Indicateurs de champs sémantiques et abréviat...

English	Abbr.	Français
mathematics	*Math*	mathématiques
medicine	*Med, Méd*	médecine
carpentry	*Menuis*	menuiserie
meteorology	*Met, Météo*	météorologie
metallurgy	*Metal, Métal*	métallurgie
masculine and feminine noun	*mf*	nom masculin et féminin
military	*Mil*	militaire
mining	*Min*	mines
mineralogy	*Miner, Minér*	minéralogie
marketing	*Mktg*	marketing
masculine plural	*mpl*	masculin pluriel
music	*Mus*	musique
mythology	*Myth*	mythologie
noun	N	nom
we	*n.*	nous
swimming	*Natation*	
nautical, naval	*Naut*	nautique, naval
negative	*neg, nég*	négatif
feminine noun	NF	nom féminin
feminine plural noun	NFPL	nom féminin pluriel
masculine noun	NM	nom masculin
masculine plural noun	NMPL	nom masculin pluriel
plural noun	NPL	nom pluriel
nuclear	*Nucl*	nucléaire
numeral	NUM	numéral
obstetrics	*Obst*	obstétrique
occasionally	*occ*	parfois
Old-fashioned	*Old-fashioned*	vieilli
optics	*Opt*	optique
computing	*Ordinat*	ordinateurs, informatique
ornithology	*Orn*	ornithologie
occasionally	*parfois*	
parliament	*Parl*	parlement
fishing	*Pêche*	
pejorative	*Pej, Péj*	péjoratif
personal	PERS	personnel
petroleum industry	*Petr, Pétr*	industrie pétrolière
pharmacy	*Pharm*	pharmacie
philosophy	*Phil*	philosophie
philately	*Philat*	philatélie
past historic	*p hist*	passé simple
photography	*Phot*	photographie
physics	*Phys*	physique
physiology	*Physiol*	physiologie
plural	*pl*	pluriel
politics	*Pol*	politique
possessive	POSS	possessif
past participle	*pp*	participe passé
present tense	*pr*	présent
prefix	PREF, PRÉF	préfixe
preposition	PREP, PRÉP	préposition
present indicative	*pr ind*	présent de l'indicatif
pronoun	PRON	pronom
proverb	*Prov*	proverbe
present participle	*prp*	participe présent
present subjunctive	*pr sub*	présent du subjonctif

English	Abbr.	Français
psychology, psychiatry		
past tense		
something		
somebody		
registered trademark	®	marque déposée
	Radio	
railways	*Rail*	chemin de fer
regionalism	*Région*	régionalisme
relative	REL	relatif
religion	*Rel*	religion
somebody	*sb*	quelqu'un
school	*Sch, Scol*	école
Scottish English	*Scot*	anglais d'Écosse
see		voir
Sewing	*Sewing*	couture
singular	*sing*	singulier
skiing	*Ski*	
slang	*Sl*	argot
often	*souvent*	
	Sport	
specialist term	*Spec, Spéc*	terme de spécialiste
Stock Exchange	*St Exch*	Bourse
something	*sth*	quelque chose
subjunctive	*sub*	subjonctif
suffix	SUFF	suffixe
Swiss French	*Suisse*	français de Suisse
superlative	*superl*	superlatif
surgery	*Surg*	chirurgie
especially	*surtout*	
Swimming	*Swimming*	natation
technical	*Tech*	technique
telecommunications	*Tel, Tél*	télécommunications
textiles	*Tex*	textiles
theatre	*Theat, Théâtre*	
very colloquial	*très Fam*	
knitting	*Tricot*	
television	*TV*	télévision
typography, printing	*Typ*	typographie, imprimerie
European Union	*UE*	Union européenne
university	*Univ*	université
usually	*usu*	généralement
verb	v	verbe
you	*v.*	vous
veterinary medicine	*Vet, Vét*	médecine vétérinaire
intransitive verb	VI	verbe intransitif
old-fashioned	*Vieilli*	
see	*voir*	
pronominal verb	VPR	verbe pronominal
transitive verb	VT	verbe transitif
inseparable transitive verb	VT INSEP	verbe transitif jamais séparé
separable transitive verb	VT SEP	verbe transitif séparable
vulgar	*Vulg*	vulgaire
zoology	*Zool*	zoologie
gloss	=	glose
cultural equivalent	≃	équivalent culturel

HARRAP'S SHORTER

DICTIONARY

English–French / French–English

DICTIONNAIRE

Anglais–Français / Français–Anglais

HARRAP

This 7th edition first published in 2004
by Chambers Harrap Publishers Ltd
7 Hopetoun Crescent, Edinburgh EH7 4AY, UK

The previous (6th) edition of the *Harrap's Shorter Dictionary* was first published
in 2000 and reprinted 2000, 2001, 2002

ISBN 0245 60727 7 (UK)
ISBN 0245 50564 4 (France)

Dépôt légal: décembre 2003

www.chambersharrap.co.uk
www.harrap.com

Designed and typeset by Chambers Harrap Publishers Ltd, Edinburgh
Printed and bound in Italy by LaTipografica Varese SPA

Contributors to 7th edition/Ont participé à la 7e édition

Project editors/Directeurs de projet

Georges Pilard
Anna Stevenson

with/avec

Bérangère Chevalier
Nadia Cornuau
Pat Dunn
Isabelle Elkaim
Stuart Fortey
Alexandra Jaton
Laurence Larroche
Kate Nicholson
Liam Rodger
Rachel Skeet

Illustrations

Glen McBeth

Prepress/Prépresse

Clair Cameron
Sharon McTeir
David Reid
Kirsteen Wright

Publishing manager/Direction éditoriale

Patrick White

Acknowledgements

The publisher would like to acknowledge the contribution made by the previous editorial teams who worked on the Harrap's Shorter and in particular that made by the team managed by Peter Terrell in the making of the fifth edition of this dictionary.

Remerciements

Les éditions Harrap tiennent à remercier tous les rédacteurs qui ont participé aux précédentes éditions du Harrap's Shorter, et tout particulièrement Peter Terrell qui dirigea la cinquième édition de cet ouvrage.

Trademarks

Words considered to be trademarks have been designated in this dictionary by the symbol ®. However, no judgement is implied concerning the legal status of any trademark by virtue of the presence or absence of such a symbol.

Marques déposées

Les termes considérés comme des marques déposées sont signalés dans ce dictionnaire par le symbole ®. Cependant, la présence ou l'absence de ce symbole ne constituent nullement une indication quant à la valeur juridique de ces termes.

7 to call sb to a. demander une explication *ou* des comptes à qn (**for sth** de qch); **to be brought to a.** devoir rendre des comptes; **to give a good a. of oneself** bien se comporter **8** *(importance)* **of no a.** *(person, matter)* insignifiant, de peu d'importance; **to take sth into a., to take a. of sth** tenir compte de qch, faire entrer qch en ligne de compte; **taking everything into a.** tout bien calculé; **to leave out of a., to take no a. of** ne pas tenir compte de; *(circumstance)* négliger **9** *(because)* **on a. of sth** en raison de qch; *(esp in negative context)* à cause de qch; **I did it on your a.** je l'ai fait pour vous; **I did it on a. of you** *(reproaching)* je l'ai fait à cause de vous; **the road was closed on a. of the accident** la route était barrée à cause *ou* en raison de l'accident; **he can't play football on a. of his health** il ne peut pas jouer au football en raison de sa santé; **on no a., not on any a.** en aucun cas; **I don't want to talk to her on any a.** je ne veux lui parler en aucun cas *ou* sous aucun prétexte; **you're not on any a. to ...** tu ne dois en aucun cas *ou* sous aucun prétexte ... **10** *(responsibility)* **to act on one's own a.** agir de sa propre initiative *ou* de soi-même; **to set up in business on one's own a.** s'établir à son compte **11** *(report)* *(of events)* récit *m*; *(of facts, actual situation)* exposé *m*; *(in newspaper)* compte rendu *m*; **to give an a. of sth** faire le récit de qch; **an interesting a. of his travels** un récit intéressant de ses voyages; **his a. of the siege of Gerona** le récit qu'il fait/faisait du siège de Gérone; **his latest book contains an amusing a. of how he learned to drive** son dernier livre relate de façon amusante la manière dont il a appris à conduire; **her a. (of the events) was slightly different** son exposé des événements était légèrement différent; **on any a.** à tous points de vue; **by all accounts** au dire de tout le monde ▪ **vT** *Fml* **to a. sb guilty** tenir qn pour coupable ▸ ▸ **a. balance** *(status)* situation *f* de compte; *Acct (after audit)* reliquat *m* de compte; *Acct* **a. book** livre *m* de comptes, registre *m* de comptabilité; **a. card** *Fin (record of charges)* fiche *f* de compte *ou* de facture; *Com (for use in department store)* carte-clients *f, pl* cartes-clients; **a. charges** frais *mpl* de tenue de compte; **a. commission** commission *f* de compte; **a. credit** avoir *m* de compte; *St Exch* **a. day** *(jour m de)* liquidation *f*, *(jour de)* règlement *m*; *Com* **a. director** *(in advertising, marketing, PR)* directeur, -trice des comptes-clients; *Am St Exch* **a. executive** agent *m* de change; **a. fee** commission de compte; *Com* **a. handler** *(in advertising, marketing, PR)* responsable *mf* des comptes-clients; **a. handling fee** commission de tenue de compte; *Banking* **a. holder** titulaire *mf*; *Banking* **a. management charges** frais de tenue de compte; **a. manager** *Banking, Fin* chargé, -ée de compte; *Com (in advertising, marketing, PR)* responsable de budget; *Banking* **a. number** numéro *m* de compte; *Acct* **a. payable** compte créditeur, dette *f* fournisseur; *Acct* **accounts payable** dettes fournisseurs; *Acct* **accounts payable book, accounts payable ledger** livre des créanciers; *Banking* **a. position** situation de compte; *Acct* **a. receivable** compte client, compte débiteur; *Acct* **accounts receivable** créances *fpl*, créances clients; **accounts receivable ledger book, accounts receivable ledger** livre des débiteurs; **a. statement** relevé *m ou* état *ou* bordereau *m* de compte ▸ **account for** **vT INSEP 1** *(one's behaviour, expense)* *(explain)* rendre compte de; *(justify)* justifier; *(circumstance)* expliquer; **that accounts for his interest in baseball** voilà qui

explique son intérêt pour le base-ball; **I can't a. for it** je ne me l'explique pas; **five people have still not been accounted for** *(after accident etc)* cinq personnes n'ont toujours pas été retrouvées; **there is no accounting for taste** chacun son goût **2** *(constitute)* constituer; **oil accounts for 10 per cent of exports** le pétrole constitue 10 pour cent des exportations; **all my time is already accounted for** mon temps est *ou* je suis déjà complètement pris **3** *(destroy)* *(plane)* abattre; *(submarine)* couler; *(troops)* tuer; *Fig* **he accounted for three batsmen** il a renversé le guichet de trois batteurs; **that accounts for him** *(striking sb off list etc)* son compte est réglé, à celui-là

accountability [əkaʊntə'bɪlɪtɪ] **N** responsabilité *f* (**to** envers); **local government a. is an important issue** la nécessité pour les municipalités de rendre compte de leurs actions est une question d'actualité

accountable [ə'kaʊntəb(ə)l] **ADJ to be a. to sb for sth** être responsable de qch envers qn; **to hold sb a.** tenir qn *(pour)* responsable (**for sth** de qch); **to be a. for a sum of money** être redevable d'une somme d'argent; **I am a. to no one** je n'ai de comptes à rendre à personne; **the police must be made more a. for their actions** la police doit rendre davantage compte de ses actions; **a. government/police force** gouvernement *m*/police *f* responsable ▸ ▸ **a. marketing** marketing *m* responsable

accountancy [ə'kaʊntənsɪ] **N** *Acct* comptabilité *f*, expertise *f* comptable, *Fam* compta *f*

accountant [ə'kaʊntənt] **N** *Acct* comptable *mf*; **chief a.** chef *m* de (la) comptabilité; **chartered a.,** *Am* **certified public a.** ≃ expert-comptable *m, pl* experts-comptables

accounting [ə'kaʊntɪŋ] **N** *Acct* comptabilité *f*, *Fam* compta *f* ▸ ▸ **a. clerk** commis *m* aux écritures; **a. control** contrôle *m* de la comptabilité; **a. day** journée *f* comptable; **a. entry** écriture *f* comptable; **a. entry form, a. entry sheet** bordereau *m* de saisie; **a. firm** cabinet *m* d'expertise comptable *ou* d'expert-comptable; **a. method** méthode *f* de comptabilité, procédé *m ou* mode *m* comptable; **a. period** exercice *m* (financier), période *f* comptable; **a. policy** politique *f* comptable; **a. procedure** pratique *f* comptable; **a. records** états *mpl* comptables; **a. system** système *m ou* plan *m* comptable; **a. year** exercice (financier), année *f* comptable

accounts [ə'kaʊnts] **NPL** comptabilité *f*, comptes *mpl*; *(department)* (service *m* de la) comptabilité; **to keep the a.** tenir les livres *ou* les écritures *ou* les comptes; **to enter sth in the a.** comptabiliser qch; **who does your a.?** qui est-ce qui fait votre comptabilité? ▸ ▸ **a. clerk** employé, -ée aux écritures; **a. department** (service de la) comptabilité; **a. ledger** grand livre *m* des comptes; *Comput* **a. software** logiciel *m* de comptabilité

accoutrements [ə'ku:trəmənts], *Am* **accouterments** [ə'ku:təmənts] **NPL** *(equipment)* équipement *m*; **all the a. of her profession** tout l'attirail propre à sa profession

accredit [ə'kredɪt] **vT 1** *(attribute)* attribuer (**to** à) **2** *(appoint, authorize)* *(ambassador, journalist)* accréditer (**to** auprès de)

accreditation [əkredɪ'teɪʃən] **N** accréditation *f*

accredited [ə'kredɪtɪd] **ADJ** *(person)* accrédité, autorisé; *(journalist)* accrédité ▸ ▸ **a. college** école *f* reconnue (par l'État)

accretion [ə'kri:ʃən] **N** accroissement *m*; *(of skills)* accumulation *f*; **an a. of fungus** une accumulation de moisissures

accrual [ə'kru:əl] **N** *Fin* accumulation *f*, *Acct*

accruals *(accrued expenses)* charges *fpl* à payer; *(accrued income)* produits *mpl* à recevoir ▸ ▸ *Acct* **a. accounting** comptabilité *f* d'engagements; **accruals concept** principe *m* d'indépendance des exercices *ou* de rattachement à l'exercice; **a. rate** taux *m* d'accumulation *ou* d'accroissement

accrue [ə'kru:] **vI 1** *Fin (of interest)* s'accumuler; **interest accrues (as) from the 5th of the month** les intérêts courent à partir du 5 du mois **2** *(of moneys, land etc)* **to a. to sb** revenir à qn ▪ **vT** *(interest)* produire ▸ ▸ **accrued benefits** *(under pension scheme)* points *mpl* de retraite; **accrued charges** effets *mpl* à payer; **accrued dividends** dividendes *mpl* accrus; **accrued expenses** frais *mpl* cumulés *ou* accumulés; **accrued income** produit *m* à recevoir; **accrued interest** intérêts *mpl* courus

accruing interest [ə'kru:ɪŋ] **N** *Fin* intérêts *mpl* à échoir

accumulate [ə'kju:mjʊleɪt] **vT** *(fortune etc)* accumuler, amasser; *(objects)* amonceler, entasser; *(heat, electricity etc)* emmagasiner; *(dust)* ramasser ▪ **vI** s'accumuler

accumulated [ə'kju:mjʊleɪtɪd] **ADJ ATTRIB** accumulé ▸ ▸ *Fin* **a. depreciation** amortissement *m* cumulé

accumulation [əkju:mjʊ'leɪʃən] **N 1** *(act)* accumulation *f*, *(of objects)* amoncellement *m*, entassement *m*; *(of heat, electricity etc)* emmagasinage *m* **2** *(result)* *(of objects, sand etc)* amas *m*, tas *m*; *(of facts, evidence)* accumulation *f*

accumulative [ə'kju:mjʊlətɪv] **ADJ** qui s'accumule; *Fin* cumulatif

accumulator [ə'kju:mjʊleɪtər] **N 1** *Tech, Constr, Elec* accumulateur *m* **2** *Horseracing* pari *m* avec report **3** *(person)* **he's an a. of useless gadgets** il accumule les gadgets inutiles ▸ ▸ *Horseracing* **a. bet** pari avec report

accuracy ['ækjʊrəsɪ] **N** *(of calculation, forecast)* exactitude *f*; *(of firearm, shot, meter)* précision *f*; *(of report, statement, scales)* justesse *f*; *(of translation, portrayal)* fidélité *f*

accurate ['ækjʊrət] **ADJ** *(calculation, forecast)* correct, exact; *(firearm, shot, meter)* précis; *(report, statement, scales)* juste; *(translation, portrayal)* fidèle; **my typing is much more a.** ma frappe est beaucoup plus précise; **to be (strictly) a. ...** pour être tout à fait exact ...

accurately ['ækjʊrətlɪ] **ADV** *(to calculate, forecast)* exactement; *(to measure, aim, report)* avec précision; *(to translate, portray)* fidèlement; *(to draw)* correctement; **very a. measured/predicted** calculé/prédit avec une grande précision; **he a. predicted that ...** il a justement prédit que ...

accurateness ['ækjʊrətnɪs] **N** exactitude *f*, précision *f*

accursed [ə'kɜ:sɪd] **ADJ** *Lit* maudit

accusation [ækjʊ'zeɪʃən] **N** accusation *f*; **to bring an a. against sb** porter *ou* déposer plainte contre qn; **an a. of bribery was made against him** on l'a accusé de corruption; **to make an a.** lancer une accusation; **he made some wild accusations about my having bugged his telephone** il m'a absurdement accusé d'avoir mis son téléphone sur écoute

accusative [ə'kju:zətɪv] *Gram* **N** (cas *m*) accusatif *m*; **in the a.** à l'accusatif ▪ **ADJ** *(case)* accusatif

accusatory [ə'kju:zətərɪ, ækjʊ'zeɪtərɪ] **ADJ** accusateur, -trice

accuse [ə'kju:z] **vT** accuser (**sb of sth** qn de

qch; **of doing sth** de faire qch); **you stand accused** vous êtes inculpé; *Iron* **no one could a. her of being punctual** on ne peut pas l'accuser d'être ponctuelle

accused [ə'kju:zd] **N** *Law* **the a.** l'inculpé, -ée; *(of offence)* le prévenu, la prévenue; *(of crime)* l'accusé, -ée

accuser [ə'kju:zər] **N** accusateur, -trice

accusing [ə'kju:zɪŋ] **ADJ ATTRIB** *(look, finger etc)* accusateur, -trice; **she pointed an a. finger at him** elle dirigea vers lui un doigt accusateur; *Fig* elle l'a mis en cause

accusingly [ə'kju:zɪŋlɪ] **ADV** *(to ask)* d'une manière accusatrice; *(to look, stare)* d'un air *ou* d'un œil accusateur

accustom [ə'kʌstəm] **VT** habituer, accoutumer (**sb to sth** qn à qch; **to do sth** à faire qch); **to a. oneself to** *(new job, country, climate etc)* s'habituer *ou* se faire *ou* s'accoutumer à; **to a. oneself to doing/being sth** s'habituer à faire/être qch

accustomed [ə'kʌstəmd] **ADJ 1 I am a. to getting up early** j'ai l'habitude de me lever de bonne heure; **they weren't a. to strangers/politeness** ils n'étaient pas habitués aux étrangers/à la politesse; **to get** *or* **grow a. to sth/to doing sth** s'habituer à qch/à faire qch; **her eyes had got a. to the dark** ses yeux s'étaient accoutumés à l'obscurité **2** *(habitual)* habituel, coutumier

AC/DC ['eɪsi:'di:si:] **N** *Elec (abbr* **alternating current/direct current)** CA/CC *m*; *Fig Fam* **to be A.** *(bisexual)* marcher à voile et à vapeur

ace [eɪs] **N 1** *Cards* as *m*; **a. of spades** as de pique; *Fam* **to have an a. up one's sleeve** avoir un atout en réserve **2** *Tennis* **(service) a.** ace *m* **3** *Fam (expert)* as *m*; **flying a.** as de l'aviation; *esp Am* **a. reporter** journaliste *mf* d'élite **4 within an a. of sth** à deux doigts de qch
ADJ *Sl (very good)* extra *inv*
VT *Am Sl* **to a. an exam** réussir un examen les doigts dans le nez

acerbic [ə'sɜ:bɪk] **ADJ** *(fruit, taste)* aigre; *Fig (person, comment)* acerbe, mordant

acerbity [ə'sɜ:bɪtɪ] **N** aigreur *f*, acerbité *f*

acetate ['æsɪteɪt] **N** *Chem, Typ* acétate *m*
▸▸**a. foil** feuille *f* d'acétate

acetic [æ'si:tɪk, -'set-] **ADJ** *Chem* acétique
▸▸**a. acid** acide *m* acétique

acetone ['æsɪtəʊn] **N** *Chem* acétone *f*

acetylene [æ'setɪli:n] **N** *Chem* acétylène *m*
▸▸**a. lamp** lampe *f* à acétylène; **a. torch** torche *f* à acétylène; **a. welding** soudure *f* autogène

acetylsalicylic acid [æsɪtaɪlsælɪ'sɪlɪk] **N** *Pharm* acide *m* acétylsalicylique

ACH [eɪsi:'eɪtʃ] **N** *Banking (abbr* **automated clearing house)** chambre *f* de compensation automatisée

ache [eɪk] **N** mal *m*, douleur *f*, *Spec* algie *f*, **stomach a.** mal de ventre; **to have (a) stomach a.** avoir mal au ventre; **she's always telling people about all her aches and pains** elle n'arrête pas de se plaindre de ses maux à tout le monde; **I've just got a few aches and pains, that's all** j'ai quelques douleurs, c'est tout; *Fig esp Lit* **I have an a. in my heart** j'ai de la peine
VI my head aches j'ai mal à la tête; **it makes my head a.** cela me donne mal à la tête; **I'm aching all over** j'ai mal partout; *Fig* **it makes my heart a.** cela me serre le cœur; **he was aching to join in the fight** il brûlait de prendre part au combat

achieve [ə'tʃi:v] **VT 1** *(accomplish) (aim, goal)* atteindre, arriver à; **to achieve a great deal** *(in life)* accomplir beaucoup de choses; *(in task)* réussir à faire beaucoup de choses; **to**

a. very little *(in life, task)* ne pas faire grandchose; **to a. one's purpose** *or* **ends** parvenir *ou* en venir à ses fins; **to a. the impossible** réussir l'impossible; **we achieved what we set out to do** nous avons rempli nos objectifs; **I feel that we have achieved something** j'ai le sentiment que nous sommes arrivés à quelque chose; **he will never a. anything** il n'arrivera jamais à rien; **this policy achieved very little** cette politique n'a pas donné de grands résultats; **what will that a.?** *(of suggestion etc)* qu'est-ce que ça fera de plus?, pour en venir à quoi? **2** *(gain) (honour, notoriety)* acquérir; *(reputation)* se faire
▸▸**achieved room rate** prix *m* total des chambres

> Note that the French verb **achever** is a false friend and is never a translation for the English verb **to achieve**. Its most common meaning is **to complete**.

achievement [ə'tʃi:vmənt] **N 1** *(feat)* exploit *m*, haut fait *m*; **their real a. lay in ...** leur véritable prouesse résida dans ...; **getting him to talk about anything is quite an a.** arriver à le faire parler de quoi que ce soit relève vraiment d'un exploit; **a lasting a.** une réalisation durable; **her many achievements** ses nombreux succès **2** *(successful completion)* accomplissement *m*, réalisation *f*

> Note that the French word **achèvement** is a false friend and is never a translation for the English word **achievement**. It means **completion**.

achievement-orient(at)ed [-'ɔ:rɪent-t(eɪt)ɪd] **ADJ to be a.** mettre l'accent sur la réussite; *Pej* être obsédé par la réussite

achiever [ə'tʃi:vər] **N** homme *m*/femme *f* performant(e), battant, -ante

Achilles [ə'kɪli:z] **N** Achille
▸▸*Myth* **A. heel** talon *m* d'Achille; *Fig* **gambling is his A. heel** le jeu est son point faible; **A. tendon** tendon *m* d'Achille

aching ['eɪkɪŋ] **ADJ** *(tooth, head etc)* qui vous/me/*etc* fait mal; *(leg, shoulder etc)* endolori; **to have an a. heart** avoir une peine de cœur; **her death left an a. void in his life** sa mort a laissé un vide douloureux dans sa vie

achromatic [ækrə'mætɪk] **ADJ** *Opt* achromatique

achromatous [ə'krəʊmətəs], **achromous** [ə'krəʊməs] **ADJ** *Phot* achrome

achy ['eɪkɪ] **ADJ** courbaturé; **I feel rather a.** j'ai mal un peu partout; **I have an a. feeling in my joints** mes jointures sont douloureuses

acid ['æsɪd] **ADJ 1** acide **2** *(tone, reply)* acerbe
N 1 acide *m* **2** *Fam (LSD)* acide *m*
▸▸**a. bath** bain *m* acide; **a. drop** *(sweet)* bonbon *m* acidulé; *Ecol* **a. rain** pluies *fpl* acides; *Chem* **a. solution** solution *f* acide; **a. test** épreuve *f* à la pierre de touche; *Fig* épreuve décisive; *Acct* **a. test ratio** ratio *m* de liquidité immédiate

acidic [ə'sɪdɪk] **ADJ** *Chem* acide; *Fig (comment etc)* acerbe

acidification [ə'sɪdɪfɪ'keɪʃən] **N** acidification *f*

acidify [ə'sɪdɪfaɪ] **VT** acidifier

acidity [ə'sɪdɪtɪ] **N 1** *Chem* acidité *f*, *Med* aigreurs *fpl*, **excessive a. in the stomach** une acidité gastrique excessive **2** *Fig (of reply)* aigreur *f*

acidly ['æsɪdlɪ] **ADV** aigrement

acidosis [æsɪ'dəʊsɪs] **N** *Med* acidose *f*

acidulous [ə'sɪdjʊləs] **ADJ** acidulé

ack-ack ['æk'æk] **N** *Mil Old-fashioned (wea-*

pon) artillerie *f* antiaérienne; *(system)* ≃ Défense *f* contre avions, DCA *f*
▸▸**a. fire** tir *m* de DCA

acknowledge [ək'nɒlɪdʒ] **VT 1** *(recognize) (mistake, debt etc)* reconnaître; *(service)* reconnaître, se montrer reconnaissant de, exprimer sa reconnaissance de; *TV, Cin (in credits)* mentionner; **to a. sth as a fact** faire la constatation de qch; **acknowledged as the** *or* **to be the best Chinese restaurant in the city** reconnu comme le meilleur restaurant chinois de la ville; **to a. oneself beaten, to a. defeat** s'avouer *ou* se reconnaître vaincu; **she acknowledged my presence** elle m'a fait signe qu'elle m'avait vu; **he didn't even a. my presence** il m'a complètement ignoré; **she never acknowledges me** *(greets)* elle fait toujours comme si elle ne me voyait pas **2** *(reply to) (courtesy, greeting etc)* répondre à; **to a. (receipt of) a letter** accuser réception d'une lettre; *Naut* **to a. a signal** faire l'aperçu
▸▸*Comput* **a. character** *(in datacomms)* caractère *m* d'accusé de réception

acknowledged [ək'nɒlɪdʒd] **ADJ ATTRIB** *(fact)* reconnu, avéré; *(expert etc)* qui fait autorité; **an a. thief** un voleur reconnu

acknowledg(e)ment [ək'nɒlɪdʒmənt] **N 1** *(of mistake, service etc)* reconnaissance *f*, *(of fact)* constatation *f*, *Comput (in datacomms)* accusé *m* de réception; **I waved/smiled at him, but received no a.** je lui ai fait signe/ai souri mais il ne m'a pas répondu; **in a. of** pour témoigner ma/sa/*etc* reconnaissance de; **acknowledgments** *(in book)* remerciements *mpl*, *(in credits)* mentions *fpl* (au générique), remerciements; **to quote an author without a.** citer un auteur sans mentionner son nom; **to give some a. to the fact that ...** reconnaître le fait que ...; **there's not enough a. of the debt he owes to Goldstein** il ne rend pas suffisamment hommage à Goldstein; **a. of debt** reconnaissance de dette **2** *(of payment)* reçu *m*, quittance *f*, **a. (of receipt)** *(of letter)* accusé *m* de réception; **a. of reservation** confirmation *f* de réservation

acme ['ækmɪ] **N** *Lit (of perfection, politeness)* comble *m*

acne ['æknɪ] **N** *Med* acné *f*

acolyte ['ækəlaɪt] **N** *Rel, Fig* acolyte *m*

Acorn® ['eɪkɔ:n] **N** *Mktg (abbr* **A Classification of Residential Neighbourhoods)** = classement *m* des différents types de quartiers résidentiels existant en Grande-Bretagne en 39 catégories, utilisé par les entreprises pour mieux cibler leurs clients potentiels lors de campagnes commerciales

acorn ['eɪkɔ:n] **N** gland *m* (de chêne)

acoustic [ə'ku:stɪk] **ADJ** acoustique
▸▸*Comput, Tel* **a. coupler** coupleur *m* acoustique; **a. engineer** acousticien, -ienne; **a. feedback** effet *m* Larsen, rétroaction *f* acoustique, bouclage *m* acoustique; *Mus* **a. guitar** guitare *f* sèche; **a. hood** capot *m* antibruit; *Anat* **a. nerve** nerf *m* acoustique *ou* auditif; **a. screen** écran *m* acoustique; **a. signal** signal *m* sonore; *Constr* **a. tile** carreau *m* acoustique

acoustically [ə'ku:stɪk(ə)lɪ] **ADV** acoustiquement

acoustics [ə'ku:stɪks] **N** acoustique *f*, **the a. in the hall are good, the hall has good a.** cette salle a une bonne acoustique **VOIR GRAMMAIRE A10**

ACPO ['ækpəʊ] **N** *(abbr* **Association of Chief Police Officers)** = syndicat *m* d'officiers supérieurs de la police britannique

acquaint [ə'kweɪnt] **VT 1** *esp Fml* **to a. sb with sth** *(his duties, situation, fact)* mettre qn au courant de qch, informer qn de qch; **to a. sb with the controls** instruire qn sur le fonctionnement des commandes; **a stay in the jungle had acquainted him with these dangers** un séjour dans la jungle l'avait familiarisé avec ces dangers; **to a. oneself with the facts/the situation** se mettre au courant des faits/de la situation; **the doctor acquainted himself with her case history** le médecin s'est informé de ses antécédents médicaux

2 to be acquainted with sb connaître qn; **to be acquainted with sth** connaître qch, être au fait *ou* au courant de qch; **to become** *or* **get acquainted** *(of two people)* faire connaissance; **to become** *or* **get acquainted with sb** faire *ou* lier connaissance avec qn; **we soon became** *or* **got acquainted** nous avons vite fait connaissance; **I got acquainted with him later** j'ai fait sa connaissance plus tard; **to become acquainted with the facts** prendre connaissance des faits

acquaintance [əˈkweɪntəns] N **1** *(person)* connaissance *f*; **he is an a. (of mine)** c'est quelqu'un que je connais; **a casual a. (of mine)** quelqu'un que je connais de loin; **to have a wide circle of acquaintances** avoir des relations très étendues **2 a. with** *(person, fact, language)* connaissance *f* de; **to make sb's a.** faire la connaissance de qn; **during our brief a.** pendant la courte période où nous avons été en contact; **his apparent lack of a. with the facts** son ignorance apparente des faits

acquiesce [ækwɪˈes] VI acquiescer, donner son assentiment (**in, to** à); **to a. in an arrangement** accepter un arrangement

acquiescence [ækwɪˈes(ə)ns] N assentiment *m*, consentement *m*, acquiescement *m* (**in, to** à)

acquiescent [ækwɪˈes(ə)nt] ADJ consentant

acquire [əˈkwaɪər] VT *(house, knowledge, experience etc)* acquérir; *(habit)* prendre, contracter; *(friend)* se faire; *(overtones)* prendre; **to a. a taste for sth** prendre goût à qch; **he acquired a stoop** son dos s'est voûté; **to a. an accent** prendre un accent; **we seem to have acquired some friends** *(are being followed etc)* on dirait que nous avons de la compagnie; **we seem to have acquired a cat** il semble qu'on ait hérité d'un chat

acquired [əˈkwaɪəd] ADJ acquis; **gin/Proust is an acquired taste** le gin c'est quelque chose/Proust est un auteur qu'on apprend à aimer

▸▸ *Psy* **a. characteristic** caractère *m* acquis; *Med* **a. immune deficiency syndrome** syndrome *m* immunodéficitaire acquis

acquirement [əˈkwaɪəmənt] N acquisition *f* (**of** de)

acquisition [ækwɪˈzɪʃən] N **1** *(act)* acquisition *f* (**of** de) **2** *(object, person)* acquisition *f*; **she could be a useful a.** elle pourrait se révéler être une acquisition utile

▸▸ *Acct* **a. accounting** = base *f* de préparation des comptes consolidés où une société a pris le contrôle d'une autre; *Acct* **a. cost** coût *m* d'acquisition

acquisitive [əˈkwɪzɪtɪv] ADJ thésauriseur, -euse; **an a. nature** une nature avide

acquit [əˈkwɪt] VT (-tt-) **1** *Law (person accused of a crime)* acquitter; **to a. sb of sth** *(mistake)* absoudre qn de qch; *(of charge)* décharger qn de qch **2** *Fin (debt)* acquitter, s'acquitter de, régler **3 to a. oneself with distinction** s'en sortir très honorablement; **he acquitted himself well/badly** il s'en est bien/mal acquitté; **how did he a. himself?** comment s'en est-il sorti?

acquittal [əˈkwɪt(ə)l] N **1** *Law (of defendant)* acquittement *m*, décharge *f*; *(of debt)* acquittement **2** *(of duty)* exécution *f*, accomplissement *m*

acquittance [əˈkwɪtəns] N *Fin (of debt)* acquittement *m*, décharge *f*, quittance *f*

acre [ˈeɪkər] N acre *f* (= 0,4 *hectare*), ≃ arpent *m*, demi-hectare *m*; **vast acres** des terres *fpl* étendues; **acres of forest** des hectares *mpl* de forêts; *Fig Fam* **acres of ...** des tas de ...; **acres of room** énormément de place

acreage [ˈeɪkərɪdʒ] N superficie *f (en mesures agraires)*

acrid [ˈækrɪd] ADJ **1** *(taste, smoke)* âcre **2** *Fig (style)* mordant; *(criticism)* acerbe

acrimonious [ækrɪˈməʊnɪəs] ADJ acrimonieux; *(person)* acariâtre; **the discussion was becoming a.** la discussion s'envenimait

acrimoniously [ækrɪˈməʊnɪəslɪ] ADV avec acrimonie

acrimony [ˈækrɪmənɪ], **acrimoniousness** [ækrɪˈməʊnɪəsnɪs] N acrimonie *f*, *(of tone, character)* aigreur *f*; **the tone of a. in his voice** l'aigreur qu'il y avait dans sa voix

acrobat [ˈækrəbæt] N acrobate *mf*

acrobatic [ækrəˈbætɪk] ADJ acrobatique; **an a. feat** une acrobatie

acrobatics [ækrəˈbætɪks] N acrobatie *f* VOIR GRAMMAIRE A10

acronym [ˈækrənɪm] N sigle *m*

Acropolis [əˈkrɒpəlɪs] N Acropole *f*

ACROSS [əˈkrɒs] ADV, PREP **1** *(from one side to the other)* en travers (de); **line drawn a. the page** ligne tirée en travers de la page; **with his arms folded a. his chest** les bras croisés sur la poitrine; **they talked to each other a. the table** ils se parlaient de part et d'autre de la table; **there was no bridge a. the river** aucun pont n'enjambait la rivière; **to find a way a. the mountain** trouver un chemin pour traverser la montagne; **a. country** à travers champs; **from a. the entire range** de toute la gamme

2 *(of motion)* **to walk a. (a street)** traverser (une rue); **we helped him a. the road** nous l'avons aidé à traverser la rue; **to swim a. a river** traverser une rivière à la nage; **to go a. a bridge** passer (sur) un pont, franchir un pont; **they got the barrel a. the river/road** ils ont fait passer le tonneau de l'autre côté de la rivière/rue; **is he a. the river/road yet?** est-ce qu'il a enfin traversé la rivière/la rue?; **she threw it a. the room/courtyard** elle l'a balancé en travers de *ou* de l'autre côté de la pièce/de la cour; **we cut a. the park** nous avons coupé à travers le parc; **to get** *or* **come a.** *(of play)* passer la rampe; **to get sth a. to sb** *(make understand)* faire comprendre qch à qn; **he doesn't come a. as an aggressive person** il ne donne pas l'impression de quelqu'un d'agressif

3 *(of distance)* **2 km a.** 2 km de large; **he is broad a. the shoulders** il est large d'épaules; **the distance a.** *(width)* la distance en largeur; *(of crossing)* la longueur de la traversée; **it's too far a.** c'est trop loin

4 *(on the other side)* **a. the street** de l'autre côté de la rue; **the woman from a. the street** la femme d'en face; **there's a supermarket just a. the road from us/our house** il y a un supermarché juste en face/en face de notre maison; **just a. the border** de l'autre côté *ou* au-delà de la frontière; **from a. the sea** par-delà la mer

5 *(in crossword)* horizontalement

across-the-board ADJ général, -aux; **an a. wage increase** une augmentation générale des salaires; **a. cuts** réduction linéaire générale

ADV de façon générale; **this applies a.** ceci s'applique à tous les niveaux

acrostic [əˈkrɒstɪk] N *Liter* acrostiche *m*

acrylic [əˈkrɪlɪk] ADJ *(fibre, paint etc)* acrylique; *(garment)* en acrylique

N **1** *(resin)* résine *f* acrylique **2** *(material)* acrylique *m*, fibre *f* acrylique **3** *(garment)* vêtement *m* en acrylique **4** *(paint)* peinture *f* acrylique

ACT [ækt]

N	acte **1, 2** ▪ numéro **3** ▪ loi **4**
VT	jouer
VI	agir **1, 2** ▪ jouer **3**

N **1** *(of justice, kindness etc)* acte *m*; *(deed)* action *f*; **an a. of folly** une folie; **an a. of despair** un acte désespéré; **the a. of a criminal/madman** l'action d'un criminel/fou; **to catch sb in the (very) a.** prendre qn sur le fait *ou* en flagrant délit; **she was caught in the a. of taking the money** on l'a surprise en train de voler l'argent

2 *(in play)* acte *m*; **A. I, scene 1** Acte I, scène I; **a one-a. play** une pièce en un acte

3 *(in cabaret, circus etc)* numéro *m*; **circus a.** numéro de cirque; **to put on an a.** *(pretend)* jouer la comédie; **it's all an a.** *(pretence)* c'est du cinéma; *Fig* **to get in on the a.** se mettre dans le mouvement; *Fig* **to be/to let sb in on the a.** être/mettre qn dans le coup; *Fam* **to have got one's a. together** *(professionally)* bien connaître son affaire; *(personally)* être un homme/une femme accompli(e); *Fam* **get your a. together!** *(professionally)* vous ne pourriez pas vous secouer, un peu!; *(personally)* prends ta vie en main!; *Am Fam* **to queer the a.** tout faire foirer

4 *Law, Pol* loi *f*; **Companies A.** = loi sur les sociétés; **factory a.** législation *f* industrielle; **land a.** loi agraire

VT *(play, character)* jouer; *(role)* jouer, tenir; **to a. Hamlet** jouer Hamlet; *Fig* **to a. the fool** faire l'imbécile; **to a. a part** jouer un rôle; *Fig* jouer la comédie, feindre; **to a. the part of an honest man** se conduire *ou* agir en honnête homme

VI **1** *(take action)* agir; **it is time to a.** il est temps d'agir; **to a. out of fear/greed/selfishness** agir sous l'emprise de la peur/par cupidité/par égoïsme; **I acted for the best** j'ai fait pour le mieux; **to a. for sb** agir au nom de qn; *(of lawyer)* représenter qn; **I'm acting for her** j'agis en son nom; **the police refused to a.** la police a refusé d'intervenir; **to a. as secretary** exercer les fonctions de secrétaire; **the stick acted as a tent pole** le bâton servit de montant pour la tente; **the smell acts as a warning for other animals** l'odeur sert d'avertissement pour les autres animaux; **the engine acts as a brake** le moteur fait fonction de frein; **to a. as a warning** servir d'avertissement; **to a. as a motivation** constituer une motivation

2 *(behave)* se comporter, agir; **they a. as if nothing had happened** ils se comportent *ou* ils font comme si rien ne s'était passé; **he acts as if he were** *or* *Fam* **like he was the boss** il se comporte comme si c'était lui le patron; **stop acting like a child!, a. your age!** arrête de faire l'enfant!

3 *Theat, Cin* jouer; *(pretend)* jouer la comédie; **he can't a.** c'est un mauvais acteur; **I always wanted to a.** j'ai toujours voulu être acteur; **to a. in a film** tourner dans un film; **to a. stupid/all innocent** faire l'idiot/l'innocent

▸▸ *Bible* **the Acts of the Apostles** les Actes des Apôtres; *Rel* **a. of faith** acte de foi; **a. of God** cas *m* de force majeure; **A. of Parliament** loi, décret *m*; **a. of war** acte de guerre

▸ **act on** VT INSEP **1** *(affect)* influer sur, agir sur; *(of remedy etc)* agir sur; **acid acts on metal** l'acide agit sur le métal; *Med* **to a. on the brain/the bowels** exercer une action sur *ou* agir sur le cerveau/l'intestin; **the rumours acted on their fears** les rumeurs ont joué sur leurs craintes

2 *(respond to)* *(advice)* agir d'après, suivre;

(order) exécuter; *(letter)* donner suite à; **acting on my lawyer's advice** conformément aux conseils de mon avocat; **the police acted on the information** la police a agi après avoir reçu l'information

▸ **act out** VT SEP **to a. out a fantasy** vivre un fantasme; **local people a. out scenes from the town's history** les gens du coin jouent des scènes de l'histoire de leur ville; **she acts out our deepest fears** elle exprime nos peurs les plus profondes

▸ **act up** VI *Fam (of child)* se conduire mal; *(of machine)* marcher mal; **the car's acting up again** la voiture recommence à faire des siennes; **don't start acting up!** conduis-toi bien!; **my knee/back is acting up again** mon genou/dos recommence à me faire souffrir

▸ **act upon** VT INSEP = **act on**

acting ['æktɪŋ] ADJ ATTRIB *(temporary)* suppléant, intérimaire

N *Theat, Cin (of actor)* jeu *m*, interprétation *f*; *(profession)* métier *m* d'acteur; **she's done some a.** elle a fait du théâtre/du cinéma; **the a. is marvellous** le jeu des acteurs est merveilleux

ACTION ['ækʃən]

action **1–3, 5, 7** ▪ acte **1** ▪ mécanisme **4** ▪ procès **5** ▪ combat **6**

N **1** *(of person, remedy etc)* action *f*; *(single act)* action, acte *m*, fait *m*; *Br* **(industrial) a.** mouvement *m* de revendication; *(strike)* grève *f*; **the a. of water** *(on river bank etc)* le travail des eaux, l'action de l'eau; **we want a. not words** nous voulons des actes non des paroles; **to take a.** agir; *(intervene)* intervenir; *Br (go on strike)* se mettre en grève; **their quick a. prevented more deaths** leur action rapide a évité d'autres morts; **course** or **line of a.** ligne *f* de conduite; **a man of a.** un homme d'action; **sphere of a.** sphère *f* d'activité; *Br* **day of a.** journée *f* d'action; **to put a plan into a.** mettre un projet à exécution; **to come into a.** entrer en action *ou* en jeu; **in a.** *(of machine)* en marche; *(of sportsman)* à l'œuvre; *Fam* **she destroys interviewers, you should see her in a.** elle a néantit les interviewers, tu l'as vue à l'œuvre?; **out of a.** *(machine, vehicle etc)* hors de service, hors d'usage; *(person)* hors de combat; **to put a machine out of a.** détraquer une machine; **the flu put** or **kept him out of a. for a month** la grippe l'a mis hors de combat pendant un mois; **impulsive a.** action irréfléchie, coup *m* de tête; **she's not responsible for her actions** elle n'est pas responsable de ses actes; *Prov* **actions speak louder than words** les actes en disent plus long que les paroles

2 *Theat, Cin, TV, Liter (of play, novel etc)* action *f*; **the a. takes place in …** l'action se passe à …; *Cin* **a.!** on tourne!, action!

3 *(movement) (of player)* action *f*; *(of horse)* allure *f*; **a song with actions** une chanson mimée

4 *Tech (of watch, clock)* mécanisme *m*; *(of pump, lock)* jeu *m*

5 *Law* action *f*; **a. at law, legal a.** action en justice; *(trial etc)* procès *m*; **a. for libel** procès *ou* plainte *f* en diffamation; **a. for damages** action en dommages et intérêts; **to bring an a. against sb** intenter une action *ou* un procès à *ou* contre qn

6 *Mil etc* combat *m*, engagement *m*; **naval a.** engagement naval, opération *f* navale; **to go into a.** entrer en action, engager le combat; **ready for a.** prêt à combattre; **to send troops into a.** faire intervenir *ou* faire donner des troupes; **to see a.** *(of soldier)* combattre; **to put a gun/plane/etc out of a.** *(destroy)* mettre un canon/avion/etc hors de combat; *(disable)* mettre un canon/un

avion/etc hors de service *ou Fam* de cause; **killed in a.** tué à l'ennemi; **as a result of enemy a.** à la suite de l'action ennemie; **a. stations!** tout le monde à son poste!; *Fig* vingt-deux!

7 *Fam (excitement)* action *f*; **there's plenty of a. in the movie** il y a plein d'action dans ce film; **they were looking for some a.** *(nightlife etc)* ils cherchaient un peu d'animation; **where's the a. around here?** où est-ce que ça bouge par ici?

8 *Sl* **they want a piece** or **slice of the a.** *(profits)* ils veulent une part du gâteau

▸▸ *Cin* **a. film,** *Cin* **a. movie** film *m* d'action; *Art* **a. painting** peinture *f* gestuelle; **a. plan** plan *m* d'action; **a. programme** plan d'action, plan de manœuvre; **a. replay** reprise *f*, *(in slow motion)* ralenti *m*

actionable ['ækʃənəb(ə)l] ADJ *Law (remarks, action)* qui expose à des poursuites

action-packed ADJ *(film, novel, match)* plein d'action; *(day, morning etc)* bien rempli

activate ['æktɪveɪt] VT **1** *(put into operation) (mechanism, alarm)* déclencher **2** *Chem* activer **3** *Phys* rendre radioactif

▸▸ *Chem* **activated carbon** charbon *m* actif *ou* activé

activation [æktɪ'veɪʃən] N activation *f*, *(of alarm)* déclenchement *m*

active ['æktɪv] ADJ **1** *(person)* actif; *(mind)* éveillé; *(imagination)* vif; **to be still a.** *(of elderly person)* être encore alerte *ou* actif; **to be/become a.** *(of volcano)* être/entrer en activité; **she's very a. in the party** elle est très active au sein du parti; **he was very a. in seeing that the measure was passed** il a contribué très activement à l'approbation de cette mesure; **to take an a. part in sth** prendre une part active *ou* effective à qch; **to take an a. dislike to sb** se prendre d'une vive aversion contre qn; *Mil* **on a. service** en service actif; **to see a. service** *(fight)* combattre; *Mil* **to be on the a. list** être en activité

2 *Gram (voice)* actif

N *Gram* actif *m*, voix *f* active; **verb in the a.** verbe *m* à l'actif *ou* à la voix active VOIR GRAMMAIRE A40

▸▸ *Comput* **a. desktop** bureau *m* actif; *Comput* **a. file** fichier *m* actif; *Comput* **a. matrix** matrice *f* active; *Comput* **a. matrix screen** écran *m* à matrice active; *Banking, Fin* **a. money** monnaie *f* circulante; *Fin, Com* **a. partner** *(in company)* associé, -ée gérant(e), commandité, -ée; *Comput* **a. program** programme *m* en cours d'exécution; *Comput* **a. window** fenêtre *f* active *ou* activée

actively ['æktɪvlɪ] ADV activement; **they were a. seeking peace** ils cherchaient activement à faire la paix; **to a. dislike sb** avoir une vive aversion pour qn

activist ['æktɪvɪst] N *Pol* activiste *mf*; **antinuclear/peace activists** activistes antinucléaires/en faveur de la paix

activity [æk'tɪvɪtɪ] N activité *f*; **economic a.** activité économique; **this week has seen a lot of a. on the Stock Market** la Bourse a été très active cette semaine; **his numerous activities leave him little leisure** ses nombreuses occupations lui laissent peu de loisirs; **activities** *(at holiday camp)* animation *f*

▸▸ *Acct* **a. accounting** comptabilité *f* par centres de responsabilité; **a. book** livre-jeu *m*, *pl* livres-jeux; **a. break** *(courtes)* vacances *fpl* actives; **a. centre** centre *m* aéré; **a. chart** graphique *m* des activités; *Br* **a. holiday** vacances actives; **a. indicator** indicateur *m* d'activité; **a. rate** taux *m* d'activité; *Acct* **a. ratio** ratio *m ou* coefficient *m* d'activité, ratio de gestion

actor ['æktər] N *Theat* acteur *m*, comédien *m*; *Cin, Fig* acteur *m*; **to be an a.** *Theat* faire du théâtre, être acteur *ou* comédien; *Cin* faire du cinéma, être acteur

actress ['æktrɪs] N *Theat* actrice *f*, comédienne *f*, *Cin* actrice; *Br Fam Hum* **he's got a huge one… as the a. said to the bishop** il en a une énorme, si j'ose dire

actual ['æktʃʊəl] ADJ *(concrete)* réel, véritable; *(case)* concret, -ète; **to give the a. figures** donner les chiffres mêmes; *Fam* **in a. fact** en fait; **her a. words were …** ce qu'elle a dit en fait, c'est …; **this is the a. house where she was born** voici en fait la maison où elle est née; *Br Fam* **the a. managing director visited us today** le directeur général nous a rendu visite en personne aujourd'hui; **the actual ceremony doesn't start until 10.30** la cérémonie même ne commence pas avant 10 h 30

▸▸ *Acct, Fin* **a. cost** prix *m* de revient *ou* d'achat; *Acct, Fin* **a. costs** coûts *mpl* constatés; **a. demand level** niveau *m* de demande réelle; **a. dollars** dollars *mpl* courants; **a. operating costs** coûts réels d'exploitation; **a. size** grandeur *f* réelle, vraie grandeur; *Cin, Radio, TV* **a. sound** son *m* direct; **a. value** valeur *f* réelle

> Note that the French adjective **actuel** is a false friend and is never a translation for the English adjective **actual**. It means **current**.

actuality [æktʃʊ'ælɪtɪ] N *Fml* **1** *(reality)* réalité *f* **2 a play that lacks a.** une pièce qui n'a aucun rapport avec la vie d'aujourd'hui

actually ['æktʃʊəlɪ] ADV **1** *(really)* réellement, en fait, en réalité; **what a. happened?** que s'est-il passé au juste?; **what he a. means is …** ce qu'il veut vraiment dire, c'est …; **I didn't a. see it myself** en réalité, je ne l'ai pas vu de mes propres yeux; **the piano's just for decoration, no one a. plays it** le piano fait partie du décor, en fait personne n'en joue; **we haven't a. decided yet** on n'a pas encore vraiment décidé; **yes, but what will the government a. do?** oui, mais que va vraiment faire le gouvernement?

2 *(even, surprisingly)* **he a. swore** il est (même) allé jusqu'à lâcher un juron; **she a. said good morning to me** à mon grand étonnement elle m'a dit bonjour; **he was a. on time for once** pour une fois il était à l'heure

3 *(in fact)* en fait; **a., yes, I do mind, very much!** à vrai dire, oui, ça m'ennuie beaucoup!; **I'm not sure, a.** je n'en suis pas certain, en fait; **what do you do? – I'm a lawyer, a.** que faites-vous? – je suis avocat; **a., I rather like it** à vrai dire, ça me plaît assez; **he's not a very nice person, a.** il n'est pas très gentil à vrai dire

> Note that the French adverb **actuellement** is a false friend and is never a translation for the English adverb **actually**. It means **at present**.

actuals ['æktʃʊəlz] NPL **1** *Acct, Fin (real figures)* chiffres *mpl* réels; **to compare budgeted amounts with a.** comparer les prévisions budgétaires et les résultats obtenus **2** *St Exch* livraisons *fpl* physiques, marchandises *fpl* livrées au comptant

actuarial [æktʃʊ'eərɪəl] ADJ actuariel

▸▸ **a. tables** tables *fpl* de mortalité

actuary ['æktʃʊərɪ] N actuaire *mf*

actuate ['æktʃʊeɪt] VT **1** *(machine etc)* mettre en action, faire marcher **2** *(person)* faire agir; **actuated by jealousy** poussé par la jalousie

actuation [æktʃʊ'eɪʃən] N *(of machine etc)* mise *f* en action

actuator ['æktʃʊeɪtər] N actionneur *m*

acuity [ə'kjuːɪtɪ] N *Fml (of mind, comment)* acuité *f*, **visual a.** acuité visuelle autre; **as much a.** deux fois autant; **half as much a.** moitié plus; **different a.** encore différent; **she was wearing something different a.** elle était encore habillée différemment; **to begin a.** recommencer; **to come a.** revenir; **he never came back a.** il n'est plus jamais revenu; **I've seen him a.** je l'ai revu; **I hope I shall find it a.** j'espère bien le retrouver; *Fam* **what was your name a.?** rappelez-moi votre nom; **what was that a.?** *(could you say that again)* comment?

2 *(rhetorical)* de plus, d'ailleurs, en outre; **a., I am not sure that …** d'ailleurs, je ne suis pas sûr que …

3 *(on the other hand)* **(then) a.** d'un autre côté; **then a., he may have forgotten** par ailleurs, il se peut qu'il ait oublié; **then a., others may disagree** d'un autre côté, certains peuvent ne pas être d'accord

AGAINST [ə'genst, *occ* ə'geɪnst] **PREP 1** *(in opposition to)* contre; **to fight a. sb** se battre contre qn; **to fight a. sth** *(against crime, cancer)* lutter contre qch; **to march a. the enemy** marcher à l'ennemi; **she was a. the idea** elle était opposée à l'idée; **to be a. abortion/nationalization** être contre l'avortement/la nationalisation; **to be a. sb** être contre qn, être opposé à qn; **what have you got a. him/going to Paris?** qu'est-ce que tu as contre lui/le fait d'aller à Paris?; **to have nothing a. sth** ne rien avoir contre qch; **the war set brother a. brother** la guerre a opposé des hommes à leurs frères; **a. my will** contre mon gré; **it was a. my instincts/principles** ça allait à l'encontre de mes instincts/principes; **to act a. the law** agir illégalement; **it's a. the law** c'est illégal *ou* contraire à la loi; **a. the rules** contraire au règlement; **conditions are a. us** les conditions nous sont défavorables; **there is no law a. it** il n'y a pas de loi qui s'y oppose; *Tex* **a. the nap** à rebrousse-poil; **it goes a. nature** c'est contre nature; **it was a race a. time** ça a été une véritable course contre la montre; **to be insured a. fire/theft** être assuré contre les incendies/le vol; **a. all risks** contre tous les risques

2 *(as protection from)* **to warn sb a. sb/sth** mettre qn en garde contre qn/qch; **protected a. the cold** protégé contre le froid; **a. this eventuality** pour parer à cette éventualité; **to vaccinate sb a. smallpox/malaria** vacciner qn contre la variole/la malaria

3 *(in contact with)* **leaning a. the wall** appuyé contre le mur; **to place sth a. a wall** adosser qch à un mur; **he banged his head a. the wall** il s'est cogné la tête contre le mur; **a cross is placed a. each name** *(beside)* une croix est placée à côté de chaque nom

4 *(in comparison)* **three deaths this year (as) a. thirty in 2002** trois morts cette année contre trente en 2002; **a. this must be set their extreme youth** en contrepartie il faut tenir compte de leur extrême jeunesse; **to check sth a. a list** vérifier qch d'après une liste; **to rise/fall a. the dollar** augmenter/chuter par rapport au dollar

5 *(in contrast to)* **to show up a. a background** se détacher sur un fond; **she was silhouetted a. the sky** sa silhouette se détachait sur le ciel; **the red stood out a. the grey** le rouge contrastait avec le gris; **a. the light** à contre-jour

6 *Fin* en contrepartie de; **to issue a ticket a. payment of …** remettre un ticket en contrepartie du paiement de …

agape [ə'geɪp] **ADV, ADJ** bouche bée; **to stand a.** rester bouche bée; **with mouth a.** bouche bée

agar(-agar) [ˈeɪgə(ˈreɪgə)r] **N** agar-agar *m*, gélose *f*

agaric [ˈægərɪk] **N** *(toadstool)* agaric *m*; **fly a.**

(amanite *f*) tue-mouches *m inv*, fausse oronge *f*

agate [ˈægət] **N** *Miner* agate *f*; **an a. brooch** une broche en agate

agave [əˈgaːvɪ] **N** *(plant)* agave *m*

AGC [eɪdʒiːˈsiː] **N** *(abbr* **Automatic Gain Control)** *(in audio)* antifading *m*

AGE [eɪdʒ] **N 1** âge *m*; **to be past middle a.** être sur le retour; **twenty years of a.** âgé de vingt ans; **what a. is she?, what's her a.?** quel âge a-t-elle?; **children of their own a.** des enfants de leur âge; **he's your a.** il a ton âge; **she's the same a. as me** *or* **as I am** elle a le même âge que moi; **they're the same a., they're of an a.** ils sont du même âge, ils ont le même âge; **when I was your a.** quand j'avais votre âge; **when you're my a.** quand vous aurez mon âge; **he doesn't look his a.** il ne fait pas son âge; *Fam* **act** *or* **be your a.!** ne fais pas l'enfant!; **at your a. you should know** à ton âge, tu devrais savoir; **at that a. children need a lot of attention** c'est un âge où les enfants demandent beaucoup d'attention; **fifteen is the worst a.** quinze ans est l'âge le plus difficile; **at the a. of thirty-three** à l'âge de trente-trois ans; **I'm at an a. where I question things more** je suis arrivé à un âge où l'on se pose davantage de questions; **to be of an a. to marry** être en âge de se marier; **people of all ages** des gens de tout âge; **people over the a. of fifty** les gens de plus de cinquante ans

2 (old) a. vieillesse *f*; **wisdom comes with a.** la sagesse vient avec l'âge; **a. has not been kind to her** l'âge ne l'a pas marquée par l'âge; **the house is falling to pieces with a.** la maison tombe de vieillesse *ou* de vétusté; **a tree of great a.** un très vieil arbre; **the car's beginning to show its a.** la voiture commence à donner des signes de vieillesse; **you're showing your a.!** *(remembering things like that etc)* tu es d'un autre âge!; *(you've lost touch)* tu te fais vieux!; *Hum* **a. before beauty** c'est le privilège de l'âge

3 *(adulthood)* **to be of a.** être majeur; **to come of a.** atteindre sa majorité; **coming of a.** entrée *f* en majorité; **to be under a.** *Law* être mineur; *(not old enough to buy alcohol etc)* ne pas avoir l'âge

4 *(era)* âge *m*, époque *f*, siècle *m*, ère *f*; **the a. we live in** notre siècle, le siècle où nous vivons; **in our a.** à notre époque; **in an earlier a. this wouldn't have been tolerated** il fut un temps où on n'aurait pas toléré cela; **she is the product of an earlier a.** elle est d'un autre temps; **in this a. of consumerism** en cette ère de consumérisme; **through the ages** à travers les âges ou les siècles; **the A. of Steam/the Dinosaurs** l'ère de la vapeur/des dinosaures

5 *Fam (a long time)* **it's ages** *or* **an a. since I saw him, I haven't seen him for ages** il y a une éternité que je ne l'ai pas vu; **I've been waiting (for) ages** cela fait une éternité que j'attends; **you'll be here for ages yet** tu en as encore pour un bon bout de temps; **it takes them ages to get dressed** ils mettent *ou* ça leur prend une éternité pour s'habiller; **it's expensive, but it lasts for ages** c'est cher, mais ça dure très longtemps

VI (**aged** [eɪdʒd], **ageing, aging** [ˈeɪdʒɪŋ]) vieillir, prendre de l'âge; **to a. ten years** vieillir de dix ans; **he had aged beyond recognition** il avait tellement vieilli qu'on ne le reconnaissait plus

VT 1 *(of clothes etc)* vieillir; **the years had aged him** il avait beaucoup vieilli

2 *Ind etc* *(wine, whisky, wood)* vieillir

▸▸ **a. of consent** = âge légal auquel on peut se marier ou avoir des rapports sexuels; **a. group** tranche *f* ou classe *f* d'âge; **the 15-to-20 a. group** le groupe *ou* la classe des 15-20 ans; **a. limit** limite *f* d'âge;

a. mix éventail *m* d'âges; *Hist* **A. of Reason** siècle des Lumières; **a. ring** *(on tree)* cerne *m*

aged¹ [ˈeɪdʒɪd] **ADJ** *Lit* âgé, vieux, *f* vieille; **an a. man** un vieillard

NPL the a. les personnes *fpl* âgées

▸▸ *Acct* **a. creditor** créancier *m* âgé; *Acct* **a. debt** créance *f* âgée

aged² [eɪdʒd] **ADJ PRED 1** *(of the age of)* **a. twenty** âgé de vingt ans **2** *(older)* **I found him greatly a.** je l'ai trouvé bien vieilli

ageing [ˈeɪdʒɪŋ] **ADJ 1** *(person, population)* vieillissant; *(industry)* déclinant; *(car)* qui prend/prenait de l'âge **2** *(making sb look older) (clothes)* qui vieillissent

N *(of person, wine etc)* vieillissement *m*; *(of person)* sénescence *f*

▸▸ **a. process** processus *m* de vieillissement

ageism [ˈeɪdʒɪz(ə)m] **N** âgisme *m*

ageist [ˈeɪdʒɪst] **ADJ** *(policy etc)* âgiste, qui défavorise les personnes âgées; **or would that be a.?** ou est-ce que ce serait de la discrimination contre les personnes âgées?

ageless [ˈeɪdʒlɪs] **ADJ 1** sans âge; *(young-looking)* toujours jeune **2** *(eternal)* éternel

agency [ˈeɪdʒənsɪ] **N 1** *Com* agence *f*; **to have the sole a. for a firm** être le représentant exclusif d'une maison; **aid a.** association *f* d'aide aux pays en voie de développement; **news** *or* **press a.** agence de presse **2** *(action)* action *f*, opération *f*; **the a. of water** l'action de l'eau; **through sb's a.** par l'entremise *ou* l'intermédiaire de qn **3** *esp Am (government department)* organisme *m* gouvernemental

▸▸ *Com* **a. agreement** accord *m* de représentation; *Com* **a. contract** contrat *m* d'agence; **a. copy** *(from press agency)* dépêche *f* d'agence; **a. fee** frais *mpl* d'agence; *Banking* commission *f* de gestion; **a. work** travail *m* pour une agence

agenda [əˈdʒendə] **N** *(of meeting)* ordre *m* du jour, programme *m*; **question on the a.** question *f* à l'ordre du jour; **what's on the a. for today?** qu'est-ce qu'il y a à l'ordre du jour?; *Fig* qu'est-ce qu'il y a de prévu aujourd'hui?; **to have a full a.** avoir un programme très chargé; *Fig* **drugs are back on the a.** la drogue revient à la une de l'actualité; **the problem of the homeless doesn't come very high on the government's a.** le problème des sans-abri ne figure pas parmi les priorités du gouvernement; **hidden a.** des projets *mpl* secrets

▸▸ **a. setting** fonction *f* d'agenda

Note that the French word **agenda** is a false friend and is never a translation for the English word **agenda**. It means **diary**.

agent [ˈeɪdʒənt] **N 1** *Com* agent *m*, représentant, -ante; *(of actor, writer etc)* agent *m*; **a. for the firm of …** représentant, -ante de la maison …; **sole a.** agent exclusif; *Pol* **(election) a.** directeur, -trice de campagne électorale; **2 (secret) a.** agent *m* secret; **double a.** agent double

3 *(instrument)* agent *m*; **to be the a. of sth** être le moteur *ou* la cause de qch; **the a. of change was the revolution** la révolution était le moteur du changement; **she was the a. of her own downfall** elle a été l'artisan de sa propre perte

4 *(chemical, therapeutic etc)* agent *m*

5 *Comput (software)* logiciel *m* client

▸▸ **a. middleman** agent intermédiaire; **a. provocateur** (agent) provocateur *m*

age-old **ADJ ATTRIB** *(custom etc)* séculaire

agglomerate¹ [əˈglɒmərət] **ADJ** *Fml* aggloméré

N *Geol* aggloméré *m*

agglomerate² [əˈglɒməreɪt] **VT** agglomérer
VI s'agglomérer

agglomeration [əglɒməˈreɪʃən] **N** agglomération f

agglutinate [əˈgluːtɪneɪt] *Physiol, Biol, Ling* **VT** agglutiner
VI s'agglutiner

agglutination [əgluːtɪˈneɪʃən] **N** agglutination f

aggrandize [əˈgrændaɪz] **VT** *(state)* agrandir; *(one's importance, role)* grossir, grandir

aggrandizement [əˈgrændɪzmənt] **N** *(of state etc)* agrandissement m; **they're doing it purely for their own a.** ils ne font cela que pour se grandir aux yeux des autres

aggravate [ˈægrəveɪt] **VT 1** *(mistake, difficulty, situation)* aggraver; *(evil)* empirer; *(wound, quarrel)* envenimer; *(indignation, pain)* augmenter **2** *Fam (annoy, anger)* (person) agacer, exaspérer

aggravating [ˈægrəveɪtɪŋ] **ADJ 1** *(circumstance)* aggravant **2** *Fam (exasperating)* exaspérant, agaçant; **I've had a very a. day** j'ai passé une journée atroce; **it's very a.** c'est vraiment agaçant

aggravation [ægrəˈveɪʃən] **N 1** *(of situation, crime, illness)* aggravation f; *(of wound, quarrel)* envenimement m **2** *Fam (of person)* exaspération f, agacement m; **he does nothing but cause a.** il ne fait qu'embêter le monde; **I don't want to give or cause any more a.** je ne veux plus embêter qui que ce soit **3** *Fam (cause of aggravation)* circonstance f aggravante

aggregate¹ [ˈægrɪgət] **ADJ ATTRIB 1** collectif; *Econ* global, -aux; **for an a. period of three years** pendant trois ans en tout **2** *Bot, Geol* agrégé
N 1 *(total)* ensemble m, total m; **world aggregates** totaux mondiaux; **a complex a. of forces** un assemblage complexe de forces; **in the a.** dans l'ensemble; *esp Sp* **on a.** au total; **Milan won on a.** c'est Milan qui a totalisé le plus de points **2** *Phys* masse f, assemblage m, agrégation f, *Chem, Miner* agrégat m **3** *Constr* granulat m
▸▸ *Fin* **a. amount** montant m global; *Com, Econ* **a. economic activity** ensemble m des activités économiques; *Fin* **a. figure** chiffre m global; *Com* **a. output** production f globale

aggregate² [ˈægrɪgeɪt] **VT 1** *Phys* agréger **2** *(group together) (various categories)* rassembler, regrouper
VI *Phys* s'agréger

aggregation [ægrɪˈgeɪʃən] **N 1** *Phys* agrégation f, agglomération f **2** *Miner* agrégat m

aggression [əˈgreʃən] **N 1** *(attack)* agression f; **an act of a.** une agression; **war of a.** guerre f d'agression **2** *(aggressiveness)* agressivité f

aggressive [əˈgresɪv] **ADJ 1** *(violent etc)* agressif (**towards** envers) **2** *(management, sales policy)* énergique, dynamique; *(chess player)* qui attaque
▸▸ *Psy* **a. impulse** impulsion f agressive

aggressively [əˈgresɪvlɪ] **ADV 1** *(to behave)* d'une manière agressive; *(to say)* d'un ton agressif; *(to look at)* d'un air agressif **2** *(to sell)* énergiquement, avec dynamisme; *(to push sth through)* avec vigueur, vigoureusement; **to play a.** avoir un jeu offensif

aggressiveness [əˈgresɪvnɪs] **N 1** *(violent nature)* agressivité f **2** *(of management style, sales policy)* dynamisme m

aggressor [əˈgresər] **N** agresseur m
▸▸ **a. nation** pays m agresseur

aggrieved [əˈgriːvd] **ADJ** *(expression, tone)* vexé; **to be** *or* **feel a.** se sentir lésé (**at, by** de); *Law* **the a. party** la partie lésée

aggro [ˈægrəʊ] **N** *Br Fam* **1** *(hassle)* enquiquinement m; **it's not worth the a.** ça ne vaut pas le coup de s'enquiquiner; **there's a. with her all the time** on s'accroche tout le temps avec elle; **don't give me any more a.** arrête de m'enquiquiner; **can you do this for once without any a.?** est-ce que pour une fois tu pourrais faire ça sans m'embêter? **2** *(fighting)* bagarre(s) f(pl), grabuge m; **to look for some a.** chercher la bagarre; **there was a bit of a. at the pub last night** il y a eu du grabuge *ou* ça a chauffé au pub hier soir

aghast [əˈgɑːst] **ADJ** horrifié (**at** de); **to stand a.** en rester *ou* en être tout pantois; **they watched a. as ...** horrifiés, ils regardaient ...

agile [ˈædʒaɪl] **ADJ** *(person, mind, limbs, movement)* agile

agilely [ˈædʒaɪllɪ] **ADV** *(to move, jump)* agilement, avec agilité; *(to argue)* adroitement

agility [əˈdʒɪlɪtɪ] **N** agilité f

aging [ˈeɪdʒɪŋ] **ADJ, N** = **ageing**

agio [ˈædʒɪəʊ] **N** *Fin* **1** *(price)* agio m **2** *(business)* commerce m du change

agitate [ˈædʒɪteɪt] **VT** *(liquid, mind)* agiter
VI to a. for/against sth mener une campagne en faveur de/contre qch

agitated [ˈædʒɪteɪtɪd] **ADJ** *(water, person)* agité; **now don't get a.!** allons, ne t'agite pas comme ça!

agitatedly [ˈædʒɪteɪtɪdlɪ] **ADV** *(to act)* de manière agitée; *(to say)* avec agitation, d'une voix agitée

agitation [ædʒɪˈteɪʃən] **N** *(of air, sea, person)* agitation f; *Pol* agitation, troubles mpl; **the a. for a change in the law** la campagne en faveur d'un changement de la loi; **in a state of a.** agité; **they arrived in a state of considerable a.** ils étaient fort agités quand ils sont arrivés

agitator [ˈædʒɪteɪtər] **N 1** *(person)* agitateur, -trice; *(for sth)* contestataire mf **2** *(machine)* agitateur m

agitprop [ˈædʒɪtprɒp] **N** *Pol* agit-prop f inv

aglitter [əˈglɪtər] **ADJ PRED** brillant; **her eyes were a. with mischief** ses yeux pétillaient de malice

aglow [əˈgləʊ] **ADJ PRED** enflammé, embrasé; **the sky was a.** le ciel était embrasé; **to be a. with colour** briller de vives couleurs; *Fig* **face a. with delight** visage rayonnant de joie *ou* tout épanoui; *Fig* **a. with health** resplendissant de santé

AGM [eɪdʒiːˈem] **N** *(abbr* **annual general meeting)** AGA f, AG f

agnostic [ægˈnɒstɪk] **ADJ, N** agnostique mf

agnosticism [ægˈnɒstɪsɪz(ə)m] **N** agnosticisme m

ago [əˈgəʊ] **ADV** **ten years a.** il y a dix ans; **he arrived an hour a.** il est arrivé il y a une heure; *(in this place)* il est là depuis une heure; **a little while a., a short time a.** tout à l'heure; **long a.** il y a longtemps; **long, long a.** il y a très, très longtemps; **not long a.** il n'y a pas longtemps; **not so long a.** il n'y a pas si longtemps; **no longer a. than the last century** pas plus loin qu'au siècle dernier; **how long a. is it since ...?** combien de temps y a-t-il que ...?; **as long a. as 1840** déjà en 1840, dès 1840; **I knew her long a.** je l'ai connue dans le temps; **that was years a.** ça fait des années de cela; **how long a. was that?** il y a combien de temps de cela?

agog [əˈgɒg] **ADV, ADJ to be all a.** (**with excitement**) être agité *ou* en émoi (**about sth** à cause de qch); **everyone was a.** tout le monde était en émoi; **he was a. to hear the latest news** il brûlait d'impatience d'apprendre les dernières nouvelles; **she was a. at**

the news elle était stupéfiée par cette nouvelle

agonize [ˈægənaɪz] **VI 1** *(worry)* se ronger les sangs, se tourmenter; **to a. over the smallest details** se tourmenter à propos du moindre détail; **you shouldn't a. so much about these decisions** tu ne devrais pas te ronger les sangs comme ça à propos de ces décisions **2** *Lit (suffer)* être au supplice *ou* au martyre

> Note that the French verb **agoniser** is a false friend and is never a translation for the English verb **to agonize**. It means **to be dying**.

agonized [ˈægənaɪzd] **ADJ** *(cry)* d'angoisse; **with an a. expression (on her face)** le visage déchiré par l'angoisse; **an a. look** un regard angoissé *ou* plein d'angoisse

agonizing [ˈægənaɪzɪŋ] **ADJ** *(pain, worry, death)* atroce; *(sight)* navrant, angoissant; *(situation, silence, wait)* angoissant; *(decision, choice, dilemma)* pénible
N angoisse f; **to come to a decision without any a. over the consequences** parvenir à une décision sans se tourmenter sur ses conséquences; **why all this a. about something that can't be helped?** pourquoi se tourmenter à propos de quelque chose qu'on ne peut pas changer?

agonizingly [ˈægənaɪzɪŋlɪ] **ADV** *(painful, difficult)* atrocement; **a. slow** d'une lenteur insupportable

agony [ˈægənɪ] **N 1** *(anguish)* angoisse f; **in an a. of fear** saisi d'une peur atroce; **to be in an a. of suspense** attendre avec angoisse; **to be in an a. of doubt** être en proie à un doute terrible; **the a. of homelessness** le calvaire des sans-abri; **the a. of watching a child die** la douleur insoutenable de voir mourir un enfant; **to suffer agonies, to be in a.** être au supplice *ou* au martyre; *Fam* **it's a. walking in these shoes** c'est un véritable supplice de marcher avec ces chaussures; *Fam* **to pile** *or* **put on the a.** forcer la dose; **it was a. to watch them lose** c'était atroce de les voir perdre **2** *Lit (death)* **a.** agonie f
▸▸ *Br* **a. aunt** = responsable mf du courrier du cœur; **a. column** courrier m du cœur

> Note that the French word **agonie** is a false friend. It means **death throes**.

agoraphobia [æg(ə)rəˈfəʊbɪə] **N** *Psy* agoraphobie f; **to have a.** souffrir d'agoraphobie

agoraphobic [æg(ə)rəˈfəʊbɪk] **ADJ, N** *Psy* agoraphobe mf; **to be (an) a.** souffrir d'agoraphobie, être agoraphobe

agrarian [əˈgreərɪən] **ADJ** *(law, measure)* agraire; *(party)* agrarien
N *Pol* agrarien, -ienne

agree [əˈgriː] **VT 1** *(reach agreement on) (price, conditions etc)* s'accorder *ou* se mettre d'accord sur; **to be agreed** *(date)* à convenir; *(price)* à débattre; **(are we) agreed?** (nous sommes) d'accord?; **unless otherwise agreed** sauf arrangement contraire; **to a. to do sth** se mettre d'accord pour faire qch; **as agreed** comme convenu
2 *(concur)* **I a. that's expensive, but ...** c'est cher, j'en conviens, mais ...; **I a. that he was mistaken, but ...** j'admets qu'il s'est trompé, mais ...; **don't you a. that ...?** ne croyez-vous pas que ...?; **everyone agrees that he's the best singer** tout le monde s'accorde à dire que c'est le meilleur chanteur
3 *(consent)* **to a. to do sth** accepter *ou* convenir de faire qch, consentir à faire qch; **to a. to differ** accepter ses différences (**on** *or* **about sth** sur qch); **everyone agrees that ...** tout le monde accepte que ...; **it is generally agreed that ...** il est généralement ad-

mis que …; **he agreed to let us go home** il nous a permis de rentrer à la maison

4 (accept, approve) (statement, plan) accepter; Acct **to a. the accounts** or **the books** faire accorder les livres; **the figures were agreed between the accountants** les chiffres ont été acceptés (d'un commun accord) par les experts-comptables

VI **1** (be of same opinion, concur) être d'accord (**about** sur); (after discussion) se mettre d'accord (**about** sur); **I quite** or **entirely a.** je suis entièrement d'accord; **everyone agrees** tout le monde est d'accord; **I'm afraid I can't a.** (with you, him etc) j'ai bien peur de ne pas être du même avis; **I think it's too expensive, and Peter agrees** je pense que c'est trop cher, et Peter est d'accord avec moi ou est du même avis; **in the end she agreed** (that it was too expensive) elle a fini par l'admettre; **it's expensive, I a., but …** c'est cher, j'en conviens ou je suis d'accord, mais …; **I couldn't a. more!** je suis tout à fait d'accord!

2 (match) (of statements, totals, facts etc) s'accorder, concorder; (of ideas, opinions) concorder, coïncider; Gram s'accorder

3 (accept) consentir (**to** à); **she'll never a.** elle n'acceptera jamais ou ne sera jamais d'accord; **how did he get them to a.?** comment a-t-il fait pour qu'ils acceptent?; Mktg **to a. and counter** approuver et contre-argumenter

▸ **agree on** VT INSEP **1** (of people) (point) être d'accord sur; (after discussion) se mettre d'accord sur; (date) se mettre d'accord sur, convenir de; **we a. on the need for research** nous concordons sur la nécessité de faire des recherches; Law **conditions agreed on** conditions fpl acceptées d'un commun accord **2** (of books, versions etc) (point) s'accorder sur

▸ **agree to** VT INSEP (accept) (condition, proposal) accepter; **to a. to sth being done** accepter que qch se fasse; **they have agreed to your visiting us** ils ont accepté que ou ils veulent bien que tu viennes nous voir

▸ **agree upon** VT INSEP = **agree on**

▸ **agree with** VT INSEP **1** (be of same opinion as) (person) être du même avis que, être d'accord avec; **he entirely agrees with you** il est entièrement d'accord avec vous, il est entièrement de votre avis; **they a. with each other** ils sont du même avis; Fam **I couldn't a. with you more!** tu l'as bien dit!; **to a. with a theory** accepter une théorie; **to a. with a decision** approuver une décision; Fam **I don't a. with all this violence on television** je n'approuve pas toute cette violence à la télé **2** (suit) convenir à, réussir à; (of food) réussir à; **the climate doesn't a. with him** le climat ne lui convient pas ou ne lui réussit pas **3** (coincide with) (what person said) concorder avec, être en accord avec; Gram **the verb agrees with the subject in number** le verbe s'accorde en nombre avec le sujet

agreeable [ə'griːəb(ə)l] ADJ **1** (pleasant) agréable (**to** à); (person) aimable (**to** envers); **if that is a. to you** si cela vous convient (**willing**) **to be a. to sth/to doing sth** consentir à qch/à faire qch, accepter qch/de faire qch; **I am (quite) a.** je veux bien

agreeably [ə'griːəblɪ] ADV agréablement

agreed [ə'griːd] ADJ (price, time etc) convenu INT entendu!, soit!, d'accord!; **it was expensive, a., but …** c'était cher, soit ou d'accord, mais …
  ▸▸ **a. statement** (in the media) déclaration f commune

agreement [ə'griːmənt] N **1** (contract) (between people, countries) accord m (**on, about** sur); **collective (wage) a.** convention f collective (des salaires); **to enter into** or **conclude an a. with sb** passer un accord ou un contrat avec qn; **to have an a. with sb**

avoir conclu ou passé un accord avec qn; **to hold sb to an a.** faire respecter un accord à qn; **our a. was that …** nous avions convenu que …; **to come to an a.** tomber d'accord; **to come to** or **arrive at** or **reach an a. with sb** se mettre d'accord avec qn; (compromise) s'accommoder ou s'arranger avec qn; **to work out an a.** parvenir à un accord; **to sign a legal agreement (to do sth)** s'engager (par) devant notaire (à faire qch); **an a. has been concluded between the two parties** un accord est intervenu entre les deux parties; Com **as per a.** comme (il a été) convenu; **by mutual a.** d'un commun accord; **marketing a.** accord de commercialisation

2 the proposal met with unanimous a. la proposition a été reçue à l'unanimité; **to be in a. with sb** être d'accord avec qn; **to be in a. with a decision** approuver une décision; **there was a. on all sides that a change would be welcome** de toute part on convenait de l'opportunité d'un changement

3 (match), Gram accord m (**with** avec); **to be in a. with** (facts) concorder avec; (rules) être conforme à, être en conformité avec; **a. of adjectives** accord des adjectifs SEE GRAMMAR B9; B38

> Note that the French word **agrément** is a false friend. Its most common meaning is **pleasure**.

agribusiness ['ægrɪbɪznɪs] N agro-alimentaire m

agrichemical [ægrɪ'kemɪk(ə)l] N esp Am = **agrochemical**

agricultural [ægrɪ'kʌltʃər(ə)l] ADJ agricole; **East Anglia is very a.** l'East Anglia est une région très agricole
  ▸▸ **a. college** = école f supérieure d'agriculture et d'agronomie; **a. economy** économie f du secteur agricole; **a. engineer** ingénieur m agronome; **a. labourer** ouvrier, -ière agricole; **a. tourism** tourisme m agricole; **a. worker** ouvrier, -ère agricole

agriculturalist [ægrɪ'kʌltʃərəlɪst] N = **agriculturist**

agriculture ['ægrɪkʌltʃər] N agriculture f

agriculturist [ægrɪ'kʌltʃərɪst] N agriculteur, -trice

agritourism ['ægrɪtʊərɪz(ə)m] N tourisme m agricole

agrochemical [ægrəʊ'kemɪk(ə)l] N Agr produit m agrochimique

agronomic [ægrə'nɒmɪk] ADJ agronomique

agronomist [ə'grɒnəmɪst] N agronome mf

agronomy [ə'grɒnəmɪ] N agronomie f

aground [ə'graʊnd] ADV Naut échoué; **to run a.** (of ship) (s')échouer; Fig (of policy, project etc) échouer

ague ['eɪgjuː] N Med, Arch fièvre f (paludéenne) intermittente

ah [ɑː] INT ah!, ha!; **ah, yes, now you come to mention it** euh, oui, maintenant que tu m'en parles

aha [ə'hɑː] INT ah! ah!

AHEAD [ə'hed] ADV **1** devant; **to send sb a.** envoyer qn en avant; **what lies a. for us?** qu'est-ce qui nous attend?, qu'est-ce que l'avenir nous réserve?; **to get a.** (of person, car etc) prendre de l'avance; Fig (in career) avancer (dans sa carrière); **to draw a.** (of runner, cyclist etc) décoller, prendre de l'avance; Sport **to be a. on points** avoir des points d'avance; **to be a. of sb** (in space) être en avant de qn; **to be a. of the bunch** mener le peloton; **to be a. of one's competitors** devancer ses concurrents; **to go on a.** prendre les devants; **to get a. of sb** dépasser qn; **to be two hours a. of sb** avoir deux heures d'avance sur qn; Sch **he is a. of his**

class il est en avance sur sa classe; **to be a. of one's time** être en avance sur son temps; **to be a. of time** (of person) arriver/avoir fini/ etc avant l'heure; **you've got your best years a. of you** vous avez vos meilleures années devant vous; **to look a.** (in front) regarder devant soi; (to the future) penser à l'avenir; **to plan a.** faire des projets; **you have to plan a. for a big wedding** il faut s'organiser à l'avance pour un grand mariage; **how far a. should one book?** combien de temps à l'avance faut-il retenir?

2 Naut **to be a.** être sur l'avant ou en avant (du navire); **the ship was right a.** le navire était droit devant; **to go a.** aller de l'avant; **full speed a.!** en avant toute!; **wind a.** vent debout; **line a.** en ligne de file, en colonne; **single line a.** ligne de file

ahem [ə'hem] INT hum!

ahoy [ə'hɔɪ] INT Naut **boat/ship a.!** oh(é) du canot/du navire!; **land a.!** terre!

AI [eɪ'aɪ] N **1** Comput (abbr artificial intelligence) IA f **2** Biol abbr artificial insemination **3** Pol abbr Amnesty International

AID [eɪaɪ'diː] N **1** Biol (abbr artificial insemination by donor) IAD f **2** Am Pol abbr Agency for International Development

aid [eɪd] N **1** (help) aide f, assistance f, secours m; (to developing countries, for disaster relief) aide; **with** or **by the a. of sb** avec l'aide de qn; **with** or **by the a. of sth** à l'aide de qch; **to go to sb's a.** aller ou se porter au secours de qn; **collection in a. of …** quête f au profit de …; Fam **what's (all) this in a. of?** c'est en quel honneur?; Fam **what's all this wiring in a. of?** ça sert à quoi tous ces fils?; Fam **what's all this noise in a. of?** qu'est-ce que c'est que tout ce bruit?; **mutual a.** entraide f; **mutual-a. society** société f de secours mutuels ou d'assistance mutuelle; **medical a.** soins mpl médicaux

2 (device) **beauty aids** produits mpl de beauté; **hearing** or **deaf a.** audiophone m; Sch **audio-visual aids** matériel m audiovisuel; **to act as an a. to international understanding** contribuer à la compréhension entre les nations

VT (person, company) aider, venir en aide à; (sb's recovery) contribuer à; (digestion) faciliter; **to a. one another** s'aider les uns les autres, s'entraider; Law **to a. and abet sb** être le complice de qn
  ▸▸ Admin **a. organization** organisme m d'aide; **a. worker** (voluntary) volontaire mf; (paid) employé, -ée d'une organisation humanitaire

AIDA [aɪ'iːdə] Mktg (abbr attention-interest-desire-action) AIDA

aide [eɪd] N aide mf, assistant, -ante; (to president etc) conseiller, -ère

aide-de-camp, pl **aides-de-camp** ['eɪd-də'kɒm] N Mil aide m de camp

aided recall ['eɪdəd] N Mktg notoriété f assistée

aide-mémoire ['eɪdmem'wɑ:r] N aide-mémoire m inv

aiding ['eɪdɪŋ] N Law **a. and abetting** complicité f

AIDS, Aids [eɪdz] N Med sida m; **A.-related** lié au sida
  ▸▸ **A. clinic** clinique f spécialisée dans le traitement du sida; **A. sufferer** sidéen, -enne, malade mf atteint(e) du sida; **the A. virus** le virus du sida

aikido [aɪ'kiːdəʊ] N Sport aïkido m

ail [eɪl] VT Arch **what ails you?** qu'avez-vous?; VI être souffrant

aileron ['eɪlərɒn] N Aviat aileron m

ailing ['eɪlɪŋ] ADJ (person) souffrant; Fig (company, economy) en mauvaise passe;

the **a. state of the economy/country** la mauvaise passe dans laquelle se trouve l'économie/le pays

ailment ['eɪlmənt] N mal m; **childish ailments** maladies mplinfantiles

AIM [eɪaɪ'em] N Br St Exch (abbr **Alternative Investment Market**) = marché m hors-cote rattaché à la Bourse de Londres

aim [eɪm] N **1** (action) action f de viser; **to miss one's a.** (with firearm etc) manquer la cible ou son coup; Fig frapper à faux; **to take a. at sb/sth** viser qn/qch; **to take a.** mettre en joue, viser; **he took careful a.** il visa avec soin; Mil **take a.!** en joue!; **her a. was good** elle visait bien

2 (goal) but m, dessein m, visées fpl; **his a. was to ...** son but était de ..., il avait pour but de ...; **with the a. of doing sth** dans le but ou le dessein de faire qch

VT **1** (stone) lancer (**at** à); (blow) porter, allonger (**at** à)

2 (gun etc) pointer (**at** sur); **to a. a gun at sb/sth** coucher qn/qch en joue avec un fusil, pointer un fusil sur qn; **to a. a camera** cadrer (**at** sur)

3 (remarks, TV programme) destiner (**at** à); **to a. a criticism at sb** adresser une critique à qn; **these measures are aimed at reducing unemployment** ces mesures visent une réduction du chômage

VI **1** (with gun etc) **to a. at sb/sth** viser qn/qch, mettre ou coucher qn/qch en joue; **I aimed at the tyres** j'ai visé (dans) les pneus

2 Fig **to a. at becoming sth, to a. to become sth** aspirer ou viser à devenir qch; **what are you aiming at?** (what do you hope to do?) quel but poursuivez-vous?; (what do you mean?) où voulez-vous en venir?; **to a. high** viser haut; Fam **I a. to go** (intend) j'ai l'intention d'y aller; **we're aiming for a six a.m. start** nous comptons partir à six heures du matin

aiming ['eɪmɪŋ] N Mil pointage m

aimless ['eɪmlɪs] ADJ sans but, sans objet; (violence) gratuit; **an a. sort of life** une vie désœuvrée; **a few a. remarks** quelques remarques en l'air

aimlessly ['eɪmlɪslɪ] ADVsans but, sans objet; **to wander about a.** aller ou errer à l'aventure

aimlessness ['eɪmlɪsnɪs] N **the a. of their existence** leur existence sans but

ain't [eɪnt] Arch, Sl CONTR **1** = am not, is not, are not, see be **2** = have not, see have

AIO [eɪaɪ'əʊ] Mktg (abbr **activities, interests and opinions**) AIO

▸▸ **A. research** étude f AIO

air [eər] N **1** air m; **a change of a. will do me good** un changement d'air me fera du bien; **we need a change of a.** nous avons besoin de changer d'air; **in the open a.** en plein air, au grand air, à ciel ouvert; **high up in the a.** très haut dans le ciel; **in the a.** en l'air, dans les airs; **to throw sth (up) in the a.** lancer qch en l'air; **to fly through the a.** voler ou voltiger en l'air; **war in the a.** guerre f aérienne

2 Fig **I can't live on fresh a.** je ne vis pas de l'air du temps; **to walk on a.** être aux anges; **to be in the a.** (of rumour) circuler; (of idea) être dans l'air; (of project) être encore vague; **everything's up in the a.** (uncertain) rien n'a été décidé pour l'instant; **the date is still up in the a.** la date n'a pas encore été fixée; **our plans are up in the a.** again et voilà nos projets qui retombent à l'eau; Fam **to go up in the a.** (explode), Fig (in anger) exploser; **there's something in the a.** il y a quelque chose dans l'air; Fam **it's all hot a.** c'est du vent; **to melt** ou **vanish into thin a.** s'évanouir, disparaître

3 Naut, Lit (wind) brise f, vent m; **there was**

no a. il n'y avait pas de vent

4 Mil, Aviat (attack, base, defence etc) aérien; **by a.** par avion

5 Radio, TV **to be on the a.** (of person) être à l'antenne; (of programme) être diffusé; (of station) émettre; **we're going on the a. in two minutes** nous sommes à l'antenne dans deux minutes; **you're on (the) a.** vous êtes à l'antenne; **the station goes off the a. at midnight** les programmes finissent à minuit; **to put a play on the a.** mettre une pièce en ondes ou sur les ondes

6 Mus air m

7 (look) air m, mine f, apparence f; **he has an a. about him** il en impose; **to give oneself** or **to put on airs (and graces)** se donner des airs

VT **1** (room) aérer, ventiler; (clothing, bedding, duvet etc) aérer, mettre à l'air

2 Fig (one's opinions, differences) exposer; (one's knowledge) faire parade de, faire étalage de; (one's feelings) donner libre cours à

3 Radio, TV (programme) passer, donner

VI **1** s'aérer

2 Radio, TV (of programme) passer

▸▸ **a. bed** matelas m pneumatique; Br Fam Hum **a. biscuit** (fart) perle f, prout m; **a. brake** frein m pneumatique; **a. broker** courtier m de l'air; **a. cargo** fret m aérien; **a. carrier** transporteur m aérien; Br Mil **a. commodore** ≃ général m de brigade aérienne, Can ≃ brigadier-général m, pl brigadiers-généraux; **a. compressor** compresseur m d'air; Mil, Aviat **a. cover** couverture f aérienne; Tech **a. duct** conduite f d'air, amenée f d'air; **a. fare** tarif m aérien; **a. filter** ≃ filtre m à air; **A. Force** Armée f de l'air, Aviation f; **a. freshener** désodorisant m (pour la maison); Tech **a. gauge** micromètre m pneumatique; **a. gun** fusil m à air comprimé; **a. hostess** hôtesse f de l'air; **a. inclusive tour** voyage m à forfait (par avion) **a. injection** injection f d'air; **a. intake** prise f d'air; Aviat **a. link** liaison f aérienne; Aviat **a. mile** mille m marin; Hist **A. Ministry** ≃ ministère m de l'Air; Tech **a. passage** conduit m aérifère; Bot **a. plant** plante f aéricole, (plante) épiphyte m; **a. pocket** Met, Aviat (affecting plane) trou m d'air; Tech (in pipe) poche f d'air; Ecol **a. pollution** pollution f atmosphérique; Mil, Aviat **a. power** puissance f aérienne; Aviat **a. rage** = comportement m agressif de certains passagers d'avion; Mil **a. raid** attaque f aérienne, raid m aérien; Tech **a. rifle** carabine f à air comprimé; Aviat **a. route** route f aérienne; Aviat **a. service** liaison aérienne; **a. show** Com (exhibition) salon m de l'aéronautique; Aviat (display) meeting m aérien; **a. strikes** frappes fplaériennes; Mil **a. supremacy** suprématie f aérienne; Met **a. temperature** température f ambiante; Aviat **a. terminal** aérogare f; Aviat **a. ticket** billet m d'avion; Aviat **a. traffic** circulation f aérienne, trafic m aérien; Aviat **a. transport** transport m aérien ou par avion; Aviat **a. travel** voyages en avion; Tech **a. valve** soupape f (pour l'air); **a. vent** aérateur m, buse f de ventilation, diffuseur m; Com **a. waybill** lettre f de transport aérien, connaissement m aérien

airbag ['eəbæg] N Air Bag® m, sac m gonflable

airborne ['eəbɔːn] ADJ **1** (particles, seeds etc) en suspension dans l'air; (disease) présent dans l'air **2** (aircraft) en vol; (balloon) en l'air; **to become a.** (of aircraft) décoller; **once we are a.** une fois que nous aurons décollé **3** Mil (troops, unit) aéroporté **4** Aviat (equipment, radar) de bord

▸▸ Mil **a. attack** attaque f exécutée par des troupes aéroportées, assaut m vertical

airbrush ['eəbrʌʃ] Art, Phot N aérographe m, pistolet m vaporisateur

VT retoucher à l'aérographe

▸ **airbrush in** VT SEP Art, Phot ajouter à l'aérographe

▸ **airbrush out** VT SEP Art, Phot effacer à l'aérographe

airbrushing ['eəbrʌʃɪŋ] N Art, Phot peinture f ou retouchage m à l'aérographe

air-bubble N bulle f d'air

airburst ['eəbɜːst] N explosion f (en plein ciel)

Airbus® ['eəbʌs] N aérobus m, Airbus® m

aircon ['eəkɒn] N Fam (abbr **air-conditioning**) clim f

air-conditioned [-kən'dɪʃənd] ADJ climatisé, à air conditionné

air-conditioning [-kən'dɪʃənɪŋ] N climatisation f, Fam clim f

air-cooled [-kuːld] ADJ refroidi par air

▸▸ Aut **a. engine** moteur m à refroidissement par air

air-cooling N refroidissement m par air

aircraft ['eəkrɑːft] N INV avion m

▸▸ Naut, Mil **a. carrier** porte-avions m inv; Aviat **a. engineering** ingénierie f aéronautique; **a. factory** usine f d'aviation; **a. grounding** interdiction f de vol; **a. identification code** code m d'identification d'avion; **a. manufacturer** constructeur m d'avions, avionneur m

aircraftman, pl **aircraftmen** ['eəkrɑːftmən] N Br = soldat m de la Royal Air Force; **leading a.** = caporal m de la Royal Air Force

aircraftwoman, pl **aircraftwomen** ['eəkrɑːftwʊmən, -wɪmɪn] N Br = femme f soldat de la Women's Royal Air Force; **leading a.** = femme f caporal de la Women's Royal Air Force

aircrew ['eəkruː] N Aviat équipage m

airdrome ['eədrəʊm] N Am aérodrome m

airdrop ['eədrɒp] N Aviat largage m (de charges)

Airedale ['eədeɪl] N (chien m) airedale m

airer ['eərər] N (for clothes) séchoir m

airfield ['eəfiːld] N champ m ou terrain m d'aviation, aérodrome m

airflow ['eəfləʊ] N Tech écoulement m d'air; **smooth/turbulent a.** écoulement régulier/turbulent

▸▸ Am Aut **a. body** carrosserie f aérodynamique; **a. meter** débitmètre m d'air

airfoil ['eəfɔɪl] N Am = aerofoil

airframe ['eəfreɪm] N Aviat cellule f d'avion, fuselage m

air-freight N fret m aérien; **send it by a.** envoyez-le par avion ou par air

VT expédier par fret aérien

▸▸ **a. consignment note** récépissé m aérien; **a. consolidator** groupeur m de fret aérien; **a. container** conteneur-avion m, pl conteneurs-avions; **a. forwarding agent** groupeur de fret aérien; **a. services** messageries fpl aériennes

air/fuel mixture N mélange m air/carburant

airhead ['eəhed] N Sl tête f de linotte, tête en l'air

airhole ['eəhəʊl] N trou m de ventilation ou d'aération

airily ['eərɪlɪ] ADV avec désinvolture; (to say) d'un ton dégagé ou désinvolte

airiness ['eərɪnɪs] N **1** (of building, flat) caractère m spacieux **2** (casualness) désinvolture f

airing ['eərɪŋ] N **1** (of room etc) ventilation f, aération f; **give the room a good a.** aère bien la pièce

2 (of clothes) **give the clothes an a. outside** mets ces habits à l'air dehors

3 (of new car etc) présentation f; **they gave**

the project/the matter an a. ils ont eu une première discussion à propos du projet/de la question; **to give one's grievances/feelings an a.** exposer ses griefs/ses sentiments
4 *Radio, TV (of programme)* diffusion *f*, transmission *f*
5 *Arch (walk)* (petite) promenade *f*; **to take an a.** prendre l'air
▸▸ **a. cupboard** = placard *m* chauffé où l'on fait sécher le linge

air-kiss vi = faire semblant de faire la bise

airless ['eəlɪs] ADJ **1** *(room, house etc)* privé d'air, qui sent le renfermé **2** *Tech* sans air **3** *(evening etc)* sans air, lourd

airlessness ['eəlɪsnɪs] N **1** *(of room)* manque *m* d'air *ou* d'aération **2** *(of weather)* lourdeur *f*

airlift ['eəlɪft] N pont *m* aérien
vT *(supplies)* transporter par avion; **to a. in/out** *(supplies)* amener/emporter par avion; *(refugees)* amener/évacuer par avion

airline ['eəlaɪn] N **1** *Aviat* ligne *f* ou compagnie *f* aérienne, compagnie d'aviation; **to be an a. pilot** être pilote de ligne **2** *(of diver)* voie *f* d'air
▸▸ *Aviat* **a. club** = programme *m* de fidélisation de la clientèle d'une compagnie aérienne; *Aviat, Com* **a. operator** compagnie aérienne; *Aviat* **a. passenger** passager, -ère des compagnies aériennes; **a. ticket** billet *m* d'avion

airliner ['eəlaɪnər] N avion *m* de ligne

airlock ['eəlɒk] N **1** *Constr (of caisson)* écluse *f* ou sas *m* pneumatique ou à air; *Naut, Astronaut* sas **2** *(in pipe)* poche *f* d'air

airmail ['eəmeɪl] ADJ *(paper, envelope)* avion
ADV par avion
N *(service)* poste *f* aérienne, service *m* postal aérien; *(letters etc)* courrier *m* par avion; **by a.** par avion
vT *(letter etc)* envoyer par avion
▸▸ **a. edition** = édition *f* imprimée sur papier très fin; **a. letter** *(letter sent by airmail)* lettre *f* par avion; *(bought at post office)* aérogramme *m*; **a. paper** papier *m* avion; **a. sticker** étiquette *f* par avion

airman, *pl* **airmen** ['eəmən] N **1** *(in general)* aviateur *m* **2** *Am Mil, Aviat* = soldat *m* de la United States Air Force
▸▸ *Am Mil, Aviat* **a. basic** = soldat *m* de la United States Air Force

airpass ['eəpɑːs] N carte *f* d'abonnement de transport aérien

airplane ['eəpleɪn] N *esp Am* avion *m*

airplay ['eəpleɪ] N *Radio* diffusion *f*; **to get** *or* **receive a.** *(of record etc)* passer sur les ondes; **that record is getting a lot of a.** on entend souvent ce disque à la radio

airport ['eəpɔːt] N *Aviat* aéroport *m*; **Geneva A.** l'aéroport de Genève
▸▸ *Mktg* **a. advertising** publicité *f* dans les aéroports; **a. apron** aire *f* de stationnement (des avions); **a. of departure** aéroport de départ; **a. of destination** aéroport de destination; **a. hotel** hôtel *m* d'aéroport; *Fin* **a. landing tax** taxe *f* d'atterrissage; **a. lounge** hall *m* d'aéroport; **a. service charge** taxe d'aéroport; **a. shop** boutique *f* d'aéroport; *Fin* **a. tax** taxe d'aéroport; **a. taxi** taxi *m* desservant l'aéroport

airprox ['eəprɒks] N quasi-collision *f* aérienne

airscrew ['eəskruː] N *Aviat Old-fashioned* hélice *f*

air-sea rescue N sauvetage *m* aéro-maritime, sauvetage aérien en mer

airship ['eəʃɪp] N dirigeable *m*

airsick ['eəsɪk] ADJ **to be a.** avoir le mal de l'air

airsickness ['eəsɪknɪs] N mal *m* de l'air

airspace ['eəspeɪs] N *Aviat* espace *m* aérien

airspeed ['eəspiːd] N *Aviat (of plane)* vitesse *f*

airstream ['eəstriːm] N courant *m* d'air

airstrike ['eəstraɪk] N *Mil* raid *m* aérien, attaque *f* aérienne

airstrip ['eəstrɪp] N *Aviat* bande *f* ou piste *f* d'atterrissage

airtight ['eətaɪt] ADJ *(seal)* hermétique; *(container etc)* hermétique, étanche (à l'air)

airtime ['eətaɪm] N **1** *Radio, TV (length of programme)* temps *m* d'antenne; **the subject didn't get much a.** *(during programme)* on n'a pas consacré beaucoup de temps au sujet pendant l'émission **2** *Radio, TV (starting time)* heure *f* où commence l'émission; **five minutes to a.** on est à l'antenne dans cinq minutes **3** *Tel* temps *m* de communication
▸▸ *Tel* **a. provider** société *f* de téléphonie mobile

air-to-air ADJ *Mil (missile etc)* air-air *inv*

air-to-ground ADJ *Mil (missile etc)* air-sol *inv*, air-terre *inv*

air-to-surface ADJ *(missile etc) Mil* air-sol *inv*, *Naut* air-surface *inv*

airwaves ['eəweɪvz] NPL *Radio, TV* ondes *fpl*, ondes hertziennes; **the best DJ on the a.** le meilleur DJ sur les ondes *ou* ondes hertziennes

airway ['eəweɪ] N **1** *Aviat (route)* route *f* ou ligne *f* ou voie *f* aérienne **2** *Med* bronches *fpl* **3** *Am Radio, TV* chaîne *f*
▸▸ *Aviat* **a. marker** balise *f* d'entrée de piste

airwoman, *pl* **airwomen** ['eəwʊmən, -wɪmɪn] N aviatrice *f*

airworthiness ['eəwɜːðɪnɪs] N *Aviat* tenue *f* en l'air, navigabilité *f*; **certificate of a.** certificat *m* de navigabilité

airworthy ['eəwɜːðɪ] ADJ *(aircraft)* en état de prendre l'air, en bon état de vol ou de navigabilité; *(certified)* muni d'un certificat de navigabilité; **to be a.** tenir l'air

airy ['eərɪ] ADJ **1** *(room, house)* clair et spacieux **2** *(dress, material)* léger; **the cake was light and a.** le gâteau était très léger **3** *(person, attitude)* insouciant, désinvolte **4** *(promises)* vain, illusoire

airy-fairy ADJ *Fam (person, idea)* farfelu

aisle [aɪl] N **1** *(between seats)* passage *m*; *(in plane)* couloir *m*; *(in bus etc)* couloir central; *(at cinema, theatre, in supermarket)* allée *f*; **he had them rolling in the aisles** il les faisait mourir de rire **2** *(in church)* allée *f*, *Fig* **to walk up the a.** se marier (à l'église)
▸▸ *Mktg* **a. end display** tête *f* de gondole; **a. seat** *(in train, plane)* siège *m* côté couloir

aitch [eɪtʃ] N *(letter)* h *m*; **to drop one's aitches** ne pas prononcer (correctement) les h

ajar [ə'dʒɑːr] ADV, ADJ PRED *(door, window)* entrouvert, entrebâillé; **to swing a.** s'entrouvrir, s'entrebâiller

aka [eɪkeɪ'eɪ] ADV *(abbr* also known as*)* alias

akimbo [ə'kɪmbəʊ] ADV **with arms a.** les (deux) poings sur les hanches

akin [ə'kɪn] ADJ **a. to sb/sth** apparenté à qn/qch; **feeling a. to fear** sentiment voisin de la peur; **this is a. to treachery** cela s'apparente à de la traîtrise

alabaster ['æləbɑːstər, -bɑː-] N albâtre *m*
ADJ ATTRIB **1** *(figurine, vase etc)* en albâtre **2** *Fig (complexion, hands etc)* d'albâtre

à la carte [ælɑː'kɑːt] ADJ, ADV à la carte

alacrity [ə'lækrɪtɪ] N empressement *m*, promptitude *f*; **he accepted with a.** il a accepté avec enthousiasme, il s'est empressé d'accepter

Aladdin [ə'lædɪn] N Aladin *m*; **the shop is an A.'s cave** *(full of wonderful things)* cette bou-

tique est une véritable caverne d'Ali Baba

alarm [ə'lɑːm] N **1** *(signal)* alarme *f*, alerte *f*, **false a.** fausse alerte; **to raise** *or* **give the a.** donner l'éveil ou l'alerte *ou* l'alarme
2 *(fright, anxiety)* alarme *f*, frayeur *f*; **there's no cause for a.** il n'y a aucune raison de s'alarmer; **he hid in a.** effrayé, il s'est caché
3 *(warning device)* avertisseur *m*, alarme *f*, *Fig* **to set (the) a. bells ringing** déclencher l'alerte; *(give rise to suspicion)* mettre la puce à l'oreille de qn
4 *(on clock)* sonnerie *f*; *(clock)* réveil *m*, réveille-matin *m inv*; **to set the a. for six o'clock** mettre le réveil à six heures; **the a. went off at six o'clock** le réveil a sonné à six heures
5 *(of bird etc)* cri *m* d'alarme
vT *(frighten)* effrayer; **to be alarmed at sth** s'alarmer *ou* s'effrayer de qch, être alarmé de qch; **don't be alarmed** ne vous effrayez pas; **there's no need to feel alarmed** inutile de s'alarmer; **the parents looked alarmed** les parents semblaient très inquiets
▸▸ **a. call** *(to wake sleeper)* réveil téléphonique; *(in hotel)* appel *m* de réveil; **a. clock** réveil, réveille-matin; **a. signal** signal *m* d'alarme

alarming [ə'lɑːmɪŋ] ADJ *(news etc)* alarmant, inquiétant

alarmingly [ə'lɑːmɪŋlɪ] ADV d'une manière alarmante *ou* très inquiétante; **the shots were coming a. close** les tirs se rapprochaient dangereusement; **to develop a. fast** se développer à une vitesse alarmante

alarmist [ə'lɑːmɪst] ADJ, N alarmiste *mf*; **don't be such an a.** ne sois pas aussi alarmiste

Alas *abbr* Alaska

alas [ə'læs] INT *Lit, Fml* hélas!

Alaska [ə'læskə] N Alaska *m*; *Culin* **baked A.** omelette *f* norvégienne

alb [ælb] N *Rel* aube *f*

Albania [æl'beɪnɪə] N Albanie *f*

Albanian [æl'beɪnɪən] ADJ albanais
N **1** Albanais, -aise **2** *Ling* albanais *m*

albatross ['ælbətrɒs] N *(bird)* albatros *m*; *Fig* **to be an a. around sb's neck** être un boulet pour qn; **this issue has become an a. around the government's neck** ce problème est devenu un gros handicap pour le gouvernement

albeit [ɔːl'biːɪt] CONJ quoique, bien que; **a brilliant, a. slipshod, writer** un écrivain brillant, bien que négligent

albinism ['ælbɪnɪz(ə)m] N *Biol* albinisme *m*

albino, *pl* **albinos** [æl'biːnəʊ, -əʊz] ADJ *(person)* albinos
N albinos *mf*; **a. rabbit** lapin *m* albinos *ou* russe

Albion ['ælbɪən] N *Lit (England)* Albion *f*, **perfidious A.** la perfide Albion

album ['ælbəm] N **1** *(for photos, comic book)* album *m* **2** *(record)* album *m*

albumen ['ælbjʊmɪn, æl'bjuːmɪn] N **1** *(in egg)* albumen *m* **2** *(in blood)* albumine *f*

albumin ['ælbjʊmɪn, æl'bjuːmɪn] N *Chem* albumine *f*

alchemist ['ælkəmɪst] N alchimiste *m*

alchemy ['ælkəmɪ] N alchimie *f*

alcohol ['ælkəhɒl] N *(drink), Chem* alcool *m*; **I never touch a.** je ne bois jamais d'alcool; **low in a.** à faible teneur en alcool; **to have an a. problem** boire trop
▸▸ **a. abuse** abus *m* d'alcool; **a. content** teneur *f* en alcool

alcoholic [ælkə'hɒlɪk] ADJ alcoolique; **a. drink** boisson *f* alcoolisée
N *(person)* alcoolique *mf*
▸▸ **Alcoholics Anonymous** Alcooliques *mpl* anonymes

alcoholism ['ælkəhɒlɪz(ə)m] N alcoolisme m

alcopop ['ælkəʊpɒp] N prémix m

alcove ['ælkəʊv] N alcôve f; (in wall) niche f; **dining a.** coin m des repas, coin salle à manger

aldehyde ['ældɪhaɪd] N Chem aldéhyde m

alder ['ɔːldər] N (tree) aune m, aulne m

alderman, pl **aldermen** ['ɔːldəmən] N Am (for city) conseiller m municipal; Br (for county) conseiller général

Alderney ['ɔːldənɪ] N Aurigny m

ale [eɪl] N bière f anglaise (légère), ale f; **pale/brown a.** bière blonde/brune

Alec(k) ['ælɪk] N Fam **a smart A.** un(e) je-sais-tout; **I've had enough of his smart A. remarks** j'en ai assez de ses remarques désobligeantes; **who's the smart A. who forgot to switch it off?** quel est le malin qui a oublié de l'éteindre?

alehouse ['eɪlhaʊs] N Arch taverne f, cabaret m

alert [ə'lɜːt] N alerte f; **to be on the a.** être sur le qui-vive, être en état d'alerte; **police were on the a. for an escaped prisoner** la police était en état d'alerte à la suite de l'évasion d'un prisonnier; **to be on the a. against an attack** veiller en prévision d'une attaque; **the navy has been put on full a.** l'alerte générale a été déclarée dans la marine; **they're always on the a. for interesting stories** ils sont toujours à l'affût d'histoires intéressantes

ADJ 1 (temporarily) alerté, vigilant, éveillé; **to be a. to a danger** être conscient d'un danger **2** (naturally) actif, vif, preste; **a. mind** esprit m vif ou éveillé

VT alerter; **troops have been alerted** les troupes sont en état d'alerte; **to a. sb to a danger** avertir qn d'un danger; **a noise alerted her to the presence of an intruder** un bruit l'avertit de la présence d'un intrus

alertness [ə'lɜːtnɪs] N **1** (of sentry etc) vigilance f **2** (of mind) vivacité f

A-level N (in England, Wales and Northern Ireland) **A-levels, A. exams** ≃ baccalauréat m; **he teaches A. physics** ≃ il est professeur de physique en terminale; **he has an A. in maths** il a un diplôme de maths niveau bac; **to take one's A-levels** ≃ passer son bac

> ## A-levels
> Cet examen, qui ouvre l'accès aux études supérieures en Grande-Bretagne, est beaucoup plus spécialisé que le baccalauréat français; il ne comprend que deux ou trois matières (exceptionnellement quatre). D'autre part, les mentions sont très importantes pour pouvoir choisir l'université où l'on souhaite faire ses études. En Écosse l'examen équivalent aux **A-levels** s'appelle le "Higher" ou "Higher Grade".

Alexander [ælɪg'zɑːndər] N
> ▸ ▸ **A. the Great** Alexandre le Grand; Med **A. technique** technique f Alexander (visant à limiter les tensions exercées sur le corps en travaillant sur le maintien et les mouvements)

Alexandria [ælɪg'zɑːndrɪə] N Alexandrie f

alexandrine [ælɪg'zɑːndraɪn] ADJ, N Liter alexandrin m

alfalfa [æl'fælfə] N (plant) luzerne f

alfresco [æl'freskəʊ] ADJ, ADV en plein air; **a. meal** repas m en plein air

alga, pl **algae** ['ælgə, 'ældʒiː] N Bot algue f

algal ['ælg(ə)l] ADJ des algues

algebra ['ældʒɪbrə] N algèbre f

algebraic(al) [ældʒɪ'breɪɪk, -ɪk(ə)l] ADJ (sign, calculation etc) algébrique

Algeria [æl'dʒɪərɪə] N Algérie f

Algerian [æl'dʒɪərɪən] ADJ algérien
> N Algérien, -ienne

Algiers [æl'dʒɪəz] N Alger m

ALGOL ['ælgɒl] N Comput algol m

algorithm ['ælgərɪð(ə)m] N algorithme m

algorithmic [ælgə'rɪðmɪk] ADJ algorithmique

alias ['eɪlɪəs] ADV alias
> N (pl **aliases** ['eɪlɪəsɪz]) nom m d'emprunt, faux nom; Comput alias m

aliasing ['eɪlɪəsɪŋ] N Comput aliassage m, crénelage m

alibi ['ælɪbaɪ] N Law alibi m; **to produce an a.** produire ou fournir un alibi; **to establish an a.** prouver ou établir son alibi; **they're using the economic crisis as an a. for their own incompetence** ils se servent de la crise économique pour déguiser leur propre incompétence
> VT trouver un alibi pour

alien ['eɪlɪən] N **1** Law étranger, -ère (non naturalisé, -ée); **illegal a.** clandestin, -ine **2** (from outer space) extra(-)terrestre mf, pl extra(-)terrestres
> ADJ **1** Law étranger **2** (from outer space) extra(-)terrestre **3** Fig (foreign) (land, territory, concept) étranger; **a. to** contraire à; **an action entirely a. to her nature** une action entièrement contraire à sa nature; **such thoughts are a. to her** de telles pensées lui sont étrangères

alienable ['eɪlɪənəb(ə)l] ADJ Law (property) aliénable

alienate ['eɪlɪəneɪt] VT **1** (supporters, electorate, readers) éloigner; **she has alienated many of her colleagues** elle s'est aliéné beaucoup de ses collègues; **to a. sb from his friends** détacher ou éloigner qn de ses amis; **to a. oneself from sb** se détacher ou s'éloigner de qn; **these young people feel alienated from society** ces jeunes gens se sentent en marge de la société; **to be or feel alienated by sb's manner** être rebuté par les manières de qn **2** Law (property etc) aliéner **3** Fin (money) détourner

alienation [eɪlɪə'neɪʃən] N **1** désaffection f **2** Law (of property) aliénation f **3** Psy mental a. aliénation f mentale
> ▸ ▸ Theat **a. effect** distanciation f

alight¹ [ə'laɪt] ADJ PRED en feu; **to keep a flame/fire a.** maintenir une flamme/un feu; **to catch a.** prendre feu; **to set sth a.** mettre le feu à qch; Fig **his face was a. with joy** son visage resplendissait de joie; Fig Fam **to set the world a.** faire sensation

alight² VI **1** Fml (from train, car etc) descendre (**from** de) **2** (of bird, eyes, glance) se poser (**on** sur)

align [ə'laɪn] VT **1** (objects, soldiers etc) aligner, mettre en ligne; (paper in printer) mettre bien droit; Comput, Typ (characters, graphics) aligner, cadrer; Tech (axes) faire coïncider; Aut (wheels) régler le parallélisme de; **to a. sth with sth** aligner qch avec qch; Aut **the wheels were badly aligned** les roues n'étaient pas centrées **2** Fin (of country) (one's currency) aligner (**on** sur) **3** **to a. oneself with sb** s'aligner sur qn; **they aligned themselves against the President/this policy** ils se sont ligués contre le président/cette politique
> VI **1** s'aligner, se mettre en ligne; Fig **to a. with sb** s'aligner sur qn **2** (of shafts etc) coïncider

alignment [ə'laɪnmənt] N **1** alignement m; (of railway etc) tracé m; Comput, Typ (of characters, graphics) alignement, cadrage m; Aut (of wheels) réglage m; **out of a.** désaligné; Constr hors d'œuvre; Typ sortant; **in a.** aligné; **to bring sth into a. with the new re-**

gulations aligner qch sur la nouvelle réglementation; **this is not in a. with current practice** ceci n'est pas conforme à ce qui se pratique actuellement **2** Fin **a. of currencies** alignement m des monnaies

alike [ə'laɪk] ADJ PRED semblable, pareil; **they are very much a.** ils se ressemblent beaucoup; **no two are a.** il n'y en a pas deux de pareils; **you are all a.!** vous êtes tous les mêmes!; **they're very a. in dress/their tastes** leur façon de s'habiller/leurs goûts se ressemble(nt) beaucoup
> ADV (to dress, treat etc) de la même façon ou manière, pareillement, de même; **we don't think a.** nous ne sommes pas d'accord, nous n'avons pas le même point de vue; **every day, summer and winter a.** tous les jours, été comme hiver; **old and young a.** les vieux comme les jeunes; **the problem affects all of us a.** ce problème nous touche tous sans exception

aliment ['ælɪmənt] N Scot Law = alimony

alimentary [ælɪ'mentərɪ] ADJ alimentaire
> ▸ ▸ Anat **a. canal** tube m digestif

alimony ['ælɪmənɪ] N Law pension f alimentaire

A-list ADJ (star, celebrity, guest) très en vue; **all the A. stars were at the première** toutes les grandes stars étaient à la première

alive [ə'laɪv] ADJ PRED **1** (person, animal, plant) **to be (still) a.** être (encore) vivant ou en vie, vivre (encore); **to keep sb a.** maintenir qn en vie; **to come a. again** (after apparent death) revenir à la vie; (after real death) ressusciter; **to stay a.** survivre; **to be burnt a.** être brûlé vif; **to be buried a.** être enterré vivant; **to be a. and well** bien se porter; **no one got out of the building a.** personne n'est sorti vivant de l'immeuble; **Mr Evans was last seen a. on 21 June** c'est le 21 juin qu'on a vu M. Evans vivant pour la dernière fois; Fam **to be a. and kicking** être plein de vie; **it feels good to be a.!** il fait bon vivre!; **dead or a.** mort ou vif; **when your father was a.** du vivant de votre père; **no one a.** personne au monde; **the oldest man a.** l'homme le plus vieux au monde
> **2** (memory, hope, custom) **in parts of the country her memory/this custom is still very much a.** dans certaines régions, son souvenir/cette coutume est encore très vivant(e); **to keep sth a.** (memory, custom) garder ou entretenir qch; (conversation) entretenir qch, ne pas laisser languir qch; **to keep a religion a.** entretenir la pratique d'une religion
> **3** (aware) **to be fully a. to sth** avoir pleine conscience de qch; **I am a. to the fact that ...** je n'ignore pas que ...; **she's very a. to the latest developments in the industry** elle est très au courant des nouveaux développements dans le secteur; **she's very a. to the world around her** elle est très ouverte au monde qui l'entoure
> **4** (full of vitality) vif, éveillé; **I've never felt so a.** je ne me suis jamais senti aussi plein de vie; **he came a. when someone mentioned food** il s'est réveillé quand quelqu'un a parlé de manger; **the evening came a. when the musicians arrived** la soirée s'est animée à l'arrivée des musiciens; **look a.!** remuez-vous (donc)!
> **5 the cheese was a. with maggots** le fromage grouillait de vers; **the street was a. with people** la rue fourmillait ou grouillait de monde
> **6** esp Am Elec **the wire was a.** le fil était sous tension

alkali ['ælkəlaɪ] N Chem alcali m
> ▸ ▸ **a. metal** métal m alcalin

alkaline [ˈælkəlaɪn] ADJ *Chem* alcalin

alkaloid [ˈælkəlɔɪd] ADJ, N *Chem* alcaloïde *m*

alky [ˈælkɪ] N *Fam* **1** (*abbr* **alcoholic**) alcolo *mf* **2** *Am* (*abbr* **alcohol**) gnôle *f*

ALL [ɔːl] VOIR GRAMMAIRE A36; B15–16 ADJ tout, *f* toute, *mpl* tous, *fpl* toutes; **a. France** toute la France; **a. men** tous les hommes; **a. the others** tous les autres; **a. four of them** tous les quatre; **to be a. things to a. men** être tout à tous; **to be a. heart** être plein de bonnes intentions; **he's a. man, isn't he?** quel homme, hein?; **a. day** toute la journée; **a. her life** toute sa vie; **(with) a. my love** (*at end of letter*) bien affectueusement; **the people/books had a. disappeared** les gens/les livres avaient tous disparus; **they are a. smokers** ce sont tous des fumeurs; **a. the way** (*of journey*) tout le long du chemin; (*of course of action*) jusqu'au bout; **he leaves the door open a. the time** il laisse tout le temps la porte ouverte; **people have been phoning a. the time you've been out** le téléphone n'a pas arrêté de sonner pendant que tu étais sorti; **I've been here a. the time** je n'ai pas bougé d'ici; **is that a. the luggage you're taking?** c'est tout ce que vous emportez comme bagages?; **for a. his wealth** en dépit de *ou* malgré sa fortune; **with a. speed** au plus vite, à toute vitesse; **by a. accounts they've had a most successful year** tout semble indiquer qu'ils ont eu une excellente année; **at a. hours** à toute heure; **in a. sorts of ways** de toutes les façons; **in a. honesty/sincerity** pour être honnête/sincère; **in a. frankness** en toute franchise; *Fml* **with a. due care (and attention)/dispatch** avec tout le soin requis/toute la promptitude requise; *Fml* **with a. due respect** avec tout le respect qui vous est dû; **what's a. that noise?** qu'est-ce que c'est que tout ce bruit?; **a. that's nonsense** tout ça, c'est des bêtises; **for a. that they say he's a genius, I think …** ils ont beau dire que c'est un génie, moi, je pense …; *Fam* **and a. that** et tout cela, et tout le reste; **you're not as ill as a. that** vous n'êtes pas aussi *ou* si malade que ça; **it's not a. that pleasant** ce n'est pas tellement agréable; **of a. the stupid things to say/do!** de toutes les idioties possibles!; **of a. times to phone!** il a bien choisi son heure pour téléphoner!; **you, of a. people, should know what I mean** toi au moins tu devrais savoir ce que je veux dire

PRON **1** (*with pl*) tous, *f* toutes; **a. are agreed that …** tous sont d'accord que …; **a. of us** nous tous; **we a. love him** nous l'aimons tous; **a. of them are blue, they are a. blue** ils sont tous bleus, tous sont bleus; **a. together** tous à la fois, tous ensemble; **a. but he** *or* **him** tous sauf *ou* excepté lui; **a. and sundry** tous sans exception

2 (*everything*) tout; **I want a. of it** je le veux en entier; **almost a.** presque tout; **I did a. I could** j'ai fait tout ce que j'ai pu; *Prov* **a. that glitters is not gold** tout ce qui brille n'est pas de l'or; *Iron Hum* **a. is forgiven** tout est pardonné; **I know it a.** (*of news etc*) je sais tout cela; (*of poem etc*) je le sais en entier; **best/worst of a., …** le mieux/pire, c'est que …; **most of a.** surtout, en particulier; **take it a.** prenez le tout; **in the middle of it a.** au milieu de tout cela; **for a. he may say** en dépit de ce qu'il dit, quoi qu'il en dise; **that's a.** c'est tout, voilà tout; **is that a.?** c'est tout?; *Iron* **c'est que ça?** if **that's a.** si c'est ne'est que cela; **that's a. well and good** tout cela est bien joli; **a.'s well** tout va bien; **a.'s well that ends well** tout est bien qui finit bien; **I think that's about a.** je crois que c'est tout; **a. I said was 'good morning'** tout ce que j'ai dit a été 'bonjour'; **that's a. they ever do, complain** c'est tout ce qu'ils savent faire, se

plaindre; **it was a. I could do not to laugh** j'avais le plus grand mal à ne pas rire; **when** *or* **after a.'s said and done** en fin de compte; *Fam* **he must be a. of sixty** il doit avoir au moins soixante ans; *Fam Iron* **it cost a. of £2** ça a coûté 2 livres et pas moins

3 once and for a. une fois pour toutes; **for a. I know** autant que je sache; **for a. I care** pour (tout) ce que cela me fait; **it's a. the same to me** ça m'est égal; **thirty men in a.** trente hommes en tout; **above a.** surtout; **most of a.** surtout, le plus; **when I was busiest of a.** au moment où j'étais le plus occupé

4 *Sl* (*everything else*) **and a.** et (tout) le reste; **I know he's been very kind and a., but …** je sais bien qu'il a été très gentil et tout, mais …

5 *Br Sl* (*nothing*) **damn** *or* **bugger** *or* **sod a.** rien du tout, que dalle; **I've done damn a. today** je n'ai rien fichu aujourd'hui

ADV **1** (*entirely*) tout; **she is a. alone** elle est toute seule; **a. on one's own** tout seul; **to be (dressed) a. in black** être habillé tout en noir *ou* tout de noir; **she is a. ears/impatience/smiles** elle est tout oreilles/impatience/sourires; **a. (a)round the room** dans toute la pièce; **I forgot a. about the meeting** j'ai complètement oublié qu'il y avait une réunion; **a. in one piece** tout d'une pièce; **are you still a. in one piece?** (*after accident*) est-ce que tu es encore en un seul morceau?; **she is a. for accepting this offer** elle est tout en faveur d'accepter cette offre; **my wife was a. for calling in a doctor** ma femme voulait à toute force *ou* à tout prix appeler un médecin; **I'm a. for it** je suis entièrement d'accord *ou* pour; **to be a. in favour of sth** être entièrement favorable à qch; **he's not a. bad** il n'est pas entièrement mauvais; **that's a. to the good!** tout va pour le mieux!; **a. the better/worse (for me)** tant mieux/pis (pour moi); **you will be a. the better for it** vous vous en trouverez (d'autant) mieux; **a. the harder** encore plus dur; **the time came a. too soon** l'heure n'arriva que trop tôt; **a. along** depuis le début; **a. at once** (*suddenly*) tout à coup, subitement; (*everything together*) tout d'un coup, tous à la fois; **a. round** (*in general*) à tous points de vue; **a. of a sudden** tout à coup, soudain; **a. over** partout; **a. over the floor/pavement** partout par terre/sur le trottoir; *Fig* **the team was a. over the place** l'équipe faisait n'importe quoi; **she was a. over him at the party** elle n'a pas arrêté de lui tourner après à la soirée; **an a. girl band** un groupe composé uniquement de femmes; **an a. new outfit** un ensemble tout neuf; **a. ready** fin prêt; **to be a. indignant about sth** être fou d'indignation à propos de qch; **it's a. mine!** c'est tout à moi!; *Fam* **to be a. in** être complètement crevé; *Fam* **he's gone a. red** il est devenu tout rouge; *Fam* **the dress was a. torn** la robe était toute déchirée; *Fam* **he's not a. there** il est un peu simplet; **to go a. out** ne pas s'épargner; **to go a. out to pass one's exams** faire son maximum pour réussir ses examens; *Fam* **a. that** (*excellent*) super, génial; *Fam* **she thinks she's a. that** elle ne se prend pas pour n'importe qui

2 (*almost*) **a. but** presque; **it's a. but done** c'est pour ainsi dire fini, c'est presque fini *ou* fait

3 (*in the slightest*) **at a.** du tout; **do you know him at a.?** est-ce que vous le connaissez (un peu)?; **I didn't speak at a.** je n'ai pas parlé du tout; **I'm not a. astonished** je n'en suis aucunement étonné; **not at a.** pas du tout, *Fam* du tout; (*when thanked*) je vous en prie; **if he comes at a.** s'il vient; **it seemed to worry him very little, if at a.** ça n'a pas eu l'air de l'inquiéter le moins du monde; **if it is at a. cold** s'il fait un (tant soit) peu froid; **if it is at a. possible** si c'était possible; **why do it at a.?** pourquoi se donner la peine de le

faire?

4 (*altogether*) **in a.** en tout; **(taking it) a. in a.** à tout prendre

5 (*in games*), *Ftbl etc* **five a.** cinq à cinq, cinq partout; *Tennis* **four (games) a.** quatre (jeux) partout; *Tennis* **fifteen a.** quinze à

N tout *m*, totalité *f*; **to stake one's a.** risquer le tout pour le tout; **I would give my a. to see her** je donnerais tout ce que j'ai pour la voir; **he was really giving his a. in the last aria** il a vraiment tout donné dans la dernière aria

all-absorbing ADJ absorbant, passionnant; **of a. interest** fascinant

Allah [ˈælə] N Allah *m*

all-American ADJ cent pour cent américain

all-around ADJ *Am* (*athlete*) complet; (*man*) universel

allay [əˈleɪ] VT **1** (*storm, anger*) apaiser, calmer **2** (*fear*) calmer; (*suspicions*) endormir, dissiper **3** (*pain*) alléger, calmer, soulager; (*thirst, hunger, temperature*) apaiser

all-clear N (signal *m* de) fin *f* d'alerte; **to give the a.** *Mil* sonner la fin de l'alerte; (*for project etc*) donner le feu vert; **he gave us the a.** (*no one was watching*) il nous a fait signe que la voie était libre

all-conquering ADJ (*love etc*) qui triomphe de tout

all-consuming [-kənˈsjuːmɪŋ] ADJ (*passion, ambition*) dévorant

all-day ADJ ATTRIB qui dure toute la journée

allegation [ælɪˈgeɪʃən] N allégation *f*; **to make an a.** alléguer *ou* avancer quelque chose

allege [əˈledʒ] VT alléguer, prétendre (**that** que); **the words alleged to have been spoken by …** les propos qui auraient été tenus par …; **he was alleged to be dead** on le prétendait *ou* disait mort; **it is alleged that …** on prétend que …

alleged [əˈledʒd] ADJ ATTRIB (*attack, motive etc*) allégué; **the a. thief** le voleur présumé

allegedly [əˈledʒɪdlɪ] ADV prétendument; **a. he's the greatest violinist since Paganini** on dit de lui qu'il est le plus grand violoniste depuis Paganini

allegiance [əˈliːdʒəns] N fidélité *f*, obéissance *f* (**to** à); **to owe a. to a party** devoir fidélité à un parti; **to renounce one's a. to a party** se détacher d'un parti; **to owe a. to a king** devoir fidélité et obéissance à un roi; **to take an oath of a.** prêter serment d'allégeance

allegorical [ælɪˈgɒrɪk(ə)l] ADJ allégorique

allegorically [ælɪˈgɒrɪklɪ] ADV allégoriquement

allegory [ˈælɪgərɪ] N allégorie *f*

allegretto [ælɪˈgretəʊ] ADV, N *Mus* allegretto *m*

allegro [əˈlegrəʊ, -ˈleɪ-] ADV, N *Mus* allegro *m*

alleluia [ælɪˈluːjə] INT, N *Rel* alléluia *m*

all-embracing [-ɪmˈbreɪsɪŋ] ADJ (*love*) qui embrasse tout; (*category*) hétéroclite; **a. knowledge** vaste érudition *f*

allen key [ˈælən] N clé *f* allen

allergen [ˈælədʒən] N *Med* allergène *m*

allergenic [æləˈdʒenɪk] ADJ allergisant

allergic [əˈlɜːdʒɪk] ADJ *Med* allergique (**to** à); *Fig* **I'm a. to him/rap music** il/le rap me hérisse

allergy [ˈælədʒɪ] N *Med, Fig* allergie *f* (**to** à)

alleviate [əˈliːvɪeɪt] VT (*pain*) alléger, soulager; (*grief*) adoucir; (*thirst*) apaiser; (*problem*) alléger, modérer

alleviation [əliːvɪˈeɪʃən] N (*of pain*) allègement *m*, soulagement *m*; (*of grief*) adoucissement *m*; (*of thirst*) apaisement *m*; (*of* *problem)* allègement

all-expenses paid ADJ tous frais payés

all-expense tour N voyage *m* à forfait

alley [ˈælɪ] N **1** *(narrow street)* ruelle *f*; **I wouldn't like to meet him in a dark a.!** je n'aimerais pas le rencontrer au coin d'un bois! **2** *Sport* **bowling a.** bowling *m*
▸▸ **a. cat** chat *m* de gouttière

alleyway [ˈælɪweɪ] N *(street)* ruelle *f*

alliance [əˈlaɪəns] N **1** alliance *f*; **to enter into an a.** s'allier (**with** avec); **electoral a.** apparentement *m*, alliance électorale; **to make a political a. with a party** s'allier à un parti; **in a. with a German firm** en association avec une firme allemande **2** *(by marriage)* alliance *f*

allied [ˈælaɪd] ADJ **1** allié (**to** à; **with** avec); *(consideration, issue)* du même ordre, de la même nature; *(subjects, disciplines, sciences)* voisin; **the A. Powers** les Puissances *fpl* alliées; **closely a. industries** industries *fpl* connexes **2** *Biol, Med etc* du même ordre, de la même nature; *Biol (species)* voisin

alligator [ˈælɪɡeɪtər] N **1** *(animal)* alligator *m* **2** *(skin)* crocodile *m*; **a. handbag** sac *m* en crocodile *ou Am Fam* en croco
▸▸ **a. clip** pince *f* alligator; **a. pear** (poire *f* d')avocat *m*

all-important ADJ capital, -aux; **speed is a.** la vitesse est capitale *ou* est de la plus grande importance

all-in ADJ *(price, tariff)* net, tout compris, forfaitaire
  ADV *Com* tout compris; **the holiday costs £500 a.** les vacances coûtent 500 livres tous frais compris
▸▸ **a. policy** *(in insurance)* police *f* tous risques; *Sport* **a. wrestler** catcheur *m*; *Sport* **a. wrestling** lutte *f* libre, catch *m*

all-inclusive ADJ *(price)* tout compris, forfaitaire; *(theory)* universel

alliteration [əlɪtəˈreɪʃən] N allitération *f*

alliterative [əˈlɪtərətɪv, -reɪt-] ADJ allitératif

all-night ADJ *(party, session etc)* qui dure toute la nuit; **to maintain an a. vigil** veiller toute la nuit
▸▸ *Mil* **a. pass** permission *f* de (la) nuit; *Admin etc* **a. service** permanence *f* de nuit; *Cin* **a. showing** = projection *f* ininterrompue durant toute la nuit

all-nighter [-ˈnaɪtər] N **it turned into another a.** finalement, ça a encore duré toute la nuit

allocate [ˈæləkeɪt] VT allouer, assigner (**to** à); **to a. duties** attribuer des fonctions (**to** à); **to a. a sum to sth** affecter *ou* assigner une somme à qch; **more money was allocated to defence** on a affecté plus d'argent à la défense; **in the time allocated** dans le temps *ou* les délais imparti(s); **you'll need to allocate your time carefully** il va falloir que tu répartisses ton temps avec précaution; **allocated budget** allocation *f* budgétaire, budget *m* alloué

allocation [æləˈkeɪʃən] N **1** *(action) (of sum of money)* allocation *f*, affectation *f*; *(of expenses, means etc)* répartition *f*; *(of capital)* affectation *f*; *(of duties)* attribution *f*; *Fin* **a. to lowest tender** adjudication *f* au mieux-disant **2** *(share)* part *f* assignée *ou* allouée; *(money)* somme *f* assignée *ou* allouée; **my a.** la part/somme qui m'est assignée *ou* allouée

allograft [ˈæləʊɡrɑːft] N *Med* allogreffe *f*

allopathic [æləˈpæθɪk] ADJ *Med* allopathique

allopathy [æˈlɒpəθɪ] N *Med* allopathie *f*

all-or-none order N *St Exch* ordre *m* 'tout ou rien'

allot [əˈlɒt] VT (**-tt-**) **1** *(assign)* attribuer, assigner (**to sb** à qn); **to a. sth to a purpose** affecter *ou* destiner qch à un but; **in the allotted time** dans le temps imparti; **allotted budget** enveloppe *f* budgétaire **2** *(distribute) (tasks, seats)* répartir, distribuer; *(shares)* attribuer, répartir

allotment [əˈlɒtmənt] N **1** *Br (land)* jardin *m* (ouvrier) **2** *(distribution) (of rooms etc)* distribution *f*, *(of tasks)* partage *m*, répartition *f*; *(of property)* lotissement *m*; *St Exch (of shares)* attribution *f*; *St Exch* **letter of a.** (lettre *f* d')avis *m* de répartition **3** *(share)* portion *f*, part *f*, *(of airplane seats)* bloc-sièges *m inv*
▸▸ *St Exch* **a. right** droit *m* d'attribution

all-out *Fam* ADJ ATTRIB *(effort, resistance)* suprême, maximum; *(attack)* tous azimuts; *(strike, war)* total, -aux
  ADV **to go a.** y aller tous azimuts *ou* à fond; **to go a. for gold** y aller tous azimuts pour avoir la médaille d'or; **we're going a. for the end of the month** on fait le maximum pour y arriver avant la fin du mois

all-over ADJ ATTRIB *(tan)* intégral, -aux; **with an a. pattern** dont le motif couvre toute la surface; **it gives a. relief** cela vous apportera un soulagement total

allow [əˈlaʊ] VT **1** *(permit)* permettre; **to a. sb sth** permettre qch à qn; **to a. sb to do sth** permettre à qn de faire qch; **to a. sb home** laisser qn rentrer chez lui; **is he allowed sweets/help?** est-ce qu'il a le droit de manger des sucreries/de recevoir de l'aide?; **gambling is not allowed** les jeux d'argent sont interdits; **no conferring is allowed** il est interdit *ou* il n'est pas permis de se consulter; **she isn't allowed alcohol** elle n'a pas le droit de boire d'alcool; **to be allowed to compete** etre admis à concourir; **I am allowed to do it** on me permet *ou* il m'est permis de le faire; **a. me!** permettez(-moi)!; **a. me to …** permettez-moi de …; **passengers are not allowed on the bridge** la passerelle est interdite aux voyageurs; **as soon as circumstances a.** dès que les circonstances le permettront; **to a. oneself to be led/deceived/persuaded** se laisser mener/tromper/convaincre; **I will not a. you to be ill-treated** je ne vous laisserai pas maltraiter **2** *(accept) (request, claim)* faire droit à; *(petition)* admettre; *Sport (penalty, goal)* accorder **3** *(grant, allocate)* accorder; **to a. sb £5,000 a year** accorder *ou* allouer à qn une rente de 5000 livres; **to a. a debtor time to pay** accorder un délai à un débiteur; **how much time/money are we allowed?** de combien de temps/d'argent disposons-nous?; **they haven't allowed enough time** ils n'ont pas laissé assez de temps; *Com, Fin* **to a. sb a discount** consentir *ou* accorder un escompte *ou* une remise à qn; **the bank allows 5% interest on deposits** la banque alloue *ou* attribue 5% d'intérêt sur les dépôts; **at the end of the six months allowed** à l'expiration du délai de six mois; **a. 20 minutes to get to the airport** comptez 20 minutes pour aller à l'aéroport **4** *(admit)* admettre (**that** que) **5** *Am Fam (maintain)* juger, opiner, affirmer (**that** que)

▸ **allow for** VT INSEP tenir compte de; *(difficulties, delay etc)* prévoir; **after allowing for** *(discount, expenses etc)* déduction faite de; **to a. for some wastage** prévoir plus large; **a. two litres for wastage** comptez deux litres de pertes en plus; **to a. so much for carriage** compter tant pour le transport; **you must a. for his being ill** il faut tenir compte de ce qu'il est malade; **has that been allowed for in your figures?** en avez-vous tenu compte dans vos estimations?

▸ **allow in** VT SEP laisser entrer; **no one is al-**

lowed in personne n'a le droit d'entrer
▸ **allow of** VT INSEP *Fml* permettre, admettre; **the facts a. of only one interpretation** les faits n'admettent qu'une seule interprétation
▸ **allow out** VT SEP **to a. sb out** permettre à qn de sortir; **no one is allowed out after dark** personne n'a le droit de sortir après la tombée de la nuit; **some prisoners are allowed out at weekends** certains détenus ont la permission de sortir le weekend

allowable [əˈlaʊəb(ə)l] ADJ **1** *(permissible)* admissible **2** *Com (claim)* recevable; *(expense)* déductible

allowance [əˈlaʊəns] N **1** *(money given)* pension *f*; *Am (pocket money)* argent *m* de poche; **his parents stopped or cut off his a.** ses parents ont arrêté de lui verser de l'argent régulièrement; *(while he was living away from home)* ses parents ont arrêté sa pension
  2 *Admin etc (compensation)* allocation *f*, **cost-of-living a.** indemnité *f* de vie chère; *Br Formerly* **family a.** allocations familiales; **supplementary allowances** majorations *fpl* de pension; *Fin* **personal a.** abattement *m* personnel (sur l'impôt); **entertainment a.** frais *mpl* de représentation; **travel or travelling a.** indemnité de déplacement; **allowances in kind** prestations *fpl* en nature
  3 *(free)* **luggage a.** *(on plane, coach etc)* bagages *mpl* en franchise; **there is an a. of one item of luggage per passenger** chaque passager a droit à un bagage; **what's the duty-free a.?** qu'est-ce qu'on a droit de ramener hors taxe?; *Sport* **time a.** rendement *m* de temps; *Horseracing* **weight a.** décharge *f*
  4 *Com, Fin (discount)* remise *f*, rabais *m*; **to make an a. on an article** faire un rabais sur un article
  5 **to make allowances or an a. for sth** tenir compte de qch; *(delays)* prévoir qch; **to make allowances for sb** avoir de l'indulgence pour qn; **some a. must be made for shrinkage** il faut tenir compte du rétrécissement
  6 *Tech* tolérance *f*

alloy[1] [ˈælɔɪ] N alliage *m*
▸▸ *Metal* **a. steel** acier *m* allié *ou* spécial; **a. wheel** jante *f* (en) alliage

alloy[2] [əˈlɔɪ] VT *(metals)* allier
  VI *(of metals)* s'allier (l'un avec l'autre)

alloyed [əˈlɔɪd] ADJ *(metal etc)* allié (**with** à, avec)

all-pervading, all-pervasive ADJ *(stench)* envahissant, qui se répand partout; *(fear, corruption, influence)* omniprésent

all-powerful ADJ tout-puissant, toute-puissante, *pl* tout-puissants, toutes-puissantes

all-purpose ADJ *(glue, cleaner)* universel; *(vehicle)* tous usages; *(building, room)* polyvalent

all right ADJ **everything's a.** tout va très bien; **it's a.** *(there's no need to worry)* tout va bien, ne vous inquiétez pas; *(to person apologizing)* je vous en prie!!; **a.!** *(expressing agreement)* bien!, entendu!; *Am (expressing great enthusiasm)* génial!!; **a., a., I'm coming** *(expressing irritation)* d'accord, d'accord, j'arrive; **are you a.?** *(are you well?)* est-ce que vous allez bien?; *(did you hurt yourself?)* vous ne vous êtes pas blessé?; *Iron* tu ne te sens pas bien?; **I'm a. again now** *(after being ill)* je suis tout à fait remis maintenant; **I'm a. until Monday** *(financially)* ça ira jusqu'à lundi; **are you a. for cash/cigarettes?** tu as assez de liquide/de cigarettes?; **it's a. for you to laugh!** ça vous va bien de rire!; **any more? – no, I'm a., thanks** tu en veux encore? – non, ça va, merci; **I'm a. at algebra** en algèbre je me débrouille *ou* je ne me défends pas trop mal; **it was a.** *(film, party etc)* ce n'était pas mal; **he's/she's a.** *(a good sort)* c'est un bon type; *Fam* **to be a bit of a.** *(of woman)* être une jolie fille; *(of man)* être un beau mec

all-risks insurance N assurance *f* tous risques

all-round ADJ ATTRIB **1** *(athlete etc)* complet, -ète; *(education)* général, -aux; *(expert)* dans tous les domaines; **a. improvement** amélioration *f* générale *ou* sur toute la ligne **2** *Aut* **car with a. vision** voiture *f* à carrosserie panoramique

all-rounder [-'raʊndər] N homme *m* universel, femme *f* universelle; *(athlete)* athlète *mf* complet(ète); *Sch* **a good a.** un élève complet, une élève complète; **she's quite an a.** elle est douée pour tout

all-seater stadium N *Sport* = stade *m* ayant uniquement des places assises

All-Share Index N *Br St Exch* = indice *m* du Financial Times et de l'Institut des actuaires britannique

allspice ['ɔːlspaɪs] N *Bot, Culin* poivre *m* de la Jamaïque

all-star ADJ ATTRIB *Theat etc* **an a. cast** une distribution prestigieuse; **a. performance** spectacle *m* à la distribution prestigieuse

all-terrain ADJ *Aut* tout-terrain *inv*

all-time ADJ ATTRIB *Fam (record)* sans précédent, inouï; **a. high/low** record le plus élevé/bas; **the a. greats of rock music** les plus grands du rock; **one of the a. hits** un des plus grands succès

allude [ə'luːd] VI **to a. to sb/sth** *(of person)* faire allusion à qn/qch; *(of phrase)* avoir trait à *ou* se rapporter à qn/qch; **I am not alluding to anybody in particular** je ne vise personne

allure [ə'lʊər] N attrait *m*; **it holds no a. for me** ça ne m'attire pas du tout
VT attirer, séduire

> Note that the French word **allure** is a false friend. It means **pace**, **speed** or **appearance**, depending on the context.

alluring [ə'lʊərɪŋ] ADJ attrayant, attirant, séduisant

allusion [ə'luːʒən] N allusion *f*; **to make an a. to sth** faire allusion à qch; **in a. to sth** par allusion à qch

allusive [ə'luːsɪv] ADJ allusif

alluvial [ə'luːvɪəl] *Geol* ADJ *(terrain)* alluvial, -aux; **a. deposits** alluvions *fpl*, dépôts alluvionnaires
N *Austr* alluvions *fpl* aurifères
> ▸ **a. plain** plaine *f* alluviale

alluvium [ə'luːvɪəm] N *Geol* limon *m*

all-weather ADJ *Aviat etc (plane, landing strip)* tous temps; *(clothes), Sport (pitch)* pour tous les temps

all-wheel drive N quatre roues *fpl* motrices

ally[1] ['ælaɪ] N *(country, person etc)* allié, -ée; *Hist* **the Allies** les Alliés *mpl*; **to become allies** s'allier (ensemble), se coaliser

ally[2] [ə'laɪ] VT allier (**to** à; **with** avec); **the country has allied itself with its neighbour** le pays s'est allié à *ou* avec l'état voisin; **we must a. ourselves with other unions** nous devons nous allier à *ou* nous associer avec d'autres syndicats; **this newspaper is allied with another** ce journal est associé avec un autre

alma mater ['ælmə'meɪtər, -'mɑːtər] N = l'université *f* ou l'école *f* où l'on a fait ses études

almanac ['ɔːlmənæk, 'æl-] N almanach *m*

almighty [ɔːl'maɪtɪ] ADJ ATTRIB *(omnipotent)* tout-puissant, toute-puissante, *pl* tout-puissants, toutes-puissantes; *Fam (scandal etc)* monstrueux, terrible; *Fam* **an a. row** *or* **din** un fracas de tous les diables

N **the A.** le Tout-Puissant, le Très-Haut
ADV *Am Fam* très; **he's a. stubborn** il est têtu comme une mule

almond ['ɑːmənd] N amande *f*; **sweet/bitter a.** amande douce/amère; **ground almonds** amandes pilées; **a.(-shaped) eyes** yeux *mpl* en amande
> ▸ *Culin* **a. essence** essence *f* d'amande; **a. grove** amandaie *f*, **a. oil** huile *f* d'amande; *Culin* **a. paste** pâte *f* d'amande; **a. tree** amandier *m*

almoner ['ɑːmənər, 'æl-] N **1** *Br (in hospital)* assistant, -ante social(e) **2** *Hist (distributor of alms)* aumônier *m*

almost ['ɔːlməʊst] ADV presque; **it's a. six (o'clock)** il est presque six heures; **a. nothing** presque rien; **a. blind** presque *ou* quasi aveugle; **he a. fell/missed the bus** il a failli tomber/rater l'autobus; **we're a. there** nous sommes presque arrivés; **you're a. there** *(in answering question)* tu y es presque; **I a. didn't see you** j'ai failli ne pas vous voir

alms [ɑːmz] NPL aumône *f*, **to give a. to sb** donner *ou* faire l'aumône à qn, faire la charité à qn
> ▸ *Hist* **a. box** tronc *m* (pour les pauvres)

almshouse ['ɑːmzhaʊs] N hospice *m*

aloe ['æləʊ] N **1** *(plant)* aloès *m* **2** *Pharm* **aloes** aloès *mpl*; **bitter aloes** amer *m* d'aloès

aloft [ə'lɒft] ADV **1** *Naut* dans la mâture **2** *(in sky)* en haut, en l'air

alone [ə'ləʊn] ADJ PRED, ADV **1** *(in isolation)* seul; **he lives (all) a.** il vit (tout) seul; **I like being a.** j'aime la solitude *ou* être seul; **I want to speak to you a.** je voudrais vous parler seul à seul; **a. at last!** enfin seul(s)!; **he was left a. when his wife died** il s'est retrouvé seul quand sa femme est morte; **we are not a. in thinking that …** nous ne sommes pas seuls à penser que …; **you a. can help me** vous êtes le seul qui puissiez m'aider, vous seul pouvez m'aider; **he a. knows …** lui seul sait …; **I did it a.** je l'ai fait tout seul; *Fam* **to go it a.** faire cavalier seul; *Bible* **man does not live by bread a.** l'homme ne vit pas que de pain; **my salary a. isn't enough** mon salaire à lui seul *ou* mon seul salaire ne suffit pas; **his shoes a. must have cost what I earn in a week** rien que ses chaussures ont dû coûter ce que je gagne en une semaine; **with that charm which is his a.** avec ce charme qui lui est propre **2** *(undisturbed)* **to let** *or* **leave sb a.** *(not touch, not disturb)* laisser qn tranquille *ou* en paix; *(not interfere with)* laisser qn tranquille; **leave me a.!** laissez-moi tranquille!, *Fam* fichez-moi la paix!; **leave her a. to get on with it** laisse-la se débrouiller toute seule; **to let** *or* **leave sth a.** *(not get involved)* ne pas se mêler de qch; **leave these things a.** *(don't touch)* ne touchez pas à tout ça; **a subject better left a.** un sujet qu'il vaut mieux ne pas aborder; **your work is all right, leave it a.** ton travail est bien, n'y touchez plus; **let a. …** encore moins …; **the soup wasn't even warm, let a. hot!** la soupe ne risquait pas d'être chaude, elle était à peine tiède!

ALONG [ə'lɒŋ] PREP le long de; **to walk a. the shore** se promener le long de la plage, longer la plage; **to go a. a street** suivre une rue; **to look a. the street/corridor** regarder dans la rue/le couloir; **to sail a. the coast** longer *ou* suivre la côte; **to crawl a. the ground** ramper à la surface du sol; *Fig* **victorious all a. the line** victorieux sur toute la ligne; **all a. the street** tout le long de la rue; **trees a. the river** arbres qui bordent la rivière; **they live somewhere a. this street** ils habitent quelque part dans cette rue; **it's somewhere a. here** c'est quelque part dans cette direction *ou* par là; **somewhere a. the way** en route, en chemin

ADV **to move a.** avancer; **move a. so I can sit down** *(in row of seats etc)* pousse-toi que je puisse m'asseoir; **to stride a.** avancer à grandes enjambées; **come a. with me** venez avec moi; *Fam* **come a. now!** *(be reasonable)* allons, sois raisonnable!; **he'll be a. in ten minutes** il va arriver dans dix minutes; **there'll be another one a. in a minute** *(of bus)* il en passera un autre dans une minute; **bring a tent a. (with you)** apportez une tente; **can I bring a friend a.?** est-ce que je peux amener un ami?; **a. with Mozart, Haydn is my favourite composer** avec Mozart, Haydn est mon compositeur favori; *SI* **get a. (with you)!** *(go away)* allez!, filez!; *(expressing astonishment, disbelief)* allons donc!; *Am* **a. about four o'clock** vers quatre heures; *Am* **the afternoon was well a.** l'après-midi tirait à sa fin; **all a.** *(all the time)* depuis toujours; **I knew that all a.** je le savais dès *ou* depuis le commencement, je l'ai toujours su; **I said so all a.** c'est ce que j'ai toujours dit; **he was lying all a.** il n'a fait que mentir, il a menti du début à la fin

alongside [ə'lɒŋ'saɪd] PREP *esp Naut (boat, quay)* accosté à, le long de; **to come a. (of) a ship** accoster *ou* aborder un navire; **the police car pulled up a. us** la voiture de police s'est arrêtée à côté de nous; **to walk a. sb** marcher côte à côte avec qn *ou* à côté de qn; **read these instructions a. the illustrations** lisez ces instructions en accompagnement des illustrations; **if you look at it a. his earlier work** si vous le comparez à ses travaux plus anciens; **a. what others have done** par rapport à ce que *ou* à côté de ce que d'autres ont fait
ADV *Naut* **to come a.** accoster; **a police car pulled up a.** une voiture de police nous/les/*etc* a accostés

aloof [ə'luːf] ADV **to keep a.** se tenir à l'écart *ou* à distance (**from sth** de qch); **to stand a. from** se tenir à l'écart de
ADJ *(person, manner)* distant; *(emphasizing coldness)* froid et distant

aloofness [ə'luːfnɪs] N attitude *f* distante, réserve *f*

alopecia [æləʊ'piːʃə] N *Med* alopécie *f*

aloud [ə'laʊd] ADV à haute voix, (tout) haut; **to read a.** lire à haute voix; **I was thinking a.** je pensais tout haut; **he says a. what others only dare to whisper** il dit tout haut ce que les autres pensent tout bas

alp [ælp] N *Geog* **1** *(pasture)* alpe *f*, pâturage *m* de montagne **2 the Alps** les Alpes *fpl*

alpaca [æl'pækə] N **1** *(animal)* alpaga *m* **2** *Tex* alpaga *m*; **a. coat/jacket** manteau *m*/veste *f* en alpaga *ou* d'alpaga; **a. wool** laine *f* d'alpaga

alpenhorn ['ælpənhɔːn] N *Mus* cor *m* des Alpes

alpha ['ælfə] N alpha *m*; *Br (mark)* A *m*; *Lit, Fig* **a. and omega** l'alpha et l'oméga
> ▸ *Zool* **a. male** mâle *m* alpha; *Fig* **he's the a. male of the group** c'est lui qui domine le groupe; *Phys* **a. rays** rayons *mpl* alpha

alphabet ['ælfəbet] N alphabet *m*
> ▸ **a. soup** *Culin* soupe *f* aux petites pâtes en forme de lettres; *Fig (speech, writing)* = charabia *m* bourré de sigles et d'abréviations

alphabetic(al) [ælfə'betɪk, -ɪk(ə)l] ADJ alphabétique; **in a. order** par ordre *ou* dans l'ordre alphabétique; **a. filing** classement *m* par ordre alphabétique

alphabetically [ælfə'betɪklɪ] ADV alphabétiquement, par ordre alphabétique

alphabetize ['ælfəbətaɪz] VT classer par ordre alphabétique; **to a. sth on sth** trier qch par ordre alphabétique sur la base de qch

alphanumeric(al) [ælfənjuːˈmerɪk, -ɪk(ə)l] ADJ *Comput* alphanumérique
▸▸ **a. code** code *m* alphanumérique; **a. field** champ *m* alphanumérique; **a. filing** classement *m* alphanumérique; **a. keyboard, a. keypad** clavier *m* alphanumérique

alphasort [ˈælfəsɔːt] *Comput* N tri *m* alphabétique; **to do an a. on sth** trier qch par ordre alphabétique
VT trier par ordre alphabétique

alphatest [ˈælfətest] *Comput* N alpha-test *m*, *pl* alpha-tests, essai *m* préliminaire
VT conduire les alpha-tests sur, conduire les essais préliminaires sur

alpine [ˈælpaɪn] N *(plant)* plante *f* alpine *ou* alpestre
ADJ *(skiing)* alpin; *(site, landscape, climate)* alpestre; *(plant)* alpin, alpestre
▸▸ **a. range** chaîne *f* de montagnes alpine

alpinism [ˈælpɪnɪz(ə)m] N alpinisme *m*

alpinist [ˈælpɪnɪst] N alpiniste *mf*

already [ɔːlˈredɪ] ADV déjà; **ten o'clock a.!** déjà dix heures!; **you've eaten enough a.** tu as déjà assez mangé

alright [ɔːlˈraɪt] ADJ = **all right**

Alsatian [ælˈseɪʃən] ADJ alsacien; *(wine)* d'Alsace
N **1** Alsacien, -ienne **2** *Br (dog)* berger *m* allemand

also [ˈɔːlsəʊ] ADV aussi; **he a. saw it, he saw it a.** *(didn't only hear it)* il l'a vu aussi; *(as well as other people)* lui aussi, il l'a vu, il l'a vu, lui aussi; *esp Am* **I study French a.** *(as well as other subjects)* j'étudie également le français; **not only … but a. …** non seulement … mais encore … *ou* mais aussi …; **it's very efficient and a. very cheap** c'est très efficace et, de plus, très bon marché; *Horseracing* **a. ran** non classés, ont couru aussi

also-ran N *Horseracing* concurrent, -ente non classé(ée); *Fam (unsuccessful person, thing)* non-valeur *f*, *pl* non-valeurs

alt [ɔːlt] N *Comput (key)* touche *f* alt
▸▸ **a. key** touche *f* alt

Alta *abbr* Alberta

altar [ˈɔːltər] N autel *m*; **to lead sb to the a.** conduire qn à l'autel; *Fig* **they were sacrificed on the a. of the party's interests** ils ont été sacrifiés dans l'intérêt du parti; **high a.** maître-autel *m*, *pl* maîtres-autels
▸▸ **a. boy** enfant *m* de chœur; **a. cloth** nappe *f* d'autel; **a. rail(s)** cancel *m*; **a. screen** retable *m*

altarpiece [ˈɔːltəpiːs] N retable *m*

alter [ˈɔːltər] VT **1** *(thing, person)* changer; *(design, one's opinion etc)* modifier; *(garment etc)* faire des retouches à; **that alters the case/the situation** voilà qui change les choses/la situation; **that doesn't a. the fact that …** cela ne change rien au fait que …; **this has not altered our determination to …** ceci n'a pas altéré notre détermination de …; *Naut* **to a. course** changer de route **2** *Am, Austr Fam (castrate)* châtrer
VI *(of person, situation)* changer; **her whole outlook has altered** elle a complètement changé d'horizon
▸▸ **a. ego** alter ego *m*

alteration [ɔːltəˈreɪʃən] N changement *m*, modification *f* (**to** apporté(e) à); *(to garment)* retouche *f* (**to** à); **subject to a.** *(programme, timetable etc)* susceptible de révisions, sauf modifications; **marginal alterations** *(written)* corrections *fpl* en marge

altercation [ɔːltəˈkeɪʃən] N *Fml* altercation *f*, querelle *f*; **to have an a.** se quereller

alternate[1] [ɔːlˈtɜːnət] ADJ **1** alterné, alternant; **she comes on a. days** elle vient tous les deux jours *ou* un jour sur deux; **they**

come on a. days *(one after the other)* ils viennent en alternance un jour sur deux; **on a. afternoons/Wednesdays** un après-midi/mercredi sur deux; **a. layers of stone and timber** couches alternées de pierre et de bois; **a. periods of calm and distress** des périodes de calme alternant avec des périodes d'angoisse; **a. airfield** aérodrome *m* de dégagement; *Aviat etc* **a. route** parcours *m* de rechange
2 *Math, Bot (angle, leaf)* alterne
3 *Liter (rhyme)* croisé
4 *Am* = **alternative**
N *esp Am* remplaçant, -ante

Attention: ne pas confondre avec **alternative**.

alternate[2] [ˈɔːltəneɪt] VT *(methods)* employer tour à tour *ou* alternativement; *(jackets etc)* mettre tour à tour *ou* alternativement; **… alternating the tomato and cucumber slices …** en faisant alterner les rondelles de tomates et de concombre; *Agr* **to a. crops** alterner les récoltes
VI alterner (**with** avec); **he alternated with his friend on watches throughout the night** son ami et lui se sont relayés toute la nuit pour monter la garde; **they alternated between welcoming his help and resenting his intrusion** tantôt ils lui étaient reconnaissants de son aide, tantôt ils lui en voulaient de son intrusion; **rain and sunshine alternated all afternoon** la pluie et le soleil se sont succédés tout l'après-midi

alternately [ɔːlˈtɜːnətlɪ] ADV alternativement, tour à tour, en alternance; **boys and girls were seated a.** les garçons et les filles étaient assis en alternance; *Bot* **leaves placed a.** feuilles *fpl* alternes

Attention: ne pas confondre avec **alternatively**.

alternating [ˈɔːltəneɪtɪŋ] ADJ **1** alternant, alterné **2** *Elec (current)* alternatif; *Tech (movement)* alternatif, de va-et-vient

alternation [ɔːltəˈneɪʃən] N alternance *f*

alternative [ɔːlˈtɜːnətɪv] ADJ ATTRIB **1** *(plan, route, course of action)* alternatif; **an a. site will have to be found** il faudra trouver un autre endroit; **we'll find you a. employment** nous vous emploierons à autre chose; **to make a. arrangements** s'arranger autrement **2** *(not conventional)* parallèle, alternatif
N *(choice)* alternative *f*; **there is no a.** il n'y a pas d'alternative; **they were given the a. of a fine or a month's imprisonment** on leur a donné le choix entre une amende et un mois de prison; **the a. would be to …** une autre solution serait de …; **to have no a.** ne pas avoir le choix; **he had no a. but to obey** il n'a pu faire autrement que d'obéir; **there are alternatives to nuclear power** le nucléaire n'est pas la seule solution possible; **the a. was starvation** c'était ça ou mourir de faim
▸▸ **a. comedy** nouvelle comédie *f*; *Br St Exch* **A. Investment Market** = marché *m* hors-cote rattaché à la Bourse de Londres; *Med* **a. medicine** médecines *fpl* douces *ou* parallèles; **a. tourism** tourisme *m* vert

Attention: ne pas confondre avec **alternate**.

alternatively [ɔːlˈtɜːnətɪvlɪ] ADV *(on the other hand)* ou bien; *(in a different way)* *(employed etc)* autrement; **a., we could go to the beach** ou bien nous pourrions aller à la plage; **he's probably in the library, a. you might try the squash courts** il est sûrement à la bibliothèque, sinon, vous pouvez essayer les courts de squash

Attention: ne pas confondre avec **alternately**.

alternator [ˈɔːltəneɪtər] N *Elec* alternateur *m*

although [ɔːlˈðəʊ] CONJ quoique, bien que + *sub*; **a. I am a father** tout père que je suis; **Paul, a. rich, was not mean** Paul, bien que riche, n'était pas avare; **a. not beautiful, she was attractive** sans être belle, elle plaisait; **it's not possible … a. …** *(considering, changing mind)* cela n'est pas possible … à moins que …

altimeter [ˈæltɪmiːtər] N *Aviat* altimètre *m*; **radio a.** radiosonde *f*

altitude [ˈæltɪtjuːd] N **1** altitude *f*; **at these altitudes** à cette altitude **2** *Astron, Geom (of star, triangle)* hauteur *f*
▸▸ *Tech* **a. recorder** enregistreur *m* d'altitude; **a. sickness** mal *m* d'altitude

alto [ˈæltəʊ] N *Mus* **1** **to sing a.** chanter la partie alto **2** *(male voice)* haute-contre *f*, *pl* hautes-contre; *(female voice)* contralto *m*, alto *f*; **I'm an a.** je suis haute-contre/alto **3** *(viola)* alto *m* (à cordes); **a. trombone/saxophone** trombone *m*/saxophone *m* alto
▸▸ **a. clef** clef *f* d'ut

altocumulus [æltəʊˈkjuːmjələs] N altocumulus *m*

altogether [ɔːltəˈgeðər] ADV **1** *(entirely)* entièrement, tout à fait; **to change sth a.** changer qch de fond en comble *ou* radicalement; **it's a. out of the question** c'est absolument impossible; **I was not a. pleased** ça ne me faisait pas exactement plaisir
2 *(in total)* en tout; **a. the bill came to £63** au total ça a fait 63 livres; **how much is that a.?** ça fait combien en tout?; **a., it was a memorable occasion** somme toute, ce fut un événement mémorable; **taking things a.** à tout prendre
N *Fam Hum* **in the a.** complètement nu, en tenue d'Adam/d'Ève

altostratus [æltəʊˈstrɑːtəs] N altostratus *m*

altruism [ˈæltrʊɪz(ə)m] N altruisme *m*

altruist [ˈæltrʊɪst] N altruiste *mf*

altruistic [æltrʊˈɪstɪk] ADJ altruiste

ALU [eɪelˈjuː] N *Comput (abbr* **arithmetic and logic unit)** unité *f* arithmétique et logique

alum [ˈæləm] N alun *m*
▸▸ *Phot* **a. bath** bain *m* aluné

alumina [əˈluːmɪnə] N *Miner* alumine *f*

aluminium [æljʊˈmɪnɪəm], *Am* **aluminum** [əˈluːmɪnəm] N aluminium *m*; *Metal* **a. alloy** alliage *m* d'aluminium; **a. saucepan** casserole *f* en aluminium
▸▸ **a. foil** papier *m* aluminium; *Chem* **a. oxide** alumine *f*

aluminize [əˈluːmɪnaɪz] VT **1** *Metal* combiner avec de l'aluminium; **aluminized steel** acier *m* à l'aluminium **2** *Tech (mirror)* aluminer **3** *Chem* aluminer; *(in dyeing)* aluner

aluminum [əˈluːmɪnəm] N *Am* = **aluminium**

alumna, *pl* **alumnae** [əˈlʌmnə, -iː] N *esp Am (of school)* ancienne élève *f*, *(of university)* ancienne étudiante *f*

alumnus, *pl* **alumni** [əˈlʌmnəs, -aɪ] N *esp Am (of school)* ancien élève *m*; *(of university)* ancien étudiant *m*; **a. association** association *f* des anciens

alveolus, *pl* **alveoli** [ælˈvɪələs, -laɪ] N *Anat* alvéole *f* pulmonaire

always [ˈɔːlwəz, -wɪz, *stressed* -weɪz] ADV **1** *(all the time)* toujours; **nearly** *or* **almost a.** presque toujours; **the office is a. open** le bureau est toujours ouvert *ou* est ouvert en permanence; **he is a. complaining** il se plaint tout le temps, il n'arrête pas de se plaindre; **I'll a. remember you!** je ne t'oublierai jamais! VOIR GRAMMAIRE A21

2 (*as alternative*) toujours; **I can a. try** je peux toujours *ou* quand même essayer; **there's a. the old age pension** il y a toujours la retraite

alyssum ['ælɪsəm] N alysse *f*

Alzheimer's, Alzheimer's disease ['æltshaɪməz] N *Med* maladie *f* d'Alzheimer

AM ['eɪ'em] N (*abbr* **amplitude modulation**) AM *f*

am¹ [æm] *see* be

am², **a.m.** ['eɪ'em] ADV (*abbr* **ante meridiem**) avant midi; **five am** cinq heures du matin; **we're leaving at six – am or pm?** nous partons à six heures – du matin ou de l'après-midi? VOIR GRAMMAIRE A80

AMA ['eɪ'em'eɪ] N **1** *Med* (*abbr* **American Medical Association**) = ordre *m* américain des médecins **2** *Mktg* (*abbr* **American Marketing Association**) = institut *m* américain de marketing

amalgam [ə'mælgəm] N *Metal, Fig* amalgame *m*

amalgamate [ə'mælgəmeɪt] VT *Metal* amalgamer; *Fig* (*ideas*) amalgamer; (*companies, industries*), *Fin* (*shares*) fusionner

▸ VI (*of metals, ideas*) s'amalgamer; (*of companies*) fusionner

amalgamation [əmælgə'meɪʃən] N (*of metals*) amalgamation *f*; (*of two companies*), *Fin* (*of shares*) fusionnement *m*; (*collection*) (*of evidence etc*) accumulation *f*

amaryllis [æmə'rɪlɪs] N (*plant*) amaryllis *f* (belle-dame)

amass [ə'mæs] VT (*wealth, objects, information etc*) amasser, accumuler

amateur ['æmətər, -tjʊər, æmə'tɜːr] N **1** (*non-professional*) amateur *m*; **a. painter/musician** peintre *m*/musicien *m* amateur; **he paints as an a.** il peint en amateur *ou* en dilettante; *Pej* **he's a real a.** ce n'est qu'un amateur, c'est un amateur; **they did a rather a. job** ils ont fait du travail d'amateur **2** *Sport* amateur *m*; **a. championship** championnat *m* amateur; *Horseracing* **a. rider** gentleman rider *m*; **a. sport** sport *m* d'amateur

amateurish ['æmətərɪʃ, æmə'tɜːrɪʃ] ADJ *Pej* (*piece of work etc*) d'amateur; (*actor, singer etc*) amateur

amateurishly ['æmətərɪʃlɪ] ADV *Pej* en amateur; (*presented, written*) avec amateurisme

amateurism ['æmətərɪz(ə)m] N **1** (*in arts*) dilettantisme *m*, *Pej* amateurisme *m* **2** *Sport* amateurisme *m*

amatory ['æmət(ə)rɪ] ADJ *Lit, Hum* (*sentiment, conquests*) amoureux; (*letter*) d'amour; (*intentions, ambitions*) galant; (*poem*) érotique

amaze [ə'meɪz] VT ébahir, stupéfier; **his courage amazed me** son courage m'a stupéfié; **I was amazed at** *or* **by the price** le prix m'a ébahi, j'étais très étonné de le *ou* du prix; **I was amazed to learn that** ça m'a ébahi *ou* stupéfié de l'apprendre; **it amazes me that he could have done such a thing** je suis stupéfait qu'il ait pu faire une telle chose; **you a. me sometimes** (*are exasperating*) tu es incroyable quelquefois; **you never cease to a. me** tu m'étonneras toujours; *Iron* **you a. me!** non, vraiment?; *Iron* **go on, a. me!** vas-y, surprends-moi!

amazement [ə'meɪzmənt] N stupéfaction *f*, stupeur *f*, grand étonnement *m*; **to listen in a.** écouter avec stupeur; **to our a.** à notre grand étonnement, à notre stupéfaction; **I heard with a. that …** j'ai été stupéfait d'apprendre que …

amazing [ə'meɪzɪŋ] ADJ stupéfiant, étonnant; (*dexterity*) prestigieux; **it's a.!** je n'en

reviens pas!; **it's a. that no one was hurt** c'est étonnant que personne n'ait été blessé; **you've been a.** tu as été formidable

amazingly [ə'meɪzɪŋlɪ] ADV étonnamment; **a. quickly** à une vitesse stupéfiante *ou* étonnante; **we were a. lucky** nous avons eu une chance formidable; **a., no one was hurt** c'est étonnant mais personne n'a été blessé; **he's doing a. well** (*in business*) il réussit à merveille; (*recovering quickly*) il se remet merveilleusement bien

Amazon ['æməz(ə)n] N **1 the (river) A.** l'Amazone *f* **2** *Myth* Amazone *f*, *Fig* femme *f* forte et athlétique

▸▸ **the A. basin** le bassin amazonien; **the A. rainforest** la forêt tropicale (humide) amazonienne

Amazonian [æmə'zəʊnɪən] ADJ **1** *Geog* de l'Amazone, amazonien **2** *Myth* d'Amazone; *Fig* (*woman*) fort et athlétique; *Fig* **I like the A. type** j'aime les femmes fortes et athlétiques

ambassador [æm'bæsədər] N (*diplomat*), *Fig* ambassadeur *m*, ambassadrice *f*, **the French A. to Japan** l'ambassadeur de France au Japon

ambassadorial [æmbæsə'dɔːrɪəl] ADJ (*duties etc*) d'ambassadeur

ambassadress [æm'bæsədrɪs] N (*diplomat*), *Fig* ambassadrice *f*

amber ['æmbər] N (*colour, stone*) ambre *m*; **yellow a.** ambre jaune; **he crossed on a.** (*traffic light*) il a traversé à l'orange

▸ ADJ **1** (*necklace*) d'ambre, en ambre; **a. varnish** vernis *m* au succin **2 a.(-coloured)** ambré

▸▸ **a. light** feu *m* orange; *Br, Austr Fam Hum* **a. nectar** bière *f*, mousse *f*

ambergris ['æmbəgriːs] N ambre *m* gris

ambidextrous [æmbɪ'dekstrəs] ADJ ambidextre

ambience, ambiance ['æmbɪəns] N ambiance *f*

ambient ['æmbɪənt] ADJ *Tech, Cin* (*temperature, noise, light etc*) ambiant

▸▸ **a. sound** son *m* d'ambiance

ambiguity [æmbɪ'gjuːɪtɪ] N **1** (*ambiguousness*) ambiguïté *f* **2** (*instance*) équivoque *f*; **his speech was full of ambiguities** son discours a été très ambigu

ambiguous [æm'bɪgjʊəs] ADJ ambigu, *f* -uë; équivoque

ambiguously [æm'bɪgjʊəslɪ] ADV d'une manière ambiguë *ou* équivoque; **an a. worded reply** une réponse formulée de façon ambiguë

ambiguousness [æm'bɪgjʊəsnɪs] N ambiguïté *f*

ambit ['æmbɪt] N *Fml* (*of law, investigations*) portée *f*; **that does not come within our a.** cela n'entre pas dans nos compétences

ambition [æm'bɪʃən] N ambition *f*; **the a. to succeed** l'ambition de réussir; **to have great ambitions** avoir de grandes ambitions *ou* de hautes visées; **it's my a. to …, my a. is to …** j'ambitionne de …; **my parents had great ambitions for me** mes parents avaient de grands projets pour moi

ambitious [æm'bɪʃəs] ADJ (*person, project etc*) ambitieux; **to be a. to do sth** ambitionner de faire qch; **they're very a. for their children** ils sont très ambitieux en ce qui concerne leurs enfants

ambitiously [æm'bɪʃəslɪ] ADV ambitieusement; **they planned a.** ils ont fait des projets ambitieux

ambitiousness [æm'bɪʃəsnɪs] N (*of project, design*) caractère *m* ambitieux; (*of person*) ambition *f*

ambivalence [æm'bɪvələns] N ambivalence *f*

ambivalent [æm'bɪvələnt] ADJ ambivalent

amble ['æmb(ə)l] N (*of horse*) amble *m*; (*of person*) pas *m* ou allure *f* tranquille; **to walk at an a.** (*of horse*) aller l'amble, ambler

▸ VI (*of horse*) aller (à) l'amble, ambler; **to make a horse a.** mettre un cheval à l'amble; **he ambled up to us** (*of person*) il s'est avancé vers nous d'un pas tranquille; **I'll just a. down to the corner shop** je vais faire un saut à l'épicerie du coin; **he just ambles in at ten o'clock** il arrive à dix heures les mains dans les poches *ou* en se baladant

▸ **amble along** VI (*of horse*) aller à l'amble; (*of person*) aller *ou* marcher d'un pas tranquille; (*without destination*) flâner

ambrosia [æm'brəʊzɪə] N *Myth* ambroisie *f*

ambrosial [æm'brəʊzɪəl] ADJ ambrosiaque

ambulance ['æmbjʊləns] N ambulance *f*

▸▸ *Am Fam Pej* **a. chaser** = avocat *m* qui ne s'occupe que d'affaires de demandes de dommages et intérêts pouvant rapporter gros; **a. crew** ambulanciers *mpl*; **a. man** (*driver*) ambulancier *m*; (*nurse*) infirmier *m* d'ambulance; (*stretcher carrier*) brancardier *m*; **a. plane** avion *m* sanitaire; **a. post** poste *m* d'ambulance; **a. ship** navire *m* hôpital; **a. train** train *m* sanitaire; **a. woman** (*driver*) ambulancière *f*, (*nurse*) infirmière *f* d'ambulance; (*stretcher carrier*) brancardière *f*

ambulant ['æmbjʊlənt] ADJ *Med* ambulatoire

ambulatory ['æmbjʊlətərɪ] ADJ **1** ambulant, mobile **2** *Med* (*treatment, sick person*) ambulatoire

▸ N promenoir *m*, préau *m*; *Archit* (*in church*) déambulatoire *m*

ambush ['æmbʊʃ] N embuscade *f*, guet-apens *m*, *pl* guets-apens; **to lie in a.** se tenir en embuscade; *Fig* être à l'affût; **to lay** *or* **set an a. for sb** tendre une embuscade à qn; **troops lying in a.** troupes embusquées; **they were caught in an a.** ils sont tombés dans une embuscade *ou* un guet-apens

▸ VT (*enemy*) attirer dans une embuscade; **to be ambushed** tomber dans une embuscade

ameba, amebic *Am* = amoeba, amoebic

ameliorate [ə'miːlɪəreɪt] *Fml* VT améliorer

▸ VI s'améliorer

amelioration [əmiːlɪə'reɪʃən] N *Fml* amélioration *f*

amen ['ɑː'men, 'eɪ'men] INT *Rel* amen, ainsi soit-il; *Fig* certes; **and we all say a. to that** c'est ce que nous souhaitons tous

amenable [ə'miːnəb(ə)l] ADJ (*subject*) sujet (**to** à); (*person*) (*to law, discipline*) soumis; (*to advice*) docile; (*child*) soumis, docile; **a. to reason** raisonnable, disposé à entendre raison; **to prove a. to a suggestion** se ranger à une suggestion; **the case is not a. to ordinary rules** ce cas n'est pas sujet aux règles ordinaires; **to be a. to treatment** (*of illness*) pouvoir être traité

amend [ə'mend] VT (*change*) modifier, amender; *Pol* (*bill*) amender; (*correct*) rectifier, corriger; **amended invoice** facture *f* rectificative

▸ VI s'amender

amendment [ə'mendmənt] N (*change*) modification *f*, *Pol* (*of bill*) amendement *m*; (*correction*) rectification *f*, correction *f*, (*of mistake*) redressement *m*, correction; *Pol* **to move an a.** proposer un amendement (**to** a bill à un projet de loi); *Am* **the third A.** (*to the Constitution*) le troisième amendement

amends [ə'mendz] NPL **to make a.** faire amende honorable; **nothing could make a. for what they had done** rien ne pouvait réparer ce qu'ils avaient fait; **to make a. to sb for sth** dédommager qn de qch

amenity [ə'miːnɪtɪ] N **1** (*usu pl*) **amenities** (*in town, city*) facilités *fpl*, aménagements *mpl; (at sports centre, campsite etc)* équipements *mpl;* **close to all amenities** *(in accommodation advertisement)* proximité tous commerces **2** *Fml, Arch (of place)* agrément *m*

amenorrhoea, *Am* **amenorrhea** [eɪmenəˈrɪə] **N** *Med* aménorrhée *f*

America [əˈmerɪkə] **N 1** *(continent)* Amérique *f;* **North/South A.** Amérique du Nord/Sud; **in A.** en Amérique; **the Americas** les Amériques **2** *(United States)* États-Unis *mpl* (d'Amérique)

American [əˈmerɪkən] **ADJ 1** *(continental)* américain **2** *(of United States)* américain **N 1** Américain, -aine; **Native A.** Amérindien, -ienne **2** *Ling* américain *m*
▸▸ **A. Automobile Association** = société *f* de dépannage pour les automobilistes, ≃ Touring Club *m* de France; **A. breakfast** petit déjeuner *m* américain; *Tex* **A. cloth** toile *f* cirée; *Fin* **A. depositary receipt** certificat *m* américain de dépôt; **A. English** (anglais *m*) américain; **A. Express**® American Express®; **to pay by A. Express**® payer par American Express®; **A. Express**® **card** carte *f* American Express®; *Br* **A. football** football *m* américain; **A. Indian** Indien, -ienne d'Amérique, Amérindien, -ienne; *Mus* **A. organ** harmonium *m; Am* **A. plan** pension *f* complète; **A. service** service *m* à l'américaine *ou* à l'assiette; *Cin* **A. shot** plan *m* américain

Americanism [əˈmerɪkənɪz(ə)m] **N** *Ling* américanisme *m*

Americanize [əˈmerɪkənaɪz] **VT** américaniser; **to become Americanized** s'américaniser

American-style option **N** *St Exch* option *f* américaine

Amerind [ˈæmərɪnd], **Amerindian** [æməˈrɪndɪən] **ADJ** amérindien **N** Amérindien, -ienne

amethyst [ˈæmɪθɪst] **N** améthyste *f*

Amex [ˈæmeks] **N 1** *(abbr* American Express®*)* Amex® carte *f* Amex® **2** *(abbr* American Stock Exchange*)* = deuxième place *f* boursière des États-Unis

amiability [eɪmɪəˈbɪlɪtɪ] **N** amabilité *f* (**to** envers)

amiable [ˈeɪmɪəb(ə)l] **ADJ** aimable (**to** envers); **to be very a.** être très aimable *ou* d'une grande amabilité

> Attention: ne pas confondre avec **amicable.**

amiably [ˈeɪmɪəblɪ] **ADV** aimablement, avec amabilité

amicability [æmɪkəˈbɪlɪtɪ] **N** nature *f ou* disposition *f* amicale; **the a. of his nature** sa nature amicale

amicable [ˈæmɪkəb(ə)l] **ADJ** *(manner, relationship, chat etc)* amical, -aux; *(separation, agreement)* à l'amiable
▸▸ *Law* **a. settlement** arrangement *m* à l'amiable

> Attention: ne pas confondre avec le terme anglais **amiable.**

amicably [ˈæmɪkəblɪ, əˈmɪk-] **ADV** amicalement; *(to part)* bons amis; *(to divorce, settle issue)* à l'amiable; **to live a. together** vivre en harmonie

AMICUS [ˈæmɪkəs] **N** = syndicat *m* industriel britannique né de la fusion de l'AEEU et du MSF

amid [əˈmɪd] **PREP** au milieu de; **the news came a. revelations of corruption** la nouvelle survint en plein milieu *ou* au moment des révélations de corruption; **the meeting ended a. some confusion** la réunion s'est terminée dans une certaine confusion

amide [ˈæmaɪd] **N** *Chem* amide *m*

amidships [əˈmɪdʃɪps] **ADV** *Naut* au milieu du navire; **cabin a.** cabine *f* par le travers; **to put the helm a.** mettre la barre droite; **helm a.!** barre à zéro!, zéro (la barre)!

amidst [əˈmɪdst] **PREP =** amid

amino-acid [æˈmiːnəʊ-] **N** *Chem* aminoacide *m*

amiss [əˈmɪs] **ADV, ADJ PRED 1** *(badly)* **to take sth a.** prendre qch de travers, mal prendre qch; **he took it very much a.** il a très mal pris la chose **2** *(out of place)* malvenu; **a cup of coffee wouldn't come** *or* **go a.** une tasse de café serait bienvenue; **a few more women presenters on TV wouldn't go a.** ce ne serait pas un mal *ou* une mauvaise chose s'il y avait plus de présentateurs femmes à la télévision; **something is a.** il y a quelque chose qui ne va pas *ou* *Fam* qui cloche; **there was nothing a. when I last saw him** tout allait bien la dernière fois que je l'ai vu

amity [ˈæmɪtɪ] **N** *Fml (between countries)* amitié *f,* concorde *f,* bons rapports *mpl;* **to live in a. with sb** vivre en bonne intelligence avec qn

ammeter [ˈæmiːtər] **N** *Elec* ampèremètre *m*

ammo [ˈæməʊ] **N** *Fam* munitions *fpl*

ammonia [əˈməʊnɪə] **N** *Chem* ammoniac *m,* gaz *m* ammoniac

ammoniac [əˈməʊnɪæk] **ADJ** ammoniac, -iaque; **sal a.** sel *m* ammoniac
N (gum) a. gomme *f* ammoniaque

ammonite [ˈæmənaɪt] **N** *(fossil)* ammonite *f*

ammonium [əˈməʊnɪəm] **N** *Chem* ammonium *m*
▸▸ **a. carbonate** carbonate *m* d'ammonium; **a. sulphate** sulfate *m* d'ammonium

ammunition [æmjʊˈnɪʃən] **N** *Mil* munitions *fpl; Fig* **the scandal provided the opposition with useful a.** le scandale a procuré à l'opposition un bon moyen d'offensive; *Fig* **protesters used the report as a.** les manifestants ont utilisé le rapport comme argument; **blank a.** munitions à blanc; **dummy a.** fausses munitions; **live a.** munitions réelles *ou* pour tir réel
▸▸ *Mil* **a. box** coffre *m* à munitions; *Mil* **a. depot, a. dump** dépôt *m* de munitions; *Mil* **a. train** train *m* de munitions

amnesia [æmˈniːzɪə] **N** *Med* amnésie *f;* **to suffer from a.** être amnésique *ou* souffrir d'amnésie

amnesiac [æmˈniːzɪæk], **amnesic** [æmˈniːzɪk] **N, ADJ** amnésique *mf*

amnesty [ˈæmnɪstɪ] **N** amnistie *f*
VT amnistier

amniocentesis [æmnɪəʊsenˈtiːsɪs] **N** *Med* amniocentèse *f*

amoeba, *Am* **ameba,** *pl* **amoebas, amoebae** [əˈmiːbə, -əz, -iː] **N** *Biol* amibe *f*

amoebic, *Am* **amebic** [əˈmiːbɪk] **ADJ** *Med* amibien
▸▸ **a. dysentery** dysenterie *f* amibienne

amok [əˈmɒk] **ADV to run a.** *(of gunman)* faire des ravages; *(of rioters, editor)*, *Fam (children)* se déchaîner

among [əˈmʌŋ], **amongst** [əˈmʌŋst] **PREP** parmi; **a house standing a. trees** une maison située au milieu des arbres *ou* entourée d'arbres; **to wander a. the ruins** errer parmi les ruines; **a. the crowd** au milieu de la foule, parmi la foule; **to live a. savages** vivre au milieu des sauvages; **we are a. friends** nous sommes entre amis; **this expression is current a. young people** cette expression est courante chez les jeunes; **a. the guests were ...** au nombre des invités qu'on a invités se trouvaient ...; **that cake won't go far a. twelve** ce gâteau ne donnera pas grand-chose, divisé entre douze person-

nes; **the orchestra is a. the finest in Europe** l'orchestre est l'un des meilleurs d'Europe; **not one a. them** pas un d'entre eux *ou* parmi eux; **a. other things, he said that ...** il a dit, entre autres, que ...; **a. ourselves** entre nous; **they quarrel a. themselves** ils se disputent entre eux

amoral [eɪˈmɒrəl] **ADJ** amoral, -aux

amorous [ˈæmərəs] **ADJ** *Lit, Hum (look, advances, adventures)* amoureux; **to be of an a. disposition** être romantique; **he became quite a.** il a commencé à me/lui/*etc* faire des avances

amorously [ˈæmərəslɪ] **ADV** amoureusement

amorphous [əˈmɔːfəs] **ADJ 1** *Chem* amorphe **2** *(mass, lump)* amorphe; *Fig (opinions, project)* vague

amortizable [əmɔːˈtaɪzəb(ə)l] **ADJ** *Com, Fin (debt)* amortissable

amortization [əmɔːtɪˈzeɪʃən] **N** *Com, Fin (of debt)* amortissement *m*

amortize [əˈmɔːtaɪz] **VT** *Com, Fin (debt)* amortir

amount [əˈmaʊnt] **N 1** *Com (sum of money)* somme *f,* *(total) (of bill etc)* montant *m,* total *m;* **please tender the exact a.** *(on bus etc)* on est prié de faire l'appoint; **(up) to the a. of ...** jusqu'à concurrence de ...; *Acct* **a. carried forward** report *m* à nouveau; **no a. (of money) could make up for what I've lost** rien ne pourrait compenser ce que j'ai perdu; **a. exclusive of VAT** montant hors TVA
2 *(quantity)* quantité *f;* **a massive a. of time** énormément de temps; **a massive a. of effort** des efforts énormes; **a certain a. of discomfort/comfort** un certain manque de confort/un certain confort; **the a. of work that an engine will do** la somme de travail que peut fournir une machine; **in small amounts** par petites quantités; **no a. of persuasion would make her stay** il n'y avait pas moyen de la persuader de rester; **a dwindling a. of funds** des fonds en quantité décroissante; **varying amounts of enthusiasm** des expressions d'enthousiasme inégales; *Fam* **he has any a. of money/friends/books** il a de l'argent/des amis/des livres tant et plus
▸ **amount to VT INSEP 1** *(of money etc)* s'élever à, se monter à; **transactions amounting to several million pounds** opérations qui se chiffrent par plusieurs millions de livres; **I don't know what my debts a. to** j'ignore le montant de mes dettes, j'ignore à combien se montent *ou* s'élèvent mes dettes
2 *(be equivalent to)* équivaloir à, se réduire à, revenir à; **these conditions a. to a refusal** ces conditions équivalent à un refus; **it amounts to the same thing** cela revient au même; **all that amounts to very little/to nothing** tout cela se réduit à peu de chose/à rien; **he'll never a. to much/to anything** il ne fera jamais grand-chose/rien

amour [əˈmʊər] **N** *Lit, Arch* intrigue *f* amoureuse, liaison *f*

A-movie **N** *Cin* film *m* projeté en exclusivité *(lors d'une séance où deux longs métrages sont projetés)*

amp [æmp] **N 1** *Elec (abbr* ampere*)* ampère *m;* **13-a. plug** fiche *f* de 13 ampères **2** *Mus Fam (abbr* amplifier*)* ampli *m*

ampere [ˈæmpeər] **N** *Elec* ampère *m*

ampersand [ˈæmpəsænd] **N** *Typ* esperluette *f*

amphetamine [æmˈfetəmɪn] **N** *Pharm* amphétamine *f;* **to be on amphetamines** *(of drug addict)* prendre des amphétamines

amphibia [æmˈfɪbɪə] **NPL** *Zool* amphibiens *mpl*

amphibian [æmˈfɪbɪən] **ADJ** amphibie **N 1** *Zool* amphibie *m* **2** *(tank)* char *m* amphibie; *(vehicle)* voiture *f* amphibie

amphibious [æmˈfɪbɪəs] ADJ (animal, plane etc) amphibie

amphitheatre, Am **amphitheater** [ˈæmfɪθɪətər] N Archit, Theat etc amphithéâtre m

amphora, pl **amphorae** [ˈæmfərə, -iː] N Antiq amphore f

ample [ˈæmp(ə)l] ADJ **1** (garment) ample, large; (bag, stomach, bosom) gros; **man of a. proportions** homme m corpulent **2** (plentiful) abondant; **this will be a.** ceci sera amplement suffisant, ceci suffira amplement; **to have a. means** avoir de gros moyens; **a. proof** de nombreuses preuves; **there are a. supplies of fish this week** (in shops) il y a de gros arrivages de poisson cette semaine; **the money we have is a. for our needs** nous avons largement assez d'argent pour subvenir à nos besoins; **to have a. time** avoir largement le temps (**to do** de faire); **you'll be given a. warning** vous serez averti longtemps à l'avance; **he was given a. opportunity to explain his actions** il a eu de nombreuses occasions d'expliquer ses actes; **you'll have a. opportunity to practise your backhand this summer** tu auras largement l'occasion de pratiquer ton revers cet été

amplification [æmplɪfɪˈkeɪʃən] N **1** (expansion) augmentation f, extension f; **if I could say something in a. of …** si je pouvais dire quelque chose pour développer … **2** (of power, current, volume etc) amplification f **3** Opt (using lens etc) grossissement m

amplifier [ˈæmplɪfaɪ] N **1** (for sound system) amplificateur m, Fam ampli m **2** Phot (lentille f) amplificatrice f
▸▸**a. circuit** circuit m d'amplification

amplify [ˈæmplɪfaɪ] VT **1** (expand) (essay, remarks etc) développer; (report etc) ajouter des détails à **2** (current, power, volume etc) amplifier

amplitude [ˈæmplɪtjuːd] N Fml (of dimensions, resources etc) ampleur f, (of space) étendue f, Astron (of star) amplitude f, Phys (of oscillations, vibrations) amplitude f; Phys **magnetic a.** déclinaison f magnétique
▸▸**a. modulation** modulation f d'amplitude

amply [ˈæmplɪ] ADV amplement; **a. proportioned** aux dimensions généreuses; **a. rewarded** largement récompensé

ampoule [ˈæmpuːl] N Med (for hypodermic injection) ampoule f

amputate [ˈæmpjʊteɪt] VT (leg etc) amputer; **his right leg was amputated** il a été amputé de la jambe droite
VI amputer

amputation [æmpjʊˈteɪʃən] N amputation f

amputee [æmpjʊˈtiː] N amputé, -ée

Amtrak [ˈæmtræk] N = société f des chemins de fer interurbains des États-Unis

amuck [əˈmʌk] ADV = amok

amulet [ˈæmjʊlet] N amulette f

amuse [əˈmjuːz] VT amuser, divertir, faire rire; **it amused her to do it** ça l'a amusée de le faire; **is something amusing you?** quelque chose vous amuse?; **to a. oneself** s'occuper, passer le temps; **to a. oneself by** or **with doing sth** (have fun) s'amuser à faire qch ou en faisant qch; (pass the time) s'occuper en faisant qch; **to a. oneself with sth** s'amuser avec qch; **to keep sb amused** (occupied) occuper qn; (entertained) amuser qn

amused [əˈmjuːzd] ADJ amusé; **to be a. at** or **by sth** s'amuser de qch, trouver qch drôle; **she wasn't at all a.** elle n'a pas du tout trouvé ça drôle; **a. smile** sourire m amusé

amusedly [əˈmjuːzɪdlɪ] ADV d'un air amusé

amusement [əˈmjuːzmənt] N **1** amusement m; **source of a.** source f d'amusement; **smile of a.** sourire m amusé; **to the great a. of the children** au grand amusement des enfants; **much to everyone's a.** au grand amusement de la compagnie **2** (occupation, pastime) amusement m, divertissement m, distraction f; **we have few amusements here** nous avons peu de distractions ici; **it offered** or **provided little a. for them** cela ne les amusait guère; **place of a.** lieu m de divertissement
▸▸**a. arcade** salle f de jeux électroniques; **a. park** parc m d'attractions

amusing [əˈmjuːzɪŋ] ADJ (person) amusant, drôle; (book, film) amusant, drôle, divertissant; **what an a. woman/idea** quelle femme/quelle idée amusante

amusingly [əˈmjuːzɪŋlɪ] ADV d'une manière amusante; **a. worded** drôle, amusant

amylase [ˈæmɪleɪz] N Biol, Chem amylase f

an see a²

ANA [eɪenˈeɪ] N Journ (abbr American Newspaper Association) = syndicat m américain de la presse écrite

anabaptist [ænəˈbæptɪst] ADJ, N Rel, Hist anabaptiste mf

anabolic [ænəˈbɒlɪk] ADJ Chem anabolisant
▸▸Pharm **a. steroid** stéroïde m anabolisant

anachronism [əˈnækrənɪz(ə)m] N anachronisme m; **she's an a.** c'est un véritable anachronisme

anachronistic [ənækrəˈnɪstɪk] ADJ anachronique

anaconda [ænəˈkɒndə] N (snake) anaconda m

anaemia, Am **anemia** [əˈniːmɪə] N anémie f; **to suffer from a.** souffrir d'anémie, faire de l'anémie

anaemic, Am **anemic** [əˈniːmɪk] ADJ Med anémique; Fig faible, mou, f molle; **to become a.** s'anémier

anaesthesia, Am **anesthesia** [ænəsˈθiːzɪə] N anesthésie f; **general/local a.** anesthésie générale/locale; **spinal a.** anesthésie rachidienne

anaesthetic, Am **anesthetic** [ænəsˈθetɪk] N (product) anesthésique m; (procedure) anesthésie f; **under a.** sous anesthésie; **under the a.** sous l'effet de l'anesthésie
ADJ anesthésique

anaesthetist, Am **anesthetist** [əˈniːsθətɪst] N anesthésiste mf

anaesthetize, Am **anesthetize** [əˈniːsθətaɪz] VT Med, Fig anesthésier

anagram [ˈænəgræm] N anagramme f

anal [ˈeɪn(ə)l] ADJ Anat anal, -aux

analeptic [ænəˈleptɪk] N, ADJ Pharm analeptique m

analgesia [ænælˈdʒiːzɪə] N Med analgésie f

analgesic [ænælˈdʒiːsɪk, -zɪk] ADJ, N Med analgésique m; Pharm antalgique m

analog [ˈænəlɒg] ADJ Comput analogique
N Am = analogue

analogical [ænəˈlɒdʒɪk(ə)l] ADJ analogique

analogically [ænəˈlɒdʒɪklɪ] ADV analogiquement, par analogie; **a. speaking** analogiquement parlant

analogous [əˈnæləgəs] ADJ analogue (**to**, **with** à)

analogously [əˈnæləgəslɪ] ADV d'une manière analogue

analogue, Am **analog** [ˈænəlɒg] N analogue m; **this is an a. of what happens on a national level** ceci est analogue à ce qui se passe au niveau national
ADJ (clock, watch) (à affichage) analogique
▸▸**a. computer** calculateur m analogique; **a. network** réseau m analogique

analogy [əˈnælədʒɪ] N analogie f (**to**, **with** avec; **between** entre); **by a. with …** par analogie avec …; **to draw an a.** faire une analogie; **on the a. of …** en comparant avec …

analyse, Am **analyze** [ˈænəlaɪz] VT (text, events), Chem, Math analyser, faire l'analyse de; (feelings, attitude) analyser; Gram (sentence) faire l'analyse logique de; Psy (person) psychanalyser

analysis, pl **analyses** [əˈnæləsɪs, -iːz] N (of text), Chem, Phys analyse f, Gram (of sentence) analyse logique; Psy psychanalyse f, **nothing abnormal showed up under a.** l'analyse n'a rien révélé d'anormal; **our a. is that …** notre analyse démontre que …; **to hold up under** or **withstand a.** résister à l'analyse; Psy **to be in a.** (of patient) être en analyse; **in the final** or **last a.** (ultimately) en fin de compte, au bout du compte
▸▸Acct **a. ledger** journal m analytique

analyst [ˈænəlɪst] N analyste mf, Psy (psych)analyste mf

analytic(al) [ænəˈlɪtɪk, -ɪk(ə)l] ADJ analytique; **a. mind** esprit m d'analyse
▸▸**a. psychology** psychologie f introspective

analyze [ˈænəlaɪz] VT Am = analyse

analyzer [ˈænəlaɪzər] N Comput analyseur m

anamorphic [ænəˈmɔːfɪk] ADJ Cin, TV anamorphique
▸▸**a. format** format m anamorphique; **a. lens** objectif m anamorphoseur

anarchic [æˈnɑːkɪk] ADJ anarchique

anarchist [ˈænəkɪst] ADJ, N anarchiste mf

anarchy [ˈænəkɪ] N anarchie f

anastigmatic [ænəstɪgˈmætɪk] ADJ Opt anastigmat(ique)

anastomosis [ænæstəˈməʊsɪs] N Med anastomose f

anathema [əˈnæθəmə] N Rel, Fig anathème m; **his name is a.** son nom est tabou; Fig **it's/ he's a. to me** c'est ma bête noire; **such theories were pronounced a.** l'anathème a été jeté sur ces théories; **their ideas were a. to him** leurs idées l'horripilaient

anathematize [əˈnæθəmətaɪz] VT Arch, Fml frapper d'anathème

anatomical [ænəˈtɒmɪk(ə)l] ADJ anatomique; **a. specimen** pièce f d'anatomie, préparation f anatomique

anatomically [ænəˈtɒmɪklɪ] ADV anatomiquement

anatomist [əˈnætəmɪst] N anatomiste mf

anatomy [əˈnætəmɪ] N **1** (of human, animal) anatomie f **2** (science) anatomie f, (textbook) cours m d'anatomie; **human a.** anatomie humaine **3** Fig analyse f, anatomie f

ANC [eɪenˈsiː] N (abbr African National Congress) ANC m

ancestor [ˈænsestər] N ancêtre m, Lit aïeul m, pl aïeux
▸▸**a. worship** culte m des ancêtres

ancestral [ænˈsestr(ə)l] ADJ **1** ancestral, -aux, héréditaire, de famille; **it's an a. right** c'est un droit ancestral; **his a. home** la demeure de ses ancêtres **2** Biol ancestral, -aux

ancestress [ˈænsestrɪs] N ancêtre f, Lit aïeule f

ancestry [ˈænsestrɪ] N **1** (descent) ascendance f, **both families were of French a.** les deux familles étaient d'ascendance française; **this custom is of more recent a.** cette coutume est d'apparition plus récente **2** (no pl) (ancestors) ancêtres mpl, ascendants mpl, aïeux mpl

anchor [ˈæŋkər] N **1** Naut etc ancre f, Fig planche f de salut; **to let go** or **drop the a.** jeter ou mouiller l'ancre; **to weigh a.** lever l'ancre, appareiller; **to lie** or **ride at a.** être à l'ancre, mouiller; **at a.** au mouillage; **to slip the a.** filer (sa chaîne) par le bout; **to drag**

her a. *(of ship)* chasser sur son ancre *ou* sur ses ancres
2 *TV (presenter)* présentateur, -trice principal(e)
vt 1 *Naut (ship)* ancrer, mouiller
2 *(fix firmly) Constr* affermir par des ancres; *Naut etc (mast etc)* hauban(n)er; *Fig* **to be anchored to the spot** *(by indecision, terror)* être cloué sur place
3 *TV (programme)* présenter
vi *Naut* jeter l'ancre, mouiller
▸▸ *Naut* **a. buoy** bouée *f* de mouillage *ou* d'ancre; *Constr* **a. iron** grappin *m*; *Constr* **a. plate** plaque *f* d'ancrage; *Constr* **a. stay** câble *m* d'ancrage; *Am* **a. store** magasin-phare *m*, *pl* magasins-phares; *Constr* **a. tie** grappin

anchorage ['æŋkərɪdʒ] **N 1** *Naut (act, place)* mouillage *m*; **to leave the a.** dérader **2** *Naut (fee)* droits *mpl* d'ancrage *ou* de stationnement **3** *Constr* ancrage *m*; *(of tie beam)* point *m* d'attache
▸▸ **a. point** *(of seatbelt)* point d'ancrage

anchored ['æŋkəd] **ADJ** *Naut* ancré, mouillé, à l'ancre; *Fig* **firmly a. faith** foi *f* solidement ancrée

anchoring ['æŋkərɪŋ] **N** *Naut* ancrage *m*, mouillage *m*

anchorite ['æŋkəraɪt] **N** *Rel* anachorète *m*

anchorman, *pl* **anchormen** ['æŋkəmən] **N 1** *Sport (of team)* dernier coureur *m* **2** *Radio, TV* présentateur *m* principal

anchorwoman, *pl* **anchorwomen** ['æŋkəwʊmən, -wɪmɪn] **N** *Radio, TV* présentatrice *f* principale

anchovy ['æntʃəvɪ, æn'tʃəʊvɪ] **N** anchois *m*
▸▸ **a. butter** beurre *m* d'anchois; **a. paste** pâte *f* d'anchois

ancient ['eɪnʃənt] **ADJ** ancien; *(monument)* historique; *(oak)* centenaire; *Fam (person)* très vieux, *f* vieille, décrépit; *Fam (car, TV etc)* antique, antédiluvien; *Fam* **this car is getting pretty a.** cette voiture est une vraie antiquité
NPL the ancients les anciens *mpl*
▸▸ *also Fig* **a. history** histoire *f* ancienne; **A. Rome** la Rome antique; **the a. world** le monde antique

ancillary [æn'sɪlərɪ] **ADJ** subordonné (**to** à); *(assisting)* auxiliaire
N *(helper)* auxiliaire *mf*, *(in hospital)* auxiliaire de service
▸▸ **a. equipment** matériel *m* annexe *ou* d'appoint, accessoires *mpl*; **a. rights** droits *mpl* dérivés; **a. staff** personnel *m* auxiliaire; *(in hospital)* personnel des services auxiliaires; *(in school)* personnel auxiliaire, auxiliaires; **a. worker** *(in hospital)* auxiliaire de service

AND [ænd] **N** *Comput*
▸▸ **A. circuit** circuit *m* ET; **A. element** élément *m* ET

AND [ænd, *unstressed* ənd, ən, n] **CONJ 1** *(connecting words)* et; **a./or** et/ou; **a knife a. fork** un couteau et une fourchette; **my father a. mother are out** mon père et ma mère sont sortis; **four a. five make(s) nine** quatre plus cinq font neuf; **ham a. eggs** des œufs au jambon; **now a. then** de temps en temps; **he came without pencils a. paper** il est venu sans crayons ni papier; **he speaks English, a. very well too** il parle anglais et même très bien; **a. (what about) the invalids?** et les malades?; **the water was nice a. warm** l'eau était bien chaude; **good a. ready** fin prêt; **a. what if I am going?** et si j'y allais?
2 *(connecting clauses)* et; **he could read a. write** il savait lire et écrire; **move (an inch) a. you're a dead man** un pas et tu es mort; *esp Br* **go a. look for it** allez le chercher; **come a. see me** venez me voir; **try a. help me** essaie de m'aider; **to look for sth a. not see it**

chercher qch sans le voir; **I waited an hour a. he still hadn't turned up** j'ai attendu une heure et il n'était toujours pas là; **they started taking drugs, so I came home – a. a good thing too!** ils ont commencé à prendre de la drogue, alors je suis rentré – tu as bien fait!
3 *(with numerals)* **two hundred a. two** deux cent deux; **four a. a half** quatre et demi; **four a. three-quarters** quatre trois quarts; **an hour a. twenty minutes** une heure vingt minutes; *Old-fashioned* **five a. twenty** vingt-cinq; *Br Arch* **three shillings a. sixpence, three a. six** trois shillings six pence
4 *(repetition)* et; **for miles a. miles** pendant des kilomètres et des kilomètres, sur des kilomètres; **better a. better** de mieux en mieux; **smaller a. smaller** de plus en plus petit; **I knocked a. knocked (again)** j'ai frappé tant et plus; **over a. over again** maintes et maintes fois
5 *(contrast)* et; **there are doctors a. (there are) doctors** il y a médecins et médecins
6 a. so on, a. so forth, a. so on a. so forth et ainsi de suite

---

Andalusia [ændə'lu:sɪə, -zɪə] **N** Andalousie *f*

andante [æn'dæntɪ] **ADV, N** *Mus* andante *m*

andantino [ændæn'ti:nəʊ] **ADV, N** *Mus* andantino *m*

Andean ['ændɪən] **ADJ** andin, des Andes

Andes ['ændi:z] **NPL the A.** les Andes *fpl*, la Cordillère des Andes

andiron ['ændaɪən] **N** chenet *m*

Andorra [æn'dɔ:rə] **N** (république *f* d')Andorre *f*; **A. (City)** Andorre-la-Vieille

Andorran [æn'dɔ:rən] **ADJ** andorran
N Andorran, -ane

androgen ['ændrədʒən] **N** *Biol* androgène *m*

androgynous [æn'drɒdʒɪnəs] **ADJ** androgyne

androgyny [æn'drɒdʒɪnɪ] **N** androgynie *f*

anecdotal [ænɪk'dəʊt(ə)l] **ADJ** anecdotique

anecdote ['ænɪkdəʊt] **N** anecdote *f*

anemia, anemic *Am* = **anaemia, anaemic**

anemometer [ænɪ'mɒmɪtər] **N** *Met* anémomètre *m*

anemone [ə'nemənɪ] **N** *(flower)* anémone *f*

aneroid ['ænərɔɪd] **ADJ** *Phys (barometer)* anéroïde

anesthesia, anesthetic *etc Am* = **anaesthesia, anaesthetic** *etc*

anesthesiologist [ænəsθi:zɪ'ɒlədʒɪst] **N** *Am Med* anesthésiste *mf*

aneurism, aneurysm ['ænjʊrɪz(ə)m] **N** *Med* anévrisme *m*, anévrysme *m*

anew [ə'nju:] **ADV 1** *(again)* de nouveau; **to begin a.** recommencer **2** *(from beginning)* à nouveau; **to create sth a.** créer qch à nouveau

angel ['eɪndʒ(ə)l] **N 1** ange *m*; **the a. of death** l'ange de la mort; **fallen a.** ange déchu; *Fam* **you a.!, you're an a.!** tu es un ange *ou* un amour!; *Fam* **be an a.** sois gentil **2** *Fam (financial backer)* bailleur *m* de fonds **3** *Aviat Fam* écho *m* radar non identifié
▸▸ *Culin* **a. cake** gâteau *m* de Savoie; *Sl* **a. dust** poudre *f* d'ange; **a. face** visage *m* d'ange *ou* angélique; *Culin* **a. food cake** gâteau de Savoie

angelfish ['eɪndʒəlfɪʃ] **N** ange *m* de mer, angelot *m*

angelic [æn'dʒelɪk] **ADJ** angélique

angelica [æn'dʒelɪkə] **N** *Bot, Culin* angélique *f*

angelically [æn'dʒelɪklɪ] **ADV** comme un ange

angelus ['ændʒələs] **N** *Rel* angélus *m*

anger ['æŋgər] **N** colère *f*; **in a fit** *or* **moment of a.** dans un accès de colère; **to speak in a.** parler sous le coup de la colère; **the cannon was never fired in a.** on ne s'est jamais servi de ce canon en temps de guerre
vt mettre en colère, irriter; **he is easily angered** il se met facilement en colère, il est irascible; **to be slow to a.** ne pas se mettre facilement en colère; **these remarks have angered Christians** ces commentaires ont exaspéré la communauté chrétienne; **he is angered by suggestions that he took bribes** cela le met en colère qu'on suggère qu'il ait pu accepter des pots-de-vin

angina [æn'dʒaɪnə] **N** *Med* angine *f* de poitrine; **to have a.** avoir une angine de poitrine
▸▸ **a. pectoris** angine de poitrine

angiology [ændʒɪ'ɒlədʒɪ] **N** *Med* angiologie *f*, angéiologie *f*

angioplasty ['ændʒɪəplæstɪ] **N** *Med* angioplastie *f*

angiosperm ['ændʒɪəʊspɜ:m] **N** angiosperme *f*

Angle ['æŋg(ə)l] **N** *Hist* Angle *mf*

angle[1] ['æŋg(ə)l] **N 1** *Math, Fig* angle *m*; *(viewpoint)* point *m* de vue; *(of newspaper article etc)* perspective *f*; **at an a. of ...** formant un angle de ...; **at an a.** de biais; **the house stands at an a. to the street** la maison fait angle sur la rue; **from a different a.** sous un angle différent, sous un autre angle; **seen from this a.** vu sous cet angle; **to study a problem from every a.** *or* **all angles** étudier un problème sur toutes ses faces *ou* sous tous les angles; **we need a new a.** *(on story)* il nous faut un éclairage *ou* un point de vue nouveau; *Fig* **what's your a. on this?** qu'est-ce que vous pensez de ceci?; **visual** *or* **viewing a.** angle de vision, angle visuel
2 *Mil* angle *m*
3 *Aviat* **critical a.** *(of attack),* **stalling a.** angle *m* critique; **listing a.** angle de gîte
4 *Constr (of room)* coin *m*, encoignure *f*, angle *m*; **cutting a.** angle de coupe
5 *Elec, Electron* angle *m*; **phase a.** angle de phase
vt 1 *(set at angle) (light beam)* orienter, diriger (**on, to** sur); **to a. a lamp onto one's book** orienter *ou* diriger le faisceau de sa lampe sur son livre; *Tennis* **to a. a shot** envoyer la balle en diagonale
2 *(report)* orienter; *(facts)* présenter d'une manière tendancieuse *ou* partiale; **it's angled towards the 16-18 age range** cela vise les 16-18 ans, c'est destiné aux 16-18 ans; **studies are angled towards exams** les études sont très axées sur les examens
▸▸ *Mil* **a. of altitude** angle de hausse *ou* de tir positif; *Aviat* **a. of ascent** *(of plane, projectile)* angle de montée; *Aviat* **a. of attack** angle d'attaque; *Constr* **a. bar** cornière *f*, équerre *f*; *Constr* **a. brace** *(tool)* foret *m* à angle; *Typ* **a. bracket** crochet *m* en chevron; **a. of climb** *(of plane, projectile)* angle de montée; *Mil* **a. of deflection** angle de dérive; *Mil* **a. of elevation** angle de hausse *ou* de tir positif; **a. gauge** goniomètre *m*; *Naut* **a. of heel** *(of ship)* angle de gîte; *Phys* **a. of incidence** angle d'incidence; *Constr* **a. iron** cornière, équerre; *Naut* **a. of list** *(of ship)* angle de gîte; *Constr* **a. plate** cornière, équerre; *Cin* **a. shot** prise *f* de vue oblique; *Mil* **a. of sight** angle de mire *ou* de visée; *Constr* **a. of torque** angle de torsion; **a. of vision** angle de vision, angle visuel

angle[2] **vi** *(fish)* pêcher à la ligne
▸ **angle for vt insep** *(fish)* pêcher; *Fig (compliments)* chercher; **to a. for promotion** chercher à être promu; **to a. for an invitation** chercher à se faire inviter

angled ['æŋg(ə)ld] **ADJ 1** **acute-a.** acutangle,

aux angles aigus **2** *(report etc)* partial, -aux, tendancieux
▸▸ *Sport* **a. shot** coup *m* en diagonale

Anglepoise® ['æŋg(ə)lpɔɪz] N
▸▸ **A. lamp** lampe *f* d'architecte

angler ['æŋglər] N **1** *(person)* pêcheur, -euse (à la ligne) **2** baudroie *f*, crapaud *m* de mer
▸▸ **a. fish** baudroie *f*, crapaud *m* de mer

Anglican ['æŋglɪkən] *Rel* ADJ anglican
N Anglican, -ane
▸▸ **the A. Church** l'Église *f* anglicane

Anglicanism ['æŋglɪkənɪz(ə)m] N *Rel* anglicanisme *m*

anglicism ['æŋglɪsɪz(ə)m] N anglicisme *m*

Anglicist ['æŋglɪsɪst] N angliciste *mf*

anglicization [æŋglɪsaɪ'zeɪʃən] N anglicisation *f*

anglicize ['æŋglɪsaɪz] VT angliciser

angling ['æŋglɪŋ] N *(fishing)* pêche *f* à la ligne

Anglo ['æŋgləʊ] N *Am* Américain, -aine d'ascendance européenne

Anglo-American ADJ anglo-américain
N Anglo-Américain, -aine, *pl* Anglo-Américains, -aines

Anglo-Catholic ADJ, N *Rel* anglo-catholique *mf*, *pl* anglo-catholiques

Anglo-French ADJ franco-britannique
N *Ling* anglo-normand *m*

Anglo-Indian ADJ anglo-indien
N **1** *(person of mixed ancestry)* métis *m*, -isse *f* d'origine anglaise et indienne **2** *(Briton who has lived in India)* Anglo-Indien, -ienne, *pl* Anglo-Indiens, -iennes

Anglo-Irish ADJ anglo-irlandais
NPL **the A.** les Anglo-Irlandais *mpl*

anglophile ['æŋgləʊfaɪl] ADJ, N anglophile *mf*

anglophobe ['æŋgləʊfəʊb] ADJ, N anglophobe *mf*

anglophobia ['æŋgləʊ'fəʊbɪə] N anglophobie *f*

Anglophone ['æŋgləfəʊn] ADJ, N anglophone *mf*

Anglo-Saxon ADJ anglo-saxon
N **1** *(person)* Anglo-Saxon, -onne, *pl* Anglo-Saxons, -onnes **2** *Ling* anglo-saxon *m*

Angola [æŋ'gəʊlə] N Angola *m*

Angolan [æŋ'gəʊlən] ADJ angolais
N Angolais, -aise

angora [æŋ'gɔːrə] N **1** *(animal)* angora *m* **2** *Tex* angora *m*; **a. jumper** pull *m* en angora; **a. wool** laine *f* angora
▸▸ **a. cat** chat *m* angora; **a. goat** chèvre *f* angora; **a. rabbit** lapin *m* angora

angostura [æŋgəs'tjʊərə] N *Pharm etc* angusture *f*
▸▸ **A. bitters®** bitter *m* à base d'angusture

angrily ['æŋgrɪlɪ] ADV *(to answer etc)* avec colère

angry ['æŋgrɪ] ADJ *(person)* en colère (**at sb** contre qn; **about sth** à cause de qch), fâché, irrité (**with** *or Am* **at sb** contre qn; **about sth** de qch); *(voice)* irrité; *(speech, letter)* furieux, virulent; **he was a. at being kept waiting** il était irrité qu'on le fît attendre; **to be a. with oneself** *(for not doing better)* être mécontent de soi; *(for giving offence, causing pain etc)* s'en vouloir; **to get a.** se mettre en colère, se fâcher, s'irriter; **to get a. with sb** se fâcher *ou* se mettre en colère contre qn; **to make sb a.** exaspérer qn, mettre qn en colère; **it makes me very a. when I hear people say that** ça m'exaspère d'entendre dire ça; **a. words were exchanged** il y eut un échange assez virulent; *Lit* **the a. sea** la mer courroucée *ou* en courroux; **a. sky** *(stormy)* ciel *m* orageux *ou* menaçant; *Med* **a. sore** plaie *f* irritée *ou* enflammée
▸▸ **a. young man** jeune *m* contestataire

angst [æŋst] N angoisse *f*

angstrom ['æŋstrəm] N *Phys* angström *m*

angsty ['æŋstɪ] ADJ *Fam* stressé

anguish ['æŋgwɪʃ] N **1** *(great anxiety)* angoisse *f*, douleur *f*; **to be in a.** être dans l'angoisse *ou* angoissé, être au supplice; **to cause sb a.** mettre qn dans l'angoisse, angoisser qn **2** *Med* angoisse *f*

anguished ['æŋgwɪʃt] ADJ angoissé

angular ['æŋgjʊlər] ADJ **1** *(rock, face)* anguleux; *(body)* maigre, osseux **2** *(movement)* saccadé **3** *Math, Phys (velocity etc)* angulaire

anhydride [æn'haɪdraɪd] N *Chem* anhydride *m*

anhydrous [æn'haɪdrəs] ADJ *Chem* anhydre

aniline ['ænɪlaɪn] N *Chem* aniline *f*
▸▸ **a. dye** colorant *m* d'aniline

animal ['ænɪm(ə)l] VOIR GRAMMAIRE A27 N animal *m*, -aux; **to behave like an a.** se comporter comme un animal; *Fig* **he's an a.** c'est une brute; *Fig* **she's not a political a.** elle n'est pas portée sur la politique; *Fig* **that's an entirely different a.** c'est tout à fait autre chose; *Fam* **there ain't no such a.** ça n'existe pas
ADJ **1** *(fat, kingdom etc)* animal, -aux **2** *(instinct, need)* animal, -aux
▸▸ **a. husbandry** élevage *m*; **a. painter** animalier, -ière; **a. rights** droits *mpl* des animaux

animalcule [ænɪ'mælkjuːl] N *Zool* animalcule *m*

animate¹ ['ænɪmət] ADJ *(alive)* vivant, animé, doué de vie; **to become a.** s'animer

animate² ['ænɪmeɪt] VT *(person, party, conversation, film)* animer

animated ['ænɪmeɪtɪd] ADJ *(discussion)* animé; **to become a.** *(of person, discussion)* s'animer
▸▸ **a. cartoon** dessin *m* animé; **a. film** film *m* d'animation; *Comput* **a. GIF** (fichier *m*) GIF *m* animé

animatedly ['ænɪmeɪtɪdlɪ] ADV *(to say)* d'un ton animé; *(to discuss, speak, gesture)* avec animation

animatic [ænɪ'mætɪk] N *(storyboard)* animatique *f*

animation [ænɪ'meɪʃən] N **1** *(of person)* animation *f*, entrain *m*; *(of style)* chaleur *f*; *(of orator)* feu *m*, véhémence *f* **2** *(act)* stimulation *f* **3** *Cin* animation *f*

animator ['ænɪmeɪtər] N *Cin* animateur, -trice

animatronic [ænɪmə'trɒnɪk] ADJ *Cin, TV* animé électroniquement

animatronics [ænɪmə'trɒnɪks] N *Cin, TV* animatronique *f*

animism ['ænɪmɪz(ə)m] N *Phil* animisme *m*

animist ['ænɪmɪst] ADJ, N *Phil* animiste *mf*

animosity [ænɪ'mɒsɪtɪ] N animosité *f*; **to feel a. against** *or* **towards sb** ressentir de l'animosité contre qn; **there was considerable a. towards this idea** cette idée soulevait une grande hostilité

animus ['ænɪməs] N *Fml* **1** *(hostility)* animosité *f* **2** *(motive, stimulus)* stimulation *f*

anion ['ænaɪən] N *Phys, Elec* anion *m*

anise ['ænɪs] N *(plant)* anis *m*; **star a.** anis étoilé

aniseed ['ænɪsiːd] N *Bot, Culin* (graine *f* d')anis *m*
▸▸ **a. ball** bonbon *m* à l'anis; **a. cake** gâteau *m* à l'anis

anisette [ænɪ'zet] N *(liqueur)* anisette *f*

ankle ['æŋk(ə)l] N cheville *f*; **a.-length dress** robe *f* qui descend jusqu'à la cheville; **to be a.-deep in water/mud** avoir de l'eau/de la boue jusqu'aux chevilles
▸▸ **a. bone** astragale *m*; **a. boot** bottine *f*; **a.**

chain bracelet *m* de cheville; **a. joint** articulation *f* du pied; **a. sock** socquette *f*; **a. strap** bride *f*; **a. support** chevillière *f*

ankle-biter N *Fam (child)* gosse *mf*

anklet ['æŋklət] N **1** *(ornament)* bracelet *m*/anneau *m* de cheville **2** *Am (sock)* socquette *f*

ankylose ['æŋkɪləʊz] *Med* VT ankyloser
VI s'ankyloser

ankylosis [æŋkɪ'ləʊsɪs] N *Med* ankylose *f*

annalist ['ænəlɪst] N annaliste *mf*

annals ['æn(ə)lz] NPL annales *fpl*

Anne [æn] N Anne; *Hist* **A. of Austria** Anne d'Autriche

anneal [ə'niːl] VT *Tech (glass)* recuire, adoucir; *(metal)* détremper, recuire, adoucir

annealing [ə'niːlɪŋ] N *Tech (of glass)* recuit *m*, recuite *f*; *Metal (of metal)* adoucissement *m*, recuit, recuite; **box** *or* **close a.** recuit en vase clos
▸▸ **a. furnace** four *m* à recuire

annex¹ ['æneks] N *Am* = **annexe**

annex² [æ'neks] VT **1** *(take possession of) (province)* annexer **2** *(attach)* annexer (**sth to sth** qch à qch)

annexation [ænek'seɪʃən] N annexion *f* (**of** de)

annexe, *Am* **annex** ['æneks] N **1** *(of building)* annexe *f* **2** *(to document)* annexe *f*

annihilate [ə'naɪəleɪt] VT *(fleet, army)* anéantir, réduire à néant; *Fam* **his opponent annihilated him** son adversaire l'a pulvérisé *ou* anéanti

annihilation [ənaɪə'leɪʃən] N **1** *(of fleet, people)* anéantissement *m* **2** *Nucl* annihilation *f*, *(of electron and positron)* dématérialisation *f*

anniversary [ænɪ'vɜːs(ə)rɪ] N anniversaire *m*; **it's our wedding a.** c'est l'anniversaire de notre mariage; **on the a. of ...** le jour (de l')anniversaire de ...; **an a. dinner** un dîner d'anniversaire; **golden/silver/ruby (wedding) a.** noces *fpl* d'or/d'argent/de rubis

anno Domini ['ænəʊ'dɒmɪnaɪ, -niː] ADV en l'an du Seigneur *ou* de grâce

annotate ['ænəteɪt] VT *(book etc)* annoter; **annotated draft** brouillon *m* annoté

annotation [ænə'teɪʃən] N annotation *f*

annotator ['ænəteɪtər] N annotateur, -trice

announce [ə'naʊns] VT annoncer; **the Prime Minister has announced his cabinet** le Premier ministre a fait connaître *ou* a annoncé la composition de son cabinet; **to a. the birth/marriage/death of sb** faire part de la naissance/du mariage/du décès de qn

announcement [ə'naʊnsmənt] N annonce *f*, *(statement)* déclaration *f*, *(of birth, marriage etc)* faire-part *m inv*; *Journ* **a. of death** avis *m* de décès; **here is a passenger a.** avis voyageurs; **here is a staff a.** appel de service

announcer [ə'naʊnsər] N annonceur, -euse; *Radio, TV* speaker *m*, speakerine *f*
▸▸ **a. booth** cabine *f* de présentation; **a. studio** studio *m* d'annonceur

annoy [ə'nɔɪ] VT *(person)* ennuyer, embêter; *(stronger)* agacer, énerver; *(by going against sb's wishes etc)* contrarier; **you're really annoying me!** ce que tu peux m'embêter!; **is the light/noise annoying you?** est-ce que la lumière/le bruit t'ennuie *ou* te dérange?; **is this man annoying you?** est-ce que cet homme vous importune?

Note that the French verb **ennuyer** often means **to bore**.

annoyance [ə'nɔɪəns] N énervement *m*, agacement *m*, *Fam* embêtement *m*; **look of a.** air *m* contrarié *ou* ennuyé; **much to his a.** à son grand déplaisir *ou* mécontentement;

source of a. désagrément *m*, cause *f* d'ennuis; **petty annoyances** petits ennuis *mpl*, petites contrariétés *fpl*; **to cause a. to everyone** énerver tout le monde; *(by going against wishes etc)* contrarier tout le monde; **she failed to hide her a. at his words** elle n'a pas réussi à cacher l'énervement *ou* l'agacement que lui inspiraient ses paroles

annoyed [ə'nɔɪd] ADJ ennuyé, *Fam* embêté (**at, about** par, à cause de); *(stronger)* agacé, énervé (**at, about** par, à cause de); *(because sb has gone against one's wishes)* contrarié; **to be a. with sb/oneself** être en colère contre qn/soi-même; **to get a. with sb/sth** se mettre en colère *ou* s'énerver contre qn/qch; **promise you won't get a.** promets-moi que tu ne vas pas te mettre en colère *ou* t'énerver

annoying [ə'nɔɪɪŋ] ADJ ennuyeux, agaçant; *(habits)* agaçant; **the a. thing about it is that ...** ce qu'il y a d'ennuyeux là-dedans c'est que ...; **how a.!** que c'est ennuyeux *ou Fam* embêtant!

annoyingly [ə'nɔɪɪŋlɪ] ADV *(irritatingly) (to behave)* d'une façon agaçante *ou* énervante; **a., he was late** il était en retard, ce qui était ennuyeux; **she's a. punctual** elle est agaçante à être aussi ponctuelle; **it's getting a. unreliable** il/elle devient de moins en moins fiable au point que c'en est agaçant; **he's so a. knowledgeable** il sait tellement de choses que c'en devient agaçant

annual ['ænjʊəl] ADJ *(holiday, payment, report etc)* annuel; **he has an a. salary of £50,000** il gagne 50 000 livres par an ▸ N1 *Bot* plante *f* annuelle 2 *(publication)* publication *f* annuelle; *(for children)* album *m* (annuel)
▸ ▸ *Acct, Fin* **a. accounts** bilan *m* annuel, comptes *mpl* de clôture *ou* de fin d'exercice; *Fin* **a. budget** budget *m* annuel; *Fin* **a. contribution** *(to pension scheme)* cotisation *f* annuelle; *Acct* **a. depreciation** dépréciation *f* annuelle, amortissement *m* annuel; *Fin* **a. earnings** *(of company)* recette(s) *f(pl)* annuelle(s); *(of person)* revenu *m* annuel; *Com* **a. general meeting** assemblée *f* générale (annuelle); **a. guaranteed salary** salaire *m* annuel garanti; **a. income** revenu annuel; **a. instalment** annuité *f*; *Admin* **a. leave** congé *m* annuel; *Fin* **a. percentage rate** taux *m* effectif global; **a. profit** profit *m* annuel; *Fin* **a. returns** déclarations *fpl* annuelles; **a. revenue** recette annuelle; **a. ring** *(of tree)* couche *f* annuelle; *Com* **a. sales figures** chiffre *m* d'affaires annuel; **a. spend** dépenses *fpl* annuelles; *Acct, Fin* **a. turnover** chiffre d'affaires annuel; *Acct* **a. writedown** dépréciation annuelle, amortissement annuel

annually ['ænjʊəlɪ] ADV *(in a year)* par an, annuellement; *(every year)* tous les ans

annuity [ə'njuːɪtɪ] N *Fin* rente *f* (annuelle); **government a.** rente sur l'État; **perpetual a.** rente perpétuelle, rente en perpétuel; **life a.** rente viagère, pension *f* viagère; **to buy an a.** placer son argent en viager *ou* à fonds perdu; **to pay sb an a.** servir *ou* faire une rente à qn; **a. in redemption of debt** annuité *f*

annul [ə'nʌl] VT (**-ll-**) *Law (contract)* annuler, résilier; *(bill)* annuler, casser; *(treaty)* dénoncer; *(marriage, will, agreement)* annuler, casser, déclarer nul; *(law)* abroger; *(decision)* infirmer

annular ['ænjʊlər] ADJ *(eclipse, finger)* annulaire

annulment [ə'nʌlmənt] N *Law (of contract etc)* annulation *f*, résiliation *f*; *(of will, marriage, bill)* annulation, cassation *f*; *(of law)* abrogation *f*; *(of decree)* abolition *f*; **decree of a.** décret *m* abolitif

annunciation [ənʌnsɪ'eɪʃən] N *Rel* **the A.** l'Annonciation *f*

anode ['ænəʊd] N *Elec* anode *f*, électrode *f* positive

anodyne ['ænəʊdaɪn] N *Med* calmant *m*, analgésique *m*
ADJ 1 *Med* antalgique, analgésique 2 *(remark, topic)* anodin

anoint [ə'nɔɪnt] VT oindre (**with** de); **to a. sb king/bishop** sacrer qn roi/évêque

anointing [ə'nɔɪntɪŋ] N onction *f*; *(of king etc)* sacre *m*

anomalous [ə'nɒmələs] ADJ anormal, -aux, irrégulier

anomaly [ə'nɒməlɪ] N anomalie *f*

anon[1] [ə'nɒn] ADV *Arch, Hum* 1 *(later)* plus tard; **more of this a.** je reviendrai sur cela 2 *(soon)* tout à l'heure, bientôt; **see you a.** à bientôt; **I'll be with you a.** je vous rejoins tout de suite

anon[2] ADJ *abbr* **anonymous**

anonymity [ænə'nɪmɪtɪ] N anonymat *m*; **to preserve one's a.** garder l'anonymat, préserver son anonymat

anonymous [ə'nɒnɪməs] ADJ 1 *(gift, letter etc)* anonyme; **to remain a.** garder l'anonymat, préserver son anonymat 2 *(building, face)* anonyme
▸ ▸ *Mktg* **a. buyer** acheteur, -euse anonyme; *Comput* **a. FTP** protocole *m* de transfert anonyme; *Comput* **a. remailer** service *m* de courrier électronique anonyme

anonymously [ə'nɒnɪməslɪ] ADV anonymement; **to write a.** écrire sous (le couvert de) l'anonymat

anopheles mosquito [ə'nɒfɪliːz] N anophèle *m*

anorak ['ænəræk] N 1 *(garment)* anorak *m* 2 *Br Fam Pej (person)* ringard *m*

anorexia [ænə'reksɪə] N *Med* anorexie *f*
▸ ▸ **a. nervosa** anorexie *f* mentale

anorexic [ænə'reksɪk] ADJ, N *Med* anorexique *mf*; **you look a.** tu n'as plus que la peau sur les os

another [ə'nʌðər] ADJ, PRON VOIR GRAMMAIRE A36–7; B15–16 1 *(one more)* encore un(e); *(second)* un(e) autre; un(e) deuxième, un(e) second(e); **we're thinking of getting a. car** *(in addition to the one we have)* nous pensons acheter une deuxième voiture; **a. cup of tea** encore une tasse de thé; **a. fifty years** encore cinquante ans; **in a. ten years** dans dix ans (d'ici); **a. hour/20 miles and we'll be there** encore une heure/une vingtaine de mil(l)es et nous y serons; **I don't want to see a. fish as long as I live** je ne veux plus voir un seul poisson de toute ma vie; **without a. word** sans (un mot de) plus; **have a. (drink)!** encore un(e)?; **this is not just a. small car** ce n'est pas seulement une petite voiture parmi d'autres; **he is a. Picasso** c'est le nouveau Picasso; **the situation could become a. Vietnam** la situation pourrait tourner en un autre Vietnam
2 *(different one)* un(e) autre; **we're thinking of getting a. car** *(to replace the car we have)* nous pensons acheter une nouvelle voiture *ou* changer de voiture; **take this cup away and bring me a. (one)** enlevez cette tasse et apportez-m'en une autre; **a. of the passengers** un autre passager; **that's (quite) a. matter** c'est (tout) autre chose; **science is one thing, art is a.** la science est une chose, l'art en est une autre; *Lit* **he loves a.** il en aime une autre; **she now has a. husband** elle a maintenant un nouveau mari; **a. athlete would have played safe** un autre athlète aurait joué la prudence; **a. time** une autre fois; **let's do it a. way** faisons autrement; *Fam* **tell me a.!** *(you're exaggerating)* ce n'est pas vrai!, à d'autres!; **one way or a.** d'une façon

ou d'une autre; **taking one thing with a., we just manage** l'un dans l'autre, on arrive à joindre les deux bouts; **what with one thing and a., I forgot** avec tout ça, j'ai oublié
3 *(reciprocal)* **one a.** l'un l'autre; *(more than two people)* les uns les autres; **to help one a.** s'entraider; **love one a.** aimez-vous les uns les autres; **he and his wife adore one a.** lui et sa femme s'adorent; **they give one a. presents** ils se donnent des cadeaux

Ansaphone® ['ɑːnsəfəʊn] N *Tel* répondeur enregistreur *m*

ANSI ['ænsɪ] N *Am (abbr* **American National Standards Institute)** = association *f* américaine de normalisation
▸ ▸ **A. character** caractère *m* ANSI

answer ['ɑːnsər] N 1 *(to question, letter)* réponse *f*; *(to criticism)* réponse, réplique *f*; **she made no a.** elle n'a pas répondu; **I knocked but there was no a.** j'ai frappé mais personne n'a répondu; *Tel* **there's no a.** ça ne répond pas; **he has an a. to everything** il a réponse à tout; **you think you know all the answers, don't you?** tu crois que tu sais tout, c'est ça?; **his only a. was to burst into tears** pour toute réponse il a fondu en larmes; **Scotland's a. to Pelé** le Pelé écossais; **they had no a. to this/this new scrum half** ils ne savaient pas quoi faire contre ça/ce nouveau demi de mêlée; **there's no a. to that!** comment répondre à ça!; **it's the a. to the government's prayers** c'est exactement ce dont le gouvernement avait besoin; **she's the a. to all his prayers** c'est la femme de ses rêves; *Fml* **in a. to your letter** en réponse à votre lettre; *Law etc* **a. to a charge** réfutation *f* à une accusation SEE GRAMMAR B64
2 *Math, Fig (to problem)* solution *f*; **the a. is 624** la réponse est 624
VT *(person, question, letter)* répondre à; **what did he a.?** qu'a-t-il répondu?; **letters to be answered** courrier *m* en cours; **letters answered** lettres *fpl* auxquelles on a répondu; **the question is not easy to a.** c'est une question à laquelle il n'est pas facile de répondre; **to a. the bell/the telephone** répondre à un coup de sonnette/au téléphone; **to a. the door** *(go)* aller ouvrir; *(come)* venir ouvrir; **to a. a prayer** exaucer une prière; *Law* **to a. a charge** répondre à *ou* réfuter une accusation; **to a. a description** répondre à un signalement; **to a. the helm** *(of ship)* obéir à la barre; **to a. a need** répondre à un besoin; **this should a. the purpose quite nicely** ceci fera très bien l'affaire; **it should a. the purposes of both students and translators** ce devrait être utile aux étudiants comme aux traducteurs; **that will a. my purpose** cela fera mon affaire
VI répondre; **it's not answering** *(phone)* ça ne répond pas
▸ ▸ *Tel* **a. mode** mode *m* réponse; *Tel* **a. tone** tonalité *f* de réponse
▸ **answer back** VI *(be impertinent)* répondre; **don't a. back!** ne réponds pas!
VT SEP *(be impertinent to)* répondre à
▸ **answer for** VT INSEP répondre de; *(sb's integrity)* se porter garant de; **to a. for one's actions** prendre la responsabilité de ses propres actes; **to a. for one's crimes** payer pour ses crimes; **he/the motor car has a lot to a. for** il/la voiture est responsable de bien des problèmes
▸ **answer to** VT INSEP 1 *(be accountable to)* être responsable envers, rendre compte à; **you'll have me to a. to** *(if you do that)* c'est à moi que vous devrez rendre des comptes; **to a. to sb for sth** être responsable de qch envers qn 2 *(correspond to) (description)* répondre à 3 **the dog answers to the name of Rover** le chien répond au nom de Rover

answerable ['ɑːnsərəb(ə)l] ADJ 1 garant, responsable (**to sb for sth** de qch envers qn); **to be a. to an authority** relever d'une autorité; **he is a. to nobody** il n'a de comptes à rendre à personne **2** *(accusation)* réfutable

answerback ['ɑːnsəbæk] N *Comput (in datacomms)* réponse *f* en retour

answering ['ɑːnsərɪŋ] ADJ **an a. cry** un cri jeté en réponse
▸▸ *Tel* **a. machine** répondeur *m* (automatique *ou* téléphonique); *Tel* **a. service** *(manned)* permanence *f* téléphonique; *(unmanned)* répondeur téléphonique

answerphone ['ɑːnsəfəʊn] N *Tel* répondeur *m* (automatique *ou* téléphonique)

ant [ænt] N fourmi *f*, *Fig Fam* **to have ants in one's pants** ne pas tenir en place, avoir la bougeotte
▸▸ **a. bear** tamanoir *m*; **a. colony** colonie *f* de fourmis; **a. hill** fourmilière *f*; **a. lion** fourmilion *m*, fourmi-lion *m*, *pl* fourmis-lions

antacid [ænt'æsɪd] ADJ, N *Med* antiacide *m*

antagonism [æn'tægənɪz(ə)m] N hostilité *f* (**to, towards** envers); *(between two people)*, *Physiol* antagonisme *m*

antagonist [æn'tægənɪst] N antagoniste *mf*, adversaire *mf*

antagonistic [æntægə'nɪstɪk] ADJ *(opposed)* opposé, contraire (**to** à); *(person, attitude)* hostile; *(parties)* antagonique; *Anat (muscle)* antagoniste

antagonize [æn'tægənaɪz] VT éveiller l'hostilité de; **to a. the public** ranger l'opinion contre soi; **don't a. him** ne te le mets pas à dos; **she only succeeded in antagonizing him further** elle n'a réussi qu'à le rendre encore plus hostile

Antarctic [æn'tɑːktɪk] ADJ antarctique
N **the A.** l'Antarctique *m*

Antarctica [æn'tɑːktɪkə] N Antarctique *m*

ante ['æntɪ] *Cards* N *(at poker)* première mise *f*, **to raise** *or* **up the a.** *Cards* lever la mise; *Fig (in dispute)* placer la barre plus haut
VI faire une mise
▸ **ante up** VI *Am Fam (pay)* casquer

anteater ['æntiːtər] N fourmilier *m*; **great a.** tamanoir *m*; **scaly a.** pangolin *m*; **spiny a.** échidné *m*

antebellum [æntɪ'beləm] ADJ d'avant la guerre; *Am* d'avant la guerre Civile

antecedence [æntɪ'siːd(ə)ns] N **1** *(precedence)* antériorité *f* **2** *(priority)* priorité *f*

antecedent [æntɪ'siːd(ə)nt] ADJ antérieur (**to** à)
N **1** *Gram, Math* antécédent *m* VOIR GRAMMAIRE A32–3; B22–3 **2 antecedents** *(of person)* *(past)* antécédents *mpl*; *(ancestors)* ancêtres *mpl*; *(of society etc)* origines *fpl*

antechamber ['æntɪtʃeɪmbər] N **1** *(room)* antichambre *f* **2** *(in engine)* préchambre *f*; **diesel engine with a.** moteur *m* diesel à chambre de précombustion

antedate [æntɪ'deɪt] VT *(precede)* précéder

antediluvian [æntɪdɪ'luːvɪən] ADJ antédiluvien

antelope ['æntɪləʊp] N *(pl* **antelopes, antelope***)* antilope *f*

ante meridian ADV *Fml* du matin

antenatal [æntɪ'neɪt(ə)l] ADJ prénatal, -als, anténatal, -als; **an a. clinic** un cours de préparation à l'accouchement

antenna [æn'tenə] N **1** *(pl* **antennae** [-iː]*) (of insect, crustacean)* antenne *f*; *(of mollusc)* tentacule *m*; *(of snail)* corne *f* **2** *(pl usu* **antennas** [-əz]*) esp Am Radio, TV* antenne *f*

antepenultimate [æntɪpə'nʌltɪmət] ADJ antépénultième; **the a. syllable** l'antépénultième *f* (syllabe *f*)

anterior [æn'tɪərɪər] ADJ **1** antérieur, -eure

(**to** à) **2** *Gram* past a. passé *m* antérieur **3** *Anat (muscle)* antérieur

anteroom ['æntɪruːm] N antichambre *f*, vestibule *m*

anthem ['ænθəm] N *Rel* motet *m*; *Lit (song of joy)* chant *m* d'allégresse; **national a.** hymne *m* national; **the party's a.** l'hymne du parti

anther ['ænθər] N *Bot* anthère *f*

anthologist [æn'θɒlədʒɪst] N anthologue *mf*

anthology [æn'θɒlədʒɪ] N anthologie *f*

anthracite ['ænθrəsaɪt] N *Min* anthracite *m*

anthrax ['ænθræks] N charbon *m*, anthrax *m*

anthropoid ['ænθrəpɔɪd] N *Zool (ape)* (singe *m*) anthropoïde *m*
ADJ **1** *(person) (apelike)* simiesque **2** *(ape) (resembling man)* anthropoïde

anthropological ['ænθrəpə'lɒdʒɪk(ə)l] ADJ anthropologique

anthropologist [ænθrə'pɒlədʒɪst] N anthropologue *mf*

anthropology [ænθrə'pɒlədʒɪ] N anthropologie *f*

anthropometry [ænθrə'pɒmɪtrɪ] N anthropométrie *f*

anthropomorphic [ænθrəpə'mɔːfɪk] ADJ anthropomorphe

anthropomorphism [ænθrəpə'mɔːfɪz(ə)m] N anthropomorphisme *m*

anthropomorphous [ænθrəpə'mɔːfəs] ADJ anthropomorphe

anthropophagous [ænθrə'pɒfəgəs] ADJ anthropophage

anthropophagy [ænθrə'pɒfədʒɪ] N anthropophagie *f*

anti ['æntɪ, *Am* 'æntaɪ] PREP anti; **she was a. the idea** elle était contre cette idée; **he's a. everything** rien ne lui plaît; **she's a. anything which involves spending money** elle est contre tout ce qui entraîne des dépenses
N opposant, -ante

anti- ['æntɪ, *Am* 'æntaɪ] PREF anti-; **anti-American** anti(-)américain

anti-abortionist N adversaire *mf* de l'avortement

anti-aircraft ADJ *(gun, defence etc)* antiaérien

anti-aliasing N *Comput* anti-crénelage *m*, anti-aliassage *m*

anti-apartheid ADJ anti(-)apartheid

antibacterial [æntɪbæk'tɪərɪəl] ADJ *Med* antibactérien

antiballistic [æntɪbə'lɪstɪk] ADJ *Mil* antiballistique, antimissile
▸▸ **a. missile** engin *m* ou fusée *f* antimissile

antibiotic [æntɪbaɪ'ɒtɪk] ADJ antibiotique
N antibiotique *m*; **to be on antibiotics** être sous antibiotiques

antibody ['æntɪbɒdɪ] N *Physiol* anticorps *m*

anti-burst lock N serrure *f* renforcée

Antichrist ['æntɪkraɪst] N Antéchrist *m*

antichristian [æntɪ'krɪstʃən] ADJ antichrétien

anticipate [æn'tɪsɪpeɪt] VT **1** *(expect) (possibility, reaction)* prévoir; *(difficulty, pleasure etc)* s'attendre à, envisager; **we don't a. any objections** nous n'envisageons pas d'objections; **we do not a. any delays** aucun retard n'est prévu; **to a. that ...** prévoir que ...; **to a. the worst** s'attendre au pire
2 *(enjoy, count on in advance) (events)* anticiper sur; *(pleasure)* savourer d'avance; *(result, vote)* escompter; **to a. one's salary** anticiper sur son salaire; *Fin* **anticipated profit** profit *m* espéré
3 *(act in advance of) (person, sb's orders)* devancer, prévenir, aller au-devant de; **you must a. your opponent's moves/other drivers' intentions** il faut que vous anticipiez

---

les mouvements de votre adversaire/les intentions des autres conducteurs; **her writing anticipated later developments in English fiction** son style présageait des développements futurs de la fiction anglaise; **don't a. me** *(in telling story)* attends la suite, laisse-moi finir
VI anticiper

anticipation [æntɪsɪ'peɪʃən] N **1** *(foresight)* prévision *f*; **in a. of trouble** en prévision de troubles; **thanking you in a.** en vous remerciant d'avance; **Brian showed great a.** *(in game)* Brian a très bien anticipé **2** *(expectation)* anticipation *f*; **they awaited his arrival with eager a.** ils l'attendaient avec beaucoup d'impatience

anticipatory pricing [æn'tɪsɪpeɪt(ə)rɪ] N fixation *f* des prix par anticipation

anticlerical [æntɪ'klerɪk(ə)l] ADJ anticlérical, -aux

anticlericalism [æntɪ'klerɪk(ə)lɪz(ə)m] N anticléricalisme *m*

anticlimax [æntɪ'klaɪmæks] N *(disappointment)* déception *f*; **the party itself was a bit of an a.** la soirée a été plutôt décevante; **after all the waiting, the news almost felt like an a.** après toute cette attente, la nouvelle n'a pas produit tout l'effet escompté

anticline ['æntɪklaɪn] N anticlinal *m*

anticlockwise [æntɪ'klɒkwaɪz] ADV, ADJ *Br* **a., in a. direction** dans le sens inverse des aiguilles d'une montre; **clockwise or a.?** dans le sens des aiguilles d'une montre ou l'inverse?

anticoagulant [æntɪkəʊ'ægjʊlənt] ADJ, N *Med* anticoagulant *m*

anticolonialism [æntɪkə'ləʊnɪəlɪz(ə)m] N anticolonialisme *m*

anticonstitutional [æntɪkɒnstɪ'tjuːʃən(ə)l] ADJ anticonstitutionnel

anti-corrosion ADJ anti-corrosion
▸▸ **a. guarantee** garantie *f* anti-corrosion; **a. primer** apprêt *m* anti-corrosion

antics ['æntɪks] NPL bouffonneries *fpl*, singeries *fpl*; **he's up to his a. again** le voilà qui fait de nouveau des siennes

anticyclone [æntɪ'saɪkləʊn] N anticyclone *m*

anti-dazzle ADJ anti-aveuglant; *(headlights)* anti-éblouissant

anti-democratic ADJ antidémocratique

antidepressant [æntɪdɪ'presənt] ADJ, N *Pharm* antidépresseur *m*

anti-dieselling valve [-'diːz(ə)lɪŋ] N *Aut* thermovalve *f*

anti-dive geometry N *Aut* géométrie *f* anti-plongée

antidote ['æntɪdəʊt] N *Med, Fig* antidote *m* (**to** contre), contrepoison *m* (**to** à)

anti-dumping ADJ *(laws, legislation)* anti-dumping *inv*

anti-establishment ADJ anticonformiste

antifascism [æntɪ'fæʃɪz(ə)m] N *Pol* antifascisme *m*

antifascist [æntɪ'fæʃɪst] ADJ, N antifasciste *mf*

antifebrile [æntɪ'fiːbraɪl] N, ADJ *Pharm* antipyrétique *m*, fébrifuge *m*

antifreeze ['æntɪfriːz] ADJ, N *Aut* antigel *m*

antigen ['æntɪdʒen] N *Med* antigène *m*

anti-glare ADJ anti-aveuglant; *(headlights)* anti-éblouissant
▸▸ **a. mirror** rétroviseur *m* jour/nuit; **a. screen** écran *m* antireflets

antiglobalization [æntɪgləʊbəlaɪ'zeɪʃən] N antimondialisation *f*

Antigua [æn'tiːgə] N Antigua *m*

anti-hero N *Liter* antihéros *m inv*

anti-heroine N *Liter* antihéroïne *f*

antihistamine [æntɪ'hɪstəmɪn] ADJ, N *Med* antihistaminique *m*

anti-icing N *Aut* antigel *m*; *Aviat* antigivrant *m*
ADJ antigivre *inv*

anti-imperialist N, ADJ anti-impérialiste *mf*

anti-inflammatory ADJ, N *Med* anti-inflammatoire *m*

anti-inflationary ADJ *(measures, policy)* anti-inflationniste

anti-knock ADJ, N *Aut* antidétonant *m*

Antilles [æn'tɪliːz] NPL **the A.** les Antilles *fpl*

anti-lock ADJ
▸▸ **a. brakes** anti-blocage *m* des freins; **a. braking system** système *m* anti-blocage des freins

antilogarithm [æntɪ'lɒgərɪð(ə)m] N *Math* antilogarithme *m*

antimacassar [æntɪmə'kæsər] N têtière *f*

antimalarial [æntɪmə'leərɪəl] N, ADJ *Pharm* antipaludique *m*, antipaludéen *m*

antimatter ['æntɪmætər] N antimatière *f*

antimilitarism [æntɪ'mɪlɪtərɪz(ə)m] N antimilitarisme *m*

anti-missile ADJ antimissile

antimony [æn'tɪmənɪ] N antimoine *m*

antinazi [æntɪ'nɑːtsɪ] ADJ, N *Pol* antinazi, -ie

anti-nuclear ADJ antinucléaire

antiparticle ['æntɪpɑːtɪk(ə)l] N *Nucl* antiparticule *f*

antipathetic(al) [æntɪpə'θetɪk, -ɪk(ə)l] ADJ antipathique; **a. to** qui a de l'aversion pour

antipathy [æn'tɪpəθɪ] N antipathie *f*; **to feel a. for sb** avoir de l'antipathie pour *ou* contre qn

antipersonnel [æntɪpɜːsə'nel] ADJ *(bomb)* antipersonnel

antiperspirant [æntɪ'pɜːspɪrənt] ADJ, N déodorant *m*

antiphon ['æntɪfɒn] N *Rel* antienne *f*

antipodean [æntɪpə'diːən] ADJ **1** *Geog* des antipodes **2** *Br (from Australia and/or New Zealand)* d'Australie/de Nouvelle-Zélande; *Hum* **our a. cousins** nos cousins d'Australie/de Nouvelle-Zélande; **the kangaroo and other a. animals** le kangourou et les autres animaux australiens
▸▸ **A. day** jour *m* méridien

antipodes [æn'tɪpədiːz] NPL *Geog* **the a.** les antipodes *mpl*; **at the a.** aux antipodes; *Br* **the A.** l'Australie *f* et/ou la Nouvelle-Zélande

anti-pollution ADJ anti-pollution

antiproton [æntɪ'prəʊtɒn] N *Nucl* antiproton *m*

antipyretic [æntɪpaɪ'retɪk] N, ADJ *Pharm* antipyrétique *m*, fébrifuge *m*

antiquarian [æntɪ'kweərɪən] ADJ *(book)* ancien; **a. bookseller/bookshop** libraire *mf*/librairie *f* spécialisé(e) dans les éditions anciennes; **a. collection** collection *f* d'antiquités
N *(dealer)* antiquaire *mf*; *(collector)* amateur *m* d'antiquités; *(scholar)* historien, -ienne

antiquary ['æntɪkwərɪ] N *(collector)* amateur *m* d'antiquités; *(dealer)* antiquaire *mf*; *(scholar)* historien, -ienne

antiquated ['æntɪkweɪtɪd] ADJ *(outmoded)* *(method)* désuet, *f* -ète, suranné; *(car, tools)* vieillot; **an a. kitchen range** une cuisinière (à charbon) d'autrefois

antique [æn'tiːk] ADJ antique, ancien; **a. furniture** meubles *mpl* anciens; *Fam* **she's got an a. gas cooker** sa cuisinière à gaz est une véritable antiquité
N *(ancient object, piece of furniture)* antiquité *f*; **a. shop** magasin *m* d'antiquités; **be**

careful with that, it's an a. fais attention, c'est ancien; *Fam* **that television's an a.** cette télévision est une antiquité
▸▸ **a. dealer** antiquaire *mf*

antiquity [æn'tɪkwɪtɪ] N **1** *(of custom)* ancienneté *f* **2** *Hist (Greek, Roman)* antiquité *f*; **the works of art of classical a.** les antiquités; **women in a.** la femme dans le monde ancien **3 Roman antiquities** *(remains)* monuments *mpl* romains

anti-rabies ADJ antirabique

antiracism [æntɪ'reɪsɪz(ə)m] N antiracisme *m*

antiracist [æntɪ'reɪsɪst] ADJ antiraciste

antiraid precautions [æntɪ'reɪd] N *St Exch* barrières *fpl* antiraid

anti-roll bar N *Aut* barre *f* antiroulis

antirrhinum [æntɪ'raɪnəm] N *(plant)* muflier *m*

anti-run-on valve N *Aut* thermovalve *f*

anti-rust ADJ antirouille *inv*; **a. treatment** traitement *m* antirouille

anti-Semite N antisémite *mf*

anti-Semitic ADJ antisémite

anti-Semitism [-'semɪtɪz(ə)m] N antisémitisme *m*

antisepsis [æntɪ'sepsɪs] N *Med* antisepsie *f*

antiseptic [æntɪ'septɪk] ADJ *Med* antiseptique; *Fig (atmosphere)* aseptisé; *(person)* froid, peu amical, -aux
N *Med* antiseptique *m*

antiserum ['æntɪsɪərəm] N *Med* antisérum *m*

antislavery [æntɪ'sleɪvərɪ] ADJ antiesclavagiste

antisocial [æntɪ'səʊʃəl] ADJ **1** *(behaviour, element, vandalism)* asocial, -aux; *(bill, measure, policy)* antisocial, -aux **2** *(unsociable) (sort of person)* qui fait bande à part, sauvage; **he's being very a.** en ce moment il n'est pas très sociable; **I don't want to be a., but …** *(I'd rather be alone)* désolé de faire bande à part, mais …; *(I have to leave, you have to leave)* je m'en voudrais de gâcher l'ambiance, mais …

antispasmodic [æntɪspæz'mɒdɪk] N, ADJ *Pharm* antispasmodique *m*

antistatic [æntɪ'stætɪk] ADJ antistatique

anti-submarine ADJ anti-sous-marin

anti-tank ADJ *Mil* antichar(s)

anti-terrorist ADJ antiterroriste

anti-theft ADJ *(lock)* antivol *inv*; **a. device** antivol *m inv*

antithesis, *pl* **antitheses** [æn'tɪθɪsɪs, -iːz] N **1** *(opposite)* antithèse *f*, opposé *m* *(of* de*)* **2** *Phil (in dialectic)* antithèse *f* *(between* entre; **to, of** de*)*

antithetical [æntɪ'θetɪk(ə)l] ADJ antithétique

antitoxin [æntɪ'tɒksɪn] N *Med* antitoxine *f*

antitrust [æntɪ'trʌst] ADJ *Econ* antitrust

antitussive [æntɪ'tʌsɪv] N, ADJ *Pharm* antitussif *m*

antivirus ['æntɪvaɪrəs] N *Comput* antivirus *m*
▸▸ **a. check** vérification *f* antivirale; **a. program** programme *m* antivirus

antivivisectionist [æntɪvɪvɪ'sekʃənɪst] N antivivisection(n)iste *mf*

antler ['æntlər] N *(of stag)* andouiller *m*; **the antlers** les bois *mpl*

antonym ['æntənɪm] N antonyme *m*

antsy ['æntsɪ] ADJ *esp Am (nervous)* agité, nerveux; *(irritable)* à cran

Antwerp ['æntwɜːp] N Anvers *m*

anus ['eɪnəs] N *Anat* anus *m*

anvil ['ænvɪl] N *(of blacksmith, in ear)* enclume *f*

anxiety [æŋ'zaɪətɪ] N **1** *(worry, concern)* inquiétude *f*; **deep a.** anxiété *f*, angoisse *f*; **to cause sb great a.** donner de grandes inquiétudes *ou* bien des soucis à qn; **there is no cause for a.** il n'y a pas de quoi s'inquiéter; **to feel a.** s'inquiéter, être anxieux *(about* à propos de*)*; **to be full of a.** être anxieux
2 *(individual concern)* souci *m*; **the report failed to remove their anxieties** le rapport ne leur a pas ôté leurs inquiétudes
3 *(desire)* désir *m*, souci *m* *(for sth* de qch*)*; **a. to help sb/please sb** désir *ou* souci d'aider qn/de plaire à qn; **in her a. not to offend** dans son souci de n'offenser personne
4 *Psy* anxiété *f*
▸▸ *Psy* **a. attack** crise *f* d'angoisse

anxious ['æŋkʃəs] ADJ **1** *(worried)* inquiet, *f* -ète, soucieux *(about* sur, de, au sujet de*)*; **what are you so a. about?** pourquoi es-tu aussi inquiet *ou* soucieux?; **very** *or* **extremely a.** angoissé; **he was a. that all his work might come to nothing** il craignait que tout son travail n'ait servi à rien; **the a. faces of relatives** le visage angoissé des membres de la famille; **to be a. for sb/sb's safety** être inquiet *ou* s'inquiéter pour qn/la sécurité de qn; **I am a. about his health** sa santé me préoccupe, je m'inquiète de sa santé
2 *(worrying)* inquiétant; **an a. moment** un moment d'anxiété; **it was an a. time for us** ça a été une période de grande inquiétude pour nous
3 *(eager)* désireux; **to be a. to do sth** tenir à faire qch, être désireux de faire qch; **why are you so a. to go?** *(impatient)* pourquoi êtes-vous si impatient de partir?; *(eager)* pourquoi tenez-vous tant à y aller?
4 *Psy* anxieux

anxiously ['æŋkʃəslɪ] ADV **1** *(worriedly)* anxieusement, avec inquiétude, avec anxiété **2** *(with concern)* avec sollicitude **3** *(with impatience)* avec impatience

ANY ['enɪ] VOIR GRAMMAIRE A34; B5; B66-7

ADJ du, de la, de l', des **1** ▪ aucun **2** ▪ n'importe quel **3** ▪ tout **4**
PRON n'importe quel
ADV ne... plus **1**

ADJ **1** *(some, one)* **have you a. milk/books?** avez-vous du lait/des livres?; **have you a. more milk?** avez-vous encore du lait?; **is there a. hope?** y a-t-il de l'espoir?; *(stressed)* y a-t-il aucun espoir?; **if you had a. sense (at all)** si tu avais ne serait-ce qu'un peu de bon sens
2 *(in neg sentences or with implied negation)* **not a.** ne … aucun; **he hasn't a. reason to complain** il n'a aucune raison de se plaindre; **he hasn't a. more money** il n'a plus d'argent; **without a. help** sans aucune aide; **she is forbidden to do a. work** tout travail lui est interdit; **it is difficult to find a. explanation for it** il est difficile d'y trouver une quelconque explication; **complaining won't do a. good** se plaindre n'avancera à rien
3 *(no particular)* n'importe quel; **come a. day (you like)** venez n'importe quel jour; **a. man, woman or child** qui que ce soit, homme, femme, ou enfant; **a. doctor will tell you that** n'importe quel médecin vous le dira; **that may happen at a. time** cela peut arriver n'importe quand; **I expect him a. moment now** je l'attends d'un instant à l'autre; **take a. two cards** prenez deux cartes quelconques; *Fam* **a. old thing** n'importe quoi; *Fam* **a. old book** n'importe quel livre; **I don't want just a. (old) wine** je ne veux pas n'importe quel vin
4 *(every)* **a. pupil who forgets his books will be punished** tout élève qui oubliera ses livres sera puni; **at a. rate, in a. case** en tout cas

PRON **I haven't got a.** je n'en ai pas; **I haven't seen a.** je n'en ai pas vu; **have you a.?** en avez-vous?; **is there a. more?** y en a-t-il encore?; **I/you/etc needn't say a. more** pas besoin d'en dire davantage; **they won't take a. less** ils n'accepteront pas moins; **few, if a., can read** peu, si ce n'est aucun, savent lire; **he has no money and no prospect of a.** il est sans argent et sans l'espoir d'en avoir; **take a. of the bottles** prends n'importe laquelle des bouteilles; **a. of us** n'importe qui d'entre vous; **I don't think a. of the guests have arrived yet** je ne pense pas qu'aucun des invités soit encore arrivé; **there was no paper in a. of the boxes** il n'y avait de papier dans aucune des boîtes

ADV 1 *(with comparative)* **I'm not a. better** je ne vais pas mieux; **I can't go a. further** je ne peux pas aller plus loin; **the weather couldn't be a. worse** le temps ne pourrait pas être pire *ou* plus mauvais; **I don't see him a. longer** *or* **more** je ne le vois plus; **I didn't do it a. more than you did** je ne l'ai pas fait plus que vous; **I don't like her a. more than you do** je ne l'aime pas plus que tu ne l'aimes

2 *Fam* **that didn't help us a.** cela ne nous a été d'aucun secours; **her attitude didn't help a.** son attitude n'a rien arrangé; **a. old how** n'importe comment

ANYBODY ['enɪbɒdɪ], **anyone** ['enɪwʌn]

| quelqu'un **1** ▪ personne **2** ▪ n'importe qui **3** |

PRON *(no pl)* (*NOTE in examples where one of the forms is preferred, the word has been printed in full*) **1** *(indeterminate)* quelqu'un; *(expecting answer 'no')* personne; **can you see a. over there?** est-ce que vous voyez quelqu'un là-bas?; **does a. mind if I close the window?** est-ce que cela gêne quelqu'un si je ferme la fenêtre?; **would a. like some more cake?** est-ce que quelqu'un voudrait reprendre du gâteau?; **does a. dare to say so?** y a-t-il personne qui ose le dire?; **he knows French if a. does** il sait le français comme pas un; **she'll know, if a. does** c'est bien elle **VOIR GRAMMAIRE A34; B67**

2 *(in neg sentences)* **not a.** ne … personne; **there isn't a. here** il n'y a personne ici; **there was hardly a.** il n'y avait presque personne; **don't speak to a.** ne parlez à personne, ne parlez pas à qui que ce soit **VOIR GRAMMAIRE A34; B67**

3 *(no particular person)* n'importe qui, tout le monde; **a. will tell you so** le premier venu *ou* n'importe qui *ou* tout le monde vous le dira; **a. would think he was mad** on le croirait fou; **a. but me** tout autre que moi; **you're not just a.** tu n'es pas n'importe qui; **a. with any sense** quiconque a un peu de bon sens; **bring along a. you like** amenez qui vous voudrez; **I challenge a. to …** je défie qui que ce soit de …; **I haven't met a. else** je n'ai rencontré personne d'autre; *Sport* **it's a.'s match** n'importe qui peut gagner, n'importe qui peut remporter la victoire; **it's a.'s guess!** qui sait?; *Hum Fam* **one drink and he's anybody's** un verre et il est prêt à repartir avec n'importe qui

4 *Fam (person with status)* **is he anybody?** est-ce que c'est quelqu'un d'important?; **he'll never be anybody** il n'arrivera jamais à rien

anyhow ['enɪhaʊ] **ADV 1** = **anyway 2** *Fam (carelessly)* **to do sth (all) a.** faire qch n'importe comment; **the clothes had been thrown on the bed just a.** les vêtements avaient été jetés n'importe comment *ou* en pagaille sur le lit

anyone *see* **anybody**

anyplace ['enɪpleɪs] **ADV** *Am Fam* = **anywhere**

ANYTHING ['enɪθɪŋ]

| **PRON** quelque chose **1** ▪ rien **2** ▪ n'importe quoi **3** ▪ tout **3** |

PRON **VOIR GRAMMAIRE A34; B67 1** quelque chose; *(with implied negation)* rien; **can I do a. for you?** est-ce que je peux faire quelque chose pour vous (aider)?; **is there a. I can do (to help)?** puis-je faire quelque chose?; **have you a. to write with?** avez-vous de quoi écrire?; **is there a. more pleasant than …?** est-il rien de plus agréable que …?; **will there be a. else, madam?** *(in shop)* désirez-vous autre chose, madame?, et avec cela, madame?; **a. bigger than that won't go through a letterbox** quelque chose de plus volumineux que ça ne passera pas par une boîte aux lettres; **have you a. smaller?** *(in different size)* est-ce que vous avez la taille en-dessous?; *(money)* vous n'avez pas plus petit?; **if a. should happen to me** s'il m'arrivait quelque chose; **do you see a. of your friend?** voyez-vous quelquefois votre ami?; **is (there) a. the matter?** y a-t-il quelque chose qui ne marche pas?

2 *(in neg sentences)* **not a.** ne … rien; **he doesn't do a.** il ne fait rien; **I shan't give you a. at all** je ne vous donnerai rien du tout; **hardly a.** presque rien; **it doesn't mean a.** cela ne veut rien dire

3 *(no matter what)* n'importe quoi, tout; **he eats a.** il mange de tout; **a. you like** tout ce que vous voudrez; **a. will do** n'importe quoi fera l'affaire; **I love a. French** j'aime tout ce qui est français; **he would do a. for me** il ferait tout *ou* n'importe quoi pour moi; **I would have given a. not to go** j'aurais tout donné *ou* j'aurais donné n'importe quoi pour ne pas y aller; **he's a. but mad** il est loin d'être fou; **he's not mad, a. but** il n'est pas fou, loin de là

4 *Fam (adv phrase, intensive)* **as easy/funny/strong as a.** facile/drôle/fort comme tout; **to work like a.** travailler comme un fou; **it's raining like a.** il pleut à verse; **it's not that you were wrong or a.** ce n'est pas du tout que vous ayez tort; **I don't want to cause a problem or a., but …** je ne veux surtout pas causer de problème, mais …

ADV she doesn't look a. like her sister elle ne ressemble pas du tout *ou* en rien à sa sœur; **is it a. like Chinese food?** est-ce que ça ressemble un peu à de la cuisine chinoise?; **it didn't cost a. like £500** *(less)* ça a coûté bien moins de 500 livres; **the weather wasn't a. like as bad as I'd expected** le temps était loin d'être aussi mauvais que ce à quoi je m'attendais; **if the food's a. like as good as it was at the last party** si on mange ne serait-ce qu'aussi bien qu'à la soirée précédente

anyway ['enɪweɪ] **ADV** en tout cas, de toute façon; **a., it's too late** en tout cas *ou* de toute façon, il est trop tard; **a., you can always try** vous pouvez toujours essayer; **a., let's get back to what we were saying** enfin *ou* bon, revenons à ce que nous disions

anywhere ['enɪweər] **ADV SEE GRAMMAR B67 1** *(no matter where)* n'importe où; **put it a.** mettez-le n'importe où; **I'd know him a.** je le reconnaîtrais entre mille; **a. else** n'importe où (ailleurs); **it's miles from a.** c'est en pleine cambrousse; **this could be a. in Europe** ce pourrait être n'importe où en Europe; **has he a. near finished?** est-ce qu'il a bientôt terminé?

2 *(in negative clauses)* **not a.** nulle part; **I've never been a.** je ne suis jamais allé nulle part; **you won't find a better curry a.** vous ne trouverez de meilleur curry nulle part; **I can't find it a.** je ne le trouve nulle part; *Fig*

we're not getting a. nous n'arrivons à rien, nous n'avançons pas

3 *(somewhere)* quelque part; **can you see it a.?** est-ce que vous le voyez?; **have you found a. to live?** avez-vous trouvé à vous loger?

AOB [eɪəʊ'biː] *(abbr* **any other business***)* divers

A-OK [eɪəʊ'keɪ] **ADJ** *Am Fam* excellent; **everything's A.** tout baigne; **he's A.** c'est un type bien

ADV parfaitement; **to go A.** se passer vachement bien

AOR [eɪəʊ'ɑːr] **N** *(abbr* **adult-orientated rock***)* rock *m* pour adultes

aorta [eɪ'ɔːtə] **N** *Anat* aorte *f*

aortic [eɪ'ɔːtɪk] **ADJ** *Anat* aortique

AP [eɪ'piː] **N** *Journ (abbr* **Associated Press***)* AP *f*

apace [ə'peɪs] **ADV** *Arch, Lit* vite, rapidement

Apache [ə'pætʃɪ] **N** Apache *mf*

apart [ə'pɑːt] **ADV 1** *(at a distance)* à l'écart; **to hold oneself** *or* **stand a.** se tenir à l'écart (**from** de); **the house was set a little way a. from the others** la maison était un peu à l'écart des autres; **the garage stands a. from the house** le garage est séparé de la maison

2 *(separated)* **they are a mile a.** ils sont à un mil(l)e l'un de l'autre; **lines 10 centimetres a.** lignes espacées de 10 centimètres; **to stand with one's feet a.** se tenir les jambes écartées; **they consider themselves in a class a.** ils se considèrent au-dessus des autres; **place set a. for worship** endroit réservé au culte; **cities as far a. as New York and Tokyo** des villes aussi éloignées que New York et Tokyo; **children born two years a.** des enfants nés à deux ans d'intervalle; **the boys and girls were kept a.** on tenait séparés les garçons et les filles; **they're never a.** ils ne se séparent jamais; **they're living a.** *(because of circumstances)* ils n'habitent pas ensemble; *(because of divorce, split-up)* ils sont séparés, ils vivent séparément; **it is difficult to tell them a.** il est difficile de les distinguer l'un de l'autre; **this problem cannot be treated a.** c'est un problème qu'on ne peut pas considérer séparément

3 *(to pieces)* **to take a machine a.** démonter *ou* désassembler une machine; **my dress is coming a. at the seams** ma robe est en train de se découdre; *Fam* **to take a room a.** fouiller une pièce à fond

4 a. from à part, sauf; **a. from the fact that …** indépendamment du fait que …, outre (le fait) que …; **a. from a few mistakes** à part *ou* sauf quelques erreurs; **a. from him, there is nobody who can do it** à part lui, personne ne peut le faire; **I don't know anyone a. from you** je ne connais personne à part toi

apartheid [ə'pɑːtaɪt, -eɪt] **N** *Pol* apartheid *m*

apartment [ə'pɑːtmənt] **N 1** *Am* appartement *m* **2** *(room)* pièce *f*; **state apartments** grands appartements *mpl*, salons *mpl* d'apparat; **(furnished) apartments to let** chambres *fpl* (meublées) à louer

▸▸ **a. block, a. building** immeuble *m* d'habitation; **a. hotel** résidence *f* hôtelière, résidence de tourisme

apathetic [æpə'θetɪk] **ADJ** apathique; **to be a. about sth** être indifférent à qch; **the response to the appeal has been a.** l'appel a été reçu dans l'apathie générale

apathetically [æpə'θetɪklɪ] **ADV** avec apathie *ou* indifférence; **to smile a.** sourire mollement *ou* sans grande conviction

apathy ['æpəθɪ] **N** apathie *f*, indifférence *f*; **an air of a.** un air apathique; **their a. about the issue** leur indifférence à l'égard de ce problème

ape [eɪp] N grand singe m (sans queue); **the higher apes** les primates mpl; Fig **he's a big a.** c'est une grande brute; Sl **to go a.** (become angry) piquer une crise (**over sb/sth** à propos de qn/qch); (enthuse) s'emballer (**over sb/sth** pour qn/qch)
VT (imitate) singer

apelike ['eɪplaɪk] ADJ (face, appearance, creature) simiesque; (noises) de singe

Apennines (the) [ðiːˈæpənaɪnz] NPL les Apennins mpl

aperient [əˈpɪərɪənt] ADJ, N Med laxatif m

aperitif [əperɪˈtiːf] N apéritif m

aperture ['æpətʃər] N orifice m; (of lens, diaphragm) ouverture f

apeshit ['eɪpʃɪt] ADV Sl **to go a.** (get angry) piquer une crise

APEX ['eɪpeks] N (abbr Advance Purchase Excursion) APEX m
►► **A. fare** tarif m APEX

apex, pl **apexes, apices** ['eɪpeks, -ɪz, 'eɪpɪsiːz] N (of triangle, building, mountain) sommet m; Fig (of career) apogée m, sommet; Br Sl Hum **to fall arse over a.** tomber cul pardessus tête

aphasia [əˈfeɪzɪə] N Med aphasie f

aphasic [əˈfeɪzɪk] ADJ, N Med aphasique mf

aphid ['eɪfɪd, 'æfɪd] N = **aphis**

aphis, pl **aphides** ['eɪfɪs, 'æfɪs, -ɪdiːz] N (insect) aphis m, puceron m

aphorism ['æfərɪz(ə)m] N aphorisme m

aphoristic [æfəˈrɪstɪk] ADJ aphoristique

aphrodisiac [æfrəʊˈdɪzɪæk] ADJ, N aphrodisiaque m

API [eɪpiːˈaɪ] N Journ (abbr American Press Institute) = association f de journalistes américains

apiarist ['eɪpɪərɪst] N apiculteur, -trice

apiary ['eɪpɪərɪ] N rucher m

apiculture ['eɪpɪkʌltʃər] N apiculture f

apiculturist [eɪpɪˈkʌltʃərɪst] N apiculteur, -trice

apiece [əˈpiːs] ADV chacun; **to cost £10 a.** (of things) coûter 10 livres (la) pièce; **he gave them 5 euros a.** (to each of them) il leur donna 5 euros chacun

aplenty [əˈplentɪ] ADV en abondance

aplomb [əˈplɒm] N aplomb m; **with great a.** avec un aplomb formidable

apnoea, Am **apnea** [æpˈniːə] N Med apnée f

apocalypse [əˈpɒkəlɪps] N Rel, Fig apocalypse f; **the four horsemen of the A.** les quatre cavaliers mpl de l'Apocalypse

apocalyptic [əpɒkəˈlɪptɪk] ADJ apocalyptique

Apocrypha (the) [ðiːəˈpɒkrɪfə] NPL Bible les livres mpl deutérocanoniques; (not in Protestant Bible) les apocryphes mpl

apocryphal [əˈpɒkrɪfəl] ADJ apocryphe; **the story's a.** je doute que l'histoire soit vraie

apogee ['æpədʒiː] N (of career, fame) apogée m

apolitical [eɪpəˈlɪtɪk(ə)l] ADJ apolitique

Apollo [əˈpɒləʊ] N Myth Apollon m

apologetic [əpɒləˈdʒetɪk] ADJ 1 (tone) d'excuse; (voice, smile) désolé, contrit; **to be very a.** se confondre en excuses; **she was quite a. about it** elle a fait beaucoup d'excuses; **he was most a. about the whole affair** il était vraiment désolé de toute cette histoire 2 (book etc) apologétique

apologetically [əpɒləˈdʒetɪklɪ] ADV (in regret) pour s'excuser, en s'excusant; **she looked/smiled at me a.** elle me regarda/sourit d'un air contrit

apologize [əˈpɒlədʒaɪz] VI s'excuser (**for sth** de qch); **to a. for doing sth** s'excuser

d'avoir fait qch; **to a. to sb for sth** s'excuser de qch auprès de qn, faire ou présenter des ou ses excuses à qn pour qch; **I was wrong, I a.** j'ai eu tort, excusez-moi ou je m'excuse; **I a. for having kept you waiting** excusez-moi de vous avoir fait attendre; **we a. for any inconvenience** veuillez nous excuser pour les désagréments occasionnés; **I had to a. for you or your behaviour** j'ai dû demander qu'on excuse ta conduite; **it's him you should be apologizing to** c'est à lui qu'il faut demander pardon, c'est auprès de lui que tu dois t'excuser; **there's no need to a.** vous n'avez pas à vous excuser

apology [əˈpɒlədʒɪ] N 1 excuses fpl; **to make/offer an a.** faire/présenter des excuses; **to make/send one's apologies** faire/envoyer ses excuses; **I owe you an a.** je vous dois des excuses; **by way of an a. (for having …)** pour s'excuser/m'excuser/etc (d'avoir …); **will you accept this gift by way of an a.?** accepterez-vous ce cadeau avec mes excuses?; **I got a very handsome a. from them** ils se sont gracieusement excusés; **did you get an a.?** est-ce qu'il s'est/ils se sont/etc excusé(s)?; **letter of a.** lettre f d'excuses; Fig **an a. for a …** un/une … lamentable; **an a. for a dinner** un semblant de dîner
2 Lit (defence) apologie f, justification f (**for** de)

> Note that the French word **apologie** is a false friend. Its most common meaning is **eulogy**.

apoplectic [æpəˈplektɪk] ADJ (person) apoplectique; (attack) d'apoplexie; **to be a. (with rage)** s'étrangler de rage; **she was a. when I told her** elle a failli avoir une attaque quand je le lui ai dit

apoplexy ['æpəpleksɪ] N Med apoplexie f

apostasy [əˈpɒstəsɪ] N apostasie f

apostate [əˈpɒstət] ADJ, N apostat, -ate

apostatize [əˈpɒstətaɪz] VI apostasier

apostle [əˈpɒs(ə)l] N (disciple), Fig apôtre m
►► **the Apostles' Creed** le Symbole des Apôtres; **a. spoon** cuiller f avec figurine d'apôtre

apostolic(al) [æpəsˈtɒlɪk, -ɪk(ə)l] ADJ Rel (benediction etc) apostolique
►► **a. succession** succession f apostolique

apostrophe [əˈpɒstrəfɪ] N Gram apostrophe f

apostrophize [əˈpɒstrəfaɪz] VT Liter apostropher

apothecary [əˈpɒθɪkərɪ] N Arch apothicaire m

apotheosis, pl **apotheoses** [əpɒθɪˈəʊsɪs, -ˈəʊsiːz] N apothéose f

app [æp] N Comput Fam (abbr application) application f

appal, Am **appall** [əˈpɔːl] VT (Br **appals,** Am **appalls;** Br, Am **appalled, appalling**) consterner; (stronger) choquer, révolter; **to be appalled at or by sb's behaviour** être choqué par le comportement de qn; **it appals me to think that …** je suis horrifié à la pensée que …; **I'm appalled!** ça me scandalise!

Appalachian [æpəˈleɪtʃən] ADJ, N **the A. Mountains, the Appalachians** les (monts mpl) Appalaches mpl

appalling [əˈpɔːlɪŋ] ADJ (behaviour, conditions, smell etc) épouvantable, effroyable; **to make an a. row** faire un bruit de tous les diables

appallingly [əˈpɔːlɪŋlɪ] ADV 1 (badly) épouvantablement, effroyablement; (to cook, play) effroyablement mal; **he speaks French quite a.** son français est épouvantable ou effroyable; **he's a. badly behaved** il se tient tellement mal que c'en est consternant; **to treat sb a.** se conduire épouvantablement

mal envers qn 2 (very) (ugly, boring, rude etc) effroyablement; **he's a. stupid** il est d'une stupidité effroyable ou extraordinaire

apparatchik [æpəˈrɑːtʃɪk] N Pol Fam apparatchik m

apparatus, pl **apparatuses** [æpəˈreɪtəs, -əsɪz] N (usu no pl) appareil m, dispositif m; **breathing a.** appareil respiratoire; **a piece of a.** un appareil; Fig **the a. of the state** l'appareil de l'État; Liter **critical a., a. criticus** (of text) appareil ou apparat m critique; Physiol **the digestive a.** l'appareil digestif; **laboratory a.** appareils de laboratoire; **mental a.** cellules fpl grises
►► Gym **a. work** (gymnastique f ou exercices mpl aux) agrès mpl

apparel [əˈpærəl] N Arch, Lit, Am vêtement(s) m(pl)

apparent [əˈpærənt] ADJ 1 (clear, obvious) apparent, manifeste, évident; **to make sth a.** indiquer qch clairement; **his indifference was a.** son indifférence était manifeste; **the truth became a. to her** la vérité lui apparut; **it was a. to me that …** pour moi, il était évident que …; **as will soon become a.** comme on le verra bientôt 2 (seeming) apparent; **with a. ease** avec une facilité apparente; **in spite of his a. indifference** malgré son air d'indifférence
►► Econ **a. consumption** consommation f apparente

apparently [əˈpærəntlɪ] ADV apparemment; **he's a. going to Venice** il paraît qu'il va aller à Venise; **a. not** il paraît que non

apparition [æpəˈrɪʃən] N (ghost, vision, appearance) apparition f

appeal [əˈpiːl] N 1 (call) appel m (**for** à); **to make or issue an a. for help** lancer un appel au secours; **to make an a. to sb** (for help, support, money) lancer un appel auprès de qn; **the president's a. for calm** l'appel au calme du président; **to make an a. to sb's generosity** faire appel à la générosité de qn; **an a. for donations** une demande de contributions; **a charity a.** un appel de la part d'une œuvre de bienfaisance
2 Law appel m (**against** de); **without a.** sans appel; **notice of a.** intimation f (d'appel); **to lodge an a.** se pourvoir en appel; **acquitted on a.** acquitté en seconde instance; **Court of A.** cour f d'appel; **Supreme Court of A.** cour de cassation; **military a. court** conseil m de révision
3 (attraction) attrait m, attraction f; **to have or hold little a. for sb** ne guère attirer qn; **to have great a.** (of thing) être très attrayant; (of person) avoir beaucoup de charme; **to have a narrow a.** (of music, politician etc) plaire à peu de gens; **their music has a wide a.** leur musique plaît à toutes sortes de gens; Com **sales a.** attraction commerciale
VI 1 (make a plea) **to a. (to sb) for help/money** demander de l'aide/de l'argent (à qn); **I a. to you to …** je vous supplie de …; **to a. to sb's generosity** faire appel à la générosité de qn
2 (attract, interest) **this appealed to his imagination** cela parlait à son imagination; **the plan/idea appeals to me** ce projet/cette idée me plaît; **it doesn't a. to me** cela ne me dit rien; **the idea did not a. to him** l'idée ne l'enchantait guère; **to a. to the emotions/the senses** faire appel aux sentiments/aux sens; **styles that a. to the young** modes qui plaisent aux jeunes
3 Law etc interjeter appel; **to a. against a judgment** faire appel d'un jugement; **to a. to another court** en appeler à un autre tribunal, introduire un recours devant un autre tribunal; **to a. against a decision** réclamer contre une décision; Law faire appel d'une décision

VT *Law (decision)* faire appel de
▸▸ *Law* **A. Court** cour d'appel

> Note that the French verb **appeler** is a false friend. Its most common meaning is **to call**.

appealing [ə'pi:lɪŋ] **ADJ 1** *(imploring) (look, tone)* suppliant **2** *(attractive) (personality, person, smile)* sympathique; *(idea, prospect)* séduisant, attrayant; **there's something very a. about him/puppies** il y a quelque chose de très attirant chez lui/les chiots

appealingly [ə'pi:lɪŋlɪ] **ADV 1** *(beseechingly) (to say)* d'un ton suppliant; *(to look)* d'un air suppliant **2** *(attractively)* de façon attrayante

appear [ə'pɪər] **VI 1** *(come into view)* paraître, apparaître, se montrer; *(in accounts, on a list etc)* figurer; **a head appeared at the window** un visage a paru ou est apparu ou s'est montré à la fenêtre; **a huge lorry suddenly appeared out of the fog** un gros camion a surgi tout à coup du brouillard; **she appeared to him in a dream** elle lui est apparue en rêve; **she only appears at meal times** elle n'apparaît qu'au moment des repas; **where did you a. from?** d'où est-ce que tu sors?; **to a. from nowhere** sortir de nulle part
2 *Law* comparaître, paraître; **to a. before a court** comparaître devant un tribunal; **to fail to a.** faire défaut; **failure to a.** défaut *m* de comparution; **to a. for sb** représenter qn; *(of counsel)* plaider pour qn
3 *Theat, Cin* paraître; **to a. on the stage** *(make entrance)* entrer en scène; *(act)* faire du théâtre; **to a. on TV** passer à la télé; *Fig* **that was when I appeared on the scene** c'est à ce moment que je suis arrivé
4 *(of book, newspaper etc)* paraître, sortir
5 *(seem)* sembler, paraître; **he appeared to hesitate** il paraissait ou semblait hésiter, il avait l'air d'hésiter; **she appears to have a lot of friends** elle semble avoir beaucoup d'amis; **there appears to be a mistake** il semble(rait) qu'il y ait erreur; **it appears not** il semble que non; **it appears to us that the situation is worse** la situation nous semble pire; **to make it a. that ...** faire croire que ...; **to a. to be lost** avoir l'air d'être perdu; **to a. sad** paraître ou sembler triste, avoir l'air triste
6 *(become apparent)* **it appeared later that ...** on a vu par la suite ou plus tard que ...; **as appears from these records** comme il ressort de ces pièces

appearance [ə'pɪərəns] **N 1** *(arrival etc)* apparition *f*, arrivée *f*; **they were startled by the a. of a teacher** ils ont été surpris par l'arrivée d'un professeur; **with the a. of fast-food restaurants** avec l'apparition ou l'arrivée de fast-foods; **to put in an a.** passer; *Iron* faire acte de présence
2 *(of actor)* entrée *f* en scène; *Sport (of athlete)* entrée sur le terrain de jeu; **first a. of Miss Kane** *(as an actress)* début *m* de Mlle Kane; **to make one's first a.** débuter, faire ses débuts; **her Olympic a.** sa participation aux jeux Olympiques
3 *Law (in court)* comparution *f*
4 *(of book, newspaper etc)* parution *f*
5 *(looks, demeanour)* apparence *f*, aspect *m*, air *m*; **she had the a. of somebody who had not slept well** elle avait l'air de quelqu'un qui a mal dormi; **from his a. one would say ...** à son air ou son extérieur on dirait ...; **you should not judge by appearances** il ne faut pas juger selon les apparences; **his beard gave him the a. of a sailor** avec sa barbe il avait l'air d'un marin; **they gave every a. of being bored** ils ont donné tous les signes possibles de l'ennui; **an a. of gaiety** un air de gaieté; **it is like a mushroom in a.**

ça ressemble à un champignon; **at first a.** à première vue; **it has all the appearances of a conspiracy** ça a toutes les apparences d'une conspiration; **appearances are against him** les apparences sont contre lui; **appearances can be deceptive** les apparences peuvent être trompeuses; **to all appearances** selon toute apparence, apparemment; **to keep up appearances** sauver les apparences

appease [ə'pi:z] **VT** apaiser; *Pej* endormir; *(anger, hunger)* apaiser

appeasement [ə'pi:zmənt] **N 1** *(of person)* apaisement *m*; *(of nation)* conciliation *f* *(of avec)*; **to aim at the a. of terrorists/one's enemies** chercher à endormir les terroristes/ses ennemis; **policy of a.** politique *f* de conciliation **2** *(of anger, hunger etc)* assouvissement *m*

appellant [ə'pelənt] **ADJ, N** *Law* appelant, -ante

appellate [ə'pelət, -leɪt] **ADJ** *Law (court)* d'appel

appellation [æpe'leɪʃən] **N** *Fml* appellation *f*, nom *m*

append [ə'pend] **VT** *(attach) (document)* joindre (**to** à); *(in writing) (one's signature)* apposer (**to** à); *(notes, comments)* ajouter; *Comput (to database)* ajouter; **to a. a document to a file** annexer ou joindre un document à un dossier
▸▸ *Comput* **a. mode** mode *m* ajout

appendage [ə'pendɪdʒ] **N** *Anat, Biol* appendice *m*; **the concert was just an a. to the main events of the day** le concert n'était qu'un prolongement des principaux événements de la journée; **I will not be treated as a mere a. of my husband** je n'existe pas qu'en fonction de mon mari, j'existe aussi par moi-même

appendectomy [æpen'dektəmɪ], **appendicectomy** [æpendɪ'sektəmɪ] **N** *Surg* appendicectomie *f*

appendicitis [əpendɪ'saɪtɪs] **N** *Med* appendicite *f*

appendix, *pl* **appendixes, appendices** [ə'pendɪks, -ɪksɪz, -ɪsi:z] **N** VOIR GRAMMAIRE A14 **1** *Anat* appendice *m*; **to have one's a. (taken) out** se faire enlever l'appendice; **have you had your a. out?** tu as encore ton appendice?; *Med* **grumbling a.** appendicite *f* chronique **2** *(of report etc)* annexe *f*, *(of book)* appendice *m*

appertain [æpə'teɪn] **VI** *Fml* **1** *(belong)* appartenir (**to** à); **lands appertaining to the Crown** terres *fpl* appartenant à ou dépendant de la Couronne **2** *(of duties, responsibilities)* incomber (**to** à)

appetite [æ'pɪtaɪt] **N 1** *(for food)* appétit *m* *(for* pour); **to have a good a.** avoir bon appétit; **to have a poor a.** ne pas avoir beaucoup d'appétit; **to have a big a.** avoir un gros ou solide appétit; **to have a small a.** avoir un petit appétit, avoir peu d'appétit; **to take away** *or* **spoil sb's a.** couper l'appétit ou la faim à qn; **to give sb an a.** donner de l'appétit à qn, mettre qn en appétit; **the walk gave him an a.** la marche lui a ouvert l'appétit; **loss of a.** manque *m* d'appétit; *Med* **inappétence** *f*
2 *Fig (for knowledge)* soif *f*, *(for travel, Chinese music etc)* goût *m*; *(for doing sth)* envie *f*; **that whetted his a. for travel** cela a aiguisé son goût des voyages; **for revenge** soif de vengeance; **she had an enormous a. for books** elle avait une immense soif de lecture, elle était avide de lecture; **to have little a. for a fight** être peu enclin à une querelle ou à se disputer; **sexual a.** appétit *m* sexuel

appetizer [æ'pɪtaɪzər] **N** *Culin, Fig* amuse-gueule *m*, *pl* amuse-gueule(s)

appetizing [æ'pɪtaɪzɪŋ] **ADJ** *(food, smell)* appétissant, alléchant; *Fig* **he doesn't look very a.** il n'est pas ragoûtant

appetizingly [æ'pɪtaɪzɪŋlɪ] **ADV** d'une façon appétissante

applaud [ə'plɔ:d] **VT** *(performer, decision)* applaudir; **to a. sb's efforts** applaudir les efforts de qn
VI *(of audience etc)* applaudir

applause [ə'plɔ:z] **N** applaudissements *mpl*; *Fig (approval)* approbation *f*; **to meet** *or* **be greeted with a.** *(of performance, decision etc)* être applaudi, soulever les applaudissements; **to win a.** *(of performance, decision etc)* être applaudi *(from* par, de)
▸▸ *TV* **a. meter** applaudimètre *m*

apple [æ'p(ə)l] **N** pomme *f*; **eating** *or* **dessert a.** pomme à couteau ou à dessert; **cooking a.** pomme à cuire; **baked a.** pomme cuite (au four); *Prov* **an a. a day keeps the doctor away** = mangez une pomme par jour et vous resterez en bonne santé; *Fig* **his son is the a. of his eye** il tient à son fils comme à la prunelle de ses yeux; *Fam* **the Big A.** = la ville de New York
▸▸ **a. core** trognon *m* de pomme; **a. green** *(colour)* vert *m* pomme; **a. juice** jus *m* de pomme; **a. orchard** pommeraie *f*, **a. pie** *(covered)* tourte *f* aux pommes; *(open)* tarte *f* aux pommes; *Am Fam* **a. polisher** lèche-bottes *mf inv*; *Am* **a. sauce** compote *f* de pommes; **a. tart** tarte aux pommes; **a. tree** pommier *m*

applecart [æ'p(ə)lkɑ:t] **N** *Fig* **to upset the a.** tout chambouler

applejack [æ'p(ə)ldʒæk] **N** *esp Am* ≃ calvados *m*

apple-pie **ADJ** *Fam* **in a. order** admirablement rangé, parfaitement en ordre
▸▸ *Br* **a. bed** lit *m* en portefeuille

applet [æ'plət] **N** *Comput* appelette *f*, appliquette *f*

appliance [ə'plaɪəns] **N 1** *(machine)* appareil *m*; **mechanical a.** engin *m* mécanique; **electrical/household appliances** appareils électriques/ménagers **2** *(fire engine)* auto-pompe *f*, pompe *f* à incendie

applicable [ə'plɪkəb(ə)l, 'æplɪkəb(ə)l] **ADJ** applicable (**to** à); **not a.** *(on form)* sans rapport; **delete where not a.** rayer les mentions inutiles

applicant [æ'plɪkənt] **N 1** *(for job)* candidat, -ate (**for** à), postulant, -ante; *(for loan, funding, patent)* demandeur, -euse (**for** de); *Fin (for shares)* souscripteur, -trice (**for** de) **2** *Law* demandeur, -deresse, requérant, -ante

application [æplɪ'keɪʃən] **N 1** *(putting on)* application *f* *(of sth to sth* de qch à ou sur qch); *Aut, Tech Fml* **a. of the brake** freinage *m*
2 *(thing applied)* application *f*, *(of paint)* couche *f*, enduit *m*
3 *(use) (of theory, principle, discovery etc)* application *f*; **practical applications of a process** applications d'un procédé
4 *(assiduousness)* assiduité *f*, application *f*; **to show a lot of a.** faire preuve d'une grande application ou assiduité; **a. to a task** application à un travail
5 *(for help, patent)* demande *f* *(for* de); *(for job)* candidature *f*; **to submit an a.** *(for help)* faire une demande; *(for job)* présenter sa candidature; **to make an a. for sth** formuler une demande pour obtenir qch; **full details on a.** informations complètes sur demande; *St Exch* **a. for shares** demande de titres en souscription; **to make an a. for shares** souscrire (à) des actions
6 *Comput* application *f*
▸▸ **a. form** *(for grant, benefits)* formulaire *m* de demande; *(for membership)* demande d'inscription; *(detailed)* dossier *m* de candi-

dature; *Univ* dossier d'inscription; *St Exch (for shares)* bulletin *m* de souscription; *Comput* **a. program** programme *m* d'application; *Comput* **a. software** logiciel *m* d'application

> Note that the French word **application** is a false friend. It never means **request**.

applicator ['æplɪkeɪtər] N *(for glue, eyeshadow, tampon)* applicateur *m*

applied [ə'plaɪd] ADJ *(maths etc)* appliqué; *(sciences)* expérimental, -aux
▸▸ **a. psychology** psychotechnique *f*

appliqué [æ'pliːkeɪ] N *Sewing (decoration)* application *f*; *(decorative work)* travail *m* d'application

apply [ə'plaɪ] VT **1** *(put on) (paint, lotion, bandage)* appliquer *(to* sur*)*; *(brake)* actionner; **to a. the brake** freiner; **to a. pressure** exercer une pression; **to a. pressure on sb** faire pression sur qn
2 *(use) (system, theory, experience)* appliquer *(to* à*)*, mettre en application; *(rule)* appliquer *(to* à*)*; **to a. one's mind to sth** s'appliquer à qch; **to a. oneself to one's work** travailler avec application; **he would like to a. his experience in IT to industry** il voudrait utiliser ses compétences en informatique dans le domaine de l'industrie
VI **1 to a. to sb for sth** s'adresser *ou* recourir à qn pour obtenir qch; **to a. for a job** faire une demande d'emploi, poser sa candidature à un emploi, *Fml* solliciter *ou* postuler un emploi; **to a. for a loan** demander un prêt; **to a. for a grant** faire une demande de bourse; **to a. within** s'adresser ici; **to a. in writing** écrire; **to a. in person** se présenter; *St Exch* **to a. for shares** souscrire (à) des actions
2 *(of law, rule, order)* s'appliquer *(to* à*)*; **that applies to all of you!** *(what I've just said)* cela s'adresse à vous tous!

appoint [ə'pɔɪnt] VT **1** *(director etc)* nommer; *(committee)* constituer, nommer; *(heir)* instituer; **to a. sb to a post** nommer *ou* désigner qn à un poste; **to a. sb to do sth** désigner qn pour faire qch; **to a. sb (to be) manager** nommer qn directeur; **newly appointed officials** fonctionnaires *mpl* entrants *ou* nouvellement nommés **2** *Fml (time, place)* fixer, désigner; *(day)* arrêter

appointed [ə'pɔɪntɪd] ADJ **1** *(official)* nommé; *(agent)* attitré **2** *Fml (agreed) (place, hour)* convenu, dit; **on the a. day** le jour convenu *ou* dit **3 a well a. house** une maison bien montée *ou* bien agencée *ou* bien installée

appointee [əpɔɪn'tiː] N personne *f* nommée; **she was an a. of the President** elle avait été nommée par le Président

appointment [ə'pɔɪntmənt] N **1** *(meeting) (at doctor's etc)* rendez-vous *m*; *(for business)* rendez-vous *m*, entrevue *f*; **to make an a. with sb** *(for oneself)* donner rendez-vous à qn; *(for sb else)* fixer un rendez-vous avec qn; **I've made an a. with the doctor for you** je t'ai pris un rendez-vous chez le docteur; **please telephone if you cannot make** *or* **keep your a.** veuillez téléphoner s'il vous est impossible de venir à votre rendez-vous; **she didn't keep our** *or* **the a.** elle n'est pas venue au rendez-vous; **I've got an a. with the doctor** j'ai rendez-vous chez le médecin; *(announcing arrival to receptionist)* j'ai rendez-vous avec le médecin; **to meet sb by a.** rencontrer qn sur rendez-vous; **by a. only** sur rendez-vous seulement; **have you got an a.?** avez-vous un rendez-vous?; *Admin* êtes-vous convoqué?; **appointments diary** carnet *m* de rendez-vous, agenda *m* **2** *(of sb to job)* nomination *f*; *Admin (of sb for task)* désignation *f*; *Mil, Naut (of sb to unit, ship)* affectation *f*; **he is a popular a.** tout le

monde est content de sa nomination *ou* qu'il ait été nommé; **by a. to His/Her Majesty** *(of company, shop etc)* fournisseur breveté *ou* attitré de Sa Majesté; *Journ* **appointments** offres *fpl* d'emploi
3 *Fml* **appointments** *(of house)* aménagement *m*

> Note that the French word **appointements** is a false friend and is never a translation for the English word **appointments**. It means **salary**.

apportion [ə'pɔːʃən] VT *(expenses, praise)* répartir; *(property)* lotir; **to a. sth to sb** assigner qch à qn; **to a. (out) a sum among several people** partager *ou* distribuer une somme entre plusieurs personnes; **to a. blame** dégager les responsabilités de chacun

apportionment [ə'pɔːʃənmənt] N *(of taxes, expenses etc)* répartition *f*, partage *m*; *(of rations etc)* allocation *f*; *(of shares, property)* distribution *f*; *(of blame)* répartition

apposite ['æpəzɪt] ADJ approprié *(to* à*)*; *(remark)* (fait) à propos, pertinent; *(observation)* juste

apposition [æpə'zɪʃən] N *Gram, Bot etc* apposition *f*; **words in a.** mots *mpl* apposés *ou* en apposition VOIR GRAMMAIRE A6; B5

appraisal [ə'preɪzəl] N *(of standards, personnel)* évaluation *f*; *(of object for insurance purposes etc)* estimation *f*, appréciation *f*; *(before auction)* prisée *f*; **to carry out an a.** conduire une expertise; **official a.** *(of object)* expertise *f*; **self a.** autocritique *f*

appraise [ə'preɪz] VT estimer, évaluer *(at so much* à tant*)*; *(situation)* évaluer; *(damage)* faire l'expertise de; **to a. the value of sth** estimer *ou* apprécier la valeur de qch; **with an appraising eye** d'un œil critique

appreciable [ə'priːʃəb(ə)l] ADJ *(difference, variation, amount, distance)* appréciable, notable; *(change, improvement)* sensible

appreciably [ə'priːʃəblɪ] ADV *(changed, improved, better)* sensiblement

appreciate [ə'priːʃɪeɪt, -sɪeɪt] VT **1** *(know the value of, attach importance to) (person, thing)* apprécier; **she was never appreciated properly** elle n'a jamais été appréciée à sa juste valeur; **no one appreciates me** personne ne m'apprécie à ma juste valeur; **to a. the value of sb/sth** reconnaître la valeur de qn/qch
2 *(be grateful for)* être reconnaissant de, être sensible à; **I greatly a. your kindness** je suis très sensible à votre gentillesse; **I a. your having done this** je vous suis reconnaissant d'avoir fait cela; **I a. it** j'en suis reconnaissant; *esp Am (thanks)* je vous en remercie
3 *(grasp, understand)* comprendre, se rendre compte de; **I fully a. (the fact) that ...** je me rends bien compte que ...; **he doesn't a. his good fortune** il ne se rend pas compte à quel point il a de la chance; **while I a. your predicament ...** tout en comprenant bien votre situation difficile ...; **we a. the risks/difficulties involved** nous sommes conscients des risques que cela implique/des difficultés que cela comporte; **I hadn't appreciated you needed one** je ne savais pas qu'il vous en fallait un
VI *(of goods, investment etc)* prendre de la valeur; *(of value)* augmenter; *(of currency)* s'apprécier; **the euro has appreciated in terms of other currencies** l'euro s'est apprécié par rapport aux autres monnaies

appreciation [əpriːʃɪ'eɪʃən, əpriːsɪ-] N **1** *(gratitude)* gratitude *f*, reconnaissance *f*; **as a sign of our a.** en témoignage de notre gratitude *ou* reconnaissance; **I should like to express my a. of your kindness** j'aimerais

vous dire combien je suis sensible à votre gentillesse; **in a. of her years of loyal service** pour témoigner de ma/notre/leur/etc reconnaissance pour ses années de bons et loyaux services; **the audience showed its a. of the performance by cheering** le public a acclamé le spectacle
2 *(understanding)* compréhension *f*; **she has no a. of what is involved** elle ne se rend pas compte de ce que ça implique
3 *Fin (increase)* accroissement *m ou* hausse *f* de valeur; **a. of assets** plus-value *f* d'actif
4 *(review)* critique *f*; **to write an a. of a new play** faire la critique d'une nouvelle pièce
5 *(evaluation) (of object)* appréciation *f*, estimation *f*; **literary a.** explication *f* de texte; **musical a.** appréciation musicale; **a literary/wine a. society** une société d'amateurs de littérature/de vin

appreciative [ə'priːʃɪətɪv, -sɪətɪv] ADJ **1** *(grateful)* reconnaissant; **I'm very a. of all you've done for me** je vous suis reconnaissant de tout ce que vous avez fait pour moi; **she's a very a. sort of person** c'est une personne qui sait faire preuve de reconnaissance *ou* de gratitude; **in a few a. words** avec quelques mots de reconnaissance
2 *(review, audience)* favorable; *(praising)* élogieux
3 *(showing liking etc)* **I gave him the present, but he wasn't very a.** je lui ai donné le cadeau, mais il n'a pas beaucoup aimé; **to be a. of music** apprécier la musique
4 *(showing understanding, awareness)* **to be a. of sth** comprendre l'importance de qch, être sensible à qch; **he was very a. of their problems** il s'est montré très sensible à leurs problèmes

appreciatively [ə'priːʃɪətɪvlɪ, -sɪətɪvlɪ] ADV **1** *(gratefully)* avec reconnaissance
2 *(showing understanding, praising) (to review etc)* en termes élogieux, favorablement; *(to listen)* avec appréciation; **they clapped a.** ils applaudirent pour montrer leur enthousiasme; **she smiled a. at his joke** elle a aimé l'histoire qui l'a fait sourire; **she smiled a.** *(approving of point made)* elle eut un sourire approbateur; **'a superb brandy,' she said a.** 'un cognac exceptionnel,' dit-elle en connaisseuse; **the performance was received a.** le spectacle a été bien *ou* favorablement reçu
3 *(showing liking)* **'excellent coffee,' he said a.** 'excellent café,' dit-il avec plaisir

apprehend [æprɪ'hend] VT **1** *Law (arrest)* appréhender **2** *Fml (understand) (facts)* comprendre; **as far as I a. it** si je comprends bien **3** *Arch, Lit (fear) (danger etc)* appréhender, craindre

apprehension [æprɪ'henʃən] N **1** *(fear)* appréhension *f*; **to give cause for a.** motiver des craintes **2** *Law (arrest)* appréhension *f*, arrestation *f*

apprehensive [æprɪ'hensɪv] ADJ *(look, smile etc)* timide, craintif; **to be a. for sb/for sb's safety** craindre pour qn/pour la sûreté de qn; **to be a. about sth/doing sth** appréhender qch/de faire qch; **there's nothing to be a. about** il n'y a aucune raison de s'inquiéter; **I'm feeling a bit a.** je me sens un peu nerveux

apprehensively [æprɪ'hensɪvlɪ] ADV avec appréhension

apprentice [ə'prentɪs] N apprenti, -ie; **carpenter's/plumber's a., a. carpenter/plumber** apprenti menuisier/plombier; **sorcerer's a.** apprenti sorcier
VT **to a. sb to sb** placer *ou* mettre qn en apprentissage chez qn

apprenticed [ə'prentɪst] ADJ en apprentissage *(to sb* chez qn*)*

apprenticeship [ə'prentɪʃɪp] N apprentissage *m*; **to serve an a.** faire un apprentissage; *Fig* **to serve one's a.** faire ses débuts

apprise [ə'praɪz] **VT** *Fml* **to a. sb of sth** apprendre qch à qn, prévenir *ou* informer qn de qch; **we were not apprised of his arrival** nous n'avons pas été informés de son arrivée

appro ['æprəʊ] **N** *Com Fam* **on a.** à l'essai

approach [ə'prəʊtʃ] **N 1** *(coming) (of person)* approche *f*, *(of spring)* venue *f*, *(of night)* tombée *f*, *(of death)* approche(s); **I could hear his a.** je l'entendais s'approcher; *Aviat* **a. end of the runway** entrée *f* de piste, seuil *m* de la piste

2 *(method)* méthode *f*, démarche *f*, **let's try a different a.** essayons une autre méthode; **her a. to the problem** sa façon d'aborder le problème; **I don't like her a.** je n'aime pas sa façon de s'y prendre

3 *Fig (to person)* avance *f*, ouverture *f*, *(for business purposes)* proposition *f*, ouverture; **to make an a. to sb** faire une proposition à qn

4 *(point of entry)* voie *f* d'accès; **the a. to a town** les abords *mpl ou* les approches *fpl* d'une ville; **all approaches to the town have been sealed off** tous les abords de la ville ont été bouclés; **a. to a harbour** atterrage *m*, accès *m* d'un port

5 *(approximation)* **a. to an apology/a smile** semblant *m* d'excuse/de sourire; **it is the nearest a. to perfection** c'est ce qui s'approche le plus de la perfection

VI approcher, s'approcher; **Christmas/spring is approaching** Noël/le printemps approche

VT 1 *(get nearer to)* approcher; *(place)* approcher de; **the town can only be approached from the north** on ne peut accéder à *ou* gagner la ville que par le nord; **I'm approaching 45** je vais sur mes 45 ans; **the wind was approaching gale force** le vent soufflait presque en tempête; **something approaching a feeling of relief** un sentiment proche du soulagement

2 *(go up to) (person)* s'approcher de, aborder, approcher; *(of company, group, team)* pressentir, faire des propositions à; **des ouvertures à; I was approached by a man in the street** j'ai été abordé par un homme dans la rue; **to a. sb on the subject of ...** approcher qn au sujet de ...; **to be easy/difficult to a.** avoir l'abord facile/difficile

3 *(question)* aborder, s'attaquer à; **she approaches the issue from the angle of ...** elle aborde la question du point de vue de ...

▸▸ *Aviat* **a. aids** moyens *mpl* d'approche; **a. shot** *Tennis* coup *m* d'approche; *Golf* approche

approachable [ə'prəʊtʃəb(ə)l] **ADJ 1** *(person)* d'un abord facile, abordable **2** *(building, place)* accessible

approaching [ə'prəʊtʃɪŋ] **ADJ** *(death)* prochain; *(storm)* qui arrive; **the a. war ...** la guerre qui approche/approchait ...; **the a. car** *(from opposite direction to one's own)* la voiture qui vient/venait en sens inverse

approbation [æprə'beɪʃən] **N** approbation *f*, **smile of a.** sourire *m* approbateur

appropriate[1] [ə'prəʊprɪət] **ADJ** *(suitable, fitting)* approprié (**to** à); *(word, expression)* juste; *(clothes)* convenable (**for** pour); *(name, site)* bien choisi; *(music)* de circonstance; *(moment)* opportun; **to take a. action** prendre les mesures indiquées; **he could have chosen a more a. time and place** il aurait pu choisir un moment et un endroit plus appropriés (**to** pour); **it seemed a. that she should have died in a theatre** cela semblait être dans l'ordre des choses qu'elle soit morte dans un théâtre

appropriate[2] [ə'prəʊprɪeɪt] **VT 1** *(take)* s'approprier, s'emparer de; *(keep for oneself)*

s'attribuer, se réserver; **to a. sb's ideas** s'approprier les idées de qn **2** *(set aside) (money, funds)* affecter, destiner (**to** à); **£4,000 has been appropriated to upgrading computers** 4000 livres ont été affectées à l'augmentation de mémoire des ordinateurs

appropriately [ə'prəʊprɪətlɪ] **ADV** *(suitably)* de manière appropriée; *(properly)* convenablement, proprement; **a. dressed** en tenue convenable

appropriateness [ə'prəʊprɪətnɪs] **N** *(of behaviour)* correction *f*, bienséance *f*, *(of remarks)* justesse *f*, à-propos *m inv*

appropriation [əprəʊprɪ'eɪʃən] **N 1** *(taking)* appropriation *f*, prise *f* de possession (**of** de) **2** *(setting aside) (of money for specific purpose)* application *f*, affectation *f* **3** *Fin* affectation *f* de fonds; *(of sum)* attribution *f*, *Pol* crédit *m* (budgétaire)

approval [ə'pruːv(ə)l] **N 1** approbation *f*, assentiment *m*, *Fml* agrément *m*; *(of dealer, distributor)* agrément; **to meet with sb's a.** recevoir *ou* obtenir l'approbation de qn; **to submit sth for a. (by sb)** soumettre qch à l'approbation (de qn); **gesture** *or* **sign of a.** geste *m ou* signe *m* d'approbation; **to nod a.** approuver d'un signe de (la) tête; **subject to a.** soumis à l'approbation

2 *Com* **on a.** à condition, à l'essai; **a book sent on a.** un livre envoyé à l'examen; *Am* **approvals** *(goods)* marchandises *fpl* envoyées à l'essai

3 *(of document, proposal)* ratification *f*, homologation *f*, **for (your) a.** *(of draft letter)* pour approbation

▸▸ **a. rating** *(of politician)* cote *f* de popularité; *Mktg (of product)* score *m* d'agrément

approve [ə'pruːv] **VT** *(action)* approuver, sanctionner; *(decision, proposal)* ratifier, homologuer; *(contract, dealer, distributor)* agréer; **read and approved** lu et approuvé; **approved by the government** agréé par l'État

VI être d'accord; **I told her what I had done and she seemed to a.** je lui ai dit ce que j'avais fait et elle a eu l'air de m'approuver

▸ **approve of VT INSEP** approuver; **I don't a. of your friends** tes amis ne me plaisent pas; **I don't a. of the plan** je ne suis pas d'accord avec ce projet; **she doesn't a. of them smoking** ça ne lui plaît pas qu'ils fument

approved [ə'pruːvd] **ADJ** approuvé, agréé; *Admin* **(officially) a.** homologué

▸▸ **a. dealer** concessionnaire *m* agréé; *Formerly* **a. school** = nom anciennement donné en Grande-Bretagne à un centre d'éducation surveillé (aujourd'hui appelé "community home"); **a. stallion** étalon *m* autorisé

approving [ə'pruːvɪŋ] **ADJ** *(look, smile)* approbateur, -trice

approvingly [ə'pruːvɪŋlɪ] **ADV** *(to look)* d'un air approbateur; *(to say)* d'un ton approbateur; **to react a.** approuver

approx *abbr* **approximately**

approximate[1] [ə'prɒksɪmɪt] **ADJ** *(calculation etc)* approximatif, approché SEE GRAMMAR B59 **2** *Biol, Phys* rapproché, proche, voisin

▸▸ **a. value** valeur *f* approximative

approximate[2] [ə'prɒksɪmeɪt] **VT to a. sth in size/cost** se rapprocher de qch par les dimensions/le prix

VI to a. in size/cost to sth se rapprocher de qch par les dimensions/le prix; **to a. to the truth** se rapprocher de la vérité

approximately [ə'prɒksɪmətlɪ] **ADV** approximativement, à peu près; **5 miles are a. 8 kilometres** 5 mil(l)es équivalent à peu près à 8 kilomètres; **his income is a. £15,000** son revenu est d'environ 15 000 livres

approximation [əprɒksɪ'meɪʃən] **N** approximation *f*, **his statement was no more than an a. of the truth** sa déclaration n'avait qu'un lointain rapport avec la réalité

appurtenance [ə'pɜːtɪnəns] **N** *(usu pl)* **appurtenances** accessoires *mpl*; *Law* **a house with all its appurtenances** un immeuble avec ses appartenances et dépendances

APR [eɪpiː'ɑːr] **N** *Fin* *(abbr* **annual percentage rate***)* TEG *m*

Apr *abbr* **April**

après-ski [æpreɪ'skiː] **N** = distractions *fpl* après une séance de ski

> Note that the French word **après-ski** is a false friend and is never a translation for the English word **après-ski**. It means **snowboot**.

apricot ['eɪprɪkɒt] **N 1** abricot *m*; **a. yoghurt/ice cream** yaourt *m*/glace *f* à l'abricot **2** *(colour)* abricot *m inv*; **a. dress** robe *f* (couleur) abricot

▸▸ **a. jam** confiture *f* d'abricots; **a. tart** tarte *f* aux abricots; **a. tree** abricotier *m*

April ['eɪprɪl] **N** VOIR GRAMMAIRE A81–2; B61 avril *m*; **in A.** en avril, au mois d'avril; **(on) the first/the seventh of A.** le premier/le sept avril

▸▸ **A. fool** *(person)* = personne *f* à qui l'on a fait un poisson d'avril; *(trick)* poisson *m* d'avril; **A. fool!** poisson d'avril!; **A. Fool's Day** le premier avril; **A. showers** ≃ giboulées *fpl* de mars

April Fool's Day

En Grande-Bretagne, le premier avril est l'occasion de farces en tous genres; en revanche, la tradition du poisson en papier n'existe pas.

a priori ['eɪpraɪ'ɔːraɪ, ˌɑːprɪ'ɔːrɪ] **ADV, ADJ** a priori

apron ['eɪprən] **N 1** *(clothing)* tablier *m*; *Fig* **to be tied to one's mother's a. strings** être pendu aux jupons de sa mère **2** *Theat* avant-scène *f*, *pl* avant-scènes **3** *Aviat* aire *f* de manœuvre *ou* de stationnement; *(for plane maintenance and repair)* tablier *m*, aire en dur

▸▸ *Theat* **a. stage** avant-scène

apropos ['æprəpəʊ] **ADJ** *(remark)* opportun, pertinent

PREP a. (of) à propos de

APS [eɪpiː'es] **ADJ, N** *Phot* *(abbr* **advanced photo system***)* APS *m*

▸▸ **A. camera** appareil *m* photo APS

apse [æps] **N** *(in church)* abside *f*

apt[1] [æpt] **ADJ 1** *(word)* juste; *(expression)* heureux, qui convient; *(description)* parlant; **it is very a. that it should end in this way** il est tout à fait approprié que cela se termine de cette manière **2 to be a. to do sth** *(of person, thing)* avoir tendance à faire qch **3** *(student etc)* intelligent, doué; **to be a. at languages** être doué en *ou* pour les langues

apt[2] *Am* *(abbr* **apartment***)* appt

aptitude ['æptɪtjuːd] **N** aptitude *f* (**for** à, pour); **to show great a.** montrer de grandes dispositions; **to have an a. for science** avoir une aptitude pour la science, avoir des dispositions scientifiques; **to have no a. for French** n'avoir aucune facilité pour le français

▸▸ **a. test** test *m* d'aptitude

aptly ['æptlɪ] **ADV** *(to say, comment)* avec justesse, à propos; *(described)* justement; **a. chosen name** nom *m* bien choisi

aptness ['æptnɪs] **N 1** *(appropriateness) (of expression, quotation etc)* justesse *f*, à-propos *m inv* **2** *(tendency)* tendance *f* (**to do sth** à faire qch)

aqualung ['ækwəlʌŋ] N scaphandre *m* autonome

aquamarine [ækwəmə'ri:n] N *(gem)* aiguemarine *f*, *pl* aigues-marines
ADJ *(dress etc)* bleu vert *inv*

aquanaut ['ækwənɔ:t] N aquanaute *mf*

aquaplane ['ækwəpleɪn] N *Sport* aquaplane *m*
VI *Sport* faire de l'aquaplane; *Aut* faire de l'aquaplaning

aquaplaning ['ækwəpleɪnɪŋ] N *Sport* aquaplane *m*; *Aut* aquaplaning *m*, effet *m* d'hydroglisseur

aquarelle [ækwə'rel] N *Art* aquarelle *f*

aquarium, *pl* **aquariums, aquaria** [ə'kweərɪəm, -ɪəmz, -ɪə] N aquarium *m*

Aquarius [ə'kweərɪəs] N *Astrol* le Verseau; **to be (an) A.** être (du) Verseau

aquarobics ['ækwə'rəʊbɪks] N aquagym *f*

aquatic [ə'kwætɪk] ADJ *(plant etc)* aquatique
▸▸**a. display** numéro *m* aquatique; **a. sports** sports *mpl* nautiques

aquatics [ə'kwætɪks] NPL sports *mpl* nautiques VOIR GRAMMAIRE A10

aquatint ['ækwətɪnt] N aquatinte *f*

aqueduct ['ækwɪdʌkt] N aqueduc *m*

aqueous ['eɪkwɪəs] ADJ aqueux
▸▸*Anat* **a. humour** humeur *f* aqueuse; *Chem* **a. solution** soluté *m*

aquilegia [ækwɪ'li:dʒɪə] N *(plant)* aquilégie *f*

aquiline ['ækwɪlaɪn] ADJ aquilin; *(nose)* aquilin, busqué, en bec d'aigle

A&R [eɪən'dɑ:r] N *(abbr* **artists and repertoire**) = service *m* d'une maison de disques chargé de recruter de nouveaux artistes
▸▸**A. man** = personne *f* qui recrute de nouveaux artistes

Arab ['ærəb] VOIR GRAMMAIRE A19 ADJ **1** arabe; **the A. world** le monde arabe **2** *(horse)* arabe
N **1** *(person)* Arabe *mf* **2** *(horse)* arabe *m*
▸▸*Pol* **the A. League** la Ligue arabe

Arab
En anglais le mot "Arab" désigne l'ensemble des ressortissants des pays de culture arabe, et surtout de l'Arabie Saoudite. Il n'a pas le sens restreint de "Maghrébin" que l'on rencontre souvent en français: "the firm was bought by a wealthy Arab family".

---

arabesque [ærə'besk] ADJ *Art (decoration)* de style arabe
N **1** *(usu pl)* *Art* arabesque *f* **2** *(in ballet)* arabesque *f*

Arabia [ə'reɪbɪə] N Arabie *f*

Arabian [ə'reɪbɪən] VOIR GRAMMAIRE A19 ADJ arabe
N *(from Arabia)* Arabe *mf*
▸▸**the A. Gulf** le golfe Arabique; *Liter* **the A. Nights** les Mille et Une Nuits; **the A. Peninsula** la péninsule d'Arabie

Arabic ['ærəbɪk] VOIR GRAMMAIRE A19 ADJ *(language, literature)* arabe; **A. scholar** arabisant, -ante
N *Ling* arabe *m*
▸▸**A. numerals** chiffres *mpl* arabes

Arabist ['ærəbɪst] N arabisant, -ante

arable ['ærəb(ə)l] ADJ *(land)* arable

arachnid [ə'ræknɪd] N *Zool* arachnide *m*

Aramaic [ærə'meɪɪk] ADJ, N *Ling* araméen *m*

arbiter ['ɑ:bɪtər] N *(of fashion etc)* arbitre *m*; **a. of taste** arbitre des élégances

arbitrage ['ɑ:bɪtrɑ:ʒ] N *Fin, St Exch* arbitrage *m*

arbitrager ['ɑ:bɪtrɑ:ʒər] N *Fin, St Exch* arbitragiste *mf*

arbitrarily ['ɑ:bɪtreərəlɪ] ADV arbitrairement

arbitrariness ['ɑ:bɪtrərɪnɪs] N *(of decision etc)* caractère *m* arbitraire

arbitrary ['ɑ:bɪtrərɪ] ADJ *(decision etc)* arbitraire

arbitrate ['ɑ:bɪtreɪt] VT *(dispute)* arbitrer, trancher
VI arbitrer (**between** entre)

arbitration [ɑ:bɪ'treɪʃən] N arbitrage *m*; **to go to a.** *(of union)* soumettre le différend à l'arbitrage; *(of dispute)* être soumis à l'arbitrage; **to refer a question to a.** soumettre une question à un arbitrage
▸▸**a. board** commission *f* d'arbitrage; **a. clause** clause *f* compromissoire; **a. committee** commission d'arbitrage; **a. court** instance *f* chargée d'arbitrer les conflits sociaux, tribunal *m* arbitral; **a. ruling** décision *f* arbitrale; **a. tribunal** instance chargée d'arbitrer les conflits sociaux, tribunal arbitral

arbitrator ['ɑ:bɪtreɪtər] N médiateur, -trice; *Law* arbitre *m*

arbor N *Am* = **arbour**

arboreal [ɑ:'bɔ:rɪəl] ADJ **1** *(relating to trees)* d'arbre(s) **2** *(living in trees) (animal)* arboricole; *(existence)* dans les arbres

arboriculture ['ɑ:bərɪkʌltʃər] N arboriculture *f*

arbour, *Am* **arbor** ['ɑ:bər] N berceau *m* de verdure, charmille *f*, *(on trellis)* tonnelle *f*; **vine a.** treille *f*

arbutus [ɑ:'bju:təs] N *(shrub)* arbousier *m*

arc [ɑ:k] N *Math etc (of circle etc)* arc *m*; **to describe an a.** décrire un arc; *Mil* **a. of fire** *(of cannon etc)* champ *m* de tir
VI (**arcing** ['ɑ:kɪŋ], **arced** [ɑ:kt]) *Elec* faire jaillir un arc, amorcer l'arc
▸▸**a. lamp, a. light** lampe *f ou* projecteur *m* à arc

arcade [ɑ:'keɪd] N *(covered passageway)* passage *m* (couvert); *(for shopping)* galerie *f* (marchande)

Arcadia [ɑ:'keɪdɪə] N Arcadie *f*

Arcadian [ɑ:'keɪdɪən] ADJ arcadien
N Arcadien, -ienne

arcane [ɑ:'keɪn] ADJ mystérieux, ésotérique; *(knowledge, practice, ritual)* secret, -ète
N **the a.** le mystérieux

arch[1] [ɑ:tʃ] N **1** *Archit, Constr* voûte *f*, arc *m*; *Constr (of bridge, viaduct)* arche *f*; **a. of a vault** arceau *m* d'une voûte **2** *Anat (of foot)* cambrure *f*, voûte *f* plantaire; **to have fallen arches** avoir les pieds plats
VT *(one's back)* arquer, courber; **the cat arched its back** le chat a fait le dos rond
VI former une voûte
▸▸*Archit* **a. stone** claveau *m*, voussoir *m*; **a. support** *(in shoes)* cambrure

arch[2] ADJ *(mischievous)* espiègle, malicieux

arch[3] ADJ *(great)* grand
PREF archi-
▸▸**a. enemy** adversaire *m ou* ennemi *m* numéro un; **a. traitor** traître *m* insigne

archaeological, *Am* **archeological** [ɑ:kɪə'lɒdʒɪk(ə)l] ADJ archéologique

archaeologically, *Am* **archeologically** [ɑ:kɪə'lɒdʒɪklɪ] ADV archéologiquement

archaeologist, *Am* **archeologist** [ɑ:kɪ'ɒlədʒɪst] N archéologue *m*

archaeology, *Am* **archeology** [ɑ:kɪ'ɒlədʒɪ] N archéologie *f*

archaic [ɑ:'keɪɪk] ADJ archaïque

archaism ['ɑ:keɪɪz(ə)m] N archaïsme *m*

archangel ['ɑ:keɪndʒ(ə)l] N archange *m*

archbishop [ɑ:tʃ'bɪʃəp] N archevêque *m*; **a.'s palace** palais *m* archiépiscopal

archbishopric [ɑ:tʃ'bɪʃəprɪk] N archevêché *m*

archdeacon [ɑ:tʃ'di:k(ə)n] N archidiacre *m*

archdiocese [ɑ:tʃ'daɪəsɪs, -si:z] N archidiocèse *m*, archevêché *m*

archduchess [ɑ:tʃ'dʌtʃɪs] N archiduchesse *f*

archduchy [ɑ:tʃ'dʌtʃɪ] N archiduché *m*

archduke [ɑ:tʃ'dju:k] N archiduc *m*

arched [ɑ:tʃt] ADJ *Archit (roof)* voûté
▸▸**a. window** *(semicircular)* fenêtre *f* cintrée; *(pointed)* fenêtre en arc brisé

archeological, archeologically *etc Am* = **archaeological, archaeologically** *etc*

archer ['ɑ:tʃər] N *Mil, Sport* archer *m*

archery ['ɑ:tʃərɪ] N tir *m* à l'arc

archetypal [ɑ:kɪ'taɪp(ə)l] ADJ **the a. English village** l'archétype *m* du village anglais

archetype ['ɑ:kɪtaɪp] N archétype *m*

archiepiscopal [ɑ:kɪɪ'pɪskəp(ə)l] ADJ archiépiscopal, -aux

Archimedes [ɑ:kɪ'mi:di:z] N Archimède
▸▸*Phys* **A.' principle** principe *m* d'Archimède; **A.' screw** vis *f* d'Archimède

archipelago, *pl* **archipelagos, archipelagoes** [ɑ:kɪ'peləgəʊ, -əʊz] N *Geog* archipel *m*

architect ['ɑ:kɪtekt] N *also Fig* architecte *mf*; **naval a.** ingénieur *m* des constructions navales *ou* du génie maritime; **to be the a. of one's own downfall** être l'artisan de sa propre ruine

architectural [ɑ:kɪ'tektʃər(ə)l] ADJ architectural, -aux

architecturally [ɑ:kɪ'tektʃərəlɪ] ADV du point de vue de l'architecture

architecture ['ɑ:kɪtektʃər] N *Constr, Comput* architecture *f*

architrave ['ɑ:kɪtreɪv] N *Archit* architrave *f*

archive ['ɑ:kaɪv] N *(usu pl)* **archives** archives *fpl*; **we'll be showing film from the archives** nous présenterons des extraits d'archives
VT mettre aux archives; *Comput* archiver
▸▸*Comput* **a. copy** copie *f* archivée; *TV* **a. footage** extraits *mpl* d'archives; **a. librarian** archiviste *mf*; **a. material** matériel *m* d'archives; *Comput* **a. site** site *m* FTP

archiving ['ɑ:kaɪvɪŋ] N archivage *m*
▸▸*Comput* **a. facility** fonction *f* d'archivage

archivist ['ɑ:kɪvɪst] N archiviste *mf*

archly ['ɑ:tʃlɪ] ADV d'un air espiègle *ou* malicieux; *(to say)* d'un ton espiègle *ou* malicieux

archness ['ɑ:tʃnɪs] N espièglerie *f*, malice *f*

archway ['ɑ:tʃweɪ] N *(entry)* porte *f* cintrée, voûte *f* d'entrée

arctic ['ɑ:ktɪk] ADJ *(territory, circle, expedition etc)* arctique
N **the A.** l'Arctique *m*; **an expedition to the A.** une expédition dans l'Arctique
▸▸**a. fox** isatis *m*

arc-weld VT *Tech* souder à l'arc (électrique)

arc-welding N *Tech* soudure *f* à l'arc

ardent ['ɑ:d(ə)nt] ADJ *(desire, love)* passionné, ardent; *(admirer, believer)* fervent

ardently ['ɑ:d(ə)ntlɪ] ADV ardemment

ardour, *Am* **ardor** ['ɑ:dər] N *(of passion, desire)* ardeur *f*, *(religious)* ferveur *f*

arduous ['ɑ:djʊəs] ADJ *(path, task)* ardu, pénible

arduously ['ɑ:djʊəslɪ] ADV péniblement

arduousness ['ɑ:djʊəsnɪs] N difficulté *f*

are [ɑ:r] *see* **be**

area ['eərɪə] N **1** *(of circle, field, room etc)* superficie *f*, aire *f*, *(of floor)* surface *f*; **the room**

has an a. of 24 square metres *or* is 24 square metres in a. la pièce a une superficie de 24 mètres carrés, la superficie de la pièce est de 24 mètres carrés; **surface a.** surface

2 *(region)* territoire *m*, région *f*; *(of town)* zone *f*, quartier *m*; *(of lung, brain, disk, surface)* zone; *(part of office, hall, playground etc)* espace *m*; *(of influence etc)* périmètre *m*; *Fig (of knowledge, research)* domaine *m*; **a. of competence** domaine de compétence; **a. of coverage** *(of satellite)* zone de couverture; **a. of expertise** domaine de compétence; **a. of operations** branche *f* d'activité; **residential a.** *(in town)* quartier résidentiel; **industrial/suburban a.** zone industrielle/suburbaine; **houses were searched over a wide a.** on a fouillé les maisons sur un large périmètre; **cotton (growing)/mining a.** région du coton/minière; **customs a.** territoire douanier; **currency a.** zone monétaire; **the Manchester a.** la région de Manchester; **the Greater London a.** l'agglomération *f* londonienne, le grand Londres; **a. of agreement** terrain *m* d'entente; *Fig* **problem a.** domaine problématique; **growth a.** secteur *m* de croissance; *Mil etc* **forward a.** zone de l'avant, zone avancée; **prohibited** *or* **restricted a.** zone prohibée; *Comput* **storage a.** zone de mémoire; *Aut* **parking a.** parking *m*; **service a.** *(on motorway)* relais *m* d'autoroute; **play a.** *(in park)* aire *f* de jeu; **dining a.** *(in living room)* coin *m* salle à manger; *(in kitchen)* coin-repas *m, pl* coins-repas

▸▸*Mil* **a. bombing** bombardement *m* sur zone; *Com* **a. manager** directeur, -trice régional(e); **A. of Outstanding Natural Beauty** = zone naturelle protégée; *Am* **a. rug** tapis *m, Can* carpette *f*; *Mktg* **a. sample** échantillon *m* par zone; *Mktg* **a. sampling** échantillonnage *m* par zone

areaway ['eəɪəweɪ] *n Am (courtyard)* cour *f* d'entrée en sous-sol

▸▸ **a. steps** escalier *m* de service *(du sous-sol)*

areca ['ærɪkə] N

▸▸ **a. nut** noix *f* d'arec; **a. palm (tree)** aréquier *m*

arena [ə'riːnə, -əz] N *(bullring etc)* arène *f*; *Fig (economic, international etc)* scène *f*; *Fig* **the political a.** l'arène politique; *Fig* **to enter the a.** entrer dans l'arène

aren't [ɑːnt] CONTR **1** = are not, *see* **be 2 a. I?** = am I not?, *see* **be**

Argentina [ɑːdʒən'tiːnə] N Argentine *f*

Argentine ['ɑːdʒəntaɪn] ADJ argentin

N **1** *Old-fashioned* **the A.** l'Argentine *f* **2** *(person)* Argentin, -ine

Argentinian [ɑːdʒən'tɪnɪən] ADJ argentin

N Argentin, -ine

argon ['ɑːgɒn] N *Chem* argon *m*

Argonaut ['ɑːgənɔːt] N **1** *Myth* Argonaute **2 a.** *(mollusc)* voilier *m*, argonaute *m*

argot ['ɑːgəʊ] N argot *m*

arguable ['ɑːgjʊəb(ə)l] ADJ **1** *(open to discussion)* discutable, contestable; **that's a.** c'est discutable; **it is a. whether it would have made any difference** on peut se demander si cela aurait changé quelque chose **2** *(capable of being maintained) (theory)* défendable; **it is a. that they didn't need our help** on pourrait soutenir qu'en fait ils n'avaient pas besoin de notre aide

arguably ['ɑːgjʊəblɪ] ADV **it's a. the city's best restaurant** on peut dire que c'est le meilleur restaurant de la ville

argue ['ɑːgjuː] VT **1** *(debate)* discuter; *(question)* débattre; **she argued the case well** elle a bien débattu la question; **he argued the case for lower taxes** il a plaidé en faveur d'une baisse des impôts

2 *(put a case)* **to a. that …** soutenir *ou* maintenir que … + *ind*

3 *Fig (of fact etc) (existence of ancient civilization etc)* témoigner de, révéler

VI **1** *(debate)* discuter (**with sb about sth** avec qn de qch); *(quarrel)* se disputer (**with sb about sth** avec qn à propos de qch); **I'm not going to a. about it** *(I refuse to discuss it)* je ne veux pas en discuter; **to a. about politics** discuter (de) politique; **those two are always arguing** ces deux-là sont toujours à se disputer; **he's always arguing** c'est un argumentateur; **don't a.!** pas de discussion!; **they're always arguing about whose turn it is to do the washing-up** ils sont toujours à se disputer pour savoir qui va faire la vaisselle

2 *(put a case)* plaider; **all this argues in his favour** tout ceci plaide *ou* témoigne en sa faveur

▸ **argue against** VT INSEP plaider contre

▸ **argue away** VT SEP *(make disappear)* nier l'importance de

VI **they've been arguing away for hours** *(quarrelling)* ils se disputent depuis des heures; *(discussing)* ils discutent depuis des heures

▸ **argue for** VT INSEP plaider pour *ou* en faveur de

▸ **argue out** VT SEP *(settle by argument)* résoudre par le débat; **I'll leave you to a. it out between you** je vous laisse résoudre la question *ou* le problème entre vous

arguing ['ɑːgjuːɪŋ] N argumentation *f*; **that's enough a.** assez discuté; *Fam* **and no a.!** pas de discussion!

argument ['ɑːgjʊmənt] N **1** *(debate)* discussion *f*, débat *m*; *(quarrel)* dispute *f*; **to have an a. about sth** *(debate)* discuter de *ou* sur qch; *(quarrel)* se disputer à propos de qch; **I don't want to have an a. about it** je ne veux pas qu'on se dispute pour ça; **to get into an a.** se disputer (**with sb** avec qn; **about sb/sth** à propos de qn/qch); **to get the best of an a.** l'emporter dans une discussion; **to obey without a.** obéir sans discuter

2 *(reasoning, case)* argument *m* (**for** en faveur de; **against** contre); **that is another a. for dismissing him** c'est une raison de plus pour le congédier; **to follow sb's (line of) a.** suivre le raisonnement de qn; **suppose for a.'s sake that …** supposons à titre d'exemple que … + *sub*

3 *Lit (of work)* argument *m*

argumentative [ɑːgjuː'mentətɪv] ADJ *(person)* raisonneur, disposé à argumenter *ou* à disputailler; *(tone)* polémique, agressif; **don't be so a.** arrête de faire le raisonneur

Argy ['ɑːdʒɪ] N *Br Offensive Sl* Argentin, -ine

argy-bargy ['ɑːdʒɪ'bɑːdʒɪ] N *Br Fam* chamailleries *fpl*

aria ['ɑːrɪə] N *Mus* aria *f*

arid ['ærɪd] ADJ *(land, subject)* aride

aridity [ə'rɪdɪtɪ], **aridness** ['ærɪdnɪs] N aridité *f*

Aries ['eəriːz] N *Astrol* le Bélier; **to be (an) A.** être (du) Bélier

aright [ə'raɪt] ADV *Arch, Lit* bien, juste; **to put** *or* **set things a.** redresser la situation

arise [ə'raɪz] VI (**arose** [ə'rəʊz]; **arisen** [ə'rɪz(ə)n]) **1** *(come about) (of situation, deficit)* se produire; *(of problem)* surgir, survenir, se présenter; *(of storm)* se lever; **if complications a.** s'il survient des complications; **if the need arises** si besoin est; **the question has not yet arisen** la question ne s'est pas encore posée; **should the occasion a.** le cas échéant

2 *(result)* émaner, provenir, résulter (**from** de); **obligations that a. from a clause** obligations qui émanent d'une clause

3 *Lit (of person)* s'élever; **a prophet arose** un prophète surgit *ou* se révéla; **a., Sir John!** *(in knighthood ceremony)* relevez-vous, Sir

John!; *Bible* **to a. from the dead** ressusciter (des morts)

aristocracy [ærɪs'tɒkrəsɪ] N *(nobility)* aristocratie *f*; *Fig* **the a. of the fashion world** le gratin de la mode

aristocrat ['ærɪstəkræt, ə'rɪs-] N aristocrate *mf*

aristocratic [ærɪstə'krætɪk] ADJ aristocratique

aristocratically [ærɪstə'krætɪklɪ] ADV aristocratiquement

Aristotelian [ærɪstɒ'tiːlɪən] ADJ *Phil* aristotélicien

Aristotle ['ærɪstɒt(ə)l] N Aristote

arithmetic [ə'rɪθmətɪk] N *(calculations)* calcul *m*; *(subject)* arithmétique *f*; **my a. is absolutely appalling** je suis nul en calcul; **your a. is spot on** tes calculs tombent pile; **it's a simple question of a.** les chiffres parlent d'eux-mêmes; **the a. is against a Labour victory** mathématiquement, les Travaillistes ont peu de chances de gagner; *Sch* **a. book** livre *m* d'arithmétique VOIR GRAMMAIRE A77; B59

arithmetic(al) [ærɪθ'metɪk, -ɪk(ə)l] ADJ arithmétique; **a. mistakes** *or* **errors** des erreurs *fpl* de calcul

arithmetically [ærɪθ'metɪklɪ] ADV arithmétiquement

Ariz *abbr* Arizona

Ark *abbr* Arkansas

ark [ɑːk] N **1** arche *f, Fam* **it looked like it had come out of the a.** il avait l'air vieux comme Hérode **2** *Rel* **the A. of the Covenant** l'Arche *f* d'alliance

arm [ɑːm] N **1** *(of person)* bras *m*; **upper a.** haut *m* du bras; **to carry a child in one's arms** porter un enfant dans ses bras; **to hold sb in one's arms** tenir qn dans ses bras; **to carry sth under one's a.** porter qch sous le bras; **to carry a basket over** *or* **on one's a.** porter un panier au bras; **with a girl on his a.** une fille à son bras; **to walk a. in a.** marcher bras dessus bras dessous; **give me your a.** donne-moi le *ou* ton bras; **to hold out one's arms** *(in front)* tendre les bras; *(to sides)* lever les bras; **to receive sb with open arms** recevoir qn à bras ouverts; **to keep sb at a.'s length** tenir qn à distance

2 *(of dress etc)* manche *f*; *(of chair)* accoudoir *m*, bras *m*; *(of sea, river, lever)* bras; **(pick-up) a.** *(on record player)* bras de lecture; *Fig* **the secular a.** le bras séculier; *Fig* **the long a. of the law** l'autorité *f* de la loi, *Fam* le représentant de la loi **3** *Mil (branch)* arme *f*

arm [ɑːm] VT **1** *(person, regiment, fortified place)* armer; **to a. oneself with an umbrella** se munir d'un parapluie; *Lit* **to a. oneself with patience** s'armer de patience **2** *(bomb, rocket, torpedo, mine)* armer

VI s'armer, prendre les armes; **the country was arming for war** le pays s'armait pour la guerre

armada [ɑː'mɑːdə] N **1** *Hist* **the (Spanish) A.** l'Invincible Armada *f* **2** *(any fleet of warships)* armada *f*

armadillo [ɑːmə'dɪləʊ] N *(animal)* tatou *m*

Armageddon [ɑːmə'ged(ə)n] N *Bible, Fig* Armageddon

armament ['ɑːməmənt] N *(weapons) (of ship, tank, plane)* artillerie *f*; **armaments** *(weapons)* armement *m*, armes *fpl*

armature ['ɑːmətʃər] N **1** *Zool* armure *f* **2** *Elec* armature *f* **3** *Constr, Art* armature *f*

armband ['ɑːmbænd] N brassard *m*; *(for swimmers)* manchon *m*; **black a.** brassard de deuil

armchair ['ɑːmtʃeər] N fauteuil *m*; **a. strategist/traveller** stratège *m*/voyageur *m* en chambre

armed [ɑːmd] ADJ *(person, conflict, torpedo, fuse)* armé; **a. to the teeth/with a gun** armé jusqu'aux dents/d'un fusil; **to offer a. resistance** résister par les armes, se défendre les armes à la main
▸▸ *Mil* **a. forces** forces *fpl* armées; *Law* **a. robbery** vol *m ou* attaque *f* à main armée; **a. truce** suspension *f* d'armes; **a. warfare** conflit *m* armé

Armenia [ɑːˈmiːnɪə] N Arménie *f*

Armenian [ɑːˈmiːnɪən] ADJ arménien
N **1** Arménien, -ienne **2** *Ling* arménien *m*

armful [ˈɑːmfʊl] N brassée *f*; **to bring armfuls of flowers** *or* **flowers by the a.** apporter des fleurs à pleins bras, apporter des brassées de fleurs

armhole [ˈɑːmhəʊl] N *Sewing* emmanchure *f*

armistice [ˈɑːmɪstɪs] N armistice *m*
▸▸ **A. Day** l'Armistice *m*

armless [ˈɑːmlɪs] ADJ sans bras

armlet [ˈɑːmlɪt] N **1** *(bracelet)* bracelet *m (porté au-dessus du coude)* **2** *(armband)* brassard *m*

armor *etc Am* = **armour** *etc*

armorial [ɑːˈmɔːrɪəl] ADJ armorial, -aux
▸▸ **a. bearings** armoiries *fpl*

armour, *Am* **armor** [ˈɑːmər] N *(no pl)* **1** *Naut (of ship)* cuirasse *f*, cuirassement *m*; *Mil (of vehicle, tank etc)* blindage *m*; *Mil (units, vehicles)* blindés *mpl* **3** *Hist (of knight etc)* armure *f*; **suit of a.** armure complète; **in full a.** armé de pied en cap
VT *Naut (ship)* cuirasser; *Mil (train etc)* blinder

armoured, *Am* **armored** [ˈɑːməd] ADJ *Naut (ship)* cuirassé; *Mil (vehicle, train)* blindé
▸▸ **a. car** voiture *f* blindée; *Mil* engin *m* blindé de reconnaissance; *(for cash, gold etc)* fourgon *m* bancaire; *Am Mil* **a. corps** blindés *mpl*; *Mil* **a. personnel carrier** véhicule *m* blindé de transport de troupes; *Mil* **a. troops** blindés

armourer, *Am* **armorer** [ˈɑːmərər] N *Ind, Mil, Naut* armurier *m*

armour-piercing, *Am* **armor-piercing** ADJ *(shell)* perforant, de rupture

armour-plated, *Am* **armor-plated** ADJ *Naut* cuirassé, blindé; *Mil* blindé

armour-plating, *Am* **armor-plating** N blindage *m*

armoury, *Am* **armory** [ˈɑːmərɪ] N **1** *(store room)* magasin *m* d'armes; *(in barracks)* armurerie *f*, *(in museum etc)* salle *f* d'armes **2** *Am (factory)* fabrique *f* d'armes; *(workshop)* armurerie *f*

armpit [ˈɑːmpɪt] N aisselle *f*, *Fam Pej* **the a. of the universe** *(place)* un coin paumé, un trou

armrest [ˈɑːmrest] N accoudoir *m*, appuie-bras *m inv*

arms [ɑːmz] NPL **1** *(weapons)* armes *fpl*; **side a.** armes blanches; **small a.** armes portatives; **call to a.** appel *m* aux armes; **nation in a.** nation *f* en armes; **100,000 men under a.** 100 000 hommes sous les drapeaux; **to take up a.** prendre les armes, s'armer (**against** contre); **to rise up in a.** se dresser en armes (**against sb/sth** contre qn/qch); *Fig* **to be up in a. about sth** s'insurger contre qch **2** *Her* armoiries *fpl*, armes *fpl*
▸▸ *Mil* **a. dealer** armurier *m*; **a. embargo** embargo *m* sur les armes; *Pol* **a. limitation talks** négociations *fpl* pour la limitation des armements; **a. manufacturer** fabricant *m* d'armes, armurier; *Mil* **a. race** course *f* aux armements; **the a. trade** le commerce des armes; **a. trader** trafiquant *m* d'armes

arm's-length ADJ *Com (relationship)* impartial, -aux; *(price)* réaliste

army [ˈɑːmɪ] N VOIR GRAMMAIRE A11 *Mil, Fig (of ants, civil servants etc)* armée *f*, *(of people)* foule *f*, multitude *f*; **he joined the A. not the Air Force** il est entré dans l'armée de terre et non pas dans l'armée de l'air; **to be in the a.** être dans l'armée, être militaire; **to go into** *or* **join the a.** *(volunteer)* s'engager, s'enrôler; *(be conscripted)* partir au régiment *ou* à l'armée; **there was enough food for an a.** il y avait assez de nourriture pour un régiment; **standing** *or* **regular a.** armée permanente *ou* active; **professional a.** armée de métier
▸▸ *Entom* **a. ant** fourmi *f* légionnaire; **a. barracks** caserne *f*, baraquement *m* militaire; **a. corps** corps *m* d'armée; *Br Mil* **A. List** annuaire *m* militaire *ou* des officiers de carrière *(de l'armée de terre)*; **a. lorry** camion *m* militaire; **a. officer** officier *m* de l'armée de terre

arnica [ˈɑːnɪkə] N *Bot, Pharm* arnica *f*

A-road N *Br Aut* ≃ route *f* nationale

aroma [əˈrəʊmə] N arôme *m*

aromatherapy [ərəʊməˈθerəpɪ] N aromathérapie *f*

aromatic [ærəʊˈmætɪk] ADJ *(herb, tea, smell)* aromatique
N **1** aromate *m* **2** *Chem* **aromatics** carbures *mpl* aromatiques *ou* à noyau

AROUND [əˈraʊnd]

| ADV | autour **1** |
| PREP | autour de **1** ▪ environ **3** |

ADV **1** autour; **all a.** tout autour, de tous côtés; **the woods (all) a.** les bois d'alentour; **for miles a.** à des kilomètres à la ronde; **people came from miles a.** les gens sont venus de partout *ou* de très loin; **the trunk was over two metres a.** le tronc faisait plus de deux mètres de circonférence
2 *(in different directions, places)* **to walk a.** marcher par-ci par-là; **I try to get a. as much as I can** j'essaie de me déplacer le plus possible; **to run a.** courir dans tous les sens; **to throw things a.** jeter des choses dans tous les sens; **swivel it a. a little** fais-le pivoter un peu; **he's now able to get a. again** il est de nouveau sur pied; *Fam* **she's been a.** *(is mature)* elle n'est pas née d'hier; *(sexually)* elle a des kilomètres au compteur, elle a des heures de vol
3 *(in existence, in the area etc)* **this product has been a. for a long time** ce produit existe *ou* est en circulation depuis longtemps; **I still see her a.** il m'arrive encore de la voir; **I haven't seen him a. for ages** ça fait longtemps que je ne l'ai vu dans les parages; **are you a. this weekend?** tu es là ce weekend?; **there aren't many good translators a.** les bons traducteurs ne courent pas les rues; **is he still a.?** *(in the area)* est-ce qu'il est encore dans les parages *ou* là?; *(alive)* est-ce qu'il est encore de ce monde?; **it's the best value a.** c'est ce qu'il y a de meilleur marché
4 *(in circular motion)* **to turn a.** se retourner; **to spin** *or* **whirl** *or* **wheel a.** faire volteface; **he was waving his arms a.** il gesticulait dans tous les sens
PREP **1** autour de; **his arms were a. her neck** il avait les bras autour de son cou; **she had her family a. her** elle a été entourée de sa famille; **the people a. him** les gens qui l'entourent; **we walked a. the lake** nous avons fait le tour du lac en marchant
2 *(in different parts)* **to travel a. the country** parcourir le pays; **there were books all a. the room** il y avait des livres dans toute la pièce; **a. town** en ville
3 *(in the region of)* environ; **at a. four o'clock** vers quatre heures, sur les quatre heures; **it cost a. £200** ça a coûté dans les 200 livres *ou* environ 200 livres

4 *(near)* **somewhere a. here** quelque part par ici; **is there anywhere a. here I can sleep?** est-ce que je peux trouver où dormir par ici?

arousal [əˈraʊz(ə)l] N *(from sleep)* éveil *m*, réveil *m*; *(of interest, suspicion)* éveil; *(of anger)* soulèvement *m*; *(sexual)* excitation *f*

arouse [əˈraʊz] VT *(person) (wake)* réveiller, éveiller; *(stir up) (from laziness, torpor)* secouer; *(sexually)* exciter; *(feeling)* exciter, éveiller; *(passions)* soulever; *(jealousy)* piquer, éveiller, provoquer; *(curiosity)* éveiller, chatouiller; *(sb's suspicion, interest)* éveiller; *(pity, enthusiasm)* inspirer; **they aroused her from her sleep** ils l'ont réveillée; **the crowd was aroused** la foule était agitée; **once (their anger was) aroused, …** une fois leur colère éveillée, …

arpeggio [ɑːˈpedʒɪəʊ] N *Mus* arpège *m*

arr *(abbr* **arrives)** *(on timetables etc)* arrive

arrack [ˈærək] N *(drink)* arac(k) *m*

arraign [əˈreɪn] VT **1** *Law* poursuivre en justice; **to a. sb before a court** traduire qn en justice *ou* devant un tribunal **2** *Lit (criticize) (declaration, action etc)* attaquer, critiquer violemment

arraignment [əˈreɪnmənt] N *Law* **1** *(of person)* mise *f* en accusation *ou* en jugement **2** *(charges)* acte *m* d'accusation

arrange [əˈreɪndʒ] VT **1** *(put in an order) (furniture etc)* disposer, arranger; *(flowers)* disposer; **the chairs were arranged in a circle** les chaises étaient disposées en cercle; **they arranged themselves around the room** ils se sont répartis dans la pièce
2 *(organize) (wedding)* arranger; *(concert, meeting etc)* organiser; *(date, time)* fixer; **an arranged marriage** un mariage de convenance; **everything is arranged** tout est en ordre; **it was arranged that …** il fut convenu que …; **try to a. it** tâchez d'arranger la chose; **that can be arranged** cela peut s'arranger; **a. it among yourselves** arrangez cela entre vous, entendez-vous là-dessus; **the meeting arranged for tomorrow** la réunion prévue pour demain; **at the time arranged** à l'heure prévue; **I've got nothing arranged** je n'ai rien de prévu; **have you arranged what to do if …?** as-tu pris tes dispositions pour le cas où …?; **what have you arranged? (with him)** qu'est-ce que vous avez prévu?; **to a. one's affairs** mettre ses affaires en ordre; *Mktg* **arranged interview** entretien *m* organisé
3 *Mus (piece)* adapter, arranger (**for (the) piano** pour piano)
VI *(organize)* **to a. to do sth** *(make preparations)* s'arranger *ou* prendre ses dispositions pour faire qch; *(with sb else)* convenir de faire qch; **to a. for sth to be done** s'arranger *ou* prendre des dispositions *ou* prendre des mesures pour que qch se fasse; **I had arranged to …** j'avais prévu de …; **we arranged to meet** nous avons prévu de nous rencontrer; **I think I'll a. to be out when he comes** je crois que je m'arrangerai pour être sorti quand il viendra; **can you a. to have it finished by Friday?** est-ce que vous pouvez vous arranger pour qu'il soit terminé vendredi?; **to a. to have sth delivered** faire le nécessaire pour que qch soit livré; **they arranged for a taxi to meet me** ils se sont arrangés pour qu'un taxi vienne me chercher

arrangement [əˈreɪndʒmənt] N **1** *(preparation)* disposition *f*, aménagement *m* (**of** de); **to make arrangements** prendre des dispositions *ou* des mesures, faire des préparatifs (**for sth/to do sth/for sth to be done** pour qch/pour faire qch/pour que qch se fasse); **to make arrangements for a journey** faire ses préparatifs pour un voyage; **I've made all the arrangements** j'ai tout arrangé

2 *(agreement)* arrangement *m*, accord *m*; *Fin (with creditors)* accommodement *m*; *Law* transaction *f*; *Com etc* **to make an a.** *or* **to come to an a. with sb** prendre un arrangement avec qn; **to come to an a. with one's creditors** parvenir à un accord avec ses créanciers; **the a. was that ...** *(I or you etc would do)* on avait prévu que ...; **price by a.** prix à débattre; **by prior a.** sur accord préalable

3 *Mus* arrangement *m*, adaptation *f* (**for (the) piano** pour piano)

arranger [ə'reɪndʒər] **N** *Mus* arrangeur, -euse

arrant ['ærənt] **ADJ ATTRIB** *(rogue, fool)* fini; *(liar)* fieffé; **don't talk such a. rubbish** comment est-ce que tu peux dire des bêtises pareilles?; **this is a. folly** c'est de la folie pure

array [ə'reɪ] **N 1** *(display)* étalage *m*, collection *f*; **a bewildering a. of salads** un étalage de salades stupéfiant; **an imposing a. of tools** une imposante collection d'outils

2 *Mil* rangs *mpl*; **in close a.** en rangs serrés; **in battle a.** en ordre de bataille

3 *Math (of figures)* tableau *m*; *Comput* matrice *f*, tableau

4 *Lit (fine clothing)* parure *f*, appareil *m*; **in rich a.** paré de ses plus beaux atours

VT 1 *(troops etc) (in battle formation)* disposer, déployer; **his medals were arrayed across his chest** ses médailles étaient étalées sur sa poitrine

2 *Lit (clothe)* revêtir, parer (**sb in sth** qn de qch)

arrears [ə'rɪəz] **NPL** arriéré *m*, arrérages *mpl*; **I'm £100 in a.** j'ai 100 livres d'arriérés; **rent a.** arriéré de loyer; **to be in a. with the rent, to let one's rent fall into a.** être en retard pour payer son loyer; **I'm a month in a.** j'ai (pris) un retard d'un mois, je suis en retard d'un mois; **to get into a.** s'arriérer; **to be getting into a. with the repayments** prendre du retard pour payer *ou* avec les versements; **work in a.** travail *m* en retard; **to be paid monthly in a.** être payé à la fin du mois; **to be in a. with one's correspondence** avoir du retard dans sa correspondance

arrest [ə'rest] **N 1** *(of wrongdoer)* arrestation *f*; *Mil, Naut* arrêts *mpl*; **to put sb/to be under a.** mettre qn/être en état d'arrestation; *Mil, Naut* mettre qn/être aux arrêts; **you're under a.!** vous êtes en état d'arrestation!; **several arrests were made** plusieurs personnes ont été arrêtées; **to make an a.** *(of police officer)* procéder à une arrestation; *Mil, Naut* **open a.** arrêts simples; *Mil, Naut* **close a.** arrêts forcés *ou* de rigueur

2 *(of movement, progress etc)* arrêt *m*, suspension *f*

3 *Law* **a. of judgment** sursis *m* à l'exécution d'un jugement

VT 1 *(capture) (person)* arrêter; *Scot, Naut (property, ship)* saisir

2 *(stop) (movement, sb's progress, thing)* arrêter; **arrested growth** *(of person)* arrêt *m* dans la croissance; *(of thing)* arrêt dans le développement

3 *Law* **to a. judgment** suspendre l'exécution d'un jugement

4 *(attention)* retenir, arrêter, fixer

► ► *Law* **a. warrant** mandat *m* d'arrêt

arrester [ə'restər] **N** *Tech* intercepteur *m*, séparateur *m*; **spark a.** pare-étincelles *m inv*

► ► **a. gear** *Aviat (on runway)* dispositif *m* d'arrêt; *Aviat, Naut (on carrier deck)* dispositif d'appontage

arresting [ə'restɪŋ] **ADJ 1** *(spectacle etc)* frappant, qui retient l'attention **2** *Law* **the arresting officer** le policier qui a effectué/qui effectue l'arrestation

N 1 *Law* arrestation *f* **2** *Tech etc* arrêt *m*

► ► *Tech* **a. device** dispositif *m* d'arrêt

arrhythmia [ə'rɪðmɪə] **N** *Med* arythmie *f*

arrival [ə'raɪv(ə)l] **N 1** arrivée *f*; *Com (of goods)* arrivage *m*; *Naut (of ship)* entrée *f*; *(of passengers)* débarquement *m*; **port of a.** port *m* d'arrivée; **on a.** à l'arrivée; *(of passengers)* au débarquement; **arrivals and departures** arrivées et départs; **to await a.** *(on letter)* ne pas faire suivre

2 *(person)* arrivant, -ante; **a new a.** un nouveau venu, une nouvelle venue; *(baby)* un nouveau-né, une nouveau-née, *pl* nouveau-nés, -ées; *(book)* une dernière parution; **late arrivals** retardataires *mpl*

► ► **a. form** fichette *f* d'arrivée; **arrivals list** liste *f* des arrivées; **arrivals lounge** salle *f* d'arrivée; **a. quay** quai *m* d'arrivée; **a. time** heure *f* d'arrivée

arrive [ə'raɪv] **VI 1** arriver (**at** à; **in** dans); **she has just arrived** elle arrive à l'instant, elle vient d'arriver; **the baby arrived at 4.37 a.m.** le bébé est né à 4 h 37 du matin; **he is expected to a. next week** on attend son arrivée pour la semaine prochaine; **as soon as he arrived** dès son arrivée; **to a. unexpectedly** survenir, arriver à l'improviste; **to a. at the age of sixty** atteindre *ou* parvenir à *ou* arriver à l'âge de soixante ans; **to a. at a decision** arriver à *ou* en venir à *ou* aboutir à une décision; **we arrived at a situation where** *or* **in which ...** nous en sommes arrivés à *ou* nous avons abouti à une situation dans laquelle ...; **to a. at a price** *(of seller)* calculer *ou* fixer un prix; *(of seller and buyer)* convenir d'un prix

2 *Fam (achieve recognition) (of person)* réussir, arriver, faire son trou; **you know you've really arrived when ...** on sait qu'on a vraiment réussi le jour où ...; **that was before the telephone had really arrived** c'était avant l'avènement du téléphone; **notebook computers have arrived in a big way** on voit des notebooks partout maintenant

arrogance ['ærəgəns] **N** arrogance *f*

arrogant ['ærəgənt] **ADJ** arrogant

arrogantly ['ærəgəntlɪ] **ADV** avec arrogance; **to a. assume that ...** avoir l'arrogance de présumer que ...

arrogate ['ærəgeɪt] **VT** *Law, Lit* **1** *(appropriate)* **to a. sth to oneself** s'arroger qch **2** *(attribute wrongly)* attribuer injustement (**to sb** à qn)

arrow ['ærəʊ] **N 1** *(missile)* flèche *f*; **to shoot** *or* **let fly an a.** lancer *ou* décocher une flèche; **to fly straight as an a.** voler droit comme une flèche **2** *(indicating direction) (on sign etc)* flèche *f*; *(of surveyor)* fiche *f* **3** *Br Fam* **arrows** *(darts)* fléchettes *fpl*

VT marquer d'une flèche, *(route, direction)* flécher

► ► *Comput* **a. key** touche *f* fléchée, touche de direction; **a. slit** *(in building)* arbalétrière *f*

► **arrow in VT SEP** *(insertion)* marquer d'une flèche

arrowhead ['ærəʊhed] **N 1** *(on missile)* tête *f* ou fer *m* ou pointe *f* de flèche **2** *(plant)* sagittaire *f*, flèche *f* d'eau

arrowroot ['ærəʊruːt] **N 1** *(plant)* marante *f* **2** *Culin* arrow-root *m*

arse [ɑːs] *Br Vulg* **N 1** cul *m*; **a kick up the a.** un coup de pied dans le cul; **to talk out of one's a.** raconter des conneries; **he fell** *or* **went a. over tit** *or* **tip** *or* **apex** il est tombé cul par-dessus tête; **get your a. in gear!** remuez-vous le cul!; **get your a. in here right now!** rapplique tout de suite!, ramène ta fraise!; **it's my a. that's on the line** ça risque de me retomber sur la gueule; **he's**

been sitting on his a. all day il n'a rien foutu de la journée; **to make an a. of sth** saloper qch; **he doesn't know his a. from his elbow** il est complètement nul; **to make an a. of oneself** se ridiculiser; **to do sth a.-backwards** faire qch à l'envers *ou* n'importe comment; **my a.!** *(I don't believe you)* mon cul!

2 *(idiot)* connard *m*, connasse *f*

VT I couldn't be arsed doing it myself ça m'a fait chier de le faire moi-même; **why don't you come with us? – I can't be arsed** tu viens avec nous? – non, j'ai trop la flemme

► **arse about, arse around VI** *Br Vulg* déconner

► **arse up VT SEP** *Br Vulg* foirer

arsehole ['ɑːshəʊl] **N** *Br Vulg* **1** *(anus)* trou *m* du cul; *Fig* **the a. of the universe** *(ugly town etc)* le trou du cul du monde **2** *Fig (stupid person)* connard *m*, connasse *f* **3** *(nasty person)* salaud *m*, salope *f*; **don't be such an a.!** arrête de faire/dire des conneries!; *(nasty person)* ne fais pas le salaud!

arseholed ['ɑːshəʊld] **ADJ** *Br Vulg (drunk)* bourré comme un coing, complètement pété

arse-licker [-lɪkər] **N** *Br Vulg* lèche-cul *mf inv*

arse-licking N *Br Vulg* **they're sick of his a.** ils en ont marre de ce lèche-cul

arsenal ['ɑːsən(ə)l] **N** arsenal *m*, -aux

arsenic ['ɑːs(ə)nɪk] **N** arsenic *m*

arsewipe ['ɑːswaɪp] **N** *Br Vulg (person)* raclure *f*

arsey ['ɑːsɪ] **ADJ** *Br Vulg (stupid)* débile; *(unfashionable)* ringard; **that was a bit of an a. thing to say** c'est un peu débile de dire un truc pareil

arson ['ɑːs(ə)n] **N** incendie *m* criminel *ou* volontaire; **to commit a.** provoquer (volontairement) un incendie; **to be charged with a.** être accusé d'avoir provoqué un incendie; **police suspect a.** la police suspecte un incendie criminel

arsonist ['ɑːsənɪst] **N** incendiaire *mf*

art [ɑːt] **N 1** art *m*; **the (fine) arts** les beaux-arts *mpl*; **arts and crafts** artisanat *m*; **a. for a.'s sake** l'art pour l'art

2 *Univ* **arts** lettres *fpl*; **faculty of arts** faculté *f* de lettres (et sciences humaines)

3 *(technique)* art *m*; **the a. of war** l'art militaire, l'art de la guerre; **it's an a. in itself** c'est tout un art; **there's an a. to doing that** c'est tout un art que de faire cela; **to get** *or* **have sth down to a fine a.** maîtriser qch jusque dans les moindres détails; **she's got time-saving down to a fine a.** elle est passée maître dans l'art de gagner du temps; **a dying a.** un art en voie de disparition; **the black arts** la magie noire

4 *Typ (illustrations)* iconographie *f*, illustrations *fpl*

5 *Pej (trick)* stratagème *m*, ruse *f*

► ► **a. cinema** cinéma *m* d'art et d'essai; **a. class** cours *m* de dessin; **a. critic** critique *mf* d'art; **a. department** service *m* création; **a. desk** bureau *m* de dessin; **a. direction** direction *f* artistique; **a. director** directeur, -trice artistique; **a. editor** rédacteur, -trice artistique; **a. exhibition** exposition *f* d'art; *Univ* **arts faculty** faculté *f* de lettres (et sciences humaines); **arts festival** festival *m* culturel; **a. form** moyen *m* d'expression artistique; **a. gallery** *(museum)* musée *m* d'art; *(shop)* galerie *f* d'art; **a. nouveau** art *m* nouveau, modern style *m*; **a. nouveau furniture** meubles *mpl* de style art nouveau; **a. object** objet *m* d'art; *Comput* **a. package** logiciel *m* de dessin; **a. paper** papier *m* couché classique; **arts programme** programme *m* culturel; **a. reviewer** critique d'art; **a. school** ≃ école *f* des Beaux-Arts; **a. student** étudiant, -ante en art; **arts student** étudiant, -ante en lettres *(et sciences humaines)*; **a. teacher** professeur *m* de dessin

art[2] *Bible, Arch (2nd pers sing pr of* be) thou **a. good** tu es bon

artefact ['ɑːtɪfækt] N **1** *Archeol* objet *m* (fabriqué *ou* façonné) **2** *(side-effect)* conséquence *f*, **to be a mere a. of sth** être simplement la conséquence de qch, découler simplement de qch

arterial [ɑːˈtɪərɪəl] ADJ *Anat, Med etc (blood etc)* artériel
▶▶ *Br Transp* **a. road** route *f ou* voie *f* à grande circulation

arteriole [ɑːˈtɪərɪəʊl] N *Anat* artériole *f*

arteriosclerosis [ɑːˌtɪərɪəʊsklə'rəʊsɪs] N *Med* artériosclérose *f*

artery ['ɑːtərɪ] N **1** *Anat* artère *f* **2** *(road, river etc)* artère *f*, **main arteries** grandes voies *fpl* de communication, grandes artères

artesian [ɑːˈtiːzɪən, -ˈtiːʒən] ADJ
▶▶ **a. well** puits *m* artésien

artful ['ɑːtfʊl] ADJ **1** *(person)* rusé, astucieux, malin, *f* -igne; **as a monkey** malin comme un singe **2** *(solution, device)* ingénieux; **an a. dodge** un truc ingénieux

artfully ['ɑːtfʊlɪ] ADV ingénieusement

artfulness ['ɑːtfʊlnɪs] N **1** *(of person)* habileté *f* (**in doing** à faire) **2** *(of thing, reply)* ingéniosité *f*

arthouse ['ɑːthaʊs] ADJ
▶▶ **a. cinema** cinéma *m* d'art et d'essai; **a. film** film *m* d'art et d'essai

arthritic [ɑːˈθrɪtɪk] ADJ, N *Med* arthritique *mf*

arthritis [ɑːˈθraɪtɪs] N *Med* arthrite *f*

arthropod ['ɑːθrəpɒd] N *Zool* arthropode *m*

arthrosis [ɑːˈθrəʊsɪs] N *Med* arthrose *f*

Arthurian [ɑːˈθjʊərɪən] ADJ *Liter, Myth (cycle etc)* d'Arthur; *(novel)* arthurien

artic [ɑːˈtɪk] N *Br Sl (lorry)* semi-remorque *m, pl* semi-remorques

artichoke ['ɑːtɪtʃəʊk] N **(globe) a.** artichaut *m*
▶▶ **a. hearts** cœurs *mpl* d'artichauts

article ['ɑːtɪk(ə)l] N **1** *(object)* objet *m*; **a. of clothing** vêtement *m*; **toilet articles** produits *mpl* de toilette **2** *Journ etc (in newspaper, magazine)* article *m* **3** *Com, Law (in agreement, treaty)* clause *f*; *Naut* **ship's articles** contrat *m* d'engagement, conditions *fpl* d'embarquement **4** *Gram* **definite/indefinite a.** article *m* défini/indéfini VOIR GRAMMAIRE A5–8; B3–5

VT *Law etc* **to a. sb to an attorney/an architect** placer qn (comme élève) chez un avoué/un architecte; **articled clerk** clerc *m* d'avoué lié par un contrat d'apprentissage
▶▶ *Law* **articles of apprenticeship** contrat d'apprentissage; *Law* **articles of association** statuts *mpl* de société; *Rel* **a. of faith** article *m* de foi; **articles of war** *Mil* code *m* (de justice) militaire; *Naut* code de justice maritime

articulate[1] [ɑːˈtɪkjʊlət] ADJ **1** *(speech)* net, distinct; **to be a.** *(of person)* s'exprimer facilement *ou* avec facilité; **try to be more a.** essaie d'être plus clair; **the child gave a very a. account** l'enfant a fait un compte rendu très clair **2** *Zool* articulé

articulate[2] [ɑːˈtɪkjʊleɪt] VT **1** *(pronounce clearly) (word etc)* articuler; **he doesn't a. his words** il n'articule pas **2** *(express clearly) (one's thoughts, idea)* exprimer clairement
VI **1** *Anat* s'articuler; **a bone that articulates or is articulated with another** un os qui s'articule *ou* est articulé avec un autre **2** *(in speaking)* articuler

articulated [ɑːˈtɪkjʊleɪtɪd] ADJ *Anat, Ling etc* articulé

▶▶ *Aut* **a. lorry** semi-remorque *m, pl* semi-remorques

articulately [ɑːˈtɪkjʊlətlɪ] ADV **1** *(to express oneself, argue)* clairement; **as you so a. put it** comme vous l'avez si bien exprimé **2** *(to speak)* distinctement

articulateness [ɑːˈtɪkjʊlətnɪs] N **1** *(of speaker)* facilité *f* d'expression; *(of writing, speech)* clarté *f* **2** *(clarity of sound)* articulation *f* nette, netteté *f* d'énonciation

articulation [ɑːˌtɪkjʊˈleɪʃən] N **1** *Biol, Ling etc* articulation *f* **2** *(of thought)* expression *f*, **you've heard his a. of the new theory** vous avez entendu sa présentation de la nouvelle théorie

artifact ['ɑːtɪfækt] N = artefact

artifice ['ɑːtɪfɪs] N **1** *(trick)* artifice *m*, ruse *f*, stratagème *m*; **a. of war** ruse *ou* artifice de guerre **2** *(skill)* habileté *f*, adresse *f*

artificial [ɑːtɪˈfɪʃəl] ADJ **1** *(conditions, light, distinction, situation)* artificiel **2** *(behaviour, person)* affecté; *(style)* factice, recherché; **she is very a.** elle manque de naturel
▶▶ **a. fibres** fibres *fpl* synthétiques; *Astron* **a. horizon** horizon *m* artificiel; **a. insemination** insémination *f* artificielle; *Comput* **a. intelligence** intelligence *f* artificielle; **a. limb** prothèse *f*, membre *m* artificiel; **a. manure** engrais *mpl* chimiques; *Med* **a. respiration** respiration *f* artificielle; **to give sb a. respiration** faire la respiration artificielle à qn; *Cin* **a. sunlight** sunlight *m*; **a. sweetener** édulcorant *m* (de synthèse)

artificiality [ɑːtɪfɪʃɪˈælɪtɪ] N **1** *(of product etc)* nature *f* artificielle **2** *(of person, smile)* manque *m* de naturel; *(of behaviour, manner)* affectation *f*

artificially [ɑːtɪˈfɪʃəlɪ] ADV artificiellement; **to behave a.** avoir un comportement affecté, manquer de naturel; **a. coloured** *(on packet etc)* contient un colorant artificiel

artillery [ɑːˈtɪlərɪ] N artillerie *f*, **heavy/light a.** artillerie lourde/légère; **to lay down an a. barrage** déployer un barrage d'artillerie
▶▶ **a. fire** tir *m* d'artillerie; **a. regiment** régiment *m* d'artillerie; **a. shell** obus *m*

artilleryman, *pl* **artillerymen** [ɑːˈtɪlərɪmən, -men] N artilleur *m*

artisan [ɑːtɪˈzæn] N artisan, -e *m*

artist ['ɑːtɪst] N *(painter)* artiste *mf*; **he is an a.** *(painter)* il est artiste, il est peintre; *(footballer etc)* c'est un véritable artiste

> Note that the French word **artiste** is not restricted to the contexts of painting or drawing and is used to describe someone who practises any kind of art.

artiste [ɑːˈtiːst] N *Theat, Cin, TV* artiste *mf*

artistic [ɑːˈtɪstɪk] ADJ *(style, taste, temperament, arrangement)* artistique; **she came from an a. family** elle venait d'une famille d'artistes; **she's the a. one in the family** c'est l'artiste de la famille; **I'm not at all a.** je n'ai aucune inclination artistique, je n'ai pas la fibre artistique
▶▶ **a. adviser** conseiller, -ère artistique; *Cin, Theat* **a. director** directeur, -trice artistique

artistically [ɑːˈtɪstɪklɪ] ADV avec art, artistiquement; **to be a. gifted/inclined** avoir des dons/la fibre artistique(s); **a. speaking** du point de vue artistique

artistry ['ɑːtɪstrɪ] N *(of painter, footballer)* art *m*; *(of painting, sb's game)* qualité *f* artistique; **his goal was sheer a.** son but, c'était du grand art

artless ['ɑːtlɪs] ADJ **1** *(natural)* naturel, sans artifice **2** *(naive)* naïf, ingénu

artlessly ['ɑːtlɪslɪ] ADV **1** *(naturally)* natu-

rellement, sans artifice **2** *(naively)* naïvement, ingénument

artlessness ['ɑːtlɪsnɪs] N **1** *(naturalness)* naturel *m*, simplicité *f* **2** *(naivety)* naïveté *f*, ingénuité *f*

artwork ['ɑːtwɜːk] N *Art (in book production) (illustrations)* illustrations *fpl*; *(layout)* mise *f* en page; *(made-up page for printing)* document *m* d'exécution; **to use sth as a.** utiliser qch dans la maquette

arty ['ɑːtɪ] ADJ *Fam (person, style, job, furniture)* artistique; *(existence)* bohème; *Pej (person)* qui donne dans le genre artiste; *(furniture etc)* qui se veut artistique; **he's an a. type** c'est le genre artiste; **the a. set** le milieu artiste

arty-crafty ADJ *Fam Hum Pej* bohème

arty-farty [-ˈfɑːtɪ], *Am* **artsy-fartsy** ['ɑːtsɪˈfɑːtsɪ] ADJ *Fam Pej* aux prétentions artistiques, soi-disant artistique; **it's a lot of a. rubbish** c'est un tas d'idioties prétendument artistiques

arum ['eərəm] N *Bot* arum *m*
▶▶ **a. lily** calla *f*

arvo ['ɑːvəʊ] N *Austr Fam (afternoon)* après-midi *m ou f inv*, aprème *m ou f*

Aryan ['eərɪən] *Ling etc* ADJ aryen
N Aryen, -enne

AS [əz, *stressed* æz]

PREP	comme
CONJ	comme **1, 2, 4** ▪ puisque **2** ▪ que **6** ▪ aussi … que (*as … as*) **8**
ADV	▪ comme **1** ▪ quant à (*as for*) **2** ▪ aussi, en plus (*as well*) **3** ▪ en plus de (*as well as*) **3** ▪ comme si (*as if*) **4**

PREP *(manner, function, role, condition)* comme; **they rose as one man** ils se levèrent comme un seul homme; **to acknowledge sb as an expert/one's equal** reconnaître qn en tant qu'expert/comme son égal; **to consider sb as a friend** considérer qn comme un ami; **to treat sb as a stranger** traiter qn en étranger; **to treat sth as a joke** tourner qch à la plaisanterie; **to recognize sb as one's son** reconnaître qn comme son fils; **I intended it as a compliment** j'ai dit ça en bien; **she was often ill as a child** enfant elle était souvent malade, elle était souvent malade dans son enfance; **to use sth as a flag** se servir de qch comme drapeau *ou* en guise de drapeau; **to send sth as a present** envoyer qch comme cadeau; *Theat* **Olivier as Hamlet** Olivier dans le rôle de Hamlet; **to act as interpreter** servir d'interprète; **I acted in my capacity as a magistrate** j'ai agi en ma qualité de magistrat; **to be dressed as a boy** être habillé en garçon; **as a very old friend of your father's** en tant que vieil ami de votre père; **the novel as social history** le roman comme témoin de l'histoire de la société; **my rights as a mother** mes droits de mère; **as one doctor to another** soit dit entre médecins; **as someone new to the place** en tant que nouveau venu; **as revenge for …** pour se venger de …

CONJ VOIR GRAMMAIRE B74–6; B58 **1** *(time)* **as I was opening the door** au moment où *ou* comme j'ouvrais la porte; **he went out (just) as I came in** il est sorti au moment (même) où *ou* comme j'entrais; **as I spoke, I could see …** tandis que je parlais, je voyais …; **as you get older** en vieillissant; **he's probably trying to contact us as we sit here** il essaie probablement de nous contacter en ce moment même; **one day as I was sitting …** un jour que j'étais assis …; **she drew back as I advanced** à mesure que j'avançais, elle reculait; **it's the last one as you come from the station** c'est le dernier en venant de la gare; **as and when required** à discrétion; **as and**

when I want à mon bon plaisir; **as (and when) is necessary** quand c'est nécessaire **2** *(reason)* puisque, comme; **as he has now left** puisqu'il *ou* comme il est maintenant parti **3** *(concessive)* **ignorant as he is** tout ignorant qu'il est; **late as it was** malgré l'heure tardive; **try as she might, she couldn't open it** elle avait beau essayer, elle n'arrivait pas à l'ouvrir; **hard as it may be to believe, …** c'est peut-être difficile à croire, mais …; **much as I like her** quelle que soit mon affection pour elle; **be that as it may** quoi qu'il en soit **4** *(manner)* comme; **do as you like** faites comme vous voulez *ou* voudrez; **it happened as I told you** cela s'est passé comme je vous l'ai dit; **as Mrs Smith remarked …** comme Mme Smith l'a fait remarquer …; **covered with dust as he was, he didn't want to come in** couvert qu'il était de poussière, il ne voulait pas entrer; **as they say, …** comme on dit, …; **why should I do as he says?** pourquoi devrais-je faire ce qu'il dit?; **as often happens** comme il arrive souvent, ainsi qu'il arrive souvent; **leave it as it is** laissez-le tel quel, laissez-le tel qu'il est; **as it is, we must … les choses étant ainsi, il nous faut …; there are too many cars as it is** il y a déjà trop de voitures; **as it were** pour ainsi dire; *Mil, Gym* **as you were!** revenez!, au temps!; **as a man lives, so he dies** comme on a vécu, ainsi l'on meurt; **as is** tel quel; *Fam* **the Apollo theatre as was** *(it now has another name)* le théâtre de l'Apollo comme on l'appelait; *(it now has another function)* l'ancien théâtre de l'Apollo **5** *(result, purpose)* **he is not so foolish as to believe it** il n'est pas assez stupide pour le croire; **put on your gloves so as to be ready** mettez vos gants pour être prêt *ou* de manière à être prêt **6 mother is well, as are the children** maman va bien, de même que les enfants; **beasts of prey, such as the lion or tiger** les bêtes fauves, telles que *ou* comme le lion ou le tigre; **he was a foreigner, as they noticed from his pronunciation** il était étranger, ce qui se remarquait à sa prononciation; **it's the same one as I was telling you about** c'est celui-là même dont je vous parlais **7** *Eng Dial* **it was her as told me** c'est elle qui me l'a dit **8** *(in comparisons)* *(also adv)* **as … as …** aussi … que …; **not as … as …** pas aussi *ou* si … que …; **you are as tall as he (is)** *or* **as him** vous êtes aussi grand que lui; **you are not as** *or* **not so tall as he (is)** *or* **as him** vous n'êtes pas aussi grand que lui; **I'm not as rich as I was** je ne suis pas aussi riche que je l'ai été; **is it as high as that?** est-ce si *ou* aussi haut que ça?; **I came down as fast as I could** je suis descendu aussi vite que possible; **I worked as hard as I could** j'ai travaillé autant que j'ai pu; **as many as you want** autant que tu veux; **he's not such a fool as he looks** il n'est pas si bête qu'il en a l'air; **a house twice as large (as this)** une maison deux fois plus grande (que celle-ci); **as white as a sheet** blanc comme un linge; **as recently as last week** pas plus tard que la semaine dernière; **as much for your sake as for mine** tant pour vous que pour moi; **she doesn't enjoy it as much as I do** elle n'aime pas ça autant que moi; **I don't know why I like her as much as I do** je ne sais pas pourquoi elle me plaît à ce point; **as soon/as much as possible** aussitôt/autant que possible; **we could go as high as 5,000, but no higher** nous pourrions monter jusqu'à 5000, mais pas au-delà

ADV 1 *(form, manner, kind)* **as per advice** suivant avis; **as per invoice** selon facture; **as promised** comme promis; **as ordered** conformément à la commande; **as reques-** **ted** comme il a été requis; **as advertised on TV** vu à la télé; **as recommended** comme il est recommandé; **the GR241, as recommended by leading experts** le GR241, modèle recommandé par les plus grands experts; **ready to use as delivered** livré prêt à fonctionner; **if used as intended** s'il est utilisé selon les recommandations; **we didn't arrive at lunch time as intended** nous ne sommes pas arrivés à l'heure du déjeuner, comme cela avait été notre intention; **as noted/discussed above** comme il est mentionné/démontré plus haut; **B as in Bombay** B comme Bombay

2 *(switching or identifying topic)* **as for that, as to that, as regards that** quant à cela, pour cela; **as for you** quant à vous; **as for money, I can lend you some** pour ce qui est de l'argent, je peux t'en prêter; **to question sb as to his/her motives** interroger qn sur ses motifs

3 as well aussi; **I don't want trouble from you as well** je ne veux pas que toi aussi tu me causes des problèmes; **as well as the rent, there was the heating to consider** en plus du loyer, il fallait penser au chauffage; **you can't expect me to cook as well as do the dishes** tu ne peux pas me demander de faire la cuisine et la vaisselle en plus; **by day as well as by night** le jour comme la nuit, de jour comme de nuit

4 as if comme si; **it was as if …** on aurait dit que …; **he winked as if** *or* **though to say …** il fit un clin d'œil, comme pour dire …; **we can't go on as if** *or* **though nothing had happened** nous ne pouvons pas continuer comme si de rien n'était; **it isn't as if** *or* **though I haven't tried** ce n'est pourtant pas manque d'avoir essayé; **it isn't as if** *or* **though it's difficult** ce n'est pourtant pas difficile; **he made as if** *or* **though to go** il a fait mine de partir; **he looked as if** *or* **though he was about to go out** on aurait dit qu'il était sur le point de sortir; **as if you didn't know!** comme si tu ne le savais pas!

ASA [eɪes'eɪ] N *Phot (abbr* **American Standards Association)** ASA *f*; **A./DIN exposure index** graduations *fpl* ASA/DIN; **an A. 100 film, a 100 A. film** une pellicule 100 ASA

asap [eɪeseɪ'piː] ADV *(abbr* **as soon as possible)** le plus tôt possible, dans les plus brefs délais; **we need to reply a.** il faut qu'on réponde dès que possible

asbestos [æs'bestəs] N amiante *m*
► ►**a. dust** poudre *f* d'amiante

asbestosis [æsbes'təʊsɪs] N *Med* asbestose *f*

ascend [ə'send] VI *Fml* monter
VT **1** *(ladder)* monter à; *(stairs)* monter, gravir; *(mountain)* gravir, faire l'ascension de; *(throne)* monter sur **2** *(river)* remonter

ascendancy, ascendency [ə'sendənsɪ] N *Fml* ascendant *m* (**over sb** sur qn); **to gain (the) a. over sb** prendre de l'ascendant sur qn

ascendant, ascendent [ə'sendənt] ADJ **1** *Astrol, Astron, Math etc* ascendant; *(power, faction)* dominant **2** *Bot (stalk)* montant
N *Astrol* ascendant *m*; **to be in the a.** être à l'ascendant; *Fig* avoir le dessus, s'affirmer; **his star is in the a.** son étoile est à l'ascendant; **his fortunes are once more in the a.** ses finances commencent à mieux se porter
► ►*Astrol* **a. star** astre *m* ascendant

ascender [ə'sendər] N *Typ (of character)* hampe *f* (montante), ascendante *f*

ascending [ə'sendɪŋ] ADJ **1** *Astrol, Astron, Math etc* ascendant; *Met (current)* ascendant; **in a. order** en ordre croissant; **steeply a. path** sentier *m* raide **2** *Bot (stalk)* montant
► ►*Law* **a. line** ascendance *f*, ligne *f* ascendante; *Mus* **a. scale** gamme *f* ascendante *ou* montante; **a. series** progression *f* crois-

sante; *Comput* **a. sort** tri *m* en ordre croissant

ascension [ə'senʃən] N ascension *f*; **her a. to the throne** son élévation *f* sur le trône
► ►*Rel* **A. Day** jour *m ou* fête *f* de l'Ascension; **A. Island** île *f* de l'Ascension

ascent [ə'sent] N **1** *(of mountain)* ascension *f*; **first a.** première *f* (ascension); **a. in a balloon** ascension en ballon; **to make an a.** faire une ascension; *Fig* **the a. of man** le progrès de l'humanité; **his a. to power** son ascension jusqu'au pouvoir **2** *Tech (of piston etc)* montée *f*, remontée *f* **3** *(slope)* montée *f*, pente *f* **4** *Law* **line of a.** ascendance *f*

> Attention: ne pas confondre avec **assent**.

ascertain [æsə'teɪn] VT *(fact)* déterminer; *(truth about sth)* s'assurer de; **to a. sth from sb** s'informer de qch auprès de qn; **I ascertained from his report that …** j'ai déduit de son rapport que …; **are we to a. from this that …?** devons-nous en déduire que …?

ascertainable [æsə'teɪnəb(ə)l] ADJ *(information, fact)* qui peut être déterminé; *(truth)* vérifiable; **that's as much detail as is a. from this distance** c'est tout ce qu'on peut distinguer avec certitude à cette distance

ascertainment [æsə'teɪnmənt] N *Fml (of fact)* détermination *f*, *(of truth)* vérification *f*

ascetic [ə'setɪk] ADJ USU ATTRIB *(life etc)* ascétique; **a thin a. face** un maigre visage d'ascète
N *esp Rel* ascète *mf*; **he led the life of an a.** il menait une vie d'ascète, il vivait en ascète

ascetically [ə'setɪklɪ] ADV ascétiquement; *(to live)* en ascète

asceticism [ə'setɪsɪz(ə)m] N ascétisme *m*

ASCII ['æskiː] N *Comput (abbr* **American Standard Code for Information Interchange)** ASCII *m*
► ►**A. code** code *m* ASCII; **A. file** fichier *m* ASCII; **A. text** texte *m* ASCII

ascorbic [ə'skɔːbɪk] ADJ *Chem (acid etc)* ascorbique

ascribable [ə'skraɪbəb(ə)l] ADJ PRED attribuable (**to** à); *(of sth negative)* imputable (**to** à); **certain parts of the text are easily a.** l'origine de certaines parties du texte est facile à déceler

ascribe [ə'skraɪb] VT attribuer (**to** à); *(sth negative)* imputer (**to** à)

ascription [ə'skrɪpʃən] N *Fml* attribution *f* (**of sth to sth** de qch à qch); *(of sth negative)* imputation *f* (**of sth to sth** de qch à qch)

asdic ['æzdɪk] N *Naut* asdic *m*

ASEAN ['æzɪæn] N *(abbr* **Association of South East Asian Nations)** ANASE *f*

asepsis [eɪ'sepsɪs] N *Med* asepsie *f*

aseptic [eɪ'septɪk] ADJ *Med* aseptique; *Fig (smile, charm)* aseptisé

asexual [eɪ'seksjʊəl] ADJ *Biol, Fig* asexué; *(flower)* neutre
► ►*Biol* **a. reproduction** reproduction *f* asexuée

ash¹ [æʃ] N *(tree, wood)* frêne *m*; **a. furniture** meubles *mpl* en *ou* de frêne
► ►**a. tree** frêne *m*

ash² N **1** *(from fire etc)* cendre(s) *f(pl)*; *Ind etc* escarbilles *fpl*; **cigar a.** cendre de cigare; **to drop a. on the carpet** laisser tomber des cendres sur la moquette; **to reduce** *or* **burn sth to ashes** réduire qch en cendres; **volcanic a.** cendres volcaniques; *Lit* **to rake over the ashes of the past** tisonner les cendres du passé; **to rise from the ashes** renaître de ses cendres; **ashes** *(of dead)* cendres; **ashes to ashes, dust to dust** *(from funeral service)* tu es poussière, et tu retourneras en poussière; *Cr* **the Ashes** = le trophée que les équipes anglaises et australiennes se disputent

2 *(colour)* cendré *m*, gris cendré *m inv*
ADJ *(in colour)* gris cendré *inv*
▶▶**a. cloud** *(above volcano)* nuée *f* de cendres; **a. heap** crassier *m*; *Rel* **A. Wednesday** mercredi *m* des Cendres

ashamed [əˈʃeɪmd] **ADJ USU PRED** honteux, confus; **to be a. of sb/sth** avoir honte de qn/qch; **I am a. of you** vous me faites honte; **to feel a.** être honteux *ou* confus; **you make me feel a.** *(of myself, you)* vous me faites honte; **I am a. to say that ...** j'avoue à ma grande honte que ...; **a. though I am to admit it, I have never been there** j'ai honte de l'avouer, je n'y suis jamais allé; **I'm not a. to admit it** je l'admets sans honte; **you ought to be a. of yourself** vous devriez avoir honte; **there is nothing to be a. of** il n'y a pas de quoi avoir honte; **... he said, with an a. look on his face** ... dit-il, l'air confus

A-share **N** *St Exch* action *f* ordinaire sans droit de vote

ash-blond(e) **ADJ** *(hair)* blond cendré *inv*
N *(person)* **she's an a.** elle a les cheveux blond cendré

ashcan [ˈæʃkæn] **N** *Am* boîte *f* à ordures, poubelle *f*

ashen [ˈæʃən] **ADJ** *(colour)* cendré; *(face)* pâle comme la mort; **his face turned a.** il devint blême, son visage blêmit

ashen-faced [ˈæʃənˈfeɪst] **ADJ** pâle comme la mort

ashlar [ˈæʃlər] **N** *Constr, Archit* **1** *(stone)* pierre *f* de taille **2** *(facing)* parements *mpl*, revêtement *m*

ashore [əˈʃɔːr] **ADV** *Naut* **1** *(on land)* à terre; **to go a.** aller *ou* descendre à terre, débarquer; **to set** *or* **put sb a.** débarquer qn **2** *(to the shore) (to swim etc)* jusqu'au rivage, jusqu'à la rive; **to be driven a.** *(of ship)* être jeté à la côte; **to run a.** *(of ship)* s'échouer, faire côte

ashpan [ˈæʃpæn] **N** *(for stove)* cendrier *m*

ashtray [ˈæʃtreɪ] **N** cendrier *m*

ashy [ˈæʃɪ] **ADJ 1** cendreux, couvert de cendres **2** *(in colour)* cendré, couleur de cendre

Asia [ˈeɪʒə] **N** Asie *f*
▶▶**A. Minor** Asie *f* Mineure

Asian [ˈeɪʒən] **ADJ** asiatique; *(Indian)* indien; *(Pakistani)* pakistanais
N Asiatique *mf*, *(Indian)* Indien, -ienne; *(Pakistani)* Pakistanais, -aise
▶▶*Fam* **A. babe** Indienne *f*/Pakistanaise *f*/ Orientale *f* super belle; *Med* **A. flu** grippe *f* asiatique

> **Asian**
> Pour les Britanniques, "Asian" désigne le plus souvent les habitants de l'Inde et des pays limitrophes: ainsi, l'expression "the Asian community in Edinburgh" fait référence aux personnes d'origine indienne, pakistanaise et bangladaise qui habitent Edimbourg.

Asiatic [eɪsɪˈætɪk] **ADJ** asiatique
N Asiatique *mf*

aside [əˈsaɪd] **ADV 1** de côté, à l'écart, à part; **to pull a.** *(curtain etc)* écarter; **to lay** *or* **put sth a.** mettre qch de côté; **to put sth a. for sb** *(in shop)* mettre qch de côté pour qn; **stand a.!** écartez-vous!; **to turn a.** se détourner *(from* de); **I took** *or* **drew him a.** je le pris à part *ou* à l'écart *ou* en particulier; **(leaving) politics a., I think ...** si on laisse de côté la politique, je pense ...; **injuries to my vanity a., it hasn't caused me much trouble** à part quelques blessures d'amour-propre, ça ne m'a pas vraiment causé de problèmes; **joking a.** blague à part; *Theat* **(words spoken) a.** *(paroles dites)* en aparté

2 *esp Am* **a. from** à part; *(except for)* excepté, sauf; **a. from my own interest** mon propre intérêt à part; **a. from being frightened, I was unhurt** j'en ai été quitte pour la peur
N *Theat, Fig* aparté *m* **(to sb** avec qn); **(purely) as an a.** soit dit entre nous

A-side **N** *(of record)* face *f* A

asinine [ˈæsɪnaɪn] **ADJ 1** *(stupid)* stupide, sot **2** *(like an ass)* asinien

ask [ɑːsk] *(asked* [ɑːskt]) **VT 1** demander; **to a. sb sth** demander qch à qn; **a. him his name/how old he is** demandez-lui son nom/son âge; **to a. the time** demander l'heure; **to a. (sb) the way** demander son chemin (à qn); **to a. (sb) a question** poser une question (à qn) *(about* sur); **it may be asked whether ...** on peut se demander si ...; **I've often asked myself whether ...** je me suis souvent demandé si ..., je me suis souvent posé la question de savoir si ...; *Fam* **if you a. me** à mon avis; *Fam* **I a. you!** je vous demande un peu!

2 *(request)* demander; **to a. sb for sth** demander qch à qn; **to a. a favour of sb, to a. sb a favour** demander une faveur à qn; **if it isn't asking too much** si ce n'est pas trop vous demander; **to a. sb's permission to do sth** demander à qn la permission de faire qch; **to a. to do sth** demander à faire qch, demander la permission *ou* l'autorisation de faire qch; **to a. to be excused** s'excuser de partir; *(in class)* demander la permission de sortir; **to a. sb to do sth** demander à qn de faire qch; **a. him to wait/to come in** priez-le d'attendre/d'entrer

3 *(charge)* **to a. 600 euros for sth** demander 600 euros pour *ou* de qch; **how much** *or* **what are you asking for it?** combien en voulez-vous?

4 *(question) (person)* interroger *(about* sur); **he asked me all about my work** il m'a interrogé longuement sur mon travail

5 *(invite)* inviter; **to a. sb to lunch** inviter qn à déjeuner; **I have asked him to come for the weekend** je l'ai invité à passer le week-end chez nous; **can I a. a friend along?** est-ce que je peux inviter un ami à se joindre à nous?

VI 1 *(inquire)* se renseigner *(about* sur); **if you don't mind me** *or* **my asking** si vous permettez que je vous le demande; **the police were asking about you** la police a posé des questions à votre sujet

2 *(request)* **all you have to do is a.!** il n'y a qu'à demander!
▶▶*St Exch* **a. price** cours *m* offert, cours vendeur

▶ **ask after VT INSEP** *(show concern for, ask for news of) (person, sb's health)* demander des nouvelles de

▶ **ask around VI** *(enquire)* demander autour de soi, se renseigner; **some odd people have been asking around after you** il y a des drôles de types qui te cherchent

▶ **ask back VT SEP** *(invite to one's home)* inviter à la maison; *(invite again)* réinviter; **do you want to a. them back for a drink?** tu veux les inviter à boire un verre à la maison?

▶ **ask for VT INSEP 1 to a. for sb** demander à voir qn; *(on the telephone)* demander à parler à qn; **to a. for sth** demander qch; **to a. for something to eat/to drink** demander (quelque chose) à manger/à boire; **to a. for more** en redemander; **to a. for sth back** *(that has been lent)* redemander qch; **when I want your opinion, I'll a. for it** lorsque j'aurai besoin de ton avis, je te le demanderai; **to be asking for trouble** aller au-devant des ennuis; *Fam* **he's been asking for it!** il l'a bien cherché!, il ne l'a pas volé!; **that's asking for a cold** tu/il/*etc* cherche(s) vraiment à

tomber malade!; *Fam* **you asked for that!** tu l'as cherché!

▶ **ask in VT SEP** *(invite in)* inviter à entrer; **I would a. you in for tea, but ...** je vous inviterais bien à (entrer) prendre le thé, mais ...

▶ **ask out VT SEP** *(to a date etc)* inviter à sortir

▶ **ask round VT SEP** *(invite to one's home)* inviter; **why don't we a. them round for dinner one night?** pourquoi ne pas les inviter à dîner un soir?

▶ **ask up VT SEP** *(invite up)* inviter à monter; **they asked us up to their flat** ils nous ont invités à monter dans leur appartement *ou* chez eux

askance [əˈskæns, -ɑːns] **ADV** *Fig* **to look a. at sb/sth** regarder qn/qch de travers *ou* avec méfiance; **she looked rather a. when I suggested Burger King** elle a fait un drôle d'air quand j'ai suggéré Burger King

askew [əˈskjuː] **ADV** de biais, de travers; *(to put one's hat on)* de guingois; *Fig* **his calculations were slightly a.** il s'était un peu trompé dans ses calculs; **I don't want anything going a.** je tiens à ce que rien n'aille de travers

asking [ˈɑːskɪŋ] **N** **it's yours for the a.** il n'y a qu'à (le) demander; **it was theirs for the a.** ils n'ont eu qu'à demander
▶▶**a. price** *Fin* prix *m* de départ, prix demandé; *Am St Exch* cours *m* offert, cours vendeur

aslant [əˈslɑːnt] **ADV** obliquement, de travers, de biais
PREP en travers de

asleep [əˈsliːp] **ADJ PRED** endormi; **to be a.** dormir; **to fall a.** s'endormir; **they lay a. on the floor** ils s'étaient endormis par terre; **to be fast** *or* **sound a.** être profondément endormi *ou* plongé dans le sommeil; **my foot is a.** j'ai le pied engourdi

ASLEF [ˈæzlef] **N** *Br abbr* Associated Society of Locomotive Engineers and Firemen

ASM [eɪˈesˈem] **N 1** *Mil abbr* air-to-surface missile **2** *Theat abbr* assistant stage manager

as-new **ADJ** comme neuf

asocial [eɪˈsəʊʃəl] **ADJ** asocial, -iaux

asp [æsp] **N** *(snake)* (vipère *f*) aspic *m*

asparagus [əˈspærəgəs] **N** *(no pl) Culin* asperges *fpl*; **a piece** *or* **spear of a.** une asperge; **a. soup** soupe *f* aux asperges
▶▶**a. fern** asparagus *m*; **a. tips** pointes *fpl* d'asperges

aspect [ˈæspekt] **N 1** *(of problem, subject etc)* aspect *m*; **the worrying a. of the situation is ...** ce qu'il y a d'inquiétant dans cette situation c'est ...; **there were amusing aspects to the situation** la situation avait des côtés amusants

2 *Fml (appearance)* air *m*; **a man of serious a.** un homme à l'air sérieux

3 *(outlook) (of house etc)* exposition *f*, orientation *f*; **to have a northern a.** être exposé au nord; **flats with southern a.** appartements *mpl* orientés au sud

4 *Astrol (of planets)* aspect *m*

5 *Gram* aspect *m* VOIR GRAMMAIRE A39
▶▶*Cin* **a. ratio** rapport *m* hauteur/largeur, format *m* de l'image

aspen [ˈæspən] **N** *(tree)* (peuplier *m*) tremble *m*
▶▶**a. leaf** feuille *f* de tremble

asperity [æˈsperɪtɪ] **N** *(of climate)* rigueur *f*, sévérité *f*, *(of character, voice)* aspérité *f*, rudesse *f*, *(of reproach)* âpreté *f*, *(of style)* aspérité

aspersion [əˈspɜːʃən] **N** *Fml, Hum* calomnie *f*, **to cast aspersions on sb/sth** calomnier qn/ qch; **to cast aspersions on sb's honour** porter atteinte à l'honneur de qn

asphalt [ˈæsfælt] **N** *Miner, Constr* asphalte *m*,

bitume *m*; **a. roadway** chaussée *f* asphaltée **vт** *Constr (road etc)* asphalter, bitumer

asphalting ['æsfæltɪŋ] **N** asphaltage *m*, bitumage *m*

asphyxia [æs'fɪksɪə] **N** asphyxie *f*; **it led to a.** cela a provoqué l'asphyxie *ou* une asphyxie

asphyxiate [æs'fɪksɪeɪt] **vт** asphyxier **vɪ** mourir d'asphyxie

asphyxiation [æsfɪksɪ'eɪʃən] **N** asphyxie *f*

aspic ['æspɪk] **N** *Culin* gelée *f*; **eggs in a.** œufs *mpl* en gelée; **chicken/salmon in a.** aspic *m* de volaille/de saumon; *Fig* **preserved in a.** mis sous verre

aspidistra [æspɪ'dɪstrə] **N** *(plant)* aspidistra *m*

aspirant ['æspɪrənt] **N** candidat, -ate

aspirate[1] ['æspɪrət] **ADJ** *Ling* aspiré

aspirate[2] ['æspɪreɪt] **vт 1** *Ling (vowel, h)* aspirer **2** *Tech (gas, liquid)* aspirer; **aspirating filter** filtre *m* à vide

aspiration [æspɪ'reɪʃən] **N 1** *Ling, Med etc* aspiration *f* **2** *(ambition)* aspiration *f*; **to have aspirations to greater things/to become a doctor** aspirer à de grandes choses/ à devenir médecin; **to have political aspirations** avoir des aspirations politiques; **to have presidential aspirations** aspirer à la présidence

aspirational [æspɪ'reɪʃən(ə)l] **ADJ** *Mktg (product)* qui fait chic; *(consumer)* qui achète des produits de prestige; *(advertising)* qui joue sur le prestige d'un produit ▸▸ **a. group** groupe *m* de référence

aspirator ['æspɪreɪtər] **N** *Phys, Med* aspirateur *m*

aspire [ə'spaɪər] **vɪ** aspirer; **to a. to** *or* **after sth** aspirer *ou* prétendre *ou* viser à qch, ambitionner qch; **to a. to do sth** aspirer à *ou* ambitionner de faire qch; **they aspired to greatness** ils aspiraient à la gloire

aspirin ['æsprɪn] **N** *(drug)* aspirine *f*, *(pill)* comprimé *m* d'aspirine

aspiring [ə'spaɪərɪŋ] **ADJ ATTRIB** *(artiste etc)* en herbe; **to be an a. doctor/dancer** aspirer à devenir médecin/danseur

ass[1] [æs] **N 1** *(animal)* âne *m*; **she a.** ânesse *f*; **a.'s milk** lait *m* d'ânesse; **wild a.** onagre *m* **2** *(idiot)* âne *m*, idiot, -ote; **don't be a silly a.** ne fais pas l'imbécile *ou* l'idiot; **to make an a. of oneself** se ridiculiser; *(make an exhibition of oneself)* se donner en spectacle

ass[2] **N** *esp Am Vulg (buttocks)* cul *m*; **she's got a great little a. on her** elle a un beau petit cul; **a nice piece of a.** *(woman)* un beau cul, une belle pépée; *see also* **arse, arse about** *etc*
▸ **ass about, ass around** **vɪ** *Am Sl* déconner

ass[3] **N** *abbr* assistant

assail [ə'seɪl] **vт** *Fml (enemy)* assaillir, attaquer; *Fig* **to a. sb with questions** accabler *ou* assaillir qn de questions; **assailed with doubts** saisi de doutes

assailant [ə'seɪlənt] **N** assaillant, -ante, agresseur *m*

assassin [ə'sæsɪn] **N** *(of head of state etc)* assassin *m*; *Hist* **Assassins** Assassins, Ismaïliens *mpl*

assassinate [ə'sæsɪneɪt] **vт** assassiner

assassination [əsæsɪ'neɪʃən] **N** assassinat *m*; **character a.** diffamation *f*
▸▸ **a. attempt** attentat *m* *(contre quelqu'un)*

assault [ə'sɔːlt] **N 1** *Law* tentative *f* de voie de fait; *(attempted rape)* tentative *f* de viol; *(rape)* viol *m*; **unprovoked a.** agression *f*; **a. and battery** voies *fpl* de fait, coups *mpl* et blessures *fpl*; **criminal a.** agression **2** *Mil* assaut *m*; *Fig (on government, person's beliefs etc)* attaque *f* (**on** contre); **to take** *or* **carry a**

town by a. prendre une ville d'assault; **to make an a. on sth** donner l'assaut à qch; *Fig (on problem, correspondence)* s'attaquer à qch
vт 1 *(attack) (person)* agresser, attaquer; *Law* se livrer à des voies de fait sur; *(sexually)* violenter; **to be assaulted** être victime d'une agression; *(sexually)* être victime d'un attentat à la pudeur **2** *Mil (town, position etc)* attaquer, assaillir, donner l'assaut à; *Fig (senses)* agresser
▸▸ *Mil* **a. course** parcours *m* du combattant; *Mil* **a. craft** engin *m* d'assaut; **a. rifle** fusil *m* d'assaut

assay [ə'seɪ] **N** *Metal (of precious metal, mineral)* essai *m*; *Chem* dosage *m*
vт 1 *Metal (precious metal, mineral)* essayer, titrer, analyser; *(metal)* faire l'essai de; *(gold, silver)* coupeller **2** *Lit (attempt)* tenter
▸▸ **a. office** laboratoire *m* d'essais

assaying [ə'seɪɪŋ] **N** *Metal (of mineral etc)* essai *m*, titrage *m*, analyse *f*, *(of gold, silver)* coupellation *f*

assemblage [ə'semblɪdʒ] **N 1** *Tech (of pieces of woodwork etc)* assemblage *m* **2** *(of objects)* collection *f*, *(of individuals)* assortiment *m*

assemble [ə'semb(ə)l] **vт 1** *(people)* rassembler, réunir; *(documents, evidence)* réunir; *(insurgents etc)* ameuter; *(parliament)* convoquer; *Mil (troops)* rassembler; **he addressed the assembled schoolchildren** il s'est adressé à l'ensemble des élèves réunis **2** *Tech (in joinery)* assembler; *(machine)* ajuster, assembler, monter; *(watch etc)* habiller
vɪ *(of people)* s'assembler, se rassembler, se réunir; *(of insurgents etc)* s'ameuter

assembler [ə'semblər] **N** *Ind* monteur, -euse; *Comput* assembleur *m*

assembly [ə'semblɪ] **N 1** *(gathering)* réunion *f*, *Br Sch etc* rassemblement *m*; **place of a.** lieu *m* de réunion; *Law* **unlawful a.** attroupement *m*; **right of a.** droit *m* à la liberté de réunion **2** *Pol etc* assemblée *f*; **the National A.** l'Assemblée nationale **3** *Ind, Cin etc (assembling)* montage *m*, assemblage *m* **4** *(group of components)* assemblage *m*
▸▸ *Mil* **a. area** zone *f* d'attente; **a. hall** = hall *m* où les enfants se réunissent le matin avant d'entrer en classe; **a. instructions** instructions *fpl* de montage *ou* d'assemblage; *Comput* **a. language** langage *m* d'assemblage; *Comput* **a. language program** programme *m* en assembleur; *Ind* **a. line** chaîne *f* de montage; *Ind* **a. plant** usine *f* de montage; **a. rooms** salle *f* des fêtes, salle de danse; *Ind* **a. shop** salle *f* de montage

assent [ə'sent] **N** assentiment *m*; *Law* agrément *m*; **to withhold one's a. from a proposal** refuser son assentiment à une proposition; **he acted with the full a. of his colleagues** il a agi avec l'approbation totale de ses collègues; **to gain the a. of sb** *or* **sb's a.** obtenir l'assentiment de qn; **the royal a.** le consentement du souverain; **by common a.** du consentement de tous
vɪ donner son assentiment (**to** à); **to a. to a bill** *(of sovereign)* sanctionner une loi

Attention: ne pas confondre avec *ascent*.

assert [ə'sɜːt] **vт 1** *(one's rights, point of view etc)* faire valoir; **to a. oneself** s'imposer, se faire entendre; **you must a. your authority** il vous faut imposer votre autorité **2** *(declare) (one's innocence etc)* protester de; **to a. that ...** affirmer *ou* prétendre *ou* soutenir que ... + *ind*

assertion [ə'sɜːʃən] **N 1** *(of right)* revendication *f* **2** *(claim)* assertion *f*, affirmation *f*; **her a. that she had never seen him was un-**

convincing elle prétendait de façon peu convaincante qu'elle ne l'avait jamais vu

assertive [ə'sɜːtɪv] **ADJ** *(tone, person, manner etc)* assuré; **don't be too a.** ne te montre pas trop autoritaire; **he's not a. enough** il n'a pas assez d'autorité, il ne s'affirme pas assez

assertiveness [ə'sɜːtɪvnɪs] **N** assurance *f*
▸▸ **a. training** stage *m* d'affirmation de soi

assess [ə'ses] **vт 1** *(value or profit)* estimer; *(quality of product)* juger de; **to a. the damage** évaluer les dégâts; *Naut* évaluer l'avarie; *Law* **to a. the damages** fixer les dommages et intérêts; *Admin* **to a. sb at so much** imposer *ou* taxer qn à tant; **to a. a property (for taxation)** évaluer une propriété; **if we a. this speech at its true worth** si nous estimons ce discours à sa juste valeur; **to a. the situation** évaluer la situation; **how do you a. the team's chances?** à votre avis, quelles sont les chances de l'équipe?, quelles chances accordez-vous à l'équipe?; **to a. the chances of sth happening** évaluer les chances que qch a de se produire **2** *Admin (tax)* répartir, établir **3** *Sch, Univ* évaluer; **students are continuously assessed** le niveau des étudiants est évalué par un contrôle continu

assessment [ə'sesmənt] **N 1** *(of value of sth)* estimation *f*, *(for insurance or tax purposes)* évaluation *f*, *Law* **. of damages** fixation *f* de dommages et intérêts; *Sch* **continuous a.** contrôle *m* continu; **they gave their a. of the situation** ils ont donné leur avis sur la situation, ils ont dit ce qu'ils pensaient de la situation; **what is your a. of their chances?** à votre avis, quelles sont leurs chances?, quelles chances leur accordez-vous? **2** *Admin (for tax) (of municipality, building)* imposition *f*, *(of taxpayer)* cotisation *f*, *(amount)* cote *f*, taxe *f* officielle; **basis of a.** assiette *f* des impôts; **notice of a.** avis *m* de contributions; **year of a.** année *f* d'imposition; **a. on landed property** cote foncière; **a. on income** impôt *m* sur le revenu **3** *Admin (of tax)* répartition *f*, assiette *f*

assessor [ə'sesər] **N 1** *(of tax)* répartiteur, -trice **2** *(for insurance)* expert *m* **3** *Law* assesseur *m*, juge *m* assesseur

asset ['æset] **N 1** *(advantage)* avantage *m*, atout *m*; **she is a great a. to the firm** c'est un grand atout pour l'entreprise **2** *Fin etc (usu pl)* **assets** actif *m*, avoir(s) *m(pl)*; *(personal)* patrimoine *m*; *Law (of inheritance, company)* masse *f*, *(on liquidation after bankruptcy)* masse active; **capital assets** actif immobilisé; **frozen assets** fonds *mpl* bloqués *ou* non liquides
▸▸ *Fin* **a. allocation** répartition *f* des actifs; *Fin* **a. management** gestion *f* de biens, gestion de capital; *(of individual's wealth)* gestion de patrimoine; *Fin* **a. swap** swap *m* d'actifs; *Fin* **a. turnover** rotation *f* des capitaux

asset-strip **vт** démembrer les actifs de

asset-stripper **N** = personne *f* spécialisée dans le démembrement d'actifs

asset-stripping [-'strɪpɪŋ] **N** démembrement *m* des actifs *(suite au rachat d'une société)*

asseverate [ə'sevəreɪt] **vт** *Fml (one's innocence)* protester de; **to a. that ...** affirmer (solennellement) que ... + *ind*

asshole ['æshəʊl] **N** *Am Vulg* **1** *(anus)* trou *m* du cul **2** *Fig (idiot)* connard *m*, connasse *f*, *(nasty person)* fumier *m*, salaud *m*, salope *f*; **don't be such an a.** ne sois pas si con

assiduity [æsɪ'djʊɪtɪ] **N** assiduité *f* (**in doing sth** à faire qch)

assiduous [ə'sɪdjʊəs] **ADJ** assidu; **she was a. in her attention to detail** elle portait une attention assidue aux détails

assiduously [əˈsɪdjʊəslɪ] ADV assidûment

assign [əˈsaɪn] VT **1** *(allocate) (task, equipment, time, function)* assigner (**to** à); *(funds)* affecter (**to** à); **to a. sb to a task** assigner une tâche à qn; **they had been assigned to guard duty** on leur avait assigné la garde; **responsibilities haven't yet been assigned** les responsabilités n'ont pas encore été réparties *ou* assignées; **to a. sb to do sth** charger qn de faire qch **2** *(ascribe)* attribuer; **to a. a reason for sth** donner la raison de qch; **to a. a meaning to a word** attribuer un sens à un mot **3** *Law (property)* céder, transférer; *(lawsuits, patent)* transmettre (**to sb** à qn)

assignation [æsɪgˈneɪʃən] N **1** *Old-fashioned (meeting)* rendez-vous *m* secret; *(with lover)* rendez-vous galant; **to have an a. with sb** avoir un rendez-vous avec qn **2** *Law* = **assignment 3 3** *Fml (allocation etc)* = **assignment 1**

assignee [æsaɪˈniː] N cessionnaire *mf*

assignment [əˈsaɪnmənt] N **1** *(of task, equipment, function)* assignation *f*; *(of funding)* affectation *f*, allocation *f*; *(of duties, responsibilities)* attribution *f*; *(sharing out)* répartition *f*; **a. of sb to a post** affectation de qn à un poste; *Mil* **he was on a. to headquarters** il était affecté au quartier général; **2** *(task) Sch etc* devoir *m*; *Journ (of individual reporter)* reportage *m* assigné; **dangerous a.** tâche *f* dangereuse; *Journ* **to be on a.** être en reportage **3** *Law etc (of property, debts etc)* cession *f*, transfert *m*; **deed of a.** acte *m* attributif, acte de transfert
▸▸ *Acct* **a. of accounts receivable** transfert de créances; *Comput* **a. table** table *f* d'affectation

assimilate [əˈsɪmɪleɪt] VT *(food, facts, immigrants etc)* assimiler
VI **1** *(become absorbed)* s'intégrer, être assimilé; *(of people)* s'intégrer **2** *(become similar)* **to a. to** *or* **with sth** s'assimiler à qch

assimilation [əsɪmɪˈleɪʃən] N *(of food, ideas, immigrants etc)* assimilation *f*

Assisi [əˈsiːzɪ, əˈsiːsɪ] N Assise *f*; **St Francis of A.** saint François d'Assise

assist [əˈsɪst] VT *(person)* aider, prêter son assistance à; *(in their work)* seconder, prêter (son) concours à; *(process)* faciliter; *(sth's growth, development)* contribuer à; **to a. sb in doing sth** aider qn à faire qch; **economic growth was assisted by lower interest rates** des taux d'intérêts plus faibles ont contribué à la croissance économique
VI **1** *(help)* aider **2** *(be present) (at ceremony etc)* assister
▸▸ **assisted suicide** suicide *m* assisté

assistance [əˈsɪstəns] N aide *f*, secours *m*, assistance *f*; **to give sb a.** prêter son aide *ou* assistance à qn; *(in work, task)* prêter (son) concours à qn; **to come to sb's a.** venir en aide à qn; **with the a. of sth/sb** à l'aide de qch/avec l'aide de qn; **can I be of any** *or* **some a.?** puis-je être utile à quelque chose?, est-ce que je peux vous aider?; **to be of as much a. as one can** prêter toute l'assistance possible; **this theatre receives financial a. from the state** ce théâtre reçoit des subventions de l'État; *Br Admin Arch* **National A.** ≃ aide sociale

assistant [əˈsɪstənt] N **1** aide *mf*, adjoint, -ointe; **(shop) a.** vendeur, -euse; **laboratory a.** laborantin, -ine **2** *Sch* assistant, -ante; **French a.** assistant, -ante de français
▸▸ **a. accountant** aide-comptable *mf*, *pl* aides-comptables; **a. cameraman** aide-opérateur, -trice, *pl* aides-opérateurs, -trices; **a. director** sous-directeur, -trice, *pl* sous-directeurs, -trices; *Cin* assistant-réalisateur *m*, assistante-réalisatrice *f*, *pl* assistants-

réalisateurs, assistantes-réalisatrices; **a. editor** *TV* assistant monteur *m*; *Cin* monteur, -euse adjoint(e); *Journ* rédacteur, -trice en chef adjoint(e); *TV* **a. floor manager** régisseur *m* de plateau adjoint; **a. housekeeper** *(in hotel)* assistante gouvernante *f*, aide-gouvernante *f*, *pl* aides-gouvernantes; *Br Univ* **a. lecturer** ≃ maître-assistant, -ante, *pl* maîtres-assistants, -antes, *Can* ≃ professeur *m* adjoint; *Com* **a. manager** sous-directeur, -trice, *pl* sous-directeurs, -trices, directeur, -trice adjoint(e); **a. producer** producteur, -trice adjoint(e); *Am Univ* **a. professor** ≃ maître-assistant, -ante, *pl* maîtres-assistants, -antes, *Can* ≃ professeur *m* adjoint; *Ftbl* **a. referee** juge *m* de touche

assize [əˈsaɪz] N *Law* **1** *(usu pl)* **(court of) assizes** (cour f d')assises *fpl*; **to be brought before the assizes** être traduit en cour d'assises **2** *Scot (trial)* jugement *m* par jury; *(jury)* jury *m*
▸▸ **a. court** (cour d')assises

associate¹ [əˈsəʊʃɪət, -sɪət] N *(in business)* associé, -ée, partenaire *mf*; *(in criminal venture)* complice *mf*; *(of society of letters, science etc)* membre *m* correspondant, associé, -ée
ADJ associé
▸▸ *Com* **a. company** société *f* affiliée; *Cin* **a. director** assistant-réalisateur *m*, assistante-réalisatrice *f*, *pl* assistants-réalisateurs, assistantes-réalisatrices; *Journ* **a. editor** rédacteur, -trice associé(e); **a. membership** *(members)* membres *mpl* associés; *(participation)* adhésion *f* en tant que membre associé; **a. producer** producteur, -trice associé(e); *Am Univ* **a. professor** ≃ maître *m* de conférences, *Can* professeur *m* agrégé

associate² [əˈsəʊʃɪeɪt, -sɪeɪt] VT **1** *(mentally)* associer (**with sb** avec qn; **with sth** à qch); **I don't a. the two things** pour moi, les deux choses sont indépendantes **2** *(in partnership etc)* **to a. oneself** s'associer (**with sb** avec qn); **to be associated with sb in an undertaking** s'associer avec qn pour une entreprise; **to be associated with sth** *(with project, research etc)* participer à qch; *(with company etc)* avoir des liens avec qch, travailler avec qch; **we are not associated in any way with that company** nous n'avons absolument rien à faire *ou* voir avec cette société
VI **1** *(frequent)* **to a. with sb** fréquenter qn; **to a. with undesirable companions** avoir de mauvaises fréquentations **2** *(join)* **to a. with sb in sth/doing sth** s'associer *ou* s'unir avec qn pour qch/pour faire qch

associated [əˈsəʊsɪeɪtɪd] ADJ associé
▸▸ *Com* **a. company** société *f* affiliée; *Journ* **A. Press** Associated Press *f (agence de presse dont le siège est à New York)*

association [əsəʊsɪˈeɪʃən] N **1** *(mental)* association *f*; **a. of ideas** association d'idées; **a land full of historic associations** un pays fertile en souvenirs historiques; **the name has unfortunate associations for her** ce nom lui évoque des pensées désagréables; **the associations of the name** ce qu'on associe à ce nom **2** *(of people)* fréquentation *f* (**with sb** de qn); **through long a. with ...** à force de fréquenter ...; **in a. with ...** associé à ...; **to do sth in a. with sb** faire qch en association avec qn; **I have no a. with that company** je n'ai pas de liens avec cette société; **it has only a tenuous a. with its original purpose** cela n'a plus qu'un rapport lointain avec l'idée de départ; **my a. with the company has now ended** ma collaboration avec cette société est maintenant terminée **3** *(organization)* association *f*, société *f*; *(of*

teachers etc) amicale *f*; **to form an a.** constituer une société; **trade a.** association professionnelle; **Young Men's/Women's Christian A.** Union *f* chrétienne de jeunes gens/de jeunes femmes; *Law* **deed of a.** acte *m* d'association
▸▸ *Br* **a. football** football *m* association; *Psy* **a. test** test *m* d'association

associative [əˈsəʊsɪətɪv] ADJ *Psy* associatif

assonance [ˈæsənəns] N *Ling* assonance *f*

assorted [əˈsɔːtɪd] ADJ **1** *(sweets, screws etc)* assorti; *(colours)* varié; **an audience of a. academics and businessmen** un public très varié, composé d'universitaires et d'hommes d'affaires **2** *(matched)* assorti; **well a. couple** époux bien assortis

assortment [əˈsɔːtmənt] N *(of sweets, tools etc)* assortiment *m*; **I did it for an a. of reasons** je l'ai fait pour des raisons diverses; **quite an a. of people** des gens de toutes sortes

asst *abbr* assistant

assuage [əˈsweɪdʒ] VT *Lit (anger, hunger)* apaiser

assume [əˈsjuːm] VT **1** *(believe without proof)* présumer, supposer; **we can't a. anything** nous ne pouvons présumer de rien; **if we a. there will be no problems, ...** en supposant qu'il n'y aura aucun problème, ...; **I a. that he will come** je présume qu'il viendra; **he was assumed to be rich** on le supposait riche; **in the absence of proof, he must be assumed to be innocent** en l'absence de preuves, il doit être présumé innocent; **don't a. that people will like you because you are rich** ne crois pas que les gens t'aimeront parce que tu es riche; **let us a. that ...** mettons *ou* supposons que ...; **assuming that the story is true** en supposant *ou* en admettant que l'histoire soit vraie; **to a. the worst** mettre les choses au pis **2** *(take over) (responsibility)* prendre sur soi, assumer; *(duty)* se charger de; *(power, command)* prendre; *(running of hotel, company etc)* prendre en main **3** *(adopt) (right, title etc)* s'attribuer, s'arroger, s'approprier; *(name)* adopter, emprunter; *Law* **to a. ownership** faire acte de propriétaire **4** *(take on) (air, appearance, tone)* prendre, se donner; *(shape, character)* affecter, revêtir; *(of problem) (importance, vast proportions)* prendre; **his voice assumed a tone of authority** sa voix prit un ton autoritaire **5** *(feign) (indifference)* feindre, simuler

> Note that the French verb **assumer** is a false friend. It never means **to suppose** or **to adopt**.

assumed [əˈsjuːmd] ADJ ATTRIB *(identity)* faux; *(cause of death, motive, rate of increase)* présumé; **with a. nonchalance** avec une nonchalance feinte
▸▸ **a. load** *(on bridge etc)* surcharge *f* hypothétique; **a. name** nom *m* d'emprunt; *(of author)* pseudonyme *m*

assumption [əˈsʌmpʃən] N **1** *(supposition)* supposition *f*, hypothèse *f*; *Phil* postulat *m*; **it's a fair a. that ...** on peut facilement supposer que ...; **I am going on the a. that ...** je me fonde sur l'hypothèse que ...; **to work on the a. that ...** se fonder sur l'hypothèse que ...; **the assumptions on which society is based** les idées de base qui servent de fondement à la société **2** *(of power, responsibility etc)* prise *f*; **a. of office** entrée *f* en fonctions; **his a. of the role of chairman** *(after nomination)* son entrée en fonctions en tant que président; *(without consent)* le fait qu'il s'arroge la fonction de président **3** *Rel (of Virgin)* assomption *f*, **Feast of the A.** fête *f* de l'Assomption

assurance [ə'ʃʊərəns] N **1** (promise) promesse f (formelle); **I can give you an a. that … je** peux vous assurer ou vous affirmer que …; **he gave us any number of assurances that …** il nous a assuré maintes et maintes fois que …; **based on their a. that delivery would be within two days** en considération de leur promesse d'une livraison dans les deux jours

2 (affirmation) affirmation f; **a. to the contrary** affirmation contraire

3 (confidence) assurance f; **I have every a. that he will help us** j'ai la ferme assurance qu'il nous aidera

4 (self-confidence) assurance f, confiance f en soi; **to lack a.** (of person, answer) manquer d'assurance; **to answer with a.** (self-confidently) répondre d'un ton assuré ou avec assurance

5 Br (insurance) assurance f; **life a.** assurance sur la vie f, assurance-vie f, pl assurances-vie

▸▸ Br **a. company** compagnie f d'assurances

assure [ə'ʃʊər] VT **1** (person) assurer; **to a. sb of the truth of sth** assurer qn de la vérité de qch; **to a. sb of a fact** assurer ou affirmer un fait à qn; **he assures me that it is true** il me certifie que c'est vrai; **he assured me he was coming** il m'a assuré qu'il viendrait; **he will do it, I (can) a. you!** il le fera, je vous assure! **2** (ensure) (peace, sb's happiness etc) assurer **3** Br (insure) (sb's life) assurer; **to a. one's life** s'assurer (sur la vie)

assured [ə'ʃʊəd] ADJ **1** (certain) (success etc) assuré; **they are a. of victory** ils sont certains de gagner; **she is a. a place in the finals** elle est certaine d'aller en finale; **you're a. of a warm welcome** on vous garantit un accueil chaleureux **2** (self-confident) (person) sûr de soi; (manner, performance) plein d'assurance, assuré **3** (in insurance) **the sum a.** la valeur assurée

N (in insurance) **the a.** l'assuré, -ée, pl les assurés, -ées

assuredly [ə'ʃʊərɪdlɪ] ADV Fml assurément, sans aucun doute; **when she returns, as she a. will, …** quand elle reviendra, ce qui ne laisse aucun doute, …

Assyria [ə'sɪrɪə] N Antiq Assyrie f

Assyrian [ə'sɪrɪən] Antiq ADJ assyrien N **1** Assyrien, -ienne **2** Ling assyrien m

AST [eɪes'tiː] N Am abbr **Atlantic Standard Time**

aster ['æstər] N (flower) aster m; **China a.** aster de Chine, reine-marguerite f, pl reines-marguerites

asterisk ['æst(ə)rɪsk] N astérisque m
VT (word etc) marquer d'un astérisque

astern [ə'stɜːn] Naut ADV à l'arrière, sur l'arrière; **two guns a.** deux canons à l'arrière ou en poupe; **to go/come a.** (of ship) faire machine ou marche arrière; **full speed a.!** en arrière à toute vitesse!, en arrière toute!; **to make a boat fast a.** amarrer un canot derrière; **to fall** or **drop a.** (of another ship) rester en arrière; **ship right a.** navire droit derrière
PREP **a. of a ship** derrière un navire, sur l'arrière d'un navire; **to pass a. of a ship** passer sur l'arrière d'un navire

asteroid ['æstərɔɪd] N Astron astéroïde m

asthma ['æsmə] N asthme m; **to have a.** avoir de l'asthme; **a. sufferer** asthmatique mf

asthmatic [æs'mætɪk] ADJ, N asthmatique mf

astigmatic [æstɪg'mætɪk] ADJ, N Opt astigmate mf

astigmatism [ə'stɪgmətɪz(ə)m] N Opt astigmatisme m

astir [ə'stɜːr] ADJ PRED Old-fashioned **1** (out of bed) debout, levé **2** (in motion) animé; **the whole town was a.** toute la ville était en émoi

ASTMS ['æztems] N Br abbr **Association of Scientific, Technical and Managerial Staffs**

astonish [ə'stɒnɪʃ] VT stupéfier, étonner; **you a. me** vous m'étonnez; **it never fails to a. me that …** ça m'étonnera toujours de voir que …; **to be astonished at seeing sth** être étonné ou s'étonner de voir qch; **I was astonished at** or **by the price** j'ai été étonné du prix; **I am continually astonished by her audacity** son audace ne cesse de m'étonner; **I am astonished that …** cela m'étonne que … + sub; **she had an astonished look on her face** elle avait l'air étonné(e) ou stupéfait(e)

astonishing [ə'stɒnɪʃɪŋ] ADJ étonnant, surprenant; **it is a. to me that …** je m'étonne que … + sub

astonishingly [ə'stɒnɪʃɪŋlɪ] ADV étonnamment; **a. enough, he arrived** chose étonnante, il est arrivé

astonishment [ə'stɒnɪʃmənt] N étonnement m, stupéfaction f; **look of a.** regard m étonné ou stupéfait; **I fell back in a.** j'ai failli en tomber à la renverse; **to my a.** à mon grand étonnement; **to everyone's a.** à la stupéfaction générale

astound [ə'staʊnd] VT abasourdir, frapper de stupeur, stupéfier; **I was astounded by it** j'en ai été stupéfait; **you a. me!** c'est stupéfiant!

astounding [ə'staʊndɪŋ] ADJ abasourdissant, renversant; **a., but true!** incroyable, mais vrai!

astrakhan [æstrə'kæn] N (fur) astrakan m; **a. coat** manteau m d'astrakan

astral ['æstrəl] ADJ Astron (body etc) astral, -aux
▸▸ **a. projection** projection f astrale

astray [ə'streɪ] ADV, ADJ PRED (lost) égaré; (morally) dévoyé; **to go a.** (of person, letter etc) s'égarer; (morally) se dévoyer, se détourner du droit chemin; **my pen seems to have gone a.** j'ai égaré mon stylo; **to come a.** (of hair) se détacher; (of wires) se débrancher; **to lead sb a.** (with false information) égarer qn, induire qn en erreur; (morally) dévoyer qn, détourner qn du droit chemin

astride [ə'straɪd] ADV Horseriding à califourchon; **to ride a.** monter à califourchon
PREP **to stand a. sb/sth** enjamber qn/qch; **to sit a. sth** être à cheval ou à califourchon sur qch

astringency [ə'strɪndʒənsɪ] N virulence f, acrimonie f

astringent [ə'strɪndʒənt] ADJ Med astringent; Fig (person, voice etc) caustique
N Med astringent m

astringently [ə'strɪndʒəntlɪ] ADV (to say) d'une voix péremptoire; **a. worded** virulent

astrologer [ə'strɒlədʒər] N astrologue mf

astrological [æstrə'lɒdʒɪk(ə)l] ADJ astrologique

astrology [ə'strɒlədʒɪ] N astrologie f

astronaut ['æstrənɔːt] N astronaute mf

astronautics [æstrə'nɔːtɪks] N astronautique f VOIR GRAMMAIRE A10

astronomer [ə'strɒnəmər] N astronome mf

astronomic(al) [æstrə'nɒmɪk, -ɪk(ə)l] ADJ (year, unit etc) astronomique; Fig **an a. price** un prix astronomique; **an a. failure/disaster** un échec/désastre aux proportions astronomiques

astronomically [æstrə'nɒmɪklɪ] ADV astronomiquement; Fig (to increase) de façon astronomique; **it's a. expensive** ça coûte les yeux de la tête

astronomy [ə'strɒnəmɪ] N astronomie f

astrophysicist [æstrəʊ'fɪzɪsɪst] N astrophysicien, -ienne

astrophysics [æstrəʊ'fɪzɪks] N astrophysique f VOIR GRAMMAIRE A10

Astro Turf® ['æstrəʊtɜːf] N pelouse f artificielle

astute [ə'stjuːt] ADJ (shrewd) astucieux; (person) astucieux, malin, f maligne

astutely [ə'stjuːtlɪ] ADV astucieusement, avec finesse; **she realized a. that …** elle a eu la finesse de se rendre compte que …

astuteness [ə'stjuːtnɪs] N astuce f, finesse f

asunder [ə'sʌndər] ADV Arch, Lit (to pieces) **to tear sth a.** mettre qch en pièces; **the family had been torn a. by war** la famille avait été déchirée par la guerre; **to break a.** se casser en deux

asylee [æsaɪ'liː] N = personne f qui a obtenu l'asile politique

asylum [ə'saɪləm] N **1** (shelter) (lieu m de) refuge m; (in church etc) asile m (inviolable); **to seek a.** chercher asile; **he was granted/ refused a.** on lui a accordé/refusé l'asile; **the right to** or **of a.** le droit d'asile; **political a.** asile politique **2** Arch (hospital etc) hospice m; (for lunatics) asile m d'aliénés

asylum-seeker N demandeur, -euse d'asile

asymmetric(al) [eɪsɪ'metrɪk, -ɪk(ə)l] ADJ asymétrique; **a charmingly a. room** une pièce dont l'asymétrie fait le charme

asymmetry [eɪ'sɪmɪtrɪ] N asymétrie f

asymptomatic [eɪsɪmptə'mætɪk] ADJ Med asymptomatique

asymptote ['æsɪmptəʊt] N Math asymptote f

asynchronous [eɪ'sɪŋkrənəs] ADJ Comput, Cin, TV asynchrone
▸▸ **a. data transmission** transmission f de données asynchrone

AT [æt, unstressed ət]

| à **1–3, 9** | ■ dans la direction de **7** | ■ en **6** |

PREP VOIR GRAMMAIRE A68; B54 **1** (place) à; **at the centre/the top** au centre/sommet; **at table/ church/school/the station** à table/l'église/ l'école/la gare; **at my side** à mes côtés, à côté de moi; **at hand** sous la main; **at Oxford** à l'université d'Oxford; **at sea** en mer; **at home** à la maison, chez soi; **at my uncle's/ the dentist's** chez mon oncle/le dentiste; **to sit at the window** être assis près de la fenêtre

2 (time) à; **at six o'clock** à six heures; **at present** à présent; **at that time** (period) à cette époque, en ce temps-là; **at all times** tout le temps; **at the weekend** (pendant ou durant) le week-end; **at a time when …** à un moment où …; **two at a time** deux par deux, deux à la fois; **at the beginning of the year** au début de l'année; **at night** la nuit, le soir; **at (the age of) 20** à 20 ans

3 (price, speed, height etc) à; **at two euros a pound** à deux euros la livre; **at 30 mph** à 30 mil(l)es l'heure; **at an altitude of 10,000 feet** à une altitude de 10 000 pieds; **at 5 feet 2 inches, he was too short** avec ses 5 pieds 2 pouces, il était trop petit; **at minus 13°** à moins 13°; **at a rate of 2 cm a year** à un rythme de 2 cm par an

4 (state, condition) **to be at war/peace** être en guerre/paix; **she's not at her best in the morning** le matin, elle n'est pas au mieux de sa forme; **Skye is at its most beautiful in early June** c'est au début juin que Skye est la plus belle; **at all events** en tout cas; **we'll leave it at that for today** nous en resterons là pour aujourd'hui

5 (resulting from) **at my request/invitation** sur ma demande/mon invitation; **at a word from her, he left the room** il a suffi qu'elle prononce un mot pour qu'il quitte la pièce

6 *(skill)* **quick at repartee** prompt à la repartie; **to be good/bad at mathematics** être fort/faible en mathématiques; **to be good at games** être sportif; **she's very good at making people feel welcome** elle est très douée pour mettre les gens à l'aise

7 *(direction)* vers, dans la direction de; **to look at sb/sth** regarder qn/qch; **to aim at sb** viser qn; **to throw sth at sb/sth** jeter qch sur qn/qch; **to laugh at sb** se moquer de qn; **to swear at sb** jurer contre qn; **to shout at sb** crier après *ou* contre qn; *Fam* **she is always (on) at him** elle est toujours après lui, elle lui casse tout le temps les pieds; *Fam* **he's been on at me to do it** il me casse les pieds pour que je le fasse; **at him!** *(to dog)* attaque!

8 *(cause)* **to be surprised/delighted at sth** être étonné/enchanté de qch; **to be angry at sb** être fâché contre qn; **I'm very excited at the idea of going to Rome** je suis très content à l'idée d'aller à Rome

9 *(activity)* **to be at work** être au travail; **to be hard at work on a project** travailler dur sur un projet; **schoolchildren at play** élèves en récréation; **he's at his beekeeping again** le revoilà à s'occuper de ses abeilles; **I've been at this all morning** je suis là-dessus depuis ce matin; **to keep sb at it** faire trimer qn; **keep at it!** continue!; **she's at it again!** voilà qu'elle recommence!, la voilà qui recommence!; **they're at it again!** *(arguing, having sex)* ils remettent ça!; **they're always at it over something** ils sont toujours à se disputer pour une chose ou pour une autre; **while we are at it** pendant que nous y sommes; **it's an old idea and a rather poor one at that!** cette idée est démodée, et d'ailleurs elle n'est pas très bonne!

10 *Fam* **where are we at?** *(situation, in book etc)* où en sommes-nous?; **where's he at politically?** *(what are his views)* politiquement, il se situe où?; **Paris is where it's at!** c'est à Paris que ça se passe!; **that's not where I'm at** *(not my style)* ce n'est pas mon genre; **jazz is not really where I'm at** le jazz, ce n'est pas vraiment mon trip; **that's where I was at musically** c'est ce que j'écoutais (à l'époque)

11 *Comput (in e-mail address)* arobase *f*, a commercial; **gwilson at transex, dot, co, dot, uk** gwilson, arobase, transex, point, co, point, uk

---

atavism ['ætəviz(ə)m] **N** atavisme *m*

atavistic [ætə'vistik] **ADJ** atavique

ataxia [ə'tæksiə], **ataxy** [ə'tæksi] **N** *Med* ataxie *f*, **locomotor a.** ataxie locomotrice progressive, tabes *m* dorsalis

ate **PT** *see* **eat**

atheism ['eiθiz(ə)m] **N** athéisme *m*

atheist ['eiθiist] **N** athée *mf*

atheistic(al) [eiθi'istik, -ik(ə)l] **ADJ** athée

Athenian [ə'θi:niən] **ADJ** athénien, d'Athènes
N Athénien, -ienne

Athens ['æθənz] **N** Athènes *f*
▸▸ *Naut* **A. Convention** Convention *f* d'Athènes

athlete ['æθli:t] **N** athlète *mf*; *Med* **a.'s foot** pied *m* d'athlète, mycose *f*

athletic [æθ'letik] **ADJ** athlétique; **she's very a.** c'est une sportive; **an a.-looking young man** un jeune homme à l'allure sportive; **I don't do anything very a.** je ne fais pas beaucoup de sport

athletically [æθ'letikli] **ADV** de façon athlétique

athletics [æθ'letiks] **NPL** *(usu with sing verb)* athlétisme *m*
▸▸ **a. club** société *f* d'athlétisme

at-home **N** réception *f*, *(in evening)* soirée *f*

---

athwart [ə'θwɔ:t] *Naut* **ADV** en travers, par le travers
PREP en travers de

atishoo [ə'tiʃu:] **INT** *(sneeze)* atchoum!

Atlantic [ət'læntik] **N the A.** l'(océan *m*) Atlantique *m*
ADJ *(coast etc)* atlantique
▸▸ *Naut* **A. liner** transatlantique *m*; **the A. Ocean** l'(océan) Atlantique; **A. Standard Time** = heure *f* d'hiver des Provinces Maritimes du Canada et d'une partie des Caraïbes

Atlantis [ət'læntis] **N** *Myth* Atlantide *f*

Atlas ['ætləs] **N** *Myth* Atlas
▸▸ *Geog* **the A. Mountains** l'Atlas *m*

atlas ['ætləs] **N 1** *(book)* atlas *m* **2** *Anat* atlas *m* **3** *Archit (pl* **atlantes** [ət'lænti:z]*)* atlante *m*, télamon *m*

ATM [eiti:'em] **N 1** *Banking (abbr* **automated teller machine***)* DAB *m* **2** *Tel (abbr* **asynchronous transfer mode***)* ATM *m*

atmosphere ['ætməsfiər] **N** *(of earth, air)*, *Phys* atmosphère *f*, *Fig* atmosphère, ambiance *f*, *Fig* **there was a bit of an a. in the office** l'atmosphère était plutôt tendue au bureau; *Fig* **there was a great a.** il y avait une de ces ambiances; *Fig* **the place has no a.** l'endroit est impersonnel

atmospheric [ætməs'ferik] **ADJ** *(pressure, condition etc)* atmosphérique; *Fig (novel)* plein d'atmosphère; *(lighting, music)* qui met dans l'ambiance; **the music was very a.** la musique vous mettait complètement dans l'ambiance

atmospherics [ætməs'feriks] **NPL** *Radio etc (interference)* (parasites *mpl*) atmosphériques *fpl*

ATOL [æ'tol] **N** *(abbr* **air travel organizer's licence***)* licence *m* d'organisateur de voyages par avion

atoll ['ætol] **N** *Geog* atoll *m*

atom ['ætəm] **N** *Phys* atome *m*; *Fig* **not an a. of common sense** pas un grain de bon sens; **smashed to atoms** réduit en miettes *ou* en poudre
▸▸ *Mil, Nucl* **a. bomb** bombe *f* atomique

atomic [ə'tomik] **ADJ** *(energy, war, weapon, explosion)* atomique, nucléaire; *Phys (weight, number etc)* atomique; **the a. age** l'ère *f* ou l'âge *m* atomique
▸▸ *Mil, Nucl* **a. bomb** bombe *f* atomique; **a. physicist** atomiste *mf*, **a. reactor** réacteur *m* nucléaire

atomization [ætəmai'zeiʃən] **N** *(of fuel)* atomisation *f*, pulvérisation *f*

atomize ['ætəmaiz] **VT** *(matter)* atomiser; *(fuel)* atomiser, pulvériser; *(in spray, liquid)* vaporiser

atomized ['ætəmaizd] **ADJ** *(life, society)* fragmenté

atomizer ['ætəmaizər] **N** atomiseur *m*; **an a. spray** un atomiseur, un vaporisateur

atonal [ei'təun(ə)l] **ADJ** *Mus* atonal, -aux

▸ **atone for** [ə'təun] **VT INSEP** *(sin, crime)* expier; *(mistake, behaviour)* racheter, réparer

atonement [ə'təunmənt] **N** *(for sin, crime)* expiation *f*, *(for mistake, behaviour)* réparation *f* *(for* de*)*; **in a. for a wrong** en réparation d'un tort; *Rel* **to make a.** expier; *Jewish Rel* **Day of A.** Fête *f* du Grand Pardon

atop [ə'top] **PREP** *esp Lit* en haut de, au sommet de; **sitting a. a suitcase** assis sur une valise

ATP [eiti:'pi:] **N** *Chem (abbr* **adenosine triphosphate***)* ATP *m*

at-risk **ADJ** **an a. group** un groupe *ou* une population à risque

atrium ['eitriəm] **N 1** *Archit* atrium *m* **2** *Anat* oreillette *f*

---

atrocious [ə'trəuʃəs] **ADJ 1** *Fam (very bad)* *(pun, weather, journey etc)* atroce, exécrable; *(hat etc)* affreux; *(behaviour, manners, mess)* ignoble; *(injuries)* atroce; **his French is a.** son français est très mauvais; **his singing is a.** il chante atrocement *ou* affreusement mal **2** *(crime)* atroce; **a. act** atrocité *f*

atrociously [ə'trəuʃəsli] **ADV 1** *Fam (very badly)* exécrablement; **a. bad** atroce, exécrable **2** *(cruelly)* atrocement

atrociousness [ə'trəuʃəsnis] **N 1** *(of crime)* atrocité *f* **2** *Fam (of pun, weather etc)* caractère *m* exécrable *ou* atroce; **we could scarcely believe the a. of the weather** nous avions peine à croire qu'il faisait un temps aussi exécrable *ou* atroce

atrocity [ə'trositi] **N 1** *(act)* atrocité *f* **2** *(of crime)* atrocité *f*

atrophied ['ætrəfid] **ADJ** atrophié

atrophy ['ætrəfi] **N** atrophie *f*
VT atrophier
VI s'atrophier

at-sign **N** *Typ* arobase *f*

attaboy ['ætəbɔi] **INT** *Fam* bravo!

attach [ə'tætʃ] **VT 1** *(join)* attacher, fixer *(to* à*)*; *(two things)* attacher; *(document)* annexer, joindre; **the climbers were attached to each other by a rope** les alpinistes étaient reliés *ou* accrochés les uns aux autres par une corde; **the attached letter** la lettre ci-jointe; **please find attached …** *(in letter)* veuillez trouver ci-joint …; *(in e-mail)* veuillez trouver ci-joint …, veuillez trouver en annexe ….; **the two pieces of paper weren't attached** *(to each other)* les deux feuilles de papier étaient indépendantes; *(enclosed)* les deux feuilles n'étaient pas jointes; **house with garage attached** maison avec garage attenant; **the kitten attached himself to her** *(followed her)* le chaton l'a adoptée

2 *(assign)* *(importance)* prêter, attacher *(to* à*)*; *(blame)* imputer *(to* à*)*; **official attached to another department** fonctionnaire détaché à un autre service; **to be attached to a unit** être affecté à une unité

3 *Law (property, salary)* mettre une saisie-arrêt sur

4 *Comput (file)* joindre *(to* à*)*; **to a. a file to an e-mail** joindre un fichier à un message électronique

VI 1 to a. to *(fix on to)* s'accrocher à; *(of appliance, shelves) (to wall)* se fixer à; *(of rope, hook)* être relié à

2 no blame attaches to the crew l'équipage n'est nullement à blâmer

attaché [ə'tæʃei] **N** attaché *m*; **military a.** attaché militaire
▸▸ **a. case** mallette *f*, attaché-case *m*, *pl* attachés-cases

attached [ə'tætʃt] **ADJ 1 to be a. to sb/sth** *(fond of)* être attaché à qn/qch; **she became very a. to the dog** elle s'est beaucoup attachée au chien **2 the only woman not a.** *(not married)* la seule femme qui soit libre; **is he a. (to anyone) at the moment?** est-ce qu'il a quelqu'un en ce moment?

attachment [ə'tætʃmənt] **N 1** *(for machine)* accessoire *m*; **lathe with drilling a.** tour *m* avec accessoire pour foret

2 *(act)* *(of object)* fixation *f* *(to* à*)*; *(of document)* annexation *f* *(to* à*)*

3 *(fastener)* attache *f*, lien *m*; **attachments of a muscle** attaches d'un muscle

4 *(secondment)* rattachement *m*, stage *m*; **to serve an a. with the French army** faire un stage dans l'armée française; **to be on a. to a department** être détaché à un service

5 *(fondness)* attachement *m* *(for sb* pour qn; *to sth* à qch*)*, affection *f* *(for* pour*)*; **to form an a. for sb** s'attacher à qn, se prendre d'affection pour qn; **because of his a. to the**

idea à cause de l'attachement qu'il portait à cette idée

6 *Law* arrêt *m*, saisie *f*, saisie-arrêt *f*, *pl* saisies-arrêts; **a. of real property** saisie immobilière

7 *Comput (of e-mail)* fichier *m* joint

attack [ə'tæk] **N 1** *Mil, Sport* attaque *f*; **combined a.** attaque combinée; **to be/come under a. from sb** être attaqué par qn; **to launch an a.** lancer une attaque; **a. is the best form of defence** l'attaque est la meilleure forme de défense

2 *(on person)* agression *f*, attaque *f* (**on** contre); *Pol* attentat *m*

3 *(strong criticism)* attaque *f* (**on sb** contre qn; **on sth** de *ou* contre qch); **an a. on freedom of speech/on the right to strike** une atteinte à la liberté d'expression/au droit de grève

4 *Med (of asthma etc)* attaque *f*, crise *f*, *(of fever)* poussée *f*; **a. of nerves** *(nervousness)* trac *m*; *(hysteria)* crise de nerfs; **to have an a. of the shakes** être pris de tremblements; **to have an a. of giddiness** être pris de vertiges; **an a. of self-doubt** une crise de doute

5 *Mus (of note)* attaque *f*

VT 1 *Mil, Sport* attaquer; **to be attacked** subir une attaque, être attaqué; *Fig* **the government is attacking our rights** le gouvernement porte atteinte à nos droits

2 *(person) (in street etc)* agresser, attaquer

3 *(criticize) (person, project etc)* attaquer; *(abuse of sth etc)* s'attaquer à

4 *(set about with energy) (task, problem etc)* s'attaquer à

5 *(of disease) (person, organ etc)* s'attaquer à, atteindre; *(of rust) (metal)* attaquer, s'attaquer à, ronger; *(of fear, doubts)* assaillir

VI attaquer

► ► **a. dog** chien *m* d'assaut

attacker [ə'tækər] **N** attaquant, -ante, agresseur *m*, assaillant, -ante; *Sport* attaquant, -ante; **could you describe your a.?** pourriez-vous décrire votre agresseur?

attacking [ə'tækɪŋ] **ADJ** attaquant; *(game, play)* d'attaque

attagirl ['ætəgɜːl] **INT** *Fam* bravo!

attain [ə'teɪn] **VT** *(great age, one's ends, success etc)* atteindre, parvenir à, arriver à; *(high rank, position)* s'élever jusqu'à, parvenir à; *(knowledge)* acquérir; *(ambition)* réaliser; *(happiness)* atteindre; **to a. a reputation** se faire une réputation (**for** de)

VI *Fml* **to a. to perfection** atteindre la perfection; **to a. to power** arriver au pouvoir

attainable [ə'teɪnəb(ə)l] **ADJ** *(dream, ambition etc)* réalisable

attainment [ə'teɪnmənt] **N 1** *(no pl) (achieving) (of goal, ambition)* réalisation *f*, *(of independence)* obtention *f*; *(of happiness)* conquête *f*; **for the a. of his purpose** pour atteindre ses fins, pour arriver à ses fins **2** *(skill, achievements) (usu pl)* **attainments** *(knowledge)* connaissance(s) *f(pl)*; *(skills)* talents *mpl*; **a man of considerable attainments** un homme qui a beaucoup d'instruction *ou* d'acquis; **her linguistic attainments** sa connaissance des langues

attempt [ə'tempt] **N 1** *(effort)* tentative *f*, essai *m*; **an a. at a smile** l'esquisse *f* d'un sourire; **was that an a. at an apology?** est-ce que c'était censé être une excuse?; **her feeble a. to justify herself** la piètre tentative qu'elle a faite pour se justifier; **without (making) any a. at concealment** sans chercher à se cacher; **they made no a. to help** ils n'ont pas essayé d'aider; **a. to escape** tentative d'évasion; **to make an a. at (doing) sth** *or* **to do sth** essayer *ou* tâcher de faire qch; **he made an a. at 'War and Peace'** il a essayé de lire 'Guerre et paix'; **to make an a. on a record** *or* **to beat a record** essayer de battre

un record; **to make an a. on Everest** tenter l'ascension de l'Everest; **first a.** coup *m* d'essai, première tentative; **it wasn't bad for a first a.** ce n'était pas mal pour une première tentative *ou* un premier essai; **at the first a.** du premier coup; **at the fourth a.** à la quatrième tentative, au quatrième coup; **to make another a.** renouveler ses tentatives, revenir à la charge; **to give up the a.** y renoncer; **he died in the a.** il est mort en essayant

2 *(attack)* attentat *m*; **a. on sb's life** tentative *f* d'assassinat; **to make an a. on sb's life** attenter à la vie de qn

VT **to a. to do sth** essayer *ou* tenter de faire qch, chercher à faire qch; **he attempted to get up** il essaya *ou* tenta de se lever; **he attempted a smile** il s'efforça de sourire; **to a. a piece of work** entreprendre un travail; **candidates must a. five questions** les candidats doivent traiter cinq questions; **to a. the impossible** tenter l'impossible; **attempted murder/theft** tentative *f* d'assassinat/de vol

attend [ə'tend] **VI 1** *(be present)* être présent; **two delegates did not a.** deux délégués étaient absents

2 *(pay attention)* faire attention

3 *Fml (serve)* **to a. on sb** servir qn, être au service de qn

VT 1 *(go to) (church, school, funeral)* aller à; *(be present at) (conference, meeting)* assister à; *(course)* suivre; **the lectures are well attended** les cours sont très suivis; **the celebrations were well attended** les cérémonies ont attiré beaucoup de monde

2 *(of doctor) (sick person)* soigner, donner des soins à

3 *Lit Fml (accompany)* accompagner; **success attended my efforts** mes efforts furent couronnés de succès; **it was attended by considerable publicity** cela s'est accompagné d'une vaste publicité

4 *Fml (serve)* **we were attended by three waiters** nous étions servis par trois garçons; **to a. a prince** suivre *ou* accompagner un prince

► **attend to VT INSEP 1** *(deal with) (matter)* s'occuper de; *(one's business)* vaquer à; *(one's interests)* veiller à; *(one's health, appearance)* soigner; *(order)* exécuter; **I shall a. to it** je m'en occuperai, je m'en chargerai **2** *(customer etc)* s'occuper de; **are you being attended to?** est-ce qu'on s'occupe de vous? **3** *(pay attention to)* faire *ou* prêter attention à; **a. to what I'm saying** écoutez attentivement ce que je dis

attendance [ə'tendəns] **N 1** *(presence) (at meeting)* présence *f*, **regular a.** assiduité *f*; **school a.** fréquentation *f* scolaire; **church attendances have fallen** le nombre de personnes qui vont à l'église a baissé; **his a. has been good/bad** il a été/il n'a pas été assidu; **poor a.** manque *m* d'assiduité

2 *(people present)* assistance *f*, **there was a good a. at the meeting** il y avait une assistance nombreuse à la réunion; **there was a record a. at the final** la finale a attiré un nombre record de spectateurs; **the evening class had to be cancelled because of poor a.** le cours du soir a dû être annulé pour manque d'élèves

3 **to be in a. on** *(of doctor) (sick person)* donner ses soins à; *(of courtier) (king etc)* être de service auprès de; **with six bodyguards in a.** accompagné de six gardes du corps; **in close a.** à proximité

► ► *Br* **a. allowance** = allocation *f* pour les handicapés; **a. list** *(for meetings)* liste *f* de présence; **a. register** registre *m* de présence; **a. sheet** *(for meetings)* feuille *f* de présence

attendant [ə'tendənt] **N 1** *(official)* surveillant, -ante; *(in public lavatory, cloakroom*

etc) préposé, -ée; *(in museum, car park etc)* gardien, -ienne; *(in theatre)* ouvreuse *f*, **(petrol-)pump a.** pompiste *mf*, **swimming pool a.** maître *m* nageur **2** *(usu pl)* **attendants** *(of king etc)* gens *mpl*, suite *f*

ADJ *Fml* **a. on sb/sth** qui accompagne qn/qch; **famine and its a. diseases** la famine et les maladies dont elle s'accompagne

► ► *Law* **a. circumstances** *(of crime etc)* circonstances *fpl* concomitantes

attending [ə'tendɪŋ] **ADJ** *Med* **the a. physician** le médecin traitant

attention [ə'tenʃən] **N 1** *(concentration, thought)* attention *f* (**to** à); **a. to details** attention portée aux détails; **a. to truth** souci *m* de vérité; **to pay a. to sth** faire attention à qch; **to pay a.** *or* **give one's a. to sb** prêter attention à qn; **she didn't pay a. in class** elle n'a pas été attentive en cours; **to give sb/sth one's full a.** consacrer toute son attention à qn/qch; **you have my undivided a.** je suis tout à vous; **the report will receive our full a.** nous prêterons une attention toute particulière à ce rapport; **your a. please, ladies and gentlemen** mesdames et messieurs, votre attention s'il vous plaît; **particular a. should be given to posture** surveillez tout particulièrement votre attitude; *Admin, Com* **for the a. of Mr Green** à l'attention de M. Green; **to turn one's a. to sth** diriger son attention vers qch, porter son attention sur qch; **she constantly switched her a. between the two conversations** elle passait sans cesse d'une conversation à l'autre; **to call** *or* **attract** *or* **draw (sb's) a. to sth** attirer l'attention (de qn) sur qch, faire remarquer qch (à qn); **to draw a. to oneself** se faire remarquer; *Fml* **it has been brought to our a. that …** il a été porté à notre connaissance que …, on nous a fait savoir *ou* remarquer que …; **to catch sb's a.** attirer *ou* capter l'attention de qn; **to attract everybody's a.** fixer tous les regards; **to hold** *or* **engage sb's a.** retenir l'attention de qn; **to get a.** *(of application, plan etc)* être considéré; **the child doesn't get much a. at home** on ne s'occupe pas beaucoup de cet enfant chez lui; **he gets all the a.** il n'y en a que pour lui; **he just does it to get a.** il ne fait ça que pour se faire remarquer; **she likes being the centre of a.** elle aime être le centre du monde; *(at party)* elle aime se faire remarquer

2 *(maintenance)* soins *mpl*, entretien *m*; **the engine needs** *or* **requires some a.** le moteur a besoin d'entretien *ou* d'être entretenu; **the batteries require daily/monthly a.** les accus exigent un entretien journalier/mensuel; **the bathroom looks as if it needs some a.** la salle de bains a besoin d'être un peu retapée

3 *Old-fashioned* **attentions** *(acts of affection)* attentions *fpl*, prévenances *fpl*, empressement *m*; **he was always paying his wife little attentions** il était toujours plein d'attentions *ou* de prévenances pour sa femme; **to pay one's attentions to a lady** faire la cour à une dame

4 *Mil* **a.!** garde-à-vous!; **to come to a.** se mettre au garde-à-vous; **to stand at a.** être *ou* se tenir au garde-à-vous

► ► *Med* **a. deficit** déficit *m* de l'attention, déficit attentionnel; *Med* **a. deficit hyperactivity disorder** syndrome *m* hyperkinétique de l'enfant, syndrome de l'enfant hyperactif; **a. span** capacité *f* de concentration

attention-seeking [-siːkɪŋ] **N** **it's just a.** il/elle/*etc* ne cherche qu'à attirer l'attention sur lui/elle/*etc*

ADJ **her a. behaviour** son besoin constant de se faire remarquer

attentive [ə'tentɪv] **ADJ 1** *(pupil, listener, audience etc)* attentif (**to** à); *(in one's work)* soigneux; **she is very a. to detail** elle porte une grande attention aux détails **2** *(anxious to please, considerate)* prévenant, empressé, attentionné; **to be very a. to sb** être très attentionné pour qn, être très empressé auprès de qn; **she was a. to his every need** elle était aux petits soins pour lui; *esp Fml* **thank you, most a.** merci, c'est très aimable à vous

> When translating **attentive**, note that **attentif** and **attentionné** are not interchangeable. **Attentif** refers to someone who pays attention and **attentionné** to someone who is considerate.

attentively [ə'tentɪvlɪ] ADV attentivement

attentiveness [ə'tentɪvnɪs] N **1** *(concentration)* attention *f* **2** *(anxiety to please)* prévenances *fpl*, empressement *m* (**to** auprès de qn); **to look after sb with a.** être plein de prévenances pour qn

attenuate [ə'tenjʊeɪt] VT **1** *(seriousness of sth etc)* atténuer; **attenuating circumstances** circonstances *fpl* atténuantes **2** *Tech (gas etc)* raréfier
  VI *Tech* s'atténuer, diminuer

attenuation [ətenjʊ'eɪʃən] N atténuation *f*

attenuator [ə'tenjʊeɪtər] N *TV etc* atténuateur *m*

attest [ə'test] VT **1** *(affirm, prove) (fact)* attester; **to a. that ...** attester que ...; **the document attests the fact that ...** le document atteste que ...; *Agr* **attested herd** troupeau *m* tuberculiné **2** *(of witness) (thing)* affirmer sous serment; *(signature)* légaliser; **attested copy** copie *f* certifiée **3** *Law (person)* assermenter
  VI **to a. to sth** *(be evidence of)* témoigner de qch; *(give evidence of)* attester qch

attestation [æte'steɪʃən] N *Law* **1** *(of witness)* déposition *f*, témoignage *m* **2** *(of fact)* attestation *f* **3** *(of signature)* légalisation *f* **4** *(oath-taking)* prestation *f* de serment

at-the-money option N *St Exch* option *f* au cours, option à la monnaie

attic ['ætɪk] N grenier *m*
  ▸▸ **a. room** mansarde *f*; **a. window** fenêtre *f* en mansarde; *(skylight)* lucarne *f*

Attica ['ætɪkə] N *Hist Lit* Attique *f*

attire [ə'taɪər] N *Fml, Hum (clothing)* tenue *f*
  VT *Arch, Lit (usu passive or reflexive)* vêtir, parer; **attired in black/silk** vêtu de noir/soie

attitude ['ætɪtjuːd] N **1** *(of mind)* attitude *f*, **what's your a. to people who say that?** que pensez-vous des gens qui disent cela?; **what's your a. to abortion?** que pensez-vous de l'avortement?, quelle est votre attitude face à l'avortement?; **old-fashioned attitudes** des idées *fpl* démodées; **their a. is that ...** leur point de vue est que ...; **she takes the a. that ...** elle considère que ...; **his whole a. is 'I don't care'** tout lui est égal; **I don't like your a.** je n'aime pas ton attitude; **well, if that's your a.** très bien, si c'est comme ça que tu le prends; **she's got an a. problem** elle n'est pas du tout coopérative; *Fam* **she's got a.** elle a du caractère; *Fam* **a car with a.** une voiture qui a du caractère **2** *(pose)* attitude *f*, pose *f*; **to strike an a.** prendre une attitude dramatique, poser **3** *Mktg (of consumer to product)* attitude *f* **4** *Aviat etc (of plane, missile etc on its trajectory)* attitude *f*
  ▸▸ *Mktg* **a. research** enquête *f* d'attitudes; **a. scale** échelle *f* d'attitudes; **a. survey** enquête *f* d'attitudes

attn *abbr* **attention**

attorney [ə'tɜːnɪ] N *Law* **1** *Am (lawyer)* avocat, -ate; *Am* **District A.** ≃ procureur *m* de la République **2** *(legal agent)* procureur *m*, fondé *m* de pouvoir(s)
  ▸▸ **A. General** *(in England, Wales and North-*

ern Ireland) = principal avocat *m* de la couronne; *(in US)* ≃ ministre *m* de la Justice; *(in Canada)* procureur général

attract [ə'trækt] VT *(of magnet, person, advert etc)* attirer (**to** à, vers); **he is not attracted to her** elle ne lui plaît pas, *Fam* elle ne lui dit rien; **I was sexually attracted to her** elle m'attirait physiquement; **what really attracts me to him is his sense of humour** ce qui me plaît chez lui, c'est son sens de l'humour; **the prospect of a week in London doesn't a. me** ça ne me dit rien d'aller passer une semaine à Londres; **how does that a. you?** qu'est-ce que tu dis de ça?

attraction [ə'trækʃən] N **1** *(act, power)* attraction *f*, attirance *f* (**to** vers); **wealth has no a. for her** elle n'est pas attirée par la richesse; **the prospect holds little/no a. for me** cette perspective ne me dit pas grand-chose/rien du tout; **I can't** *or* **don't see the a. of it** je n'en vois pas l'intérêt; **his a. to her** son attirance pour elle **2** *(thing, person)* attraction *f*; **the chief a.** *(at fair)* la grande attraction; *(in show etc)* le clou; **tourist a.** attraction pour touristes; **it's the main a. of the job** c'est ce que cet emploi a de plus attrayant **3** *(of person) (usu pl)* **physical attractions** charmes *mpl* physiques; **that's one of my attractions** cela fait partie de mes charmes

attractive [ə'træktɪv] ADJ **1** *(person, offer, manner, prospect etc)* attrayant, attirant; *(house, town, region)* beau, *f* belle; *(village)* coquet; *(price)* intéressant, attrayant, attractif; **do you find him a.?** il te plaît?, tu le trouves séduisant?; **in an a. shade of blue** dans une jolie teinte de bleu **2** *(magnet, properties)* attractif, attirant

attractively [ə'træktɪvlɪ] ADV d'une manière attrayante *ou* séduisante; **a. bound in red leather** élégamment relié de cuir rouge; **an a. laid out garden** un jardin qui est un plaisir pour les yeux; **a. priced** à un prix attrayant *ou* attractif

attractiveness [ə'træktɪvnɪs] N attrait *m*; **the a. of their prices/offer** leurs prix attrayants/leur offre attrayante

attributable [ə'trɪbjʊtəb(ə)l] ADJ *(words, success, work of art)* attribuable (**to** à); *(crime, fault etc)* imputable (**to** à)
  ▸▸ *Acct* **a. profit** bénéfices *mpl* nets

attribute[1] ['ætrɪbjuːt] N **1** *(quality)* attribut *m* **2** *Gram* épithète *f* VOIR GRAMMAIRE A17 **3** *Comput* attribut *m*

attribute[2] [ə'trɪbjuːt] VT *(work of art, success etc)* attribuer (**to** à); *(quality, words)* prêter, attribuer (**to** à); *(mistake, error, crime etc)* imputer (**to** à)

attribution [ætrɪ'bjuːʃən] N *(of words, work of art etc)* attribution *f* (**to** à); *(of crime, fault etc)* imputation *f* (**to** à)

attributive [ə'trɪbjʊtɪv] *Gram* VOIR GRAMMAIRE A17 ADJ épithète
  N épithète *f*
  ▸▸ **a. adjective** épithète *f*

attributively [ə'trɪbjʊtɪvlɪ] ADV *(word used)* avec valeur d'épithète VOIR GRAMMAIRE A17

attrition [ə'trɪʃən] N **1** *(wearing away)* usure *f* par le frottement; **policy of a.** politique *f* d'usure; **war of a.** guerre *f* d'usure **2** *Econ, Ind* attrition *f*, départs *mpl* volontaires

attune [ə'tjuːn] VT accorder, harmoniser (**to** avec); **ear attuned to every sound** oreille exercée à saisir tous les sons; **to a. oneself** *or* **become attuned to sth** se faire à qch, s'accoutumer à qch

ATW [eɪtiː'dʌb(ə)ljuː] *(abbr* **around the world)** autour du monde

atypical [eɪ'tɪpɪk(ə)l] ADJ atypique

aubergine ['əʊbəʒiːn] N *Br Culin* aubergine *f*

auburn ['ɔːbən] ADJ *(hair)* châtain roux, auburn *inv*

auction ['ɔːkʃən] N **1** *Com* **(sale by) a., a. sale** vente *f* aux enchères; *(for fish, vegetables etc)* (vente à la) criée *f*; **car a.** vente aux enchères de voitures; **to sell by a.** *or* **at a.** vendre aux enchères; *(fish etc)* vendre à la criée; **to put sth up for a.** mettre qch aux enchères; **the estate is up for a.** le domaine va être mis *ou* vendu aux enchères **2** *Cards* enchère *f*
  VT *(put up for auction)* mettre aux enchères; *(sell)* vendre aux enchères; *(foodstuffs, building by legal authority)* vendre à la criée
  ▸▸ *Cards* **a. bridge** bridge *m* aux enchères; **a. room** salle *f* des ventes; *(for fish, vegetables etc)* chambre *f* des criées
  ▸ **auction off** VT SEP vendre aux enchères

auctioneer [ɔːkʃə'nɪər] N commissaire-priseur *m*, *pl* commissaires-priseurs; *(at fish or vegetable market etc)* crieur, -euse

audacious [ɔː'deɪʃəs] ADJ **1** *(daring) (attempt, neckline)* audacieux, hardi **2** *(insolent)* effronté, hardi

audaciously [ɔː'deɪʃəslɪ] ADV **1** *(bravely)* audacieusement, avec audace **2** *(insolently)* effrontément

audacity [ɔː'dæsɪtɪ] N **1** *(bravery)* audace *f*, intrépidité *f*, hardiesse *f* **2** *(nerve)* audace *f*, effronterie *f*; **to have the a. to do sth** avoir l'audace de faire qch

audibility [ɔːdɪ'bɪlɪtɪ] N perceptibilité *f*, audibilité *f*

audible ['ɔːdɪb(ə)l] ADJ *(sound)* perceptible (à l'oreille); *(speech, voice)* audible; **he was scarcely a.** on l'entendait à peine
  ▸▸ *Phys* **a. frequency** fréquence *f* audible

audibly ['ɔːdɪblɪ] ADV *(to speak)* de façon à être entendu; *(to yawn, purr)* bruyamment

audience ['ɔːdɪəns] N **1** *(spectators, listeners)* assistance *f*; *Theat* spectateurs *mpl*, auditoire *m*, public *m*; *Radio* auditeurs *mpl*; *TV* téléspectateurs *mpl*; *Mktg (for product, advertisement)* public; **the whole a.** applauded toute la salle applaudit; **do we have any Americans in the a.?** y a-t-il des Américains dans la salle?; **to perform before a large a.** se produire devant un nombreux public VOIR GRAMMAIRE A11 **2** *Fml (with king, pope etc)* audience *f*; **to grant sb an a.** donner audience *ou* accorder une audience à qn; **to hold an a.** tenir une audience
  ▸▸ **a. chamber** salle *f* d'audience; *Mktg* **a. exposure** exposition *f* au public; *Radio, TV* **a. figures** indice *m* d'écoute; *Radio, TV* **a. measurement** mesure *f* de l'audience; **a. participation** participation *f* de l'assistance (à ce qui se passe sur la scène); *Radio, TV* **a. rating** indice d'écoute; *Mktg* **a. research** études *fpl* d'audience; *Radio, TV* **a. share** part *f* d'audience; *Radio, TV* **a. show** émission *f* en public; *Mktg* **a. size** audience *f* cumulée; *Mktg* **a. study** étude *f* d'audience

> Note that the French word **audience** is rarely a translation for the English word **audience**.

audio ['ɔːdɪəʊ] ADJ ATTRIB sonore
  N son *m*
  ▸▸ **a. book** livre *m* audio; **a. cassette** cassette *f* audio; **a. cassette recorder** magnétophone *m* à cassette; **a. CD** CD *m* audio; **a. (control) console** pupitre *m* son; **a. equipment** équipement *m* acoustique; **a. feedback** effet *m* Larsen, bouclage *m*; *Phys* **a. frequency** audiofréquence *f*; **a. library** sonothèque *f*, phonothèque *f*; **a. logo** logo *m* audio; **a. recording** enregistrement *m* sonore; **a. response** réponse *f* acoustique; **a. signal** signal *m* audio, signal son; **a. system** système *m* audio; **a. tape** bande *f* magné-

tique audio; **a. tape recorder** magnéto-phone à bande; **a. track** piste *f* son

audioconference [ˈɔːdɪəʊkɒnfərəns] **N** au-dioconférence *f*

audiometer [ˈɔːdɪəʊmiːtər] **N** *Tech* audio-mètre *m*

audiotyping [ˈɔːdɪəʊtaɪpɪŋ] **N** audiotypie *f*

audiotypist [ˈɔːdɪəʊtaɪpɪst] **N** audiotypiste *mf*

audiovisual [ɔːdɪəʊˈvɪzjʊəl] **ADJ** audiovi-suel
▸▸**a. archives** archives *fpl* audiovisuelles; **a. equipment** équipement *m* audiovisuel, matériel *m* audiovisuel

audit [ˈɔːdɪt] **N** *Fin* audit *m* (comptable), vé-rification(s) *f(pl)* comptable(s), apurement *m*; *Econ* **internal a.** contrôle *m* interne
VT 1 *Fin (accounts)* vérifier, apurer, examiner **2** *Am Univ (course)* assister en auditeur libre à
▸▸*Admin* **A. Office** ≃ Cour *f* des Comptes; **a. trail** *Comput* protocole *m* de vérification *ou* de contrôle; *Fin* vérification *f* à rebours

auditing [ˈɔːdɪtɪŋ] **N** vérification *f* et certifi-cation *f* des écritures, apurement *m*

audition [ɔːˈdɪʃən] **N** *Theat, Mus etc* audi-tion *f*; **I've got an a.** je vais passer une audi-tion; **she didn't even get an a.** elle n'a même pas obtenu d'audition
VT & VI *Theat, Mus etc* auditionner (**for a part** pour un rôle)

auditor [ˈɔːdɪtər] **N 1** *Admin* vérificateur, -trice des comptes **2** *Com, Fin* audit *m*, audi-teur, -trice; *(of company)* commissaire *m* aux comptes; *(of insurance company)* censeur *m*; **firm of auditors** cabinet *m* d'audit, cabinet comptable **3** *(at conference, lecture etc)* audi-teur, -trice; *Am Univ* auditeur, -trice libre
▸▸**auditors' report** rapport *m* des vérificateurs

auditorium [ɔːdɪˈtɔːrɪəm] **N** auditorium *m*; *(of theatre, concert hall)* salle *f*, *(lecture theatre)* amphithéâtre *m*

auditory [ˈɔːdɪtrɪ] **ADJ** *Anat (nerve etc)* au-ditif; **the a. organ** l'organe *m* de l'ouïe

AUEW [eɪjuːiːˈdʌb(ə)ljuː] **N** *Br Formerly abbr* **Amalgamated Union of Engineering Workers**

Aug *abbr* **August**

Augean [ɔːˈdʒiːən] **ADJ** *Myth* **the A. Stables** les écuries *fpl* d'Augias

auger [ˈɔːgər] **N** *Carp* tarière *f*

aught [ɔːt] **N** *Arch, Lit* quelque chose *m*, quoi que ce soit; **for a. I know** (pour) autant que je sache

augment [ɔːgˈment] **VT** *Fml* augmenter, ac-croître (**with, by** de); *Mus* **augmented inter-val** intervalle *m* augmenté; *Mktg* **augmented product** produit *m* augmenté
VI *Fml* augmenter, s'accroître

augmentation [ɔːgmenˈteɪʃən] **N** *(of for-tune etc)* augmentation *f*, accroissement *m*

augur [ˈɔːgər] *Lit* **VT** augurer, présager, pré-dire; **it augurs no good** cela ne présage *ou* n'annonce rien de bon
VI **it augurs well/ill** c'est de bon/de mauvais augure (**for** pour); **it doesn't a. well for the future** cela ne présage *ou* n'annonce rien de bon
N *(prophet)* augure *m*

augury [ˈɔːgjʊrɪ] **N 1** *Fml (sign)* augure *m*, présage *m* **2** *(practice)* science *f* des augu-res, science augurale

August [ˈɔːgəst] **N** VOIR GRAMMAIRE A81–2; B61–2
août *m*; **in A.** au mois d'août, en août; **(on) the first/the seventh of A.** le premier/le sept août

august [ɔːˈgʌst] **ADJ** *(assembly)* auguste; *(bearing, figure)* imposant, majestueux

Augustinian [ɔːgəˈstɪnɪən] **ADJ** *Rel, Hist* au-gustinien, de saint Augustin; **A. monk** *or* **friar** Augustin *m*
N *Rel* Augustin, -ine

Augustus [ɔːˈgʌstəs] **N** Auguste

auk [ɔːk] **N** *(bird)* alque *f*, **great a.** grand pin-gouin *m*

auld [ɔːld] **ADJ** *Scot* vieux, *f* vieille
▸▸*Mus* **A. Lang Syne** = chanson *f* sur l'air de "ce n'est qu'un au revoir" que l'on chante à minuit le soir du 31 décembre en Grande-Bretagne

aunt [ɑːnt] **N** tante *f*
▸▸*Br* **A. Sally** *(at fairground)* ≃ jeu *m* de massacre; *Fig (person)* tête *f* de Turc

auntie, aunty [ˈɑːntɪ] **N 1** *Fam* tatie *f*, tata *f*, tantine *f*; **A. Julia** tatie *ou* tata Julia **2** *Br Sl* **Auntie** = surnom *m* affectueux de la BBC, perçue comme une vieille tante détentrice des valeurs morales

AUP [eɪjuːˈpiː] **N** *Comput (abbr* **Acceptable Use Policy***)* = code *m* de conduite défini par un fournisseur d'accès à l'Internet

au pair [əʊˈpeər] **N** *(jeune fille f)* au pair *f*; **she's working as an a.** elle travaille au pair
ADV she's staying with them a. elle est chez eux au pair
VI travailler *ou* être au pair

aura [ˈɔːrə] **N 1** aura *f*, *(of place)* atmosphère *f*, **he's got an a. of …** une aura de … émane de lui **2** *Med* aura *f*; **epileptic a.** aura épileptique

aural [ˈɔːrəl] **ADJ** auditif, sonore
▸▸**a. comprehension** compréhension *f* orale; *Radio etc* **a. reception** réception *f* du son; **a. specialist, a. surgeon** auriste *mf*

Attention: ne pas confondre avec l'adjec-tif anglais **oral**.

aureola [ɔːˈriːələ], **aureole** [ˈɔːrɪəʊl] **N 1** *Art (of saint)* auréole *f* **2** *Astron (of sun)* auréole *f*

auricle [ˈɔːrɪk(ə)l] **N** *Anat* **1** *(of heart)* auri-cule *f* **2** *(external ear)* pavillon *m*

auricular [ɔːˈrɪkjʊlər] **ADJ** *Anat* auriculaire
▸▸*Rel* **a. confession** confession *f* auricu-laire

aurochs [ˈɔːrɒks] **N** *(animal)* aurochs *m*

Aurora [ɔːˈrɔːrə] **N** *Myth* Aurore

aurora [ɔːˈrɔːrə] **N** aurore *f*
▸▸**a. australis** aurore australe; **a. borealis** aurore boréale

auscultate [ˈɔːskəlteɪt] **VT** *Med* ausculter

auscultation [ɔːskəlˈteɪʃən] **N** *Med* auscul-tation *f*

auspices [ˈɔːspɪsɪz] **NPL** auspices *mpl*; **fa-vourable a.** d'heureux auspices; **under the a. of the United Nations** sous l'égide des Na-tions unies

auspicious [ɔːˈspɪʃəs] **ADJ** *(wind etc)* pro-pice, favorable; *(sign)* de bon augure; *(age)* heureux, prospère; **an a. start to a career** des débuts prometteurs dans une carrière; **on this a. occasion** en ce jour mémorable

auspiciously [ɔːˈspɪʃəslɪ] **ADV** sous d'heu-reux auspices, favorablement; **to begin a.** bien commencer

auspiciousness [ɔːˈspɪʃəsnɪs] **N** *(of begin-ning)* aspect *m* prometteur; **the a. of this omen** cet heureux auspice

Aussie [ˈɒzɪ] *Fam* **ADJ** australien
N 1 Australien, -ienne **2** *Ling* anglais *m* australien

austere [ɒˈstɪər] **ADJ** *(life, style, person etc)* austère; *(home)* sans luxe, d'un goût sévère, austère

austerely [ɒˈstɪəlɪ] **ADV** austèrement, avec austérité; *(to live)* dans l'austérité, austère-ment; *(furnished)* sans luxe, de façon dépouillée

austerity [ɒˈsterɪtɪ] **N** *(of life, style, person, home etc)* austérité *f*
▸▸*Econ* **a. measures** mesures *fpl* d'austérité

Australasia [ɒstrəˈleɪʒə, -ˈleɪʃə] **N** Australa-sie *f*

Australasian [ɒstrəˈleɪʒən, -ˈleɪʃən] **ADJ** australasien
N Australasien, -ienne

Australia [ɒˈstreɪlɪə] **N** Australie *f*

Australian [ɒˈstreɪlɪən] **ADJ** australien
N 1 Australien, -ienne **2** *Ling* anglais *m* australien

Austria [ˈɒstrɪə] **N** Autriche *f*

Austria-Hungary **N** *Hist* Autriche-Hon-grie *f*

Austrian [ˈɒstrɪən] **ADJ** autrichien
N Autrichien, -ienne

Austro-Hungarian [ɒstrəʊ-] **ADJ** *Hist* aus-tro-hongrois; **the A. Empire** l'empire *m* d'Au-triche-Hongrie

autarchy [ˈɔːtɑːkɪ] **N** autarchie *f*

autarky [ˈɔːtɑːkɪ] **N** autarcie *f*

auteur [ɔːˈtɜːr] **N** *Cin* auteur *m*

authentic [ɔːˈθentɪk] **ADJ** *(document, fact, story etc)* authentique

authentically [ɔːˈθentɪklɪ] **ADV** authen-tiquement

authenticate [ɔːˈθentɪkeɪt] **VT 1** *(prove genuine)*, *Law* authentifier **2** *Mil, Radio (cor-respondent)* identifier

authenticity [ɔːθenˈtɪsɪtɪ] **N** authenticité *f*

author [ˈɔːθər] **N** *(of book, plan etc)* auteur *m*; **to be an a.** être écrivain; *Lit* **to be the a. of one's own misfortunes** être l'artisan de ses malheurs; *Typ* **a.'s correction** correction *f* d'auteur

authoress [ˈɔːθəres] **N** *Old-fashioned* femme *f* auteur, écrivain *m*

authoritarian [ɔːθɒrɪˈteərɪən] **ADJ, N** auto-ritaire *mf*

Attention: ne pas confondre avec **authoritative**.

authoritative [ɔːˈθɒrɪtətɪv] **ADJ** *(statement, book, document etc)* qui fait autorité; **to have sth from an a. source** avoir qch de source autorisée *ou* de bonne source

Attention: ne pas confondre avec **authoritarian**.

authoritatively [ɔːˈθɒrɪtətɪvlɪ] **ADV 1** *(commandingly)* autoritairement; *(to look)* d'un air autoritaire **2 I can state a. that …** je puis affirmer de source sûre que …

authority [ɔːˈθɒrɪtɪ] **N 1** *(power)* autorité *f*, **those in a.** les autorités; **in a position of a.** en position d'autorité; **to be in a.** être *or* exer-cise a. **over sb** *(officially)* avoir *ou* exercer une autorité sur qn; *(have power)* avoir de l'ascendant sur qn; **an air of a.** un air auto-ritaire
2 *(authorization)* autorisation *f*, mandat *m*; **to have a. to act** avoir qualité pour agir; **to give sb a. to do sth** autoriser qn à faire qch; **they had the full a. of the law** ils ont agi avec la pleine autorité de la loi; **to act on sb's a.** agir sur l'autorité de qn; **to do sth on one's own a.** faire qch de sa propre autorité; **on what a./on whose a. did they search the house?** avec quelle autorisation/avec l'au-torisation de qui ont-ils perquisitionné la maison?
3 *(of person, book)* **to be an a.** être expert dans la matière; **to be an a. on sth** faire au-torité en matière de qch; **to have sth on good a.** tenir *ou* savoir qch de bonne part *ou* de bonne source *ou* de source autorisée; **to quote sb as one's a.** se réclamer de qn; **to quote one's authorities** citer ses sources *ou*

ses auteurs; **she spoke with a.** elle a parlé avec autorité

4 *Admin* **the authorities** les autorités *fpl*; *(government)* l'administration *f*; **the health authorities** les services *mpl* de santé; **the military authorities** les autorités militaires

authorization [ɔːθəraɪˈzeɪʃən] N autorisation *f* (**to do sth** de faire qch); *(given to official)* pouvoir *m*, mandat *m*; **to give sb/to be given a. to do sth** donner à qn/recevoir l'autorisation de faire qch

authorize [ˈɔːθəraɪz] VT *(person, thing)* autoriser (**to do sth** à faire qch); **to be authorized to act on sb's behalf** avoir qualité pour agir au nom de qn; **to a. a payment** ordonnancer un paiement; **to a. a price** homologuer un prix

authorized [ˈɔːθəraɪzd] ADJ autorisé; *(supplier etc)* agréé; *Mil etc* réglementaire; **a. to sign** habilité à signer
▸▸ *Com* **a. agent** mandataire *mf*, agent *m* mandataire; *Fin* **a. capital** capital *m* autorisé *ou* social *ou* nominal; *Admin* **a. charges** prix *mpl* homologués; **a. distributor** distributeur *m* agréé; *Banking* **a. overdraft facility** autorisation *f* de découvert; *Com* **a. representative**, agent mandataire; *St Exch* **a. share capital** capital autorisé; **a. signatory** signataire *mf* autorisé(e) *ou* accrédité(e); *Rel* **the A. Version** = la traduction anglaise de la Bible de 1611

authorship [ˈɔːθəʃɪp] N *(of book, plan etc)* paternité *f*; **to establish the a. of a book** identifier l'auteur d'un livre; **a manuscript of unknown a.** un manuscrit d'un auteur anonyme

autism [ˈɔːtɪz(ə)m] N *Med* autisme *m*

autistic [ɔːˈtɪstɪk] *Med* ADJ autistique, autiste
N autiste *mf*

auto [ˈɔːtəʊ] N *Am Fam* auto(mobile) *f*, voiture *f*; **a. accident** accident *m* de voiture

auto- [ˈɔːtəʊ] PREF auto-

auto-addresser [-ədresər] N *(on laser printer)* adressage *m* automatique

auto-answer N *Comput (in datacomms)* réponse *f* automatique

auto-antigen [-ˈæntɪdʒən] N *Med* auto-antigène *m*

autobank [ˈɔːtəʊbæŋk] N distributeur *m* automatique de billets

autobiographic(al) [ɔːtəʊbaɪəˈɡræfɪk, -ɪk(ə)l] ADJ autobiographique

autobiography [ɔːtəʊbaɪˈɒɡrəfɪ] N autobiographie *f*

autocade [ˈɔːtəʊkeɪd] N *Am* cortège *m* de voitures

autocorrect [ˈɔːtəʊkərekt] VT *Comput* corriger automatiquement

autocracy [ɔːˈtɒkrəsɪ] N autocratie *f*

autocrat [ˈɔːtəkræt] N autocrate *m*

autocratic(al) [ɔːtəˈkrætɪk, -ɪk(ə)l] ADJ *(government, policies)* autocratique; *(person)* autocrate; *(character)* absolu

autocratically [ɔːtəˈkrætɪklɪ] ADV autocratiquement

autocue [ˈɔːtəkjuː] N *TV* téléprompteur *m*

autodial [ˈɔːtəʊdaɪəl] N numérotation *f* automatique

autodialler [ˈɔːtəʊdaɪələr] N numéroteur *m* automatique

autodidact [ˈɔːtəʊdaɪdækt] N *Fml* autodidacte *mf*

auto-dissolve N *TV, Cin* fondu *m* enchaîné automatique

autoerotic [ˈɔːtəʊrɪˈrɒtɪk] ADJ autoérotique

autoexec. bat [ɔːtəʊeksekˈbæt] N *Comput* **a. (file)** fichier *m* autoexec. bat

m; **a. camera, camera with a.** appareil *m* autofocus

autogenous [ɔːˈtɒdʒɪnəs] ADJ *Biol, Metal* autogène

autogiro [ɔːtəʊˈdʒaɪrəʊ] N *Aviat* autogyre *m*

autograft [ˈɔːtəɡrɑːft] N *Med* autogreffe *f*

autograph [ˈɔːtəɡrɑːf] N autographe *m*
VT *(book, photo, programme etc)* signer, dédicacer
▸▸ **a. album** album *m* de signatures; **a. collector, a. hunter** collectionneur, -euse d'autographes

autogyro [ɔːtəʊˈdʒaɪrəʊ] = **autogiro**

auto-ignition N auto-allumage *m*

autoload [ˈɔːtəʊləʊd] VI *Comput* se charger automatiquement

automat [ˈɔːtəmæt] N *Am Old-fashioned* cafétéria *f* à distributeurs automatiques

automatable [ˈɔːtəmeɪtəb(ə)l] ADJ automatisable

automate [ˈɔːtəmeɪt] VT automatiser

automated [ˈɔːtəmeɪtɪd] ADJ automatisé
▸▸ *Banking* **a. clearing house** chambre *f* de compensation automatisée; **a. reservation** réservation *f* télématique; *Banking* **a. teller machine** distributeur *m* automatique (de billets); **a. ticket** billet *m* informatisé; *Banking* **a. withdrawal** retrait *m* automatique

automatic [ɔːtəˈmætɪk] ADJ **1** automatique; **fully a.** entièrement automatique **2** *(movement)* automatique, inconscient, machinal, -aux
N **1** *Aut* (voiture *f*) automatique *f*; **a Renault® a.** une Renault® (avec boîte de vitesses) automatique **2** *(pistol)* automatique *m*
▸▸ *Comput* **a. backup** sauvegarde *f* automatique; *Comput* **a. data processing** traitement *m* automatique des données; *Tel* **a. dialling** composition *f* automatique de numéros; *Comput* **a. feed** avance *f* automatique; *Radio, Elec* **a. gain control** antifading *m*; *Comput* **a. line break** coupure *f* automatique de fin de ligne; *Comput* **a. pagination** séparation *f* automatique des pages; *Aviat* **a. pilot** pilote *m* automatique; *Fig* **to do sth on a. pilot** faire qch mécaniquement *ou* machinalement; **a. pistol** pistolet *m* automatique, automatique; **a. search** *(on cassette player)* recherche *f* automatique (de séquences musicales); **a. ticket distributor** distributeur *m* automatique de titres de transport; **a. ticket machine** billetterie *f* automatique; *Banking* **a. transfer** virement *m* automatique; *Aut* **a. transmission** transmission *f* automatique; *Radio, Elec* **a. volume control** antifading

automatically [ɔːtəˈmætɪklɪ] ADV **1** automatiquement; **a. renewable** renouvelable automatiquement **2** *(without thinking)* sans réfléchir, automatiquement

automation [ɔːtəˈmeɪʃən] N automatisation *f*

automatization [ɔːtɒmətaɪˈzeɪʃən] N automatisation *f*

automaton, *pl* **automatons, automata** [ɔːˈtɒmətən, -ɒnz, -ə] N automate *m*

automobile [ˈɔːtəməʊbiːl] N *Am* automobile *f*, voiture *f*
▸▸ **A. Association** = société *f* de dépannage pour les automobilistes, ≃ Touring Club *m* de France; **a. club** club *m* automobile; **the a. industry** l'industrie *f* automobile; **a. manufacture** fabrication *f* d'automobiles; **a. workers** ouvriers *mpl* de l'industrie automobile

automotive [ɔːtəˈməʊtɪv] ADJ **1** *(self-propelled)* automoteur, -trice **2** *Aut* automobile
▸▸ *Am* **a. engineering** technique *f* automobile; **a. parts** pièces *fpl* d'automobile

autonomous [ɔːˈtɒnəməs] ADJ autonome

autonomy [ɔːˈtɒnəmɪ] N autonomie *f*

autopilot [ˈɔːtəʊpaɪlət] N *Aviat* pilotage *m* automatique; **to be on a.** *(of aircraft), Fig (person)* être en pilotage automatique

autopsy [ˈɔːtɒpsɪ] N autopsie *f*; **to carry out an a.** faire une autopsie; *esp Pol, Fig* faire une analyse
VT autopsier

auto-redial N renumérotation *f* automatique

auto-refresh N *Comput* autorafraîchissement *m*

autoresponder [ɔːtəʊrɪˈspɒndər] N *Comput* fonction *f* de réponse automatique

autoreverse [ɔːtəʊrɪˈvɜːs] N autoreverse *m*, inversion *f* automatique du sens de défilement

autosave [ˈɔːtəʊseɪv] N *Comput* sauvegarde *f* automatique

autosome [ˈɔːtəsəʊm] N *(in genetics)* chromosome *m* somatique

autostart [ˈɔːtəʊstɑːt] N *Comput* démarrage *m* automatique

autosuggestion [ɔːtəʊsəˈdʒestʃən] N *Psy* autosuggestion *f*

autoswitch [ˈɔːtəʊswɪtʃ] N *Comput* commutateur *m* automatique

autowinder [ˈɔːtəʊwaɪndər] N *Phot* avance *f* automatique du film

autumn [ˈɔːtəm] N automne *m*; **in a.** en automne; **a. colours** couleurs *fpl* automnales *ou* de l'automne; **a. leaves** feuilles *fpl* d'automne; **a. plants** plantes *fpl* automnales; **an a. evening** une soirée d'automne; *Lit* **he was in the a. of his years** il était à l'automne de sa vie VOIR GRAMMAIRE A81; B61
▸▸ *Bot* **a. crocus** safran *m* cultivé

autumnal [ɔːˈtʌmn(ə)l] ADJ automnal, -aux, d'automne; **there was an a. feeling in the air, it was a.** il y avait de l'automne dans l'air; **a. shades** teintes *fpl* automnales
▸▸ *Astron* **a. equinox** équinoxe *m* d'automne

auxiliary [ɔːɡˈzɪlɪərɪ, -zɪlərɪ] ADJ *(staff, troops etc)* auxiliaire; *(machine etc)* auxiliaire, de secours; *(heating, lighting)* d'appoint VOIR GRAMMAIRE A38–9; A57–61; B26–8; B39–40
N auxiliaire *mf*; *Gram* (verbe *m*) auxiliaire *m*; *Mil* **auxiliaries** (troupes *fpl*) auxiliaires *mpl*; **nursing a.** infirmier, -ière auxiliaire
▸▸ *Aut* **a. driving lamps** feux *mpl* facultatifs; *Gram* **a. verb** (verbe) auxiliaire VOIR GRAMMAIRE A38–9; A57–61; B26–8; B39–40

AV [eɪˈviː] **1** *(abbr* **Authorized Version)** = traduction *f* anglaise de la Bible de 1611 **2** *(abbr* **audiovisual)** audiovisuel

Av *(abbr* **avenue)** av.

avail [əˈveɪl] N **of no a., without a.** sans effet; **to be of little a.** être peu utile *ou* peu avantageux; **to no a.** sans résultat; **to work to little or no a.** travailler sans (grand) résultat; **their efforts were all to no a.** leurs efforts n'ont produit aucun résultat
VT **to a. oneself of sth** *(of guidebook, map)* se servir *ou* s'aider de qch; *(of offer)* profiter de qch; *(of right)* user *ou* faire usage de qch; *(of sb's services)* faire appel à qch; **to a. oneself of the opportunity to do sth** saisir l'occasion de faire qch
VI *Lit* **nothing availed against the storm** contre la tempête nous ne pouvions/il ne pouvait/*etc* rien

availability [əveɪləˈbɪlɪtɪ] N *(of materials, people etc)* disponibilité *f*; **offer subject to a.** dans la limite des stocks disponibles; *(of tickets)* dans la limite des places disponibles

available [əˈveɪləb(ə)l] ADJ *(worker, room, theatre seat etc)* disponible; **they used the time a. to evacuate the area** ils ont utilisé le temps dont ils disposaient pour évacuer le secteur; **capital that can be made a.** capitaux *mpl* mobilisables; **a. to download from our web site** peut être téléchargé à partir de notre site Web; **a. on CD-ROM/DVD** existe en CD-ROM/DVD; **a. for work** disponible; **when are you a. to start work?** à partir de quand pouvez-vous commencer à travailler?; **a. for delivery** livraison immédiate; *Com* **a. in all bookshops** en vente *ou* disponible chez tous les libraires; *Com* **also a. in white** existe également en blanc; *Com* **we regret that this offer is no longer a.** nous avons le regret de vous annoncer que cette offre n'est plus valable; **drugs are readily a. in the town** on se procure facilement de la drogue dans cette ville; **legal aid should be a. to everyone** l'assistance juridique devrait être accessible à tous; **I'm catching the first a. flight** je prends le premier avion; **they're not readily a.** il est difficile de s'en procurer; **a. means** moyens *mpl* disponibles; **to try every a. means** essayer tous les moyens possibles

▸▸*Fin* **a. assets** actif *m* disponible *ou* liquide; *Fin* **a. balance** solde *m* disponible; **a. bed capacity** capacité *f* d'accueil; *Fin* **a. capital** capitaux disponibles; *Fin* **a. cash flow** cash-flow *m* disponible; *Fin* **a. funds** fonds *mpl* liquides *ou* disponibles, disponibilités *fpl*; *Phot* **a. light** lumière *f* naturelle; *Mktg* **a. market** marché *m* effectif; *Comput* **a. memory** mémoire *f* disponible

aval [æ'væl] N *Banking* aval *m* bancaire

avalanche ['ævəlɑːntʃ] N (*of snow*), *Fig* (*of congratulations, mail etc*) avalanche *f*; **an a. of tourists** une nuée de touristes

avalize ['ævəlaɪz] VT *Banking* avaliser

avant-garde [ævɒŋ'gɑːd] N avant-garde *f, pl* avant-gardes
ADJ d'avant-garde, avant-gardiste; **a. films** films *mpl* d'avant-garde

avarice ['ævərɪs] N cupidité *f*

avaricious [ævə'rɪʃəs] ADJ cupide

avariciously [ævə'rɪʃəslɪ] ADV (*to behave*) cupidement

avast [ə'vɑːst] INT *Naut Old-fashioned* tiens bon!, tenez bon!, baste!

AVC [eɪviː'siː] N (*abbr* **additional voluntary contribution**) supplément *m* de cotisation retraite (*payé volontairement*)

Ave¹ ['ɑːvɪ] N
▸▸**A. Maria** Avé (Maria) *m inv*

Ave² (*abbr* **avenue**) av.

avenge [ə'vendʒ] VT (*person, crime*) venger; **to a. oneself for an insult/on sb** se venger d'une injure/de qn

avenger [ə'vendʒər] N vengeur *m*, vengeresse *f*

avenging [ə'vendʒɪŋ] ADJ (*angel etc*) vengeur, *f* vengeresse

avenue ['ævɪnjuː] N **1** allée *f*, (*with trees*) avenue *f*, *Fig* **to explore every a.** explorer toutes les voies; **this opens up another a. of investigation** ceci ouvre une nouvelle voie de recherche; **an a. to fame/wealth** un moyen de parvenir à la gloire/fortune **2** (*in street name*) avenue *f* **3** *esp Am* (*wide street*) boulevard *m*

aver [ə'vɜːr] VT (**-rr-**) *Lit* déclarer, affirmer (**that** que)

average ['ævərɪdʒ] N **1** moyenne *f*; **on a.** en moyenne; **to work out the a.** établir la moyenne; **that gives an a. of 6** ça fait une moyenne de 6; **above (the) a.** au-dessus de la moyenne; **to spend an a. of £85 per week** dépenser en moyenne 85 livres par semaine

2 (*in marine insurance*) avarie(s) *f(pl)*
3 *St Exch* indice *m*
ADJ (*price, time, weight etc*) moyen; **the a. Englishman** l'Anglais *m* moyen; **of a. height**

de taille moyenne; **the food is better than a.** la nourriture est au-dessus de la moyenne; **no better than a.** pas si bien que ça; **far from a.** exceptionnel; **in an a. week** dans une semaine ordinaire; **how was your day? – a.** comment s'est passée ta journée? – moyen; *Fam* **a very a. singer** un chanteur de qualité très moyenne

VT **1** (*amount to on average*) **to a. 500** atteindre une moyenne de 500; **sales a. a thousand copies a year** la vente moyenne *ou* la moyenne des ventes est de mille exemplaires par an; **to a. eight hours' work a day** travailler en moyenne huit heures par jour; **to a. 85 kph** rouler en moyenne à 85 km/h; **household spending averages £120 per week** les dépenses des ménages sont de *ou* atteignent les 120 livres par semaine en moyenne

2 (*calculate average of*) (*results, sales etc*) calculer *ou* faire la moyenne de

▸▸**a. adjuster** dispacheur *m*, expert-répartiteur *m, pl* experts-répartiteurs; **a. adjustment** dispache *f, Fin* **a. cost** coût *m* moyen; *Radio* **a. listening time** durée *f* d'écoute par auditeur, DEA *f, Fin* **a. revenue** produit *m* moyen; *Fin* **a. unit cost** coût moyen unitaire; *TV* **a. viewing time** durée d'écoute par téléspectateur, DET *f, Fin* **a. yield** rendement *m* moyen

▸**average out** VT SEP (*calculate average of*) **I've averaged out how much I spend a week** j'ai calculé combien je dépense en moyenne par semaine

VI **how does it a. out per week?** combien ça fait en moyenne par semaine?; **it'll a. out over a month** sur un mois ça s'équilibrera

▸**average out at** VT INSEP (*amount to as an average*) équivaloir en moyenne à; **what does it a. out at?** ça fait combien en moyenne?

averse [ə'vɜːs] ADJ opposé (**to** à); **to be a. to sth** (*to task, job*) répugner à qch; (*to criticism, change etc*) détester qch; **to be a. to doing sth** répugner à faire qch; **why are you so a. to the idea of helping?** pourquoi l'idée d'apporter ton aide te répugne-t-elle tant?; **he is not a. to a glass of beer** il prend volontiers un verre de bière

> Attention: ne pas confondre avec le mot anglais **adverse**.

aversion [ə'vɜːʃən] N **1** (*feeling*) aversion *f*; **to feel** *or* **have an a. to sb** ressentir de l'aversion pour *ou* envers qn; **to feel** *or* **have a great a. to sth/to doing sth** avoir horreur *f* de qch/de faire qch **2** (*thing*) objet *m* d'aversion; **my pet a.** ma bête noire

avert [ə'vɜːt] VT **1** (*eyes, one's gaze, thoughts*) détourner (**from** de) **2** (*suspicion, danger, misfortune*) écarter, éloigner, prévenir; (*catastrophe, accident, war*) éviter, parer à, conjurer; (*blow*) détourner

aviary ['eɪvɪərɪ] N volière *f*

aviation [eɪvɪ'eɪʃən] N aviation *f*; **a. history** histoire *f* de l'aviation

aviator ['eɪvɪeɪtər] N *Old-fashioned* aviateur, -trice

aviculture ['eɪvɪkʌltʃər] N aviculture *f*

avid ['ævɪd] ADJ passionné, fervent (**for** de); **to be a. for sth** être avide de qch; **a. reader** lecteur, -trice passionné(e)

avidity [ə'vɪdɪtɪ] N avidité *f* (**for** de, pour)

avidly ['ævɪdlɪ] ADV avidement, avec avidité

avionics [eɪvɪ'ɒnɪks] N avionique *f* [VOIR GRAMMAIRE A10]

avocado [ævə'kɑːdəʊ] N (*fruit*) avocat *m*; (*tree*) avocatier *m*
▸▸**a. pear** avocat

Avogadro's number [ævəʊ'gædrəʊz] N *Chem* nombre *m* d'Avogadro

avoid [ə'vɔɪd] VT (*person, thing*) éviter; (*punishment, blow etc*) se soustraire à; (*sb's attentions, blow, difficulty*) esquiver; (*truth, fact*) nier; **you've been avoiding me** tu m'évites; **to a. doing sth** éviter de faire qch; **I could not a. speaking to him** je ne pouvais faire autrement que de lui parler; **to a. (paying) tax** échapper à *ou* se soustraire à l'impôt; **to a. sb like the plague** fuir qn comme la peste; **to a. sth like the plague** éviter qch à tout prix; **he avoided doing his homework until the last possible minute** il a reculé le moment de faire ses devoirs jusqu'à la dernière minute; **the comparison is hard to a.** la comparaison est difficile à éviter; **to a. sb's eye** fuir le regard de qn; **to a. the issue** éviter *ou* contourner le problème; *Pej* (*be devious*) esquiver la question

avoidable [ə'vɔɪdəb(ə)l] ADJ évitable
▸▸*Fin* **a. costs** coûts *mpl* évitables

avoidance [ə'vɔɪdəns] N **a. of taxes** évasion *f* fiscale; **a. of payment** non-paiement *m*

avoirdupois [ævədə'pɔɪz] N **1** poids *m* du commerce; **ounce a.** once *f* avoirdupois **2** *Hum* (*stoutness*) excès *m* de poids, embonpoint *m*

avow [ə'vaʊ] VT *Fml* **1** (*declare*) **to a. oneself a socialist** se déclarer socialiste **2** (*admit*) (*mistake*) avouer, admettre; **to a. oneself beaten** s'avouer vaincu

avowal [ə'vaʊəl] N déclaration *f*

avowed [ə'vaʊd] ADJ (*enemy, believer etc*) déclaré; **a. atheist** athée *mf* de son propre aveu

avowedly [ə'vaʊɪdlɪ] ADV de son propre aveu

avuncular [ə'vʌŋkjʊlər] ADJ paternel

AWACS ['eɪwæks] N *Mil* (*abbr* **Airborne Warning and Control System**) AWACS *m*

await [ə'weɪt] VT *Lit* attendre; *Com* **awaiting your instructions** dans l'attente de vos instructions; **soldiers awaiting discharge** soldats en instance de libération; *Com* **parcel awaiting delivery** colis en souffrance; *Com* **awaiting collection** en souffrance; *Law* **to be awaiting trial** être en instance de jugement

awake [ə'weɪk] ADJ PRED éveillé; **to stay a.** rester éveillé; **he lay a. for hours worrying** l'inquiétude l'a tenu éveillé pendant des heures; **I was a.** je ne dormais pas; **drink some coffee, and that will keep you a.** bois du café, ça te tiendra éveillé; **that noise is keeping me a.** ce bruit m'empêche de dormir; **to be a. to** (*aware of*) (*possibility*) avoir conscience de; (*danger, fact etc*) se rendre compte de, avoir conscience de; (*careful of*) (*one's interests*) veiller à

VI (*pt* **awoke** [ə'wəʊk]; *pp* **awoken** [ə'wəʊkən]) s'éveiller, se réveiller; **to a. from a deep sleep** se réveiller d'un profond sommeil; **I awoke to the sound of birds singing** à mon réveil j'ai entendu chanter les oiseaux; *Fig* **to a. to** (*danger, fact etc*) se rendre compte de, prendre conscience de; (*possibility*) prendre conscience de; **to a. from** (*illusion, dream etc*) revenir de; (*trance, unconsciousness*) sortir de

VT (*person, sb's remorse*) éveiller, réveiller; (*curiosity, suspicions, interest*) éveiller; (*hope, passion*) faire naître; *Fig* **to a. sb to sth** faire prendre conscience de qch à qn

awaken [ə'weɪk(ə)n] VT & VI = **awake** VT & VI

awakening [ə'weɪk(ə)nɪŋ] N réveil *m*

award [ə'wɔːd] N **1** (*for writer, actor etc*) prix *m*; *Mil etc* distinction *f* honorifique; *Sch etc* récompense *f*; **to make/be given an a.** décerner/recevoir un prix/une récompense; **the annual awards ceremony** la cérémonie annuelle de remise des prix; **the Oscar**

awards ceremony la cérémonie de remise des Oscars **2** *Law (money)* dommages-intérêts *mpl; (decision)* décision *f* (arbitrale), adjudication *f; (of contract)* adjudication; **to make an a.** rendre un jugement (arbitral)

VT *(prize)* décerner, adjuger; *(medal)* décerner, remettre; *(contract)* adjuger; *(high office)* conférer; *(pay increase, grant, free kick)* accorder; **she was awarded first prize** on lui a décerné le premier prix; *Law* **to sb a sum as damages** allouer *ou* attribuer une somme à qn à titre de dommages-intérêts

award-winning ADJ *(film, book etc)* primé; *(writer, actor)* à qui on a décerné un prix; **his a. performance** son interprétation qui lui a valu un prix

aware [ə'weər] ADJ **1 to be a. of sth** *(fact)* avoir connaissance *ou* conscience de qch, être au courant de qch; **I wasn't a. of him** je ne m'étais pas aperçu qu'il était là; **I am a. of all the circumstances** je connais tous les détails; **I am well** *or* **fully a. that …** je n'ignore pas que …, j'ai pleinement conscience que …; **were you a. that your husband owed money?** saviez-vous que votre mari était endetté?; **not that I am a. of** pas que je sache; **as far as I'm a.** autant que je sache; **to become a. of** *(fact)* prendre connaissance de; **I became a. of a smell of burning/a presence** j'ai senti une odeur de brûlé/une présence **2** *(well-informed)* **socially/environmentally a.** au courant *ou* informé des questions sociales/de l'environnement; **politically a.** politisé

awareness [ə'weənɪs] N *(of something)* conscience *f,* **he has little a. of the situation** il n'a guère conscience de la situation

▸▸ *Mktg* **a. rating** taux *m* de notoriété; *Mktg* **a. study** étude *f* de notoriété

awash [ə'wɒʃ] ADJ **1** *Naut (of submarine etc)* à fleur d'eau; **rocks a. at high tide** roches couvertes d'eau à marée haute **2** *(flooded)* inondé; *Fig* **to be a. with money** crouler sous l'argent; **his desk was a. with complaints** son bureau croulait sous les lettres de réclamation

AWAY [ə'weɪ] ADV **1** *(in opposite direction)* **to turn (one's face) a. from sth** détourner la tête de qch; **to look a.** détourner son regard; **the signpost pointed a. from the village** le bras du poteau indiquait une direction opposée à celle du village; **to go a.** partir, s'en aller; **to walk/drive a.** partir (à pied/en voiture); **to run/fly a.** s'enfuir/s'envoler **2** *(at a distance)* **far a.** dans le lointain, au loin; **a. in the distance** tout au loin; **the town is five miles a.** la ville est à (une distance de) cinq mil(l)es; **it's less than five minutes' walk a.** c'est à moins de cinq minutes à pied; **the church was set a. from the road** l'église était située en retrait par rapport à la route; **to hold sth a. from sth** tenir qch éloigné *ou* loin de qch

3 *(absent)* **a. from home** absent (de chez soi); **he is a.** *(from home, school etc)* il est absent; **she is a. on business** elle s'est absentée pour affaires; *Sport* **to play a.** jouer à l'extérieur

4 *(disappearance)* **to melt a.** *(of snow)* fondre; **to boil a.** s'évaporer; **to fade** *or* **die a.** *(of sound)* s'éteindre; *(of protests)* se taire; **to fritter a.** *(one's money, time)* gaspiller; **put that knife a.!** range ce couteau!

5 *(continuity)* **to work a.** travailler beaucoup *ou* *(stronger)* sans relâche; **he was coughing a.** il toussait beaucoup; **to laugh/hoot a.** ne pas s'arrêter de rire/klaxonner

6 *(elliptical)* **a. with you!** *(don't be silly)* arrête!; *esp Arch, Lit* **a. with him!** emmenez-le!; *Arch, Lit* **we must a.** il nous faut partir

7 *(in motion)* **and they're a.!** *(at beginning of*

race etc)* et ils sont partis!; *Fam* **a couple of drinks and he's a.** *(talking, doing sth)* deux verres et il est parti; *Fam* **well a.** *(progressing)* bien en train; *(drunk)* soûl

8 *(without delay)* **to do sth right** *or* **straight a.** faire qch tout de suite *ou* sur-le-champ

9 *(time)* **I knew him a. back in 1980** je l'ai connu dès 1980; **that was a. back** c'était il y a longtemps; **it's two weeks a.** c'est dans deux semaines; **Christmas is only two weeks a.** il n'y a que deux semaines jusqu'à Noël, nous ne sommes qu'à deux semaines de Noël

▸▸ *Sport* **a. game** match *m* à l'extérieur; *Sport* **a. ground** terrain *m* adverse; *Sport* **a. match** match à l'extérieur; *Sport* **the a. team** l'équipe *f* qui joue à l'extérieur, les visiteurs *mpl*

AWB [eɪdʌb(ə)lju:'bi:] N *Com (abbr* **air waybill)** LTA *f*

awe [ɔː] N *(fear)* crainte *f, (respect)* respect *m,* révérence *f,* **to strike sb with a.** *(of person)* imposer à qn un respect mêlé de crainte; *(of object, phenomenon)* faire une forte impression à qn; **to be in a. of sb/sth, to hold sb/sth in a.** *(fear)* craindre *ou* redouter qn/qch; *(respect)* avoir une crainte respectueuse de qn/qch

VT *Fml (frighten)* remplir de crainte; *(make respect)* intimider, impressionner; **the children were awed by the cathedral/the tone of her voice** les enfants ont été terriblement impressionnés par la cathédrale/le ton de sa voix; **they were awed into silence** ils tombèrent dans un silence respectueux

aweigh [ə'weɪ] ADV *Naut* **with anchor a.** l'ancre dérapée; **anchors a.!** levez l'ancre!

awe-inspiring ADJ imposant, impressionnant

awesome ['ɔːsəm] ADJ **1** *(awe-inspiring)* *(height, strength)* imposant, impressionnant; *(responsibility, task)* imposant; *(prospect)* effrayant; **the a. silence of the desert** le silence imposant du désert **2** *Am Fam (wonderful)* super

awe-struck, awe-stricken ADJ *(frightened)* terrifié; *(respectful)* intimidé, impressionné; **to be a. by sb/sth** être terriblement impressionné par qn/qch

awful ['ɔːfʊl] ADJ **1** horrible, effroyable; **to die an a. death** mourir d'une mort horrible; **that's the a. part of it** c'est cela le plus terrible; **an a. silence** un silence effroyable **2** *Fam (very bad)* horrible, affreux, abominable; **it's simply a.** c'est affreux *ou* horrible; **she's an a. woman** c'est une femme épouvantable; **what a. weather!** quel temps abominable!; **he's an a. fool** il est bien bête; **an a. lot of people** énormément de gens; **I don't care an a. lot** ça ne me fait pas grand-chose

ADV *Fam* terriblement; **I'm a. glad to see you** je suis rudement content de vous voir; **an a. long time** terriblement longtemps

awfully ['ɔːflɪ] ADV **1** terriblement, effroyablement **2** *Fam (very)* énormément; **a. funny** amusant *ou* drôle comme tout; **I'm a. sorry** je regrette infiniment *ou* énormément; **I'm a. glad** je suis rudement content; *esp Old-fashioned* **thanks a.!** merci mille fois!; **he's an a. good player** il joue affreusement *ou* terriblement bien; *Fam Hum* **a. a.** = maniérisme *m* utilisé pour décrire les manières et l'accent de la haute bourgeoisie britannique

awfulness ['ɔːfʊlnɪs] N **1** *(of situation)* horreur *f* **2** *Fam* **the a. of the weather/this place** le temps/cet endroit abominable

awhile [ə'waɪl] ADV *Am, Lit* un moment, un peu

awkward ['ɔːkwəd] ADJ **1** *(clumsy) (move-*

ment, person)* gauche, maladroit, balourd; *(sentence etc)* maladroit, gauche; **to be a. with one's hands** ne pas être habile de ses mains

2 *(embarrassed)* embarrassé, gêné

3 *(embarrassing)* embarrassant; **it would be a. if we met** une rencontre serait embarrassante; **an a. silence** un silence gêné; **to arrive at an a. moment** arriver mal à propos; **to ask a. questions** poser des questions embarrassantes

4 *(difficult, not straightforward)* incommode, peu commode; *(tool)* peu maniable; *(bend)* difficile, dangereux; **the switch is in an a. place** l'interrupteur est situé à un endroit peu accessible; **their house is a. to get to** leur maison est d'un accès difficile; **I'm sorry to be a.** *(but that doesn't suit me)* je suis désolé d'être peu accommodant; **they're just trying to be a.** ils font ça pour compliquer les choses; **the a. age** l'âge *m* ingrat; *Fam* **he's an a. customer** c'est un type difficile, il n'est pas commode

awkwardly ['ɔːkwədlɪ] ADV **1** *(clumsily)* gauchement, maladroitement; **to put sth a.** mal tourner qch, dire qch d'une façon maladroite

2 *(showing embarrassment)* d'une manière embarrassée; *(to speak)* d'un ton embarrassé *ou* gêné

3 *(causing embarrassment)* d'une façon embarrassante

4 *(inconveniently)* **the lever is a. placed** le levier est mal placé; **their house is a. situated** leur maison est mal située

awkwardness ['ɔːkwədnɪs] N **1** *(clumsiness)* gaucherie *f,* maladresse *f; (lack of grace)* balourdise *f* **2** *(embarrassment)* embarras *m,* gêne *f;* **a moment of a.** un moment de gêne **3** *(inconvenience) (of situation etc)* difficulté *f,* incommodité *f*

awl [ɔːl] N alène *f,* poinçon *m,* perçoir *m*

awn [ɔːn] N *Bot (of barley etc)* barbe *f*

awning ['ɔːnɪŋ] N *(of shop etc)* store *m,* banne *f, (of cart)* bâche *f, (of theatre, hotel etc)* marquise *f, Naut* tente *f,* tendelet *m; (on deck of boat)* cabane *f,* **rain a.** taud *m,* taude *f*

▸▸ **a. blind** store à l'italienne; **a. deck** pont-abri *m, pl* ponts-abris

AWOL ['eɪwɒl] ADJ *Mil Fam (abbr* **absent without leave) to go A.** s'absenter sans permission; **to have gone A.** être absent sans permission

awry [ə'raɪ] ADV, ADJ de travers, de guingois; **to go all a.** *(of plans etc)* aller tout de travers; **services were thrown a. by the strike** les services ont été perturbés par la grève

axe, *Am* **ax,** *pl* **axes** [æks, 'æksɪz] N **1** hache *f,* **ice a.** piolet *m; Fig* **to have an a. to grind** agir dans un but intéressé **2** *Fam* **to get the a.** *(of project etc)* être abandonné; *(of employee etc)* être mis à la porte; *(of department etc)* être supprimé; **500 threatened with a.** *(newspaper headline)* 500 personnes menacées de chômage **3** *Mus Sl (guitar)* gratte *f,* râpe *f*

VT *Fam (person, worker)* renvoyer, mettre à la porte; *(project)* abandonner (pour des raisons d'économie); *(job)* supprimer; **to a. public expenditure** tailler dans les dépenses publiques

▸▸ **a. handle** manche *m* de hache; **a. head** fer *m* de hache

axial ['æksɪəl] ADJ *Geom* axial, -aux

axil ['æksɪl] N *Bot (of leaf)* aisselle *f*

axiom ['æksɪəm] N axiome *m*

axiomatic [æksɪə'mætɪk] ADJ **1** axiomatique **2** *(self-evident)* évident

axis, *pl* **axes** ['æksɪs, 'æksiːz] N **1** *Geom, Geol etc (of sphere, plant, crystal)* axe *m;* **a. of the**

earth axe de la terre; **a. of revolution** axe de révolution **2** *Anat (of neck)* axis *m* **3** *Hist* **the A.** l'Axe *m*

axle ['æks(ə)l] **N 1** *(of vehicle)* essieu *m*; *Rail* **driving a.** essieu moteur; *Aut* **front/rear a.** essieu *ou* pont *m* avant/arrière **2** *(of wheel)* tourillon *m*, arbre *m*, axe *m*
 ▸▸ **a. box** boîte *f* de l'essieu; **a. shaft** arbre *m* d'essieu; **a. tramp** rebond *m* de l'essieu; **a. tree** essieu

ay(e) [aɪ] **INT** *esp Scot* oui, mais oui; *Naut*

a. a., sir! oui, commandant/lieutenant/*etc*! **N** *(in voting)* **ayes and noes** voix *fpl* pour et contre; **the ayes have it** les voix pour l'emportent

azalea [ə'zeɪlɪə] **N** *(plant)* azalée *f*

Azerbaijan [æzəbaɪ'dʒɑːn] **N** Azerbaïdjan *m*

Azerbaijani [æzəbaɪ'dʒɑːnɪ], **Azeri** [ə'zeə-rɪ] **ADJ** azerbaïdjanais, azéri **N** Azerbaïdjanais, -aise, Azéri, -ie

AZERTY keyboard [ə'zɜːtɪ-] **N** clavier *m* AZERTY

azimuth ['æzɪməθ] **N** *Astron etc* azimut *m*

Azores (the) [ðəə'zɔːz] **NPL** les Açores *fpl*

AZT [eɪzed'tiː] **N** *Pharm* (*abbr* **azidothymi-dine**) AZT *m*

Aztec ['æztek] *Hist* **ADJ** aztèque **N 1** Aztèque *mf* **2** *Ling* aztèque *m*

azure ['æʒər, 'eɪʒər] **N** *Her, Lit* azur *m* **ADJ** d'azur, azuré

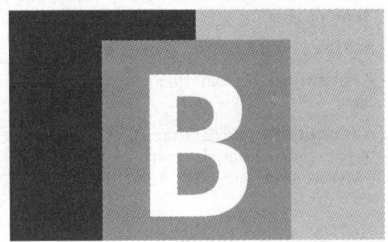

B, b¹ [biː] N **1** *(letter)* B, b *m*; **two b's** deux b; **51B** *(house number)* 51 ter; *Mil* **B company** deuxième compagnie *f* **2** *Mus* si *m*; **in B flat** en si bémol **3** *Sch (grade)* **to get a B** avoir une bonne note, ≃ avoir 14 ou 15 sur 20 **4** *Med* **B cell** lymphocyte *m* B
▸▸ *Br* **B road** route *f* secondaire; **B side** *(of record)* face *f* B

b² *(abbr* **born)** né

BA [biːˈeɪ] N *Univ (abbr* **Bachelor of Arts) to have a BA in history** ≃ avoir une licence en histoire; **John Smith, BA** ≃ John Smith, licencié ès lettres/en droit/*etc*

baa [baː] N bêlement *m*; **b.!** bêê!; **b.-lamb** *(in children's language)* petit agneau *m*
VI (**baaed, baa'd** [baːd]) bêler

baba [ˈbaːbaː] N *Culin* **rum b.** baba *m* au rhum

babble [ˈbæb(ə)l] N **1** *(incoherence)* brouhaha *m*; **the b. of voices coming from downstairs** le brouhaha qui parvenait d'en bas; **his speech was full of the usual b. about …** son discours était le verbiage habituel sur … **2** *(of stream)* murmure *m*
VI **1** *(tell secrets)* bavarder, jaser **2** *(chatter incoherently) (of baby)* babiller, gazouiller; *(of adult)* bafouiller **3** *(of stream)* murmurer, gazouiller
▸ **babble away, babble on** VI bavarder, papoter; **you were babbling away in your sleep last night** tu n'as pas arrêté de bredouiller des choses incompréhensibles dans ton sommeil cette nuit; **what are you babbling on about?** qu'est-ce que tu bafouilles encore?

babbler [ˈbæblər] N **1** *(who tells secrets)* bavard, -arde **2** *(incoherent talker)* **she's a b.** elle bafouille

babbling [ˈbæb(ə)lɪŋ] ADJ **1** *(incoherent)* bafouilleur; **I felt like a b. idiot** j'avais l'impression que je racontais n'importe quoi **2** *(stream)* murmurant
N = **babble** N

babe [beɪb] N **1** *Lit* petit enfant *m*, bambin *m*; **a b. in arms** un bébé; *Fig* un naïf, une naïve; **his mother died when he was still a b. in arms** il était encore au berceau quand sa mère mourut **2** *Fam (attractive woman)* canon *m*; **hi, b.!** salut, poupée!

Babel [ˈbeɪb(ə)l] N **the Tower of B.** la Tour de Babel; *Fig* **b. of voices** brouhaha *m*

baboon [bəˈbuːn] N *(animal)* babouin *m*; *Fig* singe *m*

baby [ˈbeɪbɪ] N **1** bébé *m*; **when I was a b.** quand j'étais bébé; **b. brother/sister** petit frère/petite sœur; **a b. boy/girl** un petit garçon/une petite fille; **b. carrots/aubergines** carottes *fpl*/aubergines *fpl* naines; **b. elephant/chimpanzee** bébé éléphant/chimpanzé; **the b. of the family** le benjamin; **you're such a b.!** tu es un vrai bébé!; **don't be such a b.** arrête de faire le bébé; **I'm not**

a **b.!** je ne suis plus un bébé!; **my b. pictures** *(of me)* des photos de moi bébé; *Fig* **to throw the b. out with the bath water** jeter le bébé avec l'eau du bain; *Fig* **to leave sb holding the b.** refiler le bébé à qn; *Fig* **the dictionary is his b.** le dictionnaire est son bébé
2 *Am Fam (girlfriend)* jeune fille *f*, nana *f*, *(boyfriend)* mec *m*; *(as form of address)* chéri, -ie; *(thing)* machin *m*; *(machine)* merveille *f*
VT (**babied**) *(person)* *Pej* *(treat as baby)* materner; *(give love and attention to)* dorloter
▸▸ **b. boom** baby boom *m*; **b. boomer** enfant *m* du baby boom; **b.'s breath** *(flower)* gypsophile *f*, *Am* **B. Buggy®** landau *m*, voiture *f* d'enfant; *Am* **b. carriage** voiture d'enfant, landau; *Mus* **b. grand** (piano *m*) demi-queue *m*, *pl* demi-queues; **b. scales** pèse-bébé *m*, *pl* pèse-bébés; *Aut* **b. seat** siège *m* auto pour bébé, siège enfant; **b. snatcher** kidnappeur, -euse; **b. snatching** enlèvement *m* ou rapt *m* d'enfant, kidnapping *m*; **b. talk** langage *m* enfantin *ou* de bébé; **b. tooth** dent *f* de lait

baby-changing area N nurserie *f*, point-bébé *m*

baby-face N visage *m* poupin; **he's a real b.** il a un visage poupin

baby-faced [-feɪst] ADJ au visage poupin

Babygro® [ˈbeɪbɪɡrəʊ] N grenouillère *f*

babyhood [ˈbeɪbɪhʊd] N petite enfance *f*

babyish [ˈbeɪbɪɪʃ] ADJ *Pej* de bébé

baby-listening service N service *m* de surveillance à distance des bébés, service babyphone

Babylon [ˈbæbɪlən] N *Antiq* Babylone *f*

Babylonia [bæbɪˈləʊnɪə] N *Antiq* Babylonie *f*

Babylonian [bæbɪˈləʊnɪən] *Antiq* ADJ babylonien
N Babylonien, -ienne

baby-minder N nourrice *f*

babyproof [ˈbeɪbɪpruːf] VT *(house, room)* sécuriser *(pour éviter qu'un bébé ne se blesse)*

baby-sit VI (**-sat, -sitting**) faire du baby-sitting, garder des/les enfants

baby-sitter N baby-sitter *mf*, *pl* baby-sitters, *Can* gardienne *f*

baby-sitting N baby-sitting *m*, garde *f* d'enfants

baby-walker N trotteur *m*

baccalaureate [bækəˈlɔːrɪət] N *Univ Am* ≃ licence *f*, *Can* baccalauréat *m*

baccara(t) [ˈbækərɑː] N *Cards* baccara *m*; **to play b.** jouer au baccara

bacchanal [ˈbækən(ə)l] *Lit* ADJ bachique
N *(orgy)* bacchanale *f*, débauche *f* bachique

bacchanalia [bækəˈneɪlɪə] NPL *Lit* bacchanales *fpl*

bacchanalian [bækəˈneɪlɪən] ADJ *Lit* bachique

baccy [ˈbækɪ] N *Old-fashioned Fam* tabac *m*

bachelor [ˈbætʃələr] N **1** célibataire *m*; **b. uncle** oncle *m* non marié **2** *Univ* ≃ licencié, -ée; *Fam* **b.'s** ≃ licence *f*, **to have a b.'s (degree) in French** ≃ avoir une licence de français; *Univ* **B. of Arts** *(person)* ≃ titulaire *mf* d'une licence de lettres; *(qualification)* licence de lettres; **B. of Laws** ≃ licencié, -ée en droit *Univ* **B. of Science** *(person)* = titulaire d'une licence de sciences; *(qualification)* licence de sciences **3** *Hist* bachelier *m* *(aspirant à la chevalerie)*; **knight b.** chevalier *m*
▸▸ *Univ* **b.'s degree** ≃ licence; **b. flat** garçonnière *f*, **b. girl** célibataire *f*

bachelorhood [ˈbætʃələhʊd], **bachelordom** [ˈbætʃələdəm] N célibat *m*, vie *f* de garçon

bacillary [bəˈsɪlərɪ] ADJ *Biol* bacillaire

bacillus, *pl* **bacilli** [bəˈsɪləs, -aɪ] N *Biol, Med* bacille *m*

BACK [bæk]

N dos **1, 2**	▪ fond **3**	▪ arrière **2, 4**
ADJ arrière **1**	▪ de derrière **1**	
ADV en arrière **1**	▪ re + *verb* **2, 3**	
VT financer **1**	▪ parier sur **2**	
▪ reculer **3**		
VI reculer		

N **1** *(of person, animal)* dos *m*; *(of chair etc)* dossier *m*; **mind your backs!** attention, s'il vous plaît!; *Fig* **to be at sb's back** *(chase, harry)* poursuivre qn; **he had two policemen at his b.** il avait deux policiers à ses trousses; **with an army at his b.** *(supporting him)* soutenu par une armée; **to do sth behind sb's b.** faire qch dans le dos de qn; **he laughs at you behind your b.** il se moque de vous quand vous avez le dos tourné; **to talk about sb behind their b.** dire du mal de qn dans son dos; **to turn one's b. on sb** tourner le dos à qn; *Fig* abandonner qn; **when my b. was turned** quand j'avais le dos tourné; **to sit/stand with one's b. to sb** tourner le dos à qn; **to sit with one's b. to the engine** s'asseoir dans le sens contraire à la marche; **sitting with one's b. to the light** assis à contre-jour; **he was sitting with his b. to the wall** il était assis, dos au mur; *Fig* **our backs were to the wall** nous étions au pied du mur; **to be glad to see the b. of sb/sth** être content d'être débarrassé de qn/qch; **I saw him only from the b.** je ne l'ai vu que de dos; **to be on one's b.** *(lying down)* être étendu sur le dos; *Fam (ill)* être alité; *Fam* **I spent three months (flat) on my b.** j'ai passé trois mois à lit; *Fam* **the boss was on my b. all day** j'ai eu le patron sur le dos toute la journée; *Fam* **get off my b.!** fiche-moi la paix!; **to live off the backs of the poor/the Third World** vivre sur le dos des pauvres/du tiers-monde; **to put** *or* **get sb's b. up** mettre qn en colère; *Fig* **to put one's b. into it** s'y mettre énergiquement; **b. pain** mal *m* de dos; **to have b. problems** avoir des problèmes de dos; **to break one's b.** se casser les reins; *Fam* **he won't break his b.** working il ne se casse pas au travail; **to break the b. of the work** faire le plus dur *ou* le plus gros du travail; **to break her b.** *(of ship)* se briser en deux, se casser

2 *(reverse)* *(of knife, book, envelope, cheque etc)* dos *m*; *(of fabric)* envers *m*; *(of page)* verso *m*; *Mus (of violin etc)* table *f* du fond; *(of medal)* revers *m*; *(of hand)* revers, dos; *(of house, clock, wardrobe etc)* arrière *m*; *also Fig* **to be at the b. of sth** être derrière qch; **outside agitators were at the b. of the trouble** des agitateurs extérieurs étaient à l'origine des troubles; *Fam* **I've parked the car round the b.** j'ai garé la voiture derrière; *Fam* **you'll feel the b. of my hand in a minute!** tu vas en prendre une!; **there was an advert on the b. of the bus** il y avait une publicité à l'arrière du bus; *Br Fam* **to have a face like the b. of a bus** être moche comme un pou; **carriage at the b. of the train** voiture en queue de *ou* du train; **the house has a garden at the b.** *or Am* **in b.** il y a un jardin derrière la maison; **the dress fastens at the b.** *or Am* **in b.** la robe s'agrafe dans le dos; **the worry was always there at the b. of his mind** ce souci lui trottait constamment dans la tête; **it was always there at the b. of his mind that …** l'idée ne le quittait pas que …; **it's something to keep at the b. of your mind** c'est quelque chose à ne pas oublier; **you have your sweater on b. to front** tu as mis ton pullover sens devant derrière *ou* à l'envers; *Fig* **she knows the system (inside out and) b. to front** elle connaît le système par cœur; **he knows London like the b. of his hand** il connaît Londres comme sa poche

3 *(rear, furthest away part)* *(of cupboard, room, stage)* fond *m*; **b. of the mouth** arrière-bouche *f*, *pl* arrière-bouches; **b. of the throat** arrière-gorge *f*, *pl* arrière-gorges; **to sit in the b.** *or Am* **in b. (of car)** monter à l'arrière; **to sit at the b.** *(of bus)* s'asseoir à l'arrière; *(of church, hall etc)* s'asseoir dans le *ou* au fond; **at the b. of the book** à la fin du livre; **the b. of beyond** le bout du monde; *Fam* **to live at the b. of beyond** habiter un trou perdu; **b. of the house** *(hotel services)* emplois *mpl* fonctionnels

4 *Sport* arrière *m*; **(full) b.** arrière; **right/left b.** arrière droit/gauche; *Rugby* **the backs** les arrières; *(three quarters)* les trois quarts *mpl*

ADJ 1 *(part, wheel, axle etc)* arrière; *(door, garden etc)* de derrière; *Fig* **to put sth on the b. burner** remettre qch à plus tard

2 *(in opposite direction) (movement)* inverse

ADV 1 *(of place)* en arrière; **to step b. a pace** faire un pas en arrière; **he left him three miles b.** il l'a laissé à trois mil(l)es d'ici; **far b.** *(seated)* dans les derniers rangs; **the house stands b. from the road** la maison est en retrait par rapport à la route; *Am* **b. of sth** derrière qch

2 *(in return, retaliation)* **if somebody hits you, hit them b.** si quelqu'un te frappe, rends-lui ses coups; **if you kick me, I'll kick you b.** si tu me donnes un coup de pied, je te le rendrai; **to get one's own b.** prendre sa revanche (**on sb** sur qn); **that's her way of getting b. at you** c'est sa façon de prendre sa revanche sur toi; **to call sb b.** *(shout, telephone)* rappeler qn

3 *(to original starting point)* **to come b.** revenir; **to arrive b.** rentrer; **to go b.** *(return)* retourner (**to** à); **to go** *or* **turn b.** *(retrace footsteps)* rebrousser chemin; **to make one's way b.** s'en retourner; **I'll be b. on Friday** je serai de retour vendredi; **I'll be b.** *(threat)* vous me reverrez; **I expect him b. tomorrow** j'attends son retour pour demain; **as soon as I am** *or* **get b.** dès mon retour; **he's just b. from a trip** il arrive de voyage; **b. home** chez

nous/lui/*etc;* **she's b. at work** elle a repris son travail; **a few pages b.** quelques pages plus haut; **b. in Britain** en Grande-Bretagne VOIR GRAMMAIRE A21

4 *(of time)* **a few years b.** il y a (déjà) quelques années; **way b. in the Middle Ages** il y a bien longtemps au Moyen Âge; **as far b. as 1914** déjà en 1914, dès 1914; **b. in 1992** en 1992; **b. when I was young** quand j'étais jeune

VT 1 *(support) (person)* soutenir, appuyer; *(in an argument)* donner raison à; *Com etc (person, project etc)* financer; *Fin (bill)* avaliser, endosser

2 *Sport etc (gamble money on) (team)* parier *ou* miser sur; *(horse)* jouer, parier *ou* miser sur; **a well-backed horse** un cheval très coté; *Horseracing, Fig* **to b. a winner** parier *ou* miser sur le gagnant; *Horseracing, Fig* **to b. the wrong horse** parier *ou* miser sur le mauvais cheval

3 *(move) (cart)* reculer; *(horse)* faire reculer; *(train)* refouler; **to b. one's car into the garage** entrer en marche arrière dans le garage; **to b. one's car into a lamppost/another car** rentrer dans un lampadaire/une autre voiture en reculant; *Naut* **to b. the oars, to b. water** ramer à rebours, dé-ramer

4 *(put backing on) (picture)* rentoiler

5 *Mus (person)* accompagner

VI *(of car, lorry)* faire marche arrière, reculer; *(of horse)* reculer; **to b. into sb** *(of person)* rentrer dans qn; *Aut* **to b. into the garage** entrer dans le garage en marche arrière; **I backed into my neighbour's car** je suis rentré dans la voiture de mon voisin en reculant; **to b. into the station** *(of train)* arriver dans la gare en marche arrière

► *Tech* **b. boiler** = ballon *m* d'eau chaude situé derrière un foyer; *Comput* **b. button** bouton *m* Précédente; *Journ* **b. copy** vieux numéro *m*; *Austr* **b. country** campagne *f*, arrière-pays *m inv*; **b. door** *(of building)* porte *f* de derrière; *Fin* financement *m* déguisé; **b. entrance** entrée *f* située à l'arrière; *Ling* **b. formation** dérivation *f* régressive; *Fin* **b. interest** arrérages *mpl*, intérêts *mpl* arriérés; *Journ* **b. issue** vieux numéro; *Cin, TV* **b. light** décrochage *m*; **b. list** *(of publisher)* = liste *f* des titres disponibles et régulièrement réimprimés; *Cin* **b. lot** plateau *m* extérieur d'un studio; **b. matter** *(in book)* annexes *fpl*, *Journ* **b. number** vieux numéro; *Banking* **b. office** back-office *m*, *pl* back-offices; *Banking* **b. office staff** personnels *mpl* de back-office; *Com* **b. orders** commandes *fpl* en souffrance; **b. page** dernière page *f*, *Ftbl* **b. pass** passe *f* en retrait; **b. passage** *Anat* rectum *m*; *(alley)* ruelle *f*, **b. pay** rappel *m* de salaire; *Aut* **b. plate** *(for brakes)* plaque-support *f*, *pl* plaques-support; *Cin, Theat* **b. projection** rétroprojection *f*, **b. rent** arriéré *m* de loyer; **b. rest** *(of seat)* dossier; **b. road** petite route *f*, **b. room** *(in house)* pièce *f* de derrière; *(in shop)* arrière-boutique *f*, *pl* arrière-boutiques; *(for research)* laboratoire *m* de recherche secret; **b. seat** siège *m* arrière; **b. shelf** *(of car)* tablette *f* arrière; **b. shift** *(people)* = équipe *f* du soir; *Ling* **b. slang** ≃ verlan *m*; **b. slapping** *(friendly behaviour)* démonstrations *fpl* d'amitié un peu exubérantes; *(congratulatory)* félicitations *fpl* un peu exubérantes; *Sport* **b. straight** *(on athletics track)* ligne *f* (droite) d'en face; *Horseracing* **b. stretch** *(on race course)* ligne d'en face; **b. yard** *(of building)* arrière-cour *f*, *pl* arrière-cours

► **back away** **VI** *(in fear)* reculer (**from** devant)

► **back down** **VI 1** *Fig (in argument)* admettre qu'on est dans son tort; *(in conflict)* faire marche arrière

2 *(from ladder etc)* descendre à reculons

► **back off** **VI 1** *(move away)* reculer

2 *Am Fig* = **back down (a)**

► **back on to** **VT INSEP** *(of building)* **the colleges b. on to the river/garden** les collèges donnent sur la rivière/le jardin à l'arrière

► **back out** **VI 1** *(of person etc)* sortir à reculons; *Aut* sortir en marche arrière

2 *Fig (withdraw)* retirer sa promesse, se dédire; *(of a responsibility)* se défiler; **to b. out of an undertaking** se dédire d'un engagement; **he's trying to b. out (of it)** il voudrait se dédire

VT SEP *(car)* sortir en marche arrière

► **back up** **VT SEP 1** *(support) (person, story, version of events)* soutenir, appuyer; **to b. sb up in an argument** donner raison à qn

2 *(car etc)* faire reculer; **the accident has backed traffic up all the way to the service station** l'accident a créé un ralentissement jusqu'à la station-service

3 *Comput (data, file)* sauvegarder (**to** sur)

VI 1 *(of car)* reculer, faire marche arrière

2 *Comput* sauvegarder (**to** sur)

3 *(of drains)* être obstrué

---

backache ['bækeɪk] **N** mal *m* de dos; **to have b.** avoir mal au dos

backbench ['bæk'bentʃ] **N 1** *Br Parl (usu pl)* **backbenches** = banc *m* des députés qui n'occupent pas de poste officiel dans le gouvernement ou dans l'opposition; **discontent on the backbenches** mécontentement parmi les députés de base; **she got b. support** elle a eu le soutien des députés de base; **b. MPs** = députés *mpl* qui n'occupent pas de poste officiel dans le gouvernement ou dans l'opposition **2** *Journ* équipe *f* de soutien; *(night desk)* équipe de nuit

backbencher ['bæk'bentʃər] **N** *Br Parl* député *m* de base *(qui n'occupe pas de poste officiel dans le gouvernement ou dans l'opposition)*

Backbencher

Les "backbenchers" sont assis aux derniers rangs de la Chambre des communes, tandis que les rangs de devant sont réservés aux ministres et aux membres du "**shadow cabinet**" (voir la note à l'entrée 'shadow').

---

backbite ['bækbaɪt] **VI** médire
VT *(person)* médire de

backbiting ['bækbaɪtɪŋ] **N** médisance *f*

backboard ['bækbɔːd] **N** *(in basketball)* panneau *m*

backbone ['bækbəʊn] **N 1** *(of person, animal)* épine *f* dorsale, colonne *f* vertébrale; *(of fish)* grande arête *f*, *Fig* **English to the b.** anglais jusqu'au bout des ongles; **he's got no b.** il n'a rien dans le ventre *ou Fam* les tripes; **he hasn't got the b. to do it** il n'a pas les tripes pour le faire; **she is the b. of the movement** c'est elle qui mène le mouvement; **tourism is the b. of the economy** le tourisme est le pivot de l'économie **2** *Comput* épine *f* dorsale

backbreaking ['bækbreɪkɪŋ] **ADJ** *(work etc)* éreintant

backburn ['bækbɜːn] **N** *Austr (to control forest fire)* contre-feu *m*, *pl* contre-feux **VI** allumer un contre-feu

backchat ['bæktʃæt] **N** *Br Fam (impudence)* impertinence *f*, **none of your b.!** ne réponds pas!

backcloth ['bækklɒθ] **N** *Br* = **backdrop**

backcomb ['bækkəʊm] **VT** *(hair)* crêper

backdate ['bækdeɪt] **VT** antidater; **an increase backdated to 1ˢᵗ July** une augmentation avec effet rétroactif au 1er juillet; **will it be backdated?** est-ce qu'il aura effet rétroactif?

backdrop ['bækdrɒp] N **1** *Theat* toile *f* de fond; *(with perspective)* découverte *f* **2** *Fig (background)* toile *f* de fond, arrière-plan *m, pl* arrière-plans; **against a b. of continuing violence** avec, comme arrière-plan *ou* toile de fond, un climat de violence permanente

-backed ['bækt] SUFF **broad-b.** *(person)* qui a le dos large; **a high-b. chair** une chaise à haut dossier

back-end load N *Am St Exch* frais *mpl* de sortie

backer ['bækər] N **1** *Horseracing* parieur, -euse **2** *Pol etc* partisan *m; Com* commanditaire *mf, Fin (of bill)* donneur *m* d'aval; *Theat etc* **we need a b.** il nous faut un mécène; **financial b.** bailleur, -eresse de fonds

backfill ['bækfɪl] *Constr* N *(of trench)* remplissage *m*
VT *(trench)* remplir
VI remplir

backfire [bæk'faɪər] N **1** *(of engine)* retour *m* de flamme; *(noise)* pétarade *f* **2** *Am (to control forest fire)* contre-feu *m, pl* contre-feux
VI **1** *Aut* avoir des retours de flamme, pétarader, avoir un raté (d'allumage); *Fig* **the plan backfired on them** le projet leur est retombé sur le dos **2** *Am (to control forest fire)* allumer un contre-feu

backgammon ['bækgæmən] N backgammon *m*
▸▸ **b. board** damier *m* de backgammon

background ['bækgraʊnd] N **1** *(position)* fond *m*, arrière-plan *m, pl* arrière-plans; *Comput* arrière-plan; **b. of mountains** fond de montagnes; **in the b.** dans le fond, à l'arrière-plan; *Comput* en arrière-plan; **b. colour** couleur *f* de fond; **music was playing in the b.** il y avait de la musique en bruit de fond; **there's a lot of noise in the b.** il y a beaucoup de bruit de fond; *Comput* **the program works in the b.** le programme est exécuté en arrière-plan; **against a dark b.** sur (un) fond sombre; *Fig* **the protests took place against a b. of repression** les manifestations se sont inscrites dans un climat de *ou* sur fond de répression; **to keep (oneself) or to stay in the b.** s'effacer; *Fig* **she stays very much in the b.** elle est très effacée; **to push sb into the b.** mettre *ou* reléguer qn au second plan; *(outshine)* prendre le pas sur qn; *Fig* **to fade/melt into the b.** disparaître/se fondre dans l'arrière-plan; **he's rather faded into the b. since then** on n'entend plus tellement parler de lui depuis
2 *(social class)* origines *fpl, (education)* formation *f, (experience)* expérience *f, (to event)* contexte *m* historique (**to** de); *(to problem)* contexte (**to** de); **a young man of good b.** un garçon de bonne famille; **to come from a middle-class/deprived b.** venir d'un milieu bourgeois/défavorisé; **what's his professional b.?** quelle expérience professionnelle a-t-il?; **he's been given a b. briefing** on lui a fait un briefing sur l'historique de l'événement; **I need a bit more b. (information)** j'ai besoin de plus de données
▸▸ *Comput* **b. job** tâche *f* de fond; **b. light** éclairage *m* d'ambiance; *Comput* **b. mode printing** impression *f* en arrière-plan; **b. music** musique *f* d'ambiance *ou* de fond; *Cin, Theat* fond *m* sonore; **b. noise** bruit *m* de fond; *Comput* **b. printing** impression en arrière-plan; *Comput* **b. processing** traitement *m* de données en tâches de fond; *Phys* **b. radiation** rayonnement *m* naturel; **b. reading** lectures *fpl* complémentaires; *TV etc* **b. sound** fond sonore; *Comput* **b. task** tâche d'arrière-plan

backhand ['bækhænd] N **1** *Tennis* revers *m*; **her b. is weak** son revers manque de puissance **2** *(writing)* écriture *f* renversée *ou* penchée à gauche

backhanded [bæk'hændɪd] ADJ *(blow)* de revers; *Fig (compliment)* équivoque

backhander ['bækhændər] N *Fam* **1** *(blow)* revers *m; Fig (attack)* attaque *f* indirecte **2** *(bribe)* pot-de-vin *m, pl* pots-de-vin

backing ['bækɪŋ] N **1** *(support) (for person)* soutien *m*, appui *m; (for picture)* entoilage *m;* **financial b.** *(for person, project etc)* financement *m;* **to give financial b. to sth** financer qch **2** *Horseracing (bets)* paris *mpl* **3** *(movement) (of car, horse, cart)* recul *m* **4** *(providing with back) (of picture)* rentoilage *m* **5** *Mus* accompagnement *m*
▸▸ *Mus* **b. track** piste *f* de fond

backlash ['bæklæʃ] N **1** *Fig (of event)* contrecoup *m; (political etc)* réaction *f*, retour *m* de manivelle (**against** contre) **2** *Aut (gearing)* jeu *m* entre-dents

backless ['bæklɪs] ADJ *(dress)* dos nu; *(seat etc)* sans dossier

backlighting ['bæklaɪtɪŋ] N *Cin, TV* éclairage *m* en contre-jour

backlit ['bæklɪt] ADJ **1** *Cin, TV* éclairé en contre-jour **2** *Comput (screen)* rétro-éclairé

backlog ['bæklɒg] N *(of work)* retard *m; Com* **b. of orders** commandes *fpl* non exécutées; **to have a b. of correspondence/work** avoir du retard dans son courrier/travail, avoir du courrier/travail en retard; **to clear a b.** se mettre à jour

backpack ['bækpæk] N sac *m* à dos
VI faire de la randonnée

backpacker ['bækpækər] N randonneur, -euse

backpacking ['bækpækɪŋ] N randonnée *f*, **to go b.** aller faire de la randonnée

back-pedal VI (-ll-, *Am* -l-) *(on bicycle)* rétropédaler; *Fig* faire marche arrière; **to b. on a promise** revenir sur une promesse

back-pedalling, *Am* **back-pedaling** ['bækped(ə)lɪŋ] N *(on bicycle)* rétropédalage *m; Fig* marche *f* arrière

back-pressure N *Aut* contre-pression *f, pl* contre-pressions

backscratcher ['bækskrætʃər] N gratte-dos *m inv*

backscratching ['bækskrætʃɪŋ] N *Fig* échange *m* de faveurs

back-seat ['bæksiːt] ADJ **I don't want any b. driving** je n'ai pas besoin de conseils pour conduire
▸▸ *Pej* **b. driver** *(in car)* = personne *f* qui donne toujours des conseils au conducteur; *(interfering person)* donneur, -euse de leçons; **b. passenger** passager, -ère arrière

backsheesh, backshish ['bækʃiːʃ] N bakchich *m*

backside [bæk'saɪd] N *Fam* derrière *m*, postérieur *m*

backsight ['bæksaɪt] N *(on rifle)* hausse *f*

backslash ['bækslæʃ] N *Comput* barre *f* oblique inversée
▸▸ **b. key** touche *f* barre oblique inversée

backslide ['bækslaɪd] VI (**backslid** ['bækslɪd]) récidiver

backsliding ['bækslaɪdɪŋ] N récidive *f*

backspace ['bækspeɪs] N espacement *m* arrière, touche *f* d'espacement arrière
VI *(on keyboard)* revenir en arrière d'un caractère; **b. twice** revenir en arrière de deux caractères
▸▸ **b. character** caractère *m* de retour arrière; **b. command** commande *f* de retour arrière; **b. key** espacement arrière, touche d'espacement arrière

backstage [bæk'steɪdʒ] ADV *Theat* derrière la scène, en coulisse, dans les coulisses; *Fig* en coulisse; *Theat* **to help b.** aider en coulisse(s)

ADJ ATTRIB *Theat (area, activity)* de derrière la scène; *Fig* en coulisse
▸▸ **b. worker** personne *f* qui travaille dans les coulisses

backstairs [bæk'steəz] N *(for servants etc)* escalier *m* de service; *(hidden)* escalier dérobé
▸▸ **b. gossip** commérages *mpl (des domestiques);* **b. influence** influence *f*

backstitch ['bækstɪtʃ] *Sewing* N point *m* de piqûre
VI coudre au point de piqûre

backstreet ['bækstriːt] N petite rue *f*; **he was brought up in the backstreets** il a été élevé dans les quartiers populaires
▸▸ **b. abortion** avortement *m* clandestin; **b. abortionist** faiseur, -euse d'anges, *Pej* avorteur, -euse

backstroke ['bækstrəʊk] N **1** *Swimming* dos *m* crawlé; **the 100 metres b.** le 100 mètres dos **2** *Tech (of piston etc)* course *f* arrière, course de retour

backtalk ['bæktɔːk] N *Am* = backchat

back-to-back ADJ *(seats, people)* dos à dos; *Br* **a row of b. houses** une rangée de maisons adossées les unes aux autres; *Sport* **to play two games b.** jouer deux parties l'une à la suite de l'autre
N *Br (house)* **a row of little back-to-backs** une rangée de petites maisons adossées les unes aux autres
▸▸ *Fin* **b. credit** crédit *m* dos-à-dos; *Fin* **b. loan** opération *f* de face à face; *Fin* **b. operation** opération de face à face

backtrack ['bæktræk] VI revenir sur ses pas; *Fig* faire marche arrière; **to b. on a promise/decision** revenir sur une promesse/une décision

backup ['bækʌp] N **1** *(support)* soutien *m*, appui *m; Mil etc* renfort *m; Med* soins *mpl* supplémentaires; **to ask for b.** *(of police etc)* demander des renforts; **we have a generator as b.** nous avons un générateur de secours **2** *Comput* sauvegarde *f*, **to do the b.** faire la sauvegarde; **the b. has failed** la sauvegarde a échoué
▸▸ **b. car** voiture *f* de rechange; *Comput* **b. copy** copie *f* de sauvegarde; *Comput* **b. device** unité *f* de sauvegarde; *Comput* **b. disk(ette)** disquette *f* de sauvegarde; *Comput* **b. drive** unité de sauvegarde; *Comput* **b. file** fichier *m* de sauvegarde; *Comput* **b. system** *(for doing the backup)* système *m* de sauvegarde; *(auxiliary system)* système de secours; **b. team** *(which provides support)* équipe *f* de soutien; *(which acts as replacement)* équipe de remplacement; *Mil* **b. troops** renforts *mpl*

back-up ADJ
▸▸ *Am Aut* **b. lights** feux *mpl* de recul

backward ['bækwəd] ADJ **1** *also Fig (movement, glance, step etc)* en arrière; **b. and forward motion** mouvement *m* de va-et-vient **2** *(child)* retardé, attardé; *(area, region)* moins développé; *(people)* attardé; **the b. state of the country** le retard dont souffre le pays; **to be b. in doing sth** être lent à faire qch; *Br Fam* **he isn't b. in coming forward** il n'a pas peur de se mettre en avant; **he isn't b. in coming forward with his ideas** il n'a pas peur de mettre ses idées en avant; **he isn't b. in coming forward to complain** il n'est jamais le dernier à se plaindre
ADV = backwards
▸▸ *Econ* **b. integration** intégration *f* en amont; *Mktg* **b. invention** invention *f* en amont; *(simplification of product)* invention rétrograde; **b. pricing** rajustement *m* des prix; *Comput* **b. search** recherche *f* arrière

backwardation [bækwəˈdeɪʃən] N *Fin* déport *m*

backward-compatible ADJ *Comput* compatible avec les versions antérieures

backwardness ['bækwədnɪs] N *(mental)* arriération *f* mentale, retard *m*; **b. in doing sth** hésitation *f* à faire qch

backwards ['bækwədz] ADV *(to jump, lean)* en arrière; *(to go, walk)* à reculons; *(to fall)* à la renverse; *(to say, read sth)* à l'envers; **to look b.** jeter un coup d'œil en arrière; *(in time)* remonter dans le passé; **to flow b.** *(of water)* couler à contre-courant; *Fig* **to know sth b.** connaître qch parfaitement; *also Fig* **a step b.** un pas en arrière; **to walk b. and forwards** aller et venir; **movement b. and forwards** mouvement *m* de va-et-vient; **to go b. and forwards** faire la navette *(entre deux endroits)*

backwash ['bækwɒʃ] N remous *m*; *Fig* conséquences *fpl* néfastes; **in the b. of the civil war** dans les remous qui ont suivi la guerre civile

backwater ['bækwɔːtər] N *(tributary)* bras *m* de décharge *(d'une rivière)*; *Fig, often Pej* **to live in a b.** habiter un trou perdu; **a secluded b.** un coin tranquille

backwoods ['bækwʊdz] NPL *esp Am* forêts *fpl* de l'intérieur; *Fig* **to live in the b.** habiter un trou perdu *ou* un bled

backwoodsman, *pl* **backwoodsmen** [bæk'wʊdzmən] N *Fam* **1** *Am (uncouth man)* rustre *m*, rustaud *m* **2** *Br Pol* = membre *m* de la Chambre des lords qui ne fait acte de présence que lorsqu'il s'intéresse à un vote

baclava [bə'klɑːvə] N *Culin* baklava *m*

bacon ['beɪkən] N bacon *m*; **b. and eggs** œufs *mpl* au bacon; **streaky b.** ≃ petit salé *m*; *Fig* **to save sb's b.** sauver la peau de qn; *Fig* **to bring home the b.** *(provide material support)* faire bouillir la marmite; *(be successful)* réussir

BACS [bæks] N *(abbr* **bankers' automated clearing services)** système *m* électronique de paiement; **to pay by B.** payer par virement automatique

bacteria [bæk'tɪərɪə] NPL bactéries *fpl*

bacterial [bæk'tɪərɪəl] ADJ bactérien

bacteriological [bæktɪərɪə'lɒdʒɪk(ə)l] ADJ bactériologique
▸▸*Biol, Mil* **b. warfare** guerre *f* bactériologique

bacteriologist [bæktɪərɪ'ɒlədʒɪst] N bactériologiste *mf*, bactériologue *mf*

bacteriology [bæktɪərɪ'ɒlədʒɪ] N bactériologie *f*

bacterium, *pl* **bacteria** [bæk'tɪərɪəm, -ɪə] N bactérie *f*

Bactrian camel ['bæktrɪən] N chameau *m* (bactrien)

BAD [bæd]

| ADJ mauvais **1–3** ▪ grave **2** |
| N mauvais |

ADJ *(* **worse** [wɜːs], **worst** [wɜːst]*)* **1** *(of poor quality)* mauvais, de mauvaise qualité; *(unfortunate, incorrect)* mauvais; **it's not b.** ce n'est pas mal; **the pay's not b.** ça ne paie pas mal; **things are not as b. as all that** ça ne va pas si mal que ça; *Br Fam* **it's not half b.** ce n'est pas mal du tout; **he's/she's not b. looking** il/elle n'est pas mal; **it was a b. buy** ce n'était pas un bon investissement; **to go b.** *(of food)* se gâter, s'avarier; **to speak b. French** parler mal le français; **b. at maths** nul en maths; **he's b. at keeping a secret** il ne sait pas garder un secret; **he's b. at helping about the house** il n'aide pas souvent aux tâches ménagères; **to have a b. effect on sth** avoir un effet néfaste sur qch; **to be** *or* **have a b. influence on sb** avoir une mau-

vaise influence sur qn; **to get into b. habits** *or* **ways** prendre de mauvaises habitudes; **b. light stopped play** *(at cricket match)* la partie a été remise à cause d'un manque de lumière; **is this a b. time to ask for leave?** peut-être n'est-ce pas le moment de demander des congés?; **am I phoning at a b. time?** je vous dérange?; **to be in a b. way** *(of person)* aller mal; **he'll come to a b. end** il finira mal; **to have a b. name** avoir (une) mauvaise réputation; **it wouldn't be a b. thing** *or* **plan** *or* **idea to …** cela ne serait pas une mauvaise idée de …; **things are going from b. to worse** les choses vont de mal en pis; **a b. apple** une pomme pourrie; *Fig* une brebis galeuse; *Fig* **one b. apple spoils the barrel** il ne faut qu'une brebis galeuse pour gâter un troupeau; *Fig* **there's b. blood/feeling between them** il y a du ressentiment *ou* de la rancune entre eux; *Fam* **he's always turning up like a b. penny** on n'arrive jamais à se débarrasser de lui; **don't worry, he'll turn up like a b. penny** ne t'en fais pas, tu sais bien qu'il revient toujours; *Fam* **I'm having a b. hair day** *(my hair's a mess)* je n'arrive pas à me coiffer aujourd'hui; *(I'm having a bad day)* aujourd'hui c'est un jour sans

2 *(unpleasant, serious) (news, smell, mood etc)* mauvais; *(cold)* gros; *(headache)* violent; *(accident, mistake etc)* grave; **it's a b. business** c'est une mauvaise affaire; **is the pain b.?** est-ce que cela fait très mal?; *Fig* **she's b. news** elle ne te/lui/*etc* apportera que des ennuis; **b. weather** mauvais temps *m*; *Naut* **to be on b. terms with sb** être mal *ou* en mauvais termes avec qn; **it's (really) too b.!, that's too b.!** c'est vraiment dommage!; *Old-fashioned* **it's too b. of him!** ce n'est vraiment pas bien de sa part!; **if you don't like it, that's just too b.** si cela ne te plaît pas, tant pis pour toi

3 *(not healthy)* **to be b. for sb/sth** ne rien valoir à qn/pour qch; **all that whisky is b. for him** tout ce whisky ne lui vaut rien; **smoking is b. for you** *or* **your health** le tabac est mauvais pour la santé; **because of my b. leg** parce que ma jambe me fait souffrir; **I have a b. heart/back** j'ai le cœur/le dos fragile; **I'm not so b.** *(I'm well)* je ne vais pas trop mal; **how's business? – not so b.** comment vont les affaires? – pas trop mal

4 *(wicked)* méchant; *Fam* **he's a b. lot** c'est un vaurien

ADV *Fam* **that looks b.** *(of injury, accident etc)* ça a l'air grave; *(in eyes of other people)* c'est mal vu; *(augurs ill)* c'est mauvais signe; **to feel b. about sth** *(regret)* avoir du remords au sujet de qch; **I feel b. about firing him but I'll have to** cela m'embête d'avoir à le renvoyer, mais il faudra bien que je le fasse; **I feel b. about not having told him sooner** je m'en veux de ne pas lui avoir dit plus tôt; *Fam* **she was taken b. yesterday** *(became ill)* elle est tombée malade hier; *Fam* **to have it b.** *(be in love)* être mordu

N **to take the b. with the good** accepter la mauvaise fortune aussi bien que la bonne; *Fam* **to go to the b.** *(of person)* mal tourner; *(of business)* être en mauvaise passe; **to be £500 to the b.** en être de 500 livres (de sa poche); *Fam* **to be in b. with sb** être en mauvais termes avec qn; *Am Fam* **my b.!** c'est ma faute!
▸▸**b. breath** mauvaise haleine *f*; *Banking* **b. cheque** chèque *m* sans provision; *Comput* **b. command** commande *f* erronée; *Fin* **b. debt** créance *f* irrécouvrable *ou* douteuse; *Fin* **b. debtor** créance *f* irrécouvrable *ou* douteuse; *Comput* **b. file name** nom *m* de fichier erroné; **b. language** gros mots *mpl*; *Comput* **b. sector** secteur *m* endommagé

badass ['bædæs] *Am Sl* N *(person)* dur *m* (à cuire)

ADJ **1** *(intimidating, tough)* **to be b.** être un dur à cuire **2** *(excellent)* super, génial, -aux; **her new sneakers are so b.** ils sont super, ses nouveaux tennis

baddie, baddy ['bædɪ] N *Fam* méchant, -ante

bade PT *see* **bid** VT & VI

badge [bædʒ] N **1** *(metal, plastic)* badge *m*; *Mil, Sch* écusson *m*; *(to indicate membership of club)* insigne *m* **2** *Fig* symbole *m*, signe *m*
▸▸**b. of office** insigne de fonction

badger ['bædʒər] N *(animal)* blaireau *m*
VT *(person)* harceler; **to b. sb with sth/to do sth** harceler qn avec qch/pour qu'il fasse qch; **to b. sb into granting a favour, to b. a favour out of sb** obtenir une faveur de qn à force de harcèlement
▸▸**b. baiting** déterrage *m* du blaireau

badinage ['bædɪnɑːʒ] N *Fml, Lit* badinage *m*

badly ['bædlɪ] ADV *(* **worse** [wɜːs], **worst** [wɜːst]*)* **1** *(poorly) (informed, dressed, behave, explain sth etc)* mal; **to do b., to come off b.** mal réussir; **he didn't do b.** il ne s'en est pas trop mal tiré; **to be very b. off** *(financially)* être dans la gêne; *Fig* **I'm very b. off for clothes** je ne suis pas riche en vêtements; **to speak English b.** parler mal l'anglais; **he took it very b.** il a très mal pris la chose; **they get on b. (with each other)** ils ne s'entendent pas; **I get on b. with him** je ne m'entends pas bien avec lui

2 *(seriously) (damaged, scratched)* très; **his arm was b. broken** il a eu une mauvaise fracture au bras; **he was b. disabled in the accident** il a été sérieusement handicapé dans l'accident; **b. wounded** gravement *ou* grièvement blessé

3 *(greatly)* **to want sth b.** avoir très envie de qch; **if you want it b. enough, you'll get it** quand on veut, on peut; **I need it b.** j'en ai bien *ou* *Fml* grand besoin; *Sport etc* **b. beaten** battu à plate(s) couture(s); **he's b. in need of a haircut** il a bien besoin de se faire couper les cheveux

bad-mannered ADJ mal élevé

badminton ['bædmɪntən] N badminton *m*
▸▸**b. court** terrain *m* de badminton; **b. player** joueur, -euse de badminton

bad-mouth VT *esp Am (person)* déblatérer sur, dire du mal de

badness ['bædnɪs] N **1** *(of cooking, writing etc)* mauvaise qualité *f* **2** *(of person)* méchanceté *f*

bad-tempered ADJ *(person)* grincheux; *(reply)* désagréable; **to be b.** *(temporarily)* être de mauvaise humeur; *(permanently)* avoir mauvais caractère

baffle ['bæf(ə)l] N **1** *Tech* chicane *f*, déflecteur *m* **2** *Radio (of loudspeaker)* écran *m*, baffle *m*
VT **1** *(mystify) (person)* laisser perplexe; **to b. the imagination** dépasser l'imagination; **it baffles the imagination why she agreed** Dieu sait pourquoi elle a accepté!; **a mystery that has baffled all investigators** un mystère qui a déjoué toutes les recherches; **the police admit they are baffled** la police admet qu'elle est perplexe; **I'm baffled as to why she said that** je ne comprends vraiment pas pourquoi elle a dit ça; **to b. definition** échapper à toute définition **2** *(foil) (plot, attempt)* déjouer
▸▸*Radio* **b. board** *(of loudspeaker)* écran, baffle; *Tech* **b. plate** plaque-chicane *f*, *pl* plaques-chicanes

baffling ['bæf(ə)lɪŋ] ADJ *(behaviour)* déconcertant; *(mystery etc)* inexplicable

BAFTA ['bæftə] N *(abbr* **British Academy of Film and Television Arts)** B. (award) = prix *m* récompensant les meilleurs films et émissions de télévision en Grande-Bretagne

bag [bæg] **N 1** *(container)* sac *m*; *(handbag)* sac à main; **travel(ling) b.** sac de voyage; *Old-fashioned, Lit* **b. and baggage** avec armes et bagages; **to pack one's bags** faire ses bagages; *Fam* **we've bags of time** on a tout le temps; *Fam* **they've bags of money** ils sont pleins aux as; *Fam* **there's bags of room** la place ne manque pas; *esp Am Sl* **that's not my b.** *(I'm not good at it)* ce n'est pas mon fort; *(I'm not interested in it)* ce n'est pas mon genre; *Fam* **bags under the eyes** poches *fpl* sous les yeux; **to let it out of the b.** vendre la mèche; *Fam* **b. of bones** sac *m* ou tas *m* d'os
2 *Br Sl Pej (woman)* **old b.** vieille toupie *f*
3 *(in hunting)* **the b.** le tableau; **to make a good b.** faire un grand abattis de gibier; *Fig (of fighter pilot)* avoir un beau tableau de chasse; *Fam* **it's in the b.** l'affaire est dans le sac
4 *Br Old-fashioned Fam* **bags** *(trousers)* pantalon *m*
VT (**-gg-**) **1** *Fam (take)* s'emparer de, mettre la main sur; *(best seats)* accaparer; *Br* **bags I go first!** c'est moi le premier!; *Br* **bags I sit in front!** c'est moi qui monte devant!
2 *(pack) (coal, potting compost)* mettre en sac; *(apples, sweets)* ensacher; *Am (purchases) (in supermarket)* emballer
3 *(kill) (game)* abattre, tuer; *Aviat Fam (enemy aircraft)* abattre
VI *(of garment)* bouffer, avoir trop d'ampleur; **trousers that b. at the knees** pantalon qui fait des poches aux genoux
▸▸ *Fam* **b. lady** clocharde *f*

bagatelle [bægə'tel] **N** *(trifle), Mus* bagatelle *f*

bagel ['beɪg(ə)l] **N** *Culin* = petit pain *m* en forme de couronne, *Can* bagel *m*

baggage ['bægɪdʒ] **N 1** *(luggage)* bagages *mpl*; **one piece of b.** un bagage; *Fig* **to have a lot of (emotional) b.** avoir accumulé les échecs sentimentaux **2** *Old-fashioned (cheeky girl)* coquine *f* **3** *Mil* bagage *m*
▸▸ **b. allowance** franchise *f* de bagages; *Am* **b. car** fourgon *m* *(d'un train)*; **b. check** *(inspection)* contrôle *m* des bagages; *Am (ticket)* ticket *m* d'enregistrement; **b. claim** retrait *m* des bagages; **b. claim area** zone *f* de livraison des bagages; **b. claim sticker** étiquette *f* autocollante d'identification de bagage; **b. container** conteneur *m* à bagages; **b. conveyor belt** tapis *m* de livraison de bagages; **b. cover** *(lid, hood)* cache-bagage *m* *inv*; *(insurance)* assurance *f* bagage(s); **b. handler** bagagiste *m*; **b. lift** ascenseur *m* à bagages; **b. reclaim** retrait des bagages; *Am* **b. room** consigne *f*; *Am* **b. tag** bulletin *m* de consigne; **b. waggon** fourgon à bagages

baggy ['bægɪ] **ADJ** *(sweater, trousers) (deliberately so)* ample, large; *(out of shape)* déformé

Baghdad [bæg'dæd] **N** Bagdad

bagpipe(s) ['bægpaɪp(s)] **NPL** cornemuse *f*
▸▸ **b. player** joueur, -euse de cornemuse

bah [bɑː] **INT** bah!

Bahama [bə'hɑːmə] **N** **the Bahamas, the B. Islands** les (îles *fpl*) Bahamas *fpl*, l'archipel *m* des Bahamas VOIR GRAMMAIRE A12

Bahrain [bɑː'reɪn] **N** Bahreïn

Bahraini [bɑː'reɪnɪ] **ADJ** bahreïni
N Bahreïni, -ie

bail¹ [beɪl] *Law* **N** *(system)* cautionnement *m*; *(money)* caution *f*; **to go** *or* **stand b. for sb** se porter garant *ou* caution de qn, fournir une caution pour qn *(pour sa libération pro-*

visoire); **to grant sb b.** *(of judge)* libérer qn sous caution; **released on b.** libéré sous caution; **to be (out) on b.** être en liberté provisoire (sous caution); *Fam* **to jump b.** se dérober à la justice *(alors qu'on jouit de la liberté provisoire)*
VT *(person) (of judge)* libérer sous caution; *(of lawyer, family member etc)* se porter caution pour

bail² **N** *Cr* **bails** barrettes *fpl*, bâtonnets *mpl*

bail³ **N** *Naut (bucket)* écope *f*
▸ **bail out** **VT SEP 1** **to b. sb out** *Law* se porter garant *ou* caution pour qn; *Fig* tirer qn d'affaire; *Fig* **to b. out a company** renflouer une entreprise **2** *(boat, water)* écoper, vider
VI écoper

bailer ['beɪlər] **N** *Naut (bucket)* écope *f*

Bailey ['beɪlɪ] **N** **the Old B.** = le tribunal principal de Londres
▸▸ *Mil* **B. bridge** pont *m* Bailey

bailiff ['beɪlɪf] **N 1** *Law* huissier *m* **2** *(of estate, farm)* régisseur *m*; **water b.** garde-pêche *m*, *pl* gardes-pêche **3** *Br Hist (sovereign's representative)* bailli *m*

bailiwick ['beɪlɪwɪk] **N** *Law* bailliage *m*; *Fig (territory)* territoire *m*; *Fig* **it's not my b.** *(field, area of expertise)* ce n'est pas mon rayon

bairn [beən] **N** *Scot* enfant *mf*

bait [beɪt] **N** *(for fish)* amorce *f*, appât *m*; *Fig* appât, leurre *m*; **ground b.** amorce de fond; **to rise to** *or* **swallow** *or* **take the b.** *(of fish)*, *Fig* mordre à l'hameçon
VT 1 *(tease) (animal)* harceler; *(person)* harceler, tourmenter **2** *(put bait on) (hook, trap etc)* amorcer (**with** avec); *(line)* mettre l'appât à

baiting ['beɪtɪŋ] **N 1** *(teasing) (of animals, person)* harcèlement *m*; *(of badger)* déterrage *m* **2** *(of hook, trap etc)* amorçage *m*

baize [beɪz] **N** feutre *m*; **green b.** tapis *m* de billard; **green b. door** porte *f* recouverte de feutre vert

bake [beɪk] **VT** *Culin* (faire) cuire au four; *Tech (bricks, porcelain etc)* cuire; **to b. bread** faire cuire le pain; **earth baked by the sun** sol durci *ou* desséché par le soleil; *Fam* **I'm baked** je crève de chaleur, je cuis
VI *(of bread etc)* cuire; *(of person) (make cakes)* faire de la pâtisserie *ou* des gâteaux; *(make bread)* faire du pain; *Fam* **I'm baking** je crève de chaleur

baked [beɪkt] **ADJ** cuit au four
▸▸ *Culin* **b. Alaska** omelette *f* norvégienne; **b. beans** *Br (in tomato sauce)* haricots *mpl* blancs à la sauce tomate; *Am (dish)* haricots au lard, *Can* fèves *fpl* au lard; **b. potato** pomme *f* de terre en robe de chambre *ou* en robe des champs

baker ['beɪkər] **N** boulanger, -ère *m*; **b.'s (shop)** boulangerie *f*
▸▸ **b.'s dozen** treize à la douzaine

bakery ['beɪkərɪ] **N** boulangerie *f*

Bakewell tart ['beɪkwel] **N** *Br Culin* = fond *m* de tarte, fourré au biscuit de Savoie, à la confiture et à la pâte d'amandes

baking ['beɪkɪŋ] **ADJ** *Fam* **b. hot** *(food, container)* brûlant; *(day)* torride; **it's b. in here** on étouffe ici; **the b. streets** les rues écrasées de chaleur
N 1 *(of bread etc)* cuisson *f*, *(of bricks etc)* cuisson, cuite *f*; **I'll do a** *or* **some b. tomorrow** demain, je ferai de la pâtisserie **2** *(batch) (of bread, cakes)* fournée *f*, *(of bricks etc)* cuite *f*
▸▸ **b. powder** levure *f* (chimique); **b. sheet** plaque *f* (de four), tôle *f*; **b. soda** bicarbonate *m* de soude; **b. tin** moule *m* à gâteau

baklava [bə'klɑːvə] **N** *Culin* baklava *m*

baksheesh ['bækʃiːʃ] **N** bakchich *m*

Balaclava [bælə'klɑːvə] **N** passe-montagne *m*, *pl* passe-montagnes
▸▸ **B. helmet** passe-montagne

balalaika [bælə'laɪkə] **N** *Mus* balalaïka *f*

BALANCE ['bæləns]

N équilibre **1** ▪ solde, reste **2**
▪ balance **2, 3**
VT mettre en équilibre **1** ▪ balancer, solder **2** ▪ équilibrer **2**
VI s'équilibrer **2** ▪ être en équilibre **3**

N 1 *(steadiness)* équilibre *m*; **there's a good b. of funny and serious articles** il y a une proportion égale d'articles amusants et sérieux; **to keep** *or* **maintain one's b.** garder l'équilibre; **to lose one's b.** perdre l'équilibre; *Fig* **to catch sb off b.** prendre qn au dépourvu; **to throw sb off b.** faire perdre l'équilibre à qn; *Fig* **to be off b.** être déséquilibré; **to put out of b.** *(scales, machine)* dérégler; *Fig* **to strike a b.** *(between two things)* trouver le juste milieu; *Pol* **the b. of power** l'équilibre des forces; *Pol* **the Liberals hold the b. of power** les Libéraux ont le pouvoir de faire pencher l'Assemblée d'un côté ou de l'autre; **while the b. of his mind was disturbed** alors qu'il n'était pas dans son état normal
2 *(remainder)* reste *m*; *Com, Fin (of account)* solde *m*; *Acct* balance *f*, bilan *m*; **credit/debit b.** solde créditeur/débiteur; *Fig* **on b.** tout bien considéré
3 *Tech (for weighing)* balance *f*, *Astron* **the B.** la Balance; *Fig* **the b. of evidence** l'ensemble *m* des preuves; *Fig* **to swing the b. (in sb's favour)** faire pencher la balance (du côté de qn); *Fig* **to hang in the b.** être en jeu
VT 1 *(object)* mettre *ou* maintenir en équilibre; *Aut, Naut* équilibrer; *(counteract weight of)* faire contrepoids à; **to b. sth on one's head** mettre qch en équilibre sur la tête; **women balancing pots on their heads** des femmes portant des pots sur la tête; **one thing balances another** une chose compense l'autre
2 *Com, Fin (account)* balancer, solder, aligner; *(debt)* compenser; *(budget)* équilibrer; **to b. the books** balancer les livres
VI 1 *(of scales)* s'équilibrer; **the two things b.** les deux choses s'équilibrent
2 *Com, Fin (of accounts)* s'équilibrer; **account that balances** compte *m* en balance; **I can't get the accounts to b.** je n'arrive pas à équilibrer les comptes
3 *(remain in stable position)* se maintenir en équilibre; *(be in stable position)* être en équilibre; **to b. on one foot** se tenir en équilibre sur un pied; **books balancing on the desk** des livres en équilibre sur le bureau
▸▸ *Gym* **b. beam** poutre *f*, *Acct* **b. brought forward** solde reporté; *(on balance sheet)* report *m*; *Acct* **b. carried forward** solde à reporter; *(on balance sheet)* report à nouveau; *Acct, Fin* **b. due** solde dû; *Econ* **b. of payments** balance des paiements; *Econ* **b. of payments deficit** déficit *m* de la balance des paiements, déficit extérieur; *Acct* **b. sheet** bilan *m*; *Acct* **b. sheet auditing** contrôle *m* du bilan; *Acct* **b. sheet consolidation** consolidation *f* de bilan; *Acct* **b. sheet item** poste *m* de bilan; *Acct* **b. sheet value** valeur *f* bilantielle *ou* d'inventaire; *Econ* **b. of trade** balance commerciale; *Tech* **b. wheel** balancier *m*; *(of clock)* roue *f* de rencontre
▸ **balance against** **VT SEP** **to b. one thing against another** comparer les avantages d'une chose par rapport à une autre; **you have to b. the advantages against the disadvantages** il faut peser le pour et le contre

▶ **balance out** VI *(of figures)* correspondre VT SEP *(match) (something)* compléter; **they b. each other out** *(because of their respective skills)* ils se complètent bien

---

Note that the French word **balance** is a false friend. Its most common meaning is **scales**.

---

balanced ['bælənst] ADJ **1** *(in weight)* équilibré, compensé; *Fig (judgment)* pondéré; *(report, account)* objectif; **to be well b.** *(of person)* être équilibré; *(in diet)* un régime (alimentaire) équilibré **2** *(in strength, value)* égal, -aux; *Fin (budget)* équilibré; **the two parties are pretty well b.** les deux parties sont à peu près égales

balancer shaft ['bælənsər] N *Aut* arbre *m* d'équilibrage

balancing ['bælənsɪŋ] N **1** mise *f* en équilibre; *Aut (of wheels)* équilibrage *m*; *Art (of elements in a painting)* balancement *m* **2** *Com, Fin* **b. of accounts** solde *m* ou alignement *m* des comptes **3** *(of two things)* ajustement *m*; *(of sth by sth)* compensation *f*
▶▶ **b. act** numéro *m* d'équilibriste; **b. pole** *(of tightrope walker)* contrepoids *m*

balcony ['bælkənɪ] N **1** *(on house)* balcon *m*; **on the b.** sur le balcon **2** *Theat, Cin* balcon *m*; **we always sit in the b.** nous prenons toujours des places au balcon; **there are two b. seats left** il reste deux places au balcon

bald [bɔːld] ADJ **1** *(person)* chauve; *(tyre)* lisse; *Fig (hillside)* nu; **his b. head** son crâne chauve; **he is going b.** il commence à perdre ses cheveux ou à devenir chauve; *Fam* **b. as a coot** or **an egg** chauve comme un œuf ou une boule de billard **2** *Fig (style etc)* dépouillé, sec, *f* sèche; **a b. statement of the facts** une simple exposition des faits
▶▶ **b. eagle** pygargue *m* à tête blanche; **b. patch** tonsure *f*

balderdash ['bɔːldədæʃ] *Old-fashioned Fam* N bêtises *fpl*, balivernes *fpl*; **to talk b.** dire des bêtises ou des balivernes; **the book is utter b.** le livre est complètement nul
INT balivernes!

bald-headed ADJ chauve; *Fig Fam* **to go b. into** or **at sth** foncer tête baissée dans qch

balding ['bɔːldɪŋ] ADJ **a b. fifty-year-old** un homme de cinquante ans avec une calvitie naissante; **he's b.** il commence à perdre ses cheveux, il devient chauve

baldly ['bɔːldlɪ] ADV *Fig (to write)* d'un style dépouillé ou sec; *(to say)* sèchement; **b. worded** *(reply)* sec; *(statement)* bref; **to put it b.** pour parler clairement; **you didn't have to put it so b.!** tu n'avais pas besoin d'être aussi brutal!

baldness ['bɔːldnɪs] N **1** *(of person)* calvitie *f*, premature **b.** calvitie précoce **2** *Fig (of style etc)* sécheresse *f*

bale[1] [beɪl] N *Com (of goods)* balle *f*, ballot *m*; *(of hay, straw)* botte *f*, **b. of paper** ballot de dix rames de papier
VT *(goods)* mettre en ballot; *(hay, straw)* botteler

bale[2] N *Naut* = **bail**[3]
▶ **bale out** VI *Aviat* sauter en parachute d'un avion en perdition; **he baled out over the Atlantic** il s'est éjecté de l'avion au-dessus de l'Atlantique
VT SEP = **bail out** VT SEP 2

Balearic [bælɪˈærɪk] ADJ **the B. Islands, the Balearics** les (îles *fpl*) Baléares *fpl*

baleen ['beɪliːn] N *(of whale)* fanon *m* de baleine

baleful ['beɪlfʊl] ADJ *Lit* sinistre, maléfique

balefully ['beɪlfʊlɪ] ADV sinistrement

---

baler[1] ['beɪlər] N **1** *Agr (machine)* botteleuse *f* **2** *(person)* emballeur, -euse

baler[2] N *Naut (bucket)* écope *f*

Bali ['bɑːlɪ] N Bali

Balinese [bɑːlɪˈniːz] ADJ balinais

baling ['beɪlɪŋ] N *(of goods)* mise *f* en balles, paquetage *m*
▶▶ *Agr* **b. machine** botteleuse *f*

balk [bɔːk] VT *Fml (person's plans)* déjouer, contrarier; *(person)* contrarier
VI *(of horse)* refuser, (se) dérober; **to b. at a fence** refuser un obstacle; *Fig* **to b. at** *(difficulty, expense)* s'arrêter ou reculer ou hésiter devant

Balkan ['bɔːlkən] ADJ **the B. States** les États *mpl* balkaniques; **the B. Peninsula** la péninsule des Balkans
NPL **the Balkans** *(region, mountains)* les Balkans *mpl*

Balkanization [bɔːlkənaɪˈzeɪʃən] N balkanisation *f*

Balkanize ['bɔːlkənaɪz] VT *(country)* balkaniser

ball[1] [bɔːl] N **1** *(for playing football, rugby, basketball etc, of child)* ballon *m*; *(for cricket, tennis, golf)* balle *f*, *(for croquet, bowling)* boule *f*, *(for billiards)* bille *f*, *(of wool, string)* pelote *f*, *Culin (of dough etc)* boulette *f*, **to wind wool into a b.** mettre de la laine en pelote; **to roll sth (up) into a b.** mettre qch en boule; **b. of earth** motte *f*, **b. of fire** boule de feu; *Fig* **to be a b. of fire** déborder d'énergie; *Tennis* **to knock the b. about** faire des balles; **to kick a b. about** s'amuser avec un ballon; *Cr* **no b.** balle nulle; **to play b.** jouer à la balle ou au ballon; *Am (baseball)* jouer au baseball; *Fig* coopérer, jouer le jeu; *Fig* **to be on the b.** *(quick-witted)* avoir de la présence d'esprit; *(knowledgeable)* connaître son affaire; *Fig* **to keep one's eye on the b.** rester très vigilant; *Fig* **to keep the b. rolling** *(in conversation)* soutenir la conversation; *Fig* **to start** or **get the b. rolling** faire démarrer les choses, mettre les choses en route; *Fig* **the b. is in your court** c'est à vous de jouer; *Fig* **to have the b. at one's feet** avoir la partie belle

2 *Vulg (testicle)* **balls** couilles *fpl*, *Fig (courage)* courage *m*; *(nonsense)* conneries *fpl*; **balls!** *(rubbish)* quelles conneries!; **to talk a lot** or **a load of balls** dire beaucoup de conneries; **balls to him!** qu'il aille se faire foutre!; *Fig* **they've got us by the balls** ils nous ont à leur merci; *Fig* **to have balls** *(courage)* avoir des couilles; **that type of thing takes balls** il faut avoir des couilles pour faire ce genre de truc

3 *Anat (of foot)* plante *f*, *(of eye)* globe *m*; *(of thumb)* partie *f* charnue, gras *m*
VT **1** **to b. one's fist** serrer le poing **2** *Am Vulg (have sex with)* **to b. sb** se faire qn
▶▶ *Tech* **b. bearing** bille de roulement; *Sport* **b. boy** ramasseur *m* de balles; **b. cock** robinet *m* ou soupape *f* à flotteur; **b. game** *(with small ball)* jeu *m* de balle; *(with large ball)* jeu de ballon; *(baseball)* match *m* de baseball; *Sport* **b. girl** ramasseuse *f* de balles; **b. joint** *Anat* articulation *f* à emboîtement ou à trois axes; *Tech* joint *m* à rotule, articulation à genouillère; *Met* **b. lightning** éclair *m* en boule; *Tech* **b. peen hammer** marteau *m* à panne ronde ou sphérique; **b. race** piste *f* des billes, chemin *m* de roulement des billes; **b. ramp** plan *m* incliné, rampe *f*, **b.-and-socket joint** *Anat* articulation à emboîtement ou à trois axes; *Tech* joint à rotule, articulation à genouillère; *Tech* **b. valve** robinet *m* à tournant sphérique
▶ **ball up** VT SEP *Am Vulg* = **balls up**

When translating **ball**, note that **balle** and **ballon** are not interchangeable.

---

ball[2] N *(dance)* bal *m*, *pl* bals; *Fam* **to have (oneself) a b.** s'éclater; **how was the party? – an absolute b.!** et la soirée, c'était comment? – génial!
▶▶ **b. dress, b. gown** robe *f* de bal

ballad ['bæləd] N **1** *Mus* romance *f* **2** *Liter* ballade *f*

ballast ['bæləst] N **1** *Naut, Aviat* lest *m*; **ship in b.(-trim)** navire *m* sur lest; **to take in b.** faire son lest; **to discharge b.** se délester, jeter du lest; *Fig* **I'm carrying a bit too much b.** j'ai un peu de poids en excédent; *Fig* **to act** or **serve as b.** apporter un équilibre **2** *Constr* pierraille *f*, cailloutage *m*; *Rail* ballast *m*, empierrement *m*
VT **1** *Naut, Aviat* lester **2** *Constr* empierrer, caillouter; *Rail* ballaster
▶▶ **b. bed** *(of railway track)* coffre *m*, empierrement; *(of road)* encaissement *m*; *Rail* **b. car** wagon *m* de terrassement; *Naut* **b. tank** *(of submarine)* ballast *m*; *Rail* **b. truck** wagon de terrassement

ballerina [bæləˈriːnə] N ballerine *f*

ballet ['bæleɪ, *esp Am* bæˈleɪ] N danse *f* classique, ballet *m*; **I'm going to the b. this evening** je vais voir un ballet ou un spectacle de danse classique ce soir; **the Bolshoi b.** le ballet Bolchoï
▶▶ **b. dancer** danseur, -euse de ballet; **b. lesson** cours *m* de danse classique; **b. school** école *f* de danse classique; **b. shoe** chausson *m* de danse

ballistic [bəˈlɪstɪk] ADJ balistique; *Fam* **to go b.** *(get angry)* piquer une crise, grimper aux rideaux
▶▶ *Mil* **b. missile** missile *m* balistique

ballistics [bəˈlɪstɪks] N balistique *f* VOIR GRAMMAIRE A10

balloon [bəˈluːn] N **1** *(toy)* ballon *m*; *Aviat* ballon (dirigeable), montgolfière *f*, *Fig* **when the b. goes up** quand il va y avoir du grabuge; *Fig* **to go down like a lead b.** *(of suggestion, joke)* tomber complètement à plat **2** *(in cartoons, comic strips)* bulle *f*, phylactère *m*
VI *(of skirt, sail etc)* ballonner; *(of cheeks)* gonfler; **to b. (up)** *(of arm, leg etc)* enfler; **she ballooned out in the last months of her pregnancy** elle avait un ventre énorme durant les derniers mois de sa grossesse
▶▶ *Chem* **b. flask** ballon *m*; **b. glass** verre *m* ballon; *Comput* **b. help** bulles *fpl* d'aide; *Psy* **b. test** test *m* de la bulle ou de frustration

ballooning [bəˈluːnɪŋ] N **1** *(sport)* ballon *m*, montgolfière *f*, **to go b.** faire du ballon ou de la montgolfière **2** *(of skirt, sail etc)* ballonnement *m*

balloonist [bəˈluːnɪst] N aérostier *m*

ballot ['bælət] N **1** *(process)* tour *m* de scrutin; *(vote)* scrutin *m*, vote *m*; **to vote by b.** voter par (voie de) scrutin; **to put sth to the b.** soumettre qch à un vote; **second b.** deuxième tour de scrutin; **to cast one's b. for sb** voter pour qn **2** *St Exch (when shares are oversubscribed)* allocation *f* d'actions par tirage au sort
VT *Pol* appeler à voter; **union members will be ballotted on Tuesday** les membres du syndicat décideront par voie de scrutin mardi
VI **1** *Pol* voter par (voie de) scrutin; **to b. for/against sb** voter pour/contre qn **2** *Arch (draw lots)* tirer au sort; **to b. for a place** tirer une place au sort
▶▶ **b. box** *(for ballot papers)* urne *f*, *Fig* système *m* électoral ou démocratique; **b. box stuffing** fraude *f* électorale *(consistant à ajouter des bulletins dans les urnes)*; **b. paper** bulletin *m* de vote; **b. rigging** fraude électorale

balloting ['bælətɪŋ] N **1** *Pol* scrutin *m* **2** *Arch (drawing of lots)* tirage *m* au sort

ballpark ['bɔːlpɑːk] N *Am* terrain *m* de baseball; *Fig* **you're not even in the b.!** tu es loin du compte!; *Fig* **are we in the same b.?** est-ce qu'on est sur la même longueur d'ondes? ▸▸ *Fig* **b. figure** estimation *f*, approximation *f*

ballplayer ['bɔːlpleɪər] N *Am Sport* joueur *m* de base-ball

ballpoint ['bɔːlpɔɪnt] N stylo *m* (à) bille ▸▸ **b. pen** stylo (à) bille

ballroom ['bɔːlruːm] N salle *f* de bal, salle de danse ▸▸ **b. dancing** danse *f* de salon; **to go b. dancing** aller danser; **b. dancing championship** championnat *m* de danses de salon

▸ **balls up** [bɔːlz] *Br Vulg* VT SEP foutre la merde *ou* le merdier dans; **don't b. things up again!** ne recommence pas à foutre la merde!
 VI merder

balls-up N *Br Vulg* merdier *m*; **to make a (right) b. of sth** foutre la merde *ou* le merdier dans qch

ballsy ['bɔːlzɪ] ADJ *Am Sl Fam* culotté

ballup ['bɔːlʌp] N *Am Vulg* = **balls-up**

bally ['bælɪ] ADJ *Old-fashioned Br Fam* sacré, satané

ballyhoo [bælɪ'huː] N *Fam Pej* **1** *(publicity)* battage *m* (publicitaire) **2** *(fuss)* blabla *m*; **to see through the b.** ne pas être dupe; **what's all the b. about?** pourquoi tout ce remue-ménage?
 VT *esp Am Fam (book, show)* faire du battage (publicitaire) pour promouvoir

balm [bɑːm] N *Pharm, Fig* baume *m*; **b. to the soul** baume au cœur

balminess ['bɑːmɪnɪs] N **1** *(mildness)* **the b. of the evening air** l'air embaumé du soir **2** *Br Fam* = **barminess**

balmoral [bɑːl'mɒrəl] N *(shoe)* balmoral *m*

balmy ['bɑːmɪ] ADJ **1** *(air, weather)* doux, *f* douce; **the air was b. with the scent of roses** l'air était embaumé du parfum des roses **2** *Br Fam* = **barmy**

balneotherapy [bælnɪəʊ'θerəpɪ] N balnéothérapie *f*

baloney [bə'ləʊnɪ] N *Am (sausage)* saucisse *f* bolognaise; *Fam* **it's all b.** *(nonsense)* c'est des bêtises; **the film/book is a load of b.** le film/livre est complètement nul; **the usual b. from the government** les boniments habituels du gouvernement; **don't give me that b.!** à d'autres!
 INT ne dites pas de bêtises!

balsa ['bɔːlsə] N balsa *m* ▸▸ **b. wood** balsa *m*; **b. wood raft** radeau *m* en bois de balsa

balsam ['bɔːlsəm] N **1** *(substance)* baume *m* **2** *(plant)* balsamine *f* ▸▸ *Bot* **b. fir** sapin *m* baumier

balsamic vinegar [bɔːl'sæmɪk] N vinaigre *m* balsamique

balti ['bɔːltɪ] N *Br Culin (container)* = récipient *m* métallique utilisé dans la cuisine indienne; *(food)* = plat *m* épicé préparé dans un balti

Baltic ['bɔːltɪk] N **the B.** la (mer) Baltique ADJ **1** *(state)* balte, baltique **2** *Br Fam* **it's b.** *(very cold)* il fait un froid de canard ▸▸ **B. port** port *m* balte; **the B. Sea** la mer Baltique; **the B. States** les pays *mpl* baltes

baluster ['bæləstər] N balustre *m*; **balusters** rampe *f* d'escalier

balustrade [bælə'streɪd] N balustrade *f*

bamboo [bæm'buː] N bambou *m*; **b. chair** chaise *f* en bambou ▸▸ **b. cane** bambou *m*; **B. Curtain** rideau *m* de bambou; **b. shoots** pousses *fpl* de bambou

bamboozle [bæm'buːz(ə)l] VT *Fam (person)* embobiner; **you've been bamboozled** tu t'es fait embobiner; **to b. sb out of sth** *(cheat)* refaire qn de qch; *(trick)* soutirer qch à qn; **to b. sb into doing sth** embobiner qn pour qu'il fasse qch

ban [bæn] N interdiction *f*, *Hist (banishment)* ban *m*, bannissement *m*, proscription *f*, *Rel* interdit *m*; **atomic test b.** interdiction des essais nucléaires; **to put** *or* **impose a b. on sth** interdire qch; **to lift the b. on sth** lever l'interdiction qui porte sur qch; **is there a b. on smoking?** est-il interdit de fumer?
 VT *(-nn-)* interdire; **b. the bomb!** non à la bombe atomique!; **to be banned from driving** se voir retirer son permis de conduire; **he should be banned for life** *(from driving)* on devrait lui retirer son permis de conduire à vie; **dogs have been banned from the beach** les chiens sont interdits sur la plage; **to be banned from a club** être exclu d'un club; **he's been banned from the restaurant/bar** il n'a plus le droit de rentrer dans ce restaurant/bar

banal [bə'næl] ADJ banal, -als, ordinaire

banality [bə'nælɪtɪ] N banalité *f*

banana [bə'nɑːnə] N banane *f*, *Fam* **to go bananas** *(become excited)* déjanter; *(become angry)* grimper aux rideaux; *Fam* **you're bananas!** *(crazy)* tu es cinglé!; *Fig Fam* **top b.** grand chef *m* ▸▸ **b. boat** bananier *m (bateau)*; **b. plantation** bananeraie *f*, *Fam* **b. republic** république *f* bananière; **b. skin** peau *f* de banane; *Culin* **b. split** banana split *m*; **b. tree** bananier

bancassurance ['bæŋkəʃʊərəns] N *Banking* bancassurance *f*

band¹ [bænd] N **1** *(round hat)* ruban *m*; *(round cigar)* bague *f*
 2 *(stripe) (of colour)* bande *f*, raie *f*, *Radio* **bands of the spectrum** bandes du spectre
 3 *Radio* bande *f* de fréquence
 4 *(range)* tranche *f*; **children in the 10–15 age b.** les enfants dans la tranche des 10–15 ans
 5 *Tech etc* bande *f*, courroie *f*
 6 *Rel, Law* **bands** *(on collar)* rabat *m*
 7 *(wedding ring)* alliance *f*, **b. of gold** alliance en or ▸▸ *Ind* **b. conveyor** tapis *m* roulant; *Tech* **b. saw** scie *f* à ruban

band² N **1** *Mus (jazz)* orchestre *m*, groupe *m*; *(rock music)* groupe; **to be** *or* **play in a b.** faire partie d'un orchestre/un groupe **2** *(group)* bande *f*, troupe *f*, *Pej* clique *f* ▸ **band together** VI *(unite)* se liguer (**to do** pour faire)

bandage ['bændɪdʒ] N *Med* bandage *m*, bande *f*, *(blindfold)* bandeau *m*; **to have** *or* **wear a b. on one's arm, to have one's arm in a b.** avoir le bras bandé; **to put a b. on sb/sth** bander qn/qch
 VT *(person, wound, leg)* bander, panser ▸ **bandage up** VT SEP *(person)* bander, panser; **I'll b. this up for you** je vais te faire un bandage; **I bandaged her up with towels** je lui ai fait un bandage avec des serviettes de toilette

bandaging ['bændɪdʒɪŋ] N **1** *(bandages)* bandage *m*, pansement *m* **2** *(action)* pansement *m*

Band-Aid® ['bændeɪd] N *esp Am* sparadrap *m*; *Fig* **a b. solution/measure** une solution/une mesure d'attente *ou* provisoire

bandan(n)a [bæn'dænə] N bandana *m*

bandbox ['bændbɒks] N *Old-fashioned Fig* **she looks as if she's just stepped out of a b.** elle est tirée à quatre épingles

banded ['bændɪd] ADJ *(striped)* rayé ▸▸ *Com* **b. pack** lot *m*; *Com* **b. pack selling** vente *f* par lot

bandit ['bændɪt] N bandit *m*, brigand *m*

banditry ['bændɪtrɪ] N brigandage *m*

bandmaster ['bændmɑːstər] N *Mil etc* chef *m* de musique; *(of brass band)* chef de fanfare

bandoleer, bandolier [bændə'lɪər] N cartouchière *f (portée en bandoulière)*

bandsman, *pl* **bandsmen** ['bændzmən] N *(in military band)* musicien *m*; *(in brass band)* fanfariste *m*

bandstand ['bændstænd] N kiosque *m* à musique

bandwagon ['bændwæg(ə)n] N char *m* des musiciens *(en tête de la cavalcade)*; *Fig* **to climb** *or* **jump on the b.** prendre le train en marche

bandwidth ['bændwɪdθ] N *Radio* largeur *f* de bande; *(of computer monitor)* bande *f* passante

bandy¹ ['bændɪ] VT *(witticisms, insults etc)* échanger; *(statistics)* se renvoyer; **they were bandying words** *(quarrelling)* ils se chamaillaient; **don't b. words with me, young man!** ne venez pas me faire la leçon, jeune homme!

bandy² ADJ aux jambes arquées; **to be b.** avoir les jambes arquées ▸▸ **b. legs** jambes *fpl* arquées; **to have b. legs** avoir les jambes arquées ▸ **bandy about, bandy around** VT SEP **her name was being bandied about as a possible candidate** son nom est revenu plusieurs fois parmi ceux des candidats possibles; **I don't like the papers bandying my name about** je n'aime pas que mon nom revienne à tout propos dans les journaux; **decentralization is a word the government bandies about a lot** la décentralisation est un mot que le gouvernement a souvent à la bouche

bandy-legged ADJ aux jambes arquées

bane [beɪn] N *Lit* plaie *f*; **she is the b. of pretentious authors** elle est la bête noire des auteurs prétentieux; *Fam* **he's the b. of my life** il m'empoisonne l'existence

baneful ['beɪnfʊl] ADJ *Lit* funeste; *(influence)* néfaste

banefully ['beɪnfʊlɪ] ADV funestement

bang¹ [bæŋ] N **1** *(blow)* coup *m* (violent); **she got a bad b. on the head** elle a reçu un mauvais coup sur la tête
 2 *(noise) (of rifle etc)* détonation *f*, *(of door)* claquement *m*; **the door shut with a b.** la porte s'est refermée en claquant; **to shut the door with a b.** claquer la porte; **to shut the windows/cupboard with a b.** fermer les fenêtres/les portes du placard en les faisant claquer; **to go off with a b.** *(of firework)* détoner; *Fam Fig* **to go (off)** *or Am* **over with a b.** être une réussite; **to end with a b.** finir en beauté
 3 *Am Sl (pleasure)* **to get a b. from doing sth** prendre son pied à faire qch; **she gets a real b. out of her grandchildren** elle retire beaucoup de plaisir de ses petits-enfants
 4 *Sl (of heroin)* shoot *m* d'héroïne
 5 *Vulg (sexual intercourse)* baise *f*
 VI **1** *(make noise) (of door, shutter)* claquer, battre; *(of gun)* retentir; **the door banged shut** la porte s'est refermée en claquant; **to b. at** *or* **on the door** frapper à la porte à grands coups; **to b. on the table with one's fist** taper du poing sur la table
 2 *Sl (of heroin addict)* se shooter
 VT **1** *(strike)* frapper (violemment); **to b. one's head** se cogner la tête; *Fig* **to b. one's head against a brick wall** perdre son temps; *Fig* **to b. a few heads together** taper du poing sur la table
 2 *(make noise with) (door, window)* (faire) claquer
 3 *Vulg (have sex with)* baiser

INT pan!, v'lan!, boum!; *Br Fam* **b. went fifty pounds!** et vlan! cinquante livres se sont envolées; *Br Fam* **b. went my hopes of a quiet weekend** pour le week-end tranquille c'était râpé

ADV **to go b.** éclater; **he crashed b. into the tree** il est rentré en plein dans l'arbre; *Fam* to **fall b. in the middle** tomber en plein milieu; *Fam* **b. on time** pile à l'heure; *Fam* **it's b. on** c'est au poil; *Fam* **b. up to date** *(equipment etc)* à la pointe de la technologie; *(reference book etc)* vraiment à jour; **to be b. up-to-date on sth** être vraiment à jour pour ce qui est de qch; *Br Fam* **to be caught b. to rights** être pris la main dans le sac

▸ **bang about, bang around** VI faire du potin

▸ **bang away** VI **1** *(with hammer)* donner des coups, taper; *(with gun)* tirer, donner des coups de feu; **to b. away at a typewriter/ piano** taper sur un clavier de machine à écrire/piano **2** *(criticize)* **they've been banging away at the government for months** cela fait des mois qu'ils s'acharnent sur le gouvernement **3** *Fam (have sex)* baiser

▸ **bang down** VT SEP *(lid)* refermer violemment; **he banged the book down on the table** il a fait claquer le livre sur la table

▸ **bang into** VT INSEP *(collide with)* foncer dans

▸ **bang on** VI *Sl* **he's always banging on about it** il n'arrête pas de bassiner tout le monde avec ça; **if I have to listen to him banging on one more time about it** s'il se remet à me casser les oreilles avec ça mal

▸ **bang out** VT SEP *(tune)* jouer tant bien que mal

▸ **bang up** VT SEP *Br Sl* **1** *(imprison)* boucler; **to be banged up** être en taule **2** *(make pregnant) (usu passive)* **to get banged up** se faire mettre en cloque

bang² N *(also* **bangs)** *(hair)* frange *f*; **to have bangs, to wear one's hair in a b.** avoir une frange

banger ['bæŋər] N *Br* **1** *Fam (sausage)* saucisse *f*; **bangers and mash** purée *f* avec des saucisses **2** *(firework)* pétard *m* **3** *Fam (car)* **old b.** vieux tacot *m*, vieille guimbarde *f*

Bangladesh [bæŋglə'deʃ] N Bangladesh *m*

Bangladeshi [bæŋglə'deʃɪ] N Bangladais, -aise

ADJ *(government, representative etc)* bangladais

bangle ['bæŋgəl] N *(for wrist)* bracelet *m* rigide; *(for ankle)* anneau *m* attaché autour de la cheville

bang-up ADJ *Br Fam (excellent)* super, génial, - aux; **she did a b. job of throwing a good party** elle avait organisé une super soirée

banish ['bænɪʃ] VT **1** *(exile) (person)* bannir, exiler, proscrire **2** *Fig (drive away) (fear, care, idea)* chasser; **to b. sth from one's thoughts** chasser qch de ses pensées; **you can b. all thoughts of a holiday** ce n'est plus la peine de compter sur des vacances

banishment ['bænɪʃmənt] N bannissement *m*, exil *m*; **to go into b.** partir pour l'exil; **to be sent into b.** être banni *ou* exilé

banisters ['bænɪstəz] NPL rampe *f* (d'escalier); **to slide down the b.** glisser le long de la rampe d'escalier

banjax ['bændʒæks] VT *Scot, Ir Fam (break)* bousiller

banjo, *pl* **banjos, banjoes** ['bændʒəʊ, -əʊz] N *Mus* banjo *m*

banjoist ['bændʒəʊɪst] N joueur, -euse de banjo, banjoiste *m*

bank¹ [bæŋk] N **1** *(of river, canal)* berge *f*, bord *m*, rive *f*; *(of lake)* bord, rive; **the banks of the Thames** les berges de la Tamise
　2 *(on side of road etc)* talus *m*; *(man-made)* terrasse *f*, levée *f* de terre; *Constr* banquette *f*, remblai *m*; *Rail* rampe *f*, *Horseracing* banquette (irlandaise)
　3 *(mass) (of fog, cloud, sand)* banc *m*; **banks of flowers** des multitudes *fpl* de fleurs; *Geog* **the Banks of Newfoundland** les Bancs de Terre-Neuve
　4 *Aviat* inclinaison *f*, *(turn)* virage *m* incliné

VT **1** *(river)* contenir par des berges; *Constr* **to b. a road** surhausser *ou* relever un virage; **banked corner** virage *m* relevé **2** *(mass, form)* **to be banked** *(of clouds, snow)* être tassé

VI *(of road)* être incliné; *Aviat* s'incliner sur l'aile; *(turn)* virer (sur l'aile)

▸ **bank up** VT SEP *(earth etc)* remblayer, terrasser; *(fire)* remettre du bois/du charbon dans

VI *(of snow, clouds, mist etc)* s'entasser, s'accumuler

bank² N **1** *Com, Fin* banque *f*, *(for coins)* tirelire *f*, **is there a b. nearby?** y a-t-il une banque par ici?; **could you tell me where the nearest Barclays® b. is?** pouvez-vous me dire où se trouve la Barclays® la plus proche?
　2 *(in game)* banque *f* (de celui qui tient le jeu); **to break the b.** faire sauter la banque; *Fig* **it won't break the b.** *(of expenditure)* ça ne va pas me/nous/etc ruiner
　3 *(store) (for blood, sperm, information)* banque *f*

VT *(money)* mettre *ou* déposer en banque

VI **to b. with sb** avoir un compte en banque chez qn; **who do you b. with?** à quelle banque êtes-vous?; **do you b. with us?** avez-vous un compte chez nous?

▸▸ **b. account** compte *m* en banque; **b. accounting note** avis *m* de la banque; **b. balance** solde *m* bancaire; **b. base rate** taux *m* de base bancaire; **b. borrowings** emprunts *mpl* bancaires, concours *m* bancaire; **b. branch code** code *m* guichet; **b. buying rate** taux de change à l'achat; **b. card** carte *f* (d'identité) bancaire; **b. charges** frais *mpl* bancaires *ou* de banque; **b. cheque** chèque *m* bancaire; **b. clerk** employé, -ée de banque; **b. commission** commission *f* bancaire; **b. credit** avoir *m* en banque, crédit *m* bancaire; **b. debts** dettes *fpl* bancaires; **b. details** relevé *m* d'identité bancaire, RIB *m*; **b. discount** escompte *m* de banque, escompte en dehors; **b. discount rate** escompte officiel; **b. draft** traite *f* bancaire; **the B. of England** la Banque d'Angleterre; **the B. of France** la Banque de France; **b. guarantee** garantie *f* bancaire, caution *f* de banque; **b. holiday** *(in UK)* jour *m* férié; *(in US)* jour de fermeture des banques; **b. interest** intérêt *m* bancaire; **b. ledger** livre *m* ou journal *m* de banque; **b. lending** concours bancaire; **b. loan** *(money lent)* prêt *m* bancaire; *(money borrowed)* emprunt *m* bancaire; **b. manager** directeur, -trice de banque; **b. money** monnaie *f* de banque, monnaie scripturale; **b. notification** avis *m* de la banque; **b. overdraft** découvert *m* bancaire; **b. rate** taux d'escompte *ou* de l'escompte, taux bancaire; **b. reconciliation** rapprochement *m* bancaire; **b. references** références *fpl* bancaires; **b. reserves** réserves *fpl* bancaires; **b. robber** cambrioleur, -euse de banque; **b. selling rate** taux de change à la vente; *St Exch* **b. shares** valeurs *fpl* bancaires; **b. sort code** code guichet; **b. statement** relevé de compte; **b. transactions** transactions *fpl* bancaires; **b. transfer** virement *m* bancaire; **b. treasurer** trésorier, -ière de banque

▸ **bank on** VT INSEP compter sur; *(event)* miser sur; **to b. on success** escompter un succès; **I wouldn't b. on her being there** ça

m'étonnerait qu'elle soit là; **don't b. on it** ne comptez pas là-dessus

bank³ N **1** *(group, series) (of switches, dials, of cylinders)* rangée *f*, *Cin (of projectors)* rampe *f*, *(of speakers, transformers etc)* groupe *m*, batterie *f*, *Comput (of chips)* banc *m* **2** *Naut (of rowers)* banc *m*; *(of oars)* rang *m*; *(of seats)* travée *f*

bankable ['bæŋkəb(ə)l] ADJ *Fin* bancable; *Fig* **to be b.** *(of film star etc)* être une valeur sûre; *Fig* **a b. idea** une idée qui vaut de l'or

bankbook ['bæŋkbʊk] N *(of account holder)* livret *m* ou carnet *m* de compte ou banque; *(for accounting)* journal *m* ou livre *m* de banque

banker ['bæŋkər] N **1** *Fin* banquier, -ière **2** *(in game)* banquier, ière; **to be b.** tenir la banque

▸▸ *Fin* **b.'s acceptance** acceptation *f* bancaire; *Fin* **Bankers' Automated Clearing System** système *m* électronique de paiement; *Fin* **b.'s card** carte *f* bancaire; *Fin* **b.'s cheque** traite *f* bancaire; *Fin* **b.'s draft** chèque *m* bancaire *ou* de banque; *Fin* **b.'s order** ordre *m* de transfert permanent

banking¹ ['bæŋkɪŋ] N **1** *Constr* remblayage *m*, *(of bend)* surhaussement *m*, relèvement *m* **2** *Aviat* inclinaison *f*, *(turning)* virage *m* incliné

banking² N **1** *(business)* affaires *fpl* ou opérations *fpl* de banque; **electronic b.** bancatique *f* **2** *(profession)* profession *f* de banquier, la banque; **she's in b.** elle travaille dans la banque

▸▸ *Am* **b. account** compte *m* en banque, compte bancaire; **b. centre** place *f* bancaire; **b. consortium** consortium *m* de banques; **b. controls** contrôle *m* bancaire; **b. hours** heures *fpl* d'ouverture des banques; **b. law** droit *m* bancaire; **b. network** réseau *m* bancaire; **b. products** produits *mpl* bancaires; **b. profession** métier *m* de banquier; **b. regulator** régulateur *m* bancaire; **b. secrecy** secret *m* bancaire; **b. services** services *mpl* bancaires; **b. terms** conditions *fpl* de banque

banknote ['bæŋknəʊt] N billet *m* de banque

bankroll ['bæŋkrəʊl] VT *Am Fam (person, project)* financer

bankrupt ['bæŋkrʌpt] N *(person)* failli, -ie; **fraudulent b.** banqueroutier, -ière

ADJ failli; **to go b.** *(of person, business)* faire faillite; *(fraudulently)* faire banqueroute; **to be b.** être en faillite; **to declare sb b.** déclarer *ou* mettre qn en faillite; *Fig* **to be morally b.** avoir perdu toute crédibilité

VT *(person)* mettre en faillite, *Fam* ruiner

bankruptcy ['bæŋkrəptsɪ] N faillite *f*, **fraudulent b.** banqueroute *f*, **to present** *or* **file one's petition for bankruptcy** déposer son bilan; **to bring sb to the verge of b.** amener qn au bord de la ruine

▸▸ *Br Law* **b. court** ≃ tribunal *m* de commerce; *Hum* **you'll have me in the b. court!** tu veux ma ruine!; **b. proceedings** procédure *f* de faillite

banner ['bænər] N *(flag)* bannière *f*, *Comput, Mktg (for advertising on Internet)* bandeau *m*, bannière publicitaire; **the Star-Spangled B.** la bannière étoilée

ADJ *Am (year etc)* excellent

▸▸ *Journ* **b. heading, b. headline** manchette *f*

bannisters ['bænɪstəz] NPL = **banisters**

banns [bænz] NPL bans *mpl*; **to read** *or* **publish the b.** = (faire) publier les bans

banoffee pie, banoffi pie [bə'nɒfɪ] N *Culin* = gâteau *m* à la banane et au caramel

banquet ['bæŋkwɪt] N banquet *m*; **b. facilities** *(notice in hotel etc)* possibilité d'organiser des banquets

VT *(person)* offrir un banquet à

VI banqueter

▸▸**b. hall** salle *f* de banquet; **b. room** salle de banquet

banqueting ['bæŋkwɪtɪŋ] N
▸▸**b. hall** salle *f* de banquet; **b. manager** responsable *mf* des banquets; **b. room** salle de banquet

banquette [bæŋ'ket] N *esp Am (seat)* banquette *f*

banshee [bæn'ʃiː] N *Myth* fée *f* de la mythologie irlandaise, qui hurle pour annoncer une mort imminente; **to wail like a b.** hurler comme un sauvage

bantam ['bæntəm] N **1** *(chicken)* = poulet *m* de petite taille **2** *Boxing* = **bantamweight**

bantamweight ['bæntəmweɪt] N poids *m* coq; **b. champion** champion *m* poids coq

banter ['bæntər] N *(jokes)* badinage *m*; *(teasing)* taquineries *fpl*

bantering ['bæntərɪŋ] ADJ *(tone etc)* taquin

Bantu ['bæntuː] ADJ bantou
N **1** Bantou, -oue **2** *Ling* bantou *m*

banyan ['bænjən] N *(tree)* banian *m*

BAOR [biːeɪəʊ'ɑːr] *abbr* British Army of the Rhine

bap [bæp] N *Br Culin* petit pain *m* rond au lait

baptism ['bæptɪz(ə)m] N baptême *m*; *Fig* **b. of fire** baptême du feu

baptismal [bæp'tɪzm(ə)l] ADJ *(register)* baptistaire; *(name)* de baptême
▸▸**b. font** fonts *mpl* baptismaux

Baptist ['bæptɪst] N **1** *Rel* baptiste *mf* **2 (St) John the B.** saint Jean-Baptiste
ADJ baptiste
▸▸**B. doctrine** doctrine *f* baptiste, baptisme *m*

baptist(e)ry ['bæptɪstrɪ] N baptistère *m*

baptize [bæp'taɪz] VT *(person, ship etc)* baptiser; **to be baptized a Catholic/(in the name of) John** être baptisé catholique/du nom de Jean

BAR¹ [bɑːr]

N barre **1, 4, 7, 9** ▪ obstacle **2**
▪ interdiction **3** ▪ le barreau **5**
▪ bar **6, 8**
VT barrer **1** ▪ interdire **2** ▪ exclure **2**
▪ mettre des barreaux à **3**

N **1** *(of iron, gold etc)* barre *f*; *(of chocolate)* tablette *f*; *(smaller)* barre; *(of electric fire)* résistance *f*; *(of medal)* barrette *f*; *(in gym)* barre; **with b.** *(medal)* ≃ avec palme; **bars** *(of window, cage, prison)* barreaux *mpl*; **to be behind (prison) bars** être derrière les barreaux

2 *(obstacle)* empêchement *m*, obstacle *m*; *(in river, harbour)* barre *f* (de sable), traverse *f*; **to be a b. to sth** faire obstacle à qch; **a colour b. anywhere is illegal** il est illégal de faire de la discrimination raciale où que ce soit

3 *(ban)* interdiction *f*; **there is a b. on bringing drink into the club** il est interdit d'introduire de l'alcool au sein du club

4 *Br Law (in court)* barre *f*; **the prisoner at the b.** l'accusé, -ée; *Fig* **to be judged at the b. of public opinion** être jugé par l'opinion publique

5 *Law (profession)* **the B.** l'Ordre *m* des avocats, le barreau; **to read for the B.** faire son droit; **to be called to the B.** être reçu au barreau, être reçu avocat

6 *(pub)* bar *m*, café *m*, *Fam* bistro *m*; *(counter)* comptoir *m*, bar; *Fam* **he's always propping up the b.** c'est un vrai pilier de bar *ou* de bistro

7 *(line)* barre *f*; *Mus* mesure *f*; *Mus* **double b.** double barre

8 *Met* bar *m*

9 *Comput (menu bar)* barre *f*
VT **(-rr-) 1** *(obstruct) (the way)* barrer; **to b.**

sb's way barrer la route à qn, être dans le chemin de qn; **he's been barred from the club** il a été exclu du club
2 *(forbid) (action)* défendre, prohiber, interdire; *(subject of conversation)* exclure; **to b. sb from doing sth** défendre à qn de faire qch; **she's been barred from playing** elle a été interdite de jeu
3 *(put bars on) (window)* mettre des barreaux à
4 *Old-fashioned (lock) (door etc)* barrer; **to b. the door against sb** barrer la porte à qn
▸▸**b. chart** histogramme *m*; **b. code** code-barres *m*, *pl* codes-barres; **b. code reader** lecteur *m* de code-barres; **b. diagram** histogramme; **b. food** = repas *mpl* simples servis dans les bars; **b. graph** histogramme; *Mus* **b. line** barre; *Rel* **b. mitzvah** bar-mitsva *f inv*; **b. staff** personnel *m* de bar

When translating **bar**, note that **barre** and **barreau** are not interchangeable.

bar² PREP *(except)* sauf, excepté, à l'exception de; **we've decided everything b. the time** nous avons tout prévu sauf l'heure; **we've finished all of them b. one** nous les avons tous terminés sauf un; **the finest/the quickest b. none** sans conteste le meilleur/le plus rapide; **it's all over b. the shouting** les jeux sont faits

barb [bɑːb] N **1** *(on fish-hook)* barbillon *m*, dardillon *m*; *(on arrow)* barbillon; *(of barbed wire)* picot *m* **2** *(on fish, animal)* barbillon *m*; *Bot* arête *f*, *(on feather)* barbe *f* **3** *Fig (gibe)* pique *f*, remarque *f* acerbe

Barbados [bɑː'beɪdɒs] N Barbade *f*

barbarian [bɑː'beərɪən] ADJ, N barbare *mf*

barbaric [bɑː'bærɪk] ADJ barbare

barbarism ['bɑːbərɪz(ə)m] N **1** *(of person, behaviour)* barbarie *f* **2** *Gram, Ling* barbarisme *m*

barbarity [bɑː'bærɪtɪ] N **1** *(cruelty)* barbarie *f*, cruauté *f* **2** *(action)* acte *m* de barbarie, atrocité *f*

barbarize ['bɑːbəraɪz] VT **to b. sb** faire de qn un monstre; **to b. the language** estropier la langue

barbarous ['bɑːbərəs] ADJ barbare

barbarously ['bɑːbərəslɪ] ADV cruellement

Barbary ['bɑːbərɪ] N
▸▸**B. ape** singe *m* de Barbarie, magot *m*; **B. horse** cheval *m* barbe; **the B. States** la Barbarie, les États *mpl* barbaresques

barbecue ['bɑːbɪkjuː] N *(fireplace, party)* barbecue *m*; **to cook sth on the b.** faire cuire qch au barbecue; **to have a b.** faire un barbecue
VT *(food)* (faire) griller au barbecue; **barbecued chicken** poulet *m* rôti *ou* grillé au barbecue
▸▸**b. sauce** sauce *f* barbecue

barbed [bɑːbd] ADJ **1** barbelé **2** *Fig (comment etc)* acerbe **3** *Bot* hameçonné
▸▸**b. arrow** flèche *f* à barbelures; **b. wire** (fil *m* de fer) barbelé *m*

barbel ['bɑːb(ə)l] N **1** *(fish)* barbeau *m* (commun) **2** *(on fish)* barbillon *m*

barbell ['bɑːbel] N *Gym* haltère *m*

barber ['bɑːbər] N coiffeur *m* pour hommes, *Old-fashioned* barbier *m*; **I'm going to the b.'s** je vais chez le coiffeur

barbershop ['bɑːbəʃɒp] N *Am* salon *m* de coiffure *(pour hommes)*
▸▸*Mus* **b. harmony** chants *mpl* à quatre voix d'hommes; *Mus* **b. quartet** = quatuor *m* d'hommes chantant en harmonie étroite

barbican ['bɑːbɪkən] N *(fortification)* barbacane *f*

Barbie® ['bɑːbɪ] N (poupée *f*) Barbie® *f*
▸▸**B. doll** (poupée) Barbie®

barbie ['bɑːbɪ] N *Br, Austr Fam* barbecue *m*

barbiturate [bɑː'bɪtjʊrət] N *Chem* barbiturique *m*
▸▸*Med* **b. poisoning** barbiturisme *m*

barbituric [bɑːbɪ'tjʊərɪk] ADJ barbiturique

barbwire [bɑːb'waɪər] N *Am* = **barbed wire**

barcarol(l)e ['bɑːkərəʊl] N *Mus* barcarolle *f*

Barcelona [bɑːsɪ'ləʊnə] N Barcelone *f*

bard¹ [bɑːd] N **1** *Arch (poet)* poète *m*; *Lit* **the B. (of Avon)** Shakespeare **2** *(Celtic)* barde *m*

bard² *Culin* N barde *f*
VT barder

bardic ['bɑːdɪk] ADJ *(poetry)* des bardes

bardolatry [bɑː'dɒlətrɪ] N *Hum Pej* = admiration *f* sans bornes pour Shakespeare et ses œuvres

bare [beər] ADJ **1** *(without covering, unadorned) (head, leg, chest, room etc)* nu; *(cupboard, shelf)* vide; *(tree)* dénudé, dépouillé; *(country)* nu, dénudé; *Elec (wire)* dénudé; **to strip a house b.** *(remove contents)* dévaliser une maison; **they stripped the car b.** *(removed wheels etc)* ils n'ont laissé que la carcasse de la voiture; **the wind stripped the tree b.** le vent a dénudé l'arbre; **the room was b. of furniture/pictures** la pièce ne comportait aucun meuble/tableau; **at this time of year, the garden is b. of flowers** à cette époque de l'année, le jardin n'a plus de fleurs; **to fight with b. hands** se battre à mains nues; **I'll kill him with my b. hands** je le tuerai de mes propres mains; **in one's b. feet** pieds nus; **to lie** *or* **sleep on the b. boards** coucher sur la dure; **the b. facts** les faits bruts; **the b. bones of the case are ...** les grandes lignes de cette affaire sont ...; **to lay b.** *(surface, mistakes, one's heart)* mettre à nu, exposer; *(secret, fraud)* dévoiler; *(foundations, roots etc)* déchausser
2 *attrib (just sufficient)* **to earn a b. living** gagner tout juste *ou* à peine de quoi vivre; **the b. minimum** le strict minimum; **the b. necessities (of life)** le strict nécessaire; *Sch* **he got a b. pass** il a eu son examen en ayant juste la moyenne; **a b. pass isn't good enough in my father's eyes** pour mon père, réussir un examen de justesse n'est pas suffisant; **b. majority** faible majorité *f*
VT mettre à nu; **to b. one's head** se découvrir; **to b. one's teeth** montrer les dents; **to b. one's heart** *or* **soul** ouvrir son cœur, mettre son âme à nu

bareback ['beəbæk] ADV **to ride b.** monter (un cheval) à nu *ou* à cru; *Sl Hum (have unprotected sex)* faire l'amour sans capote
▸▸**b. rider** cavalier, -ière qui monte à cru

barefaced ['beəfeɪst] ADJ ATTRIB *Fam Pej (lie, liar etc)* éhonté, effronté

barefoot(ed) ['beəfʊt, -ɪd] ADJ aux pieds nus
ADV nu-pieds, pieds nus; **she goes b.** elle marche pieds nus

barehanded [beə'hændɪd] ADJ aux mains nues
ADV les mains nues

bareheaded [beə'hedɪd] ADJ à la tête nue
ADV nu-tête, (la) tête nue

bare-legged ADJ aux jambes nues
ADV (les) jambes nues

barely ['beəlɪ] ADV *(just)* à peine, tout juste; **I b. know her** je la connais à peine; **he can b. read and write** c'est tout juste s'il sait lire et écrire; **you've b. got here and you're leaving** tu viens à peine d'arriver et tu es déjà reparti; **a b. furnished room** *(lacking furniture)* une pièce avec très peu de meubles

bareness ['beənɪs] N **1** *(of room)* aspect *m* dépouillé; *(of hillside, wall)* nudité *f* **2** *(of style etc)* dépouillement *m*

barf [bɑːf] VI *esp Am Fam* vomir
▸▸**b. bag** sac *m* pour vomir

barfly ['bɑːflaɪ] N *Am Fam* pilier *m* de bar

bargain ['bɑːgɪn] N **1** *(deal)* marché *m*, affaire *f*; **a good/bad b.** une bonne/mauvaise affaire; **to make** *or* **strike a b. with sb** conclure *ou* faire un marché avec qn; **I'll make a b. with you** on fait un marché; **I thought we had a b.** je croyais qu'on s'était mis d'accord; **you haven't kept your side** *or* **part of the b.** vous n'avez pas respecté notre accord; **to drive a hard b.** ne pas faire de cadeaux; **it's a b.!** c'est entendu!; **into the b.** par-dessus le marché, en plus **2** *(good buy)* occasion *f*, affaire *f*
VI négocier (**with** avec); *(in market place)* marchander (**with** avec)
► ►**b. basement** *(in shop)* = sous-sol *m* où sont regroupés les articles en solde et autres bonnes affaires; **b. break** séjour *m* discompté; **b. counter** rayon *m* des soldes; **b. hunter** chineur, -euse; **b. hunting** chasse *f* aux affaires; **b. offer** promotion *f*, offre *f* exceptionnelle; **b. price** prix *m* avantageux; **b. sale** soldes *mpl* exceptionnels; **b. store** magasin *m* bon marché
► **bargain away** VT SEP brader
► **bargain for** VT INSEP *(reaction, question)* s'attendre à, compter sur; **he got more than he bargained for** il ne s'attendait pas à cela; **you might get more than you bargained for** tu auras peut-être du fil à retordre; **I didn't b. for that** je ne m'attendais pas à cela, je ne comptais pas là-dessus
► **bargain on** VT INSEP s'attendre à, compter sur; **I hadn't bargained on him being there** je ne m'attendais pas à ce qu'il soit là, je n'avais pas compté qu'il serait là

bargaining ['bɑːgɪnɪŋ] N *(in market)* marchandage *m*; *Ind* négociations *fpl*; **to be in a good b. position**, **to have a lot of b. power** être dans une bonne position pour négocier; **this has reduced their b. power** cela a affaibli leur position dans les négociations; **to use sb/sth as a b. chip** utiliser qn/qch comme monnaie d'échange
► ►*Ind* **b. table** table *f* des négociations; **b. unit** unité *f* de négociation

barge [bɑːdʒ] N *(for transporting goods)* péniche *f*, barge *f*, chaland *m*; *(for living on)* péniche; *(ceremonial)* bateau *m* d'apparat
VT *(goalkeeper, player)* écarter d'un coup d'épaule; **to b. sb out of the way** écarter qn d'un geste brusque; **there's a lot of barging going on** *(in race)* on joue beaucoup des épaules
► **barge in** VI **1** *(enter abruptly)* faire irruption **2** *(interrupt)* intervenir mal à propos; **don't keep barging in with questions** arrête de me/nous/*etc* interrompre avec tes questions
► **barge into** VT INSEP **1** *(collide with) (person, lamppost etc)* rentrer dans; **you nearly barged into me!** tu as failli me rentrer dedans! **2** *(enter abruptly) (room)* faire irruption dans
► **barge through** VT INSEP **to b. through a door** passer une porte en trombe; **to b. through a crowd** se forcer un passage à travers la foule
VT SEP **just b. your way through** force le passage

bargee [bɑː'dʒiː], *Am* **bargeman** ['bɑːdʒmən] N marinier *m*

bargepole ['bɑːdʒpəʊl] N *(for propelling barge)* gaffe *f*; *Fig* **I wouldn't touch it with a b.** *(it's disgusting)* ça me dégoûterait d'y toucher; *(it's risky for me)* je ne veux rien avoir à faire avec ça; *(it's risky for you)* si j'étais vous, je ne m'en mêlerais pas

barhop ['bɑːhɒp] VI *Am Fam* faire la tournée des bars

baritone ['bærɪtəʊn] N *Mus (voice, singer, instrument)* baryton *m*

barium ['beərɪəm] N *Chem* baryum *m*
► ►*Med* **b. meal** bouillie *f* barytée

bark [bɑːk] N **1** *(of tree)* écorce *f*; **to strip the b. off a tree** écorcer un arbre **2** *(for tanning)* tan *m*
VT *(tree)* écorcer; *Fig* **to b. one's shins** s'écorcher *ou* s'érafler les jambes (**on** sur)

bark [bɑːk] N *(of dog)* aboiement *m*; *(of fox)* glapissement *m*; *Fig* **his b. is worse than his bite** il aboie plus qu'il ne mord
VI *(of dog)* aboyer (**at** après, contre, à); *(of fox)* glapir; *Fig (of person)* crier (**at** sur); *Fig* **to be barking up the wrong tree** faire fausse route
VT *(of person)* dire en aboyant; **to b. an order** aboyer un ordre

bark [bɑːk] N *Naut (three-master)* trois-mâts *m inv*; *Lit (any boat)* barque *f*
► **bark out** VT SEP *(something)* aboyer

barkeep(er) ['bɑːkiːp, -ər] N *Am* barman *m*

barker ['bɑːkər] N *(at fair)* aboyeur *m*

barker N *(machine)* écorceuse *f*

barking ['bɑːkɪŋ] ADJ **1** *(dog)* aboyeur; *(fox)* glapissant **2** *Fam (cough)* sec, *f* sèche **3** *Sl* **b. (mad)** complètement cinglé
N *(of dog)* aboiement *m*; *(of fox)* glapissement *m*

barley ['bɑːlɪ] N orge *f*
► ►*Culin* **b. sugar** sucre *m* d'orge; *Br* **b. water** = sirop *m* à base d'orge généralement parfumé au citron ou à l'orange

barleycorn ['bɑːlɪkɔːn] N grain *m* d'orge

barm [bɑːm] N *(of beer)* levure *f*, *(yeast)* levain *m*

barmaid ['bɑːmeɪd] N *Br* serveuse *f*, *(in a bar)*, barmaid *f*

barman, *pl* **barmen** ['bɑːmən] N barman *m*

barminess ['bɑːmɪnɪs] N *Br Fam* folie *f*

barmy ['bɑːmɪ] ADJ *Br Fam (crazy)* toqué, cinglé

barn [bɑːn] N grange *f*, *(for cows)* étable *f*, *(for horses)* écurie *f*; *Fam* **they live in an old b. of a house** ils habitent dans un vrai hangar; *Hum* **were you born in a b.?** on ne t'a jamais appris à fermer tes portes?; **he couldn't hit a b. door** *(he's a poor shot)* c'est un mauvais tireur
► ►**b. dance** = bal *m* de campagne où l'on danse des quadrilles; **b. owl** (chouette *f*) effraie *f*, chouette des clochers

barnacle ['bɑːnək(ə)l] N *(mollusc)* bernacle *f*
► ►**b. goose** *(bird)* bernache *f* (nonnette)

barnet ['bɑːnɪt] N *Br Sl (hair)* tifs *mpl*

barney ['bɑːnɪ] N *Br Fam (argument)* prise *f* de bec, dispute *f*; **I had a bit of a b. with the bus driver** j'ai eu une prise de bec avec le conducteur du bus; *Hum* **I had a bit of a b. with a bus** *(of car driver)* j'ai eu un accrochage avec un bus; **we've had a b.** nous nous sommes disputés; **to get into a b. with sb** se disputer avec qn

barnstorm ['bɑːnstɔːm] VI **1** *Br Theat* faire une tournée théâtrale **2** *Am Pol* faire une tournée électorale

barnstormer ['bɑːnstɔːmər] N *Am Pol* orateur, -trice électoral(e)

barnstorming ['bɑːnstɔːmɪŋ] ADJ *(speech, performance)* plein de brio

barnyard ['bɑːnjɑːd] N basse-cour *f*, *pl* basses-cours
► ►**b. humour** humour *m* au ras des pâquerettes

barometer [bə'rɒmɪtər] N *(instrument)*, *Fig* baromètre *m*
► ►**b. reading** hauteur *f* barométrique

barometric [bærə'metrɪk] ADJ *(pressure etc)* barométrique

baron ['bærən] N *(nobleman)* baron *m*; *Fig* **press/oil b.** magnat *m* de la presse/du pétrole; *Culin* **b. of beef** double aloyau *m*

baroness ['bærənes] N baronne *f*

baronet ['bærənet] N baronnet *m*

baronetcy ['bærənɪtsɪ] N dignité *f* de baronnet; **to be given a b.** être élevé au rang de baronnet

baronial [bə'rəʊnɪəl] ADJ baronnial, -aux
► ►**b. hall** demeure *f* seigneuriale

barony ['bærənɪ] N *(domain)* baronnie *f*

baroque [bə'rɒk] ADJ, N *Archit, Art, Mus* baroque *m*

barque [bɑːk] N *Naut* = **bark**³

barrack ['bærək] N **1** *Mil (usu pl) (with sing or pl verb)* **barracks** caserne *f*, quartier *m*; **to be confined to barracks** être consigné **2** *Pej Fam (house)* maison *f* grande et laide
VT *Mil (troops)* caserner
► ►*Mil* **b. square** cour *f* de caserne

> Note that the French word **baraque** is a false friend. Its most common meaning is **shack**.

barrack VT *Br Fam (jeer at) (person)* se moquer de

barracking ['bærəkɪŋ] N *Br Fam* mauvais accueil *m*; **to get** *or* **be given a b.** se faire malmener

barrackroom ['bærəkruːm] N chambrée *f*
► ►**b. language** langage *m* de corps de garde *ou* de caserne; **b. lawyer** chicanier, -ière

barracuda [bærə'kjuːdə] N barracuda *m*, bécune *f*

barrage ['bærɑːʒ] N *(dam)*, *Mil* barrage *m*; *Fig (of questions, insults)* torrent *m*
VT **to b. sb with** *(questions, offers of help etc)* assaillir qn de
► ►*Mil* **b. balloon** ballon *m* de barrage

barred [bɑːd] ADJ *(locked) (door)* barré; *(with bars on) (window)* muni de barreaux

barrel ['bær(ə)l] N **1** *(container) (for wine etc)* tonneau *m*, barrique *f*, fût *m*; *(for oil)* baril *m*; *(for herring etc)* caque *f*, baril; *Fam* **to have sb over a b.** avoir qn à sa merci; **they've got us over a b.** nous sommes coincés, nous sommes à leur merci **2** *Fam (large amount)* grande quantité *f* (**of** de); **she's a b. of fun** *or* **laughs** c'est un sacré boute-en-train; **he's not exactly a b. of fun** *or* **laughs** il n'est pas franchement très marrant; **it wasn't a b. of laughs** *(interview, project)* ça n'a pas été une partie de plaisir; *(film, show)* ce n'était pas très rigolo **3** *(cylinder, tube)* cylindre *m*, partie *f* cylindrique; *(of gun, lock, key)* canon *m*; *(of pump)* corps *m*, barillet *m*; *(of lock)* cylindre, barillet; *(of capstan, winch)* fusée *f*, mèche *f*, tambour *m*; *Mil (of artillery piece)* tube *m*
VT *(-ll-, Am -l-)* mettre en fût
► ►*Mus* **b. organ** orgue *m* de Barbarie; *Aviat* **b. roll** tonneau *m* en spirale; *Archit* **b. vault** voûte *f* en berceau
► **barrel along** VI *Fam (in car etc)* foncer

barren ['bær(ə)n] ADJ *(land)* stérile; *(hillside)* sans végétation; *Old-fashioned (woman)* stérile; *Lit Fig (subject)* maigre; **the area is b. of interest for the art-lover** la région ne présente aucun intérêt pour les amateurs d'art; **he's going through a b. period** *(of author)* il n'a pas beaucoup d'inspiration ces temps-ci
NPL *Am* **barrens** lande(s) *f(pl)*
► ►**b. lands** lande(s)

barrenness ['bærənnɪs] N stérilité *f*

barrette [bə'ret] N *esp Am* barrette *f*

barricade ['bærɪkeɪd, bærɪ'keɪd] N barricade *f*
VT barricader
► **barricade in** VT SEP *(person)* barricader dans une pièce *etc*; **they barricaded themselves in** ils se sont barricadés
► **barricade off** VT SEP *(street)* barrer

barrier ['bærɪər] N barrière f; *Fig* barrière (**between** entre), obstacle m (**to** à); **to break down the barriers** abattre les barrières; **language b.** barrière linguistique
▸▸ **b. cream** crème f protectrice; **b. ice** banquise f, **b. method** *(of contraception)* méthode f de contraception locale; **b. reef** barrière de corail

barring ['bɑːrɪŋ] N **1** *(of door etc)* barrage m **2** *(of action)* interdiction f; *(of person)* exclusion f
PREP *(except)* excepté, sauf; **b. accidents** sauf accident, sauf imprévu; **b. a miracle** à moins d'un miracle

barrister ['bærɪstər] N *Br Law* ≃ avocat, -ate

barrow¹ ['bærəʊ] N *(in garden etc)* brouette f, *esp Br (handcart)* voiture f *ou* charrette f à bras; *Rail* diable m
▸▸ *Br* **b. boy** marchand m ambulant

barrow² N *Archeol* tumulus m, tertre m (funéraire)

Bart *abbr* baronet

bartender ['bɑːtendər] N *Am* barman m

barter ['bɑːtər] N troc m
VT troquer; **to b. sth for sth** troquer qch contre qch
VI faire du troc
▸▸ **b. society** société f vivant du troc

Bartholomew [bɑːˈθɒləmjuː] N *Hist* **the Massacre of St B.** le Massacre de la Saint-Barthélemy

basal ['beɪsəl] ADJ basal, -aux

basalt ['bæsɔːlt] N basalte m

basaltic [bəˈsɔːltɪk] ADJ basaltique

bascule ['bæskjuːl] N *Constr* bascule f
▸▸ **b. bridge** pont m à bascule

base¹ [beɪs] N **1** *(foundation)*, *Fig* base f; *(of column, statue)* socle m; *(of machine tool etc)* sole f, embase f; *Elec (of lamp)* culot m **2** *Math, Chem etc* base f; *Ling* base, racine f **3** *Mil etc (of operations, supplies)* base f; **Glasgow is a good b. from which to explore the Highlands** Glasgow est un point idéal pour partir à la découverte des Highlands **4** *Sport (in baseball, rounders)* base f, *Fig* **you won't even get to first b. with the chairman if you don't play golf** tu n'arriveras à rien avec le président si tu ne joues pas au golf; **he didn't even get to first b. with her** *(girlfriend)* il n'est parvenu à rien avec elle; **to be (way) off b.** *(mistaken)* être (complètement) à côté de la plaque; *Am Fam (crazy)* être fou *ou* cinglé; *Am Fam* **to touch b. with sb** contacter qn; **I just thought I would call and touch b.** je me suis dit que j'appellerais pour prendre des nouvelles
VT **1** *(found) (calculation, hope)* baser, fonder (**on** sur); *(novel, film)* baser (**on** sur); *(opinion)* asseoir, fonder (**on** sur); **what are your accusations based on?** sur quoi tes accusations sont-elles fondées?; **to b. oneself on sth** se baser sur qch **2** *(have as headquarters) (usu passive)* **to be based in Bath** être basé à Bath
▸▸ *Mil* **b. camp** camp m de base; **b. coat** *(of paint)* première couche f, *Fin* **b. date** date f de base; *Sport* **b. jumping** = saut m en chute libre à partir d'un pont, d'une falaise ou d'une montagne, avec parachute plié que l'on ouvre le plus tard possible; *Banking* **b. rate** taux m de base (bancaire) *(utilisé par les banques pour déterminer leur taux de prêt)*; *TV, Radio* **b. station** station f de base; *TV, Radio* **b. studio** studio m de base; *Banking* **b. year** année f de référence

base² ADJ *Fml (ignoble) (man, accusations etc)* vil; *(reason)* bas, f basse, indigne; *(action)* ignoble, indigne
▸▸ **b. coin, b. coinage** *(counterfeit)* fausse monnaie f; **b. metals** métaux mpl vils

baseball ['beɪsbɔːl] N *Sport* base-ball m, pl base-balls
▸▸ **b. game** match m de base-ball; **b. player** joueur m de base-ball

baseboard ['beɪsbɔːd] N *Am* plinthe f
▸▸ **b. heater** plinthe électrique

Basel ['bɑːz(ə)l] N Bâle f

baseless ['beɪslɪs] ADJ sans fondement

baseline ['beɪslaɪn] N *Tennis* ligne f de fond; *Art* ligne de fuite; *Comput* ligne de base
▸▸ *Com* **b. sales** ventes fpl de base

basely ['beɪslɪ] ADV *Fml* de façon ignoble

basement ['beɪsmənt] N *(in house, shop)* sous-sol m, pl sous-sols; **in the b.** au sous-sol
▸▸ **b. flat** (appartement m en) sous-sol

baseness ['beɪsnɪs] N *Fml (of action, accusation etc)* bassesse f

bash [bæʃ] *Fam* N **1** *(blow)* coup m; *(with fist)* coup de poing m, gnon m; *Br Fam* **to have a b. at sth** *(attempt)* essayer qch; **I'll have a b. at mending it** je vais essayer de le réparer **2** *(dent)* bosse f, gnon m **3** *(party)* fête f, soirée f
VT **to b. one's head** se cogner la tête
▸ **bash about, bash around** VT SEP *Br Fam (beat) (person)* battre, maltraiter, rudoyer; *(handle roughly) (suitcase, toys etc)* maltraiter; **the parcel's been** *or* **got a bit bashed about** le colis a été un peu abîmé
▸ **bash down** VT SEP *Br Fam (smash) (door)* enfoncer
▸ **bash in** VT SEP *Br Fam (smash) (door)* enfoncer; **I'll b. your face in** je vais te défoncer la tête
▸ **bash into** VT INSEP *Br Fam (person, object)* rentrer dans
▸ **bash on** VI *Br Fam* continuer
▸ **bash up** VT SEP *Br Fam (person)* tabasser; *(car)* esquinter

bashful ['bæʃfʊl] ADJ **1** *(timid)* modeste, timide; **b. lover** amoureux m transi **2** *(modest)* modeste, pudique

bashfully ['bæʃfʊlɪ] ADV **1** *(timidly)* modestement, timidement **2** *(modestly)* pudiquement

bashfulness ['bæʃfʊlnɪs] N **1** *(timidity)* modestie f, timidité f **2** *(modesty)* pudeur f

bashing ['bæʃɪŋ] N *Fam* volée f de coups, rossée f, *Mil, Sport etc* **to take** *or* **get a b.** prendre une raclée *ou* une peignée; **queer-/Paki-b.** persécution f des homosexuels/des Pakistanais; *Fig* **Clinton-/union-b.** acharnement m contre Clinton/les syndicats

BASIC ['beɪsɪk] N *Comput* BASIC m

basic ['beɪsɪk] ADJ *(elementary) (understanding, vocabulary, agreement etc)* de base; *(fundamental) (principle etc)* fondamental, -aux; *(truth, problem)* premier; *(rudimentary) (furniture, accommodation, skills)* rudimentaire; **to learn some b. French** apprendre les bases du français; **my French is a bit b.** mon français est plutôt rudimentaire; **I've got the b. idea** je vois de quoi il s'agit en gros; **trust is b. to any human relationship** la confiance est la base des relations humaines; **these facts are b. to an understanding of the problem** ces faits sont essentiels pour comprendre le problème
NPL **basics** choses fpl essentielles, essentiel m; *(of a language, science etc)* bases fpl, rudiments mpl; **let's get down to basics** allons à l'essentiel; **to get back to basics** *(important things in life)* retourner aux choses essentielles; *Pol* **back to basics** = expression f qui suggère un retour aux valeurs traditionnelles en matière d'éducation ou de moralité, lancée par les Conservateurs comme argument de renouveau politique au début des années 90
▸▸ *Am TV* **b. cable** câble m de base; *Econ* **b.**

commodity denrée f de base; *Mktg* **b. consumer goods** denrées de consommation courante; *Ins* **b. cover** assurance f de garantie de base; **b. offer** offre f de base; *Fin* **b. pay** salaire m de base; **b. population** population-mère f, *Br Fin* **b. rate** taux m de base; *Br Fin* **b. salary** salaire de base, traitement m de base; *Fin* **b. wage** salaire de base

basically ['beɪsɪklɪ] ADV *(different, sound, right etc)* fondamentalement; **b., I think you're right** au fond, je pense que tu as raison; **I think it's b. a question of experience** je pense qu'en fait c'est une question d'expérience; **b., what he said was …** en gros, ce qu'il a dit c'est que …

basil ['bæz(ə)l, *Am* 'beɪz(ə)l] N *Bot, Culin* basilic m

basilica [bəˈzɪlɪkə] N *Archit* basilique f

basilisk ['bæzɪlɪsk] N *Myth* basilic m; *Fig Lit* a **b. stare** un regard assassin

basin ['beɪs(ə)n] N **1** *(bowl) (for washing up etc)* bassine f, cuvette f, *(of fountain)* vasque f, coupe f, **(wash-)hand b.** lavabo m **2** *(of river)* bassin m; **the Paris B.** le Bassin parisien; **coal b.** bassin houiller **3** *Naut (for mooring)* bassin m; *(in canal, river)* garage m

basinful ['beɪs(ə)nfʊl] N *(of soup)* plein bol m, bolée f, *(of water)* pleine cuvette f, *Sl* **to have had a b.** *(enough)* en avoir ras le bol, en avoir marre

basing fare ['beɪsɪŋ] N tarif m de référence

basing point N *(for establishing air fares)* point m de référence

basis, pl **bases** ['beɪsɪs, -iːz] N **1** *(of talks etc)* base f, *(of opinion etc)* fondement m; *(of tax)* assiette f, **on the b. of …** sur la base de …; **I will be taking part on an unofficial b.** je participerai à titre non officiel; **on the b. of what you told me** d'après ce que tu m'as dit; **the rumours have no b. in fact** ces rumeurs ne sont fondées sur aucun fait; *Acct* **b. for depreciation** base amortissable; **b. of calculations** base de calcul **2** *Math* matrice f de base

bask [bɑːsk] VI **to b. in the sun** se chauffer (au soleil), *Fam* lézarder; *Fig* **to b. in sb's favour** jouir de la faveur de qn

basket ['bɑːskɪt] N *(with or without handles)* corbeille f, *(with handles)* panier m; *(carried on back)* hotte f, *(for coal etc)* banne f, manne f, *(plaited shopping basket)* cabas m, couffin m; *(for carrying baby)* couffin m; *(in basketball)* panier m; *Fin* **b. of currencies** panier de monnaies; *StExch* **b. of shares** panier d'actions; *Old-fashioned Br Fam* **(you) silly b.!** espèce d'idiot!
▸▸ *Fam* **b. case** *(nervous wreck)* paquet m de nerfs; *(mad person)* cinglé, -ée, barjo mf; *Am (invalid)* grand (e) invalide mf; **she's turning into a b. case** elle est en train de devenir cinglée; **economic b. case** pays m invalide sur le plan économique; **b. chair** chaise f en osier; **b. hilt** *(of sword)* (garde f en) coquille f, **b. maker** vannier m; **b. making** vannerie f

basketball ['bɑːskɪtbɔːl] N basket-ball m, pl basket-balls, *Fam* basket m
▸▸ **b. player** basketteur, -euse

basketful ['bɑːskɪtfʊl] N plein panier m

basketry ['bɑːskɪtrɪ], **basketwork** ['bɑːskɪtwɜːk] N vannerie f

basking shark ['bɑːskɪŋ] N pèlerin m

Basle [bɑːl] N Bâle

basmati rice [bæsˈmætɪ] N *Culin* riz m basmati

Basque [bɑːsk] ADJ basque; **the B. Country** le Pays basque
N **1** Basque mf **2** *Ling* basque m

basque [bɑːsk] N *(bodice)* guêpière f, *(of jacket)* basque f

bas-relief ['bæsrɪliːf] N bas-relief m, pl bas-reliefs; **in b.** en bas-relief

bass[1] [bæs] N (fish) (freshwater) perche f commune; (saltwater) bar m; **striped b.** bar rayé

bass[2] [beɪs] N (voice, singer, instrument) basse f, (on amplifier) basses; (double bass) contrebasse f, **he sings b.** il chante dans les basses; **deep b.** basse profonde
ADJ ATTRIB Mus (voice, part) de basse; **b. tones** sons mpl graves
▸▸Mus **b. clef** clef f de fa; **b. drum** grosse caisse f, **b. guitar** guitare f basse

bass[3] [bæs] N (material) tille f, filasse f

basset ['bæsɪt] N basset m
▸▸**b. hound** basset

bassinet(te) [bæsɪ'net] N Old-fashioned **1** (cradle) moïse m **2** (pram) voiture f d'enfant

bassist ['beɪsɪst] N Mus contrebassiste mf

basso profundo ['bæsəʊprɒ'fʊndəʊ] N Mus (voix f de) basse f profonde

bassoon [bə'suːn] N Mus basson m; **double b.** contrebasson m

bassoonist [bə'suːnɪst] N Mus basson m, bassoniste mf

bast [bæst] N = **bass**[3]

bastard ['bɑːstəd] N **1** bâtard, -arde; Law enfant mf naturel(le) **2** Sl (person) salaud m; **you b.!** espèce de salaud!; **he's a stupid b.!** c'est un pauvre con!; **you lucky b.!** sacré veinard(e)!; **the poor b.** le pauvre vieux; **it's a b. of a book to translate** ce livre est vachement dur à traduire; **I can't get the b. thing to work** j'arrive pas à faire marcher cette saloperie; **a b. of a job** une saloperie de travail; **it's a b.** (of work, problem) c'est vachement difficile
ADJ (child) bâtard

bastardize ['bɑːstədaɪz] VT **1** (debase) corrompre **2** Arch (child) déclarer illégitime

bastardy ['bæstədɪ] N Arch bâtardise f

baste[1] [beɪst] VT Sewing bâtir, faufiler

baste[2] VT Culin (roast) arroser de sa graisse/de son jus

basting[1] ['beɪstɪŋ] N Sewing (action) faufilage m, faufilure f, (stitching) bâti m, faufilure
▸▸**b. thread** fil m à faufiler

basting[2] N Culin (of roast) arrosage m

bastion ['bæstɪən] N (fortification), Fig bastion m

bat[1] [bæt] N Zool chauve-souris f, pl chauves-souris; Fig **like a b. out of hell** comme un bolide; Fam **to have bats in the belfry** avoir une araignée au plafond

bat[2] N **1** (for cricket, baseball etc) batte f, (for ping-pong) raquette f, **he's a good b.** il manie bien la batte; Fam **to do sth off one's own b.** faire qch de sa propre initiative; esp Am **to do sth right off the b.** faire qch tout de suite; esp Am **to go to b. for sb** (intercede for) intervenir ou intercéder pour ou en faveur de qn **2** Am **to go on a b.** se soûler
VI (-tt-) (use bat) (in cricket, baseball etc) manier la batte; Cr (be at wicket) être au guichet; Sl **to b. for the other side** or **team** (of gay man) en être, être pédé; (of lesbian) être gouine; Sl **to b. for both sides** or **teams** (of bisexual) marcher à voile et à vapeur

bat[3] VT (one's eyelids) battre; Fig **he didn't b. an eyelid** il n'a pas sourcillé ou tiqué

batch [bætʃ] N (of bread), Fam (of people) fournée f, (of letters) tas m, paquet m; (of goods etc), Comput (of data) lot m; (of cement, concrete) gâchée f, **in batches of 20** (people) par groupes de 20; (of files etc) par lots de 20
▸▸Comput **b. command** commande f séquentielle; Comput **b. file** fichier m de commandes; Comput **b. processing** traite-

ment m par lots; Ind **b. production** production f par lots

bated ['beɪtɪd] ADJ **with b. breath** (to wait, watch) en retenant son souffle

bath, pl **baths** [bɑːθ, bɑːðz] N **1** (washing) bain m; **to take** or **have a b.** prendre un bain; **to give a child a b.** baigner ou donner un bain à un enfant; Br Old-fashioned **(public) baths** (for washing) bains publics; (for swimming) piscine f, Br **the Order of the B.** l'Ordre m du Bain **2** (tub) baignoire f, **he's in the b.** il est dans son bain; **hip b., sitz b.** bain m de siège **3** (bathroom) salle f de bain(s) **4** Phot etc cuvette f, (liquid) bain m
VT baigner, donner un bain à
VI prendre un bain
▸▸**b. mat** tapis m de bain; **b. pearls** perles fpl de bain; **b. rail** barre f de soutien; **b. salts** sels mpl de bain; **b. sheet** drap m de bain; **b. towel** serviette f de bain; **b. water** eau f du bain

bathcap ['bæθkæp] N Am bonnet m de bain

bathe [beɪð] N Old-fashioned bain m (de rivière/de mer), baignade f, **to go for a b.** (aller) se baigner
VT (wash) Med (wound) laver; Am (child) baigner; **to b. one's face** se passer de l'eau sur le visage; **a face bathed in tears** un visage baigné de larmes; **bathed in perspiration** trempé de sueur, en nage; **bathed in light** baigné de lumière
VI **1** Old-fashioned (swim) se baigner, prendre un bain (de rivière/de mer) **2** Am (have bath) prendre un bain

bather ['beɪðər] N Old-fashioned baigneur, -euse

bathers ['beɪðəz] NPL Austr Fam (swimming costume) maillot m

bathing ['beɪðɪŋ] N **1** esp Old-fashioned (swimming) bains mpl (de rivière/de mer), baignade f, **b. is prohibited** la baignade est interdite, il est interdit de se baigner; **the water is too cold for b.** l'eau est trop froide pour se baigner **2** Med (of wound etc) lavage m
▸▸**b. cap** bonnet m de bain; **b. costume** maillot m de bain; **b. place** baignade; **b. suit** maillot m de bain; Br **b. trunks** maillot de bain

bathos ['beɪθɒs] N Liter chute f du sublime au ridicule

bathrobe ['bɑːθrəʊb] N peignoir m

bathroom ['bɑːθruːm] N **1** (with bath) salle f de bain(s) **2** Am (toilet) toilettes fpl; **to go to the b.** aller aux toilettes
▸▸**b. scales** pèse-personne m, pl pèse-personnes

bathtime ['bɑːθtaɪm] N l'heure f du bain

bathtub ['bɑːθtʌb] N baignoire f

batik ['bætɪk, bə'tiːk] N batik m; **b. skirt** jupe f en batik

batman, pl **batmen** ['bætmən] N Mil ordonnance mf

baton ['bætən] N **1** (of official) bâton m; Sport (in relay race) témoin m; Mus (of conductor) baguette f, bâton; **orchestra under the b. of Jonathan Butcher** orchestre sous la direction de Jonathan Butcher **2** Br (of policeman) bâton m
▸▸Sport **b. change** passage m de témoin; **b. charge** charge f à la matraque; **b. mike** micro m tenu à la main; **b. round** balle f en plastique

bats [bæts] ADJ Br Old-fashioned Fam loufoque; **to be b. about sb/sth** être fou de qn/qch; **I'm not exactly b. about the idea** je ne raffole pas de cette idée

batsman, pl **batsmen** ['bætsmən] N Cr batteur m

battalion [bə'tæljən] N Mil **1** bataillon m;

tank b., armoured b. bataillon de chars **2** Am groupe m d'artillerie
▸▸**b. commander** commandant m de bataillon

batten ['bæt(ə)n] N Carp (for joint) couvrejoint m, pl couvre-joints; (lathe) latte f, liteau m; (in floor) planche f
VT **1** Carp latter, voliger **2** **to b. down the hatches** Naut condamner les panneaux; Fig se préparer à affronter la crise/la situation
▸**batten on** VT INSEP (live off) vivre aux crochets de
▸**batten onto** VT INSEP (person) mettre le grappin sur; (idea) se mettre dans la tête; **once he battens onto you** une fois qu'il vous a mis le grappin dessus

batter[1] ['bætər] N Cr, Baseball batteur m

batter[2] N Culin pâte f à frire; **pancake b.** pâte à crêpes

batter[3] VT **1** (child, wife etc) battre **2** Mil (town) bombarder
VI **to b. at** or **on a door** marteler une porte; **the waves battered against the coast** les vagues s'abattaient le long de la côte
▸**batter down** VT SEP (door etc) abattre, démolir; (wall) battre en brèche
▸**batter in** VT SEP (door etc) enfoncer; **the victim's skull was battered in** la victime a eu le crâne défoncé

battered ['bætəd] ADJ **1** (face) meurtri **2** (furniture, car, house etc) délabré; (hat, pan) cabossé
▸▸**b. baby, b. child** enfant mf maltraité(ée), enfant martyr(e); **b. wife** femme f battue

battering ['bætərɪŋ] N (of child, wife) mauvais traitements mpl; **that's not the first b. he's given her** ce n'est pas la première fois qu'il la bat; Fig **his confidence took a b.** sa confiance en soi en a pris un coup; Fig **to give sb a b.** (defeat) mettre une raclée à qn; Fig **to take a b.** se prendre une raclée
▸▸**b. ram** bélier m

battery ['bæt(ə)rɪ] N **1** Elec (for calculator, watch etc) pile f, (for car) batterie f, (storage) **b.** accumulateur m, Fam accu m; **to be b. operated** or **powered** (of radio, toy) fonctionner sur piles; **batteries not included** (on packaging) piles non fournies **2** Mil batterie f, Fig **a b. of criticism** un feu roulant de critiques **3** (set, group) (of furnaces, tests) batterie f **4** Law voie f de fait **5** (for poultry) batterie f **6** Sport (in baseball) **the b.** le lanceur et le receveur
▸▸Elec **b. back-up** alimentation f de secours par batterie; Elec **b. cable** câble m de batterie; Elec **b. charger** chargeur m; Elec **b. compartment** compartiment m réservé à la batterie/aux piles; Agr **b. farming** élevage m intensif ou en batterie; Agr **b. hen** poule f de batterie; Elec **b. life** durée f de vie de la batterie/des piles; Elec **b. pack** boîtier m d'alimentation par pile

batting ['bætɪŋ] N Cr etc maniement m de la batte

battle ['bæt(ə)l] N Mil, Fig bataille f, combat m; (against poverty, disease etc) lutte f (**against** contre); **to fight/win a b.** livrer/gagner une bataille; **killed in b.** tué au combat; **to do b. with sb** livrer bataille à qn; **to join b. with sb** entrer en lutte avec qn, livrer bataille à qn; Fig **that's half the b.** c'est déjà ça de gagné; **understanding the instructions is half the b.** quand on a compris les instructions, la partie est déjà à moitié gagnée; **a b. of words** une altercation; (argument) dispute f violente
VI se battre, lutter (**with sb for sth** contre qn pour qch); **to b. with** or **against a fire** combattre ou lutter contre un incendie
VT **to b. one's way through difficulties** surmonter les difficultés; **I had to b. my way to**

the top il a fallu que je me batte pour arriver au sommet
▸▸*Hist* **the B. of Britain** la bataille d'Angleterre; *Mil, Naut* **b. cruiser** croiseur *m* cuirassé; *Mil* **b. cry** cri *m* de guerre; **b. fleet** flotte *f* de ligne *ou* de combat; **b. royal** *(fight)* bagarre *f*, *(argument)* querelle *f*, *Mil* **b. zone** zone *f* de bataille *ou* d'engagement

battle-axe N hache *f* d'armes; *Pej Fig (woman)* virago *f*, mégère *f*

battledore ['bæt(ə)ldɔ:r] N *Hist, Sport* raquette *f*; **to play at b. and shuttlecock** jouer au volant

battledress ['bæt(ə)ldres] N *Mil* tenue *f* de campagne

battlefield ['bæt(ə)lfi:ld], **battleground** ['bæt(ə)lgraʊnd] N *Mil, Fig* champ *m* de bataille

battle-hardened ADJ aguerri

battlements ['bæt(ə)lmənts] NPL remparts *mpl*

battle-scarred [-skɑ:d] ADJ *(town)* qui porte les traces de combats violents; *(soldier)* qui porte encore les traces de ses blessures; *Fig (politician)* qui en a vu de rudes

battleship ['bæt(ə)lʃɪp] N *Naut* cuirassé *m*; *Hist* bâtiment *m* de ligne

batty ['bætɪ] ADJ *Fam* toqué, timbré

batwing ['bætwɪŋ] ADJ en forme d'aile de chauve-souris
▸▸**b. sleeves** manches *fpl* chauve-souris

bauble ['bɔːb(ə)l] N babiole *f*, colifichet *m*

baud [bɔːd] N *Comput* baud *m*; **at 2,400 b.** à (une vitesse de) 2400 bauds
▸▸**b. rate** débit *m* en bauds

baulk [bɔːk] VT & VI = **balk**

bauxite ['bɔːksaɪt] N *Miner* bauxite *f*

Bavaria [bə'veərɪə] N Bavière *f*

Bavarian [bə'veərɪən] ADJ bavarois
N Bavarois, -oise

bawdiness ['bɔːdɪnɪs] N *(of conversation)* grivoiserie *f*, *(of humour, joke, poetry)* paillardise *f*, grivoiserie

bawdy ['bɔːdɪ] ADJ *(conversation)* grivois; *(humour, joke, poetry etc)* paillard, grivois

bawdyhouse ['bɔːdɪhaʊs] N *Arch* maison *f* de passe

bawl [bɔːl] VI **1** *(shout)* hurler, brailler, *Fam* beugler; **to b. at sb** hurler après qn **2** *Fam (weep)* brailler
VT *(order)* gueuler
▸ **bawl out** VT SEP **1** *(shout) (order)* gueuler **2** *Fam (scold)* engueuler

bawling ['bɔːlɪŋ] N **1** *(shouting)* hurlements *mpl*, braillements *mpl* **2** *Fam (weeping)* braillement(s) *m(pl)*; **stop that b.** arrête de brailler
▸▸*Fam* **b. out** *(reprimand)* engueulade *f*

bay¹ [beɪ] N *(shrub)* **sweet b.** laurier *m* commun, laurier des poètes
▸▸**b. laurel** laurier commun, laurier des poètes; **b. leaf** feuille *f* de laurier; **b. tree** laurier; **b. wreath** couronne *f* de laurier(s)

bay² N *Geog* baie *f*, *(small)* anse *f*, **Hudson B.** la baie d'Hudson
▸▸**the B. of Biscay** le golfe de Gascogne

bay³ N *(alcove)* enfoncement *m*, renfoncement *m*
▸▸**b. window** *Archit* fenêtre *f* en saillie; *Am Fam (stomach)* gros bide *m*

bay⁴ N **to keep** *or* **hold at b.** *(the enemy)* tenir en échec; *(assailant)* tenir en respect; *(creditors, persistent caller etc)* tenir tête à; **Fam I'm managing to keep my cold at b.** jusqu'ici j'ai réussi à combattre le rhume; **to bring a stag to b.** mettre un cerf aux abois, forcer *ou* acculer un cerf; **to be at b.** *(of stag), Fig* être aux abois
VI *(of hound)* aboyer, donner de la voix; **to b. at the moon** hurler *ou* aboyer à la lune

bay⁵ ADJ, N *(horse)* bai *m*

baying ['beɪɪŋ] N *(of hound)* aboiement *m*

bayonet ['beɪənɪt] N *Mil* baïonnette *f*, **with fixed bayonets** baïonnette au canon
VT *(-t-) (person)* passer à la baïonnette
▸▸*Mil* **b. charge** charge *f* à la baïonnette; *Elec* **b. holder** *(of light-fitting)* douille *f* à baïonnette; *Tech* **b. joint** joint *m* à baïonnette; *Elec* **b. socket** *(of light-fitting)* douille à baïonnette

bayou ['baɪju:] N *Am Geog* bayou *m*

bazaar [bə'zɑ:r] N **1** *(in Middle East)* bazar *m* **2** *(in aid of charity)* vente *f* de charité

bazooka [bə'zu:kə] N *Mil* bazooka *m*

B & B [bi:ən'bi:] N *Br (abbr* **bed and breakfast)** bed and breakfast *m*

BBC [bi:bi:'si:] N *(abbr* **British Broadcasting Corporation) what's on B./on BBC1?** qu'est-ce qu'il y a sur la BBC/sur BBC 1?; **B. programme** émission *f* de la BBC
▸▸**B. English** = l'anglais *m* tel qu'il était parlé sur la BBC et qui servait de référence pour la "bonne" prononciation; **B. World Service** = émissions *fpl* radiophoniques de la BBC diffusées dans le monde entier

BBQ *abbr* = **barbecue** N

BBS [bi:bi:'es] N *Comput (abbr* **bulletin board system)** serveur *m* télématique

BC [bi:'si:] *abbr* ADV **(before Christ)** avant Jésus-Christ; **in (the year) 25 BC** en (l'an) 25 av. J.-C.
N *Geog* **(British Columbia)** C.-B. *f*

BCE [bi:si:'i:] N *(abbr* **Board of Customs and Excise)** = douane *f* britannique

BCG [bi:si:'dʒi:] N *Med (abbr* **bacille Calmette-Guérin)** BCG *m*

BE [bi:'i:] N *Fin (abbr* **Bank of England)** Banque *f* d'Angleterre

BE [bi:] *(pr ind am* [æm]*, are* [ɑ:r]*, is* [ɪz]*, pl are; past ind was* [wɒz]*, were* [wɜ:r]*, was, pl were; pr sub be; past sub were; prp being* ['bi:ɪŋ]*, pp been* [bi:n]*, imp be; I am, he is, she is, it is, we are, you are, they are can be shortened into* **I'm, he's, she's, it's, we're, you're, they're**; *is not, are not, was not, were not into* **isn't, aren't, wasn't, weren't***)*

┌─────────────────────────────────────┐
│ **VI** ▪ être **1, 2, 4, 5** ▪ aller **2** ▪ voici, voilà │
│ **2** ▪ avoir **3** ▪ faire **3** ▪ coûter **2** ▪ il y │
│ a *(there is/are)* **4** ▪ aller, venir **5** │
│ **V AUX** être **1–3, 5, 7** ▪ *in tag questions* **6** │
└─────────────────────────────────────┘

VI **1** *(specifying attribute)* être; **Mary is pretty** Marie est jolie; **the sky was blue** le ciel était bleu; **time is money** le temps c'est de l'argent; **he's a bit odd, is Bob** c'est un drôle de garçon que Bob; **his father is a doctor** son père est médecin; **he is an Englishman** il est anglais, c'est un Anglais; **are they English?** sont-ils anglais?; **if I were you** à votre place, si j'étais vous; **as it is, we must go** les choses étant ce qu'elles sont, il nous faut partir; **unity is strength** l'union fait la force; **three and two are five** trois et deux font cinq; **money isn't everything** l'argent n'est pas tout dans la vie; **you be Robin Hood and I'll be ...** tu seras Robin des Bois et moi je serai ...; *(kids playing)* on dirait que tu es Robin des Bois et moi je suis ... VOIR GRAMMAIRE A55; B66

2 *(specifying location, time, health, price)* **the books are on the table** les livres sont *ou* se trouvent sur la table; **I was at the meeting** j'ai assisté *ou* j'étais à la réunion; **where am I?** où suis-je?; **I don't know where I am** *(I am lost)* je ne sais pas où je suis; *(I have lost my place)* je ne sais pas où j'en suis; **where was I?** *(after digression when talking)* où en étais-je?; **you never know where you are with him** avec lui on ne sait jamais à quoi s'en tenir; **here I am** me voici; **ah, there you**

are! ah, vous voilà!; **how are you?** comment allez-vous?; **I am better** je vais mieux; **how much is that?** combien cela coûte-t-il?, c'est combien?; **how far is it to London?** combien y a-t-il d'ici à Londres?; **when is the concert?** quand est-ce que le concert a lieu?; **today is the tenth, it is the tenth today** nous sommes (aujourd'hui) le dix (du mois); **tomorrow is Friday** demain, c'est vendredi; **it is six o'clock** il est six heures; **it is late** il est tard; **it is a fortnight since I saw him** il y a quinze jours que je ne l'ai pas vu; **it is my birthday tomorrow** demain, c'est mon anniversaire

3 **to be cold/hot** *(of person)* avoir froid/chaud; *(of water etc)* être froid/chaud; **it is fine/cold** il fait beau (temps)/froid; **to be ashamed of sb/sth** avoir honte de qn/qch; **to be hungry/thirsty** avoir faim/soif; **to be right/wrong** avoir raison/tort; **my hands are cold** j'ai froid aux mains; **to be twenty (years old)** avoir vingt ans; **the wall is six metres high** le mur fait six mètres de haut; **he was so foolish as to do it** il a eu la sottise de le faire

4 *(exist, remain)* **to be or not to be** être ou ne pas être; **business is not what it was** les affaires ne sont plus ce qu'elles étaient; **that may be** cela se peut; **to see things as they are** voir les choses comme elles sont; **be that as it may** quoi qu'il en soit; **let me be!** laissez-moi tranquille!; **there is, there are** *(impersonal)* il y a; **there is a man in the garden** il y a un homme dans le jardin; **what is there to see?** qu'est-ce qu'il y a à voir?; **there will be dancing** on dansera; **there were a dozen of us** nous étions une douzaine

5 *(go, come)* **I have been to see David** j'ai été *ou* je suis allé voir David; **I have been to the museum** j'ai visité le musée, je suis allé au musée; **I have never been to Venice** je n'ai jamais été *ou* je ne suis jamais allé à Venise; **he was into the room like a flash** il est entré en trombe dans la pièce; **where have you been?** où étais-tu?; **has anyone been?** est-ce que quelqu'un est venu *ou* passé?; **has the postman been?** est-ce que le facteur est passé?; *Br Sl* **you've been and gone and done it!** vous en avez fait une belle!; **be off (with you)!** va-t'en!

6 *(with impers subject)* **it is easy to do it** il est facile de le faire; **it is right that ...** il est juste que + *sub* ...; **it is said that ...** on dit que ...; **it is for you to decide** c'est à vous de décider; **what is it?** *(what do you want?)* que voulez-vous?; *(what is wrong?)* qu'est-ce qu'il y a?; **as it were** pour ainsi dire, en quelque sorte; *Fam* **what's it to be?** *(in pub, bar)* qu'est-ce que vous prenez?; *(make up your mind)* décidez donc!

V AUX **1** *(forming continuous tenses)* **I am/was doing sth** je fais/faisais qch; *(be in the process of)* je suis/j'étais en train de faire qch; **they are always laughing** ils sont toujours à rire; **the house is being built** la maison est en construction; **I have been waiting for a long time** il y a longtemps que j'attends, j'attends depuis longtemps VOIR GRAMMAIRE A49–50; A51

2 *(with a few intransitive verbs as aux of perfect)* **the sun is set** le soleil est couché; **the guests were all gone** les invités étaient tous partis

3 *(forming passive)* **he was killed** il a été tué; **she is respected by all** elle est respectée de tous; **he was always being laughed at** on se moquait toujours de lui; **she is to be pitied** elle est à plaindre; **what's to be done?** que faire? VOIR GRAMMAIRE A40; A54–5; B39

4 *(denoting future)* **I am to see them tomorrow** je dois les voir demain; **he was never to see them again** il ne devait plus les revoir; **and in July 2002 when the government announced there was to be an election ...** et en juillet 2002 quand le gouvernement annonça qu'il y aurait des élections …; **there was to be an election next year but it's been cancelled** il devait y avoir des élections l'année prochaine mais elles ont été annulées; **am I to do it or not?** *(obligation)* est-ce qu'il faut que je le fasse ou non? VOIR GRAMMAIRE A51–2

5 I am all for reform je suis pour *ou* je suis partisan de la réforme; **I'm all for staying here** je ne demande qu'à rester ici; **what are you at?** que faites-vous?

6 *(in tag questions)* **so you're back, are you?** alors, vous voilà de retour?; **she is beautiful, isn't she?** elle est belle, n'est-ce pas?; **they're big, aren't they?** ils sont grands, n'est-ce pas? VOIR GRAMMAIRE A47

7 *(elliptical)* **John's very stupid – I know he is/no he isn't** John est un imbécile – je le sais bien/non, ce n'est pas un imbécile **8** *(imperatives)* **be quiet!** tiens-toi tranquille!; **don't be ridiculous!** ne sois pas ridicule! VOIR GRAMMAIRE A40; B34

beach [biːtʃ] N plage *f*; **to go to the b.** aller à la plage; *Fig* **he's not the only pebble on the b.** un de perdu, dix de retrouvés
▪ VT *(ship) (run aground)* échouer; *(pull up on to beach)* tirer à sec; **to b. itself** *(of whale)* s'échouer; **a beached whale** une baleine échouée
▸▸ **b. buggy** buggy *m*; **b. chair** chaise *f* longue; **b. hotel** hôtel *m* de plage; **b. hut** cabine *f* (de bains ou de plage); **b. tent** tente *f* de plage; **b. wear** vêtements *mpl* de plage

beachball [ˈbiːtʃbɔːl] N ballon *m* de plage
▸▸ *Comput* **b. pointer** pointeur-balle *m*, *pl* pointeurs-balles

beachcomber [ˈbiːtʃkəʊmər] N **1** *(person)* personne *f* qui ramasse les objets échoués ou laissés sur la plage **2** *(wave)* vague *f* déferlante

beachhead [ˈbiːtʃhed] N *Mil (for landing)* tête *f* de pont

beacon [ˈbiːk(ə)n] N **1** *Naut, Aviat (lighthouse)* phare *m*; *(marking channel, runway)* balise *f*; *(light, signal)* feu *m*; *(at crossing)* signal *m* lumineux; *Fig* phare; **radar b.** balise radar, radar *m* de radionavigation **2** *Arch (fire)* feu *m* (pour donner l'alarme); *(location)* tour *f*/colline *f* où un feu est allumé pour donner l'alarme
▸▸ **b. light** balise

bead [biːd] N **1** *(of glass, enamel etc)* perle *f*, **(string of) beads** collier *m*; **beads of dew** perles de rosée; **there were beads of perspiration on his forehead** la sueur perlait sur son front
2 *(for prayers)* grain *m*; **to tell one's beads** égrener *ou* dire son chapelet
3 *(on sparkling wine etc)* bulle *f*
4 *Archit, Carp (moulding)* baguette *f*
5 *(on gun)* guidon *m*, mire *f*
6 *Metal* cordon *m* de soudure
7 *Aut (on tyre)* bourrelet *m*
▪ VT **1** couvrir *ou* orner de perles **2** *Archit, Carp* appliquer une baguette sur
▪ VI *(of liquid)* perler
▸▸ *Aut* **b. apex** bord *m* de talon (de pneu); **b. curtain** rideau *m* de perles; *Aut* **b. wire** armature *m* de bourrelet

beaded [ˈbiːdɪd] ADJ *(material)* perlé
▸▸ *Archit, Carp* **b. strip** chapelet *m*

beading [ˈbiːdɪŋ] N **1** *(decoration)* garniture *f* de perles **2** *Archit, Carp* baguette *f* **3** *(of tyre)* talon *m*, bourrelet *m*

beadle [ˈbiːd(ə)l] N bedeau *m*

beady [ˈbiːdɪ] ADJ *(eyes)* petits et brillants; **a b.-eyed shopkeeper** un commerçant qui tient ses clients à l'œil dans sa boutique; *Br Fam* **I've got my b. eye on you** je t'ai à l'œil

beagle [ˈbiːg(ə)l] N beagle *m*, briquet *m*

beagling [ˈbiːglɪŋ] N chasse *f* au briquet

beak [biːk] N **1** *(of bird, tortoise, jug, vase etc)* bec *m*; *Fam Hum (of person)* tarin *m*, blair *m* **2** *Br Sl (judge)* juge *m*; *(headmaster)* dirlo *m*

beaked [biːkt] ADJ *(animal)* à bec; *(nose)* crochu
▸▸ **b. whale** hyperodon *m*

beaker [ˈbiːkər] N **1** *(container)* gobelet *m*, timbale *f* **2** *Chem* vase *m* à bec

be-all and end-all N *Fam (aim)* but *m* suprême, fin *f* des fins; **it's not the b. if it doesn't work** ce n'est pas la fin du monde si ça ne marche pas; *Hum Pej* **he thinks he's the b.** il ne se prend pas pour n'importe qui; **she thinks her son's the b.** elle pense que son fils est une petite merveille

beam [biːm] N **1** *Constr* poutre *f* (en bois), solive *f*, madrier *m*; *(small)* poutrelle *f*, **ceiling b.** doubleau *m*
2 *Gym* **(balance) b.** poutre *f* horizontale
3 *(width)* **(breadth of) b.** *(of ship)* largeur *f*, **broad in the b.** *(ship)* à larges baux; *Fam (person)* large de hanches
4 *(of ship)* travers *m*; **on the port/starboard b.** par le travers bâbord/tribord
5 *(of light, sun)* rayon *m*; *(of headlamp etc)* faisceau *m*, *Fig (smile)* grand *ou* large sourire *m*; **the headlights were on full b.** la voiture était en pleins phares
6 *Elec* faisceau *m*; **electronic/radar b.** faisceau électronique/radar; **radio b.** faisceau hertzien; *Aviat* **radio landing b.** axe *m* balisé d'atterrissage; *Fam* **you're way off b.** *(mistaken)* tu es complètement à côté de la plaque; **the calculations are way off b.** les calculs sont archifaux
▪ VT **1** *TV (pictures)* transmettre; *Tel (message)* transmettre par ondes dirigées; *Aviat* **to be beamed in on Orly** *(of aircraft)* être dirigé sur Orly **2** *Fig (of person)* **she beamed her thanks** elle a fait un grand sourire en guise de remerciement
▪ VI *(of sun)* rayonner; *(of person)* faire un grand sourire; **beaming with health** resplendissant de santé; **she beamed with pride** *(smiled)* elle a eu un sourire de fierté; **she is beaming with pride** *(radiating pride)* elle rayonne de fierté
▸▸ *Aut* **b. deflector** déflecteur *m* de faisceau, traverse *f*

beam-ends NPL *(of ship)* baux *mpl*; **to be on her b.** *(of ship)* être sur le flanc; *Fig* **to be on one's b.** être *ou* se trouver à bout de ressources

beaming [ˈbiːmɪŋ] ADJ *(sun, face)* rayonnant, radieux; *(smile)* radieux

bean [biːn] N **1** *(vegetable)* haricot *m*; **broad b.** fève *f*, **French b.**, *Am* **string b.** haricot vert, *Can* fève verte; **runner b.** haricot d'Espagne; *Br* **butter b.**, *Am* **Lima b.** haricot de Lima; **kidney b.**, **haricot b.** *(red)* haricot rouge; *(white)* haricot de Soissons; **soya b.** graine *f* de soja; *Culin* **dried beans** haricots secs; *Fam* **to be full of beans** être en pleine forme; *Fam* **it isn't worth a b.** ça ne vaut pas un radis; *Fam* **he hasn't a b.** il n'a pas un radis; *Am Fam* **not to know beans about sth** savoir que dalle sur qch; *Am Fam* **she knows how many beans make five** elle n'est pas née d'hier, c'est un vieux renard; *Old-fashioned* **old b.** *(form of address)* mon vieux
2 *(of coffee)* grain *m*; *(of cocoa)* graine *f*, fève *f*
3 *Am Sl (head)* caboche *f*
4 *Am Offensive Sl* métèque *mf* (d'origine latino-américaine)
▸▸ *Culin* **b. curd** pâte *f* de soja; **b. sprout** germe *m* de soja

beanbag [ˈbiːnbæg] N **1** *(bag)* balle *f* lestée **2** *(cushion, chair)* fauteuil *m* poire

bean-counter N *esp Am Fam Pej* comptable *mf*

beanery [ˈbiːnərɪ] N *Am* = petit restaurant *m* pas cher

beanfeast [biːnfiːst] N *Br Fam (festive occasion)* bombe *f*

beanie hat [ˈbiːnɪ] N bonnet *m*

beano [ˈbiːnəʊ] N *Br Fam* = **beanfeast**

beanpole [ˈbiːnpəʊl] N rame *f* pour haricots; *Fig (person)* échalas *m*, perche *f*

beanstalk [ˈbiːnstɔːk] N tige *f* de haricot

bear¹ [beər] N **1** *(animal)*, *Fig* ours *m*; **to be like a b. with a sore head** être d'une humeur massacrante; **the Great B. Lake** le grand lac de l'Ours; *Astron* **the Great/Little B.** la Grande/Petite Ourse; **she b.** ourse *f* **2** *St Exch* baissier, -ière, joueur, -euse à la baisse; **to go a b.** spéculer à la baisse; **to sell a b.** vendre à découvert
▪ VT **(-r-)** *St Exch* **to b. the market** chercher à faire baisser les cours
▪ VI *St Exch* spéculer à la baisse
▸▸ *St Exch* **b. closing** arbitrage *m* à la baisse; **b. cub** ourson *m*; **b. garden** *Hist* fosse *f* aux ours; *Fig* pétaudière *f*, *St Exch Fam* **b. hug** = communiqué *m* d'information annonçant une OPA immédiate; **to give sb a b. hug** serrer qn très fort dans ses bras; *St Exch* **b. market** marché *m* à la baisse *ou* baissier; *Zool* **b. pit** fosse aux ours; *St Exch* **b. speculation** spéculation *f* à la baisse; *St Exch* **b. spread** spread *m* baissier; *St Exch* **b. trading** spéculation à la baisse

BEAR² *(pt* **bore** [bɔːr]; *pp* **borne** [bɔːn])* VT **1** *(burden, arms, name, date, signature)* porter; *Lit* **to b. gifts** apporter des cadeaux; **I still b. the scars** *(of attack etc)* j'en porte encore les cicatrices; *Fig* j'en garde encore les cicatrices; **to b. all the marks of sth** être caractéristique de qch; **the murder bore all the marks of a mafia killing** le meurtre avait tout d'un crime mafieux; **to b. sth in mind** *(remember)* se souvenir de qch; *(take into account)* tenir compte de qch; **b. us in mind if ever you want to sell it** pensez à nous si jamais vous décidez de le vendre; **it bears no relation/resemblance to …** cela n'a aucun rapport/aucune ressemblance avec …; **his account bears no relation to the truth** sa version n'a rien à voir avec ce qui s'est vraiment passé; **he bore himself with dignity** il est resté très digne; **to be borne backwards/along** être refoulé/emporté; **to b. the costs** supporter *ou* assumer les frais; **we will b. the costs** nous prendrons les frais en charge; **to b. the responsibility for sth** être responsable de qch; **I refuse to b. the responsibility for that** je décline toute responsabilité à ce sujet; **she bears a heavy responsibility** elle porte une lourde responsabilité; **to b. one's troubles with patience** supporter ses malheurs avec courage
2 *(tolerate) (weight)* supporter, soutenir; *(suffering, consequences, pain)* supporter; **he can't b. being beaten** il ne supporte pas d'être battu; **he could b. it no longer** il ne pouvait plus tenir; **I can't b. this** je ne peux pas supporter ça; **his language does not b. repeating** il a été si grossier que je n'ose même pas répéter ce qu'il a dit; **I can't b. (the sight of) him** je ne peux pas le supporter; **I can't b. the idea of it** je ne peux pas en supporter l'idée; **it doesn't b. thinking about** l'idée en est insupportable
3 *Lit, Arch (give birth to)* (see also **born**) donner naissance à; **she has borne him three sons** elle lui a donné trois fils
4 *(yield)* **to b. interest** porter intérêt; **to b. fruit** *(of tree)* donner des fruits; *Fig (of work etc)* porter ses fruits; **my enquiries bore fruit** mes recherches ont été couronnées de succès *ou* ont porté leurs fruits
▪ VI **1** *(move, lie)* **to b. (to the) right/left** *(of person)* tourner à droite/à gauche, prendre

à droite/à gauche; *(of road)* tourner à droi-te/à gauche

2 pressure has been brought to b. on a exercé une pression sur lui/elle/*etc*

▸ **bear away** VT SEP *(thing)* emporter

▸ **bear down** VI *(of woman in labour)* pous-ser

VT SEP *Lit (usu passive)* **to be borne down by poverty** être accablé par la misère

▸ **bear down on, bear down upon** VT INSEP *(person, enemy, boat etc)* foncer sur

▸ **bear on** VT INSEP **1** *(weigh)* **to bring all one's strength to b. on a lever** s'appuyer de toutes ses forces sur un levier; **to bring all one's energies to b. on sth** apporter *ou* consacrer toute son énergie à qch; **to bring one's mind to b. on sth** porter son attention sur qch; **to bring influence/pressure to b. on sb** exercer une influence/une pression sur qn; **it was gradually borne in on him that …** peu à peu il s'est rendu compte que …

2 *(be relevant to)* avoir un rapport avec; **I don't see how that bears on what I'm doing** je ne vois pas le rapport que ça a avec ce que je fais

▸ **bear out** VT SEP *(confirm) (assertion)* con-firmer; **to b. sb out, to b. out what sb has said** confirmer *ou* corroborer ce que qn a dit; **I feel – and I'm sure Peter will b. me out on this –** … j'estime – et je suis sûr que Peter confirmera *ou* corroborera ce point – …

▸ **bear up** VI **1** *(of person)* **to b. up under misfortune** faire face au malheur; **she's bearing up remarkably well** elle tient drôle-ment bien le coup; **b. up!** tenez bon!, du courage!; *Br Fam* **how are you? – bearing up** comment ça va? *ou* ça va? – on fait aller

2 *(of results)* tenir

▸ **bear upon** VT INSEP = **bear on**

▸ **bear with** VT INSEP **1** *(tolerate) (sb's bad mood etc)* supporter

2 *(be patient with)* **if you'll b. with me, I'll explain** si vous patientez un instant, je vais vous expliquer; **b. with me while I finish this** je termine ceci et je suis à vous; **I won't be a minute, if you could b. with me** je suis à vous dans une minute

bearable ['beərəb(ə)l] ADJ supportable

bearably ['beərəblɪ] ADV d'une façon sup-portable; **it was hot but b. so** il faisait chaud mais c'était supportable

bear-baiting N combat *m* d'ours et de chiens

beard [bɪəd] N **1** *(of man, animal), Bot (of ear of barley etc)* barbe *f*; **to have a b.** porter la barbe; **to grow a b.** se laisser pousser la barbe; **a week's b.** une barbe de huit jours **2** *Sl (woman going out with gay man)* = femme *f* que fréquente un homosexuel de façon à dissimuler son homosexualité

VT *(person)* braver, défier; *Fig* **it was very brave of you to b. the lion in his den** c'est très courageux de ta part d'avoir été l'affronter

bearded ['bɪədɪd] ADJ *(man)* barbu

▸▸ **b. lady** femme *f* à barbe

-bearded ['bɪədɪd] SUFF **black-/white-b.** à la barbe noire/blanche

beardless ['bɪədlɪs] ADJ imberbe

bearer ['beərər] N *(of news, letter, cheque)* porteur, -euse; *(of passport)* titulaire *mf*; **the bearers** *(at funeral)* les porteurs

▸▸ *Fin* **b. bill** effet *m* *ou* billet *m* au porteur; *St Exch* **b. bond** titre *m* au porteur; *Fin* **b. cheque** chèque *m* au porteur; *Fin* **b. paper** papier *m* au porteur; *St Exch* **b. share** action *f* au porteur

bearing ['beərɪŋ] ADJ *(axle etc)* porteur

N **1** *(of arms)* port *m*

2 *(deportment)* port *m*, maintien *m*, allure *f*; **because of her dignified b. throughout** parce qu'elle est restée digne jusqu'au bout

3 *Tech* palier *m*; **self-lubricating b.** palier graisseur; **ball/roller/needle b.** roulement *m* à billes/à rouleaux/à aiguilles

4 *(direction)* orientation *f*, *(in surveying)* gi-sement *m*, azimut *m*; *Naut, Aviat* relève-ment *m*, position *f*; **true b.** *(in surveying)* azimut *ou* gisement géographique; *Naut, Aviat* relè-vement vrai; **compass b.** relèvement au compas; **to take the ship's bearings** faire le point; *Naut* **to take one's bearings** s'orienter, se repérer; **to lose one's bearings** *Naut* per-dre sa direction *ou* sa route; *Fig* ne plus s'y retrouver; **to get one's bearings** *Naut* ret-rouver sa direction *ou* sa route; *Fig* s'y ret-rouver

5 *(connection)* rapport *m* (**on a question** avec une question); **it has no b. on the mat-ter** *(of fact etc)* cela n'a aucun rapport avec l'affaire

▸▸ **b. surface** *(of beam)* surface *f* d'appui; *(of joist)* tablette *f*; *Tech* surface portante *ou* de portage; **b. wall** mur *m* d'appui

-bearing ['beərɪŋ] SUFF **fruit-b.** fructifère, qui porte des fruits; **interest-b. capital** capi-tal *m* qui rapporte; **silver-b.** argentifère; **wool-b.** lanifère

bearish ['beərɪʃ] ADJ **1** *Fig (manners)* d'ours; *(person)* bourru **2** *St Exch (market)* à la baisse, baissier; **to be b.** spéculer *ou* jouer à la baisse

▸▸ *St Exch* **b. tendency** tendance *f* à la baisse

bearskin ['beəskɪn] N **1** peau *f* d'ours **2** *Mil (helmet)* bonnet *m* à poil

▸▸ **b. rug** peau d'ours

beast [biːst] N **1** bête *f*, **wild b.** *(not domesti-cated)* bête sauvage; *(fierce)* bête féroce; *Lit* **the king of the beasts** le roi des animaux; **b. of prey** carnassier *m*; *Lit* **b. of burden** *etc)*, *Fig* bête de somme; *Bible* **the B.** l'Anté-christ *m*; **beasts** *(on farm)* bétail *m*, bestiaux *mpl* **2** *Fig (brute)* brute *f*, *Fam (unkind per-son)* vache *f*, peau *f* de vache; **the little b.** le petit diable; **he's a perfect b.!** c'est une peau de vache!; **it was a b. of a day** *(bad weather)* il a fait un temps abominable *ou* un temps de chien; **I've had a b. of a day** *(full of prob-lems)* j'ai eu une journée affreuse; **a b. of a job** *(task)* un travail pénible

beastliness ['biːstlɪnɪs] N *esp Old-fash-ioned* **the b. of his behaviour** sa conduite ignoble

beastly ['biːstlɪ] *Fam* ADJ *(person)* affreux; *(place, smell, taste)* dégoûtant; **a b. job** *(task)* un travail pénible; **what b. weather!** quel sale temps!

ADV bigrement, vachement

BEAT [biːt] N **1** *(stroke, blow) (of heart, clock, drum)* battement *m*; *Mus* mesure *f*, temps *m*; **music with a strong b.** musique avec un fort rythme

2 *Br (of policeman)* ronde *f*; **a policeman on the b.** un agent qui fait sa ronde; *Fig Fam* **it's off my b. altogether** cela ne relève pas de ma compétence, ce n'est pas de mon ressort

VT *(pt beat; pp beaten ['biːt(ə)n])* **1** *(hit) (person, rug, eggs, wood for game birds etc)* battre; **to b. sb with a stick** donner des coups de bâton à qn; **to b. one's breast** se frapper la poitrine; **to b. a drum** battre du tambour; **the world is beating a path to her door** tout le monde se rue sur elle; *Fam* **b. it!** *(go away)* file!, fiche le camp!; *Vulg* **to b. one's meat** se branler; **to b. its wings** *(of bird)* battre des ailes

2 *(defeat, conquer) (enemy)* battre, vaincre; *(record)* battre; *(get ahead of)* battre, de-vancer; **to b. sb at chess** battre qn aux échecs; *Fam* **that beats me!** ça me dépasse!; *Fam* **it beats me why he did it** je ne pige vraiment pas pourquoi il a fait ça; *Fam* **that beats everything!** ça c'est le comble *ou* le

bouquet!; *Fam* **you can't b. a good book** rien de tel qu'un bon livre; *Fam* **I got up early to b. the traffic** je me suis levé tôt pour éviter les embouteillages; *Fam* **he b. me to it** *(ar-rived, telephoned before me etc)* il m'a de-vancé; *Prov* **if you can't b. them, join them** mieux vaut s'allier aux gens que l'on ne peut pas vaincre

3 *Am Sl (cheat, get the better of)* rouler, re-faire; **to b. the customs** frauder la douane

VI **1** *(of heart, rain)* battre; **the waves are beating against the shore** les vagues dé-ferlent sur le rivage

2 *Naut* **to b. to windward** louvoyer

3 *Fig* **to b. about** *or Am* **around the bush** tourner autour du pot

ADJ *Fam* **1 you've got me b.** *(defeated)* je m'avoue vaincu; *(unable to answer)* je sèche; **I think Hingis has got Williams b.** je pense que Hingis a déjà battu Williams; **this cross-word's got me b.** je sèche sur ces mots croisés; **it's got** *or* **it has me b. why she did it** je ne comprends pas pourquoi elle a fait ça

2 *(very tired)* crevé; **dead b.** complètement crevé

▸ **beat back** VT SEP *(people, enemy troops, flames)* repousser

▸ **beat down** VT SEP *(door)* enfoncer; *(nettles, grass etc with stick)* rabattre; *(earth)* damer; *Fig* **to b. down the price of sth** *(by bargain-ing)* faire baisser le prix de qch; **to b. sb down** faire baisser le prix à qn

VI *(of rain)* tomber à verse; *(of sun)* taper; **the rain was beating down on the tin roof** la pluie s'abattait sur le toit en tôle; **the sun is beating down on our heads** le soleil nous tape sur la tête

▸ **beat in** VT SEP *(door etc)* défoncer

▸ **beat off** VT SEP *(person, assault)* repousser

VI *Am Vulg (masturbate)* se branler

▸ **beat out** VT SEP **1** *(extinguish) (flames)* étouffer

2 *(flatten) (sheet metal)* battre, aplatir; *(gold etc)* marteler; *(bodywork)* débosseler; **to b. out the dents in a car door** débosseler une porte de voiture

3 *Mus* **to b. out the rhythm**, *Fam* **to b. it out** marquer le rythme

4 *Fam* **I'll b. your brains out!** je vais te dé-molir!; *Fig* **to b. one's brains out** se creuser la tête *ou* la cervelle

5 to b. the dust out of sth battre qch pour en faire sortir la poussière

▸ **beat up** VT SEP **1** *(person)* tabasser

2 *(eggs)* battre

3 *(game)* rabattre, traquer

VI *Naut* louvoyer *ou* gagner vers la terre

▸ **beat up on** VT INSEP *esp Am Fam (hit)* bat-tre, tabasser; **stop beating up on yourself** arrête de culpabiliser

beat-'em-up N = film *m* ou jeu *m* vidéo comportant de nombreuses bagarres

beaten ['biːt(ə)n] ADJ **1** *(gold, metal)* battu, martelé; *(earth)* battu; *Fig* **off the b. track** *(house, to live)* à l'écart; **let's go somewhere a bit more off the b. track** sortons un peu des sentiers battus **2** *(enemy)* battu, vaincu

beater ['biːtər] N **1** *(person)* batteur, -euse; *(in hunting)* rabatteur, -euse **2** *(device) (for eggs)* fouet *m*

beatific [biːə'tɪfɪk] ADJ *Lit (vision)* béati-fique; *(smile)* béat

beatifically [biːə'tɪfɪklɪ] ADV *Lit* d'un air béat

beatification [biːætɪfɪ'keɪʃən] N *Rel* béati-fication *f*

beatify [biː'ætɪfaɪ] VT *Rel* béatifier

beating ['biːtɪŋ] ADJ *(heart)* battant, palpi-tant; *(rain)* battant

N **1** *(of wings, heart etc)* battement *m*; *(of game)* rabattage *m*, rabat *m*; *(of wood for game)* traque *f* **2** *(thrashing)* raclée *f*, rossée *f;* **to give sb a b.** donner une raclée à qn, rosser qn **3** *(in match etc)* défaite *f*, *Fam* raclée *f*; **to get a good b.** être battu à plate(s) couture(s); *Fam* recevoir une bonne raclée **4** *Naut* louvoyage *m*

beatitude [bi:'ætɪtju:d] N béatitude *f*; *Bible* **the Beatitudes** les Béatitudes

beatnik ['bi:tnɪk] N beatnik *mf*

beat-up ADJ *Fam (car, chair etc)* déglingué

beau, *pl* **beaus, beaux** [bəʊ, bəʊz] N **1** *Arch (dandy)* élégant *m*, dandy *m* **2** *Arch, Am (of young girl)* prétendant *m*, galant *m*

beaut [bju:t] *Fam* N **what a b.!** quelle merveille!; **what a b. of a car!** quelle voiture! ADJ *Austr* super, génial, -aux

beautician [bju:'tɪʃən] N esthéticien, -ienne; *(make-up artist)* visagiste *mf*

beautiful ['bju:tɪfʊl] ADJ **1** *(person, place, face etc)* (très) beau, (très) belle; **the b. people** le beau monde **2** *(dinner, weather etc)* magnifique

beautifully ['bju:tɪfʊlɪ] ADV *(intensifier)* admirablement, à merveille; **b. dressed** merveilleusement bien habillé

beautify ['bju:tɪfaɪ] VT embellir

beauty ['bju:tɪ] N **1** *(appearance)* beauté *f*, **the beauties of nature** les beautés de la nature; **that's the b. of it** c'est ça qu'il y a de bien; *Prov* **b. is in the eye of the beholder** ce qu'on aime est toujours beau **2** *(person, object)* **she was a b. in her day** c'était une beauté dans son temps; **B. and the Beast** la Belle et la Bête; **Sleeping B.** la Belle au bois dormant; *Fam* **isn't it a b.?** *(of flower)* n'est-ce pas qu'elle est belle?; *(of car)* n'est-ce pas qu'elle est super?; *(of mistake)* elle est bonne celle-là!; *Br Fam* **(you) b.!** super!; *Fam* **he fetched him a b. on the chin** il lui a flanqué un coup magnifique *ou* formidable au menton; *Fam* **that black eye is a real b.** c'est un bel œil au beurre noir
  ► ► **b. contest** concours *m* de beauté; **b. parlour** institut *m* de beauté; **b. products** produits *mpl* de beauté; **b. queen** reine *f* de beauté; **b. salon** institut de beauté; **b. sleep** sommeil *m* avant minuit *(considéré comme le plus réparateur)*; **b. spot** *(on skin)* grain *m* de beauté; *(artificial)* mouche *f*, *(scenic place)* site *m* touristique; **b. treatment** soins *mpl* esthétiques

beaver ['bi:vər] N **1** *(animal, fur)* castor *m*; *Fam* **to work like a b.** travailler d'arrache-pied; **b. coat/jacket** manteau *m*/veste *f* de castor **2** *Am Vulg (female genitals)* chatte *f*
  ► ► **b. lamb** mouton *m* doré
► **beaver away** VI travailler d'arrache-pied (**at** à)

becalmed [bɪ'kɑ:md] ADJ *(ship)* encalminé

became PT *see* become

because [bɪ'kɒz, -kəz] CONJ parce que; **I eat b. I'm hungry** je mange parce que j'ai faim; **I was all the more astonished b. I had been told that ...** j'en fus d'autant plus étonné qu'on m'avait assuré que ...; **b. he dashed off a sonnet, he thinks himself a poet** il se prend pour un poète simplement parce qu'il a torché un sonnet; **why? – just b.** pourquoi? – parce que
  PREP **b. of sth** à cause de qch; **b. of his illness** à cause de *ou* en raison de sa maladie

béchamel ['beʃəmel] N *Culin* béchamel *f*
  ► ► **b. sauce** sauce *f* (à la) béchamel

beck¹ [bek] N **to have sb at one's b. and call** avoir qn à ses ordres *ou* à sa disposition; **to be at sb's b. and call** obéir aux moindres volontés de qn, être aux ordres de qn

beck² N *Dial* ruisseau *m* de montagne

beckon ['bekən] VT & VI faire signe (**to sb à** qn); **to b. sb in** faire signe à qn d'entrer; *Fig* **the bright lights of the city beckoned** les lu-

mières de la ville étaient une tentation; **I can't stay, work beckons** il faut que je m'en aille, j'ai du travail; **and fame beckoned** et les portes de la gloire lui étaient ouvertes; **to b. sb** faire signe à qn de s'approcher

become [bɪ'kʌm] *(pt* **became** [bɪ'keɪm]; *pp* **become)** VI **1** *(a priest, an adult, sb's enemy etc)* devenir; **to b. king/a doctor** devenir roi/médecin; **to b. old/thin** vieillir/maigrir; **to b. suspicious of sb** commencer à avoir des soupçons à propos de qn, devenir soupçonneux à l'égard de qn; **the murmurs became louder** les murmures se faisaient plus forts; **to b. accustomed/attached/interested** s'accoutumer/s'attacher/s'intéresser; **to b. known** *(of person)* commencer à être connu; **it will soon b. clear that ...** il sera bientôt évident que ...
  2 what has b. of Tom? qu'est devenu Tom?; **what will b. of him?** que va-t-il devenir?; **I don't know what has b. of her** je ne sais pas ce qu'elle est devenue
  VT *esp Fml (person) (of behaviour etc)* être digne de; *(of clothes, colour etc)* aller bien à

becoming [bɪ'kʌmɪŋ] ADJ **1** *(proper) (behaviour)* convenable, bienséant **2** *(colour, clothes)* seyant; **red is very b. to her** le rouge lui va très bien *ou* lui sied; **green looks very b. on you** le vert te va très bien; **you look very b. in that dress** cette robe te va très bien

becquerel [bek(ə)'rel] N *Phys* becquerel *m*

BEd [bi:'ed] N *Univ abbr* **Bachelor of Education**

bed [bed] N **1** lit *m*; **to be in b.** *(to rest)* être couché, être au lit; *(through illness)* être alité, garder le lit; **to keep sb in b.** garder qn au lit; **to read in b.** lire au lit; **to get out of b.** se lever; **to get out of b. on the wrong side** se lever du pied gauche; **I'm sorry to get you out of b.** je suis désolé de vous tirer du lit; *Hum* **I wouldn't kick her out of b.** si elle voulait de moi, je ne dirais pas non; **to go to b.** se coucher; *Journ* **the paper has gone to b.** le journal est bouclé; **I'm going home to b.** je vais rentrer me coucher; **to keep to one's b.** garder le lit; *Fam* **to go to b. with a man/woman** coucher avec un homme/une femme; *Fig* **to be in b. with sb** être allié avec qn de façon officieuse; **to put a child to b.** coucher un enfant, mettre un enfant au lit; *Journ* **to put a paper to b.** boucler un journal; **she always takes her teddy to b. with her** elle emmène toujours son ours au lit avec elle; **it's time for b.** c'est l'heure d'aller au lit *ou* d'aller se coucher; **to make the b.** faire le lit; *Fig* **you've made your b. and now you must lie in it** comme on fait son lit, on se couche; **to sleep in separate beds** faire lit à part
  2 *(of river, sea)* lit *m*; *(of billiard table)* fond *m*; **filter b.** lit de filtrage; **place the roast on a b. of vegetables** placez le rôti sur un lit de légumes
  3 *(in garden) (for vegetables)* carré *m*; *(for flowers)* parterre *m*; **oyster b.** banc *m* d'huîtres; *(on oyster farm)* parc *m* à huîtres
  4 *Geol* assise *f*, couche *f*, *Miner* gisement *m* **5** *Constr etc (of concrete)* assise *f*, lit *m*; *(of stone)* assise; *Rail* infrastructure *f*
  6 *Tech (of lathe)* banc *m*
  VT *(-dd-) Fam (woman)* coucher avec
  ► ► **b. and board** pension *f* complète; **b. and breakfast** *(establishment)* chambre *f* d'hôte; chambre et petit déjeuner; *St Exch* **b. and breakfasting** aller et retour *m*; **b. head** chevet *m*, tête *f* (de lit); *Br* **b. jacket** liseuse *f*, **b. linen** draps *mpl* de lit (et taies *fpl* d'oreiller); **b. occupancy** occupation *f* des lits; **b. settee** convertible *m*, canapé-lit *m*, *pl* canapés-lits; **b. sheet** drap *m*
► **bed down** VI *(of animal)* se gîter; *Fam (of person)* se coucher
  VT SEP *(horses)* faire la litière à
► **bed out** VT SEP *(plants)* repiquer

bedbug ['bedbʌg] N punaise *f*

bedchamber ['bedtʃeɪmbər] N *Arch* chambre *f* à coucher

bedclothes ['bedkləʊðz] NPL couvertures *fpl* et draps *mpl*; **to turn down the b.** ouvrir le lit

beddable ['bedəb(ə)l] ADJ *Fam Hum* baisable

bedding ['bedɪŋ] N **1** *(for bed)* literie *f* **2** *(for animals)* litière *f*
  ► ► **b. out** *(of plants)* dépotage *m*, dépotement *m*; **b. plants** plants *mpl* à repiquer

bedevil [bɪ'dev(ə)l] VT *(-ll-, Am -l-)* **1** *(torment)* tourmenter **2** *(cause difficulties or problems for)* **industrial relations bedevilled by politics** rapports entre patrons et ouvriers empoisonnés par la politique; **the project is bedevilled by problems** le projet est en proie à de nombreuses difficultés; **the strikes which had bedevilled the industry** les grèves qui avaient affligé l'industrie; **to be bedevilled by complaints** être assailli de réclamations

bedfellow ['bedfeləʊ] N compagnon *m*/compagne *f* de lit; *Fig* **they make strange bedfellows** c'est une association inattendue, c'est un couple disparate

bedlam ['bedləm] N **1** *Fig* bazar *m*; **the meeting was absolute b.** la réunion était un véritable bazar **2** *Arch (asylum)* maison *f* de fous *ou* d'aliénés

bed-night N nuitée *f*

Bedouin ['bedʊɪn] ADJ bédouin
  N *(pl* **Bedouin)** Bédouin, -ine

bedpan ['bedpæn] N bassin *m*

bedpost ['bedpəʊst] N colonne *f* de lit

bedraggled [bɪ'dræg(ə)ld] ADJ *(muddy)* crotté, taché de boue; *(wet)* trempé; **you look a bit b.** tu es dans un piteux état

bedridden ['bedrɪd(ə)n] ADJ alité, cloué au lit; *(permanently)* grabataire

bedrock ['bedrɒk] N *Geol* roche *f* de fond; *Fig (of one's belief etc)* fondement *m*; *Fig* **to get down to b.** parler des choses sérieuses

bedroll ['bedrəʊl] N *Am* matériel *m* de couchage

bedroom ['bedru:m] N chambre *f* (à coucher); **spare b.** chambre d'ami; **b. curtains** rideaux *mpl* de chambre
  ► ► *Theat* **b. farce** comédie *f* légère, vaudeville *m*; **b. furniture** meubles *mpl* de chambre; **b. slippers** pantoufles *fpl*

-bedroom, -bedroomed ['bedru:m(d)] SUFF **a two/three-bedroom(ed) house** une maison à deux/trois chambres

Beds *abbr* **Bedfordshire**

bedside ['bedsaɪd] N chevet *m*; **to have a good b. manner** *(of doctor)* être agréable avec les malades; **I didn't think much of his b. manner** je ne l'ai pas trouvé très agréable
  ► ► **b. lamp** lampe *f* de chevet; **b. rug** descente *f* de lit; **b. table** table *f* de nuit *ou* de chevet

bedsit ['bedsɪt], **bed-sitter**, **bed-sitting-room** N *Br* chambre *f* meublée

bedsock ['bedsɒk] N chausson *m* de nuit

bedsore ['bedsɔ:r] N escarre *f*

bedspace ['bedspeɪs] N *(in hotels etc)* capacité *f* d'accueil

bedspread ['bedspred] N dessus-de-lit *m inv*

bedstead ['bedsted] N châlit *m*, bois *m* de lit

bedtick ['bedtɪk] N *Am (bug)* punaise *f*

bedtime ['bedtaɪm] N heure *f* du coucher; **b.!** c'est l'heure d'aller au lit *ou* de se coucher!; **when is your b.?** à quelle heure vous couchez-vous?; **it's past your b.** vous devriez déjà être couché; **it's long past my b.** je devrais être couché depuis longtemps;

they were allowed to stay up past their b. on leur a permis de se coucher plus tard que d'habitude; **to tell sb a b. story** raconter une histoire à qn avant qu'il ne s'endorme

bed-wetter [-wetər] N *(child)* enfant *mf* qui fait pipi au lit; **he's a b.** il fait pipi au lit

bed-wetting [-wetɪŋ] N énurésie *f* nocturne; **if b. is a problem for your child** si votre enfant fait pipi au lit

bee [bi:] N **1** abeille *f*; **bees' nest** nid *m* d'abeilles; **to keep bees** élever des abeilles; *Fig* **to be a busy b.** être très actif; *Fig* **to have a b. in one's bonnet** avoir une idée fixe; **he's got a b. in his bonnet about it** c'est pour lui une idée fixe; **he's got a b. in his bonnet about burglars** les cambrioleurs, c'est une idée fixe chez lui; *Br Fam* **she thinks she's the b.'s knees** elle ne se prend pas pour n'importe qui; *Br Fam* **she thinks he's the b.'s knees** elle le trouve formidable **2** *Am (meeting)* réunion *f (pour travaux en commun)*; **spelling b.** concours *m* (oral) d'orthographe ▸▸*Bot* **b. balm** monarde *f* d'Amérique; *Bot* **b. orchid** ophrys *f* abeille

Beeb [bi:b] N *Fam* **the B.** la BBC

beech [bi:tʃ] N *(tree)* hêtre *m*; **b. furniture** meubles *mpl* en hêtre ▸▸*Bot* **b. mast** faines *fpl (tombées par terre)*; **b. wood** bois *m* de hêtre

beechnut ['bi:tʃnʌt] N faîne *f*, faînes *fpl*

bee-eater N *(bird)* guêpier *m* (d'Europe)

beef [bi:f] N **1** *(no pl)* Culin bœuf *m*; *Fig* **to have plenty of b.** *(muscles)* avoir du muscle, être costaud; **give it some b.!** fais un petit effort!; **the team's a bit short of b.** l'équipe manque un peu de muscle **2** *Am (animal)* *(pl* **beeves** [bi:vz]*)*; **beefs** [bi:fs] bœuf(s) *m(pl)* à l'engrais; **a b.** un bœuf, une vache **3** *Fam (complaint)* *(pl* **beefs***)* plainte *f*, grief *m*; **he enjoys a good b.** il aime ronchonner *ou* rouspéter; **what's your b.?** qu'est-ce que tu as à ronchonner?; **my main b. is that ...** ce qui m'énerve le plus, c'est que ... ▸ VI *Fam* ronchonner, rouspéter ▸▸*Agr* **b. cattle** bœufs *mpl* de boucherie; **b. farm** élevage *m* de bœufs; **b. farmer** éleveur *m* de bœufs; **b. stew** ragoût *m* de bœuf, bœuf mode; **b. tea** bouillon *m* de bœuf; **b. tomato** ≃ marmande *f* ▸ **beef up** VT SEP *Fam (text, character in play etc)* étoffer, donner plus de consistance à; *(army)* renforcer; **we need to b. up our coverage of Latin America** il faut que nous couvrions l'Amérique latine davantage

beefburger ['bi:fbɜːgər] N hamburger *m*

beefcake ['bi:fkeɪk] N *Fam* beaux hommes *mpl* musclés

Beefeater ['bi:fi:tər] N *Fam* = hallebardier *m* de service à la Tour de Londres

beefing ['bi:fɪŋ] N *Fam (moaning)* ronchonnements *mpl*, rouspétances *fpl*

beefsteak ['bi:fsteɪk] N *Culin* bifteck *m* ▸▸ **b. tomato** ≃ marmande *f*

beefy ['bi:fɪ] ADJ *Fam* **1** *(muscular)* musclé, costaud **2** *(fleshy)* bien en chair

beehive ['bi:haɪv] N **1** *(for bees)* ruche *f* **2** *(hairstyle)* coiffure *f* toute en hauteur, choucroute *f*

beekeeper ['bi:ki:pər] N apiculteur, -trice

beekeeping ['bi:ki:pɪŋ] N apiculture *f*

beeline ['bi:laɪn] N *Fig* **to make a b. for sth** aller droit *ou* directement vers qch

Beelzebub [bɪ'elzɪbʌb] N *Bible* Belzébuth

beemer ['bi:mər] N *Fam (BMW)* BM *f*

been PP *see* **be**

beep [bi:p] N *(of satellite, computer, watch etc)* bip *m*, signal *m* ou bip sonore; *(of car horn)* coup *m* de klaxon; *Aut* **to give the horn a b.** klaxonner; *Aut* **to give sb a b.** klaxonner qn ▸ VI *(of satellite, computer, watch etc)* faire bip,

émettre un signal *ou* bip sonore; *(of car driver)* klaxonner; **to b. at sb** klaxonner qn ▸ VT **1** *Aut* **to b. the horn** klaxonner **2** *(person) (on pager)* appeler au récepteur d'appel; **I'm being beeped** *(of doctor etc)* on m'appelle

beeper ['bi:pər] N récepteur *m* d'appels

beeping ['bi:pɪŋ] N *(of satellite, computer, watch etc)* bip-bip *m*, *pl* bips-bips; **a sudden b. of car horns** des coups de klaxon brutaux

beer [bɪər] N bière *f*; **to go for a b.** aller boire une bière; **will you join me in a b.?** est-ce que tu prends une bière aussi?; *Fig* **life's not all b. and skittles** la vie n'est pas qu'une partie de rigolade ▸▸ **b. barrel** tonneau *m* à bière; *Fam* **b. belly** brioche *f*, bide *m*; **b. bottle** canette *f* ou bouteille *f* de bière; **b. cellar** *(bar)* brasserie *f*; **b. garden** = jardin *m* d'un pub, où l'on peut prendre des consommations; **b. glass** verre *m* à bière; *Fam* **b. gut** brioche, bide; **b. mat** sous-bock *m inv*; **b. pump** pompe *f* à bière

beery ['bɪərɪ] ADJ **1** *(atmosphere etc)* qui sent la bière **2** **b. voice** voix *f* avinée

beeswax ['bi:zwæks] N cire *f* d'abeilles ▸▸ **b. polish** cire d'abeilles

beet [bi:t] N **1** betterave *f*; **fodder b.** betterave fourragère **2** *Am* = **beetroot** ▸▸ **b. industry** industrie *f* betteravière; **b. sugar** sucre *m* de betterave

beetle¹ ['bi:t(ə)l] N *(insect)* coléoptère *m*; *Aut Fam* **(Volkswagen) B.** coccinelle *f* ▸ **beetle along** VI *Fam (hurry along)* se dépêcher, se presser; **I must be beetling along now** il faut que je mette les bouts ▸ **beetle away, beetle off** VI *Fam* décamper

beetle² N *(for beating, pounding) (large)* masse *f (en bois); (small)* maillet *m; (for paving)* hie *f*, demoiselle *f*

beetle³ VI *(of cliff)* surplomber

beetle-browed [-'braʊd] ADJ *(with overhanging eyebrows)* aux sourcils proéminents; *(with bushy eyebrows)* aux sourcils touffus

beetle-crusher [-krʌʃər] N *Fam* écrase-merde *m*, *pl* écrase-merdes

beetling ['bi:tlɪŋ] ADJ *(cliff, rock etc)* surplombant, en surplomb

beetroot ['bi:tru:t] N *Bot, Culin* betterave *f* (potagère) ▸ ADJ *(colour)* rouge foncé; **he turned b.** il est devenu rouge comme une tomate ▸▸ **b. red** rouge foncé

befall [bɪ'fɔ:l] VT *(conj like* **fall***; used only in third person)* Lit, Arch *(person)* arriver à, survenir à

befit [bɪ'fɪt] VT *(-tt-)* Lit *(used only in third person)* convenir à; **as befits her position** comme il convient à son rang; **it does not b. a man to ...** ce n'est pas le fait d'un homme de ...

befitting [bɪ'fɪtɪŋ] ADJ convenable, seyant *(for sb/sth* à qn/qch*)*, digne *(of sb* de qn*)*; **with b. modesty/generosity** avec la modestie/générosité qui convient

BEFORE	[bɪ'fɔːr]	
ADV	avant **1**	▪ devant **2**
PREP	devant **1**	▪ avant **2, 3**
CONJ	avant de, avant que **1**	▪ plutôt que de **2**

ADV **1** *(of time)* auparavant, avant; **two days b.** deux jours avant *ou* auparavant, l'avant-veille *f*, *pl* avant-veilles; **the day b.** la veille; **the year b.** l'année d'avant, un an auparavant; **she had come two years b.** elle était venue deux ans auparavant; **a moment b.** un instant plus tôt; **I have seen him b.** je l'ai déjà vu; **I have never seen him b.** je ne l'ai jamais vu *(de ma vie)*; **we've met b.** nous nous sommes déjà rencontrés; **I've told**

you b. je te l'ai déjà dit; **you should have told me so b.** vous auriez dû me le dire plus tôt; **she gave me the same advice as b.** elle m'a redonné le même conseil; **to go on as b.** faire comme avant

2 *(of place)* devant; *Lit* **to go on b.** *(at front of procession)* marcher en tête; *(in advance)* partir devant; **this page and the one b.** cette page et la précédente

PREP **1** *(of place)* devant; **b. my (very) eyes** sous mes (propres) yeux; **b. God and man** devant Dieu et les hommes; **to appear b. the judge** comparaître devant le juge; **that is the task b. us** c'est là la tâche qui nous incombe

2 *(of time)* avant; **b. that, she was a teacher** auparavant *ou* avant ça, elle était professeur; **where did you go b. that?** où est-ce que vous êtes allé avant ça?; **not b. Easter** pas avant Pâques; **it ought to have been done b. now** ce devrait déjà être fait; **to arrive an hour b. time** arriver avec une heure d'avance *ou* une heure à l'avance; *Fam* **it's not b. time, and not b. time** ce n'est pas trop tôt; **I got here b. you** je vous ai devancé, je suis arrivé avant vous; **you were b. me** *(in queue)* vous étiez avant moi; **the day b. the battle** la veille de la bataille; **two days b. Christmas** l'avant-veille de Noël; **b. answering/leaving** avant de répondre/partir; **b. tax** hors taxe, HT; *(income)* avant impôt

3 *(of order)* **b. anything else, I must have ...** il me faut avant tout ...; **death b. dishonour** plutôt la mort que le déshonneur; **ladies b. gentlemen** les dames d'abord; **this word should come b. that one** ce mot devrait être placé devant celui-là; **the welfare of the country comes b. everything** le bien de la patrie prime tout; **she puts family b. friends** pour elle, la famille est plus importante que les amis

CONJ **1** *(of time)* avant que (ne) + *sub*, **come and see me b. you leave** venez me voir avant de partir *ou* avant votre départ; **I saw him the day b. he died** je l'ai vu la veille de sa mort; **don't come in b. I call you** n'entrez pas avant que je vous appelle; **it was long b. he came** *(it happened before that)* c'était longtemps avant qu'il arrive; **how long will it be b. you hear?** quand est-ce que tu sauras?; **b. long** avant longtemps, sous peu; *Fam* **b. you know where you are, b. I/he/etc knew where I/he/etc was** en moins de rien; **b. I forget, they expect you this evening** avant que je n'oublie, il faut que je te dise qu'ils comptent sur toi ce soir

2 *(of order)* **I will die b. I yield** je préfère mourir plutôt que de céder

3 *(or else)* avant que (ne) + *sub*, **get out b. I throw you out** sortez avant que je vous jette dehors; **tell me, b. I die of curiosity** dis-le moi, je n'en peux plus de curiosité; **give it to her b. she cries** donne-le-lui avant qu'elle ne se mette à pleurer

beforehand [bɪ'fɔ:hænd] ADV à l'avance, au préalable; **to come an hour b.** venir une heure à l'avance; **I must tell you b. that ...** il faut vous dire d'avance *ou* au préalable que ...; **if I come I'll let you know b.** si je viens je vous préviendrai; **we should make sure b.** nous ferions mieux de nous en assurer au préalable

befriend [bɪ'frend] VT *(make friends with)* se lier d'amitié avec; **I was befriended by a stray dog** un chien perdu s'est attaché à moi

befuddle [bɪ'fʌd(ə)l] VT **1** *(confuse)* embrouiller; **his mind is befuddled with drink** l'alcool lui a embrouillé l'esprit **2** *(make drunk)* griser; **befuddled (with drink)** éméché

beg [beg] *(-gg-)* VI *(for money)* mendier; *(plead)* supplier; **to sit up and b.** *(of dog)* faire le beau; **to b. for mercy** demander grâce; **I b. of you!** je vous en prie!; **these jobs are going begging** ce sont des emplois qui trouvent peu d'amateurs; **there's a piece of cake going begging** il reste un morceau de gâteau

VT to b. sb to do sth supplier qn de faire qch; **to b. a favour of sb** demander instamment un service à qn; **she begged to be sent back to school** elle supplia qu'on la renvoie à l'école; *Fml* **I b. to inform you that …** j'ai l'honneur de vous faire savoir que …; **I b. your pardon** je vous demande pardon; **to b. forgiveness** implorer le pardon; **I b. to differ** permettez-moi d'être d'un autre avis; *Fml* **to b. leave to do sth** demander la permission de faire qch; **to b. the question** *(evade the issue)* ne pas aborder la question; *(in logic)* faire une pétition de principe; **wanting to climb Mount Everest rather begs the question 'why'** on serait enclin à se demander pourquoi quelqu'un aurait envie d'escalader le mont Everest

▸ **beg off** VI *(from a meeting, party etc)* demander à être excusé

beget [bɪ'get] VT *(pt* **begot** [bɪ'gɒt], *Bible* **begat** [bɪ'gæt]; *pp* **begotten** [bɪ'gɒt(ə)n]) **1** *Bible, Lit* engendrer; **Abraham begat Isaac** Abraham engendra Isaac; *Bible* **the only begotten Son of the Father** le Fils unique du Père **2** *Lit Fig* engendrer, causer

beggar ['begər] N **1** *(in street)* mendiant, -ante; *Prov* **beggars can't be choosers** il ne faut pas être difficile quand on n'a pas le choix **2** *esp Br Fam (person)* **poor b.!** pauvre diable!; **lucky b.!** chançard!, veinard!; **you little b.!** petit coquin!, petit espiègle! **VT** *(beggared* ['begəd]) **1 to b. sb** réduire qn à la mendicité; **they are beggaring themselves doing it** en faisant cela, ils vont tout droit à la ruine **2** *Fig* **to b. description** être indescriptible

beggarly ['begəlɪ] ADJ *(very poor)* minable, misérable; *(wage)* dérisoire, minable

beggar-my-neighbour N *Cards* bataille *f*

beggary ['begərɪ] N mendicité *f*

begging ['begɪŋ] N mendicité *f*; **to live by b.** vivre d'aumône
▸ ▸ **b. bowl** sébile *f (de mendiant)*; **b. letter** lettre *f* de requête *(demandant de l'argent)*

BEGIN [bɪ'gɪn] VT & VI *(pt* **began** [bɪ'gæn]; *pp* **begun** [bɪ'gʌn])* commencer; *(piece of work, new chapter)* commencer, entamer; **b. at the beginning** commencez par le commencement; **before winter begins** avant le début de l'hiver; **the day began well/badly** la journée commença bien/mal; **to b. to do sth, to b. doing sth** commencer à faire qch, se mettre à faire qch; **to b. to laugh/cry, to b. laughing/crying** se mettre à rire/à pleurer; **he soon began to complain** il ne tarda pas à se plaindre; **we began** *or* **we were beginning to get hungry** nous commencions à avoir faim; **it doesn't b. to compare with …** cela est loin d'être comparable à …; **I couldn't (even) b. to explain/describe it to you** c'est presque impossible à t'expliquer/ de te le décrire; **to b. by doing sth** commencer par faire qch; **the play begins with a prologue** la pièce commence *ou* débute par un prologue; **to b. again** recommencer
▸ **begin with** VI **to b. with** *(in the first place)* premièrement, pour commencer; *(at first)* au départ

VT INSEP commencer par; **what did you have to b. with?** *(in restaurant etc)* par quoi avez-vous commencé?

beginner [bɪ'gɪnər] N **1** *(novice)* débutant, -ante, novice *mf*; **English for beginners** anglais pour débutants; **b.'s class** cours *m* de débutants; **(it's just) b.'s luck** aux innocents les mains pleines; **she just had b.'s luck** elle

n'y connaît rien, elle a simplement eu de la chance; **complete** *or* **absolute b.** grand débutant **2** *Theat* **beginners please!** en scène!

beginning [bɪ'gɪnɪŋ] N *(of speech, career etc)* commencement *m*, début *m*; *(of the world etc)* origine *f*, naissance *f*; **in the b.** au commencement, au début; **from the b.** dès le commencement *ou* le début; **from b. to end** depuis le commencement jusqu'à la fin; **at the b. of the week** au début de la semaine; **at the b. of term** à la rentrée *(des classes)*; **the first beginnings of civilization** l'aube *f* de la civilisation; **I have the beginnings of a cold** je couve un rhume, j'ai un début de rhume; **to make a b.** commencer, débuter; **the b. of the end** le début de la fin; **to have one's beginnings in sth** avoir qch pour origine

begone [bɪ'gɒn] VI *Arch, Lit (used as imp)* va-t'en!, allez-vous-en!

begonia [bɪ'gəʊnɪə] N bégonia *m*

begrudge [bɪ'grʌdʒ] VT **1** *(be unwilling to give)* donner à contrecœur; **you don't b. me the money do you?** tu ne me donnes pas cet argent à contrecœur, n'est-ce pas?; **they b. him his food** ils le nourrissent à contrecœur; **I b. spending so much money** c'est à contrecœur que je dépense une telle somme; **I b. the money I spent on that dress** je regrette d'avoir eu à payer autant pour cette robe; **he begrudged every moment spent away from his wife** chaque minute passée loin de sa femme lui était pénible **2** *(be envious of)* **to b. sb sth** envier qch à qn; **I don't b. him his success** je ne lui en veux pas d'avoir réussi

beguile [bɪ'gaɪl] VT *Lit* **1** *(charm)* enjôler, séduire; **to b. sb with promises** bercer qn de promesses; **to b. sb into doing sth** séduire qn pour qu'il fasse qch **2** *(while away)* **to b. the time** faire passer le temps

beguiling [bɪ'gaɪlɪŋ] ADJ *(smile)* enjôleur, séduisant

begum ['beɪgəm] N bégum *f*

behalf [bɪ'hɑːf] N **on** *or Am* **in b. of sb** au nom de qn, de la part de qn; *(to sign)* au nom de qn, pour qn; **he is acting on my b.** il agit pour moi *ou* pour mon compte; **don't be uneasy on my b.** ne vous inquiétez pas à mon sujet; **speaking on my own b.** *or* **on b. of myself** en mon (propre) nom; **on b. of my husband and myself** de la part de mon mari et moi; **she accepted the award on his b.** elle a reçu le prix en son nom *ou* pour lui

behave [bɪ'heɪv] VI **1** se comporter, se conduire; *(well)* bien se comporter, bien se conduire; **to b. well/badly to(wards) sb** bien/mal agir *ou* se comporter envers qn; **what a way to b.!** quelles manières!; **to know how to b.** savoir vivre; **I'll teach him how to b.!** je lui apprendrai la politesse!; **b. yourself!** *(to husband etc)* tiens-toi comme il faut *ou* bien!; *(to child)* sois sage!, tiens-toi comme il faut *ou* bien!
2 to b. (itself) *(of machine, clock etc)* marcher, fonctionner; **the television hasn't behaved properly since** la télévision ne marche pas bien depuis

-behaved [bɪ'heɪvd] SUFF **well-b.** sage, qui se conduit *ou* se tient bien; **badly-b.** qui se conduit *ou* se tient mal

behaviour, *Am* **behavior** [bɪ'heɪvjər] N **1** *(of person)* comportement *m* (**towards** envers); *(of pupil)* conduite *f* **(to(wards) sb** avec *ou* envers qn); **good b.** bonne conduite; **to be on one's best b.** se tenir (particulièrement bien) **2** *(of machine, car)* fonctionnement *m*
▸ ▸ *Psy* **b. pattern** type *m* de comportement; *Mktg* **b. segmentation** segmentation *f* comportementale

behavioural, *Am* **behavioral** [bɪ'heɪvjər(ə)l] ADJ de comportement
▸ ▸ **b. analysis** étude *f* de comportement; **b. pattern** type *m* de comportement; **b. scientist** behavioriste *mf*; **b. study** étude de comportement

behaviourism, *Am* **behaviorism** [bɪ'heɪvjərɪz(ə)m] N *Psy* behaviorisme *m*

behaviourist, *Am* **behaviorist** [bɪ'heɪvjərɪst] N, ADJ *Psy* behavioriste *mf*

behead [bɪ'hed] VT décapiter

beheading [bɪ'hedɪŋ] N décapitation *f*

behemoth [bɪ'hiːmɒθ] N *Lit* monstre *m*

behest [bɪ'hest] N *Lit* commandement *m*, ordre *m*; **at whose b.?** sur l'ordre de qui?

BEHIND [bɪ'haɪnd]

ADV	derrière ▪ en retard	
PREP	derrière ▪ en retard sur	
N	derrière	

ADV derrière; **to attack sb from b.** attaquer qn par-derrière; **to stay** *or* **remain b.** *(be at the back)* rester *ou* demeurer en arrière; *(not leave)* ne pas partir; **I'll stay b. and wait for them** je resterai derrière pour les attendre; **the teacher kept him b.** *or* **made him stay b.** le professeur l'a retenu *ou* l'a mis en retenue; **I left my umbrella b.** *(at home)* j'ai oublié mon parapluie à la maison; *(at sb else's home)* j'ai oublié mon parapluie (chez lui/eux/etc); **to be b. with** *or* **in one's work** être en retard dans son travail; **to be b. with the rent** être en retard pour son loyer; **to get** *or* **fall b. in one's work** prendre du retard dans son travail; *Sport* **they are only three points b.** ils ne sont qu'à trois points; **to follow close b.** suivre de très près

PREP derrière; **he hid b. it** il s'est caché derrière; **look b. you** regardez derrière vous; **I'm right b. you** *(at your back)* je suis juste derrière toi; *Fig (I support you)* je suis avec toi; **to walk** *or* **follow close b. sb** suivre qn de près; *Fig* **he has the minister b. him** il a le ministre derrière *ou* avec lui, il est protégé par le ministre; *Fig* **to be b. sth** être derrière qch; **the reasons b. sth** les raisons de qch; **to be b. schedule** avoir du retard; **she's ten minutes b. the leaders** *(in race)* elle a dix minutes de retard sur le peloton de tête; **she is b. the other pupils** elle est en retard sur les autres élèves; *Fig* **to put sth b. one** ne plus penser à qch, oublier qch *(volontairement)*; **let's put it all b. us** oublions tout cela, n'y pensons plus; **it's all b. me now** tout ça, c'est du passé; **b. the times** *(country)* arriéré, attardé; **you're b. the times** *(old-fashioned)* tu n'es pas à la page; *(not aware of latest developments)* tu as un métro de retard

N *Fam (buttocks)* derrière *m*; **to kick sb's b.** botter le derrière à qn; **get up off your b. and find yourself a job!** remue-toi un peu et trouve du boulot!

behindhand [bɪ'haɪndhænd] ADV en retard; **to be b. with the rent/with one's work** être en retard pour payer le loyer/dans son travail; **I've got awfully b.** j'ai pris énormément de retard

behind-the-scenes ADJ en coulisse

behold [bɪ'həʊld] VT *(pt, pp* **beheld** [bɪ'held])* *Lit, Arch* voir; **b.!** voyez!

beholden [bɪ'həʊld(ə)n] ADJ *Fml* **to be b. to sb** être redevable à qn **(for** de)

beholder [bɪ'həʊldər] N *Prov* **beauty is in the eye of the b.** il n'y a point de laides amours

behove [bɪ'həʊv], *Am* **behoove** [bɪ'huːv] V **IMPERS** *Arch* incomber à; **it ill behoves her to criticize** ça lui va mal de critiquer

beige [beɪʒ] ADJ, N *(colour)* beige *m*

Beijing [beɪˈʒɪŋ] N Beijing

being [ˈbiːɪŋ] N **1** (existence) existence f; **to come into b.** prendre forme, prendre naissance; **the company is still in b.** la société existe toujours; **my entire b. rebels at the idea** tout mon être se révolte à cette idée; **I loathe him with all my b.** je le hais de tout mon être **2** (human) **b.** être m humain; **human being** le genre humain, les (êtres) humains mpl; **the Supreme B.** l'Être suprême; **a b. from another planet** un être venu d'une autre planète

▸ ADJ **for the time b.** pour le moment

Beirut [beɪˈruːt] N Beyrouth

bejewelled, Am **bejeweled** [bɪˈdʒuːəld] ADJ paré de bijoux

belabour, Am **belabor** [bɪˈleɪbər] VT (beat) rouer de coups; **to b. sb with insults** accabler ou abreuver qn d'injures; Fig **to b. a point** insister lourdement sur un point

Belarus [beləˈruːs] N Biélorussie f

belated [bɪˈleɪtɪd] ADJ (information, invitation etc) tardif; (guest, traveller etc) en retard; **to wish you a b. happy birthday** pour te souhaiter un bon anniversaire avec un peu de retard

belatedly [bɪˈleɪtɪdlɪ] ADV Fml en retard, avec du retard, tardivement; **he apologized, somewhat b., for his conduct** il s'est excusé de sa conduite, mais un peu tard

belay [bɪˈleɪ] VT **1** Naut (line) amarrer **2** (mountaineer) assurer

belaying [bɪˈleɪɪŋ] N **1** Naut amarrage m; **b. pin** or **cleat** cabillot m, taquet m **2** (in mountaineering) assurance f, assurage m

belch [beltʃ] N éructation f, Fam rot m; **he gave a b.** il a fait un rot

▸ VI éructer, Fam roter; **he belched all through the meal** il a roté pendant tout le repas

▸ VT Fig **the house was belching smoke and flames** la maison crachait de la fumée et des flammes

▸ **belch forth, belch out** VT SEP (flames, smoke etc) vomir, cracher

▸ VI **smoke and flames were belching out of the house** la maison crachait de la fumée et des flammes

beleaguer [bɪˈliːgər] VT (city) assiéger; Fig critiquer; (project, ideology etc) s'attaquer à; **she was beleaguered by problems** elle croulait sous les problèmes

beleaguered [bɪˈliːgəd] ADJ (city) assiégé; Fig (project, ideology) très critiqué; (government, politician) assailli de toutes parts; (parents, look, manner) accablé

belfry [ˈbelfrɪ] N beffroi m, clocher m

Belgian [ˈbeldʒən] ADJ belge; (history, ambassador) de Belgique

▸ N Belge mf

Belgium [ˈbeldʒəm] N Belgique f

belie [bɪˈlaɪ] VT (prp belying [bɪˈlaɪɪŋ]) (image, feelings) s'opposer à, être en contradiction avec; (wealth) être en contradiction avec; **his appearance belies it** il n'en a pas l'air; **his looks b. his age** il ne fait pas son âge

belief [bɪˈliːf] N **1** conviction f, Rel croyance f; **b. in ghosts** croyance aux revenants; **b. in God** croyance en Dieu; **she did it in the b. that ...** elle l'a fait en étant persuadée que ...; **it is beyond b.** c'est incroyable; **to the best of my b.** autant que je sache; **it is my b. that ...** je suis convaincu que ..., j'ai la conviction que ... **2** (trust) foi f, confiance f (in on)

believable [bɪˈliːvəb(ə)l] ADJ (story, account) croyable, crédible; (character in novel, person) crédible; **far from b.** pas du tout crédible

BELIEVE [bɪˈliːv] VT (person, news, rumour etc) croire; **I b. that it is true** je crois que c'est vrai; **I b. (that) I am right** je crois avoir raison; **I b. him to be alive** je le crois vivant; **she is believed to be in Paris** on la croit à Paris; **the house was believed to be haunted** on croyait la maison hantée; **he believes himself to have been unfairly treated** il se croit (la) victime d'une injustice; **I b. not** (I don't think so) je crois que non; **I b. so** (I think so) je crois que oui; **I don't b. a word of it** je n'en crois rien ou pas un mot; **I don't know what to b.** je ne sais que croire; **I could scarcely or hardly b. my eyes** j'en croyais à peine mes yeux; **you can't b. everything you read in the papers** il ne faut pas croire tout ce qu'on lit dans les journaux; **to make sb b. that ...** faire croire à qn que ...; **I can well b. it** je suis prêt à le croire, je veux bien le croire; **b. it or not, he fell for her!** tu le croiras si tu veux, il s'est épris d'elle!; **would you b. it!** vous vous rendez compte!; **if he is to be believed** à l'en croire, s'il faut l'en croire; **she's a smart one, b. me!** or Fam **b. you me!** c'est une maligne, crois-moi!; **I wouldn't have believed it of you** je n'aurais pas cru ça de toi; Fam **I don't b. it!** c'est pas vrai!; Fam **don't you b. it!** n'en croyez rien! VOIR GRAMMAIRE A47–8

▸ VI **to b. in (one) God** croire en (un seul) Dieu; **to b. in ghosts** croire aux revenants; **I b. in his innocence** je crois en son innocence; **to b. in sth** (support) être partisan de qch, être pour qch; **I don't b. in making promises** je ne fais jamais de promesses; **to b. in sb/oneself** croire en qn/soi; **I don't b. in doctors** je ne fais pas confiance aux médecins

believer [bɪˈliːvər] N Rel croyant, -ante; **to be a b. in sth** croire à qch; (supporter of) être partisan de qch, être pour qch; **I'm a great b. in newborn babies being breast-fed** je suis très en faveur de l'allaitement au sein pour les nouveau-nés

Belisha beacon [bəˈliːʃə] N Br Formerly = sphère f orange lumineuse (indiquant un passage clouté)

belittle [bɪˈlɪt(ə)l] VT (person) rabaisser; (person's merits, efforts) déprécier, amoindrir; **to b. oneself** (disparage) se déprécier; (demean) se déconsidérer (aux yeux de qn, auprès de qn); **a belittling remark** une remarque désobligeante

Belize [beˈliːz] N Belize m

bell¹ [bel] N **1** cloche f; (small) clochette f; (on door) sonnette f; (on bicycle) sonnette, timbre m; (for cattle etc) clochette, clarine f; (for cat) grelot m; Br Fam **to give sb a b.** (telephone) passer un coup de fil à qn; **electric b.** sonnerie f (électrique); **set of bells** (in church) sonnerie; **great b.** (of a church) bourdon m; **there's the b.** (on door) on sonne; (in school) la cloche sonne; **to ring the b.** (on door) sonner; (handbell) agiter la sonnette; Fig **that rings a b.** cela me rappelle ou me dit quelque chose; Naut **six bells** six coups (de cloche) **2** (of flower) calice m; (of trumpet etc) pavillon m; (of blast furnace) cône m, cloche f

▸ VT Fig **to b. the cat** attacher le grelot

▸ ▸ Naut **b. buoy** bouée f à cloche; Am **b. captain** chef m chasseur; Tech **b. crank lever** levier m coudé; Bot **b. heather** bruyère f cendrée; Chem **b. jar** cloche de verre; **b. pull** (in room) cordon m de sonnette; **b. push** bouton m de sonnette; **b. tent** tente f conique; **b. tower** clocher m

▸ **bell out** VI (of tube etc) s'évaser

bell² N (cry) (of stag) bramement m, brame m

▸ VI (of stag) bramer

belladonna [beləˈdɒnə] N Bot, Pharm belladone f

bell-bottomed [-bɒtəmd] ADJ **b. trousers** = **bell-bottoms**

bell-bottoms [-bɒtəmz] NPL pantalon m (à) pattes d'éléphant

bellboy [ˈbelbɔɪ] N Am groom m

belle [bel] N beauté f; **the b. of the ball** la reine du bal

bellflower [ˈbelflaʊər] N campanule f

bellhop [ˈbelhɒp] N Am Fam groom m

bellicose [ˈbelɪkəʊs] ADJ belliqueux

bellicosity [belɪˈkɒsɪtɪ] N (of speech, behaviour) caractère m belliqueux, agressivité f; (of person) humeur f belliqueuse

-bellied [-ˈbelɪd] SUFF round-/swollen-/etc **b.** au ventre rond/enflé/etc

belligerence [beˈlɪdʒərəns] N agressivité f

belligerent [beˈlɪdʒərənt] ADJ **1** (aggressive) (person, tone of voice, attitude etc) agressif, belliqueux **2** (at war) (country) belligérant

▸ N belligérant, -ante

bellow [ˈbeləʊ] N (of bull) beuglement m, mugissement m; (of person) braillement m

▸ VI (of bull) beugler, mugir; (of person) brailler; **to b. with pain** hurler de douleur; **to b. at sb** (with rage) brailler dans les oreilles de qn; **I bellowed at him but he was too far away to hear** j'ai crié dans sa direction mais il était trop loin pour m'entendre

▸ VT (order) brailler; Fam (song) beugler

▸ **bellow out** VT SEP = bellow VT

bellowing [ˈbeləʊɪŋ] N (of animal) beuglement m, mugissement m; (of person) braillement m

bellows [ˈbeləʊz] NPL **1** (for fire) (pair of) **b.** soufflet m VOIR GRAMMAIRE A10 **2** Mus (of organ) soufflerie f

bell-ringer N carillonneur, -euse

bell-ringing N (sound) carillonnement m; (art) art m du carillonnement

bell-shaped ADJ en forme de cloche

bellwether [ˈbelweðər] N (sheep) mouton m qui mène le troupeau; Fig chef m de file

belly [ˈbelɪ] N **1** (of person) ventre m, Fam bedaine f, (large) panse f, (of animal) panse; Culin **b. of pork** poitrine f de porc; **to have an empty b.** avoir l'estomac vide; **to have a full b.** avoir le ventre plein; **his eyes are bigger than his b.** il a les yeux plus gros que le ventre; **to go b. flop** (of plane) faire un plat; Fig Fam **to go b. up** (of company) faire faillite **2** (of plane, ship, jug etc) ventre m **3** Mus (of violin etc) table f d'harmonie **4** Naut (of sail) creux m, renflement m

▸ VT (of wind) (sail) enfler, gonfler

▸ VI (of sail) faire (le) sac, s'enfler, se gonfler

▸ ▸ **b. band** (around book) bande f publicitaire; **b. dance** danse f du ventre; **b. dancer** danseuse f du ventre ou orientale; Aviat **b. landing** atterrissage m sur le ventre; Fam **b. laugh** gros rire m

▸ **belly out** VT SEP, VI = belly VT & VI

bellyache [ˈbelɪeɪk] Fam N mal m au ventre

▸ VI ronchonner, rouspéter, râler; **he's always bellyaching about something** il faut toujours qu'il rouspète après qch

bellyacher [ˈbelɪeɪkər] N Fam râleur, -euse; **to be a b.** être un râleur

bellyaching [ˈbelɪeɪkɪŋ] N Fam rouspétance f, jérémiades fpl; **I don't want any b.** je n'accepterai aucune rouspétance; **your constant b. is driving me up the wall** tes jérémiades incessantes me fatiguent

bellybutton [ˈbelɪbʌt(ə)n] N Fam nombril m

belly-flop VI Fam (of diver) faire un plat

bellyful [ˈbelɪfʊl] N Fig Fam **to have had a b.** en avoir ras le bol, en avoir marre; **I've had a** or **my b. of him** j'en ai marre ou plein le dos de lui

bellyland ['belɪlænd] vi *Aviat* atterrir sur le ventre

belong [bɪ'lɒŋ] vi **1** *(be property of)* to b. to appartenir à; **that book belongs to me** ce livre m'appartient *ou* est à moi; **to b. to the Crown** *(of land etc)* dépendre de la Couronne
2 *(be connected to)* **what category do they b. to?** à quelle catégorie appartiennent-ils?; **to b. to a society** faire partie d'une société; **do you b. to this club?** êtes-vous membre de ce cercle?; **I b. here** *(come from)* je suis d'ici; *(feel at ease)* je me sens chez moi ici; **to feel that one doesn't b.** ne pas se sentir à sa place
3 *(usually go)* **this is where the spoons b.** c'est ici qu'on range les cuillers; **where does this book b.?** où va *ou* se range ce livre?; **things that b. together** choses qui vont ensemble; **to put things back where they b.** remettre les choses à leur place

belonging [bɪ'lɒŋɪŋ] N **to feel** *or* **have a sense of b.** se sentir chez soi *ou* à sa place

belongings [bɪ'lɒŋɪŋz] NPL affaires *fpl*

beloved ADJ [bɪ'lʌvd] bien-aimé; **b. by all** aimé de tous; **the b. wife of …** l'épouse bien-aimée de …
N [bɪ'lʌvɪd] bien-aimé, -ée, *pl* bien-aimés, -ées, chéri, -ie; **my b.** mon bien-aimé, ma bien-aimée; *Rel* **dearly b.** mes bien chers frères

below [bɪ'ləʊ] ADV en bas, (en-)dessous; **voices from b.** des voix qui venaient d'en bas; **the tenants (of the flat) b.** les locataires du dessous; **on the floor b.** à l'étage en dessous; *Fam* **it's ten (degrees) b.** il fait moins dix; **here b.** *(on earth)* ici-bas; *Naut* **all hands b.!** tout le monde en bas!; **the passage quoted b.** *(immediately afterwards)* le passage cité ci-dessous; *(further on)* le passage cité plus loin *ou* ci-après
PREP au-dessous de; **b. the knee** au-dessous du genou; **b. (the) average** au-dessous de la moyenne; **people b. the age of 65** les gens âgés de moins de 65 ans; *Fam* **I'm feeling a bit b. par** je ne suis pas dans mon assiette; **temperature b. normal** température inférieure à la normale; **ten degrees b. zero** dix degrés au-dessous de zéro; **b. sea level** au-dessous du niveau de la mer; **b. the surface** sous la surface; **b. the bridge** *(downstream)* en aval du pont

below-the-line N *Mktg* publicité *f* hors-média
ADJ *Acct* au-dessous de la ligne, *Mktg* hors-média
▸ ▸ *Acct* **b. accounts** comptes *mpl* de résultats exceptionnels; *Mktg* **b. advertising** publicité hors-médias; **b. costs** *Acct* coûts *mpl* au-dessous de la ligne; *Mktg* coûts hors-média; **b. expenditure** *Acct* dépenses *fpl* au-dessus de la ligne; *Mktg* dépenses hors-média; *Mktg* **b. promotion** promotion *f* hors-média

belt [belt] N **1** *(round waist)* ceinture *f*, *Mil* ceinturon *m*; **to tighten one's b.** serrer sa ceinture; *Fig* se serrer la ceinture; *Fam* **I'm a b. and braces type** *(very cautious)* je suis du genre à penser que deux précautions valent mieux qu'une; **to be a brown/black b.** *(in martial arts)* être ceinture marron/noire; *Boxing* **to hold the b.** être le champion; *Boxing* **a blow beneath the b.** un coup bas; *Fig* **to hit sb beneath** *or* **below the b.** donner à qn un coup en traître *ou* un coup bas; **that was a bit beneath** *or* **below the b.** *(of joke, remark)* c'était un coup bas; *Fig* **to have sth under one's b.** *(move, project)* en avoir fini avec qch; *(driving licence, degree)* avoir qch en poche; **once you've got a few years' experience under your b.** une fois que tu as quelques années d'expérience à ton actif

2 *Tech* courroie *f*; **b. driven** entraîné par courroie
3 *(area)* région *f*, zone *f*
4 *Fam (blow) (with hand)* gifle *f*; *(with bat, stick)* coup *m*; **he gave the ball a terrific b.** il a tapé un grand coup dans la balle; **to give sb a b. in the face** flanquer un gnon *ou* un pain dans la tronche à qn
VT *Fam (hit with belt)* donner des coups de ceinture à; *(hit with hand)* gifler; *(hit with bat, stick) (ball)* frapper dans, taper dans; *(person)* frapper; **less of your cheek or I'll b. you one!** ne sois pas insolent ou je t'en mets une!
VI *Fam* **to b. down the stairs** descendre l'escalier quatre à quatre; **she belted out of the house** elle est sortie de la maison en courant
▸ ▸ **b. buckle** boucle *f* de ceinture; *Tech* **b. conveyor** transporteur *m* à courroie *ou* à ruban *ou* à bande; *Tech* **b. drive** transmission *f* par courroie; **b. loop** passant *m (de ceinture)*
▸ **belt along** VI *Fam* courir/aller/conduire à toute vitesse
▸ **belt out** VT SEP *Fam (order etc)* vociférer, gueuler; *(song)* gueuler, brailler
▸ **belt up** VI **1** *Br Sl* se taire; **b. up!** ta gueule! **2** *Aut Fam (put on seatbelt)* attacher sa ceinture de sécurité

belted ['beltɪd] ADJ ceinturé
▸ ▸ *Aut* **b. tyre** pneu *m* à ceinture

belter ['beltər] N *Br Fam* **a b. of a film** un super film; **that last song was a b.** la dernière chanson était super

belting ['beltɪŋ] N **1** *Tech (belts)* courroie(s) *f(pl)*; *(material)* matériau *m* à courroies **2** *Fam* **to give sb a (good) b.** *(spanking)* donner une bonne fessée à qn; *(beating-up)* donner une bonne raclée à qn; *(in match, competition etc)* mettre la pâtée à qn

beltway ['beltweɪ] N *Am* périphérique *m*

beluga [bə'luːgə] N *(fish)* béluga *m*; *(whale)* béluga, dauphin *m* blanc; *(caviar)* caviar *m* de béluga

belvedere ['belvɪdɪər] N *Archit* belvédère *m*

bemoan [bɪ'məʊn] VT pleurer; **to b. the loss of sth** se lamenter de *ou* pleurer la perte de qch; **to b. one's fate** pleurer sur son sort; **she was bemoaning the fact that they had no money** elle se lamentait de ce qu'ils n'avaient pas d'argent

bemuse [bɪ'mjuːz] VT *Lit (confuse)* rendre perplexe, dérouter

bemused [bɪ'mjuːzd] ADJ perplexe

ben [ben] N *Scot Geog* sommet *m*, mont *m*
▸ ▸ **B. Nevis** = point *m* culminant de la Grande-Bretagne, en Écosse (1343m)

bench [bentʃ] N **1** *(seat) (in park, garden)* banc *m*; *(upholstered)* banquette *f*, *(in lecture hall, amphitheatre)* gradin *m*; *Sport (pour les joueurs qui ne sont pas sur le terrain)* **Law** *(for judge, magistrates)* siège *m*; *Br Law* **the B.** *(magistrates)* la magistrature; *(court)* **to be on the B.** *(as a magistrate)* être magistrat; *(as a judge)* siéger au tribunal; **to retire from the B.** prendre sa retraite; *Sport* **to be on the b.** *(waiting to play)* être remplaçant; *(as punishment)* avoir été renvoyé du terrain **2** *Tech (worktable) (for carpenter)* établi *m*; *(for fitter)* banc *m*, marbre *m*; *(in greenhouse)* tablette *f*; *Chem etc* **laboratory b.** paillasse *f*
▸ ▸ **b. seat** *(in vehicle)* banquette *f*; **b. test** essai *m* au banc

benchmark ['bentʃmɑːk] N *Comput, Fig* référence *f*, *Com* point *m* de repère; *(in surveying)* repère *m* (de nivellement)
VT comparer
▸ ▸ *Mktg* **b. market** marché *m* de référence; *Can Admin* **b. position** poste-repère *m*, *pl* postes-repères; *Comput* **b. program** programme *m* d'évaluation des performances;

Comput **b. test** test *m* d'évaluation (de programme)

benchmarking ['bentʃmɑːkɪŋ] N évaluation *f* de performances, benchmarking *m*

benchtest ['bentʃtest] N essai *m* au banc
VT faire passer au banc d'essai

BEND¹ [bend] N **1** *(curve)* courbure *f*, *(in road)* tournant *m*, virage *m*; *(in pipe)* coude *m*; *(in river)* courbe *f*; **bends for 3 kilometres** *(road sign)* virages sur 3 kilomètres; *Aut* **to take a b. at speed** prendre un virage à toute vitesse; *Fam* **to be round the b.** être fou *ou* cinglé; *Fam* **you're driving me** *or* **sending me round the b.** tu me rends dingue *ou* fou
2 *Med* **the bends** maladie *f* des caissons; **to have the bends** souffrir de la maladie des caissons
3 *(action) (of body)* inclination *f*
VT *(pt* **bent** [bent] *pp* **bent**, *Arch* **bended)** *(knee, arm etc)* plier; *(head)* baisser; *(of age) (the back)* courber; *(pipe, rail)* cambrer, cintrer; *(wood, iron) (into a specific shape)* cambrer, arquer; *(metal) (of strong man in circus)* tordre; *(bow, spring)* tendre, bander; *Phys (light)* réfracter; *(ray)* infléchir; *Fig (law, rule etc)* faire une entorse à; **to b. one's head over a book** pencher la tête sur un livre; **to b. sb to one's will** plier qn à sa volonté; **to b. a rod/a key (out of shape)** tordre une barre de fer/une clef; *Br Fam* **to b. the elbow** *(drink)* lever le coude; *Br Fam* **to b. sb's ear** casser les oreilles à qn; **thanks for letting me b. your ear** merci de m'avoir laissé m'épancher
VI *(of rod, branch etc)* plier, ployer; *(of person)* se pencher; *(of road, river)* tourner; **to b. under the strain** *(of wood, iron)* arquer; *(of steel plate etc)* s'envoiler; *(of rod, wheel)* se voiler; **an old man bending under a heavy load** un vieillard courbé sous un pesant fardeau; *Fig* **to b. (to pressure)** céder (à la pression); *Fig Lit* **to b. to sb's will** se plier à la volonté de qn; *Fig* **to b. before the wind** plier
▸ **bend back** VT SEP recourber; *(to original straight position)* détordre; *(to original bent position)* replier; *(light)* infléchir
VI *(of person)* se pencher en arrière; *(of light)* s'infléchir
▸ **bend down** VT SEP *(branch)* courber, ployer; **the tree was bent down by the weight of the fruit** l'arbre penchait sous le poids des fruits
VI *(of person)* se courber, se baisser
▸ **bend forward** VI se pencher en avant
▸ **bend over** VI *(of person)* se pencher; *Fig* **to b. over backwards** se mettre en quatre (**to do** pour faire)
VT INSEP **to b. over sb** se pencher sur qn
VT SEP *(steel plate etc)* plier

bend² N *Naut (knot)* nœud *m*

bended ['bendɪd] ADJ *Lit* **on one's b. knees, on b. knee** *(ask for sth)* à genoux; **to go down on b. knee** *or* **knees** *(kneel down)* se mettre à genoux, s'agenouiller; *Fig* **to go down on one's b. knees to sb** *(beg)* supplier qn

bender ['bendər] N **1** *Fam (drinking session)* soûlerie *f*, **to go on a b.** se soûler **2** *Sl (homosexual)* pédale *f*, tantouze *f*

bending ['bendɪŋ] N **too much b. is bad for the back** il est mauvais pour le dos de se pencher trop souvent
▸ ▸ *Tech* **b. moment** moment *m* de flexion, moment fléchissant; *Tech* **b. strength** résistance *f* à la flexion; *Tech* **b. test** essai *m ou* épreuve *f* de ployage *ou* de flexion

beneath [bɪ'niːθ] ADV dessous, au-dessous; **from b.** de dessous
PREP sous; **b. contempt** parfaitement méprisable; **to marry b. one** faire une mésalliance; **she thinks everybody's b. her** elle s'imagine que tout le monde lui est inférieur; **he would consider it b. him to**

complain il considère qu'il serait indigne de lui de se plaindre; **to be b. sb's dignity** *(of behaviour etc)* ne pas être digne de qn; **the plank gave way b. me** la planche a cédé sous mon poids

Benedictine [benɪ'dɪktɪn] N **1** *Rel* Bénédictin, -ine **2** *(also* [-tiːn]*) (liqueur)* Bénédictine *f* ADJ *Rel* bénédictin

benediction [benɪ'dɪkʃən] N bénédiction *f, (at meals)* bénédicité *m*

benefaction [benɪ'fækʃən, 'benɪ-] N *Lit* **1** *(kindness)* bienfaisance *f* **2** *(act of kindness)* bienfait *m; (donation)* don *m* charitable

benefactor, benefactress ['benɪfæktər, 'benɪfæktrɪs] N bienfaiteur, -trice

benefice ['benɪfɪs] N *Rel, Hist* bénéfice *m*

beneficence [bɪ'nefɪs(ə)ns] N *Lit* **1** *(kindness)* bienfaisance *f* **2** *(act of charity)* œuvre *f* de bienfaisance

beneficent [bɪ'nefɪsənt] ADJ *Lit* bienfaisant

beneficial [benɪ'fɪʃəl] ADJ *(doing good)* bon, bénéfique; **b. to** *(the health, business)* bon pour
▸▸ *Law* **b. owner, b. occupant** usufruitier, -ière

beneficiary [benɪ'fɪʃərɪ] ADJ, N *Law* bénéficiaire *mf,* ayant droit *m,* pl ayants droit; *(of family allowance)* allocataire *mf,* Fig **the main beneficiaries of the new law will be working mothers** ce sont les mères qui travaillent qui bénéficieront le plus de la nouvelle loi

benefit ['benɪfɪt] N **1** *(advantage)* avantage *m;* **to derive b. from sth** profiter de qch, tirer profit de qch; **in order to derive full b. from the medicine** de façon à tirer tout le profit de ce médicament; **it's no b. to me, I get** *or* **gain no b. from it** je n'en retire aucun avantage; **a performance for the b. of the blind** une représentation au profit des aveugles; **for the b. of the others** à l'intention des autres; **that remark was for my b.** cette remarque était à mon intention *ou* m'était destinée; **I'm not doing this for my own b.** *or* Fam **for the b. of my health** je ne fais pas ça pour moi; **for the b. of one's health** dans l'intérêt de sa santé; **to give sb the b. of the doubt** accorder à qn le bénéfice du doute; **she hasn't had the b. of a university education** elle n'a pas eu la chance d'aller à l'université; **to offer sb the b. of one's experience** faire profiter qn de son expérience; **b. in kind** avantage en nature; *Fin* **benefits (package)** *(to employee)* avantages sociaux
2 *Theat (performance)* représentation *f* de bienfaisance; *Sport* **a b. match to raise money for the victims' families** un match organisé au bénéfice des familles des victimes
3 *Br Admin (allowance)* indemnité *f,* allocation *f,* **social security benefits** prestations *fpl* sociales; **to be on b.** toucher l'aide sociale; **child b.** = allocations familiales; **housing b.** allocation logement; **maternity b.** allocation de maternité; **sickness b.** indemnité *f* de maladie; **unemployment b.** allocation de chômage
VT être avantageux à, profiter à; **a steady exchange rate benefits trade** un change stable est avantageux pour le commerce *ou* favorise le commerce; **who(m) does it b.?** qui en bénéficie?; **it will b. mankind** c'est l'humanité toute entière qui en profitera; **to b. the cause of disarmament** favoriser le désarmement
VI **to b. by** *or* **from sth** bénéficier de qch, profiter de qch, tirer avantage de qch; **you will b. by a holiday** un congé vous fera du bien; **who benefits most from his death?** à qui sa mort profite-t-elle le plus?; **to b. from a rise in prices** profiter *ou* tirer profit d'une hausse des prix
▸▸ *Theat* **b. performance** représentation de

bienfaisance; *Mktg* **b. segmentation** segmentation *f* par avantages recherchés

Benelux ['benɪlʌks] N *Pol* Bénélux *m*
▸▸ **the B. countries** les pays *mpl* du Bénélux

benevolence [bɪ'nevələns] N **1** *(kindness)* bienveillance *f,* bonté *f* **2** *(charitableness)* bienfaisance *f*

benevolent [bɪ'nevələnt] ADJ **1** *(kindly disposed)* bienveillant **(to** envers**) 2** *(charitable)* bienfaisant, charitable **(to** envers**)**
▸▸ *Hist* **b. despotism** despotisme *m* éclairé; *Fin* **b. fund** fonds *m* de prévoyance; *Admin* **b. society** association *f* de bienfaisance

benevolently [bɪ'nevələntlɪ] ADV avec bienveillance

BEng [biː'eŋ] N *Univ abbr* **Bachelor of Engineering**

Bengal [beŋ'gɔːl] N Bengale *m*

Bengali [beŋ'gɔːlɪ], **Bengalese** [beŋgə'liːz] ADJ bengali, bengalais
N **1** Bengali *mf,* Bengalais, -aise **2** *Ling* bengali *m*

benighted [bɪ'naɪtɪd] ADJ *Lit (country etc)* plongé dans (les ténèbres de) l'ignorance

benign [bɪ'naɪn] ADJ *(smile, look etc)* bienveillant; *(climate)* doux, *f* douce
▸▸ *Med* **b. tumour** tumeur *f* bénigne

Benin [be'niːn] N Bénin *m*

Benjamin ['bendʒəmɪn] N *Arch* **the B. of the family** le benjamin de la famille

benny ['benɪ] N *Sl (drug)* (comprimé *m* de) benzédrine *f*

bent [bent] PT, PP *see* **bend**[1]
ADJ **1** *(branch)* courbé, plié; *(axle, lever)* coudé; *(back)* voûté; *(out of shape) (aerial, coathanger)* tordu; **to become b.** *(with age)* se voûter; *Am Fig Fam* **b. out of shape** *(angry, upset)* dans tous ses états **2** *Sl (corrupt) (politician, police officer etc)* malhonnête, pourri **3** *Sl (homosexual)* homosexuel, inverti; **as b. as a nine-bob note** *or* **as a three-pound note** pédé comme un phoque **4** *(determined)* déterminé, résolu (**(up)on** doing sth à faire qch); **he is b. on seeing me** il veut absolument me voir; **the government is b. on eliminating dissent** le gouvernement est résolu à éliminer toute opposition

bentwood ['bentwʊd] ADJ *(chair)* en bois courbé

benumbed [bɪ'nʌmd] ADJ *Fml* engourdi

benzene ['benziːn] N *Chem* benzène *m*

benzin(e) ['benziːn, ben'ziːn] N *Chem, Ind* benzine *f*

benzodiazepine [benzəʊdaɪ'eɪzəpiːn] N *Pharm* benzodiazépine *f*

benzol ['benzɒl] N *Chem* benzol *m*

bequeath [bɪ'kwiːð] VT léguer **(to** à**)**

bequest [bɪ'kwest] N legs *m;* **it was a b. from my grandmother** je l'ai hérité de ma grand-mère; **she made a b. of £2,000 to her favourite charity** elle a légué 2000 livres à l'œuvre de bienfaisance qu'elle préférait

berate [bɪ'reɪt] VT *Fml (person)* réprimander; *(plan, intention)* condamner

Berber ['bɜːbər] ADJ berbère
N **1** Berbère *mf* **2** *Ling* berbère *m*

bereave [bɪ'riːv] VT *(pt, pp usu* **bereft** [bɪ'reft]*)* **he has been bereaved** *(by a death)* il est en deuil

bereaved [bɪ'riːvd] ADJ en deuil; *(family, parents etc)* du défunt, de la défunte; **the entire nation feels b.** le pays tout entier est en deuil
NPL **the b.** la famille du défunt/de la défunte

bereavement [bɪ'riːvmənt] N deuil *m;* **owing to a recent b.** en raison d'un deuil récent; **she has suffered a b.** elle a été affligée par un deuil
▸▸ *Br* **b. counsellor** = conseiller *m* qui pro-

pose une assistance psychologique aux personnes qui ont perdu un être cher

bereft [bɪ'reft] ADJ *Fml* **to be b. of sth** être privé de qch; **b. of all hope** ayant perdu tout espoir; **to leave sb b. of speech** rendre qn muet; **she collapsed into a chair, her face b. of colour** elle s'effondra sur une chaise, le visage livide

beret ['bereɪ, 'berɪ] N béret *m; Mil* **the blue berets** les casques *mpl* bleus; **the red berets** les bérets rouges, les parachutistes *mpl*

berg [bɜːg] N *Fam (iceberg)* iceberg *m*

bergamot ['bɜːgəmɒt] N *(plant)* bergamote *f*

beriberi ['berɪ'berɪ] N *Med* béribéri *m*

berk [bɜːk] N *Br Sl* andouille *f,* con *m,* conne *f,* **to make a complete b. of oneself** se conduire comme une andouille *ou* un con; **to feel a right b.** se sentir con *ou f* conne

Berks [bɑːks] *abbr* **Berkshire**

Berlin [bɜː'lɪn] N Berlin; *Formerly* **East/West B.** Berlin Est/Ouest; **the B. airlift** le pont aérien de Berlin; **the B. Wall** le mur de Berlin

Berliner [bɜː'lɪnər] N Berlinois, -oise

berm(e) [bɜːm] N **1** *(fortification)* berme *f* **2** *(path)* berme *f,* banquette *f*

Bermuda [bə'mjuːdə] N les Bermudes *fpl; Fam* **bermudas** bermuda *m*
▸▸ *Am* **B. Plan** tarif *m* chambre avec petit déjeuner anglais; *Naut* **B. rig** gréement *m* Marconi; **B. shorts** bermuda; **the B. Triangle** le triangle des Bermudes

Bern(e) [bɜːn] N Berne

Bernese [bɜː'niːz, 'bɜː-] ADJ bernois
N Bernois, -oise
▸▸ **the B. Alps** l'Oberland *m* bernois

berried ['berɪd] ADJ **1** *Bot* à baies, couvert de baies **2** *Zool (lobster etc)* œuvé

berry ['berɪ] N **1** *(fruit)* baie *f,* **to go b. picking** aller cueillir des baies **2** *Zool (of crustacean)* œuf *m;* **lobster in b.** homard *m* œuvé
VI **to go berrying** aller cueillir des baies

berserk [bə'zɜːk] ADJ *Fam* fou furieux, *f* folle furieuse; **to go b.** devenir fou furieux; **to send sb b.** rendre qn fou furieux

berth [bɜːθ] N **1** *Naut, Rail* couchette *f, Fam* **I can give you a b. for the night** tu peux pieuter ici cette nuit si tu veux **2** *Naut (for ship)* poste *m* à quai; **she left her b. this morning** il est sorti du quai ce matin; **(anchoring) b.** poste de mouillage *ou* d'amarrage **3** *(distance) Naut* **to give a ship a wide b.** éviter *ou* parer un navire, passer au large d'un navire; *Fig* **to give sb a wide b.** éviter qn **4** *Fam (job)* boulot *m;* **to find a soft** *or* **an easy b.** trouver un emploi pépère
VT *(ship) (of helmsman)* faire accoster le long du quai, amener *ou* amarrer à quai; *(of port official)* donner *ou* assigner un poste à; **where is she berthed?** à quel quai se trouve-t-il?
VI **1** *(of ship)* aborder à quai, se ranger à quai; **when do we b.?** quand accostons-nous? **2 to b. forward/aft** *(of passengers, crew)* coucher à l'avant/à l'arrière

berthing ['bɜːθɪŋ] N *(of ship)* abordage *m* à quai

beryl ['berɪl] N *Miner* béryl *m*

beryllium [be'rɪlɪəm] N *Chem* béryllium *m*

beseech [bɪ'siːtʃ] VT *(pt, pp* **besought** [bɪ'sɔːt]*) Lit* implorer, supplier, conjurer (**sb to do sth** qn de faire qch); **help me, I b. you** aidez-moi, je vous en supplie *ou* conjure

beseeching [bɪ'siːtʃɪŋ] ADJ *(air, ton)* suppliant

beset [bɪ'set] *(pt, pp* **beset;** *prp* **besetting)** VT *Fml usu passive (of misfortunes, temptations etc)* assaillir; **b. with dangers/difficulties** environné *ou* entouré de dangers/de difficultés; **to be b. by doubts** être assailli de doutes *ou* par le doute

besetting [bɪ'setɪŋ] **ADJ ATTRIB** *Fml (idea, thought etc)* obsédant; **it's his b. sin** c'est son plus grand défaut

beside [bɪ'saɪd] **PREP 1** *(place) (person)* à côté de, auprès de; *(object)* à côté de; **seated b. me** assis à côté de *ou* auprès de moi, assis à mes côtés; **a house b. the lake** une maison au bord du lac
2 *(comparison)* à côté de; **b. him, everyone else appears slow** à côté de lui, tous les autres paraissent lents; **I feel very underdressed b. you** par rapport à toi *ou* à côté de toi, je ne me sens pas assez habillée
3 *(in addition to)* en dehors de; **other people b. ourselves** d'autres (personnes) que nous
4 *(wide of)* **that is b. the point** cela n'a rien à voir (avec l'affaire en question); **whether you arrrived or not is b. the point** que tu sois arrivé ou non n'est pas le problème; **b. oneself (with joy/anger)** fou de joie/colère; **b. oneself with enthusiasm** débordant d'enthousiasme

> Attention: ne pas confondre avec **besides**.

besides [bɪ'saɪdz] **ADV 1** *(in addition)* en outre, en plus; **many more b.** encore bien d'autres; **and many more people b.** et bien d'autres gens encore **2** *(moreover)* d'ailleurs, du reste, (et) en outre
PREP *(in addition to)* excepté, hormis; **ten of us, b. myself** (nous sommes/serons/etc) dix, sans me compter; **there are others b. him** il y en a d'autres que lui; **have you got it in anything b. black?** est-ce que vous l'avez dans d'autres couleurs qu'en noir?; **what else can you do b. type?** que savez-vous faire en dehors de *ou* à part taper à la machine?; **b. watching television, I did nothing all night** à part regarder la télévision, je n'ai rien fait de la soirée; **b. his grandmother, he was the only one with blue eyes** à part sa grand-mère, il était le seul de la famille à avoir les yeux bleus; **b. being an excellent singer, she also plays the violin** c'est une excellente chanteuse, et en plus elle joue du violon; **b. which, he was unwell** sans compter qu'il était indisposé

> Attention: ne pas confondre avec **beside**.

besiege [bɪ'siːdʒ] **VT** *(city)* assiéger; *Fig (building)* faire le siège de; *(person)* assaillir; **we have been besieged with requests to …** nous avons été assaillis de demandes de …; **the public besieged the tourist office with complaints** l'office du tourisme fut inondé de plaintes de la part du public

besmirch [bɪ'smɜːtʃ] **VT** *Lit* salir, tacher; *Fig (sb's memory)* salir, entacher, ternir

besom ['biːzəm] **N 1** *(broom)* balai *m* (de jonc) **2** *Pej (woman)* bonne femme *f*

besotted [bɪ'sɒtɪd] **ADJ 1** *(in love)* entiché (**with** sb de qn); **to be b. with sth** *(car, computer etc)* adorer qch; **she was b. with the idea of going to Mexico** l'idée d'aller au Mexique l'obsédait **2** *(with drink)* abruti par l'alcool

bespatter [bɪ'spætər] **VT** éclabousser; **bespattered with mud** tout couvert de boue

bespeak [bɪ'spiːk] **VT** *Fml (be sign of)* témoigner de

bespectacled [bɪ'spektək(ə)ld] **ADJ** qui porte des lunettes, à lunettes

bespoke [bɪ'spəʊk] **ADJ USU ATTRIB** *esp Br (clothing)* (fait) sur mesure; **b. tailor/shoemaker** tailleur *m*/cordonnier, -ière à façon

besprinkle [bɪ'sprɪŋk(ə)l] **VT** saupoudrer (**with** de)

Bess [bes] **N** *(dimin of* **Elizabeth***) (in English*

history) **Good Queen B.** = la reine Élisabeth Iʳᵉ d'Angleterre

BEST [best]

| **ADJ** meilleur |
| **N** le meilleur **1, 3, 4** ▪ le mieux **1, 3, 4** ▪ pour le mieux *(for the best)* **7** |
| **ADV** mieux **1** ▪ au mieux *(at best)* **2** |

ADJ VOIR GRAMMAIRE A25; A41 *(superl of* **good***)* meilleur; **the b. man on earth** le meilleur homme du monde; **may the b. man win** que le meilleur gagne; **my b. dress** ma plus belle robe; **to be dressed in one's b. clothes** être sur son trente et un; **to be on one's b. behaviour** bien se conduire; **I am acting in your b. interests** j'agis au mieux de vos intérêts; **with the b. will in the world** avec la meilleure volonté du monde; **the b. part of the year** *(most of)* la plus grande partie de l'année; **I waited for the b. part of an hour** j'ai attendu presque une heure; **I'm b. at biology** *(it's my strongest subject)* la biologie, c'est mon point fort; *(better than others)* je suis le meilleur en biologie; **it is b. to …** le mieux, c'est de …; **the b. thing you can do** or **the b. course to take is to …** ce qu'il y a de mieux à faire, c'est de …; **it would be b. to …, the b. plan would be to …** le mieux serait de …; **to know what is b. for sb** savoir ce qui va *ou* convient le mieux à qn; **I only want what's b. for you** je ne veux que ce qu'il y a de mieux pour toi; **I thought it (would be) b. to stay** j'ai pensé qu'il valait mieux rester; **b. before …** *(on packaging)* à consommer/utiliser avant le …; **the b. years of one's life** les meilleures années de sa vie; **to put one's b. foot forward** *(do one's best)* faire de son mieux; *(make an effort)* faire un petit effort; *Fam Hum* **it's the b. thing since sliced bread** c'est ce qu'on a inventé de mieux depuis le fil à couper le beurre

N 1 *(maximum, peak)* le meilleur, la meilleure; **this is the b. there is** voici ce qu'il y a de meilleur *ou* de mieux; **I am in the b. of health** je me porte à merveille, je suis en excellente santé; **to do sth to the b. of one's ability** faire qch de son mieux; **to the b. of my belief/knowledge** à ce que je crois/autant que je sache; **the b. of it is that …** le plus beau de l'affaire, c'est que …; **to have** or **get the b. of both worlds** gagner sur les deux tableaux; **he can sing with the b. (of them)** il chante comme un dieu *ou* divinement; **she's up there with the b. of them** elle peut rivaliser avec les meilleurs; **we are the b. of friends** nous sommes les meilleurs amis du monde; **he was undemonstrative at the b. of times** même dans ses meilleurs moments, il était peu démonstratif; **let's make it the b. of five** le premier qui remporte trois jeux *ou* parties sur cinq a gagné; *Sch Old-fashioned Br Fam* **six of the b.** une correction magistrale; **to be dressed in one's Sunday b.** porter ses habits du dimanche; **I keep it for b.** *(of dress, suit etc)* je le garde pour des occasions spéciales
2 *(good wishes)* *Fam* **the b. of luck!** bonne chance!; *Fam* **all the b.** *(spoken)* toutes mes amitiés; *(written)* amitiés; **my brother sends his b.** mon frère vous dit bien des choses *ou* vous prie d'accepter toutes ses amitiés
3 *(optimum performance)* **I did my b.** j'ai fait de mon mieux; **your b. wasn't good enough** tu as peut-être fait de ton mieux, mais ça n'a pas suffi; **to do one's b.** *or* **the b. one can to …** faire de son mieux pour …; **I did my b. to comfort her** je l'ai consolée du mieux que j'ai pu, j'ai fait de mon mieux pour la consoler; **he did his b. to smile** il s'efforça de sourire; **I am doing my (level) b.** *or* **the b. I can** for you je fais tout ce que je peux pour vous; **that's the b. I can offer** c'est ce que je peux vous offrir de mieux; **is that the b. you can do?**

vous ne pouvez pas faire mieux?; **do the b. you can** *(given the circumstances)* arrangez-vous; *(in exam)* faites de votre mieux; **to bring out the b. in people** faire ressortir les bons côtés des gens; **to get the b. out of sb** tirer le maximum de qn; **to get the b. out of sth** tirer le meilleur parti de qch
4 *(appearance, condition)* **to look one's b.** être *ou* paraître à son avantage; **to be at one's b.** être en grande forme *ou* au meilleur de sa forme; **I am not at my b. in the morning** je ne suis pas au mieux de ma forme le matin; **you haven't seen the house at its b.** tu n'as pas vu la maison sous son meilleur jour; **that is Dickens at his b.** voilà du meilleur Dickens
5 *(advantage)* **to get** *or* **have the b. of it** *or* **of the bargain** faire une bonne affaire; **to have the b. of an argument** l'emporter dans une discussion; **to get the b. of sb in an argument** l'emporter sur qn dans une discussion
6 *(compromise)* **to make the b. of sth** s'accommoder de qch; **you'll just have to make the b. of it** il faudra t'y faire; **to make the b. of things** *or* **a bad job** faire avec ce qu'on a, faire contre mauvaise fortune bon cœur
7 *(result, outcome)* **to act for the b.** agir pour le mieux; **I did it for the b.** j'ai fait pour le mieux; **it's all for the b.** tout est pour le mieux; **I meant it for the b.** cela partait d'une bonne intention; **to hope for the b.** ne pas désespérer, avoir bon espoir; **we must hope for the b.** il faut être optimiste; **only the b. will do** ne fera l'affaire que ce qu'il y a de meilleur; **your parents only want the b. for you** tes parents ne veulent que ce qu'il y a de mieux pour toi

ADV *(superl of* **well***)* **1 he does it b.** c'est lui qui le fait le mieux; **I comforted her as b. I could** je la consolai de mon mieux; **I got down as b. I could** je suis descendu comme j'ai pu; **you know b.** c'est vous (qui êtes) le mieux placé pour en juger; **mother knows b.** maman a raison; **he's b. able to decide** il est le plus à même de décider; **do as you think b.** faites comme bon vous semble(ra); **he had b. agree** il ferait mieux d'accepter; **the b. dressed man** l'homme le mieux habillé; **the b. kept secret of the war** le secret le mieux gardé de la guerre; **the b. known book** le livre le mieux *ou* le plus connu; **the b.-looking women** les femmes les plus jolies; **to come off b.** *(in argument, discussion)* l'emporter, avoir l'avantage, avoir le dessus; **I like beef b.** je préfère le bœuf; **what goes down b. with the public is …** ce que le public préfère, c'est …; **these things are b. left to the police** il vaut mieux laisser à la police le soin de s'occuper de ces choses-là
2 at b. au mieux; **at b., he will get 2,000 votes** au mieux, il aura 2000 voix; **your article is at b. unhelpful, at worst obstructive** au mieux, votre article n'apporte rien d'utile, au pire il constitue un obstacle
VT *(in argument etc)* l'emporter sur, battre; **she is rarely bested in an argument** il est rare qu'elle soit battue *ou* qu'on l'emporte sur elle dans un débat
▸▸ *TV, Cin* **b. boy** aide-électricien *m, pl* aides-électriciens; *Br Culin* **b. end** *(of lamb)* = filet *m*; *Br Culin* **b. end of neck** carré *m*; **b. man** *(at wedding)* garçon *m* d'honneur; *Com* **b. practice** meilleure pratique *f*

Best Man

Dans les pays anglo-saxons, le garçon d'honneur présente l'alliance au marié et prononce un discours lors de la réception de mariage.

---

best-before date **N** date *f* limite de consommation

bestial ['bestɪəl] ADJ bestial, -aux

bestiality [bestɪˈælɪtɪ] N bestialité f

bestially ['bestɪəlɪ] ADV avec bestialité, bestialement

best-in-class N Mktg chef m de file

bestir [bɪˈstɜːr] VT (-rr-) Fml to b. oneself se démener, s'activer

best-of-breed N Mktg nec plus ultra m inv

bestow [bɪˈstəʊ] VT Lit accorder, donner (sth (up)on sb qch à qn); **to b. a favour on sb** accorder une faveur à qn

bestowal [bɪˈstəʊəl] N octroi m

bestride [bɪˈstraɪd] VT Fml (pt **bestrode** [bɪˈstrəʊd]; pp **bestridden** [bɪˈstrɪd(ə)n]) **1** (straddle) être à cheval ou à califourchon sur **2** (cross) (ditch etc) enjamber

bestseller [best'selər] N (book, record) best-seller m, pl best-sellers; **to be a b.** (of book, record) être un best-seller; (of author, musician etc) être un auteur/un musicien/etc à succès; **the month's bestsellers** les meilleures ventes du mois; **this book is the year's b.** ce livre est le plus gros succès de l'année; **it's been on the b. list for months** il est au palmarès des meilleures ventes depuis des mois

best-selling ADJ (book, author) à succès; **this is our b. item** c'est l'article que nous vendons le mieux; **it's been on the b. list for months** il est au palmarès des ventes depuis des mois

bet [bet] N pari m (**on** sur); **to win/lose a b.** gagner/perdre un pari; **to make** or **lay a b.** parier, faire un pari; Fam **your best b. would be to ...** ce que vous avez de mieux à faire, c'est de ...; **I'd take a b. on it** je serais prêt à le parier; Fam **it's my b.** or **my b. is that he'll come** je parie qu'il viendra; **all bets are off** les paris sont annulés

VT (pt **bet**; pp **bet**, occ **betted**) (sum of money) parier; **I'll b. you that ...** je vous parierais que ..., parions que ...; **to b. ten to one that ...** parier à dix contre un que ...; Fam **I'll b. you anything (you like) that ...** je te parie tout ce que tu veux que ..., j'en donnerais ou mettrais ma tête à couper que ...; Fam **you don't!** chiche (que tu ne le feras pas)!; Fam **b. you I will!** chiche (que je le fais)!; Fam **you b. I will/you did/etc!** bien sûr que oui!; **you b. I won't/you didn't/etc!** bien sûr que non!

VI **to b. on a horse** miser sur ou jouer un cheval; **to b. with sb** parier avec qn; **to b. on sth** parier sur qch; **I never b. on a sure thing** ce serait un pari perdu d'avance; **do you want to b.?** (as challenge) tu paries?; **I b.!** (expressing disbelief) sûrement!; **you b.!** bien sûr

beta-blocker ['biːtəblɒkər] N (drug) bêta-bloquant m

Betamax® cassette ['biːtəmæks] N Betamax® f

beta test ['biːtə] Comput N bêta-test m, pl bêta-tests, essai m approfondi
VT conduire les bêta-tests sur, conduire les essais approfondis sur

beta testing N Comput béta-tests mpl

betel ['biːt(ə)l] N (for chewing), Bot bétel m
▶▶ **b. nut** noix f d'arec; **b. nut palm, b. palm** arec m, aréquier m

Bethlehem ['beθlɪhem, -lɪəm] N Bethléem m ou f

betide [bɪˈtaɪd] VT Arch, Lit, Hum (used only in) **woe b. him/you/etc** malheur ou gare à lui/à toi/etc

betimes [bɪˈtaɪmz] ADV Arch de bonne heure

betoken [bɪˈtəʊkən] VT Fml dénoter

betray [bɪˈtreɪ] VT **1** (be disloyal to) (person, one's country, faith etc) trahir; **to b. sb's trust**

trahir la confiance de qn **2** (disclose) (secret, one's ignorance, emotion) révéler, trahir

betrayal [bɪˈtreɪəl] N **1** (disloyalty) trahison f (**of** de); **b. of trust** abus m de confiance **2** (disclosure) (of one's ignorance, secret etc) révélation f

betrayer [bɪˈtreɪər] N **1** (of country) traître, -esse; **she attacked her b. with a knife** elle attaqua avec un couteau celui/celle qui l'avait trahie **2** (of secret) dénonciateur, -trice

betrothal [bɪˈtrəʊðəl] N Fml fiançailles fpl

betrothed [bɪˈtrəʊðd] ADJ, N Fml, Arch fiancé, -ée

BETTER¹ ['betər]

ADJ	meilleur ▪ mieux
N	le meilleur **2**
ADV	mieux
VT	améliorer

ADJ (comp of good) meilleur; **you will find no b. hotel** vous ne trouverez pas mieux comme hôtel; **he's a b. man than you** (morally) vous valez mieux que vous; **you'd b. than I am** (at maths etc) vous êtes plus fort que moi; **she's b. at tennis than her brother** elle est meilleure que son frère au tennis; **he's b. at maths than me** il est meilleur que moi en math; **fruit juice is b. for you than coffee** le jus de fruit est meilleur pour la santé que le café; **he is no b.** (of patient) il ne va pas mieux; **he is no b. than his brother** il ne vaut pas mieux que son frère; Old-fashioned, Hum **she's no b. than she should be** elle n'a rien d'une sainte; **to appeal to sb's b. feelings** faire appel aux bons sentiments de qn; **I had hoped for b. things** j'avais espéré mieux; **to get b.** (of patient) se remettre, se rétablir; (at doing sth) faire des progrès; (of weather, situation etc) s'améliorer; (of wine etc) se bonifier; **the weather is b.** il fait meilleur; **to be b.** (in health) aller ou se porter mieux; **I hope you will soon be b.** j'espère que vous serez bientôt rétabli; **is your cold any b.?** ton rhume va mieux?; **is your headache any b.?** tu as encore mal à la tête?; **is your foot any b.?** est-ce que tu as moins mal au pied?; **it's b. that way** c'est mieux comme ça; **it's b. to do without it** mieux vaut ou il vaut mieux s'en passer; **it would be b. for you to go** (to that place) il vaudrait mieux que vous y alliez; **that's b.** voilà qui est mieux; **it would be b. if you called me tomorrow** ce serait ou il vaudrait mieux que tu m'appelles demain; **nothing could be b., it couldn't be b.** cela ne peut pas être mieux, c'est on ne peut mieux; **b. luck next time!** tu feras mieux la prochaine fois!; **for the b. part of the day** pendant la plus grande partie de la journée; Br Fam **my b. half** ma (chère) moitié, ma légitime; (man) mon homme; Br **to go one b. than sb**, Am **to go sb one b.** (r)enchérir ou surenchérir ou faire une surenchère sur qn VOIR GRAMMAIRE A25; A41

N **1 I expected b. of you** je m'attendais à mieux de ta part; **one's betters** (socially) ceux qui sont d'un rang social plus élevé; **one's elders and betters** ses aînés **2** (superior of two) le meilleur, la meilleure; **which is the b. of the two?** lequel des deux est le meilleur?; **what do you think of this wine? – I've tasted b.** comment trouvez-vous ce vin? – j'en ai bu de meilleurs; **change for the b.** changement m en bien; (in state of health) amélioration f; **he has changed for the b.** (his character has improved) il a changé à son avantage; **things are taking a turn for the b.** les choses prennent meilleure tournure; **to get the b. of sb** l'emporter sur qn, prendre le dessus sur qn; **to get the b. of** (obstacle etc) surmonter, vaincre; (one's

anger etc) maîtriser; **his anger/shyness got the b. of him** sa colère/timidité a eu raison de lui; **to be (all) the b. for doing sth** se trouver mieux d'avoir fait qch; **I'm all the b. for seeing you** ça me fait du bien de te voir; **I'd feel all the b. for a holiday** je partirais volontiers en vacances; **you will be all the b. for it** vous vous en trouverez (d'autant) mieux; **I think all the b. of you for it** je vous en estime d'autant plus; **all the b.!** tant mieux!

ADV (comp of well) mieux; **so much the b.** tant mieux; **to take sb for b. or for worse** (in marriage ceremony) s'unir à qn pour le meilleur comme pour le pire; **b. and b.** de mieux en mieux; **I know that b. than you** je sais cela mieux que vous; **I am feeling b.** je me sens mieux; **you are looking b.** tu as meilleure mine; **to know sb b.**, **to get to know sb b.** mieux connaître qn; **the more I know him, the b.** I like him plus je le connais, plus je l'aime; **I can understand it all the b. because ...** je le conçois d'autant mieux que ...; **you'd b. stay** il vaut mieux que vous restiez; **I'd b. begin by ...** je ferais bien de commencer par ...; **we'd b. be going back** il est temps de rebrousser chemin; **you'd b. not** il ne vaudrait mieux pas; **hadn't you b. phone first?** est-ce qu'il ne vaudrait pas mieux que tu appelles avant?; **to think b. of it** changer d'opinion, se raviser; **to think b. of sb for doing sth** estimer qn davantage d'avoir ou pour avoir fait qch; **that's b. still** (what you have done) c'est encore mieux; **b. still, you could come tomorrow** mieux encore, tu pourrais venir demain, ce qui serait mieux, c'est que tu viennes demain; **b. dressed** mieux habillé; **b. known** plus connu; **b. looking** (more attractive) plus beau ou joli; **he's b. tempered than his brother** il est plus agréable que son frère; **I hope you're a bit b. tempered tomorrow!** j'espère que tu seras de meilleure humeur demain!; **to be b. off** (wealthier) être plus aisé; (well situated) se trouver dans de meilleures conditions; **he's b. off where he is** il est bien mieux où il est; **you're b. off without him** tu es bien mieux sans lui; **the children of b.-off parents** les enfants dont les parents sont aisés

VT **1** (improve) améliorer; **to b. oneself** améliorer sa condition **2** (surpass) (exploit, piece of work) surpasser; Sport (time) améliorer; **the company has bettered the competition for the second year running** c'est la deuxième année consécutive que l'entreprise a fait mieux que la concurrence; **can you b. that?** pouvez-vous faire mieux que cela?

better² N (person who bets) parieur, -ieuse

betterment ['betəmənt] N Fml amélioration f

betting ['betɪŋ] N (bets) paris mpl; (price) cote f; **the b. ran high** on a parié gros; **the b. is twenty to one** la cote est à vingt contre un; **the b. is that ...** il y a fort à parier que ...; **what's the b. he doesn't turn up?** combien tu paries qu'il ne viendra pas?; **if I were a b. man** si j'étais homme à parier
▶▶ **b. book** carnet m de paris; **b. shop** bureau m de paris (appartenant à un bookmaker); **b. slip** bulletin m de pari

bettor ['betər] N = **better²**

BETWEEN [bɪˈtwiːn] PREP entre; **a table stood b. him and the door** une table le séparait de la porte; **to stand b. two opponents** s'interposer ou intervenir entre deux adversaires; **no one can come b. us** personne ne peut nous séparer; **to be b. life and death** être entre la vie et la mort; **to be something b. ... and ...** tenir autant de ... que de ...; **b. eight and nine o'clock** entre huit et neuf heures; **b. now and Monday** d'ici (à) lundi; **b. twenty and thirty** de vingt à trente; **you must**

choose **b. them** il faut choisir entre eux; **to distinguish b. A, B and C** distinguer entre A, B et C; **b. the two/the three of them** à eux deux/trois; **they scored 1,500 b. them** (of two people) ils ont marqué 1500 à eux deux; (of more than two people) ils ont marqué 1500 à eux tous; **we bought it b. us** nous l'avons acheté à nous deux/à nous trois/etc; **they shared the loot b. them** ils se sont partagé le butin; **b. ourselves …** entre nous …; **this is strictly b. ourselves** or **b. you and me** que cela reste entre nous; Fam **b. you (and) me and the gatepost** (soit dit) entre nous; **b. one thing and another …** d'une chose à l'autre …; **there's no love lost b. them** ils ne peuvent pas se souffrir ou se sentir

ADV **(in) b.** entre les deux; (in the intervening time) dans l'intervalle

between-decks Naut ADV dans l'entrepont
N entrepont m

betweentime(s) [bɪ'twiːntaɪm(z)], **betweenwhile, betweenwhiles** [bɪ'twiːnwaɪl(z)] ADV dans l'intervalle, entre-temps

betwixt [bɪ'twɪkst] ADV Fam **it's b. and between** c'est entre les deux

bevel ['bev(ə)l] N biseau m
VT (-ll-, Am -l-) biseauter, chanfreiner, tailler en biseau
VI aller en biseau
▸▸ Mining **b. cut** fausse coupe f; Carp **b. edge** biseau m; Tech **b. gear** engrenage m conique; **b. rule, b. square** fausse équerre f

bevelled, Am **beveled** ['bevəld] ADJ (edge) biseauté, en biseau, en chanfrein

bevelling, Am **beveling** ['bev(ə)lɪŋ] N biseautage m, chanfreinage m

beverage ['bevərɪdʒ] N boisson f
▸▸ Can **b. room** bar m

bevvied ['bevɪd] ADJ BrFam bourré, beurré; **to get b.** se cuiter, prendre une cuite

bevvy ['bevɪ] N BrFam **1** (alcohol) alcool m **2** (alcoholic drink) **to have a b.** boire un coup **3** (drinking session) beuverie f; **to go on the b.** aller se cuiter

bevy ['bevɪ] N **1** (group) bande f, troupe f; **b. of girls** bande de filles **2** (of larks, quail) volée f

bewail [bɪ'weɪl] VT pleurer; (one's fate) se lamenter sur

beware [bɪ'weər] VI (used only in inf and imp) (of sb) se méfier, Lit se défier (of de); (of sth) se méfier (of de), prendre garde (of à); **b.!** prenez garde!; **b. of pickpockets** attention aux pickpockets; **b. of the dog** (sign) ≃ chien méchant; **to b. of doing sth** se garder de faire qch

bewhiskered [bɪ'wɪskəd] ADJ Lit, Hum qui porte des rouflaquettes

bewilder [bɪ'wɪldər] VT **1** (puzzle) désorienter, dérouter **2** (confuse) ahurir, abasourdir

bewildered [bɪ'wɪldəd] ADJ **1** (puzzled) désorienté; (air) perplexe **2** (confused) ahuri, abasourdi

bewildering [bɪ'wɪldərɪŋ] ADJ **1** (puzzling) (problem, question) déroutant **2** (confusing) (number, variety) ahurissant

bewilderingly [bɪ'wɪldərɪŋlɪ] ADV **the problem is b. complex** le problème est d'une complexité déroutante; **even more b., …** chose encore plus ahurissante, …; **b. varied/frequent** d'une variété/fréquence ahurissante

bewilderment [bɪ'wɪldəmənt] N **1** (puzzlement) perplexité f **2** (confusion) ahurissement m

bewitch [bɪ'wɪtʃ] VT ensorceler, jeter un sort sur; Fig captiver

bewitching [bɪ'wɪtʃɪŋ] ADJ ravissant

bey [beɪ] N bey m

beyond [bɪ'jɒnd] ADV au-delà, par-delà; **the next century and b.** le siècle à venir et au-delà
PREP **1** (of place) au-delà de, par-delà; **the house is b. the church** la maison est au-delà de ou plus loin que l'église; **b. the seas** par-delà les ou au-delà des mers
2 (of time) **b. a certain date** passé une certaine date
3 (surpassing) **to live b. one's means** vivre au-dessus de ses moyens; **it's b. me** cela me dépasse, je n'y comprends rien; **it's b. me how they can do it** je ne comprends vraiment pas comment ils peuvent le faire; **circumstances b. our control** circonstances indépendantes de notre volonté; **what you're asking is b. my power** ce que vous demandez me dépasse ou dépasse mes attributions; **it's b. my power to save him** je ne peux rien pour le sauver; **b. my reach** hors de ma portée; **I'm b. caring what they do next** peu m'importe ce qu'ils feront ensuite; **frankly, I'm b. caring** franchement, ça m'est complètement égal; **b. belief** incroyable, à n'en pas y croire; **b. doubt** hors de doute, sans le moindre doute; Fml **b. measure** outre mesure, sans mesure; **b. praise** au-dessus de tout éloge; **b. reach** inaccessible, hors de portée; **b. repair** irréparable; **b. question** indiscutablement, incontestablement; **to be b. question** être indiscutable ou incontestable; **it is a fact b. doubt** or **question** c'est un fait avéré; **that's (going) b. a joke** cela dépasse les bornes (de la simple plaisanterie); **she is b. recovery** (of sick person) elle est perdue; **the agreement is b. saving** l'accord est à l'eau
4 (except) **he has nothing b. his wages** il n'a rien que son salaire
N **the b.** l'au-delà m inv

bezel ['bezəl] N **1** (of cut gem) biseau m, bezel m **2** (of ring) chaton m

BF [biː'ef] N BrSl abbr **bloody fool**

B-feature N Cin film m de série B

BFI [biːef'aɪ] N Cin (abbr **British Film Institute**) = organisme m britannique de promotion du cinéma (aide à la réalisation notamment)

bhp [biːeɪtʃ'piː] N (abbr **brake horsepower**) ch mpl, CV mpl

Bhutan [buː'tɑːn] N Bhoutan m

bi [baɪ] ADJ Fam (abbr **bisexual**) bi

bi-annual ADJ semestriel

bi-annually ADV deux fois par an

bias ['baɪəs] N **1** préjugé m, parti m pris (**against** contre; **in favour of** en faveur de); **without b.** être sans parti pris; **the b. in his remarks was obvious** il était clair à ses remarques qu'il était de parti pris **2** Sewing biais m; **material cut on the b.** étoffe coupée en ou de biais
VT (pt, pp **bias(s)ed**) rendre partial, influencer, prévenir (**towards, in favour of** en faveur de; **against** contre)
▸▸ Sewing **b. binding** biais m (ruban); Aut **b. tyre** pneu m à structure diagonale

bias(s)ed ['baɪəst] ADJ **1** (person) partial; **you're b. in her favour** tu as un parti pris pour elle; **b. opinion** opinion f préconçue **2** (bowling ball) décentré
▸▸ **b. error** (in statistics) erreur f systématique; **b. sample** (in statistics) échantillon m biaisé ou avec erreur systématique

bib [bɪb] N **1** (child's) bavette f, bavoir m **2** (of apron) bavette f; Old-fashioned Fam **in one's best b. and tucker** sur son trente et un

bible ['baɪb(ə)l] N bible f; **the B.** la Bible; Fig **this dictionary is his b.** il fait de ce dictionnaire sa bible
▸▸ **the B. Belt** = États mpl du sud des États-

Unis où l'évangélisme est très répandu; **B. class** (in school, church) classe f d'instruction religieuse; (in Catholic church) catéchisme m; **B. stories** histoires fpl tirées de la Bible

Bible-basher [-bæʃər] N FamPej grenouille f de bénitier

Bible-bashing N Fam Pej **B. preacher** évangéliste m zélé

Bible-thumper [-θʌmpər] N Fam Pej = **Bible-basher**

Bible-thumping N Fam Pej = **Bible-bashing**

biblical ['bɪblɪk(ə)l] ADJ biblique

bibliographer [bɪblɪ'ɒgrəfər] N bibliographe mf

bibliographical [bɪblɪə'græfɪk(ə)l] ADJ bibliographique

bibliography [bɪblɪ'ɒgrəfɪ] N bibliographie f

bibliophile ['bɪblɪəfaɪl] N bibliophile mf

bibulous ['bɪbjʊləs] ADJ Fml, Hum (person) qui s'adonne à la boisson; (celebration) bien arrosé

bicameral [baɪ'kæmərəl] ADJ Pol bicaméral, -aux
▸▸ **b. system** bicaméralisme m, bicamérisme m

bicarb [baɪ'kɑːb] N Fam bicarbonate m de soude

bicarbonate [baɪ'kɑːbəneɪt] N (of soda etc) bicarbonate m

bicentenary [baɪsen'tiːnərɪ], Am **bicentennial** [baɪsen'tenɪəl] ADJ, N bicentenaire m; **the b. celebrations** les cérémonies fpl du bicentenaire

biceps ['baɪseps] N Anat (muscle m) biceps m

bicker ['bɪkər] VI se chamailler, se quereller

bickering ['bɪkərɪŋ] N chamailleries fpl, querelles fpl

bickie ['bɪkɪ] N BrFam biscuit m

bicolour(ed), Am **bicolor, bicolored** ['baɪkʌlər, -ləd] ADJ bicolore

bicultural [baɪ'kʌltʃərəl] ADJ esp Am biculturel

bicycle ['baɪsɪk(ə)l] N bicyclette f, vélo m; **to go by b.** aller à ou Fam en bicyclette ou vélo; **to ride a b.** faire de la bicyclette ou du vélo; **to know how to ride a b.** savoir monter à bicyclette ou à vélo, savoir faire du vélo; **he was riding his b.** il était à bicyclette ou à vélo
VI (for exercise) faire de la bicyclette ou du vélo; (travel) aller à bicyclette ou à vélo (**to** à)
▸▸ **b. chain** chaîne f de vélo; (for securing bike) antivol m inv; **b. clip** pince f à vélo; **b. club** club m de cyclistes; Ftbl **b. kick** retourné m bicyclette; **b. path** piste f ou bande f cyclable; **b. race** course f de bicyclette; **b. rack** (on pavement) ratelier m à bicyclettes ou à vélos; (on car) porte-vélos m inv; **b. track** piste cyclable

BID [bɪd] N **1** (offer) (at auction) enchère f; **higher** or **further b.** offre f supérieure, surenchère f; **lowest/highest b.** enchère la plus basse/forte; **to make a b.** faire une offre, enchérir
2 (attempt) tentative f (**for sth** de qch; **to do sth** pour faire qch); **to make a b. for sth** tenter d'obtenir qch; **to make a b. for power** (legally) viser le pouvoir; (illegally) tenter un coup d'État; **she failed in her b. to beat the record** elle a échoué dans sa tentative de battre le record
3 Cards (in bridge) annonce f; (in solo whist) demande f; **b. of two diamonds** ouverture de deux carreaux; **no b.!** je passe!, parole!
4 (in takeover) offre f; (tender) soumission f;

to make a b. soumissionner; **to put a b. in on a flat** faire une offre pour un appartement

VT & VI (pt **bade** [bæd, beɪd], **bid**; pp **bidden** [ˈbɪd(ə)n], **bid**) **1** (pt, pp **bid**) (offer) **to b. for sth** faire une offre pour qch; **what am I b. for this table?** qu'est-ce que vous m'offrez pour cette table?; **to b. ten pounds** faire une offre de dix livres

2 Cards **to b. three diamonds** enchérir de trois carreaux

3 (in call for tenders) faire une soumission (**on sth** pour qch)

4 Fml (greet) **to b. sb welcome/good day** souhaiter la bienvenue/le bonjour à qn; **to b. sb goodbye** faire ses adieux à qn

5 Arch, Fml (seem probable) **the weather bids fair to be fine** or **to improve** le temps s'annonce beau; **he bids fair to become ...** il promet de devenir ...

6 Arch, Lit (order) commander, ordonner (**sb (to) do sth** à qn de faire qch); **to b. sb be silent** ordonner à qn de se taire, commander le silence à qn

▸▸ Fin **b. bond** caution f d'adjudication ou de soumission; St Exch **b. price** cours m acheteur

▸ **bid up** VT SEP Fin **to b. up the price of goods** enchérir sur le prix des marchandises

biddable [ˈbɪdəb(ə)l] **ADJ** (child etc) obéissant, docile

bidder [ˈbɪdər] **N** (at sale) enchérisseur, -euse; (at cards) demandeur, -euse; **there were no bidders** il n'y a pas eu de preneurs; **the highest b.** le plus offrant

bidding [ˈbɪdɪŋ] **N 1** (at auction) enchères fpl; **the b.** les enchères; **to start the b. at £5,000** commencer les enchères à 5000 livres; **to open the b.** ouvrir les enchères; **the b. is against you** est-ce que vous voulez surenchérir? **2** Fml (order) **at sb's b.** sur l'ordre de qn; **to do sb's b.** exécuter les ordres de qn; **he needed no second b.** il n'a pas eu besoin qu'on lui répète cet ordre

▸▸ Am St Exch **b. price** cours m acheteur

bide [baɪd] **VT** (pt **bided**) **to b. one's time** attendre le bon moment

bidet [ˈbiːdeɪ] **N** bidet m

bidirectional [baɪdɪˈrekʃən(ə)l] **ADJ** bidirectionnel

▸▸ Typ **b. printing** impression f bidirectionnelle

biennial [baɪˈenɪəl] **ADJ 1** (event) biennal, -aux **2** (plant) bisannuel
N Bot plante f bisannuelle

biennially [baɪˈenɪəlɪ] **ADV** tous les deux ans

bier [bɪər] **N** (for coffin, body) bière f

biff [bɪf] **N** Sl baffe f
INT v'lan!, pan!
VT Sl (hit) flanquer une baffe à

bifocal [baɪˈfəʊk(ə)l] Opt **ADJ** bifocal, -aux, à double foyer
NPL bifocals verres mpl bifocaux ou à double foyer

bifurcate [ˈbaɪfəkeɪt] **VI** Fml bifurquer

bifurcation [baɪfəˈkeɪʃən] **N** Fml bifurcation f

BIG [bɪg]

ADJ grand **1-3** ▪ gros **1-3** ▪ important **2**

ADJ (**bigger** [ˈbɪgər], **biggest** [ˈbɪgɪst]) **1** (object) (large, tall) grand; (bulky) gros; **a b. hotel** un grand hôtel; **a b. drop in prices** une forte baisse des prix; **to be doing a b. trade** faire de grosses affaires; Fam **you've got a b. mouth** (you let the secret out) tu n'es pas capable de la fermer; Fam **a b. A** un A majuscule; **to give sb a b. hand** applaudir qn bien fort

2 (serious, important) (problem, explosion, argument, difference) gros; (mistake) grave; (decision) important; **this is our b. day** c'est le grand jour pour nous; **you've got a b. day ahead of you tomorrow** tu as une journée importante devant toi demain; **you want to look your best on the b. day** tu veux être la plus belle possible le grand jour; Fam **he had b. ideas** il voyait grand; **don't get any b. ideas about doing this yourself** ne crois pas que tu vas pouvoir faire ça tout seul; Fam **I've got b. plans for you** j'ai de grands projets pour toi; **b. budget film** superproduction f, Fam **b. money** or Am **bucks** fric m; Fam **to earn b. money** gagner beaucoup d'argent; Fam **I'm talking b. money here** je te parle de beaucoup d'oseille; **a b. eater** un gros mangeur; **the b. names in the theatre world** les grands noms du théâtre; **she's a b. noise in publishing** c'est quelqu'un d'important dans le monde de l'édition; **they'll need to bring in the b. guns from New York on this one** il faudra qu'ils amènent les experts de New York sur ce coup-là; Theat, Cin **the b. battle scene** la grande scène de bataille; **this is your b. scene** (of main character) la scène est à toi; (of minor character) c'est ta scène

3 (person) (tall) grand et fort; (fat) gros; Fam (important) important; **you're a b. girl/boy now** tu es une grande fille/un grand garçon maintenant; **she's b. enough to look after herself** elle est assez grande pour se défendre; Fam **he's getting too b. for his boots** or Am **britches** il ne se sent plus; **my b. brother** mon grand frère; **to get big(ger)** (taller) grandir; (fatter) grossir; **you're the biggest fool of the lot!** c'est toi le plus bête de tous!; Arch Lit **to be b. with child** être sur le point d'enfanter

4 (idioms) **she goes for Frenchmen in a b. way** elle se pâme devant les Français; **he goes in for office memos in a b. way** il envoie des quantités de mémos; **we don't celebrate Christmas in a b. way** nous ne faisons pas tellement la fête à Noël; **you really do things in a b. way** tu ne fais pas les choses à moitié; **they've decided to get into exports in a b. way** ils ont décidé de se lancer à fond dans les exportations; also Iron **that was b. of you** c'était vraiment généreux de votre part; Fam **to be b. on sth** (keen) aimer beaucoup qch; **reality TV was b. last year** la télé réalité a eu un succès fou l'année dernière; Fam **to be in the b. time, to have made the b. time** être en haut de l'échelle, être le dessus du panier, être arrivé; Fam **to hit** or **make the b. time** réussir; Fam **once they've had a taste of the b. time** une fois qu'ils ont goûté au succès; Fam **to be into sb/sth b. time** or **in a b. way** être dingue de qn/qch; Fam **he's been doing drugs b. time** or **in a b. way** depuis quelque temps il arrête pas de se droguer; Fam **he messed up his driving test b. time** il s'est planté dans les grandes largeurs au permis

ADV Fam **to talk b.** (boast) se vanter, faire l'important; **to think b.** voir grand; **to go over** or **down b.** avoir un succès fou; **the last song went down b. with the audience** la dernière chanson a fait un tabac auprès du public; **to make it b.** réussir

▸▸ Fam **the B. Apple** = surnom m donné à la ville de New York; **the B. Bang** Br St Exch Fam = déréglementation f de la Bourse de Londres en octobre 1986; Astron le big bang; **b. bank** grande banque f, enseigne f bancaire; Comput **B. Blue** = surnom m de la société IBM; Am St Exch **the b. board** = la Bourse de New York; **B. Brother** Big Brother; Com **b. business** les grandes entreprises fpl; Zool **b. cat** fauve m, grand félin m; Fam Fig **b. cheese** gros bonnet m; Br Aut **b. end** tête f de bielle; **b. game** gros gibier m; Br Fam Hum **b. girl's blouse** (wimp) femmelette f, Fam **b. hair** =

coiffure f volumineuse et apprêtée; Am Fam **b. house** (prison) taule f, placard m; Br Journ **The B. Issue** = hebdomadaire m vendu au profit des sans-logis par ces derniers, ≃ le Réverbère; Sport **b. match** grand match m; Fam **the b. screen** le grand écran; Fam Fig **b. shot** gros bonnet; **b. spender** = personne f qui dépense beaucoup d'argent; **he's a b. spender when it comes to clothes** il dépense beaucoup d'argent en vêtements; Iron **you know what he's like, the last of the b. spenders!** tu le connais, toujours à faire des frais!; Anat **b. toe** gros orteil m; **b. top** (tent) grand chapiteau m; (circus) cirque m; **b. wheel** grande roue f, Fig Fam gros bonnet

▸ **big up** VT SEP Fam faire du battage à propos de; **to b. oneself up** se faire mousser; **all the radio stations are bigging up his new album** toutes les stations de radio font un sacré battage autour de son dernier album

Big Ben
Nom de la cloche de la Tour de l'horloge à Westminster, souvent donné à tort à la tour elle-même. Elle est considérée comme un des monuments principaux de Londres.

bigamist [ˈbɪgəmɪst] **N** bigame mf

bigamous [ˈbɪgəməs] **ADJ** bigame; **b. marriage** bigamie f; **to enter into a b. marriage** se rendre coupable de bigamie

bigamy [ˈbɪgəmɪ] **N** bigamie f, **to commit b.** être coupable de bigamie

big-bellied [-ˈbelɪd] **ADJ** (fat) ventru, pansu; **she's b.** (of pregnant woman) elle a un gros ventre

big-boned **ADJ** fortement charpenté

biggie [ˈbɪgɪ] **N** Fam **that's a b.** (fish, car etc) c'en est un(e) gros(se); **it's gonna be a b.** (book, film, record) il va faire un malheur; **there's a storm coming and it's a b.** il y a un orage qui se prépare, j'te dis pas

biggish [ˈbɪgɪʃ] **ADJ** (tall, large) assez grand; (fat) assez gros

bighead [ˈbɪghed] **N** Fam crâneur, -euse

bigheaded [bɪgˈhedɪd] **ADJ** Fam crâneur

bigheadedness [bɪgˈhedɪdnɪs] **N** Fam suffisance f, prétention f

big-hearted [-ˈhɑːtɪd] **ADJ** **to be b.** avoir le cœur sur la main; also Iron **in his usual b. way** le cœur sur la main, comme à son habitude

bight [baɪt] **N** Geog (in coastline) renfoncement m; **the Great Australian B.** la Grande Baie Australienne, le Grand Golfe Australien ou de l'Australie

bigness [ˈbɪgnɪs] **N** (of person) (tallness) grande taille f, (fatness) grosseur f, (of thing) grandes dimensions fpl; **his b. made him self-conscious** il était complexé parce qu'il était si gros

bigot [ˈbɪgət] **N** sectaire mf, fanatique mf

Note that the French word **bigot** is a false friend. It is used to describe an excessively religious person but has no overtones of sectarianism.

bigoted [ˈbɪgətɪd] **ADJ** sectaire (**against** à l'égard de); **don't be so b.** ne sois pas si borné

bigotry [ˈbɪgətrɪ] **N** sectarisme m; (religious) bigoterie f

big-ticket **ADJ** Am (expensive) cher

big-time **ADJ** Fam **a b. lawyer/executive** un avocat/cadre qui a réussi; **b. actor** acteur m de premier plan; **b. operator** gros trafiquant m

bigwig [ˈbɪgwɪg] **N** Fam Hum, Pej gros bonnet m, grosse légume f

bijou ['biːʒuː] ADJ **b. flat** or **residence** petit appartement m ravissant

bike [baɪk] Fam N (bicycle) vélo m; (motorbike) moto f; Br Sl **on your b.!** (go away) tiretoi!; (hurry up) magne-toi!; (I don't believe you, don't talk rubbish) à d'autres!, tu charries!
▪ VT (send by motorcycle courier) envoyer par coursier; **to b. sth round to sb** envoyer qch à qn par coursier
▪ VI faire du vélo; (on motorbike) faire de la moto; **we biked there** nous y sommes allés à ou en vélo/moto
▸▸**b. carrier** porte-vélo m, pl porte-vélos; **b. lane** piste f cyclable; **b. shed** cabane f ou remise f à vélos

biker ['baɪkər] N cycliste mf; (on motor bike), Pej motard, -arde; (courier) coursier, -ière

bikini [bɪˈkiːnɪ] N bikini® m

bilabial [baɪˈleɪbɪəl] ADJ, N Ling (consonne f) bilabiale f

bilateral [baɪˈlætər(ə)l] ADJ bilatéral, -aux

bilaterally [baɪˈlætər(ə)lɪ] ADV bilatéralement

bilberry ['bɪlbərɪ] N airelle f, myrtille f

bile [baɪl] N Physiol bile f; Fig Fml **to be full of b.** (bad-tempered) être plein de hargne
▸▸Anat **b. duct** canal m biliaire

bilestone ['baɪlstəʊn] N calcul m biliaire

bilge [bɪldʒ] N Naut (hold) fond m de cale; (water) eau f de cale; Fam **to talk a lot of b.** dire des bêtises; **b.!** sottises!
▸▸Naut **b. pump** pompe f de drain ou de cale; **b. water** eau de cale

bilharzia [bɪlˈhɑːtsɪə] N Med **1** (disease) bilharziose f **2** (parasite) bilharzia f, bilharzie f

biliary ['bɪlɪərɪ] ADJ Physiol biliaire

bilingual [baɪˈlɪŋgwəl] ADJ bilingue
▸▸**b. secretary** secrétaire mf bilingue

bilingualism [baɪˈlɪŋgwəlɪz(ə)m] N bilinguisme m

bilious ['bɪlɪəs] ADJ **1** Physiol bilieux; **he looks rather b.** on dirait qu'il va nous faire une crise de foie; **b. attack** crise f de foie; Fig **b. yellow/green** jaunâtre/verdâtre **2** Fig (bad-tempered) colérique

biliousness ['bɪlɪəsnɪs] N Med affection f bilieuse; Fig hargne f

bilk [bɪlk] VT Old-fashioned Fam (cheat) avoir; **he bilked her (out) of all her money** il lui a extorqué tout son argent; **you've been bilked** tu t'es fait avoir

Bill [bɪl] N Br Fam **the (Old) B.** (police) les flics mpl, les poulets mpl

bill¹ [bɪl] N **1** (notice of payment due) Com facture f; (for gas, electricity) facture, note f; (in hotel) note; Br (in restaurant) addition f; **to pay a b.** payer ou régler une facture; **to foot the b.** payer la note ou les dépenses; **to make out a b.** dresser ou rédiger une facture; **can I/we have the b., please?** (in restaurant) l'addition, s'il vous plaît; **put it on my b.** (in hotel) mettez-le sur ma note
2 Am (banknote) billet m de banque; **five-dollar b.** billet de cinq dollars
3 Com, Fin effet m (de commerce); **bills** valeurs fpl, papier m (bancable); **long(-dated)/short(-dated) bills** effets à longue/courte échéance
4 Theat etc (poster) affiche f; (for political party) affiche, placard m; **(stick) no bills!** défense d'afficher; **to head** or **top the b.** (of actor) être en tête d'affiche; Fam **that will fill** or **fit the b.** cela fera l'affaire
5 Fig **the doctor gave me a clean b. of health** le docteur m'a trouvé en parfaite santé; **the investigators gave the engine a clean b. of health** les enquêteurs ont conclu que le moteur était en parfait état
6 Pol projet m de loi; (private) proposition f

de loi; **to pass/reject a b.** adopter/repousser un projet de loi
▪ VT **1** (invoice) envoyer une facture à (**for** pour) **2** Theat **she is billed to play Ophelia** elle est à l'affiche dans le rôle d'Ophélie; Fig **he is billed as America's greatest actor** on dit que c'est le meilleur acteur américain
▸▸Fin **b. made out to bearer** effet m au porteur; Fin **b. book** livre m d'échéance; Fin **bills for collection** effets à l'encaissement; Fin **bills for collection form** formulaire m d'encaissement; **b. of entry** déclaration f d'entrée (en douane); Fin **b. of exchange** lettre f de change, effet de commerce; Fin **bills of exchange statement** lettre de change relevé, LCR f; **b. of fare** carte f (du jour); **b. of lading** Com connaissement m; Am Rail feuille f d'expédition; Acct **bills payable** effets à payer; Acct **bills payable ledger** livre ou journal m des effets à payer; Constr **b. of quantities** devis m; Acct **bills receivable** effets à recevoir; Acct **bills receivable ledger** livre ou journal des effets à recevoir; Hist **the B. of Rights** (in UK) = loi f de 1689 déterminant les droits du citoyen anglais; (in US) = les dix premiers amendements mpl à la Constitution américaine garantissant, entre autres droits, la liberté d'expression, de religion et de réunion; **b. of sale** acte m ou contrat m de vente; Fin **b. 'without protest'** traite f 'sans frais'

bill² [bɪl] N **1** (of bird) bec m **2** Geog bec m, promontoire m
▪ VI (of birds) se becqueter; Fam **to b. and coo** (of couple) se faire des mamours

billboard ['bɪlbɔːd] N esp Am panneau m ou support m d'affichage
▸▸**b. advertising** publicité f sur panneaux; **b. site** emplacement m d'affichage

billet ['bɪlɪt] N **1** Mil (requisition) billet m de logement **2** Mil (accommodation) (in sb's house) logement m; (in town) cantonnement m; (of evacuee) logement **3** Old-fashioned Br Fam (job) situation f
▪ VT (-t-) (troops, evacuee) loger (**on sb** chez qn); **to b. troops on** or **in a town** cantonner des troupes dans une ville
▪ VI loger (**with** chez)

billeting ['bɪlɪtɪŋ] N Mil (in private house) logement m chez l'habitant; (on town) cantonnement m
▸▸**b. officer** officier m de cantonnement

billfold ['bɪlfəʊld] N Am (wallet) portefeuille m

billhook ['bɪlhʊk] N (for pruning, chopping) serpe f; (small) serpette f

billiard ['bɪlɪəd] N **1** (usu pl with sing verb) **billiards** (jeu m de) billard m; **to play billiards** jouer au billard; **to have** or **play a game of billiards** faire une partie ou disputer une partie de billard; **bar billiards** billard russe **2** Am (shot) carambolage m
▸▸**b. ball** boule f de billard; **b. cue** queue f de billard; **b. room** salle f de) billard; **b. table** (table f de) billard

billing ['bɪlɪŋ] N **1** Theat, Cin affichage m; **to get** or **to have top/second b.** (of actor) être en tête d'affiche/en deuxième place à l'affiche **2** Fin facturation f
▸▸Fin **b. date** date f de facturation; Fin **b. machine** caisse f (enregistreuse); Fin **b. office** bureau m de facturation

billion ['bɪljən] N (one thousand million) milliard m; Br Old-fashioned (one million million) billion m VOIR GRAMMAIRE A76

billionaire [bɪljəˈneər] N milliardaire mf

billionth ['bɪljənθ] ADJ milliardième
▪ N **1** (ordinal) milliardième mf **2** (fraction) milliardième m

billow ['bɪləʊ] N Lit (large wave) lame f; Lit **the billows** les flots mpl; **billows of smoke** nuages mpl de fumée

▪ VI (of sea) se soulever en vagues; (of crowds, smoke etc) ondoyer; **the sails billowed in the wind** les voiles se gonflaient au vent

billowy ['bɪləʊɪ] ADJ (sea) houleux

billposter ['bɪlpəʊstər], **billsticker** ['bɪlstɪkər] N afficheur, -euse, colleur, -euse d'affiches; **billposters will be prosecuted** ≃ défense d'afficher

billposting ['bɪlpəʊstɪŋ], **billsticking** ['bɪlstɪkɪŋ] N affichage m

billy, pl **billies** ['bɪlɪ, -z] N **1** Austr, New Zealand (can) gamelle f; **to boil the b.** faire du thé **2** (club) gourdin m; Am (for police) matraque f
▸▸**b. club** gourdin

billycan ['bɪlɪkæn] N = **billy 1**

billy-goat N bouc m

billy-o(h) N Old-fashioned Br Fam **it's raining like b.** il pleut à verse; **to run like b.** courir très vite ou à toutes jambes

BIM [biːaɪˈem] N (abbr **British Institute of Management**) = organisme m britannique dont la fonction est de renseigner et de conseiller les entreprises en matière de gestion, ainsi que de promouvoir l'enseignement de cette discipline

bimbo ['bɪmbəʊ] N Pej minette f, jolie sotte f; **she's a real b.** elle n'a rien dans la tête

bimedia [baɪˈmiːdɪə] ADJ bi-média; **to be a b. reporter** être journaliste à la radio et à la télévision

bimetallic [baɪmɪˈtælɪk] ADJ Econ (system) bimétallique
▸▸**b. strip** bilame m

bimetallism [baɪˈmetəlɪz(ə)m] N Econ bimétallisme m

bimonthly [baɪˈmʌnθlɪ] ADJ **1** (every two months) bimestriel; **to appear on a b. basis** paraître tous les deux mois **2** (twice a month) bimensuel; **to appear on a b. basis** paraître deux fois par mois
▪ N (magazine) (every two months) bimestriel m; (twice monthly) bimensuel m
▪ ADV **1** (every two months) tous les deux mois **2** (twice a month) deux fois par mois

bin [bɪn] N coffre m, huche f, bac m; (dustbin) poubelle f; **wine b.** casier m à bouteilles, porte-bouteilles m inv; Sl **the b.** la maison de fous
▪ VT Fam (throw in the bin) mettre à la poubelle
▸▸**b. bag** sac m poubelle; Br **b. end** (wine) fin f de série; Br **b. liner** sac poubelle

binary ['baɪnərɪ] ADJ Math etc binaire
▪ N Astron binaire f
▸▸**b. code** code m binaire; **b. number** nombre m binaire; Comput **b. search** recherche f binaire ou dichotomique; Astron **b. star** binaire; Mil **b. weapon** arme f binaire; Comput **b. word** mot m binaire

bind [baɪnd] (pt, pp **bound** [baʊnd]) VT **1** (attach) (object) attacher, lier (**to** à); (sheaf of corn) lier; (prisoner) attacher, ligoter; **to b. sb hand and foot** lier pieds et poings à qn; Fig **to be bound hand and foot** (powerless) avoir les mains liées; **they are bound together by a close friendship** ils sont unis par les liens de l'amitié; **they are very much bound up with each other** (of lovers) ils sont très attachés l'un à l'autre; (of friends) ils sont très liés; **the present is bound up with the past** le présent est étroitement lié au passé; **to b. one's skis** fixer ses skis
2 (dress) (wound) bander, panser
3 (cover) (book) relier; **bound in boards** cartonné; **bound in cloth** relié toile
4 (cause to cohere) (sand etc) lier, agglutiner, agglomérer; **stones bound together with cement** pierres liées avec du ciment; **b. the mixture with egg white** liez le mélange avec du blanc d'œuf

5 *usu passive (of obligation, promise etc)* lier, engager; **to be bound to do sth** *(obliged)* être obligé *ou* tenu de faire qch; **to be bound by an oath** être lié par un serment; **to b. sb to pay a debt** astreindre *ou* obliger qn à payer une dette; **to b. oneself to do sth** s'engager à faire qch **6** *Sewing (coat, hat)* border; *(buttonhole)* brider

vi *(of gravel etc)* se lier, s'agglomérer, s'agglutiner

n *Fam (nuisance)* plaie *f*; **what an awful b.!** quelle plaie *ou* barbe!; **to be in a b.** *(difficult situation)* être dans une mauvaise passe; **I'm in a bit of a b.** j'ai un petit problème, je suis un peu coincé

▸ **bind over** **vt sep** *Law* **to b. sb over to keep the peace** exiger de qn sous caution qu'il ne se livrera à aucune voie de fait; **to be bound over** être sommé d'observer une bonne conduite

▸ **bind up** **vt sep 1** *(tie)* *(sheaf of corn)* lier **2** *(wound)* bander, panser

binder ['baɪndər] **n 1** *(for papers)* classeur *m* **2** *(of books)* relieur, -ieuse **3** *Agr (machine)* *(for sheaves of corn)* lieuse *f*; *(for hay)* botteleuse *f* **4** *(on sewing machine)* ourleur *m* **5** *Culin (for sauce)* liant *m*; *Constr* matériau *m* d'agrégation; *(for road surface)* liant, agglomérant *m*

bindery ['baɪnd(ə)rɪ] **n** atelier *m* de reliure

binding ['baɪndɪŋ] **adj 1** *Constr (agent)* aggloménant, agglutinant **2** *(contract etc)* obligatoire (**upon sb** pour qn), qui engage; **agreement b. (up)on sb** contrat *m* qui lie qn; **decision b. on all parties** décision *f* obligatoire pour tous **3** *Med* constipant

n 1 *Sport (on ski)* fixation *f*; **safety (release) bindings** fixations de sécurité **2** *(of book)* reliure *f* **3** *Constr* agglutination *f*, agrégation *f*, *(of road surface)* liant *m*, agglomérant *m* **4** *(of dress etc)* bordure *f*, liseré *m*

▸▸ **b. machine** *(for book)* brocheuse *f*, *Constr* **b. material** matière *f* agglomérante *ou* d'agrégation

bindweed ['baɪndwiːd] **n** *(plant)* liseron *m*

binge [bɪndʒ] *Fam* **n to go on a b.** *(of drinking)* prendre une cuite; *(of eating)* se gaver; *(of shopping)* faire une razzia; **b. drinking** excès *mpl* de brisson

vi *(drink a lot)* prendre une cuite; *(eat a lot)* s'en mettre plein la lampe, se gaver; **he binged on chocolate** il s'est gavé de chocolat

bingo ['bɪŋgəʊ] **n** bingo *m*; *Br Fam* **to go to the b.** aller jouer au bingo

int et voilà!

▸▸ **b. hall** salle *f* de bingo

Bingo

Ce jeu d'argent très populaire en Grande-Bretagne et aux États-Unis consiste à tirer des numéros et à les cocher sur une carte jusqu'à ce qu'elle soit remplie; il est souvent pratiqué dans d'anciens cinémas ou des salles municipales.

BinHex [bɪn'heks] **n** *Comput (abbr* **Binary Hexadecimal)** BinHex

binman, *pl* **binmen** ['bɪnmæn, -men] **n** *Br* éboueur *m*

binnacle ['bɪnək(ə)l] **n** *Naut* habitacle *m*

binocular [bɪ'nɒkjʊlər, baɪ-] **adj** *(vision etc)* binoculaire

binoculars [bɪ'nɒkjʊləz] **npl** jumelles *fpl*; **to look at sth through b.** regarder qch avec des jumelles VOIR GRAMMAIRE A10

binomial [baɪ'nəʊmɪəl] *Math* **adj** *(factor etc)* binôme; **the b. theorem** le binôme de Newton, le théorème de Newton

n binôme *m*

bint [bɪnt] **n** *Br Sl Pej (woman)* grognasse *f*

biochemical [baɪəʊ'kemɪk(ə)l] **adj** biochimique; **b. oxygen demand** demande *f* biochimique en oxygène

biochemist [baɪəʊ'kemɪst] **n** biochimiste *mf*

biochemistry [baɪəʊ'kemɪstrɪ] **n** biochimie *f*

biodegradability [baɪəʊdɪgreɪdə'bɪlɪtɪ] **n** biodégradabilité *f*

biodegradable [baɪəʊdɪ'greɪdəb(ə)l] **adj** biodégradable

biodiversity [baɪəʊdaɪ'vɜːsɪtɪ] **n** biodiversité *f*

bioethanol [baɪəʊ'eθənɒl] **n** *Chem* bioéthanol *m*

bioethics [baɪəʊ'eθɪks] **n** bioéthique *f*; **b. debate** débat *m* sur la bioéthique VOIR GRAMMAIRE A10

biogenesis [baɪəʊ'dʒenɪsɪs] **n** biogenèse *f*

biographer [baɪ'ɒgrəfər] **n** biographe *mf*

biographical [baɪə'græfɪk(ə)l] **adj** biographique

▸▸ **b. novel** biographie *f* romancée

biography [baɪ'ɒgrəfɪ] **n** biographie *f*

biological [baɪə'lɒdʒɪk(ə)l] **adj** biologique

▸▸ **b. clock** horloge *f* interne *ou* biologique; **my b. clock is ticking (away)** *(of woman)* si je veux des enfants il va falloir que je commence à y penser sérieusement; **my b. clock is ticking and I don't even have a boyfriend** le temps passe et je n'ai toujours pas d'enfant ni même de petit ami; **b. control** *(of insects)* élimination *f* des insectes par des méthodes biologiques; *Mil* **b. warfare** guerre *f* bactériologique

biologically [baɪə'lɒdʒɪklɪ] **adv** biologiquement

biologist [baɪ'ɒlədʒɪst] **n** biologiste *mf*

biology [baɪ'ɒlədʒɪ] **n** biologie *f*

biomass ['baɪəʊmæs] **n** biomasse *f*

biomaterial [baɪəʊmə'tɪərɪəl] **n** biomatériau *m*

biometrics [baɪəʊ'metrɪks] **n** biométrie *f* VOIR GRAMMAIRE A10

bionic [baɪ'ɒnɪk] **adj** bionique

bionics [baɪ'ɒnɪks] **n** bionique *f* VOIR GRAMMAIRE A10

biophysics [baɪəʊ'fɪzɪks] **n** biophysique *f* VOIR GRAMMAIRE A10

biopic ['baɪəʊpɪk] **n** *Cin Fam* film *m* biographique

biopiracy [baɪəʊ'paɪrəsɪ] **n** biopiratage *m*

biopsy ['baɪɒpsɪ, baɪ'ɒpsɪ] **n** biopsie *f*

biorhythm ['baɪəʊrɪð(ə)m] **n** rythme *m* biologique, biorythme *m*

BIOS ['baɪɒs] **n** *Comput (abbr* **basic input/output system)** BIOS *m*

bioscope ['baɪəskəʊp] **n** *Cin* **1** *Old-fashioned (projector)* bioscope *m* **2** *(in South Africa) (cinema)* cinéma *m*

biosphere ['baɪəsfɪər] **n** biosphère *f*

biosynthesis [baɪəʊ'sɪnθɪsɪs] **n** biosynthèse *f*

biotechnology [baɪəʊtek'nɒlədʒɪ], *Fam* **biotech** ['baɪəʊtek] **n** biotechnologie *f*

biotope ['baɪətəʊp] **n** *Biol* biotope *m*

bipartisan [baɪ'pɑːtɪzæn] **adj** *Pol etc* bipartite, biparti

bipartite [baɪ'pɑːtaɪt] **adj 1** *Biol* bipartite, biparti **2** *Law (document)* rédigé en double **3** *(agreement)* bipartite, biparti

biped ['baɪped] **adj, n** bipède *m*

biplane ['baɪpleɪn] **n** *Aviat (avion m)* biplan *m*

bipolar [baɪ'pəʊlər] **adj** *Elec, Physiol etc* bipolaire

birch [bɜːtʃ] **n 1** *(tree)* bouleau *m*; *(wood)* (bois *m* de) bouleau; *(rod)* verge *f* **2 to give sb the b.** donner le fouet à qn, fouetter qn

vt donner le fouet à, fouetter

▸▸ **b. rod** verge; **b. wood** (bois de) bouleau

birching ['bɜːtʃɪŋ] **n** correction *f (au fouet)*; **to give sb a b.** fouetter qn

bird [bɜːd] **n 1** oiseau *m*; *(farmyard)* **b.** volaille *f*, *Fam* **a little b. told me** mon petit doigt me l'a dit; *Lit* **a b. of ill omen** un oiseau de mauvais augure; *Fam* **to eat like a b.** avoir un appétit d'oiseau; *Fam* **to give sb the b.** *(hiss)* huer *ou* siffler qn; *(send packing)* envoyer qn paître; *Am (make fun of)* se foutre de la gueule de qn; *(gesture at)* faire un doigt d'honneur à qn; *Fam* **to get the b.** être hué *ou* sifflé; *Prov* **a b. in the hand is worth two in the bush** un tiens vaut mieux que deux tu l'auras; *Fig* **the b. has flown** l'oiseau s'est envolé; *Prov* **birds of a feather flock together** qui se ressemble s'assemble; **you and your father are birds of a feather** toi et ton père, vous ne valez pas mieux l'un que l'autre, toi et ton père, je vous mets dans le même sac; *Euph* **it's time you talked to him about the birds and the bees** *(facts of life)* il serait temps de lui expliquer que les bébés ne naissent pas dans les choux; *Fam* **it's (strictly) for the birds** c'est de la roupie de sansonnet **2** *Br Sl (woman)* nana *f*; **who's the b. in the corner?** c'est qui la nana au coin? **3** *Br Sl (time in prison)* taule *f*, tôle *f*; **to do b.** faire de la taule **4** *Fam (fellow)* type *m*, individu *m*; **he's a queer b.** c'est un drôle d'oiseau; **a home b.** un casanier, une casanière; *Fig* **night b.** noctambule *mf*

▸▸ *Fam Pej* **b. brain** tête *f* de linotte, écervelé, -ée; **b. call** cri *m* d'oiseau; *(device)* appeau *m*, pipeau *m*; *Br* **b. fancier** *(interested in birds)* ornithologue *mf* amateur; *(breeder)* aviculteur, -trice; **b.'s nest** nid *m* d'oiseau; *Culin* **b.'s nest soup** soupe *f* aux nids d'hirondelles; **b. of paradise** *(bird, flower)* oiseau de paradis; **b. of passage** oiseau de passage; **I'm just a b. of passage** je ne suis que de passage; **b. of prey** oiseau de proie, rapace *m*; **b. sanctuary** réserve *f ou* refuge *m* d'oiseaux; **b. shot** cendrée *f*, **b. strike** collision *f* d'un avion avec un oiseau; **b. table** *(in garden)* mangeoire *f*

birdbath ['bɜːdbɑːθ] **n** vasque *f* pour les oiseaux

bird-brained [-breɪnd] **adj** *Fam Pej* écervelé; **to be b.** avoir une cervelle d'oiseau *ou* de moineau

birdcage ['bɜːdkeɪdʒ] **n** cage *f* (à oiseaux); *(large)* volière *f*

birdcatcher ['bɜːdkætʃər] **n** oiseleur, -ière

bird-dog **vt** *Am Fam* surveiller de près

bird-house **n** *(aviary)* volière *f*

birdie ['bɜːdɪ] **n** *Fam* **1** *Golf* birdie *m* **2** *(in children's language)* gentil petit oiseau *m*; *Phot Fam* **watch the b.!** attention, le petit oiseau va sortir!

birdlike ['bɜːdlaɪk] **adj** *(appetite)* d'oiseau; **b. movements/features** mouvements *mpl*/traits *mpl* semblables à ceux d'un oiseau

birdlime ['bɜːdlaɪm] **n** glu *f*

bird-nesting **n** **to go b.** = rechercher des nids pour y prendre les œufs

birdseed ['bɜːdsiːd] **n** graines *fpl* pour oiseaux

bird's-eye ['bɜːdzaɪ] **n** *Bot* véronique *f*

▸▸ **b. mahogany** acajou *m* moucheté; **b. maple** érable *m* madré *ou* à broussin; **b. shot** *Phot* photographie *f* aérienne oblique; *Cin* (prise *f* de vue en) plongée *f*; **b. view** vue *f* aérienne; *Fig* **a b. view of the situation** une vue d'ensemble de la situation

bird-watcher **n** ornithologue *mf* amateur

bird-watching [-wɒtʃɪŋ] N observation f des oiseaux *(dans leur milieu naturel)*; **to go b.** aller observer les oiseaux

biretta [bɪˈretə] N *Cathol* barrette f

Biro® [ˈbaɪrəʊ] N *Br* stylo m (à) bille

birth [bɜːθ] N **1** *(of child, nation, industry)* naissance f; *Fig (of idea etc)* genèse f; **date/place/country of b.** date f/lieu m/pays m de naissance; **to give b. to a child** mettre un enfant au monde, donner naissance à un enfant; **she has given b. to a daughter** elle a donné naissance à une fille; **at b.** à la naissance; *Hum Fam* **he should have been drowned at b.!** on aurait dû le noyer à la naissance!; **will the father be present at the b.?** le père assistera-t-il à l'accouchement *ou* à la naissance?; **it was a difficult b.** cela a été un accouchement difficile; **Irish by b.** Irlandais de naissance; **from b.** *(to be blind, deaf etc)* de naissance; *(to be delicate)* dès *ou* depuis la naissance **2** *(of animal)* mise f bas; **to give b. to a litter** mettre bas une portée

▸▸ *Admin* **b. certificate** *(original)* acte m de naissance; *(copy)* extrait m de naissance; *Astrol* **b. chart** thème m astral; *Journ* **births column** carnet m rose; **b. control** *(contraception)* contraception f; *(family planning)* contrôle m des naissances; **b. rate** (taux m de) natalité f; **b. statistics** statistiques fpl de natalité

birthday [ˈbɜːθdeɪ] N *(anniversary)* anniversaire m; *(day of birth)* jour m de naissance; **she was 42 on her last b.** elle a 42 ans; *Fam Hum* **to be in one's b. suit** être dans le *ou* en costume d'Adam/d'Ève, être dans le plus simple appareil; **let me buy the b. girl a drink** laisse-moi te payer un verre pour ton anniversaire

▸▸ **b. card** carte f d'anniversaire; **b. cake** gâteau m d'anniversaire; **the B. Honours** = titres mpl honorifiques et autres distinctions décernés chaque année le jour de l'anniversaire officiel du souverain britannique; **b. present** cadeau m d'anniversaire; **b. party** fête f d'anniversaire

birthing [ˈbɜːθɪŋ] N

▸▸ *Br* **b. pool** piscine f d'accouchement; **b. room** salle f d'accouchement

birthmark [ˈbɜːθmɑːk] N tache f de naissance, envie f

birthplace [ˈbɜːθpleɪs] N lieu m de naissance; *Fig (of religion etc)* berceau m

birthright [ˈbɜːθraɪt] N *(something to which one is entitled)* droit m de naissance, droit du sang; *(of first-born)* droit d'aînesse; *(inheritance)*, *Fig* patrimoine m; *Fig* **clean air is everyone's b.** tout le monde a le droit de vivre dans un endroit non pollué

birthstone [ˈbɜːθstəʊn] N *Astrol etc* pierre f porte-bonheur, pl pierres porte-bonheur

biryani [bɪrɪˈɑːnɪ] N *(Indian dish)* biriani m

Biscay [ˈbɪskeɪ] N **the Bay of B.** le golfe de Gascogne

biscuit [ˈbɪskɪt] N **1** *Br* biscuit m; *Am (scone)* petit pain m; **ship's b.** biscuits de mer; **dog b.** biscuit pour chien; *Fam* **that (really) takes the b.!** ça, c'est le bouquet! **2** *Cer* biscuit m **3** *(colour)* marron m clair

▸▸ **b. barrel** boîte f à biscuits; **b. factory** biscuiterie f; *Cer* **b. ware** biscuit

bisect [baɪˈsekt] VT *Geom (line, angle)* couper *ou* diviser en deux parties égales

VI *(of road etc)* bifurquer

bisection [baɪˈsekʃən] N *Geom* bissection f

bisector [baɪˈsektər] N *Geom* bissectrice f, ligne f de bissection

bisexual [baɪˈseksjʊəl] ADJ *(attracted to both sexes)* bisexuel; *(having characteristics of both sexes)* bisexué

N bisexuel, -elle; **to be a b.** être bisexuel

bishop [ˈbɪʃəp] N **1** *Rel* évêque m; **b.'s palace** palais m épiscopal, évêché m **2** *Chess* fou m

bishopric [ˈbɪʃəprɪk] N *(office, diocese)* évêché m

bismuth [ˈbɪzməθ] N *Miner, Pharm* bismuth m

bison [ˈbaɪsən] N bison m

bisque¹ [biːsk] N *Cer* biscuit m

bisque² N *Culin (lobster etc)* bisque f

bistre [ˈbɪstər] ADJ, N bistre m

bistro [ˈbiːstrəʊ] N petit resto m

bisulphite [baɪˈsʌlfaɪt] N *Chem* bisulfite m; **sodium b.** bisulfite de sodium *ou* de soude

bisync [baɪˈsɪŋk], **bisynchronous** [baɪˈsɪŋkrənəs] ADJ *Comput* bisynchrone

bit¹ [bɪt] N **1** *(on bridle)* mors m; **to champ at the b.** *(of horse)* mâcher son mors; *(of person)* ronger son frein; **to take the b. between one's teeth** *(of horse, person)* prendre le mors aux dents **2** *(for brace)* mèche f, *(for drill)* foret m

BIT²

morceau **1, 2** ▪ bout **1** ▪ un peu **3** ▪ pièce **4**		

N **1** *(piece) (of bread, cake etc)* morceau m; *(of paper, string, old carpet etc)* bout m; *(of straw etc)* brin m; **a b. of news** une nouvelle; **a b. of luck** une chance; **a (little) b. of hope** un petit brin d'espoir

2 *(part)* partie f, morceau m; *(of book, film, report etc)* passage m; **to tear sth to bits** déchirer qch en morceaux; **smashed to bits** brisé (en mille morceaux); **to take sth to bits** démonter qch; **to come to bits** *(dismantle)* se démonter; *(break)* tomber en morceaux; *Fig* **to go to bits** *(of person)* s'effondrer, craquer; **in bits** en morceaux; **he has eaten every b.** il a tout mangé; **this is the difficult b.** c'est là où ça se complique; **made of bits and pieces** *or Fam* **bits and bobs** fait de bric et de broc; *Fam* **my bits and pieces** *or* **bobs** mes affaires

3 *(little)* **a b.** un peu (**of** de); **a tiny** *or* **little b.** un tout petit peu; **I'm a b. late** je suis un peu en retard; **I'm a b. hungry** j'ai un peu faim, *Fam* j'ai un petit creux; **she's a b. of an artist** *(paints, draws)* elle est artiste à ses heures perdues; **it was a b. of a nuisance** c'était vraiment ennuyeux; **quite a b. of sun/rain/trouble** pas mal de soleil/de pluie/d'ennuis; **I've had quite a b. to drink** j'ai un peu trop bu; *Fam* **he's a b. of a lad** *(likes a good time)* il aime faire la bringue; *(runs after women)* c'est un coureur (de jupons); **we got a b. of a shock** ça nous a fait un choc; **to give you a b. of an idea** pour te donner une petite idée; **it was a b. too much of a coincidence** c'était un peu fort comme coïncidence; **b. by b.** peu à peu, petit à petit; **not a b. (of it)!** pas du tout!; **I don't care a b.** cela m'est bien *ou* complètement égal; **it's not a b. of use** cela ne sert absolument à rien; **hold on** *ou* **wait a b.!** attendez un peu *ou* un instant!; *Fam* **in a b.** dans quelques minutes; *Fam* **after a b.** quelques minutes après; **that takes a b. of doing** ça, c'est bien difficile; **a good b. older/colder** nettement plus âgé/froid; **every b. as good/interesting** aussi bon/intéressant que; *Fam* **it's a b. much!** ça, c'est vraiment trop fort!; **we all had to do our b.** nous avons dû tous nous y mettre, nous avons dû tous y mettre du nôtre; **I did my b. too, you know** moi aussi j'ai fait ma part, tu sais; *Fam* **to make quite a b.** *(earn money)* gagner pas mal d'argent *ou* de fric; **to have a b. put away** avoir un petit pécule; **that must be worth quite a b.!** ça doit valoir pas mal d'argent!; *Fam* **she's a nice b. of stuff** *or* **skirt** c'est un beau brin de fille; **he's a b. of all right** c'est un beau mec, il est pas mal

4 *Fam (coin)* pièce f, *Br Arch* **threepenny b.** pièce de trois pence; *Am* **two bits** vingt-cinq cents

5 *Am Fam (term of imprisonment)* peine f de prison; **he did a b. in Fort Worth** il a fait de la taule à Fort Worth

▸▸ *Cin, Theat* **b. part** petit rôle m; *Cin, Theat* **b. player** acteur, -trice qui joue des petits rôles

bit³ N *Comput* bit m; **bits per second** bits par seconde

▸▸ **b. command** commande f binaire; **b. rate** débit f binaire

bit⁴ PT *see* **bite** VT & VI

bitch [bɪtʃ] N **1** *(dog)* chienne f, *(fox etc)* femelle f; **terrier b.** terrier m femelle **2** *Sl Pej (woman)* garce f **3** *Sl* **a b. of a job** un travail de chien; **life's a b.!** quelle *ou* cette chienne de vie!; **I've had a b. of a day!** j'ai eu une putain de journée!

VI *Sl (complain)* rouspéter; *Br (say nasty things)* déblatérer; **stop bitching about the weather** arrête de rouspéter après le temps; **bitching session** séance f de défoulement

bitchin [ˈbɪtʃɪn] ADJ *Am Sl* super, génial, -aux

bitchy [ˈbɪtʃɪ] ADJ *Sl (woman)* garce, vache; *(remark etc)* vache; **that was a b. thing to do!** quelle vacherie!, quel sale coup!; **to be b.** *(of woman)* être garce *ou* vache; *(of man)* être vache

BITE [baɪt] N **1** *(of person)* coup m de dent; *(in dentistry)* articulé m dentaire; *esp Am Sl* **to put the b. on sb** *(extort money from)* gruger qn; *(borrow money from)* taper qn

2 *(in fishing)* touche f, **I haven't had a b. all day** je n'ai pas eu une seule touche de toute la journée

3 *(of dog etc)* morsure f, *(of insect)* piqûre f, morsure; **the dog had given him a playful b. on the arm** le chien lui avait mordu le bras en jouant

4 *Fam (of food)* bouchée f, morceau m; **would you like a b. to eat?** voulez-vous manger quelque chose?; **I could do with a b. to eat** je mangerais bien quelque chose; **I haven't had a b. all day** je n'ai rien mangé de la journée; **come over for a b. of supper** viens manger un morceau à la maison ce soir; **can I have a b.?** *(of apple, chocolate bar)* je peux en avoir un peu?; **to take a (big) b. out of sth** mordre dans qch (à pleines dents); *Fig* **the repairs took a big b. out of our savings** les réparations ont fait un trou dans nos économies; *Fig* **you don't get two bites (at the cherry)** l'occasion ne se présente qu'une fois

5 *(of mustard, spice)* piquant m; *Fig* **your speech needs more b.** ton discours manque de mordant

VT *(pt* bit [bɪt], *pp* bitten [ˈbɪt(ə)n]) *(of animal, person)* mordre, donner un coup de dent à; *(of insect)* piquer; **the dog bit him in the leg** le chien l'a mordu à la jambe; **to b. one's lips** se mordre les lèvres; **to b. one's nails** se ronger les ongles; *also Fig* **to b. one's tongue** se mordre la langue; **to b. the dust** mordre la poussière; *Prov* **once bitten twice shy** chat échaudé craint l'eau froide; *Fig* **to b. the bullet** serrer les dents; **let's b. the bullet and give him what he wants** faisons contre mauvaise fortune bon cœur et donnons-lui ce qu'il veut; **to get bitten** *(by dog)* se faire mordre; *(by insect)* se faire piquer; *Fam* **what's biting/bitten him?** quelle mouche l'a piqué?; *Fam* **he got bitten by the skiing/chess bug at the age of six** il se passionne pour le ski/les échecs depuis l'âge de six ans; *Fig* **to b. the hand that feeds you** cracher dans la soupe; *Am Sl* **b. me!** va te faire voir!

VI **1** *(of fish)* mordre (à l'hameçon); *(of in-*

sect) piquer; **does the dog b.?** est-ce que ce chien mord?; **he bit into the apple** il a mordu dans la pomme; **are they** *or* **the fish biting (today)?** alors, ça mord?; *Fig* **don't worry, I don't b.!** n'ayez pas peur, je ne mords pas!; *Fig* **sanctions are beginning to b.** l'effet des sanctions commence à se faire sentir

2 *(of screw, file)* mordre (**on** sur); *(of tool)* mordre, s'engager; *(of anchor)* mordre, prendre fond; **a screw that won't b.** une vis qui foire

▸ **bite back VT SEP** *(reply)* ravaler

▸ **bite off VT SEP** enlever *ou* détacher d'un coup de dent(s); *Fam* **to b. sb's head off** rembarrer qn; *Fig* **to b. off more than one can chew** tenter quelque chose au-dessus de ses forces

biter ['baɪtər] **N it's a case of the b. bit** c'est l'arroseur arrosé

biting ['baɪtɪŋ] **ADJ** *(cold)* âpre, perçant; *(wind)* cinglant; *(style, wit, irony)* mordant, caustique

▸▸ *Aut* **b. point** *(of clutch)* point *m* d'attaque

bitmap ['bɪtmæp] *Comput* **N** bitmap *m*

ADJ pixélisé, bitmap

▸▸ **b. font** police *f* pixélisée *ou* bitmap

bitmapped ['bɪtmæpt] **ADJ** *Comput (image)* pixélisé, bitmap

▸▸ **b. font** police *f* pixélisée *ou* bitmap

bit-slice processor N *Comput* processeur *m* en tranches

bitten ['bɪtən] **PP** *see* **bite VT & VI**

bitter ['bɪtər] **ADJ** *(taste)*, *Fig (person, tears, experience, disappointment)* amer; *(words)* acerbe; *(wind)* glacial, -als *ou* -aux; *(weather)* rigoureux; *(cold)* glacial, cinglant; *(enemy, hatred)* implacable; *(conflict, opposition, resistance)* âpre; *(tone)* aigre, âpre; **not being promoted was a b. pill for him to swallow** ça a été dur à avaler pour lui de ne pas être promu; **to feel** *or* **be b. about sth** ressentir de l'amertume à propos de qch; **she's very b. about it** elle en est très amère, *Fam* elle l'a pas digéré; *Fig* **to go on/resist to the b. end** aller/résister jusqu'au bout

N 1 *Br (beer)* bière *f* brune **2 bitters** bitter(s) *m(pl)*, amer(s) *m(pl)*

▸▸ *Pharm* **b. aloes** aloès *m* (médicinal); **b. lemon** Schweppes® *m* au citron; *Bot* **b. orange** orange *f* amère

bitterly ['bɪtəlɪ] **ADV** *(to say)* amèrement, avec amertume; *(to cry)* amèrement; *(to argue)* aigrement; **b. disappointed** amèrement déçu; **it was b. cold** il faisait un froid de loup *ou* de canard; **I've regretted it b. ever since** je n'ai cessé de le regretter amèrement; **to be b. opposed to sth** être farouchement opposé à qch

bittern ['bɪtən] **N** *(bird)* butor *m*

bitterness ['bɪtənɪs] **N** *(of drink, pain, person)* amertume *f*; *(of weather)* rigueur *f*; *(of reproach)* âpreté *f*; *(of words, quarrel)* aigreur *f*, acrimonie *f*

bittersweet ['bɪtəswiːt] **ADJ** *also Fig* doux-amer

N *(plant)* douce-amère *f*, *pl* douces-amères

bitty ['bɪtɪ] **ADJ** *Fam (book etc)* (d'un style) décousu

bitumen ['bɪtjʊmɪn] **N 1** *Chem, Miner* bitume *m* **2** *Austr Fam (road)* route *f* goudronnée

bituminous [bɪ'tjuːmɪnəs] **ADJ** bitumineux; **b. coal** houille *f* grasse *ou* collante

bivalent [baɪ'veɪlənt] **ADJ** *Chem* bivalent

bivalve ['baɪvælv] **ADJ, N** *(mollusc)* bivalve *m*

bivouac ['bɪvʊæk] **N** bivouac *m*

VI (**bivouacked; bivouacking**) bivouaquer

biweekly [baɪ'wiːklɪ] **ADJ 1** *(every two weeks)* bimensuel **2** *(twice a week)* bihebdomadaire

---

ADV 1 *(every two weeks)* tous les quinze jours **2** *(twice a week)* deux fois par semaine

bizarre [bɪ'zɑːr] **ADJ** bizarre

bizarrely [bɪ'zɑːlɪ] **ADV** bizarrement

bizarreness [bɪ'zɑːnɪs] **N** bizarrerie *f*

bizzies ['bɪzɪz] **NPL** *Br Sl* **the b.** *(the police)* les flics *mpl*

B/L, b/l *Com (abbr* **bill of lading**) connt

blab [blæb] *Fam* **VI** (**-bb-**) **1** *(betray secret)* vendre la mèche **2** *(prattle)* jaser, bavarder

VT *(secret)* divulguer, laisser échapper

N = **blabber**

▸ **blab out VT SEP** = **blab VT**

blabber ['blæbər] *Fam* **N** bavard, -arde, jaseur, -euse

VI jacasser

blabbermouth ['blæbəmaʊθ] **N** grande langue *f*, bavard, -arde

Black [blæk] **N** Noir *m*, Noire *f*; **B.-on-B. violence** violence *f* des Noirs sur les Noirs

BLACK [blæk] **ADJ 1** *(colour)* *(coffee, dress, hair, Africa, music etc)* noir; *(cloud, sky etc)* sombre; **as b. as night** noir comme la nuit; **a b. man/woman** un Noir/une Noire; **b. with age** noirci par le temps; **it** *or* **the night was pitch b.** il faisait noir comme dans un four; **his hands were b.** il avait les mains toutes noires; *Fig* **to be in sb's b. books** être mal vu de qn; *Hum* **little b. book** *(of addresses)* carnet *m* d'adresses; *(of wrongdoers)* liste *f* noire; **is it b. tie?** *(at dinner etc)* est-ce que la tenue habillée est de rigueur?

2 *Fig (gloomy, sombre)* *(mood, thought)* noir; **to look as b. as thunder** avoir l'air furieux; **to give sb a b. look** jeter un regard noir à qn; **things are looking b.** les affaires prennent une mauvaise tournure; **to paint things blacker than they are** noircir la situation; **she's not as b. as she's painted** elle n'est pas si mauvaise qu'on le dit; **he's in one of his b. moods** il est dans un de ses mauvais jours; **it's a b. day for Britain** c'est un mauvais jour pour la Grande-Bretagne

3 *Fig (sinister, malevolent)* malveillant; **b. hearted** malveillant

4 *Fig (macabre) (humour)* noir

N 1 noir *m*; **she always wears b.** elle porte toujours du noir, elle est toujours en noir; **to work in b. and white** *(of artist)* faire du dessin à l'encre *ou* au crayon noir; **I have his consent in b. and white** j'ai son consentement par écrit; **I should like to have it in b. and white** je voudrais avoir cela noir sur blanc; **she sees everything in b. and white** pour elle, c'est tout l'un ou tout l'autre; **she would swear that b. is white to help him** elle serait prête à tout pour l'aider; **he'll swear b. is white for the price of a couple of drinks** il est prêt à jurer n'importe quoi en échange d'un verre ou deux

2 *Fin Fam* **to be in the b.** être en crédit; **to get back into the b.** sortir du rouge

3 *Sport* **the b.** *(in roulette)* le noir; *(in snooker)* la bille *ou* boule noire

VT 1 *(blacken)* **to b. one's face** se noircir le visage; **to b. sb's eye** pocher l'œil à qn

2 *Ind (boycott)* mettre à l'index

3 *(polish) (shoes)* cirer

▸▸ **b. art** sciences *fpl* occultes; **b. belt** *Sport* ceinture *f* noire; *Am Fam* = zone *f* habitée par des Noirs; *Aviat* **b. box** boîte *f* noire; *Culin* **b. bread** pain *m* de seigle; *Scot Culin* **b. bun** = sorte de pain au raisin consommé au Nouvel An; *Br Law, Hist* **the b. cap** le bonnet noir *(que coiffait le juge en prononçant une condamnation à mort)*; **b. comedy** comédie *f* noire; *Br* **the B. Country** région *f* de Birmingham; *Hist* **B. Death** peste *f* noire; **b. economy** économie *f* noire; **b. eye** œil *m* poché *ou* au beurre noir; **b. flag** drapeau *m* noir; **the B. Forest** la Forêt noire; *Astron* **b. hole** trou *m* noir; **b. ice** verglas *m*; *St Exch* **b.**

---

knight chevalier *m* noir; **b. magic** magie *f* noire; *Fam* **B. Maria** panier *m* à salade *(fourgon)*; **b. mark** mauvais point *m*; *Com* **b. marketeer** marché *m* noir; *Com* **b. marketeer** vendeur, -euse au marché noir; **B. Mass** messe *f* noire; **b. money** *(earned on black market)* argent *m* du marché noir; *(undeclared)* argent non déclaré au fisc; *Culin* **b. pudding** boudin *m* (noir); *Parl* **B. Rod** = huissier *m* chargé par la Chambre des lords britannique de convoquer les Communes; **the B. Sea** la mer Noire; **b. sheep** brebis *f* galeuse; *Br Fig* **b. spot** point noir; **b. swan** cygne *m* noir; **b. and tan** *(drink)* = mélange *m* de bière et de porter; *Hist* **the B. and Tans** = forces *fpl* armées britanniques envoyées en Irlande en 1920 pour lutter contre le Sinn Fein; **b. velvet** *(cocktail)* = cocktail *m* de champagne et de stout; **b. widow** *(spider)* veuve *f* noire

▸ **black out VI** *(faint)* perdre connaissance, s'évanouir; *(lose memory)* avoir un trou (de mémoire)

VT SEP 1 *(house etc) (completely)* éteindre les lumières dans, faire le black-out dans; *(partially)* voiler *ou* masquer les lumières dans; *Theat* **to b. out the stage** faire l'obscurité sur scène

2 *Radio, TV* **industrial action has blacked out this evening's programmes** un mouvement de grève a interrompu les programmes de la soirée

3 *(delete)* rayer *(d'un gros trait noir)*

▸ **black up VI** *Theat* se maquiller la peau en noir, se noircir le visage

black-and-blue ADJ **to beat sb b.** rosser qn, couvrir qn de bleus; **to be b. all over** être couvert de bleus, être tuméfié

black-and-tan ADJ

▸▸ **b. terrier** chien *m* noir et feu *inv*

black-and-white N *(photograph)* photo *f* noir et blanc

ADJ *(photograph, television)* noir et blanc; **b. film** film *m* en noir et blanc

blackball ['blækbɔːl] **VT** blackbouler

blackballing ['blækbɔːlɪŋ] **N** blackboulage *m*

blackbeetle ['blækbiːt(ə)l] **N** *Fam (insect)* blatte *f*, cafard *m*

blackberry ['blækb(ə)rɪ] **N** mûre *f*

▸▸ **b. bush** mûrier *m*; **b. jam** confiture *f* de mûres; **b. tart** tarte *f* aux mûres

blackberrying ['blækberɪŋ] **N** **to go b.** aller cueillir des mûres, aller à la cueillette des mûres

blackbird ['blækbɜːd] **N 1** merle *m* (noir) **2** *Am* *(variété f d')* étourneau *m*

blackboard ['blækbɔːd] **N** tableau *m* noir

black-bordered [-'bɔːdəd] **ADJ** à bordure noire

blackcock ['blækkɒk] **N** *(bird)* tétras-lyre *m*, *pl* tétras-lyres, coq *m* des bouleaux

blackcurrant [blæk'kʌrənt] **N** *(bush, fruit)* cassis *m*

blacken ['blæk(ə)n] **VT** *(wall)*, *Fig (sb's reputation)* noircir; *(sky)* obscurcir; *(paper, glass)* *(with smoke)* enfumer; *Fig* **to b. sb's character** calomnier qn

VI noircir, devenir noir; *Fig (of face)* s'assombrir

blackening ['blæk(ə)nɪŋ] **N** noircissement *m*

black-eyed pea N dolique *m*

blackfly ['blækflaɪ] **N** *Fam (insect)* mouche *f* noire

blackguard ['blægɑːd] **N** *Arch* fripouille *f*, canaille *f*

blackhead ['blækhed] **N** *(on face)* point *m* noir

blackheaded gull ['blækhedɪd] **N** mouette *f* rieuse

blacking ['blækɪŋ] N **1** *Ind (of ship, company)* mise f à l'index **2** *Arch (for shoes)* cirage m

blackish ['blækɪʃ] ADJ noirâtre, tirant sur le noir

blackjack ['blækdʒæk] N **1** *Am (weapon)* nerf m de bœuf **2** *Cards* vingt-et-un m inv
VT *Am* frapper avec un nerf de bœuf

blacklead ['blækled] VT *Old-fashioned (stove etc)* passer à la mine de plomb

blackleg ['blækleg] *Ind Fam Pej* N jaune m, briseur m de grève
VI (-gg-) briser une grève, être un briseur de grève

blacklist ['blæklɪst] N liste f noire
VT *(person, company etc)* inscrire ou mettre sur la liste noire

blackmail ['blækmeɪl] N chantage m; **emotional b.** chantage aux sentiments
VT soumettre à un chantage, *Fam* faire chanter; **to be blackmailed** être victime d'un chantage; **I'm being blackmailed for £5,000** je suis victime d'un chantage, on me réclame 5000 livres; **to b. sb into resigning** faire chanter qn pour qu'il démissionne

blackmailer ['blækmeɪlər] N maître chanteur m, pl maîtres chanteurs

blackness ['blæknɪs] N *(of hair, sky etc)*, *Fig* noirceur f

blackout ['blækaʊt] N **1** *(during war)* black-out m inv; *Fig* **to impose a news b.** interdire la divulgation d'une information; *(in general)* imposer le black-out sur l'information **2** *Elec* panne f d'électricité **3** *Theat* obscurcissement m de la scène **4** *(loss of consciousness)* évanouissement m; *(memory lapse)* trou m de mémoire

Blackshirt ['blækʃɜːt] N *Pol* chemise f noire

blacksmith ['blæksmɪθ] N forgeron m; *(who shoes horses)* maréchal-ferrant m, pl maréchaux-ferrants

blackthorn ['blækθɔːn] N **1** *(shrub)* épine f noire, prunier m épineux, prunellier m **2** *(stick)* gourdin m (en épines)

blacktop ['blæktɒp] N *esp Am* **1** *(substance)* bitume m **2** *(road)* route f bitumée

blackwater ['blækwɔːtər] ADJ
▶▶ *Med* **b. fever** hématurie f

bladder ['blædər] N **1** *(for urine)* vessie f; **to have a full b.** avoir la vessie pleine **2** *(sac)* vésicule f; **air b.** *(of fish)* vésicule aérienne; *(of seaweed)* vésicule aérocyste **3** *(of ball)* vessie f

bladdered ['blædəd] ADJ *Br Fam (drunk)* bourré, pété

bladderwort ['blædəwɜːt] N *(plant)* utriculaire f

bladderwrack ['blædəræk] N *(seaweed)* goémon m jaune vésiculeux

blade [bleɪd] N **1** *(of knife, sword, skate)* lame f; *(of guillotine)* couperet m; *(of saw)* feuille f, lame **2** *(of propeller)* pale f, *(of oar)* pelle f, pale; *(of ventilator, turbine)* ailette f; *(of waterwheel)* aube f, *(of spade)* fer m; *Aut (of windscreen wiper)* balai m, raclette f **3** *(of grass)* brin m **4** *Sl (knife)* lame f, surin m **5** *Arch (sword)* sabre m, épée f **6** *Arch, Hum* **a young b.** un jeune gaillard

bladed ['bleɪdɪd] ADJ à lame(s)/à pales; **three-b.** *(penknife)* à trois lames; *(propeller)* à trois pales

blag [blæg] *Br Fam* N *(robbery)* braquage m
VT **1** *(steal)* piquer **2** *(con)* **to b. oneself sth** obtenir qch au culot; **to b. one's way in** resquiller

blah(-blah) ['blɑː(blɑː)] N *Fam* bla-bla m inv, baratin m; **the usual b.** le baratin habituel

blame [bleɪm] N **1** *(reproof)* reproches mpl; **to deserve b.** mériter des reproches;

---

to be free from b. être irréprochable
2 *(responsibility)* responsabilité f, faute f; **to lay** or **put the b. (for sth) on sb, to lay the b. (for sth) at sb's door** rejeter ou faire retomber la responsabilité ou la faute (de qch) sur qn; **to bear** or **take the b.** endosser la responsabilité *(for sth* or *qch)*; **why is it always me that gets the b.?** pourquoi est-ce que tout retombe toujours sur moi?; **I got the b. for breaking the window** c'est moi qu'on a accusé d'avoir cassé la fenêtre; **to shift the b. onto sb** rejeter la responsabilité sur qn; **where does the b. lie?** à qui la faute?; **the b. lies with her** c'est (de) sa faute
VT *(person)* rendre responsable; **to b. sb for sth** reprocher qch à qn; *(hold responsible for)* rendre qn responsable de qch, attribuer à qn la responsabilité de qch; **he can't be blamed for the accident** on ne peut pas le rendre responsable de l'accident; **to b. sth on sb** rejeter la faute ou la responsabilité de qch sur qn; **the accident was blamed on the bad weather** on a dit que le mauvais temps était la cause de l'accident; **to b. sb for doing sth** reprocher à qn de faire ou d'avoir fait qch; **he can't be blamed for trying** on ne peut pas lui reprocher d'avoir essayé; **I have nothing to b. myself for** je n'ai rien à me reprocher; **I b. the parents** pour moi, ce sont les parents qui sont responsables; **I b. myself** je me sens responsable, c'est (de) ma faute; **don't b. me!** ne me mets pas ça sur le dos!; **don't b. me if you're late** tu ne viendras pas te plaindre que c'est de ma faute si tu es en retard; **I wouldn't b. you if you left me** si tu me quittais, je ne te le reprocherais pas; **I wouldn't b. you if you left him** je te comprendrais si tu le quittais; **she's leaving him and who can b. her?** elle le quitte et on la comprend bien; **to have only oneself to b., to have nobody to b. but oneself** n'avoir à s'en prendre qu'à soi-même; **he is to b.** c'est de sa faute; **she was in no way to b.** elle n'était en aucun cas responsable; **the bad weather was to b.** c'était à cause du mauvais temps

blamed [bleɪmd] ADJ *esp Am Euph* sacré

blameless ['bleɪmlɪs] ADJ irréprochable, *Lit* irrépréhensible; **to lead a b. life** avoir une vie irréprochable; **none of us is b.** nous sommes tous responsables

blamelessly ['bleɪmlɪslɪ] ADV de façon irréprochable

blameworthy ['bleɪmwɜːðɪ] ADJ *Fml (person)* coupable, blâmable; *(action, behaviour)* répréhensible

blanch [blɑːntʃ] VT *(vegetables, almonds)* blanchir; **blanched almonds** amandes fpl émondées
VI *(of person)* blêmir, pâlir

blancmange [bləˈmɒnʒ] N *Culin* blancmanger m, pl blancs-mangers

bland [blænd] ADJ **1** *(person, speech)* *(insipid)* insipide; *(suspiciously smooth)* doucereux, mielleux; *(smile)* de politesse **2** *(without flavour)* *(food, drink)* fade; *Fig (music, film)* insipide

blandish ['blændɪʃ] VT amadouer

blandishments ['blændɪʃmənts] NPL cajoleries fpl; **to resist sb's b.** ne pas se laisser amadouer par qn

blandly ['blændlɪ] ADV *(to reply, smile)* mielleusement

blank [blæŋk] ADJ **1** *(empty, with nothing on it)* *(paper)* blanc, f blanche; *(page)* blanc, vierge; *(tape, cassette)* vierge; *(wall)* aveugle; *(cartridge)* à blanc; *Comput (disk, screen)* vide; *(unformatted)* vierge; *Comput* **the screen suddenly went b.** soudain tout a disparu de l'écran; **to leave b.** *(part of form etc)* laisser blanc, ne pas remplir; **leave the other side of the paper b.** ne rien écrire sur

---

l'envers de la feuille; *Cards* **to be b. in clubs** ne pas avoir de trèfles dans son jeu
2 *(vacant) (look)* vide, sans expression; **my mind went b.** je me suis senti la tête vide, j'ai eu un trou; **to look b.** avoir l'air complètement déconcerté ou ahuri; **a look of b. astonishment** un air ébahi
3 *(absolute, complete) (impossibility, refusal)* absolu
N **1** *(in document etc)* blanc m, vide m; *Am (for telegram etc)* formulaire m, formule f, *Mil* cartouche f à blanc; *(on target)* blanc; **to fire blanks** tirer à blanc; *Fam Hum* **to shoot blanks** *(of man)* être stérile; **to leave blanks** laisser des blancs; **his mind is a b.** *(he has lost his memory)* il ne se souvient de rien; **I'm sorry, my mind is a b.** je suis désolé, j'ai un trou; **the rest is a b.** après cela, c'est le vide; *Cards* **to have a b. in clubs** ne pas avoir de trèfles dans son jeu
2 *(in dominoes)* blanc m; *Fig* **to draw a b.** *(be unsuccessful in search)* faire chou blanc; *Am (be unable to remember)* avoir un trou de mémoire
3 *(metal disc) (in minting coins)* flan m; *Metal, Tech* flan m, masselotte f, galette f
4 *Typ (to replace swearword etc)* tiret m
VT *Fam (ignore) (person)* ignorer; **he blanked me** il a fait comme s'il ne me voyait pas
▶▶ *Fin* **b. cheque** chèque m en blanc; *Fin* **b. credit** crédit m en blanc; *Fin* **b. endorsement** endossement m en blanc; **b. space** blanc, espace m vide; *Comput* **b. unformatted disk** disquette f vierge; *Literature* **b. verse** vers mpl blancs ou sans rime
▶ **blank out** VT SEP *(parts of text, tape etc)* effacer; **her face had been blanked out** *(on negative)* on avait effacé son visage; *(on print)* on avait caché son visage; **she's blanked out the memory** elle a effacé cet événement de sa mémoire
VI *(lose consciousness)* tomber dans les pommes

blank-endorse VT *Fin* endosser en blanc

blanket ['blæŋkɪt] N **1** *(for bed, horse)* couverture f, *Fig (of fog, mist)* manteau m; *(of snow)* couche f, *Old-fashioned Fam* **he was born on the wrong side of the b.** c'est un enfant naturel **2** *Typ* blanchet m
ADJ ATTRIB *(general) (acceptance)* général, -aux, global, -aux
VT **the mountain was blanketed in fog/snow** la montagne était couverte d'un manteau de brouillard/de neige
▶▶ *Com* **b. agreement** accord-cadre m, pl accords-cadres; **b. bath** grande toilette f *(d'un malade alité)*; **b. contract** contrat m global; *Radio, TV* **b. coverage** *(of event)* reportage m (très) complet; *Sewing* **b. stitch** point m de feston; **b. term** terme m général

blanking ['blæŋkɪŋ] N *TV* suppression f de faisceau; *(erasing)* effacement m

blankly ['blæŋklɪ] ADV *(to look at sb) (without expression)* sans expression, avec l'air de ne rien comprendre; *(in confusion)* d'un air déconcerté; **to stare b. into space** avoir le regard perdu dans le vide

blankness ['blæŋknɪs] N **1** *(of person)* air m confus ou décontenancé **2** *(of eyes, expression)* vacuité f

blare [bleər] N *(of trumpet)* beuglement(s) m(pl); *(of radio)* braillement(s) m(pl); **the b. of the brass band** le son éclatant de la fanfare; **the b. of car horns** le son discordant des klaxons de voiture
VI *(of trumpet)* sonner; *(of car horn)* retentir; *(of radio)* beugler, *Fam* gueuler, brailler; **the band blared** le son de la fanfare retentit de façon discordante
▶ **blare away** VI *(of radio etc) Fam* gueuler
▶ **blare out** VI *(of trumpet)* sonner; *(of voice)* résonner (de façon discordante)
VT SEP *(of loudspeaker, band)* faire retentir

Blarney ['blɑːnɪ] N *Fam* **to have kissed the B. Stone** avoir le don pour embobiner les gens

blarney ['blɑːnɪ] N boniments *mpl*; **don't give me any of your b.** arrête tes boniments ▪ VT *Fam* embobiner; **to b. sb into doing sth** faire faire qch à qn en l'embobinant; **to b. one's way out of trouble/into a job** se sortir d'embarras/obtenir un emploi grâce à son bagou(t)

blasé ['blɑːzeɪ] ADJ blasé

blaspheme [blæs'fiːm] VT & VI blasphémer

blasphemer [blæs'fiːmər] N blasphéma-teur, -trice

blasphemous ['blæsfəməs] ADJ *(person)* blasphémateur, -trice; *(words etc)* blas-phématoire

blasphemously ['blæsfəməslɪ] ADV de fa-çon blasphématoire; **to speak b.** blasphé-mer

blasphemy ['blæsfəmɪ] N blasphème *m*

blast [blɑːst] N **1** *(gust of wind)* coup *m* ou ra-fale *f* de vent; **b. of heat** bouffée *f* de chaleur; **b. of steam** jet *m* de vapeur

2 *(of whistle, siren)* coup *m*; **b. on the trum-pet** sonnerie *f* de trompette; **to give a b. on the whistle** donner un coup de sifflet

3 *Fig* **to be** *or* **be working at full b.** être en pleine activité, travailler à plein rendement; *Fam* **to turn the radio up full b.** faire gueuler *ou* brailler la radio

4 *(shock wave) (from explosion etc)* souffle *m*; **a lot of people were killed by the b.** beaucoup de gens ont été tués par l'explo-sion

5 *(explosion)* explosion *f*

6 *Am Fam (thrill)* **to get a b. out of doing sth** prendre son pied *ou* s'éclater en faisant qch

7 *Fam* **a b. from the past** *(song)* un vieux tube; **that's a real b. from the past** *(fashion, behaviour etc)* c'est comme autrefois; *(brings back memories)* ça me ramène des années en arrière

▪ INT mince (alors)!, zut (alors)!

▪ VT **1** *Min (with dynamite etc)* faire sauter **2** *(of frost) (plant)* brûler, flétrir; *(of light-ning) (tree etc)* foudroyer; *Fig* **to b. sb's hopes** anéantir les espoirs de qn

3 *Fam* **b. it!** zut alors!; **b. you/her!** je te/la maudis!; **b. this computer!** maudit ordina-teur!

4 *Fam (criticize)* démolir

▪ VI *(of brass instrument)* sonner; *(of radio etc)* hurler, brailler

▪ ▪ **b. furnace** *Tech* haut-fourneau *m*, *pl* hauts-fourneaux; *Mil* fourneau *m* de mine; *Min* **b. hole** pétard *m*, trou *m* de mine

▪ **blast away** VI **1** *(of radio etc)* hurler, brail-ler **2** *(with gun, rifle etc)* tirer en rafales

▪ **blast off** VI *(of rocket, missile)* décoller

blasted ['blɑːstɪd] ADJ ATTRIB **1** *(heath)* déso-lé; *(tree)* foudroyé **2** *Fam (intensifier)* sacré; **you b. idiot!** espèce d'idiot!; **it's a b. nui-sance!** c'est vraiment casse-pieds! **3** *Fam (drunk)* bourré, beurré; *(on drugs)* défoncé

blasting ['blɑːstɪŋ] N **1** *Min* travail *m* aux ex-plosifs; **beware of b.!** attention aux coups de mine! **2** *Fam (severe criticism)* critique *f* féroce *ou* violente; *(reprimand)* savon *m*; **her latest novel got a b. from reviewers** son dernier roman a été démoli par les criti-ques *ou* la critique

blastoderm ['blæstəʊdɜːm] N *Biol* blasto-derme *m*

blastoff ['blɑːstɒf] N *(of rocket)* décollage *m*; **b. is at two o'clock** la fusée décollera à deux heures

blatancy ['bleɪtənsɪ] N *(of injustice, crime etc)* caractère *m* flagrant

blatant ['bleɪtənt] ADJ *(injustice)* criant; *(lie, prejudice, disregard)* flagrant, manifeste; **a**

b. liar un fieffé menteur, un menteur éhonté; **don't be so b.** *(in your approach)* sois un peu plus diplomate; **it was a b. attempt to win him over** c'était une tentative évidente de s'assurer ses faveurs

blatantly ['bleɪtəntlɪ] ADV *(to lie etc)* d'une manière flagrante; **it's b. obvious that …** il est évident que …; **yes, that's b. obvious** oui, évidemment

blather ['blæðər] N, VI = **blether**

blaxploitation [blæksplɔɪ'teɪʃən] N *Cin* = genre *m* de cinéma qui exploitait les stéréo-types associés à l'identité noire américaine au cinéma, au cours des années 70

blaze[1] [bleɪz] N **1** *(fire)* flamme(s) *f(pl)*, feu *m*; *(in fireplace)* flambée *f*; *Fig (of sun)* flam-boiement *m*; *(of colours, diamonds etc)* éclat *m*; **many people died in the b.** beaucoup de gens ont péri dans les flammes; **in a b.** en feu, en flammes; *Fig* **b. of anger** éclat de co-lère; **in a b. of anger** enflammé de colère; **the street was a b. of light** la rue était tout illuminée; **the garden was a b. of colour** le jardin était resplendissant de couleur; **he married her in a b. of publicity** il l'a épousée sous le feu des médias; **the film was re-leased in a b. of publicity** la sortie du film a été accompagnée d'une publicité monstre; **in a b. of glory** *(to die, retire, return)* plein de gloire

2 *Old-fashioned Fam* **go to blazes!** allez au diable!; **what the blazes does he want/is he doing?** mais qu'est-ce qu'il veut/fait, bon sang?; **to work like blazes** travailler comme un forcené; **to run like blazes** courir comme un dératé

▪ VI **1** *(of fire etc)* flamber; **they had left all the lights blazing** ils avaient laissé toutes les lu-mières allumées; **the house was blazing** *(on fire)* la maison flambait; **the house was blaz-ing with lights** la maison était tout illumi-née; **his eyes were blazing with anger/passion** ses yeux lançaient des éclairs de colère/passion **2** *(of sun, colours)* flamboyer

▪ **blaze away** VI **1** flamboyer **2** *(with gun)* = **blast away 2**

▪ **blaze down** VI *(of sun)* taper; **the sun was blazing down on the beach** le soleil dardait ses rayons sur la plage

▪ **blaze up** VI *(of fire)* s'embraser, s'enflam-mer; *Fam (in anger) (of person)* s'emporter

blaze[2] N **1** *(on face of horse, ox)* marque *f* al-longée blanche **2** *(on tree)* blanchis *m*, griffe *f*

▪ VT *(tree)* griffer, blanchir; **to b. a trail** tracer un chemin; *Fig* faire œuvre de pionnier, montrer la voie; *(in science etc)* poser des ja-lons

▪ ▪ **b. mark** *(on tree)* blanchis, griffe

blazer ['bleɪzər] N *(clothing)* blazer *m*

blazing ['bleɪzɪŋ] ADJ USU ATTRIB **1** *(on fire)* en feu, enflammé; *(ship)* embrasé **2** *Fig (fire, sun)* ardent **3** *Fam* **b. row** une dispute vio-lente **4** *Fam (angry)* fou de rage; **he was b.** il fulminait, il était fou de rage

blazon ['bleɪzən] N *Her (arms)* blason *m*

▪ VT **1** *Fig* **his name was blazoned over the front pages of all the newspapers** son nom s'étalait en grosses lettres à la une de tous les journaux **2** *Her* blasonner

▪ **blazon abroad** VT SEP *Fml (news)* annon-cer à son de trompe

▪ **blazon out, blazon forth** VT SEP *Fml* an-noncer *ou* proclamer à son de trompe

bldg *abbr* **building**

bleach [bliːtʃ] N *(for hair)* décolorant *m*; **(household) b.** eau *f* de Javel

▪ VT *(clothes)* passer à l'eau de Javel; *(hair)* dé-colorer; **hair/sheets bleached by the sun** cheveux/draps décolorés par le soleil; *Phot* **to b. out** blanchir

▪ VI *Tex etc* blanchir; *Chem etc* se décolorer;

do not b. *(washing instruction)* Javel inter-dite; **the colours had bleached out** les cou-leurs étaient passées

bleachers ['bliːtʃəz] NPL *Am Sport* gradins *mpl*

bleaching ['bliːtʃɪŋ] N *Tex etc* blanchiment *m*; *(of hair)*, *Chem* décoloration *f*

▪ ▪ **b. agent** produit *m* blanchissant, déco-lorant *m*; *Chem* décolorant

bleak [bliːk] ADJ **1** *(weather)* morne, triste; *(terrain)* exposé au vent; *(wind)* froid **2** *Fig (future)* lugubre; *(smile)* pâle; **the prospects are b.** les perspectives sont peu encoura-geantes

bleakly ['bliːklɪ] ADV *(to smile, stare)* d'un air affligé *ou* désolé; *(to reply, answer)* d'un ton affligé *ou* désolé

bleakness ['bliːknɪs] N *(of weather, land-scape)* aspect *m* morne, tristesse *f*; *Fig (of fu-ture, room)* caractère *m* lugubre

blearily ['blɪərɪlɪ] ADV *(to look at sb)* les yeux troubles

bleary ['blɪərɪ] ADJ *(eyes)* trouble

bleary-eyed ADJ aux yeux troubles; **to be b. with lack of sleep** avoir des petits yeux (à cause du manque de sommeil)

bleat [bliːt] N *(of sheep)* bêlement *m*; *Fig (complaint)* plainte *f*

▪ VI *(of sheep)* bêler; *(of ram)* blatérer; *(of goat, old man etc)* chevroter; *Fig (complain)* se plaindre; **what's he bleating about?** de quoi se plaint-il?

bleating ['bliːtɪŋ] ADJ *(voice)* chevrotant

▪ N *(of sheep)* bêlement *m*; *Fig (complaining)* plaintes *fpl*

bleed [bliːd] *(pt, pp* **bled** [bled]*)* VI **1** saigner; **his nose is bleeding** il saigne du nez; **to b. to death** saigner à mort; *Iron* **my heart bleeds for you** tu me fends le cœur **2** *(of tree etc)* pleurer, perdre sa sève **3** *(of colour) (on washing)* couler

▪ VT **1** *Med* saigner; *Fam* **to b. sb white** *or* **dry** saigner qn à blanc **2** *Tech (brakes, pipes, ra-diator etc)* purger

▪ N *Typ* fond *m* perdu

▪ ▪ *Tech* **b. nipple** téton *m* de purge; *Tech* **b. screw** vis *f* de purge; *Tech* **b. valve** soupape *f* de purge

bleeder ['bliːdər] N **1** *Br Sl Pej* salaud *m*; **poor b.** pauvre type *m*; **you lucky b.!** sacré vei-nard! **2** *Tech* dispositif *m* de drainage, pur-geur *m*

bleeding ['bliːdɪŋ] ADJ **1** saignant, qui sai-gne **2** *Br Sl (intensifier)* sacré; **you b. liar!** sa-cré menteur!; **what a b. nuisance!** quelle saloperie! **3** *Typ* à fond perdu

▪ N **1** saignement *m*, hémorragie *f*; *Bot* écou-lement *m* de sève; **b. from the nose** saigne-ment de nez **2** *Med, Hist (blood-letting)* saignée *f* **3** *Tech (of brakes, radiator)* purge *f*

▪ ▪ **b. heart** *Pej (person)* sentimental *m*; *Bot* cœur-de-Jeannette *m*, *pl* cœurs-de-Jean-nette; *Lit* **with a b. heart** le cœur brisé

bleeding-heart ADJ **b. liberals** = des libé-raux *mpl* au cœur tendre

bleep [bliːp] N *(of electronic device)* bip *m*

▪ VI *(of electronic device)* faire bip

▪ VT **1** *(with pager)* appeler au moyen d'un bip; **I'm being bleeped** on m'appelle **2** *Radio, TV* **to b. words (out)** masquer des paroles (par un bip)

bleeper ['bliːpər] N bip *m*, récepteur *m* d'ap-pel *ou* de poche, Alphapage® *m*

bleeping ['bliːpɪŋ] N *(of electronic device)* bip-bip *m*, *pl* bips-bips

blemish ['blemɪʃ] N *(mark)* tache *f*; **there's not a b. on it** *(on piece of furniture etc)* il/elle n'a pas le moindre défaut; *Fig* **there's not a b. on her record** il n'y a rien à redire à ses états de service; **a reputation without b.** une réputation sans tache; **the case left her without a b. on her reputation** le procès se termina sans que sa réputation soit entachée ▪ **VT** *(work of art etc)* abîmer, gâcher; *Fig (reputation etc)* entacher, ternir; **blemished fruit** fruits *mpl* tachés

> Note that the French verb **blêmir** is a false friend and is never a translation for the English verb **to blemish**. It means **to go pale**.

blench [blentʃ] **VI** *(turn pale)* blêmir; **to b. with terror** pâlir de terreur

blend [blend] **N** *(of teas, whiskies, tobaccos etc)* mélange *m*
▪ **VT** *(teas, coffees, whiskies etc)* mélanger; **to b. sth with sth** mélanger qch à *ou* avec qch; **to b. one colour with another** *(mix)* mélanger une couleur avec une autre; *(harmonize)* allier *ou* marier deux couleurs; **to b. one colour into another** *(in painting)* fondre une couleur dans une autre
▪ **VI** se mêler, se mélanger, se confondre (**into** en); *(of voices etc)* se marier harmonieusement; *(of colours, flavours)* s'allier, se marier; *(of ideas etc)* fusionner; **oil does not b. with water** l'huile ne se mélange pas à l'eau; **the colours b. well** les couleurs se marient bien *ou* vont bien ensemble; **the new building blends into the background** le nouveau bâtiment se fond dans son environnement; *Fig* **she tends to b. into the background** elle a tendance à se fondre dans les décors
▸ **blend in** **VI** *(harmonize)* s'harmoniser, se marier (**with** avec); *(of person)* s'intégrer; **that new building doesn't b. in with its surroundings** ce nouveau bâtiment ne se marie pas bien *ou* ne va pas bien avec ce qui l'entoure
▪ **VT SEP** *(mix)* *(flour etc)* incorporer

blender ['blendər] **N** *(kitchen appliance)* mixer *m*, mixeur *m*

blending ['blendɪŋ] **N** *(of teas, tobaccos etc)* mélange *m*; *(of two characteristics)* alliance *f*; *(in wine-making)* coupage *m*

bless [bles] **VT** *(pt, pp* **blessed** [blest], *pp Arch* **blest** [blest])* **1** *(of God, priest) (people)* bénir; *(bell)* consacrer, bénir; **I b. the day I learnt to swim** béni soit le jour où j'ai appris à nager; **God b. you!** que Dieu vous bénisse!; **b. you!** *(when sb sneezes)* à vos souhaits!; *Fam* **b. you for doing the washing-up** merci bien d'avoir fait la vaisselle; **Mary, b. her, has agreed to do it** Mary, Dieu soit loué, a accepté de le faire; **b. her (heart)!** quel ange! **2** *usu passive (be fortunate in possessing)* **to be blessed with sth** jouir de qch, avoir le bonheur de posséder qch; **to be blessed with a cheerful disposition** être doté d'un heureux caractère; **they have been blessed with two fine children** ils ont deux enfants adorables; *Iron* **they are blessed with eight children** ils ont huit enfants sur les bras; *Fam* **he hasn't a penny to b. himself with** il n'a pas le sou **3** *(glorify)* **to b. God** bénir *ou* adorer Dieu **4** *Old-fashioned (expressing surprise)* **b. me!, (God) b. my soul!** mon Dieu!; **well, I'm blest!** par exemple!; **I'm blest if I know** que le diable m'emporte si je le sais

blessed ['blesɪd] **ADJ 1** *Rel (Sacrament, Virgin etc)* saint; **the late king of b. memory** le feu roi, d'heureuse mémoire; *Bible* **b. are the poor in spirit** heureux les pauvres d'esprit **2** *Fam (intensifier)* **every b. day** tous les jours que Dieu fait; **the whole b. day** toute la sainte journée; **the whole b. lot** tout le bazar, tout le bataclan; **it's a b. nuisance having to ...** quelle barbe d'avoir à ...; **I can't see a b. thing** je n'y vois rien

blessedly ['blesɪdlɪ] **ADV** parfaitement; **the speech was b. short** Dieu merci, le discours fut bref

blessedness ['blesɪdnɪs] **N** félicité *f*; *Rel* béatitude *f*

blessing ['blesɪŋ] **N 1** *(divine sanction, favour)* bénédiction *f*; **to give** *or* **pronounce the b.** donner la bénédiction; **to ask** *or* **say a b.** *(at meal)* dire le bénédicité; **the blessings of God** les grâces *fpl* de Dieu; **to give a plan one's b.** donner sa bénédiction à un projet; **it's a b. no one was hurt** c'est une bénédiction que personne n'ait été blessé **2** *(benefit, advantage)* **the blessings of civilization** les bienfaits *mpl* de la civilisation; **it turned out to be a b. in disguise** à la longue, j'ai/il a *etc* pu m'en/s'en/*etc* féliciter; **losing my job was a b. in disguise** finalement, ça a été une bonne chose de perdre mon travail; **to count one's blessings** s'estimer heureux avec ce qu'on a; **count your blessings** ne te plains pas, estime-toi heureux

blest [blest] **ADJ** bienheureux
▪ **NPL** *Rel Arch* **the B.** les bienheureux *mpl*, les saints *mpl* du Paradis

blether ['bleðər] *Fam* **N 1** *(nonsense)* paroles *fpl* en l'air, bêtises *fpl* **2** *(person)* = personne *f* qui parle à tort et à travers *ou* qui dit des bêtises
▪ **VI** parler à tort et à travers, dire des bêtises; **blethering idiot** espèce *f* d'idiot

blight [blaɪt] **N 1** *Agr (on cereals)* rouille *f*; *(on potatoes)* brunissure *f*; *(on peaches etc)* cloque *f* **2** *Fig* influence *f* néfaste; **his arrival cast a b. over the company** son arrivée a jeté un froid sur l'assistance
▪ **VT** *Agr (wheat)* rouiller; *(of wind)* flétrir; *Fig* **to b. sb's hopes** anéantir les espoirs de qn; *Fig* **a marriage blighted by money problems** un mariage assombri par des problèmes d'argent

blighter ['blaɪtər] **N** *Old-fashioned Br Fam* **1** *(fellow)* individu *m*, type *m*; **poor b.** pauvre type; **(you) lucky b.!** veinard! **2** *Pej (despicable person)* salaud *m*; **the little b.** le petit coquin

Blighty ['blaɪtɪ] **N** *Br Mil, Hist Fam (Britain)* Grande-Bretagne *f*, le pays; *(wound)* = pendant la Première Guerre mondiale, une blessure suffisamment grave pour qu'elle nécessite un rapatriement en Grande-Bretagne

blimey ['blaɪmɪ] **INT** *Br Sl* mince alors!

blimp [blɪmp] **N 1** *Aviat* (petit) dirigeable *m* de reconnaissance **2** *Br Fig (reactionary)* réactionnaire *m* endurci; **a real Colonel B.** une vraie culotte de peau, un scrogneugneu

blind [blaɪnd] **ADJ 1** *(person)*, *Fig (obedience, faith, hatred)* aveugle; **b. from birth** aveugle de naissance; **b. in one eye** borgne; **a b. man/woman** un/une aveugle; **to be struck b.** être frappé de cécité; **I'm b. without my glasses** je ne vois rien sans mes lunettes; **he's as b. as a bat** il est myope comme une taupe; **to turn a b. eye on** *or* **to sth** fermer les yeux sur qch; **to be b. to sb's faults** ne pas voir les défauts de qn, être aveugle aux défauts de qn; *Prov* **love is b.** l'amour est aveugle; *Fam* **he didn't take a b. bit of notice** il n'a pas fait la moindre attention; *Fam* **in a b. stupor** *(drunk)* bourré **2** *(bend)* masqué, sans visibilité **3** *(without exit) (window, door)* feint, aveugle
▪ **ADV** **to fire b.** tirer au jugé; *Aviat* **to fly b.** voler à l'aveuglette; *Culin* **bake b. for five minutes** cuire le fond de tarte cinq minutes; *Fam* **to go at sth b.** se lancer à l'aveuglette dans qch; **she swore b. that ...** elle a juré ses grands dieux que ...; **b. drunk** complètement ivre *ou* soûl
▪ **VT** *(person)* aveugler, rendre aveugle; *(temporarily) (of tears)* aveugler; *(dazzle)* aveugler, éblouir; **blinded ex-servicemen** aveugles *mpl* de guerre; **blinded by passion**

aveuglé par la passion; **love blinded her to his faults** aveuglée par l'amour, elle n'a pas vu ses défauts; **to b. sb to the facts** cacher les faits à qn; *Fig* **don't b. me with science** pas la peine de m'éblouir avec ta science
▪ **N 1** *Br (at window)* store *m*; *Aut (on radiator)* rideau *m*; **shop b.** *(over pavement)* banne *f* **2** *Fig (pretext)* prétexte *m*
▪ **NPL** **the b.** les aveugles *mp*
▸▸ *Br* **b. alley** impasse *f*, cul-de-sac *m*, *pl* culs-de-sac; *Fig* impasse; **b. date** *(meeting)* rendez-vous *m* *inv* *ou* rencontre *f* arrangé(e) *(avec quelqu'un qu'on ne connaît pas)*; *(person)* inconnu, -ue *(avec qui on a rendez-vous)*; *Aviat* **b. flying** vol *m* sans visibilité, vol en PSV; **b. man's buff** *(game)* colin-maillard *m*, *pl* colin-maillards; *Old-fashioned Fam* **b. school** école *f* pour aveugles *ou* pour non-voyants; **b. side** *Sport (in rugby)* côté *m* fermé; *Aut* angle *m* mort; **b. spot** *Aut (in mirror)* angle mort; *(in road)* endroit *m* sans visibilité; *Med* point *m* aveugle; *Fig (weak area)* côté faible, faiblesse *f*; *Mktg* **b. test** test *m* aveugle; *Mktg* **b. testing** tests aveugles

blinder ['blaɪndər] **N 1** *Br Sl* **to go on a b.** *(get very drunk)* se bourrer (la gueule) **2** *Sport Fam (outstanding feat)* **he played a b. (of a game)** il a eu un jeu spectaculaire; **the first goal was a b.** le premier but a été spectaculaire **3** *Am (for horse)* œillère *f*

blindfold ['blaɪndfəʊld] **ADJ** les yeux bandés
▪ **ADV** *(to enter into an undertaking)* aveuglément; *Chess (to play)* sans voir l'échiquier; **I can do it b.** *(I am very familiar with the task)* je pourrais le faire les yeux fermés
▪ **N** bandeau *m* sur les yeux; **they put a b. over my eyes** ils m'ont mis un bandeau sur les yeux
▪ **VT** **to b. sb** bander les yeux à *ou* de qn, couvrir les yeux de qn avec un bandeau; **to be blindfolded** avoir les yeux bandés, avoir un bandeau sur les yeux

blinding ['blaɪndɪŋ] **ADJ 1** *(dazzling)* aveuglant; **b. headache** mal *m* de tête effroyable; **it was a b. revelation** ça a été une véritable révélation; **the b. intensity of his criticism** l'intensité affolante de ses critiques **2** *Br Fam (excellent)* super *inv*, génial, -aux
▪ **N** *(by headlights, light etc)* éblouissement *m*

blindingly ['blaɪndɪŋlɪ] **ADV** **it's b. obvious** c'est tout à fait évident, cela saute aux yeux (**that** que)

blindly ['blaɪndlɪ] **ADV 1** *(to look at sth, sb)* sans le/la/*etc* voir; *(to grope)* à l'aveuglette **2** *Fig (to obey)* aveuglément; *(to follow)* aveuglément, sans réfléchir

blindness ['blaɪndnɪs] **N** cécité *f*; *Fig* aveuglement *m*; **b. to the facts** refus *m* d'envisager *ou* de voir les faits

blindworm ['blaɪndwɜːm] **N** orvet *m*

bling [blɪŋ], **bling-bling** ['blɪŋ('blɪŋ)] *Sl* **N** *(jewellery)* bijoux *mpl*, quincaillerie *f*
▪ **ADJ** *(ostentatious)* tape-à-l'œil; **that car is so b.!** cette voiture est vraiment tape-à-l'œil

blink [blɪŋk] **N 1** *(of eyes)* battement *m* *ou* clignement *m* de paupières **2** *(of light)* lueur *f* momentanée **3** *Br Sl* **to be on the b.** *(of television set etc)* être en panne, faire des siennes
▪ **VI 1** *(of person)* battre *ou* cligner des paupières, clignoter; *Fig* **without blinking** *(calmly, without surprise)* sans sourciller; *Fig* **he was the first to b.** *(in confrontation)* c'est lui qui a cédé le premier; **to b. at sb/sth** regarder qn/qch en clignant des yeux; **she blinked at the sight in astonishment** elle regardait et n'en croyait pas ses yeux; *Fig* **to b. at the fact that ...** *(pretend not to see)* nier le fait que ...; *Fig* **to b. at the facts** fermer les yeux sur

la vérité **2** *(of light, cursor)* clignoter
vt to b. one's eyes cligner des yeux
▸▸ *Comput* **b. rate** *(of cursor)* vitesse *f* de clignotement
▸ **blink away vt sep** *(tears)* refouler d'un battement de paupières

blinker ['blɪŋkər] **N 1** *(for horse), Fig* œillère *f* **2** *(at airfield)* phare *m* à éclats; *Aut* clignotant *m*
vt *(horse)* mettre des œillères à; *Fig* **they are very blinkered, that's very blinkered thinking on their part** ils ont des œillères

blinking ['blɪŋkɪŋ] **adj 1** *(eyes)* qui clignotent **2** *(light)* clignotant, papillotant **3** *Old-fashioned Br Fam* **what a b. nuisance!** quelle barbe!; **b. idiot!** espèce d'idiot!; **a b. good meal** un repas sacrément bon; **I b. well** did **see her there** je l'y ai vue de mes propres yeux
N 1 *(of eyes)* clignotement *m* **2** *(of light)* papillotage *m*

blintz(e) [blɪnts] **N** *Am Culin* crêpe *f* fourrée *(au fromage, aux fruits etc)*

blip [blɪp] **N** *(of radar) (on screen)* spot *m*; *(noise)* top *m* d'écho; *Fig Fam (in statistics)* écart *m* momentané; **the company suffered a b. in February when it lost that contract** l'entreprise a subi un contretemps en février lorsqu'elle a perdu ce contrat

bliss [blɪs] **N** grand bonheur *m*, béatitude *f*; **breakfast in bed, what b.!** le petit déjeuner au lit, quel bonheur!; **it was b. to plunge into the water** c'était un bonheur de plonger dans l'eau; **it's sheer b.!** c'est le bonheur total!; **isn't it b. not having your mother here!** quel bonheur de ne plus avoir ta mère ici, hein?

blissful ['blɪsfʊl] **adj** *(person)* (bien)heureux; *(holiday, weekend etc)* plein de bonheur; **we had a b. time in France** nous avons passé un merveilleux séjour en France; **... she said with a b. sigh** ... dit-elle en soupirant de bonheur; **he was in b. ignorance of what was happening** il n'avait pas la moindre idée de ce qui se passait; **I'd rather remain in b. ignorance** j'aime autant ne pas savoir

blissfully ['blɪsfʊlɪ] **adv ... she said b. ...** dit-elle, au comble du bonheur; **he smiled b.** il eut un grand sourire de bonheur; **b. happy** au comble du bonheur; **to be b. ignorant of sth** ne pas se douter le moins du monde de qch; **to be b. unaware that ...** ne pas se douter le moins du monde que ...; **the house is b. quiet without the children** la maison est merveilleusement calme sans les enfants

B-list adj *(star, celebrity, guest)* pas parmi les plus connus; **there were only B. stars among the guests** il n'y avait aucune vedette de stature internationale parmi les invités

blister ['blɪstər] **N 1** *(on skin)* ampoule *f*, cloque *f* **2** *(in paint)* cloque *f*, boursouflure *f*, *(in glass)* bulle *f*, *Metal* soufflure *f*
vt *(hand etc)* provoquer des ampoules sur
vi 1 *(of heel etc)* se couvrir d'ampoules **2** *(of paint)* cloquer
▸▸ *Br* **b. pack** *(for light bulb, pens)* blister *m*; *(for pills)* plaquette *f*

blistered ['blɪstəd] **adj** couvert d'ampoules

blistering ['blɪstərɪŋ] **adj** *(sun, heat)* brûlant, ardent; *Fig (attack)* foudroyant; **she's setting a b. pace** elle mène un train d'enfer
N 1 *(on skin)* ampoules *fpl*; **b. is inevitable** la formation d'ampoules est inévitable **2** *(of paint)* cloquage *m*

blisteringly ['blɪstərɪŋlɪ] **adv it was a b. hot day** c'était une journée d'une chaleur étouffante; **it was b. hot** il faisait une chaleur étouffante

blithe ['blaɪð] **adj** joyeux, allègre; *(irresponsible) (disregard, attitude, response etc)* désinvolte

blithely ['blaɪðlɪ] **adv** joyeusement, allègrement; *(irresponsibly)* avec désinvolture; **she b. ignored him** elle l'a ignoré avec une complète désinvolture; **he was b. unaware of the danger** il ne se doutait pas le moins du monde du danger qu'il courait

blithering ['blɪðərɪŋ] **adj** *Fam* sacré; **b. idiot!** espèce d'idiot!

BLitt [bi:'lɪt] **N** *Univ (abbr* **Bachelor of Letters)** *(diploma)* licence *f* ès lettres; *(person)* licencié, -ée ès lettres

blitz [blɪts] **N** *Mil* blitz *m*, bombardement *m* aérien; *Hist* **the B.** le Blitz; *Fig* **to have a b. on sth** s'attaquer à qch; *Fig* **the b. of holiday advertisements starts immediately after Christmas** dès que les fêtes sont finies, on est bombardé de publicité par les agences de voyages
vt bombarder; **the house was blitzed** la maison a été endommagée/détruite par un bombardement; *Fig Fam* **to b. sb with letters/complaints** bombarder qn de lettres/plaintes

blitzed [blɪtst] **adj** *Sl (drunk)* bourré; *(on drugs)* défoncé

blizzard ['blɪzəd] **N** tempête *f* de neige; *(in North America)* blizzard *m*

bloat [bləʊt] **vt** boursoufler, bouffir
vi bouffir

bloated ['bləʊtɪd] **adj** bouffi, boursouflé; *Fig (estimate, bill)* salé; **to feel b.** *(because of water retention, overeating)* se sentir ballonné *ou* gonflé; **he suffers from a b. ego** sa suffisance n'a pas de limites; **b. with pride** bouffi d'orgueil

bloater ['bləʊtər] **N** *(herring)* hareng *m* bouffi

blob [blɒb] **N** *(of colour)* tache *f*, *(of ink)* pâté *m*

bloc [blɒk] **N** *Pol etc* bloc *m*

BLOCK [blɒk] **N 1** *(slab) (of marble, paper etc)* bloc *m*; *(of wood)* tronçon *m*; *(of chocolate)* grosse tablette *f*; *(for chopping)* billot *m*; *(for getting on horse)* montoir *m*; *(for athletes)* bloc de départ; **like a b. of stone** *(transfixed)* immobile; *(unfeeling)* dur; *(not speaking)* silencieux, muet; *Am* **to be on the b.** *(up for auction)* être mis aux enchères; **blocks** *(for children)* (jeu *m* de) cubes *mpl*; *Fam* **to have been around the block a few times** ne plus être de la première jeunesse
2 *esp Am (buildings between two streets)* pâté *m* de maisons; *Austr (plot of land)* lot *m*; **he lives two blocks from us** il habite à deux rues de nous; **it's two blocks north/south of here** c'est à deux rues d'ici vers le nord/sud; **we live on the same b.** nous habitons dans le même pâté de maisons; **to walk round the b.** faire le tour du pâté de maisons; *Br* **b. of flats** immeuble *m*
3 *(obstruction)* **traffic b.** embouteillage *m*; **mental b.** blocage *m* psychologique; **I have a mental b. about computers** je fais un blocage psychologique avec les ordinateurs; *Fin* **to put a b. on an account** bloquer un compte
4 *Sl (head)* caboche *f*; **I'll knock your b. off!** je vais te casser la gueule!
5 *(of rooms)* contingent *m*; **to book a b. of four weeks** réserver quatre semaines consécutives; **b. of seats** bloc-sièges *m inv*; *Fin* **b. of shares** paquet *m* d'actions
6 *Aut* **(engine) b.** bloc-moteur *m*, *pl* blocs-moteurs; **to put a car up on blocks** mettre une voiture sur cales
7 *Comput* bloc *m*
8 *(in engraving) (wood)* planche *f*, bois *m*
9 *Tech (pulley)* poulie *f*; **b. and tackle** palan *m*

vt 1 *(passage etc)* bloquer, obstruer; *(wheel)* bloquer, enrayer; *(flow of traffic)* entraver, gêner; *(progress)* arrêter; *Fin (cheque, account)* bloquer; **to b. sb's way** barrer le passage *ou* le chemin à qn; **to b. the view** cacher la vue; *Parl* **to b. a bill** faire obstruction à un projet de loi
2 *Sport (ball)* bloquer; *Ftbl (opponent)* gêner; **the goalkeeper blocked the shot** le gardien arrêta le tir; *Tennis* **she blocked the serve magnificently** elle fit un superbe retour de service
3 *Comput (text)* sélectionner; **to b. text** sélectionner un bloc de texte; **to b. and copy** sélectionner et copier
4 *(room)* retenir, bloquer
5 *(actors)* = faire prendre leurs marques aux acteurs; *(scene, play)* prendre les marques pour
▸▸ **b. association** association *f* de riverains; **b. booking** *(of theatre tickets etc)* réservation *f* *ou* location *f* de groupe; *Typ* **b. capital** *(caractère *m*)* majuscule *f*; **in b. capitals** en majuscules; *Comput* **b. copy** copie *f* de bloc; **b. diagram** *Comput, Geog* bloc-diagramme *m*, *pl* blocs-diagrammes; *Electron* schéma *m* (de principe); *Typ* **b. letter** (caractère *m*) majuscule; **in b. letters** en majuscules; *Comput* **b. marker** délimiteur *m* de bloc; *Comput* **b. structure** *(of file)* structure *f* de bloc; *Pol, Ind* **b. vote** = mode *m* de scrutin utilisé par les syndicats britanniques par opposition au mode de scrutin "un homme, une voix"
▸ **block in vt sep** *esp Aut (person)* empêcher de sortir, bloquer le passage à; **I'm blocked in** je suis coincé
▸ **block off vt sep** *(street)* barrer
▸ **block out vt sep 1** *(prevent entry of)* empêcher d'entrer *ou* de passer; **those trees b. out all the sun** ces arbres empêchent le soleil de passer; **to b. out the memory of sb/sth** refouler le souvenir de qn/qch; **it's impossible to b. that music out** il est impossible d'ignorer cette musique
2 *(draft) (book, project)* ébaucher, esquisser
▸ **block up vt sep 1** *(close) (hole)* boucher; *(door, window)* boucher, murer
2 *(clog) (pipe etc)* obstruer, engorger; *(sink)* boucher

blockade [blɒ'keɪd] **N** *Mil, Pol* blocus *m*; **to impose/break a b.** imposer/forcer un blocus; **to raise** *or* **lift a b.** lever un blocus; *Hist* **to run the b.** forcer le blocus
vt 1 *(town, port)* bloquer, faire le blocus de; *(fortified place)* faire le blocus de **2** *Am (flow of traffic)* bloquer; *(street)* encombrer
▸▸ *Hist* **b. runner** forceur *m* de blocus

blockage ['blɒkɪdʒ] **N** *(of pipe, artery etc)* obstruction *f*, *(in street)* embouteillage *m*

blockbuster ['blɒkbʌstər] **N** *Fam (film)* superproduction *f*, *(book)* best-seller *m*, *pl* best-sellers

blocked [blɒkt] **adj** *(account, cheque, market)* bloqué; **b. up** bouché; **b. space** *(reserved)* espace *m* réservé

blockhead ['blɒkhed] **N** *Fam* lourdaud *m*

blockhouse ['blɒkhaʊs] **N** *Mil* blockhaus *m*

blocking ['blɒkɪŋ] **N 1** *(of street)* encombrement *m*, embouteillage *m*; *(of port)* blocus *m* **2** *Elec (of current)* blocage *m* **3** *(in bookbinding)* gaufrage *m*, frappe *f*
▸▸ *Comput* **b. software** logiciel *m* de filtrage

block-oriented adj *Comput* orienté bloc

blog [blɒg] **N** *Comput (abbr* **weblog)** blog *m*

bloke [bləʊk] **N** *Br Fam (man)* type *m*

blokeish ['bləʊkɪʃ] **adj** *Br Fam* = typique d'un style de vie caractérisé par de fréquentes sorties entre copains, généralement copieusement arrosées, et un goût prononcé pour le sport et les activités de groupe

blond, f blonde [blɒnd] ADJ, N blond, f blonde

blood [blʌd] N sang m; **to give b.** (of donor) donner du sang; **his b. will be on your hands** tu porteras la responsabilité de sa mort; Fig **his b. is up** il est furieux; **it makes my b. boil / run cold** cela me fait bouillir/me glace le sang; **to commit a crime in cold b.** commettre un crime de sang-froid; Fig **the committee needs new** or **fresh b.** le comité a besoin d'être rajeuni; **to shed** or **spill b.** verser le sang; Fig **it's not worth shedding** or **spilling b. over** inutile de se battre pour ça; Fig **to be out for b.** chercher à se venger; Fig **to be after** or **out for sb's b.** vouloir se venger de qn, en vouloir à qn; Fig **the boss is after your b.** le patron en a après toi; Prov **it's like trying to get b. out of a stone** c'est comme si on se heurtait à un mur; **the theatre is in her b.** elle a le théâtre dans le sang; Prov **b. is thicker than water** la famille passe avant tout; **prince of the b.** prince m du sang; **warm the milk until it is at b. temperature** chauffe le lait jusqu'à ce qu'il atteigne la température du corps

VT **1** (first-time hunter) initier (en l'aspergeant du sang de la bête morte); (hounds) donner le goût du sang à **2** esp Sp Fig initier ►► Med **b. bank** banque f du sang; **b. bath** carnage m, massacre m; **b. blister** pinçon m; **b. brother** frère m de sang; Anat **b. cell** cellule f sanguine, globule m (du sang); Med **b. count** numération f globulaire; Med **b. donor** donneur, -euse de sang; **b. doping** = transfusion f sanguine utilisée comme méthode de dopage; Med **b. group** groupe m sanguin; **b. horse** pur-sang m inv; **b. money** prix m du sang; **b. orange** (orange f) sanguine f; Biol **b. plasma** plasma m sanguin; Med **b. poisoning** septicémie f; Med **b. pressure** tension f (artérielle); Med **b. product** dérivé m du sang; Culin **b. pudding** boudin m (noir); **b. red** (colour) rouge sang m inv, **b. relation** parent, -ente par le sang; Med **b. sample** prise f de sang; Culin **b. sausage** boudin (noir); Med **b. serum** sérum m sanguin; **b. sports** chasse f, Med **b. test** analyse f de sang

blood-and-thunder ADJ (film, novel etc) sensationnel, mélodramatique

bloodcurdling [ˈblʌdkɜːdlɪŋ] ADJ (story, scream) à vous tourner les sangs, à (vous) figer le sang

-blooded [ˈblʌdɪd] SUFF **hot-/cold-b.** à sang chaud/froid

bloodhound [ˈblʌdhaʊnd] N (dog), Fig (detective) limier m

bloodiness [ˈblʌdɪnɪs] N état m sanglant; (of battle) sauvagerie f

bloodless [ˈblʌdlɪs] ADJ **1** (victory etc) sans effusion de sang **2** (pale) exsangue, pâle **3** (lifeless) sans vitalité

bloodlessly [ˈblʌdlɪslɪ] ADV sans effusion de sang

blood-letting N **1** (violent feud, bloodshed) effusion f de sang **2** Med, Hist saignée f

blood-red ADJ rouge sang inv

bloodshed [ˈblʌdʃed] N **1** effusion f de sang; **without b.** sans verser de sang **2** (slaughter) carnage m

bloodshot [ˈblʌdʃɒt] ADJ (eye) injecté de sang; **to become b.** (of eye) s'injecter

bloodstain [ˈblʌdsteɪn] N tache f de sang

bloodstained [ˈblʌdsteɪnd] ADJ taché ou souillé de sang, ensanglanté

bloodstock [ˈblʌdstɒk] N pur-sang mpl

bloodstone [ˈblʌdstəʊn] N Miner jaspe m sanguin

bloodstream [ˈblʌdstriːm] N Physiol sang m

bloodsucker [ˈblʌdsʌkər] N Zool sangsue f, Fig Fam sangsue, parasite m

bloodsucking [ˈblʌdsʌkɪŋ] ADJ ATTRIB Zool hématophage; Fig Fam vampirique

bloodthirsty [ˈblʌdθɜːstɪ] ADJ (person) sanguinaire; (film, book) très violent

bloody [ˈblʌdɪ] ADJ **1** (stained with blood) ensanglanté, taché de sang; (revolution, battle etc) sanglant; **he came home with a b. nose** il est rentré en saignant du nez; Fig **to give sb a b. nose** donner une raclée à qn **2** Br Sl (intensifier) sacré; **a b. liar** un sacré menteur; **(you) b. fool!** espèce d'imbécile!; **b. hell!** merde, bon sang!; **he wouldn't even tell me his b. name!** il n'a même pas voulu me dire son nom, cet animal!; **politicians are all the b. same!** ces foutus hommes politiques sont tous les mêmes!

ADV Br Sl **it's b. hot!** on crève de chaleur!; **he can b. well do it himself!** il n'a qu'à se démerder tout seul!; **I b. well am going out** j'ai bien l'intention de sortir (et personne ne m'en empêchera); **I'm b. tired** je suis complètement crevé; **it's not b. likely!** il n'y a pas de danger!; **I wish he'd b. stop it!** quand est-ce qu'il va s'arrêter, merde!

VT (pt, pp bloodied) (one's hands etc) ensanglanter, souiller de sang; Fig **to b. one's hands** se salir les mains

►► **B. Mary** Hist (queen) = surnom m de la reine Marie Tudor, donné par les protestants qu'elle persécuta; (cocktail) bloody mary m inv

bloody-minded ADJ Br Sl **he's just b.** c'est un mauvais coucheur; **don't be so b.** arrête d'emmerder le monde

bloody-mindedness [-ˈmaɪndɪdnɪs] N Br Sl **it's sheer b.** ce n'est rien que pour emmerder le monde; **the b. of the decision is unbelievable** la décision, prise uniquement pour emmerder le monde, est incroyable; **I admire her b.** j'admire la façon qu'elle a d'emmerder le monde

bloom [bluːm] N **1** (flower) fleur f; **to come** or **burst into b.** fleurir; **flower in b.** fleur éclose; **the roses are in b.** les roses sont ouvertes; **in full b.** épanoui; Lit **in the b. of youth** à ou dans la fleur de l'âge; **the constant arguing soon took the b. off their marriage** les disputes perpétuelles firent rapidement perdre son charme à leur mariage **2** (on grape, peach etc) velouté m, pruine f, duvet m; (of cheeks) éclat m; Chem **cobalt/zinc b.** fleur f de cobalt/zinc

VI (of plant) fleurir, être en fleur; Fig (of child) être éclatant ou resplendissant de santé

bloomer [ˈbluːmər] N Br Fam (mistake) bourde f, (in social circumstances) gaffe f

bloomers [ˈbluːməz] NPL culotte f bouffante (de femme)

blooming [ˈbluːmɪŋ] ADJ **1** (flower) éclos; Fig florissant; **b. with health** resplendissant de santé **2** Br Fam (intensifier) **you b. idiot!** espèce d'idiot!; **it's a b. lie!** ça, pour un mensonge!; **the woman's a b. genius** cette femme, c'est vraiment un génie

ADV Br Fam **I b. well will go!** et moi, je te dis que j'irai!

N floraison f, fleuraison f

blooper [ˈbluːpər] N Am Fam = bloomer

blootered [ˈbluːtəd] ADJ Scot Fam (drunk) pété, bourré

blossom [ˈblɒs(ə)m] N (of trees) fleur f, tree **in b.** arbre m en fleur(s); **apple/cherry/orange b.** fleur de pommier/de cerisier/d'oranger; **to come into b.** fleurir

VI (of tree) fleurir; Fig (of friendship, relationship) s'épanouir; **she had blossomed into a charming young woman** elle était devenue une charmante jeune femme

► **blossom out** VI = blossom VI

blossoming [ˈblɒsəmɪŋ] N fleuraison f, floraison f, Fig épanouissement m

ADJ qui commence à fleurir; Fig (friendship, partnership) en herbe

blot [blɒt] N tache f, (of ink) pâté m; Fig **a b. on sb's honour/reputation** une tache faite à l'honneur/la réputation de qn; Fig **to be a b. on the landscape** (of building) gâcher le paysage

VT (-tt-) **1** (stain) tacher, souiller; (with ink) faire des pâtés sur; Fig **to b. one's copybook (with sb)** se faire mal voir (de qn) **2** (letter etc) passer un buvard sur; (lipstick) passer un Kleenex® sur

VI (of blotting paper) boire l'encre

► **blot out** VT SEP (obliterate) (memory etc) effacer; (word) rayer, barrer; (of fog etc) (feature of landscape etc) cacher, masquer

blotch [blɒtʃ] N **1** (of ink, paint) tache f, éclaboussure f **2** (on skin) tache f, marbrure f

VT (skin) couvrir de taches; **cold blotches the skin** le froid marbre la peau; **her face was blotched with tears** son visage portait des traces de larmes

VI **this pen blotches** ce stylo fuit

blotchy [ˈblɒtʃɪ] ADJ tacheté; (complexion) brouillé, couperosé

blotter [ˈblɒtər] N **1** (for ink) (paper) buvard m; (desk pad) sous-main m inv; (with handle) tampon m buvard **2** Com Old-fashioned brouillard m, main f courante

blotting [ˈblɒtɪŋ] N séchage m au papier buvard

►► **b. pad** (bloc m) buvard m; (large) sous-main m inv; **b. paper** (papier m) buvard

blotto [ˈblɒtəʊ] ADJ Br Sl (drunk) bourré

blouse [blaʊz] N **1** (woman's) chemisier m, corsage m **2** Am (sailor's etc) vareuse f

Note that the French word **blouse** is a false friend. Its most common meaning is **overall**.

BLOW¹ [bləʊ]

N	souffle **1** ▪ coup **2**
VI	souffler **1, 2**
VT	faire bouger **1** ▪ souffler **2** ▪ jouer de **3** ▪ faire sauter **6** ▪ gâcher **7** ▪ claquer **8**

N **1** (through mouth) souffle m; **give your nose a good b.** (to child) mouche-toi bien

2 (of whistle) coup m

3 Br Sl (cannabis) shit m; Am Sl (cocaine) coke f, neige f, (heroin) héro f, blanche f

VI (pt blew [bluː], pp blown [bləʊn]) **1** (of wind) souffler; **the wind's blowing from the west** le vent souffle de l'ouest; **it was blowing a gale** le vent soufflait en tempête; **the wind was blowing down the chimney** le vent s'engouffrait dans la cheminée; **my papers blew out of the window** mes papiers se sont envolés par la fenêtre; **the door blew open** le vent a ouvert la porte

2 (of person, animal) souffler; (of whale) rejeter l'eau par les évents; (of whistle) retentir, se faire entendre; **to b. on one's fingers** souffler dans ses doigts; Fam **to b. into town** arriver en ville à l'improviste; **when did you b. into town?** quand est-ce que tu es arrivé?

3 Am Fam (boast) se vanter

4 (of fuse) sauter; (of boiler etc) exploser

5 Fam **b.!** zut!

VT **1** (of wind) faire bouger; **the wind is blowing the rain against the windows** le vent pousse la pluie contre les vitres; **to b. a ship ashore** (of wind) pousser un navire à la côte; **to be blown out to sea** être poussé au large; **he was nearly blown off his feet** (by wind, explosion) il a failli être emporté

2 (of person) souffler; **to b. one's nose** se moucher; **he blew the dust off the book** il

a soufflé sur le livre pour enlever la poussière; **to b. sb a kiss** envoyer un baiser à qn **3** *(musical instrument)* jouer de; **to b. a whistle** donner un coup de sifflet; **he blew the whistle** il donna un coup de sifflet; *Fig* **to b. the whistle on sb** balancer qn; **to b. the dust off sth** souffler sur qch pour enlever la poussière; **to b. the horn** sonner du cor; *Fig* **to b. one's own trumpet** chanter ses propres louanges, se faire mousser **4** *(soap bubbles)* faire; *(glass)* souffler; *(egg)* vider **5** *(horse etc)* essouffler **6** *(fuse, gasket, safe)* faire sauter; *Fam* **the Grand Canyon blew my mind** j'ai vraiment été époustouflé par le Grand Canyon!; *Fam* **the prices blew my mind** les prix m'ont affolé **7** *Fam (ruin, spoil)* gâcher, bousiller; *(opportunity)* louper; **that's blown it!** ça a tout gâché *ou* bousillé, ça a tout fait louper **8** *Fam (money)* claquer **(on** dans) **9** *Fam* **b. the expense!** au diable l'avarice!; **I'll be blowed if ...** je veux bien être pendu si ...; **well, I'm blowed!** ça, par exemple!; **b. it!** zut!
▸▸ *Vulg* **b. job** *(oral sex)* pipe *f*, **to give sb a b. job** tailler une pipe à qn
▸ **blow about** VI *(of leaves etc)* voler çà et là VT SEP agiter, faire voler; *(leaves etc)* disperser
▸ **blow away** VT SEP **1** *(of wind etc)* emporter **2** *Am Sl (kill)* descendre, flinguer VI *(of papers etc)* s'envoler; **his hat blew away in the wind** son chapeau s'est envolé à cause du vent; **all my cares have blown away** tous mes soucis se sont évanouis *ou* envolés
▸ **blow down** VT SEP *(of wind)* *(fence etc)* abattre, renverser; *(tree)* abattre; *Old-fashioned Fam* **well b. me down!** c'est pas Dieu possible! VI *(of fence etc)* s'abattre, se renverser; *(of tree)* s'abattre
▸ **blow in** VT SEP **1** *(of explosion, wind etc)* *(window, door)* enfoncer **2** *(of person)* souffler; **b. some more air in** souffle un peu plus d'air dedans VI **1** *(of window etc)* s'enfoncer **2 the dust is blowing in** le vent fait entrer la poussière **3** *Fam (of person)* arriver à l'improviste; **when did you b. in?** quand est-ce que tu es arrivé?
▸ **blow off** VT SEP **1** *(of wind)* *(hat, slates)* emporter; **the wind blew the papers off my desk** le vent a fait s'envoler les papiers qui étaient sur mon bureau **2** *(of person)* *(dust etc)* enlever en soufflant dessus **3** *(with gun, explosives)* faire sauter; **the gunman threatened to b. their heads off** l'homme au pistolet a menacé de leur faire sauter la cervelle; **she got her hand blown off** sa main a été arrachée dans l'explosion VI *(of hat etc)* s'envoler
▸ **blow out** VT SEP **1** *(candle)* souffler **2** *(air)* chasser, expulser; *(one's cheeks)* gonfler; **to b. one's brains out** se faire sauter la cervelle; **to b. sb's brains out** faire sauter la cervelle à qn; **to b. itself out** *(of storm)* se dissiper, se calmer VI **1** *(of candle)* s'éteindre **2** *Aut etc (of gasket)* sauter; *(of tyre)* éclater; *Elec (of fuse)* sauter
▸ **blow over** VT SEP *(of wind)* *(table etc)* renverser VI **1** *(fall down)* se renverser **2** *(come to an end)* *(of storm)* se calmer, se dissiper; *Fig (of argument)* se calmer; **the scandal soon blew over** le scandale a été vite oublié
▸ **blow up** VI *(of mine)* éclater, sauter; *(of boiler etc)* crever, exploser; *Fig (of person)* piquer une colère **(at sb** contre qn); **the ar-**

gument blew up out of nowhere la dispute a commencé sans raison; **to b. up into a crisis** *(of situation)* prendre les proportions d'une crise; **there's a gale blowing up** il se prépare une tempête; *Fig* **to b. up in sb's face** *(go wrong)* se retourner contre qn VT SEP **1** *(bomb, booby-trapped car etc)* faire sauter, (faire) exploser; *(building)* faire sauter **2** *(tyre, balloon etc)* gonfler **3** *Phot* agrandir; **I'd like this photograph blown up** j'aimerais un agrandissement de cette photo **4** *Fam (exaggerate)* *(incident etc)* exagérer; **you're blowing this up out of all proportion** tu en fais un drame

blow² N *(with fist etc)*, *Fig (of fate)* coup *m*; **at the first b.** du premier coup; **at a (single) b.** d'un (seul) coup; **to strike a b.** asséner *ou* donner un coup; *Fig* **to strike a b. for/ against sth** remporter une bataille en faveur de/contre qch; **to come to blows, to exchange blows** en venir aux coups *ou* aux mains; **to return b. for b.** rendre coup pour coup; **his death is a sad b. to his family** sa mort est un rude coup pour sa famille; **b. to sb's pride** atteinte *f* (faite) à l'amour-propre de qn

blowback ['bləʊbæk] N *Aut* retour *m* de flamme

blow-by N *Aut* fuite *f* de gaz

blow-by-blow ADJ *(account)* minutieux, détaillé

blowcock ['bləʊkɒk] N robinet *m* d'extraction *ou* de vidange

blowdart ['bləʊdɑːt] N petite flèche *f*

blow-dry N *(at hairdresser's)* brushing *m* VT *(one's hair)* sécher (avec un séchoir); **to b. sb's hair** faire un brushing à qn

blow-drying N **too much b. can damage your hair** à force d'être séchés au séchoir, les cheveux s'abîment

blower ['bləʊə(r)] N **1** *Br Fam (telephone)* bigophone *m*; **on the b.** au bigophone; **to get on the b. to sb** passer un coup de fil à qn **2** *(in ventilation system)* turbine *f* de ventilation; *(supercharger)* soufflante *f*

blowfly, *pl* **blowflies** ['bləʊflaɪ, -flaɪz] N mouche *f* de la viande, mouche bleue

blowgun ['bləʊɡʌn] N *Am (for darts)* sarbacane *f*

blowhard ['bləʊhɑːd] N *Fam (boaster)* vantard, -arde, crâneur, -euse

blowhole ['bləʊhəʊl] N **1** *Zool (of whale)* évent *m* **2** *(in ice)* = trou *m* où un phoque etc vient respirer **3** *(in tunnel)* bouche *f* d'aération

blowing ['bləʊɪŋ] N **1** *(of wind)* souffle *m*; **he could hear the b. of the wind outside** il entendait le vent souffler dehors **2** *(of glass)* soufflage *m*

blowlamp ['bləʊlæmp] N **1** *(for welding, brazing)* chalumeau *m*, lampe *f* à souder *ou* à braser **2** *(for removing paint)* brûloir *m*

blown [bləʊn] ADJ **1** *(person)* essoufflé, hors d'haleine **2** *Elec* **b. fuse** fusible *m* fondu, plomb *m* sauté
▸▸ **b. glass** verre *m* soufflé

blowout ['bləʊaʊt] N **1** *Sl (large meal)* gueuleton *m*, grande bouffe *f*; **we had a b. last night** on a fait un gueuleton hier soir **2** *Aut etc (of tyre)* éclatement *m* **3** *Min etc (of gas, oil etc)* éruption *f* au cours d'un sondage

blowpipe ['bləʊpaɪp] N **1** *(for darts)* sarbacane *f* **2** *Chem, Metal* chalumeau *m*; *(of glassblower)* fêle *f*

blowtorch ['bləʊtɔːtʃ] N *Am* = **blowlamp**

blow-up N *Fam* **1** *(argument)* dispute *f*, bagarre *f*; *(tantrum)* accès *m* de fureur; **we had a b. last night** on s'est bagarrés *ou* disputés hier soir **2** *Phot* agrandissement *m*

blow-valve N *(on steam boiler)* reniflard *m*

blowy ['bləʊɪ] ADJ *(day, weather)* de (grand) vent

blowzy ['blaʊzɪ] ADJ *(woman)* négligé

blub [blʌb] VI *Fam* (**-bb-**) = **blubber²**

blubber¹ ['blʌbə(r)] N *(of whale)* graisse *f*, lard *m*; *Fam (of person)* graisse

blubber² VI *Fam* chialer, pleurer comme un veau *ou* une madeleine (**over** sur)

blubbering ['blʌbərɪŋ] N larmoiements *mpl*

bludge [blʌdʒ] VI *Austr Fam* **1** *(shirk responsibilities)* se défiler **2** *(cadge)* quémander **3** *(live off the State)* vivre en parasite de la société

bludgeon ['blʌdʒən] N gourdin *m*, matraque *f* VT matraquer; **he was bludgeoned to death** il a été matraqué à mort; *Fig* **to b. sb into doing sth** forcer qn à faire qch par des méthodes brutales

bludger ['blʌdʒə(r)] N *Austr Fam* **1** *(shirker)* tire-au-flanc *m inv* **2** *(cadger)* pique-assiette *mf inv*, parasite *m* **3** *(who lives off the State)* parasite *m* de la société

blue¹ [bluː] ADJ **1** *(dress, sky etc)* bleu; **to go** *or* **turn b.** *(of sky, litmus paper)* virer au bleu; *(of person) (because suffocating, near death)* devenir violacé *ou* bleu; **to go** *or* **turn b. with cold** devenir bleu de froid; **her face was b. with cold** elle avait le visage violacé par le froid *ou* bleu de froid; *Fam* **I've told you until I'm b. in the face** je me tue à te le dire; *Fam* **she can complain until she's b. in the face** elle peut se plaindre autant qu'elle veut; *Fam* **to be in a b. funk** avoir une trouille bleue; *Fam* **to scream** *or* **yell b. murder** crier comme un putois, hurler comme un damné; **once in a b. moon** tous les trente-six du mois; *Fig* **to take a b. pencil to sth** censurer qch; *Am* **to talk a b. streak** tchatcher **2** *Fam (depressed)* triste, déprimé; **to feel b.** avoir le cafard **3** *Fam (indecent) (joke)* grivois, paillard; **to tell b. jokes** en dire de vertes, en raconter des vertes et des pas mûres **4** *Pol* conservateur, -trice N **1** *(colour)* bleu *m*; *Fig* **a bolt from the b.** un événement imprévu; **her resignation was** *or* **came like a bolt from the b.** sa démission a été une véritable surprise; **he arrived out of the b.** il est arrivé à l'improviste; **his resignation came out of the b.** personne ne s'attendait à ce qu'il démissionne; **you can't just fire him out of the b. like that** tu ne peux pas le renvoyer du jour au lendemain comme ça **2 the blues** *Mus* le blues; *Fam (depression)* le cafard; **to sing the blues** chanter le blues; *Am Fig (complain)* pleurnicher; **to have a fit of the blues, to get the blues** avoir le cafard; **this kind of weather gives me the blues** ce temps me donne le cafard **3** *Pol* conservateur, -trice; **a true b.** *(patriot)* un(e) patriote; *Pol* un conservateur, une conservatrice **4** *Sport* **Oxford/Cambridge b.** membre *m* d'une équipe sportive de l'université d'Oxford/de Cambridge **5** *Mil* **the Blues** *Br* la Cavalerie de la Maison du Souverain; *Am Hist* l'armée *f* du Nord
▸▸ *Med* **b. baby** enfant *mf* bleu(e); **b. blood** sang *m* bleu *ou* noble; **b. cheese** (fromage *m*) bleu; **b. chip** *St Exch (stock)* valeur *f* de père de famille *ou* de premier ordre; *Fin (investment)* placement *m* de bon rapport; **b. film** film *m* porno; **b. fox** *(animal)* isatis *m*, renard *m* bleu; *(fur)* renard bleu; **b. movie** film porno; **b. ribbon** *(first prize)* premier prix *m*; **b. rinse** rinçage *m* à reflets bleus; *Zool* **b. whale** baleine *f* bleue

blue² VT *Br Fam* **to b. one's money** claquer

son argent (**on** dans); **don't tell me you've blued the lot!** ne me dis pas que tu as tout claqué!

blue-arsed fly [-ɑːst-] N Br Sl **to run about** or **around like a b.** courir dans tous les sens

Bluebeard ['bluːbɪəd] N Barbe-Bleue m

bluebell ['bluːbel] N (flower) jacinthe f sauvage ou des bois; Scot (harebell) campanule f

blueberry ['bluːb(ə)rɪ] N (shrub, fruit) airelle f, myrtille f, Can bleuet m

bluebird ['bluːbɜːd] N rouge-gorge m bleu, pl rouges-gorges bleus

blue-black ADJ (hair, plumage) noir aux reflets bleus; (sky) bleu (de) nuit; (ink, coat) bleu-noir inv

bluebottle ['bluːbɒt(ə)l] N 1 (insect) mouche f de la viande 2 Old-fashioned Br Fam (policeman) flic m

blue-chip ADJ St Exch
▸▸ **b. company** affaire f de premier ordre; **b. stocks, b. shares** valeurs fpl de père de famille ou de tout repos

blue-collar ADJ
▸▸ **b. union** syndicat m ouvrier; **b. worker** col m bleu

blue-eyed ADJ aux yeux bleus; Br Fam **his mother's b. boy** le chouchou de sa maman, le petit chéri de sa maman; **the boss's b. boy** le chouchou du patron

bluegrass ['bluːgrɑːs, -æs] N 1 **the B. state** Kentucky m 2 Mus folklore m du Kentucky

blue-green ADJ bleu-vert inv

blueness ['bluːnɪs] N bleu m

blue-pencil VT Old-fashioned (article) censurer

blueprint ['bluːprɪnt] N plan m, Spec épure f, Fig **a b. for success** une recette ou une garantie de succès

blue-ribbon ADJ
▸▸ Am **b. committee** comité m constitué par des personnalités; Sport **b. event** épreuve f phare; Law **b. jury** jury m d'experts

bluestocking ['bluːstɒkɪŋ] N Pej (woman) bas-bleu m, pl bas-bleus

Bluetooth ['bluːtuːθ] N Tel Bluetooth m

bluff¹ [blʌf] ADJ 1 (cliff, coast) escarpé, à pic 2 (person) carré et sincère
N (cliff) cap m ou falaise f à pic, à-pic m inv

bluff² N 1 (at poker) bluff m; **to call sb's b.** (at poker) inviter qn à mettre cartes sur table; Fig prendre qn au mot 2 (deception) bluff m
VT Cards etc bluffer; Fig **he bluffed her into agreeing** il a bluffé pour la faire accepter
VI bluffer, faire du bluff; Cards bluffer
▸ **bluff out** VT SEP (use cleverness) **to b. one's way out of a tricky situation** se tirer d'affaire par un coup de bluff; **we'll just have to b. it out** nous n'aurons qu'à bluffer

bluffer ['blʌfər] N bluffeur, -euse

blunder ['blʌndər] N bévue f, Fam gaffe f
VI faire une bévue ou Fam une gaffe; **to b. along** avancer d'un pas maladroit; (in task) progresser tant bien que mal; **she was blundering about the room** elle avançait dans la pièce en se cognant contre tout ce qu'elle rencontrait; **to b. against** or **into sth** heurter qch, se heurter contre ou à qch; **to b. against** or **into sb** heurter qn; **she blundered into a situation she knew nothing about** elle s'est trouvée prise dans une situation dont elle ignorait tout; **he managed to b. through** il s'en est tiré tant bien que mal; **to b. on the truth/the solution** tomber sur la vérité/la solution par accident

blunderbuss ['blʌndəbʌs] N Hist tromblon m

blunderer ['blʌndərər] N gaffeur, -euse

blundering ['blʌndərɪŋ] ADJ maladroit
N maladresse f

blunt [blʌnt] ADJ 1 (knife, cutting edge etc) émoussé; (pencil) mal taillé; Law (instrument) contondant 2 Fig (person) brusque, carré; (question) brusque; (reply) carré; (fact) brutal, -aux; (refusal) net, carré; **to be b., ...** pour parler franchement, ...
VT 1 (knife etc) émousser; (pencil) épointer 2 Fig (sb's feelings, anger) émousser

bluntly ['blʌntlɪ] ADV (to ask) brusquement; (to reply) carrément, brutalement; **to put it b., ...** (pour parler) franchement, ...; **to speak b.** parler net ou carrément

bluntness ['blʌntnɪs] N 1 (of knife, sword etc) manque m de tranchant; **because of the b. of the pencil** parce que le crayon n'avait pas de pointe 2 Fig (of person) brusquerie f, (of question, manner, attitude) rudesse f

blur [blɜːr] N (vague shape) forme f confuse; Phot flou m; **without my glasses, everything is a b.** sans mes lunettes, je suis complètement dans le brouillard; **b. of tears** voile m de larmes; Fig **it's all a b. now** (of past events) ce n'est plus qu'un vague souvenir; **her memories were a b.** ses souvenirs étaient très vagues; **the first years of her marriage had gone by in a b.** les premières années de son mariage étaient passées à toute vitesse; **when travelling at such speeds, the countryside is little more than a b.** quand on avance à une telle vitesse, le paysage n'est qu'une suite de formes confuses
VT (-rr-) 1 (make hazy) brouiller, troubler; **eyes blurred with tears** yeux voilés ou brouillés de larmes; **the haze has blurred the outline of the mountain** la brume a estompé les contours de la montagne; **time had blurred the memory** le souvenir était devenu confus avec le temps 2 (smear) (with ink etc) barbouiller; Typ maculer, mâchurer
VI 1 (become hazy) **her memories had blurred with time** ses souvenirs s'étaient estompés avec le temps 2 (smear) (of ink) s'estomper

blurb [blɜːb] N notice f publicitaire; (on book) promotion f (en quatrième de couverture); (on front page of paper etc) accroche f

blurred [blɜːd] ADJ (photograph) flou; (contours) indécis, flou, estompé; (memories) confus, vague
▸▸ Med **b. vision** vue f trouble; **to have b. vision** voir trouble

blurring ['blɜːrɪŋ] N Phot flou m

▸ **blurt out** [blɜːt] VT SEP (secret) lâcher étourdiment, laisser échapper; **'he's dead,' she blurted out** 'il est mort', a-t-elle lâché

blush [blʌʃ] N 1 (of shyness, shame) rougeur f, **a b. rose to her cheeks** le sang lui est monté au visage; **to hide one's blushes** baisser les yeux d'embarras; **to bring a b. to sb's cheeks** faire rougir qn; Lit **the first b. of dawn** les premières rougeurs de l'aube 2 Fml **at first b.** à l'abord, au premier abord
VI (of person) rougir; **he blushed at the thought** il rougit à cette pensée; **to b. for** or **with shame** rougir de honte; **to b. crimson** devenir cramoisi; **to b. to the roots of one's hair** rougir jusqu'à la racine des cheveux; Fig **to b. to admit sth** rougir de devoir admettre qch
▸▸ **b. wine** vin m rosé très léger

blusher ['blʌʃər] N (for face) blush m, fard m à joues

blushing ['blʌʃɪŋ] ADJ (person) rougissant; **the b. bride** la mariée
N rougissement m

bluster ['blʌstər] N (of storm) fureur f, fracas m; Fig **I wasn't impressed by his b.** ses grands cris ne m'impressionnaient pas; **his threats were no more than b.** ses menaces fulminantes n'étaient en fait que du vent

VI (of wind) souffler en rafales; Fig (speak aggressively) fanfaronner
▸ **bluster out** VT SEP **to b. one's way out of a situation** se sortir d'une situation en fanfaronnant; **to b. it out** s'en sortir en fanfaronnant

blustering ['blʌstərɪŋ] ADJ (wind) violent; Fig (person, tone) fanfaron
N fanfaronnade(s) f(pl)

blustery ['blʌst(ə)rɪ] ADJ (wind) violent; (day) de (grand) vent

blvd (abbr **boulevard**) boul, bd

BMA [biːemˈeɪ] N (abbr British Medical Association) ≃ ordre m des médecins

B-movie N film m de série B; **he was a B. actor** c'était un acteur de série B

BO [biːˈəʊ] N Fam (abbr body odour) = odeur f corporelle; **to have BO** sentir (la transpiration), sentir mauvais

boa ['bəʊə] N (snake) boa m; **feather b.** (scarf) boa m
▸▸ Zool **b. constrictor** (boa) constricteur m

boar [bɔːr] N (animal) verrat m; **wild b.** sanglier m; (young) marcassin m
▸▸ Culin **b.'s head** hure f de sanglier; **b. hunting** chasse f au sanglier

board [bɔːd] N 1 (plank) planche f, (thick) madrier m; (for bread) planche à (couper le) pain; (for notices) panneau m de publicité ou d'affichage; (inscribed with information) écriteau m; Sch **to write sth on the b.** écrire qch au tableau; Theat Old-fashioned, Hum **the boards** les planches
2 Admin etc conseil m, comité m, commission f, **b. (of directors)** (of company) conseil d'administration; **to be on the b.** (of company) faire partie ou être membre du conseil d'administration; **advisory b.** comité consultatif; **disciplinary b.** conseil de discipline; **medical b.** conseil de santé
3 (table) table f, (food) table, nourriture f, **b. and lodging** pension f complète; **full b.** pension complète; Fig **to sweep the b.** faire table rase
4 (for draughts) damier m; (for chess) échiquier m
5 Aviat, Naut **on b.** à bord; **to take goods on b.** embarquer des marchandises; Fig **to take on b.** (work, responsibility) accepter; (problem) assumer; (comments) prendre note de; **to go on b.** monter à bord, s'embarquer; Fig **to go by the b.** (of plan, hopes etc) être abandonné; (of reputation) être perdu; Fig **to let sth go by the b.** abandonner qch, laisser tomber qch
6 (in bookbinding) (cardboard) carton m; **the boards** (of book) les plats mpl; **in paper boards** cartonné; **limp boards** cartonnage m souple
7 Am TV etc console f
8 Comput (in PC) carte f, (in mainframe) panneau m; **on b.** installé
VT 1 (of passengers) (ship, plane) aller ou monter à bord de; (train, bus) monter dans; Naut (come alongside) aborder, accoster; Admin (ship) (for inspection) arraisonner
2 (book) cartonner
VI 1 (lodge) être en pension; **I b. at Mrs Brown's** or **with Mrs Brown** je suis en pension chez Mme Brown; Sch **he'll start boarding when he's twelve** à douze ans, il ira en pension
2 Aviat **flight 123 is now boarding** l'embarquement a commencé pour le vol 123
▸▸ **b. of enquiry** commission d'enquête; **b. of examiners** jury m d'examen; **b. game** jeu m de société; Com **b. meeting** réunion f du conseil d'administration; Com **b. member** membre m du conseil d'administration; Com **the B. of Trade** (in UK) le ministère du Commerce; (in US) la chambre de

commerce; **b. of trustees** conseil de gestion; *TV* **b. test** animatique *f*
▸ **board in** VT SEP = board up
▸ **board out** VT SEP *(children)* mettre en pension
▸ **board up** VT SEP *(door, window)* condamner

boarder ['bɔːdər] N **1** *(lodger)* pensionnaire *mf*; *Sch* interne *mf*; **she takes in boarders** elle prend des pensionnaires **2** *Naut* abordeur *m*

boarding ['bɔːdɪŋ] N **1** *Naut, Aviat* embarquement *m*; *Naut (for inspection)* arraisonnement *m*; *Naut (by pirates, enemy)* abordage *m*; **flight 123 is now ready for b.** le vol 123 est maintenant prêt pour l'embarquement; *Aviat* **in preparation for b., please extinguish all cigarettes** veuillez éteindre vos cigarettes en vue de l'embarquement **2** *Sch* pensionnat *m*
▸ **Aviat b. bridge** (pré-)passerelle *f*; *Aviat* **b. card** carte *f* d'embarquement; *Aviat* **b. gate** porte *f* d'embarquement; **b. house** pension *f*; *Sch* internat *m*; **b. kennels** *(for dogs)* = chenil *m* où l'on peut faire garder ses chiens pendant les vacances; **b. party** *Naut (for inspection)* détachement *m* de visite; *(of pirates, enemy)* détachement d'abordage; *Aviat* **b. pass** carte d'embarquement; **b. school** internat, pensionnat

---

Boarding Schools
Les "boarding schools", traditionnellement réservées à la progéniture de la haute bourgeoisie, existent en Grande-Bretagne depuis des siècles et furent pendant très longtemps caractérisées par une discipline stricte et un confort rudimentaire. Aujourd'hui, même si les "boarding schools" prônent toujours des valeurs traditionnelles elles ont dû s'adapter à la société moderne. Elles sont maintenant très souvent mixtes et acceptent des pensionnaires d'origine sociale un peu plus variée ainsi qu'un nombre croissant d'internes à la semaine.

---

boardroom ['bɔːdruːm] N salle *f* de réunion *(du conseil d'administration)*; **there is uncertainty in boardrooms across the country** l'incertitude règne au sein des conseils d'administration de toutes les entreprises du pays; **to be promoted to the b.** être promu au conseil d'administration

boardwalk ['bɔːdwɔːk] N *Am* = passage *m* ou trottoir *m* fait de planches de bois (au bord de la mer); on the b. sur les planches

boast [bəʊst] N vantardise *f*; **it is their b. that ...** ils se vantent que ...; **it was her proud b. that she had read ...** elle se vantait d'avoir lu ...; **it turned out to be no more than an empty b.** finalement, ce n'était que des fanfaronnades
VI se vanter (**of** *or* **about sth** de qch); **without wishing to b., I ...** sans vouloir me vanter, je ...; **that's nothing to b. about** il n'y a pas de quoi se vanter
VT **1** *(to claim)* **he boasted that he could beat me** il s'est vanté de pouvoir me battre **2** *(to take pride in)* **the school boasts a fine library** l'école est fière de posséder une belle bibliothèque; **the entire town boasts just one pub** il n'y a qu'un seul pub dans toute la ville

boaster ['bəʊstər] N vantard, -arde, fanfaron, -onne

boastful ['bəʊstfʊl] ADJ vantard, fanfaron

boastfully ['bəʊstfʊlɪ] ADV avec vantardise

boasting ['bəʊstɪŋ] N vantardise *f*

boat [bəʊt] N **1** *Naut* bateau *m*; *(small)* canot *m*, embarcation *f*; **I came by b.** je suis venu en bateau *ou* par (le) bateau; *Fig* **we're all in the same b.** nous sommes tous dans le

même cas *ou* logés à la même enseigne; **b. stations!** à vos postes d'abandon! **2** *(for sauce, gravy)* saucière *f*
VI se promener en bateau; *(in rowing boat etc)* canoter, faire du canotage
▸ *Naut* **b. deck** pont *m* des embarcations; *Naut* **b. drill** manœuvres *fpl* d'évacuation; **b. neck** *(on dress, jumper)* encolure *f* bateau; *Hist* **b. people** boat people *mpl*; **b. race** *(event)* course *f* d'avirons; *Naut* régates *fpl*; *Br Sl (face)* visage *m*; **b. train** = train *m* qui assure la correspondance avec un bateau

boatbuilder ['bəʊtbɪldər] N constructeur *m* de bateaux

boater ['bəʊtər] N *(hat)* canotier *m*

boathook ['bəʊthʊk] N gaffe *f*

boathouse ['bəʊthaʊs] N hangar *m* à bateaux

boating ['bəʊtɪŋ] N canotage *m*; **to go b.** faire du canotage
▸ **b. accident** accident *m* de bateau; **b. holiday** vacances *fpl* en bateau; **b. song** barcarolle *f*

boatload ['bəʊtləʊd] N *(of wood, cars, fruit etc)* cargaison *f*; **six boatloads of refugees** six bateaux pleins de réfugiés; **to arrive by the b.** arriver par bateaux entiers

boatman, *pl* **boatmen** ['bəʊtmən, -men] N **1** *(operator)* passeur *m* **2** *(renter)* loueur *m* de canots

boatswain ['bəʊs(ə)n] N *Naut* maître *m* d'équipage, maître principal de manœuvre, bosco *m*

boatyard ['bəʊtjaːd] N chantier *m* de construction pour canots et bateaux de plaisance

Bob [bɒb] N *Fam* **and B.'s your uncle!** et ça y est!, et voilà (le travail)!

bob[1] [bɒb] N **1** *(sudden movement)* petit coup *m* **2** *(curtsey)* petite révérence *f* **3** *(on pendulum)* lentille *f*, *(on plumb line)* plomb *m*; *(on end of kite tail)* poids *m*; *(on fishing line)* bouchon *m*
VT **to b. a curtsey** faire une petite révérence
VI s'agiter; **bobbing for apples** = à Hallowe'en, jeu *m* consistant à essayer d'attraper avec les dents des pommes flottant dans une bassine d'eau; **to b. down** se baisser subitement; **to b. up** surgir brusquement; *Fig* réapparaître d'une façon inattendue; **to b. up and down** *(in one's seat)* s'agiter; **to b. up and down in the water** danser sur l'eau; **to b. under** *(of fisherman's float)* plonger

bob[2] N *(hairstyle)* (coupe *f* au) carré *m*; **to wear one's hair in a b.** avoir les cheveux coupés au carré; **to have a b.** avoir une coupe au carré, avoir un carré
VT (**-bb-**) **to have one's hair bobbed** se faire couper les cheveux au carré

bob[3] N INV *Br Old-fashioned Fam (shilling)* shilling *m*; **that must cost a few b.** ça ne doit pas être donné; **he's not short of a b. or two** il n'est pas dans l'indigence, il a de quoi

bob[4] N *Sport (sleigh)* bob(sleigh) *m*

bobbin ['bɒbɪn] N **1** *Tex (for shuttle)* bobine *f*, *(for lace)* fuseau *m* **2** *Elec* corps *m* de bobine
▸ *Tex* **b. frame** bobinoir *m*; *Tex* **b. winder** bobineuse *f*

bobble ['bɒb(ə)l] N *Fam (on hat etc)* pompon *m*

bobby ['bɒbɪ] N *Old-fashioned Br Fam (policeman)* flic *m*; **we need more bobbies on the beat** il nous faut plus de policiers dans le quartier
▸ *Am* **b. pin** pince *f* à cheveux; **b. socks** socquettes *fpl*

bobby-dazzler [-'dæzlər] N *Old-fashioned Br Fam (girl)* jolie fille *f*; **his new car's a b.** sa nouvelle voiture est vraiment extra

bobbysoxer ['bɒbɪsɒksər] N *Old-fashioned Am Fam* = jeune fille *f* portant socquettes et jupe ample, à la mode des années 50

bobcat ['bɒbkæt] N *Am (animal)* lynx *m* rufus

bobo ['bəʊbəʊ] N *Fam (abbr* **bohemian bourgeois**) bobo *mf*

bobsled ['bɒbsled], **bobsleigh** ['bɒbsleɪ] N bobsleigh *m*, *Fam* bob *m*
VI faire du bobsleigh *ou Fam* du bob
▸ **b. race** course *f* de bobsleigh

bobtail ['bɒbteɪl] N **1** *(of horse, dog)* queue *f* écourtée **2** *(dog)* bobtail *m*

bock [bɒk] N *(glass)* bock *m*; *Am (beer)* bière *f* brune (allemande)
▸ *Am* **b. beer** bière brune (allemande)

bod [bɒd] N **1** *Br Fam (fellow)* type *m*; **any old b. can do it** n'importe quel péquenaud peut le faire **2** *Fam (body)* corps *m*; **what a great b. he's got!** il est vachement bien (foutu)!

bode [bəʊd] VI **to b. well/ill** être de bon/de mauvais augure (**for** pour)
VT *Arch, Lit* présager

bodge [bɒdʒ] VT *Fam (piece of work)* bousiller, saboter; **to b. sth up** *(make temporary or unskilful repair)* rafistoler qch, faire une réparation de fortune sur qch

bodice ['bɒdɪs] N *(of dress)* corsage *m*
▸ **b. ripper** = roman *m* grivois à trame historique

-bodied ['bɒdɪd] SUFF **a large-/slender-b. man** un homme au corps gros/svelte; **a full-b. wine** un vin robuste

bodily ['bɒdɪlɪ] ADJ corporel, physique; **to be in b. fear of sb** craindre d'être attaqué par qn
ADV **1** *(forcibly)* **he was carried b. to the door** on l'a saisi (à bras-le-corps) et transporté jusqu'à la porte; **they hurled him b. through the window** ils le saisirent à bras-le-corps et le firent sortir par la fenêtre sans ménagement **2** *(as whole)* entièrement, en masse
▸ **b. functions** fonctions *fpl* corporelles; **b. needs** besoins *mpl* matériels; **b. strength** force *f* physique

bodkin ['bɒdkɪn] N *(for threading)* passelacet *m*, *pl* passe-lacets; *(for piercing)* poinçon *m*

body ['bɒdɪ] N **1** *(of person, animal)* corps *m*; *(dead body)* cadavre *m*, corps; *Fig* **to throw oneself b. and soul into sth** se jeter corps et âme dans qch; *Fig* **to have just enough to keep b. and soul together** avoir tout juste de quoi vivre; *Fam* **(it'll be) over my dead b.!** plutôt crever!; **if he comes into this house, it'll be over my dead b.!** il faudra qu'il me passe sur le corps s'il veut rentrer dans cette maison!; **this obsession with the b.** beautiful cette obsession que tout le monde a d'avoir un corps parfait
2 *(of wine)* corps *m*; *(of hair)* volume *m*; *Mus* **to give b. to the tone** nourrir le son
3 *(group)* corps *m*; *(organization)* organisme *m*; *(of laws)* recueil *m*; *(of water)* étendue *f*, **large b. of people** foule *f* nombreuse, assistance *f* nombreuse; **there is a large b. of support for the policy** un grand nombre de personnes sont en faveur de cette politique; **b. of troops** troupe *f* armée; **the main b.** *(of employees, refugees etc)* la majeure partie; *Mil* le gros des troupes; **to come in a b.** venir en masse; *Old-fashioned* **learned b.** corps savant; **public b.** corporation *f*
4 *(main part)* *(of document, building etc)* corps *m*; *(of church)* nef *f*, *(of musical instrument)* coffre *m*; *(of plane)* fuselage *m*; *(of pram)* nacelle *f*, *Law* **the b. of evidence** l'ensemble *m* des preuves
5 *Aut* carrosserie *f*

6 *Phys etc* corps *m*; *Astron* **heavenly b.** corps céleste, astre *m*
7 *(underwear)* body *m*
▸▸ **b. bag** sac *m* mortuaire; *Boxing* **b. blow** coup *m* dur; **to be a real b. blow to sb's hopes** être un véritable coup porté aux espoirs de qn; *Sport* **b. builder** culturiste *mf*; *Sport* **b. building** culturisme *m*; **b. clock** horloge *f* interne *ou* biologique; *Pol* **b. corporate** personne *f* morale; **b. count** pertes *fpl* en vies humaines; *Cin* **b. double** doublure *f*; *Psy* **b. dysmorphic disorder** dysmorphophobie *f*; **b. language** attitude *f*; **b. lotion** lait *m* corporel; **b. odour** odeur *f* corporelle; *Aut* **b. panel** panneau *m* de carrosserie; **b. part** *Aut* pièce *f* de carrosserie; *(of person)* partie *f* de corps humain; **b. piercing** piercing *m*; *Aut* **b. platform** plate-forme *f*, *pl* plates-formes; *Pol* **b. politic** corps politique; **b. popper** smurfer, -euse; **b. popping** smurf *m*; *Aut* **b. repair centre** atelier *m* (de réparation) de carrosserie; *Aut* **b. roll** roulis *m* de la caisse, mouvement *m* de caisse; **b. scrub** produit *m* exfoliant pour le corps; *Typ* **b. setting** composition *f* (des caractères); **b. shop** *Aut (for vehicles)* atelier *m* de carrosserie; *Am Fam (gym)* club *m* de gym; *Typ* **b. size** taille *f* de corps; *Hist* **b. snatcher** déterreur, -euse de cadavres; **b. stocking** body; **b. swerve** feinte *f*; **b. warmer** gilet *m* matelassé

bodycheck [ˈbɒdɪtʃek] N *Sport (in ice hockey)* interception *f*, *(in wrestling)* coup *m* de bélier
▸ VT *Sport (in ice hockey, football)* intercepter

bodyguard [ˈbɒdɪgɑːd] N **1** *(individual)* garde *m* du corps, *Fam* gorille *m* **2** *(no pl) (group)* gardes *mpl* du corps

bodylock [ˈbɒdɪlɒk] N *Aut* **b. seat restraint** blocage *m* de maintien du corps

bodyshell [ˈbɒdɪʃel] N *Aut* caisse *f*, coque *f*, carcasse *f*

body-surf VI body-surfer

body-surfer N body-surfe(u)r, -euse, *pl* body-surfe(u)rs, -euses

body-surfing N body-surfing *m*

bodywork [ˈbɒdɪwɜːk] N *Aut* **1** *(structure)* carrosserie *f* **2** *(repairs)* travail *m* de carrosserie

Boer [bɔːr] ADJ boer; **the B. War** la guerre des Boers
▸ N Boer *mf*

boffin [ˈbɒfɪn] N *Br Fam Hum* savant *m*

bog [bɒg] N **1** *(marsh)* marécage *m*; **peat b.** tourbière *f* **2** *Br Fam (lavatory)* chiottes *fpl*, gogs *mpl*, gogues *mpl*
▸▸ *Br Fam* **b. brush** brosse *f* à chiottes; *Br Fam* **b. paper** PQ *m*; *Br Fam* **b. roll** *(roll)* rouleau *m* de PQ; *(paper)* PQ; *Br Fam* **b. seat** cuvette *f* des chiottes

▸ **bog down** VT SEP *(usu passive)* **to get bogged down** *(of car etc)* s'embourber, s'enliser, s'enfoncer dans une fondrière; *Fam (of person, discussion etc)* s'enliser; **don't let's get bogged down in details** ne nous perdons pas dans les détails

▸ **bog off** VI *Br Sl* dégager; **oh, b. off!** *(go away)* dégage!; *(expressing contempt, disagreement)* tu vas te faire voir!

bogey [ˈbəʊgɪ] N **1** *(source of fear)* spectre *m*, hantise *f*; **unionization is the b. of the company** la syndicalisation est la hantise de la société **2** *Fam (source of bad luck)* chose *f* qui porte malheur; *(cause of worry)* bête *f* noire **3** *Fam (in nose)* crotte *f* de nez **4** *Golf* bogey *m* **5** *(spirit)* fantôme *m*, spectre *m* *(effrayant)*; *Arch (devil)* diable *m*
▸ VT *Golf* **to b. a hole** jouer un trou en un coup au-dessus du par

bogeyman, *pl* **bogeymen** [ˈbəʊgɪmæn, -men] N **the b.** le croque-mitaine, *pl* croque-mitaines, le Père fouettard; **the b. will get you** le Père fouettard va venir te chercher

boggle [ˈbɒg(ə)l] VI **1 to b. at doing sth** rechigner à faire qch **2 the mind boggles** ça laisse rêveur
▸ VT **it boggles the mind** *or* **the imagination** ça laisse rêveur

boggy [ˈbɒgɪ] ADJ marécageux

bogie [ˈbəʊgɪ] N *Rail* bog(g)ie *m*

bog-standard ADJ *Br Fam* tout simple

bog-trotter N *Sl* **1** *Offensive (Irish person)* Irlandais, -aise **2** *(country bumpkin)* plouc *m*, péquenaud *m*

bogus [ˈbəʊgəs] ADJ **1** *(fake)* faux, *f* fausse; **he's completely b.** *(not genuine in feelings etc)* c'est un faux jeton **2** *Am Sl (unfashionable)* ringard
▸▸ *Com* **b. company** société *f* fantôme

Bohemia [bəʊˈhiːmɪə] N **1** *Geog* Bohême *f* **2** *(unconventional life)* (vie *f* de) bohème *f*

Bohemian [bəʊˈhiːmɪən] ADJ **1** *Geog* bohémien **2** *Fig (life etc)* de bohème
▸ N **1** *Geog* Bohémien, -ienne **2** *(unconventional person)* bohème *mf*; *(gipsy)* bohémien, -ienne

boil[1] [bɔɪl] N **to come to the b.** *(of water etc)* commencer à bouillir, arriver à ébullition; **let the water come to a** *or* **the b.** attendre que l'eau arrive à ébullition; **the water is on the b.** l'eau bout; **to bring the water to the b.** amener l'eau à l'ébullition; *Fig* **their romance has gone off the b.** leur histoire tourne au ralenti, leur histoire ne marche plus très fort; **to go off the b.** *(of athlete, actor etc)* perdre son entrain
▸ VI **1** *(of liquid)* bouillir; *(violently)* bouillonner; **to begin to b.** arriver à ébullition; *Culin* **allow to b.** gently laissez mijoter; **to let the kettle b. dry** laisser évaporer complètement l'eau de la bouilloire; **the kettle's boiling** l'eau bout dans la bouilloire; **are the potatoes boiling?** est-ce que les pommes de terre bouillent?; *Fam* **to keep the pot boiling** *(bring in enough money)* faire bouillir la marmite; **it makes me** *or* **my blood b.!** ça me met hors de moi!; **to b. with rage** bouillir de colère; *Fam* **I'm boiling!** *(very hot)* je crève de chaleur *ou* de chaud! **2** *Lit (of sea)* bouillonner
▸ VT **1** *(liquid)* faire bouillir; *Culin (potatoes, vegetables, meat)* faire cuire à l'eau; *(sugar)* cuire; **to b. the kettle** *(by gas)* mettre la bouilloire sur le feu; *(by electricity)* brancher la bouilloire; **to b. an egg** faire cuire un œuf à la coque; *Hum* **he can't b. an egg** *(does not know how to cook)* il n'est même pas capable de faire cuire un œuf; *Sl* **go (and) b. your head!** va te faire cuire un œuf! **2** *(in papermaking) (fibres)* décreuser

▸ **boil away** VI **1** *(go on boiling)* continuer à bouillir **2** *(evaporate)* s'évaporer

▸ **boil down** VT SEP *(solution)* réduire; *(syrup etc)* (faire) réduire; *Fig (article)* condenser
▸ VI *(of sauce etc)* se réduire

▸ **boil down to** VT INSEP *Fam* se ramener *ou* se résumer *ou* revenir à; **what her story boils down to is that …** ce à quoi se résume son histoire, c'est que …; **this is what it all boils down to** voilà à quoi cela revient *ou* se résume

▸ **boil over** VI **1** *(of liquid)* déborder, *Fam* se sauver; *(of pot)* déborder **2** *Fam (become angry)* exploser (de colère) **3** *(worsen)* empirer; **the dispute is in danger of boiling over into a strike** le conflit risque de virer à la grève

▸ **boil up** VT SEP *(water, milk)* faire bouillir
▸ VI *(of water, milk)* monter

boil[2] N *Med* furoncle *m*

boiled [bɔɪld] ADJ bouilli; *Culin* cuit à l'eau
▸▸ *Culin* **b. egg** œuf *m* à la coque; *Culin* **b. ham** jambon *m* blanc; *Culin* **b. potatoes** pommes *fpl* de terre à l'eau *ou* bouillies; *Br* **b. sweet** bonbon *m* à sucer

boiler [ˈbɔɪlər] N **1** chaudière *f*, *Culin* **double b.** bain-marie *m*, *pl* bains-marie **2** *Culin* poule *f* (à la casserole) **3** *Sl Pej* **(old) b.** *(woman)* vieille peau *f*
▸▸ **b. maker** chaudronnier *m*; **b. room** *(in building)* salle *f* des chaudières, chaufferie *f*, *Naut (in boat)* chaufferie, chambre *f* de chauffe; *Am Fin* = organisation *f* qui vend illégalement au public des produits financiers très spéculatifs ou sans valeur; *Br Ind* **b. suit** *(for work)* bleu(s) *m(pl)* (de travail); *(fashion garment)* salopette *f*

boilerman, *pl* **boilermen** [ˈbɔɪləmən, -men] N chauffeur *m*

boiling [ˈbɔɪlɪŋ] ADJ **1** *(water)* bouillant **2** *Lit (sea)* bouillonnant
▸ ADV *Fam* **b. hot** bouillant; *Fam* **it's been a b. hot day** il a fait une chaleur à crever aujourd'hui; *Fam* **I'm b. hot** je crève de chaleur *ou* de chaud
▸ N bouillonnement *m*, ébullition *f*
▸▸ **b. point** point *m* d'ébullition

boiling-water reactor N *Nucl* réacteur *m* à eau bouillante

boil-in-the-bag ADJ *Culin (rice etc)* en sachet de cuisson

boink [bɔɪŋk] *Am Fam* N **to have a b.** *(have sex)* faire une partie de jambes en l'air
▸ VT s'envoyer en l'air avec
▸ VI faire une partie de jambes en l'air

boisterous [ˈbɔɪst(ə)rəs] ADJ *(person) (noisy)* bruyant, tapageur; *(unruly)* turbulent; *(wind)* violent; *(sea)* tumultueux; **b. spirits** gaieté *f* débordante *ou* tapageuse

boisterously [ˈbɔɪst(ə)rəslɪ] ADV bruyamment

boisterousness [ˈbɔɪst(ə)rəsnɪs] N turbulence *f*, agitation *f*

bold [bəʊld] ADJ **1** *(fearless, confident)* hardi; *(tone, look)* assuré, confiant; *(audacious) (move, plan, thinker)* audacieux; **to put on a b. front** *or* **face, to put a b. front** *or* **face on it** faire bonne figure
2 *(impudent)* impudent, effronté; *Old-fashioned, Fam* **if I may be** *or* **make so b.** si je puis me permettre; **she made so b. as to ask what my salary was** elle a eu l'effronterie de me demander combien je gagnais; *Fam* **as b. as brass** *(to do sth)* avec un culot pas possible; **he's as b. as brass** il a un culot pas possible
3 *(strong, distinctive) (style, brushstrokes)* nerveux, vigoureux; **b. colours** couleurs *fpl* vives; **b. features** traits *mpl* accusés
4 *Typ* gras
▸ N *Typ* **in b.** en gras
▸▸ *Typ* **b. character** caractère *m* gras; *Typ* **b. face** caractères gras; *Typ* **b. italics** caractères italiques gras; *Typ* **b. print, b. type** caractères gras

boldly [ˈbəʊldlɪ] ADV **1** *(confidently, fearlessly)* hardiment; *(audaciously)* audacieusement; **to state sth b.** affirmer qch avec assurance; **to deal with sth b.** *(subject, problem etc)* traiter qch de façon directe **2** *(impudently)* effrontément, avec impudence **3** *Art* avec vigueur

boldness [ˈbəʊldnɪs] N **1** *(fearlessness)* hardiesse *f*, *(audacity)* audace *f* **2** *(impudence)* effronterie *f*, impudence *f* **3** *Art (of style, brushstrokes)* nervosité *f*, vigueur *f*

bole [bəʊl] N *(of tree)* fût *m*, tronc *m*

bolero [bəˈlɛərəʊ] N **1** *(dance, music)* boléro *m* **2** *(also* [ˈbɒlərəʊ]*) (jacket)* boléro *m*

boletus [bɒˈliːtəs] N *(fungus)* bolet *m*

Bolivia [bəˈlɪvɪə] N Bolivie *f*

Bolivian [bəˈlɪvɪən] ADJ bolivien
▸ N Bolivien, -ienne

boll [bəʊl] N *Bot (of cotton, linen)* capsule *f* *(du cotonnier)*
▸▸ *Entom* **b. weevil** anthonome *m* (du cotonnier)

bollard ['bɒlɑːd] N **1** *Naut (for mooring)* bitte *f* **2** *Br (in road)* borne *f*

bollocking ['bɒlǝkɪŋ] N *Sl (reprimand)* engueulade *f*; **he got a b. from the boss** il s'est fait engueuler par le patron

bollocks ['bɒlǝks] NPL *Vulg* couilles *fpl*; **b.!** c'est des conneries!; **oh, b., I've got no money on me!** quelle merde *ou* quelle connerie, je n'ai pas d'argent sur moi!
▸ **bollocks up** VT SEP *Vulg* bousiller

Bollywood ['bɒlɪwʊd] N *Cin* = appellation *f* humoristique de l'industrie du film en Inde, formée à partir de Bombay (où sont produits la plupart des films) et Hollywood

Bologna [bǝ'lɒnjǝ] N Bologne

Bolognese [bɒlǝ'niːz, -eɪz] ADJ bolognais N Bolognais, -aise

boloney [bǝ'lǝʊnɪ] N = **baloney**

Bolshevik ['bɒlʃǝvɪk], **Bolshevist** ['bɒlʃǝvɪst] ADJ, N bolchevik *mf*, bolcheviste *mf*

Bolshevism ['bɒlʃǝvɪz(ǝ)m] N bolchevisme *m*

bolshie, bolshy ['bɒlʃɪ] *Fam* ADJ **he's b.** c'est un mauvais coucheur; **he turned b.** il a commencé à râler; **she's in a b. mood** elle est de très mauvais poil; **she was a bit b. about going to school** elle a un peu rechigné pour aller à l'école
N *Pol Old-fashioned* rouge *mf*

bolster ['bǝʊlstǝr] N *(pillow)* traversin *m* VT *(strengthen)* **to b. sb's confidence** redonner de la confiance à qn; **it bolstered his ego** ça a fait du bien à son amour-propre; **to b. one's courage** se donner du courage
▸ **bolster up** VT SEP *Fig (regime, government)* appuyer, soutenir; *(theory)* étayer; **he bolstered himself up with a few drinks** il a bu quelques verres pour se donner du courage; **bolstered up by recent successes** fort de ses récents succès; *Fin* **to b. up the pound** soutenir la livre

bolt [bǝʊlt, bɒlt] N **1** *(closing device) (for door etc)* verrou *m*; *(of lock)* pêne *m*
2 *Tech (for nut)* boulon *m*
3 *Fam (rush)* **to make a b. for it** décamper, déguerpir; **he tried to make a b. for it** il a essayé de se tailler; **she made a b. for the door** elle s'est précipitée vers la porte
4 *Met* **a b. of lightning** la foudre; *Fig* **it was** *or* **came like a b. from the blue** ce fut comme un coup de foudre
5 *(roll)* **a b. of cloth** une coupe de tissu
6 *Arch (of crossbow)* carreau *m*; *Fig* **he's shot his b.** *(is exhausted)* il est épuisé; *(of politician etc)* il a joué sa dernière carte
VT **1** *(close) (door etc)* verrouiller **2** *Tech (join)* boulonner, cheviller; **to be bolted to the floor** être fixé au sol par des boulons **3** *Fam (eat quickly) (one's dinner etc)* avaler à toute vitesse, engloutir
VI **1** *(of door etc)* se verrouiller **2** *(of horse)* s'emballer, prendre le mors aux dents; *Fam (of person)* décamper, déguerpir **3** *(of plant)* monter en graine
ADV **b. upright** droit comme un piquet
▸ **b. hole** abri *m*, refuge *m*
▸ **bolt down** VT INSEP *(stairs, street)* dévaler VT SEP **to down one's food** *or* **a meal** manger avec un lance-pierres; **don't b. your food down** ne mange pas si vite
▸ **bolt in** VI *(enter quickly)* entrer comme un bolide
VT SEP *(lock in)* enfermer (au verrou)
▸ **bolt out** VI *(leave quickly)* sortir comme un bolide; **they bolted out of the door** ils sont sortis comme des bolides
VT SEP *(lock out)* enfermer dehors

bomb [bɒm] N *Mil etc* bombe *f*; **the b.** *(atom bomb)* la bombe atomique; **to release** *or* **drop a b.** lâcher *ou* larguer une bombe; *Fam* **this room looks as if a b.'s hit it** cette

pièce est un véritable champ de bataille; *Br Fam* **to go like a b.** *(of car)* être une vraie fusée; *(of party)* être génial; *(of play, show etc)* casser la baraque, marcher très bien; *Am* **it's a b.** *(of musical, play etc)* c'est un fiasco *ou* un flop; *Fam* **it costs a b.** ça coûte les yeux de la tête; *Fam* **to make a b.** se faire un fric fou
VT **1** *(town etc)* bombarder, lancer des bombes sur; *Sl* **to b. the hell** *or* **shit out of a place** pilonner un endroit **2** *Am Fam (fail) (test)* se planter complètement à
VI *Am Fam (of play etc)* faire un flop; *(of student)* se planter complètement
▸ ▸ **b. attack** bombardement *m*; *Aviat* **b. bay** soute *f* à bombes; **b. crater** entonnoir *m*, cratère *m*; *Mil* **b. disposal** déminage *m*; *Mil* **b. expert** démineur *m*; **b. hoax** fausse alerte *f* à la bombe; **b. scare** alerte à la bombe; **b. threat** menace *f* d'attentat à la bombe
▸ **bomb along** *Fam* VI *(of car, driver)* bomber
VT INSEP **to b. along the road** bomber sur la route
▸ **bomb down** VT INSEP *Fam (of car, driver)* **to b. down the road at 100 mph** foncer à 160 (km/h)
▸ **bomb out** VT SEP **1 they have been bombed out of their homes** ils sont à la rue parce que leurs maisons ont été bombardées; **the whole street had been bombed out** toute la rue avait été détruite par les bombardements **2** *Br Fam (fail to keep appointment with)* **to b. sb out** poser un lapin à qn

bombard [bɒm'bɑːd] VT *Mil etc* bombarder; *Fig* **to b. sb with questions** bombarder qn de questions

bombardier [bɒmbǝ'dɪǝr] N **1** *Aviat* bombardier *m* **2** *Br Mil* brigadier *m*

bombardment [bɒm'bɑːdmǝnt] N *Mil* bombardement *m*

bombast ['bɒmbæst] N emphase *f*

bombastic [bɒm'bæstɪk] ADJ *(style)* ampoulé, emphatique

bombastically [bɒm'bæstɪklɪ] ADV dans un style ampoulé *ou* emphatique

Bombay mix [bɒm'beɪ] N *Culin* = mélange *m* apéritif épicé composé de cacahouètes et de lentilles

bombazine ['bɒmbǝziːn] N *Tex* bombasin *m*

bombe [bɒm] N *(ice cream)* bombe *f* glacée

bombed out [bɒmd] ADJ *Sl* **1** *(exhausted)* crevé, nase **2** *(very crowded)* plein à craquer **3** *(drunk)* bourré; *(on drugs)* défoncé

bomber ['bɒmǝr] N **1** *(aircraft)* bombardier *m* **2** *(person) Aviat* bombardier *m*; *(terrorist)* poseur, -euse de bombe(s)
▸ ▸ **b. jacket** blouson *m* d'aviateur

bombing ['bɒmɪŋ] N attentat *m* à la bombe; *Aviat* bombardement *m*
▸ ▸ **b. campaign** campagne *f* d'attentats à la bombe; **b. raid** bombardement aérien; **b. run** course *f* de visée

bombproof ['bɒmpruːf] ADJ à l'épreuve des bombes
▸ ▸ **b. shelter** abri *m* blindé

bombshell ['bɒmʃel] N **1** *Mil* obus *m*; *Fig* **the news came as a b. (to us)** cette nouvelle nous a fait l'effet d'une bombe; **to drop a b.** faire part d'une nouvelle qui fait l'effet d'une bombe **2** *Fam (attractive woman)* beauté *f*

bombsight ['bɒmsaɪt] N *Aviat* viseur *m* ou collimateur *m* de bombardement

bombsite ['bɒmsaɪt] N zone *f* bombardée; **to look like a b.** ressembler à un champ de bataille

bombthrower ['bɒmθrǝʊǝr] N **1** *(device)* lance-bombes *m inv* **2** *(person)* lanceur, -euse de bombes

bona fide ['bǝʊnǝ'faɪdɪ] ADJ *(excuse, contract, reason, agreement)* valable; *(offer)* sé-

rieux, sincère; *(agent)* agréé; *(charity)* vrai; **are you sure he was a b. salesman?** es-tu sûr que c'était vraiment un vendeur?
N **one's bona fides** [-faɪdɪz] sa bonne foi

bonanza [bǝ'nænzǝ] N *Min* riche filon *m*; *Fig* aubaine *f*; **the tourist industry has had a bit of a b.** l'industrie touristique a fait de bonnes affaires; **to strike a b.** *Min* rencontrer un riche filon; *Fig* faire une affaire en or
ADJ **b. year** année *f* exceptionnelle

Bonapartist ['bǝʊnǝpɑːtɪst] N, ADJ *Hist* bonapartiste *mf*

bonbon ['bɒnbɒn] N bonbon *m*

bonce [bɒns] N *Br Fam (head)* caboche *f*

bond [bɒnd] N **1** *(tie)* lien *m*; *Lit* **bonds (chains)** fers *mpl*, liens; *Fig* **the bonds of friendship/marriage** les liens de l'amitié/du mariage; **there is a very close b. between us** nous sommes très liés
2 *Chem* liaison *f*; *(of glue)* adhérence *f*; *Constr etc* attache *f*
3 *(commitment)* engagement *m*, contrat *m*; *Law* obligation *f*, *Fml* **my word is my b.** *(you can trust me)* je vous donne ma parole d'honneur; *(I cannot back out)* j'ai donné ma parole d'honneur
4 *Fin* bon *m*, obligation *f*; **registered b.** bon nominatif; **mortgage b.** titre *m* hypothécaire
5 *Law (for bail)* caution *f*
6 *Com (warehouse)* dépôt *m*; **to be in b.** être à l'entrepôt *ou* en dépôt; **to take goods out of b.** dédouaner des marchandises
7 *(paper)* papier *m* à lettres (de luxe)
VT **1** *(metals etc)* coller; *Constr (stones)* liaisonner **2** *Com (goods)* entreposer, mettre en dépôt *ou* à l'entrepôt **3** *Fig* **hardship had bonded them together** les privations qu'ils avaient endurées avaient créé un lien très fort entre eux
▸ ▸ *Fin* **b. equivalent yield** = rendement *m* équivalent à celui d'une obligation; *Fin* **b. holder** détenteur, -trice d'obligations; *Fin* **b. investment** placement *m* obligataire; *Fin* **b. issue** emprunt *m* obligataire; **to make a b. issue** émettre un emprunt; *Fin* **b. market** marché *m* obligataire *ou* des obligations; *Fin* **b. note** titre d'obligation; **b. paper** papier à lettres (de luxe); *Fin* **b. yield** rendement de l'obligation

bondage ['bɒndɪdʒ] N **1** *Lit (slavery)* esclavage *m*, asservissement *m* **2** *Hist (serfdom)* servage *m* **3** *(sexual practice)* bondage *m*, = pratique *f* sexuelle où l'un des partenaires est attaché

bonded ['bɒndɪd] ADJ **1** *Constr (masonry)* en liaison **2** *Com (goods)* en dépôt, en entrepôt **3** *Fin (debt)* garanti par obligations
▸ ▸ *Com* **b. warehouse** entrepôt *m* sous douane

bonder ['bɒndǝr] N *Com* entrepositaire *m*

bonding ['bɒndɪŋ] N **1** *Constr (of stones)* liaison *f* **2** *(of metals)* collage *m* **3** *Com (of goods)* entreposage *m* **4** *(emotional attachment)* lien *m* affectif; **the b. process** la formation de liens affectifs; **male b.** la formation de liens affectifs entre hommes
▸ ▸ *Chem* **b. agent** agent *m* de collage *ou* d'adhésivité; **b. scheme** *(with tour operator)* agrément *m*

bondholder ['bɒndhǝʊldǝ(r)] N *Fin* obligataire *mf*, détenteur, -trice *ou* porteur, -euse d'obligations

bondstone ['bɒndstǝʊn] N *Constr* parpaing *m*

bone [bǝʊn] N **1** *(of human, animal)* os *m*; *(of fish)* arête *f*; **the handle was made from b.** le manche était en os; **to be as dry as a b.** ou **b. dry** *(of earth)* être desséché; *(of well)* être à sec; *(of washing)* être complètement sec; *Old-fashioned* **he won't make old bones** il ne fera pas de vieux os; **chilled** or **frozen to the b.** gelé ou transi jusqu'à la moelle; **to cut expenses to the b.** réduire les dépenses au minimum; **to work one's fingers to the b.** se tuer au travail; **to be b. idle** or **lazy** être paresseux comme une couleuvre; **I feel it in my bones** je le sens; Fam **to have a b. to pick with sb** avoir un compte à régler avec qn; **to make no bones about doing sth** ne pas hésiter à faire qch; **he made no bones about it** il y est allé carrément, il n'y est pas allé par quatre chemins; **she made no bones about her displeasure** elle n'a pas caché son mécontentement; **near** or **close to the b.** (joke etc) douteux, limite

2 (of corset) baleine f

3 bones (of the dead) ossements mpl

VT **1** (meat) désosser; (fish) ôter les arêtes de **2** (corset) garnir de baleines **3** Am Vulg (have sex with) tringler

▸▸ Cer **b. china** porcelaine f tendre; **b. of contention** sujet m de dispute; Anat **b. marrow** moelle f; Med **b. marrow transplant** greffe f de moelle; Agr **b. meal** engrais m (de cendres d'os); **b. structure** ossature f

▸ **bone up on** VT INSEP Sl (study) potasser

boned [bəʊnd] ADJ **1** (meat) désossé; (fish) sans arêtes **2** (corset) baleiné

bone-dry ADJ (earth) desséché; (well) à sec; (washing) complètement sec

bonehead ['bəʊnhed] N Fam (stupid person) idiot, -ote; (stubborn person) tête f de bois

boneless ['bəʊnlɪs] ADJ (meat) sans os; (from which bones have been removed) désossé; (fish) sans arêtes

boner ['bəʊnər] N **1** Am Fam (mistake) gaffe f, **I made a real b.!** j'ai fait une de ces gaffes! **2** Vulg (erection) **to have a b.** avoir le gourdin ou la trique

boneshaker ['bəʊnʃeɪkər] N Fam esp Hum **1** (car) vieux clou m, vieille guimbarde f **2** Arch (bicycle) vélocipède m

bonfire ['bɒnfaɪər] N (with fireworks) feu m de joie; (for burning leaves etc) feu de jardin; **to make** or **build a b.** (with wood, leaves etc) faire un feu

▸▸ Br **B. Night** le 5 novembre (commémoration de la tentative de Guy Fawkes de faire sauter le Parlement en 1605)

bong [bɒŋ] N (of bell, drum) coup m

bongo ['bɒŋgəʊ] N bongo m; **a set of bongos** un bongo

bonhomie [bɒnɒ'miː] N bonhomie f

bonito [bə'niːtəʊ] N (fish) bonite f

bonk [bɒŋk] Fam N Br **to have a b.** tirer un coup

VT **1** Br (have sex with) **to b. sb** se faire qn **2** (hit) taper; **he got bonked on the head by a tennis ball** il s'est pris une balle de tennis sur la tête

VI Br (have sex) tirer un coup, s'envoyer en l'air (**with sb** avec qn)

bonkers ['bɒŋkəz] ADJ Br Sl cinglé; **it's driving me b.!** ça me rend dingue!

bonnet ['bɒnɪt] N **1** (hat) bonnet m **2** Br Aut capot m; **to have a look under the b.** jeter un coup d'œil sous le capot

▸▸ Aut **b. release** déverrouillage m du capot; Aut **b. strut** tige f (de maintien) de capot, béquille f de capot

bonny ['bɒnɪ] ADJ esp Scot joli

bonsai ['bɒnsaɪ] N bonsaï m

bonus, pl **bonuses** ['bəʊnəs, -əsɪz] N (esp at work) prime f, St Exch (on shares) dividende m supplémentaire, bonification f, **to work on a b. system** travailler à la prime; **cost-of-living b.** indemnité f de vie chère ou de cherté de vie; Com etc **Christmas b.** gratification f de fin d'année; Fig **the hot weather was an unexpected b.** le beau temps fut vraiment bienvenu étant donné qu'on ne

s'y attendait pas; **it's a real b. having a theatre close by** le fait qu'il y ait un théâtre tout près constitue vraiment un plus

▸▸ Br St Exch **b. issue** émission f d'actions gratuites; **b. number** (in lottery) numéro m complémentaire; Mktg **b. pack** prime produit en plus; Br St Exch **b. share** action f gratuite ou donnée en prime

bony ['bəʊnɪ] ADJ **1** (person, body, face) osseux; (knees, shoulders) anguleux; (fingers, arms) squelettique; (meat) plein d'os; (fish) plein d'arêtes **2** (like bone) osseux

bonzer ['bɒnzər] Austr Fam ADJ vachement bien, super, génial, -aux

INT super!, génial!

bonzo ['bɒnzəʊ] N Am Fam cinglé, fêlé

boo [buː] INT hou!; Fam **he wouldn't say b. to a goose** c'est un timide

N huée f, **her arrival was greeted with boos** elle s'est fait huer à son arrivée

VT & VI **to b. (at) sb** huer qn; **to be booed off the stage** quitter la scène au milieu des huées

boob [buːb] Fam N **1** (fool) idiot, -ote, crétin, -ine **2** Br (mistake) gaffe f **3** (breast) nichon m; **to have a b. job** se faire refaire les nichons

VI Br faire une gaffe

▸▸ Fam **b. tube** (strapless top) bustier m moulant; Am (television) télé f

boo-boo N Fam (blunder) gaffe f, bourde f, **to make a b.** faire une gaffe ou une bourde

booby ['buːbɪ] N **1** Old-fashioned (fool) idiot, -ote, crétin, -ine, nouille f **2** (bird) fou m

▸▸ **b. hatch** Naut écoutillon m; Am Fam (mental hospital) asile m de dingues; Sport **b. prize** prix m de consolation (attribué par plaisanterie au dernier); **b. trap** Mil objet m piégé; (practical joke) traquenard f

booby-trap VT (car etc) piéger

booger ['buːgər] N Am Fam crotte f de nez

boogie ['buːgɪ] VI **1** Mus (dance) danser, guincher; (party) faire la fête **2** Am (leave) mettre les bouts, s'arracher; **let's b. on out of here** on met les bouts, on s'arrache

N Mus boogie m; **to have a b.** danser, guincher

▸▸ Sport **b. board** boogie board m

boogie-woogie [-'wuːgɪ] N Mus boogie-woogie m, pl boogie-woogies

booing ['buːɪŋ] N huées fpl

BOOK [bʊk]

N	▪ livre **1** ▪ registre **2** ▪ pari **2**
	▪ carnet **3**
VT	▪ réserver **1** ▪ engager **1**
VI	▪ réserver **1**

N **1** (for reading) livre m; (of opera) livret m, libretto m; (of songs, prayers etc) recueil m; Tel annuaire m; Tel **I'm in the b.** (listed in directory) je suis dans l'annuaire; **a b. on** or **about gardening** un livre de jardinage; **old books** vieux bouquins mpl, (antiquarian) vieilles éditions fpl, **not published in b. form** inédit en librairie; **her articles have now been published in b. form** ses articles ont maintenant été publiés sous forme de livre; Fig **by** or **according to the b.** selon les règles; **to do things** or **go by the b.** suivre les règles; **to be a closed b. to sb** (of subject) être du chinois pour qn; **she's a closed b. to me** (I don't understand her) cette fille est un mystère pour moi; **she's an open b.** (her feelings etc are obvious) elle ne peut rien cacher, elle est transparente; **to read sb like an open b.** lire à livre ouvert dans la pensée de qn; **in my b.** (in my opinion) d'après moi; **that doesn't suit my b.** ça ne me convient pas; Old-fashioned **the good B.** la Bible; **to swear on the B.** prêter serment sur la Bible

2 (for writing in) Com, Fin etc registre m; Sch

cahier m; **account b.** livre m de comptes; **to keep the books of a firm** tenir les comptes d'une entreprise; Fig **he's on our books** (member of our club etc) c'est un de nos membres; (player in our team) c'est un de nos joueurs; (employee) il est dans nos fichiers; **to be in sb's good books** être dans les petits papiers de qn, être bien vu par qn; **to be in sb's bad books** être mal vu par qn; **to bring sb to b. for sth** forcer qn à rendre compte de qch; Fam **to throw the b. at sb** (tell off) passer un savon à qn; (punish) donner le maximum à qn; Horseracing **to make a b.** faire un pari; **we've opened a b. on how late he'll be** les paris sont ouverts sur le retard qu'il va avoir

3 b. of stamps/tickets carnet m de timbres/billets; **b. of matches** pochette f d'allumettes

VT **1** (seat, room, table) réserver, retenir; Rail, Aviat (ticket, seat) réserver; Theat etc (performer) engager; **I've booked you on the next flight** je vous ai réservé une place sur le prochain vol; **fully booked** (theatre, flight) complet; **I'm booked for this evening** (have engagement) je suis pris ce soir

2 Fam (of policeman) (motorist) dresser une contravention à; (of referee) (player) donner un avertissement à; **I was booked for speeding yesterday** hier j'ai eu une contravention pour excès de vitesse; **have you booked him?** (in police station) tu as pris tous ses renseignements?

3 Am Fam **to b. it** (leave) mettre les bouts, s'arracher

VI **1** Rail, Aviat, Theat réserver une place; (in restaurant, hotel) réserver; **to b. through to Nice** prendre tous les billets nécessaires pour Nice

2 Am Fam (leave) mettre les bouts, s'arracher; (move quickly) foncer

▸▸ **b. club** club m du livre; Acct **b. debts** comptes mpl fournisseurs, dettes fpl compte; **b. end** serre-livres m inv; Acct **b. entry** écriture f comptable; Acct **b. entry transfer** transfert m de compte à compte; **b. fair** salon m du livre; (secondhand) foire f aux livres; **b. matches** allumettes fpl plates; Acct **b. of original entry** livre-journal m, pl livres-journaux; **b. review** revue f littéraire; **b. reviewer** critique mf littéraire; Br **b. token** bon m d'achat de livres, chèque-livre m, pl chèques-livres; **the b. trade** l'industrie f du livre, la librairie; Fin **b. value** valeur f comptable, valeur de bilan

▸ **book in** VI (of hotel guest) se faire inscrire sur le registre

VT SEP (of receptionist) inscrire au registre

▸ **book into** VT INSEP **to b. into a hotel** prendre une chambre d'hôtel

VT SEP **I've booked myself into the best hotel in town** (in advance) j'ai réservé une chambre dans le meilleur hôtel de la ville; (on the spur of the moment) j'ai pris une chambre dans le meilleur hôtel de la ville

▸ **book out** VI (of hotel guest) quitter un/l'hôtel

VT SEP (find other hotel for) trouver un autre hôtel pour; **I booked them out at noon** (they left) ils ont réglé leur note à midi

▸ **book up** VI (make reservations) réserver; **have you booked up for your holiday?** est-ce que vous avez réservé pour vos vacances?

VT SEP (usu passive) **the hotel is all booked up** l'hôtel est complet; **I'm booked up for this evening** (have engagement) je suis pris ce soir

bookable ['bʊkəb(ə)l] ADJ Theat etc (seat) qui peut être réservé à l'avance

bookbinder ['bʊkbaɪndər] N relieur, -ieuse

bookbinding ['bʊkbaɪndɪŋ] N reliure f

bookcase ['bʊkkeɪs] N bibliothèque f

booker ['bʊkər] N *(for model, actor etc)* agent *m*

bookie ['bʊkɪ] N *Horseracing Fam* bookmaker *m*, book *m*

booking ['bʊkɪŋ] N **1** *(of order)* enregistrement *m*, inscription *f* **2** *(of room, seat etc)* réservation *f*, *(of seats, tickets)* location *f*, *Theat etc (of performer)* engagement *m*; **to make a b.** *(for theatre, plane seat etc)* réserver une place; *(for restaurant)* réserver (une table); **I have a b. in the name of Smith** *(to hotel clerk)* j'ai réservé au nom de Smith
▸▸ **b. agency** agence *f* de réservation; **b. clerk** préposé, -ée aux réservations; **bookings diary** agenda *m* de réservation; **b. fee** frais *mpl* de réservation; **b. form** feuille *f ou* fiche *f* de réservation; **b. office** bureau *m* de location; **b. status** état *m* de la réservation

bookish ['bʊkɪʃ] ADJ **1** *(studious)* studieux **2** *Pej (person, style)* pédant

book-keeper N *Com* comptable *mf*

book-keeping N *Com* comptabilité *f*

book-learning N érudition *f*, *Pej* savoir *m* livresque

booklet ['bʊklɪt] N *(pamphlet)* brochure *f*, *(small book)* plaquette *f*

booklover ['bʊklʌvər] N bibliophile *mf*

bookmaker ['bʊkmeɪkər] N *Horseracing* bookmaker *m*

bookmark ['bʊkmɑːk] N *also Comput* signet *m*
VT *Comput (web page)* créer un signet sur; **don't forget to b. this page** n'oublie pas de créer un signet sur cette page
▸▸ *Comput* **b. list** liste *f* de signets

bookmobile ['bʊkməbiːl] N *Am* bibliobus *m*

bookplate ['bʊkpleɪt] N ex-libris *m inv*

bookrest ['bʊkrest] N lutrin *m*

bookseller ['bʊkselər] N libraire *mf*; **second-hand b.** bouquiniste *mf*

bookselling ['bʊkselɪŋ] N librairie *f*, commerce *m* du livre

bookshelf, *pl* **bookshelves** ['bʊkʃelf, -ʃelvz] N rayon *m*, étagère *f*

bookshop ['bʊkʃɒp] N librairie *f*

bookstall ['bʊkstɔːl] N **1** *(selling second-hand books)* étalage *m* de livres **2** *(in station)* kiosque *m* à journaux

bookstore ['bʊkstɔːr] N *Am* librairie *f*

bookworm ['bʊkwɜːm] N **1** *(person)* mordu, -ue de lecture **2** *(insect)* anobion *m*, ptine *m*

Boolean ['buːliən] ADJ booléen
▸▸ **B. algebra** algèbre *f* booléenne; **B. function** fonction *f* booléenne; **B. operator** opérateur *m* booléen; **B. search** recherche *f* booléenne

boom[1] [buːm] N **1** *(at harbour mouth)* barrage *m* flottant, barre *f ou* estacade *f* flottante **2** *Naut (for jib)* bout-dehors *m*, *pl* bouts-dehors; **derrick b.** mât *m* de charge; **swinging b.** tangon *m* **3** *(of crane)* flèche *f*, *Cin, TV (for microphone)* perche *f*, *Fam* girafe *f*
▸▸ *Cin, TV* **b. microphone** micro *m* sur perche; *Cin, TV* **b. operator** perchiste *m*

boom[2] N *(sound)* *(of cannon, thunder, waves)* grondement *m*; *(of wind)* mugissement *m*; *(of organ)* ronflement *m*; *(of bells)* bourdonnement *m*; *Aut (of engine)* ronflement, grondement; **the b. of his voice** les éclats *mpl* de sa voix
VI *(of thunder, waves)* gronder; *(of wind)* mugir; *(of guns)* gronder, tonner; *(of organ)* ronfler; *(of bells)* résonner sourdement; *(of voice)* retentir; **'stop!' he boomed** 'arrête!' dit-il de sa voix retentissante
▸ **boom out** VI *(sound loudly)* résonner
VT SEP *(utter loudly)* *(order)* hurler

boom[3] N *Com, Fin etc* boom *m*

VI *(of trade, business etc)* être florissant
▸▸ *Econ* **b. town** ville *f* en plein essor, ville-champignon *f*, *pl* villes-champignons; *(prosperous)* ville prospère

boomerang ['buːməræŋ] N *(for throwing)*, *Fig* boomerang *m*
VI *Fig* faire boomerang; **the joke boomeranged on him** la plaisanterie lui est retombée dessus

booming ['buːmɪŋ] ADJ *(wind)* mugissant; *(thunder, voice)* retentissant

boon [buːn] N **1** *(useful item)* avantage *m*; **I found it a great b.** cela m'a rendu grand service **2** *Arch Lit (favour)* faveur *f*
▸▸ **b. companion** bon compère *m*; **they're b. companions** ils sont inséparables

boondocks ['buːndɒks], **boonies** ['buːnɪz] NPL *Am Fam* (grande) banlieue *f*; **to live in the boonies** habiter à Perpète-(les-Oies)

boondoggle ['buːndɒg(ə)l] VI *Am Fam* flemmarder, peigner la girafe

boor [bɔːr] N rustre *m*, rustaud *m*

boorish ['bɔːrɪʃ] ADJ *(manners, behaviour, person)* rustre, grossier

boorishly ['bɔːrɪʃlɪ] ADV grossièrement, de façon rustre

boorishness ['bɔːrɪʃnɪs] N grossièreté *f*

boost [buːst] N **1** **to give a b. to** *(industry, production, exports, sales etc)* relancer; *(morale)* remonter; *(product)* faire du battage pour; *Fam* **to give sb a b.** *(morally)* regonfler qn; *(in finding a job)* donner un coup de pouce à qn; *(over a wall)* soulever qn; **to give sb's confidence a b.** redonner confiance à qn; **to give sb's morale a b.** remonter le moral à qn; **that win will have given her ego a b.** cette victoire aura regonflé son amour-propre **2** *Elec* survoltage *m*; *Aviat* surpression *f*
VT **1** *(industry, production, exports etc)* relancer; *(recruitment, numbers etc)* augmenter; *(morale)* remonter; *(product)* faire du battage pour; *Fam (person) (morally)* regonfler; *(in finding job)* donner un coup de pouce à; **to b. sb's hopes/confidence** redonner de l'espoir/de la confiance à qn **2** *(speed, energy, pressure of sth)* augmenter; *Elec* survolter; *(engine)* suralimenter **3** *Am Fam (steal)* piquer, faucher; *(break into)* cambrioler

booster ['buːstər] N **1** *Elec* survolteur *m* **2** *(of missile)* propulseur *m* auxiliaire de départ, booster *m* **3** *Aviat* démarreur *m* auxiliaire, accélérateur *m* (de décollage) **4** *(supercharger)* compresseur *m*; *(on heater)* ventilateur *m*; *(for brakes)* servofrein *m* **5** *Electron* suramplificateur *m*, booster *m* **6** *Chem* renforçateur *m*
▸▸ **b. cushion** *(in car)* rehausseur *m*; *Med* **b. dose** (dose *f* de) rappel *m*; *Med* **b. injection** (injection *f* de) rappel; **b. rocket** fusée *f* de démarrage; **b. seat** *(in car)* (siège *m*) rehausseur, siège de rehausse; **b. station** *Tel* station *f* relais; *Tech* station auxiliaire de pompage

boot[1] [buːt] N **1** *(footwear)* botte *f*, *(short)* bottine *f*, *(for football, rugby)* chaussure *f*; **walking** *or* **climbing boots** chaussures de marche; **riding boots** bottes de cheval *ou* de cavalier; **... or you'll feel (the toe of) my b. up your backside** ... sinon tu vas recevoir un bon coup de pied au derrière; *Fam* **to put** *or* **stick the b. in** *(kick someone)* flanquer des coups de pied à; **they really put the b. in** *(kicked him)* ils l'ont vraiment bourré de coups de pied; *Fig* **you really know how to put the b. in!** tu es vraiment doué pour enfoncer le couteau dans la plaie!; *Fig* **the b.'s on the other foot** les rôles sont renversés *ou* inversés; *Fig* **you can bet your boots that ...** je te fiche mon billet que ...; *Fig Fam* **to give sb (the order of) the b.** *(from job)* mettre *ou* flanquer qn à la porte; *(from relationship)* plaquer qn; *Fig* **to get the b.** *(from job)* être

mis à la porte; *(from relationship)* se faire plaquer; *Fam* **as tough as old boots** *(meat)* dur comme de la semelle; *(plant)* très résistant; **to die with one's boots on** *(in battle)* mourir les bottes aux pieds; *Fig* rester fidèle au poste jusqu'à la mort; *Fig Fam* **to be too big for one's boots** avoir les chevilles qui enflent, avoir la grosse tête
2 *Br Aut* coffre *m*
3 *(kick)* coup *m* de pied; **to give a ball a b.** donner un coup de pied dans un ballon; **he needs a b. up the backside** il a besoin d'un bon coup de pied au derrière
4 *Br Fam Pej (ugly woman)* boudin *m*, cageot *m*
VT *Fam* flanquer des coups de pied à; **to b. sb out** *(dismiss)* flanquer qn à la porte; **her parents booted her out of the house** ses parents l'ont mise à la porte
VI *(of computer)* s'amorcer
▸▸ *Fam* **b. camp** *Am Mil* = camp *m* d'entraînement pour nouvelles recrues; *Br (centre for young offenders)* = centre *m* de redressement *(pour jeunes délinquants)*; *Comput* **b. disk** *(hard)* disque *m* de démarrage; *(floppy)* disquette *f* de démarrage; *Br Aut* **b. light** éclaireur *m* de coffre; *Br* **b. sale** = sorte de marché aux puces où des particuliers apportent dans leur voiture les objets de brocante qu'ils souhaitent vendre; *Comput* **b. sector** secteur *m* d'initialisation; *Comput* **b. track** piste *f* d'amorçage
▸ **boot up** *Comput* VI *(of computer)* s'amorcer, démarrer; *(of person)* démarrer
VT SEP *(computer)* amorcer, faire démarrer

boot[2] N *(only in the phrase)* **to b.** en sus, par-dessus le marché; **and a liar/a thief to b.** et par-dessus le marché c'est un menteur/un voleur

bootable ['buːtəb(ə)l] ADJ *Comput* amorçable

bootblack ['buːtblæk] N cireur, -euse, de chaussures

bootee [buː'tiː] N **1** *(short boot)* bottillon *m* **2** *(baby's)* chausson *m*

booth [buːð, buːθ] N *(at fair)* baraque *f*, *Am (at exhibition)* stand *m*; *Tel* cabine *f*, *(in restaurant)* alcôve *f*

bootjack ['buːtdʒæk] N tire-botte *m*, *pl* tire-bottes

bootlace ['buːtleɪs] N lacet *m* (de botte)

bootleg ['buːtleg] N *(cassette, video)* cassette *f* pirate
ADJ *(whisky)* de contrebande; *(record, video)* pirate
VT (**-gg-**) *(alcohol)* *(produce)* produire illégalement; *(transport)* transporter illégalement; *(sell)* vendre illégalement; *(video, tape)* pirater
VI *(deal)* *(in alcoholic drinks)* trafiquer, faire de la contrebande; *(in videos, software etc)* faire du piratage
▸▸ **b. trousers** = pantalon *m* légèrement évasé que l'on porte avec des bottes

bootlegger ['buːtlegər] N *(of videos, software etc)* personne *f* qui se livre au piratage; *Hist (of alcohol)* bootlegger *m*

bootlegging ['buːtlegɪŋ] N *(of videos, software)* piratage *m*; *(of alcohol)* contrebande *f*

bootlicker ['buːtlɪkər] N *Fam* lèche-bottes *mf inv*

bootlicking ['buːtlɪkɪŋ] N *Fam* lèche-bottes *m*; **b. is his speciality** il est spécialiste du lèche-bottes

bootloader ['buːtləʊdər] N *Comput* chargeur-amorce *m*, *pl* chargeurs-amorces

bootmaker ['buːtmeɪkər] N bottier *m*

bootstrap ['buːtstræp] N **1** *(on boot)* languette *f*, *Fig* **to pull oneself up by one's bootstraps** se faire tout seul **2** *Comput* amorce *f*, programme *m* d'amorcement

▶▶ *Comput* **b. loader** chargeur-amorce *m*, *pl* chargeurs-amorces, chargeur *m* initial; *Comput* **b. routine** routine *f* d'amorçage

booty ['buːtɪ] **N** 1 *(loot)* butin *m* 2 *Am Sl (buttocks)* cul *m*, derche *m*; **to get some b.** *(have sexual intercourse)* s'envoyer en l'air

booze [buːz] *Fam* **vi** boire, picoler; **he's gone out boozing** il est allé picoler
N boisson *f* (alcoolique); **there's no more b.** il n'y a plus rien à boire; **to go on the b.** se mettre à boire; **I'm (staying) off the b.** j'ai arrêté de boire

boozehound ['buːzhaʊnd] **N** *Am Sl* poivrot, -ote

boozer ['buːzər] **N** *Sl* 1 *(drunkard)* poivrot, -ote 2 *Br (pub)* pub *m*; **down the b.** au pub

booze-up **N** *Br Sl* bringue *f*; **we're having a b. on Friday** on fait une bringue vendredi

boozily ['buːzɪlɪ] **ADV** *Fam* **to look at sb b.** regarder qn à travers les vapeurs de l'alcool; **to say sth b.** dire qch d'une voix avinée

boozy ['buːzɪ] **ADJ** *Fam (breath)* qui sent l'alcool; *(voice)* aviné; *(look, manner)* d'ivrogne; **a b. evening** une soirée bien arrosée; **a b. old man** un vieil ivrogne

bop[1] [bɒp] **N** 1 *Mus* bop *m* 2 *Fam (at disco)* danse *f*, **to go for a b.** aller danser
vi *Fam (at disco)* danser

bop[2] *Fam* **N** *(blow)* léger coup *m*
vt *(hit)* donner un léger coup à

bo-peep [bəʊ-] **N** *Fam* cache-cache *m inv*

boracic [bəˈræsɪk] **ADJ** *Chem (acid)* borique; **b. ointment** pommade *f* boriquée

borage ['bɒrɪdʒ] **N** *Bot, Culin* bourrache *f*

borax ['bɔːræks] **N** *Chem etc* borax *m*

bordeaux [bɔːˈdəʊ] **N** *(wine)* bordeaux *m*

border ['bɔːdər] **N** 1 *(of rug, plate, picture) also Comput* bordure *f*
2 *(edge) (of path)* bord *m*; **there were flowers along the b. of the path** il y avait des fleurs sur le bord du chemin
3 *(between two countries)* frontière *f*, **to cross the b.** passer la frontière; **north of the B.** *(from viewpoint of England)* en Écosse; *(from viewpoint of the US)* au Canada; **south of the B.** *(from viewpoint of Scotland)* en Angleterre; *(from viewpoint of Canada)* aux États-Unis; *(from viewpoint of the US)* au Mexique; **the Borders** *(in Britain)* = région *f* vallonnée du sud-est de l'Écosse
4 *(hem)* bordure *f*
5 *(flowerbed)* plate-bande *f*, *pl* plates-bandes
vt 1 *(be adjacent to) (lake, garden)* border; *(country)* confiner à *ou* avec; **the countries that b. the Mediterranean** les pays qui sont en bordure de la Méditerranée 2 *Sewing* lisérer
▶▶ **b. controls** contrôles *mpl* aux frontières; **b. crossing** passage *m* de frontière; *Mil* **b. guard** garde-frontière *m*, *pl* gardes-frontières; **b. post** poste-frontière *m*, *pl* postes-frontières; **b. region** région frontalière; **b. town** ville *f* frontière *ou* frontalière
▶ **border on** **vt insep** 1 *(of territory) (another country)* confiner à; **the two countries b. on each other** les deux pays se touchent *ou* ont une frontière commune; **his estate borders on mine** ses terres touchent les miennes 2 *(be almost equivalent to) (madness, cruelty etc)* approcher de, être voisin de; **to b. on rudeness/a lie/the absurd** friser l'impolitesse/le mensonge/l'absurde; **he was bordering on sixty** il frisait la soixantaine; **emotion bordering on terror** émotion voisine de la terreur

borderer ['bɔːdərər] **N** *Br* habitant, -ante des "Borders"

bordering ['bɔːdərɪŋ] **ADJ** *(country)* contigu, *f* -uë, limitrophe

borderland ['bɔːdəlænd] **N** pays *m* frontalier *ou* limitrophe; *Fig* **the b. between sleeping and waking** l'état de demi-sommeil

borderline ['bɔːdəlaɪn] **N** *(between two categories etc)* distinction *f*; *(between two countries)* frontière *f*, *Fig* **the b. between sanity and insanity** la limite entre le bon sens et la folie; **she's on the b.** c'est un cas limite
ADJ **a b. case** un cas limite; **it's b.** c'est un cas limite

bore[1] ['bɔːr] **N** 1 *(person)* personne *f* ennuyeuse, *Fam* raseur, -euse; **what a (crashing) b. (he is)!** ce qu'il est barbant *ou* rasoir!; **he's a real b. on the subject of gardening** il est vraiment barbant quand il se met à parler de jardinage 2 *(thing)* chose *f* ennuyeuse; **the film was a bit of a b.** le film était un peu ennuyeux; **I know it's a b. but it's got to be done** je sais que ce n'est pas marrant mais il faut le faire; **what a b.!** quelle barbe!
vt ennuyer, *Fam* raser, *Fam* barber; *Fam* **it/he bores me rigid** *or* **stiff** *or* **to death** *or* **to tears** ça/il m'ennuie à mourir; *Fam* **to b. the pants off sb** ennuyer qn à mourir; **I won't b. you with the details** je vous passe les détails

bore[2] **N** 1 *(diameter)* calibre *m*; *(of pipe etc)* alésage *m*; *(of firearm)* calibre 2 *(cylinder) (of firearm)* âme *f*, **smooth/rifled b.** âme lisse/rayée 3 *Min (hole)* trou *m* de sonde, sondage *m*, forage *m*
vt *(well)* foncer; *(hole)* forer, creuser; *(cylinder)* aléser
vi **to b. into wood** *(of insect)* creuser un trou *ou* une galerie dans le bois; **to b. through sth** percer qch; *Min* **to b. for water/minerals** faire un sondage *ou* sonder pour trouver de l'eau/des minéraux

bore[3] **N** *(wave)* mascaret *m*

bore[4] **PT** *see* **bear**[2]

Boreal ['bɔːrɪəl] **ADJ** *(forest)* boréal, -als *ou* -aux

bored [bɔːd] **ADJ** *(look, sigh etc)* d'ennui; *(person)* qui s'ennuie; **you look b.** tu as l'air de t'ennuyer; **to be** *or* **get b.** s'ennuyer; **I'm never b.** je ne m'ennuie jamais; **she is b. with him/it** elle en a assez de lui/elle en a assez; **he's a bit b. with his job** il s'ennuie un peu dans son travail; **I'm getting b. with this conversation** j'en ai assez de cette conversation; *Fam* **to be b. rigid** *or* **to tears** *or* **out of one's mind** s'ennuyer à mourir

boredom ['bɔːdəm] **N** ennui *m*

borehole ['bɔːhəʊl] **N** *Min (exploratory)* trou *m* de sonde, sondage *m*; *(for mine)* trou de mine

borer ['bɔːrər] **N** *(device) (for wood, metal)* foret *m*; *Min (of well)* sonde *f*

boric ['bɔːrɪk] **ADJ** *Chem (acid etc)* borique

boring[1] ['bɔːrɪŋ] **ADJ** *(tedious)* ennuyeux, *Fam* barbant, *Fam* rasant, *Fam* rasoir

boring[2] **ADJ** *(insect)* térébrant
N *(of hole etc)* percement *m*; *Tech* forage *m*, perçage *m*; *(of cylinder)* alésage *m*; *Min* sondage *m*, forage
▶▶ *Tech* **b. machine** *(for wood)* perceuse *f*, *(for metal)* alésoir *m*

born [bɔːn] *(pp of* **bear**[2] *used in formation of passive verb)* **to be b.** naître; **I was b. in London/in 1977** je suis né à Londres/en 1977; **my mother died when I was b.** ma mère est décédée en me mettant au monde; **Queen Victoria was still on the throne when I was b.** la reine Victoria régnait toujours quand je suis né; **the house where I was b.** ma maison natale; **he is French b.** il est français de naissance; **to be b. deaf/blind** être sourd/aveugle de naissance; **to be b. lucky** être né coiffé; *Fam* **I wasn't b. yesterday** je ne suis pas né d'hier *ou* tombé de la dernière pluie; *Hum* **were you b. in a barn** *or* **a stable?**

on ne t'a jamais appris à fermer les portes?; *Fig* **it was a decision b. of necessity** cette décision était dictée par les circonstances; ... **he said, with a cynicism b. of experience** ... dit-il avec le cynisme que lui conférait l'expérience
ADJ **a b. storyteller/linguist** un conteur/linguiste né; **she's a b. liar** elle ment comme elle respire; **a b. loser** un raté irrécupérable; **a Londoner b. and bred** un vrai Londonien de Londres; **in all my b. days** de toute ma vie

born-again **ADJ** *Rel, Hum* régénéré; *Fig* **b. vegetarian** personne *f* devenue végétarienne (et qui essaye de convaincre les autres)
▶▶ **b. Christian** chrétien, -ienne régénéré(e)

borne **PP** *see* **bear**[2]

Borneo ['bɔːnɪəʊ] **N** Bornéo *m*

borough ['bʌrə] **N** *Br* 1 *(British town)* = ville *f* représentée à la Chambre des communes par un ou plusieurs députés 2 *(in London)* = une des 32 subdivisions administratives de Londres 3 *(in New York)* = une des cinq subdivisions administratives de New York
▶▶ **b. council** = conseil *m* municipal d'un "borough"

borrow ['bɒrəʊ] **vt** emprunter (**from** à); **to b. money from sb** emprunter de l'argent à qn, faire un emprunt à qn; **can I b. the car?** est-ce que je peux prendre la voiture?; **to b. an idea from sb** emprunter une idée à qn; **this word was borrowed from Latin** ce mot est un emprunt au latin
vi emprunter; **to b. from sb** *(money)* faire un emprunt à qn, emprunter de l'argent à qn
▶ **borrow against** **vt insep** *Fin* emprunter sur; **the company borrowed against its assets** l'entreprise a emprunté de l'argent en utilisant son actif comme garantie

borrowed ['bɒrəʊd] **ADJ** **the doctors say he's living on b. time** *(close to death)* les médecins disent qu'il n'en a plus pour longtemps; **the company is living on b. time** les jours de l'entreprise sont comptés; **my grandfather is living on b. time** *(is very old)* mon grand-père a de la chance d'être encore en vie; **he'd been living on b. time since he was caught stealing from his employer** *(his job was in danger)* il était en sursis depuis qu'on l'avait pris à voler son employeur
▶▶ *Fin* **b. capital** capitaux *mpl* empruntés *ou* d'emprunt

borrower ['bɒrəʊər] **N** emprunteur, -euse

borrowing ['bɒrəʊɪŋ] **N** *(action, money)* emprunt *m*; **financed by b.** financé par des emprunts
▶▶ **b. capacity** capacité *f* d'endettement, capacité à emprunter; **b. limit** maximum *m* d'emprunt, limite *f* d'endettement; **b. power** capacité de crédit *ou* d'emprunt *ou* d'endettement; **b. rate** taux *m* d'intérêt des emprunts; **b. requirements** besoins *mpl* d'emprunt

borsch [bɔːʃ] **N** *Culin* bortsch *m*

borstal ['bɔːst(ə)l] **N** *Br Formerly* maison *f* de redressement *(pour jeunes délinquants âgés de 15 à 21 ans)*
▶▶ **b. boy** jeune délinquant *m*

borzoi ['bɔːzɔɪ] **N** *(dog)* lévrier *m* russe, barzoï *m*

bosh [bɒʃ] *Old-fashioned Fam* **N** bêtises *fpl*, blagues *fpl*
INT n'importe quoi!, sottises!

bos'n ['bəʊs(ə)n] **N** = **boatswain**

Bosnia ['bɒznɪə] **N** Bosnie *f*; **B.-Herzegovina** Bosnie-Herzégovine *f*

Bosnian ['bɒznɪən] **N** Bosniaque *mf*
ADJ bosniaque

bosom ['bʊzəm] **N** *(of woman)* seins *mpl*; *Old-fashioned, Lit (of person)* poitrine *f*, *Fig*

in the b. of one's family au sein de sa famille; in the b. of the Church dans le giron de l'Église
▸▸b. friend ami, -ie intime; they're b. friends ils sont grands amis

bosomy ['bʊzəmɪ] ADJ (woman) à la poitrine opulente; she was a b. lady elle avait une poitrine opulente

Bosp(h)orus (the) [ðə'bɒsfərəs, ðə'bɒspərəs] N le Bosphore

boss[1] [bɒs] Fam N (person in charge) patron, -onne, chef m; Am (of political party) chef; the trade-union bosses les gens mpl à la tête du syndicat; show them who's (the) b. montre-leur qui commande ici; to be one's own b. être son propre patron
ADJ esp Am (excellent) épatant, merveilleux VT (person) donner des ordres à; Fig to b. the show faire la loi
▸ boss about, boss around VT SEP donner des ordres à; stop bossing me about! j'en ai assez que tu me donnes des ordres!

boss[2] N 1 (knob) protubérance f, Archit, Metal, Zool etc bosse f, (on furniture) capiton m 2 Tech mamelon m, portée f, Aviat (of propeller) moyeu m; Aut (centre of steering wheel) bossette f, centre b. (of wheel, crank) tourteau m

boss-eyed ADJ Br Fam qui louche; to be b. avoir un œil qui dit merde à l'autre

bossily ['bɒsɪlɪ] ADV Fam de façon autoritaire

bossiness ['bɒsɪnɪs] N Fam (of person, manner) façons fpl autoritaires

bossy ['bɒsɪ] ADJ Fam autoritaire; don't be so b., don't be such a b. boots arrête de jouer au petit chef

Boston matrix ['bɒstən] N Mktg matrice f BCG

bosun ['bəʊs(ə)n] N = boatswain

bot [bɒt] N Comput robot m

botanical [bə'tænɪk(ə)l] ADJ botanique
▸▸b. garden(s) jardin m botanique

botanist ['bɒtənɪst] N botaniste mf

botanize ['bɒtənaɪz] VI herboriser

botany ['bɒtənɪ] N botanique f
▸▸ Tex b. wool laine f mérinos

botch [bɒtʃ] Fam N travail m mal fait ou salopé; you've made an awful b. of it tu as complètement salopé le boulot; to make a b. of an interview/speech rater complètement un entretien/un discours; she made a terrible b. of putting up the shelves elle a mis les étagères n'importe comment
VT (job) saloper; (interview, speech) rater; he botched the shelves il a mis les étagères n'importe comment
▸ botch up VT SEP (job) saloper; (interview, speech) rater

botched [bɒtʃt] ADJ Fam a b. attempt at suicide une tentative de suicide ratée; his b. apology only made matters worse ses excuses minables n'ont fait qu'empirer la situation; a b. job un travail de sagouin

botcher ['bɒtʃər] N Fam bousilleur, -euse

botch-up N = botch h

botel ['bəʊtel] N bateau-hôtel m, pl bateaux-hotels; (on barge) péniche-hôtel f, pl péniches-hôtels

both [bəʊθ] ADJ, PRON les deux, tous (les) deux, toutes (les) deux; b. brothers, b. (of) the brothers les deux frères; b. (of them) are dead ils sont morts tous (les) deux; b. of us saw it nous l'avons vu tous les deux; he has two houses, b. of which are vacant il a deux maisons, qui sont vides toutes les deux; she kissed him on b. cheeks elle l'a embrassé sur les deux joues; to hold sth in b. hands tenir qch à deux mains; on b. sides des deux côtés; b. alike l'un comme l'autre,

look b. ways (when crossing street) regarde des deux côtés; you can't have it b. ways on ne peut pas avoir le beurre et l'argent du beurre; Naut stop b. engines stoppez partout VOIR GRAMMAIRE A5; A37
ADV b. you and I vous et moi; b. you and I know it's not that simple vous savez comme moi que cela n'est pas aussi simple; she is b. intelligent and beautiful elle est à la fois intelligente et belle

bother ['bɒðər] N 1 (trouble) ennui m; to be having a bit or a spot of b. avoir quelques ennuis (with avec); it's such a b. having to take it back c'est tellement embêtant d'avoir à le ramener; to be in b. with the police avoir des ennuis avec la police; if it's not too much b. si cela ne vous dérange pas trop; I hope I haven't put you to a lot of b. j'espère que je ne vous ai pas trop dérangé; it's a lot of b. to go to ça représente beaucoup de dérangement pour pas grand-chose; I hate to be a b., but … je suis désolé de vous déranger, mais …; it's no b. at all ça ne m'ennuie pas du tout; it's not worth the b. cela ne vaut pas la peine; to go to the b. of doing sth se donner la peine de faire qch 2 Br Sl (fighting) bagarre f; there was a bit of b. in the pub il y a eu un peu de bagarre dans le pub
VT 1 (annoy) ennuyer; (disturb) déranger; (be in the way of) gêner; does the light b. you? est-ce que la lumière vous gêne ou dérange?; my back's still bothering me (giving pain) j'ai toujours des problèmes de dos; his old wound bothers him in damp weather sa vieille blessure le fait souffrir par temps humide; I hate to b. you, but … je suis désolé de vous déranger, mais …; he didn't even b. to apologize il n'a même pas pris la peine de s'excuser; don't b. me! laissez-moi tranquille!; I can't be bothered (to do it) ça ne me dit rien (de le faire); b. (it)! zut!; b. the man! qu'il aille au diable!
2 (worry) inquiéter; to be bothered about sth s'inquiéter de qch, se faire du mauvais sang pour qch; don't b. yourself or your head about me ne vous inquiétez pas pour moi; Fam I'm not bothered cela m'est égal
VI 1 (take trouble) s'occuper (with de); (make an effort) prendre ou se donner la peine (to do sth de faire qch); don't b. to ring me up/to turn the lights off ce n'est pas la peine de me téléphoner/d'éteindre la lumière; don't b. with the dishes just now ne t'embête pas à faire la vaisselle maintenant; I'll call you next week – don't b.! (I can get on without you) je t'appellerai la semaine prochaine – te fatigue pas!
2 (worry) s'inquiéter (about de); he doesn't b. about anything il ne s'inquiète de rien

botheration [bɒðə'reɪʃən] INT Old-fashioned Fam zut!

bothersome ['bɒðəsəm] ADJ gênant

bottle ['bɒt(ə)l] N 1 bouteille f, (small) (for perfume etc) flacon m; (wide-mouthed) bocal m; (for baby) biberon m; Med urinal m, Fam pistolet m; bring your own b. (on invitation) chacun doit amener une bouteille; (notice in restaurant) = les clients peuvent apporter leur vin (étant donné que le restaurant n'a pas de licence); he drank the whole b. il a bu toute la bouteille; brought up on the b. (baby) élevé au biberon; Fam to be fond of the b. aimer la bouteille; Fam to be on the b. boire; Fam to hit or take to the b. commencer à picoler; Fam he's been hitting the b. a lot recently il picole beaucoup ces temps-ci
2 Br Sl (courage, nerve) cran m; to have a lot of b. avoir beaucoup de cran; to lose one's b. se dégonfler; (permanently) perdre son assurance
VT (wine etc) mettre en bouteilles; (jam etc)

mettre en bocal; autumn is the best time for bottling fruit l'automne est la meilleure saison pour faire des conserves de fruits
▸▸b. bank = conteneur m pour la collecte du verre usagé; Fam Pej b. blonde blonde f décolorée; b. green vert m bouteille; b. opener ouvre-bouteilles m inv, décapsuleur m; Br b. party = soirée f où chacun des invités apporte à boire
▸ bottle out VI Br Sl (be too frightened) se dégonfler; he bottled out of the fight il s'est dégonflé au dernier moment et a refusé de se battre; he bottled out of telling her the truth finalement il a eu la trouille de lui dire la vérité
▸ bottle up VT SEP (one's feelings) étouffer; (one's anger) refouler, ravaler

bottlebrush ['bɒt(ə)lbrʌʃ] N 1 (for cleaning) goupillon m 2 (plant) callistemon m

bottled ['bɒt(ə)ld] ADJ (wine, beer, gas etc) en bouteille(s); b. fruit fruits mpl en bocaux; b. water eau f minérale

bottle-fed ADJ nourri au biberon

bottle-feed VT (baby, lamb etc) nourrir au biberon

bottle-feeding N alimentation f au biberon

bottleful ['bɒt(ə)lfʊl] N a b. of sth une pleine bouteille de qch; by the b. à pleine bouteille

bottleneck ['bɒt(ə)lnek] N 1 goulot m (de bouteille) 2 Fig (in road) rétrécissement m de la chaussée; (traffic jam) embouteillage m, bouchon m; (in production etc) goulet m ou goulot m d'étranglement 3 Mus (guitar style) bottleneck m

bottlenosed dolphin ['bɒt(ə)lnəʊzd] N grand dauphin m, dauphin à gros nez

bottle-washer N (person) laveur, -euse de bouteilles; (machine) rince-bouteilles m inv

bottling ['bɒt(ə)lɪŋ] N (of wine etc) mise f en bouteille(s); (of fruit) mise en bocaux

BOTTOM ['bɒtəm] N 1 Fam (of person) derrière m
2 bottoms (of pyjamas, tracksuit) pantalon m, bas m
3 (of hill, stairs, page) bas m; (of well, box, sea) fond m; at the b. of the garden/of my bag au fond du jardin/de mon sac; he's at the b. of the class il est le dernier de sa classe; at the b. of the page au ou en bas de la page; to send a ship to the b. envoyer un bâtiment par le fond; to go to the b. (of ship) couler; to strike or touch b. (of ship) toucher le fond; to touch b. (of swimmer), Fig toucher le fond; from the b. of one's heart du fond du cœur; to get to the b. of sth (solve) tirer qch au clair; to get to the b. of things aller au fond des choses; to be at the b. of sth (be instigator) être derrière qch, être l'instigateur de qch; (be cause) être la cause de qch; at b. au fond, dans le fond
4 (of chair) siège m; Naut (of ship) carène f, fond m; the b. of my glass/plate (inside) le fond de mon verre/assiette; (outside) le dessous de mon verre/assiette; to put sth b. up(wards) mettre qch sens dessus dessous; a box with a false b. une boîte à double fond; to knock the b. out of (box etc) défoncer; Fig (argument) démolir; the b. has fallen out of the market le marché s'est effondré; Fam bottoms up! (empty your glass) cul sec!; (cheers) à votre santé!; Billiards to put b. on a ball faire de l'effet à revenir ou de l'effet rétrograde
5 Aut (gear) première f
ADJ b. half partie f inférieure; it's on the b. shelf il se trouve sur l'étagère du bas; the b. book in the pile le livre qui est en bas de la pile; b. end of the table bout m de la table; b. stair (going up) première marche f, (going

down) dernière marche; *Aut* **in b. gear** en première; *Fam* **you can bet your b. dollar that ...** vous pouvez être sûr que ...

▸▸ *Tech* **b. dead centre** point *m* mort bas; *Br* **b. drawer** *(trousseau)* trousseau *m*; **b. feeder** *(fish)* poisson *m* de fond; *Fam Fig Pej (unsuccessful person)* raté, -ée; *(team, company)* ratés *mpl*; **b. fishing** pêche *f* à la ligne de fond; *Acct, Fin* **b. line** résultat *m* net *ou* final, solde *m* final; *Fig* **the b. line is that we can't afford it** le fait est que nous ne pouvons pas nous le permettre; *Typ* **b. margin** marge *f* du bas; **b. price** prix *m* plancher

▸ **bottom out** VI *(of inflation, unemployment, prices)* atteindre son niveau le plus bas; *(of recession)* atteindre son plancher

bottomless ['bɒtəmlɪs] ADJ **1** *(well etc)* sans fond **2** *(resources, reserves)* inépuisable

▸▸ *Fig* **b. pit** gouffre *m*; **it's like pouring money into a b. pit** c'est comme jeter de l'argent par les fenêtres; **he's a b. pit** *(always hungry)* c'est un crevard

bottommost ['bɒtəmməʊst] ADJ ATTRIB *(shelf)* le plus bas, d'en bas; **the b. book in the pile** le livre qui se trouve tout en bas de la pile; *Lit* **the b. depths** le tréfonds

bottom-of-the-range N modèle *m* de base
ADJ bas de gamme

botty ['bɒtɪ] N *Fam* fesses *fpl*

botulism ['bɒtjʊlɪz(ə)n] N *Med* botulisme *m*

bouclé ['bu:kleɪ] ADJ, N *Tex* bouclé *m*; **b. sweater** pull *m* en bouclette; **b. wool** bouclette *f*

boudoir ['bu:dwɑ:r] N *Old-fashioned* boudoir *m*

bouffant ['bu:fɒn] ADJ *(hair, sleeve, skirt)* bouffant

bougainvillea [bu:gən'vɪlɪə] N *(plant)* bougainvillée *f*

bough [baʊ] N *(of tree)* branche *f*, rameau *m*

bought PT, PP *see* **buy**
▸▸ *Acct, Fin* **b. ledger** cahier *m ou* livre *m* des achats

bouillon ['bu:jɒn] N *Culin* bouillon *m*, consommé *m*
▸▸ *Am* **b. cube** cube *m* de bouillon; *Am* **b. cup** tasse *f* à bouillon *ou* à consommé

boulder ['bəʊldər] N *(gros)* bloc *m* de pierre

boulevard ['bu:ləvɑ:d] N **1** *(street)* boulevard *m* **2** *Am (on road)* terre-plein *m* (central), *pl* terre-pleins (centraux)

bounce [baʊns] N **1** *(of ball)* rebond *m*; **you get a better b. on grass** cela rebondit mieux sur l'herbe; **to catch the ball on the b.** prendre la balle au bond; *Am Fam* **to get the b.** *(from job)* se faire virer; **she gave him the b.** *(from relationship)* elle l'a plaqué; *Br Fam* **on the b.** *(consecutively)* de suite; **they won three games on the b.** ils ont gagné trois matchs de suite
2 *Fam (of person)* entrain *m*; **a shampoo to put the b. back in your hair** un shampooing qui redonnera de la vitalité à vos cheveux
VI **1** *(of ball)* rebondir; *(of breasts)* ballotter; **to b. (up and down) on a bed/trampoline** sauter sur un lit/trampoline; **the epaulettes bounced (up and down) on his shoulders** les épaulettes dansaient sur ses épaules; **to b. up and down** *(not sit still)* s'agiter; **to b. into/out of a room** *(of person)* entrer dans une/sortir d'une pièce en coup de vent *ou* en trombe; *Fam* **the cheque bounced** le chèque a été refusé (parce qu'il était sans provision)
2 *Comput (of e-mail)* revenir à l'expéditeur
VT **1** *(ball)* faire rebondir; *Fig* **to b. a few ideas around** explorer quelques idées; **to b. a baby on one's knee** faire sauter un bébé sur ses genoux; *Fam* **to b. a cheque** *(of bank)* refuser un chèque sans provision

2 *Am Fam (person) (from job, nightclub etc)* flanquer à la porte
▸▸ *Comput* **b. message** = message *m* électronique non délivré revenu à l'expéditeur

▸ **bounce back** VI *(of ball)* rebondir; *Fig (of actor etc) (after failure)* faire son retour; *(from illness, disappointment)* se remettre; *(of Stock Exchange)* reprendre, remonter; *Fin* **the pound has bounced back against the dollar** la livre a regagné du terrain par rapport au dollar

▸ **bounce off** VT SEP **to b. a ball off a wall/off the ground** faire rebondir une balle contre un mur/sur le sol; *Fig* **to b. an idea off sb** soumettre une idée à qn (pour voir sa réaction)
VT INSEP *(of ball, rain, bullets etc) (window, houses)* rebondir contre; *(roof, pavement)* rebondir sur; *Fig* **criticism bounces off him** *(does not penetrate)* les critiques ne l'atteignent pas

bouncer ['baʊnsər] N **1** *Fam (in nightclub etc)* videur *m* **2** *Sl (cheque)* chèque *m* sans provision *ou Fam* en bois **3** *Cr* balle *f* qui rebondit en hauteur

bouncing ['baʊnsɪŋ] ADJ *(ball)* rebondissant; *Fig (baby)* plein de vie et de santé

bouncy ['baʊnsɪ] ADJ **1** *(ball)* qui rebondit; *(hair)* plein de vigueur **2** *Fig (person)* plein d'entrain
▸▸ **b. castle** château *m* gonflable

bound[1] [baʊnd] N *(usu pl) (limit)* limite(s) *f(pl)*, bornes *fpl*; **out of bounds** interdit; *Mil etc* consigné; **to go beyond the bounds of reason** dépasser les bornes de la raison; **it is not beyond the bounds of possibility** c'est dans le domaine du possible; **my fury knew no bounds** je n'ai (pas) pu contenir ma fureur; **his ambition knows no bounds** son ambition ne connaît pas de bornes; **to keep within bounds** ne pas exagérer; **to keep one's imagination within (reasonable) bounds** mettre un frein à son imagination; **to keep one's spending within (reasonable) bounds** modérer *ou* limiter ses dépenses
VT *(usu passive) (area of town)* limiter, délimiter; *(country, region)* être limitrophe de; **France is bounded by Spain in the south** l'Espagne est limitrophe de la France au sud; **an area bounded by Smith Street on the west, James Avenue on the south** une zone délimitée par Smith Street à l'ouest et James Avenue au sud

bound[2] N *(jump)* bond *m*, saut *m*; **at one b.** d'un (seul) bond, d'un saut
VI *(of person, dog)* bondir; *(of ball etc)* rebondir; **he bounded across the room to greet them** il a traversé la pièce d'un bond pour venir les saluer

bound[3] ADJ **1** *Naut* **a ship b. for America** *(still in port)* un navire en partance pour l'Amérique; *(under way)* un navire en route pour l'Amérique; **a plane b. for Paris** un avion à destination de Paris; **the plane which was b. for Paris crashed** l'avion qui volait à destination de Paris s'est écrasé; **where are you b. for?** où allez-vous?
2 *(sure)* **he's b. to come** il ne peut pas manquer de venir, il viendra sûrement; **it's b. to rain tomorrow** il pleuvra sûrement demain; **it's b. to happen** c'est fatal; *Fam* **he'll come, I'll bet** il viendra, j'en suis sûr *ou* je vous le promets; *Am* **he's b. (and determined) to come and see you** il veut absolument venir vous voir
3 *Com* **b. by contract** lié par contrat
▸▸ *Ling* **b. morpheme** morphème *m* lié

bound[4] PT, PP *see* **bind**

boundary ['baʊnd(ə)rɪ] N limite *f*, *Fig (between private and professional life etc)* frontière *f*; *Cr* **to hit** *or* **score a b.** envoyer la balle jusqu'aux limites du terrain; **the boundaries**

of human knowledge les limites de la connaissance humaine
▸▸ *Br Parl* **b. change** *(of parliamentary constituency)* = modification *f* des limites d'une circonscription; **b. line** *(between properties)* limite; *Fig* frontière *f*; *Sport* ligne *f* du jeu; **to form the b. line between two estates** marquer la limite entre deux domaines; **b. stone** borne *f*, pierre *f* de bornage

bounden ['baʊndən] ADJ *Lit* **b. duty** devoir *m* impérieux

bounder ['baʊndər] N *Old-fashioned Fam* goujat *m*

boundless ['baʊndlɪs] ADJ sans bornes, illimité

bounteous ['baʊntɪəs] ADJ *Lit* **1** *(harvest etc)* abondant **2** *(person)* libéral, -aux, généreux

bounteousness ['baʊntɪəsnɪs] N *Lit* **1** *(of harvest etc)* abondance *f* **2** *(of person)* bonté *f*, générosité *f*

bountiful ['baʊntɪfʊl] ADJ *Lit* **1** *(harvest, supply etc)* abondant **2** *(person)* généreux

bounty ['baʊntɪ] N **1** *(reward)* récompense *f* **2** *Lit (of person)* bonté *f*, générosité *f*; **the b. from one's garden** les fruits *mpl ou* produits *mpl* de son jardin
▸▸ **b. hunter** chasseur *m* de primes

bouquet N **1** [bəʊ'keɪ, bu:-] *(of flowers)* bouquet *m* *(composé par un fleuriste)*; *TV* **b. of channels** bouquet de chaînes **2** [bu:'keɪ] *(of wine)* bouquet *m*

Bourbon ['bʊəb(ə)n] N *Hist* Bourbon *mf*
▸▸ *Br* **b. biscuit** = biscuit *m* au chocolat fourré de crème au chocolat

bourbon ['bɜ:b(ə)n] N *(whiskey)* bourbon *m*

bourdon ['bʊəd(ə)n] N *Mus (of organ, bagpipes)* bourdon *m*

bourgeois ['bʊəʒwɑ:] ADJ, N *usu Pej* bourgeois, -oise

bourgeoisie [bʊəʒwɑ:'zi:] N *usu Pej* bourgeoisie *f*

bout [baʊt] N **1** *(in boxing, wrestling)* combat *m* **2** *(brief attack) (of malaria, rheumatism, bronchitis etc)* accès *m*; *(of fever)* poussée *f*; *(of coughing)* quinte *f*; *(of self-pity)* crise *f*; *(of depression, intense activity)* période *f*; **she had a bad b. of flu** elle a eu une mauvaise grippe; **a b. of drinking** une période d'excès de boisson

boutique [bu:'ti:k] N boutique *f* de mode; *(in department store)* boutique

bovine ['bəʊvaɪn] ADJ *Zool* bovin; *Fig Pej (person)* lourd; **b. expression** *or* **look** regard *m* bovin; **b. stupidity** lourdeur *f*
▸▸ *Vet* **b. spongiform encephalopathy** encéphalite *f* bovine spongiforme

bovver ['bɒvər] N *Br Sl (hooliganism, rowdiness)* **to go out looking for b.** chercher la bagarre
▸▸ **b. boots** brodequins *mpl*, rangers *mpl*; **b. boys** voyous *mpl*

bow[1] [bəʊ] N **1** *(of archer)* arc *m*; **to draw a b.** bander *ou* tendre un arc; *Fig* **to have more than one string to one's b.** avoir plus d'une corde à son arc **2** *Mus (for violin etc)* archet *m*; *(movement)* coup *m* d'archet **3** *(in ribbon, shoelace)* nœud *m*
VT *Mus* jouer (avec l'archet); **bowed instrument** instrument *m* à archet
VI *Mus* jouer (de l'archet)
▸▸ **b. legs** jambes *fpl* arquées; **b. tie** nœud *m* papillon; *Br Archit* **b. window** fenêtre *f* en saillie, oriel *m*, bow-window *m*, *pl* bow-windows

bow[2] [baʊ] N *(as greeting etc)* salut *m*; *(from waist)* révérence *f*; **to make a deep** *or* **low b. to sb** saluer qn bien bas; **to take a b.** *(of performer)* saluer; **to take one's final b.** *(retire from stage etc permanently)* faire ses adieux

vi 1 *(as greeting etc)* s'incliner (**to** devant); *Pej* **to b. and scrape** faire des salamalecs *ou* des courbettes **2** *(to sb's will, decision etc)* se soumettre (**to** à); **to b. to the inevitable** s'incliner devant les faits; **I bowed to her (greater) wisdom** je me suis incliné devant tant de sagesse

vt *(head)* incliner, baisser; *(knee)* fléchir; *(sb's back, shoulders)* courber, voûter; **to become bowed** se voûter

▸ **bow down vi** *(incline one's head)* s'incliner; **to b. down before sb** faire des courbettes devant qn; *(very deeply)* se prosterner devant qn; *Fig* **the teachers b. down before the headmaster** les professeurs s'écrasent devant le directeur

vt sep *(of poverty etc)* accabler; **he is bowed down by worry** il est accablé par les soucis

▸ **bow out vi** *Fam* *(leave job, relationship etc voluntarily)* tirer sa révérence

bow³ n 1 *Naut (often pl)* avant *m*, étrave *f*, bossoir *m*; **on the port/starboard b.** par le bossoir bâbord/tribord; **to cross the bows of a ship** couper la route d'un navire **2** *(oarsman)* nageur *m* de tête *ou* de l'avant

▸▸ **b. oar** aviron *m* de l'avant; **b. rope** amarre *f* de bout *ou* de l'avant; **b. wave** lame *f* d'étrave

bowdlerize ['baʊdləraɪz] **vt** *(literary work)* expurger, couper; *Fig* **a bowdlerized version of the party** une version tronquée de la soirée

bowed [baʊd] **adj with b. head** la tête inclinée; *(with shame etc)* la tête baissée; **b. with age** courbé par le fardeau des ans

bowel ['baʊəl] **n** *Anat* intestin *m*; **bowels** intestins; **b. complaint** affection *f* intestinale; *Lit* **the bowels of the earth** les entrailles *fpl ou* le sein de la terre

▸▸ **b. movement** selles *fpl*; **have you had a b. movement today?** est-ce que vous êtes allé (à la selle) aujourd'hui?

bower ['baʊər] **n 1** *(in wood, garden)* berceau *m* de verdure, charmille *f*; *(made of trelliswork)* tonnelle *f* **2** *Lit Arch (lady's boudoir)* appartement *m*, boudoir *m*

bowerbird ['baʊəbɜ:d] **n** oiseau *m* à berceau

bowfronted [baʊ'frʌntɪd] **adj** *(piece of furniture)* pansu; *(house)* à la façade arrondie

bowhead ['baʊhed] **n** *(whale)* baleine *f* boréale

bowing¹ ['baʊɪŋ] **n** *(as greeting etc)* saluts *mpl*; *Pej* **b. and scraping** courbettes *fpl*, salamalecs *mpl*

bowing² ['baʊɪŋ] **n** *Mus* coups *mpl* d'archet; **her wonderful b.** son jeu magnifique à l'archet

bowl¹ [baʊl] **n 1** *(for soup, cereal etc)* bol *m*; *(made of crystal etc)* coupe *f*, *(for washing hands, dishes)* cuvette *f*, bac *m* (d'évier); *(plastic)* bassine *f*, *(of toilet)* cuvette *f* **2** *(of tobacco pipe)* fourneau *m*, godet *m*; *(of spoon)* cuilleron *m*; *(of stemmed glass)* coupe *f*, *(of scales)* plateau *m* **3** *Geog* cuvette *f*, bassin *m* **4** *Am (for concerts etc)* amphithéâtre *m*

bowl² **n** *Sport* boule *f*; **bowls** *(game)* *(on grass)* boules; *(in bowling alley)* bowling *m*; **to play (at) bowls** jouer aux boules/au bowling VOIR GRAMMAIRE A10

vt 1 *(hoop)* faire rouler **2** *Sport (ball)* lancer, rouler **3** *Cr (ball)* lancer, servir; *(player)* renverser le guichet à

vi 1 *(play bowls) (on grass)* jouer aux boules; *(in bowling alley)* jouer au bowling **2** *Cr* lancer *ou* servir la balle; **well bowled!** bien lancé!

▸ **bowl along vi** *(in car, train)* rouler rapidement

▸ **bowl out vt sep** *Cr* renverser le guichet de

▸ **bowl over vt sep 1** *(knock down) (skittles, person etc)* renverser **2** *Fam (astound)* époustoufler; **I was bowled over by her beauty** sa beauté m'a époustouflé, j'ai été époustouflé par sa beauté; **I was bowled over by winning first prize** j'ai été sidéré *ou* époustouflé de gagner le premier prix

bowlegged [baʊ'legɪd] **adj** aux jambes arquées

bowler¹ ['baʊlər] **n 1** *(in bowls) (on grass)* joueur, -euse de boules, bouliste *mf*, *(in bowling alley)* joueur, -euse de bowling **2** *Cr* lanceur, -euse, serveur, -euse

bowler² **n** (chapeau *m*) melon *m*

▸▸ **b. hat** (chapeau) melon

bowlful ['baʊlfʊl] **n** *(of milk, soup etc)* plein bol *m*; *(of washing-up water)* cuvette *f*

bowline ['baʊlɪn] **n** *Naut* **1** *(rope)* bouline *f* **2** *(knot)* nœud *m* de chaise *ou* d'agui

bowling ['baʊlɪŋ] **n 1** *(game) (on grass)* jeu *m* de boules; *(tenpin)* bowling *m* **2** *(action)* lancement *m* de la boule; *Cr* lancement de la balle

▸▸ **b. alley** *(building)* bowling *m*; *(single lane)* piste *f* de bowling; **b. ball** boule *f* de bowling; **b. green** terrain *m* de boules *(sur gazon)*

bowman, *pl* **bowmen** ['baʊmən] **n** *Hist* archer *m*

bowsaw ['baʊsɔ:] **n** *(tool)* scie *f* à archet *ou* à arc *ou* à chantourner

bowser ['baʊzər] **n** *Petr* camion-citerne *m*, *pl* camions-citernes

bowsprit ['baʊsprɪt] **n** *Naut* beaupré *m*

bowstring ['baʊstrɪŋ] **n** corde *f* d'arc

bow-wow ['baʊ'waʊ] **int** oua-oua!

n *Fam (dog in children's language)* toutou *m*

box¹ [bɒks] **n 1** *(container) (small)* boîte *f*; *(large)* coffre *m*, caisse *f*, *Gym (for vaulting)* plinth *m*; *(casing of computer)* boîte; **a b. of cigars/chocolates** une boîte de cigares/chocolats; **jewel b.** coffret *m* à bijoux; **safety deposit b.** coffre-fort *m*, *pl* coffres-forts; **Christmas b.** *(gratuity)* ≃ étrennes *fpl*, *Fig* **in a pine ou wooden b.** *(coffin)* dans un cercueil; *Br Sl* **to be out of one's b.** *(extremely drunk)* être complètement pété, être plein comme une barrique

2 *(postal)* **b. number 12** référence 12; **write to b. number 12** *(in newspaper advertisement)* écrire en rappelant la référence 12

3 *Fam* **the b.** *(television)* la télé; **on the b.** à la télé

4 *(enclosed space) (in stables)* stalle *f*, *Theat* loge *f*, *(on ground floor)* baignoire *f*, *Tel* cabine *f* téléphonique; *Ftbl (for penalties)* surface *f* de réparation; **my flat is a bit of a b.** mon appartement est à peu près grand comme un mouchoir de poche

5 *Tech (of axle, brake)* boîte *f*, *(of wheel)* moyeu *m*; *(of lock)* palâtre *m*, palastre *m*

6 *(printed, drawn) (to fill in on form etc)* case *f*, *(boxed text)* pavé *m*, encadré *m*; *(frame around article)* cadre *m*; *(on screen)* boîte *f*, case; *(that can be drawn)* encadré *m*; **to draw a b. round sth** encadrer qch

vt *(goods)* mettre en carton

▸▸ *Phot* **b. camera** appareil *m* photographique rudimentaire; *Am Geog* **b. canyon** cañon *m ou* canyon *m* encaissé; **b. file** boîte archive; *Constr* **b. girder** poutre-caisson *f*, *pl* poutres-caissons; *Br* **b. junction** carrefour *m* (matérialisé sur la chaussée par des bandes croisées); **b. kite** cerf-volant *m* cellulaire, *pl* cerfs-volants cellulaires; *Cin, Theat* **b. office** *(office)* bureau *m* de location; *(window)* guichet *m* (de location); **b. pleat** pli *m* creux; **b. spanner** clef *f* à douille; **b. spring** sommier *m* à ressort; **b. wrench** clef á douille

▸ **box in vt sep 1** *(surround) (person)* coincer;

the defence seem to have him boxed in la défense semble l'avoir coincé **2** *(enclose) (bath, washbasin etc)* encastrer; **don't you feel boxed in in such a small room?** tu ne te sens pas un peu à l'étroit dans une pièce aussi petite?; **to be boxed in** *(by other cars)* être coincé par d'autres voitures

box² **n** *(blow)* **b. (on the ear)** gifle *f*, claque *f*, taloche *f*; **to give sb a b. on the ear** gifler qn

vt **to b. sb's ears** gifler qn, *Fam* flanquer une gifle *ou* une claque *ou* une taloche à qn

vi *Sport* boxer, faire de la boxe; *(of two opponents)* combattre

box³ **n 1** *(tree)* buis *m* **2** *(wood)* (bois *m* de) buis *m*

▸▸ **b. tree** buis

box-calf **n** *(leather)* box-calf *m*, *pl* boxcalfs, *Fam* box *m*

boxcar ['bɒkskɑ:r] **n** *Am Rail* wagon *m*, fourgon *m*

boxed [bɒkst] **adj 1** *Com etc* en boîte; *(jewellery)* en écrin; *(person) (surrounded)* coincé; *(confined)* à l'étroit; **b. in** *(bath etc)* encastré **2** *(text)* encadré; **b. article** encadré *m*

Boxer ['bɒksər] **n** *Hist* Boxer *m* (chinois)

▸▸ **the B. Rebellion** la révolte des Boxers

boxer ['bɒksər] **n 1** *(fighter)* boxeur, -euse; *Fam* **boxers** *(underwear)* caleçon *m* **2** *(dog)* boxer *m*

▸▸ *Aut* **b. engine** moteur *m* à cylindres à plat, boxer *m*; **b. shorts** caleçon

boxful ['bɒksfʊl] **n** *(small)* pleine boîte *f*, *(large)* plein coffre *m*, pleine caisse *f*

Boxing Day **n** *Br* = le 26 décembre

boxing ['bɒksɪŋ] **n** *Sport* boxe *f*; **he loves b.** il adore la boxe

▸▸ **b. glove** gant *m* de boxe; **b. match** match *m* de boxe; **b. ring** ring *m*

box-pleated **adj** à plis creux *ou* ronds

boxroom ['bɒksru:m] **n** débarras *m*

boxwood ['bɒkswʊd] **n** (bois *m* de) buis *m*

boy [bɔɪ] **n 1** garçon *m*; **boys will be boys** les hommes et les garçons sont comme ça et on ne les changera pas

2 *Sch* élève *m*; **day b.** externe *m*

3 *Fam (man)* **a new b.** *(in company)* un nouveau; **the race was won by a local b.** c'est un jeune de la région qui a gagné la course; **a nice old b.** un vieux monsieur sympathique; *Br Old-fashioned* **I say, old b.!** dis, mon vieux!; **one of the boys** un joyeux vivant; **he's having a night out with the boys** il est sorti avec ses copains; *Br Fam* **the boys in blue** *(police)* = la police; *Sl* **he threatened to send the boys round** il a menacé d'envoyer ses gars; *Sl* **the big boys** *(important men)* les grosses légumes *fpl*, *Fig* **to play with the big boys** jouer dans la cour des grands; *esp Am* **oh b.!** ben alors!, dis donc!; *esp Am* **b., am I glad to be home!** dis donc, qu'est-ce que je suis content d'être rentré à la maison!

4 *(employee) (in Africa)* boy *m*; **office b.** garçon *m* de bureau

▸▸ **b. band** boys band *m*; *Br Fam* **b. racer** jeune conducteur *m* imprudent; **b. scout** scout *m*; **b. wonder** petit génie *m*

boycott ['bɔɪkɒt] **n** boycott *m*, boycottage *m*; **to put under a b., to put a b. on** *(goods, company, event etc)* boycotter

vt *(person, company, event etc)* boycotter

boyfriend ['bɔɪfrend] **n** *(of girl, woman)* (petit) ami *m*, *Can Fam* chum *m*

boyhood ['bɔɪhʊd] **n** *(when very young)* enfance *f*, première jeunesse *f*, *(in teens)* adolescence *f*; **b. friends** amis *mpl* d'enfance

boyish ['bɔɪɪʃ] **adj 1** *(hopes, enthusiasm)* d'enfant, enfantin **2** *(charm)* juvénile; *(tomboyish) (clothes, figure, face)* de garçon; **b. good looks** *(of man)* air *m* de beau gosse;

(of woman) air de joli garçon; **b. haircut** coupe *f* de cheveux à la garçonne **3** *(manners)* de garçon

boyishly ['bɔɪɪʃlɪ] **ADV** *(to smile, laugh)* comme un enfant; *(tomboyishly)* comme un garçon

boyishness ['bɔɪɪʃnɪs] **N** manières *fpl* de garçon *ou* de jeune homme

boy-meets-girl **ADJ b. story** *(book, film)* banale histoire *f* d'amour

bozo ['bəʊzəʊ] **N** *Am Sl (stupid man)* débile *m*, abruti *m*

bps [bi:pi:'es] **N** *Comput (abbr* **bits per second)** bps

BR [bi:'a:r] **N** *Formerly (abbr* **British Rail)** = service *m* national des chemins de fer britannique

bra [bra:] **N** soutien-gorge *m*, *pl* soutiens-gorge
▸▸ **b. top** brassière *f*

brace [breɪs] **N 1** *Constr etc* étai *m*; **cross or diagonal b.** écharpe *f*, diagonale *f*
2 *Med (on teeth)* appareil *m* dentaire; *(on leg)* armature *f* orthopédique; *(on torso)* corset *m*; **neck b.** minerve *f*
3 *Br* **braces** *(for trousers)* bretelles *fpl*
4 *(pair) (of partridges, pheasants etc)* couple *m*; *(of pistols etc)* paire *f*, **two b. of partridges** deux couples de perdrix
5 *(drill)* **b. (and bit)** vilebrequin *m* (et sa mèche); *Aut* **wheel b.** vilebrequin (à roues)
6 *Typ (bracket)* accolade *f*
VT 1 *Constr etc (construction, wall, roof)* étayer; *Aviat (wing)* croisillonner
2 *(tense) (bow)* tendre, bander; **to b. (the skin of) a drum** tendre la peau d'un tambour, bander un tambour; **the passengers braced themselves for the impact** les passagers se raidirent avant le choc; **she braced herself between two rocks** elle s'arc-bouta entre deux rochers; **b. yourself!** *(hold tight)* tiens bon!; *(be brave)* courage!; **b. yourself for a shock** prépare-toi à recevoir un choc
3 *(strengthen) (body)* fortifier; *(nerves)* tonifier; **a whisky to b. myself** un whisky pour me donner du courage; **to b. oneself to do sth** rassembler ses forces pour faire qch, s'armer de courage pour faire qch

bracelet ['breɪslɪt] **N 1** *(jewellery)* bracelet *m*; **chain b.** gourmette *f* **2** *Fam* **bracelets** *(handcuffs)* bracelets *mpl*; **put the bracelets on him** passe-lui les bracelets
▸▸ **b. watch** montre-bracelet *f* pour femme, *pl* montres-bracelets

bracer ['breɪsər] **N** *Fam* (petit verre *m* de) remontant *m*

brachial ['brækɪəl, 'breɪk-] **ADJ** *Anat* brachial, -aux

brachiopod ['brækɪəppd] **N** *(mollusc)* brachiopode *m*

brachycephalic [brækɪsɪ'fælɪk] **ADJ** brachycéphale

bracing ['breɪsɪŋ] **ADJ** *(air, climate etc)* vivifiant, tonifiant; *Fig (effect)* stimulant
▸▸ *Constr* **b. strut** jambe *f* de force

bracken ['bræk(ə)n] **N** *(plant)* fougère *f*

bracket ['brækɪt] **N 1** *Constr, Tech (for fixing or supporting)* tasseau *m*, équerre *f*, *(for holding part)* support *m*; *(for lamp)* applique *f*; *Archit* corbeau *m* **2** *Typ etc (square)* crochet *m*; *(round)* parenthèse *f*, *(connecting two lines)* accolade *f*; **in brackets** entre parenthèses/crochets/accolades **3** *Admin (level of income, tax)* tranche *f*, *(of salaries)* fourchette *f*, **the 15-to-20 age b.** le groupe *ou* la classe des 15 à 20 ans; **people in the upper income brackets** les gens dans les tranches de revenu les plus élevées; **what tax b. are you in?** dans quelle tranche d'imposition estu?
VT (-t-) 1 *(words etc)* mettre entre parenthè-

ses; *(in square brackets)* mettre entre crochets; *(in a vertical list)* réunir par une accolade **2** *Fig (two ideas)* associer; *(two candidates)* placer ex aequo; **bracketed together** *(candidates)* classé ex aequo; **his name has often been bracketed with hers** son nom a souvent été associé au sien; **he didn't want to be bracketed (together) with them** il ne voulait pas qu'on les mette dans le même sac
▸▸ **b. lamp** (lampe *f* d')applique

bracketing ['brækɪtɪŋ] **N** *(action)* mise *f* entre parenthèses; *(with square brackets)* mise entre crochets; *(in a vertical list)* réunion *f* par une accolade

brackish ['brækɪʃ] **ADJ** *(water)* saumâtre

bract [brækt] **N** *Bot* bractée *f*

brad [bræd] **N** *(nail)* clou *m* de tapissier, semence *f*

bradawl ['brædɔ:l] **N** *(tool)* alêne *f* plate, poinçon *m*

bradycardia [brædɪ'ka:dɪə] **N** *Med* bradycardie *f*

brae [breɪ] **N** *Scot* colline *f*

brag [bræg] **N 1** *(boast)* vantardise *f*, forfanterie *f* **2** *Cards* = sorte *f* de poker
VI (-gg-) *(boast)* se vanter (**of, about** de); **it's not something to b. about!** il n'y a pas de quoi s'en vanter!; **you've got nothing to b. about** tu n'as pas de quoi te vanter
VT **to b. that one has done sth** se vanter d'avoir fait qch; **he bragged that he would win** il s'est vanté de pouvoir gagner

braggadocio [brægə'dəʊtʃɪəʊ] **N** *Lit* vantardise *f*

braggart ['brægət] **N** *Old-fashioned* vantard, -arde, hâbleur, -euse

bragging ['brægɪŋ] **ADJ** vantard, hâbleur, -euse
N vantardise *f*, hâblerie *f*

Brahman ['bra:mən] **N** brahmane *mf*

Brahmanism ['bra:mənɪz(ə)m] **N** brahmanisme *m*

Brahmin ['bra:mɪn] **N 1** *(in India)* brahmane *mf* **2** *Am Fam (intellectual)* intellectuel, -elle; *(member of the upper classes)* membre *m* de la haute

braid [breɪd] **N 1** *esp Am (of hair)* tresse *f*, natte *f*, **she wears her hair in braids** elle porte *ou* se fait des nattes **2** *(on cushion, clothing etc)* galon *m*, passepoil *m*; **gold b.** *(on officer's uniform)* galon
VT 1 *(straw)* tresser; *esp Am (hair)* tresser, natter **2** *(clothing)* galonner, soutacher; *(edge of chair etc)* passementer

braiding ['breɪdɪŋ] **N 1** *esp Am (of hair)* tressage *m*, nattage *m* **2** *(decoration) (on cushion, clothing)* galon *m*, passepoil *m*

Braille [breɪl] **N** braille *m*; **to read B.** lire le braille; **in B.** en braille
▸▸ **B. alphabet** alphabet *m* braille

brain [breɪn] **N 1** *(organ)* cerveau *m*; *Culin* **brains** cervelle *f*; **to blow sb's brains out** faire sauter la cervelle à qn; *Fam* **to have money on the b.** être obsédé par l'argent; *Fam* **to have a tune on the b.** avoir un air dans la tête; **to be b. dead** *Med* être en coma dépassé; *Fam Fig (extremely stupid)* ne rien avoir dans la cervelle; **she had a b. scan** on lui a fait un scanner du cerveau
2 *(intelligence)* **brains** intelligence *f*, **he has brains** *or* **a good b.** il est intelligent; **I haven't the brains to become a doctor** je ne suis pas assez intelligent pour devenir médecin; **anyone with half a b.** n'importe qui d'un tant soit peu intelligent; **he's the brains of the family** c'est lui le plus intelligent de la famille; **she's the brains of the business** c'est elle le cerveau de l'entreprise; **use your brains** fais marcher ta cervelle

3 *Fam (intelligent person)* cerveau *m*; **to call in the best brains** faire appel à tous les talents; **she's a real b. at maths** c'est une tête en maths
VT *Sl (hit over head)* assommer; **I brained myself on the cupboard door** je me suis cogné contre la porte du placard
▸▸ *Med* **b. damage** lésions *fpl* cérébrales; *Med* **b. death** mort *f* cérébrale; **b. disease** maladie *f* cérébrale; *Fam* **the b. drain** l'exode *m ou* la fuite des cerveaux; *Old-fashioned* **b. fever** fièvre *f* cérébrale; *Anat* **b. stem** pédoncule *m* cérébral; *Med* **b. surgeon** neurochirurgien, -ienne; *Med* **b. surgery** neurochirurgie *f*, *Am* **b. trust**, *Br* **brains trust** brain-trust *m*, *pl* brain-trusts; *Med* **b. tumour** tumeur *f* au cerveau; *Br Fam* **b. wave** idée *f* de génie, idée lumineuse

> When translating **brain**, note that **cerveau** and **cervelle** are not interchangeable. **Cerveau** refers to the organ, whereas generally **cervelle** refers to brain matter.

brainbox ['breɪnbɒks] **N** *Sl* **1** *Old-fashioned (skull)* boîte *f* crânienne **2** *(intelligent person)* tête *f*, **she's a real b.** c'est une sacrée tête

brainchild ['breɪntʃaɪld] **N** *Fam* trouvaille *f*

brainless ['breɪnlɪs] **ADJ** *Fam (stupid)* stupide; **he's a b. idiot** c'est un idiot sans pareil

brainpower ['breɪnpaʊər] **N** intelligence *f*

brainstorm ['breɪnstɔ:m] **N 1** *Br* **I must have had a b.** j'ai dû avoir un moment d'égarement **2** *Am Fam (brilliant idea)* idée *f* de génie

brainstorming ['breɪnstɔ:mɪŋ] **N** brainstorming *m*, remue-méninges *m inv*; **b. session** réunion *f* de remue-méninges; **we had a b. session** nous avons eu un brainstorming

brain-teaser **N** casse-tête *m inv*

brainwash ['breɪnwɒʃ] **VT** faire un lavage de cerveau à; **to b. sb into doing sth** faire un lavage de cerveau à qn pour qu'il fasse qch; *Fig* **they've been brainwashed into believing that ...** on leur a mis dans la tête que ...; **I won't be brainwashed into buying things I don't need** je refuse de me laisser manipuler pour acheter des choses dont je n'ai pas besoin

brainwashing ['breɪnwɒʃɪŋ] **N** lavage *m* de cerveau

brainwork ['breɪnwɜːk] **N** travail *m* intellectuel

brainy ['breɪnɪ] **ADJ** *Fam (person)* intelligent; *(idea)* génial, -aux; **she's really b.** il y en a là-dedans; **I can't cope with b. stuff like that** c'est trop compliqué pour moi

braise [breɪz] **VT** *Culin* braiser, cuire à l'étouffée; **braised beef** bœuf *m* braisé; **braised chicken** poulet *m* en cocotte

braising ['breɪzɪŋ] **N** *Culin* cuisson *f* à l'étouffée
▸▸ **b. beef** bœuf *m* à braiser

brake[1] [breɪk] **N** *(on car, train etc)* frein *m*; **to apply the brake(s)** *(in traffic)* freiner; **to put the b. on** *(after parking)* mettre *ou* serrer le frein; **to slam on the brakes** écraser la pédale de frein, *Fam* piler; **to release the brake(s)** desserrer le frein; *Fig* **to put a b. or the brakes on a project** donner un coup de frein à un projet; *Fig* **b. on growth** frein à l'expansion
VI *Aut (in traffic)* freiner; **to b. hard** freiner brusquement, écraser la pédale de frein, *Fam* piler
▸▸ *Aut* **b. adjuster spanner** clé *f* de réglage des freins; *Aut* **b. block** sabot *m ou* patin *m* de frein; *Aut* **b. fade** fading *m*; *Aut* **b. fluid** liquide *m* de freins, Lockheed® *m*; *Aut* **b. horsepower** puissance *f* au frein; *Aut, Tech* **b. lever** frein à main; *Aut* **b. light** feu *m* de stop; *Aut* **b. lining** garniture *f* de frein; *Aut* **b.**

pad plaquette *f* de frein; *Aut* **b. pedal** pédale *f* de frein; *Aut* **b. shoe** mâchoire *f* de frein; *Br Rail* **b. van** fourgon *m* à frein

brake [2] N *(undergrowth)* fourré *m*, hallier *m*

brake [3] N *(vehicle)* = **break** [2]

braked trailer ['breɪkt] N remorque *f* freinée

brakelight function ['breɪklaɪt] N *Am TV, Radio* signal *m* de fin de temps de parole

brakesman, *Am* **brakeman,** *pl* **brakesmen** ['breɪk(s)mən] N *Rail etc* garde-frein(s) *m, pl* gardes-frein(s)

braking ['breɪkɪŋ] N *(in traffic)* freinage *m; (abrupt)* coup *m* de frein
▸▸ **b. distance** distance *f* de freinage

bramble ['bræmb(ə)l] N **1** *(shrub)* ronce *f ou* mûrier *m* des haies; **brambles** *(thorns)* ronces **2** *(fruit)* mûre *f* (de ronce), mûre sauvage
▸▸ **b. jelly** gelée *f* de mûres

brambly ['bræmblɪ] ADJ plein *ou* couvert de ronces

bran [bræn] N *(of oats, wheat)* son *m*
▸▸ **b. flakes** son en flocons; *Br* **b. mash** son *ou* bran *m* mouillé; *Br* **b. tub** pêche *f* miraculeuse *(jeu)*

branch [brɑːntʃ] N **1** *(of tree)* branche *f*, rameau *m*; **the branches** le branchage, les branches
2 *(of road)* embranchement *m; (of river)* bras *m; (of candlestick, family, science, industry etc, of artery)* branche *f*
3 *Admin, Com (of shop)* succursale *f; (of company)* agence *f*, succursale; *(of bank)* agence, succursale, guichet *m*; **where's the nearest b. of Harvey Nicks?** où se trouve le Harvey Nicks le plus proche?
4 *Mil (of armed forces)* division *f; (in administration)* organe *f*
5 *Comput* branchement *m*
VI **1** *(of road etc)* bifurquer; **at the point where the road branches** à l'endroit où la route bifurque **2** *(of tree)* faire des branches
▸▸ **b. banking** banque *f* à réseau; *Rail* **b. line** ligne *f* secondaire; **b. manager** *(of bank)* directeur, -trice d'agence; *(of shop)* directeur, -trice de succursale; **b. office** *(of company)* succursale; *(of bank)* agence, succursale
▸ **branch off** VI *(of road),* Fig *(in conversation etc)* bifurquer; *Fig* **then I branched off into quantum mechanics** puis j'ai bifurqué vers la mécanique quantique
▸ **branch out** VI *(of person, organization etc)* étendre ses activités, se diversifier; **to b. out into ...** étendre ses activités à ...; **I'm going to b. out on my own** je vais faire cavalier seul

branched [brɑːntʃt] ADJ **1** *Bot* branchu, rameux **2** *(candlestick)* à (plusieurs) branches

branchia, *pl* **branchiae** ['bræŋkɪə, -iː] N branchie *f*

branchiate ['bræŋkɪət] ADJ *Zool* branchié

brand [brænd] N **1** *Com, Mktg* marque *f* (de fabrique); *Fig* **he has his own b. of humour** il a un humour un peu particulier; **a good b. of cigars** une bonne marque de cigares **2** *(on cattle)* marque *f* au fer rouge; *Hist (on criminal)* flétrissure *f*, marque au fer rouge; *(branding iron)* fer *m* rouge; **the cattle have his b. on them** le bétail porte sa marque **3** *(burning wood)* brandon *m*, tison *m*
VT *(with branding iron) (person, animal, goods)* marquer au fer rouge; *Hist (criminal)* flétrir, marquer au fer rouge; *(slave)* marquer; **to b. sb (as) a liar/coward/etc** coller à qn une étiquette de menteur/lâche/*etc; Fig* **to be branded on sb's memory** *(of sight, scene)* être gravé dans la mémoire de qn; **the experience branded them for life** l'expérience les a marqués à vie
ADV **b. new** tout neuf, flambant neuf
▸▸ *Mktg* **b. advertising** publicité *f* de

marque, publicité sur la marque; **b. awareness** mémorisation *f* de la marque, notoriété *f* de la marque; **b. beliefs** croyances *fpl* vis-à-vis d'une marque; **b. competition** concurrence *f* entre marques; **b. concept** concept *m* de marque; **b. extension** extension *f* de la marque; **b. familiarity** connaissance *f* de la marque; **b. identifier** identificateur *m* de marque; **b. image** image *f* de marque; **b. imitation** imitation *f* de marque; **b. leader** marque dominante; **b. life-cycle** cycle *m* de vie de la marque; **b. loyalty** fidélité *f* à la marque; **b. manager** chef *m* de marque; **b. mapping** carte *f* perceptuelle des marques, carte des positions de marques; **b. mark** emblème *m* de marque; **b. name** marque (de fabrique); **b. name recall** mémorisation de la marque; **b. positioning** positionnement *m* de la marque; **b. preference** préférence *f* pour une marque; **b. recognition** identification *f* de la marque; **b. sensitivity** sensibilité *f* aux marques; **b. switching** changement *m* de marque

branded ['brændɪd] ADJ **1** *(cattle, criminal etc)* marqué au fer rouge **2** *(product)* de marque

branding ['brændɪŋ] N **1** *(of cattle)* marquage *m* au fer rouge **2** *Mktg* marquage *m*
▸▸ **b. iron** fer *m* à marquer

brandish ['brændɪʃ] VT *(weapon etc)* brandir

brand-led ADJ *Mktg* conditionné *ou* piloté par la marque

brand-loyal ADJ *Mktg* fidèle à la marque

brandy ['brændɪ] N *(cognac)* cognac *m; (clear spirit)* eau-de-vie, *pl* eaux-de-vie; **b. and soda** = cognac à l'eau de Seltz
▸▸ *Br Culin* **b. butter** = beurre *m* mélangé avec du sucre et parfumé au cognac; **b. glass** verre *m* à cognac; *Br Culin* **b. snap** cigarette *f* russe au gingembre

brash [bræʃ] ADJ *(person) (impudent)* effronté, présomptueux, impudent; *(showing off)* exubérant; *(manner)* présomptueux; *(colour)* cru

brashly ['bræʃlɪ] ADV *(with impudence)* effrontément, présomptueusement, impudemment; *(when showing off)* avec exubérance

brashness ['bræʃnɪs] N *(impudence)* effronterie *f*, impudence *f; (showing off)* exubérance *f*

brass [brɑːs] N **1** *(metal)* laiton *m; Fig* **to get down to b. tacks** en venir aux faits; *Br* **I haven't got a b. farthing** *(any money)* je n'ai pas un rond; *Br* **it's not worth a b. farthing** ça ne vaut pas un clou; *Mil Fam* **the top b.** les huiles *fpl; Br Sl* **it's a bit b. monkeys today** *(very cold)* on se les caille **2** *(item) (in church)* plaque *f* tombale en cuivre; **brass(es)** *(household objects etc)* cuivres *mpl;* **to do or clean the b. or brasses** faire les cuivres; **the b.** *(in band, orchestra)* les cuivres **3** *Br Fam (money)* argent *m*, galette *f* **4** *Br Fam (cheek, nerve)* culot *m;* **to have the b. to do sth** avoir le culot de faire qch
▸▸ *Mus* **b. band** fanfare *f*, orchestre *m* de cuivres; **b. foundry** fonderie *f* de cuivre; *Br Fam Fig* **b. hat** gros bonnet *m; Mus* **b. instrument** cuivre *m; Br Fam* **b. neck** *(cheek, nerve)* culot *m;* **to have a b. neck** avoir du culot, être culotté, *Can* avoir du front tout le tour de la tête; **what a b. neck!** quel culot!; **b. plate** plaque de cuivre; *(of doctor, lawyer etc)* plaque; *Art* **b. rubbing** *(picture)* décalque *m; (action)* décalquage *m* par frottement
▸ **brass off** VT SEP *Br Fam (usu passive)* **to be brassed off** en avoir marre, en avoir ras le bol; **I'm brassed off with waiting** j'en ai marre *ou* ras le bol d'attendre; **I'm brassed off with their complaints** j'en ai plein le dos de leurs récriminations

brasserie ['bræsərɪ] N *(restaurant, bar)* brasserie *f*

brassic ['bræsɪk] ADJ *Br Fam (poor)* fauché, à sec, sans un

brassica ['bræsɪkə] N *Bot* brassica *m*

brassie ['bræsɪ] N *Golf* brassie *m*

brassière ['bræzɪər, *Am* brə'zɪər] N soutien-gorge *m, pl* soutiens-gorge

brassiness ['braːsɪnɪs] N **1** *(of piece of music)* sons *mpl* cuivrés **2** *Fam (insolence)* culot *m*

brassware ['braːsweər] N dinanderie *f*

brasswork ['braːswɜːk] N dinanderie *f*, chaudronnerie *f* d'art

brassy ['braːsɪ] N *Golf* brassie *m*
ADJ **1** *Pej (yellow, blonde)* artificiel; *(cheap jewellery)* qui fait toc **2** *(sound)* cuivré **3** *Pej Fam (person)* effronté

brat [bræt] N *Pej* gamin, -ine, morveux, -euse
▸▸ *Cin* **the B. Pack** = terme désignant les jeunes acteurs américains populaires des années 80

bravado [brə'vaːdəʊ] N bravade *f*

brave [breɪv] ADJ courageux; **be b. for a little bit longer** courage, c'est presque fini; **as b. as a lion** courageux comme un lion; **to put a b. face on it** faire bonne contenance; **to make a b. effort to smile** s'efforcer bravement de sourire; **it was a b. effort, nonetheless** néanmoins, c'était un bel effort; *Fig* **a b. new world for small business** un paradis pour les petites entreprises
N *(American Indian warrior)* brave *m*
VT *(person)* braver, défier; *(danger etc)* braver, affronter

> Note that the French adjective **brave** is a false friend. Its most common meaning is **kind.**

bravely ['breɪvlɪ] ADV courageusement, vaillamment

bravery ['breɪvərɪ] N courage *m*, bravoure *f*; **she was decorated for b.** elle a été décorée pour son courage

bravo [braː'vəʊ] INT bravo!

bravura [brə'vʊərə] N *Mus* morceau *m* de bravoure

brawl [brɔːl] N rixe *f*, bagarre *f*; **drunken b.** querelle *f* d'ivrognes
VI *(of people)* se bagarrer

brawler ['brɔːlər] N bagarreur, -euse

brawling ['brɔːlɪŋ] N rixes *fpl*, bagarres *fpl*

brawn [brɔːn] N **1** *Fam* muscles *mpl*; **to have plenty of b.** avoir du biceps; **he's got more b. than brains** il a du muscle mais pas grand-chose dans la tête **2** *Br Culin* fromage *m* de tête

brawny ['brɔːnɪ] ADJ *(arm)* fort, musculeux; *(person)* musclé, bien bâti

bray [breɪ] N *(of donkey)* braiment *m*
VI *(of donkey)* braire

braze [breɪz] VT *Tech (using solder)* braser; *(using brass)* souder au laiton

brazen ['breɪz(ə)n] ADJ **1** *(shameless)* effronté, impudent; **I wish they weren't so b. about it** ils pourraient au moins faire ça discrètement; **b. lie** mensonge *m* éhonté; **a b. hussy** une effrontée **2** *Lit (made of brass) (vase, pot etc)* d'airain **3** *Mus* cuivré
▸ **brazen out** VT SEP **to b. it out** s'en tirer au culot

brazen-faced [-feɪst] ADJ effronté, impudent

brazenly ['breɪz(ə)nlɪ] ADV effrontément, impudemment

brazenness ['breɪz(ə)nnɪs] N effronterie *f*

brazier ['breɪzɪər] N brasero *m*

Brazil [brə'zɪl] N Brésil *m*

brazil [brə'zɪl] N noix *f* du Brésil
▸▸ **b. nut** noix du Brésil

Brazilian [brə'zɪlɪən] **ADJ** brésilien
N 1 *(person)* Brésilien, -ienne **2** *(wax)* épilation *f* maillot brésilien

breach [briːtʃ] **N 1** *(of regulations etc)* infraction *f*, contravention *f*; *(of law, professional secrecy etc)* violation *f* (**of** de); *(of discipline)* manquement *m* (**of** à); *(of contract)* rupture *f* (**of** de); **the company is in b. of the law** la société enfreint la législation; **the company is suing him for b. of contract** la société lui fait un procès pour rupture de contrat; **b. of good manners** manque *m* de savoir-vivre; **to commit a b. of etiquette** manquer au protocole
2 *(between two friends etc)* brouille *f*
3 *(in wall)*, *Mil (in defences)* brèche *f*; *Fig* **they found a b. in his defences** ils ont trouvé sa faille; *Mil* **to stand in the b.** monter sur la brèche; **to make a b. in the enemy's lines** percer les lignes de l'ennemi; *Fig* **to step into the b.** intervenir au bon niveau; **it was very good of you to step into the b.** c'est très aimable à vous de l'avoir remplacé(e)
VT 1 *(violate) (contract, agreement, treaty)* rompre **2** *(make hole in) (dam, wall)* ouvrir une brèche dans; *Mil (wall)* battre en brèche; *(enemy lines)* percer; **to b. the surface of the water** apparaître à la surface de l'eau; *(of rocks)* pointer à la surface de l'eau
VI *(of whale)* sauter au-dessus de la surface de l'eau
▸▸ **b. of faith** manquement à sa parole; *Law* **b. of the peace** atteinte à l'ordre public; *Parl* **b. of privilege** atteinte *f* aux privilèges parlementaires; **b. of promise** manque de parole; *(of marriage)* violation de promesse de mariage; **b. of trust** abus *m* de confiance; *Law (by trustee etc)* violation d'un des devoirs d'un mandataire

bread [bred] **N 1** pain *m*; **a loaf of b.** un pain; **b. and butter** pain beurré; **a slice of b. and butter** une tartine de beurre, une tartine beurrée; *Fig* **poetry doesn't earn you your b. and butter** la poésie ne nourrit pas son homme; *Fig* **the customers are our b. and butter** les clients sont notre gagne-pain; **to be on b. and water** être au pain (sec) et à l'eau; *Rel* **give us this day our daily b.** donne-nous aujourd'hui notre pain de ce jour; *Fig* **to earn one's (daily) b.** gagner sa vie *ou* son pain; *Fig* **to take the b. out of sb's mouth** enlever le pain de la bouche de qn; *Fig* **to put b. on the table** *(of person)* faire bouillir la marmite; **we want policies that will put b. on the table** nous voulons des politiques qui nous permettent de gagner notre pain; *Fig* **he knows which side his b. is buttered on** il sait où est son avantage *ou* son intérêt; *Fig* **b. and circuses** du pain et des jeux
2 *esp Am Old-fashioned Sl (money)* blé *m*, avoine *f*, galette *f*
VT *(fish etc)* passer à la chapelure
▸▸ **b. bin** *(horizontal)* boîte *f* à pain; *(vertical)* huche *f* à pain; **b. cutter** coupe-pain *m inv*; **b. knife** couteau *m* à pain; *Culin* **b. pudding** gâteau *m* de pain; **b. roll** petit pain; *Br Culin* **b. sauce** sauce *f* à la mie de pain; **b. slicer** coupe-pain

bread-and-butter **ADJ**
▸▸ **b. issues** problèmes *mpl* essentiels, questions *fpl* essentielles; *Fam* **b. letter** lettre *f* de remerciements; *Culin* **b. pudding** pain perdu *m (cuit au four)*

breadbasket ['bredbɑːskɪt] **N 1** corbeille *f* à pain; *esp Am Fig* **the b. of the world** la principale région productrice de céréales panifiables dans le monde **2** *Old-fashioned Sl (stomach)* estomac *m*, bedaine *f*

breadboard ['bredbɔːd] **N 1** planche *f* à pain
2 *Electron etc* montage *m* expérimental

breadcrumb ['bredkrʌm] **N** miette *f* (de pain); *Culin* **breadcrumbs** chapelure *f*; **fried**

in breadcrumbs pané; **to coat fish with breadcrumbs** passer du poisson à la chapelure
VT *(fish etc)* passer à la chapelure

breaded ['bredɪd] **ADJ** pané

breadfruit ['bredfruːt] **N** *(fruit)* fruit *m* à pain
▸▸ **b. tree** arbre *m* à pain

breadline ['bredlaɪn] **N** = file *f* d'attente pour toucher des bons de pain ou recevoir de la nourriture gratuite; *Fig* **on the b.** indigent, sans ressources

breadth [bredθ] **N 1** *(width)* largeur *f*, *(of material)* largeur, lé *m* **2** *Fig (of thought, mind, views etc)* largeur *f*, *(of style, sound)* ampleur *f*; **her b. of understanding** l'ampleur de ses connaissances

breadthwise ['bredθwaɪz], **breadthways** ['bredθweɪz] **ADV** dans le sens de la largeur

breadwinner ['bredwɪnər] **N** soutien *m* de famille

BREAK¹ [breɪk]

N cassure, brisure **1** ▪ fracture **1**		
▪ trouée **2** ▪ interruption **2** ▪ rupture **3** ▪ pause **4** ▪ évasion **5** ▪ chance **6**		
VT casser **1** ▪ briser **1, 4**		
▪ rompre **1–3** ▪ couper **1** ▪ amortir **3**		
▪ enfreindre **5**		
VI se casser **1** ▪ se briser **1** ▪ se fracturer **1**		

N 1 *(in china, glass)* cassure *f*, brisure *f*, *(in wood)* cassure, rupture *f*; *(fracture) (in limb)* fracture *f*; **b. in the voice** *Physiol (at puberty)* mue *f*, *(caused by emotion)* altération *f* de la voix; *Lit* **b. of day** point *m* du jour
2 *(interruption) (in hedge, wall etc)* trouée *f*, percée *f*, brèche *f*, *(in clouds)* trouée; *Elec (in circuit)* rupture *f*, *(in series, line)* interruption *f*; *Typ (in word)* césure *f*, *(in pagination)* fin *f* de page; *Radio, TV (commercial)* **b.** page *f* de publicité; *Radio, TV* **b. (in transmission)** interruption; **b. in** *or* **of continuity** interruption, solution *f* de continuité; **b. in the journey** arrêt *m*; **b. in the weather** changement *m* du temps; **there will be a b. in the weather tomorrow** le temps va changer demain; **without a b.** sans s'arrêter
3 *(breach) (between countries, spouses)* rupture *f*, *(between two friends)* brouille *f*; **b. with tradition** rupture avec une tradition; **in a b. with tradition** en rupture avec la tradition; **to make a b. with the past** rompre avec son passé
4 *(rest), Mus* pause *f*, *Sch (between classes)* récréation *f*, *(holiday)* vacances *fpl*; **an hour's b. for lunch** une heure de pause pour le déjeuner; **a weekend in the country makes a pleasant b.** un week-end à la campagne fait du bien; **a much needed b.** un repos indispensable; **give a b.!** *(talk about something else)* change de disque!; **give me a b.!** *(stop nagging)* fiche-moi la paix!; *(don't talk nonsense)* arrête ton char; **give work/ tennis a b. for a while** je devrais arrêter un peu de travailler/de jouer au tennis
5 *Fam (escape)* évasion *f*; **to make a b. for it** s'évader; *Fig* **to make the b.** larguer les amarres
6 *Fam (chance)* chance *f*, **a good/bad b.** une bonne/mauvaise chance; **this could be your big b.** ça pourrait être la chance de ta vie; **she's never had an even b. in her life** rien n'a jamais été facile dans sa vie; **we had a lucky b.** nous avons eu de la veine; **give him a b.** donne-lui une chance; *(he won't do it again)* donne-lui une seconde chance
7 *Billiards etc (opening shot)* acquit *m*; *(series of shots)* série *f*, suite *f* (de coups gagnants); *Tennis (of opponent's service)* break *m*; **she had a b. of serve** *(lost her serve)* elle a perdu son service; *(won her op-*

ponent's serve) elle a gagné le service de son adversaire; *Tennis* **to have two b. points** avoir deux balles de break
8 *Mus (solo jazz passage)* solo *m*; *(pause)* break *m*
VT (*pt* **broke** [brəʊk], *pp* **broken** ['brəʊk(ə)n])
1 *(fracture, shatter, sever) (glass)* casser, briser; *(egg, toy etc)* casser; *(window, ties of friendship etc)* briser; *(rope), Naut (moorings etc)* rompre; *(stick)* casser, rompre; *(skin)* entamer; *Law (seals) (illegally)* briser; *(legally)* lever; *Elec (current)* interrompre; *(circuit)* couper; *Aviat (sound barrier)* franchir; **to b. sth into pieces** mettre qch en morceaux; **to b. one's arm/neck** se casser le bras/le cou; **to b. a branch off a tree** détacher une branche d'un arbre; *Lit Arch* **to b. bread with sb** rompre le pain avec qn; *Constr* **to b. ground** donner les premiers coups de pioche; *Fig* **to b. (new or fresh) ground** faire œuvre de pionnier, innover; *Fig* **to b. the ice** rompre *ou* briser la glace; **to b. a ten-pound note** entamer un billet de dix livres; **to get broken** se casser
2 *(interrupt) (silence, fast etc)* rompre; *Typ (page)* couper; **to b. step** rompre le pas; **to b. ranks** rompre les rangs; **to b. the thread of a story** interrompre le fil d'une narration; **to b. one's journey** s'arrêter en route, faire une étape; *Naut* faire escale; *Aviat* **to b. one's journey in Singapore** faire (une) escale à Singapour
3 *(weaken impact of) (fall, force of sth)* amortir; *(wind)* arrêter; *(current)* rompre; **to b. the force of a blow** amortir un coup
4 *(overcome, destroy) (strike, person's resistance)* briser; *(person's pride)* abattre, dompter; *(person's health)* ruiner; *(alibi)* écarter; *(record)* battre; *(horse)* dresser, entraîner; *(bad habit)* corriger; **to b. sb into the work** rompre qn au travail; **to b. sb of a habit** corriger *ou* guérir qn d'une habitude; **to b. oneself of a habit** se corriger *ou* se défaire d'une habitude; **to b. sb** *(financially)* ruiner qn; *(of grief etc)* briser qn; **to b. the bank** *(when gambling)* faire sauter la banque; *Hum* **one night out won't b. the bank** une sortie ne va pas me/vous/*etc* ruiner; *Tennis* **to b. one's opponent's service** gagner le service de son adversaire; **to b. sb's heart/spirit** briser le cœur à qn/le courage de qn
5 *(fail to respect) (law, regulation, ceasefire)* enfreindre, ne pas observer; *(one's word, appointment etc)* manquer à; *(contract, agreement, treaty)* rompre; **to b. one's word to sb** manquer à sa parole envers qn; **to b. a promise** ne pas tenir sa promesse; **to b. gaol** s'évader de prison; **to b. cover** *(of animal)* débucher; *Mil, Sch* **to b. bounds** violer la consigne; **his insolence has broken all bounds** son insolence a passé les bornes
6 *(reveal, disclose)* **to b. the news of sth to sb** apprendre qch à qn; **to b. a piece of bad news gently to sb** apprendre une mauvaise nouvelle doucement à qn
7 *Physiol* **to b. wind** lâcher un vent
VI 1 *(fracture, shatter etc) (of glass)* se casser, se briser; *(of egg, toy etc)* se casser; *(of window)* se briser; *(of wood, rope)* se rompre; *(of limb)* se fracturer, se casser; *(of wave)* se briser, déferler; *(of heart)* se briser, se fendre; **my waters have just broken** *(of pregnant woman)* je suis en train de perdre les eaux; **to b. with sb/a tradition** rompre avec qn/ une tradition; **to b. in two/into pieces** se casser en deux/en morceaux; **the sea was breaking against the rocks** les vagues se brisaient sur les rochers
2 *(collapse, give way) (of health)* s'altérer; **to b. under torture** s'effondrer sous la torture
3 *(change) (of weather)* changer; *(of heatwave)* passer, prendre fin; *(of voice) Physiol* muer; *(with emotion)* se briser, s'étrangler
4 *(start) (of storm)* éclater, se déchaîner; *(of*

news, scandal) éclater; **we bring you the stories as they b.** nous transmettons les événements au fur et à mesure qu'ils arrivent; **day was beginning to b.** le jour commençait à se lever

5 *Billiards* donner l'acquit

6 *Boxing (move away from each other)* se séparer; **b.! break!,** stop!

7 *Typ (in paginating)* faire une coupure de page

8 **to b. free of one's bonds** briser ses liens
▸▸ *Comput* **b. character** caractère *m* d'interruption; *Comput* **b. key** touche *f* d'interruption; *Typ* **b. line** *(of paragraph)* dernière ligne *f*; *Elec* **b. switch** disjoncteur *m*, interrupteur *m*

▸ **break away** VT SEP détacher (**from** de)

VI **1** *(escape)* s'évader; *Sport* se détacher; **she broke away from the guards** elle a échappé à la surveillance de ses gardiens

2 *(cut ties with)* se dégager, se détacher (**from** de); *(of province) (from State)* se séparer; **when did you b. away from your family?** quand est-ce que tu as coupé les ponts avec ta famille?; *Pol* **to b. away from a party** abandonner un parti; **the year France broke away from NATO** l'année où la France a quitté l'OTAN

3 *(come off)* se détacher (**from** de)

▸ **break back** VI *Tennis* = gagner le service de son adversaire après avoir perdu son propre service

▸ **break down** VT SEP **1** *(destroy) (door)* enfoncer; *(wall etc)* abattre, démolir

2 *(overcome) (resistance)* briser; *(prejudice)* vaincre, surmonter; **to b. down all opposition** vaincre toute opposition

3 *(separate into parts)* *Fin etc (account, figures)* décomposer, ventiler; *(statistics)* analyser; *(bill, estimate)* détailler; *Chem (substance)* décomposer; *(molecules)* dissocier; *Com* **to b. down bulk** ventiler un lot; **we need to b. the figures down a bit further** il faut que nous décomposions *ou* ventilions les chiffres un peu plus; **we can b. the problem down into three parts** le problème peut se décomposer en trois parties; **the story can be broken down into two parts** on peut diviser l'histoire en deux parties

VI **1** *(fail) (of health)* se détériorer, s'altérer; *(of car, train, machinery)* tomber en panne; *(of ship)* subir une avarie; **that's where your argument breaks down** c'est là que ton argument s'effondre *ou* ne tient plus debout

2 *(collapse) (of negotiations)* échouer; *(of resistance)* s'effondrer; *(of person) (have nervous breakdown)* faire une dépression nerveuse; *(burst into tears)* éclater en sanglots, fondre en larmes; *(confess)* faire des aveux complets, passer aux aveux; **their marriage is breaking down** leur mariage se désagrège

3 *(separate)* se décomposer (**into** en)

▸ **break even** VI *(financially) (of person, company)* rentrer dans ses frais

▸ **break in** VT SEP **1** *(destroy) (door etc)* enfoncer

2 *(accustom to being used) (horse)* dresser; *(pipe)* culotter; *(new shoes)* faire, briser; *Am (car)* roder; **to b. sb/oneself in to sth** rompre qn/se rompre à qch; **I'm getting these shoes broken in at last** ces chaussures commencent enfin à se faire

VI **1** *(interrupt)* interrompre; **to b. in on sb/a conversation** interrompre qn/une conversation; **I really must b. in at this point** il faut vraiment que je vous interrompe ici

2 *(enter premises) (of burglar)* s'introduire *ou* entrer *ou* pénétrer par effraction; **I'd lost my front-door key so I had to b. in** j'avais perdu la clé de ma porte d'entrée et donc j'ai dû forcer la porte; **the police broke in through a window** la police est entrée par la fenêtre

▸ **break into** VT INSEP **1** *(house) (illegally)* en-

trer *ou* pénétrer par effraction dans; *(desk, safe)* forcer; **I had to b. into my flat through a window** j'ai dû forcer une fenêtre pour entrer chez moi; **they've been broken into three times** ils se sont fait cambrioler trois fois

2 *(begin suddenly)* **to b. into laughter** éclater de rire; **to b. into a song** se mettre à chanter; **to b. into a trot/run/sprint** se mettre au trot/à courir/à sprinter; **her face broke into a smile** son visage s'éclaira d'un sourire

3 *(use part of) (stocks, large-denomination bank note, savings)* entamer

4 *(interrupt) (conversation)* interrompre

▸ **break loose** VI *(from bonds)* se dégager; *(escape)* s'évader (**from** de); *(of ship)* partir à la dérive

▸ **break off** VT SEP **1** *(remove)* casser, rompre, détacher (**from** de); **I've broken the handle off a cup** j'ai cassé l'anse d'une tasse

2 *(end) (temporarily)* interrompre; *(permanently)* abandonner; *(negotiations)* rompre; **to b. off relations with** *(person)* cesser tout contact avec; *(country)* rompre les relations avec

3 *(romantic relationship)* rompre; **to b. it off** rompre (**with sb** avec qn)

VI **1** *(become detached)* se casser net, se détacher net, se détacher (**from** de); **the handle broke off in my hand** l'anse m'est restée dans la main

2 *(stop)* **to b. off for ten minutes** prendre dix minutes de pause; **to b. off for lunch** s'arrêter pour déjeuner; **shall we b. off for the rest of the day?** on s'arrête là pour aujourd'hui?

3 *(stop talking)* s'interrompre, se taire; **to b. off in the middle of a speech** s'arrêter *ou* s'interrompre au milieu d'un discours

▸ **break open** VT SEP *(door)* enfoncer; *(lock, safe, till)* forcer; *Fam (bottle of wine etc)* ouvrir, déboucher; **to b. a desk open** ouvrir un bureau en forçant la serrure, forcer un bureau

VI *(of box etc)* s'ouvrir

▸ **break out** VI **1** *(escape) (from prison etc)* s'échapper, s'évader (**of** de)

2 *(start) (of argument, war, riots)* éclater; *(of fire, epidemic)* se déclarer; **panic broke out in the cinema when …** ce fut la panique dans le cinéma lorsque …

3 *(develop)* **to b. out into a sweat** se mettre à transpirer; **to b. out in spots** *(of face etc)* se couvrir de boutons; **the baby is breaking out into a rash** le bébé est en train de faire une éruption; **to b. out in a laugh** éclater de rire

VT INSEP **1** *Fam (bottle of wine etc)* ouvrir, déboucher

2 *Am (prepare for use)* sortir; *(flag)* déployer

▸ **break through** VT INSEP *(barrier, police cordon etc)* enfoncer; *(wall)* faire une brèche dans; *Aviat (sound barrier)* franchir; *(of sun) (clouds)* percer; **to b. through sb's reserve** vaincre la réserve de qn

VI *(of sun)* percer

▸ **break up** VT SEP **1** *(reduce to pieces)* mettre *ou* briser en morceaux; *(building, ship etc)* démolir; *(property)* morceler; *(empire)* dissoudre; *(crowd, family)* disperser; *Com (conglomerate, trust)* scinder, diviser; *(company)* scinder; *(coalition)* rompre; *Chem (compound)* résoudre; *Agr (earth)* ameublir; **to b. a word up into syllables** décomposer un mot en syllabes

2 *(bring to an end) (marriage)* détruire; *(meeting)* dissoudre; *(conference)* mettre fin à; **to b. up a fight** séparer des combattants; *Fam* **b. it up!** la paix!

VI **1** *(disintegrate) (of ship)* se briser; *(of empire)* se dissoudre; *(of road surface)* se désagréger; *(of thawing ice)* se briser; *(of crowd, group etc)* se disperser; *(of clouds)* se

dissiper, se disperser; *Fig Fam* **I just broke up** *(with laughter)* j'ai été pris d'un fou rire

2 *(end) (of party, celebration etc)* se terminer; *Sch* être en vacances; **the meeting broke up in disorder** la réunion s'est terminée dans la pagaille; *Sch* **we b. up on the 4th** nous vacances commencent le 4, nous sommes en vacances le 4; **the schools will be breaking up for summer soon** les écoles vont bientôt fermer pour l'été; **their marriage has broken up** ils se sont séparés

3 *(end relationship)* se séparer, rompre; **they're breaking up** ils se séparent

4 *(of weather)* se gâter

break² N **1** *(carriage)* break *m* **2** *Aut* shooting **b.** break *m* (de chasse)

breakable ['breɪkəb(ə)l] ADJ cassable, fragile

NPL **breakables** objets *mpl* fragiles

breakages ['breɪkɪdʒɪz] NPL **have there been any b.?** *(was anything broken?)* est-ce qu'il y a eu de la casse?; **to pay for b.** payer la casse

breakaway ['breɪkəweɪ] N **1** sécession *f* (**from** de); **b. union/party** syndicat *m*/parti *m* dissident **2** *Ftbl (of winger etc)* échappée *f*

break-dance VI danser le smurf

break-dancer N danseur, -euse de smurf

break-dancing N smurf *m*

breakdown ['breɪkdaʊn] N **1** *(failure) (of efforts)* échec *m*; *(in negotiations, communications)* rupture *f*; *(of marriage)* échec; *(of system)* écroulement *m*; *(of service)* arrêt *m* complet

2 *(collapse) (of health)* délabrement *m*; **(nervous) b.** dépression *f* (nerveuse); **she's had a b.** *(and has not yet recovered)* elle fait une dépression; *Hum* **I'm going to have a b.** je vais craquer; **mental b.** dépression nerveuse

3 *Aut, Rail etc (mechanical)* panne *f*; **I've had a b.** je suis tombé en panne

4 *(into component parts) (of statistics etc)* analyse *f*; *(of account, figures etc)* décomposition *f*, ventilation *f*; *(of bill, costs)* détail *m*; *(of population) (by class, age etc)* répartition *f*, classement *m*; *(of script)* prédécoupage *m*; *(for recording)* dépouillement *m*; *Banking* **b. of charges/interest** décompte *m* d'agios/d'intérêts

5 *Chem* dissociation *f*
▸▸ *Aut* **b. gang** équipe *f* de dépannage; *Aut* **b. and recovery service** service *m* de remorquage et de dépannage; *Aut* **b. service** service de dépannage; *TV, Cin* **b. sheet** *(artistic)* fiche *f* artistique; *(technical)* fiche technique; **b. truck**, **b. van** dépanneuse *f*, camion *m* de dépannage

breaker ['breɪkər] N **1** *(of horses)* dresseur, -euse **2** *(wave)* (vague *f*) déferlante *f* **3** *Aut* rupteur *m*
▸▸ **b.'s yard** *(for cars, boats etc)* chantier *m* de démolition

breakeven ['breɪkiːv(ə)n] ADJ ATTRIB N seuil *m* de rentabilité; *Acct* point *m* mort; **to reach b.** atteindre le seuil de rentabilité
▸▸ *Fin* **b. analysis** analyse *f* du point mort; **b. point** seuil de rentabilité; **b. prices** prix *mpl* permettant de rentrer dans ses frais

breakfast ['brekfəst] N petit déjeuner *m*; **to have (one's) b.** déjeuner, prendre le *ou* son (petit) déjeuner; **while we were at b.** pendant que nous déjeunions; **what do you want for b.?** qu'est-ce que tu veux pour le petit déjeuner?; *Fam* **to have sb for breakfast** ne faire qu'une bouchée de qn VOIR GRAMMAIRE A7

VI déjeuner (le matin)
▸▸ **b. buffet** buffet *m* du petit déjeuner; **b. cereals** céréales *fpl* (en flocons); **b. chef** chef *m* de petit déjeuner; **b. cook** cafetier *m*; **b.**

meeting réunion f pendant le petit déjeuner; **b. room** salle f du petit déjeuner; **b. television** télévision f du matin; **b. tray** plateau m petit déjeuner

break-in N **1** (by burglar etc) effraction f **2** Tech, Am Aut rodage m

breaking ['breɪkɪŋ] N **1** (of window etc) bris m; (of silence etc) rupture f, (of journey) interruption f, Aviat (of sound barrier) franchissement m; Law **b. and entering** (into house) entrée f par effraction; Law **b. of seals** (illegal) bris m des scellés; (legal) levée f des scellés; **b. of new** or **fresh ground** Agr défrichage m, Fig (in research, science etc) œuvre f de pionnier

2 (disintegration) (of waves) déferlement m; Med (of bone etc) fracture f, **b. of the voice** Physiol mue f, (with emotion) altération f de la voix

3 (of horse) dressage m

4 (of fall, force of sth) amortissement m

5 (of strike, sb's heart) action f de briser

6 (of law, treaty etc) violation f, (of promise) rupture f

ADJ (news) de dernière minute

▸▸ Com **b. bulk** fractionnement m d'un lot; **b. point** point m de rupture; (of resistance) limite f critique; Fig (of strength etc) limite f, **she has reached b. point** elle est au bout du rouleau, elle est à bout; **their marriage has reached b. point** leur mariage a atteint le point critique; **to try sb's patience to b. point** pousser à bout la patience de qn; Tech **b. strain** tension f de rupture

breakneck ['breɪknek] ADJ **at b. speed** à une vitesse ou allure folle

break-out N (from prison etc) évasion f

breakpoint ['breɪkpɔɪnt] N Typ point m de césure

breakthrough ['breɪkθruː] N **1** Mil (of enemy lines) percée f **2** (advance, discovery, in market) percée f, (in negotiations) progrès m; **their latest b. in computing technology** leur dernière découverte en technologie informatique; **to make a b.** (discovery) faire une percée; (in negotiations) progresser; **the b. came only after a week of deadlock** la situation ne s'est débloquée qu'après une semaine

break-up N **1** (of empire, meeting) dissolution f, (of company) scission f, (of marriage etc) échec m; (of ship etc) dislocation f, **they still saw one another after the b.** ils ont continué à se voir après leur séparation **2** (of ice) débâcle f

▸▸ Fin **b. price** prix m de liquidation; Com **b. value** valeur f de liquidation

breakwater ['breɪkwɔːtər] N **1** (wall) brise-lames m inv; môle m; (jetty) jetée f **2** (of bridge) éperon m

bream [briːm] N (fish) brème f, **sea b.** dorade f

breast [brest] N **1** (of woman) sein m; **a child at the b.** un(e) enfant au sein **2** (chest) (of person) poitrine f, (of horse) poitrail m; (of bird) gorge f, (of shirt etc) devant m; Culin (of chicken) blanc m; **to make a clean b. of it** tout avouer; **b. high** or **deep** (water etc) jusqu'à la poitrine

VT Lit (storm) affronter; (hill) atteindre le sommet de; **to b. the waves** (of swimmer) fendre la lame; Sport **to b. the tape** être le premier à franchir la ligne d'arrivée

▸▸ **b. cancer** cancer m du sein; **b. enlargement** augmentation f mammaire; **b. pocket** poche f de poitrine; **inside b. pocket** poche poitrine intérieure, poche portefeuille; **b. pump** tire-lait m inv; **b. reduction** réduction f mammaire

breastbone ['brestbəʊn] N (of person, animal, bird) sternum m

breastfeed ['brestfiːd] (pt, pp **breastfed** [-fed]) VT (baby) nourrir au sein, allaiter VI allaiter

breastfeeding ['brestfiːdɪŋ] N allaitement m maternel

breastplate ['brestpleɪt] N (armour) cuirasse f

breaststroke ['bres(t)strəʊk] N (in swimming) brasse f, **I can only do** or **swim b.** je ne sais nager que la brasse

breastwork ['brestwɜːk] N Mil parapet m

breath [breθ] N (smelt) haleine f, (breathed) souffle m; **his b. smelt of onions** son haleine sentait l'oignon; **to have bad b.** avoir mauvaise haleine; **I felt his b. on my neck** j'ai senti son souffle dans mon cou; **to draw b.** respirer; **give me time to draw b.** donnez-moi le temps de souffler; **to draw** or **take a deep** or **long b.** respirer profondément ou à pleins poumons; **to pause for b.** (when speaking) s'arrêter pour reprendre sa respiration; **to draw one's last** or **dying b.** rendre le dernier soupir; **the b. of life** le souffle vital ou de la vie; Fig **music is the very b. of life to me** je ne pourrais pas vivre sans musique; **(all) in the same b.** tout d'une haleine; **he agreed and disagreed (all) in the same b.** il a dit qu'il était d'accord puis il est immédiatement revenu sur ce qu'il avait dit; **but in the next b. he said the opposite** mais quelques secondes plus tard il a dit le contraire; **they are not to be mentioned in the same b.** on ne saurait les comparer; **to hold one's b.** retenir son souffle; Fam **I wouldn't hold my b.!** je ne compterais pas trop là-dessus!; **to gasp for b.** haleter; **to waste one's b.** perdre son temps en discours inutiles, perdre sa salive; **I'm wasting my b.** je perds mon temps, je me fatigue pour rien; **save your b.** ne te fatigue pas; **to be short of b.** être essoufflé, avoir la respiration coupée; **out of b.** à bout de souffle, hors d'haleine, essoufflé; **to get** or **run out of b.** s'essouffler; **to take sb's b. away** couper la respiration ou le souffle à qn; Fig couper le souffle à qn; **to get one's b. (back), to recover** or **catch one's b.** reprendre haleine; **under one's b.** (to talk) d'une voix très basse, à voix basse; (to swear) entre ses dents; **the first b. of spring** le premier souffle du printemps; **a b. of wind/of air** un souffle de vent/d'air; **to go out for a b. of (fresh) air** sortir prendre l'air; Fig **it's/she's like a b. of fresh air** c'est/elle est comme une bouffée d'air frais; **a b. of scandal** l'ombre f d'un scandale

▸▸ **b. freshener** purificateur m d'haleine, spray m buccal; **b. test** Alcootest® m

breathalyse, Am **breathalyze** ['breθəlaɪz] VT faire subir l'Alcootest® à; **he was breathalysed** on l'a fait souffler dans le ballon

breathalyser, Am **breathalyzer** ['breθəlaɪzər] N Alcootest® m

▸▸ **b. test** Alcootest®

breathe [briːð] VI **1** respirer; **to b. hard** haleter; **to b. heavily** (noisily) respirer bruyamment; (with difficulty) respirer péniblement; **you can't b. in here** (it's too hot) on ne peut pas respirer ici; **I feel as if I can't b.** je me sens oppressé; **I need room to b.** (in relationship) j'ai besoin d'espace, il faut que je respire; **to b. (easily) again** (with relief) respirer de nouveau; **to b. on one's fingers** souffler dans ses doigts; Fam **to b. down sb's neck** (supervise) être sur le dos de qn; (look over their shoulder) regarder par-dessus l'épaule de qn; Fam **he's breathing down my neck for this translation** il me casse les pieds à propos de cette traduction; Fam **the police are breathing down our necks** (very close to arresting us) la police nous talonne; Fam **there's a police car breathing down our necks** on a une voiture de police aux fesses

2 (of voice, instrument, wind) soupirer, souffler doucement; **open the bottle to let the wine b.** ouvre la bouteille pour permettre au vin de respirer

VT **1** (air) respirer

2 (sigh) exhaler, laisser échapper; (prayer) murmurer; **to b. a sigh of relief** pousser un soupir de soulagement; Lit **to b. one's last** rendre le dernier soupir, rendre l'âme; **don't b. a word (of it)!** n'en soufflez (pas un) mot!; **to b. fire** (be very angry) cracher des flammes; **to b. new life into sth** insuffler une force nouvelle à qch; **he was breathing whisky fumes all over me** il me soufflait des relents de whisky en pleine figure

3 Ling (sound, consonant) aspirer

▸ **breathe in** VT SEP (smoke, fumes) inhaler VI inspirer

▸ **breathe out** VI expirer

breathed [briːðd] ADJ Ling (unvoiced) sourd, non voisé

breather ['briːðər] N **1** Fam (rest) pause f, **to give sb a b.** laisser souffler qn, laisser un moment de répit à qn; **to go out for a b.** aller respirer un peu d'air, sortir prendre l'air; **to take a b.** faire une pause **2** Fam (person) heavy **b.** (on telephone) = homme m qui donne des coups de téléphone anonymes

▸▸ Aut **b. pipe** (tuyau m de) reniflard m; Tech **b. port** orifice m de reniflard

breathing ['briːðɪŋ] N (of person) respiration f, **heavy b.** (noisy) respiration bruyante; (difficult) respiration pénible

▸▸ Tech **b. apparatus** (for fireman, miner etc) masque m à oxygène; (for diver) scaphandre m; **b. space** moment m de répit; Fig **I need some b. space** (in relationship) j'ai besoin de respirer ou d'espace

breathless ['breθlɪs] ADJ **1** (person) (out of breath) à bout de souffle, hors d'haleine, essoufflé; **b. from running** essoufflé d'avoir couru; **he was b. with excitement** l'exultation lui avait coupé le souffle **2** (very fast) (chase, speed) fou **3** Fig **to have sb b.** (of film etc) tenir qn en haleine; **b. silence** or **hush** silence m absolu; **b. calm** calme m plat; **b. suspense** suspense m total

breathlessly ['breθlɪslɪ] ADV **1** (out of breath) tout essoufflé **2** (to wait, listen) en retenant son souffle

breathlessness ['breθlɪsnɪs] N essoufflement m; (of patient) manque m de souffle, oppression f

breathtaking ['breθteɪkɪŋ] ADJ (beauty, imagination, audacity etc) à vous couper le souffle; **with a b. lack of tact** avec un manque de tact incroyable; **it's b.** (view) c'est à vous couper le souffle; (stupidity etc) c'est sidérant

breathtakingly ['breθteɪkɪŋlɪ] ADV (beautiful) extraordinairement; (stupid, tactless etc) incroyablement

breath-test VT faire subir l'Alcootest® à

breathy ['breθɪ] ADJ Mus (voice) qui manque d'attaque; **b. voice** voix f haletante

breech [briːtʃ] N **1** Obst (accouchement m par le) siège m **2** (of firearm) culasse f, tonnerre m; **b. action** or **mechanism** mécanisme m de culasse

▸▸ Obst **b. birth**, **b. delivery** (accouchement par le) siège; Obst **b. presentation** présentation f par le siège

breeches ['brɪtʃɪz] NPL (knee-length) haut-de-chausses mpl, culotte f, (full-length) pantalon m; **knee b.** culotte f

▸▸ Naut **b. buoy** bouée-culotte f, pl bouées-culottes

breed [briːd] N (of people, animals) race f, Fig **she is one of the new b. of executives** elle fait partie de la nouvelle race ou génération de cadres; **a new b. of modems** une nouvelle génération de modems; **thatchers are a dying b.** les couvreurs de toits en chaume sont une race en voie de disparition

VT (pt, pp **bred** [bred]) **1** (give birth to) (children, offspring) produire, procréer; Fig engendrer, donner naissance à; **dirt breeds disease** la saleté entraîne des maladies; **all these rumours are breeding insecurity** toutes ces rumeurs engendrent l'insécurité **2** (raise) (cattle, rabbits etc) élever; **they're specially bred for racing** ils sont élevés spécialement pour la course; **to be town/country bred** (of person) avoir été élevé à la ville/à la campagne; Prov **what's bred in the bone will come out in the flesh** bon chien chasse de race

VI **1** (of animals) se multiplier, se reproduire; (of people) se reproduire **2** (of animal breeder) faire de l'élevage

breeder ['briːdər] N **1** (animal) reproducteur, -trice **2** (person) (of animals) éleveur, -euse; **poultry b.** aviculteur, -trice

▸ ▸ Nucl **b. reactor** surgénérateur m, surrégénérateur m, Fam couveuse f

breeding ['briːdɪŋ] N **1** (reproduction) reproduction f, multiplication f **2** (raising) (of domestic animals etc) élevage m; **animal kept for b. purposes** (animal m) reproducteur m; **sheep b.** élevage des moutons **3** (education) (of child etc) éducation f, **(good) b.** bonne éducation, bonnes manières fpl, savoir-vivre m inv; **to lack b.** manquer de savoir-vivre ou d'éducation

▸ ▸ **b. ground** = lieu m de reproduction de certains animaux; Fig foyer m, terrain m propice; **a b. ground of anarchists** un foyer d'anarchistes; **a b. ground of crime/violence** un terrain propice au crime/à la violence; **damp areas are a b. ground for germs** les zones humides sont des foyers de microbes ou constituent un terrain propice aux microbes; **b. stock** animaux mpl élevés en vue de la reproduction

breeze[1] [briːz] N (wind) brise f, **gentle or light b.** petite ou légère brise; Naut **strong or stiff b.** vent m frais; **fresh b.** bonne brise; Fam **it was a b.** (easy) c'était simple comme bonjour, c'était un jeu d'enfant

▸ **breeze in** VI (quickly) entrer en coup de vent; (casually) entrer d'une façon désinvolte

▸ **breeze out** VI (quickly) sortir en coup de vent; (casually) sortir d'une façon désinvolte

▸ **breeze through** VI (pass exam with ease) réussir les doigts dans le nez

VT INSEP (exam) réussir les doigts dans le nez; **to b. through life** se laisser vivre

breeze[2] N

▸ ▸ **b. block**, **b. brick** parpaing m

breezeway ['briːzweɪ] N Am passage m couvert (souvent entre la maison et le garage)

breezily ['briːzɪlɪ] ADV (in lively fashion) avec verve; (casually) avec désinvolture

breezy ['briːzɪ] ADJ **1** (day, place etc) venteux **2** Fam (pleasant) jovial, -aux; (casual) désinvolte; (speech) plein de verve

brekky ['brekɪ] N Br Fam petit déj m

Bremen ['breɪmən] N Brême

Bren [bren] N Mil fusil-mitrailleur m, pl fusils-mitrailleurs

▸ ▸ **B. carrier** chenillette f porte-fusil-mitrailleur, pl chenillettes porte-fusil(s)-mitrailleur(s); **B. gun** fusil-mitrailleur

brent [brent] N bernache f cravant

▸ ▸ **b. goose** bernache cravant

brethren ['breðrɪn] NPL esp Rel frères mpl; **my dearly beloved b.** mes très chers frères

Breton ['bretɒn] ADJ breton

N **1** Breton, -onne **2** Ling breton m

breve [briːv] N **1** (accent) brève f **2** Mus double ronde f

▸ ▸ Mus **b. rest** double pause f

breviary ['briːvɪərɪ] N Rel bréviaire m

brevity ['brevɪtɪ] N **1** (of style) brièveté f, concision f, (of expression) laconisme m; Prov **b. is the soul of wit** le secret d'un bon mot d'esprit réside dans sa concision **2** (of life etc) brièveté f, courte durée f

brew [bruː] N **1** (of beer) cuvée f, **home b.** bière f/cidre m de ménage; Fig **the book is a heady b. of …** le livre est un mélange formidable de … **2** Fam (tea) thé m **3** Am Fam (beer) mousse f

VT **1** (beer) brasser; **home brewed** (beer, cider) de ménage, (fait à la maison) **2** (tea) faire (infuser)

VI (of tea) infuser; Met, Fig **there's a storm brewing** il y a de l'orage dans l'air; Fig **there's something brewing** il se trame quelque chose, il y a quelque chose qui se prépare; **there's trouble brewing** il va y avoir du grabuge

▸ **brew up** VI Br Fam faire du thé

brewer ['bruːər] N brasseur, -euse; **b.'s yeast** levure f de bière; Br Sl Hum **b.'s droop** = impuissance f due à l'alcool; **to have b.'s droop** ne pas pouvoir bander après un excès d'alcool

brewery ['bruːərɪ] N brasserie f

brewing ['bruːɪŋ] N **1** (of beer) brassage m; **the b. industry** la brasserie **2** (of tea) infusion f

brewski ['bruːskɪ] N Am Fam (beer) mousse f

brew-up N Br Fam **to have a b.** faire du thé

briar[1] ['braɪər] N **1** (shrub) bruyère f **2** (pipe) pipe f de bruyère

briar[2] N = **brier**[1]

briarroot ['braɪəruːt], **briarwood** ['braɪəwʊd] N racine f de bruyère

bribable ['braɪbəb(ə)l] ADJ corruptible

bribe [braɪb] N pot-de-vin m, pl pots-de-vin; **to take bribes** toucher des pots-de-vin

VT soudoyer, acheter, Fam graisser la patte à; **to b. sb into silence** acheter le silence de qn; **to b. sb into doing sth** soudoyer ou acheter ou Fam graisser la patte à qn pour qu'il/elle fasse qch; Fig **I bribed her with some chocolate to go to bed** je lui ai donné du chocolat pour qu'elle aille se coucher

bribery ['braɪbərɪ] N corruption f, **open/not open to b.** corruptible/incorruptible; **b. and corruption** corruption; Hum **that's b. and corruption!** c'est une tentative de corruption!

bribing ['braɪbɪŋ] N corruption f, Fam graissage m de patte; Law (of witnesses) subornation f

bric-a-brac ['brɪkəbræk] N (no pl) bric-à-brac m

brick [brɪk] N **1** brique f, **air b.** brique perforée; Fig **to invest in bricks and mortar** investir dans la pierre; Prov **you cannot make bricks without straw** on ne peut pas faire de miracles; Fam **to come down on sb like a ton of bricks** tomber sur le dos à qn; Fig **to drop a b.** faire une bourde ou une gaffe; **box of (building) bricks** (toys) jeu m de cubes ou de construction; Com, Comput **a bricks-and-clicks shop** une société qui vend ses produits en magasin et sur Internet **2** Old-fashioned Br Fam **he's a b.** c'est un chic type **3** (of ice cream) pain m; (of tea) bloc m

VT Br Fam **to b. it** (be scared) les avoir à zéro, avoir les jetons

▸ ▸ **b. kiln** four m à briques; **b. red** rouge m brique (inv, he went b. red il est devenu tout rouge; **b. wall** mur m de brique; Fig **to come up against a b. wall** se heurter à un obstacle infranchissable; **to knock one's head against a b. wall** se démener en pure perte;

it's like knocking your head against a b. wall c'est peine perdue; **it's like talking to a b. wall** (he or she etc won't listen) c'est comme parler à un mur ou à un sourd

▸ **brick up**, **brick in** VT SEP (window, doorway etc) murer

brickbat ['brɪkbæt] N Fig **she got a lot of brickbats for her performance** son interprétation lui a valu beaucoup de critiques; **the government has been receiving more brickbats than bouquets** le gouvernement a été plus critiqué qu'applaudi

brickfield ['brɪkfiːld] N briqueterie f

bricklayer ['brɪkleɪər], Br Fam **brickie** ['brɪkɪ] N maçon m

bricklaying ['brɪkleɪɪŋ] N briquetage m

brickmaker ['brɪkmeɪkər] N briquetier m

brickwork ['brɪkwɜːk] N briquetage m, maçonnerie f de brique

brickworks ['brɪkwɜːks] N (place) briqueterie f

brickyard ['brɪkjɑːd] N briqueterie f

bridal ['braɪd(ə)l] ADJ ATTRIB nuptial, -aux, de noce(s)

▸ ▸ **the b. party** la noce (les invités); **b. suite** suite f nuptiale; **b. veil** voile m de mariée

bride [braɪd] N (about to be married) future mariée f, (married) jeune mariée; **the b. and (bride)groom** (about to be married) les futurs époux mpl, (married) les jeunes mariés mpl; **with his young b.** avec sa jeune épouse; **his b. of four months** la femme avec qui il est/était marié depuis quatre mois

bridegroom ['braɪdgruːm] N (about to be married) futur marié m; (married) jeune marié

bridesmaid ['braɪdzmeɪd] N demoiselle f d'honneur

bride-to-be N future mariée f

bridge[1] [brɪdʒ] N **1** (across river etc) pont m; Fig **we'll cross that b. when we get or come to it** chaque chose en son temps

2 (in wrestling) pont m; **to make a b.** ponter **3** (in billiards etc) chevalet m **4** (on ship) passerelle f **5** (of nose) arête f, (of violin) chevalet m; (of spectacles) arcade f **6** (on teeth) bridge m **7** Cin, TV (shot) transition f, (piece of music) pont m sonore

VT (river etc) construire un pont sur; **to b. a gap** relier les bords d'une brèche; Fig (in knowledge etc) combler une lacune; (of snack) boucher un trou; **to b. the gap between two groups** réduire l'écart qui existe entre deux groupes; Com **to b. the gap** (esp for supplies) faire la soudure

▸ ▸ **b. building** construction f de ponts; Fig réconciliation f, Am Fin **b. loan** prêt-relais m, pl prêts-relais

bridge[2] N Cards bridge m; **to play b.** jouer au bridge; **game of b.** (partie f de) bridge

▸ ▸ Cards **b. partner** partenaire mf au bridge; Cards **b. player** bridgeur, -euse; Br **b. roll** petit pain m (au lait)

bridgehead ['brɪdʒhed] N Mil, Fig tête f de pont

bridgework ['brɪdʒwɜːk] N esp Am (on teeth) bridge m

bridging ['brɪdʒɪŋ] N **1** Constr **the b. of the river took several months** la construction du pont sur la rivière a pris plusieurs mois; **2** Fig (of gap) comblement m **3** Elec, Electron shuntage m

▸ ▸ Elec **b. connection** montage m en pont; Br Fin **b. loan** prêt-relais m, pl prêts-relais; Constr **b. party** équipe f de pontonniers; Constr **b. piece** entretoise f, Cin **b. title** titre m de liaison

bridle ['braɪd(ə)l] N (for horse) bride f; Fig (restraint) frein m

VT (horse) brider; Fig (one's passions) maîtriser, mettre un frein à; **to b. one's tongue** tenir sa langue

VI (of horse) redresser la tête; Fig (of person) s'indigner, se scandaliser; Fig **she bridled at the implication** elle s'est indignée en entendant l'insinuation

▸▸**b. bit** mors m de bride; **b. path** piste f cavalière

brief [bri:f] ADJ (letter, interval etc) court; (pause) petit; (discussion, explanation etc) bref, succinct, concis; (account, report) sommaire, bref; (stay etc) bref, de courte durée; **we exchanged a few b. words** nous avons échangé quelques mots; **give me a b. idea of what happened** donne-moi une petite idée de ce qui s'est passé; **I caught a b. glimpse of her** je n'ai fait que l'entrevoir; **a very b. pair of shorts** un short très court; **for a b. period** pendant peu de temps, pendant une courte période; **in b.** en bref; **to be b., ...** (in short) bref, ...; **please be b.** soyez bref, s'il vous plaît

NPL **briefs** (for man, woman) slip m; **bikini briefs** slip de bikini

N **1** Law dossier m; Am **b. (of argument)** conclusions fpl (présentées à la cour avant l'audience); **to take a b.** accepter un dossier; **to hold a b.** être chargé d'un dossier; **to hold a b. for sb** représenter qn en justice; **to hold a watching b. for sb** veiller (en justice) aux intérêts de qn; Fig **I don't hold any** or **I hold no b. for him** ce n'est pas mon affaire de plaider sa cause; Fig **I hold no b. for this policy** je n'adhère absolument pas à cette politique **2** (instructions) (of committee etc), Pol mission f **3** Br Sl (lawyer) avocat m

VT **1** Eng Law (lawyer) confier une cause à **2** Aviat, Com etc (inform) donner des informations à (about sur), faire l'exposé à (about de); (instruct) donner ou fournir des instructions ou des directives à; **have you been briefed?** (brought up to date) est-ce que vous avez été mis au courant?; (given instructions) est-ce qu'on vous a donné vos instructions?; **was the Prime Minister briefed?** est-ce que le Premier ministre a été renseigné sur la question?

briefcase ['bri:fkeɪs] N serviette f; (for carrying under arm) porte-documents m inv

briefing ['bri:fɪŋ] N **1** Eng Law **b. of a barrister** ≃ constitution f d'avoué **2** (orders) (for mission) instructions fpl, directives fpl; (meeting) réunion f d'information, Com briefing m; Aviat briefing; **they gave me a final b.** ils m'ont donné les dernières directives

▸▸**b. room** salle f de réunion

briefly ['bri:flɪ] ADV **1** (in a few words) brièvement, en peu de mots, en bref **2** (for a short time) (to work, stay) brièvement; (to pause, smile etc) un court instant; **we spoke b. on the telephone** nous avons échangé quelques mots au téléphone

| Attention: ne pas confondre avec **shortly**. |

briefness ['bri:fnɪs] N (of time, visit) brièveté f; (of speech) concision f

brier¹ ['braɪər] N **1** (wild rose) églantier m; **wild b.** églantier commun, rosier m sauvage; **sweet b.** églantier odorant **2 briers** (thorny bushes) ronces fpl

▸▸**b. rose** églantine f

brier² N = **briar¹**

brierroot ['braɪəru:t], **brierwood** ['braɪəwʊd] N = **briarroot, briarwood**

Brig [brɪg] N Mil abbr **Brigadier**

brig [brɪg] N Naut **1** (ship) brick m **2** esp Am (prison) prison f, cellule f (à bord d'un navire)

brigade [brɪ'geɪd] N Mil brigade f; Fig Hum Pej (group of people) bande f; **infantry b.** régiment m d'infanterie; Am **artillery b.** brigade d'artillerie; Fig **one of the old b.** un vieux de la vieille

brigadier [brɪgə'dɪər] N Mil général m de brigade

▸▸**b. general** général de brigade

brigand ['brɪgənd] N Old-fashioned brigand m, bandit m

brigandage ['brɪgəndɪdʒ] N Old-fashioned brigandage m

bright [braɪt] ADJ **1** (star, metal, gem etc) brillant; (sun) éclatant; (fire, light etc) vif, f vive; (eyes) lumineux, brillant; (day, weather, sound) clair; (colour) vif, éclatant; Met **it'll be brighter tomorrow** le temps sera plus clair demain; Met **to become brighter** s'éclaircir; Met **b. intervals** éclaircies fpl; **b. red** (colour) rouge m vif; **to go b. red** (blush) devenir tout rouge ou rouge comme une tomate; **b. red socks** des chaussettes rouge vif; **the company's future looks b.** cette société est très prometteuse; **it was the only b. spot in the day** c'était la seule chose positive de la journée; **the only b. spot in the play was her acting** son jeu était le seul intérêt de la pièce; **brighter days** (happier) des jours plus heureux; **the unemployment situation is looking a bit brighter** la situation de l'emploi commence à s'améliorer; **b. future** avenir m brillant ou qui promet; **to look on the b. side (of things)** prendre les choses du bon côté; Fig **the b. lights** (big city) la ville; **as soon as he could, he headed for the b. lights of the city** dès qu'il a pu, il est allé s'installer en ville **2** (cheerful, lively) vif, animé, sémillant; (face, smile) gai **3** (clever) intelligent; **a b. idea** une idée lumineuse; **she's a real b. spark** c'est une vraie lumière; Iron **some b. spark has locked the door** il y a un gros malin qui a fermé la porte à clef; **he's not very b.** ce n'est pas une lumière, il n'est pas très futé ou malin; Iron **that's b.!** c'est vraiment intelligent!

ADV **to get up/leave b. and early** se lever/partir de bonne heure

NPL Am Aut **brights** pleins phares mpl; **put the brights on** mets en (pleins) phares

brighten ['braɪt(ə)n] VT (colour) aviver; Fig (room, person) égayer

VI (of person, face) s'épanouir; (of eyes) s'allumer, briller; (of weather) s'éclaircir; (of future) s'éclaircir, devenir moins sombre; (of prospects) s'améliorer; **their mood brightened** ils se sont déridés

▸ **brighten up** VT SEP, VI = **brighten**

brightening ['braɪt(ə)nɪŋ] N **1** (of sky, weather) éclaircissement m; Fig **there was a momentary b. of her mood** elle s'est égayée un moment **2** (of colours) avivage m

bright-eyed ADJ aux yeux brillants; Fig (eager) enthousiaste; Fam **b. and bushy-tailed** (eager) très enthousiaste; (alert) en pleine forme

brightly ['braɪtlɪ] ADV **1** (coloured, to sparkle) vivement; **the sun was shining b.** le soleil était éclatant; **to burn b.** (of fire) être vif; **b. lit** (street, shop window etc) bien éclairé; **b. polished** reluisant **2** (to say) gaiement, gaîment

brightness ['braɪtnɪs] N (of sun, light, sound) éclat m; (of lighting) intensité f; (of surface) luminosité f; (of day, sound, room) clarté f; (of colour) vivacité f; (of child etc) intelligence f; (of steel) brillant m, éclat; TV luminosité f

▸▸TV **b. control** dispositif m de réglage de la luminosité

brill¹ [brɪl] N (fish) barbue f

brill² ADJ Br Fam (abbr **brilliant**) super inv

brilliance ['brɪljəns], **brilliancy** ['brɪljənsɪ] N **1** (of sun) éclat m; (of shine) brillant m, lustre m; (of sound) netteté f; Opt etc luminance f **2** (intelligence) (of person) intelligence f remarquable; (of mind, style, acting etc) génie m; (of plan, scheme) ingéniosité f; (skill) (of surgeon etc) habileté f remarquable

brilliant ['brɪljənt] ADJ **1** (lighting) intense, brillant; (sun) brillant, éclatant; (smile) radieux **2** (painter, scientist, actor etc) excellent, brillant; (speech) remarquable; (future, career) brillant; (success) éclatant; **she was b. in her last film** elle était formidable dans son dernier film; **you were b.!** tu étais formidable ou magnifique!; **he's not b.** il n'est pas brillant; Fam **I'm not feeling too b.** (I feel ill) je ne suis pas dans mon assiette

N (diamond, cut) brillant m

brilliantine ['brɪljənti:n] N (for hair) brillantine f

brilliantly ['brɪljəntlɪ] ADV **1** (coloured) vivement; **the sun was shining b.** le soleil était éclatant; **b. lit** très bien éclairé **2** (performed, played) brillamment; **b. intelligent** d'une intelligence brillante; Mus **to play b.** jouer avec brio

brim [brɪm] N (of glass, hat etc) bord m; **to fill a glass to the b.** remplir un verre à ras bord

VI (-mm-) **eyes brimming with tears** yeux noyés de larmes; **to be brimming with ideas** (of person) déborder d'idées

▸ **brim over** VI déborder, regorger (with sth de qch); Fig **brimming over with health/life/ideas** débordant de santé/de vie/d'idées

brimful ['brɪmfʊl] ADJ (glass etc) plein jusqu'au bord; **to fill a glass b.** remplir un verre à ras bord; Fig **b. of health/of life/of ideas** débordant de santé/de vie/d'idées

brimless ['brɪmlɪs] ADJ (chapeau) sans bord(s)

-brimmed [brɪmd] SUFF **broad/narrow-b.** à larges bords/à bords étroits

brimstone ['brɪmstəʊn] N **1** Arch (sulphur) soufre m (brut) **2** (butterfly) citron m

▸▸**b. butterfly** citron

brindled ['brɪnd(ə)ld] ADJ moucheté, tacheté

brine [braɪn] N **1** Culin saumure f; **tuna in b.** thon m mariné **2** (seawater) eau f de mer; Lit **the b.** (the sea) la mer, l'océan m

BRING [brɪŋ]

| amener **1** ▪ apporter **1** |
| ▪ provoquer **2** ▪ rapporter **4** |

VT (pt, pp **brought** [brɔ:t]) **1** (lead, carry) (person, animal) amener; (object, letter, news etc) apporter; **b. your friend** amenez votre ami; **she brought a lot of luggage (with her)** elle a apporté beaucoup de bagages; **what brings you to London?** qu'est-ce qui vous amène à Londres?; **to b. sth onto the market** introduire qch sur le marché; **to b. a child into the world** mettre un enfant au monde; Law **to b. before a court** (person) faire comparaître devant un tribunal; (case) soumettre ou déférer à un tribunal; Law **to b. an action** intenter une action en justice; Law **to b. an action against sb** intenter un procès contre ou à qn; Law **to b. an accusation or a charge against sb** porter une accusation contre qn

2 (lead to, cause) provoquer; **to b. sb (good) luck/bad luck** porter bonheur/malheur à qn; **the announcement brought an angry reaction** la nouvelle a suscité la colère; **production has been brought to a standstill** la production a été paralysée; **to b. new hope to sb** redonner de l'espoir à qn; **you've brought it on yourself** vous l'avez cherché;

to b. tears to sb's eyes faire venir les larmes aux yeux de qn; **to b. discord into a family** semer la discorde dans une famille; **it has brought me great happiness** cela m'a apporté un grand bonheur

3 *(cause to come to a particular condition)* **to b. sb to his senses** ramener qn à la raison; **to b. sb into the conversation** *(involve)* mêler qn à la conversation; **to b. sb's name into the conversation** mentionner le nom de qn dans la conversation; **to b. water to the boil** faire bouillir de l'eau; **to b. sth into question** mettre qch en question; **to b. sth into disrepute** discréditer qch; **to b. sth to sb's attention** attirer l'attention de qn sur qch; **to b. sth to mind** rappeler qch; **to b. to light** *(old artefacts, manuscripts etc)* déterrer; *(crime, secret)* révéler; **to b. sth to an end** mettre fin à qch; **to b. sth to a successful conclusion** faire aboutir qch; **to b. oneself to do sth** se résoudre *ou* se décider à faire qch; **he cannot b. himself to speak about it** il lui est trop pénible d'en parler

4 *(be sold for)* **the house won't b. very much** la maison ne rapportera pas beaucoup

▸ **bring about** vt sep **1** *(cause)* amener, causer, occasionner; *(reconciliation)* amener; *(person's downfall)* entraîner; *(accident etc)* provoquer, causer; *(change)* provoquer

2 *Naut (boat)* retourner, faire virer

▸ **bring along** vt sep *(person)* amener; *(object)* apporter

▸ **bring away** vt sep *(carry) (object)* rapporter; *(memories, impressions)* garder; **I brought away a lot of happy memories from my stay** j'ai gardé de mon séjour le souvenir de beaucoup de moments heureux

▸ **bring back** vt sep **1** *(carry) (object)* rapporter; *(lead) (person)* ramener; **crying won't b. him back** pleurer ne le fera pas revenir; *Law* **to b. a case back before the court** ressaisir le tribunal d'un dossier

2 *(of letter, song etc) (memories)* rappeler; **it brings back my childhood to me** cela me rappelle mon enfance

3 *(restore) (freedom, discipline, monarchy etc)* rétablir; *(confidence)* ramener; **the electors will decide whether the government should be brought back** les électeurs décideront si le gouvernement doit être maintenu; **a couple of days in bed will b. him back to normal** quelques jours au lit le remettront d'aplomb; **to b. sb back to health** rendre la santé à qn; **to b. sb back to life** ramener qn à la vie

▸ **bring down** vt sep **1** *(destroy) (tree, game bird, plane, wall etc)* abattre; *Fam* **her performance brought the house down** son interprétation lui a valu des applaudissements à tout rompre; *Fam* **the audience brought the house down** les spectateurs ont applaudi à tout rompre

2 *(cause to fall) (adversary)* terrasser; *(government)* faire tomber

3 *(lead, carry) (person)* faire descendre; *(object)* descendre (**from** de); **what brings you down to the fourth floor?** qu'est-ce qui t'amène au quatrième étage?

4 *(reduce) (price, costs, temperature)* faire baisser; *(currency)* déprécier, avilir; *(birth rate, inflation, unemployment, swelling)* réduire

5 *(land) (plane)* faire atterrir

6 *(cause to appear) (esp a person in authority)* attirer; **stop making so much noise or you'll b. the headmaster down on us** ne fais pas tant de bruit, tu vas attirer l'attention du proviseur sur nous

▸ **bring forth** vt sep **1** *Arch, Lit (young)* mettre au monde; *(of animal)* mettre bas; *(of plant) (fruit)* produire

2 *Fig (idea)* faire naître; *(suggestion)* donner lieu à; *(condemnation, objections)* provoquer; *(of research, investigations)* générer

▸ **bring forward** vt sep **1** *(carry, lead) (chair etc)* avancer; *(person)* amener, faire avancer, faire approcher; *(witness, evidence)* produire, présenter; *(argument)* avancer, présenter

2 *(in time) (meeting etc)* avancer

3 *Com (sum of money)* reporter; **brought forward** report *m*

▸ **bring in** vt sep **1** *(lead, carry) (person)* introduire, faire entrer; *(object)* rentrer; **b. him in** faites-le entrer; **to b. in the harvest** rentrer la moisson; **to b. sb in for questioning** emmener qn au poste de police pour l'interroger

2 *(introduce) (fashion etc)* introduire, lancer; *(bill)* déposer, présenter; **to b. in new measures** instaurer des mesures; **new legislation will be brought in next year** une nouvelle loi prendra effet l'an prochain

3 *(involve) (person)* faire intervenir, faire appel à; **the company is bringing consultants in** la société fait appel à des experts-conseils

4 *(earn)* **to b. in interest** rapporter, porter intérêt; **investment that brings in 10%** placement qui rapporte 10%; **this land brings her in an income of £5,000** cette terre lui procure un revenu de 5000 livres; **how much money is he bringing in?** *(earning)* combien est-ce qu'il gagne?

5 *Law* **to b. in a verdict** rendre un verdict

6 to b. in the New Year *(celebrate it)* fêter le Nouvel An

▸ **bring off** vt sep **1** *(person) (from ship)* débarquer; **the injured men will be brought off by helicopter** les blessés seront évacués en hélicoptère

2 *(complete successfully)* réussir; **they brought it off** ils ont réussi

3 *Vulg (bring to orgasm)* **to b. sb/oneself off** branler qn/se branler

▸ **bring on** vt sep **1** *(cause to appear) (illness, asthma attack)* causer, provoquer; *Hum* **what brought this on?** *(why are you offering to help with dishes etc)* qu'est-ce que tu me caches?

2 *(of sun etc) (plants)* faire pousser; *(of teacher, trainer) (person)* faire faire des progrès à

3 *Theat (person, animal)* amener sur la scène; *(object)* apporter sur la scène; **please b. on our next contestant** faites entrer le concurrent suivant

4 I brought it on myself *(it was my own fault)* c'est entièrement de ma faute

▸ **bring out** vt sep **1** *(extract, lead) (object)* sortir; *(person)* faire sortir; *Fig* **to b. sb out (of his/her shell)** *(make less shy)* faire sortir qn de sa réserve

2 *(cause to appear) (meaning of sth)* révéler, faire ressortir; *(colour, detail etc)* faire ressortir; *(publish) (book)* publier, sortir; **to b. out the best/the worst in sb** faire ressortir les qualités/les défauts de qn; **the sun has brought out the roses** le soleil a fait s'épanouir les roses; **strawberries b. her out in a rash** les fraises lui donnent de l'urticaire

▸ **bring over** vt sep *(lead, carry) (person)* amener, faire venir; *(object)* amener, apporter

▸ **bring round** vt sep **1** *(lead, carry) (person)* amener; *(object)* amener, apporter; **b. her round to meet us some time** amène-la un jour, qu'on puisse faire sa connaissance

2 *(restore to consciousness)* faire reprendre connaissance à, ranimer

3 *(restore to good mood)* rendre sa bonne humeur à

4 *(persuade)* convertir (**to an opinion** à une opinion)

5 *(steer) (conversation)* (r)amener (**to a subject** sur un sujet)

6 *Naut (ship)* faire virer

▸ **bring through** vt sep *(cure with success)*

guérir; *(lead with success)* conduire à la réussite; **his faith, which had brought him through the crisis** sa foi, qui l'avait aidé à surmonter la crise; **she brought all of us through the exam** grâce à elle, nous avons tous réussi l'examen

▸ **bring to** vt sep *(restore to consciousness)* faire reprendre connaissance à, ranimer

▸ **bring together** vt sep *(people)* réunir; *(put in touch with each other)* mettre en contact; *(documents)* rassembler, réunir; **he brought them together again** *(for meeting)* il les a réunis; *(after quarrel)* il les a réconciliés; *Law* **to b. the parties together** mettre les parties en présence

▸ **bring up** vt sep **1** *(carry, lead upstairs) (object)* monter; *(person)* faire monter; *(carry, lead forward) (object)* approcher; *(troops)* faire avancer; *(reinforcements, fresh supplies etc)* faire venir; **to be brought up before the magistrate** comparaître devant le tribunal; **to b. sb/sth up to professional standard** élever qn/qch à un niveau professionnel

2 *(vomit)* vomir; **to b. up one's food** vomir

3 *(rear) (children)* élever; **I was brought up to be polite** on m'a appris la politesse; **well/ badly brought up child** enfant bien/mal élevé; **to b. sb up the hard way** élever qn à la dure

4 *(mention) (question)* soulever, mettre sur le tapis; **to b. sth up against sb** reprocher qch à qn

5 *(stop)* **to be brought up short by a road-block/an accident** *(of car)* s'arrêter brusquement à cause d'un barrage routier/d'un accident; **to be brought up short by sb's indifference** *(when talking)* être choqué par l'indifférence de qn

---

bring-and-buy (sale) N *Br* vente *f* de charité

> **Bring-and-Buy**
> Ces brocantes sont en général destinées à réunir des fonds pour une œuvre de charité. On y vend des articles d'occasion et des produits faits maison.

bringing-up ['brɪŋɪŋ-] N *(of child)* éducation *f*

brink [brɪŋk] N *(of precipice, river)* bord *m*; *Fig* **to be on the b. of** *(tears, war, success, starvation etc)* être au bord de; *(discovery)* être à la veille de; *(death)* être à deux doigts de; *(ruin)* être au bord *ou* à deux doigts de; *Fig* **I was on the b. of telling him/of doing it** j'étais à deux doigts de le lui dire/de le faire; *Fig* **to be on the b. of extinction** *(of animal)* être en voie de disparition; *Fig* **to stand shivering on the b.** hésiter à faire le plongeon

brinkmanship ['brɪŋkmənʃɪp] N *esp Pol* politique *f* de la corde raide; **he's a master in the art of b.** c'est un maître dans l'art de savoir jusqu'où il peut aller *ou* *Iron* jusqu'où il peut aller trop loin

briny ['braɪnɪ] ADJ saumâtre
N *Lit, Hum* **the b.** la grande bleue

briquette [brɪ'ket] N *(of coal)* briquette *f*

brisk [brɪsk] ADJ **1** *(person, attitude, tone)* vif; *(to the point of curtness)* sec, *f* sèche **2** *(movement)* vif; *Com (business, trade)* actif; *(demand)* fort; **at a b. pace** à vive allure; **to take a b. walk** aller se promener d'un bon pas; **business is b.** les affaires marchent bien; **to do a b. trade** *(of shop)* marcher à plein rendement; *(of street seller)* faire de bonnes affaires; **we're doing a b. trade in this particular item** cet article se vend très bien **3** *(air)* vivifiant; *(morning, wind, weather etc)* frais, *f* fraîche

brisket ['brɪskɪt] N *Culin* poitrine *f*

briskly ['brɪsklɪ] ADV **1** *(to say)* d'un ton vif;

(to the point of curtness) sèchement **2** *(to move)* vivement; **to step out b.** marcher d'un bon pas; **to sell b.** bien se vendre

briskness ['brɪsknɪs] **N 1** *(of person, voice)* vivacité *f*, *(to the point of curtness)* brusquerie *f*, **the b. with which she goes about her job** l'extrême diligence avec laquelle elle fait son travail **2** *(of movement)* vivacité *f*, *(of business, trading)* dynamisme *m* **3** *(of air etc)* fraîcheur *f*

bristle ['brɪs(ə)l] **N 1** *(of pig, caterpillar, badger)* soie *f*, *(of brush)* soie, poil *m*; *(of beard)* poil raide; **his face was covered with bristles** il avait une barbe de trois jours **2** *Bot* soie *f*, poil *m*
VI *(of animal, hair etc)* se hérisser; *Fig* **to b. (with anger)** se hérisser (**at** à)
▸ **bristle with VT INSEP** grouiller de; **the room was bristling with security men** la pièce grouillait d'agents de sécurité; **a situation bristling with difficulties** une situation hérissée de difficultés; **bristling with machine guns** *(fort, trench)* hérissé de mitrailleuses; **soldiers bristling with weapons** des soldats bardés d'armes

bristly ['brɪslɪ] **ADJ 1** *(face)* couvert de poils raides; *(animal)* couvert de soies; *(moustache)* hérissé **2** *Bot* poilu, garni de soies

Bristol ['brɪst(ə)l] **N** *Naut, Fig* **(shipshape and) B. fashion** en bon ordre
▸▸ **B. board** bristol *m*

bristols ['brɪst(ə)lz] **NPL** *Br Old-fashioned Sl (breasts)* nichons *mpl*

Brit [brɪt] **N** *Fam (abbr* **Briton***)* Britannique *mf*, Anglais, -aise, *Pej* rosbif *mf*

Britain ['brɪt(ə)n] **N** Grande-Bretagne *f*

Britannia [brɪ'tænɪə] **N** = nom *m* symbolique de la Grande-Bretagne

Britannic [brɪ'tænɪk] **ADJ** *His/Her* **B. Majesty** Sa Majesté britannique

Britart ['brɪtɑːt] **N** = appellation *f* collective des jeunes artistes britanniques qui ont fait de Londres, depuis la fin des années 1970, un important centre d'art contemporain

Briticism ['brɪtɪsɪz(ə)m] **N** *Ling* anglicisme *m*

British ['brɪtɪʃ] VOIR GRAMMAIRE A19 **ADJ** britannique, de la Grande-Bretagne; **B. goods** produits *mpl ou* marchandises *fpl* britanniques; **the B. consul** le consul de Grande-Bretagne
NPL the B. les Britanniques *mpl*, *Fam* les Anglais *mpl*
▸▸ **B. Columbia** Colombie-Britannique *f*, **B. Council** = organisme *m* chargé de promouvoir la langue et la culture anglaises; **B. English** anglais *m* britannique; **B. Isles** îles *fpl* Britanniques; **B. Standards Institution** = association *f* britannique de normalisation; **B. Summer Time** = heure *f* d'été en Grande-Bretagne; **B. thermal unit** = 1055,06 joules *mpl*

> **British Council**
> Le British Council est un organisme chargé de promouvoir la langue et la culture anglaises, et de renforcer les liens culturels avec les autres pays.

Britisher ['brɪtɪʃər] **N** *Am* Britannique *mf*, *Fam* Anglais, -aise

Briton ['brɪt(ə)n] **N 1** Britannique *mf*, *Fam* Anglais, -aise VOIR GRAMMAIRE A19 **2** *Hist (Celt)* Breton, -onne *(de la Grande-Bretagne)*

Britpop ['brɪtpɒp] **N** = la musique pop britannique du milieu des années 90

Brittany ['brɪtənɪ] **N** Bretagne *f*

brittle ['brɪt(ə)l] **ADJ** fragile, cassant; *Fig (laugh)* un peu forcé; **to suffer from b. bones** souffrir d'ostéoporose; *Fig* **in a b. voice** *(brusque)* d'un ton cassant; *(strained)* d'une

voix tendue; **there is still a slightly b. air about the new coalition** la nouvelle coalition donne toujours une légère impression de fragilité; **a b. and rather unconvincing defence** une défense faible et peu convaincante
N = bonbon *m* croquant à base de mélasse et de noix

brittleness ['brɪt(ə)lnɪs] **N** *(of bones)* fragilité *f*, **the b. of his humour** son humour caustique

broach [brəʊtʃ] **N** *(for tapping cask)* perçoir *m*
VT *(cask)* percer; *Fig (question etc)* aborder; **I broached with your mother the subject of your leaving school** j'ai abordé la question de ton départ de l'école avec ta mère

broad [brɔːd] **ADJ 1** *(wide)* large; **the road is 15 metres b.** la route a 15 mètres de large *ou* de largeur; **to make sth broader** élargir qch; **a b. smile** un large sourire; **to have a b. back** avoir une forte carrure; *Fig* avoir bon dos; **it was already b. daylight** il faisait déjà grand jour; **in b. daylight** en plein jour; *Fig* au grand jour, devant tout le monde; *Fig* **it's as b. as it's long** cela revient au même, c'est tout un, c'est bonnet blanc et blanc bonnet; **b. views** *or* **ideas** *or* **outlook** idées *fpl* larges; **b. humour** humour *m* de mauvais goût *ou* peu délicat; **b. joke** grosse plaisanterie *f*, **to have b. tastes in literature** avoir des goûts éclectiques en littérature; *Fig* **the party is a b. church** le parti rassemble de nombreux courants différents
2 *(general) (rule, implications)* général, -aux; *(distinction)* sommaire; **term used in its broadest sense** terme employé dans un sens (très) large; **b. outline** *(of project etc)* aperçu *m*; **the project has b. support** le projet bénéficie d'un large soutien; **to be in b. agreement** être d'accord dans les grandes lignes
3 *(accent)* prononcé; **to speak b. Scots/Yorkshire** parler avec un accent écossais/du Yorkshire prononcé
N 1 **the b. of the back** le milieu du dos **2** *Br* **the Broads** la région des lacs du Norfolk **3** *esp Am Sl (woman)* gonzesse *f*
▸▸ **b. bean** fève *f*, *Am Sport* **b. jump** saut *m* en longueur; *Ling* **b. vowel** voyelle *f* large

broadband ['brɔːdbænd] **Tel, Comput N** connexion *f* à haut débit *ou* à large bande
ADJ à haut débit, à large bande

broad-brimmed **ADJ** *(hat)* à large bord

broadcast ['brɔːdkɑːst] **VT** *(pt, pp* **broadcast***)*
1 *(programme etc)* *Radio* transmettre, (radio)diffuser; *TV* transmettre, diffuser; **the match will be b. live** le match sera diffusé en direct **2** *Agr (seed)* semer à la volée; *Fig (news)* répandre; **don't b. it!** ne le crie pas sur les toits!
VI 1 *(of person) (on radio)* parler/chanter/*etc* à la radio; *(on television)* passer à la télévision **2** *(of radio or TV authority)* émettre
N *Radio, TV* émission *f*, **simultaneous/recorded/live/outside b.** émission simultanée/en différé/en direct/hors studio
ADJ 1 *Radio* (radio)diffusé; *TV* télévisé **2** *Agr* semé à la volée
ADV *Agr* **to sow b.** semer à la volée
▸▸ *TV etc* **b. antenna** antenne *f* d'émission; **b. journalism** *Radio* journalisme *m* de radiodiffusion; *TV* journalisme de télévision; *TV etc* **b. master** copie *f* antenne; **b. network** réseau *m* de transmission; *TV etc* **b. satellite** satellite *m* de radiodiffusion; *Agr* **b. sowing** semis *m* à la volée; *Mktg* **b. sponsorship** parrainage *m* audiovisuel

broadcaster ['brɔːdkɑːstər] **N** *(reporter)* *Radio* reporter *m* radio; *TV* reporter de la télévision; *(who gives talks, speaks)* personne *f* qui fait de la radio/la télévision; *Radio, TV*

independent b. *(station)* station *f* de radio/chaîne *f* de télévision privée

broadcasting ['brɔːdkɑːstɪŋ] **N 1** *Radio* radiodiffusion *f*, *TV* diffusion *f*, **she works in b.** *Radio* elle fait de la radio; *TV* elle fait de la télévision; **(television) b.** télévision *f*, **news b.** *Radio* reportage *m* (radio); *TV* téléreportage *m*, reportage (télévisé); **music/children's b.** émissions *fpl* musicales/pour les enfants; **this is the end of today's b.** voici la fin de nos émissions pour aujourd'hui **2** *Agr* semis *m* à la volée
▸▸ **b. centre** centre *m* de diffusion; **b. company** *TV* société *f* de télédiffusion; *Radio* société *f* de radiodiffusion; **B. House** = siège *m* de la BBC à Londres; **b. network** réseau *m* de diffusion; **b. rights** droits *mpl* de diffusion *ou* d'antenne; **b. station** station *f* émettrice

broadcloth ['brɔːdklɒθ] **N** *Tex* **1** *(for men's clothing)* drap *m* fin **2** *Am (poplin)* popeline *f*

broaden ['brɔːd(ə)n] **VT** élargir; **to b. sb's outlook** *or* **horizons** élargir l'horizon de qn; **travel broadens the mind** les voyages ouvrent de nouveaux horizons
VI s'élargir
▸ **broaden out VI** *(of river, road, valley)* s'élargir

broad-leaved **ADJ** *(tree)* à larges feuilles, *Spec* latifolié

broadloom ['brɔːdluːm] **N** moquette *f* grande largeur
▸▸ **b. carpet** moquette grande largeur

broadly ['brɔːdlɪ] **ADV 1** *(widely)* largement; **smiling b.** avec un large sourire **2** *(generally)* généralement; **b. speaking** généralement parlant, d'une façon générale; **to b. agree** être d'accord sur les grandes lignes **3** *(to speak)* avec un accent prononcé

broad-minded **ADJ** tolérant; **to be b.** avoir l'esprit large, être tolérant, être large d'esprit; **she takes a b. attitude to that kind of thing** elle est très tolérante pour ce genre de choses

broad-mindedness [-'maɪndɪdnɪs] **N** largeur *f* d'esprit, tolérance *f*

broadness ['brɔːdnɪs] **N 1** *(width)* largeur *f* **2** *(of accent)* **because of the b. of his Yorkshire accent** à cause de son accent du Yorkshire à couper au couteau

broadsheet ['brɔːdʃiːt] **N 1** *(newspaper)* journal *m* grand format *(de qualité)* **2** *(pamphlet)* feuille *f* imprimée
▸▸ **b. format** plein format *m*; **the b. press** les journaux grand format

broad-shouldered [-'ʃəʊldəd] **ADJ** large d'épaules, aux larges épaules

broadside ['brɔːdsaɪd] **N** *Naut* **1** *(of ship)* flanc *m*, travers *m*; **collision b. on** abordage *m* par le travers **2** *(from guns)* bordée *f*, *Fig (attack)* attaque *f* virulente; **to fire a b.** *Naut* tirer une bordée; *Fig* lancer une attaque virulente (**at** contre)

broad-spectrum **ADJ** *(antibiotic)* au spectre d'action très large

broadways, broadwise ['brɔːdweɪz, -waɪz] **ADV** dans le sens de la largeur

brocade [brə'keɪd] *Tex* **N** brocart *m*; **b. curtains/skirt** rideaux *mpl*/jupe *f* en brocart
VT brocher; **brocaded gown** robe *f* de brocart

broccoli ['brɒkəlɪ] **N** brocoli *m*; **eat your b.** mange tes brocolis

brochure ['brəʊʃʊər, -ʃər] **N** brochure *f*, *(folding)* dépliant *m*

brogue¹ [brəʊg] **N** *(shoe)* = chaussure *f* basse, ornée de petits trous

brogue² **N** *(accent)* accent *m*

broil [brɔɪl] *Am* **VT** *Culin (under grill)* passer au gril; *(over fire)* griller, (faire) cuire sur le gril

VI *Fam* **we were broiling (hot)** on grillait; **a broiling hot day** un jour où il fait une chaleur à crever

broiler ['brɔɪlər] N **1** *Am (grill)* gril *m*, rôtissoire *f*; **put it under the b.** passez-le au gril **2** *(fowl)* poulet *m* (à rôtir) **3** *Am Fam* **it's a real b. (of a day)** on crève de chaleur
▸▸ **b. fowl** poulet (à rôtir); **b. house** éleveuse *f* (de poulets)

broke [brəʊk] PT *see* **break**¹
ADJ *Fam* fauché, à sec; **to go b.** *(of company)* faire faillite; **to be (stony or dead) b.** être sans le sou, être fauché, être à sec; *Sl* **to go for b.** jouer le tout pour le tout

broken ['brəʊk(ə)n] PP *see* **break**¹
ADJ **1** *(limb, egg, stick, toy etc)* cassé; *(glass, window)* cassé, brisé; *(friendship)* brisé; *(rope), Naut (moorings etc)* rompu; *(stones)* (con)cassé **2** *(terrain)* accidenté; *(shoreline)* découpé; *(outline)* irrégulier **3** *(sleep)* interrompu; *(words)* entrecoupé; **we had rather a b. night** nous avons été réveillés plusieurs fois pendant la nuit; **a voice b. with sobs** une voix entrecoupée de sanglots; **in a b. voice** d'une voix brisée; **to speak b. English** parler un mauvais anglais **4** *(marriage, heart)* brisé; *(promise)* violé; **b. health** mauvaise santé *f*; **b. home** foyer *m ou* famille *f* désuni(e); **a b. man** *(financially)* un homme ruiné; *(by grief etc)* un homme brisé
▸▸ *Com* **b. lots** articles *mpl* dépareillés; **b. white line** *(on road)* ligne *f* discontinue

broken-down ADJ *(car etc)* en panne; *(mechanism)* détraqué; *(house, furniture)* délabré; *(horse)* fourbu; **a b. old man** un vieil homme usé

brokenhearted [brəʊk(ə)n'hɑːtɪd] ADJ au cœur brisé; **to die b.** mourir de douleur *ou* de chagrin

brokenly ['brəʊk(ə)nlɪ] ADV *(to speak)* de façon entrecoupée

broken-winded [-'wɪndɪd] ADJ *Vet (horse)* poussif

broker ['brəʊkər] N **1** *Com (for insurance etc)* courtier, ière; **insurance b.** courtier d'assurances; **wine b.** négociant, -ante en vins **2** *St Exch* courtier, ière *ou* agent *m* de change; **outside b.** courtier libre; *St Exch* **b.'s commission** (frais *mpl* de) courtage *m*; **b.'s contract** courtage
VT *Fig* **to b. an agreement** négocier un accord en tant qu'intermédiaire

brokerage ['brəʊkərɪdʒ] N *Fin (fee)* (frais *mpl* de) courtage *m*
▸▸ **b. house** *(business)* maison *f* de courtage

broking ['brəʊkɪŋ] N *Fin (profession)* courtage *m*

brolly ['brɒlɪ] N *Br Fam (umbrella)* pépin *m*, pébroc *m*

bromeliad [brəʊ'miːlɪæd] N *Bot* broméliacée *f*

bromide ['brəʊmaɪd] N **1** *Chem, Typ* bromure *m*; *Phot* papier *m* au gélatinobromure (d'argent); **potassium b.** bromure de potassium **2** *Fig (platitude)* banalité *f*
▸▸ *Phot* **b. paper** papier au gélatinobromure (d'argent)

bronchial ['brɒŋkɪəl] ADJ *Anat, Med (artery, asthma etc)* bronchique
▸▸ *Med* **b. pneumonia** broncho-pneumonie *f*, *pl* broncho-pneumonies; *Anat* **b. tubes** bronches *fpl*

bronchiole ['brɒŋkɪəʊl] N *Anat* bronchiole *f*

bronchitic [brɒŋ'kɪtɪk] ADJ, N *Med* bronchitique *mf*

bronchitis [brɒŋ'kaɪtɪs] N *Med* bronchite *f*; **she has b.** elle a une bronchite

bronchopneumonia [brɒŋkəʊnjuː'məʊ-

nɪə] N *Med* broncho-pneumonie *f*, *pl* broncho-pneumonies

bronchus, *pl* **bronchi** ['brɒŋkəs, -kiː] N *Med* bronche *f*

bronco ['brɒŋkəʊ] N cheval *m* sauvage *(dans l'ouest américain)*

broncobuster ['brɒŋkəʊbʌstər] N *Am* dresseur *m* de chevaux

brontosaurus [brɒntə'sɔːrəs] N brontosaure *m*

bronze [brɒnz] N **1** *(metal)* bronze *m* **2** *Art (object)* (objet *m* en) bronze *m* **3** *Sport etc Fam (medal)* médaille *f* de bronze
ADJ **1** *(statue)* de *ou* en bronze **2** *(colour)* (couleur) bronze *inv*
VT bronzer
▸▸ **the B. Age** l'âge *m* de bronze; *Sport etc* **b. medal** médaille de bronze

bronzed [brɒnzd] ADJ *(skin)* bronzé

bronzing ['brɒnzɪŋ] N bronzage *m*

brooch [brəʊtʃ] N broche *f*

brood [bruːd] N **1** *(of chicks)* couvée *f*, nichée *f* **2** *Fig (children)* enfants *mpl*, *Pej* marmaille *f*, **a member of the McGowan b.** un membre de la progéniture des McGowan **3** *Fig Pej (of scoundrels etc)* race *f*, engeance *f*
VI *(of hen)* couver; *Fig* broyer du noir; **to b. about or on or over** *(the past, mistakes)* remâcher; *(idea)* ruminer; **there's no point in brooding over what might have happened** ça ne sert à rien de ruminer en imaginant ce qui aurait pu se passer; **she's brooding about the exam** *(which she has sat)* elle repense à son examen; *(which she will sit)* elle n'arrête pas de penser à son examen; **stop brooding about what he said** arrête de ruminer ce qu'il a dit; **to b. about things** ruminer; *Lit* **night brooded over the castle** les ténèbres enveloppaient le château
▸▸ **b. cell** *(in beehive)* cellule *f* d'incubation; **b. hen** *(poule f)* couveuse *f*; **b. mare** *(jument f)* poulinière *f*

brooder ['bruːdər] N **1** *(hen)* *(poule f)* couveuse *f* **2** *(enclosure)* couveuse *f* (artificielle) **3** *Fig (person)* **he's such a b.** il est toujours à ruminer

broody ['bruːdɪ] ADJ *(hen)* couveuse *f*, qui demande à couver; *Fig (person)* songeur, pensif; **to feel b.** *(of woman)* être en mal d'enfant

brook¹ [brʊk] N ruisseau *m*
▸▸ *Ich* **b. trout** saumon *m* de fontaine

brook² VT *Lit (used only in neg sentences)* tolérer, supporter; **the matter brooks no delay** l'affaire n'admet aucun retard; **he will b. no insolence** il ne supporte pas d'impertinence; **I will b. no refusal** je ne tolérerai pas que tu/il/etc refuse(s)

broom [bruːm] N **1** *(shrub)* genêt *m* (à balai) **2** *(for sweeping)* balai *m*; *Fig* **new b.** = personne *f* nouvellement arrivée qui veut remanier l'organisation de l'entreprise; *Prov* **a new b. sweeps clean** = de nouveaux dirigeants mettent en œuvre de nouvelles méthodes

broomstick ['bruːmstɪk] N manche *m* à balai

Bros [brɒs] *Com (abbr* **Brothers)** Thomas B. maison *f* Thomas B.

broth [brɒθ] N *Culin (clear)* bouillon *m*; *(with vegetables etc)* potage *m*; **Scotch b.** soupe *f* (de mouton) avec orge et légumes

brothel ['brɒθ(ə)l] N maison *f* close, *Fam* bordel *m*
▸▸ *Br Fam* **b. creepers** chaussures *fpl* à semelles de crêpe; **b. keeper** tenancier, -ière de bordel

brother ['brʌðər] N **1** *(sibling)* frère *m*; **older b.** frère aîné; **younger b.** (frère) cadet *m*; *Com* **Thomas Brothers** maison *f* Thomas frè-

res **2** *Rel (in community)* frère *m*; **B. John** Frère John **3** *(fellow member)* (in guild) confrère *m*; *Sl (fellow Black American)* frère; **brothers!** (at union meeting etc) camarades! INT *esp Am Fam* bon sang!
▸▸ **brothers in arms** frères d'armes; **b. officers** officiers *mpl* de la même brigade; *Mil* officiers du même régiment

brotherhood ['brʌðəhʊd] N **1** *(relationship)* fraternité *f*; **the b. of man** la fraternité des hommes **2** *(organization)* fraternité *f*, *(religious)* confrérie *f* *esp Am (trade union)* syndicat *m* ouvrier

brother-in-law, *pl* **brothers-in-law** N beau-frère *m*, *pl* beaux-frères

brotherliness ['brʌðəlɪnɪs] N *(of relation)* amour *m* fraternel

brotherly ['brʌðəlɪ] ADJ *(love etc)* fraternel

brought [brɔːt] PP, PT *see* **bring**

brouhaha ['bruːhɑːhɑː] N brouhaha *m*

brow [braʊ] N **1** *Anat* front *m*; **to knit one's brows** froncer les sourcils **2** *(of hill)* sommet *m*; **the b. of a hill** *(on road)* le haut d'une côte

browbeat ['braʊbiːt] VT intimider; **to b. sb into doing sth** intimider qn pour qu'il fasse qch

browbeaten ['braʊbiːt(ə)n] ADJ persécuté

browbeating ['braʊbiːtɪŋ] N intimidation *f*

brown [braʊn] ADJ *(coat, shoes)* marron *inv*; *(hair)* brun, châtain; *(eyes)* brun, marron; **light b. hair** cheveux châtain clair; **to be b.** *(tanned)* être bronzé; **to be as b. as a berry** *(tanned)* être tout bronzé *ou* noir
N marron *m*
VT **1** *(of sun)* brunir, bronzer; **a face browned by the sun** un visage bruni *ou* hâlé par le soleil **2** *Culin (fish, meat etc)* faire dorer; *(butter, sauce)* faire roussir; *(almonds)* praliner
VI **1** *(in sun)* brunir **2** *Culin* dorer
▸▸ **b. ale** bière *f* brune; **b. bear** ours *m* brun; **b. bread** pain *m* complet *ou* bis; *Com* **b. goods** = biens *mpl* de consommation de taille moyenne tels que téléviseur, radio ou magnétoscope; **B. Owl** *(in Brownies)* cheftaine *f*, **b. owl** chat-huant *m*, *pl* chats-huants, chouette *f* des bois, hulotte *f*; **b. paper** papier *m* d'emballage; **b. paper bag** sac *m* en papier kraft; *Zool* **b. rat** surmulot *m*; **b. rice** riz *m* complet; **b. sugar** *Culin* cassonade *f*, sucre *m* roux; *Sl (heroin)* héro *f*; **b. trout** truite *f* de rivière

brown-bag VT & VI *Am Fam* **to b. (it)** = apporter son déjeuner (sur son lieu de travail)
▸▸ *Am* **b. seminar** = séminaire *m* où les participants apportent leur déjeuner

brown-bagger [-'bægər] N *Am Fam* = personne *f* qui apporte son déjeuner sur son lieu de travail

browned-off [braʊnd-] ADJ *esp Br Fam* **to be b.** en avoir marre *ou* ras le bol; **I'm b. with always having to do the dishes** j'en ai marre de devoir toujours faire la vaisselle; **he's very b. with you** il en a vraiment marre de toi

brown-eyed ADJ aux yeux bruns *ou* marron

brownfield site ['braʊnfiːld] N terrain *m* à bâtir *(après démolition de bâtiments préexistants)*

brown-haired ADJ aux cheveux bruns *ou* châtains

brownie ['braʊnɪ] N **1** *(elf)* lutin *m* (bienfaisant), farfadet *m* **2 B.** *(guide)* ≃ jeannette *f*, *Fig* **to win or get b. points** se faire bien voir **3** *Am Culin* brownie *m*

Browning ['braʊnɪŋ] N *(gun)* browning *m*

browning ['braʊnɪŋ] N **1** *(by sun)* brunissement *m*, bronzage *m* **2** *Culin (of almonds)* pralinage *m*; **the b. of the meat is important**

c'est important de faire rissoler la viande **3** *Br Culin (substance)* colorant *m* brun (pour les sauces)

brownish ['braʊnɪʃ] **ADJ** brunâtre

brown-nose *Am Sl* **VI** faire du lèche-cul **VT** faire du lèche-cul à

brown-noser [-nəʊzər] **N** *Am Sl* lèche-cul *mf inv*

brownout ['braʊnaʊt] **N** *Am Elec* baisse *f* de tension

Brownshirt ['braʊnʃɜːt] **N** *Hist* Chemise *f* brune

browse [braʊz] **VT** *Comput* **to b. the Web** naviguer sur le Web; **to b. the contents of one's hard disk** parcourir le contenu du disque dur **VI 1** *(of animal)* brouter, paître; **to b. on leaves** brouter des feuilles; *Fig* **I'm just browsing, thank you** *(in shop)* je regarde, merci **2** *Comput* se promener
  ▸▸ *Comput* **b. mode** mode *m* survol
▸ **browse through VT INSEP 1** *Fig* **to b. through a book/magazine** feuilleter un livre/un magazine; **to b. through sb's books/records** jeter un coup d'œil aux livres/disques de qn **2** *Comput* se promener dans, survoler

browser ['braʊzər] **N** *Comput* navigateur *m*, logiciel *m* de navigation

brucellosis [bruːsɪ'ləʊsɪs] **N** *Med, Vet* brucellose *f*

bruise [bruːz] **N** bleu *m*, contusion *f*, *Spec* ecchymose *f*, *(on fruit)* meurtrissure *f*, talure *f*; **she just has cuts and bruises** *(of accident victim)* elle n'a que quelques égratignures
  VT 1 *(part of body)* meurtrir; *(fruit)* meurtrir, taler; **to b. one's arm** se faire un bleu au bras, se meurtrir le bras; **you've bruised my arm!** tu m'as fait un bleu au bras!; *Fig* **to b. sb's pride** blesser l'amour propre de qn **2** *(crush)* *(substance)* broyer, écraser, concasser
  VI *(of person)* se faire des bleus; *(of fruit etc)* s'abîmer; **he bruises easily** il se fait des bleus très facilement; *Fig* il est très sensible

bruised [bruːzd] **ADJ** meurtri; *Fig (pride)* blessé; **badly b.** couvert de bleus

bruiser ['bruːzər] **N** *Fam (boxer)* boxeur *m*; *(bully)* cogneur *m*; *Fam* **their baby's a real b.!** *(big)* leur bébé est vraiment costaud

bruising ['bruːzɪŋ] **N 1** *(on skin)* bleus *mpl*, meurtrissures *fpl*, contusions *fpl*, *Spec* ecchymoses *fpl*; *(on fruit)* meurtrissures, talures *fpl*; *Fig* **to take a b.** *(of ego, self-confidence etc)* en prendre un coup **2** *(of substance)* broyage *m*, écrasement *m*, concassage *m*
  ADJ *Fig (hurtful to emotions, self-confidence etc)* douloureux

brumbie, brumby ['brʌmbɪ] **N** *Austr Fam* cheval *m* sauvage *ou* non dressé

Brummie ['brʌmɪ] **N** *Br Fam* = personne *f* née à ou habitant Birmingham

brunch [brʌntʃ] **N** *Fam* brunch *m*

Brunei [bruː'naɪ] **N** Brunei *m*

brunette [bruː'net] **N** brune *f*; **she's a b.** elle est brune

brunt [brʌnt] **N** *(of blow etc)* choc *m*; **the car took the b. of it** c'est la voiture qui a tout pris; *Fig* **the b. of his argument** le point principal de sa thèse; **to bear the b. of** *(attack, storm etc)* soutenir le plus fort de; *(sb's anger)* soutenir le poids de; **to bear the b. of the expense** supporter la plus grande partie des frais

brush [brʌʃ] **N 1** *(undergrowth)* broussailles *fpl*; *(scrubland)* brousse *f*
  2 *(for hair, clothes etc)* brosse *f*; *(for sweeping)* balai *m*; *(with dustpan)* balayette *f*; *(for paint, paste)* pinceau *m*; **flat b.** queue-de-morue *f*, *pl* queues-de-morue; **paste b.** pinceau à colle; **to paint with a full b.** *(of artist)* peindre dans la pâte

3 *(tail) (of fox)* queue *f*
  4 *Elec* balai *m*; **(contact) b.** frotteur *m*
  5 to give sth a b. *(clothes)* donner un coup de brosse à qch; *(floor)* donner un coup de balai à qch; **to give one's hair a b.** se donner un coup de brosse; **to give one's teeth a b.** se brosser les dents
  6 *(encounter) (with enemy)* rencontre *f*, échauffourée *f*, *Fam (with boss)* prise *f* de bec; *Fam* **to have a b. with the police** avoir des ennuis avec la police; *Fig* **to have a b. with death** frôler la mort
  7 *(light stroke)* effleurement *m*; **she felt the b. of his lips on her neck** elle a senti ses lèvres lui effleurer le cou
  VT 1 *(clothes, carpet)* brosser; **to b. one's hair** se brosser les cheveux; **to b. one's teeth** se brosser *ou* se laver les dents; **to b. sth clean** nettoyer qch avec une brosse *ou* à la brosse **2** *(touch in passing) (surface)* effleurer, raser, frôler **3** *Tex (wool, nylon)* gratter
  ▸▸ **b. fire** *(fire)* feu *m* de brousse, incendie *m* de broussailles; *Mil (minor war)* conflit *m* armé; **b. holder** porte-balai *m*, *pl* porte-balai(s)
▸ **brush against VT INSEP** frôler, effleurer
▸ **brush aside VT SEP** *(person, difficulty)* écarter; *(objection, problem)* mépriser
▸ **brush away VT SEP 1** *(remove) (from clothes)* enlever d'un coup de brosse; *(from floor)* enlever d'un coup de balai; *(tears)* essuyer; **b. the leaves away from the path** balaye les feuilles qui sont sur le chemin **2** *(treat as unimportant) (person, difficulty)* écarter; **to b. away criticism** mépriser les critiques
▸ **brush down VT SEP** *(person)* donner un coup de brosse à; *(horse)* brosser
▸ **brush off VT SEP 1** *(remove) (from clothes)* enlever d'un coup de brosse; *(from floor)* enlever d'un coup de balai; **b. those flies off** chasse ces mouches **2** *Fam (reject)* envoyer promener; **he never brushes anyone off** il n'envoie jamais les gens promener; **to b. off pleas for help** rejeter des demandes d'aide
  VI *(of dirt etc)* s'enlever à la brosse
▸ **brush over VT SEP b. the varnish over the surface** badigeonner la surface de vernis
  VT INSEP to b. over an issue *(not treat in detail)* effleurer une question; *(ignore)* ignorer une question
▸ **brush past VT INSEP** passer tout près de; **but he just brushed past me** mais il est passé à côté de moi sans s'arrêter
▸ **brush up VT SEP 1** *(collect) (crumbs etc)* ramasser (avec une brosse) **2** *Fam (subject)* *(improve knowledge of)* se remettre à; *(for exam etc)* réviser; **to b. up one's French** *(improve)* se remettre au français, remettre son français à niveau

brushdown ['brʌʃdaʊn] **N** **to give sb a b.** donner un coup de brosse à qn; **to give a horse a b.** brosser *ou* panser un cheval

brushed [brʌʃt] **ADJ** *Tex (wool, nylon)* gratté

brushing ['brʌʃɪŋ] **N** *(of hair, carpet etc)* brossage *m*; *(of floor)* balayage *m*

brushoff ['brʌʃɒf] **N** *Fam* **to give sb the b.** envoyer promener qn

brush-up N coup *m* de brosse

brushwood ['brʌʃwʊd] **N 1** *(undergrowth)* broussailles *fpl* **2** *(worthless wood)* mortbois *m*, *pl* morts-bois; *(for fire etc)* menu bois *m*; *(twigs)* brindilles *fpl*

brushwork ['brʌʃwɜːk] **N** *Art (of artist)* touche *f*

brusque [bruːsk] **ADJ** *(manner)* brusque, rude; *(tone)* rude, bourru

brusquely ['bruːsklɪ] **ADV** *(to behave)* de façon brusque, avec rudesse; *(to answer)* avec rudesse

brusqueness ['bruːsknɪs] **N** brusquerie *f*, rudesse *f*, *(of tone)* rudesse

Brussels ['brʌs(ə)lz] **N** Bruxelles
  ▸▸ **B. sprouts** choux *mpl* de Bruxelles

brutal ['bruːt(ə)l] **ADJ** brutal, -aux; **the b. truth** la vérité toute nue

brutality [bruː'tælɪtɪ] **N** brutalité *f*, *Law* sévices *mpl* (**to** envers)

brutalize ['bruːtəlaɪz] **VT 1** *(make brutal)* rendre brutal **2** *(ill-treat)* brutaliser, maltraiter

brutally ['bruːtəlɪ] **ADV** brutalement; **to be b. frank** *or* **honest with sb** être d'une franchise brutale avec qn

brute [bruːt] **N** *(animal)* bête *f*, brute *f*, *Fig (person)* brute; **you b.!** espèce de brute!; *Fam* **a b. of a job** un travail pénible
  ADJ b. beast bête *f*, brute *f*, *Fig* **b. strength** *or* **force** force *f* brutale; **by b. force** par la force; **you'll have to use b. force** il faudra user de la manière forte

brutish ['bruːtɪʃ] **ADJ** bestial, -aux; *Fig (stupid)* abruti; *(violent)* brutal, -aux

brutishly ['bruːtɪʃlɪ] **ADV** comme une brute

Brylcreem® ['brɪlkriːm] **N** = marque *f* de brillantine

bryony ['braɪənɪ] **N** *(plant)* bryone *f* couleuvrée

BS [biː'es] **N** *(abbr* **British Standard***)* = indique que le chiffre qui suit renvoie au numéro de la norme fixée par l'association britannique de normalisation

BS [2] **N** *Am Sl (abbr* **bullshit***)* conneries *fpl*

BSc [biːes'siː] **N** *Univ (abbr* **Bachelor of Science***)* **to have a BSc** ≃ être licencié, -ée en sciences; **John Smith, BSc** ≃ John Smith, licencié ès sciences

BSE [biːes'iː] **N** *Vet (abbr* **bovine spongiform encephalopathy***)* EBS *f*

B-share N *St Exch* action *f* ordinaire avec droit de vote, action à dividende prioritaire

BSI [biːes'aɪ] **N** *abbr* **British Standards Institution**

BST [biːes'tiː] **N** *abbr* **British Summer Time**

BT [biː'tiː] **N** *abbr* **British Telecom**

BTW *Comput (abbr* **by the way***) (used in e-mails)* à propos

B2B ['biːtəbiː] **ADJ** *(abbr* **business to business***)* B2B

B2C ['biːtəsiː] **ADJ** *(abbr* **business to consumer***)* B2C

bubba ['bʌbə] **N** *Am Fam* **1** *(term of address)* mec *m*, vieux *m*; **hey b., gimme a smoke!** hé, vieux! file-moi une clope! **2** *Pej (redneck)* plouc *m (du sud des États-Unis)*

bubble ['bʌb(ə)l] **N** *(of air, soap, gas etc)* bulle *f*, *(in glass)* soufflure *f*, bulle; *Metal* boursouflure *f*, **to blow bubbles** faire des bulles de savon; *Fig* **to burst sb's b.** détruire les illusions de qn; **the economic b.** l'illusion d'un miracle économique
  VI *(of boiling liquid etc)* bouillonner; *Chem, Ind (of gas through liquid)* barboter; *(of liquid poured)* faire glouglou, glouglouter
  ▸▸ **b. bath** bain *m* moussant; *Br Aut* **b. car** = petite voiture *f* à trois roues; **b. economy** économie *f* de bulle; **b. gum** bubble-gum *m*; *Comput* **b. memory** mémoire *f* à bulles; **b. pack** *Com (for toy, batteries)* blister *m*, emballage *m* bulle; *(for pills)* plaquette *f*, *Br Culin* **b. and squeak** = plat *m* à base de pommes de terre et de choux, servi réchauffé; *Com* **b. wrap** bullpack® *m*
▸ **bubble over VI** *(of soup, milk)* (bouillonner et) déborder; *(of champagne)* (mousser et) déborder; *Fig* **to b. over with vitality/with high spirits** déborder de vie/de gaieté; **to b. over with joy** pétiller de joie; **he was bubbling over with laughter** il ne se retenait pas de rire

bubble-jet printer N imprimante f à bulles

bubbling ['bʌb(ə)lɪŋ] ADJ bouillonnant
N bouillonnement m; *Chem, Ind* barbotage m; *(in paintwork)* boursouflures fpl

bubbly ['bʌblɪ] ADJ plein de bulles; *Fig (person)* pétillant, plein d'entrain; *(personality)* plein de vitalité
N *Fam (champagne)* champagne m; *(sparkling wine)* vin m mousseux

bubonic [bjuː'bɒnɪk] ADJ
▸▸ **b. plague** peste f bubonique

buccal ['bʌk(ə)l] ADJ *Anat* buccal, -aux

buccaneer [bʌkə'nɪər] N boucanier m
VI faire le boucanier

Bucharest [buːkə'rest] N Bucarest

buck[1] [bʌk] N **1** *(male deer)* daim m, chevreuil m (mâle)
2 *(male reindeer, chamois etc)* mâle m; **to have b. teeth** avoir des dents de lapin
3 *esp Am Pej (young Black)* (jeune) Noir m; *(American Indian)* (jeune) Indien m (d'Amérique)
4 *Am Fam (dollar)* dollar m; **to make a fast** or **quick b.** faire du fric
5 *(sawhorse)* chèvre f *(de sciage); Gym* cheval-d'arçons m, *pl* chevaux-d'arçons *ou* cheval-d'arçons
6 *(jump) (of horse)* saut m de mouton
VI **1** *(of horse)* faire le saut de mouton; *(of aircraft)* se cabrer **2** *Am (of person)* résister, regimber; **to b. against** or **at sth** résister à qch
VT **1** *(of horse)* **to b. sb (off)** désarçonner qn **2** *Fig* **he bucked the odds by being chosen yet again** contre toute attente, il a encore été choisi; **you can't b. the odds** tu ne peux pas forcer le destin; **you can't b. the system** on ne peut rien faire contre l'ordre établi; **to b. a trend** aller à l'encontre d'une tendance; **to b. the question** ne pas répondre à la question
▸▸ **b.'s fizz** = cocktail m fait à partir de champagne et de jus d'orange; **b. rabbit** lapin m (mâle)
▸ **buck for** VT INSEP *Am Fam (strive to achieve)* chercher à obtenir
▸ **buck up** *Old-fashioned Fam* VT SEP *(of person)* remonter le moral à; **this whisky will b. you up** ce whisky vous remontera; **getting that job has really bucked her up** ça lui a remonté le moral d'obtenir cet emploi; **to b. one's ideas up** se ressaisir, se prendre en mains
VI *(become more cheerful)* reprendre courage; *(hurry)* se grouiller, se remuer; **b. up!** *(be cheerful)* courage!; *(hurry)* remue-toi!, grouille-toi!

buck[2] N *Fig* **to pass the b.** *(shift blame)* rejeter la responsabilité sur quelqu'un d'autre; *(make sb else decide)* laisser la décision à quelqu'un d'autre; *Fam* **the b. stops here** *(with me)* en fin de compte, c'est moi qui en suis responsable *ou* c'est moi le responsable; *(with you)* en fin de compte, c'est toi qui en es responsable *ou* c'est toi le responsable

buckaroo ['bʌkəruː] N *Am* cow-boy m, *pl* cow-boys

bucked [bʌkt] ADJ *Old-fashioned Fam* enchanté; **I was really b. to hear the news** ça m'a fait vraiment plaisir d'apprendre la nouvelle

bucket ['bʌkɪt] N **1** seau m; **a b. of water** un seau d'eau; *Br Fam* **it's coming down in** or **raining buckets** il pleut à verse *ou* à seaux; *Fam* **to cry** or **weep buckets** pleurer à chaudes larmes; *Sl* **to kick the b.** *(die)* casser sa pipe **2** *Min, Ind* baluchon m, baquet m; *(of crane)* benne f; *(of water wheel)* auget m, auge f; *(of dredger)* godet m, louchet m
VI *Br Fam* **1** *(move jerkily)* cahoter; **the car**

bucketed down the street la voiture avançait en cahotant dans la rue **2** *(rain heavily)* pleuvoir à verse *ou* à seaux
▸▸ **b. chain** = chaîne f de personnes qui se passent des seaux d'eau pour éteindre un incendie; *Tech* **b. dredger** drague f à godets; *Tech* **b. elevator** élévateur m à godets, noria f; *Aut, Aviat* **b. seat** baquet m, siège-baquet m, *pl* sièges-baquets, siège m cuve; **b. shop** *Fin* bureau m *ou* maison f de contrepartie, bureau de courtier marron; *Br Com (travel agency)* = organisme m de vente de billets d'avion à prix réduit; *Tech* **b. wheel** roue f à augets
▸ **bucket along** VI *Br Fam (of car etc)* aller à une vitesse folle
▸ **bucket down** VI *Br Fam* pleuvoir à verse *ou* à seaux

bucketful ['bʌkɪtfʊl] N *(pl* bucketsful *or* bucketfuls*)* plein seau m

bucking ['bʌkɪŋ] N *(of horse)* sauts mpl de mouton

buckle ['bʌk(ə)l] N **1** *(fastener) (for strap, belt etc)* boucle f **2** *(deformation) (of wheel etc)* gauchissement m, voile m
VT **1** *(fasten) (suitcase, belt etc)* boucler; *(safety belt)* attacher; **to b. sth to sth** attacher qch à qch (à l'aide d'une boucle) **2** *(deform) (metal)* gauchir; *(wheel)* voiler; *(accumulator plate)* tordre
VI *(of wheel)* se voiler; *(of metal)* gauchir; *Fig (under attack)* céder; *(under criticism)* se décomposer; **the bridge buckled under the weight of traffic** le pont s'est déformé sous le poids des véhicules; **his knees buckled** ses jambes cédèrent sous lui; *Fig* **I'm buckling at the knees** *(exhausted)* je suis sur les rotules
▸ **buckle down** VI *(set to work)* s'y mettre; **to b. down to a task** se mettre *ou* s'atteler à un travail; **isn't it time you buckled down to your homework?** il serait peut-être temps de faire tes devoirs, non?; **he buckled down and finished cleaning the car** il s'est armé de courage et a fini de nettoyer la voiture
▸ **buckle on** VT SEP *(belt, sword)* attacher; *(armour)* revêtir, mettre
▸ **buckle to** VI = **buckle down**
▸ **buckle up** VI **1** *Aut* attacher sa ceinture de sécurité **2** = **buckle** VI
VT SEP = **buckle** VT **1**

buckled ['bʌk(ə)ld] ADJ **1** *(fastened) (belt)* bouclé **2** *(deformed) (metal)* déformé, gauchi; *(wheel)* voilé; *(accumulator plate)* tordu

buckling ['bʌk(ə)lɪŋ] N *(of metal etc)* déformation f, gauchissement m; *(of wheel, sheet iron)* voilure f

buckram ['bʌkrəm] N *Tex* bougran m

Bucks [bʌks] *abbr* Buckinghamshire

bucksaw ['bʌksɔː] N *(tool)* scie f à bûches

buckshee [bʌk'ʃiː] ADJ, ADV *Br Fam* gratis inv; **we got in b.** on est entré gratis *ou* sans payer

buckshot ['bʌkʃɒt] N *(ammunition)* chevrotine f

buckskin ['bʌkskɪn] N peau f de daim; **b. breeches, buckskins** culotte f de peau (de daim)

bucktoothed ['bʌktuːθt] ADJ *(person)* aux dents de lapin; **he gave a b. grin** il a souri en montrant ses dents de lapin

buckwheat ['bʌkwiːt] N *Agr* sarrasin m

bucolic [bjuː'kɒlɪk] ADJ *(life, poetry, poet)* bucolique
NPL *Liter* **bucolics** *(poems)* bucoliques fpl

bud[1] [bʌd] N *(on shrub, tree)* bourgeon m; *(of flower)* bouton m; **to be in b.** *(of tree)* bourgeonner
VI *(-dd-)* *(of shrub, tree)* bourgeonner; *(of flower)* être en bouton(s)

bud[2] INT *Am Fam* hey, b.! *(to stranger)* hep,

vous là-bas!; *(to friend)* salut, mon pote *ou* mon vieux!

Budapest [bjuːdə'pest] N Budapest

Buddha ['bʊdə] N Bouddha m

Buddhism ['bʊdɪz(ə)m] N bouddhisme m

Buddhist ['bʊdɪst] N bouddhiste mf
ADJ *(priest, doctrine)* bouddhiste; *(art, temple)* bouddhique

budding ['bʌdɪŋ] ADJ *(shrub, tree)* bourgeonnant; *(flower)* en bouton; *Fig (artist, lawyer, genius etc)* en herbe; *(passion, talent)* naissant
N *(of plant, tree)* bourgeonnement m

buddleia ['bʌdlɪə] N buddleia m

buddy ['bʌdɪ] N *Fam* copain m, copine f, pote m; **hey b., what are you doing in my car?** eh mec, qu'est-ce que tu fais dans ma bagnole?
▸▸ *Am* **b. movie** film m qui raconte les histoires de deux copains
▸ **buddy up** VI *Am Fam* former des groupes de deux; **do you want to buddy up (with me)?** tu veux te mettre avec moi?; *Pej* **to b. up to sb** faire de la lèche à qn

buddy-buddy ADJ *esp Am (close, friendly)* copain, f copine (**with** avec); **those two are very b.** ils sont très copain-copain

budge [bʌdʒ] VI **1** *(move)* bouger; **if you (so much as) b.** si vous faites le moindre mouvement; **the door won't b.** la porte est bloquée **2** *(give way)* céder, reculer; **to refuse to b.** refuser de céder
VT **1** *(change mind of)* **I couldn't b. him** il est resté inébranlable **2** *(move)* bouger; *Fig* **I won't b. an inch** je ne reculerai pas d'un centimètre
▸ **budge up, budge along** VI se pousser

budgerigar ['bʌdʒərɪgɑːr] N perruche f

budget ['bʌdʒɪt] N *Fin etc* budget m; *(allocated ceiling)* enveloppe f budgétaire; **we are within b.** *(at the moment)* nous n'avons pas dépassé le budget; **the museum was finished within b.** le musée a été fini sans dépasser le budget; **it was finished well below** or **within b.** c'est revenu bien moins cher que prévu; **the project is already well over b.** on a déjà largement dépassé le budget qui était alloué pour le projet; *Fam* **I'm on a b. this month** je fais des économies ce mois-ci; **family/household b.** budget familial/du ménage; *Can* **to bring down the b.** présenter le budget; *Parl* **to pass the b.** voter le budget
ADJ **1** *(inexpensive)* économique, bon marché; **b. brand/fare** marque f/tarif m économique; **b. holiday** des vacances fpl économiques *ou* pas chères; **b. meals** repas mpl bon marché; **b. prices** prix mpl raisonnables *ou* avantageux **2** *Fin (relating to budgets)* budgétaire
VI prévoir ses dépenses
VT *(time, money)* gérer
▸▸ **b. account** *(with store)* compte-crédit m, *pl* comptes-crédits; *(with bank)* ≃ compte m permanent; **b. constraint** contrainte f budgétaire; **b. cuts** coupes fpl budgétaires; *Br* **B. Day** = jour m de la présentation du budget par le Chancelier de l'Échiquier; **b. deficit** déficit m budgétaire; **b. estimates** prévisions fpl budgétaires; **b. forecast** prévisions budgétaires; **b. planning** planification f budgétaire; **b. rate** tarif budgétaire; *Br, Can* **b. speech** = discours m à l'occasion de la présentation du budget au Parlement; **b. surplus** excédent m budgétaire
▸ **budget for** VT INSEP *(allow for in accounts)* porter *ou* inscrire au budget; *(expense)* prévoir, *Spec* budgétiser; **we didn't b. for all these car repair bills** nous n'avions pas prévu toutes ces dépenses pour la réparation de la voiture; **I'm budgeting for my holidays**

je surveille mes dépenses pour pouvoir partir en vacances

budgetary ['bʌdʒɪtərɪ] **ADJ** *Fin etc* budgétaire

budgeting ['bʌdʒɪtɪŋ] **N** *Fin etc* budgétisation *f*

budgie ['bʌdʒɪ] **N** *Fam (bird)* perruche *f*

Buenos Aires ['bwenɒs'aɪrɪz] **N** Buenos Aires

buff [bʌf] **N 1** *(shine)* **to give sth a b.** faire briller qch **2** *(colour)* couleur *f* chamois **3** *Fam* **in the b.** tout nu **4** *(fan)* enthousiaste *mf*; **a film b.** c'est un cinéphile; **she's a history b.** elle est passionnée d'histoire; **computer b.** mordu, -ue *ou* passionné, -ée d'informatique

▸ **ADJ** *(coloured)* de couleur chamois; *(envelope)* kraft

▸ **VT** *(car, shoes)* lustrer; *Metal (metal etc)* polir; **to b. one's nails** se polir les ongles

▸▸ **b. stick** polissoir *m*

▸ **buff up VT SEP** *(car, shoes)* lustrer, faire briller

buffalo, *pl* **buffaloes** *or inv* ['bʌfələʊ, -əʊz] **N 1** buffle *m*; **water b.** karbau *m*; **young b.** bufflon *m* **2** *Am (bison)* bison *m*

buffer¹ ['bʌfər] **N** *Rail (at end of train)* tampon *m*; *(at end of line)* butoir *m*, heurtoir *m*; *Elec, Electron (circuit m)* tampon; *Comput* tampon, mémoire *f* intermédiaire; *Fig* **to run into the buffers** tomber à l'eau; *Fam* **to act as a b.** *(between people)* faire tampon; *Mil* **recoil b.** frein *m*, amortisseur *m* de recul ▸▸ *Comput* **b. memory** mémoire *f* tampon; *Radio* **b. stage** étage *m* tampon *ou* intermédiaire; *Pol* **b. state** état *m* tampon; *Com* **b. stock** stock *m* tampon; *Pol* **b. zone** région *f* tampon

buffer² **N** *Br Fam* **old b.** vieux *m*; *(fool)* vieille ganache *f*, vieux bonze *m*

buffer³ **N** *(for polishing)* polissoir *m*

buffering ['bʌfərɪŋ] **N** *Comput (storage)* stockage *m* en mémoire tampon; *(use)* utilisation *f* de mémoire tampon

buffet¹ ['bʌfɪt] **N** *(with fist)* coup *m*; *(slap)* gifle *f*

▸ **VT** *(person)* bourrer de coups de poing; **buffeted by the waves/the wind** *(ship)* battu *ou* ballotté par les vagues/secoué par le vent; *Fig* **to be buffeted by events** être ballotté par les événements

buffet² **N 1** ['bʌfɪt] *(piece of furniture)* buffet *m* **2** ['bʊfeɪ] *(meal, counter)* buffet *m*; **cold b.** *(on menu)* viandes *fpl* froides, assiette *f* anglaise; *(meal)* buffet froid; **b. lunch/supper** buffet

▸▸ *Rail* **b. car** wagon-restaurant *m*, *pl* wagons-restaurants; *Rail* **b. service** service *m* de restauration

buffeting ['bʌfɪtɪŋ] **N** succession *f* de coups *ou* de chocs; *(by waves)* ballottement *m*; *(by wind)* secousses *fpl*; **the ship took a b. in the storm** le navire a été violemment ballotté par la tempête; *Fig* **she's taken quite a b. in the past couple of months** elle a beaucoup enduré au cours de ces derniers mois

buffing ['bʌfɪŋ] **N** *Metal etc* polissage *m* ▸▸ **b. wheel** meule *f* à polir

buffoon [bə'fu:n] **N** bouffon *m*; **to act** *or* **play the b.** faire le pitre

buffoonery [bə'fu:nərɪ] **N** bouffonneries *fpl*

bug [bʌg] **N 1** *(insect)* **(bed) b.** punaise *f* (des lits)

2 *esp Am (any insect)* insecte *m*

3 *Med Fam* virus *m*, microbe *m*; **to catch a b.** attraper un microbe; **there's a b. going round** il y a un virus qui traîne; **she's got a stomach b. of some kind** elle a des ennuis gastriques; *Fig* **to have** *or* **have been bitten by the skiing b.** avoir la passion *ou* la folie du

ski; *Fig* **the travel b.** la passion des voyages

4 *Comput* bogue *f*

5 *(concealed listening device)* micro *m* caché; **to plant a b.** cacher un micro

▸ **VT 1** *(room)* cacher des micros dans; *(telephone) (with hidden microphone)* cacher un micro dans; *(tap)* brancher sur table d'écoute; *(conversation)* enregistrer *(de façon clandestine)* **2** *Fam (annoy) (of thing, person)* taper sur les nerfs à, embêter, *Vulg* emmerder; **stop bugging me about it** arrête de m'embêter *ou Vulg* m'emmerder avec ça; **it really bugs me to think of her having all that money** ça m'énerve vraiment de savoir qu'elle a tout cet argent; **he's been bugging me to buy it** il n'arrête pas de m'embêter pour que je l'achète

▸ **bug off, bug out VI** *Am Fam (leave hurriedly)* ficher le camp

bugaboo ['bʌgəbu:] **N** *esp Am Fig* = **bugbear**

bugbear ['bʌgbeər] **N** *Fam (goblin)* croquemitaine *m*; *Fig (cause of fear)* épouvantail *m*; **maths is my b.** les maths, c'est mon cauchemar; **inflation is the government's chief b.** l'inflation est le grand cauchemar du gouvernement

bug-eyed **ADJ** *Fam* aux yeux exorbités; **to go b. at sth** ouvrir de grands yeux ébahis devant qch

bug-free **ADJ 1** *Comput (program)* exempt d'erreurs *ou* de bogues **2** *(room) (without listening devices)* sans micros clandestins; *(having no insects)* d'où les insectes ont été chassés

bugger ['bʌgər] **N 1** *Sl (unpleasant person)* salaud *m*; *(foolish person)* couillon *m*, **silly b.!** espèce d'idiot!; **poor b.** pauvre type; **a b. of a job** un travail pénible; **this recipe's a real b. to make** cette recette est vachement compliquée; **her house is a b. to find** sa maison est vachement dure à trouver; **b. all money/thanks** pas un sou/un merci; **she knows b. all about it** elle n'y connaît foutrement rien; **he doesn't care** *or* **give a b.** il s'en fout complètement **2** *Law (pederast)* pédéraste *m*

▸ **VT 1** *Sl* **b. (it)!** merde!; **I'll be buggered if I'm going to pay for it!** pas question que je paye!; **that's really buggered it!** *(spoilt things)* ça a tout gâché; **ça l'a complètement bousillé 2** *Law* sodomiser

▸ **bugger about, bugger around** *Sl* **VI** déconner; **to b. about** *or* **around with one's car** s'amuser avec sa voiture; **stop buggering about with my computer** arrête de tripoter mon ordinateur

▸ **VT SEP** *(person)* emmerder, faire chier

▸ **bugger off VI** *Sl* se casser, foutre le camp; **b. off!** *(go away)* fous le camp!; *(leave me alone)* fous-moi la paix!

▸ **bugger up VT SEP** *Sl (spoil) (plan, holiday etc)* foutre en l'air; *(machine, TV etc)* bousiller; **having to work overtime buggered up my weekend** ça m'a foutu mon week-end en l'air de devoir faire des heures supplémentaires; **you've buggered the whole thing up** tu as tout foutu en l'air

buggeration [bʌgə'reɪʃən] **INT** *Br Sl* bordel!, putain!

buggered ['bʌgəd] **ADJ PRED** *Sl* **to be b.** *(exhausted)* être crevé; *(broken, in trouble)* être foutu; **if we don't get the money soon, we're b.** si on a pas l'argent rapidement, on est foutus

buggery ['bʌgərɪ] **N 1** *Law* sodomie *f* **2** *Sl* **to run like b.** courir ventre à terre; **my plans have been shot to b.** ça a foutu mes projets en l'air

bugging ['bʌgɪŋ] **N** *(of room)* installation *f* de micros *(pour espionner)*; *(of telephone)* mise *f* sur table d'écoute

▸▸ **b. device** appareil *m* d'écoute (clandestin)

buggy¹ ['bʌgɪ] **N 1** *(carriage)* boghei *m*, buggy *m*; **(beach) b.** buggy; **(moon) b.** jeep *f* lunaire **2** *Am (for baby)* landau *m*; *Br (pushchair)* poussette *f*

buggy² **ADJ** *Comput* plein de bogues

bughouse ['bʌghaʊs] *Am Sl* **N** *(for the insane)* maison *f* de fous

▸ **ADJ** *(insane)* fou, *f* folle

bugle¹ ['bju:g(ə)l] **N** *Mil* clairon *m*

▸▸ **b. call** sonnerie *f* de clairon

bugle² **N** *(plant)* bugle *f*

bugler ['bju:glər] **N** *(sonneur m de)* clairon *m*

bugless ['bʌglɪs] **ADJ** *Comput* sans bogues

bug-ridden **ADJ** *Comput* plein de bogues

build [bɪld] **VT** *(pt, pp* built [bɪlt]*) (house etc)* construire, bâtir; *(ship, bridge, road etc)* construire; *(temple)* édifier; *(nest)* faire; **the walls were built of granite** les murs étaient *(construits ou bâtis)* en granit; **the house is being built** la maison est en construction; **to b. one's hopes on sth** fonder *ou* baser ses espoirs sur qch; *Mktg* **to b. a brand** créer une marque

▸ **VI 1** *Constr* construire, bâtir; **to b. on a piece of land** bâtir un terrain; *Fig* **to b. on sand** bâtir sur le sable; **to b. on one's success** mettre à profit sa réussite; **to b. on an opportunity** profiter d'une occasion **2** *(increase) (of pressure)*, *Fig (of excitement, tension)* augmenter

▸ **N** *(of person)* carrure *f*, **a man of powerful b.** un homme à forte carrure; **of slight b.** fluet

▸ **build in VT SEP** *(incorporate)* intégrer, incorporer; *Constr (wardrobe, beam etc)* encastrer; **to b. in safety features** intégrer des dispositifs de sécurité

▸ **build into VT SEP** **to b. sth into a product** incorporer qch dans un produit

▸ **build on VT SEP** *(add to existing structure) (porch etc)* ajouter; **we've built on a garage** nous avons ajouté un garage; **the stables are built on to the house** les écuries sont attenantes à la maison

▸ **build up VT SEP 1** *(increase) (demand)* développer; *Mil etc (reserves)* constituer; *(forces, reinforcements etc)* mettre sur pied; *(one's strength)* reprendre; **don't b. your hopes up** ne te fais pas trop d'illusions

2 *(create) (theory, system)* bâtir, échafauder, construire; *(business)* développer; *(reputation)* se faire; *(collection, library)* constituer; **to b. up custom** *or* **a clientele** *(of company)* se faire *ou* se constituer une clientèle; **his father built the company up from nothing** son père a créé la société à partir de rien; *Med etc* **to b. up an immunity** développer une immunité

3 *(strengthen)* **the children need vitamins to b. them up** les enfants ont besoin de vitamines pour se fortifier

4 *(usu passive)* **this area has been very much built up** on a beaucoup construit par ici

5 *(publicize) (film, book, actor etc)* dire du bien de; **the film wasn't as good as it had been built up to be** le film n'était pas aussi bon qu'on le prétendait

6 *(wall) (make higher)* rehausser; *(rebuild)* réparer

▸ **VI** *(of pressure)* s'accumuler, augmenter; *(of tension)* augmenter, monter; *(of traffic)* devenir dense; *(of snow, clouds)* s'amonceler; *(of hurricane, storm)* se préparer

builder ['bɪldər] **N** *Constr* entrepreneur, -euse en bâtiment; *(of ships etc)* constructeur, -trice; *Fig (of empire etc)* créateur, -trice, fondateur, -trice

building ['bɪldɪŋ] **N 1** *(house, factory etc)* bâtiment *m*, immeuble *m*; *(large)* édifice *m*; **public b.** édifice public **2** *(action)* construction f, Fig the b. of better relations l'établissement m de meilleures relations

▸▸ b. block (toy) cube m; Fig composante f; Constr b. contractor entrepreneur, -euse (en bâtiment ou construction); b. materials matériaux mpl de construction; b. plot terrain m à bâtir; b. site chantier m (de construction); b. slip (for ship) cale f de construction; Br Fin b. society ≃ société f de crédit immobilier; the b. trade le bâtiment; b. worker ouvrier, -ière du bâtiment

Building Societies

Les "building societies" fonctionnent comme des banques mais elles n'ont pas de système de compensation. Établissements consentant des prêts immobiliers aux particuliers, elles jouent un rôle important dans la vie en Grande-Bretagne. Au cours des dernières années, de nombreuses "building societies" ont abandonné leur statut de sociétés mutuelles pour devenir des banques cotées en Bourse.

build-up N 1 (of pressure) accumulation f, augmentation f; (of tension) augmentation; the b. of traffic on the motorway la formation de bouchons sur l'autoroute; traffic b. bouchon m
2 (of system etc) élaboration f, développement m
3 Mil (of forces, reinforcements etc) mise f sur pied; (of reserves of troops, supplies etc) constitution f; there has been a b. of troops along the border on a envoyé du renfort aux troupes le long de la frontière
4 (publicity) battage m (publicitaire); her latest book is getting a lot of b. on fait beaucoup de battage autour de son dernier livre; despite the big b., the film didn't do well en dépit du battage dont il a fait l'objet, le film n'a pas bien marché
5 (preparatory period) the b. to the match la période d'avant le match; in the b. to the election, there will be ... pendant la période qui précédera les élections, il y aura ...

built [bɪlt] ADJ bâti; British b. de construction britannique; a powerfully b. man un homme à forte carrure ou charpente
▸▸ b. attraction (in tourism) centre m d'intérêt 'non-naturel'

built-in ADJ (wardrobe, bath, beam) encastré; (device, safeguard) intégré; Fig (feature) inné, ancré; Comput incorporé; Fig a b. resistance to ... une opposition viscérale à ...
▸▸ b. obsolescence obsolescence f programmée

built-to-order ADJ Comput construit sur mesure

built-up ADJ (beam) composé, rapporté; (shoulders of garment) rehaussé
▸▸ b. area agglomération f (urbaine); b. shoes chaussures fpl à semelles compensées

bulb [bʌlb] N 1 (tulip etc) bulbe m, oignon m 2 Elec ampoule f 3 Phys (of thermometer) réservoir m; Chem (flask) ballon m; Culin (of baster) poire f 4 Anat bulbe m

bulbous ['bʌlbəs] ADJ bulbeux; b. nose gros nez m

Bulgaria [bʌl'geərɪə] N Bulgarie f

Bulgarian [bʌl'geərɪən] ADJ bulgare
N 1 Bulgare mf 2 Ling bulgare m

bulge [bʌldʒ] N (in wall, ceiling) bombement m, renflement m; (on face, body, caused by a growth etc) protubérance f; (in tyre) hernie f; Mil (of front) saillant m; Econ Fam (increase) poussée f; this dress shows all my bulges cette robe révèle toutes mes rondeurs; the gun made a b. in his pocket le revolver faisait une protubérance dans sa poche

VI to b. (out) bomber, ballonner; (stick out) faire saillie; (of wall, ceiling etc) faire ventre; his eyes were bulging il avait les yeux exorbités; a sack bulging with potatoes un sac bourré de pommes de terre; I knew from the way his pocket bulged j'ai su à la protubérance que formait sa poche

bulging ['bʌldʒɪŋ] ADJ (forehead, wall, ceiling) bombé; (stomach) ballonné; (eyes) protubérant; (cheeks) bouffi; (bag, wallet etc) bourré, plein à craquer
N (of wall etc) bombement m, renflement m; (of stomach) ballonnement m

bulimia [bjuː'lɪmɪə, bʊ'l-] N Med boulimie f

bulk [bʌlk] N 1 (size) masse f, volume m; (of parcel) encombrement m 2 the b. (greater part) (of people) la masse, la plupart; (of army) le gros; (of one's property, work, money etc) la plus grosse partie 3 Comput (of information) volume m, masse f 4 Com etc to buy in b. acheter en gros ou par grosses quantités; to sell in b. vendre en gros
VI Fig to b. large occuper une place importante (in sb's eyes aux yeux de qn)
VT Com (packages) grouper; to b. sth out étoffer qch
▸▸ Com b. buying achat m par grosses quantités, achat en gros; b. cargo cargaison f en vrac; Naut b. carrier vraquier m, transporteur m de vrac; Com b. discount remise f quantitative; Com b. order grosse commande f; Com b. rate affranchissement m à forfait

bulkhead ['bʌlkhed] N (on ship etc) cloison f

bulkiness ['bʌlkɪnɪs] N 1 volume m excessif; (of parcel) encombrement m 2 (of sweater) épaisseur f

bulky ['bʌlkɪ] ADJ 1 (parcel etc) volumineux, encombrant; (book) épais 2 (sweater) gros, épais

bull¹ [bʊl] N 1 taureau m; Astron the B. le Taureau; Fig to take the b. by the horns prendre le taureau par les cornes; like a b. in a china shop comme un éléphant dans un magasin de porcelaine; to go at sth like a b. at a gate foncer tête baissée ou la tête la première dans qch
2 (male) (elephant, whale etc) mâle m
3 Br Mil Sl (polishing) fourbissage m
4 Sl (nonsense) conneries fpl; he talks a lot of b. il raconte beaucoup de conneries
5 St Exch spéculateur, -trice à la hausse, haussier, -ière
6 (of target) mouche f, mille m; he got six bulls il a fait mouche six fois, il a mis six fois dans le mille
7 (dog) bouledogue m; b. bitch/pup chienne f/chiot m de bouledogue
INT Sl foutaise!, quelle(s) connerie(s)!
VT St Exch to b. the market chercher à faire monter les cours
VI St Exch (of person) spéculer à la hausse; (of stocks) être en hausse
▸▸ Aut b. bars pare-buffles m inv; b. calf jeune taureau m, taurillon m; St Exch b. market marché m à la hausse ou haussier; b. mastiff = chien m issu d'un métissage entre le bouledogue et le mastiff; St Exch b. spread spread m haussier; b. terrier bull-terrier m, pl bull-terriers; St Exch b. trading spéculation f à la hausse; St Exch b. transaction opération f à la hausse

bull² N Rel bulle f, papal b. bulle papale

bulldog ['bʊldɒg] N bouledogue m; Fig (tenacious person) personne f très tenace; Br Univ (official) appariteur m du censeur (aux universités d'Oxford et de Cambridge)
▸▸ Br St Exch b. bond obligation f bulldog (obligation d'un emprunteur étranger à la Bourse de Londres, libellée en sterling); b. clip pince f à dessin

bulldoze ['bʊldəʊz] VT (land) dégager ou

déblayer au bulldozer; (house etc) démolir au bulldozer; Fig to b. sb into doing sth forcer qn à faire qch; I was bulldozed into it on m'a forcé à le faire; to b. sth through a committee forcer une commission à adopter qch

bulldozer ['bʊldəʊzər] N Constr bulldozer m

bulldyke ['bʊldaɪk] N Sl lesbienne f à l'allure masculine

bullet ['bʊlɪt] N 1 (from rifle, revolver) balle f, Fam to stop a b. recevoir une balle 2 Typ puce f
▸▸ Am Fin b. bond obligation f remboursable en une seule fois; b. hole impact m de balle; Typ b. point puce f; Rail b. train train m à grande vitesse (au Japon); b. wound blessure f par balle

bulleted list ['bʊlɪtɪd] N Typ liste f à puces

bullet-headed ADJ 1 à tête ronde 2 Am Fig (obstinate) entêté, têtu

bulletin ['bʊlɪtɪn] N bulletin m, communiqué m
▸▸ b. board Am tableau m d'affichage; Comput serveur m télématique, Can babillard m; Comput b. board service serveur télématique, Can babillard

bulletproof ['bʊlɪtpruːf] ADJ (glass, car) à l'épreuve des balles
▸▸ b. vest gilet m pare-balles

bullfight ['bʊlfaɪt] N course f de taureaux, corrida f

bullfighter ['bʊlfaɪtər] N torero m

bullfighting ['bʊlfaɪtɪŋ] N courses fpl de taureaux; (as art) tauromachie f

bullfinch ['bʊlfɪntʃ] N (bird) bouvreuil m

bullfrog ['bʊlfrɒg] N grenouille f taureau

bull-headed ADJ Fam 1 (impetuous) d'une impétuosité de taureau; to go at sth b. foncer la tête la première dans qch 2 (obstinate) entêté, têtu

bullhorn ['bʊlhɔːn] N Am porte-voix m inv

bullion ['bʊljən] N INV (gold) or m en barres ou en lingot(s); (silver) argent m en lingot(s); Fin métal m
▸▸ b. van fourgon m bancaire

bullish ['bʊlɪʃ] ADJ 1 St Exch (market, trend) à la hausse, haussier; to be b. spéculer à la hausse 2 Fig (optimistic) optimiste (about sth au sujet de qch, à propos de qch)

bull-necked [-nekt] ADJ au cou de taureau

bullock ['bʊlək] N bœuf m; young b. bouvillon m
▸▸ b. cart char m à bœufs

bullpen ['bʊlpen] N Am (in police station) = grande cellule f commune

bullring ['bʊlrɪŋ] N arène f

bull's-eye N 1 (of target) mouche f, mille m; to hit the or get a b. (in archery) faire mouche, mettre dans le mille; (at darts) mettre dans le mille; Fig to hit the b. (of remark) faire mouche 2 (in glass) boudine f 3 (sweet) gros bonbon m à la menthe
▸▸ b. panes carreaux mpl à boudines ou en culs-de-bouteille

bullshit ['bʊlʃɪt] Vulg N conneries fpl; don't give me that b.! ne raconte ou dis pas de conneries!; he's a real b. artist (talks a lot of nonsense) il ne dit que des conneries; (can impress people) c'est un vrai baratineur
INT foutaise!
VI dire des conneries
VT to b. one's way into a job obtenir un emploi grâce à son culot; to b. one's way through an exam réussir à un examen à force de baratin; to b. sb into doing sth baratiner qn pour qu'il fasse qch; he bullshitted her into believing he would marry her avec son baratin, il lui a fait croire qu'il l'épouserait

bullshitter ['bʊlʃɪtər] N Vulg (smooth-talker) baratineur, -euse; **he's a b.** (talks nonsense) il dit des conneries

bully[1] ['bʊlɪ] N tyran m; Sch petit tyran (qui fait subir des brimades à ses camarades); **don't be such a b.** ne sois pas si tyrannique **VT** (wife, employee) brimer; (classmates, little sister etc) brimer, persécuter; **to b. sb into doing sth** faire faire qch à qn à force de menaces ou d'intimidations; **to b. sb into submission** faire céder qn à force de menaces ▸▸ Old-fashioned Br Fam **b. beef** singe m (corned-beef)

bully[2] INT Old-fashioned Fam **b. for you!** (what luck) vous avez de la chance!; (well done) bravo!

▸ **bully off** VI (in hockey) engager (le jeu)

bullyboy ['bʊlɪbɔɪ] N voyou m, dur m; **b. tactics** manœuvres fpl d'intimidation

bullying ['bʊlɪɪŋ] ADJ brutal, -aux N brimades fpl

bully-off N (in hockey) engagement m (du jeu)

bulrush ['bʊlrʌʃ] N (plant) jonc m des marais

bulwark ['bʊlwɜːk] N **1** (fortification), Fig rempart m **2** Naut **bulwarks** bastingage m

bum[1] [bʌm] N Br Fam (bottom) derrière m ▸▸ Br **b. bag** banane f; **b. fluff** (beard) barbe f très peu fournie

bum[2] esp Am Sl ADJ moche, minable; **b. advice** des conseils mpl inutiles; **b. check** chèque m en bois
N **1** (worthless person) fainéant, -ante; (tramp) clochard, -arde, trimardeur m; **to give sb the b.'s rush** (from relationship, meeting) virer qn avec perte et fracas; **to give a suggestion/an idea the b.'s rush** ne tenir aucun compte d'une suggestion/idée **2 to be on the b.** (live off other people) vivre aux crochets des autres; (travel round country) vagabonder
VI (-mm-) Am Sl (beg) vivre aux crochets des autres, vivre en parasite
VT **to b. a cigarette from** or **off sb** taper une cigarette à qn; **to b. a ride** (from stranger) faire de l'auto-stop; **I managed to b. a ride from a lorry driver** je me suis fait prendre en auto-stop par un routier; **do you mind if I b. a ride to the station?** ça t'ennuierait de me déposer à la gare?
▸▸ **b. rap** (false charge) accusation f inventée de toutes pièces; (unfair punishment) punition f injuste; **b. steer** tuyau m percé

▸ **bum around** Sl VI glander, glandouiller; (travel) vadrouiller; **they spent three months bumming around in Mexico** ils ont passé trois mois à se balader au Mexique
VT INSEP **to b. around Europe/Paris** vadrouiller en Europe/à Paris

▸ **bum around with** VT INSEP Sl traîner avec

bumble ['bʌmb(ə)l] VI (be inefficient) s'agiter et ne rien faire d'efficace

bumblebee ['bʌmb(ə)lbiː] N bourdon m

bumbler ['bʌmb(ə)lər] N Fam **an old b.** un vieux maladroit

bumbling ['bʌmb(ə)lɪŋ] ADJ **b. fool** or **idiot** andouille f

bumboat ['bʌmbəʊt] N Naut canot m d'approvisionnement

bumf [bʌmf] N **1** Fam (useless paper) paperasse f **2** Sl (lavatory paper) papier m cul

bumfreezer ['bʌmfriːzər] N Br Sl = veste f qui arrive au ras des fesses

bumhole ['bʌmhəʊl] N Sl trou m de balle

bummed [bʌmd] ADJ Am Sl **to be b.** l'avoir mauvaise

bummer ['bʌmər] N Sl (something worthless) fiasco m; **the film's a b.** ce film est nul; **I didn't get the job – what a b.!** je n'ai pas eu

le boulot – c'est con!; **it's a real b. when you find out ...** ça en fiche un coup quand on découvre que ...

bump [bʌmp] N **1** (collision) choc m, heurt m; (jolt) secousse f, cahot m; (by boat in bumping race) heurt; **the boat hit the jetty with a b.** le bateau a cogné contre la jetée; **to sit down with a b.** s'asseoir brusquement
2 (lump) (in path, road surface etc) bosse f, (on head) (as result of being hit) bosse; (in phrenology) protubérance f, Fam bosse; Hum **he patted her b.** (unborn baby) elle a tapoté son ventre; **she's had a b. on the head** elle s'est cogné la tête; Aut **to hit a b.** passer sur une bosse
3 Fam **bumps and grinds** (of stripper) déhanchements mpl
4 Aviat (air current) trou m d'air
VT 1 (hit) cogner, frapper; (boat in front in bumping race) heurter; **to b. one's head on** or **against sth** se cogner la tête contre qch
2 Aviat Fam **to be bumped (from a flight)** perdre sa place sur un vol (pour cause de surréservation)
VI Fam **to b. and grind** (of stripper) se déhancher
ADV, INT pan!, boum!; Fam **things that go b. in the night** des bruits étranges dans la nuit
▸▸ Aut **b. steer** réversibilité f de direction

▸ **bump along** VI (in cart etc) cahoter

▸ **bump into** VT INSEP **1** (collide with) (of person) se cogner ou se heurter ou buter contre; (of vehicle) heurter **2** (meet) rencontrer par hasard

▸ **bump off** VT SEP Fam (kill) supprimer, Fam faire la peau à

▸ **bump up** VT SEP Fam (prices) gonfler (d'une façon exagérée)

bumper ['bʌmpər] N **1** Aut pare-chocs m inv; bouclier m, pare-chocs bouclier; front/rear **b.** pare-chocs avant/arrière; **the cars were b. to b.** les voitures étaient pare-chocs contre pare-chocs **2** (large measure of alcoholic drink) rasade f
ADJ **b. crop** or **harvest** récolte f magnifique ou exceptionnelle; **it's been a b. year for tourism** ça a été une année exceptionnelle pour le tourisme
▸▸ Aut **b. apron** tablier m de pare-chocs; Aut **b. guard** butoir m de pare-chocs; Aut **b. skirt** jupe f de pare-chocs

bumpety-bump ['bʌmpɪtɪ'-] ADV Fam en cahotant; **my heart went b.** mon cœur a battu à tout rompre

bumph [bʌmf] N = **bumf**

bumping ['bʌmpɪŋ] N **1** (collision) heurt(s) m(pl), choc(s) m(pl); (jolting) cahotement m **2** (of air passenger) bumping m, refus m d'embarquer suite à surréservation
▸▸ **b. race** course-poursuite f, pl courses-poursuites (dans laquelle chaque bateau doit rattraper le précédent et de son avant se heurter l'arrière)

bumpkin ['bʌmpkɪn] N **(country) b.** rustre m, rustaud m

bump-start Aut N démarrage m poussé; **to give sb a b.** pousser la voiture de qn pour la faire démarrer
VT **to b. a car** pousser une voiture pour la faire démarrer

bumptious ['bʌmpʃəs] ADJ orgueilleux, suffisant

bumpy ['bʌmpɪ] ADJ **1** (road etc) cahoteux, défoncé; **we had a b. flight** nous avons été secoués dans l'avion; Fig **we've got a b. road ahead of us** nous avons une période difficile devant nous; Fig **to give sb a b. ride** faire passer un mauvais moment à qn; **the proposals were given a b. ride** les propositions ont rencontré une vive opposition **2** (forehead etc) couvert de bosses

bun [bʌn] N **1** Culin petit pain m au lait; Fig

Fam **to have a b. in the oven** avoir un polichinelle dans le tiroir **2** (in hair) chignon m; **she wears her hair in a b.** elle se fait un chignon **3** esp Am Sl **buns** (buttocks) miches fpl; **a nice pair of buns** un beau cul, de belles miches
▸▸ Br Fam Hum **b. fight** (gathering) réception f

bunch [bʌntʃ] N **1** (of flowers) bouquet m; (of radishes, carrots etc) botte f, (of grapes) grappe f, (of herbs) touffe f, (of feathers) houppe f, (of keys) trousseau m; (of bananas) régime m; **to wear one's hair in bunches** porter des couettes **2** (of people) groupe m; Am (of livestock) troupeau m; **he's the best** or **the pick of the b.** c'est lui le meilleur (de la bande); **they're quite an intelligent b.** c'est un groupe plutôt intelligent; **the b. (of people) I work with** les gens avec qui je travaille; **what a stupid b.!** ce qu'ils peuvent être bêtes!; **they seem like a pretty nice b. of people** ils ont l'air très sympa; Sport **the b.** le peloton; Am Fam **thanks a b.** merci beaucoup; Fam **a whole b. of stuff** or **things** plein de trucs, tout un tas de choses; Br Sl **a b. of fives** un coup de poing
VT (flowers etc) mettre en bouquet; (radishes etc) mettre en bottes

▸ **bunch together** VI (of people) se serrer
VT SEP (books etc on shelf) serrer; **to be bunched together** (of runners, horses etc) être serrés

▸ **bunch up** VT **1** (dress) retrousser **2** (books etc on shelf) serrer; **to be bunched up** (of runners, horses etc) être serrés
VI (of material) se retrousser

bundle ['bʌnd(ə)l] N tas m; (secured, fastened in some way) (of washing etc) paquet m, ballot m; (of goods) ballot; (of asparagus etc) botte f, (of canes, wires etc) faisceau m; (of banknotes, papers) liasse f, (of wood) fagot m; Am Fam **to make a b.** (lots of money) faire son beurre; Am Fam **thanks a b.** merci beaucoup; Am Fam **to go a b. on sb/sth** (like) être fou de qn/qch; Fam **she's a b. of nerves** c'est un paquet de nerfs; Fam **my driving test wasn't exactly a b. of fun** passer mon permis de conduire n'a pas vraiment été une partie de plaisir; Hum **they came with their b. of joy** (new baby) ils sont venus avec leur bambin
VT **1** (make bundle of) faire un paquet de; (documents) mettre en liasses; (straw) mettre en bottes; **she bundled the baby in a blanket** elle a enveloppé le bébé dans une couverture; Mktg, Com **to b. sth with sth** offrir qch en plus de qch; Mktg, Com **to come bundled with sth** être livré avec qch **2** (put, lead hastily) **to b. papers into a drawer** fourrer des papiers dans un tiroir; **to b. sb into a car** embarquer qn dans une voiture; **he bundled me down the stairs** il m'a fait descendre les escaliers en toute hâte

▸ **bundle off** VT SEP **1** (send hastily) envoyer à la hâte ou sans attendre; **the baby was bundled off to hospital** le bébé a été envoyé à l'hôpital sans attendre; **they bundled me off the train** ils m'ont fait descendre du train en toute hâte **2** Pej (get rid of) se débarrasser de (sans cérémonie); **his father bundled him off to boarding school** son père l'a expédié en pension

▸ **bundle out** VT SEP faire sortir sans cérémonie ou ménagement

▸ **bundle up** VT SEP **1** (make parcel of) = **bundle** VT **1 2** (collect) (one's things etc) rassembler
VI (wear warm clothes) s'emmitoufler

bundling selling ['bʌndlɪŋ-] N Com vente f par lots

bung [bʌŋ] N **1** (for cask) bonde f, bondon m **2** Br Sl (money given) bakchich m
VT **1** (opening) boucher **2** Br Fam (put) met-

tre, fourrer; **b. it in a drawer** fourre-le dans un tiroir; **b. it over** *(throw it)* balance-le; **I bunged him a tenner** je lui ai filé un billet de dix livres; **they bunged him in prison** ils l'ont jeté en prison

▸ **bung up** VT SEP *Fam (block) (drain)* boucher; **I'm** *or* **my nose is all bunged up** j'ai le nez complètement bouché

bungalow ['bʌŋgələʊ] N pavillon *m*; *(in India)* bungalow *m*

bungee ['bʌndʒɪ] N *(cord)* tendeur *m*
▸▸ **b. cord** tendeur *m*; **b. jump** saut *m* à l'élastique; **b. jumping** saut à l'élastique

bunghole ['bʌŋhəʊl] N *(in cask)* bonde *f*

bungle ['bʌŋg(ə)l] N gâchis *m*, ratage *m*, *Fam* bousillage *m*; **to make a b. of sth** gâcher *ou Fam* cochonner *ou Fam* saloper qch
VT *(piece of work)* gâcher, *Fam* cochonner, *Fam* saloper; *(hold-up, operation, escape attempt)* rater
VI s'y prendre maladroitement; **someone has bungled** quelqu'un a fait une bourde

bungler ['bʌŋglər] N incapable *mf*, bon *m* à rien, bonne *f* à rien

bungling ['bʌŋglɪŋ] ADJ **b. idiot** incapable *mf*, bon *m* à rien, bonne *f* à rien
N gâchis *m*, *Fam* bousillage *m*; **your b. has cost us the contract** tes bourdes nous ont fait perdre le contrat

bunion ['bʌnjən] N *Med* oignon *m*

bunk[1] [bʌŋk] N **1** *Naut, Rail etc* couchette *f* **2** *Old-fashioned Fam (sleeping place)* logement *m*; **I can give you a b. for the night** je peux te loger pour la nuit
VI *Naut* coucher **(forward** à l'avant)
▸▸ **b. beds** lits *mpl* superposés

bunk[2] N *Br Fam* **to do a b.** déguerpir, décamper
▸ **bunk down** VI *Fam* **1** *(go to bed)* aller se coucher **2** *(sleep)* passer la nuit **(with friends** chez des amis**)**
▸ **bunk off** VI *Fam* **1** *(leave without permission) (from work)* partir avant l'heure sans en avoir l'autorisation; *(from school)* faire l'école buissonnière **2** *(leave hurriedly)* filer
VT INSEP **to b. off school** faire l'école buissonnière

bunk[3] N *Old-fashioned Fam (nonsense)* bêtises *fpl*

bunker ['bʌŋkər] N **1** *(in home) (for coal)* coffre *m* à charbon; *Naut (for coal, oil etc)* soute *f*, *(for oil)* réservoir *m*; *Com* **b. adjustment factor** ajustement *m* fret **2** *Golf* banquette *f*, bunker *m* **3** *Mil* blockhaus *m*; **nuclear b.** abri *m* antiatomique
VT **1** *Naut (fuel)* mettre en soute **2** *Golf* **to be bunkered** se trouver dans le sable
VI *Naut* se ravitailler en charbon

bunkhouse ['bʌŋkhaʊs] N *Am (for lumberjacks etc)* baraquement *m* pourvu de couchettes

bunkum ['bʌŋkəm] N *Fam* foutaise(s) *f(pl)*, âneries *fpl*

bunny ['bʌnɪ] N *Fam (rabbit)* Jeannot lapin *m*, petit lapin
▸▸ **b. girl** = employée *f* de boîte de nuit play-boy (habillée en lapin); **b. rabbit** Jeannot lapin, petit lapin

Bunsen ['bʌns(ə)n] N
▸▸ *Chem etc* **B. burner** bec *m* Bunsen

bunt [bʌnt] *Am Sp* N coup *m* retenu
VT frapper doucement
VI frapper doucement la balle

bunting[1] ['bʌntɪŋ] N *(bird)* bruant *m*

bunting[2] N *(flags)* drapeaux *mpl*, fanions *mpl*; **decorated with b.** pavoisé

buoy [bɔɪ] N *Naut* bouée *f*
VT *Naut (channel)* baliser; *(wreck)* marquer
▸ **buoy up** VT SEP *Naut (object)* faire flotter; *Fig (person, currency)* soutenir, maintenir;

Fig **buoyed up with new hope** animé *ou* soutenu par un nouvel espoir

buoyancy ['bɔɪənsɪ] N **1** *Naut, Aviat etc (of object)* flottabilité *f*, **centre of b.** centre *m* de poussée **2** *Fig* entrain *m*, allant *m*; *StExch* dynamisme *m*; *Com (of market)* fermeté *f*, *(of prices, currency)* stabilité *f*; **she has great b.** elle a un ressort incroyable
▸▸ **b. bag** ballonnet *m* de flottabilité; **b. tank** réservoir *m* de flottabilité

buoyant ['bɔɪənt] ADJ **1** *Naut, Aviat etc* qui flotte; **saltwater is more b. than fresh** l'eau salée porte mieux que l'eau douce **2** *Fig (person)* qui a du ressort; *Com (market)* soutenu, ferme; *(prices)* stable; **to be in a b. mood** être plein d'entrain; **a b. step** un pas élastique

buoyantly ['bɔɪəntlɪ] ADV avec entrain

BUPA ['buːpə] N *(abbr British United Provident Association)* = service *m* de santé privé

bur [bɜːr] N = burr[1] **1**

Burberry® ['bɜːbərɪ] N **1** *(raincoat)* imperméable *m* (de la marque Burberry®), Burberry® *m* **2** *(garment)* vêtement *m* de la marque Burberry®

burble ['bɜːb(ə)l] VI *(of stream)* murmurer; *Fig (of baby)* gazouiller; *(of person)* murmurer (des sons inarticulés); *Fam Pej (talk nonsense)* débiter des inepties
▸ **burble away, burble on** VI *Fam Pej* débiter des inepties

burbot ['bɜːbət] N *(fish)* lotte *f*, barbot *m*, barbot(t)e *f*

burbs [bɜː(r)bz] NPL *Am Fam* **the b.** la banlieue

burden ['bɜːd(ə)n] N **1** fardeau *m*, charge *f*, **b. of taxation** poids *m* de la fiscalité *ou* des impôts; *Law* **b. of proof** charge de la preuve; **the b. of proof rests with him** c'est à lui qu'il incombe d'apporter des preuves; **I'm a b. to you** je suis un fardeau pour toi; **to make sb's life a b.** rendre la vie dure à qn **2** *Fml (theme, gist) (of speech, complaint, argument)* substance *f*, *Old-fashioned (of song)* refrain *m* **3** *Naut (of ship)* charge *f*, contenance *f*
VT accabler **(sb with sth** qn de qch**)**; **to b. one's memory with useless facts** se charger *ou* s'encombrer la mémoire de faits inutiles; **I'm sorry to b. you with my worries** je suis désolé de vous accabler avec mes soucis; **a donkey burdened with wood** un âne chargé d'un fardeau de bois; **she is burdened with a retarded child** elle a un enfant handicapé à sa charge

burdensome ['bɜːd(ə)nsəm] ADJ *Fml* lourd

burdock ['bɜːdɒk] N *(weed)* bardane *f*, glouteron *m*

bureau, *pl* **bureaux** ['bjʊərəʊ, -əʊz] N **1** *(furniture)* bureau *m*; *(with roll top)* secrétaire *m*; *Am (chest of drawers)* commode *f* **2** *Am (government department)* bureau *m*, service *m*
▸▸ **b. de change** bureau de change

bureaucracy [bjʊə'rɒkrəsɪ] N *Pej* bureaucratie *f*

bureaucrat ['bjʊərəkræt] N *Pej* bureaucrate *mf*

bureaucratic [bjʊərə'krætɪk] ADJ *Pej* bureaucratique

burette, *Am* **buret** [bjʊ'ret] N *Chem* burette *f*, éprouvette *f* graduée

burg [bɜːg] N *Am Fam (village)* bled *m*; *(town)* ville *f*; **there's nothing happening in this b.** il ne se passe rien dans ce coin *ou* bled

burgeon ['bɜːdʒən] VI *Lit* fleurir

burgeoning ['bɜːdʒənɪŋ] ADJ *Lit, Fml (industry, population etc)* en expansion; **a b. talent** un talent en herbe; **the b. movement for independence** le mouvement naissant pour l'indépendance

burger ['bɜːgər] N *Fam* hamburger *m*

burgess ['bɜːdʒɪs] N **1** *Hist (in England)* citoyen *m* **2** *(in English history) (MP)* député *m (représentant une ville)* **3** *Am* = conseiller *m* municipal

burgher ['bɜːgər] N *Arch, Hum (citizen)* citoyen *m*

burglar ['bɜːglər] N cambrioleur, -euse; **b. proof** inviolable
▸▸ **b. alarm** alarme *f* antivol

burglarize ['bɜːgləraɪz] VT *Am* cambrioler

burglary ['bɜːglərɪ] N cambriolage *m*; *(breaking and entering)* vol *m* avec effraction

burgle ['bɜːg(ə)l] VT cambrioler; **it's the third time they've been burgled** c'est la troisième fois qu'ils se sont fait cambrioler

Burgundian [bɜː'gʌndɪən] ADJ bourguignon
N Bourguignon, -onne

Burgundy ['bɜːgəndɪ] N **1** *Geog* Bourgogne *f* **2** *(wine)* bourgogne *m*, vin *m* de Bourgogne **3** *(colour)* bordeaux *m*

burial ['berɪəl] N enterrement *m*, inhumation *f*, *Fig* **the b. of sb's hopes** la fin des espoirs de qn
▸▸ **b. chamber** caveau *m*; **b. ground** cimetière *m*; **b. mound** tumulus *m*; **b. place** *(lieu m de)* sépulture *f*, *(for radioactive substances)* dépôt *m* souterrain; **b. service** office *m* des morts

burin ['bjʊərɪn] N *(for engraving)* burin *m*

burk [bɜːk] N *Br Sl* **you (great) b.!** espèce d'idiot!

Burkina-Faso [bɜː'kiːnə'fæsəʊ] N Burkina *m*

burlap ['bɜːlæp] N *Tex* toile *f* d'emballage

burlesque [bɜː'lesk] ADJ burlesque
N **1** *(satire)* burlesque *m*; *(caricature)* parodie *f* **2** *Am Theat* revue *f* vulgaire
VT parodier, tourner en ridicule

burliness ['bɜːlɪnɪs] N **1** *(person's build)* forte *ou* solide charpente *f* **2** *Am (brusqueness)* brusquerie *f*

burly ['bɜːlɪ] ADJ **1** *(well-built)* bien bâti, *Fam* costaud **2** *Am (brusque)* brusque, bourru

Burma ['bɜːmə] N Birmanie *f*

Burmese [bɜː'miːz] ADJ birman
N **1** Birman, -ane **2** *Ling* birman *m*
▸▸ **B. cat** burmese *m*, chat *m* birman

BURN[1] [bɜːn] N **1** *Med etc* brûlure *f*, **the child suffered severe burns** l'enfant a subi de graves brûlures **2** *Astronaut* allumage *m*; *(of rocket)* poussée *f*, *Fig Fam* **I was doing a slow b.** la moutarde me montait au nez
VT *(pt, pp* burnt [bɜːnt], *occ* burned*)* **1** *(fuel, building)* brûler; **to b. coal/oil/gas** *(of boiler)* marcher au charbon/au mazout/au gaz; *Fig* **to b. one's boats** *or* **one's bridges** brûler ses vaisseaux; **to b. sth to ashes** réduire qch en cendres; **to b. sth to a cinder** *or* **a crisp** carboniser qch; *Old-fashioned Fam* **to be burnt** *(of police informer)* être grillé; **to be burnt alive, to be burnt to death** être brûlé vif; **the house was burned to the ground** la maison a été complètement brûlée; **to b. one's fingers** se brûler les doigts; *Fig* **he got his fingers burnt, he burnt his fingers over it** il s'est fait échauder (dans cette affaire); **to b. a hole in sth with a cigarette/the iron** faire un trou dans qch avec une cigarette/le fer à repasser; *Fig* **money burns a hole in his pocket** l'argent lui brûle les doigts; *Fig* **to have money to b.** avoir de l'argent à ne plus savoir quoi en faire; **acids b. into metal** les acides rongent le métal; **mustard burns the tongue** la moutarde pique *ou* brûle la langue; **I burned my tongue** je me suis brûlé la langue **2** *Ind (bricks, charcoal)* cuire; *(rubber)* vulcaniser, cuire

3 *Comput (CD)* graver
4 *Am Fam (swindle)* arnaquer
5 *Am Fam (anger)* foutre en rogne
 ▸ **vi 1** *(of house, forest, fire, wood)* brûler; *Culin (of meat, toast etc)* brûler; *(of sauce, milk etc)* attacher; *(of wound, eyes)* brûler, piquer; **the smell of burning rubber** l'odeur de caoutchouc brûlé; **to b. low** *(of fire)* baisser; *Fig* **to b. with** *(impatience, passion, desire)* brûler de; *(anger, hatred)* bouillonner de; **his cheeks were burning with shame** il était rouge de honte
2 *(of mixture in engine)* exploser
▸ **burn down vt sep** *(town, house etc)* brûler, incendier
 vi 1 *(of building etc)* être détruit par le feu *ou* par un incendie
2 *(of fire)* baisser
▸ **burn in vt sep** *Comput* roder
▸ **burn off vt sep 1** *(remove by burning)* *(bracken, gas)* brûler; *(paint)* décaper au chalumeau; *(rust etc)* enlever au feu
2 *(consume, use up)* *(calories)* brûler; **to b. off some energy** se dépenser
▸ **burn out vt sep** *Aut etc (brake linings or pads)* brûler; *Elec (coil)* brûler, court-circuiter; *(lamp)* griller; **the house was burnt out** le feu a complètement détruit l'intérieur de la maison; **to b. itself out** *(of fire)* s'éteindre; *Fig* **it'll b. itself out** *(of love affair)* une passion comme ça ne dure pas; *Fig* **to b. oneself out** s'épuiser (par excès de travail), se vider
 vi *(of fire, oil lamp)* s'éteindre; *(of candle)* s'éteindre, brûler jusqu'au bout; *(of light bulb)* griller
▸ **burn up vt sep 1** *(consume)* brûler (entièrement), consumer; **to b. up energy** se dépenser; *Fam* **to b. up the miles** *or* **the motorway** avaler les kilomètres
2 *(of sun)* *(leaves etc)* griller, flétrir; *Fam (make angry)* mettre en pétard
 vi 1 *Fam (get angry)* se mettre en pétard; **to b. up inside** bouillir intérieurement
2 *(of rocket)* brûler, se consumer; *(of person with high temperature)* être brûlant; **the pavement was burning up** le trottoir était brûlant

burn² **n** *Scot (stream)* ruisseau *m*

burner ['bɜːnər] **n 1** *(on stove)* brûleur *m*, feu *m* **2** *(in gas or acetylene lamp)* bec *m* **3** *Comput* graveur *m*

burn-in **n** *Comput (of machine)* rodage *m*

burning ['bɜːnɪŋ] **adj** *(fever, thirst, desire etc)* brûlant, ardent; *(coal)* embrasé, allumé, ardent; *(town, house)* incendié, enflammé, en feu; *(heat)* brûlant, torride; *(sun)*, *Fig (question)* brûlant; *Fam* **I'm b. (hot)** je crève de chaleur
 n *(of house etc)* incendie *m*; *Chem* combustion *f*; *Hist* **b. (at the stake)** supplice *m* du bûcher; **there's a smell of b.** ça sent le brûlé; **b. sensation** *(heat)* sensation *f* de chaleur (excessive); *(discomfort)* sensation de brûlure; *(pain)* douleur *f* cuisante
 ▸▸**b. bush** *Bible* buisson *m* ardent; *(shrub)* fraxinelle *f*

burnish ['bɜːnɪʃ] **n** *(on metal)* bruni *m*, poli *m*
 vt *(metal)* brunir, polir; *Phot (print)* satiner; *Lit* **her hair was like burnished gold** elle avait les cheveux d'un or cuivré

burnisher ['bɜːnɪʃər] **n** *Metal* **1** *(person)* brunisseur, -euse **2** *(instrument)* brunissoir *m*, polissoir *m*

burnishing ['bɜːnɪʃɪŋ] **n** brunissage *m*, polissage *m*

burnous(e) [bɜːˈnuːs] **n** burnous *m*

burnout ['bɜːnaʊt] **n** *Fig* saturation *f*, épuisement *m*

burnt [bɜːnt] **adj 1** *(person, object)* brûlé; *(smell, taste)* de brûlé, de roussi; **to be b. beyond recognition** être carbonisé; *Prov* **a**

b. child dreads *or* **fears the fire** chat échaudé craint l'eau froide **2** *(earth, clay)* cuit
 ▸▸**b. offering** *Rel (sacrifice)* holocauste *m*; *Hum (food)* plat *m* calciné *ou* carbonisé

burnt-out **adj 1** *(destroyed by fire)* incendié, brûlé **2** *Fam (person)* lessivé, vidé; **she was b. by thirty** elle était usée avant (l'âge de) trente ans **3** *Tech (bearings)* grippé; *Elec (coil, light bulb)* grillé

burp [bɜːp] **n** éructation *f*, *Fam* rot *m*
 vi éructer, *Fam* roter
 vt *(baby)* faire roter

burr¹ [bɜːr] **n 1** *Bot (of burdock etc)* teigne *f*; *Fig* **to stick to sb like a b.** se cramponner *ou* s'accrocher à qn **2** *(on metal)* bavure *f*, barbe *f*; **to take the burrs off metal** ébarber le métal
 ▸▸**b. walnut** ronce *f* de noyer

burr² **n 1** *Ling* grasseyement *m*; **to speak with a b.** grasseyer **2** *(of machine)* ronflement *m*
 vi **to b. one's r's** grasseyer
 vi *(of machine etc)* ronfler

burro ['bʊrəʊ] **n** *Am* âne *m*

burrow ['bʌrəʊ] **n** terrier *m*
 vi *(dig)* *(of rabbit, dog etc)* creuser (la terre); *Fig* **to b. into the archives** fouiller dans les archives; **to b. in one's pocket/bag** fourrager dans sa poche/son sac
 vt *(hole)* creuser; **to b. one's way underground** creuser (un chemin) sous terre; **to b. the ground** *(of rabbits)* creuser *ou* fouir la terre

burrowing ['bʌrəʊɪŋ] **adj** *(animal)* fouisseur; *(insect)* fossoyeur, mineur

bursar ['bɜːsər] **n** *Sch (official in charge of finance)* économe *mf*, intendant, -ante

bursary ['bɜːsərɪ] **n 1** *(office)* économat *m*, intendance *f* **2** *esp Scot (grant)* bourse *f* (d'études); **b. student** boursier, -ière

bursitis [bɜːˈsaɪtɪs] **n** *Med* bursite *f*; **I have b. in my shoulder** j'ai une bursite à l'épaule

BURST [bɜːst]

n éclatement **1** ▪ jaillissement **2**
▪ éclat **2**
vi éclater ▪ crever
vt faire éclater

n 1 *(of bomb, boiler etc)* éclatement *m*, explosion *f*
2 *(of flame)* jaillissement *m*, jet *m*; *(of gunfire, machine-gun)* rafale *f*, *(of laughter)* éclat *m*; *(of anger)* explosion *f*; *(of eloquence)* élan *m*; *(of applause)* salve *f*; *(of activity)* poussée *f*; *(of enthusiasm)* accès *m*; *Sport* **b. of speed** accélération *f*; **to put on a b. of speed** faire une accélération; *Sport* **final b.** sprint *m*
 vi *(pt, pp burst)* *(of boiler, bomb etc)* éclater, exploser; *(of dam)* éclater, céder; *(of abscess, blister)* crever, percer; *(of bubble)* crever; *(of storm, paper bag)* éclater; *Hum* **he'll b. if he eats any more** il va éclater s'il mange davantage; *Fam* **to be bursting (for the toilet)** avoir terriblement envie d'aller aux toilettes; **we've got a b. pipe** *(in house)* nous avons un tuyau qui a éclaté; *Fig* **her heart was ready to b.** *(with sorrow)* elle avait le cœur brisé; *(with happiness)* elle débordait de joie; **to be bursting at the seams** *(of dress etc)* se découdre; *Fig (of building etc)* être plein à craquer; **to be bursting with pride** crever d'orgueil; **to be bursting with health** déborder de santé; **to be bursting with impatience** bouillir d'impatience; **I was bursting to tell him so** je mourais d'envie de le lui dire; **b. from his lips** un cri s'échappa de ses lèvres; *Lit* **to b. upon sb's sight** se présenter aux yeux de qn; *Lit* **to b. upon sb's ears** *(of sound)* parvenir brusquement aux oreilles de qn

 vt *(balloon, tyre, paper bag)* faire éclater; *(boiler)* faire éclater *ou* exploser; *Lit (one's bonds)* rompre; **to b. a blood vessel** se rompre un vaisseau sanguin; *Fig* **he nearly b. a blood vessel when I told him** il a failli attraper un coup de sang quand je le lui ai dit; **to b. its banks** *(of river)* sortir de son lit
 ▸▸*Comput* **b. mode** mode *m* continu
▸ **burst in vt sep** *(door)* enfoncer
 vi *(of person)* faire irruption, entrer en trombe; **to b. in on sb** faire irruption chez qn/dans le bureau de qn; **to b. in on a conversation** interrompre brusquement une conversation
▸ **burst into vt insep 1** *(enter noisily)* **to b. into a room** faire irruption dans une pièce
2 *(suddenly start)* **to b. into flame(s)** s'enflammer brusquement; **to b. into song** entonner une chanson; **to b. into blossom** *(of tree)* commencer à fleurir; **to b. into laughter/tears** éclater de rire/fondre en larmes
▸ **burst open vt sep** *(door)* *(open suddenly)* ouvrir brusquement; *(smash open)* enfoncer, briser; *(cover, lock)* faire sauter
 vi *(of door)* s'ouvrir brusquement
▸ **burst out vi 1** *(say suddenly)* s'écrier; **to b. out laughing/crying** éclater de rire/fondre en larmes
2 *(leave noisily)* **to b. out of a room** sortir précipitamment d'une pièce
▸ **burst through vt insep** *(police cordon)* enfoncer; **to come bursting through the door** *(open it suddenly)* entrer précipitamment; *(smash it)* enfoncer la porte; **the sun b. through the clouds** le soleil creva les nuages

bursting ['bɜːstɪŋ] **n** *(of bomb, tyre etc)* éclatement *m*, explosion *f*; *(of dam)* rupture *f*

burton ['bɜːt(ə)n] **n** *Br Sl* **to have gone for a b.** *(be dead)* être mort; *(of hopes, plans etc)* être tombé à l'eau; *(be broken)* *(of plate etc)* être cassé; *(of iron, television etc)* être foutu; *(be lost)* *(of ball etc)* être perdu pour de bon; **there's another plate gone for a b.!** voilà une autre assiette de cassée!

Burundi [bəˈrʊndɪ] **n** Burundi *m*

bury ['berɪ] **vt** *(pt, pp buried)* **1** *(body)* enterrer, inhumer, ensevelir; *(at sea)* immerger; *(object)* enterrer, enfouir; **to b. sb alive** enterrer qn vivant; **to b. itself** *(of animal)* se terrer, s'enfouir; **buried treasure** trésor *m* enterré *ou* enfoui; *Elec* **buried cable** câble *m* souterrain
2 *(of snow, landslide)* *(town, house)* ensevelir; **I found the letter buried under my papers** j'ai trouvé la lettre enfouie sous mes papiers; **to b. oneself in the country** s'enterrer à la campagne; **to b. oneself in one's work** se plonger *ou* s'absorber dans son travail; **to b. one's face in one's hands** se cacher la figure dans les mains; *Fig* **to b. one's head in the sand** pratiquer la politique de l'autruche; **she always has her head buried in a book** elle est toujours plongée dans un livre; **to be buried in thought** être absorbé dans ses pensées

burying beetle ['berɪɪŋ] **n** nécrophore *m*

bus, *pl* **buses**, *Am* **busses** [bʌs, 'bʌsɪz] **n 1** bus *m*, autobus *m*; *(on long-distance services)* car *m*; **by b.** en bus; **to miss the b.** manquer *ou* rater le bus; *Fig Fam* manquer le coche; *Fam* **old b.** *(car)* vieille bagnole *f*, *(aircraft)* coucou *m*; **have you got enough money for your b. fare?** est-ce que tu as assez d'argent pour le bus? **2** *Comput, Electron* bus *m*
 vi voyager en autobus
 vt 1 *(drive in a bus)* transporter en autobus/en car; **the children are bus(s)ed to school** les enfants sont emmenés à l'école en autobus; **are you bus(s)ing it?** tu y vas en autobus? **2** *Am (restaurant tables)* débarrasser
 ▸▸**b. advertising** publicité *f* sur les auto-

bus; *Comput* **b. board** carte *f* bus; *Am* **b. boy** aide-serveur *m*, *pl* aides-serveurs; *Br* **b. conductor** receveur, -euse d'autobus; *Br* **b. conductress** receveuse *f* d'autobus; *Comput* **b. controller** contrôleur *m* de bus; **b. depot** dépôt *m* d'autobus; *(long-distance bus station)* gare froutière; **b. driver** conducteur, -trice d'autobus; **b. lane** voie *f* ou couloir *m* d'autobus; *Mktg* **b. mailing** publipostage *m* groupé, multipostage *m*; *Mktg* **b. phoning** télévente *f* groupée; **b. route** trajet *m* de bus; **are you on a b. route?** est-ce qu'il y a un bus qui passe près de chez toi?; **b. shelter** Abribus® *m*; **b. station** gare routière; **b. stop** arrêt *m* de bus; **b. ticket** ticket *m* de bus; *Comput* **b. structure** structure *f* de bus

busbar ['bʌzbɑːr] N *Electron* bus *m*

busby ['bʌzbɪ] N *Mil* bonnet *m* de hussard

bush¹ [bʊʃ] N **1** buisson *m*; **a great b. of red hair** une grosse tignasse rousse **2** *(in Africa, Australia)* **the b.** la brousse; **to take to the b.**, *Austr* **to go b.** prendre la brousse **3** *Vulg (woman's pubic hair)* barbu *m*
▸▸ **b. hat** chapeau *m* de brousse; **b. jacket** saharienne *f*; *Am Sport* **b. league** = petite équipe *f* locale de baseball; *Aviat* **b. pilot** pilote *m* de ligne opérant dans une région peu habitée *ou* dans la brousse *ou* Can dans le Grand Nord; **b. shirt** saharienne; **b. telegraph** téléphone *m* de brousse; *Br Fig Hum (grapevine)* téléphone arabe

bush² *Tech* N bague *f*, douille *f*, manchon *m*; *(between bearing and shaft)* coussinet *m*
VT baguer, manchonner; *(bearing)* mettre un coussinet à

bushbaby ['bʊʃbeɪbɪ] N galago *m*

bushed [bʊʃt] ADJ *Fam* **1** *(exhausted)* fatigué, éreinté **2** *Can (confused)* rendu déséquilibré par un isolement prolongé **3** *Austr (lost)* perdu *ou* égaré dans la brousse; *Fig (bewildered)* désorienté

bushel ['bʊʃəl] N **1** *(unit of measurement)* boisseau *m* (= *approx* 36 litres); *Fig* **to hide one's light under a b.** cacher son talent **2** *Am Fam (great amount)* grande quantité *f*

bushfire ['bʊʃfaɪər] N feu *m* de brousse

bushing ['bʊʃɪŋ] N *Tech (sleeve)* bague *f*, bague de culbuteur; *(between bearing and shaft)* coussinet *m*

Bushman, *pl* **Bushmen** ['bʊʃmən] *(in South Africa)* ADJ bochiman
N **1** Bochiman, -ane **2** *Ling* bochiman *m*

bushman, *pl* **bushmen** ['bʊʃmən] N broussard *m* *(en Australie)*

bushwhacker ['bʊʃwækər] N **1** *Am* = personne *f* qui vit dans des régions boisées et reculées; *Austr* broussard *m* **2** *Am (guerrilla)* guérillero *m*

bushy ['bʊʃɪ] ADJ **1** *(country, eyebrows)* broussailleux; *(beard)* fourni; *(hair)* touffu, embroussaillé **2** *(shrub)* épais, touffu

busily ['bɪzɪlɪ] ADV *(to prepare)* activement; *(to search)* d'un air affairé

BUSINESS ['bɪznɪs] N **1** *(affair, matter)* affaire *f*; **it's a bad** *or* **sad** *or* **sorry b.** c'est une bien triste affaire; **it's a bad** *or* **sad** *or* **sorry b. when you can't trust your own brother** c'est triste quand on ne peut même pas faire confiance à son propre frère; **I'm sick of the whole b.** j'en ai assez de toute cette affaire; **it's quite a b. finding a plumber** ce n'est pas une petite affaire que de trouver un plombier; **it was a real b. persuading him to come** j'ai/nous avons/etc eu beaucoup de mal à le persuader de venir; **what's your b. (with him)?** que (lui) voulez-vous?; **it's/it's not my b. to ...** c'est/ce n'est pas à moi de ...; **it's not your b., it's none of your b.** cela ne vous regarde pas, ce n'est pas votre affaire; **you have no b. (being) in here** vous n'avez rien à faire ici; **you had no b. telling her** ce n'était

pas à toi de le lui dire; **what b. is it of yours where she spent the night?** qu'est-ce que ça peut te faire où elle a passé la nuit?; **mind your own b.** occupez-vous de ce qui vous regarde *ou* de vos affaires; **I mind my own b.** je m'occupe de mes affaires; **I was just walking along, minding my own b., when ...** je marchais tranquillement dans la rue quand ...; **to go about one's b.** vaquer à ses occupations; *esp Fml* **I sent him about his b.** *(sent him away)* je l'ai envoyé promener; **to make it one's b. to do sth** prendre sur soi de faire qch; **... or I'll make it my b.** ... ou je vais m'en occuper personnellement; **let's get down to b.!** au travail!; **can we get down to b.?** est-ce qu'on peut commencer?, est-ce qu'on peut se mettre au travail?; **we got through a lot of b.** nous avons abattu de la besogne; **to mean b.** être sérieux; **the b. before a meeting** l'ordre *m* du jour; **(any) other b.** *(on agenda)* questions *fpl* diverses; **can we turn to the b. of who's going to be responsible?** est-ce que nous pouvons discuter de la question de qui sera responsable?; **Fam she can sing like nobody's b.** *(does it very well)* elle chante très bien; *Fam* **they're working like nobody's b.** *(very hard)* ils travaillent très dur; *Br Fam* **it's the b.** c'est impec'; *Euph* **has the dog done its b.?** est-ce que le chien a fait ses besoins?

2 *(dealings)* affaires *fpl*, *(commerce)* commerce *m*; **somebody in the antiques/restaurant b.** quelqu'un qui est dans les antiquités/la restauration; **to go into** *or* **to set up in b. as a grocer** s'établir épicier, ouvrir une épicerie; **to be in/go into b. on one's own** *or* **for oneself** être/s'établir *ou* s'installer à son compte; **to do b. with sb** faire affaire *ou* des affaires avec qn; **she's in b.** elle est dans les affaires; **the shop has been in b. for twenty years** le magasin existe depuis vingt ans; **they've been in b. together for twenty years** ils sont associés depuis vingt ans; *Fig* **now we're in b.** maintenant nous pouvons y aller; *Fig* **it looks as if we're back in b.** on dirait que les choses reprennent pour nous; **to go out of b.** fermer; **supermarkets have put many small shops out of b.** les supermarchés ont obligé beaucoup de petits magasins à fermer; **I've got some b. to discuss with him** il faut que je discute affaires avec lui; **they've put a lot of b. our way** ils nous ont donné beaucoup de travail; **to go to London on b.** aller à Londres pour affaires; **a profitable piece of b.** une affaire rentable *ou* qui rapporte; **to lose b.** perdre de la clientèle; **to do b. with sb** faire des affaires avec qn; **shop that does good b.** commerce qui marche bien; **it's good/bad for b.** c'est bon/mauvais pour les affaires; **how's b.?** comment vont les affaires?; **b. is b.** les affaires sont les affaires; **b. as usual** *(sign)* ouvert; **it's b. as usual in the town despite the floods** la vie continue dans la ville malgré les inondations; **this shop will be open for b. from tomorrow** ce magasin ouvrira demain; **hours of b.** *(sign)* heures d'ouverture; **to mix b. with pleasure** joindre l'utile à l'agréable; **you shouldn't mix b. with pleasure** il ne faut pas mélanger le travail et les loisirs; **b. before pleasure** le travail avant tout; **b. is slow** les affaires ne vont pas; **she has a good head for b.** elle a le sens des affaires; **to talk b.** parler affaires; **the tourist trade is big b.** le tourisme est une industrie qui rapporte beaucoup d'argent; **looking for b.?** *(said by prostitute)* tu viens, chéri?; **with b. experience** rompu aux affaires

3 *(company, firm)* affaire *f*, entreprise *f*; *(shop)* commerce *m*; **to run a b.** gérer une entreprise; **to carry on a b.** avoir une affaire/ un commerce; **b. for sale** commerce à vendre; **a farm is a b. like any other** une ferme est une entreprise comme les autres

4 *(trade)* métier *m*; **what's his line of b.?**, **what b. is he in?** qu'est-ce qu'il fait (comme métier)?; **I'm not in this b. for the good of my health** je ne fais pas ce métier pour le plaisir; **I'm not in the b. of solving your problems** ce n'est pas à moi de résoudre tes problèmes; **the best in the b.** le meilleur de tous

5 *Theat* jeux *mpl* de scène
▸▸ **b. account** compte *m* professionnel *ou* commercial; **b. accounting** comptabilité *f* commerciale; **b. acumen** sens *m* des affaires; **b. address** adresse *f* professionnelle; **b. administration** gestion *f* commerciale; **b. assignment** mission *f* commerciale; **b. associate** associé, -ée; **b. bank** banque *f* d'affaires; **b. banking** operations *fpl* des banques d'affaires; **b. buyer** acheteur *m* industriel; **b. card** carte *f* de visite; **b. career** carrière *f* dans les affaires; **b. centre** centre *m* des affaires; *Aviat* **b. class** classe *f* affaires; **b. computer** ordinateur *m* de bureau; **b. computing** informatique *f* de gestion; **b. concern** exploitation *f* commerciale; *Journ* **b. correspondent** correspondant, -ante financier(ière); **b. cycle** cycle *m* économique, temps *m* de cycle; *Fam* **b. end** *(of knife)* partie *f* coupante; *(of gun)* gueule *f*; **b. enterprise** entreprise commerciale; **b. environment** environnement *m* commercial; **b. ethics** déontologie *f* professionnelle; **b. expansion** extension *f* du commerce; **b. expenses** *(for individual)* frais *mpl* professionnels; *(for company)* frais généraux; **b. failure** défaillance *f* d'entreprise; **b. fare** tarif *m* affaires; *Comput* **b. graphics** graphiques *mpl* de gestion; **b. hotel** hôtel *m* d'affaires; **b. hours** *(of office)* heures *fpl* de bureau; *(of shop, public service)* heures d'ouverture; **b. incubator** pépinière *f* d'entreprises; *Comput* **b. intelligence system** réactive *f*; *Admin* **b. letter** lettre *f* commerciale; **b. lunch** déjeuner *m* d'affaires; **b. management** gestion d'entreprise *ou* des sociétés, direction *f* des entreprises; *(study)* économie *f* d'entreprise; **b. manager** *Com, Ind* directeur, -trice commercial(ale); *Sport* manager *m*; *Theat* directeur, -trice; **b. market** marché *m* industriel *ou* des entreprises; **b. meeting** rendez-vous *m* inv d'affaires; *Mktg* **b. mission** mission *f* d'activité *ou* de l'entreprise; **b. news** chronique *f* économique; **b. park** zone *f* d'activités; **b. plan** projet *m* commercial; **b. portfolio** portefeuille *m* d'activités; **b. premises** locaux *mpl* commerciaux; **b. relations** relations *fpl* d'affaires, relations commerciales; **b. reply envelope** enveloppe *f* préaffranchie; **b. school** école *f* de commerce; **b. section** *(of newspaper)* rubrique *f* des affaires; *Econ* **b. sector** secteur *m* tertiaire, secteur d'affaires; **b. services** services *mpl* du secteur tertiaire, services aux entreprises; **b. strategy** stratégie *f* d'entreprise; **b. studies** études *fpl* commerciales *ou* de commerce; **b. suit** complet *m* (-veston *m*), *pl* complets (-vestons); *Comput* **b. systems** logiciels *mpl* de bureautique; **b. tourism** tourisme *m* d'affaires; **b. travel** voyages *mpl* d'affaires; **b. traveller** = personne *f* qui voyage pour affaires; **b. trend** courant *m* d'affaires; **b. trip** voyage *m* d'affaires

businesslike ['bɪznɪslaɪk] ADJ *(person, manner)* sérieux; *(attitude, appearance)* professionnel; *(transaction)* régulier, sérieux

businessman, *pl* **businessmen** ['bɪznɪsmən] N homme *m* d'affaires; **big b.** homme d'affaires important

businesswoman, *pl* **businesswomen** ['bɪznɪswʊmən, -wɪmɪn] N femme *f* d'affaires; **she's a good b.** elle s'y connaît en affaires

busing ['bʌsɪŋ] N = **bussing**

busk [bʌsk] vi *esp Br* = chanter ou jouer d'un instrument dans les rues ou le métro

busker ['bʌskər] N *esp Br* musicien, -ienne ambulant(ante)

busman, *pl* **busmen** ['bʌsmən] N *Fam* **to take a b.'s holiday** faire la même chose pendant ses loisirs que pendant son travail; **that's a bit of a b.'s holiday** vous appelez ça des vacances!

bussing ['bʌsɪŋ] N *(of schoolchildren etc)* transport *m* par autobus *(surtout dans le cadre de la politique de déségrégation aux États-Unis)*

bust¹ [bʌst] N **1** *Anat (of woman)* poitrine *f*; **what (size) b. are you?** combien est-ce que vous faites de tour de poitrine?; **what b. is this dress?** combien cette robe fait-elle de tour de poitrine?; **to be small/big in the b.** avoir une petite/grosse poitrine; **it's too tight round the b.** c'est trop serré à la poitrine; **b. measurement** tour *m* de poitrine **2** *(by sculptor)* buste *m*

bust² *Fam* ADJ *(iron, radio etc)* foutu; **if it ain't b.,** don't fix it le mieux est l'ennemi du bien; **to go b.** faire faillite

VT **1** *(break)* casser; *(balloon etc)* crever; *Am* **to b. sb's nose** donner un coup de poing à qn sur le nez; *Fig Fam* **to b. a gut** se décarcasser, se donner un mal de chien; *Am Vulg* **to b. one's ass doing sth** se crever le cul à faire qch

2 *(arrest) (thief etc)* coffrer; *(gang of traffickers)* démanteler; **he was busted for armed robbery** il s'est fait coffrer pour vol à main armée; **you're busted** tu es fait

3 *(raid) (bar etc)* faire une descente dans

4 *Am esp Mil (reduce in rank)* rétrograder; **he's been busted to private** il a été rétrogradé au rang de simple soldat

5 *Am (wild horses)* dresser

bust³ N *Fam (by police) (of thief etc)* arrestation *f, (raid)* descente *f, (search)* perquisition *f*

▸ **bust out** vi *Fam* s'échapper

▸ **bust up** *Fam* VT SEP **1** *(marriage, friendship etc)* casser; **to b. up a meeting** interrompre une réunion **2** *(damage, destroy) (bar, flat)* saccager

VI *(of spouses, lovers)* casser; **their marriage has b. up** ils ont cassé

bustard ['bʌstəd] N *(bird)* outarde *f*

buster ['bʌstər] N *Am Fam (child)* (petit) garçon *m; (man)* homme *m*, type *m*; **hi, b.!** *(as address)* salut, mon pote!; **now listen, b. ...** écoute, mec ...

bustle¹ ['bʌs(ə)l] N *(activity)* agitation *f*; **the b. in the streets** l'animation *f* des rues

VI **to b. (about)** s'activer, s'affairer; **the streets are bustling with people** les rues grouillent de monde

VT **to b. sb out of the house** faire sortir qn précipitamment

bustle² N *(of skirt)* tournure *f*

bustling ['bʌs(ə)lɪŋ] ADJ *(person)* très actif; *(street)* animé; **the b. crowds of shoppers** la foule animée des gens qui font leurs courses

bust-up N *Fam* **1** *(of marriage, relationship)* échec *m*; **their b. was quite a shock to me** leur séparation m'a fait un choc **2** *(quarrel)* engueulade *f*, **to have a b.** se brouiller **3** *(brawl)* bagarre *f*

busty ['bʌstɪ] ADJ *Fam (woman)* à la poitrine plantureuse

busy ['bɪzɪ] ADJ (**busier, busiest**) **1** *(person)* occupé; **not now, I'm b.** pas maintenant, je suis occupé; **you have been b.!** tu as bien travaillé!; **my work keeps me b. all morning** mon travail m'occupe toute la matinée; **to keep (oneself) b.** s'occuper; **to be b. with sth** être occupé à qch; **to be b. doing sth** être

occupé à faire qch; **I suppose it's time I got b.** il est temps que je m'y mette; *Fam* **get b.!** grouille-toi!

2 *(day etc)* chargé; *Rail (line)* à grand trafic; *(street)* animé, passant; **it's a b. road** c'est une route à grande circulation; **the roads were very b. this morning** il y avait beaucoup de circulation sur les routes ce matin; **the train was very b.** il y avait beaucoup de monde dans le train; **the hotel industry is at its busiest in August** l'industrie hôtelière est au plus haut de son activité au mois d'août; **we're not b. at the moment** *(of business etc)* nous travaillons au ralenti en ce moment; **this is a b. time of year for us** *(of business etc)* nous travaillons beaucoup à cette période de l'année; **this is a b. time of year for gardeners** c'est une période de l'année où il y a beaucoup à faire pour les jardiniers

3 *esp Am Tel* occupé; **the line is b.** la ligne est occupée

4 *Comput (printer)* occupé

VT **to b. oneself with sth** s'occuper à qch; **to b. oneself (with) doing the housework/ ironing the shirts** s'occuper en faisant le ménage/en repassant les chemises; **I can always find something to b. myself with** je trouve toujours à m'occuper; **to b. oneself with other people's problems** s'occuper des problèmes des autres

▸▸ *Bot* **b. lizzie** balsamine *f*, impatiente *f*, *esp Am Tel* **b. signal** tonalité *f* occupé; **I keep getting the b. signal** ça sonne toujours occupé

busybody ['bɪzɪbɒdɪ] N curieux, -ieuse, indiscret, -ète; **he's an awful b.** il se mêle des affaires de tout le monde

BUT [bʌt]

CONJ	mais **1, 3**
ADV	ne … que
PREP	sauf **1** ▪ sans **3**

CONJ **1** *(coordinating)* mais; **he is small b. strong** il est petit mais fort; **b. I tell you I saw it!** (mais) puisque je vous dis que je l'ai vu!; **he does nothing b. complain** il n'arrête pas de se plaindre

2 *(subordinating)* **I can't go out for a minute b. something happens** je ne peux pas sortir une minute sans qu'il se passe quelque chose; *Arch, Lit* **I cannot b. believe that … il** m'est impossible de ne pas croire que …; **what could I do b. invite him?** que pouvais-je faire d'autre que de l'inviter? VOIR GRAMMAIRE A76

3 *(intensive)* **not just once b. twice** pas une fois, mais deux; **nobody, b. nobody** personne, mais absolument personne

ADV *(only)* ne … que; *esp Lit* **had I b. known!** si j'avais su!; **I can b. try** je ne peux qu'essayer; **it seems b. yesterday** c'est comme si c'était hier; **it seems b. yesterday that she was here** on dirait qu'hier encore elle était ici; *Formal* **his resignation cannot b. confirm such suspicions** sa démission ne fait que confirmer de tels soupçons; **if I could b. see him!** si seulement je pouvais le voir!; **he's b. a boy** ce n'est qu'un garçon

PREP **1** *(except)* **any day b. tomorrow** n'importe quel jour excepté *ou* sauf demain; *Arch, Lit* **all b. he** *or* **him** tous excepté *ou* sauf lui; *Arch, Lit* **none b. he** personne d'autre que lui; **nobody b. me could have done something so stupid** il n'y a que moi pour faire quelque chose d'aussi stupide; **nobody b. me knew about it** personne d'autre que moi n'était au courant; **anyone b. me** tout autre que moi; **I wish the prize had been won by anyone b. him** j'aurais voulu que n'importe qui d'autre remporte le prix plutôt que lui; **anything b. that** tout plutôt que cela; **he's anything b. a hero** c'est loin d'être un

héros; **he is anything b. happy** il n'est pas du tout heureux; **is she lazy? – anything b.!** est-ce qu'elle est paresseuse? – bien au contraire!; **it's nothing b. laziness** ce n'est que de la paresse; **there is nothing for it b. to obey** il n'y a qu'à obéir

2 **the last b. one** l'avant-dernier; **the next house b. one** la deuxième maison (à partir d'ici)

3 **b. for** sans; **b. for the rain I should have gone out** s'il n'avait pas plu je serais sorti; **he wouldn't have left b. for me** *(it was my fault for being there)* il serait resté si je n'avais pas été là; *(it was for my sake)* il ne serait pas parti si ça n'avait pas été pour moi; **b. for you I would have been killed** *(if you hadn't been there)* si vous n'aviez pas été là, j'aurais été tué

N **there is a b.** il y a un mais; **I don't want any buts!** il n'y a pas de mais!; **you're coming to dinner at our place and I don't want any buts** tu viens dîner chez nous, et je ne veux pas de discussions

butane ['bju:teɪn] N *Chem* butane *m*

butch [bʊtʃ] ADJ *Fam (man, woman)* très masculin; *(haircut, clothes)* de mec

butcher ['bʊtʃər] N **1** *(for meat)* boucher, -ère; **to go to the b.'s** aller chez le boucher; **b.'s block** billot *m* de boucher; **b.'s boy** garçon *m* boucher; **b.'s shop/trade** boucherie *f* **2** *Pej (killer)* boucher *m* **3** *Fam (surgeon)* boucher *m*, charcutier *m*

VT **1** *(animal) (kill for meat)* abattre; *(cut up)* dépecer **2** *Pej (kill) (person)* massacrer; *Fam* **he butchered that song** il a massacré cette chanson **3** *Fam (of surgeon) (patient)* charcuter

butcher's ['bʊtʃəz] N *Br Sl* **to have a b. at sb/ sth** mater qn/qch; **let's have a b. at the photos then** laisse-moi voir les photos

butchery ['bʊtʃərɪ] N **1** *(trade)* boucherie *f* **2** *Pej (bloodshed)* boucherie *f*, massacre *m*

butler ['bʌtlər] N maître *m* d'hôtel; **b.'s pantry** office *m*

butt¹ [bʌt] N **1** *(cask)* barrique *f*, futaille *f* **2** *(for rainwater)* tonneau *m*

butt² N **1** *(of cigar etc)* mégot *m* **2** *esp Am Fam (buttocks)* derrière *m*; **get off your b. and do something!** remue-toi le cul et fais quelque chose!; **move your b.!** bouge-toi! **3** *(of tool)* gros bout *m; (of fishing rod)* gros brin *m; (of rifle)* crosse *f; Fig* **the b. end of the conversation** la fin de la conversation **4** *Billiards (of cue)* masse *f*, talon *m* **5** *Carp* about *m*

▸▸ **b. end** *(of tool)* gros bout; *(of fishing rod)* gros brin; *(of rifle)* crosse; *Carp* about *mf*, **b. hinge** charnière *f; Tech* **b. joint** joint *m* abouté, soudure *f* bout à bout; **b. welding** soudure bout à bout

butt³ N **1** *Mil (mound)* butte *f* (de tir); **the butts** le champ de tir **2** *(target), Fig (of humour, joke)* cible *f*

butt⁴ N *(with head)* coup *m* de tête *ou Fam* de boule; *(of ram etc)* coup de tête

VT *(of person)* donner un coup de tête *ou Fam* de boule à; *(of ram etc)* donner un coup de tête à

▸ **butt in** vi interrompre la conversation; **if I could just b. in here** permettez-moi d'intervenir

▸ **butt into** VT INSEP **to b. into the conversation** interrompre la conversation

▸ **butt out** vi *Fam* **b. out!** ne t'en mêle pas!; **I decided to b. out** j'ai décidé de rester en dehors de ça

butter ['bʌtər] N beurre *m; Fig* **b. wouldn't melt in her mouth** on lui donnerait le bon Dieu sans confession

VT **1** *(bread)* beurrer **2** *Culin (vegetables etc)* mettre du beurre dans

▶▶ **b. bean** = sorte de haricot de Lima; **b. cream** crème *f* au beurre; **b. dish** beurrier *m*; **b. knife** couteau *m* à beurre; *EU* **b. mountain** montagne *f* de beurre

▶ **butter up** VT SEP *Fam* passer de la pommade à

butterball ['bʌtəbɔːl] N *Am Fam (plump person)* personne *f* boulotte

buttercup ['bʌtəkʌp] N renoncule *f* des champs, *Fam* bouton-d'or *m*, *pl* boutons-d'or

butterfat ['bʌtəfæt] N *(of milk)* matière *f* grasse

butterfingered ['bʌtəfɪŋgəd] ADJ *Fam* maladroit, empoté; **to be b.** tout laisser tomber

butterfingers ['bʌtəfɪŋgəz] N *Fam* maladroit, -oite, empoté, -ée *(qui laisse tout tomber)*; **b.!** espèce de maladroit!

butterfly ['bʌtəflaɪ] N **1** *(insect)* papillon *m* (diurne); *Fig (person)* papillon; *Fam* **to have butterflies (in one's stomach)** avoir l'estomac noué, avoir le trac **2** *Swimming (nage f ou brasse f)* papillon *m*
▶▶ **b. net** filet *m* à papillons; *Tech* **b. nut** papillon, écrou *m* à ailettes; *St Exch* **b. spread** spread *m* papillon; *Tech* **b. valve** (soupape *f* à) papillon; *Swimming* **b. stroke** (nage *ou* brasse) papillon

buttermilk ['bʌtəmɪlk] N babeurre *m*

butterscotch ['bʌtəskɒtʃ] N caramel *m* (dur) au beurre

buttery[1] ['bʌtərɪ] N *(esp in some English universities)* office *f*, dépense *f*, restaurant *m*
▶▶ **b. hatch** passe-plats *m inv*

buttery[2] ADJ *(taste)* de beurre; **with a b. texture** avec la consistance du beurre; **b. fingers** doigts pleins de beurre

butthead ['bʌthed] N *Am Fam* crétin, -ine

butting ['bʌtɪŋ] N *(by person)* coups *mpl* de tête; *(by ram, goat)* coups de corne; **he was disqualified for b.** il a été disqualifié pour avoir donné un/des coup(s) de tête

buttock ['bʌtək] N *fesse f*; **the buttocks** les fesses, le derrière; **cross b.** *(in wrestling)* ceinture *f* arrière *ou* à rebours, tour *m* de hanche

button ['bʌtən] N **1** *(on dress etc)* bouton *m*; **as bright as a b.** *(child)* vif, éveillé; *Am* **she's as cute as a b.** elle est trognon; *Fam* **it's not worth a b.** ça ne vaut pas un clou; *Fam* **I don't care a b.** je m'en fiche pas mal; **a b. nose** un petit nez; **chocolate buttons** *(sweets)* pastilles *fpl* de chocolat; *Br Old-fashioned* **buttons** *(pageboy)* groom *m* **2** *(for doorbell etc)* bouton *m*; *Comput (on mouse)* bouton; *(for menu selection)* case *f*, *Fam* **to be right on the b.** *(of answer)* tomber pile; *Fam* **you've hit it right on the b.** tu as mis en plein dans le mille **3** *Am (badge)* badge *m* **4** *(of foil)* bouton *m*, mouche *f*
VT **1** *(garment)* boutonner; *Fam* **b. your lip** *or* **it, keep your lip buttoned** ferme-la, la ferme, boucle-la **2** *Fencing (foil)* moucheter
VI *(of garment)* se boutonner; **a dress that buttons at the back/side** une robe qui se boutonne par derrière/sur le côté
▶▶ **b. mushroom** champignon *m* de couche *ou* de Paris

▶ **button up** VT SEP **1** *(fasten)* boutonner; **buttoned up** *(person)* boutonné jusqu'au menton **2** *Fig* **we've got the deal all buttoned up** l'affaire est dans le sac

button-down ADJ *(collar)* à pointes boutonnées; **b. shirt** chemise *f* à col boutonné

buttoned-up [bʌtənd-] ADJ *Fam (taciturn)* constipé

buttonhole ['bʌtənhəʊl] N **1** *(in garment)* boutonnière *f* **2** *Surg* boutonnière *f*, petite incision *f* **3** *(flower)* (fleur *f* portée à la) boutonnière *f*
VT *Fam* **to b. sb** coincer qn
▶▶ *Sewing* **b. stitch** point *m* de boutonnière

button-through ADJ **b. dress** robe *f* chemisier; **b. skirt** jupe *f* boutonnée jusqu'en bas

buttress ['bʌtrɪs] N *Archit* contrefort *m*; *Fig* pilier *m*, *Lit* étai *m*
VT *Constr* arc-bouter, étayer; *Fig* étayer

butty ['bʌtɪ] N *Eng Dial* sandwich *m*

buxom ['bʌksəm] ADJ *(full-bosomed)* à forte poitrine; *(plump)* bien en chair, aux formes rebondies *ou* planureuses

BUY [baɪ] N achat *m*; **a good/bad b.** un bon/mauvais achat, une bonne/mauvaise affaire
VT *(pt, pp bought* [bɔːt]) **1** acheter *(from* à); *(company)* racheter; **to b. sb sth** acheter qch à qn; **to b. sth for sb** acheter qch pour qn; **to b. sth cheap** acheter qch (à) bon marché; **money can't b. you love/health/happiness** l'amour/la santé/le bonheur ne s'achète pas; **a dearly bought advantage** un avantage chèrement payé; *Fam* **he's bought it,** *Am* **he's bought the farm** *(is dead)* il a passé l'arme à gauche; *Fig* **to b. time** gagner du temps
2 *Pej (bribe) (witness etc)* acheter
3 *Fam (believe)* gober, croire; **I won't b. that!** tu ne me feras pas gober *ou* croire ça!; **I'll b. that!** *(believe it)* je te/le/*etc* crois!; *(that's good, I agree)* d'accord!
VI acheter; *Fin* **to b. on credit** acheter à crédit *ou* à terme; **to b. forward** acheter à terme; **to b. on margin** acheter à découvert; **to b. spot** acheter au comptant
▶▶ *St Exch* **b. order** ordre *m* d'achat
▶ **buy back** VT SEP *(house etc)* racheter *(from* à)
▶ **buy in** VT SEP *(supplies etc)* s'approvisionner en
▶ **buy into** VT INSEP *(purchase share in) (business)* acheter une part de
▶ **buy off** VT SEP *Fam* acheter; **she refused to be bought off** elle refusa de se laisser acheter
▶ **buy out** VT SEP **1** *Com (partner etc)* (r)acheter la part de, désintéresser; **he was bought out for £50,000** on lui a (r)acheté sa part pour 50 000 livres **2** *Mil* racheter; **to b. oneself out** racheter son contrat avec l'armée
▶ **buy up** VT SEP *(surplus grain, wine etc)* acheter; *(in anticipation of shortages)* rafler; *Fam* **you must have bought up the entire store** tu as dû dévaliser tout le magasin

buyback ['baɪbæk] N rachat *m*
▶▶ **b. arrangement** accord *m* de reprise; **b. right** droit *m* de rachat

buyer ['baɪər] N **1** *(consumer)* acheteur, -euse **2** *(for shop)* acheteur, -euse, responsable *mf* des achats; **head b.** acheteur principal
▶▶ *Mktg* **b. behaviour** comportement *m* de l'acheteur; *Fin* **b. credit** crédit-acheteur *m*, *pl* crédits-acheteurs; *Fin* **b. credit guarantee** garantie *f* de crédit-acheteur; **b.'s market** marché *m* demandeur *ou* d'acheteurs

buyer-readiness N *Mktg* prédisposition *f* à l'achat

buying ['baɪɪŋ] N achat *m*; **b. and selling** l'achat et la vente
▶▶ *Mktg* **b. behaviour** comportement *m* d'achat; **b. centre** centrale *f* d'achat; *Mktg* **b. decision** décision *f* d'achat; **b. department** service *m* (des) achats; **b. group** centrale d'achat; **b. office** centrale *ou* bureau *m* d'achat; *Fin* **b. power** pouvoir *m* d'achat; **b. ring** groupement *m* d'achat

buy-out N *Com (of company)* rachat *m*; *(of partner)* désintéressement *m*

buy-sell agreement N *Com, Law* protocole *m ou* accord *m* d'achat et de vente

buzz [bʌz] N **1** *(of insect)*, *Fig (of conversation)* bourdonnement *m*; *(of plane)* vrombissement *m*; *Radio* ronflement *m*; **to give sb a b.** *Tel Fam* donner un coup de fil à qn; *Sl (thrill)* faire vibrer qn; *Sl* **being recognized gives him a b.** ça l'éclate d'être reconnu; *Sl* **there's nothing quite like the b. you get from skiing** rien ne vaut le frisson qu'on ressent en skiant; *Sl* **she gets a real b. out of those grandchildren of hers** elle prend beaucoup de plaisir à s'occuper de ses petits-enfants **2** *(rumour, gossip)* rumeur *f*; **the b. is that he's been fired** on murmure qu'il a été renvoyé
VI *(of insect, ears)* bourdonner; *(of aircraft)* vrombir; **the whole town was buzzing with excitement** la ville était en pleine agitation; **she is buzzing with ideas** elle a plein d'idées; **her head was buzzing with ideas** elle avait la tête bourdonnante d'idées
VT *Fam* **1** *Aviat (plane, ship)* frôler; *(building, town)* raser **2** *(call) (on telephone)* donner un coup de fil à; *(on intercom)* appeler (à l'Interphone®)
▶▶ **b. word** mot *m* en vogue
▶ **buzz about, buzz around** VI *(of bees, flies)* voler en bourdonnant; *Fam (of person)* s'activer; **I like to hear the bees buzzing about** j'aime entendre le bourdonnement des abeilles
▶ **buzz off** VI *Br Fam* décamper; **b. off!** allez, file *ou* décampe!

buzzard ['bʌzəd] N buse *f*, busard *m*

buzzcut ['bʌzkʌt] N coupe *f* en brosse

buzzer ['bʌzər] N *(device)* sonnette *f*, *(sound)* sonnerie *f*, **there's the b.** *(on machine)* ça sonne; *(at door)* on sonne

buzzing ['bʌzɪŋ] N *(of insect)*, *Med (of ears)* bourdonnement *m*; **a b. noise** un bourdonnement
ADJ *Fam (party, nightclub)* hyper animé; *(person)* speed, speedé

buzz-kill N *Am Fam* rabat-joie *mf inv*

BY [baɪ]

| PREP | par **1, 3, 4, 11** ▪ près de **2** ▪ au bord de **2** ▪ devant **5** ▪ à **4, 11** ▪ en **4** ▪ de **10, 12, 15** |
| ADV | près **1** ▪ de côté **2** |

PREP **1** *(agent)* par; **to be punished by sb** être puni par qn; **to be loved by sb** être aimé de qn; **made by hand** fait à la main; **to have a child by sb** avoir un enfant de qn; **she has a daughter by her first marriage/husband** elle a une fille de son premier mariage/mari; *Lit* **to die by one's own hand** mourir de ses propres mains; **he took me by the arm/hand** il m'a pris par le bras/la main; **to live by one's work** vivre de son travail; **what do you mean by that?** qu'entendez-vous par là?; **by force** de force; **by way of a joke** par plaisanterie; **by chance** par hasard; **by heart** par cœur
2 *(near) (person)* (au)près de, à côté de; *(thing)* près de, à côté de; *(in compass reading)* quart; **sitting by the fire** assis près du feu; **by the side of the road** au bord de la route; **by the sea** au bord de la mer; **north by east** nord quart nord-est
3 *(via)* par; **to go by the same road** aller par la même route; **by land and sea** par terre et par mer; **by land/sea** par (voie de) terre/mer
4 *(means of transport)* **to travel by rail** voyager en *ou* par le chemin de fer; **to come by car/motorcycle** venir en voiture/à motocyclette
5 *(past)* **he walked by the churchyard** il est passé devant le cimetière; **she drove by me** elle m'a dépassé *(en voiture)*
6 *(time: at or before)* **he will be here by three o'clock** il sera ici avant *ou* pour trois heures; **you will hear from us by Monday** vous aurez de nos nouvelles d'ici lundi; **he ought to be here by now** *or* **by this time** il

devrait être déjà ici; **I'll be gone by the time (that) you have finished** quand vous aurez fini, je serai parti; **you'll have it by tomorrow** vous l'aurez pour demain; **they were tired by the end of the day** ils étaient fatigués à la fin de la journée; **by 1990** *(talking about the past)* en 1990; **by 2025** *(talking about the future)* d'ici (à) 2025

7 *(during)* **by day** de jour, le jour; **by night** de nuit, la nuit; **by daylight** au jour, à la lumière du jour

8 by oneself (tout) seul; **to do sth (all) by oneself** faire qch (tout) seul

9 *(+ doing sth)* **to earn one's living by teaching** gagner sa vie en enseignant; **I shall gain/lose by (doing) it** j'y gagnerai/j'y perdrai; **to begin/end by laughing** commencer/finir par rire; **we shall lose nothing by waiting** nous n'avons rien à perdre en attendant

10 *(according to)* **to call sb by his name** appeler qn par son nom; **cheerful by nature** gai par nature, d'un naturel gai; **by my watch** à ma montre; **to set one's watch by the time signal** régler sa montre sur le signal horaire; **to judge sb by appearances** juger qn sur les apparences; **I can tell by your face** on le voit à votre visage; **he's a plumber by trade** il est plombier de son métier; **I know him by name/sight** je le connais de nom/vue

11 *(with numbers, measurements etc)* **to divide by three** diviser par trois; **three metres by two** trois mètres sur deux; **to sell sth by the pound/dozen** vendre qch à la livre/douzaine; **to rent a house by the year** louer une maison à l'année; **by degrees** par degrés; **by turns** chacun son tour, tour à tour; **they did it by turns** ils l'ont fait chacun leur tour; **he was happy and sad by turns** il était tour à tour heureux et triste; **one by one** un à un; **to come in by twos** *or* **two by two** entrer deux par deux; **little by little** peu à peu, petit à petit; **day by day** jour par jour, de jour en jour

12 *(to the extent of)* de; **longer by two metres** plus long de deux mètres; **by far** de loin; **they overcharged me by ten per cent**

ils m'ont compté dix pour cent en trop

13 *(in oaths)* **by God** au nom de Dieu; **to swear by all one holds sacred** jurer par tout ce qu'on a de plus sacré

14 *Mil* **by the right, quick march!** ≃ en avant, marche!

15 *(with regard to)* de; **to do one's duty by sb** faire son devoir envers qn; **she's Canadian by birth** elle est canadienne de naissance; **he's an actor by trade** *or* **profession** il est acteur de profession; *Fam* **it's all right by me!** ça (me) va!, d'accord!; *Fam* **if that's okay by you** si ça te va, si tu es d'accord

ADV 1 *(near)* près; **close by** tout près, ici près, tout à côté; **by and large** dans l'ensemble

2 *(aside)* **to lay** *or* **set** *or* **put sth by** mettre qch de côté; **to put** *or* **lay money by** mettre de l'argent de côté

3 to go *or* **pass by** *(elapse)* passer; **time goes by** le temps passe; **to come** *or* **stop by** *(to see sb, fetch sth)* passer

4 by and by *(soon)* bientôt, tantôt; *(in the immediate future)* tout à l'heure; **by the by(e)**, **by the way** à propos

---

bye[1] [baɪ] **N 1** *Cr* balle *f* passée **2** *Sport* **to have a b.** *(of player)* être exempt *(d'une épreuve, d'un match, dans un tournoi)* **3 by the b. ...** à propos ...

bye[2] **INT** *Fam* au revoir!, salut!; **b. for now!** à bientôt!

bye-bye *Fam* **INT** salut!, au revoir!
N *(in children's language)* **to go to b.**, **to go bye-byes** aller faire dodo

by-election N *Pol* élection *f* partielle

Byelorussia [bɪeləʊ'rʌʃə] **N** Biélorussie *f*

Byelorussian [bɪeləʊ'rʌʃən] **ADJ** biélorusse **N** Biélorusse *mf*

bygone ['baɪɡɒn] **ADJ** passé, ancien, d'autrefois; **in b. days** autrefois, dans l'ancien temps
NPL to let bygones be bygones oublier le passé

bylaw N arrêté *m* municipal; *Am*

Law **bylaws** *(of company)* statuts *mpl* de société

by-line N 1 *Journ* signature *f*; **a report under the b. of Mary Jones** un reportage signé Mary Jones **2** *Sport* limites *fpl* du terrain

BYO [biːwaɪ'əʊ] **N** *Austr* *(abbr* **bring your own)** = restaurant *m* qui ne sert pas d'alcool et où l'on peut apporter sa boisson

BYOB [biːwaɪəʊ'biː] **ADJ** *Fam abbr* **bring your own bottle**

bypass ['baɪpɑːs] **N 1** *Aut* rocade *f*; **temporary b.** déviation *f* **2** *Med* pontage *m*; **she's had a b.**, **she's had b. surgery** on lui a fait un pontage **3** *Tech* (conduit *m* de) dérivation *f* **4** *Elec* dérivation *f*
VT 1 *(town etc)* *(of motorist)* contourner, éviter; *(of road)* contourner; *Fig (middleman etc)* court-circuiter **2** *Tech (steam etc)* amener en dérivation **3** *Elec* mettre hors circuit
▸▸ *Aut* **b. filter** filtre *m* en dérivation; *Tech* **b. valve** soupape *f* ou clapet *m* de dérivation, clapet by-pass

by-play N *Theat etc (action)* jeu *m* accessoire, jeu de second plan; *(speech)* aparté *m* mimé, jeu muet

by-product N *Ind* sous-produit *m*, *pl* sous-produits, dérivé *m*; *Fig* effet *m* secondaire

byre ['baɪər] **N** *esp Scot* étable *f* à vaches

byroad ['baɪrəʊd] **N** petite route *f*

bystander ['baɪstændər] **N** spectateur, -trice

byte [baɪt] **N** *Comput* **(eight-bit) b.** octet *m*

byway ['baɪweɪ] **N** petite route *f*; *Fig* **byways of history** à-côtés *mpl* de l'histoire

byword ['baɪwɜːd] **N** *Arch* proverbe *m*, dicton *m*; *Fig* **to have become a b.** être devenu proverbial; **she is a b. for punctuality** elle est l'exemple même de la ponctualité; **she has become a b. for punctuality** sa ponctualité est devenue proverbiale

Byzantine [bɪ'zæntaɪn, baɪ-] **ADJ** *Hist, Fig* byzantin; **the B. Empire** l'Empire *m* byzantin **N** *Hist* Byzantin, -ine

Byzantium [bɪ'zæntɪəm, baɪ-] **N** *Antiq* Byzance *f*

C¹, c [siː] N **1** (*letter*) C, c *m*; **two c's** deux c **2** *Mus* do *m*, ut *m*; **in C sharp** en do dièse **3** *Sch* (*grade*) **to get a C** avoir une note moyenne, ≃ avoir entre 10 et 13 sur 20
▸▸ *Am Fam* **C note** billet *m* de cent dollars

C² (*abbr* **centigrade**) C.

c, ca (*abbr* **circa**) env.

CA [siːˈeɪ] N *Br Fin abbr* **chartered accountant**

C/A, c/a *Banking* (*abbr* **current** *or* **cheque** *or Am* **checking account**) C/C *m*, CCB *m*

CAA [siːeɪˈeɪ] N *Br Aviat, Admin* (*abbr* **Civil Aviation Authority**) = organisme *m* de réglementation de l'aviation civile

CAB *abbr* **Citizens' Advice Bureau**

cab [kæb] N **1** (*taxi*) taxi *m*; *Arch* (*horsedrawn*) fiacre *m*; **to call** *or* **hail a c.** appeler *ou* héler un taxi; **by c.** en taxi; **hansom c.** cab *m* **2** (*of truck, train, crane etc*) cabine *f*, **driver's c.** cabine *ou* poste *m* de conduite
▸▸ **c. driver** chauffeur *m* de taxi; **c. rank** station *f* de taxis

cabal [kəˈbæl] N *esp Pol, usu Pej* **1** (*plot*) cabale *f* **2** (*group*) coterie *f*

cabana [kəˈbænə] N (*room by beach/swimming pool*) cabine *f* de bain

cabaret [ˈkæbəreɪ] N **1** (*show*) spectacle *m* de music-hall *ou* de cabaret; **she's in c.** c'est une artiste de cabaret **2** (*nightclub, restaurant*) cabaret *m*
▸▸ **c. act** numéro *m* de cabaret; **c. artist** artiste *mf* de cabaret; **c. show** (*in nightclub*) spectacle *m* de music-hall *ou* de cabaret

cabbage [ˈkæbɪdʒ] N **1** chou *m*, *pl* choux; **red c.** chou rouge **2** *Fam* (*person*) légume *m*; **the accident left him a c.** l'accident en a fait un légume, il est à l'état végétatif depuis l'accident
▸▸ **c. lettuce** laitue *f* pommée; **c. palm** (*tree*) palmiste *m*; **c. rose** rose *f* centfeuilles; **c. white** (*butterfly*) piéride *f* du chou

cab(b)alistic [kæbəˈlɪstɪk] ADJ cabalistique

cabbie, cabby [ˈkæbɪ] N *Fam* chauffeur *m* de taxi

caber [ˈkeɪbər] N *Scot Sport* **tossing the c.** = concours *m* de lancer d'un tronc d'arbre (*dans les jeux des Highlands*)

cabin [ˈkæbɪn] N **1** (*hut*) cabane *f*, case *f*; *Br Rail* (*signal box*) poste *m ou* cabine *f* d'aiguillage **2** *Naut* cabine *f*, (*on barge etc*) cabane *f*; *Aviat* cabine *f*, habitacle *m* **3** *Aut* (*of passenger car*) habitacle *m*; (*of lorry*) cabine *f*
▸▸ *Aviat* **c. attendant** (*male*) steward *m*; (*female*) hôtesse *f* de l'air; *Aviat* **c. baggage** bagages *mpl* à main; *Naut* **c. boy** mousse *m*; *Aviat* **c. crew** personnel *m* de cabine; *Naut* **c. cruiser** cruiser *m*, yacht *m* de croisière; *Aviat* **c. staff** personnel *m* de cabine; **c. steward** steward *m*; **c. trunk** malle-cabine *f*, *pl* malles-cabine

cabinet [ˈkæbɪnɪt] N **1** (*piece of furniture*)

meuble *m* à tiroirs; (*for TV*) meuble télé; (*for video*) meuble vidéo; (*for stereo system*) meuble hi-fi; **filing c.** classeur *m*; (*for index cards*) fichier *m*; **bathroom c.** armoire *f* de toilette *ou* de salle de bains; **medicine c.** armoire *f* à pharmacie **2** *Pol* cabinet *m*, ministère *m*; **to form a c.** former un cabinet *ou* un ministère **3** *Arch* (*room*) cabinet *m*
▸▸ *Pol* **c. meeting** conseil *m* des ministres; *Pol* **c. minister** ministre *m* siégeant au cabinet; *Pol* **c. reshuffle** remaniement *m* ministériel

cabinet-maker N ébéniste *mf*

cabinet-making N ébénisterie *f*

cable [ˈkeɪb(ə)l] N **1** *Naut* câble *m*; **c.('s) length** (*measure*) encâblure *f* **2** *Elec* câble *m*; **to lay a c.** poser un câble; **overhead/underground/submarine c.** câble aérien/souterrain/sous-marin; **twin c.** câble à deux conducteurs **3** *Tel* câble *m*, câblogramme *m* **4** (*cable TV*) câble *m*; **it's only available on c.** ça n'existe que sur le câble **5** *Knitting* torsade *f*
▸ VT *Tel* (*message*) câbler; **to c. sb** câbler à qn, envoyer un câble à qn; **to c. sth to sb** câbler qch à qn
▸ VI *Tel* câbler; **to c. to sb** envoyer un câble à qn
▸▸ *Tel* **c. address** adresse *f* télégraphique; *TV* **c. broadcasting** télédiffusion *f* par câble; **c. car** téléphérique *m*; *TV* **c. company** câbloopérateur *m*, *pl* câblo-opérateurs; *TV* **c. distribution** câblodistribution *f*, distribution *f* par câble; *Comput* **c. modem** modem-câble *m*, *pl* modems-câble; *Knitting* **c. needle** aiguille *f* à torsades; *TV* **c. network** réseau *m* câblé; *TV* **C. News Network** = réseau d'information américain par câble et satellite; *TV* **c. operator** câblo-opérateur *m*; **c. railway** funiculaire *m*; *Phot* **c. release** déclencheur *m*; *Tel, Naut* **c. ship** câblier *m*; *Knitting* **c. stitch** point *m* de torsade; *TV* **c. television** télévision *f* par câble; *Aut* **c. terminal** cosse *f*, **c. transfer** (*of money*) virement *m* télégraphique

cabled [ˈkeɪb(ə)ld] ADJ câblé
▸▸ **c. network** réseau *m* câblé

cablegram [ˈkeɪb(ə)lgræm] N *Tel* câblogramme *m*

cableless [ˈkeɪb(ə)lɪs] ADJ sans câble

cableway [ˈkeɪb(ə)lweɪ] N téléphérique *m*

cabling [ˈkeɪb(ə)lɪŋ] N *Elec etc* (*cables*) câbles *mpl*, câblage *m*

cabman, *pl* **cabmen** [ˈkæbmən] N chauffeur *m* de taxi

caboodle [kəˈbuːd(ə)l] N *Fam* **the whole (kit and) c.** tout le bazar *ou* bataclan

caboose [kəˈbuːs] N **1** *Am Rail* (*of goods train*) fourgon *m* de queue **2** *Am Sl* (*jail*) tôle *f*, taule *f* **3** *Can* (*for loggers etc*) baraquement *m* mobile **4** *Naut* (*kitchen*) cuisine *f*, coquerie *f*

cabotage [kæbəˈtaːdʒ] N *Aviat, Naut* cabotage *m*
▸▸ **c. fare** tarif *m* de cabotage; **c. route** itinéraire *m* de cabotage

CAC 40 index [kæk] N *St Exch* indice *m* CAC 40

cacao [kəˈkɑːəʊ, kəˈkeɪəʊ] N *Bot* **1** (*tree*) cacaotier *m*, cacaoyer *m* **2** (*bean*) (graine *f* de *ou* fève *f* de) cacao *m*
▸▸ **c. bean** (graine *ou* fève de) cacao; **c. pod** cabosse *f*, **c. tree** cacaotier, cacaoyer

cache [kæʃ] N **1** (*arms, drugs etc that have been hidden*) objets *mpl* cachés; **a c. of guns/drugs** une cache d'armes/de drogues; **the c. had a value of ...** les armes/drogues/ *etc* cachées là avaient une valeur de ... **2** (*hiding place*) cache *f* **3** *Comput* antémémoire *f*, mémoire-cache *f*, *pl* mémoirescache
▸ VT **1** (*hide*) cacher **2** *Comput* (*data*) mettre en antémémoire *ou* en mémoire-cache
▸▸ *Comput* **c. memory** antémémoire, mémoire-cache

cachet [ˈkæʃeɪ] N *Pharm, Fig* cachet *m*; *Mktg* label *m*; *Fig* **to have a certain c.** avoir un certain cachet

cack [kæk] N *Br Sl* **1** (*excrement*) caca *m* **2** (*nonsense*) conneries *fpl*; **don't talk c.!** arrête de raconter n'importe quoi! **3** (*worthless things*) camelote *f*, **the film was a load of c.** le film était nul
▸ ADJ (*bad*) nul; **her music is c.** sa musique est nulle
▸ VT **he was cacking himself** (*scared*) il faisait dans son froc

cack-handed [-ˈhændɪd] ADJ *Fam* (*clumsy*) maladroit

cackle [ˈkæk(ə)l] N **1** (*of hen*) caquet *m* **2** *Fig Fam* (*talking*) caquet *m*, jacassement *m*; (*laughter*) gloussement(s) *m(pl)*; **cut the c.!** la ferme!
▸ VI **1** (*of hen*) caqueter; (*of goose*) cacarder **2** *Fig Fam* (*talk*) caqueter, jacasser; (*laugh*) glousser

cacophonous [kəˈkɒfənəs] ADJ cacophonique

cacophony [kəˈkɒfənɪ] N cacophonie *f*

cactus, *pl* **cacti** [ˈkæktəs, -tiː, -taɪ] N cactus *m*

CAD N **1** [kæd] *Comput* (*abbr* **computer-assisted design**) CAO *f* **2** [siːeɪˈdiː] *Com* (**cash against documents**) comptant *m* contre documents

cad [kæd] N *Br Old-fashioned* mufle *m*, goujat *m*

cadaver [kəˈdævər] N *esp Am Med* cadavre *m*

cadaverous [kəˈdævərəs] ADJ **1** (*pale*) (*complexion etc*) cadavéreux, cadavérique **2** (*haggard*) (*appearance, face*) cadavérique

CAD/CAM [ˈkædkæm] N *Comput* (*abbr* **computer-assisted design/computer-assisted manufacture**) CFAO *f*

caddie ['kædɪ] *Golf* N caddie *m*
VI **to c. for sb** servir de caddie à qn
▸▸ **c. car, c. cart** chariot *m* (pour crosses de golf)

caddish ['kædɪʃ] ADJ *Br Old-fashioned (behaviour)* de mufle; *(person)* mufle; **a c. thing to do** une preuve de muflerie

caddy[1] ['kædɪ] N **(tea) c.** boîte *f* à thé

caddy[2] N, VI = **caddie**

cadence ['keɪdəns] N cadence *f*, rythme *m*; *Mus* cadence

cadenza [kə'denzə] N *Mus* cadence *f*

cadet [kə'det] N *Mil etc* élève *mf* d'une école militaire, élève officier; *Sch* élève de la préparation militaire
▸▸ *Mil* **c. corps** peloton *m* d'instruction militaire; *(for police training)* corps *m* d'élèves policiers

cadge [kædʒ] *Fam, often Pej* VT mendier, quémander (**from, off** à); *(money, cigarette)* taxer, taper (**from, off** à); **can I c. a lift?** ça ne t'ennuierait pas de me déposer?
VI mendier

cadger ['kædʒər] N *Fam Pej* quémandeur, -euse; *(of cigarette, money)* tapeur, -euse

Cadiz [kə'dɪz] N Cadix

cadmium ['kædmɪəm] N *Miner* cadmium *m*

cadre [kɑ:dər] N *Mil, Pol* cadre *m*

CAE [si:eɪ'i:] N *Comput (abbr* **computer-aided engineering**) ingénierie *f* assistée par ordinateur

caecum, *pl* **caeca,** *Am* **cecum,** *pl* **ceca** ['si:kəm, -ə] N *Anat* cæcum *m*

Caesar ['si:zər] N César; **Julius C.** Jules César
▸▸ *Culin* **C. salad** = salade *f* à base de romaine, de croûtons et d'une vinaigrette additionnée d'œuf

Caesarean, Caesarian [sɪ'zeərɪən] N **1** *Obst* césarienne *f*; **it was a C.** *(of delivery)* on lui a fait une césarienne; **to be a C.** *(of baby)* être né par césarienne; **she has to have a C.** il va falloir lui faire une césarienne; **the baby was born by C.** l'enfant est né par césarienne **2** *Hist* Césarien, -ienne
ADJ césarien
▸▸ *Obst* **C. section** césarienne

caesura [sɪ'zjʊərə] N *Liter* césure *f*

café ['kæfeɪ] N *(in UK)* ≃ café-restaurant *m*, *pl* cafés-restaurants; *(in rest of Europe)* café *m*

> **Café**
> En Grande-Bretagne, le mot "café" désigne une sorte de snack où l'on peut prendre un repas léger et boire du thé ou du café.

cafeteria [kæfɪ'tɪərɪə] N *(in large store)* cafétéria *f*, *(for employees)* cantine *f* en self-service

caff [kæf] N *Br Sl* ≃ café-restaurant *m*, *pl* cafés-restaurants

caffeine ['kæfi:n] N caféine *f*

caffeine-free ADJ *(without caffeine)* sans caféine

caftan ['kæftæn] N caf(e)tan *m*

cage [keɪdʒ] N **1** *(for birds, animals etc)* cage *f* **2** *(of lift)* cabine *f* **3** *Min* cage *f* d'extraction
VT *(bird etc)* mettre en cage; **caged animal** animal *m* en cage; **I feel caged in** je me sens enfermé
▸▸ **c. bird** oiseau *m* d'agrément *ou* d'appartement

cagey ['keɪdʒɪ] ADJ *Fam (careful)* prudent, circonspect; *(not frank)* cachottier; **to be c. about one's age** ne pas vouloir avouer son âge, rester vague concernant son âge

cagily ['keɪdʒɪlɪ] ADV *(carefully)* très prudemment; **to answer c.** *(deliberately vaguely)* donner une réponse vague

caginess ['keɪdʒɪnɪs] N *(carefulness)* prudence *f*, *(deliberate vagueness)* vague *m*; **there was a certain c. in her replies** elle évitait de répondre en restant dans le vague

cagoule [kə'gu:l] N anorak *m* léger et long (avec capuche)

cahoots [kə'hu:ts] NPL *Fam* **to be in c. (with sb)** être de mèche (avec qn)

CAI [si:eɪ'aɪ] N *Comput (abbr* **computer-aided instruction**) IAO *f*

caiman ['keɪmən] N caïman *m*

Cain [keɪn] N *Bible* Caïn; *Fam* **to raise C.** *(make noise)* faire un bruit *ou* un fracas de tous les diables; *(make scene)* faire une scène monumentale

cairn [keən] N **1** *(of stones)* cairn *m*, tumulus *m* de pierres **2** *(dog)* terrier *m* cairn
▸▸ **c. terrier** terrier cairn

cairngorm [keən'gɔ:m] N *(gem)* pierre *f* de cairngorm

Cairo ['kaɪrəʊ] N Le Caire

caisson ['keɪs(ə)n] N **1** *Constr (for working underwater)* caisson *m* **2** *Naut (in dry dock)* bateau-porte *m*, *pl* bateaux-portes **3** *Mil (for ammunition)* caisson *m*
▸▸ *Med* **c. disease** maladie *f* des caissons

cajole [kə'dʒəʊl] VT enjôler; **to c. sb into/out of doing sth** persuader/dissuader qn de faire qch

cajolery [kə'dʒəʊlərɪ] N cajolerie(s) *f(pl)*

Cajun ['keɪdʒən] ADJ *(language, music, recipe)* cajun *inv*
N **1** *(person)* Cajun *mf* **2** *Ling* cajun *m*

cake [keɪk] N **1** *Culin* gâteau *m*; *(small)* pâtisserie *f*, **(small) cakes** (petits) gâteaux, pâtisseries; **fruit c.** cake *m*; *Am Fam* **that takes the c.!** ça c'est le comble *ou* le bouquet!; *Fig Fam* **it's a piece of c.** c'est simple comme bonjour, c'est du gâteau!; *Fam* **they're going** *or* **selling like hot cakes** ça se vend comme des petits pains; *Prov* **you can't have your c. and eat it** on ne peut pas avoir le beurre et l'argent du beurre; **a big c. of mud** un gros paquet de boue **2** *Old-fashioned (of soap)* pain *m*; *(of chocolate, paint)* tablette *f*
VI *(solidify)* former une croûte; *(of mud)* sécher; *(of blood etc)* coaguler
▸▸ **c. mix** préparation *f* (instantanée) pour gâteau; **c. shop** pâtisserie *f*, **c. stand** plat *m* à gâteaux; **c. tin** moule *m* à gâteau

caked [keɪkt] ADJ *(mud)* séché; *(blood)* coagulé; **c. with mud/blood** couvert de boue/sang séché(e)

cakehole ['keɪkhəʊl] N *Br Fam* bouche *f*, **shut your c.** ferme-la!, ferme ton clapet!

cakewalk ['keɪkwɔ:k] N *(dance)* cake-walk *m*, *pl* cake-walks; *Am Fig Fam* **it was a c.** *(very easy)* c'était du gâteau

CAL [kæl] N *Comput (abbr* **computer-aided learning**) EAO *m*

Cal *abbr* California

calabash ['kæləbæʃ] N **1** *(tree)* calebassier *m* **2** *(bottle)* calebasse *f*, gourde *f*
▸▸ **c. gourd** calebasse, gourde; **c. tree** calebassier

calaboose ['kæləbu:s] N *Am Sl (prison)* taule *f*, tôle *f*; **ten days in the c.** dix jours de taule *ou* tôle

calamine ['kæləmaɪn] N calamine *f*
▸▸ **c. lotion** lotion *f* calmante à la calamine

calamitous [kə'læmɪtəs] ADJ désastreux

calamity [kə'læmɪtɪ] N désastre *m*, calamité *f*
▸▸ *Fam* **C. Jane** Miss Catastrophe *f*

calcareous [kæl'keərɪəs] ADJ *Geol etc* calcaire

calceolaria [kælsɪə'leərɪə] N *(plant)* calcéolaire *f*

calcification [kælsɪfɪ'keɪʃən] N calcification *f*

calcify ['kælsɪfaɪ] *Chem etc* VT calcifier
VI se calcifier

calcium ['kælsɪəm] N *Chem* calcium *m*
▸▸ **c. carbide** carbure *m* de calcium; **c. chloride** chlorure *m* de calcium; **c. deficiency** carence *f* en calcium

calculable ['kælkjʊləb(ə)l] ADJ calculable

calculate ['kælkjʊleɪt] VT **1** *(sum, figure, amount, distance)* calculer **2** *(intend)* calculated to do sth fait pour faire qch; **the remark was calculated to shock** la remarque était délibérément choquante **3** *Am Fam (think)* croire, supposer (**that** que)
VI *esp Am (rely)* **to c. on sth/on doing sth** compter sur qch/compter faire qch

calculated ['kælkjʊleɪtɪd] ADJ *(insolence etc)* délibéré, calculé; *(crime)* prémédité; **words c. to reassure us** paroles propres à nous rassurer
▸▸ *Comput* **c. field** champ *m* calculé; **c. risk** risque *m* calculé

calculating ['kælkjʊleɪtɪŋ] ADJ **1** *Pej (person)* calculateur, -trice; **this was not the action of a c. murderer** ce n'était pas un meurtre prémédité **2** *(cautious)* prudent, mesuré
▸▸ *Math* **c. machine** machine *f* à calculer

calculation [kælkjʊ'leɪʃən] N calcul *m*; *(estimate)* estimation *f*, **to make a c.** effectuer un calcul; **to upset sb's calculations** bouleverser les calculs de qn

calculator ['kælkjʊleɪtər] N **1** *(machine)* calculatrice *f*, machine *f* à calculer; *(pocket)* calculatrice, calculette *f* **2** *(person)* calculateur, -trice

calculus ['kælkjʊləs] N *Math, Med* calcul *m*

Calcutta [kæl'kʌtə] N Calcutta

Caledonia [kælɪ'dəʊnɪə] N *Antiq, Lit (Scotland)* Calédonie *f*

Caledonian [kælɪ'dəʊnɪən] *Antiq, Lit* ADJ calédonien
N Calédonien, -ienne

calendar ['kælɪndər] N *(of dates), Rel* calendrier *m*; *(of institution, university etc)* annuaire *m*; *Law (list of cases)* rôle *m* des causes; *(in criminal law)* rôle des assises; *Am (of Congress)* ordre *m* du jour; **I'll check my c.** je vais vérifier mon agenda; **c. of (forthcoming) events** calendrier des manifestations; **the club has a full c. this month** le club a un calendrier chargé ce mois-ci; **an important date in the publishing c.** une date importante dans le calendrier de l'édition
▸▸ **c. month** mois *m* civil; **c. year** année *f* civile

calender ['kælɪndər] *Tech* N calandre *f*
VT calandrer

calendered ['kælɪndəd] ADJ *(paper)* calandré, satiné

calends ['kælɪndz] NPL *Antiq* calendes *fpl*

calf[1], *pl* **calves** [kɑ:f, kɑ:vz] N **1** *(animal)* veau *m*; **cow in** *or* **with c.** vache *f* pleine; **buffalo c.** buffletin *m*; **elephant c.** éléphanteau *m*; **sea c.** phoque *m* commun; **whale c.** baleineau *m* **2** *(leather)* veau *m* **3** *(broken off from iceberg)* glaçon *m*
▸▸ **c. binding** *(of book)* reliure *f* en veau *ou* en vélin; **c. love** premières amours *fpl*

calf[2], *pl* **calves** N *(of leg)* mollet *m*; **c.-length boots** demi-bottes *fpl*

calfskin ['kɑ:fskɪn] N (cuir *m* de) veau *m*; **c. wallet** portefeuille *m* en veau

caliber ['kælɪbər] N *Am* = **calibre**

calibrate ['kælɪbreɪt] VT *Tech (measuring instrument etc)* étalonner; *(bore)* calibrer; *(thermometer)* graduer; *Mil (piece of artillery)* vérifier le calibre de

calibration [kælɪˈbreɪʃən] N *(of measuring instrument)* étalonnage *m*; *(of bore)* calibrage *m*

calibre, *Am* **caliber** [ˈkælɪbər] N *(of firearm),* *Fig (of person)* calibre *m*; **a man of your c.** un homme de votre calibre *ou* envergure; **a very high c. translator** un traducteur de très grande envergure

calico [ˈkælɪkəʊ] N *Tex* calicot *m*; **printed c.,** *Am* **c.** calicot imprimé, indienne *f*
ADJ 1 *Tex* de calicot **2** *Am (cow)* tacheté; *(cat)* moucheté

California [kælɪˈfɔːnɪə] N Californie *f*

Californian [kælɪˈfɔːnɪən] **ADJ** californien **N** Californien, -ienne

caliper [ˈkælɪpər] N **1** *Aut* étrier *m* (de frein à disque) **2** = **calliper**

caliph [ˈkeɪlɪf] N calife *m*

caliphate [ˈkeɪlɪfɪt] N califat *m*

calisthenics [kælɪsˈθenɪks] N *esp Am* gymnastique *f* rythmique VOIR GRAMMAIRE A10

calk¹ [kɔːk] VT *Art etc* décalquer

calk² VT *(ship)* calfater, étouper

CALL [kɔːl]

N	appel **1, 2, 4** ▪ visite **5**
VT	appeler **1–6** ▪ réveiller **3**
VI	appeler **1** ▪ passer **3** ▪ s'arrêter **3**

N 1 *(shout)* appel *m*, cri *m*; *(of bird)* cri; **to give sb a c.** appeler qn
2 *(summons) (of person)* convocation *f*; *(of bugle)* sonnerie *f*; **c. for help** appel *m* au secours; **the President's c. for calm** l'appel au calme lancé par le Président; **to come at/ answer sb's c.** venir/répondre à l'appel de qn; **on c.** *(doctor)* de garde; *(interpreter, engineer etc)* disponible à tout moment; **to be within c.** être à portée de voix; **to give sb a c.** *(waken)* réveiller qn; *Euph* **to obey** *or* **answer a c. of nature** satisfaire un besoin naturel; **c. for tenders** appel d'offres
3 *Rel* vocation *f*; **he felt a c. (to the ministry)** il se sentait une vocation religieuse
4 *Tel* **(telephone) c.** coup *m* de téléphone *ou* *Fam* de fil, *Fml* appel *m* téléphonique; **to make a c.** passer un coup de téléphone *ou* *Fam* de fil; **to give sb a c.** téléphoner à qn, appeler qn (au téléphone), *Fam* passer un coup de fil à qn; **you have a c. from Canada** on vous appelle du Canada; **you had a c. from Pam** Pam t'a appelé; **there was a c. for you** il y a eu un coup de téléphone *ou* un appel pour toi; **he's on a c.** il est en ligne; **will you accept the c.?** *(when charges are reversed)* est-ce que vous prenez *ou* acceptez l'appel?; **to put a c. through** passer la communication; **to return sb's c.** rappeler qn; **local c.** appel local
5 *(visit)* visite *f*; *Com (of representative)* passage *m*; **to pay** *or* **make a c. on sb** rendre visite à qn; *Euph* **to pay a c.** *(go to toilet)* aller se laver les mains
6 *(demand)* demande *f*; **there's not much c. for …** il n'y a pas une forte demande de …; **there's not much c. for them** ce n'est pas un article très demandé
7 *(need)* besoin *m*; **there's no c. for rudeness!** pas besoin *ou* ce n'est pas la peine d'être impoli!
8 *Cards (at bridge)* appel *m*; *(at solo whist, boston)* demande *f*; **c. for trumps** invite *f* d'atout; **a c. of three diamonds** une annonce de trois carreaux
9 *Tennis, Cr (of umpire)* décision *f*
10 *Fin (for money)* demande *f*, appel *m* de fonds *ou* de versement; **c. for capital** appel de fonds; **payable at c.** remboursable sur demande *ou* à vue; **money at** *or* **on c.** prêts *mpl* au jour le jour, argent *m* à court terme

VT 1 *(attract attention of) (person)* appeler; **come quickly, he called** venez vite, a-t-il crié
2 *(say out loud)* **to c. sb's name** appeler qn;

to c. the banns publier les bans; **to c. a halt** faire halte; **to c. the roll** faire l'appel
3 *(summon) (person, fire brigade, lift)* appeler; *(meeting)* convoquer; *Law (case)* appeler; **to c. sb's attention to sth** attirer l'attention de qn sur qch; **to c. a strike** appeler à la grève; **to c. the doctor** faire venir le médecin, appeler le médecin; **I was called to the manager's office** j'ai été appelé dans le bureau du directeur; **c. me at six o'clock** *(wake me)* réveillez-moi à six heures; **to be called away on an emergency** être appelé en urgence; **she's been called away, her mother is ill** elle a dû s'absenter parce que sa mère est malade
4 *Tel (person)* téléphoner à, appeler; *(taxi)* appeler; **I called her house** j'ai téléphoné chez elle; **I got the impression it was a case of 'don't c. us, we'll c. you'** j'ai eu l'impression que ça voulait dire 'on vous écrira'
5 *(name)* appeler; **he is called Martin** *(that is his name)* il s'appelle Martin; *(by other people)* on l'appelle Martin; **c. me by my Christian** *or* **first name** appelez-moi par mon prénom; **to c. sb after sb** appeler qn comme qn; **she's called Margaret, after her grandmother** elle s'appelle Margaret, comme sa grand-mère; **to c. oneself a colonel** s'attribuer le titre de colonel; **c. yourself a carpenter!** et tu te prétends menuisier!; **and they c. themselves socialists!** et ils se disent socialistes!; **do you c. that clean?** c'est ce que tu appelles propre?; **to c. sb names** injurier qn, invectiver qn; **to c. sb a liar/a thief** traiter qn de menteur/de voleur; **we'll c. it three** mettons trois; **I c. that a dirty trick** voilà ce que j'appelle un sale tour
6 *Cards (two diamonds etc)* appeler, déclarer; **to c. spades** déclarer pique
7 *(call on)* **to c. a guarantee** faire jouer une garantie

VI 1 *(to attract attention)* **to c. to sb** appeler qn; **the bird was calling to its mother** l'oiseau appelait sa mère
2 *(summon)* **duty calls** le devoir m'appelle
3 *(visit, come to door etc)* passer; **has anyone called?** est-ce que quelqu'un est passé?; **I called at your house** je suis passé chez vous; **I must c. at the grocer's** il faut que je passe chez l'épicier; **to c. again** repasser; **the train calls at every station** le train s'arrête à toutes les gares; *Naut* **to c. at a port** *(of ship)* faire escale à un port
4 *Tel* appeler; **who's calling, please?, may I ask who's calling?** c'est de la part de qui, s'il vous plaît?; **to c. again** rappeler
5 *Cards* appeler (l'atout); *(at poker)* forcer l'adversaire à déclarer son jeu

▸▸ *Tel* **c. barring** interdiction *f* d'appels; **c. button** bouton d'appel; *Com* **c. centre** centre *m* d'appels; *Tel* **c. connection** établissement *m* d'appel; *Banking* **c. deposit** dépôt *m* à vue; *Tel* **c. diversion** transfert *m* d'appel; *Tel* **c. forwarding** redirection *f* d'appel; *Tel* **c. forwarding device** dispositif *m* de redirection d'appel; **c. girl** *(prostitute)* call-girl *f*, *pl* call-girls; *Tel* **c. holding** mise *f* en attente d'appels; *Tel* **c. key** touche *f* d'appel; *Am Radio* **c. letters** indicatif *m* d'appel *(d'une station de radio)*; *Fin* **c. money** prêts au jour le jour, argent à court terme; *St Exch* **c. option** option *f* d'achat, call *m*; *St Exch* **c. price** cours *m* du dont; *Tel* **c. screening** filtrage *m* d'appels; **c. sheet** *(in hotel etc)* feuille *f* des réveils; *Cin, TV* feuille de service; *Radio* **c. sign** indicatif d'appel *(d'une station de radio)*; *Tel* **c. waiting service** signal *m* d'appel

▸ **call back** VT SEP *(person) (summon again)*, *Tel* rappeler; *Theat (with applause)* rappeler sur scène; **to c. sb back from vacation** demander à qn de rentrer de vacances
VI 1 *(return)* repasser; **I'll c. back for it** je repasserai le prendre *ou* le chercher
2 *Tel* rappeler

▸ **call by** VI = **call round** VI **1**

▸ **call down** VT SEP **they called her down from upstairs** ils lui ont demandé de descendre; **to c. down God's wrath upon sb** appeler la colère de Dieu sur qn
VI I called down after him je l'ai appelé du haut de l'escalier/de la fenêtre/*etc*

▸ **call for** VT INSEP **1** *(summon) (person)* appeler, faire venir; *(thing)* faire apporter; *(drink etc)* commander; **to c. for help** crier au secours, appeler à l'aide
2 *(collect)* venir prendre, venir chercher; **to be called for** *(by messenger)* à remettre au messager; *(on envelope)* poste restante; *Rail* en gare
3 *(request, demand) (explanation, apology)* demander, exiger; **the opposition were calling for his resignation** l'opposition exigeait sa démission; **some union members are calling for industrial action** certains syndicalistes appellent à la grève; **the police are calling for tougher penalties** la police réclame des sanctions plus fermes; **to c. for volunteers** demander des volontaires
4 *(require) (attention, reform)* demander, réclamer, exiger; **situation that calls for tactful handling** situation qui demande à être gérée avec tact; **this calls for a celebration/ a drink!** il faut fêter/arroser ça!; **that sort of behaviour isn't called for** on se passe bien de ce genre de comportement; **that wasn't called for** ça n'était vraiment pas nécessaire

▸ **call in** VT SEP **1** *(person) (into building, office etc)* faire entrer; **c. Miss Smith, please** faites entrer Mlle Smith, s'il vous plaît; **she called the children in** *(back into the house)* elle a fait rentrer les enfants
2 *(withdraw from circulation) (coin, book)* retirer de la circulation; *(of manufacturer) (defective product)* rappeler; **to c. in one's money** faire rentrer ses fonds; **to c. in a loan** *(of bank)* demander le remboursement d'un prêt
3 *(specialist, army) (for advice, help)* faire appel à
VI 1 *(visit)* rendre visite; **to c. in at sb's house/at the grocer's** passer chez qn/chez l'épicier; **to c. in to see sb** aller/venir voir qn; **I'll c. in on my way home** je passerai en rentrant chez moi
2 *(by telephone)* passer un coup de téléphone *ou* *Fam* de fil; **nurses called in and offered to help** des infirmières ont téléphoné pour offrir leur aide; **to c. in sick** téléphoner pour prévenir qu'on est malade

▸ **call off** VT SEP **1** *(cancel) (appointment, strike, match, holiday)* annuler; *(deal)* rompre, annuler; **they were going to get married, but they called it off** ils étaient sur le point de se marier mais ils ont tout annulé; **she called it off** elle a rompu
2 *(tell to come away) (dog)* rappeler

▸ **call on** VT INSEP **1** *(request)* **to c. on sb for sth** demander instamment qch à qn, réclamer qch à qn; **to c. on sb to do sth** demander instamment à qn de faire qch, prier instamment qn de faire qch; **I c. on the government to act** je demande instamment au gouvernement d'agir; **I now c. on Mr Stewart** *(to speak)* la parole est à M. Stewart; **the limited resources the police can c. on** les ressources limitées que la police peut mettre en œuvre; **to c. on the experts/sb's services** faire appel aux *ou* avoir recours aux experts/services de qn
2 *(person) (visit)* rendre visite à; *(drop in on)* passer voir
3 *(name of God)* invoquer

▸ **call out** VT SEP **1** *(summon) (person)* faire sortir, prier de sortir; *(fire brigade)* appeler; **to c. out workers (on strike)** donner l'ordre de grève à des ouvriers
2 *(shout)* crier; **she called out the winning number** elle a annoncé le numéro gagnant

vi **1** *(shout out)* appeler; **to c. out in anger/ pain** crier de colère/douleur; **to c. out for sth** appeler pour demander qch
2 to c. out for *(urgently require)* nécessiter de façon urgente; **it's calling out for it!** c'est urgent de le faire!; *Fam* **this room is calling out for red velvet curtains** il faut à tout prix des rideaux de velours rouge dans cette pièce
▸ **call round** vi **1** *(in person)* passer; **c. round when you're in the area** passez nous/me/ *etc* voir quand vous serez dans la région
2 *(on telephone)* passer une série de coups de fil; **c. round and see if any of the local shops have any** téléphonez pour savoir si les boutiques du coin en ont
vt INSEP *(on phone)* **I've called round all her friends** j'ai appelé tous ses amis
▸ **call up** vt SEP **1** *(summon) (person)* faire monter; *Mil etc (reinforcements)* appeler
2 *(evoke) (spirit)* invoquer; *(memory)* évoquer
3 *Tel (person)* téléphoner à, appeler (au téléphone)
4 *Mil, Naut (reservist)* mobiliser; *(for military service)* appeler; **to be called up** être mobilisé/appelé
5 *Fin* **called-up capital** capital *m* appelé
6 *Comput (help screen etc)* appeler
vi **I called up after him** je l'ai appelé du bas de l'escalier/l'échelle/*etc*

callable [ˈkɔːləb(ə)l] ADJ *Fin (bond, debt)* remboursable avant échéance
▸ ▸ **c. loan** crédit *m* révocable
callbox [ˈkɔːlbɒks] N cabine *f* téléphonique
callboy [ˈkɔːlbɔɪ] N *Theat etc* avertisseur *m*
caller [ˈkɔːlər] N **1** *(visitor)* visiteur, -euse; **to be a frequent c. at sb's house** aller souvent chez qn **2** *Tel* personne *f* qui appelle (au téléphone); *Comput* appelant *m*; **did the c. say anything?** est-ce qu'il/elle a dit quelque chose?; **the vast majority of callers just need someone to talk to** la plupart des gens qui nous appellent ont juste besoin de parler; **one minute please, c.** un instant s'il vous plaît, monsieur/madame **3** *(in bingo hall)* celui/celle qui annonce les numéros gagnants
▸ ▸ *Tel* **c. display** présentation *f* du numéro de l'appelant; *Tel* **c. ID** identification *f* d'appel
calligrapher [kəˈlɪɡrəfər] N calligraphe *mf*
calligraphy [kəˈlɪɡrəfɪ] N calligraphie *f*
call-in N *Am Radio, TV* émission *f* à ligne ouverte
calling [ˈkɔːlɪŋ] N **1** *(shouting)* appel *m*; **the stallholders' c. of their wares** les cris des marchands qui vantent leurs marchandises
2 *(of meeting etc)* convocation *f* **3** *(vocation)* vocation *f* (**for** pour); **I felt no/a c. for a religious life** je n'avais pas/j'avais la vocation **4** *(profession)* profession *f*, métier *m*
▸ ▸ *Am* **c. card** *(visiting card)* carte *f* de visite; *Tel* carte téléphonique; *Fin* **c. in** *(of debt, loan)* demande *f* de remboursement immédiat; *(of currency)* retrait *m*; **c. off** *(of appointment, meeting, match, holidays)* annulation *f*, *(of deal)* rupture *f*, *(of dog, attacker)* rappel *m*; **c. up** *(of memory)* évocation *f*, *(by telephone)* appel au téléphone; *Mil* appel (sous les drapeaux)
calliper [ˈkælɪpər] N **1** *Tech* **(pair of) callipers** compas *m* de calibre *ou* à calibrer **2** *Med* attelle-étrier *f*, *pl* attelles-étriers
▸ ▸ *Tech* **c. compasses** compas de calibre *ou* à calibrer; *Med* **c. splint** attelle-étrier
callisthenics [kælɪsˈθenɪks] N gymnastique *f* rythmique VOIR GRAMMAIRE A10
callosity [kæˈlɒsɪtɪ] N *Fml* callosité *f*
callous [ˈkæləs] ADJ *(person)* dur, sans cœur; *(treatment, behaviour)* dur, brutal, -aux; *(remark)* dur; **to be c. to sb** être dur avec qn; **the**

c. way in which the government has reacted la dureté de la réaction du gouvernement; **to show a c. indifference to sth** montrer une indifférence totale pour qch
calloused [ˈkæləst] ADJ *(skin, feet, hands)* calleux
callously [ˈkæləslɪ] ADV durement
callousness [ˈkæləsnɪs] N *(of person)* dureté *f*, insensibilité *f*, manque *m* de cœur; *(of treatment, behaviour)* dureté
callout [ˈkɔːlaʊt] N *(by maintenance man)* dépannage *m*
▸ ▸ **c. charge** *(frais mpl de)* déplacement *m*; **c. maintenance insurance** assurance *f* maintenance visite
callow [ˈkæləʊ] ADJ *(youth)* sans expérience
callowness [ˈkæləʊnɪs] N manque *m* d'expérience
call-up N *Mil* appel *m* (sous les drapeaux)
▸ ▸ **c. papers** ordre *m* d'incorporation; **to receive one's c. papers** être appelé sous les drapeaux
callus [ˈkæləs] N *(on skin)* cal *m*, *pl* cals, durillon *m*
calm [kɑːm] N *(peace)*, *Naut* calme *m*; *(of person)* tranquillité *f*, sérénité *f*; **the government appealed for c.** le gouvernement appela au calme; *Naut* **flat c.** calme plat; **period of c.** accalmie *f*, *Naut, Fig* **the c. before the storm** le calme avant la tempête
ADJ *(peaceful)* calme, tranquille; *(person)* calme, posé; *(sea)* calme; *(day)* sans vent; **to remain** *or* **keep c.** rester calme; **to grow calmer** se calmer
vt *(anger, people, storm of protest etc)* calmer, apaiser; *(pain)* calmer, atténuer; **this will c. your nerves** *or* **you** cela vous calmera; **c. yourself** calmez-vous!
▸ **calm down** vi *(of person, storm)* se calmer; *(of sea, wind)* calmir, se calmer; **things have calmed down** *(after crisis, busy spell etc)* les choses se sont calmées
vt SEP *(person)* calmer
calming [ˈkɑːmɪŋ] ADJ *(effect etc)* tranquillisant, calmant
N *(of waves, anger etc)* apaisement *m*; *(of pain)* atténuation *f*
calmly [ˈkɑːmlɪ] ADV calmement; **she c. shot him** elle lui tira dessus sans sourciller; **he just c. wrote out a cheque for £50,000** il a fait un chèque de 50 000 livres sans cérémonie
calmness [ˈkɑːmnɪs] N *(of person)* tranquillité *f*, calme *m*; *(of sea)* calme
Calor Gas® [ˈkæləɡæs] N butane *m*
caloric [kəˈlɒrɪk] ADJ *Phys* calorique
calorie [ˈkælərɪ] N *Phys* calorie *f*; **to be low/ high in calories** *(of food)* être pauvre/riche en calories; **low-c. diet, c. controlled diet** régime *m* hypocalorique *ou* basses calories *ou* faible en calories; **calories per serving** nombre *m* de calories par portion; *Fam* **to watch** *or* **count the calories** surveiller sa ligne
calorific [kæləˈrɪfɪk] ADJ *Phys* calorifique
▸ ▸ *Phys* **c. value** valeur *f* calorifique
calumniate [kəˈlʌmnɪeɪt] VT *Fml* calomnier
calumny [ˈkæləmnɪ] N calomnie *f*
Calvary [ˈkælvərɪ] N **1** *(Mount)* **C.** le Calvaire
2 *Fig* **c.** calvaire *m*
calve [kɑːv] VI *(of cow)* vêler
calving [ˈkɑːvɪŋ] N *(of cow)* vêlage *m*, vêlement *m*; **at c. time** pendant le vêlement
Calvinism [ˈkælvɪnɪz(ə)m] N *Rel, Hist* calvinisme *m*
Calvinist [ˈkælvɪnɪst] N, ADJ *Rel* calviniste *mf*
calypso [kəˈlɪpsəʊ] N *Mus* calypso *m*
calyx, *pl* **calyxes, calyces** [ˈkeɪlɪks, -ɪksiːz, -ɪsiːz] N *Bot* calice *m*

CAM [kæm] N *Comput (abbr* **computer-assisted manufacture)** FAO *f*
cam [kæm] N *Tech etc* came *f*
▸ ▸ *Aut* **c. follower** poussoir *m*
camber [ˈkæmbər] N *(of road)* bombement *m*; *(of beam)* cambrure *f*, *Naut (of deck)* tonture *f*, *Aut (of wheel)* carrossage *m*; *Aviat (of wing)* flèche *f*
VT *(road surface)* bomber; *(beam)* cambrer
VI *(of road)* bomber; *(of beam)* cambrer
Cambodia [kæmˈbəʊdɪə] N Cambodge *m*
Cambodian [kæmˈbəʊdɪən] ADJ cambodgien
N **1** Cambodgien, -ienne **2** *Ling* cambodgien *m*
cambric [ˈkæmbrɪk, ˈkeɪm-] N *Tex* batiste *f*
Cambs [kæmz] *abbr* **Cambridgeshire**
camcorder [ˈkæmkɔːdər] N *Phot* caméscope® *m*
camel [ˈkæməl] N **1** *(animal)* chameau *m*; **she-c.** chamelle *f* **2** *(colour)* chameau *m inv*
▸ ▸ *Mil* **the C. Corps** les compagnies *fpl* de méharistes; **c. driver** chamelier *m*
camelhair [ˈkæməlheər] N poil *m* de chameau; **c. brush** *(for watercolour painting)* pinceau *m* en petit-gris; **c. coat** manteau *m* en poil de chameau
camellia [kəˈmiːlɪə] N camélia *m*
cameo [ˈkæmɪəʊ] N **1** *(gem)* camée *m*; **c. brooch** camée **2** *Theat, Cin (appearance)* brève apparition *f* *(par un acteur connu)*
▸ ▸ *Theat, Cin* **c. performance** brève apparition *(par un acteur connu)*; *Theat, Cin* **c. role** petit rôle *m* *(joué par un acteur connu)*
camera [ˈkæmərə] N **1** *Phot* appareil *m* photo, *pl* appareils photos; *TV, Cin* caméra *f*; **I'm no good with a c.** je ne suis pas doué pour prendre des photos; *TV, Cin* **in front of the c.** devant les caméras; *TV* **on c.** à l'écran; **off c.** hors champ; **film c.** caméra *f* **2** *Law* **in c.** à huis clos; **the trial was held in c.** le procès a eu lieu à huis clos
▸ ▸ **c. angle** angle *m* de prise de vue; **c. assistant** assistant, -ante opérateur(trice); **c. blocking** *(rehearsal)* prise *f* de repères; **c. crew** équipe *f* de tournage; **c. cue** signal *m* caméra; **c. head** tête *f* de caméra; *TV, Cin* **c. loader** clapman *m*; *TV, Cin* **c. matte** cache *m* de caméra; *Opt* **c. obscura** chambre *f* noire; **c. operator** cadreur, -euse, opérateur, -trice de prise de vue; **c. platform** plateforme *f* de prise de vue; **c. script** liste *f* des mouvements de caméra; **c. test** essai *m* (de) caméra; **c. tower** échafaudage *m* pour caméra, tour *f*, *TV, Opt* **c. tube** tube *m* analyseur; **c. unit** unité *f* de tournage
cameraman, *pl* **cameramen** [ˈkæmərəmən] N *Cin, TV* cameraman *m*, *pl* cameramen; **assistant c.** opérateur *m*
camera-ready copy N *Typ* épreuves *fpl* bonnes à filmer
camera-shy ADJ **he is c.** il n'aime pas être pris en photo; *(doesn't like being filmed)* il n'aime pas être filmé
camerawork [ˈkæmərəwɜːk] N photographie *f*, *TV, Cin* prise(s) *f (pl)* de vues, photographie; *(document)* document *m* d'exécution
Cameroon [kæməˈruːn] N **the Republic of C.** la République fédérale du Cameroun
camiknickers [ˈkæmɪnɪkəz] NPL = sousvêtement *m* féminin comprenant une culotte et une chemise
camisole [ˈkæmɪsəʊl] N caraco *m*
camomile [ˈkæməmaɪl] N *Bot, Culin* camomille *f*
▸ ▸ **c. tea** infusion *f* de camomille
camouflage [ˈkæməflɑːʒ] N *Mil etc*, *Fig* camouflage *m*
VT *Mil etc* camoufler; *Fig (one's intentions etc)* dissimuler

▸▸*Mil* **c. net(ting)** filet *m* de camouflage; **c. painting** peinture *f* de camouflage

camp¹ [kæmp] N camp *m*, campement *m*; **to break c.** lever le camp; *Fig* **to go over to the other c.** passer dans l'autre camp; *Fig* **to have a foot in both camps** avoir des intérêts dans les deux camps; **gipsy c.** camp *ou* campement de gitans; **(holiday) c.** camp de vacances; *(for children)* ≃ colonie *f* de vacances

VI camper

▸▸ **c. bed** lit *m* de camp; **c. chair** pliant *m*, chaise *f* pliante; **c. counsellor** moniteur, -trice; **c. follower** *Mil* = civil *m* qui accompagne une armée pour rendre des services; *(prostitute)* prostituée *f*, fille *f* à soldats; *Fig (supporter)* compagnon *m* de route; **c. site** camp; **c. stool** pliant, chaise pliante
▸ **camp out** VI camper

camp² *Fam* ADJ **1** *(affected)* affecté; *(suggesting homosexuality)* efféminé; *(theatrical)* théâtral, -aux; *Hum* **he's as c. as a row of tents** il fait très grande folle **2** *(kitsch) (decor)* kitsch

VT **to c. it up** forcer la dose

campaign [kæm'peɪn] N campagne *f*; **on c.** en campagne; **to lead** *or* **conduct a c. against sb** mener (une) campagne contre qn; **advertising c.** campagne publicitaire
VI *Mil* faire (une)/des campagne(s); *Pol* faire campagne; **she campaigned on an anti-drug platform** elle a axé sa campagne sur la lutte contre la drogue; **they campaigned for his release** ils ont mené une campagne pour sa libération; **campaigning journalism** journalisme *m* militant
▸▸*Mil* **c. medal** médaille *f* commémorative

campaigner [kæm'peɪnər] N *(activist)* militant, -ante; **old c.** *Mil* vieux soldat *m*, vieux troupier *m*; *Fig* vétéran *m*

campanologist [kæmpə'nɒlədʒɪst] N carillonneur, -euse

campanology [kæmpə'nɒlədʒɪ] N art *m* du carillon

campanula [kæm'pænjʊlə] N *(flower)* campanule *f*

camper ['kæmpər] N *(person)* campeur, -euse; *(vehicle)* camping-car *m*, *pl* camping-cars
▸▸ **c. van** camping-car

campfire ['kæmpfaɪər] N feu *m* de camp

camphor ['kæmfər] N camphre *m*
▸▸ **c. oil** essence *f* de camphre; **c. tree** camphrier *m*

camphorated ['kæmfəreɪtɪd] ADJ *(oil etc)* camphré

camping ['kæmpɪŋ] N camping *m*; **to go c.** faire du camping
▸▸ **c. equipment, c. gear** matériel *m ou* équipement *m* de camping; **c. ground** terrain *m* de camping; **c. holiday** vacances *fpl* (en) camping; **c. site** (terrain de) camping; **c. stove** camping-gaz® *m inv*

camping-caravanning N campage-caravanage *m*, camping-caravaning *m*

campion ['kæmpɪən] N *(plant)* lychnide *f*, lychnis *m*; **white c.** compagnon *m* blanc

campus ['kæmpəs] N campus *m* (universitaire); **they live on c.** *(of students)* ils vivent sur le campus

camshaft ['kæmʃɑːft] N *Tech* arbre *m* à came(s)
▸▸ **c. drive** entraînement *m* d'arbre à cames

can¹ [kæn] N **1** *(for drink, esp American food)* boîte *f*
2 *(for petrol, oil, water etc)* bidon *m*; *(for milk, film)* boîte *f*, *Fig Fam* **to carry the c.** payer les pots cassés; *Fam* **I'm not carrying the c. for you** je ne vais pas payer les pots cassés pour toi; *Fam* **in the c.** *(of film)* en boîte; *Fig (of deal etc)* dans la poche; *Fig*

Fam **c. of worms** problème *m* insoluble; *Fig Fam* **don't let's open up that c. of worms** ne nous occupons pas de ce problème pour le moment; *Am* **trash** *or* **garbage c.** poubelle *f*, **watering c.** arrosoir *m*
3 *Fam* **cans** *(earphones)* casque *m*
4 *Sl (prison)* taule *f*, tôle *f*
5 *Am Sl (lavatory)* **the c.** les chiottes *fpl*
6 *Am Sl (buttocks)* fesses *fpl*; **to kick sb in the c.** botter les fesses à qn
VT **(-nn-) 1** *(put in cans) (meat etc)* mettre en boîte *ou* en conserve; **canned fruit** fruits en conserve *ou* en boîte; *Am Sl* **c. it!** *(shut up!)* la ferme! **2** *Am Sl (dismiss) (person)* virer
▸▸ **c. opener** ouvre-boîtes *m inv*

CAN² *(stressed* [kæn], *unstressed* [k(ə)n]*)*

pouvoir **1, 3–6** ▪ savoir **2**

MODAL AUX V VOIR GRAMMAIRE A58–9; B39–40 *(pr* can; *neg* cannot ['kænɒt], *Am* can not ['kæn'nɒt]; *pt, cond* could [kʊd]; *no inf, prp, pp; defective parts are supplied from* to be able to; cannot *and* could not *are often contracted into* can't [kɑːnt], couldn't ['kʊdnt]) **1** *(be able to)* pouvoir; **I c. do it** je peux le faire; **we cannot** *or* *Am* **c. not possibly do it** nous ne pouvons absolument pas le faire; **I will come as soon/as often as I c.** je viendrai aussitôt/ aussi souvent que possible; **he will do what he c.** il fera ce qu'il pourra; **I will help you all I c., I will do all I c. to help you** je vous aiderai de mon mieux, je ferai tout mon possible pour vous aider; **I can't very well accept it** m'est difficile d'accepter; *Fam* **I'd like it finished by tomorrow – c. do!** j'aimerais que ce soit fini demain – aucun problème!; *Fam* **no c. do** c'est impossible; **(it) can't be helped!** tant pis!, on n'y peut rien!; **it can't be done** il est impossible de le faire; **how could he say that?** comment a-t-il pu dire cela?; **how c. you say that?** comment peux-tu dire une chose pareille?; **what c. it be?** qu'est-ce que cela peut bien être?; **c. it be true?** serait-ce vrai?; **(it) could be** c'est possible; **I never could understand maths** je n'ai jamais été capable de comprendre les maths; **what can he want?** qu'est-ce qu'il peut bien me/ nous/etc vouloir?; **how could you!** comment avez-vous pu faire une chose pareille?; **he could not have been kinder** il n'aurait pu être plus aimable
2 *(know how to)* savoir; **I c. swim** je sais nager; **a man who c. cook** un homme qui sait faire la cuisine; **she c. play the violin** elle sait jouer du violon
3 *(indicating possibility)* **you don't know how hot it c. get** vous ne savez pas à quel point il peut faire chaud; **the crossing c. be rough** il arrive que la traversée soit mauvaise; **adult animals c. grow to 20 feet** l'animal adulte peut mesurer jusqu'à 6 mètres; **you can't be serious!** tu plaisantes!
4 *(indicating permissibility)* pouvoir; **when c. I move in?** quand est-ce que je peux emménager?; **could you be quiet please?** pourriez-vous vous taire, s'il vous plaît?; **c. I ask you something?** est-ce que je peux vous demander quelque chose?; **you can't smoke in here** il est défendu de fumer ici
5 *(asking help)* pouvoir; **c. you help me?** peux-tu m'aider?; *(asking more politely)* pourrais-tu m'aider?; **could you get me some water?** pourriez-vous m'apporter de l'eau?
6 *(making suggestion)* pouvoir; **we could always telephone** nous pourrions toujours téléphoner; **you could go to the beach** tu pourrais aller à la plage; **I c. help if you like** je peux t'aider si tu veux
7 *(with 'see', 'hear' etc: not translated)* **I c. see nothing** je ne vois rien; **c. you see that hill?** est-ce que tu vois cette colline?; **I could hear them talking** je les entendais parler; **I c. see**

you don't believe me je vois bien que vous ne me croyez pas; **how c. you tell?** comment le savez-vous?
8 *(in conditional)* **he could have done it** il aurait pu le faire; **I could not have asked for anything better** je n'aurais pas désiré mieux; **I could weep/could have wept** j'ai/ j'avais envie de pleurer; **I could have smacked his face!** je l'aurais giflé!; **you could have warned me!** tu aurais pu me prévenir!
9 *(elliptically)* **I cannot but believe him** je suis bien forcé de le croire; **you c. but try** vous pouvez toujours essayer

Canada ['kænədə] N Canada *m*; **in C.** au Canada
▸▸ **C. Day** Fête *f* du Canada *(anniversaire de l'indépendance canadienne, le 1er juillet)*; *Orn* **C. goose** bernache *f* du Canada

Canadian [kə'neɪdɪən] ADJ canadien
N Canadien, -ienne
▸▸*Ling* **C. English** anglais *m* du Canada; *Ling* **C. French** français *m* du Canada

Canadianism [kə'neɪdɪənɪz(ə)m] N canadianisme *m*

canal [kə'næl] N **1** *(waterway)* canal *m*, -aux; **ship c.** canal maritime **2** *Anat etc* canal *m*, -aux; **auditory c.** conduit *m* auditif
▸▸ **c. barge** péniche *f*; **c. boat** péniche; *Geog* **the C. zone** la zone du canal de Panamá

canalization [kænəlaɪ'zeɪʃən] N canalisation *f*

canalize ['kænəlaɪz] VT *(river etc), Fig* canaliser; **to c. one's efforts/energy into sth** canaliser ses efforts/son énergie dans qch

canapé ['kænəpeɪ] N *Culin* canapé *m*

canard ['kænɑːd, kə'nɑːd] N *Lit* canard *m*, fausse nouvelle *f*

Canary [kə'neərɪ] N **the C. Islands, the Canaries** les îles *fpl* Canaries

canary [kə'neərɪ] N *(bird)* serin *m*, canari *m*
▸▸*Bot* **c. seed** millet *m*; **c. yellow** jaune *m* canari

canasta [kə'næstə] N *Cards* canasta *f*

cancan ['kænkæn] N cancan *m*
▸▸ **c. dancer** danseuse *f* de cancan

cancel ['kæns(ə)l] (**-ll-**, *Am* **-l-**) VT **1** *(meeting, reservation, message, cheque, debt)* annuler; *(order)* Com annuler; *Mil* lever; *(deal, contract)* annuler, résilier; *(train)* supprimer; *(stamp)* oblitérer; **to c. each other** *(of two book-keeping entries)* s'annuler; **500, no c. that, 350 … 500**, ou plutôt, 350 … **2** *Math (factors in fraction)* éliminer
VI **1** *(having made booking)* se décommander **2** *Comput* s'annuler; **press 'esc' to c.** appuyez sur 'Échap' pour annuler; **c. entry** *(command)* annulation d'entrée
▸▸*Comput* **c. button** case *f* 'annuler'
▸ **cancel out** VT SEP *Math (term)* annuler; **to c. each other out** s'annuler; **inflation cancelled out the increase in salary** l'inflation a annulé la hausse des salaires

cancellation [kænsə'leɪʃən] N annulation *f*, *Com (of order, sale, contract)* annulation, résiliation *f*, *(of stamp)* oblitération *f*, **there have been several cancellations** *(in restaurant, hotel)* il y a plusieurs réservations qui ont été annulées
▸▸ **c. charge** frais *mpl* d'annulation; **c. clause** clause *f* d'annulation *ou* de résiliation; **c. fee** frais d'annulation; **c. form** bon *m ou* bulletin *m* d'annulation; **c. holiday** = vacances *fpl* annulées et soldées

cancer ['kænsər] N **1** *Med* cancer *m*; **to have c.** avoir un *ou* le cancer; **c. of the lung/skin, lung/skin c.** cancer du poumon/de la peau; **c. of the pancreas** cancer du pancréas; *Fig* **we must remove the c. of militarism** il faut enrayer le cancer du militarisme **2** *Astrol* **C. Cancer** *m*; **to be (a) C.** être (du) Cancer **3**

Geog **the Tropic of C.** le tropique du Cancer
▸▸**c. patient** cancéreux, -euse; **c. research** oncologie *f*, cancérologie *f*; **c. specialist** cancérologue *mf*; *Fam Hum* **c. stick** clope *f*

cancer-causing [-kɔːzɪŋ] ADJ *(substance etc)* cancérigène

cancerous ['kæns(ə)rəs] ADJ cancéreux

candelabra, *pl* **candelabras** [kændɪ'lɑːbrə, -əz], **candelabrum,** *pl* **candelabra** [kændɪ-'lɑːbrəm, -ə] N candélabre *m*

candid ['kændɪd] ADJ franc, *f* franche, sincère
▸▸**c. camera** caméra *f* invisible *ou* cachée; **c. camera shot** = photo *f* prise à l'insu de la personne photographiée

> Note that the French word **candide** is a false friend and is never a translation for the English word **candid**. It means **ingenuous**.

candida ['kændɪdə] N *Med* candidose *f*

candidacy ['kændɪdəsɪ] N candidature *f*

candidate ['kændɪdeɪt] N *(for job, office)* candidat, -ate (**for** à); **to stand as c. for sth** se présenter comme candidat à qch, poser sa candidature à qch; **presidential c.** candidat aux élections présidentielles; **successful candidates will have …** les candidats retenus auront …

candidature ['kændɪdətʃər] N *Br* candidature *f*

candidiasis ['kændɪdɪ'eɪsɪs] N *Med* muguet *m*, candidose *f*

candidly ['kændɪdlɪ] ADV franchement, sincèrement

candidness ['kændɪdnɪs] N franchise *f*, sincérité *f*

candied ['kændɪd] ADJ *Culin* glacé, confit (au sucre)
▸▸**c. peel** zeste *m* confit

candle ['kænd(ə)l] N bougie *f*, *Old-fashioned* chandelle *f*, *(lit in church)* cierge *m*; *Fig* **to burn the c. at both ends** brûler la chandelle par les deux bouts; *Fig* **he can't hold a c. to you** il ne vous arrive pas à la cheville
▸▸**c. grease** suif *m*; **c. power** intensité *f* lumineuse

candlelight ['kænd(ə)llaɪt] N lumière *f* de bougie; **by c.** à la chandelle, à la bougie

candle-lit ADJ *(room)* éclairé à la bougie; *(meal)* aux chandelles

Candlemas ['kænd(ə)lməs] N *Rel* Chandeleur *f*

candlestick ['kænd(ə)lstɪk] N *(tall)* chandelier *m*; *(low)* bougeoir *m*

candlewick ['kænd(ə)lwɪk] N **1** *Tex* candlewick *m*, chenille *f* de coton; **c. bedspread/dressing gown** dessus *m* de lit/robe *f* de chambre en chenille de coton **2** *(of candle)* mèche *f* de bougie *ou* de chandelle

can-do ADJ dynamique, entreprenant; **c. spirit** esprit *m* de battant *ou* de gagneur

candour, *Am* **candor** ['kændər] N franchise *f*, sincérité *f*

> Note that the French word **candeur** is a false friend and is never a translation for the English word **candour**. It means **ingenuousness**.

candy ['kændɪ] N **1** *(sugar)* **c.** sucre *m* candi; **stick of (sugar) c.** sucre d'orge **2** *Am (sweet)* bonbon *m*; *(sweets)* bonbons; *Fam* **it's like taking c. from a baby** c'est simple comme bonjour
VT *(sugar)* faire candir; *(fruit)* glacer
VI *(of sugar)* se candir, se cristalliser
▸▸*Am* **c. apple** pomme *f* d'amour; *Am* **c. bar** barre *f* chocolatée; *Am* **c. store** confiserie *f*

candyfloss ['kændɪflɒs] N *Br Culin* barbe à papa

candy-striped ADJ *Tex* à raies (de deux couleurs)

candy-striper [-straɪpər] N *Am Med Fam* = bénévole *mf*

cane [keɪn] N **1** *Bot (of bamboo)* (canne *f* de) bambou *m*; *(of rattan)* rotin *m*; *(of raspberry bush)* tige *f*, **c. furniture** meubles *mpl* en rotin; **c. chair** siège *m* en rotin; **c.-seated chair** chaise *f* cannée **2** *(walking stick)* canne *f* **3** *(for punishment)* verge *f*, baguette *f*, badine *f*; **to get the c.** recevoir des coups de verge *ou* de baguette
VT **1** *(person, pupil)* *(beat)* donner des coups de verge *ou* de baguette à **2** *Sl (defeat)* démolir **3** *Br Fam* **to c. it** se bourrer *ou* se pinter la gueule **4** *(chair)* canner
▸▸**c. sugar** sucre *m* de canne

caned [keɪnd] ADJ *Br Fam (drunk)* bourré comme un coing

canine ['keɪnaɪn, 'kæ-] ADJ ATTRIB de chien; *(race, species)* canin; **c. devotion** dévotion *f* de chien
N **1** *Anat (tooth)* canine *f* **2** canines *(animals)* canidés *mpl*
▸▸*Anat* **c. tooth** canine

caning ['keɪnɪŋ] N **1** *(punishment)* coups *mpl* de verge *ou* de baguette *(comme châtiment corporel)* **2** *Sl* **to get a c.** *(be defeated)* se faire démolir **3** *(in furniture)* cannage *m*

canister ['kænɪstər] N boîte *f* (en fer blanc)

canker ['kæŋkər] N **1** *Med, Fig* chancre *m* **2** *Vet (in horse's hoof)* crapaud *m*; *(of dog etc)* gale *f* de l'oreille **3** *Bot* chancre *m*; *(in wood)* nécrose *f*

cankerworm ['kæŋkəwɜːm] N ver *m* rongeur (des plantes)

cannabis ['kænəbɪs] N cannabis *m*
▸▸**c. resin** résine *f* de cannabis

canned [kænd] ADJ **1** *TV, Cin (laughter, applause)* préenregistré; *(music)* enregistré, en conserve **2** *Sl (drunk)* soûl, beurré; **to get c.** se soûler, se beurrer

cannelloni [kænɪ'ləʊnɪ] N cannelloni *mpl*

cannery ['kænərɪ] N conserverie *f*

cannibal ['kænɪb(ə)l] N, ADJ cannibale *mf*

cannibalism ['kænɪbəlɪz(ə)m] N cannibalisme *m*

cannibalization [kænɪbəlaɪ'zeɪʃ(ə)n] N *Mktg, Aut* cannibalisation *f*

cannibalize ['kænɪbəlaɪz] VT *Tech, Aut etc (machine etc)* récupérer des pièces en bon état sur, cannibaliser; *Mktg (product)* cannibaliser; **cannibalized income** revenu *m* cannibalisé

cannily ['kænɪlɪ] ADV *esp Scot (cautiously)* prudemment, avec circonspection; *(cleverly)* avec ruse

canning ['kænɪŋ] N *(of food)* mise *f* en conserve
▸▸**c. factory** conserverie *f*, fabrique *f* de conserves; **c. industry** conserverie, industrie *f* de la conserve

cannon ['kænən] N **1** *(usu inv) Mil* canon *m*; *Am Fig* **he's a loose c.** on ne sait pas trop ce qu'il va faire **2** *Billiards* carambolage *m*; **c. off the cushion** bricole *f*
VI *Billiards* faire un carambolage, caramboler; **to c. off the cushion** *(of player)* jouer la bricole
▸▸*Mil* **c. fodder** chair *f* à canon; *Billiards* **c. shot** *(ball)* boulet *m* de canon
▸**cannon into** VT INSEP se heurter à

cannonade [kænə'neɪd] N *Mil Old-fashioned* canonnade *f*

cannonball ['kænənbɔːl] N *Mil, Fig* boulet *m* de canon; *Tennis* **c. serve** service *m* boulet de canon

cannot ['kænɒt] *see* **can²**

cannula ['kænələ] N *Med* canule *f*

canny ['kænɪ] ADJ *esp Scot (cautious)* prudent, circonspect; *(aware)* avisé; *(clever)* rusé; *(thrifty)* économe; **c. answer** réponse *f* de Normand

canoe [kə'nuː] N canoë *m*; **(dugout) c.** pirogue *f*, *Fig* **to paddle one's own c.** mener seul sa barque
VI *(pp, pt* canoed; *prp* canoeing) faire du canoë; **to c. up the river** remonter la rivière en canoë

canoeing [kə'nuːɪŋ] N canoë *m*; **to go c.** faire du canoë; **c. holiday** raid *m ou* randonnée *f* en canoë-kayak; **c. trip** voyage *m* en canoë

canoeist [kə'nuːɪst] N canoéiste *mf*

canon¹ ['kænən] N **1** *Rel (of mass etc)* canon *m* **2** *Lit (rule)* canon *m* **3** *Liter (of author)* œuvre *f*; **the literary c.** les classiques *mpl* **4** *Mus* canon *m*
▸▸*Rel* **c. law** droit *m* canon

canon² N *Rel (priest)* chanoine *m*

canonical [kə'nɒnɪk(ə)l] ADJ **1** *Rel (right, epistle, residence etc)* canonique; *Fig (accepted)* autorisé, accepté **2** *Mus (passage)* en canon
NPL **canonicals** vêtements *mpl* sacerdotaux
▸▸**c. dress** vêtements sacerdotaux; **c. hours** *(Catholic)* heures *fpl* canoniales; *(Church of England)* = heures pendant lesquelles la célébration des mariages est autorisée (entre 8 heures et 18 heures)

canonization [kænənaɪ'zeɪʃən] N *Rel* canonisation *f*

canonize ['kænənaɪz] VT *Rel* canoniser

canoodle [kə'nuːd(ə)l] VI *esp Hum* se faire des mamours

canopy ['kænəpɪ] N *(over throne)* dais *m*; *(over bed)* baldaquin *m*; *(over fireplace)* hotte *f*, *(over doorway)* auvent *m*, marquise *f*, *(of parachute)* calotte *f*, voilure *f*, *Aviat (of cockpit)* verrière *f*, *Archit (of roof, over window)* gâble *m*, gâble *m*; *Rel (above altar etc)* ciel *m*; *Fig* **c. of leaves** voûte *f* de feuillage *ou* de verdure

cant¹ [kænt] N **1** *(of thieves, beggars)* argot *m* **2** *(hypocritical talk)* langage *m* hypocrite; **c. phrase** cliché *m*
VI **1** *(of thieves, beggars etc)* parler en argot **2** *(talk hypocritically)* faire l'hypocrite

cant² N **1** *Carp, Constr etc (slope)* inclinaison *f*, dévers *m*; *Rail (of outer rail)* surélévation *f*, dévers; **to give sth a c.** incliner qch; **to have a c.** pencher **2** *Archit, Carp (edge)* chanfrein *m*, biseau *m*
VT **1** *(turn over)* renverser, retourner; *Naut (boat for repair)* chavirer **2** *(tilt) (beam, pillar)* dévoyer, incliner; *(barrel)* incliner, pencher; *Rail (outer rail)* surhausser **3** *Carp etc (edge)* biseauter, écorner
VI **1** *Carp, Constr etc* s'incliner **2** *(tilt)* se trouver incliné, pencher

can't [kɑːnt] *(abbr* **cannot)** *see* **can²**

Cantab ['kæntæb] *(abbr* **Cantabrigiensis)** de l'université de Cambridge

cantaloup(e) ['kæntəluːp] N *(melon)* cantaloup *m*

cantankerous [kæn'tæŋk(ə)rəs] ADJ *(bad-tempered)* revêche, acariâtre; *(irritable)* querelleur, -euse

cantata [kæn'tɑːtə] N *Mus* cantate *f*

canteen [kæn'tiːn] N **1** *(in school, factory etc)* cantine *f* **2** *Mil (shop)* magasin *m* à l'usage des soldats; *(water bottle)* bidon *m*; *(mess tin)* gamelle *f* **3** **c. of cutlery** ménagère *f*

canter ['kæntər] N *Horseriding* petit galop *m*; *Fig* **let's have a quick c. through tomorrow's agenda** revoyons rapidement l'emploi du temps de demain
VI *Horseriding* aller au petit galop; *Fig* **to c.**

through a speech *(do quickly)* expédier un discours; **to c. through an exam** *(do easily)* réussir un examen haut la main
▸ **vt** *(horse)* faire aller au petit galop

Canterbury ['kæntəb(ə)rɪ] **N** Canterbury; *Hist* Cantorbéry
▸▸ **C. bell(s)** *(flower)* campanule *f*

canticle ['kæntɪk(ə)l] **N** cantique *m*

cantilever ['kæntɪliːvər] **N** *Archit* encorbellement *m*; *Aviat* cantilever *m*
▸▸ *Constr etc* **c. beam** poutre *f* en porte-à-faux; **c. bridge** pont *m* cantilever

canto ['kæntəʊ] **N** *Liter (of poem)* chant *m*

canton ['kæntɒn] **N** canton *m*

cantonal ['kæntən(ə)l] **ADJ** cantonal, -aux

Cantonese [kæntə'niːz] **ADJ** cantonais
N 1 Cantonais, -aise **2** *Ling* cantonais *m*

cantonization [kæntənaɪ'zeɪʃən] **N** morcellement *m*

cantonment [kæn'tuːnmənt] **N** cantonnement *m*

cantor ['kæntɔːr] **N** *Rel* chantre *m*

Canuck [kə'nʌk, kə'nʊk] **N** *Pej* Canadien, -ienne français(e)

canula ['kænələ] **N** *Med* canule *f*

canvas ['kænvəs] **N 1** *Tex* (grosse) toile *f*; *(for tapestry)* canevas *m*; *Mil etc* **under c.** sous la tente; **c. bucket** seau *m* en toile; **c. shoes** chaussures *fpl* de toile **2** *Art (material, painting)* toile *f* **3** *Boxing* tapis *m* **4** *(sails)* voile(s) *f(pl)* **under c.** sous voiles

> Attention: ne pas confondre avec le verbe **to canvass.**

canvass ['kænvəs] **vt 1** *Pol, Com (solicit) (votes, orders)* solliciter; **to c. sb** *(for vote)* solliciter la voix de qn *(en faisant du porte-à-porte)*; *(for custom)* solliciter la clientèle de qn; *(for support in job application etc)* solliciter l'appui de qn; *Com* **to c. a client** démarcher un client; *Pol* **to c. a district** faire une tournée électorale dans une région **2** *(debate, discuss)* discuter **3** *(get opinion of)* sonder; **to c. opinions** sonder l'opinion (**on** à propos de) **4** *Am Pol (inspect) (votes)* pointer, vérifier
▸ **vi 1** *Pol* faire campagne, faire une tournée électorale; **candidates were out canvassing today** les candidats ont fait une tournée électorale aujourd'hui; **I'm canvassing on behalf of the Labour Party** je fais campagne pour le Parti travailliste **2** *Com* faire du démarchage; **to c. for customers** prospecter un quartier/une région en y recherchant la clientèle
N = canvassing

> Attention: ne pas confondre avec le nom **canvas.**

canvasser ['kænvəsər] **N** *Pol* = personne *f* qui sollicite les voix des électeurs en faisant du porte-à-porte; *Com* prospecteur, -trice; *(door-to-door)* représentant, -ante, démarcheur, -euse; **no canvassers** *(notice on door)* démarchage interdit

canvassing ['kænvəsɪŋ] **N** *Pol (of votes)* démarchage *m* électoral; *Com (of orders)* démarchage; *(for support in job application etc)* sollicitation *f* d'appui

canyon ['kænjən] **N** *Geog* canyon *m*, cañon *m*

canyoning ['kænjənɪŋ] **N** *Sport* canyoning *m*

CAP [siːeɪ'piː] **N** *EU (abbr* **Common Agricultural Policy)** PAC *f*

cap¹ [kæp] **N 1** *(headgear)* bonnet *m*; *(with peak)* casquette *f*, *(of university graduate, jockey)* toque *f*, **swimming c.** bonnet de bain; *Sport* **to win one's c.** être sélectionné

dans l'équipe nationale; *Univ* **in c. and gown** en costume d'apparat; *Fig* **to come/go c. in hand** se présenter chapeau bas *ou* humblement (**to sb** devant qn); *Fig* **if the c. fits(, wear it)!** qui se sent morveux se mouche!; *Fig* **to put on one's thinking c.** réfléchir, méditer la question; *Old-fashioned Fam* **to set one's c. at sb** jeter son dévolu sur qn
2 *(cover) (of pen, tyre valve)* capuchon *m*; *(of pump)* calotte *f*, *(of bottle)* capsule *f*, *Phot (for lens)* capuchon, bouchon *m*; *Tech (protective)* chapeau *m*; *(of bearing, valve)* chapeau, couvercle *m*; *(for tooth)* couche *f* d'émail; **(Dutch) c.** *(contraceptive)* diaphragme *m* (contraceptif)
3 *(upper part) (of column)* chapiteau *m*; *(of mushroom)* chapeau *m*
4 *(for toy gun)* amorce *f*, capsule *f*; *Am Sl (bullet)* bastos *f*, **percussion c.** amorce
5 *Orn (of bird)* capuchon *m*
6 *(spending limit)* plafond *m*
▸ **vt** (**-pp-**) **1** *(cover)* recouvrir (**sth with sth** qch de qch); *(bottle)* capsuler; **the mountain was capped with snow** le sommet de la montagne était recouvert de neige; **to c. a tooth** mettre une couche d'émail sur une dent
2 *(surpass, do better than)* surpasser; **to c. a quotation** renchérir sur une citation; **that caps everything** *or* **the lot** *or* **it all!** ça c'est le comble! *ou* le bouquet!; **c. that!** tu n'es pas cap de faire mieux!
3 *Scot, New Zealand Sch (candidate)* conférer un diplôme à
4 *Sport* **to be capped for England** être sélectionné dans l'équipe d'Angleterre
5 *Admin (impose limit on) (spending)* limiter; *(borough etc)* limiter les dépenses de
6 *Am Sl (shoot)* descendre

cap² **N** *Typ Fam* majuscule *f*; **put in small caps** à imprimer en petites capitales

capability [keɪpə'bɪlɪtɪ] **N** capacité *f* (**to do sth** de faire qch); **we have the military c. to ...** nous avons les capacités militaires de ...; **to have outstanding/limited capabilities** *(of person)* être très doué/avoir des moyens limités

capable ['keɪpəb(ə)l] **ADJ 1** capable (**of sth** de qch; **of doing sth** de faire qch); **to show what one is c. of** montrer ce dont on est capable; **c. of love** capable d'aimer; **the machine is c. of producing 300 items a minute** cette machine a une capacité de production de 300 pièces à la minute; **she's not c. of lying** elle est incapable de mentir; **that man's c. of anything** cet homme est capable de tout **2** *(competent)* capable, compétent; **the business is in c. hands** l'affaire est entre de bonnes mains **3** *Fml* **c. of improvement** susceptible d'amélioration *ou* d'être amélioré

capably ['keɪpəblɪ] **ADV** avec compétence, d'une manière compétente

capacious [kə'peɪʃəs] **ADJ** vaste, spacieux; *(clothing)* ample

capacitance [kə'pæsɪtəns] **N** *Elec* capacité *f*

capacitate [kə'pæsɪteɪt] **vt** *Law* donner pouvoir *ou* qualité à (**to act** pour agir)

capacitor [kə'pæsɪtər] **N** *Elec* condensateur *m*

capacity [kə'pæsɪtɪ] **N 1** *(of cylinder, tank, hotel, theatre, train, stadium etc)* capacité *f*; *(of barrel, drum, cask)* contenance *f*; **there was a c. crowd at the match** le stade était plein *ou* bondé pour le match; **we played to c. audiences** on a fait salle comble; **there was a c. audience at the theatre** le théâtre était comble; **the stadium has a c. of 50,000** le stade peut accueillir 50 000 personnes; *Theat, Sport etc* **to play to c.** jouer à guichets fermés; *Fam* **he has a remarkable c. for alcohol/beer** il peut absorber des quantités

extraordinaires d'alcool/de bière
2 *Ind etc (output)* rendement *m*; **to work at (full) c.** travailler à plein rendement; **production c.** capacité *f* de production
3 *Elec* capacité *f*
4 *(aptitude)* **c. for work** capacité *f* de travail; **he has no c. for love** il est incapable d'aimer; **to be beyond sb's c.** dépasser les compétences de qn; **to be within sb's c.** être dans les possibilités de qn; **to the utmost of my c.** dans la mesure de mes moyens
5 *Law* **to have c./no c. to act** avoir/ne pas avoir capacité pour agir
6 *(position)* **in the c. of ...** en qualité de ...; **to act in one's official c.** agir dans le cadre de ses fonctions; **in my c. as chairwoman** en ma qualité de présidente
▸▸ **c. occupancy** *(of hotel etc)* occupation *f* maximale; *Ind etc* **c. utilization** rentabilisation *f*

caparison [kə'pærɪs(ə)n] *Hist* **N** caparaçon *m*
▸ **vt** caparaçonner

cape¹ [keɪp] **N** *(cloak)* pèlerine *f*, cape *f*, *(small)* collet *m*; *(of priest)* camail *m*, *pl* camails

cape² **N** *Geog* cap *m*, promontoire *m*
▸▸ **C. Coloured** métis, -isse sud-africain(e); **the C. of Good Hope** le cap de Bonne-Espérance; **C. Town** Le Cap

caper¹ ['keɪpər] **N 1** *Bot, Culin (bud)* câpre *f* **2** *(plant)* câprier *m*

caper² **N 1** *(movement)* cabriole *f*, gambade *f*, **to cut a c.** faire des cabrioles **2** *(prank)* farce *f*, *Fam* bonne rigolade *f*, **I've had enough of his capers** j'en ai assez de ses bêtises; **what a c.!** *(fuss)* quel cirque! **3** *Sl (robbery)* hold-up *m inv*
▸ **vi** **to c. (about)** faire des cabrioles, cabrioler, gambader

capercaillie, capercailzie [kæpə'keɪlɪ] **N** *(bird)* grand tétras *m*, (grand) coq *m* de bruyère

capful ['kæpfʊl] **N** *(of liquid, disinfectant etc)* plein bouchon *m*

capillary [kə'pɪlərɪ] **ADJ** *(tube, pressure etc)* capillaire; *Anat* **the c. vessels** les vaisseaux *mpl* capillaires
NPL *Anat* **the capillaries** les capillaires *mpl*

capital ['kæpɪt(ə)l] **ADJ 1** *(principal)* capital, -aux; **a c. A** un A majuscule; *Fam* **he's lazy with a c. L** c'est un paresseux avec un grand P **2** *(important)* capital, -aux; **of c. importance** d'une importance capitale **3** *Old-fashioned Br Fam (excellent)* excellent
N 1 *Typ* capitale *f*, majuscule *f* **2** *(city)* capitale *f* **3** *Fin* capital *m*, capitaux *mpl*, fonds *mpl*, *(assets)* avoir *m*; **to live on one's c.** vivre sur son capital; *Fig* **to make c. out of sth** profiter *ou* tirer parti de qch; *Fig* **they're trying to make political c. out of the scandal** ils essaient de récupérer ce scandale **4** *Archit* chapiteau *m*
▸▸ *Fin* **c. assets** actif *m* immobilisé, immobilisations *fpl*; *Fin* **c. budget** budget *m* d'investissement; *Fin* **c. charge** intérêt *m* des capitaux (investis); **c. city** capitale *f*; *Fin* **c. contribution** apport *m* en capital, dotation *f* en capital, apport de capitaux; *Law* **c. crime** crime *m* capital *ou* puni de mort; *Acct* **c. employed** capital engagé, capitaux permanents; *Acct, Fin* **c. equipment** biens *mpl* d'équipement, capitaux fixes; **c. error** erreur *f* fatale; *Fin* **c. expenditure** mise *f* de fonds, investissements *mpl* (en immobilisations), dépenses *fpl* d'équipement; *Fin* **c. gain** plus-value *f* (en capital), *pl* plus-values; **to make a c. gain on sth** réaliser une plus-value sur qch; *Fin* **c. gains tax** impôt *m* sur les plus-values (en capital); *Fin* **c. goods** biens d'équipement *ou* d'investissement; *Fin* **c. grants** subventions *fpl* en capital; *Fin*

c. growth croissance *m* du capital; *Fin* **c. injection** injection *f* de capital, injection de capitaux; *Fin* **c. investment** mise de fonds; *Fin* **c. items** biens capitaux; **c. letter** (lettre *f*) capitale, (lettre) majuscule; *Fin* **c. levy** impôt *ou* prélèvement *m* sur le capital; *Fin* **c. loss** moins-value *f*, *pl* moins-values; *Fin* **c. market** marché *m* des capitaux; *Law* **c. offence** crime capital *ou* puni de mort; *Law* **c. punishment** peine *f* capitale, peine de mort; *Fin* **c. reserves** profits *mpl* mis en réserve, réserves *fpl* non distribuées; *Fin* **c. share** part *f* sociale; *Fin* **c. tax** impôt sur le capital; **c. transfer** transfert *m* de capitaux; *Fin Formerly* **c. transfer tax** droits *mpl* de mutation; *Fin* **c. turnover** rotation *f* des capitaux

capital-intensive ADJ *(industry etc)* qui nécessite un investissement important

capitalism [ˈkæpɪtəlɪz(ə)m] N capitalisme *m*

capitalist(ic) [ˈkæpɪtəlɪst, -ˈlɪstɪk] ADJ *(system, society etc)* capitaliste

capitalization [kæpɪtəlaɪˈzeɪʃən] N **1** *Fin (of interest etc)* capitalisation *f* **2** *Typ* emploi *m* des majuscules; *(putting into caps)* mise *f* en majuscules
▸▸ *Fin* **c. issue** attribution *f* d'actions gratuites; *Fin* **c. ratio** ratio *m* de capitalisation

capitalize [ˈkæpɪtəlaɪz] VT **1** *Fin (income etc)* capitaliser; **capitalized value** valeur *f* capitalisée **2** *Typ (word) (first letter)* écrire avec une majuscule; *(entire word)* écrire en majuscules
▸ **capitalize on, capitalize upon** VT INSEP *Fig (something)* tourner à son avantage

capital-output ratio N ratio *m* capital-travail

capitation [kæpɪˈteɪʃən] N *Econ* capitation *f*
▸▸ *Admin* **c. grant** allocation *f* par tête

Capitol (the) [ðəˈkæpɪtɒl] N *(of Rome, Washington etc)* le Capitole

---

Capitol Hill

Ce nom désigne, par extension, le Congrès américain. Par exemple, "The proposed bill is in danger of being rejected on Capitol Hill." ("La proposition de loi risque d'être rejetée par le Congrès américain.")

---

capitulate [kəˈpɪtjʊleɪt] VI capituler (**to** devant)

capitulation [kəpɪtjʊˈleɪʃən] N *(surrender)* capitulation *f*

capon [ˈkeɪpən] N *Culin* chapon *m*

capper [ˈkæpər] N *Am Fam* **that was the c.!** c'est la goutte d'eau qui a fait déborder le vase!

cappuccino [kæpʊˈtʃiːnəʊ] N cappucino *m*

caprice [kəˈpriːs] N **1** *(whim)* caprice *m* **2** *Mus* caprice *m*

capricious [kəˈprɪʃəs] ADJ capricieux

capriciously [kəˈprɪʃəslɪ] ADV capricieusement

Capricorn [ˈkæprɪkɔːn] N **1** *Astrol* Capricorne *m*; **to be (a) C.** être (du) Capricorne **2** *Geog* **the Tropic of C.** le tropique du Capricorne

caps [kæps] NPL *(abbr* **capital letters**) majuscules *fpl*, capitales *fpl*
▸▸ *Comput* **c. lock** verrouillage *m* des majuscules; *Comput* **c. lock key** touche *f* de verrouillage des majuscules

capsicum [ˈkæpsɪkəm] N **1** *Culin (hot)* piment *m*; *(mild)* poivron *m* **2** *(plant)* piment *m*; *(mild)* poivron *m*

capsize [kæpˈsaɪz] VI *(of boat)* chavirer; **we capsized** nous avons chaviré
VT *(boat)* faire chavirer

capstan [ˈkæpst(ə)n] N **1** *Naut etc* cabestan *m* **2** *Tech (of lathe)* revolver *m*
▸▸ *Tech* **c. lathe** tour *m* revolver

capsular [ˈkæpsjʊlər] ADJ *Biol etc* capsulaire

capsule [ˈkæpsjuːl] N capsule *f*; *Med (of drug)* gélule *f*; **space c.** capsule spatiale

Capt N *abbr* **Captain**

captain [ˈkæptɪn] N **1** *Naut, Sport* capitaine *m*; *Aviat* commandant *m* de bord; *(in fire brigade)* capitaine; *(of quiz team etc)* leader *m*; *(in Girl Guides)* cheftaine *f*; *Am (in restaurant)* maître *m* d'hôtel; *Br* **c. of the school, school c.** = élève *mf* délégué(e) qui a certaines responsabilités et représente son établissement au cours de cérémonies officielles; *Fig* **captains of industry** capitaines d'industrie
2 *(officer, rank)* capitaine *m*; *Naut* capitaine de vaisseau; *(in American police force)* = officier *m* de police responsable d'un quartier; **c. of the fleet** capitaine de pavillon; **C. James Brown** *(in title)* le capitaine James Brown; **yes, c.!** oui, mon capitaine!
VT *Sport (team)* être capitaine de; *(expedition etc)* conduire, mener; *Sport* **he captained the side in the World Cup** c'était lui le capitaine de l'équipe pour la Coupe du monde

captaincy [ˈkæptɪnsɪ] N **1** *Mil, Naut* grade *m* de capitaine; **to take over the c. of the ship** prendre le commandement du vaisseau **2** *Sport* fonction *f* de capitaine; **under** *or* **during his c.** quand il était capitaine

caption [ˈkæpʃən] N *(of cartoon, photograph, illustration)* légende *f*; *Cin (in silent film)* sous-titre *m*, *pl* sous-titres
VT *(illustration)* légender, écrire la légende de; *(film, television programme)* sous-titrer
▸▸ *TV, Cin* **c. generator** générateur *m* de caractères

captious [ˈkæpʃəs] ADJ *Fml (reasoning)* captieux; *(person)* pointilleux, chicaneur, -euse

captivate [ˈkæptɪveɪt] VT *(of story, storyteller)* captiver; *(of smile, charm etc)* séduire

captivating [ˈkæptɪveɪtɪŋ] ADJ *(person, smile)* séduisant; *(personality)* captivant, fascinant; *(smile)* enchanteur, -eresse

captivation [kæptɪˈveɪʃən] N fascination *f*

captive [ˈkæptɪv] ADJ captif; **he was taken c.** il a été fait prisonnier; **he had a c. audience** le public était forcé de l'écouter
N captif, -ive, prisonnier, -ière
▸▸ **c. audience** audience *f* captive; *Mktg* **c. market** clientèle *f* captive, marché *m* captif; *Mktg* **c. product** produit *m* lié; *Mktg* **c.-product pricing** fixation *f* du prix des produits liés; **c. state** état *m* de captivité

captivity [kæpˈtɪvɪtɪ] N captivité *f*; **animals in c.** animaux en captivité

captor [ˈkæptər] N ravisseur, -euse

capture [ˈkæptʃər] N **1** *(of ship, criminal, animal etc)* capture *f* **2** *Comput (of data)* saisie *f* **3** *(thing or person taken)* prise *f*
VT *(ship, criminal, animal etc)* capturer; *(town)* prendre, s'emparer de (**from** sur); *(sb's attention, imagination)* captiver; *(of artist, painting) (sb's likeness)* saisir; *(of film, book, director etc) (atmosphere)* rendre; *Comput (data)* saisir; **to c. the moment** *(of photographer, photograph)* saisir l'instant; **to c. sb/sth (on film)** immortaliser qn/qch (sur la pellicule); *Com* **to c. a market** accaparer un marché

Capuchin [ˈkæpʊʃɪn] N *Rel* capucin, -ine

capuchin [ˈkæpʊʃɪn] N *(monkey)* capucin *m*

car [kɑːr] N **1** *Aut (motor)* **c.** voiture *f*, automobile *f*; **to go by c.** aller en voiture **2** *Am Rail* voiture *f*, wagon *m*; **buffet** *or* **refreshment c.** voiture-bar *f*, *pl* voitures-bars **3** *(cabin) (of balloon)* nacelle *f*; *Am (of lift)* cabine *f*
▸▸ **c. bomb** voiture piégée; *Br* **c. ferry** ferry-boat *m*, *pl* ferry-boats; **c. hire** location *f* de voitures; **c. hire company** société *f* de location de voitures; **c. industry** industrie *f* automobile; **c. insurance** assurance *f* auto; **c. manufacturer** constructeur *m* automobile; *Br* **c. park** parking *m*, parc *m* de stationnement; **c. phone** téléphone *m* de voiture; **c. radio** autoradio *f*; **c. rental** location de voitures; **c. theft** vols *mpl* de voiture

---

Note that the French word **car** is a false friend and is never a translation for the English word **car**. It means **coach**.

---

carafe [kəˈræf, -ˈrɑːf] N carafe *f*; *(small)* carafon *m*

caramel [ˈkærəməl] N **1** *Culin* caramel *m* **2** *(sweet)* caramel *m* **3** *(colour)* (couleur *f*) caramel *m inv*
▸▸ *Culin* **c. cream** crème *f* caramel; *Culin* **c. custard** crème (renversée) au caramel

caramelize [ˈkærəməlaɪz] *Culin* VT caraméliser
VI se caraméliser

carapace [ˈkærəpeɪs] N *Zool* carapace *f*

carat [ˈkærət] N **1** *(for gold)* carat *m* (de fin); **eighteen-c. gold** or *m* à dix-huit carats **2** *(for diamonds)* **metric c.** carat *m* (de 200 milligrammes)

caravan [ˈkærəvæn] N **1** *Br (pulled by car)* caravane *f*; **c. holiday** vacances *fpl* en caravane **2** *(horse-drawn)* roulotte *f* **3** *(in desert)* caravane *f*; **to travel in c.** voyager en convoi
▸▸ **c. park** terrain *m* de caravaning; **c. route** piste *f* caravanière; *Br* **c. site** *(for campers)* camping *m* (pour caravanes); *(of gypsies)* campement *m*

caravanette [kærəvæˈnet] N camping-car *m*, *pl* camping-cars

caravan(n)ing [ˈkærəvænɪŋ] N caravaning *m*; **to go c., to go on a c. holiday** faire du caravaning

caravanserai [kærəˈvænsəraɪ] N caravansérail *m*

caraway [ˈkærəweɪ] N *(plant)* carvi *m*, cumin *m* des prés
▸▸ **c. seeds** (graines *fpl* de) carvi

carb [kɑːb] N *Fam* **1** *Aut* carburateur *m* **2** *(carbohydrate)* glucide *m*

carbide [ˈkɑːbaɪd] N *Chem, Ind* carbure *m*

carbine [ˈkɑːbaɪn] N *Mil* **1** *Hist* carabine *f* **2** *Am (automatic)* mitraillette *f*

carbohydrate [kɑːbəʊˈhaɪdreɪt] N **1** *Chem* hydrate *m* de carbone **2** *(in food)* **carbohydrates** glucides *mpl*

carbolic [kɑːˈbɒlɪk] ADJ *Chem* phénique
▸▸ **c. acid** phénol *m*; **c. soap** ≃ savon *m* de Marseille

carbon [ˈkɑːbən] N **1** *Chem* carbone *m* **2** *(copy, paper)* carbone *m*
▸▸ **c. copy** *(of letter etc)* double *m ou* copie *f* (au carbone); *Fig* **she is a c. copy of her mother** c'est la copie conforme de sa mère; *Aut* **c. deposit** calaminage *m*; *Chem* **c. dioxide** gaz *m* carbonique, dioxyde *m* de carbone; **c. electrode** électrode *f* de charbon; *Chem, Tex* **c. fibre** fibre *f* de carbone; *Aut* **c. filter** filtre *m* au charbon; **c.(-14) dating** *(in archaeology)* datation *f* au carbone 14; *Chem* **c. monoxide** monoxyde *m* de carbone; **c. paper** *(papier m)* carbone; *Comput* **c. ribbon** ruban *m* de carbone; *Metal* **c. steel** acier *m* carburé

carbonaceous [kɑːbəˈneɪʃəs] ADJ *Chem* carboné; *Geol* carbonifère

carbonate [ˈkɑːbəneɪt] N *Chem* carbonate *m*

carbonated [ˈkɑːbəneɪtɪd] ADJ gazéifié, gazeux
▸▸ **c. water** eau *f* gazeuse

carbonic [kɑːˈbɒnɪk] ADJ Chem carbonique

Carboniferous [kɑːbəˈnɪfərəs] ADJ, N Geol carbonifère m

carboniferous [kɑːbəˈnɪfərəs] ADJ carbonifère

carbonization [kɑːbənaɪˈzeɪʃən] N (of wood etc) carbonisation f, Aut etc encrassement m, calaminage m

carbonize [ˈkɑːbənaɪz] VT Chem carboniser; Ind (wood etc) carboniser, charbonner VI Aut etc s'encrasser, se calaminer

car-boot sale N Br = vente f à la brocante où les vendeurs exposent leurs marchandises à l'arrière de leur voiture

Carborundum® [kɑːbəˈrʌndəm] N carborundum® m

carboy [ˈkɑːbɔɪ] N bonbonne f

carbuncle [ˈkɑːbʌŋk(ə)l] N 1 Med furoncle m 2 (gem) escarboucle f

carburation [kɑːbjʊˈreɪʃən] N carburation f

carburettor, Am **carburetor** [ˈkɑːbjʊretər] N Aut carburateur m
▸▸ **c. damper** amortisseur m de commande sur carburateur

carcass [ˈkɑːkəs] N 1 (of animal) cadavre m, carcasse f 2 (of house, ship) charpente f 3 Fam Pej (of person) (corpse) macchabée m; Fam Hum (body) carcasse f, **move** or **shift your c.!** pousse-toi de là!

carcinogen [kɑːˈsɪnədʒen] N Med substance f cancérigène

carcinogenic [kɑːsɪnəʊˈdʒenɪk] ADJ Med cancérigène, cancérogène

carcinoma [kɑːsɪˈnəʊmə] N Med carcinome m

card¹ [kɑːd] N 1 Cards (playing) **c.** carte f (à jouer); **to play cards** jouer aux cartes; **to win at cards** gagner aux cartes; **to play one's cards well** bien jouer ses cartes; Fig **to play one's cards right** bien se débrouiller, bien mener sa barque; **play your cards right and you could get promoted** si tu te débrouilles bien, tu peux avoir une promotion; Fig **play one's last c.** jouer son va-tout; Fig **to hold all the (winning** or **best) cards** avoir tous les atouts dans son jeu ou en main; Fig **to keep one's cards close to one's chest** cacher son jeu; Cards, Fig **to put one's cards on the table** mettre cartes sur table; Fig **to have a c. up one's sleeve** avoir un atout dans son jeu; Fig **it is on** or Am **in the cards that ...** il est bien possible que ..., il se pourrait fort bien que ...; **I don't think that's on the cards** je ne pense pas que ce soit possible; Fig **to throw in the** or **one's cards** abandonner; Old-fashioned Fam **he's a (real) c.** or **quite a c.** c'est un original

2 (with printed information) carte f, (postcard) carte (postale); Golf carte du parcours; Sport (list of races) programme m des courses; **here's my c.** voici ma carte; Br Fam **to get** or **be given one's cards** être renvoyé; **birthday/Christmas c.** carte d'anniversaire/de Noël

3 (for card index) fiche f

4 (for holding wool, buttons) carte f

5 (cardboard) carton m

6 Comput carte f

7 (plastic) carte f, **banker's c., cheque c.** carte (d'identité) bancaire; **smart c.** carte à puce
▸▸ **c. catalogue** fichier m (de bibliothèque); **c. file** fichier; **c. game** jeu m de cartes; **c. index** fichier; **c. key** carte-clé f, pl cartes-clés; **c. player** joueur, -euse de cartes; **c. reader** lecteur m de cartes; Comput **c. slot** emplacement m pour carte; **c. table** table f de jeu; **c. trick** tour m de cartes; Br **c. vote** vote m sur carte (chaque voix représentant le nombre de voix d'adhérents représentés)

card² Tex N (tool) carde f, peigne m
VT (wool etc) carder, peigner

cardamom [ˈkɑːdəməm] N cardamome f

cardan joint [ˈkɑːdən] N Aut joint m de cardans

cardboard [ˈkɑːdbɔːd] N carton m; (thin) bristol m
▸▸ **c. box** (boîte f en) carton; Fig **c. character** (in play, novel etc) personnage m sans aucune profondeur; **c. city** quartier m des sans-abri; **c. cutout** personnage m découpé dans le carton

card-carrying ADJ
▸▸ **c. member** adhérent, -ente (of à)

cardiac [ˈkɑːdiæk] ADJ Anat, Med cardiaque
▸▸ **c. arrest** arrêt m cardiaque; **he suffered c. arrest** il a eu un arrêt cardiaque; **c. massage** massage m cardiaque

cardigan [ˈkɑːdɪɡən] N cardigan m, gilet m

cardinal [ˈkɑːdɪn(ə)l] ADJ 1 (importance, significance) capital, -aux; **c. error** erreur f fondamentale VOIR GRAMMAIRE A76; B58-9 2 (colour) pourpre, rouge cardinal inv
N Rel cardinal m, -aux
▸▸ **c. numbers** nombres mpl cardinaux; **the c. points** les (quatre) points mpl cardinaux; Rel **c. sin** péché m capital; **the c. virtues** les (quatre) vertus fpl cardinales

carding [ˈkɑːdɪŋ] N Tex cardage m, peignage m
▸▸ **c. machine** cardeuse f

cardiogram [ˈkɑːdɪəʊɡræm] N Med cardiogramme m

cardiograph [ˈkɑːdɪəʊɡrɑːf] N Med cardiographe m

cardiologist [kɑːdɪˈɒlədʒɪst] N Med cardiologue mf

cardiology [kɑːdɪˈɒlədʒɪ] N Med cardiologie f

cardiovascular [kɑːdɪəʊˈvæskjʊlər] ADJ Med (disease) cardio-vasculaire, pl cardio-vasculaires

card-operated lock N (in hotel etc) serrure f à carte perforée

cardphone [ˈkɑːdfəʊn] N Tel publiphone® m ou téléphone m à carte

cardsharp(er) [ˈkɑːdʃɑːp, -ər] N tricheur, -euse professionnel(elle)

cardy [ˈkɑːdɪ] N Fam = **cardigan**

CARE [keər]

N souci 1 ▪ soin 2, 3	
VI se soucier ▪ aimer	
VT vouloir 2	

N 1 (worry) souci m, inquiétude f, **to be full of cares** avoir beaucoup de soucis; **to be free of** or **from c.** être insouciant; **a life of c.** une vie pleine de soucis; **she doesn't have a c. in the world** elle n'a aucun souci; **cares of State** responsabilités fpl d'État

2 (attention) soin(s) m(pl), attention f, **constant c.** soins continuels ou assidus; **to do sth with great c.** faire qch avec beaucoup de soin; **to put a lot of c. into sth** apporter beaucoup de soin à qch; **to put a lot of c. into doing sth** mettre beaucoup de soin à faire qch; **to drive without due c.** conduire de façon imprudente; **with c.** (on parcel etc) fragile; **they didn't receive the proper c. in hospital** ils n'ont pas reçu les soins appropriés à l'hôpital; **to take c. of** (invalid, child, customer, problem etc) s'occuper de; **he doesn't take c. of his bicycle** il ne prend pas soin de son vélo; **to take good c. of sb/sth** prendre bien soin de qn/qch; **to take c. of oneself** savoir se débrouiller tout seul; (healthwise) prendre soin de sa santé; **take c. of yourself** (look after yourself) soignez-vous bien; **to take c. of one's health** ménager sa santé; **to take c. of itself** s'arranger tout seul ou de soi-même; **this should take**

c. of that stain cela devrait venir à bout de cette tache; **to take c. to do sth** avoir (bien) soin ou prendre (bien) garde de faire qch; **take c. when you cross the road** fais attention en traversant la rue; **take c.!** (look out!) faites attention!, prenez garde!; **take c., bye** à bientôt

3 (looking after) (of teeth, hair etc) soin(s) m(pl); (of machine, shoes, clothes etc) entretien m; Br Admin **children in c.** enfants confiés aux services sociaux; **to be in/go into c.** (of child) être/être confié à l'Assistance publique; **to put a child in c.** confier un enfant à l'Assistance publique; **to put sb/sth in sb's c.** confier qn/qch à qn; **to be in** or **under sb's c.** être sous la responsabilité de qn; **to be under a doctor's c.** se faire soigner par un médecin; **write to me c. of Mrs Smith** or **c/o Mrs Smith** or Am **in c. of Mrs Smith** écrivez-moi aux bons soins de Mme Smith ou chez Mme Smith

VI (be concerned) se soucier, se préoccuper (about de); **people who c.** des gens compatissants; **no one seems to c.** tout le monde s'en moque; **no one seems to c. about the environment/the elderly** personne ne semble se préoccuper ou se soucier de l'environnement/des personnes âgées; **to care about** or **for sb** aimer qn; **of course we c. about you!** mais bien sûr qu'on t'aime; **that's all he cares about** il n'y a que cela qui l'intéresse; **who cares?** qu'est-ce que ça peut faire?; **do you really c.?** (how I am, what my feelings are etc) est-ce que ça t'intéresse vraiment?; **she just doesn't c.** elle s'en moque complètement, Fam elle n'en a rien à faire; **for all I c.** pour ce que ça me fait; **I don't c.!** ça m'est égal!, je m'en fiche!; **as if I cared!** I **couldn't c. less** je m'en fiche éperdument, je m'en fous; **couldn't-c.-less attitude** je-m'en-foutisme m

VT 1 (mind) **I don't c. what he says** peu m'importe ce qu'il dit; **what do I c.?** qu'est-ce que ça peut bien me faire?; **I don't c. whether he likes it or not** que cela lui plaise ou non, ça m'est parfaitement égal

2 (like) **would you c. to come with me?** voulez-vous m'accompagner?, aimeriez-vous m'accompagner?; **if you c. to join us** si vous voulez vous joindre à nous
▸▸ Br Admin **c. in the community** = système m de soins prodigués aux malades mentaux en dehors du milieu hospitalier; **c. label** (on garment) conseils mpl d'entretien; **c. parcel** (for famine relief etc) colis m d'aide humanitaire
▸ **care for** VT INSEP 1 (tend) (patients, children) soigner; **to look well cared for** (of animal, child, hair etc) avoir l'air soigné ou une apparence soignée; (of car, garden etc) avoir l'air bien entretenu

2 (like) **I don't c. for this music** je n'aime pas tellement cette musique; **he doesn't c. for her** elle ne lui plaît pas; **would you c. for some tea?** voulez-vous du thé?

3 (love) (person) aimer, tenir à

careen [kəˈriːn] VT Naut 1 (make keel over) (boat) abattre ou mettre en carène 2 (clean) caréner
VI 1 Naut (of ship) se coucher 2 Am (of car etc) pencher sur le côté

careening [kəˈriːnɪŋ] N Naut (cleaning) carénage m

career¹ [kəˈrɪər] N (working life, profession) carrière f, **his dancing c.** sa carrière de danseur; **a job with c. prospects** un emploi qui offre des perspectives; **it's a good/bad c. move** c'est bon/mauvais pour ta/sa/etc carrière
▸▸ **c. break** interruption f de carrière; **c. diplomat** diplomate mf de carrière; **careers officer** conseiller, -ère d'orientation; **careers service** service m d'orientation profession-

nelle; **c. woman** = femme *f* ambitieuse *ou* qui ne pense qu'à sa carrière

career [2] **vi to c. (along)** aller à toute vitesse; **to c. into a lorry** *(of vehicle)* foncer dans un camion; **the car careered off the road** la voiture a quitté la route à vive allure

careerist [kə'rɪərɪst] **n** *usu Pej* carriériste *mf*

carefree ['keəfriː] **adj** sans souci

careful ['keəfʊl] **adj 1** *(taking pains)* soigneux (**of** de), attentif (**of** à); **a c. worker** un travailleur méticuleux; **c. speakers would avoid this usage** les gens qui parlent correctement éviteraient cet usage; **to be c. of** *(appearance)* être soucieux de; **be c. of his feelings** ne heurte pas ses sentiments; **to be c. with one's money** regarder à la dépense; **to be c. to do sth** avoir soin de faire qch, veiller à faire qch; **she was c. not to mention this** elle a fait bien attention de ne pas mentionner cela; **(be) c.!** faites attention!; **be c. you don't fall** *or* **not to fall** faites attention de ne pas tomber; **be c. what you say** faites attention à ce que vous dites; **we are very c. (about) who we employ** nous faisons très attention quand nous engageons quelqu'un; **c. consideration of a question** examen *m* attentif *ou* approfondi d'une question **2** *(prudent)* prudent, circonspect; **you can't be too c. these days** de nos jours, on n'est jamais trop prudent; **a c. answer** une réponse bien pesée *ou* réfléchie; **a c. driver** un conducteur prudent

carefully ['keəfʊlɪ] **adv 1** *(painstakingly)* soigneusement, avec soin; *(to choose)* avec soin; *(to listen)* attentivement; **a c. worded document** un document aux termes choisis avec soin **2** *(to drive, approach sb)* prudemment

carefulness ['keəfʊlnɪs] **n 1** *(taking pains)* soin *m*, attention *f* **2** *(prudence)* prudence *f*

careless ['keəlɪs] **adj 1** *(negligent)* négligent; *(work)* négligé; *(error, moment)* d'inattention; **accused of c. driving** accusé d'imprudence au volant; **to be c. about one's appearance** être négligé de sa personne; **she's very c. about her things** elle n'est pas soigneuse avec ses affaires **2** *(unconcerned)* insouciant, peu soucieux (**of**, **about** de); *Fml* **to be c. of sb's feelings** manquer de délicatesse avec qn; **a c. remark** une observation inconsidérée *ou* irréfléchie; **with a c. wave of her hand** en faisant un léger geste de la main

carelessly ['keəlɪslɪ] **adv 1** *(negligently)* négligemment, sans soin **2** *(casually)* avec insouciance; **he threw the towel c. over his shoulder** il balança nonchalamment la serviette sur son épaule

carelessness ['keəlɪsnɪs] **n 1** *(negligence)* négligence *f* **2** *esp Lit (lack of concern)* insouciance *f*, inattention *f*

carer ['keərər] **n** *(professional)* aide *mf* à domicile; *(relative)* = personne *f* s'occupant d'un parent malade ou âgé

caress [kə'res] **n** caresse *f*
vt caresser

caret ['kærət] **n** *Typ* signe *m* d'insertion

caretaker ['keəteɪkər] **n** *(of building, school)* concierge *mf*, gardien, -ienne; *(of museum etc)* gardien, -ienne
▸▸ *Pol* **c. government** gouvernement *m* intérimaire

careworn ['keəwɔːn] **adj** *(face etc)* rongé *ou* usé par les soucis

cargo, *pl* **cargoes** ['kɑːgəʊ, -əʊz] **n** *Naut, Aviat* cargaison *f*, chargement *m*; **full c.** plein chargement; **general** *or* **mixed c.** cargaison mixte
▸▸ **c. afloat** cargaison flottante; **c. floor** *(of truck)* plancher *m* de chargement; **c. insur-**

-ance assurance *f* sur facultés; **c. list** bordereau *m* de chargement; **c. plane** avion-cargo *m*, *pl* avions-cargos; **c. ship** cargo *m*; **c. space** espace *m* cargo; **c. vessel** cargo

Note that the French word **cargo** is a false friend and is never a translation for the English word **cargo**. It means **cargo ship**.

Caribbean [kærɪ'biːən, *Am* kə'rɪbɪən] **n the C.** *(area)* les Antilles *fpl*, *(sea)* la mer des Caraïbes *ou* des Antilles; **in the C.** dans les Caraïbes, aux Antilles
adj des Caraïbes
▸▸ **the C. islands** les Antilles; **the C. Sea** la mer des Caraïbes *ou* des Antilles

caribou ['kærɪbuː] **n** caribou *m*, *pl* -ous

caricature ['kærɪkətjʊər] **n** caricature *f*
vt caricaturer

caricaturist [kærɪkə'tjuːrɪst] **n** caricaturiste *mf*

caries ['keəriːz] **n** *Med* carie *f*

carillon [kə'rɪljən] **n** *Mus* carillon *m*

caring ['keərɪŋ] **adj** *(society)* humain; **she's a c. person** c'est une personne très humaine *ou* généreuse; **a c. family atmosphere** une atmosphère familiale chaleureuse; **the c. professions** = les professions *fpl* médicales et paramédicales

carjacking ['kɑːdʒækɪŋ] **n** = vol *m* de voiture sous la menace d'une arme

carless ['kɑːlɪs] **adj** sans voiture

carload ['kɑːləʊd] **n 1** *Aut* pleine voiture *f*; **a c. of people/furniture** une voiture pleine de passagers/de meubles; **to arrive by the c.** arriver par voitures entières **2** *Am Rail* plein wagon *m*

Carmelite ['kɑːməlaɪt] **n** *(nun)* carmélite *f*, *(friar)* carme *m*
adj carmélite

carmine ['kɑːmaɪn] **n** carmin *m*
adj carmin *inv*

carnage ['kɑːnɪdʒ] **n** carnage *m*

carnal ['kɑːn(ə)l] **adj** charnel
▸▸ **c. knowledge** connaissance *f* charnelle; **to have c. knowledge of sb** *Bible, Lit* connaître qn; *Law* avoir des relations sexuelles avec qn; **c. sins** péchés *mpl* de la chair

carnation [kɑː'neɪʃən] **n 1** *(flower)* œillet *m* **2** *(colour)* incarnat *m*
adj *(colour)* incarnat

carnet ['kɑːneɪ] **n** *Com (customs pass)* carnet *m* de passage en douanes

carnival ['kɑːnɪv(ə)l] **n 1** *(festive occasion)* carnaval *m*, -als, fête *f*; **during C.** pendant le Carnaval; **a c. atmosphere** une ambiance de fête *ou* de carnaval **2** *(funfair)* fête *f* foraine **3** *Rel (before Lent)* carnaval *m*, -als

carnivora [kɑː'nɪvərə] **npl** *Zool* carnivores *mpl*

carnivore ['kɑːnɪvɔːr] **n** *(animal)* carnivore *m*

carnivorous [kɑː'nɪv(ə)rəs] **adj 1** *(animal)* carnivore, carnassier **2** *(person, plant)* carnivore

carob ['kærəb] **n 1** *(tree)* caroubier *m* **2** *Culin* caroube *m*

carol ['kær(ə)l] **n** chant *m*, chanson *f*; **(Christmas) c.** (chant de) Noël *m*; **to go c. singing** aller chanter des chants de Noël
vi (**-ll-**, *Am* **-l-**) **1** *(sing carols)* chanter des chants de Noël **2** *Lit (sing)* chanter (joyeusement); *(of lark)* chanter
vt chanter joyeusement; **I'll be with you in a minute, she carolled** je suis à vous dans un instant, lança-t-elle gaiement
▸▸ **c. service** = office *m* religieux qui précède Noël; **c. singer** = personne *f* qui, à l'époque de Noël, va chanter et quêter au profit des bonnes œuvres

Carol Service
Le "Carol Service" se tient juste avant Noël et se compose surtout de chants de Noël et de lectures de la Bible.

Carolina [kærə'laɪnə] **n** Caroline *f*; **South/ North C.** Caroline du Sud/du Nord; **the Carolinas** la Caroline du Sud et la Caroline du Nord

Carolingian [kærə'lɪndʒɪən] *Hist* **adj** carolingien
n Carolingien, -ienne

carom ['kærəm] **n** *Am Billiards* carambolage *m*

carotid [kə'rɒtɪd] *Anat, Med* **adj** *(artery)* carotide; *(nerve, system)* carotidien
n (artère *f*) carotide *f*
▸▸ **c. artery** artère carotide

carousal [kə'raʊz(ə)l] **n** *Old-fashioned, Hum* beuverie *f*

carouse [kə'raʊz] **vi** *Old-fashioned, Hum* faire la fête *ou* *Fam* la bombe

carousel [kærə'sel] = **carrousel**

carp [1] [kɑːp] **n** *inv* *(fish)* carpe *f*

carp [2] **vi** se plaindre; **to c. about sb/sth** se plaindre de qn/qch

carpal ['kɑːp(ə)l] **adj** carpien
n carpe *m*

Carpathian [kɑː'peɪðɪən] **adj, n the C. Mountains, the Carpathians** les (monts *mpl*) Carpates *mpl*

carpel ['kɑːp(ə)l] **n** *Bot* carpelle *m*, carpophylle *m*

carpenter ['kɑːpɪntər] **n** charpentier *m*, menuisier *m* en bâtiments; *(making smaller objects)* menuisier
vt charpenter

carpentry ['kɑːpɪntrɪ] **n** *Constr* charpenterie *f*, *(for smaller items)* menuiserie *f*; **that's a nice piece of c.** *(chair, table, etc)* c'est un beau travail de menuiserie

carpet ['kɑːpɪt] **n 1** tapis *m*; *(fitted, in car)* moquette *f*; **to lay a c.** poser un tapis/une moquette; *Fig* **to sweep sth under the c.** enterrer qch; *Fig* **to be on the c.** *(of question)* être sur le tapis; *(of person)* être sur la sellette; *Fig* **to have** *or* **put sb on the c.** réprimander qn **2** *Fig (of flowers, leaves etc)* tapis *m*
vt 1 *(floor)* recouvrir d'un tapis; *(with fitted carpet)* recouvrir d'une moquette; *(room)* moquetter; **all the rooms are carpeted** il y a de la moquette dans toutes les pièces; *Fig* **the pond was carpeted with weed** le bassin était tapissé d'algues **2** *Fam (person)* réprimander
▸▸ *Mil* **c. bombing** bombardement *m* intensif; **c. cleaner** *(product)* produit *m* nettoyant pour moquette; *(machine)* shampouineuse *f*, **c. shampoo** shampooing *m* pour moquette; **c. slippers** pantoufles *fpl*; **c. tack** fixe-tapis *m inv*; **c. tile** carreau *m* de moquette

Note that the French word **carpette** is a false friend and is never a translation for the English word **carpet**. It means **small rug**.

carpetbagger ['kɑːpɪtbægər] **n 1** *esp Am Pol Fam* candidat, -ate étranger(ère) à la circonscription **2** *Am Hist* profiteur, -euse venu(e) d'un état nordiste *(après la guerre de Sécession)*

carpeting ['kɑːpɪtɪŋ] **n 1** *(laying of carpet)* pose *f* de(s) tapis/de(s) moquette(s) (**of** dans) **2** *(carpets)* moquette *f* **3** *Fam (severe reprimand)* réprimande *f*; **to give sb a c.** passer un savon à qn

carpet-sweeper **n** balai *m* mécanique

carping ['kɑ:pɪŋ] ADJ (person) très critique, pointilleux; (criticism) malveillant
N critiques fpl

carport ['kɑ:pɔ:t] N Aut auvent m pour voitures

carpus ['kɑ:pəs] N Med carpe m

carriage ['kærɪdʒ] N 1 (vehicle) voiture f, (together with horses and driver) équipage m; open/closed c. voiture découverte/fermée; invalid c. voiture d'infirme; c. and pair voiture à deux chevaux
 2 Br Rail voiture f, wagon m
 3 Tech (of lathe, typewriter etc) chariot m; Mil gun c. affût m
 4 (transport) transport m; Com (cost) (frais mpl de) port m; c. forward (en) port dû, port avancé; c. free franc de port, franco; c. insurance paid port payé, assurance comprise; c. paid (en) port payé
 5 (bearing) (of person) port m, maintien m
 ▸▸ Br c. clock pendulette f (à boîtier rectangulaire muni d'une poignée); c. entrance porte f cochère; Typ c. release arm (on typewriter) levier m de dégagement du chariot; Typ c. return retour m de chariot; esp Am the c. trade la clientèle haut de gamme

carriageway ['kærɪdʒweɪ] N Br Aut chaussée f

carrier ['kærɪər] N 1 Med etc (of disease, germs etc) porteur, -euse
 2 Com (company) transporteur m; Law voiturier m
 3 (container) (on bicycle etc) (basket) panier m; (behind the saddle) porte-bagages m inv; (for homing pigeon) cartouche f
 4 Ind (mechanism) transporteur m
 5 (aircraft) c. porte-avions m inv
 6 Tel (fréquence f) porteuse f
 ▸▸ c. bag sac m en plastique; c. pigeon pigeon m voyageur; Comput c. signal signal m de détection de porteuse; Tel c. tone tonalité f

carrier-based [-'beɪst] ADJ Aviat, Naut embarqué

carrion ['kærɪən] N (no pl) charogne f
 ▸▸ Orn c. crow corneille f noire

carrot ['kærət] N carotte f, Fig a pay rise is the c. management is holding out to the unions le patronat tente d'amadouer les syndicats en promettant une hausse des salaires; the c. and the stick la carotte et le bâton; Fam carrots, c. top (hair) cheveux mpl roux ou carotte; (person) rouquin, -ine, poil m de carotte

carroty ['kærətɪ] ADJ Fam (person, hair) roux, f rousse

carrousel [kærə'sel] N 1 (for slides) magasin m 2 (at airport) carrousel m (pour bagages) 3 Am (at fairground) chevaux mpl de bois, manège m

CARRY ['kærɪ] (pt & pp **carried**)

VT porter **1, 2, 7, 8** ▪ transporter **1** ▪ transmettre **1** ▪ adopter **5** ▪ vendre **6** ▪ retenir **9**
VI porter **1**

VT 1 (of person, wind) (burden, bag, child, scent etc) porter; (goods, passengers etc) transporter; Med (disease) véhiculer; (of wires etc) (sound etc) conduire, transmettre; (of pipes) (water etc) amener, transporter; (revolver, watch etc) (on one's person) porter (sur soi); I don't c. much money about or on me je n'ai jamais beaucoup d'argent sur moi; the current carried the raft out to sea le courant a emporté le radeau au large; rats c. diseases les rats sont porteurs de maladies; a memory that he will c. with him to the grave un souvenir qu'il n'oubliera jamais; the bus carried us to our destination l'autobus nous a conduits jusqu'à notre des-

tination; we were carrying livestock (of ship) nous avions du bétail à bord; to c. sth in one's head avoir qch en mémoire; Fig the other team members have to c. him les autres membres de l'équipe doivent le porter; he's being carried by the other members of the team il se repose sur les autres membres de l'équipe; his strong constitution carried him through his illness sa forte constitution lui a permis de surmonter sa maladie; to c. a child (be pregnant) porter un enfant, être enceinte; I can't c. a tune je suis incapable de chanter sans faire de fausses notes
 2 (involve) porter, comporter; to c. (no) conviction (ne pas) être convaincant; to c. a guarantee être garanti; to c. a fine/penalty être passible d'amende/d'une peine; to c. a risk comporter un risque; to c. responsibility comporter des responsabilités; to c. weight/authority (of person, opinion) avoir du poids/de l'autorité; to c. significance (for sb/sth) avoir de l'importance (pour qn/qch); to c. interest (of money) porter intérêt
 3 (take, lead, extend) to c. an argument to its logical conclusion aller au bout d'un raisonnement; to c. sth too far pousser qch trop loin; to c. the battle or fight into the enemy's camp Mil faire du territoire ennemi le lieu du conflit; Fig attaquer l'ennemi sur son propre terrain
 4 (capture, win) (fortress) enlever; (position) emporter d'assaut; to c. all before one (be successful) remporter tous les prix; (win support, approval) vaincre toutes les résistances, triompher sur toute la ligne; Hum she carries all before her (has large bosom) il y a du monde au balcon; to c. the day l'emporter; to c. several states l'emporter dans plusieurs états; to c. one's point établir la validité de son argument
 5 (proposal) (pass) adopter; (secure passage of) faire adopter ou passer; the bill was carried le projet a été adopté
 6 Com (keep in stock) (article) faire, vendre, avoir; (goods) avoir en magasin ou en dépôt; to c. an advertisement/article (of newspaper etc) comporter une publicité/un article; do you c. bathroom accessories? (to sales assistant) est-ce que vous vendez des accessoires pour salles de bain?
 7 (hold) to c. oneself well/badly se tenir bien/mal; to c. one's head high porter la tête haute
 8 Archit, Constr (beam, vault) porter, supporter
 9 Math c. two je retiens deux, on retient deux

VI 1 (of sound, gun etc) porter; her voice carries well elle a une voix qui porte bien
 2 Sl (possess drugs) avoir de la drogue sur soi; he was arrested for carrying il a été arrêté parce qu'il avait de la drogue sur lui

▸ **carry along** VT SEP emporter, entraîner; (of stream etc) (mud etc) charrier

▸ **carry away** VT SEP 1 (take) (object) emporter, enlever; (person) entraîner, emmener
 2 (make excited, over-enthusiastic) he let his enthusiasm c. him away il s'est laissé emporter par son enthousiasme; I got carried away je me suis emballé; don't get carried away! ne te laisse pas emporter!; Iron Fam ne t'emballe pas!

▸ **carry back** VT SEP 1 (bring) (object) rapporter; (person) ramener
 2 (take) (object) reporter; (person) remmener; that carries me back to my youth cela me ramène à l'époque de ma jeunesse

▸ **carry down** VT SEP 1 (from upstairs etc) (person, thing) descendre
 2 (usu passive) (tradition) transmettre

▸ **carry forward** VT SEP Acct to c. an item forward reporter un article; carried forward report, à reporter; carried forward from the

previous year report de l'exercice précédent; carried forward to the next year report à l'exercice suivant

▸ **carry off** VT SEP 1 (bring, take) (object) emporter; (person) emmener
 2 (win) (prize) remporter
 3 (be successful in) (sth unusual) faire passer, faire accepter; to c. it off réussir le coup; they managed to c. the robbery off ils ont mené à bien le cambriolage; it's a difficult role and he didn't quite c. it off c'est un rôle difficile, et il n'a pas su se montrer à la hauteur
 4 Old-fashioned (of disease) emporter

▸ **carry on** VT SEP (task) poursuivre, continuer; (tradition) continuer; (business, trade) exercer; (correspondence) entretenir; they were carrying on a conversation ils étaient en train de parler
 VI 1 (continue) continuer; to c. on doing sth continuer à faire qch; just c. on with what you were doing continuez ce que vous étiez en train de faire; c. on! continuez!; Mil c. on, sergeant! vous pouvez disposer, sergeant; I shall c. on to the end j'irai jusqu'au bout; will you be able to c. on during my absence? (assume responsibility) pourras-tu prendre les choses en main pendant mon absence?
 2 Fam (behave) se comporter; I don't like the way she carries on je n'aime pas ses façons; from the way he carries on anyone'd think that … vu la façon dont il se comporte, on croirait vraiment que …
 3 Fam (behave badly) faire des scènes, s'emporter; don't c. on like that! ne vous emballez pas comme ça!
 4 Fam (have an affair) avoir une liaison (with avec)

▸ **carry out** VT SEP 1 (bring, take) (object) porter dehors/hors de la salle/etc; (person) transporter dehors
 2 (do, execute) (plan, threat, decision) mettre à exécution; (experiment) effectuer; (instructions, order) exécuter; (idea, order etc) donner suite à; (wish) satisfaire à; (responsibilities) assumer; (job) mener à bonne fin; (task, duty) s'acquitter de; the police carried o la police a effectué une perquisition; to c. out a procedure suivre une procédure

▸ **carry over** VT SEP (take, bring) transporter de l'autre côté; Com, Math (figure, sum) reporter; (practice, tradition) continuer; to c. over one's holiday entitlement/tax allowance to the next year reporter ses congés/son abattement fiscal sur l'année suivante; that will have to be carried over to the next meeting il faudra poursuivre ce point lors de la prochaine réunion
 VI (of effect, implications) avoir des répercussions (into sur); the right carries over to future owners les futurs propriétaires conservent ce droit

▸ **carry through** VT SEP 1 (complete) (undertaking) mener à bien ou à bonne fin ou à bon terme; (task) exécuter
 2 his strong constitution carried him through sa forte constitution lui a permis de s'en sortir

▸ **carry up** VT SEP monter

carryall ['kærɪɔ:l] N (sac m) fourre-tout m inv

carrycot ['kærɪkɒt] N porte-bébé m inv

carrying ['kærɪŋ] ADJ
 ▸▸ Tech c. axle (of locomotive) essieu m porteur; c. capacity (of vehicle) charge f utile; (of tourist attraction) capacité f d'accueil; Com c. charge Am (extra charge) supplément m (que l'on paye lorsqu'on achète à crédit); Br (transport costs) frais mpl de transport; Acct c. forward report m

carrying-on N Fam (foolish behaviour) (of child) cirque m; (of unfaithful spouse, lover) écart m de conduite

carry-on¹ N *Fam* cinéma *m*; **what a c. just to buy a ticket!** quelle histoire *ou* quel cinéma rien que pour acheter un billet!

carry-on² ADJ *(luggage)* à main

carry-out *Scot, Am* N *(meal)* repas *m* à emporter; *(restaurant)* restaurant *m* qui fait des plats à emporter; *(alcohol)* = alcool *m* acheté (surtout) dans un pub pour être consommé à l'extérieur
  ADJ ATTRIB *(meal, food)* à emporter
  ▸▸ **c. menu** liste *f* des plats à emporter

carryover ['kærɪəʊvər] N **it's a c. from my childhood** *(habit, tradition)* c'est une habitude qui vient de mon enfance; *(fear, phobia)* c'est une peur qui vient de mon enfance

carsick ['kɑːsɪk] ADJ **to be/get c.** avoir mal au cœur en voiture

carsickness ['kɑːsɪknɪs] N mal *m* de la route

cart¹ [kɑːt] N charrette *f (à deux roues)*; *(small)* carriole *f*, *(with four wheels)* chariot *m*; *Fig* **to put the c. before the horse** mettre la charrue avant les bœufs
  VT **1** *Fam (carry)* trimballer **2** *(transport by cart)* charrier, voiturer
  ▸▸ **c. track** chemin *m* de terre
 ▸ **cart about, cart around** VT SEP *Fam (parcels etc)* trimbal(l)er
 ▸ **cart away, cart off** VT SEP *Fam (rubbish etc)* enlever, emporter; *(person)* emmener; **he was carted away** *or* **off to prison** ils sont venus le chercher pour l'emmener en prison

cart² N *(abbr* **cartridge)** cartouche *f*, cassette *f*
  ▸▸ **c. tape** bande *f* magnétique en cartouche

cartage ['kɑːtɪdʒ] N **1** *(transport) (in cart)* charroi *m*, charriage *m*; *(in lorry)* camionnage *m* **2** *(cost) (by cart)* (coût *m* de) charriage *m*; *(by lorry)* (coût de) camionnage *m*

carte blanche ['kɑːt'blɑːʃ] N **to give sb c. (to do sth)** donner carte blanche à qn (pour faire qch)

cartel [kɑː'tel] N *Com* cartel *m*; **oil/steel c.** cartel du pétrole/de l'acier; **to form a c.** former un cartel
  ▸▸ **c. laws** lois *fpl* anti-trust

carter ['kɑːtər] N charretier *m*

Cartesian [kɑː'tiːzɪən] ADJ, N *Phil* cartésien, -ienne

carthorse ['kɑːthɔːs] N cheval *m* d'attelage

Carthusian [kɑː'θjuːzɪən] ADJ **1** *Rel* chartreux **2** *Br Sch* de l'école de Charterhouse
  N **1** *Rel* chartreux, -euse **2** *Br Sch* élève *m/* ancien élève de l'école de Charterhouse

cartilage ['kɑːtɪlɪdʒ] N cartilage *m*

cartload ['kɑːtləʊd] N charretée *f*, voiturée *f* (**of** de); *(transported in tip cart)* tombereau *m*

cartographer [kɑː'tɒgrəfər] N cartographe *mf*

cartographic(al) [kɑːtə'græfɪk, -ɪk(ə)l] ADJ cartographique

cartography [kɑː'tɒgrəfɪ] N cartographie *f*

cartomancy ['kɑːtəmænsɪ] N cartomancie *f*

carton ['kɑːtən] N **1** *(box)* (boîte *f* en) carton *m* **2** *(container) (for yoghurt, cream etc)* pot *m*; *(for milk, orange juice etc)* brick *m*; **a c. of cigarettes** une cartouche de cigarettes

cartoon [kɑː'tuːn] N **1** *(in newspaper etc)* dessin *m* humoristique *ou* satirique; *Cin* dessin animé; **(strip) c.** bande *f* dessinée, BD *f* **2** *(caricature)* caricature *f* **3** *Art (sketch)* carton *m*
  ▸▸ **c. character** personnage *m* de bande dessinée *ou* de dessin animé; **c. strip** bande dessinée, BD

cartoonist [kɑː'tuːnɪst] N **1** *(in newspaper etc)* dessinateur, -trice de dessins humoristi-

ques *ou* satiriques; *(of strip cartoons)* dessinateur de bandes dessinées; *(for films)* dessinateur de dessins animés, animateur, -trice **2** *(caricaturist)* caricaturiste *mf*

cartridge ['kɑːtrɪdʒ] N **1** *Mil (for firearm)* cartouche *f* **2** *(container, unit) (of film, ink, fuse etc)* cartouche *f*; *(on record-player)* cellule *f* de lecture; *(for tape recorder)* cassette *f*. **3** *Phot* chargeur *m* (d'appareil photo)
  ▸▸ **c. belt** *(for hunter, soldier)* cartouchière *f*, *(for machine gun)* bande *f* (de mitrailleuse), bande-chargeur *f* souple *ou* articulée, *pl* bandes-chargeurs; **c. clip** chargeur *(d'une arme à feu)*; **c. paper** papier *m* à cartouche; **c. pen** stylo *m* à cartouche; **c. tape** bande *f* magnétique en cartouche

cartwheel ['kɑːtwiːl] N roue *f* de charrette; *Gym* **to turn cartwheels** faire la roue; **to do a c.** faire une roue

cartwright ['kɑːtraɪt] N charron *m*

carve [kɑːv] VT **1** *(wood, stone)* sculpter; *(design, name on marble etc)* graver, ciseler; **to c. a statue in** *or* **out of marble** sculpter une statue dans le marbre; **carved lion** lion *m* sculpté; *Fig* **carved in stone** *or* **tablets of stone** *(instructions, orders etc)* auquel on doit obéir à la lettre; **her recommendations are not carved in stone** il n'est pas nécessaire d'obéir à la lettre à ses recommandations **2** *(meat, poultry)* découper
  VI **1** *(sculpt)* sculpter (**in** dans) **2** *(of material)* **wood that carves well/badly** bois qui se prête bien/mal à la sculpture **3** *(at meal)* découper
 ▸ **carve out** VT SEP *(cut out) (piece of wood etc)* tailler, découper; *(sculpt) (statue etc)* sculpter; *Fig* **the company carved out a niche in the market** la société s'est taillé une place sur le marché; **to c. out a career for oneself** se faire une carrière
 ▸ **carve up** VT SEP **1** *(cut) (meat, poultry)* découper; *Fig Fam* **to c. sb up** *(disfigure)* défigurer qn; *Fig* **Europeans carved up the continent (among themselves)** les Européens se sont partagé le continent **2** *Aut Fam (overtake dangerously)* faire une queue de poisson à; **did you see how that idiot carved me up?** tu as vu la queue de poisson que m'a faite cet imbécile?

carver ['kɑːvər] N **1** *(sculptor)* sculpteur *m* **2** *(knife)* couteau *m* à découper **3** *Br (chair)* fauteuil *m* de table *(qu'occupe le chef de famille)*

carvery ['kɑːvərɪ] N grill *m*

carving ['kɑːvɪŋ] N **1** *Art (technique, object)* sculpture *f*, *(on wood, metal)* gravure *f*, *(on metal, stone)* ciselure *f*, **wood c.** sculpture sur bois **2** *(of meat)* découpage *m*
  ▸▸ **c. fork** fourchette *f* à découper; **c. knife** couteau *m* à découper; **c. set** service *m* à découper; **c. table** table *f* à découper

carwash ['kɑːwɒʃ] N *Aut* lave-auto *m*, *pl* lave-autos

caryatid [kærɪ'ætɪd] N *Archit* cariatide *f*

cascade [kæs'keɪd] N *(waterfall)*, *Fig* cascade *f*
  VI *(of water etc)*, *Fig (of balloons, hair)* tomber en cascade; **the tins came cascading down** les boîtes de conserve sont tombées les unes après les autres

cascading menu [kæs'keɪdɪŋ] N *Comput* menu *m* en cascade

CASE [keɪs] N *Comput (abbr* **computer-aided software engineering)** ingénierie *f* des systèmes assistée par ordinateur

CASE¹ [keɪs]

cas **1, 2, 4** ▪ affaire **3** ▪ arguments **3**

N **1** *(instance, situation)* cas *m*; **a c. in point** un cas d'espèce; **to put the c. clearly** exposer

clairement le cas *ou* la situation; **if that's the c.** dans ce cas-là, *Fml* s'il en est ainsi; **should that be the c.** le cas échéant; **it's a c. of now or never** il s'agit de saisir l'occasion *ou* de faire vite; **in c. of emergency/accident/ need** en cas d'urgence/d'accident/de besoin; **in c. he isn't there** au cas où il ne serait pas; **just in c.** à titre de précaution, *Fam* au cas où; **just in c. it rains I'll take an umbrella** je prends un parapluie, juste au cas où il pleuvrait; **I'll take an umbrella, just in c.** je prends un parapluie au cas où; **in any c.** *(at any rate)* en tout cas; *(besides)* de toute façon; **in that c.** dans ce cas; **in such a c., in such cases** en pareil cas, en pareille circonstance; **in these cases it's best to wait** dans de telles circonstances, il vaut mieux attendre; **in his c.** dans son cas; **let's take the c. of Mrs Smith** prenons le cas de Mme Smith; **or not, as the c. may be** ou non, suivant le cas; **in most cases** dans la plupart des cas; **it appears to be a c. of mistaken identity** il semble y avoir erreur sur la personne; **if it's a c. of not having enough money** si c'est une question d'argent; *Fam* **he's always on my c.** je l'ai tout le temps sur le dos; *Fam* **get off my c.!** lâche-moi les baskets!, oublie-moi!

2 *Med (of jaundice, scarlet fever etc)* cas *m*; *(patient)* malade *mf*; **heart c.** cardiaque *mf*; *Fam* **he's a c.** *(odd)* c'est un drôle de type

3 *Law etc* affaire *f*, **famous cases** causes *fpl ou* affaires célèbres; **the police are working on the c.** la police enquête sur cette affaire; **the c. will be heard on January 5th** l'audience aura lieu le 5 janvier; **to state the c.** faire l'exposé des faits; *Fig* **to state** *or* **put one's c.** plaider sa cause; **to put the c. for the defence** présenter la défense du prévenu; **the c. for the Crown** *(in criminal trial)* l'accusation *f*; **there is no c. against you** vous êtes hors de cause; **the judge ruled that there was no c. to answer** le juge a rendu un non-lieu; *Fig* **the c. for sb/sth** les arguments *mpl* en faveur de qn/qch; **to put up a strong c. for sb** *(defend)* prendre le parti de qn, défendre qn; *(recommend)* recommander qn très chaudement; **divorce c.** procès *m* en divorce

4 *Gram* cas *m*
  ▸▸ *Gram* **c. ending** désinence *f*, **c. history** antécédents *mpl*; **c. law** jurisprudence *f*, droit *m* jurisprudentiel; *Law* **c. load** (nombre *m* de) dossiers *mpl* à traiter; **c. study** étude *f* de cas

case² N **1** *(large)* **(packing) c.** caisse *f*, boîte *f* (d'emballage); **c. of wine** caisse de vin

2 *(for specific object) (for spectacles, cigarettes, musical instrument etc)* étui *m*; *(for jewellery)* coffret *m*, écrin *m*; *(for pencils, geometry etc instruments)* trousse *f*, **(display** *or* **glass) c.** vitrine *f*, **record c.** mallette *f* porte-disques; **dressing c.** nécessaire *m ou* trousse *f* de toilette; **card c.** porte-cartes *m inv*

3 *(suitcase)* valise *f*, *(briefcase)* porte-documents *m inv*

4 *(outer part) (of piano)* coffre *m*, caisse *f*, *(of organ)* buffet *m*; *(of clock)* caisse; *(of watch etc)* boîtier *m*; *(of lock)* palastre *m*, coffre; *(of cartridge)* douille *f*, étui *m*; *(of engine cylinder)* chemise *f*, enveloppe *f*, *(of turbine)* bâche *f*, *Aut (of differential etc)* carter *m*

5 *(in bookbinding)* couverture *f* cartonnée

6 *Typ* casse *f*, **lower c.** bas *m* de casse; **lower-c. letter** minuscule *f*, **upper c.** haut *m* de casse; **upper-c. letter** (lettre *f*) majuscule *f*, (lettre) capitale *f*, *Comput* **c. insensitive** qui ne distingue pas les majuscules des minuscules; *Comput* **c. sensitive** qui distingue les majuscules des minuscules; **this e-mail address is c. sensitive** cette adresse électronique tient compte des majuscules

VT 1 *(put in box) (goods)* mettre en caisse(s) **2** *(put outer layer on)* envelopper (**with** de); *(boiler, cylinder)* chemiser; *(turbine)* bâcher **3** *(in bookbinding) (book)* cartonner **4** *Sl* **to c. the joint** *(before burglary)* examiner les lieux

casebook ['keɪsbʊk] N **1** *Law* recueil *m* de jurisprudence **2** *Med* dossier *m* médical

casebound ['keɪsbaʊnd] ADJ *(book)* cartonné

cased [keɪst] ADJ *(edition)* cartonné

case-harden VT *Metal (steel)* tremper *ou* durcir à la surface

case-hardened ADJ *Metal* trempé à la surface; *Fam (person)* endurci

case-hardening N *Metal (of steel)* cémentation *f*

casein ['keɪsɪɪn] N *Chem, Ind* caséine *f*

casement ['keɪsmənt] N *(frame)* châssis *m* de fenêtre à deux battants
▸▸ **c. window** fenêtre *f* à battant *ou* battants, croisée *f*

casework ['keɪswɜːk] N *Med* traitement *m* individuel; *(social work)* assistance *f* individuelle

caseworker ['keɪswɜːkər] N assistant, -ante social(e)

cash [kæʃ] N *(no pl) (coins, banknotes)* argent *m*, liquide *m*; *(in commerce)* liquide, espèces *fpl*, *Fam (money)* argent, *Fam* fric *m*; **I haven't got any c.** *(no money)* je n'ai pas d'argent; *(no change)* je n'ai pas de monnaie; *Fam* **I'm short of c.** je suis à sec; **that's an awful lot of c.** c'est beaucoup d'argent *ou Fam* de fric; **to pay (in) c.** payer comptant; *(money not cheque)* payer en liquide *ou* en espèces; **will that be c. or shall I charge it to your account?** *(not credit)* vous payez comptant ou est-ce que je le mets sur votre compte?; *(money not cheque)* vous payez en liquide ou est-ce que je le mets sur votre compte?; **c. (purchases) only** *(notice at checkout)* paiements en liquide seulement; *Com* **c. against documents** comptant contre documents; *Acct* **c. at bank** avoir *m* en banque; **c. on delivery** paiement à la livraison; **c. in hand** fonds *mpl* en espèces *ou* argent en caisse; **it's all c. in hand in this sort of work** dans cette branche, tout se paye de la main à la main; *Acct* **c. in till** encaisse *f*, *Acct* **c. on hand** argent en caisse; *Com* **c. with order** paiement *m* à la commande, envoi *m* contre paiement; **discount for c.** escompte *m* de caisse

VT *(cheque, postal order etc)* toucher, encaisser; **to c. a cheque for sb** verser à qn le montant d'un chèque
▸▸ **c. account** compte *m* de caisse; **c. advance** avance *m* en numéraire; **c. balance** *(status)* situation *f* de caisse; *(amount remaining)* solde *m* actif, solde de caisse; *Acct* **c. basis accounting** comptabilité *f* de caisse *ou* de gestion; **c. benefits** avantages *mpl* en espèces; **c. bonus** prime *f* en espèces; **c. book** livre *m* ou journal *m* de caisse; **c. box** caisse *f*; **c. budget** budget *m* de trésorerie; **c. card** carte *f* de retrait; *Br* **c. and carry** libre-service *m* de gros, *pl* libres-services; *Acct* **c. contribution** apport *m* en numéraire *ou* en espèces; *Mktg* **c. cow** vache *f* à lait; *Agr* **c. crop** culture *f* de rapport *ou* commerciale; *Com* **c. deal** marché *m* au comptant; **c. deficit** déficit *m* de trésorerie; **c. deposit** versement *m* en espèces; **c. desk** caisse; **c. discount** escompte de caisse; **c. dispenser** distributeur *m* (automatique) de billets, DAB *m*, *Suisse* bancomat *m*; **c. dividend** dividende *m* en espèces; *Acct* **c. expenditure** dépenses *fpl* de caisse; **c. incentive** stimulation *f* financière; *Acct* **c. inflow** rentrées *fpl* de fonds; *Banking* **c. machine** distributeur de

billets; **c. management** gestion *f* de trésorerie; *Acct* **c. order** ordre *m* au comptant; *Acct* **c. outflow** sorties *fpl* de trésorerie; *Acct* **c. overs** excédent *m* de caisse; **c. payment** *(immediate)* paiement comptant; *(in cash)* paiement en espèces *ou* en liquide; *Banking* **c. point** distributeur *ou* guichet *m* automatique; *Acct* **c. position** situation de caisse; **c. price** prix *m* comptant; **c. purchase** achat *m* au comptant, achat contre espèces; *Acct* **c. ratio** ratio *m* de trésorerie; *Com* **c. rebate** remboursement *m*; *Acct* **c. receipt** reçu *m* pour paiement en espèces, reçu d'espèces; *Acct* **c. received** *(balance sheet item)* entrée *f* d'argent; **c. register** caisse (enregistreuse); *Acct* **c. report** *(form)* situation de caisse; **c. reserves** réserves *fpl* en espèces; *St Exch* **c. settlement** liquidation *f* en espèces; *Fin* **c. shortage** insuffisance *f* de trésorerie; *Acct* **c. statement** état *m* ou relevé *m* de caisse; *Acct* **c. surplus** restant *m* en caisse; **c. transaction** transaction *f* ou opération *f* au comptant; *Mktg* **c. trap** poids *m* mort; *Acct* **c. unders** manque *m* de caisse; *Fin* **c. voucher** pièce *f* de caisse, PC *f*; **c. withdrawals** retraits *mpl* d'espèces
▸ **cash in** VT SEP *Fin (exchange for money)* **to c. in savings stamps** se faire rembourser des timbres-épargne; *Sl* **to c. in one's chips** *or* **checks** *(die)* casser sa pipe
▸ **cash in on** VT INSEP *Fam (derive benefit from)* profiter de, tirer profit de
▸ **cash up** VI *Br* faire les comptes

cashable ['kæʃ(ə)bl] ADJ *(bill etc)* encaissable

cashback ['kæʃbæk] N *Br* = espèces *fpl* retirées à la caisse d'un magasin lors d'un paiement par carte

cashew [kæ'ʃuː] N *(tree)* anacardier *m*; *(nut)* (noix *f* de) cajou *m*
▸▸ **c. nut** (noix de) cajou; **c. nut tree** anacardier

cashflow ['kæʃfləʊ] N *Fin* cash-flow *m*, *pl* cash-flows, trésorerie *f*; *Acct (in cashflow statement)* marge *f* brute d'autofinancement; *Fam* **I've got a c. problem** j'ai des problèmes d'argent
▸▸ **c. forecast** prévision *f* de trésorerie; **c. management** gestion *f* de trésorerie; *Acct* **c. statement** état *m* des mouvements de la trésorerie

cashier[1] [kæ'ʃɪər] N caissier, -ière; *Am* **c.'s check** chèque *m* de banque; **c.'s desk** comptoir-caisse *m*, *pl* comptoirs-caisses; **c.'s office** bureau *m* du caissier

cashier[2] VT *Mil, Naut (dismiss)* casser

cashless ['kæʃlɪs] ADJ **the c. society** la société où l'argent liquide n'est plus utilisé; **c. transaction** transaction *f* sans argent

cashmere ['kæʃmɪər] N *Tex* cachemire *m*; **c. shawl** (châle *m* de) cachemire; **c. sweater** pull *m* en cachemire

casing ['keɪsɪŋ] N **1** *(process) (of goods)* encaissage *m*, mise *f* en caisses; *(of book)* cartonnage *m*; *(of mine shaft etc)* tubage *m*, cuvelage *m* **2** *(outer layer) (of pump etc)* enveloppe *f*, garniture *f*; *(of cylinder)* blindage *m*, chemise *f*; *(of turbine)* huche *f*, bâche *f* fermée; *(of machine)* cage *f*, coquille *f*; *Constr (for reinforced concrete)* coffrage *m*; *Aut (of differential)* carter *m*; *(of clutch)* boîte *f*, caisse *f*, carter; **tyre c.** enveloppe (extérieure) de pneu

casino [kə'siːnəʊ] N casino *m*

cask [kɑːsk] N fût *m*, tonneau *m*; *Com* **wine in the c.** vin *m* en fût

casket ['kɑːskɪt] N **1** *(for jewellery)* coffret *m*, cassette *f*; *(for money)* cassette **2** *esp Am (coffin)* cercueil *m* **3** *(for ashes)* urne *f*

CASM ['kæz(ə)m] N *Comput (abbr* **computer-aided sales and marketing***)* vente *f* et marketing *m* assistés par ordinateur

Caspian ['kæspɪən] ADJ caspien; **the C. Sea** la mer Caspienne

Cassandra [kə'sændrə] N *Myth* Cassandre *f*, *Fig* oiseau *m* de malheur

cassata [kə'sɑːtə] N *Culin* cassate *f*

cassava [kə'sɑːvə] N *Bot* cassave *f*, manioc *m*
▸▸ **c. flour** farine *f* de manioc

casserole ['kæsərəʊl] N **1** *Br (pan)* cocotte *f* **2** *(food)* ragoût *m* en cocotte; **beef c.** ragoût de bœuf
VT *(meat etc)* cuire à la cocotte

> Note that the French word **casserole** is a false friend and is never a translation for the English word **casserole**. It means **saucepan**.

cassette [kə'set] N **1** *(audio, video etc)* cassette *f* **2** *Phot* chargeur *m*
▸▸ **c. case** étui *m* de cassette; **c. deck** lecteur *m* de cassettes; *Comput* **c. drive** lecteur de cassettes; **c. head cleaner** cassette autonettoyante; **c. library** cassettothèque *f*, **c. player** lecteur de cassettes; **c. recorder** magnétophone *m* à cassettes

cassock ['kæsək] N *Rel* soutane *f*

cassowary ['kæsəweərɪ] N *(bird)* casoar *m*

CAST [kɑːst]

N	acteurs **1** ▪ coup **2** ▪ plâtre **3**
	▪ moulage **3**
VT	projeter **1** ▪ jeter **1** ▪ distribuer les rôles de **3** ▪ mouler **5**

N **1** *Theat, Cin, TV* distribution *f*, acteurs *mpl*; **the c. is Italian** tous les acteurs sont italiens; **the members of the c. include …** parmi les acteurs; *esp Radio* **other parts were played by members of the c.** les autres rôles étaient tenus par les comédiens déjà nommés; **he was in the c. of …** il a joué dans …; *Theat* **to have a c. of three** être joué par trois acteurs; *Cin* **a c. of thousands** des milliers d'acteurs; **c. and credits** générique *m* **2** *(of dice, net)* coup *m*; *(in fishing) (of line, fly, net)* lancer *m* **3** *Med* plâtre *m*; *Art, Metal etc (mould)* moule *m* en creux; *(item)* pièce *f* moulée; *(of plaster)* plâtre; **plaster c.** *Art* moulage *m* au plâtre; *Med* plâtre; **to take a c. of sth** mouler qch; **the dentist took a c. of my teeth** le dentiste a fait un moulage en plâtre de mes dents; **they took a c. of the footprints** ils ont relevé les empreintes de pas; **to have one's arm in a c.** avoir le bras dans le plâtre **4** *(squint)* **to have a c. in one's eye** avoir une coquetterie dans l'œil **5** *Lit* **a man of his c.** un homme de sa trempe; **c. of mind** mentalité *f* **6** *(of earthworm)* déjections *fpl* **7** *(skin of insect, snake)* dépouille *f* **8** *(regurgitated food)* pelote *f* régurgitée *(par les hiboux, les faucons)*

VT *(pt, pp* **cast***)* **1** *(shadow)* porter, projeter; *Fml (stone etc)* jeter, lancer; *(net, line)* lancer; *Fml* **she c. her eyes over the letter** elle a parcouru la lettre; *Naut* **to c. anchor** jeter l'ancre; **to c. doubt on sth** jeter le doute sur qch; **this cast doubt on his ability** cela jeta un doute sur ses capacités; **to c. its skin** *(of reptile)* muer; **to c. a shoe** *(of horse)* perdre un fer; **to c. a spell over sb** ensorceler qn, envoûter qn
2 *Pol etc* **to c. a vote**, **to c. one's vote** voter (**for** pour); **the numbers of votes c. for …** le nombre de voix pour …
3 *Theat, Cin, TV (play, film)* distribuer les rôles de; **to c. sb for a part** attribuer un rôle à qn; **she was c. as** *or* **in the role of Desdemona** on lui a donné le rôle de Desdémone; *Fig* **to c. sb in the role of the villain** donner à qn le rôle du méchant

4 *(horoscope)* faire
5 *Art, Metal etc (metal)* fondre; *(cylinder etc)* mouler, couler; *(medal)* sabler; *(statue)* couler; **the statue had been cast in bronze** la statue avait été coulée dans le bronze; **cast in one piece** coulé en bloc
vi lancer; **to c. for fish** pêcher au lancer
ADJ *Art, Metal* coulé, fondu
▸▸ **c. iron** fonte *f*; **c. list** *Cin, TV* générique; *Theat* distribution; **c. steel** acier *m* moulé; *Cer* **c. ware** pièces coulées
▸ **cast about, cast around** *vi* chercher; **to c. around for sth** chercher qch
▸ **cast aside** *vt sep* jeter sur le côté; *Fig (wife, friends, doubts)* abandonner, se défaire de; **to c. aside one's fears** oublier ses craintes; **to c. aside one's former life** changer de vie; **are you going to c. all this aside for a foolish dream?** est-ce que tu vas renoncer à tout ça pour une chimère?
▸ **cast away** *vt sep* *Naut* **to be c. away** faire naufrage
▸ **cast back** *vt sep* **to c. one's mind back** revenir en arrière; **to c. one's mind back to sth** se rappeler qch; **c. your mind back a year** souvenez-vous ou rappelez-vous l'année dernière
▸ **cast down** *vt* sep **1** *(eyes)* baisser; *(weapons)* déposer
2 *Lit* **to be c. down** *(dejected)* être abattu ou découragé ou déprimé
▸ **cast off** *vt sep* **1** *(reject) (person)* rejeter
2 *(clothes)* enlever, se dépouiller de; *(bonds etc)* se défaire de, se libérer de; *Fig (shyness etc)* se débarrasser de
3 *Knitting (stitches)* arrêter
4 *Naut (moorings)* larguer
vi 1 *Naut (of ship)* larguer les amarres
2 *Knitting* arrêter les mailles
▸ **cast on** *Knitting* *vt sep* *(stitches)* monter
vi monter les mailles
▸ **cast out** *vt sep* **1** *(reject) (person)* rejeter
2 *(exorcise) (evil spirits)* chasser, exorciser
▸ **cast up** *vt sep* **1** **to c. sth up to sb** *(as reproach)* reprocher qch à qn
2 *(of sea)* rejeter

castanets [kæstə'nets] **NPL** **(pair of) c.** (paire *f* de) castagnettes *fpl*

castaway ['ka:stəweɪ] **N** naufragé, -ée

caste [ka:st] **N** caste *f*; **high/low-c.** de haute/basse caste; *Fig* **to lose c.** se discréditer

casteless ['ka:stlɪs] **ADJ** sans caste

castellated ['kæstɪleɪtɪd] **ADJ** *Archit* crénelé; *(with turrets)* à tourelles

caster ['ka:stər] **N 1** *Metal etc (machine)* fondeuse *f* **2** *(for sugar, cocoa)* saupoudroir *m*
▸▸ *Aut* **c. action** *(of steering)* effet *m* de chasse; *Br* **c. sugar** sucre *m* en poudre

castigate ['kæstɪgeɪt] **VT 1** *Old-fashioned (punish) (person)* châtier, corriger **2** *Fml (criticize) (person, book etc)* critiquer sévèrement, étriller

castigation [kæstɪ'geɪʃən] **N 1** *Old-fashioned (punishment)* châtiment *m*, correction *f* **2** *Fml (criticism)* critique *f* sévère

Castile [kæ'sti:l] **N** Castille *f*; **New C.** Nouvelle-Castille *f*

Castilian [kæs'tɪlɪən] **ADJ** castillan
N 1 *(person)* Castillan, -ane **2** *Ling* castillan *m*

casting ['ka:stɪŋ] **N 1** *(in fishing)* lancer *m* **2** *Art, Metal etc (process)* moulage *m*, fonte *f*; *(individual item)* pièce *f* coulée, pièce de fonte; **heavy castings** grosses pièces; **die c.** *(item)* pièce moulée sous pression; **sand c.** *(process)* coulée *f* en sable **3** *Cin, Theat* distribution *f* des rôles, casting *m*; *Fam* **she got the part through the c. couch** elle a eu le rôle parce qu'elle a couché avec le metteur en scène
▸▸ *Cin, Theat* **c. director** directeur, -trice de

casting, régisseur *m* de distribution; *Fishing* **c. net** épervier *m*; *Knitting* **c. off** arrêt *m* (de mailles); *Knitting* **c. on** montage *m* (de mailles); **c. vote** voix *f* prépondérante; **the chairman has the c. vote** la voix du président est prépondérante

castle ['ka:s(ə)l] **N 1** château *m*; *(fortress)* château fort; *Fig* **to build castles in the air** *or* **in Spain** bâtir des châteaux en Espagne
2 *Chess* tour *f*
vi *Chess* roquer

castling ['ka:s(ə)lɪŋ] **N** *Chess* roque *f*

cast-off **N 1** *(item of clothing)* vieux vêtement *m*; **I used to wear my brother's cast-offs** je portais les vieilles nippes de mon frère **2** *Fig (person) (male)* laissé-pour-compte *m*, *pl* laissés-pour-compte; *(female)* laissée-pour-compte *f*, *pl* laissées-pour-compte; **one of society's cast-offs** un laissé-pour-compte de la société; **the manager had built a team from other clubs' cast-offs** le directeur sportif avait formé une équipe avec les joueurs dont les autres équipes ne voulaient pas; **I'm not going out with one of his cast-offs** je ne veux pas sortir avec une copine dont il ne veut plus **3** *Typ (in printing)* calibrage *m*
ADJ dont personne ne veut; **c. clothing** vieux vêtements

castor ['ka:stər] **N** *(on chair, bed etc)* roulette *f*; **the desk is on castors** le bureau est sur roulettes
▸▸ **c. oil** huile *f* de ricin

castrate [kæs'treɪt] **VT** *(animal, man)* châtrer, castrer; *Fig (text etc)* mutiler, expurger

castration [kæs'treɪʃən] **N** *(of animal, man)* castration *f*; *Fig (of text etc)* mutilation *f*, expurgation *f*

castrato, *pl* **castrati** [kæ'stra:təʊ, -tɪ] **N** *Mus* castrat *m*

casual ['kæʒʊ(ə)l] **ADJ 1** *(remark)* en passant, désinvolte; *(glance)* au hasard; **it was just a c. remark** j'ai/il a *etc* dit ça en passant; **to engage in c. conversation** parler de choses et d'autres ou de la pluie et du beau temps; **to throw out a c. suggestion** suggérer quelque chose en passant; **to the c. observer** pour un observateur non-averti
2 *(relaxed) (person, manner, approach)* décontracté; **they were very c. about the danger** ils ne se sont pas souciés du danger
3 *(not serious, not taking sth seriously)* insouciant; **your attitude's too c.** tu es trop insouciant; **I found the police very c. about the whole situation** j'ai trouvé que la police a manqué de sérieux dans cette affaire
4 *(jacket etc)* sport *inv*; décontracté
5 *(employment, worker)* temporaire
6 *(encounter)* fortuit, accidentel
N *Br Fam (football supporter)* jeune supporter *m* de foot *(soucieux de sa mise et souvent responsable de violences)*
NPL casuals *(shoes)* mocassins *mpl*
▸▸ **c. clothes** tenue *f* sport *inv* ou décontractée; **c. employment** *(temporary)* emploi *m* temporaire; *(without social benefits)* = emploi précaire sans avantages sociaux; **c. labour** main-d'œuvre *f* occasionnelle ou temporaire, *pl* mains-d'œuvre; **c. sex** rapports *mpl* sexuels de rencontre; **c. wear** tenue sport ou décontractée; **c. worker** *(temporary)* employé, -ée ou travailleur, -euse temporaire; *(without social benefits)* = employé qui ne bénéficie d'aucun avantage social

casualisation [kæʒʊ(ə)laɪ'zeɪʃən] **N** **the c. of labour** la précarisation de l'emploi

casually ['kæʒʊ(ə)lɪ] **ADV 1** *(to remark, suggest)* en passant
2 *(to walk, do sth)* avec décontraction; **she told him, quite c., that she had ...** elle lui a dit, tout tranquillement, qu'elle avait ...

3 *(not seriously enough) (to treat sth)* avec trop de décontraction; **they're treating this far too c.** il y a un manque de sérieux
4 **to dress c.** s'habiller décontracté ou *Fam* décontract; **you're much too c. dressed to ...** tu es habillé de façon bien trop décontractée pour ...
5 *(to meet)* par hasard

casualness ['kæʒʊ(ə)lnɪs] **N 1** *(of remark)* désinvolture *f* **2** *(of style of dress, approach)* décontraction *f* **3** *(lack of seriousness)* manque *m* de sérieux

casualty ['kæʒʊəltɪ] **N 1** *(victim) (in accident, fire, earthquake etc)* victime *f*, *(in war)* blessé, -ée; *(in road accident)* blessé, accidenté, -ée; **to be a c. of sth** être la victime de qch; **there were no casualties** il n'y a pas eu de victimes; *Mil* **casualties** pertes *fpl*; *Fig* **the party had many casualties in the last election** le parti a perdu beaucoup de députés aux dernières élections; **freedom of speech was one of the first casualties** la liberté d'expression a été une des premières choses à disparaître; **these children are the casualties of divorce** ces enfants sont les victimes du divorce **2** *Br (hospital department)* urgences *fpl*; **she was taken to c.** elle a été emmenée aux urgences
▸▸ *Br* **c. department** *(of hospital)* service *m* des urgences; *Mil* **c. list, c. return** état des pertes

casuist ['kæzjʊɪst] **N** casuiste *m*

casuistry ['kæzjʊɪstrɪ] **N** casuistique *f*

CAT [kæt] **N** *Med (abbr* **computerized axial tomography)** TDM *f*
▸▸ **C. scan** scanographie *f*

cat [kæt] **N 1** *(male)* chat *m*; *(female)* chatte *f*; **tom c.** matou *m*; **ginger** *or Fam* **marmalade c.** chat roux tigré; **wild c.** chat sauvage; **the big cats** *(lions, tigers etc)* les grands félins *mpl*; **it smelled of cats** ça sentait le pipi de chat; *Fam* **that looks like something the c.'s brought in** ça, c'est dégoûtant; *Fam* **you look like something the c.'s brought in** tu es dans un état lamentable; **to fight like c. and dog** s'entendre comme chien et chat; *Fam* **c. got your tongue?** tu as perdu ta langue?; *Fam* **he thinks he's the c.'s whiskers** il se croit sorti de la cuisse de Jupiter; *Fig* **to see which way the c. jumps** voir d'où vient le vent; **to play a c.-and-mouse game with sb** jouer au chat et à la souris avec qn; *Prov* **when the c.'s away the mice will play** quand le chat n'est pas là, les souris dansent; *Prov* **a c. may look at a king** = un chien regarde bien un évêque; *Fam* **to be like a c. on hot bricks** *or* **on a hot tin roof** ne pas tenir en place; *Fam* **to let the c. out of the bag** vendre la mèche; *Fam* **to put** *or* **set the c. among the pigeons** jeter un pavé dans la mare; *Fam* **there's no** *or* **there isn't enough room to swing a c.** on ne peut pas se tourner
2 *Pej (woman, girl)* sale vache *f*
3 *Am Sl (man)* type *m*, individu *m*
▸▸ **c. burglar** monte-en-l'air *m inv*; **c.'s cradle** *(game)* = jeu *m* qui consiste à faire des figures avec une ficelle; *Aut* **c.'s eyes®** catadioptres *mpl*, cataphotes® *mpl*, yeux *mpl* de chat; **c. flap** chatière *f*; **c. litter** litière *f* (pour chats); **c. show** exposition *f* féline

cataclysm ['kætəklɪz(ə)m] **N** cataclysme *m*

cataclysmic [kætə'klɪzmɪk] **ADJ** cataclysmique

catacombs ['kætəku:mz] **NPL** catacombes *fpl*

catafalque ['kætəfælk] **N** catafalque *m*

Catalan ['kætəlæn] **ADJ** catalan
N 1 *(person)* Catalan, -ane **2** *Ling* catalan *m*

catalepsy ['kætəlepsɪ] **N** *Med* catalepsie *f*

cataleptic [kætə'leptɪk] **ADJ, N** *Med* cataleptique *mf*

catalogue, *Am* **catalog** ['kætəlɒg] N 1 *Com (book)* catalogue *m* 2 *(list) (of books, works etc)* catalogue *m*; *Fig* **the holiday was a c. of disasters** les vacances ont été une suite de catastrophes; **subject c.** catalogue thématique

▪ VT cataloguer

►► **c. number** référence *f*; *(for library book)* référence bibliographique; *Com* **c. price** prix *m* catalogue; *Com* **c. selling** vente *f* par catalogue

cataloguing, *Am* **cataloging** ['kætəlɒgɪŋ] N catalogage *m*

Catalonia [kætə'ləʊnɪə] N Catalogne *f*

catalysis [kə'tælɪsɪs] N *Chem* catalyse *f*

catalyst ['kætəlɪst] N *Chem, Fig* catalyseur *m*

catalytic [kætə'lɪtɪk] ADJ *Chem* catalytique; *Fig* catalyseur

►► *Aut* **c. converter** pot *m* catalytique

catamaran [kætəmə'ræn] N *Naut* catamaran *m*

cataplasm ['kætəplæz(ə)m] N *Med* cataplasme *m*

catapult ['kætəpʌlt] N 1 *Br (for stones etc)* fronde *f* 2 *(on aircraft carrier)* catapulte *f* ▪ VT catapulter, projeter; *Tech (plane)* catapulter; **he catapulted the stone over the wall** il a lancé la pierre par-dessus le mur; *Fig* **these reforms catapulted the country into the 20th century** ces réformes ont propulsé le pays dans le vingtième siècle; **to c. sb to stardom** *(of film etc)* propulser qn vers la célébrité

▪ VI entrer en trombe (**into a room** dans une pièce)

cataract ['kætərækt] N *(in river), Med* cataracte *f*

catarrh [kə'tɑːr] N *Med* catarrhe *m*; **bronchial c.** bronchite *f*

catarrhal [kə'tɑːr(ə)l] ADJ *(cough, person)* catarrheux

catastrophe [kə'tæstrəfɪ] N catastrophe *f*; **to head for/end in c.** aller vers la/se terminer en catastrophe

catastrophic [kætə'strɒfɪk] ADJ *(effect etc)* catastrophique

catastrophically [kætə'strɒfɪklɪ] ADV d'une façon catastrophique

catatonia [kætə'təʊnɪə] N *Med* catatonie *f*

catatonic [kætə'tɒnɪk] N, ADJ *Med* catatonique *mf*

catcall ['kætkɔːl] N *Theat etc* sifflet *m* de mécontentement; **there were catcalls from the audience** le public a sifflé en signe de mécontentement

▪ VT *(actor)* siffler

▪ VI *(of audience)* siffler (en signe de mécontentement)

CATCH [kætʃ]

N	prise 1 ▪ pêche 2 ▪ loquet 4 ▪ piège 5
VT	attraper 1, 2, 6 ▪ saisir 3 ▪ attirer 4 ▪ se prendre 5
VI	se prendre 4

N 1 *(of ball etc)* prise *f* au vol; **that was a good c.** bien joué!; **to make an easy/a difficult c.** attraper une balle facile/difficile; **to play c.** *(of children)* jouer au ballon

2 *(in fishing)* pêche *f*; **to have a good c.** faire (une) bonne pêche; **the day's c.** la pêche de la journée

3 *(person as marriage partner)* parti *m*; **he's/she's no great c.** ce n'est pas un bon parti

4 *(fastening) (on door etc)* loquet *m*, loqueteau *m*; *(of window)* loqueteau; *(to permit dismantling, opening etc)* crochet *m*; *(to limit movement of mechanism, drawer etc)* taquet *m*

5 *(disadvantage)* piège *m*; **there's a c. in it** il y

a un truc *ou* un piège; **that's** *or* **there's the c.** voilà le hic;

6 **with a c. in one's voice** la voix pleine d'émotion

7 *Mus* canon *m*

8 *(in rowing)* attaque *f*

▪ VT *(pt, pp* **caught** [kɔːt]*)* 1 *(ball etc)* attraper, saisir; *(fish, thief etc)* attraper, prendre; **c.!** *(when throwing sth to sb)* attrape!; **well caught!** bien joué!; *Ftbl* le beau blocage!; *(said by sports coach etc)* excellente réception de la balle!; *Naut* **to c. the wind** *(of sail etc)* prendre le vent; **I caught him as he fell** je l'ai retenu *ou* attrapé au moment où il tombait; **I caught him by the hand** je l'ai attrapé par la main; **to c. sb in the act** *or* **red-handed** prendre qn sur le fait *ou* la main dans le sac; **don't get caught!** ne te fais pas prendre!; **you'll be in trouble if your mother catches you** gare à toi si ta mère t'attrape; **caught you!** je t'y prends!; **to c. sb doing sth** prendre *ou* surprendre qn en train de faire qch; *Fam* **you won't c. me doing that again** on ne m'y reprendra plus; **to be caught in a storm** être surpris par un orage; **you might c. her if you run** vous pouvez la rattraper si vous courez; **you're unlikely to c. her at home** je ne pense pas que tu la trouveras chez elle; **you caught me just as I was going into a meeting** tu m'as parlé au moment où j'allais en réunion; **we caught him in a good mood** il était de bonne humeur quand nous l'avons vu; **to c. sb napping** prendre qn au dépourvu; *Fam* **c. you later!** on se voit plus tard!

2 *(not miss) (train etc)* attraper, prendre; *Fam (manage to see) (film)* voir; *Fam (manage to hear) (radio programme)* écouter; *Fam* **c. this outstanding singer next month** ne manquez pas ce chanteur étonnant le mois prochain

3 *(perceive) (sounds)* saisir, percevoir; **to c. a glimpse of sth, to c. sight of sth** apercevoir qch; **I caught a few words** j'ai entendu *ou* j'ai saisi quelques mots; **I didn't c. what you were saying** je n'ai pas entendu ce que vous disiez; **I caught a hint of bitterness** *(in what she said)* j'ai senti un peu d'amertume dans ses paroles; **the author has caught the mood of the time** l'auteur a su rendre l'ambiance de l'époque

4 *(make impression on) (sb's attention)* attirer; **to c. sb's eye** attirer l'attention de qn; **nothing in the shop caught my fancy** je n'ai rien trouvé qui me plaisait dans la boutique; **their story caught the imagination of the public** leur histoire a passionné le public *ou* retenu l'attention du public

5 *(entangle)* **I caught my dress on a nail** j'ai fait un accroc à ma robe avec un clou; **he caught his foot on a root and fell** il s'est pris le pied dans une racine et il est tombé; **don't c. your fingers in the door!** ne te coince pas les doigts dans la porte!; **there's something caught in the door** il y a quelque chose de coincé dans la porte

6 *(contract) (illness)* attraper; *Fig (habit)* prendre; **to c. (a) cold** s'enrhumer, attraper un rhume; **I caught this cold from you** c'est toi qui m'as passé ce rhume; **to c. fire** *or* **light** prendre feu

7 *(of blow, object)* **the punch caught me in the chest** j'ai reçu le coup de poing en plein dans la poitrine; **the stone caught her on the arm** elle a reçu la pierre sur le bras; *Boxing* **he caught him with a left to the chin** il lui a porté un gauche au menton; *Fam* **you'll c. it!** ça va être ta fête!

8 **to c. the sun** *(of person)* prendre des couleurs; **the sun caught her hair/the drops of dew** le soleil brilla dans ses cheveux/les perles de rosée; **my bedroom catches the sun** le soleil donne dans ma chambre; **the garden really catches the sun in the afternoon** le jardin est très ensoleillé l'après-midi

9 *Fam (fool)* attraper, avoir; **you won't c. me!** ça ne prend pas (avec moi)!

▪ VI 1 attraper; **(here) c.!** tiens, attrape!; **I'm**

hopeless at catching *(ball etc)* je n'arrive jamais à rien attraper

2 *(of gears)* s'enclencher

3 *(of fire)* prendre, s'allumer

4 *(become entangled) (in door, machinery etc)* se prendre; *(on thorn, nail etc)* s'accrocher; **my fingers caught in the drawer** je me suis coincé les doigts dans le tiroir

5 *Am* **to c. on fire** prendre feu

►► *Agr* **c. crop** culture *f* dérobée; **c. question** question-piège *f*, *pl* questions-pièges, colle *f*; *Fig* **c. 22** cercle *m* vicieux

► **catch at** VT INSEP *(grab at)* essayer de saisir; *(hold on to)* s'accrocher à; **to c. at an opportunity** saisir une opportunité

► **catch on** VI 1 *(of fashion etc)* avoir du succès; *(of tune)* accrocher; **the game never caught on in Europe** ce jeu n'a jamais pris en Europe *ou* eu de succès en Europe

2 *Fam (understand)* saisir, piger; **he still hasn't caught on** il n'y est toujours pas; **to c. on quickly** comprendre vite

► **catch out** VT SEP *(trap) (by difficult question)* prendre, piéger; *(of circumstances)* surprendre; **the police caught her out when they asked her ...** la police l'a piégée en lui demandant ...; **to c. sb out in a lie** prendre *ou* surprendre qn à mentir; **a lot of investors got caught out when the stock market collapsed** beaucoup d'investisseurs se sont fait piéger quand la Bourse s'est effondrée; **we got caught out by the rain** nous avons été surpris par la pluie

► **catch up** VI *(close gap, get closer)* rattraper son retard; **to c. up with sb** rattraper qn; **caught up with them at the lights** nous les avons rattrapés au feu rouge; **the runners behind are catching up** les coureurs qui sont derrière se rapprochent; **to c. up on** *or* **with one's work/sleep** rattraper du travail/du sommeil en retard; *Fam* **it will c. up with you (one of these days)** ça va te retomber sur le nez

▪ VT SEP 1 *(reach) (person, car in front etc)* rattraper

2 *(entangle)* **I got caught up in a discussion** j'ai été entraîné dans une discussion; **she got really caught up in the electoral campaign** elle s'est laissé complètement absorber par la campagne électorale; **they were caught up in a traffic jam for hours** ils ont été bloqués dans un embouteillage pendant des heures; **to be caught up in a wave of enthusiasm** être entraîné dans un mouvement d'enthousiasme

3 *(snatch up) (object)* saisir; *(baby, child)* prendre au bras

catch-all N *Fam* fourre-tout *m inv*

►► **c. category** catégorie *f* fourre-tout; **c. clause** clause *f* fourre-tout

catch-as-catch-can N *(wrestling)* catch *m*, lutte *f* libre

catcher ['kætʃər] N 1 attrapeur, -euse; **rat c.** *(person, dog)* preneur *m* de rats 2 *Baseball* attrapeur *m*, receveur *m*; **c.'s mitt** gant *m* de baseball

catching ['kætʃɪŋ] ADJ *(disease, habit etc)* contagieux; *(enthusiasm)* communicatif

N 1 *(of ball)* réception *f*; **I'm no good at c.** je ne suis pas doué pour rattraper les balles qu'on m'envoie 2 *(of toothed wheel)* engrenure *f*, *(of gearing)* enclenchement *m*

catchline ['kætʃlaɪn] N accroche *f*, *(identification for story)* intitulé *m*

catchment ['kætʃmənt] N *(of water)* captation *f*, captage *m*

►► **c. area** *Geog (drainage area)* bassin *m* hydrographique; *Admin (for hospital)* = circonscription *f* hospitalière; *(for school)* secteur *m* de recrutement scolaire; *Geog* **c. basin** bassin hydrographique

catchpenny ['kætʃpenɪ] ADJ *(book, ornaments)* racoleur; **c. scheme** *or* **show** attrape-nigaud *m*, *pl* attrape-nigaud(s)

catchphrase ['kætʃfreɪz] N *(of comedian)* formule f *(comique)*; *(political)* slogan m; *(in advertising)* accroche f

catchword ['kætʃwɜːd] N **1** *Pol* slogan m **2** *Theat (cue)* réplique f

catchy ['kætʃɪ] ADJ *(tune)* entraînant, facile à retenir; *(slogan)* facile à retenir

catechism ['kætɪkɪz(ə)m] N catéchisme m

catechist ['kætəkɪst] N catéchiste mf

catechize ['kætəkaɪz] VT **1** *Rel* catéchiser **2** *Fig (question)* interroger, questionner

categoric(al) [kætɪ'gɒrɪk, -ɪk(ə)l] ADJ catégorique; *Phil* **categorical imperative** impératif m catégorique

categorically [kætɪ'gɒrɪklɪ] ADV *(to answer, refuse etc)* catégoriquement

categorization [kætɪɡəraɪ'zeɪʃ(ə)n] N catégorisation f

categorize ['kætɪɡəraɪz] VT classer par catégories; **I don't like being categorized** je n'aime pas qu'on me colle une étiquette

category ['kætɪɡərɪ] N catégorie f
▸▸ *Mktg* **c. leader** *(product)* chef m de file dans sa catégorie

cater ['keɪtər] VT **to c. a party** fournir le repas d'une soirée; **we're having the meal catered** nous faisons fournir le repas
▸ **cater for** VT INSEP **1** *(provide with food) (people, function etc)* fournir les repas à, préparer les repas pour **2** *(provide with special requirement)* **parties catered for** *(notice in hotel etc)* = banquets, noces; **hotel that caters for English visitors** hôtel qui s'adresse surtout à la clientèle anglaise; **the hotel doesn't c. for children** l'hôtel ne prévoit pas d'aménagements pour les enfants; **to c. for all tastes** satisfaire tous les goûts; **I hadn't catered for that** *(allowed for)* je n'avais pas prévu ça
▸ **cater to** VT INSEP *(needs)* satisfaire à

cater-corner(ed) ADJ, ADV *Am* diamétralement opposé

caterer ['keɪtərər] N *Com* traiteur m

catering ['keɪtərɪŋ] N restauration f; *Aviat* service m traiteur m; **who did the c. at your wedding?** qui a préparé le repas/le buffet à votre mariage?
▸▸ **c. company** société f de restauration; **c. contract** contrat m de restauration; **c. industry** industrie f de la restauration; **c. manager** chef m ou responsable mf de la restauration; **c. staff** personnel m de restauration

caterpillar ['kætəpɪlər] N **1** chenille f **2** *Tech* chenille f
▸▸ *Tech* **C®. track** chenille; **C®. tractor** tracteur m à chenilles; **C®. tread** chenille

caterwaul ['kætəwɔːl] VI **1** *(of cat)* feuler **2** *Fig (of person)* hurler

caterwauling ['kætəwɔːlɪŋ] N **1** *(of cats)* feulements mpl **2** *Fig (of person)* hurlements mpl

catfish ['kætfɪʃ] N **1** silure m, poisson-chat m, pl poissons-chats **2** *(wolffish)* blennie f

catgut ['kætɡʌt] N **1** *Mus* corde f de boyau; **c. strings** *(for violin)* cordes en boyau de chat **2** *Med* catgut m

catharsis [kə'θɑːsɪs] N catharsis f

cathartic [kə'θɑːtɪk] ADJ cathartique

cathedral [kə'θiːdrəl] N cathédrale f
▸▸ **c. city** ville f épiscopale, évêché m

Catherine ['kæθrɪn] N *Hist* **C. the Great** la Grande Catherine
▸▸ **C. wheel** *(firework)* soleil m

catheter ['kæθɪtər] N *Med* cathéter m; **indwelling c.** sonde f intérieure ou à demeure; **he has to have a c.** il faut qu'on lui pose un cathéter

cathode ['kæθəʊd] N *Elec* cathode f, **photo-(electric) c.** cathode photoélectrique
▸▸ *Elec* **c. beam** faisceau m cathodique; *Elec* **c. rays** rayons mpl cathodiques; *Elec* **c. ray tube** tube m cathodique; *Elec* **c. ray tube monitor** moniteur m à tube cathodique; *Elec* **c. screen** écran m cathodique

Catholic ['kæθlɪk] *Rel* ADJ catholique
N catholique mf; **she has become a C.** elle est devenue catholique

catholic ['kæθlɪk] ADJ *(wide-ranging)* éclectique; *(broad-minded)* à l'esprit large; *(universal)* universel; **to be c. in one's tastes** avoir des goûts éclectiques

Catholicism [kə'θɒlɪsɪz(ə)m] N *Rel* catholicisme m

cathouse ['kæthaʊs] N *Am Sl (brothel)* bordel m

catkin ['kætkɪn] N *Bot* chaton m

catlick ['kætlɪk] N *Fam* **to give oneself** or **have a c.** se laver le bout du nez, faire une toilette de chat

catmint ['kætmɪnt] N *(plant)* cataire f, herbe f aux chats

catnap ['kætnæp] *Fam* N petite sieste f, somme m; **to take** or **have a c.** faire une petite sieste
VI (-pp-) faire une petite sieste ou un somme

catnip ['kætnɪp] N *(plant)* cataire f, herbe f aux chats

cat-o'-nine-tails N chat m à neuf queues

catspaw, cat's-paw ['kætspɔː] N *Old-fashioned* **to be sb's c.** être le pigeon de qn; **to be made a c. of** être dupé

catsuit ['kætsuːt] N combinaison f

catsup ['kætsəp] N *Am* = ketchup

cattery ['kætərɪ] N pension f pour chats

cattiness ['kætɪnɪs] N *Fam* vacherie f, rosserie f

cattle ['kæt(ə)l] N *(no pl)* bétail m, bestiaux mpl; **horned c.** bêtes fpl à cornes, bovins mpl; **we were herded onto trucks like c.** on nous a entassés dans des camions comme du bétail VOIR GRAMMAIRE A11
▸▸ **c. breeding** élevage m *(du bétail)*; *Am* **c. car** wagon m à bétail ou bestiaux; **c. crossing** passage m de troupeaux; **c. market** marché m ou foire f aux bestiaux; **c. prod** aiguillon m électrique; **c. truck** wagon à bétail ou bestiaux

cattle-cake N tourteau m

cattle-grid N = grille f placée sur un fossé pour empêcher le passage du bétail

cattleman, pl **cattlemen** ['kæt(ə)lmən] N *Am* bouvier m

catty ['kætɪ] ADJ *Fam* **1** *(esp woman)* vache, rosse; **c. remark** vacherie f, rosserie f **2** *(like a cat)* **there's a c. smell** ça sent le pipi de chat

catty-corner(ed) ADJ, ADV *Am* diamétralement opposé

catwalk ['kætwɔːk] N passerelle f, *Naut* coursive f, *(for fashion models)* passerelle f de défilé de mode; **on the c.** *(model)* sur la passerelle du défilé

Caucasian [kɔː'keɪʒən, -'keɪzɪən] ADJ **1** *Geog, Ling* caucasien **2** *(in ethnology)* caucasien
N Caucasien, -ienne; *(white person)* blanc m, blanche f

Caucasus (the) [ðə'kɔːkəsəs] N le Caucase

caucus ['kɔːkəs] N *esp Pol* **1** *(group)* bloc m **2** *(meeting)* réunion f du bloc

caudal ['kɔːd(ə)l] ADJ *Zool* caudal, -aux
▸▸ **c. fin** *(nageoire f)* caudale f

caught PT, PP *see* **catch**

caul [kɔːl] N coiffe f *(de nouveau-né)*; **born with a c.** né coiffé

cauldron ['kɔːldrən] N chaudron m

cauli ['kɒlɪ] N *Br Fam* chou-fleur m, pl choux-fleurs

cauliflower ['kɒlɪflaʊər] N chou-fleur m, pl choux-fleurs
▸▸ *Culin* **c. cheese** chou-fleur au gratin; **c. ear** oreille f en chou-fleur

caulk [kɔːk] VT *(boat)* calfater, étouper

caulking ['kɔːkɪŋ] N calfatage m
▸▸ **c. iron** calfait m, burin m

causal ['kɔːz(ə)l] ADJ causal, -als ou -aux

causality [kɔː'zælɪtɪ] N causalité f; **what's the c.?** quelles sont les causes?

causally ['kɔːzəlɪ] ADV **to be c. connected** avoir un rapport de cause à effet

causation [kɔː'zeɪʃən] N causalité f

causative ['kɔːzətɪv] ADJ *Gram (verb)* causatif

cause [kɔːz] N **1** *(origin)* cause f, **c. and effect** la cause et l'effet; **to be the c. of an accident** être la cause d'un accident
2 *(reason)* raison f, motif m, sujet m; **I have c. to be thankful** j'ai lieu d'être reconnaissant; **you've no c. to be indignant** vous n'avez pas lieu d'être indigné, vous n'avez pas de quoi être indigné; **to have good c. for doing sth** avoir de bonnes raisons de faire qch; **to give c. for complaint** susciter des plaintes; **his condition is giving c. for concern** son état est inquiétant; **and with good c.** et pour cause; **without c.** sans raison
3 *(purpose etc)* cause f, **to win sb over to one's c.** gagner qn à sa cause; **to make common c.** faire cause commune *(with* avec*)*; **in the c. of justice** pour *(la cause de)* la justice; **to work for a good c.** travailler pour une bonne cause; **it's for a good c.** c'est pour une bonne cause; *Fam* **it's all in a good c.** ce n'est pas du temps perdu
4 *Law* cause f, **to plead sb's c.** plaider la cause de qn
VT *(misfortune, delay etc)* causer, occasionner; *(accident)* provoquer, causer; *(mirth, quarrel, surprise)* provoquer; **to c. a fire** provoquer un incendie; **to c. grief** causer du chagrin; **to c. trouble** *(disturbance)* semer la perturbation; *(problems)* causer des ennuis; **to c. a sensation** faire sensation; **all the worry you've caused us** toute l'inquiétude que tu nous as causée; **to c. sb/sth to do sth** faire faire qch à qn/qch; **a dog caused him to swerve** un chien lui a fait faire une embardée; **to c. sb to be punished** faire punir qn; **to c. sth to be done** faire faire qch; **something caused him to change his mind** quelque chose l'a fait changer d'avis

causeway ['kɔːzweɪ] N *(over marshy area)* chaussée f

caustic ['kɔːstɪk] ADJ *(substance)* caustique; *Fig (humour, joke etc)* caustique, décapant
N *Chem, Med* caustique m
▸▸ *Chem* **c. soda** soude f caustique

cauterization [kɔːtəraɪ'zeɪʃən] N *Med* cautérisation f

cauterize ['kɔːtəraɪz] VT *Med* cautériser

caution ['kɔːʃən] N **1** *(prudence)* prudence f, précautions fpl; **with great c.** avec beaucoup de prudence ou de précautions; **c. is advised** on conseille la prudence **2** *(warning)* avis m, avertissement m; **c.! steep gradient/pressurized container** attention! descente rapide/récipient sous pression **3** *Law, Sport etc (reprimand)* réprimande f, **he has been let off with a c.** il s'en est tiré avec une réprimande; **to be given a c.** se faire réprimander **4** *Old-fashioned Fam (amusing person)* numéro m, phénomène m
VT **1** *(warn)* avertir, mettre en garde; *Sport (player, boxer)* mettre en garde; **to c. sb against sth** mettre qn en garde contre qch; **to c. sb against doing sth** déconseiller à qn de faire qch **2** *Law* **to c. a suspect** = prévenir un suspect que tout ce qu'il dira pourra être

utilisé contre lui lors du procès **3** *Law (reprimand)* réprimander

---

Note that the French word **caution** is a false friend and is never a translation for the English word **caution**. Its most common meaning is **deposit, guarantee**. Note also that the French verb **cautionner** is a false friend. It never means **to warn**.

---

cautionary ['kɔːʃənərɪ] ADJ **a c. tale** une histoire édifiante

cautious ['kɔːʃəs] ADJ circonspect; *(driver, remark)* prudent; **to be c. in doing sth** faire qch avec prudence *ou* précaution; **to play a c. game** jouer serré; **c. optimism** optimisme *m* prudent

cautiously ['kɔːʃəslɪ] ADV *(to proceed)* avec prudence *ou* précaution; *(to drive)* prudemment; **to be c. optimistic** faire preuve d'un optimisme prudent

cautiousness ['kɔːʃəsnɪs] N *(of driver, remark etc)* prudence *f*

cavalcade [kævəl'keɪd] N cortège *m*; *(on horseback)* cavalcade *f*

Cavalier [kævə'lɪər] N *(in English history)* royaliste *m*; **the Cavaliers and Roundheads** les Cavaliers *mpl* et les Têtes *fpl* rondes

cavalier [kævə'lɪər] ADJ *(attitude etc)* cavalier, désinvolte; **with a c. air** avec désinvolture

cavalry ['kævəlrɪ] N cavalerie *f*
▸▸ *Mil* **c. officer** officier *m* de cavalerie

cavalryman, *pl* **cavalrymen** ['kævəlrɪmən] N *Mil* cavalier *m*, soldat *m* de cavalerie

cave[1] [keɪv] N caverne *f*, grotte *f*
VI *Sport* faire de la spéléologie
▸▸ **c. art** art *m* rupestre; **c. dweller** *(in prehistory)* homme *m* des cavernes; *(troglodyte)* troglodyte *m*; **c. dwelling** maison *f* troglodyte; **c. paintings** peintures *fpl* rupestres
▸ **cave in** VI **1** *(of ground, structure etc)* céder, s'affaisser, s'effondrer **2** *Fam (of person, government)* céder, s'avouer vaincu; *(of team, defence)* s'effondrer

---

Note that the French word **cave** is a false friend and is never a translation for the English word **cave**. It means **cellar**.

---

cave[2] ['keɪvɪ, 'kaːveɪ] INT *Br Sch Arch Fam* attention!, pet!

caveat ['kævɪæt] N **1** *Fml* mise *f* en garde *(against* contre*)* **2** *Law* opposition *f (* **to** à*)*

cave-in N *(of ground, structure etc)* affaissement *m*, effondrement *m*; *Fam (of person, government)* capitulation *f*

caveman, *pl* **cavemen** ['keɪvmæn, -men] N *(prehistoric man)* homme *m* des cavernes; *Fig Hum* primitif *m*

caver ['keɪvər] N spéléologue *mf*

cavern ['kævən, -əːn] N caverne *f*

cavernous ['kævənəs] ADJ *(room etc)* immense et vide; *(yawn)* à se décrocher la mâchoire; **a monster with a c. mouth** un monstre à la gueule immense

caviar(e) ['kævɪɑːr] N caviar *m*; *Prov* **(it's) c. to the general** c'est donner de la confiture aux cochons

cavil ['kævɪl] VI (**-ll-,** *Am* **-l-**) *Fml* chicaner, ergoter (**at** *or* **about sth** sur qch)

caving ['keɪvɪŋ] N *Sport* spéléologie *f*

cavity ['kævɪtɪ] N cavité *f*, creux *m*; *Med (abdominal, thoracic)* cavité *f*; **(dental) c.** cavité dentaire
▸▸ **c. wall** mur *m* creux *ou* à double paroi; **c. wall insulation** isolation *f* en murs creux

cavort [kə'vɔːt] VI faire des cabrioles; *Fig* batifoler

cavy ['keɪvɪ] N *(animal)* cobaye *m*, cochon *m* d'Inde

---

caw [kɔː] VI *(of crow etc)* croasser
N *(of crow etc)* croassement *m*

cawing ['kɔːɪŋ] N *(of crow etc)* croassement *m*

cayenne [keɪ'en] N cayenne *m*
▸▸ **c. pepper** (poivre *m* de) cayenne

cayman ['keɪmən] N *(animal)* caïman *m*
▸▸ **C. Islands** îles *fpl* Caïmans

CB [siː'biː] N *(abbr* **Citizens' Band**) CB *f*

CBC [siːbiː'siː] N *TV, Radio (abbr* **Canadian Broadcasting Corporation**) (société *f*) Radio-Canada *f*

CBE [siːbiː'iː] N *abbr* **Commander of the Order of the British Empire**

CBI [siːbiː'aɪ] N *Br (abbr* **Confederation of British Industry**) ≃ Medef *m*

CBS [siːbiː'es] N *abbr* **Columbia Broadcasting System**

CC [siː'siː] N *abbr* **County Council**

cc [siː'siː] N **1** *(on memorandum) (abbr* **carbon copy**) copie **2** *(abbr* **cubic centimetres**) cm³
VT envoyer une copie à

CCA [siːsiː'eɪ] N *Acct (abbr* **current cost accounting**) comptabilité *f* en coûts actuels

CCI [siːsiː'aɪ] N *(abbr* **Chamber of Commerce and Industry**) CCI *f*

CCTV [siːsiːtiː'viː] N *(abbr* **closed circuit television**) télévision *f* en circuit fermé

CD [siː'diː] N **1** *Comput (abbr* **compact disc**) CD *m*; **on CD** sur CD **2** *Admin (abbr* **Corps Diplomatique**) CD *m*; **a car with CD plates** une voiture avec des plaques du Corps diplomatique
▸▸ **CD burner** graveur *m* de CD; **CD library** CD thèque *f*; **CD player** lecteur *m* laser; **CD rewriter** graveur *m* de CD réinscriptibles; **CD stacker** meuble *m* à CD; **CD system** chaîne *f* laser; **CD video** CD vidéo *m*; **CD writer** graveur de CD

CDI, CD-I [siːdiː'aɪ] N *Comput (abbr* **compact disc interactive**) CD-I *m*

CDR, CD-R [siːdiː'ɑːr] *Comput* N **1** *(abbr* **compact disc recorder**) graveur *m* de disque compact **2** *(abbr* **compact disc recordable**) CD-R *m*

Cdr N *Mil abbr* **Commander**

Cdre N *Naut abbr* **Commodore**

CD-ROM [siːdiː'rɒm] N *Comput (abbr* **compact disc-read only memory**) CD-ROM *m*, CD-Rom *m*; **available on C.** existe en CD-ROM
▸▸ **C. burner** graveur *m* de CD-ROM; **C. drive** lecteur *m* de CD-ROM, lecteur *m* de disque optique; **C. newspaper** journal *m* sur CD-ROM; **C. reader** lecteur de CD-ROM; **C. recorder** graveur de CD-ROM; **C. rewriter** graveur de CD-ROM réinscriptible; **C. writer** graveur de CD-ROM

CD-RW [siːdiːɑː'dʌb(ə)ljuː] N *Comput (abbr* **compact disc rewritable**) CD *m* réinscriptible
▸▸ **C. drive** lecteur *m* de CD réinscriptible

CDT [siːdiː'tiː] N *(abbr* **Central Daylight Time**) = heure *f* d'été du centre des États-Unis

CDV [siːdiː'viː] N *Comput (abbr* **compact disc video**) vidéodisque *m*

cease [siːs] N *Fml* **without c.** sans cesse
VI cesser; **hostilities have ceased** les hostilités ont cessé; **they have ceased to exist** ils n'existent plus; **it never ceases to amaze me that ...** cela m'étonne toujours que ...; **without ceasing** sans arrêt; **we will not c. from campaigning for her release** nous ne cesserons pas de nous battre pour sa libération
VT cesser; **to c. doing sth** cesser de faire qch; *Mil* **to c. fire** cesser le feu; *Com* **to c. trading** cesser ses activités, cesser toute activité commerciale

cease-fire N cessez-le-feu *m inv*

---

ceaseless ['siːslɪs] ADJ incessant, continuel

ceaselessly ['siːslɪslɪ] ADV sans cesse, continuellement

cecum ['siːkəm] N *Am* = **caecum**

cedar ['siːdər] N *(tree)* cèdre *m*; **c. panelling** lambris *mpl* en cèdre
▸▸ *Am* **c. closet** *(for protecting clothes etc against moths)* placard *m* en cèdre; **c. of Lebanon** cèdre du Liban; *Bot* **c. tree** cèdre

cede [siːd] VT *Law (property, province, debt)* céder (**to** à); **to c. a point** *(in argument)* concéder un point

cedilla [sɪ'dɪlə] N *Ling* cédille *f*

Ceefax® ['siːfæks] N *TV* Ceefax® *m*

ceilidh ['keɪlɪ] N = bal *m* folklorique écossais ou irlandais

ceiling ['siːlɪŋ] N **1** *(of room etc)* plafond *m*; *Fam* **to hit the c.** *(become angry)* péter les plombs **2** *Econ etc* plafond *m*; *Fin* **to have a c. of** être plafonné à; **to reach a c.** *(of prices etc)* plafonner **3** *Aviat* plafond *m*; **to fly at the c.** plafonner **4** *Met* plafond *m* (nuageux)
▸▸ **c. light** plafonnier *m*; *Fin* **c. price** prix *m* plafond; **c. tile** dalle *f* pour plafond

celadon ['selədɒn] N *(porcelain)* céladon *m*
▸▸ **c. green** (vert *m*) céladon

celandine ['seləndaɪn] N *(flower)* **greater c.** chélidoine *f*, grande éclaire *f*; **lesser c.** ficaire *f*, petite éclaire

celeb [sə'leb] N *Fam* célébrité *f*

celebrant ['selɪbrənt] N *Rel* célébrant *m*, officiant *m*

celebrate ['selɪbreɪt] VT **1** *(mark with festivity) (event)* fêter, célébrer; **the city is celebrating the anniversary of its founding** la ville fête l'anniversaire de sa fondation; **to c. sb's birthday** fêter l'anniversaire de qn; **let's open a bottle of wine to c. the occasion** ouvrons une bouteille de vin pour fêter ça **2** *Rel (mass, wedding, feast)* célébrer
VI faire la fête; **let's c. with a new car/a weekend in Paris** achetons une nouvelle voiture/allons passer un week-end à Paris pour fêter ça; **will you be celebrating tonight?** tu vas arroser ça ce soir?; **let's c. with some champagne** on va arroser ça au champagne

celebrated ['selɪbreɪtɪd] ADJ célèbre (**for** sth par qch)

celebration [selɪ'breɪʃən] N **1** *(party, drink etc)* fête *f*, festivités *fpl*; **the Independence Day celebrations** les festivités à l'occasion de l'anniversaire de l'Indépendance; **this calls for a c.!** il faut fêter ça!, ça s'arrose!; **a party in c. of sth** une fête pour célébrer qch **2** *Rel (of communion, feast)* célébration *f*

celebratory [selɪ'breɪtərɪ] ADJ *(dinner)* de fête; *(marking official occasion)* commémoratif; *(atmosphere, mood)* de fête, festif

celebrity [sɪ'lebrɪtɪ] N **1** *(person)* célébrité *f*; **2** *(fame)* célébrité *f*, renommée *f*
▸▸ **c. magazine** magazine *m* people

celeriac [sɪ'lerɪæk] N céleri-rave *m*, *pl* céleris-raves

celerity [sɪ'lerɪtɪ] N *Fml* célérité *f*

celery ['selərɪ] N céleri *m*; **head of c.** pied *m* de céleri; **stick of c.** branche *f* de céleri; **c. soup** soupe *f* au céleri

celestial [sɪ'lestɪəl] ADJ céleste

celiac ['siːlɪæk] ADJ, N *Am* = **coeliac**

celibacy ['selɪbəsɪ] N *(sexual abstinence)* abstinence *f* sexuelle, chasteté *f*; *(not being married)* célibat *m*; *Rel* **to take a vow of c.** faire vœu de chasteté

celibate ['selɪbət] ADJ *(person) (chaste)* qui n'a pas de rapports sexuels, chaste; *(life) (by choice)* de chasteté; *(forced)* sans rapports sexuels
N personne *f* qui n'a pas de rapports sexuels

Note that the French word **célibataire** is a false friend and is never a translation for the English word **celibate**. It means **unmarried**.

cell [sel] N **1** *(in prison)* cellule f; **they spent a night in the cells** ils ont passé la nuit en cellule
2 *(of monk, hermit)* cellule f
3 *(in beehive)* cellule f, alvéole m
4 *Elec, Electron etc (of battery)* cellule f; **dry c.** pile f sèche; **wet c.** pile à liquide; **photoelectric/photovoltaic c.** cellule photoélectrique/photovoltaïque; **solar c.** pile solaire, photopile f
5 *Biol* cellule f; **blood c.** globule m; **cancer c.** cellule cancéreuse
6 *Pol* **communist c.** cellule f communiste
7 *Comput (on spreadsheet)* cellule f
8 *Am Fam (cellphone)* portable m, *Belg* GSM m, *Suisse* Natel® m, *Can* cellulaire m
▸▸ *Biol* **c. wall** paroi f cellulaire

cellar ['selər] N cave f; *(of wine merchant)* chai m; **to keep a good c.** avoir une bonne cave

Note that the French word **cellier** is a false friend. It means **storeroom**.

cellarman, *pl* **cellarmen** ['seləmən] N sommelier m

cellist ['tʃelɪst] N *Mus* violoncelliste mf

cello ['tʃeləʊ] N *Mus* violoncelle m
▸▸ **c. concerto** concerto m pour violoncelle

Cellophane ® ['seləfeɪn] N *Br* cellophane® f

cellphone ['selfəʊn] N téléphone m cellulaire, radiotéléphone m; *Am (mobile phone)* (téléphone m) portable m, *Belg* GSM m, *Suisse* Natel® m, *Can* cellulaire m

cellular ['seljʊlər] ADJ *Biol (structure etc)* cellulaire
▸▸ *Tex* **c. blanket** couverture f alvéolaire; **c. board** *(cardboard)* carton m ondulé; *Electron, Tel* **c. logic** logique f cellulaire; **c. phone** téléphone m cellulaire, radiotéléphone m

cellulite ['seljʊlaɪt] N cellulite f

Celluloid® ['seljʊlɔɪd] N *(no pl)* celluloïd® m; *Cin* **on c.** sur la pellicule

cellulose ['seljʊləʊs] ADJ celluleux
N cellulose f

Celsius ['selsɪəs] ADJ Celsius; **ten degrees C.** dix degrés Celsius
▸▸ **C. thermometer** thermomètre m de Celsius

Celt [kelt] N Celte mf

Celtic ['keltɪk] *Ling* ADJ celtique, celte
N *(ancient)* celtique m; *(modern)* langues fpl celtiques *ou* celtes

cement [sɪ'ment] N **1** *Constr* ciment m; **Portland c.** ciment de Portland; **quick-setting c.** ciment à prise rapide; **c. path** allée f en ciment **2** *(for tooth)* amalgame m **3** *(glue)* colle f
VT **1** *(join) (stones, bricks)*, *Fig (friendship)* cimenter **2** *(in dentistry)* obturer
▸▸ **c. mixer** bétonnière f; **c. powder** poudre f à ciment

cementation [si:men'teɪʃən] N cimentation f

cemetery ['semətrɪ] N cimetière m

cenotaph ['senətɑ:f] N cénotaphe m

censer ['sensər] N *Rel* encensoir m

censor ['sensər] N **1** *Admin, Mil* censeur m; **the film c.** la censure cinématographique; *Mil, Cin etc* **to get past the c.** échapper à la censure **2** *Antiq* censeur m
VT **1** *(ban) (book, film, article etc)* interdire, censurer; *(scene)* supprimer, couper; *(line, word)* supprimer **2** *(cut parts of) (film, article,*

newspaper) censurer; *(play, book, scenario)* censurer, expurger
▸▸ *TV, Radio* **c. bleep** bip m de censure

Attention: ne pas confondre avec le verbe **to censure**.

censoring ['sensərɪŋ] N censure f

censorious [sen'sɔ:rɪəs] ADJ *Fml* sévère (**of** vis-à-vis de)

censorship ['sensəʃɪp] N censure f; **there is no longer any c. of his films** ses films ne sont plus censurés
▸▸ **c. laws** censure

censurable ['senʃərəb(ə)l] ADJ *Fml* censurable, blâmable

censure ['senʃər] *Fml* N critiques fpl; *Law* réprimande f; **he deserves c.** il mérite des reproches; *Pol* **vote of c.** motion f de censure
VT blâmer, critiquer

Note that the French verb **censurer** is a false friend and is never a translation for the English verb **to censure**. It means **to censor**.

Attention: ne pas confondre avec le verbe **to censor**.

census ['sensəs] N recensement m; **to take a c.** faire un recensement; **c. of population** recensement de la population
▸▸ *Am* **C. Bureau** Bureau m des statistiques; **c. return** formulaire m de recensement; **c. taker** agent m recenseur

cent [sent] N *(coin, sum)* cent m; *Fam (smallest amount of money)* sou m; **to pay to the last c.** payer jusqu'au dernier sou

centaur ['sentɔ:r] N *Myth* centaure m

centenarian [sentɪ'neərɪən] N *(person)* centenaire mf
ADJ centenaire

centenary [sen'ti:nərɪ] N *(anniversaire m)* centenaire m; **c. celebrations** célébrations fpl du centenaire
ADJ centenaire

centennial [sen'tenɪəl] ADJ centenaire
N *Am* = **centenary** N

center, centerboard etc *Am* = **centre, centreboard** etc

centering ['sent(ə)rɪŋ] N *Typ* centrage m

centigrade ['sentɪɡreɪd] ADJ centigrade; **ten degrees c.** dix degrés centigrades
▸▸ **c. thermometer** thermomètre m centigrade

centigramme, *Am* **centigram** ['sentɪɡræm] N centigramme m

centilitre, *Am* **centiliter** ['sentɪli:tər] N centilitre m

centimetre, *Am* **centimeter** ['sentɪmi:tər] N centimètre m; **square/cubic c.** centimètre carré/cube

centipede ['sentɪpi:d] N mille-pattes m inv; *Spec* scolopendre f

central ['sentr(ə)l] ADJ **1** *(in location)* central, -aux; **in a c. position** situé au centre; **the office is very c.** *(in town)* le bureau est situé en plein centre **2** *(in importance)* central, -aux; **the c. character** le personnage central; **c. to the debate is the question of safety** la question de la sécurité se situe au cœur du débat; **of c. importance** d'une importance capitale
N *Am Tel Old-fashioned* central m (téléphonique)
▸▸ *Banking* **c. account** compte m centralisateur; **C. America** Amérique f centrale; **c. bank** banque f centrale; *Com* **c. buyer** acheteur, -euse principal(ale); *Com* **c. buying group** centrale f d'achat(s); **c. government** gouvernement m central; **c. heating** chauffage m central; *Br Parl* **C. Lobby** = hall m principal de la Chambre des communes;

Aut **c. locking** verrouillage m central; *Anat* **c. nervous system** système m nerveux central; *Admin* **C. Office of Information** = organisme m chargé d'organiser les campagnes d'information du gouvernement britannique; **c. point** centre m; *Comput* **c. processing unit** unité f centrale (de traitement), processeur m central; *Com* **c. purchasing** achats mpl centralisés; *Com* **c. purchasing department** *(in company)* centrale d'achat(s); *Com* **c. purchasing group** centrale d'achat(s); *Com* **c. purchasing office** centrale d'achat(s); *Br Aut* **c. reservation** *(with grass)* terre-plein m central, pl terre-pleins centraux, *Belg, Suisse* berme f centrale; *(with barrier)* bande f médiane; **c. reservations** réservations fpl centralisées; **c. reservations office** centrale de réservation; **C. Standard Time** heure f d'hiver du centre des États-Unis

centralize ['sentrəlaɪz] VT centraliser

centralized ['sentrəlaɪzd] ADJ *(power, planning etc)* centralisé
▸▸ *Comput* **c. data capture** saisie f centralisée; **c. management** gestion f intégrée; **c. purchasing** achats mpl centralisés; *Comput* **c. storage** mémoire f centrale

centrally ['sentrəlɪ] ADV centralement; **c. heated** avec chauffage central; **the flat is c. heated** l'appartement a le chauffage central; **c. situated** situé dans le centre, central, -aux

centre, *Am* **center** ['sentər] N **1** *(of circle, earth, town etc)* centre m; *(of table etc)* milieu m; *(of wheel)* corps m, centre; *Med (of infection)* foyer m; **in the c.** au centre, au milieu; **the great urban centres** les grandes agglomérations fpl urbaines; **commercial/industrial c.** centre commercial/industriel; **civic/community c.** centre civique/social; **shopping c.** centre commercial; **sports c.** centre sportif; *Phys* **c. of gravity** centre de gravité; **c. of attraction** *Phys* centre d'attraction *ou* de gravitation; *Fig* centre d'attraction
2 *Pol* centre m; **the c. party** le parti du centre; **to be left/right of c.** être du centre gauche/droit
3 *Sport (player)* centre m
4 *Tech etc (of lathe)* pointe f; **out of c.** décentré; **ten centimetres c. to c.** dix centimètres centre à centre
VT **1** *(text, wheel, sth on lathe etc)* centrer **2** *Cin, Phot (image)* centrer, cadrer **3** *Ftbl etc (ball etc)* centrer
▸▸ *Ftbl* **c. forward** avant-centre m, pl avant(s)-centres; *Ftbl* **c. half** demi-centre m, pl demi-centres; *Journ* **c. page** page f centrale; *Tech* **c. punch** pointeau m; *Typ* **c. spread** double page centrale
▸ **centre on, centre round** VT INSEP être centré *ou* axé sur
VT SEP *(usu passive)* **to be centred on sb/sth** se concentrer sur qn/qch

centreboard, *Am* **centerboard** ['sentəbɔ:d] N *Naut* dérive f

centrefold, *Am* **centerfold** ['sentəfəʊld] N *(in magazine, newspaper)* double page f centrale détachable; *(nude picture)* photo f de pin-up; **to do a c.** *(nude picture)* poser comme pin-up; **c. girl** pin-up f inv

centrepiece, *Am* **centerpiece** ['sentəpi:s] N *(on table)* décoration f centrale d'une table; *Fig* pièce f de résistance

centre-point steering N *Aut* direction f à point milieu

centrifugal [sentrɪ'fjʊɡ(ə)l] ADJ *(force, pump etc)* centrifuge

centrifuge ['sentrɪfju:dʒ] VT *(liquid)* centrifuger
N centrifugeur m, centrifugeuse f

centring, *Am* **centering** ['sent(ə)rɪŋ] N **1** *(of* sth on lathe, of text etc) centrage m **2** Cin, Phot cadrage m

▸▸ **c. tool** centreur m

centripetal [sen'trɪpɪtəl] ADJ (force etc) centripète

centrist ['sentrɪst] Pol N centriste mf ADJ centriste

centuries-old ['sentʃərɪz-] ADJ vieux/f vieille de plusieurs siècles

century ['sentʃərɪ] N **1** siècle m; in the nineteenth c. au dix-neuvième siècle; the wedding of the c. le mariage du siècle; trees centuries old arbres mpl séculaires ou centenaires **2** Cr (one hundred runs) centaine f, série f de cent

▸▸ Am Fam **c. note** billet m de cent dollars

CEO [siːiː'əʊ] N Com (abbr chief executive officer) ≃ directeur m général; President and C. ≃ président-directeur général m, P-DG m

cephalic [se'fælɪk] ADJ (vein, index etc) céphalique

ceramic [sə'ræmɪk] ADJ céramique
NPL **ceramics** céramique f
▸▸ Br **c. hob** plaque f vitrocéramique; **c. tiles** carrelage m

cereal ['sɪərɪəl] N céréale f; (breakfast) cereals céréales
▸▸ **c. bowl** assiette f creuse, bol m à céréales; **c. crops** céréales

cerebellum [serɪ'beləm] N Anat cervelet m

cerebral ['serɪbrəl, Am sə'riːbrəl] ADJ **1** Anat cérébral, -aux **2** (intellectual) cérébral, -aux
▸▸ Med **c. death** mort f cérébrale; Anat **c. hemisphere** hémisphère m cérébral; Med **c. palsy** paralysie f cérébrale

cerebrospinal fluid [serebrəʊ'spaɪn(ə)l] N Anat liquide m céphalo-rachidien

cerebrum ['serɪbrəm] N Anat cerveau m

ceremonial [serɪ'məʊnɪəl] ADJ de cérémonie
N cérémonial m

ceremonially [serɪ'məʊnɪəlɪ] ADV en grande cérémonie

ceremonious [serɪ'məʊnɪəs] ADJ cérémonieux

ceremoniously [serɪ'məʊnɪəslɪ] ADV cérémonieusement, avec cérémonie

ceremony ['serɪmənɪ] N cérémonie f; the marriage c. la cérémonie du mariage; with c. avec cérémonie, cérémonieusement; without c. sans cérémonies; we don't stand on c. nous ne faisons pas de cérémonies

cert [sɜːt] N Fam (certainty) a dead c. une certitude (absolue); Horseracing un gagnant sûr; he's a dead c. for the job à tous les coups, il a le poste; if one thing's a c. it's that ... s'il y a une chose qui est sûre c'est que ...

cert. N Cin (abbr certificate) certificat m; a c. 18 film un film interdit aux moins de 18 ans

certain ['sɜːt(ə)n] ADJ **1** (sure) (success, failure etc) certain, assuré; (cure, solution) infaillible; they face c. dismissal ils seront renvoyés à coup sûr; they face c. death ils sont condamnés; it's absolutely c. c'est sûr et certain; there is c. to be some opposition to the bill il est sûr que la loi rencontrera une opposition; he is c. to come il viendra à coup sûr; to my c. knowledge, they are ... je sais pertinemment qu'ils sont ...; in the c. belief that he was right convaincu qu'il avait raison; I am almost c. j'en suis presque sûr; I am c. that he will come je suis certain ou sûr qu'il viendra; to know sth for c. être certain de qch; I can't say for c. je ne peux pas vous dire de façon certaine; you'll have it tomorrow for c. vous l'aurez demain sans faute; to make c. that ... (find out, ensure) s'assurer que ...; I'd better make c. je ferais mieux de m'en assurer; to make c. of sth (find out) s'assurer de qch; (make sure to get

sth) s'assurer qch; I made c. of the date je me suis assuré de la date; to make c. of a seat s'assurer une place; don't worry, I made c. of that! ne t'inquiète pas, j'ai pris toutes les dispositions!

2 (particular) certain; women of a c. age les femmes d'un certain âge; a c. person une certaine personne; c. people (de) certaines gens, certains mpl; a c. Mr Thomas un certain M. Thomas; he used to write to me on a c. day il m'écrivait à jour fixe

certainly ['sɜːtənlɪ] ADV **1** (definitely) certainement; (admittedly) certes; she c. knows her facts elle sait parfaitement de quoi elle parle; you shall c. have it tomorrow vous l'aurez demain sans faute; it c. won't be ready tomorrow ça ne sera jamais prêt pour demain; may I? – c.! or you c. may! vous permettez? – je vous en prie! ou certainement!; will you tell him? – c. not! tu vas lui dire? – certainement pas!; did you tell him? – c. not! tu lui as dit? – bien sûr que non!

> Note that the most common meaning of the French word **certainement** is **probably**.

certainty ['sɜːtəntɪ] N **1** (sureness) (of future event) certitude f; there is no c. that we will win il n'est absolument pas certain que nous gagnions **2** (thing) I know it for a c. je le sais parfaitement; we now know for a c. that he was here last night nous avons maintenant la preuve qu'il était là hier soir; it's a dead c. c'est une certitude absolue **3** (conviction) certitude f, conviction f; she said it with some c. elle a dit cela avec une certaine conviction

certifiable ['sɜːtɪfaɪəb(ə)l] ADJ **1** (insane) (person) dont l'état nécessite l'internement psychiatrique; Fam he's c. il est fou à lier **2** (document, fact etc) que l'on peut certifier

certificate [sə'tɪfɪkət] N **1** certificat m; birth/marriage/death c. certificat de naissance/mariage/décès; Fin etc bearer c. titre m au porteur; (government) savings c. bon m d'épargne; Aut test c. ≃ certificat de contrôle technique **2** (professional, educational) diplôme m; teaching/nursing c. diplôme d'enseignement/d'infirmière; coaching/first aid c. brevet m d'entraîneur/ de secourisme; Naut master's c. brevet de capitaine **3** Cin visa m de censure
▸▸ Aviat **c. of airworthiness** certificat de navigabilité; Fin **c. of deposit** certificat de dépôt; Acct **c. of dishonour** certificat de non-paiement; Com **c. of incorporation** certificat d'enregistrement de société; **c. of insurance** attestation f d'assurance; Com **c. of origin** certificat d'origine; Com **c. of quality** certificat de qualité; Br Sch Formerly **C. of Secondary Education** = ancien brevet de l'enseignement secondaire en Grande-Bretagne, aujourd'hui remplacé par le "GCSE", ≃ BEPC m; Fin **c. of transfer** acte m de cession; Com **c. of value** certificat de valeur

certificated [sə'tɪfɪkeɪtɪd] ADJ diplômé

certification [sɜːtɪfɪ'keɪʃən] N certification f, authentification f; (of product) homologation f

certified ['sɜːtɪfaɪd] ADJ **1** (having certificate) diplômé **2** (guaranteed) **c. by a notary** notarié **3** (declared insane) dont l'état nécessite l'internement psychiatrique
▸▸ **c. accounts** comptes mpl approuvés; Am Fin **c. cheque** chèque m certifié; **c. copy** copie f certifiée conforme, copie authentique; Com **c. invoice** facture f certifiée; Am **c. letter** lettre f recommandée; Am **c. public accountant** ≃ expert-comptable m, pl experts-comptables; Am Sch **c. teacher** (in state school) professeur m diplômé; (in private school) professeur habilité

certify ['sɜːtɪfaɪ] VT **1** (confirm) certifier, attester; (death) constater; to c. that sth is true certifier que qch est vrai; this is to c. that A. Gooch has ... (on certificate) ce document certifie que A. Gooch a ...; to c. sb insane (of doctor) déclarer que l'état de santé de qn nécessite l'internement psychiatrique; Fam you ought to be certified tu es complètement fou **2** (guarantee) (document) authentifier, homologuer, légaliser; Acct to c. the books viser les livres de commerce
VI to c. to sth attester qch

certitude ['sɜːtɪtjuːd] N certitude f

cervical ['sɜːvɪk(ə)l, sɜː'vaɪk(ə)l] ADJ Anat **1** (of the cervix) du col de l'utérus **2** (of the neck) cervical, -aux
▸▸ **c. cancer** cancer m du col de l'utérus; **c. collar** minerve f; **c. smear** frottis m vaginal; **c. vertebra** vertèbre f cervicale

cervix, pl **cervices** ['sɜːvɪks, -vɪsiːz] N Anat **1** (of uterus) col m de l'utérus **2** (neck) cou m
▸▸ **c. uteri** col de l'utérus

cessation [se'seɪʃən] N cessation f, arrêt m

cession ['seʃən] N (of territory) cession f; Law (to creditors) cession de biens

cesspit ['sespɪt] N = cesspool

cesspool ['sespuːl] N (for sewage) fosse f d'aisances; Fig cloaque m; the district is a c. of drug-dealing and prostitution le quartier est un cloaque où règnent le trafic de drogue et la prostitution

CET [siːiː'tiː] N EU (abbr common external tariff) tarif m externe commun

Ceylon [sɪ'lɒn] N Hist Formerly Ceylan m

C & F [siːænd'ef] Com (abbr cost and freight) C et F

cf [siː'ef] (abbr confer) cf

CFC [siːef'siː] N (abbr chlorofluorocarbon) CFC m inv

CFO [siːef'əʊ] N Am (abbr Chief Financial Officer) chef m comptable, chef de la comptabilité

CFSP [siːefes'piː] N (abbr Common Foreign and Security Policy) PESC f

cg (abbr centigramme) cg

CGI [siːdʒiː'aɪ] N Comput **1** (abbr common gateway interface) interface f commune de passerelle, CGI f **2** (abbr computer-generated images) images fpl créées par ordinateur

CH [siː'eɪtʃ] (abbr central heating) c. c., ch. c.

ch (abbr chapter) chapitre m

cha [tʃɑː] N Old-fashioned Br Fam (tea) thé m

Chad [tʃæd] N Tchad m

chaebol ['tʃeɪbɒl] N Econ chaebol m

chafe [tʃeɪf] VT **1** (make worn) (rope, collar) user; (make sore) (skin) irriter; the boots chafed her ankles les bottes lui blessaient les chevilles; apply to chafed skin (of lotion etc) appliquer sur la peau irritée **2** Fig (annoy) irriter, agacer **3** (warm) (sb's limbs etc) frictionner
VI **1** (of skin) être irrité; his skin chafed under the coarse material sa peau était irritée à cause du tissu rugueux **2** Fig (of person) to c. at or under sth s'énerver contre qch, s'irriter de ou contre qch; to c. under restraint ronger son frein

chafed [tʃeɪft] ADJ (rope, shirt) usé; (skin) irrité

chaff[1] [tʃɑːf] N **1** Agr (husks) balle f; Fig the bulk of his collected poems is mere c. la plupart de ses poèmes ne valent pas grand-chose **2** Electron ruban m métallique antiradar

chaff[2] VT (tease) taquiner

chaffinch ['tʃæfɪntʃ] N (bird) pinson m

chafing ['tʃeɪfɪŋ] N **1** (of skin) irritation f **2**

(warming) (of limbs) friction f
▸▸ **c. dish** chauffe-plats *m inv*

chagrin ['ʃægrɪn] N *Fml* dépit *m*; **much to my c.** à mon grand dépit
VT *esp Lit* dépiter; **to be chagrined at sth** être contrarié par qch

chain [tʃeɪn] N **1** chaîne f, *(small) (for medallion etc)* chaînette f; **to put a dog on a c.** attacher un chien à une chaîne; **a prisoner in chains** un prisonnier enchaîné; *Fig* **to break** *or* **burst one's chains** rompre ses chaînes; *Fig* **to have nothing to lose but one's chains** n'avoir rien d'autre à perdre que ses chaînes; **to form a c.** *(to pass buckets of water etc)* former *ou* faire la chaîne; **to pull the c.** *(in WC)* tirer la chasse d'eau; **a c. of events** un enchaînement de faits; *Com* **c. of distribution** circuit *m* de distribution, réseau *m* de distribution; *Naut* **anchor c.** chaîne d'ancrage; **bicycle c.** chaîne de bicyclette; *Aut* **(snow) chains** chaînes
2 *Geog (of mountains)* chaîne f
3 *Com (of stores, restaurants)* chaîne f, **fast food c.** chaîne de restauration rapide
4 *Phys, Chem etc* chaîne f
5 *Arch (measurement)* = 20,12 m; **surveyor's c., measuring c.** chaîne f d'arpenteur *ou* d'arpentage
VT *(door etc)* fermer avec une chaîne; **to c. sb** enchaîner qn (**to sth/sb** à qch/qn); **to c. sth to sth** attacher qch à qch avec une chaîne/des chaînes; **she chained herself to the railings** elle s'est enchaînée à la grille; *Fig* **chained to one's desk** rivé à son bureau; *Fig* **she's chained to the kitchen sink** elle ne sort pas de sa cuisine
▸▸ **c. armour** mailles *fpl*, *(suit)* cotte f de mailles; *Tech* **c. drive** transmission f par chaîne; **c. gang** chaîne de forçats; **c. guard** caiter *m (de bicyclette)*; *Aut* **c. guide** guide *m* chaîne; **c. letter** lettre f faisant partie d'une chaîne; **c. link** chaînon *m ou* maillon *m* de chaîne; **c. mail** mailles, *(suit)* cotte de mailles; *Phys, Chem, Fig* **c. reaction** réaction f en chaîne; **c. saw** tronçonneuse f, *Sewing* **c. stitch** point *m* de chaînette; **c. store** magasin *m* à succursales (multiples); *(individual store)* succursale f; *Aut* **c. tensioner** tendeur *m* de chaîne
▸ **chain down** VT SEP *(cargo on ship)* attacher avec des chaînes; *(person)* enchaîner; *Fig* **to be chained down by one's work** être esclave de son travail
▸ **chain up** VT SEP *(dog)* attacher à une chaîne; *(person)* enchaîner; *(bike, gate)* mettre une chaîne à; **I left it chained up** j'ai mis le cadenas

chaining ['tʃeɪnɪŋ] N *Comput* chaînage *m*

chain-smoke VT **he chain-smokes untipped cigarettes** il fume des cigarettes sans filtre du matin au soir; **he was chain-smoking Gitanes** il fumait Gitane sur Gitane
VI fumer cigarette sur cigarette

chain-smoker N personne f qui fume cigarette sur cigarette

chair [tʃeər] N **1** chaise f, *(armchair)* fauteuil *m*; **folding c.** chaise pliante, pliant *m*; **easy c.** fauteuil; **invalid c., Old-fashioned bath c.** voiture f de malade, fauteuil roulant
2 *Univ (of professor)* chaire f
3 *(in meeting)* fauteuil *m* de président; *(chairperson)* président, -ente; **to be in the c.** présider (la séance); **to address the c.** s'adresser au président
4 *Am Fam* **the c.** *(electric chair)* la chaise électrique; **to go to the c.** passer sur *ou* à la chaise électrique
VT **1** *(preside over) (meeting)* présider **2** *(person) (after victory etc)* porter en triomphe
▸▸ **c. attendant** *(in park etc)* loueur, -euse de chaises, chaisier, -ière

chairback ['tʃeəbæk] N dossier *m* de chaise

chaircover ['tʃeəkʌvə(r)] N housse f de fauteuil

chairlift ['tʃeəlɪft] N *Ski* télésiège *m*

chairman, *pl* **chairmen** ['tʃeəmən] N *(of committee, meeting)* président, -ente; *(of party)* secrétaire *m* général; *Com (of company)* président-directeur *m* général; **c. and managing director** président-directeur général, P-DG *m*; **c. of the board** Président du conseil; **to act as c.** présider (la séance); **Mr C.** Monsieur le Président; **Madam C.** Madame la Présidente

chairmanship ['tʃeəmənʃɪp] N *(of committee, meeting)* présidence f, *(of party)* secrétariat *m* général; **under the c. of Mr Stevens** sous la présidence de M. Stevens

chairperson ['tʃeəpɜːsən] N *(of committee, meeting)* président, -ente; *(of party)* secrétaire mf général(ale)

chairwoman, *pl* **chairwomen** ['tʃeəwʊmən, -wɪmɪn] N *(of committee, meeting)* présidente f, *(of party)* secrétaire f générale

chalet ['ʃæleɪ] N chalet *m*
▸▸ **c. girl** = jeune femme f qui s'occupe de l'entretien d'un chalet de sports d'hiver; **c. park** parc *m* résidentiel de loisirs

chalice ['tʃælɪs] N **1** *Rel* calice *m* **2** *Arch, Lit* coupe f

chalk [tʃɔːk] N *(for writing etc)*, *Geol, Billiards* craie f, **they are as different as c. and cheese** c'est le jour et la nuit; *Br Fam* **not by a long c.** loin s'en faut; *Br Fam* **by a long c.** de beaucoup; **a set of coloured chalks** un assortiment de craies de couleur; **c. hills/cliffs** collines *fpl*/falaises *fpl* crayeuses; *Sewing* **French c.** craie de tailleur
VT *(mark)* marquer à la craie; *(write)* écrire (à la craie); *Carp etc* **to c. a line** tringler une ligne; *Billiards* **to c. one's cue** mettre de la craie sur sa queue de billard
▸▸ **c. drawing** dessin *m* à la craie; **c. line** *(drawn)* trait *m* à la craie; *Carp (string)* cordeau *m*; *(made by string)* ligne f faite au cordeau
▸ **chalk up** VT SEP **1** *(write)* écrire à la craie **2** **c. it up** *(give credit in shop)* mettez-le sur mon ardoise **3** *(put down to)* **you'll just have to c. it up to experience** maintenant, tu sauras; **they chalked their defeat up to lack of practice** ils ont mis leur défaite sur le compte du manque d'entraînement **4** *(achieve) (victory, success, points)* remporter

chalkboard ['tʃɔːkbɔːd] N *Am* tableau *m* (noir)

chalkdust ['tʃɔːkdʌst] N poussière f de craie

chalkpit ['tʃɔːkpɪt] N carrière f de craie, crayère f

chalky ['tʃɔːkɪ] ADJ **1** *(terrain, soil)* crayeux; *(deposit)* calcique **2** *(colour)* pâle, terreux; *(texture, taste)* plâtreux; **c. white** *(complexion, houses)* blanc, f blanche; *(because of illness, shock etc)* pâle comme un linge

challenge ['tʃælɪndʒ] N **1** défi *m*; *Sport* défi, challenge *m*; *Mil (by sentry)* interpellation f; **to throw down** *or* **issue a c.** lancer un défi; **to accept** *or* **take up a c.** relever un défi; *Pol* **a c. to his leadership** une tentative pour le supplanter à la tête du parti; **to enjoy a c.** aimer les défis; **I find the work a real c.** ce travail est une vraie gageure pour moi; **environmental problems are the major c. for our generation** les problèmes d'environnement constituent la principale gageure *ou* le principal défi de notre génération
2 *Law (of jury member)* récusation f
VT **1** **to c. sb** *(to a fight)* provoquer qn; **to c. sb to do sth** défier qn de faire qch; **to c. sb to single combat** provoquer qn en combat singulier; **to c. sb to a game of chess/to a game of tennis** proposer une partie d'échecs/de

tennis à qn; *(with serious intent to beat them)* défier qn aux échecs/au tennis
2 *(statement etc)* protester contre, disputer; *(sb's word)* mettre en question *ou* en doute *ou* en cause; *(sb's qualifications, account, figures)* contester; **their position was challenged by younger artists** leur position a été remise en question par des artistes plus jeunes; **to c. sb's right to do sth** contester à qn le droit de faire qch
3 *(stimulate)* **you need a job that will c. you** il te faut un travail stimulant
4 *Mil (of sentry)* interpeller
5 *Law (member of jury)* récuser
▸▸ *Sport* **c. cup** coupe-challenge f, *pl* coupes-challenges; *Sport* **c. match** challenge

challenger ['tʃælɪndʒər] N *(to a fight)* provocateur, -trice; *Sport* challengeur *m*; *Mktg* challengeur, prétendant *m*

challenging ['tʃælɪndʒɪŋ] ADJ **1** *(look, remark etc)* provocateur, -trice; *(air)* de défi **2** *(job)* stimulant

chamber ['tʃeɪmbər] N **1** *(hall, room)* chambre f; *Pol (upper, lower)* Chambre
2 *Law* **chambers** *(of barrister, judge)* cabinet *m*; **in chambers** en chambre du conseil; **to hear a case in chambers** juger une cause en référé
3 *Metal (of furnace)* laboratoire *m*; *Phys (for ionization, expansion)* chambre f, *(of revolver)* chambre; **air c.** *(in pump)* chambre à air
4 *Anat* cavité f
5 *Arch, Lit (room)* salle f, *Lit* **(bed-)c.** chambre f (à coucher); **council c.** salle du conseil
▸▸ **C. of Commerce** Chambre de commerce; **C. of Commerce and Industry** Chambre de commerce et d'industrie; **c. music** musique f de chambre; *Mus* **c. orchestra** orchestre *m* de chambre; **c. pot** pot *m* de chambre

chamberlain ['tʃeɪmbəlɪn] N chambellan *m*

chambermaid ['tʃeɪmbəmeɪd] N *(in hotel)* femme f de chambre

chameleon [kə'miːlɪən] N *(animal)*, *Fig* caméléon *m*

chamfer ['tʃæmfər] *Carp etc* N biseau *m*, chanfrein *m*
VT *(beam etc)* biseauter, chanfreiner; *(cut grooves in) (column etc)* canneler

chammy ['ʃæmɪ] N *Fam* = **chamois 2**

chamois N **1** ['ʃæmwɑː] *(deer)* chamois *m* **2** ['ʃæmɪ] *(cloth for washing car)* chamois *m*, peau f de chamois; **c. jacket** veste f en peau de chamois
▸▸ **c. leather** *(for washing car)* chamois, peau f de chamois

champ[1] [tʃæmp] N *Sport Fam* champion, -ionne

champ[2] VT *(of horse etc) (fodder)* mâcher bruyamment; *(bit)* ronger, mâcher, mâchonner
VI *Fig Fam* **to c. at the bit** *(of person)* ronger son frein

champagne [ʃæm'peɪn] N **1** *(drink)* champagne *m* **2** *(colour)* champagne *m inv*
ADJ *(colour)* champagne *inv*; **a c.-coloured sofa** un canapé couleur champagne
▸▸ **c. flute** flûte f à champagne; **c. glass** *(tall)* flûte à champagne; *(broad)* coupe f à champagne; **c. reception** réception f avec champagne

champers ['ʃæmpəz] N *Fam (champagne)* champ *m*

champion ['tʃæmpɪən] N **1** *Sport* champion, -ionne; **world c.** champion du monde; **a c. footballer** un champion du football **2** *(of cause)* champion, -ionne
ADJ *Br Dial* formidable
VT *(cause)* se faire le champion de; *(person)* soutenir

championship ['tʃæmpɪənʃɪp] N **1** *Sport etc* championnat *m* **2** *(of cause)* défense *f*
▸▸ *Sport* **c. match** match *m* de championnat

CHANCE [tʃɑːns]

N	chance **1, 3** ▪ hasard **1**
	▪ occasion **2** ▪ risque **4**
ADJ ATTRIB	fortuit
VT	risquer

N **1** *(luck)* hasard *m*, chance *f*; **by c.** par hasard; **somebody I met by c.** quelqu'un que j'ai rencontré par hasard; **do you by any c. know his address?** est-ce que par hasard tu connaîtrais son adresse?; **to leave nothing to c.** ne rien laisser au hasard; **to leave everything to c.** s'en remettre entièrement au hasard; *Fam* **to have an eye to** *or* **for the main c.** chercher à tirer profit de toutes les occasions; *Fam* **c. would be a fine thing!** ah, si seulement je pouvais!

2 *(opportunity)* occasion *f*; **now's your c.** c'est maintenant qu'il faut y aller; **it's your last c.** c'est ta dernière chance; **it's a c. in a million** c'est une occasion qui ne se présentera pas deux fois; **I had a c. to work in the States** j'ai eu l'occasion de travailler aux États-Unis; **I go to the theatre when I get the c.** je vais au théâtre quand j'en ai l'occasion; **can you translate this for me when you get a c.?** est-ce que tu pourras me traduire ça quand tu auras le temps?; **there are no second chances, there is no second c.** tu n'as pas droit à l'erreur; **to give sb a c.** *(in job)* mettre qn à l'essai; *(to do better)* donner une chance à qn; **give me another c.** donne-moi une autre chance; **you didn't give me a c.!** *(to tell you)* tu ne m'en as pas laissé le temps!; *Fam* **given half a c. she'd play tennis every day** si elle pouvait elle jouerait au tennis tous les jours

3 *(possibility)* **to have** *or* **stand a c.** *(of succeeding)* avoir des chances de succès; **he never had a c., the truck was coming straight at him** il n'avait aucune chance de s'en sortir, le camion est arrivé droit sur lui; **she stands a good c. of being chosen** elle a de bonnes chances d'être choisie; **he hasn't the slightest c.** *or Fam* **a c. in hell of succeeding** il n'a pas la moindre chance de réussir; **they have an even** *or* **a fifty-fifty c. of winning** ils ont une chance sur deux *ou* cinquante pour cent de chances de gagner; **there's little/ no/a good c. of that happening** il y a peu de chance/aucune chance/de bonnes chances que cela se produise; *Fam* **do you think they'll win? – no c.!** est-ce que tu crois qu'ils vont gagner? – aucune chance!; *Fam* **can I stay the night? – no c.!** est-ce que je peux passer la nuit ici? – pas question!; **(the) chances are (that) he'll forget** il y a fort à parier qu'il oubliera

4 *(risk)* risque *m*; **she takes too many chances** elle prend trop de risques; **to take a c.** prendre un risque; **he took a c. on them not finding out** il a pris le risque en espérant qu'ils ne le découvrent pas; **I'll have to take a c. on that** j'en prends le risque; **I'm taking no chances** je ne veux pas prendre de risques; **to take a sporting c.** tenter le coup; **to take one's chances** tenter sa chance

ADJ ATTRIB c. customer client *m* imprévu; **c. discovery** découverte *f* accidentelle *ou* fortuite; **c. meeting** rencontre *f* fortuite

VI *Lit (happen)* **to c. to do sth** faire qch par hasard; **only when she chanced to visit him was the body discovered** c'est en passant chez lui par hasard qu'elle a découvert le corps

VT *(risk)* risquer; *Fam* **to c. it** *or* **one's luck** *or* **one's arm** risquer *ou* tenter le coup; **to c. doing sth** prendre le risque de faire qch

▸ **chance on, chance upon** VT INSEP *(find by accident)* tomber (par hasard) sur

> Note that the French noun **chance** is a false friend. Its most common meaning is **luck**.

chancel ['tʃɑːns(ə)l] N *Archit* chœur *m*
▸▸ **c. screen** jubé *m*

chancellery ['tʃɑːnsələrɪ] N chancellerie *f*

chancellor ['tʃɑːnsələr] N **1** *Univ, Rel* chancelier *m* **2** *Br Pol* **C.** chancelier *m*; *Br Pol* **C. (of the Exchequer)** Chancelier de l'Échiquier, = ministre *m* des Finances; *Br Law* **the Lord (High) C.** le Grand Chancelier, = le ministre de la Justice

chancer ['tʃɑːnsər] N *Br Sl (opportunist)* filou *m*; **he's a real c.** il n'en rate pas une

chancery ['tʃɑːnsərɪ] N **1** *Law Br* **(Court of) C.** cour *f* de la chancellerie; *Am* **(court of) c.** cour d'équité **2** *(of embassy)* chancellerie *f*

chancre ['ʃæŋkər] N *Med* chancre *m*

chancy ['tʃɑːnsɪ] ADJ *Fam* risqué

chandelier [ʃændə'lɪər] N lustre *m*

> Note that the French word **chandelier** is a false friend and is never a translation for the English word **chandelier**. Its most common meaning is **candlestick** or **candelabra**.

chandler ['tʃɑːndlər] N *Com* **ship('s) c.** fournisseur *m* de navires; **corn c.** marchand *m* de blé *ou* de grains

CHANGE [tʃeɪndʒ]

N	changement **1** ▪ monnaie **2**
VT	changer **1–4**
VI	changer **1, 3** ▪ se changer **2**

N **1** *(alteration)* *(of air, job etc)* changement *m*; *(in expression, voice)* altération *f*; *(modification)* modification *f*; **c. of address** changement de domicile *ou* d'adresse; **to have a c. of opinion** *or* **of heart** changer d'avis; **c. for the better/worse** *(of health etc)* amélioration *f*/détérioration *f*; **there's been a c. in the weather** il y a eu un changement de temps; **there's been a c. in the law** la loi a été modifiée; **sudden c. of fortune** revirement *m* de fortune; **there is no/little c. in the situation** il n'y a pas/il y a peu de changement dans la situation; **there are going to be some changes in this office!** il va y avoir du nouveau *ou* du changement dans ce bureau!; **some changes were made to the train timetable** il y a eu des changements *ou* des modifications dans les horaires de train; **you need a c.** tu as besoin de changer d'air; **the c. will do you good** le changement te fera du bien; *Prov* **a c. is as good as a rest** changer de décor fait autant de bien que partir en vacances; **this trip will be** *or* **make a bit of a c. for you** ce voyage vous changera un peu; **you must find it a bit of a c. living in the country** vous devez trouver un drôle de changement à vivre à la campagne; **he was early for a c.** pour une fois, il était en avance; **why don't you wash the dishes for a c.?** si tu faisais la vaisselle, pour une fois?; **it** *or* **that makes a c.** ça change un peu; **yes, it makes a (nice) c., doesn't it?** oui, ça change (un peu) (de l'ordinaire) n'est-ce pas?; **it was a c. from the old system** ça changeait du système précédent; **the c. of life,** *Fam* **the c.** *(of woman)* le retour d'âge; *Fam* **to go through the c.** *(of woman)* traverser la ménopause; *Mus* **chord c.** changement d'accord; *Theat* **scene c.** changement de décor; **c. of clothes** vêtements *mpl* de rechange

2 *(money)* monnaie *f*; **small** *or* **loose c.** petite *ou* menue monnaie; **to get c.** faire de la monnaie; **to get c. for £5** faire la monnaie de 5 livres; **have you got c. for a £10 note?** est-ce que tu as de la monnaie sur un billet de 10 livres?; **keep the c.** gardez la monnaie; **the machine doesn't give c.** cet appareil ne rend pas la monnaie; *Fam* **you won't get much c. out of £100** *(if you buy that)* il ne va pas te rester grand-chose sur tes 100 livres; *Fam* **he won't get much c. out of me** il en sera pour ses frais avec moi

3 *(in bell-ringing)* **to ring the changes** carillonner avec variations *ou* avec permutations; *Fig* **to ring the changes on** *(subject)* ressasser, rabâcher, broder des variations sur; *(menu, programme etc)* varier, introduire des changements dans

VT **1** *(alter)* *(one's plans, lifestyle etc)* changer, modifier; **to c. water into wine** changer l'eau en vin; **you can't c. a dictatorship into a democracy overnight** on ne transforme pas une dictature en démocratie en une nuit; **the witch changed him into a frog** la sorcière l'a transformé en crapaud; **to c. one's ways** *or* **habits** changer (ses habitudes); **to c. one's mind** *or* **opinion** changer d'avis; **to c. the subject** changer de sujet; **don't c. the subject!** ne détourne pas la conversation!; **to c. colour** changer de couleur

2 *(replace)* *(sheets)* changer; **to c. one's clothes** se changer; **to c. one's dress/one's shoes** changer de robe/de chaussures; **to c. the baby** changer le bébé; *Aut* **to c. a tyre** changer *ou* remplacer un pneu; *Aut* **to c. the oil** faire la *ou* une vidange; *Aut* **to c. gear** changer de vitesse; **to c. channels** *(on TV)* changer de chaîne; **to c. trains/one's seat** changer de train/de place; **I've changed doctors** j'ai changé de médecin

3 *(exchange)* **to c. one thing for another** changer une chose pour *ou* contre une autre; **to c. places** *or* **seats with sb** changer de place avec qn; *Fig* **I wouldn't (like to) c. places with him** je ne changerais pas avec lui; *Fig* **to c. sides** changer de camp, virer de bord; *Mil* **to c. the guard** relever la garde

4 *(money)* changer; **to c. a note into coins** faire la monnaie sur un billet; **to c. dollars into euros** changer des dollars contre des euros *ou* en euros; **they won't c. pounds** ils ne changeront pas des livres

VI **1** *(alter)* changer; *(of moon)* changer de quartier; *(of luck, wind)* tourner; **she's changed since I last saw her** elle a changé depuis la dernière fois que je l'ai vue; **some things never c.** certaines choses ne changent jamais; **to c. for the better** changer en mieux, s'améliorer; *(of weather)* tourner au beau; **the situation has changed for the worse** la situation s'est détériorée; **to c. beyond recognition** être méconnaissable; **to c. into sth** *(by magic, through biological transformation)* se transformer en qch; **he changed into a psychopath** il est devenu psychopathe; **the country had changed from dictatorship to democracy overnight** en une nuit, le pays était passé de la dictature à la démocratie; **the lights changed from green to amber** les feux sont passés du vert à l'orange; **to c. from one system to another** passer d'un système à un autre

2 *(put on other clothes)* se changer; **to c. into another dress** changer de robe; **to c. into trousers** se mettre en pantalon; **to c. into something more comfortable/less formal** mettre un vêtement plus confortable/moins habillé; **to c. out of a wet shirt** enlever *ou* quitter une chemise mouillée

3 *Rail etc (of passenger)* changer; **we had to c. twice** nous avons eu deux correspondances; *(in underground)* nous avons eu deux changements; **all c.!** tout le monde descend!

4 *(of sentries, shifts)* se relever

▸▸ **c. machine** distributeur *m* de monnaie

▸ **change down** VI *Aut (use lower gear)* rétrograder; **to c. down (in)to second** passer en seconde

▸ **change over** VI (convert) **the UK changed over to decimal currency in 1971** le Royaume-Uni est passé à la monnaie décimale en 1971; **we c. over next year** on passe au nouveau système l'an prochain

2 (switch) **let's c. over** (exchange places etc) on change?; (exchange jobs, roles etc) on échange?; TV **to c. over (to another channel)** passer sur une autre chaîne; TV **c. over for the news** change de chaîne pour regarder les informations; TV **why don't you c. over to ITV?** et si on mettait ITV?

3 Sport (change ends) changer de côté; (in relay race) passer le témoin

▸ **change up** VI Aut (use higher gear) passer à la vitesse supérieure; **to c. up (in)to third** passer en troisième

changeability [tʃeɪndʒəˈbɪlɪtɪ], **changeableness** [ˈtʃeɪndʒəb(ə)lnɪs] N (of weather etc) variabilité f; (of moods) changements mpl

changeable [ˈtʃeɪndʒəb(ə)l] ADJ changeant; (weather) variable, instable; (wind) inégal, -aux; **c. character** caractère m changeant ou instable

changeless [ˈtʃeɪndʒlɪs] ADJ (rituals, landscape) immuable

changeling [ˈtʃeɪndʒlɪŋ] N = enfant mf que les fées ont substitué(ée) à un(e) autre

changeover [ˈtʃeɪndʒəʊvər] N **1** (to new system) changement m, passage m **2** (after election etc) relève f **3** Sport changement m de côté; (in relay race) passage m du témoin **4** Cin changement m de bobine

changing [ˈtʃeɪndʒɪŋ] ADJ (nature, world, mood) changeant

N changement m

▸▸ Aut **c. down** (of gears) rétrogradage m; **the C. of the Guard** la relève de la garde; Br **c. room** (in sports centre, gym) vestiaire m; (in shop) cabine f d'essayage; **c. table** table f à langer

channel [ˈtʃæn(ə)l] N **1** (of river) lit m; (waterway) chenal m; **the (English) C.** la Manche; **on the other side of the C.** outre-Manche

2 (of distribution) canal m, circuit m; (for complaint, inquiry etc) voie f; **to go through (official) channels** suivre la filière ou la voie hiérarchique; **through diplomatic channels** par voie diplomatique; **channels of communication** canaux de communication; **there were still channels of communication open** la communication n'était pas totalement interrompue; **channels of communication are still open** (between us) nous sommes toujours en relation, le dialogue continue

3 TV chaîne f; Radio station f

4 Elec, Electron etc voie f; Comput canal m; (on stereo) sortie f

5 (for irrigation) canal m

6 (groove) (in wood) rainure f; (on column) cannelure f

VT (-ll-, Am -l-) **1** (direct) (effort, energy, information) canaliser (**towards** vers; **into** dans); (resources, aid etc) acheminer; **she channelled all her energy into charity work** elle a investi toute son énergie dans des œuvres de bienfaisance **2** (cut channels in) (ground) creuser des rigoles dans

▸▸ Com **c. of distribution** circuit de distribution, canal de distribution; **C. Four** = chaîne de télévision privée britannique à vocation culturelle; **the C. Islands** les îles fpl Anglo-Normandes; Mktg **c. management** gestion f du circuit de distribution; **C. port** port m sur la Manche; **the C. Tunnel** le tunnel sous la Manche

channel-hop VI TV zapper

channel-hopper N TV zappeur, -euse

channel-hopping N TV zapping m

chant [tʃɑːnt] N **1** (of demonstrators) slogans mpl (scandés); **the c. went up ... on** commença à scander ... **2** Mus, Rel psalmodie f; **Gregorian c.** chant m grégorien

VT **1** (slogans, name etc) scander **2** Rel psalmodier

VI **1** (of demonstrators, crowd etc) scander des slogans **2** Rel psalmodier

> Note that the French verb **chanter** is a false friend and is never a translation for the English verb **to chant**. It means **to sing**.

chantey [ˈʃæntɪ] N Am chanson f de marin

chanting [ˈtʃɑːntɪŋ] ADJ (voice etc) monotone, traînant

N **1** (of demonstrators) slogans mpl (scandés) **2** Rel chants mpl, psalmodie f

chantry [ˈtʃɑːntrɪ] N Rel Arch chantrerie f, chanterie f

chaos [ˈkeɪɒs] N chaos m; (in filing system, sb's life) pagaille f, Fam bordel m; **it'll be c. if you try to introduce these changes** ça va être la pagaille si tu fais ces changements; **the country is in a state of c.** le pays est dans un état de confusion totale; Journ **c. on roads as bus drivers strike** la grève des chauffeurs de bus entraîne le chaos sur les routes; **it was in the post office** c'était la pagaille au bureau de poste; **it's just c.!** c'est la confusion totale!

▸▸ **c. theory** théorie f du chaos

chaotic [keɪˈɒtɪk] ADJ chaotique; (office, filing system) en désordre; **in a c. state** en pagaille; **a c. love life** une vie amoureuse chaotique

chaotically [keɪˈɒtɪklɪ] ADV en pagaille; **clothes all c. piled into one drawer** des vêtements tous mis en pagaille dans un tiroir; **a c. disorganized life** une vie totalement chaotique

chap¹ [tʃæp] N Fam (man) type m, mec m; **a good c.** un type bien; **an odd c.** un drôle de type; **be a good c.** sois sympa; Old-fashioned **I say, old c.!** dis, mon vieux!

chap² N (on skin) gerçure f, crevasse f

VT (-pp-) (skin) gercer; **chapped lips** lèvres fpl gercées

VI se gercer

chapel [ˈtʃæp(ə)l] N **1** (of school etc) chapelle f; (private) oratoire m; (in cathedral etc) chapelle latérale **2** Rel (protestant) temple m; Scot Cathol **to go to c.** aller à la messe **3** (of print union, NUJ) branche f syndicale (dans l'industrie du livre et de l'édition); **Father/ Mother of C.** président/présidente de la branche syndicale

▸▸ **c. of rest** = chambre f mortuaire dans une entreprise de pompes funèbres

chaperone [ˈʃæpərəʊn] N (for young girl), Hum chaperon m; **to act as c.** servir de chaperon; **the foreign journalists had a c.** les journalistes étrangers étaient accompagnés partout où ils allaient

VT (girl, young woman) chaperonner

chaplain [ˈtʃæplɪn] N Rel aumônier m

chaplaincy [ˈtʃæplɪnsɪ] N aumônerie f

chappie [ˈtʃæpɪ] N Fam (man) type m, gus m; (little boy, baby) petit gars m

Chaps [tʃæps] N Banking (abbr **clearing house automated payment system**) Sit m

chapter [ˈtʃæptər] N **1** (of book), Fig chapitre m; Fig **to give c. and verse for sth** citer les références exactes de qch; **a new c. in East-West relations** un nouveau chapitre dans les relations est-ouest; **what a c. of accidents!** quelle série noire! **2** Rel (of canons, monks) chapitre m **3** (of society etc) groupe m; **a Hell's Angel c.** une bande de Hell's Angels

char¹ [tʃɑːr] (-rr-) VT (wood, bones) carboniser, réduire en cendres; **the charred remains of a building** les restes carbonisés d'un bâtiment

VI se carboniser

char² N Br Sl (tea) thé m

char³ Br Fam N (charlady) femme f de ménage

VI (work as charlady) faire des ménages

char⁴ N (fish) omble m (chevalier)

charabanc [ˈʃærəbæŋ] N Br Hist char m à bancs; Hum (sightseeing coach) car m de touristes

character [ˈkærɪktər] N **1** Liter, Theat etc personnage m; **a c. straight out of a novel** un vrai personnage de roman; **Chaplin plays two different characters in 'The Great Dictator'** Chaplin joue deux rôles différents dans 'Le Dictateur'; **characters in order of appearance** (in credits) distribution par ordre d'entrée en scène

2 (distinctive quality) (of person, race, book etc) caractère m; **her face is full of c.** son visage a beaucoup de caractère; **to have c.** avoir du caractère; **this region has a c. of its own** cette région a un caractère particulier; **books of this c.** les livres de ce genre; **his behaviour/remark was in/out of c.** la façon dont il s'est conduit/la remarque qu'il a faite lui correspond bien/ne lui correspond pas

3 (moral qualities) caractère m; (reputation) réputation f; **a man of (strong) c.** un homme de caractère ou de volonté; **to be lacking in c.** manquer de caractère; Fml **a person of good c.** une personne honorable; **a place of very dubious c.** un endroit mal famé

4 (person) **a suspicious c.** un individu suspect ou louche; **he's quite a c.!** (odd, remarkable) c'est un sacré numéro!, c'est un personnage!

5 Comput, Typ caractère m; **in Greek characters** en caractères grecs; **special/binary c.** caractère spécial/binaire; **characters per inch** caractères par pouce; **characters per second** caractères par seconde

▸▸ Cin, Theat **c. actor** acteur m de genre; **c. assassination** diffamation f; Comput **c. code** code m de caractère; Comput **c. count** nombre m de caractères; **to do a c. count** compter les caractères; Comput, Typ **c. font** fonte f de caractère; Comput **c. generator** générateur m de caractères; Comput **c. insert** insertion f de caractère; Mktg **c. licensing** cession f de licence sur un personnage; Comput **c. map** tableau m des caractères; Comput **c. mode** mode m caractère; Cin, Theat **c. part** rôle m de composition; Comput **c. recognition** reconnaissance f de caractères; **c. reference** des références f pl; Comput **c. set** jeu m de caractères; **c. sketch** portrait m ou description f rapide; Comput **c. smoothing** lissage m de caractères; Comput **c. space** espace m; Comput **c. spacing** espacement m des caractères; Comput **c. string** chaîne f de caractères; Law **c. witness** témoin m de moralité

character-building, character-forming ADJ qui forme le caractère; **it's c.** ça forme le caractère

characteristic [kærɪktəˈrɪstɪk] ADJ (sign, taste etc) caractéristique; **this attitude is c. of him** cette attitude lui correspond bien, c'est bien de lui

N **1** caractéristique f, trait m caractéristique **2** Math (of logarithm) caractéristique f

characteristically [kærɪktəˈrɪstɪklɪ] ADV de façon caractéristique; **he was c. blunt/ evasive** comme à son habitude, il a été abrupt/vague

characterization [kærɪktəraɪˈzeɪʃən] N **1** *(description)* caractérisation *f* **2** *Cin, Liter, Theat* représentation *f ou* peinture *f* des personnages

characterize [ˈkærɪktəraɪz] VT **1** *(of writer)* *(person)* caractériser; *(century etc)* dépeindre **2** *(be characteristic of)* être caractéristique de, caractériser; **the long pauses that c. his speech** les longs silences qui caractérisent son discours

characterless [ˈkærɪktəlɪs] ADJ sans caractère

charade [ʃəˈrɑːd] N **1** *(farce)* mascarade *f* **2** *(game)* **to play charades** jouer aux charades mimées

> Note that the French word **charade** is a false friend. It is a type of word game.

charcoal [ˈtʃɑːkəʊl] N **1** charbon *m* de bois **2** *Art* fusain *m*
▸▸**c. drawing** (dessin *m* au) fusain; **c. filter** filtre *m* à charbon

charcoal-broiled [-ˈbrɔɪld] ADJ *(steak etc)* grillé au charbon de bois

charcoal-burner N **1** *(person)* charbonnier *m* **2** *(stove)* réchaud *m* à charbon de bois

chard [tʃɑːd] N *Bot, Culin* **Swiss c.** bette *f*, blette *f*

CHARGE [tʃɑːdʒ] N **1** *(cost)* frais *mpl*; *Admin* droits *mpl*; *Law* privilège *m*, droit *m*; *(to an account)* imputation *f*; **list of charges** tarif *m*; **scale of charges** barème *m* des prix; **no c. for admission** *(in museum etc)* entrée gratuite; **there is no extra c. for installation** l'installation est comprise dans le prix; **to make a c. for sth** faire payer qch; **free of c.** gratis, (à titre) gratuit, à titre gracieux; *Com, Banking* exempt de frais, sans frais; *esp Am* **will that be cash or c.?** vous payez comptant ou vous le portez à votre compte?; **service c.** prestation *f* de service; **extra c.** supplément *m* (de prix); **bank charges** frais bancaires, agios *mpl*; **minimum c.** *(in taxi)* prise *f* en charge; *(in café, restaurant)* = prix *m* minimum à payer; *Banking* **c. over business assets** nantissement *m* de fonds de commerce
2 *(accusation)* accusation *f*; *Law* chef *m* d'accusation, acte *m* d'accusation; *(by public prosecutor)* réquisitoire *m*; **to bring** *or* **lay a c. against sb** porter une accusation *ou* porter plainte contre qn; **on a c. of having …** accusé d'avoir …; **what's the c.?** de quoi est-il/suis-je/*etc* accusé?; **he denies the c.** il nie les accusations
3 *(responsibility)* garde *f*, soin *m*; **to place sth in sb's c.** confier qch à qn *ou* à la garde de qn *ou* aux mains de qn; **to have c. of sth** avoir la garde de qch; **to take c. of sth/sb** se charger de qch/qn; **I'll take c. while the director is sick** je m'occupe de tout pendant que le directeur est malade; **to be in c. of** piloter; **Jane is in c. of sales** Jane est chargée *ou* responsable des ventes; **he is in overall c. of the project** il est responsable du projet dans son ensemble; **he was put in c. of 100 men** on a mis 100 hommes sous sa responsabilité; **who is in c.?** qui est le responsable?; **look, I'm in c. here!** écoute, c'est moi le patron ici!; **I want to speak to the person in c.** je veux parler au responsable *ou* à la personne responsable; **who was in c. of the vehicle?** *(driving)* qui était au volant?; *Law* **to take sb in c.** arrêter qn
4 *(person, thing entrusted)* = personne *f*/ chose *f* confiée à la garde de qn; **the nanny is out for a walk with her charges** la nourrice est partie se promener avec les enfants qu'elle garde *ou* dont elle a la charge
5 *Mil* charge *f*, attaque *f*; **to sound the c.** sonner la charge
6 *Elec, Phys (of cartridge, bomb, battery)* charge *f*; *Fig* **the word has an emotional c.** le mot a une charge affective; *Am Fam Fig* **to get a c. out of sth/doing sth** *(thrill)* s'éclater *ou* prendre son pied avec qch/en faisant qch
VT **1** *(price)* faire payer; *Com, Fin (account)* charger (**with** de); **he charged me £15** il m'a fait payer 15 livres; *Fam* **they charged me a fortune for this haircut** j'ai payé une fortune pour me faire couper les cheveux; **how much do you c. for an hour?** combien prenez-vous de l'heure?; *Tel* **calls charged for conversations** *fpl* taxées; **to c. the postage to the customer** faire payer les frais d'envoi au client; **commission charged by the bank** commission prélevée par la banque; **c. it to my account/the bill** mettez-le sur mon compte/la note
2 *(accuse)* accuser (**with sth** de qch; **with doing** de faire *ou* d'avoir fait); *Law* inculper (**with a crime** d'un crime); *Am* **to c. that …** alléguer que …
3 *(entrust, order)* **to c. sb to do sth** ordonner à qn de faire qch; **to c. sb with a task** confier une tâche à qn
4 *(of troops, forwards, bull etc)* charger
5 *Elec (electrical conductor, battery etc)* (re)charger (**with** de); *Fig* **a highly charged atmosphere** une atmosphère très tendue; **charged with emotion** chargé d'émotion
VI **1** *Mil* charger, faire une charge; *(of animal)* charger; *Fam (run heavily) (of person)* se précipiter, foncer; *Mil* **c!** chargez!; **he charged in** il s'est précipité dans la maison/ la pièce/*etc*; **the crowd charged across the square** la foule s'est ruée à travers la place; **stop charging around, you kids, this is a living room!** arrêtez de courir dans tous les sens, les enfants, ici c'est un salon!
2 *(require payment)* faire payer (**for sth** qch); **do you c. for delivery?** est-ce qu'il y a des frais de livraison?
3 *(of battery)* se (re)charger
▸▸*Am Com, Fin* **c. account** compte *m* crédit d'achats, compte accréditif; *Com, Fin* **c. card** carte *f* de paiement; *Br* **c. hand** sous-chef *m* d'équipe, *pl* sous-chefs d'équipe; *Br* **c. nurse** infirmier, -ière en chef; *Br Law* **c. sheet** procès-verbal *m*, *pl* procès-verbaux *(établi par la police avant le passage d'un prévenu devant un tribunal)*

▸ **charge down** VT SEP *Rugby (ball)* contrer
▸ **charge off** VT SEP *Am Fin (capital)* amortir, imputer à l'exercice; **we were obliged to c. the whole operation** il a fallu imputer l'intégralité du coût de l'opération à l'exercice
▸ **charge up** VT SEP **1** *(in shop etc)* **to c. sth up to sb's account** mettre qch sur le compte de qn; **could you c. it up?** pourriez-vous le mettre sur mon compte?
2 *(battery)* (re)charger
VI *(of battery)* se (re)charger

chargeable [ˈtʃɑːdʒəb(ə)l] ADJ **1** *Law (person)* **we would be c. with fraud** on nous accuserait de fraude; **a c. offence** un délit **2** *Com etc (to an account)* imputable; **to be c. to sb** *(payable by)* être à la charge de qn, être pris en charge par qn; **is it c.?** est-ce qu'il y a des frais?; **a small fee is c. for delivery and installation** il y a quelques frais de livraison et d'installation; **who is it c. to?** c'est à la charge de qui?; **could you make that c. to …?** est-ce que vous pourriez facturer …?; **is this a c. expense?** est-ce que c'est frais facturable?
▸▸**c. distance** *(in taxi)* distance *f* tarifaire; *Fin* **c. gain** bénéfice *m* imposable; *Com* **c. weight** poids *m* de taxation

charge-cooled [-kuːld] ADJ *Aut (engine)* suralimenté refroidi

chargé d'affaires [ˈʃɑːʒeɪdæˈfeər] N chargé *m* d'affaires

charger [ˈtʃɑːdʒər] N **1** *Elec (for battery)* chargeur *m* **2** *(horse)* cheval *m* de bataille, destrier *m*

charily [ˈtʃeərɪlɪ] ADV *(cautiously)* avec précaution, avec prudence

chariot [ˈtʃærɪət] N char *m*

charioteer [tʃærɪəˈtɪər] N conducteur *m* de char

charisma [kəˈrɪzmə] N charisme *m*; **to have c.** avoir du charisme

charismatic [kærɪzˈmætɪk] ADJ charismatique

charitable [ˈtʃærɪtəb(ə)l] ADJ **1** *(person, action)* charitable; *Fig* **the critics were not c.** les critiques n'ont pas été très tendres *ou* bienveillants **2** *(organization)* caritatif, de bienfaisance, de charité; *(work)* de bienfaisance, de charité
▸▸**c. donation** don *m* à une œuvre de bienfaisance; **c. society** organisation *f* caritative; **c. status** statut *m* d'organisation caritative; **c. trust** fondation *f* d'utilité publique

charitably [ˈtʃærɪtəblɪ] ADV avec charité

charity [ˈtʃærɪtɪ] N **1** *(money, food)* charité *f*, aumônes *fpl*; **to live on c.** vivre d'aumônes; **I don't want your c.** je ne veux pas que tu me fasses la charité **2** *(organization)* organisation *f* caritative; **registered c.** œuvre *f* reconnue d'utilité publique; **we're not a c.!** nous ne sommes pas des philanthropes *ou* une organisation de bienfaisance! **3** *(kindness)* charité *f*; **out of c.** par charité; *Prov* **c. begins at home** charité bien ordonnée commence par soi-même
▸▸**c. ball** bal *m* de bienfaisance; *Br* **the C. Commission** = commission *f* gouvernementale britannique contrôlant les associations caritatives; **c. organization** association *f* caritative, œuvre de bienfaisance; **c. run** = course *f* à pied au profit d'une œuvre de bienfaisance; **c. shop** = magasin *m* dont les employés sont des bénévoles et dont les bénéfices servent à subventionner une œuvre d'utilité publique; **c. work** bénévolat *m*

charlady [ˈtʃɑːleɪdɪ] N *Br* femme *f* de ménage

charlatan [ˈʃɑːlət(ə)n] N charlatan *m*

charleston [ˈtʃɑːlstən] N *(dance)* charleston *m*

Charley, Charlie [ˈtʃɑːlɪ] N *Br Fam* **I felt a right** *or* **a proper C.** j'ai vraiment eu l'air bête

charley horse N *Am Fam* **to have a c.** avoir des crampes

charlie [ˈtʃɑːlɪ] N *Sl (cocaine)* coke *f*, neige *f*

charlotte [ˈʃɑːlət] N *Culin* **apple c.** charlotte *f* aux pommes

charm [tʃɑːm] N **1** *(attractiveness)* charme *m*, agrément *m*; *(of youth etc)* charme, attrait *m*; **a film of great c.** un film plein de charme; **the village has a quiet c.** le village a un charme tranquille; **to be devoid of c.** manquer de charme; *Fam* **to turn on the c.** faire du charme; **(physical) charms** *(of person)* charmes, attraits; **the c. of this system is that it's so easy to use** ce qu'il y a de bien avec ce système, c'est qu'il est facile à utiliser; *Iron* **what c. school did you go to?** oh, comme tu parles bien!
2 *(spell)* charme *m* (**against** contre), sortilège *m*, sort *m*, enchantement *m*; **to be under a c.** être envoûté; *Fam* **it worked like a c.** ça a marché à merveille
3 *(talisman)* amulette *f*, fétiche *m*; **(lucky) c.** porte-bonheur *m inv*
VT *(person) (delight)* charmer, enchanter; *(snake)* charmer; **she charmed them into signing** elle a obtenu leur signature à force de charme; **he leads a charmed life** c'est un veinard
▸▸**c. bracelet** bracelet *m* à breloques; **c. offensive** offensive *f* de charme

charmer [ˈtʃɑːmər] N charmeur, -euse; **he's quite a c.** c'est un charmeur; **snake c.** charmeur de serpents

charming ['tʃɑːmɪŋ] **ADJ** *(person, child, village, story), Iron* charmant; **Prince C.** le Prince Charmant

charmingly ['tʃɑːmɪŋlɪ] **ADV** d'une façon charmante

charnel ['tʃɑːn(ə)l] **N** *(for corpses)* charnier *m*

▸▸**c. house** *(for bones)* ossuaire *m*

charring ['tʃɑːrɪŋ] **N** carbonisation *f*

chart [tʃɑːt] **N 1** *Math etc (graph)* graphique *m*; *(diagram)* diagramme *m*; *(table)* tableau *m*; *Med* **temperature c.** feuille *f* de température; *Com* **colour c.** nuancier *m* **2** *Mus* **(pop) charts** hit-parade *m*, *pl* hit-parades; **she's (got a record) in the charts** elle est au hit-parade; **it's number one in** *or* **it's top of the charts** c'est le numéro un au hit-parade **3** *Naut, Aviat (for navigation)* carte *f*

VT 1 *Naut (sea etc)* hydrographier, faire l'hydrographie de; *(rock etc)* porter sur une carte **2** *(patient's temperature etc)* porter sur la feuille; *(plot graph of) (series of readings etc)* établir le graphique de; **this graph charts sales over the last ten years** ce graphique montre l'évolution des ventes au cours des dix dernières années; *Fig* **the book charts the rise of the labour movement** ce livre retrace la montée du mouvement travailliste

VI *Mus Fam (of record)* être classé; **it charted at number 16** il a été classé 16ᵉ

▸▸*Acct* **c. of accounts** plan *m* comptable général; **c. analyst** analyste *mf* sur graphiques; *Naut* **c. room** cabine *f* des cartes; *Mus* **c. topper** numéro *m* un

charter ['tʃɑːtər] **N 1** *Hist, Law (of town, university etc)* charte *f*, *(of company)* statuts *mpl*; *Pol* **the Atlantic C.** la Charte de l'Atlantique **2** *(of plane, ship, bus)* affrètement *m*; **on c.** *(to company)* affrété

VT 1 *(hire) (ship, plane)* affréter, noliser; *(ship)* prendre à fret; *(coach)* affréter **2** *(company etc)* accorder une charte à

▸▸**c. flight** (vol *m*) charter *m*; **c. plane** (avion *m*) charter

chartered ['tʃɑːtəd] **ADJ 1** *(ship, plane)* affrété, nolisé; *(coach)* affrété **2** *(company, bank)* privilégié

▸▸*Br* **c. accountant** expert-comptable *m*, *pl* experts-comptables; **c. surveyor** expert *m* immobilier

charterer ['tʃɑːtərər] **N** *Naut, Aviat* affréteur *m*

chartering ['tʃɑːtərɪŋ] **N** *(of plane, ship, coach)* affrètement *m*; *(of plane, boat)* nolisation *f*, *(at reduced rates)* chartérisation *f*

▸▸**c. broker** courtier *m* d'affrètement

charwoman, *pl* **charwomen** ['tʃɑːwʊmən, -wɪmɪn] **N** *Br* femme *f* de ménage

chary ['tʃeərɪ] **ADJ** *(cautious)* prudent, circonspect; **to be c. of doing sth** hésiter à faire qch; **to be c. of praise** *(sparing with it)* être avare de compliments

chase¹ [tʃeɪs] **N 1** *(pursuit)* chasse *f*, poursuite *f*; **to give c. to sb** se lancer à la poursuite de qn; **in c. of sb** à la poursuite de qn; **a car c.** une poursuite en voitures; **paper c.** rallye-paper *m*, *pl* rallye-papers **2** *Horseracing* steeple *m* **3** **the c.** *(hunting)* la chasse à courre

VT 1 *(pursue) (thief, enemy etc)* poursuivre, donner la chasse à; *(hunt) (deer)* chasser; **to c. a dog away** chasser un chien; **to c. sb out of the house** chasser qn de la maison **2** *Fam (court) (man, woman)* courir après

VI I've been chasing around all day j'ai couru toute la journée; **the kids were chasing all over the house** les gosses passaient leur temps à courir partout dans la maison

▸**chase after VT INSEP** *Fam (man, woman)* courir après; *(car, animal etc)* être à la poursuite de, poursuivre; **we've been all over town chasing after that spare part** nous avons dû faire tout le tour de la ville pour trouver cette pièce détachée

▸**chase away VT SEP** chasser

▸**chase up VT SEP 1** *(insistently contact or try to contact)* relancer; **I'll c. them up about those files** je vais leur réclamer ces fichiers; **to c. up a debtor** relancer un débiteur **2** *(payment)* réclamer; **I'll c. the matter up for you** je vais tenter d'activer les choses pour vous

> Note that the French verb **chasser** is a false friend. Its most common meaning is **to hunt**.

chase² **VT 1** *(engrave) (gold, silver)* ciseler; **chased work** ouvrage *m* ciselé **2** *(emboss) (metal)* repousser; **chased silver** argent *m* repoussé

chaser ['tʃeɪsər] **N** *Fam* **1** *(drink)* = alcool *m* bu après une bière ou vice versa **2** **woman c.** coureur *m* de jupons

chasing ['tʃeɪsɪŋ] **N 1** *(engraving) (of gold, silver)* ciselage *m*, ciselure *f* **2** *(embossing) (of metal)* repoussage *m*

chasm ['kæz(ə)m] **N** *(abyss)* abysse *m*, abîme *m*, gouffre *m* béant; *Fig (between two people)* abîme *m*; **the c. between their political viewpoints** l'abîme qui sépare leurs opinions politiques

chassis ['ʃæsɪ] **N** *Aut, Aviat etc, Sl (of woman)* châssis *m*; *Hum* **she's got a classy c.** elle est super bien balancée *ou* carrossée

▸▸**c. number** numéro *m* de châssis

chassisless construction ['ʃæsɪlɪs] **N** *Aut* carrosserie *f* autoporteuse

chaste [tʃeɪst] **ADJ 1** *(sexually)* chaste **2** *Lit (speech, taste, style)* sobre, simple

chastely ['tʃeɪstlɪ] **ADV 1** *(in sexual sense)* chastement **2** *Lit (soberly)* sobrement

chasten ['tʃeɪs(ə)n] **VT** *esp Lit (of providence, suffering etc) (person)* éprouver; *(humble)* rabattre la présomption *ou* l'orgueil de; *(subdue)* assagir; **he was in a chastened mood** il était abattu; **my son returned from Bangladesh chastened by what he had seen** le voyage de mon fils au Bangladesh, et ce qu'il y a vu, lui a mis du plomb dans la tête

chasteness ['tʃeɪstnɪs] **N** *(sexual)* chasteté *f*

chastening ['tʃeɪs(ə)nɪŋ] **ADJ** salutaire; **it had a c. effect on her** ça l'a assagie

chastise [tʃæs'taɪz] **VT 1** *(reprimand, criticize)* réprimander **2** *Old-fashioned, Fml (punish)* châtier; *(beat) (child)* corriger

chastisement [tʃæs'taɪzmənt] **N** *Old-fashioned, Fml (punishment)* châtiment *m*; *(beating) (of child)* correction *f*

chastity ['tʃæstɪtɪ] **N** *(sexual)* chasteté *f*; **to take a vow of c.** faire vœu de chasteté

▸▸**c. belt** ceinture *f* de chasteté

chasuble ['tʃæzjʊb(ə)l] **N** *Rel* chasuble *f*

chat [tʃæt] **N** petite conversation *f*, causette *f*, *Comput* bavardage *m*; **to have a c. with sb** bavarder avec qn; *(about a problem, their work performance etc)* dire un mot à qn; **it's time we had a little c.** il est temps que nous ayons une petite discussion; **the c. at work is all about cars** au travail, on ne discute que de voitures

VI (-tt-) causer, bavarder; *Comput* bavarder; **to c. with sb** bavarder avec qn, faire la causette avec qn; **to c. about one thing and another** parler de choses et d'autres

▸▸*Comput* **c. room** site *m* de bavardage, salon *m*, *Can* bavardoir *m*; *Br TV* **c. show** causerie *f* télévisée, talk-show *m*, *pl* talk-shows; *Br TV* **c. show host** présentateur, -trice de talk-show

▸**chat up VT SEP** *Fam (talk flirtatiously to)* baratiner, draguer; *Fig* **to c. up a client** baratiner un client

chattel ['tʃæt(ə)l] **N** *Law* bien *m* meuble, bien mobilier; **chattels** biens; **goods and chattels** biens et effets *mpl*

chatter ['tʃætər] **N** *(of people)* bavardage *m*; *(of birds)* caquet(age) *m*; *(of monkeys)* babil *m*; *(of teeth)* claquement *m*; *(of machine-gun)* martèlement *m*

VI *(of person)* bavarder, jaser; *(of birds)* caqueter, jacasser; *(of monkeys)* babiller; *(of teeth)* claquer; **my teeth were chattering** je claquais des dents

chatterbox ['tʃætəbɒks] **N** *Fam* moulin *m* à paroles

chatterer ['tʃætərər] **N** = chatterbox

chattering ['tʃætərɪŋ] **N** *(of people)* bavardage *m*; *(of birds)* caquetage *m*; *(of monkeys)* babil *m*; *(of teeth)* claquement *m*; *(of machine-gun)* martèlement *m*

▸▸*Pej* **the c. classes** les intellectuels *mpl* qui s'écoutent parler *(terme journalistique appliqué, dès le début des années 80, à une poignée de personnes qui pensent que leurs opinions ont de l'importance mais qui ne représentent guère l'opinion de la majorité)*

chatty ['tʃætɪ] **ADJ** *(person)* bavard; *(letter)* plein de bavardages; *(article etc)* écrit sur le ton de la conversation; **Mr Smith was very c.** *or* **in a very c. mood today** M. Smith était très bavard aujourd'hui; **the interview with the President was rather too c.** il y avait un peu trop de bavardage dans l'entretien avec le Président

chat-up line N *Fam* **that's his standard c.** c'est son baratin habituel quand il drague

chauffeur ['ʃəʊfər] **N** chauffeur *m*; **c.-driven** *(car)* avec chauffeur

VT *(person)* accompagner, conduire; *(car)* conduire; **we were chauffeured to the airport** on nous a conduits à l'aéroport

chauvinism ['ʃəʊvɪnɪz(ə)m] **N** *Pej* **1** *(patriotism)* chauvinisme *m* **2 (male) c.** machisme *m*

chauvinist ['ʃəʊvɪnɪst] *Pej* **N 1** *(patriot)* chauvin, -ine **2** *Fam* **(male) c.** macho *m*, machiste *m*

ADJ 1 *(patriotic)* chauvin **2** *Fam* **(male) c.** macho, machiste; **male c. pig** phallocrate *m*

> Note that the French word **chauvin** only refers to patriotism.

chauvinistic [ʃəʊvɪ'nɪstɪk] **ADJ** *Pej* **1** *(patriotic)* chauvin **2** *Fam (of male chauvinist)* macho, machiste

> Note that the French word **chauvin** only refers to patriotism.

cheap [tʃiːp] **ADJ 1** *(inexpensive)* bon marché *inv*, pas cher; **it's c. to run** *(car)* elle est économique à l'entretien; **a cheaper model** un modèle moins cher *ou* meilleur marché; **it works out cheaper to take a whole bottle** cela revient moins cher de prendre la bouteille entière; **the cheapest** le meilleur marché, le moins cher; *Fam* **he's very c.** *(shopkeeper)* il n'est pas cher; **to do sth on the c.** *(at little cost)* faire qch à peu de frais; *(meanly)* faire qch chichement; **it's c. at the price** c'est une affaire; **c. and cheerful** sans prétentions

2 *Pej (of little worth)* de peu de valeur; *(emotion)* superficiel; **life is c.** la vie a peu de valeur là-bas; **it's c. and nasty** c'est de la camelote; **a c. remark** une remarque facile; **that was a c. thing to do** ça n'était pas bien de faire ça; *Fam* **to feel c.** avoir honte; *Fam* **to make oneself c.** s'abaisser

3 *Pej (mean)* pingre

ADV to go c. se vendre bon marché; **he got off c.** il s'en est tiré à bon compte

►► *Br* **c. day return** = aller-retour *m* à tarif réduit valable une journée; **c. fare** tarif *m* réduit; *Fin* **c. money** argent *m* à bon marché; **c. rate** tarif réduit

cheapen ['tʃiːp(ə)n] VT **1** *(degrade) (something)* diminuer la valeur de; **to c. oneself** s'abaisser **2** *(lower price of)* (ra)baisser *ou* faire baisser le prix de

cheapjack ['tʃiːpdʒæk] *Pej Fam* N camelot *m* ADJ *(goods)* de la camelote; *(solution)* facile; *(remark)* facile, mesquin

cheaply ['tʃiːplɪ] ADV *(to buy)* (à) bon marché, à bas prix; *(to do sth, to travel)* à peu de frais; **to eat out c.** manger dehors pour pas cher; **the room was c. furnished** *(at little cost)* la pièce avait été meublée à moindre frais; *(nastily)* le mobilier de la pièce était de mauvaise qualité

cheapness ['tʃiːpnɪs] N **1** *(low price)* bas prix *m* **2** *Pej (low worth)* peu *m* de valeur, mauvaise qualité *f*; *(of remark)* bassesse *f*

cheapo ['tʃiːpəʊ] *Fam* ADJ *(inexpensive)* bon marché, pas cher
N **it's a real c.** c'est un truc pas cher

cheapskate ['tʃiːpskeɪt] *Pej Fam* N radin, -ine
ADJ *(remark)* facile, mesquin

cheat [tʃiːt] N **1** *(at games)* tricheur, -euse **2** *(dishonest person)* escroc *m* **3** *(deception)* triche *f*
VT *(be dishonest to)* tromper, *Fam* rouler; *(defraud)* frauder; **I felt cheated** je me suis senti dupé; **to c. sb out of sth** escroquer qch à qn; **to c. sb into doing sth** faire faire qch à qn en le trompant; **I feel as if I've been cheated of my chance to represent my country** *(because of injury, illness)* j'ai l'impression d'avoir été privé de la possibilité de représenter mon pays
VI **1** *(at games)* tricher **2** *(be dishonest)* tricher, frauder
► **cheat on** VT INSEP **1** *(be unfaithful to)* (wife, husband) tromper **2** *(be dishonest about)* (expenses) tricher sur

cheating ['tʃiːtɪŋ] N **1** *(dishonesty)* tromperie *f* **2** *(in games)* tricherie *f*, *Fam* triche *f*; **that's c.!** c'est de la triche!

CHECK¹ [tʃek]

| Ⓝ contrôle **1** ▪ coche **2** ▪ addition **3** ▪ frein **7** ▪ échec **9** |
| Ⓥ vérifier **1** ▪ contrôler **2** ▪ enregistrer **3** ▪ cocher **4** |
| Ⓥ vérifier **1** |

N **1** *(inspection)* contrôle *m*, vérification *f*; *(of accounts etc)* vérification; **to keep a c. on sth** contrôler qch; **to run a c. on sb/sth** enquêter sur qn/vérifier qch
2 *Am (tick)* coche *f*; **there's a c. mark against his name** son nom a été coché
3 *Am (bill in restaurant etc)* addition *f*, note *f*
4 *Am (for deposited item)* billet *m*, ticket *m*; *Rail etc* **luggage c.** bulletin *m* de bagages *ou* d'enregistrement; **cloakroom c.** bulletin de consigne
5 *Am (gambling chip)* jeton *m*
6 *Am Fin* = **cheque**
7 *(restraint)* frein *m*; **to keep** *or* **hold the enemy in c.** tenir l'ennemi en échec; **to keep one's feelings in c.** se contraindre, se contenir; *Pol* **a system of checks and balances** un système reposant sur l'équilibre des pouvoirs; **there is no effective c. on presidential power** il n'y a pas de limitation réelle du pouvoir du président
8 *(reversal)* revers *m*; **her plans had suffered a c.** ses projets avaient été contrariés
9 *Chess* échec *m*; **c.!** échec au roi!
VT **1** *(verify, examine) (account, pressure etc)* vérifier; *(against the original) (document)* compulser sur l'original; *Typ (proofs) (go*

over) réviser; *(compare)* comparer; **I'll c. the arrival time/when they're supposed to arrive** je vérifierai l'heure d'arrivée/quand ils sont censés arriver; **to c. the names on a list** *(mark off)* pointer les noms sur une liste; *(by calling out)* faire l'appel des noms sur une liste; **to c. sth against sth** comparer qch à qch; **c. these names against the ones on the list** vérifie que ces noms sont les mêmes que ceux de la liste; *Sch* **c. your work before handing it in** relisez votre travail avant de le rendre; *Com* **to c. the books** pointer les écritures; **checked and double checked** vérifié et revérifié; **to c. that …** vérifier *ou* s'assurer que … + *ind*
2 *(officially inspect) (tickets)* contrôler
3 *Am (hand in) (baggage)* (faire) enregistrer; *(at restaurant etc) (hat, raincoat)* mettre au vestiaire; *(take in) (baggage)* enregistrer; *(hat, raincoat)* prendre; **checked baggage** bagages *mpl* enregistrés
4 *Am (mark with tick)* cocher; **c. the appropriate box** cocher la case appropriée
5 *(halt)* faire échec à, arrêter net; *(crisis, price rise)* enrayer; *(attack)* arrêter; **to c. inflation** juguler l'inflation
6 *(restrain) (tears, anger)* refouler, retenir; *(passion, emotion)* réprimer, refréner
7 *Chess (king)* mettre en échec, faire échec à
8 *Scot (reprimand)* réprimander
VI **1** *(verify)* vérifier; **they usually have vacancies, but it's a good idea to c.** d'ordinaire, ils ont de la place, mais il vaut mieux s'en assurer *ou* vérifier; **we checked with the university** nous avons vérifié auprès de l'université; **you'd better c. with her** vous feriez mieux de lui demander
2 *(halt)* hésiter, s'arrêter (**at** devant)
3 *(match)* **that checks with what we were told** cela confirme ce qu'on nous a dit; *Am* **c.!** *(confirming data etc)* d'accord!
►► *Comput* **c. bit** bit *m* de contrôle; *Comput* **c. box** case *f* de pointage, case d'option; *Comput* **c. byte** octet *m* de contrôle; **c. list** liste *f* de contrôle; *Aviat* **check-list** *f*, *pl* check-lists; *Mktg* **c. question** question *f* de contrôle, question filtre; *Mktg* **c. sample** échantillon *m* témoin
► **check in** VI **1** *(at hotel)* remplir la fiche d'entrée *ou* le registre; **have you checked in yet?** *(not said by receptionist)* est-ce que tu es passé à l'hôtel?
2 *(at airport)* se faire enregistrer
VT SEP **1** *(of receptionist)* enregistrer l'arrivée de; **I checked them in myself** c'est moi-même qui les ai accueillis
2 *(make reservation for)* faire une réservation pour; **they checked the actress into a four-star hotel** ils ont fait une réservation pour l'actrice dans un hôtel quatre étoiles; **I've checked myself into a hotel for the night** je suis descendu dans un hôtel pour la nuit
3 *(at airport etc) (baggage)* enregistrer
► **check off** VT SEP **1** **to c. sth off** *(against sth)* vérifier qch (avec qch); *Com* **to c. off goods** recenser des marchandises
2 *Am (name etc)* cocher
► **check on** VT INSEP *(information etc)* vérifier, recouper; **to c. on sb** *(for security reasons etc)* enquêter sur qn, prendre des renseignements sur qn
► **check out** VI **1** *(leave hotel)* quitter l'hôtel; *Fam Euph (die)* caner
2 *Fam (of story, statement)* tenir debout; **it doesn't c. out** ça ne tient pas debout, ça ne marche pas
VT SEP **1** *(investigate) (information etc)* vérifier, recouper; *(person) (for security reasons etc)* enquêter sur; *esp Am Fam* **there's a new club we could c. out** il y a une nouvelle boîte que nous pourrions essayer; *Fam* **c. it out!** regarde un peu ça!, *Fam* vise un peu ça!

2 *(of hotel receptionist)* **to c. sb out** encaisser la note de qn *(avant son départ)*
► **check over** VT SEP *(look over)* vérifier
► **check through** VT SEP **1** *(examine) (baggage etc)* contrôler, examiner
2 *(send by plane)* faire envoyer (par avion); **I'd like my luggage checked through to Los Angeles** je voudrais faire envoyer directement mes bagages à Los Angeles
► **check up** VI *(make sure)* vérifier
► **check up on** VT INSEP = **check on**

check² N *Tex* carreau *m*; **c. material/shirt** tissu *m*/chemise *f* à carreaux

checkbook ['tʃekbʊk] N *Am* = **chequebook**

check-control N *Aut* appareil *m* de signalisation des défauts

checked [tʃekt] ADJ *(material etc)* à carreaux, quadrillé

checker¹ ['tʃekər] N *(person)* contrôleur, -euse; *Comput* **grammar/spelling c.** correcteur grammatical/orthographique

checker² VT *Am* = **chequer**

checkerboard ['tʃekəbɔːd] N *Am* damier *m*

checkered ['tʃekəd] ADJ *Am* = **chequered**

checkers ['tʃekəz] NPL *Am* jeu *m* de dames
VOIR GRAMMAIRE A10

check-in N *Aviat* **1** *(of passengers)* enregistrement *m* **2** *(desk)* guichet *m ou* comptoir *m* d'enregistrement
►► **c. desk** guichet *ou* comptoir d'enregistrement; **c. time** *(at airport, hotel)* heure *f* d'enregistrement

checking ['tʃekɪŋ] N *(verification, examination)* contrôle *m*, vérification *f*; *(more detailed)* pointage *m*
►► *Am Banking* **c. account** compte *m* courant

checklist ['tʃeklɪst] N liste *f* de contrôle

checkmark ['tʃekmɑːk] N *Am* coche *f*

checkmate ['tʃekmeɪt] *Chess* N échec *m* et mat; *Fig* **it was c.** *(we won)* ce fut une victoire; *(we lost)* ce fut un échec
VT *(king)* faire échec et mat à; *Fig* échec à; *(sb's plans)* contrecarrer, déjouer

checkout ['tʃekaʊt] N **1** *(in supermarket)* caisse *f* **2** *(in hotel)* heure *f* de départ
►► **c. desk** caisse; **c. display** devant *m* de caisse, nez *m* de caisse; **c. display item** article *m* de caisse; **c. girl** caissière *f*, **c. operator** caissier, -ière; **c. point** caisse; **c. time** heure de départ; **c. time is 12 noon** les clients doivent libérer la chambre avant midi

checkpoint ['tʃekpɔɪnt] N contrôle *m*

checkroom ['tʃekruːm] N *Am* vestiaire *m*
►► **c. ticket** ticket *m* de vestiaire

checksum ['tʃeksʌm] N *Comput* somme *f* de contrôle

checkup ['tʃekʌp] N **1** *Med* examen *m* médical (complet), bilan *m* de santé, check-up *m inv*; **to give sb a c.** faire le bilan de santé de qn; **to have a c.** se faire faire un check-up; **it's just a c.** c'est juste une visite de routine **2** *(inspection)* vérification *f*, inspection *f*; *(of machinery)* révision *f*

cheddar ['tʃedər] N *(fromage m de)* cheddar *m*

cheek [tʃiːk] N **1** *Anat* joue *f*; **to dance c. to c.** danser joue contre joue; *Fig* **c. by jowl with sb** coude à coude avec qn; *Fig* **to turn the other c.** tendre l'autre joue **2** *Fam (buttock)* fesse *f* **3** *Br Fam (impudence)* toupet *m*, culot *m*; **he's got a c.!** il est culotté *ou* gonflé!; **that's enough of your c.!** j'en ai assez de cette impertinence!; **the c. (of it)!, some c.!** quel culot *ou* toupet!
VT *Br Fam* dire des impertinences à, faire l'insolent avec

cheekbone ['tʃiːkbəʊn] N pommette *f*, *Spec* os *m* malaire; **high/prominent cheekbones** pommettes hautes/saillantes

cheekily ['tʃiːkɪlɪ] ADV *Br Fam (to do sth)* d'une manière impertinente *ou* effrontée; *(to say)* d'un air impertinent *ou* effronté

cheekiness ['tʃiːkɪnɪs] N *Br Fam* effronterie *f*

cheeky ['tʃiːkɪ] ADJ *Br Fam* effronté, impertinent; **don't be c.!** pas d'impertinence!; **a c. little wine** un bon petit pinard

cheep [tʃiːp] N *(of bird)* piaulement *m*; *Fam* **you can't get a c. out of her** elle ne dit jamais mot
▸ VI *(of bird)* piauler

cheer [tʃɪər] N 1 *(shout)* hourra *m*; **cheers** acclamations *fpl*, bravos *mpl*; **to give three cheers** pousser trois hourras; **three cheers for Mary!** un ban pour Mary!, vive Mary! 2 *Fam* **cheers!** *(toast)* (à votre) santé!; *Br (at parting)* à bientôt!; *Br (thanks)* merci! 3 *Lit (good spirits)* bonne disposition *f* (d'esprit); **be of good c.!** prenez courage!; **we were of good c.** nous étions de bonne humeur
▸ VT 1 *(shout for)* acclamer 2 *(encourage, make happier)* remonter le moral à
▸ VI *(shout)* pousser des hourras *ou* des acclamations
▸ **cheer on** VT SEP *(support)* encourager
▸ **cheer up** VI *(become more cheerful)* s'égayer, devenir plus gai; **the weather's cheered up** le temps s'est arrangé; **c. up!** courage!
▸ VT SEP 1 *(make more cheerful)* réjouir, remonter le moral à 2 *(make brighter) (room etc)* égayer

cheerful ['tʃɪəfʊl] ADJ *(person)* gai, de bonne humeur; *(face)* souriant, riant; *(room)* gai, d'aspect agréable; *(conversation, music etc)* joyeux; *(news etc)* encourageant; **that's a c. thought!** ça c'est encourageant!; *Iron* comme vous êtes optimiste!; **you're (very) c. this morning** tu es de bonne humeur ce matin

cheerfully ['tʃɪəfʊlɪ] ADV 1 *(happily)* gaiement, avec entrain, allègrement 2 *(willingly)* de bon cœur, volontiers 3 *(without compunction)* sans remords; **she would c. leave the work for the others** elle laisserait sans remords le travail aux autres; **I could quite c. strangle him** je l'étranglerais volontiers

cheerfulness ['tʃɪəfʊlnɪs] N *(of person)* gaieté *f*, bonne humeur *f*; *(of room)* aspect *m* agréable

cheerily ['tʃɪərɪlɪ] ADV gaiement, avec gaieté

cheering ['tʃɪərɪŋ] N acclamations *fpl*, bravos *mpl*
ADJ *(sight, display)* réjouissant; *(piece of news, conversation)* qui remonte le moral

cheerio [tʃɪərɪ'əʊ] INT *Br Fam (at parting)* salut!, ciao!; *(in drinking a toast)* à la vôtre/tienne!; **it's c. 2003** bye-bye 2003

cheerleader ['tʃɪəliːdər] N *Am* = majorette *f* qui stimule l'enthousiasme des supporters des équipes sportives, surtout aux États-Unis

cheerless ['tʃɪəlɪs] ADJ morne, triste, sombre

cheery ['tʃɪərɪ] ADJ *(person, smile, wave, colour)* joyeux, gai

cheese [tʃiːz] N 1 fromage *m*; **blue c.** (fromage) bleu *m*; **cream c.** fromage frais; **cottage c.** fromage blanc *(salé et grenu)*; **cauliflower/macaroni c.** chou-fleur *m*/macaronis *mpl* au gratin; **toasted c.** toast *m* au fromage; **c. sandwich/omelette** sandwich *m*/omelette *f* au fromage; **the c. industry** l'industrie *f* fromagère; *Phot Fam* **(say) c.!** souriez! 2 *(individual piece of cheese)* (*pl* **cheeses**) **a c.** un fromage (entier), une meule (de fromage)
▸ **c. biscuit** *(for cheese)* biscuit *m* salé; *(cheese-flavoured)* biscuit au fromage; **c. grater** râpe *f* à fromage; **c. maker**, **c. manufacturer** fromager, -ère; **c. mite** mite *f* du fromage; **c. straw** allumette *f* au fromage
▸ **cheese off** VT SEP *(usu passive) Br Fam* **to be cheesed (off)** en avoir marre (**with** de)

cheeseboard ['tʃiːzbɔːd] N 1 *(for cutting cheese)* plateau *m* à fromage 2 *(as part of meal)* plateau *m* de fromages; **a selection from our** *or* **the c.** *(in restaurant etc)* une sélection de fromages

cheeseburger ['tʃiːzbɜːɡər] N *Culin* cheeseburger *m*

cheesecake ['tʃiːzkeɪk] N 1 *Culin* cheesecake *m* 2 *(no pl) Fam Hum (attractive women)* belles nanas *fpl*; *(in photo)* pin-up *f inv*; *Br* **she's a real c.** elle est vraiment bien foutue

cheesecloth ['tʃiːzklɒθ] N *(for cheese)* gaze *f*, étamine *f*; *Tex* crépon *m*

cheeseparing ['tʃiːzpeərɪŋ] ADJ parcimonieux
N économies *fpl* de bouts de chandelle

cheesy ['tʃiːzɪ] ADJ 1 *(in taste)* qui a un goût de fromage; *(in smell)* qui sent le fromage 2 *Am Fam (poor quality)* moche 3 *Fam* **a c. grin** un large sourire

cheetah ['tʃiːtə] N guépard *m*

chef [ʃef] N chef *m* (de cuisine)

chemical ['kemɪk(ə)l] ADJ chimique
N produit *m* chimique
▸ **c. company** compagnie *f* de produits chimiques; **c. dependency** toxicodépendance *f*, **c. engineer** ingénieur *m* chimiste; **c. engineering** génie *m* chimique; **c. reaction** réaction *f* chimique; **c. toilet** W-C *mpl* chimiques; **c. warfare** guerre *f* chimique; **c. weapons** armes *fpl* chimiques

chemically ['kemɪk(ə)lɪ] ADV chimiquement

chemist ['kemɪst] N 1 *esp Br Com* pharmacien, -ienne; **c.'s (shop)** pharmacie *f* 2 *(scientist)* chimiste *mf*

chemistry ['kemɪstrɪ] N chimie *f*; **organic/inorganic c.** chimie organique/minérale; **industrial c.** chimie industrielle; *Fig* **there was a certain c. between the members of the band** il y avait une certaine affinité entre les musiciens; *Fig* **the c.'s right/wrong** ça passe bien/mal (entre nous/eux/*etc*); *Fig* **the c.'s missing** le courant ne passe pas, on n'a pas d'atomes crochus
▸ **c. set** panoplie *f* de chimiste

chemotherapy [kiːmə'θerəpɪ], *Fam* **chemo** ['kiːməʊ] N *Med* chimiothérapie *f*; **to have c.** suivre un traitement de chimiothérapie

cheque, *Am* **check** [tʃek] N *Fin* chèque *m*; **to pay by c.** payer par chèque; **to cash a c.** toucher un chèque; **to stop a c.** faire opposition à un chèque; **to write sb a c.** faire un chèque à qn; **who should I make the c. out to?** à quel ordre dois-je faire *ou* écrire le chèque?; **will you take a c.?** est-ce que vous acceptez les chèques?; **c. for £20** chèque de vingt livres; **c. made out to bearer** chèque au porteur; *Fam* **dud c.** chèque en bois
▸ *Br* **c. account** compte *m* chèques; *Br* **c. guarantee card** carte *f* bancaire; **c. number** numéro *m* de chèque; **c. stub** talon *m* de chèque, souche *f*

chequebook, *Am* **checkbook** ['tʃekbʊk] N carnet *m* de chèques, chéquier *m*
▸ **c. account** compte *m* (de) chèques; **c. journalism** = dans les milieux de la presse, pratique qui consiste à payer des sommes importantes pour le témoignage d'une personne impliquée dans une affaire

chequer, *Am* **checker** ['tʃekər] VT *(variegate with colour)* diaprer, bigarrer

chequered, *Am* **checkered** ['tʃekəd] ADJ 1 *(pattern)* quadrillé, à carreaux; *(two colours only)* en damier 2 *(variegated)* diapré, bigarré; *Fig (life)* plein de vicissitudes; **she's had a somewhat c. career** *(varied)* elle a fait toutes sortes de métiers; *(ups and downs)* elle a eu une carrière en dents de scie; **this text has had a fairly c. history** ce texte a eu une histoire assez compliquée

cherish ['tʃerɪʃ] VT 1 *(hope)* bercer, caresser; *(past, occasion, memory, possessions, gift)* chérir; *(idea, opinion)* nourrir, entretenir; **to c. illusions** se nourrir d'illusions; **his most cherished hopes** ses espérances les plus chères 2 *(love) (person)* chérir

cheroot [ʃə'ruːt] N petit cigare *m*

cherry ['tʃerɪ] N 1 *(fruit)* cerise *f*, *(tree)* cerisier *m*; *Fam* **you don't get two bites at the c.** il n'y a pas de deuxième chance; *Prov* **life is just a bowl of cherries** il faut voir la vie en rose 2 **wild c.** *(fruit)* merise *f*, *(tree)* merisier *m* 3 *(colour)* cerise *f*, **c.-red** rouge *m* cerise 4 *Sl (virginity)* **to lose one's c.** perdre sa fleur 5 *Am Fam (newcomer)* bleu *m*
ADJ 1 cerise *inv*; **c.-red** rouge cerise *inv* 2 *Am Fam (in perfect condition)* en parfait état, impec
▸ **c. brandy** cherry *m*; **c. orchard** cerisaie *f*, **c. stone** noyau *m* de cerise; **c. tart** tarte *f* aux cerises; **c. tomato** tomate *f* cerise; **c. tree** cerisier

cherry-pick VT **to c. the best** sélectionner ce qu'il y a de mieux

cherub, *pl* **cherubs**, *Bible* **cherubim** ['tʃerəb, -z, -əbɪm] N *Bible* chérubin *m*; *Art* angelot *m*, ange *m* joufflu; *Fig* **a little c.** *(child)* un petit ange

cherubic [tʃɪ'ruːbɪk] ADJ *Bible, Art* de chérubin; *Fig (smile, face etc)* d'ange

chervil ['tʃɜːvɪl] N *Bot, Culin* cerfeuil *m*

Ches *abbr* Cheshire

Cheshire ['tʃeʃər] N **to grin like a C. cat** sourire jusqu'aux oreilles
▸ *Culin* **C. cheese** fromage *m* de Chester, chester *m*

chess [tʃes] N échecs *mpl*; **a c. game, a game of c.** une partie d'échecs; **to play c.** jouer aux échecs
▸ **c. player** joueur, -euse d'échecs

chessboard ['tʃesbɔːd] N échiquier *m*

chessman, *pl* **chessmen** ['tʃesmən], **chesspiece** ['tʃespiːs] N pièce *f* (du jeu d'échecs)

chest [tʃest] N 1 *Anat* poitrine *f*, *(of horse)* poitrail *m*; *Fig* **to get it off one's c.** dire ce qu'on a sur le cœur 2 *(box)* coffre *m*, caisse *f*, **tea c.** caisse à thé **medicine c.** (coffret *m* de) pharmacie *f*
▸ **c. cold** rhume *m* de poitrine; **c. of drawers** commode *f*; **c. expander** extenseur *m (pour développer les pectoraux)*; **c. infection** infection *f* des voies respiratoires; **c. pains** douleurs *fpl* dans la poitrine; **c. size** tour *m* de poitrine; **what c. size are you?** quel est votre tour de poitrine?

chesterfield ['tʃestəfiːld] N *(sofa)* canapé *m* capitonné

chestnut ['tʃesnʌt] N 1 *(sweet or Spanish)* **c.** *(fruit)* châtaigne *f*, *(when cooked)* marron *m*; *(tree)* châtaignier *m*; **(horse) c.** *(fruit)* marron (d'Inde); *(tree)* marronnier *m* (d'Inde); *Fam* **an old c.** *(joke)* une plaisanterie usée; *Fig* **to pull sb's chestnuts out of the fire** tirer les marrons du feu à qn 2 *(wood)* châtaignier *m* 3 *(colour)* châtain *m* 4 *(horse)* alezan *m*
ADJ 1 *(hair)* châtain 2 *(colour)* châtain 3 *(horse)* alezan
▸ **c. puree** purée *f* de marrons; **c. tree** châtaignier

chesty ['tʃestɪ] ADJ *Fam* **to be c.** être bronchitique; **a c. cough** une toux de poitrine

cheval glass [ʃə'væl] N psyché *f*

chevron ['ʃevrən] N *Her, Mil* chevron *m*

Chevvy ['ʃevɪ] N *Fam* Chevrolet® *f*

chew [tʃuː] N **1** *(action)* **to have a c. at sth** mâchonner qch **2** *(tobacco)* chique *f*; *(sweet)* bonbon *m*

▸ VT *(food)* mâcher, mastiquer; *(tobacco)* chiquer; *(cigar, end of pen etc)* mâchonner; **to c. one's nails** se ronger les ongles; **to c. the cud** *(of cow)* ruminer; *Fam* **to c. the rag** *or* **the fat** *(chat)* discuter le coup; *(complain)* ronchonner, râler

▸ VI *(food)* mâcher, mastiquer; **the rats had chewed through the rope** les rats avaient coupé la corde en la rongeant

▸**chew on** VT INSEP **1** *(gnaw)* mâchouiller, ronger; **he chewed on his pipe** il mâchouillait sa pipe **2** *Fam (consider)* réfléchir sur; **how much longer do you need to c. on it?** combien te faut-il encore de temps pour réfléchir à la question?

▸**chew out** VT SEP *Am Fam (reprimand)* engueuler

▸**chew over** VT SEP *Fam (think over)* réfléchir à; *(discuss)* discuter de

▸**chew up** VT SEP *(damage by chewing)* abîmer à force de mâchonner; *Fig (damage) (bank card, tape etc)* endommager; **the dog has chewed up the newspaper** le chien a mangé le journal; **his arm had been badly chewed up by the machinery** son bras avait été déchiqueté par la machine

chewing ['tʃuːɪŋ] N mastication *f*, mâchement *m*, mâchonnement *m*

▸▸**c. gum** chewing-gum *m*; **c. tobacco** tabac *m* à chiquer

chewy ['tʃuːɪ] ADJ **1** *Pej (meat etc)* difficile à mâcher **2** *(sweet)* mou, *f* molle, tendre

chiaroscuro [kɪɑːrəˈskʊərəʊ] N *Art* clairobscur *m*

chic [ʃiːk, ʃɪk] ADJ élégant, chic
▸ N chic *m*

chicane [ʃɪˈkeɪn] N *Aut, Sport, Cards* chicane *f*

chicanery [ʃɪˈkeɪnərɪ] N chicanerie *f*, chicane *f*

chicano [tʃɪˈkɑːnəʊ] N *Am* citoyen, -enne d'origine mexicaine

chichi ['ʃiːʃiː] *Fam* ADJ prétentieux
▸ N prétention *f*

chick [tʃɪk] N **1** *(young bird)* oisillon *m*; *(of fowl)* poussin *m*; *Fig (child)* poussin **2** *Fam (young woman)* fille *f*, nana *f*
▸▸**c. flick** = film ou qui plaît particulièrement aux femmes; **c. lit** = genre *m* romanesque destiné à un public de jeunes femmes et qui est censé refléter leurs préoccupations

chickadee [tʃɪkəˈdiː] N *Am (bird)* mésange *f* (à tête noire)

chicken ['tʃɪkɪn] N **1** *(bird)* poulet *m*; *Prov* **don't count your chickens before they are hatched** il ne faut pas vendre la peau de l'ours avant de l'avoir tué; **prairie c.** *Am* tétras *m* cupidon, cupidon *m* des prairies, *Can* poule *f* des prairies **2** *Fam (coward)* lâche *mf*, froussard, -arde **3** *Am Fam (young person)* mineur, -eure, gamin, -ine; **she's no (spring) c.** elle n'est plus de la première jeunesse
▸ ADJ *Fam (cowardly)* lâche, froussard
▸▸**c. breast** blanc *m* (de poulet); **c. farm** élevage *m* de poulets, élevage avicole; **c. farmer** éleveur, -euse de volailles, aviculteur, -trice; *Am Sl* **c. hawk** pédophile *m*; **c. liver** foie *m* de volaille; **c. run** enclos *m* (d'un poulailler); **c. soup** *(clear)* potage *m* au poulet; *(creamy)* velouté *m* ou crème *f* de volaille; **c. wire** grillage *m*
▸**chicken out** VI *Fam* se dégonfler; **she chickened out of going** elle s'est dégonflée; **she chickened out of her dental appointment**

elle avait rendez-vous chez le dentiste mais elle s'est dégonflée

chickenfeed ['tʃɪkɪnfiːd] N nourriture *f* pour volaille; *Fig* **it's c.** c'est de la gnognote; **£2,000 is c.** 2 000 livres, c'est pas grand-chose

chickenhearted [tʃɪkɪnˈhɑːtɪd], **chicken-livered** [tʃɪkɪnˈlɪvəd] ADJ *Old-fashioned Fam* poltron, froussard

chickenpox ['tʃɪkɪnpɒks] N *Med* varicelle *f*; **to have c.** avoir la varicelle

chickenshit ['tʃɪkɪnʃɪt] ADJ *Am Vulg* dégonflé

chickpea ['tʃɪkpiː] N pois *m* chiche

chickweed ['tʃɪkwiːd] N *(plant)* mouron *m* des oiseaux, morgeline *f*

chicory ['tʃɪkərɪ] N **1** *(plant)* endive *f* **2** **(ground) c.** chicorée *f* (en poudre)

chide [tʃaɪd] VT *Arch, Lit (pt* **chided** ['tʃaɪdɪd] *or* **chid** [tʃɪd], *pp* **chided** *or* **chidden** ['tʃɪd(e)n]*)* réprimander, gronder

chief [tʃiːf] N *(pl* **chiefs***) (of tribe, gang)* chef *m*; *Am* **fire/police c.** chef des pompiers/de la police; *Fam* **the c.** *(boss)* le patron; *Fig Fam* **he's the big white c.** c'est lui le grand patron; **in c.** en chef; *Mil, Naut* **commander-in-c.** commandant *m* en chef; **editor in c.** rédacteur *m* en chef; *Prov* **too many chiefs and not enough Indians** trop de gens qui donnent des ordres et pas assez pour les exécuter
▸ ADJ *(most important)* principal, -aux; *(in rank)* (en) chef; **my c. assistant** mon principal collaborateur; **the c. reason for doing sth** la raison majeure *ou* principale pour faire qch
▸▸*Am Pol* **the C. Executive** le président des États-Unis, le chef de l'exécutif; *Com, Ind* **c. executive officer** président-directeur *m* général, *pl* présidents-directeurs généraux; *Am* **C. Financial Officer** chef comptable, chef de la comptabilité; *Br* **C. Inspector** *(of police)* inspecteur *m* principal; **c. justice** président, -ente de la Haute cour de justice; *Am* juge *m* de la Cour suprême; **c. photographer** *(on newspaper)* photographe *m* en chef; **c. reporter** grand reporter *m*; *Br Pol* **C. Secretary to the Treasury** ≃ ministre *m* du Budget; **c. of staff** *Mil* chef d'état-major; *Am (at White House)* secrétaire *m* général de la Maison Blanche

chiefly ['tʃiːflɪ] ADV principalement, surtout

chieftain ['tʃiːftən] N *(of clan)* chef *m*

chiffon ['ʃɪfɒn] N mousseline *f* de soie

chignon ['ʃiːnjɒn] N chignon *m*

chihuahua [tʃɪˈwɑːwɑː] N chihuahua *m*

chilblain ['tʃɪlbleɪn] N *Med* engelure *f*; **to have chilblains** avoir des engelures

child, *pl* **children** [tʃaɪld, 'tʃɪldrən] N enfant *mf*; **to treat sb like a c.** traiter qn en enfant; **I'm not a c.!** je ne suis pas un enfant!; *Old-fashioned* **come here, c.!** viens ici, (mon/ma) petit(e)!; **the c. in all of us** l'enfant qui est en chacun de nous; **ever since I was a c.** depuis mon enfance; *Old-fashioned* **I have known him from a c.** *(when he was a child)* je l'ai connu enfant; *(when I was a child)* je le connais depuis mon enfance; **it's c.'s play** *(easy)* c'est un jeu d'enfant; **our children's children** les enfants de nos enfants; **children's shoes/clothes** chaussures/vêtements pour enfants; **children's literature** littérature *f* enfantine *ou* pour enfants; **children's television** émissions *fpl* pour enfants; *Bible* **the children of Israel** les enfants d'Israël; **children's area** *(in restaurant etc)* coin *m* enfants
▸▸**c. abuse** mauvais traitements *mpl* à enfant; *(sexual)* abus *m* sexuel sur enfant; **c. abuser** = personne *f* coupable de mauvais traitements à enfant; *(sexual)* = personne

coupable d'abus sexuel sur enfant; **c. actor** acteur *m* enfant, actrice *f* enfant; *Br Admin* **c. benefit** allocation *f* familiale, allocations *fpl* familiales *(pour un enfant)*; *Aut* **c. booster cushion** réhausseur *m*; *Aut* **c. booster seat** siège *m* réhausseur; **c. bride** femme *f* enfant; **I was his c. bride** j'étais une enfant quand il m'a épousée; **c. labour** travail *m* des enfants; *Aut* **c. lock** sécurité-enfants *f*, *pl* sécurités-enfants; **I put the c. lock on** j'ai mis la sécurité; **c. poverty** pauvreté *f* des enfants, pauvreté infantile; *Aut* **c. restraint** dispositif *m* de retenue pour enfant, ceinture *f* pour enfant; **c. seat** siège-auto *m*, *pl* sièges-auto *(pour enfant)*; **c. welfare** protection *f* de l'enfance

child-bearing N maternité *f*; **after 20 years of c.** après 20 ans de maternités successives; **of c. age** en âge d'avoir des enfants; **past c. (age)** *(woman)* trop âgée pour avoir des enfants; **to have c. hips** avoir les hanches larges

childbirth ['tʃaɪldbɜːθ] N accouchement *m*; **to die in c.** mourir en couches

childcare ['tʃaɪldkeər] N **1** *(day care)* garde *f* d'enfants; **we haven't decided on c. arrangements yet** nous n'avons pas encore pris de décision quant à la garde des enfants **2** *Br Admin* protection *f* de l'enfance

child-friendly ADJ *(area, city)* aménagé pour les enfants; *(furniture, house)* pas dangereux pour les enfants

childhood ['tʃaɪldhʊd] N enfance *f*; **to be in one's second c.** être retombé en enfance
▸▸**c. memory** souvenir *m* d'enfance; **c. sweetheart** amour *m* d'enfance

childish ['tʃaɪldɪʃ] ADJ **1** *Pej (person, behaviour, remarks)* puéril; **don't be so c.** ne faites pas l'enfant, ne soyez pas aussi puéril **2** *(of children, childlike) (laughter, curiosity, innocence)* enfantin; *(ailment)* infantile; *(question)* naïf, *f* naïve; **c. games** jeux enfantins *ou* d'enfant

childishness ['tʃaɪldɪʃnɪs] N *Pej* enfantillage *m*, puérilité *f*

childless ['tʃaɪldlɪs] ADJ sans enfant(s); *(marriage)* stérile; **she died c.** elle est morte sans enfants

childlike ['tʃaɪldlaɪk] ADJ enfantin; *(question)* naïf, *f* naïve; *(smile)* d'enfant; **he was c. in his curiosity** il avait une curiosité enfantine *ou* d'enfant

child-minder N gardienne *f* d'enfants

child-minding ['tʃaɪldmaɪndɪŋ] N garde *f* d'enfants

childproof ['tʃaɪldpruːf] ADJ *(lock etc)* ne pouvant être ouvert par les enfants, de sécurité; *(not breakable)* ne pouvant être cassé par les enfants

children *see* **child**

Chile ['tʃɪlɪ] N Chili *m*

Chilean ['tʃɪlɪən] ADJ chilien
▸ N Chilien, -ienne

chili ['tʃɪlɪ] N *esp Am* = **chilli**

chill [tʃɪl] N **1** *Med* coup *m* de froid; **to catch a c.** prendre froid; **c. of fear** frisson *m* de peur; **his laugh sent a c. down my spine** son rire m'a fait froid dans le dos **2** *(of water, marble etc)* froideur *f*, fraîcheur *f*; **there's a c. in the air** le fond de l'air est frais; **to take the c. off** *(water)* (faire) tiédir; *(wine)* chambrer; *Fig* **to cast a c. over the company** jeter un froid sur l'assemblée
▸ ADJ froid, glacé; *(wind)* froid
▸ VT **1** *(of wind) (person, air)* refroidir, glacer; **chilled to the bone** gelé jusqu'aux os; *Fig* **chilled with fear** transi de peur **2** *(put in fridge) (wine, melon, dessert etc)* mettre au frais
▸ VI **1** *(food, drink)* refroidir **2** = **chill out**
▸▸**c. cabinet** armoire *f* réfrigérante

▶ **chill out** VI *Fam* se détendre; **I wish he'd c. out a bit** ça serait bien qu'il soit un peu plus cool; **he likes chilling out at home** il aime bien être chez lui, peinard; **c. out!** relax!, calmos!

chilled [tʃɪld] ADJ **1** *Culin* refroidi; **best served c.** *(on label)* servir glacé *ou* très frais; **c. meat** viande *f* réfrigérée *ou* frigorifiée; **c. products** produits *mpl* frigorifiés **2** *Fam (relaxed)* relax

chilli ['tʃɪlɪ] N *Culin (vegetable)* piment *m* (rouge); *(dish)* chili *m*
▶▶ **c. con carne** chili con carne; **c. pepper** piment (rouge); **c. powder** chili; **c. sauce** sauce *f* aux tomates et piments

chilliness ['tʃɪlɪnɪs] N *(of air)* froid *m*, froideur *f*; *Fig (of person, welcome)* froideur

chilling ['tʃɪlɪŋ] ADJ *(wind, welcome)* glacial, -als *ou* aux; *(story, events)* qui donne la chair de poule

chill-out room N *Fam (in nightclub)* espace *m* chill-out

chilly ['tʃɪlɪ] ADJ **1** *(cold) (weather etc)* frais, *f* fraîche; **to feel c.** *(of person)* avoir froid; **it's** *or* **it feels c. this morning** il fait frais *ou Fam* frisquet ce matin **2** *(person) (feels the cold a lot)* frileux **3** *Fig (person, manner, welcome)* froid; *(politeness)* glacial, -als *ou* aux

chime [tʃaɪm] N **c.** *(of bells)* carillon *m*; **the chimes of St. Mary's** le carillon de St. Mary; **to ring the chimes** carillonner; **(door) chimes** carillon de porte
VI *(of clock, bells)* carillonner
VT **1** *(bells)* sonner en carillon **2** *(of clock) (the hour)* sonner
▶ **chime in** VI *Fam* **1** *(intervene)* placer son mot, intervenir; **they all chimed in at once** ils sont tous intervenus en même temps **2** *(agree)* **his story chimes in with what we already know** sa version correspond à ce que nous savons déjà

chimera [kaɪ'mɪərə, kɪ-] N *Myth, Lit Fig* chimère *f*; *Lit Fig* **to pursue a c.** poursuivre des chimères

chiming ['tʃaɪmɪŋ] ADJ carillonnant; *(clock)* à carillon
N carillonnement *m*, carillon *m*

chimney ['tʃɪmnɪ] N **1** *(of house, factory)* cheminée *f*; *Fam* **to smoke like a c.** *(of person)* fumer comme un sapeur **2** *(in mountaineering)* cheminée *f* **3** *Geol* cheminée *f*
▶▶ **c. breast** manteau *m* de (la) cheminée; **c. corner** coin *m* du feu; **c. stack** *(of house)* tuyau *m* de cheminée; *(of factory)* cheminée (d'usine); **c. sweep** ramoneur *m*

> Note that the French word **cheminée** also means **fireplace** and **mantelpiece**.

chimneypiece ['tʃɪmnɪpiːs] N *esp Br* (manteau *m* de) cheminée *f*

chimneypot ['tʃɪmnɪpɒt] N mitre *f*

chimpanzee [tʃɪmpæn'ziː, *Am* tʃɪm'pænzɪ:], *Fam* **chimp** [tʃɪmp] N chimpanzé *m*

chin [tʃɪn] N menton *m*; *Fig* **to keep one's c. up** tenir bon, tenir le coup; *Fig* **to take sth on the c.** encaisser qch sans broncher; **she took the news on the c.** elle a écouté la nouvelle sans broncher
▶▶ **c. strap** *(on helmet)* jugulaire *f*

China ['tʃaɪnə] N Chine *f*
▶▶ **the C. Sea** la mer de Chine; **C. tea** thé *m* de Chine

china ['tʃaɪnə] N **1** *(no pl) (material)* porcelaine *f*, *(plates etc)* vaisselle *f* (de porcelaine); **made of c.** en porcelaine; **c. plate** assiette *f* en porcelaine **2** *Br Sl (friend)* pote *m*; **my old c.!** mon vieux!
▶▶ **c. clay** kaolin *m*; **c. doll** poupée *f* en porcelaine

Chinagraph® ['tʃaɪnəgrɑːf] N *(pencil)* crayon *m* gras

Chinaman, *pl* **Chinamen** ['tʃaɪnəmən] N *Old-fashioned* Chinois *m*

Chinatown ['tʃaɪnətaʊn] N quartier *m* chinois; **in C.** dans le quartier chinois

chinaware ['tʃaɪnəweər] N porcelaine *f*

chinchilla [tʃɪn'tʃɪlə] N *(rodent, fur)* chinchilla *m*; **c. coat/jacket** manteau *m*/veste *f* en chinchilla

chin-chin INT *Fam (as a toast)* santé!, à la vôtre/la tienne!

chine [tʃaɪn] N *Anat, Culin* échine *f*

Chinese [tʃaɪ'niːz] ADJ chinois; **the C. Ambassador** l'ambassadeur *m* de Chine
N **1** Chinois, -oise **2** *Ling* chinois *m* **3** *Fam (food)* **I feel like a C. tonight** j'ai envie de manger chinois ce soir
▶▶ *Bot, Culin* **C. cabbage** chou *m* chinois; **C. checkers** dames *fpl* chinoises; *Bot, Culin* **C. gooseberry** kiwi *m (fruit)*; **C. lantern** lanterne *f* vénitienne; *Bot, Culin* **C. leaves** chou chinois; **C. white** blanc *m* de Chine

Chink [tʃɪŋk] N *Offensive Sl (Chinese)* Chinetoque *mf*

chink¹ [tʃɪŋk] N *(gap) (in wall etc)* fente *f*, crevasse *f*, lézarde *f*, *(in door)* entrebâillement *m*; *Fig* **to have a c. in one's armour** avoir une faiblesse; **the c. in sb's armour** le talon d'Achille de qn

chink² N *(sound)* tintement *m*
VT *(money)* faire sonner *ou* tinter; *(glasses etc)* faire tinter
VI sonner (sec)

Chinky ['tʃɪŋkɪ] N *Offensive Fam* **1** *(restaurant)* (restaurant *m*) chinois *m*; *(meal)* repas *m* chinois **2** *(person)* Chinetoque *mf*

chinless ['tʃɪnlɪs] ADJ au menton fuyant
▶▶ *Br Fam Hum* **c. wonder** = individu *m* de bonne famille dépourvu de volonté et d'intelligence

chino ['tʃiːnəʊ] N *Tex* chino *m*; **chinos** *(trousers)* chinos *mpl*

chintz [tʃɪnts] N *Tex* chintz *m*, indienne *f*; **c. curtains** rideaux *mpl* de chintz

chinwag ['tʃɪnwæg] N *Br Fam* causette *f*; **to have a c.** tailler une bavette (**with** avec)

chip [tʃɪp] N **1** *(small piece) (of wood)* éclat *m*, copeau *m*; *(of marble)* écaille *f*, éclat; *(of chocolate)* pépite *f*; *Culin* **diamond chips** semence *f* de diamants; *Fig* **he's a c. off the old block** c'est son père tout craché; *Fig* **to have a c. on one's shoulder** être aigri, en vouloir à tout le monde; **get rid of that c. on your shoulder** cessez d'en vouloir à tout le monde
2 *(piece missing) (in plate)* ébréchure *f*, *(in knife blade)* brèche *f*; **this cup has a c.** cette tasse est ébréchée
3 *Br Culin (French fry)* (pomme de terre *f*) frite *f*
4 *Am Culin (crisp)* chips *f inv*
5 *Cards etc* jeton *m*; *Fig* **when the chips are down** aux moments critiques; *Fig Fam* **he's had his chips** il est cuit *ou* fichu
6 *Comput* **(silicon) c.** puce *f*
7 *Sport (shot)* pichenette *f*
VT (-pp-) **1** *(cut at)* tailler
2 *(damage) (knife, plate)* ébrécher; *(furniture)* écorner; *(enamel)* écailler; *(tooth)* casser
3 *Sport (ball)* prendre en dessous, donner une pichenette à; **he chipped the ball over the net** d'une pichenette, il a envoyé la balle au-dessus du filet
VI *(of stone, china)* s'ébrécher
▶▶ *Br* **c. basket** panier *m* à frites; *Br* **c. cutter** coupe-frites *m inv*; *Comput* **c. manufacturer** fabricant *m* de pastilles de silicium; *Br* **c. pan** friteuse *f*; *Br* **c. shop** = boutique *f* où l'on vend des frites ainsi que du poisson frit, des saucisses etc; *Comput* **c. technology** technologie *f* des puces

> Note that the French word **chips** is a false friend for British English speakers. It means **crisps**.

▶ **chip away** VT SEP *(plaster etc)* décaper, enlever petit à petit
VI *(of plaster)* s'écailler

▶ **chip away at** VT INSEP **to c. away at the old paintwork** enlever la vieille peinture petit à petit; **to c. away at sb's authority** grignoter l'autorité de qn; **just keep chipping away at him until he changes his mind** continuez à le travailler au corps jusqu'à ce qu'il change d'avis

▶ **chip in** VI **1** *Fam (contribute) (in collection)* participer; *(in discussion)* intervenir; *Pej (interrupt)* s'emmêler, mettre son grain de sel; **they chipped in to buy her a present** ils ont tous participé à l'achat de son cadeau; **if everyone chips in with an idea** si chacun proposait une idée **2** *Cards* miser
VT SEP *Fam (contribute)* donner; **everyone chipped in £5** tout le monde a donné 5 livres

▶ **chip off** VI *(fall off, break off) (of paint etc)* s'écailler
VT SEP *(break off)* enlever; **somebody had chipped the nose off the statue** quelqu'un avait cassé le nez de la statue; **to c. a piece off a plate** ébrécher une assiette

chipboard ['tʃɪpbɔːd] N *Carp* aggloméré *m*; **a piece of c.** un panneau d'aggloméré

chipmunk ['tʃɪpmʌŋk] N tamia *m* rayé, écureuil *m* rayé, *Can* suisse *m* rayé *ou* barré

chipolata [tʃɪpə'lɑːtə] N *esp Br Culin* chipolata *f*
▶▶ **c. sausage** chipolata

chipped [tʃɪpt] ADJ *(knife, plate)* ébréché; *(furniture)* écorné; *(enamel)* écaillé; *(tooth)* cassé
▶▶ *Am Culin* **c. beef** ≃ émincé *m* de bœuf; *Br Culin* **c. potatoes** (pommes de terre *fpl*) frites *fpl*

chipper ['tʃɪpər] ADJ *Fam (person)* gai, vif

chippings ['tʃɪpɪŋz] NPL *(of stone, marble)* éclats *mpl*, **(wood) c.** copeaux *mpl* (de bois); **loose c.** *(road sign)* gravillons *mpl*, *Can* gravelle *f*

chippy ['tʃɪpɪ] N *Br Fam* **1** *(fish and chip shop)* = boutique *f* où l'on vend des frites ainsi que du poisson frit, des saucisses, etc **2** *Old-fashioned (carpenter)* charpentier *m*

Chips [tʃɪps] N *Banking (abbr* **clearing house interbank payment system)** Sit *m*

chipset [tʃɪpset] N *Comput* ensemble *m* de puces

chiromancer ['kaɪrəʊmænsər] N chiromancien, -ienne

chiromancy ['kaɪrəʊmænsɪ] N chiromancie *f*

chiropodist [kɪ'rɒpədɪst] N *Med* pédicure *mf*

chiropody [kɪ'rɒpədɪ] N *Med* pédicurie *f*

chiropractic [kaɪrə'præktɪk] N *Med* chiropraxie *f*

chiropractor ['kaɪrəpræktər] N *Med* chiropracteur *m*, chiropracticien, -ienne

chirp [tʃɜːp] N *(of birds)* pépiement *m*, gazouillement *m*, gazouillis *m*; *(of chick)* piaulement *m*; *(of grasshopper)* chant *m*
VT & VI **1** *(of bird)* pépier, gazouiller; *(of chick)* piauler; *(of grasshopper)* chanter **2** *(of person)* babiller

chirpily ['tʃɜːpɪlɪ] ADV *Fam* gaiement

chirpiness ['tʃɜːpɪnɪs] N *Fam* humeur *f* joyeuse

chirpy ['tʃɜːpɪ] ADJ *Fam* d'humeur joyeuse

chirrup ['tʃɪrəp] N, VT & VI = **chirp**

chisel ['tʃɪz(ə)l] N ciseau *m*, burin *m*; **wood**

c. ciseau à bois; **hollow c.** gouge f; **cold c.** ciseau à froid, burin

VT (**-ll-**, Am **-l-**) **1** (wood, stone) ciseler; (metal) buriner, ciseler; **to c. sth off** enlever qch au burin **2** Sl (cheat) rouler; **to c. sb out of sth** rouler qn de qch

chiselled ['tʃɪz(ə)ld] **ADJ delicately c. features** visage délicatement ciselé

chiseller ['tʃɪz(ə)lər] **N** Sl **1** (swindler) escroc m **2** Ir (child) gosse mf, môme mf

chit [tʃɪt] **N** Old-fashioned Fam (child) mioche mf, gosse mf, gamin, -ine; (girl) jeune fille f ou femme f

chit [²] **N** (note) petit mot m, billet m; (for money owed) note f

chitchat ['tʃɪttʃæt] **N** Fam bavardage m, papotage m

chitterlings ['tʃɪtəlɪŋz], **chitlings** ['tʃɪtlɪŋz], **chitlins** ['tʃɪtlɪns] **NPL** Culin Old-fashioned tripes fpl

chivalrous ['ʃɪvəlrəs] **ADJ** courtois; Hist (worthy of a knight) chevaleresque

chivalrously ['ʃɪvəlrəslɪ] **ADV** courtoisement; Hist chevaleresquement

chivalry ['ʃɪvəlrɪ] **N 1** (of medieval knight) chevalerie f, **in the days of c.** aux temps de la chevalerie **2** (courteous behaviour) courtoisie f, esp Hum **it's nice to see c. is not dead** ça fait plaisir de voir que la galanterie n'a pas entièrement disparu

chives [tʃaɪvz] **NPL** ciboulette f, civette f

chiv(v)y ['tʃɪvɪ] **VT** Br Fam (pester) harceler; **to c. sb into doing sth** harceler qn jusqu'à ce qu'il fasse qch; **you'll have to c. them along** il faudra que tu les presses un peu; **go and c. them along** va leur dire de se dépêcher

chlamydia [klə'mɪdɪə] **N** Med chlamydia f

chloral ['klɔ:r(ə)l] **N** Chem chloral m

chlorate ['klɔ:reɪt] **N** Chem chlorate m

chloric ['klɔ:rɪk] **ADJ** Chem (acid etc) chlorique

chloride ['klɔ:raɪd] **N** Chem chlorure m
▸▸ **c. of silver** chlorure d'argent

chlorinate ['klɒrɪneɪt] **VT** (water) chlo(ru)rer

chlorinated ['klɔ:rɪneɪtɪd] **ADJ** (water) chloré

chlorination [klɒrɪ'neɪʃən] **N** chloration f
▸▸ **c. plant** usine f de chloration; **c. works** usine de chloration

chlorine ['klɔ:ri:n] **N** Chem chlore m

chlorite ['klɔ:raɪt] **N 1** Chem chlorite m **2** Miner chlorite m

chlorofluorocarbon [klɒrəflʊərəʊ'kɑ:bən] **N** chlorofluorocarbone m

chloroform ['klɒrəfɔ:m] **N** chloroforme m
VT chloroformer

chlorophyl(l) ['klɒrəfɪl] **N** Chem, Bot chlorophylle f

chloroquine ['klɔ:rəʊkwi:n] **N** Med chloroquine f

choc [tʃɒk] **N** Fam **a box of chocs** une boîte de chocolats

chocaholic [tʃɒkə'hɒlɪk] **N** Fam accro mf du chocolat

choc-ice **N** esquimau® m

chock [tʃɒk] **N** (under car wheel, door etc) cale f; Aviat **to remove the chocks** enlever les cales; Aviat **chocks away!** enlevez les cales!
VT 1 (barrel, wheel, door) caler **2** (in engineering etc) (part) coincer

chock-a-block **ADJ** Fam plein à craquer, bourré (**with** de)

chock-full **ADJ** Fam bourré (**of** de)

chocolate ['tʃɒklət] **N** (also drink) chocolat m; **bar of c.** tablette f de chocolat; **white c.** chocolat blanc; **cooking c.** chocolat à cuire;

drinking c. (drink) chocolat; (powder) chocolat en poudre; **hot c.** chocolat chaud; **a c.** un chocolat; **c. biscuit/ice cream/cake** biscuit m/glace f/gâteau m au chocolat

ADJ 1 (coloured) chocolat inv **2** (made of chocolate) en chocolat; (chocolate-flavoured) au chocolat, chocolaté
▸▸ **c. bar** barre f chocolatée; **c. brown** chocolat m inv; **c. chip cookie** biscuit m aux pépites de chocolat ou Can brisures de chocolat; **c. factory** chocolaterie f

choice [tʃɔɪs] **N 1** (act of choosing) choix m; **to make** or **take one's c.** faire son choix, choisir; **a difficult/easy c.** un choix difficile/facile; **by** or **out of c.** par choix; **to do sth of one's own c.** faire qch volontairement
2 (thing chosen) choix m; **the red wine was her c.** c'est elle qui avait choisi le vin rouge; **Spain would be my c.** je choisirais l'Espagne
3 (alternative) choix m; **to have the c. of two evils** avoir le choix entre deux maux; **what c. did she have?** (rhetorical) qu'est-ce qu'elle pouvait faire d'autre?; **you have no c. in the matter** vous n'avez pas le choix
4 (selection) assortiment m, choix m; **available in a c. of colours** disponible en plusieurs couleurs; **there isn't much c.** il n'y a pas grand choix; **to have a wide c.** avoir amplement de quoi choisir

ADJ 1 (well chosen) bien choisi; **in a few c. sentences** en quelques phrases bien choisies; Hum **she used some c. language** elle a juré comme un charretier
2 (of good quality) (article) de choix; (wine) fin
▸▸ Mktg **c. set** ensemble m de considérations, éventail m de choix

choir ['kwaɪər] **N 1** Mus chœur m, chorale f; **male voice c.** chœur ou chorale d'hommes
VOIR GRAMMAIRE A11 **2** Archit (of church) chœur m
▸▸ **c. practice** répétition f de la chorale; **c. school** maîtrise f; **c. screen** jubé m; **c. stall** stalle f

choirboy ['kwaɪəbɔɪ] **N** Rel jeune choriste m

choirmaster ['kwaɪəmɑ:stər] **N** Rel maître m de chapelle ou de chœur

choke [tʃəʊk] **N 1** Aut starter m; (on carburettor) buse f; **to pull out the c.** mettre le starter; **you've given it too much c.** tu as mis trop de starter **2** (in voice) étranglement m **3** Elec (coil of wire) bobine f d'impédance, self f **4** (of artichoke) foin m

VT 1 (strangle) étouffer, suffoquer; (of weeds) (flowers) étouffer; **voice choked with sobs** voix entrecoupée par les sanglots **2** (block) (pipe etc) obstruer, boucher (**with** de); **the streets were choked with traffic** les rues étaient congestionnées

VI 1 (become stifled) étouffer; **I choked on a bone** je me suis étranglé avec un os; **he was choking with anger** il suffoquait de colère; **to c. with laughter** s'étrangler de rire **2** Sl (die) clamser
▸▸ **c. cable** câble m de starter; **c. chain** (for dog) collier m étrangleur; Elec **c. coil** bobine d'impédance, self

▸ **choke back** **VT SEP** (suppress) (tears, words, anger) refouler, ravaler

▸ **choke up** **VT SEP** (block) boucher, obstruer; **the drain is all choked up with leaves** la bouche d'égout est complètement obstruée par les feuilles; **she was all choked up** (upset) elle était bouleversée ou toute émue

choked [tʃəʊkt] **ADJ** Br Fam (disappointed) déçu; (annoyed) ennuyé

choker ['tʃəʊkər] **N** (necklace) collier m de chien

choking ['tʃəʊkɪŋ] **ADJ** étouffant, suffocant; **he made a c. sound** il a fait un bruit comme quelqu'un qui s'étouffe
N étouffement m, suffocation f

cholera ['kɒlərə] **N** choléra m; **to have c.** avoir le choléra

choleric ['kɒlərɪk, kə'lerɪk] **ADJ** Fml colérique, coléreux

cholesterol [kə'lestərɒl] **N** Med cholestérol m; **with a high/low c. content** riche/pauvre en cholestérol
▸▸ **c. level** taux m de cholestérol

chomp [tʃɒmp] **VT & VI** mâcher bruyamment
N mâchonnement m bruyant

choo-choo ['tʃu:tʃu:] **N** Br Fam (in children's language) petit train m; **the train goes c.** le train fait tchou-tchou

chook [tʃʊk] **N** Austr Fam (chicken) poulet m

choose [tʃu:z] (pt chose [tʃəʊz], pp chosen ['tʃəʊz(ə)n]) **VT** choisir; **there is nothing to c. between them** l'un vaut l'autre, ils se valent; **I didn't c. to go there** je n'ai pas choisi d'y aller; **since you chose not to accept** puisque vous avez décidé de ne pas accepter; **well if you will c. to ignore my advice** bon, si tu préfères ne pas tenir compte de mes conseils

VI choisir; **c. for yourself** je vous laisse le choix; **c. to pick and c.** se montrer difficile, faire le/la difficile; **I'll do as I c.** je ferai comme il me plaît ou comme bon me semble; **to c. from** or **between several people** choisir entre ou parmi plusieurs personnes

chooser ['tʃu:z(ə)r] **N** Comput sélecteur m

choosing ['tʃu:zɪŋ] **N** choix m; **it was none of my c.** ce n'est pas moi qui l'ai choisi; **the circumstances were not of his c.** les circonstances n'étaient pas de son fait

choosy ['tʃu:zɪ] **ADJ** Fam difficile; **I'm not c.** (at this moment) ça m'est égal; (in general) je ne suis pas difficile; **don't be so c.** ne fais pas le difficile; **he isn't too c. who he does business with** il n'est pas très difficile quant aux gens avec lesquels il traite

chop [¹] [tʃɒp] **N 1** (blow) (with axe etc) coup m; Fam **to get the c.** (of person) se faire saquer, être mis à la porte; (of project) être annulé; (of chapter, part of text, film etc) être supprimé **2** Culin (pork, lamb) côtelette f **3** (in karate etc) coup m porté avec le tranchant de la main

VT (**-pp-**) **1** (wood) couper, fendre; (meat, vegetables etc) couper en morceaux; **to c. sth in(to) pieces** couper qch en morceaux; **to c. sth finely** hacher qch menu; **to c. logic** couper les cheveux en quatre **2** Tennis (ball) couper

VI Fam **c., c.!** vite, vite!
▸▸ Culin **c. suey** chop suey m

▸ **chop at** **VT INSEP** (something) (with axe, knife etc) donner des coups à; (aim blow at) tenter de porter un coup à

▸ **chop down** **VT SEP** (tree etc) abattre

▸ **chop off** **VT SEP** trancher, couper; **to c. sb's head off** trancher la tête à qn

▸ **chop up** **VT SEP** couper en morceaux, hacher

chop [²] **VI** **to c. and change** changer sans cesse; **he's always chopping and changing** (changing his mind) il change d'opinion à tout bout de champ; (changing policy/approach) il change de politique/méthode tout le temps

chophouse ['tʃɒphaʊs] **N** grill m

chopper ['tʃɒpər] **N 1** (tool) couperet m, hachoir m **2** (person) (of wood) fendeur, -euse **3** Fam (helicopter) hélico m **4** (motorcycle) chopper m; (bicycle) vélo m cross **5** Vulg (penis) bite f

choppers ['tʃɒpəz] **NPL** Fam (false teeth) râtelier m; (teeth) ratiches fpl

chopping ['tʃɒpɪŋ] **N** (of wood) coupe f
▸▸ **c. block** billot m; **c. board** planche f à découper; **c. knife** couperet m, hachoir m

choppy ['tʃɒpɪ] ADJ *(sea, lake)* agité

chops [tʃɒps] NPL *Fam* bajoues *fpl*; **he had a smile all over his fat c.** un large sourire lui couvrait la tronche; **to lick one's c.** se lécher les babines

chopsticks ['tʃɒpstɪks] NPL baguettes *fpl*

choral ['kɔ:r(ə)l] ADJ *Mus* choral, -als ▸ ▸ **c. society** chorale *f*; **c. symphony** symphonie *f* avec chœur

choral(e) [kə'rɑ:l] N *Mus* **1** *(hymn)* choral *m*, *pl* -als **2** *Am (choir)* chorale *f*

chord¹ [kɔ:d] N *Mus (group of notes)* accord *m*; **a c. sequence** une suite d'accords ▸ ▸ **c. progression** progression *f* harmonique

chord² N **1** *(of harp)* corde *f*; *Fig* **to strike a c., to strike the right c.** faire vibrer la corde sensible; **his words struck a c. with the audience** ses paroles ont trouvé un écho auprès du public **2** *Math (of arc)* corde *f*

chore [tʃɔ:r] N **1** *(usu pl)* **chores** *(in household)* travaux *mpl* ménagers; **the daily chores** les travaux quotidiens; **to do the chores** faire le ménage **2** *(unwelcome task)* corvée *f*

choreograph ['kɒrɪəgrɑ:f] VT *(ballet, show)* faire la chorégraphie de

choreographer [kɒrɪ'ɒgrəfər] N chorégraphe *mf*

choreographic [kɒrɪə'græfɪk] ADJ chorégraphique

choreography [kɒrɪ'ɒgrəfɪ] N chorégraphie *f*

chorister ['kɒrɪstər] N choriste *mf*

chortle ['tʃɔ:t(ə)l] N gloussement *m* (de joie); **she gave a c.** elle a gloussé, elle a poussé un gloussement de joie
VI glousser (de joie), pousser un gloussement de joie
VT **oh, no, he chortled** ah non, dit-il dans un gloussement

chorus, *pl* -uses ['kɔ:rəs, -əsɪz] N **1** *(of song)* refrain *m*; **to join in the c.** *(of several people)* chanter le refrain en chœur; *(of one person)* se joindre aux autres pour le refrain **2** *(group of singers, actors)* chœur *m*; **in the c.** *(of musical)* dans les chœurs VOIR GRAMMAIRE A11 **3 to sing in c.** chanter en chœur; **no!, they shouted in c.** non!, se sont-ils exclamés en chœur; **c. of praise** concert *m* de louanges; **a c. of criticism** une avalanche de critiques; **they greeted him with a c. of cheers** ils l'accueillirent avec des hourras
VT (-s-) dire en chœur; *(song)* chanter en chœur; **yes please!, they chorused** volontiers, ont-ils répondu en chœur ▸ ▸ *Theat, Mus* **c. girl** girl *f*

chorusmaster ['kɔ:rəsmɑːstər] N maître *m* de chant

chosen ['tʃəʊz(ə)n] PP *see* choose
ADJ choisi; **the c. people** les élus *mpl*; **the c. few** les heureux élus
NPL **the c.** les élus *mpl*

chough [tʃʌf] N *(bird)* crave *m* à bec rouge

choux [ʃu:] Culin N *(pastry)* pâte *f* à choux ▸ ▸ **c. bun** chou *m* à la crème; **c. pastry** pâte à choux

chow [tʃaʊ] N **1** *(dog)* chow-chow *m*, *pl* chows-chows **2** *Fam (food)* boustifaille *f* ▸ **chow down** VI *Am Fam* bouffer

chow-chow N *(dog)* chow-chow *m*, *pl* chows-chows

chowder ['tʃaʊdər] N *Culin* = potage *m* épais contenant du poisson ou des fruits de mer

Christ [kraɪst] N le Christ, Jésus-Christ *m*; **the C. Child** l'Enfant Jésus *m*
INT *Fam* bon Dieu!; **C. Almighty!** nom de Dieu!

christen ['krɪs(ə)n] VT **1** *(person, ship)* baptiser; *(nickname)* surnommer; **to c. a child George** baptiser un enfant Georges **2** *(use for first time)* étrenner

Christendom ['krɪs(ə)ndəm] N chrétienté *f*, **throughout C.** dans toute la chrétienté; **he's the biggest fool in C.** c'est l'homme le plus bête du monde

christening ['krɪs(ə)nɪŋ] N baptême *m* ▸ ▸ **c. ceremony** cérémonie *f* du *ou* de baptême; **c. robe** *(for baby)* robe *f* de baptême

Christian ['krɪstʃən] *Rel* N chrétien, -ienne; **to be a C.** être chrétien
ADJ **1** chrétien; **C. burial** sépulture *f* en terre sainte; **C. charity** charité *f* chrétienne **2** *(good, kind)* chrétien, de chrétien; **that wasn't very C. of you** ce n'était pas très aimable de ta part; **that's not a very C. attitude** ce n'est pas une attitude très chrétienne ▸ ▸ **the C. era** l'ère *f* chrétienne; **C. name** prénom *m*; **C. Scientist** scientiste *mf* chrétien, -ienne

Christianity [krɪstɪ'ænɪtɪ] N christianisme *m*; **in a spirit of C.** en chrétien

Christianize ['krɪstʃənaɪz] VT christianiser, convertir au christianisme

Christmas ['krɪsməs] N Noël *m*; **at C.** à (la) Noël; **to spend C. at home** passer Noël chez soi; **Merry** *or* **Happy C.!** joyeux Noël!; **Father C.** le père Noël ▸ ▸ *Br* **C. box** étrennes *fpl (offertes à Noël)*; **C. cake** gâteau *m* de Noël *(cake décoré au sucre glace)*; **C. card** carte *f* de Noël; **C. carol** chant *m* de) Noël; **C. Day** jour *m* de Noël; **on C.** le jour de Noël; **C. dinner** repas *m* de Noël; **C. Eve** veille *f* de Noël; **C. present** cadeau *m* de Noël; **C. pudding** pudding *m* de Noël, plum-pudding *m*, *pl* plum-puddings; *Bot* **C. rose** rose *f* de Noël; **C. stocking** = chaussette *f* que les enfants suspendent à la cheminée pour que le père Noël y dépose les cadeaux; **C. tree** sapin *m* de Noël

Christmassy ['krɪsməsɪ] ADJ *Fam* typique de Noël; **to be in a C. mood** être dans l'ambiance de Noël; **not in a C. mood** pas d'humeur à supporter Noël; **it all looks so C.** c'est tout décoré pour Noël

Christmastide ['krɪsməstaɪd] N *Old-fashioned* période *f* de Noël; **at C.** à la Noël

Christopher Columbus ['krɪstəfər] N Christophe Colomb

chromatic [krəʊ'mætɪk] ADJ *Mus, Phys* chromatique

chromatography [krəʊmə'tɒgrəfɪ] N chromatographie *f*

chrome [krəʊm] N chrome *m*; *Br Fam Hum* **he's a c. dome** il a une casquette en peau de fesse
ADJ *(taps, handles etc)* chromé ▸ ▸ **c. nickel** nickel-chrome *m*; **c. steel** acier *m* chromé *ou* au chrome; **c. tape** bande *f* magnétique chromée; *Art* **c. yellow** jaune *m* de chrome

chromium ['krəʊmɪəm] N *Chem* chrome *m* ▸ ▸ **c. plating** chromage *m*

chromium-plated ADJ chromé

chromosome ['krəʊməsəʊm] N *Biol* chromosome *m*; **X-c.** chromosome X

chronic ['krɒnɪk] ADJ **1** *Med, Fig* chronique; **c. unemployment** chômage *m* chronique; **c. invalid** invalide *mf* chronique; **to suffer from c. ill health** être de santé fragile; *Fig* **a c. drunkard/liar** un buveur/menteur invétéré **2** *Br Fam (very bad)* atroce; **their singing was c.** ils chantaient atrocement mal; **my back was hurting something c.** mon dos me faisait un mal de chien ▸ ▸ *Med* **c. fatigue syndrome** encéphalomyélite *f* myalgique, syndrome *m* de fatigue chronique

chronically ['krɒnɪklɪ] ADV chroniquement

chronicity [krɒ'nɪsɪtɪ] N *Med* chronicité *f*

chronicle ['krɒnɪk(ə)l] N chronique *f*, *Fig* **a c. of disasters** une suite de catastrophes; *Bible* **(the Book of) Chronicles** les Chroniques *fpl*
VT **to c. events** faire la chronique d'événements

chronicler ['krɒnɪklər] N chroniqueur *m*

chronological [krɒnə'lɒdʒɪk(ə)l] ADJ *(order etc)* chronologique

chronologically [krɒnə'lɒdʒɪklɪ] ADV chronologiquement, par ordre chronologique

chronology [krə'nɒlədʒɪ] N chronologie *f*

chronometer [krə'nɒmɪtər] N chronomètre *m*

chronometry [krə'nɒmɪtrɪ] N chronométrie *f*

chrysalid ['krɪsəlɪd], **chrysalis**, *pl* **chrysalises** ['krɪsəlɪs, 'krɪsəlɪsɪz] N *Entom* chrysalide *f*

chrysanthemum [krɪ'sænθəməm] N chrysanthème *m*

chub [tʃʌb] N *(fish)* chevesne *m*, meunier *m*

chubbiness ['tʃʌbɪnɪs] N *(of person)* apparence *f* potelée

chubby ['tʃʌbɪ] ADJ *(person)* potelé, boulot, dodu, grassouillet; *(hands)* potelé; *(face)* joufflu; *(cheeks)* rebondi; **c.-cheeked** aux joues rebondies
N **come on, c.!** allez, gros dodu!

chuck¹ [tʃʌk] VT **1** *Fam (throw) (stone etc)* balancer; **c. me that hammer** balance-moi le marteau; **to c. one's money about** *or* **around** gaspiller son argent
2 *Fam (finish with) (job)* lâcher, laisser tomber; *(girlfriend, boyfriend)* plaquer
3 *Fam (throw away)* balancer, foutre en l'air
4 *Br Fam* **c. it!** *(stop it!)* arrête!
5 to c. sb under the chin donner une petite tape à qn sous le menton
N **1** *Fam* **to give sb the c.** *(from job)* virer *ou* sa(c)quer qn; *(from relationship)* plaquer qn
2 *(under the chin)* petite tape *f*
3 *(steak)* morceau *m* de bœuf dans le paleron ▸ ▸ **c. steak** morceau de bœuf dans le paleron; **c. wagon** cantine *f* ambulante *(pour les cow-boys)*

▸ **chuck away** VT SEP *Fam* balancer, flanquer *ou* foutre en l'air; **that's just chucking money away** ça, c'est flanquer l'argent par les fenêtres

▸ **chuck down** VT SEP *Br Fam* **it's chucking it down** *(raining)* il tombe des cordes

▸ **chuck in** VT SEP *Fam (finish with) (job)* lâcher, laisser tomber; *(person)* plaquer, virer; **he chucked it all in and bought a farm** il a tout plaqué pour acheter une ferme; **to c. one's hand in** *Cards* jeter ses cartes sur la table; *Fig (admit defeat)* s'avouer vaincu

▸ **chuck off** VT SEP *Fam* virer; **he was chucked off the team** il s'est fait virer de l'équipe

▸ **chuck on** VT SEP *Fam (clothes, aftershave)* mettre

▸ **chuck out** VT SEP *Fam* **1** *(throw away)* jeter **2** *(from pub, house etc)* flanquer à la porte, vider

▸ **chuck up** *Fam* VT SEP *(finish with) (job)* lâcher, laisser tomber; **she chucked everything up and became a nurse** elle a tout plaqué pour devenir infirmière
VI *esp Am (vomit)* vomir, rendre

chuck² N *Tech (for lathe, drill)* mandrin *m*

chucker-out ['tʃʌkər-] N *Br Fam (in disco etc)* videur *m*

chucking-out ['tʃʌkɪŋ-] N *Br Fam* **c. time** l'heure *f* de la fermeture (des pubs)

chuckle ['tʃʌk(ə)l] N rire *m* étouffé, petit rire; **to give a c.** lâcher un petit rire

vi rire tout bas *ou* en soi-même (**at, over** de)

chuff¹ [tʃʌf] **vi** *(of train)* haleter

chuff² N *Br Vulg* **1** *(vagina)* craquette *f*, fente *f*; **to be as tight as a nun's c.** *(miserly)* avoir des oursins dans le porte-monnaie, les lâcher avec des élastiques **2** *(anus)* trou *m* de balle

chuffed [tʃʌft] **ADJ** *Br Fam* tout content (**about** de); **he's dead c. with his present** il est super content de son cadeau; **I'm really c. with myself** je suis tout content de moi

chuffing [ˈtʃʌfɪŋ] **ADJ** *Br Sl* foutu, sacré; **that c. idiot** ce sombre crétin

chug [tʃʌg] N *(of steam engine)* souffle *m*
vi (**-gg-**) *(of steam engine)* souffler, haleter
▸ **chug along vi** *Fam (move slowly)* avancer doucement; **the guy in front was chugging along at 30 km/h** le type devant moi se traînait à 30 à l'heure

chum [tʃʌm] N *Fam* camarade *mf*, copain *m*, copine *f*
▸ **chum up with vt INSEP** (**-mm-**) *Fam* copiner avec

chummy [ˈtʃʌmɪ] **ADJ** *Fam* (bon) copain, *f* (bonne) copine; **she's quite c. with the boss** elle est assez copine avec le patron; **he's a c. sort of bloke** c'est un type sympa (et sociable); **he's a bit too c. for my liking** il est un peu trop familier à mon goût

chump [tʃʌmp] N **1** *Fam (foolish person)* idiot, -ote **2** *Culin (end of mutton)* selle *f* d'agneau **3** *Fam (head)* **off one's c.** timbré, maboul
▸▸*Am Fam* **c. change** *(small amount of money)* cacahuètes *fpl*; *Br Culin* **c. chop** côtelette *f* d'agneau *(coupée dans le gigot)*

chunder [ˈtʃʌndər] **vi** *Br, Austr Sl (vomit)* dégueuler

chunk [tʃʌŋk] N *(of bread, cheese etc)* gros morceau *m*; *(of bread)* quignon *m*; *(of wood)* tronçon *m*

chunky [ˈtʃʌŋkɪ] **ADJ** *Fam* **1** *(person)* trapu **2** *(pullover)* gros; *(glass)* solide

Chunnel [ˈtʃʌn(ə)l] N *Fam* **the C.** le tunnel sous la Manche, l'Eurotunnel *m*

▸ **chunter away, chunter on** [ˈtʃʌntər] **vi** *Fam* papoter; **he's still chuntering away about it** il continue son baratin; **with those two chuntering away in the background** avec ces deux-là qui papotent/papotaient dans le fond

church [tʃɜːtʃ] N ◼ VOIR GRAMMAIRE A6–7 **1** *(building)* église *f*; *(French Protestant)* temple *m*; **to go to c.** aller à l'église; *(of Catholic)* aller à l'église *ou* à la messe; *(of French Protestant)* aller au temple; **I saw her in c. on Sunday** je l'ai vue à l'église dimanche **2** *(institution)* **the C.** l'Église *f*; **the Anglican C.** l'Église anglicane; **to go into the C.** *(take orders)* entrer dans les ordres; **to leave the C.** quitter l'église; **High C.** = section *f* de l'Église anglicane qui se rapproche du catholicisme en matière de rituel; **Low C.** = section de l'Église anglicane qui se distingue par la simplicité du rituel; **the (Roman) Catholic C.** l'Église catholique; **C. of England** Église anglicane
▸▸ **C. Fathers** Pères *mpl* de l'Église; **c. hall** salle *f* paroissiale; **c. leader** chef *m* de l'église; **c. service** office *m*, culte *m*; **c. wedding** mariage *m* religieux

churchgoer [ˈtʃɜːtʃɡəʊər] N *Rel* pratiquant, -ante; **an occasional c.** une personne qui va à l'église de temps en temps

churchgoing [ˈtʃɜːtʃɡəʊɪŋ] *Rel* **ADJ** pratiquant; **the c. public** les gens qui vont à l'église
N fréquentation *f* des églises; **c. is not regarded as an essential part of ...** aller à l'église n'est pas considéré comme une part essentielle de ...

Churchillian [tʃɜːˈtʃɪljən] **ADJ** churchillien

churchman, *pl* **churchmen** [ˈtʃɜːtʃmən] N *Rel* **1** *(clergyman)* homme *m* d'église **2** *(member of a church)* membre *m* d'une église

churchwarden [tʃɜːˈtʃwɔːd(ə)n] N **1** *Rel* marguillier *m*, bedeau *m* **2** *(pipe)* longue pipe *f (en terre)*, pipe hollandaise
▸▸ **c. pipe** longue pipe *(en terre)*, pipe hollandaise

churchwoman, *pl* **churchwomen** [ˈtʃɜːtʃwʊmən, -wɪmɪn] N *Rel* **1** *(clergywoman)* femme *f* d'église **2** *(member of a church)* femme *f* membre d'une église

churchy [ˈtʃɜːtʃɪ] **ADJ** *Fam* calotin, bondieusard

churchyard [ˈtʃɜːtʃjɑːd] N *(graveyard)* cimetière *m*; *(grounds)* enclos *m* d'église

churl [tʃɜːl] N rustre *m*

churlish [ˈtʃɜːlɪʃ] **ADJ** *(rude)* grossier; *(surly)* *(behaviour, person)* revêche; **it would be c. to refuse** ce serait mal élevé de refuser

churlishly [ˈtʃɜːlɪʃlɪ] **ADV** *(rudely)* avec grossièreté; *(in a surly way)* de façon revêche

churlishness [ˈtʃɜːlɪʃnɪs] N *(rudeness)* grossièreté *f*; *(surliness)* attitude *f* revêche; **he agreed, but with his usual c.** il accepta, revêche comme à l'ordinaire

churn [tʃɜːn] N **1** *Agr (for butter)* baratte *f* **2** *Agr (for milk)* bidon *m* à lait **3** *Mktg* perte *f* de clients passés à la concurrence
vt *(milk, cream)* baratter; *(butter)* battre; **to c. water** *(of propellor etc)* faire des remous
vi *(of sea)* bouillonner; *Fig* **my stomach's churning** *(with nerves, excitement)* j'ai l'estomac noué
▸ **churn out vt SEP** *Fam (produce in large numbers) (books etc)* produire en série, *Fam* pondre en série; *(objects)* produire en série
▸ **churn up vt SEP** *(mud)* remuer; **to c. up water** faire bouillonner l'eau; *Fig* **I felt all churned up** *(nervous)* j'étais tout retourné; *(excited)* j'étais tout excité

churning [ˈtʃɜːnɪŋ] N *(of cream)* barattage *m*

chute [ʃuːt] N **1** *(for parcels etc)* glissière *f*; *(for coal)* déversoir *m*; *(rubbish or Am garbage)* **c.** vide-ordures *m inv* **2** *Sport (for sleds)* piste *f*; *(in swimming pool, playground)* toboggan *m* **3** *(waterfall)* chute *f* d'eau **4** *Fam (parachute)* parachute *m*

chutney [ˈtʃʌtnɪ] N *Culin* chutney *m*

chutzpah [ˈhʊtspə] N culot *m*

chyme [kaɪm] N *Med* chyme *m*

C & I [siːændˈaɪ] N *Com (abbr* **cost and insurance***)* c et a

CIA [siːaɪˈeɪ] N *Am (abbr* **Central Intelligence Agency***)* CIA *f*

ciborium, *pl* **ciboria** [sɪˈbɔːrɪəm, -ɪə] N *Rel (vessel)* ciboire *m*

cicada [sɪˈkɑːdə, -ˈkeɪdə] N *(insect)* cigale *f*

cicatrice [ˈsɪkətrɪs], **cicatrix** [ˈsɪkətrɪks] N *Fml* cicatrice *f*

Cicero [ˈsɪsərəʊ] N Cicéron

cicerone [sɪsəˈrəʊnɪ] N *Old-fashioned* cicérone *m*

CID [siːaɪˈdiː] N *Br (abbr* **Criminal Investigation Department***)* ≃ P J *f*; **Joanna Smith, C.** ≃ Joanna Smith, de la P J

cider [ˈsaɪdər] N **1** *Br (alcoholic drink)* cidre *m* **2** *Am (apple juice)* jus *m* de pommes; **hard c.** cidre *m*
▸▸ **c. apple** pomme *f* à cidre; **c. press** pressoir *m* à cidre; **c. vinegar** vinaigre *m* de cidre

cif [siːˈaɪef] *Com (abbr* **cost, insurance and freight***)* CAF

cigar [sɪˈɡɑːr] N cigare *m*
▸▸ **c. butt** mégot *m* de cigare; **c. case** étui *m* à cigares; **c. cutter** coupe-cigares *m inv*; **c. holder** fume-cigare *m inv*; **c. lighter** allume-cigare *m inv*

cigarette, *occ Am* **cigaret** [sɪɡəˈret] N cigarette *f*
▸▸ **c. advertising** publicité *f* pour les cigarettes; **c. ash** cendre *f* de cigarette; **c. butt** mégot *m* de cigarette; **c. card** = image *f* offerte autrefois avec chaque paquet de cigarettes; **c. case** étui *m* à cigarettes, porte-cigarettes *m inv*; **c. end** mégot; **c. holder** fume-cigarette *m inv*; **c. lighter** briquet *m*; **c. machine** *(vending machine)* distributeur *m* automatique de cigarettes; *(for rolling cigarettes)* rouleuse *f*; **c. packet** paquet *m* de cigarettes; **c. paper** papier *m* à cigarettes; **c. smoke** fumée *f* de cigarette; **c. smoker** fumeur, -euse (de cigarettes)

ciggie [ˈsɪɡɪ] N *Br Fam* tige *f*, clope *f*

CIM [siːaɪˈem] N *Comput (abbr* **computer-integrated manufacturing***)* CFAO *f*

CIM waybill N *Com* lettre *f* de voiture CIM

C-in-C, C in C [siːɪnˈsiː] N *Mil, Naut (abbr* **Commander in Chief***)* commandant *m* en chef

cinch [sɪntʃ] N **1** *Fam (something very easy)* **it's a c.** c'est simple comme bonjour, c'est un jeu d'enfant **2** *Fam (certainty)* certitude *f*; **it's a c.** c'est certain *ou* couru **3** *Am (for horse)* sangle *f*, sous-ventrière *f*, *pl* sous-ventrières

cinder [ˈsɪndər] N cendre *f*; **burnt to a c.** *(meat, toast etc)* complètement carbonisé
▸▸ *Am* **c. block** parpaing *m*; **c. track** *(piste f)* cendrée *f*

Cinderella [sɪndəˈrelə] N *Liter* Cendrillon *f*; *Fig* **poetry has always been the C. of the arts** la poésie a toujours été le parent pauvre des arts

Cinders [ˈsɪndəz] N *Fam* Cendrillon *f*

cine [ˈsɪnɪ] PREF *Br*
▸▸ **c. camera** caméra *f*; **c. film** film *m*; **c. projector** projecteur *m* de cinéma

cineaste, cineast [ˈsɪnɪæst] N cinéphile *mf*

cinema [ˈsɪnəmə] N **1** *(art)* cinéma *m*; **French c.** le cinéma français **2** *esp Br (place)* cinéma *m*; **to go to the c.** aller au cinéma;
▸▸ *Mktg* **c. advertising** publicité *f* au cinéma; *TV* **c. channel** chaîne *f* de cinéma

cinemagoer [ˈsɪnəməɡəʊər] N cinéphile *mf*; **he's not much of a c.** ce n'est pas un grand amateur de cinéma

cinema-going N fréquentation *f* des salles de cinéma
ADJ the c. public les cinéphiles *mpl*

Cinemascope® [ˈsɪnəməskəʊp] N Cinémascope® *m*

cinematic [sɪnəˈmætɪk] **ADJ** cinématique; **the novel has a c. quality** le roman utilise des effets qui rappellent le cinéma

cinematograph [sɪnəˈmætəɡræf] N *Br Old-fashioned* cinématographe *m*

cinematographer [sɪnəməˈtɒɡrəfər] N directeur *m* de la photographie, chef opérateur *m*

cinematographic [sɪnəmætəˈɡræfɪk] **ADJ** cinématographique

cinematography [sɪnəməˈtɒɡrəfɪ] N **1** *(technique)* cinématographie *f* **2** *(camerawork)* prises *fpl* de vue

cinephile [ˈsɪnɪfaɪl] N *Am* cinéphile *mf*

Cinerama® [sɪnəˈrɑːmə] N Cinérama® *m*

cineraria [sɪnəˈreərɪə] N *(plant)* cinéraire *f*

cinnabar [ˈsɪnəbɑːr] N *Miner* cinabre *m*

cinnamon [ˈsɪnəmən] N **1** *Culin (spice)* cannelle *f* **2** *Bot (tree)* cannelier *m*
ADJ *(colour)* cannelle *inv*
▸▸ **c. stick** bâton *m* de cannelle; *Bot* **c. tree** cannelier

cinq(ue)foil [ˈsɪŋkfɔɪl] N **1** *(plant)* potentille *f* rampante, quintefeuille *f* **2** *Archit* quintefeuille *m*

cipher [ˈsaɪfər] N **1** *(secret writing)* chiffre *m*,

code *m*; *(message)* message *m* chiffré *ou* codé; **to write a message in c.** chiffrer un message; **2** *(monogram)* chiffre *m* **3** *Math* zéro *m*; *Fig* **he's a mere c.** c'est un zéro *ou* une nullité
vt *(message)* chiffrer
▸▸ **c. clerk** chiffreur, -euse

circa ['sɜːkə] **prep** *(of time)* aux alentours de; *(of amount)* environ

circadian [sɜː'keɪdɪən] **adj** circadien

circle ['sɜː(ə)l] **n 1** *Math etc* cercle *m*; **to draw a c.** tracer un cercle; **to stand in a c.** *(of people)* se tenir en cercle; **the chairs were arranged in a c.** les chaises étaient disposées en cercle; *Fig* **to go round in circles** tourner en rond; **to have circles under one's eyes** avoir les yeux cernés, avoir des cernes sous les yeux; **Arctic/Antarctic C.** cercle (polaire) arctique/antarctique; *Gym* **to do a c. (on the horizontal bar)** faire le (grand) soleil; *Archeol* **stone c.** cercle de pierres
2 *(movement)* *(of planet)* révolution *f*, orbite *f*; **to come full c.** *(of planet)* compléter son orbite; *(of argument, person walking)* revenir à son point de départ; *(of fashion, history)* revenir au même point
3 *Theat* **first c.** (premier) balcon *m*, corbeille *f*; **upper c.** deuxième balcon
4 *(group)* cercle *m*, groupe *m*; **a c. of friends** un cercle d'amis; **the family c.** le cercle familial; **in certain circles** dans certains milieux; **in theatrical circles** dans le monde du théâtre; **the inner c.** *(of friends)* le cercle intime
vt 1 *(go round)* tourner autour de, faire le tour de
2 *(surround)* entourer (**with** de)
vi *(of plane, tiger around prey)* tourner; *(of birds)* tourner, tournoyer; **to c. round sth** tourner/tournoyer autour de qch; **the planes are circling overhead** les avions décrivent des cercles au-dessus de nos têtes; *Fig* **she circled round the issue** elle tournait autour du pot

circlet ['sɜːklɪt] **n** bandeau *m*

circlip ['sɜːklɪp] **n** *Tech* circlip *m*
▸▸ **c. pliers** pince *f* à circlip

circuit ['sɜːkɪt] **n 1** *Elec* circuit *m*; **in/out of c.** en/hors de circuit
2 *(journey, movement around)* *(of sun)* révolution *f*, *(of assizes judge)* tournée *f*; **to make one c. of the track** faire un tour de circuit; **to make a c. of the estate** faire le tour du domaine; **to make a wide c.** faire un grand détour; *Law* **to go on c.** *(of judge)* aller en tournée
3 *(route, places visited)* *(of assizes judge)* circonscription *f* de tournée, ressort *m*; *(series of venues etc)* circuit *m*; **the hottest act on the club c.** le meilleur numéro du circuit
4 *Sport* *(in motor racing)* circuit *m*, parcours *m*
▸▸ *Elec* **c. board** plaquette *f* (de circuits imprimés); *Elec* **c. breaker** disjoncteur *m*; *Law* **c. court** = tribunal *m* en service dans les principales villes de province lors du passage du "circuit judge"; *Law* **c. judge** = juge *m* itinérant; *Sport* **c. training** programme *m* d'exercices en salle

circuitous [sə'kjuːɪtəs] **adj** *(route)* détourné, indirect; *(reasoning)* long et compliqué; **by c. means** par des moyens détournés *ou* indirects

circuitously [sə'kjuːɪtəslɪ] **adv** *(to reach destination etc)* par le chemin le plus long; *(to reason etc)* avec beaucoup de circonvolutions; **the path winds c. to the summit** le chemin monte en lacets jusqu'au sommet

circuitry ['sɜːkɪtrɪ] **n** *(no pl)* *Electron* circuits *mpl*; **the c. on this board is really simple** le montage de cette plaquette est vraiment simple

circular ['sɜːkjʊlər] **adj** *(movement, argument)* circulaire

n (lettre *f*) circulaire *f*, *(publicity material)* prospectus *m*; *Br Journ* **Court c.** rubrique *f* de la Cour *(décrivant les engagements de la famille royale)*
▸▸ *Econ* **c. flow of income** flux *m* circulaire des revenus; *Tech* **c. saw** scie *f* circulaire

circularity [sɜːkjʊ'lærɪtɪ] **n** circularité *f*

circularize ['sɜːkjʊləraɪz] **vt** *(customers etc)* *(letter)* envoyer une/des circulaire(s); *(publicity material)* envoyer un/des prospectus à

circulate ['sɜːkjʊleɪt] **vi** *(of rumour, person at party, money)* circuler
vt 1 *(air, wine etc)* faire circuler **2** *(money)* mettre en circulation; *(news)* répandre, faire circuler

circulating ['sɜːkjʊleɪtɪŋ] **adj** circulant
▸▸ *Acct* **c. assets** actif *m* circulant; *Fin* **c. capital** capitaux *mpl* circulants; **c. library** *(mobile library)* bibliothèque *f* ambulante *ou* mobile; *Am* *(lending library)* bibliothèque *f* de prêt

circulation [sɜːkjʊ'leɪʃən] **n 1** *(of air, liquid, news)* circulation *f*; **to put a book into c.** mettre un livre en circulation; **for private c.** *(in publishing)* hors commerce; **the memo was for internal c. only** c'était une note de service à usage interne uniquement; **newspaper with a large c.** journal à grand tirage; *Journ* **a c. of 500,000** un tirage de 500 000 exemplaires
2 *Physiol* *(of blood etc)* circulation *f*; **to have poor** *or* **bad c.** avoir une mauvaise circulation; **to restore the c. in one's legs** se dégourdir les jambes
3 *(of currency)* circulation *f* (de la monnaie); **to put forged notes into c.** mettre de faux billets en circulation; **notes in c.** billets en circulation; **to be in c.** être en circulation; *Fig* **to be in/out of c.** *(of person)* être/ne plus être dans le circuit; **to withdraw sth from c.** retirer qch de la circulation
▸▸ *Journ* **c. figures** chiffres *mpl* de diffusion

Note that the French word **circulation** also means **traffic**.

circulatory [sɜːkjʊ'leɪt(ə)rɪ, 'sɜːkjʊlət(ə)rɪ] **adj** *Anat etc* circulatoire, de (la) circulation

circumcise ['sɜːkəmsaɪz] **vt** *(boy)* circoncire; *(girls)* exciser

circumcised ['sɜːkəmsaɪzd] **adj** *(boy)* circoncis; *(girl)* excisée

circumcision [sɜːkəm'sɪʒən] **n** circoncision *f*; **female c.** excision *f*; *Rel* **the C.** la (fête de la) Circoncision

circumference [sə'kʌmfərəns] **n** circonférence *f*; **to be thirty metres in c.** avoir trente mètres de circonférence

circumflex ['sɜːkəmfleks] *Gram* **n** accent *m* circonflexe
adj *(accent)* circonflexe; **it's spelt with an "e" c.** ça s'écrit avec un "e" accent circonflexe

circumlocution [sɜːkəmlə'kjuːʃən] **n** circonlocution *f*, périphrase *f*, **without c.** sans ambages

circumlocutory [sɜːkəmlə'kjuːt(ə)rɪ] **adj** périphrastique

circumnavigate [sɜːkəm'nævɪgeɪt] **vt** faire le tour de *(par la mer)*

circumnavigation [sɜːkəmnævɪ'geɪʃən] **n** circumnavigation *f*

circumscribe ['sɜːkəmskraɪb] **vt 1** *(limit)* *(powers, field of operations)* limiter, restreindre **2** *Geom* *(circle etc)* circonscrire

circumscribed ['sɜːkəmskraɪbd] **adj 1** *(limited)* restreint, limité **2** *Geom* *(circle etc)* circonscrit

circumscription [sɜːkəm'skrɪpʃən] **n 1** *(limitation)* restriction *f*, limitation *f* **2** *Geom* circonscription *f*

circumspect ['sɜːkəmspekt] **adj** *(person,*

conduct) circonspect, avisé, prudent; *(speech etc)* mesuré

circumspection [sɜːkəm'spekʃən] **n** circonspection *f*

circumspectly ['sɜːkəmspektlɪ] **adv** avec circonspection

circumstance ['sɜːkəmstəns] **n 1** *(situation)* *(usu pl)* **circumstances** circonstances *fpl*; **in** *or* **under the circumstances** dans ces circonstances, en de telles circonstances; **in** *or* **under no circumstances** en aucun cas, sous aucun prétexte; **it depends on the circumstances** cela dépend des circonstances, *Fam* c'est selon; **he was the victim of c.** *or* **circumstances** il a été la victime des circonstances; **due to circumstances beyond our control** en raison de circonstances indépendantes de notre volonté; **by force of circumstances** par la force des choses
2 *(financial situation)* **in easy circumstances** à l'aise; **if his circumstances allowed** si ses moyens le permettaient
3 **with pomp and c.** en grande cérémonie, en grand apparat

circumstantial [sɜːkəm'stænʃəl] **adj 1** *(incidental)* accidentel, fortuit; **it's all a bit c.** il n'y a rien de concret **2** *(detailed)* détaillé, circonstancié
▸▸ *Law* **c. evidence** preuves *fpl* indirectes

circumstantiate [sɜːkəm'stænʃɪeɪt] **vt** *Fml* *(report)* donner des détails circonstanciés sur

circumvent [sɜːkəm'vent] **vt** circonvenir; **to c. the law** contourner la loi

circumvention [sɜːkəm'venʃən] **n** *(of law etc)* contournement *m*

circus, pl circuses ['sɜːkəs, -əsɪz] **n** *(show, troupe, Antiq, Fig* cirque *m*; **to join a c.** entrer dans un cirque; *Aviat* **flying c.** parade *f* aérienne itinéraire; **travelling c.** cirque forain
▸▸ **c. act** numéro *m* de cirque

cirrhosis [sɪ'rəʊsɪs] **n** *Med* cirrhose *f*, **c. of the liver** cirrhose du foie; **to have c.** avoir une cirrhose

cirrus, pl cirri ['sɪrəs, -raɪ] **n** *Met* cirrus *m*

CIS [siːaɪ'es] **n** *(abbr* **Commonwealth of Independent States)** CEI *f*

cisalpine [sɪs'ælpaɪn] **adj** cisalpin
▸▸ **C. Gaul** Gaule *f* cisalpine

cissy ['sɪsɪ] **n, adj** *Fam Pej* = **sissy**

Cistercian [sɪ'stɜːʃən] **n, adj** *Rel* cistercien, -ienne; **the C. Order** l'ordre *m* de Cîteaux

cistern ['sɪstən] **n** *(in attic)* réservoir *m* d'eau; *(in lavatory)* réservoir de chasse d'eau; *(underground)* citerne *f*, *(of pump)* réservoir

citadel ['sɪtədəl, -del] **n** citadelle *f*

citation [saɪ'teɪʃən] **n 1** *(from author)* citation *f* **2** *Mil* citation *f* (à l'ordre du jour) **3** *Law* *(summons)* citation *f* à comparaître

cite [saɪt] **vt 1** *(quote)* *(passage, author, example)* citer **2** *Mil* *(soldier for heroism)* citer **3** *Law* **to c. sb before a court** citer qn devant un tribunal

citizen ['sɪtɪzən] **n 1** *(of nation)* citoyen, -enne; *(of city, town)* habitant, -ante; **c. of the world** citoyen du monde; **a private c.** un simple particulier **2** *Am* *(as opposed to person in army, navy)* civil *m*
▸▸ *Br* **Citizens' Advice Bureau** = service *m* gratuit d'aide juridique; **c. army** armée *f* de citoyens; **c.'s arrest** = arrestation *f* effectuée par un individu en vertu du droit commun; **citizens' band (radio)** (radio *f* de la) citizen band *f*; **c. rights** droits *mpl* civiques

citizenry ['sɪtɪzənrɪ] **n** ensemble *m* des habitants

citizenship ['sɪtɪzənʃɪp] **n** *(of nation)* citoyenneté *f*, *(of city, town)* droit *m* de cité *ou* de bourgeoisie; **to be granted full c. of a**

country se voir accorder la citoyenneté d'un pays; **good c.** civisme *m*

citrate ['sɪtreɪt] N *Chem* citrate *m*

citric ['sɪtrɪk] ADJ *Chem (acid etc)* citrique

citron ['sɪtrən] N *(fruit)* cédrat *m*; *(tree)* cédratier *m*
➤➤ **c. tree** cédratier

citronella [sɪtrə'nelə] N *(plant)* citronnelle *f*

citrus fruit ['sɪtrəs] N agrume *m*

City ['sɪtɪ] N *Br* **the C.** *(district)* la Cité de Londres; *(financial world)* le monde de la finance
➤➤ *Journ* **C. editor** rédacteur, -trice en chef pour les nouvelles financières; *Journ* **C. pages** pages *fpl* financières

> **City**
> La City, quartier financier de la capitale, est une circonscription administrative autonome de Londres ayant sa propre police.

city ['sɪtɪ] N (grande) ville *f*, *Lit* cité *f*; *Br* **cathedral c.** ville épiscopale, évêché *m*; **the Holy C.** la Ville sainte; **the Celestial C.** la Cité céleste; **the Eternal C.** la Ville éternelle; **the C. of Manchester** la ville de Manchester SEE GRAMMAR B7
➤➤ **c. break** *(holiday)* court séjour *m* en ville; *Br* **c. centre** centre *m* de la ville, centre-ville *m*, *pl* centres-villes; **c. council** ≃ conseil *m* d'arrondissement; *Am* **c. editor** rédacteur, -trice en chef pour les nouvelles locales; **c. fathers** édiles *mpl* locaux; *Am* **c. hall** hôtel *m* de ville; *Fig* **you can't win against c. hall** on ne peut pas gagner contre la bureaucratie; *Acct* **c. ledger** *(in hotels, business)* débiteurs *mpl* divers; **c. terminal** *(of airline)* terminal *m* urbain

cityscape ['sɪtɪskeɪp] N paysage *m* urbain

city-state N état-cité *m*, *pl* états-cités

civet ['sɪvɪt] N *(animal, scent)* civette *f*

civic ['sɪvɪk] ADJ *(authority, building)* municipal, -aux; *(duty, pride etc)* civique; **the c. authorities** les autorités *fpl* municipales
➤➤ **c. centre** = centre *m* administratif d'une ville, parfois complété par des équipements de loisirs, ≃ cité *f* administrative; **c. rights** droits *mpl* civils

civics ['sɪvɪks] N *Sch* instruction *f* civique
VOIR GRAMMAIRE A10

civies ['sɪvɪz] NPL *Fam* vêtements *mpl* civils

civil ['sɪv(ə)l] ADJ **1** *(of community, non-military)* civil **2** *(polite)* poli, *Vieilli* civil; **he was very c. to me/to them** il s'est montré très aimable; **keep a c. tongue in your head!** soyez plus poli!; **that's very c. of you** c'est aimable (de votre part)
➤➤ *Law* **c. action** action *f* civile; **c. aircraft** appareil *m* de l'aviation civile; **c. airline** compagnie *f* d'aviation civile; **c. aviation** aviation *f* civile; **c. commotion** agitation *f* sociale; *Mil* **c. defence** protection *f* civile; **c. engineer** ingénieur *m* des travaux publics; **c. engineering** génie *m* civil; **c. law** droit *m* civil; *Br* **C. List** liste *f* civile *(allouée à la famille royale britannique)*; *Law* **c. proceedings** action *f* civile; **c. rights** droits *mpl* civils *ou* civiques; *Admin* **c. servant** fonctionnaire *mf*; *Admin* **c. service** fonction *f* publique, administration *f*; **c. war** guerre *f* civile

civilian [sɪ'vɪljən] N civil, -ile
ADJ civil; **in c. life** dans le civil
➤➤ **c. clothes** tenue *f* civile

civility [sɪ'vɪlɪtɪ] N courtoisie *f*, politesse *f*; **exchange of civilities** échange *m* d'amabilités

civilization [sɪvɪlaɪ'zeɪʃən] N civilisation *f*; *Fam* **it's miles from c.** c'est à des kilomètres de toute civilisation

civilize ['sɪvɪlaɪz] VT civiliser

civilized ['sɪvɪlaɪzd] ADJ *(life, people)* civilisé; **the little girl is really quite c.** la petite fille est très bien élevée; **they have real coffee in their office – very c.** ils ont du vrai café dans leur bureau – la classe!; **their divorce was a very c. affair** ils ont divorcé comme des gens civilisés; **let's be c. about this** restons civilisés; **can't you eat in a c. manner?** tu ne peux pas manger convenablement?

civilizing ['sɪvɪlaɪzɪŋ] ADJ **the c. influence of …** l'influence civilisatrice de …; **the new teacher has had a c. influence on them** le nouveau professeur semble les avoir calmés

civvies ['sɪvɪz] NPL *Fam* vêtements *mpl* civils

civvy ['sɪvɪ] ADJ *Fam* **to get back to c. street** rentrer dans le civil; **on c. street** dans le civil

CJD [siːdʒeɪ'diː] N *(abbr* Creutzfeldt-Jakob disease) MCJ *f*; **new variant C.** nouveau variant *m* de MCJ

cl *(abbr* centilitre) cl

clack [klæk] N *(sound)* bruit *m* sec, claquement *m*; **click-c.** clic-clac *m*
VI *(make sound)* cliqueter

clacking ['klækɪŋ] N *(noise)* claquement *m*

clad[1] [klæd] PT, PP *see* clothe

clad[2] VT *(-dd-)* *Tech (wall, metal plate etc)* revêtir (**with** de)

cladding ['klædɪŋ] N *Tech* revêtement *m*

claim [kleɪm] N **1** *(demand)* *(for damages, compensation etc)* revendication *f*, réclamation *f*; **to make** *or* **put in a c. for damages** demander une indemnité, réclamer des dommages-intérêts; **to put in a c.** *(in insurance)* demander à être indemnisé; **pay c.** revendications *fpl* salariales
2 *(right)* droit *m* (**to sth** à qch); **legal c. to sth** titre *m* juridique à qch; **to put in a c.** faire valoir ses droits; **to have a c. to sth** avoir droit à qch; **what is her c. to the throne?** quel est son titre à la couronne?; **they have no c. to the land** ils n'ont aucun droit sur le terrain; **to lay c. to** *(property etc)* prétendre à, revendiquer son droit à; *(skills)* s'attribuer; *Fig* **to have a c. on sb** avoir prise sur qn; *Fig* **I have many claims on my time** je suis très pris; **his only c. to fame** la seule chose notable qu'il ait faite
3 *(assertion)* déclaration *f*; **she makes no c. to being original** elle ne prétend pas être originale; **exaggerated claims have been made for this medicine** on a exagéré l'efficacité de ce médicament
4 *Min* concession *f* (minière)
VT **1** *(demand as a right)* *(right, territory)* revendiquer; *(respect, attention)* exiger, demander; **to c. sth from sb** réclamer qch à qn; **to c. damages** réclamer des dommages et intérêts; **to c. a privilege** prétendre à un privilège; **have you claimed your allowance?** est-ce que tu as réclamé ton allocation?; **to c. the right to do sth** revendiquer le droit de faire qch; **to c. responsibility for an attack** *(of terrorist)* revendiquer un attentat
2 *(assert)* **to c. that …** prétendre *ou* affirmer que … + *ind*; **he claims knowledge of their plans** il prétend *ou* affirme qu'il connaît leurs projets; **to c. acquaintance with sb** prétendre connaître qn; **he claims to be an expert** il se prétend expert; **I don't c. to be an expert** je ne prétends pas être un expert
3 *(collect, take)* *(baggage)* récupérer; *(lost property)* réclamer; **has anyone arrived to c. her?** *(lost child)* est-ce que quelqu'un est venu la chercher?; **the sea claims many victims** la mer fait de nombreuses victimes
VI *(in insurance)* demander à être indemnisé

➤➤ **claims adjuster** répartiteur *m*; **claims book** livre *m* des réclamations; **claims cover** garantie *f* de recours; **c. form** *(for insurance)* formulaire *m* de déclaration de sinistre; *(for expenses)* note *f* de frais
➤ **claim back** VT SEP *(expenses, cost)* se faire rembourser

claimant ['kleɪmənt] N *(for social security, insurance etc)* demandeur, -eresse; *(to throne)* prétendant, -ante; **rightful c.** ayant droit *m*, *pl* ayants droit

clairvoyance [kleə'vɔɪəns] N **1** *(second sight)* voyance *f*, don *m* de seconde vue **2** *(shrewdness)* clairvoyance *f*

clairvoyant [kleə'vɔɪənt] ADJ **1** doué de seconde vue **2** *(shrewd)* clairvoyant
N voyant, -ante, extra-lucide *mf*, *pl* extra-lucides

clam [klæm] N **1** *(mollusc)* palourde *f*, clam *m*; **to shut up like a c.** refuser de dire quoi que ce soit **2** *Am Fam (dollar)* dollar *m*
➤➤ *Culin* **c. chowder** = potage *m* épais aux palourdes
➤ **clam up** VI *(-mm-)* *Fam* se fermer comme une huître; **don't c. up on me** parle-moi

clambake ['klæmbeɪk] N *Am (picnic)* = pique-nique *m* où l'on mange des fruits de mer; *Fam (noisy gathering)* grande réunion *f* tapageuse

clamber ['klæmbər] N **it was quite a c.** c'était une sacrée grimpette
VI escalader; **to c. up a wall** escalader un mur; **he clambered over the pile of bricks** il a escaladé le tas de briques; **they clambered out of the car** ils se sont extirpés de la voiture

clamminess ['klæmɪnɪs] N *(of skin)* moiteur *f* froide; *(of air)* humidité *f* froide

clammy ['klæmɪ] ADJ *(hands, skin)* moite; *(atmosphere)* froid et humide

clamor ['klæmər] N, VI *Am* = clamour

clamorous ['klæmərəs] ADJ *esp Lit* bruyant; *(crowd)* vociférant

clamorously ['klæmərəslɪ] ADV *esp Lit* bruyamment

clamour ['klæmər] N **1** *(noise)* clameur *f*, cris *mpl*, vociférations *fpl* **2** *(protest)* tollé *m*; **there was a great c.** ça a été un tollé général
VI vociférer, crier; **to c. for sth** réclamer *ou* demander qch à grands cris

clamp [klæmp] N **1** crampon *m*, presse *f*; *(of vice)* mordache *f*; *(for wire)* pince *f*; *Surg* clamp *m*; *Aut* **(wheel) c.** sabot *m* de Denver **2** *Agr (for potatoes)* silo *m* (temporaire)
VT **1** *(fasten)* cramponner; *(precision instrument)* bloquer; *Surg* clamper; **to c. two pieces of wood together** cramponner deux morceaux de bois **2** *(car)* mettre un sabot à **3** *Agr (potatoes)* mettre en silo
➤ **clamp down** VT SEP fixer par un crampon
VI *Fam (become stricter)* sévir (**on sb/sth** contre qn/qch); **the police are clamping down on illegal parking** la police sévit contre *ou* devient plus sévère avec les automobilistes en stationnement interdit

clampdown ['klæmpdaʊn] N renforcement *m* des mesures (de répression) (**on** contre); **as a result of the c.** suite au mesures de répression

clamping ['klæmpɪŋ] N *(of cars)* immobilisation *f* des voitures au moyen de sabots de Denver

clamshell ['klæmʃel] N *(mobile phone)* téléphone *m* portable avec couvercle

clan [klæn] N *Scot (of tribe)* clan *m*; *Fig* bande *f*, clique *f*; **the head of the c.** le chef de *ou* du clan; *Fig* **gathering of the clans** réunion *f* d'adhérents *ou* de partisans
➤➤ **c. name** nom *m* du clan; **c. tartan** couleurs *fpl* du clan

clandestine [klæn'destɪn] ADJ clandestin

clandestinely [klæn'destɪnlɪ] ADV clandestinement

clang [klæŋ] N son *m ou* bruit *m* métallique ▪ VI retentir, résonner, rendre un son métallique; **the gate clanged shut** le portail s'est refermé avec un bruit métallique ▪ VT *(bell etc)* faire résonner; **she clanged the gate shut** elle ferma le portail bruyamment

clanger ['klæŋər] N *Br Fam* bourde *f*; **to drop a c.** faire une gaffe *ou* une boulette, gaffer

clank [klæŋk] N *(of chains etc)* bruit *m* métallique ▪ VI *(of chain, bucket)* rendre un bruit métallique

clannish ['klænɪʃ] ADJ *Pej (person)* qui a l'esprit de clan; *(group)* fermé

clansman, *pl* **clansmen** ['klænzmən, -mən] N = membre *m* d'un clan

clanswoman, *pl* **clanswomen** ['klænzwʊmən, -wɪmɪn] N = membre *f* d'un clan

clap[1] [klæp] N *(with hands)* **to give sb a c.** applaudir qn; **to give sb a big c.** applaudir qn bien fort; **she got a c. for that** on l'a applaudie pour ça; **to give sb a c. on the back** donner une tape sur le dos de qn; **a c. of thunder** un coup de tonnerre ▪ VT (**-pp-**) **1 to c. one's hands** battre des mains; **to c. a performer** applaudir un artiste; **to c. sb on the back** donner à qn une tape sur le dos **2** *(put)* mettre, *Fam* coller; **to c. sb in irons** mettre qn aux fers; **to c. sb in prison** fourrer qn en prison; *Fam* **to c. eyes on sb/sth** voir qn/qch; *Fam* **I've never clapped eyes on her before** je ne l'ai jamais vue de ma vie ▪ VI *(of person, audience etc)* applaudir
▶ **clap on** VT SEP **he clapped his hat on** il a enfoncé son chapeau sur sa tête; *Naut* **to c. on more sail** augmenter de toile

clap[2] N *Sl (gonorrhoea)* chaude-pisse *f*; **he's got a dose of the c.** il a la chaude-pisse; **to give sb the c.** passer la chaude-pisse à qn

clapboard ['klæpbɔːd] N *Am Constr* planche *f* à clin; *(house)* maison *f* à clins; **c. house** maison à clins

Clapham ['klæpəm] N *Br* **the man on the C. omnibus** le citoyen lambda; **it's like C. Junction in here** c'est un vrai moulin ici

clapometer [klæ'pɒmɪtər] N *TV etc* applaudimètre *m*

clapped out [klæpt] ADJ *Br Fam (person)* crevé, éreinté; *(car, television etc)* pourri

clapper ['klæpər] N **1** *(of bell)* battant *m* **2** *Agr (for scaring birds)* moulin *m* à claquet; *Br Fam* **like the clappers** *(to work)* comme un enragé; *(to run)* comme un dératé; *(to drive)* comme un fou
▶▶ **c. valve** (soupape *f* à) clapet *m*

clapperboard ['klæpəbɔːd] N *TV, Cin* clap *m*, claquette *f*

clapping ['klæpɪŋ] N *(applause)* applaudissements *mpl*

claptrap ['klæptræp] N **1** *Fam* sottises *fpl*; **to talk c.** raconter des histoires; **what c.!** quel tissu d'âneries *ou* de sottises! **2** *TV, Cin (clapperboard)* clap *m*

claque [klæk] N *Theat* claque *f*

claret ['klærət] N **1** *(wine)* bordeaux *m* rouge **2** *(colour)* bordeaux *m inv* ▪ ADJ *(coloured)* bordeaux *inv*

clarification [klærɪfɪ'keɪʃən] N **1** *(further explanation)* clarification *f*, *(of question etc)* éclaircissement *m*, élucidation *f*; **to ask for c.** demander des éclaircissements **2** *(of butter, stock)* clarification *f*, *(of wine)* collage *m*

clarify ['klærɪfaɪ] VT **1** *(thinking)* clarifier; *(mind, views, opinions)* éclaircir; *(question)* élucider **2** *(butter, stock)* clarifier; *(wine)* coller ▪ VI *(of liquid, one's thoughts)* se clarifier, s'éclaircir

clarinet [klærɪ'net] N clarinette *f*

clarinettist [klærɪ'netɪst] N clarinettiste *mf*

clarion ['klærɪən] N *Lit* clairon *m*; *Fig* **the speech was a c. call to …** le discours était un appel à …

clarity ['klærɪtɪ] N clarté *f*

clash [klæʃ] N **1** *(noise)* fracas *m*; *(of swords etc)* cliquetis *m*; *(of cymbals)* son *m* assourdissant **2** *(conflict)* *(of colours, styles)* discordance *f*, *(of opinions)* conflit *m*, choc *m*; *(of doctrines)* opposition *f*, *(between people)* affrontement *m*; *(between mobs)* échauffourée *f*; **a c. of interests** un conflit d'intérêts; **we had a slight c. of opinions** nous avons eu un léger désaccord; **clashes on the border** des affrontements à la frontière; **there was a c. (between them) over the methods to be used** il y a eu un conflit entre eux quant aux méthodes à utiliser; **c. of personalities, personality c.** incompatibilité *f* de caractères ▪ VI **1** *(of cymbals)* résonner (bruyamment); *(of swords etc)* s'entrechoquer **2** *(come into conflict)* entrer en conflit, s'affronter; **police clashed with protestors** il y a eu des heurts entre la police et les manifestants; **they clashed over how to solve the problem** ils sont entrés en conflit quant à la manière de résoudre le problème; **their personalities c.** leurs personnalités se heurtent, il y a incompatibilité entre leurs caractères **3** *(of colours)* jurer, détonner; *(of evidence, explanations etc)* ne pas correspondre; *(of literary styles)* être discordant; *(of events, appointments)* tomber le même jour/la même heure ▪ VT *(cymbals)* faire résonner

clashing ['klæʃɪŋ] ADJ **1** *(sound)* bruyant, retentissant **2** *(opinions)* opposé; *(colours, styles)* discordant

clasp [klɑːsp] N **1** *(fastener)* *(on brooch, medal etc)* agrafe *f*, *(on book, necklace, handbag)* fermoir *m*; **2** *(grip)* étreinte *f* ▪ VT **1** *(fasten)* *(bracelet etc)* fermer **2** *(grip)* *(in hand)* serrer; *(in arms)* *(person)* étreindre, enlacer; *(object)* prendre dans ses bras; **to be clasped in each other's arms** se tenir étroitement enlacés; **to c. sb's hand** serrer la main à qn; **to c. one's hands** joindre les mains; **to c. one's knees** entourer ses genoux de ses bras
▶▶ **c. knife** couteau *m* pliant

class [klɑːs] N **1** *(in social hierarchy)* classe *f* **2** *Fam (quality)* classe *f*; **to have c.** avoir de la classe **3** *Sch (lesson)* cours *m*; *(group of pupils)* classe *f*; **the French c.** le cours de français; **evening c.** cours du soir; **day release classes** scolarité *f* à temps partiel; **in c.** en classe **4** *Am Sch (students in year)* promotion *f*; **the c. of '89** la promotion 1989 **5** *(category)* catégorie *f*, classe *f*, *Rail, Aviat, Naut, Biol* classe; **to be in a c. of one's own, to be in a c. by oneself** *(of person, thing)* être unique, être de loin le/la meilleur(e); *Iron* **what c. are you travelling?** en quelle classe est-ce que vous voyagez?; *Br Univ* **what c. (of) degree did you get?** quelle mention est-ce que tu as eu (à ton diplôme)?; **of Olympic c.** digne de participer aux Jeux olympiques ▪ ADJ *Fam (excellent)* classe *inv*; **a c. car** une voiture classe; **a c. player** un joueur hors pair; **she's a real c. act** elle est vraiment classe ▪ VT classer; **to c. sb/sth with …** assimiler qn/qch à …; **classed first** classé premier
▶▶ *Am Law* **c. action** recours *m* collectif en justice; **c. distinctions** distinctions *fpl* entre les classes; **c. prejudice** préjugés *mpl* sociaux; **c. struggle** lutte *f* des classes; **c. traitor** personne *f* qui renie ses origines sociales; **c. war** lutte des classes

class-conscious ADJ conscient des différences de classe

class-consciousness N conscience *f* des différences de classe

classic ['klæsɪk] ADJ classique; **c. records of the sixties** des classiques de la musique des années soixante; *Fam* **a c. example** un exemple classique *ou* typique ▪ N *(book etc)* classique *m*; *Horseracing* classique *f*; **a c. of romantic poetry** un classique de la poésie romantique; *Fam* **it was a c.!** ça payait!; **classics** *(usu with sing verb)* *(subject)* les langues *fpl* classiques, les humanités *fpl*; **a classics degree** une licence en latin et (en) grec
▶▶ *Horseracing* **c. race** course *f* classique

classical ['klæsɪk(ə)l] ADJ **1** *(civilization etc)* de l'antiquité; **the c. world** le monde de l'antiquité; **in c. times** dans l'antiquité; **c. Greece** la Grèce antique; **c. scholar** humaniste *mf* **2** *Mus, Art, Liter etc* classique
▶▶ *Econ* **c. economics** économie *f* classique

classically ['klæsɪk(ə)lɪ] ADV classiquement; **c. trained** *(pianist etc)* ayant reçu une formation classique

classicism ['klæsɪsɪz(ə)m] N **1** *Art, Liter, Archit etc* classicisme *m* **2** *Ling* tour *m ou* locution *f* emprunté(e) aux langues classiques

classicist ['klæsɪsɪst] N humaniste *mf*, *(advocate of classical studies)* partisan, -ane des études classiques

classification [klæsɪfɪ'keɪʃən] N **1** *(action)* *(of plants, animals)* classification *f*, *(of papers, competitors, books etc)* classement *m* **2** *(category)* classification *f*, classe *f*

classified ['klæsɪfaɪd] ADJ **1** *(arranged)* classé **2** *(secret)* *(document, information)* confidentiel
▶▶ *Journ* **c. advertisements** petites annonces *fpl*; *Sport* **c. results** résultats *mpl* et classements *mpl*

classifieds ['klæsɪfaɪdz] NPL *Journ* **the c.** les petites annonces *fpl*

classifier ['klæsɪfaɪər] N *(person)* classificateur, -trice

classify ['klæsɪfaɪ] VT **1** classer; **their music is classified as jazz** leur musique est classée comme étant du jazz **2** *(make secret)* *(document etc)* classer confidentiel

classless ['klɑːslɪs] ADJ *(society)* sans classes; *(accent)* neutre

classmate ['klɑːsmeɪt] N **1** *Sch (in same class)* camarade *mf* de classe **2** *Am Univ (in same year)* camarade *mf* de promotion

classroom ['klɑːsruːm] N *Sch* (salle *f* de) classe *f*

classy ['klɑːsɪ] ADJ *Fam (person)* qui a de la classe, classieux; *(restaurant)* chic *inv*, *(car, hotel)* de luxe

clatter ['klætər] N bruit *m*, vacarme *m*, fracas *m*; *(of typewriters)* claquement *m*; *(of machine)* ferraillement *m*; **the c. of dishes** les bruits de vaisselle ▪ VI faire du bruit; **we could hear him clattering about in the attic** on l'entendait qui faisait un bruit de tous les diables dans le grenier; **the old cart clattered by** le vieux chariot est passé en faisant du bruit; **to come clattering down** dégringoler avec fracas ▪ VT faire résonner; **don't c. your spoons!** ne faites pas de bruit avec vos cuillers!

Claudius ['klɔːdɪəs] N *Hist* Claude

clause [klɔːz] N **1** *Law (of treaty, law)* clause *f*, article *m*; *(of will)* disposition *f*, **c. of a/the contract** clause contractuelle **2** *Gram* proposition *f* VOIR GRAMMAIRE A4; B2

claused bill [klɔːzd] N *Com* connaissance *m* clausé

claustrophobia [klɔːstrə'fəʊbɪə, klɒs-] N claustrophobie *f*

claustrophobic [klɔːstrə'fəʊbɪk, klɒs-] ADJ *(person)* claustrophobe; **this room feels quite c.** cette pièce donne une impression de claustrophobie; **I feel c.** j'ai un sentiment de claustrophobie

clavichord ['klævɪkɔːd] N *Mus* clavicorde *m*

clavicle ['klævɪk(ə)l] N *Anat* clavicule *f*

claw [klɔː] N **1** *(of cat etc)* griffe *f*, *(of bird of prey)* serre *f*, *(of lobster)* pince *f*; **to sharpen its claws** *(of cat)* se faire les griffes; **to show its/one's claws** *(of cat)*, *Fig* sortir ses griffes; **to draw in its/one's claws** *(of cat)*, *Fig* rentrer ses griffes, faire patte de velours; **c.-footed** *(table etc)* à pied de griffon; *Fig* **to get one's claws into sb** *(trap)* mettre le grappin sur qn; **she's got her claws in me** *(dislikes me)* elle a une dent contre moi **2** *Tech (of hammer)* panne *f* fendue

▸▸ VT *(scratch)* griffer, donner un coup de griffe à; *Fig* **to c. one's way to the top** arriver au sommet par tous les moyens

▸▸ VI **to c. at sth** *(of cat)* saisir qch avec ses griffes, s'accrocher à qch; *(grip)* s'accrocher à qch, agripper qch; *(try to grip)* essayer de s'accrocher à qch *ou* d'agripper qch; **she clawed at my face** *(scratched me)* elle m'a griffé au visage; *(tried to scratch me)* elle a essayé de me griffer au visage

▸▸ **c. hammer** marteau *m* à pied-de-biche, marteau fendu; **c. marks** griffures *fpl*

▸ **claw back** VT SEP **1** *Fin (expenditure)* récupérer **2** *(regain)* regagner péniblement; **she clawed her way back to a prominent position** à force de persévérance, elle a réussi à regagner une position influente

clawback ['klɔːbæk] N *Fin* récupération *f*

clay [kleɪ] N argile *f*, (terre-)glaise *f*, **(modelling) c.** pâte *f* à modeler; *Lit* **idol with feet of c.** idole aux pieds d'argile; *Lit* **mortal c.** le corps humain; *Tennis* **to play on c.** jouer sur terre battue; *Tennis* **to be good on c.** jouer bien sur la terre battue

▸▸ *Tennis* **c. court** court *m* en terre battue; **c. pigeon** pigeon *m* d'argile *ou* de ball-trap; *Am Fam Fig (sitting duck)* cible *f* facile; **c. pigeon shooting** ball-trap *m*, *pl* ball-traps **c. pipe** pipe *f* de *ou* en terre; **c. pit** glaisière *f*, **c. soil** terre *f* glaise

clayey ['kleɪɪ] ADJ *(soil)* argileux, glaiseux

claymation [kleɪ'meɪʃən] N *Br Cin*, *TV* = animation *f* de figurines en pâte à modeler

claymore ['kleɪmɔːr] N *Scot Hist* = sabre *m* écossais à deux tranchants

CLEAN [kliːn]

ADJ	propre **1** ▪ net **1, 2** ▪ pur **1**
ADV	complètement
N	nettoyage
VT	nettoyer ▪ vider
VI	se nettoyer **2** ▪ nettoyer **3**

ADJ 1 propre, net; *(clothes)* propre; *(water)* pur, propre; *(sheet of paper)* blanc, *f* blanche; *(break)* franc, net; *(wound)* pas infecté; *(joke)* décent; **to keep sth c.** tenir qch propre; *Fam* **keep it c.!** *(the joke, story etc)* pas de grossièretés!; *Fig Fam* **to be c.** *(innocent)* n'avoir rien à se reprocher; *(without incriminating material)* n'avoir rien sur soi; *(not carrying drugs)* ne pas avoir de drogue sur soi; *(not carrying weapons)* ne pas être armé; *(no longer addicted to drugs)* avoir décroché; **good c. fun** jeu *m* innocent; **to make a c. break** *(in relationship)* en finir une bonne fois pour toutes; *Fig* **to show sb a c. pair of heels** *(run away)* s'enfuir devant qn; **he's showing the other runners a c. pair of heels** il a pris une belle avance sur les autres concurrents; **to make a c. copy of sth** mettre qch au net; **he made a c. sweep of the medals/prizes** il a raflé toutes les médailles/tous les prix; **c. (driving) licence** permis *m* de conduire vierge; *Com* **c. on board** net de réserves à bord; **c. living** vie *f* saine; **the doctor gave him a c. bill of health** le docteur l'a trouvé en parfaite santé

2 *(sharp, well-defined)* **c. (out)lines** contours *mpl* nets; **car with c. lines** voiture aux lignes élégantes

3 *Sport Fam (honest) (player, boxer)* fair-play *inv*; qui joue franc jeu

ADV *Fam (completely)* **I c. forgot** j'ai complètement oublié; **they got c. away** ils se sont échappés sans laisser de traces; **we're c. out of sugar** nous n'avons plus de sucre du tout; **to cut c. through sth** couper *ou* traverser qch de part en part; **to come c.** avouer, dire toute la vérité

N nettoyage *m*; **to give sth a c.** nettoyer qch

VT *(floor, house etc)*, *Med (sore, ulcer)* nettoyer; *Culin (fish, poultry)* vider; *(boiler)* décrasser; **to c. one's teeth** se laver les dents; **to c. one's nails** se nettoyer *ou* se curer les ongles; **to c. the mud off one's shoes** enlever la boue de ses chaussures; **to c. one's plate** *(eat everything on it)* finir son assiette; *Am* **to c. house** faire le ménage

VI 1 *(do the cleaning)* faire le ménage

2 *(of pan etc)* se nettoyer

3 *(of cleaning product, detergent)* nettoyer

▸▸ **c. bill** *Fin* effet *m* libre, traite *f* libre; *Com* connaissement *m* net; *St Exch* **c. float** taux *mpl* de change libres *ou* flottants; *Typ* **c. proof** *(with few corrections)* épreuve *f* peu chargée; *(final)* épreuve pour bon à tirer; **c. room** *Med* pièce *f* aseptisée; *Comput* salle *f* blanche

▸ **clean out** VT SEP **1** *(cupboard etc)* nettoyer; *(furnace, boiler)* curer, décrasser; *(ditch)* vidanger

2 *Fam (leave without money)* nettoyer, laisser sans un rond; **they cleaned out the safe** ils ont vidé le coffre; **cleaned out** *(penniless)* nettoyé (à sec), fauché

3 *(buy, take all of)* **to c. a shop out of sugar** dévaliser un magasin de son stock de sucre

▸ **clean up** VT SEP **1** *(dirt etc)* enlever; *(room etc)* nettoyer; *(make less polluting) (engine)* dépolluer; *Fig (television)* assainir; **to c. oneself up** se débarbouiller; *Fig* **to c. up a town** *(get rid of enemy, gangsters etc)* nettoyer une ville; **to c. up one's act** *(of lewd comedian)* rendre son spectacle moins choquant; *(of corrupt or inefficient organization)* faire le ménage; *(of unsatisfactory employee, pupil)* s'améliorer

2 *Am Sl (obtain)* **to c. up a thousand dollars** gagner *ou* ramasser mille dollars

VI 1 *(in room, building etc)* nettoyer; *(wash oneself)* se débarbouiller

2 *(put back in order)* nettoyer, ranger, remettre tout en ordre; **he expects us to c. up after him** il compte sur nous pour nettoyer après lui

3 *(repair damage)* réparer les dégâts

4 *Fam (make a lot of money)* ramasser une fortune

clean-cut ADJ *(lines)* d'une grande netteté; *(man)* à l'apparence très soignée

cleaner ['kliːnər] N **1** *(person)* employé, -ée du service de nettoyage; *(in home)* personne *f* qui fait le ménage; *(woman)* femme *f* de ménage; **(dry) c.** teinturier, -ière; **to take sth to the c.'s** donner qch à nettoyer *ou* au nettoyage; *Fam* **to take sb to the c.'s** *(cheat)* nettoyer qn, plumer qn; *(defeat)* battre qn à plates coutures **2** *(device, machine)* **(vacuum) c.** aspirateur *m*; **pipe c.** cure-pipe *m*, *pl* cure-pipes **3** *(product)* produit *m* nettoyant *ou* pour nettoyer; *(for clothes)* détachant *m*

cleaning ['kliːnɪŋ] N nettoyage *m*; *(in household)* ménage *m*; *(of boiler)* décrassage *m*; *Culin (of fish)* vidage *m*

▸▸ **c. fluid** produit *m* nettoyant; **c. lady** femme *f* de ménage; **c. materials** produits *mpl* d'entretien; **c. staff** personnel *m* de nettoyage; **c. up** *(of room)*, *Fig (of neighbourhood)* nettoyage *m*; *(of exhaust gases)* dépollution *f*, **c. woman** femme de ménage

clean-limbed [kliːn'lɪmd] ADJ bien proportionné

cleanliness ['klenlɪnɪs] N propreté *f*, **c. of habit** habitudes *fpl* de propreté; *Prov* **c. is next to godliness** la propreté du corps s'apparente à la pureté de l'âme

clean-living ADJ *(person)* réglé, qui mène une vie réglée

cleanly[1] ['kliːnlɪ] ADV proprement, nettement; **to break c.** se casser net

cleanly[2] ['klenlɪ] ADJ *(person)* propre (par habitude)

cleanness ['kliːnnɪs] N *(of habits, language, apartment etc)* propreté *f*, *(of water)* pureté *f*, *(of lines)* netteté *f*, pureté

clean-out N nettoyage *m*; **to give a room a c.** nettoyer une pièce

clean-room clothing N *Comput* vêtements *mpl* de salle blanche

cleanse [klenz] VT *(face)* démaquiller; *(wound)* nettoyer; *(blood)* purifier; *(air)* épurer; *Arch*, *Lit (heart, soul)* purifier

cleanser ['klenzər] N *(for skin)* démaquillant *m*

clean-shaven ADJ *(man, face)* glabre

cleansing ['klenzɪŋ] N *(of face)* démaquillage *m*; *(of blood, soul)* purification *f*

▸▸ **c. cream** crème *f* démaquillante; *Br Admin* **c. department** service *m* du nettoyage; **c. lotion, c. milk** *(for skin)* lait *m* démaquillant; **c. pads** disques *mpl* démaquillants

cleanup ['kliːnʌp] N *(of room)*, *Fig (town)* nettoyage *m*; **to give sth a c.** nettoyer qch

CLEAR [klɪər]

ADJ	clair **1–3** ▪ tranquille **1** ▪ net **2, 3, 5** ▪ évident **2** ▪ certain **4** ▪ libre **6**
VT	débarrasser **1** ▪ innocenter **2** ▪ franchir **6** ▪ autoriser **9** ▪ clarifier **11**
VI	s'éclaircir **1**

ADJ 1 *(sky, complexion, eye, sound etc)* clair; *(weather)* clair, dégagé; *(water)* clair, limpide; **on a c. day** par temps clair; *TV* **the picture was very c.** l'image était très nette; **to have c. skin** avoir la peau nette; **a c. conscience** une conscience tranquille; **my conscience is c.** j'ai la conscience tranquille; **c. voice** voix *f* claire *ou* nette

2 *(unmistakeable, manifest)* clair, net; *(sign)* évident; **a c. case of bribery** un cas manifeste de corruption; **the meaning of the sentence was c.** le sens de la phrase était clair; **to make one's meaning** *or* **oneself c.** se faire comprendre; **have I made myself c.?** est-ce que je me suis bien fait comprendre?; **to make it c. to sb that ...** bien faire comprendre à qn que ...; **she made it quite c. that ...** elle lui/nous/*etc* a bien fait comprendre que ...; **the letter doesn't make it c. when they will arrive** la lettre n'indique pas clairement quand ils vont arriver; **I want to be quite c. on this point** je tiens à ce qu'il n'y ait aucun malentendu sur ce point; **is that c.?** *(do you understand?)* c'est clair?; **it is c. that ...** il est clair *ou* évident que ...; **it was not c. who had won** on ne savait pas exactement qui avait gagné; **it is not yet c. whether ...** on ne sait pas encore si ...; **as c. as daylight** *or* **crystal** clair comme le jour *ou* comme de l'eau de roche

3 *(not confused) (description, explanation, argument, style)* clair, net; *(reasoning)* lucide, clair; *(instructions)* clair; **c. thinker/ mind** esprit *m* lucide; **c. thinking is essential** la clarté de pensée est essentielle; **to keep a c. head** garder les idées claires

4 *(certain)* **to be c. about sth** être certain de qch; **are you c. about what you have to do?** es-tu sûr de ce que tu as à faire?; **there's something I'm not c. about** il reste quelque chose dont je ne suis pas sûr; **I wasn't c. what she meant** je n'étais pas sûr de ce qu'elle voulait dire

5 *(unqualified)* **c. profit** bénéfice *m* net; **a c. ten thousand pounds a year** un revenu net de dix mille livres; **c. majority** majorité *f* absolue; *Sport* **c. winner** vainqueur *m* incontesté; **there wasn't a c. winner** on ne pouvait pas dire qui l'avait emporté; *Law* **three c. days** trois jours francs

6 *(unobstructed, free)* libre; *(view etc)* dégagé; **his latest X-rays are c.** ses dernières radios ne montrent rien d'anormal; **to be c. of sth** *(rid of)* être débarrassé de qch; **he was c. of all signs of the disease** il ne montrait aucun symptôme de la maladie; **we were c. of the last checkpoint** nous avions passé le dernier poste de contrôle; **the sea is c. of ice** la mer est libre; **the exhaust pipe is 30 cm c. of the ground** le tuyau d'échappement est à 30 cm du sol; *Aviat* **you are c. to take off** vous êtes autorisé à *ou* vous pouvez décoller; **all c.!** *(there's no traffic, no-one is watching)* vous pouvez y aller, la voie est libre; *Mil* fin d'alerte

ADV we could hear them c. across the valley on les entendait de l'autre bout de la vallée; **to jump five centimetres c. of the bar** franchir la barre avec cinq centimètres de reste; **to hang c. of the ground** être suspendu de manière à ne pas toucher le sol; **to stand c.** s'écarter (**of** de); **stand c. of the doors!** attention aux portes!; *Rail* ≃ attention au départ!; **to keep** *or* **steer c. of sth** éviter qch; *Naut* **to steer c. of a rock** passer au large d'un écueil; **they pulled him c. of the wreckage** ils l'ont dégagé de l'épave; **she was thrown c. of the car** elle a été éjectée de la voiture; **to get c. of sb** échapper à qn; **to get c.** s'échapper; *Sport* **to punch the ball c.** écarter le ballon d'un coup de poing

N 1 to be in the c. *(of person) (free from suspicion)* être lavé de tout soupçon; *(free from debt)* ne pas avoir de dettes; *(out of danger)* être hors de danger

2 *Mil etc* **despatch sent in c.** *(not coded)* dépêche *f* en clair

VT 1 *(free of obstacles) (road, area, entrance)* dégager; *(room etc)* débarrasser, désencombrer; *(forest)* défricher; *(streets, room) (of people)* faire évacuer; *(pipe)* déboucher; *Law* **to c. the court** faire évacuer la salle; **to c. one's conscience** décharger sa conscience; **to c. one's throat** se racler la gorge; **he cleared a space on the floor** il a dégagé un espace sur le plancher; **they cleared 20 acres of forest** ils ont défriché 8 hectares de forêt; **to c. a way** *or* **a passage for sb** frayer un passage à qn; *Fig* **to c. the way for sth** ouvrir la voie pour qch; **to c. a way for oneself** se frayer un passage; **to c. the table** *(after meal)* débarrasser la table; **to c. one's desk** *(tidy)* débarrasser son bureau; *(complete pending tasks)* régler les affaires en suspens; *Naut* **to c. the decks for action** faire le branle-bas de combat; *Fig* **to c. the decks** déblayer le terrain; *Comput* **to c. the screen** vider l'écran; **the rain had cleared the streets** la pluie avait vidé les rues; **to c. slums** assainir des taudis; *Mil* **to c. an area of mines** déminer un terrain; **fresh air clears the head** un peu d'air frais vous éclaircit les idées; *Com* **to c. goods** *(in sale etc)* solder *ou* liquider des marchandises; *Rail* **to c. the line**

dégager la voie; *(after an accident)* déblayer la voie

2 *(exonerate)* disculper, innocenter; **he was cleared of all blame** il a été entièrement disculpé; **to c. oneself** se justifier; **to c. one's name** se disculper; **to clear sb's name** disculper qn

3 *(make less dense) (fog etc)* dissiper; **to c. the air** *(of thunderstorm)* rafraîchir l'air; *(of discussion etc)* mettre les choses au point

4 *(remove)* **to c. sth from** *or* **off sth** enlever qch de qch; **c. all this out of here** débarrassez-moi de tout cela

5 *(empty)* **to c. the postbox** lever le courrier; *Med* **to c. the bowels** purger les intestins

6 *(go past, over etc without touching)* **to c. a barrier (by 10 centimetres)** franchir une barrière (avec 10 centimètres de marge); **to c. a ditch** sauter *ou* franchir un fossé; *Naut* **to c. the harbour** sortir du port, quitter le port; **the ship just cleared the bottom** le bateau a évité le fond de justesse

7 *(make a profit of)* **to c. 10%** faire un bénéfice net de 10%; **I cleared a hundred pounds** j'ai touché cent livres net

8 *Banking (cheque)* compenser, virer

9 *Admin (authorize) (ship)* expédier; *(goods through customs)* dédouaner; **to c. customs** être dédouané; **cleared through customs** dédouané; **to c. sb** *(for security purposes)* attribuer à qn un certificat de sécurité; **he's been cleared** l'enquête de sécurité a été favorable; **to c. sth with sb** *(obtain permission for)* obtenir de qn la permission de faire qch; **I'll need to c. it with the boss** il faut que j'obtienne la permission du patron; **to c. an article for publication** *(ask for authorization)* demander l'autorisation de publier un article; *(authorize)* autoriser la publication d'un article; **the plane was cleared for take-off** l'avion a été autorisé à décoller, l'avion a reçu l'autorisation de décoller

10 *Fin (debt)* acquitter; *(mortgage)* purger; *(account)* solder; **to c. one's property of debt** purger son bien de dettes

11 *(free from impurities) (liquid)* clarifier; *(blood)* purifier

12 *Sport (ball)* dégager; **to c. the ball with one's head** écarter le ballon d'un coup de tête

VI 1 *(of the weather)* s'éclaircir; *(of mist)* se dissiper; *(of sky)* se dégager; **her face cleared** son visage se détendit

2 *(of cheque)* être viré

3 *(of liquid)* se clarifier

4 *Sport (of goalkeeper, fullback)* dégager; **he cleared off the line with his head** il a écarté le ballon de la ligne des buts d'un coup de tête

▶ **clear away VT SEP** *(remove)* enlever, ôter; *(obstacle)* écarter; *(one's things)* ranger
VI *(of mist)* se dissiper

▶ **clear off VT SEP** *(remove)* retirer, enlever
VI *Br Fam (leave)* filer, déguerpir, se tirer; **my wife cleared off** ma femme s'est tirée; **c. off!** tire-toi!, casse-toi!, dégage!
VT INSEP dégager de; **he told them to c. off his land** il leur a dit de dégager de sa propriété

▶ **clear out VT SEP** *(empty) (cupboard)* vider; *(garage, shed)* débarrasser; *Fam (leave without money)* nettoyer
VI *Br Fam (leave building, room etc)* filer, déguerpir; *(leave home) (of spouse etc)* se tirer; **c. out!** filez!, dehors!

▶ **clear up VT SEP 1** *(tidy) (room)* (re)mettre en ordre; *(one's things)* ranger; **we had to c. up the mess** *(after party)* il a fallu tout ranger *ou* nettoyer; *Fig* il a fallu tout arranger

2 *(misunderstanding)* dissiper; *(mystery, doubt, problem)* éclaircir; *(difficulty)* résoudre; **to c. up a matter** tirer une affaire au clair

3 *(cure)* guérir

VI 1 *(of weather)* se (re)mettre au beau
2 *(of rash, headache etc)* disparaître
3 *(tidy up)* ranger; *(after flood, earthquake, bombing etc)* déblayer

clearance ['klɪərəns] **N 1** *(slum)* **c.** assainissement *m* des taudis

2 *(of land)* défrichement *m*; *Hist* **the (Highland) Clearances** = l'expulsion *f* des habitants des Highlands aux XVIIIᵉ et XIXᵉ siècles pour faire paître les moutons

3 *Banking (of a cheque)* compensation *f*

4 *(authorization)* autorisation *f*; *(by customs)* dédouanage *m*, dédouanement *m*; **we got c. to inspect the documents** nous avons eu l'autorisation d'examiner les documents; *Aviat* **(flight) c.** autorisation de vol; *Admin, Mil* **(security) c.** autorisation

5 *Tech (space)* espace *m* (libre); *(of piston etc)* jeu *m*; *Constr (under bridge, doorway etc)* hauteur *f* libre

6 *Ftbl* dégagement *m*

7 *Med (of kidneys)* clairance *f*

▶ ▶ *Com* **c. sale** liquidation *f*, soldes *mpl*

clear-cut ADJ *(outline, feature)* net; *(opinion)* bien défini, tranché, net; *(order)* précis; *(division, dividing line)* net; **it's not quite as c. as that** ce n'est pas aussi simple que ça

clear-headed ['klɪə'hedɪd] **ADJ** lucide

clearing ['klɪərɪŋ] **N 1** *(unblocking, freeing of obstacles) (of track)* dégagement *m*, déblaiement *m*; *(of ground)* défrichement *m*; *(of ditches)* curage *m*

2 *(removal) (of rubbish)* enlèvement *m*

3 *(emptying) (of room)* évacuation *f*

4 *Fin (of debts)* acquittement *m*

5 *Banking* compensation *f*, clearing *m*; **under the c. procedure** par voie de compensation

6 *(in forest)* clairière *f*

▶ ▶ *Banking, Fin* **c. account** compte *m* de compensation; *Br* **c. bank** banque *f* de compensation; **c. house** *Banking, Fin* chambre *f* de compensation; *(for information, materials)* bureau *m* central; *St Exch* **c. member** adhérent-compensateur *m*, *pl* adhérents-compensateurs, membre *m* de compensation; **c. price** cours *m* de compensation; *Mil* **c. station** *(for wounded)* centre *m* de triage *ou* d'évacuation; *Banking, Fin* **c. system** système *m* de compensation; **c. up** *(of house etc)* remise *f* en ordre; *(after earthquake, flood, bombing etc)* déblaiement *m*; **c. up operations have started** les opérations de déblaiement ont commencé

clearly ['klɪəlɪ] **ADV 1** *(to see)* clair; *(to explain, write, speak)* clairement, d'une manière claire; *(to hear)* distinctement; *(to distinguish)* clairement, nettement; **you're not thinking very c.** tu raisonnes de travers; **is that c. understood?** c'est bien compris?; **c. legible** bien lisible **2** *(obviously, plainly)* évidemment; **he is c. wrong** il est évident qu'il a tort; **they are c. different** il est évident qu'ils sont différents; **c., this can't be right** c'est faux, il n'y a aucun doute là-dessus; **c., we'll have to pay** nous devrons payer, c'est certain; **this is c. unacceptable** c'est tout à fait inacceptable; **c. not** manifestement pas

clearness ['klɪənɪs] **N 1** *(of water, atmosphere etc)* clarté *f*, limpidité *f* **2** *(of image)* netteté *f* **3** *(of ideas, explanations)* clarté *f*

clearout ['klɪəraʊt] **N this room needs a good c.** cette pièce a besoin d'un bon nettoyage par le vide; **to have a c.** faire le nettoyage par le vide; **to give the cupboards a c.** faire le nettoyage par le vide dans les placards; *Fig* **the party has had a c.** le parti s'est débarrassé de quelques-uns de ses membres

clear-sighted ADJ 1 *(having good judge-*

ment) lucide, clairvoyant **2** *(having good sight)* qui a une bonne vue

clear-sightedness [-'saɪtɪdnɪs] N *(good judgement)* lucidité *f*, clairvoyance *f*

clear-up N *(of room etc)* remise *f* en ordre; **this place needs a good c.** cet endroit a bien besoin d'être remis en ordre; **c. rate (for crimes)** pourcentage *m* d'affaires élucidées par la police

clearway ['klɪəweɪ] N *Br Aut* grande route *f* à stationnement interdit

cleat [kliːt] N *esp Naut* taquet *m (de tournage)*

cleavage ['kliːvɪdʒ] N **1** *(of woman)* décolleté *m*; **what a c.!** quel décolleté!; **it fell down her c.** c'est tombé dans son décolleté; **to show a lot of c.** *(of woman)* avoir un décolleté plongeant; *(of dress)* être très décolleté **2** *(split) (in party)* clivage *m* **3** *(splitting)* *Tech* fendage *m*; *Geol, Chem* clivage *m*; *Biol* division *f*

cleave [kliːv] *(pt* **cleaved, cleft** [kleft], *Lit* **clove** [kləʊv], *pp* **cleaved, cleft,** *Lit* **cloven** ['kləʊv(ə)n]) VT *Lit (wood, waters)* fendre
VI **1** *Lit* **to c. (asunder)** se fendre, se feuilleter **2** *(of crystals)* se cliver
▸ **cleave to** VT INSEP *(pt, pp* **cleaved)** *Lit (person, party, principle)* être fidèle à

cleaver ['kliːvər] N fendoir *m*; *(for meat)* couperet *m*; *(for wood)* merlin *m*

clef [klef] N *Mus* clef *f*, **bass c.** clef de fa; **C c.** clef d'ut

cleft [kleft] N fente *f*, fissure *f*, crevasse *f*
ADJ fendu
▸▸ *Med* **c. palate** palais *m* fendu; **c. stick** branche *f* fourchue; *Fig* **to be in a c. stick** se trouver dans une impasse

clematis ['klemətɪs, klə'meɪtɪs] N clématite *f*

clemency ['klemənsɪ] N **1** *(mercy)* clémence *f*, indulgence *f* **(to** envers); **to show c.** faire preuve de clémence **2** *(of weather)* douceur *f*

clement ['klemənt] ADJ *Fml* **1** *(person)* clément, indulgent **(to** envers, pour) **2** *(weather)* doux, clément

clementine ['klemənti:n, -aɪn] N clémentine *f*

clench [klen(t)ʃ] VT *(teeth, fist)* serrer; **between clenched teeth** *(to say)* les dents serrées; **to c. sth in one's hand** serrer qch dans la main
VI *(of teeth, hands)* se serrer

Cleopatra [klɪə'pætrə] N *Antiq* Cléopâtre
▸▸ **C.'s needle** l'Obélisque *m* de Cléopâtre

clerestory ['klɪəstɔːrɪ] N *Archit* claire-voie *f*, *pl* claires-voies

clergy ['klɜːdʒɪ] N *(no pl) Rel* clergé *m* **VOIR GRAMMAIRE A11**

clergyman, *pl* **clergymen** ['klɜːdʒɪmən] N *Rel* ecclésiastique *m*; *(protestant)* pasteur *m*; *(catholic)* prêtre *m*

clergywoman, *pl* **clergywomen** ['klɜːdʒɪwʊmən, -wɪmɪn] N *Rel* femme *f* pasteur

cleric ['klerɪk] N *Rel* ecclésiastique *m*

clerical ['klerɪk(ə)l] ADJ **1** *(work)* d'écritures, de bureau; *(staff)* de bureau **2** *Rel* clérical, -aux; *(dress)* ecclésiastique
▸▸ **c. assistant** employé, -ée de bureau; **c. error** *(in document)* faute *f* de copiste; *(in accounting)* erreur *f* d'écriture

clericalism ['klerɪk(ə)lɪz(ə)m] N *Rel* cléricalisme *m*

clerk [klɑːk, *Am* klɜːrk] N **1** *(in office)* employé, -ée de bureau; *(of solicitor)* clerc *m*; **bank c.** employé, -ée de banque; **filing c.,** *Am* **file c.** *Am* au classement; **records c.** archiviste *mf*, **shipping c.** expéditionnaire *mf*, employé, -ée de l'expédition
2 *Am (in shop)* vendeur, -euse
3 *Am (receptionist)* réceptionniste *mf*

---

4 *Rel* **c. in holy orders** ecclésiastique *m*
VI *Am* **1** *(work in office)* travailler comme employé, -ée de bureau
2 *(in shop)* travailler comme vendeur, -euse
3 *Am Pol, Law* **to c. for a senator/a judge** être assistant d'un sénateur/d'un juge
▸▸ *Sport* **c. of the course** commissaire *m* de piste; **C. of the Court** greffier, -ière (du tribunal); *Constr* **c. of (the) works** conducteur *m* des travaux

clever ['klevər] ADJ **1** *(intelligent)* intelligent; *(plan, gadget)* ingénieux, astucieux; *Sch* **c. at mathematics** fort en mathématiques; **he was too c. for us** il s'est montré plus malin que nous; *Pej* **he's/she's too c. by half** il/elle est bien trop malin/maligne; **don't get c. with me** ne fais pas le malin avec moi; *Fam* **a c. Dick** un petit malin **2** *(skilful)* habile, adroit; **to be c. with one's hands** être adroit *ou* habile de ses mains; **c. at doing sth** habile à faire qch; *Fam* **to play it c.** jouer serré

cleverly ['klevəlɪ] ADV **1** *(intelligently)* avec intelligence, intelligemment; *(planned)* ingénieusement; **the dog had c. worked out how to …** le chien avait astucieusement découvert comment … **2** *(skilfully)* habilement, adroitement

cleverness ['klevənɪs] N **1** *(intelligence)* intelligence *f*, *(of invention etc)* ingéniosité *f* **2** *(with hands)* adresse *f*, dextérité *f*

cliché ['kliːʃeɪ] N cliché *m*

clichéd ['kliːʃeɪd] ADJ rebattu; **that's very c.** c'est un vrai cliché

cliché-ridden ADJ bourré *ou* truffé de clichés

click [klɪk] N *(sound)* bruit *m* sec, déclic *m*, clic *m*; *(of camera)* déclic; *Comput (of keys, mouse)* clic; *(with tongue)* claquement *m* de langue; *Ling* **he gave a c. of the tongue** il fit claquer sa langue; *Fig Fam* **something went c.** il y a eu comme un déclic, et puis ça a été le déclic
VI **1** *(make a sound)* faire un petit bruit sec; *Comput (with mouse)* cliquer; *Comput* **to c. on sth** cliquer sur qch; *Comput* **to c. and drag** cliquer et glisser; **she clicked along the pavement in her high heels** ses hauts talons faisaient de petits bruits secs sur le trottoir; **cameras were clicking** on entendait le déclic des appareils; **to c. together** *(of two parts)* s'emboîter (avec un bruit sec); **to c. shut** *(of door etc)* se refermer avec un bruit sec
2 *Fig (become clear)* faire tilt; **now it's clicked** *(of one thing)* ça a fait tilt; *(of something more complicated)* tout s'est mis en place; **it'll c. if you work at it** tu finiras par comprendre si tu t'y mets
3 *Fam (of two people)* **we clicked right away** nous nous sommes tout de suite entendus à merveille; **to c. with the public** *(of play, film)* avoir du succès auprès du public
VT **to c. one's heels** *(when saluting)* (faire) claquer les talons; **to c. one's tongue** claquer la langue
▸▸ *Ling* **c. language** langue *f* à clics; *Com, Comput* **clicks-and-mortar company** = société *f* qui vend ses produits en magasin et sur Internet
▸ **click away** VI *(take photos)* prendre sans cesse des photos; **the photographers were clicking away furiously** les photographes s'en donnaient à cœur joie
▸ **click on** VI *Br Fam (understand)* piger
VT INSEP *Comput* cliquer, cliquer sur

clickable ['klɪkəbəl] ADJ *Comput* cliquable
▸▸ **c. image** image *f* cliquable; **c. image map** image cliquable

clicking ['klɪkɪŋ] N *(noise)* cliquetis *m*

client ['klaɪənt] N *(of shop, lawyer)* client, -ente
▸▸ *Banking* **c. account** compte *m* client;

Com, Mktg **c. base** clientèle *f*; *Com, Mktg* **c. file** dossier *m* client, fichier *m* client; *Pej* **c. government** gouvernement *m* à la solde d'un autre; *Com, Mktg* **c. list** liste *f* de clients; *Pej* **c. state** état *m* à la solde d'un autre

clientele [kliːɒn'tel] N *(of shop, lawyer etc)* clientèle *f*

client-server ADJ *Comput* client-serveur *inv*
▸▸ **c. database** base *f* de données client-serveur; **c. model** modèle *m* client-serveur

cliff [klɪf] N falaise *f*, *(in mountains)* à-pic *m*, *pl* à-pics

cliffhanger ['klɪfhæŋər] N *(film, novel etc)* film *m*/roman *m*/etc à suspense; *(situation)* situation *f* qui vous tient en haleine; **it was a real c.** ça m'a/nous a tenu en haleine jusqu'à la fin; **a real c. of an ending** une fin qui vous tient en haleine; **the election/race was a c.** le résultat de l'élection/de la course est resté incertain jusqu'à la dernière minute

climacteric [klaɪ'mæktərɪk] N climatère *m*

climactic [klaɪ'mæktɪk] ADJ *(scene)* qui constitue le paroxysme; **the c. moment of the film** le paroxysme du film

> Attention: ne pas confondre avec l'adjectif **climatic**.

climate ['klaɪmət] N *Met, Fig* climat *m*
▸▸ *Aut* **c. control (system)** climatiseur *m*

climatic [klaɪ'mætɪk] ADJ climatique

> Attention: ne pas confondre avec l'adjectif **climactic**.

climatologist [klaɪmə'tɒlədʒɪst] N climatologue *mf*

climatology [klaɪmə'tɒlədʒɪ] N climatologie *f*

climax ['klaɪmæks] N **1** *(highest point)* paroxysme *m*; *(of play, piece of music etc)* point *m* culminant; *(of career)* apogée *f*, point culminant; **the c. of the festivities** l'apogée des réjouissances; **to reach a c.** *(of music)* atteindre son point culminant; **to work up to a c.** *(in rhetoric)* procéder par gradation (ascendante); *Theat etc* corser l'action; **as a c. to the entertainment …** comme bouquet de la fête … **2** *(sexual)* orgasme *m*
VI **1** *(reach climax)* atteindre son paroxysme *ou* point culminant; **to c. in a firework display** finir en beauté par un feu d'artifice **2** *(have an orgasm)* jouir

climb [klaɪm] N *(of rock face)* montée *f*, ascension *f*, *(of mountain)* ascension, course *f*, *(steep slope) (of road etc)* côte *f*, montée; *Fig* ascension; *Sport, Aut* **hill c.** course de côte; **to go for a c.** faire de l'escalade; *Aviat* **rate of c.** vitesse *f* ascensionnelle *ou* de montée; **a short c. takes you to the village** une petite montée vous mène au village
VI **1** grimper; **to c. on(to) the roof** monter *ou* grimper sur le toit; **to c. over the wall** escalader le mur; **to c. out of a hole** se hisser hors d'un trou; **to c. into bed** grimper dans son lit; *Fig* **to c. to power** gravir tous les échelons qui mènent au pouvoir; **to c. (socially or in the world)** s'élever (au-dessus de sa condition)
2 *Sport (go mountain climbing)* faire de l'alpinisme; *(go rock climbing)* faire de la varappe
3 *(rise) (of road)* monter; *(of prices)* monter, augmenter, *Fam* grimper
4 *Aviat* prendre de l'altitude, monter; **the plane climbed 200 feet** l'avion a pris 60 mètres d'altitude
VT *(tree)* grimper à *ou* dans; *(ladder)* monter *ou* grimper à; *(cliff, mountain)* escalader
▸ **climb down** VI **1** *(descend)* descendre; **to**

c. down out of a tree descendre d'un arbre **2** *Fig (in negotiations etc)* reculer ▪ **vt insep** descendre
▸ **climb up vt insep** = **climb vt**

climb-down N *Fig* reculade *f*

climber ['klaɪmər] N **1** *(of mountain)* alpiniste *mf*; *(of rock face)* varappeur, -euse; *(leopard, koala etc)* grimpeur, -euse; *Fig Pej* **(social) c.** arriviste *mf* **2** *Bot* plante *f* grimpante

climbing ['klaɪmɪŋ] ADJ *(plant)* grimpant; *(animal)* grimpeur ▪ N escalade *f*, *Sport* alpinisme *m*; **(rock) c.** varappe *f*, *Pej* **social c.** arrivisme *m* ▸▪ *Br* **c. frame** cage *f* à poules *(jeu)*; **c. irons** *(for mountaineer)* grappins *mpl*; *(on boots)* crampons *mpl*; *(for climbing trees, poles)* étriers *mpl*; *Sport* **c. wall** mur *m* d'escalade

clime [klaɪm] N *Lit (climate)* climat *m*; **they have gone to sunnier** *or* **warmer climes** ils sont partis sous des cieux plus cléments; **in these climes** sous ces climats

clinch [klɪntʃ] N **1** *Fam (embrace)* étreinte *f*, **to go into a c.** *(of lovers)* s'étreindre **2** *Boxing* clinch *m*; **to break a c.** briser un corps à corps; **to go into a c.** se prendre corps à corps ▪ **vt** *(settle) (deal)* conclure, clore; *(argument)* confirmer; **that clinches it!** c'est terminé!; **that was what clinched it for me** c'est ce qui m'a décidé ▪ **vi 1** *Boxing* en venir aux prises, se prendre corps à corps **2** *Fam (of lovers)* s'étreindre

clincher ['klɪntʃər] N *Fam* **1** *(argument)* argument *m* irréfutable; **that was the c. for me** *(that realization, experience etc)* c'est ce qui m'a décidé **2** *Sport* but *m*/point *m* décisif

cling [klɪŋ] **vi** *(pt, pp* **clung** [klʌŋ]*)* *(of child)* s'accrocher, se cramponner (**to sth/sb** à qch/qn); *Fig Pej* coller (**to sb** qn); *(of plant) (to wall)* s'accrocher (**to** à); **to c. to the figure** *(of garment)* mouler le corps; **he clung to the rope for dear life** il s'agrippa à la corde de toutes ses forces; **the two children were clinging to each other** les deux enfants étaient serrés l'un contre l'autre; *Fig* **to c. (on) to one's children/wife/ideas** s'accrocher à ses enfants/sa femme/ses idées; **to c. to an opinion** persister dans une opinion; **to c. to a hope** se raccrocher à un espoir ▸▪ **c. peach** pavie *f*

clingfilm ['klɪŋfɪlm] N *Br* film *m* alimentaire

clinging ['klɪŋɪŋ] ADJ *(plant)* qui s'accroche; *(garment)* collant, qui colle; *(material)* qui moule le corps; *(perfume)* tenace; *Fam (person)* collant; *(parent, boyfriend etc)* possessif ▸▪ *Am Fam Fig* **c. vine** pot *m* de colle

clingy ['klɪŋɪ] ADJ *Pej* collant; **she's so c.** *(child)* elle est toujours dans mes pattes; **he's the c. type** c'est le genre collant

clinic ['klɪnɪk] N *Med* **1** *(for outpatients)* dispensaire *m*, centre *m* médical **2** *Br (nursing home)* clinique *f*

clinical ['klɪnɪk(ə)l] ADJ **1** *Med* clinique **2** *Fig (analysis, approach)* froid ▸▪ *Med* **c. psychology** psychologie *f* clinique; *Med* **c. thermometer** thermomètre *m* médical

clinically ['klɪnɪklɪ] ADV **1** *Med* cliniquement; **c. dead** cliniquement mort **2** *Fig (coldly, in detached way)* froidement

clinician [klɪ'nɪʃ(ə)n] N clinicien, -ienne

clink¹ [klɪŋk] N *(sound)* tintement *m* ▪ **vt** *(of glasses etc)* tinter ▪ **vt** faire tinter; **to c. glasses** choquer les verres, trinquer

clink² N *Br Sl (prison)* taule *f*, tôle *f*; **to be in (the) c.** être en taule *ou* tôle

clinker ['klɪŋkər] N **1** *Constr (for tiling)* brique *f* hollandaise; *(vitrified)* brique vitrifiée, brique à four **2** *(cinders) (of forge etc)* mâchefer *m*

clinker-built ADJ *Naut* bordé à clin(s)

clip [klɪp] N **1** *(for attaching, holding)* pince *f*; *(brooch)* clip *m*; *(hair ornament)* barrette *f*; **(paper) c.** trombone *m*; **bicycle** *or* **trouser c.** pince à pantalon, pince-pantalon *m inv* **2** *Elec (of wire, cable)* cosse *f* **3** *(cut) (of dog etc)* tondage *m*; **to give a hedge a c.** couper *ou* tailler une haie; **to give one's nails a c.** se couper les ongles **4** *Fam (blow)* **c. (on the ear)** taloche *f* **5** *Cin (of film, programme etc)* extrait *m* **6** *Am (from newspaper)* coupure *f* ▪ **vt** (**-pp-**) **1** *(fasten)* **to c. (together)** *(papers)* attacher (avec un trombone); **to c. one document to another** attacher un document à un autre; **to c. a brooch on a blouse** accrocher une broche à un chemisier; **to c. a microphone to sb's tie** attacher *ou* fixer un micro à la cravate de qn **2** *(cut) (dog, lawn)* tondre; *(hedge)* couper, tailler; *(metal plate)* couper, cisailler; **to c. the wings of a bird** rogner les ailes à un oiseau; *Fig* **to c. sb's wings** rogner les ailes à qn; **to c. ten seconds off a record** améliorer un record de dix secondes **3** *Rail etc (ticket)* poinçonner **4** *(hit) Tennis* **to c. the line** *(of ball)* mordre la ligne; *Fam* **to c. sb's ear** flanquer une taloche à qn; **I just clipped the wall** j'ai effleuré le mur ▸▪ *Comput* **c. art** clipart *m*; *Fam* **c. joint** = boîte *f* de nuit où l'on pratique des prix excessifs; *TV, Radio* **c. mike** micro-cravate *m*, *pl* micros-cravates
▸ **clip on vt sep** attacher ▪ **vi** s'attacher

clipboard ['klɪpbɔːd] N planchette *f* porte-papiers; *Comput* presse-papiers *m inv*; bloc-notes *m*, *pl* blocs-notes ▸▪ *Comput* **c. file** fichier *m* presse-papiers

clip-clop ['klɪpklɒp] N bruit *m* de sabots; **the horse went c. down the street** on entendit le bruit des sabots du cheval qui descendait la rue

clip-on ADJ qui s'attache avec une pince ▪ N *(earring)* clip *m* ▸▪ **c. earring** clip; **c. microphone** micro-cravate *m*, *pl* micros-cravates; **c. tie** cravate *f* à système

clipped [klɪpt] ADJ *(pronunciation, speech)* saccadé

clipper ['klɪpər] N *Naut* clipper *m* ▸▪ *Aviat* **c. class** classe *f* affaires

clippers ['klɪpəz] NPL *(for the hair etc)* tondeuse *f*, **(hedge) c.** taille-buissons *m inv*; **(nail) c.** coupe-ongles *m inv*

clippie ['klɪpɪ] N *Old-fashioned Br Fam* receveuse *f* (d'autobus)

clipping ['klɪpɪŋ] N **1** *(from newspaper)* coupure *f* de presse **2** **clippings** *(from nails)* rognures *fpl*; *(from hair)* mèches *fpl* (de cheveux coupés); *(from hedge)* bouts *mpl* de branches

clique [kliːk] N *Pej* coterie *f*, clique *f*

cliqu(e)y ['kliːkɪ], **cliquish** ['kliːkɪʃ] ADJ *Fam* qui a l'esprit de clique

clitoral ['klɪtərəl] ADJ clitoridien

clitoridectomy [klɪtərɪ'dektəmɪ] N clitoridectomie *f*

clitoris ['klɪtərɪs] N clitoris *m*

Cllr *abbr* **Councillor**

cloak [kləʊk] N *(grande)* cape *f*, *Fig Lit* **under the c. of night** sous le couvert de la nuit ▪ **vt** couvrir *ou* revêtir d'une (grande) cape; *Fig* **cloaked in mystery** enveloppé de mystère

cloak-and-dagger ADJ *(film, novel)* de cape et d'épée; **it was all very c.** c'était très mystérieux; **what's all this c. stuff about?** qu'est-ce que c'est que ce mystère?

cloakroom ['kləʊkruːm] N *(for coats etc)* vestiaire *m*; *Br (lavatory)* toilettes *fpl*; *Br* **ladies' c.** *(lavatory)* toilettes des dames ▸▪ **c. attendant** préposé, -ée au vestiaire; *Br (in lavatory)* préposé, -ée aux cabinets de toilette

clobber¹ ['klɒbər] N *Br Fam* **1** *(clothes)* frusques *fpl*, fringues *fpl* **2** *(belongings)* bazar *m*, fourbi *m*

clobber² **vt** *Br Fam (hit)* tabasser; *(defeat heavily)* flanquer une raclée à; *(penalize)* écraser, accabler; **the new tax legislation will c. small businesses** les nouvelles lois fiscales vont saigner à blanc les petites entreprises

clobbering ['klɒbərɪŋ] N *Br Fam* **to get a c.** *(be beaten up)* prendre une dérouillée *ou* une raclée; *(be heavily defeated)* se prendre une pâtée; **to give sb a c.** *(beat up)* tabasser qn, flanquer une raclée à qn; *(defeat)* flanquer une raclée à qn

cloche [klɒʃ] N cloche *f*

clock [klɒk] N **1** horloge *f*, *(small)* pendule *f*, *Fam* **to watch the c.** *(of employee)* avoir les yeux rivés sur l'horloge, ne penser qu'à l'heure de la sortie; **I don't pay you to come in here and watch the c.** je ne vous paie pas pour que vous passiez votre temps à ne rien faire; **a full hour by the c.** une bonne heure d'horloge; **to work round the c.** travailler vingt-quatre heures sur vingt-quatre; **a race against the c.** une course contre la montre; **to beat the c.** arriver/finir avant l'heure; **to put** *or* **turn the clocks back** *(in autumn)* retarder les pendules; *Fig* **to put the c. back** revenir en arrière, *Pej* régresser; **the measures will turn the c. back to Victorian times** les mesures nous feront retourner à l'époque victorienne; *Aut* **dashboard c.** pendule de tableau de bord **2** *Aut (milometer)* compteur *m*; *(in taxi)* compteur horokilométrique, taximètre *m*; **15,000 miles on the c.** 15 000 mil(l)es au compteur **3** *Comput* horloge *f* ▪ **vt** *Fam* **1** *Sport etc (measure speed of) (runner etc)* chronométrer **2** *(reach speed)* faire; *Aut* **to c. ninety** faire du 150 chrono; **the fastest time he's clocked this year** son meilleur temps cette année **3** *Br Sl (notice)* repérer; **she clocked him as soon as he walked in** elle l'a repéré dès qu'il est entré ▸▪ **c. golf** jeu *m* de l'horloge; *Comput* **c. rate** fréquence *f* d'horloge; *Comput* **c. speed** fréquence d'horloge; *Comput* **c. speed doubler** doubleur *m* de fréquence (d'horloge)
▸ **clock in vi 1** *Sport (have a time of)* **for the 100 metres she clocked in at nine seconds** elle a fait neuf secondes aux 100 mètres; **the last of the marathon runners clocked in at six hours** le dernier marathonien a effectué le parcours en six heures **2** *Ind (record arrival at work)* pointer (en arrivant); **you clocked in 10 minutes late** vous avez pointé avec 10 minutes de retard ▪ **vt sep** *Ind* **to c. sb in** pointer pour qn
▸ **clock off** *Ind* **vi** *(record departure from work)* pointer (en partant) ▪ **vt sep** **to c. sb off** pointer pour qn
▸ **clock on vi, vt sep** = **clock in vi 2, vt sep**
▸ **clock out vi, vt sep** = **clock off**
▸ **clock up vt sep** *(achieve)* (parvenir à) atteindre; **she has clocked up 700 kilometres in two days** elle a fait 700 kilomètres en deux jours

clock-doubled [-dʌb(ə)ld] ADJ *Comput* à fréquence d'horloge doublée

clocking-in ['klɒkɪŋ] N *Ind* pointage *m* à l'arrivée
▸ ▸ **c. card** fiche *f* de pointage
clocking-off N *Ind* pointage *m* à la sortie
clocking-on N *Ind* = **clocking-in**
clocking-out N *Ind* = **clocking-off**
clocklike ['klɒklaɪk] ADJ *(regularity)* d'horloge
clockmaker ['klɒkmeɪkər] N horloger, -ère
clock-watcher [-wɒtʃər] N *Fam* = employé, -ée qui ne pense qu'à l'heure de sortie
clockwise ['klɒkwaɪz] ADV, ADJ dans le sens des aiguilles d'une montre
clockwork ['klɒkwɜːk] N mouvement *m* d'horloge; *(in toy etc)* mécanisme *m* à ressort; **as regular as c.** réglé comme du papier à musique; **everything's going like c.** tout va *ou* marche comme sur des roulettes; **the hotel runs like c.** l'hôtel marche sans problème ADJ *(toy)* mécanique; *(mechanism)* qui se remonte; **everything is done with c. precision** tout est réglé comme du papier à musique; *Sl* **as queer as a c. orange** *(homosexual)* pédé comme un phoque
clod [klɒd] N **1** *(of earth)* motte *f* **2** *Fam (stupid person)* lourdaud, -e; **you great c.!** espèce de lourdaud!
clodhopper ['klɒdhɒpər] N *Fam* **1** *(person)* lourdaud, -aude **2 clodhoppers** *(shoes)* (grosses) godasses *fpl*
clog¹ [klɒg] N *(shoe)* gros brodequin *m* à semelle de bois; **(wooden) c.** sabot *m*; *Fam* **to pop one's clogs** *(die)* casser sa pipe
▸ ▸ **c. dance** = danse *f* où les participants marquent le rythme avec leurs sabots
clog² (-gg-) VT **1** *(block) (artery, pipe etc)* boucher, obstruer; *(firearm, machine)* encrasser; *(filter)* boucher, encrasser; **our boots got clogged with mud** nos bottes se sont crottées dans la boue **2** *(prevent from moving) (animal)* entraver; *Fig (enterprise etc)* entraver, gêner
VI *(of artery, pipe etc)* se boucher, s'obstruer; *(of firearm, machine)* s'encrasser; *(of filter)* se boucher, s'encrasser
▸ **clog up** VT SEP, VI = **clog** VT **1**, VI
cloister ['klɔɪstər] N **1** *Archit (usu pl)* **cloisters** *(of convent, church etc)* cloître *m* **2** *Rel (monastery)* monastère *m*
VT cloîtrer
cloistered ['klɔɪstəd] ADJ **1** *(life)* de cloître, cloîtré; *Fig* **a c. childhood** une enfance protégée; **to lead a very c. life** mener une vie très protégée **2** *Archit* entouré d'un cloître
clone [kləʊn] N *Bot, Biol, Comput etc* clone *m*; **a Tom Cruise/Marilyn Monroe c.** un sosie de Tom Cruise/Marilyn Monroe
VT *Bot, Biol, Comput* cloner
cloner ['kləʊnər] N *Mktg* cloneur *m*
cloning ['kləʊnɪŋ] N *Bot, Biol, Comput* clonage *m*

CLOSE¹ [kləʊs]

ADJ proche **1, 2** ▪ près **1** ▪ soutenu **3**
▪ lourd **5** ▪ serré **6, 7**
ADV près

ADJ **1** *(in distance, time)* proche; *(to each other)* rapproché; *(ties)* étroit; **we must be c. now** nous devons être près maintenant; **our office is c. to the town hall** notre bureau est près de la mairie; **he was c.** *(of person guessing)* il brûlait; **in c. proximity to sth** dans le voisinage immédiat de *ou* tout près de qch; **to be c. to tears** être au bord des larmes; **to be (very) c. to victory** être (tout) près de la victoire; **at c. intervals** à intervalles rapprochés; **I saw him at c. quarters** je l'ai vu de près; **to fire at c. range** tirer à bout portant

2 *(in relationship)* proche; **to be c. to sb** être proche de qn; **he and his brother are very c.** lui et son frère sont très proches; **Italian is c. to French** l'italien est proche du français; **to be in c. contact** être en contact étroit; **a c. friend** un ami intime; **a c. relative** un parent proche, un proche
3 *(careful) (attention)* soutenu; *(observer)* attentif; *(study)* minutieux; **on closer examination** en y regardant de plus près; **after c. consideration** après mûre réflexion; **to keep (a) c. watch on sb/sth** surveiller qn/qch de près; **a c. copy of sth** une bonne imitation de qch
4 *(secret)* intime; **to keep sth a c. secret** garder le secret absolu sur qch; **to keep sth c.** *(be secretive)* ne rien dire de qch; **to play a c. game** jouer serré
5 *(weather)* lourd; **it's c. in here** *(stuffy)* on étouffe ici; **it's c. today** il fait lourd aujourd'hui
6 *(dense)* serré, dense; *(thicket, woods)* épais, touffu; **c. grain** *(of metal, stone, wood etc)* grain *m* serré *ou* fin; **c. texture** *(of metal, stone etc)* (con)texture *f* serrée, tissu *m* serré; *Mil* **in c. order** *or* **ranks** en rangs serrés
7 *(contest)* serré; **c. election** élection *f* vivement contestée; *Sport* **c. finish** arrivée *f* serrée; **c. match** match *m* serré; **a c. shave** un rasage de près; *Fig* **that was a c. shave** *or* **thing** *or* **call** nous l'avons/ils l'ont/*etc* échappé belle, *Fam* c'était moins une *ou* cinq
8 *Fam* **to be c. with money** être près de ses sous
ADV *(near)* près, de près; **to be** *or* **follow c. behind sb** suivre qn de près; **to stand c. against a wall** se coller contre un mur; **houses c. together** maisons serrées les unes contre les autres; **to sit/stand c. together** être/se tenir serrés; **to keep c.** rester tout près; **it keeps c. to the original** cela reste proche de l'original; **c. to** *or* **by sb/sth** (tout) près de *ou* à proximité de qn/qch; **to keep c. to sb** se tenir tout près de qn; **he lives c. to here** il habite tout près *ou* à deux pas (d'ici); **to come** *or* **draw c./closer to sb** s'approcher/ se rapprocher de qn; **it's brought us closer** ça nous a rapprochés; **put it closer to the door** mets-le plus près de la porte; **c. to the ground** au ras *ou* près du sol; **to cut c.** *(hair)* couper ras; **to keep c. to the text** rester près du texte; **she came c. to losing her job** elle a failli perdre son emploi; **to come c. to death** frôler la mort; **to come c. to the world record** frôler le record du monde; **c. at hand, c. by** tout près, tout contre; **c. on nine (o'clock)** tout près de neuf heures; **to be c. on fifty** *(age)* friser la cinquantaine
N **1** *Br (street)* impasse *f*, cul-de-sac *m*, *pl* culs-de-sac
2 *(of cathedral)* enceinte *f*
▸ ▸ *Mil* **c. combat** corps à corps *m*; *Mus* **c. harmony** tessiture *f* limitée; *Cin, TV* **c. shot** plan *m* rapproché; *Mktg* **c. substitute** substitut *m* rapproché

CLOSE² [kləʊz] N *(end)* fin *f*, conclusion *f*, *(of year)* fin; *(of meeting, session)* clôture *f*, levée *f*; *St Exch* **at c. of business** à la *ou* en clôture; *Lit* **at c. of day** à la tombée du jour; *Cr* **at c. of play** à la fin de la journée; **to draw to a c.** tirer à sa fin
VT **1** *(door, eyes, book, shop etc)* fermer; *(road)* barrer; **a road closed to motor traffic** une route interdite à la circulation automobile; **cold closes the pores** le froid resserre les pores; *Fig* **to c. ranks** serrer les rangs, faire bloc; **the party closed ranks around its leader** le parti a fait bloc autour de son leader
2 *(bring to an end) (matter)* conclure, terminer; *(meeting, session)* lever, clore; *(debate)* fermer; *(account)* fermer, clôturer; **to**

declare the discussion closed prononcer la clôture des débats
3 *(shut down) (factory, shop, railway line etc)* fermer (définitivement)
4 *(finalize) (sale)* conclure; *(deal)* arrêter
5 *Acct* **to c. the books** régler les livres; **to c. an account** arrêter un compte
6 *St Exch (operation)* liquider; *(position)* couvrir
VI **1** *(of door etc)* (se) fermer; *(of wound, hole etc)* se refermer; **the theatre will c. for a month** le théâtre fermera pendant un mois; **theatres c. on Good Friday** les théâtres font relâche le vendredi saint
2 *(end)* finir, se terminer; **I must c. now** *(in letter writing)* je dois te quitter; **I will c. with a story** pour terminer, je vais vous raconter une histoire
3 *(shut down) (of factory, shop, railway line etc)* fermer (définitivement)
4 *St Exch* clôturer; **the shares closed at £1.57** les actions ont clôturé à 1,57 livre; **the share index closed two points down** l'indice (boursier) a clôturé en baisse de deux points
▸ ▸ *Comput* **c. box** case *f* de fermeture; *Br* **c. season** *(in hunting)* fermeture *f* de la chasse; *(in fishing)* fermeture de la pêche; *Ftbl* **intersaison** *f*; *Ling* **c. vowel** voyelle *f* fermée
▸ **close down** VT SEP *(factory etc)* fermer (définitivement)
VI **1** *(of factory, shop etc)* fermer (définitivement), fermer ses portes; *(of shopkeeper)* fermer boutique
2 *Radio, TV* terminer ses émissions
▸ **close in** VI **1** *(approach) (of night)* tomber; **the police/his creditors are closing in** l'étau de la police/de ses créanciers se resserre
2 *(get shorter) (of days)* raccourcir
VT SEP *(enclose) (land etc)* clôturer
▸ **close in on** VT INSEP *(person)* encercler, cerner; **darkness closed in on us** la nuit nous enveloppa
▸ **close off** VT SEP fermer; *(road)* barrer; *Acct* **to c. off an account** arrêter un compte
▸ **close out** VT SEP *St Exch* **to c. a position** boucler *ou* clore *ou* fermer une position
▸ **close round** VT INSEP *(person)* cerner, se presser autour de
▸ **close up** VI **1** *(of aperture)* s'obturer; *(of wound, hole etc)* se refermer
2 *(of people)* se serrer, se tasser; *Mil etc* **c. up!** serrez (les rangs)!
3 *(of shopkeeper)* fermer
VT SEP **1** *(seal) (opening etc)* boucher, obturer
2 *(shop, house)* fermer
3 *Typ (characters)* rapprocher; *Mil etc (ranks)* serrer; **the car accelerated to c. up the gap** la voiture accéléra pour réduire l'écart
▸ **close with** VT INSEP **1** *Com* **to c. with sb** conclure un/le marché avec qn
2 *(in fighting)* **to c. with sb** se battre avec qn

close-cropped [-'krɒpt] ADJ *(hair)* coupé ras; *(grass)* rasé, tondu ras

closed [kləʊzd] ADJ *(door, electrical circuit etc)* fermé; **c. (notice)** *Theat* relâche; *(on shop)* fermé; **behind c. doors** *(of official meeting etc)* à huis clos; **with eyes c.** les yeux fermés; **to have a c. mind** être hermétique aux idées des autres *ou* aux idées nouvelles; **it remains a c. book to me** je n'y comprends rien; **road c. (notice)** rue barrée
▸ ▸ **c. question** question *f* fermée; *Br* **c. season** *(in hunting)* fermeture *f* de la chasse; **c. set** *Math* ensemble *m* fermé; *Cin, TV* plateau *m* fermé; *Ind* **c. shop** *(practice)* = système *m* selon lequel une entreprise n'embauche que des travailleurs syndiqués; *(establishment)* = entreprise *f* qui n'embauche que des travailleurs syndiqués; **c. shop policy**

exclusivité *f* syndicale; *Comput* **c. user group** groupe *m* fermé d'utilisateurs

closed-circuit television N télévision *f* à *ou* en circuit fermé

closed-end ADJ
▸▸ *Fin* **c. (investment) fund** société *f* d'investissement à capital fixe; **c. mortgage** prêt *m* hypothécaire à montant fixe

close-down N **1** *(of factory etc)* fermeture *f* **2** *TV, Radio* fin *f* des émissions

close-fisted [-'fɪstɪd] ADJ avare, pingre

close-fitting ADJ *(dress etc)* bien ajusté

close-knit ADJ *(community etc)* étroitement lié, très uni

closely ['kləʊslɪ] ADV **1** *(to examine, watch)* de près, attentivement; *(to listen)* attentivement; *(to resemble)* beaucoup; *(followed, observed)* de près; *(connected, guarded, related)* étroitement; **c. contested** très disputé; **c. cut** tondu ras **2** *(densely)* **a c. planted forest** une forêt très dense; **c. packed in a box** serré dans une boîte; **two c. written pages** deux pages d'une écriture serrée; **a c. printed book** un livre imprimé très petit; **a c. reasoned argument** une argumentation très détaillée; **c. packed** *(people)* entassé

closeness ['kləʊsnɪs] N **1** *(nearness)* proximité *f* (**to** de)
2 *(of relationship, contact etc)* intimité *f* (**to sb** avec qn)
3 *(of description)* exactitude *f*, *(of translation)* fidélité *f*, exactitude
4 *(stuffiness)* manque *m* d'air
5 *(of weather)* lourdeur *f*
6 *(reserve, secretiveness) (of person)* réserve *f*, caractère *m* réservé
7 *(meanness)* avarice *f*, pingrerie *f*

close-range ADJ
▸▸ *Mil* **c. weapon** arme *f* à courte portée

close-run ADJ *(election, race)* serré; **we won in the end, but it was a c. thing** on a fini par gagner, mais il s'en est fallu d'un cheveu; **he may not be as boring as Thomas but it's a c. thing** il n'est peut-être pas aussi ennuyeux que Thomas, mais presque

close-set ADJ *(eyes)* rapproché

close-shaven ADJ rasé de près

closet ['klɒzɪt] N **1** *esp Am (cupboard)* placard *m*, armoire *f*; *Fam* **to come out of the c.** *(of homosexual)* se déclarer homosexuel, révéler (publiquement) qu'on est homosexuel; *Fam* **many economists are coming out of the c. as Keynesians** beaucoup d'économistes se révèlent keynésiens; *Fam* **many country music fans are now coming out of the c.** bien des fans de country avouent maintenant leur passion **2** *Arch (room)* cabinet *m* de travail, bureau *m* **3** *Old-fashioned* **(water) c.** waters *mpl*, cabinets *mpl*
ADJ *(secret) (discussions etc)* confidentiel; **c. homosexual** = homosexuel, -elle qui n'ose pas s'avouer
VT (**-t-**) **to be closeted with sb** être enfermé avec qn

close-up N *Cin, TV* gros plan *m*, plan serré; **in c.** en gros plan; *Fig* **the programme gives us a c. of life in prison** l'émission nous donne en gros plan de la vie carcérale
ADJ *(shot, photograph, picture)* en gros plan
▸▸ **c. lens** bonnette *f*

closing ['kləʊzɪŋ] ADJ *(final)* dernier, final, -als *ou* -aux; **the c. bid** la dernière enchère
N **1** *(shutting) (of shops, factory, theatre etc)* fermeture *f* **2** *(ending) (of meeting, session)* levée *f*, *(of conference)* clôture *f* **3** *Fin, Admin (of account)* arrêté *m*, règlement *m*; *(of bank account)* fermeture *f*; *St Exch* **c. of a position** clôture *f* d'une position
▸▸ *Typ* **c. bracket** parenthèse *f* fermante; *Cin, TV* **c. credits** générique *f* de fin; **c. date**

(for applications) date *f* limite de dépôt; *(for project)* date de réalisation *(d'une opération)*; **c. down** *(of factory, shop, business)* fermeture (définitive); *Acct* **c. entry** écriture *f* d'inventaire *ou* de clôture; **c. headlines** *(in news programme)* rappel *m* des titres; **c. off** *Acct (of accounts)* arrêté; *Comput (of bad sector)* fermeture; *Am* **c. out** *(of factory, shop, business)* fermeture (définitive); *St Exch* **c. prices** cours *mpl* de clôture; *St Exch* **c. quotation** cotes *fpl* en clôture; **c. remarks** observations *fpl* finales *(à la fin d'une conférence etc)*; **c. speech** discours *m* de clôture; **c. time** heure *f* de fermeture; *St Exch* **c. trade** transactions *fpl* de clôture

closure ['kləʊʒər] N **1** *(of factory etc)* fermeture *f* (définitive); *St Exch* **c. by repurchase** clôture *f* par rachat **2** *Parl* clôture *f*, **to move the c.** voter la clôture **3** *(of crisis, conflict)* résolution *f*, **it gave him a sense of c.** ça lui a permis de tourner la page

clot [klɒt] N **1** *(of blood)* caillot *m* **2** *Br Fam (stupid person)* patate *f*, andouille *f*
VI (**-tt-**) *(of blood)* (se) coaguler
VT *(cream)* caillebotter; *(blood)* coaguler

cloth, *pl* **cloths** [klɒθ, klɒθs] N **1** *(material)* étoffe *f*, *(linen, cotton)* toile *f*; **c. of gold** drap *m* d'or; *Br Fam* **hey, c. ears, didn't you hear me?** espèce de sourdingue, tu n'as pas entendu ce que j'ai dit?; *Fig* **to be cut from the same c.** être coulé dans le même moule **2** *(individual piece)* linge *m*; *(for cleaning)* chiffon *m*; *(tablecloth)* nappe *f*, *Theat* toile *f* *(de décor)* **3** *Rel Fam* **the c.** *(the clergy)* le clergé; **a man of the c.** un membre du clergé
▸▸ **c. binding** reliure *f* en toile; **c. cap** casquette *f* *(symbole de la classe ouvrière britannique)*; **the Labour Party wants to get rid of its c. cap image** les travaillistes veulent se débarrasser de leur image 'prolo'

cloth-bound ADJ relié toile

clothe [kləʊð] VT *(pt, pp* **clad** [klæd], **clothed** [kləʊðd]) *(dress)* vêtir, habiller (**in, with** de); **three children to feed and c.** trois enfants à nourrir et à habiller; **warmly/lightly clad** chaudement/légèrement vêtu

cloth-eared ADJ *Br Fam (deaf)* dur de la feuille

clothes [kləʊðz] NPL vêtements *mpl*, habits *mpl*; **in one's best c.** (tout) endimanché; **to put on/take off one's c.** s'habiller/se déshabiller; **to go to bed with one's c. on** *or* **in one's c.** se coucher tout habillé; **with no c. on** (tout) nu; **dirty c.** *(washing)* linge *m* sale
▸▸ **c. basket** panier *m* à linge; **c. brush** brosse *f* à habits; *Am* **c. closet** penderie *f*, **c. hanger** cintre *m*; **c. hook** patère *f*, **c. peg** pince *f* à linge; **c. pole** poteau *m* de corde à linge; **c. prop** perche *f* de corde à linge; *Am* **c. rack** séchoir *m*

clotheshorse ['kləʊðhɔːs] N séchoir *m* (à linge); *esp Am Fig Fam* **she's a c.** à part les fringues, rien ne l'intéresse

clothesline ['kləʊðzlaɪn] N corde *f* à linge

clothespin ['kləʊðzpɪn] N *esp Am* pince *f* à linge

clothier ['kləʊðɪər] N *Com* **1** *(clothes seller)* marchand, -ande de confections **2** *(cloth seller)* marchand, -ande de drap; *(cloth maker)* fabricant, -ante de drap

clothing ['kləʊðɪŋ] N *(no pl) (clothes)* habillement *m*, vêtements *mpl*; **warm c.** vêtements chauds; **articles of c.** vêtements; **the c. trade** l'industrie *f* du vêtement
▸▸ **c. allowance** indemnité *f* vestimentaire

clotted ['klɒtɪd] ADJ
▸▸ *Br Culin* **c. cream** = crème *f* très épaisse typique du sud-ouest de l'Angleterre

clotting ['klɒtɪŋ] N *(of blood)* coagulation *f*

cloud [klaʊd] N **1** *Met* nuage *m*, *Lit* nuée *f*, *Fig* **to have one's head in the clouds** être dans

les nuages *ou* dans la lune; *Fam* **to be on c. nine** être aux anges; *Prov* **every c. has a silver lining** à quelque chose malheur est bon; *Fig* **to be under a c.** *(suspected)* être *ou* faire l'objet de soupçons; *(out of favour)* être en défaveur; **he left the firm under a c.** il a quitté la société dans une atmosphère de scandale étouffé; **this was not enough to remove the c. of suspicion hanging over him** cela ne suffit pas à faire oublier la méfiance à son égard
2 *(of smoke, dust)* nuage *m*, voile *m*
3 *(swarm) (of locusts etc)* nuée *f*
VT *(liquid)* troubler, rendre trouble; *(mirror)* ternir; *(by breathing on it)* embuer; *(sb's happiness)* troubler; *(reputation)* ternir; **a clouded sky** un ciel plein de nuages; **eyes clouded with tears** yeux voilés de larmes; **to c. the issue** embrouiller la question
VI *(of sky)* se couvrir *ou* se voiler (de nuages)
▸▸ *Met* **c. bank** banc *m* de nuages; *Nucl* **c. chamber** chambre *f* de détente *ou* d'ionisation

▸ **cloud over** VI *(of sky)* se couvrir *ou* se voiler (de nuages); *Fig (of face)* s'assombrir; **it clouded over in the afternoon** ça s'est couvert dans l'après-midi

▸ **cloud up** VI **it's clouding up** ça se couvre; **the mirror had clouded up** le miroir s'était couvert de buée
VT SEP *(windows)* embuer

cloudburst ['klaʊdbɜːst] N trombe(s) *f(pl)* d'eau, averse *f* violente

cloud-cuckoo-land N **you're living in c. if you think ...** tu te fais des idées *ou* tu rêves doucement *ou Can* tu rêves en couleurs si tu penses que ...; **that's c.** il rêve/tu rêves/*etc*

clouded ['klaʊdɪd] ADJ *(sky)* couvert (de nuages); *(liquid)* trouble; **to become c.** *(of sky)* se couvrir; *(of mind)* s'obscurcir

cloudiness ['klaʊdɪnɪs] N **1** *(of sky)* aspect *m* nuageux **2** *(of liquid)* turbidité *f*

cloudless ['klaʊdlɪs] ADJ *(sky)* sans nuages

cloudy ['klaʊdɪ] ADJ **1** *(weather)* couvert; *(sky)* nuageux; **it's c.** le temps est couvert; **a c. day** un jour nuageux **2** *(liquid)* trouble; *Med (urine)* chargé

clout [klaʊt] N **1** *Fam (influence)* influence *f*, *(power)* poids *m*; **to have (plenty of) c.** *(be powerful)* être puissant; *(be influential)* avoir de l'influence *ou* le bras long **2** *Fam (blow)* coup *m*, taloche *f*, **to give sb/sth a c.** flanquer une taloche à qn/qch **3** *Br Old-fashioned, Dial (cloth)* chiffon *m*
VT *Fam* flanquer une taloche à

clove[1] [kləʊv] N *Bot, Culin* **c. of garlic** gousse *f* d'ail

clove[2] N **1** *Bot, Culin* clou *m* de girofle; **oil of cloves** essence *f* de girofle **2** *Bot (flower)* œillet-giroflée *m*, *pl* œillets-giroflées, œillet *m* des fleuristes; *(tree)* giroflier *m*
▸▸ *Bot* **c. pink** œillet-giroflée, *pl* œillets-giroflées, œillet des fleuristes; *Bot* **c. tree** giroflier

clove[3] PT *see* **cleave**
▸▸ **c. hitch** demi-clef *f*, *pl* demi-clefs, nœud *m* de cabestan

cloven ['kləʊv(ə)n] ADJ fendu, fourchu
▸▸ **c. foot, c. hoof** *(of ruminant)* sabot *m* fendu; *(of devil)* pied *m* fourchu

cloven-footed, cloven-hoofed ['kləʊv(ə)n'fʊtɪd, -'huːft] ADJ *(ruminant)* aux sabots fendus; *(devil)* aux pieds fourchus

clover ['kləʊvər] N *(plant)* trèfle *m*; *Fam* **to be** *or* **live in c.** être *ou* vivre comme un coq en pâte
▸▸ **c. honey** miel *m* de trèfle

cloverleaf, *pl* **cloverleafs, cloverleaves** ['kləʊvəliːf, -liːfs, -liːvz] N *Bot* feuille *f* de trèfle; *Aut* croisement *m ou* carrefour *m* en trèfle

▸▸*Aut* **c. intersection** croisement *ou* carrefour en trèfle

clown [klaʊn] N *(in circus), Fig* clown *m*; *Theat* bouffon *m*; **to act the c.** faire le clown; **to make a c. of oneself** se ridiculiser

VI = **clown about**

▸ **clown about, clown around** VI faire le clown *ou* le pitre

clowning ['klaʊnɪŋ] N *Theat, Fig* bouffonneries *fpl*, pitreries *fpl*

clownish ['klaʊnɪʃ] ADJ clownesque

cloy [klɔɪ] VI *Lit* **delights that never c.** plaisirs dont on ne se lasse pas

cloying ['klɔɪɪŋ] ADJ *(cake, taste etc), Fig* écœurant

club [klʌb] N **1** *(political, literary, gentlemen's etc)* club *m*, cercle *m*; *(sporting)* club; **football/tennis/yacht c.** club de football/tennis/yachting; **I've got a cold – join the c.!** j'ai un rhume – on est deux!; *Fam* **to be in the (pudding) c.** *(pregnant)* avoir un polichinelle dans le tiroir

2 *(nightclub)* boîte *f* de nuit; **the London c. scene** les milieux nocturnes londoniens

3 *(weapon etc)* massue *f*, gourdin *m*; *Golf* club *m*, crosse *f*, *Gym* **(Indian) c.** massue de gymnastique

4 *Cards* trèfle *m*; **ace of clubs** as *m* de trèfle

VT **(-bb-)** *(hit)* frapper avec une massue *ou* avec un gourdin; **to c. sb to death** tuer qn à coups de gourdin

▸▸**c. chair** club; *Aviat* **c. class** classe *f* club, classe affaires; *Med* **c. foot** pied *m* bot; **c. sandwich** sandwich *m* mixte (à trois étages); **c. tie** = cravate *f* aux couleurs d'une association sportive

▸ **club together** VI se cotiser, mettre son argent en commun; **to c. together to buy sth** se cotiser pour acheter qch

Clubs

Les "clubs" britanniques sont des lieux de rencontre et de détente très fermés, qui jouent un rôle important dans la vie sociale des milieux aisés en Grande-Bretagne. Traditionnellement ces institutions (notamment les "gentlemen's clubs" londoniens, tels que l'Athenaeum ou le Carlton Club) étaient interdites aux femmes, mais récemment cette tendance a commencé à changer.

clubbable ['klʌbəb(ə)l] ADJ *Old-fashioned* sociable

clubber ['klʌbər] N *Fam* fêtard *m*, adepte *mf* des boîtes de nuit

clubbing ['klʌbɪŋ] N *Fam* **to go c.** aller en boîte

clubfooted ['klʌbfʊtɪd] ADJ *Med* qui a un pied bot

clubhouse ['klʌbhaʊs] N *Golf, Tennis etc* pavillon *m*

clubland ['klʌblənd] N **1** *(area of gentlemen's clubs)* = quartier *m* des alentours de Saint James où se trouvent la plupart des clubs sélects de Londres **2** *(nightclub area)* = quartier *m* des boîtes de nuit

cluck [klʌk] N *(of hens)* gloussement *m*
VI *(of hen)* glousser; *(of person)* faire claquer sa langue

clucking ['klʌkɪŋ] N *(of hens), Fig (of scandalized person)* gloussement *m*

clue [kluː] N **1** *(indication, hint)* indication *f*, indice *m*; *(to crime)* indice; **to get** *or* **find the c. to sth** trouver *ou* découvrir la clef de qch; **her hat provides a c. to her profession** on devine sa profession à son chapeau; **to give sb a c.** donner un indice à qn, mettre qn sur la voie *ou* sur la piste; *Fam* **I haven't got a c.** je n'en sais absolument rien, je n'en

ai pas la moindre idée; *Fam* **he hasn't got a c. what he's doing** il fait n'importe quoi; *Fam* **when it comes to physics I haven't got a c.** je ne pige rien à la physique **2** *(in crossword)* définition *f*; **what's the c. to 13 down?** quelle est la définition du 13 vertical?

▸ **clue in** VT SEP *Fam (inform)* renseigner, mettre au courant *ou* au parfum

▸ **clue up** VT SEP *Fam (usu passive)* **I'm not very clued up on astrophysics** je ne suis pas très calé en astrophysique

clueless ['kluːlɪs] ADJ *Fam* **he's quite c.** il ne sait rien de rien

clump [klʌmp] N **1** *(cluster) (of trees)* groupe *m*, bouquet *m*; *(of bushes, flowers)* massif *m* **2** *(lump) (of earth)* motte *f* **3** *(sound)* bruit *m* de pas lourd(s); **the c. of his footsteps** le bruit lourd de ses pas

VI **1** *(group)* se grouper en masse compacte **2** **to c. (about** *or* **around)** *(of person)* marcher lourdement; **with the neighbours clumping about upstairs** avec les voisins qui font du potin en haut

VT grouper en masse compacte; *(bushes, flowers)* planter en massif

clumsily ['klʌmzɪlɪ] ADV **1** *(to move)* maladroitement, gauchement **2** *(drawn)* grossièrement; **c. built** mal bâti **3** *(to break bad news etc)* maladroitement, gauchement, sans tact

clumsiness ['klʌmzɪnɪs] N **1** *(of person, movement etc)* maladresse *f*, gaucherie *f* **2** *(of shape)* grossièreté *f*, lourdeur *f*; *(of sentence)* lourdeur, maladresse *f* **3** *(lack of tact)* manque *m* de tact, maladresse *f*

clumsy ['klʌmzɪ] ADJ **1** *(person, movement etc)* maladroit, gauche; **these boots are really c.** ce sont de vrais godillots, ces bottes **2** *(heavy) (phrase)* maladroit, gauche; *(shape)* lourd, disgracieux; **3** *(tactless) (person, excuse, remark)* maladroit, gauche

clung PT, PP *see* **cling**

clunk [klʌŋk] N bruit *m* sourd

cluster ['klʌstər] N *(of flowers, cherries)* bouquet *m*; *(of grapes)* grappe *f*, *(of stars)* amas *m*; *(of people, islands, houses, diamonds)* groupe *m*; *Comput* cluster *m*, bloc *m* *(d'information sur disque)*; *(of terminals)* grappe

VI **to c. round sb/sth** *(of people)* se grouper *ou* se rassembler autour de qn/qch; **to c. together** *(of particles etc)* se conglomérer

▸▸*Mktg* **c. analysis** analyse *f* par segments; **c. bomb** bombe *f* à fragmentation; *Mktg* **c. sample** échantillon *m* aréolaire, échantillon par grappes; *Mktg* **c. sampling** échantillonnage *m* aréolaire, échantillonnage par grappes

clutch[1] [klʌtʃ] N **1** *Aut etc* embrayage *m*; **to let in the c.** embrayer; **to release** *or* **let out the c.** débrayer **2** *(action)* prise *f*, étreinte *f*; **to make a c. at sth** essayer de saisir qch **3** *(claw) (of animal)* griffe *f*, *(of bird of prey)* serre *f*; **to fall into sb's clutches** tomber sous la patte *ou* la griffe *ou* entre les griffes de qn; **to escape from sb's clutches** se tirer des pattes *ou* des griffes de qn

VT *(to hold tightly)* tenir fermement; *(to seize)* agripper; **to c. hold of sth** s'agripper *ou* se cramponner à qch

VI **to c. at sth** tenter de s'agripper *ou* se cramponner à qch; *Fig* **to c. at straws** se raccrocher à n'importe quoi

▸▸**c. bag** pochette *f*, *Aut* **c. cone** cône *m* d'embrayage; *Aut* **c. disc** disque *m* d'embrayage; *Aut* **c. fluid** fluide *m* d'embrayage; *Aut* **c. housing** carter *m* d'embrayage; *Aut* **c. pedal** pédale *f* d'embrayage *ou* de débrayage; *Aut* **c. plate** plateau *m* d'embrayage; *Am* **c. purse** pochette; *Aut* **c. slip** patinage *m* de l'embrayage; *Aut* **c. start** démarrage *m* à l'embrayage

clutch[2] N *(of eggs, chicks)* couvée *f*

clutter ['klʌtər] N encombrement *m*, désordre *m*, *Fam* pagaille *f*, *Fam* pagaïe *f*, *(of furniture etc)* entassement *m*; **the Victorians loved c.** les Victoriens adoraient accumuler des objets dans leurs maisons; **among the c. on her desk** au milieu du désordre *ou Fam* de la pagaille qu'il y a sur son bureau; **everything's in a c.** tout est en désordre *ou Fam* en pagaille

VT *(room, desk)* encombrer *(with* de*)*; **to c. one's mind with useless facts** s'encombrer la mémoire de faits inutiles

▸ **clutter up** VT SEP = **clutter** VT

cluttered ['klʌtəd] ADJ encombré *(with* de*)*; **the c. appearance of the room** l'impression d'encombrement qui se dégageait de la pièce

cm *(abbr* **centimetre)** cm

Cmdr *abbr* **Commander**

CMOS ['siːmɒs] ADJ *Comput (abbr* **complementary metal oxide silicon)** CMOS

CMR waybill [siːemˈɑː] N *Com* lettre *f* de voiture CMR

CMYK [siːemwaɪˈkeɪ] N *Typ, Comput (abbr* **cyan, magenta, yellow, black)** CMJN

CND [siːenˈdiː] N *Br (abbr* **Campaign for Nuclear Disarmament)** = mouvement *m* pour le désarmement nucléaire

CNN [siːenˈen] N *TV (abbr* **Cable News Network)** = réseau *m* d'information américain diffusé par câble et satellite

CO [siːˈəʊ] N *Mil* **1** *abbr* **Commanding Officer 2** *abbr* **conscientious objector**

Co, co [kəʊ] *Com (abbr* **company)** Cie; *Fig* **Jane and co** Jane et compagnie

.co [dɒtˈkəʊ] *Comput* = abréviation *f* désignant les entreprises commerciales dans les adresses électroniques britanniques

c/o *(abbr* **care of)** aux bons soins de, chez

coach [kəʊtʃ] N **1** *Br (motor vehicle)* car *m* **2** *Rail* voiture *f*, wagon *m* **3** *(trainer) Sport* entraîneur, -euse, *Fam* coach *m*; *Sch* répétiteur, -trice **4** *(horse-drawn)* carrosse *m*; *Hist* **(stage) c.** diligence *f*; **c. and four** carrosse à quatre chevaux; *Fig* **to drive a c. and horses through sth** démolir qch (en le critiquant), tailler qch en pièces

VT *Sch* donner des leçons particulières à; *Sport (person, team)* entraîner; **to c. sb in French** donner des leçons particulières en français à qn; *Theat* **to c. sb for a part** faire répéter son rôle à qn; **the police coached the witness** la police a préparé le témoin à la déclaration; **he had been carefully coached in what to say** on lui avait bien expliqué quoi dire

▸▸*Am Aviat* **c. class** classe *f* économique; *Am Aviat* **c. fare** tarif *m* économique; **c. house** remise *f (pour carrosse ou voiture)*; **c. party** groupe *m* voyageant en autocar; **c. shuttle** autocar *m* navette; *Br* **c. station** gare *f* routière; **c. tour** circuit *m* (touristique) en car, voyage *m* en autocar; *(excursion)* excursion *f* en car; **c. tour operator** autocariste *m*; **c. trip** excursion en car

coachbuilder ['kəʊtʃbɪldər] N *Aut* carrossier *m*

coaching ['kəʊtʃɪŋ] N *Sport* entraînement *m*; *Sch* leçons *fpl* particulières

▸▸*Hist* **c. inn** relais *m*

coachman, *pl* **coachmen** ['kəʊtʃmən] N cocher *m*

coachwork ['kəʊtʃwɜːk] N *Aut* carrosserie *f*

coagulant [kəʊˈægjʊlənt] N coagulant *m*

coagulate [kəʊˈægjʊleɪt] VT coaguler
VI (se) coaguler

coagulation [kəʊægjʊˈleɪʃən] N coagulation *f*

coal [kəʊl] N charbon *m*; *(ore)* houille *f*; **a piece** *or* **lump of c.** un morceau de charbon;

the **c. (mining) industry** l'industrie *f* minière *ou* houillère; *Fig* **to carry coals to Newcastle** porter de l'eau à la rivière; *Fig* **to haul sb over the coals** réprimander qn vertement; **live coals** braise *f*, charbons *mpl* ardents

vt *Naut (ship)* approvisionner en charbon; **to c. ship** charbonner

vi *Naut* charbonner

►► *Br* **c. bunker** coffre *m* à charbon; *Naut* soute *f* à charbon; **c. cellar** cave *f* à charbon; *Min* **c. cutter** *(person)* haveur *m*; *(machine)* haveuse *f*; **c. gas** gaz *m* de houille; **c. merchant** charbonnier, -ière, marchand, -ande de charbon; **c. mine** mine *f* de charbon *ou* de houille, houillère *f*; **c. miner** mineur *m*; **c. mining** exploitation *f* du charbon *ou* de la houille; **c. scuttle** seau *m* à charbon; **c. shovel** pelle *f* à charbon; **c. strike** grève *f* des mineurs; **c. tar** coaltar *m*, goudron *m* de houille

coal-black ADJ noir comme du charbon

coalesce [kəʊə'les] VI *(of parties, movements)* s'unir, fusionner; *Chem* se combiner

coalescence [kəʊə'lesəns] N union *f*, fusion *f*

coalface ['kəʊlfeɪs] N *Min* front *m* de taille

coalfield ['kəʊlfiːld] N *Min* bassin *m* houiller

coal-fired [-faɪəd] ADJ (alimenté) au charbon

coalition [kəʊə'lɪʃən] N coalition *f*; *Pol* **to form a c.** former une coalition, se coaliser; **a c. government** une coalition gouvernementale

coalman, *pl* **coalmen** ['kəʊlmən] N (petit) marchand *m* de charbon, charbonnier *m*

coalshed ['kəʊlʃed] N hangar *m* à charbon

coal-tar soap N savon *m* au coaltar

coaltit ['kəʊltɪt] N *(bird)* mésange *f* noire

coarse [kɔːs] ADJ **1** *(vulgar)* grossier, vulgaire; *(language, joke)* grossier **2** *(material)* gros, grossier; *(skin, hands)* rugueux, rêche; *(hair)* rêche; *(features)* grossier, lourd **3** *(food, drink)* ordinaire, commun; **this is a fairly c. wine** ce vin n'est pas très fin; **c. red wine** du gros rouge

►► **c. cut marmalade** marmelade *f* avec des écorces d'orange; **c. fish** poisson *m* d'eau douce *(sauf truite et saumon)*; **c. fishing** pêche *f* à la ligne en eau douce; **c. grain** gros grain *m*; **c. salt** gros sel *m*; **c. sandpaper** papier de verre *m* épais; **c. weave** texture *f* grossière

coarsely ['kɔːslɪ] ADV **1** *(vulgarly)* grossièrement, vulgairement **2** *(ground)* grossièrement; *(chopped etc)* gros

coarsen ['kɔːs(ə)n] VT rendre (plus) grossier VI devenir (plus) grossier

coarseness ['kɔːsnɪs] N **1** *(vulgarity)* grossièreté *f*, vulgarité *f* **2** *(roughness) (of skin, hair)* rudesse *f*, *(of material)* texture *f* grossière

coast [kəʊst] N *(of sea)* côte *f*, rivage *m*; *(extensive)* littoral *m*; *Br* **the c.** *(seaside)* la côte; **from c. to c.** d'un bout à l'autre du pays; **the country's Caribbean c.** la côte caraïbe du pays; **two miles off the c. of France** *or* **the French c.** à deux mil(l)es de la côte française; **the country has no sea c.** le pays n'est bordé par aucune mer; **we took the c. road** nous avons pris la route qui longe la mer; *Fig* **the c. is clear** le champ *ou* la voie est libre

VI *(on bicycle, in car etc)* avancer en roue libre; *(downhill)* descendre en roue libre; *(on sledge)* descendre en luge; *Fig* **he coasted home** *(in race)* il a gagné sans effort; **she coasted through her exams** elle a passé ses examens sans difficulté *ou Fam* les doigts dans le nez; *Fig* **you're coasting** *(not working hard)* tu te la coules douce

coastal ['kəʊst(ə)l] ADJ côtier, littoral, -aux

►► **c. defence** défense *f* côtière; **c. naviga-**

tion navigation *f* côtière, cabotage *m*; **c. resort** station *f* balnéaire; **c. waters** eaux *fpl* littorales

coaster ['kəʊstər] N **1** *Naut (ship)* cabotier *m*, caboteur *m* **2** *(for wine bottle/carafe)* dessous *m* de bouteille/de carafe; *(for glass)* dessous de verre

coastguard ['kəʊstgɑːd] N **1** *(no pl) (force)* garde-côtes *mpl*; **he's in the c.** il est garde-côte; **a c. official** un garde-côte **2** *(person)* garde-côte *m*, *pl* garde-côtes

►► **c. cutter** garde-côte; **c. station** bureau *m* de la gendarmerie maritime; **c. vessel** garde-côte

coastguard(s)man, *pl* **-men** [kəʊst'gɑːd(z)mən] N garde-côte *m*, *pl* garde-côtes

coasting ['kəʊstɪŋ] N *Naut* navigation *f* côtière

►► **c. vessel** caboteur *m*

coastline ['kəʊstlaɪn] N littoral *m*

coat [kəʊt] N **1** *(short)* veste *f*, *(long)* manteau *m*; *(for men)* manteau, pardessus *m*; *esp Am (of man's suit)* veston *m*; **morning c.** jaquette *f*, **car c.** manteau trois quarts; **lab c.** blouse *f* blanche

2 *(of dog, horse)* robe *f*, *(of big cat)* pelage *m* **3** *(of snow etc)* manteau *m*, couche *f* **4** *(of paint, varnish, tar etc)* couche *f*, application *f*

VT *(with paint, tar etc)* enduire, couvrir; *(with chocolate etc)* enrober; *(cable)* revêtir, armer *(with* de); *(paper)* coucher; **to c. with sugar** enrober de sucre; *(pill)* dragéifier; *(almonds)* recouvrir de sucre; **to c. sth with dust** couvrir qch de poussière

►► *Her* **c. of arms** blason *m*, armoiries *fpl*; **c. hanger** cintre *m*; **c. hook** patère *f*, *Hist* **c. of mail** cotte *f* de mailles; **c. rack** portemanteau *m*

coated ['kəʊtɪd] ADJ *(with dust, mud)* (re)couvert *(with* de); *(with sugar, chocolate)* enrobé *(with* de); *(tongue)* chargé, pâteux; *(paper)* couché

coati [kəʊ'ɑːtɪ] N *Zool* coati *m*

coating ['kəʊtɪŋ] N *(of paint, varnish etc)* couche *f*, *(of chocolate)* couche, enrobage *m*

coat-tails NPL basques *fpl ou* pan *m* d'un habit; *(of tail coat)* queue-de-pie *f*, *Fig* **to ride** *or* **hang on sb's c.** profiter de l'influence de qn

co-author N coauteur *m*

VT *(book)* écrire en collaboration; **a book co-authored by Marsh and Brown** un livre écrit conjointement par Marsh et Brown

coax [kəʊks] VT *(person)* enjôler; **to c. sb into doing sth** amener qn à faire qch en l'enjôlant *ou* par les cajoleries; **to c. sth out of sb** obtenir qch de qn en l'enjôlant *ou* par les cajoleries

coaxial [kəʊ'æksɪəl] ADJ *Elec (cable etc)* coaxial, -aux

coaxing ['kəʊksɪŋ] ADJ *(tone etc)* cajoleur, enjôleur

N cajoleries *fpl*; **he took a lot of c.** il s'est bien fait tirer l'oreille; **no amount of c. would get him to agree** malgré les efforts pour l'enjôler, on n'a pas réussi à le faire accepter

cob [kɒb] N **1** *(horse)* cob *m*

2 *(swan)* cygne *m* mâle

3 *(hazelnut)* aveline *f*, grosse noisette *f*

4 (corn) c. *(with grain)* épi *m* de maïs; *(without grain)* rafle *f*, *Culin* **corn on the c.** maïs *m* en épi

5 *Br (type of loaf)* pain *m* rond, miche *f* de pain

►► **c. swan** cygne mâle

cobalt ['kəʊbɔːlt] N **1** *Chem* cobalt *m* **2** *(colour)* bleu *m* de cobalt

►► **c. bloom** fleur *f* de cobalt; **c. blue** bleu de cobalt; *Chem* **c. bomb** bombe *f* au cobalt

cobber ['kɒbə] N *Austr Fam* copain *m*, pote *m*

cobble ['kɒb(ə)l] N *(of roadway)* pavé *m*

VT **1** *(road etc)* paver **2** *Br Old-fashioned (shoes)* réparer

► **cobble together** VT SEP *(make hastily, get together) (bookcase, newspaper article, team etc)* bricoler

cobbled ['kɒb(ə)ld] ADJ *(path, street)* pavé

cobbler ['kɒblər] N **1** *Br (shoe repairer)* cordonnier, -ière; *(maker of shoes)* bottier *m* **2** *Am Culin* = dessert *m* chaud à base de fruits recouvert d'une génoise

cobblers ['kɒbləz] *Br Sl* NPL **1** *(rubbish)* conneries *fpl*; **that's c.** c'est des conneries tout ça **2** *Vulg (testicles)* couilles *fpl*

INT quelles foutaises!

cobblestone ['kɒb(ə)lstəʊn] N *(on roadway)* pavé *m*

cobloaf ['kɒbləʊf] N *Br* pain *m* rond, miche *f* de pain

cobnut ['kɒbnʌt] N aveline *f*, grosse noisette *f*

COBOL ['kəʊbɒl] N *Comput (abbr* **Common Business-Oriented Language)** Cobol *m*

cobra ['kəʊbrə] N cobra *m*

co-branding N *Mktg* alliance *f* de marque, co-branding *m*

cobweb ['kɒbweb] N *(web)* toile *f* d'araignée; *(thread)* fil *m* d'araignée; *Fig* **to go for a walk to blow away the cobwebs** prendre l'air pour se rafraîchir les idées; *Fig* **to brush the cobwebs off sth** ressortir qch

coca ['kəʊkə] N *Bot* coca *m or f*, *Pharm* coca *f*

cocaine [kə'keɪn] N cocaïne *f*, **c. addict** cocaïnomane *mf*

coccyx ['kɒksɪks] N *Anat* coccyx *m*, rachis *m* coccygien

cochineal ['kɒtʃɪniːl] N cochenille *f*

cock [kɒk] N **1** *(male fowl)* coq *m*; *(male bird)* *(oiseau m)* mâle *m*; **fighting c.** coq de combat; *Fig* **c. of the walk** *or* **of the roost** coq de village; **at university he was the c. of the walk** à l'université, c'était un vrai petit coq (de village)

2 *Vulg (penis)* bit(t)e *f*

3 *Tech etc (in plumbing)* robinet *m*

4 *(on firearm)* chien *m*; **at full c.** au cran de l'armé; *Fig* **to go off at half c.** rater; *(of person)* démarrer au quart de tour

5 *Br Sl (form of address)* **wotcher c.!** salut, mon vieux!

VT **1** **to c. one's eye at sb/sth** donner un coup d'œil à qn/qch; **to c. one's hat** *(put on one side)* mettre son chapeau de côté

2 **to c. (up) its ears** *(of horse, dog)* dresser les oreilles

3 *(gun)* armer

►► **c. canary** serin *m*; **c. lobster** homard *m* mâle; **c. pheasant** coq faisan *m*; **c. sparrow** moineau *m* mâle

► **cock up** *Br Sl* VT SEP bousiller

VI merder

cockade [kɒ'keɪd] N cocarde *f*

cock-a-doodle-doo ['kɒkəduːd(ə)l'duː] INT cocorico!

cock-a-hoop [kɒkə'huːp] ADJ jubilant; *(having done sth)* triomphant; **all c.** fier comme Artaban

cock-a-leekie [kɒkə'liːkɪ] N *Scot Culin* = bouillon *m* de volaille aux poireaux et à l'avoine

►► **c. soup** = bouillon de volaille aux poireaux et à l'avoine

cock-and-bull N *Fam* balivernes *fpl*

►► **c. story** histoire *f* à dormir debout

cockatoo [kɒkə'tuː] N cacatoès *m*

cockchafer ['kɒktʃeɪfər] N *(beetle)* hanneton *m*

cockcrow ['kɒkkrəʊ] N chant *m* du coq; **to rise at c.** se lever au (premier) chant du coq *ou* à l'aube

cocked [kɒkt] **ADJ**
▸▸ **c. hat** chapeau *m* à cornes; *Fam* **to knock sb into a c. hat** *(defeat)* battre qn à plate(s) couture(s), démolir qn; *(be better than)* dépasser qn de très loin, *Fam* enfoncer qn; **as for cooking, she knocks me into a c. hat** pour ce qui est de la cuisine, je ne lui arrive pas à la cheville

cocker [ˈkɒkər] **N** *(dog)* cocker *m*
▸▸ **c. spaniel** cocker

cockerel [ˈkɒk(ə)r(ə)l] **N** jeune coq *m*, coquelet *m*

cockeyed [ˈkɒkaɪd] **ADJ** *Fam* **1** *(absurd)* farfelu; *(story)* qui ne tient pas debout **2** *(person)* qui a un œil qui dit zut à l'autre

cockfight [ˈkɒkfaɪt] **N** combat *m* de coqs

cockfighting [ˈkɒkfaɪtɪŋ] **N** combats *mpl* de coqs

cockiness [ˈkɒkɪnɪs] **N** assurance *f* excessive; **because of his c.** parce qu'il était trop sûr de lui

cockle [ˈkɒk(ə)l] **N** *(mollusc)* coque *f*, fausse praire *f*, *Fig* **that will warm the cockles of your heart** voilà qui vous réchauffera le cœur

cockleshell [ˈkɒk(ə)lʃel] **N 1** *(boat)* coquille *f* de noix **2** *(of mollusc)* coquille *f* de coque

Cockney [ˈkɒknɪ] **ADJ** cockney
N 1 *(person)* Cockney *mf* *(des quartiers de l'est de Londres)* **2** *(dialect)* cockney *m*

cockpit [ˈkɒkpɪt] **N 1** *(of plane)* poste *m* de pilotage, cockpit *m*; *(of racing car)* cockpit **2** *(in cockfighting)* arène *f* de combats de coqs

cockroach [ˈkɒkrəʊtʃ] **N** *(insect)* blatte *f*, cafard *m*

cockscomb [ˈkɒkskəʊm] **N** *(on bird)* crête *f* de coq

cocksure [kɒkˈʃʊər] **ADJ** trop sûr de soi

cocktail [ˈkɒkteɪl] **N** *(drink)*, *Fig* cocktail *m*
▸▸ **c. bar** bar *m*; **c. cabinet** bar *(meuble)*; **c. dress** robe *f* de cocktail; **c. lounge** bar; **c. mixer** shaker *m*; **c. party** cocktail *(fête)*; **c. sausage** petite saucisse *f* (à apéritif); **c. shaker** shaker; **c. stick** pique *f* à apéritif

cockup [ˈkɒkʌp] **N** *Br Sl* connerie *f*, cagade *f*; **the mission was a complete c.** la mission a complètement merdé *ou* foiré; **to make a c. of sth** *(exam, interview, speech, relationship)* foutre qch en l'air

cocky [ˈkɒkɪ] **ADJ** *Fam* trop sûr de soi, culotté; **don't get c.!** ne prends pas tes airs supérieurs

cocoa [ˈkəʊkəʊ] **N** *(powder, drink)* cacao *m*
▸▸ **c. bean** graine *f* de cacao; **c. butter** beurre *m* de cacao

coconut [ˈkəʊkənʌt] **N** *(noix f de)* coco *m*
▸▸ **c. butter** beurre *m* de coco; **c. fibre** fibre *f* de coco, coir *m*; **c. matting** tapis *m* en fibres de noix de coco; **c. milk** lait *m* de coco; **c. oil** huile *f* de coco; **c. palm** cocotier *m*; **c. shy** jeu *m* de massacre *(où l'on essaie d'abattre des noix de coco)*; **c. tree** cocotier

cocoon [kəˈkuːn] **N** *(silkworm etc)* cocon *m*
VT envelopper *(in dans)*; *Fig* **workers in the public sector have been cocooned from unemployment** les travailleurs du secteur public ont été protégés du chômage

cocooning [kəˈkuːnɪŋ] **N** cocooning *m*

COD, cod [siːəʊˈdiː] *Com (abbr cash or Am collect on delivery)* contre remboursement, paiement à la livraison

cod² [kɒd] **N 1** *(fish)* morue *f*; **fresh c.** morue fraîche, cabillaud *m*; **dried c.** morue sèche, merluche *f*; **c.'s roe** œufs *mpl* de morue **2** *Br Sl (nonsense)* foutaises *fpl*

coda [ˈkəʊdə] **N** *Mus* coda *f*

coddle [ˈkɒd(ə)l] **VT 1** *(spoil)* choyer, dorloter; **to c. oneself** se dorloter **2** *Culin (eggs)* à

peine faire cuire; **coddled eggs** des œufs *mpl* à peine cuits

code [kəʊd] **N 1** *Tel, Comput* code *m*; *Tel* **(dialling) c.** indicatif *m*; **the terrorist used a c. word** le terroriste a utilisé un code; *Comput* **computer c.** code machine
2 *(secret writing)* code *m*, chiffre *m*; **to write a message in c.** coder *ou* chiffrer un message; **the letter was in c.** la lettre était codée **3** *(rules etc)* code *m*; **c. of conduct** déontologie *f*, code de conduite; **c. of criminal procedure** code d'instruction criminelle; **c. of honour** code *ou* règles *fpl* de l'honneur; **c. of practice** règlements *mpl* et usages, déontologie
VT 1 *(message etc)* coder, mettre en code *ou* en chiffre **2** *Comput* coder
▸▸ **c. book** *(for encoding)* code *ou* carnet *m* de chiffrement; *(for decoding)* code *ou* carnet de déchiffrement; **c. letter** lettre *f* code; **c. message** message *m* codé *ou* chiffré; **c. name** nom *m* de code; **c. translation** transcodage *m*

▸ **code up VT SEP** *Typ (text)* insérer les codes dans

coded [ˈkəʊdɪd] **ADJ 1** *(message etc)* codé, chiffré **2** *Comput* codé
▸▸ *Aut* **c. engine immobilizer** antidémarrage *m* codé, ADC *m*; **c. signal** *(in video)* signal *m* codé

co-defendant **N** *Law* coaccusé, -ée; *(in civil law)* codéfendeur, -eresse

codeine [ˈkəʊdiːn] **N** *Pharm* codéine *f*

coder [ˈkəʊdər] **N** *(device)* codeur *m*

code-sharing **N** partage *m* de code, code sharing *m*

codex, *pl* **codices** [ˈkəʊdeks, -ɪsiːz] **N** manuscrit *m* (ancien)

codger [ˈkɒdʒər] **N** *Br Fam* **an old c.** un vieux bonhomme

codicil [ˈkɒdɪsɪl] **N** *Law (of will)* codicille *m*

codification [kəʊdɪfɪˈkeɪʃən] **N** codification *f*

codify [ˈkəʊdɪfaɪ] **VT** *(laws etc)* codifier

coding [ˈkəʊdɪŋ] **N 1** *(putting into code)* codification *f*, codage *m* **2** *Comput (providing codes)* codage *m*; *(system of codes)* codes *mpl*
▸▸ *Comput* **c. error** erreur *f* de codage; *Comput* **c. line** ligne *f* de programmation; *Comput* **c. sequence** séquence *f* programmée

co-director **N** codirecteur, -trice

cod-liver oil **N** huile *f* de foie de morue

codpiece [ˈkɒdpiːs] **N** braguette *f*

co-driver **N** *Sport* copilote *mf*

codswallop [ˈkɒdzwɒləp] **N** *Br Sl* foutaises *fpl*; **it's a load of (old) c.** c'est un tas de foutaises

co-ed [ˈkəʊˈed] *Fam* **ADJ** *(school)* mixte; **to go c.** *(school)* devenir mixte
N 1 *Br (school)* école *f* mixte **2** *Am (pupil)* élève *f* d'une école mixte

coeducation [ˈkəʊedjʊˈkeɪʃən] **N** enseignement *m* mixte

coeducational [ˈkəʊedjʊˈkeɪʃənəl] **ADJ** mixte

coefficient [kəʊɪˈfɪʃənt] **N** *Math, Phys* coefficient *m*

coelacanth [ˈsiːləkænθ] **N** cœlacanthe *m*

coeliac, *Am* **celiac** [ˈsiːlɪæk] *Med* **ADJ** cœliaque
N = personne *f* atteinte de maladie cœliaque
▸▸ **c. disease** maladie *f* cœliaque

coerce [kəʊˈɜːs] **VT** forcer, contraindre *(sb into doing sth* qn à faire qch)

coercion [kəʊˈɜːʃən] **N** coercition *f*, contrainte *f*; *Law* coaction *f*; **to act under c.** agir sous la coercition; **to use c. to obtain a**

confession utiliser la contrainte pour obtenir une confession

coexist [ˈkəʊɪgˈzɪst] **VI** coexister *(with avec)*

coexistence [ˈkəʊɪgˈzɪstəns] **N** coexistence *f* *(with avec)*; *Pol* **peaceful c.** coexistence pacifique

coexistent [ˈkəʊɪgˈzɪstənt] **ADJ** coexistant *(with avec)*

C of E [siːəʊˈviː] **ADJ** *Rel (abbr* **Church of England)** anglican

coffee [ˈkɒfɪ] **N 1** *(drink)* café *m*; **two coffees, please!** deux cafés, s'il vous plaît!; **black c.** café noir; *Br* **white c.**, *Am* **c. with milk** café crème, crème *m* **2** *(colour) (dark)* café *m inv*, *(light)* café au lait *inv*
ADJ *(colour) (dark)* café *inv*; *(light)* café au lait *inv*
▸▸ *Br* **c. bar** café, cafétéria *f*; **c. bean** grain *m* de café; **c. break** pause-café *f*, *pl* pauses-café; **c. cream** *(chocolate)* chocolat *m* fourré au café; **c. cup** tasse *f* à café; **c. grinder** moulin *m* à café; **c. grounds** marc *m* de café; **c. machine** cafetière *f* électrique; *(in café)* percolateur *m*; *(drinks dispenser)* machine *f* à café; **c. mill** moulin à café; **c. pot** cafetière; **c. shop** *(small restaurant)* ≃ café-restaurant *m*, *pl* cafés-restaurants; *(shop selling coffee)* magasin *m* spécialisé dans le café; **c. spoon** cuillère *f ou* cuiller *f* à café, petite cuillère *ou* cuiller; *(smaller)* cuillère *ou* cuiller à moka; **c. table** table *f* basse; **c. tree** caféier *m*

coffee-coloured **ADJ** *(dark)* café *inv*; *(light)* café au lait *inv*

coffee-maker **N** cafetière *f* électrique

coffee-table book **N** = livre *m* de grand format abondamment illustré *(destiné à être feuilleté plutôt que véritablement lu)*

coffer [ˈkɒfər] **N 1** *(chest)* coffre *m*; *Fig* **the coffers** *(of country, organization etc)* les caisses *fpl*; *Fig* **to swell the State coffers** renflouer les caisses de l'État **2** *Archit (of ceiling)* caisson *m* **3** *(in dam, lock etc)* chambre *f*, bassin *m*, sas *m* **4** = **cofferdam**
VT 1 *Min, Constr (well)* coffrer **2** *(ceiling)* diviser en caissons; **coffered ceiling** plafond *m* à caissons

cofferdam [ˈkɒfədæm] **N** *Tech* coffre *m*, batardeau *m*, caisson *m* hydraulique

coffering [ˈkɒfərɪŋ] **N** *Min etc* coffrage *m*

coffin [ˈkɒfɪn] **N 1** cercueil *m*, bière *f*, *Fam* **that's another nail in his c.** *(he's closer to death)* c'est (pour lui) un pas de plus vers la tombe; *(he's closer to defeat, disaster etc)* c'est un autre coup funeste pour lui **2** *(of horseshoe)* cavité *f* du sabot
▸▸ *Br Fam Pej* **c. dodger** *(old person)* croulant, -ante; *Fam Hum* **c. nail** *(cigarette)* clope *m ou f*, tige *f*

cofounder [kəʊˈfaʊndər] **N** cofondateur, -trice

cog [kɒg] **N 1** *(of cogwheel)* dent *f*; **the cogs** la denture; *Fig* **I'm only a c. in the machinery** je ne suis qu'un rouage de la machine **2** *(wheel)* pignon *m*, roue *f* dentée
▸▸ **c. rail** crémaillère *f*; *Am* **c. railroad** chemin *m* de fer à crémaillère; *Br* **c. railway** chemin *m* de fer à crémaillère

cogency [ˈkəʊdʒənsɪ] **N** force *f*, puissance *f*

cogent [ˈkəʊdʒənt] **ADJ** *(argument)* convaincant; *(reason)* valable, convaincant

cogently [ˈkəʊdʒəntlɪ] **ADV** avec force, puissamment

cogitate [ˈkɒdʒɪteɪt] **VI** *Fml* méditer, réfléchir *(on, over* sur)

cogitation [kɒdʒɪˈteɪʃən] **N** réflexion *f* *(on, over* sur)

cognac [ˈkɒnjæk] **N** cognac *m*

cognate [ˈkɒgneɪt] **N 1** *Ling* mot *m* de même origine **2** *Law* cognat *m*
ADJ *Fml* apparenté; *Ling* de même origine

cognition [kɒg'nɪʃən] **N** cognition f, connaissance f

cognitive ['kɒgnɪtɪv] **ADJ** cognitif

cognizance ['kɒgnɪzəns, 'kɒnɪzəns] **N 1** Fml (knowledge) connaissance f; **to take c. of sth** prendre connaissance de qch **2** Law (of a court) compétence f; **within** or **under the c. of a court** de la compétence ou du ressort d'une cour

cognizant ['kɒgnɪzənt, 'kɒnɪzənt] **ADJ 1** Fml ayant connaissance (**of** de); **to be c. of a fact** être instruit ou avoir connaissance d'un fait **2** Law court **c. of an offence** tribunal m compétent pour juger un délit

cognoscenti [kɒnjəʊ'ʃentɪ, kɒgnə-] **NPL** connaisseurs mpl, spécialistes mpl

COGS [kɒgz] **N** Acct (abbr **cost of goods sold**) coût m des produits vendus

cogwheel ['kɒgwiːl] **N** roue f à dents ou dentée, roue d'engrenage

cohabit [kəʊ'hæbɪt] **VI** vivre maritalement (**with** avec)

cohabitation [kəʊhæbɪ'teɪʃən] **N** vie f maritale, union f libre (**with** avec)

cohabitee [kəʊhæbɪ'tiː] **N** compagnon m, compagne f

cohere [kəʊ'hɪər] **VI** (of whole, of parts) tenir ensemble; (of argument, style) se suivre (logiquement), être cohérent; **they don't c. as a team** ils ne forment pas une équipe unie

coherence [kəʊ'hɪərəns] **N** (of argument, style) suite f (logique), cohérence f

coherent [kəʊ'hɪərənt] **ADJ** (whole) cohérent; (plan, speech, thinker etc) cohérent, logique; (argument) qui se tient, logique; Fam **the man wasn't c.** il racontait n'importe quoi, il était incohérent

coherently [kəʊ'hɪərəntlɪ] **ADV** d'une manière cohérente, avec cohérence

cohesion [kəʊ'hiːʒən] **N** cohésion f
▸▸ EU **c. policy** politique f de cohésion

cohesive [kəʊ'hiːsɪv] **ADJ** cohésif; Phys (force) de cohésion

cohort ['kəʊhɔːt] **N** Antiq, Mil cohorte f; Fig **he was there with his cohorts** il était là avec toute une armée de suiveurs; **a c. of lawyers** une armée d'avocats

coiffure [kwɑː'fjʊər] **N** coiffure f

coil [kɔɪl] **N 1** (roll) (of rope) rouleau m; (of wire) rouleau m, torque f
2 (single loop) (of rope) pli m, repli m; (of snake) anneau m; (of hair) boucle f
3 (in hairdressing) rouleau m (de cheveux), chignon m
4 Med (contraceptive) stérilet m
5 Elec bobine f
VT (en)rouler; Elec (wire) bobiner; **to c. sth around sth** enrouler qch autour de qch; **to c. itself up** (of snake) s'enrouler, se lover
VI serpenter; (of snake) se lover
▸▸ Aut **c. ignition system** circuit m d'allumage par bobine

coiled [kɔɪld] **ADJ** (en)roulé; (spring) en spirale; (snake) lové; Fig **like a c. spring** tendu, prêt à l'action

coin [kɔɪn] **N 1** pièce f de monnaie; **a 10p c.** une pièce de 10 pence **2** (no pl) (currency) monnaie f; Fig **to pay sb back in their own c.** rendre à qn la monnaie de sa pièce
VT 1 to c. money frapper de la monnaie; Fig Fam **he's simply coining money** or **coining it** il fait des affaires en or **2** (invent) (new word) inventer, créer; **to c. a phrase** inventer une phrase; Iron **..., to c. a phrase** ... pour employer le cliché habituel

coinage ['kɔɪnɪdʒ] **N 1** (coins) monnaie(s) f(pl), Spec numéraire m **2** (coining) (of money) frappe f **3** (invention) **the word is a recent c.** c'est un mot nouveau, c'est un néo-

logisme **4** (currency) (of country) système m monétaire

coincide [kəʊɪn'saɪd] **VI 1** (in space, time) coïncider (**with** avec) **2** (agree) (of interests, opinions etc) coïncider, s'accorder (**with** avec)

coincidence [kəʊ'ɪnsɪdəns] **N** coïncidence f; **what a c.!** quelle coïncidence!; **it is no c. that ...** ce n'est pas une coïncidence si ...

coincidental [kəʊɪnsɪ'dent(ə)l] **ADJ** it was more than merely **c. that ...** ce n'était pas une coïncidence si ...; **this had the c. effect of ...** par coïncidence, cela a eu le résultat de ...; **any similarity with ... is purely c.** toute ressemblance avec ... ne serait que pure coïncidence

coincidentally [kəʊɪnsɪ'dentlɪ] **ADV** par (pure) coïncidence

coiner ['kɔɪnər] **N** (of word, expression) inventeur, -trice

coin-op N Fam laverie f automatique

coin-operated [-ɒpəreɪtɪd] **ADJ** automatique
▸▸ **c. laundry** laverie f automatique

co-insurance N coassurance f

co-insurer N coassureur m

coitus ['kəʊɪtəs, 'kɔɪ-] **N** Fml coït m
▸▸ **c. interruptus** coït m interrompu

Coke® [kəʊk] **N** Fam Coca® m

coke¹ N (fuel) coke m; **c. oven** four m à coke
VT (coal) cokéfier, convertir en coke
VI (of coal) se cokéfier, se convertir en coke

coke² N Fam (cocaine) neige f, blanche f, coke f

cokehead ['kəʊkhed] **N** Fam **to be a c.** marcher à la coke

coking ['kəʊkɪŋ] **ADJ** (coal) cokéfiable
N cokéfaction f, coké(i)fication f

Col 1 (abbr **Colonel**) Col **2** abbr **Colombia 3** abbr **Colorado**

col¹ [kɒl] **N** Geog col m

col² (abbr **column**) col

COLA ['kəʊlə] **N** Am Admin (abbr **cost-of-living adjustment** or Can **allowance**) = augmentation f de salaire indexée sur le coût de la vie, Can IVC f, indemnité f de vie chère

colander ['kʌləndər, 'kɒl-] **N** passoire f

cold [kəʊld] **ADJ 1** (weather, bath, meal, engine etc) froid; **it's c.** (ice-cream, food, object etc) c'est froid; (weather) il fait froid; **to get** or **grow c.** se refroidir; **it's getting c.** (weather) le temps se refroidit, il commence à faire froid; **it's getting colder** (weather) la température baisse; **to be** or **feel c.** (of person) avoir froid; Fam **out c.** sans connaissance, inanimé; **to knock sb out c.** étendre qn raide; esp Am **you'll knock them c.!** (with your performance) tu vas faire un tabac!; **you're c.** (in game) tu gèles; **my hands are c.** j'ai les mains froides, j'ai froid aux mains; **my feet are as c. as ice** j'ai les pieds glacés; Fig **to have c. feet** avoir la frousse; **the scent had gone c.** (in hunting) Fig on avait perdu sa/leur/etc trace
2 Fig (person, manner, welcome etc) froid; **to be c. with sb** se montrer froid avec qn; **to give sb the c. shoulder** tourner le dos à qn, snober qn; Fam **that leaves me c.** cela me laisse froid; Fam **he's a c. fish** c'est un pisse-froid
ADV 1 Am Fam **to turn sb down c.** envoyer promener qn **2** (without preparation) à froid; Surg **to operate c.** opérer à froid
N 1 (of the weather etc) froid m; **I feel the c.** je suis très frileux; Fig **to leave sb out in the c.** laisser qn à l'écart; Fig **to be left out in the c.** rester sur le carreau; Fig **to come in from the c.** rentrer en faveur ou en grâce
2 Med (common) **c.** rhume m; **to have a c.** être enrhumé, avoir un rhume; **a bad** or

heavy c. un gros rhume; **c. in the head, head c.** rhume de cerveau; **c. on the chest, chest c.** rhume de poitrine; **to catch (a) c.** s'enrhumer, attraper un rhume
▸▸ **c. buffet** buffet m froid; Com, Mktg **c. call** visite f à froid; (on phone) appel m à froid; Com, Mktg **c. calling** visites à froid; (on phone) appels à froid; Tech **c. chisel** ciseau m à froid; **c. cream** crème f de beauté, cold-cream m; Am Culin **c. cuts** viandes fpl froides; (on menu) assiette f anglaise; **c. drink** boisson f fraîche; Met **c. front** front m froid; Culin **c. meats** viandes froides; (on menu) assiette anglaise; **c. remedy** remède m contre le rhume; Tech **c. riveting** rivure f à froid; Com, Mktg **c. selling** vente f à froid; **c. snap** vague f de froid; **c. sore** bouton m de fièvre; Can feu m sauvage; Aut, Comput **c. start** démarrage m à froid; Aut **c. start protection** protection f de démarrage à froid; **c. storage** conservation f par le froid; **c. storage dock** dock m frigorifique; **c. store** (room) chambre f froide ou frigorifique; (warehouse) entrepôt m frigorifique; **c. tap** robinet m d'eau froide; Fam **c. turkey** (drugs withdrawal) manque m; Pol **c. war** guerre f froide; Pol **c. warrior** partisan, -ane de la guerre froide

cold-blooded [-'blʌdɪd] **ADJ 1** (animal) à sang froid; **reptiles are c.** les reptiles sont des animaux à sang froid **2** Fig (unemotional) froid, insensible; (murderer etc) sans pitié; (murder etc) (commis) de sang-froid

cold-bloodedly [-'blʌdɪdlɪ] **ADV** (unemotionally) froidement; (to murder) de sang-froid, froidement

cold-bloodedness [-'blʌdɪdnɪs] **N** froideur f, insensibilité f

coldcock ['kəʊldkɒk] **VT** Am Fam (knock out) assommer, estourbir

cold-hearted [-'hɑːtɪd] **ADJ** (person) froid, insensible; (words) dur; (action) impitoyable; **that was a c. thing to do/say** c'était faire preuve d'insensibilité que de faire/dire ça

coldly ['kəʊldlɪ] **ADV** froidement; (to look at sb, sth) avec froideur

coldness ['kəʊldnɪs] **N 1** (of climate etc) froideur f **2** Fig (of welcome, person etc) froideur f; **there is a c. between them** il y a un froid entre eux

cold-pressed ADJ embouti à froid; (olive oil) pressé à froid

cold-rivet VT Tech riveter à froid

cold-shoulder VT (somebody) tourner le dos à, snober, se montrer très froid avec; **the party continues to be cold-shouldered by the electorate** le parti est toujours boudé par les électeurs

coleslaw ['kəʊlslɔː] **N** Culin = salade f de chou blanc à la mayonnaise

colic ['kɒlɪk] **N** Med, Vet colique f

coliform bacteria ['kɒlɪfɔːm] **NPL** colibacilles mpl

colitis [kə'laɪtɪs] **N** Med colite f

collaborate [kə'læbəreɪt] **VI** (in work), Pej collaborer (**with** avec; **on** à)

collaboration [kəlæbə'reɪʃən] **N** (in work), Pej collaboration f; **in c. with** en collaboration avec

collaborator [kə'læbəreɪtər] **N** (in work), Pej collaborateur, -trice

collage ['kɒlɑːʒ] **N** Art collage m

collagen ['kɒlədʒən] **N** collagène m

collapse [kə'læps] **N 1** (of building) effondrement m, écroulement m; (of land) éboulement m; Fig (of hopes, moral values, market, economy) effondrement m; (of country, institution) effondrement m, débâcle f, (of prices) effondrement m, chute f subite; (of the dollar etc) effondrement m, Fam dégringolade f

2 *Med (of lungs)* collapsus *m*; **she's had a c.** elle a perdu connaissance

VI 1 *(of building, institution etc)* s'écrouler, s'effondrer; *(of screen, bookshelf etc)* s'écrouler; *(of resistance, support, prices, economy)* s'effondrer; *(of bridge, axle etc)* s'effondrer, s'affaisser

2 *(of person)* s'effondrer, s'affaisser subitement; **I collapsed from the heat** je me suis évanoui tellement il faisait chaud; **he collapsed into an armchair** il s'effondra dans un fauteuil; **I feel like I'm about to c.** j'ai l'impression que je vais m'effondrer; *Med* **her lung has collapsed** elle a eu *ou* fait un collapsus pulmonaire

3 *(be collapsible)* se (re)plier

VT 1 *(table etc)* plier **2** *(merge) (paragraphs, entries)* mettre ensemble, fusionner

collapsed lung [kə'læpst] **N** *Med* collapsus *m* pulmonaire

collapsible [kə'læpsəb(ə)l] **ADJ** *(chair, boat etc)* pliant, repliable; *(handle etc)* rabattable; *Aut (steering column)* rétractile, rétractable
► ► *Aut* **c. hood** capote *f* pliante *ou* rabattable

collar ['kɒlər] **N 1** *(of shirt etc)* col *m*; *(for dog)* collier *m*; **to seize** *or* **grab sb by the c.** prendre *ou* saisir qn au collet; *Fig* **to get hot under the c.** *(angry)* se mettre *ou Fam* se ficher en rogne; *(embarrassed)* se sentir gêné; **detachable c.** faux col **2** *Tech* bague *f*; *(of pipe)* collet *m* **3** *Zool (marking) (on bird, animal)* collier *m*
VT *(seize by the collar)* saisir *ou* prendre au collet; *Fig Fam (catch)* pincer

collarbone ['kɒləbəʊn] **N** clavicule *f*

collate [kə'leɪt] **VT 1** *(assemble) (documents, data)* rassembler; *Comput (documents)* interclasser; *(in bookbinding) (sheets)* assembler, collationner **2** *(compare) (text)* collationner (**with** avec)

collateral [kə'lætər(ə)l] **N** *Fin* nantissement *m*; **what can you provide as c.?** qu'est-ce que vous pouvez fournir en nantissement?
ADJ 1 *(secondary)* accessoire, subsidiaire **2** *(parallel)* parallèle; *(fact)* concomitant; *Law* collatéral, -aux **3** *(branch, family), Med (artery)* collatéral, -aux
► ► *Mil* **c. damage** dégâts *mpl* collatéraux; *Fin* **c. loans** crédits *mpl* sur nantissement; *Fin* **c. security** nantissement

collateralize [kə'lætərəlaɪz] **VT** *Banking* garantir

collation [kə'leɪʃən] **N 1** *(assembling) (of documents, data)* rassemblement *m*; *(in bookbinding) (of sheets)* assemblage *m*, collationnement *m* **2** *(comparing) (of texts)* collation *f* **3** *Culin Old-fashioned, Fml* collation *f*

collator [kə'leɪtər] **N** *(on photocopier)* interclasseuse *f*

colleague ['kɒliːg] **N** collègue *mf*, *(doctor, lawyer)* confrère *m*, consœur *f*

collect¹ [kə'lekt] **VT 1** *(as pastime) (stamps, books etc)* collectionner, faire collection de; **she has collected more than 2,000 records** elle a une collection de plus de 2 000 disques

2 *(gather) (crowd, one's belongings, material)* rassembler; *(friends, documents)* réunir; *(data, news)* recueillir; *(of post office) (letters)* faire la levée de; *Mil (wounded)* ramasser; **he had collected six parking fines** il avait ramassé six P.V.; **he collects parking fines** il collectionne les P.V.; **that tray is there to c. the drips** ce plateau sert à recueillir les gouttes

3 *Fig (one's thoughts, strength)* rassembler; **to c. oneself** se reprendre, se calmer

4 *(pick) (flowers)* cueillir; *(mushrooms)* ramasser

5 *Fin (salary)* toucher; *(debt)* recouvrer; **to c. taxes** percevoir *ou* lever des impôts

6 *(recover, call for) (luggage, ticket, car)* aller chercher, aller prendre; *(goods)* enlever; **I'll c. you at midday** je passerai vous prendre à midi

VI 1 *(of people)* s'assembler, se rassembler, se réunir; *(of things)* s'amasser **2** *(gather money)* faire la quête, quêter (**for** pour)

ADV *Am* **to send a telegram c.** envoyer un télégramme en port dû; *Tel* **to call (sb) c.** appeler (qn) en PCV, *Can* faire un appel à frais virés (à qn)
► ► *Am Tel* **c. call** appel *m* en PCV, *Can* appel à frais virés

collect² ['kɒlekt] **N** *Rel (prayer)* collecte *f*

collectable [kə'lektəb(ə)l] **ADJ 1** *(sought-after)* prisé par les collectionneurs **2** *(debt)* recouvrable
N objet *m* de collection

collected [kə'lektɪd] **ADJ 1** *(assembled)* réuni; **the c. works of Jane Austen** les œuvres complètes de Jane Austen **2** *(calm)* plein de sang-froid; **to remain calm and c.** garder son sang-froid

collectible [kə'lektəb(ə)l] **ADJ, N** = **collectable**

collecting [kə'lektɪŋ] **N** **he does a lot of c. for the blind** il quête beaucoup *ou* il fait de nombreuses quêtes pour les aveugles
► ► *Banking, Fin* **c. agency** banque *f* de recouvrement; *Banking, Fin* **c. bank** banque de recouvrement

collection [kə'lekʃən] **N 1** *(of stamps, butterflies etc)* collection *f*, *(of songs, poems)* recueil *m*; **spring c.** *(in fashion industry)* collection de printemps

2 *(act of collecting) (of sum of money, debts)* recouvrement *m*; *(of taxes)* perception *f*, *(of water, electric current)* captage *m*; *(of data)* collecte *f*; **c. times are 8.45 and 17.30** *(from letterbox)* les levées sont à 8h45 et 17h30; **c. and delivery** enlèvement *m* et livraison *m*; **c. of customs duties** perception douanière

3 *(group, accumulation) (of people)* assemblée *f*, rassemblement *m*; *(of things)* amas *m*; *(ordered)* assemblage *m*; **a c. of rubbish had built up outside the door** des ordures s'étaient amassées devant la porte

4 *(in church)* quête *f*, *(for charity etc)* collecte *f*, quête; **to take up a c.** faire la quête

5 *Fin (of bill)* encaissement *m*; **to send sth for c.** envoyer qch à l'encaissement

6 *(picking up) (of foods)* enlèvement *m*; **your watch will be ready for c. tomorrow** votre montre sera prête demain

7 *(removal) (of garbage)* ramassage *m*
► ► **c. box** caisse *f*, *(in church)* tronc *m*; *Com* **c. charge** commission *f* d'encaissement; **c. department** service *m* de recouvrement; *Com* **c. fee** commission d'encaissement; **c. plate** *(in church)* corbeille *f*, *Fin* **c. rate** tarif *m* d'encaissement

collective [kə'lektɪv] **ADJ** collectif
N 1 *Gram* collectif *m* VOIR GRAMMAIRE A11; B8 **2** *(farm etc)* coopérative *f*
► ► *Ind* **c. agreement** convention *f* collective; *Ind* **c. bargaining** = négociations *fpl* pour une convention collective; *Agr* **c. farm** ferme *f* collective; *Ling* **c. noun** collectif; *Law* **c. ownership** propriété *f* collective; *(of building)* copropriété *f*, *Mktg* **c. promotion** communication *f* collective

collectively [kə'lektɪvlɪ] **ADV** collectivement; **c. owned** mis en commun; **c. owned building** immeuble *m* en copropriété

collectivism [kə'lektɪvɪz(ə)m] **N** collectivisme *m*

collectivist [kə'lektɪvɪst] **ADJ, N** collectiviste *mf*

collectivity [kɒlek'tɪvɪtɪ] **N** collectivité *f*

collectivization [kəlektɪvaɪ'zeɪʃən] **N** collectivisation *f*

collectivize [kə'lektɪvaɪz] **VT** collectiviser

collector [kə'lektər] **N 1** *(of paintings, stamps etc)* collectionneur, -euse; **c.'s item** pièce *f* de collection **2** *(for charity)* quêteur, -euse; **c. of taxes** percepteur *m* **3** *Tech etc (for oil, steam etc)* collecteur *m*; *(of overflow)* récepteur *m*

colleen ['kɒliːn] **N** *(in Ireland)* jeune fille *f*

college ['kɒlɪdʒ] **N 1** *(of further or higher education)* établissement *m* d'enseignement supérieur; *(technical)* IUT *m*, collège *m* technique; *(be a student there)* faire des études supérieures; **I've got to go off to c. now** il faut que j'aille en cours maintenant; **c. of art** école *f* des beaux-arts; *Br* **C. of Education** ≃ institut *m* de formation des maîtres; **c. of music** conservatoire *m* (de musique); **agricultural c.** institut *m* agronomique; **military/navy c.** école militaire/navale; **technical c.** collège technique VOIR GRAMMAIRE A6–7

2 *(part of British university)* collège *m* *(comme ceux d'Oxford)*; **the c. team** l'équipe du collège; **he played rugby for his c.** il a joué au rugby pour son collège *ou* dans l'équipe de son collège

3 *Rel* collège *m*

4 *Pol* **electoral c.** collège *m* électoral
► ► **the C. of Cardinals** le Collège des cardinaux, le Sacré Collège; **c. education** études *fpl* supérieures; **c. student** étudiant, -ante

collegiate [kə'liːdʒɪət] **ADJ** *(system)* des collèges; *(life)* dans un collège/les collèges; *(university)* organisé en collèges
► ► *Rel* **c. church** collégiale *f*

collide [kə'laɪd] **VI** *(of vehicles etc)* se heurter, se tamponner, entrer en collision; **to c. with** *(of vehicle)* heurter, tamponner, entrer en collision avec; *(ship)* aborder; **to c. with sb** *(of person)* se heurter à *ou* contre qn; *Fig* **the two countries have collided over the issue of human rights** les deux pays se sont heurtés sur la question des droits de l'homme

collie ['kɒlɪ] **N** *(dog)* colley *m*, chien *m* de berger écossais

collier ['kɒlɪər] **N 1** *(ship)* (navire *m*) charbonnier *m* **2** *Min (person)* mineur *m* *(de charbon)*

colliery ['kɒlɪərɪ] **N** *Min* houillère *f*, mine *f* de charbon

collision [kə'lɪʒən] **N 1** collision *f*, *(of ships)* abordage *m*, collision; *Fig (of interests etc)* conflit *m*; **to come into c. with sth** *(with moving object)* entrer en collision avec qch; *(with stationary object)* rentrer dans qch; *(of ship)* aborder qch; *Naut* **to be on a c. course** être sur un cap de collision; *Fig* **they are on a c. course** ils vont se rentrer dedans; *Fig* **to be on a c. course with sb** avoir toutes les chances de rentrer en conflit avec qn; *Fig* **to avoid a c. with sb** éviter les heurts avec qn **2** *Phys (of particles)* choc *m*, collision *f*
► ► *Aut* **c. damage waiver** = suppression *f* de franchise pour les dommages causés aux véhicules

colloid ['kɒlɔɪd] **N** colloïde *m*

colloquial [kə'ləʊkwɪəl] **ADJ** familier, parlé

colloquialism [kə'ləʊkwɪəlɪz(ə)m] **N** expression *f* familière

colloquially [kə'ləʊkwɪəlɪ] **ADV** familièrement, en style familier; **known c. as ...** communément appelé ...

collude [kə'luːd] **VI** être de connivence (**with sb** avec qn)

collusion [kə'luːʒən] **N** collusion *f*; **to act in c. with sb** agir de connivence avec qn; **to do sth in c. with sb** faire qch de connivence avec qn; **to be in c. with sb** être d'intelligence *ou* de connivence avec qn

collywobbles ['kɒlɪwɒb(ə)lz] **NPL** *Fam* **to**

have the c. *(an upset stomach)* avoir mal au ventre; *(be nervous)* avoir la frousse; **he gives me the c.** il me fiche la frousse

Colo *abbr* **Colorado**

cologne [kə'ləʊn] N eau *f* de Cologne

Colombia [kə'lɒmbɪə] N Colombie *f*

Colombian [kə'lɒmbɪən] ADJ colombien N Colombien, -ienne

colon[1] ['kəʊlən] N *Anat* côlon *m*

colon[2] N *(punctuation mark)* deux-points *m inv*

colonel ['kɜːn(ə)l] N *Mil, Am Aviat* colonel *m*

colonial [kə'ləʊnɪəl] ADJ colonial, -aux; *Am Archit etc (style)* du dix-huitième siècle, colonial; **in c. times** au *ou* du temps des colonies N colonial, -ale

colonialism [kə'ləʊnɪəlɪz(ə)m] N colonialisme *m*

colonialist [kə'ləʊnɪəlɪst] ADJ, N colonialiste *mf*

colonic [kə'lɒnɪk] ADJ du côlon ►► *Med* **c. irrigation** lavement *m*

colonist ['kɒlənɪst] N colon *m*

colonization [kɒlənaɪ'zeɪʃən] N colonisation *f*

colonize ['kɒlənaɪz] VT coloniser

colonizer ['kɒlənaɪzər] N colonisateur, -trice

colonnade [kɒlə'neɪd] N *Archit* colonnade *f*

colony ['kɒlənɪ] N *(also of animals, writers)* colonie *f*; **to live in the colonies** vivre aux colonies; *Hist* **the Colonies** les Colonies *fpl*; **the English c. in Paris** la colonie anglaise de Paris

colophon ['kɒləfən] N *Typ (of publisher, printer)* logo *m*

color, color-blind *etc Am* = **colour, colour-blind** *etc*

Colorado [kɒlə'rɑːdəʊ] N Colorado *m* ►► **C. beetle** doryphore *m*, *Can* bête *f* à patates

coloration [kʌlə'reɪʃən] N coloration *f*, coloris *m*

coloratura [kɒlərə'tʊərə] N *Mus* coloratura *f* ►► **c. aria** air *m* de colorature; **c. soprano** *(soprano f)* coloratura

colored *Am* = **coloured**

colossal [kə'lɒs(ə)l] ADJ colossal, -aux

colossus, *pl* **colossi**, **colossuses** [kə'lɒsəs, -aɪ, -əsɪz] N colosse *m*; **the C. of Rhodes** le colosse de Rhodes

colostomy [kə'lɒstəmɪ] N *Surg* colostomie *f*; **to have a c.** subir une colostomie ►► **c. bag** poche *f*

colour, *Am* **color** ['kʌlər] N VOIR GRAMMAIRE A7; B10 **1** couleur *f*; **what c. is it?** de quelle couleur est-ce?; **it's the c. of a ripe cherry** ça a *ou* c'est de la couleur d'une cerise mûre; **a dark grey c.** une couleur gris foncé; **it's a sort of greenish c.** c'est d'une couleur un peu verdâtre; **local c.** couleur locale; **the political c. of a journal** la couleur politique d'un journal; **to give** *or* **lend c. to a story** rendre une histoire plus vivante; *Fig* **I've still to see the c. of his money** je n'ai pas encore vu la couleur de son argent

2 *Art etc (tones)* coloris *m*; **light colours** coloris clairs

3 *(pigment)* matière *f* colorante, couleur *f*; **box of colours** boîte *f* de couleurs

4 *(complexion)* teint *m*, couleurs *fpl*; **she had a lot of c. in her cheeks** ses joues avaient de belles couleurs; **to lose c.** perdre ses couleurs; **a week in the country will bring the c. (back) to her cheeks** une semaine à la campagne, et elle reprendra des couleurs; **indignation brought the c. to his cheeks** l'indignation colorait ses joues; *Br*

to be off c. ne pas être dans son assiette; *Fig* **the joke was a bit off c.** la plaisanterie était d'un goût douteux

5 *(race)* couleur *f*; **to discriminate against sb on the basis of c.** faire de la discrimination contre qn en fonction de sa couleur de peau; **the c. problem** les problèmes *mpl* raciaux

6 colours *(insignia etc) (of party)* couleurs *fpl*; *Naut* pavillon *m*, couleurs; *Mil* **the (regimental) colours** le fanion du régiment; **to serve with the colours** servir sous les drapeaux; **with colours flying** (à) enseignes déployées; *Fig* **to pass with flying colours** *(in exam)* être reçu brillamment *ou* haut la main; **to sail under false colours** naviguer sous un faux pavillon; *Fig* **to show oneself in one's true colours** se révéler tel que l'on est; **to see sb in his/her true colours** voir qn sous son vrai jour; *Fig* **to nail one's colours to the mast** afficher ses opinions

7 *Sport, Horseracing* **colours** *(of jockey, team)* couleurs *fpl*; *Sport, Sch* **to get one's colours** recevoir une haute distinction sportive

VT **1** colorer; *(card, drawing)* colorier; *(etching)* enluminer; **to c. sth blue** colorer *ou* colorier qch en bleu

2 *(description) (exaggerate)* exagérer; *(enliven)* rendre plus vivant; *(with false details)* enjoliver

3 *(bias, distort) (fact, view of reality, judgement)* influencer; *(stronger)* déformer

VI *(of person) (become embarrassed)* rougir ►► *Phot* **c. balance** équilibre *m* des couleurs; *Br* **c. bar** discrimination *f* raciale; **c. bearer** porte-drapeau *m*, *pl* porte-drapeaux; **c. blindness** daltonisme *m*; **c. chart** nuancier *m*; *Comput* **c. display** affichage *m* couleur; **c. film** *(for camera)* pellicule *f* (en) couleur; *(movie)* film *m* en couleur; *Phot* **c. filter** filtre *m* coloré; *Comput* **c. graphics** graphisme *m* en couleur; **c. line** discrimination *ou* ségrégation *f* raciale; *Comput* **c. monitor** moniteur *m* couleur; *Mil* **c. party** garde *f* du drapeau; **c. photocopying** photocopie *f* en couleurs; **c. photography** photographie *f* en couleur(s); *Typ* **c. plate** planche *f* en couleur; *Typ, Phot* **c. positive** positif *m* (en) couleur; *Typ* **c. print** reproduction *f* en couleurs; *Typ* **c. printer** imprimante *f* couleur; *Typ* **c. printing** impression *f* couleur; *Typ* **c. scheme** palette *f* ou combinaison *f* de couleurs; *Comput* **c. screen** écran *m* couleur; *Typ* **c. separation** séparation *f* des couleurs, séparation quadrichromique; *Br Mil* **c. sergeant** ≃ sergent-chef *m*, *pl* sergents-chefs *(de la garde du drapeau)*; *Br Journ* **c. supplement** supplément *m* illustré; **c. television** télévision *f* couleur; *Art* **c. value** valeur *f* chromatique

► **colour in**, *Am* **color in** VT SEP *(add colour to black and white illustration)* colorier; *(film, photo)* coloriser

colour-blind, *Am* **color-blind** ADJ daltonien

colour-coded, *Am* **color-coded** ADJ repéré par des couleurs; **everything is c.** on classe tout par un système de couleurs

colour-coding, *Am* **color-coding** N système *m* de classement par couleurs; **what's their c.?** de quelle couleur sont-elles dans le classement?

Coloured, *Am* **Colored** ['kʌləd] N (Cape) C. *(in South Africa)* métis, -isse

coloured, *Am* **colored** ['kʌləd] ADJ **1** coloré; *(drawing)* colorié; *(shirt)* de couleur; **gaily c. butterfly** papillon multicolore; **brightly c. clothing** des vêtements aux couleurs vives; *Fig* **highly c. narrative** récit *m* coloré **2** *(person etc)* de couleur

coloureds, *Am* **coloreds** ['kʌlədz] NPL **1** *(clothes)* couleurs *fpl*; **separate whites and**

c. *(washing instruction)* lavez les couleurs et le blanc séparément **2** *(people)* gens *mpl* de couleur

colourful, *Am* **colorful** ['kʌləfʊl] ADJ *(sky etc)* coloré; *(style)* coloré, pittoresque; **a c. character** un original; **c. language** langage *m* coloré

colouring, *Am* **coloring** ['kʌlərɪŋ] N **1** *(act)* coloration *f*, *(of children's pictures)* coloriage *m* **2** *(shade) (of painting, style)* coloris *m* **3** *(complexion) (of person)* teint *m* ►► **c. book** album *m* à colorier

colouring-in, *Am* **coloring-in** N coloriage *m* ►► **c. book** album *m* à colorier

colourist, *Am* **colorist** ['kʌlərɪst] N *Art* coloriste *mf*

colourization, *Am* **colorization** [kʌləraɪ'zeɪʃən] N *Cin* colorisation *f*

colourize, *Am* **colorize** ['kʌləraɪz] VT *Cin* coloriser

colourless, *Am* **colorless** ['kʌlələs] ADJ **1** *(clear)* sans couleur, incolore **2** *(pale)* terne, incolore; *(face)* blême; *(complexion)* pâle, délavé; *(light)* pâle, falot **3** *Fig (dull) (style)* insipide, fade; *(voice)* terne; *(person)* sans caractère

colourlessness, *Am* **colorlessness** ['kʌlələsnɪs] N **1** absence *f* de couleur; *(of complexion)* pâleur *f* **2** *Fig (of style)* fadeur *f*, *(of person)* manque *m* de personnalité

colourway, *Am* **colorway** ['kʌləweɪ] N coloris *m*

colt [kəʊlt] N *(horse)* poulain *m*, jeune cheval *m* mâle

coltish ['kəʊltɪʃ] ADJ **1** *(immature)* sans expérience **2** *(playful)* folâtre

coltsfoot ['kəʊltsfʊt] N *(plant)* pas-d'âne *m inv*

Columbia [kə'lʌmbɪə] N **British C.** Colombie-britannique *f*, **(District of) C.** (District *m* fédéral de) Columbia *f*

Columbine ['kɒləmbaɪn] N *Theat* Colombine *f*

columbine ['kɒləmbaɪn] N *(plant)* ancolie *f*

Columbus [kə'lʌmbəs] N **(Christopher) C.** Christophe Colomb

column ['kɒləm] N **1** *(of building, smoke, figures etc)* colonne *f*; **putting into columns** colonnage *m*; *Aviat* **control c.** levier *m* de commande

2 *Mil, Naut (formation)* colonne *f*; **to march in c./in two columns** marcher en colonne/en deux colonnes; **supply/relief c.** colonne de ravitaillement/de secours

3 *Journ* colonne *f*, *(feature)* rubrique *f*, **six-c. page** page de six colonnes; **sports c.** rubrique *ou* chronique *f* sportive

4 *Comput, Typ* colonne *f* ►► *Journ* **c. centimetre** *(for advertisement)* centimètre-colonne *m*, *pl* centimètres-colonne; *Aut* **c. change** levier *m* de vitesses sur colonne de direction; *Comput, Typ* **c. graph** histogramme *m*; *Comput, Typ* **c. header** en-tête *m* de colonnes, *pl* en-têtes; *Journ* **c. inch** = unité *f* de mesure des espaces publicitaires équivalant à une colonne sur un pouce; ≃ centimètre-colonne; **it got a lot of c. inches** *(of story)* on lui a consacré beaucoup d'espace dans le journal; *Comput, Typ* **c. mode** mode *m* colonne; *Comput, Typ* **c. printing** impression *f* en colonnes; *Journ* **c. space** colonnage *m*; *Comput, Typ* **c. spacing** espacement *m* des colonnes

columnist ['kɒləmnɪst] N *Journ* chroniqueur, -euse, courriériste *mf*, **sports c.** chroniqueur sportif, chroniqueuse sportive

colza ['kɒlzə] N *(plant)* colza *m* ►► **c. oil** huile *f* de colza

COM [kɒm] N *Comput (abbr* **Computer Output Microfilm***)*

▸▸**C. plotter** traceur *m* COM; **C. printer** imprimante *f* sur microfilm; **C. unit** unité *f* d'impression sur microfilm

.com [dɒtˈkɒm] *Comput* = abréviation *f* désignant les entreprises commerciales dans les adresses électroniques

coma [ˈkəʊmə] **N** *Med* coma *m*; **to go into/be in a c.** entrer/être dans le coma

co-management **N** cogérance *f*

comatose [ˈkəʊmətəʊs] **ADJ** *Med* comateux; **to be c.** être dans le coma; *Fam (fast asleep)* en écraser

comb [kəʊm] **N 1** *(for hair, wool etc)* peigne *m*; *(for horse)* étrille *f*; **to run a c. through one's hair, to give one's hair a c.** se donner un coup de peigne **2** *(of cock)* crête *f* **3** *(honeycomb)* rayon *m*; **honey in the c.** miel *m* en rayon
vt 1 *(sb's hair)* peigner; **to c. one's hair** se peigner; **to c. down a horse** étriller un cheval **2** *Tex etc (wool etc)* carder; **combed cotton** coton peigné **3** *(search thoroughly) (area, town etc)* ratisser, passer au peigne fin (**for sb** pour (re)trouver qn); **she combed the book for references to the crisis** elle a passé le livre au peigne fin *ou* au crible pour trouver des références à la crise
▸ **comb out vt sep 1** *(hair)* peigner; *(untangle)* démêler; **to c. the knots out of one's hair** démêler ses cheveux **2** *(wool)* peigner **3** *(remove) (fleas)* retirer avec un peigne

combat [ˈkɒmbæt] **N** combat *m*; **in c.** au combat; **single c.** combat singulier; **women are now used in a c. role** on envoie maintenant les femmes dans des situations de combat
vt (-t-) *(disease, prejudice, crime)* lutter contre, combattre
vi combattre (**against** contre)
▸▸**c. dress** tenue *f* de combat; *Psy* **c. fatigue** psychose *f* traumatique, syndrome *m* commotionnel; **c. jacket** veste *f* de treillis; **c. mission** mission *f* de combat; **c. troops** troupes *fpl* de combat; **c. trousers** battle-dress *m inv*, pantalon *m* multi-poches; **c. zone** zone *f* de combat

combatant [ˈkɒmbətənt] **ADJ, N** combattant, -ante

combative [ˈkɒmbətɪv] **ADJ** combatif

combi [ˈkɒmbɪ] **N** *Austr Fam* **c. (van)** camping-car *m*, *pl* camping-cars

combination [kɒmbɪˈneɪʃən] **N 1** combinaison *f*, *(of circumstances)* concours *m*; *Chem* combiné *m*, combinaison; **nitrogen in c. with oxygen** l'azote combiné avec l'oxygène; **an interesting c. of flavours** un mélange intéressant de parfums **2** *(of people, workers etc)* association *f*; **to enter into a c. with …** s'associer avec … **3** *(for lock)* combinaison *f* **4** *Br Old-fashioned (clothing)* **(pair of) combinations** combinaison-culotte *f*, *pl* combinaisons-culottes
▸▸**c. lock** serrure *f* à combinaison; **c. rate** *(in advertising)* couplage *m*, tarif *m* couplage; **c. skin** peau *f* mixte; *Tech* **c. spanner** clé *f* mixte; *Med* **c. therapy** trithérapie *f*

combine¹ [ˈkɒmbaɪn] **N 1** *Com, Fin* cartel *m* **2** *Agr* moissonneuse-batteuse *f*, *pl* moissonneuses-batteuses
▸▸*Agr* **c. harvester** moissonneuse-batteuse, *pl* moissonneuses-batteuses

combine² [kəmˈbaɪn] **vt** combiner (**with** à); *(qualities etc)* allier (**with** à); **to c. forces** joindre ses forces (**with** à); **to c. strength of body with strength of mind** allier la force du corps à celle de l'âme; **to c. business with pleasure** joindre l'utile à l'agréable; **the play combines drama and music** la pièce allie intrigue et musique
vi *(of people)* s'unir, s'associer, s'allier; *(ag-*

gressively) se liguer (**against** contre); *(of workers)* se syndiquer; *Pol (of parties)* s'allier; *(merge)* fusionner; *Chem (of elements)* se combiner; **everything combined to give me this impression** tout concourait à me donner cette impression

combined [kəmˈbaɪnd] **ADJ** *(efforts)* réuni; **the c. sound of a pneumatic drill and the traffic** le bruit d'un marteau-piqueur additionné à celui de la circulation
▸▸*Naut* **c. fleets** flottes *fpl* combinées; *Mil* **c. force** force *f* mixte; *Mil etc* **c. operation** *(by several nations)* opération *f* alliée; *(by forces of one nation)* opération interarmées; *Com* **c. transport bill of lading** connaissement *m* de transport combiné; **c. transport company** entrepreneur *m* de transport combiné, ETC *m*

combining [kəmˈbaɪnɪŋ] **N** combinaison *f*
▸▸*Gram* **c. form** affixe *m*

combo [ˈkɒmbəʊ] **N 1** *Mus* petite formation *f* musicale **2** *Fam (combination)* combinaison *f*, *(mixture)* mélange *m*
▸▸*Comput* **c. box** équipement *m* de jonction

combust [kəmˈbʌst] **vi** brûler

combustible [kəmˈbʌstɪb(ə)l] **ADJ** combustible
N matière *f* inflammable; *(fuel)* combustible *m*

combustion [kəmˈbʌstʃən] **N** combustion *f*
▸▸**c. chamber** chambre *f* de combustion; **c. gases** gaz *mpl* de combustion

COME [kʌm] **vi** *(pt* came [keɪm]*, pp* come) **1** venir; *(arrive)* venir, arriver (**to** à; **from** de); **to c. from France/Edinburgh** venir de France/d'Édimbourg; **here c. the children** voici les enfants qui arrivent; **here he comes!** le voilà qui arrive!; **I'm coming with you** je viens avec vous, je vous accompagne; **she comes this way every week** elle vient par ici chaque semaine; **what way do you usually c.?** par où passes-tu d'habitude?; **they don't c. here often** ils ne viennent pas souvent ici; **we're coming to a crossroads** nous arrivons à un croisement; **c. here!** venez ici!, arrive ici!; *(to dog)* au pied!; **coming!** j'arrive!; **ok ok, I'm coming!** d'accord, je viens!; **(are you) coming?** *(with me, us etc)* tu viens?; **c. and see/do** viens voir/faire; **to c. for sb/sth** venir chercher qn/qch; **to c. to sb for advice** venir demander conseil à qn; **you've c. to the wrong person** vous vous adressez à la mauvaise personne; **you've c. to the wrong place** vous vous êtes trompé de chemin, vous faites fausse route; **if you're looking for sun, you've c. to the wrong place** si c'est le soleil que vous cherchez, il ne fallait pas venir ici; **to c. to the end of sth** arriver à la fin de qch; **I was coming to the end of my stay** j'arrivais à la fin de mon séjour; **when you c. to the last coat of paint …** quand tu en seras à la dernière couche de peinture …; **to c. to the throne** monter sur le trône; **a crisis is coming** une crise se prépare; **the fireworks c. next** le feu d'artifice est après; **what comes after the performance?** qu'est-ce qu'il y a après la représentation?; **what are things coming to (when …)?** où allons-nous (si …)?; **letters came pouring in** ce fut une avalanche de lettres; **he has c. a long way** il vient de loin; *Fig* il a fait du chemin; **computers have c. a long way** les ordinateurs ont beaucoup évolué; *Fig* **they saw you coming (a mile off)** ils t'ont vu venir (de loin); **to c. and go** aller et venir; **the idea came to me that …** il m'est venu à l'esprit que …; **suddenly it came to me** *(I remembered)* tout d'un coup, je m'en suis souvenu; *(I had idea)* tout d'un coup, j'ai eu une idée; **the idea came to me one morning** l'idée m'est venue à l'esprit un matin; **a smile came to her lips** un

sourire parut sur ses lèvres *ou* lui vint aux lèvres; **c. now!, c., c.!** allons!, voyons!; *Fam* **she's as obstinate/intelligent as they c.** il n'y a pas plus têtue/intelligente qu'elle; *Fam* **he had it coming to him** il n'a eu que ce qu'il méritait; *Fig* **I don't know whether I'm coming or going** je perds la tête *ou Fam* les pédales; **c. summer (and) we'll all meet again** quand viendra l'été, on se retrouvera tous; **she'll be ten c. January** elle aura dix ans en janvier; **I've got £500 coming to me** je vais (bientôt) toucher 500 livres; **we mustn't let a small disagreement c. between us** nous n'allons pas nous disputer à cause d'un petit malentendu; **a woman came between them** ils se sont disputés à cause d'une femme; **she won't let anything c. between her and her work** son travail passe avant tout
2 *(happen)* **we must take things as they c.** il faut prendre les choses comme elles viennent; **c. what may, we'll get it finished** quoi qu'il arrive, nous finirons; **how did the door c. to be open?** comment se fait-il que la porte soit ouverte?; *Fam* **how c.?** pourquoi?; *(how)* comment se fait-il?; **now that I c. to think of it** maintenant que j'y pense
3 *(originate)* venir; **word that comes from Latin** mot qui vient du latin; **that's surprising coming from him** cela étonne de sa part, venant de lui, c'est étonnant; **to c. from** *or* **of a good family** être issu *ou* venir d'une bonne famille
4 *(be)* **that comes easy/natural(ly) to him** cela lui est facile/naturel, ça lui vient facilement/naturellement; **it came as a shock/a relief to me** cela a été un choc/un soulagement pour moi; **gold watches don't c. cheap** les montres en or ne sont pas données; **that doesn't c. within my duties** cela ne rentre pas dans mes fonctions
5 *(become)* **to c. undone/untied/loose** *(of tie, knot, bootlaces etc)* se dénouer/se délacer/se défaire
6 in the years/days to c. dans les années/les jours à venir; **that will not be for some time to c.** cela va prendre un peu de temps
7 *(of teeth)* sortir
8 *Fam* **that's coming it a bit strong** ça, c'est un peu fort; **don't c. the big boss with me** ne prends pas ce ton autoritaire avec moi; **don't c. it with me** *(don't pretend)* à moi, on ne me la fait pas!; *(as threat)* arrête!; **don't even think about coming it with me!** ne joue pas à ça avec moi!
9 *Fam (reach orgasm)* jouir; *(ejaculate)* prendre son pied, décharger
N *Fam (semen)* sperme *m*, *Vulg* foutre *m*
▸ **come about vi 1** *(of event, occurrence etc)* arriver, se passer, se produire; **it came about that …** il arriva *ou* il advint que …
2 *(of ship)* virer de bord; *(of wind)* tourner
▸ **come across vt insep** *(find) (person)* rencontrer par hasard, tomber sur; *(object)* trouver par hasard, tomber sur
vi 1 *(make an impression)* **to c. across well/badly** *(at interview)* faire une bonne/mauvaise impression, bien/mal passer; *(on TV)* bien/mal passer; **they c. across as nice people** ils ont l'air gentils; **the story doesn't c. across so well on the screen** l'histoire ne rend pas très bien à l'écran; **how did her story c. across?** quelle impression est-ce que son histoire t'a faite *ou* laissée?
2 *Fam (pay up)* payer ce que l'on doit
▸ **come across with vt insep** *Fam (supply) (money)* cracher
▸ **come after vt insep 1** *(chase)* poursuivre
2 *(follow)* venir *ou* être après, suivre; **n comes after k in the alphabet** le n vient après le k dans l'alphabet; **what comes after the dancing?** qu'est-ce qu'il y a après la danse?
vi *(follow)* suivre, venir après

► **come along** vi **1 c. along!** *(hurry)* allons-y!; *(come here)* allons, viens par ici!

2 *(make progress)* **how's the work coming along?** comment ça avance, le travail?; **the preparations are coming along fine** les préparatifs avancent bien

3 *(arrive)* arriver; **everything was peaceful until he came along** tout était calme avant qu'il n'arrive; **these things c. along when you least expect them** ces choses-là arrivent quand on s'y attend le moins

4 *(come as well)* **the children came along** les enfants sont venus avec moi/nous *ou* aussi; **would you like to c. along?** tu voudrais venir?

► **come apart** vi *(fall to pieces)* tomber en morceaux; *Fig (of person)* craquer; *(of plans etc)* aller à la catastrophe; **to c. apart at the seams** *(of garment)* se défaire aux coutures

► **come at** vt insep **1** *(attack)* attaquer; **criticisms/jibes were coming at me from all sides** des critiques/quolibets arrivaient sur moi de tous côtés

2 *(approach)* **to c. at a problem from a different angle** aborder un problème sous un angle différent

► **come away** vi **1** *(leave)* partir, s'éloigner; **why not c. away with us to Paris for the weekend?** pourquoi ne pas venir avec nous à Paris ce week-end?; **c. away from that cat** éloigne-toi de ce chat

2 *(become detached)* se détacher; *(when glued)* se décoller, se détacher; *(when nailed)* se déclouer, se détacher; **the handle came away in his hand** l'anse lui est restée dans la main

► **come back** vi **1** *(return)* revenir; **to c. back (home)** rentrer; **it's all coming back to me** cela me revient (à la *ou* en mémoire); **her name will c. back to me later** son nom me reviendra plus tard; **to c. back to what I was saying …** pour en revenir à ce que je disais …

2 *(of fashion)* revenir; *(of long skirts etc)* revenir (à la mode)

3 *(from losing position etc)* revenir; **to c. back from a defeat/setback** revenir après une défaite/un échec

4 *Fam (retort)* répliquer, riposter

► **come by** vt insep *(acquire)* **how did you c. by this camera/those bruises?** comment as-tu fait pour avoir cet appareil-photo/ces bleus?; **how did she c. by all that money?** comment s'est-elle procuré tout cet argent?; **how did you c. by your fortune?** d'où vient ta fortune?; **how did you c. by your Nordic looks?** d'où vient que tu as l'air nordique?

vi *(past, visit)* passer

► **come down** vi **1** *(descend)* *(from ladder, stairs)* descendre; *(from mountain etc)* descendre, faire la descente; *(of plane)* *(crash)* s'écraser; *(land)* atterrir; *(of rain)* tomber; **to c. down to breakfast** descendre déjeuner *ou* prendre le petit déjeuner; **the plane came down in the sea** *(crashed)* l'avion est tombé en mer; *(landed)* l'avion a amerri; **hemlines are coming down this year** les jupes rallongent cette année; *Fig* **to c. down (in the world)** déchoir; *Fig* **to c. down to earth** descendre des nues

2 *(decrease)* *(of temperature, prices)* baisser; **he'll c. down a few pounds if you bargain** il baissera son prix de quelques livres si tu marchandes

3 *(decide)* se décider; **to c. down in favour of sb/sth** se décider en faveur de qn/qch; **to c. down on sb's side** décider en faveur de qn

4 *(reach)* **her hair came down to her waist** les cheveux lui tombaient *ou* descendaient jusqu'à la taille; **the curtains should c. right down to the floor** les rideaux devraient tomber jusqu'au sol

5 *(be an inheritance)* être laissé en héritage *ou* légué (**to sb** à qn; **from** par); *(of tale, tradition)* être transmis (**from** par); **the necklace came down to her from her great-aunt** elle tient ce collier de sa grand-tante; **the tales that have c. down to us** les contes qui nous sont parvenus

6 *(collapse)* *(of tree etc)* s'abattre; *(of structure)* s'écrouler

7 *(be removed)* être défait *ou* décroché; **that wallpaper will have to c. down** il va falloir enlever ce papier peint; **the Christmas decorations are coming down today** aujourd'hui, on enlève les décorations de Noël; **that disgusting poster is coming down now!** enlève-moi tout de suite cet affreux poster!; **the tree will have to c. down** *(be felled)* il faut abattre cet arbre; **these houses are coming down soon** on va bientôt démolir ces maisons

8 *(be a question of)* **to c. down to** se résumer *ou* se réduire à; **the whole difficulty comes down to this question** toute la difficulté se réduit à cette question; **it all comes down to money** ce n'est qu'une question d'argent

9 *Am Fam (to happen)* se préparer

vt insep *(stairs, street)* descendre

► **come down on** vt insep *Fam (criticize, punish)* tomber sur le dos de; **one mistake and he'll c. down on you like a ton of bricks** si tu fais la moindre erreur, il te tombera sur le dos; **she came down on me for not having told her about it earlier** elle m'est tombée dessus parce que je ne lui en avais pas parlé plus tôt

► **come down with** vt insep *(succumb to)* *(cold, flu etc)* attraper

► **come forward** vi *(present oneself)* se proposer; **no one has c. forward with any alternative ideas** personne n'a rien proposé d'autre; **the police have appealed for witnesses to c. forward** la police a demandé aux témoins de se faire connaître; **to c. forward as a candidate** poser sa candidature, se porter candidat; *Hum* **he's not backward in coming forward** il ne se gêne pas

► **come in** vi **1** *(enter)* entrer; **to c. in again** rentrer; **c. in!** entrez!; *(on radio)* répondez!; *Br Fam* **Mrs Brown comes in twice a week** *(to clean)* Madame Brown vient (faire le ménage) deux fois par semaine; **Mr Jones isn't coming in today** *(to office etc)* M. Jones n'est pas là aujourd'hui; *Cin, Fig* **this is where we came in** on a déjà vu ça; *Radio, TV* **c. in Barry Stewart from New York** *(begin to speak)* à vous, Barry Stewart à New York

2 *(of tide)* monter; *(of ship)* arriver; *Pol (of party)* arriver *ou* parvenir au pouvoir; *Cr (of batsman)* venir prendre son tour au guichet; **we don't have much money coming in** il n'y a pas beaucoup d'argent qui rentre; *Sport* **to c. in first/second** arriver premier/second; **this fashion is coming in again** cette mode revient *ou* reprend; **reports of a coup are coming in** on nous annonce qu'il y a eu un coup d'état

3 *(have a role)* *(in matter)* avoir un rôle à jouer; **and where do I c. in?** et moi, quel sera mon rôle?; **that's where I c. in** *(to help)* voilà où je peux vous aider, voilà où j'interviens; **to c. in useful** *(to sb/for sth/for doing sth)* servir (à qn/à qch/à *ou* pour faire qch); **extra money always comes in useful** *ou* **handy** il est toujours utile d'avoir de l'argent en plus

4 *(join an enterprise etc)* **to c. in with sb** s'associer à qn; **they were the founder members, the others didn't c. in till later** ce sont les membres fondateurs, les autres ne s'y sont associés que plus tard

► **come in for** vt insep **to c. in for praise** être félicité; **to c. in for criticism** être critiqué, être en butte aux critiques; **the government came in for a lot of criticism over its handling of the crisis** le gouvernement a été très critiqué pour la façon dont il gère la crise; **to**

c. in for a share of sth avoir part à qch

► **come in on** vt insep *(be given a part in)* prendre part à; **they let him c. in on the deal** ils l'ont laissé prendre part à l'affaire

► **come into** vt insep **1** *(enter)* *(room)* entrer dans; **to c. into the world** venir au monde; **to c. into power** *(of party, person etc)* arriver *ou* parvenir au pouvoir; **to c. into force** *or* **effect** *(of law, ruling etc)* entrer en vigueur; **when does the law c. into force** *or* **effect?** quand la loi prend-elle effet *ou* entre-t-elle en vigueur?; **to c. into possession of sth** entrer en possession de qch; **how did this painting c. into your possession?** comment êtes-vous entré en possession de ce tableau?; **to c. into sb's mind** *(of idea)* venir à l'esprit de qn

2 *(inherit)* *(money, property etc)* hériter (de); *(inheritance)* entrer en possession de, recueillir; **to c. into some money** *(inherit it)* faire un héritage; *(win it)* gagner le gros lot

3 *(be involved in)* **luck doesn't c. into it** la chance n'a rien à voir là-dedans

► **come of** vt insep **1** *(result from)* **what will c. of it?** qu'en adviendra-t-il?, qu'en résultera-t-il?; **no good will c. of it** cela tournera mal; **that's what comes of being too ambitious** voilà ce qui arrive quand on est trop ambitieux

2 **to c. of age** *(reach legal status)* atteindre la *ou* sa majorité

► **come off** vi **1** *(become detached)* *(of button etc)* se détacher, sauter; *(of paint, stain etc)* s'enlever, partir; *(become unstuck)* se décoller; **does this bit c. off?** est-ce que ça s'enlève?; **the colour came off on my dress** la couleur a déteint sur ma robe; **the chain has c. off** *(of bicycle)* la chaîne a sauté; **the top of the pen had c. off** le bouchon du stylo avait sauté

2 *(fall from horse, motorbike etc)* tomber

3 *(take place)* *(of meeting etc)* avoir lieu

4 *(succeed)* réussir, aboutir; **did it c. off all right?** ça s'est bien passé?; **my little trip abroad didn't c. off** mon petit voyage à l'étranger est tombé à l'eau; **the experiment came off** l'expérience a réussi

5 *(acquit oneself)* **to c. off badly** mal s'en tirer; **you'll c. off worst** tu auras le dessous

6 *Sl (reach orgasm)* jouir

vt insep **1** *(climb down from, leave)* *(wall, ladder etc)* descendre de; **to c. off a ship/ plane** débarquer d'un navire/d'un avion; **I've just c. off the night shift** *(finished work)* je viens de quitter l'équipe de nuit; *(finished working nights)* je viens de finir le travail de nuit

2 *(fall from)* *(horse, motorbike etc)* tomber de

3 *(become detached from)* **the handle has c. off the knife** le manche s'est détaché du couteau

4 *(be removed from)* **that stain will never c. off the carpet** cette tache sur le tapis ne partira jamais

5 *Fam* **c. off it!** arrête ton baratin!; **c. off it, he's not 21!** arrête de dire n'importe quoi, il n'a pas 21 ans!

► **come on** vi **1 c. on!** *(with motion, encouraging, challenging)* vas-y!, allez!; *Fam (expressing incredulity)* tu rigoles!; **c. on, hurry!** allez, dépêche-toi!; **c. on, let's have a game!** allons! faisons une partie!; **c. on Scotland!** allez l'Écosse!

2 *(make progress)* *(of plants etc)* se développer; *(of people)* faire des progrès; **Jackie's French is really coming on** le français de Jackie s'améliore vraiment; **Jackie is really coming on with her French** Jackie fait de gros progrès en français; **how's the work coming on?** est-ce que le travail avance?; **the building work is coming on fine** la construction avance bien

3 *(start)* *(of winter etc)* venir, arriver; *(of*

night) tomber; (of symptoms) apparaître; **I feel a cold coming on** je sens que je suis en train de m'enrhumer; **I have a sore throat coming on** je commence à avoir mal à la gorge

4 *Theat (appear)* entrer en scène; *Sport (on to field)* (r)entrer

5 *(be shown) (of film etc)* passer; **the play/ film is coming on next week** on va donner la pièce/le film va passer la semaine prochaine; **when does that programme c. on?** quand passe cette émission?; **the film's coming on** le film va commencer

6 *Fam* **to c. on to sb** *(make sexual overtures to)* draguer qn

7 *Br Sl (start menstruating)* avoir ses ragnagnas

▸ **come out** VI **1** *(from room, prison, hospital etc)* sortir; **to c. out of a place/a room** sortir d'un lieu/d'une pièce

2 *(become detached)* partir; *(of screw)* se dévisser; *(of tooth)* tomber; *(of page)* se détacher; **my filling has c. out** j'ai perdu mon plombage

3 *esp Br Ind* **to c. out (on strike)** se mettre en grève

4 *(emerge)* **to c. out of an affair badly/well** mal/bien se tirer d'une affaire; **they came out of the business looking rather foolish** à la suite de cette affaire, ils avaient l'air plutôt ridicule; *Sch* **to c. out first/second** sortir premier/second, être reçu premier/second

5 *(appear) (of sun, stars)* paraître; *(of buds)* éclore; *(of pimple)* sortir; *(of rash)* apparaître; **to c. out in a rash** *(of person)* se couvrir de boutons, avoir une éruption

6 *(become known) (of the truth)* être découvert; *(of election, sports results etc)* être révélé *ou* communiqué; **as soon as the news came out …** dès qu'on a su la nouvelle …; **it came out that …** il s'avéra que …, il se trouva que …

7 *(be published, issued) (of book, journal)* paraître, sortir; *(of record, film)* sortir

8 *(of photo)* **he always comes out well** il est toujours bien sur les photos; **these photos have c. out well** ces photos sont bien sorties

9 *(be removed) (of stain)* s'enlever; *(of colour, dye)* déteindre; **when do your stitches c. out?** quand est-ce qu'on t'enlève les points?

10 *Math (be solved)* **I can't get this sum to c. out** je n'y arrive pas, la somme ne tombe pas juste; **it won't c. out** ça ne marche pas; **to c. out at …** *(of total etc)* être de …, se monter à …; *(of average)* être de …; **it comes out at …** le résultat est de …; *Fig* **everything will c. out (all) right in the end** tout finira par s'arranger

11 *Br (of debutante)* débuter, faire son entrée dans le monde

12 *Fam (as gay or lesbian)* se déclarer homosexuel

13 *(decide)* **to c. out strongly** se prononcer avec vigueur (**for** pour; **against** contre); **we've c. out against the idea of moving** nous avons renoncé à déménager; **the committee came out in her favour** le comité s'est décidé en sa faveur

14 *Comput (exit)* sortir; **to c. out of a document** sortir d'un document

▸ **come out with** VT INSEP *(say)* sortir, dire; *(remark)* sortir, faire; **I'm always wondering what he'll c. out with next** je me demande toujours ce qu'il va sortir; **she finally came out with what was bothering her** elle a fini par dire ce qui la tracassait

▸ **come over** VI **1** *(travel, walk etc across)* traverser; **a lot of Americans came over during the war** de nombreux Américains sont venus (en Europe) pendant la guerre; **friends are coming over from Canada** des amis arrivent du Canada; **some friends are coming over** *(who live not far away)* des amis viennent me/nous/*etc* voir; **c. over to-**

morrow passe demain; **he came over and spoke to me** il est venu me parler

2 *(change allegiance)* **to c. over to sb's side** passer dans le camp de qn *ou* du côté de qn; **to c. over to sb's way of thinking** se rallier à l'opinion de qn

3 *(make impression)* **how did she c. over?** quelle impression vous a-t-elle faite?; **he doesn't c. over well on television** il ne passe pas bien à la télévision, il n'est pas très médiatique; **her voice comes over well** sa voix passe *ou* rend bien; **he comes over as (being) rather pompous** il a l'air (d'être) assez solennel

4 *Fam (suddenly become)* **to c. over (all) funny** être pris d'un malaise

VT INSEP *(affect) (of mood etc) (person)* envahir, gagner; **a change has c. over him** il a bien changé; **what's c. over you?** qu'est-ce qui te prend?

▸ **come round** VI **1** *(travel)* faire le tour; **the road is blocked, I had to c. round by the village** la route est bloquée, j'ai dû faire un détour par le village

2 *(visit)* **c. round and see me one day** venez me voir un de ces jours

3 *(arrive)* **the weekend will soon c. round** ce sera bientôt le week-end; **birthdays seem to c. round more often after you're 40** les anniversaires semblent revenir plus souvent quand on a dépassé la quarantaine

4 *(regain consciousness)* reprendre connaissance, revenir à soi

5 *(change one's mind)* changer d'avis; **to c. round to sb's way of thinking** se ranger à l'avis de qn; **they soon came round to the idea** ils se sont faits rapidement à cette idée; **he's c. round** il a cédé

6 *Naut (of ship)* venir dans le vent; *(of wind)* remonter

▸ **come through** VI **1** *(penetrate) (of tooth)* percer; *(of water)* pénétrer

2 *(survive)* **he came through without a scratch** il s'en est tiré indemne

3 *(arrive) (of message etc)* arriver, parvenir; **my visa is taking a long time to c. through** mon visa met du temps à arriver *ou* à me parvenir

VT INSEP **1** *(penetrate)* **water is coming through the roof** l'eau s'infiltre par le toit; **the nail has c. through the wood** le clou a traversé le bois

2 *(survive)* survivre à; **he came through the war without a scratch** il a survécu à la guerre sans une égratignure; **I'm sure you will c. through this crisis** je suis sûr que tu te sortiras de cette crise; **she came through her exams with flying colours** elle a réussi brillamment (à) ses examens

▸ **come to** VI **1** = **come round 4**

2 *Naut (of ship)* lofer, venir dans le vent

VT INSEP **1** *(amount to)* s'élever à; **the bill came to $80** la note s'éleva à 80 dollars; **how much does it c. to?** combien cela fait-il?; **the plan never came to anything** le projet n'a abouti à rien; **that nephew of yours will never c. to anything** ton neveu n'arrivera jamais à rien

2 *(be a question of)* **when it comes to …** en ce qui concerne …; **when it comes to music I haven't got a clue** je ne m'y connais absolument pas en musique; **c. to that, what are you doing here?** au fait, qu'est-ce que vous faites ici?; **if it comes to that …** à ce compte-là …; **let's hope it won't c. to that** espérons que nous n'en arrivions pas là; **when it comes to buying a car, find yourself a reputable dealer** si vous voulez acheter une voiture, adressez-vous à un concessionnaire de bonne réputation

3 *(get as far as)* en venir à; **I wish she'd c. to the point** si seulement elle en venait au fait; **if it comes to a fight, we outnumber them** si on en vient à se battre, nous sommes plus

nombreux qu'eux; **it's really c. to something when …** ce n'est pas malheureux que …; **what is the world coming to?** où est-ce qu'on va!

▸ **come together** VI **1** *(gather)* s'assembler, se réunir; *(of troops)* opérer une jonction

2 *(meet)* se rencontrer; **the two roads c. together at this point** les deux routes se rejoignent à cet endroit

▸ **come up** VI **1** *(by stairs, on ladder, up a hill etc)* monter; **would you like to c. up for tea?** *(to my room etc)* vous voulez monter prendre un thé?; **a man came up from the office downstairs** un homme est monté du bureau d'en-dessous; **to c. up after a dive** revenir à la surface après un plongeon

2 *Br* **to c. up to town** venir en ville

3 *(approach)* **a man came up (to me) and started talking** un homme est venu vers moi *ou* s'est approché de moi et a commencé à me parler; **a police car came up alongside ours** une voiture de police s'est mise à la hauteur de la nôtre; **it's coming up to 10 o'clock** il est presque 10 heures; *Tennis* **to c. up to the net** monter au filet

4 *(appear)* apparaître; *(of plant)* sortir de terre, pousser; *(of sun)* se lever; **some words came up on the screen** quelques mots sont apparus sur l'écran; *Naut* **to c. up on the horizon** *(of land etc)* paraître à l'horizon; **there's a cabaret act coming up (next)** il y a un numéro de cabaret tout de suite après; **there are some interesting films coming up on television** il y a quelques films intéressants qui vont passer à la télévision; **one coffee, coming up!** *(in café)* un café, oui m'sieur/ m'dame!

5 *(arise) (of opportunity, question etc)* se présenter; *(of problem etc)* survenir, surgir; **to deal with problems as they c. up** traiter les problèmes au fur et à mesure; **have any vacancies c. up recently?** est-ce que des postes se sont libérés récemment?; **I'll let you know if anything comes up** *(if I find further information)* s'il y a du nouveau, je vous tiendrai au courant; *(anything that is suitable)* je vous tiendrai au courant si je vois quelque chose qui vous convienne; **call me if something comes up that you can't handle** appelle-moi s'il y a quelque chose qui te pose problème; *Law* **to c. up before the court** comparaître (devant le tribunal); **the case comes up (for trial)** tomorrow la cause sera entendue demain; **two houses in our street are coming up for sale soon** dans notre rue, deux maisons seront bientôt à vendre; **the question has never yet c. up** cette question n'a encore jamais été soulevée; **the subject came up twice in the conversation** le sujet est revenu deux fois dans la conversation; **your name came up twice** on a mentionné votre nom deux fois

6 *(shine, look clean)* **the sideboard came up beautifully** le buffet a retrouvé toute sa splendeur

VT INSEP *(stairs)* monter; *(street)* remonter

▸ **come up against** VT INSEP **1** *(encounter)* se heurter à; **the reformers came up against some pretty strong opposition** les réformateurs se sont heurtés à une opposition plutôt violente; **who does she c. up against in the next round?** qui doit-elle affronter dans la prochaine manche?

2 *(hit, come into contact with)* rencontrer; **his hand came up against something cold** sa main rencontra quelque chose de froid; **the tunnellers came up against solid rock** les ouvriers qui creusaient le tunnel se sont retrouvés face à un mur de roche dure

▸ **come upon** VT INSEP *(find) (person, object)* tomber sur

▸ **come up to** VT INSEP **1** *(reach) (something)* atteindre; **the water came up to my knees** l'eau m'arrivait jusqu'aux genoux; **I only c.**

up to her shoulder je ne lui arrive qu'aux épaules; **we're coming up to the halfway mark** nous atteindrons bientôt la moitié **2** *(equal)* égaler; **to c. up to sb's expectations** répondre à l'attente de qn; **to c. up to standard** être au niveau
▸ **come up with** VT INSEP *(produce)* *(solution, money)* trouver; *(idea, theory)* proposer; *(suggestion)* faire; **unless someone comes up with a better idea** à moins que quelqu'un ait une meilleure idée

comeback ['kʌmbæk] N **1** *(return)* retour *m* (en vogue); *(of politician)* retour au pouvoir; *(of actor)* retour à la scène/à l'écran, comeback *m inv*; *(of sports person)* retour, comeback; **to make a c.** faire un come-back; **70's fashions are making a c.** la mode des années 70 revient **2** *Fam (reply)* réplique *f* **3** *(justification for complaint)* **to have no c.** n'avoir aucun recours

Comecon ['kɒmɪkɒn] N *(abbr* **Council for Mutual Economic Aid)** COMECON *m*

comedian [kə'miːdɪən] N comique *mf, Fig (amusing person)* comique; *(practical joker)* farceur, -euse

Note that the French word **comédien** is a false friend and is never a translation for the English word **comedian**. It means **actor**.

comedienne [kəmiːdɪ'en] N actrice *f* comique

comedown ['kʌmdaʊn] N *Fam (loss of status)* déchéance *f*; **isn't that a bit of a c. for you?** c'est un peu la dégringolade pour toi, non?

comedy ['kɒmɪdɪ] N **1** *(genre)* comédie *f*, genre *m* comique **2** *(play, film)* comédie *f*; *TV* **(situation) c.** comédie de situation, sit-com *m ou f*; *Fig* **it was a c. of errors from start to finish** ce fut une farce grotesque du début à la fin; *Fig* **we weren't taken in by her little c.** sa petite comédie n'a pas pris
▸ ▸ **c. actor** acteur *m* de comédie; **c. actress** actrice *f* de comédie; **c. drama** comédie dramatique; **c. of manners** comédie de mœurs

come-hither ADJ *Fam (look)* aguichant

comely ['kʌmlɪ] ADJ *Lit (person)* avenant

come-on N *Fam* incitation *f*, **it was a c. to get buyers interested** c'était pour attirer les clients; **to give sb the c.** *(sexually)* faire du gringue à qn

comer ['kʌmər] N **open to all comers** ouvert à tous; **I'm ready to take on all comers** je suis prêt à me battre avec n'importe qui

comestible [kə'mestɪb(ə)l] ADJ *esp Am* comestible
NPL *Old-fashioned, Fml* **comestibles** comestibles *mpl*

comet ['kɒmɪt] N *Astron* comète *f*

come-to-bed ADJ **c. eyes** regard *m* aguichant *ou* suggestif

comeuppance [kʌm'ʌpəns] N *Fam* **he got his c.** il n'a eu que ce qu'il mérite

comfort ['kʌmfət] N **1** *(ease)* confort *m*; **to live in c.** être aisé; **the boots are fur-lined for extra c.** les bottes sont fourrées pour plus de confort; **to do sth in the c. of one's own home** faire qch confortablement chez soi
2 comforts commodités *fpl*; **tobacco was one of the soldiers' few comforts** le tabac était l'un des seuls plaisirs des soldats
3 *(consolation)* réconfort *m*, consolation *f*, **to give sb c.** réconforter qn; **to take c. from** *or* **in sth** trouver du réconfort *ou* de la consolation dans qch; **that's cold c.** c'est là une piètre consolation; **to get too close for c.** *(of ship, truck)* devenir trop dangereux; **the deadline's getting a bit too close for c.** la

date limite est un peu trop proche à mon goût; **it was a great c. to him** ça lui a été d'un grand réconfort, ça l'a beaucoup soulagé; *Iron* **some c. you are/that is!** tu parles d'une consolation!; **there was little c. in the news that the strike would continue** la nouvelle selon laquelle la grève allait continuer était peu réconfortante
VT *(console)* réconforter, consoler; *(of beverage etc)* réconforter; **they comforted the wounded** ils ont réconforté les blessés; **it comforted him to know she had had a decent burial** ça l'a réconforté de savoir qu'elle avait eu un enterrement décent
▸ ▸ **c. eating** = fait *m* de manger pour se remonter le moral; **c. food** = chose *f* que l'on mange pour se remonter le moral; *Am* **c. station** toilettes *fpl* publiques *(sur le bord d'une route)*

comfortable ['kʌmfətəb(ə)l] ADJ **1** *(bed, armchair, hotel, garment etc)* confortable; *(warmth, sensation)* agréable, doux, *f* douce; **you will be more c. in this armchair** vous serez mieux dans ce fauteuil; **to make oneself c.** se mettre à son aise; **to be c.** *(of person)* être à l'aise *ou* à son aise; **to feel c.** se sentir bien *ou* à son aise; **I wouldn't feel c. accepting that money** ça me mettrait mal à l'aise d'accepter cet argent; **he couldn't get c. in bed** il ne savait pas comment se mettre dans le lit pour être à l'aise; **she makes people feel c.** elle met les gens à l'aise
2 *(not in pain)* **to be c.** ne pas souffrir; **he had a c. night** il a passé une bonne nuit
3 *(substantial) (majority, lead, income)* confortable; **to be in c. circumstances** mener une vie aisée; **two hours will give you a c. margin** en deux heures, tu auras largement le temps

comfortably ['kʌmfətəblɪ] ADV **1** *(to sit etc)* confortablement; *(warm etc)* agréablement **2** *(in financial, material sense)* **to be c. off** être à l'aise; **to live c.** être à l'aise, vivre dans l'aisance **3** *(without difficulty) (to win)* facilement; **we can get there c. in an hour** une heure suffira amplement pour y aller

comforter ['kʌmfətər] N **1** *(person)* consolateur, -trice **2** *Am (quilt)* édredon *m* **3** *Br Old-fashioned (scarf)* cache-nez *m inv* **4** *(baby's dummy)* tétine *f*, sucette *f*

comforting ['kʌmfətɪŋ] ADJ réconfortant

comfortless ['kʌmfətlɪs] ADJ *(room etc)* sans confort, peu confortable; *(prospect, thought)* décourageant; **he was left alone and c.** il s'est retrouvé seul et sans réconfort

comfy ['kʌmfɪ] ADJ *Fam* = **comfortable 1**

comic ['kɒmɪk] ADJ *(song etc)* comique
N **1** *(performer) (man)* comique *m*; *(woman)* actrice *f* comique **2** *(magazine)* bande *f* dessinée, BD *f* **3** *Am Fam (in newspaper)* **comics** (page *f* des) bandes *fpl* dessinées
▸ ▸ **c. actor** acteur *m* comique; **c. actress** actrice *f* comique; **c. book** bande dessinée, BD; **c. opera** opéra-comique *m*, *pl* opéras-comiques; **c. relief** *Theat* intervalle *m* comique; *Fig* moment *m* de détente (comique); **to provide some c. relief** décrisper l'atmosphère; **c. strip** bande dessinée

comical ['kɒmɪk(ə)l] ADJ comique, drôle; **what a c. idea!** quelle drôle d'idée!

comically ['kɒmɪklɪ] ADV de façon comique; **they tried, c., to distract her attention** ils essayaient de détourner son attention et c'était comique

coming ['kʌmɪŋ] ADJ *(year, week)* qui vient; *(trials, difficulties, elections)* à venir; *(storm)* qui approche
N *(of person)* venue *f*, arrivée *f*; *(of night)* approche *f*; *(of the Messiah)* avènement *m*, venue *f*; *Rel* **the Second C.** le second avènement; **comings and goings** allées *fpl* et venues

Coming of Age
À sa majorité, c'est-à-dire à 18 ans, un(e) jeune Britannique acquiert le droit de voter, de faire partie d'un jury, de boire de l'alcool dans les pubs et de se marier sans le consentement de ses parents.

comma ['kɒmə] N virgule *f*, **inverted commas** guillemets *mpl*; **to put a word in inverted commas** mettre un mot entre guillemets; *Comput* **c.-separated values format** format *m* valeurs séparées par des virgules

command [kə'mɑːnd] N **1** *(order)* ordre *m*, commandement *m*; **to give a c.** donner un ordre; **to do sth at sb's c.** faire qch sur les ordres de qn; **to be at sb's c.** être aux ordres de qn; **word of c.** commandement
2 *Mil (authority) (of army, expedition)* commandement *m* (**of** de; **over** sur); *(of fort, town etc)* gouvernement *m*; **he was given (the) c. of a division/fleet** on lui a confié le commandement d'une division/d'une flotte; **to be in c. of a battalion** avoir le commandement d'un bataillon, commander un bataillon; **it was my first c.** c'était la première fois que j'étais au commandement; **to be in c. of a pass** *(hold it)* commander un défilé; **c. of the seas** maîtrise *f* des mers; *Fig* **c. over oneself** maîtrise *f* de soi; **who is in c.?** qui est-ce qui commande?; **to be first/second in c.** commander en premier/en second; **under (the) c. of ...** sous le commandement de ...
3 *Mil (troops)* **to be responsible for one's c.** être responsable de ses troupes; **they were my first c.** c'est la première section que j'ai commandée; **bomber/fighter c.** aviation *f* de bombardement/de chasse
4 *Mil (area)* **Scottish/Northern c.** région *f* militaire d'Écosse/du Nord; **air/naval c.** région aérienne/maritime
5 *(knowledge) (of language)* connaissance *f*, maîtrise *f*, **to have a c. of several languages** parler plusieurs langues couramment; **she has a good c. of English** *or* **of the English language** elle a une bonne maîtrise de l'anglais
6 *Comput* commande *f*; *(from menu options)* article *m*
VT **1** *(order)* ordonner, commander (**sth** qch; **sb to do sth** à qn de faire qch); **he did what** *or* **as I commanded him** il a fait ce que je lui ai demandé; **do as I c.!** fais ce que je te demande!; *esp Lit* **we are yours to c.** nous sommes à vos ordres
2 *Mil (be in command of) (ship, regiment)* commander
3 *(have at one's disposal)* avoir à sa disposition; **all the skill he could c.** toute l'habileté qu'il possédait
4 *(inspire) (respect, admiration)* inspirer; *(attention)* forcer; **to c. a high price** se vendre très cher
5 *(of fort etc) (town, entry to pass)* dominer; **window that commands a view over the valley** fenêtre qui donne sur la vallée
VI commander
▸ ▸ *Comput* **c. button** case *f* de commande; *Comput* **c. code** code *m* de commande; **c. economy** économie *f* planifiée; *Comput* **c. file** fichier *m* de commande; *Comput* **c. key** touche *f* de commande; *Comput* **c. language** langage *m* de commande; *Comput* **c. line** ligne *f* de commande; **c. module** *(of spacecraft)* module *m* de commande; *Br Theat* **c. performance** = représentation *f* (d'un spectacle) à la requête du monarque; *Comput* **c. processor** interpréteur *m* de commandes; *Comput* **c. sequence** séquence *f* de commandes

commandant [kɒmənˈdænt] N *Mil (of camp etc)* commandant *m*

commandeer [kɒmənˈdɪər] VT *Mil* réquisitionner; *Fig* **the boss commandeered our photocopier** le patron a fait main basse sur notre photocopieuse

commander [kəˈmɑːndər] N *Mil (of army, company etc)* commandant *m*; *(of section)* chef *m*; *Aviat* chef de bord; *Naut* capitaine *m* de frégate; **one of the great commanders of history** un des grands chefs de l'histoire

commander-in-chief, *pl* **commanders-in-chief** N commandant *m* en chef

commanding [kəˈmɑːndɪŋ] ADJ **1** *(in command)* qui commande **2** *(tone)* d'autorité, impérieux; *(air)* imposant; *(beauty)* majestueux **3** *(position, height)* dominant; *(lead)* considérable
▸▸*Mil* **c. officer** commandant *m*

commandment [kəˈmɑːndmənt] N *Rel* commandement *m*; **the Ten Commandments** les Dix Commandements *mpl*; **to keep the commandments** observer les commandements

commando [kəˈmɑːndəʊ] N *Mil* commando *m*

command-orientated [-ɔːrɪənteɪtɪd] ADJ *Comput (program)* orienté commande

commemorate [kəˈmeməreɪt] VT *(person, person's memory)* commémorer

commemoration [kəmeməˈreɪʃən] N commémoration *f*; **in c. of sb/sth** en commémoration de qn/qch

commemorative [kəˈmemərətɪv] ADJ commémoratif (**of** de); **c. issue of a stamp** émission *f* d'un timbre commémoratif

commence [kəˈmens] VT & VI *Am, Br Fml* commencer; **he commenced speaking** il commença à parler

commencement [kəˈmensmənt] N **1** *Fml (beginning)* commencement *m*, début *m* **2** *Univ (in US, Canada, at Cambridge, in Trinity College, Dublin)* remise *f* des diplômes
▸▸*Univ* **C. Day** *(in US, at Cambridge)* jour *m* de la remise des diplômes

commend [kəˈmend] VT **1** *(praise)* *(person)* faire l'éloge de, louer; **to c. sb for bravery** faire l'éloge de la bravoure de qn
2 *(recommend)* *(something)* recommander; **a course of action that did not c. itself to me** une façon de faire que je ne pouvais pas approuver; **the train journey has little to c. it** je ne vous recommande pas le voyage en train; **the hotel has little to c. it apart from the cooking** il n'y a pas grand-chose de bien à dire sur cet hôtel à part la cuisine
3 *Lit (entrust)* **to c. sth to sb's care** recommander *ou* confier qch aux soins de qn; **to c. one's soul to God** recommander son âme à Dieu
4 *Arch, Fml (remember)* **c. me to Dr Smith** rappelez-moi au bon souvenir du Docteur Smith

commendable [kəˈmendəb(ə)l] ADJ louable; *(action)* digne d'éloges; **with c. promptness** avec une rapidité digne d'éloges

commendably [kəˈmendəblɪ] ADV d'une manière louable

commendation [kɒmenˈdeɪʃən] N *(praise)* éloge *m* (**of** de); *(award in competition)* mention *f* spéciale; **worthy of c.** digne d'éloges

commensurable [kəˈmensərəb(ə)l, -ʃər-] ADJ **1** *Math* commensurable (**with, to** avec)
2 = **commensurate 2**

commensurate [kəˈmensərət, -ʃər-] ADJ **1** *(of same proportions)* coétendu (**with** à) **2** *(proportionate)* proportionnel (**to, with** à); **the salary offered will be c. with experience** le salaire sera proportionné à l'expérience; **there was no post c. with his abilities** aucun

poste ne correspondait à ses compétences; **of c. value** d'une valeur équivalente

comment [ˈkɒment] N observation *f*, commentaire *m*; **to make a c. on sth** faire des observations sur qch; **no c.** sans commentaire; **to refrain from c.** s'abstenir de faire des commentaires
VT **to c. that …** (faire) remarquer *ou* (faire) observer que … +*ind*
VI **1** faire un/des commentaire(s); **I'd rather not c.** je préfère m'abstenir de tout commentaire; **to c. on sth** faire des observations *ou* des commentaires sur qch; **nobody commented on it** personne n'a fait de commentaire à ce sujet **2** *Liter* **to c. on a text** commenter un texte
▸▸**c. card** fiche *f* d'observations

commentary [ˈkɒmənt(ə)rɪ] N **1** *Radio, TV* commentaire *m*; **with c. by Terry Davis** commenté par Terry Davis **2** *Liter (on text etc)* commentaire *m* **3** *(remarks)* commentaire *m*, observations *fpl*
▸▸*Radio, TV* **c. booth** cabine *f* du commentateur; *Radio, TV* **c. box** tribune *f* des journalistes

commentate [ˈkɒmənteɪt] VI *Radio, TV* faire le commentaire; **to c. on an event** faire le commentaire d'un *ou* commenter un événement

commentator [ˈkɒmənteɪtər] N **1** *Radio, TV* commentateur, -trice; **(sports) c.** commentateur sportif, commentatrice sportive **2** *Journ* journaliste *mf (de la presse écrite)*; **political c.** journaliste politique **3** *Liter (on text)* commentateur, -trice

commerce [ˈkɒmɜːs] N **1** *(trade)* commerce *m*; **Chamber of C.** Chambre *f* de commerce **2** *Fml (social relations)* relations *fpl*, rapports *mpl* (**between** entre)

commercial [kəˈmɜːʃəl] ADJ **1** commercial, -aux; *(port, tribunal etc)* de commerce; *(value)* marchand; **a course in c. French** un cours de français commercial **2** *also Pej (profit-orientated)* *(mind)* mercantile, commercial, -aux; *(record, music)* commercial; *(mainstream)* *(film)* grand public *inv*; **his films are terribly c.** ses films sont vraiment commerciaux **3** *(radio, television)* commercial, -aux
N *Radio, TV* publicité *f*, pub *f*, spot *m* publicitaire
▸▸**c. agency** agence *f* commerciale; **c. artist** graphiste *mf*; **c. attaché** attaché *m* commercial; **c. bank** banque *f* commerciale; *Fin* **c. bill** effet *m* de commerce; *Radio, TV* **c. break** page *f* de publicité; **c. channel** *Écon* circuit *m* commercial; *TV* chaîne *f* commerciale; **c. contract** contrat *m* commercial; **c. directory** annuaire *m* du commerce; **c. documents** papiers *mpl* d'affaires; **c. law** droit *m* commercial; **c. loan** prêt *m* commercial; *Fin* **c. paper** billet *m* de trésorerie; *Old-fashioned* **c. traveller** voyageur *m ou* représentant *m* de commerce, VRP *m*; **c. vehicule** véhicule *m* utilitaire, commerciale *f*

commercialism [kəˈmɜːʃəlɪz(ə)m] N esprit *m* commercial; *Pej (obsession with profit)* mercantilisme *m*

commercialization [kəmɜːʃəlaɪˈzeɪʃən] N *also Pej* commercialisation *f*

commercialize [kəˈmɜːʃəlaɪz] VT *Pej* commercialiser

commercially [kəˈmɜːʃəlɪ] ADV commercialement

commie [ˈkɒmɪ] N, ADJ *Fam Pej (communist)* coco *mf*, communiste *mf*

commis [ˈkɒmɪ] ADJ
▸▸**c. chef** commis *m*, commis cuisinier, commis de cuisine; **c. waiter** commis

commiserate [kəˈmɪzəreɪt] VI **to c. with sb** être désolé pour qn

commiseration [kəmɪzəˈreɪʃən] N commisération *f*, compassion *f* (**with** pour); **commiserations are in order, I think** *(for you)* j'avoue que vous n'avez pas de chance

commissariat [kɒmɪˈseərɪət] N *Mil (department)* commissariat *m* de l'armée de terre, *Old-fashioned* intendance *f*

commissary [ˈkɒmɪsərɪ] N *Am Mil (store)* dépôt *m* de vivres; *(officer)* officier *m* d'intendance

Commission [kəˈmɪʃən] N *EU* Commission *f*

commission [kəˈmɪʃən] N **1** *Com (payment)* commission *f*; *(on exchange)* commission de change; **sale on c.** vente *f* à la commission; **three per cent c.** trois pour cent de commission; *Com* **c. only** rémunération *f* à la commission
2 *Com etc (order)* commande *f*, mission *f*; **work done on c.** travail fait sur commande; **to carry out a c.** s'acquitter d'une commande
3 *(investigating body)* commission *f*; **fact-finding c.** commission d'enquête
4 *Naut etc (of ship)* armement *m*; **to put a ship into c.** armer un navire; **in c.** *(ship)* en commission; *(plane, factory)* en service; **out of c.** *(ship)* désarmé; *(car, machine)* hors service; **you'll be out of c. for six weeks** vous serez obligé de suspendre vos activités pendant six semaines
5 *Mil* brevet *m* (d'officier); **to resign one's c.** démissionner, donner sa démission; **to get a** *or* **one's c.** être nommé officier
6 *(of a crime)* perpétration *f*
VT **1** *(order)* *(person)* commissionner (**to do sth** pour faire qch); *(book, painting)* commander; **to c. an artist to paint a portrait** commander un portrait à un artiste; **to be commissioned to do sth** être chargé de faire qch
2 *(appoint)* préposer *ou* déléguer à une fonction; *Mil (officer)* nommer à un commandement; *Mil* **to be commissioned** être nommé officier
3 *Naut etc (ship)* armer; *(plane, factory)* mettre en service
▸▸*Com* **c. agent** commissionaire *mf*; *Acct* **c. note** note *f* de commission

commissionaire [kəmɪʃəˈneər] N portier *m*

commissioned [kəˈmɪʃənd] ADJ **1** *Naut (ship)* armé **2** *(operative)* en service
▸▸*Mil* **c. officer** officier *m*

commissioner [kəˈmɪʃənər] N **1** *(member of a commission)* commissaire *m*, membre *m* d'une/de la commission **2** *(of police) Br* ≃ préfet *m* de police; *Am* ≃ (commissaire *m*) divisionnaire *m*
▸▸*Law* **c. for oaths** = officier *m* ayant qualité pour recevoir les déclarations sous serment

commissioning [kəˈmɪʃənɪŋ] N **1** *Mil (of officer)* nomination *f* à un commandement **2** *Naut etc (of ship)* armement *m*; *(of new power plant etc)* mise *f* en service *ou* en exploitation
▸▸**c. editor** directeur, -trice éditorial(e) *(chargé(e) notamment de commander de nouveaux ouvrages aux auteurs)*

commit [kəˈmɪt] VT (**-tt-**) **1** *(carry out)* *(crime)* commettre; **to c. suicide** se suicider
2 *(promise)* **to c. oneself** s'engager; **to c. oneself to sth/to doing sth** s'engager à qch/à faire qch; **without committing myself** sans m'engager; **to c. sth to sth** *(funds to project etc)* engager qch dans qch; **he had committed 2,000 troops to the defence of the village** il avait assigné 2 000 soldats à la défense du village
3 *(entrust)* confier, remettre (**sb/sth to sb's care** qn/qch aux soins *ou* à la garde de qn); **to c. sb's body to the earth/the deep** porter

un corps en terre/confier un corps aux flots; **to c. one's soul to God** rendre son âme à Dieu; **to c. sth to writing** coucher qch par écrit; **to c. sth to memory** apprendre qch par cœur

4 *(confine)* **she has been committed** *(to mental institution)* on l'a fait interner; **to c. sb (to prison)** envoyer qn en prison

5 *Law* **c. sb for trial** mettre qn en accusation; *(send to assizes)* renvoyer qn aux assises

6 *Pol (bill)* renvoyer à une commission

commitment [kə'mɪtmənt] **N 1** *(obligation)* engagement *m*; **family commitments** obligations *fpl* familiales; **I cannot do it because of other commitments** d'autres obligations m'empêchent de le faire; **there are no teaching commitments attached to this job** ce poste ne comporte pas d'heures d'enseignement obligatoires; **my teaching commitments this term** les heures d'enseignement que je dois assurer ce trimestre; **without any c. on your part** sans aucun engagement de votre part

2 *(to a political party, union etc)* engagement *m* (**to** pour); **his c. to the proposed reform of the tax system** son soutien pour la réforme du système fiscal qui a été proposée; **so many men avoid c. in relationships** il y a tellement d'hommes qui refusent de s'investir dans les relations amoureuses; **I found her lacking in c.** je trouvais qu'elle ne s'investissait pas assez; **to make a c.** s'engager

3 *Law* emprisonnement *m*

4 *(act of entrusting) (of document to notary etc)* dépôt *m*

▶▶ *Banking* **c. fee** commission *f* d'engagement

committal [kə'mɪt(ə)l] **N 1** *Law* emprisonnement *m*, mise *f* en prison; *(of insane person)* internement *m* dans un hôpital psychiatrique **2** *(of corpse)* mise *f* en terre; **the c. of a body to the ground/the deep** la mise en terre/l'immersion *f* d'un mort

▶▶ *Law* **c. order** mandat *m* de dépôt; *Law* **c. proceedings** = mise en accusation afin de décider si une affaire doit être renvoyée devant un tribunal de plus grande instance; *Law* **c. for sentence** = fait de renvoyer une affaire devant un tribunal de plus grande instance pour une condamnation qui reflète la gravité du crime; *Law* **c. for trial** = fait de renvoyer une affaire devant un tribunal de plus grande instance

committed [kə'mɪtɪd] **ADJ** engagé (**to** dans); **a c. socialist** un socialiste engagé; **he didn't seem very c.** son engagement ne semblait pas être très ferme; **to be c. to an idea** être attaché à une idée

▶▶ *Acct* **c. costs** coûts *mpl* engagés

committee [kə'mɪtɪ] **N** comité *m*, commission *f*; *Parl* commission *f*; **to be** *or* **sit on a c.** être membre *ou* faire partie d'un comité *ou* d'une commission; **in c.** en commission; **standing c.** commission permanente **VOIR GRAMMAIRE A11**

▶▶ **c. meeting** réunion *f* de comité; **c. member** membre *m* d'un/du comité *ou* d'une/de la commission; *Br Parl* **c. stage** = stade *m* de discussion d'un projet de loi par une commission; *Br Parl* **C. of Ways and Means** commission *f* du budget

committeeman, *pl* **committeemen** [kə-'mɪtɪmæn, -men] **N** *esp Am* homme *m* membre d'un/de plusieurs comité(s)

committeeperson [kə'mɪtɪpɜ:sən] **N** *esp Am* membre *m* d'un/de plusieurs comité(s)

committeewoman, *pl* **committee-women** [kə'mɪtɪwʊmən, -wɪmɪn] **N** *esp Am* femme *f* membre d'un/de plusieurs comité(s)

commode [kə'məʊd] **N 1** *(with drawers)* commode *f* **2** *(toilet)* chaise *f* percée

commodious [kə'məʊdɪəs] **ADJ** spacieux

commodity [kə'mɒdɪtɪ] **N** *Com, Econ* marchandise *f*, produit *m*; **primary** *or* **basic c.** produit de base

▶▶ *St Exch* **c. broker, c. dealer** courtier, -ière en matières premières; *St Exch* **c. futures** opérations *fpl* à terme sur matières premières; *St Exch* **c. market** marché *m* des matières premières; **c. money** monnaie *f* de marchandise; **c. tax** impôt *m* sur les denrées

commodore ['kɒmədɔ:r] **N** *Naut* chef *m* de division; *(of convoy)* chef de convoi; *(in merchant navy)* capitaine *m* le plus ancien; *(of yacht club)* président *m*

common ['kɒmən] **ADJ 1** *(frequent, widespread)* ordinaire, courant; **mixed marriages are c. here** les mariages mixtes sont courants ici; **in c. use** d'usage courant; **it is c. (practice) to ...** il est courant de ...; **it is c. knowledge** tout le monde le sait; **the agreement is c. knowledge** l'accord est connu de tous; **c. or garden cabbage** chou *m* commun; *Hum* **I'm just a c. or garden journalist** je ne suis qu'un journaliste ordinaire *ou* un journaliste parmi tant d'autres; **you may think this just a c. or garden wristwatch but ...** tu as peut-être l'impression que c'est une montre ordinaire *ou* comme les autres mais ...; **c. prostitute** vulgaire prostituée *f*; **c. thief** vulgaire voleur *m*; **c. decency** les convenances *fpl* (sociales)

2 *(shared)* commun; **he was, by c. consent ...** il était, de l'avis de tous, ...; **by c. consent, it has been decided to ...** d'un commun accord, on a décidé de ...; *Law* **c. land** champs *mpl* communs; **c. ownership** copropriété *f*; **c. staircase** escalier *m* commun; **c. wall** mur *m* commun *ou* mitoyen; **to make c. cause with sb** s'allier à qn; **we have c. interests** nous avons des intérêts communs

3 *(average)* **the c. people** les gens *mpl* ordinaires; **the c. man** l'homme *m* de la rue; **he lacks the c. touch** il ne sait pas parler aux gens; **he's nothing but a c. criminal** ce n'est qu'un vulgaire criminel

4 *Pej (vulgar) (person, manners, language, style, joke)* vulgaire; *(accent)* populaire; **he's rather a c. little man** il est plutôt commun

N 1 to have sth in c. with sb/sth avoir qch en commun avec qn/qch; **they have nothing in c.** ils n'ont rien en commun

2 *(land)* terrain *m* communal; **the village c.** les terrains communaux, les communaux *mpl*

3 *Law* **(right of) c.** droit *m* de (vaine) pâture

▶▶ *EU* **C. Agricultural Policy** politique *f* agricole commune; **c. carrier** *(of goods)* transporteur *m* public, entreprise *f* de transport public; **c. cold** rhume *m*; *Math, Fig* **c. denominator** dénominateur *m* commun; *Math* **c. divisor** diviseur *m* commun; *EU* **c. external tariff** tarif *m* externe commun; *Math* **c. factor** facteur *m* commun; *EU* **C. Fisheries Policy** politique commune de la pêche; *Comput* **c. gateway interface** interface *f* commune de passerelle; **c. ground** *(in interests)* intérêt *m* commun; *(for discussion)* terrain *m* d'entente; *Fig* **there is no c. ground between them** il n'y a pas de terrain d'entente entre eux; **c. interest group** groupe *m* d'intérêt commun; **c. law** droit *m* coutumier, common law *f*; *EU* **the C. Market** le marché commun; **c. name** *(of plant)* nom *m* vulgaire; *Gram* **c. noun** nom *m* commun; *Aviat* **c. rated fare** tarif *m* commun; *Br Sch, Univ* **c. room** *(for students)* salle *f* commune; *(for staff)* salle des professeurs; **c. salt** sel *m* ordinaire; **c. sense** bon sens *m*, sens commun; *Am St Exch* **c. stock** actions *fpl* ordinaires; *Mus* **c. time** mesure *f* à quatre temps

commoner ['kɒmənər] **N 1** *(not noble)* roturier, -ière **2** *Law* usager, -ère du droit de vaine pâture **3** *Univ (at Oxford)* étudiant, -ante ordinaire *(qui ne reçoit pas de bourse)* **4** *Br Parl* député *m*, membre *m* de la Chambre des communes

common-law **ADJ** *Law* **c. husband** concubin *m*; **c. wife** concubine *f*; **c. marriage** concubinage *m*, union *f* libre; **the children of c. marriages** les enfants issus d'unions libres

commonly ['kɒmənlɪ] **ADV 1** *(frequently)* communément, ordinairement; **what is c. known as ...** ce qu'en langage courant on appelle ... **2** *Pej (vulgarly)* vulgairement, de façon vulgaire

commonness ['kɒmənnɪs] **N 1** *(frequency)* fréquence *f* **2** *Pej (vulgarity)* vulgarité *f*

commonplace ['kɒmənpleɪs] **N** *(thing)* banalité *f*; *(saying)* lieu *m* commun, platitude *f* **ADJ** banal, -als; **such operations are becoming c.** de telles opérations deviennent de plus en plus banales

▶▶ *Old-fashioned* **c. book** recueil *m* de pensées

commons ['kɒmənz] **NPL 1** *(people)* **the c.** le peuple; **the (House of) C.** la Chambre des Communes **2** *Old-fashioned (food)* **to be on short c.** faire maigre chère

commonweal ['kɒmənwi:l] **N** *Lit* bien *m* commun

Commonwealth ['kɒmənwelθ] **N 1 the (British) C. (of Nations)** le Commonwealth **2** *Br Hist* = période *f* de l'histoire britannique de 1649 (mort de Charles I) à 1660 (rétablissement de la monarchie)

▶▶ **the C. of Australia** le Commonwealth d'Australie; **C. country** pays *m* du Commonwealth; *Br* **C. Development Group** = organisme *m* gouvernemental dont le rôle est de répartir l'aide aux pays en voie de développement; **the C. of Massachusetts** l'État *m* du Massachusetts; **the C. of Pennsylvania** l'État de Pennsylvanie

commotion [kə'məʊʃən] **N** *(noise)* agitation *f*, commotion *f*; **in a state of c.** en émoi; **to create a c.** faire du bruit; **what's all the c. about?** pourquoi toute cette agitation?

comms [kɒmz] **N** *Comput* communication *f*

▶▶ **c. package** logiciel *m* de communication; **c. port** port *m* de communication

communal ['kɒmjʊn(ə)l] **ADJ 1** *(shared) (bathroom, garden etc)* commun; *Law* **c. estate** communauté *f* (conjugale); **c. property** biens *mpl* en commun *ou* en copropriété **2** *(of community)* communautaire, collectif; **c. life** la vie commune *ou* communautaire; **c. violence** violence *f* entre communautés

communally [kə'mju:nəlɪ] **ADV** en commun; **c. owned** en copropriété

commune¹ ['kɒmju:n] **N 1** *(of hippies etc)* communauté *f*; *Hist* **the Paris C.** la Commune (de Paris) **2** *Admin (in France, Belgium, Italy etc)* commune *f*

commune² [kə'mju:n] **VI 1** *Lit* communiquer (**with** sb avec qn); **to c. with nature** être en communion avec la nature **2** *Am Rel* communier

communicable [kə'mju:nɪkəb(ə)l] **ADJ** *(disease)* transmissible; *(idea)* communicable

communicant [kə'mju:nɪkənt] **N** *Rel* communiant, -ante

communicate [kə'mju:nɪkeɪt] **VI 1** communiquer; **to c. with sb** communiquer avec qn; **to c. by letter** communiquer par lettre; **he finds it difficult to c.** il a du mal à communiquer; **we can't seem to c.** on ne se comprend pas; **we've stopped communicating** on a cessé toute communication; **to c. well/badly** avoir de grandes qualités relationnelles/manquer de qualités relationnelles **2** *(connect) (of rooms)* communiquer; **rooms that**

c. with one another chambres qui communiquent **3** *Rel* communier, recevoir la communion
VT *(news etc)* communiquer, faire parvenir; *(illness)* passer; *(emotion, heat etc)* communiquer

communicating [kə'mjuːnɪkeɪtɪŋ] ADJ *(room)* communicant; *(door)* de communication

communication [kəmjuːnɪ'keɪʃən] N **1** *(contact)* **to be in c. with ...** être en relation avec ...; **to be in close c. with one another** être en relation constante; **we haven't had any c. for six months** nous ne sommes plus en relation(s) depuis six mois; **to break off all c. with sb** rompre toutes relations avec qn; **communications between the two have broken down** ils ne sont plus en relation; **line of c.** lien *m*; *Mil* ligne *f* de communication
2 *(message etc)* communication *f*; **no official c. of his death has yet been received** on n'a encore reçu aucune communication officielle de sa mort
3 *(of information, feeling etc)* communication *f* (**to sb** à qn); **means of c.** moyens *mpl* de communication; **c. gap** manque *m* de communication; **c. problem** problème *m* de communication
4 communications *(technology)* communications *fpl*; *Mil (system)* transmissions *fpl*, liaison(s) *f(pl)*; **radio communications** liaison (par) radio
▸▸ *Br* **c. cord** sonnette *f* d'alarme *(dans les trains)*; **communications director** directeur, -trice de la communication, dircom *m*; **communications link** liaison *f* de communications; **communications manager** directeur, -trice de la communication, dircom; **c. network** réseau *m* de communication; **communications satellite** satellite *m* de communications; **communications sector** secteur *m* des communications; **c. skills** *(of person)* qualités *fpl* relationnelles; **to have good c. skills** avoir des talents de communication, être un bon communicateur; *Comput* **communications software** logiciel *m* de communication; *Mil* **c. trench** boyau *m*; *Br* **C. Workers Union** = syndicat *m* des travailleurs des postes et des télécommunications

communications-intensive ADJ utilisant intensivement les moyens de communication

communicative [kə'mjuːnɪkətɪv] ADJ communicatif; *(skills)* en matière de communication; **she's not very c.** elle n'est pas très communicative

communion [kə'mjuːnjən] N **1** *Rel* **(Holy) C.** sainte communion *f*; **to administer Holy C. to sb** administrer la sainte communion à qn; **to take (Holy) C.** communier; **the c. of saints** la communion des saints **2** *Lit* communication *f* (**with sb** avec qn)
▸▸ *Rel* **c. cup** calice *m*; *Rel* **c. wafer** hostie *f*; *Rel* **c. wine** vin *m* de messe

communiqué [kə'mjuːnɪkeɪ] N communiqué *m*

communism ['kɒmjʊnɪz(ə)m] N communisme *m*

communist ['kɒmjʊnɪst] ADJ, N communiste *mf*

Community [kə'mjuːnɪtɪ] ADJ *EU* communautaire
▸▸ **C. law** droit *m* communautaire

community [kə'mjuːnɪtɪ] N **1** *(group)* communauté *f*; **the international c.** la communauté internationale; **the Greek c. in Paris** la communauté grecque de Paris
2 *(village etc)* communauté *f*; **a small mining c.** une petite communauté minière; **a c. of 2,000** une communauté de 2 000 habitants

3 *Rel* communauté *f* *(religieuse)*
4 *(public)* **the c.** le public; **harmful to the c.** nuisible à la communauté
5 *(something shared)* *(of possessions, interests etc)* communauté *f*, *(of tastes)* communauté, identité *f*; **there's no c. of values between them** il n'y a pas de communauté de valeurs entre eux
▸▸ *Admin* **c. care** = système *m* britannique de soins et d'aide au niveau local; **c. centre** foyer *m* municipal, centre *m* social; *Am TV* **c. channel** = chaîne *f* du réseau câblé sur laquelle des particuliers peuvent diffuser leurs propres émissions; *Br Admin Formerly* **c. charge** = impôt *m* local; *Am Fin* **c. chest** fonds *m* commun *(à des fins sociales)*; **c. policing** ≃ îlotage *m*, *Can* services *mpl* de police communautaires, patrouille *f* pédestre de quartier; **c. radio** radio *f* communautaire; *Law* **c. service** ≃ travail *m* d'intérêt général; **c. singing** chansons *fpl* populaires *(reprises en chœur)*; **c. spirit** esprit *m* de groupe

commutable [kə'mjuːtəb(ə)l] ADJ **1** *Law (sentence)* commuable **2** *(interchangeable)* permutable, interchangeable

commutation [kɒmjʊ'teɪʃən] N commutation *f*, *Law* **c. of sentence** commutation de peine
▸▸ *Am* **c. ticket** *(for public transportation)* carte *f* d'abonnement

commutator ['kɒmjʊteɪtər] N *Elec* commutateur *m*

commute [kə'mjuːt] VI faire la navette entre sa résidence et son travail; **I c. here every day** je fais le trajet tous les jours; **to c. by train/car** se rendre à son travail en train/voiture
VT **1** *(exchange)* échanger (**for, into** pour, contre); **to c. an annuity into** or **for a lump sum** racheter une rente par un versement global **2** *Law* **to c. a penalty into** or **for another** commuer une peine en une autre **3** *(interchange)* interchanger **4** *Metal* transformer
N *Am* trajet *m* *(entre travail et domicile)*; **it's an easy c.** c'est un trajet commode

commuter [kə'mjuːtər] N *(from suburbs)* banlieusard, -arde *(qui fait la navette entre sa résidence et son travail)*, *Belg* navetteur, -euse; **I've been a c. for fifteen years** ça fait quinze ans que je fais la navette *(entre chez moi et le travail)*; **the problems caused by c. traffic** les problèmes provoqués par l'utilisation de la voiture pour se rendre au travail; **c. traffic is very heavy this evening** la circulation en direction de la banlieue est très dense ce soir
▸▸ **c. airline** compagnie *f* d'aviation court-courrier; *Br* **the c. belt** la grande banlieue; *Rail* **c. line** ligne *f* de banlieue; **c. plane** commuter *m*; **c. town** cité-dortoir *f*, *pl* cités-dortoirs; **c. train** train *m* de banlieue

commuterland [kə'mjuːtəlænd] N = grande banlieue *f* considérée comme un pays à part, où l'on ne fait rien d'autre que dormir

commuting [kə'mjuːtɪŋ] N trajets *mpl* réguliers, migrations *fpl* quotidiennes *(entre le domicile, généralement en banlieue, et le lieu de travail)*; **I'm tired of c.** j'en ai assez de faire le trajet jusqu'à mon travail tous les jours

comp [kɒmp] N **1** *Typ (compositor)* metteur *m* (en pages) **2** *(ticket)* exonéré *m*

compact¹ [kɒm'pækt, 'kɒmpækt] ADJ **1** *(dense, closely packed)* *(snow, ground etc)* compact; *(style)* concis **2** *(small)* *(apartment, kitchen etc)* petit mais fonctionnel; *(telephone, computer, camera etc)* compact; *Am (car)* petit et économique; *(person)* trapu; **to have a c. build** être trapu
▸▸ **c. disc** *(disque m)* compact *m*, CD *m*; **c. disc interactive** CDI *m*; **c. disc player** platine *f* CD; **c. disc recorder** graveur *m* de disque

compact; **c. disc rewritable** CD réinscriptible; **c. disc video** CD vidéo *m*

compact² ['kɒmpækt] N **1** *(for powder)* *(in handbag)* poudrier *m* **2** *Am Aut* voiture *f* petite et économique **3** *Fml (agreement)* convention *f*, accord *m*

compact³ [kɒm'pækt] VT rendre compact; *(snow)* tasser; *Constr* compacter

compacting [kəm'pæktɪŋ] N *Comput* compression *f*

compactly [kəm'pæktlɪ] ADV d'une manière compacte

compactness [kəm'pæktnɪs] N **1** *(of earth, snow, muscles)* dureté *f*, *(of style)* concision *f* **2** *(smallness)* *(of computer, design, camera etc)* compacité *f*; **the c. of the kitchen** la cuisine petite mais fonctionnelle

Companies Act ['kɒmpənɪz] N *Law* Loi *f* sur les sociétés

Companies House N *Br Com* = institut *m* où sont enregistrées toutes les informations concernant les entreprises du pays

companion¹ [kəm'pænjən] N **1** *(male)* compagnon *m*; *(female)* compagne *f*, **(lady) c.** dame *f* de compagnie; **c. in arms** compagnon d'armes; **a drinking/travelling c.** un compagnon de boisson/voyage **2** *(other of a pair)* *(of book etc)* pendant *m* (**of** à) **3** *(in titles)* compagnon *m*; **C. to English Literature** guide *m* de la littérature anglaise
▸▸ **c. fare** *(for additional person)* tarif *m* par personne supplémentaire

companion² N *Naut*
▸▸ **c. hatch** capot *m*; **c. ladder** échelle *f* de commandement

companionable [kəm'pænjənəb(ə)l] ADJ sociable

companionship [kəm'pænjənʃɪp] N compagnie *f*, *(comradeship)* camaraderie *f*, **the dog provides c. for her** le chien lui fait de la compagnie *ou* lui tient compagnie

companionway [kəm'pænjənweɪ] N *Naut* escalier *m* des cabines

company ['kɒmpənɪ] N **1** compagnie *f*, **in sb's c.** en compagnie de qn; **I like his c.** j'aime sa compagnie, j'aime être avec lui; **to keep sb c.** tenir compagnie à qn; **he's very good c.** c'est un compagnon agréable, il est de bonne compagnie; **it's nice to have c.** c'est agréable d'avoir de la compagnie; **she needs the c. of children of her own age** elle a besoin d'être avec des enfants de son âge; **to be fond of one's own c.** aimer être seul; *Prov* **two's c., three's a crowd** = vous seriez/nous serions/*etc* mieux tous les deux; **to part c. with sb** *(split up)* se séparer de qn; *(disagree)* ne plus être d'accord avec qn
2 *(acquaintances)* compagnie *f*, société *f*, **I don't like the c. he keeps** je n'aime pas ses fréquentations; **to get into bad c.** avoir de mauvaises fréquentations
3 *(people present)* assemblée *f*, personnes *fpl* présentes; **to do sth in c.** faire qch en public; **present c. excepted** à part les personnes ici présentes; **the most intelligent of the c. were in agreement** les plus intelligentes des personnes présentes étaient d'accord
4 *(guests)* invités *mpl*, **are you expecting c.?** vous attendez de la visite?; *Fam* **we've got c.!** *(there's someone else here, we're being followed)* nous avons de la compagnie
5 *Com, Ind* entreprise *f*, société *f*, **to form** or **incorporate a c.** constituer une société; **insurance c.** compagnie *f* d'assurances; **(the firm of) Thomas and C.** (la maison) Thomas et Cie; **on** or **in c. time** *(to make telephone call etc)* pendant les heures de travail **VOIR GRAMMAIRE A11**
6 *Theat* compagnie *f*

7 *Naut* **the ship's c.** l'équipage *m* (au complet, y compris les officiers)
8 *Mil* compagnie *f*
9 (of girl guides) compagnie *f*
10 (guild) corporation *f* de marchands
▸▸ **c. car** voiture *f* de fonction; **c. credit card** carte *f* de crédit professionnelle; **c. director** directeur, -trice; **c. doctor** (medical) médecin *m* du travail; (businessperson) redresseur *m* d'entreprises; **c. funds** fonds *m* social; **c. law** droit *m* des sociétés; **c. lawyer** avocat, -ate d'une/de l'entreprise *ou* d'une/ de la société; *Mil* **c. officer** officier *m* de compagnie; **c. policy** politique *f* de la maison *ou* de la société; **it isn't c. policy** ce n'est pas la politique de la maison *ou* de la société; **c. savings scheme** plan *m* d'épargne entreprise; **c. secretary** secrétaire *mf* général(e) (d'une entreprise)

comparability [kɒmpərə'bɪlɪtɪ] N comparabilité *f*

comparable ['kɒmpərəb(ə)l] ADJ comparable (**with** avec; **to** à)

comparative [kəm'pærətɪv] ADJ **1** (comparing) comparatif; **c. rating scale** échelle *f* d'évaluation comparative; **c. methodology** méthodologie *f* comparative; **a c. study** une étude comparative **2** (relative) (cost, comfort, wealth etc) relatif; **he's a c. stranger to me** je ne le connais pratiquement pas
N *Gram* comparatif *m*; **in the c.** au comparatif VOIR GRAMMAIRE A24–7; B11; B13–14
▸▸ *Econ* **c. advantage** avantage *m* comparé; *Gram* **c. adverb** adverbe *m* de comparaison *ou* comparatif; *Am* **c. advertising** publicité *f* comparative; *Econ* **c. cost** loi *f* des avantages comparés; *Gram* **the c. degree** le comparatif; **c. grammar** grammaire *f* comparée; **c. linguistics** linguistique *f* comparée; *Mktg* **c. test** test *m* comparatif

comparatively [kəm'pærɪtɪvlɪ] ADV **1** (in comparison) comparativement, par comparaison **2** (relatively) (easy, expensive etc) relativement

compare VT (facts, ideas) comparer; **to c. sth to sth** (liken) comparer qch à qch; (contrast) comparer qch avec qch; **to c. sth with sth** (contrast) comparer qch avec qch; **compared with** *or* **to …** en comparaison de …, à côté de …, par rapport à …; **compared with last year's figures** par rapport aux chiffres de l'année dernière; **to c. notes** (exchange impressions) échanger ses impressions
VI être comparable (**with** à); **he can't c. with you** on ne peut pas le comparer à vous; **nothing compares to you** tu es unique; **other brands of washing powder just can't c.** les autres marques de lessive ne sont pas à la hauteur de celle-ci; **to c. favourably with sth** ne le céder en rien à qch; **the French car compares well with the Italian one** la voiture française supporte la comparaison avec l'italienne
N *Lit* **beyond c.** sans comparaison; **beauty without c.** beauté sans pareille

comparison [kəm'pærɪs(ə)n] N comparaison *f*; **to make** *or* **draw a c. between sth and sth** faire la comparaison de qch avec qch; **in** *or* **by c.** en comparaison; **in c. with … comparé à …; without c., beyond all c.** sans comparaison; **there is no c.** il n'y a pas de comparaison; **to stand** *or* **bear c.** supporter la comparaison; **that's a rather unfair c.** ce n'est pas très juste de me/le/etc comparer à lui/elle/etc; *Gram* **degrees of c.** degrés *mpl* de comparaison
▸▸ *Mktg* **c. advertising** publicité *f* comparative; *Mktg* **c. shopping** achats *mpl* comparatifs

compartment [kəm'pɑːtmənt] N **1** *Rail* compartiment *m*; **sleeping c.** compartiment lit (dans un wagon-lit) **2** (of a drawer etc) case *f*, compartiment *m*

compartmentalize [kɒmpɑːt'ment(ə)laɪz] VT compartimenter

compass ['kʌmpəs] N **1** (in surveying), Naut etc (with moving needle) boussole *f*, (with moving card) compas *m* **2** *Geom* **(pair of) compasses** compas *m* **3** *Fml* (scope) (of knowledge, powers) étendue *f*, (of inquiry, reforms) cadre *m*; (of time) espace *m*; (of mind) portée *f*, *Mus* (of voice) étendue, diapason *m*, registre *m*; **to be beyond the c. of the human mind** dépasser les limites de l'entendement humain
▸▸ *Naut* **c. bearing** relèvement *m* au compas; **to take a c. bearing** prendre un relèvement au compas; *Naut* **c. card** rose *f* des vents; *Naut* **c. dial** rose des vents; *Naut* **c. error** erreur *f ou* variation *f* du compas

compassion [kəm'pæʃən] N compassion *f*, pitié *f*, **to arouse c.** faire pitié, exciter la compassion; **to show c.** montrer de la compassion; **you have no c.** tu n'as pas de pitié
▸▸ **c. fatigue** = lassitude *f* du public à l'égard des nécessiteux

compassionate [kəm'pæʃənət] ADJ compatissant (**to** à; **towards** pour); **on c. grounds** pour des raisons personnelles *ou* familiales (en cas de décès d'un proche etc)
▸▸ **c. leave** congé *m* exceptionnel; *Mil* permission *f* exceptionnelle (pour raisons personnelles)

compassionately [kəm'pæʃənətlɪ] ADV avec compassion

compatibility [kəmpætə'bɪlɪtɪ] N (of people), Comput compatibilité *f*

compatible [kəm'pætəb(ə)l] ADJ (person), Comput compatible (**with** avec); **IBM-c.** compatible IBM

compatibly [kəm'pætəblɪ] ADV d'une manière compatible (**with** avec)

compatriot [kəm'pætrɪət, -'peɪ-] N compatriote *mf*

compel [kəm'pel] VT (-ll-) contraindre, forcer, obliger (**to do sth** à faire qch); **to be compelled to do sth** être contraint *ou* obligé de faire qch; **don't feel compelled to do it** ne vous sentez pas obligé de le faire; **to c. sb's admiration/respect** forcer l'admiration/le respect de qn

compelling [kəm'pelɪŋ] ADJ (force, curiosity, urge, desire etc) irrésistible; (film, performance) captivant; **her book makes c. reading** son livre est captivant *ou* prenant; **a c. speaker** un orateur qui subjugue *ou* captive son auditoire

compellingly [kəm'pelɪŋlɪ] ADV irrésistiblement

compendium, *pl* **compendiums** [kəm'pendɪəm, -z] N (summary) abrégé *m*, précis *m*, compendium *m*
▸▸ **c. of games** boîte *f* de jeux; *Law* **c. of laws** recueil *m* des lois

compensable [kəm'pensəb(ə)l] ADJ indemnisable
▸▸ *Acct* **c. loss** perte *f* indemnisable

compensate ['kɒmpənseɪt] VT **1** (make amends for/to) dédommager, indemniser (**for** de) **2** *Tech* (pendulum etc) compenser; **to c. one another** (of factors etc) se compenser
VI **1 to c. for sth** compenser qch; **experience may c. for lack of qualifications** l'expérience peut compenser le manque de qualifications **2** *Psy* compenser

compensated ['kɒmpənseɪtɪd] ADJ *Elec etc* compensé

compensating ['kɒmpənseɪtɪŋ] ADJ compensateur
▸▸ **c. errors** erreurs *fpl* compensatoire

compensation [kɒmpən'seɪʃən] N compensation *f*, (for loss, injury, damage) dédommagement *m*, indemnisation *f*, **all of the victims will receive c.** toutes les victimes recevront une indemnité; **in c.** à titre compensatoire *ou* de compensation *ou* de dédommagement; **c. for loss of custom** indemnité *f* de clientèle; **c. for wrongful dismissal** indemnité de rupture abusive; **c. in lieu of notice** indemnité compensatrice de préavis
▸▸ **c. package** *Br* (for redundancy) prime *f* de licenciement; *Am* (when starting new job) avantages *mpl* sociaux; *Com* **c. plan** mode *m* de rémunération

compensator ['kɒmpenseɪtər] N *Tech*
▸▸ **c. arm** bras *m* compensateur; **c. valve** valve *f* de compensation

compensatory [kɒmpən'seɪt(ə)rɪ] ADJ compensatoire

compère ['kɒmpeər] *Theat, TV etc* N animateur, -trice, présentateur, -trice
VT (programme) présenter, animer

compete [kəm'piːt] VI rivaliser (**with sb** avec qn; **for sth** pour qch); *Com* (of one company) faire de la concurrence (**with** à); (of two companies) se faire concurrence; **we can't c.** (are not competitive) nous ne sommes pas concurrentiels; **children here aren't encouraged to c.** ici, les enfants ne sont pas encouragés à la compétition; **the player had competed for every point** le joueur s'était battu sur chaque point; **to c. with one another** se faire concurrence; *Sport* **to c. against sb** concourir avec qn; **France is competing against several countries for the contract** la France est en compétition avec plusieurs autres pays pour décrocher ce contrat; **to c. for a prize** concourir pour un prix; **to c. with sb for a prize** disputer un prix à qn; **her cooking can't c. with yours** sa cuisine ne peut pas rivaliser avec la tienne

competence ['kɒmpɪtəns] N **1** (ability) compétences *fpl*, capacités *fpl* (**in** *or* **for sth** en qch; **in doing** pour faire) **2** *Fml* (scope of functions) (of civil servant) attributions *fpl*, *Law* compétence *f*, **to be within/beyond the c. of a court** être/ne pas être de la compétence *ou* du ressort d'un tribunal

competency ['kɒmpɪtənsɪ] N = competence

competent ['kɒmpɪtənt] ADJ **1** (able) (doctor, worker etc) compétent, capable; **a c. piece of work** du bon travail; **c. to do sth** capable de faire qch; (qualified) apte à faire qch, qualifié pour faire qch; **he's quite c. at French** il a un bon niveau de français; **c. knowledge of English** bonne connaissance *f* de l'anglais **2** *Law* (tribunal) compétent; **c. to inherit** habilité à succéder

competently ['kɒmpɪtəntlɪ] ADV avec compétence

competition [kɒmpɪ'tɪʃən] N **1** (rivalry) rivalité *f*, concurrence *f*, **to be in c.** être en compétition; **to enter into c. with sb** concurrencer qn, faire concurrence à qn; **there was a lot of c. for the job** il y avait beaucoup de concurrence pour cette place **2** (contest) concours *m*; *Sport* compétition *f* (sportive); **a poetry c.** un concours de poésie; **to win a prize in open c.** remporter un prix dans un concours ouvert à tous; **to take part in competitions** faire de la compétition; **that's him out of the c.** le voilà hors compétition **3** *Com, Econ* concurrence *f*, **free c.** libre concurrence **4 the c.** (rivals) *Com* la concurrence; *Sport* les concurrents, -entes *ou* adversaires *mfpl*; (for a job) les autres candidats, -ates; **you're up against some tough c.** (in race) vous êtes en face d'adversaires de taille; (for job, uni-

versity) la concurrence est rude; **the company has to stay ahead of the c.** l'entreprise doit rester plus compétitive que les autres
➤➤ **c. car** *(in motor racing)* voiture *f* de compétition

competitive [kəm'petɪtɪv] **ADJ 1** *(person)* qui a l'esprit de compétition, qui aime la compétition; *(atmosphere, environment)* de compétition; **a c. school/society** une école/société où l'on met l'accent sur la compétition; **he's so c.** il a vraiment l'esprit de compétition **2** *Com, Econ (price)* concurrentiel, compétitif; *(product)* concurrent; *(firm, company, industry)* compétitif; **to offer c. terms** proposer des prix très compétitifs; **in a c. marketplace** dans un marché de concurrence; **industry must get more c.** l'industrie doit devenir plus compétitive
➤➤ *Com* **c. advantage** avantage *m* concurrentiel; *Com* **c. awareness** sensibilité *f* compétitive; *Com* **c. discounting** remise *f* compétitive; **c. edge** (léger) avantage concurrentiel; *Com* **c. equilibrium price** prix *m* d'équilibre concurrentiel; **c. examination** concours *m*; **c. position** position *f* concurrentielle; *Mktg* **c. positioning** positionnement *m* concurrentiel; **c. scope** domaine *m* concurrentiel, champ *m* concurrentiel; **c. spirit** esprit *m* de compétition; **c. sports** sports *mpl* de compétition; **c. strategy** stratégie *f* concurrentielle

competitively [kəm'petɪtɪvlɪ] **ADV** dans un esprit de compétition; *Com, Econ* **c. priced** à un prix concurrentiel *ou* compétitif

competitiveness [kəm'petɪtɪvnɪs] **N 1** compétitivité *f* **2** *Com, Econ (of product)* concurrence *f*, *(of firm, company)* compétitivité *f*

competitor [kəm'petɪtər] **N** *Sport, Com* concurrent, -ente

compilation [kɒmpɪ'leɪʃən] **N 1** *(activity)* compilation *f* **2** *(list)* compilation *f*
➤➤ **c. album** compilation *f*

compile [kəm'paɪl] **VT** compiler

compiler [kəm'paɪlər] **N** *(of dictionary etc)* compilateur, -trice, rédacteur, -trice; *Comput* compilateur

complacency [kəm'pleɪsənsɪ] **N** contentement *m* de soi; **there is no room for c.** il n'y a pas de quoi faire de l'autosatisfaction; **this is no time for c.** ce n'est pas le moment de faire de l'auto-satisfaction

complacent [kəm'pleɪsənt] **ADJ** *(person)* content de soi; *(look, remark)* très satisfait; **to be c. about sth** faire de l'auto-satisfaction à propos de qch; **we shouldn't become c. about unemployment just because of a few successes** nous ne devons pas relâcher notre effort dans la lutte contre le chômage sous prétexte que nous avons marqué quelques points

> Attention: ne pas confondre avec l'adjectif anglais **complaisant**.

complacently [kəm'pleɪsəntlɪ] **ADV** *(to smile, reply)* d'un air suffisant; **some of our managers have been sitting c. behind their desks** certains de nos dirigeants se sont un peu trop reposés sur leurs lauriers

complain [kəm'pleɪn] **VI 1** se plaindre (**about** de; **to** à); *(officially)* se plaindre (**to** auprès de); **he's always complaining** il se plaint toujours; **to c. that ...** se plaindre que *ou* de ce que ... + *ind*; **don't come complaining to me about it** tu ne viendras pas te plaindre à moi; **I can't c.** je n'ai pas à me plaindre **2** *(of sore throat, headaches etc)* se plaindre (**of** de)

complainant [kəm'pleɪnənt] **N** *Law* plaignant, -ante

complaint [kəm'pleɪnt] **N 1** *(grievance)*

plainte *f*; **I have no cause** *or* **grounds for c.** je n'ai aucun motif de plainte; **do you have any complaints about the company?** est-ce que vous avez à vous plaindre de l'entreprise?; **her latest c. was that ...** la dernière chose dont elle s'est plainte a été que ...; **I've got no c. against you** je n'ai rien à te reprocher **2** *(official)* plainte *f*, réclamation *f*; **to lodge** *or* **make a c. against sb** porter plainte contre qn **3** *(illness)* maladie *f*; **liver c.** maladie *ou* affection *f* du foie
➤➤ **complaints book** cahier *m* de réclamations; **complaints office** bureau *m ou* service *m* des réclamations

complaisance [kəm'pleɪzəns] **N** *Fml* complaisance *f*

complaisant [kəm'pleɪz(ə)nt] **ADJ** *Fml* complaisant

> Attention: ne pas confondre avec l'adjectif **complacent**.

complement ['kɒmplɪmənt] **N 1** *(of bus etc) (passengers)* charge *f* complète; *Naut (crew etc)* effectif *m*; *Naut* **full c.** effectif complet; **have we got a full c.?** *(in office, team etc)* est-ce que nous sommes au complet? **2** *Math (of angle etc)* complément *m*; *Gram (of verb)* complément; *(following 'to be', 'to seem' etc)* attribut *m*
VT compléter; *(of wine, sauce etc)* mettre en valeur; **they c. each other well** *(of two people)* ils se complètent parfaitement

complementary [kɒmplɪ'ment(ə)rɪ] **ADJ** *(angle, colour)* complémentaire
➤➤ **c. medicine** médecine *f* douce; *Comput* **c. MOS** MOS *m* complémentaire

complete [kəm'pliːt] **ADJ 1** complet, -ète, entier; *(surprise, failure)* total, -aux; **I need a c. break from teaching** j'ai besoin de vraies vacances où je ne penserai plus du tout à mes cours; **is the pack c.?** *(of cards)* le jeu est-il complet?; *Com* **c. with battery** livré avec pile; **my happiness is c.** mon bonheur est total, rien ne manque à mon bonheur; **a visit to Brussels would not be c. without a meal here** la visite de Bruxelles ne serait pas complète sans un repas ici; **to give a c. account** donner tous les détails; **a c. (and utter) failure** un échec total; **the operation has been a c. success** l'opération a pleinement réussi; **she is a c. fool** elle est complètement idiote; **he's a c. stranger** c'est un total inconnu
2 *(finished)* terminé, achevé
VT 1 *(finish) (job, task)* achever, terminer; *(training, apprenticeship)* accomplir **2** *(fill missing parts of) (collection, number, tea service)* compléter **3** *(fill in) (form, questionnaire)* remplir

completely [kəm'pliːtlɪ] **ADV** complètement, totalement; **I c. understand your frustration** je comprends tout à fait ta frustration

completeness [kəm'pliːtnɪs] **N** état *m* complet; **there's a c. to it** *(to novel, film etc)* il a un caractère abouti; **they added a final volume for c.** ils ont ajouté un dernier volume pour que l'ensemble soit complet

completion [kəm'pliːʃən] **N** *(of work)* achèvement *m*; **in the process of c.** en (cours d')achèvement; **near c.** près d'être achevé; **to reach c.** *(of project etc)* s'achever; **occupation on c. (of contract)** *(of property)* prise *f* de possession des lieux à la signature du contrat
➤➤ **c. date** *(for building, repair work)* date *f* d'achèvement; *Com (for sale)* date d'exécution; **c. guarantee** caution *f* de bonne fin

complex ['kɒmpleks] **ADJ** *(question, phrase)* complexe
N 1 *(building(s))* complexe *m*; **industrial c.** complexe industriel; **shopping c.** centre *m*

commercial **2** *Psy* complexe *m*; *Fam* **he has a c. about his teeth** il fait un complexe à cause de *ou* pour ses dents; *Fam* **you'll give her a c.** tu vas lui donner un complexe
➤➤ *Math* **c. number** nombre *m* complexe

complexion [kəm'plekʃən] **N 1** teint *m*; **to have a dark/fair c.** avoir le teint mat/clair; **to have a good** *or* **clear c.** avoir une belle peau **2** *Fig* nature *f*, caractère *m*; **that puts a new** *or* **a different c. on it** voilà qui change la situation

complexity [kəm'pleksɪtɪ] **N** complexité *f*

compliance [kəm'plaɪəns] **N** observation *f* (**with** de); **in c. with your wishes** conformément à vos désirs
➤➤ *Com* **c. test** test *m* de conformité

compliant [kəm'plaɪənt] **ADJ 1** complaisant, accommodant **2** *Pej (submissive)* servile

complicate ['kɒmplɪkeɪt] **VT** compliquer (**with** de); **that complicates matters** cela complique les choses

complicated ['kɒmplɪkeɪtɪd] **ADJ** compliqué; **to become c.** *(of situation etc)* se compliquer

complication [kɒmplɪ'keɪʃən] **N** complication *f*; *Med* **if no complications set in** s'il ne survient pas de complications; **you're always creating complications!** tu compliques toujours les choses!

complicity [kəm'plɪsɪtɪ] **N** complicité *f* (**in** dans)

compliment ['kɒmplɪmənt] **N 1** compliment *m*; **to pay a c. to sb, to pay sb a c.** faire *ou* adresser un compliment à qn; **to return the c.** retourner le compliment; **my compliments to the chef** mes compliments au chef; **with the compliments of the chef** avec les compliments du chef; **compliments of the season** meilleurs vœux de fin d'année; **with compliments** avec nos compliments **2** *Old-fashioned (greetings)* **to pay one's compliments to sb** faire une visite (de politesse) à qn; **to present** *or* **send one's compliments to sb** se rappeler au bon souvenir de qn
VT complimenter, féliciter, faire des compliments à; **to c. sb on sth/on doing sth** féliciter qn de qch/d'avoir fait qch; **she complimented him on his English/haircut** elle l'a félicité *ou* elle lui a fait des compliments pour son anglais/sa coupe de cheveux
➤➤ **compliments slip** papillon *m* présentant les compliments de la société

complimentary [kɒmplɪ'ment(ə)rɪ] **ADJ 1** flatteur, -euse (**about** à l'égard de); **they weren't very c. about my paintings** ils ne se sont pas montrés très flatteurs à l'égard de mes tableaux; **c. remarks** compliments *mpl*, félicitations *fpl* **2** *(free)* gratuit, gracieux
➤➤ **c. copy** *(of book)* exemplaire *m* offert à titre gracieux; **c. ticket** billet *m* de faveur

comply [kəm'plaɪ] **VI** **to c. with** *(code, specifications, rule etc)* se conformer à; *(contract)* respecter; *(law)* se soumettre à; *(request)* accepter; *(wish)* satisfaire; *(order)* obéir à; **we asked them to move on but they did not c.** nous leur avons demandé de circuler mais ils n'ont pas obéi

component [kəm'pəʊnənt] **ADJ** composant, constituant
N *Ind, Phys, Chem* composant *m*; *Fig (of program, education, system etc)* élément *m*
➤➤ **c. part** *(of machine)* pièce *f* détachée; *(of theory)* composante *f*

comport [kəm'pɔːt] *Fml* **VT** **to c. oneself** se comporter
VI concorder (**with** avec)

comportment [kəm'pɔːtmənt] **N** *Fml* conduite *f*, comportement *m*

compose [kəm'pəʊz] **VT 1** *(poem, symphony etc)*, *Typ* composer **2** *(constitute)* composer, constituer; **to be composed of sth** se composer *ou* être composé *ou* être constitué de qch **3** *Art (people in painting)* composer **4** *(calm) (mind)* calmer, tranquilliser; **to c. one's thoughts** mettre de l'ordre dans ses pensées; **she composed her features into a smile** elle réussit à esquisser un sourire; **c. yourself!** calmez-vous! **5** *Fml (settle) (difference)* régler

  vi *Mus* composer

composed [kəm'pəʊzd] **ADJ** *(calm)* calme

composer [kəm'pəʊzər] **N** *Mus* compositeur, -trice

composing [kəm'pəʊzɪŋ] **N 1** *(of letter, musical or literary work)* composition *f*, création *f* **2** *Typ* composition *f*
  ▸▸ *Typ* **c. room** (salle *f* de) composition

composite ['kɒmpəzɪt] **ADJ** composite; *Bot* composé
  N composé *m*; *Bot* composée *f*, *Pol* = proposition *f* discutée au niveau national; **my main character is a c. of several people** mon personnage principal est un mélange de plusieurs personnes
  ▸▸ *St Exch* **c. index** indice *m* composé *ou* composite; *Cin* **c. shot** impression *f* combinée

composition [kɒmpə'zɪʃən] **N 1** *(of symphony, poem etc)* composition *f*; **a sonata of his own c.** une sonate de sa composition
  2 *(piece of music)* composition *f*
  3 *(constitution) (of air, water, committee etc)* composition *f*
  4 *Art (distribution of elements)* composition *f*
  5 *(mixture)* mélange *m*, composé *m*
  6 *Sch (essay)* dissertation *f*, rédaction *f*, *Old-fashioned* **prose c.** thème *m*
  7 *Com (settlement) (with creditors)* arrangement *m*, accommodement *m*; *(on bankruptcy)* concordat *m* préventif; **to make a c.** composer

compositor [kəm'pɒzɪtər] **N** *Typ* compositeur, -trice, metteur *m* en pages

compos mentis ['kɒmpɒs'mentɪs] **ADJ** *Law* sain d'esprit; **to be c.** *(not drunk, not half asleep)* être en possession de toutes ses facultés; **I'm not c. yet** je suis encore à moitié endormi

compost ['kɒmpɒst] **N** *(for garden)* compost *m*, terreau *m*
  vt *(treat with compost)* composter *(une terre)*; *(make compost from)* faire du compost à partir de
  ▸▸ **c. heap** tas *m* de compost

composure [kəm'pəʊʒər] **N** calme *m*, sang-froid *m*; **to regain** *or* **recover one's c.** retrouver son sang-froid, se calmer

compote ['kɒmpɒt] **N** *Culin* compote *f*

compound¹ ['kɒmpaʊnd]   VOIR GRAMMAIRE   A14   **ADJ** composé, combiné; *Gram (word, noun)* composé; *Mus (time)* composé; *Surg (fracture)* compliqué; *Math (number)* complexe
  N 1 *(combination) Chem* (corps *m*) composé *m*; *Tech* composition *f*, mastic *m*; *Gram* mot *m* composé; **chemical c.** composé chimique **2** *(of palace etc)* enceinte *f*, *(of prison)* cour *f* **3** *(in South Africa) (for miners)* quartier *m* des noirs; *(for livestock)* parc *m* à bétail
  ▸▸ *Acct* **c. entry** *(in bookkeeping)* article *m* composé; *Biol* **c. eye** œil *m* composé *ou* à facettes; *Math* **c. fraction** fraction *f* composée; *Fin* **c. interest** intérêts *mpl* composés

compound² [kəm'paʊnd] **vt 1** *(worsen) (problem etc)* aggraver **2** *Chem, Pharm (elements)* combiner; *(drug)* préparer **3** *(settle) (difference)* régler, arranger; **to c. a debt** faire une transaction pour le règlement d'une dette
  vi 1 *Fml* s'arranger, composer (**with sb** avec

qn) **2** *Com (with one's creditors)* arriver à un concordat

comprehend [kɒmprɪ'hend] **vt** *(understand, include)* comprendre

comprehensible [kɒmprɪ'hensəb(ə)l] **ADJ** compréhensible, intelligible

comprehensibly [kɒmprɪ'hensəblɪ] **ADV** d'une manière compréhensible *ou* intelligible

comprehension [kɒmprɪ'henʃən] **N 1** *(understanding)* compréhension *f*; **it is above** *or* **beyond my c.** cela dépasse mon compréhension **2** *Sch (of text etc)* compréhension *f*, **a reading/listening c.** un exercice de compréhension écrite/orale
  ▸▸ *Sch* **c. test** test *m* de compréhension

comprehensive [kɒmprɪ'hensɪv] **ADJ** *(wide-ranging) (answer, introduction, coverage, list etc)* complet, ète; *(study, view)* d'ensemble; *(defeat, victory)* écrasant; **c. knowledge** vastes connaissances *fpl*; **c. measures** mesures *fpl* d'ensemble
  N *Br Sch* = établissement *m* secondaire d'enseignement général
  ▸▸ *Br* **c. insurance** assurance *f* tous risques; *Br* **c. policy** police *f* tous risques, police multirisque; *Br* **c. school** = établissement secondaire d'enseignement général; **c. site insurance** assurance tous-risques chantiers

---

Note that the French word **compréhensif** is a false friend and is never a translation for the English word **comprehensive**. Its most common meaning is **understanding**.

Comprehensive Schools

Les "comprehensive schools" ont été introduites en Grande-Bretagne dans les années 60 dans le but d'assurer l'égalité des chances pour tous les enfants, quel que soit leur origine sociale. Aujourd'hui 90 pour cent des élèves du secondaire fréquentent ce type d'établissement scolaire. Cependant l'insuffisance des crédits alloués à l'éducation ainsi que la persistance d'un système d'enseignement privé dont ne peuvent bénéficier que les classes aisées rendent très aléatoire la réalisation d'un projet de démocratisation de l'enseignement.

---

comprehensively [kɒmprɪ'hensɪvlɪ] **ADV** de façon complète; **c. beaten** *or* **defeated** battu à plate(s) couture(s)

comprehensiveness [kɒmprɪ'hensɪvnɪs] **N** *(of answer, treatment of subject)* caractère *m* complet

compress¹ ['kɒmpres] **N** *Med* compresse *f*

compress² [kəm'pres] **vt 1** *(gas, air, spring)* comprimer; *(of compressor) (air etc)* refouler; **to c. one's lips** serrer *ou* pincer les lèvres **2** *(speech, detail etc)* condenser; **to c. 3,000 years of history into a 45-minute video** condenser 3 000 ans d'histoire en une vidéo de 45 minutes **3** *Comput (file)* compresser
  vi *Tech (of gas, spring etc)* se comprimer

compressed [kəm'prest] **ADJ** *(lips)* serré, pincé; *(style)* condensé
  ▸▸ **c. air** air *m* comprimé

compression [kəm'preʃən] **N 1** *(of gas, spring etc)* compression *f* **2** *(of thought, style etc)* concentration *f* **3** *Comput (of file)* compression *f*
  ▸▸ **c. chamber** chambre *f* de compression; *Aut* **c. ignition** allumage *m* par compression; **c. period** période *f* de compression; **c. pump** pompe *f* de compression; *Tech* **c. ratio** taux *m* de compression; *Tech* **c. stroke** *(in engine)* (temps *m* de) compression

compressive [kəm'presɪv] **ADJ** compressif, de compression
  ▸▸ *Tech* **c. strain** déformation *f* occasionnée par la compression; *Tech* **c. strength** résistance *f* à la compression; *Tech* **c. stress** contrainte *f* de compression

compressor [kəm'presər] **N** *Anat, Tech (of gas, air etc)* compresseur *m*
  ▸▸ *Comput* **c. program** programme *m* de compression

comprise [kəm'praɪz] **vt** être composé de, comprendre; **the flat is comprised of** *or* **comprises three rooms** l'appartement comprend trois pièces; **a meal comprising meat and vegetables** un repas composé de viande avec des légumes

compromise ['kɒmprəmaɪz] **N** compromis *m*; **to agree to a c.** accepter un compromis; **to make** *or* **reach** *or* **arrive at a c.** faire *ou* parvenir à un compromis (**with sb** avec qn); **policy of no c.** politique *f* intransigeante; **there must be no c.** il ne faut pas faire de compromis
  vt *(person, one's principles)* compromettre; **to c. oneself with sb** se compromettre avec qn
  vi transiger, composer (**with sb** avec qn); **if he agrees to c.** s'il accepte un compromis; **let's c.** faisons un compromis, transigeons

compromising ['kɒmprəmaɪzɪŋ] **ADJ** *(situation etc)* compromettant

comptroller [kən'trəʊlər] **N** *Admin* contrôleur, -euse; *(of accounts)* vérificateur, -trice

compulsion [kəm'pʌlʃən] **N 1** *(obligation)* contrainte *f*; **under c.** sous la contrainte; **to be under c. to do sth** être astreint à faire qch; **there's no c. to do it** il n'y a pas d'obligation à le faire **2** *Psy (urge)* compulsion *f*; **to feel a c. to do sth** avoir une envie irrésistible de faire qch

compulsive [kəm'pʌlsɪv] **ADJ** *Psy (behaviour)* compulsif; *(smoker, gambler, liar)* invétéré; **I am a c. eater** je suis boulimique; **c. eating is a sign of stress** la boulimie est un signe de stress; **I found it c. reading/viewing** j'ai trouvé que c'était absolument captivant *ou* prenant

compulsively [kəm'pʌlsɪvlɪ] **ADV** **to smoke/lie/talk c.** ne pas pouvoir s'empêcher de fumer/de mentir/de parler; **to eat c.** être boulimique; **it's c. readable/watchable** c'est passionnant

compulsorily [kəm'pʌlsərɪlɪ] **ADV** obligatoirement; *Admin* **to be retired c.** être mis à la retraite d'office

compulsory [kəm'pʌlsərɪ] **ADJ 1** *(obligatory)* obligatoire; **military service/Latin is c.** le service militaire/le latin est obligatoire; **c. school attendance** présence *f* obligatoire à l'école **2** *(coercive)* coercitif
  ▸▸ *Fin* **c. liquidation** liquidation *f* forcée; **c. powers** pouvoirs *mpl* coercitifs; **c. purchase** expropriation *f* pour cause d'utilité publique; **c. purchase order** ordre *m* d'expropriation; **c. redundancy** licenciement *m* sec; **c. retirement** mise *f* à la retraite d'office; *Law* **c. sale** adjudication *f* forcée; **c. schooling** scolarisation *f* obligatoire; *Pol* **c. voting** vote *m* obligatoire

compunction [kəm'pʌŋkʃən] **N** remords *m*, scrupule *m*; **without c.** sans remords *ou* scrupules

computation [kɒmpjʊ'teɪʃən] **N** *Fml* calcul *m*; **to make a c. of** faire le calcul de, calculer

computational [kɒmpjʊ'teɪʃən(ə)l] **ADJ** *Comput* de calcul
  ▸▸ **c. linguistics** linguistique *f* computationnelle

compute [kəm'pjuːt] **vt** calculer
  vi faire des calculs; *Fam* **it doesn't c.** ce n'est pas logique

computer [kəm'pjuːtər] N ordinateur *m*; **to be c. literate** avoir des connaissances en informatique; **she's in computers** elle est dans l'informatique; **to have sth on c.** avoir qch sur ordinateur; **to put sth on c.** mettre qch sur ordinateur; **analog/digital c.** calculateur *m* analogique/numérique; **to go on a c. course** suivre un cours d'informatique

▸▸ **the c. age** l'ère *f* des ordinateurs *ou* de l'informatique; **c. analyst** analyste *mf*, **c. animation** animation *f* par ordinateur; **c. art** dessin *m* par ordinateur; *Am* **c. camp** colonie *f* de vacances centrée sur l'informatique; **c. centre** centre *m* informatique, infocentre *m*; **c. code** code *m* d'ordinateur; **c. crime** fraude *f* informatique; **c. dating** = rencontres *fpl* sélectionnées par ordinateur; **c. dealer** revendeur *m* informatique; **c. department** service *m* informatique; **c. diagram** diagramme *m* réalisé par *ou* sur ordinateur; **c. engineer** ingénieur-informaticien, -ienne, *pl* ingénieurs-informaticiens, -iennes; **c. equipment** équipment *m* informatique; **c. expert** informaticien, -ienne; **c. fraud** fraude informatique; *Fam* **c. freak** *(enthusiast)* dingue *mf* d'informatique; **c. game** jeu *m* informatique; *Fam* **c. geek** allumé, -ée de l'informatique; **c. generation** génération *f* d'ordinateur; **c. genius** génie *m* de l'informatique; **c. graphics** graphiques *mpl*, *(technique)* infographie *f*; **c. hacker** pirate *mf* informatique; **c. hardware** matériel *m* informatique; **c. instruction** instruction *f* machine; **c. keyboard** clavier *m* d'ordinateur; **c. language** langage *m* de programmation; **c. link-up** liaison *f* informatique; **c. literacy** compétence *f* informatique; **c. manager** directeur, -trice informatique; **c. manufacturer** constructeur *m* informatique; **c. model** modèle *m* informatique; **c. modelling** réalisation *f* de modèles sur ordinateur; **c. network** réseau *m* informatique; **c. operator** opérateur, -trice (sur ordinateur); **c. output** sortie *f* d'ordinateur; **c. printout** sortie papier; *(continuous)* listing *m*, listage *m*; **c. processing** traitement *m* sur ordinateur; **c. program** programme *m* informatique; **c. programmer** programmeur, -euse; **c. programming** programmation *f*; **c. revolution** révolution *f* informatique; **c. room** salle *f* des ordinateurs; **c. science** informatique *f*; **c. scientist** informaticien, -ienne; **c. simulation** simulation *f* par ordinateur; **c. supplier** fournisseur *m* informatique; **c. system** système *m* informatique; **c. technician** technicien, -ienne en informatique; **c. terminal** terminal *m* informatique; **c. translation** traduction *f* par ordinateur; **c. typesetting** composition *f* par ordinateur; **c. virus** virus *m* informatique

computer-aided [-'eɪdɪd] ADJ assisté par ordinateur

▸▸ **c. design** conception *f* assistée par ordinateur; **c. engineering** ingénierie *f* assistée par ordinateur; **c. instruction** enseignement *m* assisté par ordinateur; **c. learning** enseignement assisté par ordinateur; **c. manufacturing** fabrication *f* assistée par ordinateur; **c. presentation** présentation *f* assistée par ordinateur; **c. sales and marketing** vente *f* et marketing *m* assistés par ordinateur; **c. trading** commerce *m* assisté par ordinateur; **c. translation** traduction *f* assistée par ordinateur

computer-assisted [-ə'sɪstɪd] ADJ assisté par ordinateur

▸▸ **c. interviewing** entretien *m* assisté par ordinateur

computer-controlled ADJ contrôlé par ordinateur

▸▸ **c. lock** serrure *f* électronique

computer-enhanced [-ɪn'hɑːnst] ADJ *(graphics etc)* amélioré par ordinateur

computer-generated [-'dʒenəreɪtɪd] ADJ généré par ordinateur

▸▸ **c. image** image *f* de synthèse

computer-integrated manufacturing N *Comput* fabrication *f* intégrée par ordinateur

computerizable [kəmpjuːtə'raɪzəb(ə)l] ADJ informatisable

computerization [kəmpjuːtəraɪ'zeɪʃən] N *(of organization, records etc)* informatisation *f*

computerize [kəm'pjuːtəraɪz] VT *(organization, filing system etc)* informatiser

computerized [kəm'pjuːtəraɪzd] ADJ informatisé

▸▸ **c. accounts** compatabilité *f* informatisée; **c. banking** informatique *f* bancaire; **c. data** données *fpl* informatiques; **c. key** clé *f* magnétique; *St Exch* **c. trading system** système *m* informatique de cotation; **c. typesetting** composition *f* par ordinateur

computer-to-computer ADJ *(transmission)* d'ordinateur à ordinateur

computer-typeset VT & VI composer sur ordinateur

computing [kəm'pjuːtɪŋ] N 1 *(calculating)* calcul *m* 2 *(science)* informatique *f*; **he works in c.** il travaille dans l'informatique

▸▸ **c. centre** centre *m* de calcul; **c. course** stage *m* d'informatique; **c. machine** machine *f* à calcul; **c. power** puissance *f* de calcul; **c. skills** connaissances *fpl* en informatique

comrade ['kɒmreɪd, -rəd] N camarade *mf*, compagnon *m*; *Pol* camarade; *Mil, Fig* **comrades in arms** compagnons d'armes; **C. Jones** le/la camarade Jones

comradeship ['kɒmreɪdʃɪp, -rəd-] N camaraderie *f*

COMSAT® ['kɒmsæt] N satellite *m* de communication

Con *Pol abbr* **Conservative**

con[1] [kɒn] *Fam* N *(trick)* arnaque *f*, escroquerie *f*; **what a c.!** quelle arnaque!

VT *(-nn-)* *(trick)* arnaquer, escroquer; **I've been conned** je me suis fait arnaquer; **they were conned out of £500** ils se sont fait arnaquer de cinq cents livres; **to c. sb into doing sth** persuader qn de faire qch par la ruse

▸▸ **c. artist** arnaqueur, -euse, escroc *m*; **c. man** arnaqueur, escroc; **c. woman** arnaqueuse *f*, **c. trick** arnaque, escroquerie

con[2] N **the pros and cons** le pour et le contre

con[3] N *Sl (convict)* taulard *m*, tôlard *m*; **an ex-c.** un ancien taulard

con[4] VT *(-nn-)* *Old-fashioned (study)* consulter

concatenated [kɒn'kætəneɪtɪd] ADJ *Comput* concaténé

concatenation [kɒnkætə'neɪʃən] N *Comput* enchaînement *m*

concave ['kɒnkeɪv] ADJ concave, incurvé

concavity [kɒn'kævɪtɪ] N concavité *f*

conceal [kən'siːl] VT *(object, intentions, truth etc)* cacher, dissimuler; *(thoughts)* cacher, voiler; **to c. oneself** se cacher; **to c. one's intentions** cacher *ou* déguiser ses intentions *ou* son jeu; **to c. sth from sb** *(hide, not tell)* cacher qch à qn

concealed [kən'siːld] ADJ caché; *(bend)* masqué; *(lighting)* indirect; *Aut* **danger!** **entrance** *(notice)* danger! sortie de véhicules

concealment [kən'siːlmənt] N dissimulation *f*; **to keep sb in c.** cacher qn; **place of c.** cachette *f*; *Fin* **c. of assets** dissimulation d'actif

concede [kən'siːd] VT *(privilege, corner etc)* concéder; *Pol, Sport etc* **to c. defeat** s'avouer vaincu; **to c. that one is wrong** reconnaître qu'on a tort

conceit [kən'siːt] N 1 *(vanity)* vanité *f*, suffisance *f*; **eaten up with c.** pétri *ou* pourri de vanité 2 *Liter* métaphore *f* astucieuse

conceited [kən'siːtɪd] ADJ suffisant, vaniteux; **I don't want to sound c. but ...** je ne veux pas avoir l'air prétentieux mais ...; **he is unbearably c.** il est d'une suffisance insupportable

conceitedly [kən'siːtɪdlɪ] ADV avec suffisance, avec vanité; **he c. imagined that ...** il a eu la prétention d'imaginer que ...

conceivable [kən'siːvəb(ə)l] ADJ concevable, imaginable; **it is c.** cela se conçoit; **it is c. that ...** il est concevable que ... + *sub*; **by every c. means** par tous les moyens possibles et imaginables; **what c. reason could I have?** quelle raison pourrais-je bien avoir?

conceivably [kən'siːvəblɪ] ADV **she could c. have done it, it's c. possible that she did it** il n'est pas exclu qu'elle l'ait fait; **I don't see how it's c. possible** ce n'est pas concevable; **this is c. the best/worst ...** c'est peut-être le meilleur/pire ...; **is he capable of it? – c.** en est-il capable? – c'est fort possible

conceive [kən'siːv] VT 1 *(form) (plan)* concevoir; **to c. a dislike for sb** prendre qn en aversion 2 *(imagine)* **I cannot c. why ...** je n'arrive pas à imaginer pourquoi ...; **it is difficult to c. how ...** il est difficile de concevoir *ou* d'imaginer comment ... 3 *(child)* concevoir; **to be conceived** *(of child)* être conçu

VI *(become pregnant)* concevoir

▸ **conceive of** VT INSEP imaginer; **I can c. of him having done it** je peux très bien imaginer qu'il l'ait fait

concentrate ['kɒnsəntreɪt] N *(of tomatoes, orange juice etc)* concentré *m*; *(mineral)* minerai *m* concentré; **made from c.** *(orange juice etc)* fait à base de concentré

VT *(troops, attention, efforts)* concentrer (**on** sur); **the presence of danger helped to c. our minds** la présence du danger nous a aidés à nous concentrer; **with concentrated fury** avec une fureur intense; **industry is concentrated in the south** l'industrie est concentrée dans le sud

VI 1 *(mentally)* se concentrer; **to c. on sth** se concentrer sur qch; **to c. on doing sth** s'appliquer à faire qch 2 *(specialize)* **to c. on sth** se concentrer sur qch 3 *(group)* se concentrer, être groupé; **the population tends to c. in cities** la population tend à se concentrer dans les villes

concentration [kɒnsən'treɪʃən] N 1 *(mental)* concentration *f*, application *f*; **to lose one's c.** se déconcentrer; **the work requires c.** le travail demande de la concentration; **c. span** concentration *f*; **she has a poor c. span** elle n'arrive pas à se concentrer très longtemps

2 *(specializing)* spécialisation *f*; **in view of their recent c. on other areas of the market** étant donné qu'ils se sont récemment concentrés sur d'autres secteurs du marché

3 *(grouping) (of troops etc)* concentration *f*; **there was a c. of cases of food poisoning in the area** il y a eu plusieurs cas d'intoxication alimentaire dans le quartier; **c. of effort** convergence *f* des efforts; *Chem* **(degree of) c.** *(of acid etc)* titre *m*; **the large urban concentrations** les grandes agglomérations *fpl* urbaines

▸▸ **c. camp** camp *m* de concentration

concentric [kən'sentrɪk] ADJ *Geom* concentrique

concept ['kɒnsept] N concept *m*; **this is a difficult c. for children** c'est un concept difficile à comprendre pour les enfants

▸▸ **c. car** concept-car *m*, *pl* concept-cars; *Mktg* **c. test** test *m* de concept

conception [kən'sepʃən] N 1 *(action) (of child, idea etc)* conception *f* 2 *(idea)* conception f, idée f; **to have a clear c. of sth** se représenter clairement qch dans la pensée; **he has no c. of how long the work takes** il ne se rend absolument pas compte du temps que prend le travail

concept-testing N *Mktg* tests *mpl* de concept

conceptual [kən'septjʊəl] ADJ conceptuel

conceptualize [kən'septjʊəlaɪz] VT & VI conceptualiser

CONCERN [kən'sɜːn] N **1** (*interest*) intérêt *m* (**in** dans); **it's no c. of mine/yours** cela ne me/vous regarde pas; **this is a matter of public c.** c'est une affaire qui nous concerne tous **2** (*worry, compassion*) inquiétude *f*, souci *m*; (*stronger*) anxiété *f*; **to show c.** se montrer inquiet; **there is growing c. for her safety** on est de plus en plus inquiet à son sujet *ou* sur son sort; **there is growing c. that ...** on craint de plus en plus que ...; **my only c. has been to ensure that ...** ma seule préoccupation a été de m'assurer que ...; **there is no cause for c.** il n'y a pas de raison de s'inquiéter; **to express c. about sth** exprimer de l'inquiétude au sujet de qch; **thank you for your c.** tu es gentil de m'avoir posé la question/de me l'avoir proposé/*etc* **3** *Com, Ind* entreprise *f*; **a large publishing c.** une grande maison d'édition

VT **1** (*apply to, affect*) (*person, matter*) concerner, toucher; (*be the business of*) (*person*) regarder, être l'affaire de; **matters that c. the public** choses qui intéressent le public; **to whom it may c.** à qui de droit; **to c. oneself with** *or* **about sth** s'intéresser à qch, s'occuper de qch; **don't c. yourself with that for the moment** ne t'occupe pas de cela pour l'instant; **where work is/children are concerned** en ce qui concerne le travail/les enfants, pour ce qui est du travail/des enfants; **to be concerned with sth** s'occuper de qch; **the parties/people concerned** les intéressés *mpl*; *Com etc* **the department concerned** le service compétent; **as far as I am concerned** en ce qui me concerne, quant à moi; **as far as this question is concerned** en ce qui concerne cette question, pour ce qui est de cette question **2** (*be about*) traiter de; **the book is concerned with politics** ce livre traite de politique; **it concerns your mother** c'est au sujet de votre mère **3** (*usu passive*) (*worry*) **to be concerned about sb/sth** s'inquiéter *ou* être inquiet de qn/qch; **I am concerned for his health** son état de santé m'inquiète

concerned [kən'sɜːnd] ADJ (*smile, look*) inquiet, soucieux; **we feel very c. about this** cela nous préoccupe au plus haut point, cela nous inquiète beaucoup; **he didn't seem at all c.** il n'avait pas du tout l'air inquiet *ou* de s'inquiéter

concerning [kən'sɜːnɪŋ] PREP concernant, au sujet de; **information c. the crime** des informations au sujet du *ou* concernant le délit

concert¹ [ˈkɒnsət] N **1** *Mus* concert *m*; **Bob Dylan in c.** Bob Dylan en concert; **to give a c.** donner un concert; **2** *Fml* (*association*) concert *m*; **to act in c.** agir de concert (**with** avec)
▸▸ *Mus* **c. grand** piano *m* de concert; **c. hall** salle *f* de concert; *St Exch* **c. party** action *f* de concert; *Mus* **c. performer** concertiste *mf*; *Mus* **c. pianist** pianiste *mf* de concert; *Mus* **c. pitch** diapason *m* (de concert); *Mus* **c. tour** tournée *f*

concert² [kən'sɜːt] VT (*measures etc*) concerter

concerted [kən'sɜːtɪd] ADJ (*plan, effort etc*) concerté; **c. action** action *f* concertée *ou* d'ensemble

concertgoer [ˈkɒnsətgəʊər] N amateur, -trice de concerts

concertina [kɒnsə'tiːnə] N *Mus* concertina *m*
VI (**concertinaed** [-nəd]) (*of car etc in collision*) se plier en accordéon

concertmaster [ˈkɒnsətmɑːstər] N *Am* (*of orchestra*) premier violon *m*

concerto [kən'tʃɑːtəʊ] N *Mus* concerto *m*; **piano/violin c.** concerto pour piano/violon

concession [kən'seʃən] N **1** (*allowance*) concession *f*; **to make concessions** faire des concessions; **the only c. the film makes to reality is ...** la seule concession que le film fasse à la réalité est ... **2** *Com* concession *f*; **she has a c. in a department store** elle a une concession dans un grand magasin **3** *Min* (*mining*) **c.** concession *f* minière **4** *Br* (*reduction*) tarif *m* réduit; **price: £4.50 (concessions £3)** prix des billets: 4,50 livres (tarif réduit 3 livres); **we offer a 10% c. to retailers** nous accordons une remise de 10% aux détaillants
▸▸ *Com* **c. close** conclusion *f* par concession; *Br* **c. ticket** (*for theatre, cinema*) billet *m* à prix réduit

concessionary [kən'seʃən(ə)rɪ] *Com* ADJ (*company etc*) concessionnaire; *Br* (*fare, rate etc*) réduit
N = **concession(n)aire**

concession(n)aire [kənseʃə'neər] N *Com* concessionnaire *mf*

conch [kɒŋk, kɒn(t)ʃ] N (*mollusc*) conque *f*

conchie, conchy [ˈkɒntʃɪ] N *Old-fashioned Fam* (*abbr* **conscientious objector**) objecteur *m* de conscience

concierge [kɒnsɪ'eərʒ] N (*in hotel*) concierge *mf*; **c.'s desk** comptoir *m* du concierge

conciliate [kən'sɪlɪeɪt] VT **1** (*win over*) apaiser; **she refused to be conciliated** elle refusait la conciliation **2** (*reconcile*) (*theories, beliefs*) concilier, réconcilier
VI *Fml* **to c. between two people/countries** réconcilier deux peuples/pays

conciliation [kənsɪlɪ'eɪʃən] N conciliation *f*
▸▸ **c. board, c. service** (*in industrial dispute*) conseil *m* d'arbitrage, ≃ conseil des prud'hommes

conciliator [kən'sɪlɪeɪtər] N conciliateur, -trice; (*in industrial dispute*) médiateur, -trice

conciliatory [kən'sɪlɪət(ə)rɪ] ADJ conciliant; (*spirit*) de conciliation; *Law* conciliatoire

concise [kən'saɪs] ADJ concis; (*style*) concis, dense; (*dictionary*) abrégé

concisely [kən'saɪslɪ] ADV brièvement, avec concision

conciseness [kən'saɪsnɪs], **concision** [kən'sɪʒən] N concision *f*; **to aim at c.** (*in one's style*) essayer d'être concis

conclave [ˈkɒnkleɪv] N **1** (*meeting*) conseil *m*, réunion *f*; **to be in c. with sb** tenir conseil avec qn **2** *Cathol* conclave *m*

conclude [kən'kluːd] VT **1** (*finish*) (*speech, book, programme*) conclure, finir, achever; (*session*) clôturer; (*meal*) terminer **2** (*infer*) conclure; **from this I c. that ...** de ceci je conclus que ... **3** (*sign etc*) (*peace, treaty*) conclure; (*deal, contract*) arranger, régler
VI **1** (*of play, evening, book etc*) s'achever, se terminer (**with** avec) **2** (*at end of speech etc*) conclure; **to c. ...** en conclusion ..., pour conclure ...

concluding [kən'kluːdɪŋ] ADJ (*chapter, episode*) dernier; (*concert*) de clôture; **he made a few c. remarks** il a fait quelques remarques finales

conclusion [kən'kluːʒən] N **1** (*inference*) conclusion *f*; **to draw a c. from sth** tirer une conclusion de qch; **draw your own conclusions** tirez vos propres conclusions; **to come to** *or* **reach the c. that ...** conclure que ... + *ind*, (en) arriver à la conclusion que ... + *ind*; **without coming to any c.** sans arriver à une conclusion; **you're jumping to conclusions** tu tires une conclusion hâtive; **don't jump to conclusions!** réfléchis avant de conclure!; **he jumped to the wrong c.** il a tiré une conclusion erronée **2** (*end*) (*of essay, film*) conclusion *f*, (*of session*) clôture *f*; **in c.** pour conclure, en conclusion; **to bring a matter to a successful c.** mener une affaire à bonne fin **3** (*signing etc*) (*of treaty etc*) conclusion *f*

conclusive [kən'kluːsɪv] ADJ (*argument*) concluant, décisif; (*test*) probant

conclusively [kən'kluːsɪvlɪ] ADV (*to argue, show*) de façon concluante

concoct [kən'kɒkt] VT **1** (*make*) (*cocktail*) préparer; (*dish*) concocter **2** (*think up*) (*plan*) imaginer, élaborer, concocter; (*plot*) machiner

concoction [kən'kɒkʃən] N **1** (*action*) (*of food etc*) confection *f* **2** (*drink, dish etc*) mélange *m*, concoction *f* **3** (*of plan*) élaboration *f*, (*of plot*) machination *f*; **a c. of lies** un tissu de mensonges

concomitant [kən'kɒmɪtənt] *Fml* ADJ concomitant (**with** de)
N **the concomitants of old age/marriage** ce qui va de pair avec la vieillesse/le mariage

concord [ˈkɒŋkɔːd] N **1** *Fml* (*between people*) entente *f*, harmonie *f*, *Lit* **to live in c.** vivre en harmonie (**with** avec) **2** *Gram* concordance *f* **3** *Mus* accord *m* consonant

concordance [kən'kɔːdəns] N **1** *Fml* accord *m*, concordance *f* (**with** avec); **to be in c. with ...** être en accord avec ... **2** *Mus* consonance *f* **3** *Liter* (*of Bible*) index *m*, concordance *f*

concordant [kən'kɔːdənt] ADJ **1** en accord, concordant (**with** avec) **2** *Mus* consonant

concordat [kɒn'kɔːdæt] N concordat *m*

Concorde [ˈkɒnkɔːd] N *Aviat* Concorde *m*

concourse [ˈkɒnkɔːs] N **1** (*of railway station*) hall *m* **2** *Fml* (*gathering place*) lieu *m* de rassemblement **3** *Fml* (*crowd*) foule *f*, rassemblement *m*

concrete [ˈkɒnkriːt] N *Constr* béton *m*; **reinforced c.** béton armé
ADJ (*example, term, noun*) concret, -ète; (*suggestion, proposal*) concret, pratique
VT *Constr* (*wall etc*) bétonner
▸▸ *Fig* **c. jungle** univers *m* de béton; *Constr* **c. mixer** bétonnière *f*; **c. music** musique *f* concrète; **c. poem** calligramme *m*; **c. poetry** calligrammes *mpl*
▸ **concrete over** VT SEP (*garden, field etc*) bétonner

concreting [ˈkɒnkriːtɪŋ] N *Constr* bétonnage *m*

concretion [kən'kriːʃən] N *Med, Geol etc* concrétion *f*

concubinage [kɒn'kjuːbɪnɪdʒ] N concubinage *m*

concubine [ˈkɒnkjʊbaɪn] N concubine *f*

concur [kən'kɜːr] VI (**-rr-**) **1** (*agree*) (*of person*) être d'accord (**with sb/sth** avec qn/qch), être du même avis (**with sb** que qn); **to c. with sb's views/opinions/conclusions** partager le point de vue/l'opinion/les conclusions de qn; **he proposed a different approach and she concurred** il a proposé une approche différente et elle a approuvé **2** (*of findings, results of experiment*) concorder (**with** avec) **3** *Fml* (*of events*) coïncider; **to c. in a result** concourir à un résultat

concurrence [kən'kʌrəns] N *(agreement)* accord *m*; *(assent)* assentiment *m*, consentement *m* (in à); *Fml* **c. of events** concours *m* de circonstances

concurrent [kən'kʌrənt] ADJ **1** *(in time)* simultané; *Math* concourant **2** *(in agreement) (views etc)* qui concordent
▸▸ *Law* **c. cause** cause *f* contribuante; *Law* **c. sentences** confusion *f* des peines

concurrently [kən'kʌrəntlɪ] ADV simultanément (with avec); *Law* **the two sentences to run c.** avec confusion des deux peines

concuss [kən'kʌs] VT commotionner; **she was badly concussed in the accident** elle a subi de graves commotions lors de l'accident

concussion [kən'kʌʃən] N commotion *f* cérébrale; **suffering from c.** souffrant de commotion cérébrale

condemn [kən'dem] VT **1** *(sentence)* condamner; **to c. sb to death** condamner qn à mort; **to be condemned to sth/to do sth** être condamné à qch/à faire qch; **she was condemned to a life of poverty** elle était condamnée à vivre dans la pauvreté **2** *(declare unsafe) (building)* déclarer inhabitable; **this meat has been condemned** cette viande a été jugée impropre à la consommation **3** *(censure) (person, policy, abuse etc)* condamner; **she condemned the remarks as pure prejudice** elle a condamné les remarques comme étant de purs préjugés

condemnation [kɒndem'neɪʃən] N **1** *(of prisoner)* condamnation *f* **2** *(of building)* condamnation *f* **3** *(censure)* condamnation *f*

condemned [kən'demd] ADJ **1** *Law (sentenced)* condamné; **the c. man** le condamné **2** *(building)* condamné; *(meat)* jugé impropre à la consommation
▸▸ **c. cell** cellule *f* des condamnés

condensation [kɒnden'seɪʃən] N *(of gas, liquid, text etc)* condensation *f*, *(on windows)* buée *f*

condense [kən'dens] VT *(gas, liquid, text etc)* condenser; **to c. a chapter into a single paragraph** condenser un chapitre en un seul paragraphe
VI se condenser

condensed [kən'denst] ADJ concentré, condensé
▸▸ **c. book** livre *m* condensé; **c. milk** lait *m* concentré; *Comput* **c. mode** mode *m* condensé; *Comput, Typ* **c. print** impression *f* condensée; **in c. print** en caractères étroits

condenser [kən'densər] N *Elec* condensateur *m*; *(for condensing liquids)* condenseur *m*
▸▸ **c. microphone** microphone *m* électrostatique

condensing [kən'densɪŋ] N condensation *f*

condescend [kɒndɪ'send] VI **1** *(agree, accept with reluctance)* condescendre (**to do sth** à faire qch), daigner (**to do sth** faire qch) **2** *(be condescending)* se montrer condescendant (**to sb** envers qn)

condescending [kɒndɪ'sendɪŋ] ADJ condescendant

condescendingly [kɒndɪ'sendɪŋlɪ] ADV d'une manière condescendante, avec condescendance

condescension [kɒndɪ'senʃən] N condescendance *f* (**to** envers, pour)

condiment [ˈkɒndɪmənt] N condiment *m*
▸▸ **c. set** poivrier *m* et salière *f*

condition [kən'dɪʃən] N **1** *(state)* état *m*; **in good c.** en bon état; **in bad c., in a poor c.** en mauvais état; **you're in no c. to drive** *(you're ill, tired, drunk)* tu n'es pas en état de

conduire; **in your c.** *(to pregnant woman)* dans ton état; **to keep oneself in c.** se maintenir en forme; **I'm out of c.** je n'ai pas la condition physique; **he's in excellent c.** sa condition physique est excellente
2 *(circumstance) (usu pl)* condition *f*, **working conditions** *(in factory etc)* conditions de travail; **normal operating conditions** *(of machine)* régime *m* de fonctionnement normal; **weather conditions** conditions météorologiques; **road** or **driving conditions** état *m* des routes; **drive with particular care as conditions on the roads are hazardous** soyez prudents sur les routes: le mauvais temps rend la circulation très dangereuse; **the human c.** la condition humaine
3 *(term)* condition *f*, **to impose conditions on sb** (im)poser des conditions à qn; **conditions of sale/carriage** conditions de vente/transport; **conditions of a contract** stipulations *fpl* ou termes *mpl* d'un contrat; **on c. that …** à (la) condition que … + *sub*; **you can borrow the book, on one c.** tu peux emprunter le livre, à une condition; **it was a c. of the lease that …** l'une des stipulations du bail était que …; **under these conditions** dans ces conditions
4 *(illness) (of heart, liver etc)* maladie *f*, affection *f*, **to have a heart c.** avoir une maladie du cœur
VT **1** *Psy (subject)* conditionner (**to do** à faire); **a conditioned reflex** un réflexe conditionné
2 **to c. one's hair** utiliser de l'après-shampooing
3 *(subject to a condition) (usu pass)* déterminer; **to be conditioned by** dépendre de

conditional [kən'dɪʃən(ə)l] ADJ *(offer, agreement), Gram (tense)* conditionnel; **c. on sth** dépendant de qch; **my promise was c.** j'ai promis sous certaines conditions
N *Gram* conditionnel *m*; **in the c.** *(verb)* au conditionnel VOIR GRAMMAIRE A52–3; B34
▸▸ **c. acceptance** acceptation *f* sous réserve; **c. access television** télévision *f* à accès conditionnel

conditionally [kən'dɪʃən(ə)lɪ] ADV de façon conditionnelle

conditioner [kən'dɪʃənər] N **air c.** climatiseur *m*; **(fabric) c.** adoucissant *m*; **(hair) c.** après-shampoing *m*, démêlant *m*

conditioning [kən'dɪʃənɪŋ] N *Psy* conditionnement *m*

condo [ˈkɒndəʊ] N *Am Fam* = **condominium 2**

condole [kən'dəʊl] VI *Fml* **to c. with sb** faire ou exprimer ses condoléances à qn

condolence [kən'dəʊləns] N condoléances condoléances *fpl*, **to offer sb one's condolences** présenter ses condoléances à qn; **a letter of c.** une lettre de condoléances

condom [ˈkɒndəm] N préservatif *m*

condominium [kɒndə'mɪnɪəm] N **1** *(shared sovereignty)* condominium *m*; **the territory was made a c.** le territoire fut placé sous un régime de condominium **2** *Am (building)* immeuble *m* en copropriété; *(apartment)* appartement *m* dans un immeuble en copropriété; *(ownership)* copropriété *f*

condone [kən'dəʊn] VT trouver des excuses pour, excuser; **I am not condoning the crime** je ne cherche pas à excuser le crime

condor [ˈkɒndɔːr] N condor *m*

conduce [kən'djuːs] VI *Fml (of action or thing)* contribuer (**to** à)

conducive [kən'djuːsɪv] ADJ **c. to sth** favorable à qch; **this weather is not c. to work** ce temps n'incite pas au travail

conduct¹ [ˈkɒndʌkt] N **1** *(behaviour)* conduite *f* (**towards sb** à l'égard de ou avec ou envers qn) **2** *(management)* conduite *f*,

gestion *f*, **the lawyer's c. of the case** la manière dont l'avocat a mené l'affaire

conduct² [kən'dʌkt] VT **1** *(manage, direct) (business, operations, orchestra, religious service)* diriger; *(carry out) (campaign, survey)* mener; *(experiment)* effectuer; *Law* **to c. one's own case** plaider soi-même sa cause; **to c. the traffic** faire la circulation
2 **to c. oneself** se comporter, se conduire
3 *(lead)* **to c. sb round a building/factory/museum** faire visiter un bâtiment/une usine/un musée à qn; **conducted tours** visites *fpl* guidées; **to give sb a conducted tour** faire faire une visite guidée à qn
4 *Elec, Phys (heat, electricity)* conduire, être conducteur de
VI *Mus* diriger; *(work as conductor)* être chef d'orchestre; **who's conducting?** qui est le chef d'orchestre?, qui dirige?

conducting [kən'dʌktɪŋ] N *Mus* direction *f* d'orchestre

conduction [kən'dʌkʃən] N *Phys, Elec* conduction *f*

conductive [kən'dʌktɪv] ADJ *Phys, Elec* conducteur, -trice

conductivity [kɒndʌk'tɪvɪtɪ] N *Phys, Elec* conductivité *f*

conductor [kən'dʌktər] N **1** *Br (on bus)* receveur *m*; *Am Rail* chef *m* de train **2** *Mus* chef *m* d'orchestre **3** *Phys, Elec (of electricity etc)* conducteur *m*
▸▸ *Rail* **c. rail** rail *m* conducteur ou sous tension; **c. wire** fil *m* conducteur

> Note that the French word **conducteur** is not always a translation for the English word **conductor**.

conductress [kən'dʌktrɪs] N *Br (on bus)* receveuse *f*

conduit [ˈkɒndjʊɪt] N *Tech (for fluid)* conduit *m*, canalisation *f*, *Elec* tube *m*; *Fig (for money)* intermédiaire *mf*

condyle [ˈkɒndɪl] N *Med* condyle *m*

cone [kəʊn] N *(of light, volcano, retina etc)* cône *m*; *(of pine)* pomme *f* de pin, cône; *(for ice cream)* cornet *m*; **(traffic) c.** cône ou balise *f* de signalisation
▸▸ *Aut* **c. clutch** embrayage *m* à cône
▸ **cone off** VT SEP **to c. off two lanes of a motorway** fermer la circulation sur deux voies d'une autoroute *(avec des cônes de signalisation)*

cone-bearing ADJ conifère

cone-shaped ADJ en forme de cône, conique

coney [ˈkəʊnɪ] N *Old-fashioned* lapin *m*; **c. skin** peau *f* de lapin

confab [ˈkɒnfæb] N *Fam (conversation)* discussion *f*, **to have a c. (about sth)** *(discuss)* discuter (de qch), se consulter (sur qch)

confection [kən'fekʃən] N **1** *esp Am Culin (cake, sweet)* friandise *f* **2** *Fml (act)* confection *f*

confectioner [kən'fekʃənər] N *(selling sweets)* confiseur, -euse; *(making, selling cakes)* pâtissier, -ière; **c.'s** confiserie *f*, **J. Smith bakers & confectioners** boulangerie-pâtisserie J. Smith
▸▸ **c.'s custard** crème *f* pâtissière; **c.'s shop** confiserie; *Am* **c.'s sugar** sucre *m* glace

confectionery [kən'fekʃən(ə)rɪ] N *(sweets)* confiserie *f*

confederacy [kən'fed(ə)rəsɪ] N *(alliance)* confédération *f*, *Am Hist* **the C.** les États *mpl* Confédérés

confederate¹ [kən'fed(ə)rət] ADJ confédéré
N confédéré *m*; *(in crime)* complice *mf*
▸▸ *Hist* **the C. States** les États *mpl* Confédérés

confederate² [kən'fedəreɪt] VT *(states)*

confédérer; **to c. oneself with ...** se liguer avec ...

VI *(join)* se confédérer (**with** avec); *(conspire)* conspirer (**with** avec; **against** contre)

confederation [kənfedəˈreɪʃən] **N** confédération *f*

▸▸ **C. of British Industry** = patronat *m* britannique, ≃ Medef *m*

confer [kənˈfɜːr] (**-rr-**)- **VT** *(title, rank, powers)* conférer (**on** à); *(degree, diploma)* remettre (**on** à)

▸ **VI** s'entretenir (**with** avec; **on, about** sur); **contestants are not allowed to c.** les concurrents n'ont pas le droit de se consulter

conference [ˈkɒnfərəns] **N 1** conférence *f*; **press** *or* **news c.** conférence de presse; **to be in c.** *(with several people)* être en conférence (**with** avec); *(with one or two people)* être en réunion (**with** avec); **round-table c.** table *f* ronde; **we hope to get management to the c. table** nous espérons réunir la direction en table ronde **2** *(of professional association etc)* congrès *m*; *Pol* **Party C.** congrès annuel du parti

▸▸ **c. call** téléconférence *f*; **c. centre** *(building)* centre *m* de congrès; *(town)* = ville *f* pouvant accueillir des congrès; **c. coordinator** responsable *mf* des congrès; **c. delegate** congressiste *mf*; *Naut,Com* **c. line** ligne *f* maritime de conférence; **c. organizer** organisateur, -trice de conférences *ou* de congrès; **c. pack** = dossier *m* offert aux conférenciers avec informations générales sur la conférence, petits cadeaux etc; **c. room** salle *f* de conférence; *Naut, Com* **c. ship** navire *m* de conférence

conferment [kənˈfɜːmənt] **N** *(of rank, powers)* attribution *f*; *(of title, diploma)* remise *f*

confess [kənˈfes] **VI 1** *(of criminal)* avouer, faire des aveux; **to c. to a crime** avouer un crime

2 *(admit)* **to c. to sth** avouer qch; **to c. to doing** *or* **having done sth** avouer avoir fait qch; **I c. to not liking her** j'avoue que je ne l'aime pas; **to c. to a liking for ...** avouer avoir un penchant *ou* un faible pour ...

3 *Rel* se confesser (**to sb** à qn, auprès de qn)

VT 1 *(admit) (fault)* avouer, confesser; **to c. that ...** avouer *ou* confesser que ... + *ind*; **I must c. that ...** je dois avouer que ..., je dois reconnaître que ...; **I was wrong, I c.** j'admets que j'ai eu tort; **I don't understand either, I must c.** je dois avouer que je ne comprends pas non plus; **medical experts c. themselves helpless** les médecins s'avouent impuissants

2 *Rel (of sinner) (sins)* confesser, se confesser; *(of priest) (penitent)* confesser; **to c. oneself** se confesser (**to sb** à qn, auprès de qn)

confession [kənˈfeʃən] **N 1** *(admission)* aveu *m*, confession *f*; **to make a full c.** faire des aveux complets; **I have a c. to make** j'ai un aveu à faire; **on their own c.** de leur propre aveu; **that would be a c. of failure** cela reviendrait à s'avouer vaincu **2** *Rel* confession *f*; **to go to c.** aller se confesser; **to hear sb's c.** *(of priest)* entendre la confession de qn, entendre qn en confession, confesser qn; **c. of faith** confession de foi; **the seal of c.** le secret de la confession *ou* du confessionnal

confessional [kənˈfeʃən(ə)l] **ADJ** confessionnel

N *Rel* confessionnal *m*

confessor [kənˈfesər] **N** *Rel (priest)* confesseur *m*; *(sinner)* personne *f* qui se confesse; *Hist* **Edward the C.** Édouard le Confesseur

confetti [kənˈfetɪ] **NPL** confettis *mpl* VOIR
GRAMMAIRE A14

---

confidant, *f* **confidante** [kɒnfɪˈdænt] **N** confident, -ente

> Attention: ne pas confondre avec l'adjectif anglais **confident**.

confide [kənˈfaɪd] **VT** *(secret)* confier (**to sb** à qn); **she confided to me that ...** elle m'a confié que ...; **to c. sth to sb's care** confier qch à la garde de qn

▸ **confide in VT INSEP** se confier à

confidence [ˈkɒnfɪdəns] **N 1** *(trust)* confiance *f* (**in** en); **to place** *or* **put one's c. in sb/sth** placer *ou* mettre sa confiance en qn/qch, faire confiance à qn/qch; **have a bit more c.!** *(in me)* fais-moi un peu plus confiance; **to win sb's c.** gagner la confiance de qn; **to have every c. in sb** faire entièrement confiance à qn, avoir toute confiance en qn; **I have every c. that ...** je ne doute pas un instant que ...; **she has no c. in her own ability** elle n'a aucune confiance en elle; **with complete c.** en toute confiance; **vote of c.** vote *m* de confiance; *Pol* **motion of no c.** motion *f* de censure

2 *(certainty)* confiance *f*; **because of their c. that it would work** parce qu'ils étaient sûrs que ça marcherait

3 *(self-assurance)* assurance *f*, confiance *f* en soi; **full of c.** *(person)* plein d'assurance *ou* de confiance en soi; *(performance)* plein d'assurance; *(letter, article)* qui dénote une grande assurance; **with c.** *(to act etc)* avec assurance

4 in c. confidentiellement, en confidence; **remarks made in c.** des remarques formulées confidentiellement; **to take sb into one's c.** se confier à qn; **to be in sb's c.** partager les secrets de qn

5 *(secret)* confidence *f*; **to exchange confidences** échanger des confidences

▸▸ **c. trick** escroquerie *f*, abus *m* de confiance; **c. trickster** escroc *m*

> Note that the French word **confidence** never means **trust** or **self-assurance**.
>
> When translating **confidence**, note that the French words **confiance** and **confidence** are not interchangeable. **Confiance** means **trust** and **confidence** is only used in the sense of a **secret**.

confident [ˈkɒnfɪdənt] **ADJ** sûr (**of** de); *(self-assured)* sûr de soi, assuré; *(remark, performance)* plein d'assurance; **are you feeling c.?** tu te sens sûr de toi?; **we are c. that it will work** nous sommes sûrs *ou* persuadés que ça marchera; **I'm c. about this translation** je suis sûr que cette traduction est bonne; **c. of success** sûr de réussir; **be c.!** aie confiance en toi!

> Attention: ne pas confondre avec le nom anglais **confidant**.

confidential [kɒnfɪˈdenʃəl] **ADJ 1** *(information, report, tone etc)* confidentiel; **keep it c.** n'en parlez à personne **2** *(attached to one person) (position)* de confiance; *(secretary)* particulier

▸▸ **c. agent** homme *m* de confiance

confidentiality [kɒnfɪdenʃɪˈælɪtɪ] **N** *(of information, report)* caractère *m* confidentiel, confidentialité *f*

confidentially [kɒnfɪˈdenʃəlɪ] **ADV** *(to tell sb sth)* confidentiellement, en confidence; **c., I don't trust him** entre nous, je ne lui fais pas confiance

confidently [ˈkɒnfɪdəntlɪ] **ADV** *(with trust)* avec confiance, en toute confiance; *(with self-assurance)* avec assurance

confiding [kənˈfaɪdɪŋ] **ADJ** confiant

config. sys, config. sys file [kɒnˈfɪgˈsɪs] **N** *Comput* fichier *m* config. sys

---

configurable [kənˈfɪgjʊrəb(ə)l] **ADJ** *Comput* configurable, paramétrable

configuration [kənfɪgjʊˈreɪʃən] **N** *(shape)* configuration *f*, *Comput* configuration, paramétrage *m*

configure [kənˈfɪgər] **VT** *Comput* configurer, paramétrer

confine [kənˈfaɪn] **VT 1** *(in prison etc)* enfermer; **to be confined to one's room** (être obligé de) garder la chambre; **confined to bed** alité; *Mil* **confined to barracks** consigné; **confined space** espace restreint **2** *(limit)* **to c. oneself to sth/to doing sth** se limiter *ou* s'en tenir à qch/à faire qch; **let us c. ourselves to the question of ...** tenons-nous-en à la question de ...; **c. your answer to the matter in hand** limitez votre réponse au sujet qui nous occupe **3** *Obst Old-fashioned* **to be confined** accoucher

confinement [kənˈfaɪnmənt] **N 1** *(in prison)* emprisonnement *m* **2** *(limitation)* limitation *f*, restriction *f* (**to** à) **3** *Obst Old-fashioned* couches *fpl*, accouchement *m*

confines [ˈkɒnfaɪnz] **NPL** *Lit (of a place etc)* confins *mpl*; **within the c. of this subject** dans les limites de ce sujet; **within/beyond the c. of human knowledge** dans/au delà des limites de la connaissance humaine

confirm [kənˈfɜːm] **VT 1** *(corroborate) (news, suspicions)* confirmer, corroborer; *(reservation)* confirmer; *Aviat* **flight confirmed** vol confirmé; **to be confirmed** *(notice) (concert, film etc)* à confirmer; **to c. that ...** confirmer que ... + *ind*

2 *(reinforce) (power)* raffermir, consolider; *(person's reputation, position)* consolider; **to c. sth as sth** confirmer qch comme étant qch; **to c. sb's fears** confirmer les craintes de qn

3 *(approve, validate) (treaty, result)* confirmer; *(nomination)* approuver; *(decision)* entériner; *(election)* valider

4 *Rel* confirmer, donner la confirmation à; **to be confirmed** recevoir la confirmation

VI confirmer; **please c. in writing** veuillez confirmer par écrit

confirmation [kɒnfəˈmeɪʃən] **N 1** *(of news, doubts, reservation etc)* confirmation *f*; **there has been no c. of the rumour** la rumeur n'a pas été confirmée; **in c. of** en confirmation de

2 *(reinforcement) (of person's authority)* raffermissement *m*, consolidation *f*

3 *(validation) (of treaty, result)* confirmation *f*; *(of nomination)* approbation *f*, *(of decision)* entérinement *m*; *(of election)* validation *f*, **in c. of ...** *(booking)* pour confirmer ...; **she wrote in c. of her acceptance** elle a écrit pour confirmer qu'elle acceptait

4 *Rel* confirmation *f*

▸▸ *Com* **c. of receipt** accusé *m* de réception

confirmed [kənˈfɜːmd] **ADJ 1** *(habit, liar, womanizer etc)* invétéré; *(drunkard)* incorrigible, invétéré; **he's a c. bachelor** c'est un célibataire endurci **2** *Rel* confirmé

▸▸ *Fin* **c. credit** crédit *m* confirmé; *Fin* **c. irrevocable letter of credit** lettre *f* de crédit irrévocable confirmé; **c. letter of credit** lettre de crédit confirmé; *Aviat* **c. seat** place *f* confirmée

confirming [kənˈfɜːmɪŋ] **ADJ**

▸▸ **c. bank** banque *f* confirmatrice; **c. house** organisme *m* confirmateur

confiscate [ˈkɒnfɪskeɪt] **VT** confisquer (**from sb** à qn)

confiscation [kɒnfɪsˈkeɪʃən] **N** confiscation *f*

confiscatory [kɒnfɪsˈkeɪtərɪ] **ADJ** *(power)* de confiscation

conflagration [kɒnfləˈgreɪʃən] **N** *Fml (fire)*, *Fig* conflagration *f*

conflate [kənˈfleɪt] **VT** *(issues, reports)* amalgamer

conflation [kənˈfleɪʃən] **N** fusion *f*

conflict [ˈkɒnflɪkt] **N** *(between people, of feelings etc)* conflit *m*; **c. of interests** conflit d'intérêts; **a c. of interest situation** une situation présentant un conflit d'intérêts; **to come into/be in c.** entrer/être en conflit (**with** avec); **this was in c. with her principles** c'était en conflit *ou* en contradiction avec ses principes

conflict [kənˈflɪkt] **VI** être en conflit *ou* en désaccord (**with sth** avec qch); **this conflicts with his earlier statement** ceci est en contradiction avec sa déclaration précédente; **duties that c. with each other** charges incompatibles; **it conflicts with another appointment** j'ai/elle a/*etc* un autre rendez-vous à cette heure

conflicting [kənˈflɪktɪŋ] **ADJ** *(opinions)* opposé; *(advice, evidence)* contradictoire
▸▸ **c. interests** des intérêts *mpl* qui s'opposent

confluence [ˈkɒnfluəns] **N** *Geog (place)* confluent *m*; *(action) (of two rivers, glaciers)* confluence *f*

conform [kənˈfɔːm] **VI** se conformer (**to** *or* **with sth** à qch); **to c. to a standard** *(of equipment)* être conforme à *ou* répondre à une norme; **to c. to the law** obéir aux lois; **to c. (in shape) to another part** être identique à une autre pièce; **this conforms with what we were told/we expected** ceci est conforme à ce que l'on nous avait dit/nos attentes; **to c. to fashion** suivre la mode
VT conformer (**sth to sth** qch à qch)

conformism [kənˈfɔːmɪz(ə)m] **N** conformisme *m*

conformist [kənˈfɔːmɪst] **ADJ, N** conformiste *mf*

conformity [kənˈfɔːmɪtɪ] **N** conformité *f* (**to, with** à); **in c. with ...** conformément à ...; **their action was in c. with the law** ce qu'ils ont fait était en conformité avec la loi

confound [kənˈfaʊnd] **VT 1** *(confuse, surprise)* confondre; **they were confounded by this news** cette nouvelle les a consternés; **he confounded his critics** il a fait mentir les gens qui le critiquaient **2** *(bring to nothing) (sb's plans etc)* renverser; *(hopes)* réduire à néant **3** *Lit (put in confusion)* mettre la confusion dans; **to c. sth with sth** confondre qch avec qch **4** *Old-fashioned Fam (curse)* **c. him!** la peste soit de lui!; **c. it!** la barbe!

confounded [kənˈfaʊndɪd] **ADJ** *Old-fashioned Fam* sacré; **you c. idiot!** espèce d'idiot!

confraternity [kɒnfrəˈtɜːnɪtɪ] **N** association *f*

confront [kənˈfrʌnt] **VT** *(enemy, danger, problem, situation)* affronter, faire face à; **to c. the issue** faire face au problème; **to c. sb with** *(witness etc)* confronter qn avec; *(something)* mettre qn en face de; **she confronted him with his responsibilities** elle l'a mis face à ses responsabilités; **a difficult situation confronts them** ils doivent faire face à une situation difficile; **to be confronted by** *(somebody, something)* être en face de, se trouver en présence de; **to be confronted by** *or* **with a difficulty** se trouver face à une difficulté

confrontation [kɒnfrʌnˈteɪʃən] **N 1** *(of two people, armies etc)* affrontement *m* (**with** avec) **2** *(bringing into contact) (of witnesses etc)* confrontation *f*

confrontational [kɒnfrʌnˈteɪʃən(ə)l] **ADJ** *(situation)* d'affrontement; *(policy)* de confrontation; *(management style)* agressif; **he's quite c.** il aime la confrontation

Confucian [kənˈfjuːʃən] **ADJ** *Phil* confucéen, confucianiste

confuse [kənˈfjuːz] **VT 1** *(bewilder) (person)* embrouiller; *(animal)* troubler; **to get confused** s'embrouiller, s'y perdre **2** *(put into disorder)* **to c. the issue, to c. things** *or* **matters** compliquer les choses **3** *(mix up) (dates, names etc)* confondre; **he always confuses the two** il confond toujours les deux; **to c. sth/sb with** *or* **and sth/sb** confondre qch/qn avec qch/qn

confused [kənˈfjuːzd] **ADJ 1** *(person) (because not understanding sth)* embrouillé; *(not knowing what to do)* perdu; *(after blow on head, anaesthetic etc)* sonné, groggy; *(mind)* troublé; **to get c.** *(of person)* s'embrouiller; **I'm c.** *(don't understand)* je suis perdu, je n'y comprends rien; **I'm still a little c. as to why he did it** je ne comprends toujours pas très bien pourquoi il a fait cela; **the old lady's a bit c.** *(mentally)* la vieille dame ne sait plus trop où elle en est *ou* est un peu perdue **2** *(disordered) (mass, speech, logic, reasoning)* confus

> Note that the most common meaning of the French word **confus** is **embarrassed**.

confusedly [kənˈfjuːzɪdlɪ] **ADV** confusément

confusing [kənˈfjuːzɪŋ] **ADJ** *(unclear, causing lack of understanding)* embrouillé, confus; **it's very c.** on s'y perd; **it's too c. for the user** l'utilisateur s'y perdra; **I hope my explanation wasn't too c.** j'espère que mon explication ne vous a pas trop embrouillé; **there's a c. number of different makes** il y a tant de marques différentes qu'on s'y perd

confusingly [kənˈfjuːzɪŋlɪ] **ADV** *(unclearly, causing lack of understanding)* de manière embrouillée, confusément; **c., they both had the same name** ils avaient le même nom, ce qui provoquait souvent des confusions

confusion [kənˈfjuːʒən] **N 1** *(bewilderment)* confusion *f*, *Med* confusion *f* mentale; **in his c. he forgot his hat** dans sa confusion il a oublié son chapeau; **to add to the c. ...** pour ajouter à la confusion ...; **this news added to her c.** cette nouvelle a ajouté à sa confusion; **there's still some c. about the exact number killed** on ne connaît toujours pas le nombre de victimes; **it will only lead to c.** ce ne va faire qu'embrouiller les choses **2** *(disorder)* confusion *f*, désordre *m*; **everything was in c.** tout était en désordre, tout était pêle-mêle; **to spread c. everywhere** jeter partout le désordre *ou* la confusion **3** *(mixing up)* **c. of sth with** *or* **and sth** confusion *f* de qch avec qch **4** *(embarrassment)* confusion *f*; **to be covered in c.** être rempli de confusion

confute [kənˈfjuːt] **VT** *Fml (disprove) (argument, person)* réfuter

conga [ˈkɒŋgə] **N** conga *f*
VI danser la conga

congeal [kənˈdʒiːl] **VI** *(of fat, oil)* se figer; *(of blood)* se coaguler, se figer
VT *(blood)* faire coaguler; *(oil)* faire figer

congenial [kənˈdʒiːnɪəl] **ADJ** *(person, character)* sympathique, aimable; *(work)* agréable (**to** à); **I find his company c.** je le trouve d'une compagnie agréable; **an evening spent in c. company** une soirée passée en compagnie de gens sympathiques

congenital [kənˈdʒenɪt(ə)l] **ADJ** *(defect, idiot etc)* congénital, -aux

congenitally [kənˈdʒenɪtlɪ] **ADV** congénitalement; **to be c. insane** souffrir de folie congénitale

conger [ˈkɒŋgər] **N** congre *m*, anguille *f* de mer
▸▸ **c. eel** congre, anguille *f* de mer

congest [kənˈdʒest] **VT 1** *(traffic, roads etc)* encombrer, embouteiller **2** *Med (with blood, mucus)* congestionner

congested [kənˈdʒestɪd] **ADJ 1** *(street, road, airport etc)* encombré; *(room) (with furniture)* encombré; *(with people)* plein; **the c. state of the roads** l'encombrement *m* des routes; **the traffic gets c. at ...** il y a des encombrements à ... **2** *Med (lungs)* congestionné; **I'm feeling really c.** j'ai les bronches très prises

congestion [kənˈdʒestʃən] **N 1** *(of traffic etc)* encombrements *mpl*; **the new road will relieve the c. in the town** la nouvelle route va décongestionner la ville **2** *Med* congestion *f*
▸▸ **c. charge** taxe *f* anti-embouteillages

conglomerate [kənˈglɒmərət] **N** *Econ* conglomérat *m*; *Geol* conglomérat, aggloméré *m*

conglomerate [kənˈglɒməreɪt] **VI** *Geol, Ind* s'agglomérer

conglomeration [kənglɒməˈreɪʃən] **N** conglomération *f*; *(of rocks etc)* agrégat *m*; *Fig* **a c. of ideas** un mélange d'idées

Congo [ˈkɒŋgəʊ] **N** **the (River) C.** le Congo; **the C.** *(state)* le Congo

Congolese [kɒŋgəˈliːz] **N** Congolais, -aise
ADJ congolais

congrats [kənˈgræts] **NPL** *Br Fam* = **congratulations**

congratulate [kənˈgrætjʊleɪt] **VT** *(person)* féliciter (**on** de); **I c. you** je vous félicite, (je vous fais) mes compliments; **to c. oneself on sth/on having done sth** se féliciter de qch/d'avoir fait qch; **they are to be congratulated** ils méritent d'être félicités

congratulations [kəngrætjʊˈleɪʃənz] **NPL** félicitations *fpl*; **give her my c.** transmets-lui mes félicitations, félicite-la de ma part; **c.!** félicitations!; **c. on passing your exams** félicitations pour tes examens; **warmest c. on your promotion!** *(on card)* toutes nos félicitations pour votre promotion!; **c. are in order, I hear** au fait, félicitations!

congratulatory [kənˈgrætjʊleɪtərɪ] **ADJ** *(letter etc)* de félicitation(s)

congregate [ˈkɒŋgrɪgeɪt] **VI** se rassembler, s'assembler

congregation [kɒŋgrɪˈgeɪʃən] **N 1** *(in church)* assemblée *f* des fidèles, assistance *f*; **I'm not a member of your c.** je ne fais pas partie de votre paroisse, je ne viens pas à l'église ici **2** *(group, action of grouping)* rassemblement *m* **3** *Br Univ (at Oxford, Cambridge) (of professors etc)* assemblée *f* générale

congregational [kɒŋgrɪˈgeɪʃən(ə)l] **ADJ** *Rel* en assemblée; **the C. Church** l'Église *f* congrégationaliste; **c. worship** culte *m* public

Congress [ˈkɒŋgres] **N** *Am Pol* Congrès *m*

Congress
Le Congrès, organe législatif américain, est constitué du Sénat et de la Chambre des représentants. Une proposition de loi doit obligatoirement être approuvée séparément par ces deux Chambres.

congress [ˈkɒŋgres] **N 1** *(conference)* congrès *m* **2** *Fml (sexual intercourse)* rapports *mpl* sexuels

Congressional [kənˈgreʃən(ə)l] **ADJ** *Am Pol (committee, election)* du Congrès

Congressman, *pl* **Congressmen** [ˈkɒŋgresmən] **N** *Am Pol* membre *m* du Congrès

Congresswoman, *pl* **Congresswomen** [ˈkɒŋgreswʊmən, -wɪmɪn] **N** *Am Pol* membre *f* du Congrès

congruence ['kɒŋgrʊəns] N **1** *Fml* adéquation *f* (**with** avec) **2** *Geom* congruence *f* (**with** à)

congruent ['kɒŋgrʊənt] ADJ **1** *Fml* conforme (**with** à) **2** *Geom (triangle)* congruent

congruity [kɒŋ'gruːɪtɪ] N *Fml* = **congruence 1**

congruous ['kɒŋgrʊəs] ADJ *Fml* = **congruent 1**

conic ['kɒnɪk] ADJ *Geom* conique

conical ['kɒnɪk(ə)l] ADJ conique; **a c. paper hat** un chapeau pointu en papier
▸▸ **c. projection** *(in mapmaking)* projection *f* conique

conifer ['kɒnɪfər] N conifère *m*

coniferous [kə'nɪfərəs] ADJ conifère; *(forest)* de conifères

conjectural [kən'dʒektʃər(ə)l] ADJ conjectural, -aux

conjecture [kən'dʒektʃər] N conjecture *f*; **to hazard a c.** risquer une hypothèse *ou* une supposition; **it's a matter of c.** cela relève de l'hypothèse *ou* de la conjecture; **it's sheer c.** ce ne sont que des suppositions
▪ VT supposer
▪ VI faire des conjectures

conjoin [kən'dʒɔɪn] VT *Fml* unir, réunir

conjoint [kən'dʒɔɪnt] ADJ *Fml* conjoint, associé

conjointly [kən'dʒɔɪntlɪ] ADV *Fml* conjointement, ensemble

conjugal ['kɒndʒʊg(ə)l] ADJ conjugal, -aux

conjugate ['kɒndʒʊgeɪt] VT *Gram (verb)* conjuguer
▪ VI *Gram, Biol* se conjuguer

conjugation [kɒndʒʊ'geɪʃən] N *Gram, Biol* conjugaison *f* SEE GRAMMAR B24–7

conjunction [kən'dʒʌŋkʃən] N **1** *(combination)* conjonction *f*, **in c. with sb** conjointement avec qn; **these factors, in c. with others, were responsible for ...** ces facteurs combinés à d'autres furent responsables de ... **2** *Gram* conjonction *f* VOIR GRAMMAIRE A73–6; B57–8 **3** *Astron* conjonction *f*, **in c.** *(planets)* en conjonction
▸▸ *Aviat* **c. tickets** billets *mpl* complémentaires

conjunctive [kən'dʒʌŋktɪv] ADJ *(tissue etc)* conjonctif

conjunctivitis [kəndʒʌŋktɪ'vaɪtɪs] N *Med* conjonctivite *f*; **to have c.** avoir de la conjonctivite

conjure ['kʌndʒər] VI faire des tours de passe-passe *ou* de prestidigitation; *Fig* **a name to c. with** un nom qui fait rêver
▪ VT **1** *(produce)* **they conjured a bottle of wine out of nowhere** *or* **thin air** ils ont fait apparaître une bouteille de vin comme par enchantement **2** [kən'dʒʊər] *Fml (entreat)* conjurer (**sb to do sth** qn de faire qch)
▸ **conjure up** VT SEP **1** *(call to mind) (images, memories)* évoquer **2** *(call up) (spirit etc)* faire apparaître **3** *(produce)* **they conjured up some armchairs** ils ont déniché des fauteuils d'on ne sait où; **she conjured up an incredible meal out of almost nothing** elle a réussi à préparer un repas fantastique avec presque rien; **I'll c. something up** *(to eat)* je vais me débrouiller pour préparer quelque chose avec ce que j'ai; **I can't just c. extra staff up out of thin air!** je ne peux pas sortir du personnel supplémentaire de mon chapeau!

conjurer, conjuror ['kʌndʒərər] N prestidigitateur *m*, illusionniste *mf*

conjuring ['kʌndʒərɪŋ] N prestidigitation *f*
▸▸ **c. trick** tour *m* de passe-passe *ou* de prestidigitation

conk [kɒŋk] *Sl* N *Br (nose)* blair *m*, pif *m*
▪ VT *(hit)* foutre un gnon à

▸ **conk out** VI *Fam* **1** *(of machine, television etc)* tomber en panne **2** *(lose consciousness)* tomber dans les pommes **3** *(go to sleep)* s'endormir, s'écrouler **4** *Am (die)* clamser, clamecer

conker ['kɒŋkər] N *Br Fam* marron *m* (d'Inde); **conkers** *(game)* = jeu *m* qui consiste à faire éclater le marron que son adversaire tient au bout d'une ficelle

Conn *abbr* **Connecticut**

connect [kə'nekt] VT **1** *(join) (something)* relier, rattacher (**to** à); *Tech (two shafts)* embrayer; *(pipes)* joindre; *Elec (circuits)* interconnecter; *(wires)* connecter; **a road connects the two cities, the two cities are connected by a road** une route relie les deux villes, les deux villes sont reliées par une route; **a corridor connects the room to the library** il y a un couloir qui relie la pièce à la bibliothèque; **we were connected with the studio by radio** nous étions en liaison radio avec le studio; **the telephone/electricity hasn't been connected** le téléphone/l'électricité n'a pas été branché(e); **c. this wire to the other terminal** connectez ce fil à l'autre borne
2 *Tel (caller)* mettre en ligne *ou* en communication (**with** avec); **will you c. me with reservations, please?** est-ce que vous pouvez me passer votre service des réservations?; **to c. two subscribers** mettre deux abonnés en communication
3 *(link, associate)* associer (**sb/sth with sb/sth** qn/qch avec qn/à qch); **there is nothing to c. the two crimes** il n'y a aucun lien entre les deux crimes; **at first I didn't c. the name with the face** au début je n'ai pas fait le lien *ou* le rapprochement entre le nom et le visage; **to be connected with ...** *(of person)* avoir des relations *ou* un lien avec ...; *(of thing)* se rattacher *ou* se rapporter à ...; **the questions were connected with another subject** les questions étaient relatives *ou* se rapportaient à un autre sujet; **to be connected with** *or* **to a family** *(be related to)* avoir un lien de parenté avec une famille
▪ VI **1** *(of wires)* être reliés (**with** à); *(of roads)* se rejoindre; *(of rooms)* communiquer (**with** avec); **this road connects with the motorway** cette route rejoint l'autoroute; **the tunnels don't c.** les deux tunnels ne sont pas reliés *ou* ne communiquent pas
2 to c. with a train/a flight *(of train, plane)* assurer la correspondance avec un train/un vol; *(of person)* prendre la correspondance
3 *Fam (of blow)* atteindre son but; *(of boxer)* frapper *ou* atteindre son adversaire; *(of tennis player, cricketer, racket, bat)* frapper la balle
▪ N *Comput* connexion *f*
▸▸ *Comput* **c. time** durée *f* (d'établissement) de la connexion
▸ **connect up** VT SEP *(pipes)* raccorder; *(wires)* connecter; *Comput (to Internet)* connecter

connected [kə'nektɪd] ADJ *(linked) (facts, events etc)* connexe, lié; **to be well c.** *(of person)* avoir des relations

connecting [kə'nektɪŋ] ADJ *(cable, wire)* de connexion
▸▸ **c. door** porte *f* de communication; **c. flight** correspondance *f*, *Tech* **c. piece** pièce *f* de raccordement; *Tech* **c. pipe** tuyau *m* de raccordement *ou* de jonction; *Tech* **c. rod** bielle *f*, **c. rooms** *(in hotel)* pièces *fpl* communicantes; **c. time** *(for travel)* temps *m* de correspondance; **c. train** correspondance *f*

connection [kə'nekʃən] N **1** *(link, association)* rapport *m*, lien *m* (**between** entre **with** avec); **I didn't make the c.** je n'ai pas fait le rapprochement; **in c. with ...** à propos de ...; **in this c.** à ce propos, à cet égard

2 *(personal relationship)* relations *fpl*, rapports *mpl*; **I have broken off all c. with him** j'ai cessé toutes relations avec lui; **to establish a business c. with a firm** établir des relations commerciales avec une entreprise
3 *(acquaintance)* relation *f*, *Sl (drug dealer)* dealer *m*; **she has important connections** elle a des relations en haut lieu; **I have some useful connections within the police** j'ai des relations très utiles dans la police
4 *(family relationship)*, **to form a c. by marriage with a good family** s'allier à *ou* avec une bonne famille; **there's no c. with the Yorkshire Smythes** il n'y a pas de lien de parenté avec les Smythe du Yorkshire; **my family has Scottish connections** il y a des Écossais dans ma famille
5 *Tech etc* connexion *f*, *(of pipes, wires etc)* assemblage *m*, raccordement *m*; *(of machine parts)* accouplement *m*, engrenage *m*; *Elec* raccordement, connexion, branchement *m*; *Comput* connexion, liaison *f*, *Tel* communication *f*; *Elec* **the c. is loose** il y a un faux contact; *Tel* **we had a very bad c.** la communication était très mauvaise
6 *Elec (connecting device)* **earth** *or Am* **ground c.** prise *f* de terre
7 *(in journey) (train, plane, boat etc)* correspondance *f*, **I missed my c.** j'ai manqué *ou* raté ma correspondance
▸▸ *Tech* **c. kit** kit *m* d'accès *ou* de connexion

connective [kə'nektɪv] ADJ *Gram (word, phrase)* conjonctif
▪ N *Gram* conjonction *f* de coordination
▸▸ *Anat* **c. tissue** tissu *m* conjonctif

connectivity [kɒnek'tɪvɪtɪ] N *Comput* connectivité *f*

connector [kə'nektər] N *Elec* connecteur *m*; *Tech etc* raccord *m*
▸▸ **c. kit** kit *m* d'accès *ou* de connexion

connexion [kə'nekʃən] N = **connection**

conning tower ['kɒnɪŋ] N *(of submarine)* kiosque *m*

conniptions [kə'nɪpʃənz] N *Am Fam* **to have c.** piquer une crise (**about sth** à propos de qch)

connivance [kə'naɪvəns] N connivence *f*, **c. at** *or* **in a crime** complicité *f* dans un crime; **to be in c. with sb** être de connivence avec qn

connive [kə'naɪv] VI *(scheme, plot)* être de connivence (**with** avec; **to do** pour faire); **to c. at** *(abuse, irregularity etc)* se rendre complice de

conniving [kə'naɪvɪŋ] ADJ ATTRIB malhonnête; **you c. bastard!** espèce de pourri!

connoisseur [kɒnə'sɜːr] N connaisseur, -euse (**of** en); **to be a c. of sth** s'y connaître en qch, être un connaisseur en matière de qch

connotation [kɒnə'teɪʃən] N *(of term)* connotation *f*

connote [kɒ'nəʊt] VT *Fml (of word) (notion, idea)* suggérer, comporter; **the word connotes courage** le mot suggère une idée de courage

connubial [kə'njuːbɪəl] ADJ *Fml* conjugal, -aux

conquer ['kɒŋkər] VT *(country, world, sb's heart, market)* conquérir; *(difficulty, one's shyness, fears)* vaincre, surmonter; *(inflation, illness)* vaincre; **Everest was conquered in 1953** l'Everest a été conquis en 1953

conquering ['kɒŋkərɪŋ] ADJ *(army, hero)* conquérant, victorieux

conqueror ['kɒŋkərər] N **1** *(of country)* conquérant *m*; *Hist* **(William) the C.** Guillaume le Conquérant **2** *(victor)* vainqueur *m*

conquest ['kɒŋkwest] N *(victory, prize)*, *Fig* conquête *f*, *Hist* **the (Norman) C.** la conquête de l'Angleterre; *Fig* **his many**

conquests ses nombreuses conquêtes; *Fig* **to make a c. of sb** faire la conquête de qn

conrod ['kɒnrɒd] N *Aut* bielle *f*

Cons *Pol abbr* **Conservative**

consanguinity [kɒnsæŋ'gwɪnɪtɪ] N *Fml* consanguinité *f*

conscience ['kɒnʃəns] N conscience *f*; **to have a clear** *or* **an easy c.** avoir la conscience tranquille; **to have a guilty** *or* **bad c.** avoir mauvaise conscience; **to have sth on one's c.** avoir qch sur la conscience; **it's on my c.** je l'ai sur la conscience; **it's on my c. that I left him alone** je l'ai laissé tout seul et j'ai mauvaise conscience; **I can't sleep with that on my c.** je ne peux pas dormir avec ça sur la conscience; **he had no c. about abandoning them to their fate** il n'avait aucun scrupule à les abandonner à leur sort; **a matter of c.** une affaire de conscience; **freedom of c.** liberté *f* de conscience; **one cannot in all c. believe that ...** on ne peut pas raisonnablement croire que ...
▶▶**c. clause** clause *f* de conscience; **c. money** argent *m* restitué *(pour soulager sa conscience)*

conscience-stricken ADJ pris de remords

conscientious [kɒnʃɪ'enʃəs] ADJ *(worker, work)* consciencieux; **to be c. about time-keeping** être très ponctuel
▶▶**c. objection** objection *f* de conscience; **c. objector** objecteur *m* de conscience

conscientiously [kɒnʃɪ'enʃəslɪ] ADV *(to work)* consciencieusement

conscientiousness [kɒnʃɪ'enʃəsnɪs] N minutie *f*, conscience *f*

conscious ['kɒnʃəs] ADJ **1** *Med* **to be c.** être conscient; **to become c.** reprendre connaissance; **he's not c. yet** il n'a pas encore repris connaissance; *Hum (he's still in bed)* il n'a pas encore fait surface
2 *(aware)* conscient; **to be c. of sth** avoir conscience de qch, être conscient de qch; **to become c. of sth** s'apercevoir de qch; **I wasn't c. of having annoyed you** je ne m'étais pas rendu compte que je t'avais énervé; **to be c. that ...** être conscient du fait que ...
3 *(intentional)* conscient; **it was not a c. decision** ce n'était pas une décision prise de façon consciente; **it required a c. effort to ...** il fallait se forcer pour ...
4 *Phil, Psy* conscient; **the c. mind** la conscience; **to have a c. dislike of sb** éprouver une aversion consciente pour qn
N *Phil, Psy* **the c.** le conscient

-conscious SUFF **fashion-c.** qui suit de près la mode; **clothes-c.** qui s'habille avec soin; **health-c.** qui se préoccupe de sa santé; **safety-c.** soucieux de sécurité

consciously ['kɒnʃəslɪ] ADV consciemment; *(deliberately)* sciemment

consciousness ['kɒnʃəsnɪs] N **1** *Med* conscience *f*, connaissance *f*; **to lose c.** perdre connaissance *ou* conscience; **to regain c.** reprendre connaissance, revenir à soi **2** *(awareness)* conscience *f* (**of** de); **the organization aims to raise people's c. of these problems** l'organisme a pour objet de sensibiliser les gens à ces problèmes **3** *Phil, Psy* conscience *f*
▶▶**c. raising** sensibilisation *f*

conscript¹ ['kɒnskrɪpt] N *Mil* conscrit *m*
▶▶**c. army** armée *f* de conscrits

conscript² [kən'skrɪpt] VT *Mil* enrôler, appeler (sous les drapeaux); **to be conscripted** être appelé (sous les drapeaux); *Fig* **I've been conscripted to do the dishes** on m'a enrôlé pour faire la vaisselle

conscription [kən'skrɪpʃən] N *Mil* conscription *f*

consecrate ['kɒnsɪkreɪt] VT **1** *Rel (church,*

communion bread) consacrer; *(king, bishop)* sacrer **2** *(dedicate)* consacrer; **to c. one's life to sth** consacrer sa vie à qch, se vouer à qch; **the day was consecrated to the memory of the country's dead** la journée a été dédiée à la mémoire des morts du pays

consecrated ['kɒnsɪkreɪtɪd] ADJ *Rel (church, bread)* consacré; **in c. ground** en terre sainte *ou* bénite

consecration [kɒnsɪ'kreɪʃən] N **1** *(of church, communion bread)* consécration *f*, *(of king, bishop)* sacre *m* **2** *(dedication)* **the c. of her life to helping the poor** le fait de consacrer sa vie à aider les pauvres

consecutive [kən'sekjʊtɪv] ADJ consécutif; **on three c. days** trois jours de suite, trois jours consécutifs

consecutively [kən'sekjʊtɪvlɪ] ADV **two days c.** deux jours de suite, deux jours consécutifs; **to deal with problems c.** traiter les problèmes l'un après l'autre

consensual [kən'sensjʊəl] ADJ consensuel

consensus [kən'sensəs] N *(of opinion, evidence etc)* consensus *m*; **to reach a c.** arriver à un consensus; **a c. was beginning to emerge** un consensus commençait à apparaître; **the c. was that the new road was unnecessary** l'opinion générale était que la nouvelle route n'était pas nécessaire; **what is the c. of opinion?** quelle est l'opinion générale?
▶▶**c. management** gestion *f* par consensus; **c. politics** politique *f* de consensus

consent [kən'sent] N consentement *m*, accord *m*, assentiment *m*; **to give/withhold one's c. to sth** donner/ne pas donner son consentement à qch; **I'll never give my c.** je n'y consentirai jamais, je ne donnerai jamais mon accord; **do I have your c.?** est-ce que j'ai votre accord?; **by common c.** de l'aveu de tout le monde; **by mutual c.** de gré à gré; *(divorce)* par consentement mutuel; *Law* **age of c.** âge *m* nubile
VI **to c. to sth/to do sth** consentir à qch/à faire qch; **I c.** j'y consens

consenting [kən'sentɪŋ] ADJ *Law (adult)* consentant; *Hum* **she is a c. adult, after all** elle est majeure et vaccinée après tout

consequence ['kɒnsɪkwəns] N **1** *(result)* conséquence *f*, suites *fpl*; **the c. is that ...** il en résulte *ou* il s'ensuit que ...; **in c., as a c.** par conséquent; **in c. of ...** par suite de ...; **this decision had dire consequences for the region** cette décision a eu des conséquences terribles pour la région; **unforeseen consequences** conséquences imprévues; **to take the consequences** accepter les conséquences
2 *(importance)* importance *f*; **it is of no c.** cela n'a pas d'importance, cela ne fait rien; **it is of some c. to me** ça a de l'importance pour moi; **he is of no c.** il ne compte pas; **a woman of c.** une femme avec qui il faut compter
3 *Br* **consequences** *(game)* (jeu *m* des) petits papiers *mpl*

consequent ['kɒnsɪkwənt] ADJ **1** *(resulting)* résultant; **c. upon sth** qui est la conséquence de qch, qui résulte de qch; **a glut and the c. drop in prices** un surplus et la baisse des prix qui en résulte **2** *(in logic)* conséquent

consequential [kɒnsɪ'kwenʃəl] ADJ *(resulting)* conséquent, consécutif (**to** à); **c. effects** *(of action)* répercussions *fpl*
▶▶*Law* **c. damages** dommages *mpl* indirects

consequently ['kɒnsɪkwəntlɪ] ADV, CONJ par conséquent, donc

conservancy [kən'sɜːvənsɪ] N *Br (for protection of forest, river etc)* commission *f* de conservation

conservation [kɒnsə'veɪʃən] N **1** conservation *f*; **c. of energy** économies *fpl* d'énergie **2** *(of environment)* protection *f* de l'environnement; **c. expert** expert *m* de la protection de l'environnement
▶▶**c. area** zone *f* protégée *(d'un point de vue architectural ou historique)*

conservationist [kɒnsə'veɪʃənɪst] N partisan, -ane de la protection de l'environnement

conservatism [kən'sɜːvətɪz(ə)m] N conservatisme *m*

conservative [kən'sɜːvətɪv] ADJ **1** conservateur, -trice; *(evaluation)* prudent; **at a c. estimate** au minimum, au bas mot **2** *Pol* conservateur, -trice
N *Pol* conservateur, -trice; **the Conservatives** les conservateurs
▶▶*Br* **C. Central Office** = siège *m* du parti conservateur britannique; **the C. Party** le parti conservateur

conservatively [kən'sɜːvətɪvlɪ] ADV *(to dress)* de façon classique; **it was c. estimated at £5,000** selon des estimations prudentes, cela devrait coûter 5 000 livres

conservatoire [kən'sɜːvətwɑːr] N *Mus* conservatoire *m*

conservatory [kən'sɜːvətrɪ] N **1** *(attached to house)* véranda *f* **2** = **conservatoire**

conserve¹ ['kɒnsɜːv] N *Culin (jam)* confiture *f*

conserve² [kən'sɜːv] VT *(ancient monument etc)* conserver, préserver; **to c. water/energy** faire des économies d'eau/d'énergie; **they had to c. their water supplies to get across the desert** il a fallu qu'ils économisent l'eau pour pouvoir traverser le désert

consider [kən'sɪdər] VT **1** *(reflect on, think over) (matter)* considérer; *(facts, proposal, offer)* étudier; **I'll c. it** j'y réfléchirai; **he was considering whether to go out when ...** il se demandait s'il allait sortir quand ...; **have you considered (buying) a larger model?** est-ce que vous avez envisagé d'acheter un modèle plus grand?; **the jury retired to c. its verdict** le jury se retira pour délibérer; **to c. sb for a job** envisager de donner un poste à qn
2 *(take into account) (sb's feelings)* avoir égard à; *(expense)* regarder à; *(possibility)* envisager; **she never considers anybody but herself** elle ne fait jamais attention aux autres; **when you c. that ...** quand on pense *ou* songe que ...; **c. the cost!** pensez au coût!; **you ought to have considered my feelings** tu aurais dû penser à moi; **all things considered** tout bien considéré, tout compte fait
3 *(regard)* considérer; **I c. him a friend** je le considère comme un ami; **c. it done** considérez cela comme fait; **c. yourself dismissed** tenez-vous pour congédié; **to c. oneself happy** s'estimer heureux; **I c. it my duty to ...** j'estime qu'il est de mon devoir de ...; **I would c. it an honour** ce serait pour moi un honneur; **we c. it likely that ...** nous estimons qu'il est probable que ...

considerable [kən'sɪdərəb(ə)l] ADJ **1** *(great)* considérable; **a c. number of ...** un nombre considérable de ...; **the new car attracted c. attention** la nouvelle voiture a fait l'objet d'une attention considérable; **she only found the house after c. difficulty** elle n'a trouvé la maison qu'avec beaucoup de difficulté **2** *(worthy of attention)* digne d'attention; *(person)* notable, important

considerably [kən'sɪdərəblɪ] ADV considérablement

considerate [kən'sɪdərət] ADJ prévenant, plein d'égards (**towards, to** pour, envers); **it's very c. of you** c'est très aimable de votre part, c'est très gentil de ta part; **try to be more c.** essaie d'être un peu plus prévenant

considerately [kən'sɪdərətlɪ] **ADV** avec considération, avec prévenance

consideration [kənsɪdə'reɪʃən] **N 1** *(deliberation)* **under c.** *(question, candidate etc)* à l'étude; **to give a. to a question** mettre une question à l'étude; **I'll give it some c.** j'y penserai; **after due c.** après mûre réflexion; **to take sth into c.** prendre qch en considération, tenir compte de qch, prendre qch en ligne de compte; **taking all things into c.** tout bien considéré; **taking her age into c.** si l'on tient compte de son âge; **to leave sth out of c.** ne pas tenir compte de qch

2 *(factor)* facteur *m*; **there is another c.** il y a autre chose dont il faut tenir compte; **money is always the first c.** la question d'argent vient toujours en premier; **on no c.** à aucun prix; **money is no c.** l'argent n'entre pas en ligne de compte

3 *(regard)* considération *f*; **to have no c. for anyone** n'avoir de considération pour personne; **show some c.!** fais preuve d'un peu de considération!; **out of c. for sb** par égard pour qn; **to treat sb with c.** traiter qn avec considération

4 *(payment)* compensation *f*, rémunération *f*; *Com etc* **for a c.** moyennant paiement; **he'll do it for a c.** il le fera si vous le payez; **in c. of your services** en récompense de vos services

▸▸ *Mktg* **c. set** ensemble *m* de considérations

considered [kən'sɪdəd] **ADJ 1** *(thought out)* **it is my c. opinion that ...** après mûre réflexion je pense que ...; **is that your c. opinion?** est-ce ainsi que vous voyez les choses? **2** *(thought of)* **to be highly** *or* **well c.** être très estimé

considering [kən'sɪdərɪŋ] **PREP** étant donné, vu; **c. his age/the circumstances** étant donné *ou* vu son âge/les circonstances

CONJ étant donné que, vu que; **c. (that) he is so young** étant donné son jeune âge

ADV *Fam* après tout, malgré tout; **it's not so bad, c.** ce n'est pas si mauvais après tout *ou* malgré tout

consign [kən'saɪn] **VT 1** *(entrust)* confier, remettre (**sth to sb's care** qch à qn); **to c. a body to the grave** livrer un corps à la tombe **2** *Com (goods)* expédier (**to sb** à qn)

consignee [kɒnsaɪ'niː] **N** destinataire *mf*, réceptionnaire *mf*; *Com (of goods on consignment)* consignataire *mf*

consignment [kən'saɪnmənt] **N** *Com* **1** *(goods)* livraison *f*; *(incoming)* arrivage *m*, livraison **2** *(act) (of goods)* envoi *m*, expédition *f*; *Com* **on c.** en consignation; **to send sb goods on c.** livrer à qn une marchandise en dépôt permanent

▸▸ **c. note** bordereau *m* d'expédition

consignor [kən'saɪnər] **N** *Com* expéditeur, -trice

▸ **consist in** [kən'sɪst] **VT INSEP** consister en; **to c. in doing sth** consister à faire qch

▸ **consist of** **VT INSEP** consister en, se composer de; **her inheritance consisted of a house** son héritage consistait en une maison

consistency [kən'sɪstənsɪ] **N 1** *(of liquid etc)* consistance *f*; **to be the c. of sth** avoir la consistance de qch **2** *(internal logic)* cohérence *f*; *(in ideas)* logique *f*; **to lack c.** *(of statements, views etc)* manquer de suite *ou* de cohérence **3** *(staying the same) (of quality of work, ideas)* constance *f*, *(of athlete, performance)* régularité *f*, **4** *(compatibility) (of result with theory)* concordance *f*

▸▸ **c. check** contrôle *m* d'uniformité; *Acct* **c. concept** principe *m* de la permanence (des méthodes)

consistent [kən'sɪstənt] **ADJ 1** *(having internal logic) (reasoning, behaviour, person)* conséquent, cohérent, logique; **she was c. in her choice of partners** elle a toujours fait preuve de cohérence dans le choix de ses partenaires

2 *(staying the same) (quality of work, ideas)* constant; *(refusal, failure)* persistant; *(athlete, performer)* régulier; **because of her c. denial of the accusation** du fait qu'elle a toujours nié être coupable

3 *(compatible)* compatible (**with** avec); **the results are c. with the theory** les résultats concordent avec la théorie; **this action is not c. with his character** cette action n'est pas en harmonie avec son caractère; **her behaviour is c. with a diagnosis of ...** son comportement est caractéristique d'un diagnostic de ...

> Note that the French word **consistant** is a false friend and is never a translation for the English word **consistent**. Its most common meaning is **substantial**.

consistently [kən'sɪstəntlɪ] **ADV 1** *(with logic)* de manière cohérente *ou* conséquente **2** *(with regularity) (to play, perform, work)* avec régularité; *(to fail, maintain)* constamment; **she has c. denied the accusation** elle a toujours nié cette accusation; **he has been c. better than the others** il a constamment été meilleur que les autres

consistory [kən'sɪstərɪ] **N** *Rel (pontifical)* consistoire *m*

▸▸ **C. Court** tribunal *m* ecclésiastique

consolation [kɒnsə'leɪʃən] **N** consolation *f*, **words of c.** paroles *fpl* consolatrices; **that's one c.** c'est déjà une consolation; **if it's any c.** si ça peut te consoler; **it wasn't much c. to reflect that tomorrow was her birthday** c'était une piètre consolation de penser que son anniversaire était le lendemain

▸▸ **c. prize** prix *m* de consolation

console¹ [kən'səʊl] **VT** consoler (**for** de); **c. yourself with the thought that it's Friday tomorrow** console-toi en pensant que demain c'est vendredi

console² ['kɒnsəʊl] **N 1** *(control panel)* console *f*, pupitre *m*; *Aviat* tableau *m* de bord; *Comput* pupitre *m* de commande **2** *Radio, TV (cabinet)* meuble *m* (pour téléviseur, chaîne hi-fi) **3** *Mus (of organ)* console *f*

▸▸ **c. table** console *f*

consolidate [kən'sɒlɪdeɪt] **VT** *(foundations)* consolider, renforcer; *Mil (position)* raffermir; *Fig (position, lead)* conforter; *Com (orders, deliveries)* grouper; *Fin (debt)* consolider; *St Exch (shares)* regrouper; **to c. one's power** asseoir son pouvoir; **the company has consolidated its position as the market leader** la société a conforté sa position de leader sur le marché

VI se consolider

consolidated [kən'sɒlɪdeɪtɪd] **ADJ** *Fin* consolidé; *Com (orders, deliveries)* groupé

▸▸ *Acct* **c. accounts** comptes *mpl* consolidés; *Fin* **c. annuities** fonds *mpl* consolidés; *Acct* **c. balance sheet** bilan *m* consolidé; *Fin* **c. debt** dette *f* consolidée; *Acct* **c. entry** écriture *f* de consolidation; *Br Pol* **c. fund** = compte du gouvernement à la Banque d'Angleterre, qui sert à régler toutes les dépenses publiques; *Br Fin* **c. funds** fonds consolidés; **c. loan** emprunt *m* consolidé; **c. subsidiary** filiale *f* consolidée

consolidation [kənsɒlɪ'deɪʃən] **N 1** *(of foundations, power etc)* consolidation *f*, renforcement *m*; *(of public opinion)* raffermissement *m* **2** *Fin (of national debt)* consolidation *f*; *St Exch (of shares)* regroupement *m*; *Law (of laws)* unification *f* **3** *Com (of orders, deliveries)* groupage *m*, **c. for export** groupement *m* à l'export

consolidator [kən'sɒlɪdeɪtər] **N** *Com* groupeur *m*

consoling [kən'səʊlɪŋ] **ADJ** consolateur, -trice

consols ['kɒnsɒlz, kən'sɒlz] **NPL** *Br Fin* (fonds *mpl*) consolidés *mpl*

consonance ['kɒnsənəns] **N 1** *Mus, Ling* consonance *f* **2** *Fml (of ideas etc)* accord *m*, conformité *f*

consonant ['kɒnsənənt] **N** *Ling* consonne *f*
ADJ *Fml* en accord; **to be c. with** *or* **to sth** être en accord avec qch

consort ['kɒnsɔːt] **N** *(spouse) (of ruler etc)* époux, -ouse; **prince c.** prince *m* consort

▸ **consort with** [kən'sɔːt] **VT INSEP** frayer avec, fréquenter

consortium [kən'sɔːtɪəm] **N** *Com, Fin* consortium *m*

conspicuous [kən'spɪkjʊəs] **ADJ 1** *(easily visible)* bien visible, apparent, manifeste; *(monument, landmark)* bien visible; *(uniform etc)* voyant; **in a c. position** bien en évidence; **to make oneself c.** se faire remarquer (**by, through par**) **2** *(obvious) (failure, lack)* manifeste, évident; *(striking) (bravery, intelligence)* remarquable, frappant; **c. gallantry** acte *m* de bravoure insigne; **to be c. by one's absence** *(of person, quality)* briller par son absence

▸▸ **c. consumption** consommation *f* ostentatoire

conspicuously [kən'spɪkjʊəslɪ] **ADV 1** *(visibly)* visiblement, manifestement; **to be c. absent** briller par son absence **2** *(remarkably)* remarquablement; *(dressed)* de façon (un peu) ostentatoire

conspicuousness [kən'spɪkjʊəsnɪs] **N 1** *(visibility)* caractère *m* bien visible; *(of uniform etc)* caractère voyant **2** *(striking nature) (of action)* caractère *m* insigne *ou* remarquable

conspiracy [kən'spɪrəsɪ] **N** conspiration *f*, conjuration *f*, complot *m*; *Law* association *f* de malfaiteurs; **c. of silence** conspiration du silence; **c. to obtain documents illegally** conspiration pour obtenir des documents de façon illégale; **there's a c. against me** il y a un complot contre moi; **it's a c.** c'est un complot

▸▸ **c. theorist** partisan *m* de la thèse *ou* théorie du complot; **c. theory** thèse *f* *ou* théorie *f* du complot

conspirator [kən'spɪrətər] **N** conspirateur, -trice

conspiratorial [kənspɪrə'tɔːrɪəl] **ADJ** *(air)* de conspirateur; **she gave me a c. wink** elle m'a jeté un coup d'œil complice

conspire [kən'spaɪər] **VI 1** *(of person)* conspirer (**against** contre; **with** avec); **to c. to do sth** comploter de faire qch **2** *(of events etc)* concourir, contribuer; **everything conspired to make him late** tout a contribué à le mettre en retard; **circumstances conspired against me** les circonstances se sont liguées contre moi

constable ['kʌnstəb(ə)l, 'kɒn-] **N** *Br (in police)* agent *m* de police; *(rural)* gendarme *m*; **good evening, c.** bonsoir, monsieur l'agent; **special c.** auxiliaire *m* de police; **chief c.** ≃ commissaire *m* divisionnaire

constabulary [kən'stæbjʊlərɪ] **N** *(no pl)* *Br* police *f*, **the Kent C.** la Gendarmerie du Kent

constancy ['kɒnstənsɪ] **N** *(of character, temperature)* constance *f*, *(of friend)* fidélité *f*, *(of wind etc)* régularité *f*

constant ['kɒnstənt] **ADJ 1** *(unchanging) (temperature, price, pressure)* constant; *(friend)* fidèle; **to remain c.** *(of temperature,* *price*) rester constant **2** *(unceasing) (attention)* continuel; *(doubts, questions, complaining)* incessant; *(care)* continuel, assidu, soutenu; **through c. repetition** à force de répéter; **there was c. pressure for reform** il y avait une pression continuelle pour qu'une réforme soit mise en œuvre; **a c. stream of insults** un flot d'injures ininterrompu

N *Math, Phys* constante *f*; **time c.** constante de temps

constantly ['kɒnstəntlɪ] **ADV** constamment, continuellement

constant-velocity joint N *Aut* joint *m* de cardan, joint homocinétique

constellation [kɒnstə'leɪʃən] **N** constellation *f*

consternation [kɒnstə'neɪʃən] **N** consternation *f*; **a look of c.** un air consterné; **they looked at each other in c.** ils se regardaient atterrés; **to our c.** à notre consternation

constipate ['kɒnstɪpeɪt] **VT** *Med* constiper

constipated ['kɒnstɪpeɪtɪd] **ADJ** *Med, Fig* constipé; *Fig* **his rather c. prose style** son style plutôt empesé *ou* guindé

constipation [kɒnstɪ'peɪʃən] **N** *Med* constipation *f*

constituency [kən'stɪtjʊənsɪ] **N** *Pol* **1** *(voters)* électeurs *mpl* *(d'une circonscription)* **2** *(district)* circonscription *f* électorale; *Br* **the c. party** la section locale du parti

constituent [kən'stɪtjʊənt] **ADJ** constitutif
N 1 *Pol (of MP)* électeur, -trice **2** *(part)* élément *m* constitutif, composant *m*; *Ling* constituant *m*
▸▸*Pol* **c. assembly** assemblée *f* constituante

constitute ['kɒnstɪtjuːt] **VT 1** *(make up, form)* constituer; *(sb's happiness etc)* faire; **to c. a threat to …** constituer une menace pour …; **the countries that c. the EU** les pays qui constituent l'UE; **factors that c. an offence** éléments constitutifs d'un délit; **that, to me, constitutes happiness** pour moi, c'est ça le bonheur **2** *Fml (appoint)* **to c. sb arbitrator** constituer qn arbitre

constitution [kɒnstɪ'tjuːʃən] **N 1** *Pol (of state, organization)* constitution *f* **2** *(of person)* constitution *f*; **to have a strong/an iron c.** avoir une bonne constitution/une santé de fer **3** *(composition)* constitution *f*, composition *f*

constitutional [kɒnstɪ'tjuːʃən(ə)l] **ADJ 1** *Pol etc (monarchy, regime, reform)* constitutionnel; **the president's actions are not c.** les actions du président sont anticonstitutionnelles **2** *Med (disorder)* diathésique
N *(short walk)* (petite) promenade *f*

constitutionally [kɒnstɪ'tjuːʃən(ə)lɪ] **ADV 1** *Pol (act)* constitutionnellement **2** *(by nature) (lazy, weak, strong)* de *ou* par nature

constitutive [kən'stɪtjuːtɪv] **ADJ** constitutif

constrain [kən'streɪn] **VT 1** *(compel) (person)* contraindre, forcer (**to do** à *ou* de faire); **to find oneself constrained to do sth** se voir contraint de faire qch **2** *(restrict movement of) (of clothing etc)* gêner; *(of person)* contenir; **she did not feel constrained by the conventions of her time** elle ne se sentait pas obligée d'obéir aux conventions sociales de son époque

constrained [kən'streɪnd] **ADJ** *(air)* contraint, gêné; *(voice)* forcé; *(smile)* contraint

constraint [kən'streɪnt] **N 1** *(compulsion, restriction)* contrainte *f*; *Law* coercition *f*; **to do sth under c.** faire qch sous la contrainte **2** *(of manner)* gêne *f*, contrainte *f* **3** *(self-control)* retenue *f*; **to speak about sth without c.** parler librement de qch

constrict [kən'strɪkt] **VT** *(opening)* resserrer,

rétrécir; *(of clothing) (movements)* entraver
VI se resserrer

constricted [kən'strɪktɪd] **ADJ** *(opening, passage)* étroit

constriction [kən'strɪkʃən] **N** resserrement *m*, rétrécissement *m*; *Med* constriction *f*

constrictor [kən'strɪktər] **N** *Anat* (muscle *m*) constricteur *m*; **boa c.** boa *m* constricteur

construct¹ [kən'strʌkt] **VT** *(building, machine, novel)* construire; **well/badly constructed** *(phrase, play)* bien/mal agencé *ou* construit

construct² ['kɒnstrʌkt] **N** *Phil (idea)* concept *m*

construction [kən'strʌkʃən] **N 1** *(of building, ship, machine etc)* construction *f*; **under c.** en (cours de) construction **2** *(thing constructed)* construction *f* **3** *Gram* construction *f* **4** *(interpretation) (of action etc)* interprétation *f*; **to put a good/bad c. on sb's words/actions** interpréter en bien/en mal les paroles/actions de qn; **to put another c. on sth** interpréter qch d'une autre façon
▸▸**the c. industry** le bâtiment; **c. site** chantier *m* (de construction); **c. worker** ouvrier *m* du bâtiment

constructional [kən'strʌkʃən(ə)l] **ADJ** de construction; *(technique)* mécanique
▸▸*Tech* **c. engineering** construction *f* mécanique

constructive [kən'strʌktɪv] **ADJ 1** *(criticism, remark)* constructif; *(mind)* créateur **2** *(relating to construction)* de construction
▸▸*Ind* **c. dismissal** = démission *f* provoquée par la conduite de l'employeur

constructively [kən'strʌktɪvlɪ] **ADV** *(to criticize)* d'une manière constructive

constructor [kən'strʌktər] **N** constructeur, -trice

construe [kən'struː] **VT** *(interpret) (sb's words)* interpréter; **the phrase can be construed to mean two things** on peut interpréter l'expression de deux manières différentes

consul ['kɒns(ə)l] **N** *(diplomat)* consul *m*
▸▸**c. general** consul *m* général

consular ['kɒnsjʊlər] **ADJ** consulaire
▸▸*Com* **c. fees** frais *mpl* consulaires; *Com* **c. invoice** facture *f* consulaire

consulate ['kɒnsjʊlət] **N** *(office)* consulat *m*
▸▸**c. general** consulat général

consult **VT** *(doctor, dictionary etc)* consulter (**on, about** sur)
VI consulter (**with sb** qn); **to c. together** se consulter
N *Fam* = **consultation**

consultancy [kən'sʌltənsɪ] **N 1** *(company)* cabinet *m* d'expert-conseil; *(advice)* assistance *f* technique; **to do c. work** être consultant **2** *Br Med (post)* poste *m* de médecin/chirurgien consultant
▸▸**c. fees** frais *mpl* de conseil; **c. firm** cabinet *m* d'expert-conseil; **c. service** service *m* d'assistance technique

consultant [kən'sʌltənt] **N 1** *Com, Ind etc* consultant, -ante; **engineering c.** ingénieur *m* conseil; **beauty c.** esthéticien, -ienne; *(for face)* visagiste *mf*; **financial c.** conseiller, -ère financier(ière) **2** *Br Med* médecin *m*/chirurgien, -ienne spécialiste, consultant, -ante

consultation [kɒnsəl'teɪʃən] **N** *(of person, dictionary etc), Law* consultation *f*; *(as a group)* délibération *f*; **in c. with sb** en consultation avec qn; **to hold a c.** délibérer, conférer

consultative [kən'sʌltətɪv] **ADJ** *(committee)* consultatif; **to play a c. role** avoir un rôle de consultant *ou* de conseil

consulting [kən'sʌltɪŋ] **ADJ** *(doctor)* consultant; *(engineer)* conseil

▸▸*Med* **c. room** cabinet *m* de consultation; **c. service** (service *m* de) conseil *m*

consumable [kən'sjuːməb(ə)l] **N** produit *m* ou article *m* ou bien *m* de consommation; *Comput* **computer consumables** petit matériel *m* informatique
ADJ consommable
▸▸*Com, Econ* **c. goods** produits *mpl* de consommation

consume [kən'sjuːm] **VT** *(food, drink, fuel etc)* consommer; *(exhaust)* épuiser; *(of fire) (building etc)* consumer, dévorer; **the discussion consumed many hours** la discussion a pris de nombreuses heures; **to be consumed with** *(desire)* brûler de; *(jealousy, envy, curiosity)* être en proie à

> When translating **to consume**, note that the French verbs **consommer** and **consumer** are not interchangeable. **Consommer** always refers to consumer activity, while **consumer** is used to describe the process of being eaten up or destroyed, especially by fire.

consumer [kən'sjuːmər] **N** consommateur, -trice; **gas/electricity consumers** abonnés *mpl* au gaz/à l'électricité
▸▸**c. advocate** défenseur *m* des intérêts des consommateurs; *Mktg* **c. behaviour** comportement *m* du consommateur; *Mktg* **c. benefit** bénéfice *m* consommateur; *Com, Mktg* **c. brand** marque *f* grand public; *Com, Mktg* **c. credit** crédit *m* à la consommation; *Com, Econ* **c. debt** endettement *m* des consommateurs; *Com, Mktg* **c. demand** demande *f* des consommateurs; *Com, Econ* **c. durables** biens *mpl* de consommation durables; **c. expenditure** dépenses *fpl* de consommation; **c. goods** biens de consommation durables; *Com, Econ* **c. industry** industrie *f* de consommation; **c. journalism** journalisme *m* dans le cadre de la défense des consommateurs; **c. loan** prêt *m* à la consommation; **c. magazine** magazine *m* pour les consommateurs; *Com, Econ* **c. market** marché *m* de la consommation; *Com, Econ* **c. nondurables** biens de grande consommation; *Com* **c. organization** organisme *m* de défense des consommateurs; *Mktg* **c. panel** groupe-témoin *m*, *pl* groupes-témoins, panel *m* de consommateurs; *Com, Econ* **c. price index** indice *m* des prix à la consommation; *Com, Econ* **c. protection** défense *f* des consommateurs; **c. protection agency** bureau *m* d'accueil des consommateurs; *Mktg* **c. research** étude *f* de marché; *Mktg* **c. resistance** résistance *f* ou réticence *f* des consommateurs; **c. society** société *f* de consommation; *Mktg* **c. survey** étude auprès des consommateurs finaux; *Mktg* **c. welfare** intérêt *m* du consommateur

consumerism [kən'sjuːmərɪz(ə)m] **N** consumérisme *m*

consummate¹ ['kɒnsəmɪt, kən'sʌmɪt] **ADJ** *(art)* consommé, achevé; *(liar)* fieffé; *(snob, hypocrite)* parfait; *(linguist, cook, musician etc)* de premier ordre; **she was c. in the art of concealing her feelings** elle était maître dans l'art de cacher ses sentiments; **to be a c. master of one's craft** connaître à fond son métier

consummate² ['kɒnsjəmeɪt] **VT** *(marriage, relationship)* consommer

consummation [kɒnsə'meɪʃən] **N 1** *(of marriage, relationship)* consommation *f* **2** *(of ambition, career)* aboutissement *m*

consumption [kən'sʌmpʃən] **N 1** *(of goods, heat, coal, petrol etc)* consommation *f*; **unfit for human c.** impropre à la consommation; *Econ* **home c.** consommation intérieure; *Fig* **the president's remarks were strictly for domestic c.** les remarques du président ne s'adressaient qu'à son pays **2** *Med Old-fashioned* consumption *f*, phtisie *f*

▸▸ *Econ* **c. expenditure, c. spending** dépenses *fpl* de consommation

consumptive [kən'sʌmptɪv] **ADJ, N** *Med Old-fashioned* phtisique *mf*

cont 1 *abbr* **contents 2** (*abbr* **continued**) suite

contact ['kɒntækt] **N 1** (*act of touching*) contact *m*; **to come into c. with** entrer en contact avec, toucher; **the substance must not come into c. with the air** la substance ne doit pas être exposée à l'air; **point of c.** (*of two curves etc*) point *m* de contact

2 (*between people*) rapport *m*, contact *m*; **to be in/come into c. with sb** être/entrer en contact ou en rapport avec qn; **are you still in c.?** (*of two people*) est-ce que vous êtes toujours en contact?; **the two leaders are in close c.** les deux dirigeants sont en contact étroit; **he didn't get in c. (with me/them/etc)** il n'est pas entré en contact (avec moi/eux/*etc*) il ne m'a/les a/*etc* pas contacté(s); **to put sb in c. with sb** mettre qn en rapport avec qn; **she hadn't come into c. with poverty** elle ne s'était pas trouvée au contact de la pauvreté; **anyone who has come into c. with the sick man** quiconque s'est trouvé au contact du malade; **to make c. with sb** (*by radio etc*) contacter qn, prendre contact avec qn; **after three days they made c. with civilization** après trois jours ils ont pris contact avec la civilisation; **to make eye c. with sb** rencontrer le regard de qn; **we made eye c.** nos regards se sont croisés; *Mil* **to establish c. with the enemy** prendre contact avec l'ennemi

3 (*contact lens*) verre *m* ou lentille *f* de contact; **to wear contacts** porter des lentilles de contact

4 *Med* (*person*) = personne *f* ayant approché un malade contagieux; **sexual c.** partenaire *mf* sexuel(elle)

5 (*acquaintance etc*) relation *f*; **I have a c. who may be able to help you** je connais quelqu'un qui pourrait vous aider; **who's our c. in Paris?** qui est notre contact à Paris?

6 *Elec etc* (*state, part*) contact *m*

VT se mettre en contact ou en rapport ou en relation avec, *Fam* contacter; **I can be contacted at this address** on peut me contacter à cette adresse

▸▸ *Elec* **c. breaker** disjoncteur *m*; *Elec* **breaker plate** plateau *m* porte-rupteur; *Elec* **c. breaker points** contacts *mpl* rupteur; **c. lens** lentille *f* de contact; *Phot* **c. print** planche *f* contact, épreuve *f* par contact; **c. sport** sport *m* de contact

contactable [kɒn'tæktəb(ə)l] **ADJ** joignable

contagion [kən'teɪdʒən] **N** *Lit, Fig* contagion *f*

contagious [kən'teɪdʒəs] **ADJ** (*disease*) contagieux; *Fig* (*laughter*) communicatif, contagieux

contagiousness [kən'teɪdʒəsnɪs] **N** contagiosité *f*, *Fig* **the c. of laughter** la contagion du rire

contain [kən'teɪn] **VT 1** (*hold*) contenir

2 (*include*) (*of book, medicine etc*) contenir; **the ore contains a high percentage of iron** le minerai a une forte teneur en fer; **the document contains a reference to …** le document contient une référence à …

3 (*control*) (*rage, emotion, inflation*) contenir, maîtriser; *Mil* (*enemy*) contenir; (*epidemic, spread of an idea*) circonscrire; **he was unable to c. his laughter** il ne pouvait pas s'empêcher de rire; **I could no longer c. myself** je ne pouvais plus me contenir davantage

container [kən'teɪnər] **N 1** récipient *m* **2** (*for transport*) conteneur *m*

▸▸ **c. depot** entrepôt *m* de conteneurs, dépôt *m* pour conteneurs; **c. lorry** = camion *m* adapté au transport des conteneurs; **c. port** port *m* pour conteneurs; **c. premium** prime *f* contenant; **c. ship** navire *m* porte-conteneurs, porte-conteneurs *m inv*; **c. terminal** terminal *m* à conteneurs; **c. truck** = camion *m* adapté au transport des conteneurs

containerization [kənteɪnəraɪ'zeɪʃən] **N** conteneurisation *f*, (*of port*) conversion *f* à la conteneurisation

containerize [kən'teɪnəraɪz] **VT** mettre en conteneur, conteneuriser; (*port*) convertir à la conteneurisation

containerized freight [kən'teɪnəraɪzd] **N** fret *m* par conteneur

containment [kən'teɪnmənt] **N 1** (*of disease, ideology*) action *f* de circonscrire; **a policy of c.** une politique d'endiguement **2** *Nucl* confinement *m*

contaminate [kən'tæmɪneɪt] **VT** contaminer; **contaminated air** air *m* vicié; *Fig* **he has been contaminated by contact with political activists** il a été contaminé au contact d'activistes

contamination [kəntæmɪ'neɪʃən] **N** (*bacterial, radioactive etc*) contamination *f*

contango, *pl* **contangoes** [kən'tæŋgəʊ, -əʊz] **N** *Br St Exch* report *m*; (*percentage*) taux *m* du report

contd (*abbr* **continued**) suite; **c. on p.14** suite à la page 14; **to be c.** à suivre

contemplate ['kɒntempleɪt] **VT 1** (*look at*) contempler **2** (*think about, consider*) (*the universe, the past, one's life*) réfléchir à, méditer sur **3** (*envisage*) envisager; **to c. doing sth** envisager de ou songer à faire qch; **it's too awful to c.** c'est insupportable rien que d'y penser; **to c. suicide** songer au suicide; **that was never contemplated** il n'a jamais été question de cela

VI se recueillir, méditer

contemplation [kɒntem'pleɪʃən] **N 1** (*of painting, shop window etc*) contemplation *f* **2** (*thinking about*) **they sat in silent c. of …** ils méditaient en silence sur … **3** (*meditation*) contemplation *f*

contemplative [kən'templətɪv] **ADJ** *Rel* (*life, order*) contemplatif

contemporaneous [kəntempə'reɪnɪəs] **ADJ** contemporain (**with** de)

contemporaneously [kəntempə'reɪnəslɪ] **ADV** **c. with …** à la même période ou époque que …

contemporary [kən'temp(ə)rərɪ] **ADJ** (*of same time*) contemporain (**with** de) **2** (*present day*) contemporain, actuel, moderne

N **our contemporaries** nos contemporains *mpl*; **she and I are contemporaries** elle et moi sommes de la même génération; **a c. of mine at school** quelqu'un qui était dans la même année que moi à l'école

contempt [kən'tempt] **N** mépris *m*, dédain *m*; **to hold sb/sth in c.** mépriser qn/qch; **to treat sb/sth with c.** traiter qn/qch avec dédain ou mépris; **it is/he is beneath c.** c'est/il est tout ce qu'il y a de plus méprisable; **her c. for the law/our opinions** son mépris de la loi/nos opinions; **I have nothing but c. for him** je n'éprouve que du mépris pour lui; *Law* **c. of court** outrage *m* au tribunal, offense *f* à la cour

contemptible [kən'temptəb(ə)l] **ADJ** méprisable

contemptibly [kən'temptɪblɪ] **ADV** (*to say, to look at*) avec mépris; **a c. small amount** une quantité dérisoirement faible

contemptuous [kən'temptjʊəs] **ADJ** (*air, person*) méprisant; (*gesture, word*) de mépris, méprisant; **to be c. of sth** mépriser qch

contemptuously [kən'temptʊəslɪ] **ADV** avec mépris, avec dédain

contend [kən'tend] **VI** (*struggle*) affronter, lutter (**with, against** contre); (*argue*) se disputer (**with** avec; **about** sur); **the difficulties I have to c. with** les difficultés que je dois affronter; **they still had the perimeter fence to c. with** il leur restait encore à régler le problème de la clôture d'enceinte; **I have a lot to c. with** je dois faire face à beaucoup de problèmes; **several candidates were contending for the job** plusieurs candidats étaient en compétition pour le poste

VT (*maintain, argue*) **to c. that …** prétendre ou soutenir que …

contender [kən'tendər] **N** concurrent, -ente; (*in election*) candidat, -ate; *Sport etc* (*for title*) challenger *m* (**for sth** de qch); **he is the main c. in the battle for the leadership** c'est le grand favori dans la lutte pour la position de leader

contending [kən'tendɪŋ] **ADJ** **the c. parties** les concurrents *mpl*; **the c. armies** les armées *fpl* opposées

content [¹ ['kɒntent] **N** VOIR GRAMMAIRE A10 **1** *Chem, Miner etc* teneur *f*; **gold/moisture c.** teneur en or/humidité; **high protein/fibre/fat c.** haute teneur en protéines/fibres/lipides; **peanut butter has a high protein c.** le beurre de cacahuètes est riche en protéines **2** (*of book, film, speech*) contenu *m*; (*meaning*) teneur *f*, fond *m*; **there is more emphasis on style than on c.** une plus grande importance est accordée au style qu'au fond

▸▸ *Comput* **c. provider** fournisseur *m* de contenu

content [² [kən'tent] **ADJ** content, satisfait (**with** de); **they were poor but c.** ils étaient pauvres mais heureux; **to be c. with sth** se contenter de qch; **he's quite c. to stay at home** il ne demande pas mieux que de rester à la maison; **she's never c. to just watch a film, she has to make comments** il ne lui suffit pas de regarder un film, il faut qu'elle fasse des commentaires; **not c. with having ruined our evening, he came round next day** non content d'avoir gâché notre soirée, il revint le lendemain

VT contenter, satisfaire; **to c. oneself with (doing) sth** se contenter de (faire) qch

N = contentment

contented [kən'tentɪd] **ADJ** content, satisfait (**with** de); (*smile*) de satisfaction; **he's a very c. baby** il est toujours content, ce bébé

contentedly [kən'tentɪdlɪ] **ADV** avec contentement; **to live c.** vivre heureux

contentedness [kən'tentɪdnɪs] **N** contentement *m*

contention [kən'tenʃən] **N 1** (*struggle*) lutte *f*, (*argument*) dispute *f* **2** (*competition*) **to be in c.** être en compétition (**for sth** pour qch); **the teams in c.** les équipes concurrentes ou rivales **3** (*opinion*) affirmation *f*, **my c. is that …** je soutiens que …

contentious [kən'tenʃəs] **ADJ 1** (*issue etc*) controversé **2** (*person, mood*) querelleur

contentment [kən'tentmənt] **N** contentement *m*; **a smile of c.** un sourire de satisfaction

contents ['kɒntents] **NPL** (*of box, drawer, house etc*) contenu *m*; **(table of) c.** (*of book*) table *f* des matières VOIR GRAMMAIRE A10

▸▸ **c. insurance** assurance *f* mobilier; **c. list** liste *f* du contenu; **c. page** table des matières

contest [¹ ['kɒntest] **N 1** (*competition*) concours *m*, *Sport* compétition *f*, *Boxing etc* combat *m*; *Pol* **presidential c.** élection *f* présidentielle; *Fig* **there's simply no c.** il n'y a aucune comparaison; **beauty c.** concours de beauté **2** (*struggle*) combat *m*, lutte *f* (**with**

avec, contre; **between** entre) **3** *Am Law* **no c.** pas de témoins à charge

contest² [kən'test] **VT 1** *(call into question) (right, ability, will, inheritance)* contester; **to c. sb's right to do sth** contester à qn le droit de faire qch; *Fin* **contested debt** créance *f* litigieuse **2** *Pol (seat in Parliament)* se porter candidat pour; **to c. an election** disputer *ou* se présenter à une élection; *Sport* **to c. a race** participer à une course; *Pol* **a hotly contested seat** un siège très disputé

contestant [kən'testənt] **N** concurrent, -ente; *(in boxing, wrestling etc)* combattant *m*

contestation [kɒntes'teɪʃən] **N** *Fml (of right etc)* contestation *f*

context ['kɒntekst] **N** contexte *m*; **in this c.** *(regard)* à ce propos; **in/out of c.** en/hors contexte; **she was quoted out of c.** on a cité ses paroles hors de leur contexte; **in the c. of** dans le contexte de; **to put sth into c.** replacer qch dans son contexte

context-dependent **ADJ** **to be c.** dépendre du contexte

context-sensitive **ADJ** *Comput (spellchecker)* contextuel

contextual [kən'tekstjuəl] **ADJ** contextuel

contextualize [kən'tekstjuəlaɪz] **VT** *(historical event, film etc)* placer dans son contexte; *(word, expression)* contextualiser, donner dans un contexte

contextually [kən'tekstjuəlɪ] **ADV** *(to examine)* dans son contexte; **to be c. dependent** dépendre du contexte

contiguous [kən'tɪgjuəs] **ADJ** *Fml* contigu, -uë (**to** à, avec)

continence ['kɒntɪnəns] **N 1** *Physiol (control of bladder, bowel)* continence *f* **2** *Fml (sexual)* chasteté *f*

continent¹ ['kɒntɪnənt] **N** *Geog* continent *m*; *Br* **the C.** l'Europe *f* continentale; *Br* **on the C.** en Europe (continentale)

continent² **ADJ 1** *(in control of bladder, bowel)* continent **2** *Fml (sexually)* chaste

continental [kɒntɪ'nent(ə)l] **ADJ 1** *Geog* continental, -aux **2** *Br (European)* de l'Europe continentale

N *Br (European)* continental, -ale, habitant, -ante de l'Europe (continentale)

▶▶ **c. breakfast** petit déjeuner *m* à la française; *Geol* **c. drift** dérive *f* des continents; *Am* **c. plan** *(at hotel)* tarif *m* chambre avec petit déjeuner à la française; **c. quilt** couette *f*, duvet *m*; *Geol* **c. shelf** plateau *m* continental, plate-forme *f* continentale, *pl* plates-formes continentales

---

Continental Breakfast

Ce terme désigne un petit déjeuner léger, par opposition au breakfast anglais, beaucoup plus copieux et comportant un plat chaud.

---

contingency [kən'tɪndʒənsɪ] **N 1** *(unexpected event)* éventualité *f*; **to provide for every c.** parer à toute éventualité; **contingencies** *(item on balance sheet)* frais divers; **prepared for all contingencies** préparé à toutes les éventualités; **to allow for contingencies** parer aux imprévus **2** *Fml (uncertainty) (of events)* contingence *f*

▶▶ *Fin* **c. fund** fonds *mpl* de prévoyance; **c. plan** plan *m* d'urgence; **c. tax** impôt *m* imprévu

contingent [kən'tɪndʒənt] **ADJ 1** *(conditional)* conditionnel; **c. on sth** sous réserve de qch; **to be c. (up)on sth** *(of event)* dépendre de qch **2** *Phil* contingent

N *Mil etc* contingent *m*; **a c. of holiday-makers** un contingent de vacanciers

▶▶ *Acct* **c. liability** passif *m* éventuel *ou* exigible; *St Exch* **c. order** ordre *m* conditionnel

---

continual [kən'tɪnjuəl] **ADJ** continuel, incessant

> Attention: ne pas confondre avec l'adjectif **continuous**.

continually [kən'tɪnjuəlɪ] **ADV** continuellement, sans cesse

> Attention: ne pas confondre avec l'adverbe **continuously**.

continuance [kən'tɪnjuəns] **N 1** *(continuation)* continuation *f*; **the c. of these abuses is a scandal** il est scandaleux que ces abus puissent continuer **2** *Am Law* ajournement *m*

continuation [kəntɪnjʊ'eɪʃən] **N 1** *(action) (of work, project etc)* continuation *f*; *(of road)* prolongement *m* **2** *(result) (of wall, road etc)* prolongement *m*; *(of novel)* suite *f*; **to be a c. of …** faire suite à … **3** *St Exch* report *m*

continue [kən'tɪnjuː] **VT 1** *(work, activity etc)* continuer, poursuivre; *(straight line)* prolonger; *(journey)* poursuivre; *(conversation)* continuer; *(after interruption)* reprendre; *(species, tradition)* perpétuer; **to c. one's studies** poursuivre ses études; *(later in life)* reprendre ses études; **to c. to do sth** *or* **doing sth** continuer à *ou* de faire qch; **after lunch we continued working** nous avons repris notre travail; *Journ* **to be continued** à suivre; **continued on page 30** suite à la page 30

2 *Am Law (trial)* ajourner

VI 1 continuer; *(of line)* se prolonger; **the situation cannot c.** la situation ne peut pas durer; **the situation continued into the 1990s** la situation s'est prolongée jusque dans le courant des années 1990; **to c. in office** garder sa charge; *(of political party)* rester au pouvoir; **she will c. as director until December** elle gardera les fonctions de directrice jusqu'en décembre; **his bad luck continues** ses malheurs se poursuivent; **to c. on one's way** continuer son chemin; **they continued to Rome** ils ont poursuivi leur chemin jusqu'à Rome

2 *(resume talking)* continuer; **'and then', he continued** 'et puis', continua-t-il

continued [kən'tɪnjuːd] **ADJ** *(effort, interest)* soutenu

continuing [kən'tɪnjuːɪŋ] **ADJ** continu; *(interest)* soutenu; **the c. story of a small American town** *(TV serial etc)* l'histoire *f* d'une petite ville américaine

▶▶ **c. education** formation *f* permanente *ou* continue; **c. education class** cours *mpl* de formation permanente *ou* continue

continuity [kɒntɪ'njuːɪtɪ] **N 1** continuité *f*; **to ensure c.** assurer la continuité (**between** entre) **2** *Cin, TV* continuité *f*

▶▶ *TV, Radio* **c. announcement** annonce *f* de continuité; *TV, Radio* **c. announcer** speaker, -ine (de transition); *Cin, TV* **c. girl** scripte *f*, *Cin, TV* **c. man** scripte *m*

continuous [kən'tɪnjuəs] **ADJ 1** *(uninterrupted)* continu, ininterrompu; *(unbroken)* continu **2** *Gram* progressif VOIR GRAMMAIRE A49–51; B30

▶▶ *Sch, Univ* **c. assessment** contrôle *m* continu; *Mktg* **c. innovation** innovation *f* continue; *Comput* **c. mode** mode *m* continu; *Comput* **c. paper** papier *m* (en) continu; *Cin* **c. performance** cinéma *m* permanent; *Comput* **c. stationery** papier (en) continu

> Attention: ne pas confondre avec l'adjectif **continual**.

continuously [kən'tɪnjuəslɪ] **ADV** continuellement, continûment, sans interruption

---

▶▶ *Aut* **c. variable transmission** transmission *f* à réglage continu, transmission CVT

> Attention: ne pas confondre avec l'adverbe **continually**.

contort [kən'tɔːt] **VT** *(features etc)* tordre; **face contorted by pain** visage tordu par la douleur

VI **his face contorted with rage/pain** il grimaçait de rage/de douleur

contortion [kən'tɔːʃən] **N** *(of features etc)* crispation *f*; *(of body)* contorsion *f*; *Fig* **he went through all sorts of contortions to justify this decision** il a fait des pieds et des mains pour justifier cette décision

contortionist [kən'tɔːʃənɪst] **N** contorsionniste *mf*; **a c. act** un numéro de contorsionnisme; **you have to be a c. to get into this car!** il faut faire toute une gymnastique *ou* tout un tas de contorsions pour monter dans cette voiture

contour ['kɒntʊər] **N** *(line)* courbe *f* de niveau; *(of object)* contour *m*; **the contours of the hill** les contours de la colline

▶▶ **c. line** *(on map)* courbe de niveau, courbe hypsométrique; **c. map** carte *f* topographique

Contra ['kɒntrə] **N** *Pol* Contra *m*

contra ['kɒntrə] **PREP** contre

N *Acct* **per c.** par contre; **as per c.** en contre-partie, porté ci-contre

VT *Acct* contrepasser

▶▶ *Acct* **c. account** compte *m* de contrepartie *ou* d'autre part; *Acct* **c. entry** article *m ou* écriture *f* inverse, contre-passation *f*, *pl* contre-passations

contraband ['kɒntrəbænd] **N** contrebande *f*; **c. goods** marchandises *fpl* de contrebande

contrabass ['kɒntrəbeɪs] **N** *Mus* contrebasse *f*

contrabassoon [kɒntrəbə'suːn] **N** *Mus* contrebasson *m*

contraception [kɒntrə'sepʃən] **N** contraception *f*; **method of c.** méthode *f* contraceptive *ou* de contraception

contraceptive [kɒntrə'septɪv] *Med* **N** contraceptif *m*

ADJ contraceptif

▶▶ **c. advice** conseils *mpl* sur la contraception; **c. device** contraceptif; **c. method** méthode *f* contraceptive *ou* de contraception; **c. pill** pilule *f* contraceptive; **c. sponge** éponge *f* contraceptive

contract¹ ['kɒntrækt] **N** contrat *m*; *(of sale)* acte *m* de vente; **marriage c.** contrat de mariage; **to draw up a c.** dresser *ou* rédiger un contrat; **to bind oneself by c.** s'engager par contrat; **to sign a c.** signer un contrat; **to break one's c.** rompre son contrat; **that isn't in my c.** ce n'est pas dans mon contrat; **to be under c.** être sous contrat (**to** avec); **to enter into a c.** *(of person)* passer (un) contrat (**with** avec); **they were given a c. to build the new road** ils se sont vu attribuer le contrat pour construire la nouvelle route; **to put work out to c.** faire effectuer un travail en sous-traitance; **to tender for a c.** soumissionner à une adjudication; **conditions of c.** *(in tender)* cahier *m* des charges; **breach of c.** rupture *f* de contrat; **you are in breach of c.** vous violez *ou* vous ne respectez pas votre contrat; *Sl* **there was a c. out on him** *(he was to be murdered)* un tueur à gages avait été engagé pour le tuer

▶▶ *St Exch* **c. bond** garantie *f* d'exécution; *Cards* **c. bridge** bridge *m* contrat; **c. killer** tueur *m* à gages; **c. labour** main-d'œuvre *f* contractuelle; **c. law** droit *m* des contrats; *St Exch* **c. note** avis *m* d'exécution, avis d'opération sur titre; **c. staff** personnel *m* en contrat à durée déterminée *ou* en CDD;

(in public sector) contractuels *mpl*; **c. work** travail *m* en sous-traitant

contract² [kən'trækt] **VT 1** *(obligation, illness)* contracter; *(habit)* prendre; **to c. debts** s'endetter **2** *Com* **to c. to do sth** s'engager (par contrat) à faire qch; **she has contracted to make two films** elle a signé un contrat pour faire deux films **3** *(muscles)* contracter; *(features)* crisper; *Physiol (tissues)* resserrer; *Ling* **'shall not' into 'shan't'** contracter 'shall not' en 'shan't'

VI 1 *Com* **to c. for a supply of sth** s'engager à fournir qch; **to c. for work** entreprendre des travaux à forfait **2** *(of metal, muscle etc)* se contracter; *(of opening, material)* rétrécir; **the pupil contracts in bright light** la pupille se contracte à la lumière intense; *Ling* **'cannot' contracts into 'can't'** 'cannot' se contracte en 'can't' VOIR GRAMMAIRE A66

▸ **contract in** **VI** *Br (into insurance scheme)* souscrire; *Hist (into trade union)* s'inscrire au syndicat

▸ **contract out** **VI** *Br (out of insurance policy, pension plan)* arrêter de souscrire (**of** à); *(of hospital)* se retirer du service public; *Hist (of union member)* cesser de payer sa cotisation au syndicat

VT SEP *Com (work)* donner en sous-traitance (**to** à)

contract-awarding party [-əwɔːdɪŋ] **N** adjudicateur *m*

contracting [kən'træktɪŋ] **ADJ**
▸▸ **c. company** *(party to a contract)* contractant *m*; *(sub-contractor)* sous-traitant *m*, *pl* sous-traitants *mpl*; **c. parties** contractants *mpl*

contraction [kən'trækʃən] **N 1** *(of metal, pupil etc)* contraction *f*; *(of muscle)* contraction, contracture *f*; *(of material)* rétrécissement *m*; *Physiol (of tissues)* resserrement *m*; *Obst* **contractions have begun** les contractions ont commencé **2** *Ling (of two words)* contraction *f*; *(word)* mot *m* contracté **3** *Fml* **c. of debts** endettement *m*

contractor [kən'træktər] **N 1** *(firm of builders)* entrepreneur *m* (en bâtiment); *(building worker)* ouvrier *m* en bâtiment; **the contractors haven't finished yet** les ouvriers n'ont pas encore fini **2** *(company, supplier)* haulage **c.** entreprise *f* de transports; **arms c.** fournisseur *m* d'armement **3** *(party to a contract)* entrepreneur *m*

contractual [kən'træktjʊəl] **ADJ** *(agreement, obligations etc)* contractuel; **on the present c. basis** selon les stipulations actuelles du contrat
▸▸ *Acct* **c. allowance** indemnité *f* conventionnelle; **c. cover** *(in insurance)* garantie *f* conventionnelle; *Com, Fin* **c. date** date *f* contractuelle; *Com, Fin* **c. guarantee** garantie contractuelle; *Com, Fin* **c. liability** responsabilité *f* contractuelle; *Com, Fin* **c. price** prix *m* contractuel

contractually [kən'træktjʊəlɪ] **ADV** *(bound, obliged)* par contrat; *(stipulated)* dans le contrat; **I'm c. forbidden to …** le contrat m'interdit de …

contradict [kɒntrə'dɪkt] **VT** *(person)* contredire; *(rumour)* démentir; **to c. oneself** se contredire; **the statements of the witnesses c. each other** les dépositions des témoins se contredisent

contradiction [kɒntrə'dɪkʃən] **N** contradiction *f*; **this was a c. of what they had previously said** c'était un démenti de ce qu'ils avaient dit auparavant; **in c. with** en contradiction avec; **it's a c. in terms** c'est parfaitement contradictoire, c'est une contradiction dans les termes; **he's full of contradictions** il est plein de contradictions

contradictory [kɒntrə'dɪktərɪ] **ADJ 1** *(statement etc)* contradictoire (**to** à) **2** *Fam (per-*

son) raisonneur; **don't be so c.** ne sois pas aussi raisonneur

contradistinction [ˌkɒntrədɪs'tɪŋkʃən] **N** *Fml* **in c. to …** contrairement à …

contra(-)flow **N** *Br Aut* contre-courant *m*, *pl* contre-courants
▸▸ **c. system** système *m* de circulation à contre-sens

contraindication [ˈkɒntraɪndɪ'keɪʃən] **N** *Med* contre-indication *f*, *pl* contre-indications

contralto [kən'træltəʊ] *Mus* **N** contralto *m*
ADJ de contralto

contraption [kən'træpʃən] **N** *Fam* machin *m*, engin *m*, truc *m*

contrapuntal [ˌkɒntrə'pʌnt(ə)l] **ADJ** *Mus (piece, accompaniment etc)* en contrepoint

contrarily [kən'treərɪlɪ] **ADV** de façon contrariante

contrariness [kən'treərɪnɪs] **N** esprit *m* de contradiction

contrariwise [ˈkɒntrərɪwaɪz] **ADV 1** *(on the other hand)* au contraire **2** *(in the opposite direction)* dans le sens opposé **3** [kən'treərɪwaɪz] *(perversely)* par esprit de contradiction

contrary¹ [ˈkɒntrərɪ] **N** contraire *m*; **on the c.** au contraire; **unless you hear to the c.** sauf avis contraire
ADJ 1 *(opposite)* contraire (**to** à); *(interests etc)* opposé (**to** à); **c. to nature** contre nature; **c. to reason** contraire à la raison; **c. to the terms of the contract** contraire aux termes du contrat **2** *Fml (winds)* contraire **3** [kən'treərɪ] *(person)* contrariant, qui a l'esprit de contradiction; *(remark)* formulé par esprit de contradiction
ADV contrairement (**to** à); **to act c. to instructions** contrevenir aux ordres reçus; **c. to my expectations** contre mon attente; **c. to what I was told** contrairement à ce qu'on m'a dit

contrast¹ [ˈkɒntrɑːst] **N** *(difference)*, *Comput, TV, Phot, Art* contraste *m* (**between** entre); **in c. with** or **to sth/sb** par contraste avec qch/qn; **by c. the president was almost optimistic** par contraste, le président était presque optimiste; **to form a c. to …** faire contraste avec …; **as a c. to …** comme contraste à …
▸▸ **c. button** bouton *m* de contraste; **c. control** réglage *m* du contraste

contrast² [kən'trɑːst] **VT** faire contraster, mettre en contraste (**with** avec); **it was impossible not to c. her attitude with her brother's** c'était impossible de ne pas comparer son attitude à celle de son frère
VI contraster (**with** avec); **to c. strongly** trancher (**with** sur)

contrasting [kən'trɑːstɪŋ] **ADJ** *(colours)* contrasté; *(opinion, attitude, temperament)* opposé; **the c. yellow on the wall opposite** le jaune qui fait contraste sur le mur d'en face

contrasty [ˈkɒntrɑːstɪ] **ADJ** *Phot* contrasté

contravene [ˌkɒntrə'viːn] **VT** *(law etc)* transgresser, enfreindre; *(rule)* être en contravention avec

contravention [ˌkɒntrə'venʃən] **N** *(of law)* infraction *f*; **to act in c. of the law** enfreindre la loi

contribute [kən'trɪbjuːt] **VT** donner; *(money)* donner, verser; **to c. one's time** donner de son temps; **to c. one's share** payer sa part; **she contributed $50,000 to the cause** elle a versé 50 000 dollars au profit de la cause; **he didn't c. anything to the discussion** il n'a rien apporté à la discussion; **to c. an article to a newspaper** écrire un article pour un journal

VI 1 contribuer; **if everyone contributes**

we'll be able to get a bigger present si tout le monde participe, nous pourrons acheter un cadeau plus important; **he rarely contributes to discussions** il contribue rarement aux discussions; **to c. to a charity** donner à une œuvre de charité; **to c. to a newspaper** collaborer à un journal; **to c. to the success** contribuer au succès; **everything contributed to make him happy** tout contribuait à le rendre heureux **2** *(to pension scheme etc)* cotiser (**to** à)

contribution [ˌkɒntrɪ'bjuːʃən] **N 1** contribution *f*; *(to meal, present etc)* contribution, participation *f*; **I've already made a c.** *(to sb collecting for charity)* j'ai déjà donné; **contributions welcome** *(to charity)* toutes les contributions sont les bienvenues; **their c. to the carnival was a brass band** leur participation au carnaval s'est concrétisée par une fanfare
2 *Journ (article)* article *m*
3 *Fin (to pension plan, NIC etc)* cotisation *f*
4 *Acct (in management accounting)* marge *f* (brute); **c. in kind** apport *m* en nature
▸▸ *Acct* **c. margin** marge sur les coûts variables

contributor [kən'trɪbjʊtər] **N 1** *(to charity)* donateur, -trice; **the contributors to the meal/the present** les personnes *fpl* qui ont contribué au repas/au cadeau **2** *Journ* collaborateur, -trice (**to a paper** d'un journal)

contributory [kən'trɪbjʊtərɪ] **ADJ** *(cause, factor etc)* concourant; **to be a c. factor in sth** contribuer à qch; **the weather may have had a c. effect, but …** le temps a peut-être joué un rôle mais …
▸▸ *Law* **c. negligence** imprudence *f*, faute *f* (avant un accident)

contrite [kən'traɪt, 'kɒntraɪt] **ADJ** contrit

contritely [kən'traɪtlɪ] **ADV** d'un air contrit, avec contrition

contrition [kən'trɪʃən] **N** contrition *f*, pénitence *f*

contrivance [kən'traɪvəns] **N 1** *(device)* appareil *m*, dispositif *m*, engin *m* **2** *esp Fml (invention) (of scheme, plan)* invention *f*; **I was fairly sure the scheme was of George's c.** j'étais presque certain que c'était un stratagème de George **3** *(inventiveness)* ingéniosité *f* **4** *Pej (scheme)* stratagème *m*

contrive [kən'traɪv] **VT** *(device etc)* inventer, concevoir; **to c. to do sth** trouver le moyen de faire qch; **she contrived to get herself mentioned in the article** elle a réussi à faire en sorte qu'on parle d'elle dans l'article

contrived [kən'traɪvd] **ADJ** forcé, qui manque de naturel

CONTROL [kən'trəʊl]

N contrôle **1, 2, 4** ▪ maîtrise **1**		
▪ direction **1** ▪ témoin **3**		
▪ commande **4**		
VT contrôler **1–3** ▪ diriger **1**		
▪ maîtriser **2**		

N 1 *(power)* contrôle *m*; *(over oneself)* maîtrise *f*; *(of country, organization)* direction *f*; **to take c.** prendre le contrôle (**of** de); **to have c. over sth/sb** avoir le contrôle de qch/qn; **the state has no c. over the media** l'état n'a aucun contrôle sur les médias; **she has no c. over the children** elle n'a aucune autorité sur les enfants; **to be in c. of sth/sb** avoir le contrôle de qch/qn; **the government is now firmly back in c.** le gouvernement a maintenant fermement repris le contrôle; **to have c. of a business** être à la tête d'une entreprise, diriger une entreprise; **things/the situation had got out of c.** les choses étaient/la situation était devenue(s) incontrôlable(s); **the children/the horses were out of c.** les enfants/les chevaux étaient incontrôlables; **she soon had the horse under c.** elle est vite parvenue à maîtriser le cheval; **to keep one's feelings under c.** contrôler *ou* maîtriser ses émotions; **everything is under c.** *(organized, in hand)* tout est en bonne voie; *(there's no need to panic)* tout va bien; **to bring under c.** *(fire etc)* maîtriser; *(illness)* enrayer; **circumstances beyond our c.** circonstances indépendantes de notre volonté; **these things are beyond our c.** ces choses-là ne dépendent pas de notre volonté; **to lose c. (of oneself)** ne plus être maître de soi; **to regain c. of oneself** se ressaisir; **to exercise strict c. over sth** exercer un contrôle strict sur qch; **to exercise strict c. over sb** tenir la bride serrée à qn

2 *Econ etc (of exchange rates, rents)* contrôle *m*; **to impose controls on rents/prices** contrôler les loyers/prix; **new government controls on financial practices** nouvelles réglementations *fpl* gouvernementales sur les pratiques financières

3 *(used in experiment)* témoin *m*
4 *(action) (of mechanism)* commande *f*, *(of power, volume)* réglage *m*; **to lose c. of one's car** perdre le contrôle de sa voiture; **the driver/pilot lost c.** le conducteur/pilote a perdu le contrôle; **the truck went out of c.** le chauffeur a perdu le contrôle de son camion; **the ship was out of c.** le navire n'était plus manœuvrable; **temperature c.** régulation *f* thermique; **automatic c.** réglage automatique; **dual c.** double commande; **remote c.** télécommande *f*, commande à distance
5 *Tech (device)* (organe *m* de) commande *f*, **the controls** les commandes; **to be at the controls** être aux commandes; *Aviat* **flying controls** commandes de vol; *Radio etc* **volume c.** bouton *m* de (réglage de) volume

VT 1 *(be in charge of, direct) (business, production)* diriger; *(of troops) (area etc)* contrôler; *(action of machine)* commander; **to c. the traffic** réglementer la circulation
2 *(master, restrain) (horse)* maîtriser; *(child, pupils, class)* avoir de l'autorité sur, tenir; *(one's passions)* dompter; *(one's reactions etc)* contrôler, maîtriser; *(one's tears)* retenir; *(price increases, inflation)* contenir, enrayer; *Med (diabetes etc)* équilibrer; *(vehicle)* maîtriser, garder le contrôle de; **to c. oneself** se contrôler, se maîtriser; **to try to c. oneself** faire un effort sur soi-même; **he can't c. his pupils** il ne tient pas ses élèves, il manque d'autorité sur ses élèves; **couldn't you c. that child a little better?** tu ne crois pas que tu pourrais avoir un peu plus d'autorité sur cet enfant?
3 *(check) (quality etc)* contrôler
▸▸ *Comput* **c. bit** bit *m* de contrôle; *Aut* **c. box** régulateur *m* de charge; *Comput* **c. bus** bus *m* de contrôle; *Comput* **c. character** caractère *m* de contrôle; *Comput* **c. code** code *m* de commande; **c. column** manche *m* à balai; **c. experiment** expérience *f* de contrôle; **c. freak** = personne *f* qui veut tout contrôler; *Tech* **c. gear** appareils *mpl* ou organes *mpl* de commande; **c. group** groupe *m* témoin; *Comput* **c. key** touche *f* contrôle; *Comput* **c. knob** molette *f* de réglage; *Mktg* **c. market** marché *m* témoin; **c. mechanism** appareil *m* de commande; *TV* **c. monitor** écran *m* de contrôle; **c. panel** *Aviat* tableau *m* de bord; *Comput* panneau *m* de configuration; *Sport, Aut* **c. point** contrôle *m*; *Comput* **c. program** programme *m* de contrôle; *Mktg* **c. question** *(in market research)* question *f* de contrôle; *Nucl* **c. rod** barre *f* de commande; **c. room** salle *f* des commandes; *Naut* poste *m* de commande; *Radio, TV* (cabine *f* de) régie *f*; **c. tower** tour *f* de contrôle; *Comput* **c. unit** unité *f* de commande, contrôleur *m*; *Aut* **c. valve** valve *f* modulatrice

controllable [kən'trəʊləb(ə)l] ADJ *(speed, heat, brightness)* réglable; *(economic growth, inflation, mechanism)* qui peut être contrôlé; *(moods)* maîtrisable; **it's c. by the user** cela peut être réglé par l'utilisateur; **if you find that the class is just not c.** si vous trouvez que la classe est vraiment intenable; **the spread of the disease is c.** la progression de la maladie peut être maîtrisée *ou* enrayée; **the more easily c. aspects of the project** les aspects du projet les plus faciles à contrôler

controlled [kən'trəʊld] ADJ *(person)* qui sait se maîtriser *ou* se contrôler; *(market)* réglementé; *(experiment)* contrôlé; *Med (diabetes etc)* équilibré; **to remain c.** *(of person)* garder son sang-froid; **the transition to democracy must take place in a c. manner** le passage à la démocratie doit se faire dans l'ordre
▸▸ *Econ* **c. economy** économie *f* dirigée *ou* planifiée; **c. explosion** neutralisation *f* (d'un explosif); **c. parking zone** zone *f* de stationnement réglementé; *Econ* **c. price** taxe *f*, **to sell goods at the c. price** vendre des marchandises à la taxe

controller [kən'trəʊlər] N *(person)* contrôleur, -euse; *Fin, Comput* contrôleur; *(of TV channel)* directeur, -trice d'antenne; *Aviat* **flight c.** contrôleur de vol; *Comput* **disk c.** contrôleur de disques
▸▸ *Comput* **c. card** carte *f* contrôleur

controlling [kən'trəʊlɪŋ] ADJ *(power)* dirigeant
▸▸ *Fin, Com* **c. factor** facteur *m* déterminant; *Fin* **c. interest, c. stake** *(in company)* participation *f* majoritaire

controversial [kɒntrə'vɜːʃəl] ADJ controversé; **he's trying to be c.** il cherche la controverse; **I only said that to be c.** je n'ai dit cela que pour provoquer la controverse

controversy ['kɒntrəvɜːsɪ, kən'trɒvəsɪ] N controverse *f*; **to avoid c.** éviter la controverse; **to court c.** inviter à la controverse; **to be the subject of c.** être sujet à controverse; **the decision was surrounded by c.** la décision a soulevé beaucoup de controverses

contumacious [kɒntjʊ'meɪʃəs] ADJ *Fml* désobéissant

contumacy ['kɒntjʊməsɪ, kən'tjuː-] N **1** *Law* contumace *f* **2** *Fml (disobedience)* désobéissance *f*

contumely ['kɒntjuːmlɪ] N *Fml (scorn)* mépris *m*

contusion [kən'tjuːʒən] N *Med* contusion *f*

conundrum [kə'nʌndrəm] N **1** *(riddle)* devinette *f* **2** *(mystery)* énigme *f*

conurbation [kɒnɜː'beɪʃən] N conurbation *f*

convalesce [kɒnvə'les] VI *Med* se remettre (d'une maladie); *(be resting)* être en convalescence

convalescence [kɒnvə'lesəns] N *Med* convalescence *f*

convalescent [kɒnvə'lesənt] *Med* N convalescent, -ente
ADJ convalescent
▸▸ **c. home** maison *f* de convalescence *ou* de repos

convection [kən'vekʃən] N *Phys, Elec* convection *f*
▸▸ **c. drier** séchoir *m* à convection; **c. drying** séchage *m* par convection; **c. heater** convecteur *m*, radiateur *m* à convection

convector [kən'vektər] N *(heater)* convecteur *m*, radiateur *m* à convection

convene [kən'viːn] VT *(meeting)* convoquer
VI se réunir

convener [kən'viːnər] N **1** *Br (of trade union)* délégué, -ée (syndical(e)) **2 he was the c. of the meeting** c'est lui qui a demandé la réunion

convenience [kən'viːnɪəns] N **1** commodité *f*, **at your c.** quand cela vous conviendra; *Com* **at your earliest c.** dans les meilleurs délais; **at your own c.** à votre convenance; **for c. I use tinned fruit** j'utilise des fruits en conserves pour des raisons de commodité; **a bus service is provided for our customers' c.** un service d'autobus est à la disposition de nos clients; **marriage of c.** mariage *m* de convenance; *Naut* **flag of c.** pavillon *m* de complaisance **2** *(installation)* **(public) c.** W.-C. *mpl* (publics), toilettes *fpl*; **the rooms are fitted with all modern conveniences** les chambres ont tout (le) confort moderne
▸▸ *Com* **c. brand** marque *f* pratique; **c. food** aliments *mpl* prêts à consommer, plats *mpl* cuisinés; *Com* **c. goods** produits *mpl* d'achat courant, produits de consommation courante; **c. store** = supérette *f* de quartier qui reste ouverte tard le soir, *Can* dépanneur *m*

convenient [kən'viːnɪənt] ADJ commode, pratique; *(time)* opportun; **if it is c. for you** si cela vous convient, si vous n'y voyez pas d'inconvénient; **2 o'clock isn't very c. (for me)** 14 heures ne m'arrange pas; **a c. place to stop** un endroit commode pour s'arrêter; **to find a c. opportunity to do sth** trouver l'occasion de faire qch; **we climbed through a c. hole in the fence** un trou bien situé nous a permis de traverser la clôture; **the ticket collector wasn't there – how very c.!** le contrôleur n'était pas là – ça tombait très bien!; **the flat is very c. for the shops** l'appartement est bien situé pour les commerces

conveniently [kən'viːnɪəntlɪ] ADV commodément; *(to arrive)* opportunément, à propos; **the house is c. situated near the town centre** la maison est située près du centreville, ce qui est bien pratique; *Iron* **someone had c. forgotten to lock the door** *(accidentally)* quelqu'un avait oublié de fermer la porte, ce qui était bien pratique; *(deliberately)* comme par hasard, quelqu'un avait oublié de fermer la porte

convenor [kən'viːnər] N = **convener**

convent ['kɒnvənt] N *Rel* couvent *m*; **to enter a c.** entrer au couvent; **she went to c. school** elle est allée à l'école chez les sœurs

convention [kən'venʃən] N **1** *(conference)* assemblée *f*, convention *f*, congrès *m*; *Am Pol* convention; **medical c.** congrès médical **2** *(agreement)* accord *m*; *(international)* convention *f* (**on** relative à) **3** *(established practice)* usage *m*; *Mus, Theat etc* convention *f*; **the c. is that …** la convention veut que …; **there is a c. that Ministers do not answer such questions** l'usage est que les ministres ne répondent pas à ce genre de questions; **to be a slave to c.** être l'esclave des usages **4** *(custom) (usu pl)* **conventions** convenances *fpl*; **to observe the conventions** respecter les convenances; **social conventions** conventions *fpl* sociales
▸▸ **c. centre** palais *m* des congrès

conventional [kən'venʃən(ə)l] ADJ **1** *(normal) (person, upbringing)* conventionnel, *Pej* sans originalité; *(beauty, good looks)* classique **2** *(established, traditional) (method)* classique, traditionnel; **the c. wisdom is that …** la sagesse populaire veut que …
▸▸ *Constr* **c. material** matériau *m* traditionnel; *Comput* **c. memory** mémoire *f* conventionnelle; **c. propriety** les convenances *fpl*; *Mil* **c. warfare** guerre *f* conventionnelle; *Mil* **c. weapon** arme *f* conventionnelle

conventionality [kənvenʃə'nælɪtɪ] N *(of person, upbringing)* caractère *m* conventionnel *ou* ordinaire

conventionally [kən'venʃən(ə)lɪ] ADV **1** *(in accepted fashion)* conventionnellement, *Pej* sans originalité; **she's not c. beautiful** elle n'est pas d'une beauté classique **2** *(traditionally)* d'une manière classique

conventioneer [kənven∫ə'nɪər] N *Am* congressiste *mf*

converge [kən'vɜ:dʒ] VI **1** *Opt, Phys* converger (**on** vers) **2** *(of people)* se diriger (**on** vers); **over a hundred had converged on the town** plus de cent s'étaient rassemblés dans la ville; **three armies were converging on Paris** trois armées convergeaient sur Paris

convergence [kən'vɜ:dʒəns] N *(of lines, opinions), EU* convergence *f; Math* focalisation *f*

convergent [kən'vɜ:dʒənt] ADJ convergent
▸▸ *Opt* **c. lens** lentille *f* convexe *ou* convergente

conversant [kən'vɜ:sənt] ADJ **to be c. with sth** *(with French grammar, the law etc)* s'y connaître en qch; *(with type of engine etc)* connaître qch; *(with recent developments etc)* être au courant de qch

conversation [kɒnvə'seɪ∫ən] N **1** conversation *f;* **to hold** *or* **have a c. with sb** avoir une conversation avec qn; **to get into c. (with sb)** entamer une conversation (avec qn); **she was just making c.** elle parlait par politesse; **from my c. with him I got the impression that ...** lorsque je me suis entretenu avec lui, j'ai eu l'impression que ...; **his c. was very dull** sa conversation était sans aucun intérêt; **I'm not good at (making) c.** je ne suis pas très doué pour faire la conversation **2** *Comput* dialogue *m*
▸▸ *Fam* **c. killer** = **c. stopper;** *Comput* **c. mode** mode *m* conversationnel *ou* dialogue; **c. piece** objet *m* qui suscite des commentaires; **the vase is quite a c. piece** le vase alimente bien des conversations; **c. skills** l'art *m* de la conversation; *Fam* **c. stopper** remarque *f*/sujet *m* qui arrête net les conversations; *Fam* **that was a c. stopper** cela a arrêté net la conversation

conversational [kɒnvə'seɪ∫ən(ə)l] ADJ **1** *(tone, voice)* de la conversation; *(style)* familier; **in a c. tone** sur le ton de la conversation **2** *Comput (mode)* dialogue

conversationalist [kɒnvə'seɪ∫ənəlɪst] N **to be a c.** *(like talking)* aimer la conversation; *(be a good talker)* bien parler; **I'm not much of a c.** je ne suis pas brillant causeur

conversationally [kɒnvə'seɪ∫ən(ə)lɪ] ADV sur le ton de la conversation

converse¹ [kən'vɜ:s] VI *Fml* converser (**on, about** sur), deviser (**on, about** de)

converse² ['kɒnvɜ:s] ADJ *(results, theory etc)* contraire; *Math* réciproque
N inverse *m,* contraire *m; (in logic)* proposition *f* converse; *Math* proposition réciproque

conversely ['kɒnvɜ:slɪ, kən'vɜ:slɪ] ADV réciproquement, inversement

conversion [kən'vɜ:∫ən] N **1** *Rel, Fig* conversion *f* (**to** à)
2 *(adaptation, alteration)* conversion *f* (**of sth into sth** de qch en qch); **the c. of a house into flats** l'aménagement *m ou* la transformation d'une maison en appartements
3 *(in American football, rugby)* transformation *f*
4 *(in converted building)* = appartement *m* aménagé dans un ancien hôtel particulier, entrepôt, atelier etc
5 *Law* conversion *f;* **improper c. of funds** détournement *m* de fonds
6 *(of bonds, securities, loan stock)* conversion *f*
▸▸ *Fin* **c. loan** emprunt *m* de conversion; *Fin* **c. order** ordre *m* de conversion; *Fin* **c. premium** prime *f* de conversion; *Fin* **c. price** prix *m* de conversion; *Comput* **c. program** pro-

gramme *m* de conversion; *Fin* **c. rate** taux *m* de conversion; *Fin* **c. right** droit *m* de conversion; *Comput* **c. software** logiciel *m* de conversion; **c. table** table *f* de conversion; *Comput* **c. utility** utilitaire *m* de conversion

convert¹ ['kɒnvɜ:t] N *Rel, Fig* converti, -ie; **to become a c. to sth** se convertir à qch; **to make a c. of sb** convertir qn; **she's made another c.** elle a encore converti quelqu'un

convert² [kən'vɜ:t] VT **1** *Rel, Fig* convertir (**to** à); **to be converted to Christianity** se convertir au christianisme; *Fig* **she converted them to her way of thinking** elle les a amenés à voir les choses à sa manière
2 *(alter, adapt)* transformer, convertir (**sth into sth** qch en qch); **the car has been converted to run on unleaded petrol** la voiture a été modifiée pour rouler à l'essence sans plomb; **her studio was a converted barn** son studio était une grange aménagée; **to c. miles into kilometres** convertir les mil(l)es en kilomètres; *Fin* **to c. loan stock/securities** convertir un emprunt/des valeurs; *Fin* **converted share** action *f* convertie
3 *Rugby* **to c. a try** transformer un essai
4 *Law* **to c. funds to another purpose** affecter des fonds à un autre usage; **to c. funds to one's own use** détourner des fonds
VI **1** *Rel* se convertir (**to** à); *Fig* **she converted to a belief in capitalism** elle s'est mise à croire au capitalisme
2 *(of settee etc)* se transformer (**into a bed** en lit); **we've converted to electricity** nous sommes passés à l'électricité

converter [kən'vɜ:tər] N *(person), Metal, Elec, Radio, Comput* convertisseur *m;* **steel c., Bessemer c.** convertisseur Bessemer;
▸▸ *Aut* **c. clutch** convertisseur-embrayage *m, pl* convertisseurs-embrayages; *Nucl* **c. reactor** réacteur *m* convertisseur

convertibility [kənvɜ:tə'bɪlɪtɪ] N convertibilité *f*

convertible [kən'vɜ:təb(ə)l] ADJ **1** *(thing)* convertible (**into** en); *(settee etc)* transformable **2** *Aut* décapotable **3** *Fin (bond, security, money)* convertible
N *Aut (voiture f)* décapotable *f*
▸▸ *Fin* **c. currency** monnaie *f ou* devise *f* convertible; **c. loan stock** emprunt *m* obligataire convertible; **c. money of account** monnaie *f* de compte convertible

convex ['kɒnveks] ADJ **1** *Phys* convexe **2** *(road, road surface)* bombé

convexity [kɒn'veksɪtɪ] N *Phys* convexité *f*

convey [kən'veɪ] VT **1** *(communicate) (order)* transmettre, donner; *(one's thoughts, news)* transmettre, communiquer (**to** à); **please c. my good wishes to the young couple** veuillez transmettre tous mes vœux aux jeunes époux; **to c. one's meaning** communiquer sa pensée; **his writing conveys the mood of the country** sa manière d'écrire évoque l'atmosphère du pays; **does that name c. anything to you?** est-ce que ce nom vous dit quelque chose? **2** *(transport)* transporter; *(person)* transporter, (a)mener; *(of air) (sound, smell)* transmettre **3** *Law (of property)* transfert *m,* cession *f,* disposition *f; (document)* acte *m* translatif de propriété, acte de cession

conveyancing [kən'veɪənsɪŋ] N *Law* **1** *(procedure)* procédure *f* translative de propriété **2** *(drawing up documents)* rédaction *f* des actes de cession *ou* des actes translatifs de propriété

conveyor [kən'veɪər] N **1** *Ind* (appareil *m*)

transporteur *m; Min* convoyeur *m; (belt)* convoyeur, tapis *m* roulant; **bucket c.** transporteur à godets **2** *Fml (person) (of letter, parcel)* porteur, -euse
▸▸ **c. belt** tapis *m* roulant

convict¹ ['kɒnvɪkt] N *(convicted person)* détenu, -ue; *Old-fashioned (prisoner)* forçat *m,* bagnard *m;* **former c.** repris *m* de justice

convict² [kən'vɪkt] VT **to c. sb (of a crime)** déclarer qn coupable (d'un crime); **he was convicted** il fut reconnu coupable; **you stand convicted by your own words** vos propres paroles vous condamnent

> Attention: ne pas confondre avec le verbe **to convince.**

conviction [kən'vɪk∫ən] N **1** *Law* condamnation *f;* **previous convictions** condamnations antérieures; **c. for murder** condamnation pour meurtre **2** *(belief)* conviction *f;* **to act from c.** agir par conviction; **to have the courage of one's convictions** avoir le courage de ses opinions; **to carry c.** *(of voice, manner)* être convaincant; **to lack c.** *(of person, voice, manner)* manquer de conviction

convince [kən'vɪns] VT convaincre, persuader (**of** de; **that ...** que ...); **to allow oneself to be convinced** se laisser convaincre; **you'll never c. me of that** tu ne me feras jamais croire cela

> Attention: ne pas confondre avec le verbe **to convict.**

convinced [kən'vɪnsd] ADJ convaincu; **to be c. (that) ...** être convaincu que ... + *ind;* **I'm not c.** je ne suis pas convaincu

convincing [kən'vɪnsɪŋ] ADJ *(argument, theory, performance etc)* convaincant; *(victory)* décisif; **she wasn't very c. as Juliet** elle n'était pas convaincante dans le rôle de Juliette; **the battle scenes were very c.** les scènes de bataille étaient très réalistes

convincingly [kən'vɪnsɪŋlɪ] ADV d'une manière convaincante; *(to win)* d'une manière décisive

convivial [kən'vɪvɪəl] ADJ *(person)* bon vivant; *(atmosphere)* convivial, -aux, joyeux; **to have a c. evening** passer une soirée conviviale

conviviality [kənvɪvɪ'ælɪtɪ] N convivialité *f,* esprit *m* de société

convocation [kɒnvə'keɪ∫ən] N **1** *(of meeting)* convocation *f* **2** *(meeting)* assemblée *f; Br Rel* assemblée, synode *m*

convoke [kən'vəʊk] VT *Fml (meeting)* convoquer

convoluted ['kɒnvəlu:tɪd] ADJ **1** *(complicated)* compliqué, *Fam* emberlificoté **2** *Biol* convoluté

convolution [kɒnvə'lu:∫ən] N **1** *(complication) (of argument etc)* méandre *f* **2** *(twist)* circonvolution *f; Anat* **cerebral convolutions** circonvolutions cérébrales

convolvulus, *pl* **convolvuluses** [kən'vɒlvjʊləs, -əsɪz] N volubilis *m,* belle-de-jour *f, pl* belles-de-jour

convoy ['kɒnvɔɪ] *Mil, Naut, Aut* N convoi *m;* **ship under** *or* **in c.** bâtiment *m* convoyé *ou* en convoi; **to drive in c.** *(of lorries)* rouler en convoi; *(of private cars)* se suivre; **to be on c. duty** *(of ship)* assurer un convoi
VT convoyer, escorter

convulse [kən'vʌls] VT **1** *(of sobs, spasms etc) (person)* secouer; *Fig (disrupt) (sb's life)* bouleverser; **to be convulsed with laughter/pain** se tordre de rire/douleur; **scene that convulses the audience** scène qui fait tordre de rire toute la salle **2** *Med (muscle)* convulsionner

VI *(of person)* avoir des convulsions; *(of face, body etc)* se contracter

convulsion [kən'vʌlʃən] **N** *Med (usu pl)* **convulsions** convulsions *fpl*; *Fam* **to be in convulsions** *(laughing)* se tordre de rire; *Fig* **political convulsions** bouleversements *mpl* politiques

convulsive [kən'vʌlsɪv] **ADJ** *(movement etc)* convulsif; *(transition)* brutal, -aux; **the most c. years in the country's history** les années les plus agitées dans l'histoire du pays

convulsively [kən'vʌlsɪvlɪ] **ADV** convulsivement

coo¹ [ku:] **INT** *Br Sl* tiens!, ça alors!

coo² **VI** *(of dove)* roucouler; *(of baby)* gazouiller; **the neighbours came to c. over the baby** les voisins sont venus s'extasier sur le bébé
> **VT** *(of person)* dire (d'un ton attendri); *(greeting, endearment etc)* murmurer, susurrer; **what a beautiful baby, he cooed** quel beau bébé, s'est-il extasié
> **N** *(of dove)* roucoulement *m*

cooing ['ku:ɪŋ] **N** *(of dove)* roucoulement *m*; *(of baby)* gazouillement *m*; *(of person)* mots *mpl* attendris

cook [kʊk] **N** cuisinier, -ère; *Naut* coq *m*; **to be a good/bad c.** être bon/mauvais cuisinier; **head c.** chef *m* (de cuisine); *Fam Hum* **chief** *or* **head c. and bottlewasher** factotum *m*; *Prov* **too many cooks spoil the broth** on ne parvient jamais à rien quand tout le monde met son grain de sel
> **VT** *(meal)* faire, préparer; *(meat etc)* (faire) cuire; **half-cooked** demi-cuit, à moitié cuit; **the meat should be cooked all the way through** la viande doit être bien cuite; *Fig Fam* **to c. the accounts** *or* **the books** falsifier *ou* truquer les comptes
> **VI** *(of food)* cuire; *(of person)* faire la cuisine, cuisiner; **can you c.?** est-ce que tu sais faire la cuisine?; *Fig Fam* **what's cooking?** *(happening)* qu'est-ce qui se passe?; *Fig Fam* **to be cooking with gas** marcher très fort
> ► **cook up VT SEP** *Fam (fabricate) (excuse etc)* inventer, imaginer

cookbook ['kʊkbʊk] **N** livre *m* de cuisine

cook-chill **ADJ** cuisiné (et réfrigéré)

cooked [kʊkt] **ADJ** cuit; **c. breakfast** petit déjeuner *m* à l'anglaise; **I always have a c. meal in the evening** je mange toujours un repas chaud le soir

cooker ['kʊkər] **N 1** *(stove)* cuisinière *f*; **gas/electric c.** cuisinière à gaz/électrique; **pressure c.** cocotte-minute® *f*, *pl* cocottes-minute **2** *Br Fam (apple)* pomme *f* à cuire

cookery ['kʊkərɪ] **N** cuisine *f*
> ► ► **c. book** livre *m* de cuisine; **c. course** stage *m* de cuisine; **c. programme** émission *f* de cuisine

cookhouse ['kʊkhaʊs] **N** cuisine *f*

cookie ['kʊkɪ] **N 1** *esp Am (sweet biscuit)* biscuit *m*; *Fam* **that's the way the c. crumbles!** c'est la vie (que veux-tu)! **2** *esp Am Fam (person)* **a tough c.** un dur à cuire; **a smart c.** un petit malin **3** *Comput* cookie *m*, mouchard *m* électronique

cooking ['kʊkɪŋ] **N 1** *(process)* cuisson *f*; **method of c.** cuisson **2** *(style, activity)* cuisine *f*; **plain** *or* **home c.** cuisine bourgeoise; **my mother's c.** la cuisine de ma mère; **do you like c.?** est-ce que tu aimes faire la cuisine?; **to do the c.** faire la cuisine **3** *Fam (falsification)* **c. of the books** *or* **accounts** falsification *f* des comptes
> ► ► **c. apple** pomme *f* à cuire; **c. chocolate** chocolat *m* à cuire; **c. fat** matière *f* grasse pour la cuisine; **c. foil** papier *m* d'aluminium; **c. oil** huile *f* de cuisine; **c. time** temps *m* de cuisson; **c. utensils** batterie *f* de cuisine

cool [ku:l] **ADJ 1** *(wind, weather etc)* frais, *f* fraîche; *(drink)* frais, rafraîchissant; *(coffee, bathwater etc)* tiède; **it's c.** *(weather)* il fait frais; **it's getting c.** *(weather)* le temps se rafraîchit; *Com etc* **keep in a c. place** tenir au frais
2 *(calm)* calme; **to keep c., calm and collected** rester calme, garder son sang-froid; **keep c.!** du calme!; **to keep a c. head** garder la tête froide, garder son sang-froid
3 *(unfriendly) (person, reception etc)* froid
4 *Fam (unruffled)* sans gêne; **I call that c.!** ça, c'est du toupet!; **well, you're a c. customer!** eh bien, vous avez du culot *ou* du toupet!
5 *Fam (of money)* **I lost a c. thousand** j'ai perdu mille livres bien comptées
6 *Fam (fashionable, sophisticated)* super *inv*; **you look c. in that jacket** tu es super avec cette veste; **he thinks he's so c.** il se croit vraiment super; **it's not c. to smoke** ce n'est pas cool de fumer
7 *Fam (nice, excellent)* sympa *inv*; cool *inv*; **my sister's c.** ma sœur est sympa *ou* cool
8 *Fam (allowed, acceptable)* **is it c. to smoke dope here?** est-ce que c'est OK de fumer de l'herbe ici?
> **N 1** fraîcheur *f*; **in the c. of the evening** dans la fraîcheur du soir **2** *Fam (calm)* **to keep/lose one's c.** garder/perdre son sang-froid
> **ADV** *Fam* **to play it c.** *(act calm)* jouer décontracté; *(be calm)* être décontracté
> **VT** *(water, air)* rafraîchir, refroidir; **to c. sb's ardour** refroidir l'ardeur de qn; *Fam* **c. it!** calme-toi!, on se calme!; **to c. one's heels** poireauter, faire le pied de grue; **he was put in jail overnight to c. his heels** on l'a gardé au poste pour la nuit histoire de le calmer
> **VI** *(of liquid)* se rafraîchir, (se) refroidir; *Fig (of friendship etc)* se refroidir; **his anger soon cooled** sa colère a vite passé
> ► **cool down VI 1** *(of person) (become calm)* s'apaiser, se calmer; **we'll talk about it when you've cooled down** nous en parlerons quand tu te seras calmé; **he still hasn't cooled down** il ne s'est pas encore calmé, il n'a pas encore décoléré **2** *(of weather)* se rafraîchir; *(of liquid)* (se) refroidir, se rafraîchir; *Fig* **things have cooled down between them** les relations se sont refroidies entre eux
> **VT SEP 1** *(make calm)* calmer, apaiser **2** *(of cold drink)* rafraîchir
> ► **cool off VI** *(of person) (by going for a swim etc)* se rafraîchir; *(of food)* refroidir; *Fig (of affection, enthusiasm)* se refroidir; *(of angry person)* se calmer

coolant ['ku:lənt] **N** *Tech* liquide *m* de refroidissement
> ► ► **c. inlet** arrivée *f* de liquide de refroidissement; **c. outlet** sortie *f* de liquide de refroidissement

cooler ['ku:lər] **N 1** *Am (refrigerator)* réfrigérateur *m* **2** *Tech* (appareil *m*) refroidisseur *m* **3** *Sl (prison)* taule *f*, tôle *f*

cool-headed [-'hedɪd] **ADJ** *(person)* calme, imperturbable

coolie ['ku:lɪ] **N** coolie *m*

cooling ['ku:lɪŋ] **ADJ** *(breeze, drink)* rafraîchissant; *Ind etc* réfrigérant
> **N** *(of temperature etc)* refroidissement *m*; **there had been a c. in their relationship** leurs relations s'étaient refroidies
> ► ► *Tech* **c. fan** ventilateur *m* de refroidissement; *Aut* **c. fin** ailette *f* de refroidissement; *Tech* **c. jacket** chemise *f* d'eau; *Fig* **c. off period** période *f* de réflexion; *Tech* **c. system** système *m* de refroidissement; *Tech* **c. tower** refroidisseur *m*; *Aut, Nucl* **c. water** eau *f* de refroidissement

coolly ['ku:lɪ] **ADV 1** *(calmly) (to act)* avec calme; **she walked c. out of the room** elle a calmement quitté la pièce **2** *Fam (impudently)* effrontément **3** *(to welcome)* froidement

coolness ['ku:lnɪs] **N 1** *(of air)* fraîcheur *f* **2** *(calm)* calme *m*, sang-froid *m* **3** *(of reception)* froideur *f*

coon [ku:n] **N 1** *Am Fam (raccoon)* raton *m* laveur **2** *Offensive Sl (Negro)* nègre *m*, négresse *f*

coonskin ['ku:nskɪn] **N** *Am Fam* peau *f* de raton laveur

coop [ku:p] **N (hen** *or* **chicken) c.** cage *f* à poules, poulailler *m*; *Fig* **to fly the c.** prendre la fuite, filer
> ► **coop up VT SEP** *(usu passive)* **to c. sb up** tenir qn enfermé; **we were cooped up for hours in a tiny room** nous sommes restés enfermés pendant des heures dans une pièce minuscule; **to feel cooped up** se sentir à l'étroit

co(-)op ['kəʊɒp] **N** coopérative *f*

cooper ['ku:pər] **N** tonnelier *m*

cooperage ['ku:pərɪdʒ] **N** tonnellerie *f*

co(-)operate [kəʊ'ɒpəreɪt] **VI** coopérer (**with sb in sth** avec qn à qch); **the two governments are co-operating in the drug war** les deux gouvernements coopèrent dans la lutte contre la drogue; **if you c. your sentence may be reduced** si vous coopérez, votre peine pourra être réduite

co(-)operation [kəʊɒpə'reɪʃən] **N** coopération *f*; **your c. would be appreciated** nous vous serions reconnaissants de votre coopération

co(-)operative [kəʊ'ɒp(ə)rətɪv] **ADJ 1** *(activity, work)* coopératif; **c. dairy** coopérative laitière **2** *(person, attitude)* coopératif; **to be c.** se montrer coopératif
> **N** *Com (agricultural, viticultural etc)* coopérative *f*
> ► ► **c. advertising** publicité *f* coopérative *ou* associée; **c. credit society** coopérative de crédit; **c. exporting** exportation *f* collective; **c. group** coopérative (de consommateurs); **c. selling** vente *f* en coopération; **c. society** société *f* coopérative

co(-)opt [kəʊ'ɒpt] **VT 1** *(onto committee)* coopter (**onto** à) **2** *Fam (commandeer)* réquisitionner; **I've been co-opted to help with the spring cleaning** j'ai été réquisitionné pour le nettoyage de printemps

co(-)ordinate¹ [kəʊ'ɔ:dɪnət] **ADJ** *Gram, Math* coordonné
> **N** *Math, Astron etc* coordonnée *f*
> ► ► *Gram* **c. clause** proposition *f* coordonnée

co(-)ordinate² [kəʊ'ɔ:dɪneɪt] **VT** coordonner (**with** à, avec)

co(-)ordinated [kəʊ'ɔ:dɪneɪtɪd] **ADJ** *(physically, in movements)* coordonné; **you look very c. for a change** pour une fois tu portes des couleurs qui vont bien ensemble *ou* qui ne jurent pas; **to give sth a more c. appearance** donner à qch une apparence plus harmonieuse

co(-)ordinates **NPL** *(clothes)* coordonnés *mpl*

co(-)ordinating [kəʊ'ɔ:dɪneɪtɪŋ] **ADJ** coordinateur, -trice
> ► ► *Gram* **c. conjunction** conjonction *f* de coordination VOIR GRAMMAIRE A73–4; B57–8

co(-)ordination [kəʊɒdɪ'neɪʃən] **N** coordination *f*; **you need good c. to play tennis** il faut avoir une bonne coordination pour jouer au tennis

co(-)ordinator [kəʊ'ɔ:dɪneɪtər] **N** coordinateur, -trice

coot [ku:t] **N 1** *(bird)* **(common** *or* **bald) c.** foulque *f* (macroule), *Can* foulque noire **2** *Old-fashioned Fam (fool)* idiot, -ote

cooties ['ku:tɪz] **NPL** *Am Fam* poux *mpl*

co-owner ['kəʊ'əʊnər] **N** *(of building etc)* copropriétaire *mf*

co-ownership [ˈkəʊˈəʊnəʃɪp] N copropriété f

cooze [ku:z] N Am Vulg (female genitals) craquette f, fente f; (women) nanas fpl, cuisse f

cop [kɒp] N 1 Fam (policeman) flic m; **speed c.** motard m; **to play cops and robbers** jouer aux gendarmes et aux voleurs 2 Br Sl (arrest) **it's a fair c.!** je suis fait 3 Br Sl **it's not much c.** (not very good) ça ne vaut pas grand-chose

▸ VT Sl (catch) (person) attraper, pincer; **c. this!** (listen) écoute-moi ça!; (look) regarde-moi ça!; **to get copped** (by police etc) se faire pincer; Br **to c. it** (be caught and punished) se faire pincer; (get injured) être blessé; (die) clamser; **to c. hold of sth** attraper qch; **to c. some zeds** or Am **zees** roupiller; Law **to c. a plea** plaider coupable (pour éviter une charge plus grave)

▸ Fam **c. shop** (police station) poste m de police; TV Fam **c. show** série f policière
▸ **cop off** VI Br Sl **to c. off with sb** lever ou emballer qn; **did you c. off last night?** t'as réussi à lever quelqu'un hier soir?
▸ **cop out** VI Sl (avoid responsibility) se défiler; (choose easy solution) choisir la solution de facilité

co-partner [ˈkəʊˈpɑːtnər] N coparticipant, -ante, coassocié, -ée

co-partnership [ˈkəʊˈpɑːtnəʃɪp] N coparticipation f

cope¹ [kəʊp] N Rel chape f

cope² VT Constr (wall) chaperonner, mettre un couronnement à

cope³ VI se débrouiller, s'en tirer, s'en sortir; **to c. with** (situation, danger, job, debt) faire face à; (difficulty) venir à bout de; (troublemaker) se charger de; (look after) (children) s'occuper de; (put up with) (children, noise etc) supporter; **to be able to c. with a job** être à la hauteur d'une tâche; **I can't c. with her when she gets angry** je ne sais pas comment la prendre quand elle se met en colère; **the engine couldn't c. with the extra weight** le moteur n'était pas assez puissant pour supporter cette charge supplémentaire; **I just can't c.** je n'y arrive plus; **that's all right, thanks, I can c.** ça va, merci, j'y arriverai; **I'll c. with it** (take care of it) je m'en chargerai; **I'll c.** je me débrouillerai; **he seems to be coping** il a l'air de se débrouiller ou de s'en sortir

Copenhagen [kəʊpənˈheɪg(ə)n] N Copenhague

copiable [ˈkɒpɪəb(ə)l] ADJ Comput copiable

copier [ˈkɒpɪər] N 1 (person) copiste mf 2 Pej (imitator) imitateur, -trice 3 (device) duplicateur m, copieur m; (photocopying machine) (photo)copieuse f

copilot [ˈkəʊpaɪlət] N Aviat copilote m

coping [ˈkəʊpɪŋ] N Constr (of wall etc) chaperon m
▸ Tech **c. saw** scie f découper ou à chantourner; Constr **c. stone** couronnement m, chaperon

copious [ˈkəʊpɪəs] ADJ copieux, abondant; **we drank c. amounts of beer** nous avons bu des quantités de bière

copiously [ˈkəʊpɪəslɪ] ADV abondamment

co-plaintiff [ˈkəʊˈpleɪntɪf] N Law co-demandeur, -eresse

cop-out N Sl 1 (act) solution f de facilité; **that's a bit of a c.** c'est la solution de facilité 2 Am (person) personne f qui se défile

copper [ˈkɒpər] N 1 (metal, colour) cuivre m 2 Br Fam (coin) sou m; **coppers** petite monnaie f; **to give a beggar a few coppers** donner quelques sous à un mendiant 3 Br (for washing) cuve f à lessive 4 Fam (policeman) flic m
▸ ADJ (colour, hair) cuivré

▸ VT (in metalwork) cuivrer
▸ Bot **c. beech** hêtre m pourpre; **c. wire** fil m de cuivre

copper-bottomed [-bɒtəmd] ADJ (pot, saucepan etc) à fond en cuivre; Fig (guarantee) sûr

copper-coloured ADJ cuivré

copperhead [ˈkɒpəhed] N (snake) trigonocéphale m

copperplate [ˈkɒpəpleɪt] N 1 Typ (plate) cuivre m 2 (plate) plaque f (de cuivre); (in engraving) taille-douce f, pl tailles-douces 3 (handwriting) écriture f moulée; **written in c.** calligraphié
▸ **c. engraving** taille-douce

coppersmith [ˈkɒpəsmɪθ] N chaudronnier, -ière

copperware [ˈkɒpəweər] N ustensiles mpl en cuivre

coppery [ˈkɒpərɪ] ADJ (colour) cuivré

coppice [ˈkɒpɪs] N taillis m, hallier m

copra [ˈkɒprə] N Com copra(h) m

co-presenter [ˈkəʊprɪzentər] N coprésentateur, -trice

co-processor [kəʊˈprəʊsesər] N Comput coprocesseur m; **maths c.** coprocesseur arithmétique

coproduce [kəʊprəˈdju:s] VT Cin etc coproduire

coproducer [kəʊprəˈdju:sər] N Cin etc coproducteur, -trice

coproduction [kəʊprəˈdʌkʃən] N Cin etc coproduction f

copse [kɒps] N taillis m

copter [ˈkɒptər] N Aviat Fam hélico m

Coptic [ˈkɒptɪk] ADJ coptique, copte ▸ Ling copte m

copula [ˈkɒpjʊlə] N Gram etc copule f

copulate [ˈkɒpjʊleɪt] VI copuler, s'accoupler (**with** avec)

copulation [kɒpjʊˈleɪʃən] N Physiol copulation f, coït m

copulative [ˈkɒpjʊlətɪv] ADJ Gram etc copulatif; Physiol, Anat copulateur, -trice

copy [ˈkɒpɪ] N 1 (reproduction) copie f; (of statue etc) reproduction f, copie; **this picture is only a c.** ce tableau n'est qu'une copie 2 (of handwritten letter, text) copie f; (of typewritten letter, text) double m; **rough c.** brouillon m; **fair c.** copie (au net); **certified c.** copie authentique; **true c.** copie conforme 3 (of book) exemplaire m; (of newspaper) numéro m; **5,000 copies of the book were printed** le livre a été tiré à 5000 exemplaires 4 Typ (written material for printing) manuscrit m, copie f; (in advertisement) texte m; Journ copie; **this would make good c.** voilà un bon sujet d'article; **he wrote some brilliant c.** (articles) il a écrit d'excellents articles ou Fam papiers

5 Comput **c. and paste** copier-coller m inv ▸ VT 1 (work of art, drawing etc) copier, imiter 2 (model oneself on) copier; (sb's walk) copier, imiter; Art, Liter, Mus (sb's style) copier, pasticher 3 (write out) (letter etc) (re)copier 4 Sch (in order to cheat) copier (**from sb** sur qn; **from sth** dans qch) 5 Comput copier; **to c. sth to disk** copier qch sur disquette; **to c. and paste sth** faire un copier-coller sur qch 6 (send copy to) envoyer une copie à; **to c. sb with sth** faire parvenir une copie de qch à qn
▸ VI Sch copier (**from another pupil** sur un autre élève)
▸ Comput **c. block** copie de bloc; Comput **c. check** contrôle m par duplication; Comput **c. command** commande f de copie; Journ **c. deadline** tombée f, dernière heure f; Comput

c. disk disquette f de copie; **c. editor** Journ secrétaire mf de rédaction; (in publishing) préparateur, -trice de copie; Comput **c. protection** protection f contre la copie; **c. taster** premier lecteur m; Mktg **c. test** pré-test m publicitaire, pl pré-tests publicitaires; Mktg **c. testing** pré-tests mpl publicitaires; **c. typist** dactylographe mf, dactylo mf
▸ **copy out** VT SEP recopier; **to c. out a passage from a book** transcrire ou recopier un passage d'un livre

copybook [ˈkɒpɪbʊk] N cahier m d'écriture; Fig **to blot one's c.** ternir sa réputation (**with** sb auprès de qn); **he really blotted his c. when he suggested that …** il a fait une vraie bourde lorsqu'il a proposé que …; **a c. example** un exemple classique

copycat [ˈkɒpɪkæt] N Fam copieur, -euse; **they're just copycats** ce ne sont que des copieurs
▸ **c. crime** crime m inspiré par un autre

copy-edit Typ VI corriger les épreuves
▸ VT (proofs) corriger

copy-editing N Typ correction f d'épreuves

copy-holder N (for keyboarder) porte-copies m, bras m porte-copies

copying [ˈkɒpɪɪŋ] N (imitation) imitation f; Sch (cheating) copiage m
▸ **c. machine** duplicateur m; (photocopier) photocopieuse f; Comput **c. program** programme m de copie

copyist [ˈkɒpɪɪst] N copiste mf

copy-protect VT Comput protéger contre la copie

copy-protected ADJ Comput protégé contre la copie

copyreader [ˈkɒpɪri:dər] N secrétaire mf de rédaction, correcteur, -trice

copyright [ˈkɒpɪraɪt] N droit m d'auteur, copyright m; **it's still subject to c.** c'est toujours soumis au droit d'auteur; **breach or infringement of c.** violation f du droit d'auteur; **to hold the c.** or **to have c. on sth** avoir le droit d'auteur sur qch; **it's his c.** c'est lui qui détient les droits d'auteur; **c. Lawrence Durrell** copyright, Lawrence Durrell; **out of c.** (tombé) dans le domaine public
▸ ADJ (book) qui est protégé par des droits d'auteur; (article) dont le droit de reproduction est réservé; **c. (in all countries)** tous droits de reproduction et de traduction réservés (pour tous pays)
▸ VT (book) réserver les droits de
▸ **c. library** bibliothèque f de dépôt légal; **c. notice** mention f de réserve

copyrighted [ˈkɒpɪraɪtɪd] ADJ (book, music) déposé

copytaker [ˈkɒpɪteɪkər] N Journ opérateur, -trice

copywriter [ˈkɒpɪraɪtər] N rédacteur, -trice publicitaire

copywriting [ˈkɒpɪraɪtɪŋ] N rédaction f publicitaire

coquetry [ˈkəʊkɪtrɪ, ˈkɒk-] N esp Lit coquetterie f

coquette [kəʊˈket, kɒk-] N esp Lit coquette f

coquettish [kəˈketɪʃ, kɒk-] ADJ 1 (woman) flirteuse 2 (smile etc) aguichant

cor¹ [kɔːr] N
▸ Mus **c. anglais** cor m anglais

cor² INT Br Sl ça alors!

coracle [ˈkɒrək(ə)l] N (boat) coracle m

coral [ˈkɒr(ə)l] ADJ 1 (island) de corail, corallien; (necklace) de corail 2 (colour) corail
▸ N 1 corail m, -aux 2 (colour) corail m
▸ **c. red** rouge m corail; **c. reef** récif m de corail; **the C. Sea** la mer de Corail; Zool **c. snake** serpent m corail

corbel ['kɔːb(ə)l] N *Archit* corbeau *m*, console *f*

cord [kɔːd] N **1** *(string)* grosse ficelle *f*; *(for curtains)* cordon *m*; *(of pyjama trousers)* cordon, ficelle; *(of dressing gown)* ceinture *f* **2** *Anat* **(umbilical) c.** cordon *m* (ombilical) **3** *Tex (corduroy)* velours *m* côtelé; **(pair of) cords** *(trousers)* pantalon *m* en *ou* de velours côtelé **4** *Am Elec* cordon *m*, fil *m*

cordage ['kɔːdɪdʒ] N *Naut* cordage *m*

corded ['kɔːdɪd] ADJ *Tex* côtelé, à côtes

cordial ['kɔːdɪəl] ADJ cordial, -aux N *(drink)* cordial *m*, sirop *m*

cordiality [kɔːdɪˈælɪtɪ] N cordialité *f*; *Fml* **exchange of cordialities** échange *m* de cordialités

cordially ['kɔːdɪəlɪ] ADV cordialement; *Am* **c. yours** *(at end of letter)* bien cordialement

cordite ['kɔːdaɪt] N cordite *f*

cordless ['kɔːdlɪs] ADJ sans fil
▸▸*Comput* **c. keyboard** clavier *m* sans fil; **c. mouse** souris *f* sans fil; **c. telephone** téléphone *m* sans fil

cordon ['kɔːd(ə)n] N **1** *(barrier)* cordon *m*; **police c.** cordon de police **2** *Bot (tree)* cordon *m*
▸▸*Bot* **c. tree** cordon
▸**cordon off** VT SEP *(close) (road)* barrer; *(area etc)* boucler; **the street was cordoned off by the police** *(they ordered it closed)* la police a barré la rue; *(they acted as a barrier)* on a isolé la rue par un cordon de police

cordon bleu [-blɜː] *Culin* N *(cookery, chef)* cordon bleu *m*
ADJ de cordon bleu

corduroy ['kɔːdərɔɪ] N *Tex* velours *m* côtelé; **(pair of) corduroys** pantalon *m* en *ou* de velours côtelé
ADJ de velours côtelé
▸▸**c. road** chemin *m* de rondins

core [kɔːr] N **1** *(of mass)* centre *m*, partie *f* centrale; *(of apple etc)* trognon *m*, cœur *m*; *(of argument)* essentiel *m*; *(of organization)* noyau *m*; *Fig* **hard c.** noyau *m* dur; **selfish to the c.** d'un égoïsme foncier; *Fam* **he's rotten to the c.** il est pourri jusqu'à la moelle; **it shocked us to the c.** cela nous a complètement bouleversés; **the c. issue** la question centrale **2** *Geol (of the earth)* noyau *m* **3** *Tech (of cable)* mèche *f*, *Elec (of electromagnet)* noyau *m*; *Nucl (of reactor)* cœur *m*
VT *(apple etc)* enlever le cœur de, évider
▸▸*Com, Mktg* **c. brand** marque *f* phare; *Com* **c. business** activité *f* principale; **c. competence** principale compétence *f*; *Sch* **c. curriculum** tronc *m* commun; *Tech* **c. hole** *(in engine block)* trou *m* de coulée *ou* d'usinage; **c. hours** *(in flexitime scheme)* plage *f* fixe; *Mktg* **c. market** marché *m* principal, marché de référence; *Comput* **c. memory** mémoire *f* à tores (magnétiques); *(main memory)* mémoire centrale; *Com, Mktg* **c. message** *(in advertising)* message *m* principal; *Aut* **c. plug** obturateur *m* de trou de coulée *ou* de trou d'usinage; *Geol* **c. sample** carotte *f*; **c. time** *(in flexitime scheme)* plage fixe; **c. values** valeurs *fpl* principales; *Ling* **c. vocabulary** vocabulaire *m* de base

coreligionist [kəʊrɪˈlɪdʒ(ə)nɪst] N coreligionnaire *mf*

corer ['kɔːrər] N **(apple) c.** vide-pomme *m*, *pl* vide-pommes

co-respondent [kəʊrɪˈspɒndənt] N *Law (in divorce suit)* complice *mf*

Corfu [kɔːˈfuː] N Corfou *f*

corgi ['kɔːgɪ] N corgi *m*

coriander [kɒrɪˈændər] N *Bot, Culin* coriandre *f*
▸▸**c. seeds** graines *fpl* de coriandre

Corinthian [kəˈrɪnθɪən] ADJ **1** *Geog* corin-

thien **2** *Archit (column etc)* corinthien
N *Geog* Corinthien, -ienne

cork [kɔːk] N **1** *(material)* liège *m* **2** *(stopper)* bouchon; *Br Fam* **put a c. in it!** *(shut up)* la ferme!
VT **1** *(bottle)* boucher **2** *(blacken)* **to c. one's face** se noircir le visage avec un bouchon brûlé
▸▸**c. charge** *(in restaurant)* droit *m* de bouchon; *Bot* **c. oak** chêne-liège *m*, *pl* chênes-lièges
▸**cork up** VT SEP **the genie had been corked up in the bottle for years** le génie avait été enfermé dans la bouteille pendant des années; *Fig* **to c. up one's feelings** refouler ses émotions

corkage ['kɔːkɪdʒ] N *(in restaurant)* droit *m* de bouchon

corked [kɔːkt] ADJ *(wine)* bouchonné, qui sent le bouchon; **the wine tasted c.** le vin était bouchonné

corker ['kɔːkər] N *Br Sl* **1** *(thing, action)* chose *f*/action *f* qui vous en bouche un coin; **that was a c. of a goal** c'était un super but; **that joke was a c.** elle était super cette blague!; **a c. of a lie** un énorme mensonge **2** *Old-fashioned (man)* type *m* épatant; *(pretty woman)* canon *m*; **when it comes to telling lies he's a c.** comme menteur il se pose là

corking ['kɔːkɪŋ] ADJ *Old-fashioned Br Sl (wonderful)* épatant, fameux

corkscrew ['kɔːkskruː] N tire-bouchon *m*, *pl* tire-bouchons
VI **to c. (up/down)** *(of staircase)* monter/descendre en colimaçon; **the plane corkscrewed into the sea** l'avion est descendu en vrille et s'est écrasé dans la mer
▸▸**c. curl** mèche *f* en tire-bouchon

cork-tipped ADJ *(cigarette)* à bout de liège

corkwood ['kɔːkwʊd] N liège *m*

corm [kɔːm] N *Bot* bulbe *m* (solide)

cormorant ['kɔːmərənt] N *(bird)* cormoran *m*

corn¹ [kɔːn] N **1** *(no pl) Br (cereal)* blé(s) *m(pl)*; **winter c.** semis *m* d'hiver **2** *esp Am (maize)* maïs *m*; **c. on the cob** maïs en épi **3** *(seed)* grain *m* (de plante céréalière) **4** *Fam (sentimentality)* mièvrerie *f*; *(lack of originality)* banalité *f*; **that film was pure c.** ce film était d'une mièvrerie affligeante; **his routine was pure c.** *(of comedian)* son spectacle manquait totalement d'originalité
▸▸*Geog* **c. belt** plaines *fpl* du centre des Etats-Unis *(où est cultivé le maïs)*; **c. bread** pain *m* à la farine de maïs; *Orn* **c. bunting** bruant *m*; **c. chandler** marchand, -ande de blé *ou* de grains; **c. dolly** figurine *f* en paille tressée; **C. Exchange** halle *f* aux blés; **c. meal** farine *f* de maïs; **c. merchant** marchand, -ande de blé *ou* de grains; **c. oil** huile *f* de maïs; **c. poppy** coquelicot *m*; *Bot, Culin* **c. salad** mâche *f*; *Bot* **c. silk** barbe *f*; *Am* **c. whiskey** whisky *m* de maïs

corn² N *Med (on toe etc)* cor *m*; *Fig Fam* **to tread on sb's corns** froisser qn
▸▸**c. plaster** pansement *m* (pour cors)

cornball ['kɔːnbɔːl] *Am Fam* **1** N personne *f* gnangnan
ADJ cucul, gnangnan

corncob ['kɔːnkɒb] N épi *m* de maïs; *(pipe)* pipe *f* en épi de maïs
▸▸**c. pipe** pipe en épi de maïs

corncockle ['kɔːnkɒk(ə)l] N *(plant)* nielle *f* des blés

corncrake ['kɔːnkreɪk] N *(bird)* râle *m* des genêts

cornea ['kɔːnɪə] N *Anat (of eye)* cornée *f*

corneal ['kɔːnɪəl] ADJ *Anat* cornéen
▸▸*Med* **c. graft** greffe *f* de la cornée

corned [kɔːnd] ADJ
▸▸*Culin* **c. beef** corned beef *m*

cornelian [kɔːˈniːlɪən] N *(gem)* cornaline *f*

CORNER ['kɔːnər]

N coin **1–3, 6, 7** ▪ angle **3** ▪ virage **4** ▪ corner **5**	
VT coincer **1** ▪ accaparer **2**	
VI prendre un virage	

N **1** *(of page, screen)* coin *m*; **to turn down the c. of a page** corner une page; **bottom left-hand c.** *(of page, photograph etc)* coin en bas à gauche
2 *(of room etc)* coin *m*; **the four corners of the earth** les quatre coins du monde; **to search every c. of the house** chercher dans tous les coins et recoins de la maison; **to put a child in the c.** mettre un enfant au coin; *Fig* **to drive sb into a c.** acculer qn, mettre qn au pied du mur; *Fig* **driven into a c.** acculé, au pied du mur; *Fig* **to be in a tight c.** être dans une mauvaise passe; *Fig* **to paint oneself into a c.** se mettre dans une impasse
3 *(on street)* coin *m*, angle *m*; **situated at** *or* **on the c.** situé au coin *ou* à l'angle; **the house on the c.** la maison qui fait l'angle, la maison au coin; **you'll find the grocer's round the c.** tournez au coin de la rue et vous verrez l'épicerie; **it's just round the c.** c'est au coin de la rue; *Fig* **spring is just around the c.** ce sera bientôt le printemps; **with the elections just round the c.** avec les élections qui approchent; **another rise in mortgage rates is just round the c.** une autre augmentation des taux de prêt se prépare; **you never know what's around the c.** on ne sait jamais ce qui peut se produire; **to hang around street corners** traîner dans les rues; **to turn the c.** tourner le coin; *Fig (of economy, company)* passer le moment critique; *(of sick person)* commencer à se rétablir
4 *(bend in road)* tournant *m*; *Aut* virage *m*; *Aut* **to take a c.** prendre un virage; **to cut a c. (close)** couper un virage; *Fig* **to cut corners** *(economize excessively)* faire des économies exagérées; *(not follow rules)* contourner les règlements; **if you cut corners now you'll just have more work to do later on** si tu fais les choses trop vite maintenant, tu auras plus à faire plus tard; **we had to cut a few corners to get the job finished on time** il nous a fallu simplifier un peu les choses pour finir ce travail à temps
5 *Ftbl* corner *m*; **to take a c.** faire un corner
6 *(of eye)* coin *m*; *(of lips)* coin *m*, commissure *f*; **to look out of the c. of one's eye** regarder du coin de l'œil
7 a little c. of Normandy un petit coin de Normandie; **they had created a little c. of France in Rome** ils avaient recréé un petit coin de France à Rome
VT **1** *(drive into a corner)* acculer, coincer; *Fig* coincer, mettre au pied du mur
2 *Com (market)* accaparer, *Belg* s'accaparer *(in de)*
VI *Aut* prendre un virage; **the car corners well** cette voiture prend bien les virages
▸▸**c. cupboard** armoire *f* de coin; *Sport* **c. flag** drapeau *m* de corner; *Ftbl* **c. kick** corner; *Ftbl* **c. post** piquet *m* de corner; *Br* **c. shop** magasin *m* de quartier

cornered ['kɔːnəd] ADJ *(driven into a corner)* acculé, coincé; *Fig* coincé, au pied du mur; **you've got me c.** là, tu m'as coincé; **we've got him c.** *(criminal etc)* nous l'avons coincé

cornering ['kɔːnərɪŋ] N **1** *Com (of market)* accaparement *m* **2** *Aut (of driver)* façon *f* de prendre les virages; *(of car)* stabilité *f* dans les virages; **the car is good at c.** la voiture prend bien les virages

cornerstone ['kɔːnəstəʊn] N *Constr, Fig* pierre *f* angulaire

cornet ['kɔːnɪt, *Am* kɔːˈnet] N **1** *Mus (instru-*

ment) cornet *m* à pistons; *(player)* cornet-tiste *mf* **2** *(of paper)* cornet *m* (en papier) **3** *Br* **(ice-cream) c.** cornet *m* de glace

cornet(t)ist [kɔːˈnetɪst] N *Mus* cornettiste *mf*

cornfield [ˈkɔːnfiːld] N *Br* champ *m* de blé; *Am* champ de maïs

cornflakes [ˈkɔːnfleɪks] NPL *Culin* flocons *mpl* de maïs, cornflakes *mpl*

cornflour [ˈkɔːnflaʊər] N *Br Culin* farine *f* de maïs

cornflower [ˈkɔːnflaʊər] N **1** *(plant)* bleuet *m*, barbeau *m inv* **2** *(colour)* bleu *m* centaurée
▸ ADJ *(colour)* bleu centaurée *inv*
▸▸ **c. blue** bleu centaurée

cornice [ˈkɔːnɪs] N *(of wardrobe, snow)*, *Archit* corniche *f*

Cornish [ˈkɔːnɪʃ] ADJ *Geog* cornouaillais
▸ N *Ling* cornique *m*
▸▸ *Br Culin* **C. pasty** = chausson *m* à la viande et aux légumes

Cornishman, *pl* **Cornishmen** [ˈkɔːnɪʃmən] N Cornouaillais *m*

Cornishwoman, *pl* **Cornishwomen** [ˈkɔːnɪʃwʊmən, -wɪmɪn] N Cornouaillaise *f*

cornstarch [ˈkɔːnstɑːtʃ] N *Am Culin* farine *f* de maïs

cornucopia, *pl* **cornucopias** [kɔːnjʊˈkəʊpɪə, -əz] N *Myth, Fig* corne *f* d'abondance

Cornwall [ˈkɔːnw(ə)l] N Cornouailles *f*

corny [ˈkɔːnɪ] ADJ *Fam (poor) (joke)* nul; *(sentimental) (story, film, novel)* tarte; **don't be so c.** ne sois pas aussi tarte

corolla [kəˈrɒlə] N *Bot* corolle *f*

corollary [kəˈrɒlərɪ] N corollaire *m* (**of** à)

corona, *pl* **coronae** [kəˈrəʊnə, -ɪ] N *Astron, Bot, Elec, Phys* couronne *m*;
▸▸ *Phys* **c. discharge** effluve *f* électrique; *Phys* **c. shielding** dispositif *m* anti-effluves

coronary [ˈkɒrən(ə)rɪ] *Med* ADJ coronarien
▸ N infarctus *m* (du myocarde); **to have a c.** avoir un infarctus (du myocarde); *Fam* **I just about had a c. when I saw the bill** j'ai failli avoir une attaque quand j'ai vu l'addition
▸▸ **c. artery** artère *f* coronaire; **c. bypass** pontage *m* coronaire; **c. thrombosis** infarctus du myocarde, thrombose *f* coronarienne

coronation [kɒrəˈneɪʃən] N couronnement *m*
▸▸ *Culin* **c. chicken** = morceaux *mpl* de poulet froid à la mayonnaise parfumée au curry; *Br* **c. mug** = tasse *f* haute fabriquée spécialement à l'occasion d'un couronnement et décorée sur ce thème

coroner [ˈkɒrənər] N *Law* coroner *m (officier civil chargé d'instruire, assisté d'un jury, en cas de mort violente ou subite)*; **c.'s inquest** enquête *f* du coroner

coronet [ˈkɒrənɪt] N *(petite)* couronne *f*, *(lady's)* diadème *m*

corp, Corp 1 *Com (abbr* **corporation)** Cie **2** *Mil abbr* **corporal**

corporal¹ [ˈkɔːpər(ə)l] ADJ corporel
▸▸ **c. punishment** châtiment *m* corporel

corporal² N *Mil (in infantry, air force)* caporal-chef *m*, *pl* caporaux-chefs; *(in cavalry, artillery)* brigadier-chef *m*, *pl* brigadiers-chefs

corporate [ˈkɔːp(ə)rət] ADJ *Com* **1** *(of a specific company)* corporatif, de société; *(of companies in general)* d'entreprise; *(taxation)* sur les sociétés; **I mean 'we' in the c. sense** par 'nous' j'entends la société; **we have a number of c. customers** certains de nos clients sont des entreprises; **to be a good c. citizen** *(of company)* avoir le sens des responsabilités civiques **2** *(forming a single body)* constitué (en corps), formant

(un) corps; *Law* **body c.** corps *m* constitué, corporation *f*, *(considered as an individual)* personne *f* morale **3** *(of a group of people)* de corporation, de corps; **c. feeling** esprit *m* de corps
▸▸ **c. advertising** publicité *f* institutionnelle, publicité d'entreprise; *Am* **c. apartments** = appartements *mpl* destinés au personnel d'une société; **c. banking** banque *f* d'entreprise; *Law* **c. body** corps constitué, corporation; *(considered as an individual)* personne morale; **c. budget** budget *m* de l'entreprise; **c. culture** culture *f* d'entreprise; **c. image** image *f* de marque de l'entreprise; **the company cares about its c. image** la société se préoccupe de son image; **our c. image demands that ...** notre image en tant que société exige que ...; **c. income** revenu *m* de société; **c. income tax** impôt *m* sur les bénéfices des sociétés; **c. law** droit *m* des sociétés *ou* des entreprises; **c. lawyer** juriste spécialisé(e) en droit des sociétés; *Fin* **c. lending** crédit *m* aux entreprises; **c. literature** = brochures *fpl* décrivant une société; **c. member** *(of association)* société-membre *f*, *pl* sociétés-membres; **c. name** raison *f* sociale; *St Exch* **c. raider** attaquant *m*; **c. sponsorship** sponsoring *m*, parrainage *m* d'entreprises; **c. strategy** stratégie *f* de l'entreprise; **c. tax** impôt sur les sociétés

corporation [kɔːpəˈreɪʃən] N **1** *Com Am* société *f*, compagnie *f*; *Br* **public c.** entreprise *f* publique **2** *Br* **municipal c.** *(council)* conseil *m* municipal, municipalité *f* **3** *Law* personne *f* morale **4** *Old-fashioned Fam (paunch)* bedaine *f*, bedon *m*
▸▸ *Am Fin* **c. income tax** impôt *m* sur les sociétés; *Br Fin* **c. tax** impôt *m* sur les sociétés

corporeal [kɔːˈpɔːrɪəl] ADJ corporel, matériel

corps [kɔːr, *pl* kɔːz] N INV corps *m*; *Mil* corps d'armée; **the diplomatic c.** le corps diplomatique; **tank c.** blindés *mpl*

corpse [kɔːps] N cadavre *m*
▸ VI *Theat (of actor)* avoir le fou rire sur scène

corpulence [ˈkɔːpjʊləns] N corpulence *f*

corpulent [ˈkɔːpjʊlənt] ADJ corpulent

corpus [ˈkɔːpəs] N **1** *(of writings)* corpus *m* **2** *(main body)* corpus *m* **3** *Ling* corpus *m*
▸▸ *Cathol* **C. Christi** la Fête-Dieu; *Law* **c. delicti** corps *m* du délit

corpuscle [ˈkɔːpʌs(ə)l] N *Biol* corpuscule *m*; **red/white blood corpuscles** globules *mpl* rouges/blancs

corral [kɒˈrɑːl] N corral *m*, *pl* -als
▸ VT *(livestock, horses etc)* renfermer dans un corral; *Fig (demonstrators)* isoler; **to c. sb into doing sth** amener qn à faire qch

correct [kəˈrekt] VT **1** *(translation, homework, proofs)* corriger
2 *(rectify) (error, imbalance, oversteer)* rectifier, corriger; *(instrument setting)* modifier; **to c. a misunderstanding** dissiper un malentendu; **to c. a squint** *(of glasses)* corriger un strabisme
3 *(put right) (person)* reprendre, corriger; **he had the nerve to c. my grammar/English/pronunciation** il a eu le culot de corriger *ou* de me reprendre sur ma grammaire/mon anglais/ma prononciation; **I said it was 2 o'clock but someone corrected me** j'ai dit qu'il était 2 heures mais quelqu'un m'a corrigé; **to c. oneself** se reprendre; **c. me if I'm wrong, but ...** reprenez-moi si je me trompe, mais ...; **I stand corrected** j'avais tort
4 *Old-fashioned (punish) (guilty person)* punir, infliger une correction à
▸ ADJ **1** *(exact)* correct, exact, juste; **the c. time** l'heure exacte; **c. to a millimetre** exact à un millimètre près; **am I c.?** je ne me trompe pas?; **his prediction proved c.** sa pré-

diction s'est vérifiée; **you must be Mr Jones – that's c.** vous devez être M. Jones – c'est exact; **if my memory is c.** si j'ai bonne mémoire; **figures c. at time of going to press** chiffres exacts au moment de la publication **2** *(appropriate) (behaviour)* convenable, correct; *(person)* convenable, comme il faut; **it's the c. thing to send a letter of thanks** la politesse veut que l'on envoie une lettre de remerciements; **it's the c. thing to do** c'est ce qu'il convient de faire; **as is only c.** comme il se doit, comme il convient

correcting fluid [kəˈrektɪŋ] N liquide *m* correcteur

correction [kəˈrekʃən] N **1** *(of proofs, homework)*, *Tech* correction *f*, *(statement in newspaper)* mise *f* au point, rectificatif *m*; **to make corrections to a text** apporter des corrections à un texte; **subject to c.** sous toutes réserves **2** *Old-fashioned (punishment)* correction *f*, punition *f*; *Arch* **house of c.** maison *f* de correction *ou* de redressement
▸▸ **c. fluid** liquide *m* correcteur

corrective [kəˈrektɪv] N rectificatif *m*, correctif *m*; *Med (for teeth)* appareil *m* dentaire; *(for deformed limb)* appareil orthopédique
▸ ADJ *(action, measure)* rectificatif, correctif; *(exercises, treatment)* correctif; *(lens, make-up)* correcteur, -trice

correctly [kəˈrektlɪ] ADV **1** *(to answer, report, predict)* correctement; **or (to put it) more c.** ou pour mieux dire **2** *(to behave)* correctement

correctness [kəˈrektnɪs] N **1** *(of description, answer)* exactitude *f*, justesse *f* **2** *(of dress, behaviour)* correction *f*

correlate [ˈkɒrɪleɪt] VI correspondre (**with** à), être en corrélation (**with** avec)
▸ VT corréler, mettre en corrélation (**with** avec); **poverty and ill-health are closely correlated** il y a une corrélation étroite entre la pauvreté et la maladie

correlation [kɒrɪˈleɪʃən] N corrélation *f* (**with** avec; **between** entre)

correlative [kɒˈrelətɪv] ADJ corrélatif
▸ N corrélatif *m*

correspond [kɒrɪˈspɒnd] VI **1** *(conform)* correspondre, être conforme (**with, to** à); **to c. with** *or* **to reality** correspondre à la réalité **2** *(be equivalent)* correspondre (**to** à), être l'équivalent de (**to** à), équivaloir (**to** à); **the gendarmes roughly c. to our motorway police** les gendarmes sont à peu près l'équivalent de notre 'motorway police' **3** *(write letters)* correspondre (**with** avec); **they corresponded for many years** ils ont correspondu *ou* ils se sont écrit pendant des années

correspondence [kɒrɪˈspɒndəns] N **1** *(relationship)* correspondance *f* (**with, to** avec), rapport *m* (**with, to** entre) **2** *(letter writing)* correspondance *f*; **to be in c. with sb** être en correspondance avec qn, correspondre avec qn; **they kept up a c. for many years** ils sont restés en correspondance pendant des années; **to do one's c.** faire sa correspondance **3** *(mail)* courrier *m*; **I don't get much c.** je ne reçois pas beaucoup de courrier
▸▸ *Journ* **c. column** courrier *m* des lecteurs; **c. course** cours *m* par correspondance; **c. tray** bac *m* à correspondance

correspondent [kɒrɪˈspɒndənt] N correspondant, -ante; *Journ* **our London c.** notre correspondant à Londres; **parliamentary c.** *Journ* rédacteur, -trice parlementaire; *TV* correspondant, -ante parlementaire; **special c.** envoyé, -ée spécial(e)
▸▸ **c. bank account** compte *m* de correspondant

corresponding [kɒrɪˈspɒndɪŋ] ADJ correspondant (**to** à); **as compared with the c. period last year** par rapport à la même période l'année dernière

▸ ▸ **c. member** (of society, club) membre m correspondant

correspondingly [kɒrɪˈspɒndɪŋlɪ] ADV (to react, respond, adjust) en conséquence; (as a consequence) donc, par conséquent; **prices are c. more expensive** les prix sont proportionnellement plus élevés

corridor [ˈkɒrɪdɔːr] N couloir m, corridor m; Aviat (air) couloir aérien; Hist **the Polish C.** le couloir ou le corridor de Dantzig; Fig **the corridors of power** les hautes sphères fpl du pouvoir

▸ ▸ **c. train** train m à couloir

corroborate [kəˈrɒbəreɪt] VT (evidence, confession) corroborer, confirmer

corroboration [kərɒbəˈreɪʃən] N corroboration f, confirmation f; **in c. of** à l'appui de …

corroborative [kəˈrɒb(ə)rətɪv] ADJ (evidence, statement) qui confirme ou corrobore

corrode [kəˈrəʊd] VT (metal) corroder, attaquer; Fig (society) miner; (optimism) entamer

VI se corroder

corroded [kəˈrəʊdɪd] ADJ corrodé, attaqué; **badly c. metal** métal très corrodé ou attaqué

corrosion [kəˈrəʊʒən] N corrosion f

corrosion-resistant ADJ anti-corrosion inv

corrosive [kəˈrəʊsɪv] ADJ, N corrosif m, corrodant m

corrugated [ˈkɒrʊgeɪtɪd] ADJ (cardboard, paper) ondulé

▸ ▸ **c. cardboard** carton m ondulé; **c. iron** tôle f ondulée; **c. iron roof** toit m en tôle ondulée

corrupt [kəˈrʌpt] ADJ **1** (dishonest) (official, politician) corrompu **2** (depraved) corrompu, dépravé; **c. morals** immoralité f **3** Comput (disk, file) corrompu, altéré, endommagé; **to go c.** s'endommager **4** Liter (text) corrompu, altéré

VT **1** (deprave) (youth) corrompre; **to c. sb's morals** dépraver qn; **to be corrupted by power** être corrompu par le pouvoir **2** Comput corrompre, altérer, endommager **3** Liter (text etc) corrompre, altérer

corruptible [kəˈrʌptəb(ə)l] ADJ corruptible

corrupting [kəˈrʌptɪŋ] ADJ dépravant, corrupteur, -trice; **c. influence** influence f corruptrice

corruption [kəˈrʌpʃən] N **1** (giving and taking bribes) corruption f; **bribery and c.** corruption **2** (act of making depraved) corruption f, dépravation f **3** Comput corruption f, altération f, dommage m **4** Liter (of text) corruption f, altération f

corruptive [kəˈrʌptɪv] ADJ corrupteur, -trice

corruptly [kəˈrʌptlɪ] ADV d'une manière corrompue

corsage [kɔːˈsɑːʒ] N **1** fleur f (portée au corsage, à la taille ou au poignet) **2** (bodice of dress) corsage m

corsair [ˈkɔːseər] N Hist (pirate, ship) corsaire m

corset [ˈkɔːsɪt] N corset m; **orthopaedic** or **surgical c.** corset orthopédique

Corsica [ˈkɔːsɪkə] N Corse f

Corsican [ˈkɔːsɪkən] ADJ corse

N **1** (person) Corse mf **2** Ling corse m

cortège [kɔːˈteʒ] N cortège m; **funeral c.** convoi m ou cortège funèbre

cortex, pl **cortices** [ˈkɔːteks, -ɪsiːz] N Bot, Anat cortex m

corticosteroids [kɔːtɪkəʊˈsterɔɪdz] NPL Med corticoïdes mpl

cortisone [ˈkɔːtɪzəʊn] N Biol, Chem, Med cortisone f

corundum [kəˈrʌndəm] N Miner corindon m

coruscate [ˈkɒrəskeɪt] VI Lit scintiller

coruscating [ˈkɒrəskeɪtɪŋ] ADJ Lit brillant, scintillant; Fig (wit) brillant, étincelant

corvette [kɔːˈvet] N Naut corvette f

cos¹ [kɒz] N Math (abbr cosine) cosinus m

cos² CONJ Fam = **because**

cos³ [kɒs] N Br (lettuce) (laitue f) romaine f

▸ ▸ **c. lettuce** (laitue) romaine

cosh [kɒʃ] Br N matraque f

VT assommer, matraquer

cosignatory [ˈkəʊˈsɪgnətərɪ] N cosignataire mf (**to** de)

cosily [ˈkəʊzɪlɪ] ADV (warmly) confortablement, douillettement; **c. wrapped up** bien emmitouflé

cosine [ˈkəʊsaɪn] N Math cosinus m

cosiness [ˈkəʊzɪnɪs] N **1** (of armchair, room) confort m **2** Fig (of arrangement) caractère n combinard

cosmetic [kɒzˈmetɪk] N cosmétique m; **cosmetics** produits mpl de beauté, cosmétiques mpl; **the cosmetics industry/counter** l'industrie f/le rayon des cosmétiques ou des produits de beauté

ADJ **1** (for beautifying) cosmétique **2** (superficial) superficiel; **the policy change is c. rather than real** le changement de politique est plutôt un changement de forme que de fond; **the alterations they made to the translation are purely c.** les changements qu'ils ont apportés à la traduction sont très superficiels

▸ ▸ **c. surgery** chirurgie f esthétique

cosmetician [kɒzmɪˈtɪʃən] N esthéticien, -ienne

cosmetologist [kɒzməˈtɒlədʒɪst] N cosmétologue mf

cosmetology [kɒzməˈtɒlədʒɪ] N cosmétologie f

cosmic [ˈkɒzmɪk] ADJ (ray, dust) cosmique; Fig gigantesque

cosmogony [kɒzˈmɒgənɪ] N cosmogonie f

cosmology [kɒzˈmɒlədʒɪ] N cosmologie f

cosmonaut [ˈkɒzmənɔːt] N cosmonaute mf

cosmopolitan [kɒzməˈpɒlɪt(ə)n] N cosmopolite mf

ADJ (city etc) cosmopolite

cosmos [ˈkɒzmɒs] N cosmos m

Cossack [ˈkɒsæk] ADJ cosaque

N Cosaque m

cosset [ˈkɒsɪt] VT dorloter, choyer

cossie [ˈkɒzɪ] N Br, Austr Fam maillot m de bain

COST [kɒst] N **1** (price) coût m, frais mpl; Law **costs** frais d'instance, dépens mpl; Law **they were ordered to pay costs** ils ont été condamnés aux dépens; **at little/great c.** à peu de/à grands frais; **to sell at c.** vendre au prix coûtant; **for the c. of a room in a hotel you could …** pour le prix d'une chambre à l'hôtel, vous pourriez …; **the c. of money** le loyer de l'argent; **c., insurance and freight** coût, assurance, fret; **c. and freight** coût et fret; Acct **c. of goods purchased** coût d'achat; Acct **c. of goods sold** coût des ventes, coût des marchandises vendues; Mktg **c. per thousand** coût par mille, CPM m; Acct **c. of sales** coût des marchandises vendues

2 Fig **to count the cost(s) of sth** calculer le coût de qch; **at any c., at all costs** à tout prix, à n'importe quel prix, coûte que coûte; **I learnt it to my c.** je l'ai appris à mes dépens; **as I know to my c.** comme je l'ai appris à mes dépens; **at the c. of one's life** au prix de sa vie; **the c. in human life** (of disaster etc) le prix en vies humaines

VT **1** (pt, pp cost) coûter; **it costs \$25** ça coûte 25 dollars; **it c. me £30 a night to stay here** ça m'a coûté 30 livres par nuit ici; **how much does it c.?** combien cela coûte-t-il?; **it costs nothing to join the library** l'inscription à la bibliothèque est gratuite; **that will c. him a great deal of money/trouble** cela lui coûtera beaucoup d'argent/de peine; **to c. a fortune** or **the earth** coûter une fortune, coûter les yeux de la tête; Br Fam **if you go by air it'll c. you** si tu y vas par avion, tu vas le sentir passer; **the attempt c. him his life** cette tentative lui a coûté la vie; **it must have c. her something to admit that** il a dû lui en coûter de l'avouer

2 (pt, pp costed) Com, Ind (estimate cost of) (article) établir le prix de revient de; (job) évaluer le coût de; **how much was it costed at?** (of work) à combien est-ce que le coût a été évalué?

▸ ▸ **c. accounting** comptabilité f analytique ou d'exploitation; Acct **c. allocation** imputation f des charges; Fin **c. analysis** analyse f des coûts, analyse du prix de revient; **c. assessment** évaluation f du coût; **c. budget** budget m des charges; Acct **c. centre** centre m d'analyse; Fin **c. curve** courbe f des coûts; **c. equation** équation f de coût; **c. factor** facteur m coût; **c. of living** coût de la vie; Fin **c. management** gestion f des coûts; **c. overrun** dépassement m de coût; **c. price** prix m coûtant ou de revient; Acct **c. pricing** méthode f des coûts marginaux

▸ **cost out** VT SEP = **cost** VT **2**

Costa Brava [ˈkɒstəˈbrɑːvə] N Costa Brava f

Costa del Crime [ˈkɒstədelˈkraɪm] N Br Fam Hum = appellation f humoristique de la Costa del Sol, par allusion au grand nombre de criminels britanniques qui y résident

Costa del Sol [ˈkɒstədelsɒl] N Costa del Sol f

co-star [ˈkəʊstɑːr] Cin N partenaire mf à l'écran

VI partager la vedette (**with** avec)

VT **the film co-stars Tom Cruise and Nicole Kidman** le film met en scène Tom Cruise et Nicole Kidman dans les rôles principaux ou vedettes; **co-starring Gwyneth Paltrow** (in credits) avec Gwyneth Paltrow

Costa Rica [ˈkɒstəˈriːkə] N Costa Rica m

Costa Rican [ˈkɒstəˈriːkən] ADJ costaricien

N Costaricien, -ienne

cost-benefit analysis N Fin analyse f coûts-bénéfices

cost/benefit ratio N Fin rapport m coût/profit

cost-competitive ADJ (product) à prix compétitif; **we're not c.** nos prix ne sont pas compétitifs

cost-conscious ADJ qui fait attention aux dépenses; **to be c.** contrôler ses dépenses

cost-cutting N réduction f des frais ou des dépenses; **further c. may be necessary** d'autres compressions ou réductions des coûts pourraient s'avérer nécessaires

ADJ de réduction des frais ou des dépenses; **c. measures** mesures fpl visant à réduire les frais ou les dépenses

cost-effective ADJ rentable; **the project must be made c.** il faut rentabiliser le projet

cost-effectiveness N Com rentabilité f

coster(monger) [ˈkɒstər, ˈkɒstəmʌngər] N Br Old-fashioned marchand, -ande des quatre saisons

costing [ˈkɒstɪŋ] N Ind, Com (of article) établissement m du prix de revient; (of job) évaluation f du coût

costive [ˈkɒstɪv] ADJ Med constipé

costliness [ˈkɒstlɪnɪs] N cherté f; Fig **the c. of an error** les conséquences fpl d'une erreur

costly ['kɒstlɪ] ADJ cher, coûteux, onéreux; *Fig* **it was a c. mistake** c'est une erreur qui a coûté cher

cost-plus ADJ *Fin* à coût majoré
▸▸ **c. pricing** fixation *f* du prix en fonction du coût

cost-push inflation N inflation *f* par les coûts

cost-reduce VT *Com* réduire le coût de

costume ['kɒstjuːm] N **1** costume *m*; *Theat* **to be (dressed) in c.** porter un costume (de scène); **national c.** costume national; *Br* **(bathing** *or* **swimming) c.** maillot *m* de bain **2** *Old-fashioned (woman's suit)* tailleur *m*
▸▸ *Theat* **c. department, costumes department** service *m* des costumes; **c. designer** costumier, -ière; **c. drama** dramatique *f* en costumes d'époque; **c. jewellery** bijoux *mpl* fantaisie; **c. party** bal *m* costumé

costum(i)er [kɒ'stjuːm(ɪ)ər] N costumier, -ière

cosy, *Am* **cozy** ['kəʊzɪ] ADJ **1** *(room, pub)* confortable, douillet; **to feel** *or* **be c.** *(of person in room)* être confortablement *ou* douillettement installé; *(in coat, blankets etc)* être bien emmitouflé; **it's c. here** c'est confortable ici **2** *Fig* **a c. little job** *(undemanding)* un travail pépère; **a c. little arrangement** une bonne petite combine; **at university it's all very c.** à l'université, c'est pépère; **the c. relationship between government and the employers** les relations très privilégiées entre le gouvernement et le patronat; **it's all a bit too c. for my liking** *(of relationship between union and management etc)* c'est un peu trop copain-copain à mon goût
N *(egg)* **c.** couvre-œuf *m*, *pl* couvre-œufs; **(tea) c.** couvre-théière *m*, *pl* couvre-théières
▸ **cosy up to** VT INSEP *(ingratiate oneself with)* se mettre dans les petits papiers de

cot [kɒt] N *(for child)* lit *m* d'enfant; *esp Am (folding bed)* lit d'enfant pliant; *(camp bed)* lit de camp; *Naut* cadre *m* à l'anglaise
▸▸ *Br* **c. death** mort *f* subite du nourrisson

cotangent ['kəʊ'tændʒ(ə)nt] N *Math* cotangente *f*

cotel ['kɒtel] N *Am* auberge *f* de jeunesse

coterie ['kəʊtərɪ] N coterie *f*

co-trustee ['kəʊtrʌs'tiː] N *Law* co-administrateur, -trice

cottage ['kɒtɪdʒ] N **1** petite maison *f* (à la campagne), cottage *m*; *Am (for holidays)* petite maison de vacances, *Can* chalet *m*; **(thatched) c.** chaumière *f* **2** *Br Sl (for homosexuals)* = toilettes *fpl* publiques utilisées comme lieu de rencontre par les homosexuels
▸▸ **c. cheese** fromage *m* blanc (égoutté), cottage cheese *m*; *Br* **c. flat** = appartement *m* situé dans un pavillon; *Br* **c. hospital** petit hôpital *m* de campagne; **c. industry** industrie *f* artisanale; *(small-scale, at home)* industrie familiale; *Br* **c. loaf** = miche *f* de pain en forme de brioche; *Br* **c. pie** hachis *m* parmentier

cottager ['kɒtɪdʒər] N **1** *Br (in countryside)* = habitant, -ante d'un cottage **2** *Am (in holiday resort)* = propriétaire *mf*/locataire *mf* d'une maison de campagne

cottaging ['kɒtɪdʒɪŋ] N *Br Sl* = relations *fpl* homosexuelles dans les toilettes publiques

cotter ['kɒtər] N *Tech (wedge)* goupille *f*, *(pin)* clavette *f*
▸▸ **c. pin** clavette

cotton ['kɒt(ə)n] N **1** *(crop)* coton *m*; **to pick c.** cueillir le coton **2** *(cloth)* (toile *f* de) coton *m*; **is this dress c.?** *(made of cotton)* cette robe est-elle en coton?; **c. goods** cotonnades *fpl*; **put it with the rest of the cottons** *(garments made of cotton)* mets-le avec le reste du (linge en) coton **3** *(for sewing)* fil *m* à coudre

▸▸ *Geog* **C. Belt** = région *f* du coton dans le sud des États-Unis; *Br* **c. bud** coton-tige® *m*, *pl* cotons-tiges; *Bot* **c. bush** cotonnier *m*; *Am* **c. candy** barbe *f* à papa; **c. field** champ *m* de coton; **c. growing** culture *f* du coton; **c. grass** linaigrette *f*, lin *m* des marais; **c. mill** filature *f* de coton; **c. picker** *(person)* cueilleur, -euse de coton; **c. plant** cotonnier; **c. plantation** plantation *f* de coton; *Am* **c. swab** coton-tige®; *Br* **c. wool** coton hydrophile, ouate *f*, **c. yarn** coton filé, fil de coton
▸ **cotton on** VI *Fam (understand)* piger; **to c. on to sth** piger qch
▸ **cotton to** VT INSEP *Am Fam* **1** *(take a liking to)* se prendre d'amitié pour **2** *(approve of) (person)* avoir à la bonne; *(behaviour, suggestion)* voir d'un bon œil; **I don't c. to that kind of behaviour** je n'approuve pas ce genre de comportement

cotton-picking [-'pɪkɪŋ] ADJ *Am Fam (intensifier)* sacré; **that's a c. lie!** ce n'est qu'un mensonge!; **get your c. hands off me!** enlève tes sales pattes!

cottonseed ['kɒt(ə)nsiːd] N graine *f* de coton
▸▸ **c. oil** huile *f* de coton

cottontail ['kɒt(ə)nteɪl] N *Am* lapin *m* (de garenne)

cotyledon [kɒtɪ'liːd(ə)n] N *Bot* cotylédon *m*

couch [kaʊtʃ] N *(sofa)* canapé *m*, divan *m*, sofa *m*; *(in psychiatrist's office)* divan; *Fig* **to be on the c.** *(in psychoanalysis)* être en analyse
VT *(express) (phrase, comment)* formuler, rédiger; **the complaint was couched in very polite language** la plainte avait été formulée très poliment
▸▸ *Bot* **c. grass** chiendent *m*; *Fam* **c. potato** mollasson, -onne *(toujours affalé devant la télévision)*; **he's a real c. potato** il est toujours affalé devant la télé

couchette [kʊ'ʃet] N *Rail, Naut* couchette *f*
▸▸ *Rail* **c. car** voiture-couchette *f*, *pl* voitures-couchettes

cougar ['kuːɡər] N *(animal)* puma *m*

cough [kɒf] N toux *f*; **I've got a c.** je tousse; **he gave a c. to warn me** il toussota pour m'avertir; **he cleared his throat with a c.** il toussota pour s'éclaircir la voix *ou Fam* la gorge; **dry c.** toux sèche
VI *(of person, animal), Fam (engine)* tousser; *(to warn sb)* toussoter
▸▸ **c. drop** pastille *f* contre la toux *ou* antitussive; **c. lozenge** pastille contre la toux *ou* antitussive; **c. mixture** sirop *m* antitussif *ou* contre la toux; **c. sweet** pastille contre la toux *ou* antitussive; **c. syrup** sirop contre la toux *ou* antitussif
▸ **cough up** VT SEP **1** *(produce by coughing)* cracher (en toussant), expectorer; **to c. up phlegm/blood** cracher des glaires/du sang **2** *Fam (pay)* sortir; **I had to c. up £50 for the meal** j'ai dû sortir 50 livres pour le repas
VI *Fam (pay)* casquer, cracher, raquer; **come on, c. up!** *(money owed me)* allez! file-moi mon argent!; *(pay your share)* allez! allonge!

coughing ['kɒfɪŋ] N toux *f*, **fit of c., c. fit** quinte *f* de toux; **your c. woke me up** tu m'as réveillé en toussant

could PT *see* **can²**

couldn't-care-less ['kʊd(ə)ntkeə'les] ADJ **c. attitude** laisser-aller *m*, *Fam* je-m'enfichisme *m*, *Fam* je-m'en-foutisme *m*

coulomb ['kuːlɒm] N *Elec* coulomb *m*, ampère-seconde *m*

council ['kaʊnsəl] N **1** *(group of people)* conseil *m*; **the UN Security C.** le Conseil de sécurité des Nations unies
2 *Br Admin (elected local body) (people)* conseil *m*; *(government)* municipalité *f*, **the c. sent a repairman** la municipalité a envoyé

un réparateur; **to be on the c.** être au conseil municipal
3 *Rel* concile *m*
4 *(meeting)* conseil *m*; *Mil, Fig* **to hold a c. of war** tenir un conseil de guerre
▸▸ *Am Pol* **C. of Economic Advisers** = groupe *m* de conseillers nommés par le président des États-Unis pour formuler la politique économique du pays; **c. estate** cité *f*, **C. of Europe** Conseil de l'Europe; *Br* **c. flat** ≃ habitation *f* à loyer modéré, HLM *f*; *Br* **c. house** ≃ habitation à loyer modéré, HLM; **c. meeting** réunion *f* du conseil municipal; *EU* **C. of Ministers** Conseil des ministres; **c. offices** bureaux *mpl* de la municipalité

> Attention: ne pas confondre avec le nom **counsel.**

councillor, *Am* **councilor** ['kaʊnsɪlər] N conseiller, -ère, membre *m* du conseil; **C. John Smith** M. John Smith, membre du conseil

> Attention: ne pas confondre avec le nom **counsellor.**

councillorship, *Am* **councilorship** ['kaʊnsɪləʃɪp] N **1** *(rank)* dignité *f* de conseiller **2** *(period in office)* période *f* d'exercice des fonctions de conseiller; **during his c.** pendant la période où il a exercé en tant que conseiller

counsel ['kaʊns(ə)l] N **1** *Fml (advice)* conseil *m*, avis *m*; **to take c. with sb** consulter qn *(about,* au sujet de*)* **2 to keep one's (own) c.** *(about one's plans, intentions)* garder ses projets pour soi; *(about one's opinions)* garder son opinion pour soi **3** *(no pl) Br Law (in court)* avocat *m*; *(adviser)* conseil *m* juridique; **to be represented by c.** être représenté par un avocat; **to take the advice of c.** suivre les conseils d'un avocat; **c. for the defence** défenseur *m*; *(in criminal law)* avocat de la défense; **c. for the prosecution** procureur *m*; **King's/Queen's c.** conseiller *m* du Roi/de la Reine, conseiller de la Couronne
VT (-ll-, *Am* -l-) *(patience, prudence)* conseiller; **to c. sb to do sth** conseiller à qn de faire qch

> Attention: ne pas confondre avec le nom **council.**

counselling ['kaʊns(ə)lɪŋ] N *(activity, profession)* activité *f* de conseil; *(advice)* conseils *mpl*; **he needs (professional) c.** *(psychological)* il a besoin d'un soutien psychologique; **to offer c. for alcoholics/people suffering from AIDS** offrir un soutien psychologique et moral aux alcooliques/aux malades du SIDA

counsellor, *Am* **counselor** ['kaʊns(ə)lər] N **1** *(diplomatic)* conseiller, -ère d'ambassade **2** *(social, psychological)* conseiller, -ère **3** *Am Law* avocat, -ate

> Attention: ne pas confondre avec le nom **councillor.**

COUNT¹ [kaʊnt] N **1** *(act of counting)* compte *m*, comptage *m*; *(of votes)* dépouillement *m*; *(of people)* dénombrement *m*, comptage; **to keep c.** tenir le compte (**of** de); **to lose c.** perdre le compte; **I've lost c. of how many times I've asked you to ...** je t'ai demandé je ne sais combien de fois de ...; **we'll have to do another c.** il faudra qu'on recompte; **a quick c. revealed that half were car owners** un comptage rapide a révélé que la moitié étaient propriétaires de voitures; **at the last c.** au dernier comptage
2 *(total, result of count)* compte *m*, total *m*; **what was the c.?** quel était le total?; **this is**

short of the **c.** cela ne fait pas le compte

3 *Boxing* compte *m* (de dix secondes); **to take the c.** rester au tapis pour le compte, être knock-out; *Boxing, Fig* **to be out for the c.** être K.O.

4 *Law* chef *m* d'accusation; **not guilty on the first c.** non coupable au premier chef; *Fig* **I'm angry with them on both counts** je suis fâché avec eux pour les deux raisons; **to fail on a number of counts** *(of project etc)* échouer à plusieurs égards

VT 1 *(enumerate) (people, vehicles, animals etc)* dénombrer, compter; *(money)* compter; **to c. the votes** *(at election)* dépouiller le scrutin; **I counted three wrecked cars** j'ai compté trois voitures démolies; **to c. sheep** *(in order to go to sleep)* compter les moutons

2 *(include)* compter; **there were four of us, counting the dog** nous étions quatre en comptant le chien; **without** *or* **not counting …** sans compter …

3 *(consider)* compter (**as** comme); **I don't c. him as a friend** je ne le considère pas comme un ami; **to c. sb among one's friends** compter qn parmi ses amis; **to be counted as a member** compter parmi les membres; **I c. it (as) one of my triumphs** je considère cela comme un de mes triomphes; **c. yourself lucky you weren't killed** estime-toi heureux de n'avoir pas été tué

VI 1 compter; **to c. on one's fingers** compter sur ses doigts; **to c. (up) to 100** compter jusqu'à 100; **to c. from 1 to 100** compter de 1 à 100; **counting from tomorrow** à compter de demain

2 *(be considered)* compter (**among** parmi); **he counts among my best friends** il compte parmi mes meilleurs amis; **two children c. as one adult** deux enfants comptent pour un adulte; **he's under five so he doesn't c.** il a moins de cinq ans, donc il ne compte pas; **marks in this exam c. towards your degree** les notes de cet examen comptent pour votre licence

3 *(be of importance)* compter; **I don't c. around here** je ne compte pas ici; **every vote counts** chaque voix compte; **every minute counts** il n'y a pas une minute à perdre; **experience counts for more than qualifications** l'expérience compte plus que les diplômes; **doesn't that c. for anything?** est-ce que ça ne compte pas, ça?

▸▸ *Gram* **c. noun** nom *m* comptable

▸ **count against VT INSEP** jouer contre

▸ **count down VI** *(for rocket launch)*, *Fig* faire le compte à rebours

▸ **count in VT SEP** *(include)* compter; **c. me in!** je suis de la partie, *Fam* je suis partant

▸ **count on VT INSEP 1** *(depend on)* compter sur; **we're counting on you to give a speech** nous comptons sur vous pour faire un discours; **you can always c. on him to be late** tu peux compter sur lui pour être en retard, tu peux être sûr qu'il sera en retard; **I wouldn't c. on the train arriving on time** je ne compterais pas sur le fait que le train soit à l'heure; **can we c. on your vote?** pouvons-nous compter sur votre voix?

2 *(expect)* compter; **I didn't c. on seeing you** je ne comptais pas te voir

▸ **count out VT SEP 1** *(add up) (money)* compter; **he counted me out twenty £1 coins** il m'a compté vingt pièces d'une livre

2 *(exclude)* ne pas compter; **he's teetotal, so you can c. him out** il ne boit pas, donc ne le compte pas; **no thanks, c. me out!** non merci, ne comptez pas sur moi

3 *Boxing* **to be counted out** rester au tapis pour le compte, être (mis) knock-out

▸ **count up VT SEP** *(add up)* compter

count² N *(nobleman)* comte *m*

countable ['kaʊntəb(ə)l] *Gram* **ADJ** *(noun)* dénombrable, comptable ▐VOIR GRAMMAIRE A9–12▌

▸▸ **c. noun** nom *m* dénombrable *ou* comptable

countdown ['kaʊntdaʊn] N *(for rocket launch)* compte *m* à rebours; *Fig* **the c. to Christmas has begun** on commence à compter les jours qui nous séparent de Noël

countenance ['kaʊntɪnəns] N *esp Lit* **1** *(face)* (expression *f* du) visage *m*, mine *f*; **to lose c.** se décontenancer, perdre contenance; **to be out of c.** avoir perdu contenance, être décontenancé **2** *(support)* **to give** *or* **lend c. to sb/sth** apporter son appui *ou* son soutien à qn/qch, appuyer qn/qch

VT approuver, appuyer; **she wouldn't c. borrowing money** elle n'approuverait pas le fait d'emprunter de l'argent

counter¹ ['kaʊntər] N **1** *(in shop)* comptoir *m*; *(in supermarket)* rayon *m*; *(in bank etc)* guichet *m*; **payable over the c.** payable au guichet; **you can get these drugs over the c.** on peut acheter ces médicaments sans ordonnance, ces médicaments sont en vente libre; *Fin* **to buy shares over the c.** acheter des actions sur le marché hors cote; **sold over the c.** *(not pre-packaged)* vendu au détail; **to sell under the c.** vendre sous le manteau

2 *(token in games) (square)* fiche *f*, *(round)* jeton *m*; **the hostage was being used as a bargaining c.** l'otage a été utilisé comme monnaie d'échange

3 *Comput etc (device)* compteur *m*

▸▸ *Br* **c. hand** vendeur, -euse; *Banking* **c. services** services *mpl* de caisse; *Banking* **c. staff** employés, -ées du guichet, guichetiers, -ières; *Banking* **c. transactions** opérations *fpl* de caisse

counter² N *Fencing, Boxing* contre *m*

ADJ 1 *(contrary)* contraire, opposé (**to** à) **2** *(in compounds)* contre-

ADV en sens inverse; **to act c. to one's orders** agir contrairement aux ordres (que l'on a) reçus; **to run c. to sth** aller à l'encontre de qch

VT *(person, thing)* aller à l'encontre de; *(sb's intentions)* contrecarrer; *(accusation, criticism)* répondre à; **measures have been taken to c. the threat of the disease** des mesures ont été prises pour lutter contre la menace que représente la maladie; *Boxing* **to c. a blow** contrer un coup; *(ward off)* parer un coup; **to c. that …** riposter *ou* rétorquer que … + *ind*

VI riposter, contre-attaquer; *Boxing, Fencing* contrer; *(ward off)* parer

▸▸ **c. declaration** contre-déclaration *f*, *pl* contre-déclarations; *Med* **c. indication** contre-indication *f*, *pl* contre-indications; **c. reaction** contre-réaction *f*, *pl* contre-réactions

counteract [kaʊntə'rækt] **VT** *(act against)* contrecarrer; *(neutralize) (influence, effects of drug)* neutraliser

counter-appraisal N *Am Com* contre-expertise *f*, *pl* contre-expertises

counterattack ['kaʊntərətæk] *Mil, Fig* N contre-attaque *f*, *pl* contre-attaques
VT & VI contre-attaquer

counterattraction ['kaʊntərə'trækʃən] N attraction *f* concurrente; *(on TV)* émission *f* concurrente

counterbalance¹ ['kaʊntəbæləns] N contrepoids *m*

counterbalance² [kaʊntə'bæləns] **VT** contrebalancer, faire contrepoids à

counterbid ['kaʊntəbɪd] N *Fin* suroffre *f*, surenchère *f*; *(during takeover)* contre-OPA *f inv*

counterblast ['kaʊntəblɑːst] N contre-attaque *f*, *pl* contre-attaques

countercharge ['kaʊntətʃɑːdʒ] N *Law*

contre-accusation *f*, *pl* contre-accusations, contre-plainte *f*, *pl* contre-plaintes

countercheck ['kaʊntətʃek] **VT** vérifier (une seconde fois)

counterclaim ['kaʊntəkleɪm] N demande *f* reconventionnelle
VI *Law* faire une demande reconventionnelle *(en dommages-intérêts)*

counterclockwise [kaʊntə'klɒkwaɪz] **ADV, ADJ** *esp Am* en sens inverse des aiguilles d'une montre

counterculture ['kaʊntəkʌltʃər] N contre-culture *f*, *pl* contre-cultures

counterespionage [kaʊntər'espɪənɑːʒ] N contre-espionnage *m*

counterfeit ['kaʊntəfɪt] **ADJ** *(banknote, document)* faux; *(piece of jewellery)* contrefait; *Fig (emotions)* feint
N *(banknote, document)* contrefaçon *f*, faux *m*; *(piece of jewellery)* faux
VT *(banknote, document, piece of jewellery)* contrefaire; *Fig (emotions)* feindre

counterfeiter ['kaʊntəfɪtər] N faussaire *mf*; *(of money)* faux-monnayeur *m*, *pl* faux-monnayeurs

counterfoil ['kaʊntəfɔɪl] N *Br (of cheque, receipt)* souche *f*, talon *m*
▸▸ **c. book** carnet *m* à souches

counter-guarantee N *St Exch* contre-garantie *f*, *pl* contre-garanties

counterinsurgency ['kaʊntərɪn'sɜːdʒənsɪ] N contre-insurrection *f*, *pl* contre-insurrections

counterintelligence ['kaʊntərɪn'telɪdʒəns] N contre-espionnage *m*

counterintuitive ['kaʊntərɪn'tjuːɪtɪv] **ADJ** qui va contre l'intuition

countermand ['kaʊntə'mɑːnd] **VT** *(order)* annuler

countermarketing ['kaʊntəmɑːkətɪŋ] N contremarketing *m*, contremercatique *f*

countermeasure ['kaʊntəmeʒər] N contre-mesure *f*, *pl* contre-mesures

countermove ['kaʊntəmuːv] N contre *m*

counteroffensive ['kaʊntərə'fensɪv] N *Mil* contre-offensive *f*, *pl* contre-offensives

counter-offer N contre-offre *f*, *pl* contre-offres

counterorder ['kaʊntərɔːdər] N contrordre *m*

counterpane ['kaʊntəpeɪn] N couvre-lit *m*, *pl* couvre-lits; *(quilted)* courtepointe *f*

counterpart ['kaʊntəpɑːt] N **1** *(person)* homologue *mf* **2** *(corresponding system)* équivalent *m*; *(of pair of works of art)* pendant *m*; *(piece that corresponds)* pièce *f* qui va de pair

counterparty risk ['kaʊntəpɑːtɪ] N *Banking* risque *m* de contrepartie

counterplot ['kaʊntəplɒt] N contre-ruse *f*, *pl* contre-ruses

counterpoint ['kaʊntəpɔɪnt] N *Mus* contre-point *m*

counterpoise ['kaʊntəpɔɪz] N *also Fig* contrepoids *m*; **in c.** en équilibre; **his sense of organization served as a c. to …** son sens de l'organisation contrebalançait …
VT contrebalancer, faire contrepoids à

counterproductive ['kaʊntəprə'dʌktɪv] **ADJ** qui a des effets contraires; **that would be c.** cela irait à l'encontre du but recherché

counterproposal ['kaʊntəprə'pəʊz(ə)l] N contre-proposition *f*, *pl* contre-propositions

counterpurchase ['kaʊntəpɜːtʃɪs] N contre-achat *m*, *pl* contre-achats

Counter-Reformation N *Rel, Hist* **the C.** la Contre-Réforme

counter-revolution N *Pol* contre-révolution *f*, *pl* contre-révolutions

counter-revolutionary *Pol* N contre-révolutionnaire *mf, pl* contre-révolutionnaires
ADJ contre-révolutionnaire

countersegmentation ['kaʊntəsegmen-'teɪʃən] N *Mktg* contre-segmentation *f*, stratégie *f* d'indifférenciation

countershaft ['kaʊntəʃɑ:ft] N *Aut (layshaft)* arbre *m* intermédiaire

countersign ['kaʊntəsaɪn] VT *(order etc)* contresigner, signer en second, viser

countersignature ['kaʊntə'sɪgnətʃər] N contreseing *m*

countersink ['kaʊntəsɪŋk] N **1** *(tool)* fraise *f* **2** *(for head of screw)* noyure *f*, *(of hole)* fraisure *f*
VT *(pt, pp* **countersunk**) *(head of screw)* noyer; *(hole)* fraiser
▸▸ **c. bit** *(tool)* fraise

counterstroke ['kaʊntəstrəʊk] N *Mil, Fig* contre-offensive *f, pl* contre-offensives

countersunk ['kaʊntəsʌnk] ADJ *(screw)* fraisé, noyé

countertenor ['kaʊntətenər] N *Mus (person)* haute-contre *m, pl* hautes-contre, contre-ténor *m, pl* contre-ténors

counterterrorism ['kaʊntə'terərɪz(ə)m] N contre-terrorisme *m*

counterterrorist ['kaʊntə'terərɪst] ADJ contre-terroriste

countertop ['kaʊntətɒp] N *Am* plan *m* de travail

countertrade ['kaʊntətreɪd] N commerce *m* d'échange, troc *m*

countertrading [kaʊntə'treɪdɪŋ] N troc *m*

countervailing [kaʊntə'veɪlɪŋ] ADJ ATTRIB *Fml* compensatoire
▸▸ *Econ* **c. duty** droit *m* compensateur

countervaluation ['kaʊntəvælju'eɪʃən] N contre-expertise *f, pl* contre-expertises

counterweight ['kaʊntəweɪt] N contrepoids *m*

countess ['kaʊntɪs] N comtesse *f*

counting ['kaʊntɪŋ] N compte *m*; *(of vote)* dépouillement *m*; *(of people)* compte, dénombrement *m*

countless ['kaʊntlɪs] ADJ innombrable, sans nombre

countrified ['kʌntrɪfaɪd] ADJ aux allures campagnardes; **it's very c. here** c'est comme à la campagne ici

country ['kʌntrɪ] N **1** *(political entity)* pays *m*; **in this c.** dans ce pays; **the Prime Minister isn't in the c.** le premier ministre est à l'étranger; **to die for/love one's c.** mourir pour/aimer sa patrie; *esp Br Pol* **to go to the c.** *(call election)* se présenter aux suffrages des électeurs; **c. of destination** pays de destination VOIR GRAMMAIRE A12
2 *(opposed to town)* campagne *f*; **in the c.** à la campagne
3 *(opposed to capital)* province *f*; **a quiet little c. town** une petite ville tranquille de province
4 *(region)* pays *m*, région *f*; **rough c.** terrain *m* accidenté; **open c.** rase campagne *f*; **flat c.** pays *ou* terrain plat; **wheat-growing c.** région à blé; **this is Proust c.** c'est le pays de Proust
▸▸ *Fam Pej* **c. bumpkin** péquenaud, -aude, plouc *mf*; **c. club** = club *m* sportif ou de loisirs situé à la campagne; **the c. code** = code *m* de conduite à respecter lorsqu'on se promène dans la campagne, qu'on y pique-nique etc; *Pej* **c. cousin** cousin, -ine de province; **c. dancing** danse *f* folklorique; **c. gentleman** gentilhomme *m* campagnard; **c. house** = grande maison *f* de campagne, souvent historique; **c. inn** auberge *f* rurale *ou* de campagne; *Comput* **c. keyboard** cla-vier *m* national; **c. life** vie *f* à la campagne; *Br* **c. park** parc *m* naturel; **c. seat** *(of noble family)* manoir *m*; *Mktg* **c. version** *(of a product)* version *f* nationale; *Mus* **c. and western** country *m* ou *f inv*

countryfolk ['kʌntrɪfəʊk] NPL gens *mpl* de la campagne

countryman, *pl* **countrymen** ['kʌntrɪmən] N **1** *(not living in town)* campagnard *m* **2** *(compatriot)* compatriote *m*

countryside ['kʌntrɪsaɪd] N campagne *f*; **beautiful c.** beau paysage *m*; **there's some beautiful c. around Bath** il y a de beaux paysages autour de Bath; **the voters in the c.** les électeurs des régions rurales

country-specific ADJ *Comput (keyboard)* particulier à un pays

country-style ADJ **c. cooking** cuisine *f* campagnarde

countrywoman, *pl* **countrywomen** ['kʌntrɪwʊmən, -wɪmɪn] N **1** *(not living in town)* campagnarde *f* **2** *(compatriot)* compatriote *f*

county ['kaʊntɪ] N **1** *(political entity)* comté *m*; *Br* **the c. of Kent** le comté du Kent; *Am* **New York C.** le comté de New York **2** *(population)* habitants *mpl* du comté
ADJ *(rural upper class)* **the c. set** la noblesse campagnarde; **she's very c.** elle fait très femme de la noblesse campagnarde
▸▸ *Br* **c. council** ≃ conseil *m* général; *Br* **c. councillor** ≃ conseiller, -ère général(e); *Br* **c. cricket** = grands matches *mpl* de cricket disputés par les équipes du comté; *Am* **c. line** frontière *f* délimitant un/le comté; *Br* **c. society** l'aristocratie *f* et la haute bourgeoisie du comté; **c. town** *(in England)* chef-lieu *m* de comté, *pl* chefs-lieux de comté

coup [ku:] N **1** coup *m* (audacieux); **to bring off a c.** réussir un joli coup **2** *(overthrow of government)* coup *m* d'État
▸▸ **c. d'état** coup d'État

coupé ['ku:peɪ] N *Aut* coupé *m*

couple ['kʌp(ə)l] N **1 a c.** *(a few)* quelques-uns, *f* quelques-unes; *(two)* deux; **a c. of** *(a few)* quelques; *(two)* deux; **a c. of seconds** deux secondes; *Fam* **to have a c.** *(of drinks)* prendre un verre ou deux **2** *(two people, dancers)* couple *m*; **the married c.** les (deux) époux *mpl*; **the newly married c.** les nouveaux *ou* jeunes mariés *mpl*; **they make a lovely c.** ils font un beau couple; **a married c.** un couple marié
VT **1** *(bring together) (oxen)* (ac)coupler; *(male and female)* accoupler; *(names, ideas etc)* associer; **common sense coupled with intelligence** le bon sens allié à l'intelligence; **the course couples theory with practical work** le cours allie la théorie à la pratique **2** *(two engines, batteries)* accoupler; *Rail* **to c. (up) a carriage** atteler *ou* accrocher un wagon
VI *(of male and female)* s'accoupler

coupler ['kʌplər] N *Comput* coupleur *m*

couplet ['kʌplɪt] N *Liter* distique *m*; **rhyming couplets** distiques qui riment

coupling ['kʌp(ə)lɪŋ] N **1** *(bringing together)* accouplement *m*; *(of ideas, names)* association *f* **2** *Rail (of carriages)* attelage *m*; *(of batteries)* couplage *m* **3** *(static device)* raccord *m*, joint *m*; *Rail* attelage *m*; *(device for transmitting motion)* accouplement *m*, embrayage *m* **4** *(mating)* accouplement *m*
▸▸ *Aut* **c. bar** barre *f* d'accouplement

coupon ['ku:pɒn] N *(to be filled in)* coupon *m*; *(exchangeable voucher)* bon *m*; *Fin (on bearer bond)* coupon; *Br Admin* **petrol c.** bon *m* d'essence; *Br Sport* **football** *ou* **pools c.** = formulaire *m* de concours de pronostics de football
▸▸ *Fin* **c. bond** obligation *f* au porteur; *Com* **c. offer** offre *f* de bon de réduction; *Fin* **c. yield** rendement *m* coupon

couponing ['ku:pənɪŋ] N *Mktg* couponing *m*, couponnage *m*

courage ['kʌrɪdʒ] N courage *m*; **to have the c. to do sth** avoir le courage de faire qch; **to take one's c. in both hands** prendre son courage à deux mains; **to restore sb's c.** redonner du courage à qn

courageous [kə'reɪdʒəs] ADJ courageux

courageously [kə'reɪdʒəslɪ] ADV courageusement, avec courage

courgette [kʊə'ʒet] N *Br* courgette *f*

courier ['kʊrɪər] N **1** *(messenger)* messager *m*; *Com* coursier *m*; **to send sth/arrive by c.** envoyer qch/arriver par coursier; **(motorcycle) c.** messager/coursier en moto; **she was a c. for drug dealers** elle transportait de la drogue pour le compte de trafiquants **2** *(in tourism)* accompagnateur, -trice

COURSE [kɔ:s]

ⓝ cours **1, 5** ▪ bien sûr *(of course)* **2**
▪ route **3** ▪ ligne de conduite **4**
▪ plat **7** ▪ terrain **8**

N **1** *(process) (of river, time, business, events etc)* cours *m*; *(of illness)* évolution *f*; **in the c. of conversation/the evening** au cours de la conversation/de la soirée; **in the c. of time** *(gradually)* à la longue; *(eventually)* finalement; **the building is in the c. of completion** le bâtiment est en cours d'achèvement; **to be in the c. of doing sth** être en train de faire qch; **in the ordinary** *or* **normal c. of things** *or* **events** normalement; **in due c.** en temps utile; **to let nature take its c.** laisser la nature faire les choses; **let things take** *or* **run their c.** laisser les choses suivre *ou* se faire leur cours; **it's best to let the fever run its c.** il vaut mieux laisser la fièvre évoluer normalement; **that is a matter of c.** cela va sans dire; **as a matter of c.** tout naturellement, automatiquement; **blood tests are carried out as a matter of c.** des examens sanguins sont effectués automatiquement
2 *of c.* bien sûr, bien entendu, naturellement; **of c. not!** bien sûr que non!; **of c. she was angry!** bien sûr qu'elle était fâchée!; **he forgot, of c.** bien entendu, il a
3 *(route)* route *f*, direction *f*; **to keep one's c.** ne pas dévier de sa route; *Naut* maintenir son cap; **to change (one's) c.** changer de direction; *Naut* changer le cap; *Naut, Fig* **to be on c.** suivre le cap fixé; **to be driven off c.** *(of ship)* être dévié de son cap, dévier de son cap
4 c. *(of action)* ligne *f* de conduite; **to take a c. of action** adopter une ligne de conduite; **it is the only c. open to me** c'est la seule chose que je puisse faire; **there is no other c. open to us** nous n'avons pas d'autre solution; **the best c. would be to ...** la meilleure chose à faire *ou* le mieux serait de ...; **his best c. would be to ...** le mieux pour lui serait de ...; **the right c.** la bonne voie
5 *Sch, Univ* cours *m*; **to give a c. of lectures** donner une série de cours; **to take** *or* **follow** *or* **do a c. (in sth)** suivre un cours (de qch); **a degree c.** un cours de licence; **he has published a French c.** il a publié une méthode de français
6 *Med* **c. (of treatment)** traitement *m*; **a c. of injections** une série de piqûres
7 *(of meal)* plat *m*; **first c.** entrée *f*; **four-c. dinner** dîner *m* de quatre plats
8 *Sport etc (for races)* parcours *m*; *(for motor-racing)* circuit *m*; **(golf) c.** terrain *m* de golf, golf *m*; **to finish the c.** finir la course; *Fig* finir
9 *Constr (of bricks)* assise *f*
VI **1** *(of liquids)* ruisseler; **the blood coursed**

through her veins le sang courait dans ses veines; **tears were coursing down my face** j'avais le visage ruisselant de larmes
2 *(in hunting)* courir le lièvre
VT *(hare)* courir

courseware ['kɔ:sweər] **N** *Comput* didacticiel *m*

coursing ['kɔ:sɪŋ] **N 1** *(hunting)* chasse *f* à courre au lièvre **2** *(racing hounds)* = concours *m* de vitesse entre lévriers lâchés sur un lièvre en champ clos

court [kɔ:t] **N 1** *Law* cour *f*, tribunal *m*; *(courtroom)* auditoire *m* de tribunal; **civil/criminal c.** tribunal civil/criminel; *Br* **county c.** tribunal de grande instance; **International C. of Justice** Cour internationale de justice; **to go to c.** aller en justice; **to take sb to c.** faire un procès à qn; **are you prepared to say that in c.?** est-ce que vous seriez prêt à le jurer devant le tribunal?; **in open c.** en plein tribunal; **case before the c.** affaire *f* en cause; **to come before the c.** *(of person)* comparaître devant le tribunal; *(of case)* être jugé; **to settle a case out of c.** arranger une affaire à l'amiable; **we've decided to settle out of c.** nous avons décidé d'arranger ça à l'amiable; **tell the c. what you saw** veuillez dire à la cour ce que vous avez vu; **sale by order of the c.** vente *f* judiciaire; **this is a matter for the courts, not the government** c'est à la justice d'en décider, pas au gouvernement
VOIR GRAMMAIRE A6–7
2 *(for tennis, squash etc)* court *m*; **tennis c.** court (de tennis), tennis *m*; **grass c.** court sur gazon; **hard c.** court en dur; **he was on c. for three hours** il a été sur le court pendant trois heures
3 *(royal etc)* cour *f*; **to pay c. to the king** faire sa cour au roi; **to hold c.** *(of celebrity etc)* s'entretenir avec toute une cour d'admirateurs
4 *(courtyard)* cour *f*; *(in names of blocks of flats)* ≃ résidence *f*; *(in names of palaces)* château *m*, palais *m*
5 *Old-fashioned* **to pay c. to a woman** faire la cour à une femme
VT 1 *(seek)* *(sb's friendship)* (re)chercher, solliciter; *(sb's favour)* briguer; *(failure)* aller au-devant de; *(death)* braver; **to c. popularity** chercher à se faire bien voir (**with** auprès de); **to c. disaster** aller à la catastrophe; **to c. the electorate** chercher à gagner les voix des électeurs
2 *Old-fashioned (seek in marriage) (woman)* courtiser, faire la cour à; **they had been courting one another for nearly a year** ils se fréquentaient depuis presque un an
VI *Old-fashioned* **to be courting** *(of individual)* fréquenter; *(of couple)* se fréquenter; **courting couple** couple *m* d'amoureux
▸▸ *Law* **C. of Appeal** cour d'appel; *Law* **c. appearance** *(of accused)* comparution *f* en justice; *EU* **C. of Auditors** Cour des comptes européenne; *Br Cards* **c. card** figure *f*; *Law* **c. case** procès *m*, affaire *f*; *Br Journ* **c. circular** rubrique *f* d'un journal indiquant les engagements officiels de la famille royale; *Journ* **c. correspondent** correspondant, -ante à la cour royale; *Law* **c. of first instance** juridiction *f* de première instance; *Br* **c. of inquiry** *(body of people)* commission *f* d'enquête; *(investigation)* enquête *f*; **c. of law** tribunal *m*; *Mil* **c. martial** cour martiale; *Law* **c. reporter** chroniqueur, -euse judiciaire; *Law* **c. ruling** décision *f* de justice; *Br* **c. shoe** escarpin *m*; *Am* **c. tennis** jeu *m* de paume

courteous ['kɜ:tɪəs] **ADJ** courtois, poli (**to, towards** envers)

courteously ['kɜ:tɪəslɪ] **ADV** courtoisement, poliment

courtesan [kɔ:tɪ'zæn] **N** courtisane *f*

courtesy ['kɜ:təsɪ] **N** courtoisie *f*, politesse *f*; **common c.** la politesse la plus élémen-

taire; **he didn't have the c. to reply to my letter** il n'a pas eu la politesse de répondre à ma lettre; **by c. of …** avec la gracieuse permission de …; **exchange of courtesies** échange *m* de politesses
▸▸ **c. bus** navette *f* gratuite; **c. call** visite *f* de politesse; **to pay sb a c. call** faire une visite de politesse à qn; **c. car** *(from hotel)* voiture *f* de courtoisie; *(from garage)* voiture de remplacement; *Aut* **c. light** plafonnier *m*, éclairage *m* intérieur; *Aut* **c. mirror** miroir *m* de courtoisie; *Br* **c. title** titre *m* de courtoisie

courthouse ['kɔ:thaʊs] **N** *esp Am* palais *m* de justice, tribunal *m*

courtier ['kɔ:tɪər] **N** courtisan *m*

courtly ['kɔ:tlɪ] **ADJ** *(polite)* courtois, d'une politesse raffinée
▸▸ *Hist* **c. love** amour *m* courtois

court-martial **VT** (-**ll**-, *Am* -**l**-) *(soldier)* faire passer en cour martiale; **to be court-martialled** passer en cour martiale

court-ordered **ADJ** *(sale)* judiciaire

courtroom ['kɔ:tru:m] **N** *Law* salle *f* d'audience; *(people)* auditoire *m* d'un/du tribunal; **his c. performances** ses performances *fpl* devant la cour
▸▸ *Cin, TV* **c. drama** drame *m* judiciaire

courtship ['kɔ:tʃɪp] **N** *(of woman)* cour *f*; **during their c.** à l'époque où il lui faisait la cour
▸▸ *Zool* **c. display** parade *f* nuptiale

courtyard ['kɔ:tjɑ:d] **N** *(of house etc)* cour *f*

couscous ['ku:sku:s] **N** couscous *m*

co-user ['kəʊju:zər] **N** *Comput* co-utilisateur *m*

cousin ['kʌz(ə)n] **N** cousin, -ine; **first c., full c.** cousin, -ine germain(e); **second c.** cousin, -ine issu(e) de germains; *Fig* **our American cousins** nos cousins américains; **a distant c. of the sparrow** un cousin éloigné du moineau

couth [ku:θ] **ADJ** *Br Hum* **he's not very c.** il n'est pas très raffiné

couture [ku:'tʊər] **N** couture *f*; **haute c.** haute couture

couturier, *f* **couturière** [ku:'tjʊərɪeɪ, -ɪeər] **N** *(grand)* couturier *m*, (grande) couturière *f*; *(head of company)* directeur, -trice d'une maison de haute couture

covalent [kəʊ'veɪlənt] **ADJ** *Chem* covalent

cove[1] [kəʊv] **N** *Geog* anse *f*, crique *f*

cove[2] **N** *Old-fashioned Br Fam (fellow)* type *m*; **a queer c.** un drôle de pistolet

coven ['kʌv(ə)n] **N** bande *f* ou réunion *f* de sorcières

covenant ['kʌvənənt] **N 1** *Law* convention *f*, contrat *m* **2** *Pol* pacte *m*, traité *m* **3** *Bible (of Jews)* alliance *f*
VT *Law* promettre par contrat; **to c. to do sth** convenir de faire qch; **to c. a sum of money** s'engager par contrat à payer une somme d'argent
VI *Law* **to c. with sb for sth** convenir (par contrat) de qch avec qn

Coventry ['kɒvəntrɪ] **N** *Br Fam* **to send sb to C.** mettre qn en quarantaine

COVER ['kʌvər]

N	couvercle **1**	▪ couvre-lit **2**
	▪ couverture **3, 8, 9**	▪ abri **5, 6**
VT	couvrir **1-10**	▪ recouvrir **2**
	▪ parcourir **6**	▪ marquer **12**

N 1 *(lid) (for pot etc)* couvercle *m*
2 *(soft covering) (bedspread)* couvre-lit *m*, *pl* couvre-lits; *(for umbrella)* fourreau *m*; *(for car, boat, furniture, computer)* housse *f*; **covers** *(on bed)* couvertures *fpl*; *Met* **cloud c.** couverture nuageuse
3 *(of book, magazine)* couverture *f*, *(in*

bookbinding) plats *mpl*; **to read a book from c. to c.** lire un livre d'un bout à l'autre; **(front) c.** couverture; **hard/soft covers** couverture rigide/souple
4 *(envelope)* **under plain/separate c.** sous pli ordinaire/séparé
5 *(shelter from weather)* abri *m*; **to take c.** *(from the rain etc)* se mettre à l'abri; **the rocks gave us some c.** les rochers nous ont fourni un abri; **to be under c.** être à couvert *ou* à l'abri
6 *Mil etc (from gunfire etc)* couvert *m*, abri *m*; *(firing)* tir *m* de couverture *ou* de protection; **under c.** à couvert, à l'abri; **to take c.** se mettre à couvert, s'abriter; **to give sb c.** *(of aircraft, artillery etc)* couvrir qn; **the rocks provided c. for snipers** les rochers ont fourni des abris pour les tireurs isolés; **without c.** à découvert; **air/radar c.** couverture *f* aérienne/radar
7 *(in hunting)* couvert *m*, fourré *m*, gîte *m*, *Old-fashioned* remise *f*; **to take c.** se remiser; **to break c.** *(of game)* débusquer; *Fig (of person)* sortir de sa retraite
8 *(something that conceals)* voile *m*, masque *m*; *(for spy, police officer etc)* couverture *f*; **under the c. of** *(friendship etc)* sous le couvert *ou* le masque de; **under (the) c. of darkness** à la faveur de la nuit; **to go under c.** *(of police officer etc)* adopter une identité d'emprunt *(pour les besoins d'une enquête)*; **to blow sb's c.** *(in espionage, undercover police work)* démasquer qn
9 *(in insurance)* couverture *f*, provision *f*; **with c.** avec couverture; **without c.** à découvert; **full c.** garantie *f* totale
10 *(in restaurant)* couvert *m*
VT 1 *(person, object)* couvrir (**with, in** de); **covered in** *or* **with snow** couvert de neige *ou* par la neige; **to c. one's head** se couvrir (la tête); **to c. one's ears** *(so as not to hear)* se boucher les oreilles; **writing covered the page** la page était couverte d'écriture; **the scarf covered her mouth** l'écharpe lui couvrait la bouche; **to be well covered** *(warmly dressed)* être bien couvert; *Fam (plump, fat)* être bien en chair; **to c. oneself with glory** se couvrir de gloire; **to c. sb with ridicule** couvrir qn de ridicule; **covered with shame** couvert de honte
2 *(in order to protect)* recouvrir (**with** de); *(in bookbinding) (book)* couvrir; **a wire covered with plastic** un fil électrique recouvert de plastique
3 *(hide) (one's anxiety, confusion etc)* couvrir, dissimuler; **to c. one's tracks** brouiller les pistes
4 *Mil etc (protect)* protéger; *(person)* couvrir; **I've got you covered** *(I have a gun aimed at you)* j'ai mon fusil/revolver braqué sur toi
5 *(deal with, take into account)* couvrir; **the course covers the first half of the century** le cours couvre la première moitié du siècle; **to c. all eventualites** parer à toute éventualité; **that's not covered** ce n'est pas traité; **it's covered in some detail** c'est traité en détail
6 *(travel) (a distance)* couvrir, parcourir; **we covered 100 kilometres before breakfast** nous avons fait cent kilomètres avant le petit déjeuner; **to c. a lot of ground** *(travel great distance)* faire beaucoup de chemin; *(search etc over a wide area)* parcourir un champ très vaste; *Fig (of book, author etc)* couvrir de nombreux domaines; *(of meeting etc)* traiter bien des problèmes
7 *(in insurance) (risk)* couvrir; *Fin* **to be covered** *(of creditor)* être couvert; **we're not covered for** *or* **against theft** nous ne sommes pas couverts contre le vol; **to c. oneself** se couvrir *(against a risk* d'un risque)*; *Fig* **the president covered himself by saying that …** le président s'est couvert en disant que …
8 *(of money) (expenses, cost etc)* couvrir;

£100 won't c. the cost of a new carpet 100 livres ne couvriront pas le coût d'une moquette neuve; **to c. a deficit** combler un déficit; *Acct* **to c. a loss** couvrir un déficit; **to c. an overdraft** couvrir un découvert; **will that c. it?** est-ce que ça suffira?
9 *Journ, TV, Radio (sports event etc)* couvrir
10 *(in breeding) (female)* couvrir, saillir
11 *Mus* **to c. a song** faire une reprise d'une chanson
12 *Sport (mark) (player)* marquer
▸ VI **paint that covers well** peinture qui couvre bien *ou* bien couvrante
▸▸ **c. charge** *(in restaurant)* couvert *m*; *Am (in bar)* entrée *f*, prix *m* d'entrée; **c. clause** clause *f* de garantie; **c. girl** cover-girl *f*, *pl* cover-girls; *Am* **c. letter** *(for job application)* lettre *f* de motivation; *(sent with invoice etc)* lettre d'accompagnement; **c. mount** = cadeau *m* offert avec un magazine; *Br* **c. note** *(in insurance)* attestation *f* provisoire; **c. page** *(of fax)* page *f* de garde; **c. price** *(of magazine)* prix *m*; **c. sheet** *(of fax)* page de garde; *Journ* **c. story** article *m* principal (faisant la couverture); *Mus* **c. version** reprise *f*
▸ **cover for** VT INSEP *(replace)* remplacer; *(provide excuses for)* couvrir; **I refuse to c. for you with the boss** je refuse de te couvrir auprès du patron
▸ **cover in** VT SEP *(fill in) (trench)* remplir
▸ **cover up** VT SEP **1** *(conceal)* recouvrir; *(truth, illegal act)* dissimuler
2 *(with blanket etc)* couvrir, recouvrir; **keep the baby covered up** garde le bébé bien couvert; **they covered up the bodies** ils ont recouvert les corps; **that dress is a bit too low – c. yourself up a bit** cette robe est trop décolletée – couvre-toi un peu
▸ VI *(conceal the truth)* cacher la vérité; **the government has been accused of covering up** on a accusé le gouvernement de vouloir étouffer l'affaire; **to c. up for sb** protéger qn; **architects and builders are covering up for each other** les architectes et les entrepreneurs se protègent les uns les autres

coverage ['kʌvərɪdʒ] N **1** *Journ etc* couverture *f* (médiatique); **some people objected to XTV's c. of these events** certaines personnes ont protesté contre la manière dont XTV a traité ces événements; *TV* **there was no c. of the match** on n'a pas retransmis ce match; **the c. given to the elections was biased** le compte-rendu des élections était partial; **the book gives good c. of the coup** le livre décrit bien la façon dont le coup d'État s'est déroulé; **sports get too much c. on TV** la télé consacre trop de temps au sport
2 *(in insurance)* couverture *f*, provision *f*
3 *Tel (of mobile phone network)* couverture *f*

coverall(s) ['kʌvərɔːl, -z] N(PL) *Am* bleu(s) *m(pl)* (de travail)

covered ['kʌvəd] ADJ **1** *(market, way etc)* couvert **2** *(by insurance policy) (risk)* couvert; *(person)* assuré
▸▸ *St Exch* **c. position** position *f* couverte; *St Exch* **c. short position** position courte couverte; **c. wagon** chariot *m* (à bâche)

covering ['kʌvərɪŋ] ADJ **1** *(document, note)* d'accompagnement **2** *Mil (forces, troops)* de couverture
▸ N **1** *(protective) (for floor)* revêtement *m*; *(for plants, object in trailer)* bâche *f*, *(on furniture)* housse *f* **2** *(of snow, dust, chocolate)* couche *f*
▸▸ *Mil* **c. fire** tir *m* de couverture; *Br* **c. letter** lettre *f* d'accompagnement; *(sent with job application)* lettre de motivation

coverlet ['kʌvəlɪt] N dessus-de-lit *m inv*

cover-line N *Journ* titraille *f*, titre *m* de rappel

covert ['kʌvət] ADJ *(threat etc)* caché, voilé;

(action etc) secret, clandestin
▸ N *(in hunting)* couvert *m*, fourré *m*

covertly ['kʌvətlɪ] ADV secrètement

cover-up N *(of irregularity etc)* dissimulation *f*; **the president denied there had been a c.** le président a nié qu'on ait tenté d'étouffer l'affaire; **in a c. attempt that went wrong** dans une tentative ratée pour étouffer l'affaire

covet ['kʌvɪt] VT *(-t-)* convoiter; **a highly coveted prize** un prix très convoité

covetous ['kʌvɪtəs] ADJ *(person)* avide (**of** de); *(gaze)* de convoitise; **to be c. of sb's property** convoiter les biens d'autrui

covetously ['kʌvɪtəslɪ] ADV avec convoitise

covetousness ['kʌvɪtəsnɪs] N *(greed)* cupidité *f*, avidité *f*; *(for particular thing)* convoitise *f*

covey ['kʌvɪ] N *(of partridges etc)* compagnie *f*, vol *m*

cow [kaʊ] N **1** vache *f*, *Fig Fam* **till the cows come home** *(to wait)* jusqu'à la Saint-Glinglin; *(to argue, talk)* à n'en plus finir **2** *Pej Fam (woman)* peau de vache; **old c.** vieille bique *f*, vieux chameau *m*; **silly c.** espèce *f* d'idiote; **poor c.!** la pauvre!; **lucky c.!** la veinarde! **3** *(female elephant)* éléphant *m* femelle, éléphante *f*, *(female seal)* phoque *m* femelle; *(female whale)* baleine *f* femelle
▸ VT intimider; **to look cowed** avoir l'air d'un chien battu; **to c. sb into submission** intimider qn jusqu'à ce qu'il/elle se soumette
▸▸ *Bot* **c. parsley** cerfeuil *m* sauvage

coward ['kaʊəd] N lâche *mf*, poltron, -onne; **I'm a terrible c. in the dark** j'ai très peur du noir; **he's a moral c.** c'est un lâche, il n'a pas le courage de ses opinions

cowardice ['kaʊədɪs], **cowardliness** ['kaʊ-ədlɪnəs] N lâcheté *f*, poltronnerie *f*, **moral c.** lâcheté

cowardly ['kaʊədlɪ] ADJ lâche

cowbell ['kaʊbel] N clochette *f* (pour bétail)

cowboy ['kaʊbɔɪ] N **1** cow-boy *m*, *pl* cowboys; **to play cowboys and indians** jouer aux cow-boys et aux indiens **2** *Br Fam Pej (careless or dishonest workman)* fumiste *m*; **a bunch of cowboys, a c. outfit** des petits rigolos *mpl*, **what c. did this plumbing?** quel est le petit rigolo qui s'est occupé de la plomberie?
▸▸ **c. boots** bottes *fpl* de cow-boy, santiags *fpl*; **c. film, c. movie** film *m* de cow-boys

cowcatcher ['kaʊkætʃər] N *Am Rail* chasse-pierres *m inv*

cower ['kaʊər] VI se tapir (à terre); **to c. before sb** *(show fear)* trembler devant qn

cowhand ['kaʊhænd] N vacher *m*

cowherd ['kaʊhɜːd] N vacher *m*, bouvier *m*

cowhide ['kaʊhaɪd] N peau *f ou* cuir *m* de vache

cowl [kaʊl] N **1** *Rel (hood)* capuchon *m*; *(habit)* habit *m* à capuchon **2** *(on chimney)* capuchon *m*, abat-vent *m inv*; *Aviat, Naut (on engine, funnel)* capot *m*
▸▸ **c. neck** *(on sweater)* col *m* cagoule *ou* boule

cowled [kaʊld] ADJ (en)capuchonné

cowlick ['kaʊlɪk] N *Fam* épi *m* (de cheveux)

cowling ['kaʊlɪŋ] N *(on chimney)* capuchonnement *m*; *Aviat (on engine)* capot *m*; *Aut* capot de ventilateur

cowman, *pl* **cowmen** ['kaʊmən] N vacher *m*; *Am (rancher)* propriétaire *m* d'un/du ranch

co-worker ['kəʊ'wɜːkər] N collègue *mf*

cowpat ['kaʊpæt] N bouse *f* de vache

cowpoke ['kaʊpəʊk] N *Am Fam* cow-boy *m*, *pl* cow-boys

cowpox ['kaʊpɒks] N *Vet* cowpox *m*, vaccine *f*

cowpuncher ['kaʊpʌntʃər] N *Am Fam* cow-boy *m*, *pl* cow-boys

cowrie, cowry ['kaʊrɪ] N *(mollusc)* porcelaine *f*, *(shell)* cauri *m*

cowshed ['kaʊʃed] N étable *f*

cowslip ['kaʊslɪp] N coucou *m*, primevère *f* commune

cox [kɒks] *Sp* N *(in rowing)* barreur, -euse
▸ VT & VI *(in rowing)* gouverner, barrer

coxless four ['kɒkslɪs] N quatre *m* sans barreur

coxswain ['kɒksw(ə)n] N barreur, -euse

coy [kɔɪ] ADJ *(shy)* timide; *Pej (affectedly shy)* qui fait la sainte-nitouche; *(seductive)* qui fait des mines; **a c. look** un air de sainte-nitouche; **to go all c.** *(of child)*, *Pej* faire le/la timide; **with a c. little smile** avec un petit sourire séducteur; **why be so c. about accepting?** pourquoi faire semblant d'hésiter?; **he was rather c. about the price** il était plutôt évasif quant au prix; **the rather c. treatment of the sex scenes** la façon un peu mièvre dont sont traitées les scènes de sexe

coyly ['kɔɪlɪ] ADV timidement; *Pej* en faisant le/la timide; **to reply c.** *(evasively)* faire une réponse évasive

coyness ['kɔɪnɪs] N *(shyness)* timidité *f*, *Pej (affected shyness)* fausse timidité *f*; **... he said, with a certain c.** *(evasively and vaguely)* ... dit-il, restant dans le vague

coyote [kɔɪ'jəʊtɪ] N coyote *m*

coypu ['kɔɪpuː] N coypou *m*, ragondin *m*

coziness ['kəʊzɪnɪs] N *Am* = **cosiness**

cozy ['kəʊzɪ] ADJ *Am* = **cosy**

cp *(abbr* compare*)* comparer

CPA [siːpiːˈeɪ] N *Am (abbr* **Certified Public Accountant** *)* expert-comptable *m*, *pl* experts-comptables

cpa [siːpiːˈeɪ] N *(abbr* **critical path analysis***)* analyse *f* du chemin critique

cpi [siːpiːˈaɪ] *Comput (abbr* **characters per inch***)* cpp

Cpl *Mil abbr* **Corporal**

CP/M [siːpiːˈem] N *Comput (abbr* **control program/monitor***)* CP/M *m*

cps [siːpiːˈes] *Comput (abbr* **characters per second***)* cps

CPU [siːpiːˈjuː] N *Comput (abbr* **central processing unit***)* unité *f* centrale

CR [siːˈɑːr] N *Comput (abbr* **carriage return***)* retour *m* chariot

crab[1] [kræb] N **1** *(crustacean)* crabe *m* **2** *(louse)* morpion *m*; **to have crabs** avoir des morpions **3** *Astron* **the C.** *(constellation)* le Cancer; *(nebula)* le Crabe **4** *Cin, TV* travelling *m* latéral
▸ VI **1** *esp Am Fam (grumble)* ronchonner (**about** contre) **2** *Cin, TV* faire un travelling latéral; **to c. right/left** faire un travelling latéral vers la droite/gauche
▸▸ *Med* **c. louse** morpion *m*; *Culin* **c. paste** beurre *m* de crabe; **c. pot** casier *m* à crabes

crab[2] N *(apple)* pomme *f* sauvage
▸▸ **c. apple** *(fruit)* pomme sauvage; *(tree)* pommier *m* sauvage

crabbed ['kræbɪd, kræbd] ADJ **1** *(writing)* en pattes de mouche **2** *(grumpy)* maussade, grincheux

crabby ['kræbɪ] ADJ maussade, grincheux

CRACK [kræk]

N fente **1**	fissure **1**	fêlure **1**
crevasse **1**	craquement **3**
claquement **3**	coup **5**
plaisanterie **6**
VT fêler **1**	crevasser **1**	faire craquer **2**	faire claquer **2**
assommer **3**
VI se fêler **1**	se crevasser **1**
craquer **3, 4**	claquer **4**

N 1 *(split)* fente *f*, fissure *f*; *(in bone)* fêlure *f*; *(in skin)* crevasse *f*, gerçure *f*; *(in wall, ground)* crevasse, lézarde *f*; *(in varnish, enamel)* craquelure *f*; *(in glass, pottery, bell etc)* fêlure; *Fig (in policy, argument)* fissure, faiblesse *f*; **cracks were beginning to appear in the coalition** la coalition commençait à se fissurer

2 *(of door etc)* entrebâillement *m*; **open the window a c.** ouvrez la fenêtre un petit peu; *Fig* **at the c. of dawn** à la pointe du jour

3 *(sound) (of branches, ice etc)* craquement *m*; *(of whip)* claquement *m*; *(of rifle)* détonation *f*, claquement sec; *Fig Fam* **to get a fair c. of the whip** avoir toutes ses chances; *Fam* **to give sb a fair c. of the whip** donner toutes ses chances à qn

4 *Fig Fam (attempt)* **to have a c. at sth** s'essayer à qch; **I'll have a c. (at it)** je vais tenter le coup; **to give sb** *or* **let sb have a c. at sth** laisser qn essayer de faire qch

5 *Fam (blow)* **c. on the head** coup *m* sec sur la tête

6 *Fam (gibe)* plaisanterie *f*; **to make a c.** faire une plaisanterie, lancer une vanne; **a cheap c. about short people** une plaisanterie facile sur les gens de petite taille; **nasty c.** plaisanterie acerbe *ou* acérée

7 *Sl (drug)* crack *m*

8 *Ir Fam* **there was some good c.** on s'est bien marré

ADJ *Fam* d'élite; *Sport* **c. player** as *m*, crack *m*; **c. regiment** régiment *m* d'élite

INT crac!, clac!

VT 1 *(damage, break etc) (glass, plate, bone, tooth)* fêler; *(lip)* gercer; *(wall, earth)* lézarder, crevasser; *(stone etc)* fendre; *(varnish, paint, plastic)* fendiller, craqueler

2 *(make sound with) (whip)* faire claquer; *(one's fingers)* faire craquer

3 *Fam (hit)* **to c. sb over the head** assommer qn; **he cracked his head against the wall** il s'est cogné au mur

4 *(solve) (problem)* résoudre; *(code)* décrypter; **I think I've cracked it** je crois que j'y suis arrivé

5 *(break open) (safe)* percer; *(nut)* casser; *Com (market)* percer sur; *Fam* **to c. a bottle of wine (with sb)** boire une bouteille de vin (avec qn)

6 *(make)* **to c. a joke** raconter une blague; **it's not the sort of thing you can c. jokes about** ce n'est pas le genre de choses sur lequel on peut plaisanter; **where are you going, the North Pole?, he cracked** où est-ce que tu vas, au pôle Nord?, a-t-il plaisanté

7 *Ind (heavy oil)* fractionner

VI 1 *(become cracked) (of glass, plate, bone etc)* se fêler; *(of wall)* se crevasser, se lézarder; *(of skin, lips)* se gercer; *(of paint, varnish)* se fendiller, se craqueler

2 *(of voice)* se casser; *(at puberty)* muer

3 *(of person) (under pressure)* craquer; *(of resistance)* lâcher; *Hum* **the boss has finally cracked** *(gone mad)* le patron a fini par craquer

4 *(make sound)* craquer; *(of whip)* claquer; **a rifle cracked** un coup de fusil a claqué

▸▸ **c. house** = lieu *m* où l'on achète, vend et consomme du crack; **c. shot** tireur, -euse d'élite

▸ **crack down** VI sévir

▸ **crack down on** VT INSEP *(become stricter about)* prendre des mesures plus sévères *ou* énergiques contre; *(punish) (drunk driving etc)* sévir contre

▸ **crack up** VI **1** *(break)* se briser en morceaux; **the ice is cracking up** la glace se brise

2 *Fam (of person) (have nervous breakdown)* craquer; *(of marriage, organization)* aller à la ruine

3 *Br Fam (be helpless with laughter)* s'écrouler (de rire); *(get angry)* péter les plombs

VT SEP 1 *Fam (cause to be helpless with laugh-*

ter) **it really cracked me up when I heard about it** je me suis vraiment écroulé de rire quand j'ai entendu parler de ça

2 *Fam (praise)* **it's not all it's cracked up to be** ce n'est pas tout ce qu'on en dit

crackbrained ['krækbreɪnd] **ADJ** *Fam (person)* fêlé, complètement dingue; *(idea, plan etc)* complètement dingue

crackdown ['krækdaʊn] **N** mesures *fpl* énergiques (**on sth** contre qch); **the government c. on reporting** les restrictions *fpl* gouvernementales concernant les reportages

cracked [krækt] **ADJ** *Fam (crazy)* dingue, cinglé

cracker ['krækər] **N 1** *(biscuit)* biscuit *m* salé, cracker *m*

2 *Br Fam (excellent thing)* merveille *f*; *(pretty woman)* canon *m*; **the first goal was an absolute c.** le premier but était une pure merveille; **she's an absolute c.** elle est canon; **it's a c. of a joke!** cette histoire est à se tordre!

3 *(firework)* pétard *m*; *(at Christmas)* diablotin *m*; **to pull a c.** faire éclater un diablotin

4 *(for nuts)* casse-noisette(s) *m inv*, casse-noix *m inv*

5 *Am Sl (poor white person)* blanc *m* pauvre *(du sud des États-Unis)*

6 *Comput* pirate *m* informatique

▸▸ *Am* **c. barrel** boîte *f* à biscuits

cracker-barrel **ADJ** *Am Fam (wisdom, philosophy etc)* populaire

crackers ['krækəz] **ADJ** *Br Fam* **he's c.** il est cinglé; **to go c.** perdre la boule

crackhead ['krækhed] **N** *Sl (drug addict)* drogué, -ée au crack, consommateur, -trice de crack

cracking ['krækɪŋ] *Fam* **ADJ** excellent, épatant; **to be in c. (good) form** être en super forme, avoir la pêche; **at a c. pace** à fond de train

ADV *Fam* **to get c.** s'y mettre; **they got c. with their work** ils se sont mis au travail; **get c.!** grouille-toi!

N 1 *(sound)* craquement *m*; *(of whip)* claquement *m* **2** *(of paint)* craquelure *f*, craquelage *m* **3** *Ind (of oil)* fractionnement *m*, craquage *m* **4** *Comput* piratage *m* informatique

crackle ['kræk(ə)l] **N 1** *(sound) (of dry leaves, twigs)* craquement *m*; *(of shots)* crépitement *m*, crépitation *f*; *(of something frying)* grésillement *m*; *(of fire)* crépitement, pétillement *m*; *Radio* crachotement *m*, crachements *mpl*; *Tel* **there's a bit of a c. on the line** il y a de la friture sur la ligne **2** *(finish) (of paint, porcelain)* craquelure *f*

VI *(of dry leaves, twigs etc)* craquer; *(of shots)* crépiter; *(of something frying)* grésiller; *(of fire)* crépiter, pétiller; *Radio* crachoter

▸▸ **c. finish** *(of porcelain)* craquelage *m*

crackleware ['kræk(ə)lweər] **N** *Cer* craquelé *m*

crackling ['kræklɪŋ] **ADJ** pétillant, crépitant

N 1 *Br Culin (of roast pork)* = peau *f* de porc grillée **2** *Old-fashioned Br Sl* **a nice bit of c.** *(woman)* une belle pépée

crackpot ['krækpɒt] *Fam* **N** fêlé, -ée, cinglé, -ée; **he's a c.** il est fêlé *ou* cinglé

ADJ *(idea, scheme)* dingue

crackup ['krækʌp] **N 1** *Fam (nervous breakdown)* dépression *f* nerveuse **2** *(of system)* débâcle *f*; *(of civilization)* effondrement *m*

cradle ['kreɪd(ə)l] **N 1** *(of child), Fig (of civilization)* berceau *m*; **from the c.** dès le berceau; **from the c. to the grave** du berceau à la tombe; *Med* **to have c. cap** *(of baby)* avoir les croûtes de lait; *Fam* **he's/she's a c. snatcher** il/elle les prend au berceau *ou* au biberon

2 *Ind etc (of machine etc)* berceau *m*, cadre

m; *(for window cleaner)* nacelle *f*; *Constr, Min* pont *m* volant; *(for painter)* sellette *f*

3 *Med (over bed)* cerceau *m*, arceau *m*

4 *Tel (for receiver)* support *m*

VT 1 *(in cradle) (baby)* mettre *ou* coucher dans un berceau; *Fig* **cradled in luxury** bercé dans le luxe; **the village was cradled in a valley** le village était blotti au fond d'une vallée

2 *(in one's arms) (person)* bercer; *(object)* tenir délicatement; **to c. a child in one's arms** bercer un enfant dans ses bras; **he cradled the rifle in his arms** il serrait le fusil contre lui

cradlesong ['kreɪd(ə)lsɒŋ] **N** *Mus* berceuse *f*

cradle-to-grave **ADJ 1** *(health cover, welfare system)* qui prend l'individu en charge tout au long de sa vie **2** *(service, support)* de bout en bout; **c. management** *or* **control of toxic waste** gestion *f* de bout en bout des déchets dangereux

▸▸ *Mktg* **c. marketing** = type de marketing qui vise les enfants dès le plus jeune âge

craft [krɑːft] **N 1** *(art)* art *m*; *(occupation)* métier *m* (manuel); *(professional skill) (of teacher etc)* métier; *Sch* travaux *mpl* manuels; **the c. of weaving** l'art du tissage; **painter who is master of his c.** peintre qui maîtrise parfaitement son art **2** *(skill)* habileté *f*, adresse *f*; *Pej (cunning)* ruse *f* **3** *Naut (pl craft)* embarcation *f*, petit navire *m*; **small c.** *(small boats)* canots *mpl*, petits bateaux *mpl*

▸▸ **c. centre** centre *m* d'artisanat; *Sch* **c. teacher** professeur *m* de travaux manuels

craftily ['krɑːftɪlɪ] **ADV** *(cleverly)* astucieusement, ingénieusement, *Pej* avec ruse *ou* roublardise

craftiness ['krɑːftɪnɪs] **N** ingéniosité *f*, *Pej* ruse *f*, roublardise *f*

craftsman, *pl* **craftsmen** ['krɑːftsmən] **N 1** *(artisan)* artisan *m* **2** *(artist)* artiste *m*; **this is the work of a real c.** c'est l'œuvre de quelqu'un qui s'y connaît

craftsmanship ['krɑːftsmənʃɪp] **N** *(skill)* habileté *f* (manuelle); *(knowledge, experience)* (connaissance *f* du) métier *m*; **a wonderful piece of c.** un chef-d'œuvre extraordinaire; **think of the c. that has gone into making this table!** songe à l'habileté qu'il a fallu pour faire cette table!

craftswoman, *pl* **craftswomen** ['krɑːftswʊmən, -wɪmɪn] **N** artisane *f*

craftwork ['krɑːftwɜːk] **N** artisanat *m*

crafty ['krɑːftɪ] **ADJ** astucieux, ingénieux, malin, *f* maligne; *Pej* rusé, roublard; **you c. old thing!** espèce de vieux renard!

crag [kræg] **N** rocher *m ou* flanc *m* de montagne escarpé, rocher à pic; **overhanging c.** rocher en surplomb

craggy ['krægɪ] **ADJ 1** *(rocky)* rocailleux **2** *(face)* anguleux, taillé à coups de serpe

cram [kræm] (-mm-) **VT 1** *(force)* fourrer, entasser (**sth into sth** qch dans qch); **they crammed 60 people into the bus** ils ont entassé 60 personnes dans le bus; **to c. food into one's mouth** se fourrer la nourriture dans la bouche, se gaver de nourriture, *Fam* s'empiffrer

2 *(fill)* bourrer (**sth with sth** qch de qch); **to c. sb with food** bourrer *ou* gaver qn de nourriture; **cupboards crammed with linen** armoires bourrées de linge; **at school they crammed our heads with facts** à l'école, ils nous ont bourré le crâne (d'informations)

3 *Sch Fam (candidate for exam)* faire bachoter; **to c. maths** *(of student)* potasser ferme les maths

4 *Agr (poultry)* appâter, gaver

VI 1 *(enter)* s'entasser; **we all crammed into the car** nous nous sommes tous entassés dans la voiture

2 *Sch Fam* potasser, se bourrer le crâne; **to c. for an exam** bachoter

▸ **cram in** VT SEP *(force in)* fourrer, entasser; **you certainly crammed a lot in in two weeks** *(did a lot)* vous avez fait des tas de choses en deux semaines

VI *(enter)* s'entasser; **100 people crammed in** 100 personnes se *ou* s'y sont entassées

cram-full ADJ *(train, room etc)* bondé; **the streets were c. of people** les rues grouillaient de monde

crammer ['kræmər] N *Fam (school)* boîte *f* à bac

cramming ['kræmɪŋ] N *Fam (for an exam)* bachotage *m*, bourrage *m* de crâne

cramp [kræmp] N *Med* crampe *f*; **to have (an attack of) c.** être pris d'une crampe, avoir une crampe; **to get c.** *(frequently)* avoir des crampes; *Am* **to have cramps** *(period pains)* avoir des maux de ventre

VT *(hinder) (movements)* gêner; **to be cramped up in a small space** être à l'étroit; *Fam* **to c. sb's style** priver qn de ses moyens

cramp² N **1** *Carp* serre-joint *m*, *pl* serre-joints **2** *Constr (cramp iron)* crampon *m*, clameau *m*

VT **1** *Constr (stones etc)* cramponner, agrafer **2** *Carp* serrer *(au serre-joint)*

▸▸ *Constr* **c. iron** crampon, clameau

cramped [kræmpt] ADJ *(room)* exigu, *f* exiguë; *(writing)* serré; **it's very c. in this office** on est très à l'étroit dans ce bureau; **to live/ work in c. conditions** vivre/travailler dans un espace restreint; **to be c. for space** être *ou* se sentir à l'étroit

crampon ['kræmpɒn] N crampon *m* à glace

cranberry ['krænbərɪ] N canneberge *f*

▸▸ **c. juice** jus *m* de canneberge; **c. sauce** sauce *f* à la canneberge

crane [kreɪn] N **1** *Tech etc* grue *f*; *Cin* grue (de prise de vue) **2** *(bird)* grue *f*

VT *(one's neck)* tendre, allonger

VI **to c. forward** tendre *ou* allonger le cou

▸▸ *Tech etc* **c. driver** conducteur, -trice de grue, grutier, -ière *f*; *Entom* **c. fly** tipule *f*; *Tech etc* **c. operator** conducteur, -trice de grue, grutier, -ière *f*; *Cin* **c. shot** prise *f* de vue sur grue

crane's-bill, cranesbill ['kreɪnzbɪl] N bec-de-grue *m*, *pl* becs-de-grue, géranium *m*

cranial ['kreɪnɪəl] ADJ *Anat (nerve etc)* crânien; *(fracture)* du crâne

craniology [kreɪnɪ'ɒlədʒɪ] N craniologie *f*

cranium, pl crania ['kreɪnɪəm, -ɪə] N *Anat* crâne *m*

crank¹ [kræŋk] N *Tech, Aut* manivelle *f*; *(crankpin)* maneton *m*

VT *(engine)* démarrer, lancer; *(with cranking handle)* faire démarrer à la manivelle

▸ **crank out** VT SEP *Fam* produire laborieusement

▸ **crank up** VT SEP *(engine)* lancer *ou* faire partir à la manivelle; *Fig Fam (person in morning)* mettre en route

crank² N *Fam* **1** *(eccentric)* excentrique *mf*; **a health food/religious c.** un dingue des aliments naturels/de religion **2** *Am (bad-tempered person)* grincheux, -euse

crankcase ['kræŋkkeɪs] N *Aut* carter *m*

crankiness ['kræŋkɪnɪs] N *Fam* **1** *(eccentricity)* excentricité *f*; *(whimsicality)* humeur *f* capricieuse **2** *Am (bad temper)* humeur *f* difficile

cranking ['kræŋkɪŋ] ADJ *Aut*

▸▸ **c. handle** manivelle *f*; **c. speed** vitesse *f* du démarreur, régime *m* de démarrage; **c. torque** couple *m* de démarrage

crankpin ['kræŋkpɪn] N *Aut* maneton *m*

crankshaft ['kræŋkʃɑːft] N *Aut* vilebrequin *m*

▸▸ **c. sensor** capteur *m* sur vilebrequin

cranky ['kræŋkɪ] ADJ *Fam* **1** *(eccentric)* excentrique; *(whimsical)* capricieux **2** *Am (bad-tempered)* grincheux

cranny ['krænɪ] N *(crack)* fente *f*, lézarde *f*

crap¹ [kræp] N *Sl* **1** *(excrement)* merde *f*, *Vulg* **to have** *or* **take a c.** chier

2 *Fig (worthless thing(s))* camelote *f*, saloperie *f*; *(nonsense)* foutaise(s) *f(pl)*, connerie(s) *f(pl)*; *(dirty, disgusting substance)* saloperie; **he's listening to that classical c. again** il est encore en train d'écouter ces conneries classiques; **he eats nothing but c.** il ne bouffe que des saloperies; **get all this c. off the table** enlève tout ce bordel *ou* toute cette merde de la table; **you don't believe all that c. about witches, do you?** tu ne crois quand même pas à toutes ces conneries sur les sorcières, hein?; **that's c.!, she never said that!** c'est de la connerie!, elle n'a jamais dit ça!; **what a load of c.!** quelles conneries!

ADJ *Sl (bad)* merdique; *(stupid)* con; **these books are c.** ces bouquins, c'est de la connerie *ou* de la merde

VT *Vulg* **to c. oneself** *(defecate, be scared)* faire dans son froc

VI *Vulg* chier

▸ **crap out** VT INSEP *Sl (lose one's nerve about)* **to c. out of sth** se défiler devant qch; **he crapped out of telling her she was fired** il aurait dû lui dire qu'on voulait la virer, mais il s'est défilé; **you can't c. out of it this time** tu ne peux pas te défiler cette fois-ci

crap² N *Am* = **craps**

▸▸ **c. game** jeu *m* de dés, craps *m*

crape [kreɪp] N **1** *(fabric)* crêpe *m* **2** *(for people in mourning)* crêpe *m* noir (de deuil)

▸▸ *Med* **c. bandage** bande *f* Velpeau®

crapper ['kræpər] N *Sl* **1** *(lavatory)* chiottes *fpl* **2** *(coward)* trouillard, -arde

crappy ['kræpɪ] ADJ *Sl* **1** *(dirty)* cradingue, crade **2** *(bad, stupid)* = **crap¹** ADJ

craps [kræps] NPL *(often with sing verb) Am* jeu *m* de dés, craps *m*; **to shoot c.** jouer aux dés

crapshooter ['kræpʃuːtər] N *Am* joueur, -euse de dés

crapulous ['kræpjʊləs], **crapulent** ['kræpjʊlənt] ADJ *Lit* intempérant

Note that the French word **crapuleux** is a false friend. It means **villainous** or **dissolute**.

CRASH [kræʃ]

| N fracas **1** ▪ accident **2** ▪ krach **3** |
| ▪ panne **4** |
| INT patatras |
| VI retentir **1** ▪ s'écraser **2, 3** |
| ▪ s'effondrer **4** ▪ tomber en panne **5** |
| VT avoir un accident avec **1** ▪ faire tomber en panne **2** |

N **1** *(noise)* fracas *m*; **there was a c. as the vase hit the ground** il y a eu un fracas quand le vase est tombé par terre; **the c. of thunder** le fracas du tonnerre; **there was a c. of thunder** il y eut un violent coup de tonnerre; **to fall with a c.** tomber avec fracas

2 *(accident)* accident *m*; **car/train/plane c.** accident de voiture/ferroviaire/d'avion; **we were in a c.** *(car accident)* nous avons eu un accident de voiture; **this car has been in a c.** cette voiture a eu un accident; **the force of the c.** la force de l'impact

3 *Fig (disaster)* catastrophe *f*, débâcle *f*; **(financial) c.** débâcle financière, krach *m*; *Fin* **the Wall Street C.** le krach de Wall Street

4 *(of computer)* panne *f*

INT patatras!; **c. went the vase** le vase tomba avec un grand fracas; **he drove c. into the wall** il est allé s'écraser contre le mur

VI **1** *(make sound)* retentir; *(of waves)* s'écra-

ser; **the thunder crashed** *(once)* il y eut un violent coup de tonnerre; *(repeatedly)* le tonnerre retentit

2 *(move)* **to c. (down)** tomber avec fracas; **the bottle crashed against the wall** la bouteille s'est écrasée contre le mur; **the bookcase came crashing down** la bibliothèque s'est écroulée avec fracas; **the vase crashed to the ground** le vase s'est écrasé par terre avec fracas; **the mast came crashing down** le mât s'abattit; **to c. through sth** passer à travers *ou* traverser qch avec fracas

3 *Aut, Rail* entrer en collision; *Aviat* s'écraser au sol; **the two cars crashed head on** les deux voitures se sont tamponnées de front; **to c. into a tree** s'écraser contre un arbre, rentrer dans un arbre; **to c. into sb** rentrer dans qn; **I crashed into him** je lui suis rentré dedans

4 *(of business)* faire faillite; *St Exch* s'effondrer

5 *(of network, system etc)* sauter; *(of computer)* tomber en panne

6 *Sl (sleep)* roupiller, pioncer; *(go to sleep)* se mettre à roupiller; **can I c. at your place tonight?** je peux pioncer chez toi ce soir?; **he crashed on the floor** il a roupillé par terre

VT **1** *(plane)* écraser au sol; **to c. one's car** *(accidentally)* avoir un accident avec sa voiture; *(deliberately)* démolir sa voiture

2 *Comput* faire tomber en panne

3 *(make noise with)* **to c. the gears** faire grincer la boîte de vitesses; **he crashed the books down on the table** il a posé les livres sur la table avec fracas

4 *Fam* **to c. a party** aller à une réception sans être invité

▸▸ **c. barrier** glissière *f* de sécurité; **c. course** cours *m* intensif; **c. diet** régime *m* choc; **c. dive** *(of submarine)* plongée *f* raide; *(of plane)* plongeon *m*; **c. helmet** casque *m* (de protection); **c. landing** atterrissage *m* forcé *ou* en catastrophe; *Fam* **c. pad** piaule *f* de dépannage; *Admin* **c. programme** programme *m* choc *ou* d'urgence; *Aut* **c. sensor** détecteur *m* de collision *ou* de choc; **c. test dummy** mannequin-test *m*, *pl* mannequins-test

▸ **crash out** VI *Sl* **1** *(go to sleep)* s'endormir; *(suddenly, when drunk etc)* s'écrouler; **he was crashed out on the sofa** il roupillait sur le divan

2 *(spend night, sleep)* pioncer

crash-dive *Naut* VT *(submarine)* faire plonger raide

VI plonger raide

crashing ['kræʃɪŋ] ADJ *Fam* **a c. bore** *(person)* une personne assommante; *(task)* une besogne assommante; *(party)* une soirée assommante; **to be a c. bore** être assommant

crashingly ['kræʃɪŋlɪ] ADV *Fam (boring)* incroyablement, terriblement

crash-land *Aviat* VI atterrir brutalement

VT *(plane, helicopter)* faire atterrir brutalement

crash-test VT **to c. a car** tester une voiture en situation d'accident

crashworthiness ['kræʃwɜːðɪnɪs] N *(of vehicle, helicopter)* résistance *f* aux chocs

crass [kræs] ADJ *(comment, person)* lourd; *(stupidity, behaviour)* grossier; *(ignorance)* grossier, crasse

crassly ['kræslɪ] ADV *(to behave, say)* avec grossièreté; **he's so c. stupid** il est d'une stupidité effarante

crassness ['kræsnɪs] N grossièreté *f*

crate [kreɪt] N **1** *(for wine, whisky etc)* caisse *f*; *(for apples, oranges etc)* cageot *m*; *(for glass, china)* harasse *f*; *(for bottles)* casier *m*

2 *Fam (car)* caisse *f*, *Old-fashioned (aircraft)* coucou *m*

VT *(goods)* mettre dans une caisse/des caisses

crater ['kreɪtər] **N** *Geol (of volcano, moon)* cratère *m*; *(shell hole)* entonnoir *m*, cratère; **the explosion had left a c. 20 feet wide** l'explosion avait laissé un cratère de 6 mètres de large

VT creuser; **a street cratered by shellfire** une rue défoncée par des éclats d'obus; **cratered face** visage *m* crevassé

▸► **c. lake** lac *m* de cratère

cravat [krə'væt] **N** foulard *m*

crave [kreɪv] **VT 1** *(long for, need)* désirer ardemment, réclamer; **child that craves affection** enfant qui a un grand besoin d'affection; **she craves tobacco** elle a une envie furieuse de fumer **2** *Lit (beg)* **to c. sb's pardon** demander pardon à qn; **to c. indulgence** solliciter l'indulgence

VI to c. for sth désirer ardemment qch, réclamer qch

craven ['kreɪv(ə)n] **ADJ** *Lit* lâche

cravenly ['kreɪv(ə)nlɪ] **ADV** *Lit* avec lâcheté, lâchement

craving ['kreɪvɪŋ] **N** désir *m* ardent, appétit *m* insatiable (**for** de); **c. for alcohol** passion *f* de l'alcool; *(need)* besoin *m* d'alcool; **I have a c. for chocolate** *(at this moment)* j'ai une envie furieuse de chocolat; *(in general)* j'ai la passion du chocolat; **pregnant women get strange cravings** les femmes enceintes ont souvent d'étranges envies

craw [krɔ:] **N** *(of bird)* jabot *m*; *Fig* **it sticks in my c.** ça me reste en travers de la gorge

crawfish ['krɔ:fɪʃ] **N** *esp Am* = **crayfish**

crawl [krɔ:l] **N 1** *(action)* **the baby went for a c. along the floor** le bébé a rampé sur le sol **2** *(slow pace)* **to go along at a c.** *(on foot, in vehicle)* avancer très lentement; **the traffic had slowed to a c.** la circulation avait ralenti et on roulait au pas **3** *Swimming* crawl *m*; **to do the c.** nager le crawl, crawler **4** *TV (roller captions)* générique *m* sur déroulant

VI 1 *(of person) (on belly)* ramper, se traîner; *(on hands and knees)* marcher à quatre pattes; *(of snake, worm)* ramper; **to c. on one's hands and knees** aller à quatre pattes; **she was crawling about on the carpet** elle était à quatre pattes sur la moquette; **to c. into a hole** *(of reptile etc)* se glisser dans un trou; *(of person)* se traîner jusque dans un trou; **to c. to the door** aller jusqu'à la porte en rampant/à quatre pattes **2** *(move slowly)* avancer lentement; *Aut Fam* faire du surplace **3** *(be infested)* **to be crawling with vermin** grouiller de vermine; *Fam* **the streets were crawling with troops** les rues fourmillaient *ou* grouillaient de militaires; **to make sb's skin c.** donner un frisson de dégoût à qn **4** *Fam (be obsequious)* **to c. to sb** s'aplatir devant qn, lécher les bottes à qn; **I refuse to c.** je refuse de m'aplatir **5** *Swimming* crawler, nager le crawl

crawler ['krɔ:lər] **N 1** *Fam (obsequious person)* lèche-botte *m*, *pl* lèche-bottes **2** *Comput* araignée *f*

▸► *Br Aut* **c. lane** file *f* ou voie *f* pour véhicules lents

crawlers **NPL** *(baby's overalls)* grenouillère *f*

crawling ['krɔ:lɪŋ] **ADJ 1** *(baby)* qui marche à quatre pattes; **he's just got to the c. stage** il commence à marcher à quatre pattes; *Fig* **compared with the Japanese, we're still at the c. stage** comparés aux Japonais, nous en sommes encore aux balbutiements **2** *(infested)* grouillant (**with** de) **3** *Fam (obsequious)* lèche-bottes *inv*

N *Fam (obsequiousness)* **that's just c.** c'est du lèche-botte

crayfish ['kreɪfɪʃ] **N (freshwater) c.** écrevisse *f*, **(sea) c.** langouste *f*

crayon ['kreɪɒn, -ən] *Art* **N** *(pencil)* crayon *m* de couleur; *(pastel)* crayon *m* pastel; *(wax)* crayon *m* de cire

VT 1 *(draw)* dessiner au crayon/au pastel/au crayon de cire **2** *(colour in) (sketch)* colorier

craze [kreɪz] **N** manie *f* (**for sth** de qch); *(fad)* engouement *m*; **this is the latest dance c.** c'est la dernière danse à la mode

VT 1 *Lit (drive insane)* rendre fou **2** *Cer (porcelain)* craqueler

VI *Cer* se craqueler

crazed [kreɪzd] **ADJ 1** *(with grief)* fou, *f* folle (**with** de); *(with fear)* affolé (**with** par) **2** *Cer* craquelé

-crazed [kreɪzd] **SUFF** rendu fou par; **drug/power-c.** rendu fou par la drogue/le pouvoir; **he was half-c. with grief** la douleur l'avait rendu à moitié fou

crazily ['kreɪzɪlɪ] **ADV 1** follement; *(to behave)* bizarrement; **c., they ...** ce qui est complètement fou, ils ... **2** *(to lean)* bizarrement

craziness ['kreɪzɪnɪs] **N** *(of person)* folie *f*, démence *f*

crazy ['kreɪzɪ] **ADJ 1** *(person)* fou, *f* folle, *Fam* dingue; **c. with fear** fou de terreur; **to go c.** devenir fou *(with anger* de colère); **to drive** *or* **send sb c.** rendre qn fou; **you're c.!** vous êtes fou!; **but that's c., we've only just arrived!** mais c'est dingue, nous venons juste d'arriver!; **to be c. about** *or* **over sb/sth** être fou de qn/qch; **like c.** comme un enragé **2** *(odd) (dress, building, angle etc)* bizarre **3** *esp Am Sl (very good)* fou, *f* folle, dément **4** *esp Am Sl (person)* original, -ale

▸► *Am* **c. bone** petit juif *m*; **c. golf** minigolf *m*; *Am Sl* **c. house** asile *m* ou maison *f* de fous; *Br* **c. paving** = dallage *m* irrégulier en pierres plates

CRB [si:ɑ:'bi:] **N** *(abbr* **Criminal Records Bureau***)* identité *f* judiciaire

CRC [si:ɑ:'si:] **N** *Typ (abbr* **camera-ready copy***)* épreuves *fpl* bonnes à filmer

CRE [si:ɑ:'ri:] **N** *Br Admin (abbr* **Commission for Racial Equality***)* commission *f* pour l'égalité raciale

creak [kri:k] **N** *(of hinge)* grincement *m*; *(of floor, chair, new shoes etc)* craquement *m*; **to give a c.** grincer/craquer

VI *(of hinge)* grincer; *(of floor, chair, shoes)* craquer; *Fig (of plot etc)* être boiteux; **the chair creaked under his weight** la chaise a craqué sous son poids

creaking ['kri:kɪŋ] **ADJ** *(hinge)* qui grince; *(timber, shoes)* qui craque

N *(of hinge)* grincement *m*; *(of timber, shoes)* craquement *m*

creaky ['kri:kɪ] **ADJ** *(hinge)* qui grince; *(timber, shoe)* qui craque; *Fig (dialogue, plot etc)* boiteux

cream [kri:m] **N 1** *(of milk)* crème *f*, *(used in cakes etc)* crème (fraîche); **single/double c.** crème fluide *ou* fleurette/épaisse; **strawberries and c.** fraises *fpl* à la crème; **c. of tomato/asparagus soup** crème de tomates/d'asperges **2** *Fig* **the c.** *(best part etc)* la crème, le dessus du panier; **they're the c. of the crop** *(of students, job applicants etc)* c'est le dessus du panier, c'est la crème; **the c. of society** la crème de la société **3** *(filling for chocolates, biscuits)* fondant *m*; *(individual chocolate)* chocolat *m* fourré à la crème **4** *(sauce)* **c. of horseradish** épaisse sauce *f* au raifort

5 *(for face, shoes)* crème *f* **6** *(colour)* crème *f*

ADJ *(colour)* crème *inv*; *Br Sl* **c. crackered** *(exhausted)* crevé, lessivé, naze

VT 1 *(remove cream from) (milk)* écrémer **2** *(add cream to) (coffee etc)* ajouter de la crème à **3** *(beat) (butter)* battre en crème; **to c. potatoes** réduire les pommes de terre en purée; **c. the butter and sugar** *(in recipe)* battre le beurre et le sucre jusqu'à ce qu'ils forment un mélange mousseux *ou* crémeux **4** *Am Fam (person) (beat up)* casser la figure à; *(defeat)* battre à plate couture, mettre la pâtée à **5** *Vulg* **to c. one's jeans** *(ejaculate in)* juter dans son froc; *(of woman)* mouiller

VI *Vulg (ejaculate)* décharger

▸► **c. bun** = petit pain *m* au lait servi avec de la crème chantilly; **c. cake** gâteau *m* à la crème; **c. cheese** ≃ fromage *m* frais; *Br* **c. cracker** biscuit *m* sec; **c. jug** pot *m* à crème; **c. puff** chou *m* à la crème; **c. sherry** sherry *m* *ou* xérès *m* doux; *Culin* **c. of tartar** crème de tartre; *Br* **c. tea** = goûter *m* composé de thé et de scones servis avec de la confiture et de la crème

▸ **cream off** **VT SEP** *(remove)* écrémer; **to c. off the best part of sth** écrémer *ou* prélever la meilleure partie de qch; **the universities c. off the best students** les universités écrèment toujours les meilleurs étudiants

cream-coloured, *Am* **cream-colored** **ADJ** crème *inv*

creamed [kri:md] **ADJ** *Culin (chicken etc)* à la crème

▸► **c. potatoes** purée *f* de pommes de terre

creamer ['kri:mər] **N 1** *Am (jug)* pot *m* à crème **2** *(for coffee)* succédané *m (de lait)* **3** *(machine)* écrémeuse *f*

creamery ['kri:mərɪ] **N** *(dairy)* laiterie *f*, *(shop)* crémerie *f*

▸► **c. butter** beurre *m* laitier

creamy ['kri:mɪ] **ADJ** *(containing cream, resembling cream)* crémeux; **rich c. sauce** sauce *f* onctueuse

crease [kri:s] **N 1** *(made on purpose)* pli *m*; *(accidental)* faux pli *m*; **to remove the creases from sth** enlever les faux plis de qch; **to put a c. in a pair of trousers** faire le pli d'un pantalon **2** *Cr (batting)* **c.** ligne *f* du batteur

VT 1 *(on purpose)* plisser, faire des plis à; *(accidentally)* froisser, chiffonner; *(accidentally with iron)* faire un/des faux pli(s) à; **well-creased trousers** pantalon avec un pli impeccable; **to c. one's brow** froncer les sourcils **2** *(of bullet) (scalp etc)* érafler

VI 1 *(become creased)* se froisser **2** *Br Fam* = **crease up** **VI**

▸ **crease up** *Br Fam* **VI** *(laugh uncontrollably)* se tordre (de rire)

VT SEP *(make laugh uncontrollably)* faire rire à se tordre

crease-resistant **ADJ** infroissable

create [kri:'eɪt] **VT** *(world, peer, jobs, role, difficulties etc)* créer; *(impression)* faire, produire; **she created a studio out of a shed** elle a créé un studio à partir d'une cabane; **if opportunities do not exist you must c. them** si les occasions n'existent pas, il faut les créer; **to c. a scene** *(fuss)* faire une scène; *Law* **to c. a disturbance** troubler l'ordre public

VI 1 *(be creative)* créer **2** *Br Fam (make a scene)* faire du tapage, faire une scène *(about* à propos de)

creation [kri:'eɪʃən] **N 1** *(action) (of the world, a title etc)* création *f*, **job c.** création d'emplois **2** *(product)* création *f*, **the latest creations** *(fashions)* les dernières créations **3** *(universe)* création *f*, *Rel* **the C.** la Création

creative [kri:'eɪtɪv] **ADJ** *(professional artist,*

designer etc) créateur, -trice; *(activity, child, amateur artist etc)* créatif; **I don't do anything c.** je ne fais rien de créatif
▸▸ *Euph* **c. accounting** *(manipulation of accounts)* comptabilité *f* fantaisiste; **c. brief** *(in advertising)* plan *m* de travail créatif, PTC *m*; **c. copy strategy** *(in advertising)* copie *f* stratégie créative; **c. department** service *m* de création; **c. director** directeur, -trice de la création; **c. instinct** instinct *m* créatif; **c. team** équipe *f* de création; **c. writing** techniques *fpl* de l'écriture; **c. writing workshop** atelier *m* d'écriture

creatively [krɪ'eɪtɪvlɪ] **ADV** avec créativité; **more c.** avec plus de créativité, de façon plus créative

creativeness [krɪ'eɪtɪvnɪs], **creativity** [kriːə'tɪvɪtɪ] **N** créativité *f*

creator [krɪ'eɪtər] **N** *(of a fashion, role etc)* créateur, -trice; *Rel* **the C.** le Créateur

creature ['kriːtʃər] **N 1** *(living being)* créature *f*, être *m* (vivant); **creatures from outer space** extra-terrestres *mpl* **2** *(animal)* animal *m*, bête *f* **3** *(person)* **poor c.!** le/la pauvre!; *Pej* **c. of the government** créature *f* du gouvernement; **man is the c. of circumstances** l'homme dépend des circonstances; **I am a c. of habit** je suis un homme/une femme d'habitude
▸▸ **c. comforts** confort *m* matériel; **to like one's c. comforts** aimer ses aises

crèche [kreɪʃ, kreʃ] **N 1** *Br (nursery)* crèche *f*, *(in shopping centre, leisure complex)* garderie *f* **2** *Rel* crèche *f*
▸▸ **c. facilities** garderie *f*

cred [kred] **N** *Fam see* **street cred**

credence ['kriːdəns] **N** croyance *f*, foi *f*; **to give** *or* **attach c. to sth** ajouter foi à qch; **letters of c.** lettres *fpl* de créance

credentials [krɪ'denʃəlz] **NPL 1** *(proof of identity)* pièces *fpl* justificatives d'identité; *(of a diplomat etc)* lettres *fpl* de créance **2** *(proof of ability)* références *fpl*; **what are your c.?** quelles sont vos références?; *Fig* **a film director with excellent c.** un metteur en scène aux excellents antécédents

credibility [kredɪ'bɪlɪtɪ] **N** *(of person, policy)* crédibilité *f*; **the government has lost c. in the eyes of** *or* **with the public** le gouvernement a perdu sa crédibilité aux yeux du public; **the president's actions gave him some c.** les actions du président lui ont conféré une certaine crédibilité
▸▸ **c. gap** manque *m* de crédibilité

credible ['kredɪb(ə)l] **ADJ** crédible; **it is hardly c. that …** il est difficile à croire que … + *sub*

credibly ['kredɪblɪ] **ADV** de façon crédible

CREDIT ['kredɪt]

| **N** crédit **1** ▪ croyance **2** ▪ mérite **3** |
| ▪ générique **4** ▪ unité de valeur **5** |
| **VT** créditer **1** ▪ attribuer **2** ▪ croire **3** |

N 1 *Com, Fin* crédit *m*; *(in an account)* avoir *m*; **to be in c.** avoir de l'argent sur son compte; *(of account)* être créditeur; **my account is still in c.** j'ai toujours de l'argent sur mon compte, *esp Spec* mon compte est toujours créditeur; **to get back into c.** rembourser un découvert; *(of account)* redevenir créditeur; **to give sb c.** faire crédit à qn; **we do not give c.** *(of shop)* la maison ne fait pas crédit; **to sell on c.** vendre à crédit; **to live on c.** vivre à crédit; **to enter a sum to sb's c.** porter une somme au crédit *ou* à l'actif de qn, créditer qn d'une somme; **his c. is good** *Fin* il a une bonne réputation de solvabilité; *Fig (he is trusted)* on lui fait toute confiance; *Fig* **he still has c. with the trade unions** les syndicats lui font encore confiance; *Am* **line of c.** ligne *f* de crédit

2 *(belief)* croyance *f*; **to give c. to** *or* **place c. in a rumour** ajouter *ou* accorder foi à un bruit; **facts that lend c. to a rumour** faits qui accréditent une rumeur; **to gain c.** *(of theory etc)* être accepté

3 *(merit)* mérite *m*, honneur *m*; **to give sb c. for sth** reconnaître le mérite de qn dans qch; **you'll have to give him c. for that** il faudra bien que tu reconnaisses son mérite là-dedans; **I gave him c. for more sense** je lui supposais plus de jugement; **she's shrewder than most people give her c. for** elle est plus perspicace que la plupart des gens ne le pensent; **give me c. for some common sense!** fais-moi l'honneur de croire que j'ai un peu de bon sens!; **to take the c. for an action** s'attribuer le mérite d'une action; **they took the c., but she did all the work** ils se sont attribué le mérite, mais c'est elle qui a fait tout le travail; **I can't claim much of the c. for the project's success** je ne peux pas m'attribuer grand mérite pour la réussite du projet; **most of the c. should go to the actors** c'est aux acteurs que devrait revenir le plus grand mérite; **c. where c.'s due** il faut rendre à César ce qui lui appartient; **OK, but c. where c.'s due, it was he who …** d'accord mais il faut bien reconnaître que c'est lui qui …; **with c.** honorablement; *Sch (in an examination)* avec mention assez bien; **it must be said to her c. that …** il faut porter à son crédit que …; **the team have three wins to their c.** l'équipe compte trois victoires à son actif; **it does him c.** cela lui fait (grand) honneur; **your children do you c. or are a c. to you** vos enfants vous font honneur; **she is a c. to the school** elle fait honneur à l'école

4 *Cin, TV* **credits** générique *m*; **to give sb a c.** *(in a book)* mentionner le nom de qn dans le liste des collaborateurs

5 *Univ* unité *f* de valeur

VT 1 *Com, Fin* **to c. sb/an account with a sum** créditer qn/un compte d'une somme; **to c. a sum to an account** porter une somme au crédit d'un compte

2 *(attribute)* attribuer, prêter (**sb with a quality** une qualité à qn); **to c. sb with superior intelligence** créditer qn d'une intelligence supérieure; **I credited you with more sense** je vous croyais *ou* supposais plus de jugement; **to be credited with having done sth** passer pour avoir fait qch

3 *(believe)* croire; **I wouldn't have credited it** je ne l'aurais pas cru possible; **you wouldn't c. it!, would you c. it!** tu te rends compte?
▸▸ **c. account** *Banking* compte *m* créditeur; *Br Com (with shop)* compte client; **c. advice** avis *m* de crédit; **c. agency** institution *f* de crédit; **c. agreement** accord *m* ou convention *f* de crédit; **c. balance** solde *m* créditeur; **c. bank** banque *f* de crédit; **c. broker** courtier, -ière en crédits *ou* en prêts; **c. card** carte *f* de crédit; **c. card reader** lecteur *m* de cartes; **c. ceiling** plafond *m* de crédit; *Acct* **c. column** colonne *f* créditrice; **c. control** *(government restrictions)* resserrement *m* ou encadrement du crédit; *(monitoring)* surveillance *f* des crédits; **c. controller** contrôleur, -euse du crédit; **c. freeze** blocage *m* du crédit; **c. history** profil *m* crédit; **to obtain information on sb's c. history** établir des renseignements de solvabilité sur qn; **c. insurance** assurance-crédit *f*; *Am* **c. line** ligne *f* de crédit; *Br* **c. note** *(in business)* facture *f* ou note *f* d'avoir; *(in shop)* avoir; **c. period** délai *m* de crédit; **c. rating** *(of person, company)* degré *m* de solvabilité; *(awarded by credit reference agency)* notation *f*; **c. rating agency** agence *f* de notation; **c. risk** risque *m* de crédit; *Acct* **c. side** crédit; *Fig* **on the c. side, it must be said he was honest enough to own up** il faut dire en sa faveur

qu'il a eu l'honnêteté d'avouer; **c. squeeze** restriction *f* ou encadrement du crédit; **c. union** société *f* ou caisse *f* de crédit; **c. voucher** chèque *m* de caisse

creditable ['kredɪtəb(ə)l] **ADJ** *(action)* estimable, digne d'éloges

creditably ['kredɪtəblɪ] **ADV** honorablement, avec honneur

creditor ['kredɪtər] **N** créancier, -ière; **creditors' meeting** réunion *f* des créanciers
▸▸ **c. account** compte *m* créditeur; *Econ* **c. nation** nation *f* créditrice

creditworthiness ['kredɪtwɜːðɪnɪs] **N** solvabilité *f*

creditworthy ['kredɪtwɜːðɪ] **ADJ** solvable

credo, *pl* **credos** ['kriːdəʊ, 'kreɪ-, -əʊz] **N** credo *m*

credulity [krɪ'djuːlɪtɪ] **N** crédulité *f*; **his story stretched c.** son histoire était vraiment difficile à croire

credulous ['kredjʊləs] **ADJ** crédule

creed [kriːd] **N 1** *Rel* credo *m inv*; **the (Apostles') C.** le Credo **2** *(beliefs)* croyance *f*, foi *f*; **political c.** credo *m* ou profession *f* de foi politique

creek [kriːk] **N** *esp Br (small bay)* crique *f*, anse *f*, *Am, Austr, New Zealand (stream)* ruisseau *m*, petit cours *m* d'eau; *Fam* **to be up the c. (without a paddle)** être dans le pétrin

creel [kriːl] **N** panier *m* de pêche

creep [kriːp] **N 1** *Sl (person) (disgusting)* personnage *m* répugnant, salopard *m*, saligaud *m*; *(obsequious)* lèche-bottes *m inv*, lèche-cul *m inv*; **that c. she's married to** son salopard de mari

2 *Fam* **the creeps** la chair de poule; **to get the creeps** avoir la chair de poule; **to give sb the creeps** *(scare)* donner la chair de poule à qn; *(annoy)* horripiler qn

3 *Aut* rampage *m*

VI *(pt, pp* **crept** [krept]*)* **1** *(of insect, animal)* ramper; *(of person)* se glisser; **to c. into bed** se glisser dans son lit; **he crept into the room** il entra furtivement *ou* à pas de loup dans la chambre; *Fig* **a moralizing tone has crept into her writing** un ton moralisateur s'est insidieusement glissé dans ses écrits; **a feeling of uneasiness crept over me** un sentiment de gêne commençait à me gagner; **to make sb's flesh c.** donner la chair de poule à qn

2 *Fam (be obsequious)* ramper *(devant les grands)*; **she's always creeping to the teacher** elle est toujours en train de ramper devant le professeur

3 *(of plant)* ramper; *(upwards)* grimper

▸ **creep along VI** *(stealthily)* s'avancer furtivement, marcher à pas de loup; *(move slowly, in car etc)* se traîner

▸ **creep away VI** s'éloigner à pas de loup

▸ **creep by VI** passer furtivement; **time** *or* **the hours crept slowly by** les heures passaient lentement

▸ **creep up VI 1** *(approach stealthily)* approcher furtivement (**to** de); **she crept up behind me** elle est arrivée derrière moi tout doucement **2** *(of inflation, prices etc)* monter petit à petit; **the speedometer crept up to 120** l'aiguille de l'indicateur de vitesse est montée tout doucement jusqu'à 120

▸ **creep up on VT INSEP** surprendre, prendre par surprise; **don't c. up on me like that!** ne m'arrive pas comme ça dessus sans prévenir!; **old age has crept up on me** j'ai vieilli sans m'en rendre compte

creeper ['kriːpər] **N 1** *(plant)* plante *f* rampante; *(climbing)* plante grimpante **2 creepers** *(shoes)* chaussures *fpl* à semelles de crêpe; *Am (crampons)* crampons *mpl* à verglas **3** *Am* **creepers** *(child's garment)* barboteuse *f*

creeping ['kri:pɪŋ] ADJ **1** *(animal)* rampant **2** *Fam (obsequious)* servile, rampant **3** *(plant) (along the ground)* rampant; *(upwards)* grimpant
N *Fam (obsequiousness)* servilité f
▶▶ *Med* **c. paralysis** paralysie f progressive

creepy ['kri:pɪ] ADJ *Fam* **1** *(film, story, person)* qui donne la chair de poule; **it was c.** c'était à vous donner la chair de poule; **a c. old house** une vieille maison sinistre **2** **I could feel something c. on my leg** je sentais quelque chose qui rampait sur ma jambe

creepy-crawly [-'krɔ:lɪ] *Fam* N insecte m rampant, bestiole f rampante
ADJ **a c. feeling** une sensation de fourmillement

cremate [krɪ'meɪt] VT *(dead person)* incinérer

cremation [krɪ'meɪʃən] N incinération f, crémation f

crematorium, pl **crematoria** [-'tɔ:rɪəm, -ɪə] N crématorium m

crematory ['kri:mətɔ:rɪ] N Am crématorium m

crenellated, Am **crenelated** ['krenəleɪtɪd] ADJ *(wall etc)* crénelé

Creole ['kri:əʊl] N **1** *(person)* Créole mf, Am *(in Louisiana)* = descendant, -ante des colons français ou espagnols de la Louisiane **2** *Ling* créole m
ADJ créole; *Am (in Louisiana)* = qui descend des colons français ou espagnols de la Louisiane

creosote ['krɪəsəʊt] N créosote f
VT *(wood)* créosoter

crêpe [kreɪp, krep] N **1** *Tex* crêpe m; **c. skirt** jupe f en crêpe **2** *(crêpe rubber)* crêpe m **3** *(crêpe paper)* papier m crépon **4** *Culin (pancake)* crêpe f
▶▶ **c. bandage** bande f Velpeau®; **c. de Chine** crêpe m de Chine; **c. paper** papier crépon; **c. rubber** crêpe m; **c. soles** semelles fpl de crêpe

crêpe-soled [-səʊld] ADJ à semelle(s) de crêpe

crept PP, PT *see* **creep** VI

Cres *(abbr* **Crescent)** rue *(en croissant)*

crescendo, pl **crescendos** [krɪ'ʃendəʊ, -əʊz] N *Mus, Fig* crescendo m inv; **to build up to a c.** aller crescendo; *Fig* **to reach a c.** atteindre son paroxysme
ADV *Mus* crescendo

crescent ['kresənt] N *(shape)* croissant m; *(street)* rue f en croissant
ADJ *(shaped)* en forme de croissant ou de demi-lune
▶▶ **c. moon** croissant m de la lune

cress [kres] N cresson m

crest [krest] N *(of chicken, reptile)* crête f, *(of bird)* huppe f, *(of peacock)* aigrette f, *Anat (of bone)* crête, arête f, *(of helmet)* cimier m, crête; *(of hill, wave)* crête, sommet m; *(of roof)* faîte m; *(coat of arms)* armoiries fpl; *(insignia)* écusson m; *Fig* **to be on the c. of a wave** être à son meilleur niveau; **she rode to power on the c. of a wave of popular enthusiasm** elle a été portée au pouvoir par l'enthousiasme populaire
VT *(wave, hill)* arriver au sommet de

crested ['krestɪd] ADJ **1** *(animal)* à crête; *(with feathered crest)* à huppe, huppé; **white-c. waves** moutons mpl, vagues fpl aux crêtes blanches **2** *(helmet)* orné d'un cimier; *(plumed)* panaché **3** *Her (coat of arms)* armorié; *(insignia)* orné d'un écusson

crestfallen ['krestfɔ:l(ə)n] ADJ *(person)* abattu, découragé; *(look)* déconfit, abattu, découragé

cretaceous [krɪ'teɪʃəs] ADJ crétacé
N **the C.** le crétacé

Cretan ['kri:t(ə)n] ADJ crétois
N Crétois, -oise

Crete [kri:t] N Crète f

cretin ['kretɪn] N *Med Old-fashioned, Fam* crétin, -ine

cretinism ['kretɪnɪz(ə)m] N *Med Old-fashioned, Fam* crétinisme m

cretinous ['kretɪnəs] ADJ *Med Old-fashioned, Fam* crétin

cretonne [kre'tɒn, 'kretɒn] N *Tex* cretonne f

Creutzfeldt-Jakob disease ['krɔɪtsfelt-'jækɒb] N *Med* maladie f de Creutzfeldt-Jakob

crevasse [krɪ'væs] N crevasse f *(glaciaire)*

crevice ['krevɪs] N fente f, *(in wall)* lézarde f, *(in rock)* crevasse f, fissure f

crew [kru:] N VOIR GRAMMAIRE A11 **1** *(of ship, plane)* équipage m; *(in rowing)* équipe f; *(gang, team)* équipe; **ambulance/camera c.** équipe d'ambulanciers/de cameramen; *Aviat* **ground c.** personnel m au sol; *Ind* **maintenance c.** équipe d'entretien **2** *Fam (group of people)* bande f, troupe f; **sorry c.** triste engeance f; **they're a good c. to work with** c'est une bonne équipe avec qui travailler
VT *(ship)* armer d'un équipage; *(plane)* fournir un équipage à; **yacht that can't be crewed by less than six** yacht qui exige un équipage de six au moins; *Naut* **crewed charter** location f de bateau avec équipage
VI **to c. for sb** servir d'équipier à qn
▶▶ **c. cut** coupe f de cheveux en brosse; **c. member** membre mf d'équipage; **c. neck** col m ras le ou du cou, ras-le-cou m inv

crib [krɪb] N **1** *(cradle)* berceau m; *Am (cot)* lit m d'enfant; *Rel (in Nativity)* crèche f **2** *Agr (for feeding animals)* mangeoire f, râtelier m **3** *Br Fam (plagiarism)* plagiat m; *Sch* antisèche f, *(translation)* traduction f *(employée subrepticement)*
VT *(-bb-)* *(passage from a book)* reproduire, copier; *Sch* **to c. an exercise from sb** pomper un exercice sur qn
VI *(-bb-)* *Sch* pomper; **to c. from an author** plagier un auteur
▶▶ *Am* **c. death** mort f subite *(du nourrisson)*

cribbage ['krɪbɪdʒ] N *Cards* = jeu m de cartes où l'on compte les points en enfonçant des chevilles dans une planche de bois

crick [krɪk] N **c. in the back** tour m de reins; **c. in the neck** torticolis m
VT **to c. one's neck** attraper un torticolis; **to c. one's back** se faire un tour de reins

cricket¹ ['krɪkɪt] N *(insect)* grillon m

cricket² N *Sport* cricket m; **to play c.** jouer au cricket; *Old-fashioned Br Fig* **that's not c.** cela n'est pas de jeu, cela ne se fait pas
▶▶ **c. ball** balle f de cricket; **c. bat** batte f de cricket; **c. field, c. pitch** terrain m de cricket

cricketer ['krɪkɪtər] N joueur, -euse de cricket

crier ['kraɪər] N **town c.** crieur m public ou municipal

crikey ['kraɪkɪ] INT *Br Sl* mince alors!

crim [krɪm] N *Br, Austr Fam (criminal)* criminel, -elle

Crimbo ['krɪmbəʊ] N *Br Fam (Christmas)* Noël m

crime [kraɪm] N *(act)* crime m; *Law (minor offence)* délit m; *(phenomenon)* criminalité f; **to commit a c.** commettre un crime/un délit; **a c. against nature/humanity** un crime contre nature/l'humanité; *Law* **a c. of passion** un crime passionnel; *Fig* **it's a c. to cut down this tree** c'est un crime d'abattre cet arbre; *Fig* **it's not a c. to …** ce n'est pas un crime de …
▶▶ **c. figures** chiffres mpl de la criminalité;

c. rate taux m de (la) criminalité; *Journ* **c. reporter** journaliste mf qui couvre les affaires criminelles; **c. scene** lieu m du crime; **c. series** série f policière; **c. story** *(novel)* roman m noir; *(detective novel)* roman policier; **c. wave** vague f de criminalité; **c. writer** auteur m de romans policiers

Crimea (the) [ðaɪ'kraɪmɪə] N la Crimée

Crimean [kraɪ'mɪən] ADJ de Crimée; *Hist* **the C. War** la guerre de Crimée

criminal ['krɪmɪn(ə)l] N criminel, -elle
ADJ *Law* criminel; *Fig* **it would be c. to cut down these trees** ce serait un crime d'abattre ces arbres; **to take c. proceedings against sb** poursuivre qn en justice; **to bring a c. action against sb** intenter une action en justice contre qn
▶▶ **c. act** action f criminelle; *Law* **c. case** affaire f criminelle; *Law* **c. conversation** adultère m; *Law* **c. court** ≃ cour f d'assises; *Br* **C. Investigation Department** = police f judiciaire britannique, ≃ PJ f; **c. law** droit m pénal ou criminel; **c. lawyer** avocat, -ate au criminel, pénaliste m; *Law* **c. liability** responsabilité f pénale, majorité f pénale; *Law* **c. negligence** négligence f coupable ou criminelle; *Law* **c. offence** délit m; *Law* **c. record** casier m judiciaire, *(document)* extrait m de casier judiciaire; **c. suit** action criminelle, procès m criminel

criminalization [krɪmɪnəlaɪ'zeɪʃən] N criminalisation f

criminalize ['krɪmɪnəlaɪz] VT criminaliser

criminally ['krɪmɪn(ə)lɪ] ADV criminellement; **to be c. insane** être dément; *(of man)* être un fou dangereux; **the c. insane** les fous dangereux; **this is c. negligent** c'est une négligence criminelle; **it's c. wasteful** c'est un crime de gaspiller comme ça

criminologist [krɪmɪ'nɒlədʒɪst] N criminologue mf

criminology [krɪmɪ'nɒlədʒɪ] N criminologie f

crimp [krɪmp] N *(in hair)* frisure f, *(in sheet)* pli m
VT *(hair)* crêper; *(pastry)* gaufrer; *(material)* plisser, crêper

Crimplene® ['krɪmpli:n] N = synthétique m infroissable semblable au crêpe de Chine

crimson ['krɪmz(ə)n] ADJ, N cramoisi m; **to blush c.** devenir cramoisi; **c. with rage** rouge de colère

cringe [krɪndʒ] VI **1** *(flinch)* avoir un mouvement de recul; **the dog cringed in the corner** le chien se blottit dans le coin; **he stayed cringing in the background** il se fit tout petit **2** *(be servile)* s'humilier, ramper, s'aplatir *(before sb* devant qn) **3** *Fam (be embarrassed)* avoir envie de rentrer sous terre; **her singing makes me c.** quand elle chante, ça me donne envie de rentrer sous terre; **it makes you c.** c'est très pénible **4** *(be disgusted)* avoir un sentiment de dégoût

cringe-making ADJ *Br Fam* qui donne envie de rentrer sous terre

cringing ['krɪndʒɪŋ] ADJ **1** *(afraid)* craintif **2** *(servile)* servile, obséquieux

crinkle ['krɪŋk(ə)l] N pli m, ride f
VT *(paper)* froisser, chiffonner; **to c. one's nose** froncer le nez
VI se froisser; *(of apples)* se rider; **his nose crinkled at the smell** l'odeur lui fit froncer le nez

crinkle-cut ADJ *(crisps, chips)* dentelé

crinkly ['krɪŋklɪ] ADJ *(skin)* ridé; *(paper)* froissé, chiffonné; **my fingers have gone all c.** la peau de mes doigts est toute fripée

crinoline ['krɪn(ə)lɪn] N crinoline f

cripes ['kraɪps] INT *Old-fashioned Br Sl* mince alors!

cripple ['krɪp(ə)l] N estropié, -ée, infirme mf,

invalide *mf*; *Fig* **emotional c.** handicapé, -ée sur le plan affectif

VT 1 *(person)* estropier; **those who were crippled in the war** les mutilés *mpl* de guerre **2** *Fig (machine)* empêcher de fonctionner; *(ship)* désemparer; *(tank)* mettre hors de combat; *(industry, system)* paralyser

crippled ['krɪp(ə)ld] **ADJ 1** *(person)* estropié, infirme; **c. with rheumatism** perclus de rhumatismes; **a c. arm** un bras malade **2** *Fig (ship)* désemparé; *(tank)* hors de combat; **the country is c. with debt** le pays est paralysé par les dettes

crippling ['krɪplɪŋ] **ADJ 1** *(illness)* qui rend infirme **2** *Fig (taxation, strike etc)* paralysant; **the c. effect of the blockade** l'effet paralysant du blocus

crisis, *pl* **crises** ['kraɪsɪs, -iːz] **N** *(in business, one's personal life etc)* crise *f*; **in c.** en pleine crise; **things are coming to a c.** la situation devient critique; **to go through a c.** traverser une crise; **a minor family c.** un petit problème familial

▸▸ **c. management** gestion *f* des crises; **c. point** point *m* critique; **to reach c. point** atteindre un point critique

crisp [krɪsp] **ADJ** *(biscuit, pastry etc)* croquant, croustillant; *(apple, lettuce)* croquant, craquant; *(bacon)* croustillant; *(air)* vif; *(style)* vif et précis; *(tone)* tranchant; **the snow was c. underfoot** la neige craquait sous mes/nos/etc pas; **a c. five-pound note** un billet de cinq livres tout neuf; **a c. white shirt** *(appearance)* une chemise blanche impeccable; *(texture)* une chemise blanche fraîchement lavée

N 1 cooked **to a c.** rôti à point pour croquer sous la dent; **burnt to a c.** carbonisé **2** *Br (potato)* **crisps** (pommes *fpl*) chips *fpl*; **one c.** une chips

VT *(meat etc)* donner du croustillant *ou* du croquant à

crispbread ['krɪspbred] **N** pain *m* suédois

crisper ['krɪspər] **N** *(in refrigerator)* bac *m* à légumes

crisply ['krɪsplɪ] **ADV** *(to speak)* d'un ton tranchant; *(to write)* d'un style vif et précis

crispness ['krɪspnɪs] **N** *(of biscuit, pastry etc)* croustillant *m*, croquant *m*; *(of apple, lettuce)* craquant *m*; *(of bacon)* croustillant; *(of snow)* dureté *f*, *(of air)* fraîcheur *f*, *(of style)* vivacité *f* et précision *f*; **to lose its c.** *(of fabric etc)* perdre sa raideur

crispy ['krɪspɪ] **ADJ** croustillant

criss-cross ['krɪs-] **ADJ** *(pattern etc)* entrecroisé

N entrecroisement *m*

VT *(threads etc)* entrecroiser; **a brow criss-crossed with wrinkles** un front craquelé de rides; **a network of streets criss-crosses the town** un réseau de rues parcourt la ville dans tous les sens

VI s'entrecroiser

crit [krɪt] **N** *Fam (criticism)* critique *f*; *lit* **c.** critique littéraire

criterion, *pl* **criteria** [kraɪ'tɪərɪən, -ɪə] **N** critère *m*; **what criteria do you apply** *or* **what are your criteria when selecting candidates?** sur quels critères vous fondez-vous *ou* quels sont vos critères lorsque vous sélectionnez des candidats?

critic ['krɪtɪk] **N** *(in general)* critiqueur, -euse; *(of other people's behaviour)* censeur *m*; *Cin, Liter etc* critique *mf*; **she has her critics** il y en a qui la critiquent; **there are few critics of the policy** peu de gens critiquent la politique; **music/drama/literary c.** critique musical/dramatique/littéraire; **film c.** critique de cinéma

critical ['krɪtɪk(ə)l] **ADJ 1** *(criticizing)* critique; **a c. audience** un public exigeant; **to**

be c. of sb/sth *(of person)* se montrer *ou* être critique à l'égard de qn/qch; *(of report, article etc)* être critique à l'égard de qn/qch; **stop being so c.** arrête de critiquer

2 *Cin, Liter etc (essay, study)* critique; **the film received c. acclaim** le film a été salué unanimement par les critiques, le film a fait l'unanimité de la critique

3 *(decisive)* *(situation, moment, age etc)* critique; *Med* **she is in a c. condition** elle est dans un état critique; **she is going through a c. time** elle subit *ou* traverse une crise en ce moment; **the next few days will be c.** les prochains jours seront décisifs

▸▸ *Phys* **c. angle** angle *m* critique; *Phys* **c. mass** masse *f* critique; *Com, Tech* **c. path** chemin *m* critique; *Com, Tech* **c. path analysis** analyse *f* du chemin critique; *Com, Tech* **c. path method** méthode *f* du chemin critique; *Com, Tech* **c. path model** modèle *m* du chemin critique

critically ['krɪtɪklɪ] **ADV 1** *(to consider sth)* en critique; *(to look at sth)* d'un œil critique **2** *(acclaimed etc)* par les critiques **3** *(seriously)* gravement; *Med* **she is c. ill** elle est gravement malade, elle est dans un état critique; **the c. ill** les grands malades *mpl*

criticism ['krɪtɪsɪz(ə)m] **N 1** *(action, act of criticizing)* critique *f*; **it wasn't meant as a c.** ce n'était pas une critique; **to lay oneself open to c.** s'exposer à la critique; **the report contained strong c. of this department** le rapport contenait de graves critiques de ce service **2** *Cin, Liter etc* critique *f*; **to write a c. of a book** écrire la critique d'un livre

criticize ['krɪtɪsaɪz] **VT 1** *(express disapproval of)* *(person, behaviour etc)* critiquer; **to c. sb for sth** critiquer qn pour qch; **to c. sb for doing sth** critiquer qn d'avoir fait qch; **they have been criticized for not trying** on leur a reproché de ne pas avoir essayé; **his report has been criticized for being too ...** on a reproché à son rapport d'être trop ...; **to c. sth severely** se répandre en critiques sur qch **2** *(film, book etc)* critiquer, faire la critique de

VI critiquer; **stop criticizing** arrête de critiquer *ou* de faire des critiques

critique [krɪ'tiːk] **N** critique *f*, *(of book etc)* article *m* critique

critter ['krɪtər] **N** *Am Dial* = **creature**

CRN [siːɑː'ren] **N** *Com (abbr* **customs registered number)** numéro *m* d'enregistrement douanier

croak [krəʊk] **N** *(of frog)* coassement *m*; *(of raven)* croassement *m*; **..., he said in a c.** ..., dit-il d'une voix rauque

VI 1 *(of frog)* coasser; *(of raven)* croasser; *(of person)* parler d'une voix rauque **2** *Sl (die)* crever, claquer

VT *(words, warning etc)* proférer d'une voix rauque; **I'm not well, she croaked** ça ne va pas, dit-elle d'une voix rauque

croaking ['krəʊkɪŋ] **N** *(of frog)* coassement *m*; *(of raven)* croassement *m*

croaky ['krəʊkɪ] **ADJ** *(voice)* rauque, enroué

Croat ['krəʊæt] **ADJ** croate

N 1 Croate *mf* **2** *Ling* croate *m*

Croatia [krəʊ'eɪʃə] **N** Croatie *f*

Croatian [krəʊ'eɪʃən] **ADJ** croate

N 1 Croate *mf* **2** *Ling* croate *m*

croc [krɒk] **N** *Fam* crocodile *m*

crochet ['krəʊʃeɪ, -ʃɪ] **N** (travail *m* au) crochet *m*

VT *(shawl, tablecloth etc)* faire au crochet; **crocheted sweater** pull au crochet

VI faire du crochet

▸▸ **c. hook** crochet; **c. work** travail au crochet

crocheting ['krəʊʃeɪɪŋ, -ʃɪ-] **N** (travail *m* au) crochet *m*

crock [krɒk] **N 1** *(pot)* pot *m* de terre; *(jug)* cruche *f*; *Vulg* **it's a c. of shit** *(nonsense)* c'est un tas de conneries **2** *(in gardening)* tesson *m* *(pour couvrir le trou d'un pot de fleurs)* **3** *Fam* **old c.** *(person)* vieux bonhomme *m* fini, croulant *m*; *(car)* vieux clou *m*, vieille bagnole *f*

crockery ['krɒkərɪ] **N** *(no pl) (tableware)* vaisselle *f* de table *ou* de cuisine

crocodile ['krɒkədaɪl] **N 1** *(animal)* crocodile *m* **2** *(skin)* peau *f* de crocodile, *Fam* croco *m* **c. handbag** sac *m* à main en crocodile *ou Fam* en croco **3** *Br Fam (line of pupils)* élèves *mpl* marchant en colonne par deux

▸▸ **c. clip** pince *f* crocodile; **c. skin** peau de crocodile, *Fam* croco; **c. tears** larmes *fpl* de crocodile

crocus, *pl* **crocuses** ['krəʊkəs, -əsɪz] **N** crocus *m*

croft [krɒft] **N** *esp Scot* petite ferme *f*

crofter ['krɒftər] **N** *esp Scot* petit fermier *m*

Crohn's disease [krəʊnz] **N** *Med* maladie *f* de Crohn

crone [krəʊn] **N** *Pej* **old c.** vieille bique *f*

crony ['krəʊnɪ] **N** copain *m*, copine *f*; **a Labour c. is believed to have got the top advisory job** le principal poste de conseiller aurait été attribué à un membre du parti travailliste proche du pouvoir

▸▸ **c. capitalism** capitalisme *m* de copinage

cronyism ['krəʊnɪɪzəm] **N** *Pej* copinage *m*

crook [krʊk] **N 1** *Fam (criminal, rogue)* escroc *m* **2** *(of shepherd)* houlette *f*, *(of bishop)* crosse *f* **3** *(curve)* **in the c. of her arm** dans le creux de son bras

VT courber, recourber; *(arm)* plier; **to c. one's finger** recourber son doigt

ADJ *Austr Fam* **1** *(ill)* malade; *(furious)* furieux; **to go c.** piquer une rage *(*at sb* contre qn)*; **to feel a bit c.** ne pas se sentir dans son assiette **2** *(broken down) (machinery etc)* en panne **3** *(poor) (thing, place etc)* moche

crooked ['krʊkɪd] **ADJ 1** *Fam (lawyer, salesman etc)* véreux; **c. means** moyens *mpl* douteux **2** *(not straight)* courbe; *(limb, tree)* déjeté; *(nose)* crochu; *(leg)* tors; **the painting was c.** le tableau était de travers; **his hat was on c.** son chapeau était de travers; **a c. smile** un sourire forcé **3** [krʊkt] *(with a hooked end)* **c. stick** bâton *m* recourbé

crookedly ['krʊkɪdlɪ] **ADV 1** *Fam (to deal)* malhonnêtement **2** *(to hang)* de travers

crookedness ['krʊkɪdnɪs] **N 1** *Fam (dishonesty)* malhonnêteté *f* **2** *(of outlines etc)* irrégularité *f*, *(of smile)* fausseté *f*

croon [kruːn] **VT 1** *(song)* chantonner, fredonner **2** *(say)* dire d'une voix charmeuse

VI chantonner

crooner ['kruːnər] **N** *(singer)* chanteur, -euse de charme, crooner *m*

crop [krɒp] **N 1** *Agr (of cereals)* récolte *f*, moisson *f*, *(of fruit, potatoes etc)* récolte; **a poor/good c.** une mauvaise/bonne récolte; **to harvest the crops** faire la récolte *ou* la moisson; *Fig* **a fine c. of hair** une belle chevelure; **this year's c. of films** les films de cette année **2** *(haircut)* coupe *f* (de cheveux); **to give sb a close c.** couper ras les cheveux de qn **3** *(handle of whip)* manche *m*; **(riding) c.** cravache *f*, **hunting c. stick** *m* de chasse **4** *(of bird etc)* jabot *m*

VT *(-pp-)* **1** *(cut) (animal's ears, tail)* écourter, couper; *(hair)* couper ras; *Comput (graphic)* rogner; *(photograph)* couper **2** *(of cattle) (grass)* brouter **3** *Agr (potatoes etc)* cultiver; **to c. land with corn** mettre une terre en blé

VI *(-pp-)* *(of land)* donner une récolte; **to c. well** donner une bonne récolte

▸▸ **c. circle** = motif *m* circulaire tracé dans un champ, attribué par certains à l'intervention d'extraterrestres; *Agr* **c. rotation** assolement *m*, rotation *f* des cultures

▸**crop up** VI *(arise)* se présenter, surgir; **her name cropped up in the conversation** son nom a surgi dans la conversation; **did anything c. up while I was away?** est-ce qu'il s'est passé quelque chose pendant mon absence?; **something has cropped up** *(I'll be late etc)* j'ai un empêchement

cropper ['krɒpər] N **1** *Fam* **to come a c.** *(fall)* faire une chute, *Fam* se prendre *ou* se ramasser une pelle; *Fig (fail)* se planter; **to come a c. over sth** se casser les dents sur qch **2** *Agr (person)* cultivateur, -trice **3** *(plant)* **good/bad c.** plante *f* qui donne de bonnes/de mauvaises récoltes *ou* qui donne bien/mal

cropping ['krɒpɪŋ] N *Comput (of graphics)* rognage *m*, recadrage *m*

croquet ['krəʊkeɪ, -kɪ] N *Sport* croquet *m*; **to play c.** jouer au croquet
▸▸**c. mallet** maillet *m*; **c. player** joueur, -euse de croquet

croquette [krɒ'ket] N *Culin* croquette *f*; **potato c.** croquette de pomme de terre

crosier ['krəʊzɪər] N *Rel* crosse *f (d'évêque)*

CROSS [krɒs]

N croix **1** ▪ hybride **2**	
VT croiser **1, 5** ▪ traverser **2** ▪ contrarier **3**	
VI se croiser **1** ▪ traverser **2**	
ADJ fâché **1** ▪ transversal **2**	

N **1** *(sign, shape)* croix *f*, *Fig* **everyone has their c. to bear** chacun a sa croix à porter; *Rel* **to make the sign of the c.** faire le signe de (la) croix; **market c.** croix de la place du marché; **St Andrew's C.** croix de Saint-André; **Military C.** Croix de Guerre; **to sign with a c.** signer d'une croix
2 *(hybrid)* hybride *m*, croisement *m*; **a c. between a horse and a donkey** un croisement *ou* hybride du cheval et de l'ânesse; *Fig* **to be a c. between sth and sth** être un mélange de qch et de qch; **it's a c. between a car and a van** c'est un compromis entre une voiture et une camionnette
3 *Boxing* cross *m*, coup *m* croisé
VT **1** *(form into the shape of a cross) (two sticks etc)* croiser; **to c. one's legs/arms** (se) croiser les jambes/les bras; **to c. one's eyes** loucher, faire exprès de loucher; *Fig* **to c. swords** croiser le fer (**with** avec); **let's keep our fingers crossed** croisons les doigts; **I've got my fingers crossed for you** je croise les doigts pour toi; *Rel* **to c. oneself** faire le signe de croix, se signer; *Fam* **c. my heart (and hope to die)** croix de bois croix de fer (si je mens, je vais en enfer); *Fig* **we must have got our wires crossed** nous avons dû mal nous comprendre; *Prov* **c. my palm with silver** *(said by fortune-teller)* une petite pièce, s'il vous plaît
2 *(go across) (sea, river)* traverser, passer; *(street etc)* traverser; *(frontier)* traverser, franchir; *(threshold)* franchir; *(bridge)* passer (sur), traverser; **the bridge that crosses the river** le pont qui traverse *ou* enjambe la rivière; **to c. sb's path** se trouver sur le chemin de qn; *Br Pol* **to c. the floor (of the House)** changer de parti (politique); *Naut* **to c. the line** passer l'équateur; **to c. sb's mind** *(of thought)* traverser l'esprit de qn, venir à l'esprit *ou* à l'idée de qn; **didn't it c. your mind that she might have been lying?** est-ce qu'il ne t'est pas venu à l'idée qu'elle ait pu mentir?
3 *(oppose) (person, person's plans)* contrarier, contrecarrer; *(go against) (person)* s'opposer à; **to be crossed in love** avoir une déception amoureuse
4 *(in writing) (cheque)* barrer; **to c. one's t's** mettre les barres à ses t

5 *(in breeding etc)* croiser; *Fig (two styles)* mélanger, marier
VI **1** *(of roads, letters etc)* se croiser; *(of lines)* se croiser, s'entrecroiser
2 *(go across)* traverser; **to c. from Dover to Calais** faire la traversée de Douvres à Calais; **look before you c.** regarde avant de traverser
ADJ **1** *(angry)* fâché; **he looks c.** il a l'air fâché; **to get c.** se fâcher (**with** contre; **about** de); **Mummy's very c. with you!** Maman est très fâchée!; **don't be c. with me** il ne faut pas m'en vouloir; **to be c. with oneself** s'en vouloir; **you never hear a c. word from her** avec elle, on n'entend jamais un mot plus haut que l'autre; **we've never had a c. word** nous ne nous sommes jamais disputés
2 *(transverse)* transversal
▸▸*Opt* **c. hairs** = fils *mpl* croisés d'une lunette qui déterminent la ligne de visée; *St Exch* **c. hedge** couverture *f* croisée; **c. section** coupe *f ou* section *f* transversale; **in c. section** en coupe transversale; *Fig* **a c. section of life** une tranche de vie; *Fig* **a c. section of the population** un groupe représentatif de la population; *Am* **c. street** rue *f* transversale
▸**cross off** VT SEP *(remove) (name)* rayer, barrer; **to c. a name off a list** rayer un nom d'une liste
▸**cross out** VT SEP *(word, phrase etc)* biffer, barrer, rayer
▸**cross over** VT INSEP *(street)* traverser
VI *(go across street, sea, frontier etc)* traverser; **they crossed over to Cherbourg in their yacht** ils ont fait la traversée jusqu'à Cherbourg dans leur yacht

crossbar ['krɒsbɑːr] N *(barre f de)* traverse *f*, entretoise *f*, *(on man's bike)* barre; *Ftbl, Rugby etc* barre transversale

crossbeam ['krɒsbiːm] N *Constr* sommier *m*, traverse *f*, *(on piles)* chapeau *m*; *Gym* portique *m*

cross-bencher [-bentʃər] N *Br Parl* (député *m*) non-inscrit, -ite, *pl* non-inscrit(e)s

crossbill ['krɒsbɪl] N *(bird)* bec-croisé *m*, *pl* becs-croisés

crossbones ['krɒsbəʊnz] NPL **skull and c.** tête *f* de mort *(du pavillon des pirates)*

cross-border ADJ transfrontières *inv*, transfrontalier
▸▸**c. talks** négociations *fpl* transfrontalières; **c. trade** commerce *m* transfrontalier

crossbow ['krɒsbəʊ] N arbalète *f*

crossbred ['krɒsbred] ADJ *(animal)* croisé; *(plant)* hybride

crossbreed ['krɒsbriːd] N croisement *m*; *(person)* métis, -isse
VT *(pt, pp* **crossbred***)* croiser; *(humans)* métisser; *(plants)* hybrider

cross-Channel ADJ *(ferry)* trans-Manche *inv*

crosscheck ['krɒs'tʃek] N vérification *f* par recoupement
VT vérifier par recoupement; **I crosschecked my list against yours** j'ai vérifié que ma liste et la vôtre sont identiques, j'ai vérifié qu'il n'y a pas de disparités entre ma liste et la vôtre

cross-compiler N *Comput* compilateur *m* croisé

cross-country ADJ *(walk)* à travers champs; *(vehicle)* tout-terrain *inv*
N *Sport* **1** *(race, racing)* cross *m*, cross-country *m*, *pl* cross-countrys *ou* cross-countries
2 *(skiing)* ski *m* de fond
▸▸**c. runner** coureur, -euse de cross, crossman, *pl* crossmen, crosswoman *f*, *pl* crosswomen; **c. running** cross; **c. skier** fondeur, -euse; **c. skiing** ski de fond

cross-cultural ADJ interculturel

cross-currency swap N *St Exch* crédit *m* croisé

cross-current N *(in air, water)* contre-courant *m*, *pl* contre-courants

crosscut ['krɒskʌt] N **1** coupe *f* en travers **2** *Cin, TV* montage *m* alterné
▸▸**c. file** lime *f* à taille croisée; **c. saw** scie *f* passe-partout

crosscutting ['krɒskʌtɪŋ] N *Cin, TV* montage *m* alterné

cross-dressing N travestisme *m*

crossed [krɒst] ADJ croisé; *Tel* **we seem to have a c. line** il y a des interférences sur la ligne; **the regimental badge is two c. rifles** le badge du régiment représente deux fusils croisés
▸▸**c. cheque** chèque *m* barré

cross-examination N *Law* contre-interrogatoire *m*, *pl* contre-interrogatoires; *Fig* interrogatoire *m* serré

cross-examine VT *Law* soumettre à un contre-interrogatoire; *Fig* soumettre à un interrogatoire serré

cross-eyed ADJ qui louche; **to be c.** loucher

cross-fade N *Radio* fondu *m* enchaîné (sonore); *Cin, TV* fondu enchaîné

cross-fertilization N hybridation *f*, pollinisation *f* croisée; *Fig* échanges *mpl*

cross-fertilize VT *Bot* hybrider; *Fig (ideas)* échanger
VI *Bot* s'hybrider; *Fig (of teams, people at conference etc)* échanger des idées

crossfire ['krɒsfaɪər] N *Mil* feu *m* croisé; **to be caught in the c.** *Mil* être pris dans le feu croisé; *Fig (in argument)* être pris entre deux feux

cross-flow radiator N *Aut* radiateur *m* à flux transversal

cross-grained [-greɪnd] ADJ **1** *(wood)* aux fibres irrégulières, à fibres torses **2** *Fig (person)* difficile, acariâtre

crosshair pointer ['krɒsheər] N *Comput* pointeur *m* en croix

crosshatch ['krɒshætʃ] VT *(in drawing)* hachurer en croisillons

crosshatching ['krɒshætʃɪŋ] N *(système m de)* hachures *fpl* croisées *ou* en croisillons

cross-headed ADJ *Tech (screw, screwdriver)* cruciforme

cross-holding N *Fin* participation *f* croisée

cross-impact analysis N *Mktg* analyse *f* d'interférence

crossing ['krɒsɪŋ] N **1** *(of sea)* traversée *f*, *(of river, the Alps)* traversée, passage *m*; *Mil (of river)* franchissement *m*; **we had a fine** *or* **good c.** nous avons eu *ou* fait une belle traversée; **a sea c.** une traversée maritime **2** *(for pedestrians)* passage *m* pour piétons, passage clouté **3** *(of roads)* croisement *m*, intersection *f*, carrefour *m*; *Rail* **level** *or Am* **grade c.** passage *m* à niveau

cross-legged ADJ **in a c. position** les jambes croisées
ADV les jambes croisées; **to sit c.** être assis en tailleur

crossly ['krɒslɪ] ADV *(with annoyance)* avec mauvaise humeur; *(angrily)* d'un air/d'un ton fâché

cross-member N *Aut* traverse *f*

crossover ['krɒsəʊvər] N **1** croisement *m*; *(of roads)* (croisement par) pont *m* routier; *(for pedestrians)* passage *m* clouté; *Rail* voie *f* de croisement **2** *(singer)* = chanteur, -euse qui est passé(e) d'un style de musique à un autre
ADJ *Mus (music)* qui associe deux styles; *(singer)* = qui est passé d'un style de musique à un autre
▸▸*Mus* **c. album** album *m* hybride

cross-party ADJ *Pol*

▶▶ **c. agreement** accord *m* entre partis; **c. support** = soutien *m* au-delà des clivages politiques; **c. talks** négociations *fpl* entre partis

crosspatch ['krɒspætʃ] N *Fam* ronchon, -onne

crosspiece ['krɒspiːs] N (barre *f* de) traverse *f*

cross-ply tyre N *Aut* pneu *m* à structure diagonale

cross-post VT *Comput* faire un envoi multiple de

cross-posting N *Comput* envoi *m* multiple

cross-pricing N fixation *f* de prix croisés

cross-purposes ['krɒs'pɜːpəsɪz] N **to be (talking) at c.** ne pas parler de la même chose

cross-question VT = **cross-examine**

cross-refer VT (-rr-) renvoyer; **the reader is cross-referred to page 332** il y a un renvoi à la page 332

cross-reference N renvoi *m*
VT (*book*) établir les renvois de; **to c. X to Y** renvoyer de X à Y; **it's cross-referenced** (*to another article*) il y a un renvoi à un autre article
▶▶ *Comput* **c. table** table *f* de références

crossroad ['krɒsrəʊd] N *Am* (*across a road*) = route *f* qui en coupe une autre; (*between main roads*) route secondaire, route départementale

crossroads ['krɒsrəʊdz] N (*with sing verb*) carrefour *m*, croisement *m*; *Fig* **the city is at the c. of Europe** la ville est au carrefour de l'Europe; *Fig* **we are now at the c.** (*decisive moment*) c'est l'heure des décisions irrévocables

cross-stitch N *Sewing* point *m* de croix

crosstalk ['krɒstɔːk] N **1** *Br* série *f* de répliques du tac au tac **2** *Tel* diaphonie *f*

cross-town ADJ *Am* (*bus, trolley*) qui traverse la ville

cross-trainer N (*gym equipment*) cross-trainer *m*, *pl* cross-trainers

cross-training N *Sport* = entraînement *m* dans d'autres disciplines afin d'améliorer ses performances dans sa discipline principale

crosswalk ['krɒswɔːk] N *Am* passage *m* clouté, passage pour piétons

crossway ['krɒsweɪ] N *Am* = **crossroad**

crosswind ['krɒswɪnd] N vent *m* de travers

crosswise ['krɒswaɪz] ADV (*at right angles*) à angle droit; (*diagonally*) en travers

crossword ['krɒswɜːd] N (*puzzle*) mots *mpl* croisés
▶▶ **c. puzzle** mots croisés

crotch [krɒtʃ] N (*of person*) entrejambe *m*; (*of trousers*) entrejambe, *Spec* fourche *f*

crotchet ['krɒtʃɪt] N *Mus* noire *f*

crotchety ['krɒtʃətɪ] ADJ (*person*) grognon; (*mood*) difficile, acariâtre

croton ['krəʊt(ə)n] N (*plant*) croton *m*

crouch [kraʊtʃ] N accroupissement *m*
VI (*of animal*) se tapir; (*of person*) s'accroupir; **the tiger was crouching for a spring** le tigre, tapi, était sur le point de sauter
▶ **crouch down** VI = **crouch** VI

croup[1] [kruːp] N (*of horse*) croupe *f*

croup[2] N *Med* croup *m*; **to have c.** avoir le croup

croupier ['kruːpɪər] N croupier *m*

crow[1] [krəʊ] N (*bird*) corneille *f*, *Am Fig* **to eat c.** s'humilier (*en reconnaissant qu'on s'est trompé*); **as the c. flies** à vol d'oiseau
▶▶ **c.'s nest** nid *m* de corneille; *Naut* nid-de-pie *m*, *pl* nids-de-pie

crow[2] N (*of cock*) chant *m* du coq, *Fam* cocorico *m*; *Fig* **he let out a c. of triumph** il a

---

crié victoire, *Fam* il a poussé un cocorico, il a fait cocorico
VI **1** (*of cock*) chanter; *Fig* chanter victoire, *Fam* faire cocorico (**about** à propos de) **2** (*of baby*) gazouiller

crowbar ['krəʊbɑːr] N pince *f* (à levier)

crowd [kraʊd] N **1** (*large number of people*) foule *f*; (*in building*) foule, affluence *f*; **to come in a c.** or **in crowds** venir en foule; **to draw a c.** attirer la foule; **that's what happens when you get a c. of boys together** c'est ce qui se produit quand tout un groupe de garçons se trouve rassemblé; **there wasn't much of a c. at the game** il n'y avait pas grand monde au match; **there was quite a c. in the square** il y avait pas mal de monde dans le square; *Fig* **the c.** la foule; **to stand out from the c.** se distinguer (de la foule); *Fig* **to follow the c.** suivre le mouvement; *Theat, Cin* **the c.** les figurants *mpl*; *Theat, Cin* **to be a c. puller** attirer les foules
2 *Fam* (*group*) bande *f*, clique *f*; **they're a good c.** ce sont de braves types; **they stick to their own c.** ils font bande à part
VT **1** (*force in, on*) (*people, objects*) entasser; (*fill*) remplir, bourrer (**with** de); **they crowded 10,000 people into the square** ils ont entassé 10 000 personnes sur la place; **too many books had been crowded onto the shelf** on avait entassé trop de livres sur l'étagère; **the tourists crowding the streets** les touristes qui se pressaient dans les rues
2 (*come too close to*) *Sport* (*competitor*) tasser; (*another car*) serrer; *Am* (*debtor*) importuner; **don't c. me!** (*don't pressure me*) ne me pousse pas!; **to be crowded off the pavement** être forcé de quitter le trottoir
VI **to c. (together)** se serrer; **they all crowded into the room** ils se sont tous entassés dans la pièce; **to c. round sb** se presser autour de qn; **they all crowded round** ils se sont tous amassés
▶▶ *Cin, TV* **c. scene** scène *f* de foule; **c. surfing** = pratique *f* courante dans les concerts pop ou rock, qui consiste à se laisser transporter, allongé, au-dessus de la foule
▶ **crowd in on** VT INSEP assaillir; **memories c. in on me here** ici, des souvenirs m'assaillent en foule
▶ **crowd out** VT SEP (*force out*) (*person, object*) ne pas laisser de place à; **to c. sb out of a deal/a market** exclure qn d'une affaire/ d'un marché

crowded ['kraʊdɪd] ADJ (*train, cinema, restaurant etc*) bondé; (*street*) (*with people*) bondé; (*with cars*) encombré; (*day*) chargé; **they lived in a room c. with furniture** ils vivaient dans une pièce encombrée de meubles; **it's a bit c. in here** il y a un peu trop de monde ici; **crowded together** pressés *ou* serrés l'un contre l'autre; **we are too crowded here** on est trop serrés ici; **the hall was crowded with people** la salle était bondée; **the c. events of that day** les nombreux événements de cette journée

crowfoot ['krəʊfʊt] N (*pl usu* **crowfoots**) (*plant*) renoncule *f* (âcre)

crowing ['krəʊɪŋ] N (*of cock*) chant *m*; *Fig* fanfaronnades *fpl*

crown [kraʊn] N **1** (*of monarch, martyr, made of flowers etc*) couronne *f*; **c. of thorns** couronne d'épines; **to wear the c.** porter la couronne
2 *Pol* **the C.** *or* **c.** la Couronne (*symbole de l'État monarchique*)
3 (*of tooth, natural or artificial*) couronne *f*
4 (*coin*) couronne *f*
5 (*highest part*) (*of vault*) clef *f*; (*of bridge, road*) bombement *m*; (*of hill*) crête *f*; (*of roof*) faîte *m*; **the c. (of the head)** le sommet de la tête
6 (*of hat*) fond *m*

VT **1** (*person, person's head*) couronner (**with** de); **to c. sb king** couronner qn roi; **they crowned her head with a garland of flowers** ils lui ont couronné la tête d'une guirlande de fleurs; **the crowned heads of Europe** les têtes *fpl* couronnées d'Europe; *Br Fam* **I'll c. you!** (*hit you*) je vais te flanquer un de ces coups sur la tête!
2 *Fig* (*person's happiness*) combler, couronner; (*person's efforts*) récompenser; *Br Fam* **to c. it all** pour comble de malheur
3 (*be at summit of*) couronner; **the woods that c. the hill** les bois qui couronnent la colline
4 (*in dentistry*) (*tooth*) couronner
5 (*at draughts*) **to be crowned** aller à dame
▶▶ *Br* **c. cap** capsule *f* (de bouteille); *Br* **c. colony** colonie *f* de la Couronne; *Can* **C. corporation** société *f* d'État; *Br* **C. Court** ≃ Cour *f* d'assises; **c. estates** terres *fpl* domaniales *ou* appartenant à la Couronne; **c. gear** *Tech* roue *f* plate; *Aut* grande couronne; **c. jewels** (*crown, sceptre etc*) joyaux *mpl* de la Couronne; *Sl Hum* (*man's genitals*) bijoux *mpl* de famille; **c. lands** terres domaniales *ou* appartenant à la Couronne; **c. prince** prince *m* héritier; **C. rating system** (*for hotels*) système *m* de classement (des hôtels britanniques); **c. wheel** *Tech* roue plate; *Aut* grande couronne; *Law* **c. witness** témoin *m* à charge

crowning ['kraʊnɪŋ] ADJ (*ambition, achievement*) suprême; **the c. moment** l'apothéose *f*
N (*of monarch etc*) couronnement *m*
▶▶ *Hum* **c. glory** (*hair*) chevelure *f*; **the red hair that was her c. glory** la belle crinière rousse qui faisait l'admiration de tout le monde

crow's-foot, *pl* **crow's-feet** N (*wrinkle*) patte *f* d'oie

crozier ['krəʊzɪər] N *Rel* (*of bishop*) crosse *f*

CRT [siːɑːˈtiː] N **1** (*abbr* **cathode ray tube**) tube *m* cathodique **2** *Comput* (*abbr* **carriage return**) retour *m* chariot

crucial ['kruːʃ(ə)l] ADJ **1** (*point etc*) crucial, -aux, décisif, critique; **the c. test** l'épreuve *f* décisive; **to be c. to sth** être crucial pour qch **2** *Sl* (*excellent*) d'enfer, supergénial

crucible ['kruːsɪb(ə)l] N *Metal, Chem, Ind, Fig* creuset *m*; *Fig* **their friendship was forged in the c. of war** leur amitié fut forgée pendant les temps difficiles de la guerre

crucifix ['kruːsɪfɪks] N crucifix *m*, christ *m*; (*at roadside*) calvaire *m*

crucifixion [kruːsɪˈfɪkʃən] N crucifixion *f*, crucifiement *m*

cruciform ['kruːsɪfɔːm] ADJ cruciforme

crucify ['kruːsɪfaɪ] VT **1** (*execute*) crucifier; **Christ Crucified** le Crucifié **2** *Sl* (*person*) (*defeat*) flanquer *ou* mettre la pâtée à; (*criticize*) descendre en flammes; **we were crucified** (*in match*) ils nous ont mis la pâtée; **my mum will c. us if she finds out!** ma mère va nous étriper si elle découvre ça!

crud [krʌd] N *Sl* (*dirt*) saletés *fpl*; (*nonsense*) bêtises *fpl*; (*person*) ordure *f*, saloperie *f*

cruddy ['krʌdɪ] ADJ *Sl* (*dirty*) cradingue; (*very bad*) merdique

crude [kruːd] ADJ **1** (*unsophisticated, unrefined*) (*method, idea, style etc*) grossier; (*tool etc*) grossier, primitif; **a c. statement of the facts** un exposé brutal des faits **2** (*vulgar*) (*language, joke*) grossier, cru; (*manners*) grossier
N *Petr* (*crude oil*) (pétrole *m*) brut *m*
▶▶ *Petr* **c. oil** (pétrole) brut

crudely ['kruːdlɪ] ADV **1** (*in an unrefined, unsophisticated manner*) d'une manière grossière, grossièrement; **a c. constructed canoe** un canoë construit sommairement;

to put it c. *(bluntly)* pour être tout à fait franc **2** *(vulgarly)* crûment, grossièrement

crudeness [ˈkruːdnɪs], **crudity** [ˈkruːdɪtɪ] N **1** *(lack of refinement) (of style)* nature f grossière; *(of tool etc)* caractère m grossier *ou* primitif **2** *(vulgarity) (of expression etc)* crudité f; *(of manners etc)* grossièreté f

cruel [ˈkruəl] ADJ *(person, joke, treatment, winter)* cruel; **to be c. to sb** être cruel envers qn; **a c. blow** un coup dur; *Prov* **you have to be c. to be kind** qui aime bien châtie bien

cruelly [ˈkruəlɪ] ADV cruellement

cruelty [ˈkruəltɪ] N cruauté f (**to** envers); *Law* sévices mpl (**to sb** envers qn); **an act of c.** une cruauté

cruet [ˈkruːɪt] N **1** *(for oil, vinegar)* petit flacon m **2** *Culin (set of condiments)* service m à condiments **3** *Rel* burette f
▸▸ *Culin* **c. stand** service m à condiments

Cruft's [krʌfts] N = très importante exposition f canine qui se tient à Londres

cruise [kruːz] N **1** *Naut* croisière f; **(pleasure) c.** croisière; **to go on a c.** partir en croisière **2** *Mil (missile)* missile m de croisière
VI **1** *Naut (of yacht, liner)* croiser, être en croisière; *(of passenger)* être en croisière **2** *(of taxi, car)* marauder, être en maraude; **he was cruising up and down the high street** il montait et redescendait la rue principale; **we went cruising around the streets in search of ...** nous avons roulé dans les rues à la recherche de ...; *Fam* **you're cruising for a bruising** tu vas droit vers les ennuis **3** *Aviat, Aut etc (maintain constant speed)* aller à une vitesse de croisière; **we were cruising at 60** nous allions à une vitesse de croisière de 60 **4** *Sl (look for sexual partner)* draguer
VT **1** *(of ship)* croiser dans; *(of ship's passenger)* être en croisière dans **2** *Sl* **he was out cruising the streets** il se baladait en voiture **3** *Sl* **to c. the bars** draguer dans les bars
▸▸ *Aut* **c. control** régulateur m d'allure; **c. missile** missile de croisière; **c. ship** bateau m de croisière

cruiser [ˈkruːzər] N **1** *Naut* **(battle) c.** croiseur m; **(cabin) c.** yacht m de croisière *(à moteur)* **2** = **cruiserweight**

cruiserweight [ˈkruːzəweɪt] N *Br Boxing* poids m mi-lourd

cruising [ˈkruːzɪŋ] N *Naut* croisière(s) f(pl)
▸▸ *Aviat* **c. altitude** altitude f de croisière; **c. holiday** croisière; *Aviat* **c. range** autonomie f à vitesse de croisière; *Aviat* **c. speed** vitesse f de croisière

crumb [krʌm] N **1** *(small piece) (of bread)* miette f; *(opposed to crust)* mie f *(de pain)*; *Fig* **they make the profit and we get the crumbs from their table** ils réalisent les bénéfices et nous récupérons les miettes; **c. of comfort** brin m de consolation; **crumbs of news** fragments mpl d'information **2** *Fam (contemptible person)* minable mf
VT *Culin (cutlet, fish)* paner, couvrir de chapelure

crumble [ˈkrʌmb(ə)l] VI *(of stone, earth etc)* s'effriter; *(of bread, pastry)* s'émietter; *Fig (of empire, opposition, prices)* s'effondrer; **everything is crumbling to dust** tout tombe en poussière; **her world was crumbling (to pieces) around her** tout son univers s'effondrait autour d'elle
VT *(bread)* émietter; *(stone)* désagréger
N *Br Culin* **apple/rhubarb c.** = dessert m aux pommes/à la rhubarbe recouvert de pâte sablée

crumbling [ˈkrʌmblɪŋ] ADJ *(stone, earth)* qui s'effrite; *(wall etc)* qui s'écroule, croulant; *Fig (empire, opposition, resistance)* qui s'effondre

N *(of stone, earth)* effritement m; *Fig (of empire, opposition, resistance, prices etc)* effondrement m

crumbly [ˈkrʌmblɪ] ADJ *(cake, bread)* friable, qui s'émiette *(trop)*; *(cheese)* qui s'émiette; *(stone, brick)* friable, qui se désagrège
N *Br Fam (old person)* croulant, -ante

crumbs [krʌmz] INT *Br Fam* ça alors!, zut!

crummy [ˈkrʌmɪ] ADJ *Fam (film, job, idea etc)* minable; **what a c. joint!** quel endroit minable!; **to feel c.** *(ill)* ne pas se sentir dans son assiette; *(unhappy, upset)* ne pas se sentir fier *(about doing d'avoir fait)*

crump [krʌmp] N *(of shells)* détonation f assourdie

crumpet [ˈkrʌmpɪt] N **1** *Culin* = petite galette fronde et spongieuse que l'on sert avec du beurre, de la confiture etc **2** *(no pl) Br Sl (women)* nanas fpl; **a nice bit of c.** une belle nana; *Hum (man)* un beau gars *ou* garçon *ou* type; *Hum* **he's the thinking woman's bit of c.** il est le chéri des femmes intelligentes

crumple [ˈkrʌmp(ə)l] VT *(material, dress etc)* froisser, friper, chiffonner; **to c. paper** chiffonner *ou* froisser du papier; *(make into a ball)* faire une boule avec du papier; **to get crumpled** se froisser *ou* friper
VI *(of fabric)* se friper, se froisser, se chiffonner; *(of leaves, parchment)* se ratatiner; *(of mudguard, car)* se plier; *(of face)* se décomposer; *Fig (of opposition)* s'effondrer; **he crumpled as the bullet hit him** il s'est écroulé au moment où la balle l'a atteint
▸▸ *Aut* **c. zone** zone f d'absorption
▸ **crumple up** VT SEP *(screw up into a ball) (paper)* faire une boule avec
VI *(of person)* s'écrouler; *(of car)* se plier

crumpled [ˈkrʌmp(ə)ld] ADJ *(paper)* froissé, chiffonné; *(skirt etc)* froissé, fripé, chiffonné; *(car)* à la tôle froissée; *(car wing)* froissé

crunch [krʌntʃ] N **1** *(sound)* craquement m; *(of snow, gravel etc)* crissement m **2** *Fig (critical moment)* **when it comes to the c.** au moment critique *ou* crucial; **when it came to the c. he let them down** il les a laissés tomber au moment critique *ou* crucial; **if it comes to the c. we can sell the car** au pire nous pourrons vendre la voiture **3** *(exercise)* exercice m pour les abdominaux; **to do crunches** faire des abdominaux
VT *(with teeth)* croquer; *Comput (numbers, data)* traiter à grande vitesse
VI craquer, crisser; **the hard snow crunched underfoot** la neige durcie crissait sous les pieds; **they crunched through the snow** ils avançaient dans la neige qui crissait sous leurs pas; **he was crunching on an apple** il croquait dans une pomme
▸ **crunch up** VT SEP *(crush)* broyer; **the car had been crunched up** la voiture avait été broyée

crunching [ˈkrʌntʃɪŋ] N = **crunch** N **1**

crunchy [ˈkrʌntʃɪ] ADJ *(food)* croquant, croustillant; *(snow)* qui craque (sous les pas)

crupper [ˈkrʌpər] N **1** *(part of harness)* croupière f, culière f **2** *(of horse)* croupe f

crusade [kruːˈseɪd] N *Hist, Fig* croisade f; **to go on a c.** partir en croisade; **a one-man c. against drug-dealing** une croisade contre la drogue menée par un seul homme; **to start a c.** lancer une croisade (**against** contre)
VI **1** *Hist* partir en croisade **2** *Fig* mener une campagne (**against** contre; **for** pour); **she spent her life crusading against injustice/for women's rights** elle a passé sa vie à se battre contre l'injustice/pour les droits de la femme

crusader [kruːˈseɪdər] N **1** *Hist* croisé m **2** *Fig*

champion, -ionne (**for sth** de qch); **a c. against injustice** un champion de la lutte contre l'injustice
▸▸ *Hist* **c. castle** château m de croisé

crush [krʌʃ] N **1** *(crowd)* foule f; **there was a terrible c.** il y a eu une terrible bousculade; **two people were injured in the c.** deux personnes ont été blessées dans la bousculade **2** *Br (drink)* **orange c.** orangeade f; **lemon c.** citronnade f **3** *Fam (infatuation)* béguin m; **to have a c. on sb** avoir le *ou* un béguin pour qn, en pincer pour qn
VT **1** *(person, object)* écraser; *(grapes etc)* exprimer le jus de; *(of boa constrictor) (victim)* comprimer; *(dress)* froisser; *(ice)* piler; *Min etc (ore)* broyer, concasser; **crushed together** *(people)* entassés, serrés; **we were nearly crushed to death** on a failli être écrasés; **he crushed the clothes into the suitcase** il a tassé les vêtements dans la valise **2** *(destroy) (enemy)* écraser; *(revolt)* étouffer, écraser; **to c. sb's hopes** réduire les espoirs de qn à néant; **this remark crushed her** *(humiliated her)* cette remarque l'a profondément humiliée
VI *(in order to get into a place)* se presser en foule, se bousculer
▸▸ *Theat* **c. bar** bar m des spectateurs; **c. barrier** barrière f de sécurité

crushing [ˈkrʌʃɪŋ] ADJ *(news, defeat etc)* écrasant; *(reply, remark etc)* cinglant, humiliant; **to be dealt a c. blow** *(of army, hopes etc)* en prendre un sacré coup; **to treat sb with c. contempt** écraser qn de son mépris
N *(of grapes)* pressage m; *(of ore)* broyage m, concassage m; *(of rebellion, uprising)* écrasement m; *(of hopes)* anéantissement m

crust [krʌst] N **1** *(of bread, pie)* croûte f; **there was not a c. to eat in the house** il ne restait absolument rien à manger dans la maison; *Fam* **we manage to earn a c.** nous arrivons à gagner notre croûte **2** *(of the earth, of ice etc)* croûte f **3** *(of wine)* dépôt m **4** *(on wound)* croûte f
▸ **crust over** VI *(become covered with a crust)* se couvrir d'une croûte; *(of wound etc)* former une croûte

crustacean [krʌsˈteɪʃən] ADJ crustacéen
N crustacé m

crusted [ˈkrʌstɪd] ADJ **to be c. with ice** être couvert d'une croûte de glace

crusty [ˈkrʌstɪ] ADJ **1** *Culin (bread, roll)* croustillant **2** *(person)* bourru
N *Br Fam* jeune hippie mf crado

crutch [krʌtʃ] N **1** *(support)* béquille f; *Fig* soutien m; *Fig* **a c. to lean on** un soutien; **to go about** *or* **walk on crutches** marcher avec des béquilles **2** = **crotch**

crux, pl cruxes [krʌks, ˈkrʌksɪz] N *(of discussion etc)* cœur m; **the c. of the matter** le nœud de la question

cry [kraɪ] N **1** *(call) (of person, animal)* cri m; **to give** *or* **utter a c.** pousser un cri; **a c. of pain** un cri de douleur; *also Fig* **a c. for help** un appel au secours; **there were cries of 'down with the king!'** on criait 'à bas le roi!'; **their c. was 'one man, one vote'** leur slogan était 'un homme, une voix'; **to be in full c.** *(of hounds etc)*, *Fig* être lancé dans une poursuite acharnée (**after** de); **it's a far c. from what they promised us** cela n'a rien à voir avec ce qu'ils nous avaient promis; **it's still a far c. from what I asked for** cela reste loin de ce que j'avais demandé **2** *(weeping)* **to have a c.** pleurer; **to have a good c.** pleurer un bon coup
VI *(pt, pp* **cried** [kraɪd]*)* **1** *(weep)* pleurer; **big girls don't c.** les grandes filles ne pleurent pas, on ne pleure pas quand on est une grande fille; **to c. over sth** pleurer *ou* verser des larmes sur qch; **to c. for joy** pleurer de

joie; **I laughed until I cried** j'ai ri aux larmes **2** *(shout, call)* crier, pousser un cri/des cris; **to c. aloud** pousser de grands cris; **to c. for help** appeler au secours *ou* à l'aide; **to c. for mercy** demander grâce

vt 1 *(exclaim) (name etc)* crier; **that's not true!, he cried** ce n'est pas vrai!, s'écria-t-il; *Old-fashioned* **to c. one's wares** vendre sa marchandise à la criée **2 to c. one's eyes** *or* **one's heart out** pleurer toutes les larmes de son corps; **she cried herself to sleep** elle s'est endormie en pleurant

▸ **cry down** vt sep *(person, thing)* décrier, dénigrer

▸ **cry off** vi *(cancel acceptance of invitation)* se décommander

▸ **cry out** vi *(shout)* pousser un cri; *Fam* **for crying out loud!** nom de nom!, mais bon sang!

vt sep *(name etc)* crier; **stop!, she cried out** arrêtez!, s'écria-t-elle

▸ **cry out for** vt insep **1** *(shout out for)* réclamer à grands cris **2** *Fig (need desperately)* avoir désespérément besoin de; **that wall is crying out for a coat of paint** ce mur a besoin d'un bon coup de peinture

▸ **cry up** vt insep **1** *(publicize, praise) (book, film)* vanter **2** *(exaggerate)* **to c. up one's opponent's chances** exagérer la force de son adversaire

crybaby ['kraɪbeɪbɪ] N *Fam* pleurnicheur, -euse

crying ['kraɪɪŋ] ADJ *(need etc)* urgent; **it's a c. shame that …** il est scandaleux que … + *sub* N **1** *(weeping)* pleurs *mpl* **2** *(shouting, calling)* cris *mpl*

cryogenics [kraɪə'dʒenɪks] N *(with sing verb)* cryogénie *f*

cryonics [kraɪ'ɒnɪks] N *(with sing verb)* cryoconservation *f*

cryosurgery [kraɪəʊ'sɜːdʒərɪ] N cryochirurgie *f*

crypt [krɪpt] N *(in church)* crypte *f*

cryptic ['krɪptɪk] ADJ *(message, silence, smile, look)* mystérieux, énigmatique; *(remark)* sibyllin; **he was very c. about his future plans** il a été très mystérieux sur ses projets d'avenir

▸▸ **c. crossword** = mots *mpl* croisés dont les définitions sont des énigmes qu'il faut résoudre

cryptically ['krɪptɪklɪ] ADV mystérieusement; *(to speak)* à mots couverts; **the book ends c.** le livre se termine de façon énigmatique *ou* sur une énigme

crypto- ['krɪptəʊ] PREF crypto-; **c.-communist** cryptocommuniste

cryptogram ['krɪptəgræm] N cryptogramme *m*

cryptographer [krɪp'tɒgrəfər] N cryptographe *mf*

cryptographic [krɪptə'græfɪk] ADJ cryptographique

cryptography [krɪp'tɒgrəfɪ] N cryptographie *f*

crystal ['krɪst(ə)l] N **1** *Chem, Miner* cristal *m*; **as clear as c.** clair comme le jour *ou* comme de l'eau de roche **2** *(chip)* cristal *m*; **salt crystals** cristaux *mpl* de sel; **in c. form** sous forme cristalline **3** *(on watch)* verre *m* de montre **4** *Electron etc* cristal *m*

ADJ *(clear)* limpide, cristallin; *(vase, glass)* de cristal

▸▸ **c. ball** boule *f* de cristal; **c. factory** cristallerie *f*; **c. gazing** divination *f* par la boule de cristal; *Radio* **c. set** poste *m* à galène

crystal-clear ADJ limpide, cristallin; *Fig (argument)* clair comme le jour *ou* de l'eau de roche; **it's all c. to me now** ça me paraît clair comme de l'eau de roche maintenant; **to make sth c.** rendre qch bien clair

crystalline ['krɪstəlaɪn] ADJ cristallin

▸▸ *Opt* **c. lens** cristallin *m*

crystallization [krɪstəlaɪ'zeɪʃən] N cristallisation *f*

crystallize ['krɪstəlaɪz] *Chem, Fig* vt cristalliser; **crystallized fruits** fruits *mpl* confits

vi se cristalliser

crystallography [krɪstə'lɒgrəfɪ] N cristallographie *f*

CS ['si:'es] N

▸▸ **CS gas** gaz *m* lacrymogène

CSD [si:es'di:] N *Banking, St Exch* (abbr **Central Securities Depository**) depositaire *m* national de titres

CSE [si:es'i:] N *Br Sch Formerly* (abbr **Certificate of Secondary Education**) = diplôme *m* sanctionnant la fin des études du premier cycle dans l'enseignement secondaire

C-section N *Obst* césarienne *f*

CST [si:es'ti:] N *Am* (abbr **Central Standard Time**) = heure *f* du centre de l'Amérique du Nord

CSV [si:es'vi:] NPL *Comput* (abbr **comma-separated values**) valeurs *fpl* séparées par des virgules

cub [kʌb] N **1** *(of fox)* renardeau *m*; *(of bear)* ourson *m*; *(of lion)* lionceau *m*; *(of wolf)* louveteau *m*; *Fig* **that impertinent young c.!** cette espèce de blanc-bec! **2** *(scout)* louveteau *m*; **he goes to Cubs on Fridays** il va à la réunion des louveteaux le vendredi

▸▸ **c. reporter** jeune journaliste *mf*; **C. scout** louveteau

Cuba ['kju:bə] N Cuba *m*; **in C.** à Cuba

Cuban ['kju:bən] ADJ cubain

N Cubain, -aine

▸▸ **C. heel** talon *m* cubain

cubbyhole ['kʌbɪhəʊl] N *(room)* cagibi *m*; *(cupboard)* placard *m*

cube [kju:b] N **1** *Math, Geom* cube *m*; **27 is the c. of three** 27 est le cube de trois **2** *(piece) (of bread, meat etc)* dé *m*; *(of sugar)* morceau *m*; **cut the meat into cubes** coupez la viande en dés

vt **1** *Math* élever au cube; **27 cubed** 27 au cube **2** *(meat etc)* couper en dés

▸▸ *Math* **c. root** racine *f* cubique

cubic ['kju:bɪk] ADJ **1** *(measurement)* cube **2** *(cube-shaped)* cubique

▸▸ **c. capacity** volume *m*, cube *m*; *(of engine)* cylindrée *f*; **c. centimetre** centimètre *m* cube; **c. measure** mesure *f* de volume; **c. metre** mètre *m* cube

cubicle ['kju:bɪk(ə)l] N *(in swimming pool)* cabine *f*; *(for trying on clothes)* cabine d'essayage; *(in dormitory)* box *m*; *(of public toilet)* W.-C. *mpl*; **his office was little more than a c.** son bureau n'était pas plus grand qu'un box

cubism ['kju:bɪz(ə)m] N *Art* cubisme *m*

cubist ['kju:bɪst] ADJ, N *Art* cubiste *mf*

cuckold ['kʌkəld] *esp Lit* N cocu *m*

vt cocufier, faire cocu

cuckoo ['kʊku:] N *(bird)* coucou *m*

ADJ *Fam (mad)* dingue; **to go c.** devenir dingue, perdre la boule

INT coucou!

▸▸ **c. clock** coucou *m (pendule)*; *Bot* **c. spit** crachat *m* de coucou

cucumber ['kju:kʌmbər] N concombre *m*; *Fig* **to be (as) cool as a c.** *(in a crisis etc)* être d'un calme imperturbable; **…, she said, cool as a c.** … dit-elle avec un calme imperturbable; *(without showing any remorse)* … dit-elle comme si de rien n'était; *Zool* **sea c.** concombre de mer

▸▸ **c. sandwich** = petit sandwich *m* au pain de mie et au concombre *(l'expression est parfois utilisée pour évoquer certains milieux bourgeois)*

cud [kʌd] N *(of ruminant)* bol *m* alimentaire; **to chew the c.** *(of cow etc)* ruminer; *Fig (of person)* ruminer une idée, méditer

cuddle ['kʌd(ə)l] N câlin *m*; **to give sb a c.** faire un câlin à qn

vt *(person)* serrer dans ses bras, câliner; **to c. one another** se faire des câlins; **children need lots of cuddling** les enfants ont besoin d'être beaucoup câlinés

vi *(of two people)* se faire des câlins, se câliner; **two young people kissing and cuddling** deux jeunes gens en train de s'embrasser et de se faire des câlins

▸ **cuddle up** vi *(lie, sit etc closely)* se pelotonner; **to c. up to sb** se blottir *ou* se pelotonner contre qn; **they cuddled up to each other for warmth** ils se sont pelotonnés *ou* blottis l'un contre l'autre pour se tenir chaud; **c. up if you're cold** *(to me)* pelotonne-toi si tu as froid; *(to each other)* serrez-vous *ou* pelotonnez-vous l'un contre l'autre si vous avez froid

cuddly ['kʌdlɪ] ADJ *(teddy bear etc)* tout doux, *f* toute douce; *(child, animal etc)* mignon à croquer; *Hum (plump)* dodu

▸▸ **c. toy** peluche *f*

cudgel ['kʌdʒ(ə)l] N gourdin *m*, trique *f*; *Fig* **to take up the cudgels on sb's behalf** prendre fait et cause pour qn

vt *(-ll-, Am -l-) (person)* donner des coups de bâton à; *Fig Fam* **to c. one's brains** se creuser les méninges *ou* la cervelle

cue¹ [kju:] N *(signal)* signal *m*, top *m*; *Theat (verbal)* réplique *f*; *Mus (for instrument)* indication *f* de rentrée; **to miss one's c.** *Theat* manquer la réplique; *TV, Cin* rater le signal; *Theat, Fig* **to give sb his/her c.** donner à qn la réplique *ou* le signal; *Fig* **he nodded, and that was my c. to make the coffee** il a hoché la tête pour me faire signe de faire le café; **I suppose that's my c. to leave?** je dois comprendre que c'est le moment que je parte?; *Fig* **to take one's c. from sb** prendre exemple sur qn; *Fig* **(right) on c.** au bon moment

vt donner le signal à; *Theat (verbally)* donner la réplique à; **c. and cut!** moteur! et coupez!

▸▸ **c. card** carton *m* aide-mémoire; *Radio, TV* **c. sheet** feuille *f* de conducteur, feuille de mixage

▸ **cue in** vt sep **1** donner le signal à; *Theat (verbally)* donner la réplique à **2** *esp Am (inform) (person)* mettre à la page

cue² N *(in billiards, snooker, pool)* queue *f*

▸▸ **c. ball** *(ball)* bille *f* de joueur; *Am Fam (bald person)* chauve *mf*; **c. rack** porte-queues *m inv*

cuff [kʌf] N **1** *(of shirt)* poignet *m*; *(that takes cuff links)* manchette *f*; *(of coat sleeve)* parement *m*; **double c.** poignet mousquetaire; *Fam* **off the c.** *(discours etc)* impromptu; *Fam* **to do sth off the c.** faire qch au pied levé; *Fam* **I can't tell you off the c.** je ne peux pas te le dire comme ça *ou* tout de suite **2** *Am (of trousers)* revers *m* de pantalon **3** *Fam* **cuffs** = **handcuffs 4** *(blow)* taloche *f*, calotte *f*; **he gave me a c. on the head** il m'a mis une taloche sur la tête

vt **1** *(hit) (person)* talocher, calotter **2** *Fam (put handcuffs on)* mettre les menottes à

▸▸ **c. link** bouton *m* de manchette

cuisine [kwɪ'zi:n] N cuisine *f*

cul-de-sac ['kʌldəsæk] N *(pl* **culs-de-sac, cul-de-sacs)** cul-de-sac *m, pl* culs-de-sac, impasse *f*; *Fig* impasse

culinary ['kʌlɪnərɪ] ADJ *(skill, delight, purpose)* culinaire; *(implement)* de cuisine; *(herb)* pour la cuisine; **the c. art** l'art *m* culinaire

cull [kʌl] N **1** *(killing) (of deer, wild boar)* battue *f*; *(of seals)* abattage *m* **2** *(animal) (before killing)* bête *f* à abattre; *(after killing)* bête abattue

vt 1 *(reduce by killing) (herd of deer, seal colony)* réduire la taille de; *(kill) (deer, seals)* abattre **2** *(choose)* choisir (**from** dans); **the poems have been culled from her early work** les poèmes ont été choisis parmi ses premières œuvres; **information culled from various sources** des renseignements pris à differentes sources

culminate ['kʌlmɪneɪt] **vi to c. in sth** *(undesirable)* se terminer en *ou* par qch; *(desirable)* aboutir à qch; **the protests culminated in a battle with the police** ces manifestations se sont terminées par un affrontement avec la police; **the excavations culminated in the discovery of a temple** les fouilles ont abouti à la découverte d'un temple

culminating ['kʌlmɪneɪtɪŋ] **adj** *(point, moment)* culminant

culmination [kʌlmɪ'neɪʃən] **n** *(of events etc)* point *m* culminant, sommet *m*

culottes [kuː'lɒts] **npl** *(garment)* jupe-culotte *f*, *pl* jupes-culottes

culpability [kʌlpə'bɪlɪtɪ] **n** *Fml* culpabilité *f*

culpable ['kʌlpəb(ə)l] **adj** *Law, Fml (negligence etc)* coupable

culprit ['kʌlprɪt] **n** *(guilty person)*, *Fig* coupable *mf*, responsable *mf*; *(event)* cause *f*; **I'm the c.** c'est moi le coupable; **poor housing is the main c.** ce sont les mauvaises conditions de logement qui sont principalement responsables

cult [kʌlt] **n 1** *Rel, Fig (worship)* culte *m* (**of** de); **to make a c. of sth** avoir un culte pour qch; **a personality c., a c. of personality** un culte de la personnalité; **the film/band has a c. following** c'est un film-/groupe-culte; **c. book** livre *m* culte; **c. film** film *m* culte **2** *(sect)* secte *f*
▸▸ **c. figure** idole *f*

cultivate ['kʌltɪveɪt] **vt 1** *(earth, field, vegetables etc)* cultiver **2** *Biol (bacillus)* faire une culture de **3** *(develop) (an art)* cultiver; *(friends, person's friendship, reputation, accent)* cultiver; *(approach, manner)* adopter

cultivated ['kʌltɪveɪtɪd] **adj 1** *Agr (land, plant)* cultivé **2** *(educated) (voice, manner)* qui témoigne d'une bonne éducation; *(mind)* cultivé

cultivation [kʌltɪ'veɪʃən] **n** culture *f*; **a field under c.** un champ cultivé

cultivator ['kʌltɪveɪtər] **n** *Agr* **1** *(machine) (for farm)* cultivateur *m*; *(for garden)* motoculteur *m* **2** *(person)* cultivateur, -trice

cultural ['kʌltʃər(ə)l] **adj** *(institute, development, attaché etc)* culturel
▸▸ **c. anthropology** culturologie *f*; **c. event** manifestation *f* culturelle; **c. exchange** échange *m* culturel; **c. heritage** patrimoine *m* culturel

culture ['kʌltʃər] **n 1** *(artistic activity)* culture *f* **2** *(society)* culture *f*; **in Polynesian cultures** dans les cultures polynésiennes **3** *(refinement)* culture *f*; **he lacks it** il n'a aucune culture **4** *Biol* culture *f*
vt *Biol (bacillus)* faire une culture de
▸▸ *Biol* **c. medium** milieu *m* de culture; **c. shock** choc *m* culturel; *Fam Hum* **c. vulture** fana *mf* de culture, culturophage *mf*

cultured ['kʌltʃəd] **adj 1** *(educated)* cultivé **2** *(pearl)* de culture

culvert ['kʌlvət] **n** *Constr* canal *m* souterrain; *(for cable)* conduit *m* souterrain

cum¹ [kʌm] **prep** avec; **spare room c. study** chambre-bureau *f*, *pl* chambres-bureaux; **a translation c. rewrite** tout autant une réécriture qu'une traduction
▸▸ *St Exch* **c. dividend** coupon *m* attaché

cum² [kʌm] *Sl* = **come n**

cumbersome ['kʌmbəsəm] **adj** *(clothing, luggage)* encombrant, gênant; *(system)* lourd, pesant; *(sentence)* lourd

cumin ['kʌmɪn, 'kjuː-] **n** *Bot, Culin* cumin *m*

cummerbund ['kʌməbʌnd] **n** ceinture *f* de smoking

cumulative ['kjuːmjʊlətɪv] **adj** cumulatif; *Com (error)* cumulé
▸▸ *Fin* **c. balance** solde *m* cumulé; *Law* **c. evidence** preuve *f* par accumulation de témoignages; *Fin* **c. interest** intérêts *mpl* cumulatifs; *St Exch* **c. preference share** action *f* privilégiée; *Fin* **c. profit** bénéfice *m* cumulé; **c. total** cumul *m*; *Pol* **c. voting** vote *m* plural

cumulatively ['kjuːmjʊlətɪvlɪ] **adv** de façon cumulée

cumulonimbus ['kjuːmjʊləʊ'nɪmbəs] **n** *Met* cumulo-nimbus *m inv*

cumulus, *pl* **cumuli** ['kjuːmjʊləs, -laɪ] **n** *Met* cumulus *m*

cuneiform [kjʊ'neɪɪfɔːm] **n** écriture *f* cunéiforme
adj cunéiforme

cunnilingus [kʌnɪ'lɪŋgəs] **n** cunnilingus *m*

cunning ['kʌnɪŋ] **n 1** *(deviousness)* ruse *f*, roublardise *f* **2** *(ingenuity)* astuce *f*, ingéniosité *f*
adj 1 *(devious)* rusé, roublard; *(look)* sournois; **c. as a fox** rusé comme un renard **2** *(ingenious) (device etc)* ingénieux, astucieux

cunningly ['kʌnɪŋlɪ] **adv 1** *(deviously)* avec ruse **2** *(ingeniously)* ingénieusement, astucieusement

cunt [kʌnt] **n** *Vulg* **1** *(vagina)* con *m*, chatte *f* **2** *(woman, women)* **he was out looking for c.** il cherchait une femme à baiser **3** *(unpleasant person)* salaud *m*, salope *f*

cup [kʌp] **n 1** tasse *f*, *(metal)* gobelet *m*, timbale *f*, *(paper, plastic)* gobelet; **coffee/tea c.** tasse à café/à thé; **c. of coffee/of tea** tasse de café/de thé; *Fig Fam* **that's just my c. of tea** c'est tout à fait le genre de choses que j'aime; **science-fiction is not my c. of tea** la science-fiction n'est pas ma tasse de thé; **that's not everyone's c. of tea** tout le monde n'aime pas; **they're not my c. of tea** *(of people)* ils ne sont pas mon genre; *Culin* **cider/fruit c.** boisson *f* glacée au cidre/avec des fruits
2 *(measurement)* tasse *f*; **two cups of flour** deux tasses de farine
3 *Sport* coupe *f*; **to win a c.** remporter *ou* gagner une coupe; **the Davis C.** la coupe Davis; **c. winners** vainqueurs *mpl* de coupe
4 *Lit (goblet)* coupe *f*; *Rel* calice *m* (*du saint Sacrement)*; *Fig* **my c. runneth over** je déborde de joie; *Old-fashioned* **to be in one's cups** être gris
5 *(of flower)* calice *f*, *(of bra, swimming costume)* bonnet *m*; **what size c. do you take?** *(in bra etc)* quelle profondeur de bonnet est-ce que vous mettez?
vt (-pp-) **with one's chin cupped in one's hand** le menton dans le creux de la main; **to c. one's hand behind one's ear** mettre sa main en cornet; **to c. one's hands round one's mouth** mettre les mains en porte-voix; **she scooped up the water with her cupped hands** elle a recueilli l'eau dans ses mains jointes
▸▸ *Sport* **c. final** finale *f* de la coupe; **c. holder** *(in car)* support *m* de tasse; *Sport* **c. tie** match *m* de coupe

cup-and-ball joint n *Tech* joint *m* à rotule

cupbearer ['kʌpbeərər] **n** *Hist* échanson *m*

cupboard ['kʌbəd] **n** placard *m*; **store c.** placard *ou* armoire *f* à provisions;
▸▸ *Br* **c. love** amour *m* intéressé

cupcake ['kʌpkeɪk] **n** *Culin* petit gâteau *m* *(dans une caissette en papier)*

cupful ['kʌpfʊl] **n** tasse *f* (**of** de); **add two cupfuls of milk** ajouter deux tasses de lait

Cupid ['kjuːpɪd] **n** Cupidon *m*; *Art etc* Cupidon, Amour *m*

cupidity [kjuː'pɪdɪtɪ] **n** *Fml* cupidité *f*

cupola ['kjuːpələ] **n 1** *Archit (ceiling, roof)* coupole *f*, dôme *m*; *(tower)* belvédère *m* **2** *Naut (gun turret)* coupole *f* **3** *(furnace)* cubilot *m*
▸▸ **c. furnace** cubilot

cuppa ['kʌpə] **n** *Br Fam* tasse *f* de thé

cupping glass ['kʌpɪŋ] **n** *Med* ventouse *f*

cupric ['kjuːprɪk] **adj** *Chem (acid)* cuprique

cup-shaped adj *Bot* cupulaire

cur [kɜːr] **n** *Lit* **1** *(dog)* sale cabot *m* **2** *(despicable man)* homme *m* méprisable, mufle *m*

curable ['kjʊərəb(ə)l] **adj** *Med*, *Fig* guérissable

curacy ['kjʊərəsɪ] **n** *Rel* vicariat *m*

curare [kjʊə'rɑːrɪ] **n** curare *m*

curate¹ ['kjʊərət] **n** *Rel* vicaire *m*; **c. in charge** desservant *m*; *Fig* **his latest book/film is a bit of a c.'s egg** il y a du bon et du mauvais dans son dernier livre/film

curate² [kjʊə'reɪt] **vt** *(exhibition)* organiser

curative ['kjʊərətɪv] **adj** *(powers, effect, medicine)* curatif

curator [kjʊə'reɪtər] **n** *(of museum, gallery)* conservateur, -trice

curb [kɜːb] **n 1** *(check)* frein *m*; **to put a c. on sb's enthusiasm** mettre un frein à l'enthousiasme de qn; **to put a c. on one's passions** refréner ses passions, mettre un frein à ses passions **2** *Horseriding (chain)* gourmette *f* **3** *Am (of pavement etc)* bordure *f*, rebord *m*
vt 1 *(one's anger)* réprimer, refréner; *(one's passions)* maîtriser, brider; *(impatience, enthusiasm, tendency)* modérer; *(inflation etc)* freiner; **you must learn to c. your tongue!** tu dois apprendre à tenir ta langue! **2** *(horse)* mettre la gourmette à
▸▸ *Horseriding* **c. bit** *(on harness)* mors *m*; *Horseriding* **c. chain** gourmette

curbstone ['kɜːbstəʊn] **n** *Am (of pavement)* pierre *f* de rebord

curd [kɜːd] **n** *(lait m)* caillé *m*; **curds and whey** lait caillé sucré

curdle ['kɜːd(ə)l] **vi** *(of milk)* se cailler; *Fig* **my blood curdled** mon sang s'est glacé *ou* figé
vt *(milk)* cailler; *Fig (blood)* glacer, figer; *Fam* **he had a face that would c. milk** il avait l'air aimable comme une porte de prison

cure [kjʊər] **n 1** *(remedy)*, *Fig* remède *m* (**for** contre); **there is no known c. for the condition** on ne connaît pas encore de remède pour cette maladie; **rest c.** cure *f* de repos; **to take a c.** faire une cure; **beyond** *or* **past c.** *(person)* incurable; *(situation)* irrémédiable; **the c. is worse than the disease** le remède est pire que le mal **2** *Rel* **c. of souls** cure *f ou* charge *f* d'âmes
vt 1 *(person) (of illness)* guérir (**of** de); *(of bad habit)* guérir, corriger; **this experience cured him of his infatuation** cette expérience l'a guéri de son engouement; *Prov* **what can't be cured must be endured** il faut savoir prendre son mal en patience **2** *(prepare) (food) (by salting)* saler; *(by smoking)* fumer; *(by drying)* faire sécher; *(hides)* traiter

cure-all n panacée *f*

curettage [kjʊə'retɪdʒ] **n** *Med* curet(t)age *m*

curfew ['kɜːfjuː] **n** couvre-feu *m*, *pl* couvre-feux; **to ring the c. (bell)** sonner le couvre-feu; *esp Am Fig* **to be under c.** *(of teenager)* devoir rentrer à une heure précise

curing ['kjʊərɪŋ] **n** *(preparation) (by salting)* salaison *f*, *(by smoking) (of meat)* fumage *m*;

(of herring) saurissage *m; (by drying)* séchage *m*

curio ['kjʊərɪəʊ] N curiosité *f*, bibelot *m*

curiosity [kjʊərɪ'ɒsɪtɪ] N **1** curiosité *f*; **out of or from c.** par curiosité; **I was dying of c.** je mourais de curiosité; *Prov* **c. killed the cat** = la curiosité est un vilain défaut **2** *(object)* curiosité *f*, bibelot *m*

curious ['kjʊərɪəs] ADJ **1** *(inquisitive)* curieux, *Pej* indiscret, -ète; **to be c. to see/ know** être curieux de voir/savoir; **they didn't seem at all c. as to** or **about how it had happened** ils n'avaient pas du tout l'air curieux de savoir comment cela s'était produit **2** *(strange) (way, circumstances)* curieux, singulier; **the two of them made a c. sight** ils formaient un étrange tableau tous les deux; **a c.-looking object** un objet bizarre

curiously ['kjʊərɪəslɪ] ADV **1** *(inquisitively)* avec curiosité, *Pej* indiscrètement **2** *(strangely)* curieusement, singulièrement; **c. enough …** chose curieuse ou singulière …

curl [kɜːl] N **1** *(of hair)* boucle *f; (of smoke)* spirale *f;* **in curls** *(hair)* bouclé, frisé; **to fall in curls** *(of hair)* tomber en boucles **2** *(action)* action *f* de se recourber; **with a c. of the lip** avec une moue dédaigneuse

VT *(hair) (loosely)* boucler; *(tightly)* friser; **to c. one's lip** faire une moue dédaigneuse; **to c. sth round sth** enrouler qch autour de qch; **to c. oneself into a ball** *(of animal, person)* se rouler en boule

VI *(of hair)* boucler; *(of paper)* rebiquer; *(of smoke)* s'élever en spirales; *(of waves)* onduler, déferler; *(of lip)* se relever avec dédain; *Fig* **stories that make your hair c.** histoires qui font dresser les cheveux sur la tête; **his language would make your hair c.** il jure comme un charretier; *Fig* **it made my toes c.** *(with embarrassment)* c'était vraiment pénible; *(with pleasure)* ça m'a donné des frissons de plaisir; **to c. round sth** *(of plant etc)* s'enrouler autour de qch

2 *Sport* jouer au curling

▸ **curl up** VI **1** *(lie, sit comfortably)* se blottir, se pelotonner; **I like to c. up in bed with a good book** j'aime me blottir au lit avec un bon livre; **to sleep curled up** dormir en chien de fusil; **curled up in bed** pelotonné dans son lit

2 *(form a curl)* se rouler en boule, se recroqueviller; **hedgehogs c. up into a ball for protection** les hérissons se roulent en boule pour se protéger

3 *(of leaves, paper)* se recroqueviller

4 *Fig Fam (be embarrassed)* être extrêmement gêné; **I wanted to c. up and die** je ne savais plus où me mettre

VT SEP *(form into a curl)* **to c. oneself up** se rouler en boule, se recroqueviller; **to c. itself up** *(of cat etc)* se rouler en boule

curler ['kɜːlər] N **1** *(for hair)* bigoudi *m;* **in her curlers** avec ses bigoudis sur la tête, en bigoudis **2** *Sport* joueur, -euse de curling

curlew ['kɜːljuː] N *(bird)* courlis *m*

curlicue ['kɜːlɪkjuː] N trait *m* de plume en parafe

curliness ['kɜːlɪnɪs] N *(of hair) (loose)* boucles *fpl; (tight)* frisure *f*

curling ['kɜːlɪŋ] N *Sport* curling *m*

▸▸ **c. irons** fer *m* à friser; *Sport* **c. stone** pierre *f* de curling; **c. tongs** fer à friser

curly ['kɜːlɪ] ADJ *(hair) (loosely)* bouclé; *(tightly)* frisé; *(long piece of paper etc)* en spirale; **the dried leaves had gone c.** les feuilles séchées s'étaient recroquevillées

N *Fam* **1 to have sb by the short and curlies** pouvoir faire ce qu'on veut de qn; **they've got us by the short and curlies** ils nous tiennent **2** *(person with curly hair)* **hi there, c.** salut, le/la frisé(e)

▸▸ *Typ* **c. bracket** accolade *f*; **c. endive** frisée

f; **c. lettuce** (laitue *f*) frisée; *Br Typ* **c. quotes** guillemets *mpl* anglais

curly-headed, curly-haired ADJ *(with loose curls)* à la tête bouclée, aux cheveux bouclés; *(with tight curls)* aux cheveux frisés

currant ['kʌrənt] N **1** *(dried grape)* raisin *m* de Corinthe, raisin sec **2** *(soft fruit)* groseille *f*

▸▸ **c. bun** petit pain *m* aux raisins; **c. bush** groseiller *m*

currency ['kʌrənsɪ] N **1** *Fin (unit) (of a country)* unité *f* monétaire, monnaie *f*, devise *f; (specie)* numéraire *m;* **foreign c.** devise étrangère; **to buy foreign c.** acheter des devises étrangères; **hard/soft c.** devise forte/ faible; **the world's major currencies** les principales monnaies du monde; **to buy c.** acheter des devises

2 *(circulation) (of ideas)* circulation *f*, cours *m;* **to give c. to a rumour** *(of person, newspaper etc)* faire courir un bruit; **to gain c.** *(of news)* s'accréditer; *(of expression, habit)* devenir de plus en plus courant; *(of ideas)* se répandre; **the expression is common c.** l'expression est monnaie courante; **this view had some c. at one time** cette opinion était accréditée à un moment donné

▸▸ *Fin* **c. adjustment factor** correctif *m* d'ajustement monétaire; **c. appreciation** appréciation *f* d'une monnaie; *Fin* **c. conversion** conversion *f* de monnaies; *Fin* **c. dealer** cambiste *mf*; **c. depreciation** dépréciation *f* monétaire; *Fin* **c. fluctuation** mouvement *m* des devises; *Econ, Fin* **c. market** marché *m* monétaire; *Fin* **c. risk** risque *m* de change; *Fin, St Exch* **c. speculation** spéculation *f* sur les devises; *Fin, St Exch* **c. speculator** spéculateur, -trice sur devises; *Fin, St Exch* **c. swap** échange *m* de devises; *Fin, St Exch* **c. transfer** transfert *m* de devises; **c. unit** unité *f* monétaire

current ['kʌrənt] ADJ **1** *(existing, present) (feeling, tendency, situation)* actuel; **the c. theory is that …** la théorie actuelle est que …; **which is still c.** qui est toujours d'actualité; **the c. treasurer** le trésorier actuel (de l'association)

2 *(accepted, used)* courant, admis, reçu; **to be c.** avoir cours; **in c. use** d'usage courant; **the word is in c. use** le mot s'emploie couramment; **c. issue** *(of magazine)* dernier numéro *m;* **the c. month** le mois en cours

N **1** *(of river, tide etc)* courant *m; Met* **air c.** courant d'air; *Fig* **the c. of opinion is against him** il y a un courant d'opinion contre lui; **to drift on the c.** se laisser aller au fil de l'eau, se laisser porter par le courant; *Fig* **to go with the c.** suivre le courant; **to swim against the c.** nager contre le courant ou à contre-courant; *Fig* **to go** or **swim against the c.** aller à contre-courant

2 *Elec* courant *m*

▸▸ *Br* **c. account** *Banking* compte *m* courant; *St Exch* liquidation *f* courante; **c. affairs** actualités *fpl; TV, Radio* **c. affairs programme** émission *f* d'actualités; *Acct* **c. assets** actif *m* de roulement; *Com, Fin* **c. cost** prix *m* courant ou du marché; *Acct* **c. cost accounting** comptabilité *f* en coûts actuels; *Acct* **c. earnings** bénéfices *mpl* de l'exercice, revenus *mpl* actuels; **c. expenditure** dépenses *fpl* courantes; *Br Acct* **c. financial year** exercice *m* en cours; *Am Acct* **c. fiscal year** exercice *m* en cours; **c. income** *(in accounts)* produits *mpl* courants; *(actual earnings)* revenu *m* actuel; *Acct* **c. liabilities** passif *m* exigible à court terme; **c. net value** valeur *f* actuelle nette, VAN *f*; *St Exch* cours *m* instantané; **c. price** prix courant; *Acct* **c. ratio** coefficient *m* de liquidité; *Comput* **c. smoother** régulateur *m* de tension; *Acct* **c. value** valeur actuelle

Note that the most common meaning of the French adjective **courant** is **common**.

currently ['kʌrəntlɪ] ADV *(at present)* actuellement, en ce moment; **she is c. appearing in Othello** elle apparaît en ce moment dans Othello; **c. showing** *(at cinema)* à l'affiche

curriculum, *pl* **curricula** [kə'rɪkjʊləm, -ə] N *Sch* programme *m* (d'enseignement); **on the c.** au programme

▸▸ *Br* **c. vitae** curriculum *m* (vitae) *inv*

curry¹ ['kʌrɪ] *Culin* N *(spices, dish)* curry *m*, cari *m;* **beef/chicken/vegetable c.** bœuf *m*/ poulet *m*/légumes *mpl* au curry, cari de bœuf/poulet/légumes

VT *(chicken etc)* apprêter au cari ou au curry; **curried chicken** poulet *m* au curry, cari *m* de poulet

▸▸ **c. powder** curry, cari

curry² VT **1** *Pej* **to c. favour with sb** s'insinuer dans les bonnes grâces de qn **2** *(groom) (horse)* étriller

currycomb ['kʌrɪkəʊm] N étrille *f*

curse [kɜːs] N **1** *(evil spell)* malédiction *f*, mauvais sort *m;* **to put a c. on sb** jeter un sort à qn; **a c. on …!** maudit soit …!; *Fig* **I feel as if I'm under a c.** j'ai l'impression qu'on m'a jeté un sort **2** *Old-fashioned (swearword)* imprécation *f*, juron *m;* **to let out a c.** lâcher un juron; *Hum* **curses!** diantre! **3** *(scourge)* fléau *m;* **rabbits are a c. here** ici les lapins sont un fléau; *Old-fashioned Fam* **to have the c.** *(be menstruating)* avoir ses règles

VT *(person, object)* maudire; **he is cursed with a violent temper** il est affligé d'un mauvais caractère; **c. it!** le diable l'emporte!; **he cursed his luck** il a maudit son sort; **you'll c. the day you came here** tu maudiras le jour où tu es venu ici

VI *(swear)* jurer; **to c. and swear** jurer comme un charretier; **to c. at sb** injurier qn

▸▸ *Am* **c. word** juron *m*

cursed ADJ **1** [kɜːst] *(under a curse)* maudit **2** ['kɜːsɪd] *Fam (annoying)* sacré, satané; **it's a c. nuisance** c'est bigrement embêtant

cursing ['kɜːsɪŋ] N jurons *mpl*

cursive ['kɜːsɪv] ADJ cursif; **c. handwriting** écriture cursive

N écriture *f* cursive

cursor ['kɜːsər] N *(on slide rule), Comput* curseur *m; Comput* **move the c. to the right/left** déplacez le curseur vers la droite/gauche; *Comput* **the word at the c.** le mot pointé

▸▸ *Comput* **c. blink rate** vitesse *f* de clignotement du curseur; **c. control** contrôle *m* du curseur; **c. key** touche *f* de curseur; **c. movement** déplacement *m* du curseur; **c. position** position *f* du curseur

cursorily ['kɜːsərɪlɪ] ADV *(to examine, look at)* superficiellement

cursoriness ['kɜːsərɪnɪs] N caractère *m* sommaire

cursory ['kɜːsərɪ] ADJ *(glance, examination, remarks)* superficiel

curt [kɜːt] ADJ *(manner)* brusque; *(tone, person)* cassant; *(reply, command)* sec, *f* sèche

curtail [kɜː'teɪl] VT **1** *(shorten) (visit)* abréger, écourter **2** *(limit) (person's freedom, privileges, spending)* réduire, restreindre; *(person's authority, powers)* diminuer

curtailment [kɜː'teɪlmənt] N *(of freedom, privileges, spending etc)* réduction *f*, restriction *f; (of authority, powers)* diminution *f*

curtain ['kɜːt(ə)n] N **1** *Br (on window etc)* rideau *m;* **to draw the curtains** *(open)* ouvrir les rideaux; *(close)* tirer ou fermer les rideaux **2** *Theat* rideau *m;* **safety c.** rideau de fer; *Fig Fam* **it's curtains for him** il est fichu

VT *(alcove etc)* garnir de rideaux

▸▸ *Theat* **c. call** rappel *m;* **c. hook** crochet *m* de rideau; **c. material** tissu *m* à rideaux; **c. rail** tringle *f* à rideau; **c. ring** anneau *m* de rideau; **c. rod** tringle à rideau; **c. wall** *Archit*

mur-rideau *m*, *pl* murs-rideaux; *Constr* enceinte *f*
▸ **curtain off** VT SEP *(conceal)* *(part of room)* séparer par un rideau

curtain-raiser N *Theat* *(play)* lever *m* de rideau; *Fig* préambule *m*

curtainsider [ˈkɜːt(ə)nsaɪdər] N *Aut* camion *m* bâché

curtly [ˈkɜːtlɪ] ADV *(to say)* brusquement, d'un ton cassant; **a c. worded letter** une lettre au ton sec

curtness [ˈkɜːtnɪs] N *(of manner, words)* brusquerie *f*, *(of person)* ton *m* cassant; *(of letter)* ton sec

curts(e)y [ˈkɜːtsɪ] N révérence *f*; **to make a c. to sb** faire une révérence à qn
VI *(of woman, girl)* faire une révérence (**to** à)

curvaceous [kɜːˈveɪʃəs] ADJ *(woman)* qui a de jolies formes, *Fam* bien roulée; **c. figure** silhouette *f* de vamp

curvature [ˈkɜːvətʃər] N *(of the earth etc)* sphéricité *f*; *Phys, Opt* *(of space)* courbure *f*; *Med* **c. of the spine** courbure (de la colonne) vertébrale

curve [kɜːv] N courbe *f*; *(in road)* tournant *m*, virage *m*; **the c. of the bay** la courbe de la baie; **curves** *(of woman)* rondeurs *fpl*, formes *fpl*; *Am Fig* **to throw sb a c. (ball)** *(give unpleasant surprise to)* prendre qn par surprise; *(mislead)* induire qn en erreur
VI se courber; **the road curves round the castle** la route fait le tour du château; **to c. down(wards)/up(wards)** monter/descendre en courbe
VT courber, recourber; *(pipe, surface etc)* cintrer
▸▸ *Comput* **c. smoothing** lissage *m* de courbes

curved [kɜːvd] ADJ *(intentionally bent)* courbe; *(bent out of shape)* courbé, cintré; *(nose)* busqué

curvilinear [kɜːvɪˈlɪnɪər] ADJ curviligne

curvy [ˈkɜːvɪ] ADJ **1** *(curved)* courbé, cintré **2** *Fam* *(woman)* qui a des formes

cushion [ˈkʊʃən] N **1** coussin *m*; **the mattresses acted as a c. when he fell** les matelas ont amorti sa chute; *Fig* **the annual increase in salary acts as a c. against inflation** l'augmentation annuelle des salaires amortit les effets de l'inflation **2** *Billiards* bande *f*; **off the c.** par la bande **3** *Tech* *(of air etc)* coussin *m*
VT *(reduce effect of)* *(blow, impact, fall etc)* amortir; **they have been cushioned against unemployment** ils ont été protégés contre le chômage

cushioning [ˈkʊʃənɪŋ] N *Tech* matelassage *m*; **as a c. against inflation** pour amortir les effets de l'inflation

cushy [ˈkʊʃɪ] ADJ *Fam* *(life etc)* pépère, peinard; **c. job** *or* **number** boulot *m* peinard

cusp [kʌsp] N **1** *Astron* *(of moon)* corne *f* **2** *Math* *(of curve)* sommet *m* **3** *(of tooth)* cuspide *f*

cuspidor [ˈkʌspɪdɔːr] N *Am* crachoir *m*

cuss [kʌs] N *Fam* **1** *(swear word)* juron *m*; **it isn't worth a (tinker's) c.** ça ne vaut pas un clou **2** *(person)* individu *m*, type *m*; **an awkward c.** un mauvais coucheur; **a stubborn c.** une tête de lard

cussed [ˈkʌsɪd] ADJ *Fam* *(annoying)* sacré, satané; *(stubborn)* entêté; **it's a c. nuisance** c'est bigrement embêtant

cussedness [ˈkʌsɪdnɪs] N *Fam* entêtement *m*; **out of sheer c.** par esprit de contradiction

custard [ˈkʌstəd] N *Culin* crème *f* anglaise; **baked c.** crème cuite au four
▸▸ **c. apple** anone *f*; **c. cream** biscuit *m* fourré à la crème; **c. pie** tarte *f* à la crème; **c.**

powder ≃ crème *f* anglaise instantanée; **c. tart** tarte à la crème

custodial [kʌˈstəʊdɪəl] ADJ *Law* de prison
▸▸ **c. sentence** peine *f* de prison *ou* de détention

custodian [kʌˈstəʊdɪən] N **1** gardien, -ienne; *(of museum etc)* conservateur, -trice; **the police are the custodians of law and order** la police est la garante de l'ordre public **2** *Am St Exch* dépositaire *mf*, conservateur, -trice de titres

custody [ˈkʌstədɪ] N **1** *(guardianship)* *(of children etc)* garde *f*; **the court awarded c. (of the children) to the father** le tribunal a confié la garde des enfants au père; **to have c. of sb/sth** avoir la garde de qn/qch; **in safe c.** sous bonne garde **2** *Law* détention *f*; **to take sb into c.** arrêter qn; **to be in c.** être en détention préventive

custom [ˈkʌstəm] N **1** *(practice)* coutume *f*, usage *m*; *(of individual)* habitude *f*; **according to c.** selon l'usage; **it is the c. of the country** c'est la coutume du pays; **it is their c. to fast on that day** leur coutume veut qu'ils jeûnent ce jour-là; **it was a c. with him to …**, **it was his c. to …** il avait l'habitude de …; **the manners and customs** *(of a country)* les us *mpl* et coutumes **2** *Law* *(of a country)* droit *m* coutumier, coutume *f* **3** *Com* *(of a company, shop)* clientèle *f*; **to lose sb's c.** perdre la clientèle de qn; **I'll take my c. elsewhere** je vais aller voir ailleurs, *Fam* je vais changer de crémerie
▸▸ **c. car** voiture *f* customisée, custom *m*

customarily [ˈkʌstəmərɪlɪ] ADV habituellement, d'habitude; *(normally)* ordinairement

customary [ˈkʌstəm(ə)rɪ] ADJ **1** habituel, d'usage; **at the c. hour** à l'heure habituelle; **it is c. to …** il est d'usage de …, c'est la coutume de …; **as is c.** comme il est d'usage; **her c. politeness** sa politesse habituelle *ou* coutumière **2** *Law* coutumier
▸▸ *Law* **c. law** droit *m* coutumier; *Law* **c. right** droit d'usage

custom-built ADJ fait *ou* fabriqué sur commande; *Aut* **c. body** carrosserie *f* customisée

customer [ˈkʌstəmər] N **1** *(of shop etc)* client, -ente; **regular c.** *(of restaurant etc)* habitué, -ée; *Prov* **the c. is always right** le client a toujours raison, le client est roi **2** *Fam* *(person)* individu *m*, type *m*; **an awkward c.** un type pas commode; **a queer c.** un drôle de type; **an ugly c.** un sale type
▸▸ *Com, Mktg* **c. acceptance test** test *m* d'acceptabilité auprès des consommateurs; *Com, Mktg* **c. base** base *f* de clientèle; **c. credit** crédit *m* client; *Com, Mktg* **c. satisfaction** satisfaction *f* de la clientèle; *Com, Mktg* **c. service** service *m* clientèle; *Com, Mktg* **c. service department** service clientèle; *Com, Mktg* **c. support service** service à la clientèle

customization [kʌstəmaɪˈzeɪʃən] N personnalisation *f*

customize [ˈkʌstəmaɪz] VT *(vehicle)* customiser; *(kitchen, computer etc)* personnaliser; **customized marketing** marketing *m* 'à la carte'
▸▸ *Comput* **c. option** option *f* 'personnaliser'

custom-made ADJ *(car etc)* fait *ou* fabriqué sur commande; *(clothes etc)* fait sur mesure

customs [ˈkʌstəmz] N *Admin* douane *f*; **to go through (the) c.** passer la douane; **at c.** à la douane; *Br* **C. and Excise** ≃ la Régie
▸▸ **c. agent** commissionnaire *mf* en douane; **c. allowance** tolérance *f* *ou* franchise *f* douanière; **c. barriers** barrières *fpl* douanières; **c. broker** agréé *m* en douane; **c. clearance** dédouanement *m*; **c. clearance**

area aire *f* de dédouanement; **c. clearance authorization** autorisation *f* de dédouanement; **c. control** contrôle *m* douanier; **c. declaration** déclaration *f* de *ou* en douane; **c. drawback** ristourne *f* de droits de douane; **c. duties** droits *mpl* de douane; **c. examination** contrôle douanier; **c. formalities** formalités *fpl* douanières; **c. house** (poste *m ou* bureau *m* de) douane; **c. inspector** inspecteur, -trice des douanes; **c. invoice** facture *f* douanière; **c. manifest** manifeste *m* de douane; **c. nomenclature** nomenclature *f* douanière, nomenclature générale des produits; **c. office** bureau de douane; **c. officer** douanier, -ière; **c. papers** dossier *m* de douane; **c. permit** permis *m* de douane; **c. procedure** procédure *f* douanière; **c. receipt** acquit *m* de douane; **c. regulations** réglementation *f* douanière; **c. system** régime *m* *ou* système *m* douanier; **c. tariff** tarif *m* douanier; **c. union** union *f* douanière; **c. value** valeur *f* en douane

CUT [kʌt]

N coupure **1, 4**	▪ réduction **1**		
▪ coup **2**	▪ coupe **5, 9**	▪ morceau **6**	
VT couper **1-3, 6, 7, 9-11**	▪ tondre **1**		
▪ trancher **1**	▪ réduire **3**	▪ monter **5**	
▪ graver **7**	▪ percer **8**		
VI couper **1-3**			
ADJ coupé **1**	▪ réduit **2**		

N **1** *(in an object)* entaille *f*; *Com etc* *(in price, spending)* réduction *f*; *Cin, TV* *(in film etc)* coupure *f*; **to make a clean c.** trancher net; **power** *or* **electricity c.** coupure de courant; *Cin* **the sudden c. from the battlefield to the dinner scene** la coupure brutale entre le champ de bataille et la scène du dîner; **to make a c. in a text** faire une coupure dans un texte; **a two-hundred word c.** une réduction de deux cents mots; **wage cuts** réductions de salaires; **to take a c. in one's wages** accepter une réduction de salaire; **everyone has agreed to take a c. in their wages** tout le monde a accepté de voir son salaire réduit
2 *(blow)* *(with knife, sword)* coup *m*; *Cr, Tennis* coup tranchant; **c. with a whip** coup de fouet; *Fig* **the unkindest c. of all** le coup le plus dur; **she revels in the c. and thrust of debate** elle prend plaisir aux joutes oratoires
3 *(of machine tool)* passe *f*; **(saw) c.** trait *m* de scie
4 *(wound)* coupure *f*; *(gash)* balafre *f*; *Surg* incision *f*; **c. across the cheek** balafre à la joue
5 *(style)* *(of garment, hair)* coupe *f*; *(of jewel)* taille *f*
6 *(meat)* **c. off the joint** tranche *f* de rôti; **prime c.** morceau *m* de (premier) choix; **cheap cuts** bas morceaux
7 *Fig Fam* *(portion)* commission *f*, *Fam* gratte *f*; **he gets his c.** il a sa part
8 **short c.** raccourci *m*; *Fig* solution *f* de facilité; **to take a short c.** couper au plus court, prendre (par) un raccourci; *Fig* utiliser la solution de facilité
9 *Cards* coupe *f*
10 *Fam* **to be a c. above sb/sth** être un cran au-dessus de qn/qch
11 *(of tobacco)* **I prefer a finer/coarser c. of tobacco** je préfère le tabac plus fin/grossier
VT *(pt, pp* cut, *prp* cutting) **1** couper; *(in slices)* trancher; *(rope)* couper, sectionner; *(hay)* faucher; **to c. the grass** *(with mower)* tondre le gazon; *(with shears)* couper le gazon; **to c. one's finger** se couper le doigt; **to c. one's nails** se couper les ongles; **to c. one's throat** se trancher la gorge; **to c. sb's throat** trancher la gorge de qn; **to have one's hair c.** se faire couper les cheveux; *Fig* **this remark**

c. him to the quick cette parole l'a piqué au vif

2 (*separate*) **to c. sth in two** *or* **in half** couper qch en deux; **to c. a slice of cake** couper une tranche de gâteau; **to c. to pieces** (*object*) couper en morceaux; (*army*) tailler en pièces; **to c. one's way through the wood** se frayer un chemin à travers le bois; **to c. a dog loose** libérer un chien en coupant sa laisse; **to c. a horse loose** libérer un cheval en coupant sa longe; *Fig* **to c. oneself loose from sth** se libérer de qch

3 (*shorten, reduce*) (*film, scene, text etc*) couper; (*speech*) abréger, raccourcir; (*numbers, spending*) réduire; (*production*) diminuer; **the film was c. to 100 minutes** le film a été ramené à 100 minutes; **prices/wages have been c. by 10%** les prix/salaires ont été réduits de 10%; **this cuts their journey time by 20 minutes** cela réduit la durée de leur trajet de 20 minutes; **it helps to c. costs** cela permet de réduire les frais; **to c. a speech/a visit short** écourter un discours/une visite; **to c. sb short** couper la parole à qn; **to c. a long story short …** bref …; *Fig* **it's cutting it** *or* **things fine** cela va faire juste

4 (*omit, remove*) supprimer; **this scene was later c.** cette scène a été supprimée par la suite; *Sl* **c. the crap!** arrête tes conneries!

5 (*edit*) (*film*) monter

6 *Comput* couper; **to c. and paste sth** faire un couper-coller sur qch

7 *Tech etc* (*stone, glass etc*) couper, tailler; (*canal*) percer, creuser; (*characters on metal or stone*) tailler, ciseler; (*garment*) tailler, couper; *Mus* (*record*) graver; *Fig* **to c. one's coat according to one's cloth** faire avec ce que l'on a

8 to c. a tooth (*of child*) percer une dent; *Fig* **to c. one's teeth on sth** (*of lawyer etc*) se faire les dents sur qch

9 *Cards* **to c. the cards** (*in general*) couper les cartes; (*to decide who deals etc*) tirer une carte pour savoir qui fera la donne/*etc*

10 *Cr, Tennis* (*ball*) couper

11 *Elec etc* (*turn off*) couper

12 to c. sb (dead) (*ignore*) faire semblant de ne pas voir qn, ignorer qn complètement

13 *Sch Fam* (*class*) sécher

14 to c. an elegant/a noble/a romantic figure être très élégant/noble/romantique

VI 1 (*of knife, person*) couper; **those scissors don't c. very well** ces ciseaux ne coupent pas très bien; **cloth that cuts easily** tissu qui se coupe facilement; **that wind cuts like a knife** le vent te transperce; **to c. into a cake** entamer un gâteau; **to c. into the bark** inciser l'écorce; *Lit* **to c. through the waves** fendre les eaux; **that's an argument that cuts both ways** c'est un argument à double tranchant; *Am* **to c. loose** (*free oneself*) s'émanciper; (*escape*) s'évader; *Fam* **to c. and run** filer (en vitesse), décamper, se sauver

2 *Cin, TV, Theat* (*change scene*) **the action cuts to the street** l'action passe à la rue; *Cin* **c.!** coupez!

3 *Cards* couper

ADJ 1 (*crystal, diamond*) taillé; **well/elegantly c. suit** complet bien coupé/de coupe élégante; **c. and dried** (*opinions*) tout fait; **everything was c. and dried** (*decided*) tout était déjà décidé; **it's not as c. and dried as that** ce n'est pas aussi simple que ça

2 (*reduced, shortened*) réduit; **the c. version of the film** la version raccourcie du film

▸▸ **c. glass** cristal *m* taillé; **a c. glass jug** une cruche en cristal taillé; *Br Fig* **a c. glass accent** un accent bourgeois; *Comput* **c. sheet feed** dispositif *m* d'alimentation feuille à feuille; (*act*) alimentation *f* feuille à feuille; *Comput* **c. sheet feeder** dispositif d'alimentation feuille à feuille

▸ **cut across** VT INSEP (*playing field, forest etc*) couper à travers; *Fig* **concern for the envi-**ronment **cuts across party lines** les préoccupations écologiques transcendent les clivages politiques

▸ **cut along** VI *Old-fashioned Br Fam* filer

▸ **cut away** VT SEP (*remove*) couper, ôter; **they had to c. away the wreckage to reach the victim** ils ont dû découper l'épave pour atteindre la victime; **c. away the fat** ôtez le gras

▸ **cut back** VT SEP **1** (*prune*) (*rosebush, undergrowth etc*) tailler; (*tree*) élaguer

2 (*reduce*) (*prices*) baisser; (*production etc*) diminuer; **arms spending has been c. right back** les dépenses d'armement ont été nettement réduites

VI **1** (*financially*) économiser, réduire les dépenses

2 (*go back*) s'en retourner, rebrousser chemin

3 *Cin* (*of action*) revenir en arrière; **we c. back to the scene in the kitchen** nous revenons à la scène de la cuisine

▸ **cut back on** VT INSEP (*financially*) économiser sur; (*time*) réduire; **we've already c. back on production** nous avons déjà diminué la production; **you'll have to c. back on the cakes** il faudra que vous mangiez moins de gâteaux; **to c. back on one's smoking** fumer moins

▸ **cut down** VT SEP **1** (*fell*) (*tree*) couper, abattre; (*wheat*) couper

2 (*kill*) abattre; *Lit* **to be c. down in one's prime** être fauché à la fleur de l'âge

3 (*shorten, reduce*) (*speech etc*) abréger; (*book for publication*) raccourcir; (*spending*) couper, réduire; **to c. sth down to about 150,000 words** réduire qch à environ 150 000 mots; **we've been asked to c. down the amount of time we devote to sports** on nous a demandé de consacrer moins de temps au sport; **to c. trousers down** (*to make shorts*) transformer un pantalon en short

4 (*cut through ropes*) **to c. down a hanged man** couper la corde d'un pendu; **the parachutist had to be c. down from the tree** pour décrocher le parachutiste de l'arbre il a fallu couper les cordes de son parachute

VI (*make reductions*) réduire; **I drink too much coffee so I'm trying to c. down** je bois trop de café, alors j'essaie de réduire

▸ **cut down on** VT INSEP **we had to c. down on expenditure** nous avons dû réduire nos dépenses; **to c. down on the amount of time spent doing sth** passer moins de temps à faire qch; **try to c. down on the swearing** essayez de jurer un peu moins

▸ **cut in** VI **1** (*interrupt conversation*) intervenir dans la conversation; *Tel* interrompre la conversation; **she c. in (on me)** elle m'a coupé la parole; **you're wrong, she c. in** tu as tort, interrompit-elle

2 *Aut* faire une queue de poisson; **he c. in in front of me** il m'a fait une queue de poisson

3 (*at a dance*) **mind if I c. in?** vous permettez que je vous emprunte votre partenaire?

4 *Tech* (*of mechanism, safety device*) entrer en action

VT SEP *Fam* (*include in a deal*) **to c. sb in (on the deal)** donner à qn sa part du gâteau; **we could c. him in for £5,000** nous pourrions lui filer 5 000 livres

▸ **cut into** VT INSEP **1** (*interrupt*) **to c. into a conversation** intervenir dans *ou* interrompre brusquement la conversation

2 (*use*) **to c. into one's savings** entamer ses économies; **this work cuts into my free time** ce travail empiète sur mes heures de loisir

3 (*hurt*) blesser; **the rope was cutting into his arm/skin** la corde lui blessait le bras/lui entaillait la peau; **the string is cutting into me** le cordon me coupe la chair

▸ **cut off** VT SEP **1** (*remove by cutting*) (*piece*) couper, découper; **pages with the corners** c. off pages dont les coins ont été coupés; **he's had all his hair c. off** il s'est fait couper les cheveux tout court; **to c. off sb's head** trancher la tête à qn; *Lit* **to be c. off in one's prime** être emporté *ou* fauché à la fleur de l'âge

2 (*isolate*) (*personne*) couper (du monde); **to c. off the enemy** couper la ligne de retraite de l'ennemi; **to c. off sb's retreat** couper la retraite à qn; **to be c. off** (*by snow, floods*) (*of person, village etc*) se trouver isolé; **the village is c. off from the outside world by snow** le village est coupé du monde par la neige; **I feel c. off** je me sens coupé du monde; **to c. oneself off from the world** se retirer du monde; **she c. herself off from her family** elle s'est coupée de sa famille

3 *Tel* (*person*) couper; **he's been c. off** (*during conversation*) il a été coupé; (*disconnected*) on lui a coupé le téléphone

4 (*electricity, steam, ignition*) couper; **to c. off sb's water/supplies** couper *ou* supprimer l'eau/les vivres à qn; **it c. off the supply of blood to the brain** cela a stoppé l'irrigation du cerveau

5 (*disinherit*) (*person*) déshériter; **the old man c. his son off without a penny** le vieillard n'a pas laissé un sou à son fils

▸ **cut out** VT SEP **1** (*remove by cutting*) couper, enlever; *Surg* (*tumour etc*) enlever; **to c. a picture out of a magazine** découper une photo dans un magazine

2 (*shape by cutting*) (*pictures*) découper; (*garment*) couper, tailler; (*neckline*) échancrer; **to c. a statue out of wood** tailler une statue dans le bois; *Fig* **to be c. out for sth** être fait pour qch, avoir des dispositions pour qch; **he's not c. out to be a leader** il n'a pas l'étoffe d'un dirigeant; **he's not c. out for it** il n'est pas fait pour cela; *Fig* **I've really got my work c. out** j'ai du pain sur la planche; **she's got her work c. out (for her) with those four kids** elle a de quoi faire avec ces quatre gamins

3 (*eliminate*) supprimer, éliminer; **to c. out luxuries** se passer du luxe; **to c. out smoking** arrêter de fumer; **I wish he'd c. out the jokes** j'aimerais bien qu'il arrête ses plaisanteries; *Fam* **c. it out!** ça suffit maintenant!, ça va comme ça!; **the new building cuts out a lot of the light** le nouveau bâtiment coupe une bonne partie de la lumière

4 (*oust*) **to c. sb out of a deal** évincer qn dans une affaire; **his father c. them out of his will** son père les a déshérités

VI (*stop*) (*of engine*) caler; (*of machine*) s'arrêter; (*of pilot light*) s'éteindre

▸ **cut through** VT INSEP **1** (*rope*) couper; *Fig* **to c. through red tape** éviter la paperasserie

2 (*take as a short cut*) **to c. through the park** couper par le parc

▸ **cut up** VT SEP **1** (*chop up*) (*wood, meat*) couper, débiter; (*chicken etc*) découper, dépecer; (*vegetables etc*) hacher, émincer; (*body*) couper en morceaux; **to c. sth up into small pieces** couper qch en petits morceaux

2 *Fam* (*usu passive*) (*upset*) **to be very c. up** être profondément affecté *ou* affligé (**about sth** par qch)

VI *Br Fam* **to c. up rough** (*physically*) devenir violent; (*verbally*) monter sur ses ergots

cut-and-paste *Comput* N couper-coller *m*
  VT & VI couper-coller

cutaneous [kjuːˈteɪnɪəs] ADJ cutané

cutaway [ˈkʌtəweɪ] N **1** (*coat*) jaquette *f* **2** *Tech* (*drawing*) vue *f* en coupe **3** *Cin, TV* changement *m* de plan
  ▸▸ **c. coat** jaquette; *Tech* **c. model** maquette *f* en coupe; *Cin, TV* **c. shot** changement de plan

cutback [ˈkʌtbæk] N (*in production, budget*) réduction *f*, dégonflement *m*

cute [kjuːt] ADJ *Fam* **1** *(attractive)* mignon; **what a c. little kitten** quel mignon petit chaton **2** *(clever)* malin, *f* maligne; *(idea)* original, -aux; **don't get c. with me!** ne fais pas le malin avec moi!

cuteness ['kjuːtnɪs] N *Fam* **1** *(attractiveness)* charme *m* **2** *(cleverness)* finesse *f*

cuticle ['kjuːtɪk(ə)l] N *Anat, Bot* cuticule *f*
▸▸ **c. pen** repousse-peaux *m inv*

cutie(-pie) ['kjuːtɪ(paɪ)] N *Fam* **1** *(baby, child)* mignon, -onne; *(girl, woman)* beauté *f* **2** *(shrewd person)* malin *m*, maligne *f*

cutlass ['kʌtləs] N *Naut* sabre *m* d'abordage

cutler ['kʌtlər] N coutelier, -ière *f*

cutlery ['kʌtlərɪ] N *(eating utensils)* couverts *mpl*; *Com, Ind* coutellerie *f*
▸▸ **c. drawer** tiroir *m* à couverts

cutlet ['kʌtlɪt] N *Culin* **1** *(of lamb, veal)* côtelette *f* **2** *(croquette) (of chicken etc)* croquette *f*

cutoff ['kʌtɒf] N **1** *Am (short cut)* raccourci *m* **2** *Electron* déconnexion *f*, mise *f* hors de contact, mise hors circuit **3** *(stopping point)* limite *f* **4** cutoffs *(shorts)* = jean *m* transformé en short
▸▸ **c. date** date *f* limite; **c. point** limite; **we've taken a score of 370 as the c. point in deciding who to interview** *(no less than)* les candidats doivent avoir au minimum 370 points pour pouvoir passer l'entretien; **the c. point for remedial lessons is 150** *(no more than)* seuls les élèves qui obtiennent 150 points ou en deçà pourront bénéficier de cours de rattrapage

cutout ['kʌtaʊt] N **1 a cardboard c. of Humphrey Bogart** une silhouette en carton de Humphrey Bogart **2** *Elec* coupe-circuit *m inv*; disjoncteur *m*
▸▸ *Aut* **c. device** dispositif *m* de coupure; *Aut* **c. valve** conjoncteur-disjoncteur *m*, *pl* conjoncteurs-disjoncteurs, disjoncteur

cut-price, *Am* **cut-rate** ADJ *Com (goods)* à prix réduit; *(as special offer)* bradé; **at cut-price rates** à un tarif réduit
▸▸ **c. shop** solderie *f*

cutter ['kʌtər] N **1** *(person) (of garments)* coupeur, -euse; *(of stone, diamonds)* tailleur *m*; *Cin* monteur, -euse, découpeur, -euse **2** *(tool, device)* lame *f*, couteau *m*; **rotary c.** roue *f* à couteaux; **coal c.** haveuse *f* **3** *Naut* canot *m* *(d'un bâtiment de guerre)*

cutthroat ['kʌtθrəʊt] N *(murderer)* assassin *m*; *(razor)* rasoir *m* à main
ADJ féroce; *(competition)* acharné; *(prices)* très compétitif; **it's a c. business** la concurrence est acharnée
▸▸ *Cards* **c. bridge** bridge *m* à trois; **c. razor** coupe-choux *m inv*, rasoir à main

cutting ['kʌtɪŋ] ADJ **1** *(wind)* cinglant, glacial, -aux; *(rain)* cinglant **2** *(remark etc)* mordant, blessant; *(criticism)* incisif; **she was rather c. about them** elle a dit des choses un peu dures sur eux
N **1** *(act)* coupe *f*, *(of jewel, stone)* taille *f*, *(film editing)* montage *m*; *(of trees)* coupe, abattage *m*
2 *(piece cut off) (from newspaper)* coupure *f*, *(of plant)* bouture *f*, *(of vine)* sarment *m*; **to grow a plant from a c.** faire pousser une plante à partir d'une bouture; **to take a c.** faire une bouture; **cuttings** *(of wood, metal etc)* rognures *fpl*, recoupes *fpl*, *(of carpet)* chutes *fpl*
3 *(railway)* **c.** *(voie f* en) déblai *m*
▸▸ *Tech* **c. action** cisaillement *m*; *Tech* **c. an-**

gle angle *m* de coupe; **c. back** *(of tree)* élagage *m*; *(of production, budget)* réduction *f*; *Cin* **c. copy** copie *f* de montage *ou* de travail; **c. edge** tranchant *m*; *Fig* **to be at the c. edge (of technology)** être à la pointe; *Journ* **cuttings file** fichier *m* de coupures; *Journ* **cuttings library** archives *fpl* de coupures de presse; *Cin* **c. point** point *m* de coupe; *Cin* **c. room** salle *f* de montage; *Cin* **c. table** table *f* de montage; **c. tool** outil *m* tranchant

cuttingly ['kʌtɪŋlɪ] ADV *(to say)* d'un ton caustique; **c. brief** bref et caustique

cuttlebone ['kʌt(ə)lbəʊn] N os *m* de seiche

cuttlefish ['kʌt(ə)lfɪʃ] N seiche *f*

CV [siː'viː] N *(abbr* **curriculum vitae)** CV *m*

CV joint N *Aut (abbr* **constant velocity joint)** joint *m* de cardan

CVP [siːviː'piː] N *Fin (abbr* **cost-volume-profit)** étude *f* de coût-efficacité

cwo *Com (abbr* **cash with order)** envoi contre paiement

cwt *abbr* **hundredweight**

CWU [siːdʌb(ə)ljuː'juː] N *(abbr* **Communication Workers Union)** = syndicat *m* des travailleurs des postes et des télécommunications

cyan ['saɪən] N cyan *m*

cyanide ['saɪənaɪd] N *Chem* cyanure *m*; **potassium c.** cyanure de potassium

cyanosis [saɪə'nəʊsɪs] N *Med* cyanose *f*

cyber ['saɪbər] N *Comput* cyber *m*

cyberbanking ['saɪbəbæŋkɪŋ] N transactions *fpl* bancaires en ligne

cybercafé ['saɪbəkæfeɪ] N cybercafé *m*

cybercrime ['saɪbəkraɪm] N cybercrime *m*

cyberculture ['saɪbəkʌltʃər] N cyberculture *f*

cybermall ['saɪbəmɔːl] N centre *m* commercial électronique, galerie *f* marchande électronique

cybernaut ['saɪbənɔːt] N cybernaute *m*

cybernetic [saɪbə'netɪk] ADJ cybernétique

cybernetics [saɪbə'netɪks] N VOIR GRAMMAIRE A10 *(with sing verb)* cybernétique *f*

cyberpunk ['saɪbəpʌŋk] N cyberpunk *m*

cybersex ['saɪbəseks] N amour *m* virtuel

cyberspace ['saɪbəspeɪs] N cyber(e)space *m*

cybersquatter ['saɪbəskwɒtər] N *Comput* cybersquatteur *m*

cybersquatting ['saɪbəskwɒtɪŋ] N *Comput* cybersquatting *m*, cybersquattage *m*

cyberstalking ['saɪbəstɔːkɪŋ] N *Comput* cybertraque *f*, cyberharcèlement *m*

cyclamen ['sɪkləmən] N *Bot* cyclamen *m*

cycle ['saɪk(ə)l] N **1** *(pattern) (of movements etc)* cycle *m*; *Aut* **four-stroke c.** cycle à quatre temps; *Astron* **lunar c.** cycle lunaire; **trade c.** cycle économique **2** *(bicycle)* bicyclette *f*, vélo *m* **3** *Am* = **motorcycle**
VI faire de la bicyclette *ou* du vélo; **to c. to/from school** aller à/revenir de l'école à bicyclette *ou* à vélo
▸▸ **c. lane** piste *f* cyclable; **c. path** piste *ou* bande *f* cyclable; **c. racing** courses *fpl* cyclistes; **c. racing track** vélodrome *m*; **c. shop** magasin *m* de cycles; **c. track** piste cyclable

cycler ['saɪklər] N *Am* cycliste *mf*

cyclic(al) ['sɪklɪk, -ɪk(ə)l] ADJ *(movement etc)* cyclique
▸▸ **c. unemployment** chômage *m* conjoncturel

cycling ['saɪklɪŋ] N cyclisme *m*
▸▸ **c. club** club *m* de cyclisme; **c. holidays** cyclotourisme *m*; **c. shorts** cuissard *m*; **c. track** piste *f* cyclable

cyclist ['saɪklɪst] N cycliste *mf*

cyclone ['saɪkləʊn] N *Met* cyclone *m*

cyclonic [saɪ'klɒnɪk] ADJ cyclonique, cyclonal

cyclorama [saɪkləʊ'rɑːmə] N cyclorama *m*
▸▸ **c. light** éclairage *m* de cyclorama

cyclostyle ['saɪkləʊstaɪl] VT *Old-fashioned* polycopier

cyclotron ['saɪklətrɒn] N *Nucl* cyclotron *m*

cygnet ['sɪgnɪt] N *(bird)* jeune cygne *m*

cylinder ['sɪlɪndər] N **1** *Geom* cylindre *m* **2** *Tech, Comput etc* cylindre *m*; *(of pump, revolver)* barillet *m*; **to be firing on all cylinders** *(of engine)* tourner rond; *Fig (company)* fonctionner à plein régime; *(of person)* être en pleine forme; **four/eight-c. engine** moteur *m* à quatre/huit cylindres; **the engine isn't firing on all cylinders** le moteur boite; *Fig* **he's only firing on three cylinders, he's not firing on all cylinders** il n'est pas tout à fait dans son assiette
▸▸ *Aut* **c. bank** rangée *f* de cylindres; *Tech* **c. block** bloc-cylindres *m*, *pl* blocs-cylindres; **c. bore** alésage *m* de cylindre; *Tech* **c. head** culasse *f* *(d'un moteur)*; **c. head gasket** joint *m* de culasse; **c. wall** paroi *f* des cylindres

cylindrical [sɪ'lɪndrɪk(ə)l] ADJ cylindrique

cymbal ['sɪmb(ə)l] N *Mus* cymbale *f*

Cymru ['kʌmrɪ] N = nom gallois du pays de Galles

cynic ['sɪnɪk] N cynique *mf*; *Antiq, Phil* cynique *m*

cynical ['sɪnɪk(ə)l] ADJ cynique

cynically ['sɪnɪklɪ] ADV cyniquement

cynicism ['sɪnɪsɪz(ə)m] N cynisme *m*

cypher ['saɪfər] N, VT = **cipher**

cypress ['saɪprəs] N *(tree)* cyprès *m*

Cypriot ['sɪprɪət] ADJ chypriote
N Chypriote *mf*

Cyprus ['saɪprəs] N Chypre *f*

Cyrillic [sɪ'rɪlɪk] ADJ cyrillique
N **in C.** en caractères cyrilliques

cyst [sɪst] N **1** *Biol, Anat* sac *m* **2** *Med* kyste *m*

cystic fibrosis ['sɪstɪk] N *Med* mucoviscidose *f*

cystitis [sɪs'taɪtɪs] N *Med* cystite *f*; **to have c.** avoir une cystite

cytological [saɪtə'lɒdʒɪk(ə)l] ADJ *Med* cytologique

cytology [saɪ'tɒlədʒɪ] N *Biol* cytologie *f*

cytomegalovirus [saɪtəʊ'megələʊvaɪrəs] N *Med* cytomégalovirus *m*

czar [zɑːr] N = **tsar**

czarevitch ['zɑːrəvɪtʃ] N = **tsarevitch**

czarina [zɑː'riːnə] N = **tsarina**

czarist ['zɑːrɪst] ADJ, N = **tsarist**

Czech [tʃek] ADJ tchèque
N **1** Tchèque *mf* **2** *Ling* tchèque *m*
▸▸ **C. Republic** République *f* tchèque

Czechoslovak [tʃekəʊ'sləʊvæk], **Czechoslovakian** [tʃekəʊsləʊ'vækɪən] *Formerly* ADJ tchécoslovaque
N Tchécoslovaque *mf*

Czechoslovakia [tʃekəʊslə'vækɪə] N *Formerly* Tchécoslovaquie *f*

D¹, d¹ [di:] N **1** (letter) D, d m; **two d's** deux d **2** Mus ré m **3** Sch **to get a D** avoir une mauvaise note, ≃ avoir entre 7 et 9 sur 20

D² Am Pol abbr **Democrat**

d² **1** (abbr **deceased**) m. **2** Br Hist (abbr **denarius**) pence

DA [di:'eɪ] N Am Law abbr **district attorney**

dab¹ [dæb] N **1** (touch) petit coup m; **a d. with a cloth** un petit coup de chiffon **2** (portion) (of ink, paint) tache f; (of butter) petit morceau m; (of colour) touche f; (of perfume) goutte f; (of glue) point m; **a few dabs of mustard** un peu de moutarde; **just give it a d. of paint** mets-y un coup de peinture **3** Br Old-fashioned Fam **dabs** (fingerprints) empreintes fpl digitales

VT (-bb-) (touch) donner un petit coup à; (with pad etc) tamponner; (daub) tapoter; **she dabbed the lump on her forehead with a wet facecloth** elle a tamponné la bosse qu'elle avait sur le front avec un linge humide; **to d. one's eyes (with a handkerchief)** se tamponner les yeux; **to d. paint on sth** donner un coup de peinture à qch

▶ **dab off** VT SEP ôter en tamponnant

▶ **dab on** VT SEP (paint, antiseptic etc) appliquer

dab² N (fish) limande f

dab³ ADJ Fam **to be a d. hand at (doing) sth** être doué pour (faire) qch

dabble ['dæb(ə)l] VT (one's hands etc in water) tremper; **she dabbled her feet in the brook** elle se trempa les pieds dans le ruisseau

VI Fam **to d. on the Stock Exchange** boursicoter; **to d. in politics** faire un peu de politique; **to d. in art/music** être un peu artiste/musicien; **to d. in black magic** toucher à la magie noire

dabbler ['dæblər] N often Pej (amateur) amateur m; **d. on the Stock Exchange** boursicoteur, -euse

dace [deɪs] N (fish) vandoise f, dard m

dacha ['dætʃa] N dacha f

dachshund ['dækshʊnd] N (dog) teckel m

dactyl ['dæktɪl] N Liter dactyle m

dad [dæd] N Fam papa m

Dada ['dɑ:dɑ:] N Art, Liter dada m, dadaïsme m

Dadaism ['dɑ:dɑ:ɪz(ə)m] N Art, Liter dadaïsme m

daddy ['dædɪ] N Fam papa m

daddy-longlegs [-'lɒŋlegz] N Fam (insect) cousin m

dado ['deɪdəʊ] N Archit **1** (of pedestal) dé m **2** (of wall) lambris m (d'appui)

daemon ['di:mən] N Arch, Lit démon m

daff [dæf] N Br Fam = **daffodil** N

daffodil ['dæfədɪl] N (flower) jonquille f

ADJ (colour) jonquille inv

▶▶ **d. yellow** jonquille inv

daffy ['dæfɪ] ADJ Fam (person) timbré, toqué; (idea, notion) débile

daft [dɑ:ft] ADJ Br Fam (person) timbré, toqué; (remark, idea, plan etc) débile; **to act d.** faire l'idiot; **to go d.** devenir cinglé; (become angry) devenir fou de rage; **don't be d.!** ne sois pas bête!; **don't talk d.!** ne dis pas de bêtises!; **to be d. about sb/sth** être fou de qn/qch

daftie ['dɑ:ftɪ] N Br Fam, Dial toqué, -ée

daftness ['dɑ:ftnɪs] N Br Fam stupidité f

dag [dæg] N Austr Fam **1** (unfashionable person) ringard, -arde **2** (untidy man) type m négligé; (untidy woman) bonne femme f négligée

dagger ['dægər] N **1** poignard m, Lit dague f; Fig **to be at daggers drawn** être à couteaux tirés (**with** avec); **to look daggers at sb** foudroyer qn du regard **2** Typ croix f

dago ['deɪgəʊ] N Offensive Sl métèque m

dahlia ['deɪlɪə] N (flower) dahlia m

Dáil [dɑ:l] N = Chambre f des députés de la République d'Irlande

daily ['deɪlɪ] ADJ ATTRIB quotidien; (report, wage, output) journalier; **on a d. basis** (paid, employed, calculated) à la journée; (used) tous les jours, de façon quotidienne; **d. takings** recette f journalière; **d. visitors** visiteurs mpl journaliers; **to earn one's d. bread** gagner son pain quotidien; Rel **give us this day our d. bread** donne-nous aujourd'hui notre pain de ce jour

ADV (to phone, visit, happen) tous les jours; **twice d.** deux fois par jour; **news of their defeat is awaited d.** on s'attend à apprendre leur défaite d'un jour à l'autre

N **1** Journ quotidien m **2** Br Fam (for housework) femme f de ménage **3** TV, Cin **dailies** rushes mpl

▶▶ Admin **d. allowance** indemnité f journalière; Acct **d. balance interest calculation** méthode f à échelles ou par échelles; Br Old-fashioned Fam **d. dozen** gym f quotidienne; Fam **the d. grind** métro m boulot dodo; **I've had enough of the d. grind** j'en ai assez du métro boulot dodo; Br **d. help** femme f de ménage; St Exch **D. Official List** cours mpl de clôture quotidiens; **d. paper** quotidien m; **d. press** presse f quotidienne; Fin **d. trading report** rapport m de situation journalière; Br **d. woman** femme de ménage

daintily ['deɪntɪlɪ] ADV délicatement

daintiness ['deɪntɪnɪs] N (of movement, way of working etc) délicatesse f; (of taste) raffinement m

dainty ['deɪntɪ] ADJ **1** (dish, food) fin; (morsel) de choix **2** (person) (in manners) délicat; (in build) menu; **short d. steps** petits pas délicats **3** (choosy) délicat, difficile; **these animals are d. feeders** ces animaux sont délicats sur la nourriture **4** (delicate) (porcelain, ornament) fin, délicat

dairy ['deərɪ] N **1** (on farm) laiterie f **2** (shop) crémerie f

▶▶ **d. butter** beurre m laitier; **d. cow** vache f laitière; **d. farm** ferme f laitière; **d. farming** industrie f laitière; **d. herd** troupeau m de vaches laitières; **d. ice cream** glace f à la crème; **d. produce** produits mpl laitiers

dairymaid ['deərɪmeɪd] N fille f de laiterie

dairyman, pl **dairymen** ['deərɪmən] N **1** (on farm) employé m de laiterie **2** (who sells dairy products) laitier m

dais ['deɪɪs] N estrade f

daisy ['deɪzɪ] N (flower) pâquerette f; (bigger) marguerite f; **as fresh as a d.** frais/fraîche comme une rose; Sl **he's pushing up the daisies** il mange les pissenlits par les racines

▶▶ **d. chain** guirlande f de pâquerettes; Comput **d. chaining** connexion f en boucle; Comput, Typ **d. wheel** marguerite f; **d. wheel printer** imprimante f à marguerite

daisy-chain VT Comput connecter en boucle

Dak abbr **Dakota**

Dalai Lama ['dælaɪ 'lɑ:mə] N dalaï-lama m, pl dalaï-lamas

dale [deɪl] N vallée f; (smaller) vallon m

dalliance ['dælɪəns] N Lit badinage m

dally ['dælɪ] VI **1** Old-fashioned (trifle) folâtrer (**with sb** avec qn); **to d. with an idea** caresser une idée **2** (dawdle) lambiner, traînasser; **to d. over sth** s'attarder à qch

Dalmatian [dæl'meɪʃən] N (dog) dalmatien, -ienne

dam¹ [dæm] N Tech (of reservoir) barrage m; (of canal) digue f; **storage d.** barrage-réservoir m, pl barrages-réservoirs

VT (-mm-) **to d. (up)** (valley) construire un barrage en aval de; (river, lake) endiguer; (gutter) obstruer; Fig (one's feelings etc) contenir

dam² N Agr, Lit mère f

damage ['dæmɪdʒ] N **1** (physical) dégâts mpl; (to engine, ship etc) avarie(s) f(pl); **to pay for the d.** payer les dégâts; **smoking can cause serious d. to your health** le tabac nuit gravement à la santé; Br Fam **what's the d.?** (how much do I owe?) ça fait combien?; **there's no great d. done** il n'y a pas trop de mal; **d. to property** dommage m matériel **2** (harm) préjudice m; **to cause sb d.** porter préjudice à qn; **the d. is done** le mal est fait; **to do d. to a cause** faire du tort à une cause; **d. suffered** préjudice subi **3** Law **damages** dommages-intérêts mpl, intérêts mpl compensatoires; **to be liable for damages** être tenu au versement de dommages-intérêts; **to sue sb for damages** poursuivre qn en dommages et intérêts; **to be awarded damages of £5,000** or **£5,000 in damages** obtenir 5000 livres de dommages-intérêts

VT **1** (physically) (engine, machine) endommager; *(goods)* avarier; *(furniture)* endommager, abîmer; **the storm damaged a lot of trees** de nombreux arbres ont été endommagés par la tempête; *Com* **damaged in transit** abîmé en cours de route; **damaged goods** marchandises *fpl* avariées

2 *(harm) (chances)* compromettre; *(person)* faire du tort à; *(sb's interests)* léser; *(sb's reputation)* porter atteinte à, ternir

▸▸ **d. control, d. limitation** fait *m* de limiter les dégâts; **we have to do some d. limitation** il faut limiter les dégâts; **d. report** déclaration *f* de sinistre, constat *m* de dommages

damaging ['dæmɪdʒɪŋ] ADJ *(revelation, scandal, remark etc)* préjudiciable; **it's a d. blow to his re-election prospects/career** cela compromet sérieusement ses chances d'être réélu/sa carrière

Damascus [də'mɑːskəs] N Damas *m*; *Fig* **a conversion on the road to D.** une conversion subite

damask ['dæməsk] N **1** *Tex* damas *m* **2** *(colour)* rose foncé *m inv*

▸▸ **d. rose** rose *f* de Damas; **d. silk** soie *f* damassée; *Metal* **d. steel** acier *m* damassé

dame [deɪm] N **1** *Am Fam (woman)* femme *f*; *Br (in pantomime)* vieille femme comique *(dont le rôle est joué par un homme)* **2** *Br (title)* = titre *m* honorifique donné à certaines femmes en signe de distinction

dammit ['dæmɪt] INT *Fam* nom de Dieu; **it was as near as d.** il était moins une

damn [dæm] N *Fam* **I don't give** *or* **care a d.** m'en fiche éperdument, je n'en ai rien à fiche; **I don't give a d. about the money** je me fiche pas mal de l'argent; **he doesn't give a d. about anything** il se fiche de tout; **it's not worth a d.** ça ne vaut rien

VT **1** *(book, play etc) (criticize severely)* éreinter; *(condemn)* condamner; **to d. sb/ sth with faint praise** faire de tièdes éloges de qn/qch, louer qn/qch avec si peu d'ardeur que cela revient à condamner; **you're damned if you do and damned if you don't** quoique tu fasses tu es perdant **2** *Rel* damner **3** *Fam* **well I'll be damned!** ça alors!; **I'm** *or* **I'll be damned if I'll do it** si tu crois que je vais le faire!; **d. the expense** au diable l'avarice; **d. the consequences** tant pis pour les conséquences

INT **d. (it)!** zut!; **d. you!** va te faire fiche!; **d. and blast (it)!** sacré nom d'un chien!

ADJ *Fam* = **damned** ADJ **2**

ADV *Fam* **1 he's doing d. all** il n'en fout pas une (rame); **she knows d. all about it** elle y connaît que dal(l)e; **there's d. all in the fridge** il y a que dal(l)e dans le frigo; **it's got d. all to do with you** ça n'a absolument rien à voir avec toi; **what can you see? – d. all!** tu vois quelque chose? – que dalle! **2** = **damned** ADV

damnable ['dæmnəb(ə)l] ADJ **1** *Rel* damnable **2** *Fam (detestable)* maudit

damnably ['dæmnəblɪ] ADV *Old-fashioned Fam (difficult, expensive, rude etc)* diablement, rudement

damnation [dæm'neɪʃən] N *Rel* damnation *f*, eternal **d.** la peine du dam

INT *Fam* **d.!** enfer et damnation!

damned [dæmd] ADJ **1** *Rel* damné **2** *Fam (intensifier)* **you d. fool!** espèce d'idiot!; **you have to be a d. fool to do that!** il faut être un sacré abruti pour faire ça!; **he's a d. nuisance!** ce qu'il peut être casse-pieds!; **well I'm d.!** elle est bien bonne celle-là!; **it's one d. thing after another** tout va de travers

NPL *Rel* **the d.** les damnés *mpl*; **to suffer the tortures of the d.** souffrir comme un damné

ADV *Fam* rudement, vachement; **it's d. hot** il fait rudement chaud; **I should d. well hope so** ah, ben j'espère bien!; **you can do what you d. well like!** fais ce que tu veux, je m'en

fiche!; **you know d. well what I mean** tu sais très bien ce que je veux dire; **they're d. good players** ils jouent vachement bien

damnedest ['dæmdest] *Fam* N **to do one's d.** faire tout son possible; **he did his d. to ruin the party** il a vraiment fait tout ce qu'il pouvait pour gâcher la soirée

ADJ **if that isn't the d. thing!** c'est vraiment bizarre!, c'est incroyable!

damnfool ['dæm'fuːl] ADJ ATTRIB *Fam* idiot

damning ['dæmɪŋ] ADJ *(fact, evidence etc)* accablant; *(admission)* préjudiciable; **he was pretty d. about the film** il a été très critique vis-à-vis du film

Damocles ['dæməkliːz] N **the sword of D.** l'épée *f* de Damoclès

damp [dæmp] N *(of air)* humidité *f*, *(of skin)* moiteur *f*

ADJ *(cloth, house, heat etc)* humide; *(skin)* moite; **d. patch** tache *f* d'humidité; **his hands are always d.** il a toujours les mains moites; *Fig* **to be a d. squib** faire l'effet d'un pétard mouillé

VT *(diminish) (fire, sound)* étouffer; *(shocks)* amortir; **to d. down a furnace** boucher un haut fourneau

dampcourse ['dæmpkɔːs] N revêtement *m* d'étanchéité

dampen ['dæmp(ə)n] VT **1** *(wet) (cloth)* humecter **2** *(diminish) (enthusiasm)* refroidir; **to d. sb's spirits** décourager qn; **that dampened his ardour** cela a freiné son ardeur

damper ['dæmpər] N **1** *(on enthusiasm)* douche *f* froide; **to act as a d. on sb's spirits** saper le moral de qn; **the news put rather a d. on the celebrations/the company** la nouvelle a jeté un froid sur les réjouissances/la compagnie **2** *Mus (of piano, sound)* étouffoir *m* **3** *Tech (of hearth, chimney, furnace)* registre *m*; *(of stove pipe)* soupape *f* de réglage *ou* à papillon; *Aut* amortisseur *m*, damper *m*; *Elec* amortisseur; *Radio* sourdine *f*

▸▸ *Mus* **d. pedal** *(of piano)* pédale *f* forte

damping ['dæmpɪŋ] N *Aut* amortissement *m*

dampish ['dæmpɪʃ] ADJ un peu humide

dampness ['dæmpnɪs] N humidité *f*, *(of skin)* moiteur *f*

damp-proof ADJ hydrofuge

▸▸ **d. course** revêtement *m* d'étanchéité

damp-proofing N isolation *f* contre l'humidité

damsel ['dæmz(ə)l] N *Arch, Lit* demoiselle *f*; *Hum* **a d. in distress** une belle éplorée; **to do the d. in distress act** jouer les belles éplorées

▸▸ **d. fly** *(insect)* demoiselle *f*

damson ['dæmz(ə)n] N prune *f* de Damas

▸▸ **d. tree** prunier *m* de Damas

dance [dɑːns] N **1** *(art form, steps)* danse *f*, *Mus* (air *m* de) danse; **will you have a d. with me?** voulez-vous danser?; *Fig Fam* **to lead sb a (merry) d.** donner du fil à retordre à qn **2** *(ball) (for teenagers)* soirée *f*, *(for older people)* soirée dansante; *(formal)* bal *m*, *pl* bals; **her parents are giving a d. for her birthday** ses parents organisent un bal pour son anniversaire

VI danser; **are you dancing?** vous dansez?; **to d. with sb** danser avec qn; **to d. for joy** danser de joie; **to d. about** gambader; **they danced down the road with glee** ils descendaient la rue en dansant de joie

VT *(waltz etc)* danser; **he danced the last dance with Claudia** il a fait la dernière danse avec Claudia; *esp Lit* **to d. attendance on sb** faire l'empressé auprès de qn

▸▸ **d. band** orchestre *m* de bal; **d. floor** piste *f* de danse; **d. hall** salle *f* de danse; **d. music** musique *f* dansante; *(modern)* dance *f*

dancer ['dɑːnsər] N danseur, -euse

dancing ['dɑːnsɪŋ] ADJ ATTRIB *(bear)* dansant; *Fig* **her d. eyes** son regard vif

N danse *f*; **to go d.** aller danser

▸▸ **d. dervish** derviche *m* tourneur; **d. girl** danseuse *f*; **d. partner** cavalier, ière; **d. school** école *f* de danse; **d. shoes** chaussures *fpl* de danse

dandelion ['dændɪlaɪən] N pissenlit *m*

▸▸ **d. clock** aigrettes *fpl* de pissenlits

dander ['dændər] N *Fam* **to get sb's/one's d. up** mettre qn/se mettre en colère

dandified ['dændɪfaɪd] ADJ *Pej (dress, manner etc)* de dandy; **he had become rather d. in his dress** il s'habillait de plus en plus comme un dandy

dandle ['dænd(ə)l] VT *(child) (on knees)* faire sauter; *(in arms)* bercer

dandruff ['dændrəf] N pellicules *fpl*; **he has very bad d.** il a beaucoup de pellicules

▸▸ **d. shampoo** shampooing *m* antipelliculaire

dandy ['dændɪ] N *Old-fashioned usu Pej* dandy *m*, élégant *m*

ADJ *Am Fam* épatant, chouette; **everything's just (fine and) d.** tout marche à merveille; **that's all fine and d., but ...** c'est très joli tout ça, mais ...

Dane [deɪn] N Danois, -oise VOIR GRAMMAIRE A19

dang [dæŋ] INT, ADJ, ADV *Old-fashioned Euph* = **damn**

danger ['deɪndʒər] N danger *m*; **out of d.** hors de danger; **to keep out of d.** rester à l'abri du danger; **d. keep out** *(on sign)* danger; **to be in d. of doing sth** risquer de faire qch, courir le risque *ou* être en danger de faire qch; **in d. of (losing) his life** en danger de mort; **to put sb/sth in d.** mettre qn/qch en danger; **there is some d. that ...** il y a un risque que ... + *subj*; **there is some d. that the engine will explode** *or* **of the engine exploding** le moteur risque d'exploser; **there is no d. that ...** il n'y a pas de danger que ... + *subj*; **there's no d. that he'll forget** *or* **of his forgetting** il ne risque pas d'oublier, il n'y a pas de danger qu'il oublie; **he's a d. to society** c'est un danger public; *Med* **to be on the d. list** être dans un état critique; *Med* **to be off the d. list** être hors de danger

▸▸ *Br* **d. money** prime *f* de risque; *Fig* **d. sign** signal *m* d'alarme; **d. signal** *Rail* signal d'arrêt; *Fig* signal d'alerte *ou* d'alarme

dangerous ['deɪndʒərəs] ADJ **1** dangereux; *(illness)* grave; **you are (treading) on d. ground** vous vous engagez sur un terrain dangereux **2** *(example, maxim)* pernicieux

▸▸ *Law* **d. driving** conduite *f* dangereuse; **d. goods** marchandises *fpl* dangereuses

dangerously ['deɪndʒərəslɪ] ADV dangereusement; **he came d. close to accusing me of lying** il m'a presque traité de menteur; **he came d. close to falling** il a failli tomber; **d. ill** gravement malade; **his energy was at a d. low ebb** ses forces avaient dangereusement diminué

dangle ['dæŋg(ə)l] VI pendiller; **with one's legs dangling** les jambes ballantes; **you can't keep him dangling like that** *(in state of uncertainty)* il ne faut pas le laisser dans l'incertitude

VT *(object)* balancer; **to d. one's fingers/ feet in the water** tremper les doigts/pieds dans l'eau; *Fig* **to d. sth in front of sb** faire miroiter qch à qn

Danish ['deɪnɪʃ] ADJ danois; *(ambassador, embassy, history)* du Danemark VOIR GRAMMAIRE A19

N **1** *Ling* danois *m* **2** *Culin (pastry)* = sorte de chausson fourré

▸▸ **D. blue (cheese)** bleu *m* du Danemark; **D. pastry** = sorte de chausson fourré

dank [dæŋk] ADJ *(weather, dungeon)* humide (et froid)

Dantean ['dæntɪən, dæn'tiːən], **Dantesque** [dæn'tesk] ADJ dantesque

Danube (the) [ðə'dænjuːb] N le Danube

dapper ['dæpər] ADJ *(man, suit)* coquet; *(beard)* soigné

dapple ['dæp(ə)l] N **1** *(on horse's coat)* tache f de couleur **2** *(horse)* pommelé m
  VT tacheter; **a wall dappled with sunlight** un mur tacheté de lumière

dapple-grey N *(horse)* gris m pommelé

Darby and Joan ['dɑːbɪ] N = couple m uni de personnes âgés
  ▶▶ **D. club** club m du troisième âge *(en Grande-Bretagne)*

dare [deər] VOIR GRAMMAIRE A61; A41; B35 MO-DAL AUX v *(third sg pr* **dare**; *pt, pp* **dared**; **d. not** *contracted to* **daren't)** oser; **I d. not** *or* **daren't speak to him** je n'ose pas lui parler; **don't you d. touch him!** ne touche pas un cheveu de sa tête!; **don't you d. (do that)!** ne t'avise pas de faire ça!; **how d. you!** comment oses-tu!, quelle audace!; **I d. say that ...** je suppose que ...; **I d. say** sans doute, c'est bien possible; **your opponent, d. I say it, has never been beaten** votre adversaire, si je puis me permettre de vous le faire remarquer, n'a jamais été battu
  VT *(third sg pr* **dares**; *pt, pp* **dared**) **1** oser; **to d. to do sth** oser faire qch; **to d. to be different** oser avoir le courage d'être différent, oser être différent; **let him do it if he dare(s)!** qu'il le fasse s'il l'ose! **2** *(challenge)* **to d. sb to do sth** défier qn de faire qch; **I d. you!** fais-le si tu oses!, chiche! **3** *Fml (danger, death etc)* braver
  N défi m; **to do sth for** *or* **as a d.** faire qch pour relever un défi

daredevil ['deədev(ə)l] N casse-cou m inv
  ADJ *(pilot, driver)* casse-cou inv; *(escape, exploits)* audacieux

daring ['deərɪŋ] ADJ *(person)* audacieux, hardi; *(attempt, attack, escape etc)* audacieux; *(dress, film, writer)* provocant
  N audace f

daringly ['deərɪŋlɪ] ADV de manière audacieuse; **a d. low dress** une robe au décolleté audacieux; **to be d. different** *(of person)* avoir le courage d'être différent, oser être différent; **this is a d. different film** avec ce film, le metteur en scène ose être différent

dark [dɑːk] ADJ **1** *(without light)* sombre, obscur; **it's d.** *(outside)* il fait nuit, il fait noir; *(inside)* il fait sombre; **it's getting** *or* **growing d.** il commence à faire sombre *ou* à faire nuit; **everything suddenly went d.** soudain ce fut le noir complet; **the d. side of the moon** la face cachée de la lune
  2 *(colour)* foncé, sombre; **d. blue dresses** robes fpl bleu foncé
  3 *(eyes)* foncé; **to be d.** *(of white person)* être mat (de peau); *(of black person)* être très noir, avoir la peau très foncée; **she has d. hair** elle est brune
  4 *(unhappy)* *(thought etc)* triste; *(future, days)* sombre; *(angry)* *(look)* sombre, noir; **to look on the d. side of things** voir tout en noir; **to mutter d. threats** marmonner des menaces; **to harbour d. designs** nourrir de noirs desseins; **d. powers** puissances fpl occultes
  5 *(secret)* mystérieux, secret, -ète; **to keep sth d.** tenir qch secret; *Fig* **a d. horse** *(unknown competitor)* un concurrent inconnu; *(unexpected competitor)* un concurrent que l'on ne croyait pas dangereux; **he's a d. horse** *(a stranger)* on ne sait rien de lui; *(gave nothing away)* il a bien caché son jeu
  6 *Hum* **they live in darkest Somerset** ils habitent au fin fond du Somerset
  N ténèbres fpl, obscurité f; **the child is afraid of the d.** l'enfant a peur du noir; **after d.** à la tombée de la nuit; **until d.** jusqu'à ce qu'il fasse nuit; **in the d.** dans le noir; *Fig* **to be (kept) in the d.** être (laissé) dans l'ignorance; **we kept her in the d. about it** on ne lui en a rien dit
  ▶▶ *Hist* **the D. Ages** le haut Moyen Âge; *Fig* **we're still in the D. Ages** nous en sommes encore au Moyen Âge; *Hist* **the D. Continent** le Continent noir, l'Afrique f; **d. glasses** lunettes fpl noires

darken ['dɑːk(ə)n] VT *(room, sky)*, *Fig (future etc)* assombrir; *(colour)* foncer; *Fig Lit* **her life had been darkened by her son's death** la mort de son fils l'avait plongée dans la nuit; *Old-fashioned, Hum* **never d. my door again!** ne remettez plus les pieds chez moi!
  VI *(of sky, thoughts)* s'assombrir; *(of colour)* se foncer, s'assombrir; *(of skin)* brunir; **his face** *or* **brow darkened** il *ou* son visage s'assombrit

darkening ['dɑːk(ə)nɪŋ] ADJ *(sky)*, *Fig (face)* qui s'assombrit; **he looked up at the d. sky** il regarda le ciel qui s'assombrissait
  N *(of sky, painting)* assombrissement m

dark-eyed ADJ aux yeux foncés

dark-haired ADJ aux cheveux foncés

darkie ['dɑːkɪ] N *Old-fashioned Offensive Sl* moricaud, -aude

darkish ['dɑːkɪʃ] ADJ un peu sombre

darkly ['dɑːklɪ] ADV **1** *(dimly, not clearly)* obscurément; **the house loomed d. in the fog** la maison se dessinait, sombre dans le brouillard **2** *(to look at sb, to say)* d'un air sombre; **she contemplated the future d.** elle avait une sombre vision de l'avenir

darkness ['dɑːknɪs] N **1** obscurité f; **d. had fallen** il faisait sombre; **the room was in complete d.** il faisait tout à fait noir dans la pièce; **the house/village was in d.** *(no lights were on)* la maison/le village était dans l'obscurité f **2** *(of colour)* teinte f foncée; *(of skin)* *(caused by weather)* hâle m; *(of white person)* teint m mat; *(of black person)* peau f très noire **3** *Arch (ignorance)* ignorance f

darkroom ['dɑːkruːm] N *Phot* chambre f noire

dark-skinned ADJ à la peau mate

darky ['dɑːkɪ] N = **darkie**

darling ['dɑːlɪŋ] N chéri, -ie; **(my) d.!** *(to male)* mon chéri!, mon chou!; *(to female)* ma chérie!, mon chou!; **she's a little d.** c'est un petit amour; **be a d. and get it for me** tu serais un amour si tu allais me le chercher; **a d. little place** un petit endroit charmant; **he's his mother's d.** c'est le chouchou de sa maman; **the d. of the people** l'idole f du peuple; **to be the d. of the court/media/public** être la coqueluche de la cour/des média/du public

darn¹ [dɑːn] N *(in stocking etc)* reprise f
  VT *(stocking etc)* repriser

darn² *Fam* VT & VI **d. (it)!** zut!; **d. this car!** satanée voiture!; **d. him!** qu'il aille au diable!; **d. your father and his ideas!** ah ton père et ses satanées idées!
  ADJ sacré; **it's a d. nuisance** c'est vachement embêtant; **the d. car won't start** cette sacrée bagnole ne veut pas démarrer
  ADV vachement; **it's d. late** c'est vachement tard; **we were d. lucky** on a eu une sacrée veine; **don't be so d. stupid!** ce que tu peux être bête!

darned [dɑːnd] ADJ, ADV = **darn²**

darning ['dɑːnɪŋ] N reprise f
  ▶▶ **d. egg** œuf m à repriser; **d. needle** aiguille f à repriser; **d. wool** laine f à repriser

dart [dɑːt] N **1** *(weapon)* flèche f courte; **paper d.** avion m en papier **2** *(in games)* fléchette f; **darts** *(game)* fléchettes fpl; **do you want a game of darts?** tu veux faire une par-tie de fléchettes? VOIR GRAMMAIRE A10 **3** *Sewing* pince f **4** *(movement)* mouvement m soudain; **to make a sudden d.** foncer, se précipiter *(for, towards* sur, vers)
  VT *(look)* lancer; *(tongue)* darder
  VI se précipiter, foncer *(at* sb/sth sur qn/qch)*; **to d. in/out** entrer/sortir comme une flèche; **he darted across the road** il a traversé la rue comme une flèche; **her eyes darted from one face in the crowd to another** son regard passait rapidement d'un visage à l'autre dans la foule

dartboard ['dɑːtbɔːd] N cible f *(de jeu de fléchettes)*

dash [dæʃ] N **1** *(drop)* goutte f, *(of cognac etc)* larme f, *(of lemon juice, vinegar)* filet m, goutte; **add a d. of lemon** ajoutez-y un filet de citron; **d. of colour** *(in painting)* touche f de couleur; *Fig* **a d. of humour/cynicism** un rien d'humour/de cynisme
  2 *(of pen, in Morse alphabet)* trait m; *Typ* tiret m
  3 *(run)* course f à toute vitesse; *Am Sport* sprint m; **to make a d. forward** s'élancer en avant; **a quick d. across to Paris** un petit saut à Paris; **to make a d. at sb** se précipiter sur qch; **to make a d. at sb** foncer sur qn; **to make a d. for it** saisir l'occasion de s'enfuir
  4 *(style)* élan m, entrain m; *Old-fashioned* **to cut a d.** faire de l'épate
  5 *Aut Fam (dashboard)* tableau m de bord
  VT **1** *(throw)* heurter violemment; **to d. sth to the ground** jeter qch par terre; **the ship was dashed against a rock** le navire a été jeté sur un écueil; **to d. sth to pieces** fracasser qch
  2 *Fig (destroy)* *(sb's hopes)* détruire; *(enthusiasm)* refroidir; **to d. sb's spirits** abattre le courage de qn; **he saw his hopes dashed** il a vu tomber à l'eau ses espérances
  3 *(rush)* **to d. sb to hospital** emmener qn à l'hôpital en urgence
  4 *Fam* **d. (it)!** zut!
  VI **to come dashing in** entrer comme un bolide, entrer en trombe; **to d. up to sb** se précipiter vers qn; **to d. up/down the stairs** monter/descendre l'escalier quatre à quatre; **to d. into the room** entrer précipitamment *ou* en coup de vent dans la salle; **I'm just going to d. home and ...** je vais faire un saut chez moi et ...; **to d. across the road** traverser la route en courant; **I've been dashing around like a mad thing all day** j'ai couru toute la journée; *Fam* **I must d.** il faut que je file
  ▶ **dash away** VI partir comme une flèche, filer à toute vitesse
  ▶ **dash off** VI *(leave quickly)* partir comme une flèche, filer à toute vitesse
     VT SEP *(make or do quickly)* faire en vitesse; *(letter)* écrire en vitesse
  ▶ **dash out** VI sortir à toute vitesse; **she dashed out into the road** elle s'est précipitée sur la route; **I forgot my briefcase when I dashed out of the house** je suis sorti de chez moi à toute vitesse et j'ai oublié ma mallette; **I'll d. out to the garden/the shop for some parsley** je vais faire un saut au jardin/au magasin chercher du persil

dashboard ['dæʃbɔːd] N *Aut* tableau m de bord

dashed [dæʃt] *Old-fashioned Br Fam* ADJ sacré; **what a d. nuisance!** quel empoisonnement!
  ADV vachement; **it's d. hot** il fait vachement chaud

dashing ['dæʃɪŋ] ADJ *(person)* fringant; *(coat, jacket etc)* élégant; **to cut a d. figure** avoir fière allure; **a d. young man** un beau jeune homme

dashingly ['dæʃɪŋlɪ] ADV avec élégance; **d. handsome** d'une beauté sublime

dashpot ['dæʃpɒt] N *Aut* dash-pot *m, pl* dash-pots

dastardly ['dæstədlɪ] ADJ *Old-fashioned, Lit* **1** *(person)* lâche **2** *(crime, plan, intentions)* infâme, ignoble

DAT [diːeɪˈtiː] N *(abbr* **digital audio tape)** DAT *m*
▸▸ **D. cartridge** cartouche *f* DAT; **D. drive** lecteur *m* DAT, lecteur *m* de bande audionumérique; **D. recorder** magnétophone *m* numérique

data ['deɪtə, 'dɑːtə] N informations *fpl*; *Comput* données *fpl*; **an item of d.** une information; **what little d. we do have suggests that ...** le peu d'informations que nous avons semble montrer que ...; **to collect d. on sb/sth** recueillir des informations sur qn/qch
VOIR GRAMMAIRE A11
▸▸ **d. acquisition** collecte *f* de données, saisie *f* de données; **d. analysis** analyse *f* de données; **d. bank** banque *f* de données; **d. block** bloc *m* de données; **d. buffer** mémoire *f* tampon; **d. bus** bus *m* de données; **d. capture** saisie *f* de données; **d. carrier** support *m* de données; **d. collection** recueil *m* de données, collecte *f* de données; **d. communications** communication *f* ou transmission *f* de données, télématique *f*; **d. compression** compression *f* de données; **d. conversion** conversion *f* de données; **d. decryption** déchiffrement *m* de données; **d. encryption** cryptage *m* ou codage *m* de données; **d. entry** entrée *f* de données; **d. entry form** fiche *f* d'imputation; **d. exchange** échange *m* de données; **d. flow** flux *m* de données; **d. format** format *m* des données; **d. gathering** collecte de données; **d. input** entrée *f* de données; **d. integrity** intégrité *f* des données; **d. loss** perte *f* de données; **d. management** gestion *f* de données; **d. manipulation** manipulation *f* de données; **d. memory** mémoire *f* (pour les données); **d. mining** data mining *m*; **d. path** chemin *m* d'accès aux données; **d. pattern** modèle *m* de données; **d. pen** crayon *m* électronique; **d. privacy** secret *m* ou protection *f* des données; **d. processing** *(science)* informatique *f*; **d. processor** *(machine)* ordinateur *m*; *(person)* informaticien, -ienne; **d. protection** protection *f* de l'information; **d. protection act** ≃ loi *f* informatique et libertés; **d. reader** lecteur *m* de données; **d. reading system** système *m* de lecture de données; **d. recovery** récupération *f* de données; **d. security** sécurité *f* des données; **d. set** ensemble *m* de données; **d. storage** stockage *m* de données; **d. stream** flot *m* de données; **d. switch** commutateur *m* de données; **d. systems technology** technologie *f* informatique; **d. terminal** terminal *m* de traitement de données; **d. transfer** transfert *m* ou transmission *f* de données; **d. transfer protocol** protocole *m* de transfert de données; **d. transfer rate** taux *m* de transfert de données; **d. transmission** transmission *f* de données; **d. type** type *m* de données

database ['deɪtəbeɪs] N base *f* de données; **to have/put sth in a d.** avoir/mettre qch dans une base de données
VT intégrer dans une base de données
▸▸ **d. file** fichier *m* de base de données; **d. integration** intégration *f* de bases de données; **d. management** gestion *f* de base de données

datacomms ['deɪtəkɒms, 'dɑːtəkɒms] N *Comput* communication *f* ou transmission *f* de données, télématique *f*
▸▸ **d. linkup** liaison *f* télématique; **d. network** réseau *m* de communication de données; **d. software** logiciel *m* de communication

dataglove ['deɪtəglʌv] N *Comput* gant *m* de données

dataset ['deɪtəset, 'dɑːtəset] N *Comput* ensemble *m* de données

DATE¹ [deɪt]

N	date **1**	terme **2**	rendez-vous **3**
	ami **3**		
VT	dater **1**	sortir avec **2**	
VI	dater **1**	se démoder **2**	

N **1** date *f*; *(on coins, books etc)* millésime *m*; **d. of birth** date de naissance; **d. of departure** date de départ; **d. of dispatch** date d'envoi *ou* d'expédition; **d. of issue** date d'émission; **what's the d. (today)?** le combien sommes-nous aujourd'hui?; **to fix a d. for sth** prendre date *ou* fixer une date pour qch; **shall we fix a d. now?** est-ce que nous prenons date *ou* fixons une date maintenant?; **have you set a d. yet?** *(for wedding)* est-ce que vous avez déjà décidé de la date du mariage?; **I'm not free on that d.** je ne suis pas libre à cette date; **(on) what dates are you free?** à quelles dates êtes-vous libre?; **to be up to d.** *(with work, reading)* être à jour (**with** dans); *(with what's happening)* être au courant (**with** de); *(in fashion)* être à la page; **to bring one's diary up to d.** mettre à jour son journal; **my assistant will bring you up to d.** mon assistant vous mettra au courant; **to d.** à ce jour VOIR GRAMMAIRE A81; B61
2 *Com, Fin* terme *m*, échéance *f*; **d. of maturity, due d.** *(date f d')* échéance; **three months after d., at three months' d.** à trois mois de date *ou* d'échéance
3 *Fam (appointment)* rendez-vous *m inv*; *(boyfriend, girlfriend)* ami, -ie; **to make a d.** fixer un rendez-vous; **I have a d. tonight** j'ai un rendez-vous ce soir; *(with boyfriend etc)* je sors avec quelqu'un ce soir; *Am* **I don't have a d. for the prom** je n'ai pas de cavalier/de cavalière pour le bal de fin d'année; **where's your d.?** où est la personne qui t'accompagne?; **my d. didn't show up** on m'a posé un lapin
VT **1** *(letter, work of art etc)* dater; *(bottle of wine etc)* millésimer; *(with machine) (ticket)* composter; **the letter is dated the 12th** la lettre est datée du 12; **your letter dated ...** votre lettre en date du ...; **to d. back** antidater; **his clothes d. him** ses vêtements démodés montrent qu'il n'est pas jeune; **that dates you** *(shows how old you are)* ça montre ton âge
2 *(go out of fashion)* se démoder; **his style is beginning to d.** son style commence à dater
3 *Fam (of couple)* sortir ensemble, se fréquenter
▸▸ **d. rape** = viol *m* commis par une connaissance, un ami etc; **d. stamp** timbre *m* à date, tampon *m* ou timbre dateur

---

Date
Pour donner une date en anglais, on n'emploie pas l'article à l'écrit. En anglais britannique, on écrira donc "Monday 25th December 2000" ou, de plus en plus souvent, "Monday 25 December 2000", et, en abrégé, "25.12.00". Notez cependant qu'à l'oral, on prononce "Monday the twenty-fifth of December". En anglais américain, le mois est indiqué avant le jour. On écrira ainsi "Monday December 25 2000" et, en abrégé, "12.25.00", et on prononcera "December twenty-five".

---

date² N *(fruit)* datte *f*
▸▸ *Bot* **d. palm** palmier *m* dattier

datebook ['deɪtbʊk] N *Am* agenda *m*

dated ['deɪtɪd] ADJ démodé; **his style is rather d.** son style commence à dater **2** *Fin* **long-/short-d.** à longue/courte échéance

dateless ['deɪtlɪs] ADJ **1** *(timeless) (dress, style etc)* intemporel **2** *(not dated) (document, letter)* non daté

dateline ['deɪtlaɪn] N *Journ (of report etc)* date *f* de rédaction, dateline *f*

date-stamp VT composter

date-stamping N compostage *m*

dating ['deɪtɪŋ] N **1** *(of document etc)* datation *f*, datage *m*; *(of ticket) (with machine)* compostage *m* **2** *Archeol etc* datation *f*
▸▸ **d. agency** agence *f* matrimoniale

dative ['deɪtɪv] ADJ, N *Gram* datif *m*; **in the d.** au datif
▸▸ **d. case** datif

datum ['deɪtəm] N *(pl* **data)** *Fml* donnée *f*
VOIR GRAMMAIRE A11
▸▸ **d. point** *(in robotics)* point *m* de référence

daub [dɔːb] N **1** *Pej (picture)* croûte *f*, barbouillage *m* **2** *Constr* torchis *m*
VT **1** *Art Pej (painting, canvas)* barbouiller **2** *(smear)* barbouiller (**with** de)

daughter ['dɔːtər] N fille *f*

daughterboard ['dɔːtəbɔːd] N *Comput* carte *f* fille

daughter-in-law N belle-fille *f, pl* belles-filles, bru *f*

daunt [dɔːnt] VT *(somebody)* intimider; *Fml, Hum* **nothing daunted** intrépide(ment)

daunting ['dɔːntɪŋ] ADJ *(task etc)* impressionnant, intimidant

dauntless ['dɔːntlɪs] ADJ intrépide

dauntlessly ['dɔːntlɪslɪ] ADV intrépidement

davenport ['dævənpɔːt] N *Am* canapé(-lit) *m, pl* canapés(-lits)

davit ['dævɪt] N *Naut* bossoir *m* d'embarcation

Davy ['deɪvɪ] N *Naut Fam* **to go to D. Jones's locker** *(drown)* boire à la grande tasse; **he's in D. Jones's locker** il a bu à la grande tasse

dawdle ['dɔːd(ə)l] VI traînasser, lambiner
▸ **dawdle away** VT SEP **to d. the time away** passer le temps; *(waste)* perdre son temps

dawdler ['dɔːdlər] N traînard, -arde, lambin, -ine

dawdling ['dɔːdlɪŋ] N lambineries *fpl*, traînasseries *fpl*
ADJ traînard

dawn [dɔːn] N aube *f*, aurore *f*; *Fig (of life, civilization, new age)* aube *f*; **at d.** à l'aube; **at the crack of d.** à la pointe du jour; **from d. to dusk** du lever au coucher du soleil; **until d.** jusqu'à l'aube, jusqu'au petit jour
VI *(of day, morning)* se lever; *Fig (commencer à)* paraître; **day is dawning** le jour point *ou* se lève; *Fig* **when the truth dawned on him** quand il a compris la vérité; *Fig* **it dawned on me that ...** j'ai commencé à me rendre compte que ...; **another thought dawned on him** une autre pensée lui est venue à l'esprit
▸▸ **the d. chorus** le chant des oiseaux à l'aube; **d. raid** descente *f* à l'aube; *(by police)* descente *ou* rafle *f* à l'aube; *St Exch* raid *m* *(mené dès l'ouverture de la Bourse)*; *St Exch* **d. raider** raider *m* *(qui opère dès l'ouverture de la Bourse)*

dawning ['dɔːnɪŋ] ADJ *(day)* naissant
N aube *f*

DAY [deɪ]

jour **1–5, 7**	journée **2**	temps **8**

N **1** *(calendar unit)* jour *m*; **d. of the month** quantième *m* du mois; **what d. (of the week) is it (today)?** quel jour (de la semaine) sommes-nous?; **on this (d.) of all days!** justement aujourd'hui!; **of all (the) days to choose for a conference!** quelle idée d'avoir choisi de faire une conférence justement aujourd'hui!; **to take/get a d. off** prendre/obtenir un jour de congé; *Law etc* **ten clear days' notice** préavis *m* de dix jours francs; *Com* **d. of grace** jour de grâce; *Com* **days of grace** délai *m* de grâce VOIR GRAMMAIRE A81; B61

2 *(referring to duration)* journée *f*; **it's been a sunny/rainy d.** il a fait une journée de soleil/pluie; **on wet days we stay in** les jours où il pleut nous restons à la maison; **all d. (long)** toute la journée; **what sort of d. have you had?** tu as passé une bonne journée?; **to work/be paid by the d.** travailler/être payé à la journée; **it's all in a d.'s work** ça fait partie de la routine; **eight-hour d.** journée de huit heures; **in the course of the d.** dans la journée; **at the end of the d.** à la fin de la journée; *Fig* en fin de compte, au bout du compte; **to carry** *or* **win the d.** gagner la journée *ou* la bataille; *Lit* **d. is done** le jour s'achève VOIR GRAMMAIRE B61

3 *(time, frequency)* **the d. before/after he came** la veille/le lendemain de son arrivée; **two days previously** *or* **before** deux jours avant; **two days before/after his wedding** l'avant-veille/le surlendemain de son mariage; **the d. before yesterday** avant-hier; **the d. after tomorrow** après-demain; **the d. before yesterday was Sunday** il y a deux jours c'était dimanche; **two days later** deux jours après *ou* plus tard, le surlendemain; **I met him one d.** je l'ai rencontré un jour; **one d., some d., one of these days** *(future)* un jour (ou l'autre), un de ces jours; **the baby's due any d. now** le bébé va naître d'un jour à l'autre; **the other d.** l'autre jour; **a year ago to the d.** il y a un an jour pour jour; **I remember it to this (very) d.** je m'en souviens encore aujourd'hui; **until the d. I die, until my dying d.** jusqu'à ma mort; *Fam* **from d. one** dès le début; **from that d. on(wards)** depuis ce jour; **from this d. forth** dorénavant, à compter de ce jour; **once/twice a d.** une/deux fois par jour; **every other d.** tous les deux jours, un jour sur deux; **d. after d., d. in d. out** jour après jour; **d. by d.** jour après jour; **from d. to d. de jour en jour, d'un jour à l'autre; to live from d. to d.** vivre au jour le jour; **d.-old** *(chicks, baby)* d'un jour; *(bread)* de la veille

4 *(as distinguished from night)* **to work d. and night** travailler nuit et jour; **to travel by d.** voyager de jour; *Theat, Fam Hum* **don't give up the d. job** je ne crois pas que tu es prêt pour une carrière professionnelle; *Ind* **to be on days** *(of worker)* être de jour

5 *(dawn)* jour *m*; **before d.** avant le jour; **at break of d.** au point du jour; **they were waiting for d. to break** ils attendaient que le jour pointe

6 *(idioms)* *Fam* **he's sixty if he's a d.** il a soixante ans bien sonnés; **he doesn't look a d. older than 40/you** il n'a pas l'air d'avoir plus de 40 ans/d'être plus vieux que toi; **he doesn't look a d. older than when I last saw him** il n'a pas vieilli d'un poil depuis la dernière fois que je l'ai vu; **you've made my d.!** c'est la meilleure nouvelle de la journée; **it's not my d.!** c'est pas mon jour; *Fig* **let's call it a d.** *(finish work)* ça suffit pour aujourd'hui; *(end relationship)* finissons-en; *Fam* **let's make a d. of it!** allons faire la fête!; *Fam* **that'll be the d.!** j'aimerais voir ça!; **to pass the time of d. with sb** échanger quelques paroles de politesse avec qn

7 *(anniversary, celebration)* fête *f*; **Mother's/ Father's D.** la fête des Mères/des Pères; **Saint David's D.** la Saint-David; **All Saints' D.** la

Toussaint; **All Souls' D.** le Jour des Morts; **Christmas D.** le jour de Noël; **to name the d.** *(of wedding)* fixer le jour du mariage; *Rel* **the D. of Judgement** le jour du jugement

8 *(time)* **the good old days** le bon vieux temps; **in the days of …** au *ou* du temps de …; **in my young days** au *ou* du temps de ma jeunesse; **in those days** en ce temps-là, à cette époque, alors; **these days** de notre temps, **in this d. and age** de nos jours; **those were the days** c'était la belle vie (alors); **in his d.** *(when he was young)* en son temps; *(when he was alive)* de son vivant; **she was a great actress in her d.** c'était une grande actrice à son époque; **he ended his days in poverty** il a fini ses jours pauvre; **in days to come** à l'avenir; **to have had its d.** *(of theory, fashion etc)* être démodé; *(of car, TV)* avoir fait son temps; **to have seen better days** *(of person)* avoir connu des jours meilleurs; *(of car, shoes)* avoir fait son temps; *Fam (of food)* avoir perdu de sa fraîcheur

▸▸ *Mktg* **d.-after recall** mémorisation *f* un jour après; *Mktg* **d.-after recall test** test *m* du lendemain; **d. bed** lit *m* de repos; *Fin* **d. bill** effet *m* à date fixe; **d. cream** crème *f* de jour; **d. labourer** journalier, -ière; **d. nurse** = infirmier, -ière qui est de service de jour; **d. nursery** garderie *f*; *St Exch* **d. order** ordre *m* valable pour la journée; *Sch* **d. pupil** (élève *mf*) externe *mf*; **d. rate** tarif *m* journalier; *Br Ind* **d. release** formation *f* continue en alternance; *Br Rail* **d. return** aller-retour *m* valable pour la journée *pl* allers-retours; **d. school** externat *m*; **d. shift** *(period worked)* service *m* de jour; *(workers)* équipe *f* de jour; *Met* **d. temperature** température *f* diurne; **d. tour** excursion *f* d'une journée; **d. trade** opération *f* de journée; **d. trip** excursion (d'une journée); **d. tripper** excursionniste *mf*; **d. visitor** excursionniste

---

When translating **day**, note that **jour** and **journée** are not interchangeable. **Jour** is used to refer to a day as a distinct unit of time, while **journée** emphasizes duration.

---

daybook ['deɪbʊk] N *Com* journal *m*, -aux; *Acct* livre *m* de main-courante, main *f* courante, brouillard *m*

dayboy ['deɪbɔɪ] N *Sch* externe *m*

daybreak ['deɪbreɪk] N point *m* du jour, lever *m* du jour; **at d.** au lever du jour, au point du jour

daycare ['deɪkeər] N *(for elderly, disabled)* service *m* d'accueil de jour; *(for children)* service de garderie; **the children go to d.** les enfants vont à la garderie

▸▸ **d. centre** *(for elderly, disabled)* = centre *m* d'animation et d'aide sociale; *(for children)* garderie *f*; **d. facilities** *(for elderly, disabled)* service d'accueil de jour; *(for children)* service de garderie

daydream ['deɪdriːm] N rêverie *f*
VI rêvasser; **to d. about the future** rêver à l'avenir

daydreaming ['deɪdriːmɪŋ] N rêverie *f*, rêvasserie *f*; **d. will get you nowhere** les rêveries ne te mèneront nulle part

daygirl ['deɪgɜːl] N *Sch* externe *f*

daylight ['deɪlaɪt] N **1** jour *m*, lumière *f* du jour; **it was still d.** il faisait encore jour; **there were still two hours of d. left** il ferait jour pendant deux heures encore; *Fig* **to put d. between oneself and sb** distancer qn; *Fig* **to (begin to) see d.** *(come to the end of a task)* entrevoir la fin; *(understand)* (commencer à) voir clair **2** *(dawn)* aube *f*, point *m* du jour; **before d.** avant l'aube **3** *Fam* **to beat the living daylights out of sb** rosser qn, tabasser qn; **to scare** *or* **frighten the living daylights out of sb** flanquer la

trouille *ou* une peur bleue à qn

▸▸ **d. hours** heures *fpl* durant lesquelles il fait jour

daylight-saving N

▸▸ **d. time** heure *f* avancée d'été

daylong ['deɪlɒŋ] ADJ d'une journée

daytime ['deɪtaɪm] N jour *m*, journée *f*; **in the d.** pendant la journée, de jour; **d. classes** cours *mpl* pendant la journée

▸▸ **d. TV** émissions *fpl* télévisées pendant la journée

day-to-day ADJ *(task)* courant, quotidien; *(worry, concern)* quotidien; **d. management of a company** administration courante d'une entreprise; **on a d. basis** au jour le jour

daze [deɪz] N **1** *(caused by drug, blow)* étourdissement *m*; **to be in a d.** être étourdi; *(stronger)* être hébété **2** *(caused by news)* ahurissement *m*; **to be in a d.** être hébété *ou* ahuri; **he was left in a d. by the news** la nouvelle l'a hébété *ou* ahuri
VT **1** *(of drug, blow)* étourdir; *(stronger)* hébéter **2** *(bewilder)* abasourdir, ahurir

dazed [deɪzd] ADJ **1** *(by blow, lack of sleep)* tout étourdi, hébété **2** *(bewildered)* abasourdi, sidéré, hébété; **she had a d. look on her face, she looked d.** elle avait l'air abasourdi, elle paraissait abasourdie

dazzle ['dæz(ə)l] N *(of headlights)* lueur *f* éblouissante *ou* aveuglante; *Fig* éclat *m*
VT éblouir, aveugler; *Fig* éblouir; **dazzled with** *or* **by the light** aveuglé par la lumière; *Fig* **she was quite dazzled by him** il l'a complètement éblouie

dazzling ['dæzlɪŋ] ADJ *(light)* aveuglant, éblouissant; *(beauty, performance)* éblouissant; *(success)* éclatant

dazzlingly ['dæzlɪŋlɪ] ADV **d. beautiful** d'une beauté éblouissante; **d. bright** éblouissant, aveuglant

dB *(abbr* **decibel)** dB

DBMS [di:bi:em'es] N *Comput (abbr* **database management system)** SGBD *m*

DBS [di:bi:'es] N *Tel abbr* **direct broadcasting satellite**

DC [di:'si:] N **1** *Elec abbr* **direct current 2** *Am Fam (abbr* **District of Columbia)** DC

D & C [di:ən'si:] N *Med (abbr* **dilatation and curettage)** dilatation *f* et curetage *m*

DD [di:'di:] N **1** *Univ abbr* **Doctor of Divinity 2** *Comput (abbr* **double density)** double densité *f*

D-day N le jour J

DDE [di:di:'i:] N *Comput (abbr* **dynamic data exchange)** DDE *m*

DDT [di:di:'ti:] N *Chem* DDT *m*

DEA [di:i:'eɪ] N *Am abbr* **Drug Enforcement Agency**

deacon ['di:kən] N *Rel* diacre *m*

deaconess ['di:kənɪs] N *Rel* diaconesse *f*

deactivate [di:'æktɪveɪt] VT désactiver

deactivation [di:æktɪ'veɪʃən] N désactivation *f*

DEAD [ded]

| ADJ | mort **1–3** ▪ engourdi **2** ▪ éteint **3** |
| ADV | vachement **1** ▪ absolument **2** |

ADJ **1** *(person, tree, flower)* mort; **he is d.** il est mort *ou* décédé; **the d. man** le mort; **the d. woman** la morte; *Fam* **over my d. body!** moi vivant, jamais!; **it'll be over my d. body!** il faudra me tuer d'abord!; **to step into a d. man's shoes** être promu à la suite du décès de son supérieur; *Prov* **d. men tell no tales** les morts ne parlent pas; **to shoot sb d.** tuer qn net (d'un coup de revolver); *Fam* **d. as a doornail, d. as mutton** mort et bien mort; **d. and gone, d. and buried** mort et enterré; **half**

d. with fright à moitié mort de peur; **d. or alive** mort ou vif; **more d. than alive** plus mort que vif; **to leave sb for d.** laisser qn pour mort; *Fig* **I wouldn't be seen d. wearing it** je ne porterais ça pour rien au monde; *Fig* **I wouldn't be seen d. there** je n'irais pour rien au monde; *Fam* **to be d. from the neck up** être idiot; *Fam* **you're a d. man** tu es un homme mort; *Fam* **if Dad finds out, you're d. or a d. duck** si Papa l'apprend, gare à toi!; **the plan's a d. duck** c'est un plan foireux

2 *(lacking sensitivity) (finger)* mort, engourdi; **to go d.** *(of limb)* s'engourdir; **to be d. to the world** *(asleep)* être profondément endormi; *(in drunken stupor)* être complètement hébété; **d. to all sense of honour** insensible à tout sentiment d'honneur

3 *(lacking power, energy, activity, validity etc) (fire)* mort; *(voice, eyes)* éteint; *(colour)* terne; *(sound)* mat; *Elec (wire)* hors ou sans tension; *(battery)* épuisé; *(town)* mort; **this place is d. in winter** cet endroit est mort l'hiver; *Tel* **the phone is** *or* **has gone d.** il n'y a pas de tonalité; **the line is** *or* **has gone d.** la ligne a été coupée; **the d. hand of tradition** le poids de la tradition

4 *(absolute, total)* **to fall into a d. faint** tomber en pâmoison, s'évanouir; *Naut* **by d. reckoning** à l'estime; *Fam* **to make a d. set at sb** chercher à tout prix à mettre le grappin sur qn; *Fam* **to make a d. set at sth** vouloir obtenir qch à tout prix

NPL *(deceased)* **the d.** les morts *mpl;* **to rise from the d.** ressusciter des morts

N *(depths)* **at d. of night** au plus profond de la nuit; **in the d. of winter** au plus fort de l'hiver

ADV 1 *Fam (very)* **d. easy/simple** facile/simple comme tout; **d. clever/interesting** super *ou* vachement intelligent/intéressant; **d. boring** vraiment rasoir

2 *(completely)* absolument; **d. beat** crevé; *Fam* **d. broke** fauché; **d. certain** sûr et certain, absolument certain; **d. drunk** ivre mort; **to be d. (set) against sth** être absolument opposé à qch; **with the tide running d. against us** avec le courant en plein contre nous; **d. ahead (of sb)** droit devant (qn); *Naut* **wind d. ahead** vent droit debout; **d. on the hour/half-past six** à l'heure/six heures et demi tapante(s); **he was d. right** il avait absolument raison; **d. slow** aussi lentement que possible; *(road sign)* au pas; *Hum* **he has two speeds – d. slow and stop** il a deux vitesses – la première et le point mort; **d. smooth surface** surface parfaitement plane; **d. sure** absolument certain, sûr et certain; **d. tired** mort de fatigue; **to be d. wrong** avoir complètement tort, se tromper du tout au tout; **to stop d.** s'arrêter net

▸▸*Radio* **d. air** temps *m* mort; *Mil* **d. angle** angle *m* mort; *Ftbl* **d. ball** ballon *m* mort; *Naut* **d. calm** calme *m* plat; *Tech* **d. centre** point *m* mort; *(of lathe)* centre *m* fixe; **d. end** *(road)* cul-de-sac *m*, *pl* culs-de-sac, impasse *f*, voie *f* sans issue; *(of pipe)* bout *m* aveugle; *Fig* **to reach** *or* **come to a d. end** arriver à une impasse; **d.-end job** emploi *m* sans avenir; **d. heat** = course *f* dont les vainqueurs sont déclarés ex aequo; *Horseracing* dead-heat *m*, *pl* dead-heats; **it was a d. heat** il y a eu une arrivée exæquo; **d. language** langue *f* morte; **d. letter** lettre *f* de rebut; **to become a d. letter** *(of regulation)* tomber en désuétude; **d.-letter office** bureau *m* des rebuts; **d. level** niveau *m* parfait; **d. load** *Constr* poids *m* mort; *Aut* poids utile; *Br* **d. loss** *Com* perte *f* sèche; *Fam (person)* propre *mf* à rien; **this is a bit of a d. loss** *(party, meeting)* on perd notre temps ici; *Fig* **d. man** *(empty bottle)* cadavre *m*; **d. man's fingers** *(coral)* alcyon *m*; **d. man's handle** *(on train controls)* manette *f*, homme *m* mort; **d. march** marche *f* funèbre; *Fam* **d. ringer** sosie *m* (**for** de);

they're d. ringers ils se ressemblent comme deux gouttes d'eau; **the D. Sea** la mer Morte; **d. silence** silence *m* complet *ou* de mort; **d. stop** arrêt *m* brutal; **d. water** eau *f* stagnante; *Naut* remous *m* de sillage **d. weight** *Constr* poids mort; *Aut* poids utile; *Fig* **he's a d. weight** c'est un poids mort

dead-and-alive **ADJ** mort, triste; **a d. hole** un trou perdu, *Sl* un bled

deadbeat ['dedbi:t] **N** *esp Am Fam Pej (good-for-nothing)* bon *m* à rien, bonne *f* à rien; *(tramp)* épave *f*, loque *f*, *(parasite)* pique-assiette *mf*, *pl* pique-assiettes

deaden ['ded(ə)n] **VT** *(blow)* amortir; *(pain)* endormir; *(sound)* assourdir, étouffer; *(senses)* émousser; *(feeling)* étouffer; **they had become deadened to …** ils étaient devenus insensibles à …

deadening ['ded(ə)nɪŋ] **N** *(of blow)* amortissement *m*; *(of noise, sound)* assourdissement *m*
ADJ *(conformity, task)* engourdissant

deadhead ['dedhed] **N** *Fam* **1** *esp Am (dullard)* nullité *f* **2** *Am (person with free ticket)* *(in theatre)* personne *f* en possession d'un billet de faveur; *(on train)* personne en possession d'un titre de transport gratuit
VT **to d. flowers** *(in garden)* enlever les fleurs fanées
▸▸ **d. flight** parcours *m* à vide

deadline ['dedlaɪn] **N** *(day)* date *f* limite; *(time)* heure *f* limite; *(of journalist)* délai *m* de remise; **to work to a d.** travailler en fonction d'une date/heure limite; **the d. for returning your essays** la date limite *ou* la dernière limite pour rendre vos dissertations; **Monday is the absolute d.** c'est pour lundi dernier délai *ou* dernière limite; **to meet a d.** respecter un délai

deadliness ['dedlɪnɪs] **N 1** *(of poison etc)* nature *f* mortelle; *Fig (of wit, repartee)* mordant *m*, causticité *f* **2** *Fam (boredom)* ennui *m* mortel; **the utter d. of her style is difficult to describe** son style est tellement ennuyeux qu'on a peine à le décrire

deadlock ['dedlɒk] **N 1** impasse *f*, *Comput* interblocage *m*, impasse; **to reach d.** arriver à une impasse; **to break the d.** sortir de l'impasse **2** *Tech* serrure *f* à pêne dormant; *Aut* serrure passive
VT **talks are deadlocked** les discussions ont atteint une impasse, les discussions sont au point mort

deadly ['dedlɪ] **ADJ 1** *(mortal) (poison, blow, enemy etc)* mortel; *(weapon)* meurtrier; *(hatred)* implacable, mortel; *(combat)* à mort; *Fig (pallor, silence etc)* de mort; *(wit, satire)* mordant, caustique; *also Fig* **to d. effect** de façon dévastatrice; **the seven d. sins** les sept péchés *mpl* capitaux **2** *Fam (boring)* mortel, rasant
ADV 1 *(pale)* comme un linge **2** *(completely)* **d. accurate** extrêmement précis; **d. boring** mortellement ennuyeux; *Fam* **d. dull** rasant; **to be d. serious** être tout à fait sérieux; **to speak in d. earnest** être absolument sincère
▸▸ *Bot* **d. nightshade** belladone *f*

deadpan ['dedpæn] **ADJ** *(face)* impassible, figé; *(humour)* de pince-sans-rire

deadweight ['dedweɪt] **N** *Com* port *m* en lourd
▸▸ **d. tonnage** *(of ship)* tonnage *m* port en lourd

deadwood ['dedwʊd] **N** *Fig (person)* personne *f* improductive; *(thing)* chose *f* inutile; **there is too much d. in this office** il y a trop de gens payés à ne rien faire dans ce bureau

deaf [def] **ADJ** sourd; **to go d.** devenir sourd; **d. in one ear** sourd d'une oreille; **d. and dumb** sourd-muet, *f* sourde-muette, *pl* sourds-muets, sourdes-muettes; **d. as a**

(door)post sourd comme un pot; *Prov* **there are none so d. as those that will not hear** il n'y a pire sourd que celui qui ne veut (pas) entendre; *Fig* **d. to entreaties** sourd aux supplications; **to turn a d. ear to** *(person)* refuser d'écouter; *(pleas)* rester sourd à; **to fall on d. ears** ne pas être entendu
NPL **the d.** les sourds *mpl*

deaf-aid **N** appareil *m* acoustique

deafen ['def(ə)n] **VT** *(somebody)* assourdir, rendre sourd; **you're deafening me** vous me cassez les oreilles

deafening ['def(ə)nɪŋ] **ADJ** *(noise)* assourdissant

deaf-mute **N** sourd-muet, *f* sourde-muette, *pl* sourds-muets, sourdes-muettes

deafness ['defnɪs] **N** surdité *f*; *Fig* **their d. to any appeal** le fait qu'ils sont restés sourds à tout appel

---

DEAL [di:l]

N	affaire **1** ▪ donne **2**
VT	donner **1**
VI	négocier **1** ▪ donner **2** ▪ dealer **3**

N 1 *Com etc* affaire *f*, marché *m*; **d. on the Stock Exchange** coup *m* de Bourse; **big d.** grosse affaire; *Fam Iron* la belle affaire!; **it's no big d.** *(no problem)* c'est pas un problème; **don't make such a big d. out of it!** c'est pas la peine d'en faire tout un plat; **cash d.** transaction *f* au comptant; *Hist* **the New D.** le New Deal; **package d.** contrat *m* global; **to do a d.** conclure une affaire *ou* un marché (**with sb** avec qn); **it's a d.!** d'accord!, entendu!; *Pol* **d. between parties** accord *m* entre partis; **to give sb a fair d.** offrir un bon prix à qn; *Fig* offrir un traitement équitable à qn

2 *Cards* donne *f*, **whose d. is it?** à qui de donner?; **your d.!** à vous la donne!

3 **a good d.** *(a lot)* beaucoup; **I have a great/good d. to do** j'ai beaucoup de/bien des choses à faire; **there's a great d. of truth in that** il y a beaucoup de vrai là-dedans; **a good d. of my time** une bonne partie de mon temps; **I think a great d. of him** je l'estime beaucoup; **not a great d.** pas énormément

VT *(pt, pp dealt* [delt]*)* **1** *(cards)* donner, distribuer

2 **to d. sb a blow** porter un coup à qn; **the news dealt a serious blow to her hopes of winning** la nouvelle a sérieusement entamé ses chances de gagner

3 *Fam (drugs)* dealer

VI 1 *(trade)* négocier, traiter; **the firm has been dealing for over 50 years** cette société est en activité depuis plus de 50 ans; **to d. in leather/in options** faire le commerce des cuirs/des primes

2 *Cards* faire la donne, *Fam* faire

3 *(in drugs)* dealer

▸ **deal in** **VT SEP** **to d. sb in** *Cards* donner *ou* distribuer des cartes à qn, servir qn; *Fig (in criminal activity)* inclure qn dans l'affaire; *Fig* **d. me in!** je suis partant!

▸ **deal out** **VT SEP** *(supplies)* distribuer (**to, among** entre); *(cards)* donner, distribuer; **to d. out justice** rendre la justice; **to d. out criticism** critiquer à tour de bras

▸ **deal with** **VT INSEP** **1** *(do business with)* avoir affaire à *ou* avec; *Com* traiter *ou* négocier avec; *(get supplies from) (grocer etc)* se fournir chez; **man easy/difficult to d. with** homme commode/peu commode

2 *(be about) (subject)* traiter de

3 *(handle) (person, problem, situation)* s'occuper de; *Com (order)* donner suite à; **I know how to d. with him** je sais m'y prendre avec lui; **I'll d. with this** je m'en occupe

dealbreaker ['di:lbreɪkər] ɴ = événement *m* ou décision *f* qui rend impossible toute poursuite des négociations

dealer ['di:lər] ɴ **1** *Cards* donneur, -euse **2** *Com* négociant *m* (**in** en); *(supplier)* fournisseur *m* (**in** de); *St Exch* marchand, -ande de titres; *Aut etc* concessionnaire *m*, distributeur *m*; *(in drugs)* dealer *m*, trafiquant, -ante ► ► *Com* **d. brand** marque *f* de revendeur; *Mktg* **d. test** test *m* auprès des distributeurs

dealership ['di:ləʃɪp] ɴ *Aut* concession *f*

dealing ['di:lɪŋ] ɴ *St Exch* transactions *fpl*; *(in drugs)* vente *f* ► ► **d. out** *(of supplies)* distribution *f*; *St Exch* **d. room** salle *f* de marchés

dealings ['di:lɪŋz] ɴᴘʟ relations *fpl*, rapports *mpl*; *Pej* tractations *fpl* (**with** avec); *Com* transactions *fpl*; **to have d. with sb** avoir des rapports avec qn; *Com* faire *ou* traiter des affaires avec qn

dean [di:n] ɴ *Rel, Univ* doyen *m*

deanery ['di:nərɪ] ɴ *Rel* résidence *f* du doyen

dear [dɪər] ᴀᴅᴊ **1** *(loved)* cher, *f* chère (**to** à); **he is d. to me** il m'est cher; **a d. friend of mine** un de mes chers amis; **my dearest wish is that …** mon vœu le plus cher est que …; **a place d. to the hearts of …** un endroit qui est cher à …; *Old-fashioned* **my d. chap** *or* **fellow, …** mon cher ami, …; **all that I hold d.** tout ce qui m'est cher; **what a d. little child!** quel amour d'enfant!; **a d. little house** une petite maison coquette; *Fam* **to run for d. life** courir aussi vite que possible **2** *(in letter)* **D. Sir** Monsieur; **D. Madam** Madame; **D. Sir or Madam** Monsieur, Madame; **D. MrThomas** Cher Monsieur; **D. John Smith** Cher Monsieur Smith; **D. Alice** (Ma) chère Alice; **D. Alan and Avril** Chers Alan et Avril; *esp Am Fam* **a D. John letter** une lettre de rupture **3** *(costly)* cher, *f* chère, coûteux; **to get** *or* **become dearer** augmenter; **don't get the d./dearest ones!** ne prends pas les chers/plus chers!

ɴ *(friend)* cher *m*, chère *f*; *(darling)* chéri, -ie; **you poor d.** mon/ma pauvre; **my d.** *(adult friend)* cher ami, *f* chère amie; *(darling)* mon chéri, *f* ma chérie; *(child)* mon petit chou; *Fam* **old d.** grand-mère *f*, *pl* grand(s)-mères; **you're a d.!** tu es un amour!; **be a d. and …** sois gentil/gentille et …

ᴀᴅᴠ *(to buy, sell, pay)* cher; *Fig* **he sold his life d.** il vendit chèrement sa vie

ɪɴᴛ **d. d.!, d. me!** mon Dieu, mon Dieu!; **(dear) oh d.!** *(what have I done)* oh là là!; *(that's a pity)* hélas!; **oh d. no!** (oh) que non! ► ► *Fin* **d. money** argent *m* cher

dearie ['dɪərɪ] *Fam* ɴ mon (petit) chéri, *f* ma (petite) chérie ɪɴᴛ **d. me!** mon Dieu!

dearly ['dɪəlɪ] ᴀᴅᴠ **1** *(very much)* **I love him d.** je l'aime tendrement *ou* de tout mon cœur; **he d. loves to play jokes on people** il trouve tout son plaisir à jouer des tours aux gens; **I would d. like to meet her** je souhaite de tout mon cœur la rencontrer **2** *Fml (at great cost)* cher; **their success was d. won** leur victoire leur a coûté cher; **you shall pay d. for this** cela vous coûtera cher

dearness ['dɪənɪs] ɴ **1** *(expensiveness) (of foodstuffs etc)* cherté *f*; **the d. of the prices** les prix élevés **2** *(lovableness)* **her d. to me** l'affection *ou* l'attachement que j'ai pour elle

dearth [dɜ:θ] ɴ *Fml (of supplies, books etc)* disette *f*, pénurie *f*; *(of ideas, information)* pénurie, pauvreté *f*

DEATH [deθ] ɴ **1** *(end of life)* mort *f*, *Law, Admin* décès *m*; *Journ* **deaths** nécrologie *f*; **six food-poisoning deaths have been reported** on a signalé six décès par intoxication ali-

mentaire; **there has been a d. in the family** il y a eu un décès dans la famille; **to die a violent d.** mourir de mort violente; **he died an easy d.** il n'a pas souffert; **at (the time of) his d.** à sa mort; **until d.** pour la vie; **till d. us do part** *(in marriage ceremony)* jusqu'à ce que la mort nous sépare; **a fight to the d.** une lutte à mort; **he fell to his d.** il a fait une chute mortelle; **to send sb to his/her d.** envoyer qn à la mort; **to be at d.'s door** *or* **on the verge of d.** être sur le point de mourir; **to drink/smoke oneself to d.** se tuer à force de boire/fumer; **to stab sb to d.** tuer qn à coups de couteau; **to work sb to d.** tuer qn à force de surmenage; **to be burnt to d.** *(accidentally)* périr dans les flammes; *(as form of martyrdom)* périr sur le bûcher; **to starve sb to d.** faire mourir qn de faim; **to beat sb to d.** battre qn à mort; **one false move could mean d.** *(for trapeze artist etc)* un faux mouvement pourrait entraîner la mort; **d. to traitors!** à mort les traîtres!

2 *(execution)* **to put sb to d.** mettre qn à mort, exécuter qn; **condemned to d., under sentence of d.** condamné à mort

3 *Fam (indicating exaggeration)* **to be sick to d. of sth** en avoir marre de qch; **you'll catch your d. (of cold)** vous allez attraper la crève; **that play has been done to d.** cette pièce a été beaucoup trop jouée; **he'll be the d. of me (yet)** il me fera mourir; **that car will be the d. of her** elle va se tuer avec cette voiture; **it would be the d. of him** ce serait sa mort; **to look like d. (warmed up)** avoir une mine de déterré

4 *Fig (end)* **the d. of one's hopes/plans** la fin de ses espoirs/projets; **to be in at the d.** assister au dénouement ► ► *Zool* **d. adder** acanthopis *m*, serpent *m* de la mort; *Fin* **d. benefit** capital *m* décès; **d. camp** camp *m* de la mort; *Bot* **d. cap** amanite *f* phalloïde; **d. cell** cellule *f* de condamné à mort; **d. certificate** acte *m* ou certificat *m* de décès; **deaths column** rubrique *f* nécrologique; *Formerly* **d. duties** droits *mpl* de succession; **d. knell** glas *m*; *Fig* **to sound the d. knell (for)** sonner le glas (de); **d. mask** masque *m* mortuaire; **d. penalty** peine *f* de mort, peine capitale; **d. rate** taux *m* de mortalité; **d. rattle** râle *m* d'agonie; **d. row** quartier *m* des condamnés à mort; *Am, Austr Fam* **d. seat** *(in a vehicle)* place *f* du mort; **d. squad** escadron *m* de la mort; *Am* **d. taxes** droits *mpl* de succession; **d. throes** agonie *f*; *(painful)* affres *fpl* de la mort; *Fig* **it was agonizing to watch her d. throes** c'était atroce de la voir à l'agonie; *Fig* **the project was in its d. throes** le projet était à ses dernières heures; **d. toll** nombre *m* de morts; **D. Valley** la Vallée de la Mort; **d. warrant** ordre *m* d'exécution; *Fig* **you've just signed your own d. warrant** tu viens de signer ton arrêt de mort; *Psy* **d. wish** désir *m* de mort

deathbed ['deθbed] ɴ lit *m* de mort; **d. confession** confession *f* faite sur le lit de mort

deathblow ['deθbləʊ] ɴ coup *m* mortel *ou* fatal; *Fig* **marriage was** *or* **dealt a d. to her career** le mariage a porté un coup mortel à sa carrière

deathless ['deθlɪs] ᴀᴅᴊ *Lit* impérissable, immortel; *Hum Iron* **d. prose** prose *f* immortelle

deathlike ['deθlaɪk] ᴀᴅᴊ *(pallor etc)* de mort

deathly ['deθlɪ] ᴀᴅᴊ *(pallor)* de mort, cadavérique; *(calm)* sépulcral, -aux; **d. silence** silence *m* de mort

ᴀᴅᴠ comme la mort; **d. pale** d'une pâleur mortelle, mortellement pâle

death's-head ['deθshed] ɴ tête *f* de mort ► ► **d. moth** (sphinx *m*) atropos *m*

deathtrap ['deθtræp] ɴ *(place)* endroit *m*

dangereux; *(vehicle)* véhicule *m* dangereux; **the house is a d.** cette maison est dangereuse

deathwatch beetle ['deθwɒtʃ] ɴ *Entom* grande *ou* grosse vrillette *f*, horloger *m* de la mort

deb [deb] ɴ *Br Fam* débutante *f*; **d.'s delight** beau parti *m*

debacle [deɪ'bɑ:k(ə)l] ɴ débâcle *f*

debag [di:'bæg] ᴠᴛ (**-gg-**) *Old-fashioned Br Fam* déculotter

debar [di:'bɑ:r] ᴠᴛ (**-rr-**) **to d. sb from sth** exclure qn de qch, interdire qch à qn; **to d. sb from doing sth** interdire à qn de faire qch; **to be debarred from membership of sth** se voir refuser l'adhésion à qch

debase [dɪ'beɪs] ᴠᴛ **1** *(degrade) (person)* avilir, dégrader; *(one's style)* rabaisser **2** *(make less valuable) (metal)* altérer; *(currency)* déprécier

debasement [dɪ'beɪsmənt] ɴ **1** *(of person)* avilissement *m* **2** *(of currency)* dépréciation *f*

debatable [dɪ'beɪtəb(ə)l] ᴀᴅᴊ contestable, discutable; **it's d. whether he is to blame or she is** il est difficile de dire si c'est lui ou elle qui est à blâmer

debate [dɪ'beɪt] ɴ discussion *f*, *(esp formal, parliamentary)* débat *m*; **after much d.** après bien des discussions; **there has been some d. over the effectiveness of the treatment** l'efficacité du traitement a été mise en doute; **he was a tough opponent in d.** c'était un rude adversaire dans les débats; **the issue has been in** *or* **under d. for some time** cette question est débattue depuis un certain temps

ᴠᴛ *(question etc)* débattre, discuter, agiter; *(subject)* mettre en discussion; **a much/ fiercely debated question** une question fort controversée/vivement débattue; **we don't have time to d. the issue now** on n'a plus le temps de discuter le problème; **I was debating (with myself** *or* **in my mind) whether to go or not** je délibérais si j'irais ou non

ᴠɪ discuter (**with sb on sth** avec qn sur qch); *(take part in a debate)* prendre part à un débat; **she frequently debated for her university** elle prenait souvent part à des débats pour son université

debater [dɪ'beɪtər] ɴ spécialiste *mf* des débats

debating [dɪ'beɪtɪŋ] ɴ **she took up d. at university** elle a pris part à des débats formels à l'université ► ► **d. society** société *f* de débats contradictoires

debauch [dɪ'bɔ:tʃ] ɴ débauche *f*; **it degenerated into a drunken d.** ça a tourné à l'ivrognerie

ᴠᴛ *Old-fashioned (person)* débaucher; *(taste)* corrompre

debauched [dɪ'bɔ:tʃt] ᴀᴅᴊ *(person)* débauché; *(morals, tastes)* corrompu; *(life)* de débauche

debauchee [dɪbɔ:'tʃi:] ɴ *Arch* débauché, -ée

debauchery [dɪ'bɔ:tʃərɪ] ɴ débauche *f*; **drunken d.** ivrognerie *f*; **his numberless debaucheries** ses innombrables descentes dans la débauche

debenture [dɪ'bentʃər] *Fin* ɴ obligation *f* ᴀᴅᴊ obligataire ► ► **d. bond** titre *m* d'obligation, *Can* débenture *f*; **d. holder** obligataire *mf*, détenteur, -trice d'obligations; **d. issue** émission *f* d'obligations; **d. loan** emprunt *m* obligataire; **d. stock** obligation *f* sans garantie

debilitate [dɪ'bɪlɪteɪt] ᴠᴛ débiliter

debilitating [dɪ'bɪlɪteɪtɪŋ] ᴀᴅᴊ *(climate, heat)* débilitant; *(illness)* affaiblissant; **it**

had a d. effect on her concentration cela a provoqué une baisse de sa concentration

debility [dɪ'bɪlɪtɪ] N Méd débilité f, asthénie f

debit ['debɪt] Fin N débit m; **to the d. of** au débit de; **d. and credit** doit m et avoir m
VT (account) débiter; **to d. sb with a sum** porter une somme au débit de qn, débiter qn d'une somme; **to d. an amount to an account** porter un montant au débit d'un compte, débiter un compte d'un montant; **has this cheque been debited to my account?** est-ce que ce chèque a été débité de mon compte?
▸▸**d. account** compte m débiteur; Fin **d. advice** avis m de débit; **d. balance** solde m débiteur ou déficitaire; Banking (of account) position f débitrice; Banking **d. card** = carte f de paiement à débit immédiat; Acct **d. column** colonne f débitrice ou des débits; **d. entry** Acct écriture f passée au débit; Banking article m porté au débit d'un compte; Fin **d. interest** intérêts mpl débiteurs; Acct **d. item** poste m débiteur; Fin **d. note** note f de débit; Acct **d. side** débit m; **to enter sth on the d. side of an account** porter qch au débit d'un compte; Fig **on the d. side** sur le plan négatif

debonair [debə'neər] ADJ (person) d'une élégance nonchalante; (smile, charm) nonchalant; **you look very d.** tu es vraiment élégant

debouch [dɪ'baʊtʃ] VI Geog, Mil déboucher (**into** dans)

debrief [diː'briːf] VT Mil, Aviat etc (pilot etc) faire faire un compte-rendu (de fin de mission) à; **to be debriefed** faire un rapport

debriefing [diː'briːfɪŋ] N rapport m (de fin de mission), debriefing m

debris ['debriː] N débris mpl; Fig (after party) détritus mpl; Fig **to salvage something from the d. of one's marriage** sauver quelque chose des restes de son mariage

debt [det] N dette f, (to be recovered) créance f; **bad d.** mauvaise créance; **to be in d.** être endetté, avoir des dettes; **to be £12,000 in d.** avoir 12 000 livres de dettes; **to be in d. to sb** être en dette envers qn; **to repay a d.** régler une dette; **to be out of d.** n'avoir plus de dettes, être quitte; **to get or run into d.** s'endetter, faire des dettes; Fam **to be up to the or one's ears in d.** être criblé de dettes; Fig **I shall always be in your d.** je vous serai toujours redevable; **to owe sb a d. of gratitude** avoir une dette de reconnaissance envers qn; **d. of honour** dette d'honneur
▸▸**d. capacity** capacité f d'endettement; **d. chasing letter** lettre f de poursuite, lettre de relance des impayés; Fin **d. collection** recouvrement m ou récupération f des créances; **d. collection agency** bureau m de recouvrement ou récupération des créances; **d. collector** agent m de recouvrement; **d. due** créance f exigible; St Exch **d. equity swap** échange m de créances contre actifs; **d. financing** financement m par endettement; **d. instrument** titre m de créance; **d. rating** rating m de la dette; **d. ratio** ratio m d'endettement; **d. rescheduling** rééchelonnement m des dettes; **d. servicing** service m de la dette; **d. swap** échange m de créances

debtor ['detər] N débiteur, -trice
▸▸Acct **d. account** compte m débiteur; **d. nation** pay m débiteur; Acct **d. side** débit m, doit m

debug [diː'bʌg] VT 1 (remove faults in) Comput (program) déboguer; (prototype etc) éliminer les erreurs de; (machine) dépanner 2 (remove microphones from) (room) débarrasser des microphones clandestins
▸▸Comput **d. facility** option f de débogage, programme m débogueur

debugger [diː'bʌgər] N Comput (programme m) débogueur m

debugging [diː'bʌgɪŋ] N Comput débogage m

debunk [diː'bʌŋk] VT Fam (somebody) déboulonner, ridiculiser; (theory) discréditer; **to d. a myth** détruire un mythe

debut ['deɪbjuː] N début m; (in society) entrée f dans le monde; **to make one's d.** (of actor etc) débuter, faire ses débuts (**as** dans le rôle de)
VI esp Am débuter; **she debut'd** ['deɪbjuːd] **in the role of ...** elle a fait ses débuts ou a débuté dans le rôle de ...

debutante ['debjʊtɑːnt, -tænt] N Br débutante f

Dec abbr December

decade ['dekeɪd] N 1 (ten years) décennie f, (of French republican calendar) décade; **a few decades ago** il y a quelques dizaines d'années 2 Rel (of rosary) dizaine f 3 Comput décade f

> Note that the French word **décade** is a false friend. It usually refers to a period of ten days.

decadence ['dekədəns] N 1 (of society etc) décadence f 2 Liter, Art décadentisme m

decadent ['dekədənt] ADJ décadent; **to become d.** tomber dans la décadence; Hum **how d.!** quelle décadence!
N Liter, Art décadent m

decaf ['diːkæf] N Fam déca m

decaffeinate [diː'kæfineɪt] VT décaféiner

decaffeinated [diː'kæfɪneɪtɪd] ADJ décaféiné

decagram(me) ['dekəgræm] N décagramme m

decal [dɪ'kæl, 'diːkæl] N Am Fam décalcomanie f

decalcification [diːkælsɪfɪ'keɪʃən] N décalcification f

decalcify [diː'kælsɪfaɪ] VT (bones etc) décalcifier

Decalogue ['dekəlɒg] N Bible Décalogue m

decamp [dɪ'kæmp] VI Mil lever le camp; Fam (leave) aller s'installer ailleurs; (leave suddenly, secretively etc) décamper, filer, ficher le camp; **to d. to another room** aller s'installer dans une autre pièce

decant [dɪ'kænt] VT (liquid) transvaser; (bottle of wine) décanter dans une carafe etc; Fam (move, transfer) (people to a different district etc) transférer

decanter [dɪ'kæntər] N (for wine etc) carafe f

decapitate [dɪ'kæpɪteɪt] VT décapiter

decapitation [dɪkæpɪ'teɪʃən] N décapitation f

decapod ['dekəpɒd] N (crustacean) décapode m

decarbonize [diː'kɑːbənaɪz] VT 1 Metal (steel etc) décarburer, décarboniser 2 Aut (cylinder head) décalaminer

decathlete [dɪ'kæθliːt] N Sport décathlonien, -ienne

decathlon [dɪ'kæθlɒn] N Sport décathlon m

decay [dɪ'keɪ] N 1 (rot) (of wood etc) pourriture f, corruption f, décomposition f, (of teeth) carie f 2 (decline) (of family, country etc) décadence f, déchéance f, (of beauty etc) déclin m; (of faculties) dégradation f, (of building) délabrement m; **moral d.** déchéance morale; **to fall into d.** (of house) tomber en ruine, se délabrer; **in a state of d.** (tooth) carié; (body) en état de décomposition; (building) délabré
VT (teeth) carier

VI 1 (rot) (of meat, fruit) se gâter, pourrir; (of timber) pourrir; (of teeth) se carier 2 (decline) (of nation, family) tomber en décadence; (of building) tomber en ruine, se délabrer; (of empire) décliner; (of beauty) (se) passer, se flétrir
▸▸Phys **d. time** période f d'extinction

decayed [dɪ'keɪd] ADJ 1 (civilization) en ruines; (building, part of town) délabré 2 (wood, fruit, flesh) pourri; (tooth) carié

decaying [dɪ'keɪɪŋ] ADJ 1 (in decline) (empire, civilization) sur le déclin; (building, part of town) qui se délabre; **his d. fortunes** ses richesses qui s'amenuisent 2 (rotting) pourrissant; (teeth) en train de former des caries

decease [dɪ'siːs] Law, Admin N décès m
VI décéder

> Attention: ne pas confondre avec le nom **disease**.

deceased [dɪ'siːst] ADJ décédé; **son of Robert Martin, d.** fils de feu M. Robert Martin
N **the d.** le défunt/la défunte/les défunt(e)s

decedent [dɪ'siːdənt] N Am Law défunt, -unte

deceit [dɪ'siːt] N 1 (action) supercherie f, tromperie f, Law fraude f; **to practice d. on sb** user de tromperie ou de fourberie envers qn 2 = **deceitfulness**

deceitful [dɪ'siːtfʊl] ADJ trompeur, -euse, fourbe; **to be d.** (of person) être faux; **it was very d. of her** c'était très malhonnête de sa part

deceitfully [dɪ'siːtfʊlɪ] ADV avec duplicité; **to obtain sth d.** obtenir qch en usant de duplicité; **the message was d. worded** le message avait été rédigé de manière à tromper; **d.,** she omitted to mention the fact par duplicité, elle s'est gardée de mentionner ce fait

deceitfulness [dɪ'siːtfʊlnɪs] N fausseté f, duplicité f

deceive [dɪ'siːv] VT (person) tromper, abuser; (one's wife, husband) tromper; (sb's hopes) tromper, décevoir; **don't be deceived** ne vous y fiez pas; **to be deceived by appearances** se laisser tromper par les apparences; **to d. oneself** s'abuser, se méprendre; **don't d. yourself that it will be easy** ne croyez pas que ce sera facile; **to d. sb into thinking sth** faire croire qch à qn; **they deceived the electorate into voting for them by promising tax cuts** ils ont persuadé les électeurs de voter pour eux en promettant de diminuer les impôts; **I thought my eyes were deceiving me** je ne pouvais pas en croire mes yeux
VI tromper; **it was not done with intent to d.** cela n'a pas été fait dans l'intention de tromper

> Note that the French verb **décevoir** is a false friend and is never a translation for the English verb **to deceive**. It means **to disappoint**.

deceiver [dɪ'siːvər] N trompeur, -euse

decelerate [diː'seləreɪt] VI ralentir

deceleration [diːselə'reɪʃən] N ralentissement m, décélération f
▸▸**d. lane** voie f de décélération

December [dɪ'sembər] N VOIR GRAMMAIRE A81–2; B60–2 décembre m; **in D.** en décembre, au mois de décembre; **(on) the first/the seventh of D.** le premier/le sept décembre

decency ['diːsənsɪ] N 1 (of dress etc) décence f 2 (convention) bienséance f, convenances fpl, **common d.** les convenances (sociales); **he didn't even have the (common) d. to let us know** il n'a pas eu la bienséance élémentaire de nous informer; **the decencies** les convenances; **to observe the decencies** observer les convenances

decent ['di:sənt] ADJ 1 *(suitable)* bienséant, convenable; *(respectable)* décent, honnête; *Fam* **are you d.?** est-ce que tu es visible?; *Old-fashioned* **to do the d. thing** *(do what is required)* faire le nécessaire; *(marry sb)* faire son devoir *(et épouser la femme qu'on a mise enceinte)*; *Mil (commit suicide)* faire la seule chose possible dans les circonstances 2 *(acceptable)* passable; **this wine is quite d.** ce vin est très buvable *ou* se laisse boire; **the flat is quite a d. size** l'appartement est d'une taille raisonnable; **I earn a d. wage** je gagne un salaire décent; **wait until you have a d. amount of money** attends d'avoir suffisamment d'argent 3 *Fam (kind)* **a d. (sort of) chap** un bon type; **it's very d. of you** c'est très gentil de votre part

decently ['di:səntlɪ] ADV 1 *(respectably)* décemment, convenablement; **I can't d. ...** décemment je ne peux pas ... 2 *Fam (acceptably well)* pas trop mal; **he pays quite d.** il ne paie pas mal 3 *(honourably)* de façon correcte, correctement; **he's treated me really d.** il m'a traité de façon vraiment correcte

decentralization [di:sentrəlaɪ'zeɪʃən] N décentralisation f

decentralize [di:'sentrəlaɪz] VT décentraliser; *Comput* **decentralized processing** traitement m décentralisé

decent-sized ADJ *(house etc)* de bonnes dimensions

deception [dɪ'sepʃən] N tromperie f, supercherie f; **to obtain sth by d.** obtenir qch en usant de tromperie *ou* de supercherie; **thanks to their d. of the enemy** parce qu'ils étaient parvenus à tromper l'ennemi

> Note that the French word **déception** is a false friend and is never a translation for the English word **deception**. It means **disappointment**.

deceptive [dɪ'septɪv] ADJ *(thing, appearance)* trompeur, -euse; **he** *or* **his manner is very d.** on ne peut jamais deviner ce qu'il va faire/dire

deceptively [dɪ'septɪvlɪ] ADV **he has a d. quiet manner** il a un air tranquille (bien) trompeur; **d. worded/written** trompeur; **it looks d. simple** *ou* **easy** ce n'est pas aussi simple *ou* facile que ça en a l'air; **the mountains seem d. close** les montagnes paraissent plus proches qu'elles ne le sont en réalité; **the chair is d. light** en dépit de sa légèreté, la chaise est très robuste

deceptiveness [dɪ'septɪvnɪs] N *(of sth)* caractère m trompeur

decibel ['desɪbel] N *Phys* décibel m
▸▸ **d. level** niveau m en décibels

decide [dɪ'saɪd] VT *(question)* trancher; *(result of match, sb's fate, career etc)* décider de; **nothing has been** *or* **is decided yet** il n'y a encore rien de décidé; **that decided me** cela me décida (**to do** à faire); **to d. to do sth** se décider *ou* se résoudre à faire qch, décider *ou* résoudre de faire qch; **it was decided to wait for his reply** on a décidé d'attendre sa réponse

VI **have you decided?** êtes-vous décidé?; **you d.** décide, toi; **to d. on** *(plan of action)* arrêter; *(work procedure)* déterminer; *(day)* fixer; **have you decided on a date/a name?** vous êtes-vous décidés sur une date/un nom?; **I've decided on Greece for my holiday** j'ai décidé d'aller passer mes vacances en Grèce; **to d. on doing sth** décider de faire qch; **to d. against sth** *(give verdict)* se prononcer contre qch; **we've decided against a holiday this year** nous avons décidé de ne pas prendre de vacances cette année

decided [dɪ'saɪdɪd] ADJ 1 *(tone)* résolu; *(re-*

fusal) catégorique, net; *(opinion)* ferme; **they are quite d. about it** ils sont tout à fait décidés 2 *(distinct) (difference)* marqué, prononcé; *(change)* sensible; *(success)* incontestable; *(preference)* net, f nette; **it's a d. improvement** c'est nettement mieux

decidedly [dɪ'saɪdɪdlɪ] ADV 1 *(to answer, say)* d'un ton résolu 2 *(distinctly)* franchement

> Note that the French word **décidément** is a false friend and is never a translation for the English word **decidedly**.

decider [dɪ'saɪdər] N *(factor)* facteur m décisif; *Sport (goal)* but m décisif; *(point)* point m décisif; **the d.** *(game, match)* la belle

deciding [dɪ'saɪdɪŋ] ADJ *(factor, vote)* décisif; *Sport* **the d. game/set/match** la belle; **the chairman has the d. vote** la voix du président est décisive *ou* prépondérante

deciduous [dɪ'sɪdjʊəs] ADJ *Bot* à feuilles caduques; *Zool (antlers etc)* caduc

decilitre, *Am* **deciliter** ['desɪli:tər] N décilitre m

decimal ['desɪm(ə)l] VOIR GRAMMAIRE A76; B59
ADJ *(fraction, system, coinage etc)* décimal, -aux; *Comput* **position f décimale; correct to five d. places** exact jusqu'à la cinquième décimale; *Fam* **to go d.** adopter le système décimal
N **fraction f** décimale
▸▸ **d. coding** codification f décimale; *Math* **d. place** décimale f; *Math* **d. point** virgule f

decimalization [desɪməlaɪ'zeɪʃən] N décimalisation f

decimate ['desɪmeɪt] VT *(of disease etc) (population etc)* décimer

decimation [desɪ'meɪʃən] N décimation f

decimetre, *Am* **decimeter** ['desɪmi:tər] N *(unit of measurement)* décimètre m

decipher [dɪ'saɪfər] VT *(hieroglyphs, difficult handwriting)* déchiffrer; *(coded message)* déchiffrer, décoder

decipherable [dɪ'saɪf(ə)rəb(ə)l] ADJ déchiffrable; **easily d.** facile à déchiffrer

decision [dɪ'sɪʒən] N 1 *(of question, to do sth)* décision f; *(on question)* vote m; **to give a d.** se prononcer; **to make a d.** prendre une décision; **the judge's d. is final** *(in competition etc)* la décision du juge est irrévocable; **to come to** *or* **arrive at** *or* **reach a d.** arriver à une décision (**about** quant à, touchant); **d. by arbitration** décision f arbitrale 2 *(decisiveness)* résolution f, fermeté f; **..., he said with d.** ..., dit-il fermement
▸▸ **d. model** modèle m décisionnel *ou* déterministe *ou* de décision; **d. theory** théorie f de la décision; **d. tree** modèle m de décision en arborescence

decision-maker N décideur, -euse; **to be a good/bad d.** savoir/ne pas savoir prendre des décisions

decision-making N prise f de décisions
▸▸ **d. tool** outil m d'aide à la décision; **d. unit** unité f de prise de décision(s)

decision-tree analysis N analyse f d'un modèle de décision en arborescence

decisive [dɪ'saɪsɪv] ADJ 1 *(question, battle, proof etc)* décisif; *(experiment etc)* concluant 2 *(manner, tone, person etc)* décidé; *(approach)* tranché

decisively [dɪ'saɪsɪvlɪ] ADV 1 *(conclusively)* d'une façon décisive 2 *(resolutely) (to act)* de façon décidée; *(to say)* d'un ton décidé

decisiveness [dɪ'saɪsɪvnɪs] N 1 *(of battle, question)* caractère m décisif; *(of experiment)* caractère concluant 2 = **decision 2**

deck [dek] N 1 *Naut* pont m; **on d.** sur le pont; **below deck(s)** dans l'entrepont; **after d.** pont arrière; **lower/upper d.** pont inférieur/

supérieur; **to come/go on d.** monter sur le pont; **to clear the decks (for action)** faire le branle-bas de combat; *Fig* se préparer à agir; *Fam* **to hit the d.** *(to avoid injury)* tomber à plat ventre; *(get out of bed)* se lever; **hit the d.!** *(fall to the ground)* tout le monde à plat ventre!; *(get out of bed)* debout!; *also Fig* **all hands on d.!** tous sur le pont!
  2 *(of vehicle)* plate-forme f, pl plates-formes; **top d.** *(of bus)* impériale f
  3 *Constr* tablier m; *(of bridge)* plancher m; *Am (terrace)* terrasse f
  4 *esp Am* **d. of cards** jeu m de cartes; *Fam* **he's not playing with a full d.** *(isn't very bright)* il a quelques cases de vides
  5 *(for records etc)* platine f, **cassette d.** platine à cassette; **tape d.** platine à bande magnétique
  6 *Am Aut (space behind back seat)* coffre m; *(cover of space)* plage f arrière
VT 1 *(decorate)* parer, orner (**sth with sth** qch de qch); **to d. oneself out** s'endimancher; **I decked myself out in my Sunday best** j'ai mis mes habits du dimanche; **they were decked out in their best clothes** ils étaient sur leur trente et un
  2 *Naut (ship)* ponter
  3 *esp Am Fam (knock to ground) (person)* flanquer par terre
  ▸▸ *Naut* **d. cargo** pontée f, **d. hand** matelot m de pont; **d. load** pontée f; **d. officer** officier m de pont

deckchair ['dektʃeər] N transat m

deckhouse ['dekhaʊs] N *Naut* rouf m

deckle ['dek(ə)l] N *(frame) (in papermaking)* cadre m volant, rebord m
  ▸▸ **d. edge** *(on paper)* bord m frangeux, barbes fpl

deckle-edged ADJ *(paper)* à barbes

declaim [dɪ'kleɪm] *Fml* VI déclamer (**against** contre)
VT *(verse etc)* déclamer

declamation [deklə'meɪʃən] N déclamation f

declamatory [dɪ'klæmətərɪ, -trɪ] ADJ *(style etc)* déclamatoire

declaration [deklə'reɪʃən] N 1 *(of love, faith, war etc)* déclaration f 2 *Cards* annonce f
  ▸▸ **d. of bankruptcy** jugement m déclaratif de faillite, déclaration de faillite; *St Exch* **d. of dividend** déclaration de dividende; *Fin* **d. of income** déclaration de revenu; *Hist* **the D. of Independence** la Déclaration d'indépendance (américaine); **d. of intent** déclaration d'intention; **d. of solvency** déclaration de solvabilité; **d. of value** déclaration de valeur

declare [dɪ'kleər] VT 1 *(formally announce)* déclarer (**sth to sb** qch à qn); **to d. a change of policy** annoncer un changement de politique; **to d. war** déclarer la guerre (**on, against** à); **the two countries have declared war** *(on each other)* les deux pays se sont déclaré la guerre; **to d. a moratorium** décréter un moratoire; **to d. a strike** proclamer la grève; **she was declared the winner** elle a été déclarée vainqueur; *Fin* **to d. a dividend of ten per cent** déclarer un dividende de dix pour cent; **to d. sb guilty/innocent** déclarer qn coupable/innocent; **to d. sb bankrupt** prononcer la faillite de qn; **to d. a business bankrupt** déclarer une entreprise en faillite
  2 *Cards (make public) (trumps, suit)* appeler; *Fig* **to d. one's hand** avouer ses intentions; **to d. oneself** prendre parti; *(of lover)* se déclarer, faire sa déclaration; **have you anything to d.?** *(at customs)* avez-vous quelque chose à déclarer?; **to d. an interest** déclarer un intérêt; **to d. itself** *(of disease)* se déclarer
  VI *Cr* fermer son jeu (avant la chute des dix guichets); *Cards* annoncer son jeu; *Old-*

fashioned **well I d.!** ciel!, ça alors!; **to d. for/ against sth** se déclarer pour/contre qch

declared [dɪˈkleəd] ADJ avoué, déclaré

declassification [diːklæsɪfɪˈkeɪʃən] N *(of information, document)* levée *f* du sceau du secret (**of** portant sur)

declassify [diːˈklæsɪfaɪ] VT *(secret document etc)* lever le sceau du secret qui porte sur, déclassifier

declension [dɪˈklenʃən] N *Gram* déclinaison *f*

declinable [dɪˈklaɪnəb(ə)l] ADJ *Gram* déclinable

declination [deklɪˈneɪʃən] N **1** *Astron* déclinaison *f* **2** *Am (refusal)* refus *m* courtois et formel

decline [dɪˈklaɪn] N *(of day, empire)* déclin *m*; *(in price, number, enthusiasm)* baisse *f*; *(of business)* ralentissement *m*; **sales have shown a rapid d. over the last six months** on a observé une forte chute des ventes au cours des six derniers mois; **to go into a d.** *(of health, patient)* décliner; *(of company shares, economy)* chuter; **to be on the d.** *(of crime, birth rate)* être sur le déclin, décliner, être en baisse; *(of prices)* être en baisse, être en diminution; *(of patient)* décliner
▸ VT **1** *(refuse) (honour, invitation)* décliner; *(sb's help)* repousser; **to d. to do sth** refuser de faire qch **2** *Gram (noun etc)* décliner
▸ VI **1** *(refuse)* refuser **2** *(go down, come to end) (of sun)* décliner; *(of day)* décliner, tirer à sa fin; *(of health, influence etc)* décliner, baisser; *Com (of prices, business)* être en baisse; **to d. in importance** perdre de l'importance
▸▸ *Mktg* **d. stage** *(of product)* phase *f* de déclin

declining [dɪˈklaɪnɪŋ] ADJ **1** *(sun)* couchant; *Lit* **in one's d. years** au déclin de la vie; **she spent her d. years in a nursing home** elle a passé la fin de ses jours dans une maison de retraite **2** *Econ (industry)* déclinant, sur le déclin; *(market)* en baisse; **d. demand** demande *f* déclinante; **d. sales** ventes *fpl* en baisse

declivity [dɪˈklɪvɪtɪ] N *Fml* déclivité *f*, pente *f*

declutch [diːˈklʌtʃ] VI *Aut* débrayer

decoction [dɪˈkɒkʃən] N *Tech Fml* décoction *f*

decode [diːˈkəʊd] VT *(message)* déchiffrer, décoder, transcrire en clair; *Comput, TV* décoder; *Fig* déchiffrer; **decoded message** message transcrit en clair; **the file is automatically decoded when it is received** le fichier est décodé automatiquement à la réception

decoder [diːˈkəʊdər] N *(person, machine)* décodeur *m*, déchiffreur *m*; *Comput, TV* décodeur

decoding [diːˈkəʊdɪŋ] N *(of message)* déchiffrement *m*, décodage *m*, transcription *f* en clair; *Comput, TV* décodage

decoke [diːˈkəʊk] *Aut Fam* N **the car needs a d.** la voiture a besoin d'un décalaminage *ou* d'être décalaminée
▸ VT décalaminer
▸▸ **d. machine** machine *f* de décalaminage

décolletage [deɪkɒlˈtɑːʒ] N décolleté *m*

décolleté [deɪˈkɒlteɪ] ADJ *(dress, woman)* décolleté
▸ N décolleté *m*

decolonization [diːkɒlənaɪˈzeɪʃən] N décolonisation *f*

decolonize [diːˈkɒlənaɪz] VT décoloniser

decommission [diːkəˈmɪʃən] VT *(nuclear reactor, plant)* mettre hors service

decommissioning [diːkəˈmɪʃənɪŋ] N *(of nuclear reactor, plant)* mise *f* hors service

decompose [diːkəmˈpəʊz] VI *(of organic matter)* se décomposer, entrer en décomposition
▸ VT *(matter, compound, light etc)* décomposer

decomposition [diːkɒmpəˈzɪʃən] N décomposition *f*

decompress [diːkəmˈpres] VT *Tech (gas etc)* décomprimer; *Med (diver)* faire séjourner dans une chambre de décompression; *Comput* décompresser

decompression [diːkəmˈpreʃən] N *Comput, Tech* décompression *f*
▸▸ **d. chamber** chambre *f* de décompression; *Med* **d. illness, d. sickness** *(suffered by divers)* maladie *f* des caissons; *Comput* **d. software** logiciel *m* de décompression

decompressor [diːkəmˈpresər] N *Comput* logiciel *m* de décompression

decongestant [diːkənˈdʒestənt] ADJ, N *Med* décongestionnant *m*

decongestion [diːkənˈdʒestʃən] N *Med* décongestion *f*

deconsecrate [diːˈkɒnsəkreɪt] VT *Rel (church)* désaffecter

deconsignment [diːkənˈsaɪnmənt] N *Com* déconsignation *f*

decontaminate [diːkənˈtæmɪneɪt] VT décontaminer

decontamination [diːkəntæmɪˈneɪʃən] N décontamination *f*; **d. measures** mesures *fpl* de décontamination

decontrol [diːkənˈtrəʊl] N *(of prices, trade)* libération *f*
▸ VT libérer des contraintes du gouvernement; *(prices, trade)* libérer; *(wages)* débloquer

décor, decor [ˈdeɪkɔːr] N *Theat etc* décor *m*; *Fam* **he's part of the d.** *(has been here for a long time)* il fait partie des meubles

decorate [ˈdekəreɪt] VT **1** *(room, streets)* décorer, orner *(with sth* de qch*)*; *(cake, Christmas tree)* décorer **2** *(paint and wallpaper etc) (room)* peindre et tapisser, décorer **3** *(person) (with medal)* décorer, remettre une décoration à; **she was decorated for bravery** elle a été décorée pour son courage

decorating [ˈdekəreɪtɪŋ] N décoration *f*; **to do the d.** *(in flat, house)* faire les travaux (de décoration)

decoration [dekəˈreɪʃən] N **1** *(of room, cake, Christmas tree etc)* décoration *f*; **decorations** *(in town for festival etc)* décorations **2** *(with paint and wallpaper etc) (of room)* peinture *f* et pose *f* de la tapisserie, décoration *f*; **we did all the d. ourselves** nous avons fait tous les travaux nous-mêmes **3** *(with medal)* remise *f* d'une décoration *(of sb* à qn*)*; *(medal)* décoration *f*, médaille *f*

decorative [ˈdek(ə)rətɪv] ADJ *(art, ornament)*, *Fam (woman)* décoratif; **the house is in excellent d. order** la décoration de la maison est en excellent état

decoratively [ˈdek(ə)rətɪvlɪ] ADV décorativement

decorator [ˈdekəreɪtər] N décorateur, -trice *m*; *Br* **(painter and) d.** peintre *m* décorateur; *Br* **we're having the decorators in next week** les peintres viennent la semaine prochaine

decorous [ˈdekərəs] ADJ bienséant, convenable

decorously [ˈdekərəslɪ] ADV avec bienséance, convenablement

decorticate [diːˈkɔːtɪkeɪt] VT *Fml* décortiquer

decorum [dɪˈkɔːrəm] N décorum *m*, bienséance *f*; **a breach of d.** une inconvenance; **to have no sense of d.** ne pas avoir le sens du décorum; **her sense of d.** son sens des convenances *ou* du décorum; **to behave with d.** se comporter comme il faut

decouple [dɪˈkʌp(ə)l] VT *Elec* découpler

decoupling [dɪˈkʌplɪŋ] N *Elec* découplage *m*

decoy¹ [ˈdiːkɔɪ] N **1** *(in hunting)* appât *m*, leurre *m*; *(bird)* moquette *f*, *(oiseau m)* appelant *m* **2** *Fig (person)* appât *m*; *(phone call)* piège *m*; **police d.** *(to trick criminal)* policier *m* en civil
▸▸ **d. bird** moquette, *(oiseau)* appelant

decoy² [dɪˈkɔɪ] VT *(birds, person)* leurrer; **to d. sb into a trap** attirer qn dans un piège; **to d. sb into doing sth** leurrer qn pour qu'il fasse qch; **the phone call decoyed her away from the office** le coup de téléphone était un piège pour la faire sortir du bureau

decrease¹ [ˈdiːkriːs] N *(in unemployment, crime, population)* diminution *f*, *(in prices, strength, value, number)* baisse *f*, *(in political power)* affaiblissement *m*; **to be on the d.** *(of crime etc)* baisser; **d. in speed** ralentissement *m*; **d. in stocks** *(profit and loss item)* déstockage *m* de production

decrease² [dɪˈkriːs] VI *(of population, unemployment, crime, inflation)* diminuer, baisser, décroître; *(of value, strength, prices, output)* diminuer, baisser; *(of power)* s'affaiblir; *Knitting* diminuer, faire une/des diminution(s)
▸ VT diminuer, réduire; *(prices) (of government)* baisser; *(of economic forces)* faire baisser; *Knitting* **d. three stitches** diminuer de trois mailles, faire trois diminutions; **to d. the pain** faire diminuer la douleur

decreasing [dɪˈkriːsɪŋ] ADJ *(number, population, value, strength)* décroissant; *(prices, unemployment, crime, output)* en baisse; *(influence, importance)* déclinant, en déclin; **in d. order of importance** par ordre d'importance décroissante
▸▸ *Fin* **d. costs** frais *mpl* dégressifs; *Acct* **d. rate** taux *m* dégressif

decreasingly [dɪˈkriːsɪŋlɪ] ADV de moins en moins

decree [dɪˈkriː] N **1** *Admin* décret *m*, arrêté *m*; **to issue a d.** promulguer un décret; **to rule by d.** régner par décret **2** *Rel* décret *m* **3** *Law* décision *f*, arrêt *m*, jugement *m*
▸ VT *(order)* décréter, ordonner; *Law* arrêter (**that** que); **fate decreed that ...** le sort avait voulu que ...; **the film was decreed a threat to public morals** on a décrété que le film était une menace pour la morale publique
▸▸ *Law* **d. absolute** jugement définitif (de divorce); *Law* **d. nisi** jugement provisoire (de divorce)

decrepit [dɪˈkrepɪt] ADJ **1** *(person)* décrépit **2** *(car, house, furniture etc)* délabré

decrepitude [dɪˈkrepɪtjuːd] N *Fml* **1** *(of person)* décrépitude *f* **2** *(of car, house etc)* délabrement *m*

decriminalization [diːkrɪmɪnəlaɪˈzeɪʃən] N *Law (of drug possession)* dépénalisation *f*

decriminalize [diːˈkrɪmɪnəlaɪz] VT *Law (possession of drugs)* dépénaliser

decry [dɪˈkraɪ] VT *Fml* décrier, dénigrer; **the union has decried the suggested increase as an insult** le syndicat a qualifié l'augmentation proposée d'insulte; **his intervention has been decried as worsening the problem** on l'a accusé, en intervenant, d'avoir aggravé le problème

decrypt [diːˈkrɪpt] VT *Comput* déchiffrer

decryption [diːˈkrɪpʃən] N *Comput* déchiffrement *m*

dedicate [ˈdedɪkeɪt] VT **1** *(assign) (church)* dédier, consacrer; **to d. oneself** *or* **one's life to sb** se consacrer à qn, consacrer sa vie à qn; **to d. oneself** *or* **one's life to sth** se vouer à qch, se consacrer à qch **2** *(book, record)* dédicacer (**to** à)

dedicated [ˈdedɪkeɪtɪd] ADJ **1** *(to one's pro-*

fession) consciencieux; (*doctor, nurse, teacher*) dévoué; (*socialist, supporter*) convaincu; **to be d. to one's job** être dévoué à son travail; **she was d. to the cause** elle se consacrait à cette cause; **d. to the cause of freedom** engagé dans la lutte pour la liberté **2** (*assigned for special purpose*) dédié, spécialisé

▸▸ **d. circuit** circuit *m* dédié; *Tel* **d. line** ligne *f* spécialisée; *Comput* **d. word processor** machine *f* exclusivement destinée au traitement de texte

dedication [dedɪˈkeɪʃən] **N 1** (*of church*) consécration *f*, *Am* (*of building*) inauguration *f* **2** (*of book*) dédicace *f*; **to write a d. in a book** dédicacer un livre; **to read out the dedications** (*of disc jockey*) lire les dédicaces **3** (*devotion*) (*to a cause*) attachement *m*, dévouement *m* (**to** à); (*to country, company*) dévouement; **a life of d.** une vie de dévouement; **to work with d.** travailler avec dévouement; **I admire your d. (to your work)** j'admire ton dévouement (à ton travail); **to work with great d. for the cause of freedom** travailler avec dévouement pour la liberté

deduce [dɪˈdjuːs] **VT** déduire (**from** de); **I d. therefore that you will not be there** j'en conclus donc que vous ne serez pas là

deduct [dɪˈdʌkt] **VT** déduire (**from** de); (*from a bill, amount*) décompter; **to d. £50/10% from the price** rabattre 50 livres/10% sur le prix; **to d. a commission** prélever une commission; **to be deducted** à déduire; **tax is deducted at source** l'impôt est retenu *ou* prélevé à la source

deductibility [dɪdʌktɪˈbɪlɪtɪ] **N** déductibilité *f*

deductible [dɪˈdʌktɪb(ə)l] **ADJ** déductible

deduction [dɪˈdʌkʃən] **N 1** (*subtraction*) déduction *f* (**from a quantity** sur une quantité); (*from pay*) retenue *f*, prélèvement *m*; **d. of a sum** décompte *m* d'une somme; *Fin* **d. at source** retenue *f* à la source; **d. of tax at source** retenue *f* salariale à la source; **after deductions, I'm left with a salary of …** une fois les prélèvements *ou* les retenues décompté(e)s, il me reste un salaire de … **2** (*conclusion*) déduction *f* (**from** de); **by a process of d.** par déduction; **there is only one d. that can be made** on ne peut déduire qu'une seule chose

deductive [dɪˈdʌktɪv] **ADJ** (*reasoning*) déductif, par déduction

deed [diːd] **N 1** (*action*) action *f*, acte *m*; **to do one's good d. for the day** faire sa bonne action *ou* sa B. A. quotidienne; *Lit* **d. of valour** haut fait *m* **2** *Law* (*document*) acte *m* notarié; **mortgage** *f*, acte hypothécaire; **to change one's name by d. poll** changer légalement son nom; **the deeds to the house** les titres de propriété de la maison

VT *esp Am Law* (*transfer by deed*) transférer par un acte

▸▸ *Law* **d. of arrangement, d. of assignment** acte de transfert; **d. box** classeur *m* à documents; **d. of acknowledgment** acte récognitif; **d. of covenant** = déclaration *f* par laquelle on s'engage à verser régulièrement une certaine somme à un particulier, une association caritative, etc; **d. of partnership** acte constitutif *ou* de société; **d. of sale** acte de vente; **d. of transfer** acte de cession

deejay [ˈdiːdʒeɪ] **N** *Mus Fam* disc-jockey *m*, *pl* disc-jockeys

deem [diːm] **VT** *Arch, Lit* **I do not d. it necessary/proper to …** je ne juge pas *ou* ne crois pas *ou* ne considère pas nécessaire/convenable de …; **it is deemed necessary/proper to …** on juge *ou* croit nécessaire/convenable de …; **if it is deemed necessary** si c'est jugé nécessaire; **I d. it a great honour** je

considère cela comme un grand honneur; **he was deemed (to be) the winner** il a été considéré comme étant le vainqueur

---

DEEP [diːp]

ADJ profond **1**
ADV profondément
N océan

ADJ 1 (*water, wound, sleep, despair*), *Tennis* (*serve*), *Fig* (*thinker*) profond; (*shelf*) large, profond; **to be ten metres d.** avoir dix mètres de profondeur, avoir une profondeur de dix mètres; **to take a d. breath** respirer profondément; *Fig* respirer un grand coup; **to be in d. water** (*in serious difficulties*) être dans de sales draps, être en mauvaise posture; **I think we're getting into d. water here** je crois que nous sommes en train de nous engager sur un terrain dangereux; *Fam* **you're in d. trouble, my lad** tu as de sérieux problèmes, mon gars; **d. in debt** criblé de dettes; **he got deeper and deeper in debt** il s'est endetté de plus en plus; **d. in thought** plongé dans ses pensées; **to inflict a d. wound** (*of weapon*) pénétrer très profondément; **two/four d.** sur deux/quatre rangs; **his d. learning** ses connaissances profondes; **in deepest sympathy** (*on card*) avec toute ma sympathie; **d. concern** sincère *ou* vive préoccupation; *Hum* **in deepest Yorkshire** au fin fond du Yorkshire

2 (*colour*) foncé, sombre; (*sound*) grave; **d. blue** bleu foncé; **in a d. voice** d'une voix profonde

3 *Fam* (*not readily understandable*) **he's a d. one** il est plutôt mystérieux

ADV profondément; **the harpoon sank d. into the flesh** le harpon a pénétré très profondément dans la chair; **to walk d. into the forest** pénétrer profondément dans la forêt; **to look d. into sb's eyes** pénétrer qn du regard; **to work d. into the night** travailler tard dans la nuit; *Fam* **we're in too d. to pull out now** nous sommes trop impliqués pour faire marche arrière maintenant; *Fml* **to drink d.** boire à longs traits; **d.-lying causes** causes profondes; **d. down he's very kind** au fond, il est très gentil; **to run d.** être profond

N *Lit* **the d.** l'océan *m*; **to commit a body to the d.** immerger un mort

▸▸ *Com* **d. discount** forte remise *f*; **d. end** (*of swimming pool*) côté *m* le plus profond, grand bain *m*; *Cin, TV* **d. focus** grande profondeur *f* de champ; **the D. South** (*of the United States*) le sud profond; *Fam* **d. throat** (*informer*) informateur *m*, indicateur *m*

deep-dish **ADJ**
▸▸ *Am Culin* **d. pie** tourte *f*

deepen [ˈdiːp(ə)n] **VT 1** (*well etc*) approfondir, creuser; (*love, hatred, resentment etc*) rendre plus intense, accroître; **that only deepened his conviction** cela n'a fait que le conforter dans sa conviction **2** (*colour*) foncer; (*sound*) rendre plus grave

VI 1 (*of river, silence etc*) devenir plus profond; (*of conviction, belief*) augmenter; (*of mystery*) s'épaissir **2** (*of colour*) devenir plus foncé; (*of sound, voice*) devenir plus grave; (*of shadows*) s'épaissir

deep-fat frying **N** cuisson *f* en bain de friture

deep-freeze **N** congélateur *m*; *Fig* **to put sth in the d.** mettre qch au frigidaire
VT (*food*) congeler, surgeler

deep-frozen **ADJ** surgelé

deep-fry **VT** (*fish etc*) faire cuire dans la friture

deep-fryer **N** friteuse *f*

deep-laid **ADJ** (*plan, scheme*) habilement comploté

deeply [ˈdiːplɪ] **ADV** profondément; **to sigh**

d. pousser un profond soupir; **they gazed d. into each other's eyes leurs regards étaient plongés dans les yeux l'un de l'autre; *Fig* **to go d. into sth** pénétrer *ou* entrer profondément dans qch, approfondir qch; **she can't have looked into it very d.** elle n'a pas dû s'en occuper très sérieusement; **to fall d. in love with sb** tomber profondément amoureux de qn; **to care d. about sb** être profondément attaché à qn; **I care d. about your happiness/this country's future** ton bonheur/l'avenir de ce pays est très important pour moi; **d. interesting** fort intéressant; **d. offended** gravement offensé; **to be d. insulting** être très insultant

deepness [ˈdiːpnɪs] **N** (*of voice etc*) profondeur *f*, *Mus* (*of sound*) gravité *f*

deep-pan **ADJ**
▸▸ *Culin* **d. pizza** pizza *f* à pâte épaisse

deep-rooted **ADJ** (*tree*) profondément enraciné, aux racines profondes; (*affection, prejudice, dislike, antagonism etc*) profond; (*habit*) ancré

deep-sea **ADJ** (*plant, animal*) pélagique
▸▸ **d. diver** plongeur, -euse sous-marin(e); **d. fisherman** pêcheur *m* hauturier *ou* en haute mer; **d. fishery, d. fishing** pêche *f* hauturière

deep-seated [-ˈsiːtɪd] **ADJ** (*aversion*) profond, bien enraciné; (*affection, prejudice, conviction etc*) profond

deep-set **ADJ** (*eyes*) enfoncé

deep-six **VT** *Am Fam* (*throw away*) balancer; **we deep-sixed the project** on a balancé cette idée de projet

deep-vein thrombosis **N** *Med* thrombose *f* veineuse profonde

deer [dɪər] **N INV** cerf *m*
▸▸ **d. park** chasse *f* gardée pour le cerf

deerhound [ˈdɪəhaʊnd] **N** (*dog*) lévrier *m* d'Écosse

deerskin [ˈdɪəskɪn] **N** peau *f* de daim; *Com* daim *m*; **d. gloves** gants *mpl* en daim

deerstalker [ˈdɪəstɔːkər] **N 1** (*hunter*) chasseur *m* (de cerf) à l'approche **2** (*hat*) chapeau *m* de chasse (à la Sherlock Holmes)

deerstalking [ˈdɪəstɔːkɪŋ] **N** chasse *f* (au cerf) à l'approche

de-escalate [diːˈeskəleɪt] **VT** (*tension, bombing*) diminuer; (*crisis*) désamorcer
VI (*of tension*) diminuer; **the crisis shows no sign of de-escalating** la situation de crise ne semble pas se détendre

de-escalation [diːeskəˈleɪʃən] **N** (*of arms sales*) diminution *f*, (*of crisis, tension*) détente *f*

def [def] **ADJ** *Sl* (*excellent*) super, génial

deface [dɪˈfeɪs] **VT** (*statue*) dégrader; (*poster, walls*) barbouiller; (*book*) (*of child*) gribouiller; (*to express dissatisfaction with contents*) noircir

de facto [deɪˈfæktəʊ] **ADJ, ADV** *Law, Lit* de facto; *Law* **d. and de jure** de droit et de fait; *Law* **d. possession** possession *f* de fait

defamation [defəˈmeɪʃən] **N** diffamation *f*, **that's d. of character** c'est de la diffamation; **to sue for d. of character** engager des poursuites en diffamation, faire un procès en diffamation; **to sue sb for d. of character** poursuivre qn en diffamation

defamatory [dɪˈfæmət(ə)rɪ] **ADJ** (*remark etc*) diffamatoire, diffamant

defame [dɪˈfeɪm] **VT** (*person*) diffamer

default [dɪˈfɔːlt] **N 1** *Law* (*failure to appear in court*) défaut *m*, non-comparution *f*, (*in criminal law*) contumace *f*, **judgment by d.** jugement *m* par contumace; **by d.** (*if not otherwise specified*) implicitement; *Tech* par défaut; *Comput* **which is the d.?** quelle est la configuration/police/etc par défaut?; *Sport*

match won **by d.** match gagné par forfait; **the machine sets itself to 1 by d.** la machine se réglera sur 1 par défaut
2 *Com* défaut *m*, défaillance *f*; **d. in paying** défaut de paiement; *Fig* **in d. of ...** à défaut de ..., faute de ...
3 *Tennis* disqualification *f*
vt *Tennis (player)* disqualifier
vi 1 *Law (fail to appear in court)* ne pas comparaître; *(in criminal law)* être en état de contumace
2 *(fail to pay) St Exch* manquer à ses engagements; **to d. on alimony payments** manquer aux versements de pension alimentaire
3 *Comput* **to d. to sth** sélectionner qch par défaut
▸▸ *Comput* **d. drive** lecteur *m* par défaut; *Comput* **d. font** police *f* par défaut; *Fin* **d. interest** intérêts *mpl* moratoires; *Comput* **d. setting** configuration *f* par défaut; *Comput* **d. value** valeur *f* par défaut

defaulter [dɪˈfɔːltər] **n 1** *Law* défaillant, -ante; *(in criminal law)* contumace *mf* **2** *(debtor)* débiteur *m* défaillant; **d. on a fine** = personne *f* qui ne paie pas une amende **3** *Mil, Naut* retardataire *m*, réfractaire *m*; *(undergoing punishment)* consigné *m*

defaulting [dɪˈfɔːltɪŋ] **adj** *Law* défaillant

defeasance [dɪˈfiːzəns] **n** *Banking, Law* defeasance *m*

defeat [dɪˈfiːt] **n 1** *(of army, team, government)* défaite *f*; **to suffer a d.** essuyer une défaite; **..., he said with an air of d.** ..., dit-il d'un air de vaincu; **to admit d.** s'avouer vaincu **2** *(of plan)* échec *m*, renversement *m*; *Parl (of measure)* rejet *m*
vt 1 *(army, opponent)* battre, vaincre; *(government)* mettre en minorité; **they were defeated by their own lack of preparation** ils ont été battus ou vaincus à cause de leur manque de préparation; **it defeats me** *(I don't understand)* cela me dépasse **2** *(plan, attempt to do sth)* déjouer, faire échouer; *(hope)* frustrer; *(of meeting) (proposal)* rejeter; *Parl (measure)* faire échouer, rejeter; **to d. the ends of justice** contrarier la justice; **to d. one's own ends** aller à l'encontre de ses propres intentions; **that does rather d. the object of the exercise** cela va plutôt à l'encontre du but de l'opération

defeatism [dɪˈfiːtɪz(ə)m] **n** défaitisme *m*; **an air/mood of d.** un air/une atmosphère défaitiste ou de défaite

defeatist [dɪˈfiːtɪst] **adj, n** défaitiste *mf*

defecate [ˈdefəkeɪt] **vi** *Fml* déféquer

defecation [defəˈkeɪʃən] **n** *Fml* défécation *f*

defect¹ [ˈdiːfekt] **n** *(in construction, physical)* défaut *m*; *Com* vice *m*; *(mental)* déficience *f*

defect² [dɪˈfekt] **vi** *Mil, Pol* passer à l'ennemi; *Pol Fig (of MP)* passer dans le camp adverse; *Pol Hist* **to d. to the West** passer à l'ouest; **she defected from the USSR in 1973** elle a quitté l'URSS en 1973; *Pol Fig* **to d. from the party** abandonner le parti; *Pol Fig* **to d. to the government** passer dans le camp du gouvernement; *Com Fig* **she's defected to our main competitor** elle est passée chez notre concurrent principal

defection [dɪˈfekʃən] **n** *Mil, Pol* défection *f*; **there have been a number of defections to the West** un certain nombre de gens sont passés à l'ouest

defective [dɪˈfektɪv] **adj 1** *(machine)* défectueux; *(theory)* imparfait; *(memory)* infidèle; *(brakes)* en mauvais état; *(reasoning)* défectueux, mauvais; *(hearing, method)* mauvais; **to be d. in sth** manquer de qch; *Ind* **d. part** pièce *f* défectueuse **2** *Gram (verb etc)* défectif

Attention: ne pas confondre avec l'adjectif anglais **deficient**.

defector [dɪˈfektər] **n** *Mil, Pol etc* transfuge *mf*

defence, *Am* **defense** [dɪˈfens] **n 1** *(action)* défense *f*; **to put up a stubborn d.** se défendre avec obstination; **I carry a knife for d.** je porte un couteau pour me défendre; **he killed the man in d. of his wife** il a tué l'homme pour défendre sa femme; **to come to sb's d.** venir à la défense de qn
2 *(means)* **defences** *(of country)* moyens *mpl* de défense; **Holland's defences against the flood waters** les défenses dont dispose la Hollande contre les inondations; **the body's natural defences** les défenses naturelles du corps; *Sport* **the d.** les défenseurs; **seaward defences** *(of port)* ouvrages *mpl* de défense face à la mer
3 *(argument)* défense *f*, justification *f*; *Law* défense; **to speak in d. of sb** défendre qn; **I must say, in my own d., that ...** je dois dire pour ma propre défense que ...; **to appear for the d.** *(of barrister)* représenter la défense; **to conduct one's own d.** défendre soi-même sa cause
▸▸ *Law* **d. counsel** défenseur *m*; *(in civil law)* avocat, -ate de la défense; **d. electronics** électronique *f* de défense; *Med* **d. mechanism** défenses *fpl* immunitaires; *Psy* mécanisme *m* de défense; *Pol* **d. spending** dépenses *fpl* pour la défense; *Law* **d. witness** témoin *m* à décharge

defenceless, *Am* **defenseless** [dɪˈfenslɪs] **adj** sans défense

defend [dɪˈfend] **vt 1** *(person, border, country etc)*, *Sport (title)* défendre (**from, against** contre) **2** *(opinion)* défendre, justifier; **to d. one's actions** justifier ses actions **3** *Law (defendant)* défendre
vi 1 *Law* assumer ou soutenir la défense **2** *Sport* défendre

defendant [dɪˈfendənt] **n** *Law* défendeur, -eresse; *(on appeal)* intimé, -ée; *(in criminal case)* accusé, -ée

defender [dɪˈfendər] **n** défenseur *m*
▸▸ **D. of the Faith** Défenseur *m* de la foi

defending [dɪˈfendɪŋ] **adj 1** *Sport* **d. champion** champion, -ionne en titre **2** *Law* de la défense
▸▸ *Law* **d. counsel** défenseur *m*

defense *Am* = **defence**

defensible [dɪˈfensəb(ə)l] **adj** *(cause)*, *Mil* défendable; *(position, point of view)* tenable; *(opinion, behaviour)* défendable, justifiable; **the town was easily d.** la ville était facile à défendre

defensive [dɪˈfensɪv] **adj** défensif, de défense; **don't be so d.!** ne te mets pas sur la défensive comme ça!; **to get d.** se montrer défensif (**about** au sujet de), se mettre sur la défensive
n défensive *f*; **to be/go on the d.** se tenir/se mettre sur la défensive
▸▸ *Mil* **d. action** action *f* défensive; **d. position** position *f* de défense; *St Exch* **d. stocks** titres *mpl* de placement, valeurs *fpl* d'investissement

defensively [dɪˈfensɪvlɪ] **adv** *(to say)* d'un ton défensif; *(to react)* d'une manière défensive

defensiveness [dɪˈfensɪvnɪs] **n** when she reacted/spoke with such d. quand elle a réagi/parlé d'une manière aussi défensive; **her d. in the face of criticism** la façon qu'elle a de se mettre sur la défensive quand on la critique

defer [dɪˈfɜːr] **(-rr-) vt 1** *(delay, postpone) (question, case)* différer, ajourner, remettre; *(meeting, decision)* remettre, reporter; *(pay-*

ment) reculer, renvoyer; *(verdict)* suspendre; **to d. sth to a later date** remettre ou reporter qch à plus tard; **to d. doing sth** différer de faire qch **2** *Mil etc (person)* mettre en sursis (d'appel); **to d. sb on medical grounds** réformer qn
vi *(yield) (to sb's opinion)* se ranger (**to** à); *(to sb's wishes)* se soumettre (**to** à); *(to sb's knowledge)* s'en remettre (**to** à)

deference [ˈdefərəns] **n** déférence *f*; **to pay** or **show d. to sb,** **to treat sb with d.** témoigner de la déférence à ou envers qn; **out of** or **in d. to ...** par déférence pour ..., par égard pour ...

deferential [defəˈrenʃəl] **adj** *(air, tone)* de déférence, respectueux; *(behaviour)* respectueux; *(person)* déférent, respectueux; **to be d. to sb** se montrer plein de déférence ou de respect pour ou envers qn, se montrer respectueux envers qn

deferentially [defəˈrenʃəlɪ] **adv** *(to speak, look at)* avec déférence, avec respect; *(to behave)* avec déférence, respectueusement

deferment [dɪˈfɜːmənt] **n 1** *(of case)* ajournement *m*, remise *f*; *(of payment)* renvoi *m* **2** *Mil etc (for health reasons)* réforme *f*; **to apply for d. (of call-up)** faire une demande de report d'appel

deferral [dɪˈfɜːrəl] **n** = **deferment**

deferred [dɪˈfɜːd] **adj** ajourné, retardé; *(shares)* différé
▸▸ *Fin* **d. depreciation** amortissements *mpl* différés; *Fin* **d. income** produit *m* constaté d'avance; *Fin* **d. payment** paiement *m* différé; *(in instalments)* paiement par versements échelonnés; *Law* **d. sentence** = jugement *m* dont le prononcé est suspendu, jugement ajourné

deffo [ˈdefəʊ] **adv** *Br Fam* absolument; **are you coming tonight? – d.!** tu viens ce soir? – je veux!

defiance [dɪˈfaɪəns] **n** défi *m*; **a gesture of d.** un geste de défi; **in d. of** *(the law, an order)* au mépris de

defiant [dɪˈfaɪənt] **adj** *(gesture, look, remark)* de défi, provocant; *(person)* audacieux, *Pej* irrévérencieux

defiantly [dɪˈfaɪəntlɪ] **adv** *(to say)* d'un ton provocant; *(to look at)* d'un air provocant ou de défi

defibrillation [dɪfɪbrɪˈleɪʃən] **n** *Med* défibrillation *f*

defibrillator [dɪˈfɪbrɪleɪtər] **n** *Med* défibrillateur *m*

deficiency [dɪˈfɪʃənsɪ] **n 1** *(lack)* manque *m*, insuffisance *f* (**of** de); *Med (of minerals, vitamins)* carence *f* (**in, of** de); *(of function, organ)* déficience *f* **2** *(flaw, defect)* défaut *m*, imperfection *f* **3** *(deficit)* manquant *m*, déficit *m*; *Com* découvert *m*; *Pol* déficit budgétaire
▸▸ *Med* **d. disease** maladie *f* de carence

deficient [dɪˈfɪʃənt] **adj** *(faulty)* défectueux; *(lacking)* insuffisant, incomplet; **to be d. in sth** manquer de qch

Attention: ne pas confondre avec l'adjectif **defective**.

deficit [ˈdefɪsɪt] **n** *Fin, Com* déficit *m*; **to be in d.** être en déficit; **budget d.** budget déficitaire; **to make up the d.** combler le déficit

defile¹ [ˈdiːfaɪl] **n** *(pass)* défilé *m*

defile² [dɪˈfaɪl] **vi** *Mil etc (of troops etc)* défiler

defile³ **vt** *(memory of sb, sth)* salir; *(sacred place, tomb)* profaner; *(painting, poster) (with racist etc remarks)* vandaliser; **they've defiled my home** *(entered uninvited)* ils ont violé l'intimité de ma maison; **I feel defiled** *(after rape)* je me sens souillé

defilement [dɪ'faɪlmənt] N *(of sacred place, tomb)* profanation f; *(of sb's memory) (action)* fait m de salir; *(result)* souillure f

Note that the French word **défilement** is a false friend and is never a translation for the English word **defilement**.

definable [dɪ'faɪnəb(ə)l] ADJ définissable; **the border is not easily d.** la frontière n'est pas facile à déterminer

define [dɪ'faɪn] VT **1** *(word, object)* définir **2** *(specify) (difference)* définir; *(one's attitude, position etc)* préciser; *(objectives etc)* formuler; *(scope, extent of sth)* déterminer; *(powers)* délimiter; **to d. what it means to be French** définir ce qu'être français signifie; **well-defined limits** limites bien déterminées **3 well-defined outlines** contours nettement dessinés *ou* dégagés **4** *Comput (value)* déclarer

defining [dɪ'faɪnɪŋ] ADJ **1** *(decisive)* décisif; **a d. moment in history** un tournant de l'histoire **2** *(distinctive)* déterminant

definite ['defɪnɪt] ADJ **1** *(distinct) (views, opinions)* bien arrêté; *(shape)* défini, bien déterminé; *(taste)* bien déterminé; **I can't put my finger on anything d.** je n'arrive pas à mettre le doigt sur quoi que ce soit de précis; **it shows a d. lack of ...** cela montre un manque évident de ...; **it's a d. advantage being a woman** c'est un véritable avantage d'être une femme; **there has been a d. improvement in her condition/work** il y a eu une amélioration certaine de son état/travail **2** *(sure, certain) (date)* définitif, certain; *(response)* précis, catégorique; *Com (order)* ferme; **it's not d. yet** ce n'est pas encore définitif *ou* sûr; **at a d. time** à une heure déterminée; **and that's d.!** et c'est sûr!; **she is very d. about it** elle est tout à fait sûre de cela; **I'm d. it was him** je suis certain *ou* sûr que c'était lui; **he's d. about getting married** il est décidé à se marier **3** *Gram (article)* défini; **past d.** passé m défini VOIR GRAMMAIRE A6–8; B3–4

Attention: ne pas confondre avec l'adjectif **definitive**.

definitely ['defɪnɪtlɪ] ADV **1** *(distinctly) (improved, superior)* nettement; *(to need, lack sth)* décidément **2** *(without doubt, certainly)* à coup sûr, sans aucun doute; **the meeting will d. be held next Monday** la réunion aura bien lieu lundi prochain; **he is d. mad/the man I saw** il n'y a pas de doute qu'il est fou/que c'est l'homme que j'ai vu, il est fou/c'est l'homme que j'ai vu, c'est sûr *ou* certain; **she's d. innocent** elle est innocente, c'est sûr *ou* certain; **are you going? – d.!** est-ce que vous y allez? – absolument!; **I'll d. be there** j'y serai à coup sûr; **I'll almost d. be there** j'y serai presque certainement, il est presque certain que j'y serai; **d. not!** certainement pas!; **I'll d. call you** je te téléphonerai sans faute; **that's d. my last offer** cette fois-ci, c'est ma dernière offre **3** *(clearly, without ambiguity)* **he told me very d. that he didn't want to come** il m'a dit très clairement qu'il ne voulait pas venir

Attention: ne pas confondre avec l'adverbe **definitively**.

definition [defɪ'nɪʃən] N **1** *(meaning) (of word)* définition f; **by d.** par définition; **to give a d. of sth** donner une définition de qch, définir qch **2** *(specifying) (of powers, border etc)* délimitation f; *(of objectives)* formulation f **3** *(of image)* Opt netteté f; TV définition f

definitive [dɪ'fɪnɪtɪv] ADJ *(verdict, result)* définitif; *(authoritative) (biography, edition)* qui fait autorité; *(production of play)* inégalable; **she was, for me, the d. Juliet** pour moi, c'est une Juliette inégalable

Attention: ne pas confondre avec l'adjectif **definite**.

definitively [dɪ'fɪnɪtɪvlɪ] ADV définitivement

Attention: ne pas confondre avec l'adverbe **definitely**.

deflate [di:'fleɪt] VT **1** *(ball, tyre)* dégonfler; *Fig (person)* remettre à sa place; **to d. sb's ego** porter un coup à l'orgueil de qn; **he looked quite deflated** *(had lost his self-esteem)* il était penaud; **I felt rather deflated** *(disappointed)* j'étais assez déçu **2** *Fin, Econ* **to d. the currency** provoquer la déflation de la monnaie; **to d. the economy** pratiquer une politique déflationniste; **to d. prices** faire baisser les prix

▸ VI **1** *(of tyre etc)* se dégonfler **2** *Fin, Econ* provoquer la déflation de la monnaie; **since the government started deflating** depuis que le gouvernement pratique une politique déflationniste

deflation [di:'fleɪʃən] N **1** *(of ball, tyre)* dégonflement m; *Fig (of person)* fait m de se dégonfler; **... which resulted in the d. of his ego** ... ce qui l'a complètement abattu **2** *Fin, Econ* déflation f

deflationary [di:'fleɪʃən(ə)rɪ] ADJ *Econ* déflationniste

deflect [dɪ'flekt] VT *(ball, bullet)* (faire) dévier; *(light)* défléchir; *(sound)* renvoyer; *Fig (person)* détourner (**from** de); **to d. criticism** détourner la critique; **the government will not be deflected from its aims** le gouvernement ne se laissera pas détourner de ses objectifs; **to be deflected** *(of projectile)* dériver; **the ball was deflected into the net** le ballon a rebondi dans le filet

▸ VI *(of projectile)* dévier; *(of light)* être défléchi; **the ball deflected off the post** le ballon a rebondi contre le poteau

deflection [dɪ'flekʃən] N *(of light)* déflexion f; *(of compass needle)* déviation f; *(of projectile)* déviation, détournement m; *(of criticism)* détournement m; *Elec, Electron (of voltmeter etc)* déviation, déflexion; **it was a lucky d. off the post** heureusement la balle a été déviée par le montant du but; **he scored from a d. off the post** il a marqué un but après que le ballon ait rebondi contre le poteau

deflector [dɪ'flektər] N *Tech* déflecteur m; **sound d.** abat-son m inv

deflexion [dɪ'flekʃən] N = **deflection**

defloration [deflə'reɪʃən] N *Arch, Lit (of virgin)* défloration f

deflower [di:'flauər] VT *Arch, Lit (virgin)* déflorer

deflowering [di:'flauərɪŋ] N *Arch, Lit (of virgin)* défloration f

defocus [di:'fəukəs] VI passer au flou

defoliant [di:'fəulɪənt] N défoliant m

defoliate [di:'fəulɪeɪt] VT *(trees etc)* défeuiller

defoliation [di:fəulɪ'eɪʃən] N défoliation f

deforest [di:'fɒrɪst] VT *(region)* déboiser

deforestation [di:fɒrɪ'steɪʃən] N *(of region)* déboisement m

deform [dɪ'fɔ:m] VT déformer

deformation [di:fɔ:'meɪʃən] N *(of bone etc)* déformation f

deformed [dɪ'fɔ:md] ADJ *(person)* malformé; *(limb)* difforme, malformé; **the baby was born d.** le bébé est né avec une malformation

deformity [dɪ'fɔ:mɪtɪ] N *(of body)* difformité f

DEFRA ['defrə] N *Br Admin (abbr* **Department of the Environment, Food and Rural Affairs)** = ministère m de l'Agriculture et de l'Environnement

defragment [di:fræg'ment] VT *Comput* défragmenter

defragmentation [di:frægmen'teɪʃən] N *Comput* défragmentation f

defragmenter [di:fræg'mentər] N *Comput* défragmenteur m

defraud [dɪ'frɔ:d] VT *(taxman)* frauder; *(bank, employer)* escroquer; **to d. sb of sth** escroquer qch à qn, frustrer qn de qch

▸ VI *Law* **conspiracy to d.** entente f délictueuse dans le but de frauder

defrauder [dɪ'frɔ:dər] N fraudeur, -euse

defray [dɪ'freɪ] VT **to d. sb's expenses** rembourser les frais de qn, défrayer qn; **to d. the cost of sth** couvrir les frais de qch

defrayal [dɪ'freɪəl] N **d. of expenses** remboursement m des frais

defrock [di:'frɒk] VT *Rel (priest)* défroquer

defrost [di:'frɒst] VT **1** *(refrigerator)* dégivrer **2** *(meat etc)* décongeler

▸ VI **1** *(of refrigerator)* dégivrer **2** *(of meat)* se décongeler

defroster [di:'frɒstər] N *Aut* dégivreur m

deft [deft] ADJ adroit, habile

deftly ['deftlɪ] ADV adroitement, habilement

deftness ['deftnɪs] N adresse f, habileté f, dextérité f

defunct [dɪ'fʌŋkt] ADJ *(person)* défunt, décédé; *Fig (industry)* défunt; *(project, practice, law)* révolu; *(company)* dissous, f dissoute

defuse [di:'fju:z] VT *(bomb)*, *Fig (crisis)* désamorcer

Attention: ne pas confondre avec le verbe **to diffuse**.

defy [dɪ'faɪ] VT *(somebody, the elements)* défier, braver; *(order, law)* braver; **to d. description** échapper à toute description, défier toute description; **I d. him to prove it** je le défie de le prouver

degearing [di:'ɡɪərɪŋ] N *Fin* désendettement m

degeneracy [dɪ'dʒenərəsɪ] N dégénérescence f

degenerate¹ [dɪ'dʒen(ə)rət] ADJ, N dégénéré, -ée

degenerate² [dɪ'dʒenəreɪt] VI dégénérer (**from** de; **into** en); **the discussion degenerated into a fight** la discussion a dégénéré en bagarre

degeneration [dɪdʒenə'reɪʃən] N dégénérescence f; *Med* **fatty d.** dégénérescence graisseuse

degenerative [dɪ'dʒenərətɪv] ADJ *Med (disease)* dégénératif; **she has a d. heart condition** elle a des troubles cardiaques qui s'aggravent

degradation [deɡrə'deɪʃən] N **1** avilissement m, dégradation f; **to live a life of d.** vivre dans la dégradation **2** *Phys* dégradation f; *Geol* désagrégation f **3** *Mil* dégradation f

degrade [dɪ'ɡreɪd] VT **1** *(person)* avilir, dégrader; **I won't d. myself by answering that** je ne m'abaisserai pas à répondre à ça **2** *Phys (energy)* dégrader; *Geol (rocks)* désagréger **3** *Mil (officer)* dégrader, casser

degrading [dɪ'ɡreɪdɪŋ] ADJ *(experience)* avilissant, dégradant

degree [dɪ'ɡri:] N **1** *(extent)* degré m; **to**

some or **a (certain) d.** à un certain degré, (jusqu')à un certain point; **she's right to a d.** elle a raison jusqu'à un certain point ou dans une certaine mesure; **to** or **in a high d.** éminemment; **in the highest d.** au plus haut ou au dernier degré; **to such a d. that …** à tel point que …; **by degrees** petit à petit, graduellement; **to feel a d. of optimism** ressentir un certain optimisme; Law **marriage within the prohibited** or **forbidden degrees** mariage entre parents ou alliés au degré prohibé

2 Phys, Geog, Met etc degré m; Met **it's 25 degrees** il fait 25 degrés; **we can expect temperatures of 15 to 20 degrees** nous pouvons nous attendre à des températures de 15 à 20 degrés; **degrees Fahrenheit/Celsius** degrés Fahrenheit/Celsius; **ten degrees of frost/below zero** dix degrés au-dessous de zéro; Geom **angle of 30 degrees, 30-d.** angle angle m de 30 degrés; Math **equation of the second/third d.** équation f du second/troisième degré; Phys **d. of humidity** titre m d'eau ou d'humidité

3 Univ diplôme m (universitaire); **to take** or **do a d.** passer un diplôme (**in** en); **when did you do** or **take your d.?** quand as-tu eu ton diplôme?

▸▸ Gram **d. of comparison** degré m de comparaison

-degree [də'griː] SUFF **first/second/etc-d. burn** brûlure f du premier/deuxième/etc degré; Am **first/second-d. murder** meurtre m avec/sans préméditation

dehire [diː'haɪər] VT Am Euph (employee) remercier

dehumanize [diː'hjuːmənaɪz] VT déshumaniser; **it was a dehumanizing experience** c'était une expérience déshumanisante

dehumidification [diːhjuːmɪdɪfɪ'keɪʃən] N déshumidification f

dehumidifier [diːhjuː'mɪdɪfaɪər] N déshumidificateur m

dehumidify [diːhjuː'mɪdɪfaɪ] VT déshumidifier

dehydrate [diːhaɪ'dreɪt] VT déshydrater; **to become dehydrated** se déshydrater
VI (of person) se déshydrater

dehydrated [diːhaɪ'dreɪtɪd] ADJ (person, foodstuffs) déshydraté; (milk, eggs) en poudre

dehydration [diːhaɪ'dreɪʃən] N déshydratation f

dehydrator [diːhaɪ'dreɪtər] N déshydrateur m

de-ice [diː'aɪs] VT Aut, Aviat dégivrer

de-icer [diː'aɪsər] N Aut, Aviat dégivreur m

de-icing [diː'aɪsɪŋ] N Aut, Aviat dégivrage m

deification [diːɪfɪ'keɪʃən, deɪ-] N déification f

deify ['diːɪfaɪ, 'deɪ-] VT déifier

deign [deɪn] VT **to d. to do sth** condescendre à faire qch, daigner faire qch

deindex [diː'ɪndeks] VT Fin (salaries) désindexer par rapport au coût de la vie

deindustrialization [diːɪndʌstrɪəlaɪ'zeɪʃən] N désindustrialisation f

deinstall [diːɪn'stɔːl] VT Comput désinstaller

deinstallation [diːɪnstə'leɪʃən] N Comput désinstallation f

deinstaller [diːɪn'stɔːlər] N Comput désinstallateur m

deionized water [diː'aɪənaɪzd] N eau f déminéralisée

deism ['diːɪz(ə)m, 'deɪ-] N déisme m

deity ['diːɪtɪ, 'deɪ-] N **1** (god) dieu m, déesse f, déité f, divinité f; Rel **the D.** la Divinité, Dieu m **2** (divinity) (of Christ etc) divinité f

déjà vu ['deɪʒæ'vuː] N **I had a feeling of d.** j'ai eu une impression de déjà vu

deject [dɪ'dʒekt] VT (person) abattre, décourager

dejected [dɪ'dʒektɪd] ADJ abattu, découragé; **to become d.** se décourager

dejectedly [dɪ'dʒektɪdlɪ] ADV d'un air abattu ou découragé

dejection [dɪ'dʒekʃən] N découragement m

de jure ['diː'dʒʊərɪ] ADV Law, Lit de jure

dekko ['dekəʊ] N Br Sl coup m d'œil; **let's have a d.** fais/faites voir; **to take a d.** jeter un (coup d')œil (**at** sur)

Del abbr Delaware

delay [dɪ'leɪ] N retard m; **d. in delivery** retard à la livraison; **without d.** sans retard ou délai m; **without (any) further d.** sans plus tarder; **after much d.** après un long moment; **an hour's d.** une heure de retard; **all flights are subject to d.** tous les vols ont du retard; **delays of four hours can be expected** on peut s'attendre à des retards de quatre heures; **the road works caused traffic delays** les travaux ont retardé la circulation
VT **1** (postpone) (one's departure) retarder, remettre; (payment) différer, arriérer; **she delayed leaving until the last possible moment** elle a repoussé ou retardé son départ jusqu'au dernier moment; **I delayed writing to you until I knew the exact date** j'ai attendu de savoir la date exacte pour t'écrire
2 (hold up) (somebody) retenir, retarder; (progress, traffic) entraver, retarder; **they've been delayed by fog** ils ont été retardés par le brouillard; **she's suffering from delayed shock** elle souffre d'un choc après coup ou a posteriori
VI tarder (**in doing sth** à faire qch); Mil **delaying action** action f retardatrice; **don't d., book your holiday now** ne tardez pas, réservez vos vacances maintenant; **stop delaying and come to a decision!** arrête de remettre à plus tard ta décision!

> Note that the French word **délai** is a false friend and is never a translation for the English word **delay**. Its most common meaning is **deadline**.

delayed-action [dɪ'leɪd-] ADJ (fuse, shutter) à retardement

delayed cut-off N (of courtesy light etc) extinction f retardée

delayering [diː'leɪərɪŋ] N Com suppression f d'échelons

del credere [del'kreɪdərɪ] N Com ducroire m
▸▸ **d. agent** commissionnaire m ducroire; **d. clause** clause f ducroire

delectable [dɪ'lektəb(ə)l] ADJ délectable, délicieux

delectation [diːlek'teɪʃən] N Fml délectation f

delegate¹ ['delɪgət] N délégué, -ée; **a d. to a conference** un membre d'une conférence; **a d. conference** une conférence de délégués syndicaux

delegate² ['delɪgeɪt] VT **1** (appoint) (person) déléguer (**to do sth** pour faire qch) **2** (powers) déléguer
VI déléguer; **she's not very good at delegating** elle ne sait pas déléguer

delegation [delɪ'geɪʃən] N (act, representatives) délégation f; **d. of power** délégation de pouvoir; **to send a d.** envoyer une délégation

delete [dɪ'liːt] VT (erase) effacer (**from** de); (cross out) rayer; Comput effacer, supprimer; **d. where applicable, d. as appropriate** (on form) rayer les mentions inutiles
VI Comput effacer

N **1** Comput touche f d'effacement **2** Typ (symbol) déléatur m

▸▸ Comput **d. character** caractère m d'effacement; Comput **d. command** commande f d'effacement; Comput **d. key** touche d'effacement

deleterious [delɪ'tɪərɪəs] ADJ Fml (to health) nuisible, délétère

deleting [dɪ'liːtɪŋ] N effacement m

deletion [dɪ'liːʃən] N **1** (action) (of word, paragraph etc) suppression f, effacement m **2** (passage/word deleted) passage m/mot m effacé ou supprimé; **without deletions or additions** sans ratures ni surcharges

delft [delft] N Cer faïence f de Delft
▸▸ **d. blue** bleu m de faïence

Delhi belly ['delɪ] N Br Fam Hum **to have D.** avoir la courante

deli ['delɪ] N Fam = delicatessen

deliberate¹ [dɪ'lɪb(ə)rət] ADJ **1** (intentional) (mistake, lie, rudeness) délibéré, intentionnel, voulu; (insolence) calculé; (insult) prémédité; **it was quite d.!** c'était voulu, c'était fait exprès!; **it wasn't d.** ce n'était pas voulu **2** (unhurried) (person) circonspect, avisé; (movement etc) mesuré; (voice) posé; **she has a very d. way of working** elle travaille de manière très réglée

deliberate² [dɪ'lɪbəreɪt] VI (of individual) délibérer, réfléchir (**on** sur); (of people, committee etc) débattre, délibérer, réfléchir (**on** sur); **to d. over** or **on a question** délibérer d'une question; **they deliberated whether or not to let him go** ils délibéraient de le laisser partir ou non
VT (question) délibérer de

deliberately [dɪ'lɪb(ə)rətlɪ] ADV **1** (intentionally) intentionnellement, exprès, à dessein; **I d. didn't invite her** c'est intentionnellement que je ne l'ai pas invitée **2** (unhurriedly) avec mesure; **he paused d.** il fit une pause calculée

deliberation [dɪlɪbə'reɪʃən] N **1** (thought, discussion) délibération f; **after due d.** après mûre délibération; **the deliberations of an assembly** les débats mpl d'une assemblée **2** (lack of haste) mesure f; **with d.** (to say sth) posément; (to do sth) de façon réfléchie; (to walk) d'un pas mesuré; (to act) avec circonspection

deliberative [dɪ'lɪbərətɪv] ADJ (function) délibératif; (assembly) délibérant

delicacy ['delɪkəsɪ] N **1** (fineness) (of embroidery, carving, fingers, features) délicatesse f
2 (sensitivity) (of instrument, mechanism) sensibilité f; (tactfulness) délicatesse f, tact m; **she showed great d. of feeling** elle a fait preuve d'une grande délicatesse ou sensibilité; **negotiations of the utmost d.** négociations très délicates
3 (gentleness, lightness) (of touch) légèreté f
4 (fragility) (of health, fabric) fragilité f
5 (subtlety) (of colour, flavours) délicatesse f
6 (food) mets m délicat

delicate ['delɪkət] ADJ **1** (fine) (embroidery, carving, fingers) délicat; (feature) fin, délicat
2 (sensitive) (mechanism, matter, situation etc) délicat; (question) épineux; (feelings) sensible; (person) (over-refined, easily shocked) précieux; (tactful) délicat, sensible; **it's a matter that needs d. handling** c'est une affaire qui doit être traitée avec délicatesse; **we're at a very d. stage in our negotiations** nous en sommes à une étape très délicate de nos négociations; **to tread on d. ground** toucher à des questions délicates
3 (gentle, light) (touch) délicat
4 (fragile) (person, glass) délicat; (health, fabric) fragile, délicat
5 (subtle) (colour, flavour) délicat
NPL **delicates** linge m délicat

delicately ['delɪkətlɪ] ADV **1** (finely) (carved,

embroidered etc) délicatement, finement **2** (sensitively) (to handle question, approach a subject etc) avec délicatesse; **the mechanism is very d. balanced** le réglage du mécanisme est très sensible **3** (gently, lightly) (to put sth down, pick sth up etc) délicatement **4** (with subtlety) (coloured) délicatement; **d. flavoured** aux saveurs délicates

delicateness ['delɪkətnɪs] N = **delicacy 1, 2, 3, 4, 5**

delicatessen [delɪkə'tesən] N **1** (shop) épicerie f fine, traiteur m **2** (food) plats mpl cuisinés

delicious [dɪ'lɪʃəs] ADJ délicieux, exquis

deliciously [dɪ'lɪʃəslɪ] ADV délicieusement

delight [dɪ'laɪt] N **1** (source of pleasure) délice m; **the film is a d.** le film est un délice; **he is a d. to work with** c'est un plaisir de travailler avec lui; **it is such a d. to ...** c'est si bon de ...; **a d. to the eye** un bonheur pour les yeux; **to be sb's d.** faire le bonheur de qn; **the delights of the countryside** les délices fpl de la campagne **2** (pleasure) plaisir m; **much to the d. of ..., to the great d. of ...** au grand plaisir de ..., à la grande joie de ...; **to take d. in (doing) sth** prendre grand plaisir à faire qch; **I take no d. in telling you this, but ...** ce n'est pas de gaieté de cœur que je dois vous annoncer que ...
VT (somebody) enchanter, ravir; **to d. the ear/the eye** charmer les oreilles/enchanter la vue
▶ **delight in** VT INSEP se délecter de, aimer beaucoup; **to d. in doing sth** se délecter à ou aimer beaucoup faire qch; **he delights in the new baby** il est aux anges devant le bébé; **he delights in being a father** il est ravi d'être père

delighted [dɪ'laɪtɪd] ADJ ravi, enchanté (with de); **I'm d. to make your acquaintance** je suis ravi ou enchanté de faire votre connaissance; **I am d. for you** je suis ravi pour vous; **I'd be d. to!** j'en serais ravi!

delightedly [dɪ'laɪtɪdlɪ] ADV avec ravissement

delightful [dɪ'laɪtfʊl] ADJ (person, smile) délicieux, ravissant, charmant; (meal) délicieux, exquis; (place) ravissant, charmant; (weekend, evening, sense of humour) délicieux; **a d. child** un enfant charmant; **they have a d. home** ils ont une maison ravissante

delightfully [dɪ'laɪtfʊlɪ] ADV délicieusement; **he sings d.** il chante à ravir

delimit [di:'lɪmɪt] VT délimiter

delimitation [dɪlɪmɪ'teɪʃən] N délimitation f

delimiter [di:'lɪmɪtər] N Comput délimiteur m

delineate [dɪ'lɪnɪeɪt] VT **1** (draw) (triangle etc) tracer; Fml (sb's features) dessiner; (profile) délinéer **2** (describe) (plan, proposal) présenter en détails; (character in novel) faire le portrait de

delineation [dɪlɪnɪ'eɪʃən] N **1** (drawing) (of triangle etc) dessin m, tracé m **2** (description) (of plan, proposal etc) présentation f en détails; (of character in novel) portrait m

delinquency [dɪ'lɪŋkwənsɪ] N **1** Law délinquance f **2** Fin défaillance f, défaut m de paiement

delinquent [dɪ'lɪŋkwənt] N **1** Law délinquant, -ante **2** Fin défaillant, -ante
ADJ **1** Law (behaviour etc) délinquant **2** Fin (person) défaillant; (taxes) impayé
▶▶ Banking **d. account** compte m en souffrance

delirious [dɪ'lɪrɪəs] ADJ Med en délire, délirant; Fig en délire; Med **to be d.** délirer; Fig **to be d. with joy** délirer de joie, être délirant de

joie; Fig **I'm d.** je suis ravi; Fig **I'm d. at** or **about the prospect** cette perspective me rend fou de joie; Fig **she's d. about being pregnant** elle est ravie d'être enceinte; Fig **I'm not exactly d. about the prospect** la perspective ne m'enchante guère

deliriously [dɪ'lɪrɪəslɪ] ADV **to talk d.** délirer; Fig **to cheer d.** applaudir frénétiquement ou avec frénésie; **d. happy** délirant de joie

delirium [dɪ'lɪrɪəm] N Med délire m; **to be in a d.** être en plein délire; Fig Lit **to be in a d. of joy** être transporté de joie;
▶▶ Med **d. tremens** delirium tremens m

delist [di:'lɪst] VT Com, Mktg (product) déréférencer; St Exch (company) radier de la cote

delisting [di:'lɪstɪŋ] N Com, Mktg (of product) déréférencement m; St Exch (of company) radiation f de la cote

deliver [dɪ'lɪvər] VT **1** (parcel, telegram etc) remettre (to à); (letters) distribuer (to à); (goods) livrer (to à); **do you want your newspaper (to be) delivered?** est-ce que vous voulez qu'on vous livre votre journal?, est-ce que vous voulez que votre journal vous soit livré?; **do you have your milk delivered?** est-ce que vous vous faites livrer votre lait?, est-ce qu'on vous livre votre lait?; **to d. a message** faire une commission; **to d. sth to sb's house** Com livrer qch au domicile de qn; (non-commercial) porter qch chez qn; Com **d. to domicile** livrer à domicile; **to d. the goods** livrer les marchandises; Fig remplir ses engagements; (of new product etc) tenir ses promesses
2 Obst **to d. a child** mettre un enfant au monde; Old-fashioned **to d. a woman (of a child)** accoucher une femme; Old-fashioned **to be delivered of a child** accoucher d'un enfant
3 (blow) porter, donner; (ball etc) lancer; Ftbl **to d. a pass** faire une passe
4 (speech) faire, prononcer; (lecture) faire; Law (verdict) prononcer, rendre
5 (provide) (service) assurer; (of machine, dynamo etc) (power) débiter, fournir; Aut (hp) développer; Fin **to d. a profit** rapporter ou faire un profit; Fin **to d. shares** délivrer des valeurs
6 (fulfil) **can the party d. its election promises?** est-ce que le parti arrivera à tenir ses promesses électorales?
7 Fml (rescue) (person) délivrer (**from his enemies** de ses ennemis); **to d. sb from death** sauver qn de la mort; Rel **us from evil** délivre-nous du mal
VI (of supplier) livrer; Fig (of new product supplier, political party etc) tenir ses promesses; **it/he just doesn't d.** il n'est pas à la hauteur; **can Brown d. on reform?** est-ce que Brown pourra tenir ses promesses en ce qui concerne les réformes?
▶ **deliver up** VT SEP (surrender) (town) restituer, rendre (to à); (hostage, prisoner) remettre, livrer (to à)

deliverance [dɪ'lɪv(ə)rəns] N Fml (rescue) délivrance f (from de)

delivered [dɪ'lɪvəd] ADJ Com **d. at domicile** rendu à domicile; **d. free** livraison franco; **d. free at domicile** livré franco domicile; **d. free on board** rendu franco bord; **d. at frontier** rendu à la frontière

deliverer [dɪ'lɪvərər] N **1** Fml (saviour) libérateur, -trice, sauveur m **2** (of goods) livreur m

delivery [dɪ'lɪv(ə)rɪ] N **1** (of parcel, goods etc) livraison f; (of letter) remise f; (of mail) distribution f; **to take delivery of sth** prendre livraison de qch; **charge for d.** (frais mpl de) port m; **parcels awaiting d.** colis mpl en souffrance; **free d.** livraison franco; **to pay on d.** payer à ou sur livraison; Com **d. duty**

paid/unpaid droits mpl acquittés/non acquittés
2 Obst accouchement m; **it was an easy d.** l'accouchement a été facile
3 (of speech) prononciation f; (of speaker) diction f; **to have a good d.** avoir un bon débit
4 Sport (of ball) lancement m, envoi m; (of player) manière f de lancer (la balle); Mil (of rocket etc) lancement
5 (of water, power etc) débit m; (of pump) refoulement m
6 (of prisoner) reddition f, Law (of property) tradition f, (of bequest etc) délivrance f (**to** à); **for d.** (of stocks) au comptant
▶▶ **d. address** adresse f de livraison; **d. boy** livreur m; **d. charges** frais mpl de livraison; **d. conditions** conditions fpl de livraison; **d. date** date f de livraison; **d. deadline** terme m de livraison; **d. girl** livreuse f; **d. man** livreur m; **d. note** bon m ou bordereau m ou bulletin m de livraison; **d. point** lieu m de livraison; **d. schedule** planning m de livraison; **d. time** délai m de livraison; **d. van** camion m de livraison; (smaller) camionnette f de livraison

dell [del] N vallon m

delouse [di:'laʊs] VT (something) ôter les poux de; (somebody) épouiller, ôter les poux de

delphinium [del'fɪnɪəm] N (flower) pied-d'alouette m, pl pieds-d'alouette

delta ['deltə] N **1** (in Greek alphabet) delta m inv **2** (of river) delta m
▶▶ Aviat **d. wing** aile f (en) delta

delude [dɪ'lu:d] VT (somebody) tromper, induire en erreur; **to d. oneself** se faire des illusions; **he deluded himself/me into thinking she would agree** il s'est/m'a persuadé qu'elle accepterait

deluded [dɪ'lu:dɪd] ADJ qui se fait des illusions

deluge ['delju:dʒ] N **1** (flood) déluge m; **a d. of rain** une pluie diluvienne **2** Fig (of words) déluge m; (of letters, questions etc) avalanche f
VT (flood), Fig inonder (with de)

delusion [dɪ'lu:ʒən] N illusion f, Psy fantasme m; (bordering on insanity) délire m; **to be under a d.** se faire des illusions, s'abuser; **to suffer from delusions** être sujet à des hallucinations; Psy **delusions of grandeur** folie f des grandeurs; Hum **you're suffering from delusions of grandeur!** tu te fais des illusions!

de luxe [dɪ'lʌks] ADJ de luxe; (apartment) (de) grand standing; **d. room** chambre f catégorie 'luxe'

delve [delv] VI fouiller; **to d. in(to) one's pocket** fouiller dans sa poche; **to d. into** (the past) remonter dans, fouiller dans; (person's past) fouiller dans; (records, archives) explorer

Dem [dem] Am Pol abbr **Democrat**

demagnetize [di:'mægnɪtaɪz] VT démagnétiser

demagogic [demə'gɒgɪk] ADJ démagogique

demagogue ['deməgɒg] N démagogue m

demand [dɪ'mɑ:nd] N **1** (request) demande f, réclamation f; **d. for payment** demande de paiement; **final d.** (notice) dernier rappel m; **payable on d.** payable sur demande
2 Econ demande f; **to be in (great) d.** être (très) demandé ou recherché; **to be much in d. as ...** (of person) être très demandé en tant que ...; **there's not much d. for it** ce n'est pas très demandé, ce n'est pas très recherché
3 demands (of workers, kidnappers) exigences fpl; (of a situation, job etc) nécessités fpl,

exigences *fpl*; **to give in to sb's demands** céder aux exigences de qn; **you make too many demands on her** tu exiges trop d'elle; **to make great demands on sb's patience** exiger de qn beaucoup de patience; **I have many demands on my time** je suis très pris; **with all of these demands on your time, how do you manage to …** tu es tellement pris, comment fais-tu pour …

VT 1 *(something)* réclamer (**of, from** à); **to d. payment from sb** sommer qn de payer; **they're demanding payment** ils réclament le paiement; **to d. an apology/explanation** exiger des excuses/une explication; **I d. to speak to the manager** j'exige de parler au directeur; **to d. to know whether …** insister pour savoir si …; **to d. that …** exiger que … + *sub*

2 *(of situation, job etc)* demander, exiger; **the matter demands great care** l'affaire exige *ou* réclame beaucoup de soin

▸▸ *Com, Mktg* **d. analysis** analyse *f* de la demande; **d. curve** courbe *f* (d'évolution) de la demande; *Am Banking* **d. deposit** dépôt *m* à vue; *Am Banking* **d. deposit account** compte *m* à vue; *Com, Mktg* **d. driver** dynamisant *m* de la demande; *Com, Mktg* **d. forecasting** prévision *f* de la demande; **d. function** fonction *f* de demande; *Com* **d. management** contrôle *m* de la demande; *Fin* **d. note** bon *m* à vue

> Note that the most common meaning of the French word **demande** is **request** and that the most common meaning of the French verb **demander** is **to ask** or **to request**.

demanding [dɪˈmɑːndɪŋ] ADJ *(person)* exigeant; *(job)* exigeant, astreignant; *(task)* astreignant; **being a physiotherapist is physically d.** être kinésithérapeute est physiquement astreignant; **children are at their most d. between the ages of two and four** les enfants demandent le plus d'attention entre deux et quatre ans

demand-led ADJ *Econ* tiré par la demande

demand-pull inflation N *Econ* inflation *f* par la demande

demarcation [diːmɑːˈkeɪʃən] N démarcation *f*, délimitation *f*
▸▸ **d. dispute** conflit *m* d'attributions; **d. line** ligne *f* de démarcation

demarket [ˈdiːmɑːkɪt] VT retirer du marché

demarketing [diːˈmɑːkɪtɪŋ] N démarketing *m*

demean [dɪˈmiːn] VT **to d. oneself** s'abaisser, s'avilir; **it was very demeaning having to …** c'était très avilissant de devoir …; **to d. one's office** rabaisser sa charge

demeanour, *Am* **demeanor** [dɪˈmiːnər] N *(behaviour)* comportement *m*, attitude *f*, conduite *f*; *(bearing, mien)* air *m*

demented [dɪˈmentɪd] ADJ fou, *f* folle; *Med* dément; **to become d.** tomber en démence; **to be d. with grief/anger/worry** être fou de douleur/de colère/d'inquiétude; *Fig* **like one d.** *(to scream etc)* comme un fou

dementia [dɪˈmenʃɪə] N *Med* démence *f*

demerara [deməˈreərə] N cassonade *f*
▸▸ **d. sugar** cassonade

demerger [diːˈmɜːdʒər] N scission *f*; **several new companies were formed after the d. of the holding group** plusieurs entreprises nouvelles ont été créées à la suite de la scission du holding

demerit [diːˈmerɪt] N **1** *Fml (fault)* démérite *m*, tort *m* **2** *Am Sch* blâme *m*

demesne [dəˈmeɪn] N **1** *Law (possession)* possession *f* **2** *Hist Fml (land)* domaine *m*

demigod [ˈdemɪɡɒd] N demi-dieu *m*, *pl* demi-dieux

demijohn [ˈdemɪdʒɒn] N *Ind etc* dame-jeanne *f*, *pl* dames-jeannes, bonbonne *f*

demilitarization [diːmɪlɪt(ə)raɪˈzeɪʃən] N démilitarisation *f*

demilitarize [diːˈmɪlɪtəraɪz] VT démilitariser

demi-pension [dəmɪˈpɑ̃sjɔ̃] N demi-pension *f*, *pl* demi-pensions

demise [dɪˈmaɪz] N *Admin (of sb)* décès *m*, mort *f*; *Fig (of newspaper, empire etc)* disparition *f*; **this meant the d. of our hopes** cela a mis fin à nos espoirs

demisemiquaver [ˈdemɪsemɪkweɪvər] N *Mus* triple croche *f*

demist [diːˈmɪst] VT désembuer

demister [diːˈmɪstər] N *Aut (dispositif m)* antibuée *m*, désembueur *m*

demisting [diːˈmɪstɪŋ] N *Aut* désembuage *m*

demo [ˈdeməʊ] N *Fam* **1** *(protest)* manif *f* **2** *(of singer, musician)* disque *m*/cassette *f*/vidéo *f* de démonstration
▸▸ *Comput* **d. disk** disquette *f* de démonstration *ou* d'évaluation; **d. tape** bande *f* démo; *Comput* **d. version** version *f* de démonstration *ou* d'évaluation

demob [diːˈmɒb] *Old-fashioned Br Mil Fam* VT **(-bb-)** démobiliser
N démobilisation *f*

demobilization [diːməʊbɪlaɪˈzeɪʃən] N *Mil* démobilisation *f*

demobilize [diːˈməʊbɪlaɪz] VT & VI *Mil* démobiliser

democracy [dɪˈmɒkrəsɪ] N démocratie *f*; **people's d.** démocratie populaire

democrat [ˈdeməkræt] N démocrate *mf*; *Am Pol* **the Democrats** le parti démocrate

democratic [deməˈkrætɪk] ADJ démocratique
▸▸ **d. deficit** déficit *m* démocratique; **d. government** la démocratie *f*; **the D. Party** le parti *m* démocrate (américain); **d. socialism** socialisme *m* démocratique

democratically [deməˈkrætɪklɪ] ADV *(elected etc)* démocratiquement

democratize [dɪˈmɒkrətaɪz] VT démocratiser
VI se démocratiser

demodulation [diːmɒdjʊˈleɪʃən] N *Electron (of signal etc)* démodulation *f*

demodulator [diːˈmɒdjʊleɪtər] N *Comput* démodulateur *m*

demographer [dɪˈmɒɡrəfər] N démographe *mf*

demographic [deməʊˈɡræfɪk] ADJ démographique
▸▸ **d. analysis** analyse *f* démographique; **d. profile** profil *m* démographique; **d. segment** segment *m* démographique; **d. segmentation** segmentation *f* démographique; **d. trends** tendances *fpl* démographiques

demographics [deməʊˈɡræfɪks] N statistiques *fpl* démographiques; **the d. show that …** selon les statistiques démographiques …
VOIR GRAMMAIRE A10

demography [dɪˈmɒɡrəfɪ] N démographie *f*

demolish [dɪˈmɒlɪʃ] VT *(building, wall, argument)* démolir; *Fam (cake, meal etc)* dévorer; *Fig* **to d. sb** *(in argument)* démolir qn; *(in competition, fight)* mettre la pâtée à qn

demolition [deməˈlɪʃən] N démolition *f*
▸▸ **d. contractor** démolisseur *m*; *Sport* **d. derby** = course de voitures au cours de laquelle celles-ci sont délibérément détruites; **d. squad** équipe *f* de démolition; **d. work** travail *m* de démolition

demon [ˈdiːmən] N démon *m*, diable *m*; **the d. drink** le démon de l'alcool; *Fig* **that child's**

a little d. cet enfant est un petit démon; *Fig* **he's a d. for work** c'est un monstre de travail; *Fig* **she's a d. for punctuality** elle insiste énormément sur la ponctualité

demonetize [dɪˈmʌnɪtaɪz] VT *Fin (currency)* démonétiser

demoniac [dɪˈməʊnɪæk] ADJ, N démoniaque *mf*

demoniacal [diːməˈnaɪək(ə)l] ADJ démoniaque

demonic [dɪˈmɒnɪk] ADJ *(cruelty, rage)* démoniaque
▸▸ **d. possession** possession *f* diabolique

demonology [diːməˈnɒlədʒɪ] N démonologie *f*

demonstrable [dɪˈmɒnstrəb(ə)l, ˈdemən-] ADJ *(fact)* démontrable; **that is d. nonsense** c'est clairement absurde

demonstrably [dɪˈmɒnstrəblɪ, ˈdemən-] ADV **d. true/false statement** affirmation *f* visiblement *ou* manifestement vraie/fausse; **that's d. false** c'est faux de toute évidence; **that is d. not the case** de toute évidence *ou* manifestement ce n'est pas le cas

demonstrate [ˈdemənstreɪt] VT **1** *(prove) (truth)* démontrer; **that just demonstrates how stupid he is** ça ne fait que démontrer à quel point il est stupide **2** *(show, explain) (machine, alarm system etc)* donner une démonstration pratique du fonctionnement de; *(one's skills, use of sth)* faire une démonstration de; **to d. how sth works** montrer comment qch fonctionne
VI *Pol etc* manifester, faire une manifestation (**against** contre; **for, in favour of** pour, en faveur de)

demonstration [demənˈstreɪʃən] N **1** *(of truth)* démonstration *f* **2** *(of machine, alarm system)* démonstration *f* pratique; *Sch (séance f* de) démonstration; **to give sb a d. of one's skills** faire une démonstration de ses talents à qn; **would you like a d.?** est-ce que vous voulez que je vous fasse une démonstration?; **a d. of affection** une manifestation *ou* un témoignage d'affection; **a d. of power** une démonstration de force **3** *(political etc)* manifestation *f*; **to hold** *or* **stage a d.** manifester
▸▸ **d. car** voiture *f* de démonstration; *Sch* **d. class** *(séance de)* démonstration

> Note that the French word **démonstration** is never used to describe a protest.

demonstrative [dɪˈmɒnstrətɪv] ADJ **1** *(person)* démonstratif **2** *(argument etc)* démonstratif **3** *Gram (adjectif etc)* démonstratif VOIR GRAMMAIRE A30–1; B14–15

demonstrator [ˈdemənstreɪtər] N **1** *(of machine etc)* démonstrateur, -trice; *Sch* **science d.** préparateur, -trice en science **2** *Am (car)* voiture *f* de démonstration **3** *(political etc)* manifestant, -ante

demoralization [dɪmɒrəlaɪˈzeɪʃən] N démoralisation *f*

demoralize [dɪˈmɒrəlaɪz] VT démoraliser

demoralizing [dɪˈmɒrəlaɪzɪŋ] ADJ démoralisant

demote [dɪˈməʊt] VT *(person)* rétrograder; *Mil* **he's been demoted to private** il a été rétrogradé au grade de simple soldat; **she's been demoted to assistant manager** elle a été rétrogradée au poste de directeur-adjoint

demotic [dɪˈmɒtɪk] ADJ *Fml* populaire, du peuple; *Ling (Greek)* démotique

demotion [dɪˈməʊʃən] N rétrogradation *f*

demotivate [diːˈməʊtɪveɪt] VT démotiver

demotivation [diːməʊtɪˈveɪʃən] N démotivation *f*

demur [dɪˈmɜːr] N *Fml* objection *f*; **without d.** sans faire d'objection

vi (**-rr-**) **1** *Fml* soulever des objections (**at, to** contre) **2** *Law* opposer une exception

demure [dɪ'mjʊər] **ADJ** modeste, réservé; *Pej* d'une modestie affectée

demurely [dɪ'mjʊəlɪ] **ADV** d'un air modeste *ou* réservé; *Pej* avec une modestie affectée

demureness [dɪ'mjʊənɪs] **N** modestie *f*, réserve *f*; *Pej* modestie affectée

demurrage [dɪ'mʌrɪdʒ] **N** *Com* surestarie *f*

demystify [diː'mɪstɪfaɪ] **VT** démystifier

demythologize [diːmɪ'θɒlədʒaɪz] **VT** démythifier

den [den] **N 1** *(of wild animal)* tanière *f*, antre *m*; *Fig (of criminals, brigands)* nid *m*, repaire *m*; *Fig* **d. of thieves** repaire de voleurs; **gambling d.** maison *f* de jeu; **d. of iniquity** lieu *m* de débauche *ou* de perdition **2** *esp Am (in home)* petit salon *m* familial
▸▸ *Am* **d. mother** *(in scout group)* cheftaine *f*

denationalization [diːnæʃənəlaɪ'zeɪʃən] **N** dénationalisation *f*

denationalize [diː'næʃənəlaɪz] **VT** dénationaliser

denature [diː'neɪtʃər] **VT** *(product)* dénaturer

dengue ['deŋgɪ] **N** *Med* dengue *f*
▸▸ **d. fever** dengue

denial [dɪ'naɪəl] **N 1** *(of right, request)* refus *m*; **d. of justice** déni *m* de justice **2** *(of truth of sth, guilt)* démenti *m*; **absolute** *or* **flat d.** dénégation *f* absolue *ou* catégorique; **to issue a d.** publier un démenti **3** *Psy* dénégation *f*; **to be in d.** refuser de se rendre à l'évidence **4** *Bible* **Peter's d. of Christ** le reniement de Pierre

denier ['denɪər] **N** *Tex (of hosiery)* denier *m*; **a 30-d. stocking** un bas 30 deniers

denigrate ['denɪgreɪt] **VT** *Lit* dénigrer

denim ['denɪm] **N 1** *(fabric)* (toile *f* de) jean *m*; **d. skirt** jupe *f* en jean **2 denims** *(overalls)* bleus *mpl* (de travail); *(jeans)* jean *m*

denizen ['denɪzən] **N** *Lit, Hum* habitant, -ante, hôte *mf*; **denizens of the deep** hôtes *ou* habitants des profondeurs

Denmark ['denmɑːk] **N** Danemark *m*

denominate [dɪ'nɒmɪneɪt] **VT 1** *Fml (name)* dénommer **2** *Fin* libeller; **denominated in dollars** libellé en dollars

denomination [dɪnɒmɪ'neɪʃən] **N 1** *Rel* culte *m*, confession *f* **2** *Fin* valeur *f*, *(of share, of banknote)* coupure *f*; **in denominations of** en coupures de; **coins of all denominations** pièces *fpl* de toutes valeurs; **(notes of) small denominations** petites coupures **3** *Fml (name)* dénomination *f*

denominational [dɪnɒmɪ'neɪʃən(ə)l] **ADJ** confessionnel

denominator [dɪ'nɒmɪneɪtər] **N** *Math* dénominateur *m*; *also Fig* **lowest common d.** plus petit dénominateur commun; *also Fig* **to have a common d.** avoir un dénominateur commun

denotation [diːnəʊ'teɪʃən] **N** *(indication)* indication *f*, *(meaning)* signification *f*

denote [dɪ'nəʊt] **VT 1** *(indicate)* dénoter, montrer, indiquer (**sth** qch; **that** que) **2** *(mean)* signifier; *Ling* dénoter

denouement [deɪ'nuːmɒn] **N** *(of play, situation)* dénouement *m*

denounce [dɪ'naʊns] **VT 1** *(inform against) (criminal, crime)* dénoncer; **to d. sb to the authorities** signaler qn à la justice; **to d. sb as an impostor** taxer qn d'imposture **2** *(protest about) (abuse, government action, drugtaking etc)* dénoncer, s'élever contre; *(modern art etc)* condamner; **they have been denounced as nothing more than murderers** ils ont été accusés de n'être rien de moins

que des assassins **3** *(declare termination of) (treaty)* dénoncer

dense [dens] **ADJ 1** *Phys (body, metal etc)* dense **2** *(smoke, fog etc)* épais, *f* -aisse; *(crowd)* compact; *(population)* nombreux; *(text, argument)* dense **3** *Fam (stupid)* stupide, bête

densely ['denslɪ] **ADV d. wooded country** pays couvert de forêts épaisses; **d. populated region** région très peuplée; **to be d. packed together** être serrés les uns contre les autres; **d. written** écrit dans un style dense

denseness ['densnɪs] **N 1** *(of fog)* épaisseur *f*, *(of text, writing)* densité *f*; **in spite of the d. of the crowd** bien que la foule fût si compacte **2** *Fam (of person)* stupidité *f*

density ['densɪtɪ] **N 1** *Phys, Chem, Elec, Phot etc* densité *f*; *Tech* masse *f* volumique; *Nucl* **ion/neutron d.** densité ionique/neutronique **2** *(of population, traffic)* densité *f*
▸▸ **d. chart** *(in hotel)* feuille *f* d'occupation journalière

dent [dent] **N** *(in saucepan etc)* bosse *f*, *(in ground)* trou *m*; *(in pillow, cushion)* creux *m*; **there's a d. in the car** la voiture a une bosse; *Fig* **to make a d. in one's fortune** faire une brèche à sa fortune; *Fig* **to make** *or* **put a d. in sb's self-confidence** entamer la confiance en soi *ou* l'assurance de qn; *Fig* **to make** *or* **put a d. in one's savings/budget** faire un trou dans ses économies/son budget
VT bosseler, cabosser; *Fig* **to d. sb's self-confidence** entamer la confiance en soi *ou* l'assurance de qn; **my self-confidence has been dented** mon assurance en a pris un coup

dental ['dent(ə)l] **ADJ 1** *Med* dentaire **2** *Ling* dental, -aux
▸▸ **d. appointment** rendez-vous *m* *inv* chez le dentiste; **d. care** soins *mpl* dentaires; *Ling* **d. consonant** (consonne *f*) dentale *f*; **d. floss** fil *m* dentaire; **d. hygiene** hygiène *f* dentaire; **your d. hygiene is poor** vous avez une mauvaise hygiène dentaire; **d. hygienist** ≃ assistant, -ante de dentiste *(qui s'occupe du détartrage etc)*; **d. nurse** assistant, -ante dentaire; *Am* **d. office** cabinet *m* dentaire; *Am* **d. practice** cabinet dentaire; **d. spa** = cabinet *m* dentaire proposant des soins tels que manucures ou soins de la peau afin de permettre aux patients de se détendre; *Br* **d. surgeon** chirurgien-dentiste *m*, *pl* chirurgiens-dentistes; **d. surgery** cabinet dentaire

dented ['dentɪd] **ADJ** bosselé, cabossé

dentifrice ['dentɪfrɪs] **N** *Old-fashioned* dentifrice *m*

dentine ['dentiːn] **N** dentine *f*

dentist ['dentɪst] **N** dentiste *mf*; **to go to the d.'s** aller chez le dentiste; *Fam* **the d.'s chair** le fauteuil du dentiste

dentistry ['dentɪstrɪ] **N** dentisterie *f*

dentition [den'tɪʃən] **N** dentition *f*

dentures ['dentʃəz] **NPL** dentier *m*, prothèse *f* dentaire; **to wear d.** porter un dentier

Note that the French word **denture** is a false friend and is never a translation for the English word **dentures**. It means **set of teeth**.

denude [dɪ'njuːd] **VT** dénuder, dépouiller; **a landscape denuded of trees** un paysage sans arbres

denunciation [dɪnʌnsɪ'eɪʃən] **N 1** *(of accomplice etc)* dénonciation *f* **2** *(condemnation) (of person, abuse, modern art etc)* condamnation *f* **3** *(of treaty)* dénonciation *f*

Denver ['denvər] **N**
▸▸ *Fam* **D. boot** sabot *m* de Denver

deny [dɪ'naɪ] **VT 1** *(fact, truth)* nier, refuser d'admettre; *(report)* démentir; *(accusation)*

repousser; *(statement)* opposer un démenti à; **the accused denies the charge** l'accusé nie; **to d. having done sth** nier avoir fait qch; **there is no denying the fact** c'est un fait indéniable; **there's no denying that ...** on ne saurait nier que ...; **to d. all knowledge of sth** nier avoir connaissance de qch **2** *(person, one's faith)* renier **3** *(request etc)* refuser; **to d. sb sth** *or* **sth to sb** refuser qch à qn; **to have one's request denied** se voir refuser sa demande; **to be denied access to sth/sb** se voir refuser l'accès à qch/qn; **to d. oneself sth** se priver de qch; **to d. oneself for one's children** se priver pour ses enfants

deodorant [diː'əʊdərənt] **N** *(for body)* déodorant *m*; *(for room)* désodorisant *m*; **d. spray** déodorant/désodorisant en bombe

deodorize [diː'əʊdəraɪz] **VT** désodoriser

deodorizer [diː'əʊdəraɪzə(r)] **N** *(for home)* désodorisant *m*

deontology [diːɒn'tɒlədʒɪ] **N** *Phil* déontologie *f*

deoxidize [diː'ɒksɪdaɪz] **VT** *Chem, Ind* désoxyder

deoxyribonucleic [diː'ɒksɪraɪbəʊnjuː'kleɪɪk] **ADJ** désoxyribonucléique
▸▸ **d. acid** acide *m* désoxyribonucléique

dep *(abbr* **departure/departs)** dép

depart [dɪ'pɑːt] **vi 1** *Fml (leave)* partir; **they departed for Canada from Portsmouth** ils sont partis pour le Canada depuis Portsmouth; **departing from** en partance de; **the train departing from platform four** le train au départ quai numéro quatre **2** *(differ, deviate)* **to d. from** *(version of events)* différer de, s'écarter de; *(custom)* abandonner; *(subject)* sortir de, s'écarter de; *(truth)* manquer à; **to d. from sb's wishes** ne pas respecter la volonté de qn
VT *Lit* **to d. this life** *or* **earth** quitter cette vie *ou* ce monde

departed [dɪ'pɑːtɪd] **ADJ 1** *(glory etc)* passé, évanoui **2** *(dead)* mort, défunt, décédé
N the d. le mort/la morte/les mort(e)s

department [dɪ'pɑːtmənt] **N 1** *(in company, organization)* département *m*, service *m*; *(in shop)* rayon *m*; *Univ* département *m*; **the French d.** *(at school)* la section de français; **personnel/accounts d.** service du personnel/de la comptabilité; *Fig* **that's not (really) my d.** ce n'est pas mon rayon **2** *(of government)* ministère *m* **3** *Geog (in France)* département *m*
▸▸ *Am* **D. of Agriculture** ministère de l'Agriculture; *Br* **D. of Culture, Media and Sport** ministère de la Culture, de la Communication et des Sports; *Am* **D. of Defense** ministère de la Défense; *Am* **D. of Education**, *Br* **D. for Education and Skills** ≃ ministère de l'Éducation nationale; *Am* **D. of Energy** = ministère américain de l'Énergie; *Br* **D. of the Environment, Food and Rural Affairs** ≃ ministère de l'Agriculture et de l'Environnement; *Br* **D. of Health** ministère de la Santé; *Am* **D. of Health and Human Services** ministère de la Santé; *Am Formerly* **D. of Housing and Urban Development** ministère du logement et de la ville; *Am* **D. of the Interior** ≃ ministère de l'Intérieur; *Br* **D. for International Development** ≃ secrétariat *m* d'État à la Coopération; *Am* **D. of Justice** ministère de la Justice; *Am* **D. of Labor** ≃ ministère de l'Emploi et de la Solidarité; *Br* **D. of Public Works** ≃ ministère de l'Équipement; *Br* **D. of Social Security** ≃ ministère des Affaires sociales; *Am* **D. of State** Département d'État, ≃ ministère des Affaires étrangères; **d. store** grand magasin *m*; *Am* **D. of Trade** ministère du Commerce; *Br* **D. of Trade and Industry** ministère du Commerce et de l'Industrie; *Br* **D. of Transport**, *Am* **D. of Transportation** ministère des Transports; *Am* **D.**

of Veterans Affairs ministère des Anciens combattants; *Br* **D. of Work and Pensions** ≃ ministère de l'Emploi et de la Solidarité

departmental [diːpɑːˈtment(ə)l] **ADJ** départemental

▸▸ **d. head** chef *m* de service; *Univ* chef du département; **d. manager** chef de service; **d. meeting** réunion *f* de service

departure [dɪˈpɑːtʃər] **N 1** *(from place) (of person, train etc)* départ *m*; *Aviat* **there's only one d. a day for Montreal** il n'y a qu'un départ par jour pour Montréal; *Fml* **to take one's d.** prendre congé; **her unexpected d. from politics** son départ inattendu de la scène politique **2** *Fig* déviation *f* (**from** de); *(from general rule)* exception *f*, *(from truth)* manquement *m* (**from** à); *(from normal procedure)* dérogation *f* à la procédure habituelle; **this type of holiday is something of a d. for him** ce type de vacances représente un grand changement pour lui; **a d. from his usual habits** une action contraire à ses habitudes; **politics is a new d. for her** la politique constitue un nouveau départ pour elle

▸▸ **departures book** *(in hotel)* registre *m* des départs; **d. date** date *f* de départ; **d. gate** *(in airport)* porte *f* (d'embarquement); **d. list** liste *f* des départs; **d. lounge** salle *f* d'embarquement; **d. quay** quai *m* de départ; **d. tax** taxe *f* de départ; **d. time** heure *f* de départ

depend [dɪˈpend] **VI** dépendre (**on** de); **that depends, it all depends** ça dépend; **that depends entirely on you** cela ne tient qu'à vous; **it depends on the weather** ça dépend du temps; **it depends on how much money I have** ça dépend de combien d'argent j'ai; **depending on whether …** suivant que …; **it depends on whether she accepts** ça dépend si elle accepte

▸ **depend on VT INSEP** *(rely on) (person)* compter sur, faire confiance à; *(car, alarm system, weather etc)* compter sur; **we need somebody who can be depended on to be discreet** il nous faut quelqu'un dont on sait qu'il sera discret; **he can be depended on not to become discouraged** on peut être sûr qu'il ne se découragera pas; *Iron* **you can d. on him to be late** on peut être sûr qu'il arrive en retard; **you can never d. on what he says** on ne peut pas se fier à ce qu'il dit; **you can d. on it** tu peux compter dessus; **to d. on imports from abroad** être tributaire de l'étranger; **to d. financially/emotionally on sb** dépendre de qn financièrement/sur le plan affectif

dependability [dɪpendəˈbɪlɪtɪ] **N** *(of person)* sérieux *m*; *(of information)* véracité *f*; *(of machine)* fiabilité *f*; **I'm still not convinced of his d.** je ne suis pas encore convaincu de son sérieux *ou* qu'on peut compter sur lui

dependable [dɪˈpendəb(ə)l] **ADJ** *(person)* digne de confiance, sur qui l'on peut compter; *(information)* sûr; *(machine)* d'un fonctionnement sûr, fiable; **he is not d.** on ne peut pas compter sur lui; **to be a d. source of income** fournir un revenu régulier

dependance [dɪˈpendəns] **N** *Am* = **dependence**

dependant [dɪˈpendənt] **N** personne *f* à charge

> Attention: ne pas confondre avec l'adjectif **dependent**.

dependence, *Am* **dependance** [dɪˈpendəns] **N 1** *(reliance)* dépendance *f* (**on** de) **2** *(trust)* confiance *f* (**on** en) **3** *Med* (état *m* de) dépendance *f* (**on heroin** (à l'égard) de l'héroïne)

dependency [dɪˈpendənsɪ] **N 1** *esp Am* = **dependence 2** *(territory) (of country)* dépendance *f*

▸▸ **d. culture** = situation *f* d'une société dont les membres ont une mentalité d'assistés

dependent [dɪˈpendənt] **ADJ 1** dépendant (**on** de); *Law* relevant (**on** de); **to be d. on** *(somebody, something)* dépendre de; *(financially) (somebody)* dépendre (financièrement) de; **institution d. on voluntary contributions** institution soutenue par des contributions bénévoles; **two d. children** deux enfants à charge **2** *Med* **to be d. on heroin/drugs** être héroïnomane/toxicomane; **to be d. on insulin** être insulinodépendant **3** *Gram (clause)* subordonné

> Attention: ne pas confondre avec le nom **dependant**.

depict [dɪˈpɪkt] **VT** dépeindre, représenter

depiction [dɪˈpɪkʃən] **N** peinture *f*, description *f*

depilatory [dɪˈpɪlət(ə)rɪ] **ADJ, N** dépilatoire *m*

deplane [diːˈpleɪn] **VI** *Am* descendre d'avion, débarquer

deplete [dɪˈpliːt] **VT** réduire; **stocks are very depleted** les stocks sont très bas

depleted uranium [dɪˈpliːtɪd] **N** *Chem* uranium *m* appauvri

depletion [dɪˈpliːʃən] **N** réduction *f*

deplorable [dɪˈplɔːrəb(ə)l] **ADJ** déplorable, lamentable

deplorably [dɪˈplɔːrəblɪ] **ADV** déplorablement, lamentablement

deplore [dɪˈplɔːr] **VT** déplorer, regretter vivement; **to d. the fact that** déplorer le fait que

deploy [dɪˈplɔɪ] **VT** *(troops, resources)*, *Fig (argument)* déployer; **I think your talents would be better deployed elsewhere** je pense que vos talents seraient mieux utilisés ailleurs

VI se déployer

deployment [dɪˈplɔɪmənt] **N** *Mil, Fig* déploiement *m*

depolarization [diːpəʊlərɪˈzeɪʃən] **N** *Opt, Elec* dépolarisation *f*

depolarize [diːˈpəʊləraɪz] **VT** *Opt, Elec* dépolariser

deponent [dɪˈpəʊnənt] **N 1** *Gram* verbe *m* déponent **2** *Law* témoin *m* déposant

ADJ *Gram (verb)* déponent

depopulate [diːˈpɒpjʊleɪt] **VT** *(country)* dépeupler; **to become depopulated** se dépeupler

depopulation [diːpɒpjʊˈleɪʃən] **N** *(of country)* dépopulation *f*, dépeuplement *m*; **rural d.** dépeuplement des campagnes

deport [dɪˈpɔːt] **VT** *(foreigner)* expulser; *(political prisoner etc)* déporter

deportation [diːpɔːˈteɪʃən] **N** *(of foreigner)* expulsion *f*, *(of political prisoner etc)* déportation *f*

▸▸ **d. order** arrêt *m* d'expulsion

deportee [diːpɔːˈtiː] **N** *(foreigner)* expulsé, -ée; *(political prisoner etc)* déporté, -ée

deportment [dɪˈpɔːtmənt] **N** tenue *f*, maintien *m*

depose [dɪˈpəʊz] **VT 1** *(monarch)* déposer, détrôner; *Fig (champion, head of party)* détrôner, destituer **2** *Law (testify)* attester (**that** que)

VI *Law* faire une déposition

deposit [dɪˈpɒzɪt] **N 1** *Banking* dépôt *m*; **to make a d.** déposer de l'argent; **to make a d. of £500** déposer 500 livres en banque; **bank d.** dépôt bancaire *ou* en banque; **on d.** en dépôt

2 *Com (first payment)* acompte *m*; *(not returnable)* arrhes *fpl*, *(returnable)* caution *f*,

(on bottle) consigne *f*; **to pay** *or* **put down a d. on sth** verser un acompte/des arrhes sur qch; *Br Pol* **to lose one's d.** *(of candidate)* perdre sa caution

3 *(of minerals)* gisement *m*, couche *f*

4 *(material)* dépôt(s) *m(pl)*, précipité *m*; **alluvial deposits** alluvions *fpl*

5 *(coating) (of wine etc)* dépôt *m*; *Tech* apport *m*; **d. of silver** précipité *m* d'argent

VT 1 *(money in bank)* déposer; *(document) (with a bank)* mettre en dépôt *(with* dans); *(with a solicitor etc)* confier (**with** à); *Fin* **to d. as security** nantir, gager; *Fin* **to d. security** déposer une caution

2 *(put down)* déposer, poser (**sth on sth** qch sur qch)

3 *(of liquid) (sediment)* déposer; **the flood waters deposited a layer of mud** les inondations ont laissé un dépôt de boue

▸▸ *Br Banking* **d. account** compte *m* livret, compte de dépôt; *(when notice has to be given before withdrawal)* compte à terme; *Banking* **d. bank** banque *f* de dépôt; *Banking* **d. book** livret *m* ou carnet *m* de dépôt; *Banking* **d. money** monnaie *f* de banque, monnaie scripturale; *Banking* **d. receipt** récépissé *m* de dépôt

deposition[1] [diːpəˈzɪʃən] **N 1** *(of monarch)* déposition *f* **2** *Law* déposition *f*, témoignage *m*

deposition[2] **VT** *Mktg (product)* dépositionner

depositor [dɪˈpɒzɪtər] **N** *Banking* déposant, -ante

depository [dɪˈpɒzɪt(ə)rɪ] **N** dépôt *m*, magasin *m*, entrepôt *m*; **furniture d.** gardemeubles *m inv*

depot [ˈdepəʊ] **N 1** *Mil* dépôt *m*; *Com etc* dépôt *m*, entrepôt *m*; **goods d.** dépôt de marchandises; **supply/ammunition d.** dépôt de ravitaillement/munitions **2** *Am (station)* **(railroad) d.** gare *f* (de chemin de fer); **bus d.** gare routière; **freight d.** gare des marchandises

depravation [deprəˈveɪʃən] **N** dépravation *f*

deprave [dɪˈpreɪv] **VT** dépraver, corrompre

depraved [dɪˈpreɪvd] **ADJ** *(person, taste)* dépravé, corrompu

depravity [dɪˈprævɪtɪ] **N** dépravation *f*, perversion *f*

deprecate [ˈdeprɪkeɪt] **VT** *(action)* désapprouver; **stop deprecating yourself** arrêtez de vous dévaloriser

deprecating [ˈdeprɪkeɪtɪŋ] **ADJ 1** *(disapproving)* désapprobateur, -trice **2** *(apologetic)* modeste

deprecatingly [ˈdeprɪkeɪtɪŋlɪ] **ADV 1** *(disapprovingly)* avec désapprobation **2** *(apologetically)* avec modestie, modestement

deprecatory [ˈdeprɪkeɪtərɪ] **ADJ 1** *(modest) (smile etc)* de modestie; *(remark)* modeste **2** *(disapproving)* désapprobateur, -trice; **to be d. about sth/sb** désapprouver qch/qn

depreciate [dɪˈpriːʃɪeɪt] **VT 1** *Com (value of sth)* déprécier, rabaisser; *Fin (currency)* dévaloriser, déprécier; *Com, Ind (property, equipment etc)* amortir **2** *(denigrate)* dénigrer, déprécier

VI *(of property etc)* se déprécier, diminuer de valeur; *(of prices, shares etc)* baisser; *(of equipment)* se dévaluer, s'avilir; **the pound has depreciated against the dollar** la livre a reculé par rapport au dollar; **the tractor depreciated by £200** la valeur du tracteur a baissé de 200 livres

depreciated [dɪˈpriːʃɪeɪtɪd] **ADJ** *Acct* amorti; *(currency)* déprécié

depreciation [dɪpriːʃɪˈeɪʃən] **N 1** *(of money)*, *Ind (equipment etc)* dépréciation *f*; *Acct (of property, equipment)* amortissement *m*; *Fin (of currency)* dépréciation, dévalorisation f, (amount) moins-value f **2** (denigration) dénigrement m, dépréciation f

▸▸**d. charges** frais mpl d'amortissement; **d. period** période f d'amortissement; Acct **d. rate** taux m d'amortissement; Acct **d. schedule** tableau m ou plan m d'amortissement

depreciatory [dɪ'priːʃɪət(ə)rɪ] ADJ (remark etc) de dénigrement, critique

depredation [deprɪ'deɪʃən] N (usu pl) (of war) déprédation(s) f(pl); (by soldiers, looters etc) pillage m

depress [dɪ'pres] VT **1** (sadden, dishearten) (person) déprimer, décourager **2** Tech (press down) (a)baisser; Aut etc (pedal) appuyer sur **3** (cause to fall) (trade) faire languir; (price of sth) faire baisser

depressant [dɪ'presənt] N Med (drug) calmant m

depressed [dɪ'prest] ADJ **1** (person) déprimé; **to feel d.** être déprimé, Fam avoir le cafard; **the winter makes me feel d.** l'hiver me déprime **2** Com (market) languissant, déprimé; **one of the most d. sectors of the economy** un des secteurs économiques les plus touchés par la crise; **the economy has been in a d. state for nearly three years** l'économie est dans un état de marasme depuis bientôt trois ans; **d. area** région touchée par la crise

depressing [dɪ'presɪŋ] ADJ **1** (gloomy) déprimant; (countryside) triste; **the unemployment figures make for d. reading** les chiffres du chômage sont plutôt déprimants **2** Com **to have a d. effect on the economy** déprimer l'économie

depressingly [dɪ'presɪŋlɪ] ADV d'une manière déprimante

depression [dɪ'preʃən] N **1** (of person) dépression f; Med **state of d.** état m dépressif; Med **to suffer (from) acute d.** être en pleine dépression **2** Com (in business, region of country) crise f; (in industry) crise, marasme m; **economic d.** dépression f économique; Hist **the (Great) D.** la crise de 29 **3** Tech (pressing down) (of sth) abaissement m; Aut (of pedal) enfoncement m; Mil **angle of d.** angle m de dépression **4** Met dépression f **5** (sunken area) (in ground) dépression f, enfoncement m, creux m

depressive [dɪ'presɪv] ADJ **1** Psy (tendencies, person) dépressif **2** Com **to have a d. effect on the economy** déprimer l'économie
N Psy dépressif, -ive

depressor [dɪ'presər] N Med (for tongue) abaisse-langue m inv

depressurize [diː'preʃəraɪz] Aviat VT dépressuriser
VI se dépressuriser

deprivation [deprɪ'veɪʃən] N **1** (hardship) privation f; **to suffer deprivations** souffrir de privations; **emotional d.** carence f affective **2** (removal) (of rights, freedom etc) privation f; (of job, duties) destitution f

deprive [dɪ'praɪv] VT **to d. sb of sth** priver qn de qch, enlever qch à qn; **to d. oneself** se priver; **I won't d. you of the pleasure of telling him about it** je ne te priverai pas du plaisir de le lui dire; **to d. sb of office** déposséder qn de sa charge

deprived [dɪ'praɪvd] ADJ (child) déshérité; **she had a d. childhood** elle a eu une enfance défavorisée

deprogram [dɪ'prəʊgræm] VT déprogrammer

dept N abbr **department**

depth [depθ] N **1** (of river, thought etc) profondeur f; (of love, feelings, passion) profondeur, intensité f; **in d.** en profondeur; (to study sth) à fond; **a study in d. of ...** une étude approfondie ou très poussée de ...; **at a d. of 50 feet** par 50 pieds de fond; **to dive to a d. of 50 feet** descendre ou plonger à 50 pieds de fond; **I hadn't realised the d. of her feelings** je ne m'étais pas rendu compte de la profondeur de ses sentiments; also Fig **to go** or **get out of one's d.** perdre pied; **to be out of one's d.** (of swimmer) ne plus avoir pied; Fig avoir perdu pied, ne plus être sur son terrain; **I think she's a bit out of her d. in the new job** je crois qu'elle est un peu dépassée dans son nouveau travail; Tech **d. of cut** (of machine tool) profondeur de passe ou de coupe; Opt **d. of field/focus** profondeur de champ/de foyer
2 (of sound) gravité f, (of colour) vigueur f, intensité f
3 (of forest etc) fond m; (of night) milieu m; **in the depths of winter** en plein hiver; **the depths** (of ocean etc) les profondeurs fpl; (of ignorance etc) les ténèbres fpl; **in the depths of despair** dans le plus profond désespoir; **the lowest depths** (of shame etc) le dernier degré
4 Tech (of piston etc) hauteur f, (of layer) épaisseur f
5 Mktg (of product, range) profondeur f
6 Typ (of text) encombrement m
▸▸ Naut **d. charge** grenade f sous-marine; Tech **d. finder** sondeur m; Aut **d. indicator** (for tyres) témoin m indicateur d'usure; Mktg **d. interview** (in market research) entretien m en profondeur

deputation [depjʊ'teɪʃən] N **1** (representatives) députation f **2** (action) (of sb) députation f, délégation f

depute¹ [dɪ'pjuːt] VT **1** (person) députer, déléguer (**to do sth** pour faire qch) **2** (powers) déléguer (**to** à)

depute² [depjuːt] N Scot = **deputy**

deputize ['depjʊtaɪz] VI **to d. for sb** remplacer qn, faire l'intérim de qn, suppléer qn

deputy ['depjʊtɪ] N (second in command) adjoint, -ointe; (temporary replacement) remplaçant, -ante; (political representative) député m; **to act as d. for sb** suppléer ou remplacer qn
▸▸ **d. director** directeur m adjoint; Journ **d. editor** rédacteur m en chef adjoint; **d. governor** sous-gouverneur m; Sch **d. head** directeur adjoint; **d. judge** juge m suppléant; Pol **D. Leader** (of political party) adjoint, -ointe du chef; **d. manager** directeur adjoint; **d. managing director** directeur général adjoint; **d. mayor** adjoint, -ointe au maire; Can Admin **D. Minister** Sous-Ministre m; Pol **D. Prime Minister** vice-Premier-Ministre m; Parl **D. Speaker** = adjoint m du président de l'Assemblée

DEQ [diːiːˈkjuː] Com (abbr **delivered ex quay**) DEQ

derail [dɪ'reɪl] VT (train) faire dérailler; Fig (project, negotiations) faire avorter; **to be derailed** (train) dérailler; Fig avorter; **the discussions were derailed by their insistence on ...** les pourparlers ont avorté parce qu'ils ont insisté sur ...
VI dérailler

derailment [dɪ'reɪlmənt] N (of train) déraillement m; Fig (of plans, negotiations etc) échec m; **in spite of the d. of talks by their insistence on ...** bien que les pourparlers aient avorté suite à leur insistance sur ...

derange [dɪ'reɪndʒ] VT (person) déranger; **she has been quite deranged by the experience** cette expérience l'a profondément dérangée

deranged [dɪ'reɪndʒd] ADJ dérangé; **he** or **his mind is d.** il est dérangé, c'est un esprit dérangé

derangement [dɪ'reɪndʒmənt] N Med aliénation f mentale

Derby N **1** ['dɑːbɪ] Br Horseracing **the D.** le derby d'Epsom; **donkey D.** course f d'ânes; Ftbl **local d.** derby **2** ['dɜːbɪ] Am **d.** (hat) chapeau m melon

deregulate [diːˈregjʊleɪt] VT Com (industry, air transport, bus services) déréglementer; (prices) libérer

deregulation [diːregjʊˈleɪʃən] N Com (of industry, air transport, bus services) déréglementation f, (of prices) libération f; **d. of trade** libération f des échanges commerciaux

derelict ['derəlɪkt] ADJ **1** (car) abandonné; (house) abandonné, (tombé) en ruines **2** Fml **to be d. (in one's duty)** être négligent de son devoir
N (person) épave f humaine

dereliction [derɪ'lɪkʃən] N **1 d. of duty** manquement m au devoir **2** (abandonment) abandon m

derestricted [diːrɪ'strɪktɪd] ADJ (road) sans limitation de vitesse

derestriction sign [diːrɪ'strɪkʃən] N Aut fin f de limitation de vitesse

deride [dɪ'raɪd] VT (person) se moquer de, railler; (something) tourner en dérision

Note that the French verb **dérider** is a false friend and is never a translation for the English verb **to deride**.

derision [dɪ'rɪʒən] N dérision f, **object of d.** objet m de dérision

derisive [dɪ'raɪsɪv] ADJ moqueur, -euse

derisively [dɪ'raɪsɪvlɪ] ADV (to look at) d'un air moqueur ou de dérision; (to say) d'un ton de dérision

derisory [dɪ'raɪsərɪ] ADJ **1** (offer) dérisoire **2** = **derisive**

derivation [derɪ'veɪʃən] N **1** dérivation f, **d. of a word from Latin** dérivation d'un mot du latin; **what is the d. of ...?** quelle est l'origine de ...? **2** Math (of function) dérivation f

derivative [dɪ'rɪvətɪv] ADJ Gram (word) dérivé; Pej **his work is very d.** (of author) il n'a pas encore trouvé son style propre, il emprunte beaucoup aux autres; **I find his paintings rather d.** je trouve que ses peintures ne sont pas très originales
N Gram, Chem, Ind dérivé m; Math dérivée f, St Exch produit m dérivé; **petroleum d.** dérivé du pétrole; **to be a d. of sth** être un dérivé de qch
▸▸ St Exch **d. market** marché m à terme des instruments financiers

derive [dɪ'raɪv] VT (origin, income, profit) tirer (**from** de); (pleasure) prendre (**from** à); (satisfaction) trouver, tirer; (ideas) trouver, puiser; **to be derived from** dériver de, (pro)venir de; **income derived from an investment** revenu provenant d'un placement; Chem **to d. one compound from another** dériver un composé d'un autre; **word derived from Latin** mot qui vient du latin; Mktg **derived demand** demande f dérivée
▸ **derive from** VT INSEP dériver de, (pro)venir de

dermatitis [dɜːmə'taɪtɪs] N dermite f, dermatite f

dermatologist [dɜːmə'tɒlədʒɪst] N dermatologue mf, dermatologiste mf

dermatology [dɜːmə'tɒlədʒɪ] N dermatologie f

derogate ['derəgeɪt] VI Fml déroger (**from** à)

derogation [derə'geɪʃən] N Fml **1** dérogation f (**of a law** à une loi) **2 d. from a right** atteinte f portée à un droit

derogatory [dɪ'rɒgət(ə)rɪ] ADJ (disrespectful) (meaning of word) péjoratif; **d. remark** remarque f désobligeante; **to be d. to sb** se montrer désobligeant envers qn

derrick ['derɪk] N **1** *Petr* derrick *m*, tour *f* de forage **2** *Naut (crane)* mât *m* de charge

derring-do ['derɪŋ'duː] N *Arch* bravoure *f*; **deeds of d.** hauts faits *mpl*

derv [dɜːv] N *Br Aut* gazole *m*

dervish ['dɜːvɪʃ] N derviche *m*; **whirling** or **dancing d.** derviche tourneur

DES [diːiːˈes] Com (*abbr* **delivered ex ship**) DES

desalinate [diːˈsælɪneɪt] VT dessaler

desalination [diːsælɪˈneɪʃən] N *(of sea-water)* dessalement *m*, dessalaison *f*
➤➤ **d. plant** usine *f* de dessalement

descale [diːˈskeɪl] VT *(kettle etc)* détartrer

descant ['deskænt] N *Mus* déchant *m*

descend [dɪˈsend] VI descendre; *(of rain)* tomber; **as darkness descended** pendant que l'obscurité descendait; **a feeling of sadness descended upon him** un sentiment de tristesse s'empara de lui; **an air of gloom descended on the whole house** un sentiment de tristesse envahit la maison; **to d. on** *(attack) (group of people)* s'abattre *ou* tomber sur; *(village, town)* faire une descente sur; *Fig* **to d. on sb** *(intrude on) (without warning)* arriver chez qn à l'improviste; *(be unwelcome)* s'imposer chez qn; **to d. to sb's level/to doing sth** s'abaisser au niveau de qn/(jusqu')à faire qch; **to d.** or **be descended from sb** descendre de qn; **to d. from sb to sb** *(of property)* passer de qn à qn
VT *(hill, stairs)* descendre

descendant [dɪˈsendənt] N descendant, -ante

descender [dɪˈsendər] N *Typ (of character)* descendante *f*, jambage *m*

descending [dɪˈsendɪŋ] N **1** *(scale etc)* descendant; *Math (progression)* décroissant; **in d. order** en ordre décroissant **2** *(movement)* de descente
➤➤ *Comput* **d. sort** tri *m* en ordre décroissant

descent [dɪˈsent] N **1** *(of mountaineer, plane etc)* descente *f* **2** *(path, road etc)* descente *f*, pente *f* **3** *(origins)* descendance *f*; **to trace one's d. back to ...** faire remonter sa famille à ...; **to be of Norman d.** descendre des Normands **4** *Fig (attack, intrusion)* irruption *f* (**on** dans, sur) **5** *Law (of property)* transmission *f* par droit de succession *ou* par héritage

descramble [diːˈskræmb(ə)l] VT *Comput (message)* déchiffrer

descrambler [diːˈskræmblər] N *(for telephone)* déchiffreur *m*; *TV* désembrouilleur *m*

describe [dɪsˈkraɪb] VT **1** *(somebody, something)* décrire; *(person wanted by police)* donner le signalement de; *Com (goods etc)* désigner; **can you d. the man?** pouvez-vous décrire cet homme?; **she described him as being tall and ...** d'après sa description, il était grand et ...; **the book describes how they escaped** le livre décrit la façon dont ils se sont évadés; **to d. sb/sth as stupid/as intelligent** qualifier qn/qch de stupide/d'intelligent; *Pej* **to d. oneself as an actor** se présenter comme acteur, se dire acteur **2** *(draw) (circle, line)* décrire; *(triangle)* tracer

description [dɪsˈkrɪpʃən] N **1** description *f*; *(for police purposes, on passport)* signalement *m*; *Com (of goods)* désignation *f*; **to be beyond d.** être indescriptible; **to give a d. of sb/sth** décrire qn/qch; **to answer (to)** or **fit the d.** répondre au signalement **2** *(sort, kind)* sorte *f*, espèce *f*; **people of this d.** les gens *mpl* de cette espèce; **people of all descriptions** les gens de toutes sortes

descriptive [dɪsˈkrɪptɪv] ADJ descriptif

descriptor [dɪˈskrɪptər] N *Comput* descripteur *m*

descry [dɪsˈkraɪ] VT *Lit* discerner

desecrate ['desɪkreɪt] VT profaner, souiller

desecration [desɪˈkreɪʃən] N profanation *f*

desegregate [diːˈsegrɪgeɪt] VT *(country, school etc)* = mettre fin à la ségrégation raciale dans; **desegregated school** = école où la ségrégation raciale n'est plus pratiquée

desegregation [diːsegrɪˈgeɪʃən] N déségrégation *f*

deselect [diːsɪˈlekt] VT **1** *Br Pol* ne pas resélectionner *(comme candidat à une élection)* **2** *Comput* désactiver

deselection [diːsɪˈlekʃən] N *Br Pol* = fait *m* de ne pas sélectionner *(comme candidat à une élection)*

desensitize [diːˈsensɪtaɪz] VT *Phot, Med etc* désensibiliser

desert[1] ['dezət] N désert *m*; **the Sahara D.** le désert du Sahara
ADJ *(region, flora etc)* désertique
➤➤ **d. boots** = chaussures *fpl* en daim à lacets; **d. island** île *f* déserte; **d. rat** *Zool* gerboise *f*; *Br Mil Fam* = soldat *m* britannique combattant en Afrique du Nord *(pendant la Seconde Guerre mondiale)*

desert[2] [dɪˈzɜːt] VT *(place)* déserter, quitter; *(person)* abandonner; *Mil* **to d. one's post** déserter *ou* abandonner son poste; *Pol* **to d. one's party** tourner casaque; **to d. sb** *(of courage)* abandonner qn; **her sense of humour has deserted her** elle a perdu son sens de l'humour
VI *Mil* déserter; **to d. from the army** déserter l'armée; **to d. to the enemy** passer à l'ennemi

deserted [dɪˈzɜːtɪd] ADJ *(person)* abandonné; *(place)* désert; **the streets were d.** les rues étaient désertes

deserter [dɪˈzɜːtər] N *Mil* déserteur *m*; **to be shot as a d.** être fusillé pour désertion

desertification [dɪzɜːtɪfɪˈkeɪʃən] N *(of land)* désertification *f*

desertion [dɪˈzɜːʃən] N **1** *(of sb)* abandon *m*, délaissement *m*; *Law* abandon du domicile conjugal; **he divorced her for d.** il a demandé le divorce parce qu'elle avait abandonné le domicile conjugal **2** *Mil* désertion *f*

deserts [dɪˈzɜːts] NPL mérites *mpl*, dû *m*; **he has got his (just) d.** il n'a que ce qu'il mérite

deserve [dɪˈzɜːv] VT *(something)* mériter; *(praise)* être digne de; **the idea deserves serious consideration** cette idée mérite qu'on y réfléchisse sérieusement; **she thoroughly deserves it!** elle ne l'a pas volé!; **she deserves better** elle mérite mieux que ça; **he deserves to be punished** il mérite qu'on le punisse; **he deserved to win (and did)** il méritait de gagner; *(but did not)* il aurait mérité de gagner

deserved [dɪˈzɜːvd] ADJ *(bien)* mérité

deservedly [dɪˈzɜːvɪdlɪ] ADV justement, à juste titre

deserving [dɪˈzɜːvɪŋ] ADJ *(person)* méritant, de mérite; *(action, cause)* méritoire; *Old-fashioned, Br Hum* **the d. poor** les pauvres méritants; **to be d. of** *(sympathy, recognition)* mériter; *(praise, respect)* être digne de

desiccate ['desɪkeɪt] VT dessécher; **desiccated coconut** noix *f* de coco déshydratée

desiderata [dɪzɪdəˈrɑːtə] NPL *Lit* desiderata *mpl*

design [dɪˈzaɪn] N **1** *(intention)* dessein *m*, intention *f*; **by d.** à dessein, volontairement; **to have designs on sb/sth** avoir des desseins *ou* visées sur qn/qch
2 *(pattern) (on sweater, carpet etc)* motif *m*, dessin *m*

3 *(plan) (of novel etc)* plan *m*; *(for painting etc)* grandes lignes *fpl*, ébauche *f*; *Ind (for machine)* étude *f*, avant-projet *m*, *pl* avant-projets; *(of car, flat, house etc)* design *m*; **to study d.** étudier le design; **the sofa was made to** or **is of her own d.** le canapé a été fabriqué sur mesure pour elle; **industrial d.** esthétique *f* industrielle

4 *(arrangement of parts) (in machine etc)* dessin *m*; **machine of faulty d.** machine de construction défectueuse; *Com* **our latest d.** notre dernier modèle
VT **1** *(intend)* destiner (**for** à); **machine designed for a special purpose** machine conçue pour un but spécial; **a speech designed to inspire confidence** un discours fait pour inspirer la confiance
2 *(project)* préparer
3 *(by drawing etc) (building, plane, kitchen etc)* concevoir; *(dress, hat etc)* créer; *(syllabus etc)* mettre au point
➤➤ **d. centre** centre *m* d'exposition (de modèles); **d. department** service *m* d'études; **d. engineer** ingénieur *m* d'études; **d. office** bureau *m* d'études; **d. stage** phase *f* de conception; **d. team** équipe *f* des concepteurs

designate[1] ['dezɪgnət] ADJ désigné

designate[2] ['dezɪgneɪt] VT *(person)* désigner, nommer (**to an office** à une fonction); *(funds)* destiner; **to d. sb as one's successor** désigner qn comme son successeur; **the town is a designated special development area** la ville a été désignée *ou* classée zone de développement; **this area has been designated a no-smoking zone** cette zone est destinée aux non-fumeurs; *Aviat* **designated carrier** = compagnie *f* aérienne désignée dans un accord bilatéral pour assurer les liaisons entre deux pays

designation [dezɪgˈneɪʃən] N **1** *(of successor)* désignation *f*, nomination *f*; *(of funds)* désignation; **d. to a post** nomination à un emploi; **because of the d. of this building as a no-smoking zone** parce que le bâtiment est décrété zone non-fumeur **2** *(title, name)* désignation *f*, nom *m*

designedly [dɪˈzaɪnɪdlɪ] ADV à dessein, exprès

designer [dɪˈzaɪnər] N **1** *(of project)* auteur *m*, inventeur, -trice **2** *Art, Ind* dessinateur, -trice; *(of clothes)* styliste *mf*, créateur, -trice; *(of books, magazines)* maquettiste *mf*; *Theat, Cin* décorateur, -trice; **d. jeans/bed-linen/jewellery** jean *m*/literie *f*/bijoux *mpl* de marque;
➤➤ **d. drugs** drogues *fpl* de synthèse; **d. goods** produits *mpl* de marque; **d. label** griffe *f* de grande marque; *Hum* **d. stubble** barbe *f* de deux jours *(faisant partie d'un look étudié, faussement négligé)*

designing [dɪˈzaɪnɪŋ] ADJ *Pej (scheming)* intrigant

desirability [dɪzaɪərəˈbɪlɪtɪ] N **1** caractère *m* désirable *ou* souhaitable; **she referred to the d. of change/improvement** elle a fait référence au fait que des changements/améliorations étaient désirables *ou* souhaitables **2** *(sexual)* attrait *m*

desirable [dɪˈzaɪərəb(ə)l] ADJ **1** *(worth having)* souhaitable; *(change, improvement)* désirable; **a knowledge of French is d.** *(in job advert)* connaissance du français souhaitée **2** *(sexually)* attrayant, désirable
➤➤ *Com* **d. property** *(house)* belle maison *f*; *(flat)* bel appartement *m*

desire [dɪˈzaɪər] N **1** désir *m*, souhait *m* (**for** de); **to have a d. for sth** désirer qch; **to have one's heart's d.** obtenir ce que l'on désire le plus (au monde); **to have a d. to do sth** avoir le désir *ou* avoir envie de faire qch; **to express the** or **a d.** exprimer le désir (**that** que; **to do** de faire); **I feel no d. to ...** je n'ai aucune envie de … **2** *(sexual)* désir *m*

VT 1 *(something)* désirer, avoir envie de; **to d. to do sth** désirer faire qch; **what he desired most was to …** ce qu'il désirait le plus au monde, c'était de …; **it is to be desired that …** il est souhaitable que … + *subj*; **it leaves much** *or* **a lot to be desired** cela laisse beaucoup à désirer; **it leaves nothing to be desired** cela ne laisse rien à redire; *Lit* **to d. sth of sb** *(request)* demander qch à qn; *(want)* désirer qch de qn; **to d. sb to do sth** *(make request)* prier qn de faire qch; **it was clear that she desired him to leave** il était clair qu'elle voulait qu'il parte; **I d. nothing of you but your friendship** je ne désire rien d'autre de vous que votre amitié **2** *(sexually)* désirer

desirous [dɪˈzaɪərəs] **ADJ** *Fml* désireux (**of** de)

desist [dɪˈzɪst] **VI** *Lit* cesser (**from doing** de faire)

desk [desk] **N 1** *(in office, of teacher)* bureau *m*; *(for writing at)* secrétaire *m*; *(pupil's)* pupitre *m*; **to have a d. job** avoir un travail de bureau; **I couldn't stand being stuck behind a d. all day** je ne pourrais pas supporter de rester assis à un bureau toute la journée; **reading d.** pupitre; *Rel* lutrin *m*; *Comput etc* **control d.** pupitre de commande **2** *(in shop)* caisse *f*; *(in hotel)* réception *f*, **please leave your keys at the d.** *(in hotel)* prière de laisser les clefs à la réception; **pay at the d.** *(in shop)* payez à la caisse **3** *Journ* *(office)* **the news/sports d.** le service des informations/ des sports; *Br* **Latin America d.** direction *f* des affaires latino-américaines
▸▸ *Am* **d. clerk** réceptionniste *mf*, **d. copy** *(of book)* livre *m* spécimen; **d. diary** agenda *m* de bureau; *Journ* **d. editor** rédacteur, -trice; **d. lamp, d. light** lampe *f* de bureau; **d. microphone** micro *m* de table; **d. pad** bloc *m* de bureau; **d. research** recherche *f* documentaire

deskill [diːˈskɪl] **VT** *(process, job)* automatiser; *(workforce)* déqualifier

deskman [ˈdeskmæn] **N** *Journ* deskman *m*

desktop [ˈdesktɒp] **N** *Comput* *(screen area)* bureau *m*
▸▸ **d. calculator** calculatrice *f*, **d. computer** ordinateur *m* de bureau *ou* de table; *Comput* **d. model** modèle *m* de table; *Comput* **d. publishing** publication *f* assistée par ordinateur, microédition *f*, *Can* éditique *f*, *Comput* **d. publishing package** logiciel *m* de mise en page

desolate¹ [ˈdesələt] **ADJ 1** *(house)* abandonné; *(place)* désert, vide; *(future, prospect)* sombre **2** *(person, look)* affligé; *(cry)* de désolation

desolate² [ˈdesəleɪt] **VT 1** *(region etc)* *(of invaders, natural catastrophe)* ravager; *(of epidemic)* ravager, dépeupler; *(of recession, unemployment)* dévaster **2** *(person)* accabler, affliger

desolately [ˈdesələtlɪ] **ADV** *(to say)* d'un ton désolé; *(to look at)* d'un air désolé

desolation [desəˈleɪʃən] **N 1** *(of defeated country etc)* désolation *f*, dévastation *f* **2** *(of landscape etc)* désolation *f* **3** *(of person)* désolation *f*, chagrin *m*

despair [dɪˈspeər] **N** désespoir *m*; … **she said in d.** …, dit-elle, désespérée; **to be in d.** être au désespoir; **to be in d. over** *or* **about sth** être désespéré par qch; **in d., she took the children and left** désespérée *ou* par désespoir, elle prit les enfants et partit; **to do sth out of d.** faire qch par désespoir; **to drive sb to d.** réduire qn au désespoir, désespérer qn; **child who is the d. of his parents** enfant qui fait le désespoir de ses parents
VI (se) désespérer, perdre espoir; **I d. of you** tu me désespères; **don't d.** ne désespère

pas; **to d. of doing sth** désespérer de faire qch; **I d. of her ever speaking French well** je désespère de la voir enfin parler français correctement; *Fml* **they d. of his life** ils craignent pour sa vie

despairing [dɪˈspeərɪŋ] **ADJ** désespéré

despairingly [dɪˈspeərɪŋlɪ] **ADV** désespérément, avec désespoir

despatch [dɪˈspætʃ] **N, VT** = **dispatch**

desperado [despəˈrɑːdəʊ] **N** desperado *m*, hors-la-loi *m*

desperate [ˈdesp(ə)rət] **ADJ 1** *(very serious)* *(condition)* désespéré; **they are in d. need of food** ils ont désespérément besoin de nourriture **2** *(characterized by despair)* *(struggle, remedy, attempt)* désespéré; *(resistance, fight, defence)* acharné; **refugees d. to save their children besieged the consulate** tenant désespérément à sauver leurs enfants, les réfugiés assiégèrent le consulat; **a d. man** un désespéré; **to do something d.** faire un malheur; **she made a d. attempt to save him** elle a tenté désespérément de lui sauver la vie; **to be d. for money/a job** avoir un besoin désespéré d'argent/de travail; **I'm d., it's d.** c'est urgent; *Fam* **I'm d. for a cup of tea** je meurs d'envie de boire une tasse de thé

desperately [ˈdesp(ə)rətlɪ] **ADV 1** *(with despair)* *(to fight, plead etc)* désespérément **2** *(extremely)* extrêmement; *(in love)* éperdument; **to be in love with sb** aimer qn à la folie; **d. ill** gravement malade; **to be d. sorry** être navré

desperation [despəˈreɪʃən] **N** désespoir *m*; **to drive sb to d.** pousser qn à bout, réduire qn au désespoir; **in d.** en désespoir de cause; **out of d.** par désespoir; **an act of d.** un acte de désespoir

despicable [dɪˈspɪkəb(ə)l] **ADJ** méprisable

despicably [dɪˈspɪkəblɪ] **ADV** bassement

despise [dɪˈspaɪz] **VT** *(person, attitude, cowardice etc)* mépriser; *(offer, proposal)* dédaigner; **these things are not to be despised** cela n'est pas à dédaigner

despite [dɪˈspaɪt] **PREP** en dépit de, malgré; **d. what she says** quoi qu'elle dise; **I did it d. myself** je l'ai fait malgré moi

despoil [dɪˈspɔɪl] **VT** *Fml* dépouiller, piller, spolier

despondency [dɪˈspɒndənsɪ] **N** découragement *m*, abattement *m*

despondent [dɪˈspɒndənt] **ADJ** découragé, abattu; **to become d.** se laisser abattre; **try not to be too d. about losing** ne te laisse pas trop abattre *ou* décourager par cette défaite

despondently [dɪˈspɒndəntlɪ] **ADV** d'un air découragé *ou* abattu; *(to say)* d'un ton découragé *ou* abattu

despot [ˈdespɒt] **N** *also Fig* despote *m*

despotic [dɪˈspɒtɪk] **ADJ** *also Fig* despotique

despotically [dɪˈspɒtɪklɪ] **ADV** *also Fig* despotiquement

despotism [ˈdespətɪz(ə)m] **N** despotisme *m*

des res [ˈdezˈrez] **N** *Fam* *(house)* jolie petite maison *f*, *(flat)* joli petit appartement *m*

dessert [dɪˈzɜːt] **N** dessert *m*; **what did you have for d.?** qu'est-ce que tu as eu comme dessert?
▸▸ **d. apple** pomme *f* à couteau; **d. knife** couteau *m* à dessert; **d. plate** assiette *f* à dessert; **d. spoon** cuillère *f* à dessert; **d. trolley** chariot *m* de desserts; **d. wine** vin *m* doux

dessertspoon [dɪˈzɜːtspuːn] **N** cuillère *f* à

destabilization [diːsteɪbəlaɪˈzeɪʃən] **N** *(of government, economy)* déstabilisation *f*

destabilize [diːˈsteɪbəlaɪz] **VT** *(government, economy)* déstabiliser

destination [destɪˈneɪʃən] **N** destination *f*, **to reach one's d.** arriver à sa destination
▸▸ *Comput* **d. disk** *(hard disk)* disque *m*; *(floppy disk)* disquette *f* cible; *Comput* **d. drive** lecteur *m* de destination; **d. file** fichier *m* de destination; *Mktg* **d. purchase** achat *m* prévu

destine [ˈdestɪn] **VT** destiner (**for** à; **to a calling** à une carrière)

destined [ˈdestɪnd] **ADJ 1** *(meant)* destiné; **he was d. for the Church** il était destiné à l'église; **d. to do sth** destiné à faire qch; **she is d. to be successful** elle est destinée au succès; **he was d. never to see her again** il ne devait plus la revoir; **the marriage wasn't d. to last** leur mariage ne devait pas durer **2** *(of plane etc)* **d. for** à destination de

destiny [ˈdestɪnɪ] **N** destin *m*, sort *m*; **such was his d.** tel fut son destin

destitute [ˈdestɪtjuːt] **ADJ 1** *(needy)* indigent, sans ressources; **to be utterly d.** être dans la misère **2** *Fml* *(lacking)* dépourvu, dénué (**of** de)
NPL the d. les indigents *mpl*

destitution [destɪˈtjuːʃən] **N** *(extreme poverty)* indigence *f*, misère *f*

destock [ˈdiːˈstɒk] **VT** *(goods)* déstocker

destocking [ˈdiːˈstɒkɪŋ] **N** déstockage *m*

destroy [dɪˈstrɔɪ] **VT 1** *(demolish, wreck)* *(building, marriage, character of a place, letter etc)* détruire; *(sb's hopes, happiness, chances of doing sth)* anéantir; *(faith in sb)* détruire, anéantir; *(life, career)* gâcher; *(theory)* démentir; *(of failure, guilt etc)* *(person)* détruire, ravager; **to d. one's health** se détruire la santé; **to d. oneself with guilt** être ravagé par un sentiment de culpabilité **2** *(kill)* *(animal)* tuer, abattre; *(dog)* piquer

destroyer [dɪˈstrɔɪər] **N 1** *Naut* contre-torpilleur *m*, destroyer *m* **2** *(person or event causing destruction)* destructeur, -trice

destruct [dɪˈstrʌkt] **VI** s'autodétruire; **d. button/mechanism** bouton *m*/mécanisme *m* de destruction

destructible [dɪˈstrʌktɪb(ə)l] **ADJ** destructible

destruction [dɪˈstrʌkʃən] **N 1** *(of building)* destruction *f*, anéantissement *m*; *(of hopes, happiness, chances)* anéantissement **2** *(damage)* ravages *mpl*; **the d. caused by the fire/storm** les ravages du feu/de la tempête; **the army left a trail of d. in its wake** l'armée a tout détruit sur son passage; **the trail of d. left by soldiers on exercise** les dommages laissés par les soldats en exercice

destructive [dɪˈstrʌktɪv] **ADJ** destructeur, -trice; **d. child** enfant qui détruit tout
▸▸ **d. criticism** critique *f* négative *ou* non constructive; *Comput* **d. read** lecture *f* destructive

destructively [dɪˈstrʌktɪvlɪ] **ADV** d'une manière destructrice

destructiveness [dɪˈstrʌktɪvnɪs] **N** *(of explosive etc)* effet *m* destructeur *ou* destructif, pouvoir *m* destructeur *ou* destructif; *(of child etc)* penchant *m* à détruire, tendance *f* destructrice

desuetude [dɪˈsjuːɪtjuːd] **N** *Lit* désuétude *f*, **to fall into d.** tomber en désuétude

desultorily [ˈdesəltrɪlɪ] **ADV** *(to converse)* d'une manière décousue

desultory [ˈdesəlt(ə)rɪ] **ADJ** *(conversation)* décousu, sans suite; *(attempt)* peu convaincant; *(manner)* désinvolte

detach [dɪˈtætʃ] **VT 1** détacher; *(carriages)* dételer; *(trailer)* décrocher; *(stamp etc)* décoller; **to d. sth from sth** détacher *ou* séparer qch de qch; **she managed to d. herself**

from the rest of the group elle a réussi à s'éloigner du reste du groupe; **it took me a quarter of an hour to d. myself from him** ça m'a pris un quart d'heure pour me débarrasser de lui; **if you can bear to d. yourself from her** si tu pouvais t'arracher à elle **2** *Mil, Naut (troops, ship etc)* détacher **VI** *(of handle etc)* se détacher

detachable [dɪˈtætʃəb(ə)l] **ADJ** amovible

detached [dɪˈtætʃt] **ADJ 1** *(separate)* détaché, séparé (**from** de); **to become d.** *(of stamp), Med (retina)* se décoller; *(of price tag, carriage)* se détacher; *(of trailer)* se décrocher; **to become d. from the rest of the group** se détacher accidentellement du reste du groupe **2** *Mil (officer)* en affectation spéciale **3** *(objective) (view, person)* objectif; *(disinterested) (person)* désintéressé; *(manner)* désinvolte; *(air)* détaché, indifférent; **you have to be d. in this job** il faut savoir garder ses distances dans ce travail
▸▸ *Br* **d. house** maison *f* individuelle, pavillon *m*; *Med* **d. retina** rétine *f* décollée

detachment [dɪˈtætʃmənt] **N 1** *(separation)* action *f* de détacher, séparation *f* (**from** de); *(of carriages)* dételage *m*; *(of stamp), Med (of retina)* décollement *m* **2** *Mil* détachement *m*; **on d.** détaché **3** *(objectivity, lack of involvement)* distance *f*, détachement *m* (**from** envers); *(lack of interest)* désintérêt *m*; *(of priest) (from worldly matters)* détachement (**from** envers); **I admire your d.** j'admire ton détachement; **with an air of d.** avec un air distancié *ou* détaché

detail [ˈdiːteɪl] **N 1** détail *m*; **down to the last d.** jusqu'au moindre détail; **I'll remember every single d. of this day** je me souviendrai de cette journée dans les moindres détails; **the d. of the carving** le détail *ou* les détails de la sculpture; **to pay attention to d.** faire attention aux détails; **to go** *or* **enter into d.** *or* **(the) details** entrer dans *ou* donner tous les détails; **in d.** en détail; **in greater d.** plus en détail; **in every d.** dans le moindre détail; **in the fullest d.** dans le plus grand détail; **points** *or* **questions of d.** questions de détail; **minor details** petits détails (sans importance); **that's just a minor d.** ça n'a pas d'importance; **I can't give you any details** je ne peux vous donner aucune précision; **I'll send you the details of the property** je vous enverrai les informations concernant la propriété; **for further details please contact ...** pour plus de renseignements, veuillez contacter ...; **let me take down your details** laissez-moi vos coordonnées
2 *Mil (duty)* extrait *m* de l'ordre du jour; **details** l'ordre *m* du jour
3 *Mil (group of soldiers)* détachement *m*
VT 1 *(describe)* exposer en détail
2 *Mil etc* **to d. sb for a duty** désigner qn pour un service, affecter qn à un service
▸▸ *Cin, TV* **d. shot** très gros plan *m*

detailed [ˈdiːteɪld] **ADJ** *(description)* détaillé; *(account)* détaillé, circonstancié; *(work)* minutieux; **to give a d. account of sth** raconter qch en détail

detailing [ˈdiːteɪlɪŋ] **N** *Art etc (details)* détail *m*

detain [dɪˈteɪn] **VT** *(person) (in prison)* détenir; *(in hospital)* garder; *(hold back)* retenir, arrêter; *(prevent from leaving)* empêcher de partir; *Sch (pupil)* consigner; **this question need not d. us** cette question ne nous retiendra pas; **police have detained a man for questioning** la police a mis un homme en garde à vue; **I won't d. you for long** je ne vous garderai *ou* retiendrai pas longtemps; **I'm afraid I've been detained** *(when cancelling appointment)* je suis désolé, je suis retenu; **I'm sorry I'm late, I got detained** je suis désolé d'être en retard, j'ai été retenu

detainee [diːteɪˈniː] **N** détenu, -ue

detect [dɪˈtekt] **VT 1** *(notice) (of person) (sound, change)* percevoir; *(movement)* apercevoir; *(of alarm system etc)* détecter; **to d. a note of irony in sb's voice** déceler une nuance d'ironie dans la voix de qn **2** *(find) (pulse)* sentir; *(source of a problem, missile)* détecter; *(weakness)* déceler

detectable [dɪˈtektəb(ə)l] **ADJ** perceptible, discernable

detection [dɪˈtekʃən] **N 1** *(discovery)* découverte *f*, **to escape d.** *(of mistake, burglar etc)* passer inaperçu **2** *(location, finding) (of mines, planes etc)* détection *f* **3** *(by detective)* travail *m* de détective

detective [dɪˈtektɪv] **N** *(police officer)* agent *m* de la police judiciaire; *(private investigator)* détective *m* (privé)
▸▸ *Br* **d. chief inspector** ≃ inspecteur, -trice divisionnaire; *Br* **d. constable** ≃ inspecteur, -trice de police; *Br* **d. film** film *m* policier; *Br* **d. inspector** ≃ inspecteur, -trice de police principal(e); **d. series** série *f* policière; **d. story** roman *m* policier, polar *m*

detector [dɪˈtektər] **N** *(device)* détecteur *m*; **sound d.** détecteur par le son
▸▸ *Br* **d. van** ≃ voiture-radar *f* utilisée pour la détection des postes de télévision non déclarés

détente [deɪˈtɒnt] **N** *Pol* détente *f*

detention [dɪˈtenʃən] **N 1** *Law (in prison)* détention *f*; **d. without trial** détention arbitraire; *Mil* **six weeks' d.** six semaines de prison **2** *Sch* retenue *f*; **to give a pupil d.** consigner un élève; **to be in d.** être consigné *ou* en retenue **3** *Naut (of ship)* arrêt *m*
▸▸ *Mil* **d. barracks** locaux *mpl* disciplinaires; *Br Law* **d. centre** = jusqu'en 1988, centre de détention pour jeunes délinquants (aujourd'hui appelé "young offenders' institution"); *Law* **d. order** ordre *m* de détention

deter [dɪˈtɜːr] **VT** (**-rr-**) dissuader (**from doing sth** de faire qch); **why should that d. you from going?** pourquoi est-ce que ça t'empêche d'y aller?

detergent [dɪˈtɜːdʒənt] **N** détergent *m*, lessive *f*
ADJ détersif
▸▸ **d. additive** additif *m* détergent; **d. oil** huile *f* détergente

deteriorate [dɪˈtɪərɪəreɪt] **VI** *(of relations, weather, economy, building)* se détériorer; *(of health, product)* se détériorer, s'altérer; *(of work, situation)* se dégrader; **her condition has deteriorated** *(of patient)* son état s'est aggravé; **the house has been allowed to d.** on a laissé la maison se détériorer; **to d. even further** *(of situation, work, condition, weather etc)* encore empirer; *(of building)* se détériorer encore davantage

deterioration [dɪtɪərɪəˈreɪʃən] **N** *(of relations, weather, economy, building)* détérioration *f*, *(of health, product)* détérioration *f*, altération *f*; **despite the continuing d. of the situation** bien que la situation continue à empirer; **d. in quality** baisse *f* de qualité

determinant [dɪˈtɜːmɪnənt] **N** facteur *m* déterminant

determination [dɪtɜːmɪˈneɪʃən] **N 1** *(resoluteness)* détermination *f*, résolution *f*; **air of d.** air résolu *ou* décidé *ou* déterminé **2** *(establishment) (of date, position of planet)* détermination *f* **3** *Law (decision, finding)* décision *f* **4** *Law (termination) (of contract etc)* résolution *f*, résiliation *f*

determine [dɪˈtɜːmɪn] **VT 1** *(resolve)* se décider, se déterminer, se résoudre (**to do** à faire)
2 *(establish) (nature, size of sth)* déterminer; *(date, price)* déterminer, fixer; *(border)* délimiter; **once I've determined the cost** *(found*

out) une fois que je saurai le prix
3 *(question etc)* décider, résoudre; *(point of dispute)* régler; **the magistrate determined that they were guilty** le magistrat les a déclarés coupables; **to d. sb's fate** décider du sort de qn; **this set will d. the outcome of the match** cette manche va déterminer le résultat du match
4 *Law (terminate) (contract, lease)* résoudre, résilier
VI 1 *(of person)* se décider, se déterminer, se résoudre (**on doing** à faire)
2 *Law (of contract)* être nul

determined [dɪˈtɜːmɪnd] **ADJ** *(person, attempt)* déterminé; *(effort)* résolu; **I'm d. that this year I'll learn how to ride a horse** je suis décidé *ou* résolu à apprendre à monter à cheval cette année; **I'm d. that he'll go to university** je suis déterminé *ou* décidé à ce qu'il aille à l'université; **with a d. air** d'un air déterminé *ou* résolu

determiner [dɪˈtɜːmɪnər] **N** *Gram* déterminant *m* VOIR GRAMMAIRE A32

determining [dɪˈtɜːmɪnɪŋ] **ADJ** *(factor)* déterminant

deterrence [dɪˈterəns] **N** dissuasion *f*, **nuclear d. is indispensable to national security** une force de dissuasion nucléaire est indispensable pour la sécurité nationale

deterrent [dɪˈterənt] **N 1 to act as** *or* **be a d.** *(of penalty etc)* exercer un effet dissuasif (**to crime** contre le crime) **2** *(weapon)* arme *f* de dissuasion
ADJ *(effect) (of nuclear bomb, policy)* dissuasif

detest [dɪˈtest] **VT** détester, *Fml* abhorrer; **I d. having to wait** je déteste attendre

detestable [dɪˈtestəb(ə)l] **ADJ** détestable

detestably [dɪˈtestəblɪ] **ADV** détestablement

detestation [diːtesˈteɪʃən] **N** *Fml* **1** *(hatred)* haine *f* **2** *(object of hatred)* chose *f* détestable, abomination *f*; **that's my particular d.** c'est ma bête noire

dethrone [dɪˈθrəʊn] **VT** détrôner

dethronement [dɪˈθrəʊnmənt] **N** détrônement *m*

detonate [ˈdetəneɪt] **VT** *(explosive)* faire détoner; *(bomb)* faire exploser; *(mine)* faire sauter
VI détoner

detonation [detəˈneɪʃən] **N** détonation *f*, explosion *f*

detonator [ˈdetəneɪtər] **N 1** *(for explosive)* détonateur *m*, amorce *f*, **percussion d.** détonateur à percussion **2** *Rail (fog signal)* détonateur *m*

detour [ˈdiːtʊər] **N** détour *m*; *(on sign)* déviation *f*, **to make a d.** faire un détour; **he took us on an elaborate d.** il nous a fait faire un détour très compliqué
VI faire un détour
VT *(traffic)* (faire) dévier

detox [ˈdiːtɒks] **N** *Fam* désintoxication *f*
▸▸ **d. centre** centre *m* de désintoxication; **d. programme** cure *f* de désintoxication

detoxification [diːtɒksɪfɪˈkeɪʃən] **N** désintoxication *f*, sevrage *m*
▸▸ **d. centre** centre *m* de désintoxication; **d. programme** cure *f* de désintoxication

▸ **detract from** **VT INSEP** *(sb's pleasure, beauty of sth)* diminuer, porter atteinte à; *(sb's worth, achievements)* déprécier; **it rather detracted from my enjoyment of the film** cela m'a quelque peu empêché d'apprécier le film

detractor [dɪˈtræktər] **N** détracteur, -trice

detrain [diːˈtreɪn] **VT** *(troops)* débarquer (du train)
VI *Mil (of troops)* débarquer *ou* descendre

(du train); *Am (of passengers)* descendre du train

detriment ['detrɪmənt] **N** détriment *m*, préjudice *m*; **to the d. of …** au détriment de …; **without d. to …** sans porter préjudice à …

detrimental [detrɪ'ment(ə)l] **ADJ** nuisible, préjudiciable (**to** à); **to have a d. effect on** *(health, chances etc)* nuire à; *(paintwork, tyres, skin)* être mauvais pour; **to have a d. effect on sb** *(of treatment, stress etc)* être mauvais pour qn; **it would be d. to my interests** cela desservirait mes intérêts; **smoking is d. to your health** fumer est mauvais pour la santé

detritus [dɪ'traɪtəs] **N** *Geol* débris *mpl* de roches

de trop [də'trəʊ] **ADJ PRED** de trop

Dettol® ['detɒl] **N** = solution *f* antiseptique

deuce¹ [dju:s] **N 1** *(of dice, dominoes, cards)* deux *m* **2** *Tennis* égalité *f*, quarante à, quarante partout; **to be at d.** être à égalité; **there were 16 deuces** il y a eu 16 égalités

deuce² **N** *Old-fashioned Fam* **what the d. does he mean?** que diable veut-il dire?; **what the d.!** bon sang!; **there's the d. of a difference** il y a une sacrée différence

deuced ['dju:sɪd, -u:st] *Old-fashioned Br Fam*
ADJ sacré
ADV sacrément

devaluation [di:væljʊ'eɪʃən] **N** *Econ* dévaluation *f*

devalue [di:'vælju:] **VT** *Econ* dévaluer; *Fig (person, achievements, efforts)* dévaloriser

devastate ['devəsteɪt] **VT** *(crops, village)* dévaster, ravager; *Fig (of news) (person)* terrasser; *(hopes)* anéantir, briser; **I was devastated when I found out he'd been lying to me** ça m'a anéanti d'apprendre qu'il m'avait menti

devastating ['devəsteɪtɪŋ] **ADJ** *(storm, effect, accuracy etc)* dévastateur, -trice, ravageur, -euse; *(argument, news, admission etc)* accablant, dévastateur, écrasant; *(criticism, attack)* cinglant; *(discovery)* dévastateur; *(charm, beauty etc)* irrésistible; *(shock etc)* foudroyant

devastatingly ['devəsteɪtɪŋlɪ] **ADV** *(handsome, funny)* terriblement, irrésistiblement; **d. beautiful** d'une beauté irrésistible; **d. accurate fire** tir(s) *m(pl)* d'une précision dévastatrice

devastation [devəs'teɪʃən] **N** dévastation *f*, ravages *mpl*; **a scene of utter d.** un spectacle de dévastation complète

develop [dɪ'veləp] **(-p-** [dɪ'veləpt]**) VT 1** *(expand) (skills, theme etc)* développer; *(theory, argument)* développer, exposer; *(thought)* développer, élargir; **to d. one's muscles** développer ses muscles, se muscler **2** *Econ (region)* mettre en valeur, développer; *Tech (new design, model etc)* mettre au point, réaliser; *Constr (site)* aménager; **to d. sth into sth** transformer qch en qch; **less developed countries** pays *mpl* moins développés; **developed countries** pays développés **3** *(acquire) (infection, bad habit, mannerism)* contracter; *(cold, flu)* attraper; *(symptoms)* manifester; **to d. a temperature** *or* **a fever** (se mettre à) avoir *ou* faire de la température; **he has developed cancer/Parkinson's disease** il est atteint de cancer/de la maladie de Parkinson; **to d. a dislike/taste** *or* **liking for sth** se mettre à détester/aimer *ou* apprécier qch; **to d. a tendency to do sth** prendre l'habitude de faire qch; **the machine has developed a fault** la machine s'est mise à mal fonctionner; **to d. a stoop** se voûter; **when did she d. the rash?** quand l'éruption s'est-elle déclenchée?; **I've developed a rash on my chest** j'ai fait une éruption sur la poitrine

4 *Phot (film)* développer
5 *Math (surface, function)* développer
6 *Phys etc (heat)* engendrer
VI 1 *(of body, the faculties etc)* se développer; **she has developed into a fine-looking young woman/a gifted pianist** elle est devenue une ravissante jeune femme/une pianiste douée **2** *Econ (of country, region)* se développer; **to d. into** devenir **3** *(become apparent)* se manifester, se révéler; *(of argument, crisis)* se produire; *(of fever)* se déclarer; **to d. into sth** devenir qch; *(bronchitis, riot)* se transformer en **4** *Phot* se développer

developer [dɪ'veləpər] **N 1** *Econ* promoteur *m* **2** *Sch* **late d.** enfant *mf* qui se développe tard **3** *Phot (chemical)* (agent *m*) révélateur *m*; *(for laser printer)* développeuse *f*
▸▸ *Phot* **d. kit** *(for laser printer)* kit *m* développeur

developing [dɪ'veləpɪŋ] **ADJ** *(business)* en expansion; *(region)* qui se développe, en expansion; *(country)* en voie de développement; *(crisis)* en cours; **a d. interest in …** un intérêt grandissant pour …; **the d. situation in Iraq** la situation jour après jour en Irak
N 1 = **development 2** *Phot* développement *m*
▸▸ *Phot* **d. bath** (bain *m*) révélateur *m*; *Phot* **d. tank** cuve *f* à développement; *Phot* **d. tray** cuvette *f*

development [dɪ'veləpmənt] **N 1** *(growth, expansion) (of body, faculties, concept)* développement *m*; *(of theme)* développement *m*; *(of subject)* développement, amplification *f*, *(of idea)* élargissement *m* **2** *Econ (of region etc)* développement *m*, mise *f* en valeur; *(of area, land)* aménagement *m*, construction *f*, *(of Third World country)* développement; *Tech (of new design etc)* réalisation *f*, mise au point **3** *(progress, change)* développement *m*; *(of events etc)* déroulement *m*; *(of events, thought)* évolution *f*, **to await further developments** attendre la suite des événements; **a surprising d. in the situation** un développement étonnant de la situation; **the latest developments in the former Soviet Union** les derniers événements survenus dans l'ex-Union Soviétique; **the latest developments in medical research** les dernières découvertes médicales **4** *Phot* développement *m* **5** *Math (of surface, function)* développement *m*; *(of spiral)* développée *f*
▸▸ **d. aid** crédits *f* aux pays en voie de développement; *Br* **d. area** = zone *f* économiquement sinistrée bénéficiant d'aides publiques en vue de sa reconversion; **d. assistance** crédits *mpl* de développement; *Fin* **d. capital** capital-développement *m*; **d. costs** coûts *mpl* de développement; **d. grant** subvention *f* pour le développement; **d. loan** crédits *mpl* de développement; *Mktg* **d. stage** *(of product)* phase *f* de développement

deviant [di:vɪənt] **ADJ, N** *Psy* déviant, -ante

deviate ['di:vɪeɪt] **VI** *(from instructions, plans, intentions etc)* s'écarter (**from** de); *(from a path, course of action, line)* dévier (**from** de)

deviation [di:vɪ'eɪʃən] **N** *(from norm, principles, standard procedure)* écart *m* (**from** par rapport à); *(of magnetic needle, from path, course of action, line)* déviation *f* (**from** de)

deviationism [di:vɪ'eɪʃənɪz(ə)m] *n Pol* déviationnisme *m*

deviationist [di:vɪ'eɪʃənɪst] **ADJ, N** *Pol* déviationniste *mf*

device [dɪ'vaɪs] **N 1** *(fitting, part of a ma-*

chine etc) dispositif *m*; *(machine, gadget)* appareil *m*, dispositif; *Comput (peripheral)* unité *f* périphérique, périphérique *m*; **locking d.** système *m* de verrouillage; **safety d.** dispositif de sécurité; **explosive/nuclear d.** engin *m* explosif/nucléaire **2** *(plan)* stratagème *m*, procédé *m*; **to leave sb to their own devices** *(alone)* laisser qn s'occuper comme bon lui semble; *(without help)* laisser qn se débrouiller **3** *Lit (on shield, flag etc)* emblème *m*, devise *f*
▸▸ *Comput* **d. driver** pilote *m* de périphérique; *Comput* **d. manager** gestionnaire *m* de périphériques

DEVIL ['dev(ə)l] **N 1** *(evil being)* diable *m*, démon *m*; **the D.** le Diable **2** *(person)* diable *m*; **he's a bit of a d.** *(awkward to deal with)* il est un peu enquiquineur; *(not always honest)* il est un peu malhonnête; *(not always reliable)* on ne peut pas compter sur lui; **poor d.!** pauvre diable!; **the silly d.!** quelle espèce d'idiot!; **you little d.!** petit diable!; *(annoyed)* petit garnement!; *(to little girl)* petite diablesse!; *(annoyed)* petite peste!; *Br Fam* **go on, be a d.!** allez, laisse-toi tenter! **3** *(in phrases)* **to be (caught) between the d. and the deep (blue) sea** être pris entre deux feux; **talk of the d.!** quand on parle du loup (on en voit la queue); **to have the d.'s own luck, to have the luck of the d.** avoir une veine de cocu; *Old-fashioned* **d. take it!** que le diable l'emporte!; *Fam* **go to the d.!** allez au diable!; **to play the d. with sth** mettre la confusion dans qch; **to give the d. his due …** pour être honnête, il faut admettre que …; *Fam* **there'll be the d. to pay** ça va barder; **(and) d. take the hindmost** sauve qui peut; *Prov* **d. looks after his own** il y en a qui ont de la chance; *Prov* **better the d. you know than the d. you don't** mieux vaut se contenter de ce qu'on a plutôt que de risquer de trouver pire; *Prov* **the d. finds work for idle hands to do** l'oisiveté est la mère de tous les vices **4** *Fam (as intensifier)* **what the d. are you doing?** que diable faites-vous là?; **how the d. …?** comment diable …?; **like the d.** *(to work)* avec acharnement; **to have the d. of a job** *or* **the d.'s own job (to do sth)** avoir un mal de chien *ou* un mal de tous les diables (à *ou* pour faire qch); **he's got the d. of a temper** il a un fichu caractère
VI (-ll-, *Am* **-l-)** *Br Fam* **to d. for sb** *(lawyer etc)* servir de nègre à qn
VT *Culin (meat)* faire griller et poivrer fortement; **devilled eggs** œufs durs à la diable
▸▸ **d.'s advocate** avocat *m* du diable; **to play d.'s advocate** se faire l'avocat du diable

---

devilfish ['dev(ə)lfɪʃ] **N 1** *(fish)* raie *f* manta **2** *(octopus)* pieuvre *f*

devilish ['dev(ə)lɪʃ] **ADJ** *also Fig* diabolique
ADV *Old-fashioned Fam* rudement

devilishly ['dev(ə)lɪʃlɪ] **ADV** diaboliquement; **d. clever/cruel** d'une habileté/cruauté diabolique

devil-may-care ADJ insouciant, *Fam* je-m'en-foutiste; **d. spirit** *(reckless)* esprit *m* téméraire; *(carefree)* esprit insouciant

devilment ['dev(ə)lmənt], **devilry** ['dev(ə)l-rɪ] **N 1** *(mischief)* malice *f*, diablerie *f*, espièglerie *f*, **to do sth out of** *or* **for sheer d.** faire qch par pure malice *ou* espièglerie; **a piece of d.** une diablerie, une espièglerie; **what d. is he up to now?** qu'est-ce qu'il nous prépare comme sottise? **2** *(wickedness)* méchanceté *f*

devil's food cake N *Am Culin* = gâteau *m* au chocolat

devious ['di:vɪəs] **ADJ** *(person)* retors; *(mind)* retors, tortueux; *(way, means, route)* détourné, tortueux; *(scheme)* tortueux; **that was a bit d. of you** c'était un peu sournois de ta part

deviously [di:vɪəslɪ] **ADV** *(to achieve sth)* d'une façon détournée *ou* tortueuse, par des voies détournées *ou* tortueuses; *(to act, behave)* d'une façon tortueuse; **d. worded** rédigé d'une façon tortueuse

deviousness ['di:vɪəsnɪs] **N** *(devious behaviour)* détours *mpl*; *(of person)* caractère *m* retors; *(of scheme, mind)* caractère tortueux; **the increasing d. of their attempts** leurs efforts de plus en plus tortueux

devise [dɪ'vaɪz] **N** *Law* legs *m* (immobilier) **VT 1** *(plan)* combiner, imaginer; *(solution, excuse, gadget)* inventer, imaginer; *(explanation, punishment, means of escape)* imaginer; *(plot)* tramer **2** *Law (real estate)* léguer

devising [dɪ'vaɪzɪŋ] **N a scheme of his own d.** un plan qu'il avait imaginé lui-même

devitalize [di:'vaɪtəlaɪz] **VT** *(economy, country)* affaiblir

devoid [dɪ'vɔɪd] **ADJ PRED** dénué, dépourvu (**of** de)

devolution [di:və'lu:ʃən] **N 1** *(of power, authority to individual)* délégation *f*, transmission *f*; *Pol* décentralisation *f* (administrative) **2** *Law* dévolution *f*, transmission *f* par succession

Devolution
Ce terme désigne la décentralisation parlementaire au sein du Royaume Uni, processus engagé depuis l'élection du gouvernement travailliste de Tony Blair en 1997. Après cette victoire, le nouveau gouvernement organisa des référendums en Écosse et au Pays de Galles, à la suite de quoi un parlement écossais fut instauré à Édimbourg et une assemblée nationale galloise à Cardiff, répondant ainsi aux attentes des nombreux Écossais et Gallois qui revendiquaient depuis longtemps un plus grand degré d'autonomie. (*Voir aussi encadrés sous* "**Scottish Parliament**" et "**Welsh Assembly**".)

devolve [dɪ'vɒlv] **VT** *(functions, powers)* déléguer, transmettre (**to sb** à qn)
▸ **devolve on, devolve to VT INSEP** *Fml* **1** *(of responsibility, duty etc) (somebody)* revenir à, incomber à **2** *Law (of property) (somebody)* être dévolu à

devote [dɪ'vəʊt] **VT** *(money, efforts)* consacrer (**to** à); *(time)* consacrer, accorder (**to** à); *(attention)* accorder (**to** à); **review specially devoted to history** revue entièrement consacrée à l'histoire; **to d. oneself to** *(occupation)* se vouer à, se consacrer à; *(study)* s'adonner à, se livrer à; **to d. oneself to sb/a cause** se dévouer à qn/une cause

devoted [dɪ'vəʊtɪd] **ADJ** *(father, daughter, service, care etc)* dévoué (**to** à); *(follower, fan)* fervent; *(couple)* uni; **they are d. to each other** ils sont dévoués l'un à l'autre

devotedly [dɪ'vəʊtɪdlɪ] **ADV** avec dévouement

devotee [devəʊ'ti:] **N** *(of person)* partisan, -ane; *(of sport)* passionné, -ée; *(of method)* adepte *mf*; *(of theory)* défenseur *m*; *(of god)* adorateur, -trice; **a d. of Haydn** un fervent *ou* un grand amateur de Haydn; **a d. of classical music** un passionné de musique classique

devotion [dɪ'vəʊʃən] **N 1** *(to a god)* dévotion *f* (**to** à) **2** *(prayers)* **devotions** dévotions *fpl*, prières *fpl* **3** *(to friend, family)* dévotion *f*, attachement *m* (**to** à); *(to leader of party, boss, cause)* dévouement *m* (**to sb** à *ou* pour

qn; **to sth** à qch); **d. to duty** dévouement *m*; **d. to work** assiduité *f ou* ardeur *f* au travail

When translating **devotion**, note that the French words **dévotion** and **dévouement** are not interchangeable. **Dévotion** usually refers to religious fervour and **dévouement** expresses the idea of dedication.

devotional [dɪ'vəʊʃən(ə)l] **ADJ** *Rel (book, articles etc)* de dévotion, de piété; *(writings, literature)* religieux

devour [dɪ'vaʊər] **VT** dévorer; *Fig* **to d. sb with one's eyes** dévorer qn des yeux; *Fig* **to d. a book** dévorer un livre; *Fig* **to be devoured by jealousy/hatred** être dévoré par la jalousie/la haine

devouring [dɪ'vaʊərɪŋ] **ADJ ATTRIB** *Fig (passion)* dévorant; *(enthusiasm)* débordant

devout [dɪ'vaʊt] **ADJ 1** *(person)* dévot, pieux; **a d. Catholic/Muslim** un catholique/musulman fervent **2** *(wish etc)* fervent, sincère; **it is my d. wish that …** c'est mon vœu le plus sincère que …

devoutly [dɪ'vaʊtlɪ] **ADV 1** *(to pray)* avec dévotion; *(to live)* dans la dévotion **2** *(to wish, hope)* sincèrement; **it is d. to be wished that …** il faut sincèrement espérer que …

devoutness [dɪ'vaʊtnɪs] **N** dévotion *f*, piété *f*

dew [dju:] **N (morning) d.** rosée *f*, **evening d.** serein *m*
▸▸ *Met* **d. point** point *m* de rosée

dewclaw ['dju:klɔ:] **N** *Zool (of dog etc)* ergot *m*

dewdrop ['dju:drɒp] **N** goutte *f* de rosée

dewlap ['dju:læp] **N** *(of cow)* fanon *m*; *(of person) (under chin)* plis *mpl* sous le menton, chairs *fpl* flasques sous le menton

dewy ['dju:ɪ] **ADJ** couvert *ou* humide de rosée; *Fig* **d. complexion** teint *m* frais

dewy-eyed **ADJ 1** *(look)* humide; **she gets all d. about her husband/France** elle est tout émue quand elle parle de son mari/de la France **2** *(naive) (person)* naïf, -ïve, ingénu; *(optimism, enthusiasm)* naïf; **don't act the d. innocent with me** ne fais pas l'ingénu avec moi

dexterity [deks'terɪtɪ] **N** *(mental)* dextérité *f*, doigté *m*; *(physical)* habileté *f*, adresse *f*, manual **d.** habileté manuelle

dext(e)rous ['dekstrəs] **ADJ** adroit, habile (**in doing sth** à faire qch)

dext(e)rously ['dekstrəslɪ] **ADV** adroitement, avec dextérité

dextrin ['dekstrɪn] **N** *Chem, Ind* dextrine *f*

dextrose ['dekstrəʊs] **N** *Chem* dextrose *m*

DFC [di:ef'si:] **N** *Br abbr* **Distinguished Flying Cross**

DFM [di:e'fem] **N** *Br abbr* **Distinguished Flying Medal**

DG [di:'dʒi:] **N** *Admin abbr* **Director General**

dhoti ['dəʊtɪ] **N** dhoti *m*

dhow [daʊ] **N** = petit bateau *m* arabe à une voile

DHSS [di:eɪtʃe'ses] **N** *Br Admin Formerly (abbr* **Department of Health and Social Security**) = ministère *m* de la Santé

diabetes [daɪə'bi:ti:z] **N** *Med* diabète *m*; **to have d.** avoir du diabète
▸▸ **d. mellitus** diabète pancréatique

diabetic [daɪə'betɪk] *Med* **N** diabétique *mf* **ADJ** diabétique; **to be in a d. coma** être *ou* être en coma diabétique; **d. biscuits/jam** biscuits/confiture pour diabétiques

diabolic [daɪə'bɒlɪk] **ADJ** *(cruelty etc)* diabolique, atroce; *(plot)* infernal, -aux; *(laugh)* satanique

diabolical [daɪə'bɒlɪk(ə)l] **ADJ** *Br Fam* **1**

(very bad) épouvantable, atroce; **it's d.!** *(of price)* c'est scandaleux!; **this wine tastes d.** ce vin est infect **2** *(intensifier)* **what a d. liberty** quel culot!

diabolically [daɪə'bɒlɪklɪ] **ADV 1** diaboliquement, de façon diabolique **2** *Br Fam (very badly)* de façon épouvantable; **it's d. expensive** c'est vachement cher

diacritic [daɪə'krɪtɪk] *Gram* **N** (signe *m*) diacritique *m*
ADJ *(sign)* diacritique

diacritical [daɪə'krɪtɪk(ə)l] **ADJ** *(sign)* diacritique

diadem ['daɪədem] **N** diadème *m*

diaeresis, *Am* **dieresis**, *pl* **diaereses** [daɪ'erəsɪs, -əsi:z] **N** *Gram* tréma *m*

diagnose ['daɪəgnəʊz] **VT** *(illness)* diagnostiquer, faire le diagnostic de; *(engine problem etc)* diagnostiquer; **the doctor has diagnosed pneumonia** le médecin a diagnostiqué une pneumonie; **she has been diagnosed as a schizophrenic** d'après le diagnostic, elle est schizophrène; **the book attempts to d. the causes of the crisis** le livre tente de faire le diagnostic de la crise

diagnosis, *pl* **diagnoses** [daɪəg'nəʊsɪs, -si:z] **N** *Med, Fig* diagnostic *m*; **to make** *or* **give a d.** faire un diagnostic; **d. is not her strong point** le diagnostic n'est pas son point fort

diagnostic [daɪəg'nɒstɪk] **ADJ** diagnostique; **d. skill/ability** talent *m*/capacité *f* à diagnostiquer
N diagnostic *m*
▸▸ *Com* **d. audit** audit *m* de diagnostic; *Aut* **d. bay** station *f* diagnostic; *Comput* **d. disk** disquette *f* de diagnostic; *Med* **d. kit** trousse *f* diagnostique; *Comput* **d. program** programme *m* de diagnostic; *Med, Comput, Sch* **d. test** test *m* de diagnostic

diagnostician [daɪəgnɒ'stɪʃən] **N** diagnostiqueur *m*; **she's an excellent d.** elle fait de très bons diagnostics

diagnostics [daɪəg'nɒstɪks] **N** *Med* diagnostique *f* VOIR GRAMMAIRE A10

diagonal [daɪ'ægən(ə)l] **ADJ** diagonal, -aux; *Constr (beam etc)* en écharpe
N diagonale *f*
▸▸ **d. ply** *(of tyre)* pli *m* diagonal

diagonally [daɪ'ægən(ə)lɪ] **ADV** diagonalement, en diagonale; **d. opposite sth** diamétralement opposé à qch

diagonal-ply tyre **N** pneu *m* à carcasse diagonale

diagram ['daɪəgræm] **N** diagramme *m*, schéma *m*; *Geom* figure *f*; *Phys etc (of temperature etc)* graphique *m*, courbe *f*; *Tech (of engine etc)* diagramme, caractéristique *f*; **to make a d. of sth** faire un schéma de qch, schématiser qch; *Fig* **do I need to draw you a d.?** est-ce que je dois te faire un dessin?

diagrammatic [daɪəgrə'mætɪk] **ADJ** schématique

dial ['daɪəl] **N** *(of clock, scientific instrument)* cadran *m*; *Tel* cadran (d'appel); *Radio Old-fashioned Fam* **don't touch that d.** *(announcement)* restez avec nous
VT (-**ll**-, *Am* -**l**-) *Tel (number)* composer, faire; **to d.** *Br* **999** *or Am* **911** ≃ appeler Police Secours; **d.-a-recipe/-horoscope** recette/horoscope par téléphone
VI composer *ou* faire le numéro
▸▸ *Tel* **d. gauge, d. indicator** comparateur *m*; *Tel* **d. phone** téléphone *m* à cadran; *Am* **d. tone** tonalité *f*

dialect ['daɪəlekt] **N** dialecte *m*; **provincial d.** patois *m*

dialectic(al) [daɪə'lektɪk, -ɪk(ə)l] **ADJ** *Phil* dialectique;
▸▸ **d. materialism** matérialisme *m* dialectique

dialectic(s) [daɪəˈlektɪk, -s] N (pl) Phil dialectique f

dialler [ˈdaɪələr] N composeur m de numéros

dialling, Am **dialing** [ˈdaɪəlɪŋ] N Tel composition f du numéro, numérotation f
▸▸ **d. code** indicatif m; **d. tone** tonalité f; **I can't get a d. tone** je n'arrive pas à avoir la tonalité

dialogue, Am **dialog** [ˈdaɪəlɒg] N dialogue m; Pol **to enter into a d.** entamer le dialogue (**with sb** avec qn)
▸▸ Comput **d. box** zone f ou boîte f de dialogue; **d. coach** répétiteur, -trice de dialogues; TV, Cin **d. looping** doublage m du dialogue (en boucle); Comput **d. mode** mode m dialogue; Comput **d. screen** écran m de dialogue; TV, Cin **d. writer** dialoguiste mf

dial-up access N Comput accès m commuté

dial-up account N Comput compte m d'accès par ligne commutée

dial-up connection N Comput accès m commuté

dial-up line N Tel ligne f commutée

dial-up modem N modem m réseau commuté

dial-up service N service m de télétraitement

dialyse [ˈdaɪəlaɪz] VT Chem dialyser

dialysis, pl **dialyses** [daɪˈælɪsɪs, -iːz] N Chem, Med dialyse f; **she's in d.** elle est sous dialyse; **to have d. (treatment)** être sous dialyse
▸▸ **d. machine** dialyseur m

diamanté [daɪəˈmænteɪ, dɪə-] N broderie f diamantée

diameter [daɪˈæmɪtər] N diamètre m; **the wheel is 60 cm in d.** la roue a 60 cm de diamètre; **internal d.** (of tube) calibre m; (of cylinder etc) alésage m

diametric(al) [daɪəˈmetrɪk, -ɪk(ə)l] ADJ in **d. opposition** (opinion etc) diamétralement opposé (**to** à)

diametrically [daɪəˈmetrɪklɪ] ADV **d. opposed** (opinion etc) diamétralement opposé (**to sth** à qch)

diamond [ˈdaɪəmənd] N **1** (gem) diamant m; Tech (cutting) **d.** diamant de vitrier; **industrial d.** diamant industriel; **rough/cut d.** diamant brut/taillé; Fig **he's a rough d.** ses manières frustes cachent beaucoup de qualités; **d. necklace/ring** collier m/bague f de diamants **2** (shape) losange m; **d. pattern** dessin m en losanges **3** Cards carreau m; **the six of diamonds** le six de carreau **4** Sport terrain m de base-ball
ADJ Br Fam (excellent) super, génial, -aux; **he's a d. geezer** c'est un type super
▸▸ **d. cutter** (person) tailleur m de diamants; **d. cutting** taille f du diamant; **d. drill** foreuse f à pointe de diamant; **d. jubilee** (célébration f du) soixantième anniversaire m; **d. merchant** diamantaire m; **d. mine** mine f de diamants; **d. wedding (anniversary)** noces fpl de diamant

diamond-shaped ADJ en losange

diapason [daɪəˈpeɪsən] N Mus **1** (of organ) principaux jeux mpl de fond **2** (tuning fork) diapason m

diaper [ˈdaɪəpər] N Am (for baby) couche f, lange m

diaphanous [daɪˈæfənəs] ADJ diaphane

diaphragm [ˈdaɪəfræm] N **1** Anat diaphragme m **2** (membrane) diaphragme m, membrane f; Phot diaphragme **3** (contraceptive) diaphragme m (contraceptif)

diarist [ˈdaɪərɪst] N auteur m d'un journal (intime), diariste mf

diarrhoea, Am **diarrhea** [daɪəˈrɪə] N Med diarrhée f; **to have d.** avoir la diarrhée

diary [ˈdaɪərɪ] N **1** (recording events) journal m (intime); **to keep a d.** tenir un journal (intime) **2** (for appointments) agenda m; (showing a week at a time) semainier m; **desk d.** (loose leaf) bloc m calendrier; (bound) agenda
▸▸ Journ **d. column** billet m, rubrique f d'échos; Journ **d. job** reportage m prévu

Diaspora (the) [ðəˈdaɪˈæspərə] N Rel la Diaspora

diastole [daɪˈæstəlɪ] N Med diastole f

diatom [ˈdaɪətəm] N Biol diatomée f

diatonic scale [daɪəˈtɒnɪk] N Mus gamme f diatonique

diatribe [ˈdaɪətraɪb] N diatribe f (**against** contre)

dibber [ˈdɪbər] N = **dibble**

dibble [ˈdɪb(ə)l] N (for bulbs etc) plantoir m
VT (seeds) semer au plantoir; (plants) repiquer au plantoir
VI semer/repiquer au plantoir

dibs [dɪbz] NPL (game) osselets mpl

dice [daɪs] N INV (pl of **die**) **1** (in game) dé m; **to throw the d.** lancer le(s) dé(s); Am Fig Fam **no d.** pas question VOIR GRAMMAIRE A13 **2** Culin cube m
VI jouer aux dés; **to d. with death** risquer sa vie
VT Culin (vegetables etc) couper en cubes

dicey [ˈdaɪsɪ] ADJ esp Br Fam (uncertain) hasardeux; (dangerous) risqué

dichotomous question [daɪˈkɒtəməs] N question f fermée à choix unique

dichotomy [daɪˈkɒtəmɪ] N dichotomie f

dick [dɪk] N **1** esp Am Fam (detective) détective m, flic m **2** Vulg (penis) bite f, queue f **3** Vulg (contemptible man) trou m du cul

dickens [ˈdɪkɪnz] N Fam **what the d. are you doing?** que diable fais-tu?; **the or a d. of a row** un bruit de tous les diables; **we had the or a d. of a time getting here** on a eu un mal fou pour arriver ici

Dickensian [dɪˈkenzɪən] ADJ (scene, Christmas etc) à la Dickens; (conditions) qui sort d'un roman de Dickens

dicker [ˈdɪkər] VI Am Fam marchander; **to d. for sth** marchander qch

dickface [ˈdɪkfeɪs] N Vulg (idiot) trou m du cul

dickhead [ˈdɪkhed] N Br Vulg (idiot) trou m du cul

dicky [ˈdɪkɪ] Fam N **1** (of shirt) faux plastron m **2** Br Aut Old-fashioned (seat) spider m
ADJ Br (defective) défectueux; (heart) malade, qui flanche; **to feel d.** se sentir tout chose
▸▸ Br **d. bird** (in children's language) (petit) oiseau m, zoziau m; **did you hear anything? – not a d. bird** est-ce que tu as entendu? – non, rien du tout; Br **they haven't heard a d. bird from her** elle n'a pas fait signe de vie; Br **not a d. bird to anyone about this** pas un mot de tout ça à quiconque; Br **d. bow** nœud m papillon

dicotyledon [daɪkɒtɪˈliːdn] N dicotylédone f

Dictaphone® [ˈdɪktəfəʊn] N Dictaphone® m

dictate [ˈdɪkteɪt] N ordre m; **to follow the dictates of one's conscience** écouter sa conscience; **the dictates of fashion** les exigences de la mode
VT **1** (letter, passage) dicter **2** (conditions of peace etc) dicter **3** (determine) déterminer; (of circumstances) imposer, demander; **the size of the harvest will be dictated by the weather** l'importance de la moisson dépendra du temps

VI **1** (lay down law) faire la loi; **I won't be dictated to** on ne me donne pas d'ordres **2** (to secretary etc) dicter

dictating [dɪkˈteɪtɪŋ] N
▸▸ **d. machine** machine f à dicter

dictation [dɪkˈteɪʃən] N dictée f; **to take d. from sb** écrire sous la dictée de qn; **to give d.** dicter; Sch **to do d.** faire la dictée
▸▸ **d. speed** vitesse f de dictée

dictator [dɪkˈteɪtər] N Pol, Fig dictateur m

dictatorial [dɪktəˈtɔːrɪəl] ADJ **1** (power) dictatorial **2** (tone) impérieux, autoritaire; (person) autoritaire

dictatorially [dɪktəˈtɔːrɪəlɪ] ADV **1** (to govern) de façon dictatoriale **2** (to say) impérieusement, autoritairement; **to be d. inclined** avoir des tendances dictatoriales

dictatorship [dɪkˈteɪtəʃɪp] N dictature f

diction [ˈdɪkʃən] N **1** (pronunciation) diction f **2** (choice of words) style m

dictionary [ˈdɪkʃ(ə)rɪ] N dictionnaire m (**of** de); **English-French d.** dictionnaire anglais-français; **d. of quotations** dictionnaire de citations

dictum, pl **dictums, dicta** [ˈdɪktəm, -əmz, -ə] N **1** (statement) affirmation f, dire m **2** (saying) maxime f, dicton m

did [dɪd] PT see **do**[1]

didactic [dɪˈdæktɪk] ADJ didactique

didactically [dɪˈdæktɪklɪ] ADV didactiquement

diddle [ˈdɪd(ə)l] VT Fam **1** (con) duper, refaire, rouler; **he diddled me out of £500** il m'a refait ou roulé de 500 livres; **you've been diddled** tu t'es fait avoir ou rouler; **they diddled me into selling the house** ils ont réussi à m'embobiner et à me faire vendre la maison **2** Am Vulg (have sex with) baiser

diddler [ˈdɪdlər] N Fam escroqueur, -euse

diddly(-squat) [ˈdɪdlɪ-] N Am Fam que dalle; **I don't know d. about computers** l'informatique, j'y connais rien

didn't [ˈdɪd(ə)nt] CONTR = **did not**, see **do**[1]

DIE[1] [daɪ] (pt, pp **died** [daɪd], prp **dying** [ˈdaɪɪŋ])

VI	mourir **1, 2** ▪ caler **2** ▪ s'éteindre **2**
VT	mourir

VI **1** mourir; **to be dying** être en train de mourir; **to d. of cancer** mourir d'un cancer; **to d. of grief/starvation** mourir de chagrin/faim; **he died yesterday** il est mort hier; **to d. in one's sleep** mourir pendant son sommeil; **to d. rich/a millionaire** mourir riche/millionaire; **they died like heroes** ils sont morts en héros; **to d. from or of a wound** mourir des suites d'une blessure; **to d. in bed** mourir dans son lit; **to d. by one's own hand** se suicider, se donner la mort; Fam **never say d.!** (don't give up) il ne faut jamais désespérer; (stay cheerful) courage!, tenez bon!; Fam **I thought I would d. of boredom/of curiosity** j'ai cru mourir d'ennui/de curiosité; Fam **I nearly died laughing/of shame** j'étais mort de rire/de honte; Fam **we were dying of cold** nous mourions de froid; Fam **to be dying to do sth** brûler ou mourir d'envie de faire qch; Fam **I'm dying for a drink/cigarette** je meurs de soif/d'envie de fumer une cigarette
2 (of engine) caler; (of TV picture) disparaître; (of lights) s'éteindre; (of battery) se mettre à plat; (of love, passion, hopes, enthusiasm) mourir; **old superstitions d. hard** les vieilles superstitions ont la vie dure; **the engine died on me/us/etc** le moteur a calé; Lit **day is dying** le jour s'en va; **their love died** leur amour s'est éteint; **his secret died with him** il a emporté son secret dans le tombeau
VT **to d. a natural death** (not be murdered)

mourir de mort naturelle; *(of old age)* mourir de sa belle mort; *(of fashion etc)* passer de mode; **to d. a violent death** mourir de mort violente; **to d. a hero's death** mourir héroïquement *ou* en héros; *Fig* **to d. the death** *(of play)* faire un four; *(be embarrassed)* être mortellement embarrassé; **to d. a thousand deaths** souffrir mille morts

▸ **die away** VI *(of sound)* s'affaiblir; *(of voice)* s'éteindre; *(of wind)* tomber; *Mus* **to let the sound d. away** éteindre le son

▸ **die back** VI *(of plant)* (se) faner

▸ **die down** VI *(of fire etc)* baisser; *(of wind)* tomber; *(of sound)* s'éteindre; *(of excitement, storm, scandal)* se calmer; *(of applause)* mourir

▸ **die off** VI mourir; **they're dying off like flies** ils meurent les uns après les autres *ou* comme des mouches

▸ **die out** VI *(of family etc)* s'éteindre; *(of species)* disparaître

die² N **1** *(pl dice) (for playing, gambling)* dé *m*; *Fig* **the d. is cast** le sort est jeté, les dés sont jetés VOIR GRAMMAIRE A13 **2** *(pl dies* [daɪz]*) Metal (mould)* matrice *f*, **stamping** *or* **embossing d.** matrice *ou* machine *f* à estamper; **screw-cutting d.** mère *f* (de filet de vis) **3** *Metal (tool)* poinçonneuse *f* (à main)

▸▸ **d. casting** moulage *m* en coquille; **d. plate** *(for tickets)* plaque *f* d'imprimante de billets; **d. sinker** graveur *m* d'estampes *ou* de matrices; **d. stamping** matriçage *m*

die-hard N réactionnaire *mf*; *Pol* ultra-conservateur *m*

ADJ ATTRIB pur et dur; **d. policy** politique *f* réactionnaire; **his d. resistance to change** sa résistance obstinée au changement

dieresis [daɪˈerəsɪs] N *Am* = **diaeresis**

diesel [ˈdiːz(ə)l] ADJ *(engine, train)* diesel
N *(vehicle)* diesel *m*; *(oil, fuel)* gazole *m*, diesel, gasoil *m*

▸▸ *Aut* **d. emissions test** contrôle *m* des émissions de moteurs diesel; *Aut* **d. fuel** gazole, gasoil; *Aut* **d. injection** injection *f* diesel; *Aut* **d. knock** cognement *m* (du moteur) diesel; **d. oil** gazole, gasoil

diesel-electric ADJ diesel-électrique, *pl* diesel-électriques

dieselling [ˈdiːz(ə)lɪŋ] N *Aut* auto-allumage *m*

diet¹ [ˈdaɪət] N **1** *(what is eaten)* alimentation *f*, **their d. consists mainly of fish** leur nourriture se compose principalement de poisson; **to survive on a d. of fresh fruit and vegetables** survivre en se nourrissant de fruits et de légumes frais **2** *(for medical reasons)* régime *m*, diète *f*, *(to lose weight)* régime; **to be/go on a d.** être/se mettre au régime; **to put sb on a d.** mettre qn au régime; **d. drink** boisson *f* à basses calories **d. foods** *(for people with special requirements)* aliments *mpl* diététiques

VI être au régime; **he needs to d.** il faut qu'il se mette au régime

▸▸ **d. pill** pastille *f* amaigrissante

diet² N *Pol* diète *f*

dietary [ˈdaɪət(ə)rɪ] ADJ alimentaire
N *Fml (of patient, prison etc)* régime *m* (alimentaire)

▸▸ **d. fibre** cellulose *f* végétale

dietetic [daɪəˈtetɪk] ADJ diététique

dietetics [daɪəˈtetɪks] N diététique *f* VOIR
GRAMMAIRE A10

dietician, dietitian [daɪəˈtɪʃən] N diététicien, -ienne

differ [ˈdɪfər] VI **1** *(be different)* différer *(from* de*)*, être différent *(from* de*)*; **to d. in size/shape/colour** être de tailles/de formes/de couleurs différentes; **to d. in price** différer de prix; **how do the two species d.?** en quoi est-ce que les deux espèces diffè-

rent?, qu'est-ce qui différencie les deux espèces? **2** *(disagree)* être d'opinion différente *ou* d'avis différent; **I beg to d.** permettez-moi d'être d'un autre avis; **to agree to d.** garder chacun son opinion; **let's agree to d.** acceptons de dépasser nos différences; **that's where we d.** c'est sur ce point que nous sommes en désaccord; **I d. with her about** *or* **on** *or* **over the diagnosis** je ne suis pas d'accord avec elle sur le diagnostic

difference [ˈdɪf(ə)rəns] N **1** différence *f*, écart *m* **(between** entre*)*; *(between two numbers etc)* différence; **d. in age/in altitude** différence d'âge/d'altitude; **d. in temperature** écart de température; **differences in price** différences de prix; **there's a d. of two years between me and my brother** il y a une différence d'âge de deux ans entre mon frère et moi; **a world of d.** une différence énorme; **the d. in you is amazing** c'est incroyable à quel point tu as changé; **to notice a (big) d. in sb** remarquer que qn a (énormément) changé; **I don't quite see the d.** je ne saisis pas la nuance; **she doesn't make any d. between the children** *(of parent, teacher etc)* elle ne fait pas de distinction entre les enfants; **it doesn't make any d.** cela ne fait aucune différence; **it makes no d. (to me)** cela ne (me) fait rien, cela m'est parfaitement égal; **to make a d.** *(improve society)* faire avancer les choses; **the new colour scheme makes a big** *or* **all the d.** les nouvelles couleurs font toute la différence; **that makes all the d.** voilà qui change complètement les choses; **he's a businessman, but with a d.** c'est bien un homme d'affaires, mais pas comme les autres; **to split the d.** *(price, fee etc)* couper la poire en deux; **to pay** *or* **settle the d.** *(price, fee etc)* payer *ou* régler la différence; *Hum* **it's the same d.!** cela revient au même

2 *(disagreement)* désaccord *m*, différend *m* (**about** sth au sujet de qch*)*; **d. of opinion** différence *f* d'opinion; désaccord; **to have a d. of opinion with sb** se disputer avec qn; **settle a d.** *(of two people)* régler un différend, se mettre d'accord; **we have our differences** nous ne sommes pas toujours d'accord

different [ˈdɪf(ə)rənt] ADJ **1** différent *(from, Am also* than de*)*; **she feels a d. person** elle ne se sent plus la même; **that dress makes you look d.** cette robe vous change; **I do it in a d. way** je m'y prends tout autrement; **that's quite a d. matter** ça c'est une autre affaire **2** *(various)* divers; **d. colours** couleurs diverses *ou* variées; **d. kinds of ...** diverses *ou* différentes espèces de ...; **at d. times** à différentes *ou* diverses reprises; **I talked to d. people about it** j'en ai parlé à plusieurs personnes; **d. people say d. things** les avis diffèrent **3** *(unusual)* hors de l'ordinaire; **he just wants to be d.** tout ce qu'il veut c'est être différent, *Pej* il cherche à se faire remarquer; **it's certainly d.** c'est original

differential [dɪfəˈrenʃəl] ADJ différentiel
N *Math* différentielle *f*, *Aut* différentiel *m*; *(in prices, salaries)* écart *m*; **weight d.** différence *f* de poids; **wage** *or* **pay differentials** hiérarchie *f* salariale

▸▸ *Math* **d. calculus** calcul *m* différentiel; *Aut* **d. gear** différentiel *m*, engrenage *m* différentiel; **d. pricing** établissement *m* des prix différentiels, tarification *f* différentielle; **d. tariff** tarif *m* différentiel

differentially [dɪfəˈrenʃəlɪ] ADV *(to pay)* à des taux différentiels

differentiate [dɪfəˈrenʃɪeɪt] VT *also Math* différencier **(sth from sth** qch de qch*)*
VI **1** *(distinguish)* faire la différence **(between two things** entre deux choses*)* **2** *(discriminate)* **to d. between male and female employees** traiter les employés hommes différemment des employées femmes

differentiation [dɪfərenʃɪˈeɪʃən] N différenciation *f*

differently [ˈdɪf(ə)rəntlɪ] ADV différemment

differently-abled ADJ *(in politically correct usage)* handicapé

difficult [ˈdɪfɪkəlt] ADJ **1** *(task, problem etc)* difficile; **she's at a d. age** elle est à l'âge ingrat; **this question is d. to answer** il est difficile de répondre à cette question; **I find it d.** *or* **it is d. for me to ...** j'ai de la peine à ..., j'ai du mal à ...; **it is d. to believe that ...** on a peine à croire que ... + *sub*; **why do you have to make life d. for people?** quel besoin as-tu de compliquer la vie aux gens?; **it makes life d. not knowing how long they'll be staying for** cela n'arrange pas les choses de ne pas savoir combien de temps ils vont rester; **he seems to have a habit of making things d. for himself** il semble avoir le chic pour se compliquer les choses

2 *(person)* difficile; **he's d. to get on with** il n'est pas commode; **don't be so d.!** ne fais pas le/la difficile!; **you're just being d.** tu fais le/la difficile; **why do you have to be d. about everything?** pourquoi faut-il que tout soit aussi compliqué avec toi?; **she's very d. to talk to** il est très difficile de lui parler

difficulty [ˈdɪfɪkəltɪ] N **1** difficulté *f*, **to have d. in doing sth** avoir du mal *ou* des difficultés à faire qch; **to have d. (in) breathing** avoir du mal à respirer; **with d.** avec difficulté, avec du mal; **without much d.** sans grande difficulté

2 *(obstacle, problem)* difficulté *f*; **the d. is to ...** ce qui est difficile, c'est de ...; **I see no d. about it** je n'y vois pas d'inconvénient; **the real d. is how to keep both sides happy** le plus difficile c'est de satisfaire les deux parties; **there will be no d. about that** cela ne fera pas de difficultés; **to raise** *or* **make difficulties** soulever des objections; **there's the d.!** voilà la difficulté!; **to run into a d.** rencontrer une difficulté; **to be in d.** *or* **difficulties** *(of swimmer)* être en difficulté; *Fig (of company, marriage)* connaître des difficultés; **ship in difficulties** navire *m* en difficulté; **financial difficulties** embarras *m* pécuniaire; **to get into difficulties** se mettre dans un mauvais pas; **to get out of one's difficulties** se tirer d'affaire

diffidence [ˈdɪfɪdəns] N manque *m* de confiance en soi, manque d'assurance

diffident [ˈdɪfɪdənt] ADJ *(person)* qui manque d'assurance *ou* de confiance en soi; *(smile)* timide; *(manner, air)* peu assuré; **to be d. about doing sth** hésiter à faire qch; **to be d. about one's abilities** se montrer modeste en ce qui concerne ses propres capacités

diffidently [ˈdɪfɪdəntlɪ] ADV *(to smile)* timidement, d'un air peu assuré; *(to express oneself, say sth)* sur un ton peu assuré

diffract [dɪˈfrækt] VT *Opt (light)* diffracter

diffraction [dɪˈfrækʃən] N *Opt (of light)* diffraction *f*

diffuse¹ [dɪˈfjuːs] ADJ *(light, style etc)* diffus; *(sense of unease)* indéfini

diffuse² [dɪˈfjuːz] VT *(light)* diffuser, répandre; *Fml (news etc)* répandre
VI *(of light, gas etc)* se diffuser; *Fml (of knowledge)* se répandre

> Attention: ne pas confondre avec le verbe **to defuse**.

diffused [dɪˈfjuːzd] ADJ
▸▸ **d. lighting** éclairage *m* diffus *ou* indirect

diffuseness [dɪˈfjuːsnɪs] N *(of style)* prolixité *f*, caractère *m* diffus

diffuser [dɪˈfjuːzər] N *(for hairdryer, light)*

diffuseur *m*; *TV, Cin (on a light)* (écran *m*) diffuseur *m*

diffusion [dɪ'fjuːʒən] **N** *(of liquid, style, news etc)* diffusion *f*; *(of ideas)* rayonnement *m*; *Phys (of rays)* dispersion *f*

diffusive [dɪ'fjuːsɪv] **ADJ 1** *(property, characteristic)* diffusif **2** *(style)* diffus, prolixe

dig [dɪg] **N 1** *(in garden etc)* coup *m* de bêche; *Archeol* fouille *f*; **give the ground a good d.** retournez bien le sol; *Archeol* **to go on a d.** faire des fouilles; **a d. in the ribs** un coup de coude dans les côtes
2 *(remark)* remarque *f* désobligeante (**at sb** à qn); **to get a d. in at sb, to have a d. at sb** lancer une remarque désobligeante à qn; **that's a d. at you** cette remarque t'est destinée
VT *(pt, pp* **dug** [dʌg], *prp* **digging** ['dɪgɪŋ]) **1** *(hole, grave, well etc)* creuser; *(soil, garden)* bêcher; *Fig* **to d. one's own grave** creuser sa propre tombe
2 *(thrust)* enfoncer (**in** dans); **to d. sb in the ribs** donner un coup de coude à qn
3 *Old-fashioned Sl (understand)* comprendre, piger; *(like)* bien aimer; **she really digs you** *(likes you)* elle en pince vraiment pour toi; **I d. that** *(like it)* ça me plaît *ou* me botte, j'aime bien ça
VI *(of workmen, dog etc)* creuser; *(of gardener)* bêcher; *Archeol* faire des fouilles; **to d. for gold** faire des fouilles pour trouver de l'or; **the dog was digging for its bone** le chien creusait pour trouver son os
▸ **dig in** **VT SEP** *(compost etc)* enterrer; *Fig* **to d. one's heels** *or* **toes in** s'entêter; **she dug her heels in over the question** elle s'est montrée très intransigeante sur la question; **to d. oneself in** *Fam* s'incruster; *Mil* s'établir dans des tranchées
VI 1 *Mil (by digging trenches)* s'établir **2** *Fam (eat)* manger; *(start eating)* attaquer
▸ **dig into** **VT INSEP 1** *Fam (eat) (pie, tart etc)* manger **2** *(search) (sb's past, files)* fouiller dans **3** *(press into)* **my rucksack's digging into my back** mon sac à dos me blesse dans le dos
VT SEP enterrer dans; **to d. compost into the garden** enterrer du compost dans le jardin
▸ **dig out** **VT SEP 1** *(remove) (bullet, splinter etc)* extraire; *(person from ruins, snow drift etc)* dégager **2** *Fam (find) (address, person etc)* dénicher
▸ **dig over** **VT SEP** retourner
▸ **dig up** **VT SEP** *(plant etc)* déraciner; *(treasure)* mettre à jour; *(road)* piocher; *(body)* déterrer, exhumer; *Fam (find)* dénicher

digest¹ ['daɪdʒest] **N 1** *(short account)* condensé *m*, *Fam* digest *m* **2** *Comput* synthèse *f*

digest² [dɪ'dʒest, daɪ-] **VT** *Physiol (food)* digérer; *Fig (insult)* digérer; *(reading matter)* digérer, assimiler

digestible [dɪ'dʒestəb(ə)l, daɪ-] **ADJ** digestible; **easily d.** digeste

digestion [dɪ'dʒestʃən, daɪ-] **N** *Physiol* digestion *f*, *Fig (of what one has read)* digestion, assimilation *f*; **to have a good d.** ne pas avoir de problèmes de digestion; **a glass of wine helps the d.** un verre de vin facilite la digestion *ou* aide à digérer

digestive [dɪ'dʒestɪv, daɪ-] **ADJ** digestif; **d. troubles** troubles *mpl* digestifs *ou* de digestion
N 1 *Pharm etc* digestif *m* **2** *Br (biscuit)* = sorte de sablé
▸▸ *Br* **d. biscuit** = sorte de sablé; **d. system** système *m* digestif; **d. tract** tube *m* digestif

Digger ['dɪgər] **N** *Fam (Australian)* Australien, -ienne; *(New Zealander)* Néo-Zélandais, -aise

digger ['dɪgər] **N 1** *Constr (mechanical)* **d.** excavateur *m* **2** *(person) (with spade)* per-

sonne *f* qui bêche; *(for gold etc)* chercheur *m* **3** *(wasp)* guêpe *f* fouisseuse
▸▸ **d. wasp** guêpe fouisseuse

digging ['dɪgɪŋ] **N** *(of soil)* bêchage *m*, labour *m* à la bêche; *(of well, ditches etc)* creusement *m*; *Archeol* fouilles *fpl*

digibox ['dɪdʒɪbɒks] **N** décodeur *m* numérique

digicam ['dɪdʒɪkæm] **N** *(abbr* **digital camera)** caméra *f* numérique

digit ['dɪdʒɪt] **N 1** *Math* chiffre *m* (arabe); **double d. inflation** taux *m* d'inflation à deux chiffres **2** *(on hand)* doigt *m*; *(on foot)* orteil *m*; *Br Hum* **extract the d.!** grouille-toi!
▸▸ *Comput* **d. selector** sélecteur *m* d'indice

digital ['dɪdʒɪt(ə)l] **ADJ 1** *Comput, Tel* numérique **2** *Anat* digital, -aux
▸▸ **d. analog(ue) converter** convertisseur *m* analogique numérique; **d. audio broadcasting** diffusion *f* audio numérique; **d. audio tape** cassette *f* numérique; **d. camera** appareil *m* photo numérique; **d. cash** argent *m* électronique *ou* virtuel; *TV* **d. channel** chaîne *f* numérique; **d. clock** horloge *f* à affichage numérique; **d. computer** calculateur *m* numérique; **d. display** affichage *m* numérique; **d. economy** netéconomie *f*, **d. frequency display** affichage digital des fréquences; **d. graphics card** carte *f* graphique numérique; **d. imaging** photographie *f* numérique; **d. music** musique *f* en enregistrement numérique; **d. radio** radio *f* numérique; **d. readout** affichage digital; **d. recording** enregistrement *m* numérique; **d. signal** signal *m* numérique; *Comput* **d. signature** signature *f* électronique; **d. sound** son *m* numérique; **d. tape** bande *f* numérique; **d. television, d. TV** télévision *f* numérique; *Comput* **d. versatile disk** disque *m* vidéo numérique; **d. video** vidéo *f* numérique; **d. video disk** disque vidéo numérique; *Comput* **d. wallet** porte-monnaie *m inv* électronique; **d. watch** montre *f* à affichage numérique

digitalis [dɪdʒɪ'teɪlɪs] **N 1** *Bot* digitale *f* **2** *Pharm* digitaline *f*

digitalization [dɪdʒɪtəlaɪ'zeɪʃən] **N** numérisation *f*

digitalize ['dɪdʒɪtəlaɪz] **VT** numériser

digitally ['dɪdʒɪtəlɪ] **ADV** numériquement; **d. recorded/remastered** enregistré/remixé en numérique

digitization [dɪdʒɪtaɪ'zeɪʃən] **N** numérisation *f*

digitize ['dɪdʒɪtaɪz] **VT** convertir en numérique, numériser

digitizer ['dɪdʒɪtaɪzər] **N** *Comput* numériseur *m*

diglossia [daɪ'glɒsɪə] **N** *Ling* diglossie *f*

dignified ['dɪgnɪfaɪd] **ADJ** *(person)* digne, plein de dignité; *(air, silence)* digne; **to have a d. manner** avoir de la dignité dans ses manières

dignify ['dɪgnɪfaɪ] **VT** *(something)* donner de la dignité à; **to d. sb with the name of ...** honorer qn du nom de ...; **I won't d. that remark with a response** je ne m'abaisserai pas à répondre à cette remarque

dignitary ['dɪgnɪt(ə)rɪ] **N** dignitaire *m*

dignity ['dɪgnɪtɪ] **N** dignité *f*; **a woman of great d.** une femme d'une grande dignité; **to be** *or* **stand on one's d.** se retrancher derrière sa dignité; **to consider sth beneath one's d.** considérer que qch est en-dessous de soi; **it was beneath my d. even to respond** je me serais abaissé à seulement répondre; **the d. of labour** la dignité du travail

digress [daɪ'gres] **VI** faire une digression/des digressions; **to d. from a subject** s'écarter d'un sujet; **I'd like to d. for a moment** j'aimerais faire une parenthèse

digression [daɪ'greʃən] **N** digression *f*, **by way of a d.** par parenthèse

digs [dɪgz] **NPL** *Br Fam (lodgings)* logement *m*; **to live in d.** loger en meublé; **where are your d.?** où est-ce que tu crèches?

dihedral [daɪ'hiːdrəl] **N** dièdre *m*
ADJ *(angle)* dièdre

dike [daɪk] **N, VT** = **dyke¹**

dilapidated [dɪ'læpɪdeɪtɪd] **ADJ** *(building, car etc)* délabré, dans un état de délabrement; *Hum (hat, suit)* dépenaillé

dilapidation [dɪlæpɪ'deɪʃən] **N** *(of building, car etc)* délabrement *m*, dégradation *f*, **in a state of d.** dans un état de délabrement

dilate [daɪ'leɪt] **VT** dilater
VI *(of eyes etc)* se dilater
▸ **dilate on** **VT INSEP** *Fml (subject)* s'étendre sur

dilation [daɪ'leɪʃən] **N** dilatation *f*; **d. and curettage** (dilatation *f* et) curetage *m*

dilatoriness ['dɪlət(ə)rɪnɪs] **N** lenteur *f* (à agir)

dilatory ['dɪlət(ə)rɪ] **ADJ** *Fml (person)* lent (à agir); *(action)* tardif; *(answer)* dilatoire; **to be d. in doing sth** tarder à faire qch

dildo ['dɪldəʊ] **N 1** *(device)* godemiché *m* **2** *Sl (stupid person)* abruti, -ie

dilemma [daɪ'lemə] **N** embarras *m*; *(in logic)* dilemme *m*; **to be in a d.** être bien embarrassé; **you place** *or* **put me in a d.** tu me mets dans l'embarras; **to be in a d. over a decision** être pris dans un dilemme au sujet d'une décision; **she's in a bit of a d. over whether to tell him or not** elle ne sait pas trop si elle doit le lui dire ou non; **to be on the horns of a d.** être pris dans un dilemme

dilettante, *pl* **dilettanti** [dɪlɪ'tɑːntɪ] **N** dilettante *mf*
ADJ **in a d. manner** *(to do sth)* en dilettante

dilettantism [dɪlɪ'tɑːntɪz(ə)m] **N** dilettantisme *m*

diligence ['dɪlɪdʒ(ə)ns] **N** assiduité *f*, application *f*, zèle *m*

diligent ['dɪlɪdʒ(ə)nt] **ADJ** *(student, work)* assidu, appliqué; *(employee)* consciencieux, zélé; *(inquiries, search)* consciencieux, minutieux

diligently ['dɪlɪdʒ(ə)ntlɪ] **ADV** *(to study)* avec assiduité, assidûment; *(to work)* consciencieusement, avec zèle

dill [dɪl] **N 1** *(herb)* aneth *m* **2** *Austr Fam* andouille *f*

dilly-dally ['dɪlɪ'dælɪ] **VI** **(dilly-dallied)** *Fam* **1** *(loiter)* traîner, traînasser, lambiner **2** *(vacillate)* hésiter, tergiverser; **to d. about whether to do sth** se tâter pour savoir si on fait qch

dilute [daɪ'luːt, dɪ-] **VT 1** *(orange juice, acid)* diluer (**with** avec); *(sauce)* allonger (**with** de); **to d. wine with water** couper du vin avec de l'eau; **d. to taste** *(written on bottle)* diluer à votre convenance; **to become diluted** se diluer **2** *Fig (theory etc)* édulcorer; **diluted radicalism** radicalisme *m* à l'eau de rose
ADJ *(orange juice, acid)* dilué, étendu

dilution [daɪ'luːʃən, dɪ-] **N** dilution *f*, *Fig (of theory)* édulcoration *f*, *Fin* **d. of equity** dilution du bénéfice par action

dim [dɪm] **ADJ** **(dimmer, dimmest)** *(light)* faible, pâle; *(eyesight)* faible, trouble; *(forest, room, lighting)* sombre; *(outline, memory)* vague, faible, estompé; *Fam (chances, prospects)* faible, mince; *(person)* bête; **to grow d.** *(of light, faculties)* baisser; *(of recollection)* s'effacer; *(of eyesight)* se troubler; *(of outline)* s'effacer, s'estomper; *Fam* **to take a d. view of sth** avoir une piètre opinion de qch, désapprouver qch
VT **(-mm-)** *(light)* atténuer, réduire; *(sight)*

obscurcir; *(memory, intelligence)* troubler; *(beauty, surface of a mirror)* ternir; *Fig (sb's glory)* éclipser; **to d. the lights** baisser les lumières; *Am Aut* **to d. one's headlights** se mettre en code; **dimmed headlights** phares *mpl* code

vi *(of light)* baisser; *(of eyes)* s'obscurcir; *(of outline)* s'effacer, s'estomper

dimbo [ˈdɪmbəʊ] **n** *Fam* ballot *m*, nigaud, -e

dim-dip **n** *Aut* veilleuses-codes *fpl*

dime [daɪm] **n** *Am* dime *f (un dixième de dollar)*; **it's not worth a d.** ça ne vaut pas un clou; *Fig* **they're a d. a dozen** il y en a à la pelle; **arts graduates are a d. a dozen** des licenciés ès lettres, il y en a à la pelle, les licenciés ès lettres courent les rues

► ► *Am* **d. store** supérette *f* de quartier

dimension [daɪˈmenʃən, dɪ-] **n** dimension *f*, **what are the dimensions of the room?** quelles sont les dimensions de la pièce?; **of large dimensions** de grandes dimensions; **the fourth d.** la quatrième dimension; *Fig* **there's another d. to the problem** le problème a une autre dimension [SEE GRAMMAR 859]

dimensional [daɪˈmenʃən(ə)l, dɪ-] **adj** dimensionnel

-dimensional **suff** **two/three-d.** à deux/ trois dimensions

diminish [dɪˈmɪnɪʃ] **vt** *(power, enthusiasm)* diminuer, réduire; *(sound, light)* diminuer, baisser; *(reputation)* diminuer, affaiblir; **to d. the importance of sth** diminuer l'importance de qch

vi *(of power, enthusiasm, reputation)* diminuer, s'affaiblir; *(of sound, light)* diminuer, s'atténuer, baisser

diminished [dɪˈmɪnɪʃt] **adj** *(power, reputation)* diminué, affaibli; *(light)* atténué; *Mus (interval)* diminué; **he's greatly d.** *(physically)* il est très diminué

► ► *Law* **d. responsibility** responsabilité *f* atténuée

diminishing [dɪˈmɪnɪʃɪŋ] **adj** *(light, power etc)* décroissant, qui diminue; *(value)* à la baisse; *(popularity)* en baisse

► ► *Econ* **d. marginal utility** utilité *f* marginale décroissante; **d. returns** rendements *mpl* décroissants; *Econ, Fig* **law of d. returns** loi *f* des rendements décroissants

diminuendo [dɪmɪnjʊˈendəʊ] **n** *Mus* diminuendo *m*

diminution [dɪmɪˈnjuːʃən] **n** diminution *f*, réduction *f* (**in** de)

diminutive [dɪˈmɪnjʊtɪv] **n** *Gram* diminutif *m*

adj **1** *(tiny)* tout petit, minuscule **2** *Gram* diminutif

dimly [ˈdɪmlɪ] **adv** *(to see)* indistinctement; *(to sense, remember)* vaguement; **d. lit room** pièce mal éclairée

dimmed [dɪmd] **adj** *Comput (command)* en grisé, estompé

► ► *Comput* **d. icon** icône *f* estompée

dimmer [ˈdɪmər] **n** *Elec* variateur *m*; *Cin* obscurateur *m* de salle; *Am Aut* **dimmers** *(headlights)* (phares *mpl*) codes *mpl*, *(parking lights)* feux *mpl* de position

► ► **d. bulb** ampoule *f* veilleuse; **d. switch** *Elec* variateur; *Cin* obscurateur de salle

dimness [ˈdɪmnɪs] **n** *(of lighting, sight)* faiblesse *f*, *(of room)* obscurité *f*, *(of memory)* imprécision *f*, vague *m*; *Fam (of person)* stupidité *f*, bêtise *f*

dimple [ˈdɪmp(ə)l] **n 1** *(on cheek, chin)* fossette *f* **2** *(on surface of water)* ride *f*

vt 1 *(of smile) (sb's cheeks)* creuser des fossettes dans **2** *(of wind) (surface of water)* rider

vi 1 *(of cheeks)* se creuser de fossettes **2** *(of water)* onduler

dimpled [ˈdɪmp(ə)ld] **adj** *(cheeks)* à fossettes

dimwit [ˈdɪmwɪt] **n** *Fam* idiot, -ote; **you d.!** imbécile!

dimwitted [dɪmˈwɪtɪd] **adj** *Fam* idiot, bête

din [dɪn] **n** tapage *m*, vacarme *m*, boucan *m*; **the d. of the traffic** le vacarme *ou* le boucan que fait/faisait/*etc* la circulation; **to make** *or* **kick up a d.** faire du tapage *ou* du boucan *ou* du vacarme

► **din into** **vt sep** **to d. sth into sb** enfoncer qch dans le crâne à qn; **to d. manners/the rules of the road into sb** inculquer les bonnes manières/le code de la route à qn

dinar [ˈdiːnɑːr] **n** *(monetary unit)* dinar *m*

dine [daɪn] **vi** dîner

► **dine in** **vi** *(of hotel guest)* dîner à l'hôtel

► **dine off** **vt insep 1** *(use) (porcelain, silver)* manger dans **2** *(eat)* manger au dîner

► **dine on** **vt insep** *(eat)* manger au dîner

► **dine out** **vi** *(in restaurant)* dîner en ville *ou* dans un restaurant; *(of hotel guest)* dîner dehors; *(at friends' home)* dîner chez des amis; *Fig* **you'll be dining out on that for years** ça te fera une bonne histoire à raconter pendant des années

diner [ˈdaɪnər] **n 1** *(person)* dîneur, -euse; **the restaurant serves two hundred diners every evening** ce restaurant sert deux cents repas chaque soir; **there were only a few late diners left in the restaurant** il n'y avait plus que quelques clients attardés dans le restaurant *m* **2** *Am (restaurant)* petit restaurant *m*; *Rail* wagon-restaurant *m*, *pl* wagons-restaurants

dinette [daɪˈnet] **n** coin-repas *m*, *pl* coins-repas

ding-a-ling [ˈdɪŋəlɪŋ] **n** *Fam* **1** *(of bell, phone)* sonnerie *f*; **to go d.** sonner, faire ding-ding-ding **2** *Am (penis)* quéquette *f*, zizi *m*; *(idiot)* andouille *f*

dingbat [ˈdɪŋbæt] **n 1** *Am, Austr Fam* crétin *m*; **don't be such a d.!** quel crétin tu fais! **2** *Comput* symbole *m* Dingbat

ding-dong [ˈdɪŋˈdɒŋ] **n 1** *(of bells)* tintement *m*, sonnerie *f*, *(of doorbell)* sonnerie; **to go d.** faire ding-ding-dong **2** *Fam (fight)* bagarre *f*

adj *Fam* **to have a d. argument** *(of two people)* se disputer violemment; **d. match** partie *f* vivement disputée

dinghy [ˈdɪŋ(g)ɪ] **n** dinghy *m*, *pl* dinghies; **(ship's) d.** youyou *m*; **sailing d.** dinghy à voile; **rubber** *or* **inflatable d.** canot *m* pneumatique

> Attention: ne pas confondre avec le terme **dingy**.

dinginess [ˈdɪndʒɪnɪs] **n** *(dirtiness)* aspect *m* miteux; *(darkness)* aspect sombre

dingo [ˈdɪŋgəʊ] **n** *(animal)* dingo *m*

dingy [ˈdɪndʒɪ] **adj** *(room, furniture etc)* défraîchi; *(colour)* terne; *(hotel)* miteux

> Attention: ne pas confondre avec le terme **dinghy**.

dining [ˈdaɪnɪŋ] **n**

► ► *Rail* **d. car** wagon-restaurant *m*, *pl* wagons-restaurants; **d. hall** réfectoire *m*, salle *f* à manger; **d. room** salle à manger; **d.(-room) table** table *f* de salle à manger

dink [dɪŋk] **n** *Hum (abbr* **double income, no kids)** = couple *m* sans enfants, qui touche deux salaires

dinkum [ˈdɪŋkəm] **adj** *Austr Fam (person)* sincère; *(object)* authentique; **fair d.** vrai de vrai

dinky [ˈdɪŋkɪ] **adj** *Br Fam (dainty)* mignon

n *Hum (abbr* **double income, no kids yet)** = membre *m* d'un couple à deux revenus qui n'a pas encore d'enfant

dinner [ˈdɪnər] **n** [VOIR GRAMMAIRE A7] **1** *(evening meal)* dîner *m*, *Can, Belg, Suisse* souper *m*; **what's for d.?** qu'y a-t-il au dîner?; **to go out to d.** *(in restaurant)* dîner en ville *ou* dans un restaurant; *(at friend's home)* dîner chez des amis; **to invite sb to d.** *(in restaurant)* inviter qn à dîner au restaurant; *(in one's home)* inviter qn à dîner; **at** *or* **during d.** au *ou* pendant le dîner; **to give the dog his d.** donner à manger au chien; **public d.** banquet *m*; *Mil* **regimental d.** repas de corps; **to discuss sth at the d. table** parler de qch autour d'un repas; **when was the last time we all sat down at the d. table together?** à quand remonte la dernière fois où nous nous sommes assis ensemble autour de la table de la salle à manger? **2** *Fam (midday meal)* déjeuner *m*, *Can* dîner *m*

► ► **d. hour** *(at work)* heure *f* du déjeuner; *(at school)* pause *f* de midi; **d. jacket** smoking *m*; *Br* **d. lady** = employée *f* d'une cantine scolaire; **d. party** dîner *(sur invitation)*; **d. service**, **d. set** service *m* de table; **d. time** heure *f* du dîner; **(it's) d. time!** à table!; **d. trolley** chariot *m* à repas

dinner-dance **n** dîner-dansant *m*, *pl* dîners-dansants

dinnerware [ˈdɪnərweər] **n** vaisselle *f*

dinosaur [ˈdaɪnəsɔːr] **n** dinosaure *m*

dint [dɪnt] **n** *Fml* **by d. of (doing) sth** à force de (faire) qch; **it was by d. of her efforts that …** c'est grâce à ses efforts que …

diocese [ˈdaɪəsɪs] **n** *Rel* diocèse *m*

diode [ˈdaɪəʊd] **n** *Electron* (lampe *f*) diode *f*

dioptre, *Am* **diopter** [daɪˈɒptər] **n** *Opt* dioptrie *f*

dioxide [daɪˈɒksaɪd] **n** *Chem* dioxyde *m*, bioxyde *m*

dioxin [daɪˈɒksɪn] **n** *Chem* dioxine *f*

Dip *abbr* **diploma**

dip [dɪp] **n 1** *(in ground)* inclinaison *f*, dépression *f*, *(in road)* descente *f*, *(in prices etc)* baisse *f*

2 *(swim)* baignade *f*; **I'm going for a d.** je vais faire un petit tour dans l'eau

3 *Culin* = sauce *f* dans laquelle on trempe les crudités etc

4 *Agr* **(sheep) d.** bain *m* parasiticide (pour moutons)

5 *Naut (with flag)* salut *m*

6 *Sl (pickpocket)* pickpocket *m*

vt (-pp-) **1** *(insert, put) (hands etc)* plonger (**into** dans); *Ind (metal)* immerger, décaper; *Agr* **to d. sheep** baigner les moutons

2 *(lower)* baisser subitement; *Br Aut* **to d. one's headlights** se mettre en code; *Naut* **to d. a flag** (faire) marquer un pavillon

vi 1 *(in water etc)* plonger; **her head dipped below the surface** sa tête disparut sous l'eau

2 *(of ground)* descendre, être incliné; *(of prices, temperature etc)* baisser; *(of scale)* pencher; **the road dips sharply** la route descend brusquement; **the sun dipped below the horizon** le soleil est descendu derrière l'horizon; **shares dipped on the London Stock Market yesterday** les actions ont baissé à la Bourse des valeurs de Londres hier

► ► *Br Aut* **d. switch** basculeur *m* de phares

► **dip into** **vt insep 1** *(use part of) (one's capital)* prendre dans; **I'm always dipping into my pocket** je suis toujours à débourser **2** *(read or study parts of) (book)* feuilleter; *(subject)* effleurer

D. Ed [ˈdiːˈed] **n** ≃ CAPES *m*

diphtheria [dɪfˈθɪərɪə] **n** *Med* diphtérie *f*, **to have d.** être atteint de la diphtérie

diphthong [ˈdɪfθɒŋ] **n** *Ling* diphtongue *f*

diploid [ˈdɪplɔɪd] **adj** *Biol* diploïde

diploma [dɪˈpləʊmə] **n** diplôme *m* (**in** de, **en**); **to sit a d.** passer l'examen d'obtention d'un diplôme; **d. course** cours *m* conduisant à un diplôme

diplomacy [dɪˈpləʊməsɪ] **N 1** *Pol* diplomatie *f* **2** *(tactfulness)* diplomatie *f*, tact *m*; **to attain one's ends by d.** user d'adresse pour atteindre son but

diplomat [ˈdɪpləmæt] **N** diplomate *mf*

diplomatic [dɪpləˈmætɪk] **ADJ 1** *Pol* diplomatique **2** *(tactful) (person)* diplomate; *(answer)* diplomatique; **you should have been more d.** tu aurais dû être plus diplomate; **he knows how to be d.** il sait être diplomate *ou* agir avec diplomatie

▸▸ *Pol* **d. bag** valise *f* diplomatique; *Pol* **d. corps** corps *m* diplomatique; *Pol* **d. immunity** immunité *f* diplomatique; *Am* **d. pouch** valise diplomatique; **d. service** service *m* diplomatique, diplomatie *f*

diplomatically [dɪpləˈmætɪklɪ] **ADV** diplomatiquement

diplomatist [dɪˈpləʊmətɪst] **N** diplomate *mf*

dipole [ˈdaɪpəʊl] **N** *Elec* dipôle *m*

dipped [dɪpt] **ADJ** *(sloping)* incliné

▸▸ *Br Aut* **d. headlights** codes *mpl*, feux *mpl* de croisement

dipper [ˈdɪpər] **N 1** *(bird)* cincle *m* plongeur **2** *Am Astron* **the Great** *or* **Big D.** la Grande Ourse; **the big d.** *(at fairground)* les montagnes *fpl* russes **3** *Br Aut* basculeur *m* de phares **4** *(ladle)* cuillère *f* à pot, louche *f*

▸▸ *Br Aut* **d. switch** basculeur de phares

dipping [ˈdɪpɪŋ] **N 1** *(plunging)* plongée *f*, immersion *f*; *Metal* décapage *m*; *Agr (of sheep)* baignage *m* **2** *Br Aut (of headlights)* mise *f* en code

dippy [ˈdɪpɪ] **ADJ** *Old-fashioned Fam* toqué

dipso [ˈdɪpsəʊ] **N** *Sl (drinker)* poivrot, -ote

dipsomania [dɪpsəˈmeɪnɪə] **N** dipsomanie *f*

dipsomaniac [dɪpsəˈmeɪnɪæk] **N** dipsomane *mf*

dipstick [ˈdɪpstɪk] **N 1** *Aut* jauge *f* (de niveau) d'huile; *Med (for urine test etc)* bandelette *f* réactive **2** *Fam (idiot)* abruti, -ie

DIP switch [ˈdɪpswɪtʃ] **N** *Comput* interrupteur *m* DIP

dir *abbr* **1** *Admin* **director 2** *Comput* **directory**

dire [ˈdaɪər] **ADJ 1** *(foreboding)* lugubre; **d. necessity** dure nécessité; **to be in d. need of sth** avoir un besoin urgent de qch; **to be in d. straits** être dans une très mauvaise passe **2** *Fam (bad) (meal, book etc)* épouvantable

---

DIRECT [dɪˈrekt, daɪ-]

> **VT** adresser **1** ▪ diriger **1–3** ▪ réaliser **3** ▪ ordonner **4** ▪ instruire **4**
> **VI** faire de la réalisation
> **ADJ** direct **1, 2**
> **ADV** directement

VT 1 *(send, aim) (letter, remarks etc)* adresser (**to sb** à qn); *(light)* diriger (**at sth** sur qch); *(funds)* consacrer (**at sth** à qch); **to d. sb's attention to sth** appeler *ou* attirer l'attention de qn sur qch; **accusation directed against sb** accusation visant *ou* qui vise qn; **to d. one's steps towards …** diriger ses pas *ou* se diriger vers …; **can you d. me to the station?** pouvez-vous m'indiquer le chemin de la gare?; **to d. one's efforts at doing sth** consacrer ses efforts à faire qch

2 *(manage) (company, the economy)* diriger, mener, gérer; *(army, one's affairs)* conduire; **to d. traffic** régler la circulation

3 *Theat (play)* mettre en scène; *TV, Cin, Radio* réaliser; *(actors etc)* diriger; **directed by:** … *Theat* mise *f* en scène: …; *TV, Cin, Radio* réalisation *f*: …; **who directed it?** *(the play)* qui est le metteur en scène?; *(the*

film) de qui est la mise en scène?, de qui est ce film?

4 *(instruct) (somebody)* ordonner à, dire à (**to do** de faire); **as directed** *(as ordered)* conformément aux ordres; *(as instructed)* selon les instructions; **to d. the jury** *(of judge)* instruire le jury (sur un point de droit)

VI *Cin, Radio, TV* faire de la réalisation; *Theat* faire de la mise en scène

ADJ 1 *(straight, immediate) (route, control, influence, flight etc)* direct; *(cause)* immédiat; **to be a d. descendant of sb** descendre de qn en ligne directe

2 *(blunt)* direct; *(refusal)* catégorique; **in d. contradiction** en contradiction directe

ADV *(to go)* directement, tout droit; **to travel d. from London to Edinburgh** prendre un train/un vol/*etc* direct de Londres à Édimbourg; **to dispatch goods d. to sb** expédier des marchandises directement à qn; *Radio, TV* **the concert will be broadcast d. from Paris** ce concert sera transmis en direct de Paris

▸▸ **d. advertising** publicité *f* directe; **d. air link** liaison *f* aérienne directe; **d. banking** banque *f* à distance; *Tel* **d. broadcast satellite** satellite *m* de télédiffusion directe; **d.-comparison advertising** publicité comparative directe; **d. competition** concurrence *f* directe; **d. costing** méthode *f* des coûts variables *ou* proportionnels; **d. costs** charges *fpl* directes, frais *mpl* directs; *Elec* **d. current** courant *m* continu; *Br Banking, Fin* **d. debit** prélèvement *m* automatique; **to pay by d. debit** payer par prélèvement automatique; **d. debit advice** avis *m* de prélèvement; **d. democracy** démocratie *f* directe; *Tel* **d. dialling** automatique *m*; *Aut* **d. gear** prise *f* directe; **d. hit** coup *m* au but; **d. investment** investissement *m* direct; **d. labour** main-d'œuvre *f* directe; *Tel* **d. line** ligne *f* directe; *Com, Mktg* **d. mail** publipostage *m*; **d. mail advertising** publicité directe, publicité par publipostage; **d. mail campaign** campagne *f* de publicité directe; **d. marketing** marketing *m* direct; *Comput* **d. memory access** accès *m* direct à la mémoire; *Gram* **d. object** complément *m* (d'objet) direct; **d. purchasing** achats *mpl* directs; *Pol* **d. rule** = contrôle *m* direct du maintien de l'ordre par le gouvernement britannique en Irlande du Nord imposé en 1972; **d. response advert** publicité à réponse directe; **d. response television** télévision *f* à réponse directe; **d. sale** vente *f* directe; **d. selling** vente directe; *Br Gram* **d. speech** discours *m ou* style *m* direct; *Fin* **d. tax** impôt *m* direct; *Fin* **d. taxation** imposition *f* directe

direct-dial number **N** *Tel* numéro *m* direct

direct-dial telephone **N** ligne *f* téléphonique directe, téléphone *m* direct

direction [dɪˈrekʃən, daɪ-] **N 1** *(management) (of company etc)* direction *f*, administration *f*; *(of traffic)* réglementation *f*; *Theat* mise *f* en scène; *TV, Cin, Radio* réalisation *f*; **under the d. of …** *(of orchestra)* sous la direction de …; *(of company)* dirigé par …

2 *(way)* direction *f*, sens *m*; **in the d. of …** dans la direction de …, en direction de …; *Aut* **d. of travel** sens *m* de la marche; **I'm going in your d.** je vais dans la même direction que toi; **we were going in the d. of Paris** nous nous dirigions vers Paris; **in every d.** dans tous les sens; **in all directions** dans tous les sens, dans tous les sens; **you are not looking in the right d.** vous ne regardez pas dans la bonne direction *ou* du bon côté; *Fig* **a step in the right d.** un pas dans la bonne direction; **in the opposite d.** en sens inverse; **in which d.?** de quel côté?; **to have a good/bad sense of d.** avoir un bon/mauvais sens de l'orientation; **to lose one's sense of d.** perdre le sens de l'orientation; **to lack d.** *(in*

life) ne pas avoir de but; *(of novel, play)* ne mener nulle part; **change of d.** changement *m* de direction; *Aviat, Naut* changement de cap; *Fig* **improvements in many directions** améliorations sous bien des rapports

3 directions *(instructions)* instructions *fpl*; **directions (for use)** notice *f* (explicative), mode *m* d'emploi; **you have been given the wrong directions** on vous a mal renseigné; **to give sb directions to a place** indiquer à qn comment aller à un endroit; **to ask for directions** *(to a place)* demander son chemin; *Theat* **stage directions** indications *fpl* scéniques; *Law* **d. to the jury** = exposé *m* de la loi fait par le juge au jury

▸▸ **d. finder** radiogoniomètre *m*; *Aut* **d. sign** panneau *m* de signalisation

directional [dɪˈrekʃən(ə)l, daɪ-] **ADJ** directionnel

▸▸ *Electron* **d. aerial, d. antenna** antenne *f* directionnelle *ou* directive; *TV, Cin* **d. cut** montage *m* directionnel; *Aut* **d. indicator** indicateur *m* (de changement) de direction

directive [dɪˈrektɪv, daɪ-] **N** *Mil etc* directive *f*; **to issue a d.** donner une directive

directly [dɪˈrektlɪ, daɪ-] **ADV 1** *(to go)* directement; *(to be descended from sb)* en ligne directe; **I'm flying d. from Glasgow** j'ai un vol direct au départ de Glasgow; **I am not d. concerned** je ne suis pas directement concerné; **d. opposite the church** juste en face de l'église; **to come d. to the point** aller droit au fait; **her views are d. opposite to my own** ses vues sont diamétralement opposées aux miennes **2** *(bluntly) (to answer, speak)* franchement; *(to attack, criticize)* directement **3** *(soon)* tout de suite, immédiatement; **I'm coming d.** je viens de suite **CONJ** aussitôt que, dès que; **I'll come d. I've finished** je viendrai dès que j'aurai fini

directness [dɪˈrektnɪs, daɪ-] **N** *(of answer etc)* franchise *f*; *(of criticism, questions)* caractère *m* direct; **his d. of speech** son franc-parler

director [dɪˈrektər, daɪ-] **N 1** *(of company etc)* directeur, -trice; *(board member)* administrateur, -trice; **d. of music** maître *m* de chapelle; *Mil etc* chef *m* de musique; *Sch* personne *f* chargée de l'organisation du programme d'études **2** *Theat* metteur *m* en scène; *TV, Cin, Radio* réalisateur, -trice

▸▸ **d.'s chair** régisseur *m*; *Cin* **d.'s cut** version *f* du réalisateur, director's cut *f*; *Fin* **d.'s fees** *(for attending meetings)* jetons *mpl* de présence; *Acct* **d.'s loan account** compte *m* courant d'administrateur; *Cin* **d. of photography** directeur, -trice de la photographie; *Radio, TV* **d. of programmes** directeur, -trice des programmes; *Br Law* **D. of Public Prosecutions** ≃ procureur *m* général; **directors' report** rapport *m* annuel; *Br Univ* **d. of studies** = enseignant *m* qui suit la scolarité d'un étudiant tout au long de son cursus universitaire

directorate [dɪˈrektər(e)ɪt, daɪ-] **N** conseil *m* d'administration

directorial [daɪrekˈtɔːrɪəl] **ADJ** de mise en scène; *Cin* **his d. début** son premier film derrière la caméra

directorship [dɪˈrektəʃɪp, daɪ-] **N 1** *(position)* poste *m ou* fonctions *fpl* de directeur; **she holds directorships in several companies** elle fait partie du conseil d'administration de plusieurs entreprises **2** *(term of office)* **during my d.** *(in past)* pendant que j'étais directeur; *(in present)* depuis que je suis directeur

directory [dɪˈrektərɪ, daɪ-] **N** *Tel* annuaire *m*; *(of addresses)* répertoire *m* d'adresses; *Comput* répertoire *m*; **street d.** guide *m* des rues; **commercial d.** annuaire du commerce

▸▸ *Tel Am* **d. assistance,** *Br* **d. enquiries** renseignements *mpl*; *Comput* **d. path** arborescence *f*, *Comput* **d. structure** structure *f* arborescente, structure du répertoire; *Comput* **d. tree** arborescence *f* des répertoires

dirge [dɜːdʒ] N hymne *m ou* chant *m* funèbre

dirigible ['dɪrɪdʒɪb(ə)l] N, ADJ *Fml* (*balloon*) dirigeable *m*

dirk [dɜːk] N *Scot* poignard *m*

dirt [dɜːt] N 1 saleté *f*, (*earth*) terre *f*, (*mud*) boue *f*, (*on unwashed object, hands etc*) crasse *f*, (*excrement*) crotte *f*, (*in machine, solution etc*) corps *mpl* étrangers, saletés; **hands ingrained with d.** mains encrassées; **covered in d.** crasseux, couvert de crasse; **to show the d.** (*of material*) être salissant; *Fig* **to treat sb like d.** traiter qn comme le dernier des derniers; *Am Fam* **to be d. poor** être vachement pauvre; *Am Sl* **to do sb d.** (*treat meanly*) faire un sale coup à qn 2 *Fam* (*obscenities*) cochonneries *fpl*; **to talk d.** dire des obscénités, raconter des cochonneries 3 (*gossip*) ragot *m*; **to dig the d. on sb** chercher à salir qn

▸▸ *Am* **d. farmer** exploitant *m* agricole; *Am* **d. farming** exploitation *f* agricole; **d. road** chemin *m* de terre *ou* non goudronné; **d. track** chemin *m* de terre; *Sport* (*piste f*) cendrée *f*, *Aut* **d.-track racing** courses *fpl* (motocyclistes) sur cendrée

dirtbag ['dɜːtbæg] N *Am Fam* nullard, -arde

dirt-cheap *Fam* ADJ vraiment pas cher; **that's d.** c'est donné

ADV pour trois fois rien; **I got it d.** je l'ai eu pour trois fois rien

dirtily ['dɜːtɪlɪ] ADV 1 (*to eat*) salement 2 (*crudely*) grossièrement 3 (*to play, fight*) déloyalement

dirtiness ['dɜːtɪnɪs] N saleté *f*

dirty ['dɜːtɪ] ADJ 1 sale; (*with mud*) crotté, (*valise, piston etc*) encrassé; **d. dishes** vaisselle *f* sale; **to get d.** (*of child, clothes etc*) se salir; **to get one's hands d.** se salir les mains; 2 (*sexually*) cochon; (*story etc*) cochon, sale; (*book, film*) pornographique; **you've got a d. mind** tu as l'esprit mal tourné, tu as l'esprit entre le nombril et les genoux; **d. joke** blague *f* cochonne *ou* obscène; **to tell d. stories** raconter des cochonneries *ou* des obscénités; **d. word** ragot *m*; *Fig* **competitiveness is a d. word nowadays** le mot 'compétitivité' est tabou de nos jours 3 (*nasty*) **it's a d. business** c'est une sale affaire; **d. job** sale boulot *m* 4 *Com* (*bill of lading*) clausé

N *Br Fam* **to do the d. on sb** jouer un sale tour *ou* coup à qn

ADV 1 *Fam* (*intensive*) **a d. great lorry** un énorme camion 2 **to talk d.** (*swearing*) dire des gros mots; (*sexually*) dire des trucs cochons

VT (*one's clothes etc*) salir; **to d. one's hands** se salir les mains; *Fig* **to d. one's reputation** entacher *ou* salir sa réputation

VI se salir, se souiller; **to d. easily** (*of material, car etc*) se salir facilement, être salissant

▸▸ *Typ* **d. copy** manuscrit *m* brouillé *ou* peu clair; *St Exch* **d. float** taux *mpl* de change concertés; **d. look** (*angry*) sale coup *m* d'œil; **to give sb a d. look** regarder qn d'un sale œil *Fin* **d. money** argent *m* sale *ou* mal acquis; *Fam* **d. old man** vieux cochon *m*; *Br Fam Hum* **d. stop-out** débauché, -ée (*qui découche*); **d. trick** (*malicious act*) sale tour *m*; **d. weather** sale temps *m*; *Naut* gros temps; *Fam* **d. weekend** week-end *m* coquin; **d. work** (*unpleasant*) travail *m* salissant; *Fam* (*dishonest*) sale boulot *m*

dis [dɪs] VT (**-ss-**) *Am Sl* (*disparage*) débiner

disability [dɪsə'bɪlɪtɪ] N 1 (*infirmity*) infirmité *f*, *Admin* invalidité *f*, (*work-related*) incapacité *f* de travail; *Fig* (*handicap*) handicap *m* 2 *Law* incapacité *f* légale, inhabilité *f* (**to do** à faire)

▸▸ **d. allowance, d. pension** pension *f* d'invalidité

disable [dɪ'seɪb(ə)l] VT *Mil* (*person*) mettre hors de combat; (*maim*) estropier; (*ship*) désemparer; (*machine*) mettre hors de service; (*function, feature*) désactiver

disabled [dɪ'seɪb(ə)ld] ADJ (*infirm*) infirme, handicapé, (*as result of accident etc*) handicapé, estropié; (*ship*) désemparé; **d. exserviceman** mutilé *m* de guerre

NPL **the d.** (*people*) les handicapés; **facilities for the d.** aménagements *mpl* pour les handicapés

▸▸ **d. access** facilité *f* d'accès pour personnes handicapées

disablement [dɪ'seɪb(ə)lmənt] N 1 (*physical handicap*) invalidité *f*, *Admin* **degree of d.** coefficient *m* d'invalidité 2 (*action*) *Mil* mise *f* hors de combat; (*of machine*) mise hors service

disabuse [dɪsə'bjuːz] VT détromper; **to d. sb of sth** (*of idea*) détromper qn de qch; (*of illusion*) faire perdre qch à qn

disadvantage [dɪsəd'vɑːntɪdʒ] N désavantage *m*, inconvénient *m*; **the d. of the plan is that ...** l'inconvénient de ce projet est que ...; **to be at a d.** être désavantagé (**owing to sth** par qch); **to put sb at a d.** désavantager qn

VT désavantager

disadvantaged [dɪsəd'vɑːntɪdʒd] ADJ défavorisé

NPL **the d.** les défavorisés *mpl*; **the educationally d.** les personnes *fpl* défavorisées en matière d'éducation

disadvantageous [dɪsædvən'teɪdʒəs] ADJ désavantageux (**to** pour), défavorable (**to** à)

disaffected [dɪsə'fektɪd] ADJ (*supporters, troops etc*) mécontent (**with** de)

disaffection [dɪsə'fekʃən] N mécontentement *m*, insatisfaction *f*; **d. among the troops is growing** le mécontentement grandit au sein des troupes

disagree [dɪsə'griː] VI 1 (*of person*) ne pas être d'accord (**with** avec); (*quarrel*) se disputer, se brouiller (**with** avec); **to d. with sb** ne pas être du même avis que qn, ne pas être d'accord avec qn; **I d.** je ne suis pas de cet avis; **I can't say I d. with her** (*in opinion etc*) je ne peux pas dire que je ne suis pas de son avis; (*as regards an action*) je ne peux pas dire que je la désapprouve 2 (*not correspond*) (*of accounts, figures*) ne pas concorder 3 (*be unsuitable*) ne pas convenir (**with** à); **red wine disagrees with me** je ne supporte pas le vin rouge; **the climate disagrees with him** le climat ne lui convient pas *ou* ne lui va pas; **hard work disagrees with me** je ne suis pas fait pour les gros labeurs; **children d. with me** les enfants et moi, ça fait deux

disagreeable [dɪsə'griːəb(ə)l] ADJ (*person, job, smell*) désagréable; (*remark*) désobligeant; **he was very d. to her** il s'est montré très désagréable envers elle; **to make a d. impression on sb** faire une impression défavorable sur qn

disagreeableness [dɪsə'griːəb(ə)lnɪs] N (*of situation*) caractère *m* désagréable; (*of person*) mauvaise humeur *f*, (*of remark*) désobligeance *f* (**to** envers)

disagreeably [dɪsə'griːəblɪ] ADV désagréablement; **to behave d. to(wards) sb** se montrer désagréable envers qn

disagreement [dɪsə'griːmənt] N 1 (*of figures*) différence *f* (**between** entre) 2 (*failure to agree*) désaccord *m* (**with sb about sth** avec qn sur qch), conflit *m* d'opinions; **we are in d.** nous sommes en désaccord; **to be in d. with sb** ne pas partager l'avis de qn,

être en désaccord avec qn 3 (*quarrel*) brouille *f*, différend *m*; **to have a d. with sb** se disputer avec qn

disallow [dɪsə'laʊ] VT 1 (*reject*) (*hypothesis etc*) ne pas admettre, ne pas reconnaître; *Law* (*testimony*) rejeter 2 *Ftbl etc* (*goal, try*) annuler

disambiguate [dɪsæm'bɪgjʊeɪt] VT désambiguïser

disappear [dɪsə'pɪər] VI disparaître (**from a place** d'un endroit); **to d. in** *or* **into the crowd** se perdre dans la foule; **since she disappeared** depuis sa disparition

disappearance [dɪsə'pɪərəns] N disparition *f*

disappearing [dɪsə'pɪərɪŋ] ADJ (*race, species*) en voie de disparition; **where's that d. programme changer?** où est-ce que la télécommande a encore été se cacher?; **to do a d. act** (*of conjurer*) (*make sb/sth disappear*) faire disparaître quelqu'un/quelque chose; (*make self disappear*) disparaître; *Fig Fam* (*sneak away*) s'esquiver, s'éclipser; *Fam* **the scissors have done a d. act** les ciseaux ont disparu; **he's done his famous d. act again** il s'est encore éclipsé

disappoint [dɪsə'pɔɪnt] VT (*person*) décevoir; (*after promising*) manquer de parole à; (*person's hopes*) tromper

disappointed [dɪsə'pɔɪntɪd] ADJ (*person*) déçu; (*candidate*) refusé; **we were all d. that you couldn't come** nous avons tous été très déçus que tu ne puisses pas venir; **he was d. at** *or* **about not being invited** il a été déçu de ne pas être invité; **I am d. in** *or* **with you** tu m'as déçu; **I was d. with it** cela m'a déçu; **he was bitterly d.** il a eu une grande déception; **d. customers** clients insatisfaits; **to be d. in love** avoir des chagrins d'amour

disappointing [dɪsə'pɔɪntɪŋ] ADJ décevant; **how d.!** quelle déception!

disappointingly [dɪsə'pɔɪntɪŋlɪ] ADV **the unemployment figures are still d. high** il est décevant de constater que les chiffres du chômage restent élevés

disappointment [dɪsə'pɔɪntmənt] N déception *f*, **it was a bit of a d.** (*of film, holiday etc*) c'était un peu décevant; **bitter d.** vive contrariété *f*; **to suffer many disappointments** essuyer bien des déboires; **you've been a great d. to your parents** tu as beaucoup déçu tes parents; **to their great d., she did not come** à leur grande déception, elle n'est pas venue; **book early to avoid d.** réservez bien à l'avance pour ne pas être déçu

disapprobation [dɪsæprəʊ'beɪʃən] N *Fml* désapprobation *f* (**of** à l'égard de)

disapproval [dɪsə'pruːv(ə)l] N désapprobation *f* (**of** de); **look of d.** regard désapprobateur; **to look at sb with d.** regarder qn avec désapprobation; **much to our d.** bien que nous n'approuvions pas

disapprove [dɪsə'pruːv] VI **I d.** je ne suis pas d'accord; (*stronger, in principle*) je désapprouve; **to d. of sth** désapprouver qch; **to d. of sth being done** désapprouver que l'on fasse qch; **she disapproves of her son-inlaw** son gendre n'est pas à son goût; **your mother disapproves of me** ta mère ne m'aime pas

disapproving [dɪsə'pruːvɪŋ] ADJ (*look, tone etc*) désapprobateur, -trice; **he was a stern, rather d. man** c'était un homme sévère, qui portait sur toutes choses un œil désapprobateur

disapprovingly [dɪsə'pruːvɪŋlɪ] ADV (*to look*) d'un air désapprobateur; (*to say*) d'un ton désapprobateur

disarm [dɪs'ɑːm] VT (*prisoner, country etc*) désarmer; (*bomb etc*) désamorcer; *Fig* **her**

frankness quite disarmed us sa franchise nous a complètement désarmés
vi désarmer

disarmament [dɪs'ɑːməmənt] **N** désarmement *m*

disarming [dɪs'ɑːmɪŋ] **ADJ** *(smile, honesty etc)* désarmant

disarmingly [dɪs'ɑːmɪŋlɪ] **ADV he was d.
frank** il montrait une franchise désarmante; **to smile d.** sourire de façon désarmante

disarrange [dɪsə'reɪndʒ] **VT** *Fml* déranger, mettre en désordre; **to d. sb's plans** déranger *ou* bouleverser les projets de qn

disarrangement [dɪsə'reɪndʒmənt] **N** dérangement *m*

disarray [dɪsə'reɪ] **N** désordre *m*; **in complete d.** *(of person)* en plein désarroi; *(of objects, room, life)* en désordre; *(of troops)* en déroute; **the news threw the company into complete d.** cette nouvelle a semé la panique dans l'entreprise

disassemble [dɪsə'semb(ə)l] **VT** démonter

disassembler [dɪsə'semblər] **N** *Comput* désassembleur *m*

disassociate [dɪsə'səʊʃɪeɪt] **VT** = **dissociate**

disassociation [dɪsəsəʊsɪ'eɪʃən] **N** = **dissociation**

disaster [dɪ'zɑːstər] **N** *also Fig Fam* désastre *m*; *(by shipwreck, fire, earthquake etc)* sinistre *m*; *Fam (person)* catastrophe *f*; **our journey was a series of disasters** notre voyage n'a été qu'une suite de malheurs; **they were near the summit when d. struck** ils avaient presque atteint le sommet quand la catastrophe a eu lieu; **he is heading for d.** il court à sa perte; **it would be a d.!** ce serait le désastre!; **to finish** *or* **end in d.** tourner à la tragédie; *Fig* **the party was an absolute d.** la soirée a été un vrai désastre; **air/railway d.** catastrophe aérienne/ferroviaire; **financial d.** désastre financier
▸▸ **d. area** région *f* sinistrée; *Fig* champ *m* de bataille; **d. fund** fonds *m* de secours; **d. movie** film *m* catastrophe

disastrous [dɪ'zɑːstrəs] **ADJ** désastreux; **just how d. would that be?** est-ce que ce serait vraiment une catastrophe?

disastrously [dɪ'zɑːstrəslɪ] **ADV** désastreusement; **the performance went d. wrong** la représentation a tourné au désastre; **the estimates were d. inaccurate** l'inexactitude des prévisions s'est révélée désastreuse; **his attitude was d. complacent** son attitude complaisante a eu des effets désastreux; **d. bad** désastreux; **d. optimistic** terriblement optimiste

disavow [dɪsə'vaʊ] **VT** *Fml* désavouer, renier

disavowal [dɪsə'vaʊəl] **N** *Fml* désaveu *m*

disband [dɪs'bænd] **VT** *(troops etc)* licencier; *(committee etc)* dissoudre
vi *(of troops)* se débander; *(on instructions)* être licencié; *(of committee etc)* être dissout

disbar [dɪs'bɑː] **VT** *(-rr-)* *Law (lawyer)* rayer du barreau *ou* du tableau de l'ordre

disbarment [dɪs'bɑːmənt] **N** *Law (of lawyer)* radiation *f* du tableau de l'ordre *ou* de la liste du barreau

disbelief [dɪsbɪ'liːf] **N** incrédulité *f* (**in sth** à l'égard de qch); **she looked at him in d.** elle l'a regardé, incrédule

disbelieve [dɪsbɪ'liːv] **VT** *(somebody, something)* ne pas croire
vi *Fml* **to d. in sb/sth** ne pas croire à qn/qch

disbeliever [dɪsbɪ'liːvər] **N** *esp Rel* incrédule *mf*

disbelieving [dɪsbɪ'liːvɪŋ] **ADJ** *(look)* incrédule

disbud [dɪs'bʌd] **VT** *Bot (fruit tree)* ébourgeonner

disburse [dɪs'bɜːs] **VT** *Fml (money)* débourser

disbursement [dɪs'bɜːsmənt] **N 1** *(paying out)* déboursement *m* **2** *(money)* débours *m*
▸▸ *Fin* **d. voucher** bon *m* de décaissement

disc, *Am* **disk** [dɪsk] **N 1** *(record)* disque *m*
2 *Comput* = **disk**
3 *(of moon etc)* disque *m*; *Tech* disque, plateau *m*; *(made of cardboard etc)* rondelle *f*; *Mil etc* **identity** *or* **identification d.** plaque *f* d'identité; *Aut* **parking d.** disque de stationnement; *Aut* **(tax) d.** vignette *f*
4 *Anat* disque *m*; **intervertebral d.** disque intervertébral; *Med* **slipped d.** hernie *f* discale; **to slip a d.** se faire une hernie discale
▸▸ *Aut* **d. brakes** freins *mpl* à disque; *Phot* **d. camera** appareil *m* photo à disque; *Aut* **d. clutch** embrayage *m* monodisque; *Phot* **d. film** disque *m*; *Agr* **d. harrow** pulvériseur *m*; **d. jockey** animateur, -trice; *(on radio, in club)* disc-jockey *m*, *pl* disc-jockeys; *Agr* **d. plough** charrue *f* à disques; *Tech* **d. valve** clapet *m* disque; **d. wheel** roue *f* pleine *ou* à voile plein

discard ['dɪskɑːd] **N 1** *Cards (action, card) (at cribbage)* écart *m*; *(at bridge)* défausse *f* **2** *Ind (rejected part)* pièce *f* de rebut
VT 1 *(object)* se débarrasser de; *(person, project)* abandonner; *(item of clothing, old car etc)* mettre au rebut; **one of her discarded lovers** un de ses amants abandonnés; **his discarded coat still lay on the sofa** son manteau était toujours sur le canapé, tel qu'il l'y avait jeté **2** *Cards (at cribbage) (card)* écarter; *(at bridge etc) (suit)* se défausser de
vi *Cards (at bridge)* se défausser

discern [dɪ'sɜːn] **VT** distinguer, discerner, percevoir; **to d. a distant object** discerner *ou* reconnaître un objet dans le lointain

discernible [dɪ'sɜːnɪb(ə)l] **ADJ** perceptible

discernibly [dɪ'sɜːnɪblɪ] **ADV** perceptiblement

discerning [dɪ'sɜːnɪŋ] **ADJ** *(person)* éclairé, plein de discernement; *(intelligence)* pénétrant; *(taste)* délicat; **with a d. eye** d'un œil averti; **a house/car for the d. buyer** une maison/voiture pour l'acheteur avisé; **for the d. reader** pour le lecteur averti

discernment [dɪ'sɜːnmənt] **N** *(judgement)* discernement *m*, jugement *m*

discharge¹ ['dɪstʃɑːdʒ] **N 1** *(release)*, *Med (of patient)* renvoi *m*; *Law (of prisoner)* mise *f* en liberté, libération *f*; *(of the accused)* acquittement *m*; *Fin (of bankrupt)* réhabilitation *f*; **to apply for one's d.** *(of bankrupt)* demander sa réhabilitation
2 *(dismissal) (of employee)* renvoi *m*; *(of servant)* congé *m*; *Mil (after active service)* démobilisation *f*; *Mil, Naut (for unfitness)* réforme *f*; *Mil, Naut* **to take one's d.** prendre son congé
3 *(firing) (of firearm, artillery)* décharge *f*
4 *(emission) (of water etc)* décharge *f*, évacuation *f*; *(of gas)* décharge, dégagement *m*; *(of steam)* échappement *m*; *(from pump)* débit *m*; *Elec (of electricity, battery)* décharge; *Med (of blood)* perte *f*, *(of pus)* écoulement *m*; *(vaginal)* pertes *fpl*; *Ind (water from factory etc)* eaux *fpl* usées
5 *(performance, fulfilment) (of duty)* accomplissement *m*; *(of debt)* paiement *m*; **in the d. of his duties** dans l'exercice de ses fonctions
6 *(unloading) (of ship, cargo)* déchargement *m*
▸▸ *Tech* **d. nozzle** buse *f* de sortie; **d. pipe** tuyau *m* de décharge *ou* de débit; **d. pump** pompe *f* d'extraction *ou* d'épuisement

discharge² [dɪs'tʃɑːdʒ] **VT 1** *(release) (patient)* renvoyer; *(prisoner)* libérer, mettre en

liberté; *(the accused)* acquitter; *Law (bankrupt)* réhabiliter, décharger; *(debtor)* libérer; **he was discharged from hospital yesterday** il est sorti de l'hôpital hier; **to d. oneself from hospital** signer sa propre décharge; *Law* **to d. the jury** congédier les jurés; *Fin* **discharged bankrupt** failli *m* réhabilité; **to d. sb from an obligation** décharger *ou* acquitter qn d'une obligation
2 *(dismiss) (employee)* congédier, renvoyer; *(workman)* débaucher; *(civil servant)* destituer; *(troops)* licencier; *(soldier)* congédier, donner son congé à, désenrôler; *Mil, Naut (for unfitness) (enlisted man)* réformer; **to be discharged from the force** être congédié
3 *(firearm)* décharger, faire partir; *(missile)* lancer; *Elec (battery etc)* décharger
4 *(emit) (steam)* dégager; *(of chemical reaction) (gas)* dégager; *(of gland) (hormones)* sécréter; *(of reservoir etc) (water)* déverser; *(of pump)* débiter; **to d. pus** *(of abscess)* suppurer; **river that discharges its water into a lake** rivière qui déverse ses eaux dans un lac
5 *(perform, fulfil) (one's duties)* accomplir, s'acquitter de; *Fin (debt)* liquider, solder; *(fine)* payer; *(account, obligation)* apurer
6 *(unload) (ship, tank etc)* décharger; *(cargo)* décharger, débarquer; *(of vehicle) (passengers)* déposer
vi 1 *(of gun)* partir, se décharger
2 *Med (of abscess, wound)* suppurer
3 *(of river)* se jeter, déboucher (**into a lake** dans un lac)
4 *Elec (of battery)* se décharger

disciple [dɪ'saɪp(ə)l] **N** *Rel, Fig* disciple *m*

disciplinarian [dɪsɪplɪ'neərɪən] **N** partisan, -ane d'une forte discipline; **he is a strict d.** il est strict en matière de discipline

disciplinary ['dɪsɪplɪnərɪ] **ADJ** *(measures, committee)* disciplinaire; *(problems)* de discipline; **to take d. action** *(of employer)* prendre des mesures disciplinaires
▸▸ **d. board** conseil *m* de discipline; **d. hearing** séance *f* du conseil de discipline; **d. procedure** procédure *f* disciplinaire

discipline ['dɪsɪplɪn] **N 1** discipline *f*; **iron d.** discipline de fer; **to keep d.** *(of teacher)* maintenir la discipline **2** *(branch of learning)* discipline *f*
VT 1 *(pupils, troops)* discipliner; *(punish)* punir; **to d. oneself** se discipliner **2** *(character)* former

disciplined ['dɪsɪplɪnd] **ADJ** discipliné; *(showing self-control)* contrôlé

disclaim [dɪs'kleɪm] **VT 1** *(deny) (knowledge, responsibility)* nier **2** *(reject) (person's authority)* démentir, renier **3** *Law (right etc)* se désister de, renoncer à

disclaimer [dɪs'kleɪmər] **N 1** *(denial)* démenti *m*; *(of responsibility)* dénégation *f*; **to issue a d.** publier un démenti; **d. of authorship** désaveu *m* **2** *Law* désistement *m*, renonciation *f* (**of a right** à un droit)

disclose [dɪs'kləʊz] **VT 1** *(make known) (secret, information etc)* divulguer, révéler; **to d. that …** révéler que … **2** *(show)* révéler

disclosure [dɪs'kləʊʒər] **N 1** *(of one's thoughts etc)* révélation *f*; *(of secret)* divulgation *f*, révélation **2** *(fact disclosed)* révélation *f* **3** *(of truth, fact)* mise *f* à jour
▸▸ *St Exch* **d. threshold** seuil *m* d'annonce obligatoire

disco ['dɪskəʊ] **N** *Fam (place)* discothèque *f*; *(event)* soirée *f* disco; **we're having a d. at the party** il y aura une animation disco à la soirée
▸▸ **d. dancer** danseur, -euse de disco; **d. dancing** disco *m*; **d. music** musique *f* disco, disco

discography [dɪs'kɒɡrəfɪ] **N** discographie *f*

discolour, *Am* **discolor** [dɪs'kʌlər] **VT** *(fabric* *etc*) ternir, délaver; **to become discoloured** se décolorer; *(of fabric)* se ternir; **discoloured by tobacco** jauni par le tabac **VI** *(of fabric)* se ternir

discolo(u)ration, *Am* **discoloration** [dɪskʌlə'reɪʃən] **N** *(of fabric)* ternissure *f*, *(of teeth)* jaunissement *m*

discombobulate [dɪskəm'bɒbjʊleɪt] **VT** *Am Fam* déconcerter, confondre

discomfit [dɪs'kʌmfɪt] **VT** *Fml (confuse)* déconcerter

discomfiture [dɪs'kʌmfɪtʃər] **N** *Fml (confusion)* embarras *m*, trouble *m*; **he showed signs of d.** il avait l'air embarrassé; **much to his d.** à son grand embarras

discomfort [dɪs'kʌmfət] **N 1** *(lack of comfort)* inconfort *m* **2** *(pain)* malaise *m*, gêne *f*; **to be in some d.** *(of patient)* éprouver une sensation de gêne; **to cause (sb) d.** *(of stitches, wound etc)* gêner (qn)

discomposure [dɪskəm'pəʊʒər] **N** *Fml* trouble *m*, agitation *f*; *(of mind)* perturbation *f*

disconcert [dɪskən'sɜːt] **VT** déconcerter, troubler; **I don't want to d. you, but …** je ne veux pas vous alarmer, mais …

disconcerting [dɪskən'sɜːtɪŋ] **ADJ** *(news, attitude, habit etc)* déconcertant, troublant

disconcertingly [dɪskən'sɜːtɪŋlɪ] **ADV** d'une manière déconcertante; **they were d. eager to see him** go la hâte qu'ils avaient de le voir partir était déconcertante

disconnect [dɪskə'nekt] **VT 1** *(gas, water supply, electricity, phone)* couper; *Tel* **I've been disconnected** *(I cannot continue the call)* on a coupé la communication; *(because I haven't paid the bill)* ils m'ont coupé le téléphone *ou* la ligne; **to get the telephone disconnected** faire débrancher le téléphone **2** *(separate)* disjoindre, séparer, détacher; **sth from sth** qch de qch); *(carriages)* décrocher; *(machine etc)* débrayer, désembrayer; *Elec (battery, kettle etc)* déconnecter, débrancher; **to d. a waterpipe from the main supply** isoler un tuyau d'eau de l'arrivée

disconnected [dɪskə'nektɪd] **ADJ 1** *Elec* débranché; *Tech* débrayé **2** *(style etc) (lacking flow)* décousu; *(deliberately staccato)* entrecoupé **3** *(separate)* détaché, isolé

disconnection, disconnexion [dɪskə'nekʃən] **N 1** *(action) (of phone, gas, water, in phone call)* coupure *f*, *(of battery, kettle)* débranchement *m* **2** *(of carriage)* décrochage *m*; *(of part of machine)* démontage *m* **3** *(state)* séparation *f* (**between** entre)

disconsolate [dɪs'kɒnsələt] **ADJ** *(person)* tout triste, inconsolable; *(sigh, look, face)* accablé

disconsolately [dɪs'kɒnsələtlɪ] **ADV** tristement, désespérément

discontent [dɪskən'tent] **N** mécontentement *m*

discontented [dɪskən'tentɪd] **ADJ** mécontent (**with** de)

discontinue [dɪskən'tɪnjuː] **VT 1** *(service)* interrompre; *(practice)* abandonner; *(one's subscription)* résilier; *Com* **that item has been discontinued** cet article n'est plus suivi; *Com* **discontinued** *(on label)* fin de série; *Com* **discontinued line** fin de série **2** *Law (trial)* abandonner

discontinuity [dɪskɒntɪ'njuːɪtɪ] **N** *also Math* discontinuité *f*

discontinuous [dɪskən'tɪnjʊəs] **ADJ** *(with interruptions)*, *Ling* discontinu; *(intermittent)* intermittent

discord ['dɪskɔːd] **N 1** *(disagreement)* discorde *f*; **there was some d. over it** cela a été la source d'un certain désaccord, cela a été

un sujet de discorde; **industrial/civil d.** dissensions *fpl* ouvrières/sociales **2** *Mus* dissonance *f*

discordance [dɪs'kɔːdəns] **N 1** *(of opinions etc)* discordance *f* **2** *(of sounds)* discordance *f*

discordant [dɪs'kɔːdənt] **ADJ 1 d. opinions** opinions opposées *ou* discordantes; **a d. atmosphere** une atmosphère de discorde **2** *(sound)* discordant; *(voice)* discordant, criard **3** *Mus* dissonant

discotheque ['dɪskətek] **N** discothèque *f*

discount[1] ['dɪskaʊnt] **N 1** *Com* remise *f*, rabais *m*; **to sell sth at a d.** vendre qch au rabais; **cash d.** escompte *m* de caisse; **trade d.** remise d'usage; **to allow a d. of 10%** consentir un rabais de 10%; **d. for early payment** escompte *m* de règlement *f Fin* escompte *m*; **discounts and allowances** remise, rabais, ristourne *f*, RRR; **to be at a d.** *(of shares)* être en perte, se trouver en moins-value; *Fig (of politeness etc)* être en défaveur

▸ ▸ **d. bank** banque *f* d'escompte; *St Exch* **d. bond** obligation *f* émise au dessous du pair; *Com* **d. card** carte *f* de réduction; **d. coach card** carte de réduction sur les lignes d'autocars; **d. house** comptoir *m* d'escompte; *Fin* **d. loan** prêt *m* escompté; **d. price** prix *m* réduit; *Fin* **d. rate** taux *m* d'escompte; *Com* **d. store** solderie *f*, magasin *m* de vente au rabais; **d. tariff** tarif *m* réduit; **d. ticket agency** agence *f* spécialisée dans la vente de billets bradés; **d. travel card** carte de réduction pour les transports; *Com* **d. voucher** bon *m* de réduction

discount[2] [dɪs'kaʊnt, 'dɪskaʊnt] **VT 1** *Fin* escompter; *(bill)* prendre à l'escompte **2** *(not consider) (somebody, something)* ne pas tenir compte de; *(ignore) (sb's advice, warning)* faire peu de cas de; *(fact, importance of sth)* négliger; **you must d. half of what he says** il ne faut croire que la moitié de ce qu'il dit; **police have discounted the possibility of suicide** la police a écarté la thèse du suicide

▸ ▸ *Fin* **discounted bill** effet *m* escompté; *Acct* **discounted cashflow** valeur *f* actualisée nette

discountable [dɪs'kaʊntəb(ə)l] **ADJ** *Fin* escomptable

discounted rate N *Fin* taux *m* d'escompte

discounted value N *Acct* valeur *f* actualisée

discounting [dɪs'kaʊntɪŋ] **N** remise *f*, *Fin* **d. of a bill** escompte *m* commercial

discourage [dɪs'kʌrɪdʒ] **VT 1** *(cause to lose heart)* décourager, abattre; **to become discouraged** se décourager; **don't get discouraged** ne te décourage pas **2** *(put difficulties in the way of) (project, suitor etc)* décourager; **to d. sb from (doing) sth** décourager qn de (faire) qch; **they were discouraged from going by the weather/the price** le temps/prix les a dissuadés d'y aller; **we (actively) d. smoking** nous essayons de dissuader les gens de fumer; **you should d. it** tu devrais l'en/les en dissuader

discouragement [dɪs'kʌrɪdʒmənt] **N 1** *(state)* découragement *m* **2** *(act of discouraging)* dissuasion *f*; **their d. of the use of this drug** le fait qu'ils déconseillent l'utilisation de ce médicament **3** *(something that discourages)* source *f* de découragement; **I hope this won't be a d. to you** j'espère que ceci ne te découragera pas; **to act as a d.** avoir un effet dissuasif

discouraging [dɪs'kʌrɪdʒɪŋ] **ADJ** décourageant; **he was very d. about my chances** il n'était pas du tout encourageant quant à mes chances

discourse ['dɪskɔːs] **N 1** *Lit (conversation)*

conversation *f*, entretien *m*; *Ling* discours *m*; **2** *Lit (dissertation)* dissertation *f* (**on** sur)

▸ ▸ *Ling* **d. analysis** analyse *f* du discours

▸ **discourse on, discourse upon VT INSEP** *Lit (speak of)* discourir sur **2** *(discuss)* parler de, s'entretenir de

discourteous [dɪs'kɜːtɪəs] **ADJ** discourtois, impoli

discourteously [dɪs'kɜːtɪəslɪ] **ADV** impoliment, d'une façon impolie

discourtesy [dɪs'kɜːtəsɪ] **N** incivilité *f*, impolitesse *f*

discover [dɪ'skʌvər] **VT** *(the truth, a planet, the cause of a disease, actor etc)* découvrir; **we have discovered a good gardener** nous avons déniché un bon jardinier; **I discovered too late that …** je me suis rendu compte trop tard que …

discoverer [dɪ'skʌvərər] **N** découvreur *m*; **the d. of America** celui qui a découvert l'Amérique

discovery [dɪ'skʌvərɪ] **N** découverte *f*, *(thing found by chance)* trouvaille *f*; **he's quite a d.** *(of new actor, soccer player etc)* c'est une vraie révélation; **voyage of d.** voyage *m* d'exploration; **to make a d.** faire une découverte

discredit [dɪs'kredɪt] **N 1** *(doubt)* **to throw d. on a statement** mettre une affirmation en doute **2** *(dishonour)* **to be a d. to one's family** être une honte pour sa famille; **it does you no d. to admit you were mistaken** il n'y a aucune honte à admettre que tu t'es trompé; **much to their d.** ce qui ne leur faisait pas du tout honneur; **to bring d. on sb/sth** jeter le discrédit sur qn/qch, discréditer qn/qch; **to bring sth into d.** discréditer qch; **to bring d. on oneself** se discréditer

VT 1 *(rumour) (not believe)* ne pas croire; *(not trust)* mettre en doute; **such theories/ methods have long been discredited** ces théories/méthodes sont discréditées depuis longtemps **2** *(lower in esteem) (person, opinion)* discréditer; **his conduct has discredited him with the public** sa conduite lui a fait perdre la considération du public

discreditable [dɪs'kredɪtəb(ə)l] **ADJ** peu digne, peu honorable; **conduct d. to a barrister** conduite *f* indigne d'un avocat; **there's nothing d. about being poor** il n'y a pas de honte à être pauvre

discreet [dɪ'skriːt] **ADJ** discret, -ète (**about** sur); **can you trust him to be d.?** peut-on compter sur sa discrétion?; **to maintain a d. silence** observer un silence discret; **a d. smile** un petit sourire contenu

> Attention: ne pas confondre avec l'adjectif **discrete**.

discreetly [dɪ'skriːtlɪ] **ADV** discrètement, avec discrétion; *(to dress, be situated)* discrètement

discrepancy [dɪ'skrepənsɪ] **N** désaccord *m* (**between** entre); *(between accounts)* différence *f*, *(between statements)* divergence *f*, *(between styles, source text and target text)* décalage *m*; **there is a d. between the two stories** les deux récits ne cadrent pas; *Fin* **there is a d. in the accounts** les comptes ne concordent pas

discrete [dɪs'kriːt] **ADJ** *Math etc* discret, -ète

> Attention: ne pas confondre avec l'adjectif **discreet**.

discretion [dɪ'skreʃən] **N 1** *(liberty of action)* discrétion *f*, **I shall use my own d.** je ferai comme je jugerai à propos; **to leave sth to sb's d.** laisser qch à la discrétion de qn; **at the manager's d.** comme le directeur le décidera; **at your d.** comme vous jugerez bon, comme vous voudrez; *Law* **fine at** *or* **left to**

the d. of the judge amende laissée à l'appréciation du juge **2** *(good sense)* jugement *m*, prudence *f*; **the age of d.** l'âge *m* de raison; *Prov* **d. is the better part of valour** prudence est mère de sûreté **3** *(tact)* discrétion *f*, réserve *f*; **he is the soul of d.** il est la discrétion même

discretionary [dɪˈskreʃən(ə)rɪ] ADJ *Law* discrétionnaire
▸▸ *Banking* **d. account** compte *m* sous mandat de gestion; *St Exch* **d. order** ordre *m* à appréciation

discriminate [dɪˈskrɪmɪneɪt] VI **to d. between one thing and another** distinguer une chose d'une autre, établir une distinction entre une chose et une autre; **to d. in favour of sb** favoriser qn
VT distinguer (**from** de, d'avec)
▸ **discriminate against** VT INSEP faire de la discrimination envers; **to be (sexually/racially) discriminated against** être victime de discrimination (sexuelle/raciale)

discriminating [dɪˈskrɪmɪneɪtɪŋ] ADJ **1** *(person)* plein de discernement, capable de juger; *(buyer)* avisé, averti; *(audience, eye)* averti; *(ear, judgement)* fin **2** *Admin (duty, tariff)* différentiel

discrimination [dɪskrɪmɪˈneɪʃən] N **1** *(unfair treatment)* discrimination *f*; **without d.** sans distinction; **race** *or* **racial/sexual/religious d.** discrimination raciale/sexuelle/religieuse **2** *(in matters of taste)* jugement *m*, discernement *m* **3** *(of differences etc)* discrimination *f*, discernement *m* (**between … and …** entre … et …)

discriminatory [dɪˈskrɪmɪnət(ə)rɪ] ADJ *Pej (law etc)* discriminatoire
▸▸ **d. pricing** tarification *f* discriminatoire

discursive [dɪˈskɜːsɪv] ADJ *(style etc)* discursif

discus [ˈdɪskəs] N *Sport* disque *m*; **the d.** *(event)* le lancer du disque
▸▸ *Sport* **d. thrower** lanceur, -euse de disque

discuss [dɪˈskʌs] VT *(problem etc)* discuter, débattre; *(matter, question)* délibérer de; *(of book) (subject)* traiter de; **to d. a price** discuter *ou* débattre un prix; **I know they were discussing me** je sais qu'on parlait de moi; **I refuse to d. it** je refuse d'en parler; **have you discussed it with your parents?** est-ce que tu en as discuté avec tes parents?; **we were discussing what to do about the problem** nous discutions de ce qui devrait être fait pour résoudre le problème; **d.** *(in exam questions)* discutez

discussion [dɪˈskʌʃən] N discussion *f*; **a subject for d.** un sujet de discussion; **question under d.** question en discussion; **after much d. of sth** après avoir longtemps discuté qch; **the matter is not up for d.** le sujet n'est pas ouvert à la discussion
▸▸ *Comput* **d. list** *(on Internet)* liste *f* de diffusion; *Radio, TV* **d. programme** table *f* ronde; **d. table** table ronde

disdain [dɪsˈdeɪn] N dédain *m* (**of** de)
VT *(somebody, something)* dédaigner; **to d. to do sth** dédaigner de faire qch

disdainful [dɪsˈdeɪnfʊl] ADJ dédaigneux (**of** de)

disdainfully [dɪsˈdeɪnfʊlɪ] ADV dédaigneusement

disease [dɪˈziːz] N maladie *f*; **to die of a d.** mourir d'une maladie; **skin d.** maladie de la peau

Attention: ne pas confondre avec le nom **decease**.

diseased [dɪˈziːzd] ADJ *also Fig* malade
disembark [dɪsemˈbɑːk] VT & VI débarquer (**from** de)

disembarkation [dɪsembɑːˈkeɪʃən] N débarquement *m*

disembodied [dɪsɪmˈbɒdɪd] ADJ *(spirit)* désincarné

disembowel [dɪsɪmˈbaʊəl] VT éventrer, éviscérer

disenchant [dɪsɪnˈtʃɑːnt] VT désillusionner; **a disenchanting experience/encounter** une expérience/rencontre décevante

disenchanted [dɪsɪnˈtʃɑːntɪd] ADJ désillusionné; **she's d. with her job** son travail la déçoit beaucoup, elle n'a plus d'illusions quant à son travail

disenchantment [dɪsɪnˈtʃɑːntmənt] N désillusion *f*

disencumber [dɪsɪnˈkʌmbər] VT *Fml* **to d. oneself of sth** *(of coat etc)* se débarrasser de qch; *(of one's responsibilities, burdens)* s'affranchir de qch

disenfranchise [dɪsɪnˈfræntʃaɪz] VT *(person)* priver du droit électoral *ou* de ses droits civiques; *(borough)* priver de ses droits de représentation

disenfranchisement [dɪsɪnˈfræntʃɪzmənt] N *(of person)* déchéance *f* de ses droits civiques; *(of borough)* déchéance de ses droits de représentation

disengage [dɪsɪnˈgeɪdʒ] VT dégager, débarrasser (**sb/sth from sth** qn/qch de qch); *Tech (cogwheel)* désengrener; *(part, component)* débrayer, désembrayer; **to d. oneself from sb's embrace** se dégager de l'étreinte de qn; **to d. oneself from the struggle** se retirer de la lutte
VI *(of person)* se dégager; *Tech (of catch etc)* se déclencher, se défaire; *Mil (of troops)* se retirer

disengaged [dɪsɪnˈgeɪdʒd] ADJ *Tech* débrayé
disengagement [dɪsɪnˈgeɪdʒmənt] N **1** *(of person)* détachement *m* (**from** de); *Tech (of part, component)* débrayage *m* **2** *Pol, Mil* désengagement *m*

disentangle [dɪsɪnˈtæŋg(ə)l] VT débarrasser (**sb/sth from sth** qn/qch de qch); *(piece of string)* débrouiller, démêler; *(plot, mystery)* dénouer; **to d. itself** *(of rope etc)* se démêler; **to d. oneself from sth** se libérer *ou* se dégager de qch; *Fig (from scandal etc)* se sortir de qch

disequilibrium [dɪsiːkwɪˈlɪbrɪəm] N déséquilibre *m*
▸▸ *Econ* **d. price** prix *m* de déséquilibre

disestablish [dɪsɪˈstæblɪʃ] VT *(the Church)* séparer de l'État

disestablishment [dɪsɪˈstæblɪʃmənt] N **d. of the Church** séparation *f* de l'Église et de l'État

disfavour, *Am* **disfavor** [dɪsˈfeɪvər] N défaveur *f*; **to regard** *or* **view** *or* **look on sth with d.** être défavorable à qch; **to fall into d.** tomber en disgrâce; **to fall into d. with sb** perdre le soutien *ou* les faveurs de qn; **to be in d. with sb** être en disgrâce auprès de qn; **at the risk of incurring sb's d.** au risque de déplaire à qn

disfigure [dɪsˈfɪgər] VT *(person, statue etc)* défigurer; *(of buildings etc) (landscape)* gâter, enlaidir; **a disfiguring disease** une maladie qui défigure

disfigured [dɪsˈfɪgəd] ADJ *(person, statue etc)* défiguré; *(landscape)* enlaidi

disfigurement [dɪsˈfɪgəmənt] N *(of person, statue)* défiguration *f*; *(of landscape)* enlaidissement *m*

disfranchise [dɪsˈfræntʃaɪz] VT = **disenfranchise**

disgorge [dɪsˈgɔːdʒ] VT *(smoke, information)* dégorger; *(food)* rendre
VI **river that disgorges into …** rivière qui se déverse dans …

disgrace [dɪsˈgreɪs] N **1** *(disfavour)* disgrâce *f*, défaveur *f*; **to be in d.** *(out of favour)* être en disgrâce; *(of child)* être en pénitence; **she is in d. with the party** elle n'est pas en faveur auprès du parti **2** *(shame)* honte *f*, déshonneur *m*; **there is no d. in doing that** il n'y a pas de honte à faire cela; **to bring d. on one's family** déshonorer sa famille; **to be a d. to one's family** être la honte de sa famille, faire honte à sa famille; **it's a d.!** c'est une honte *ou* un scandale!; **you're a d.** tu me fais honte!; **house prices are a d.** c'est une honte de vendre les maisons si cher; **the state of their house is a d.!** leur maison est dans un état honteux!
VT **1** *(esp in passive)* **to be disgraced** *(out of favour)* être disgrâcié (**for** pour) **2** *(shame) (person)* déshonorer, faire déshonneur à; **to d. oneself** se couvrir de honte; **you disgraced me in front of all those people** tu m'as couvert de honte devant tous ces gens

disgraceful [dɪsˈgreɪsfʊl] ADJ honteux, infâme; **it's d.** c'est scandaleux *ou* honteux

Note that the French word **disgracieux** is a false friend and is never a translation for the English word **disgraceful**. It means **ungainly**.

disgracefully [dɪsˈgreɪsfʊlɪ] ADV honteusement; *(late, rude, expensive)* scandaleusement

disgruntled [dɪsˈgrʌnt(ə)ld] ADJ *(discontented)* mécontent (**at** de); *(sulky)* maussade; **what are you looking so d. about?** pourquoi cet air mécontent?, pourquoi est-ce que tu fais la tête?

disguise [dɪsˈgaɪz] N *(costume)* déguisement *m*; **put this on as a d.** déguise-toi avec ça; **in d.** déguisé; **in the d. of a policeman** déguisé en agent de police
VT **1** *(change appearance of) (person)* déguiser, travestir; *(the truth, one's thoughts, feelings)* déguiser; *(one's voice, writing)* déguiser, contrefaire; **to d. oneself as a clown** se déguiser en clown; **there is no disguising the fact that …** il faut avouer que … **2** *(hide) (one's feelings, motives)* cacher, dissimuler; *(smell)* masquer; **to d. one's disappointment** cacher sa déception

disgust [dɪsˈgʌst] N **1** *(physical)* dégoût *m* (**at, for, towards** pour) **2** *(moral)* écoeurement *m*, dégoût *m*; **that kind of attitude fills me with d.** ce genre d'attitude me dégoûte *ou* m'écoeure; **she turned away from him in d.** dégoûtée *ou* écoeurée, elle s'est détournée de lui; **much to my d.** à mon grand dégoût
VT **1** *(physically)* dégoûter, donner la nausée à **2** *(morally)* écoeurer, dégoûter; **to be disgusted at** *or* **with** *or* **by sb/sth** être écoeuré par qn/de qch; **he is disgusted that …** cela l'écoeure *ou* le dégoûte que … + *subj*; **I feel disgusted with myself for not having protested** je me dégoûte de ne pas avoir protesté

disgusting [dɪsˈgʌstɪŋ] ADJ *(sight, smell, prospect, behaviour, carpet)* dégoûtant, écoeurant, répugnant, *Fam* dégueulasse; *(bad quality) (music, souvenirs)* épouvantable; *(salary) (very low)* ridicule; *(very high)* écoeurant; **it's d.!** c'est dégoûtant *ou Fam* dégueulasse!

disgustingly [dɪsˈgʌstɪŋlɪ] ADV **1 d. dirty** d'une saleté répugnante; **d. sweet/bad** épouvantablement sucré/mauvais; **d. rich/underpaid** scandaleusement riche/sous-payé; **a joke in d. bad taste** une blague d'un mauvais goût détestable **2** *Fam* **d. good-looking/well-read** beau/instruit c'est pas permis; **you look d. fit** vous avez l'air vachement en forme; **he makes it look d. easy** on dirait que c'est facile comme tout quand il le fait

dish [dɪʃ] **N 1** *(for food)* plat *m*; *(earthenware casserole)* terrine *f*; **vegetable d.** légumier *m*; **butter d.** beurrier *m*; **to wash** *or* **do the dishes** faire la vaisselle; **a d. of strawberries** un plat de fraises

2 *(food)* plat *m*, mets *m*; **it's not a d. I often make** ce n'est pas une recette *ou* un plat que je prépare souvent

3 *TV* antenne *f* parabolique

4 *Old-fashioned Fam (female)* belle fille *f*; *(male)* beau mec *m*; **she's/he's a real d.** ce qu'elle est belle/ce qu'il est beau

5 *(container)* récipient *m*; *Phot* cuvette *f*

VT *Fam* **1 to d. sb's chances** gâcher les chances de qn **2 to d. the dirt on sb** faire des révélations sur qn

▸▸ *Br* **d. aerial,** *Am* **d. antenna** antenne *f* parabolique

▸ **dish out VT SEP** *Fam (meat etc)* servir; *(give) (sweets, money)* distribuer; **to d. out punishment to** *(of boxer)* assener des coups à; *(of schoolmaster)* punir; **to d. out advice** prodiguer des conseils; **he is really dishing it out** *(of boxer)* il en assène; **she can really d. it out** *(be very critical)* quand elle s'y met, c'est une vraie langue de vipère

▸ **dish up VT SEP** *(course, meal)* servir; *Fig Fam (of programme planners etc)* proposer, sortir

VI *Culin* servir; **shall I d. up?** je peux servir?, je sers?

disharmonious [dɪshɑːˈməʊnɪəs] **ADJ** *(sound)* dissonant; *(relationship)* qui manque d'harmonie, peu harmonieux

disharmony [dɪsˈhɑːmənɪ] **N 1** *(disagreement)* désaccord *m*, discorde *f*, manque *m* d'harmonie **2** *(of sound)* dissonance *f*

dishcloth [ˈdɪʃklɒθ] **N** *(for washing)* lavette *f*; *(for drying)* torchon *m* à (essuyer la) vaisselle

dishearten [dɪsˈhɑːt(ə)n] **VT** *(person)* décourager, abattre; **to become disheartened** perdre courage, se décourager

disheartening [dɪsˈhɑːt(ə)nɪŋ] **ADJ** décourageant

dishearteningly [dɪsˈhɑːt(ə)nɪŋlɪ] **ADV** de façon décourageante; **d. brief** d'une brièveté décourageante; **d. few people turned up** peu de monde est venu, ce qui était décourageant

dished [dɪʃt] **ADJ** *Tech* concave

dishevelled [dɪˈʃev(ə)ld] **ADJ** *(person)* échevelé, dépeigné; **his d. appearance** son air échevelé; **d. hair** cheveux ébouriffés

dishmop [ˈdɪʃmɒp] **N** lavette *f* (à vaisselle)

dishonest [dɪsˈɒnɪst] **ADJ** malhonnête

dishonestly [dɪsˈɒnɪstlɪ] **ADV** malhonnêtement

dishonesty [dɪsˈɒnɪstɪ] **N** malhonnêteté *f*; **an act of d.** un acte malhonnête, une malhonnêteté

dishonour, *Am* **dishonor** [dɪsˈɒnər] **N 1** *(shame, source of shame)* déshonneur *m*; **to bring d. on one's family** déshonorer sa famille; **to his eternal d.** à son grand déshonneur **2** *Fin (of cheque)* non-paiement *m*, refus *m* de paiement; *(of bill)* non-acceptation *f*

VT 1 *(shame) (one's family)* déshonorer **2** *(promise, agreement)* ne pas respecter; *Fin (bill)* ne pas accepter, refuser de payer; **dishonoured cheque** chèque impayé

dishonourable, *Am* **dishonorable** [dɪsˈɒnərəb(ə)l] **ADJ** *(person)* sans honneur; *(action, conduct)* honteux, indigne; **there's nothing d. about losing** perdre n'a rien de honteux; *Mil* **to receive a d. discharge** être renvoyé de l'armée pour manquement à l'honneur

dishonourably, *Am* **dishonorably** [dɪsˈɒnərəblɪ] **ADV** de façon déshonorante; *Mil*

to be d. discharged être renvoyé de l'armée pour manquement à l'honneur

dishpan [ˈdɪʃpæn] **N** *esp Am* cuvette *f*, bassine *f*; **to have d. hands** avoir les mains abîmées à force de faire la vaisselle

dishrag [ˈdɪʃræg] **N** lavette *f*

dishtowel [ˈdɪʃtaʊ(ə)l] **N** torchon *m* à (essuyer la) vaisselle

dishwasher [ˈdɪʃwɒʃər] **N 1** *(person)* plongeur, -euse **2** *(machine)* lave-vaisselle *m inv; Can* laveuse *f* à vaisselle; **d. safe** *(glass, plate etc)* garanti lave-vaisselle

dishwashing liquid [ˈdɪʃwɒʃɪŋ] **N** *Am* produit *m* à vaisselle

dishwater [ˈdɪʃwɔːtər] **N 1** eau *f* de vaisselle **2** *Fig Fam (tasteless soup, coffee etc)* lavasse *f*

dishy [ˈdɪʃɪ] **ADJ** *Br Fam* séduisant, sexy; **he's/she's very d.** ce qu'il est beau/ce qu'elle est belle

disillusion [dɪsɪˈluːʒən] **VT** désillusionner

N = **disillusionment**

disillusioned [dɪsɪˈluːʒənd] **ADJ** désillusionné, désenchanté; **I'm very d. with her** elle me déçoit beaucoup; **to become d.** perdre ses illusions

disillusionment [dɪsɪˈluːʒənmənt] **N** désillusionnement *m*, désenchantement *m*

disincentive [dɪsɪnˈsentɪv] **N** *Econ etc* facteur *m* décourageant; **heavy taxation is a d. to expansion** les taxes élevées découragent toute expansion; **to act as a d. to sth** avoir un effet dissuasif sur qch

disinclination [dɪsɪŋklɪˈneɪʃən] **N because of his d. to …** parce qu'il est/était peu enclin à …; **to have** *or* **show a d. to do sth** montrer peu d'empressement *ou* être peu enclin à faire qch

disinclined [dɪsɪnˈklaɪnd] **ADJ** peu disposé, peu enclin (**to do sth** à faire qch)

disinfect [dɪsɪnˈfekt] **VT** désinfecter

disinfectant [dɪsɪnˈfektənt] **N** désinfectant *m*

disinfection [dɪsɪnˈfekʃən] **N** désinfection *f*; **d. of the wound is vital** il est vital de désinfecter la plaie

disinflation [dɪsɪnˈfleɪʃən] **N** *Econ* désinflation *f*, déflation *f*

disinflationary [dɪsɪnˈfleɪʃənərɪ] **ADJ** *Econ* désinflationniste

disinformation [dɪsɪnfəˈmeɪʃən] **N** désinformation *f*

▸▸ **d. campaign** campagne *f* de désinformation

disingenuous [dɪsɪnˈdʒenjʊəs] **ADJ** *(person)* qui manque de franchise, peu sincère; **it was utterly d. of her to pretend that …** ce n'était pas du tout honnête de sa part de prétendre que …

disingenuously [dɪsɪnˈdʒenjʊəslɪ] **ADV** peu franchement; **d. worded** formulé en termes peu sincères

disingenuousness [dɪsɪnˈdʒenjʊəsnɪs] **N** manque *m* de franchise

disinherit [dɪsɪnˈherɪt] **VT** *(one's son)* déshériter

disintegrate [dɪsˈɪntɪgreɪt] **VI** *(of stone etc)* se désagréger, se désintégrer, s'effriter; *(of exploding plane, crashing train etc)* se désintégrer; *(of calm, confidence)* s'effriter; *(of health)* se dégrader, s'effriter; *Nucl* se désintégrer; **her family was disintegrating around her** sa famille se désagrégeait autour d'elle

VT désagréger

disintegration [dɪsɪntɪˈgreɪʃən] **N** *(of stone etc)* désagrégation *f*, désintégration *f*, effritement *m*; *(of health)* dégradation *f*; *(of organization, family)* désagrégation *f*; *Nucl* désintégration

disinter [dɪsɪnˈtɜːr] **VT** (**-rr-**) *(corpse, antiques)* déterrer, exhumer; *Fig (scandal)* déterrer; **to d. sth from the archives** aller repêcher qch dans les archives

disinterest [dɪsˈɪnt(ə)rɪst] **N** = **disinterestedness**

disinterested [dɪsˈɪnt(ə)rɪstɪd] **ADJ** *(unbiased)* désintéressé, impartial

> Attention: ne pas confondre avec l'adjectif **uninterested**.

disinterestedness [dɪsˈɪnt(ə)rɪstɪdnɪs] **N 1** *(lack of bias)* désintéressement *m* **2** *(indifference)* indifférence *f* (**in** à)

disintermediation [dɪsɪntəmiːdɪˈeɪʃən] **N** désintermédiation *f*

disinterment [dɪsɪnˈtɜːmənt] **N** déterrement *m*, exhumation *f*

disinvest [dɪsɪnˈvest] **VT & VI** désinvestir (**from, in** de)

disinvestment [dɪsɪnˈvestmənt] **N** *(from a country)* désinvestissement *m*

disjointed [dɪsˈdʒɔɪntɪd] **ADJ** *(speech)* sans suite, incohérent; *(style)* haché, décousu; *(movements, delivery of speech)* entrecoupé

disk [dɪsk] **N 1** *Comput* disque *m*; *(floppy)* disquette *f*; **to put sth on d.** enregistrer qch sur disque/disquette **2** *Am* = **disc**

▸▸ **d. access time** temps *m* d'accès disque; **d. box** boîte *f* à disquettes; **d. capacity** capacité *f* de disque/disquette; **d. controller** contrôleur *m* de disque; **d. controller card** carte *f* contrôleur de disque; **d. drive** lecteur *m* de disquettes; **d. file** fichier *m* disque; **d. mailer** pochette *f* d'expédition de disquette; **d. memory** mémoire *f* à disque; **d. operating system** système *m* d'exploitation de disques; **d. space** espace *m* disque

disk-based [-beɪst] **ADJ** *Comput* conçu pour disque; *(for floppy)* conçu pour disquettes

diskcopy [ˈdɪskkɒpɪ] **N** *Comput* copie *f* de disquette

diskette [dɪsˈket] **N** *Comput* disquette *f*

▸▸ **d. box** boîte *f* à disquettes; *Am* **d. drive** lecteur *m* de disquettes

diskless [ˈdɪsklɪs] **ADJ** *Comput* sans disque, sans unité de disque

▸▸ **d. workstation** station *f* de travail sans unité de disque

dislike [dɪsˈlaɪk] **N** aversion *f* (**of, for** pour); **they have the same likes and dislikes** ils ont les mêmes goûts et dégoûts; **to have a d. of sth** ne pas aimer qch; **to take a d. to** *or* **conceive a d. for sb** prendre qn en grippe; **to take a d. to** *or* **conceive a d. for sth** prendre qch en horreur

VT ne pas aimer; **I don't d. him** il ne me déplaît pas; **to d. doing sth** détester *ou* ne pas aimer faire qch; **to get oneself disliked** se rendre antipathique

dislocate [ˈdɪsləkeɪt] **VT 1** *Med (shoulder, knee)* luxer, démettre, disloquer; **to d. one's jaw** se décrocher la mâchoire **2** *(business)* désorganiser; *(plan)* bouleverser

dislocation [dɪsləˈkeɪʃən] **N 1** *Med (of shoulder, knee)* luxation *f*, déboîtement *m*, dislocation *f*; *(of jaw)* déboîtement **2** *(of business)* désorganisation *f*; *(of plan etc)* bouleversement *m*

dislodge [dɪsˈlɒdʒ] **VT** *(enemy troops)* déloger, débusquer (**from** de); *(brick etc)* détacher; *(sth stuck)* dégager; **several bricks had become dislodged** plusieurs briques s'étaient détachées; **now he's been made manager nobody is ever going to d. him** maintenant qu'il a été nommé au poste de directeur, personne ne l'en fera jamais sortir; *Fig* **nothing would d. him from his position on arms control** rien ne pouvait ébranler sa conviction sur le contrôle des armements

disloyal [dɪs'lɔɪəl] **ADJ** *(to one's king, friendship)* infidèle (**to** à); *(behaviour)* déloyal (**to** envers)

disloyalty [dɪs'lɔɪəltɪ] **N** déloyauté *f*

dismal ['dɪzməl] **ADJ** *(face, person)* lugubre, sombre, triste; *(countryside, future)* morne; *(failure, performance)* lamentable; *(weather)* maussade; **my prospects look d.** mes chances sont maigres; *Hum* **the d. science** = l'économie *f*

dismally ['dɪzməlɪ] **ADV** *(to say)* tristement; *(to fail, perform)* lamentablement

dismantle [dɪs'mænt(ə)l] **VT** *(machine, rifle etc)* démonter; *(fortress, network)* démanteler

dismast [dɪs'mɑːst] **VT** *Naut (ship)* démâter

dismay [dɪs'meɪ] **N** consternation *f*; **in d.** consterné, atterré; **to my d.** à ma grande consternation; **to be filled with d.** être consterné *ou* atterré

 VT consterner; **we were dismayed at** *or* **by the news** cette nouvelle nous jeta dans la consternation; **the dismaying news** la nouvelle accablante *ou* consternante

dismember [dɪs'membər] **VT** *also Fig* démembrer

dismemberment [dɪs'membəmənt] **N** démembrement *m*

dismiss [dɪs'mɪs] **VT 1** *(cease employing)* *(employee, servant)* congédier, renvoyer, licencier; *(civil servant)* révoquer; *Mil* **to d. sb from the service** *(career member)* rayer qn des cadres de l'armée; *(on military service)* réformer qn **2** *(send away)* *(person)* congédier, donner la permission de se retirer à; *(door-to-door salesman etc)* congédier, éconduire; *(meeting)* dissoudre; *Mil* **to d. a parade** faire rompre les rangs (aux troupes); *Mil* **d.!** rompez (les rangs)!; *Cr* **dismissed for ten** *(of batsman)* mis hors jeu quand il n'a marqué que dix points; **you are dismissed** vous pouvez vous retirer **3** *(cease or refuse to consider)* *(topic of conversation etc)* quitter, abandonner; *(threat, rumours)* ne pas tenir compte de; *(danger)* mépriser; *(theory, explanation)* rejeter; **to d. sth from one's mind** chasser *ou* éloigner qch de ses pensées; **the incident was dismissed as a mere schoolboy prank** on n'a vu dans cet incident qu'une simple farce d'écolier; **she is dismissed as an intellectual lightweight** on la considère comme une non-valeur sur le plan intellectuel **4** *(reject)* *(proposal)* écarter; *Law (request, appeal)* rejeter; **to d. a case** *(of judge)* rendre une fin de non-recevoir; **to d. a charge** rendre une ordonnance de non-lieu

dismissal [dɪs'mɪs(ə)l] **N 1** *(of employee)* congédiement *m*, renvoi *m*, licenciement *m*; *(of civil servant)* révocation *f*; **unfair d.** licenciement non justifié; **d. with/without notice** licenciement avec/sans préavis **2** *(of danger)* mépris *m*; *(of theory, explanation)* rejet *m* **3** *Law (of case)* fin *f* de non-recevoir; *(of request, appeal)* rejet *m*

dismissive [dɪs'mɪsɪv] **ADJ** *(laugh, person)* méprisant, dédaigneux; *(gesture)* de rejet; **to be d. about** *or* **of sth** *(of danger)* mépriser qch; *(of proposal)* ne pas accorder la moindre valeur à qch; **he was d. about** *or* **of my chances of winning** il pensait que je n'avais pas la moindre chance de gagner; **you shouldn't be so d. about the proposal** tu ne devrais pas condamner la proposition aussi vite

dismissively [dɪs'mɪsɪvlɪ] **ADV** *(to reply, comment etc)* dédaigneusement

dismount [dɪs'maʊnt] **VI** *(from horse, bicycle)* descendre

 VT 1 *(rider)* démonter, désarçonner **2** *(cannon, machine)* démonter

disobedience [dɪsə'biːdɪəns] **N** désobéissance *f* (**to sb** à qn); **civil d.** résistance *f* passive

disobedient [dɪsə'biːdɪənt] **ADJ** *(dog, child)* désobéissant; **to be d. to sb** désobéir à qn; **that was very d. of you** c'était très désobéissant de ta part

disobey [dɪsə'beɪ] **VT** *(person, order)* désobéir à; *(order, the law)* enfreindre

disobliging [dɪsə'blaɪdʒɪŋ] **ADJ** désobligeant (**to** envers)

disobligingly [dɪsə'blaɪdʒɪŋlɪ] **ADV** avec désobligeance; **someone had very d. left the doors locked** quelqu'un avait eu l'extrême désobligeance de laisser les portes verrouillées

disorder [dɪs'ɔːdər] **N 1** *(confusion)* désordre *m*; **in d.** en désordre; **in a terrible state of d.** terriblement en désordre; **to throw sth into d.** *(room etc)* mettre du désordre dans qch; *(plans)* bouleverser qch; **they fled in d.** ils se sont enfuis en débandade **2** *(unrest)* désordre *m*, trouble *m*; **serious disorders have broken out** de graves désordres ont éclaté **3** *Med* trouble(s) *m(pl)*; **heart d.** troubles cardiaques; **nervous d.** troubles nerveux, affection *f* nerveuse; **personality d.** trouble caractériel *ou* de la personnalité

 VT déranger, mettre en désordre; **the crisis had disordered his thoughts** la crise avait mis de la confusion dans ses idées

disordered [dɪs'ɔːdəd] **ADJ** *(room, existence)* désordonné; *(mind)* malade; *(stomach)* dérangé

disorderliness [dɪs'ɔːdəlɪnɪs] **N 1** *(untidiness)* désordre *m*; **the d. of the room** le désordre dans lequel se trouvait la pièce; **the d. of their life** leur vie désordonnée **2** *(of mob)* turbulence *f*

disorderly [dɪs'ɔːdəlɪ] **ADJ 1** *(untidy)* *(person, work etc)* désordonné; *(room etc)* en désordre **2** *(unruly)* *(mob etc)* turbulent, tumultueux; *(person, behaviour)* désordonné, déréglé; **to lead a d. life** mener une vie désordonnée *ou* déréglée; *Law* **to charge sb with being drunk and d.** inculper qn pour ivresse et atteinte à l'ordre public

  Law **d. conduct** conduite *f* portant atteinte à l'ordre public; *Law* **d. house** *(brothel)* maison *f* de débauche; *(gaming house)* maison de jeu

disorganization [dɪsɔːgənaɪ'zeɪʃəl] **N** désorganisation *f*

disorganize [dɪs'ɔːgənaɪz] **VT** désorganiser

disorganized [dɪs'ɔːgənaɪzd] **ADJ** *(person)* désorganisé; *(room)* désordonné; *(memories, ideas)* confus, désordonné

disorientate [dɪs'ɔːrɪənteɪt], **disorient** [dɪs'ɔːrɪənt] **VT** désorienter; **to be disorient(at)ed** être désorienté; **with disorient(at)ing speed** à une vitesse hallucinante

disorientation [dɪsɔːrɪən'teɪʃən] **N** désorientation *f*

disorienting [dɪs'ɔːrɪəntɪŋ] **ADJ** déroutant

disown [dɪs'əʊn] **VT** *(novel, painting)* désavouer; *(person)* renier; **to d. a child** *(deny paternity)* désavouer (la paternité d') un enfant; **if you go out looking like that I'll d. you!** si tu sors habillé comme ça, je ne te connais plus!

disparage [dɪs'pærɪdʒ] **VT** *(somebody, something)* déprécier, décrier, dénigrer

disparagement [dɪs'pærɪdʒmənt] **N** dénigrement *m*, dépréciation *f*

disparaging [dɪs'pærɪdʒɪŋ] **ADJ** *(term)* de dénigrement; **d. remark** remarque désobligeante; **he was extremely d. about the**

whole idea il s'est montré extrêmement méprisant à l'égard de cette idée

disparagingly [dɪs'pærɪdʒɪŋlɪ] **ADV** *(to say)* d'un ton méprisant; *(to look at)* d'un air méprisant; **to speak d. of sb** parler de qn en termes de mépris, faire des remarques désobligeantes à l'égard de qn

disparate ['dɪspərɪt] **ADJ** *Fml* disparate

disparity [dɪs'pærɪtɪ] **N** *(of wealth, status etc)* disparité *f*, écart *m* (**of** entre); *(between ideas, opinions)* différence *f* (**between** entre); *(between accounts, stories)* contradiction *f* (**between** entre); **d. of age** différence d'âge; **the d. in their ages** la différence d'âge entre eux

dispassionate [dɪs'pæʃənət] **ADJ 1** *(calm)* sans passion, dépassionné, calme **2** *(impartial)* impartial, -aux; **to take a d. view of things** juger impartialement les choses

dispassionately [dɪs'pæʃənətlɪ] **ADV 1** *(calmly)* sans passion **2** *(impartially)* sans parti pris, impartialement

dispatch [dɪs'pætʃ] **N 1** *(sending)* *(of object)* expédition *f*, envoi *m*

 2 *Old-fashioned (speed)* promptitude *f*; **with (all due) d.** promptement

 3 *(message, report)* *(diplomatic, by journalist)* dépêche *f*, *Com, Mil etc* **to be mentioned in dispatches** être cité à l'ordre (du jour)

 4 *(finishing off)* *(of a piece of business)* expédition *f*

 5 *(execution)* *(of condemned man)* exécution *f*

 VT 1 *(send)* *(messenger, squadron)* dépêcher; *(letter)* expédier; **to d. an order** envoyer une commande

 2 **to d. a piece of business/a job** expédier une affaire/un travail

 3 *Fam (eat up) (meal)* expédier

 4 *(kill)* *(animal)* achever; *(person)* expédier dans l'autre monde

  d. box *(for documents)* boîte *f* à documents; *Br Parl* tribune *f*; **d. case** serviette *f*, porte-documents *m inv*; **d. department** expéditions *fpl*; **d. note** bordereau *m* d'expédition; **d. rider** estafette *f*

dispatcher [dɪs'pætʃər] **N 1** *Com etc* expéditeur, -trice **2** *Rail, Aviat etc* régulateur *m*, contrôleur *m*

dispel [dɪs'pel] **VT** *(-ll-)* *(doubt, clouds, fear)* chasser, dissiper; **to d. sb's illusions** faire perdre ses illusions à qn

dispensable [dɪs'pensəb(ə)l] **ADJ** dont on peut se passer; **nobody here is d.** il n'y a personne ici dont on peut se passer, il n'y a personne en trop ici; **I felt I had become d.** j'avais l'impression qu'on pouvait se passer de moi

dispensary [dɪs'pensərɪ] **N 1** *(of pharmacy)* officine *f* **2** *(in hospital)* pharmacie *f*

dispensation [dɪspen'seɪʃən] **N 1** *Law, Rel (exemption)* **d. from sth** dispense *f* de qch; **d. from fasting** dispense du jeûne **2** *Fml (distributing) (of prizes, alms)* distribution *f*; *(of justice)* administration *f*, exercice *m* **3** *(of Providence)* décret *m*, arrêt *m* **4** *(organization, way of running things)* système *m*; **under the present d.** dans le système actuel

dispense [dɪs'pens] **VT 1** *(administer) (justice)* administrer, rendre; **to d. charity** faire la charité; **to d. advice** donner des conseils **2** *(of vending machine etc) (chocolate, condoms)* distribuer; *(change)* donner **3** *Pharm (medication, prescription)* préparer **4** *(exempt) (person)* dispenser, exempter (**from doing** de faire); *Rel* **to d. sb from fasting** dispenser qn du jeûne

  dispense with VT INSEP se passer de; **let's d. with the formalities** passons-nous des formalités; *Euph* **we've dispensed with her services** *(dismissed her)* nous nous sommes passés de ses services; **to d. with the need for sth** rendre qch superflu

dispenser [dɪ'spensər] N **1** *Pharm* pharmacien, -ienne **2** *(machine) (for cigarettes, sweets etc)* distributeur *m* **3** *Rel (of alms)* dispensateur, -trice, distributeur, -trice

dispensing [dɪ'spensɪŋ] ADJ
▸▸ *Br* **d. chemist** pharmacien *m* diplômé; **d. machine** distributeur *m*; **d. optician** = opticien, -ienne ne pouvant fournir que des montures de lunettes (et non pas des verres)

dispersal [dɪ'spɜːs(ə)l] N dispersion *f*

dispersant [dɪ'spɜːs] N dispersant *m*

disperse [dɪ'spɜːs] VT **1** *(scatter) (crowd, seeds etc)* disperser, éparpiller; *(clouds)* dissiper, chasser; *Med (tumour)* résoudre, dissoudre; *(of prism etc) (light)* disperser; *(knowledge, information)* faire circuler **2** *(arrange) (troops etc)* disperser
▸ VI *(of crowd, troops etc)* se disperser, s'éparpiller; *(of light)* se disperser; *(of darkness, clouds)* se dissiper

dispersing agent [dɪ'spɜːsɪŋ] N agent *m* dispersant

dispersion [dɪ'spɜːʃən] N **1** *(of light)* dispersion *f* **2** *Rel* **the D.** la Diaspora

dispirit [dɪ'spɪrɪt] VT *(person)* décourager, abattre

dispirited [dɪ'spɪrɪtɪd] ADJ découragé, abattu, démoralisé

dispiritedly [dɪ'spɪrɪtɪdlɪ] ADV *(to say)* d'un ton découragé *ou* abattu; *(to look)* d'un air découragé *ou* abattu; *(to play, do sth)* sans enthousiasme

dispiriting [dɪ'spɪrɪtɪŋ] ADJ décourageant, démoralisant

dispiritingly [dɪ'spɪrɪtɪŋlɪ] ADV de façon décourageante *ou* démoralisante; **their reply was d. unenthusiastic** le manque d'enthousiasme de leur réponse était décourageant *ou* démoralisant; **d., no-one had come to meet them** personne n'était venu à leur rencontre, ce qui les démoralisait

displace [dɪs'pleɪs] VT **1** *(shift)* déplacer; **weight of water displaced by a body** poids de l'eau déplacée par un corps; *Pol* **displaced persons** personnes déplacées; *Med* **to d. a bone** se déplacer un os **2** *(supplant)* remplacer (**by** par); *(person)* évincer; *(in sb's affections)* supplanter

displacement [dɪs'pleɪsmənt] N **1** *(of water, people)* déplacement *m*; *Naut (of ship)* déplacement; **ship of 5,000 tons d.** navire d'un déplacement de 5 000 tonnes **2** *(substitution)* **d. of A by B** remplacement *m* de A par B **3** *Psy* déplacement *m*
▸▸ *Psy* **d. activity** activité *f* de déplacement; *Aut* **d. volume** cylindrée *f*

displacer unit [dɪs'pleɪsər] N *Aut* amortisseur *m* à déplacement de fluide

display [dɪ'spleɪ] N **1** *Com (of merchandise)* étalage *m*, exposition *f*; **for d. only** *(on product)* en démonstration uniquement; **on d. is merchandise from all over the world** des produits du monde entier sont exposés
2 *(show)* **the treasures are on d. in the museum** les trésors sont exposés dans le musée; **you'll have a fine d. of flowers** vous aurez un beau déploiement de fleurs
3 *Fig (of feelings, opinions etc)* affichage *m*, étalage *m*; *(of affection)* étalage; *(of strength, skill, incompetence)* démonstration *f*; *(of luxury)* étalage; **to be fond of d.** aimer l'ostentation
4 *(event) (of paintings etc)* exposition *f*, *(of regional dances, handicraft)* démonstration *f*
5 *Typ* lignes *fpl* en vedette
6 *Comput etc (screen)* écran *m*; *(screen, display unit)* afficheur *m* *(text appearing)* affichage *m*
7 *(of bird)* parade *f*

▸ VT **1** *(put on show) (merchandise)* étaler, exposer; *(notice)* afficher; **to d. prices** afficher les prix
2 *(exhibit) (ignorance, bad manners)* afficher, étaler; *(talent, irritation, interest)* manifester; *(courage, tact)* faire preuve de
3 *Typ (line)* mettre en vedette
4 *Comput etc* afficher, visualiser
▸ VI *(of bird)* parader
▸▸ **d. ad(vertisement)** pavé *m* *ou* placard *m* publicitaire; **d. area** *Comput* surface *f* d'affichage, zone *f* d'affichage; *Mktg (in store)* espace *m* d'exposition; **d. cabinet** *(in shop)* étalage, vitrine *f*; *(in home)* vitrine; **d. case** *(in shop)* étalage, vitrine; *(in home)* vitrine; **d. copy** *(of book)* exemplaire *m* de démonstration; *Comput* **d. driver** pilote *m* d'affichage; **d. furniture** mobilier *m* de présentation; **d. material** matériel *m* de présentation; *Com, Mktg* **d. pack** emballage *m* de présentation, emballage présentoir; *Aut* **d. panel** tableau *m ou* panneau *m* d'affichage; **d. rack** présentoir *m*; **d. screen** écran *m* de visualisation; **d. shelf** présentoir *m*; **d. space** surface *f* d'exposition; **d. staff** étalagistes *mpl*; **d. stand** présentoir *m*; **d. unit** *Comput* unité *f* de visualisation *ou* d'affichage; *(for goods)* présentoir; **d. window** *(of shop)* vitrine, étalage; *(of calculator)* viseur *m*

displease [dɪs'pliːz] VT *(person)* fâcher, contrarier; **to be displeased at** *or* **with sb/sth** être mécontent de qn/de qch; *(stronger)* être fâché contre qn/de qch

displeasing [dɪs'pliːzɪŋ] ADJ déplaisant, désagréable (**to** à)

displeasure [dɪs'pleʒər] N mécontentement *m*, déplaisir *m*; **much to my/his/etc d.** à mon/son/etc grand déplaisir; **to incur sb's d.** s'attirer le mécontentement de qn

disport [dɪs'pɔːt] VT & VI *Lit* **to d. (oneself)** s'amuser, s'ébattre

disposable [dɪ'spəʊzəb(ə)l] ADJ **1** *(towel, lighter, nappy etc)* jetable, à jeter; *(bottle)* non consigné; *(wrapping, packaging)* perdu **2** *Fin (funds, assets)* disponible
▸ N *Fam (nappy)* couche *f* jetable
▸▸ **d. camera** appareil *m* photo jetable; *Fin* **d. income** revenus *mpl* disponibles (après impôts)

disposal [dɪ'spəʊz(ə)l] N **1** *(getting rid of)* mise *f* au rebut; *(of rubbish etc)* enlèvement *m*; **(refuse) d. plant** dépotoir *m*; **waste d.** traitement *m* des ordures; **waste d. unit** broyeur *m* d'ordures; **for the d. of the body, they …** pour se débarrasser du corps, ils …
2 *(availability)* **to be at sb's d.** être à la disposition de qn; **I am entirely at your d.** je suis à votre entière disposition; **to put sth at sb's d.** mettre qch à la disposition de qn; **to have a sum of money at one's d.** disposer d'une somme; **to have a boat at one's d.** avoir un bateau à sa disposition; **with the limited means at our d.** avec les moyens limités qui sont à notre disposition
3 *(of goods, property)* aliénation *f*, **for d.** à vendre; **d. of assets** cession *f* d'actifs; **d. of stocks** écoulement *m* de stocks; **I will decide on the d. of my property** *(who my heirs will be)* c'est moi qui prendrai les dispositions testamentaires relatives à ma propriété
4 *Fml (arrangement)* disposition *f*

dispose [dɪ'spəʊz] VT **1** *(make willing)* disposer, porter *(sb to (do) sth* qn à (faire) qch); **I am not disposed to help him** je ne suis pas disposé à l'aider **2** *Fml (arrange) (objects)* disposer, arranger; *(troops)* disposer, placer; **they had disposed themselves around the room** ils s'étaient répartis dans la pièce
▸ VI *Prov* **man proposes, God disposes** l'homme propose et Dieu dispose

▸ **dispose of** VT INSEP **1** *(get rid of)* se débarrasser de, mettre au rebut
2 *Com (merchandise)* écouler; *(item)* vendre; *(a business, lease)* céder
3 *(settle) (matter)* régler
4 *Fam (eat) (food)* liquider; *(kill) (person)* liquider; *(beat) (opponent)* mettre la pâtée à
5 *Fml (use) (one's time)* employer
6 *Fml (have at one's disposal)* disposer de

> Note that the French **disposer de** only means **to have at one's disposal**.

disposed [dɪ'spəʊzd] ADJ **d. to sth** enclin *ou* porté à qch; **d. to do sth** porté à faire qch

-disposed SUFF well/ill-disposed bien/mal intentionné (**to, towards** envers, pour)

disposition [dɪspə'zɪʃən] N **1** *(temperament)* nature *f*, humeur *f*, **child of a pleasant d.** enfant d'un bon naturel; **she is of** *or* **has a kindly d.** c'est une bonne nature **2** *Fml (arrangement) (of furniture)* disposition *f*, arrangement *m*; *(of troops)* disposition **3** *Law* disposition *f* testamentaire **4** *(inclination)* désir *m*, intention *f* (**to do sth** de faire qch); *(tendency)* tendance *f*, inclination *f* (**to sth** à qch; **to do sth** à faire qch)

dispossess [dɪspə'zes] VT *(person)* déposséder; *(of house, land)* exproprier; **to d. sb of sth** déposséder *ou* Law dessaisir qn de qch

dispossession [dɪspə'zeʃən] N dépossession *f*, Law dessaisissement *m*; *(of house, land)* expropriation *f*

disproportion [dɪsprə'pɔːʃən] N disproportion *f*

disproportionate [dɪsprə'pɔːʃənət] ADJ disproportionné (**to** à)

disproportionately [dɪsprə'pɔːʃənətlɪ] ADV d'une façon disproportionnée; **d. long/expensive** d'une longueur/d'un prix disproportionné(e)

disprove [dɪs'pruːv] VT *(pp disproved, Law disproven* [dɪs'prəʊv(ə)n]*) (statement, hypothesis etc)* réfuter

disputable [dɪ'spjuːtəb(ə)l] ADJ contestable, discutable

disputant [dɪ'spjuːtənt, 'dɪspjʊtənt] N **1** *Fml* personne *f* participant à un débat **2** *Am Law* partie *f* en litige

disputation [dɪspjʊ'teɪʃən] N *Fml* **1** *(debate)* discussion *f* **2** *(argument)* controverse *f*, débat *m*

dispute[1] ['dɪspjʊt, dɪ'spjuːt] N **1** *(debate)* contestation *f*, controverse *f*; **the matter in d.** l'affaire contestée *ou* en contestation; **the fact is beyond d.** le fait est incontestable; **there's some d. about their true intentions** il y a un doute quant à leurs véritables intentions; **it's open to d.** c'est contestable **2** *(argument)* querelle *f*, dispute *f* (**as to** relative à); **to settle a d.** régler une querelle; **industrial d.** conflit *m* du travail; **wages** *or* **pay d.** conflit salarial; **to be in d.** être en conflit (**with** avec)

dispute[2] [dɪ'spjuːt] VI se disputer, se quereller
▸ VT *(subject)* discuter; *(statement etc)* contester; **to d. (the possession of) sth with sb** disputer qch à qn; **I'm not disputing that** je ne conteste pas cela, je ne dis pas le contraire

disqualification [dɪskwɒlɪfɪ'keɪʃən] N **1** *(from competition)* disqualification *f* **2** *(disqualifying factor)* cause *f* d'incapacité (**for** à) **3** *Law* inhabilité *f* (**to act** à agir); **a year's d. (from driving)** un retrait de permis d'un an

disqualify [dɪs'kwɒlɪfaɪ] VT *Sport (player)* disqualifier; *(from military service)* rendre inapte à; **he was disqualified (from the competition) for failing to turn up on time**

il a été éliminé *ou* exclu (de la compétition) pour ne s'être pas présenté à l'heure; **her youth disqualifies her from participating** son jeune âge ne l'autorise pas à participer; **it automatically disqualifies you from standing for election/for the job** ceci vous met automatiquement dans l'incapacité de vous présenter aux élections/d'accéder à ce poste; **being a woman doesn't d. me from expressing an opinion** le fait que je suis une femme ne m'interdit pas de donner mon avis; **to d. sb from driving** retirer son permis de conduire à qn; **she was fined for driving while disqualified** on lui a mis une amende pour avoir conduit alors qu'on lui avait retiré son permis; *Law* **disqualified from making a will** inhabile à tester

disquiet [dɪs'kwaɪət] *Lit* N inquiétude *f*
   VT inquiéter, troubler

disquieting [dɪs'kwaɪətɪŋ] ADJ (*news, development etc*) inquiétant, troublant

disregard [dɪsrɪ'gɑːd] N (*for facts, one's own safety*) mépris *m* (**of, for** de); (*of the law, convention*) inobservation *f*; **to show complete d. for the feelings of others** ne pas du tout prendre les sentiments des autres en considération; **with a complete d. for his own safety he …** au mépris total du danger qu'il courait, il …
   VT (*somebody, warning, fact*) ne tenir aucun compte de; (*regulations*) mépriser; (*an order*) enfreindre; *Mil* (*orders*) manquer à; **I'll d. what you've just said** je ne tiendrai pas compte de ce que vous venez de dire

disremember [dɪsrɪ'membər] VT *Am* ne pas se souvenir de

disrepair [dɪsrɪ'peər] N (*no pl*) délabrement *m*; **to fall into d.** (*of building*) tomber en ruine, se délabrer; **the building is in d.** le bâtiment est délabré

disreputable [dɪs'repjʊtəb(ə)l] ADJ **1** (*action, methods*) déshonorant, peu honorable; (*life*) peu honorable **2** (*person*) de mauvaise réputation; (*neighbourhood, pub*) mal famé; **to look d.** avoir l'air louche; (*untidy*) être peu soigné; **she has some d. friends** elle a des amis pas très fréquentables

disreputably [dɪs'repjʊtəblɪ] ADV honteusement, d'une façon peu honorable

disrepute [dɪsrɪ'pjuːt] N **to bring sb into d.** ruiner la réputation de qn; **to bring the law/game into d.** discréditer la loi/le sport; **to fall into d.** tomber en discrédit; **to be in d.** être en défaveur (**with, among** auprès de)

disrespect [dɪsrɪ'spekt] N irrévérence *f*, irrespect *m*, manque *m* de respect (**for** envers); **to treat sb/sth with d.** manquer de respect à qn/pour qch; **I mean no d.** je ne veux pas paraître irrespectueux; **no d., but isn't that a bit daft?** sans vouloir vous manquer de respect *ou* sauf votre respect, n'est-ce pas un peu idiot?

disrespectful [dɪsrɪ'spektfʊl] ADJ irrespectueux, irrévérencieux; **to be d. to sb** manquer de respect à qn

disrespectfully [dɪsrɪ'spektfʊlɪ] ADV (*to speak of sb, behave*) d'une manière irrespectueuse *ou* irrévérencieuse

disrobe [dɪs'rəʊb] VT (*judge, priest*) aider à se dévêtir de sa robe
   VI (*take off robe*) se dévêtir de sa robe; *Fml, Hum* (*undress*) se déshabiller

disrupt [dɪs'rʌpt] VT (*administration, plan etc*) désorganiser; (*railway, bus service, traffic*) perturber; (*meeting*) (*of power failure etc*) interrompre; (*of hecklers etc*) perturber; (*life, routine*) (*seriously*) bouleverser; (*less seriously*) déranger

disruption [dɪs'rʌpʃən] N (*of railway, bus service, traffic*) perturbation *f*; (*of meeting*) (*by power failure etc*) interruption *f*; (*by

hecklers etc) perturbation; (*of life, routine*) (*major*) bouleversement *m*; (*minor*) dérangement *m*; **there were several disruptions to the meeting** la réunion a été perturbée/interrompue à plusieurs reprises; **all the disruptions to everyday life caused by the earthquake** tous les bouleversements de la vie quotidienne provoqués par le tremblement de terre; **we apologize to viewers for the d. to this evening's programmes** nous prions les téléspectateurs de bien vouloir nous excuser pour les changements intervenus dans les programmes de la soirée

disruptive [dɪs'rʌptɪv] ADJ (*element*) perturbateur; (*pupil*) turbulent; **she has** *or* **is a d. influence on the class** c'est un élément perturbateur dans la classe
  ▸▸ **d. strike** grève *f* paralysante

dissatisfaction [dɪssætɪs'fækʃən] N insatisfaction *f*, mécontentement *m* (**with** de)

dissatisfied [dɪs'sætɪsfaɪd] ADJ mécontent, insatisfait (**with** de); **I am very d. with the service I received** je suis très mécontent *ou* je ne suis pas du tout satisfait du service que j'ai reçu; **the meal/explanation left me d.** le repas/l'explication m'a laissé sur ma faim

dissaving [dɪs'seɪvɪŋ] N *Econ* désépargne *f*

dissect [dɪ'sekt, daɪ-] VT *also Fig* disséquer

dissecting [dɪ'sektɪŋ, daɪ-] ADJ ATTRIB (*table, room*) de dissection
  ▸▸ **d. knife** scalpel *m*

dissection [dɪ'sekʃən, daɪ-] N *also Fig* dissection *f*

dissemble [dɪ'semb(ə)l] *Fml* VT (*one's feelings, intentions etc*) dissimuler, cacher
   VI dissimuler

disseminate [dɪ'semɪneɪt] VT (*opinions etc*) disséminer, propager, répandre; (*information*) diffuser

disseminated [dɪ'semɪneɪtɪd] ADJ
  ▸▸ *Med* **d. sclerosis** sclérose *f* en plaques

dissemination [dɪsemɪ'neɪʃən] N (*of opinions, beliefs*) dissémination *f*, propagation *f*; (*of information*) diffusion *f*

dissension [dɪ'senʃən] N dissension *f*; **to sow d.** semer la dissension *ou* le désaccord

dissent [dɪ'sent] N **1** (*opposition*) dissensions *fpl*; **d. within the party** dissensions au sein du parti; **d. from the party line** désaccord *m* par rapport à la politique du parti; **to express one's d. from sth** exprimer son désaccord par rapport à qch; **voices of d.** voix discordantes **2** *Rel, Hist* dissidence *f*
   VI **1** différer (**from sb about sth** de qn sur qch); **to d. from a report** avoir une opinion contraire à celle exprimée dans un rapport; **I'd like to d. from the idea** j'aimerais exprimer mon désaccord par rapport à cette idée **2** *Rel, Hist* être dissident

dissenter [dɪ'sentər] N **1** dissident, -ente **2** *Rel, Hist* personne *f* qui n'appartient pas à l'Église anglicane

dissenting [dɪ'sentɪŋ] ADJ ATTRIB (*opinion, voice*) dissident

dissertation [dɪsə'teɪʃən] N *Univ* mémoire *m*, *Am* thèse *f*, *Fig* (*long explanation etc*) exposé *m*

disservice [dɪs'sɜːvɪs] N mauvais service *m*; **to do sb a d.** rendre un mauvais service à qn; **to do oneself a d.** se faire du tort

dissidence [dɪsɪdəns] N *Pol* dissidence *f*; (*disagreement*) désaccord *m*, divergence *f*

dissident [dɪsɪdənt] ADJ, N *Pol* dissident, -ente

dissimilar [dɪ'sɪmɪlər] ADJ dissemblable (**to** à, de); **they are not d.** ils se ressemblent; **a proposal not at all d. to your own** une proposition qui ne diffère pas énormément de la vôtre

dissimilarity [dɪsɪmɪ'lærɪtɪ] N dissemblance *f*, dissimilarité *f* (**to** de; **between** entre)

dissimulate [dɪ'sɪmjʊleɪt] *Fml* VT dissimuler
   VI dissimuler, feindre

dissimulation [dɪsɪmjʊ'leɪʃən] N *Fml* dissimulation *f*

dissipate [dɪsɪpeɪt] VT (*clouds, heat, fears, suspicions etc*) dissiper; (*fortune, one's energy*) gaspiller, dissiper
   VI (*of cloud, heat, fears suspicions etc*) se dissiper; *Phys* (*of energy*) se dégrader

dissipated [dɪsɪpeɪtɪd] ADJ (*life*) dissipé; (*person*) débauché; **to be d.** (*of person*) vivre dans la dissipation *ou* la débauche

dissipation [dɪsɪ'peɪʃən] N **1** (*of person*) vie *f* dissipée *ou* désordonnée **2** *Fml* (*of fog, one's assets*) dissipation *f*; (*of fortune*) gaspillage *m*, dissipation

dissociate [dɪ'səʊsɪeɪt] VT **1** dissocier (**from** de); **the two functions have become dissociated** ces deux fonctions se sont dissociées; **to d. oneself from sb/a policy** se désolidariser de qn/d'une politique **2** *Chem* (*compound etc*) dissocier
   VI *Chem* se dissocier

dissociation [dɪsəʊsɪ'eɪʃən] N dissociation *f*

dissolute [dɪsəluːt] ADJ (*person*) dissolu, débauché; (*conduct*) licencieux; (*life*) dissolu, déréglé; **to lead a d. life** vivre dans la débauche, mener une vie dissolue

dissoluteness [dɪsəluːtnɪs] N débauche *f*, dissolution *f*

dissolution [dɪsə'luːʃən] N (*of parliament, marriage etc*) dissolution *f*

dissolve [dɪ'zɒlv] N *Cin, TV* fondu *m* enchaîné
   VT (*sugar*) (faire) dissoudre, faire fondre; (*cloud, illusion*) dissiper; (*marriage, partnership, Parliament*) dissoudre
   VI **1** (*of sugar, metal in acid*) se dissoudre, fondre; (*of cloud, illusion*) se dissiper; (*of crowd*) se disperser; *Pol* (*of Parliament, opposition*) se dissoudre; *Fig* **to d. into tears** fondre en larmes; *Fig* **to d. into thin air** partir *ou* s'en aller en fumée **2** *Cin, TV* faire un fondu enchaîné

dissonance [dɪsənəns] N *Mus* dissonance *f*, *Fig* (*of views*) discordance *f*

dissonant [dɪsənənt] ADJ *Mus* dissonant; *Fig* (*voice, opinion*) discordant

dissuade [dɪ'sweɪd] VT **to d. sb from doing sth** dissuader qn de faire qch; **to d. sb from a particular course of action** dissuader qn de suivre une certaine ligne de conduite

dissuasion [dɪ'sweɪʒən] N dissuasion *f* (**from** de); **no amount of d. would have convinced him to stay** rien n'aurait pu le persuader de rester

distaff [dɪstɑːf] N quenouille *f*, *Fig* **on the d. side** (*of family*) du côté maternel

DISTANCE [dɪstəns] N **1** distance *f*, **at a d. of … ** à une distance de …; **within five minutes' walking d.** à cinq minutes de marche; **a short d. away** tout près, à deux pas; **some d. away** assez loin; **it is quite a d. (away)** (*of house etc*) ce n'est pas tout près; **to see sth from a d.** voir qch de loin; **to see sth in the d.** voir qch au loin; **in the middle d.** au second plan; *Mil* **within striking d.** (*of target*) à portée de fusil/de canon/*etc*; (*of own forces*) à portée de l'ennemi SEE GRAMMAR B59

2 (*between two places*) distance *f*; (*between two things*) distance, intervalle *m*; (*in time*) intervalle; **to go part of the d. on foot** faire une partie du trajet à pied; **to keep sb at a d.** tenir qn à distance; **at this d. in time** à cet intervalle de temps

3 *Sport* parcours *m*; *(of boxing match)* durée *f*; **long-/medium-d. race/runner** course *f*/coureur *m* de fond/de demi-fond; *Sport, Boxing, Fig* **to go** *or* **last** *or* **stay the d.** tenir la distance; **the fight went the d.** le combat est allé jusqu'à la limite

4 *(reserve)* réserve *f*, air *m* distant; **to keep one's d.**, **to keep at a d.** *(from other people)* se tenir sur la réserve, garder ses distances; *(from sth dangerous, infectious)* garder ses distances, ne pas s'approcher; **to keep sb at a d.** se tenir sur la réserve avec qn, garder la distance avec qn

VT *(competitor)* distancer; *Fig* **to d. oneself from sb/sth** prendre ses distances à l'égard de qn/par rapport à qch

▸▸ **d. banking** banque *f* à distance; **d. education**, **d. learning** enseignement *m* à distance *ou* par correspondance; *Aut* **d. table** tableau *m* des distances entre les villes

distant ['dɪstənt] **ADJ 1** *(place, object, relation)* éloigné; *(country, memory, resemblance)* lointain; *(in time)* éloigné, lointain; **in the d. future** dans un avenir lointain; **in the not too d. future** dans un futur relativement proche; **in the (dim and) d. past** dans le temps, il y a bien longtemps **2** *(reserved) (person, manner)* réservé, distant; **to be d. with sb** se montrer réservé *ou* distant avec qn; **d. look** regard perdu dans le vague

ADV three miles d. à trois mil(l)es de distance; **not far d. from ...** à peu de distance de ...

▸▸ *Rail* **d. signal** signal *m* à distance

distantly ['dɪstəntlɪ] **ADV 1** *(in the distance)* au loin; **he could d. hear ...** il entendait ... au loin; **d. related** d'une parenté éloignée; **to be d. related to sb** avoir un lien de parenté éloigné avec qn **2** *(to treat sb)* d'un air réservé, avec réserve

distaste [dɪs'teɪst] **N** dégoût *m* (**for** de), répugnance *f* (**for** pour); **she was unable to hide her d. for his attitude** il lui était impossible de cacher le dégoût que lui inspirait son attitude; **if you could only overcome your initial d. for opera** si seulement tu parvenais à surmonter ta répugnance pour l'opéra

distasteful [dɪs'teɪstfʊl] **ADJ** *(task, thought etc)* désagréable, déplaisant; *(joke)* de mauvais goût

distastefulness [dɪs'teɪstfʊlnɪs] **N** *(of task, thought etc)* caractère *m* désagréable *ou* répugnant; *(of joke)* mauvais *m* goût

distemper¹ [dɪ'stempər] **N** *Vet* maladie *f* des jeunes chiens, maladie de Carré

distemper² [dɪ'stempər] **N** *Art* détrempe *f*

VT *(wall)* badigeonner en couleur; *Art (painting, wall)* peindre à la *ou* en détrempe

distend [dɪ'stend] **VT** *(cheeks)* gonfler; *(nostrils)* dilater; *(stomach)* distendre, ballonner **VI** *(of cheeks)* se gonfler; *(of nostrils)* se dilater; *(of stomach)* se ballonner, se distendre

distension [dɪ'stenʃən] **N** dilatation *f*, distension *f*

distich ['dɪstɪk] **N** *Liter (couplet)* distique *m*

distil, *Am* **distill** [dɪ'stɪl] (-ll-) *Chem, Ind* **VT** *(water etc)* distiller **VI** *(of liquid, secretion etc)* distiller (**from** de) ▸ **distil off, distil out VT SEP** *Chem, Ind* chasser par la distillation

distillate ['dɪstɪleɪt] **N** *Chem, Ind* distillat *m*

distillation [dɪstɪ'leɪʃən] **N 1** *Chem, Ind (process)* distillation *f* **2** *(result) Chem, Ind* produit *m* de la distillation; *Fig (of ideas, theories)* condensé *m*

distilled water [dɪ'stɪld] **N** eau *f* distillée

distiller [dɪ'stɪlər] **N** *Ind* distillateur *m*

distillery [dɪ'stɪlərɪ] **N** *Ind* distillerie *f*

distinct [dɪ'stɪŋkt] **ADJ 1** *(different)* distinct,

différent (**from** de); **to keep two things d.** faire la distinction entre deux choses; **women, as d. from men** les femmes, par opposition aux hommes **2** *(clear)* distinct; *(difference)* net, *f* nette, clair; *(memory)* clair, net, précis; *(order)* formel, précis; *(promise)* formel; *(preference)* marqué; *(impression)* net; **to have a d. memory of sth** se souvenir clairement de qch; **the coast becomes more d.** la côte se précise

> Attention: ne pas confondre avec l'adjectif **distinctive**.

distinction [dɪ'stɪŋkʃən] **N 1** *(difference)* distinction *f* (**between** entre); **to make** *or* **draw a d. between two things** faire une distinction entre deux choses; **without d. of age** sans distinction d'âge; **class d.** distinction de classes **2** *(honour)* distinction *f*; **academic distinctions** distinctions académiques **3** *(excellence)* distinction *f*; *Univ* mention *f*, **to gain d.** se distinguer; **man of d.** homme distingué; *Univ* **with d.** *(thesis etc)* avec mention

distinctive [dɪ'stɪŋktɪv] **ADJ** *(feature, style)* distinctif, -ive; **to be d. of sth** être caractéristique de qch

> Attention: ne pas confondre avec l'adjectif anglais **distinct**.

distinctively [dɪ'stɪŋktɪvlɪ] **ADV** de manière distinctive *ou* caractéristique

> Attention: ne pas confondre avec l'adverbe **distinctly**.

distinctly [dɪ'stɪŋktlɪ] **ADV 1** *(clearly) (to speak, hear, see)* distinctement, clairement; **I d. remember telling you** je me rappelle clairement te l'avoir dit; **I told him d.** je le lui ai dit expressément **2** *(definitely)* décidément; **she is d. better** elle va sensiblement mieux; **by now the weather was d. cold** à présent il faisait vraiment froid

> Attention: ne pas confondre avec l'adverbe **distinctively**.

distinctness [dɪ'stɪŋktnɪs] **N 1** *(clearness)* clarté *f*, netteté *f* **2** *(separate nature)* spécificité *f*; **not to lose sight of the d. of these two issues** ne pas perdre de vue le fait que ces deux questions sont distinctes

distinguish [dɪ'stɪŋgwɪʃ] **VT 1** *(recognize) (object, sound)* distinguer, discerner; **I could not d. him among the crowd** je n'ai pu le distinguer dans la foule **2** *(characterize, differentiate)* distinguer, différencier (**from** de); **reason distinguishes man from the other animals** la raison sépare l'homme des autres animaux; **to d. oneself by ...** se distinguer par ...

VI to d. between two things faire la distinction entre deux choses

distinguishable [dɪ'stɪŋgwɪʃəb(ə)l] **ADJ 1** *(recognizable)* reconnaissable; *(sound, difference)* perceptible; *(improvement)* sensible; **the coast was hardly d.** c'est à peine si l'on distinguait la côte **2** *(that can be differentiated)* que l'on peut distinguer, qui se distingue (**from** de); **the two ideas are barely d.** les deux idées diffèrent à peine

distinguished [dɪ'stɪŋgwɪʃt] **ADJ** *(air, appearance)* distingué; *(author etc)* de distinction; *(performance)* brillant; **to look d.** avoir l'air distingué

distinguishing mark [dɪ'stɪŋgwɪʃɪŋ] **N** signe *m* distinctif

distort [dɪ'stɔːt] **VT 1** *(physically) (metal)* déformer; *(features, face)* décomposer, déformer; *(limbs)* distordre; *(surface)* fausser, déjeter *Fig (the truth)* déformer; *(facts, words)* fausser, dénaturer; **to d. the mean-**

ing of a text dénaturer un texte **3** *Electron, Radio (reception etc)* déformer **VI 1** *(of metal, wood)* se déformer, se fausser **2** *Electron, Radio* se déformer

distorted [dɪ'stɔːtɪd] **ADJ 1** *(physically)* tordu, déformé; *(features, face)* déformé; **face d. by rage** visage convulsé de fureur **2** *Fig (version, account of event)* déformé, faussé **3** *Radio, TV* déformé

distorting [dɪ'stɔːtɪŋ] **ADJ** déformant; *Fig* **those changes had a d. effect on the inflation index** ces changements ont faussé l'indice de l'inflation

▸▸ **d. mirror** glace *f* déformante

distortion [dɪ'stɔːʃən] **N 1** *(physical)* distorsion *f*; *(of features)* altération *f*, *(of body)* contorsion *f* **2** *Fig (of text)* altération *f*, *(of facts, truth)* déformation *f* **3** *Electron, Radio, Opt (of transmission)* distorsion *f*, déformation *f*; *(of sound)* distorsion sonore; *(of magnetic field)* déviation *f*; *Tech (of part)* distorsion

distract [dɪ'strækt] **VT 1** *(mind, attention)* distraire, détourner (**from** de); **stop distracting me!** arrête de me distraire!; **I don't want to d. you if you're working** je ne veux pas te déranger si tu travailles; **see if you can d. him from his problems** essaie de le distraire de ses problèmes **2** *(trouble)* préoccuper

distracted [dɪ'stræktɪd] **ADJ** préoccupé; *(look)* absent

> Note that the French word **distrait** is a false friend and is never a translation for the word **distracted**. Its most common meaning is **absent-minded**.

distractedly [dɪ'stræktɪdlɪ] **ADV** *(to pace about, look about)* d'un air préoccupé; *(to answer)* distraitement

distracting [dɪ'stræktɪŋ] **ADJ** qui distrait l'attention; **I find noise d. when I'm working** le bruit me dérange quand je travaille; **she has a d. influence on him** elle le distrait

distraction [dɪ'strækʃən] **N 1** *(interruption) (when working etc)* distraction *f*; **I could do without the d. of you asking me that every five minutes** ça m'aiderait si tu ne me dérangeais pas pour me demander ça toutes les cinq minutes **2** *(amusement)* distraction *f*, divertissement *m*; **he's seeking d.** il cherche à se distraire **3** **to drive sb to d.** rendre qn fou/*f* folle, faire perdre la tête à qn; **to love sb to d.** aimer qn éperdument *ou* à la folie

distrain [dɪ'streɪn] **VI** *Law* **to d. upon sb** contraindre qn par saisie de biens; **to d. upon a debtor** exécuter une saisie sur un débiteur

distraint [dɪ'streɪnt] **N** *Law* saisie *f*, (saisie-)exécution *f*, *pl* (saisies-) exécutions

distraught [dɪ'strɔːt] **ADJ** bouleversé; **he is d. over his wife's illness** la maladie de sa femme le bouleverse; **d. with grief/anger** fou/*f* folle de douleur/colère

distress [dɪ'stres] **N 1** *(mental suffering)* angoisse *f*, *(physical suffering)* douleur *f*; **to be in a state of great d.** *(unhappy)* être désespéré; *(anxious)* être fou/*f* folle d'angoisse; **to cause sb d.** *(unhappiness)* faire de la peine à qn; *(anxiety)* alarmer qn **2** *(difficulty)* détresse *f*, embarras *m*; *Naut* **ship in d.** navire en détresse **3** *Law (action)* saisie *f*, *(goods)* biens *mpl* saisis

VT 1 *(somebody)* affliger, angoisser, faire de la peine à **2** *(piece of furniture)* vieillir

▸▸ *Com* **d. merchandise** = marchandises *fpl* écoulées à bas prix parce qu'elles sont endommagées ou pour permettre de régler des dettes importantes; *Com* **d. sale** = vente *f* d'articles à bas prix parce qu'ils sont endommagés ou pour permettre de régler des dettes importantes; **d. signal** signal *m* de détresse; *Law* **d. warrant** mandat *m* de saisie

distressed [dɪ'strest] ADJ **1** *(suffering)* affligé, désespéré; **to be d. about sth** *(unhappy)* être affligé par qch; *(anxious)* être angoissé par qch **2** *(in difficulty)* dans la détresse **3** *(piece of furniture)* vieilli **4** *Law* saisi

distressing [dɪ'stresɪŋ] ADJ affligeant, pénible

distribute [dɪ'strɪbjuːt] VT **1** *(give out) (alms, prizes, leaflets)* distribuer; *(property)* répartir, partager; *Com, Cin (be distributor of)* distribuer; *(books, newspapers)* distribuer, diffuser; *Fin (dividend)* répartir **2** *(spread out) (over a surface etc)* disperser, répartir; **evenly distributed load** charge uniformément répartie

distributed database [dɪ'strɪbjuːtɪd] N *Comput* base *f* de données répartie

distribution [dɪstrɪ'bjuːʃən] N **1** *Com, Cin* distribution *f*; *(of books, newspapers)* distribution, diffusion *f*; **d. of profits** distribution *ou* répartition *f* des bénéfices **2** *(of population, manpower etc)* répartition *f*; *(of property)* répartition, partage *m*; **d. of wealth** distribution *f* des richesses
▸▸*Elec* **d. board** tableau *m* de distribution; *Elec* **d. box** boîte *f* de dérivation *ou* de jonction; *Com* **d. centre** centre *m* de distribution; *Com* **d. chain** chaîne *f* de distribution; *Com* **d. channel** canal *m* de distribution; *Com* **d. contract** contrat *m* de distribution; *Com* **d. costs** frais *mpl* de distribution, coût *m* de la distribution; *Com* **d. depot** dépôt *m* de distributeur; *Com* **d. market** marché *m* de la distribution; **d. method** mode *m* de distribution; *Com* **d. network** réseau *m* de distribution, circuit *m* de distribution; *Com* **d. outlet** point *m* de distribution; *Cin* **d. rights** droits *mpl* de distribution; *Elec* **d. switchboard** tableau *m* de distribution; **d. system** système *m* de distribution

distributive [dɪ'strɪbjʊtɪv] ADJ, N *Gram* distributif *m*

distributor [dɪ'strɪbjʊtər] N **1** *(person)* distributeur, -trice; *(of particular make of car etc)* concessionnaire *m*; *Cin* distributeur *m* **2** *Elec, Aut etc (device)* distributeur *m*
▸▸*Elec* **d. box** boîte *f* de dérivation *ou* de jonction; *Com* **d. brand** marque *f* de distributeur; *Aut* **d. cap** tête *f* de Delco® *ou* d'allumeur; *Com* **d. discount** remise *f* au distributeur; *Com* **d.'s margin** marge *f* du distributeur; *Com* **d. panel** panel *m* de distributeurs

distributorship [dɪ'strɪbjʊtəʃɪp] N *Com* **to have the d. for ...** distribuer ...

district ['dɪstrɪkt] N **1** *(of country)* région *f*, territoire *m*; *Admin* district *m*, secteur *m*; **electoral d.,** *Am* **congressional d.** circonscription *f* électorale; **mining d.** région minière; **postal d.** secteur postal; **urban d.** district urbain **2** *(of town)* quartier *m*; *Admin (of city)* ≃ arrondissement *m*
▸▸*Am Law* **d. attorney** ≃ procureur *m* de la République; *Br Admin* **d. council** conseil *m* municipal; *Am Law* **d. court** ≃ tribunal *m* d'instance (fédéral); *Com* **d. manager** directeur, -trice régional(e); *Br* **d. nurse** infirmière *f* visiteuse

distrust [dɪs'trʌst] N méfiance *f*, défiance *f* (**of** de); **to have a d. of sth** se méfier *ou* se défier de qch
▸VT se méfier de, se défier de; **to d. one's own eyes** ne pas en croire ses propres yeux

distrustful [dɪs'trʌstfʊl] ADJ méfiant, défiant (**of** de); **he was d. of his own capabilities** il ne croyait pas à *ou* manquait de foi en ses propres capacités; **to be d. of a policy/ sb's intentions** ne pas se fier à une politique/ à qn

disturb [dɪ'stɜːb] VT **1** *(interrupt) (person)* déranger; *(criminal)* surprendre; *(sb's rest etc)* troubler; *Phys (magnetic field)* perturber; **to d. the peace** troubler l'ordre public; **do not d.** ne pas déranger **2** *(disarrange) (papers, room)* déranger; *(surface, ground)* agiter, remuer **3** *(worry) (somebody)* inquiéter, troubler; *Law (interfere with the rights of)* inquiéter *ou* troubler dans la jouissance d'un droit; **I am disturbed by his apparent indifference** l'indifférence qu'il montre m'inquiète *ou* me trouble

disturbance [dɪ'stɜːbəns] N **1** *(interruption)* dérangement *m* **2** *(disarrangement)* trouble *m*; **atmospheric d.** perturbation *f* atmosphérique; **emotional disturbances** troubles *mpl* émotifs **3** *(noise)* bruit *m*, tumulte *m*; *(fight)* bagarre *f*, *(riot)* émeute *f*, **political disturbances** troubles *mpl* politiques; **to cause** *or* **create a d.** troubler l'ordre public; *(at meeting etc)* semer la confusion; **it will cause major disturbances to traffic** cela perturbera énormément la circulation **4** *Law (interference with rights)* trouble *m* de jouissance

disturbed [dɪ'stɜːbd] ADJ **1** *(night, sleep etc)* agité **2** *(mentally, emotionally) (at a particular time)* perturbé; *(as a characteristic)* qui souffre de troubles du comportement; *Psy* **d. behaviour** troubles *mpl* du comportement

disturbing [dɪ'stɜːbɪŋ] ADJ *(news, development etc)* inquiétant, troublant; *(stronger)* perturbant, dérangeant

disunite [dɪsjʊ'naɪt] VT *(family etc)* désunir, jeter la désunion dans; *(party)* diviser

disunited [dɪsjʊ'naɪtɪd] ADJ *(family)* désuni; *(party)* divisé

disunity [dɪs'juːnɪtɪ] N désunion *f*

disuse [dɪs'juːs] N *(of term etc)* désuétude *f*; *(of machine etc)* abandon *m*, mise *f* au rancart; **to fall into d.** *(of word, custom)* tomber en désuétude

disused [dɪs'juːzd] ADJ *(machine)* mis au rancart; *(public building)* désaffecté; *(mine, well, railway line)* abandonné

disyllabic [dɪsɪ'læbɪk] ADJ dissyllabe, dissyllabique

ditch [dɪtʃ] N fossé *m*; *(between fields)* douve *f*, *Aviat Sl (sea)* baille *f*; **drainage d.** rigole *f* d'écoulement
▸VT *Fam (get rid of) (object)* jeter, se débarrasser de; *(car, project etc)* abandonner; *(inconvenient person)* se débarrasser de; *(boyfriend, girlfriend)* plaquer; *(friend)* laisser tomber
▸VI **1** *Aviat* faire un amerrissage forcé **2** *Agr* creuser un fossé

ditcher ['dɪtʃər] N personne *f* qui creuse des fossés

ditching ['dɪtʃɪŋ] N *Aviat* amerrissage *m* forcé

ditchwater ['dɪtʃwɔːtər] N *(of ditch)* eaux *fpl* stagnantes; *Fam* **as dull as d.** ennuyeux comme la pluie *ou* un jour de pluie

dither ['dɪðər] *Fam* N **to be all of a** *or* **in a d.** ne plus savoir où donner de la tête, paniquer
▸VI hésiter; **stop dithering!** décide-toi!; **she was dithering over whether to come or not** elle n'arrivait pas à décider si elle viendrait ou pas

ditherer ['dɪðərər] N *Fam* indécis, -ise; **don't be such a d.!** allez, décide-toi!

dithery ['dɪðəri] ADJ *Fam* indécis

ditto ['dɪtəʊ] ADV idem, de même; *Com* dito; *Fam* **I'm hungry – d.** j'ai faim – moi aussi *ou* moi pareil *ou* moi de même

ditty ['dɪtɪ] N *Fam* chanson *f*, chansonnette *f*

ditz [dɪts] N *Am Fam* courge *f*, andouille *f*

ditzy ['dɪtsɪ] ADJ *Am Fam* étourdi

diuretic [daɪjʊ'retɪk] ADJ, N *Med* diurétique *m*

diurnal [daɪ'ɜːn(ə)l] ADJ *Astron, Biol* diurne
N *Rel* diurnal *m*, -aux

div [dɪv] N *Br Fam (idiot)* abruti, -ie

diva ['diːvə] N *Mus* diva *f*

divan [dɪ'væn] N divan *m*
▸▸**d. base** sommier *m*; **d. bed** divan-lit *m*, *pl* divans-lits

dive [daɪv] N **1** *Swimming* plongeon *m*; *(of submarine, deep-sea diver)* plongée *f*, *Aut (on braking)* plongée (au freinage); *Swimming* **high d.** plongeon de haut vol; *Aviat* **vertical d., nose d.** piqué *m*; *Aviat* **to go into a d.** faire un piqué; *Aviat* **to pull out of a d.** effectuer un rétablissement; **he made a d. for the shelter** il s'est précipité vers l'abri; **the goalie made a d. for the ball** le goal a plongé pour attraper le ballon; **to take a d.** *(of boxer)* se coucher; *(of salary, exchange rate)* plonger, chuter
2 *Fam Pej (place)* bouge *m*
VI (*pt* **dived,** *Am Fam* **dove** [dəʊv], *pp* **dived**) plonger (**into** dans); *(of submarine)* plonger, effectuer une plongée; *(of aircraft)* piquer, descendre en piqué; **to d. (for the ball)** *(of goalkeeper)* plonger pour attraper le ballon; **to d. for pearls** pêcher des perles; *Aviat* **to d. down on an enemy** piquer de haut sur un ennemi; **to d. into one's pocket** plonger la main dans sa poche; **to d. into a doorway for shelter** se précipiter dans une entrée pour s'abriter; *Fam* **they all dived into the pub** ils se sont précipités dans le pub
▸▸*Aviat* **d. bomber** chasseur *m* bombardier; *Aviat* **d. bombing** bombardement *m* en piqué
▸ **dive in** VI **1** *(into water)* plonger **2** *Fam (start eating)* attaquer **3** *Fam (start doing sth)* s'y mettre; *(do sth without preparation)* se jeter à l'eau

dive-bomb VT *Aviat* attaquer en piqué

diver ['daɪvər] N **1** plongeur, -euse; *(in deep sea)* scaphandrier *m* **2** *Orn (bird)* plongeon *m*, plongeur *m*

diverge [daɪ'vɜːdʒ] VI *(of rays, lines etc)* diverger, s'écarter; *(of roads)* s'écarter; *(of opinions, persons)* diverger; *Fig* **our paths diverged** nos chemins se sont séparés
VT *(rays etc)* faire diverger

divergence [daɪ'vɜːdʒəns] N divergence *f*

divergent [daɪ'vɜːdʒənt], **diverging** [daɪ'vɜːdʒɪŋ] ADJ divergent; **we take d. views on certain points** nos opinions divergent *ou* diffèrent sur certains points

diverging beam [daɪ'vɜːdʒɪŋ] N *Aut* faisceau *m* divergent

divers ['daɪvəz] ADJ *Arch (several)* divers, plusieurs

diverse [daɪ'vɜːs] ADJ **1** *(different)* divers, différent; **they are very d. in their approach** ils ont une approche très différente **2** *(varied)* divers, varié

diversely [daɪ'vɜːslɪ] ADV diversement

diversification [daɪvɜːsɪfɪ'keɪʃən] N **1** *(of company etc)* diversification *f* **2** *(of tastes etc)* diversification *f*

diversify [daɪ'vɜːsɪfaɪ] VI *(of company etc)* se diversifier; **to d. into furniture** se diversifier et commencer à fabriquer *ou* produire/ vendre/etc des meubles; **to d. into software/banking** se diversifier en pénétrant le secteur du logiciel/le secteur bancaire
VT diversifier; **we must aim to d. our product portfolio** il nous faut essayer de diversifier notre portefeuille de produits

diversion [daɪ'vɜːʃən] N **1** *(of traffic etc)* déviation *f*; *(of plane, funds)* détournement *m*; *Elec* dérivation *f*; **to create** *or* **make a d.** *(to distract attention)* faire diversion **2** *(amusement)* distraction *f*, divertissement *m*; **to**

seek **d. from sth** chercher à se distraire de qch **3** *Mil* diversion *f*

diversionary [daɪ'vɜːʃən(ə)rɪ] ADJ **1** *(activity)* destiné à faire diversion **2** *Mil (man-œuvre)* de diversion

diversity [daɪ'vɜːsɪtɪ] N diversité *f*, variété *f*

divert [daɪ'vɜːt] VT **1** *(river, traffic)* détourner, dériver; *(blow)* parer, écarter; *(criticism)* parer; *(attention, conversation, sb from course of action, funds)* détourner (**from** de); *Elec (current)* dévier; *Naut* dérouter; *Aviat (plane, flight)* détourner; **I managed to d.** his attention from the problem j'ai réussi à détourner son attention de ce problème **2** *(amuse)* divertir, amuser; **to d. one-self by doing sth** faire qch pour se distraire

diverting [daɪ'vɜːtɪŋ] ADJ divertissant, amusant

divest [daɪ'vest] VT **1** *Fml (person)* priver, dénuer (**of** de); **to d. oneself of** *(one's coat)* enlever; *(one's authority)* se dévêtir de; *(a duty)* se désinvestir de; *(right)* renoncer à **2** *Law (somebody)* déposséder (**of** de)

divestment [daɪ'vestmənt] N *Fin* **d. of assets** scission *f* d'actifs

divide [dɪ'vaɪd] VT **1** *(split) (inheritance etc)* diviser; *(kingdom)* démembrer; *(land)* morceler; *(meat etc)* détailler; *(family)* mettre le désaccord dans, désunir; *(party)* diviser, scinder; **to d. sth in two** couper *ou* diviser qch en deux; **to d. sth into parts** diviser qch en parties

2 *(distribute)* partager, répartir (**among** entre); *(spending, one's time, resources)* répartir; **to d. proportionally** répartir au prorata; **to d. profits among shareholders** répartir les bénéfices entre les actionnaires; **we d. the work among us** nous nous partageons le travail

3 *Math* diviser

4 *(separate)* séparer (**from** de); **the mountains that d. France from Spain** les montagnes qui séparent la France de l'Espagne VI **1** se diviser, se partager (**into** en); *(of political party)* se scinder, se diviser; *(of road)* bifurquer

2 *Pol (of House)* aller aux voix

3 *Math* **twelve divides by three** douze est divisible par trois; **they're learning to d.** ils apprennent à faire des divisions

N *Geog* ligne *f* de partage des eaux; *Fig (racial, political, emotional etc)* fossé *m*; **the North-South d.** le fossé entre le nord et le sud

▸ **divide off** VT SEP séparer

▸ **divide out** VT SEP *(distribute)* partager, répartir (**among** entre)

▸ **divide up** VT SEP partager; **they divided the area/work up between them** ils se sont partagé le secteur/travail

divided [dɪ'vaɪdɪd] ADJ **1** *(territory etc)* divisé; *(attention)* distrait; **we are d. on this issue** nous sommes partagés sur ce sujet; **opinions are d.** les avis sont partagés; **house/family d. against itself** maison/famille désunie; **a (political) party d. against itself** un parti divisé **2** *(work)* partagé **3** *(scale, thermometer etc)* gradué

▸ ▸ *Am* **d. highway** route *f* à quatre voies; **d. skirt** jupe-culotte *f*, *pl* jupes-culottes

dividend ['dɪvɪdend] N *Math, Fin* dividende *m*; *Fin* **d. on shares** dividende d'actions; **the company has declared a d. of 10%** la société a déclaré un dividende de 10%; *Fig* **to pay dividends** *(of action etc)* porter des fruits

▸ ▸ **d. cover** taux *m* de couverture du dividende; **d. share** action *f* de jouissance; **d. tax** impôt *m* sur les dividendes; **d. warrant** chèque-dividende *m*, *pl* chèques-dividendes, coupon *m* d'arrérages; **d. yield** taux *m* de rendement des actions

divider [dɪ'vaɪdər] N *(in room)* cloison *f* de séparation; *(for files)* intercalaire *m*

dividers [dɪ'vaɪdəz] NPL *(instrument)* compas *m* à pointes sèches

dividing [dɪ'vaɪdɪŋ] ADJ

▸ ▸ *Elec* **d. box** boîte *f* de dérivation; **d. line** ligne *f* de démarcation; *Fig* séparation *f*, distinction *f*; **she has crossed the d. line between confidence and arrogance** elle a franchi la limite entre confiance en soi et arrogance; **d. wall** mur *m* de séparation, cloison *f*

divination [dɪvɪ'neɪʃən] N divination *f*

divine [dɪ'vaɪn] ADJ *(judgement, worship etc)*, *Fig* divin; **to attend d. service** aller à l'église; *Fig Fam* **you look d. in that dress** vous êtes divine *ou* adorable dans cette robe

N théologien *m*

VT **1** *(the future, sb's intentions)* deviner **2** *(water)* découvrir, détecter

▸ ▸ *Fig* **d. inspiration** inspiration *f* divine; *Hist* **the d. right of kings** la monarchie de droit divin

divinely [dɪ'vaɪnlɪ] ADV *also Fig* divinement; **she was looking d. beautiful** elle était divine

diviner [dɪ'vaɪnər] N devin *m*, devineresse *f*; **(water) d.** radiesthésiste *mf*, sourcier *m*

diving ['daɪvɪŋ] N *(underwater)* plongée *f* (sous-marine); *(from diving board)* plongeon *m*

▸ ▸ **d. bell** cloche *f* à plongeur *ou* de plongée; **d. board** plongeoir *m*; *Naut* **d. rudder** *(of submarine)* gouvernail *m* de profondeur; **d. suit** scaphandre *m*

divining [dɪ'vaɪnɪŋ] N divination *f*, **(water) d.** radiesthésie *f*

▸ ▸ **d. rod** baguette *f* de sourcier

divinity [dɪ'vɪnɪtɪ] N **1** *(divine nature, god)* divinité *f*; **the D.** la Divinité **2** *(subject)* théologie *f*; *Univ* **Doctor of D.** docteur *m* en théologie **3** *Sch* instruction *f* religieuse

divisible [dɪ'vɪzɪb(ə)l] ADJ divisible (**by** par)

division [dɪ'vɪʒən] N **1** *(splitting)* division *f*, partage *m* (**into** en); *(of party)* scission *f*, *(of land)* morcellement *m*; *(of scale etc)* graduation *f*, *(distribution)* (*of profit etc)* répartition *f*, partage *m*; **d. of labour** division du travail; **d. of votes** partage de voix

2 *(discord)* division *f*, désunion *f*, **to sow d.** semer la zizanie *ou* la discorde

3 *Math* division *f*, **long d.** = division décomposée en ses différentes étapes VOIR GRAMMAIRE A77; B59

4 *Parl* vote *m*; **to come to a d.** voter; **without a d.** sans avoir à voter

5 *(section)*, *Ftbl, Mil* division *f*; *Biol* groupe *m*, classe *f*; *Law (of court)* section *f*, *esp Am Rail* section de ligne; *(of scale, thermometer etc)* degré *m*; *Pol* **parliamentary d.** *(area)* circonscription *f* électorale

6 *Constr etc* cloison *f*, séparation *f*

▸ ▸ *Br Pol* **d. bell** = sonnerie *f* à la Chambre des communes prévenant les députés qu'il faut venir voter; *Br Pol* **d. list** = liste *f* des députés qui ont voté pour ou contre une motion; *Br Pol* **d. lobby** = nom *m* des deux salles dans lesquelles les députés britanniques se répartissent pour voter; *Math* **d. sign** symbole *m* de division

divisional [dɪ'vɪʒən(ə)l] ADJ de la division

▸ ▸ **d. account** compte *m* divisionnaire; **d. director** directeur, -trice de division

divisive [dɪ'vaɪsɪv] ADJ qui divise, qui crée des divisions

divisor [dɪ'vaɪzər] N *Math* diviseur *m*

divorce [dɪ'vɔːs] N **1** *Law* divorce *m*; **I want a d.** je veux divorcer; **to get a d.** divorcer; **to ask for a d.** demander le divorce; **d. case** cas *m* de divorce; **to specialize in d. (cases)** *(of lawyer)* se spécialiser dans les cas de di-

vorce; **to sue for (a) d.**, *Am* to file a petition **for d.** demander le divorce; **their marriage ended in d.** ils ont divorcé; **one in three marriages ends in d.** un couple sur trois divorce **2** *Fig* divorce *m*, séparation *f* (**between sth and sth** de qch et de qch)

VT **1** *Law (of judge) (two people)* prononcer le divorce de; **to get divorced from sb, to d. sb** divorcer d'avec qn **2** *Fig* **you cannot d. form from content** on ne peut pas séparer le fond et la forme

VI *(of husband and wife)* divorcer

▸ ▸ **d. proceedings** action *f* en divorce

divorced [dɪ'vɔːst] ADJ divorcé; **she is divorced from him** elle est divorcée d'avec lui; *Fig* **d. from reality** *(life, idea)* chimérique; **passage d. from the context** passage isolé du contexte; **d. from commonsense** dénué de bon sens

divorcee [dɪvɔː'siː] N divorcé, -ée

divot ['dɪvət] N motte *f* de terre

divulge [daɪ'vʌldʒ] VT divulguer; **to d. sb's whereabouts** divulguer l'endroit où se trouve qn

divvy ['dɪvɪ] N *Br Fam* **1** *Fin* dividende *m* **2** *(idiot)* abruti, -ie; **stop being such a d.** arrête tes bêtises

▸ **divvy up** VT SEP *Fam* partager

dixie, dixy ['dɪksɪ] N *esp Mil Fam* gamelle *f*

dixieland ['dɪksɪlænd] N *Mus* dixieland *m*

▸ ▸ **d. jazz** dixieland

DIY [diːaɪ'waɪ] *Br (abbr* do-it-yourself*)* N bricolage *m*

ADJ ATTRIB de bricolage; **a D. expert** un spécialiste du bricolage

dizzily ['dɪzɪlɪ] ADV **1** *(to stagger etc)* pris de vertige **2** *(to rise) (of cliffs, share prices etc)* vertigineusement **3** *Fig (to behave, laugh)* étourdiment

dizziness ['dɪzɪnɪs] N étourdissement *m*, vertige(s) *m(pl)*, malaise *m*; **fit of d.** éblouissement *m*

dizzy ['dɪzɪ] ADJ **1** *Med* pris de vertige; **to feel d.** avoir le vertige; **to make sb d.** donner le vertige à qn; **d. with desire/fear** fou/folle de désir/peur **2** *Fig (height, speed etc)* vertigineux **3** *Fig (scatterbrained)* écervelé

▸ ▸ **d. blonde** blonde *f* évaporée; **d. spell** éblouissement *m*, malaise *m*

DJ [diː'dʒeɪ] N **1** *abbr* disc jockey **2** *Fam abbr* dinner jacket

Djibouti [dʒɪ'buːtɪ] N Djibouti

D Lit(t) [diː'lɪt] N *abbr* Doctor of Letters

DNA [diːeˈneɪ] N *Chem (abbr* deoxyribonucleic acid*)* ADN *m*

D-notice N *Journ* = consigne *f* donnée par le gouvernement britannique à la presse pour empêcher la diffusion d'informations touchant à la sécurité du pays

DNS [diːeˈnes] N *Comput (abbr* Domain Name System*)* système *m* de nom de domaine, DNS *m*

DO¹ [duː] *(he does* [dʌz], *pt did* [dɪd], *pr sub sg, pl do; pp done* [dʌn], *in the aux use* **don't** [dəʊnt], **didn't** ['dɪd(ə)nt] *are common for* **do not, did not; doesn't** ['dʌz(ə)nt] *for* **does not***)*

V AUX in questions **1** ▪ in negative statements **1** ▪ for emphasis **2** ▪ in tag questions **6** ▪ elliptically **6**	
VT faire **1–6** ▪ étudier **1**	
VI aller **2, 3**	

V AUX **1** *(usual form in questions and negative statements except with* have, *but see* have²,be, *and modal verbs; also in negative commands)* **did you see him?** l'avez-vous vu?; **we do not know** nous ne le savons pas; **do not speak!** ne parlez pas!; **don't do it!** n'en faites rien!; **don't be afraid** n'ayez pas peur; **do you mind?** ça ne vous fait rien?; *Iron* vous permettez? VOIR GRAMMAIRE A46–8

2 *(used for emphasis)* **he did go** il y est bien allé; **I do believe he is a thief** je crois vraiment que c'est un voleur; **it doesn't matter – it does (matter)!** ça ne fait rien – si, ça fait quelque chose!; **why don't you work? – I do (work)!** pourquoi ne travaillez-vous pas? – mais si, je travaille!; **do you remember him? – do I remember him** *or* **do I!** vous souvenez-vous de lui? – si je m'en souviens!; **do sit down** asseyez-vous donc!; **yes, people did live there** oui, des gens ont vécu là; **I don't like coffee, but I do like tea** je n'aime pas le café, mais j'aime bien le thé; **rarely does it happen that …** il arrive rarement que … VOIR GRAMMAIRE A57

3 *(replacing vi)* **they work in the fields as their fathers did** ils travaillent aux champs comme le faisaient leurs pères; **he writes better than I do** il écrit mieux que moi; **they have always existed and still do** ils ont toujours existé et existent encore; **if you want to speak to him, do it now** si vous désirez lui parler, faites-le maintenant VOIR GRAMMAIRE A57

4 *(replacing vt and taking its construction)* **he envies me as much as I do him** il m'envie autant que je l'envie

5 *(replacing vt and object)* **if you understood the question as well as I do** si vous compreniez la question aussi bien que moi

6 *(in replies, tag questions etc)* **may I open these letters? – (please) do** puis-je ouvrir ces lettres? – je vous en prie!; **did you see him? – I did** l'avez-vous vu? – oui(, je l'ai vu); **do you like her? – no I don't** tu l'aimes bien? – non(, je ne l'aime pas); **you don't like it – yes I do** vous ne l'aimez pas – mais si; **you like him, don't you?** vous l'aimez bien, n'est-ce pas?; **she lives here, doesn't she?** elle habite ici, n'est-ce pas?; **that does you good, doesn't it?** ça fait du bien, hein?; **he doesn't believe that, does he?** il ne croit pas ça, hein?; **you like Paris? so do I** vous aimez Paris? moi aussi VOIR GRAMMAIRE A47

7 *Law* **charged that he did on the 15th of August utter threats** accusé d'avoir proféré des menaces le 15 août

VT 1 *(carry out, complete)* *(good deed, one's duty, housework, calculation etc)* faire; *Math (problem)* résoudre; **she's doing medicine** *(studying it)* elle étudie la médecine; **to do the interpreting** faire l'interprète; **to do ten years (in prison)** faire dix ans de prison; **the car was doing sixty** la voiture faisait du soixante

2 *(with reference to general activity)* **what do you do (for a living)?** qu'est-ce que vous faites (dans la vie)?; **what are you doing?** qu'est-ce que vous faites?; **it gives me something to do** cela me donne de l'occupation; **don't do it again!** ne recommencez pas!; **don't!** ne faites pas ça!; **do as you're told** fais ce qu'on te dit; **what is to be done?** que faire?; **it can't be done** cela n'est pas possible, c'est impossible; **there's nothing to be done** il n'y a rien à faire; **it's as good as done** c'est une affaire faite; **she did nothing but cry** elle n'a fait que pleurer; **I don't know what to do** je ne sais que faire, je ne sais pas quoi faire; **what can I do for you?** que puis-je faire pour vous?; **what are you going to do about it?** que proposez-vous de faire?; **what would he do without you?** que deviendrait-il sans vous?; **it was all I could do to lift it** c'est à peine si j'ai pu le soulever; **it was all I could do not to laugh** j'ai eu du mal à ne pas rire; *Fam* **that's done it!** ça y est! VOIR GRAMMAIRE A46–8

3 *(with reference to behaviour, conduct)* **to do right/wrong** bien/mal faire; **to do right/wrong by sb** bien/mal agir envers qn; **you would do well to …** vous feriez bien de

…; **well done!** très bien!, bravo!; **it isn't done** *(is not the practice)* cela ne se fait pas; **it is quite commonly done** c'est de pratique courante

4 *(arrange, fix)* **to do sb's/one's hair** coiffer qn/se coiffer; **to do one's teeth** se brosser les dents; **he does repairs** il fait des réparations; **she's doing the flowers for the wedding** c'est elle qui s'occupe des fleurs pour le mariage

5 *Fam (look around)* *(town, museum)* visiter, faire

6 *Theat (Hamlet etc)* faire

7 *Fam (with reference to crime, dishonest conduct)* **to do sb** *(cheat)* refaire qn, faire qn; *(beat up)* casser la figure à qn, mettre une raclée à qn; **he got done last night** *(arrested)* il s'est fait ramasser la nuit dernière; **I've been done!** *(cheated)* j'ai été roulé!, on m'a eu!; **they did three other houses in the neighbourhood** *(burgled them)* ils sont passés dans trois autres maisons dans le quartier

8 *Fam (use)* **to do drugs** se droguer; **I don't do drugs** je ne me drogue pas, je ne prends pas de drogues

9 **let's do lunch** il faudra qu'on déjeune ensemble un de ces jours

10 *Fam (provide, serve, help)* Old-fashioned **they do you very well at this hotel** on est très bien servi dans cet hôtel; *Com* **we can do you this article at …** nous pouvons vous faire cet article à …; **that dress/hairstyle does something/nothing for you** cette robe/coiffure t'arrange *ou* te met en valeur/ne t'arrange pas *ou* ne te met pas du tout en valeur; **this music doesn't do anything for me** cette musique ne me dit rien, je n'aime pas cette musique

11 *(in perfect tenses and past participle)* **to have done** *(finished)* avoir fini; *Lit* **day is done** la journée tire à sa fin; **have you done shouting?** as-tu fini de crier?; **done!** *(after a bargain made)* entendu!, marché conclu!; **to be done** *(of meat, vegetable)* être prêt *ou* cuit; **meat well done** viande bien cuite; **done to a turn** cuit à point

VI 1 **how do you do?** *(on first introduction)* enchanté (de faire votre connaissance); **to be doing well** *(of patient)* être sur la voie de la guérison; *(in business)* être en bonne voie, faire de bonnes affaires; *(of business)* bien aller, réussir; *(of plant)* bien pousser; **that young man will do well** c'est un garçon qui réussira; **he did brilliantly** il a réussi brillamment; **to do very well** *or* **nicely for oneself** *(prosper)* s'en tirer pas mal du tout

2 *(serve, suffice)* **that will do** *(is satisfactory)* c'est bien (comme cela), c'est bon; *(stop it)* ça suffit, c'est assez; **tea will do** *(if you haven't got coffee)* du thé fera l'affaire; **this room will do for the office** cette pièce ira bien pour le bureau; **will this one do?** ceci fera l'affaire?; **that will never do** cela n'ira jamais, ça ne va pas du tout; **to make do with what one has** s'arranger avec ce qu'on a; **we'll just have to make do** il faudra faire avec; **that will do me** cela fera mon affaire; **it would never do for them to see me** il ne faudrait pas qu'ils me voient

3 *(happen)* **let's see what's doing next door** allons voir ce qui se passe à côté; **there's never anything doing at this time of year** il ne se passe jamais rien à cette période de l'année; **nothing doing!** *(I, she etc won't)* rien à faire!, ça ne prend pas!

N 1 **the do's and don'ts** ce qu'il faut faire et ce qu'il ne faut pas faire; **the do's and don'ts of society** ce qui se fait et ce qui ne se fait pas dans le monde; *Fam* **come on, fair do's!** *(I want my share)* dis donc, donne-moi ma part!; *(be fair)* dis donc, sois juste!

2 *(party etc)* réception *f*

3 *Old-fashioned Fam (state of affairs)* **it's a poor do!** c'est triste!

▸ **do away with** VT INSEP **1** *(abolish)* *(custom)* abolir, abandonner; *(death penalty, monarchy)* abolir; *(practice, paperwork, homework)* supprimer; **we've done away with the typists** *(got rid of them)* nous nous sommes défait des dactylos; *Fam* **they should do away with school** ils devraient supprimer l'école

2 *Fam (kill)* supprimer; **she has threatened to do away with herself** elle a menacé de se supprimer

▸ **do by** VT INSEP *Fam (treat)* **to do well** *or* **right/badly** *or* **wrong by sb** bien/mal agir *ou* se conduire envers qn; **she did very well by her granddaughter at Christmas** *(gave her lots of gifts)* elle a gâté sa petite-fille à Noël; **he has been hard done by** il a été traité durement; **he'll feel very hard done by if you don't at least send him a birthday card** il se sentira vraiment blessé si tu ne lui envoies même pas de carte d'anniversaire; *Prov* **do as you would be done by** ne fais pas aux autres ce que tu ne voudrais pas qu'ils te fassent

▸ **do down** VT SEP **1** *(swindle)* estamper

2 *(say bad things about)* dire du mal de; **to do oneself down** se rabaisser; **there's always someone ready to do you down** il y a toujours des gens prêts à dire du mal des autres

▸ **do for** VT INSEP *Fam* **1** *(murder)* tuer, faire son affaire à; **he's done for** *(will be killed)* c'est un homme mort; *(is ruined)* il est fini *ou Fam* fichu; **if he keeps on treating her this way, she'll do for him** s'il continue à la traiter de cette façon, elle va le descendre

2 *(exhaust)* épuiser; **it was that last hill that did for me** c'est la dernière colline qui m'a épuisé

3 *(clean house for)* faire *ou* tenir le ménage de; **who does for you?** qui fait votre ménage?

VT SEP *(charge with, convict of)* **to do sb for sth** *(murder, shoplifting)* condamner qn pour qch; **they'll do you for double-parking** ils vont te mettre une amende si tu restes garé en double file; *Hum* **she'll get done for child-molesting if she goes out with him** on va l'accuser de les prendre au berceau si elle sort avec lui

▸ **do in** VT SEP *Fam* **1** *(murder)* descendre, faire son affaire à; **somebody on our street was done in last night** quelqu'un de notre rue a été descendu cette nuit

2 *(exhaust)* crever; **I'm absolutely done in** je suis crevé *ou* vanné

3 *(injure, damage)* *(of shoes etc)* *(toes etc)* faire mal à; **to do one's back/knee in** se niquer le dos/genou; *Sl* **that girl really does my head in** *(annoys me)* cette fille, elle me prend la tête

▸ **do out** VT SEP **1** *(clean)* *(the kitchen, a room)* faire, nettoyer; *(drawer, cupboard)* ranger

2 *(decorate)* *(room)* faire (**in** en); *(woodwork)* peindre (**in** en)

▸ **do out of** VT SEP *Fam (cheat)* **to do sb out of sth** soutirer *ou* carotter qch à qn; *(money)* refaire *ou* escroquer qn de qch; **to do sb out of a job** *(of person)* prendre le travail de qn; **all this automation is doing people out of jobs** toute cette automatisation supprime des emplois; **the new structure did him out of his job** la nouvelle structure lui a fait perdre son travail; **you've done me out of a possible job** tu m'as fait perdre un emploi; **she's been done out of her share of the money** elle s'est fait escroquer de sa part de l'argent

▸ **do over** VT SEP **1** *Am (redecorate)* *(house)* refaire la décoration de

2 *Br Fam (beat up)* *(person)* casser la figure à, mettre une raclée à

3 *Fam (search)* *(flat etc)* retourner; **their place really got done over while they were**

away *(burgled)* on a tout retourné chez eux pendant qu'ils étaient partis

4 *Am (repeat) (homework)* refaire

▸ **do up** VT SEP **1** *(fasten) (jacket, skirt, button, zip)* fermer; *(laces)* faire; *(hair)* relever

2 *(wrap) (parcel)* faire; *(objects)* emballer, empaqueter

3 *(improve appearance of)* remettre à neuf; *(room, inside of house etc)* décorer; *Fam* to do oneself up se faire beau/belle; **to be done up to the nines** être sur son trente et un

VI *(of clothes)* s'agrafer

▸ **do with** VT SEP **1 what did you do with my umbrella?** qu'avez-vous fait de mon parapluie?; **she didn't know what to do with herself** *(to keep busy)* elle ne savait que faire *ou* à quoi s'occuper; *(for joy)* elle ne se tenait pas de joie; *(for awkwardness)* elle était gênée, elle ne savait plus où se mettre; **I can't do a thing with my hair** je n'arrive pas à me coiffer; **I'll see if Bob can do anything with the car** je vais voir si Bob peut faire quelque chose à la voiture; **I can't do a thing with him** *(child)* je ne sais plus quoi faire

2 *(need) (usually formed with could)* **I could do with a cup of tea** je prendrais bien une tasse de thé; **we can do with your help** vous n'êtes pas de trop; **you could do with a haircut** une coupe de cheveux ne te ferait pas de mal; **the house could do with a lick of paint** la maison aurait bien besoin d'un coup de pinceau; **we could do with something like that for the spare room** ce serait bien si on avait quelque chose comme ça pour la chambre d'ami

3 *(be connected with)* **she's something to do with insurance** elle est dans les assurances; **it has to do with your mother, I'm afraid** j'ai bien peur que ça concerne ta mère; **I want nothing to do with him** je ne veux pas avoir affaire à lui; **to have nothing to do with sth** *(not be involved in or responsible for)* n'être pour rien dans qch, n'avoir rien à voir avec qch; *(not be connected with)* n'avoir rien à faire avec qch; **you should have nothing to do with it** *(don't get involved)* tu ne devrais pas t'en mêler; **I had nothing to do with it** je n'y suis pour rien; **it's nothing to do with the colour of your skin** cela n'a rien à voir avec la couleur de la peau; **it's nothing to do with you** vous n'avez rien à voir là-dedans

4 *(finish)* **to have done with sth** en avoir fini avec qch; **I've done with trying to help people** j'en ai fini d'aider les gens; **let's have done with it!** finissons-en!; **to have done with sb** *(terminated relationship with lover, girlfriend etc)* avoir rompu avec qn; *(with friend)* en avoir fini avec qn; **I haven't done with him yet!** *(haven't finished scolding him)* je n'en ai pas encore fini avec lui!; **that's all over and done with!** c'est fini, tout ça!

5 *Fam (finish using) (newspaper, scissors etc)* finir avec; **once you've done with it** quand tu auras fini

6 *Fam (with negative) (not like)* **I can't be doing with getting up early** je n'aime pas me lever tôt; **I can't be doing with television** je n'aime pas la télévision; **I can't be doing with her** je ne l'aime pas

▸ **do without** VT INSEP *(manage without) (something)* se passer de; **to do without food** se passer de nourriture; *Fam* **I could do without him** je me passerais bien de lui; **we can do without the sarcasm** on n'a pas besoin de ces sarcasmes; **you could do without the heavy eye make-up** tu serais mieux avec moins de maquillage sur les yeux; **you'll just have to do without** il faudra s'en passer

do² [dəʊ] N *Mus (fixed)* do *m*, ut *m*; *Scot Fam* **to be up to high do** être dans tous ses états

DOA [diːəʊˈeɪ] ADJ *Med (abbr* **dead on arri-**

val) **to be D.** être mort avant son arrivée à l'hôpital

doc [dɒk] N *(abbr* **doctor)** *Fam* toubib *m*; **thanks d.** merci docteur

▸▸ **D. Martens®** *(shoes)* Doc Martens® *fpl*

docile [ˈdəʊsaɪl] ADJ docile

docility [dəʊˈsɪlɪtɪ] N docilité *f*

dock¹ [dɒk] N *Naut (of port)* bassin *m*; **to go into d.** entrer au bassin; **the docks** les docks *mpl*; *Fam* **in d.** *(of car, plane)* en réparation; **floating d.** dock flottant, chantier *m* à flot **2** *Theat* **scene d.** remise *f* à décors

VT **1** *Naut (ship)* faire entrer au bassin *ou* à quai; *(for repairs)* faire entrer en cale sèche; *(on canal, river) (barge etc)* garer **2** *(two spacecraft)* arrimer

VI **1** *(of ship)* entrer *ou* arriver au port *ou* aux docks *ou* à quai; *(for repair)* entrer en cale sèche; **when do we d.?** quand arrivons-nous à quai?; **we'll be docking at New York** nous entrerons à quai à New York **2** *(of two spacecraft)* s'arrimer

▸▸ **d. strike** grève *f* des dockers; **d.-warehouse** dock *m* entrepôt

dock² N *Law* banc *m* des accusés *ou* des prévenus; **prisoner in the d. Murphy** accusé Murphy

dock³ VT **1** *(sb's pay)* diminuer; **to d. two pounds from sb's wages** supprimer deux livres du salaire de qn **2** **to d. a horse('s tail)/a dog('s tail)** couper la queue à un cheval/un chien

dock⁴ N *(weed)* patience *f*

docker [ˈdɒkər] N *Br* docker *m*, débardeur *m*; **dockers' strike** grève *f* des dockers

docket [ˈdɒkɪt] N **1** *(piece of paper) (accompanying parcel, file)* bordereau *m* **2** *Law (summary)* registre *m* des jugements rendus; *Am (list of cases)* rôle *m* des causes **3** *Br (customs document)* récépissé *m* de douane

VT **1** *Law (decision)* enregistrer; *Am (case)* porter sur le rôle des causes **2** *(file, merchandise)* étiqueter

docking [ˈdɒkɪŋ] N **1** *Naut* mise *f* au bassin; *(for repairs)* radoub *m* **2** *(of two spacecrafts)* arrimage *m*

▸▸ **d. manoeuvre** accostage *m*; *Comput* **d. station** *(for notebook)* station *f* d'accueil

dockland [ˈdɒklænd] N quartiers *mpl* des docks

dockyard [ˈdɒkjaːd] N chantier *m* naval *ou* de constructions navales; **naval d.** arsenal *m* maritime

doctor [ˈdɒktər] N **1** *Med* médecin *m*, docteur *m*; **to go to the doctor('s)** aller chez le docteur; **the d. will see you now** le docteur va vous recevoir maintenant; **good morning d.** bonjour docteur; *Br Fam* **to be under the d. for sth** être suivi par le docteur pour qch; **I would like to see D. Brown** j'aimerais voir le docteur Brown; **I am a d.** je suis médecin; **woman d.** femme *f* médecin; **family d.** médecin de famille; **ship's d.** médecin de bord; **army d.** médecin militaire; *Br* **National Health (Service) d.** ≃ médecin conventionné; *Fig Fam* **that's just what the d. ordered** c'est exactement ce qu'il me fallait

2 *Univ* docteur *m*; **D. of Divinity/Law/Medicine** docteur en théologie/droit/médecine; **D. of Literature/Science** docteur ès lettres/sciences; *Rel* **Doctors of the Church** docteurs *mpl* de l'Église; **d.'s degree** doctorat *m*

VT **1** *Pej Fam (falsify, adulterate) (text)* falsifier; *(accounts, evidence)* falsifier, fausser; *(dice, cards)* piper; *(wine etc)* frelater

2 *(drug) Horseracing (horse)* doper; **to d. sb's drink** mettre de la drogue dans le verre de qn *(à son insu)*

3 *Old-fashioned (patient)* soigner

4 *Vet Fam (cat etc)* châtrer

doctoral [ˈdɒktər(ə)l] ADJ *(thesis, research etc)* de doctorat; *(robes)* de docteur

doctorate [ˈdɒktərɪt] N *Univ* doctorat *m*; **to have a d. in history** avoir un doctorat en histoire

doctoring [ˈdɒktərɪŋ] N **1** *Pej Fam (of text etc)* falsification *f* **2** *(of horse)* doping *m* **3** *Med Fam (profession)* profession *f* de médecin **4** *(care)* soins *mpl* *(of sb* donnés à qn) **5** *Vet (of cat etc)* castration *f*

doctrinaire [dɒktrɪˈneər] ADJ *Pej* doctrinaire

doctrinal [dɒkˈtraɪn(ə)l] ADJ doctrinal

doctrine [ˈdɒktrɪn] N doctrine *f*

docudrama [ˈdɒkjʊdraːmə] N *TV* docudrame *m*

document [ˈdɒkjʊmənt] N document *m*; **legal d.** acte *m* authentique; *Com* **documents against acceptance/payment** documents *mpl* contre acceptation/paiement; *Law* **documents relating to a case** dossier *m* d'une affaire; *Law* **to draw up a d.** rédiger un acte

VT documenter; *(of photographer)* faire un reportage sur; **the film documents the lives of the long-term unemployed** le film montre en détail la vie des chômeurs de longue durée; **well-documented book** livre bien documenté; **his involvement in the affair is well documented** on dispose de nombreux témoignages montrant qu'il a été impliqué à cette affaire; **the first documented case of ...** le premier cas établi de ...

▸▸ **d. case** porte-documents *m inv*; **d. collator** unité *f* de classement de documents; **d. cover** pochette *f*; *Comput* **d. file** fichier *m* document; **d. handling** manipulation *f* de documents; **d. holder** *(for keyboarder)* bras *m* porte-copies; *Comput* **d. reader** lecteur *m* de documents; *Law* **d. of title** acte *m* de propriété

documentary [dɒkjʊˈment(ə)rɪ] ADJ *(film)* documentaire; *(proof)* littéral, -aux

N *Cin, TV* documentaire *m*

▸▸ *Com, Fin* **d. bill** traite *f* documentaire; **d. charges** frais *mpl* de crédit documentaire; **d. credit** crédit *m* documentaire; **d. credit application** demande *f* d'ouverture de crédit documentaire; **d. credit department** service *m* des crédits documentaires; **d. evidence** preuve *f* littérale; **d. interview** interview-document *f, pl* interviews-documents; **d. letter of credit** lettre *f* de crédit documentaire; **d. maker** documentariste *mf*; **d. remittance** remise *f* documentaire

documentation [dɒkjʊmenˈteɪʃən] N documentation *f*

docusoap [ˈdɒkjʊsəʊp] N docu-soap *m*

dodder [ˈdɒdər] VI *(walk)* marcher d'un pas branlant; *Hum* **I'm doddering along** je vais mon petit bonhomme de chemin; **he's beginning to d. a bit** *(mentally)* il commence à devenir un peu gâteux

dodderer [ˈdɒdərər] N *Pej* croulant, -ante

doddering [ˈdɒdərɪŋ] ADJ **1** *(walk)* branlant **2** *Pej (person)* gaga *inv*, gâteux; **a d. old fool** un vieux gâteux

doddery [ˈdɒdərɪ] ADJ *Fam (shaky)* branlant, tremblotant; **I still feel a bit d. (on my feet)** *(after illness)* je ne me sens pas encore d'aplomb; *Pej* **a d. old fool** un vieux croulant

doddle [ˈdɒd(ə)l] N *Br Fam* **it's a d.** *(easy)* c'est simple comme bonjour

dodge [dɒdʒ] N **1** *(to avoid sth)* saut *m* de côté; **she made a d. to the left** elle a fait un saut vers la gauche **2** *Fam usu Pej (trick)* truc *m*, combine *f*; **he's up to all the dodges** il connaît toutes les combines; **tax d.** combine pour payer moins d'impôts

VI *(step aside)* se jeter de côté; *Boxing, Ftbl* esquiver; **to d. behind a tree** se glisser prestement derrière un arbre vⱻ **1** (blow) esquiver; (person) éviter; (police, search party) échapper à, se dérober à **2** Fam Pej (difficulty) esquiver, éluder; (question) éluder, escamoter; **to d. doing one's duty** se dérober à son devoir; **to d. doing the housework/buying one's round** se défiler pour ne pas faire le ménage/payer sa tournée; **to d. military service** couper au service militaire; **stop dodging the issue** arrête d'éluder le problème

dodgem® ['dɒdʒəm] ADJ, N Br **d. cars, dodgems®** autos fpl tamponneuses; **to have a ride** or **a go on the dodgems®** faire un tour d'autos tamponneuses

dodger ['dɒdʒər] N Fam (shirker) tire-au-flanc m inv; Old-fashioned **an artful d.** un fin matois; **fare d.** voyageur, -euse sans billet; **they're after tax dodgers** ils cherchent à coincer ceux qui fraudent le fisc

dodgy ['dɒdʒɪ] ADJ Br Fam **1** (risky, dangerous) (plan, idea) risqué; **the house is nice, but it's in a really d. area** la maison est bien mais elle est dans un quartier vraiment craignos; **investing money in a scheme like that is just too d.** c'est vraiment trop risqué d'investir dans ce genre de truc; **the weather looks pretty d.** (unreliable) le temps a l'air plutôt douteux ou menaçant **2** (untrustworthy) (person) louche; (scheme) douteux, suspect; **he's OK, but all his friends are well d.** lui, ça va, mais ses amis craignent vraiment; **they were involved in a couple of d. business deals** ils ont été impliqués dans des transactions plutôt louches **3** (not working properly, unstable) merdique; **the brakes are really d.** les freins sont très douteux; **the engine sounds a bit d.** le moteur fait un bruit suspect; **don't sit on that chair, it's a bit d.** ne t'assieds pas sur cette chaise, elle est un peu branlante; **the ceiling looks a bit d.** le plafond n'a pas l'air en très bon état; **my stomach's been a bit d. for the last couple of days** ça fait deux jours que j'ai l'estomac un peu dérangé

dodo, pl **dodoes, dodos** ['dəʊdəʊ, -z] N **1** (bird) dronte m, dodo m; Fig **(as) dead as a d.** mort et enterré **2** Fam (fool) andouille f **3** Mktg poids m mort, produit m dodo

DOE [di:əʊ'i:] N Br Admin Formerly (abbr **Department of the Environment**) ≃ ministère m de l'Environnement

doe [dəʊ] N **1** (deer) biche f; (of fallow deer) daine f; **d.-eyed** aux yeux de biche **2** (of rabbit) lapine f; (of wild rabbit, hare) hase f

doer ['du:ər] N (dynamic person) personne f dynamique; **she's a d.** c'est une femme très active; **we need a d. rather than a talker** c'est un homme d'action qu'il nous faut plutôt qu'un orateur

doeskin ['dəʊskɪn] N peau f de daim; **d. glove** gant en peau de daim

doesn't ['dʌz(ə)nt] CONTR = does not, see do[1]

doff [dɒf] VT Lit, Hum (one's hat) enlever, ôter; **to d. one's cap/hat to sb** se découvrir devant qn

DOG [dɒg] N **1** (animal) chien m; **beware of the d.** (sign) (attention) chien méchant; **to set the dogs on sb** lancer les chiens sur qn; **sporting d.** chien de chasse; Br Sport Fam **the dogs** les courses fpl de lévriers
2 Zool (of certain animals) mâle m
3 Old-fashioned (person) **you lucky d.!** veinard!; **sly d.** fin renard m; **gay d.** coureur m (de jupons); **dirty d.** salaud m, sale type m
4 Am Sl (failed film, party etc) fiasco m; Pej (ugly woman) cageot m; **dogs** (feet) panards mpl
5 Mktg (product) poids m mort, gouffre m financier
6 Tech (pawl) cliquet m

7 (idioms) **to die like a d.** mourir comme un chien; **to treat sb like a d.** traiter qn comme un chien; **to follow sb about like a d.** suivre qn comme un petit chien; Fig **he's a d. in the manger** il fait l'empêcheur de tourner en rond; **to lead a d.'s life** mener une vie de chien; **to lead sb a d.'s life** faire mener une vie de chien à qn; **it's a d.'s life being a teacher** c'est une vie de chien que d'être professeur; Prov **you can't teach an old d. new tricks** = on ne peut pas apprendre un nouveau métier etc à quelqu'un qui a dépassé un certain âge; Prov **every d. has his day** à chacun sa chance; Prov **give a d. a bad name (and hang him)** = il est très difficile de se débarrasser de sa mauvaise réputation, qu'elle soit méritée ou non; Br Fam **to give sb d.'s abuse** traiter qn de tous les noms; Fam **what a d.'s breakfast or dinner!** quel gâchis!; (of text) quel torchon!; Fam **to make a d.'s breakfast or dinner of sth** gâcher qch; Br Fam **to be dressed up like a d.'s dinner** être habillé comme un clown; esp Am Fam **to put on the d.** (put on airs and graces) prendre des grands airs; (spend a lot of money) faire des frais; Fam **he doesn't stand a d.'s chance** il n'a pas la moindre chance; Fam **I'm going to see a man about a d.** (going to the toilet) je vais aux toilettes; (going somewhere unspecified) j'ai un truc à faire; **it's a case of d. eat d.** les loups se mangent entre eux; **it's a d.-eat-d. world** c'est un monde où les loups se mangent entre eux, c'est la loi de la jungle; **to go to the dogs** (of business, country) aller à la ruine; **he's really gone to the dogs** c'est la déchéance totale pour lui; **this restaurant has gone to the dogs since he took over** ce restaurant ne vaut plus rien du tout depuis qu'il l'a racheté

VT (-gg-) [dɒgd] (person) suivre à la trace; **to d. sb's footsteps** marcher sur les talons de qn; **he is dogged by misfortune** il est poursuivi par la malchance; **she has been dogged by injury for the last year** elle a eu blessure sur blessure au cours de l'année passée

▸▸ **d. biscuit** biscuit m pour chien; **d. breeder** éleveur, -euse de chiens; **d. breeding** élevage m de chiens; Tech **d. clutch** embrayage m à crabot, crabot m; **d. collar** (for dog) collier m pour ou de chien; Fam (of clergyman) col m d'ecclésiastique; **d. days** canicule f; **d. fox** renard m mâle; **d. handler** maître-chien m, pl maîtres-chiens; **d. Latin** latin m de cuisine; Br **d. licence** = permis m de posséder un chien; **d. paddle** nage f du petit chien; **d. racing** courses fpl de lévriers; **d. rose** (flower) églantine f, (bush) églantier m, rosier m sauvage; **d. show** exposition f canine; **D. Star** Sirius f; **d. tag** (for dog, soldier) plaque f d'identification

dogcart ['dɒgkɑːt] N (vehicle) dog-cart m, pl dog-carts

dog-catcher N = employé m municipal qui est chargé d'attraper les chiens errants

doge [dəʊdʒ] N Hist doge m

dog-eared ADJ (book) aux pages cornées; (page) corné; **I'm afraid your book got a bit d.** je crois bien que les pages de ton livre se sont un peu cornées

dog-end N Fam mégot m

dogfight ['dɒgfaɪt] N combat m de chiens; Mil, Aviat combat aérien; Fig (brawl) bagarre f

dogfish ['dɒgfɪʃ] N chien m de mer, roussette f

dogfood ['dɒgfuːd] N pâtée f (pour chiens)

dogged ['dɒgɪd] ADJ (person) résolu, tenace; (research, refusal, pursuit) tenace; (attachment) fidèle

doggedly ['dɒgɪdlɪ] ADV avec ténacité, ré-

solument; **to work d.** travailler sans relâche; **to be d. intent on doing sth** avoir la ferme intention de faire qch

doggedness ['dɒgɪdnɪs] N ténacité f

doggerel ['dɒgərəl] N (silly and comical) poésie f burlesque; (worthless, mediocre) vers mpl de mirliton

▸▸ **d. verse** (silly and comical) poésie burlesque; (worthless, mediocre) vers de mirliton

doggie ['dɒgɪ] N Fam toutou m, chienchien m; **to do it d. fashion** (sex) faire l'amour en levrette

▸▸ **d. bag** = petit sac m fourni par certains restaurants pour emporter les restes; **d. paddle** nage f à la chien

doggo ['dɒgəʊ] ADV Br Fam **to lie d.** se tenir coi

doggone ['dɒgɒn] Am Fam INT **d. (it)!** zut!, nom d'un chien!
ADJ fichu; **I've lost the d. car keys** j'ai perdu ces saletés de clés de bagnole
ADV vachement; **it's so d. hot!** il fait une chaleur à crever!

doggy ['dɒgɪ] ADJ **1** (smell etc) de chien **2** Fam (person) qui adore les chiens
N Fam = doggie

doghouse ['dɒghaʊs] N esp Am chenil m; Fig **to be in the d.** être en défaveur ou en disgrâce; **you're in the d. with Mum** tu n'es pas en odeur de sainteté avec Maman

dogleg ['dɒgleg] N (in pipe, road, golf course) coude m
VI (of pipe, road, on golf course) faire un coude

doglike ['dɒglaɪk] ADJ (devotion) de chien

dogma, pl **dogmas** ['dɒgmə, -əz] N dogme m

dogmatic [dɒg'mætɪk] ADJ dogmatique

dogmatically [dɒg'mætɪklɪ] ADV dogmatiquement; (to say) d'un ton dogmatique

dogmatism ['dɒgmətɪz(ə)m] N (of opinion, person etc) dogmatisme m

dogmatist ['dɒgmətɪst] N dogmatique mf

dogmeat ['dɒgmiːt] N viande f pour chiens

do-gooder ['duː'gʊdər] N Fam Pej âme f charitable, faiseur, -euse de bonnes œuvres

dog-paddle VI nager comme un chien

dogsbody ['dɒgzbɒdɪ] N Fam factotum m; **she's the general d.** c'est la bonne à tout faire

dogsled ['dɒgsled] N luge f tirée par des chiens

dog's-tooth ['dɒgztuːθ] N = dogtooth

dog-tired ADJ Fam claqué, crevé, mort de fatigue

dogtooth ['dɒgtuːθ] N (tooth) canine f
▸▸ Tex **d. check** pied m de poule; Bot **d. violet** érythrone m, dent-de-chien f, pl dents-de-chien

dogtrot ['dɒgtrɒt] N petit trot m; **to go somewhere at a d.** aller quelque part au petit trot

dogwatch ['dɒgwɒtʃ] N Naut petit quart m

dogwood ['dɒgwʊd] N Bot cornouiller m

DOH [di:əʊ'eɪtʃ] N Br Admin (abbr **Department of Health**) ≃ ministère m de la Santé

doh[1] [dəʊ] N Mus = do[2]

doh[2] INTERJ **d!** que je suis bête!

doily ['dɔɪlɪ] N **1** (underneath plate etc) petit napperon m **2** (on plate) dessus m d'assiette

doing ['duːɪŋ] N **talking is one thing, d. is another** c'est bien beau de parler, encore faudrait-il agir; **that takes some d.** ça ne se fait pas en un tour de main; **this is his d.** c'est son ouvrage; **all this is your d.** c'est vous qui êtes la cause de tout cela; **it was none of my d.** ce n'est pas moi qui suis responsable; Br Fam **to give sb a d. (over)** casser la figure à qn, mettre une raclée à qn; **d. up** *(renovation)* remise *f* à neuf

doings ['duːɪŋz] NPL **1** *(of person)* ce qu'on fait, *Pej* agissements *mpl*; **to be informed of sb's d.** être au courant des faits et gestes de qn **2** *Fam (events)* événements *mpl*; **there have been great d. at their house** il y a eu bien du mouvement chez eux **3** *Br Fam (gadget etc)* machin *m*, truc *m*

do-it-yourself N bricolage *m*; **d. enthusiast** passionné, -ée de bricolage
▸▸ **d. shop, d. store** magasin *m* de bricolage

do-it-yourselfer [-jə'selfər] N bricoleur, -euse

dol *(abbr* **dollar)** dol(l)

Dolby® ['dɒlbɪ] N Dolby® *m*;
▸▸ **D. system** système *m* Dolby® stéréo

doldrums (the) ['dɒldrəmz] NPL *Naut* la zone calme; *Fig* le cafard, les idées *fpl* noires; **to be in the d.** *(of person)* avoir le moral à zéro, être au trente-sixième dessous; *(of business, market)* être dans le marasme

dole [dəʊl] N *Br Fam (money)* indemnité *f* de chômage; **to be on the d.** être au chômage; **to go on the d.** s'inscrire au chômage; **d. queues are lengthening** le nombre des chômeurs s'accroît
▸▸ **d. money** indemnité *f* de chômage
▸ **dole out** VT SEP *Fam (money, food, clothing)* distribuer; **I'm tired of doling out sympathy to everyone** j'en ai assez de réconforter tout le monde

doleful ['dəʊlfʊl] ADJ *(expression, look, song)* lugubre; *(cry)* plaintif; *(person)* triste, affligé

dolefully ['dəʊlfʊlɪ] ADV tristement

doll [dɒl] N **1** *(for child)* poupée *f*, *(of ventriloquist)* marionnette *f*; **baby d.** baigneur *m*; **to play with a d.** jouer à la poupée **2** *Fam (woman)* poupée *f*; *(pretty woman)* belle poupée **3** *Am Fam (kind person)* amour *m*
▸▸ **d.'s house** maison *f* de poupée; *Fig* jolie petite maisonnette *f*
▸ **doll up** VT SEP *Fam (person)* bichonner; **to d. oneself up** *(of woman)* se pomponner; *(of man)* se faire beau; **to be all dolled up** être sur son trente et un; **they've dolled their house up** ils ont retapé leur maison

dollar ['dɒlər] N dollar *m*; **dollars in real terms** dollars *mpl* constants
▸▸ *Econ, Fin* **d. area** zone *f* dollar; **d. sign** (signe *m* du) dollar

dollop ['dɒləp] N *Fam (of butter)* gros morceau *m*; *(of cream, mashed potato)* bonne cuillerée *f*, *(of mud)* tas *m*; **a good d. of cream** une bonne cuillerée de crème

dolly ['dɒlɪ] N **1** *Fam (for child)* poupée *f* **2** *Old-fashioned Br Fam (young woman)* **d.(-bird)** poupée *f* **3** *TV, Cin* travelling *m*, chariot *m* **4** *(for clothes)* agitateur *m*
VI *TV, Cin* faire un travelling; **to d. in/out** faire un travelling avant/arrière
▸▸ *TV, Cin* **d. operator** machiniste *m* caméra; **d. tub** *(for laundry)* baquet *m* à lessive

dolman ['dɒlmən]
▸▸ **d. sleeve** manche *f* chauve-souris

dolmen ['dɒlmen] N *Archeol* dolmen *m*

dolomite ['dɒləmaɪt] N *Miner* dolomite *f*, *Geol (rock)* dolomie *f*

Dolomites (the) [ðə'dɒləmaɪts] NPL les Dolomites *fpl*

dolphin ['dɒlfɪn] N *(mammal)* dauphin *m*

dolphinarium [dɒlfɪ'neərɪəm] N aquarium *m* pour dauphins

dolt [dəʊlt] N sot *m*, nigaud *m*, gourde *f*

doltish ['dəʊltɪʃ] ADJ sot, *f* sotte, bête

domain [də'meɪn] N **1** *(property)*, *Fig* domaine *m*; *Fig* **that is outside my d.** ce n'est pas mon domaine **2** *Math, Phys (of function)* domaine *m* **3** *Comput* domaine *m*

▸▸ *Comput* **d. name** nom *m* de domaine; **D. Name System** système *m* de nom de domaine

dome [dəʊm] N **1** *Archit* dôme *m*, coupole *f* **2** *Fig (of sky)* dôme *m*, voûte *f*, *(of hill)* dôme; *(of skull)* calotte *f*, *Fam (head)* tête *f* **3** *Metal (of furnace)* dôme *m*, voûte *f*
▸▸ *Am* **d. fastener** bouton-pression *m*, *pl* boutons-pression, pression *f*

domed [dəʊmd] ADJ **1** *(building)* à dôme, à coupole **2** *(shaped like a dome)* en forme de dôme; *(skull)* ovoïde

Domesday ['duːmzdeɪ] N
▸▸ *Hist* **D. Book** = (livre *m* du) cadastre *m* de l'Angleterre *(établi en 1086 par Guillaume le Conquérant)*

domestic [də'mestɪk] ADJ **1** *(misfortune, problem)* domestique; *(fuel)* de ménage; **she does d. work** *(to earn a living)* elle fait des ménages; **to be in d. service** être employé(e) de maison; **newlyweds living in d. bliss** des jeunes mariés au comble du bonheur **2** *(trade, dissent, flight etc)* intérieur; *(production, currency)* national, -aux **3** *(person)* casanier
N domestique *mf*
▸▸ *Aviat* **d. airline** ligne *f* intérieure; **d. animal** animal *m* domestique; **d. appliances** appareils *mpl* ménagers; **d. duties** travaux *mpl* ménagers; *Old-fashioned* **d. economy** économie *f* domestique; **d. excursionist** excursionniste *mf* (dans son propre pays); **d. life** vie *f* de famille; *Am* **d. mail** correspondance *f* à destination de l'intérieur; *Com, Econ* **d. market** marché *m* intérieur; *Com, Econ* **d. products** denrées *fpl* du pays; *Aviat* **d. route** ligne intérieure; **d. sales** ventes *fpl* domestiques; *Br Sch Formerly* **d. science** enseignement *m* ménager; **d. servant** domestique; **d. tasks** travaux ménagers; **d. tourism** tourisme *m* national; **d. tourist** touriste *m* national; **d. travel** voyages *mpl* domestiques; **d. virtues** talents *mpl* de femme/d'homme d'intérieur; **d. visitor** touriste *m* du pays

domestically [də'mestɪk(ə)lɪ] ADV à l'intérieur du pays

domesticate [də'mestɪkeɪt] VT **1** *(tame) (animal)* domestiquer, apprivoiser **2** *(naturalize) (animal, plant)* acclimater **3** **to be domesticated** *(of person)* être casanier, aimer la vie d'intérieur; **to become domesticated** prendre goût à la vie d'intérieur; **her husband is quite domesticated** son mari fait sa part des travaux ménagers

domesticity [dəʊme'stɪsɪtɪ] N **1** *(liking for home)* attachement *m* au foyer **2** *(home life)* vie *f* de famille; **the cosy d. of their life** leur petite vie tranquille

domicile ['dɒmɪsaɪl] N *Com, Law, Fin* domicile *m*
VT **1** *Fml (usu passive) (person)* **domiciled at Leeds** domicilié *ou* demeurant à Leeds **2** *Com* domicilier; *Fin* **domiciled bill** effet *m* domicilié; **bills domiciled in France** traites *fpl* payables en France; *Fin* **to d. acceptances** domicilier des acceptations

domiciliary [dɒmɪ'sɪlɪərɪ] ADJ *Fml (visit etc)* domiciliaire; *(assistance)* à domicile

domiciliation [dɒmɪsɪlɪ'eɪʃən] N *Fin* domiciliation *f*
▸▸ **d. papers** dossier *m* de domiciliation

dominance ['dɒmɪnəns] N *(of disease, gene etc)* dominance *f*, *(of race, political party)* prédominance *f*; **Manchester's d. of English football** la suprématie exercée par Manchester sur le football anglais

dominant ['dɒmɪnənt] ADJ *(character, gene, force etc)* dominant; *(person)* dominateur, -trice
N *Mus* dominante *f*

▸▸ *Mus* **d. chord** accord *m* de dominante; *Mus* **d. seventh** septième *f* de dominante

dominantly ['dɒmɪnəntlɪ] ADV d'une manière dominante

dominate ['dɒmɪneɪt] VT **1** *(person, a people)* dominer (sur); **to d. a match/game** *(of player, team)* dominer un match/un jeu; **to be dominated by sb** subir la loi de qn; **man dominated by ambition** homme en proie à l'ambition; **the wedding dominated his thoughts to the exclusion of everything else** le mariage prédominait sur toute autre chose dans ses pensées **2** *(of mountain etc) (landscape)* dominer; **the fortress dominates the town** la forteresse domine *ou* commande la ville

dominating ['dɒmɪneɪtɪŋ] ADJ *(feature, colour etc)* dominant; *(personality)* dominateur, -trice

domination [dɒmɪ'neɪʃən] N domination *f* (over sur); **to be under sb's d.** être dominé par qn; **Manchester's d. of English football** la suprématie exercée par Manchester sur le football anglais

domineer [dɒmɪ'nɪər] VI se montrer autoritaire
▸ **domineer over** VT INSEP tyranniser

domineering [dɒmɪ'nɪərɪŋ] ADJ *(person, character etc)* dominateur, -trice, autoritaire

Dominica [də'mɪnɪkə] N la Dominique

dominical [də'mɪnɪk(ə)l] ADJ *Rel* dominical, -aux

Dominican[1] [də'mɪnɪkən] ADJ, N *Rel* dominicain, -aine

Dominican[2] *Geog* ADJ dominicain
▸▸ **the D. Republic** la République Dominicaine
N Dominicain, -aine

dominion [də'mɪnjən] N **1** *(rule)* autorité *f*, empire *m*; **to have** *or* **hold d. over ...** exercer son empire *ou* dominer sur ... **2** *(land)* dominion *m*

domino, *pl* **dominoes** ['dɒmɪnəʊ, -əʊz] N **1** *(in game)* domino *m*; **dominoes** *(game)* (jeu *m* de) dominos; **to play dominoes** jouer aux dominos VOIR GRAMMAIRE A10 **2** *(mask)* domino *m*
▸▸ **d. effect** effet *m* d'entraînement; *Pol, Fig* **the d. theory** la théorie des dominos

don[1] [dɒn] N **1** *Br Univ* professeur *m* (d'université) *(surtout à Oxford et Cambridge)* **2** *(Spanish title)* Don *m*

don[2] VT (-nn-) *Fml (uniform, clothes)* revêtir, endosser; *(hat)* mettre, coiffer

donate [dəʊ'neɪt] VT faire un don de; *Med* **to d. blood** donner du *ou* son sang; **how much did you d.?** combien est-ce que tu as donné?; **to d. one 's time** faire don de son temps
VI faire un don

donation [dəʊ'neɪʃən] N donation *f*, don *m*; **all donations are tax-deductible** tous les dons sont déductibles des impôts; **to make a d. to a charity** faire un don *ou* une donation à une œuvre de bienfaisance

donator [dəʊ'neɪtər] N donateur, -trice

done PP *see* **do**[1]

doner kebab ['dɒnə, 'dəʊnə] N chiche-kebab *m*

dong [dɒŋ] N *Vulg (penis)* bite *f*, queue *f*

dongle ['dɒŋg(ə)l] N *Comput* fiche *f* gigogne, clé *f* gigogne

donkey ['dɒŋkɪ] N **1** *(animal)* âne *m*, *Fam* baudet *m*; *(female)* ânesse *f*, *Fam* **he would talk the hind legs off a d.** il est bavard comme une pie; *Fam* **it happened d.'s years ago** ça s'est passé il y a des années; *Fam* **I haven't seen him for d.'s years** je ne l'ai pas vu depuis une éternité **2** *Fig (idiot)* âne *m*, imbécile *mf*

▶▶*Naut* **d. boiler** chaudière *f* auxiliaire; *Tech* **d. engine** moteur *m* auxiliaire; *Br* **d. jacket** = veste *f* longue en tissu épais, généralement bleu foncé; **d. race** course *f* d'ânes

donkey-work N *(drudgery)* travail *m* pénible

donnish ['dɒnɪʃ] ADJ *(person, air, tone)* intellectuel, -elle, *Pej* pédant; **he's a bit d.** il a un petit air professoral

donor ['dəʊnər] N **1** *Med (of blood, organ etc)* donneur, -euse **2** *(to charity etc)* donateur, -trice
▶▶**d. card** carte *f* de don d'organe

don't [dəʊnt] CONTR = **do not**, *see* **do**[1]
▶▶*Fam* **d. know** *(voter)* indécis, -ise

donut ['dəʊnʌt] N *esp Am Culin* beignet *m*, *Can* beigne *m*

doobie ['duːbɪ] N *Fam (cannabis cigarette)* joint *m*

doodah ['duːdɑː] N *Fam* truc *m*, machin *m*

doodle ['duːd(ə)l] N *Fam* gribouillis *m*, griffonnage *m*
VT griffonner *ou* gribouiller (distraitement)
VI griffonner *ou* gribouiller (distraitement); *Fig (on piano)* pianoter

doodlebug ['duːd(ə)lbʌg] N *Hist Fam* bombe *f* volante

doo-doo ['duːduː] N *Fam* **1** *(excrement)* crotte *f*, caca *m*; **the dog's done a d. on the doormat** le chien a fait sa crotte sur le paillasson **2** *(trouble)* pétrin *m*; **we're in deep d.!** on est vraiment dans le pétrin!

doofus ['duːfəs] N *Am Fam (idiot)* andouille *f*

doolally [duː'lælɪ] ADJ *Sl (crazy, confused)* timbré

doom [duːm] N destin *m* (funeste), sort *m* (malheureux); **an air/a feeling of d.** un air/sentiment funeste; *Lit* **he met his d.** il trouva la mort; *Fig* **to be full of** *or* **all d. and gloom** *(of person, forecast etc)* être pessimiste; **the situation's not all d. and gloom** la situation n'est pas aussi sombre qu'il y paraît
VT condamner (**to** à); **doomed** *(town)* condamné; *(person)* perdu; *(ship, aircraft)* marqué par le destin; **an attempt doomed to failure** une tentative condamnée à l'insuccès *ou* vouée à l'échec

doom-laden ADJ *(forecast, words etc)* funeste, lugubre

Doomsday ['duːmzdeɪ] N **D. Book** *see* **Domesday**

doomsday ['duːmzdeɪ] N le (jour du) jugement dernier; *Fam* **till d.** indéfiniment; **to put off sth till d.** renvoyer qch aux calendes grecques

door [dɔːr] N *(of house, refrigerator etc)* porte *f*, *(of train, car etc)* portière *f*, porte; *(of wardrobe)* porte, battant *m*; **two doors away** deux portes plus loin; **the house next d.** la maison à côté; **I live next d.** j'habite à côté; **the journey takes twenty-five minutes d. to d.** le voyage prend vingt-cinq minutes de porte à porte; **will you answer the d.?** tu peux aller ouvrir (la porte)?; **it was Bob who answered the d. (to me)** c'est Bob qui m'a ouvert (la porte); **to show sb the d.** éconduire *ou* congédier qn; **to show sb to the d.** conduire qn à la porte, reconduire qn; **out of doors** dehors, en plein air; **to shut the d. in sb's face** fermer la porte au nez de qn; *Fig* **doors kept being closed in our faces** tout le monde nous a fermé la porte au nez; **to leave the d. open to** *or* **for negotiations** laisser la porte ouverte à des négociations; **to close** *or* **shut the d. on any discussion** rendre impossible toute discussion; **behind closed doors** *(discussions etc)* entre quatre murs, à huis-clos; **to meet behind closed doors** se rencontrer à huis-clos; **to lay a charge at sb's d.** imputer qch à qn; **to put one's foot in the d.** mettre le pied dans l'em-

brasure de la porte; **the foot in the d. technique** *(of salesman)* = la vente (en porte-à-porte) forcée
▶▶**d. attendant** portier *m*, *Aut* **d. bin** vide-poche *m*, *pl* vide-poches; **d. chain** chaînette *f* de sûreté; **d. curtain** portière *f*, *Mktg* **d. drop** distribution *f* à domicile; **d. handle** poignée *f* de porte; *Aut* poignée de portière; **d. knocker** marteau *m* de porte, heurtoir *m*; *Aut* **d. mirror** rétroviseur *m* extérieur; *Aut* **d. pocket** vide-poche

doorbell ['dɔːbel] N sonnette *f*; **to ring the d.** sonner à la porte

do-or-die ADJ *(effort, attempt etc)* acharné; **this d. attitude** cette attitude de détermination inébranlable

doorframe ['dɔːfreɪm] N chambranle *m ou* châssis *m* de porte

doorjamb ['dɔːdʒæm] N montant *m* de porte

doorkeeper ['dɔːkiːpər] N portier *m*, concierge *mf*

doorknob ['dɔːnɒb] N poignée *f* (ronde) de porte

doorman, *pl* **doormen** ['dɔːmən] N portier *m*

doormat ['dɔːmæt] N **1** *(for door)* paillasson *m* **2** *Fig (person)* lavette *f*, chiffe *f* molle; **don't be such a d.** ne te laisse pas marcher sur les pieds comme ça; **to treat sb like a d.** traiter qn comme une chose insignifiante

doornail ['dɔːneɪl] N *Fam* **(as) dead as a d.** mort et bien mort

doorpost ['dɔːpəʊst] N montant *m* de porte

doorstep ['dɔːstep] N **1** seuil *m*, pas *m* (de la porte); **don't leave him standing on the d.** ne le laisse pas sur le pas de la porte; *Fig* **there are shops and a library on your d.** tu as des boutiques et une bibliothèque à ta porte **2** *Br Fam (slice of bread)* grosse tranche *f* de pain
VI *(of canvasser)* faire du porte-à-porte

doorstepping ['dɔːstepɪŋ] N *Journ Fam* = technique *f* des journalistes qui importunent les gens à leur domicile

doorstop ['dɔːstɒp] N *(fixed)* butoir *m*; *(wedge)* cale-porte *m*, *pl* cale-portes

door-to-door ADJ
▶▶**d. canvassing** porte-à-porte *m*; **to do d. canvassing** faire du porte-à-porte; **d. salesman** vendeur *m* à domicile; **d. selling** porte-à-porte; **to do d. selling** faire du porte-à-porte

doorway ['dɔːweɪ] N *(baie f de)* porte *f*, *(frame)* encadrement *m* de la porte; **in the d.** dans l'embrasure de la porte

dopamine ['dəʊpəmɪn] N dopamine *f*

dope [dəʊp] N **1** *(drugs)* drogue *f*, *Sport* doping *m*, stimulant *m*
2 *Sl (cannabis)* shit *m*
3 *Fam (idiot)* crétin, -ine; **what a d.!** quelle nouille!, quel andouille!
4 *Old-fashioned Sl (information)* rencard *m*, tuyau *m*; **to give sb the d. on sth** rencarder qn sur qch
5 *Aviat, Aut (varnish)* enduit *m*
6 *(in petrol)* additif *m*, dopant *m*; *(for explosives)* absorbant *m*
ADJ *Am Fam (excellent)* génial, -aux, super
VT **1** *(drug) (person, horse) (to prevent from winning)* droguer; *(to increase chances)* doper; *(drink)* verser une drogue dans
2 *Aviat, Aut (varnish)* enduire
3 *Aut* **doped fuel** carburant dopé *ou* additionné d'anti-détonant
▶▶**d. test** test *m* antidopage *ou* antidoping; **to fail/take a d. test** être déclaré positif à/subir un test antidopage *ou* antidoping

dopehead ['dəʊphed], **doper** ['dəʊpər] N *Sl (drug user)* camé, -ée; *(heavy cannabis user)*

= personne *f* qui fume beaucoup de cannabis

dopey ['dəʊpɪ] ADJ *Fam* **1** *(drugged)* drogué; *(from sleep)* endormi **2** *(stupid)* stupide; **what a d. thing to say** que c'était stupide de dire une chose pareille

doping ['dəʊpɪŋ] N **1** *(to incapacitate)* administration *f* d'un narcotique (**of** à); *(to increase chances of winning)* dopage *m*, doping *m* **2** *Aviat, Aut (varnishing)* enduisage *m* **3** *Petr (of fuel)* dopage *m*

Doppler effect ['dɒplər] N *Phys* effet *m* Doppler

do-re-mi [dəʊreɪ'miː] N *Am Fam (money)* fric *m*, blé *m*

Doric ['dɒrɪk] ADJ, N *Archit* dorique *m*; *Ling* = dialecte *m* de l'anglais parlé dans le nord-est de l'Écosse

dork [dɔːk] N *Fam (idiot)* abruti, -ie

dorky ['dɔːkɪ] ADJ *Fam* ringard, nul, *f* nulle

dorm [dɔːm] N *Sch Fam* dortoir *m*

dormant ['dɔːmənt] ADJ **1** *(passion etc)* assoupi, endormi; *(conflict)* latent; **to lie d.** être en sommeil **2** *(plant, bud)* dormant **3** *(volcano)* en repos
▶▶*Banking* **d. account** compte *m* sans mouvement

dormer (window) ['dɔːmər] N fenêtre *f* en mansarde

dormitory ['dɔːmɪt(ə)rɪ] N **1** dortoir *m* **2** *Am Univ (residence)* maison *f ou* foyer *m* d'étudiants
▶▶**d. town** cité-dortoir *f*, *pl* cités-dortoirs

dormouse, *pl* **dormice** ['dɔːmaʊs, -maɪs] N *Zool* loir *m*

dorsal ['dɔːs(ə)l] ADJ dorsal, -aux; *Anat (towards back of body)* postérieur
▶▶**d. fin** nageoire *f* dorsale

dory ['dɔːrɪ] N **1** *(fish)* **(John) D.** dorée *f*, saint-pierre *m inv* **2** *Am (boat)* doris *m*

DOS [dɒs] N *Comput (abbr* **disk operating system)** DOS *m*
▶▶**D. command** commande *f* du DOS; **D. prompt** indicatif *m* (du) DOS, invite *f* du DOS; **D. switch** clé *f ou* paramètre *m* du DOS

dosage ['dəʊsɪdʒ] N *(of medicine)* dosage *m*, posologie *f*

dose [dəʊs] N **1** *Med, Nucl* dose *f*; *Fig* **she's bearable in small doses** elle est supportable à petites doses; *Fam* **to get through sth like a d. of salts** faire qch en deux temps trois mouvements *ou* en deux coups de cuillère à pot; **that curry went through me like a d. of salts** ce curry est passé tout droit **2** *Fam (bout) (of flu etc)* attaque *f* **3** *Sl (venereal disease)* vérole *f*
VT **1** *(person)* administrer un médicament à; **to d. oneself with quinine** se bourrer de quinine **2** *(medicine)* doser
▶ **dose up** VT *Fam* bourrer (**with** de)

dosh [dɒʃ] N *Br Sl (money)* fric *m*

doss [dɒs] N *Br Sl* **1** *(bed)* lit *m*, pieu *m*; **I'm looking for a d. for tonight** je cherche un endroit où dormir ce soir **2** *(sleep)* somme *m*, roupillon *m*; **to have a d.** faire un somme **3** **it was a real d.** *(easy)* c'était de la tarte *ou* du gâteau
VI *(sleep)* pieuter; *(in doss house)* coucher à l'asile de nuit
▶ **doss around** VI *Br Sl (hang around)* se la couler douce
▶ **doss down** VI *Br Sl (sleep)* se coucher, se pieuter; **do you mind dossing down on the floor?** est-ce que ça t'embête de coucher par terre?; **I need somewhere to d. down for the night** j'ai besoin d'un endroit où coucher cette nuit

dosser ['dɒsər] N *Br Sl* **1** *(person)* clochard, -arde **2** *(place)* asile *m* de nuit

doss-house N *Br Sl* asile *m* de nuit

dossier ['dɒsɪeɪ, -ɪər] N dossier *m*; **to keep a d. on sb** avoir un dossier sur qn

dot [dɒt] N *(in dotted line, over the letter i etc)*, *Comput* point *m*; *Mus* point d'augmentation; **'i' with two dots** 'i' surmonté de deux points; **dots and dashes** *(Morse code)* points et traits; *Comput* **"gwilson at transex, dot, co, dot, uk"** gwilson at *ou* arobase transex, point, co, point, uk; *Fam* **on the d.** *(to arrive)* à l'heure tapante; **on the d. of three o'clock, at three o'clock on the d.** à trois heures pile; *Fam* **since the year d.** depuis des siècles; *Fam* **that was in the year d.** c'était il y a une éternité; *Fam* **but she left early, d. d. d.** mais elle est partie de bonne heure, si vous voyez ce que je veux dire

▶ VT *(-tt-)* **1** *(an i)* mettre un point sur; *Fig* **to d. one's i's (and cross one's t's)** mettre les points sur les i

2 *(surface)* marquer de points; *(drawing)* pointiller; **dotted with flowers/etc** *(of surface etc)* parsemé de fleurs/*etc*; **his shirt was dotted with flecks of tomato sauce** sa chemise était tachetée de sauce tomate; **the islands are dotted all round the coast** les îles sont éparpillées tout autour de la côte

3 *Mus (note)* pointer

4 *Old-fashioned Fam* **to d. and carry one** *(when walking)* boiter

5 *Sl* **to d. sb one** *(hit)* flanquer un gnon à qn

▶ ▶ *Comput* **d. com** *(company)* start-up *f* inv; *Comput* **d. command** commande *f* avec point; *Comput* **d. matrix** imprimante *f* matricielle, matricielle *f*; *Comput* **d. prompt** repère *m* de saisie de commandes

dotage ['dəʊtɪdʒ] N gâtisme *m*; **to be in one's d.** être gâteux

dote [dəʊt] VI être gâteux
▶ **dote on, dote upon** VT INSEP *(somebody)* adorer

doting ['dəʊtɪŋ] ADJ ATTRIB *(parents, grandparents)* qui vivent une tendresse ou une indulgence exagérée; **a d. husband** un mari qui gâte sa femme

dotted ['dɒtɪd] ADJ **1** *(contour)* pointillé; **2** *Mus (note)* pointé
▶ ▶ **d. line** *(on form)* ligne *f* en pointillés; *Aut* ligne discontinue; **to sign on the d. line** *(on form)* signer à l'endroit indiqué; *Fig* donner son consentement; **tear along the d. line** déchirer en suivant les pointillés

dottle ['dɒt(ə)l] N *(in pipe)* culot *m*

dotty ['dɒtɪ] ADJ *Fam* toqué, piqué; **he's d. about her** il est toqué *ou* fou d'elle; **I'm not d. about him** je ne raffole pas de lui; **she wasn't d. about moving house** l'idée de déménager ne l'enchantait pas

---

DOUBLE ['dʌb(ə)l]

ADJ	double **1, 2**
ADV	en deux ▪ deux fois
N	double **1, 3–6**
VT	doubler **1, 2, 4** ▪ plier en deux **2** ▪ contrer **3**
VI	doubler **1**

ADJ 1 *(having two, two together)* double; **'all' is spelt 'a, d. l'** 'all' s'écrit 'a, deux l'; **d. two d. three** *(when giving telephone number, address)* vingt-deux trente-trois; **to reach d. figures** *(of inflation etc)* atteindre les deux chiffres; *Br Univ* **she took a d. first in English and History** elle a deux licences avec mention très bien, une en anglais et l'autre en histoire; *Am* **to go on a d. date** sortir à deux couples; *Comput* **d.-sided** *(disk etc)* à deux faces, à double face; **to have a d. yolk** *(of egg)* avoir deux jaunes; **a d. whisky** un double whisky

2 *(misleading, ambiguous)* double; **with a d. meaning** à deux *ou* double sens; *(ambiguous)* ambigu, -uë; **to play a d. game** jouer

double jeu; **to lead a d. life** mener une double vie; **to apply a d. standard** utiliser deux poids, deux mesures

▶ ADV **to see d.** voir double; **to fold a sheet (of paper) d.** plier une feuille (de papier) en deux; **bent d.** *(of person)* courbé en deux; **bent d. with pain/laughter** plié en deux de douleur/rire; **d. the number** le double, deux fois autant; **it took me d. the time I expected** ça m'a pris le double du temps que je pensais; **to pay d. (the price)** payer le double (du prix); **I am d. your age** je suis deux fois plus âgé que vous, j'ai deux fois votre âge

▶ N **1** *(of person)* double *m*, *Fam* sosie *m*; *Theat, Cin* doublure *f*

2 *Fam (hotel room)* chambre *f* à deux personnes

3 *(measure of drink)* double *m*; **make mine a d.** un double pour moi

4 *Tennis* **men's/women's/mixed doubles** double *m* messieurs/dames/mixte; **a doubles match** un double; **to play doubles** jouer des doubles

5 *Horseracing* pari *m* couplé; **to bring off a d.** réussir un double

6 *Cards (at bridge)* contre *m*; *(at dominoes)* double *m*; *Billiards* doublé *m*; **d. or quits** quitte ou double

7 on *or* **at the d.** *Mil* au pas de gymnastique, au pas de course; *Fig (quickly)* en moins de deux; *(immediately, right away)* tout de suite, sur-le-champ

▶ VT **1** *(increase) (amount, salary etc)* doubler; *(figure)* porter au double, multiplier par deux; **to d. the stakes** doubler la mise

2 *(fold) (paper, blanket etc)* plier en deux; *(thread)* doubler

3 *Cards (at bridge)* contrer; *Billiards* **to d. the red** doubler la rouge

4 *Naut (headland)* doubler

▶ VI **1** *(of population, salary etc)* doubler; **to d. in value** doubler de valeur

2 to d. as servir de; **the smallest bedroom doubles as my study** la chambre la plus petite me sert également de bureau; *Theat* **to d. as sb** jouer qn en plus d'un rôle principal

▶ ▶ **d. ace** *(in dice game, dominoes)* double-as *m*, *pl* doubles-as; **d. agent** agent *m* double; *Mus* **d. bass** contrebasse *f*, *Mus* **d. bassoon** contrebasson *m*; **d. bed** grand lit *m*, lit à deux places; **d. bedroom** chambre *f* pour deux personnes; **d. bill** *Cin* = séance *f* avec deux longs métrages à la suite; *TV* = programmation *f* de deux longs métrages à la suite; *Psy* **d. bind** double contrainte *f*, *Br* **d. bluff** = technique *f* consistant à faire croire qu'on bluffe alors qu'on dit la vérité; **d. boiler** casserole *f* à double fond; **d. chin** double menton *m*; *Comput* **d. click** double-clic *m*, *pl* doubles-clics; *Br* **d. cream** crème *f* épaisse, *Can* crème à fouetter, *Suisse* double crème; *Typ* **d. dagger** diésis *m*; **d. Dutch** *Br Fam* charabia *m*, baragouin *m*; *Am (game)* double dutch *m*; **d. entendre** mot *m* *ou* expression *f* à double sens; *Acct* **d. entry book-keeping** comptabilité *f* en partie double; *Phot* **d. exposure** surimpression *f*; *Sport* **d. fault** double faute *f*, *Cin* **d. feature** = séance avec deux longs métrages à la suite; **d. helix** double hélice *f*, *Med* **d. incontinence** incontinence *f* double; *Am Ins* **d. indemnity** = clause *f* d'une assurance-vie qui stipule qu'en cas de mort accidentelle de l'assuré la prime est doublée; **d. knitting** grosse laine *f*, *Gram* **d. negative** double négation *f*, **d. occupancy** *(of hotel room)* occupation *f* double; *St Exch* **d. option** stellage *m*; *Journ* **d. page spread** page *f* centrale, double page; *(advert)* pub *f* double page; **d. parking** stationnement *m* en double file; *Med* **d. pneumonia** pneumonie *f* double; **to have d. pneumonia** faire une pneumonie double; *Typ* **d. quotes** guillemets *mpl*; *Br* **d. saucepan** casserole *f* à double fond; **d. sink** évier *m* à

deux bacs; *Typ* **d. spacing** double interligne *m*; *Comput* **d. strike** double passage *m* (de la tête d'impression); **d. strike printing** impression *f* à double frappe; *TV, Cin* **d. take** double prise *f*, *Fam* **to do a d. take** marquer un temps d'arrêt *(par surprise)*; **he did a d. take when I told him** lorsque je le lui ai dit il a marqué un temps d'arrêt; **d. talk** propos *mpl* ambigus *ou* équivoques; *Fin* **d. taxation** double imposition *f*, **d. time** *(pay)* salaire *m* double; *Mil* **pas** *m* redoublé; *Mus* mesure *f* double; **in d. time** *Mil* au pas de gymnastique, au pas de course; *Fam (very quickly)* en moins de rien; *(immediately, right away)* tout de suite, sur-le-champ; *Typ* **d. underlining** double soulignement *m*; *Med* **d. vision** double vision *f*, *Fam* **d. whammy** double coup *m* de malchance; *Br* **d. white line** *(on road)* double ligne *f* blanche *(d'interdiction de doubler)*; *Typ* **d. yellow line** *(on road)* double ligne jaune *(qui indique une zone de stationnement interdit)*

▶ **double back** VT SEP *(blanket etc)* replier, rabattre
▶ VI **to d. back (on one's tracks)** *(of person, hunted animal etc)* revenir sur ses pas; **to d. back on itself** *(of road)* tourner en épingle à cheveux

▶ **double for** VT INSEP remplacer; *Theat* doubler; *Cin (of stuntman)* être la doublure de

▶ **double over** VI se plier; **to d. over with pain** se plier en deux de douleur, se tordre de douleur
▶ VT SEP replier, rabattre

▶ **double up** VI **1** *(bend over)* se plier (en deux), se courber (en deux); **to d. up with laughter/pain** se tordre de rire/douleur
2 *(share room)* partager une chambre
▶ VT SEP **1** *(paper, material etc)* plier en deux
2 *(of blow, pain etc) (person)* faire plier en deux

---

double-acting ADJ *Tech* à double effet

double-barrelled [-'bærəld] ADJ *(shotgun)* à deux coups
▶ ▶ *Br* **d. name** = nom *m* de famille composé (p.ex. Burnes-Jones) indiquant souvent une origine aristocratique

double-blind ADJ *Med (test)* test *m* à double insu

double-book VT *(seat, room)* réserver pour deux personnes différentes, sur-réserver; **we've been double-booked again** nous sommes encore en double réservation; **I've double-booked myself for next Friday** *(doing two things)* je me suis engagé à faire deux choses différentes vendredi prochain
▶ VI *(of hotel, airline)* faire une/des double(s) réservation(s)

double-booking N double réservation *f*

double-bottomed [-'bɒtəmd] ADJ *(saucepan, suitcase etc)* à double fond; *(dinghy etc)* à double coque

double-breasted [-'brestɪd] ADJ *(jacket)* croisé

double-check VT & VI revérifier

double-click VT cliquer deux fois sur, double-cliquer
▶ VI *Comput* cliquer deux fois, faire un double-clic

double-clutch VI *Am Aut* faire un double débrayage

double-cross *Fam* VT doubler, trahir
▶ N trahison *f*, tromperie *f*

double-crosser ['dʌb(ə)l'krɒsər] N traître, -esse

double-dealer N fourbe *m*

double-dealing N duplicité *f*
▶ ADJ déloyal, -aux

double-decker ['dʌbəl'dekər] N **1** *Br (bus)* autobus *m* à impériale **2** *esp Am (sandwich)* sandwich *m* double

double-declutch VI *Br Aut* faire un double débrayage

double-declutching [ˈdʌb(ə)ldiˈklʌtʃɪŋ] N *Br Aut* double débrayage *m*

double-density ADJ *Comput (disk)* à double densité

double-edged ADJ *(sword, compliment, argument)* à deux tranchants

double-faced [-ˈfeɪst] ADJ **1** *Tex* réversible **2** *Pej (person)* à double face, hypocrite

double-glaze VT **to have the windows double-glazed** poser du double vitrage; **they've just had their house double-glazed** ils viennent de faire poser du double vitrage chez eux

double-glazed ADJ à double vitrage

double-glazing N double vitrage *m*; **to put in d.** installer *ou* poser du double vitrage

double-headed ADJ à deux têtes, *Spec* bicéphale; *TV (programme)* animé par deux présentateurs
▸▸ **d. coin** pièce *f* de monnaie à deux faces; *Her* **d. eagle** aigle *f* à deux têtes

double-header N *Am Sl* = deux matchs *mpl* disputés l'un après l'autre

double-jointed ADJ *(person, limb)* désarticulé

double-lock VT *(door etc)* fermer à double tour

double-park VT & VI *Aut* stationner en double file

double-pointed ADJ *Knitting (needle)* à double pointe

double-quick ADJ, ADV **in d. time, d.** *Mil* au pas de gymnastique, au pas de course; *Fam (very quickly)* en moins de rien; *(immediately, right away)* tout de suite, sur-le-champ

double-space VT *(write/type) (text)* écrire/taper en double interligne, mettre en double interligne; **double-spaced** en double interligne

double-speak N propos *mpl* ambigus *ou* équivoques; **rationalization is just d. for more unemployment** rationalisation n'est qu'un euphémisme pour plus de chômage

double-speed ADJ *Comput (CD-ROM)* double vitesse

double-stop VI (-pp-) *Mus (on violin)* faire des doubles-cordes

double-stopping N *Mus* double-corde *f*

doublet [ˈdʌblɪt] N **1** *Ling* doublet *m* **2** *Hist (jacket)* pourpoint *m*, justaucorps *m*

double-think N raisonnement *m* contradictoire

doubling [ˈdʌblɪŋ] N *(of number etc)* doublement *m*

doubly [ˈdʌb(ə)lɪ] ADV doublement; **to be d. careful/interested** redoubler de prudence/d'intérêt

doubt [daʊt] N doute *m*; **to be in d.** *(of person)* être en *ou* dans le doute; *(of future, event)* être douteux *ou* incertain; **I'm in no d. as to** ... je ne doute absolument pas de ...; **to raise doubts in sb's mind** soulever des doutes dans l'esprit de qn; **the whole thing raised doubts about his abilities** toute cette affaire a mis ses capacités en question; **when in d.** dans le doute; **to cast doubt(s) on sth** mettre qch en doute; **to have one's doubts about sth** avoir des doutes sur *ou* au sujet de qch; **I have my doubts whether this is true** je doute que cela soit vrai; **beyond (a shadow of a) d.** sans aucun doute; **the facts have been established beyond (all) d.** ces faits ont été avérés sans le moindre doute; **no d. he will come** il viendra sans aucun doute; **there is** *or* **seems to be no d. that** ... il ne semble faire aucun doute que ...; **there is no d. about her guilt** il n'y a au-

cun doute sur sa culpabilité; **there is some d. about her guilt** il y a des doutes quant à sa culpabilité; **is there any d. in your mind?** est-ce qu'il y a un doute dans votre esprit?; **do you have any doubts?** est-ce que vous avez des doutes?; *(about getting married etc)* est-ce que vous hésitez?; **I have no doubts** je n'ai aucun doute; **to leave no (room for) d.** ne laisser aucun doute (**that** sur le fait que); **without (a** *or* **any** *or* **the slightest) d.** sans aucun doute
▸ VT *(person)* douter de; *(person's word)* douter de, mettre en doute; **I d. we'll be hearing** *or* **I d. if we'll hear from him again** je doute que nous entendions à nouveau parler de lui; **I d. it** j'en doute; **he made me d. the evidence of my own eyes** il m'a fait douter de ce que je voyais de mes propres yeux; **I d. whether** *or* **if he will come** je doute qu'il vienne
▸ VI *(have doubts)* douter

doubter [ˈdaʊtər] N sceptique *mf*

doubtful [ˈdaʊtfʊl] ADJ **1** *(undecided) (person)* indécis, incertain; *(future, outcome, weather)* incertain; **to be d. of** *or* **about sth** avoir des doutes sur qch; **I'm d. about going** j'hésite à y aller; **I'm d. about the wisdom/advisability of it** je doute que ce soit bien sage/conseillé; **John's a bit d. for Saturday** il n'est pas sûr qu'on puisse compter sur John samedi; **she's a d. starter (for the race)** il n'est pas certain qu'elle prenne le départ (de la course); **it is d. whether** ... il est douteux *ou* à douter que ... **2** *(questionable) (character, appearance)* équivoque, suspect; *(origin, decision, food)* douteux; **in d. taste** d'un goût douteux
▸▸ *Fin* **d. debt** créance *f* douteuse; **d. loan** prêt *m* douteux

doubtfully [ˈdaʊtfʊlɪ] ADV *(to say)* d'un ton dubitatif, dubitativement; *(to watch)* d'un air dubitatif; *(to stand etc)* en hésitant, d'une façon indécise

doubting [ˈdaʊtɪŋ] ADJ incrédule, sceptique
▸▸ **d. Thomas** incrédule *mf*; **you're always such a d. Thomas** tu es toujours tellement sceptique

doubtless(ly) [ˈdaʊtlɪs(lɪ)] ADV **1** *(certainly)* sans aucun doute **2** *(probably)* sans doute, sûrement

douche [duːʃ] N **1** *(cleansing)* douche *f*, *Med* lavage *m* interne; *(as contraceptive)* douche vaginale; **to be like a d. of cold water** faire l'effet d'une douche froide **2** *Med (instrument)* poire *f* à injection
▸ VT doucher

dough [dəʊ] N **1** *(for bread etc)* pâte *f* **2** *Old-fashioned Sl (money)* fric *m*, pognon *m*

doughboy [ˈdəʊbɔɪ] N *Hist* = soldat *m* américain de la première guerre mondiale

doughnut [ˈdəʊnʌt] N *Culin* beignet *m*, *Can* beigne *m*; **jam d.** beignet à la confiture

doughty [ˈdaʊtɪ] ADJ *Arch, Lit* vaillant

doughy [ˈdəʊɪ] ADJ **1** *(bread)* pâteux **2** *Fig (face)* terreux

dour [dʊər] ADJ austère, sévère

douse [daʊs] VT **1** *(splash) (person, object)* arroser, asperger (**with** de); *(plunge)* plonger, tremper; **he doused himself with** *or* **in aftershave** il s'est aspergé d'après-rasage **2** *(extinguish) (light, fire)* éteindre

dove [dʌv] N **1** *(bird)* colombe *f*, *(pigeon m)* ramier *m*, palombe *f*; **d. of peace** colombe de la paix; *Pol* **the doves and the hawks** les colombes et les faucons
▸ ADJ **d.(-coloured** *or* **-grey)** colombin, gorge-de-pigeon *inv*

dovecote [ˈdʌvkɒt] N colombier *m*, pigeonnier *m*

Dover [ˈdəʊvər] N Douvres; **the Straits of D.** le Pas de Calais

dovetail [ˈdʌvteɪl] N *Carp* queue-d'aronde *f*, *pl* queues-d'aronde
▸ VT *Carp* assembler à queue-d'aronde; *Fig* **to d. two schemes (together** *or* **into each other)** harmoniser deux projets
▸ VI *(of schemes etc)* se rejoindre, se raccorder (**with** à)
▸▸ **d. joint** assemblage *m* à queue-d'aronde

dovish [ˈdʌvɪʃ] ADJ *esp Am Pol (person)* partisan de la manière douce; *(speech)* conciliateur

dowager [ˈdaʊədʒər] N douairière *f*
▸▸ **d. duchess** duchesse *f* douairière; *Fam* **d.'s hump** = bosse *f* qui se développe chez les femmes d'un certain âge suite à une carence de calcium, bosse de sorcière

dowdiness [ˈdaʊdɪnɪs] N manque *m* d'élégance *ou* de chic

dowdy [ˈdaʊdɪ] ADJ peu élégant; *(dress, image)* démodé

dowel [ˈdaʊəl] N *Carp, Tech (location device)* téton *m* (de positionnement)
▸▸ **d. pin** *(wooden)* cheville *f*, goujon *m*, tourillon *m*

dowelling [ˈdaʊəlɪŋ] N *(material)* bois *m* à goujons *ou* tourillons

dower [ˈdaʊər] N
▸▸ *Br* **d. house** petit manoir *m* (de douairière)

Dow-Jones [ˈdaʊˈdʒəʊnz] N *St Exch* index *m* Dow Jones
▸▸ **D. average, D. index** index Dow Jones

Down [daʊn] N
▸▸ *Med* **D.'s syndrome** mongolisme *m*, *Spec* trisomie *f* 21; **D.'s syndrome baby** bébé *m* mongolien *ou* *Spéc* trisomique

DOWN¹ [daʊn]

ADV	vers le bas **1** ▪ en bas **3**
PREP	le long de ▪ en bas de
ADJ	déprimé
VT	abattre **1** ▪ descendre **2**

ADV **1** *(motion)* vers le bas; **I'll be d. in a minute** je descends dans une minute; **to lay d. one's arms** mettre bas les armes; **to shoot** *or* **bring d. an aircraft** abattre *ou* *Fam* descendre un avion; **to fall d.** tomber à terre *ou* par terre; **d. to the ground** jusqu'à terre; *Fam* **it suits me d. to the ground** ça me va parfaitement; **d. with traitors!** à bas les traîtres!; **d. with it!** *(of medicine etc)* avalez!; **d.!** *(to dog)* couché!; **d. you go!** allez, descends!

2 *(in crossword)* verticalement; **I can't get five d.** je ne trouve pas le cinq vertical

3 *(position, level)* **d. below** en bas, en contre-bas; **d. here** ici; *Am* **d. South** dans les États du sud; *Br Fam* **d. under** aux antipodes *(toujours en référence à l'Australie et à la Nouvelle-Zélande)*; **d. there** là-bas; **further d.** plus bas; **the blinds were d.** les stores étaient baissés; **to lay sth face d.** placer qch face en dessous *ou* à l'envers; **head d.** la tête en bas; *Fig* **to hit a man when he's d.** frapper un homme à terre; **she's d. with flu** elle est grippée; *Fam* **that gets me d.** ça me déprime; *Tel* **the lines are d.** les lignes sont coupées; **the wind is d.** le vent est tombé *ou* s'est apaisé; **the river is d.** la rivière est basse; **the price of gold is d.** le prix de l'or a baissé; **he's £20 d. on the deal** il en est pour 20 livres de sa poche; **bookings are d. on last week's** les réservations sont en baisse par rapport à la semaine dernière; **takings are several hundred pounds d. on last year** les recettes ont baissé de plusieurs centaines de livres par rapport à l'année dernière; *Fin* **to be d. 12% on last year** être en baisse de 12% par rapport à l'année précédente; **your team is five-two d.** ton équipe est en train de perdre par cinq à deux

4 *(order, time)* **everyone from the boss d.**

tout le monde, y compris le patron; **from prince d. to beggar** du prince jusqu'au mendiant; **I'm d. to my last cigarette/cheque** j'en suis à ma dernière cigarette/mon dernier chèque; **d. to recent times** jusqu'au temps présent; **d. to here** (en descendant) jusqu'ici; **one d., nine to go!** un de moins, plus que neuf!

5 (in writing) to put or get sth d. (in writing) coucher ou mettre qch par écrit; **if I was you, I'd get that d. in writing** or **on paper** (as opposed to taking sb's word for it) à ta place, j'essaierais d'obtenir ça noir sur blanc; **there's nothing d. on paper yet** il n'y a encore rien d'officiel; **but there's nothing d. on paper to that effect** mais il n'y a aucun écrit à cet effet; **she's d. for 20 boxes** (has reserved) elle a réservé 20 boîtes; **she's d. for £20** (has agreed to donate) elle est inscrite pour une cotisation de 20 livres; **he's d. for the 100 metres** il est inscrit pour le 100 mètres; **I've got you d. to present the bouquet** tu as été désigné pour offrir le bouquet

6 (phrases) **to be d. on sb** en vouloir à qn; Comput **to be d.** être en panne; **it's d. to you whether or not we go** (it's your decision) c'est à toi de décider si nous y allons ou pas; **this is all d. to you!** (your fault) tout cela est de ta faute!; **our lack of cash is all d. to the repairs to the roof** (is attributable to) notre manque d'argent est entièrement dû aux réparations du toit; **it was d. to his hard work that we managed to finish** c'est grâce à son travail acharné que nous avons réussi à terminer; **money d., cash d.** argent (au) comptant ou sur table; **you can have it for £50 d.** c'est à vous pour 50 livres au comptant; **to go d. by the bows** (of ship) piquer de l'avant

PREP **to slide d.** sth glisser le long de qch; **the tears ran d. his face** les larmes lui coulaient le long des joues; **d. the side of his trousers/the box** le long de son pantalon/de la boîte; **to go d. the street/a hill** descendre la rue/une colline; **to fall d. the stairs** tomber en bas de l'escalier; Fam **get that d. you** (food, drink) avale ça!; Fam **he's gone d. the pub** il est allé au pub; Fam **to go d. the shops** aller faire des courses; **they live further d. the street** ils habitent plus bas dans cette rue; Lit **d. the centuries/years** au long des siècles/années; Rail **d. the line** en aval

ADJ (depressed) découragé, déprimé; **to be d. (in the mouth)** être découragé ou déprimé; **you look very d.** tu as l'air très déprimé

N Fam **to have a d. on sb** en vouloir à qn

VT **1** (person) terrasser; Boxing (opponent) abattre; (aircraft) descendre, abattre

2 Ind **to d. tools** cesser le travail

3 Fam **to d. a drink** s'envoyer un verre; **he downed his beer and left** il a descendu sa bière et est parti; **to d. sth in one (go)** or **in a oner** avaler qch d'un coup

▸▸ Comput **d. arrow** flèche f vers le bas; Comput **d. arrow key** touche f de déplacement vers le bas; Fin **d. payment** acompte m; **d. time** (of machine) temps m de non-disponibilité ou d'immobilisation; Rail Old-fashioned **d. train** train m descendant

down² N (on bird, person, fruit) duvet m; (on plant) poil m, coton m, duvet

down³ N Geog (usu pl) **downs** chaîne f de collines crétacées; Br **the (North/South) Downs** les Downs mpl

down-and-out ADJ **to be d.** être sans le sou
N clochard, -arde

down-at-heel ADJ **1** (shoe) éculé **2** (person) miteux

downbeat ['daʊnbiːt] N Mus (temps m) frappé m
ADJ Fam **1** (gloomy) (ending, story) triste;

(speech, person) pessimiste **2** (relaxed) relaxe

downcast ['daʊnkɑːst] ADJ **1** (person) abattu, déprimé; **there's no need to be so d.** il ne faut pas se laisser abattre ou se décourager comme ça; **to look d.** avoir l'air découragé **2** (look, eyes etc) baissé

downdraught, Am **downdraft** ['daʊndrɑːft] N Met courant m d'air descendant
▸▸ Aut **d. carburettor** carburateur m inversé

downer ['daʊnər] N Sl **1** (drug) tranquillisant m **2** (depressing situation, experience) **to be on a d.** avoir le moral à zéro, être au trente-sixième dessous; **she's a real d.** elle vous met le moral à zéro; **it was a real d. to find out I hadn't even got an interview** ça m'a mis le moral complètement à zéro de savoir que je n'avais même pas obtenu d'entretien

downfall ['daʊnfɔːl] N (of person) ruine f; (of government etc) écroulement m, effondrement m; **drink brought about** or **was his d.** la boisson l'a perdu

downgrade ['daʊngreɪd] VT (move to lower position) (employee) rétrograder, déclasser à une échelle de salaire inférieure; (goods) classer dans une catégorie inférieure; **he was downgraded to area manager** il a été rétrogradé au rang de responsable régional; **the hurricane has been downgraded to a storm** l'ouragan n'est maintenant plus qu'une tempête
N esp Am descente f, déclivité f; Fig **to be on the d.** baisser, être sur le déclin ou Fam sur le retour

downgrading ['daʊngreɪdɪŋ] N (of employee) = déclassement m à une échelle de salaire inférieure, rétrogradation f; (of goods) classement m dans une catégorie inférieure

downhearted [daʊn'hɑːtɪd] ADJ découragé, déprimé; **don't be d.!** ne te décourage pas!, ne te laisse pas abattre!; **to become d.** se décourager

downhill ['daʊn'hɪl] N **1** descente f, pente f **2** Ski descente f
ADJ (slope) descendante; **the d. journey** la descente
ADV **to go d.** (of road, car) descendre; Fig Fam (of person) être sur le déclin; (of business etc) péricliter; (of sb's work) devenir moins bon; **it's d. all the way** ça descend tout le long du chemin; Hum **it's d. all the way after you're 40** après 40 ans, on ne fait que décliner; **after January it'll be d. all the way** (easier) après janvier le pire sera passé
▸▸ **d. skier** descendeur, -euse; **d. skiing** ski m alpin

Downing Street ['daʊnɪŋstriːt] N Br Pol = résidence f officielle du Premier ministre (n° 10) et du ministre des Finances (n° 11); **there has been no confirmation from D.** le Premier ministre n'a pas apporté de confirmation

> ### Downing Street
> C'est à Downing Street à Londres que se trouvent les résidences officielles du Premier ministre, au n° 10, et du ministre des Finances, au n° 11. Le terme "Downing Street" est souvent employé pour désigner le gouvernement.

download ['daʊnləʊd] Comput N téléchargement m
VT télécharger
VI effectuer un téléchargement; **graphic files take a long time to d.** le téléchargement de fichiers graphiques est très lent
▸▸ **d. font** police f téléchargeable

downloadable [daʊn'ləʊdəb(ə)l] ADJ Comput téléchargeable

downloading [daʊn'ləʊdɪŋ] N Comput téléchargement m

down-low N Am Fam **on the d.** (confidential) confidentiel; **I'm telling you this on the d.** je te dis ça, mais c'est entre nous

down-market ADJ (car, house etc) bas de gamme; (person) ordinaire; (district, accent) populaire
ADV **to move d.** passer au bas de gamme; (go to a cheap restaurant etc) donner dans le populaire

downpipe ['daʊnpaɪp] N Constr tuyau m de descente

downplay [daʊn'pleɪ] VT minimiser

downpour ['daʊnpɔːr] N averse f

downright ['daʊnraɪt] ADV (idiotic etc) tout à fait, complètement; (rude, disgusting, nosy) carrément
ADJ **1** (complete, absolute) (stupidity, carelessness, dishonesty) absolu; (lie) éclatant; **d. fool** parfait ou franc imbécile **2** (blunt, frank) (person, language) direct, franc, f franche

downshift ['daʊnʃɪft] VI **1** Am Aut rétrograder **2** (change one's lifestyle) = passer à un emploi moins stressant

downshifting ['daʊnʃɪftɪŋ] N = passage m à un emploi moins stressant

downside ['daʊnsaɪd] N désavantage m (to sth de qch); **there's a d. to everything** toute médaille a son revers; **on the d., however, the situation has worsened in the South** mais par contre la situation a empiré dans le sud; **on the d., we'll have to sleep in the train** le désavantage, c'est que nous devrons dormir dans le train
▸▸ St Exch **d. potential** potentiel m de baisse; St Exch **d. risk** risque m de baisse

downsize [daʊn'saɪz] VT Electron microniser; (project) réduire l'envergure de; (of designers) (car) réduire les dimensions de; **downsized car** voiture aux dimensions réduites
VI (of company) réduire ses effectifs

downsizing [daʊn'saɪzɪŋ] N **1** Electron micronisation f **2** (of company) réduction f des effectifs

downspout ['daʊnspaʊt] N tuyau m de descente

downstage ['daʊnsteɪdʒ] Théâtre ADV, ADJ sur le devant (de la scène), à l'avant-scène; **to stand d. of sb** se tenir plus en avant que qn sur la scène; **take two paces d.** fais deux pas vers le devant de la scène
N avant-scène f

downstairs ADV [daʊn'steəz] **1** (down the stairs) en bas; **to come/go d.** descendre (l'escalier); **to run d.** descendre (l'escalier) en courant **2** (on a lower floor) en bas; **our neighbours d.** nos voisins d'en-dessous
ADJ ['daʊnsteəz] **the d. rooms** les pièces d'en bas ou du bas
N ['daʊnsteəz] l'étage m du bas

downstate ['daʊnsteɪt] Am ADJ **in d. New York** dans le sud de l'État de New York
ADV au sud de l'État

downstream ADV [daʊn'striːm] en aval, à l'aval (from de); **a few miles d. from here** quelques miles en aval d'ici
ADJ ['daʊnstriːm] d'aval
▸▸ TV **d. keyer** incrustateur m après mélange; Petr **d. operations** opérations fpl en aval

downstroke ['daʊnstrəʊk] N **1** (in writing) plein m **2** Tech course f descendante; (of piston) mouvement m de descente **3** Orn (of wing) abaissée f

downswept ['daʊnswept] ADJ Aviat (wings) surbaissé

downswing ['daʊnswɪŋ] N *(in economy etc)* tendance *f* à la baisse

down-to-earth ADJ *(person, approach, attitude)* terre(-)à(-)terre *inv;* réaliste

downtown ['daʊn'taʊn] *Am* ADV dans/vers (le centre de) la ville; **he gave me a lift d.** il m'a descendu en ville; **to live d.** habiter en ville
  ADJ **d. New York** le centre de New York; **d. theatres** théâtres *mpl* du centre
  N *(of town)* centre *m*

downtrodden ['daʊntrɒd(ə)n] ADJ **1** *Fig (people, wife etc)* opprimé **2** *(grass etc)* piétiné

downturn ['daʊntɜːn] N *(in inflation, unemployment figures)* baisse *f*, *(in economy)* ralentissement *m*; **to take a d.** *(of economy)* ralentir; *(of inflation, unemployment)* baisser; **their fortunes took a sudden d. when ...** leur fortune a connu un soudain revers quand ...

downward ['daʊnwəd] ADJ *(movement, path)* descendant; **to take a d. glance** *or* **look at sth** jeter un coup d'œil par en dessous à qch; *Fig* **to be on the d. path** aller à sa perte; *Fin* **d. movement** mouvement *m* de baisse; **d. trend** *(in prices etc)* tendance *f* à la baisse
  ADV = **downwards**

downward-compatible ADJ *Comput* compatible vers le bas

downwards ['daʊnwədz] ADV vers le bas, en descendant; *(on river)* en aval; *(to look)* en bas; **to slope d.** descendre; **to lay sth face d.** placer qch face en dessous; **from the twelfth century d.** à partir du *ou* depuis le douzième siècle; **children of five and d.** enfants de cinq ans et au-dessous; **every member of the cabinet, from the Prime Minister d.** tout le monde, du Premier ministre au dernier membre du gouvernement

downwind ADV [daʊn'wɪnd] *Aviat (to land)* vent arrière; **to move d. of an animal** se déplacer sous le vent d'un animal; *Hum* **it's best to stand d. of old Mr Wilson** il vaut mieux ne pas trop s'approcher du vieux M. Wilson
  ADV ['daʊnwɪnd] *Aviat (landing)* vent arrière

downy ['daʊnɪ] ADJ duveteux, duveté; *(fruit)* velouté, duveté

dowry ['daʊrɪ] N dot *f*

dowse[1] [daʊz] VI faire de la radiesthésie; **to d. for water** chercher de l'eau à l'aide d'une baguette de sourcier

dowse[2] [daʊs] VT = **douse**

dowser ['daʊzər] N sourcier *m*, radiesthésiste *mf*

dowsing ['daʊzɪŋ] N radiesthésie *f*
  ▸▸ **d. rod** baguette *f* (de sourcier)

doyen ['dɔɪjən] N doyen *m* (d'âge)

doyenne ['dɔɪjen] N doyenne *f* (d'âge)

doz *(abbr* **dozen)** d(ou)z

doze [dəʊz] N petit somme *m*; **to have a d.** faire un petit somme; **to fall into a d.** s'assoupir
  VI somnoler
  ▸ **doze off** VI s'assoupir

dozen ['dʌz(ə)n] N VOIR GRAMMAIRE A12–13; B60 **1** *(inv)* douzaine *f*; **a d. eggs** une douzaine d'œufs; **half a d., a half d.** une demi-douzaine; **£5 a d./half d.** cinq livres la douzaine/demi-douzaine; **six d. bottles of wine** six douzaines de bouteilles de vin; **by the d.** à la douzaine **2** *(pl* **dozens)** **they arrived in their dozens** ils arrivèrent par douzaines; **dozens of people have asked me about it** des dizaines de personnes me l'ont demandé; **to have dozens of things to do** avoir des tas de choses à faire; **dozens and dozens of times** maintes et maintes fois; **a baker's d., thirteen to the d.** treize à la douzaine;

Fam **to talk nineteen to the d.** bavarder comme une pie

dozenth ['dʌz(ə)nθ] ADJ douzième

dozily ['dəʊzɪlɪ] ADV *(to watch)* d'un œil somnolent; *(to answer)* d'une voix endormie

doziness ['dəʊzɪnɪs] N **1** somnolence *f* **2** *Br Fam (stupidity)* bêtise *f*

dozy ['dəʊzɪ] ADJ **1** somnolent, assoupi; **to feel d.** avoir envie de dormir **2** *Br Fam (stupid)* nunuche

DP [diː'piː] N *Comput (abbr* **data processing)** traitement *m* des données, informatique *f*; **DP manager** chef *m* des traitements

D Phil [diː'fɪl] N *Univ abbr* **Doctor of Philosophy**

dpi [diːpiː'aɪ] *Comput (abbr* **dots per inch)** dpi, ppp

DPP [diːpiː'piː] N *Br Law abbr* **Director of Public Prosecutions**

dpt *abbr* **department**

Dr 1 *(abbr* **doctor)** Dr. **2** *(abbr* **Drive)** av.

drab [dræb] ADJ **1** *(colour)* terne; *(clothing)* de couleur terne **2** *Fig (surroundings, routine)* morne, monotone; *(existence)* terne, monotone; *(person)* insignifiant
  N **1** *(colour)* olivâtre *m* **2** *(material) (grey)* tissu *m* gris; *(brown)* tissu brun

drably ['dræblɪ] ADV de façon terne; **d. coloured** aux couleurs ternes *ou* mornes

drabness ['dræbnɪs] N *(of surroundings, existence)* monotonie *f*; **the d. of her clothes** ses vêtements ternes

drachm [dræm] N *(measurement)* drachme *f*

drachma, *pl* **drachmas** ['drækmə, -məz] N *Formerly* drachme *f*

draconian [drə'kəʊnɪən] ADJ draconien, -ienne

draft[1] [drɑːft] N **1** *(of letter)* brouillon *m*; *(of law)* projet *m*; *(of treaty)* avant-projet *m*, *pl* avant-projets; *Archit, Tech etc* dessin *m* schématique, tracé *m*; *rough* **d.** *(of map etc)* ébauche *f*, **do you want it in d.?** tu le veux au brouillon?; **first d. of a novel** premier jet *m* d'un roman
  2 *Com* traite *f*, **banker's d.** chèque *m* bancaire
  3 *Am Mil (conscription)* conscription *f*, **to be d. age** être en âge de faire son service
  4 *Mil (group) (of troops)* détachement *m*; *(of recruits)* contingent *m*
  VT **1** *(letter)* faire le brouillon de; *(deed, project)* rédiger; *Pol* **to d. a bill** établir un projet de loi
  2 *Am Mil (conscript)* appeler sous les drapeaux
  3 *Mil (detach) (troops)* détacher, envoyer en détachement; *(soldier)* affecter (**to** à); **to d. troops into ...** faire passer des troupes dans ...; *Fig* **could we d. in some outside help?** est-ce que nous pourrions obtenir de l'aide à l'extérieur?; **she had been drafted in from the Foreign Office** on l'avait fait venir du ministère des affaires étrangères
  ▸▸ **d. agreement** projet *m* de contrat; *Am Mil* **d. board** conseil *m* de révision; **d. budget** projet de budget; *Am Mil* **d. card** ordre *m* d'incorporation; **d. contract** projet de contrat; *Am Mil* **d. dodger** réfractaire *m*; *Am Mil* **d. dodging** insoumission *f*, **d. legislation** projet d'acte législatif; *Br Comput* **d. mode** mode *m* rapide *ou* brouillon; *Comput* **d. printout** brouillon *m*; *Br Comput* **d. quality** qualité *f* brouillon; *Comput* **d. quality printing** impression *f* en qualité brouillon; *Comput* **d. version** version *f* brouillon

draft[2] N *Am* = **draught**[1]

draftsman, **draftsmanship** *etc Am* = **draughtsman**, **draughtsmanship** *etc*

drafty ['drɑːftɪ] ADJ *Am* = **draughty**

drag [dræg] N **1** *(in aerodynamics)* résistance

f de l'air; *Aviat* traînée *f*, *Billiards* effet *m* rétrograde
  2 *Fam (bore) (person)* raseur, -euse; **it's an awful d.** c'est la barbe, c'est barbant; **the party was a d.** la soirée était rasante; **I don't want to be a d. but ...** je ne voudrais pas être rasoir, mais ...; **what a d. for you!** quelle barbe!
  3 *Sl* **to have a d.** *(on cigarette)* tirer une taffe; **she took a quick d. on her cigarette** elle tira vivement sur sa cigarette
  4 *Sl (women's clothes worn by man)* costume *m* féminin (porté par un homme); **he was in d.** il portait des vêtements de femme
  5 *esp Am Fam* **the (main) d.** la rue principale
  6 *Am Fam* **to have d.** *(influence)* avoir du piston
  7 *(in hunting)* voie *f* artificielle
  8 *(brake)* **to put a d. on a wheel** enrayer une roue; *Fig* **she was a d. on his career** elle entravait sa carrière, elle le freinait dans sa carrière; **I don't want to be a d. on you** *(in career, on walk, climb etc)* je ne veux pas te freiner
  9 *(trek)* **it's a long d. to the top of the hill** c'est une sacrée tirée jusqu'en haut de la colline
  10 *(for dredging)* drague *f*, *(for retrieving lost object)* araignée *f*, *Naut* grappin *m* à main; *(for helping drowning person)* gaffe *f* de sauvetage
  VT *(-gg-)* **1** *(pull)* traîner, tirer; *(by force) (person)* entraîner de force *ou* contre sa volonté; **to d. one's feet** traîner les pieds; *Fig* **to d. one's feet** *or* **heels** tarder (**over doing** à faire); **she dragged her feet over the decision** elle a tardé à se décider; *Fig* **I wish you'd stop dragging your feet** je voudrais bien que tu arrêtes d'atermoyer; **he dragged himself to the door** il se traîna jusqu'à la porte; **to d. its anchor** *(of ship)* déraper; *Fig* **I don't want to d. you through it** je ne veux pas te faire subir ça; *Fig* **he dragged me to the football match** il m'a traîné au match de football; *Fig* **to d. sb through the courts** traîner qn devant les tribunaux
  2 *(search) (pond, river)* draguer
  3 *Comput (with mouse)* faire glisser; **d. and drop** glisser-lâcher
  VI **1** *(of skirt etc)* traîner (à terre)
  2 *(progress slowly) (of lawsuit), Theat (of scene etc)* traîner en longueur; *(of conversation)* languir; *(of work)* se traîner; **time is dragging** les heures se traînent; **the meeting finally dragged to a close at 10 pm** la réunion s'est enfin terminée à 10 heures
  3 *Tech* offrir de la résistance; *(of brakes)* frotter (sur les roues)
  4 *Fam* **to d. on** *or* **at a cigarette** tirer des bouffées d'une cigarette
  5 *(search)* draguer (**for sth** pour retrouver qch)
  6 *Fishing* pêcher à la drague; **to d. for oysters** pêcher les huîtres à la drague
  7 *Comput* **to d. and drop** faire un glisser-lâcher
  ▸▸ **d. act** numéro *m* de travesti(s); **d. artist** travesti *m*; **d. coefficient** coefficient *m* aérodynamique, coefficient de pénétration dans l'air, Cx *m*; **d. factor** coefficient de traînée; **d. hunt** chasse *f* à courre où la meute suit une piste artificielle, drag *m*; *Aut* **d. link** biellette *f* de direction; *Aut* **d. link bar** bielle *f* pendante; *Fam* **d. queen** travelo *m*; *Am Aut* **d. race** concours *m* d'accélération; **d. show** spectacle *m* de travesti
  ▸ **drag along** VT SEP *(somebody, something)* traîner
  VI *(of dress)* traîner; *(of person)* être à la traîne
  ▸ **drag apart** VT SEP séparer
  ▸ **drag away** VT SEP *(person)* entraîner, emmener de force; *(somebody, something)* arra-

cher (**from** de); **I couldn't d. myself away** j'étais cloué sur place; **if you could d. yourself away from the television** si tu pouvais t'arracher de devant la télévision

▸ **drag behind** VT SEP traîner derrière (soi) VI être à la traîne; **stop dragging behind** arrête de traîner comme ça

▸ **drag down** VT SEP **1** (*person, object*) entraîner en bas; (*by force*) (*person*) faire descendre de force; *also Fig* **he dragged me down with him** il m'a entraîné dans sa chute; **to d. sb down to one's level** faire descendre qn à son niveau **2** (*of illness etc*) (*person*) déprimer

▸ **drag in** VT SEP **1** (*pull in*) traîner; (*by force*) faire entrer de force **2** *Fam* (*refer to*) faire allusion à; **why do you always have to d. in my one mistake?** pourquoi est-ce que tu te crois obligé de faire sans arrêt allusion à ma seule erreur?

▸ **drag into** VT SEP (*involve*) **don't d. me into this!** ne me mêle pas à ça!; **he keeps dragging her name into the conversation** il n'arrête pas de glisser son nom dans la conversation

▸ **drag off** VT SEP = **drag away**

▸ **drag on** VI (*of meeting, business etc*) s'éterniser, traîner en longueur; **to let a matter d. on** laisser traîner une affaire; **the play dragged on and on** la pièce n'en finissait pas; **the exams seemed to d. on for ages** les examens semblaient n'en plus finir

▸ **drag out** VT SEP **1** (*heavy object, person*) traîner à l'extérieur; (*by force*) (*person*) faire sortir de force; **to d. sb out of bed** tirer qn de son lit; **to d. the truth/a confession out of sb** arracher la vérité/des aveux à qn; **I finally managed to d. out of him the reason why he was so upset** j'ai finalement réussi à lui faire dire pourquoi il était si retourné **2** (*speech, presentation, matter*) faire traîner; *Lit* **to d. out a wretched existence** traîner une existence misérable

▸ **drag up** VT **1** (*object, person*) entraîner *ou* tirer jusqu'en haut; *Fam* **you dragged me up to London for this?** et c'est pour ça que tu m'as fait venir à Londres? **2** *Fam* (*refer to*) (*old story*) déterrer **3** *Fam* (*raise badly*) **those children are being dragged up** ces enfants sont élevés n'importe comment; **where were you dragged up?** où as-tu été élevé?

drag-and-drop N *Comput* glisser-lâcher *m inv*

dragging ['drægɪŋ] ADJ **d. step** pas *m* traînant

N **1** (*of something heavy behind one etc*) traînement *m*; *Naut* **d. of the anchor** dérapage *m* **2** (*of pond, river*) dragage *m*

draggy ['drægɪ] ADJ *Fam* **1** (*boring*) (*evening, party*) ennuyeux, barbant **2** (*listless*) pas dans son assiette; **to feel a bit d.** ne pas être dans son assiette

draglift ['dræglɪft] N tire-fesses *m inv*

dragnet ['drægnet] N **1** (*organized by police*) cordon *m* de police; **twenty suspects were picked up in the d.** vingt personnes suspectes furent arrêtées dans la rafle **2** *Fishing* seine *f*, drège *f*

dragon ['drægən] N *Myth, Fig Fam* dragon *m*; *Sl* **to chase the d.** (*smoke heroin*) chasser le dragon **2** (*lizard*) dragon *m*
▸▸ *Mil* **d.'s teeth** (*anti-tank defence*) rangées *fpl* de tétraèdres de béton

dragonfly ['drægənflaɪ] N libellule *f*

dragoon [drə'guːn] N *Mil* dragon *m*
VT **to d. sb into doing sth** forcer qn à faire qch

dragrope ['drægrəʊp] N **1** *Mil* bricole *f*, combleau *m* **2** *Aviat* (*of hot-air balloon*) guide-rope *m*, *pl* guide-ropes

dragster ['drægstər] N *Aut* dragster *m*

drain [dreɪn] N **1** (*in street*) égout *m*; (*of house*) canalisation *f* sanitaire; **a smell of drains** une odeur d'égout; **the drains are overflowing** les égouts débordent; **to pour sth down the d.** (dé)verser qch dans les égouts; *Fig* **to throw money down the d.** jeter son argent par la fenêtre; *Fam* **that's five years' work down the d.** voilà cinq années de travail perdues; *Fam* **that's my holiday down the d.** mes vacances sont à l'eau; *Fam* **to laugh like a d.** rire à gorge déployée **2** (*loss*) (*of energy etc*) perte *f*, fuite *f*; (*of capital etc*) drainage *m*; **this constant d. on our resources** cette hémorragie continuelle de nos ressources; **the car is a continual d. on our resources** la voiture nous cause constamment des dépenses; **the brain d.** l'exode *m ou* la fuite des cerveaux **3** *Tech etc* tuyau *m* d'écoulement; *Med* drain *m*; **overflow d.** (tube *m* de) trop-plein *m*, *pl* trop-pleins

VT **1** (*liquid*) (*from field, pond*) évacuer; **d. the water from the vegetables** égoutter les légumes; *Med* **to d. pus from a wound** faire sortir le pus d'une blessure; *Fig* **to d. wealth from a country** drainer les richesses d'un pays **2** (*glass, pond, radiator etc*) vider; (*land, swamp*), *Med* (*wound, abscess*) drainer; (*sump*) vidanger; *Culin* (*vegetables etc*) égoutter; *Agr* **well/poorly-drained soil** sol *m* perméable/peu perméable; *Fig* **to d. a country of its wealth** épuiser les richesses d'un pays; **the company is being drained of its top executives** la société perd ses cadres supérieurs **3** *Fig* (*person*) épuiser; **to d. sb's energy** épuiser qn; **to feel drained** (*of energy*) être épuisé; (*of emotions*) être vidé; **to be drained of emotion** ne plus ressentir aucune émotion; **to d. sb of their strength** épuiser les forces de qn

VI (*of dishes*) égoutter; (*of sink, washing machine*) se vider; **the river drains into the sea** la rivière se jette dans la mer; **the colour drained from her face** elle est devenue blême
▸▸ **d. hole** vis *m* de purge, trou *m* d'évacuation; *Aut etc* **d. plug** bouchon *m* de vidange

▸ **drain away** VT SEP (*remove*) (*oil, water etc*) faire couler
VI (*of water*) s'écouler; (*of strength, enthusiasm, energy etc*) s'épuiser; (*of fear, tension*) s'envoler, s'en aller

▸ **drain off** VT SEP (*water, oil*) évacuer
VI (*of water*) s'écouler

drainage ['dreɪnɪdʒ] N **1** = **draining 2** *Constr* (*for draining land etc*) système *m* d'écoulement des eaux; (*drains*) système d'égouts; **main d.** tout-à-l'égout *m inv*; *Agr* **soil with good d.** sol *m* perméable; **to improve the d. of the soil** rendre le sol plus perméable **3** (*water*) eaux *fpl* de surface; (*sewage*) eaux d'égout
▸▸ *Geog* **d. area, d. basin** bassin *m* hydrographique; *Agr* **d. ditch** fossé *m* d'écoulement; *Med* **d. tube** drain *m*

drainer ['dreɪnər] N égouttoir *m*

draining ['dreɪnɪŋ] N (*of water*) écoulement *m*; (*of swamp*) drainage *m*, assèchement *m*; *Agr* (*of land*) drainage, assainissement *m*; (*of bottles etc*) égouttement *m*; (*of sump etc*) vidange *f*; *Med* (*of wound*) drainage
▸▸ **d. board** égouttoir *m* (d'évier)

drainpipe ['dreɪnpaɪp] N tuyau *m* d'écoulement *ou* de drainage; *Fam* **drainpipes** pantalon *m* étroit *ou* en tuyau de poêle
▸▸ **d. trousers** pantalon étroit *ou* en tuyau de poêle

drake [dreɪk] N (*bird*) canard *m* mâle; **wild d.** malard *m*

DRAM ['diːræm] N *Comput* (*abbr* **dynamic random access memory**) DRAM *f*

dram [dræm] N **1** *Pharm* drachme *f* (= un seizième d'once, = 1,77 grammes) **2** *esp Scot Fam* (*of whisky*) goutte *f*, **to take a d.** prendre un petit verre (de whisky)

drama ['drɑːmə] N **1** *Theat* (*play*), *Fig* drame *m*; *Fig* **to make a d. out of sth** faire un drame de qch; **there's no need to make such a d. out of it** ce n'est pas la peine d'en faire tout un drame; **she always has to make a d. out of everything** elle est toujours à dramatiser **2** (*art form*) l'art *m* dramatique, le théâtre; **the masterpieces of French d.** les chefs-d'œuvre du théâtre français; **to teach d.** donner des cours d'art dramatique *ou* de théâtre **3** *Fig* (*excitement*) action *f*; **packed with d., full of d.** (*film etc*) plein d'action *ou* de rebondissements; **the d. of the situation is heightened by the fact that …** le caractère dramatique de la situation est renforcé par le fait que …
▸▸ *TV* **d. documentary** docudrame *m*; *Fam Pej* **d. queen** comédien, -ienne; **don't be such a d. queen!** arrête ton cinéma!; **d. school** école *f* d'art dramatique, école de théâtre; *TV* **d. series** série *f* dramatique; **d. student** étudiant, -ante en art dramatique; **d. studio** studio *m* d'enregistrement

> Note that the French word **drame** also means **tragedy, disaster**.

dramadoc ['drɑːmədɒk] N *TV Fam* docudrame *m*

dramatic [drə'mætɪk] ADJ **1** (*book, ending, actor etc*) dramatique; **the d. works of Corneille** le théâtre de Corneille **2** *Fig* (*substantial*) (*developments, rise, decline, change etc*) considérable, très important **3** *Fig* (*theatrical*) (*gesture, effect*) théâtral **4** (*spectacular*) (*landscape, scenery, skyline*) spectaculaire

> Note that the most common meaning of the French word **dramatique** is **tragic**.

dramatically [drə'mætɪklɪ] ADV **1** *Theat* (*to end*) sur un coup de théâtre; **d., the play doesn't work** du point de vue dramatique, la pièce ne tient pas debout **2** *Fig* (*substantially*) considérablement **3** *Fig* (*theatrically*) théâtralement; **the room is decorated rather d. in red and black** la pièce est décorée avec beaucoup d'effet en rouge et noir

> Note that the French word **dramatiquement** is a false friend and is never a translation for the English word **dramatically**.

dramatics [drə'mætɪks] N amateur **d.** théâtre *m* amateur; *Pej* **this is no time for d.** ce n'est pas le moment de faire un drame *ou* de dramatiser VOIR GRAMMAIRE A10

dramatis personae ['dræmətɪspɜː'səʊnaɪ] NPL *Theat* personnages *mpl*

dramatist ['dræmətɪst] N *Theat* auteur *m* dramatique, dramaturge *mf*

dramatization [dræmətaɪ'zeɪʃən] N *Radio, TV, Theat* (*of novel etc*) adaptation *f*; *Fig* (*of event*) dramatisation *f*

dramatize ['dræmətaɪz] VT *Radio, TV, Theat* (*novel*) adapter; *Fig* (*event*) dramatiser; **there's no need to d. it** il ne faut pas en faire un drame
VI **novel that would d. well** (*for stage/screen/radio*) roman qui s'adapterait bien à la scène/à l'écran/à la radio; *Fig* **there's no need to d.** il ne faut pas en faire un drame; **he tends to d.** il a tendance à dramatiser

drape [dreɪp] VT (*table, window, neckline, material*) draper (**with, in** de); **to d. sth over sth** draper qch sur qch; **the hall was draped in black** la salle était tendue de noir; **she was draped over the sofa** elle s'était étalée sur le canapé; **she draped herself round him** elle l'a enlacé; **he had a coat draped over his**

arm il avait un manteau sur le bras
vi *(of material)* se draper
N 1 *(of dress etc)* drapé *m* **2 drapes** tentures *fpl*; *Am (curtains)* rideaux *mpl*

draper ['dreɪpər] **N** *Old-fashioned Br* marchand, -ande de tissus; **d.'s shop** magasin *m* de tissus

drapery ['dreɪpərɪ] **N 1** *Old-fashioned Br (trade)* commerce *m* des tissus; *(shop)* magasin *m* de tissus **2** *(hangings)* tentures *fpl*

drastic ['dræstɪk] **ADJ** *(action)* énergique; *(measures, solution, change)* radical, drastique; *(cuts)* draconien, -ienne, sombre; *(remedy)* drastique; *(decline, rise, improvement, change)* dramatique; *(shortage)* dramatique, critique; *(need)* urgent; **things are getting d.** la situation devient critique; **that's quite a d. haircut you've got** tu as la boule à zéro; **d. reductions** *(sign)* soldes monstres; **that's a bit d.** *(of proposal etc)* c'est un peu exagéré

drastically ['dræstɪklɪ] **ADV** *(to act)* énergiquement; *(shortened, improved etc)* radicalement; **to be d. short of sth** manquer dramatiquement de qch; **they're not d. different** ils ne sont pas fondamentalement différents; **d. reduced prices** prix *mpl* cassés

drat [dræt] **INT** *Old-fashioned Fam* **d. (it)!** sacristi!, nom de nom!; **d. the child!** au diable cet enfant!

dratted ['drætɪd] **ADJ** *Old-fashioned Fam (boy etc)* maudit

draught¹, *Am* **draft** [drɑːft] **N 1** *(wind)* courant *m* d'air; **I'm in a d., I feel a d.** je suis dans un courant d'air; **d.-proof** à l'épreuve des courants d'air; *Fig Fam* **we're (all) feeling the d.** les choses vont mal (pour tout le monde) **2** *(of chimney)* tirage *m* **3** *Lit (drink)* trait *m*, gorgée *f*; **he took a long d. of beer** il a bu une grande gorgée de bière **4** *Med Arch* potion *f*; **poisoned d.** potion empoisonnée **5** *Naut (of ship)* tirant *m* d'eau **6 beer on d., d. beer** bière *f* à la pression **7** *(for playing draughts)* pion *m*
▸▸ **d. animal** bête *f* de trait; *Br* **d. excluder** bourrelet *m* (de porte)

draught² **N**, **VT** = **draft¹**

draughtboard ['drɑːftbɔːd] **N** damier *m*

draughts [drɑːfts] **N** *Br* (jeu *m* de) dames *fpl*; **to play d.** jouer aux dames; **a game of d.** une partie de dames VOIR GRAMMAIRE A10

draughtsman, *Am* **draftsman**, *pl* **draughtsmen** ['drɑːftsmən] **N 1** *Ind (of plans, drawings etc)* dessinateur *m* industriel **2** *Art* dessinateur *m*

draughtsmanship, *Am* **draftsmanship** ['drɑːftsmənʃɪp] **N 1** *Ind* l'art *m* du dessin industriel **2** *(ability to draw well)* talent *m* de dessinateur; **a fine piece of d.** un très bon dessin; **the d. is excellent** c'est très bien dessiné; **d. was never his strong point** le dessin n'a jamais été son fort

draughtswoman, *Am* **draftswoman**, *pl* **draughtswomen** ['drɑːftswʊmən, -wɪmɪn] **N 1** *Ind (of plans, drawings etc)* dessinatrice *f* industrielle **2** *Art* dessinatrice *f*

draughty, *Am* **drafty** ['drɑːftɪ] **ADJ** *(room, corridor etc)* plein de courants d'air; *(street corner)* exposé à tous les vents; **it's d. here** il y a des courants d'air ici

DRAW [drɔː]

N	partie nulle **1** ▪ loterie **2**
	▪ attraction **3**
VT	dessiner **1** ▪ tirer **2, 3, 7** ▪ attirer **2,**
	6 ▪ retirer **3** ▪ toucher **5**
VI	dessiner **1** ▪ faire partie nulle **2**
	▪ faire ex æquo **2** ▪ tirer **4**

N 1 *(game)* partie *f* nulle; *Ftbl, Boxing* match *m* nul; **it ended in a d.** ils ont fait partie/

match nul(le); *(of competition)* ils ont fini à égalité; *Ftbl* **a one-all/nil-nil d.** un match nul un à un/zéro à zéro; **it's a d. so far** pour l'instant, ils sont à égalité
2 *(lottery)* loterie *f*, tombola *f*; *(selection of winners, competitors)* tirage *m* (au sort); *Sport (list)* = tableau *m* des concurrents à chaque tour d'une série d'épreuves de championnat etc; **an easy/difficult d.** un tirage favorable/défavorable; *Ftbl* **the d. for the World Cup** le tirage de la Coupe du Monde; *Fam* **that's just the luck of the d.** c'est la vie!
3 *(attraction)* attraction *f*; *Theat* pièce *f* qui fait recette; **the match/film was a big d.** le match/film a remporté un grand succès; **she was a big d.** elle a attiré beaucoup de monde
4 to take a d. at one's pipe tirer une bouffée de sa pipe; **she had a quick d. on her cigarette** elle tira vivement sur sa cigarette; *Fam* **to be quick on the d.** *(with gun)* avoir la gâchette facile; *(with answers)* avoir la repartie facile; **to be a fast d.** avoir la gâchette facile; **the fastest d. in the West** le tireur le plus rapide de l'Ouest
5 *Br Sl (cannabis)* shit *m*

VT *(pt* **drew** [druː], *pp* **drawn** [drɔːn]*)* **1** *Art (landscape, figure etc)* dessiner; *Geom (circle, plan)* tracer; *(triangle, hexagon)* tracer, construire; *(line)* tirer, tracer; **to d. a map** dessiner une carte; *(of surveyor)* dresser une carte; **to d. sb's picture** faire le portrait de qn; *Fig* **the author has drawn the characters skilfully** l'auteur a tracé les personnages avec adresse
2 *(pull) (person)* attirer (**towards** vers); *(cart)* tirer; *(bow)* tendre; *(blind)* baisser; **to d. the curtains** tirer les rideaux; **drawn by a locomotive** remorqué par une locomotive; **to d. breath** souffler; *Fig* **I haven't drawn breath all day** *(I've been very busy)* je n'ai pas arrêté de la journée; **she drew his head down towards her** elle attira sa tête vers elle; **to d. a comb/brush through one's hair** se donner un coup de peigne/brosse
3 *(extract)* retirer, ôter (**sth from** or **out of sth** qch de qch); *(screw)* ôter, enlever; *(cork)* retirer, tirer, faire sauter; *(tooth, nail etc)* arracher; **to d. one's sword** tirer l'épée, dégainer; **to d. one's revolver** *(from holster/pocket)* sortir son revolver de l'étui/de sa poche, dégainer; **to d. a gun on sb** sortir un revolver et le pointer sur qn; **to d. a knife (on sb)** sortir un couteau (et en menacer qn); *Cards* **to d. a card (from the pack)** tirer une carte; *Cards* **to d. trumps** faire tomber les atouts; **to d. money from the bank** retirer de l'argent de la banque; **to d. blood** *(of weapon)* faire couler le sang; *(of dog)* mordre jusqu'au sang; *(of cat)* griffer jusqu'au sang; *Fig (of remark, criticism)* avoir un effet dévastateur; **to d. water from the river/the well** puiser *ou* tirer de l'eau à la rivière/au puits; **to d. wine (from a barrel)** tirer du vin (d'un tonneau); **to d. lots for sth** tirer qch au sort; **to d. straws** tirer à la courte paille; **to be drawn** *(of winning number, bonds)* sortir au tirage; **to d. a team/player against another** tirer une équipe/un joueur au sort contre un(e) autre; **it was the second time Czechoslovakia had been drawn against Scotland** c'était la deuxième fois que la Tchécoslovaquie tombait contre l'Écosse; **to d. a confession from sb** arracher un aveu à qn; **to d. a conclusion from sth** tirer *ou* déduire une conclusion de qch
4 *Sport* **to d. a game with sb** faire match nul avec qn; *(in chess etc)* faire partie nulle avec qn; **the match was drawn** ils ont fait match nul
5 *(receive) (salary)*, *Mil (rations)* toucher; **to d. supplies from sb** s'approvisionner chez qn

6 *(attract) (criticism, praise, person's gaze)* attirer; **to d. a crowd** *(of incident)* créer un attroupement; *(of play)* attirer le public; **to feel drawn to sb** se sentir attiré par qn; *Mil* **to d. the enemy's fire** attirer sur soi le feu de l'ennemi; **to d. sb's fire** *(of policeman)*, *Fig (deliberately)* faire diversion; *Fig (accidentally)* s'attirer les foudres de qn; **his accusation drew an instant denial** son accusation provoqua un démenti immédiat; **the government refused to be drawn** le gouvernement refusa de se commettre; **she would not be drawn on what she intended to do** elle a refusé de faire connaître ses intentions
7 *(take, derive) (strength, comfort, consolation etc)* tirer (**from** de); **our members are drawn from all walks of life** nos membres appartiennent à tous les milieux
8 *Fin (cheque)* libeller, rédiger; **to d. a cheque on** tirer *ou* disposer un chèque sur; **to d. a bill on** tirer une traite sur
9 *Culin (chicken etc)* vider
10 *Naut* **to d. twenty feet of water** *(of ship)* tirer *ou* jauger vingt pieds d'eau, avoir vingt pieds de tirant d'eau
11 *Med (abscess)* faire aboutir
12 *Metal (wire, tubes etc)* étirer, tirer
13 to d. tea faire infuser du thé

VI 1 *Art* dessiner
2 *Sport* faire match nul; *(in chess etc)* faire partie nulle; **they drew two all** ils ont fait deux partout; **they drew for third place** ils ont fait troisième ex æquo
3 *(move)* **to d. ahead of sb** devancer qn; **to d. level with a competitor** arriver à (la) hauteur d'un concurrent; **to d. to an end** tirer *ou* toucher à sa fin; **to d. near** *(of elections, Christmas)* se rapprocher; *(of person)* se rapprocher, s'approcher (**to sb** de qn); **the bird flew away as they drew near** à leur approche l'oiseau s'est envolé; **as they drew nearer, they could see ...** en s'approchant, ils ont vu ...; **to d. to a halt** *(stop)* s'arrêter
4 *(of chimney, pipe etc)* tirer; *(of pump)* aspirer
5 *(in dominoes)* **to d. (from the pool)** piocher
6 *(infuse) (of tea)* infuser
7 *Fin* **to d. at sight** tirer à vue

▸ **draw alongside** **VT INSEP** *(and stop)* se ranger à côté de; *(keep moving)* rouler à la hauteur de; **the train drew alongside the platform** le train s'est rangé le long du quai
VI *(of vehicle)* **to d. alongside of a car/the platform** *(and stop)* se ranger à côté d'une voiture/le long du quai; **the police car drew alongside and signalled him to stop** la voiture de police a roulé à sa hauteur et lui a fait signe d'arrêter

▸ **draw apart** **VT SEP** séparer, écarter
VI *(of people)* se séparer, s'écarter; *(in relationship)* s'éloigner l'un de l'autre; **they drew apart from the rest of the crowd** ils se sont écartés du reste de la foule

▸ **draw aside** **VT SEP** *(person)* tirer *ou* prendre à l'écart; *(chair, suitcase)* tirer en arrière; *(curtain, sheet)* tirer, écarter
VI s'écarter

▸ **draw away** **VT SEP** *(person)* entraîner, détourner (**from sth** de qch); **she drew us away from the other guests** elle nous a entraîné à l'écart des autres invités; **to d. one's hand away** retirer sa main
VI 1 *(of car etc)* s'éloigner; *Sport* **the first half-dozen runners are now beginning to d. away** les six premiers coureurs commencent à devancer les autres; *Sport* **to d. away from a competitor** prendre de l'avance sur un concurrent **2** *(recoil)* reculer, avoir un mouvement de recul

▸ **draw back** **VT SEP 1** *(pull) (table, chair etc)* tirer en arrière; *(sheet, veil etc)* tirer, écarter; *Mil (troops)* retirer; **she drew her hand back**

from the fire elle a retiré sa main du feu; **to d. back the curtains** ouvrir les rideaux **2** *(attract back)* **what drew you back to your home town?** qu'est-ce qui t'a poussé à revenir dans ta ville natale?; **I'm increasingly being drawn back to folk music** je reviens de plus en plus à la musique folk

vt 1 *(recoil)* reculer; **to d. back from making a decision** ne pas vouloir prendre une décision; **caution made him d. back from telling anyone about his new job** par prudence il résista à l'envie de parler à quiconque de son nouveau travail **2** *(from commitment etc)* faire marche arrière

▶ **draw in vt sep 1** *(net)* haler à bord; *(of cat etc) (claws)* rentrer, rétracter; *(of horseman) (reins, bridle)* serrer; *Fig Fam* **to d. in one's horns** faire des économies **2** *(air)* aspirer **3** *(involve) (person)* impliquer; **they're arguing and I don't want to be drawn in** ils se disputent et je ne veux pas y être mêlé

vi 1 *(of days, nights)* diminuer, raccourcir **2** *(of train, bus)* arriver

▶ **draw into vt insep** *(arrive at)* **the train drew into the station** le train entra en gare; **a car drew into the kerb** une voiture s'est rangée le long du trottoir

vt sep *(involve)* **to get drawn into an argument** être mêlé à une dispute; **to d. sb into conversation** entamer une conversation avec qn; **to d. sb into the conversation** faire entrer qn dans la conversation

▶ **draw off vt sep** *(liquid)* soutirer

▶ **draw on vt insep** *(use)* se servir de; **to d. on one's savings** prendre sur ses économies; **to d. on the reserves** puiser dans les réserves; **to d. on sb's experiences for a novel** s'inspirer des expériences de qn pour un roman **2** *(pipe, cigarette)* tirer sur **3** *Fam* **to d. on sb** sortir un revolver et le pointer sur qn

vt sep *(put on)* mettre; **she drew on a pair of gloves** elle a enfilé une paire de gants

vi 1 *(approach)* approcher; **evening was drawing on** la nuit approchait **2** *(go past slowly)* s'avancer; **as the day gradually drew on** au fur et à mesure que la journée avançait; **as time drew on his health improved** avec le temps sa santé s'améliora

▶ **draw out vt sep 1** *(sth from sth)* sortir, retirer; *(nail)* arracher; **to d. money out (of the bank)** retirer de l'argent (de la banque) **2** *(person)* faire sortir de sa réserve; **I managed to d. her out (of herself)** j'ai réussi à la faire sortir de sa réserve **3** *(prolong) (meal, speech)* prolonger; *(situation)* tirer en longueur, (faire) traîner; *Mus (note)* tenir; **they drew the meeting out on purpose** ils ont fait exprès de faire traîner la réunion **4** *Metal (stretch) (iron)* étirer; *(gold)* étendre

vi 1 *(of bus, train etc)* partir; **the train drew out of the station** le train a quitté la gare; *Aut* **to d. out in order to overtake** déboîter pour doubler **2** *(of days)* se prolonger

▶ **draw to vt sep** *(curtains)* tirer, fermer

▶ **draw together vt sep** *(people, objects)* rassembler, réunir; **the child's illness had drawn them together** la maladie de l'enfant les avait rapprochés

vi se rassembler

▶ **draw up vt sep 1** *(pull)* tirer vers le haut; *(heavy object)* hisser; *(water from well)* tirer; **he drew the blankets up to his chin** il ramena les couvertures jusqu'à son menton; **to d. oneself up** se redresser; **she drew herself up to her full height** elle s'est dressée de toute sa hauteur; *Naut* **to d. up a boat (on the beach)** tirer un bateau à sec; **to d. up a chair** approcher une chaise (**to** de)

2 *(prepare) (document)* dresser, rédiger; *(account, budget, itinerary)* établir; *(programme, procedure)* dresser, établir; *(plan)* élaborer; **document drawn up before a lawyer** acte passé devant (un) notaire; *Law* **to d. up a will** dresser un testament; **to d. up**

a commercial bill créer un effet de commerce; **to d. up an invoice** rédiger une facture

3 *(arrange in formation) (troops, chairs)* ranger, aligner

vi 1 *(of car etc)* s'arrêter, stopper; **to d. up at the kerb** se ranger le long du trottoir

2 *(of troops)* se mettre en rang, s'aligner; **to d. up in line** se mettre en ligne

3 **to d. up to the table** s'approcher de la table

---

drawback ['drɔːbæk] **n 1** *(disadvantage)* inconvénient *m*, désavantage *m* (**to** de) **2** *Admin* remboursement *m* (à la sortie) des droits d'importation

drawbar ['drɔːbɑː] **n** *Aut* crochet *m* (d'attelage)

drawbridge ['drɔːbrɪdʒ] **n 1** *(over moat)* pont-levis *m*, *pl* ponts-levis **2** *Constr* pont *m* basculant *ou* à bascule

drawcord ['drɔːkɔːd] **n** *(of curtains etc)* cordon *m*

drawdown ['drɔːdaʊn] **n** *Fin* tirage *m*

drawee [drɔːˈiː] **n** *Com (of bill of exchange)* tiré *m*, payeur *m*

drawer ['drɔːər] **n 1** *Art* dessinateur, -trice; **she's a good d.** *(of child, amateur)* elle dessine bien **2** *Fin* tireur *m*; *(of bill)* souscripteur *m* **3** *(of water)* puiseur, -euse **4** [drɔːr] tiroir *m*; **chest of drawers** commode *f*, *Old-fashioned* **bottom d.** *(trousseau)* trousseau *m* (de mariage); *Old-fashioned Fam* **they're not really (out of the) top d.** ils n'appartiennent pas vraiment à l'élite; *Com* **cash d.** tiroir-caisse *m*, *pl* tiroirs-caisses

drawers ['drɔː(ə)z] **npl** *Old-fashioned* **(pair of) d.** *(for women)* culotte *f*, *(for men)* caleçon *m*

drawing ['drɔːɪŋ] **n 1** *Art (picture, art)* dessin *m*; **to make a d. of sth** dessiner qch; **her talent for d.** son talent pour le dessin; **line d.** dessin au trait; **rough d.** ébauche *f*, croquis *m*; **pencil d.** dessin au crayon; *Ind, Tech* **engineering d.** dessin industriel; **sectional d.** (vue *f* en) coupe *f* **2** *(pulling) (of cart)* tirage *m* **3** *(extraction) (of water)* puisage *m*; *(of teeth)* extraction *f*; *(of lots)* tirage *m* **4** *(attraction)* attraction *f* (**towards** vers) **5** *Com, Fin* **drawings** prélèvements *mpl*, levées *fpl* **6** *Culin (of poultry)* vidage *m* **7** *Metal (of metal)* étirage *m*

▶▶ **d. board** planche *f* à dessin; **d. book** cahier *m* de dessin; **d. card** *Com* valeur *f* sûre; *Am Fig (of festival etc)* attraction *f*, clou *m*; **she's always a big d. card** elle attire toujours beaucoup de monde; **d. off** *(of liquid)* soutirage *m*; **d. office** atelier *m* *ou* bureau *m* d'études; **d. paper** papier *m* à dessin; *Br* **d. pin** punaise *f* (à papier); **d. power** pouvoir *m* d'attraction; *Comput* **d. program** programme *m* de dessin, logiciel *m* de dessin; *Fin* **d. rights** droits *mpl* de tirage; **d. room** *(living room)* salon *m*, *(reception room)* salle *f* *ou* salon de réception; *Am Rail* compartiment *m* privé; **d. up** *(of deed, document, will)* rédaction *f*, *(of constitution, plan)* élaboration *f*, *(of bill, list, budget, itinerary)* établissement *m*

drawl [drɔːl] **n** voix *f* traînante; **to speak with a d./a Texan d.** parler d'une voix traînante/avec un accent Texan; **to speak with an affected d.** traîner la voix avec affectation

vi traîner la voix en parlant, parler d'une voix traînante

vt **...,, he drawled** ..., dit-il d'une voix traînante; **to d. one's vowels** traîner sur les voyelles

▶ **drawl out vt sep** = **drawl vt**

drawling ['drɔːlɪŋ] **adj** *(voice, tone)* traînant **n** affectation *f* de langueur dans le débit

drawn [drɔːn] **adj 1** *(face)* hagard; *(features)* tiré; **to look d.** avoir les traits tirés **2 with d. sword(s)** sabre *m* au clair **3** *(battle)* indécis

▶▶ *Sport* **d. match** match *m* nul; *Sewing* **d.(-thread) work** ouvrage *m* *ou* travail *m* à jour(s)

drawsheet ['drɔːʃiːt] **n** *Med* alaise *f*, alèse *f*

drawstring ['drɔːstrɪŋ] **n** cordon *m*; **d. trousers, trousers with a d. waist** = pantalon *m* qui se ferme par un cordon autour de la taille

dray [dreɪ] **n** *(cart)* haquet *m*, camion *m*

drayhorse ['dreɪhɔːs] **n** cheval *m* de roulage

drayman, *pl* **draymen** ['dreɪmən] **n** conducteur *m* de haquet

dread [dred] **n** terreur *f*, épouvante *f*; **I have a d. of dentists** j'ai la hantise des dentistes; **she has a terrible d. of heights** elle a effroyablement peur du vide; **I have this d. that he'll find out where I am** j'ai la hantise qu'il apprenne où je suis; **she waited in d. for the phone to ring** angoissée, elle attendait que le téléphone sonne; **to be** *or* **stand in d. of sb/sth** craindre *ou* redouter qn/qch

adj attrib *Old-fashioned* redouté

vt redouter, appréhender, craindre; **I'm dreading Monday** je redoute la journée de lundi; **I'm dreading my driving test** j'appréhende de passer le permis de conduire; **to d. that ...** redouter que (ne) ... + *subj*, **I d. to think!** je n'ose même pas y penser!; **I d. having them both here** j'appréhende de les avoir tous les deux en même temps; **the dreaded Monday finally arrived** le lundi si redouté est finalement arrivé; **she said the dreaded words** elle prononça les mots tant redoutés

dreadful ['dredfʊl] **adj 1** *(pain, noise etc)* atroce, épouvantable; **it is d. that nothing can be done** c'est affreux qu'on ne puisse rien faire; **to feel/look d.** ne pas se sentir/avoir l'air bien du tout; **I really feel d. about it!** ça m'ennuie terriblement!; **the shops were d.** *(very busy)* c'était l'horreur dans les magasins; **I'm a d. dancer** je danse atrocement mal; **to be d. at maths** être nul en maths **2** *Fam (intensive)* terrible; **it's a d. bore!** c'est assommant!; **it's a d. pity** *or* **shame** c'est vraiment dommage **3** *Fml (causing dread)* terrible, redoutable

dreadfully ['dredfʊlɪ] **adv 1** terriblement, horriblement; **I was d. frightened** j'avais horriblement peur; **the children behaved d.** les enfants se sont terriblement *ou* horriblement mal conduits; **she suffers d. from backache** son dos la fait atrocement souffrir **2** *Fam (intensive)* terriblement; **d. ugly** affreusement laid; **our neighbours are d. noisy** nos voisins sont terriblement bruyants; **I am d. sorry** je regrette infiniment

dreadlocks ['dredlɒks], **dreads** [dredz] **npl** dreadlocks *fpl*

dream [driːm] **n** rêve *m*, songe *m*; **to have a d.** faire un rêve; **to have a d. about sb/sth** rêver de qn/qch; **to have beautiful/bad dreams** faire de beaux/mauvais rêves; **sweet dreams!** faites de beaux rêves!; **to see sth in a d.** voir qch en rêve *ou* en songe; **to go about in a d.** être comme dans un rêve; **my d. house, the house of my dreams** la maison de mes rêves; **a d. holiday** les vacances de rêve; **it's my d. to go to Australia** je rêve d'aller en Australie; **I've always had this d. that one day I would have ...** j'ai toujours rêvé d'avoir ...; **it's everybody's d. to win the lottery** tout le monde rêve de gagner à la loterie; **I've long cherished a d. to be my own boss** je caresse depuis longtemps le rêve de me mettre à mon compte; *Fam* **a d. of a car** la voiture rêvée; **it's a d.** c'est le rêve; **it's a d. come true** c'est un rêve devenu réalité, mon rêve s'est réalisé; **it worked like a d.** cela a réussi à merveille; *Fam* **in your dreams!** tu peux toujours rêver!; *Austr* **in the d. time** *(of native people)* au temps où l'homme n'était pas encore arrivé sur la terre; *Fig Fam* il y a des siècles

VI *(pt, pp* **dreamt** [dremt]**, dreamed** [driːmd]*)* **1** *(in sleep, daydream)* rêver; **to d. of** *or* **about sb/sth** rêver de qn/qch; **you must have been dreaming!** vous l'avez rêvé!; **to d. of one's youth** rêver à sa jeunesse; *Fam* **d. on!** tu peux toujours rêver! **2** *(think)* **I wouldn't d. of doing it** jamais je ne m'aviserais de faire cela; **I wouldn't d. of it!** je n'y songerais même pas!; **no one would have dreamt of suspecting him** personne n'aurait songé à le soupçonner

VT I dreamt (that) you were ill j'ai rêvé que vous étiez malade; **little did I d. that ...** je ne songeais guère que ...; **I never dreamt you would take me seriously** je n'aurais jamais pensé que tu me prendrais au sérieux; **you must have dreamt it!** vous l'avez rêvé!

▸ *Cin* **d. sequence** séquence *f* onirique; *Sport* **d. team** équipe *f* rêvée; *Pol* **d. ticket** combinaison *f* rêvée; **d. world** monde *m* imaginaire

▸ **dream away** **VT SEP** *(one's time)* passer à rêver; **he'll d. his whole life away** il passera sa vie à rêver

▸ **dream up** **VT SEP** *Fam (idea etc)* inventer, imaginer; **what have you dreamed up now?** qu'est-ce que tu as encore inventé?

dreamboat ['driːmbəʊt] **N** *Old-fashioned Fam (attractive man, woman)* canon *m*

dreamer ['driːmər] **N** rêveur, -euse

dreamily ['driːmɪlɪ] **ADV** *(to look at, smile)* d'un air rêveur; *(to say)* d'un ton rêveur; *(to wander)* comme dans un rêve; **to think d. of the future** rêvasser à l'avenir

dreaming ['driːmɪŋ] **N** rêves *mpl*; **this d. will get you nowhere** ça ne te mènera à rien de rêver comme ça

dreamland ['driːmlænd] **N** le pays *ou* le monde des rêves, le pays des songes

dreamless ['driːmlɪs] **ADJ** *(sleep)* sans rêves

dreamlessly ['driːmlɪslɪ] **ADV** *(to sleep)* d'un sommeil sans rêves

dreamlike ['driːmlaɪk] **ADJ** *(unreal)* onirique

dreamy ['driːmɪ] **ADJ 1** *(person, mood)* rêveur, -euse, songeur, -euse; **d. look/smile** air/sourire rêveur; **the d. look in her eye** son regard rêveur **2** *Fam (wonderful)* magnifique, superbe

drearily ['drɪərɪlɪ] **ADV** tristement; *(to look at)* d'un air morne; *(to say)* d'un ton morne

dreariness ['drɪərɪnɪs] **N** *(of life, countryside etc)* caractère *m* morne, *(of book, speech etc)* platitude *f*, monotonie *f*; **the d. of the weather** la grisaille

dreary ['drɪərɪ] **ADJ** *(weather, countryside)* triste, morne; *(speech, routine, person etc)* morne, ennuyeux; *(diet)* monotone; **we had a d. time (of it)** ce n'était pas très gai

dredge¹ [dredʒ] **N 1** *(boat)* (bateau *m*) dragueur *m* **2** *(machine)* drague *f* **3** *Fishing (net)* (filet *m* de) drague *f*

VT *(canal)* draguer, dévaser; **to d. away mud** enlever la vase avec une drague; **to d. one's memory for sth** chercher qch dans ses souvenirs *ou* sa mémoire

VI to d. for sth draguer à la recherche de qch

▸ **d. bucket** godet *m* de drague; *Fishing* **d. net** (filet *m* de) drague

▸ **dredge up** **VT SEP** *(silt)* enlever avec une drague; *(submerged object)* pêcher *ou* recueillir avec une drague; *Fig (scandal)* déterrer; **to d. sth up out of one's memory** ressortir qch de sa mémoire; **where did you**

d. these old photographs up from? où as-tu été repêcher ces vieilles photos?

dredge² **VT** *Culin* saupoudrer (**with** de); **to d. flour over meat** saupoudrer la viande de farine

dredger¹ ['dredʒər] **N 1** *(boat)* (bateau *m*) dragueur *m* **2** *(machine)* drague *f*, **bucket d.** drague à godets; **grab d.** drague à benne piocheuse **3** *(person)* (ouvrier *m*) dragueur *m*; **oyster d.** dragueur d'huîtres

dredger² **N** *Culin (for sugar etc)* saupoudroir *m*

dredging ['dredʒɪŋ] **N** *(of canal etc)* dragage *m*

dregs [dregz] **NPL 1** *(solid particles)* *(in glass)* lie *f*, fond *m*; *(of coffee)* marc *m*; **to drink sth to the d.** boire qch jusqu'à la lie; *Fig* **the d. of society** les bas-fonds *mpl* de la société **2** *(remainder, residue)* fond *m*

drench [drentʃ] **VT** *(soak)* tremper, mouiller (**with** de); *(earth)* *(of gardener)* arroser abondamment; *(of rain)* détremper; **to d. sb with water/a hosepipe** arroser qn d'eau/avec un tuyau; **to get drenched (with rain)** se faire tremper, *Fam* se faire saucer; **drenched to the skin** trempé jusqu'aux os; **to be drenched with sweat** être en nage

drenching ['drentʃɪŋ] **ADJ** *(rain)* battant, diluvien, -ienne

N we got a d. nous avons été trempés, *Fam* nous nous sommes fait saucer

Dresden ['drezdən] **N** Dresde; *(china)* porcelaine *f* de Saxe

▸ **D. china** porcelaine de Saxe

dress [dres] **N 1** *(for woman)* robe *f*, **ball d.** robe de bal

2 *(attire)* costume *m*; **to wear Western d.** s'habiller à l'occidentale; **evening d.** tenue *f* de soirée; **to be casual in one's d.** s'habiller de façon décontractée; **to have good d. sense** savoir s'habiller; **to have no d. sense** ne pas savoir s'habiller; *Mil* **mess d., formal d.** uniforme *m* de cérémonie *ou* de soirée; **in full d.** *(of men)* en grande tenue; *(of women)* en grande toilette; *Mil* en grande tenue, en uniforme de parade; *Mil* **full d. parade** parade *f* en grande tenue

VT (**dressed** [drest]) **1** *(put clothes on)* *(person)* habiller, vêtir; *Theat (play)* costumer; **to d. oneself, to get dressed** s'habiller; **to be dressed in black/silk** être vêtu de noir/soie; **dressed in rags** vêtu *ou* couvert de haillons; **dressed for the country/for climbing** en tenue de campagne/d'escalade; **I'm not dressed for it** je ne suis pas habillé pour; **well/badly dressed** bien/mal habillé; **to be plainly** *or* **simply dressed** avoir une mise simple, être simplement vêtu; *esp Mil* **to be improperly dressed** ne pas porter la tenue réglementaire; **dressed as a clown/a witch** *(for a party)* déguisé en clown/en sorcière; *Fam* **dressed to kill** sur son trente et un

2 *(decorate)* orner, parer (**sth with sth** qch de qch); *Naut (ship)* pavoiser; **dressed over all** *(of ship)* sous le grand pavois; *Com* **to d. the window** faire la vitrine; *TV etc* **to d. set** habiller le décor; *Old-fashioned* **to d. sb's hair** coiffer qn

3 *Mil (troops, tents etc)* aligner

4 *Med (wound)* panser

5 *Tech (prepare, finish)* *(surface, hide)* apprêter; *(land, fields)* engraisser; *(leather)* corroyer; *(stone)* dresser, tailler; *(wood)* dresser, corroyer; *(ore)* trier; *Culin (poultry, meat)* habiller; *(dish)* accommoder; *(salad)* assaisonner, garnir; **dressed poultry** volaille prête à cuire *ou* parée; **dressed crab** crabe tout préparé pour la table; **dressed timber** bois dégrossi

VI s'habiller; **she dresses like a man** elle s'habille comme un homme; **to d. in black** s'habiller de noir; **to d. (for dinner)** *(of man)*

se mettre en habit; *(of woman)* se mettre en robe du soir; **they always d. for dinner** ils s'habillent toujours pour le dîner

▸ *Theat* **d. circle** premier balcon *m*, corbeille *f*, **d. designer** modéliste *mf*, dessinateur, -trice de mode; *(famous)* couturier, -ière; **d. material** tissu *m* pour robes; *Theat* **d. rehearsal** *(répétition f)* générale *f*, *Fig (practice)* répétition générale; **d. shield** dessous-de-bras *m inv*; **d. shirt** chemise *f* de soirée; **d. suit** habit *m*, tenue *f* de soirée; **d. uniform** uniforme de cérémonie *ou* de soirée

▸ **dress down** **VT SEP** *Fam (reprimand)* passer un savon à

VI s'habiller plus simplement qu'à l'accoutumée

▸ **dress up** **VT SEP 1** *(put elegant clothes on)* **to d. oneself up** se faire beau/belle, s'habiller; **to be all dressed up, to be dressed up to the nines** être sur son trente et un **2** *(put fancy dress on)* **you could d. yourself up as Batman** tu pourrais te déguiser en Batman; **to d. sb up** costumer qn, déguiser qn (**as sth** en qch); *Fig* **we'll have to d. it up a bit** il faudra améliorer un peu la présentation; *Fig* **however you d. it up** de quelque façon qu'on le présente

VI 1 *(wear elegant clothes)* se faire beau/belle, s'habiller **2** *(wear fancy dress)* se déguiser

dressage ['dresɑːʒ] **N** *Horseriding* dressage *m* (supérieur)

dress-down Friday **N** = journée *f* du vendredi où, contrairement au reste de la semaine, les employés sont libres de s'habiller comme ils le souhaitent

dresser ['dresər] **N 1** *(for plates etc)* buffet *m*; **(Welsh) d.** vaisselier *m* **2** *Am (dressing table)* table *f* de toilette, coiffeuse *f* **3** **to be a smart d.** s'habiller avec chic **4** *Theat, Cin, TV* habilleur, -euse **5** *(tool)* *(for wood)* raboteuse *f*, *(for stone)* rabotin *m*

dressing ['dresɪŋ] **N 1** *(putting clothes on)* habillement *m*

2 *Naut (of ship)* pavoisement *m*

3 *Mil (of troops)* alignement *m*

4 *Med (of wound)* pansement *m*; **to apply a d.** mettre *ou* faire un pansement; **surgical d. case** trousse *f* de pansement

5 *Agr* engrais *m*; **a heavy d. of manure** un gros apport de fumier; **surface d., top d.** engrais en couverture, couche *f* d'engrais

6 *Culin (salad)* d. assaisonnement *m*, sauce *f*, **French d.** vinaigrette *f*

7 *Tech (of hide)* apprêt *m*; *(of stone)* dressage *m*, taille *f*, *(of wood)* dressage, corroyage *m*; *(of ore)* préparation *f* mécanique; *Tex* apprêt, empois *m*; *Culin (of poultry)* habillage *m*; *(of dish)* assaisonnement *m*

8 *Am Culin (stuffing)* farce *f*

▸ *Old-fashioned* **d. case** trousse *f* de toilette, nécessaire *m* de toilette; **d. gown** robe *f* de chambre, peignoir *m*; **d. room** *(at home)* dressing-room *m*, pl dressing-rooms, dressing *m*, vestiaire *m*; *(at gym, sports ground)* vestiaire; *Theat* loge *f* (d'acteur); *Am (in shop)* cabine *f* d'essayage; *Mil* **d. station** poste *m* de secours; **d. table** coiffeuse *f*, (table *f* de) toilette *f*; **d.-table set** garniture *f* de toilette; **d. up** *(children's activity)* déguisement *m*

dressing-down **N** *Fam* verte semonce *f*, savon *m*; **to give sb a d.** passer un savon à qn; **to get a d.** se faire passer un savon

dressmaker ['dresmeɪkər] **N** couturier, -ière

dressmaking ['dresmeɪkɪŋ] **N** *(by tailor, dress designer)* couture *f*, *Ind* confection *f* de robes

dress-run **N** *TV, Theat etc* répétition *f* générale

dressy ['dresɪ] **ADJ 1** *(clothes)* chic, élégant;

(party) habillé; **it's a bit d. for a barbecue** c'est un peu trop habillé pour un barbecue; **I wanted something a bit more d.** je cherchais quelque chose d'un peu plus habillé **2** *Pej (person)* trop (élégamment) habillé

drib [drɪb] **N** *only used in* **in dribs and drabs** petit à petit, peu à peu

dribble ['drɪb(ə)l] **N 1** *(of water etc)* petite(s) goutte(s) *f(pl)*; *Fig* **supplies are coming through in dribbles** les approvisionnements sont livrés au compte-gouttes; **there's only a d. left** il n'en reste que quelques gouttes
2 *(of person, dog)* bave *f*
3 *Ftbl etc* dribble *m*
VI 1 *(of water etc) (drop by drop)* dégoutter, tomber goutte à goutte; *(in a trickle)* dégouliner; **the wine dribbled down his chin** le vin lui dégoulina le long du menton; **half the flour/water had dribbled out** la moitié de la farine/l'eau s'était échappée; *Fig* **to d. in/out** *(of people)* entrer/sortir au compte-gouttes; **news has started to d. back** des nouvelles commencent à filtrer
2 *(of baby etc)* baver
3 *Ftbl etc* dribbler
4 *Billiards* **to d. into the pocket** *(of ball)* rouler doucement dans la blouse
VT 1 **to d. (out)** *(liquid)* laisser couler goutte à goutte; **I had dribbled juice all down my tie** je m'étais mis plein de jus de fruit sur la cravate; **d. some oil over it** versez des gouttes d'huile dessus
2 *Ftbl etc (ball)* dribbler
3 *Billiards* **to d. the ball into the pocket** faire rouler tout doucement la bille dans la blouse

dribbler ['drɪblər] **N** *Ftbl etc* dribbleur *m*

dribbling ['drɪblɪŋ] **N 1** *(of baby etc)* écoulement *m* de bave; **people were disgusted by his d.** les gens étaient dégoûtés de le voir baver comme ça **2** *Ftbl etc* dribbling *m*

driblet ['drɪblɪt] **N** *(of water etc)* gouttelette *f*, petite goutte *f*; *Fig* petite somme *f* d'argent; **in driblets** goutte à goutte, au compte-gouttes; *Fig* au compte-gouttes

dried [draɪd] **ADJ** séché

dried-up ADJ *(river bed, lake etc)* asséché; *(grass, bread)* sec; *Fig Pej* **a d. old maid** une vieille bique au cœur aride

drier ['draɪər] **N** = **dryer**

drift [drɪft] **N 1** *(movement)* mouvement *m*; *(of current)* direction *f*, sens *m*; *(of business, events)* cours *m*; *(of plane, ship)* dérive *f*; *(of missile etc)* dérivation *f*; *Constr (of borehole)* déviation *f*; *Electron* glissement *m*; **carried along by the d. of the current** emporté par le courant; *Fig* **policy of d.** politique *f* de laisser-faire; **the d. towards war** la descente vers la guerre; **the d. from the land** la lente désertification des campagnes; **the d. towards the cities** l'exode *m* rural; *Sch* **the d. away from science** le désintéressement envers la science
2 *(meaning) (of person's words)* sens *m* général, portée *f*; **I catch** *or* **follow his d.** je vois où il veut en venir; *Fam* **I get the/your d.** je pige
3 *(of sand, leaves etc)* amoncellement *m*; *Geog* apport(s) *mpl*; *(of snow)* congère *f*
4 *Min (of gallery)* direction *f*; *(passage)* (galerie *f* de) chassage *m*; *(exploratory)* galerie d'exploration
VI 1 *(of boat)* dériver, aller à la dérive; *Aviat* déporter; *(of questions, events)* tendre (**towards sth** vers qch); *Fig* **she's been drifting** elle ne s'est pas fixée; **you can't go on drifting like this** tu ne peux pas continuer à te laisser porter par les événements comme ça; **to d. from job to job** aller d'un travail à un autre; **to let things d.** laisser aller les choses; **to d. apart** *(of friends)* se perdre de

vue; *(of married couple)* devenir peu à peu des étrangers l'un pour l'autre; **wisps of smoke were drifting across the sky** la fumée formait des traînées dans le ciel; **conversation drifted from one subject to another** la conversation passait d'un sujet à un autre; **a few tramps had drifted in** in search of **warmth** attirés par la chaleur, quelques vagabonds étaient entrés; **the cigarette smoke was drifting into his eyes** la fumée de cigarette lui venait dans les yeux; **to d. into war/ crime** être entraîné dans la guerre/vers le crime; **the yacht drifted onto a sandbank** le yacht a dérivé et s'est échoué sur un banc de sable; **the audience started to d. towards the exit** les spectateurs se dirigeaient lentement vers la sortie; **to d. with the current** se laisser aller au fil de l'eau; *Fig* se laisser porter par les événements
2 *(of sand, snow etc)* s'amonceler, s'amasser; *(of snow)* se former en congères, s'amasser; **some snow had drifted in through the open door** de la neige s'était infiltrée par la porte ouverte
VT 1 *(logs)* flotter; *(of current) (something)* entraîner **2** *(of wind) (snow, sand)* amonceler, entasser; **the wind was drifting snow in through the window** de la neige entrait par la fenêtre, portée par le vent
▶▶ **d. ice** glaces *fpl* flottantes *ou* en dérive; *Fishing* **d. net** filet *m* traînant
▶ **drift off VI to d. off (to sleep)** s'assoupir
VT INSEP *Naut, Aviat* **to d. off course** dévier de son cap

drifter ['drɪftər] **N 1** *Fishing* bateau *m* de pêche à filets traînants **2** *Fig* personne *f* qui se laisse aller; **he's been a d. all his life** il ne s'est jamais fixé; **she's a bit of a d.** elle n'a pas vraiment de but dans la vie

drifting ['drɪftɪŋ] **ADJ** *(ship etc)* à la dérive; *(cloud)* traînant; **d.** snow neige *f* soulevée par le vent; **d. banks of fog/cloud** des traînées de brouillard/de nuages
N *(caused by current)* entraînement *m* par le courant; *(caused by wind)* entraînement par le vent; *(formation of drifts) (of snow)* amoncellement *m*; **caused by the d. of the snow across the road** causé par la neige soulevée par le vent en travers de la route

driftwood ['drɪftwʊd] **N** *(in the sea)* bois *m* flottant *ou* flotté; *(on the shore)* bois rejeté *ou* refoulé par la mer

drill¹ [drɪl] **N 1** *Carp, Metal (for wood, metal)* foret *m*, mèche *f*; *(for metal)* foreuse *f*, drille *f*; *(power-driven)* perceuse *f*; *(of dentist)* fraise *f*, **electric d.** perceuse électrique; **hand d.** perceuse à main; **percussion d.** perceuse à percussion; **spoon d.** cuiller *f*, cuillère *f* **2** *Min, Constr* perforateur *m*, perforatrice *f*; *(for taking borings)* sondeuse *f*, sonde *f*; *(for oil)* trépan *m* **3** *(training)* exercice(s) *mpl*; *Fig* **to know the d.** savoir ce qu'il faut faire *ou* comment s'y prendre; *Fam* **what's the d.?** *(what do you want me to do?)* qu'est-ce qu'il y a à faire?; *(for working the photocopier etc)* comment on fait?; *Sch* **verb d.** exercices *mpl* oraux sur les verbes; *Mil*
firing d. instruction *f* du tir; **recruit d.** école *f* du soldat; **rifle d.** maniement *m* du fusil
VT 1 *(well etc)* forer; *(wood, metal)* faire un trou dans; *(hole)* percer; *(tooth)* fraiser **2** *Min (rock etc)* (per)forer **3** *Gym etc (people)* faire faire l'exercice à; *Mil (soldiers)* instruire, exercer; *Naut* **well-drilled crew** équipage bien exercé; *Fam* **to d. sb (in what to do/say)** faire la leçon à qn (sur ce qu'il faut faire/dire); **I can't d. (it) into him that ...** je ne peux pas lui faire comprendre que ...; **it had always been drilled into her that ...** on lui avait enfoncé dans la tête que ...; **to d. good manners into sb** enseigner les bonnes manières à qn; *Sch* **to d. pupils in French**

verbs faire faire aux élèves des exercices oraux sur les verbes français
VI 1 *Petr* forer; **to d. for oil** forer pour trouver du pétrole **2** *(do exercises)* s'exercer, s'entraîner; *(of troops)* faire l'exercice
▶▶ **d. bit** foret, mèche; **d. chuck** mandrin *m* *(de tour)* porte-mèche; **d. ground** terrain *m* d'exercice *ou* de manœuvres; **d. hole** trou *m* à la foreuse; *Petr* trou de forage; *Mil* **d. sergeant** sergent *m* instructeur

drill² *Agr* **N 1** *(row)* rayon *m*, sillon *m*; **to sow the grain in drills** semer la graine en rayons **2** *(machine)* semoir *m* (à cuillers)
VT semer en rayons
▶▶ **d. harrow** herse *f* à semer

drill³ **N** *Tex* coutil *m*; *(for denims etc)* treillis *m*

drilling ['drɪlɪŋ] **N 1** *Metal* forage *m*, perçage *m*; *Min (of rock etc)* perforation *f*, *Min (of well)* forage, sondage *m* **2** *Petr* forage *m* **3** *(of tooth)* fraisage *m* **4** *Mil* exercices *mpl*, manœuvres *fpl*
▶▶ **d. machine** foreuse *f*, **d. mud** boue *f* (de forage); **d. operations** opérations *fpl* de forage; *Petr* **d. platform** plate-forme *f* (de forage), *pl* plates-formes; *Petr* **d. rig** *(on land)* derrick *m*, tour *f* de forage; *(at sea)* plate-forme (de forage)

drily ['draɪlɪ] **ADV = dryly**

DRINK [drɪŋk]

N boisson **1** ▪ verre **1** ▪ alcool **1**
VT boire
VI boire **1, 2**

N 1 boisson *f*, *(said by waiter, barkeeper etc)* consommation *f*; *(alcoholic)* verre *m*, *Fam* pot *m*; **to give sb food and d.** donner à boire et à manger à qn; **to give sb a d.** donner à boire à qn; **to have a d.** boire *ou* prendre quelque chose; **I'd love a d. of water** je voudrais bien un verre d'eau; **will you join me in a d.?** tu prends un verre avec moi?; **pour yourself a d.** sers-toi un verre *ou* à boire; **we're going for a d.** nous allons prendre un verre *ou Fam* un pot; **how about a d. after work?** on prend un verre *ou Fam* un pot après le travail?; **to pay for the drinks** payer les consommations; **I haven't had a d. in six months** je n'ai pas bu d'alcool depuis six mois; **long d.** = gin/vodka/*etc* allongé de jus d'orange *ou* de limonade/*etc*; **short d.** = gin/whisky/*etc* non dilué; **strong d.** *(spirits)* boissons fortes; **soft drinks** boissons sans alcool; **to take to d.** s'adonner à la boisson, se mettre à boire; **to have a d. problem** *(trop)* boire; **to smell of d.** sentir l'alcool; **to be the worse for d.** être plein *ou* ivre; **he can't hold his d.** *(gets drunk quickly)* il ne tient pas l'alcool; *(vomits)* il vomit le moindre verre d'alcool; *Fam* **I didn't mean it, it was the d. talking** je n'étais pas sérieux, j'avais juste un peu trop bu; **to be under the influence of d.** avoir trop bu; *Law* **to drive a car while under the influence of d.** conduire en état d'ébriété; **to drive sb to d.** pousser qn à l'ivrognerie; **drinks dispenser** *or* **machine** distributeur *m* automatique de boissons
2 *Fam* **the d. (sea)** la baille; **to fall into the d.** tomber à la baille
VT *(pt* **drank** [dræŋk], *pp* **drunk** [drʌŋk], *Arch* **drunken** ['drʌŋkən] *(water etc)* boire; **will you have something to d.?** voulez-vous boire *ou* prendre quelque chose?; **what are you drinking?** qu'est-ce que tu prends *ou* bois?; **to d. sb's health** boire à la santé de qn; **to d. sb under the table** faire rouler qn sous la table; **the wine is best drunk at room temperature** ce vin se boit chambré; **fit to d.** bon à boire, potable
VI 1 *(take in liquid)* boire; **to d. straight from the bottle** boire à la bouteille
2 *(take alcohol)* boire, être adonné à la

boisson; **I don't d.** je ne bois pas; **to d. heavily** s'alcooliser; **you're drinking yourself to death** l'alcool est en train de te détruire; **to d. oneself into debt** s'endetter à cause de la boisson; **don't d. and drive** ≃ boire ou conduire, il faut choisir; **to d. like a fish** boire comme un trou; **to d. to sb** boire à la santé de qn; **to d. to sth** arroser qch; **I'll d. to that!** et comment!

3 *(of wine)* the wine is now drinking superbly ce vin a atteint toute sa saveur; **it won't d. quite as well in two years' time** dans deux ans il aura perdu de sa saveur

▸ **drink away** VT SEP *(one's pay)* boire

▸ **drink down** VT SEP *(water etc)* boire, avaler

▸ **drink in** VT SEP *(person's words)* boire; *(scenery, fresh air)* se délecter de, se repaître de

▸ **drink off** VT SEP *(glass)* boire d'un coup; *(bottle)* avaler

▸ **drink up** VT SEP finir (de boire); **I want you to d. that all up!** *(not leave any)* bois tout! VI **d. up!** videz votre verre/vos verres!

drinkable ['drɪŋkəb(ə)l] ADJ buvable; *(water)* potable; **the wine's very d.** ce vin se laisse boire

drink-driver N *Br Fam* conducteur, -trice ivre; **he's a notorious d.** tout le monde sait qu'il conduit souvent en état d'ébriété

drink-driving N *Br Fam* **he was arrested for d.** il a été arrêté pour conduite en état d'ivresse

drinker ['drɪŋkər] N buveur, -euse; **I'm not much of a d.** je ne bois pas beaucoup; **wine/beer/tea drinkers** buveurs de vin/de bière/de thé; **he's a heavy** *or* **hard d.** il boit beaucoup; **she's a social d.** elle ne boit que pour les grandes occasions

drinking ['drɪŋkɪŋ] ADJ **I'm not a d. man** je n'ai pas l'habitude de boire

N **1** boire *m* **2** *(to excess)* ivrognerie *f*, alcoolisme *m*; **d. bout** beuverie *f*; **they'd been doing some heavy d.** ils avaient beaucoup bu; **it was her d. that destroyed the marriage** c'est son alcoolisme qui a détruit leur mariage; **d. companions** compagnons *mpl* de boisson;

▸▸ **d. chocolate** chocolat *m* à boire; *(powder)* chocolat *m* en poudre; *(hot drink)* chocolat *m* chaud; **d. fountain** *(in street)* fontaine *f* publique; *(in corridor, public conveniences)* jet *m* d'eau potable; **d. laws** = lois *fpl* sur les débits de boissons; **d. song** chanson *f* à boire; **d. straw** paille *f*; **d. trough** abreuvoir *m*; **d. water** eau *f* potable

drinking-up time N *Br* = dans les pubs, temps *m* accordé aux clients pour finir leur verre après l'heure de fermeture officielle

drip [drɪp] N **1** *(sound)* **the d. of water** le bruit de l'eau qui s'écoule; **the d. of a tap** le bruit d'un robinet qui goutte **2** *(drop)* goutte *f*; **there's a d. coming from the ceiling** le plafond goutte, il tombe des gouttes du plafond; **you're getting drips all over the floor** tu fais tomber des gouttes partout sur le sol; **the drips from the trees** les gouttes qui tombent/tombaient des arbres; **the d. method of making coffee** la méthode filtre de faire le café **3** *Med* goutte-à-goutte *m inv*; **he's on a d.** il est sous perfusion **4** *Sl (feeble person)* **he's/she's a d.** c'est un mou/une molle, c'est un ramolli/une ramollie

VI (-pp-) *(of rain, water)* tomber goutte à goutte, (dé)goutter; **the perspiration was dripping from his forehead** la sueur lui dégouttait du front, son front était ruisselant de sueur; **just leave it to d.** *(of shirt etc)* laisse-le s'égoutter; **the tap has been dripping all night** le robinet a fui *ou* goutté toute la nuit

VT *(liquid)* faire dégoutter, laisser tomber goutte à goutte; **you're dripping water/**

paint everywhere! tu mets des gouttes d'eau/de peinture partout!; **the ceiling was dripping water** le plafond gouttait, des gouttes d'eau tombaient du plafond

▸▸ *Mktg* **d. advertising** publicité *f* continue, publicité goutte à goutte; *Tech* **d. feed** *(for oil)* distributeur *m* compte-gouttes; *Tech* **d.-feed lubricator** (graisseur *m*) compte-gouttes *m inv*; **d. mat** dessous-de-verre *m inv*

drip-dry ADJ *Tex (shirt etc)* ne nécessitant aucun repassage

drip-feed VT *(pt, pp* **drip-fed**) *Med (patient)* nourrir *ou* alimenter par perfusion

drip-feeding N alimentation *f* par perfusion

dripping ['drɪpɪŋ] ADJ ruisselant; *(tap)* qui goutte; **to be d. wet** être trempé; **d. with perspiration/blood** ruisselant de sueur/sang; *Fig* **to be d. with jewels** être couvert de bijoux

N **1** égouttement *m* **2** *Br Culin* graisse *f* de rôti; **bread and d.** tartine *f* à la graisse;

▸▸ *Br Culin* **d. pan** lèchefrite *f*

drippy ['drɪpɪ] ADJ *Fam (person)* mou, *f* molle; *(film, novel) (inane)* plat, fade; *(sentimental)* mélo

DRIVE [draɪv]

N promenade en voiture **1**	• conduite **2–4** • dynamisme **6** • campagne **7** • allée **9**
VT conduire **1, 2**	• pousser **3** • surmener **4** • faire marcher **7**
VI conduire **1**	• aller en voiture **1** • rouler **1**

N **1** *Aut (trip)* promenade *f* en voiture; *(in taxi)* course *f*; **a 50-km d.** un parcours *ou* un trajet de 50 km; **it's an hour's d. away** c'est à une heure en voiture; **to go for** *or* **take a d.** aller faire une promenade *ou* un (petit) tour en voiture, faire une promenade en voiture; **it's a very pleasant d. to the coast** la route est très belle jusqu'à la côte; *Aut* **test d.** conduite *f* d'essai

2 *(of cattle)* conduite *f*, *(of deer)* battue *f*, *Am (guiding of logs)* (transport *m* du bois par le) flottage *m*, *Can* drave *f*, *(logs)* train *m* (de bois flotté)

3 *Tech (mouvement m de)* propulsion *f*, *(by component)* commande *f*, transmission *f*, actionnement *m*; *Aut (for any shaft)* entraînement *m*; *(on automatic gearbox)* conduite *f* normale; **belt/chain d.** entraînement *ou* transmission par courroie/chaîne; **gear d.** commande par engrenages; *Aut* **direct d.** prise *f* directe; *(for interdependent parts)* courroie de commande

4 *Aut (location of steering wheel)* conduite *f*, **left-hand d.** conduite à gauche; **car with left-hand d.** voiture *f* avec conduite à gauche

5 *(shot) Golf, Tennis* drive *m*; *Cr* coup *m* droit long et appuyé

6 *Fig (initiative)* énergie *f*, dynamisme *m*; **to have plenty of d.** être énergique *ou* entreprenant

7 *(campaign) (to increase sales etc)* campagne *f*, *(against stronghold, abuse)* offensive *f*, **membership d.** campagne *f* pour attirer des membres

8 *Psy (urge) (sexual etc)* pulsions *fpl*

9 *(of house)* allée *f*; **the car's sitting in the d.** la voiture est garée dans l'allée

10 *Cards (for bridge, whist)* tournoi *m*

11 *Comput (for disk)* lecteur *m*, unité *f*; **d. a:/ b:** unité de disque a:/b:

VT *(pt* **drove** [drəʊv]*, pp* **driven** ['drɪv(ə)n]*)* **1** *(car, train)* conduire; *(racing car)* conduire, piloter; *Horseracing (trotting horse)* driver; **can you d. a car?** savez-vous conduire?; **to d. sb to a place** conduire qn en voiture

quelque part; **I haven't driven all this way just to …** je n'ai pas fait tout ce chemin juste pour …

2 *(cattle)* conduire, mener; *(deer etc)* rabattre; *(prisoners)* faire aller (devant soi); *(log train)* diriger; **thousands of people have been driven from their homes** des milliers de personnes ont été obligées de quitter leur maison; **to d. the enemy from his position** déloger l'ennemi; **the wind is driving the rain against the window panes** le vent rabat la pluie contre les vitres; **the waves drove the ship onto the rocks** les vagues ont poussé le navire contre les rochers

3 *(force) (sb to do sth)* pousser; **I was driven to resign** j'ai été forcé de démissionner; **he won't be driven** on ne le mène pas comme on veut; **to d. sb mad** *or* **out of his/her mind** rendre qn fou/folle; **she drove me to it** c'est elle qui m'y a poussé; **to d. sb to despair** réduire qn au désespoir; **to be driven by ambition** être mû par l'ambition

4 *(one's employees)* surmener; **to d. oneself too hard** se surmener; **she drives herself as hard as she drives us** elle se surmène autant qu'elle nous surmène

5 to d. a bargain conclure un marché; **to d. a hard bargain** chercher à gagner le dernier centime, négocier serré

6 to d. the ball *Cr* chasser la balle; *Tennis* jouer un drive, driver; *Golf* driver

7 *Tech (machine)* actionner, faire marcher; *(of part) (component)* actionner; *Comput (of program)* commander, piloter; **to be driven by electricity** fonctionner à l'électricité

VI **1** *Aut* conduire; **can you d.?** savez-vous conduire?; **I don't d.** *(I never learned)* je n'ai pas mon permis; **who was driving?** qui était au volant?; **to d. to work** aller ou se rendre au travail en voiture; **to d. slowly/fast** rouler lentement/vite; **to d. on the right (of the road)** circuler à droite, tenir la droite; **car that drives well** voiture facile à conduire

2 the rain driving against the window panes la pluie qui fouette les vitres; *Lit* **to d. before the wind** *(of clouds etc)* chasser devant le vent

▸▸ *Aut* **d. belt** courroie *f* d'entraînement; *Comput* **d. door** porte *f* de l'unité de disquette; *Aut* **d. shaft** arbre *m* d'entraînement *ou* de commande

▸ **drive along** VI rouler (en voiture); **I was driving along slowly** je roulais lentement; **to d. along the road** rouler sur la route

▸ **drive at** VT INSEP **what are you driving at?** où voulez-vous en venir?; **what do you think she was driving at?** où croyez-vous qu'elle voulait en venir?

▸ **drive away** VT SEP **1** *(dog, intruder)* chasser, éloigner, écarter; *(lover, spouse)* faire partir; *(friend)* éloigner; *(doubt, suspicion)* écarter; *(fear)* chasser

2 *Aut (person)* emmener en voiture; **the men came in a car and drove her away** des hommes sont arrivés et l'ont emmenée en voiture; **they were driven away in a taxi** ils ont été conduits en taxi

VI partir *ou* s'en aller en voiture; *(of car, bus)* s'éloigner; **he jumped into his car and drove away** il a sauté dans sa voiture et s'en est allé

▸ **drive back** VT SEP **1** *(repel) (attack, demonstrators)* repousser; *(of flames)* faire reculer

2 *Aut (person)* reconduire *ou* ramener en voiture

VI *Aut* rentrer en voiture

▸ **drive down** VT SEP **1** *Econ (prices, inflation etc)* faire baisser

2 *Aut* **to d. sb down to London** conduire qn à Londres

VI *Aut (from north to south)* se rendre en voiture; **how did you get here? – we drove down** comment êtes-vous venus? – nous sommes venus *ou* descendus en voiture; **to d. down to Marseilles** descendre à Marseille en voiture; **she had driven down from Inverness the day before** elle était descendue d'Inverness en voiture la veille

▸ **drive home** VT SEP **1** *(nail)* enfoncer, renfoncer

2 *(make understood)* **to d. sth home to sb** faire comprendre qch à qn, *Fam* faire rentrer qch dans la tête de qn; **d. it home to them that they mustn't speak to strangers** faisleur comprendre qu'ils ne doivent pas parler à des inconnus

3 *Aut* **to d. sb home** reconduire qn chez lui

▸ **drive in** VT SEP *(nail)* enfoncer

VI *Aut (into garage)* entrer (en voiture); **he had driven in from the countryside** il était venu de la campagne en voiture

▸ **drive into** VT SEP **to d. a nail into the wall** enfoncer un clou dans le mur; **he drove his fist into the other man's face** il a mis un coup de poing à l'autre

VT INSEP *Aut (garage)* entrer dans (en voiture); **I'm driving into town** je vais en ville en voiture

▸ **drive off** VT SEP **1** *(repel) (attack, attackers)* repousser; *(mosquitoes)* chasser

2 *Aut (person)* emmener en voiture; **they were driven off in a taxi** ils ont été conduits en taxi

VI **1** *Aut* partir *ou* s'en aller en voiture; *(of car, bus)* s'éloigner; **he jumped into his car and drove off** il a sauté dans sa voiture et s'en est allé

2 *Golf* commencer la partie

▸ **drive on** VT SEP *(somebody)* pousser (**to do sth** à faire qch)

VI *Aut* continuer (sa route); **the policeman told us to d. on** le gendarme nous a dit de circuler

▸ **drive out** VT SEP *(somebody, something)* chasser; **I will not be driven out of my home** on ne me chassera pas de ma maison; **we're being driven out of business by the supermarkets** les supermarchés nous font faire faillite

VI *Aut* **he had driven out from Glasgow** il était venu de Glasgow en voiture; **he drove out of the petrol station** il est sorti de la station d'essence

▸ **drive through** VT SEP *Constr* **to d. a tunnel through rock** percer *ou* forer un tunnel dans le rocher; *Constr* **to d. a railway through the desert** tracer *ou* construire une ligne de chemin de fer à travers le désert; **to d. one's sword through sb's body** passer son sabre à travers le corps à qn

VT INSEP *Aut (town)* traverser en voiture

VI *Aut* passer en voiture; **we'll just d. through** *(not stop)* nous ne ferons que passer en voiture

▸ **drive up** VT SEP *Econ (prices, inflation etc)* faire monter

VI *Aut* s'approcher; **they've just driven up** ils viennent de s'approcher; **a car drove up to the door** une voiture vint s'arrêter devant la porte

driveability [draɪvəˈbɪlɪtɪ] N *(of vehicle)* facilité *f ou* agrément *m* de conduite

drive-in N *(cinema)* = cinéma *m* en plein air auquel on assiste en voiture, drive-in *m inv*, *Can* ciné-parc *m, pl* cinés-parcs; *(restaurant)* = restaurant *m* où les clients sont servis dans leurs voitures; *(bank)* = banque *f* dont les guichets sont accessibles aux clients depuis leur voiture

drivel [ˈdrɪv(ə)l] *Fam* N bêtises *fpl*, balivernes *fpl*; **to talk d.** radoter; **the film was absolute d.** le film n'était qu'un tas de balivernes

VI (**-ll-,** *Am* **-l-**) radoter; **what are you drivelling (on) about?** qu'est-ce que tu radotes?

driveline [ˈdraɪvlaɪn] N *Aut* chaîne *f* cinématique

drivelling, *Am* **driveling** [ˈdrɪv(ə)lɪŋ] ADJ *Fam* radoteur, -euse; **you d. idiot!** espèce d'idiot!

driven [ˈdrɪv(ə)n] ADJ **1** *(person)* mû comme par une obsession **2** *Tech* **electrically d.** actionné par l'électricité

▸▸ **d. snow** neige *f* vierge

driver [ˈdraɪvər] N **1** *(of car, bus)* conducteur, -trice, chauffeur, -euse; *(of taxi, truck)* chauffeur, -euse; *(of train)* mécanicien, -ienne; *(of tram)* mécanicien, -ienne, wattman *m*; *(of horse-drawn vehicle)* conducteur, -trice; *(of horse-drawn carriage)* cocher *m*; *Horseracing (of trotting horse)* driver *m*; **he's a very good/bad d.** il conduit très bien/mal **2** *Comput (software)* programme *m* de gestion, pilote *m*, gestionnaire *m* (de périphérique) **3** *(of cattle)* conducteur *m* **4** *log* **d.** flotteur *m*, driver *m*, *Can* draveur *m* **5** *Golf* driver *m*

▸▸ *Am* **d.'s license** permis *m* de conduire; **d.'s seat** siège *m* du conducteur; *Fig* **to be in the d.'s seat** mener l'affaire; **that win really puts them in the d.'s seat** cette victoire les met dans une position dominante

drive-time programme N *Radio* = émission *f* aux heures de grande écoute en voiture

drivetrain [ˈdraɪvtreɪn] N *Aut* chaîne *f* cinématique

driveway [ˈdraɪvweɪ] N *(of house)* allée *f*

driving [ˈdraɪvɪŋ] ADJ **1** *Tech (wheel etc)* moteur, -trice **2** *(rain)* battant; **d. snow** neige *f* fouettée par le vent

N **1** *(of car etc)* conduite *f*; **d. is fun** c'est amusant de conduire; **his d. is awful** il conduit affreusement mal **2** *log* **d.** flottage *m* du bois, *Can* drave *f*

▸▸ *Aut* **d. axle** essieu *m* moteur; *Tech* **d. belt** courroie *f* de commande; **d. conditions** conditions *fpl* de conduite; *Tech* **d. force** force *f* motrice; *Fig* **the d. force behind the scheme** le moteur du projet; **d. gear** (engrenage *m* de) transmission *f*, pignon *m* d'entraînement; *Br* **d. instructor** moniteur, -trice de conduite *ou* d'auto-école; *Golf* **d. iron** grand fer *m*, driver *m*; **d. lamp** feu *m* de route; **d. lessons** leçons *fpl* de conduite; *Br* **d. licence** permis *m* de conduire; **d. mirror** rétroviseur *m*; **d. school** auto-école *f, pl* autoécoles; **d. seat** place *f* du conducteur; *Tech* **d. shaft** arbre *m* moteur; **d. test** examen *m* du permis de conduire; *Tech* **d. wheel** roue *f* motrice; *(of locomotive etc)* roue de transmission

drizzle [ˈdrɪz(ə)l] N bruine *f*, crachin *m*; **the rain came down in a steady d.** il tombait un crachin persistant

VI bruiner; **it was drizzling** il bruinait

drizzly [ˈdrɪz(ə)lɪ] ADJ *(day)* bruineux

drogue [drəʊɡ] N **1** *Naut* cône-ancre *m, pl* cônes-ancres **2** *Aviat (for slowing descent)* parachute *m* de queue

droll [drəʊl] ADJ drôle, comique; *Iron* **oh, very d.!** très drôle!

dromedary [ˈdrɒməd(ə)rɪ] N dromadaire *m*

drone [drəʊn] N **1** *(bee)* abeille *f* mâle, fauxbourdon *m, pl* faux-bourdons; *Fig Pej (parasite)* fainéant *m*, parasite *m* **2** *(noise) (of bee, conversation, traffic)* bourdonnement *m*; *(of engine)* ronronnement *m*; *Mus (of bagpipe)* bourdon *m*; *Fig (of speaker etc)* débit *m* monotone **3** *Mil, Aviat* avion *m* téléguidé, drone *m*

VI *(of bee etc)* bourdonner; *(of engine)* ronronner; *Fig (of person)* parler d'un ton monotone; **a droning sound** un bourdonnement; **a droning voice** une voix monotone

VT dire d'un ton monotone

▸ **drone away, drone on** VI **he droned on for hours** il n'a pas cessé de parler de sa voix

monotone; **to d. on** *or* **away about sth** parler de qch ad nauseam

drongo [ˈdrɒŋɡəʊ] N *Austr Fam (idiot)* abruti, -ie

drool [druːl] VI *(dribble)* baver; *Fig (gloat)* baver d'admiration; *Fig* **the sight of her in her bikini made him d.** ça le faisait baver de la voir dans son bikini®

▸ **drool over** VT INSEP *(something)* baver d'admiration à la vue de

droop [druːp] N **he could tell from the d. of her shoulders/head** il savait à ses épaules tombantes/à la façon dont elle penchait la tête

VI *(of head)* (se) pencher; *(of shoulders, moustache)* tomber; *(of eyelids)* s'abaisser; *(of feathers)* pendre; *(of flower)* commencer à se faner; *Fig (of person)* languir; **his spirits drooped at the thought** cette pensée le démoralisa

VT *(head)* baisser, pencher

drooping [ˈdruːpɪŋ] ADJ *(shoulders, moustache)* tombant; *(head)* baissé, penché; *(eyelids)* abaissé; *(flower)* qui commence à faner; *Fig (person)* languissant; **to revive sb's d. spirits** remonter le moral à qn

droopy [ˈdruːpɪ] ADJ *(moustache)* tombant; *Fig (weak, not very well)* patraque, mal fichu

DROP [drɒp]

N	goutte **1** ▪ baisse **2** ▪ chute **2**
VI	tomber **1–3** ▪ se laisser tomber **1** ▪ baisser **3**
VT	laisser tomber **1, 4** ▪ baisser **2** ▪ déposer **3** ▪ abandonner **4** ▪ omettre **5** ▪ perdre **6**

N **1** *(of water, blood)* goutte *f*, *(of wine)* doigt *m*, larme *f*, *(of vinegar)* filet *m*; *(of necklace, chandelier etc)* pendant *m*, pendeloque *f*; **d. by d.** goutte à goutte; *Fig* **it's only a d. in the ocean** *or* **bucket** ce n'est qu'une goutte d'eau dans la mer; *Pharm* **drops** gouttes; *Fam* **to take a d.** boire un verre; **you've had a d. too much (to drink)** tu as un peu trop bu; **he likes a wee d.** il aime bien prendre la goutte; **I haven't touched a d. since** je n'y ai pas touché depuis; **acid d.** bonbon *m* acidulé; **chocolate d.** pastille *f* de chocolat

2 *(fall) (in price, enrolments etc)* chute *f*, baisse *f*, *(in pressure)* perte *f*, chute; **a d. of a couple of inches** une différence de niveau de quelques centimètres; **a d. of a hundred metres** *(sharp)* un à-pic de cent mètres; **careful, it's a long d.** attention, c'est haut; **d. in the ground** dénivellation *f* du terrain; *Fig* **at the d. of a hat** sans hésiter, sans la moindre hésitation; *(without any warning)* sur-lechamp, immédiatement; **he gets angry at the d. of a hat** il se met en colère pour un oui pour un rien

3 *Aviat* parachutage *m*, droppage *m*

4 *Old-fashioned Fam* **the d.** *(hanging)* la potence; **he's for the d.** il est bon pour la potence; *Fig Hum* **son compte est bon**

5 *(for spies to leave letters etc)* boîte aux lettres *f*, planque *f*

6 *Fam* **to have/get the d. on sb** *(have advantage)* avoir/prendre l'avantage sur qn

7 *(length) (of curtain, blind, earring)* hauteur *f*

VI (**-pp-** [drɒpt]) **1** *(of object)* tomber; *(of person)* se laisser tomber; *(of ground)* s'abaisser, s'affaisser; *Med (of womb etc)* descendre; **the book dropped from** *or* **out of her hands** le livre lui tomba des mains; **his jaw dropped** il en est resté bouche bée; **to d. into a chair** s'affaler dans un fauteuil; **I'm ready to d.** *(with fatigue)* je tombe de fatigue, je ne tiens plus sur mes jambes; *(with sleep)* je tombe de sommeil; **people are dropping like flies** *(succumbing quickly to flu etc)* les gens tombent comme des mouches; **to d. (down)**

dead tomber (raide) mort; *Sl* **d. dead!** va te faire voir!; **he can d. dead for all I care** il peut aller se faire voir; **he's dropped to sixth place** il est descendu à la sixième place; **to d. to the rear** passer à l'arrière; *Fam* **let it d.!** n'en parlons plus!; **I'm not going to let it d.** *(grievance etc)* je ne vais pas laisser passer cela

2 *(of liquid)* tomber doucement (**from** de); *(of rain)* tomber

3 *(of prices, temperature, voice etc)* baisser; *(of share prices)* reculer; *(of wind)* tomber; *(of speed)* diminuer; **the pound dropped three points against the dollar** la livre a reculé de *ou* a perdu trois points par rapport au dollar; **interest rates have dropped by 1%** les taux d'intérêt ont baissé de 1%

vt 1 *(object)* laisser tomber, lâcher; *(bomb, parachutist)* lâcher; *Naut (anchor)* jeter, mouiller; *Comput (icon)* lâcher; **d. it!** *(to dog)* lâche ça!; **he dropped it from the balcony to his accomplice** il l'a lancé à son complice depuis le balcon; **to d. a word in sb's ear** glisser *ou* couler un mot à l'oreille de qn; **to d. a letter into the pillar box** mettre une lettre à la poste; **to d. sb a line/a card** envoyer *ou* écrire un mot/une carte à qn

2 *(lower) (one's eyes, veil, curtain)* baisser; *(one's arms)* laisser tomber; **to d. a curtsey** faire une révérence; **to d. the hem of a dress** allonger une robe; *Aviat* **to d. a wing** piquer de l'aile

3 *(set down) Aut (person)* déposer, descendre *(de voiture)*; *Naut (pilot)* débarquer

4 *(give up, stop) (work)* abandonner, délaisser; *(pursuit)* cesser, lâcher; **to d. the idea of doing sth** renoncer à (l'idée de) faire qch; **I've dropped the idea** j'y ai renoncé; **let's d. the subject** ne parlons plus de cela!; *Fam* **d. it!** en voilà assez!; **just d. it, okay?** laisse tomber, hein?; **to d. everything** laisser tout tomber; *Sch* **to d. maths** arrêter les maths; **to d. sb** laisser tomber qn; *Fam* **to d. sb like a hot brick** *or* **potato** laisser tomber qn du jour au lendemain; *Sport* **to d. a player** laisser tomber un équipier; **she's been dropped from the team** elle a été écartée de l'équipe; *Law* **to d. the charges** abandonner l'accusation *(against* contre)

5 *(omit) (letter, syllable)* omettre, supprimer; *(when speaking) (the r etc)* ne pas prononcer; **cases in which the article is dropped** cas où l'on supprime l'article; **you can d. the 'sir' when we're on our own** inutile de m'appeler 'monsieur' quand nous sommes seuls

6 *(lose) (money, Sport points, serve, stitch)* perdre

7 *Zool (of sheep etc) (young)* mettre bas

▸▸ *Aut* **d. arm** bielle *f* pendante; *Theat* **d. curtain** rideau *m* d'entr'acte; *Metal* **d. forge** marteau-pilon *m*, *pl* marteaux-pilons; *Sport* **d. goal** *(in rugby)* drop-goal *m*, *pl* drop-goals, drop *m*; *Metal* **d. hammer** marteau-pilon, *pl* marteaux-pilons; **d. handlebars** guidon *m* renversé; *Sport* **d. kick** *(in rugby)* coup *m* de pied tombé; **d.-leaf table** table *f* à battants; *Comput, Typ* **d. letter** lettrine *f*; *Tennis* **d. shot** amorti *m*; *Aut* **d. test** essai *m* de chute

▸ **drop away** *vi (of support, attendance etc)* diminuer

▸ **drop back** *vi* = **drop behind** *vi*

▸ **drop behind** *vi (in race)* se laisser distancer; *(with work)* prendre du retard (**with** dans); **she dropped behind to talk to John** elle est passée vers l'arrière pour parler à John

vt insep *(somebody)* se laisser distancer par

▸ **drop by** *vi* passer (chez qn); **I thought I'd d. by for a chat** je me suis dit que je passerais pour bavarder deux minutes

▸ **drop down** *vi* **1** *(of person) (accidentally)* tomber par terre; *(deliberately)* se mettre par *ou* à terre; **to d. down dead** tomber (raide) mort; **they dropped down into the Second Division** ils sont descendus en deuxième division

2 *(of flap etc)* s'abaisser

▸ **drop in** *vt sep (something)* laisser tomber dedans, mettre dedans; **d. this letter in the box for me** mets cette lettre à la boîte; *Fam* **you dropped me right in it** tu m'as mis dans la merde

vi to d. in at the butcher's passer chez le boucher; **to d. in on sb** *(arrive unexpectedly)* venir en visite chez qn à l'improviste; **I'll d. in on my way home** *(to see you)* je passerai (chez toi) en rentrant; **they're always dropping in on us** ils nous tombent toujours dessus à l'improviste

▸ **drop off** *vt sep* **1** *(deposit) (letter, parcel etc)* déposer

2 *(let out of car) (person)* déposer; **where do you want to be dropped off?** où veux-tu que je te dépose?

vi 1 *(fall, become detached) (of leaves etc)* tomber, se détacher; **I feel as if my arm is going to d. off** *(because this case is so heavy etc)* j'ai l'impression que mon bras va lâcher

2 *Fam* **to d. off (to sleep)** s'assoupir, s'endormir; **it was two o'clock before I finally dropped off** je ne me suis pas endormi avant deux heures du matin; **she dropped off for a few hours** elle a dormi quelques heures

3 *(decline) (of membership, attendance etc)* diminuer

▸ **drop out** *vt sep* laisser tomber dehors; **he dropped it out of the window** il l'a laissé tomber par la fenêtre

vi 1 *(from pocket, briefcase etc)* tomber

2 *Fam (from school)* abandonner ses études; *(from class)* abandonner *ou* laisser tomber (un cours); *(from contest)* se retirer; *(from society)* rejeter la société; **he dropped out at the age of 14** il a abandonné ses études à 14 ans; **to d. out of university** laisser tomber l'université

▸ **drop round** *vi* = **drop in** *vi*

drop-dead gorgeous *adj Fam* hyper canon

drop-deadline *n Fam* délai *m* de rigueur

drop-down menu *n Comput* menu *m* déroulant

drop-forge *vt Metal* étamper, estamper

drop-forging *n Metal* **1** *(process)* estampage *m* **2** *(result)* pièce *f* emboutie *ou* étampée

drophead ['drɒphed] *n Aut* capote *f* rabattable

▸▸ **d. coupé** coupé *m* décapotable *ou* cabriolet

drop-in centre *n Br* centre *m* de permanence *(où on est reçu sans rendez-vous)*

droplet ['drɒplɪt] *n* gouttelette *f*

dropout ['drɒpaʊt] *n* **1** *Sch, Univ Fam* étudiant, -ante qui abandonne ses études; *(from society)* marginal, -ale **2** *(on a tape)* blanc *m*, perte *f* de signal

dropped [drɒpt] *adj Aut etc (axle etc)* surbaissé

▸▸ *Sport* **d. goal** *(in rugby)* drop-goal *m*, *pl* drop-goals

dropper ['drɒpər] *n* compte-gouttes *m inv*

dropping ['drɒpɪŋ] *n* **1** *(of object)* descente *f*, chute *f*; *Aviat (of parachutist, package)* largage *m*, droppage *m*

2 *(reduction) (of prices)* baisse *f*, chute *f*

3 *(omission) (of word)* suppression *f*

4 *(abandonment) (of project, course)* abandon *m*

5 *Aut (of chassis)* surbaissement *m*

6 *Vet* **d.** *(of young)* mise *f* bas

▸▸ **d. off** *(of membership, attendance etc)* diminution *f*, *Fam* **d. out** *(of school, university)* abandon *m*; *(from society)* désinsertion *f* sociale; *Aviat* **d. zone** zone *f* de largage *ou* de droppage

droppings ['drɒpɪŋz] *npl (of animals, birds)* fiente *f*; *(of sheep)* crottes *fpl*

dropsical ['drɒpsɪk(ə)l] *adj Med* hydropique

dropsy ['drɒpsɪ] *n Med* hydropisie *f*

dross [drɒs] *n* **1** *Metal* scories *fpl*, crasse *f* **2** *(waste)* impuretés *fpl*, déchets *mpl*; *Fam (rubbish)* rebut *m*

drought [draʊt] *n* sécheresse *f*

drove [drəʊv] *n* **1** *(of cattle etc)* troupeau *m* en marche **2** **droves** *(of people)* foules *fpl* (de personnes en marche); **to arrive** *or* **come in droves** *(of sightseers, tourists etc)* arriver en foule

drover ['drəʊvər] *n* conducteur *m ou* toucheur *m* de bestiaux

drown [draʊn] *vt* **1** *(kill)* noyer; **to d. oneself** se noyer; **to be drowned** *(by accident)* se noyer; *(on purpose)* être noyé; **drowned at sea** noyé en mer; *Fig* **to d. one's sorrows (in drink)** noyer son chagrin dans la boisson **2** *(flood) (meadow, city)* inonder, submerger; **eyes drowned in tears** yeux noyés de larmes; **don't d. it!** *(when adding water etc to alcoholic drink)* ne le noie pas! **3** *(make inaudible) (sound)* étouffer; **the noise of the waterfall drowned her voice** le bruit de la cascade a couvert sa voix

vi se noyer; *Fig (be unable to cope)* être dépassé; **I'm drowning in a sea of paper** je suis dans la paperasse jusqu'au cou

▸ **drown out** *vt sep (sound)* couvrir; *(person)* couvrir la voix de

drowned [draʊnd] *adj* **1** *(person, animal)* noyé; **a d. man/woman** un noyé/une noyée; *Fig* **he came home like a d. rat** il est rentré trempé comme une soupe **2** *(land)* inondé

drowning ['draʊnɪŋ] *adj* **a d. man** un homme qui se noie

n 1 *(case of)* **d.** noyade *f*; **to save sb from d.** sauver qn qui se noie, sauver qn de la noyade **2** *(of fields)* inondation *f*

drowse [draʊz] *vi* somnoler

drowsily ['draʊzɪlɪ] *adv (to look at)* d'un air somnolent, à demi endormi; *(to say)* d'une voix endormie *ou* ensommeillée, à demi endormi; *(to think, reflect)* à moitié endormi

drowsiness ['draʊzɪnɪs] *n* somnolence *f*; **may cause d.** *(notice on bottle of cough mixture etc)* peut entraîner une somnolence

drowsy ['draʊzɪ] *adj (person)* somnolent; *(atmosphere)* engourdi; *(voice)* endormi, ensommeillé; **to be** *or* **feel d.** avoir envie de dormir, avoir sommeil

drub [drʌb] *vt* **(-bb-)** *(somebody, the enemy)* battre, rosser

▸ **drub into** *vt sep* **to d. sth into sb** faire entrer qch de force dans la tête de qn

drubbing ['drʌbɪŋ] *n (with stick, fists)* volée *f* de coups; *Fig* défaite *f*; **to give an opponent a d.** battre un adversaire à plates coutures

drudge [drʌdʒ] *n* bête *f* de somme; **the household d.** la bonne à tout faire

vi trimer, peiner

drudgery ['drʌdʒərɪ] *n* travail *m* pénible *ou* ingrat, corvée(s) *f(pl)*; **just two more weeks of d.** plus que deux semaines à trimer; **the d. of housework** le caractère pénible *ou* ingrat des tâches ménagères

drug [drʌg] *n* **1** *(medication)* médicament *m*, drogue *f* **2** *(narcotic)* drogue *f*, stupéfiant *m*; **hard/soft drugs** drogues dures/douces; **to take** *or* **be on** *or Fam* **do drugs** se droguer; **to be arrested on d. charges** *(for using/possessing/dealing)* être arrêté pour utilisation/possession/trafic de stupéfiants; **athletes who take drugs** les athlètes qui se dopent;

the whole question of drugs in sport tout le problème du dopage dans le sport; *Fig* **computer games are a d.** les jeux électroniques sont une véritable drogue; *Mktg Fig* **d. on the market** produit *m* invendable; **to be a d. on the market** être invendable; **truth d.** sérum *m* de vérité

VT (**-gg-**) *(person, guard dog, wild animal, horse)* droguer; *(horse) (to increase performance)* doper; **they had drugged his wine/food** on avait mis un narcotique dans son vin/sa nourriture; *Fam* **he's drugged up to the eyeballs** *(after operation)* il est bourré de médicaments; **to be in a drugged sleep** dormir profondément sous l'effet d'un narcotique

▸ ▸ **d. abuse** usage *m* de stupéfiants; **d. addict** drogué, -ée, toxicomane *mf*; **d. addiction** toxicomanie *f*; **d. baron** gros bonnet *m* de la drogue; **d. company** compagnie *f* de produits pharmaceutiques; **d. dealer** dealer *m*; **d. dependency** dépendance *f* à l'égard des drogues, toxicomanie, *Spec* pharmacodépendance *f*; **d. money** argent *m* de la drogue; **d. peddler** revendeur, -euse de drogue; **d. peddling** trafic *m* de drogue; **d. pusher** revendeur, -euse de drogue **d. pushing** trafic de drogue; **d. smuggler** trafiquant, -ante de drogue; **d. smuggling** trafic de drogue; **d. squad** *(of police force)* brigade *f* des stupéfiants; **d. taking** dopage *m*; **d. trafficker** narco-trafiquant, -ante; **d. trafficking** trafic de drogue

druggist ['drʌgɪst] **N** *Am* pharmacien, -ienne; **wholesale d.** pharmacien, -ienne en gros

druggy ['drʌgɪ] **N** *Fam* camé, -ée

drugstore ['drʌgstɔːr] **N** *Am* drugstore *m*

druid ['druːɪd] **N** druide *m*

drum [drʌm] **N 1** *Mus* tambour *m*; **the drums** la batterie; **to beat the d.** battre du tambour; **to play the drums** jouer de la batterie; **big or bass d.** grosse caisse *f*; *Fig* **to bang or beat the d. for sb/sth** battre le tambour pour qn/qch **2** *(container)* tonneau *m* en fer, fût *m*; *(for oil)* bidon *m*, tambour *m* **3** *Tech etc* tambour *m*; *(of winch)* cylindre *m*; **concrete mixing d.** mélangeur *m* à béton, bétonnière *f*; **cable d.** tambour, dévidoir *m* *(de câble électrique)* **4** *(for laser printer)* tambour *m*

VI (**-mm-**) *Mus* jouer de la batterie; *Mil* battre du tambour; **he drummed with or for the Beatles** il était batteur *ou* il jouait de la batterie pour les Beatles; **to d. on the window panes** *(of person, rain)* tambouriner sur les vitres; **her fingers were drumming on the table** elle tapotait sur la table

VT to d. a tune on sth tambouriner un air sur qch; **she was drumming her fingers on the table** elle tapotait sur la table

▸ ▸ **d. kit** batterie *f*; *Mil* **d. major** tambour-major *m*, *pl* tambours-majors; *Am* **d. majorette** majorette *f*; **d. plotter** traceur *m* à tambour; **d. roll** roulement *m* de tambour

▸ **drum into** **VT SEP** **to d. sth into sb** enfoncer qch dans la tête de qn; **d. it into them that they mustn't take sweets from strangers** mets-leur bien dans la tête qu'ils ne doivent pas accepter de bonbons offerts par des inconnus

▸ **drum out** **VT SEP 1** *Mil, Hist (soldier)* renvoyer (**of** de) **2** *Fig (from a club etc) (person)* expulser avec ignominie

▸ **drum up** **VT SEP** *(supporters)* racoler; *(friends)* battre le rappel de; **to d. up customers** rechercher de la clientèle; **to d. up support for sth** rechercher du soutien pour qch

drumbeat ['drʌmbiːt] **N** coup *m* de tambour

drumhead ['drʌmhed] **N** *Mus* dessus *m* de tambour

▸ ▸ *Mil* **d. court-martial** conseil *m* de guerre

(tenu sur le champ de bataille); *Mil, Rel* **d. service** office *m* divin en plein air

drumlin ['drʌmlɪn] **N** drumlin *m*

drummer ['drʌmər] **N** *(of drum)* tambour *m*; *(of kettle-drum)* timbalier *m*; *(playing jazz, rock)* batteur *m*; *Fig* **to march to a different d.** suivre son propre chemin

▸ ▸ **d. boy** tambour

drumming ['drʌmɪŋ] **N 1** *(sound) (of rain, fists)*, *Mus* tambourinage *m*; **the d. of her fingers on the table was driving me crazy** la façon qu'elle avait de tapoter sur la table me rendait fou **2** *(action) (of woodpecker)* tambourinage *m*; *Mus* **his d. has improved** il s'est amélioré à la batterie

drumstick ['drʌmstɪk] **N 1** *Mus* baguette *f* de tambour *ou* de timbale **2** *Culin (of chicken)* pilon *m*

drunk [drʌŋk] **PP** *see* **drink**

ADJ ivre, soûl, gris; *Fig* enivré (**with success** par le succès); **to get d.** se soûler (**on sth** à qch); **to make** *or* **get sb d.** soûler qn; **d. as a lord** soûl comme un Polonais; *Law* **d. and disorderly** = en état d'ivresse manifeste dans un lieu public; *Fig* **d. with joy/power** ivre de joie/puissance; **he is d. with power** le pouvoir lui a monté à la tête

N homme *m* soûl/femme *f* soûle; *(habitual)* ivrogne *mf*; **the city centre was full of drunks** le centre-ville était plein de gens soûls *ou* ivres; **some old d. came up to me** un vieil ivrogne s'est approché de moi

▸ ▸ **d. driver** = personne *f* qui conduit en état d'ivresse

drunkard ['drʌŋkəd] **N** ivrogne *mf*

drunken ['drʌŋkən] **ADJ** *(person)* ivre; *(fury, stupor)* alcoolique; *(party, celebration)* bien arrosé; *(laughter, voice)* d'ivrogne; **d. brawl** querelle *f* d'ivrognes; **d. state** état *m* d'ivresse

drunkenly ['drʌŋkənlɪ] **ADV** *(to sing, speak)* d'une voix d'ivrogne; **to stagger d.** tituber; **to quarrel d.** avoir une querelle d'ivrognes; **he slumped d. onto his chair** complètement soûl, il s'est affalé sur sa chaise

drunkenness ['drʌŋkənnɪs] **N** ivresse *f*, *(habitual)* ivrognerie *f*

drunkometer [drʌŋˈkɒmɪtər] **N** *Am* alcootest® *m*

drupe [druːp] **N** *Bot* drupe *f*

dry [draɪ] **ADJ** (**drier, driest**) **1** *(weather, cold, bread, clothing etc)* sec, *f* sèche; *(well, spring)* tari, à sec; *(river)* asséché; *Ind, Chem etc (process, analysis)* par voie sèche; **tomorrow will be d. and bright** demain sera une journée sans pluie et ensoleillée; **to be** *or* **feel d.** *(of thirsty person)* avoir la gorge sèche; **to pump a well d.** épuiser l'eau d'un puits; **to run** *or* **go d.** *(of river)* s'assécher; *(of spring, well)* s'épuiser, (se) tarir; *(of pump)* se désamorcer; **to run d.** *(of speaker)* être à sec; **I've run d.** *(of author)* mon inspiration s'est tarie; **to be kept d.** *(notice on container)* garder au sec; *Fam* **as a bone, bone d.** sec comme une allumette; **d. country** pays *m* aride; *Fig* pays sec *(où les boissons alcoolisées sont prohibées)*; *Fig* **to go d.** *(prohibit alcohol)* prohiber la consommation des boissons alcoolisées; **there wasn't a d. eye in the house** tout le monde pleurait; **to have d. skin** avoir la peau sèche; *Med* **d. spell** éclaircie *f*; **d. work** *(causing thirst)* travail *m* qui donne soif

2 *(wine)* sec; **medium-d.** demi-sec; **extra d. champagne** champagne *m* brut

3 *(dull, boring) (subject)* aride; *(book, lecture)* ennuyeux; **to be as d. as dust** être ennuyeux comme la pluie

4 *(ironic) (person)* pince-sans-rire *inv*; *(wit, humour)* teinté d'ironie; **he has a d. manner** il est plutôt pince-sans-rire

5 *Br Pol Fam* dur

N 1 *Br Pol Fam* dur, *f* dure

2 *Austr Fam* **the d.** la saison sèche

3 to stay in the d. rester au sec *ou* à couvert

VT (**dried** [draɪd]) sécher; *(clothes)* faire sécher; *(skin)* dessécher; **to d. the dishes** essuyer la vaisselle; **to d. one's eyes** s'essuyer les yeux; **to d. one's hair** se sécher les cheveux; **to d. one's tears** sécher ses larmes

VI 1 *(of clothes, paint, cement)* sécher; *(of skin)* se dessécher; **to put sth out to d.** mettre qch à sécher dehors; **it's my turn to d.** *(when doing the dishes)* c'est à moi d'essuyer la vaisselle; **ink that dries black** encre qui vire au noir en séchant

2 *Fam (of actor)* oublier son texte

▸ ▸ **d. battery, d. cell** pile *f* sèche; *Naut* **d. dock** cale *f* sèche; *Fishing* **d. fly** mouche *f* sèche; *Com* **d. goods** *Br* marchandises *fpl* sèches; *Am* tissus *mpl* et articles *mpl* de bonneterie; **d. ice** neige *f* carbonique; **d. land** terre *f* ferme; *Aviat, Naut* **d. lease** location *f* d'avion/de bateau sans carburant ni équipage; **d. martini** martini *m* dry; **d. measure** = unité *f* de mesure des matières sèches; **d. rot** *(in wood, potatoes)* pourriture *f* sèche; **d. run** *(trial, practice)* coup *m* d'essai, test *m*; *Mil* entraînement *m* avec tir à blanc; **d. stone walling** murs *mpl* en pierres sèches; *(process)* construction *f* en pierres sèches; **d. weather tyre** pneu *m* temps sec

▸ **dry off** **VT SEP** *(person)* sécher; **come and d. yourself off in front of the fire** viens te sécher devant le feu

VI *(of varnish, paint etc)* sécher; *(of person)* se sécher

▸ **dry out** **VT SEP 1** *Fam (alcoholic)* désintoxiquer **2** *(water)* faire évaporer; *(skin)* dessécher; *(ground, football pitch, wood)* sécher

VI 1 *Fam (of alcoholic)* se faire désintoxiquer **2** *(of moisture)* s'évaporer, sécher; *(of skin, wooden furniture)* se dessécher; *(of soil, wood)* sécher; **leave your wet things in the bathroom to d. out** laisse tes affaires à sécher dans la salle de bain

▸ **dry up** **VT SEP** *(dishes)* essuyer; *(roads, ground)* sécher; *(skin)* dessécher

VI *(of well, pool etc)* se dessécher, tarir; *Fig (of funds, conversation)* tarir; *(of inspiration)* se tarir; *(of author etc)* épuiser son inspiration; *(of speaker, actor etc)* oublier son texte; **the well has dried up** le puits est à sec; *Sl* **d. up!** *(be quiet!)* la ferme!, ta gueule!

dryad ['draɪæd] **N** *Myth* dryade *f*

dry-clean **VT** nettoyer à sec

dry-cleaner **N** nettoyeur *m* à sec, teinturier *m*; **take it to the d.'s** portez-le à la teinturerie *ou* au pressing

dry-cleaning **N 1** *(process)* nettoyage *m* à sec; **d. is not recommended** *(on label)* le nettoyage à sec n'est pas recommandé **2** *(clothes)* vêtements *mpl* laissés chez le teinturier; **pick up the d. for me** va me chercher les vêtements chez le teinturier

dry-dock **VT** *(ship)* mettre en cale sèche

VI *(of ship)* entrer en cale sèche

dryer ['draɪər] **N 1** *(device)* *Ind* sécheur *m*, séchoir *m*; **hair d.** *(hand-held)* séchoir (à cheveux), sèche-cheveux *m inv*; *(on stand)* casque *m* sèche-cheveux; **clothes-d.** *(hanging from ceiling, folding etc)* séchoir; **spin d.** essoreuse *f* (centrifuge); **tumble d.** séchoir rotatif (à air chaud); *Phot* **plate d.** sèche-cliché *m*, *pl* sèche-clichés **2** *(in paint etc)* siccatif *m*

dry-eyed **ADJ** les yeux secs, l'œil sec

drying ['draɪɪŋ] **ADJ 1** *(wind)* desséchant; **a good d. wind** *(for drying clothes)* un bon vent pour sécher le linge **2** **quick-d.** *(oil, varnish)* siccatif

N séchage *m*; *(of skin)* dessèchement *m*; *(with a cloth)* essuyage *m*

►►*Fam* **d. out** *(of alcoholic)* désintoxication *f*; **d. rack** séchoir *m*; **d. up** *(of stream, river etc)* tarissement *m*

dryly ['draɪlɪ] ADV *(with irony)* avec une pointe d'ironie, d'un air de pince-sans-rire

dryness ['draɪnɪs] N **1** *(of region, weather, ground)* sécheresse *f* **2** *(of speech)* aridité *f* **3** *(of tone)* ironie *f*; **the d. of her wit** son humour pince-sans-rire

dry-roasted [draɪ'rəʊstɪd] ADJ *(peanuts)* grillé à sec

DSC [di:es'si:] N *Br Mil abbr* **Distinguished Service Cross**

D. Sc. [di:es'si:] N *Univ abbr* **Doctor of Science**

DSL [di:e'sel] N *Comput (abbr* **Digital Subscriber Line)** ligne *f* d'abonné numérique, DSL *m*

DSM [di:e'sem] N *Br Mil abbr* **Distinguished Service Medal**

DSO [di:e'səʊ] N *Br Mil abbr* **Distinguished Service Order**

DSS [di:e'ses] N *Br Admin Formerly abbr* **Department of Social Security**

DST [di:es'ti:] N *Am (abbr* **daylight saving time)** HAE *f*

DTI [di:ti:'aɪ] N *Br Admin abbr* **Department of Trade and Industry**

DTP [di:ti:'pi:] N *Comput (abbr* **desktop publishing)** PAO *f*
►►**D. operator** opérateur, -trice *de* PAO; **D. software** logiciel *m de* PAO

DTs [di:'ti:z] NPL *Fam (abbr* **delirium tremens) to have the D.** *(of alcoholic)* faire une crise de delirium tremens

DTT [di:ti:'ti:] N *(abbr* **digital terrestrial television)** TNT *f*

dual ['dju:əl] ADJ **1** double; **to have d. nationality** avoir la double nationalité; **to have a d. function** *or* **purpose** avoir une double fonction **2** *Math* dual
►►*Br Aut* **d. carriageway** route *f* à quatre voies; *Aut* **d.-control car** voiture *f* à double commande; **d. currency** deux monnaies *fpl*; **d. economy** économie *f* duale; *St Exch* **d. listing** cotation *f* sur deux Bourses; *Br* **d. ownership** copropriété *f*; *Psy* **d. personality** dédoublement *m* de la personnalité; **d. pricing** régime *m* du double prix; *(display)* double affichage *m (des prix)*; *Aut* **d. wheels** roues *fpl* jumelées

> Attention: ne pas confondre avec le nom anglais **duel**.

dual-band ADJ *Tel* bi-bande

dualism ['dju:əlɪz(ə)m] N dualité *f*; *Phil* dualisme *m*

duality [dju:'ælɪtɪ] N dualité *f*; *Psy (of personality)* dédoublement *m*

dual-mode ADJ *Tel* Dual Mode

dual-purpose ADJ à double emploi

dual-venturi ['dju:əlven'tjʊərɪ] ADJ *Aut* à double venturi

dub¹ [dʌb] *Cin, TV* N *(sound)* repiquage *m*; *(video)* copie *f*; *(action)* doublage *m*
VT **(-bb-)** *(film) (into foreign language)* doubler (**into** en); *(original voice soundtrack)* sonoriser; *(sound)* post-synchroniser; *(video)* faire une copie dans un autre format

dub² VT **(-bb-) 1 to d. sb (a) knight** armer *ou* adouber qn chevalier; *Fig* **he was dubbed the king of tennis** on l'a surnommé le roi du tennis **2** *(leather)* préparer au dégras

dubbin ['dʌbɪn] N *(for leather)* dégras *m*
VT *(shoes)* enduire de dégras

dubbing ['dʌbɪŋ] N *Cin, TV (into foreign language)* doublage *m*; *(of original voice soundtrack)* sonorisation *f*; *(of sound)* post-synchronisation *f*, repiquage *m* du son, mixage *m*

►►**d. mixer** mélangeur *m* de son, ingénieur *m* du son; **d. suite** studio *m* de doublage

dubiety [dju:'baɪətɪ] N *Fml* = **dubiousness**

dubious ['dju:bɪəs] ADJ **1** *(uncertain) (person)* qui doute; *(outcome)* incertain; **she looked d.** elle avait l'air d'avoir des doutes; **d. as to what he should do** ne sachant trop ce qu'il devait faire; **I'm still a bit d.** j'ai encore quelques doutes; **we were d. about the scheme** nous avions des doutes sur le projet; **d. expression** air *m* de doute; **it is d. whether they will succeed in persuading him** il n'est pas certain qu'ils réussiront à le persuader **2** *Pej (suspect, questionable) (origin)* douteux; *(advantage)* contestable; *(distinction, honour)* triste; *(compliment)* équivoque; *(company)* douteux, louche

dubiously ['dju:bɪəslɪ] ADV *(to say)* d'un ton de doute; *(to look at)* d'un air de doute

dubiousness ['dju:bɪəsnɪs] N **1** *(uncertainty) (of outcome)* incertitude *f*; *(in voice, of expression)* doute *m*; **their increasing d. about the whole enterprise** leurs doutes croissants à propos de toute cette affaire **2** *(suspect nature) (of origin, proposal, person's background)* caractère *m* douteux; *(of advantage)* caractère contestable; *(of compliment etc)* caractère équivoque; **the d. of this distinction** ce triste honneur

Dubliner ['dʌblɪnə(r)] N = personne *f* née ou habitant à Dublin

ducal ['dju:k(ə)l] ADJ USU ATTRIB ducal, -aux

ducat ['dʌkət] N *Hist (coin)* ducat *m*; *Am Fam (money)* fric *m*, blé *m*

duchess ['dʌtʃɪs] N duchesse *f*

duchesse ['du:ʃes] N
►►*Culin* **d. potatoes** pommes *fpl* (de terre) duchesse

duchy ['dʌtʃɪ] N duché *m*

duck¹ [dʌk] N **1** *(bird)* canard *m*; *(female)* cane *f*; *Culin* canard; **wild d.** canard sauvage; *Culin* **Peking d.** canard à la Pékinoise; *Culin* **Bombay d.** poisson *m* sec assaisonné de cari; **d.-egg blue** bleu-vert *m* pâle; *Fig* **to take to sth like a d. to water** mordre à qch; **criticism runs off him like water off a d.'s back** les critiques glissent sur lui comme de l'eau sur les plumes d'un canard; **to play at ducks and drakes** faire des ricochets (sur l'eau); *Fig* **to play ducks and drakes with one's money** jeter l'argent par les fenêtres;
2 *Eng Dial (form of address)* **what do you want, ducks?** *(to woman)* et pour vous, ma petite dame?; *(to man)* et pour le monsieur, qu'est-ce que ce sera?
3 *Cr* zéro *m*; **to be out for a d., to make a d.** faire chou blanc; **to break one's d.** marquer son premier point
►►*Sl* **d.'s arse** *(hairstyle)* = coiffure *f* masculine populaire dans les années cinquante *(cheveux courts plaqués vers l'arrière)*; **d. pond** mare *f* aux canards

duck² VI **1** *(to avoid being hit)* baisser la tête, se baisser; **to d. behind a tree/car** se cacher derrière un arbre/une voiture; **to d. out of sight** se cacher **2** *(under water)* plonger sous l'eau; **he ducked under the surface** il a plongé sous la surface de l'eau
VT **1** *(one's head)* baisser subitement; **to d. a blow** esquiver un coup **2** *Fig (obligations, embarrassing question etc)* se dérober à; *(problem)* contourner; **to d. the issue** s'esquiver; *(in reply)* user de faux-fuyants; **to d. a challenge** ne pas relever un défi **3** *(under water) (person)* plonger dans l'eau, faire le plongeon à
N *(movement) (to avoid being hit etc)* mouvement *m* instinctif de la tête; *Boxing* esquive *f*

►**duck out** VI se défiler; **to d. out of doing sth** éviter de faire qch; **I managed to d. out**

of it j'ai réussi à me défiler, j'ai réussi à y couper

duck³ N *Tex* coutil *m*; *Old-fashioned* **ducks** *(trousers)* pantalon *m* de coutil *ou* de toile

duck-billed [-bɪld] ADJ
►►**d. platypus** ornithorynque *m*

duckboards ['dʌkbɔ:dz] NPL caillebotis *m*

duckie ['dʌkɪ] N, ADJ = **ducky**

ducking ['dʌkɪŋ] N *(under water)* plongeon *m* (involontaire); **to give sb a d.** faire boire la tasse à qn; **to get** *or* **take a d.** boire la tasse

duckling ['dʌklɪŋ] N canardeau *m*; *(male)* caneton *m*; *(female)* canette *f*; *Culin* caneton; **the Ugly D.** le vilain petit Canard

duckweed ['dʌkwi:d] N *(plant)* lentille *f* d'eau

ducky ['dʌkɪ] N *Eng Dial (to man)* mon petit chou; *(to woman)* ma cocotte
ADJ *Am Fam* tout mignon

duct [dʌkt] N **1** *(tube)* conduit *m*; *Constr etc (for cables etc)* caniveau *m*; **air d.** manche *f* à air, gaine *f* de ventilation **2** *Anat* canal *m*, vaisseau *m*; **tear d.** conduit *m* lacrymal
►►**d. tape** ruban *m* adhésif en toile

ductile ['dʌktaɪl] ADJ *(metal)* ductile; *Fig Lit (character)* malléable

ductility [dʌk'tɪlɪtɪ] N *(of metal)* ductilité *f*; *Fig Lit (of character)* malléabilité *f*

dud [dʌd] *Fam* N *(person)* incapable *mf*; *Mil (shell)* obus *m* non éclaté; **several fireworks were duds** plusieurs pièces d'artifice ont foiré; **I'm a d. at history** je suis nul en histoire; **the note was a d.** le billet était faux
ADJ **it was a d. idea** c'était nul comme idée
►►**d. cheque** chèque *m* en bois; **d. note** faux billet *m*; *Mil* **d. shell** obus *m* non éclaté

dude [dju:d, du:d] N *Am Fam* **1** *(dandy)* gommeux *m* **2** *(man)* type *m*; **a real cool d.** un type formidable **3** *(vacationer on ranch)* hôte *m* d'un ranch qui propose des activités touristiques
►►*Am* **d. ranch** = ranch *m* qui propose des activités touristiques

dudgeon ['dʌdʒən] N *only used in* **in high d.** sur ses grands chevaux

duds [dʌdz] NPL *Fam (clothes)* fringues *fpl*

DUE [dju:] ADJ **1** *(owed) Com, Fin (debt)* exigible; *(bill)* échu; **bill d. on 1st May** effet payable le premier mai; **balance d.** solde *m* dû; **debts d. to us** dettes *fpl* actives; **debts d. by us** dettes passives; **bond d. for repayment** obligation *f* amortie; **to fall** *or* **become d.** *(of bill etc)* échoir, devenir payable; **falling d.** échéance *f*; **are you d. any money from him?** est-ce qu'il te doit de l'argent?; **the money d. to you** l'argent qui vous est dû; **on the d. date** à l'échéance, à terme échu; **redemption before d. date** remboursement *m* anticipé; **you're d. an apology** je vous dois/il vous doit/*etc* une excuse; **they are d. our thanks** ils méritent nos remerciements; **I'm (still) d. three days' holiday** on me doit encore trois jours de congé à prendre; **I'm d. (for) a rise** j'attends une augmentation de salaire
2 *(merited, proper)* dû, juste, mérité; **to give sb d. warning** avertir qn dans les formes; **with d. care** avec tout le soin requis; **he was received with d. ceremony** il fut reçu avec tout le cérémonial qui lui était dû; **in d. form** en bonne et due forme, en due forme; **after d. consideration** après mûre réflexion; **with all d. respect** avec tout le respect que je vous dois; **to treat sb with d. respect** *or* **the respect d. to him/her** traiter qn avec le respect qui lui est dû; **all in d. time** chaque chose en son temps; **in d. course** *(be told about something, learn of decision etc)* en temps voulu; *(come into inheritance, sit an exam)* le moment venu; **the impostor was unmasked in d. course** l'imposteur a finalement été démasqué

3 d. to *(caused by)* causé par, attribuable à, à cause de; *(as a result of)* par suite de, en raison de; **it is d. to his negligence** c'est sa négligence qui en est (la) cause, c'est dû à sa négligence; **what is it d. to?** à quoi cela tient-il?, à quoi est-ce que c'est dû?; **d. to fog the boat arrived late** par suite du brouillard, le bateau est arrivé en retard; **d. to circumstances beyond our control** en raison de circonstances indépendantes de notre volonté

4 *(expected)* **the train/he is d. (to arrive) at two o'clock** le train/il doit arriver à deux heures; **there's a bus d. now** un bus doit arriver d'un moment à l'autre; **when is the baby d.?** pour quand la naissance est-elle prévue?, quand le bébé doit-il naître?

ADV d. north droit vers le nord, plein nord

N *(what is owed)* dû *m*; **to give sb their d.** donner à qn ce qui lui est dû ou ce qui lui revient; *Fig* **to give him his d., he did apologize** pour lui rendre justice, il faut reconnaître qu'il s'est excusé

NPL dues *(for membership)* droits *mpl*, frais *mpl*; *(club subscription)* cotisation *f* annuelle; *(in publishing) (books on order)* livres *mpl* en commande; *esp Am Fig* **she's paid her dues** *(merits respect)* elle mérite le respect; *(has worked hard)* elle a peiné pour en arriver où elle en est; *Naut* **harbour dues** droits de port

▸▸ **d. date** *(of bill, payment)* échéance *f*, *(of baby)* date *f* prévue pour la naissance

duel [ˈdjʊəl] **N** duel *m*; *Fig* lutte *f*, **a d. to the death** un duel à mort; **to fight a d.** se battre en duel

VI (-**ll**-, *Am* -**l**-) se battre en duel

> Attention: ne pas confondre avec l'adjectif **dual**.

duelling, *Am* **dueling** [ˈdjʊəlɪŋ] **N** le duel
▸▸ **d. pistols** pistolets *mpl* de duel

duellist, *Am* **duelist** [ˈdjʊəlɪst] **N** duelliste *m*

duet [djuːˈet] **N** duo *m*; *(for piano)* morceau *m* à quatre mains

duettist [djuːˈetɪst] **N** *Mus* duettiste *mf*

duff [dʌf] **N 1** *Culin* **(plum) d.** pudding *m* aux raisins **2** *Br Fam* **up the d.** *(pregnant)* en cloque; **to get sb up the d.** mettre qn en cloque **3** *Am Fam (buttocks)* cul *m*, derche *m* **ADJ** *Br Fam* nul; **it was a d. idea** c'était nul comme idée

▸ **duff up VT SEP** *Br Sl (beat up)* rosser; **to get duffed up** se faire rosser

duffel [ˈdʌf(ə)l] **N**
▸▸ **d. bag** sac *m* marin; **d. coat** duffle-coat *m*, *pl* duffle-coats, *Can* corvette *f*

duffer [ˈdʌfər] **N** *Fam* **1** *(incompetent person)* bousilleur, -euse; *Sch* cancre *m*; **to be a d. at** *(history etc)* être nul en **2 an old d.** *(old man)* un vieux croulant

duffle [ˈdʌf(ə)l] **N = duffel**

dug¹ [dʌg] **PT, PP** *see* **dig**

dug² **N** *(of cow)* pis *m*; *Pej (of woman)* mamelle *f*, tétine *f*

dugout [ˈdʌgaʊt] **N 1** *(canoe)* canot *m* creusé dans un tronc d'arbre, pirogue *f* **2** *(shelter)* *Mil* tranchée-abri *f*, *pl* tranchées-abris; *Ftbl* banc *m* abri de touche

DUI *abbr* **driving under the influence**

duke [djuːk] **N 1** duc *m* **2** *Old-fashioned Sl* **dukes** *(fists)* poings *mpl*, **put up your dukes** en garde!

▸ **duke out VT SEP** *Am Old-fashioned* **to d. it out** se bagarrer (**with** avec)

dukedom [ˈdjuːkdəm] **N 1** *(territory)* duché *m* **2** *(title)* titre *m* de duc; *(rank)* dignité *f* de duc

dulcet [ˈdʌlsɪt] **ADJ ATTRIB** *Lit, Iron (sound)* doux, *f* douce, suave, agréable; **to say sth in d. tones** dire qch d'un ton suave; *Hum* **I recognize those d. tones** je reconnais le son harmonieux de cette voix

dulcimer [ˈdʌlsɪmər] **N** *Mus* tympanon *m*

dull [dʌl] **ADJ 1** *(not intelligent) (person)* lent, lourd; **to be d.-witted** être lent d'esprit; *Prov* **all work and no play makes Jack a d. boy** on s'abrutit à ne penser qu'au travail

2 *(boring) (book, film, person)* ennuyeux; *(life)* monotone; *(party)* assommant; *(style)* terne; **things have been pretty d. since she left** c'est plutôt monotone depuis qu'elle est partie; **as d. as ditchwater** ennuyeux comme la pluie; **deadly d.** abrutissant, assommant; **it's deadly d. here** on s'ennuie à mourir ici; **never a d. moment!** pas le temps de s'ennuyer!

3 *(not sharp) (pain)* sourd; *(sound)* sourd, étouffé; *(blunt) (edge)* émoussé; **to become d.** *(of tool, senses etc)* s'émousser

4 *(not bright) (colour, surface)* terne, mat; *(glow)* faible, terne; *(eyes)* sans éclat; *(voice)* terne; *(weather, sky, cloud)* sombre; **paper with a d. finish** papier mat *ou* non satiné

5 *Com, Fin (market)* calme, inactif; **business is d.** les affaires ne marchent pas fort

VT 1 *(the mind)* engourdir, alourdir

2 *(make less sharp) (pain)* endormir, calmer; *(pleasure)* rendre moins vif; *(sound)* amortir, assourdir; *(tool, the senses)* émousser; **sorrow is dulled by the passage of time** le temps émousse la douleur

3 *(make less bright) (colours)* ternir; *(surface)* dépolir; *(metal)* mater; *(eyes)* faire perdre son éclat à; *(voice)* ternir

VI 1 *(become less sharp) (of senses, eyesight)* s'émousser

2 *(become less bright) (of colour)* se ternir; *(of metal etc)* se dépolir; *(of eyes)* perdre son éclat

dullard [ˈdʌləd] **N** *Fml* lourdaud, -aude; *Sch* cancre *m*

dullness [ˈdʌlnɪs] **N 1** *(of mind)* lourdeur *f* d'esprit **2** *(tedium)* ennui *m*, tristesse *f*, *(of life, speech)* monotonie *f*; **a film of such d.** un film aussi ennuyeux **3** *(lack of sharpness) (of blade etc)* manque *m* de tranchant; *(of point, senses)* émoussement *m*; *(of pain)* caractère *m* sourd **4** *(lack of brightness) (of colour, eyes)* manque *m* d'éclat; *(of sound, light)* faiblesse *f*, *(of voice)* caractère *m* terne; **the d. of the weather** la grisaille **5** *Com, Fin (of business)* stagnation *f*, *(of market)* inactivité *f*

dully [ˈdʌllɪ] **ADV 1** *(stupidly)* lourdement, lentement **2** *(boringly)* d'une manière ennuyeuse **3** *(not sharply) (to echo)* sourdement, faiblement; *(to throb)* sourdement **4** *(not brightly) (lit, to gleam)* faiblement; **..., she said d. ...**, dit-elle d'une voix terne

Dulux dog [ˈdjuːlʌks] **N** *Br Fam* bobtail *m*

duly [ˈdjuːlɪ] **ADV 1** *(properly)* dûment; **d. appointed** *(member)* régulièrement désigné **2** *(as expected)* comme prévu; **rent d. paid** loyer payé exactement; **and all the shops were d. shut** et tous les magasins étaient bien entendu fermés

dumb [dʌm] **ADJ 1** *(unable or unwilling to speak)* muet, *f* muette; **I was struck d. with astonishment** la stupeur m'a rendu muet *esp Am Fam (stupid) (person, mistake)* bête; *(worthless)* nul, *f* nulle; **to play** *or* **act d.** faire le niais; **I don't want to go to some d. theatre!** je ne veux pas aller au théâtre, c'est nul!

▸▸ **d. animal** bête *f*; *Pej* **d. blonde** blonde *f* évaporée; *Fam* **d. cluck** imbécile *mf*; **d. insolence** silence *m* insolent; **d. show** = pantomime *m* faisant partie d'une pièce de théâtre; *Comput* **d. terminal** terminal *m* passif

▸ **dumb down VT SEP** *(education, news programme)* faire baisser le niveau de

dumbass [ˈdʌmæs] *Am Sl* **N** taré, -ée, débile *mf*, abruti, -ie
ADJ débile

dumbbell [ˈdʌmbel] **N 1** *(weight)* haltère *m* **2** *esp Am Sl (idiot)* lourdaud, -aude

dumbfound [dʌmˈfaʊnd] **VT** abasourdir, ahurir, ébahir

dumbfounded [dʌmˈfaʊndɪd] **ADJ** abasourdi, ahuri, ébahi (**at** de); **I'm d.** je n'en reviens pas; **we were d. at the news** la nouvelle nous frappa de stupeur

dumbing down [ˈdʌmɪŋ] **N** *(of education, news programme)* baisse *f* de niveau

dumbly [ˈdʌmlɪ] **ADV** *(to follow, stare)* sans rien dire; **to be d. obedient** obéir silencieusement

dumbness [ˈdʌmnɪs] **N 1** mutisme *m*; **deaf and d.** surdi-mutité *f* **2** *Fam (stupidity)* sottise *f*, bêtise *f*

dumbo [ˈdʌmbəʊ] **N** *Fam* andouille *f*, imbécile *mf*

dumbstruck [ˈdʌmstrʌk] **ADJ = dumbfounded**

dumbwaiter [dʌmˈweɪtər] **N** *(food stand)* guéridon *m*; *(revolving)* plateau *m* tournant; *(lift)* monte-plats *m inv*

dumdum [ˈdʌmdʌm] **N 1** *Mil (bullet)* (balle *f*) dum-dum *f*, *pl* dum-dums **2** *Fam (idiot)* idiot, -ote

▸▸ *Mil* **d. bullet** (balle) dum-dum *f*, *pl* dum-dums

dummy [ˈdʌmɪ] **N 1** *(in clothes shop window), Sewing* mannequin *m*; *(of ventriloquist)* marionnette *f*, *Fam* **standing there like a stuffed d.** planté comme un piquet **2** *(imitation object)* objet *m*/paquet *m*/bouteille *f*/etc factice; *(book)* maquette *f*; **it's just a d.** ce n'en est pas un vrai **3** *Offensive (person who cannot speak)* muet, *f* muette; *Fig Pej (idiot)* abruti, -ie, lourdaud, -aude **4** *Br (for baby)* tétine *f* **5** *Cards (player or hand at bridge, whist)* mort *m*; **to be** *or* **play d.** faire le mort **6** *Ftbl etc* feinte *f*

ADJ *(fake)* factice

▸▸ **d. bridge** bridge *m* à trois personnes; **d. run** *(trial)* essai *m*; *Fig Fam* coup *m* d'essai; *Aviat, Mil* attaque *f* simulée *ou* d'entraînement; **d. whist** whist *m* avec un mort

dump [dʌmp] **N 1** *(for refuse)* (lieu *m* de) décharge *f*, **refuse** *or* **rubbish** *or Am* **garbage d.** décharge

2 *Fam (house etc)* taudis *m*; **what a d.!** *(of place)* quel trou!, quel bled!; *(of office etc)* quelle saloperie de boîte!

3 *(store)* dépôt *m*; *Mil* **ammunition d.** dépôt de munitions, parc *m* à munitions;

4 *Comput* cliché *m* mémoire; **(memory) d.** vidage *m* (de) mémoire; **(screen) d.** impression *f* écran

5 *Sl* **to take** *or* **have a d.** *(defecate)* chier

VT 1 *(put down) (lorryload of sand etc)* décharger, déverser; *(package etc)* laisser tomber lourdement; *(somebody, something) (on chair etc)* déposer rudement; *Aviat (cargo)* se délester de; **I'm just going home to d. my suitcase** je vais déposer ma valise chez moi; **d. your bags in the corner** déposez *ou* laissez vos sacs dans le coin; **can we d. the kids here for the weekend?** est-ce que nous pouvons laisser les enfants ici ce week-end?

2 *(throw away, dispose of) (refuse)* jeter à la voirie; *(waste in the sea)* déverser; *Fam (car, unwanted object etc)* se débarrasser de; *(lover, boyfriend etc)* plaquer

3 *Com* **to d. goods on a foreign market** faire du dumping, écouler des marchandises à perte à l'étranger

4 *Comput (memory)* vider

VI *Com* faire du dumping

▸▸ *Mktg* **d. bin** panier *m* de présentation en vrac, panier présentoir; *Am Rail* **d. car** wagon *m* à bascule; **d. truck** dumper *m*, tombereau *m*

▸ **dump on** VT INSEP *Am Fam* **1** *(criticize)* *(somebody, something)* s'en prendre à **2** *(tell one's problems to) (somebody)* se décharger de ses problèmes sur

dumper ['dʌmpər] N *Br* tombereau *m*, dumper *m*

▸▸ **d. truck** tombereau, dumper

dumping ['dʌmpɪŋ] N **1** '**no d.**' *(sign)* 'décharge interdite' **2** *Com (of goods)* dumping *m* **3** *Comput (of memory)* vidage *m*

▸▸ **d. ground** *(for rubbish)* décharge *f*, dépôt *m* d'ordures; *Fig (for inferior goods)* dépotoir *m*; *Fig* **people use the home as a d. ground for their elderly parents** les gens utilisent la maison de retraite pour se débarrasser de leurs parents âgés; **they just use this house as a d. ground** ici ce n'est qu'un dépôt pour eux

dumpling ['dʌmplɪŋ] N **1** *Culin (in stew)* boulette *f* de pâte; **apple d.** pomme *f* enrobée dans de la pâte et cuite au four **2** *Fig Fam (plump person)* boulot, -otte, petit gros, *f* petite grosse; **he's become a bit of a d.** il est devenu un peu boulot

dumps [dʌmps] NPL *Fam (depression)* cafard *m*, idées *fpl* noires; **to be down in the d.** broyer du noir, avoir le cafard

dumpster ['dʌmpstər] N *Am* benne *f* à ordures

dumpy ['dʌmpɪ] ADJ *(person etc)* boulot, -otte

dun[1] [dʌn] ADJ brun grisâtre; *(horse)* gris louvet

N *(horse)* cheval *m* gris louvet

dun[2] VT (-nn-) *Old-fashioned (debtor)* importuner, harceler; **dunned by his creditors** pressé par ses créanciers; **a dunning letter** une lettre de relance *ou* de poursuite

dunce [dʌns] N *Sch* cancre *m*; **the d. of the class, the class d.** le dernier de la classe; **to be a d. at physics** être nul en physique; **d.'s cap** bonnet *m* d'âne

dunderhead ['dʌndəhed] N *Fam* imbécile *mf*

dune [dju:n] N **(sand) d.** dune *f*

▸▸ **d. buggy** buggy *m*

dung [dʌŋ] N **1** *(excrement)* crotte *f*, *(of wild animal)* fumées *fpl*; *(of cow)* bouse *f*, *(of horse)* crottin *m* **2** *Agr (manure)* fumier *m*, engrais *m*

▸▸ **d. beetle** bousier *m*

dungaree [dʌŋgə'ri:] N **1 dungarees** *(with bib)* salopette *f*, *(workman's)* bleu(s) *m(pl)* (de travail); **to be wearing (a pair of) dungarees** porter une salopette, être en salopette; *(workman's)* porter un *ou* des bleu(s) (de travail), être en bleu(s) (de travail) **2** *Tex* treillis *m*

dungeon ['dʌndʒ(ə)n] N **1** *(prison)* cachot *m* **2** *Hist (tower)* donjon *m*

dunghill ['dʌŋhɪl] N tas *m* de fumier, fumier *m*

dunk [dʌŋk] VT *(bread, croissant) (in coffee etc)* tremper

VI faire trempette

Dunkirk [dʌn'kɜːk] N Dunkerque

dunlin ['dʌnlɪn] N *(bird)* bécasseau *m* variable

dunno [dʌ'nəʊ] CONTR *Sl* = **don't know** j'sais pas!

dunnock ['dʌnək] N *(bird)* accenteur *m* mouchet

dunny ['dʌnɪ] N *Austr Fam (toilet)* chiottes *fpl*

duo ['dju:əʊ] N **1** *Mus* duo *m* **2** *(two people)* couple *m*

duodecimal [dju:əʊ'desɪm(ə)l] ADJ duodécimal

NPL **duodecimals** *(system)* système *m* de numérotation duodécimal

duodenal [dju:əʊ'di:n(ə)l] ADJ *Anat, Med (ulcer etc)* duodénal

duodenum, *pl* **duodena, duodenums** [dju:əʊ'di:nəm, -nə, -nəmz] N *Anat* duodénum *m*

dupe [dju:p] N dupe *f*

VT duper, tromper; **to be duped** se laisser duper; **to d. sb into doing sth** duper qn pour qu'il fasse qch; **she duped him into believing that …** elle lui a fait gober que …

duple ['dju:p(ə)l] ADJ

▸▸ *Mus* **d. time** rythme *m* binaire *ou* à deux temps

duplex ['dju:pleks] ADJ **1** *Elec, Tel (line)* duplex *inv*; *(operation etc)* en duplex **2** *Am (apartment)* duplex

N *Am (apartment)* (appartement *m*) duplex *m*; *(house)* maison *f* jumelée

▸▸ *Am* **d. house** maison jumelée

duplicate[1] ['dju:plɪkət] ADJ (en) double; **I have a d. key** j'ai un double de la clé; **d. set of tools** outils *mpl* de rechange; **d. receipt** quittance *f* double

N *(of work of art etc)* double *m*; *(of cheque etc)* duplicata *m*; *(of written document)* double, contrepartie *f*; **in d.** en double (exemplaire), en deux exemplaires, *Fml* en duplicata

duplicate[2] ['dju:plɪkeɪt] VT **1** *(make a copy of) (key)* faire un double de; *(document)* copier, reproduire en double exemplaire **2** *(on duplicator)* reprographier, polycopier; **to d. sth** tirer plusieurs exemplaires de qch au duplicateur, polycopier qch **3** *(do again)* refaire; **that's just duplicating what they've already done** cela revient à refaire ce qu'ils ont déjà fait

duplicating ['dju:plɪkeɪtɪŋ] N *(of document)* reproduction *f*

▸▸ **d. machine** duplicateur *m*, machine *f* à polycopier

duplication [dju:plɪ'keɪʃən] N reproduction *f*; **unnecessary d. of work** répétition *f* inutile du travail

duplicator ['dju:plɪkeɪtər] N duplicateur *m*, machine *f* à polycopier

duplicity [dju:'plɪsɪtɪ] N duplicité *f*

durability [djʊərə'bɪlɪtɪ] N durabilité *f*, *Ind* résistance *f*

durable ['djʊərəb(ə)l] ADJ *(peace)* durable; *(fabric)* résistant

NPL *Com* **(consumer) durables** biens *mpl* durables

▸▸ *Com* **d. goods** biens durables *ou* non périssables

duration [djʊ'reɪʃən] N durée *f*, *(of life)* étendue *f*; **the peace was of short d.** la paix fut de courte durée; **for the d.** *Mil (to enlist)* pour la durée de la guerre; *Fig* jusqu'à la Saint-Glinglin

duress [djʊ'res] N *Law* contrainte *f*, coercition *f*; **to act under d.** agir sous la contrainte

Durex® ['djʊəreks] N préservatif *m*

during ['djʊərɪŋ] PREP pendant, durant; **d. the whole week** toute la semaine; **d. the winter** au cours de *ou* pendant l'hiver; **d. the journey** en cours de route; **d. the last year** dans le courant de l'année dernière; **killed d. a brawl** tué au cours d'une rixe; **d. that time** pendant ce temps

durum ['djʊərəm] N

▸▸ **d. wheat** blé *m* dur

dusk [dʌsk] N crépuscule *m*; **at d.** à la nuit tombante, à la tombée de la nuit

duskiness ['dʌskɪnɪs] N **1** *(darkness of skin)* teint *m* mat **2** *Lit (dimness)* demi-jour *m*, pénombre *f*

dusky ['dʌskɪ] ADJ **1** *(dark) (complexion)*

mat; *(dark-skinned)* au teint mat **2** *Lit (dim)* crépusculaire

dust [dʌst] N **1** *(dirt, powder)* poussière *f*, *(of marble)* sciure *f*; **these ornaments just collect the d.** ces bibelots ne sont que des nids à poussière; **to raise a cloud of d.** soulever un nuage de poussière; *Fig* **to bite the d.** *(die, fail)* mordre la poussière; *(of hopes)* s'envoler; *Fig* **to throw d. in sb's eyes** jeter de la poudre aux yeux à qn; *Fig* **to blow the d. off sth** dépoussiérer qch; *Old-fashioned Fam* **to kick up** *or* **raise a d.** *(a fuss)* faire du foin; *Fig* **once the d. has settled** une fois que les choses seront revenues à la normale, une fois que la situation se sera apaisée; **all their hopes had turned to d. and ashes** tous leurs espoirs s'étaient anéantis; *Fam* **when there's work to be done you can't see him for d.!** dès qu'il y a du travail, il n'y a plus personne!; **… or you won't see me for d.!** … ou tu ne me reverras pas de sitôt!; **brick d.** poussière de brique; *Phys* **cosmic d.** poussière cosmique; **to take a d. bath** *(of bird)* s'ébrouer dans la poussière

2 *(action)* **to give the table a d.** passer un coup de chiffon sur la table (pour enlever la poussière)

VT **1** *(remove dust from) (room, furniture)* épousseter

2 *(sprinkle)* **to d. a cake with sugar, to d. sugar over a cake** saupoudrer un gâteau de sucre; **sugar-dusted doughnuts** beignets saupoudrés de sucre; *Fam* **to d. a gun for fingerprints** examiner un revolver pour y relever des empreintes digitales

▸▸ **d. bag** *(for vacuum cleaner) (disposable)* sac *m* à poussière; *(fixed)* sac tissu; *Am* **d. ball** mouton *m*; *Geog* **d. bowl** zone *f* semi-désertique; **the D. Bowl** *(in US)* le Dust Bowl; *Am* **d. bunny** mouton; **d. cap** capuchon *m* anti-poussière; *Am* **d. cloth** chiffon *m* à poussière; **d. coat** cache-poussière *m inv*; *Tech* **d. collector** capteur *m* de poussières; **d. cover** *(for book)* jaquette *f*, *(for machine)* housse *f* de rangement; *(for furniture)* housse de protection; **d. devil** tourbillon *m* de poussière; **d. jacket** *(for book)* jaquette; *Am* **d. kitten** mouton; **d. storm** tempête *f* de poussière; **d. trap** nid *m* à poussière; *Ind* **attrape-poussières** *m inv*

▸ **dust down, dust off** VT SEP *(furniture)* épousseter; *Fig (legislation, lecture)* dépoussiérer; *(one's French etc)* rafraîchir, dérouiller; **to d. oneself off** *or* **down** se brosser (pour enlever la poussière); **she dusted the crumbs off the chair** elle brossa la chaise pour en enlever les miettes

dustbin ['dʌstbɪn] N *Br* poubelle *f*

dustcart ['dʌstkɑːt] N *Br* camion *m* d'enlèvement des ordures ménagères, camion des éboueurs

dustcloud ['dʌstklaʊd] N nuage *m* de poussière

duster ['dʌstər] N **1** *Br (cloth)* chiffon *m* (à poussière); *Sch (for blackboard) (cloth)* chiffon *m* (à effacer); *(pad)* tampon *m* (à effacer); **feather d.** plumeau *m* **2** *Naut Sl (flag)* pavillon *m*; **red d.** = pavillon de la marine marchande britannique **3** *(coat)* manteau *m* léger

▸▸ **d. coat** manteau léger

dustiness ['dʌstɪnɪs] N état *m* poudreux *ou* poussiéreux

dusting ['dʌstɪŋ] N **1** *(of room, furniture etc)* époussetage *m*; **to give a room a d.** épousseter une pièce; **have you done the d.?** tu as fait les poussières? **2** *(of cake etc)* saupoudrage *m*; **the cake had a d. of chocolate powder** le gâteau était saupoudré de chocolat; **there was a d. of snow on the pavement** le trottoir était saupoudré de neige

▸▸ **d. powder** talc *m*

dustman, *pl* **dustmen** ['dʌstmən] **N** *Br* éboueur *m*, *Fam* boueur *m*, boueux *m*

dustpan ['dʌstpæn] **N** pelle *f* (à poussière)

dustproof ['dʌstpruːf] **ADJ** imperméable à la poussière

dustsheet ['dʌstʃiːt] **N** *(for furniture)* housse *f*

dust-up N *Fam (quarrel)* coup *m* de torchon, querelle *f*; *(brawl)* bagarre *f*; **to have a d. with sb** se quereller/se bagarrer avec qn; **they've had a bit of a d.** le torchon a brûlé entre eux

dusty ['dʌstɪ] **ADJ** poussiéreux, couvert de poussière; **to get d.** se couvrir de poussière; *Old-fashioned Sl* **it's not so d.** *(not bad)* c'est pas mal du tout; *Old-fashioned Fam* **a d. answer** une réponse un peu sèche

Dutch [dʌtʃ] **ADJ 1** hollandais; *(cheese etc)* de Hollande; *(government)* néerlandais; *Fig Fam* **to talk to sb like a D. uncle** faire la morale à qn **2** *Am* **(Pennsylvania) D.** allemand de Pennsylvanie
N 1 the D. (people) les Hollandais *mpl* **2** *Ling* hollandais *m*; **Cape D.** afrikaans *m*
ADV *Fam* **to go D.** payer son écot; **let's go D.** payons chacun notre part
▸▸ **D. auction** vente *f* à la baisse; *Br* **D. barn** hangar *m* à récoltes; *Br* **D. cap** diaphragme *m (contraceptif)*; *Fam* **D. courage** = courage *m* trouvé dans la boisson; **I'll need a little D. courage** il faut que je boive un peu pour me donner du courage; *Am* **D. door** porte *f* à deux vantaux; **D. elm disease** maladie *f* de l'orme, graphiose *f*; **D. oven** *(casserole)* marmite *f*, fait-tout *m inv*; *Fam* **D. treat** = sortie *f* où chacun paye son écot; **as long as it's a D. treat** tant que chacun paie sa part *ou* son écot

dutch [dʌtʃ] **N** *Br Sl (wife)* **my old d.** ma femme, ma vieille

Dutchman, *pl* **Dutchmen** ['dʌtʃmən] **N** Hollandais *m*, Néerlandais *m*; *Fam* **if that's a real diamond (then) I'm a D.** si c'est un vrai diamant je mange mon chapeau

Dutchwoman, *pl* **Dutchwomen** ['dʌtʃwʊmən, -wɪmɪn] **N** Hollandaise *f*, Néerlandaise *f*

dutiable ['djuːtɪəb(ə)l] **ADJ** *(goods purchased abroad)* soumis aux droits de douane, imposable, taxable

dutiful ['djuːtɪfʊl] **ADJ** *(son, daughter)* obéissant; **a d. husband** un mari plein d'égards pour sa femme

dutifully ['djuːtɪfʊlɪ] **ADV** avec soumission

duty ['djuːtɪ] **N 1** *(obligation)* devoir *m* (**to** envers); **to do one's d.** faire son devoir; **to fail in one's d.** manquer à son devoir (**as** a de); **to do one's d. by sb** remplir son devoir envers qn; **I shall make it my d. to …** je considérerai de mon devoir de …; **it is your d. to …** il est de ton devoir de …; **from** *or* **out of a sense of d.** par devoir; **to have no sense of d.** n'avoir aucun sens du devoir; *Hum* **I must go, d. calls** je dois y aller, le devoir m'appelle; **to pay a d. call** faire une visite de politesse
2 *(task) (usu pl)* **duties** fonctions *fpl*, attributions *fpl*; *Mil* mission *f*; **public duties** fonctions publiques; **to take up** *or* **assume one's duties** entrer en fonctions *ou* en charge; **to hand over one's duties** *(resign)* résigner ses fonctions; *(transfer them)* remettre ses fonctions (**to** à); **to carry out** *or* **perform one's duties** exercer ses fonctions
3 to be on d. être de service; *(in factory, playground etc)* être de surveillance; *Naut* être de service *ou* de corvée; *Mil, Naut* **while on d.** pendant le service; **to be off d.** ne pas être de service; **to do d. for sb** remplacer qn (dans son service); **to do d. for sth** servir de qch; *Mil* **tour of d.** tour *m* de service; *Am* **active d.** service actif; **fatigue d.** corvée *f*
4 *Fin (tax)* droit *m*; **customs d.** droit(s) *m(pl)* de douane; **liable to d.** passible de droits; **d. paid** franc de douane, droits acquittés; **to pay d. on sth** payer une taxe sur qch
▸▸ **d. chart** tableau *m* de service; *Journ* **d. editor** rédacteur, -trice en chef de service; **d. manager** directeur, -trice de service; **d. officer** officier *m* de service; **d. roster** tableau *m* de service

duty-bound **ADJ PRED** tenu; **you are d. to do it** votre devoir vous y oblige, vous y êtes tenu; **I feel d. to …** je me sens tenu par mon devoir de …

duty-free **ADJ** exempt de droits (de douane); *(wine, cigarettes etc for personal use)* hors taxe
N *(purchase)* achat *m* hors taxe
ADV **how much wine can I bring back d.?** quelle quantité de vin est-ce que j'ai le droit de ramener hors taxe?
▸▸ **d. allowance** quantité *f* de marchandises hors taxe autorisée; **d. entry** admission *f* en franchise; **d. goods** marchandises *fpl* franches de douane, marchandises hors taxe; **d. sales** ventes *fpl* hors taxe; **d. shop** magasin *m* hors taxe; **d. zone** zone *f* en franchise

duty-paid goods NPL marchandises *fpl* libérées *ou* acquittées

duvet ['duːveɪ] **N** couette *f*, *Suisse* duvet *m*
▸▸ **d. cover** housse *f* de couette; *Fam* **d. day** = journée *f* de congé supplémentaire pouvant être prise de façon impromptu

dux [dʌks] **N** *Scot Sch* premier, -ière de la classe/l'école

DV [diːˈviː] **ADV** *(abbr* **deo volente***)* si Dieu le veut

DVD [diːviːˈdiː] **N** *Comput (abbr* **Digital Versatile Disk, Digital Video Disk***) (format)* DVD *m*; *(player)* lecteur *m* de DVD; *(disk)* DVD *m*; **on DVD** sur DVD; **D. recordable** DVD enregistrable; **D. rewritable** DVD réinscriptible
▸▸ **D. drive** lecteur *m* (de) DVD; **D. player** lecteur (de) DVD

DVD-R [-ɑːr] **N** *Comput (abbr* **digital video disk-recordable***)* DVD-R *m*

DVD-ROM **N** *Comput (abbr* **digital video disk-read only memory***)* DVD-ROM *m*
▸▸ **D. drive** lecteur *m* (de) DVD-ROM

DVD-RW [-ɑːˈdʌb(ə)ljuː] **N** *Comput (abbr* **digital video disk-rewritable***)* DVD-RW *m*

DVT [diːviːˈtiː] **N** *(abbr* **deep-vein thrombosis***)* TVP *f*

dwarf, *pl* **dwarfs, dwarves** [dwɔːf, dwɔːvz] **N** *(person)*, *Myth* nain, *f* naine
ADJ *(plant, tree)* nain
VT 1 écraser; *Fig (sb's achievements, success)* éclipser; **tower that dwarfs the main building** tour dont la hauteur écrase le corps de bâtiment; **the church is dwarfed by the skyscraper** l'église est écrasée par le gratte-ciel; **at nearly six feet, Jack dwarfed his classmates** avec son mètre 80, Jack semblait un géant par rapport à ses camarades de classe **2** *(stunt growth of) (plant)* rabougrir

dwarfish ['dwɔːfɪʃ] **ADJ** *(legs)* de nain; *(man, stature)* très petit

dweeb [dwiːb] **N** *Am Fam* crétin, -ine, abruti, -ie

dwell [dwel] **VI** *(pt, pp* **dwelt** [dwelt]*)* **1** *Lit* habiter, demeurer; **he dwells in Edinburgh/in Spain** il habite à Édimbourg/en Espagne **2** *Fig (remain)* rester; **to let one's eye d. on sb** arrêter son regard sur qn; *Lit* **this hope dwells within our hearts** cet espoir repose dans notre cœur
N *Tech* dwell *m*
▸▸ **d. angle** angle *m* de dwell *ou* de fermeture

▸ **dwell on, dwell upon** **VT INSEP** *(brood about)* remâcher, ressasser; *(memories)* s'attarder sur; *(discuss) (in speech, book)* s'appesantir sur; *(syllable etc)* appuyer sur; **don't d.** *or* **don't let your mind d. on it** essaie de ne pas y penser

dweller ['dwelər] **N** habitant, -ante (**in, on** de); **city-d.** citadin, -ine; **flat-d.** personne *f* qui habite dans un appartement

dwelling[1] ['dwelɪŋ] **N** *Lit* lieu *m* de séjour; *Admin* domicile *m*, demeure *f*
▸▸ *Law* **d. house** maison *f* d'habitation; **d. place** domicile, demeure

-dwelling[2] **SUFF** tree-d. arboricole, qui vit sur les arbres; ocean-/cave-d. qui vit dans l'océan/dans les caves

DWEM [dwem] **N** *(abbr* **dead white European male***)* = écrivain/musicien/*etc* européen blanc mort depuis longtemps

DWI **N** *Am (abbr* **driving while intoxicated***)* conduite *f* en état d'ivresse

dwindle ['dwɪnd(ə)l] **VI to d. (away)** diminuer; **to d. to nothing** se réduire à rien

dwindling ['dwɪnd(ə)lɪŋ] **ADJ** *(audience, funds, membership)* en baisse; *(enthusiasm)* faiblissant; **a d. number of people** de moins en moins de gens
N *(of supplies, enthusiasm, support)* baisse *f*, diminution *f*; *Fin (of capital)* déperdition *f*

dye [daɪ] **N** *(for clothes, hair)* teinture *f*; **fast d.** *(on label)* bon teint; *Lit* **villain of the deepest d.** fieffé coquin *m*
VT teindre; **to d. sth black/red** teindre qch en noir/rouge; **to have a dress dyed** faire teindre une robe; **to d. one's hair** se teindre les cheveux
VI (se) teindre; **material that dyes well** tissu qui prend bien la teinture
▸▸ *Phot* **d. solution** bain *m* colorant

dyed-in-the-wool [daɪd-] **ADJ** *Fig* invétéré, inébranlable; **a d. Englishman/conservative** un Anglais/conservateur bon teint

dyeing ['daɪɪŋ] **N 1** *(of material, hair)* teinture *f* **2** *(trade)* teinturerie *f*

dyer ['daɪər] **N** teinturier *m*; **d. and cleaner** teinturier dégraisseur

dyestuff ['daɪstʌf] **N** matière *f* colorante, colorant *m*

dyeworks ['daɪwɜːks] **NPL** *(usu with sing verb)* teinturerie *f*

dying ['daɪɪŋ] **ADJ** *(person)* mourant, agonisant; *Fig (industry, ideology)* agonisant; *(traditions)* en voie de disparition; **d. words** dernières paroles; **in a d. voice** d'une voix éteinte; **with his d. breath** de sa voix agonisante; **it was my mother's d. wish that …** les dernières volontés de ma mère étaient que …; **I shall remember it to my d. day** je m'en souviendrai jusqu'à la mort; *Fig Fam* **to look like a d. duck (in a thunderstorm)** avoir l'air pitoyable
N *(death throes)* agonie *f*, *(death)* mort *f*
NPL the dead and the d. les morts *mpl* et les moribonds *mpl*; **prayers for the d.** prières *fpl* des agonisants

dyke[1] [daɪk] **N 1** *Tech* digue *f*, levée *f*, *(embankment)* chaussée *f* surélevée *ou* en remblai **2** *(ditch)* fossé *m*, chenal *m*, -aux
VT *Tech (river)* endiguer; *(land)* protéger par des digues

dyke[2] **N** *Fam (lesbian)* gouine *f*

dynamic [daɪˈnæmɪk] **ADJ** *Phys, Fig* dynamique; *Fig* **to have a d. personality** être plein de dynamisme
N dynamique *f*
▸▸ *Comput* **d. data exchange** échange *m* dynamique de données; *Comput* **d. RAM** mémoire *f* RAM dynamique

dynamically [daɪˈnæmɪklɪ] **ADV** dynamiquement

dynamics [daɪˈnæmɪks] NPL *(usu with sing verb)* *Phys, Fig* dynamique *f*; **the d. of change/progress** la dynamique du changement/progrès VOIR GRAMMAIRE A10

dynamism [ˈdaɪnəmɪz(ə)m] N *Phys, Fig* dynamisme *m*

dynamite [ˈdaɪnəmaɪt] N dynamite *f*; *Fam* **subject that is political d.** sujet explosif sur le plan politique; **it/she could be political d. for the Government** ça/elle pourrait faire des dégâts au niveau du gouvernement; *Fam* **this information is d.** cette information c'est de la dynamite; *Fam* **it's d.!** *(marvellous)* c'est du tonnerre!; *Fam* **this new band is d.** ce nouveau groupe déménage
▪ VT *(rocks etc)* faire sauter à la dynamite; *(building etc)* dynamiter

dynamiting [ˈdaɪnəmaɪtɪŋ] N dynamitage *m*

dynamo, *pl* **dynamos** [ˈdaɪnəməʊ, -əʊz] N *Elec* dynamo *f*; *Fig* **she's a human d.** elle a une énergie extraordinaire

dynastic [dɪˈnæstɪk] ADJ dynastique

dynasty [ˈdɪnəstɪ, *Am* ˈdaɪnəstɪ] N dynastie *f*

dyne [daɪn] N *Phys (unit of force)* dyne *f*

dysentery [ˈdɪsəntrɪ] N *Med* dysenterie *f*; **to have d.** avoir la dysenterie

dysfunction [dɪsˈfʌŋkʃən] N *Med (of organ)* insuffisance *f*

dysfunctional [dɪsˈfʌŋkʃənəl] ADJ **a d. family** une famille à problèmes

dyslectic [dɪsˈlektɪk] = **dyslexic**

dyslexia [dɪsˈleksɪə] N *Med* dyslexie *f*; **to have d.** être dyslexique

dyslexic [dɪsˈleksɪk] ADJ, N *Med* dyslexique *mf*

dysmenorrhoea, *Am* **dysmenorrhea** [dɪsmenəˈrɪə] N *Med* dysménorrhée *f*

dyspepsia [dɪsˈpepsɪə] N *Med* dyspepsie *f*; **acid d.** aigreurs *fpl*

dyspeptic [dɪsˈpeptɪk] N *Med* dyspepsique *mf*, dyspeptique *mf*
▪ ADJ **1** *Med* dyspepsique, dyspeptique **2** *Fig (bad-tempered)* ronchon, -onne, grognon, -onne

dysphasia [dɪsˈfeɪzɪə] N *Med* dysphasie *f*

dystrophy [ˈdɪstrəfɪ] N *Med* dystrophie *f*

E, e [i:] **N 1** *(letter)* E, e *m*; **two e's** deux e **2** *Mus* mi *m*; **in E flat** en mi bémol **3** *Sch* **to get an E** avoir une très mauvaise note, ≃ avoir une note inférieure à 7 sur 20 **4** *Sl (ecstasy)* ecsta *f*, X *f* **5** *Fam* **to give sb the big E** *(reject)* plaquer qn

e [2] *(abbr east)* E.

EACH [i:tʃ] VOIR GRAMMAIRE A35–6; B15–16

> | **ADJ** chaque |
> | **PRON** chacun **1** |

ADJ chaque; **e. day** chaque jour, tous les jours; **e. one of us** chacun/chacune de nous *ou* d'entre nous

PRON 1 *(both or all)* chacun, -une; **e. of us** chacun/chacune de nous *ou* d'entre nous; **we e. earn £10, we earn £10 e.** nous gagnons 10 livres chacun; **peaches at 25p e.** pêches à 25 pence chacune *ou* 25 pence pièce; **a little of e.** un peu de chaque **2** *(reciprocal)* **e. other** l'un l'autre, l'une l'autre, *pl* les uns les autres, les unes les autres; **separated from e. other** séparés l'un de l'autre/les uns des autres; **to fight e. other** se battre; **we can help e. other** nous pouvons nous aider l'un l'autre, nous pouvons nous aider mutuellement, nous pouvons nous entraider; **they flatter e. other** ils se flattent réciproquement *ou* mutuellement

eager [ˈiːgər] **ADJ** *(desire, hope)* vif; *(look)* avide; *(voice, face)* exalté; *(supporter)* fervent; **to be e. for sth** désirer qch vivement; **the crowd were e. for blood** la foule était assoiffée de sang; **the audience were still e. for more when the show ended** le public en voulait encore quand le spectacle s'est terminé; **to be e. to do sth** être impatient de faire qch; **to be e. to please** être très désireux de plaire; **they were e. to learn** ils étaient avides d'apprendre; **I didn't want to seem too e.** *(in relationship etc)* je ne voulais pas sembler trop empressé; *Fam* **to be an e. beaver** être zélé; **I've never seen such an e. beaver** je n'ai jamais vu quelqu'un d'aussi zélé

eagerly [ˈiːgəlɪ] **ADV** *(to listen)* avidement; *(to ask, smile)* avec empressement; *(to wait)* impatiemment; *(to study, work)* avec passion; **to desire sth e.** désirer qch passionnément; **her e. awaited second album** son deuxième album très attendu

eagerness [ˈiːgənɪs] **N** *(to see sb)* impatience *f*; *(to make oneself useful etc)* empressement *m*; *(to learn sth etc)* vif désir *m*; **to show e. in doing sth** montrer un intérêt très vif à faire qch; **to show** *or* **have no e. for sth** n'avoir aucunement envie de qch; **he thought he detected a certain lack of e. in her voice** il lui sembla déceler un certain manque d'ardeur dans sa voix; **e. to succeed** ardent désir de réussir

eagle [ˈiːg(ə)l] **N 1** *(bird)* aigle *m* **2** *Her* aigle *f*,

double-headed e. aigle à deux têtes **3** *Am Mil* aigle *f (= insigne de grade de colonel)* **4** *Golf* eagle *m*, *Can* aiglon *m*
> ▸ ▸ *Rel* **e. lectern** aigle *m*

eagle-eyed **ADJ** aux yeux d'aigle

eaglet [ˈiːglɪt] **N** *(bird)* aiglon *m*

ear [ɪər] **N 1** oreille *f*, *Anat* **the external** *or* **outer/middle/internal** *or* **inner e.** l'oreille externe/moyenne/interne; **deaf in one e.** sourd d'une oreille; **she was smiling** *or* **grinning from e. to e.** elle avait un sourire épanoui jusqu'aux oreilles; **to go in one e. and out the other** *(of words)* entrer par une oreille et sortir par l'autre; **your ears must have been burning** les oreilles ont dû vous siffler; **up to one's ears in work** accablé de travail; **up to one's ears in debt** endetté jusqu'au cou; *Fam* **to be (thrown) out on one's e.** se faire jeter dehors *ou* sur le pavé; **after only two months in the job he found himself out on his e. again** après seulement deux mois de travail il s'est retrouvé de nouveau sur le pavé **2** *(hearing)* **to have sharp ears** avoir l'ouïe fine; *Mus* **to have a good/poor e.** avoir de l'oreille/ne pas avoir d'oreille; **to have an e. for music** avoir de l'oreille pour la musique; *Mus* **to play by e.** jouer sans notes; *Fig* **to play it by e.** aller au pifomètre, improviser; **to have an e. for poetry** avoir le sens de la poésie; **to have an e.** *or* **a good e. for languages** avoir une bonne oreille pour les langues; **to have sb's e.** être dans les faveurs *ou* les petits papiers de qn; **to keep one's ears open** *or* **one's e. to the ground** se tenir aux écoutes; **I'm all ears** je suis tout ouïe; **to close one's ears to the truth** fermer l'oreille à la vérité; **word reached their ears of the enemy's plan** les projets de l'ennemi leur sont venus à l'oreille **3** *Tech (of vase)* anse *f*, oreille *f*, *(of bell)* anse *f* **4** *(of seashell)* oreillette *f* **5** *(of wheat etc)* épi *m*; **wheat in the e.** blé *m* en épi
> ▸ ▸ *Anat* **e. lobe** lobe *m* de l'oreille; *Med* **e., nose and throat specialist** oto-rhino(-laryngologiste) *mf*, *pl* oto-rhinos(-laryngologistes); **e., nose and throat department** service *m* d'oto-rhino-laryngologie; **e. protector** *(against cold)* protège-tympan *m inv*; *(against noise)* casque *m* anti-bruit; **e. trumpet** cornet *m* acoustique

earache [ˈɪəreɪk] **N** mal *m* d'oreille(s); *Med* otalgie *f*; **to have e.** avoir mal à l'oreille/aux oreilles

earbashing [ˈɪəbæʃɪŋ] **N** *Br* **to give sb an e.** passer un savon à qn, souffler dans les bronches à qn; **to get an e.** se faire passer un savon, se faire souffler dans les bronches

eardrops [ˈɪədrɒps] **NPL** *Med* gouttes *fpl* pour les oreilles

eardrum [ˈɪədrʌm] **N** *Anat* tympan *m*

-eared [ˈɪəd] **SUFF** **long/short-e.** aux oreilles longues/courtes

earflap [ˈɪəflæp] **N** *(of cap)* oreillette *f*

earful [ˈɪəfʊl] **N** **I got an e. of water** j'ai pris de l'eau plein l'oreille; *Fam* **to give sb an e.** *(reprimand)* donner une verte semonce à qn, passer un savon à qn; *Fam* **a right** *or* **real e.** un bon savon; *Fam* **get an e. of this!** écoute un peu ça!

earhole [ˈɪəhəʊl] **N** *Br Fam* trou *m* de l'oreille

earl [ɜːl] **N** comte *m*

earldom [ˈɜːldəm] **N 1** *(land)* comté *m* **2** *(title)* titre *m* de comte

EARLY [ˈɜːlɪ] *(earlier, earliest)*

> | **ADJ** matinal **1** ▪ premier **2, 3** ▪ en avance **4** ▪ précoce **5** |
> | **ADV** de bonne heure **1** ▪ en avance **3** |

ADJ 1 *(in the day)* matinal, -aux; **in the e. morning** de bon matin; **e. morning walk** promenade matinale; **I'm not a great believer in e. rising** se lever de bonne heure, ce n'est pas pour moi; **to be an e. riser** être matinal, se lever de bon matin; **an e. bird** un lève-tôt, un matinal; *Prov* **the e. bird catches the worm** l'avenir appartient à ceux qui se lèvent tôt; **e. morning call** appel *m* matinal; **e. morning tea** thé du matin **2** *(at beginning of period of time)* **in (the) e. summer, in the e. part of summer** dans les *ou* aux premiers jours de l'été, au début de l'été; **in the e. afternoon** au début de l'après-midi; **to have an e. night** dîner de bonne heure; **I'm going to have an e. night** je vais me coucher de bonne heure; **in the e. nineteenth century** au début du XIXᵉ siècle; **in the e. sixties** au début des années soixante; **e. youth** première jeunesse *f*, **e. medieval music** musique *f* du début du Moyen Âge; **e. Debussy/Racine** première(s) œuvre(s) *f(pl)* de Debussy/Racine; **at an e. age** tout jeune; **from the earliest age** dès la plus tendre enfance; **from (the) earliest times** depuis les temps les plus reculés; **it's e. days yet** il est encore tôt **3** *(first)* **the e. Church** l'Église *f* primitive; **the e. Christians** les premiers chrétiens *mpl*, **the earliest legends** les premières légendes *fpl*; **a very e. example of ...** un des premiers exemples de ...; **this e. pottery** ces exemples des premières formes de poterie; *Art* **the e. masters** les primitifs *mpl*, **e. radios didn't have loudspeakers** les premières radios n'avaient pas de haut-parleurs; **my earliest recollections** mes souvenirs les plus lointains; **he received his e. education at ...** il reçut sa première éducation à ... **4** *(ahead of time)* **you're e.** tu es en avance; **I am half an hour e.** je suis en avance d'une demi-heure **5** *(premature)* précoce, hâtif; *(death)* prématuré; **e. beans** haricots de primeur; **e. vegetables/fruit/produce** primeurs *fpl*; **we're having an e. winter** l'hiver est précoce; **Easter is e. this year** Pâques est tôt cette année

6 *(future)* **at an e. date** prochainement, à une date prochaine; **at an earlier date** à une date plus rapprochée; **to take an e. opportunity to do sth** faire qch à la première occasion; **at the earliest possible moment** le plus tôt possible; **at your earliest convenience** dès que possible

7 *(previous)* **at an earlier date** à une date antérieure

ADV 1 *(in the day)* de bonne heure, tôt; **e. in the morning** le matin de bonne heure, de grand matin; **e. in the evening** tôt dans la soirée; **to get up e.** se lever de bonne heure; **as e. as possible** le plus tôt possible

2 *(at beginning of period of time etc)* **e. in the winter** au début *ou* à l'entrée de l'hiver; **e. in the year** au début de l'année; **e. on, it was apparent that …** dès l'abord, il est apparu que …; **e. in (his) life** dans ses jeunes années, dans sa jeunesse; **e. in his career** au début de sa carrière; **as e. as the tenth century** dès le dixième siècle; **e. in the list** tout au commencement de la liste

3 *(ahead of time)* en avance; **too e.** trop tôt; **to arrive five minutes (too) e.** arriver avec cinq minutes d'avance; **they left the party e.** ils ont quitté la soirée tôt

4 *(prematurely)* **to die e.** *(young)* mourir jeune; *(sooner than expected)* mourir prématurément; **this flower blooms very e.** cette fleur s'épanouit très précocement

5 *(soon)* **next week at the earliest** la semaine prochaine au plus tôt

6 *(previously)* **earlier** plus tôt; **as I mentioned earlier** *(in time)* comme je l'ai mentionné plus tôt; *(in writing)* comme je l'ai mentionné ci-dessus *ou* plus haut

▸▸*Mktg* **e. adopter** réceptif *m* précoce, adopteur *m* précoce; *Br Com* **e. closing** = jour *m* où les magasins ferment tôt; **e. edition** *(of newspaper)* première édition *f*, premier tirage *m*; *Mktg* **e. follower** suiveur *m* immédiat; *Mktg* **e. majority** majorité *f* innovatrice; **e. music** *(baroque)* musique *f* ancienne; *(earlier)* première forme *f* de musique; *Fin* **e. redemption** amortissement *m* anticipé; **to take e. retirement** prendre la retraite anticipée; *Mil* **e. warning system** réseau *m* de radars de guet *ou* de pré-alerte

early-closing ADJ
▸▸*Br Com* **e. day** = jour *m* où les magasins ferment tôt

early-purchase discount N *Mktg* discompte *m* sur achat dans un bref délai

earmark ['ɪɑmɑːk] N *Agr (of sheep etc)* marque *f* à l'oreille; *Fig* **to have all the earmarks of embezzlement/another of her silly ideas** porter tous les signes d'un détournement de fonds/d'une de ses idées stupides
VT 1 *(assign) (funds)* donner à une affectation spéciale; **to e. funds for a project** assigner des fonds à un projet; **the land has been earmarked for a new school** le terrain a été affecté à la construction d'une nouvelle école; **the building is earmarked for closure** il est prévu que ce bâtiment soit fermé; *Fam* **to e. sth for oneself** se réserver qch **2** *(mark the corner of) (document, cheque)* faire une marque au coin de **3** *Agr (sheep etc)* marquer à l'oreille

earmuff ['ɪɑmʌf] N protège-oreilles *m inv*, cache-oreilles *m inv*

earn [ɜːn] VT **1** *(money)* gagner; **how much do you e.?** combien gagnez-vous?; **to e. one's living by writing** gagner sa vie de sa plume; *Fin* **to e. interest** *(of money)* produire des intérêts **2** *(deserve) (rest, respite)* mériter; *(sb's affection, respect)* gagner; **to e. sb's love** gagner le cœur de qn; **you've earned it** *(this break, rise etc)* tu l'as bien mérité; **his**

conduct earned him universal praise/many votes sa conduite lui valut les éloges de tous/de nombreuses voix; **it earned her nothing but criticism** cela ne lui a valu que des critiques; **this action earned her many enemies** cette action lui a valu de nombreux ennemis, par cette action elle s'est attiré de nombreux ennemis; **her attitude has earned her a lot of friends/supporters** son attitude lui a gagné de nombreux amis/partisans

earned [ɜːnd] ADJ
▸▸*Com* **e. income** revenus *mpl* salariaux; *Fin* **e. interest** revenu *m* des intérêts; *Acct* **e. surplus** bénéfices *mpl* non distribués

earner ['ɜːnər] N **1** *(person)* **(wage) e.** salarié, -ée; **she's not a big e.** elle ne gagne pas beaucoup; **the high/low earners** les gros/petits salaires *mpl* **2** *Br Fam (activity, business)* **a nice little e.** une bonne petite affaire, un bon plan

earnest ['ɜːnɪst] ADJ *(person, effort, discussion)* sérieux; *(expression)* pénétré, grave; *(demand, voice)* pressant; *(request)* fervent; *(desire, wish)* profond
N 1 in e. sérieusement; **to be in e.** être sérieux; **are you in e.?** *(in what you're saying)* parlez-vous sérieusement?; **to speak in e.** parler sérieusement; **she's leaving him in e. this time** cette fois elle le quitte pour de bon; **to set to work in e.** se mettre sérieusement à l'ouvrage **2** *Com etc Old-fashioned* arrhes *fpl*

earnestly ['ɜːnɪstlɪ] ADV *(to speak, discuss, consider)* sérieusement; *(to hope, believe)* sincèrement; *(to desire)* profondément; *(to pray)* avec ferveur

earnestness ['ɜːnɪstnɪs] N *(of discussion)* caractère *m* sérieux; *(of tone, person)* gravité *f*, sérieux *m*; *(of hope, desire)* sincérité *f*; *(of request)* ferveur *f*

earning ['ɜːnɪŋ] N *(act)* gain *m*
▸▸**e. capacity, e. power** *(of business)* rapport *m*; *(of person)* revenu *m* potentiel

earnings ['ɜːnɪŋz] NPL **1** *(salary)* salaire *m*; **my e.** ce que je gagne; **e. related** *(pensions, benefits etc)* proportionnel au salaire **2** *(profits)* profits *mpl*, bénéfices *mpl*
▸▸*Fin* **e. forecast** résultats *mpl* prévisionnels; *Fin* **e. growth** accroissement *m ou* augmentation *f* des bénéfices; *Fin* **e. before interest and tax** bénéfices avant impôts et charges; *Fin* **e. retained** bénéfices non distribués

earphone ['ɪəfəʊn] N *Radio, Tel* écouteur *m*

earpiece ['ɪəpiːs] N *Tel (of handset)* écouteur *m*; *(in TV studio)* écouteur auriculaire

ear-piercing ADJ *(scream)* à vous percer les tympans
N *(for earrings)* **do you know anywhere in town that does e.?** connais-tu un endroit en ville où l'on peut se faire percer les oreilles?

earplug ['ɪəplʌg] N *(for sleeping)* boule *f* Quiès®; *(for protection from noise)* protège-tympan *m inv*

earring ['ɪərɪŋ] N boucle *f* d'oreille

earshot ['ɪəʃɒt] N **within/out of e.** à portée/hors de portée de voix

ear-splitting ADJ à vous déchirer *ou* crever les tympans

earth [ɜːθ] N **1** *(planet)* terre *f*, *(world)* monde *m*; **the e.** *or* **E.** *(planet)* la Terre; **the e.'s crust/atmosphere** l'écorce *f*/l'atmosphère *f* terrestre; **on e.** sur terre; *Bible* **on e. as it is in heaven** sur la terre comme au ciel; *Fam* **where/why on e. …?** où/pourquoi diable …?; **what on e. have you done to your hair?** que diable as-tu fait à tes cheveux?; *Fam* **how on e. should I know?** comment veux-tu que je le sache?; *Fam* **to look like nothing on e.** ne

ressembler à rien; *Fam* **to feel like nothing on e.** ne vraiment pas être dans son assiette; **there's no reason on e.** il n'y a absolument aucune raison; **it wouldn't cost the e.** ça ne coûterait pas les yeux de la tête; **to pay the e. for sth** payer qch les yeux de la tête; **he promised people the e.** il a promis la lune aux gens

2 *(ground)* sol *m*; *Fig* **to come back to e. (with a bump)** revenir (brutalement) sur terre; **it brought her down to e. with a bit of a bump** ça l'a ramenée sur terre un peu brutalement; **the e. moved** la terre a tremblé; *Hum* **did the e. move for you?** *(while making love)* est-ce que tu as eu le grand frisson?

3 *Agr etc (soil)* terre *f*; **e. floor** *(of hut etc)* sol *m* en terre battue; **loose/heavy e.** terre(s) meuble(s)/lourde(s)

4 *Br Elec* terre *f*, masse *f*, *(terminal)* mise *f* à terre; **dead e.** contact *m* parfait avec le sol; **e. to frame** *(of car etc)* contact à la masse; *Aut* **câble** *m* de masse

5 *(of fox)* terrier *m*, tanière *f*; **to go to e.** *(of fox, fugitive)* se terrer; **I've been trying to get in touch with him but he seems to have gone to e.** j'ai essayé de le joindre mais on dirait qu'il s'est volatilisé; **to run to e.** *(fox)* chasser jusqu'à son terrier; *(fugitive)* dépister; *(person)* dénicher; *(mistake in the figures)* découvrir la source de

VT 1 *Br Elec* mettre à la terre **2** *(in hunting)* poursuivre jusqu'à son terrier **3** = **earth up**
VI *(of fox)* se terrer
▸▸*Br Elec* **e. cable** câble *m* de terre; *Br Elec* **e. connection** prise *f* de terre; **e. creature** *(in science fiction)* créature *f* terrestre; *Astron* **e. orbit** *(of satellite)* orbite *f* terrestre; *Astron* **e. satellite** satellite *m* terrestre; **e. sciences** sciences *fpl* de la terre; *TV* **e. station** station *f* terrestre; *Br Elec* **e. wire** fil *m* de terre
▸ **earth up** VT SEP *(in gardening) (plant)* butter, chausser

earthbound ['ɜːθbaʊnd] ADJ **1** *(mundane)* terre à terre *inv* **2** **e. spirit** esprit *m* qui ne peut pas quitter le monde des vivants **3** *(heading towards earth)* qui se dirige vers la terre

earthen ['ɜːθ(ə)n] ADJ **1** *(crockery etc)* en *ou* de terre (cuite) **2** *(floor)* en terre battue

earthenware ['ɜːθ(ə)nweər] N poterie *f* (de terre); **e. jug** cruche *f* en *ou* de terre (cuite); **glazed e.** faïence *f*, *(stoneware)* grès *m* flambé

earthfall ['ɜːθfɔːl] N éboulement *m* de terres

earthiness ['ɜːθɪnɪs] N truculence *f*, *Pej* grossièreté *f*

earthlight ['ɜːθlaɪt] N *Astron (of moon)* lumière *f* cendrée

earthling ['ɜːθlɪŋ] N *(in science fiction)* habitant, -ante de la terre, terrien, -enne

earthly ['ɜːθlɪ] ADJ terrestre; **the E. Paradise** le Paradis terrestre; *Fam* **there's no reason for …** il n'y a absolument aucune raison pour que …; *Fam* **it's of no e. use to me** ça ne me sert *ou* ne me servirait absolument à rien; *Fam* **he hasn't got an e. chance** *or* **hope** il n'a pas la moindre chance
N *Br Fam* **he hasn't got an e.** il n'a pas la moindre chance

earthman, *pl* **earthmen** ['ɜːθmæn, -men] N *(in science fiction)* terrien *m*

earthmover ['ɜːθmuːvər] N bulldozer *m*

earthmoving ['ɜːθmuːvɪŋ] N
▸▸**e. equipment** engins *mpl* de terrassement

earthquake ['ɜːθkweɪk] N *also Fig* tremblement *m* de terre, séisme *m*; **e. survivor** survivant *m ou* rescapé *m* d'un tremblement de terre

earth-shaking ['ɜːθʃeɪkɪŋ] ADJ = **earth-shattering**

earth-shattering ADJ **1** *(discovery, news)* stupéfiant; *(defeat)* accablant **2** *(explosion, crash etc)* assourdissant

earthwoman, *pl* **earthwomen** ['ɜːθwʊmən, -wɪmɪn] N *(in science fiction)* terrienne *f*

earthwork ['ɜːθwɜːk] N e. embankment terrassement *m* en remblai; **earthworks** *(banked earth)* travaux *mpl* en terre *ou* de terrassement; *(prehistoric), Mil* fortifications *fpl* en terre

earthworm ['ɜːθwɜːm] N lombric *m*, ver *m* de terre

earthy ['ɜːθɪ] ADJ **1** terreux; **to have an e. smell** sentir la terre **2** *(coarse) (person)* truculent; *(humour, language)* truculent, vert; **an e. laugh** un gros rire **3** e. common sense sens *m* pratique

earwax ['ɪəwæks] N cire *f (sécrétée par les oreilles), Fml* cérumen *m*

earwig ['ɪəwɪg] N *(insect)* perce-oreille *m*, *pl* perce-oreilles
▸ VT *Fam* écouter de façon indiscrète
▸ VI *Fam* écouter aux portes

ease [iːz] N **1** *(facility) (when speaking, moving etc)* facilité *f*, *(of manners, movements etc)* aisance *f*; **the e. with which they adapted** la facilité avec laquelle ils se sont adaptés; **with e.** *(to defeat, adapt)* facilement; *(to answer)* aisément; *(to speak)* avec facilité; **with the utmost** *or* **the greatest of e.** avec la plus grande facilité, le plus facilement du monde; **the e. with which we entered the building** la facilité avec laquelle nous sommes entrés dans le bâtiment; **e. of use** confort *m ou* facilité d'emploi
2 *(peace) (mental)* tranquillité *f*, *(physical)* repos *m*, bien-être *m*; **to be at e.** *(mentally)* avoir l'esprit tranquille; **to be at e. with sb/ in a place** être à l'aise avec qn/dans un endroit; **to be** *or* **feel ill at e.** *(awkward)* être mal à l'aise; *(worried)* être inquiet (**about** au sujet de); **a nation at e. with itself** une nation qui s'accepte; **to be at one's e.** *(relaxed)* être à son aise; *(calm)* être tranquille; **to put sb at e.** mettre qn à l'aise; **set your mind at e.** rassurez-vous, soyez tranquille; **to take one's e.** se mettre à l'aise; *Mil etc* **to stand at e.** se mettre *ou* se tenir au repos; **at e.!** repos!
3 *(leisure)* loisir *m*; *(idleness)* oisiveté *f*, **a life of e.** une vie d'oisiveté
▸ VT **1** *(alleviate) (suffering, pain)* adoucir, calmer, soulager; *(the mind)* tranquilliser; **to e. sb's anxiety/fears** calmer les inquiétudes/ craintes de qn
2 *(free)* débarrasser, délivrer (**sb of** *or* **from sth** qn de qch); **to e. oneself of a burden** se soulager d'un fardeau
3 *(relax) (rope, spring)* détendre, relâcher; *(screw)* desserrer; *(pressure)* soulager; *(tension)* réduire; **to e. the congestion in a street** décongestionner la circulation d'une rue
4 *(move carefully, slowly)* déplacer doucement; **to e. a box open** ouvrir doucement une boîte; **to e. one's way through the crowd** se faufiler à travers la foule
5 *Sewing (dress, item of clothing)* donner plus d'ampleur à; *Tech (part)* donner du jeu à
▸ VI *(of pain, pressure etc)* s'atténuer; *(of tension), St Exch (market etc)* se détendre; **the wind/rain has eased** le vent/la pluie s'est calmé(e); **the situation has eased** la situation s'est détendue
▸ **ease off** VT SEP **1** *(release)* enlever doucement; **she eased the lid off the jar** elle a doucement enlevé le couvercle de sur le pot
2 *Naut (let out) (rigging)* filer, choquer
▸ VI **1** *(work less)* moins travailler, *Pej* se relâcher

2 *(diminish) (of pain)* s'atténuer; *(of rain)* se calmer; *St Exch (of rates)* se détendre
3 *Naut* s'éloigner un peu du rivage
▸ **ease up** VI **1** = **ease off** VI **1, 2**
2 *(slow down)* ralentir

easel ['iːz(ə)l] N *(of painter)* chevalet *m*

easily ['iːzɪlɪ] ADV **1** *(without difficulty)* facilement, sans difficulté; **you can e. imagine my disappointment** vous concevez sans peine ma déception; **he is not e. satisfied** il n'est pas facile à satisfaire; *Sport etc* **he came in first e.** il est arrivé bon premier; **the car holds six people e.** six personnes tiennent à l'aise dans cette voiture; **that's e. said** c'est vite dit **2** *(in relaxed manner)* à son aise; **to take things** *or* **life e.** prendre les choses comme elles viennent, prendre la vie comme elle vient, *Pej* se laisser vivre, se la couler douce **3** *(undoubtedly)* **e. larger** largement plus grand; **e. the best/worst/biggest** de loin le meilleur/le pire/le plus gros; **he is e. forty** il a bien quarante ans; **it's e. 20 kilometres to the next village** il y a bien 20 kilomètres jusqu'au prochain village **4** *(possibly)* **the information could e. be wrong** les informations pourraient très bien être fausses

easiness ['iːzɪnɪs] N **1** *(of task)* facilité *f*, **I was surprised at the e. with which the door opened** j'ai été surpris par la facilité avec laquelle la porte s'est ouverte **2** *(easy-going nature) (of person)* décontraction *f*, *(of approach)* caractère *m* décontracté; **his e. with children** la facilité de ses rapports avec les enfants

easing ['iːzɪŋ] N **1** *(of suffering, pressure)* atténuation *f*, *(caused by medication)* soulagement *m*; *(of beam etc)* allègement *m* **2** *(relaxation) (of conflict, pressure)* atténuation *f*, *(of restrictions)* allègement *m*; **e. of tension** *(political etc)* détente *f*, *Com* **e. of the market** détente du marché
▸ **e. off** *(of pain)* atténuation *f*, *(from work)* relâchement *m*

east [iːst] N est *m*; **the house faces the e.** la maison est orientée à l'est; **on the e., to the e.** à l'est de); **the E.** *(the Orient)* l'Orient *m*; **the Middle E.** le Moyen-Orient; **the Far E.** l'Extrême-Orient; **the e. of England** l'est de l'Angleterre; **to pray to the e.** prier en direction de l'est
▸ ADV à l'est; **to travel e.** voyager vers l'est; **e. of the Rhine** à l'est du Rhin
▸ ADJ est *inv*, *(wind)* d'est; *(wall, window)* qui fait face à l'est; **the e. coast** la côte est
▸▸ **E. Africa** Afrique *f* orientale; **E. End** *(of city)* = quartiers *mpl* est de; **the East End** = quartier industriel de Londres, connu pour ses docks et, autrefois, pour sa pauvreté; *esp Am* **E. Europe** Europe *f* de l'Est; *Formerly* **E. Germany** Allemagne *f* de l'Est; *Hist* **E. India Company** compagnie *f* des Indes Orientales; *Hist* **the E. Indies** les Indes *fpl* orientales; **the E. Side** l'East Side *m (quartier situé à l'est de Manhattan)*

eastbound ['iːstbaʊnd] ADJ *(traffic)* en direction de l'est; *(lane, carriageway)* de l'est; *(road)* vers l'est; **e. traffic is subject to delays** la circulation est ralentie dans le sens est; **there's a jam on the e. carriageway** il y a un bouchon en direction de l'est

Easter ['iːstər] N Pâques *m*; **at E.** à Pâques; **to celebrate E.** fêter Pâques
▸▸ **E. Day** le jour de Pâques; **E. egg** œuf *m* de Pâques; **E. Island** l'île *f* de Pâques; **E. Monday** le lundi de Pâques; **E. Sunday** le dimanche de Pâques; **E. week** *(following Easter)* la semaine de Pâques; *(Holy Week)* la semaine sainte

easterly ['iːstəlɪ] ADJ *(wind)* d'est, qui vient de l'est; *(current)* qui se dirige vers l'est; **e.**

point point situé à *ou* vers l'est; **in an e. direction** vers l'est
▸ ADV vers l'est
▸ N vent *m* d'est

eastern ['iːstən] ADJ est *inv*, de l'est; *(of Far East)* oriental, -aux; **the e. side of the country** la partie est du pays
▸▸ *Rel* **the E. Church** l'Église *f* d'Orient; **E. Europe** Europe *f* de l'Est; **E. Standard Time** heure *f* d'hiver de New York; **the E. Townships** *(of Canada)* les Cantons *mpl* de l'Est

Easterner ['iːstənər] N *(from Far East)* oriental, -ale; *(in US)* = personne *f* qui vient de l'est des États-Unis

Eastertide ['iːstətaɪd] N Pâques *m*

east-facing ['iːstfeɪsɪŋ] ADJ orienté à l'est

eastward ['iːstwəd] ADJ vers l'est, en direction de l'est
▸ ADV = **eastwards**

eastwards ['iːstwədz] ADV vers l'est, en direction de l'est

EASY ['iːzɪ] **(easier, easiest)** ADJ **1** *(not difficult) (work)* facile, aisé; *(question, test)* facile; *(method, solution)* simple; **e. to please** pas difficile; **to be e. to annoy/upset** s'énerver/ se vexer facilement; **he's e. to keep entertained** on l'amuse, rien l'amuse; **e. to get on with** d'un commerce facile; **e. to live with** facile à vivre; **don't worry, it's e. to do on your first day** ne t'inquiète pas, ça arrive à tout le monde le premier jour; **that is e. to see** cela se voit; **it is e. for him to …** il lui est facile de …; **it's e. to say …** on a vite fait de dire …; **this will make your job easier** ceci vous facilitera la tâche; **it makes life much easier not having to fill in these forms** ça facilite bien les choses de ne pas avoir à remplir ces formulaires; **within e. reach of …** à distance commode de …; **it's within e. walking distance** on peut facilement y aller à pied; *Fam* **as e. as ABC** *or* **as falling off a log** *or* **as pie** simple comme bonjour; **it isn't e. being a mother** ce n'est pas facile d'être mère; **the e. way out** *or* **option** la solution de facilité; **there are no e. answers** c'est un problème qui est loin d'être facile à résoudre; **to have an e. time (of it)** se la couler douce; **by e. stages** *(travel)* à petites étapes; **learn how to drive/French in five e. steps** *or* **stages** apprendre à conduire/le français sans peine en cinq leçons; **the film is very e. on the eye** le film est reposant à regarder; **he's/she's e. on the eye** il/elle n'est pas mal du tout; *Com* **by e. payments, on e. terms** avec facilités de paiement; *Sport etc* **to come in an e. first** arriver bon premier
2 *(easy-going, relaxed) (person)* d'un caractère facile; *(manners etc)* libre, dégagé; *(style)* facile, naturel; *(grace)* naturel; **they're usually fairly e. about deadlines** d'habitude ils sont assez accommodants sur les délais; **the e. familiarity of her welcome instantly reassured them** la familiarité dégagée de son accueil les a immédiatement rassurés; *Fam* **I'm e.!** *(I don't mind)* ça m'est égal!; *Old-fashioned* **woman of e. virtue** femme *f* de mœurs faciles *ou* légères; *Sl* **an e. lay** une femme/fille facile
3 *(movement)* aisé, souple; *(of jeans, clothes)* lâche, de coupe confortable; *Tech* **e. fit** ajustage *m* lâche; **my coat is an e. fit** mon manteau est de coupe confortable
4 *(comfortable) (pace)* tranquille; *(life)* sans souci; **to be e. in one's mind** avoir l'esprit tranquille; **at an e. pace** tranquillement; **with an e. conscience** la conscience tranquille; *Fam* **to be on e. street** ne pas avoir de problèmes financiers
5 *Com (market)* tranquille; **prices are (getting) easier** on accuse une détente dans les prix; **cotton was easier** le coton a accusé une détente

ADV **1 to take things** or **it e.** (in relaxed manner) prendre les choses en douceur; **to take things** or **life e.** (lead a life of ease) mener une vie tranquille; (not overdo things) ralentir; **take it e.!** doucement!; (don't get upset) ne vous en faites pas!; **you'll have to go e. for a bit** il va falloir ralentir ou freiner un peu; **to go e. with sb/sth** ménager qn/qch; **e. does it!** (allez-y) doucement!; **go e. on the electricity/the curry powder** allez-y doucement avec l'électricité/le curry; **e. (ahead)!** (in rowing) (en avant) doucement!; Mil **stand e.!** repos!

2 Fam (without difficulty) **I can do it e.** cela me sera facile; **(it's) easier said than done** c'est plus facile à dire qu'à faire; Prov **e. come e. go** ce qui vient de la flûte s'en va par le tambour

▸▸ **e. chair** fauteuil m; Mus **e. listening** variété f; Fam **e. money** argent m gagné sans peine

easy-going ADJ **1** (not given to anger) qui prend les choses tranquillement; (not worrying) qui ne se fait pas de bile, décontracté; (undemanding) accommodant, coulant, peu exigeant; (permissive) qui a la conscience élastique; **the police take an e. attitude to such cases** dans de tels cas, la police se montre assez conciliante **2** (horse) à l'allure douce

eat [iːt] (pt **ate** [et, esp Am eɪt], pp **eaten** ['iːt(ə)n]) VT **1** (bread, soup etc) manger; **to e. one's breakfast** déjeuner, prendre son petit déjeuner; **to e. one's dinner/supper** dîner/souper; **to e. a good dinner** faire un bon dîner; **to e. a card** (credit card) avaler une carte; **fit to e.** bon à manger, mangeable; **I don't e. meat** je ne mange pas de viande; **to e. one's fill** manger à sa faim; **he won't e. you** il ne vous mangera pas; Fam **(I'm so hungry) I could e. a horse!** j'ai une faim de loup!; Fam **we e. teams like you for breakfast** nous ne faisons qu'une seule bouchée d'équipes comme la vôtre; Am Fam Fig **to e. sb's lunch** (defeat) battre qn à plates coutures; **to e. one's words** se rétracter; **if it comes off, I'll e. my hat** si ça réussit, je mange mon chapeau; **to e. sb out of house and home** ruiner qn en nourriture; **she ate her way through six packets of biscuits** elle a réussi à engloutir six paquets de biscuits; Am Vulg **e. shit!** va te faire voir!

2 Fam (trouble) **what's eating you?** qu'est-ce qui vous inquiète ou tracasse?

VI **1** manger; **to e. like a horse** manger comme un ogre; **to e. like a bird** avoir un appétit d'oiseau, manger trois fois rien; **he eats out of my hand** (of bird) il vient manger dans ma main; Fig (of person) il fait tout ce que je veux; **treat them right and you'll have them eating out of your hand** traite-les bien et ils te mangeront dans la main

2 (have meal) dîner; **we e. at seven** nous dînons à sept heures; **to e. well** bien manger; **let's e.!** on mange?; **have you eaten?** est-ce que tu as mangé?

▸ **eat away** VT SEP (erode) (rocks, cliff, self-confidence) éroder, miner; (foundations) saper; (part of body) ronger; (of acid) dissoudre

▸ **eat away at** VT INSEP = **eat away, eat into**
▸ **eat in** VI (of hotel guest) consommer sur place

▸ **eat into** VT INSEP **1** (attack) ronger; **rust had eaten into the metal** la rouille avait rongé le métal; **to e. into wood** (of insect, worm) ronger le bois **2** (diminish) entamer; **these expenses had eaten into their savings** ces dépenses avaient entamé leurs économies

▸ **eat off** VT SEP Fam **to e. one's head off** s'empiffrer

▸ **eat out** VI **1** (eat in restaurant) manger au restaurant **2** (of hotel guest) déjeuner/dîner à l'extérieur

VT SEP Fam **to e. one's heart out** se ronger le cœur; **e. your heart out, USA!** = dommage pour les États-Unis!

▸ **eat up** VT SEP **1** (eat completely) (cake etc) manger jusqu'à la dernière miette; **e. up your bread!** finis ton pain! **2** (consume) consumer sans profit; Fam **stove that eats up the coal** poêle qui mange beaucoup de charbon; **to e. up the miles** (of car etc) dévorer la route; **jealousy is eating him up** la jalousie le dévore; **to be eaten up with** (pride) être dévoré de; (ambition) être consumé par **3** (exhaust) (provisions) épuiser

VI (eat everything) finir son assiette; **e. up! (there's lots more)** vas-y, mange!

eatable ['iːtəb(ə)l] ADJ comestible; (fit to eat) mangeable, bon à manger; **fruit that is quite e.** fruit qui se laisse manger

NPL esp Hum **eatables** provisions fpl de bouche, comestibles mpl

eater ['iːtər] N **1** (person) mangeur, -euse; **he isn't as good an e. as his sister** il ne mange pas aussi bien que sa sœur; **to be a fussy e.** être difficile (sur la nourriture); **to be a messy e.** manger salement; **small/big e.** petit/gros mangeur **2** (apple) pomme f à couteau ou de dessert

eatery ['iːtərɪ] N Fam (café-)restaurant m, pl (cafés-)restaurants

eating ['iːtɪŋ] N manger m; **healthy e.** alimentation f saine; **these birds make good e.** ces oiseaux sont bons à manger

▸▸ **e. apple** pomme f à couteau; **e. habits** habitudes fpl alimentaires; **e. house, e. place** restaurant m

eats [iːts] NPL Fam bouffe f; **plenty of e.** plein à bouffer; **let's get some e.** allons chercher de la bouffe

eau-de-Cologne ['əʊdəkə'ləʊn] N eau f de Cologne

eaves [iːvz] NPL Constr avant-toit m

eavesdrop ['iːvzdrɒp] VI (-pp-) écouter aux portes; **to e. on a conversation** tendre l'oreille pour écouter une conversation privée; **I found myself eavesdropping on their conversation** j'ai entendu leur conversation sans le vouloir; **stop eavesdropping!** arrête d'espionner le monde!

eavesdropper ['iːvzdrɒpər] N oreille f indiscrète

ebb [eb] N **1** (of tide) reflux m; **the e. and flow** le flux et le reflux; **the e. and flow of marital life** les hauts et les bas de la vie conjugale; **the e. and flow of political change** les fluctuations de la vie politique; **the tide is on the e.** la marée baisse **2** (of fortune, life) déclin m; **to be at a low e.** (of patient) être très bas; (be depressed) être déprimé; (of business) être au ralenti; **her spirits were at a low e./their lowest e.** elle était abattue/très abattue; **their funds were at a low/their lowest e.** ils étaient à bout de ressources

VI **1** (of tide) baisser; **to e. and flow** monter et baisser **2** = **ebb away**

▸▸ **e. tide** marée f descendante

▸ **ebb away** VI (of enthusiasm, courage, strength) faiblir, baisser; (of rage, indignation) se calmer; (of support) s'amenuiser; (of time, water) s'écouler; **his life was ebbing away** il baissait d'heure en heure

ebbing ['ebɪŋ] ADJ **1** (water) qui reflue **2** (fortunes etc) sur le déclin; (popularity) en baisse; (strength, enthusiasm) faiblissant

EBIT [iːbiːaɪ'tiː, 'ebɪt] N Fin (abbr earnings before interest and tax) bénéfices mpl avant impôts et charges

EBITDA [ebiːt'daː] N Fin (abbr earnings before interest, tax, depreciation and amortization) EBITDA m

ebonics [ə'bɒnɪks] N Ling = anglais m parlé

par une partie de la communauté Noire américaine

ebony ['ebənɪ] N **1** (wood) (bois m d') ébène f, **e. box** boîte f en bois d'ébène **2** (tree) ébénier m **3** (colour) ébène f; **e. skin** peau f noire d'ébène

▸▸ **e. tree** ébénier m

e-book N livre m numérique, livre électronique, e-book m

EBRD [iːbiːɑː'diː] N (abbr European Bank for Reconstruction and Development) BERD f

e-broker N St Exch courtier, -ière électronique

e-broking N St Exch courtage m électronique

ebullience [ɪ'bʌlɪəns] N bouillonnement m, effervescence f; **the e. of youth** l'exubérance f de la jeunesse

ebullient [ɪ'bʌlɪənt] ADJ enthousiaste, exubérant; **they were in (an) e. mood** or **in e. spirits** ils étaient d'une humeur exubérante

e-business N Comput commerce m électronique

EC [iː'siː] N (abbr European Community) CE f; **EC directive** directive f européenne

ADJ ATTRIB de la CE

e-cash N Comput argent m électronique, argent virtuel, e-cash m

ECB [iːsiː'biː] N (abbr European Central Bank) BCE f

eccentric [ek'sentrɪk] ADJ **1** (person, behaviour) excentrique **2** Math, Astron (circle, orbit etc) excentrique; Tech (camshaft) excentré

N **1** (person) excentrique mf, original, -ale **2** Tech excentrique m

▸▸ Tech **e. shaft** arbre m à excentrique

eccentrically [ek'sentrɪklɪ] ADV Tech excentriquement; (to dress, behave) de manière excentrique, excentriquement

eccentricity [eksen'trɪsɪtɪ] N **1** (of character, behaviour etc) excentricité f, **eccentricities** (of person) excentricités **2** Math (of ellipse) excentricité f, Tech excentricité, désaxage m

ecclesiastic [ɪkliːzɪ'æstɪk] N Fml ecclésiastique m

ecclesiastical [ɪkliːzɪ'æstɪk(ə)l] ADJ ecclésiastique

ECE [iːsiː'iː] N abbr Economic Commission for Europe

ECG [iːsiː'dʒiː] N Med **1** (abbr electrocardiogram) ECG m **2** (abbr electrocardiograph) électrocardiographe m

ECGD [iːsiːdʒiː'diː] N (abbr Export Credit Guarantee Department) COFACE f

echelon ['eʃəlɒn] N **1** (level) **the higher** or **upper echelons of industry/the Civil Service** les niveaux supérieurs de l'industrie/de l'administration **2** Mil échelon m; **in e.** en échelon

echinacea [ekɪ'neɪʃə] N Bot, Med échinacée f

echo, pl **echoes** ['ekəʊ, -əʊz] N écho m; **this room has a bit of an e./a good e.** il y a un peu d'écho/un bon écho dans cette pièce; **to cheer sb to the e.** applaudir qn à tout rompre; Fig **there are echoes of the 18th century in this novel** il y a des accents du XVIIIe siècle dans ce roman; **echoes of Churchill/Godard** du Churchill/du Godard; **her words found an e. in many hearts** ses mots ont fait vibrer la corde sensible dans beaucoup de cœurs

VT répéter (en écho); **to e. sb's words** répéter ce que qn a dit; **to e. sb's opinions** se faire l'écho des opinions de qn; **'we're going to the beach', she said – 'the beach?' he echoed** 'nous allons à la plage', dit-elle – 'à la plage?', répéta-t-il; Fig **the yellow of the** walls is **echoed in the curtains** le jaune des murs se trouve rappelé dans les rideaux **vi** faire écho; **the woods echoed with the songs of birds** les bois retentissaient des chants des oiseaux; **his voice echoes through the room** sa voix résonne dans la salle

►► **e. chamber** chambre f de réverbération; **e. sounder** échosondeur m; **e. sounding** sondage m par ultrasons

ECHR [i:si:eɪtʃ'ɑ:r] **N** (abbr **European Court of Human Rights**) CEDH f

éclair [eɪ'kleər] **N** Culin éclair m; **chocolate e.** éclair au chocolat

eclectic [ɪ'klektɪk] **ADJ, N** éclectique mf; **an e. blend** un mélange varié

eclecticism [ɪ'klektɪsɪz(ə)m] **N** éclectisme m

eclipse [ɪ'klɪps] **N 1** Astron éclipse f; **solar/lunar e.** éclipse de soleil/de lune; **total/partial e.** éclipse totale/partielle **2** Naut (of lighthouse) éclipse f **3** Fig (overshadowing) éclipse f; **the e. of this team by a younger one** l'éclipse de cette équipe par une équipe plus jeune; **to suffer** or **go into an e.** être éclipsé

vt 1 Astron, Naut etc éclipser **2** Fig (overshadow, supersede) éclipser

Ecofin ['i:kəʊfɪn] **N** (abbr **Economic and Financial Council of Ministers**) (Conseil m) Ecofin m

ecofreak ['i:kəʊfri:k] **N** Fam écologiste mf enragé(e)

eco-friendly ['i:kəʊ-] **ADJ** (product) qui ne nuit pas à l'environnement; (lifestyle, person) qui respecte l'environnement

ecological [i:kə'lɒdʒɪk(ə)l] **ADJ** écologique

ecologically [i:kə'lɒdʒɪklɪ] **ADV** écologiquement; **to be e. harmful/sound** nuire/ne pas nuire à l'environnement

ecologist [ɪ'kɒlədʒɪst] **N** écologiste mf

ecology [ɪ'kɒlədʒɪ] **N** écologie f

e-commerce N Comput commerce m électronique

►► **e. site** site m marchand

econometric [ɪkɒnə'metrɪk] **ADJ** économétrique

►► **e. model** modèle m économétrique; **e. modelling** modélisation f économétrique

econometrics [ɪkɒnə'metrɪks] **N** économétrie f VOIR GRAMMAIRE A10

economic [i:kə'nɒmɪk] **ADJ 1** Econ économique **2** Br (profitable) rentable; **to make sth e.** rentabiliser qch **3** Fam (inexpensive) économique

►► **e. adviser** conseiller, -ère économique; **e. aid** aide f économique; **e. analysis** analyse f économique; **e. analyst** analyste mf économique; **e. appraisal** évaluation f économique; **e. circumstances** conjoncture f; EU **E. Commission for Europe** Commission f économique pour l'Europe; **e. cost** coût m économique; **e. crisis** crise f économique; **e. development** croissance f par habitant ou per capita; **e. forecast** prévisions fpl économiques; **e. forecasting firm** = organisme m spécialisé dans les prévisions économiques; **e. geography** géographie f économique; **e. goods** biens mpl économiques; **e. indicator** indicateur m économique; EU **E. and Monetary Union** union f économique et monétaire; **e. pressure** pression f économique; **e. rate of return** taux f de rentabilité économique; **e. recovery** reprise f ou redressement m économique; **e. sanctions** sanctions fpl économiques; **e. situation** conjoncture f économique; EU **E. and Social Committee** Comité m Économique et Social; **e. trend** tendance f ou conjoncture f économique; **e. zone** zone f économique

---

Il faut noter que les adjectifs **economic** et **economical** ne sont pas interchangeables. **Economic** signifie qui se rapporte à l'économie, alors que **economical** signifie qui permet d'économiser.

---

economical [i:kə'nɒmɪk(ə)l] **ADJ** (person) économe; (machine, method, approach) économique; (style) concis, sobre; **to be e. with sth** économiser qch; **to be e. with the truth** dire la vérité avec parcimonie; **it's more e. to buy larger packets** c'est plus économique d'acheter des paquets plus grands

►► **e. speed** (of ship etc) vitesse f économique

Voir note ci-dessus.

---

economically [i:kə'nɒmɪklɪ] **ADV** économiquement; **to use sth e.** (electricity, fuel) économiser qch; **e. viable** économiquement viable, rentable; **e. written** écrit avec concision

economics [i:kə'nɒmɪks] **N** VOIR GRAMMAIRE A10 **1** Econ les sciences fpl économiques; **socialist/supply-side e.** économie f socialiste/de l'offre **2** (financial aspects) aspects mpl économiques ou financiers; (profitability) rentabilité f; **we must consider the e. of the project before making any decisions** nous devons considérer l'aspect financier du projet avant de prendre une décision

economist [ɪ'kɒnəmɪst] **N** Econ économiste mf

economize [ɪ'kɒnəmaɪz] **vi** économiser, faire des économies; **to e. on sth** économiser sur qch

vt (time, money etc) économiser, ménager

economizer [ɪ'kɒnəmaɪzər] **N** Aut économiseur m

economy [ɪ'kɒnəmɪ] **N 1** (careful use, saving) (of money, resources etc) économie f; **to practise e.** économiser; **to make economies** faire des économies; **it's a false e.** ça revient aussi cher; **with e. of effort** sans effort m inutile; **e. of style** concision f de style; **economies of scale** économies fpl d'échelle **2** Econ (of country) économie f, régime m économique; **Old-fashioned political e.** économie politique; **(centrally) planned e.** économie planifiée

►► Com **e. brand** marque f économique; **e. class** classe f touriste; **e. drive** (of company, government) politique f de réduction des dépenses; **e. fare** tarif m économique; **e. measure** mesure f de réduction des dépenses; Aut **e. mode** (with automatic gears) mode m économique; Com **e. pack** paquet m économique; Com **e. size** format m économique

ECOSOC ['i:kəʊsɒk] **N** EU (abbr **Economic and Social Committee**) CES m

ecosphere ['i:kəʊsfɪər] **N** écosphère f

ecosystem ['i:kəʊsɪstəm] **N** écosystème m

ecotax ['i:kəʊtæks] **N** taxe f écologique, écotaxe f

ecoterrorist ['i:kəʊ'terərɪst] **N** = militant, -ante écologiste ayant recours à des actions violentes

ecotourism [i:kəʊ'tʊərɪz(ə)m] **N** tourisme m écologique

ecowarrior ['i:kəʊwɒrɪər] **N** écoguerrier, -ière

ecru ['ekru:] **N, ADJ** Tex écru m

ECSC [i:si:es'si:] **N** Admin (abbr **European Coal and Steel Community**) CECA f

ecstasy ['ekstəsɪ] **N 1** (joyful feeling) joie f délirante, ravissement m; **an e. of delight** un transport de joie; **to be in an e. of joy** se pâmer de joie; **to go into/be in ecstasies over sth** s'extasier/être en extase devant qch; **to send sb into ecstasies** faire tomber

---

qn en extase **2** Rel, Psy etc extase f **3** Sl (drug) ecstasy f

ecstatic [ek'stætɪk] **ADJ** extatique; **he was e. about** or **over the news/their arrival** la nouvelle/leur arrivée le rendait fou de joie

ecstatically [ek'stætɪklɪ] **ADV** avec extase; (to look at) d'un air extasié; **e. happy** heureux jusqu'au ravissement

ECT [i:si:'ti:] **N** (abbr **electroconvulsive therapy**) = traitement m par électrochocs

ectopic [ek'tɒpɪk] **ADJ**

►► Obst **e. pregnancy** grossesse f extra-utérine, grossesse ectopique

ectoplasm ['ektəʊplæz(ə)m] **N** (in spiritualism) ectoplasme m

ECU N 1 ['eɪkju:, occ i:si:'ju:] Formerly (abbr **European Currency Unit**) écu m **2** [i:si:'ju:] abbr **European Customs Union 3** [i:si:'ju:] abbr **electronic control unit**

Ecuador ['ekwədɔ:r] **N** (la République de) l'Équateur m

Ecuadoran [ekwə'dɔ:rən], **Ecuadorian** [ekwə'dɔ:rɪən] **ADJ** équatorien, équatorien **N** Équatorien, -ienne, Équatorien, -ienne

ecumenical [i:kjʊ'menɪk(ə)l] **ADJ** Rel (council) œcuménique

ecumenism [i:'kju:mənɪz(ə)m], **ecumenicism** [i:kju:'menɪsɪz(ə)m] **N** Rel œcuménisme m

eczema ['eksɪmə] **N** Med eczéma m; **to have** or **suffer from e.** avoir ou faire de l'eczéma

ed 1 (abbr **edition**) éd(it) **2** abbr **editor 3** abbr **edited**

EDC [i:di:'si:] **N** (abbr **European Defence Community**) CED f

eddy ['edɪ] **N** (of water, wind) remous m, tourbillon m, (of leaves, dust) tourbillon m

vi (of water) faire des remous; (of wind, smoke, snow) tourbillonner, tournoyer; (of crowds) tournoyer

►► Elec **e. currents** courants mpl de Foucault

edelweiss ['eɪd(ə)lvaɪs] **N** (plant) edelweiss m

edema [ɪ'di:mə] **N** Am œdème m

Eden ['i:d(ə)n] **N** Bible (the Garden of) **E.** l'Éden m, le Paradis terrestre

EDF [i:di:'ef] **N** (abbr **European Development Fund**) FED m

EDGE [edʒ] **N 1** (of blade) fil m, tranchant m; (of tool) angle m; (of skate) carre f, (of stone etc) arête f, angle; **sharp/rounded e.** arête vive/mousse; **inside/outside e.** dedans m/dehors m; **knife with a keen e.** couteau à tranchant aigu; **to put an e. on a tool** aiguiser ou affiler un outil; **to take the e. off** (blade, appetite etc) émousser; (pleasure) gâter; (argument) couper tout l'effet de

2 (rim, border, limit) (of table) bord m, rebord m; (of plank, medal, book) tranche f, (of wood) lisière f, bordure f, orée f, (of river) bord, rive f, (of plain) limite f, (of road, path) bordure, bord; (sewn onto material) liséré m; **it fell off the e. of the table** il est tombé de la table; **it fell off the e.** il est tombé; **gilt edges** tranches dorées; **with gilt edges** doré sur tranches; **to be on the e. of ...** (new age) être à l'orée de ...; (final conflict, great discoveries) être au bord de ...; **at the e. of the road** au bord ou en bordure de la route; **the flag had a golden fringe round the e.** le drapeau était bordé d'une frange dorée; Phot **e. white e.** (of print) liséré blanc; **at the water's e.** au bord de l'eau; **at the e. of a precipice** au bord d'un précipice; **on e.** (of brick) de chant, de can; **to set sth on e.** (tilt) mettre qch de chant ou de can

3 (idioms) Fam **to have an** or **the e. on sb** être avantagé par rapport à qn; **to have an e. to one's voice** avoir une voix coupante; **to**

speak with a sarcastic/nervous/contemptuous e. to one's voice parler avec une pointe de sarcasme/de nervosité/de mépris dans la voix; **on e.** *(of person)* énervé, nerveux; **to set sb on e.** crisper qn, énerver qn; **to set** *or* **put sb's teeth on e.** faire grincer des dents à qn; **to set sb's nerves on e.** taper sur les nerfs de qn; **to send sb over the e.** porter le coup de grâce à qn; **a movie that will have you on the e. of your seat** un film au suspense insoutenable; **to give sb the rough e. of one's tongue** dire son fait à qn

VT 1 *Tech (sharpen) (knife, tool)* affiler, aiguiser; *(millstone)* repiquer

2 *(border) (material)* border (**with** de); *(skirt etc)* lisérer

3 *(move slowly)* **to e. one's way into a room/through the crowd** se faufiler dans une pièce/à travers la foule; **to e. one's chair nearer** rapprocher *ou* avancer sa chaise peu à peu

VI *(move slowly)* **to e. towards sb/sth** s'approcher tout doucement de qn/qch; **to e. through the crowd/past the guards** se faufiler à travers la foule/devant les gardes; **could you possibly e. a little closer?** pourriez-vous vous rapprocher un petit peu?; **the drivers were edging forwards in the traffic jam** les conducteurs avançaient lentement dans l'embouteillage

▸▸ **e. cutter, e. trimmer** *(for grass)* coupe-bordure(s) *m, pl* coupe-bordures

▸ **edge away** **VI** *(move away slowly)* s'éloigner *ou* s'écarter tout doucement (**from sb** de qn)

▸ **edge out** **VI** *(move cautiously)* **I opened the window and edged out** j'ai ouvert la fenêtre et me suis doucement glissé dehors; **the driver/car edged out** le conducteur/la voiture se dégagea lentement

VT SEP 1 **to e. one's way out** se frayer un chemin; **she edged her way out onto the ledge** elle gagna le rebord de la fenêtre avec précaution

2 *(supplant)* évincer; **to e. sb out of the chairmanship** évincer qn de la présidence

▸ **edge past** **VI** *(move past cautiously)* passer prudemment

VT INSEP **I edged past her** je suis passé discrètement à côté d'elle

▸ **edge up** **VI** *(climb slowly) (of prices)* grimper petit à petit

VT SEP **they edged their way up the cliff** ils ont escaladé la falaise à grand peine

edged [edʒd] **ADJ** *(tool, weapon etc)* tranchant, acéré

-edged [edʒd] **SUFF** **double-e.** à double tranchant; *Fig* **a double-e. weapon** une arme à double tranchant; **sharp-e.** au tranchant affilé *ou* bien aiguisé; **a razor-e. knife/tongue** un couteau/une langue bien affilé(e)

edgeways ['edʒweɪz], **edgewise** ['edʒwaɪz] **ADV 1** *(on its edge)* de chant; **to lay** *or* **set a plank e.** placer une planche de chant; *Fam* **I can't get a word in e.** je n'arrive pas à placer un mot (dans la conversation) **2** *(from side)* latéralement, de côté; **seen e. (on)** vu de côté

edginess ['edʒɪnɪs] **N** nervosité *f*

edging ['edʒɪŋ] **N 1** *(action) (of dress)* pose *f* d'un liséré *ou* d'une ganse; *(of lawn)* entretien *m* de la bordure **2** *(border) Sewing* liséré *m*, passement *m*, ganse *f*, *(of flower bed)* bordure *f*

▸▸ **e. shears** cisaille *f* à gazon; **e. tool** coupe-gazon *m inv*, molette *f*

edgy ['edʒɪ] **ADJ** *(person)* énervé; **to get e.** s'énerver

EDI [iːdiːˈaɪ] **N 1** *Comput (abbr* **Electronic Data Interchange)** EDI *m* **2** *Fin (abbr* **European Data Interchange)** EED *m*

edible ['edɪb(ə)l] **ADJ** comestible; *(fit to eat)*

bon à manger, mangeable; **it was so hot it was barely e.** c'était si chaud que c'était à peine mangeable; **it's very e.** c'est très bon

▸▸ **e. oil** huile *f* comestible

edict ['iːdɪkt] **N** *Law, Pol* édit *m*

▸▸ *Hist* **the E. of Nantes** l'Édit de Nantes

edification [edɪfɪˈkeɪʃən] **N** *Fml* édification *f*, instruction *f*, *esp Iron* **for your e.** pour votre édification

edifice ['edɪfɪs] **N** édifice *m*

edify ['edɪfaɪ] **VT** *Fml* édifier

edifying ['edɪfaɪɪŋ] **ADJ** *Fml (spectacle, book etc)* édifiant

Edinburgh ['edɪnbrə] **N** Édimbourg

edit ['edɪt] **VT 1** *(in publishing), Journ (prepare)* préparer pour la publication; *(work)* donner une édition annotée de; *(series of texts etc)* diriger; *(be in charge of) (newspaper, magazine)* rédiger, diriger; **edited by ...** *(series, newspaper etc)* sous la direction de ... **2** *(film, TV programme, tape)* monter; **edited master** master *m* monté, montage *m* original **3** *Comput (text on screen)* éditer

N *(in publishing)* révision *f*, *TV* point *m* de montage; *(in newspaper, text)* correction *f*, révision; *Comput (menu heading)* Edition *f*

▸▸ *Comput* **e. key** touche *f* de modification; *Comput* **e. mode** mode *m* Edition; *TV* **e. suite** régie *f* *ou* salle *f* de montage

---

Note that the French verb **éditer** is a false friend. It means **to publish**.

▸ **edit in** **VT SEP** insérer

▸ **edit out** **VT SEP** *(scene)* couper; *(from text)* supprimer; *(write out of TV series)* faire disparaître; **he was edited out of the film when he broke his contract** on a coupé toutes les scènes du film où il apparaissait quand il a rompu son contrat

editable ['edɪtəb(ə)l] **ADJ** pouvant être édité

editing ['edɪtɪŋ] **N 1** *(in publishing) (of text)* préparation *f*, édition *f*, *(of newspaper, magazine)* rédaction *f*, **a book on e.** un manuel d'édition **2** *(of film, TV programme, tape)* montage *m*; *(removal) (of scene, passage etc)* suppression *f* **3** *Comput* édition *f*

▸▸ *TV* **e. desk** table *f* *ou* banc *m* de montage; *Comput* **e. function** fonction *f* d'édition; *TV* **e. table** table *f* de montage; *TV* **e. terminal** terminal *m* de montage; *Comput* **e. window** fenêtre *f* d'édition

edition [ɪˈdɪʃən] **N** *(in publishing), Journ* édition *f*; **the earlier editions of the newspapers** les premières éditions des journaux; **this error was corrected in later editions** cette erreur a été corrigée dans les éditions ultérieures; **the hardback/paperback e.** l'édition reliée/de poche; **in Tuesday's e. of the programme** dans l'émission de mardi; **school e.** édition scolaire; **cheap e.** édition populaire; **book in its fourth e.** livre à sa quatrième édition

▸▸ **e. time** *(for newspaper)* bouclage *m*, heure *f* de l'édition, tombée *f*

Note that the French word **édition** also means **publishing**.

---

editor ['edɪtər] **N 1** *(in publishing), Journ (of text)* éditeur, -trice; *(of critical edition)* auteur *m*; *(in charge of publication)* surveillant *m* de la publication; *(of series)* directeur, -trice; *(of magazine, newspaper)* rédacteur, -trice en chef, directeur; *(of dictionary)* rédacteur *m*; **news e.** rédacteur au service des informations; **series e.** directeur de la publication; **sports/political/fashion e.** rédacteur sportif/politique/de mode; **2** *Cin (of film)* monteur *m*; *TV, Radio* **programme e.** réalisateur *m* **3** *Comput (software)* éditeur *m*

▸▸ **editors' conference** conférence *f* de ré-

daction; **e.'s note** note *f* de la rédaction; *Comput* **e. program** programme *m* éditeur

editorial [edɪˈtɔːrɪəl] **ADJ** *(in publishing), Journ* de rédaction; **that's an e. decision** c'est une décision qui appartient à la rédaction

N *Journ* éditorial *m*, *Fam* édito *m*;

▸▸ **e. advertisement** reportage *m* publicitaire; **e. advertising** publicité *f* rédactionnelle; **e. changes** corrections *fpl*; **e. column** colonne *f* rédactionnelle; **e. conference** conférence *f* de rédaction; **e. content** contenu *m* rédactionnel; **e. department** service *m* de la rédaction, rédaction *f*, direction *f* de la rédaction; **e. director** *(of newspaper)* rédacteur, -trice en chef, directeur, -trice de la rédaction; *(of publishing company)* directeur, -trice de la rédaction; **e. freedom** liberté *f* des rédacteurs; **e. interference** ingérence *f* rédactionnelle; **e. office** (salle *f* de) rédaction; **e. opinion** *(in press)* avis *m* éditorial; **e. policy** politique *f* éditoriale; *(in press)* politique de la rédaction; **the e. staff** la rédaction; **e. writer** éditorialiste *mf*

editorialist [edɪˈtɔːrɪəlɪst] **N** *Am* éditorialiste *mf*

editorialize [edɪˈtɔːrɪəlaɪz] **VI** émettre des opinions personnelles, être subjectif; **as the Times editorialized, ...** comme l'affirmait l'éditorial du Times, ...

editorially [edɪˈtɔːrɪəlɪ] **ADV** du point de vue de la rédaction

editor-in-chief, *pl* **editors-in-chief** **N** rédacteur, -trice en chef

editorship ['edɪtəʃɪp] **N** rédaction *f*, direction *f*; **during her e.** quand elle dirigeait la rédaction; **the series was produced under the general e. of ...** la série a été produite sous la direction générale de ...

EDP [iːdiːˈpiː] **N** *(abbr* **electronic data processing)** informatique *f*

▸▸ **E. department** service *m* informatique

educable ['edjʊkəb(ə)l] **ADJ** éducable

educate ['edjʊkeɪt] **VT 1** *Sch (person)* donner de l'instruction à, instruire; **he was educated in France/at Oxford** il a fait ses études en France/à Oxford; **to have one's child educated** faire faire des études à son enfant; **to be impossible to e.** être inéducable **2** *(train, develop) (person, sb's taste/mind)* former; **the series aims to e. the viewers in the ways of this strange people** cette série a pour objectif d'instruire les téléspectateurs sur les coutumes de ce peuple étrange; **she was educated always to think of others before herself** on lui a enseigné à toujours penser aux autres avant elle-même

educated ['edjʊkeɪtɪd] **ADJ** *(person)* instruit, lettré; **half-e.** peu instruit; **an e. guess** une supposition éclairée; **self-e.** autodidacte; **he was well e. in the ways of the locals** il était bien renseigné sur le mode de vie des gens de la région

education [edjʊˈkeɪʃən] **N 1** *(instruction)* enseignement *m*, instruction *f*, **to study E.** étudier les Sciences de l'Éducation; **the e. of young people in the use of birth control methods** l'éducation des jeunes pour l'utilisation des méthodes contraceptives; **he has had a good e.** il a reçu une bonne instruction; **to receive a classical/literary e.** recevoir une éducation *ou* un enseignement classique/littéraire; **to get oneself an e.** faire des études; **he never completed his e.** il n'a jamais fini *ou* terminé ses études; *Iron* **it was an e. working over there** c'était instructif de travailler là-bas; **adult e.** enseignement des adultes; **compulsory e.** enseignement obligatoire; **full-time e.** enseignement à temps complet; **further e.** enseignement post-scolaire; **higher** *or* **university e.** *(system)* enseignement supérieur; *(of person)* études *fpl* supérieures; **pri-**

mary/secondary e. enseignement primaire/secondaire; *Br* **Department for Education** = Ministère *m* de l'Éducation nationale; *Br* **(local) e. authority** = Direction *f* de l'enseignement **2** *(learning)* éducation *f*; **a man without e.** un homme sans éducation; **gaps in one's e.** des lacunes dans son éducation ▸▸ **E. Act** ≃ réforme *f* (de l'Éducation); *Journ* **e. correspondent** correspondant, -ante chargé(e) des problèmes d'enseignement; **e. page** page *f* éducation; **e. supplement** supplément *m* éducation

> Note that the French noun **éducation** refers both to education and to upbringing.

educational [edʒʊ'keɪʃən(ə)l] ADJ *(institution, work)* d'éducation, d'enseignement; *(role, function)* éducatif, éducateur, -trice; *(film)* éducatif; *(programme, publisher)* scolaire; *(method)* éducatif, pédagogique; **working over there was very e.** c'était très instructif de travailler là-bas; **it was an e. experience/visit** c'était une expérience/visite instructive; **for e. purposes** dans un but pédagogique ▸▸ **e. adviser** conseiller, -ère d'orientation; **e. holiday** vacances *fpl* studieuses; **e. psychologist** *(practical)* psychologue *mf* scolaire; *(academic)* psychopédagogue *mf*, **e. qualification** diplôme *m*; *Comput* **e. software** logiciel *m* didactique; **e. tour** ≃ Éductour *m*, voyage *m* d'études

education(al)ist [edʒʊ'keɪʃənɪst, -əlɪst] N éducateur, -trice, pédagogue *mf*

educationally [edʒʊ'keɪʃən(ə)lɪ] ADV du point de vue de l'éducation *ou* de l'enseignement; **e. subnormal** *(child)* arriéré

educative ['edʒʊkətɪv] ADJ *(function, purpose)* éducatif; *(experience, remark)* instructif

educator ['edʒʊkeɪtər] N *esp Am* éducateur, -trice

edutainment [edju:'teɪnmənt] N apprentissage *m* par le jeu, édutainment *m* ADJ ludo-éducatif

Edwardian [ed'wɔ:dɪən] ADJ qui a rapport à l'époque du roi Édouard VII; **the E. era** ≃ la Belle Époque

Edward the Confessor ['edwəd] N Édouard *m* le Confesseur

EEA [i:i:'eɪ] *(abbr* **European Economic Area)** N EEE *m*

EEC [i:i:'si:] N *Formerly (abbr* **European Economic Community)** CEE *f*

e-economy N économie *f* en ligne

EEG [i:i:'dʒi:] N *Med* **1** *(abbr* **electroencephalogram)** EEG *m* **2** *(abbr* **electroencephalograph)** appareil *m* à EEG

eejit ['i:dʒɪt] N *Ir, Scot* andouille *f*, couillon *m*

eel [i:l] N anguille *f*; **e. basket** *or* **pot** nasse *f* à anguilles; *Br Culin* **jellied eels** anguilles en gelée

eelworm ['i:lwɜ:m] N anguillule *f*

EEPROM ['i:prɒm] N *Comput (abbr* **electrically erasable programmable ROM)** EEPROM *f*

eerie ['ɪərɪ] ADJ *(calm, sound)* inquiétant, sinistre; *(atmosphere)* qui donne des frissons; **an e. silence** *(after explosion, in empty house etc)* un silence de mort; **I had the e. feeling that I was being watched** j'avais l'étrange impression qu'on m'observait; **it was e. to think that …** cela donnait des frissons *ou* la chair de poule de penser que …

eerily ['ɪərɪlɪ] ADV étrangement, à donner des frissons; **the cat's eyes glowed e. in the dark** les yeux du chat brillaient d'une lueur surnaturelle dans le noir; **e. quiet** *(house etc)* d'un calme inquiétant; **the whole town was e. silent** dans toute la ville régnait un silence inquiétant *ou* sinistre

eeriness ['ɪərɪnɪs] N *(of place, sound etc)* étrangeté *f* surnaturelle

eery ['ɪərɪ] ADJ = **eerie**

eff [ef] VI *Br Sl Euph* **he's always effing and blinding** il n'arrête pas de jurer
▸ **eff off** VI *Br Sl Euph* **e. off!** va te faire foutre!; **she told him to e. off** elle lui a dit d'aller se faire foutre

efface [ɪ'feɪs] VT effacer; *(memory of sth)* oblitérer, effacer; *(remnants of past)* faire disparaître; **to e. oneself** s'effacer

effacement [ɪ'feɪsmənt] N effacement *m*

effect [ɪ'fekt] N **1** *(result)*, *Phys* effet *m*; *(of deed)* résultat *m*, conséquence *f*; **the e. of heat on metals** l'action de la chaleur sur les métaux; **the e. of this action was to bring prices down** cette action a eu pour effet de faire baisser les prix; **to have an e. on sb/sth** faire *ou* produire de l'effet sur qn/qch, affecter qn/qch; **to have no e.** ne faire *ou* ne produire aucun effet; **let's see what e. the addition of hydrogen has** voyons l'effet que produit l'addition d'hydrogène; **to take e.** *(of regulation, law etc)* entrer en vigueur; *(of drug)* agir, opérer; *(of vaccination)* prendre; **law that comes into e. today** loi qui entre en vigueur à partir d'aujourd'hui; **to no e.** en vain, sans résultat; **to put sth into e.** *(plan)* mettre qch à exécution; *(decision)* donner suite à qch **2** *(purpose, meaning) (of document)* sens *m*, teneur *f*; **to the e. that …** *(clause)* portant que …; **we have made provisions to this e.** nous avons pris des dispositions dans ce sens; **that is what he said, or words to that e.** voilà ce qu'il a dit, ou quelque chose d'approchant **3** *(simulation)* **moonlight e.** effet *m* de lune; **clever use of lighting created the e. of a thunderstorm** une utilisation adroite de la lumière donnait l'impression qu'il y avait un orage; **stage effects** jeux *mpl* scéniques; *Cin, TV etc* **(special) effects** trucage *m*, effets spéciaux; **sound effects** bruitage *m* **4** *(impression)* effet *m*, impression *f*; **the combination of colours creates or has a pleasing e.** le mélange des couleurs laisse une impression agréable; **for e.** *(to impress)* pour faire de l'effet; **words meant for e.** phrases à effet **5** **in e.** en fait, en réalité; **that is in e. a refusal** c'est de fait un refus **6** *(always pl) (belongings) Fml* **personal effects** effets *mpl ou* biens *mpl* personnels; **household effects**, *Law* **movable effects** biens mobiliers
VT *(repair, change)* effectuer; *(plan, wish, saving)* réaliser; *(plan, law)* exécuter; *(reconciliation)* parvenir à; **to e. an entry** entrer de force; **to e. a cure for sth** apporter un remède à qch; **to e. a solution to sth** apporter une solution à qch; *Mil* **to e. a retreat** battre en retraite; **to e. a payment** effectuer un paiement

effective [ɪ'fektɪv] ADJ **1** *(efficient, having desired effect)* efficace; *(speech)* qui fait de l'effet; *(response)* plein d'à-propos; **the medicine was e.** le médicament a produit son effet; **an e. argument** un argument de poids; **she is an e. speaker** ses paroles font de l'effet *ou* portent **2** *(actual) Econ etc (yield, return)* effectif; *(value)* réel; *Elec (charge)* efficace; *(frequency)* utile; **this resulted in the e. silencing of all opposition** *(was tantamount to)* cela a eu en effet pour résultat de faire taire les opposants **3** *(striking) (contrast)* frappant, saisissant **4** **to become e.** *(of law etc)* entrer en vigueur; **e. as from 10 October** applicable à partir du 10 octobre
NPL *Mil* **effectives** effectifs *mpl*
▸▸ *Fin* **e. annual rate** taux *m* annuel effectif; *Admin* **e. date** date *f* d'entrée en vigueur; *Econ* **e. demand** demande *f* effective; *Tech*

e. power rendement *m*; **e. range** *(of firearm, missile)* portée *f* utile; *Aviat* rayon *m* d'action; *Electron* étendue *f* de mesure; *Fin* **e. tax rate** taux *m* d'imposition effectif

effectively [ɪ'fektɪvlɪ] ADV **1** *(really, in effect)* en fait, en réalité; **the country was e. ruled by the military** en fait *ou* en réalité, le pays était dirigé par les militaires; **the match was e. over** c'était comme si le match était déjà terminé **2** *(efficiently)* efficacement; **the building has been designed very e.** le bâtiment a été conçu avec un grand souci d'efficacité; **he spoke e. in favour of the government's motion** il a fait un éloge percutant *ou* persuasif de la motion du gouvernement **3** *(strikingly)* d'une façon frappante

> Note that the French word **effectivement** is a false friend and is never a translation for the English word **effectively**. It means **actually**.

effectiveness [ɪ'fektɪvnɪs] N **1** *(efficiency)* efficacité *f* **2** *(of colour scheme, design)* effet *m* percutant; **the e. of the white houses outlined against a darkening sky** l'effet de contraste percutant *ou (stronger)* saisissant des maisons blanches qui se découpaient sur un ciel de plus en plus sombre

effectual [ɪ'fektjʊəl] ADJ **1** *Fml* efficace **2** *Law (contract)* valide; *(ruling)* en vigueur

effectually [ɪ'fektjʊəlɪ] ADV efficacement

effeminacy [ɪ'femɪnəsɪ] N caractère *m* efféminé

effeminate [ɪ'femɪnət] ADJ efféminé

effervesce [efə'ves] VI **1** être en effervescence; *(start to effervesce)* entrer en effervescence; *(of drinks)* pétiller **2** *Fig (of person)* pétiller de joie *ou* d'animation

effervescence [efə'vesəns] N **1** *(of liquid)* effervescence *f* **2** *Fig (of youth etc)* pétillement *m*

effervescent [efə'vesənt] ADJ **1** effervescent; *(drink)* gazeux, pétillant **2** *Fig (person, mood)* effervescent; **to be e. with enthusiasm/joy** pétiller d'enthousiasme/de joie

effete [ɪ'fi:t] ADJ *(person)* mou, *f* molle veule; *(nation, civilization etc)* amorphe

efficacious [efɪ'keɪʃəs] ADJ *Fml* efficace

efficacy ['efɪkəsɪ], **efficaciousness** [efɪ'keɪʃəsnɪs] N efficacité *f*

efficiency [ɪ'fɪʃənsɪ] N *(of method, organization)* efficacité *f*; *(of machine, business etc) (output)* rendement *m*; *(functioning)* bon fonctionnement *m*; *(of person)* capacité *f*, compétence *f*
▸▸ **e. expert** expert *m* en organisation

efficient [ɪ'fɪʃənt] ADJ *(method, work, organization)* efficace; *(machine) (productive)* à bon rendement, performant; *(functioning well)* d'un fonctionnement sûr; *(person)* performant, capable, compétent; *(software)* performant; **to be e. at sth** faire qch avec compétence; **to be e. in one's work** se montrer capable dans son travail; **e. use of one's time** utilisation rationnelle de son temps; **energy e.** *(machine)* qui ne consomme pas beaucoup d'énergie

efficiently [ɪ'fɪʃəntlɪ] ADV *(effectively)* efficacement; *(competently)* avec compétence; **to organize one's time e.** utiliser son temps de manière rationnelle; **this car runs more e. than any of its competitors** cette voiture a un meilleur rendement que toutes ses concurrentes

effigy ['efɪdʒɪ] N effigie *f*; **to burn/hang sb in e.** brûler/pendre qn en effigie

effing ['efɪŋ] *Br Sl Euph* ADJ foutu; **this e. weather** ce temps de merde
ADV **how e. stupid!** quelle connerie!

N *(swearing)* **there's too much e. and blinding** on entend trop de grossièretés

efflorescence [eflə'resns] N **1** *Bot* floraison f **2** *Chem, Med etc* efflorescence f

efflorescent [eflə'resənt] ADJ *Bot, Chem* efflorescent

effluence ['efluəns] N *Lit* émanation f, effluence f

effluent ['efluənt] ADJ effluent
N effluent m

effluvium, pl **effluvia** [e'flu:vɪəm, -ɪə] N effluve m, émanation f, *Pej* émanation désagréable ou fétide

effort ['efət] N **1** effort m; **physical e.** effort physique; **without e.** sans effort; **to make an e. to do sth** faire (un) effort pour faire qch; **he made no e. to contact us** il n'a fait aucun effort pour nous joindre; **put some e. into it!** fais un effort!; **she put all her e. into her work** elle s'est jetée corps et âme dans son travail; **their efforts were rewarded** leurs efforts ont été récompensés; *Fml* **we make every e. to ensure our products reach you in perfect condition** nous faisons tout ce qui est en notre pouvoir pour que nos produits vous parviennent en bon état; *Fam* **it's an e. to get up so early** il faut vraiment faire un effort pour se lever si tôt; **wasted e.** peine f perdue

2 *Fam (attempt)* tentative f; **that's not a bad e.** ce n'est pas mal réussi; **some of my first efforts at making pots were pretty awful** certains de mes premiers essais en poterie étaient plutôt ratés; **literary/artistic e.** œuvre f littéraire/artistique; *Fam* **what do you think of his latest e.?** qu'est-ce que vous pensez de sa dernière performance?

3 *Phys (of traction etc)* effort m, poussée f, travail m

4 *Sl (thing, gadget)* truc m; **there's this sort of lever e.** il y a une espèce de levier

effortless ['efətlɪs] ADJ *(victory, success etc)* facile; *(skill, grace)* aisé; **she won with an almost e. ease** elle a gagné avec une facilité presque absolue

effortlessly ['efətlɪslɪ] ADV sans effort; **to be e. graceful/skilful** être naturellement gracieux/talentueux; **her voice soars e. to the high notes** elle peut chanter très haut sans aucun effort

effrontery [ɪ'frʌntərɪ] N effronterie f; **she had the e. to correct me!** elle a eu l'audace de me corriger!

effusion [ɪ'fju:ʒən] N effusion f

effusive [ɪ'fju:sɪv] ADJ *(person)* démonstratif, expansif; *(style)* exubérant; *(compliments)* sans fin; *(welcome, speech)* enthousiaste; **to be e. in one's thanks** se confondre en remerciements; **to be e. in one's praise/congratulations** louer/féliciter qn avec grand enthousiasme

effusively [ɪ'fju:sɪvlɪ] ADV avec effusion; **to thank sb e.** se confondre en remerciements; **to praise/congratulate/welcome sb e.** louer/féliciter/accueillir qn avec enthousiasme

effusiveness [ɪ'fju:sɪvnɪs] N effusion f; **the e. of his praise** l'enthousiasme m de ses louanges

E-fit® N portrait-robot m électronique

EFL [i:ef'el] N *Sch (abbr* **English as a Foreign Language)** anglais m langue étrangère; **to have an E. qualification** avoir une qualification en anglais langue étrangère

EFT [i:ef'ti:] N *Comput (abbr* **electronic funds transfer)** transfert m de fonds électronique

EFTA ['eftə] N *(abbr* **European Free Trade Association)** AELE f

EFTPOS ['eftpɒs] N *Comput (abbr* **electronic funds transfer at point of sale)** transfert m

de fonds électronique sur point de vente

eg [i:'dʒi:] *(abbr* **exempli gratia)** ex

EGA [i:dʒi:'ei] N *Comput (abbr* **enhanced graphics adaptor)** EGA m

egalitarian [ɪgælɪ'teərɪən] ADJ égalitaire
N égalitariste mf

egalitarianism [ɪgælɪ'teərɪənɪz(ə)m] N égalitarisme m

e-generation N génération f électronique, E-génération f

egg [eg] N *(of hen, animal, insect etc)* œuf m; *(of louse)* lente f; **bacon and eggs** œufs au bacon; **e. sandwich** sandwich m à l'œuf; *Fam* **as sure as eggs is eggs** aussi sûr que deux et deux font quatre; *Fam* **you've got e. on your chin** *(fly is undone)* ta braguette est ouverte; *Fig Fam* **to have e. on one's face** s'être couvert de ridicule; *Old-fashioned Fam* **a bad e.** *(person)* un vaurien; *Old-fashioned Fam* **a good e.** *(man)* un gars épatant; *(woman)* une fille épatante; *Prov* **don't put all your eggs in one basket** il ne faut pas mettre tous ses œufs dans le même panier
▸▸ **e. cup** coquetier m; *Br Culin* **e. custard** ≃ crème f anglaise; **e. flip** *(with milk)* lait m de poule; *(with alcohol)* lait de poule alcoolisé; **e. mayonnaise** œufs mpl mayonnaise; **e. nog** lait de poule alcoolisé; **e. spoon** cuillère f à œufs (à la coque); **e. timer** sablier m; **e. tooth** dent f d'éclosion; **e. white** blanc m d'œuf; **e. yolk** jaune m d'œuf
▸ **egg on** VT SEP **to e. sb on (to do sth)** pousser ou inciter qn (à faire qch); **don't e. him on** ne l'encourage pas

egg-and-spoon ADJ
▸▸ **e. race** = course f dans laquelle les coureurs doivent porter un œuf dans une cuillère

eggbeater ['egbi:tər] N **1** *Culin* batteur m ou fouet m à œufs **2** *Am Fam (helicopter)* hélico m

eggbox ['egbɒks] N boîte f à œufs

egghead ['eghed] N *Hum, Pej* intello mf, cerveau m

egg-laying ADJ ovipare
N ponte f

eggplant ['egplɑ:nt] N *esp Am* aubergine f

egg-shaped ADJ ovoïde, ovoïdal, -aux

eggshell ['egʃel] N **1** coquille f (d'œuf); **e. finish** *(on paint)* fini m coquille d'œuf **2** *(colour)* (couleur f) coquille f d'œuf, blanc m cassé
▸▸ **e. blue** bleu m pâle; *Cer* **e. china** coquille d'œuf

eggwhisk ['egwɪsk] N = **eggbeater**

eggy ['egɪ] ADJ *Fam (stained)* taché ou souillé de jaune d'œuf; **an e. taste/smell** un goût/une odeur d'œuf

egis ['i:dʒɪs] N *Am* = **aegis**

eglantine ['egləntaɪn] N *(plant)* églantier m

EGM [i:dʒi:'em] N *(abbr* **extraordinary general meeting)** AGE f

ego ['i:gəʊ, 'egəʊ] N **the e.** l'ego m inv; *Psy* le moi, l'ego; **you've got an enormous e.** tu as un ego démesuré; **it gave my e. a boost** mon ego en est ressorti gonflé; **his bruised e.** son ego blessé; **to feed/deflate sb's e.** entretenir/rabaisser l'ego de qn; *Fam* **it was a real e. trip for her** c'était une occasion pour elle de donner libre cours à sa vanité

egocentric [i:gəʊ'sentrɪk] ADJ égocentrique

egocentricity [i:gəʊsen'trɪsɪtɪ] N égocentrisme m

egoism ['i:gəʊɪz(ə)m] N égoïsme m

egoist ['i:gəʊɪst] N égoïste mf

egoistic(al) [i:gəʊ'ɪstɪk, -ɪk(ə)l] ADJ égoïste

egoistically [i:gəʊ'ɪstɪklɪ] ADV égoïstement

egomania [i:gəʊ'meɪnɪə] N manie f égocentrique

egotism ['i:gəʊtɪz(ə)m] N égotisme m

egotist ['i:gəʊtɪst] N égotiste mf

egotistic(al) [i:gəʊ'tɪstɪk, -ɪk(ə)l] ADJ égotiste

egregious [ɪ'gri:dʒəs] ADJ *Fml Pej (error, mistake)* monumental, -aux, énorme; *(lie)* énorme; *(cowardice, incompetence)* extrême

egress ['i:gres] N **1** *Fml (exit)* sortie f, issue f **2** *Astron* émersion f

egret ['i:grɪt] N *(bird)* aigrette f

Egypt ['i:dʒɪpt] N Égypte f

Egyptian [ɪ'dʒɪpʃən] ADJ égyptien, d'Égypte
N Égyptien, -ienne

eh [eɪ, e] INT eh!, hé!, hein?

EIB [i:aɪ'bi:] N *(abbr* **European Investment Bank)** BEI f

eider ['aɪdər] N eider m à duvet
▸▸ **e. duck** eider m à duvet

eiderdown ['aɪdədaʊn] N **1** *(quilt)* édredon m **2** *(feathers)* duvet m d'eider

eight [eɪt] N **1** *(number, numeral)* huit m inv; **e. and e. are sixteen** huit et huit font seize; **to be e.** *(in age)* avoir huit ans; **it's e. o'clock** il est huit heures; **it's five past e.** il est huit heures cinq; **to reach the last e.** *(in knockout competition)* être en huitième de finale; *Br* **to have had one over the e.** avoir bu plus que son compte **2** *Sport (in rowing)* huit m *(de pointe)*
PRON huit; **there are e. (of them)** *(people)* ils sont huit; *(objects)* il y en a huit
NUM ADJ huit; **to work an e.-hour day** travailler huit heures par jour, faire des journées de huit heures
▸▸ *Am* **e. ball** *(ball)* bille f numéro huit; *(game)* = variante du billard; *Fig Fam* **to be behind the e. ball** être dans une situation délicate; *Am* **e. hundred number** ≃ numéro m vert

eight-bit byte N *Comput* octet m

eight-bit character N *Comput* caractère m à huit bits

eighteen [eɪ'ti:n] NUM ADJ, N dix-huit m; **she is e. (years old)** elle a dix-huit ans; **at e. thirty (hours)** à dix-huit heures trente

eighteenth [eɪ'ti:nθ] ADJ dix-huitième; **Louis the E.** Louis Dix-huit
N **1 (on) the e. of May** le dix-huit mai; **on the e.** le dix-huit **2** *(fraction)* dix-huitième m

eightfold ['eɪtfəʊld] ADJ octuple; **an e. increase** une augmentation à l'octuple
ADV huit fois autant; **to increase e.** octupler

eighth [eɪtθ] ADJ huitième; **in the e. place** huitièmement; **Henry the E.** Henri Huit
N **1 (on) the e. of April** le huit avril; **on the e.** le huit **2** *(fraction)* huitième m; **three eighths** trois huitièmes
▸▸ *Am Mus* **e. note** croche f

eightieth ['eɪtɪɪθ] ADJ, N quatre-vingtième m, *Suisse, Belg* huitantième m, *Suisse, Can* octantième m

eighty ['eɪtɪ] NUM ADJ, N quatre-vingts m, *Suisse, Belg* huitante m, *Suisse, Can* octante m; **e.-one** quatre-vingt-un; **page e.** page quatre-vingt; **in the eighties** *(decade)* dans les années quatre-vingt; **she is in her eighties** elle a quatre-vingts ans passés SEE GRAMMAR B58–9

eighty-six *Am Sl* ADJ **to be e. on sth** *(in restaurant, bar)* être à court de qch; **tell the customer we're e. on the chicken** dis au client qu'il n'y a plus de poulet
VT **1** *(eject)* vider **2** *(kill)* buter, refroidir

Eire ['eərə] N Eire f

eisteddfod [aɪ'stedfəd] N = festival m gallois de poésie et de musique

either ['aɪðər, *esp Am* 'i:ðər] ADJ, PRON VOIR

GRAMMAIRE A37 1 *(each of the two)* l'un(e) et l'autre; **on e. side** de chaque côté, des deux côtés

2 *(one or other)* l'un(e) ou l'autre; **e. of them** soit l'un(e), soit l'autre; **I don't believe e. of you** je ne vous crois ni l'un ni l'autre; **I do not want e. of them** je ne veux ni l'un(e) ni l'autre; **e. candidate may win** l'un ou l'autre candidat pourra l'emporter; **there is no evidence e. way** les preuves manquent de part et d'autre

CONJ, ADV 1 e. … or … (ou) … ou …, soit …, soit …; **e. you or your brother** (ou) vous ou votre frère, soit vous, soit votre frère; **it's e. that motorbike or me!** c'est cette moto ou moi!; **e. come in or go out!** entrez ou sortez! **VOIR GRAMMAIRE A73–4**

2 not … e. ne … non plus; **if you don't go, I won't go e.** si vous n'y allez pas, je n'irai pas non plus; **she's caught a cold, and she isn't very strong e.** elle s'est enrhumée, elle qui n'est déjà pas si forte

either-or ADJ **an e. situation** = une situation dans laquelle il faut choisir entre deux maux le moindre

ejaculate [ɪ'dʒækjʊleɪt] VI **1** *Physiol* éjaculer **2** *Old-fashioned, Lit (exclaim)* s'écrier
▸ VT *(cry)* pousser; **'help!', he ejaculated** 'à l'aide!', s'écria-t-il

ejaculation [ɪdʒækjʊ'leɪʃən] N **1** *Physiol* éjaculation *f* **2** *Old-fashioned, Lit (exclamation)* cri *m*, exclamation *f*, **an e. of surprise/joy/horror** un cri de surprise/de joie/d'horreur

eject [ɪ'dʒekt] VT **1** *(troublemaker etc)* expulser *(***from** de*)* **2** *(of volcano etc) (lava)* projeter; *(flames etc)* jeter, émettre; *(of tape recorder, rifle)* éjecter
▸ VI *Aviat (of pilot)* s'éjecter

ejection [ɪ'dʒekʃən] N **1** *(of person)* expulsion *f*, *(of tape, cartridge, pilot)* éjection *f* **2** *(by volcano) (of flames, lava)* projection *f*
▸▸ *Am* **e. seat** siège *m* éjectable; **to use the e. seat** s'éjecter

ejector [ɪ'dʒektər] N *(on firearm)* éjecteur *m*
▸▸ *Br* **e. seat** siège *m* éjectable; **to use the e. seat** s'éjecter

▸ **eke out** [iːk] VT SEP **1 to e. out a living** gagner péniblement sa vie; **they eked out a miserable existence on the barren land** ils tiraient leur maigre subsistance du sol aride **2** *(supplement) (one's income etc)* suppléer à l'insuffisance de **3** *(make last) (rations)* économiser, faire durer

El [el] N *Am Rail (abbr* **elevated railroad)** chemin *m* de fer *ou* métro *m* aérien

elaborate[1] [ɪ'læbərət] ADJ *(style)* travaillé; *(plan, arrangements, inspection etc)* minutieux; *(description, explanation)* détaillé; *(dress etc)* recherché; *(hairstyle, pattern, design)* compliqué; *(work)* soigné; *(excuse)* alambiqué; *(apparatus, network etc)* complexe; *(meal, dish)* élaboré; **I haven't cooked anything e.** je n'ai pas préparé quelque chose de compliqué; **the cake was a very e. affair** c'était un gâteau très élaboré

elaborate[2] [ɪ'læbəreɪt] VI donner plus de détails (**on** sth sur qch); **could you e.?** est-ce que vous pouvez être plus précis?
▸ VT *(formulate) (plan)* élaborer; *(flesh out)* développer

elaborately [ɪ'læbərətlɪ] ADV *(planned, drawn)* minutieusement, de façon détaillée; *(designed)* avec recherche

elaboration [ɪlæbə'reɪʃən] N *(working out from scratch)* élaboration *f*, *(fleshing out)* développement *m*

élan [eɪ'lɑːn] N *Lit* élan *m*, impétuosité *f*

eland [ˈiːlənd] N *(animal)* éland *m*; **common e.** éland du Cap

elapse [ɪ'læps] VI *(of time)* s'écouler, passer;

years have elapsed since then des années ont passé depuis

elapsed time N *Comput* temps *m* écoulé

elastic [ɪ'læstɪk] ADJ *Phys (body)* élastique; *(movement)* souple; *Econ (supply, demand)* élastique; *Pej* **e. conscience** conscience *f* élastique
▸ N **1** élastique *m* **2** *esp Am (rubber band)* élastique *m*, caoutchouc *m*
▸▸ *Br* **e. band** élastique, caoutchouc

elasticated [ɪ'læstɪkeɪtɪd] ADJ *(clothing)* extensible

elasticity [iːlæs'tɪsɪtɪ] N *Phys (of body)* élasticité *f*, *(of wood, metal)* flexibilité *f*, *Med (of muscles)* tonicité *f*, **e. of interpretation** *(of law)* élasticité; *Econ* **the e. of supply and demand** l'élasticité de l'offre et de la demande

elastomer [ɪ'læstəmər] N *Chem* élastomère *m*

Elastoplast® [ɪ'læstəplɑːst] N sparadrap *m*

elate [ɪ'leɪt] VT exalter

elated [ɪ'leɪtɪd] ADJ transporté, exalté; **to feel e.** se sentir plein de joie; **to be e. with success** être enivré de succès

elation [ɪ'leɪʃən] N exaltation *f*

Elba [ˈelbə] N **(the island of) E.** l'île *f* d'Elbe

elbow [ˈelbəʊ] N *(of arm, sleeve, pipe)* coude *m*; **to lean one's e. on sth** s'accouder sur qch; *Fig* **to stand e. to e.** être coude à coude; **to be at sb's e.** être *ou* se tenir aux côtés de qn; **to be out at the elbows** *(of person)* être déguenillé; *(of jacket etc)* être troué aux coudes; **I'm up to my elbows in work** je suis submergé de travail; **to rub elbows with all sorts of people** fréquenter *ou* coudoyer toutes sortes de gens; *Fam* **to give sb the e.** *(of employer)* virer qn; *(of boyfriend etc)* plaquer qn; *Fam* **to get the e.** *(of employee)* se faire jeter; *(of boyfriend etc)* se faire plaquer; *Fam* **to bend** *or* **lift the e.** *(drink)* lever le coude
▸ VT pousser du coude; **to e. sb aside** écarter qn d'un coup de coude; **to e. one's way through the crowd** se frayer un passage à travers la foule en jouant des coudes; *Fig* **she just elbowed aside anyone in the office who might have opposed her** elle a joué des coudes pour écarter quiconque au bureau se serait opposé à elle
▸▸ *Fam* **e. grease** huile *f* de coude; **use a bit of e. grease!** mets un peu d'huile de coude!; **e. joint** *Anat* articulation *f* de coude; *Tech* raccord *m* de coude; **e. patch** coude *m*

▸ **elbow out** VT SEP *(remove) (person)* évincer; **there have been attempts to e. him out as chairman** on a essayé de l'évincer de la présidence

elbow-length ADJ **e. gloves** gants *mpl* longs *(montant jusqu'au coude)*

elbow-rest N accoudoir *m*

elbowroom [ˈelbəʊrʊm] N *Fig* **to have (enough) e.** avoir ses coudées franches; **give me some more e.** laisse-moi les coudées franches

El Cheapo [el'tʃiːpəʊ] *Hum Fam* N article *m* bas de gamme
▸ ADJ bas de gamme

elder[1] [ˈeldər] **VOIR GRAMMAIRE A26–7** ADJ *(of two people)* aîné, plus âgé; **my e. brother** mon frère aîné; **Pliny the E.** Pline l'Ancien
▸ N **1** aîné, -ée; **he is my e. by two years** il est de deux ans mon aîné; **children should obey their elders** les enfants devraient obéir à leurs aînés **2** *Hist, Rel (of tribe, church, village)* ancien *m*
▸▸ **e. statesman** vétéran *m*; *(politician)* vétéran de la politique

elder[2] N sureau *m*
▸▸ **e. tree** sureau

elderberry [ˈeldəberɪ] N *(fruit)* baie *f* de sureau
▸▸ **e. wine** vin *m* de sureau

elderflower [ˈeldəflaʊər] N fleur *f* de sureau

elderly [ˈeldəlɪ] ADJ âgé; *Fig* **an e. typewriter** une machine à écrire qui a fait son temps
▸ NPL **the e.** les personnes *fpl* âgées

eldest [ˈeldɪst] ADJ aîné; **my e. daughter** ma fille aînée, mon aînée; **their e. son** leur fils aîné **VOIR GRAMMAIRE A26–7**
▸ N aîné, -ée

elect [ɪ'lekt] VT **1** *Pol* élire; **to e. sb to the presidency** élire qn à la présidence; **to get elected** être élu; **she was elected president** elle a été élue présidente **2** *Fml (choose)* choisir (**to do** de faire)
▸ ADJ élu; **the president e.** le président élu
▸ NPL *Rel* **the e.** les élus *mpl*

elected [ɪ'lektɪd] ADJ *Pol* élu
▸▸ **e. dictatorship** = gouvernement *m* élu qui se comporte comme une dictature

election [ɪ'lekʃən] N *(of candidate etc)* élection *f*, **to hold an e.** procéder à une élection; **to stand for e.** se présenter aux élections; **on the e. trail** en tournée électorale
▸▸ **e. agent** directeur, -trice de campagne électorale; **e. campaign** campagne *f* électorale; **e. committee** comité *m* électoral; **e. day** jour *m* des élections; **e. programme** programme *m* électoral; **e. promise** promesse *f* électorale; **e. results** résultat *m* des élections; **e. speech** discours *m* électoral

electioneer [ɪlekʃə'nɪər] VI faire de la propagande électorale

electioneering [ɪlekʃə'nɪərɪŋ] N propagande *f* électorale

elective [ɪ'lektɪv] ADJ *Pol* **1** *(office etc)* électif; *(body etc)* électoral **2** *esp Am Sch, Univ (subject)* facultatif
▸ N *esp Am Sch, Univ (course)* cours *m* facultatif; **I'm taking two electives in psychology** je suis deux cours facultatifs en psychologie
▸▸ **e. surgery** chirurgie *f* de confort

elector [ɪ'lektər] N électeur, -trice, votant, -ante; *Hist (of Holy Roman Empire)* électeur

electoral [ɪ'lektər(ə)l] ADJ électoral, -aux
▸▸ **e. body** corps *m* électoral; **e. college** collège *m* électoral *(qui élit le président des États-Unis)*; *Br* **E. Commission** commission *f* électorale; **e. district** circonscription *f* électorale; **e. pact** pacte *m* électoral; **e. process** processus *m* électoral; *Br* **e. reform** réforme *f* électorale; **e. roll** liste *f* électorale; **e. system** système *m* électoral, régime *m* électoral

electorate [ɪ'lektərət] N *Pol* corps *m* électoral, électeurs *mpl*

electret microphone [ɪ'lektrət] N microphone *m* à électret

electric [ɪ'lektrɪk] ADJ *(light, cooker, car etc)* électrique; *Fig* **the atmosphere of the meeting was e.** l'atmosphère de la réunion était électrique; **the effect of her words was e.** ses mots ont eu un effet électrisant
▸▸ *Br* **e. blanket** couverture *f* chauffante; **e. blue** bleu *m* électrique; **e. chair** chaise *f* électrique; **e. charge** charge *f* électrique; **e. eel** anguille *f* électrique; **e. eye** œil *m* électrique; **e. fence** clôture *f* électrique; **e. field** champ *m* électrique; **e. generator** générateur *m*, génératrice *f*, **e. guitar** guitare *f* électrique; **e. heater** appareil *m* de chauffage électrique; **e. motor** moteur *m* électrique; **e. power station** centrale *f* électrique; **e. ray** torpille *f*, **e. shock** décharge *f* électrique; **e. wave** onde *f* électrique; *Aut* **e. window** glace *f ou* vitre *f* électrique

electrical [ɪ'lektrɪk(ə)l] ADJ électrique
▸▸ **e. appliance** appareil *m* électrique; **e. engineer** ingénieur *m* électricien; **e. engineering** électrotechnique *f*, **e. failure** panne *f* d'électricité; **e. fault** défaut *m* dans le système électrique

electrically [ɪ'lektrɪklɪ] ADV électriquement; *Fig* an e. charged atmosphere une atmosphère électrique; e. controlled window vitre *f* à commande électrique; *Comput* e. erasable ROM mémoire *f* morte effaçable électriquement

electrician [ɪlek'trɪʃən] N électricien, -ienne
▸▸ e.'s screwdriver tournevis *m* d'électricien

electricity [ɪlek'trɪsɪtɪ] N électricité *f*; lit by e. éclairé à l'électricité; many homes are without e. *(temporarily)* de nombreux foyers sont privés d'électricité; *(not installed)* de nombreux foyers n'ont pas l'électricité; *Fig* you could feel the e. in the air il y avait de l'électricité dans l'air
▸▸ *Br Formerly* E. Board ≃ EDF *f* (Électricité de France); e. meter compteur *m* d'électricité

electrics [ɪ'lektrɪks] NPL *Br Fam (of car etc)* circuits *mpl* électriques

electrification [ɪlektrɪfɪ'keɪʃən] N *(of railways etc)* électrification *f*

electrify [ɪ'lektrɪfaɪ] VT **1** *(convert to electricity) (railway line etc)* électrifier **2** *(charge with electricity) (fence), Fig (auditorium)* électriser

electrifying [ɪ'lektrɪfaɪɪŋ] ADJ *(effect etc)* électrisant

electroacoustic [ɪ'lektrəʊə'ku:stɪk] ADJ électroacoustique

electrocardiogram [ɪlektrəʊ'ka:dɪəʊgræm] N *Med* électrocardiogramme *m*

electrocardiograph [ɪlektrəʊ'ka:dɪəʊgræf] N *Med* électrocardiographe *m*

electrocardiography [ɪlektrəʊka:dɪ'ɒgrafɪ] N *Med* électrocardiographie *f*

electrochemical [ɪ'lektrəʊ'kemɪkl] ADJ électrochimique

electrochemistry [ɪlektrəʊ'kemɪstrɪ] N électrochimie *f*

electroconvulsive [ɪlektrəʊkən'vʌlsɪv] ADJ
▸▸ *Med* e. therapy traitement *m* par électrochocs

electrocute [ɪ'lektrəkju:t] VT électrocuter; to e. oneself s'électrocuter

electrocution [ɪlektrə'kju:ʃən] N électrocution *f*

electrode [ɪ'lektrəʊd] N électrode *f*
▸▸ e. gap écartement *m* des électrodes; e. holder porte-électrodes *m inv*

electrodynamics [ɪlektrəʊdaɪ'næmɪks] N électrodynamique *f* VOIR GRAMMAIRE A10

electroencephalogram [ɪlektrəʊen'd sefələʊgræm] N *Med* électroencéphalogramme *m*

electroencephalograph [ɪlektrəʊen'd sefələʊgræf] N *Med* appareil *m* à EEG

electrolysis [ɪlek'trɒlɪsɪs] N électrolyse *f*

electrolyte [ɪ'lektrəʊlaɪt] N *Elec* électrolyte *m*

electrolytic [ɪlektrəʊ'lɪtɪk] ADJ électrolytique

electromagnet [ɪlektrəʊ'mægnɪt] N électro-aimant *m, pl* électro-aimants

electromagnetic [ɪlektrəʊmæg'netɪk] ADJ *(field, wave etc)* électromagnétique

electromagnetism [ɪlektrəʊ'mægnɪtɪz(ə)m] N électromagnétisme *m*

electromotive [ɪlektrəʊ'məʊtɪv] ADJ électromoteur, -trice
▸▸ e. force force *f* électromotrice

electron [ɪ'lektrɒn] N *Phys* électron *m*; positive/negative e. électron positif/négatif
▸▸ e. beam faisceau *m* d'électrons; e. gun canon *m* électronique *ou* à électrons; *Biol* e. microscope microscope *m* électronique

electronic [ɪlek'trɒnɪk] ADJ électronique
▸▸ *Comput* e. banking banque *f* électronique; e. book livre *m* numérique, livre électronique, e-book *m*; e. brain cerveau *m* électronique; e. business commerce *m* électronique; e. card lock serrure *f* à carte perforée; *Comput* e. cash argent *m* électronique, argent virtuel; *Comput* e. catalogue catalogue *m* en ligne; *Comput* e. commerce commerce électronique; *Comput* e. computer calculateur *m* électronique; e. control unit centrale *f* électronique; *Comput* e. data interchange échange *m* de données informatisé; *Comput* e. data processing traitement *m* électronique de l'information; *Phot* e. flash flash *m* électronique; *Aut* e. fuel injection injection *f* à commande numérique, injection électronique; *Fin, Comput* e. funds transfer transfert *m* de fonds électronique; *Fin, Comput* e. funds transfer at point of sale transfert de fonds électronique au point de vente; *Comput* e. journal journal *m* en ligne; e. keycard carte-clé *f, pl* cartes-clés; e. lock serrure *f* électronique; *Comput* e. mail courrier *m* électronique; *Comput* e. mailbox boîte *f* à *ou* aux lettres électronique; e. media médias *mpl* électroniques; *Comput* e. money argent *m* électronique, argent virtuel; *(concept)* monétique *f*; e. music musique *f* électronique; *TV* e. news gathering journalisme *m* électronique de télévision; e. newssheet bulletin *m* électronique; *Mus* e. organ orgue *m* électronique; *Com* e. payment paiement *m* électronique; *Comput* e. point of sale point *m* de vente électronique; *Comput* e. publishing édition *f* électronique, éditique *f*; *Comput* e. purse porte-monnaie *m inv* électronique; *Aut* e. ride control contrôle *m* électronique de confort; *Aut* e. route finder guide *m* électronique d'itinéraire; *Comput* e. shopping téléachat *m*, achats *mpl* en ligne; e. tagging étiquetage *m* électronique; *St Exch* e. trading transactions *fpl* boursières electroniques; e. wallet porte-monnaie *m* électronique

electronically [ɪlek'trɒnɪklɪ] ADV électroniquement

electronics [ɪlek'trɒnɪks] N **1** électronique *f* **2** *(of machine)* système *m* électronique VOIR GRAMMAIRE A10
▸▸ e. company société *f* d'électronique; e. engineer ingénieur *m* électronicien, électronicien, -ienne; e. industry industrie *f* électronique

electroplate [ɪ'lektrəʊpleɪt] *Metal* N **1** *(material)* (métal *m*) plaqué *m* **2** *(no pl) (articles)* articles *mpl* plaqués; *(plated with silver)* articles argentés
VT plaquer; *(with silver)* argenter

electroplated [ɪ'lektrəpleɪtɪd] ADJ plaqué *(par électrodéposition)*

electro-sensitive [ɪ'lektrəʊ'-] ADJ électrosensible

electroshock [ɪ'lektrəʊʃɒk] ADJ *Med* e. therapy *or* treatment traitement *m* par électrochocs

electrostatic [ɪlektrəʊ'stætɪk] ADJ *Phys (generator etc)* électrostatique

electrostatics [ɪlektrəʊ'stætɪks] N *Phys* électrostatique *f* VOIR GRAMMAIRE A10

electrotechnic(al) [ɪlektrəʊ'teknɪk, -ɪk-(ə)l] ADJ *Elec* électrotechnique

electrotherapy [ɪlektrəʊ'θerəpɪ] N *Med* électrothérapie *f*

electrotype [ɪ'lektrəʊtaɪp] *Typ* N galvanotype *m*
VT galvanotyper

elegance ['elɪgəns] N élégance *f*

elegant ['elɪgənt] ADJ **1** *(appearance, person etc)* élégant; e. furniture meubles *mpl* d'un goût raffiné **2** *Am Fam (excellent)* excellent, de premier ordre

elegiac [elɪ'dʒaɪək] *Lit* ADJ élégiaque
NPL elegiacs vers *mpl* élégiaques

elegy ['elɪdʒɪ] N élégie *f*

element ['elɪmənt] N **1** *(aspect)* e. of uncertainty/danger/chance part *f* d'incertitude/de danger/de chance; there is an e. of risk involved cela comporte un risque; disturbing e. élément *m* d'instabilité; the personal/time e. le facteur humain/temps; the film has all the elements of a hit movie le film a tous les ingrédients d'un film à succès; a key e. in selling is … un des facteurs clés dans la vente est …
2 *(part of whole)* élément *m*, partie *f*; *Elec (of kettle, fire etc)* résistance *f*; elements *(basics) (of science)* rudiments *mpl*; *Comput* data e. élément d'information; the hooligan e. (in our society/in a football crowd) les hooligans (dans notre société/parmi les spectateurs d'un match de football); undesirable elements (in society) éléments indésirables (de la société)
3 *Chem* corps *m* simple
4 *Met* the four elements les quatre éléments *mpl*; to brave the elements braver les éléments; exposed to the elements exposé aux intempéries; *Fig* to be in one's e. être dans son élément; *Fig* to be out of one's e. ne pas être dans son élément
5 *Rel* the elements (of bread and wine) les espèces *fpl*

elemental [elɪ'ment(ə)l] ADJ **1** *(belonging to the elements)* qui appartient aux éléments *ou* aux forces de la nature; *(spirit)* élémentaire; *(rage, fury)* déchaîné **2** *(primitive)* élémentaire, primitif **3** *Chem* élémentaire **4** *(basic)* fondamental, -aux, essentiel; to be e. to sth être essentiel à qch
▸▸ e. forces éléments *mpl*

elementary [elɪ'ment(ə)rɪ] ADJ élémentaire; *Sch* e. algebra rudiments *mpl* d'algèbre
▸▸ *Am* e. school école *f* primaire

elephant ['elɪfənt] N éléphant *m*; *Fam* baby e. éléphanteau *m*
▸▸ e. calf éléphanteau *m*; e. seal éléphant *m* de mer

elephantiasis [elɪfæn'taɪəsɪs] N *Med* éléphantiasis *m*

elephantine [elɪ'fæntaɪn] ADJ *(proportions etc)* éléphantesque; *(movement etc)* lourd et gauche; *Fig (humour)* lourd

elevate ['elɪveɪt] VT **1** *(raise)* élever, hausser; *Mil (gun)* pointer en hauteur; *Rel (host, mind)* élever; to e. sb to a high rank élever qn à un haut rang **2** *(exalt) (person)* exalter; *(sb's soul)* élever; they had elevated their legends into a religion ils avaient élevé leurs légendes au rang de religion

elevated ['elɪveɪtɪd] ADJ **1** *(raised, exalted)* élevé; e. thoughts hautes pensées *fpl*; he has an e. opinion of himself il a une haute opinion de lui-même **2** *(overhead)* surélevé
▸▸ e. motorway autoroute *f* surélevée; e. position position *f* élevée; *Br* e. railway, *Am* e. railroad chemin *m* de fer *ou* métro *m* aérien; *Cin, TV* e. shot plongée *f*

elevating ['elɪveɪtɪŋ] ADJ *(discourse etc)* édifiant; the experience was far from e. l'expérience n'a rien eu de bien inspirant
N élévation *f*, levage *m*

elevation [elɪ'veɪʃən] N **1** *(of sth to certain height, of sb to superior position)* élévation *f*; *Rel* the E. (of the Host) l'Élévation **2** *Geog (height)* altitude *f*, hauteur *f*; e. above sea level altitude *f ou* hauteur *f* au-dessus du niveau de la mer **3** *(hill)* élévation *f*, éminence *f* **4** *Astron (of star)* élévation *f* **5** *Mil (of gun)* hausse *f*, pointage *m* en hauteur; angle of e. angle *m* de hausse **6** *Archit etc* élévation *f*; front e. façade *f*; side e. façade latérale; rear e. derrière *m* **7** *(nobility, refine-*

ment) (of style) élévation *f*, dignité *f*; *(of character)* noblesse *f*, grandeur *f*
▸▸**e. mechanism** dispositif *m* de pointage en hauteur

elevator ['elɪveɪtər] **N 1** *(lifting device)* élévateur *m*; *Am (for goods)* monte-charge *m inv*; **bucket e.** élévateur à godets; **grain e.** élévateur *m* à grains; *(silo)* silo *m* **2** *Am (lift)* ascenseur *m*; *Fam Hum* **the e. doesn't go up to the top floor** c'est pas une lumière **3** *Aviat* gouvernail *m* de profondeur *ou* d'altitude
▸▸**e. angle** angle *m* de braquage; *Am* **e. attendant** liftier *m*; **e. shoe** chaussure *f* à semelle compensée

eleven [ɪ'lev(ə)n] **NUM ADJ, N 1** *(numeral)* onze *m*; **the e. o'clock train** le train de onze heures **2** *Sport (team)* onze *m*; **the French e.** le onze de France

elevenses [ɪ'lev(ə)nzɪz] **NPL** *Br Fam* collation *f ou* casse-croûte *m inv (de onze heures du matin)*

eleventh [ɪ'lev(ə)nθ] **ADJ** onzième; *Fig* **at the e. hour** au dernier moment, à la dernière minute
N 1 **on the e. of May** le onze mai; **on the e.** le onze **2** *(fraction)* onzième *m*

eleventh-hour ADJ de la dernière heure *ou* chance, de dernière minute; **an e. rescue attempt** une tentative de sauvetage de dernière heure

elf, *pl* **elves** [elf, elvz] **N** *Myth* elfe *m*, lutin *m*, lutine *f*

elfin ['elfɪn] **ADJ** *(grace, features)* d'elfe, de lutin; *(music)* féerique

elfish ['elfɪʃ] **ADJ 1 = elfin 2** *(mischievous)* espiègle

elicit [ɪ'lɪsɪt] **VT 1** *(extract) (truth)* découvrir; *(facts)* tirer au clair; *(answer from sb)* obtenir; **to e. sth from sb** tirer qch de qn **2** *(give rise to) (response)* provoquer

elide [ɪ'laɪd] **VT** *Ling* élider

eligibility [elɪdʒɪ'bɪlɪtɪ] **N 1** *(as a candidate)* éligibilité *f*; *(for grant, benefit)* droit *m* (**for** à) **2** *(of suitor etc)* acceptabilité *f*

eligible ['elɪdʒɪb(ə)l] **ADJ 1** *(entitled)* éligible; **to be e.** avoir droit (**for** à); **she wasn't e. for a tax rebate/early retirement** elle n'avait pas droit à une réduction d'impôts/la retraite anticipée; **e. for promotion** qualifié pour une promotion **2** *(worthy of being chosen)* digne d'être élu *ou* choisi, acceptable; **e. bachelor/young man** bon parti *m*

eliminate [ɪ'lɪmɪneɪt] **VT** *(toxic substances, names from list, poverty etc)* éliminer; *(hypothesis, possible explanation)* écarter; *(possibility of error, risk etc)* supprimer; *Euph (kill)* supprimer; *Math* **to e. x** éliminer x; **the police have eliminated him from their enquiries** la police l'a écarté de son enquête; *Sport* **they were eliminated in the first round** ils ont été éliminés au premier tour

eliminating [ɪ'lɪmɪneɪtɪŋ] **ADJ ATTRIB** éliminateur, -trice
▸▸*Sport* **e. heats, e. rounds** épreuves *fpl* éliminatoires

elimination [ɪlɪmɪ'neɪʃən] **N** élimination *f*, **in spite of her e. from the list** bien qu'elle ait été éliminée de la liste; **by (a) process of e.** en procédant par élimination

eliminator [ɪ'lɪmɪneɪtər] **N** éliminateur *m*; **the next match will be the e.** le prochain match décidera de qui sera éliminé

elision [ɪ'lɪʒən] **N** *Ling (of vowel etc)* élision *f*

élite, elite [eɪ'liːt] **N** élite *f*; **the é. of society** l'élite de la société; *Mil* **é. regiment** corps *m* d'élite

elitism [eɪ'liːtɪz(ə)m] **N** élitisme *m*; **the e. of his attitude** son attitude élitiste

elitist [eɪ'liːtɪst] **ADJ, N** élitiste *mf*

elixir [ɪ'lɪksər] **N** élixir *m*; **the e. of life** l'élixir de longue vie

Elizabethan [ɪlɪzə'biːθ(ə)n] **ADJ** *(house, literature etc)* élisabéthain
N = Anglais, -aise vivant sous le règne de la reine Élisabeth 1ʳᵉ

Elizabeth I [ɪ'lɪzəbəθðə'fɜːst] **N** Élisabeth *f*1ʳᵉ

elk [elk] **N** **(Scandinavian) e.** élan *m*; **(American) e.** wapiti *m*, orignal *m*

ell [el] **N** *Arch (measurement)* aune *f*

ellipse [ɪ'lɪps] **N** *Math* ellipse *f*

ellipsis, *pl* **ellipses** [ɪ'lɪpsɪs, -siːz] **N 1** *Gram* ellipse *f* **2** *Typ* points *mpl* de suspension

ellipsoid [ɪ'lɪpsɔɪd] **N** *Math* ellipsoïde *m*

elliptic(al) [ɪ'lɪptɪk, -ɪk(ə)l] **ADJ** *Gram, Math, Fig* elliptique

elliptically [ɪ'lɪptɪklɪ] **ADV** elliptiquement

elm [elm] **N** *(tree, wood)* orme *m*
▸▸**e. grove** ormaie *f*

elocution [elə'kjuːʃən] **N** élocution *f*, diction *f*; **e. lessons** cours *mpl* de diction

elocutionist [elə'kjuːʃənɪst] **N** *(teacher)* professeur *m* de diction

elongate ['iːlɒŋgeɪt] **VT** allonger, étendre; *(line, platform)* prolonger
VI s'allonger, s'étendre

elongated ['iːlɒŋgeɪtɪd] **ADJ** allongé

elongation [iːlɒŋ'geɪʃən] **N 1** allongement *m*; *(of line)* prolongement *m* **2** *Astron* élongation *f*

elope [ɪ'ləʊp] **VI** s'enfuir (pour se marier); **they eloped together** ils se sont enfuis pour se marier

elopement [ɪ'ləʊpmənt] **N** fuite *f*

eloquence ['eləkwəns] **N** éloquence *f*

eloquent ['eləkwənt] **ADJ** éloquent; **to be an e. speaker** être éloquent, avoir de l'éloquence; *Fig* **an e. gesture** un geste éloquent; **the state of the economy is an e. indictment of this policy** la situation économique en dit long sur cette politique

eloquently ['eləkwəntlɪ] **ADV** éloquemment; **to pause e.** faire une pause éloquente

ELSE [els] **ADV** **or e.** *(otherwise)* autrement; *(if not, then)* ou bien; **come tomorrow or e. it will be too late** venez demain, autrement il sera trop tard; **he must be joking, or e. he's mad** il plaisante, ou bien alors il est fou; **do what I tell you, or e.!** fais ce que je te dis, sinon!
ADJ, ADV 1 *(with -one/-body)* **anyone** *or* **anybody e.** toute autre personne, n'importe qui d'autre; **he is no more stupid than anyone e.** il n'est pas plus bête qu'un autre; **can I speak to anyone e.?** y a-t-il quelqu'un d'autre à qui je puisse parler?; **it couldn't be anyone e.'s** ça ne pouvait être celui de personne d'autre; **I couldn't find anyone e. to help me** je n'ai pu trouver personne d'autre pour m'aider; **someone** *or* **somebody e.** quelqu'un d'autre; **you are taking me for someone e.** vous me prenez pour quelqu'un d'autre; **everyone** *or* **everybody e. knows it** tous les autres le savent; **you're kind to everyone e., why are you so horrible to me?** tu es gentil avec tout le monde, pourquoi es-tu si horrible avec moi?; **no one e., nobody e.** personne d'autre, aucun autre; **I knew nobody e. would do it for me** je savais que personne d'autre ne le ferait pour moi; **no one e. could do it** il n'y a que lui/elle *etc* qui puisse le faire
2 *(with -thing)* **anything e.** n'importe quoi d'autre; **have you anything e. to do?** avez-vous autre chose à faire?; **he wouldn't accept anything e.** il n'a rien voulu accepter d'autre; **anything e. I produce is impossible to sell** tout ce que je fais d'autre est invendable; **anything e., madam?** *(in shop)* et avec cela, madame?; **something e.** quelque chose d'autre, autre chose; **is there something**

e. you want me to do? y a-t-il quelque chose d'autre *ou* autre chose que tu voudrais que je fasse?; **I was thinking of something e.** je pensais à autre chose; *Fam* **she's/it's something e.!** elle est/c'est génial!; **everything e.** tout le reste; **nothing e.** rien d'autre; **nothing e., thank you** c'est tout, merci
3 *(with -where)* **somewhere e.** autre part, ailleurs; **I'm sure somewhere e. will give them a room** je suis sûr qu'ailleurs on leur donnera une chambre; **anywhere e.** n'importe où (ailleurs); **anywhere e. would have turned them away** n'importe où ailleurs on les aurait renvoyés; **can I find some anywhere e.?** puis-je en trouver ailleurs?; **everywhere e.** partout ailleurs; **everywhere e. was shut** *(other shops)* tous les autres magasins étaient fermés; **nowhere e.** nulle part ailleurs; **nowhere e. was willing to accept them** nulle part ailleurs on ne voulait les accepter
4 *(with interr pronouns)* **who e.?** qui d'autre?, qui encore?; **do you think they'll give the prize to Whippleton? – who e.?** tu crois qu'ils attribueront le prix à Whippleton? – à qui d'autre veux-tu qu'ils le donnent?; **what e.?** quoi encore?, quoi de plus?; **do you use fresh pasta for this dish? – what e.?** utilises-tu des pâtes fraîches pour ce plat? – que veux-tu que j'utilise d'autre?; **what e. can I say?** qu'est-ce que je peux dire de plus?; **where e.?** *(did you go, look etc)* où encore?; *(did you think you would find it, her etc)* où est-ce que tu pensais le/la/*etc* trouver sinon là?; **when e.?** à quel autre moment/date?; **when e. has this happened?** quand cela est-il déjà arrivé?; **how e.?** de quelle autre manière?; **did you come by taxi? – how e.?** tu es venu en taxi? – comment serais-je venu sinon?; **why e.?** pour quelle autre raison?
5 *(with little/(not) much)* **little e.** pas grand-chose d'autre; **he eats bread but little e.** il ne mange guère que du pain; **there isn't much e. to be done** il ne reste pas beaucoup à faire; *(we've no choice)* il n'y a pas grand chose d'autre à faire; *Fml* **much e. could be said on this topic** on pourrait encore en dire long sur ce sujet; *Fml* **much e. remained to be done** il restait encore beaucoup à faire

elsewhere ['elsweər] **ADV** ailleurs, autre part; **e. the weather will be fine** ailleurs, il fera beau; **her ambitions lie e.** ses ambitions se situent à un autre niveau

ELT [iːel'tiː] **N** *Sch (abbr* **English Language Teaching)** = enseignement *m* de l'anglais à des étudiants étrangers

elucidate [ɪ'luːsɪdeɪt] **VT** élucider, éclaircir; *(reference)* clarifier, éclaircir
VI s'expliquer, être plus clair; **can you e.?** peux-tu être plus clair?

elucidation [ɪluːsɪ'deɪʃən] **N** élucidation *f*, éclaircissement *m* (**of** de)

elude [ɪ'luːd] **VT** *(question)* éluder; *(blow)* esquiver, éviter; *(death, police, capture)* échapper à; *(justice)* se soustraire à; **to e. sb's grasp** échapper aux mains de qn; *Fig* **to e. sb** *(mentally)* échapper à qn

elusive [ɪ'luːsɪv] **ADJ** *(enemy, happiness)* insaisissable; *(answer)* évasif; *(concept)* flottant; *(memories)* fugitif; *(scent, perfume)* indéfinissable; **but, for him, success remained e.** mais le succès lui a échappé

elusiveness [ɪ'luːsɪvnɪs] **N** *(of enemy, happiness)* nature f insaisissable; *(of answer)* caractère *m* évasif; *(of scent, perfume)* caractère indéfinissable; **a concept of great e.** un concept extrêmement flottant

elver ['elvər] **N** *(young eel)* civelle *f*

elvish ['elvɪʃ] **ADJ = elfish**

Elysian [ɪ'lɪzɪən] **ADJ** *Myth* Élyséen
▸▸**E. fields** champs *mpl* Elysées

em [em] N *Typ* cadratin *m*
▸▸ **em dash** tiret *m* cadratin

'em [əm] PRON *Fam* = **them**

emaciate [ɪ'meɪsɪeɪt] VT *(body)* émacier, dessécher

emaciated [ɪ'meɪsɪeɪtɪd] ADJ émacié, décharné

emaciation [ɪmeɪsɪ'eɪʃən] N *(of body)* émaciation *f*, dessèchement *m*

e-mail, email ['iːmeɪl] N e-mail *m*, *Can* courriel *m*; **to send an e. to sb** envoyer un e-mail à qn; **to send sth by e.** envoyer qch par courrier électronique; **to check one's e.** consulter sa boîte à lettres électronique
VT **to e. sth to sb** envoyer qch à qn par courrier électronique; **can I e. you?** est-ce que je peux vous contacter par courrier électronique?; **e. us at...** envoyez-nous vos messages à l'adresse suivante...
▸▸ **e. account** compte *m* de courrier électronique; **e. address** adresse *f* électronique; **e. bomb** bombe *f* e-mail; **e. box** boîte *f* à ou aux lettres électronique; **e. program** programme *m* de courrier électronique; **e. software** logiciel *m* de courrier électronique

emanate ['eməneɪt] VI émaner (**from** de); *(of light)* provenir (**from** de)
VT dégager

emanation [emə'neɪʃən] N émanation *f*, *(of light)* émission *f*

emancipate [ɪ'mænsɪpeɪt] VT *(minor, women etc)* émanciper; *(slave)* affranchir; **an emancipating realization** une réflexion émancipatrice

emancipated [ɪ'mænsɪpeɪtɪd] ADJ émancipé; *(slave)* affranchi

emancipation [ɪmænsɪ'peɪʃən] N émancipation *f*, *(of slave)* affranchissement *m*

e-marketing N marketing *m* électronique

emasculate [ɪ'mæskjʊleɪt] VT émasculer, châtrer; *Fig* émasculer

emasculation [ɪmæskjʊ'leɪʃən] N émasculation *f*, castration *f*

embalm [ɪm'bɑːm] VT embaumer

embalmer [ɪm'bɑːmər] N embaumeur *m*

embalming [ɪm'bɑːmɪŋ] N embaumement *m*
▸▸ **e. fluid** fluide *m* de thanatopraxie

embankment [ɪm'bæŋkmənt] N *Rail etc* talus *m*, remblai *m*; *(to contain river)* digue *f*, *(alongside river etc)* berge *f*, quai *m*

embargo, *pl* **embargoes** [em'bɑːgəʊ, -əʊz] N embargo *m*; **to be under (an) e.** être sous embargo; *(of ship)* être séquestré; **to put an e. on** *(goods etc)* mettre un embargo sur; **to lift the e.** lever l'embargo; **trade/oil/arms e.** embargo commercial/pétrolier/sur les armes
VT mettre l'embargo sur

embark [em'bɑːk] VT *Naut* embarquer, prendre à bord
VI *Naut, Aviat* s'embarquer; *Fig* **to e. (up)on** *(adventure etc)* s'embarquer dans

embarkation [embɑː'keɪʃən] N *Naut, Aviat* embarquement *m*
▸▸ **e. card** carte *f* d'accès à bord ou d'embarquement

embarrass [ɪm'bærəs] VT embarrasser

embarrassed [ɪm'bærəst] ADJ embarrassé, gêné; **an e. silence** un silence embarrassé

embarrassing [ɪm'bærəsɪŋ] ADJ embarrassant, gênant; **a financially e. situation** un embarras financier; **how e.!** comme ça a dû être/c'est/ce serait embarrassant!

embarrassingly [ɪm'bærəsɪŋlɪ] ADV d'une manière embarrassante ou gênante; **there were e. few in the audience** le public était si réduit que c'en était embarrassant; **e., we seem to have omitted the principal's name** il semble que nous ayons oublié le nom du directeur, ce qui est plutôt embarrassant

embarrassment [ɪm'bærəsmənt] N **1** *(feeling)* embarras *m*, gêne *f*; **much to my e.** à mon grand embarras; **blushing with e.** rouge de confusion; **to be in a state of financial e.** avoir des embarras d'argent **2** *(person, thing)* source *f* d'embarras

embassy ['embəsɪ] N *(building)* ambassade *f*, **the French E.** l'ambassade de France
▸▸ **e. official** fonctionnaire *mf* d'ambassade; **e. staff** personnel *m* d'ambassade

embattled [ɪm'bæt(ə)ld] ADJ *(engaged in battle)* pris d'assaut; *Fig (under attack)* assiégé

embed [ɪm'bed] VT *(-dd-)* **1** *(nail in wall)* enfoncer; *(frame in wall)* encastrer; *(diamond in gold etc)* incruster; **to be embedded in sth** *(of hook, tooth etc)* être enfoncé dans qch; **embedded in concrete** noyé dans le béton; **to be embedded in sb's memory** être gravé dans la mémoire de qn; **to be embedded in sb's mind** être ancré dans l'esprit de qn; **to be embedded in sb's personality** être enraciné dans la personnalité de qn
2 *Comput* intégrer, imbriquer

embedded [ɪm'bedɪd] ADJ **a deeply e. feeling of inferiority** un sentiment d'infériorité profondément ancré
▸▸ *Gram* **e. clause** proposition *f* enchâssée; *Comput* **e. command** commande *f* intégrée; *Journ* **e. journalist** = journaliste *mf* incorporé(e) à une unité combattante

embellish [ɪm'belɪʃ] VT orner, embellir; *(prose)* embellir; *Fig (account, story)* enjoliver

embellishment [ɪm'belɪʃmənt] N embellissement *m*, ornement *m*; *(of story)* enjolivure *f*

ember ['embər] N *(usu pl)* **embers** braise *f*, charbons *mpl* ardents

embezzle [ɪm'bez(ə)l] VT *(funds)* détourner, distraire, s'approprier
VI commettre des détournements de fonds

embezzlement [ɪm'bezəlm(ə)nt] N détournement *m* de fonds, appropriation *f* de fonds

embezzler [ɪm'bezlər] N escroc *m*

embitter [ɪm'bɪtər] VT *(person)* aigrir, remplir d'amertume; *(character)* aigrir; *(quarrel etc)* envenimer

embittered [ɪm'bɪtəd] ADJ *(person)* aigri (**by** par); *(laugh)* amer

embittering [ɪm'bɪtərɪŋ] ADJ *(experience)* qui aigrit

emblazon [ɪm'bleɪz(ə)n] VT *Her* blasonner, décorer d'armoiries; **emblazoned with the arms of the town** peint aux armes de la ville; **she didn't want to see her name emblazoned across the front page of the Sun** elle ne voulait pas voir son nom étalé en première page du Sun

emblem ['embləm] N *(symbol)* emblème *m*; *Her* emblème, devise *f*, *Aut (on radiator)* écusson *m*; **sporting e.** insigne *m* sportif

emblematic [emblə'mætɪk] ADJ emblématique

embodiment [ɪm'bɒdɪmənt] N incarnation *f*, personnification *f*, **he is the e. of kindness** il est la bonté même

embody [ɪm'bɒdɪ] VT *(embodied; embodying)* **1** *(give form to)* incarner **2** *(personify)* personnifier **3** *(incorporate) (quality)* personnifier **3** *(incorporate) (clause in law)* incorporer; *(principles in treatise)* renfermer, rédiger

embolden [ɪm'bəʊldən] VT **1** enhardir (**sb to do sth** qn à faire qch) **2** *Typ (characters)* renforcer, graisser

embolism ['embəlɪz(ə)m] N *Med* embolie *f*

embolus ['embələs] N *Med* embole *m*

embonpoint [ɒmbɒn'pwæn] N *Hum* embonpoint *m*, rondeurs *fpl*

emboss [ɪm'bɒs] VT *(leather, metal)* estamper, repousser; *(cloth, paper)* gaufrer

embossed [ɪm'bɒst] ADJ *(leather, metal)* estampé, repoussé; *(cloth, paper)* gaufré

embossing [ɪm'bɒsɪŋ] N **1** *(technique, activity) (of leather, metal)* estampage *m*, repoussage *m*; *(of cloth, paper)* gaufrage *m* **2** *(result) (on metal)* estampage *m*, repoussé *m*; *(on cloth, paper)* gaufrure *f*
▸▸ **e. press** *(in paper making)* presse *f* à imprimer en relief; **e. punch** repoussoir *m*

embrace [ɪm'breɪs] N étreinte *f*, *(of lovers)* étreinte amoureuse; **to hold sb in a warm e.** étreindre qn chaleureusement; *Lit* **winter's iron e.** l'étreinte glacée de l'hiver
VT **1** *(person)* étreindre; *(in official ceremony)* donner une accolade à; **to e. one another tenderly** s'étreindre tendrement **2** *(adopt) (religion)* embrasser; *(cause)* adopter **3** *(include)* embrasser, contenir (**in** dans); *(subjects)* comprendre; **the view from the terrace embraces the whole valley** de la terrasse la vue s'étend sur toute la vallée ou embrasse toute la vallée
VI *(of two people)* s'étreindre

> Note that the most common meaning of the French verb **embrasser** is **to kiss**.

embrasure [ɪm'breɪʒər] N **1** *Archit* embrasure *f*, ébrasement *m* **2** *Mil* embrasure *f*, sabord *m*

embrocation [embrə'keɪʃən] N *Med* embrocation *f*

embroider [ɪm'brɔɪdər] VT **1** *Sewing* broder **2** *(exaggerate) (account, report)* enjoliver
VI **1** *Sewing* broder **2** *(exaggerate)* broder, enjoliver, *Fam* en rajouter
▸ **embroider on** VT INSEP *(truth, facts)* enjoliver

embroidering [ɪm'brɔɪdərɪŋ] N = **embroidery**

embroidery [ɪm'brɔɪdərɪ] N **1** *Sewing* broderie *f* **2** *(added details) (of account, report)* enjolivement *m*, fioriture *f*, **their e. of the facts** les enjolivements qu'ils avaient apportés aux faits
▸▸ **e. frame** métier *m* à broder; *Sewing* **e. thread** fil *m* à broder

embroil [ɪm'brɔɪl] VT *(usu passive) (involve)* **embroiled in a quarrel** entraîné dans une querelle; **to become** or **get embroiled in sth** se trouver impliqué dans qch; **I wouldn't get embroiled with her if I was you** à ta place je ne me compliquerais pas la vie avec elle, *Fam* à ta place je ne me laisserais pas embringuer avec elle

embroilment [ɪm'brɔɪlmənt] N *(involvement)* implication *f*

embryo, *pl* **embryos** ['embrɪəʊ, -əʊz] N *Biol, Fig* embryon *m*; **in e.** *(foetus, plan)* à l'état embryonnaire;
▸▸ **e. research** recherche *f* portant sur les embryons

embryogenesis [embrɪəʊ'dʒenɪsɪs] N *Med* embryogenèse *f*

embryology [embrɪ'ɒlədʒɪ] N embryologie *f*

embryonic [embrɪ'ɒnɪk] ADJ *Biol* embryonnaire; *Fig (plan, idea etc)* à l'état embryonnaire

embus [ɪm'bʌs] *Mil* VT *(troops)* embarquer dans un autocar
VI monter dans un autocar

emcee ['em'siː] *Fam* N maître *m* de cérémonies; *Radio, TV* animateur, -trice
VT *(show)* animer

emend [ɪ'mend] VT corriger

emendation [iːmen'deɪʃən] N **1** *(action) (of*

text) correction *f* **2** *(proposed alteration)* variante *f* proposée

emerald ['em(ə)rəld] N **1** *Miner* émeraude *f* **2** *(colour)* *(vert m* d.')émeraude *m*
▸▸ **e. green** (vert d.')émeraude; *Lit* **the E. Isle** la verte Irlande

emerge [ɪ'mɜːdʒ] VI *(appear)* *(from liquid, the shadow, fog)* émerger *(* **from** de); *(from hole, from behind sth etc)* déboucher *(* **from** de); *(from house, hole, darkness)* sortir; *(arise)* *(of difficulty etc)* se dresser, surgir; *(of truth, facts)* émerger, se faire jour; **the moon is emerging from behind the clouds** la lune sort de derrière les nuages; **she emerged as an important politician** elle est devenue une personnalité politique importante; **from these facts it emerges that …** de ces faits il ressort que …; **it later emerged that …** il est apparu par la suite que …; **he was soon to e. from his father's shadow** il allait bientôt sortir de l'ombre de son père

emergence [ɪ'mɜːdʒəns] N *(of theory etc)* émergence *f*, *(of new state, new leader)* apparition *f*; **they still awaited the e. of a convincing account of the events** ils attendaient encore qu'un récit convaincant des événements se fasse jour

emergency [ɪ'mɜːdʒənsɪ] N circonstance *f* critique, cas *m* urgent; *Med* urgence *f*; **to provide for emergencies** parer aux éventualités *ou* à l'imprévu; **this is an e.** c'est une urgence; **to meet an e.** faire face à une situation critique; **in an e., in case of e.** en cas d'urgence; **state of e.** état *m* d'urgence; **to declare a state of e.** déclarer l'état d'urgence; **national e.** catastrophe *f* nationale
▸▸ **e. aid** secours *mpl* d'urgence; *Aut* **e. brake** frein *m* de secours; *Am (handbrake)* frein *m* à main; *Br Parl* **e. debate** débat *m* d'urgence; **e. exit** sortie *f* *ou* issue *f* de secours; **e. fund** fonds *m* de secours; **e. goods** produits *mpl* de dépannage; *Aviat* **e. landing** atterrissage *m* forcé; *Cin etc* **e. lighting** éclairage *m* de sécurité; *Med* **e. operation** opération *f* à chaud; **e. rations** vivres *mpl* de secours *ou* de réserve; **e. regulations** mesures *fpl* d'exception; **e. repairs** réparations *fpl* d'urgence; **e. services** services *mpl* d'urgence; **e. supply** réserve *f*, *Aviat* **e. tank** réservoir *m* auxiliaire; *Fin* **e. tax** impôt *m* extraordinaire; **e. telephone** téléphone *m* d'urgence, poste *m* d'appel d'urgence; *Br Med* **e. ward** salle *f* des urgences

emergent [ɪ'mɜːdʒənt] ADJ *(talent, ability)* naissant;
▸▸ **e. nation** nation *f* en voie de développement

emerging market [ɪ'mɜːdʒɪŋ] N *Econ* marché *m* émergeant

emeritus [ɪ'merɪtəs] ADJ
▸▸ *Univ* **e. professor** professeur *m* honoraire

emery ['emərɪ] N émeri *m*
▸▸ **e. board** lime *f* à ongles; **e. cloth** toile *f* (d.')émeri; **e. paper** papier *m* (d.')émeri; **e. powder** poudre *f* d'émeri; **e. wheel** meule *f* (en) émeri

emetic [ɪ'metɪk] ADJ, N *Med* émétique *m*

EMF [iːeˈmef] N **1** *Elec* *(abbr* **electromotive force)** force *f* électromotrice **2** *Econ, Pol* *(abbr* **European Monetary Fund)** FME *m*

EMI [iːeˈmaɪ] N *Econ, Pol* *(abbr* **European Monetary Institute)** IME *m*

emigrant ['emɪɡrənt] ADJ émigré
N émigrant, -ante

emigrate ['emɪɡreɪt] VI émigrer

emigrating ['emɪɡreɪtɪŋ] ADJ émigrant

emigration [emɪˈɡreɪʃən] N émigration *f*

emigré ['emɪɡreɪ] N émigré, -ée; **e. writer** écrivain *m* émigré

eminence ['emɪnəns] N **1** *(position of impor-*

tance) position *f* éminente; *(of office)* grandeur *f*, distinction *f*; **to rise to e.** parvenir à une haute position **2** *(raised ground)* éminence *f*, élévation *f* **3** *Rel* **E.** *(title of cardinal)* Éminence *f*; **Your E.** Votre Éminence

eminent ['emɪnənt] ADJ éminent; **in view of his e. suitability for the job** du fait qu'il convient tout à fait pour le poste

eminently ['emɪnəntlɪ] ADV éminemment; **an e. respectable family** une famille éminemment honorable *or* des plus honorables; **an e. suitable place** un endroit *ou* une place parfaitement adapté(e) *(* **for** à); **what an e. sensible idea!** quelle sage idée!; **an e. believable story** une affaire tout à fait crédible

emir [e'mɪər] N émir *m*

emirate ['emɪreɪt] N émirat *m*

emissary ['emɪsərɪ] N émissaire *m*

emission [ɪ'mɪʃən] N **1** *(action)* *(of gas, heat, light etc)* émission *f*, dégagement *m*; *(of pollutant)* émission; *Banking etc (of bank notes)* émission **2** *(substance)* émanation *f*, **nocturnal emissions** pollutions *fpl* nocturnes
▸▸ *Aut* **e. limit** seuil *m* d'émission

emit [ɪ'mɪt] VT *(heat, light etc)* émettre, dégager; *(signal, sigh, cry)*, *Banking (paper money)* émettre; *(smell)* exhaler, dégager; *(sparks)* lancer, jeter; *(sound)* rendre

emitter [ɪ'mɪtər] N *Nucl* émetteur *m*

Emmy ['emɪ] N *Am TV* ≃ Sept *m* d'Or

emollient [ɪ'mɒlɪənt] ADJ, N *Med* émollient *m*

emolument [ɪ'mɒljʊmənt] N *(usu pl)* émoluments émoluments *mpl*, appointements *mpl*, honoraires *mpl*

e-money N monnaie *f* électronique

emote [ɪ'məʊt] VI donner dans l'emphase

emoticon [ɪ'məʊtɪkɒn] N *Comput* emoticon *m*, *Can* binette *f*

emotion [ɪ'məʊʃən] N émotion *f*, **to show one's emotions** laisser paraître ses émotions; **to appeal to the emotions** faire appel aux sentiments; **to be in control of one's emotions** maîtriser ses émotions; **full of emotions** plein d'émotion, ému; **she felt a mixture of emotions** ses sentiments étaient partagés

emotional [ɪ'məʊʃən(ə)l] ADJ **1** *(reaction)* émotif; *(problems)* émotionnel; *(motive)* affectif; **she's an e. wreck** elle a de gros problèmes émotionnels; **e. shock** choc *m* émotif *ou* émotionnel; **he was something of an e. cripple** il était quelque peu handicapé sur le plan affectif; **to have** *or* **carry a lot of e. baggage** avoir accumulé les échecs sentimentaux; **why is my life such an e. mess?** pourquoi ma vie affective est-elle si compliquée?; **for e. reasons** pour des raisons émotives **2** *(liable to emotion)* émotif; **to be e.** *(of person)* s'attendrir facilement; **he got very e.** *(tearful)* il a pris ça très à cœur; *(tearfully angry)* il a pris ça très mal **3** *(full of emotion)* *(plea, ceremony etc)* émouvant
▸▸ **e. blackmail** chantage *m* affectif

emotionalism [ɪ'məʊʃənəlɪz(ə)m] N sentimentalisme *m*; **it's a piece of e.** c'est du sentimentalisme; **the e. of his writing** son style sentimentaliste

emotionally [ɪ'məʊʃən(ə)lɪ] ADV **1 to be e. involved with sb** être attaché à qn; **I'm too e. involved with the whole situation** cette situation me touche de trop près; **I don't want to get e. involved** je ne veux pas m'attacher; **e. deprived** en manque d'affection **e. disturbed/exhausted** troublé/vidé sur le plan émotionnel **2** *(with strong emotion)* avec beaucoup d'émotion

emotionless [ɪ'məʊʃənlɪs] ADJ *(person)* in-

différent; *(face, look)* impassible; *(style)* sobre

emotive [ɪ'məʊtɪv] ADJ qui déchaîne les passions; **e. speech/language** discours *m*/langage *m* sensationnaliste; **racism is a very e. issue** le racisme est un sujet qui déchaîne les passions; **an e. word** un mot chargé

empanel [ɪm'pæn(ə)l] VT *(-ll-, Am -l-)* *Law* **to e. a juror** inscrire un juré sur la liste du jury

empathetic [empə'θetɪk] ADJ compatissant; **to feel e. towards sb** éprouver de la compassion pour qn

empathetically [empə'θetɪklɪ] ADV avec compassion

empathize ['empəθaɪz] VI compatir; **to e. with sb** avoir de la compassion pour qn; **to e. with sb's suffering/problems** compatir à la souffrance/aux problèmes de qn

empathy ['empəθɪ] N empathie *f*; **to feel e. for sb** éprouver de l'empathie pour qn

emperor ['empərər] N empereur *m*
▸▸ **e. moth** saturnie *f*, paon *m* de nuit; **e. penguin** manchot *m* empereur

emphasis ['emfəsɪs] N **1** *(insistence)* insistance *f*; **to lay** *or* **place e. on** *(fact)* appuyer *ou* insister sur; *(word)* souligner; **too much e. is placed on individualism** l'individualisme l'emporte trop souvent; **the e. is on written work** l'accent est mis sur le travail écrit **2** *(stress)* *(in words)* force *f*, accentuation *f*, *Gram* mise *f* en relief; *Ling* accent *m*

emphasize ['emfəsaɪz] VT *(stress)* *(word, fact)* accentuer, appuyer sur; *(draw attention to)* *(fact)* attirer l'attention sur; *(quality etc)* faire ressortir, mettre en relief; **she emphasized the need for caution** elle a bien insisté sur la nécessité d'être prudent; **you should e. the first syllable** il faut accentuer la première syllabe

emphatic [ɪm'fætɪk] ADJ **1** *(manner, gesture)* énergique; *(speaker)* vigoureux; *(refusal, response)* positif, net, *f* nette; *(victory)* net; **he was quite e. on that point** il s'est montré très catégorique sur ce point **2** *Ling (syllable)* accentué

emphatically [ɪm'fætɪk(e)lɪ] ADV **1** *(to say)* énergiquement; *(to refuse)* carrément, catégoriquement; *(to deny)* catégoriquement; **they had been e. defeated** ils avaient été largement battus **2** *(intensive)* **he is most e. a leader** c'est un chef s'il en fut jamais; **e. yes!** tout à fait, oui!

emphysema [emfɪ'siːmə] N *Med* emphysème *m*; *(pulmonary)* emphysème pulmonaire

empire ['empaɪər] N empire *m*; *Hist* **the (British) E.** l'Empire britannique; *Fig* **a shipbuilding e.** un empire dans le monde de la construction navale; *Br Hist* **E. troops** *(of British Empire)* armée *f* coloniale; **E. furniture** meubles *mpl* Empire; *Archit etc* **E. style** style *m* Empire

empire-builder N *also Fig* constructeur *m* d'empires

empire-building N *also Fig* construction *f* d'empires

empiric [em'pɪrɪk] ADJ = **empirical**
N empiriste *mf*

empirical [em'pɪrɪk(ə)l] ADJ empirique; **e. evidence** preuve *f* empirique

empiricism [em'pɪrɪsɪz(ə)m] N empirisme *m*

emplacement [ɪm'pleɪsmənt] N *Mil (of gun)* emplacement *m*

emplane [ɪm'pleɪn] *Mil* VI monter en avion
VT *(person, troops)* faire monter en avion

employ [ɪm'plɔɪ] VT **1** *(give work to)* employer; **to e. sb as secretary** employer qn comme secrétaire **2** *(occupy)* **to e. oneself, to be employed** s'occuper, être occupé *(in* doing sth à faire qch); **she employed herself by tidying up the room** elle s'est occupée en rangeant la pièce **3** *(use) (means, time, technique)* employer; *(force, argument)* se servir de; *(one's skills, tact)* user de

▪ N *Fml* emploi *m*; **to be in sb's e.** être au service de qn, être employé par qn

employable [ɪmˈplɔɪəb(ə)l] ADJ employable, susceptible d'être employé; **qualifications make you more e.** il est plus facile de se faire embaucher quand on a des qualifications

employed [ɪmˈplɔɪd] ADJ employé

▪ NPL **employers and e.** le patronat et le salariat

employee [ɪmplɔɪˈiː, emˈplɔɪiː] N employé, -ée; **employees** effectif *m*, salariés *mpl*; **relations between management and employees** relations entre la direction et le personnel

▸ ▸ **e. association** comité *m* d'entreprise; *Fin* **e. buyout** reprise *f* de l'entreprise par les salariés, RES *f*; *Fin* **e. contributions** cotisations *fpl* salariales, charges *fpl* sociales salariales; **e. file** fichier *m* salarié; *Fin* **e. profit-sharing scheme** intéressement *m* aux résultats; **e. representative** délégué, -ée du personnel; **e. share ownership plan** plan *m* d'actionnariat des salariés

employer [ɪmˈplɔɪər] N patron, -onne, *Fml* employeur, -euse; **she's a good e. (to work for)** c'est une bonne patronne; **this company is the town's largest e.** c'est cette entreprise qui emploie le plus de gens dans la ville; **(body of) employers** patronat *m*

▸ ▸ **employers' association** organisation *f* patronale, syndicat *m* patronal; **e.'s contributions** cotisations *fpl* ou retenues *fpl* patronales; **e.'s liability** responsabilité *f* patronale; **e.'s organization** organisation patronale, syndicat patronal

employment [ɪmˈplɔɪmənt] N **1** *(work)* emploi *m*, travail *m*; **to be looking for e.** chercher un emploi *ou* du travail; **to be without e.** être sans emploi *ou* sans travail; **to be in e.** avoir un emploi; **the firm gives e. to 2,000 (people)** l'entreprise emploie 2 000 personnes **2** *(act of giving work)* embauche *f*; **the e. of 200 more staff** l'embauche de 200 employés supplémentaires **3** *(use) (of money, force etc)* usage *m*

▸ ▸ **e. agency, e. bureau** bureau *m* ou agence *f* de placement; *(for manual workers)* service *m* d'embauche; **e. law** code *m* ou législation *f* du travail; **e. protection** protection *f* de l'emploi; **e. tax** taxe *f* sur les salaires

emporium [ɪmˈpɔːrɪəm] N *Old-fashioned, Lit (shop)* grand magasin *m*

empower [ɪmˈpaʊər] VT **1** *(person)* donner du pouvoir à; *Law* donner pouvoir *ou* procuration à **2** *(authorize)* **to e. sb to do sth** autoriser qn à faire qch, donner *ou* conférer plein(s) pouvoir(s) à qn pour faire qch

empress ['emprɪs] N impératrice *f*

emptiness ['emptɪnɪs] N *(of room, existence etc)* vide *m*; *(of feelings, way of life, words)* vacuité *f*; **to feel an e.** *(after bereavement, divorce etc)* sentir un vide

empty ['emptɪ] ADJ **1** vide (**of** de); *(street)* désert; *(building)* inoccupé; *(stomach)* vide; *(wagon)* sans chargement; **to come back e.** *(of lorry etc)* revenir à vide; **you shouldn't run on an e. stomach** tu ne devrais pas courir à jeun **2** *Fig (existence)* vide; *(words, threats, pleasure)* vain; **word e. of meaning** mot vide de sens; **to feel e.** *(after bereavement etc)* sentir un vide

▪ N *Com (crate)* caisse *f* vide; *(bottle)* bouteille *f* vide; **returnable empties** *(bottles)* bouteilles consignées

▪ VT *(glass etc)* vider (**into** dans); *(truck)* décharger; *Min* verser; *(streets)* dépeupler;

(cesspool, tank etc) vidanger; **he emptied (the contents of) the bucket over her head** il a vidé le seau sur sa tête; **she emptied the cigarette butts into a plant pot** elle a versé les mégots dans un pot de fleurs; **she emptied the water out of her boots** elle a vidé l'eau qui était dans ses bottes

▪ VI *(of river etc)* se déverser (**into** dans); *(of theatre etc)* se vider; **the crowd emptied onto the streets** la foule s'est répandue dans les rues

▸ ▸ **e. weight** poids *m* à vide

▸ **empty out** VT SEP *(pockets)* vider; **he emptied (the contents of) his pockets out onto the table** il a vidé le contenu de ses poches sur la table

empty-handed ADV les mains vides; **to leave e.** repartir les mains vides; **to return e.** rentrer les mains vides, rentrer bredouille

empty-headed ADJ sans cervelle

emptying ['emptɪɪŋ] N *(of glass etc)* vidage *m*; *(of barrel etc)* vidange *f*, *(of wagon)* déchargement *m*; *(of streets)* dépeuplement *m*

EMS [iːeˈmes] N **1** *Formerly (abbr European Monetary System)* SME *m* **2** *(abbr engine management system)* EMS *f* **3** *Comput (abbr expanded memory specification)* = mémoire *f* paginée, spécifications *fpl* de la mémoire paginée **4** *Comput (abbr enhanced messaging service)* EMS *m*

EMU [iːemˈjuː] N *Econ, Pol (abbr Economic and Monetary Union)* UME *f*

emu ['iːmjuː] N *(bird)* émeu *m*

emulate ['emjʊleɪt] VT *(imitate)* imiter; *(try to equal or surpass) (person)* être l'émule de; *Comput* émuler; **to e. sb's success** égaler le succès de qn

emulation [emjʊˈleɪʃən] N *also Comput* émulation *f*

emulator ['emjʊleɪtər] N *also Comput* émulateur *m*

emulsifier [ɪˈmʌlsɪfaɪər] N émulsifiant *m*

emulsify [ɪˈmʌlsɪfaɪ] VT émulsionner

emulsion [ɪˈmʌlʃən] N **1** émulsion *f*, *Phot* **plate e.** émulsion pour plaques **2** *(paint)* peinture *f* mate

▸ ▸ **e. paint** peinture mate

en [en] N *Typ* demi-cadratin *m*, *pl* demi-cadratins

▸ ▸ **en dash** tiret *m* demi-cadratin

enable [ɪˈneɪb(ə)l] VT **1** **to e. sb to do sth** mettre qn à même *ou* en état de faire qch; *Law* habiliter qn à faire qch; **this legacy enabled him to retire** cet héritage lui permit de prendre sa retraite **2** *(option)* activer

enabled [ɪˈneɪb(ə)ld] ADJ *Comput (option)* activé

enabling [ɪˈneɪb(ə)lɪŋ] ADJ *Law* habilitant

▸ ▸ **e. act** loi *f* d'habilitation; **e. legislation** décret *m* d'application

enact [ɪˈnækt] VT **1** *(act out) (tragedy, play)* jouer, représenter; **the political drama currently being enacted** le drame politique qui se joue *ou* se déroule actuellement **2** *Law (law)* décréter; *(measure)* ordonner, décréter

enactment [ɪˈnæktmənt] N **1** *(of play)* représentation *f* **2** *Law (of law)* établissement *m*, promulgation *f*, *(decree)* ordonnance *f*, décret *m*; **by legislative e.** par un texte législatif

enamel [ɪˈnæm(ə)l] N **1** *Art etc* émail *m*, *pl* émaux; **e. saucepan** casserole *f* émaillée **2** *Anat (of teeth)* émail *m* **3** *(varnish)* vernis *m*, émail *m*, *pl* émails

▪ VT *(-ll-, Am -l-)* émailler

▸ ▸ **e. paint** peinture *f* laquée *ou* vernie; **e. ware** ustensiles *mpl* en fer émaillé; **e. work** émaillure *f*, *(painting on enamel)* peinture sur émail

enamelled [ɪˈnæm(ə)ld] ADJ *(covered with enamel) (brick etc)* émaillé; *(tile)* vernissé; **e. saucepan** casserole *f* émaillée **2** *(painted)* peint en émail

enamelling [ɪˈnæm(ə)lɪŋ] N *(art)* émaillure *f*, *(painting)* peinture *f* en émail

enamour [ɪˈnæmər] VT **his behaviour did little to e. me of him** son comportement ne me l'a guère rendu plus sympathique

enamoured [ɪˈnæməd] ADJ passionné (**of sth** pour qch), amoureux (**of sb** de qn); **to become e. of sb** s'éprendre de qn; **I am scarcely e. of the suggestion** cette suggestion ne m'enchante guère

encage [ɪnˈkeɪdʒ] VT *Fml (animal)* encager

encamp [ɪnˈkæmp] VT *(army)* (faire) camper; **the army had been encamped outside the city for nearly three months** l'armée campait aux portes de la ville depuis près de trois mois

▪ VI camper

encampment [ɪnˈkæmpmənt] N campement *m*, camp *m*; **an army e.** un campement militaire

encapsulate [ɪnˈkæpsjʊleɪt] VT **1** *(summarize)* résumer; **this film encapsulates the atmosphere of the times** ce film contient *ou* renferme l'atmosphère de l'époque **2** *Pharm* capsuler

encase [ɪnˈkeɪs] VT **1** *(provide with covering)* envelopper; **encased in concrete** noyé dans le béton **2** *(put in case)* encaisser, enfermer (**in** dans)

encash [ɪnˈkæʃ] VT *Br Banking (cheque)* encaisser

encashment [ɪnˈkæʃmənt] N *Br Banking (of cheque)* encaissement *m*

encaustic [enˈkɔːstɪk] ADJ *Art (painting etc)* à l'encaustique; *(paint)* encaustique

▪ N *Art* encaustique *f*

▸ ▸ *Cer* **e. tile** carreau *m* céramique

encephalitis [ensefəˈlaɪtɪs] N *Med* encéphalite *f*

encephalopathy [ensefəˈlɒpəθɪ] N encéphalopathie *f*

enchant [ɪnˈtʃɑːnt] VT **1** *(delight)* enchanter, ravir; **he was less than enchanted by the prospect** l'idée ne l'enchantait guère **2** *(put under a spell)* ensorceler

enchanted [ɪnˈtʃɑːntɪd] ADJ **1** *(delighted)* enchanté (**with** de) **2** *(under a spell, magic)* enchanté, ensorcelé; **an e. wood** une forêt enchantée

enchanter [ɪnˈtʃɑːntər] N enchanteur *m*

enchanting [ɪnˈtʃɑːntɪŋ] ADJ *(smile, scenery)* enchanteur, -eresse; *(voice, person)* ravissant, charmant; *(idea, thought)* délicieux; **an e. little cottage** une charmante petite maison de campagne

enchantingly [ɪnˈtʃɑːntɪŋlɪ] ADV à ravir; *(to sing, to smile etc)* de façon enchanteresse; **she looked quite e. beautiful** elle était belle à ravir

enchantment [ɪnˈtʃɑːntmənt] N **1** *(delight)* ravissement *m*, enchantement *m*; **he professed his e.** il a déclaré qu'il était enchanté; *Lit* **distance lends e. (to the view)** tout paraît beau (vu) de loin; **it filled us with a sense of e.** cela nous a remplis de ravissement *ou* jetés dans le ravissement **2** *(placing under spell)* enchantement *m*, ensorcellement *m*

enchantress [ɪnˈtʃɑːntrɪs] N enchanteresse *f*

enchilada [entʃɪˈlɑːdə] N **1** *(food)* enchilada *f*, *Fam* **big e.** *(person)* huile *f*; **the whole e.** *(everything)* tout le tremblement

encircle [ɪnˈsɜːk(ə)l] VT *(of roads, walls)* entourer, ceindre; *(of army, police)* encercler, cerner; **she encircled him with her arms** elle a mis ses bras autour de lui

encirclement [ɪn'sɜːkəlmənt] N encerclement m

▸▸ *Mktg* e. **attack** attaque f par encerclement; *Mktg* e. **strategy** stratégie f d'encerclement

encircling [ɪn'sɜːk(ə)lɪŋ] N encerclement m
ADJ *Mil* e. **movement** manœuvre f d'encerclement

encl (*abbr* **enclosure**) p. j.

enclave ['enkleɪv] N enclave f

enclose [ɪn'kləʊz] VT **1** (*include*) inclure, (r)enfermer (**in** dans); **to e. sth in a letter** joindre qch à une lettre; **letter enclosing a cheque** lettre contenant un chèque; **enclosed herewith** sous ce pli; **enclosed please find …** veuillez trouver ci-inclus *ou* ci-joint … **2** (*surround*) (*field*) clôturer (**with** de); (*the new, town*) entourer, investir; **garden enclosed with** *or* **in** *or* **by high walls** jardin entouré *ou* ceint de hauts murs **3** (*cover*) (*electric motor etc*) blinder; (*mechanism*) enfermer (*dans un carter*)

enclosed [ɪn'kləʊzd] ADJ **1** (*in letter*) joint, ci-joint, ci-inclus; **the e. documents** les pièces jointes **2** (*field etc*) clos, enclos; (*army*) entouré, cerné; (*city*) investi; *Rel* (*order, monk etc*) cloîtré; (*existence, way of life*) reclus; **e. space** espace m clos **3** *Tech etc* (*covered*) recouvert, enfermé; (*mechanism*) en carter

enclosure [ɪn'kləʊʒər] N **1** (*area*) enclos m, clos m, enceinte f; *Br Hist* enclosure f; *Horseracing* la e. le pesage; **the public enclosures** la pelouse **2** (*fence, wall etc*) enceinte f, clôture f **3** *Com* (*in letter*) pièce f annexée *ou* incluse, annexe f; **enclosures** pièces jointes

encode [en'kəʊd] VT (*text etc*) chiffrer; *Comput* encoder

encoder [en'kəʊdər] N *Comput* encodeur m

encoding [en'kəʊdɪŋ] N *Comput* codage m, encodage m

encomium, *pl* **encomia** [ɪn'kəʊmɪəm, -ɪə] N *Lit* apologie f, panégyrique m

encompass [ɪn'kʌmpəs] VT **1** (*include*) englober, envelopper, renfermer (**with, within** dans); **their repertoire encompasses most musical styles** leur répertoire englobe la plupart des genres musicaux; **the state education system encompasses children of all ability levels** le système d'éducation nationale regroupe des enfants de tous les niveaux d'aptitude **2** *Fml* (*surround*) entourer (**with** de); (*of army, enemy*) encercler, cerner

encore ['ɒŋkɔːr] *Théâtre* N **1** (*song etc*) = chanson f ou morceau m exécuté(e) à la fin d'un spectacle ou d'un concert etc par un artiste que l'on a bissé; **to call for an e.** (*of audience*) bisser; **to give an e.** (*of pianist, singer etc*) bisser; **to play/sing an e.** jouer/chanter un morceau supplémentaire; (*repeating sth*) bisser un morceau **2** (*shout*) bis m
INT **e.!** bis!
VT (*passage, actor etc*) bisser

encounter [ɪn'kaʊntər] N **1** (*meeting*) (*of friends etc*) rencontre f **2** (*confrontation*) rencontre f (hostile); (*fight*) combat m; *Sport, Journ* confrontation f; **the e. between colonised and colonizer** la confrontation entre colonisés et colonisateurs
VT (*person, obstacle*) rencontrer; (*difficulties*) éprouver; (*the enemy*) affronter; (*resistance*) rencontrer, trouver; (*storm, objection*) essuyer
▸▸ *Psy* e. **group** = séance f de psychothérapie de groupe

encourage [ɪn'kʌrɪdʒ] VT **1** (*person*) encourager; **to e. sb to do sth** encourager *ou* inciter qn à faire qch; **don't e. him!** ne l'encourage pas! **2** (*support*) (*good works*) appuyer; (*the arts, commerce*) favoriser;

(*belief*) encourager; **they encouraged their daughter's ambition** ils ont encouragé leur fille à réaliser ses ambitions

encouragement [ɪn'kʌrɪdʒmənt] N encouragement m; **to give** *or* **offer sb e.** encourager qn; **to get** *or* **receive e. from sb** être encouragé par qn; **her success was a great e. to us** sa réussite nous a beaucoup encouragés; *Iron* **he doesn't need any e.** il n'a pas besoin qu'on l'encourage; **to draw e. from sth** trouver des motifs d'encouragement dans qch

encouraging [ɪn'kʌrɪdʒɪŋ] ADJ (*news, person*) encourageant; **he wasn't very e. to me** il ne s'est pas montré très encourageant à mon égard; **it is e. to see the progress that has been made** c'est encourageant de constater les progrès qui ont été faits

encouragingly [ɪn'kʌrɪdʒɪŋlɪ] ADV (*to say sth*) d'une manière encourageante; (*to smile*) d'un air encourageant; **he looked e. healthy** sa bonne mine était encourageante

▸**encroach on, encroach upon** [ɪn'krəʊtʃ] VT INSEP (*land etc*) empiéter sur; (*sb's rights*) usurper; *Law* léser; **the sea is encroaching on the land** la mer gagne du terrain

encroachment [ɪn'krəʊtʃmənt] N **1** e. **upon sb's rights** usurpation f des droits de qn, empiètement m sur les droits de qn **2** (*of sea*) ingression f

encrust [ɪn'krʌst] VT **1** (*decorate*) **encrusted with diamonds** incrusté de diamants **2** (*cover with hard outer layer*) couvrir (d'une croûte), incruster (**with** de); **encrusted with mud/blood** couvert de boue/sang

encrypt [en'krɪpt] N *Comput* crypter, chiffrer

encryption [en'krɪpʃən] N *Comput* chiffrement m
▸▸ e. **key** clé f de chiffrement; e. **software** logiciel m de chiffrement

encumber [ɪn'kʌmbər] VT **1** encombrer (**with** de); (*person, movement*) gêner; **the party remains encumbered by the legacy of its Stalinist past** le parti pâtit encore du legs encombrant de son passé stalinien **2** *Law* **encumbered estate** (*with debts*) propriété f grevée de dettes; (*with mortgage*) propriété grevée d'hypothèques

encumbrance [ɪn'kʌmbrəns] N **1** embarras m; **to be an e. to sb** (*physically*) encombrer qn; (*financially*) être à la charge de qn; **to be an e. to sb's plans** gêner les projets de qn; **the suitcase was something of an e.** la valise était plutôt encombrante **2** *Law* (*of inheritance*) charges fpl; **to free an estate from encumbrances** dégrever une propriété

encyclic [ɪn'sɪklɪk] ADJ *Cathol* encyclique

encyclical [ɪn'sɪklɪk(ə)l] *Cathol* N encyclique f
ADJ (*letter*) encyclique

encyclop(a)edia [ɪnsaɪklə'piːdɪə] N encyclopédie f; **an e. entry** un article d'encyclopédie

encyclop(a)edic [ɪnsaɪklə'piːdɪk] ADJ encyclopédique

encyclop(a)edist [ɪnsaɪklə'piːdɪst] N encyclopédiste mf

END [end]

N	bout **1** • fin **2, 3** • but **3**
VT	terminer
VI	se terminer **1, 2**

N **1** (*extremity, limit etc in space*) (*of stick, road etc*) bout m, extrémité f; (*of football pitch*) camp m; (*limit*) limite f, borne f; (*of book*) fin f; (*of procession etc*) queue f; (*of beam*) about m; (*of mast*) tronçon m; (*of cable*) tronche f, (*remnant*) (*of candle*) bout; (*of cigarette*) bout, mégot m; **the e. of the**

table le bout de la table; **to the ends of the earth** jusqu'au bout du monde; **from one e. of the country to the other** d'un bout à l'autre du pays; **to come to the e. of the road** arriver au bout de la route; (*in one's career*) arriver au bout de sa carrière; (*in one's life*) arriver au bout de sa vie; (*be unable to make progress*) être dans une impasse; *Ftbl etc* **to change ends** changer de camp; **the third from the e.** le troisième avant la fin; *Tel* **the other e. of the line** à l'autre bout de la ligne, au bout du fil; **what's the weather like at your e.?** quel temps fait-il chez vous?; **the problem's at the supplier's e.** le problème est chez le fournisseur; **it's at the other e. of town** c'est à l'autre bout de la ville; **at the northern e. of the park/town/lake** à l'extrémité nord du parc/de la ville/du lac; **e. to e.** bout à bout; **from e. to e.** d'un bout à l'autre; **e. on** bout à bout; **on e.** (*of barrel etc*) debout, sur bout; **to stand a box (up) on e.** dresser une boîte debout; **the deep/shallow e.** (*of swimming pool*) le grand/le petit bain **2** (*limit in time, quantity etc*) fin f, (*of process etc*) terme m; **five hours on e.** cinq heures de suite ou d'affilée; **for hours on e.** pendant des heures et des heures; *Fig* **we shall never hear the e. of it** on n'a pas fini d'en entendre parler; **and that's the e. of it!** et voilà tout!; **let that be an e. to the matter!** qu'on en finisse là!, qu'on n'en parle plus!; **there's no e. to it** cela n'en finit pas; *Fam* **no e. of …** infiniment de …; *Fam* **it'll do you no e. of good** ça te fera énormément de bien; *Fam* **it helped me no e.** ça m'a énormément aidé; **to make an e. of, to put an e. to** (*something*) en finir avec; (*evil etc*) mettre fin à; (*competition*) supprimer; **to draw to an e.** tirer *ou* toucher à sa fin; **to come to an e.** prendre fin; **to come to an abrupt e.** terminer abruptement; **to come to the e. of the supplies/what one wants to say** arriver au bout des réserves/de ce qu'on a à dire; **to come to a bad** *or Fam* **sticky e.** mal finir; **to bring sth to an e.** mettre fin à qch; **the war was at an e.** la guerre était terminée; **to be at the e. of one's resources** être au bout de ses ressources; **I am at the e. of my patience** je suis à bout de patience; **at the e. of** (*month, winter, century, contract, class*) à la fin de; (*six months etc*) au bout de; **at the e. of the day** à la fin de la journée; *Fig* en fin de compte, au bout du compte; **in the e.** à la longue, à la fin; **you'll get used to it in the e.** tu t'y habitueras à la longue; **she gave me the money back in the e.** elle m'a rendu l'argent à la fin, elle a fini par me rendre l'argent; **he always pays me back in the e.** il finit toujours par me rendre ce qu'il me doit; **e. of the world** fin du monde; **it's not the e. of the world** ce n'est pas la fin du monde; *Rel* **world without e.** pour les siècles des siècles; **until the e. of time** jusqu'à la fin des temps; **the e. of one's life** la fin *ou* le terme de la vie; **to meet one's e.** trouver la mort; **e. of the financial year** clôture f de l'exercice **3** (*aim, purpose*) fin f, but m, dessein m; **an e. in itself** une fin en soi; **to attain** *or* **achieve one's end(s)** en arriver *ou* parvenir à ses fins, atteindre son but; **to this e.** à ces fins; **to no good e.** avec de mauvaises intentions; **with this e. in view** avec cet objectif en vue; *Fml* **to what e.?** dans quel but?; *Prov* **the e. justifies the means** la fin justifie les moyens **4** (*technical uses*) **east e.** (*in church architecture*) chevet m; *Aut* **big e.** tête f de bielle; *Aut* **small e.** pied m de bielle; *Rail* **the e. carriage** le wagon de queue; *Rail* **e. of line** tête f de ligne **5** (*idioms*) **his hair was standing on e.** ses cheveux se dressaient sur sa tête ou se hérissaient; *Fam* **to keep one's e. up** (*stay cheerful*) ne pas se laisser démonter; (*contribute*) y mettre du sien; *Fig* **to make (both)**

ends meet joindre les deux bouts; *Fig* **to get hold of the wrong e. of the stick** mal comprendre; *Fig* **to begin at the wrong e.** ne pas commencer par le commencement; *Fig* **I don't know one e. of a tennis racket/a computer from the other** je ne sais même pas à quoi ressemble une raquette de tennis/un ordinateur; *Fam* **you're the e.!** tu es impossible!; *Br Vulg* **to get one's e. away** tremper son biscuit

vt *(work, task etc)* finir, terminer, achever; *(speech)* conclure; *(meeting)* clore; **to e. one's days peacefully** terminer ses jours en paix; **to e. a speech with a quotation** terminer un discours avec une citation; *Fam* **to e. it all** en finir; **the war to e. all wars** la dernière des dernières (guerres), la der des ders; **it's the horror film to e. all horror films** c'est le nec plus ultra des films d'horreur; **a headache to e. all headaches** une migraine de première

vi 1 finir, se terminer (**in** dans, en); *(of subscription)* expirer; **to e. happily** *(of story)* avoir une fin heureuse, bien se terminer; **the path ends at the lakeside** le chemin aboutit au bord du lac; **to e. in a point** *(of stick)* se terminer en pointe; **it ended in a fight** ça a fini en bagarre, ça s'est terminé par une bagarre; **this will e. in tears!** ça va se finir par des larmes!; **to e. in bitterness/acrimony** se terminer dans l'amertume/l'acrimonie; **his extravagance will e. by ruining him** son extravagance aboutira à sa ruine; **I must e. by thanking Mr Brown** pour conclure, je dois remercier M. Brown; **the film ends with her saying …** le film se termine sur elle disant …; **let us e. with a song** finissons par une chanson; **the story ends on a happy note** l'histoire se termine sur une note gaie; **how will it all e.?** *(what is the world coming to?)* comment tout cela va-t-il se terminer?; **will this torment/the bad weather never e.?** ce tourment/ce mauvais temps n'en finira donc jamais?; *Prov* **all's well that ends well** tout est bien qui finit bien

2 *(of word)* se terminer (**in -er** *etc* en -er *etc*); **a word ending in s** un mot qui se termine par s

▸▸ *Comput* **e. key** touche *f* fin; *Publishing, Typ* **e. matter** parties *fpl* annexes; *Tech* **e. piece** embout *m*; **e. product** *Com, Ind* produit *m* final; *Fig* résultat *m*; **e. result** résultat final; *Cin, TV* **e. titles** générique *m* de fin

▸ **end up vi** *(finish)* finir; **no one thought she'd e. up in prison** personne ne pensait qu'elle finirait en prison; **we ended up going to see a movie** en fin de compte, nous sommes allés voir un film; **he ended up dead** il a fini par se faire tuer; **our luggage ended up in Hong Kong** nos bagages se sont retrouvés à Hongkong; **she'll e. up killing someone if she carries on driving like that** elle finira par tuer quelqu'un si elle continue à conduire comme ça

end-all **N** *see* be-all and end-all

endanger [ɪnˈdeɪndʒər] **vt** *(somebody, something)* mettre en danger; *(one's life)* exposer, risquer; *(interests, health, chances)* compromettre

endangered [ɪnˈdeɪndʒəd] **ADJ ATTRIB** menacé; **an e. way of life** un mode de vie qui menace de disparaître

▸▸ **e. species** espèce *f* en voie de disparition

end-consumer **N** utilisateur *m* final; *(of foodstuffs)* consommateur *m* final, utilisateur final

endear [ɪnˈdɪər] **vt** *(somebody, something)* rendre cher (**to** à); **he has endeared himself to all** il s'est fait aimer de tous; **her outspokenness did not e. her to the régime** sa franchise ne l'a pas rendue populaire auprès du régime; **the melancholy of his songs endears him to many a listener** la mélancolie de ses chansons le fait apprécier de nombreux auditeurs

endearing [ɪnˈdɪərɪŋ] **ADJ** *(person, smile, look)* attachant; *(quality)* sympathique; *(word)* tendre; **he has a less than e. habit of …** il a l'habitude peu plaisante de …

endearingly [ɪnˈdɪərɪŋlɪ] **ADV** d'une manière attachante; **he's e. coy/modest** il est d'une pudeur/modestie attachante

endearment [ɪnˈdɪəmənt] **N** **term of e.** terme *m* affectif; **endearments** mots *mpl* tendres

endeavour, *Am* **endeavor** [ɪnˈdevər] **N** effort *m*; **to wish sb good luck in their endeavours** souhaiter bonne chance à qn dans ses entreprises; **to use** *or* **make every e. to …** faire tout son possible *ou* tous les efforts possibles pour …; **in an e. to persuade them** dans une tentative pour les persuader; **in the field of human e.** dans l'histoire des réussites humaines

vt to e. to do sth s'efforcer *ou* tenter de faire qch, chercher à faire qch

endemic [enˈdemɪk] **ADJ** *Bot, Med, Fig* endémique

N *Med* endémie *f*

endgame [ˈendɡeɪm] **N** *Chess* fin *f* de partie; *Mktg* objectif *m* (mercatique)

ending [ˈendɪŋ] **N 1** *(of nuclear tests etc)* cessation *f*; *(of restrictions)* levée *f* **2** *(of story etc)* fin *f*, conclusion *f*; **happy e.** dénouement *m* heureux; **a surprise e.** une fin surprenante **3** *Gram (of word)* terminaison *f*, désinence *f*; **feminine/masculine/neuter e.** terminaison féminine/masculine/neutre; **accusative/genitive/***etc* **e.** désinence de l'accusatif/du génitif/*etc*; **verb/noun/***etc* **e.** désinence *ou* flexion *f* verbale/nominale/*etc*; **case e.** flexion casuelle

endive [ˈendaɪv] **N** *Culin* **1** *(curly)* **e.** chicorée *f* frisée **2** *Am (chicory)* endive *f*

endless [ˈendlɪs] **ADJ 1** *(in space)* infini, sans bornes; *(journey, list etc)* interminable, sans fin; *Tech (cable, screw)* sans fin; **e. space** l'infini *m* **2** *(in time)* interminable, sans fin; *(discussion, meeting)* à n'en plus finir, interminable; *(pain)* continuel, incessant; *(chatter)* intarissable; **it's an e. task, it's e.** cela n'en finit pas; **after what seemed like an e. wait** après une attente qui m'a/lui a/*etc* semblé une éternité **3** *(in number)* innombrable; **a seemingly e. number of …** un nombre apparemment infini de …; **to take e. pains to do sth** se donner une peine infinie à faire qch; **the possibilities are e., there are e. possibilities** les possibilités sont innombrables

endlessly [ˈendlɪslɪ] **ADV** *(to speak, discuss)* interminablement; *(to repeat, revise sth)* sans cesse; *(to stretch out)* à l'infini, à perte de vue

endnote [ˈendnəʊt] **N** *Comput* note *f* de fin de document, NfD *f*

endocardium [endəʊˈkɑːdɪəm] **N** *Anat* endocarde *m*

endocarp [ˈendəʊkɑːp] **N** *Bot* endocarpe *m*

endocranium, *pl* **endocrania** [endəʊˈkreɪnɪəm, -ɪə] **N** endocrâne *m*

endocrine [ˈendəʊkraɪn] *Physiol* **ADJ** *(gland)* endocrine

N *(glande f)* endocrine *f*

endocrinology [endəʊkraɪˈnɒlədʒɪ] **N** *Med* endocrinologie *f*

end-of-month **ADJ** de fin de mois

▸▸ *Fin* **e. balance** solde *m* de fin de mois; *Fin* **e. payments** échéances *fpl* de fin de mois; *Fin* **e. statement** relevé *m* de fin de mois

end-of-year **ADJ** de fin d'année

▸▸ *Com* **e. bonus** gratification *f* de fin d'année

endogamy [enˈdɒɡəmɪ] **N** endogamie *f*

endogenous [enˈdɒdʒɪnəs] **ADJ** endogène

endometrium [endəʊˈmiːtrɪəm] **N** *Anat* endomètre *m*

endomorph [ˈendəʊmɔːf] **N** endomorphe *mf*

endorphin [enˈdɔːfɪn] **N** *Physiol* endorphine *f*

endorse [ɪnˈdɔːs] **vt 1** *Admin, Fin etc (document, cheque)* endosser; *(passport)* viser; *(bill)* avaliser **2** *Br Admin* **to e. a driving licence** = décompter des points sur un permis de conduire **3** *(approve) (action)* appuyer, sanctionner; *(decision)* souscrire à; *(opinion)* souscrire à, sanctionner; *Law (appeal)* approuver; *Pol* **to e. sb as a candidate, to e. sb's candidature** appuyer la candidature de qn; *(by party)* investir qn; **I e. all you have done** j'approuve tout ce que vous avez fait; *Com* **our products are endorsed by leading athletes** nos produits sont signés par les plus grands athlètes

endorsee [endɔːˈsiː] **N** *Fin* endossataire *mf*

endorsement [ɪnˈdɔːsmənt] **N 1** *Admin, Fin etc (of cheque)* endossement *m*, endos *m*; *(of bill)* aval *m*; *(on passport)* mention *f* spéciale; *(in insurance)* avenant *m* **2** *Br Admin (on driving licence)* contravention *f* inscrite sur le permis de conduire **3** *(approval) (of action)* approbation *f*; *(of opinion)* adhésion *f* (**of** à)

▸▸ *Fin* **e. fee** commission *f* d'endos

endorser [ɪnˈdɔːsər] **N** *Fin (of document, cheque)* endosseur *m*; *(of bill)* avaliste *mf*, avaliseur *m*

endoscope [ˈendəʊskəʊp] **N** *Med* endoscope *m*

endoscopic [endəʊˈskɒpɪk] **ADJ** *Med* endoscopique

endoscopy [enˈdɒskəpɪ] **N** *Med* endoscopie *f*

endoskeleton [ˈendəʊskelətən] **N** *Zool* endosquelette *m*

endosperm [ˈendəʊspɜːm] **N** *Bot* endosperme *m*

endow [ɪnˈdaʊ] **vt 1** doter; **endowed with great talents** doué de grands talents; **woman endowed with great beauty** femme dotée d'une grande beauté; *Fam Hum* **to be well endowed** *(of man, woman)* avoir tout ce qu'il faut **2** *Fin (person, company)* doter (**with** de); *(hospital bed, university chair etc)* fonder

endowment [ɪnˈdaʊmənt] **N 1** *Fin (action, fund)* dotation *f*; *(bequeathed to home)* fondation *f*; **(ordinary) e. assurance** assurance *f* mixte; **(pure) e. assurance** *or* **policy** assurance en cas de vie, assurance à capital différé **2** *(talent)* don *m* (naturel), talent *m*

▸▸ *Fin* **e. fund** fonds *m* de dotation; *Fin* **e. mortgage** = prêt-logement *m* lié à une assurance-vie

endpaper [ˈendpeɪpər] **N** *(of book)* page *f* de garde

endue [ɪnˈdjuː] **vt** *Lit* revêtir (**with** de)

endurable [ɪnˈdjʊərəb(ə)l] **ADJ** supportable

endurance [ɪnˈdjʊərəns] **N** résistance *f*, physical e. endurance *f* (physique); **to have great powers of e.** avoir une grande endurance; **beyond e.** insupportable, intolérable; **it was boring/irritating him beyond e.** cela l'ennuyait/l'irritait atrocement *ou* insupportablement;

▸▸ **e. test** épreuve *f* d'endurance; *Fig* **this is a real e. test** c'est une véritable épreuve d'endurance

endure [ɪnˈdjʊər] **vt** endurer; *(insults etc)* supporter; **it was more than she could e.**

c'était plus qu'elle ne pouvait supporter; **it is something I (just) can't e.** c'est une chose que je ne supporte pas; **these days she just endures him** à présent elle le souffre avec patience

VI rester; *(of relationship)* durer; *(of work of art)* (bien) supporter le passage du temps; **monuments which e. to this day** des monuments qui subsistent jusqu'à ce jour; **their names will e. forever in our hearts** leurs noms resteront pour toujours dans nos cœurs

enduring [ɪn'djʊərɪŋ] **ADJ** *(influence, memory, friendship)* durable, qui dure, permanent; *(peace)* stable; *(evil)* persistant, qui persiste

enduro [ɪn'djʊərəʊ] **N** *(motor race)* enduro *m*

end-user **N** utilisateur *m* final; *(of foodstuffs)* consommateur *m* final, utilisateur final

▸▸ *Mktg* **e. specialist** spécialiste *mf* du marché utilisateur final

endways ['endweɪz], **endwise** ['endwaɪz] **ADV 1** *(end up)* de chant, debout; **e. on** avec le bout en avant; **I could only see the object e. on** je ne voyais que la face latérale de l'objet; **the house stands e. on to the road** la maison est perpendiculaire à la route **2** *(end to end)* bout à bout; **to put things together e.** mettre des choses bout à bout **3** *(lengthways)* longitudinalement; **we'll have to take it through e.** il faudra que nous le passions dans le sens de la longueur

enema ['enəmə] **N** *Med* lavement *m*; **they gave him an e.** ils lui ont administré un lavement

enemy ['enəmɪ] **N** ennemi, -ie; **to be one's own (worst) e.** se desservir soi-même; **to make enemies** se faire des ennemis; *Mil etc* **the e.** *(no pl)* l'ennemi; *Fig* **the e. at the gates** l'ennemi qui menace VOIR GRAMMAIRE A11

ADJ *(country, ship etc)* ennemi

▸▸ **e. alien** ressortissant, -ante d'un pays ennemi

enemy-occupied **ADJ**

▸▸ *Mil* **e. territory** territoire *m* occupé par l'ennemi

energetic [enə'dʒetɪk] **ADJ** *(person, action)* énergique; **I'll join you later if I'm feeling e.** je vous rejoindrai plus tard si je m'en sens l'énergie; **I'm not feeling very e.** je ne me sens pas beaucoup d'énergie

energetically [enə'dʒetɪklɪ] **ADV** énergiquement, avec énergie; *(to deny, reply etc)* énergiquement

energetics [enə'dʒetɪks] **N** *Phys* énergétique *f* VOIR GRAMMAIRE A10

energize ['enədʒaɪz] **VT 1** *(person)* donner de l'énergie à, stimuler; **an energizing effect** un effet énergisant *ou* stimulant **2** *Elec* alimenter; *(dynamo)* amorcer; *(core of coil)* aimanter

energy ['enədʒɪ] **N 1** *(vitality)* énergie *f*, vigueur *f*; **to have no e.** ne pas avoir d'énergie; **I don't have the e.** *(to do it, go out etc)* je n'en ai pas l'énergie; **to run out of e.** ne plus avoir d'énergie; **I am running out of e.** je n'ai plus beaucoup d'énergie; **man of considerable e.** homme très énergique; **to devote** *or* **apply all one's e.** *or* **energies to a task** consacrer *ou* apporter *ou* appliquer tous ses efforts *ou* toute son énergie à une tâche; **to shout/ work/etc with all one's e.** crier/travailler/etc de toutes ses forces; **to conserve one's energies** économiser ses forces **2** *Phys* énergie *f*; **e. consumed** puissance *f* absorbée; **kinetic e.** énergie cinétique; **atomic e.** énergie atomique; **to save e.** faire des économies d'énergie; **the e. crisis** la crise de l'énergie

▸▸ **e.-absorbing bumper** pare-chocs *m inv*

à absorption d'énergie; *Pol* **E. Minister** ministre *m* de l'Énergie; *Pol* **E. Secretary** ministre de l'Énergie

energy-saving **ADJ** *(device)* d'économie d'énergie, pour économiser l'énergie, qui économise l'énergie

enervate ['enəveɪt] **VT** *(body, the will)* affaiblir

enervating ['enəveɪtɪŋ] **ADJ** *(climate)* débilitant

enervation [enə'veɪʃən] **N** *(state)* mollesse *f*

enfeeble [ɪn'fiːb(ə)l] **VT** *(of pain, age)* affaiblir

enfilade ['enfɪleɪd] *Mil* **N** tir *m* d'enfilade

VT enfiler, prendre en enfilade

enfold [ɪn'fəʊld] **VT** envelopper (**sth in sth** qch dans qch); **to e. sb in one's arms** étreindre qn, serrer qn dans ses bras

enforce [ɪn'fɔːs] **VT 1** *(put into effect)* *(a law etc)* mettre en vigueur, appliquer; *(rights)* faire valoir; *(the law)* faire respecter, faire obéir; *(ruling)* imposer, faire observer; **such a law would be impossible to e.** une telle loi serait impossible à appliquer; **to e. compliance with the law/regulations** faire respecter la loi/les réglementations; **to e. obedience** se faire obéir **2** *Fml (reinforce)* *(argument)* donner de la force à, faire valoir

enforceable [ɪn'fɔːsəb(ə)l] **ADJ** *(ruling, policy)* applicable; *(contract)* exécutoire

enforced [ɪn'fɔːst] **ADJ** *(silence, inactivity etc)* forcé

enforcement [ɪn'fɔːsmənt] **N** *Law (of law)* exécution *f*, mise *f* en vigueur, application *f*; **law e. officers** fonctionnaires *mpl* chargés de l'application de la loi

enfranchise [ɪn'fræntʃaɪz] **VT 1** *(give vote to)* admettre au suffrage, accorder le droit de vote à **2** *(free)* *(slave)* affranchir

enfranchisement [ɪn'fræntʃaɪzmənt] **N 1** *Pol (of citizen)* admission *f* au suffrage **2** *(freeing)* *(of slave)* affranchissement *m*

ENG [iːenˈdʒiː] **N** *(abbr* **electronic news gathering***)* journalisme *m* électronique de télévision

engage [ɪn'geɪdʒ] **VT 1** *Fml (employ, hire)* *(domestic employee etc)* engager; *(workers)* embaucher; *Naut (men)* recruter; **to e. sb's services** employer les services de qn **2** *(occupy)* *(person)* occuper; *(attention)* fixer; *(sb's affection)* attirer, gagner; **to e. sb in conversation** entrer en conversation avec qn, engager la conversation avec qn; **to be engaged in doing sth** être occupé à faire qch **3** *Mil* **to e. the enemy** attaquer l'ennemi; **to e. an enemy aircraft** ouvrir le feu sur un appareil ennemi **4** *Tech (cog, gear)* mettre en prise; **to e. first (gear)** mettre en première (vitesse); **to e. the clutch** embrayer **5** *Fml (pledge)* **to e. oneself to do sth** s'engager à faire qch

VI 1 *(take part)* **to e. in** *(sport etc)* s'adonner à; **to e. in conversation** commencer une conversation **2** *Mil* attaquer; **to e. in an action** se lancer dans une action **3** *Tech (of cog wheel)* (s')engrener, (s')engager (**with** avec); *(of clutch)* s'embrayer **4** *Fml (pledge)* s'engager (**to do** à faire)

engaged [ɪn'geɪdʒd] **ADJ 1 to be e.** *(to be married)* être fiancé(e); **to get e.** se fiancer; **the e. couple** les fiancés *mpl* **2** *(busy)* **heavily e.** très occupé; **to be deeply e. in conversation** être en pleine conversation; **I am (otherwise) e.** je suis pris **3** *Br Tel* **the number is e.** la ligne est occupée; **to get the e. tone** *or* **signal** entendre le signal de ligne occupée **4** *(on lavatory door)* occupé **5** *Tech (gear wheels)* en prise

engagement [ɪn'geɪdʒmənt] **N 1** *(to be married)* fiançailles *fpl* **2** *(meeting etc)* rendez-vous *m*; **owing to a previous** *or* **prior e.**

en raison d'un engagement antérieur; **public e.** engagement *m* à paraître en public; **she has many social engagements** elle est très demandée; **to have an e.** être pris, être occupé **3** *(obligation)* engagement *m*, promesse *f*, obligation *f*; **to make an e./a formal e. to do sth** s'engager/s'engager formellement à faire qch; *Com* **to carry out** *or* **meet one's engagements** faire face à ses engagements, remplir ses engagements **4** *Mil (action)* combat *m*, engagement *m*; *(of unit)* intervention *f* **5** *Tech* mise *f* en prise; *(of clutch)* embrayage *m*; *(of pinion with wheel etc)* prise *f* **6** *(employment)* *(of domestic staff, actor)* engagement *m*; *Naut (of men)* recrutement *m*

▸▸ **e. book** agenda *m*; **e. ring** bague *f* de fiançailles

engaging [ɪn'geɪdʒɪŋ] **ADJ** *(smile)* engageant, attrayant, attirant; *(tone)* liant, engageant; **to have an e. manner** être liant

engagingly [ɪn'geɪdʒɪŋlɪ] **ADV** d'une manière engageante; *(to smile)* gentiment; **e. honest/modest** d'une honnêteté/modestie engageante

engender [ɪn'dʒendər] **VT** *(effect)* faire naître, produire; *(illness, feeling)* engendrer; **it engendered some respect for her among her colleagues** cela fit naître chez ses collègues un certain respect à son égard

engine ['endʒɪn] **N 1** *Tech etc* moteur *m*; *(for ship)* machine *f*, *Comput (in laser)* mécanique *f*, base *f*, cœur *m*; *Fig* **the e. of progress/reform/etc** le moteur du progrès/de la réforme/etc; **car e.** moteur de voiture; *Br* **petrol** *or Am* **gas e.** moteur à essence; *Aut* **e. trouble** panne *f* de moteur **2** *(Br* **railway** *or Am* **railroad)* **e.** locomotive *f*; **circular e. shed** rotonde *f* **3** *Arch (machine, device)* machine *f*, appareil *m*

▸▸ *Aut* **e. block** bloc-moteur *m*, *pl* blocs-moteurs; *Aut* **e. braking** frein *m* moteur; *Aut* **e. bulkhead** pare-feu *m inv* de moteur; *Aut* **e. compartment** compartiment *m* moteur; *Br Rail* **e. driver** mécanicien, -ienne, conducteur, -trice; **e. house** bâtiment *m* des machines *ou* des moteurs; *(for fire engines)* dépôt *m*; *Aut* **e. immobilizer** *(dispositif m)* antidémarrage *m*; **e. management system** commande *f* électronique du moteur; *Tech* **e. mounting** support *m* moteur; **e. oil** huile *f* à *ou* de moteur; *Naut* **e. room** salle *f* des machines; *Rail* **e. shed** dépôt *(des locomotives)*; *(circular)* rotonde *f*

> Note that the French word **engin** is a false friend and is rarely a translation for the English word **engine**. Its most common meaning is **machine**.

engineer [endʒɪˈnɪər] **N 1** *(technical specialist)* ingénieur *m*; *(mechanic, repairman)* dépanneur *m*; **civil e.** ingénieur civil; **marine e.** ingénieur du génie maritime; **mechanical e.** ingénieur mécanicien; **mining e.** ingénieur des mines; **consulting e.** ingénieur conseil; **production e.** ingénieur (chargé de la production; *Tel* **telephone e.** technicien *m* des télécommunications *ou* du téléphone **2** *Naut (of ship)* mécanicien *m*; **chief e.** chef *m* mécanicien; **second e.** officier *m* mécanicien en second **3** *Aviat* **flight e.** *(on military aircraft)* mécanicien *m* navigant; *(on civil aircraft)* mécanicien de bord; **aircraft e.** mécanicien de piste **4** *Mil* soldat *m* du génie, sapeur *m*; **the engineers** le génie, l'arme *f* du génie; *Br* **the Royal Engineers,** *Am* **the Corps of Engineers** = le Génie **5** *Am Rail (driver)* *(of locomotive)* conducteur *m*, mécanicien *m* **6** *Fig (instigator)* *(of plan, plot)* âme *f*, instigateur *m*; **her ex-husband was the e. of her downfall** son ex-mari a été l'instigateur de sa ruine

vt 1 usu Pej (cause, bring about) (coup, sb's downfall, defeat) machiner; (situation) manigancer; Sport (goal) amener; **she engineered his escape** elle a organisé son évasion; **he had carefully engineered the seating arrangements** il avait disposé les convives avec soin **2** (build) (bridges, roads) construire (en qualité d'ingénieur); **the bridge has been superbly engineered** le pont est un superbe travail d'ingénierie
▸▸ **e. officer** ingénieur mécanicien

> Note that the French word **ingénieur** is never used to mean repairman.

engineering [endʒɪ'nɪərɪŋ] **N 1** Tech ingénierie f, technique f ou science f de l'ingénieur; **a degree in e.** une licence en ingénierie; **a tremendous feat of e.** une remarquable prouesse technique; **agricultural e.** génie m agricole ou rural; **civil e.** génie civil; **industrial e.** organisation f industrielle; **light e.** petite mécanique f; **marine e.** génie maritime; **mechanical e.** mécanique; **precision e.** mécanique de précision; **production e.** technique de la production **2** usu Pej (planning) machinations fpl, manœuvres fpl; **he had participated in the e. of her downfall** il avait participé aux machinations ou manœuvres qui ont conduit à sa ruine
▸▸ Mktg **e. attributes** qualités fpl techniques; **e. consultant** ingénieur-conseil m, pl ingénieurs-conseils; **e. department** service m technique; **e. and design department** bureau m d'études; **e. test** test m technique; **e. works** atelier m de constructions mécaniques

engineman, pl **enginemen** ['endʒɪnmən, -men] **N** Am Rail mécanicien m

England ['ɪŋglənd] **N** l'Angleterre f; **in E.** en Angleterre; **to go to E.** aller en Angleterre; Sport **the E. team** l'équipe d'Angleterre; **an E. player** un joueur de l'équipe d'Angleterre

English ['ɪŋglɪʃ] **adj** anglais; **E. born** or **by birth** de naissance anglaise; Archit **early E.** (style) premier style m gothique; **E. history** histoire f d'Angleterre
NPL the E. les Anglais mpl
N Ling anglais m; **she speaks excellent E.** elle parle un anglais excellent, son anglais est excellent; **E. E., British E.** l'anglais d'Angleterre; **American/Australian/Indian/Nigerian E.** l'anglais américain/australien/indien/nigérian; **the King's/Queen's E.** l'anglais correct; **to study E.** étudier l'anglais; **to speak E.** parler anglais; **E. speaking** anglophone, de langue anglaise; **in E.** en anglais; **E. teacher** professeur m d'anglais
▸▸ **E. breakfast** petit déjeuner m anglais ou à l'anglaise, breakfast m; **the E. Channel** la Manche; Am **E. muffin** muffin m; Fig **E. rose** = le type idéal de la femme anglaise; **E. service** (in restaurant) service m à l'anglaise

> **English Breakfast**
> Le petit déjeuner traditionnel anglais se compose d'un plat chaud (des œufs au bacon, par exemple), de céréales ou de porridge, et de toasts à la marmelade d'oranges, le tout accompagné de café ou de thé; aujourd'hui il est généralement remplacé par une collation plus légère.

Englishman, pl **Englishmen** ['ɪŋglɪʃmən] **N** Anglais m; Prov **an E.'s home is his castle** tout homme est maître chez lui

Englishwoman, pl **Englishwomen** ['ɪŋglɪʃwʊmən, -wɪmɪn] **N** Anglaise f

engrave [ɪn'greɪv] **vt** graver; **to e. on wood** graver sur bois; **engraved on the memory** gravé dans la mémoire; Fig **to be engraved on tablets of stone** être parole d'évangile

engraved [ɪn'greɪvd] **adj attrib** gravé

engraver [ɪn'greɪvər] **N** (person) graveur m

engraving [ɪn'greɪvɪŋ] **N** (process, print) gravure f; (print) estampe f; **line e.** gravure au burin

engross [ɪn'grəʊs] **vt 1** (person) absorber, occuper; **engrossed in her reading** plongée dans sa lecture, toute à sa lecture; **to become engrossed in sth** s'absorber ou s'abstraire dans qch **2** Law (document) (draw up) rédiger; (copy) grossoyer

engrossing [ɪn'grəʊsɪŋ] **adj** (study, article, work) absorbant; (film, account, book) captivant

engrossment [ɪn'grəʊsmənt] **N 1** (absorption) (of attention) absorption f (**in** dans); **her total e. in the project meant she ...** ce projet l'absorbait tellement qu'elle ... **2** Law rédaction f de la grosse

engulf [ɪn'gʌlf] **vt** engloutir, engouffrer; **to be engulfed by the waves** sombrer dans les flots; **engulfed by the flames** englouti par les flammes; **the house was suddenly engulfed in darkness** la maison a été soudain plongée dans l'obscurité; **a feeling of despair engulfed him** le désespoir l'a terrassé

enhance [ɪn'hɑːns, -'hæns] **vt** (quality of life, performance, chances) améliorer; (sth's worth) rehausser; (ability, effect) renforcer; (pleasure) accroître; (sb's beauty) mettre en valeur; (reputation) agrandir; Fin (pension) augmenter; Comput améliorer

enhancement [ɪn'hɑːnsmənt, -'hæns-] **N** (of value) rehaussement m; (of pleasure) augmentation f; Comput **computer e.** amélioration f par ordinateur

enharmonic [enhɑː'mɒnɪk] **adj** Mus enharmonique

enigma [ɪ'nɪgmə] **N** énigme f; (person) personne f énigmatique ou mystérieuse

enigmatic [enɪg'mætɪk] **adj** énigmatique, mystérieux

enigmatically [enɪg'mætɪklɪ] **adv** énigmatiquement, mystérieusement

enjoin [ɪn'dʒɔɪn] **vt** Fml enjoindre (**sth on sb** qch à qn); **to e. sb to do sth** enjoindre à qn de faire qch

enjoy [ɪn'dʒɔɪ] **vt 1** (take pleasure from) aimer, prendre plaisir à; (pipe, meal) savourer; (music, film, play etc) aimer; **I don't think you would e. the concert** je ne pense pas que tu aimerais le concert ou que le concert te plairait; **I couldn't e. the film knowing what was really happening there** je n'ai pas pu apprécier le film en sachant ce qui se passait réellement là-bas; **you won't e. the party** tu ne t'amuseras pas à la soirée; **he's someone who really enjoys his food** c'est quelqu'un qui aime la bonne chère; **to e. the fine weather** jouir du beau temps; **to e. life** profiter de la vie; **to e. oneself** s'amuser, se divertir; **they enjoyed themselves hiding in the bushes** ils se sont amusés à se cacher dans les buissons; **e. yourself!** amusez-vous bien!; **to e. doing sth** aimer faire ou trouver du plaisir à faire qch; **I e. cooking** j'aime (bien) faire la cuisine; **I enjoyed seeing them make fools of themselves** j'ai pris plaisir à les voir se ridiculiser; **I don't e. being woken up in the middle of the night** je n'aime pas qu'on me réveille en plein milieu de la nuit
2 esp Fml (benefit from) (wealth, sb's confidence) jouir de, posséder; **to e. good health/a high standard of living** jouir d'une bonne santé/d'un haut niveau de vie; Hum **to e. bad health** se complaire dans ses maux
vi Am **e.!** (before meal) bon appétit!

enjoyable [ɪn'dʒɔɪəb(ə)l] **adj** (stay, trip, wine) agréable; **that was a very e. meal**

c'était très bon; **we had a most e. evening** nous avons passé une soirée des plus agréables

enjoyably [ɪn'dʒɔɪəblɪ] **adv** agréablement; **we spent the week most e.** nous avons passé une semaine des plus agréables

enjoyment [ɪn'dʒɔɪmənt] **N 1** (pleasure) plaisir m; **to get e. out of sth/doing sth** retirer du plaisir de qch/à faire qch; **to take great e. in doing sth** prendre un grand plaisir à faire qch; **the noise spoiled our e. of the music** le bruit nous a empêchés de profiter pleinement de la musique **2** Fml (benefit) (of right etc) jouissance f

enlarge [ɪn'lɑːdʒ] **vt 1** (increase in size) agrandir; (property) étendre; (wealth) accroître, augmenter; (hole) élargir; Med (heart, liver) hypertrophier; Phot (photograph) agrandir; **to have** or **get a photograph enlarged** faire agrandir une photo **2** (develop) (idea) développer
vi 1 (increase in size) s'agrandir; (of property) s'étendre; (of wealth) augmenter; (of hole) s'élargir, s'agrandir; Med (of heart, liver) s'hypertrophier **2** (speak or write at greater length) **to e. on** (subject, importance of sth) s'étendre sur

enlarged [ɪn'lɑːdʒd] **adj** (majority) accru; (photograph) agrandi; Med (tonsil, liver) hypertrophié
▸▸ **e. edition** (of reference book) édition f augmentée

enlargement [ɪn'lɑːdʒmənt] **N 1** (increase) agrandissement m; (of property) extension f; (of wealth) accroissement m; (of EU) élargissement m; (of hole) élargissement m **2** Phot (print, action) agrandissement m **3** Med (of heart, spleen) hypertrophie f

enlarger [ɪn'lɑːdʒər] **N** Phot agrandisseur m

enlighten [ɪn'laɪt(ə)n] **vt** (person) éclairer (**on, as to** sur); **can somebody e. me as to what is going on?** est-ce que quelqu'un peut m'expliquer ce qui se passe?; **the programme didn't really e. me as to why ...** l'émission ne m'a pas vraiment éclairé sur la raison pour laquelle ...

enlightened [ɪn'laɪt(ə)nd] **adj** (person, criticism) éclairé; **to be sexually e.** (liberal) avoir les idées larges sur le plan de la sexualité; (knowledgeable) avoir de bonnes connaissances en matière de sexualité
▸▸ Hist **e. despot** despote m éclairé

enlightenment [ɪn'laɪt(ə)nmənt] **N 1** éclaircissement m (**on** sur); **for your e.** pour votre édification **2** Hist **the (Age of) E.** le Siècle des lumières

enlist [ɪn'lɪst] **vt** (supporters) recruter; Mil (soldier) enrôler, engager; (sb's support, help, sympathy) s'assurer; **to e. sb's support for a cause** rallier qn à une cause; **she enlisted the help of two bystanders** elle a obtenu de l'aide de la part de deux spectateurs
vi Mil (of soldier) s'engager

enlisted [ɪn'lɪstɪd] **adj** Mil enrôlé, engagé, appelé (sous les drapeaux);
▸▸ Am Mil **e. man** (simple) soldat m

enlistment [ɪn'lɪstmənt] **N** Mil engagement m

enliven [ɪn'laɪv(ə)n] **vt** (person, conversation) animer; (party) égayer, animer; **she had been enlivened by the visit of her grandson** la visite de son petit-fils l'avait égayée

en masse ['ɒn'mæs] **adv** en masse, tous ensemble

enmesh [ɪn'meʃ] **vt** (person) prendre dans un piège; (in net) prendre au filet; Fig **to be enmeshed in a situation** être empêtré dans une situation

enmity ['enmɪtɪ] **N** inimitié f, hostilité f; **she felt no e. for** or **towards him** elle ne ressentait aucune inimitié *ou* hostilité à son égard; **religious and ethnic enmities** hostilités religieuses et ethniques

ennoble [ɪˈnəʊb(ə)l] **VT 1** *(raise to the nobility) (commoner)* anoblir **2** *(make nobler) (person, character)* ennoblir

ennoblement [ɪˈnəʊb(ə)lmənt] **N 1** *(of commoner)* anoblissement *m* **2** *(of character etc)* ennoblissement *m*

ennobling [ɪˈnəʊblɪŋ] **ADJ** *(effect, experience)* ennoblissant

ennui [ɒnˈwiː] **N** ennui *m*; **this feeling of e.** cet ennui

enormity [ɪˈnɔːmɪtɪ] **N** *(of crime)* énormité *f*; **enormities** atrocités *fpl*

enormous [ɪˈnɔːməs] **ADJ** *(building, hands, sum, difference, improvement)* énorme; *(gratitude, patience)* immense; *(power, intelligence)* colossal, -aux; *(loss)* gigantesque; *(idiot, stupidity)* monumental, -aux

enormously [ɪˈnɔːməslɪ] **ADV** énormément; **I was e. grateful** j'étais infiniment reconnaissant

enormousness [ɪˈnɔːməsnɪs] **N** immensité *f*; *(of problems)* énormité *f*

ENOUGH [ɪˈnʌf]

ADJ, N assez ▪ assez de	
ADV assez **1**	

ADJ, N assez (de); **(not) e. money** (pas) assez d'argent; **will this be e.?** est-ce que ça suffira?; **I've had e. of it/them** *(fed up with)* j'en ai assez; **I've had e. to drink** j'ai assez bu; **that's e. for me** cela me suffit; **that's e.** *(to eat, drink)* c'est assez, ça suffit; *(of your behaviour)* en voilà assez!, ça suffit!; **e. is e.** il ne faut pas exagérer; **he started to help her but then decided that e. was e.** il a d'abord essayé de l'aider mais il a ensuite décidé qu'il en avait déjà assez fait; **more than e.** plus qu'il n'en faut, plus que suffisant; **there was more than e.** il y en avait de reste; **you've said more than e. already** tu en as déjà largement assez dit; **have you e. to pay?** avez-vous de quoi payer?; **wages that are not e. to live on** salaire qui ne suffit pas pour vivre; **he has e. to live on** il a de quoi vivre; **e. said!** assez parlé!; **e. of this nonsense!** assez de ces bêtises!; **one word was e. to prove that ...** il a suffi d'un mot pour prouver que ...; **it was e. to drive you crazy** c'était à vous rendre fou; *Prov* **e. is as good as a feast** assez vaut *(un)* festin

ADV VOIR GRAMMAIRE A23 **1** *(sufficiently)* assez; **good e.** assez bon; **fair e.!** ça va!, d'accord!; **it's a good e. reason** c'est une raison comme une autre; **she is not strong e.** elle n'est pas assez forte; **to be near e. to see** être assez près pour voir; **I haven't been here long e. to say** cela ne fait pas assez longtemps que je suis ici pour le savoir; **he didn't try (hard) e.** il n'a pas assez essayé
2 *(intensive)* **you know well e. what I mean** vous savez très bien ce que je veux dire; **curiously** *or* **oddly e., nobody knew anything about it** chose curieuse, personne n'en savait rien

en passant [ɒnpæˈsɒn] **ADV** *Chess, Fig* en passant

enplane [enˈpleɪn] **VT** embarquer

enprint [ˈenprɪnt] **N** *Phot* format *m* normal

enquire [ɪŋˈkwaɪər] **VT & VI** = **inquire**

enquiry [ɪŋˈkwaɪ(ə)rɪ] **N** = **inquiry**

enrage [ɪnˈreɪdʒ] **VT** *(person)* rendre furieux; **she was enraged by the government's complacency** la complaisance du gouvernement la rendait furieuse

enrapture [ɪnˈræptʃər] **VT** éblouir, émerveiller

enraptured [ɪnˈræptʃəd] **ADJ** ébloui, émerveillé

enrich [ɪnˈrɪtʃ] **VT** *(person, language, text etc)* enrichir; *(soil)* fertiliser, amender; *Aut* **to e. the mixture** enrichir le mélange

enriched [ɪnˈrɪtʃd] **ADJ** enrichi; **e. with gold** rehaussé d'or; **e. with vitamin C** enrichi à la vitamine C
  ▸▸ *Phys* **e. uranium** uranium *m* enrichi

enriching [ɪnˈrɪtʃɪŋ] **ADJ** *(experience)* enrichissant

enrichment [ɪnˈrɪtʃmənt] **N** enrichissement *m*; *(of soil)* fertilisation *f*, amendement *m*

enrol, *Am* **enroll** [ɪnˈrəʊl] **(enrolled; enrolling) VT** *(recruits)* enrôler, encadrer; *(workers)* embaucher; *(students)* immatriculer; **to e. oneself** *(in army)* s'enrôler, s'engager (**in** dans); *(in a society)* s'inscrire
VI s'enrôler, s'engager; *(in a society)* s'inscrire (**in** dans); *(for course)* s'inscrire (**for** à); **to e. for a course of lectures** s'inscrire pour une série de conférences

enrolment, *Am* **enrollment** [ɪnˈrəʊlmənt] **N** *(of soldiers etc)* enrôlement *m*; *(of workers)* embauche *f*, *(of students)* immatriculation *f*

Ens *abbr* **Ensign**

ensconce [ɪnˈskɒns] **VT** **to e. oneself** *(in armchair)* s'installer confortablement; *(in corner)* se nicher; **she was ensconced in her favourite chair** elle était confortablement installée dans son fauteuil préféré

ensemble [ɒnˈsɒmb(ə)l] **N** *(clothing etc), Mus* ensemble *m*

enshrine [ɪnˈʃraɪn] **VT** *Rel* enchâsser (**in** dans); *Fig* **this right is enshrined in the constitution** ce droit fait partie intégrante de la constitution

ensign [ˈensaɪn] **N 1** *(flag)* drapeau *m*; *Naut* pavillon *m* national; *Br Naut* **white e.** = pavillon de la Marine anglaise et du Royal Yacht Squadron; *Br Naut* **red e.** = pavillon marchand **2** *Am (officer)* enseigne *m* *(de vaisseau de deuxième classe)*

ensilage [enˈsaɪlɪdʒ] **N** *Agr* ensilage *m*, silotage *m*

enslave [ɪnˈsleɪv] **VT** réduire à l'esclavage, asservir

enslavement [ɪnˈsleɪvmənt] **N** *(of nation etc)* réduction *f* à l'esclavage, asservissement *m*

ensnare [ɪnˈsneər] **VT** *(animal)* prendre au piège; *Pej (of woman) (lover)* attirer dans ses filets; **she used her beauty to e. him into marrying her** elle s'est servi de sa beauté comme d'un appât pour qu'il l'épouse; **he was ensnared by her charms** il a été enjôlé par ses charmes

ensue [ɪnˈsjuː] **VI** s'ensuivre; **a long silence ensued** il se fit un long silence

ensuing [ɪnˈsjuːɪŋ] **ADJ** *(in the past)* qui a/ ont suivi, suivant; *(in the future)* qui suivra/ suivront; *(negotiations)* ultérieur, postérieur

en suite [ˈɒnswiːt] **N** *(bathroom)* salle *f* de bain particulière
  ADV **with a bathroom e.** avec salle de bain particulière
  ADJ *(bathroom)* particulier

ensure [ɪnˈʃʊər] **VT** assurer; **I have taken steps to e. that ...** j'ai pris des mesures pour que ... + *subj*; **it is the police's job to e. that the public are protected** c'est à la police de faire en sorte que le public soit protégé

ENT [iːenˈtiː] **N** *Med (abbr* **ear nose and throat)** O.R.L. *f*

entail[1] [ˈenteɪl] **N 1** *Law (act)* substitution *f* **2** *(property)* bien *m* substitué **3** *(inheritance)* héritage *m* inéluctable

entail[2] [enˈteɪl] **VT 1** *(involve) (expenditure)* entraîner, occasionner; *(a lot of work)* impo-

ser; *(difficulties)* comporter; *(in logic)* entraîner; **it entailed my going to London** cela exigeait que je me rende à Londres; **the job entails working unsociable hours** ce travail nécessite que l'on travaille en dehors des heures régulières **2** *Law* **to e. an estate** substituer un bien (**on sb** au profit de qn); **entailed estate** bien *m* substitué

entangle [ɪnˈtæŋg(ə)l] **VT 1** *(catch)* empêtrer; **to get** *or* **become entangled in sth** *(of person, animal)* s'empêtrer dans qch; *(of string, raincoat belt, hair)* s'enchevêtrer dans qch **2** *(mix up) (hair, thread)* emmêler; *(wire)* enchevêtrer; **to get** *or* **become entangled** s'emmêler, s'embrouiller **3** *Fig* embarrasser, empêtrer; **to become entangled in lies/sb's problems** s'empêtrer dans des mensonges/ les problèmes de qn; **to get entangled with sb** *(emotionally)* avoir une liaison avec qn; **he got himself entangled with criminals** il s'est retrouvé mêlé à *ou Fam* embringué avec des criminels

entanglement [ɪnˈtæŋg(ə)lmənt] **N 1** emmêlement *m*, enchevêtrement *m*; *Mil* **barbed wire e.** réseau(x) *m(pl)* de fil de fer barbelé **2** *Fig* **e. with the law/the police** accrochage *m* avec la loi/la police; **emotional entanglements** complications *fpl* sentimentales; **an e. with a woman** une liaison avec une femme

entente [ɒnˈtɒnt] **N** entente *f*
  ▸▸ **e. cordiale** entente *f* cordiale

ENTER [ˈentər]

VT entrer dans **1, 2** ▪ s'inscrire à **2**	
▪ inscrire **4** ▪ entrer **6**	
VI entrer **1** ▪ s'inscrire **2**	

VT (-r-) **1** *(go or come into) (house, country etc)* entrer dans; **to e. the war** entrer en guerre; **the bullet had entered his heart** la balle lui avait pénétré dans le cœur; **it never entered my head that ...** il ne m'est pas venu à l'esprit que ...
2 *(join) (university)* s'inscrire à, se faire inscrire à; *(profession)* entrer dans; **to e. the Army/Navy** entrer dans l'armée/dans la marine; **to e. the Church** entrer dans les ordres; **to e. a university/convent** entrer dans un université/dans un couvent; **to e. politics** se lancer dans la politique; **to e. sb's service** entrer au service de qn
3 *(begin)* **to e. one's sixtieth year** entrer dans sa soixantième année
4 *(include, register)* **to e. a name on a list** inscrire *ou* porter un nom sur une liste; **to e. sb for an exam** inscrire qn à un examen; **to e. sb for a race** inscrire qn au nombre des participants d'une course; **to e. a horse for a race** engager un cheval dans une course; *Com* **to e. goods** *(in customs)* déclarer des marchandises en douane; *Acct* **to e. an item in the ledger** inscrire *ou* porter un article au grand livre; *Acct* **to e. sth to** *or* **against sb** porter *ou* inscrire qch au compte de qn; *Acct* **to e. sth in the accounts** compatibiliser qch; **to e. a protest** protester formellement
5 *(take part in) (race, competition)* participer à
6 *Comput (data)* entrer, introduire
  VI 1 entrer (**through** par); *Theat* **e. Hamlet** entre Hamlet
2 *(register)* s'inscrire; **she entered for the race/for the exam** elle s'est inscrite pour la course/à l'examen; **are you going to e.?** *(for competition, exam)* est-ce que tu vas te présenter?
  N *Comput* touche *f* (d')entrée; **press e.** appuyer sur la touche entrée
  ▸▸ *Comput* **e. key** touche *f* (d')entrée
▸ **enter into** **VT INSEP 1** *(begin) (service, relationship)* entrer en; *(business, dispute)* entrer dans; *(negotiations)* engager; *(agreement)*

conclure, passer; *(contract)* passer; **to e. into partnership with sb** s'associer avec qn; *Lit* **to e. into holy matrimony** se marier; **to e. into (a) conversation with sb** engager une conversation avec qn
2 *(have part in) (decision)* peser sur, influencer; **money doesn't e. into it** l'argent n'entre pas en jeu *ou* en ligne de compte
3 to e. into the spirit of the game entrer dans le jeu
▸ **enter on** VT INSEP **1** *(commence)* débuter (dans), commencer, entamer; **she has entered on a new career** elle a commencé une nouvelle carrière
2 *Law (property)* entrer en possession de, prendre possession de
▸ **enter up** VT SEP **to e. up an item in the ledger** inscrire *ou* porter un article au grand livre
▸ **enter upon** VT INSEP = **enter on**

enteric [en'terɪk] ADJ *Med* entérique
▸▸ **e. fever** (fièvre *f*) typhoïde *f*

entering ['entərɪŋ] N *Comput (of command, character)* entrée *f*, *(of data)* entrée *f*, introduction *f*, **e. of an order** enregistrement *m* d'une commande

enteritis [entə'raɪtɪs] N *Med* entérite *f*

enterprise ['entəpraɪz] N **1** *(undertaking)* entreprise *f* (difficile) **2** *Com (business)* entreprise *f*, **free e.** la libre entreprise; **private e.** l'entreprise privée **3** *(initiative)* **to show e.** faire preuve d'un esprit entreprenant; **man of great e.** homme entreprenant; **to lack e.** manquer d'initiative; **to be full of e., to have a lot of e.** être très entreprenant
▸▸ *Br* **e. area** = zone *f* d'encouragement à l'implantation d'entreprises dans les régions économiques défavorisées; *Com* **e. culture** = attitude *f* favorable à l'essor de l'esprit d'entreprise; *Econ* **e. economy** = type d'économie qui facilite la création d'entreprises; *Br* **e. zone** = zone *f* d'encouragement à l'implantation d'entreprises dans les régions économiques défavorisées

enterprising ['entəpraɪzɪŋ] ADJ entreprenant; *(imaginative)* plein d'imagination; *(solution)* imaginatif, ingénieux

enterprisingly ['entəpraɪzɪŋlɪ] ADV d'une façon entreprenante; *(to repair sth)* ingénieusement

entertain [entə'teɪn] VT **1** *(amuse)* divertir, amuser; **she entertained us with stories of her travels** elle nous a divertis en nous racontant ses histoires de voyages; **to keep sb entertained** divertir *ou* amuser qn **2** *esp Fml* **to e. guests** recevoir (des invités); **we are entertaining them to dinner next Tuesday** nous les avons invités à dîner mardi prochain **3** *(consider, accept) (proposition, opinion)* admettre, accueillir; *(request)* faire un accueil favorable à; **he wasn't prepared to e. the idea** il se refusait à considérer cette idée **3** *(harbour) (fears, suspicions)* éprouver; *(hope, idea, doubts)* nourrir; *(illusion)* chérir, caresser
VI offrir une réception; **they e. a great deal** ils reçoivent beaucoup (de monde)

Note that the French verb **entretenir** is a false friend and is never a translation for the English verb **to entertain**. Its most common meaning is **to maintain**.

entertainer [entə'teɪnər] N **1** *Theat etc* artiste *mf* de cabaret, fantaisiste *mf*, *(comedian)* comique *mf*; **TV e.** animateur, -trice de la télé **2** *(of guests)* **they never were big entertainers** ils n'ont jamais beaucoup reçu

entertaining [entə'teɪnɪŋ] ADJ divertissant; *(funny, amusing)* amusant
N *(of guests)* réception *f*, **they do a lot of e.** ils reçoivent beaucoup; **he never liked e.** il n'a jamais aimé recevoir

entertainingly [entə'teɪnɪŋlɪ] ADV d'une manière divertissante; *(in funny or amusing way)* d'une manière amusante

entertainment [entə'teɪnmənt] N **1** *(amusement)* divertissement *m*, amusement *m*; **much to the e. of the crowd** au grand amusement de la foule; **to be good e. value** être amusant *ou* divertissant **2** *Theat etc* spectacle *m*, divertissement *m*; **the e. business** l'industrie *f* du spectacle **3** *(hospitality)* hospitalité *f*, *(reception)* réception *f*, fête *f*
▸▸ *Com* **e. allowance** frais *mpl* de représentation; **e. centre** système *m* audio-vidéo; **entertainments director** *(at holiday centre etc)* directeur *m* de l'animation; *Com* **e. expenses** frais de représentation; **entertainments guide** guide *m* des spectacles; **entertainments officer** *(on ship)* = officier *m* chargé des spectacles, animateur *m*; **entertainments team** équipe *f* d'animation; **e. system** système audio-vidéo; **e. tax** taxe *f* sur les spectacles

enthral, *Am* **enthrall** [ɪn'θrɔːl] VT **(enthralled; enthralling)** *(of spectacle, speaker)* captiver, passionner; *(of object, beauty)* fasciner; *(of prospect, idea)* enthousiasmer, exalter; **we were enthralled by his stories** nous étions captivés par ses histoires

enthralling [ɪn'θrɔːlɪŋ] ADJ *(spectacle, speaker etc)* captivant, passionnant; *(object, beauty)* fascinant; *(prospect, idea)* exaltant, enthousiasmant

enthrallingly [ɪn'θrɔːlɪŋlɪ] ADV d'une manière captivante; **e. beautiful** d'une beauté fascinante

enthrone [ɪn'θrəʊn] VT *(king)* mettre sur le trône; *(bishop)* introniser

enthronement [ɪn'θrəʊnmənt] N intronisation *f*

enthuse [ɪn'θjuːz] VI s'enthousiasmer (**over, about** pour)
VT enthousiasmer

enthusiasm [ɪn'θjuːzɪæz(ə)m] N enthousiasme *m* (**for, about** pour); **to show/feel little e. for sth** faire preuve de/se sentir peu d'enthousiasme pour qch

enthusiast [ɪn'θjuːzɪæst] N enthousiaste *mf*, *(of golf etc)* fanatique *mf*, *(of music)* passionné, -ée; **Harold, long an e. of privatization** Harold, partisan *ou* adepte de longue date de la privatisation; **a great Shakespeare e.** un grand amateur de Shakespeare

enthusiastic [ɪnθjuːzɪ'æstɪk] ADJ enthousiaste; *(angler etc)* passionné; **to be very e. about sth** être très enthousiaste à l'égard de qch; **to become e. about sth** s'enthousiasmer pour qch; *Iron* **don't sound so e.!** tu pourrais te montrer un peu plus enthousiaste!

enthusiastically [ɪnθjuːzɪ'æstɪklɪ] ADV avec enthousiasme; **to accept e.** accepter d'enthousiasme

entice [ɪn'taɪs] VT attirer, séduire; **to e. sb to do sth** convaincre *ou* persuader qn de faire qch; **she'll never be able to e. him away from his wife** elle n'arrivera jamais à le séduire au point de lui faire quitter sa femme; **to e. sb away from a company** appâter qn pour qu'il quitte une entreprise; **they used a prostitute to e. him into the bar** ils se sont servi d'une prostituée pour le séduire et l'attirer dans le bar; **she used it to e. the mouse out from under the cooker** elle s'en est servi pour faire sortir la souris de sous la cuisinière

enticement [ɪn'taɪsmənt] N **1** *Law (act)* séduction *f* **2** *(charm)* attrait *m*, charme *m* **3** *(lure)* appât *m*; **to offer an e.** offrir une gratification

enticing [ɪn'taɪsɪŋ] ADJ *(offer, idea etc)* séduisant, tentant, attrayant; *(publicity pos-*

ter) tentant; *(dish)* alléchant; *(smile)* charmeur, séduisant; **the water doesn't look very e.** l'eau n'est pas très tentante

enticingly [ɪn'taɪsɪŋlɪ] ADV d'une manière séduisante *ou* attrayante; **the sky was e. blue** le ciel était d'un bleu tentant; **she smiled at him e.** elle lui adressa un sourire charmeur *ou* séduisant; **the food smelt e. good** la nourriture dégageait une odeur alléchante; **the holiday was e. cheap** le prix de ces vacances était tentant *ou* attrayant

entire [ɪn'taɪər] ADJ **1** *(whole)* entier, tout; **the e. population** la population (tout) entière; **the e. day** toute la journée; **she read the e. book in an afternoon** elle a lu le livre en entier *ou* tout le livre en l'espace d'un après-midi; **she didn't say one new thing in the e. speech** elle n'a pas dit une seule chose nouvelle dans tout le discours; **the e. business had proved to be a complete waste of time** toute l'affaire s'est résumée à une pure perte de temps; **to enjoy sb's e. confidence** jouir de l'entière confiance de qn **2** *(intact)* entier, intact

entirely [ɪn'taɪəlɪ] ADV entièrement, tout à fait, complètement; **to agree e. with sb** être entièrement *ou* tout à fait d'accord avec qn; **almost e.** presque entièrement *ou* complètement; **you are e. mistaken** vous vous trompez du tout au tout

entirety [ɪn'taɪərətɪ] N intégralité *f*, intégrité *f*, *(of domain etc)* totalité *f*, **in its e.** en entier, intégralement, dans son entier; **to consider sth in its e.** considérer qch dans son entier; **the skeleton had been preserved in its e.** le squelette avait été intégralement conservé

entitle [ɪn'taɪt(ə)l] VT **1** *(give right to)* donner le droit à (**to** à); **to e. sb to do sth** donner (le) droit à qn de faire qch; **to be entitled to sth** avoir droit à qch; **to be entitled to do sth** avoir le droit de faire qch; **the very least I am entitled to is an explanation!** je pourrais quand même avoir une explication, c'est la moindre des choses!; *Law* **to be entitled to inherit** être apte *ou* habilité à hériter **2** *(give title to) (book, chapter, song etc)* intituler **3** *(give aristocratic title to)* **to e. sb duke/prince/etc** donner à qn le titre de duc/prince/etc

entitlement [ɪn'taɪt(ə)lmənt] N = ce qui revient de droit à qn; *(money)* allocation *f* (à laquelle on a droit) ; **(annual) holiday e.** congé *m* annuel (auquel on a droit)

entity ['entɪtɪ] N entité *f*

entomb [ɪn'tuːm] VT *(bury)* mettre dans la tombe, mettre au tombeau; *(of ruins etc) (person)* ensevelir

entombment [ɪn'tuːmmənt] N mise *f* au tombeau; *(by ruins)* ensevelissement *m*

entomological [entəmə'lɒdʒɪk(ə)l] ADJ entomologique

entomologist [entə'mɒlədʒɪst] N entomologiste *mf*

entomology [entə'mɒlədʒɪ] N entomologie *f*

entourage [ɒntʊ'rɑːʒ] N entourage *m*

entr'acte ['ɒntrækt] N *Theat* entracte *m*

entrails ['entreɪlz] NPL entrailles *fpl*, *Fig* **to study the e.** prendre les augures

entrain [ɪn'treɪn] *Mil* VT *(troops etc)* embarquer, faire embarquer en train
VI s'embarquer (en train)

entrance [1] ['entrəns] N **1** *(way in)* entrée *f*, main. e. entrée principale; **the e. is at the rear** *(of bus etc)* l'entrée s'effectue par l'arrière **2** *(act of entering)* entrée *f*, *Theat, Fig* **to make one's e.** faire son entrée; **to force an e. into a house** forcer l'entrée d'une maison; **to gain e. to a building** s'introduire *ou* pénétrer dans un immeuble **3** *(admission)*

(to association, club etc) admission *f; (to cinema)* entrée *f;* **to refuse sb e.** *(to association, restaurant)* refuser l'accès à qn
➤➤ **e. examination** *(for school)* examen *m* d'entrée; *(for job)* concours *m* de recrutement; **e. fee** *(to exhibition, fair etc)* droit *m* d'entrée; *Br (to club, organization etc)* droit *ou* frais *mpl* d'inscription; **e. gate** grille *f* d'entrée; **e. hall** *(in house)* vestibule *m;* (in *hotel)* hall *m; Univ* **e. qualifications, e. requirements** conditions *fpl* d'admission

entrance² [ɪnˈtrɑːns] **VT** *(person)* extasier, ravir, transporter; **to be entranced by ...** s'extasier sur ..., être en extase devant ...; **I was entranced by the music** j'étais transporté par la musique; **they all sat entranced** ils étaient tous fascinés

entrancing [ɪnˈtrɑːnsɪŋ] **ADJ** *(beauty, sight)* enchanteur, -eresse; *(story)* passionnant; *(melody)* ravissant

entrancingly [ɪnˈtrɑːnsɪŋlɪ] **ADV** à ravir; *(to sing, to smile etc)* de façon enchanteresse; **to be e. beautiful** être beau à ravir

entrant [ˈentrənt] **N** *(in race, competition)* inscrit, -ite; *(in examination)* candidat, -ate; *(in profession)* débutant, -ante; *Com (on market)* acteur *m*

entrap [ɪnˈtræp] **VT** (-pp-) *also Am Law* prendre au piège, piéger; **to e. sb into doing sth** prendre qn au piège *ou* piéger qn pour qu'il fasse qch; **he claimed that his client had been entrapped into committing a crime** il prétendait que son client avait été piégé et forcé à commettre un crime

entrapment [ɪnˈtræpmənt] **N** *Am Law* = coup *m* monté par la police pour piéger un criminel; *Journ* = fait, pour un journaliste, d'inciter quelqu'un à commettre un délit dans le cadre d'un reportage

entreat [ɪnˈtriːt] **VT** **to e. sb to do sth** prier *ou* implorer *ou* supplier qn de faire qch; **they entreated him to stay** ils l'implorèrent *ou* le supplièrent de rester; *Lit* **be merciful, I e. you** ayez pitié, je vous en implore *ou* supplie

entreating [ɪnˈtriːtɪŋ] **ADJ** *(tone, look)* suppliant, implorant

entreatingly [ɪnˈtriːtɪŋlɪ] **ADV** d'un air suppliant *ou* implorant

entreaty [ɪnˈtriːtɪ] **N** *Fml* prière *f,* supplication *f;* **at sb's urgent e.** sur les vives instances de qn; **look of e.** regard suppliant

entrée [ˈɒntreɪ] **N 1** *Culin (dish before the main course)* entrée *f; Am (as main course)* plat *m* de résistance **2** *(right of entry)* entrée *f* (**to, into** dans)

entrench [ɪnˈtrentʃ] **VT** *Mil, (camp, town)* retrancher; *Fig* **to e. oneself behind** *or* **in sth** se retrancher *ou* se terrer derrière qch

entrenched [ɪnˈtrentʃt] **ADJ** *Mil, Fig* retranché; *(views, ideas)* arrêté; *(customs)* enraciné; **an e. position** une position de retranchement

entrenchment [ɪnˈtrentʃmənt] **N** *Mil, Fig* retranchement *m*

entrepôt [ˈɒntrəpəʊ] **N** entrepôt *m*

entrepreneur [ɒntrəprəˈnɜːr] **N** entrepreneur, -euse

entrepreneurial [ɒntrəprəˈnɜːrɪəl] **ADJ** *(skills, talents)* d'entrepreneur; *(person, class)* qui a l'esprit d'entreprise; **his e. success** son succès en tant qu'entrepreneur

entrepreneurship [ɒntrəprəˈnɜːʃɪp] **N** esprit *m* d'entreprise

entropy [ˈentrəpɪ] **N** entropie *f*

entrust [ɪnˈtrʌst] **VT** **to e. sth to sb** confier qch à qn; **to e. a secret/a child to sb** confier un secret/un enfant à qn; **to e. sb with** *(task etc)* charger qn de; *(mission)* investir qn de; **to e. sb with the task** *or* **job of doing sth** charger qn de faire qch; **to e. sb with the**

care of sth commettre qch à la garde de qn; **to be entrusted with the sale of sth** être chargé de la vente de qch

entry [ˈentrɪ] **N 1** *(act of entering)* entrée *f* (**(in)to** dans); *(to world of politics etc)* début *m* (**(in)to** dans); **to gain e. to a house** pénétrer dans une maison; *Law* **illegal e. (of a dwelling)** violation *f* de domicile; **to make one's e.** faire son entrée; *(of actor)* entrer en scène; *(of new politician, artist)* faire ses débuts; **right of free e.** droit *m* de passer librement les frontières; **no e.** entrée interdite; *(in one way street)* sens interdit
2 *(way in)* entrée *f* (**to** de)
3 *(writing down) (of a record)* enregistrement *m; (of name in a list, in bookkeeping)* inscription *f, (item)* article *m,* poste *m,* écriture *f, (in dictionary, encyclopedia)* article; *Acct* **single/double e.** comptabilité *f* en partie simple/double; **to make an e.** *(in bookkeeping)* porter un article à compte; *(in journal etc)* inscrire quelque chose; **author/subject entries** *(in cataloguing)* fiches *fpl* auteur/sujet; *Naut* **e. in the log** élément *m* du journal de bord
4 *Sport etc (of competitor)* inscription *f, (list of competitors)* liste *f* de concurrents; **there are twenty entries** il y a vingt participants; **a big/small e.** une forte/faible participation
➤➤ **e. card** *(for entry to a country)* fiche *f* de police *(au débarquement);* **e. form** feuille *f* d'inscription; **e. tax** taxe *f* d'entrée; **e. visa** visa *m* d'entrée

entryism [ˈentrɪɪz(ə)m] **N** *Pol* entrisme *m,* noyautage *m*

entryist [ˈentrɪɪst] **N, ADJ** *Pol* entriste *mf*

entry-level **ADJ** *(car, computer)* d'entrée de gamme

Entryphone® [ˈentrɪfəʊn] **N** Interphone® *m*

entwine [ɪnˈtwaɪn] **VT** **to e. sth round sth** enlacer qch autour de qch; **to become entwined** *(of one thing, ribbon etc)* s'enlacer; *(of two or more things, ribbons etc)* s'entrelacer; **with arms entwined** les bras entrelacés; **her hair was entwined with ribbons** ses cheveux étaient entrelacés de rubans
VI s'enlacer (**round** autour de); *(of two or more things)* s'entrelacer

E-number **N** additif *m* *(dont le code commence par E)*

enumerate [ɪˈnjuːməreɪt] **VT** *(reasons, one's services etc)* énumérer, détailler, dénombrer

enumeration [ɪnjuːməˈreɪʃən] **N** énumération *f,* dénombrement *m,* recensement *m*

enunciate [ɪˈnʌnsɪeɪt] **VT 1** *(pronounce clearly) (sounds, words)* prononcer, articuler **2** *(state clearly) (opinion etc)* énoncer, déclarer
VI **to e. clearly** articuler distinctement

enunciation [ɪnʌnsɪˈeɪʃən] **N 1** *(pronunciation)* articulation *f, (of word)* prononciation *f* **2** *Fml (of opinion etc)* énonciation *f, Math (of problem)* énoncé *m*

enuresis [enjʊˈriːsɪs] **N** *Med* énurésie *f*

envelop [ɪnˈveləp] **VT** (-p-) envelopper (**in** dans, de); **enveloped in mist/cloud** *(countryside)* enveloppé *ou* voilé de brume/par les nuages

envelope [ˈenvələʊp, *occ* ˈɒnvələʊp] **N 1** *(for letter)* enveloppe *f,* **window e.** enveloppe à fenêtre; **to put a letter in an e.** mettre une lettre sous enveloppe; **in a sealed e.** sous pli cacheté; **in the same e.** sous le même pli **2** *(covering)* enveloppe *f, Biol (of organ)* enveloppe, tunique *f*
➤➤ **e. file** chemise *f* (de carton)

envelopment [ɪnˈveləpmənt] **N** enveloppement *m*

envenom [ɪnˈvenəm] **VT** envenimer

enviable [ˈenvɪəb(ə)l] **ADJ** enviable, digne

d'envie; **in the e. position of being offered two jobs** dans la position enviable de se voir proposer deux emplois

enviably [ˈenvɪəblɪ] **ADV** d'une manière enviable; **e. rich/well-read** d'une richesse/culture enviable

envious [ˈenvɪəs] **ADJ** envieux; **I'm so e.!** comme je t'/l'/*etc* envie!; **my sister's got a big house, but I'm not e.** ma sœur a une grande maison, mais je ne l'envie pas; **to be e. of sb/sth** envier qn/qch; **e. glances** regards *mpl* d'envie; **to look at sb with e. eyes** regarder qn d'un œil jaloux; **to make sb e.** rendre qn jaloux

enviously [ˈenvɪəslɪ] **ADV** *(to speak)* avec envie; *(to look at sth)* d'un œil jaloux

environment [ɪnˈvaɪrənmənt] **N 1** *(surroundings)* milieu *m;* **in an office/a hospital e.** dans un bureau/milieu hospitalier; **natural e.** milieu naturel **2** *Ecol* **the e.** l'environnement *m;* **Department** *or* **Ministry of the Environment** ≃ ministère *m* de (la Protection de la Nature et de) l'Environnement **3** *Comput* environnement *m*

environmental [ɪnvaɪrənˈment(ə)l] **ADJ** *(conditions)* qui ont rapport à l'environnement; *(change)* de l'environnement; *(brought about by the environment)* produit par l'environnement; **chemicals that cause e. damage** produits chimiques nuisibles à l'environnement; **the company must improve its e. performance** la société doit améliorer ses performances en matière d'environnement;
➤➤ **e. audit** = rapport *m* sur l'impact des activités d'une entreprise sur l'environnement; **e. economics** économie *f* de l'environnement; **e. impact** impact *m* sur l'environnement; **e. (protection) group** groupe *m* écologiste, groupe de protection de l'environnement

environmentalist [ɪnvaɪrənˈmentəlɪst] **N** écologiste *mf*
ADJ *(issues, politics)* écologique

environmentally [ɪnvaɪrənˈmentəlɪ] **ADV** du point de vue de l'environnement; **e. friendly** qui ne nuit pas à l'environnement, non polluant, non nuisible à l'environnement
➤➤ **E. Sensitive Area** = zone *f* de protection de la nature désignée par l'Union européenne où les agriculteurs doivent utiliser des méthodes traditionnelles

environment-friendly **ADJ** *(product)* qui ne nuit pas à l'environnement; **to be e.** ne pas nuire à l'environnement

environs [ɪnˈvaɪrənz] **NPL** *(of town)* environs *mpl,* alentours *mpl;* **New York and its e.** New York et ses environs

envisage [ɪnˈvɪzɪdʒ] **VT** *(difficulty etc)* envisager; **I can easily e. something of the kind happening** j'envisage sans peine qu'arrive une chose de ce genre

envision [enˈvɪʒən] **VT** *Am* envisager

envoy [ˈenvɔɪ] **N** *(person)* envoyé, -ée

envy [ˈenvɪ] **N 1** envie *f,* jalousie *f;* **to be green with e.** être dévoré d'envie; **to do sth out of e.** faire qch par envie *ou* jalousie; **to excite sb's e.** exciter *ou* s'attirer l'envie de qn **2** *(object of envy)* **to be the e. of sb** être un objet d'envie pour qn
VT *(person)* envier, porter envie à; **I don't e. you** je ne t'envie pas; **to e. sb sth** envier qch à qn; **I don't e. him having to catch such an early train** je ne l'envie pas d'avoir à prendre le train de si bonne heure; **a job to e.** un travail que beaucoup aimeraient avoir

enzyme [ˈenzaɪm] **N** *Biol, Chem* enzyme *f,* diastase *f*

EOC [iːəʊˈsiː] **N** *Br Admin (abbr* **Equal Opportunities Commission)** = organisme *m* désigné par le gouvernement pour veiller à l'application des dispositions relatives aux droits des femmes au travail

Eocene ['i:əʊsi:n] **ADJ, N** Geol éocène m

E & OE [i:ənd'əʊi:] Com (abbr **errors and omissions excepted**) s. e. & o.

eon ['i:ən] **N** Am = **aeon**

EONIA [i:'əʊnɪɑ] **N** Fin (abbr **Euro Overnight Index Average**) EONIA m, TEMPÉ m

EP [i:'pi:] **N** (abbr **extended-play (record)**) disque m double durée

EPA [i:pi:'eɪ] **N** Am (abbr **Environmental Protection Agency**) ≃ Agence f pour la Protection de l'Environnement

epaulette, ** Am **epaulet [epə'let] **N** Mil épaulette f

ephedrine ['efɪdrɪn] **N** Pharm éphédrine f

ephemera, pl **ephemerae, ephemeras** [ɪ'femərə, -i:, -əz] **N 1** chose f éphémère **2** (insect) éphémère m

ephemeral [ɪ'femərəl] **ADJ** éphémère; (passion) fugitif; (beauty) passager, -ère

ephemerid [ɪ'femərɪd] **N** (insect) éphémère m

epic ['epɪk] **ADJ** épique
   N (poem) poème m épique, épopée f; (film) film m à grand spectacle

epicarp ['epɪkɑ:p] **N** Bot épicarpe m

epicene ['episi:n] **ADJ** Fml androgyne

epicentre, Am **epicenter** ['episentər] **N** (of earthquake) épicentre m

epicure ['epɪkjʊər] **N** (gourmet) gourmet m, gastronome mf

epicurean [epɪkjʊ'ri:ən] **ADJ, N** Phil, Fig épicurien, -ienne

epicyclic [epi'saɪklɪk] **ADJ**
   ▸▸ Tech **e. gear** engrenage m épicycloïdal

epidemic [epɪ'demɪk] **ADJ** (disease) épidémique; Fig **corruption has reached e. proportions** la corruption prend des allures d'épidémie
   N Med, Fig épidémie f

epidemiological [epɪdi:mɪə'lɒdʒɪk(ə)l] **ADJ** Med (evidence, research, study) épidémiologique

epidemiologist [epɪdi:mɪ'ɒlədʒɪst] **N** Med épidémiologiste mf

epidemiology [epɪdi:mɪ'ɒlədʒɪ] **N** Med épidémiologie f

epidermis [epɪ'dɜ:mɪs] **N** Anat épiderme m

epidural [epɪ'djʊər(ə)l] **ADJ** Anat épidural
   N Med péridurale f; **she had an e.** on lui a fait une péridurale

epiglottis [epɪ'glɒtɪs] **N** Anat épiglotte f

epigram ['epɪgræm] **N** Liter épigramme f

epigrammatic [epɪgrə'mætɪk] **ADJ** épigrammatique

epigraph ['epɪgrɑ:f] **N** épigraphe f

epilepsy ['epɪlepsɪ] **N** épilepsie f

epileptic [epɪ'leptɪk] **N** épileptique mf
   ADJ épileptique
   ▸▸ e. fit crise f d'épilepsie

epilogue ['epɪlɒg] **N** Liter, Fig épilogue m

Epiphany [ɪ'pɪfənɪ] **N** Rel Épiphanie f

epiphyte ['epɪfaɪt] **N** Bot (plante f) épiphyte m

episcopacy [ɪ'pɪskəpəsɪ] **N** Rel épiscopat m

Episcopal [ɪ'pɪskəp(ə)l] **ADJ** Rel
   ▸▸ Am, Scot **the E. Church** l'Église f épiscopale

episcopal [ɪ'pɪskəp(ə)l] **ADJ** Rel épiscopal, -aux
   ▸▸ e. palace évêché m; **e. ring** anneau m pastoral

Episcopalian [ɪpɪskə'peɪlɪən] **N** Rel Am Scot membre m de l'Église épiscopale
   ADJ de l'Église épiscopale

episcopalian [ɪpɪskə'peɪlɪən] Rel **ADJ, N** épiscopalien, -ienne

episcopate [ɪ'pɪskəpeɪt] **N** Rel épiscopat m

episiotomy [əpi:zɪ'ɒtəmɪ] **N** Obst épisiotomie f

episode ['epɪsəʊd] **N** (of story etc) épisode m; (incident) incident m

episodic [epɪ'sɒdɪk] **ADJ** épisodique

epistemic [epɪ'sti:mɪk] **ADJ** Phil, Ling épistémique

epistemology [ɪpɪstɪ'mɒlədʒɪ] **N** Phil épistémologie f

epistle [ɪ'pɪs(ə)l] **N 1** Rel épître f **2** Arch, Hum (letter) épître f, lettre f
   ▸▸ e. side (of altar) côté m de l'épître

epistolary [ɪ'pɪstələrɪ] **ADJ** (style, novel) épistolaire

epitaph ['epɪtæf] **N** épitaphe f

epithelium [epɪ'θi:lɪəm] **N** Anat épithélium m

epithet ['epɪθet] **N** épithète f VOIR GRAMMAIRE A17

epitome [ɪ'pɪtəmɪ] **N 1** (perfect example) **to be the e. of sth** incarner qch; **he is the e. of elegance** il est l'élégance même **2** Arch (summary) épitomé m, abrégé m

epitomize [ɪ'pɪtəmaɪz] **VT** (embody) incarner; **this situation epitomizes what we're up against** cette situation est le parfait exemple de ce contre quoi nous luttons

epizootic [epɪzəʊ'ɒtɪk] Vet **ADJ** (disease) épizootique
   N épizootie f

EPO [i:pi:'əʊ] **N** (abbr **European Patent Office**) OEB m

epoch ['i:pɒk] **N** époque f, âge m; **to mark an e.** faire époque, faire date

epoch-making ADJ (discovery, event) qui fait époque, qui fait date

eponymous [ɪ'pɒnɪməs] **ADJ** Lit éponyme

EPOS ['i:pɒs] **N** Com (abbr **electronic point of sale**) point m de vente électronique

epoxy [ɪ'pɒksɪ] Chem **N** époxyde m
   ▸▸ Chem **e. resin** résine f époxyde ou époxy

EPROM ['i:prɒm] **N** Comput (abbr **erasable programmable ROM**) EPROM f, mémoire f morte programmable et effaçable

eppy ['epɪ] **N** Br Fam **to have an e.** (lose one's temper) péter une durite, péter les plombs

EPS [i:pi:'es] **N 1** Fin (abbr **earnings per share**) BPA m **2** Comput (abbr **encapsulated PostScript**) EPS

Epsom ['epsəm] **N**
   ▸▸ E. salts sel m d'Epsom, epsomite f

e-publishing N édition f électronique

equability [ekwə'bɪlɪtɪ, i:k-] **N** (of climate, temperature) uniformité f; (of moods) égalité f

equable ['ekwəb(ə)l] **ADJ** (climate, temperature) uniforme, régulier, -ière; **e. temperament** humeur égale; **an e. companion** un compagnon/une compagne à l'humeur égale

equably ['ekwəblɪ] **ADV** d'humeur égale; (to reply, say) calmement

equal ['i:kwəl] **ADJ 1** (same) égal (**to, with** à); **e. numbers of boys and girls** un nombre égal de garçons et de filles; **to finish e. first/second** finir premier/deuxième ex æquo; **on e. terms** à conditions égales; **to be on e. terms** or **on an e. footing with sb** être sur un pied d'égalité avec qn; **in e. measure** en quantité égale; **e. distribution of taxes** péréquation f de l'impôt; **all things** or **other things being e.** si tout se déroule normalement, si tout va bien; **to be an e. opportunity employer** offrir des chances égales d'emploi à tous; **e. pay for e. work** à travail égal, salaire égal;

2 (of sufficient calibre etc) **to be e. to (doing) sth** être à la hauteur de (faire) qch; **I don't feel e. to (doing) it** (I'm too tired etc) je ne m'en sens pas le courage ou la force; (I'm not good enough) je ne m'en sens pas à la hauteur; **a cinema e. to any in London** un cinéma à l'instar des cinémas de Londres
   N égal, -ale; **the service is the e. of a five star hotel** le service est du niveau d'un hôtel cinq étoiles; **your equals** vos pareils, vos égaux; **you won't find her e.** vous ne trouverez pas son semblable; **she's easily his e. at tennis/chemistry** elle l'égale facilement au tennis/en chimie; **to treat sb as an e.** traiter qn d'égal à égal
   VT (-ll-, Am -l-) **1** (be equal to) égaler, être égal à (**in** en); **nothing can e. this splendour** rien ne saurait égaler cette splendeur; **no one has equalled her record** personne n'a égalé son record; **not to be equalled** sans égal, qui n'a pas son égal; **her clumsiness is only equalled by her lack of manners** sa maladresse n'a d'égal que ses mauvaises manières; **I've never seen anything to e. it** je n'ai jamais rien vu qui l'égale
   2 Math (total) faire; **four fives e.** or **four times five equals twenty** quatre fois cinq font vingt; **let x e. 20** soit x égal à 20
   ▸▸ e. rights égalité f des droits; Math **e. sign** signe m égal ou d'égalité; Radio, TV **e. time** droit m de réponse

equality [i'kwɒlɪtɪ] **N** égalité f (**with sb** avec qn); **e. of opportunity** égalité des chances

equalization [i:kwəlaɪ'zeɪʃən] **N 1** égalisation f; Fin (of taxes, wealth) péréquation f; (of dividends) régularisation f **2** Tech équilibrage m
   ▸▸ Fin **e. fund** fonds m de parité; Fin **e. payment** soulte f

equalize ['i:kwəlaɪz] **VT** égaliser (**sth with sth** qch avec qch); (taxes, wealth) faire la péréquation de; (dividends) régulariser; (chances) équilibrer; (forces etc) compenser, équilibrer
   VI Sport égaliser

equalizer ['i:kwəlaɪzər] **N 1** Elec égaliseur m de potentiel; (for sound) égaliseur; Tech compensateur m **2** Sport (point) point m égalisateur; (goal) but m égalisateur **3** Am Fam (handgun) flingue m

equalizing ['i:kwəlaɪzɪŋ] **ADJ** (current etc) compensateur, -trice; (pressure) de compensation; Sport **the e. goal** le but égalisateur

equally ['i:kwəlɪ] **ADV 1** (to an equal degree) tout aussi; **it would be e. wrong/mistaken/rash** etc **to …** ce serait tout aussi faux/erroné/imprudent etc de …; **I'm e. interested in the Baroque period** la période baroque m'intéresse tout autant; **she worked e. hard** elle a travaillé tout aussi dur **2** (in equal amounts) **to contribute e. to the expenses** contribuer pour une part égale à la dépense; **the money was divided e. between the children** l'argent a été partagé de façon égale entre les enfants **3** (likewise) **e., they may be telling the truth** il se pourrait tout aussi bien qu'ils disent la vérité

equals sign N signe m égal

equanimity [i:kwə'nɪmɪtɪ, ek-] **N** Fml égalité f d'âme, équanimité f; **to disturb sb's e.** troubler la sérénité de qn; **to recover one's e.** se ressaisir; **with e.** d'une âme égale, avec équanimité

equate [ɪ'kweɪt] **VT 1** (make equal) rendre égal (**to, with** à); Math (two expressions etc) mettre en équation **2** (think of as equal) **I e. communism with the Soviet Union** j'assimile le communisme à l'Union Soviétique; **to e. Jupiter with Zeus** donner Jupiter comme l'équivalent de Zeus; **to e. Picasso**

with Michelangelo voir en Picasso l'égal de Michel-Ange

equating [ɪˈkweɪtɪŋ] N **1** *(making equal)* égalisation *f; Math* mise *f* en équation **2** *(thinking of as equal)* assimilation *f*

equation [ɪˈkweɪʒən] N **1** *Math, Chem, Astron* équation *f; Math* **simple/quadratic e.** équation du premier/deuxième degré **2** *(making equal) (of expenditure to income etc)* égalisation *f* **3** *(thinking of as equal)* assimilation *f;* **the e. of fame with success** l'assimilation de la célébrité au succès

equator [ɪˈkweɪtər] N équateur *m* (de la terre); **at the e.** sous l'équateur

equatorial [ekwəˈtɔːrɪəl] ADJ équatorial

equerry [ˈekwərɪ] N écuyer *m*

equestrian [ɪˈkwestrɪən] ADJ USU ATTRIB *(statue etc)* équestre; **e. performances** exercices *mpl* d'équitation
N cavalier, -ière; *(in circus)* écuyer, -ère
▸▸ *Sport* **e. event** tournoi *m* équestre

equidistant [iːkwɪˈdɪstənt] ADJ *Fml* équidistant (**from** de)

equilateral [iːkwɪˈlæt(ə)rəl] ADJ *Geom* équilatéral, -aux

equilibrium [iːkwɪˈlɪbrɪəm] N **1** équilibre *m*, aplomb *m;* **stable/unstable e.** équilibre stable/instable; **to lose one's e.** perdre l'équilibre; **to maintain one's (inner) e.** garder son équilibre; **to keep sth in e.** maintenir qch en équilibre; **in a state of e.** en équilibre **2** *Econ* équilibre *m*
▸▸ *Econ* **e. price** prix *m* d'équilibre

equine [ˈiːkwaɪn, ˈekwaɪn] ADJ équin; *(race, face)* chevalin
N équidé *m*

equinoctial [iːkwɪˈnɒkʃəl, ek-] ADJ *Met (line, year etc)* équinoxial, -aux; *(storm etc)* d'équinoxe; **e. tides** marées *fpl* d'équinoxe, grandes marées

equinox [ˈiːkwɪnɒks, ˈek-] N *Met* équinoxe *m;* **spring** or **vernal e.** équinoxe du printemps, point *m* vernal; **autumn(al) e.** équinoxe d'automne

equip [ɪˈkwɪp] VT (**-pp-**) **1** *(provide with equipment) (soldier, expedition, kitchen etc)* équiper; *(house)* meubler, monter; *(factory)* outiller, monter; **to e. sb with sth** munir *ou* équiper qn de qch; **to e. oneself with sth** s'équiper *ou* se munir de qch **2** *(prepare)* préparer (**to do sth** pour faire qch); **her training had not equipped her for such an eventuality** sa formation ne l'avait pas parée à une telle éventualité

equipage [ˈekwɪpɪdʒ] N *Horseriding (vehicle)* équipage *m*

equipment [ɪˈkwɪpmənt] N **1** *(items)* équipement *m; (in house)* appareils *mpl; (in factory)* installations *fpl*, matériel *m;* **camping e.** matériel de camping; **electrical e.** équipement électrique; **emergency e.** matériel *ou* installations de secours; **heavy e.** matériel lourd; **kitchen e.** ustensiles *mpl* de cuisine; **laboratory/office e.** matériel de laboratoire/bureau; *Mil* **regulation** or **standard e.** matériel réglementaire; **sports e.** équipement sportif; **surplus e.** matériel en excédent; **2** *Fig* **intellectual e.** capacité *f* intellectuelle **3** *(act) (of expedition)* équipement *m; (of house)* aménagement *m; (of factory)* outillage *m; (of laboratory etc)* installation *f*
▸▸ **e. allowance** subvention *f* pour l'achat de matériel

equipped [ɪˈkwɪpt] ADJ **1** *(soldier, expedition etc)* équipé (**with** de); **the aircraft is e. to take aerial photographs** or **for aerial photography** l'avion est équipé pour prendre des photos aériennes **2** *(prepared)* préparé; **she is well e. to succeed/for the job** elle est préparée pour réussir/pour ce travail; *(pos-*

sessing adequate skills) elle a les qualités requises pour réussir/pour ce travail

equitable [ˈekwɪtəb(ə)l] ADJ équitable

equitably [ˈekwɪt(ə)blɪ] ADV équitablement

equitation [ekwɪˈteɪʃən] N *Fml* équitation *f*

Equity [ˈekwɪtɪ] N = principal syndicat *m* britannique des gens du spectacle

equity [ˈekwɪtɪ] N **1** *(fairness)* équité *f* **2** *Law* équité *f* **3** *Fin (of shareholders)* capitaux *mpl ou* fonds *mpl* propres, avoir *m* des actionnaires; *(of company)* capital *m* actions; **equities** actions *fpl* ordinaires
▸▸ *Fin* **e. dilution** dilution *f* du capital; *Fin* **e. financing** financement *m* par actions, financement par capitaux propres; *Fin* **e. investment** placement *m* en actions; *Fin* **e. issue** augmentation *f* du capital par émission d'actions; *Fin* **e. loan** prêt *m ou* titre *m* participatif; *Fin* **e. market** marché *m* des actions ordinaires; *Fin* **e. risk premium** prime *f* de risque de variation du prix des actions; *Fin* **e. share capital** capital en actions ordinaires; *Fin* **e. trading** marché des actions, courtage *m* sur actions; *Fin* **e. unit trust** SICAV *f* actions

equity-linked ADJ *Fin (policy)* libellé, investi en actions

equivalence [ɪˈkwɪvələns] N équivalence *f*

equivalent [ɪˈkwɪvələnt] ADJ équivalent; **to be e. to sth** être équivalent à qch, équivaloir à qch; **to be e. in meaning/weight to sth** avoir un sens/un poids équivalent à celui de qch; **that would be e. to saying that …** cela reviendrait à dire que …
N équivalent *m;* **to drink the e. of one glass of wine** boire la valeur d'un verre de vin; **the Soviet e. of the FBI** l'équivalent soviétique du FBI; **to be an acceptable e.** être un substitut acceptable

equivocal [ɪˈkwɪvək(ə)l] ADJ **1** *(ambiguous) (reply, attitude)* équivoque, ambigu, -uë; *(word)* à double sens, équivoque; **he was rather e.** il s'est montré plutôt ambigu **2** *(uncertain)* incertain, douteux

equivocally [ɪˈkwɪvəklɪ] ADV d'une manière équivoque

equivocate [ɪˈkwɪvəkeɪt] VI user d'équivoque, tergiverser

equivocation [ɪkwɪvəˈkeɪʃən] N tergiversation *f;* **to resort to equivocation(s)** user d'équivoque, tergiverser

ER [iːˈɑːr] **1** *Br (abbr* **Elizabeth Regina)** la Reine Élisabeth **2** *Am (abbr* **Emergency Room)** urgences *fpl*

er [ər, ɜːr] INT euh

ERA [iːɑːˈreɪ] N *Am (abbr* **Equal Rights Amendment)** = modification *f* proposée à la constitution relative aux droits des citoyens, indépendamment de leur race ou de leur religion

era [ˈɪərə] N *Hist, Geol etc* ère *f;* **the end of an e.** la fin d'une époque; **to mark an e.** faire date; **the post-war e.** l'après-guerre *m*

eradicate [ɪˈrædɪkeɪt] VT *(prejudice, evil)* extirper, déraciner; *(disease)* éradiquer, faire disparaître; *(resistance, poverty)* éliminer

eradication [ɪrædɪˈkeɪʃən] N *(of prejudice, evil etc)* extirpation *f; (of disease)* éradication *f; (of resistance, poverty)* élimination *f*

erasable [ɪˈreɪzəbl] ADJ effaçable

erase [ɪˈreɪz] VT *(written material, sth on tape, disk, file)* effacer; *(with eraser)* gommer; *(memory)* oblitérer
▸▸ **e. button** bouton *m* d'effacement; **e. head** tête *f* d'effacement

eraser [ɪˈreɪzər] N *(rubber)* gomme *f* (à effacer); **ink e.** gomme à encre

erasing [ɪˈreɪzɪŋ] N effacement *m*

erasure [ɪˈreɪʒər] N **1** *(act)* effacement *m* **2** *(what is erased)* mot *m*/chiffre *m/etc* effacé; **there were a number of mysterious erasures** un certain nombre de choses avaient été mystérieusement effacées

ERDF [iːɑːdiːˈef] N *(abbr* **European Regional Development Fund)** FEDER *m*

ere [eər] *Arch, Lit* PREP avant; *(by this time)* déjà; **e. long** bientôt; **e. now** *(in the past)* auparavant
CONJ avant que + *subj;* **e. you forget** avant que tu (n')oublies

erect [ɪˈrekt] ADJ *(person)* droit, debout; *(carriage)* droit; *(penis, nipples etc)* en érection; *(dog's ears)* dressé; **with head e.** la tête haute *ou* relevée; **to stand e.** se tenir droit
VT *(building, theory)* ériger; *(statue)* élever (**to** à); *(scaffolding, altar, mast)* dresser; *(machine)* installer; *(tent)* monter

erectile [ɪˈrektaɪl] ADJ *Physiol (tissue)* érectile
▸▸ *Med* **e. dysfunction** troubles *mpl* érectiles

erection [ɪˈrekʃən] N **1** *(act) (of building)* construction *f*, érection *f; (of statue)* érection; *(of mast)* dressage *m; (of machine)* installation *f* **2** *Physiol (of organ)* érection *f*, **to have/get an e.** avoir une érection **3** *often Pej (building, structure)* bâtisse *f*, construction *f*, édifice *m*

erectness [ɪˈrektnɪs] N attitude *f* droite; **the e. of his bearing** sa posture droite

erector [ɪˈrektər] N **1** *(person) (of buildings)* constructeur *m* **2** *Anat (muscle)* (muscle *m*) érecteur *m*
▸▸ *Anat* **e. muscle** (muscle *m*) érecteur

erg [ɜːg] N *Phys* erg *m*

ergo [ˈɜːgəʊ, ˈeəgəʊ] ADV *Fml, Hum* ergo, donc

ergonomic [ɜːgəˈnɒmɪk] ADJ ergonomique

ergonomically [ɜːgəˈnɒmɪklɪ] ADV **e. designed** *(chair etc)* d'une conception ergonomique

ergonomics [ɜːgəˈnɒmɪks] N ergonomie *f*
VOIR GRAMMAIRE A10

ergot [ˈɜːgɒt] N *Agr, Pharm* ergot *m*

ergotism [ˈɜːgətɪz(ə)m] N *Med* ergotisme *m*

Erie [ˈɪərɪ] N *Geog* **Lake E.** le lac Érié

erigeron [ɪˈrɪdʒərən] N *Bot (plant)* érigéron *m*

Erin [ˈerɪn] N *Arch, Lit* la verte Érin

Eritrea [erɪˈtreɪə] N Érythrée *f*

Eritrean [erɪˈtreɪən] N Érythréen, -enne

ERM [iːɑːˈrem] N *Fin Formerly (abbr* **Exchange Rate Mechanism)** mécanisme *m* de change

erm [ɜːm] INT euh

ermine [ˈɜːmɪn] N hermine *f*

erode [ɪˈrəʊd] VT *(of elements)* éroder; *(of acid, corrosive substance)* ronger, corroder; *(confidence)* miner, entamer; *Fig* **the power of the church has been eroded** le pouvoir de l'église a été miné; **our savings have been eroded by inflation** nos économies se sont trouvées grignotées par l'inflation
VI *(of metal)* s'éroder, se corroder; *(of confidence, popularity)* baisser, se détériorer; *(of prices)* s'effriter

erogenous [ɪˈrɒdʒɪnəs] ADJ érogène
▸▸ **e. zone** zone *f* érogène

Eros [ˈɪərɒs] N Éros *m*

erosion [ɪˈrəʊʒən] N *(marine etc)* érosion *f; Fig (of confidence, popularity)* détérioration *f;* **wind e.** érosion éolienne; **soil e.** érosion du sol; *Fig* **the e. of real earnings by inflation** la diminution du salaire réel causée par l'inflation; **e. of prices** effritement *m* des prix

erosive [ɪˈrəʊzɪv] ADJ érosif

erotic [ɪˈrɒtɪk] ADJ *(art, book, film etc)* érotique

erotica [ɪ'rɒtɪkə] NPL écrits mpl/dessins mpl/etc érotiques

erotically [ɪ'rɒtɪklɪ] ADV érotiquement; **to be e. charged** avoir un contenu érotique

eroticism [ɪ'rɒtɪsɪz(ə)m] N érotisme m

err [ɜːr] VI **1** (make mistake) faire erreur, esp Lit errer; **to e. in one's judgement** faire une erreur de jugement; Prov **to e. is human** l'erreur est humaine **2** (sin) pécher; **he does not e. on the side of modesty** il ne pèche pas par excès de modestie; **let's e. on the side of caution and do …** par mesure de prudence, faisons …; **it's better to e. on the side of generosity** il vaut mieux pécher par générosité, il vaut mieux être trop généreux que pas assez **3** (stray) s'égarer, s'écarter (**from** de); Hum **to e. from the straight and narrow** s'égarer du droit chemin

errand ['erənd] N commission f, course f, **to send sb on an e.** envoyer qn faire une commission ou une course; **to go on** ou **run errands** (aller) faire des commissions ou des courses; Lit **e. of mercy** mission f humanitaire
▶▶ **e. boy** garçon m de courses

errant ['erənt] ADJ (erring) dévoyé; **e. husband** mari m infidèle **e. ways** vie f dévoyée

errata [ɪ'rɑːtə] NPL Typ errata mpl

erratic [ɪ'rætɪk] ADJ **1** (irregular) irrégulier, -ière; (light) intermittent, discontinu; Aut **e. driving** conduite mal assurée **2** (person) capricieux, bizarre, velléitaire; (life) désordonné; (changes of mood) imprévisible; **her playing is e.** (of sportswoman, musician) son jeu est inégal; **the road/river follows an e. course** la route/rivière suit un cours irrégulier **3** Med (pain) erratique

erratically [ɪ'rætɪklɪ] ADV sans méthode, sans règle; **to work e.** (of person) travailler irrégulièrement; (of machine) fonctionner irrégulièrement ou par à-coups; **to play e.** (of sportsman, musician) avoir un jeu inégal; Aut **to drive e.** conduire d'une façon mal assurée

erratum, pl **errata** [ɪ'rɑːtəm, -tə] N erratum m, pl errata

erring ['ɜːrɪŋ] ADJ (sinning) dévoyé, égaré; (mistaken) tombé dans l'erreur; (husband, wife) infidèle; **e. ways** vie f dévoyée

erroneous [ɪ'rəʊnɪəs] ADJ esp Fml (calculation, premise, conclusion) erroné, faux, f fausse; (supposition) faux

erroneously [ɪ'rəʊnɪəslɪ] ADV esp Fml à tort; **e. accused of …** accusé à tort de …

erroneousness [ɪ'rəʊnɪəsnɪs] N esp Fml erreur f, fausseté f

error ['erər] N **1** (mistake) erreur f, faute f, **to make an e.** faire ou commettre une erreur; **to make an e. in one's calculations** faire une erreur de calcul; **e. of judgement** erreur de jugement; printing ou printer's **e.** faute d'impression; Com **errors and omissions excepted** sauf erreur ou omission **2** Tech erreur f, aberration f, déviation f; Comput erreur f; **allowable e.** erreur permise, tolérance f **3** (being wrong) **to do sth in e.** faire qch par erreur; **to be in e.** être dans l'erreur, avoir tort; **to fall into e.** tomber dans l'erreur **4** (wrongdoing) écart m (de conduite); **errors of youth** erreurs fpl ou écarts de jeunesse; **he has seen the e. of his ways** il est revenu de ses égarements; **to show sb the e. of his ways** montrer à qn qu'il est dans le mauvais chemin
▶▶ Comput **e. checking** vérification f d'erreurs; Comput **e. code** code m d'erreur; Comput **e. correction** correction f d'erreur; Comput **e. message** message m d'erreur; Comput **e. routine** sous-programme m de correction d'erreurs, pl sous-programmes de correction d'erreurs

ersatz [eə'zæts, 'ɜːzæts] N ersatz m, succédané m
ADJ Pej **e. coffee** succédané m de café; Fig **e. religion** ersatz m de religion

Erse [ɜːs] Ling N **1** (Gaelic) erse m, gaélique m **2** (Irish Gaelic) irlandais m
ADJ (see n) **1** gaélique **2** irlandais

erstwhile ['ɜːstwaɪl] ADJ ATTRIB Arch, Lit (pupil, friend, belief etc) ancien

eructate ['iːrʌkteɪt] VI Fml éructer

eructation [iːrʌk'teɪʃən] N Fml éructation f

erudite ['erʊdaɪt] ADJ érudit, savant

erudition [erʊ'dɪʃən] N érudition f, **work of monumental e.** vrai monument d'érudition

erupt [ɪ'rʌpt] VI **1** (of volcano) entrer en éruption **2** (of violence, anger, sound) éclater; (of person) exploser; **the stadium erupted in a huge roar** le stade a éclaté d'un énorme rugissement **3** (of teeth) percer; (of spot) sortir; **his face erupted in spots** son visage s'est couvert de boutons

eruption [ɪ'rʌpʃən] N **1** (of volcano) éruption f, **volcano in e.** volcan m en éruption **2** (of anger, joy etc) éruption f, éclat m **3** (of teeth) éruption f, (of spots) éruption, poussée f

erysipelas [erɪ'sɪpɪləs] N Med érysipèle m

erythema [erɪ'θiːmə] N Med érythème m

erythrocyte [e'rɪθrəʊsaɪt] N Physiol érythrocyte m

ESA [iːeˈseɪ] N (abbr European Space Agency) ASE f

escalate ['eskəleɪt] VI **1** (of prices etc) monter (en flèche) **2** (of conflict etc) s'aggraver; **small incidents can easily e. into a world war** de simples incidents (militaires) peuvent facilement mener à une guerre mondiale
VT intensifier; **to e. the situation** aggraver la situation

escalation [eskə'leɪʃən] N **1** (of prices etc) augmentation f (rapide), montée f en flèche; (of interest rates) escalade f **2** (of war, situation) escalade f

escalator ['eskəleɪtər] N **1** (moving stairway) escalier m mécanique, escalator m **2** Econ clause f d'échelle mobile
▶▶ Econ **e. clause** clause f d'échelle mobile

escalope ['eskəlɒp] N Culin escalope f

escapade ['eskəpeɪd] N escapade f, frasque f, fredaine f

escape [ɪs'keɪp] N **1** (flight) fuite f, évasion f, **to make one's e.** s'échapper, se sauver; **to make good one's e.** réussir à s'échapper; **to have a narrow e.** l'échapper belle; **to have a miraculous e.** échapper comme par miracle; Fig **the cinema provided an e. from their daily routine** le cinéma leur offrait un moyen de s'évader de leur routine quotidienne **2** (of gas, water etc) échappement m, fuite f, dégagement m **3** Tech déversoir m **4** Comput échappement m
VI **1** (of person) échapper, s'échapper, prendre la fuite; **to e. from prison** s'évader de prison; **escaped prisoner** évadé, -ée; **the lion escaped from the zoo** le lion s'est échappé du zoo; **to e. by the skin of one's teeth** échapper tout juste; **to e. uninjured** s'en tirer indemne; **he escaped with a fright** il en a été quitte pour la peur; **he was lucky to e. with his life** il a eu de la chance de s'en sortir vivant; Fig **to e. from reality** s'évader ou s'échapper de la réalité **2** (of gases, fluids) s'échapper, fuir
VT **1** (of person, animal) (danger) échapper à; **he narrowly escaped death** il a échappé tout juste à la mort; **he just escaped being killed** il a bien failli être tué, il a manqué (de) se faire tuer; **they escaped punishment/justice** ils ont échappé à la punition/ justice **2** (go unnoticed by) échapper à; noth-

ing escapes her eagle eye rien n'échappe à son regard perçant; **to e. notice** échapper à l'attention, passer inaperçu **3** (of name, date etc) échapper à; **his name escapes me** son nom m'échappe **4** (of sound) **a cry escaped him** un cri lui a échappé
▶▶ Law **e. clause** clause f échappatoire; **e. hatch** trappe f de secours; Comput **e. key** touche f d'échappement, touche Echap; **e. road** talus m de protection; **e. route** (from fire) itinéraire m de sortie de secours; (of criminal) itinéraire ménagé pour s'échapper; Tech **e. valve** soupape f d'échappement; Astron **e. velocity** vitesse f de libération; Tech **e. wheel** roue f d'échappement

escapee [eskeɪ'piː] N évadé, -ée

escapement [ɪs'keɪpmənt] N (of clock, piano etc) échappement m

escaper [ɪs'keɪpər] N fugitif, -ive

escapism [ɪs'keɪpɪz(ə)m] N évasion f (de la réalité); **the movie is pure e.** ce film permet de s'évader totalement de la réalité

escapist [ɪs'keɪpɪst] N **she had always been a bit of an e.** elle avait toujours un peu cherché à s'évader de la réalité
ADJ (film, story) qui permet de s'évader de la réalité; **e. literature** littérature f d'évasion

escapologist [eskə'pɒlədʒɪst] N prestidigitateur m spécialiste de l'évasion

escapology [eskə'pɒlədʒɪ] N art m de l'évasion

escarpment [ɪs'kɑːpmənt] N escarpement m

ESCB [iːessiˈbiː] N (abbr European System of Central Banks) SEBC m

eschatology [eskə'tɒlədʒɪ] N Rel eschatologie f

eschew [ɪs'tʃuː] VT Lit (notions, ideas) éviter; **to e. violence** s'abstenir de recourir à la violence; **to e. sb's company** fuir ou éviter qn

e-science N e-science f

esc key N Comput touche f d'échappement, touche Echap

escort[1] ['eskɔːt] N **1** (for convoy etc) escorte f, (for tourists etc) guide m; (woman from agency) hôtesse f, Old-fashioned (to woman) cavalier m; (to man) cavalière f, (ship) escorteur m, bâtiment m d'escorte; **a police e.** une escorte de police **2** (act of escorting) escorte f, **under the e. of …** sous l'escorte de …; **to conduct a prisoner under e.** conduire un prisonnier sous escorte
▶▶ **e. agency** service m ou bureau m d'hôtesses; Mil **e. duty** service d'escorte; Aviat, Mil **e. fighter** chasseur m d'escorte; **e. girl** hôtesse

escort[2] [ɪs'kɔːt] VT (convoy) escorter, faire escorte à, servir d'escorte à; (lady) servir de cavalier à; (prisoner) conduire sous escorte; **to be escorted to safety** être escorté jusqu'à un lieu sûr

escrow ['eskrəʊ] N Banking dépôt m fiduciaire; **to put money in e.** placer de l'argent en dépôt fiduciaire
▶▶ Law **e. account** compte m bloqué; **e. agent** dépositaire mf légal(e)

escutcheon [ɪs'kʌtʃ(ə)n] N Her écu m, écusson m

ESF [iːeˈsef] N (abbr European Social Fund) FSE m

e-signature N Comput signature f électronique, e-signature f

Eskimo, pl **Eskimos, Eskimo** ['eskɪməʊ, -əʊz] ADJ esquimau (occ -aude in feminine), -aux, eskimo inv
N Esquimau, -aude

ESL [iːeˈsel] N Sch (abbr English as a Second Language) anglais m deuxième langue

ESOP [iːeəsəʊˈpiː] N (abbr employee Br share or Am stock ownership plan) plan m d'actionnariat des salariés

esophagus [ɪ'sɒfəgəs] N Am Anat œso-phage m

esoteric [esəʊ'terɪk] ADJ ésotérique

ESP [iːes'piː] N 1 (abbr **extrasensory perception**) perception f extra-sensorielle 2 Sch (abbr **English for Specific or Special Purposes**) anglais m appliqué

esp (abbr **especially**) spécialt

espadrille ['espədrɪl] N espadrille f

espalier [ɪs'pælɪər, -ɪeɪ] N Bot espalier m

esparto [es'pɑːtəʊ] N Bot sparte m, alfa m
▸▸ Bot **e. grass** sparte, alfa

especial [ɪs'peʃəl] ADJ spécial, -aux, particulier; **of e. importance** d'une importance toute particulière

especially [ɪs'peʃəlɪ] ADV surtout; **we were e. lucky with the weather** le temps nous a été particulièrement favorable; **he likes birds, e. parrots** il aime les oiseaux, spécialement les perroquets; **I did it e. for you** je l'ai fait spécialement ou exprès pour vous; **I was e. pleased to hear about your success** cela m'a fait tout particulièrement plaisir d'apprendre la nouvelle de votre succès; **these figures are surprisingly good, e. given recent developments** ces chiffres sont étonnamment bons, surtout si l'on considère les derniers développements

Attention: ne pas confondre avec **specially**.

Esperanto [espə'ræntəʊ] N Ling espéranto m

espionage ['espɪɒnɑːʒ] N espionnage m

esplanade [esplə'neɪd] N esplanade f, (in seaside town) digue f

espousal [ɪs'paʊz(ə)l] N **the e. of a cause** l'adhésion f à une cause

espouse [ɪs'paʊz] VT (cause, belief etc) épouser, embrasser

espresso [es'presəʊ] N (café m) expresso m
ADJ expresso
▸▸ **e. machine** machine f à express

espy [ɪs'paɪ] VT Arch, Lit apercevoir, aviser

Esq Old-fashioned abbr **Esquire**

Esquire [ɪs'kwaɪər] N Old-fashioned (respectful title) **David Thomas, E.** = Monsieur David Thomas

essay[1] ['eseɪ] N 1 (piece of writing) Liter essai m; Sch composition f, (for younger students) rédaction f 2 Fml (attempt) essai m, tentative f (at de)

essay[2] [e'seɪ] VT Fml tenter; **to e. a smile** tenter de sourire

essayist ['eseɪɪst] N Liter essayiste mf, auteur m d'essais

essence ['esəns] N 1 Phil, Rel etc essence f, (of question) fond m; (of speech) essentiel m; **the very e. of authority/bravery/stupidity** l'autorité/le courage/la stupidité même; **in e.** essentiellement; **speed/time is of the e.** la vitesse/le temps est le facteur prioritaire; **diplomacy is of the e.** la diplomatie s'impose ou est de rigueur; **the e. of the matter is that ...** le fond de l'affaire, c'est que ... 2 Chem, Culin etc essence f, extrait m; **meat e.** extrait de viande; **vanilla e.** extrait de vanille

essential [ɪ'senʃəl] ADJ 1 (basic) (difference etc) essentiel 2 (indispensable) essentiel, indispensable; **an e. part or feature** un élément essentiel; **it is e. to do that** il est essentiel ou absolument nécessaire de faire cela; **the e. thing** l'essentiel m; **prudence is e.** la prudence s'impose
N (usu pl) **reduced to its essentials** dépouillé; **to concentrate on the essentials** s'attacher à l'essentiel; **one of the essentials of a business man** une des qualités indis-

pensables à un homme d'affaires
▸▸ **e. foodstuffs** denrées fpl de première nécessité; **e. information** (on package label) mentions fpl obligatoires; **e. oil** huile f essentielle

essentially [ɪ'senʃ(ə)lɪ] ADV essentiellement; **her analysis is e. correct** pour l'essentiel son analyse est correcte

Essex man ['esɪks-] N Br Fam = stéréotype du réactionnaire bête et vulgaire

Essex
Il s'agit de stéréotypes sociaux apparus au cours des années 80. L'"Essex Girl" (originaire de l'Essex, comté situé à l'est de Londres) est censée être une jeune femme d'origine modeste aux mœurs légères, vulgaire, bruyante, et peu intelligente. L'"Essex Man" est lui aussi vulgaire et bruyant; de plus, il est réactionnaire et inculte.

EST [iːes'tiː] N Am (abbr **Eastern Standard Time**) HNE f

est 1 Com (abbr **established**) établi, fondé; **A. Jones, e. 1885** A. Jones, établi en 1885 2 (abbr **estimated**) estimatif

establish [ɪs'tæblɪʃ] VT 1 (set up) (government) établir; (system) établir, édifier; (business) fonder; (agency) créer; (company) constituer; (peace) mettre sur pied; **to e. close relations with sb** nouer des relations avec qn; **to e. oneself in business** s'établir dans les affaires; Pej **to e. oneself in sb's house** s'installer ou s'incruster chez qn; Com **established 1885** établi en 1885 2 (make firm) (one's faith) affermir; (power) asseoir; (rule of law) instaurer; Law (will) confirmer, ratifier; **to e. one's right** faire apparaître son bon droit; **to e. a reputation** se faire une réputation; **to e. sb's reputation as an author** faire la réputation de qn comme auteur; **the film established her as an important director** avec ce film, elle s'est affirmée comme un metteur en scène important 3 (prove, become clear about) (fact, sb's innocence etc) établir; **research has established links between the two diseases** la recherche a permis d'établir des liens entre les deux maladies 4 Rel, Pol (Church) ériger en Église d'État

established [ɪs'tæblɪʃt] ADJ établi; (friendship) solide; (fact) avéré; (reputation) solide, bien établi; **once the company becomes e.** quand la société sera bien établie; **when you become e. as an opera singer** quand ta réputation de chanteur d'opéra sera faite; **e. scientific fact** fait acquis à la science; Rel, Pol **the e. Church** l'Église f établie; **the e. religion** la religion d'État; **the e. order** l'ordre m établi

establishing shot [ɪs'tæblɪʃɪŋ] N TV, Cin plan m de situation ou de mise en place ou d'ensemble

establishment [ɪs'tæblɪʃmənt] N 1 (established order) **the E.** (national institutions) les institutions fpl; (dominant group) l'establishment m; (prevailing values) l'ordre m établi; **the liberal/academic/etc E.** les sommités fpl libérales/académiques/etc; **E. figure** membre m de la classe dirigeante; **to be against the E., to be anti-E.** être anticonformiste; **to revolt against the E.** se révolter contre l'ordre établi; Rel **the (Church) E.** l'Église f établie 2 Com (company etc) établissement m; **business e.** maison f de commerce; **a family e.** (hotel, restaurant) un établissement familial 3 (staff) personnel m; Mil etc (of unit etc) effectif m; Fml **to be on the e.** faire partie du personnel; Mil **peacetime e.** effectifs mpl de paix 4 Pol (of government, Church) établissement m; (of system) création f, Com (of busi-

ness) fondation f, (of company) constitution f 5 (of fact etc) constatation f, (of one's faith) affermissement m; Law (of will) homologation f

estate [ɪs'teɪt] N 1 Law (possessions) bien m; (of deceased person) succession f, biens mpl; (of bankrupt) actif m 2 (land) terre f, propriété f, **country house and e. for sale** à vendre château et domaine; Br **(housing) e.** lotissement m; (council houses) cité f HLM; Br **(industrial) e.** zone f industrielle 3 Br (car) break m 4 Lit, Arch (state) état m, condition f, **man's e.** l'âge m d'homme; **of high/low e.** (social condition) de haut rang/d'humble condition 5 Pol **the third e.** le tiers (état); **the fourth e.** le quatrième pouvoir; Hist **the Estates (of the Realm)** les états mpl, les ordres mpl (de l'ancien régime)
▸▸ Br **e. agency** agence f immobilière; Br **e. agent** (salesperson) agent m immobilier; (manager) intendant m, régisseur m; Br **e. car** break m; Br **e. duty,** Am **e. tax** droits mpl de succession

esteem [ɪs'tiːm] N estime f, considération f, **to hold sb in high e.** avoir qn en haute estime; **to hold sb in low e.** avoir peu d'estime ou de considération pour qn; **to go up/down in sb's e.** monter/baisser dans l'estime ou la considération de qn
VT 1 (regard highly) (person) estimer; (something) priser; **to e. sth lightly** faire peu de cas de qch; **highly esteemed** (person) fort estimé 2 Fml (consider) estimer, regarder (sth as sth qch comme qch); **to e. it an honour that ...** se sentir honoré que ...; **I would e. it a favour if you did this** je vous serais reconnaissant de le faire
▸▸ Mktg **e. needs** besoin m d'estime

ester ['estər] N Biol, Chem ester m

esthete, esthetic etc Am = **aesthete, aesthetic** etc

estimable ['estɪməb(ə)l] ADJ estimable, digne d'estime

estimate[1] ['estɪmət] N 1 (rough calculation) (of contents of sth, of force of sth) appréciation f, évaluation f, calcul m; **it's only an e.** ce n'est qu'une estimation; **rough e.** approximation f grossière; **at a rough e.** à vue de nez; **at the lowest e.** au bas mot 2 Com devis m (estimatif); **to ask for an e.** demander un devis; **to give or put in an e. for decorating work** donner un devis pour des travaux de décoration, soumissionner des travaux de décoration; Pol **the Estimates** les prévisions fpl budgétaires; **building e.** devis de construction; **free e.** devis gratuit; **preliminary e.** devis de prévision

estimate[2] ['estɪmeɪt] VT (costs etc) estimer, évaluer; **to e. sth at £10,000** estimer ou calculer qch à 10 000 livres; **his fortune is estimated at ...** on évalue sa fortune à ...; **I e. that it will take three years** j'estime que cela prendra trois ans

estimated ['estɪmeɪtɪd] ADJ (cost) estimatif; (value) estimé; **it will cost an e. £500,000** on estime que cela coûtera 500 000 livres; **it is only an e. figure** ce n'est qu'une estimation; **e. time of arrival** heure f d'arrivée prévue

estimation [estɪ'meɪʃən] N 1 (rough calculation) estimation f, appréciation f, évaluation f, (of costs etc) calcul m 2 (judgement) jugement m; **in my e.** d'après moi, à mon avis 3 (regard) estime f, considération f, **she is rising in the e. of the public** elle monte dans l'estime du public; **he's gone down in my e.** il est descendu dans mon estime ou ma considération

estimator ['estɪmeɪtər] N Fin expert m

Estonia [es'təʊnɪə] N Estonie f

Estonian [es'təʊnɪən] ADJ estonien
N Estonien, -ienne

estrange [ɪs'treɪndʒ] **VT** s'aliéner l'affection de; **to become estranged from sb** se détacher de qn; **the quarrel estranged her from her family** cette dispute l'a brouillée avec sa famille

estranged [ɪs'treɪndʒd] **ADJ an e. couple** des époux séparés; **her e. husband** son mari dont elle est séparée; **their e. son** leur fils avec qui ils sont brouillés

estrangement [ɪs'treɪndʒmənt] **N** (of person) aliénation f; (of two people) brouille f (**between** entre); (of married couple) séparation f

estrogen ['i:strədʒən] **N** Am Biol, Chem œstrogène m

estrous ['i:strəs] **ADJ** Am Biol (cycle) œstral

estrus ['i:strəs] **N** Am Biol œstrus m

estuary ['estjʊ(ə)rɪ] **N** estuaire m; **the Thames e.** l'estuaire de la Tamise
▸▸ **e. English** = accent m standard teinté d'accent Cockney, prédominant à Londres et dans le sud-est de l'Angleterre, ne permettant pas d'identifier l'appartenance sociale du locuteur

ETA [i:ti:'eɪ] **N** Aviat (abbr **estimated time of arrival**) heure f d'arrivée prévue

e-tail N vente f en ligne

et al [et'æl] (abbr **et alii**) et autres

etc [et'setrə] **ADV** (abbr **et cetera**) etc; Fam **you have to fill in the form in duplicate e. e.** il faut remplir le formulaire en deux exemplaires etc, etc

et cetera [et'setrə] **ADV** et cætera

etceteras [et'setrəs] **NPL** extras mpl

etch [etʃ] **VT** Art, Typ (drawing etc) graver à l'eau-forte; (plate) graver; **to e. away the metal** enlever le métal à l'eau-forte; Fig **the scene was etched in his memory** la scène était gravée dans sa mémoire
VI faire de la gravure à l'eau-forte

etcher ['etʃər] **N** Art graveur m à l'eau-forte

etching ['etʃɪŋ] **N** Art (art) art m de graver à l'eau-forte; (individual work) gravure f à l'eau-forte, eau-forte f, pl eaux-fortes; Hum **come up and see my etchings** monte, je vais te montrer ma collection d'estampes japonaises

ETD [i:ti:'di:] **N** (abbr **estimated time of departure**) = heure f de départ prévue

eternal [ɪ'tɜ:n(ə)l] **ADJ** éternel; (continual) continuel, sans fin; **e. life** la vie éternelle; **e. quarrelling/complaints/gossip** querelles/ plaintes/commérages incessant(e)s
N the E. l'Éternel m
▸▸ Fig **the e. triangle** l'éternel triangle m

eternally [ɪ'tɜ:n(ə)lɪ] **ADV** éternellement; **I shall be e. grateful to you** je vous serai éternellement reconnaissant

eternity [ɪ'tɜ:nɪtɪ] **N** éternité f; Fam **I waited an e.** j'ai attendu pendant une éternité
▸▸ **e. ring** = bague f entièrement sertie de pierres symbolisant l'éternité du mariage

ethane ['i:θeɪn] **N** Chem éthane m

ether ['i:θər] **N 1** Phys, Chem éther m **2** Arch, Lit **the e.** (heavens) la voûte éthérée, l'éther m

ethereal [ɪ'θɪərɪəl] **ADJ** éthéré; (form) léger, impalpable

ethereally [ɪ'θɪərɪəlɪ] **ADV e. beautiful** d'une beauté éthérée

etherize ['i:θəraɪz] **VT** Med éthériser

Ethernet® ['i:θənet] **N** Comput Ethernet® m

ethic ['eθɪk] **ADJ**
N (set of values) éthique f, **work e.** conception f du travail
▸▸ Gram **e. dative** datif m éthique

ethical ['eθɪk(ə)l] **ADJ** éthique, moral, -aux; **it's not e.** (morally wrong) ce n'est pas moral;

the doctor's behaviour was not e. (against professional ethics) le comportement du médecin n'était pas conforme au code déontologique
▸▸ Pharm **e. drug** = remède m vendu uniquement sur l'ordonnance d'un médecin; Fin **e. investment** investissement m éthique; Liter **e. writer** moraliste m

ethically ['eθɪklɪ] **ADV** d'après (les doctrines de) l'éthique; **she has behaved quite e.** son comportement a été tout à fait éthique ou moral; **e. questionable** d'une éthique douteuse

ethics ['eθɪks] **N** Phil éthique f, morale f; (of profession) déontologie f; **e. code, code of e.** code m déontologique **VOIR GRAMMAIRE A10**

Ethiopia [i:θɪ'əʊpɪə] **N** Éthiopie f

Ethiopian [i:θɪ'əʊpɪən] **ADJ** éthiopien
N Éthiopien, -ienne

ethnic ['eθnɪk] **ADJ** ethnique
N Am membre m d'une minorité ethnique
▸▸ **e. cleansing** purification f ethnique, nettoyage m ethnique; **e. community** communauté f ethnique; **e. minority** minorité f ethnique; **e. tourism** (travel to ancestral country) tourisme m ethnique

ethnically ['eθnɪklɪ] **ADV** du point de vue ethnique

ethnicity [eθ'nɪsɪtɪ] **N** appartenance f ethnique

ethnocentric [eθnəʊ'sentrɪk] **ADJ** ethnocentrique

ethnographer [eθ'nɒgrəfər] **N** ethnographe mf

ethnography [eθ'nɒgrəfɪ] **N** ethnographie f

ethnological [eθnə'lɒdʒɪk(ə)l] **ADJ** ethnologique

ethnologically [eθnə'lɒdʒɪklɪ] **ADV** ethnologiquement

ethnologist [eθ'nɒlədʒɪst] **N** ethnologue mf

ethnology [eθ'nɒlədʒɪ] **N** ethnologie f

ethological [i:θə'lɒdʒɪk(ə)l] **ADJ** éthologique

ethology [ɪ'θɒlədʒɪ] **N** éthologie f

ethos ['i:θɒs] **N** (of people) génie m; (of company, class) culture f

Ethyl® ['eθɪl] **N** Chem éthyle m
▸▸ **e. alcohol** alcool m éthylique, éthanol m

ethylene ['eθɪli:n] **N** Chem éthylène m

etiolate ['i:tɪəʊleɪt] **VT** (plant) étioler

etiological [i:tɪə'lɒdʒɪk(ə)l] **ADJ** Am étiologique

etiology [i:tɪ'ɒlədʒɪ] **N** Am étiologie f

etiquette ['etɪket] **N** étiquette f, **court e.** cérémonial m de cour; **e. demands that ...** l'étiquette veut ou exige que ...; **professional e.** usages mpl professionnels

Etonian [i:'təʊnɪən] **N** Sch élève m (du collège) d'Eton; **Old E.** ancien élève d'Eton

Etruscan [ɪ'trʌskən] Antiq **ADJ** étrusque
N Étrusque mf

etymological [etɪmə'lɒdʒɪk(ə)l] **ADJ** étymologique

etymologically [etɪmə'lɒdʒɪklɪ] **ADV** étymologiquement

etymologist [etɪ'mɒlədʒɪst] **N** étymologiste mf

etymology [etɪ'mɒlədʒɪ] **N** étymologie f

EU [i:'ju:] **N** (abbr **European Union**) UE f, **EU legislation** législation f européenne

eucalyptus, pl **eucalypti, eucalyptuses** [ju:kə'lɪptəs, -taɪ, -təsɪz] **N** (tree) eucalyptus m
▸▸ **e. oil** essence f d'eucalyptus

Eucharist (the) [ðə'ju:kərɪst] **N** Rel l'eucharistie f, **to receive the E.** recevoir l'eucharistie

Euclidean [ju:'klɪdɪən] **ADJ** (geometry) euclidien

eugenics [ju:'dʒenɪks] **N** eugénique f, eugénisme m **VOIR GRAMMAIRE A10**

eulogist ['ju:lədʒɪst] **N** panégyriste mf

eulogize ['ju:lədʒaɪz] **VT** (person, thing) faire l'éloge ou le panégyrique de

eulogy ['ju:lədʒɪ] **N** panégyrique m; **to pronounce a e. on sb** faire l'éloge ou le panégyrique de qn

eunuch ['ju:nək] **N** eunuque m

euphemism ['ju:fɪmɪz(ə)m] **N** euphémisme m

euphemistic [ju:fɪ'mɪstɪk] **ADJ** euphémique

euphemistically [ju:fɪ'mɪstɪklɪ] **ADV** par euphémisme; **e. known as ...** auquel on se réfère par euphémisme sous le terme de ...

euphonious [ju:'fəʊnɪəs] **ADJ** euphonique

euphonium [ju:'fəʊnɪəm] **N** Mus saxhorn m basse, basse f (des cuivres)

euphony ['ju:fənɪ] **N** euphonie f

euphorbia [ju:'fɔ:bɪə] **N** Bot (plant) euphorbe f

euphoria [ju:'fɔ:rɪə] **N** euphorie f

euphoric [ju:'fɒrɪk] **ADJ** euphorique

Eurasia [jʊə'reɪʃə, -ʒə] **N** Eurasie f

Eurasian [jʊə'reɪʃən, -ʒən] **ADJ** eurasien; (fauna etc) eurasiatique
N Eurasien, -ienne

eureka [ju:'ri:kə] **INT** eurêka

eurhythmics [ju:'rɪðmɪks] **N** gymnastique f rythmique **VOIR GRAMMAIRE A10**

EURIBOR ['jʊərɪbɔ:r] **N** Fin (abbr **Euro Interbank Offered Rate**) EURIBOR m, TIBEUR m

euro ['jʊərəʊ] **N** euro m
▸▸ **E. area** zone f euro; **E. MP** membre m du Parlement européen; **E. zone** zone euro

Euro- PREF euro-

Eurobank ['jʊərəʊbæŋk] **N** eurobanque f

Eurobarometer [jʊərəʊbə'rɒmɪtər] **N** Eurobaromètre m

Eurobond ['jʊərəʊbɒnd] **N** euro-obligation f

eurocard ['jʊərəʊkɑ:d] **N** Banking eurocarte f

Eurocheque ['jʊərəʊtʃek] **N** Banking eurochèque m

Eurocommunism [jʊərəʊ'kɒmjʊnɪz(ə)m] **N** Pol eurocommunisme m

Eurocrat ['jʊərəʊkræt] **N** eurocrate mf

eurocredit ['jʊərəʊkredɪt] **N** Com eurocrédit m

eurocurrency ['jʊərəʊkʌrənsɪ] **N** eurodevise f
▸▸ **e. market** marché m des eurodevises

Eurodollar ['jʊərəʊdɒlər] **N** eurodollar m

Euro-election N the Euro-elections les élections fpl européennes

Eurofranc ['jʊərəʊfræŋk] **N** eurofranc m

Euroland ['jʊərəʊlænd] **N** Euroland(e) f

Euroloan ['jʊərəʊləʊn] **N** eurocrédit m

Euromarket ['jʊərəʊmɑ:kɪt] **N** marché m des eurodevises

Europe ['jʊərəp] **N** Europe f; **in E.** en Europe

European [jʊərə'pi:ən] **ADJ** européen
N Européen, -éenne
▸▸ Fin **E. Central Bank** Banque f centrale européenne; Pol **E. Coal and Steel Community** Communauté f européenne de charbon et de l'acier; **E. Commission** Commission f européenne; Pol **E. Community** Communauté f européenne; **E. Convention for the Protection of Human Rights and Fundamental Freedoms** Convention f européenne de sauvegarde des droits de l'homme et des libertés fondamentales; **E. Court of Human Rights** Cour européenne des droits de

l'homme; **E. Court of Justice** Cour européenne de justice; *Fin Formerly* **E. Currency Unit** Unité *f* monétaire européenne; **E. Customs Union** Union *f* douanière européenne; *Fin* **E. Development Fund** Fonds *m* européen de développement; *Pol* **E. Economic Area** Espace *m* économique européen; *Formerly* **E. Economic Community** Communauté économique européenne; *Fin Formerly* **E. Exchange Rate Mechanism** mécanisme *m* de change européen; **E. Free Trade Association** Association *f* européenne de libre-échange; *Fin* **E. Investment Bank** Banque européenne d'investissement; *Fin* **E. Monetary Institute** Institut *m* monétaire européen; *Fin Formerly* **E. Monetary System** Système *m* monétaire européen; **E. Parliament** Parlement *m* européen; **E. Patent Office** Office *m* européen des brevets; *Am* **E. plan** (*in hotel*) chambre *f* sans pension; **E. Political Cooperation** coopération *f* en matière de politique étrangère; **E. Regional Development Fund** Fonds européen de développement régional; *Fin* **E. Social Fund** Fonds social européen; **E. Standards Commission** Comité *m* européen de normalisation; **E. Union** Union européenne

Europeanize [ˈjʊərəˈpiːənaɪz] *vt* européaniser

European-style option *n* *St Exch* option *f* européenne

Eurosceptic [ˈjʊərəʊskeptɪk] *n* eurosceptique *mf*

Eurotourism [ˈjʊərəʊtʊərɪz(ə)m] *n* eurotourisme *m*

Eurotunnel [ˈjʊərəʊtʌnəl] *n* Eurotunnel *m*

Eurovision [ˈjʊərəvɪʒən] *n* Eurovision *f*; **the E. song contest** le concours Eurovision de la chanson

euroyen [ˈjʊərəʊjen] *n* *Fin* euroyen *m*

Eustachian [juːˈsteɪʃən] *adj*
▸▸ *Anat* **E. tube** trompe *f* d'Eustache

euthanasia [juːθəˈneɪzɪə] *n* euthanasie *f*

EVA [iːviːˈeɪ] *n* (*abbr* **economic value added**) VAE *f*

evacuate [ɪˈvækjʊeɪt] *vt* (*place, population*) évacuer; *Tech* (*exhaust gases*) refouler; *Phys* (*create vacuum in*) faire le vide dans; **children were evacuated to the countryside** les enfants ont été évacués vers la campagne; *Physiol* **to e. the bowels** vider les intestins

evacuation [ɪvækjʊˈeɪʃən] *n* (*of place, people, bowels*) évacuation *f*; *Tech* (*of exhaust gases*) refoulement *m*; *Phys* (*creation of vacuum*) production *f* du vide

evacuee [ɪvækjʊˈiː] *n* évacué, -ée; **e. children** enfants évacués

evade [ɪˈveɪd] *vt* (*blow*) éviter, esquiver; (*danger*) éviter; (*creditors*) esquiver; (*justice, responsibility*) se soustraire à; (*obstacle, the law*) éviter, tourner; (*question, problem*) éluder; (*sb's vigilance*) déjouer; (*one's pursuers, detection*) échapper à, se dérober à; **to e. customs duty on sth** passer qch en fraude; **to e. tax** frauder le fisc; **success evades him** le succès lui échappe

Note that the French verb **s'évader** is a false friend and is never a translation for the English verb **to evade**. It means **to escape**.

evader [ɪˈveɪdər] *n* **tax e.** fraudeur, -euse du fisc

evaluate [ɪˈvæljʊeɪt] *vt* (*danger, strength*) évaluer; (*damages*) évaluer, estimer le montant de

evaluation [ɪvæljʊˈeɪʃən] *n* évaluation *f*

evanescent [evəˈnesənt] *adj* évanescent, éphémère

evangelical [iːvænˈdʒelɪk(ə)l] *Rel* *adj* (*rela-*

ting to Gospels) évangélique; **an e. Christian/ church/sect** un chrétien/une église/une secte évangélique; **he's one of these e. Christians** c'est un de ces évangélistes; **e. preacher** évangéliste *mf*, **e. zeal** zèle *m* religieux; *Fig* **an e. vegetarian/communist** un végétarien/communiste à tout crin
n protestant, -ante évangélique

evangelicalism [iːvænˈdʒelɪkəlɪz(ə)m] *n* *Rel* évangélisme *m*

evangelism [ɪˈvændʒɪlɪz(ə)m] *n* *Rel* évangélisme *m*, prédication *f* de l'Évangile

evangelist [ɪˈvændʒɪlɪst] *n* *Rel* évangéliste *mf*

evangelize [ɪˈvændʒɪlaɪz] *Rel* *vt* évangéliser; (*person*) prêcher l'Évangile à
vi prêcher l'Évangile; *Fig* **to e. for a cause** prêcher une cause; **he has been evangelizing about jazz for years** il prêche les mérites du jazz depuis des années

evaporate [ɪˈvæpəreɪt] *vt* (*liquid*) (faire) évaporer; **evaporated milk** lait *m* condensé (non sucré)
vi (*of liquid etc*) s'évaporer; (*of acid*) se volatiliser; *Fig* (*of money*) disparaître comme par enchantement; (*of enthusiasm, hope etc*) s'envoler

evaporation [ɪvæpəˈreɪʃən] *n* (*of liquid*) évaporation *f*; (*of acid*) volatilisation *f*; (*of fears*) disparition *f*

evaporator [ɪˈvæpəreɪtər] *n* *Ind* évaporateur *m*

evasion [ɪˈveɪʒən] *n* **1** (*act of dodging a commitment*) dérobade *f*, **by skilful e. of the more difficult questions** en se dérobant adroitement aux questions plus difficiles; **tax e.** évasion *f* fiscale **2** (*subterfuge*) subterfuge *m*, échappatoire *f*, faux-fuyant *m*, *pl* faux-fuyants; **without e.** sans détours

Note that the French word **évasion** is a false friend and is rarely a translation for the English word **evasion**. Its most common meaning is **escape**.

evasive [ɪˈveɪsɪv] *adj* (*person*) évasif; (*personality*) fuyant; **to give an e. answer** faire une réponse évasive, répondre évasivement; *Mil etc* **to take e. action** faire une manœuvre d'évitement

evasively [ɪˈveɪsɪvlɪ] *adv* (*to answer*) évasivement

evasiveness [ɪˈveɪsɪvnɪs] *n* caractère *m* évasif; **her e. increased our suspicions** ses propos évasifs ont renforcé nos soupçons

EVC [iːviːˈsiː] *n* *Mktg* (*abbr* **economic value to the customer**) valeur *f* économique apporté au consommateur

Eve [iːv] *n* Ève; *Br Culin* **E.'s pudding** compote *f* de pommes recouverte de génoise

eve [iːv] *n* **1** (*day before*) veille *f*, **Christmas E.** la veille de Noël; **New Year's E.** la Saint-Sylvestre; **on the e. of ...** à la veille de ...; *Fig* **to be on the e. of success** être à la veille du succès **2** *Arch, Lit* (*evening*) soir *m*

EVEN [ˈiːv(ə)n]

ADJ plat **1** ▪ égal **1–3** ▪ pair **5**
ADV même **1, 3** ▪ encore **2**
VT égaliser

ADJ 1 (*surface, ground etc*) (*level*) plat, plan; (*smooth*) uni, égal, -aux; **to be e. with sth** être au niveau de *ou* à ras de qch; **to make e.** (*foundations of building*) araser; (*surface*) aplanir; (*edges of two planks etc*) affleurer **2** (*regular*) (*pulse*) égal, régulier; **to make e.** (*spacing*) égaliser; **e. temperature** température égale; **e. disposition** caractère *m* calme **3** (*equal*) égal, -aux; **he has an e. chance of succeeding** il a une chance sur deux de réus-

sir; **the chances** *or* **odds are about e. that ...** il y a à peu près une chance sur deux que ...; *Sport* **to be e.** être à égalité; **they are an e. match** ils sont à partie égale; *Fig* **to get e. with sb** prendre sa revanche sur qn; **to be e. with sb** être quitte avec qn; **I'll get e. with him yet** je la lui rendrai; *Sl* **to be e. Stevens** être quitte; *Sl* **to go e. Stevens with sb** partager fifty-fifty avec qn
4 (*fair*) **with an e. hand** impartialement; **e. bargain** marché *m* équitable *ou* juste
5 (*number*) pair; **odd or e.** pair ou impair
ADV 1 même; **it isn't e. amusing any more** ce n'est même plus amusant; **or e. ...** ou même ...; **e. the cleverest** même les plus habiles; **e. the children knew** même les enfants savaient; **I never e. saw it** je ne l'ai même pas vu; **without e. speaking** sans même dire un mot; **e. then she wouldn't believe me** même alors elle ne voulait pas me croire; **this would be sad, tragic e.** ça serait triste, tragique même
2 (*with comparatives*) encore; **e. more/less** encore plus/moins; **that would be e. worse/better** ce serait encore pis/mieux; **bring a friend – e. better, bring two** amène un ami – mieux encore, amène-en deux; **e. sadder than usual** encore plus triste que d'habitude
3 (*giving conditions*) même; **e. supposing that ...** même en supposant que ...; **e. if** même si; **e. if she came** même si elle venait; **e. though** même que **e. though he has a car** bien qu'il ait une voiture; **e. with a computer, the work would take months** même avec un ordinateur, le travail prendrait des mois; **e. so** cependant, quand même
4 (*with time*) **e. as I speak** au moment même où je parle; **e. now** à l'instant même; **e. now, four years later, I still haven't got over it** aujourd'hui encore, quatre ans plus tard, je ne m'en suis pas encore remis; **e. then** (*already*) déjà (à cette époque)
VT 1 (*make smooth*) (*surface etc*) aplanir, niveler, égaliser; (*two planks etc*) affleurer; (*foundations of a wall*) araser
2 (*make equal*) rendre égal; *Typ* (*spacing*) égaliser; **to e. the odds** égaliser les chances
▸▸ *Horseracing* **e. money** pari *m* avec enjeu égal; **horse quoted at e. money** cheval coté à égalité; *Fig* **I'll give you e. money that ...** je te parie que ..., je suis prêt à te parier que ...; *Comput* **e. parity** parité *f*
▸ **even out** *vi* (*become smooth, flat*) s'aplanir, s'égaliser, se niveler; (*of curve on graph*) s'aplanir; **the road goes uphill and then evens out** la route monte, puis s'aplanit; **prices finally evened out** les prix ont fini par s'égaliser; **that should e. out over the lifetime of the entire project** cela devrait s'équilibrer sur la durée totale du projet
VT SEP (*make more equal, fairer*) (*taxation etc*) répartir également; **that evens things out** on est quitte(s)
▸ **even up** *vt sep* **1** (*make equal*) (*score etc*) égaliser; **that will e. things up** (*financially*) on sera quitte(s); (*in competition*) cela équilibera les choses
2 (*sum*) arrondir au chiffre supérieur; **let's e. it up to a pound** arrondissons la somme à une livre

even-handed [-ˈhændɪd] *adj* équitable, juste, impartial, -aux

evening [ˈiːvnɪŋ] *n* **1** soir *m*; (*duration*) soirée *f*, **tomorrow e.** demain soir; **yesterday e.** hier soir; **in the e.** le soir; **what do you do in the evenings?** qu'est-ce que vous faites le soir?; **at nine o'clock in the e.** à neuf heures du soir; **I'm going out this e.** je sors ce soir; **to have an e. out** sortir; (**on**) **that e.** ce soir-là; (**on**) **the e. before,** (**on**) **the previous e.** la veille au soir; **the next e.** le lendemain soir; **one** *or* **on a fine summer e.** (par) un beau soir d'été; **long winter evenings** longues soirées d'hiver; **every e.** tous les soirs; **every Monday e.** tous les lundis soir; **on the e. of Monday, 29th March** dans la soirée du lundi 29 mars; **all (the) e.** toute la soirée; **during the e.** pendant la soirée; *Fig Lit* **in the e. of life** au déclin de la vie SEE GRAMMAR B61 **2** *(evening party)* soirée *f*; **musical/cultural e.** soirée musicale/culturelle

▸▸**e. class** cours *m* du soir; **e. dress** *(for men)* tenue *f* de soirée; *(for women)* robe *f* du soir; **in e. dress** en tenue de soirée; *Sport* **e. fixture** nocturne *f*; **e. gown** robe *f* de soirée *ou* du soir; *Sport* **e. match** nocturne; **e. paper** journal *m* du soir; *Theat* **e. performance** représentation *f* de soirée; *Rel* **e. prayers** office *m ou* service *m* du soir; **e. primrose oil** huile *f* d'onagre; *Rel* **e. service** office *ou* service du soir; *Astron* **e. star** étoile *f* du berger; **e. wear** *(for men)* tenue de soirée; *(for women)* robe du soir; **in e. wear** en tenue de soirée

When translating **evening**, note that **soir** and **soirée** are not interchangeable. **Soir** is used to refer to the evening as part of the day as opposed to the morning or the afternoon. For **soirée**, the emphasis is on duration.

evenly ['iːv(ə)nlɪ] ADV **1** *(to stretch, knit)* uniment; **spread the glue e.** étaler la colle régulièrement **2** *(to breathe)* régulièrement; *(to say sth)* calmement **3** *(fairly) (to divide)* également; **e. matched** *(of equal size)* de grandeur égale; *(of equal strength)* de force égale

evenness ['iːvənnɪs] N **1** *(smoothness)* caractère *m* plat *ou* égal *ou* nivelé **2** *(regularity)* égalité *f*; *(of movement)* régularité *f* **3** *(calm) (of character)* calme *m*; *(of mood)* égalité *f*

even-numbered ['iːvən'nʌmbəd] ADJ (portant un nombre) pair

evens ['iːv(ə)nz] NPL *(in betting)* **to lay e.** parier à l'égalité; **horses quoted at e.** chevaux cotés à égalité; **the bookmakers are offering e.** les bookmakers offrent un enjeu égal

evensong ['iːv(ə)nsɒŋ] N *Church of Eng* office *m* du soir

event [ɪ'vent] N **1** *(occurrence)* événement *m*; **it is going to be quite an e.** ça va être un véritable événement; **in the course of events** par la suite; **to be swept along by the tide** *or* **course of events** être emporté par le cours des événements; **as recent events have shown** comme l'ont montré de récents événements; *Fam* **a happy e.** *(birth)* un heureux événement; **when's the happy e.?** quand l'heureux événement doit-il avoir lieu? **2** *(outcome)* issue *f*, résultat *m*; **in either e.** dans l'un ou l'autre cas; **wise after the e.** sage après coup; **at all events, in any e.** en tout cas; **in the e. of his refusing** au cas *ou* dans le cas où il refuserait, pour le cas où il refuserait; **in the e. of (his) death** en cas de décès; **in the e. of rain** au cas où il pleuvrait, en cas de pluie **3** *Sport (meeting)* réunion *f* sportive; *(individual category, contest)* épreuve *f*, *Boxing, Fencing etc* rencontre *f*; **sporting e.** manifestation *f* sportive; **what was your best e.?** quelle a été ta meilleure discipline? ▸▸*Mktg* **e. advertising** publicité *f* par l'événement; **e. management, events management** gestion *f* d'événements; **e. manager, events manager** organisateur, -trice d'événements; *Mktg* **e. promotion** communication *f* événementielle

even-tempered ADJ *(person)* d'humeur égale; **of an e. disposition** d'humeur égale

eventer [ɪ'ventər] N *Horseriding* participant, -ante au concours complet

eventful [ɪ'ventfʊl] ADJ *(life, journey, day)* mouvementé, plein d'incidents

eventide ['iːv(ə)ntaɪd] N *Lit* soir *m* ▸▸*Br* **e. home** maison *f* de retraite

eventing [ɪ'ventɪŋ] N *Horseriding* concours *m* complet d'obstacles

eventual [ɪ'ventjʊəl] ADJ **1** *(final)* final, -als *ou* -aux, définitif; **the e. ruin** sa prodigalité et sa ruine finale **2** *Com (possible)* éventuel; **the e. profits from his new deal** les profits éventuels de sa nouvelle affaire

Note that the French word **éventuel** is a false friend and is never a translation for the English word **eventual**. It means **possible**.

eventuality [ɪventjʊ'ælɪtɪ] N éventualité *f*; **in that e.** dans cette éventualité

eventually [ɪ'ventjʊəlɪ] ADV *(in the end)* finalement, en fin de compte; *(at future date)* par la suite; **he e. became a judge** il finit par être nommé juge; **they e. reached the castle** ils ont fini par arriver au château; **I'll get round to mending that door e.** je finirai par réparer cette porte un de ces jours; **don't worry, I will do it e.** ne t'en fais pas, tôt ou tard je le ferai

Note that the French word **éventuellement** is a false friend and is never a translation for the English word **eventually**. It means **possibly**.

▸ **eventuate in** [ɪ'ventjʊeɪt] VT INSEP *Fml* conduire à

EVER ['evər]

- jamais **1** - toujours **2**

ADV **1** jamais; **I don't know if I'll e. see him again** je ne sais pas si je le reverrai un jour; **have you e. eaten caviar?** as-tu déjà mangé du caviar?; **I seldom, if e., read French** je lis rarement du français, pour ne pas dire jamais; **if I e. catch him** si jamais je l'attrape; **nothing e. happens** il n'arrive jamais rien; **hardly e., scarcely e.** presque jamais; **he's a liar if e. there was one** c'est un menteur s'il en fût jamais; **it started to rain faster than e.** il s'est mis à pleuvoir de plus belle; **without e. having thought of it** sans jamais y avoir pensé; **the best mother that e. was** la meilleure mère qui fût jamais; **it was the best/worst e.** c'était le meilleur/pire de tous; *Sl* **did you e.!** par exemple! **2** *(always)* toujours; **all she e. does is criticize** elle ne fait que critiquer; **e.-increasing influence** influence toujours plus grande; **e. the gentleman, he opened the door for her** en gentleman, comme toujours, il lui a ouvert la porte; **she was as cheerful as e.** elle était aussi gaie qu'à l'habitude; **for e.** pour toujours, à jamais; **to go away for e.** partir sans retour *ou* pour toujours; *Rel* **for e. and e.** à tout jamais, pour l'éternité; **Scotland for e.!** vive l'Écosse!; **to live for e.** vivre éternellement; **they lived happily e. after** ils vécurent heureux à tout jamais; *Old-fashioned* **yours e., e. yours** *(letter ending)* bien cordialement à vous, tout(e) à vous **3** *(intensive)* **it was the funniest sight e.** c'était à se tordre; *Fam* **e. so pretty** joli comme tout; *Fam* **it was e. so long ago** ça fait tellement longtemps; *Fam* **e. so many times** je ne sais combien de fois; *Fam* **thank you e. so much, thanks e. so** merci mille fois; *Fam* **I'm e. so pleased** j'en suis tellement content; *Fam* **e. so slightly ...** légèrement ...; *Fml* **be he e. so clever/handsome** si intelligent/beau qu'il soit; *Fam* **such a lot of money** une somme d'argent tellement importante; *Fam* **as if I e. would!** comme si

j'étais capable d'une chose pareille!; *Old-fashioned* **as quickly as e. you can** aussi vite que possible

4 *(in what/where/etc questions)* **what e. shall we do?** qu'est-ce que nous allons bien faire?; **what e.'s the matter with you?** mais qu'est-ce que vous avez donc?; **what e. can it be?** qu'est-ce que ça peut bien être?; **when e. will he come?** quand donc viendra-t-il?; **where e. have you been?** d'où venez-vous donc?; **who e. told you that?** qui est-ce qui a bien pu vous dire cela?; **why e. not?** mais pourquoi pas?; **how e. are we going to get back?** comment allons-nous bien pouvoir rentrer?; **how e. you manage I don't know** je me demande comment vous faites

5 **e. since (then)** dès lors, depuis; **I have been here e. since lunch** je suis là depuis le déjeuner; **he came to Scotland in 1990 and he's been here e. since** il est arrivé en Écosse en 1990 et il y est toujours resté

6 *esp Am Sl* **is he/she/it/etc e.!** *(generous, stupid, a beautiful day etc)* et comment!; **was I e. grateful for your help!** je te suis vraiment reconnaissant de m'avoir donné un coup de main!

evergreen ['evəgriːn] ADJ *Bot* à feuilles persistantes; *Fig* **e. topic** question *f* toujours d'actualité

N *(tree)* arbre *m* à feuilles persistantes; *(song)* classique *m* ▸▸*Fin* **e. facility** possibilité *f* de crédit permanent; *Fin* **e. fund** fonds *m* de crédit permanent non confirmé; **e. oak** chêne *m* vert

everlasting [evə'lɑːstɪŋ] ADJ **1** *(eternal)* éternel; *Bible* **the e. Father** le Père éternel; **Henry, to his e. credit, said nothing** Henry n'a rien dit, ce qui est tout à son honneur **2** *(material)* inusable, solide **3** *(continual)* perpétuel, continuel, sans fin

N **the E.** l'Éternel *m* ▸▸*Bot* **e. flower** immortelle *f*, *Bot* **e. pea** pois *m* vivace

everlastingly [evə'lɑːstɪŋlɪ] ADV *(eternally)* éternellement; *(continually)* perpétuellement

evermore [evə'mɔːr] ADV *Lit* toujours; **for e.** à jamais

EVERY ['evrɪ]

- chaque **1, 2** - tout **1** - tous les ... **1**
- chacun **2, 4**

ADJ VOIR GRAMMAIRE A35-6; B15-16 **1** *(indicating regular occurrence)* chaque, tout, tous les ...; **e. week** toutes les semaines, chaque semaine; **e. day** chaque jour, tous les jours; **it's not e. day you get married** ce n'est pas tous les jours qu'on se marie; **confidence is increasing e. day** la confiance s'accroît de jour en jour; **e. other** *or* **second day** tous les deux jours, un jour sur deux; **e. other Sunday** un dimanche sur deux; **e. other line/page** une ligne/page sur deux, toutes les deux lignes/pages; **e. second or third day** tous les deux ou trois jours; **e. third man was chosen** on choisissait un homme sur trois; **at e. quarter past the hour** toutes les heures, au quart; **e. few minutes** toutes les cinq minutes; **e. so often, e. now and again** *or* **then** de temps en temps, de temps à autre; **e. mile/few miles or so** tous les miles/deux ou trois miles **2** *(each)* chaque; **e. one** chacun, *f* chacune; **e. one of us was there** nous étions tous là; **they are my friends, e. one of them** ils sont tous mes amis; **I've checked e. single one** j'ai vérifié chacun d'entre eux; **at e. opportunity** chaque fois que c'est/c'était possible; **from e. side** de tous (les) côtés; **of e. kind** *or* **sort** de toute sorte; **of e. variety/age** de toutes les variétés/tous les âges; **e. word he says is a lie** tout ce qu'il dit est mensonge; **I have co-**

pied e. word of it je l'ai copié mot pour mot; **e. time (that) she comes** chaque fois qu'elle vient; **perseverance wins e. time** la persévérance l'emporte toujours; **e. man for himself** chacun pour soi; *(in danger)* sauve qui peut!; **e. person has this right** chacun a ce droit; **e. man Jack of them** tous sans exception

3 *(intensive)* **he was e. inch a republican** il était républicain jusqu'au bout des ongles; **I have e. reason to believe that …** j'ai tout lieu de croire que …; **you have e. right to be angry** tu as tout à fait le droit d'être en colère; **e. bit as good/intelligent as …** tout aussi bon/intelligent que …; **she's e. bit as much to be pitied as he is** elle est tout autant à plaindre que lui; **I shall give you e. assistance** je vous aiderai de tout mon pouvoir; **I look forward with e. confidence to the future** j'envisage l'avenir avec une pleine confiance; **there's e. chance that he'll pull through** il a toutes les chances de s'en sortir; **we have e. hope that …** nous avons grand espoir que …; *Am* **e. which way I look** où que je regarde; *Am* **to look e. which way for sb** chercher qn partout; *Am* **(from) e. which way** de tous les côtés

4 *esp Fml* **her e. action** chacune de ses actions; **they hung on his e. word** ils ne perdaient pas un seul mot de ce qu'il disait; **his desire to meet your e. wish** son désir d'aller au-devant de chacun de vos désirs

everybody ['evrɪbɒdɪ] **INDEF PRON** tout le monde; **e. has his/her** *or* **their own way of doing things** chacun/chacune a sa manière de faire les choses; **I don't know about e. else, you guys, but I'm going home** je ne sais pas ce que vous comptez faire, les mecs, mais moi je rentre chez moi; **I don't know about e. else, but I'll be there** je ne sais pas ce que les autres comptent faire, mais moi je serai là; **e. knows that** tout le monde *ou* n'importe qui sait cela; **not e. can do it** ce n'est pas tout le monde qui pourrait le faire; **e. who is anybody** toutes les personnes importantes; **e. else** tous les autres; **e. seems to know e. else** tout le monde semble se connaître VOIR GRAMMAIRE A36

everyday ['evrɪdeɪ] **ADJ ATTRIB 1** *(daily)* journalier, quotidien; *(ordinary)* fait banal; **e. occurrence** *(happening every day)* fait *m* journalier; **it's an e. occurrence** cela arrive tous les jours; **e. life** la vie quotidienne; **e. routine** train-train *m* quotidien **2** *(used every day)* de tous les jours; **for e. wear** pour porter tous les jours **3** *(ordinary)* usuel, ordinaire; **e. English** l'anglais de tous les jours; **e. expression** expression *f* courante; **words in e. use** mots d'usage courant

everyone ['evrɪwʌn] **INDEF PRON** = **everybody**

everyplace ['evrɪpleɪs] **ADV** *Am Fam* = **everywhere**

everything ['evrɪθɪŋ] **INDEF PRON** tout; **he has eaten e.** il a tout mangé; **e. good** tout ce qu'il y a de bon; **e. I did seemed to go wrong** tout ce que je faisais semblait mal tourner; **(a place for e. and) e. in its place** chaque chose à sa place; **they sell e.** on y vend de tout; *Com* **e. for cyclists** tout ce qui concerne le cyclisme; **money is not e.** l'argent n'est pas tout; **beauty isn't e.** il n'y a pas que la beauté (qui compte); **she's e. to me** elle est tout pour moi; *Fam* **to call sb e.** traiter qn de tous les noms; *Fam* **we're in a bad way with strikes and e.** ça marche mal à cause des grèves et de tout ça VOIR GRAMMAIRE A36; B15–16

everywhere ['evrɪweər] **ADV** partout, en tous lieux; **to look e. for sb/sth** chercher qn/qch partout; **e. you go** partout où vous allez, où que vous alliez; **e. you look there is poverty** de quelque côté que l'on se

tourne, on voit la pauvreté; **e. in France** partout en France

evict [ɪ'vɪkt] **VT** *(tenant)* évincer, expulser (**from** de); *(from meeting, court-room)* expulser; **evicted tenant** locataire *m* évincé

eviction [ɪ'vɪkʃən] **N** *Law (of tenant)* éviction *f*, expulsion *f*; **e. notice, e. order** avis *m* d'expulsion

evidence ['evɪdəns] **N 1** *(reason for belief)* preuve *f*; **there was clear e. that …** il était clair *ou* manifeste que …; **there is no e. to suggest a link between the two diseases** il n'y a aucune preuve suggérant qu'il y ait un lien entre les deux maladies; **they gave no e. of this** ils n'en laissaient paraître aucun signe; **on the e. of their past performances** si l'on en juge par leurs performances passées; **on this e., the answer would seem to be 'yes'** autant qu'on puisse en juger ici, la réponse semblerait être 'oui'

2 *(indication)* signe *m*, marque *f*; **to bear e. of sth** porter la marque de qch; **there was no e. of his stay in the house** rien ne montrait qu'il eût séjourné dans la maison; **the books were e. of her interest in the subject** les livres étaient le signe *ou* l'indication de son intérêt pour le sujet; **to be in e.** *(of person, thing)* être en évidence; **the army was much in e. on the streets** l'armée était très fortement présente dans les rues

3 *Law* preuves *fpl*; *(testimony)* témoignage *m*; **there wasn't enough e. to convict them** il n'y avait pas suffisamment de preuves pour qu'on les condamne; **internal e.** preuves intrinsèques; **external e.** preuves extrinsèques; **oral e.** preuve orale; **written/documentary e.** preuve littérale/documentaire; **to give e.** témoigner, déposer (en justice); **to give e. in sb's favour** témoigner en faveur de qn; **to call sb in e.** appeler qn à la barre des témoins; **the e. was strongly against him** les témoignages pesaient contre lui; **whatever you say may be given in e.** tout ce que vous direz pourra être retenu contre vous; **to turn** *Br* **King's/Queen's** *or Am* **State's e.** témoigner contre ses complices *(sous promesse de pardon)*

VT *Fml* témoigner de; **as evidenced by …** comme en témoigne …

Note that the French noun **évidence** is a false friend and is never a translation for the English word **evidence**. It means **obviousness**.

evident ['evɪdənt] **ADJ** évident, manifeste; *(fact, truth)* patent; **it was e. that …** il était évident *ou* clair que …; **that was far from e.** c'était loin d'être évident

evidently ['evɪdəntlɪ] **ADV 1** *(clearly)* à l'évidence, manifestement; **he was e. afraid** il était évident *ou* clair qu'il avait peur; **e. worried** manifestement inquiet; **e., such a dangerous criminal must be caught** il est évident qu'un criminel aussi dangereux doit être arrêté; **I got held up – e.** j'ai été retardé – c'est ce qu'il semblerait **2** *(apparently)* apparemment; **e. he's been away** apparemment il a été absent, il semblerait qu'il ait été absent; **e. not** il semble bien que non, apparemment non

Note that the French word **évidemment** is a false friend and is never a translation for the English word **evidently**. It means **of course**.

evil ['iːvəl] **ADJ 1** *(person, look)* mauvais, malveillant; *(spirit)* malfaisant, malin; *(moment)* funeste; **the E. One** le Malin; **to silence e. tongues** faire taire la médisance; **house of e. repute** lieu *m* mal famé; *Lit* **to fall on e. days** tomber dans l'infortune *ou* dans le malheur; *Fam* **to put off the e. hour** *(of visit to*

dentist etc) repousser le moment fatal; **e. influence** influence *f* néfaste; **e. intentions** mauvaises intentions *fpl*; **e. omen** présage *m* de malheur; **e. tongue** mauvaise langue *f*

2 *(smell)* mauvais, nauséabond

N mal *m*, *pl* maux; **to choose the lesser of two evils** choisir entre deux maux le moindre; **a social e.** une plaie sociale; **to speak e. of sb** dire du mal de qn; **the evils of drink** les effets néfastes de la boisson

▸▸ **the e. eye** le mauvais œil

evildoer ['iːv(ə)lduːər] **N** *Lit* malfaiteur *m*

evil-looking ['iːv(ə)llʊkɪŋ] **ADJ** *(man)* louche; *(knife)* vilain

evilly ['iːvɪlɪ] **ADV** *(to laugh, leer etc)* avec malveillance; *(to look at sb)* d'un mauvais œil, d'un air méchant

evil-minded **ADJ** malintentionné, malveillant

evil-smelling **ADJ** nauséabond

evince [ɪ'vɪns] **VT** *Fml (quality, talent etc)* faire montre de, témoigner; *(curiosity, enthusiasm etc)* manifester

Note that the French verb **évincer** is a false friend and is never a translation for the English verb **to evince**. It means **to oust**.

eviscerate [ɪ'vɪsəreɪt] **VT 1** éviscérer, éventrer **2** *Fig (literary work etc)* émasculer

evisceration [ɪvɪsə'reɪʃən] **N** éviscération *f*

evocation [evə'keɪʃən] **N** évocation *f*

evocative [ɪ'vɒkətɪv] **ADJ** évocateur, -trice (**of** de)

evoke [ɪ'vəʊk] **VT 1** *(conjure up) (memory)* évoquer **2** *(provoke)* **this remark evoked a smile** cette observation a provoqué *ou* suscité un sourire

evoked set [ɪ'vəʊkt] **N** *Mktg* ensemble *m* évoqué

evolution [iːvə'luːʃən] **N 1** *Biol, Fig (of species, project etc)* évolution *f*, développement *m*; **the theory of e.** la théorie de l'évolution des espèces; *Fig* **the e. of events** le déroulement des événements; **her e. from journalist to revolutionary leader** son passage de la carrière de journaliste à celle de dirigeante d'un groupe révolutionnaire **2** *(manoeuvre) (of acrobat, troops etc)* évolution *f*

evolutionary [iːvə'luːʃən(ə)rɪ] **ADJ** *Biol (character, symptom, disease)* évolutif

evolutionism [iːvə'luːʃənɪz(ə)m] **N** *Biol* évolutionnisme *m*

evolutionist [iːvə'luːʃənɪst] **ADJ, N** *Biol* évolutionniste *mf*

evolve [ɪ'vɒlv] **VT** *(plan)* dérouler, développer; *(theory, truth)* développer, déduire (**from** de); **some species evolved wings** des ailes se sont développées chez certaines espèces

VI *(of events)* se dérouler; *(of situation, race etc)* se développer, évoluer; **the scheme evolved from a pilot project** ce programme a été développé à partir d'un projet-pilote; **medicine has evolved into a sophisticated science** la médecine est devenue une science sophistiquée

ewe [juː] **N** brebis *f*

ewer ['juːər] **N** *Old-fashioned* pot *m* à eau; *(on washstand)* broc *m* de toilette

ex [eks] **PREP 1** *Com (out of)* **ex quay** à quai; **ex ship** à bord; **ex warehouse** à (prendre à) l'entrepôt, en entrepôt; **ex works** départ usine, sortie d'usine; **price ex works** prix ex départ usine, prix sortie d'usine **2** *Fin (without)* **ex all, ex allotment** ex-répartition *f*; **ex bonus** ex-capitalisation *f*; **ex cap, ex capitalisation** ex-capitalisation; **ex coupon** ex-coupon *m*, coupon *m* détaché; **ex dividend** ex-dividende *m*, dividende *m* détaché; **ex in-**

terest sans *ou* exonéré d'intérêts; **ex rights** ex-droit *m*

N *Fam (former husband, girlfriend etc)* ex *mf inv*

ex- [eks] **PREF** *(former)* ancien, ex-; **ex-minister** ex-ministre *m*; **an ex-teacher** un ancien professeur; **ex-wife** ex-femme *f*; **ex-husband** ex-mari *m*; **all her ex-boyfriends** tous ses ex

exacerbate [eg'zæsəbeit] **VT 1** *(pain, situation, sb's difficulties etc)* exacerber, aggraver **2** *(person)* irriter, exaspérer

exact [ıg'zækt] **ADJ** exact, précis; **at the e. moment when …** au moment précis *ou* au moment même où …; **she was very e. in her reporting of events** elle a été très précise dans son compte-rendu des événements; **in the south of France, the Dordogne, to be more e.** dans le sud de la France, en Dordogne, pour être plus précis; **to give e. details** donner des détails précis *ou* des précisions, préciser; **an e. replica** une réplique exacte; **those were her e. words** c'est ce qu'elle a dit mot pour mot; **the e. word to describe Joanna** le mot juste pour décrire Joanna; **that wasn't the e. word he used** ce n'est pas exactement le mot qu'il a employé; **to tender the e. amount** *(on bus)* faire l'appoint; **the e. opposite** exactement le contraire; **Fml to be e.** *(in payments)* être exact; *(in business)* être strict **VT** *(tax) (tax)* exiger (**from** de); *(ransom, promise)* extorquer (**from** à); *(insist on) (obedience)* exiger, réclamer (**from** de)
▸▸ **e. sciences** sciences *fpl* exactes

exacting [ıg'zæktıŋ] **ADJ** *(person)* exigeant; *(work)* astreignant

exaction [ıg'zækʃən] **N** *Fml (of taxes, money)* exaction *f*, *(of promise)* extorsion *f*

exactitude [ıg'zæktıtjuːd] **N** *Fml (of report)* exactitude *f*, précision *f*, *(of reasoning, calculation)* exactitude, justesse *f*, **to say sth with e.** dire qch précisément *ou* exactement

exactly [ıg'zæktlı] **ADV 1** exactement, précisément; *(of time)* juste; **I don't know e. what happened** je ne sais pas au juste ce qui est arrivé; **I don't e. know where he is** je ne sais pas exactement où il se trouve; **I'm not e. sure what you mean** je ne suis pas tout à fait sûr de ce que tu veux dire; **where e. in France did you go?** où exactement êtes-vous allés en France?; **that's e. right!** c'est exactement cela!; **but that's e. what I mean!** mais c'est précisément ce que je veux dire!; **it's e. the same thing** c'est exactement la même chose; **at e. the right/wrong moment** exactement *ou* juste au bon/mauvais moment; **e.!** précisément!, parfaitement!; **e. so!** exactement!; **it is e. five** il est cinq heures juste; **not e.** pas précisément; **she didn't e. agree, but …** elle n'était pas vraiment d'accord, mais …; **he is not e. a scholar** ce n'est pas précisément un savant
2 *(with precision)* précisément, exactement; **e. calibrated** précisément étalonné

exactness [ıg'zæktnıs] **N** exactitude *f*

exaggerate [ıg'zædʒəreit] **VT** exagérer **VI** exagérer; **let's not e.!** n'exagérons rien!

exaggerated [ıg'zædʒəreitid] **ADJ** exagéré; *(praise)* outré; **e. behaviour** comportement *m* excessif; **to have an e. opinion of oneself** avoir une trop haute opinion de soi-même; **to attach e. importance to sth** prêter une importance excessive à qch

exaggeratedly [ıg'zædʒəreitidlı] **ADV** exagérément

exaggeration [ıgzædʒə'reıʃən] **N** exagération *f*; **it would be no e. to say that …** on pourrait dire sans exagérer *ou* sans exagération que …; **without e.** sans exagération; **that's an e.!** vous exagérez!/ils exagèrent!/*etc*

exalt [ıg'zɔːlt] **VT 1** *(praise) (sb's virtues)* exalter, vanter; **to e. sb to the skies** porter qn jusqu'aux nues **2** *(raise in rank)* élever

exalted [ıg'zɔːltıd] **ADJ 1** *(sentiment)* exalté; *(tone)* élevé **2** *(rank)* élevé; *(person)* haut placé

exam [ıg'zæm] **N** = **examination 1**

examination [ıgzæmı'neıʃən] **N 1** *Sch etc* examen *m*; **to take or sit an e.** passer *ou* subir un examen; **to pass/fail an e.** être reçu/refusé à un examen
2 *(inspection)* examen *m*; *Med (of vagina, rectum)* toucher *m*; *(of machines etc)* inspection *f*, visite *f*, *(of accounts)* vérification *f*, *(of report)* dépouillement *m*; *Law (of files etc)* compulsation *f*; **on e.** après examen, examen fait; **on further e.** après un examen plus approfondi; **the matter is under e.** l'affaire est à l'étude; **to undergo a medical e.** passer une visite médicale
3 *Law (of accused)* interrogatoire *m*; *(of witness)* audition *f*, *(of case)* instruction *f*, **to be put under e.** *(accused)* subir un interrogatoire; *(witness)* être entendu; **he admitted, under e., …** il a admis, lors de l'interrogatoire/l'audition, …
▸▸ **e. paper** *(set of questions)* sujet *m* d'examen; *(written answer)* copie *f* (d'examen)

examine [ıg'zæmın] **VT 1** *(inspect) (machine)* examiner, inspecter; *(in Customs) (baggage)* fouiller, examiner; *(accounts)* vérifier; *(passport)* contrôler; *(files etc)* compulser, étudier, examiner; *(inventory, account)* dépouiller; *Med (patient)* examiner; **to e. one's conscience** faire son examen de conscience; **to e. a question thoroughly** examiner une question à fond
2 *Sch etc (pupil)* examiner, faire passer un examen à; **to e. a candidate in Latin** examiner un candidat en latin
3 *Law etc (accused)* interroger, faire subir un interrogatoire à; *(witness)* interroger, entendre; *(case)* instruire

examinee [ıgzæmı'niː] **N** *Sch etc* candidat, -ate

examiner [ıg'zæmınər] **N 1** *(of baggage etc)* inspecteur, -trice; *(of files etc)* compulseur *m* **2** *Sch etc* examinateur, -trice; **the examiners** le jury (d'examen)

examining [ıg'zæmınıŋ] **ADJ**
▸▸ **e. body** jury *m* d'examen; *Br Law* **e. magistrate** juge *m* d'instruction

example [ıg'zɑːmp(ə)l] **N 1** exemple *m*; **to give an e.** donner un exemple; **to give just one e., …** pour ne donner *ou* citer qu'un exemple, …; **to quote sth as an e.** citer qch à titre d'exemple; **she showed me some examples of her work** elle m'a montré des spécimens de son travail; **a perfect e. of what not to do in a crisis** un exemple parfait de ce qu'il ne faut pas faire dans une crise; **for e.** par exemple; **large towns, (as) for e. London** les grandes villes, telles que Londres (par exemple); **by way of e.** en guise d'exemple
2 *(model)* exemple *m*; **to set an e.** donner l'exemple; **to set a good/bad e. for sb** donner le bon/mauvais exemple à qn; **I wish you would set a better e. for your sister** j'aimerais bien que tu donnes un peu mieux l'exemple à ta sœur; **to be an e. or a good e. to sb** être un exemple *ou* un bon exemple pour qn; **their father wasn't a very good e.** leur père n'a pas été un très bon exemple; **let that be an e. to you!** que ça te serve d'exemple!; **to make an e. of sb** faire un exemple de qn, punir qn pour l'exemple; **to take sb as an e.** prendre exemple sur qn; **to follow sb's e.** suivre l'exemple de qn

exasperate [ıg'zɑːspəreit] **VT** exaspérer, irriter; **exasperated at** *or* **by his insolence**

exaspéré par son insolence; **an exasperated look/voice** un regard/une voix exaspéré(e); **an exasperated gesture** un geste d'exaspération

exasperating [ıg'zɑːspəreitıŋ] **ADJ** exaspérant, irritant

exasperatingly [ıg'zɑːspəreitıŋlı] **ADV** d'une manière exaspérante *ou* irritante; **to be e. slow/obstinate** être d'une lenteur/obstination exaspérante; **they had come e. close to winning** ils avaient frôlé la victoire de si près que c'en était exaspérant

exasperation [ıgzɑːspə'reıʃən] **N** exaspération *f*, **to drive sb to e.** pousser qn à bout; **'shut up!', she screamed in e.** 'tais-toi!', cria-t-elle, exaspérée

excavate ['ekskəveit] **VT** *(tunnel)* excaver, creuser; *(soil)* fouiller, *(canal)* approfondir; *(ruins etc)* déterrer; *Archeol* **to e. a site** faire des fouilles
VI *Archeol* faire des fouilles; *Constr* procéder à une/des excavation(s)

excavation [ekskə'veıʃən] **N 1** *(action)* excavation *f*, *(of ground, soil)* approfondissement *m*; **the e. of a site** les fouilles *fpl* conduites dans un site **2** *(site)* terrain *m* excavé; *Archeol* fouille *f*; **the excavations at Pompeii** les fouilles de Pompéi

excavator ['ekskəveitər] **N 1** *Constr (machine)* excavateur *m*, excavatrice *f*, pelleteuse *f* **2** *Archeol (person)* personne *f* qui fait des fouilles

exceed [ık'siːd] **VT** *(limits etc)* excéder, dépasser; *(hopes, fears, ambitions)* dépasser; *(other products)* surpasser (**in** en); **not exceeding ten pounds** ne dépassant pas dix livres; **not exceeding 250 g** *(parcels etc)* jusqu'à 250 g; **do not expose to temperatures exceeding 50°C** ne pas exposer à des températures excédant 50°C; **to e. one's instructions** aller au-delà des instructions reçues; **to e. one's rights/one's powers** outrepasser ses droits/sa compétence; *Aut* **to e. the speed limit** dépasser *ou* excéder la limitation de vitesse; **he was fined for exceeding the speed limit** il a eu une contravention pour excès de vitesse; **the outcome exceeded all our hopes** le résultat a dépassé toutes nos espérances; **demand exceeded supply** la demande a excédé l'offre

exceedingly [ık'siːdıŋlı] **ADV** extrêmement

excel [ık'sel] (**-ll-**) **VI** exceller (**at doing sth** à faire qch); **to e. at a game** exceller à un jeu; **at school, she excelled in chemistry** à l'école, elle excellait en chimie
VT *(person)* surpasser; **to e. oneself** se surpasser; *Iron* **he's excelled himself this time** il s'est surpassé cette fois-ci

excellence ['eksələns] **N** qualité *f*, supériorité *f*, excellence *f*, **students are expected to strive for e.** on demande aux étudiants de s'efforcer à atteindre l'excellence; **centre of e.** centre *m* d'excellence

excellency ['eksələnsı] **N** *(title)* **Your E.** Votre Excellence *f*, **his E. the French Ambassador** Son Excellence l'ambassadeur de France

excellent ['eksələnt] **ADJ** excellent, parfait

excellently ['eksələntlı] **ADV** admirablement; **she had done e. in her exams** elle avait excellé à ses examens, elle avait obtenu d'excellents résultats à ses examens

except¹ [ık'sept] **PREP** sauf, excepté, à l'exception de; **nobody e. him** personne excepté *ou* sauf lui; **all e. the doctor** tous, à l'exception du docteur, tous, sauf le docteur; **nobody heard it e. (for) me** personne ne l'a entendu sauf moi; **e. by agreement between the parties** sauf accord entre les parties; **they could do nothing e. pray** ils ne pouvaient rien faire d'autre que prier; **e.**

when sauf quand; **e. for** à part, si ce n'est; **e. for getting a few scratches, she came out of it uninjured** à part quelques égratignures, elle s'en est tirée indemne; **we would have lost e. for you** sans toi nous aurions perdu; **the dress is ready e. for the buttons** la robe est prête, à l'exception des boutons; **you cannot obtain such permission e. by paying a bribe to local officials** on ne peut obtenir une telle permission qu'en soudoyant les autorités locales

CONJ **e. (that)** excepté que, si ce n'est que; **he came out of it unscathed, e. that he lost his hat** il en est sorti indemne, si ce n'est qu'il a perdu son chapeau; **I would go, e. I'm busy** j'irais bien, mais je suis occupé

except ² VT excepter, exclure (**from** de); **present company excepted** les présents exceptés

excepting [ɪk'septɪŋ] PREP à l'exception de, sauf; **not e. my wife** sans excepter ma femme

exception [ɪk'sepʃən] N **1** exception f; **to make an e. (of sth/for sb)** faire une exception (pour qch/qn); *Prov* **the e. proves the rule** l'exception confirme la règle; **without e.** sans (aucune) exception; **with the e. of ...** à l'exception de ..., exception faite de ...; **with a few exceptions** sauf de rares exceptions, à quelques exceptions près; **with certain exceptions** sauf exceptions **2 to take e. to sth** *(object)* trouver à redire à qch; *(take offence)* se formaliser *ou* s'offenser de qch; **to take e. to sb's doing sth** trouver mauvais que qn fasse qch; **I take great e. to that remark** je trouve cette remarque très offensante

exceptionable [ɪk'sepʃənəb(ə)l] ADJ *Fml (usu with negative)* critiquable; *(offensive)* offensant; **nothing e.** rien de critiquable/ d'offensant; **to find nothing e. in sth** ne rien trouver à redire à qch; *(offensive)* ne rien trouver d'offensant à qch

exceptional [ɪk'sepʃən(ə)l] ADJ *(unusual, outstanding)* exceptionnel
  ▸▸ *Acct* **e. item** poste *m* extraordinaire

exceptionally [ɪk'sepʃən(ə)lɪ] ADV *(unusually)* exceptionnellement, extraordinairement; **e. cheap** d'un prix exceptionnellement bas; **an e. fine day** un jour exceptionnellement beau; **e., no bail was granted** à titre exceptionnel, il n'a pas été accordé de remise en liberté sous caution; **e. gifted child** enfant remarquablement doué; **an e. well-made film** un film d'une qualité exceptionnelle

excerpt ['eksɜːpt] N *Liter, Mus* extrait *m* (**from** de)

excess [ɪk'ses] N **1** *(of light, enthusiasm etc)* excès *m*; **to eat/drink to e.** manger/boire à l'excès; **indulgence carried to e.** indulgence poussée trop loin; **to commit excesses** commettre des excès; *(cruel acts)* commettre des cruautés; **to be given to e.** avoir le goût des excès; **to indulge in e.** tomber dans l'excès **2** *(quantity, sum etc)* excédent *m*; **to pay the e. (on one's ticket)** prendre un supplément; **sum in e.** somme *f* en surplus; **sum in e. of 50** somme au-dessus de 50; **there has been an e. of expenditure over revenue** les dépenses ont excédé les recettes **3** *Br Fin (in insurance)* franchise *f*
  ▸▸ **e. baggage** *(on plane)* excédent de bagages; *Br* **e. fare** supplément *m* de prix; **e. luggage** *(on plane)* excédent de bagages; **e. profit** surprofit *m*; **e. supply** suroffre *f*; **e. weight** excédent de poids

excessive [ɪk'sesɪv] ADJ *(heat, fine, expenses, amount)* excessif; *(zeal, desire)* immodéré; *(virtue)* outré, exagéré; *(ambition)* démesuré; **to be an e. drinker/smoker** boire/fumer à l'excès

excessively [ɪk'sesɪvlɪ] ADV *(expensive, hot)* excessivement; *(clever, stupid, polite)* extrêmement, particulièrement; *(to eat, drink)* à l'excès; **it was hot/damaged, but not e. so** il faisait chaud/il était endommagé, mais pas trop; **to be e. generous** être (par) trop généreux; **he's not e. intelligent** il n'est pas particulièrement intelligent

exchange ¹ [ɪks'tʃeɪndʒ] N **1** *(of prisoners, blows etc)* échange *m*; **e. of views** échange de vues; **we had an angry** *or* **heated e.** nous avons eu des mots; **in e. (for sth)** en échange (de qch); **car taken in part e.** reprise *f*; *Admin* **e. of posts** *(of two officials, civil servants)* permutation *f*, **2** *Fin (of currency)* change *m*; **foreign e.** change; **dollar e.** change du dollar *ou* en dollars; *Am* **exchanges** *(bills)* lettres *fpl* de change, traites *fpl*; **(foreign) e. broker** cambiste *mf*; **(foreign) e. office** bureau *m* de change; **(foreign) e. reserves** réserves *fpl* en devises (étrangères); **at the current rate of e.** au cours du jour, au taux du change du jour **3** *Fin* **(Stock) E.** Bourse *f* (des valeurs); **commodities e.** bourse de commerce; **corn e.** bourse des céréales; *Am Mil* **post e.** économat *m* de l'armée **4 (telephone) e.** central *m* téléphonique; **local e. area** = réseau *m* urbain
  ▸▸ **e. bank** = banque *f* s'occupant d'opérations de change; *Br Fin* **e. control** contrôle *m* des changes; *Fin* **e. dealer** cambiste *mf*, agent *m* de change, courtier, -ière de change; *Fin* **e. gain** gain *m* de change; *Fin* **e. index** indice *m* boursier; *Fin* **e. loss** perte *f* de change; *Fin* **e. market** marché *m* des changes; **e. office** bureau *m* central (téléphonique); *Fin* **e. premium** prime *f* de change; *Fin* **e. rate** taux *m* de change, cours *m* de change; *Fin Formerly* **E. Rate Mechanism** mécanisme *m* (des taux) de change (du SME); **e. rate parity** parité *f* du change; **e. rate stability** stabilité *f* des changes; *Nucl* **e. reaction** réaction *f* d'échange; *Fin* **e. restrictions** contrôle des changes; *Sch, Univ* **e. student** = étudiant qui participe à un échange; *Fin* **e. transaction** opération *f* de change; *Med* **e. transfusion** transfusion *f* d'échange; *Fin* **e. value** contre-valeur *f*, *pl* contrevaleurs, valeur *f* d'échange; *Sch* **e. visit** échange *m*

exchange ² VT *(blows, words, prisoners)* échanger; *(foodstuffs etc)* troquer; **to e. sth for sth** échanger/troquer qch pour *ou* contre qch, faire un échange de qch pour *ou* contre qch; **records exchanged for money** *(sign)* rachat de disques; **to e. glances** échanger un regard/des regards; **to e. views** échanger ses vues; *Admin* **to e. posts with sb** permuter avec qn

exchangeable [ɪks'tʃeɪndʒəb(ə)l] ADJ échangeable (**for** pour, contre); **a voucher which is e. for goods** un bon qui peut être échangé contre des marchandises

exchequer [eks'tʃekər] N *Br Admin* **the E.** *(money)* le Trésor public; *(government department)* ≃ le Ministère des Finances; **the Chancellor of the E.** le Chancelier de l'Exchiquier, ≃ le Ministre des Finances
  ▸▸ *Fin* **e. bill** bon *m* du Trésor

excise ¹ ['eksaɪz] N *Admin (tax)* contributions *fpl* indirectes, *Belg* accise *f*, *(department)* service *m* des contributions indirectes, régie *f*, *Br* **Customs and E.** la Régie
  ▸▸ **e. documents** documents *mpl* administratifs de régie; **e. duties** droits *mpl* de régie; **e. officer** receveur *m* des douanes

excise ² [ɪk'saɪz] VT *Surg (tumour etc)* exciser; *Fig (passage)* couper (**from a book** d'un livre)

exciseman, *pl* **excisemen** ['eksaɪzmən] N *Br Hist* employé *m* de l'excise *ou* de la régie

excision [ɪk'sɪʒən] N excision *f*, coupure *f*; *Surg* excision, abscission *f*, ablation *f*

excitable [ɪk'saɪtəb(ə)l] ADJ **1** *(person, temperament)* émotif; **young children tend to be easily e.** les jeunes enfants ont tendance à être facilement surexcités; **they are an easily e. people** c'est un peuple exubérant; **be careful with him, he's rather easily e.** fais attention avec lui, il est assez excitable **2** *Elec, Physiol* excitable

excite [ɪk'saɪt] VT **1** *(get worked up)* agiter, énerver, surexciter; **don't e. him** ne l'énerve pas; **easily excited** surexcitable **2** *(arouse enthusiasm in)* enthousiasmer, *Fam* emballer; **the idea/prospect clearly excited them** il était évident que l'idée/la perspective les animait *ou* enthousiasmait; **it really excites me** ça m'emballe vraiment; **what excites you in life?** qu'est-ce qui vous passionne dans la vie? **3** *(stimulate)* exciter, animer; *(feeling, passion)* stimuler; *(sexually)* exciter; *Physiol (nerve)* exciter, stimuler **4** *(give rise to)* provoquer, exciter, soulever; *(feeling, admiration, fear)* inspirer, provoquer; *(interest)* susciter; *(sb's curiosity)* piquer **5** *Elec (dynamo, relay etc)* exciter, amorcer

excited [ɪk'saɪtɪd] ADJ **1** *(worked up)* énervé, surexcité, agité; *(impatient)* impatient; *(upset)* troublé; **e. children** enfants surexcités; **e. crowd** foule surexcitée *ou* en émoi; *(impatient)* foule impatiente; **to get e.** s'exciter; *(to get angry)* s'énerver; **don't get e.!** ne vous énervez pas!, du calme!; **he gets e. over nothing** il s'emballe pour un rien; **it's nothing to get e. about** il n'y a pas de quoi en faire toute une histoire
  2 *(enthusiastic)* animé, enthousiaste; **she was very e. about her trip to Canada** elle était très excitée *ou* animée à l'idée de son voyage au Canada; **the medical world is very e.** *(by discovery etc)* le monde médical est très enthousiaste; **doctors are e. by this discovery** les médecins sont enthousiasmés par cette découverte; **she was not in the least bit e.** at the thought of his visit/about going to university elle n'était pas du tout enthousiaste *ou Fam* emballée à l'idée de sa visite/à l'idée d'aller à l'université; **I can't get e. about it** ça ne me dit vraiment rien; **I don't understand what everyone's getting so e. about** je ne comprends pas ce qu'ils ont tous à s'exciter *ou Fam* s'emballer comme ça; **he was e. at the prospect of earning all this money** la perspective de gagner tout cet argent l'enthousiasmait *ou Fam* l'emballait
  3 *Elec, Physiol* excité; **e. state** *Nucl Phys* état *m* excité *ou* d'excitation; *Elec* état d'amorçage

excitedly [ɪk'saɪtɪdlɪ] ADV *(to speak, laugh)* avec animation; *(to wait)* avec une impatience fébrile; **she was jumping up and down e.** elle sautait dans tous les sens, très animée; **she was watching the road e., waiting for the car to appear** elle regardait la route anxieusement, guettant la voiture; **he was waving his arms e.** il agitait les bras frénétiquement

excitement [ɪk'saɪtmənt] N **1** *(agitation)* agitation *f*; **he mustn't have too much e.** il ne faut pas qu'il s'agite; **to avoid e.** éviter les sensations fortes; **to be in a state of e.** *(of person)* être surexcité
  2 *(enthusiasm, excited state)* animation *f*, enthousiasme *m*; **the thirst for e.** la soif des sensations fortes; **the e. of departure** l'émoi *m* du départ; **to cause great e.** faire (grande) sensation; **there is some e. in the city** il y a un certain émoi dans la ville; **a sense** *or* **feeling of e.** un sentiment d'exaltation; **there was an air of e. surrounding the event** l'événement baignait dans une atmosphère exaltée; **in the e. of the moment** dans l'exci-

tation du moment; **we had a bit of e. at the office this morning** il y a eu de l'animation au bureau ce matin; **I wouldn't want to miss the e.** je ne veux pas rater ça; **it put the e. back into life for him** ça a remis du sel dans sa vie; **all the e. has gone out of my life** ma vie a perdu tout son piquant

3 *Physiol (of organ)* surexcitation *f*

exciting [ɪkˈsaɪtɪŋ] ADJ *(film, story, person etc)* passionnant; *(idea, prospect, proposal)* enthousiasmant; *(situation, scene)* sensationnel; *(full of suspense)* plein de suspense; **e. developments in medical research** développements passionnants dans la recherche médicale; **it was e. for him to be involved in such a project** c'était exaltant *ou* excitant pour lui de faire partie d'un tel projet; *Sport* **an e. finish** une arrivée palpitante; **an e. game** une partie mouvementée

▸▸ *Elec* **e. coil** bobine *f* inductrice; *Elec* **e. dynamo** dynamo *f* d'excitation

excitingly [ɪkˈsaɪtɪŋlɪ] ADV d'une manière sensationnelle; *(to dress)* avec originalité; **e. different** d'une originalité enthousiasmante *ou* électrisante; **the most e. dangerous thing she has ever done** la chose la plus dangereuse et la plus excitante qu'elle ait jamais faite; **the match finished as e. as it had started** le match s'est terminé de façon aussi palpitante qu'il avait commencé; **e., nobody knew exactly what might happen** ce qui était excitant *ou* exaltant, c'est que personne ne savait ce qui allait se passer

exclaim [ɪksˈkleɪm] VI s'écrier, s'exclamer; **to e. in anger/surprise/delight** pousser une exclamation de colère/surprise/ravissement

VT **'leave me alone!',** he exclaimed 'laissez-moi!', s'est-il écrié

exclamation [ekskləˈmeɪʃən] N exclamation *f*

▸▸ *Br* **e. mark,** *Am* **e. point** point *m* d'exclamation

exclamatory [eksˈklæmət(ə)rɪ] ADJ exclamatif

exclude [ɪksˈkluːd] VT exclure (**from** de); *(draught)* empêcher d'entrer; *(doubt, suspicion)* écarter; **to e. sb from a society** *(expel)* exclure qn d'une société; *(not allow to join)* refuser à qn l'entrée d'une société; **the figures e. deaths from other causes** ces chiffres ne tiennent pas compte des morts provoquées par d'autres causes; **to e. sb from voting/working** dénier le droit de vote/de travailler à qn; **excluding ...** à l'exclusion de ...; **this excludes all possibility of doubt** le doute n'est plus permis

exclusion [ɪksˈkluːʒən] N **1** exclusion *f* (**from** de); **to the e. of ...** à l'exclusion de ... **2** *(refusal to allow to join)* refus *m* d'admission (**from** à); **the e. of blacks from certain jobs** l'exclusion des noirs de certains postes; **the e. of women from voting** la dénégation du droit de vote aux femmes

▸▸ **e. order** ordre *m* d'exclusion

exclusive [ɪksˈkluːsɪv] ADJ **1** *(right etc)* exclusif; **to have e. rights in a production** avoir l'exclusivité d'une production; **you don't have an e. right to use this park!** vous n'avez pas l'exclusivité de ce parc! **2** *(only)* seul, unique; **it has been his e. occupation for ten years** cela a été son occupation unique pendant dix ans **3** *(expensive, upper-class)* huppé; *(club, social circle etc)* très fermé; *(boutique)* de luxe; *(clothing, jewellery)* de grande marque **4** *(in logic)* exclusif; **two qualities that are mutually e.** deux qualités qui s'excluent **5** *(with numbers, dates etc)* exclusivement; **chapters one to twenty e.** chapitres un à vingt exclusivement **6** *(not including extras)* sans compter les extras; **rent £10,000 a year e.** loyer 10 000 livres

par an, contributions et charges non comprises **7** *(not including)* **e. of** non compris; **e. of wrappings** sans compter l'emballage, emballage non compris; **price of dinner e. of wine** prix du dîner, vin non compris; **all prices are e. of postage and packing** les prix indiqués ne tiennent pas compte des frais d'envoi et d'emballage; **e. of tax** hors taxe, HT

N *Journ* article *m* en exclusivité; *(interview)* interview *f* exclusive; **aTimes e.** une exclusivité du Times

▸▸ *Com* **e. distribution** distribution *f* exclusive; *Journ* **e. interview** interview exclusive

exclusively [ɪksˈkluːsɪvlɪ] ADV exclusivement; **to be published e. in the Sunday Express** paraître en exclusivité dans le Sunday Express; **brought to you e. on ITV** diffusé en exclusivité sur ITV

exclusivity [eksklu:ˈsɪvɪtɪ] N **1** *(of restaurant, area)* caractère *m* huppé; *(of club, social circle)* caractère fermé **2** *Com (of dealership etc)* exclusivité *f*

▸▸ *Com* **e. arrangement** accord *m* d'exclusivité; *Com* **e. clause** clause *f* d'exclusivité

excommunicate[1] [ekskəˈmju:nɪkeɪt] VT excommunier

excommunicate[2] [ekskəˈmju:nɪkət] ADJ, N excommunié, -ée

excommunication [ekskəmju:nɪˈkeɪʃən] N excommunication *f*

ex-con N *Sl* ancien taulard *m*

excrement [ˈekskrɪmənt] N excrément *m*

excrescence [eksˈkresəns] N excroissance *f*

excrescent [eksˈkresənt] ADJ *Fml* **1** *(outward-growing)* qui forme une excroissance **2** *(superfluous)* superflu, redondant

excreta [eksˈkri:tə] NPL excrétions *fpl*

excrete [ɪksˈkri:t] VT excréter; *(of plant)* sécréter

excretion [ɪksˈkri:ʃən] N excrétion *f*, *(of plant)* sécrétion *f*

excruciating [ɪksˈkru:ʃɪeɪtɪŋ] ADJ *(pain)* atroce, horrible; *Fam (music, TV programme)* atroce; **she was in e. pain** elle souffrait atrocement *ou* horriblement

excruciatingly [ɪksˈkru:ʃɪeɪtɪŋlɪ] ADV atrocement; *Fam* **e. boring** à en mourir d'ennui; **e. embarrassing/shy** horriblement embarrassant/timide; *Fam* **e. funny** *(story)* tordant; **e. painful** atrocement douloureux

exculpate [ˈekskʌlpeɪt] VT *Fml* disculper, exonérer (**from** de)

exculpation [ekskʌlˈpeɪʃən] N *Fml* disculpation *f*, exonération *f* (**from** de)

excursion [ɪksˈkɜ:ʃən] N **1** *(journey)* excursion *f*, *Aut, Cycling etc* randonnée *f*, **to make** *or* **go on an e.** faire une excursion; **a shopping e.** un tour dans les magasins **2** *(digression) (in speech)* digression *f*, **after a brief e. into sculpture, she returned to painting** après une brève incursion dans la sculpture, elle est retournée à la peinture

▸▸ *Br Rail Formerly* **e. ticket** billet *m* circulaire *(bénéficiant de tarifs réduits)*

excursionist [ɪksˈkɜ:ʃənɪst] N excursionniste *mf*

excusable [ɪksˈkju:zəb(ə)l] ADJ *(error etc)* excusable, pardonnable

excusably [ɪksˈkju:zəblɪ] ADV de manière excusable; **she was e. reluctant to help** on pouvait l'excuser de ne pas vouloir aider

excuse[1] [ɪksˈkju:s] N **1** *(justification)* excuse *f*, there is no e. for his behaviour sa conduite est inexcusable; **there was no e. for doing that** il n'y avait aucun prétexte à faire cela; **ignorance of the law is no e.** nul n'est censé ignorer la loi; **that's no e.!** ce n'est pas une excuse!

2 *(pretext)* excuse *f*, prétexte *m*; **poor** *or*

feeble **e.** faible excuse; **I'm not interested in excuses** tes excuses ne m'intéressent pas; **their e. was that they'd forgotten** leur prétexte était qu'ils avaient oublié; **to make excuses** s'excuser; **I make no excuses for these views** je ne ressens pas le besoin de justifier ces opinions; **stop making excuses for him** arrête de lui trouver des excuses; **to look for an e.** chercher des excuses; *(in order not to do sth)* chercher un faux-fuyant *ou* une échappatoire; **to look for an e. to celebrate** chercher un prétexte pour faire la fête; **to find an e. for sth** trouver une excuse à qch; **any e. to get out of the house!** tout prétexte est bon pour sortir de la maison!; **he's just using his broken leg as an e. to ...** il se sert du fait qu'il a une jambe cassée comme excuse pour ...

3 *(example)* **a poor e. for a letter** un semblant de lettre; **a poor e. for a car** un vieux tacot délabré

excuse[2] [ɪksˈkju:z] VT **1** *(forgive)* excuser, pardonner; **to e. sb's laziness, to e. sb's being lazy** excuser la paresse de qn; **e. my being late** excusez-moi d'être en retard; **e. me yawning** je vous demande pardon si je bâille; **to e. sb's absence** excuser l'absence de qn; **he may be excused for laughing** il est excusable d'avoir ri; **you could be excused for thinking it was spring** on aurait pu facilement penser que c'était le printemps; **if you will e. the expression** si vous voulez me pardonner l'expression; **if you will e. me, I have to finish my work** si vous voulez bien m'excuser, il faut que je finisse mon travail; **e. me!** *(let me past, sorry)* pardon!, excusez-moi!; **e. me?** *(what did you say?)* pardon?; **e. me, it was yesterday that ...** *(expressing contradiction)* pardon, c'était hier que ...

2 *(exempt)* exempter, dispenser (**from doing sth** de faire qch); **to e. sb from attendance** excuser qn; **may I be excused?** *(leave the table)* puis-je sortir de table?; *Sch* est-ce que je peux sortir?; *Mil, Naut* **to be excused a fatigue** être exempté d'une corvée

3 *(justify)* excuser; **his youth excuses him** sa jeunesse l'excuse *ou* peut lui servir d'excuse

4 **to e. oneself** *(give excuse)* s'excuser; **I excused myself** *(apologized for leaving)* je me suis excusé de devoir partir

excuse-me N = danse *f* où on change de partenaire lorsque quelqu'un s'approche en disant 'excusez-moi'

ex-directory ADJ *Br Tel* **they** *or* **their number must be e.** ils doivent être sur la liste rouge; **to go e.** *(of subscriber)* se faire inscrire sur la liste rouge

▸▸ **e. number** numéro *m* ne figurant pas dans l'annuaire, numéro se trouvant sur la liste rouge

ex dividend ADV coupon échu

execrable [ˈeksɪkrəb(ə)l] ADJ exécrable, abominable

execrably [ˈeksɪkrəblɪ] ADV exécrablement, abominablement

execrate [ˈeksɪkreɪt] VT *Fml* **1** *(abhor)* exécrer **2** *(curse)* maudire

execration [eksɪˈkreɪʃən] N *Fml* **1** *(abhorrence)* exécration *f* (**of** de); **to hold sb/sth in e.** avoir qn/qch en exécration **2** *(curse)* malédiction *f*

executable file [ˈeksɪkju:təb(ə)l] N *Comput* fichier *m* exécutable

execute [ˈeksɪkju:t] VT **1** *(carry out)* *(task, order)* exécuter; *(plan)* mettre à exécution; *(operation)* accomplir; *Fin (transfer)* effectuer; *Law (will)* exécuter; *(deed)* souscrire, signer; *Mus (piece)* exécuter, jouer; *Admin* **executed on ...** fait le ... **2** *(put to death)* exécuter **3** *Comput* exécuter

▶▶*Comput* e. **cycle** cycle *m* d'exécution; *Comput* e. **file** fichier *m* exécutable

execution [eksɪˈkjuːʃən] N **1** *(of project, order)* exécution *f*; *(of purpose, goal etc)* accomplissement *m*; *Law (of deed)* souscription *f*; *(of will)* exécution *m*; *Mus (of piece of music)* exécution *f*; *(of musician)* jeu *m*; **to put** *or* **carry a plan into e.** mettre un projet à exécution; **in the e. of one's duty** dans l'exercice de ses fonctions; *St Exch* e. **at market** exécution *f* au prix du marché **2** *Law (seizure of property)* saisie-exécution *f*, *pl* saisies-exécutions **3** *(killing) (of criminal)* exécution *f*; e. **by firing squad** exécution par un peloton d'exécution **4** *Comput* exécution *f*

executioner [eksɪˈkjuːʃənər] N bourreau *m*

executive [ɪgˈzekjʊtɪv] ADJ **1** *(in business) (post etc)* de cadre; *(in politics) (power)* exécutif; *Pol* **chief e. officer** président-directeur *m* général **2** *(luxury)* de luxe
▸ N **1** *(in business)* cadre *m*; **executives** encadrement *m*, cadres *mpl*; ; **sales e.** directeur *m* commercial **2** *(of government)* (pouvoir *m*) exécutif *m* **3** *(of political party, union)* bureau *m*, comité *m* central; **the union's national e.** le bureau national du syndicat
▶▶*Am Pol* e. **agreement** accord *m* en forme simplifiée *(qui ne nécessite pas l'approbation du Sénat)*; *Com* e. **board** directoire *m*; e. **briefcase** attaché-case *m*, *pl* attachés-cases; e. **chef** cuisinier *m* en chef, maître-coq *m*, *pl* maîtres-coqs; *Aviat* e. **class** classe *f* affaires; e. **committee** comité *m* de direction; e. **decision** décision *f* prise par un cadre; *Fig* décision capitale; *Com* e. **director** directeur *m* exécutif; *Mil* e. **duties** service *m* de détail; e. **housekeeper** *(in hotel)* gouvernante *f* générale; e. **jet** jet *m* privé; e. **model** *(of car etc)* modèle *m* de (grand) luxe; *Com* e. **officer** cadre *m* supérieur; *Cin* e. **producer** producteur *m* délégué; e. **recruitment agency** association *f* pour l'emploi des cadres, APEC *f*; *Com* e. **secretary** secrétaire *mf* de direction; *Am Pol* e. **session** *(of Senate)* séance *f* à huis clos; e. **suite** *(in hotel)* suite *f* de luxe; *(in company)* bureaux *mpl* de la direction; e. **travel** voyages *mpl* d'affaires

executor [ɪgˈzekjʊtər] N *Law* exécuteur *m* testamentaire; **literary e.** exécuteur littéraire

executrix, *pl* **executrices** [ɪgˈzekjʊtrɪks, -trɪsiːz] N *Law* exécutrice *f* testamentaire

exegesis [eksɪˈdʒiːsɪs] N exégèse *f*

exegetical [eksɪˈdʒetɪk(ə)l] ADJ exégétique

exemplary [ɪgˈzemplərɪ] ADJ **1** *(outstanding) (conduct)* exemplaire; *(husband)* modèle **2** *(serving as example) (punishment)* exemplaire
▶▶*Law* e. **damages** dommages-intérêts *mpl* exemplaires *ou* à titre exemplaire

exemplification [ɪgzemplɪfɪˈkeɪʃ(ə)n] N exemplification *f*; **in e. of his remarks** pour exemplifier ses remarques

exemplify [ɪgˈzemplɪfaɪ] VT **1** *(show by example)* exemplifier, illustrer **2** *(serve as example of) (rule)* servir d'exemple à; *(problem)* être un exemple de

exempt [ɪgˈzempt] ADJ exempt, dispensé, exempté (**from** de); *(from tax)* exempt, franc, *f* franche; **he was declared e. from any blame** il a été délivré de toute responsabilité; *Mil* **to be e. from fatigues** être dispensé *ou* exempté des corvées
▸ VT exempter, dispenser (**from** de); **to e. sb from doing sth** exempter *ou* dispenser qn de faire qch; *Mil* **exempted from military service** exempté *ou* dispensé du service militaire; **to e. books from VAT** exempter les livres de TVA; **to e. sb from responsibility for sth** délivrer qn de la responsabilité de qch

exemption [ɪgˈzem(p)ʃən] N *(from tax, military service)* exemption *f*, dispense *f*; e. **from customs duty** franchise *f* douanière; e. **from liability** exonération *f* de responsabilité; e. **from VAT** exonération *f* de TVA
▶▶*Law* e. **clause** clause *f* de non-responsabilité

exercise [ˈeksəsaɪz] N **1** *(physical)* exercice *m*; **outdoor e.** exercice au grand air; **to take e.** prendre de l'exercice; **I don't get much e.** je ne fais pas beaucoup d'exercice; *Gym* **physical exercises** exercices physiques; **breathing exercises** gymnastique *f* respiratoire, exercices respiratoires **2** *(mental, educational)* exercice *m*; **school/grammar e.** exercice scolaire/de grammaire; **piano exercises** exercices pour piano **3** *Mil, Naut* exercice *m*; **tactical exercises** évolutions *fpl* tactiques; **to be on e.** être à l'exercice **4** *(activity)* **religious exercises** pratiques *fpl* religieuses; **it was an interesting e.** c'était une expérience intéressante; **sending an ambassador would be a pointless e.** envoyer un ambassadeur ne servirait à rien; **it was just an e. in public relations** ce n'était que pour les apparences *ou* pour l'effet d'annonce **5** *(use, practice) (of faculty, duty)* exercice *m*; *(of profession, religion)* pratique *f*; **in the e. of one's duties/rights** dans l'exercice de ses fonctions/droits; *St Exch* e. **of an option** levée *f* d'une prime
▸ VT **1** *(train etc) (body, mind)* exercer; *(troops)* faire faire l'exercice à; **to e. a horse** exercer un cheval; *(take for a walk)* promener un cheval **2** *(practise) (right)* exercer, user de; *(profession)* exercer, pratiquer; **to e. one's influence in sb's favour** user de son influence en faveur de qn; **to e. one's will/authority** faire acte de volonté/d'autorité; **we must e. caution/restraint** nous devons user de prudence/de retenue; *Fin* **to e. an option** lever une prime, exercer une option **3** *Fml (bother) (person)* tracasser; *Old-fashioned (sb's patience)* mettre à l'épreuve
▸ VI prendre de l'exercice; *(train)* s'entraîner
▶▶e. **bike** vélo *m* d'appartement; e. **book** *(for writing in)* cahier *m* d'exercices; *(containing exercises)* livre *m* d'exercices; e. **class** cours *m* de gymnastique; *St Exch* e. **date** date *f* d'échéance; *St Exch* e. **notice** avis *m* de levée; *St Exch* e. **price** *(of share)* prix *m* d'exercice, cours *m* de base; e. **yard** *(in prison)* cour *f*, préau *m*

exerciseable [ˈeksəsaɪzɪb(ə)l] ADJ *St Exch* exerçable

exert [ɪgˈzɜːt] VT **1** *(use) (force)* employer, faire usage de; *(influence, pressure, authority)* exercer **2** **to e. oneself** se remuer, se donner du mal; **to e. oneself to do sth** faire des efforts pour faire qch; *Iron* **don't e. yourself!** ne te donne pas trop de mal, surtout!

exertion [ɪgˈzɜːʃən] N **1** *(of force)* usage *m*, emploi *m*; **he was accused of undue e. of influence** il a été accusé d'exercer une influence abusive **2** *(effort)* effort *m*

exeunt [ˈeksɪənt] VI *Theat* e. **Romeo and Juliet** Roméo et Juliette sortent

exfoliant [eksˈfəʊlɪənt] N exfoliant *m*

exfoliate [eksˈfəʊlɪeɪt] VI *Biol, Geol* s'exfolier

exfoliating [eksˈfəʊlɪeɪtɪŋ] ADJ *Biol, Geol* exfoliant
▶▶e. **cream** crème *f* exfoliante

exfoliation [eksfəʊlɪˈeɪʃən] N *Biol, Geol* exfoliation *f*

ex gratia [eksˈgreɪʃɪə] ADJ, ADV *Law, Fml* à titre de faveur, à titre gracieux; **ex gratia payment** paiement *m* à titre gracieux

ex-growth N *Com (decline)* baisse *f*; **to go e.** être en déclin

exhalation [eksəˈleɪʃən] N **1** *(of breath)* ex-

piration *f*; **on e.** lors de l'expiration **2** *(thing exhaled)* effluve *m*, exhalaison *f*

exhale [eksˈheɪl] VT *(air from lungs)* expirer; *(one's last breath, smoke, gas etc)* exhaler
▸ VI expirer

exhaust [ɪgˈzɔːst] N **1** *Aut, Tech* échappement *m*; *(what is ejected)* gaz *m* d'échappement; **2** *(pipe)* (tuyau *m* d')échappement *m*
▸ VT **1** *(tire) (person)* épuiser, éreinter, exténuer; **to e. oneself in useless efforts** se consumer en efforts inutiles; **this/he is exhausting me** cela/il m'épuise **2** *(use up) (reserves, topic of conversation)* épuiser; **to e. sb's patience** venir à bout de la patience de qn
▶▶*Aut* e. **emission** émission *f* de gaz d'échappement; *Aut* e. **fumes** gaz *mpl* d'échappement; *Aut* e. **manifold** collecteur *m* d'échappement; *Br Aut* e. **pipe** pot *m* ou tuyau d'échappement; *Aut* e. **stroke** *(in internal combustion engine)* temps *m* d'échappement

exhausted [ɪgˈzɔːstɪd] ADJ **1** *(person)* épuisé, exténué, éreinté; **I'm e.** je n'en peux plus, je suis épuisé *ou* exténué; **this baby's got me e.** ce bébé m'épuise **2** *(land, resources)* épuisé; **my patience is e.** je suis à bout de patience

exhaustible [ɪgˈzɔːstɪb(ə)l] ADJ limité; **her patience is easily e.** elle est vite à bout de patience

exhausting [ɪgˈzɔːstɪŋ] ADJ *(effort, climate)* épuisant; *(work, person)* épuisant, éreintant

exhaustion [ɪgˈzɔːstʃən] N **1** *(of person, animal)* **(state of) e.** épuisement *m*; **mental e.** extrême fatigue *f* mentale; **to be in a state of complete e.** être complètement à bout de forces; **I was ready to drop with e.** je tombais de fatigue **2** *(of resources, land)* épuisement *m* **3** *Phys (of gas)* aspiration *f*

exhaustive [ɪgˈzɔːstɪv] ADJ *(list)* exhaustif; *(analysis, description)* détaillé, minutieux; *(investigation, enquiry, search)* approfondi; **in e. detail** très en détail; **to make an e. study of a subject** traiter un sujet à fond

exhaustively [ɪgˈzɔːstɪvlɪ] ADV *(detailed, to list)* exhaustivement; *(to describe)* minutieusement; *(to study)* à fond; **this is an e. researched book** ce livre est le résultat de recherches approfondies *ou* très poussées

exhibit [ɪgˈzɪbɪt] N **1** *Art etc* objet *m* exposé; **how many exhibits will there be?** combien d'objets seront exposés?; **we'll need more exhibits** nous aurons besoin d'autres objets à exposer **2** *Law (in criminal proceedings)* pièce *f* à conviction
▸ VT **1** *Art etc (of artist) (paintings etc)* exposer **2** *Law (items of supporting evidence)* exhiber, produire **3** *(show) (object)* exhiber, montrer, faire voir; *(in shop window)* exposer; *(courage, bad grace etc)* faire preuve de; **to e. signs of stress/anxiety** donner des signes de tension/d'anxiété; **parking permits must be clearly exhibited on the windscreen** les permis de stationnement doivent être disposés bien en vue derrière le pare-brise; **he exhibited no remorse** il n'a manifesté aucun remords
▸ VI *(of artist)* exposer

exhibition [eksɪˈbɪʃən] N **1** *(event)* exposition *f*; **Ideal Home Exhibition** ≃ Salon *m* des Arts ménagers; **2** *(display) (of merchandise etc)* exposition *f*, étalage *m*; *(of talent)* manifestation *f*; *(of procedure etc)* démonstration *f*; *Law (of items in evidence)* production *f*; *Fam* **to make an e. of oneself** se donner en spectacle; **it was a disgraceful e.** ce fut un spectacle de mauvais goût; **to give an e. of bad manners/bad temper** faire montre d'impolitesse/de mauvaise humeur; **I've never seen such an e. of bad manners** je n'ai jamais vu une telle impolitesse **3**

Am Sch = séance *f* musicale etc donnée par les élèves et à laquelle sont invités les parents **4** *Br Univ (award)* bourse *f*

▶▶ **e. centre** centre *m* d'expositions; **e. hall** salle *f* ou hall *m* d'exposition; **e. insurance** assurance *f* foire; **e. stand** stand *m* (d'exposition)

> Note that the French word **exhibition** is a false friend and is never a translation for the English word **exhibition**.

exhibitionism [eksɪˈbɪʃənɪz(ə)m] N **1** *(showing off)* désir *m* de se faire remarquer **2** *Psy (exposing oneself)* exhibitionnisme *m*

exhibitionist [eksɪˈbɪʃənɪst] N **1** he's an e. *(shows off)* il aime se faire remarquer **2** *Psy* exhibitionniste *mf*

exhibitor [ɪgˈzɪbɪtər] N **1** *Art (at exhibition)* exposant, -ante **2** *Br Cin* exploitant, -ante

exhilarate [ɪgˈzɪləreɪt] VT *(of mountain air)* vivifier; *(of experience, news etc)* faire exulter; **they had been exhilarated by the thought that ...** ils exultaient à la pensée que ...

exhilarated [ɪgˈzɪləreɪtɪd] ADJ exultant, fou, *f* folle de joie; *(laugh, cry)* d'exultation; **they felt e. by the news** la nouvelle les faisait exulter; **to feel e.** *(physically, after sauna etc)* se sentir grisé

exhilarating [ɪgˈzɪləreɪtɪŋ] ADJ *(air, wind, walk etc)* vivifiant; *(experience, ride)* grisant; *(news)* réjouissant

exhilaration [ɪgzɪləˈreɪʃən] N gaieté *f* de cœur, joie *f* de vivre; **a mood/an atmosphere of e.** une humeur/une atmosphère joyeuse; **the thought filled him with e.** cette pensée le faisait exulter; **this feeling of e.** cette exultation

exhort [ɪgˈzɔːt] VT *(person)* exhorter, encourager (**to do** à faire); **to e. sb to greater efforts** exhorter qn à plus d'efforts

exhortation [ɪgzɔːˈteɪʃən] N exhortation *f* (**to do** à faire)

exhumation [ekshjuːˈmeɪʃən] N exhumation *f*

▶▶ **e. order** permis *m* d'exhumer

exhume [eksˈhjuːm] VT exhumer, déterrer

exigency [ˈeksɪdʒənsɪ] N *Fml* **1** *(necessity)* exigence *f*, nécessité *f* **2** *(situation)* cas *m* pressant, situation *f* urgente **3** exigencies *(requirements)* exigences *fpl*, impératifs *mpl*

exigent [ˈeksɪdʒənt] ADJ *Fml* **1** *(urgent)* urgent, pressant **2** *(demanding)* exigeant

exiguity [eksɪˈgjuːɪtɪ] N *Fml (of accommodation etc)* exiguïté *f*; *(of income etc)* modicité *f*

exiguous [ɪgˈzɪgjʊəs] ADJ *Fml* exigu, -uë, fort petit; *(diet)* maigre; *(income)* modique

exile [ˈeksaɪl] N **1** *(banishment)* exil *m*, bannissement *m*; **to send sb into e.** envoyer qn en exil, bannir qn; **to go into e.** partir en exil *ou* pour l'exil; *(voluntarily)* s'exiler; **he lives in e. in Madrid** il vit en exil à Madrid; **government in e.** gouvernement en exil **2** *also Fig (person)* exilé, -ée
VT exiler (**from** de)

exist [ɪgˈzɪst] VI **1** *(be in existence)* exister; *(of conditions etc)* régner; **fairies don't e.** les fées n'existent pas; **a legend/tradition exists that ...** il y a une légende/tradition selon laquelle ...; **to cease to e.** cesser d'exister; **to continue to e.** subsister; **the Institute exists to carry out research** la raison d'être de l'Institut est d'effectuer des recherches; **these old shops still e. in a few places** ces vieilles boutiques existent encore dans quelques endroits; *Fam* **as far as you're concerned, I don't e., do I?** en ce qui te concerne, c'est comme si je n'existais pas, hein? **2** *(live)* se

maintenir en vie; **I can't e. on that** cela ne me suffit pas pour vivre; **they managed to e. on a handful of rice a day** ils parvenaient à se maintenir en vie avec une poignée de riz par jour

existence [ɪgˈzɪstəns] N **1** *(state of existing)* existence *f*; **the e. of these laws is not enough** l'existence de ces lois ne suffit pas; **to be in e.** exister; **the oldest manuscript in e.** le plus ancien manuscrit existant; **it's the only one still in e.** c'est le seul qui existe encore; **to come into e.** naître; *Lit* **to call sth into e.** créer qch; **to spring into e.** naître soudainement; **to go out of e.** disparaître, cesser d'exister **2** *(life)* existence *f*, vie *f*; **to lead a pleasant e.** mener une existence agréable

existent [ɪgˈzɪstənt] ADJ **1** *(that exists)* existant; **these conditions have been e. since ...** ces conditions existent depuis ... **2** *(current)* actuel

existential [egzɪsˈtenʃəl] ADJ *Phil* existentiel

existentialism [egzɪsˈtenʃəlɪz(ə)m] N *Phil* existentialisme *m*

existentialist [egzɪsˈtenʃəlɪst] ADJ, N *Phil* existentialiste *mf*

existing [ɪgˈzɪstɪŋ] ADJ existant, actuel, -elle; *(equipment)* existant; **in e. circumstances** dans les circonstances actuelles *ou* présentes

▶▶ *Mktg* **e. customer** client *m* actuel; *Mktg* **e. market** marché *m* existant, marché actuel

exit [ˈeksɪt] N **1** *(way out) (from theatre etc)* sortie *f*, issue *f*; *(from highway)* sortie; *(roadway)* bretelle *f* de sortie; **e. only** *(passage etc)* réservé à la sortie **2** *(act of going out)* sortie *f*; **to make a hurried e.** sortir en vitesse; *Theat* **to make one's e.** sortir, quitter la scène; **the audience must have free e. at all times** le public doit pouvoir sortir librement à tout moment; **3** *Comput* sortie *f*
VI (**-t-**) **1** *Theat* faire sa sortie; **e. Macbeth** Macbeth sort **2** *(leave)* sortir **3** *Comput* sortir
VT *Comput (program, session etc)* sortir de

▶▶ **e. barrier** *(in store)* barrière *f* à la sortie; *Fin* **e. charges** frais *mpl* de sortie; **e. door** porte *f* de sortie; *Com* **e. interview** = entretien *m* entre un employeur et son employé lors du départ de ce dernier; *Br* **e. permit** permis *m* de sortie; *Pol* **e. poll** = sondage *m* effectué lorsque les électeurs viennent de voter; *Comput* **e. routine** routine *f* de sortie; **e. sign** panneau *m* indiquant une/la sortie; **e. staircase** escalier *m* de sortie; **e. visa** visa *m* de sortie

exocrine [ˈeksəʊkraɪn] ADJ *Physiol* exocrine
▶▶ **e. gland** glande *f* exocrine

exodus [ˈeksədəs] N **1** *Bible (of the Jews etc)* exode *m*; **(the Book of) E.** l'Exode **2** *Fml, Hum (departure) (of group of people etc)* départ *m*, sortie *f*; **a mass e. towards the beaches** un exode en direction des plages; **there was a general e.** il y eut une sortie générale; *Fin* **e. of capital** évasion *f* ou fuite *f* des capitaux

ex officio [eksəˈfɪʃɪəʊ] *Admin* ADJ *(member)* de droit, à titre d'office
ADV *(to act)* d'office

exonerate [ɪgˈzɒnəreɪt] VT **1** *(absolve)* **to e. sb (from blame)** disculper *ou* justifier qn **2** *(exempt)* exonérer, décharger (**sb from an obligation** qn d'une obligation)

exoneration [ɪgzɒnəˈreɪʃən] N **1** **e. (from blame)** disculpation *f*, justification *f* **2** *(exemption)* exonération *f*, décharge *f* (**from** de)

exorbitance [ɪgˈzɔːbɪt(ə)ns] N *(of prices, demands)* énormité *f*

exorbitant [ɪgˈzɔːbɪt(ə)nt] ADJ exorbitant,

exagéré, excessif; *(interest)* usuraire; **e. price** prix exorbitant

exorbitantly [ɪgˈzɔːbɪt(ə)ntlɪ] ADV *(priced)* d'une manière exorbitante; **e. expensive** excessivement cher, d'un prix exorbitant

exorcism [ˈeksɔːsɪz(ə)m] N *Rel* exorcisme *m*

exorcist [ˈeksɔːsɪst] N *Rel* exorciste *m*

exorcize [ˈeksɔːsaɪz] VT *Rel* exorciser; *(demon, possessed etc)* conjurer; *(spirit, fears)* faire disparaître

exoskeleton [ˈeksəʊskelətən] N *Zool* exosquelette *m*, cuticule *f*

exotic [ɪgˈzɒtɪk] ADJ exotique; **a taste for the e.** le goût de l'exotique; **she is e.-looking** elle a un charme exotique; **an e.-sounding name** un nom aux consonances exotiques
N *Bot* plante *f* exotique

exotica [ɪgˈzɒtɪkə] NPL objets *mpl* exotiques

exotically [ɪgˈzɒtɪklɪ] ADV exotiquement; **e. flavoured/coloured** aux saveurs/couleurs exotiques

exoticism [ɪgˈzɒtɪsɪz(ə)m] N exotisme *m*

expand [ɪksˈpænd] VT *(production, output)* augmenter; *(gas)* dilater; *(boundaries of empire)* étendre; *(idea, algebraic formula, chest)* développer; *(mind, circle of friends, range of products)* élargir; *(wings)* déployer; **it's an idea that could easily be expanded into a novel** c'est une idée qu'on pourrait facilement développer pour en faire un roman; **the police force is to be expanded** les effectifs de la police doivent être augmentés
VI **1** *(of solid, air, gas)* se dilater; *(of balloon)* se gonfler; *(of steam)* se détendre; *(of chest)* se développer; *(of sail etc)* s'étendre, se déployer; *(of company)* s'agrandir; *Tech (of belt)* s'allonger; **they want to e. into plastics** ils veulent se développer en s'introduisant sur le marché des plastiques; **as the Empire expanded** à mesure que l'Empire grandissait *ou* s'étendait **2** *(talk, write at greater length)* préciser sa pensée; **could you e.?** est-ce que vous pourriez préciser ce que vous voulez dire par là?

▶ **expand on, expand upon** VT INSEP *(talk, write at greater length about)* développer; **I'd like to e. on that** j'aimerais développer ce point

expandable [ɪksˈpændɪb(ə)l] ADJ *Comput* extensible; **4MB e. to 64MB** 4 Mo extensible à 64 Mo

expanded [ɪksˈpændɪd] ADJ étendu; *(wings)* déployé;
▶▶ *Comput* **e. keyboard** clavier *m* étendu; *Comput* **e. memory** mémoire *f* paginée *ou* expansée; *Comput* **e. memory specification** spécifications *fpl* de la mémoire paginée; **e. polystyrene** polystyrène *m* expansé

expander [ɪksˈpændər] N **1** *Gym* **(chest) e.** extenseur *m* **2** *Aut (in brake drum)* came *f* de frein

expanding [ɪksˈpændɪŋ] ADJ **1** *(market, sector, field)* en expansion; *(gas)* qui se dilate; *(balloon etc)* qui se gonfle, qui enfle; *(commerce)* qui se développe, qui prend de l'extension; *(demand, production)* croissant; *(interests, circle of friends)* qui s'élargit; **the e. universe** l'univers *m* en expansion **2** *(watch strap, headband)* extensible; *(suitcase)* à soufflets

expanse [eksˈpæns] N *(of country, water etc)* étendue *f*; **a vast e.** *(of water, snow etc)* une vaste étendue; *(of sand)* une mer; **a wide e. of cloudless sky** une immensité de ciel sans nuages

expansion [ɪksˈpænʃən] N **1** *(making larger) (of gas)* dilatation *f*; *(of subject, chest etc)* développement *m* **2** *(becoming larger) (of solid, liquid, commerce etc)* expansion *f*; *(of gas, metal etc)* dilatation *f*; *(of flower, heart)* épanouissement *m*; *Econ* relance *f*, colo-

nial/territorial e. expansion coloniale/territoriale

▸▸**e. bit** foret *m ou* mèche *f* extensible; *Comput* **e. board, e. card** carte *f* d'extension; *Tech* **e. joint** joint *m* de dilatation; *Comput* **e. slot** emplacement *m ou* logement *m* pour carte d'extension; *Constr* **e. tank** réservoir *m* d'expansion

expansionism [ɪks'pænʃənɪz(ə)m] N *Pol* expansionnisme *m*

expansionist [ɪks'pænʃənɪst] *Pol* ADJ, N expansionniste *mf*

expansive [ɪks'pænsɪv] ADJ **1** *(force)* expansif; *(gas)* expansible, dilatable **2** *(person)* expansif; **in an e. mood** en veine d'épanchement; **to welcome sb with an e. gesture** accueillir qn à bras ouverts

> Attention: ne pas confondre avec l'adjectif **expensive**.

expansively [ɪks'pænsɪvlɪ] ADV *(to welcome)* chaleureusement; **to gesture e. towards the skyline/paintings** désigner l'horizon/les tableaux d'un grand geste

expansiveness [ɪks'pænsɪvnɪs] N **1** *(of gas)* expansibilité *f* **2** *(of person)* expansivité *f*, nature *f* expansive

expat [eks'pæt] ADJ, N *Br Fam* expatrié, -ée

expatiate [eks'peɪʃɪeɪt] VI *Fml* discourir (longuement) (**on** sur)

expatriate¹ [eks'pætrɪət] N expatrié, -ée; **an e. Scot** un Écossais expatrié

expatriate² [eks'pætrɪeɪt] VT *(person)* expatrier

expatriation [eks'pætrɪ'eɪʃən] N expatriation *f*

expect [ɪks'pekt] VT **1** *(anticipate)* *(person, letter, phone call etc)* attendre; *(event)* s'attendre à; *(sb's arrival etc)* compter sur; **to e. sb for dinner** attendre qn à dîner; **the delivery isn't expected until Thursday** on n'attend pas la livraison avant jeudi; **I expected as much** je m'y attendais; **I expected more from you** je m'attendais à mieux de ta part; **I knew what to e.** je savais à quoi m'attendre; **to e. the worst** s'attendre au pire; **as one might e., as might be expected** comme on doit s'y attendre, comme de raison; **she played with the brilliance (which) we have come to e. (from her)** elle a joué avec le brio auquel elle nous a maintenant habitués; **to e. that sb will do sth/that sth will happen** s'attendre à ce que qn fasse qch/à ce que qch arrive; **I half expected him to say no** je m'attendais plus ou moins à ce qu'il dise non; **I fully expected him to agree** je comptais bien qu'il soit d'accord; **to e. to do sth** compter *ou* espérer faire qch; **I don't e. them to be pleased** je ne m'attends pas à ce qu'ils soient contents; **the movie was better than I expected (it to be)** le film était meilleur que je ne m'y attendais; **she was angry – well, what did you e.?** elle était en colère – et alors, ça t'étonne?; **some slight initial difficulty is to be expected** il faut s'attendre à rencontrer quelques légères difficultés initiales; **that's only to be e.** ce n'est pas du tout surprenant; **he is not expected to recover** on ne s'attend pas à ce qu'il se rétablisse; **they arrived later than expected** ils sont arrivés plus tard que prévu; **she's expecting a baby** elle attend un bébé

2 *(require)* **to e. sth from sb** exiger qch de qn; **I e. you to be punctual** je vous demande d'arriver à l'heure; **I don't e. you to be perfect** je ne te demande pas d'être parfait; **it is expected that the candidate will be willing to undertake some travel** on attend du candidat qu'il soit disposé à voyager; **how do you e. me to do it?** comment voulez-vous que je le fasse?; **where do they e. them to**

go if there's nowhere else? où veulent-ils qu'ils aillent si c'est le seul endroit?; **is it too much to e. a little courtesy?** est-ce qu'un peu de courtoisie est trop demander?; **it's too much to e. of a child** c'est trop attendre d'un enfant; **I know what is expected of me** je sais ce qu'on attend de moi; **people e. too much from marriage** les gens attendent trop du mariage

3 *(suppose)* **to e. (that)** penser que; **I e. he'll pay** je pense qu'il payera; **I e. so/not** je crois bien que oui/que non

VI *Fam* **she's expecting** elle attend un bébé

expectancy [ɪks'pektənsɪ] N **1** *(expectation)* attente *f*; **an air/atmosphere of e.** un air/une atmosphère d'expectative *f*; **a look of e.** un regard plein d'espoir; **eager e.** vive impatience *f*; **life e.** espérance *f* de vie; *Mktg* **e.-value model** modèle *m* de valeur attendue **2** *Law (of inheritance etc)* expectative *f*

expectant [ɪks'pekt(ə)nt] ADJ **1** *(expecting)* (qui est) dans l'attente (**of sth** de qch); *(crowd, face)* impatient; *(air, hush)* d'expectative; **the e. look on the children's faces** l'expectative qui se lisait sur le visage des enfants **2** *Law (property, heir etc)* en expectative

▸▸**e. mother** future maman *f*

expectantly [ɪks'pekt(ə)ntlɪ] ADV dans l'expectative, dans l'attente; **fans waiting e. at the stage door** des fans qui attendent à la sortie des artistes, pleins d'espoir; **he looked at me e.** il m'a regardé avec l'air d'attendre quelque chose

expectation [ekspek'teɪʃən] N **1** *(thing expected)* attente *f*, espérance *f*; **to come up to/fall short of sb's expectations** remplir *ou* répondre à/tromper l'attente de qn; **it didn't come up to e.** il n'a pas été à la hauteur de ce qu'on attendait; **to succeed beyond one's expectations** réussir au-delà de ses espérances; **contrary to all expectations** contrairement à *ou* contre toute attente; **to have high expectations of sb/sth** attendre beaucoup de qn/qch; **in (the) e. of** dans l'attente de **2** *(anticipation)* **with eager e.** avec une vive impatience; **to live in e.** vivre dans l'expectative **3** *Law* expectative *f* d'héritage; **expectations** espérances *fpl*; **uncle from whom one has expectations** oncle *m* à héritage **4** *(probability) (of event)* probabilité *f*; **there is every/no e. that we shall be seeing them again soon** il y a de grandes chances/peu de chance pour que nous les revoyions bientôt; **e. of life** espérance *f* de vie

expected [ɪks'pektɪd] ADJ attendu; *(hoped for)* espéré

▸▸*Mktg* **e. product** produit *m* attendu; *Mktg* **e. service** service *m* attendu

expectorant [ɪks'pektərənt] ADJ, N *Med* expectorant *m*

expectorate [eks'pektəreɪt] *Med, Fml* VT *(mucus)* expectorer

VI cracher

expectoration [ekspektə'reɪʃən] N *Med, Fml* expectoration *f*

expedience [ɪks'piːdɪəns], **expediency** [ɪks'piːdɪənsɪ] N **1** *(convenience) (of measure etc)* convenance *f*, opportunité *f*; **I questioned the e. of doing ...** j'ai douté qu'il soit opportun de faire ...; **on grounds of e.** pour des raisons de convenance **2** *Pej (opportunism)* opportunisme *m*

expedient [ɪks'piːdɪənt] ADJ **1** *(convenient)* expédient, convenable; **do what you think e.** faites ce que vous jugerez à propos **2** *Pej (opportunist)* opportun

N expédient *m*, moyen *m*

expedite ['ekspɪdaɪt] VT **1** *Fml (hasten) (measure)* activer, pousser, hâter; *(procedure)* accélérer; **I'll do what I can to e. matters** je ferai ce que je pourrai pour accélérer

les choses **2** *Old-fashioned (deal with speedily) (matter)* expédier, dépêcher

expedition [ekspə'dɪʃən] N **1** *(trip)* expédition *f*; **an e. to the North Pole** une expédition au pôle Nord; *Fam* **a shopping e.** une expédition dans les magasins; *Fam* **getting here was quite an e.** ça a été toute une expédition pour arriver jusqu'ici **2** *Old-fashioned, Fml (promptness)* promptitude *f*

expeditionary [ekspə'dɪʃ(ə)nərɪ] ADJ *Mil (unit etc)* expéditionnaire

expeditious [ekspə'dɪʃəs] ADJ *Fml (procedure)* expéditif; *(reply)* prompt

expeditiously [ekspə'dɪʃəslɪ] ADV *Fml* promptement

expel [ɪks'pel] VT (-ll-) *(person)* expulser; *(foreign body, enemy etc)* chasser, expulser; *(liquid, gas)* chasser, refouler; *(breath)* exhaler; *Admin (foreigner)* expulser, refouler; **to e. a pupil (from school)** renvoyer un élève (de l'école)

expend [ɪks'pend] VT *(time, resources)* consacrer, employer; *(money)* employer; *(ammunition)* utiliser; **to e. one's energies on sth** consacrer ses énergies à qch; **all our stocks have been expended** toutes nos réserves sont épuisées

expendable [ɪks'pendəb(ə)l] ADJ **he/it is e.** il n'est pas irremplaçable *ou* indispensable; **the general considered these troops to be e.** le général considérait qu'on pouvait sacrifier ces troupes

expenditure [ɪks'pendɪtʃər] N **1** *(of money, energy etc)* dépense *f* **2** *(of ammunitions)* consommation *f* **2** *(amount)* dépense(s) *f(pl)*; **heavy e.** une forte dépense, de fortes dépenses; **e. on arms** les dépenses pour l'armement

expense [ɪks'pens] N **1** *(cost)* dépense *f*, frais *mpl*, *(of energy)* dépense; *(of funds)* utilisation *f*, *(of fuel, ammunition)* consommation *f*; **regardless of e.** sans regarder à la dépense; **at great/little e.** à grands/peu de frais; **at no extra e.** sans supplément de frais; **at my own e.** à mes propres frais; **book published at the author's e.** livre édité à compte d'auteur; **to go to great e.** faire beaucoup de dépenses; **they didn't want to go to the e. of hiring a car** ils ne voulaient pas faire les frais de louer une voiture; **it's not worth the e.** c'est trop cher pour ce que c'est; **don't go to any e. over ...** ne faites pas de frais pour ...; **they went to considerable e.** ils ont dépensé des sommes considérables; **to put sb to e.** faire faire des dépenses à qn; **no e. was spared to ...** on n'a pas regardé à la dépense pour ...; *Fig* **a joke at my e.** une plaisanterie à mes dépens; **at the e. of the poor/his social life** aux dépens des pauvres/de sa vie sociale

2 *Com* **expenses** frais *mpl*, dépenses *fpl*; **to meet/cover sb's expenses** rembourser/couvrir les frais de qn; **it's on expenses** c'est la société qui paie, ça va sur la note de frais; **to offer sb £100 and expenses** offrir à qn 100 livres, plus les frais; **travelling expenses** frais de déplacement, indemnité *f* de voyage; **living expenses** frais de séjour; **general expenses** frais généraux; **incidental expenses** faux frais; **to incur expenses** faire des dépenses; **to cut down on e.** réduire les frais; **to have all expenses paid** être défrayé de tout; **an all-expenses-paid trip to Paris** un voyage à Paris tous frais payés

3 *(financial burden)* **to be a great e. to sb** être une grande charge pour qn

▸▸**e. account** note *f* de frais; **expenses claim form** note *f* de frais

expensive [ɪks'pensɪv] ADJ *(object)* cher, *f* chère, coûteux; *(shop, restaurant)* cher; *(procedure, habit)* dispendieux; *(pastime, treatment)* onéreux; *(mistake)* qui coûte cher; **he has e. tastes** il a des goûts dispendieux *ou* de luxe; **that butcher's very e.** ce boucher est très cher; **to be** *or* **come e.** revenir cher; **that can be e.** ça peut être cher; **travelling is e.** les voyages coûtent cher

> Attention: ne pas confondre avec l'adjectif **expansive**.

expensively [ɪks'pensɪvlɪ] ADV *(to dress)* coûteusement; *(to eat, decorate)* à grands frais; **to live e.** mener la vie large, vivre dispendieusement; **e. priced** coûteux, cher

expensiveness [ɪks'pensɪvnɪs] N *(of commodity, life etc)* cherté *f*; **the e. of his tastes** ses goûts dispendieux

experience [ɪks'pɪərɪəns] N **1** expérience *f*; **to gain e. of life** faire l'apprentissage de la vie; **practical e.** pratique *f*; **driving e.** expérience de la route; **he still lacks e.** il manque encore de pratique; **she has several years' e.** elle a plusieurs années d'expérience; **have you had any previous e.?** avez-vous déjà travaillé dans ce métier?; **I have enough business e. to …** j'ai assez de pratique des affaires pour …; **a man of e.** un homme d'expérience; **e. shows that …** l'expérience démontre que …; **to know sth from e.** savoir qch par expérience; **to learn from e.** tirer les leçons de l'expérience; **I know from bitter e. that …** je sais, pour l'avoir éprouvé cruellement, que …; **he was clearly speaking from e.** de toute évidence, il parlait en connaissance de cause *ou* il parlait d'expérience; **in my e.** d'après mon expérience; **my e. has been that** *or* **in my e. people appreciate politeness** j'en ai fait l'expérience, les gens apprécient la politesse; **I had no e. of looking after disabled people** je ne m'étais jamais occupé de personnes handicapées; **the black e. in this country** la condition des noirs dans ce pays; **I lost a lot of money, but I'll just have to put it down to e.** j'ai perdu beaucoup d'argent, mais au moins ça me servira de leçon; **well, it's all e.** voilà qui est à mettre au compte de l'expérience

2 *(individual event)* expérience *f*; **to have a nasty e.** faire une mauvaise expérience; **the journey was an e.** le voyage a été enrichissant; *Iron* le voyage a été une drôle d'expérience; **it was his first e. of love** c'était la première fois qu'il tombait amoureux

VT *(emotions, feeling, pain)* ressentir; *(real hunger, poverty, success)* connaître, faire l'expérience de; *(difficulties, problems)* avoir

▸▸ *Mktg* **e. curve** courbe *f* d'expérience; *Mktg* **e.-curve pricing** tarification *f* en fonction de la courbe d'expérience; *Mktg* **e. quality** qualité *f* reconnue après achat

experienced [ɪks'pɪərɪənst] ADJ qui a de l'expérience, expérimenté, chevronné; *(observer)* averti; *(eye)* exercé; **to be e. in sth** avoir l'expérience de qch, s'y connaître en qch; **to be politically e.** avoir de l'expérience en matière de politique; **e. in business** rompu aux affaires; **a more e. doctor** un médecin plus expérimenté; **sexually e.** qui a de l'expérience en matière de sexualité

experiment [ɪks'perɪmənt] N expérience *f*; **to carry out** *or* **do an e.** faire *ou* procéder à une expérience; **as an e., by way of e.** à titre d'essai *ou* d'expérience

VI expérimenter, faire une expérience/des expériences (**on** sur); **an artist should be prepared to e.** un artiste devrait être prêt à toutes les expériences; **to e. with** *(new technique, style)* s'essayer à; *(philosophy, religion)* goûter à; **to e. with drugs** faire l'expérience de la drogue; **to e. with smoking** goûter à la cigarette

experimental [ɪksperɪ'ment(ə)l] ADJ **1** *(subject)* d'expérience; *(physics, evidence, method)* expérimental, -aux; **e. rocket** fusée

expérimentale; **this new reactor is at the e. stage** ce nouveau réacteur est à l'essai *ou* en cours d'expérimentation **2** *(based on experiment)* *(knowledge)* expérimental, -aux, fondé sur l'expérience

▸▸ **e. research** recherche *f* (expérimentale)

experimentally [ɪksperɪ'ment(ə)lɪ] ADV **1** *(as experiment)* à titre d'essai **2** *(to discover sth)* expérimentalement

experimentation [ɪksperɪmen'teɪʃən] N expérimentation *f*

expert ['ekspɜːt] ADJ expert, habile; **to be e. in** *or* **at sth** être expert en qch; **to be e. in** *or* **at doing sth** être habile à faire qch; **an e. opinion** une opinion avisée

N spécialiste *mf*; *(professional, with qualifications)* expert *m*; **I'm no e.** je ne suis pas un expert; *Law* **medical e.** médecin *m* légiste; **according to the experts** selon les experts; **to be an e. at doing sth** être habile à faire qch; **she is an e. in this field** elle est expert en la matière; **the eye of an e.** un œil expert

▸▸ **e. advice** avis *m* autorisé; **e. panel** commission *f* d'experts; **e.'s report** expertise *f*; *Comput* **e. system** système *m* expert; *Law* **e. witness** expert *m inv* (appelé comme témoin)

expertise [ekspɜː'tiːz] N *(technical, financial etc)* connaissances *fpl*; *(as a cook, carpenter etc)* savoir-faire *m inv*; adresse *f*, habileté *f* (**in** à)

expertly ['ekspɜːtlɪ] ADV habilement, de manière experte

expiate ['ekspɪeɪt] VT *(sin)* expier

expiation [ekspɪ'eɪʃən] N expiation *f*; **in e. of his crime** pour expier *ou* en expiation de son crime

expiration [ekspɪ'reɪʃən] N **1** *(expiry)* *(of lease)* cessation *f*, expiration *f*; *(of option)* échéance *f*; *(of term)* fin *f*; *(of insurance policy)* expiration, déchéance *f*; **date of e.** *(of guarantee etc)* date *f* d'expiration **2** *Physiol (of air from lungs)* expiration *f*

expire [ɪks'paɪər] VI **1** *(of law, treaty, deadline etc)* expirer, venir à expiration; **expired policy** *(in insurance)* police déchue; **this passport expires on …** ce passeport expire le …; **expired passport** passeport périmé **2** *Lit (die)* expirer, mourir; *(of hope)* s'évanouir

VT *Physiol (air from lungs)* expirer, exhaler

expiring [ɪks'paɪərɪŋ] ADJ **1** *Law (lease, contract)* qui expire, qui est à son terme **2** *Lit (dying)* expirant, qui se meurt; **with an e. voice** d'une voix mourante

expiry [ɪks'paɪərɪ] N *(of term, contract, deadline)* expiration *f*, fin *f*; *(of period)* terme *m*

▸▸ **e. date** *(of contract, lease, insurance policy)* date *f* d'expiration *ou* d'échéance; *(of visa, passport)* date d'expiration; *(on food labels)* date limite de consommation; *(on ticket, on voucher)* à utiliser avant le, valable jusqu'au; *(on bank card)* valable jusqu'au

explain [ɪks'pleɪn] VT **1** *(make clear)* expliquer; **that explains everything** voilà qui explique tout; **that is easily explained** cela s'explique facilement; **that explains his embarrassment** cela explique son embarras; **she explained to us how the system works** elle nous a expliqué comment le système fonctionne; **I explained that we were tourists** j'ai expliqué que nous étions des touristes **2** *(justify) (one's behaviour etc)* justifier **3** **to e. oneself** *(make oneself understood)* s'expliquer; *(justify oneself)* se justifier; **I don't understand, please e. yourself** je ne comprends pas, veuillez vous expliquer

VI donner des explications; **you'd better e.** allons, expliquez-vous

▸ **explain away** VT SEP donner une explica-

tion satisfaisante de; **how did he manage to e. away the broken vase?** quelle raison a-t-il trouvée pour expliquer que le vase soit cassé?; **he tried to e. away the women's underwear in the car** il a essayé de fournir une raison expliquant la présence de dessous féminins dans la voiture; **e. that away, if you can!** explique donc ça!; **he tried to e. away his absence from the meeting** il a essayé de justifier son absence à la réunion

explainable [ɪks'pleɪnəb(ə)l] ADJ *(behaviour etc)* explicable; **it's easily e.** cela s'explique facilement; **to become e.** s'expliquer

explanation [eksplə'neɪʃən] N explication *f*, éclaircissement *m*; **to give explanations** fournir des explications; **to give an e. of one's behaviour** justifier sa conduite; **one e. is that …** l'une des explications est que …; **the e. is that …** cela s'explique par le fait que …; **I hope you've got a good e. for this!** j'espère que vous avez une explication satisfaisante à me donner à propos de ceci!; **she wasn't able to offer any e. of why it had happened** elle a été incapable d'expliquer pourquoi c'était arrivé

explanatory [ɪks'plænət(ə)rɪ] ADJ explicatif; **e. notes** commentaires *mpl*

expletive [ɪks'pliːtɪv] N **1** *(swearword)* juron *m* **2** *Gram etc* particule *f* explétive, explétif *m*

ADJ *Gram etc* explétif

explicable [eks'plɪkəb(ə)l] ADJ explicable; **to become e.** s'expliquer; **this phenomenon is not e. by sociological factors alone** ce phénomène ne peut s'expliquer par les seuls facteurs sociologiques

explicit [eks'plɪsɪt] ADJ explicite; **to be more e. (in one's statements)** préciser (ses affirmations); **to make sth e.** rendre qch explicite; **e. language** *(vulgar)* langage susceptible d'offenser la pudeur; **e. sex and violence** *(on television etc)* de la violence et du sexe montrés de façon explicite; **sexually e. scenes** scènes au contenu sexuel non voilé

explicitly [eks'plɪsɪtlɪ] ADV explicitement, de manière explicite

explode [ɪks'pləʊd] VT **1** *(detonate etc)* *(shell)* faire éclater; *(mine)* faire sauter; *(gas)* faire exploser **2** *(show to be false)* démontrer la fausseté de; *(theory)* discréditer; *(myth)* détruire **3** *(in diagram)* éclater

VI *(of boiler, shell etc)* éclater; *(of mine)* sauter; *(of gas, dynamite etc)* exploser, détoner; *(of car, plane etc)* exploser; *Fig* **to e. with laughter** éclater de rire; *Fig* **he'll e.** *(with anger)* il va exploser (de colère), il va sortir de ses gonds; *(with repressed feeling)* il va craquer; *(with overeating)* il va éclater; *Fig* **the population exploded after the war** il y a eu une explosion démographique après la guerre

exploded [ɪks'pləʊdɪd] ADJ **1** *(shell)* éclaté; *(mine)* qui a sauté **2** *(theory)* abandonné, reconnu pour faux

▸▸ *Phot, Tech* **e. view** vue *f* éclatée

exploit[1] ['eksplɔɪt] N exploit *m*, haut fait *m*

exploit[2] [eks'plɔɪt] VT **1** *(take unfair advantage of)* exploiter; **immigrant workers are being exploited** les travailleurs immigrés se font exploiter **2** *(use) (mine, forest etc)* exploiter; *(talents)* mettre à profit; *(scandal)* exploiter

exploitation [eksplɔɪ'teɪʃən] N exploitation *f*

exploration [eksplə'reɪʃən] N **1** *(trip)* exploration *f*, voyage *m* d'e.; **Magellan called here on his explorations** au cours de ses explorations, Magellan est passé par ici **2** *(act) (of terrain)* exploration *f*, reconnaissance *f*; **e. work** travaux *mpl* de recherches; **the e. of a possibi-lity** l'étude d'une possibilité **3** *Med (of wound)* exploration *f*

explorative [ɪks'plɒrətɪv] **ADJ** explorateur, -trice

exploratory [ɪks'plɒrət(ə)rɪ] **ADJ** *(well, poll)* d'exploration; *(voyage)* de découverte; *(dialogue)* préliminaire
▸▸ *Med* **e. surgery** opération *f* exploratoire; *Med* **e. test** exploration *f*

explore [ɪks'plɔːr] **VT 1** *(region, town)* explorer; *(continent)* aller à la découverte de; *(country)* faire l'exploration de; *(terrain)* tâter; *(possibility, idea)* étudier; *(theory)* étudier en détail; **to e. sth with one's hands/tongue** explorer qch de ses mains/de la langue; *Com* **to e. the market** prospecter le marché **2** *Med (wound)* explorer, sonder

explorer [ɪks'plɔːrər] **N** *(person)* explorateur, -trice

explosion [ɪks'pləʊʒən] **N** *(of gases, shell etc)* explosion *f*; *(of gas)* déflagration *f*; *(noise)* détonation *f*; *Fig (of anger, joy)* débordement *m*; *(of laughter, artistic creativity, new writing)* explosion; **to cause an e.** provoquer une explosion; *Fig* **population e.** explosion démographique

explosive [ɪks'pləʊsɪv] **ADJ 1** explosif, détonant; **e. mixture** mélange *m* détonant; *Fig* **an e. situation/combination** une situation/combinaison explosive **2** *Ling (consonant)* explosif
N 1 *(material)* explosif *m* **2** *Ling* (consonne *f*) explosive *f*
▸▸ **e. device** dispositif *m* explosif; *Nucl* **e. fission** fission *f* explosive

exponent [ɪks'pəʊnənt] **N 1** *(of system etc)* interprète *mf*; *(of theory, idea, opinion)* avocat, -ate, défenseur *m*; *Mus (of work)* interprète, exécutant, -ante; *(of sport)* protagoniste *mf*; **the leading exponents of this genre** les principaux représentants de ce genre **2** *Math (of quantity)* exposant *m*

exponential [ekspəʊ'nenʃəl] **ADJ** exponentiel
▸▸ *Math* **e. curve** courbe *f* exponentielle

exponentially [ekspəʊ'nenʃəlɪ] **ADV** de manière exponentielle

export[1] ['ekspɔːt] **N 1** *(product)* article *m* d'exportation; **coffee is an important e.** le café est une des exportations principales; **exports** *(of country)* exportations *fpl*; **visible/invisible exports** exportations visibles/invisibles **2** *(trade)* exportation *f*; **the e. of coal** l'exportation de charbon; **for e. only** réservé à l'exportation
▸▸ **e. agent** commissionnaire *m* exportateur; **e. ban** interdiction *f* d'exporter; **e. bid** offre *f* export; **e. company** entreprise *f* exportatrice; **e. credit** crédit *m* à l'exportation; **e. credit guarantee** garantie *f* de crédit à l'exportation; **E. Credit Guarantee Department** COFACE *f*; **e. department** service *m* des exportations, service export; **e. director** directeur *m* export; **e. drive** = campagne *f* visant à stimuler l'exportation; **e. duty** droit *m* de sortie *ou* d'exportation; **e. earnings** revenus *mpl ou* recettes *fpl* de l'exportation; **e. financing** financement *m* des exportations; **e. guarantee** garantie *f* à l'exportation; **e. licence** permis *m* d'exportation; **e. management company** société *f* de portage; **e. manager** directeur *m* export; **e. market** marché *m* à l'export, marché à l'exportation; **e. order** commande *f* export; **e. quota** contingent *m* d'exportation; **e. reject** produit *m* impropre à l'exportation; **e. restrictions** restrictions *fpl* aux exportations; **e. sales** ventes *fpl* export *ou* à l'exportation; **e. sales director** directeur des ventes export; **e. tariff** tarif *m* export; **e. tax** taxe *f* à l'exportation; **e. tourism** tourisme *m* d'exportation;

e. trade commerce *m* d'exportation **a flourishing e. trade** une exportation florissante

export[2] [eks'pɔːt] **VT 1** *(goods)*, *Fig (way of life)* exporter **2** *Comput* exporter
VI exporter; **exporting country** pays *m* exportateur

exportable [eks'pɔːtəb(ə)l] **ADJ** exportable

exportation [ekspɔː'teɪʃən] **N** exportation *f*

exporter [eks'pɔːtər] **N** exportateur, -trice (**of** de)

expose [ɪks'pəʊz] **VT 1** *(put in unprotected position)* exposer; *(new-born child)* abandonner; *Phot (film)* exposer; **to be exposed to the weather** être exposé aux intempéries; **to e. sb/oneself to danger** exposer qn/s'exposer au danger; **to e. one's flank to the enemy** prêter le flanc à l'ennemi; **to e. oneself to ridicule/sb's anger** s'exposer à la risée publique/à la colère de qn **2** *(lay bare)* *(wire etc)* mettre à découvert *ou* à nu *ou* à jour **3** *(display)* *(one's ignorance, feelings)* afficher; *(goods for sale)* étaler; *Rel (the Blessed Sacrament)* exposer; **to e. oneself** faire de l'exhibitionnisme; **a man exposed himself to her** un exhibitionniste l'a approchée **4** *(reveal)* *(secret)* éventer; *(crime)* dévoiler; *(criminal activity, network)* mettre à jour; *(traitor)* démasquer; **they're trying to e. him as …** ils essaient de démontrer que c'est …; **he feared being exposed as a homosexual** il craignait que son homosexualité ne soit découverte *ou* mise à jour

exposé [eks'pəʊzeɪ] **N** *(article, documentary, book etc)* exposé *m*; *(of scandal etc)* révélation *f*; **the newspaper's e. of the MP's activities** l'enquête du journal sur les activités du parlementaire

exposed [ɪks'pəʊzd] **ADJ 1** *(to sight, elements)* exposé; *(gears)* à découvert; *Phot (film)* exposé, impressionné; *Mil* **e. position** endroit exposé; *Fig* **this leaves the Prime Minister in an e. position** cela laisse le Premier ministre dans une position fragile; *Mil* **to be e.** *(of troops)* être en l'air **2** *(laid bare)* à nu

exposition [ekspə'zɪʃən] **N 1** *(explanation)* exposé *m*, exposition *f*, présentation *f*; *(in novel)*, *Mus* exposition **2** *(exhibition)* exposition *f* **3** *Rel* exposition *f*

expostulate [ɪks'pɒstjʊleɪt] **VI** vitupérer (**about** contre); **to e. with sb about sth** faire des remontrances à qn sur *ou* à propos de qch

expostulation [ɪkspɒstjʊ'leɪʃən] **N** *(to person)* vitupérations *fpl*, remontrance(s) *f(pl)*

exposure [ɪks'pəʊʒər] **N 1** *(to air, cold, danger)* exposition *f*; *(of new-born child)* abandon *m*; *Fin* exposition *f* aux risques; **to die of e.** mourir de froid; *Nucl* **e. (to radiation)** irradiation *f* **2** *(display)* *(of goods for sale)* exposition *f*, étalage *m*; *(on market)* exposition; *Law* **indecent e.** outrage *m* public à la pudeur **3** *Journ etc* **press e.** couverture *f* médiatique; **to get a lot of e.** recevoir une importante couverture médiatique; **politicians eager for e.** les hommes politiques anxieux de paraître dans les médias **4** *(of crime etc)* dévoilement *m*; *(of crook)* dénonciation *f*; **to threaten sb with e.** menacer de mettre à jour les activités de qn **5** *Phot (shot)* prise *f* de vue; **time e.** pose *f*; **a 36-e. film** une pellicule 36 poses **6** *(outlook of building, place)* exposition *f*, orientation *f*
▸▸ *Phot* **e. counter** compteur *m* de prises de vue; *Phot* **e. meter** exposimètre *m*, posemètre *m*; *Phot* **e. time** temps *m* de pose

expound [ɪks'paʊnd] **VT** *(doctrine, principles)* exposer; *Rel (Holy Scriptures)* interpréter

express [ɪks'pres] **ADJ 1** *(clear)* *(law, stipulation etc)* exprès, *f* expresse; *(order)* formel, explicite; **for this e. purpose** dans ce but

même; **it was her e. instruction that we …** elle nous a formellement *ou* explicitement demandé de … **2** *(image)* exact, fidèle (**of** de)
ADV sans arrêt; **to send a letter e.** envoyer une lettre par *ou* en exprès; **lift that goes e. to the twentieth floor** ascenseur qui monte directement au vingtième étage
N 1 *(train)* express *m*, rapide *m* **2** *Am Fam (freight company)* compagnie *f* de messageries

VT 1 *(one's feelings, intention)* exprimer; *(one's will, desire)* manifester; *(opinion)* émettre; *(wish)* formuler; *(gratitude)* témoigner; **a millionaire has expressed an interest in (buying) the castle** un millionaire s'est déclaré intéressé par le château; **well/badly expressed** bien/mal rendu; **to e. oneself** s'exprimer; *Math* **to e. sth as an equation** exprimer qch sous forme d'équation **2** *(remove)* *(oil etc)* extraire (**out of, from** de); *(milk)* exprimer **3** *(letter)* envoyer par *ou* en exprès; *Am (package) (by freight company)* envoyer *ou* expédier par les messageries
▸▸ *Am* **e. company** entreprise *f* de livraison exprès; **e. delivery** envoi *m* par exprès; **e. freight** fret *m* express; **e. letter** lettre *f* exprès; **e. messenger** messager *m* exprès; *Rail* **e. train** train *m* express, express *m*

expression [ɪks'preʃən] **N 1** *(of face, eyes)* expression *f*; **he had a strange e. (on his face)** il avait une drôle d'expression **2** *(phrase)* expression *f*, locution *f*; **it's just an e.** ce n'est qu'une expression; *Math* **algebraical e.** expression *ou* formule *f* algébrique **3** *(act of expressing)* *(of thought, joy etc)* expression *f*, manifestation *f*; **beyond e.** au delà de toute expression, inexprimable; **freedom of e.** liberté *f* d'expression; **these feelings found e. in her poetry** sa poésie a su exprimer ces sentiments; **he raised his fist in an e. of defiance** il brandit le poing en signe de défi **4** *(feeling)* **with e.** *(to sing, act)* avec expression

expressionism [ɪks'preʃənɪz(ə)m] **N** *Art* expressionnisme *m*

expressionist [ɪks'preʃənɪst] **ADJ, N** *Art* expressionniste *mf*

expressionless [ɪks'preʃənlɪs] **ADJ** *(voice)* sans expression; *(face)* impassible, sans expression; **there was something rather e. about her performance** quelque chose dans sa performance manquait d'expression

expressive [ɪks'presɪv] **ADJ** *(face, eyes)* expressif, plein d'expression; *(gesture, silence)* éloquent; *(person)* démonstratif; *(language)* expressif; **attitude e. of disdain** attitude qui exprime le dédain

expressively [ɪks'presɪvlɪ] **ADV** avec expression

expressiveness [ɪks'presɪvnɪs] **N** *(of face etc)* caractère *m* expressif, force *f* d'expression

expressly [ɪks'preslɪ] **ADV 1** *(clearly)* expressément, formellement; **e. forbidden** expressément *ou* formellement défendu; **I e. told you to buy a lettuce** je t'ai bien dit d'acheter une salade **2** *(with a clear purpose)* **to do sth e. to …** faire qch dans le seul but de …

expressway [ɪks'presweɪ] **N** *Am* autoroute *f*, voie *f* rapide

expropriate [eks'prəʊprɪeɪt] **VT** *(owner, property)* exproprier

expropriation [eksprəʊprɪ'eɪʃən] **N** expropriation *f*

expulsion [ɪks'pʌlʃən] **N** *(from country, political party etc)* expulsion *f*; *(from school)* renvoi *m*

expunge [ɪks'pʌndʒ] **VT** *Fml (name from list)* effacer, rayer; *(passage from book)* supprimer; *(memory, thought)* effacer

expurgate ['ekspɜːɡeɪt] **VT** *(book)* expurger; *(text)* épurer; *(passage etc)* supprimer; **expurgated edition** édition expurgée

expurgation [ekspɜː'ɡeɪʃən] **N** *(of book)* expurgation *f*, *(of text)* épuration *f*, *(of passage)* suppression *f*

exquisite ['ekskwɪzɪt] **ADJ 1** *(food, wine, afternoon)* exquis; *(pleasure etc)* vif, *f* vive; **the relief was e.** ce fut un merveilleux soulagement **2** *(delicate)* très sensible, délicat, subtil **3** *(torture)* raffiné; *(pain)* exquis

exquisitely [eks'kwɪzɪtlɪ] **ADV 1** *(delightfully)* d'une manière exquise; **e.** *done (of needlework etc)* perlé; **an e. warm afternoon** un après-midi délicieusement chaud **2** *(intensely)* extrêmement

exquisiteness [eks'kwɪzɪtnɪs] **N 1** *(delicacy, subtlety)* *(of work of art)* perfection *f* délicate; *(of hearing)* finesse *f* **2** *(extreme degree)* *(of pleasure etc)* caractère *m* vif; *(of pain)* acuité *f*

ex-serviceman, *pl* **ex-servicemen N** militaire *m* en retraite

ex-servicewoman, *pl* **ex-servicewomen N** femme *f* militaire en retraite

ex ship ADV ex navire

ext *Tel abbr* **extension**

extant [eks'tænt] **ADJ** existant encore, qui existe encore

extemporaneous [ɪkstempə'reɪnɪəs] **ADJ** *Fml* improvisé, impromptu

extemporaneously [ɪkstempə'reɪnɪəslɪ] **ADV** *Fml (to speak etc)* impromptu

extempore [ɪks'tempərɪ] *Fml* **ADV** *(to speak)* impromptu, sans préparation **ADJ** *(speech)* improvisé, impromptu; *(speaker)* qui parle sans préparation

extemporization [ɪkstempəraɪ'zeɪʃən] **N** improvisation *f*

extemporize [ɪks'tempəraɪz] **VT** *(speech)* improviser **VI** *(speak)* improviser, parler à l'impromptu; *Mus* improviser (**on the organ/etc** à l'orgue/ etc)

extend [ɪks'tend] **VT 1** *(stretch) (body, arm)* étendre, allonger; **the giraffe extended its neck** la girafe a allongé *ou* tendu le cou; **to e. an aerial/telescope** développer une antenne/un télescope **2** *(prolong) (period of time, rail ticket, contract)* prolonger; *Com (expiry of bill)* proroger; *(research)* continuer; **the deadline has been extended until 25 May** la date limite a été repoussée au 25 mai **3** *(broaden, lengthen, increase) (line)* prolonger; *(boundaries)* étendre, porter plus loin; *(sense of word)* étendre; *(knowledge)* accroître; *(power, lands)* agrandir, augmenter; *(agreement, scope)* élargir; *(house, room)* agrandir; *(frontiers of state)* reculer; **we are going to e. our premises** nous allons nous agrandir **4** *(offer) (hand)* tendre; *(thanks, sympathy)* présenter; *(support)* offrir; **to e. a welcome to sb** souhaiter la bienvenue à qn; *Banking* **to e. credit to sb** accorder un crédit à qn **5** *Sport etc (push to limit) (horse, runner etc)* faire rendre son maximum à, pousser; **to e. oneself** donner son maximum; **they haven't really been extended by any of their opponents** aucun de leurs adversaires ne les a vraiment poussés au bout de leurs limites **VI 1** *(in space)* s'étendre, s'allonger; **to e. beyond the wall** s'avancer au-delà du mur; **the government's concern with austerity does not e. to its own departments** la volonté du gouvernement de mener une politique d'austérité ne s'étend pas jusqu'à ses propres départements **2** *(of period of time)* se prolonger, continuer; **enquiries extending over a number**

of years investigations prolongées pendant un grand nombre d'années

extendable [ɪks'tendɪb(ə)l] **ADJ** *(aerial, pole)* télescopique; *(ladder)* à coulisse; *(contract of employment)* renouvelable

extended [ɪks'tendɪd] **ADJ 1** *(body, arm)* étendu, allongé; *Mil* **in e. order** en ordre dispersé **2** *(in time) (long)* long, prolongé; *(prolonged)* prolongé **3** *(increased)* augmenté, agrandi
▸▸ *Comput* **e. ASCII** ASCII *m* étendu; **e. coverage** *(in insurance)* couverture *f* multirisque; *Radio, TV* = informations *fpl* détaillées sur un événement; **e. family** famille *f* élargie; **e. maintenance insurance** assurance *f* maintenance étendue; *Comput* **e. memory** mémoire *f* étendue; *Horseriding* **e. trot** trot *m* allongé; **e. warranty** garantie *f* prolongée

extended-play record N disque *m* double durée

extender lens [ɪks'tendər] **N** bague *f* rallonge

extending [ɪks'tendɪŋ] **ADJ** *(table)* à rallonges; *(ladder)* à coulisse

extension [ɪks'tenʃən] **N 1** *(act of stretching out) (of arm)* extension *f*, *(of canal, railway etc)* prolongement *m*; *(of factory etc)* agrandissement *m*, extension; *Surg (of broken leg)* extension; *Aviat (of landing gear)* sortie *f*, *(of table, jack etc)* (r)allonge *f*
2 *(development)* extension *f*, accroissement *m*; **there has been a considerable e. of his business** son commerce a pris une extension considérable
3 *(extra part) (of table etc)* (r)allonge *f*, *(of cable)* allonge *f*, *(on building)* annexe *f*; **we're having an e. built (onto the house)** nous faisons agrandir la maison; **an e. is being added to the museum** on construit une annexe au musée
4 *Tel* poste *m* supplémentaire; *Tel* **e. 35** poste 35
5 *Gram (of subject, attribute)* complément *m*
6 *(in time) (of leave, railway ticket etc)* prolongation *f*, **to get/give an e.** *(of deadline)* obtenir/accorder un délai
7 *Comput (of file)* extension *f*
▸▸ **e. cable** câble *m* de raccordement; *Sch etc* **e. courses** formation *f* continue; **e. ladder** échelle *f* à coulisse; **e. loudspeaker** haut-parleur *m* séparé, *pl* haut-parleurs séparés; *Tel* **e. number** numéro *m* de poste; *Tech* **e. piece** pièce *f* formant un prolongement

extensive [ɪks'tensɪv] **ADJ 1** étendu, vaste; *(repairs, alterations, reworking)* considérable, important; **there was e. damage to both wings** les deux ailes ont été très endommagées; **e. knowledge** vastes connaissances *fpl*; **e. research** travaux *mpl* approfondis; **to make e. use of sth** faire un usage considérable de qch **2** *(agriculture)* extensif

extensively [ɪks'tensɪvlɪ] **ADV** *(to travel, read etc)* énormément; *(rewritten, revised etc)* largement; **to use sth e.** se servir beaucoup de qch, faire un usage considérable de qch; **it was e. damaged/repaired** il a subi des dommages/réparations considérables

extensor [ɪks'tensər] **N** *Anat (muscle)* extenseur *m*

extent [ɪks'tent] **N** *(of lands, knowledge etc)* étendue *f*, *(of damage etc)* importance *f*; *Typ (of book)* nombre *m* de pages; **credit to the e. of £500** crédit jusqu'à concurrence de 500 livres; **to an e., to a certain e., to some e.** jusqu'à un certain point, dans une certaine mesure; **to a great e., to a large e.** en grande partie, dans une large mesure; **to such an e. that ...** à tel point que ...; **to what e. is this true?** jusqu'à quel point est-ce vrai?; **to the e. that he can play a few tunes, he is a musician** dans la mesure où il peut jouer quel-

ques airs, c'est un musicien; **the e. to which the strike affected production is unclear** les conséquences de la grève sur la production sont mal définies

extenuate [ɪks'tenjʊeɪt] **VT** *(crime)* atténuer, amoindrir

> Note that the French verb **exténuer** is a false friend and is never a translation for the English verb **to extenuate**. It means **to exhaust**.

extenuating [ɪks'tenjʊeɪtɪŋ] **ADJ**
▸▸ **e. circumstances** circonstances *fpl* atténuantes

extenuation [ɪkstenjʊ'eɪʃən] **N** **to say sth in e. of an offence/an act** dire qch pour atténuer la gravité d'un délit/d'un acte

exterior [ɪks'tɪərɪər] **ADJ** extérieur (**to** à), en dehors (**to** de)
N 1 extérieur *m*, dehors *mpl*; **on the e.** à l'extérieur; **house with an imposing e.** maison aux dehors imposants; **despite her stern e., she is very likeable** malgré un extérieur *ou* une apparence sévère, elle est très sympathique **2** *Theat, Cin* extérieur *m*
▸▸ *Math* **e. angle** angle *m* externe; **e. wall** mur *m* extérieur

exteriorize [ɪks'tɪərɪəraɪz] **VT** extérioriser

exterminate [ɪks'tɜːmɪneɪt] **VT** *(insects, population etc)* exterminer; *(belief, disease)* supprimer

extermination [ɪkstɜːmɪ'neɪʃən] **N** extermination *f*, *(of belief)* suppression *f*, *(of disease)* éradication *f*

exterminator [ɪks'tɜːmɪneɪtər] **N** *(person)* exterminateur, -trice; **a rodent e.** un employé de la dératisation

extern [eks'tɜːn] **N** *Am Med* externe *mf*

external [ɪks'tɜːn(ə)l] **ADJ** *(wall, reality, world, trade, debt)* extérieur; *(angle, damage)* externe; *(interference, pressure)* du dehors, de l'extérieur; *(affairs)* étranger, -ère, extérieur; *(student)* libre; **in e. appearance** en apparence; **to judge sth by (its) e. appearance** juger qch d'après ses apparences; *Med* **for e. use only** à usage externe
N *(usu pl)* **1** *(appearance)* **externals** extérieur *m*, formes *fpl* extérieures, dehors *mpl*; **to judge by externals** juger les choses selon les apparences **2** *(inessential things)* **externals** choses *fpl* secondaires
▸▸ *Banking* **e. account** compte *m* d'étranger, *Can* compte de non-résident; *Fin* **e. audit** audit *m* externe; *Fin* **e. auditing** vérification *f* externe, audit externe; *Fin* **e. auditor** audit *ou* auditeur, -trice externe; *Comput* **e. command** commande *f* externe; *Fin* **e. deficit** déficit *m* extérieur; *Comput* **e. device** dispositif *m* externe, périphérique *m*; *Comput* **e. drive** unité *f* (de disque) externe; *(printer)* imprimante *f*; *Univ* **e. examiner** examinateur, -trice venant de l'extérieur; *Fin* **e. financing** financement *m* externe, fonds *mpl* extérieurs; *Comput* **e. hard disk** disque *m* dur externe; *Comput* **e. modem** modem *m* externe

externality [ekstɜː'nælɪtɪ] **N** *Econ* externalité *f*

externalize [ɪks'tɜːnəlaɪz] **VT** *(feelings)* exprimer

externally [ɪks'tɜːn(ə)lɪ] **ADV** *(damaged, calm)* extérieurement; **to apply e.** appliquer en usage externe

extinct [ɪks'tɪŋkt] **ADJ** *(animal, plant)* disparu, qui n'existe plus; *(office, title)* aboli, tombé en désuétude; *(volcano, passion)* éteint; **to become e.** *(of race)* s'éteindre, disparaître; *(of way of life)* disparaître, se perdre

extinction [ɪks'tɪŋkʃən] **N** *(of fire, race)* extinction *f*, *(of hope)* anéantissement *m*; **to**

hunt an animal to e. chasser un animal jusqu'à extinction de la race; **race threatened with e.** race f en passe de disparaître

extinguish [ɪks'tɪŋgwɪʃ] VT (fire, cigarette, candle) éteindre; (hope, race) anéantir

extinguisher [ɪks'tɪŋgwɪʃər] N **1** (for fire) (appareil m) extincteur m (d'incendie), appareil d'extinction; **foam e.** extincteur à mousse **2** (for candle) éteignoir m

extirpate ['ekstɜ:peɪt] VT Fml (evil) extirper, déraciner

extirpation [ekstɜ:'peɪʃən] N Fml (of evil) extirpation f, éradication f

extn Tel (abbr **extension**) poste m

extol, Am **extoll** [ɪks'təʊl] VT (Br & Am **extolled, extolling**) esp Lit exalter, vanter, prôner; (sb's beauty) célébrer, chanter; **she was extolling the virtues of central heating** elle vantait les vertus du chauffage central; **to e. sb to the skies** porter qn aux nues

extort [ɪks'tɔ:t] VT (money etc) extorquer (**from sb** à qn); (promise, confession) arracher (**from sb** à qn)

extortion [ɪks'tɔ:ʃən] N (of money etc) extorsion f, (of promise, confession) arrachement m; **£15 for this? that's sheer e.!** 15 livres pour ça? c'est du vol!

extortionate [ɪks'tɔ:ʃənɪt] ADJ **1** (price) exorbitant **2** (person) rapace

extortioner [ɪks'tɔ:ʃənər], **extortionist** [ɪks'tɔ:ʃənɪst] N extorqueur, -euse

extra ['ekstrə] ADJ **1** (additional) de plus, supplémentaire; **an e. pint of milk** une pinte de lait supplémentaire ou de plus; **it costs 15p e.** ça coûte 15 pence de plus; **I took an e. £5, just in case** j'ai pris 5 livres de plus, au cas où; **500 e. police officers** 500 officiers de police supplémentaires; **no e. charge** sans supplément de prix; **at no e. cost** sans supplément; **e. pay** prime f, supplément m de salaire; Mil, Naut supplément de solde; **e. work** (hours) heures fpl supplémentaires; (work) surcroît m de travail; Br Sport prolongation f, Br Sport **to go into e. time** jouer les prolongations; **as an e. precaution** pour plus de précaution; **to make an e. effort** faire un surcroît d'effort **2** (spare) de réserve, de rechange; **bring some e. batteries** prends des piles de rechange; **these ones are e., take them!** ceux-là sont en trop, prends-les!
ADV **1** (more than usual) plus que d'ordinaire, extra-; **to be e. kind/polite** être particulièrement gentil/poli; **an e. special wine for those e. special occasions** un grand vin pour les grandes occasions; **this is an e. special cake for your birthday** voici un gâteau exceptionnel pour ton anniversaire; **e. strong binding/rope** reliure f/corde f extra-solide; **e. smart** ultra-chic; **e. white/fast** extra-blanc/-rapide; **e. large** (clothing) grand patron **2** (in addition) en plus; **meals taken in the bedroom are charged (for) e.** il y a un supplément pour les repas servis dans la chambre; **I had to pay e. for the sunroof** il a fallu que je paye un supplément pour le toit ouvrant; **packing e.** emballage en sus; **a few e.** quelques-uns en plus
N **1** (on restaurant bill) supplément m; (of newspaper) édition f spéciale; (on car) option f **2** Cin, Theat (actor) figurant, -ante; **to be** ou **work as an e.** faire de la figuration **3** extras (expenses) frais mpl ou dépenses fpl supplémentaires; (on invoice) suppléments mpl; **extras bill** facture f des extras **4** (luxuries) little extras petits à-côtés mpl, extras mpl
▸▸ **e. charge** supplément (de prix); Sch **e. subject** matière f facultative; **e. time** (to pay, finish) délai m; Sport prolongations fpl

extra- ['ekstrə] PREF (outside) extra-; **extra-galactic** extragalactique; **extravascular** extravasculaire

extract¹ ['ekstrækt] N **1** (of substance) extrait m, concentré m; **malt/beef e.** extrait de malt/de bœuf; **meat e.** concentré de viande **2** Liter etc extrait m; **selected extracts** (from author, works) morceaux mpl choisis

extract² [ɪks'trækt] VT (tooth) extraire, arracher; (oil, metal, data, passage from book etc) extraire (**from** de); (letter from pocket etc) tirer (**from** de); (passage from book) extraire (**from** de); **to e. money/a confession from sb** arracher de l'argent/un aveu à qn, tirer de l'argent/un aveu de qn; Math **to e. the square root of a number** extraire la racine carrée d'un nombre

extraction [ɪks'trækʃən] N **1** (removal) (of juice from lemon etc) extraction f, (of nail, tooth) arrachage m; **she needs two extractions and three fillings** il faut lui arracher deux dents et en plomber trois; **e. of stone from a quarry** extraction de la pierre d'une carrière **2** (origin) extraction f, origine f, **of humble e.** de basse extraction; **of Italian e.** d'origine italienne

extractor [ɪks'træktər] N **1** (tool) pince f, (in dentistry) davier m; Surg (of stones etc) extracteur m **2** (person) (of teeth etc) extracteur m
▸▸ **e. fan** ventilateur m, aérateur m; **e. hood** (on stove) hotte f aspirante

extracurricular ['ekstrəkə'rɪkjʊlər] ADJ Sch hors-programme inv
▸▸ **e. activities** activités fpl extrascolaires; Fig Hum frasques fpl

extraditable ['ekstrədaɪtəb(ə)l] ADJ (person) passible d'extradition; (crime, offence) qui justifie l'extradition

extradite ['ekstrədaɪt] VT Law (criminal) (hand over) extrader; (obtain extradition of) obtenir l'extradition de; **the authorities were unable to e. him from the USA** les autorités n'ont pas réussi à obtenir son extradition des États-Unis

extradition [ekstrə'dɪʃən] N extradition f, **the Spanish government is seeking/has obtained his e.** le gouvernement espagnol a demandé/obtenu son extradition
▸▸ **e. treaty** accord m d'extradition

extra-dry ADJ (wine) très sec

extra-fine ADJ extra-fin

extrajudicial ['ekstrədʒu:'dɪʃəl] ADJ extrajudiciaire

extramarital ['ekstrə'mærɪt(ə)l] ADJ extraconjugal

extramural ['ekstrə'mjʊər(ə)l] ADJ **e. course** cours m de formation continue; Br Univ **e. lecturer** = conférencier m en dehors de la Faculté accrédité pour certains cours; Br Univ **Department of E. Studies** Département m de la formation continue

extraneous [ɪks'treɪnɪəs] ADJ (considerations) en dehors de la question; (details) sans rapport; **to be e. to sth** n'avoir aucun rapport avec qch

extraordinarily [ɪks'trɔ:d(ə)nərɪlɪ] ADV extraordinairement; **it was an e. brave/foolish action** c'était un acte particulièrement courageux/inconscient

extraordinary [ɪks'trɔ:d(ə)nrɪ] ADJ **1** (remarkable) (extent, success, coincidence, story) extraordinaire; (behaviour, suggestion, idea) surprenant, singulier, étrange; (appearance) surprenant, bizarre; **the e. thing is that …** ce qu'il y a d'étrange ou de singulier, c'est que …; **that's e., he was here only an hour ago!** c'est incroyable, il était là il y a une heure à peine!; **I find it e. that you did not inform the police** je trouve incroyable ou extraordinaire que vous n'ayez pas prévenu la police; **they went to e. lengths to conceal the truth** ils se sont

donné un mal fou pour cacher la vérité **2** (special) extraordinaire; **ambassador e.** ambassadeur m extraordinaire
▸▸ Com **e. general meeting** assemblée f générale extraordinaire; Acct **e. income** produits mpl exceptionnels; Acct **e. item** poste m extraordinaire; Acct **e. loss** résultats mpl exceptionnels (pertes); **e. powers** pouvoirs mpl extraordinaires; **e. profit** résultats mpl exceptionnels (profits)

extrapolate [ek'stræpəleɪt] VT & VI extrapoler; **to e. from sth** extrapoler à partir de qch; **we can e. a prediction** nous pouvons extrapoler et établir une prévision

extrapolation [ɪkstræpə'leɪʃən] N extrapolation f

extrasensory ['ekstrə'sensərɪ] ADJ extrasensoriel
▸▸ **e. perception** perception f extrasensorielle; **to have e. perception** avoir des dons de perception extra-sensorielle

extraterrestrial ['ekstrətɪ'restrɪəl] ADJ, N extraterrestre mf

extraterritorial ['ekstrəterɪ'tɔ:rɪəl] ADJ (privilege) d'exterritorialité

extravagance [ɪks'trævəgəns] N **1** (excessive, wasteful expenditure) folles dépenses fpl, prodigalités fpl; **the e. of your tastes** tes goûts dispendieux ou fous; **it was real e.** c'était de la folie; **she accused the government of e.** elle a accusé le gouvernement de dilapider le trésor public; **a piece of e., an e.** une dépense inutile, une folie **2** (exaggeration) extravagance f

> Note that the most common meaning of the French word **extravagance** is **eccentricity**.

extravagant [ɪks'trævəgənt] ADJ **1** (wasteful) (person) dépensier, gaspilleur; (tastes) dispendieux; **it was very e. of them to come by taxi** ils ont fait une folie en venant en taxi; **don't be so e. with the butter** ne gaspillez pas le beurre; **he considered two baths a week (to be) e.** il trouvait que deux bains par semaine, c'était du gaspillage **2** (exaggerated) extravagant; (claim) exagéré, déraisonnable; (praise) outré; (style) exagéré; (price) exorbitant, prohibitif; **e. claims have been made for the drug** certaines propriétés ont été attribuées abusivement à ce médicament

> Note that the most common meaning of the French word **extravagant** is **eccentric**.

extravagantly [ɪks'trævəgəntlɪ] ADV **1** (excessively) **e. priced items** des articles à des prix exorbitants; **he spent money e.** il jetait l'argent par la fenêtre; **to live e.** vivre sur un grand pied, dépenser sans compter; **e. furnished house** maison meublée avec un luxe exagéré **2** (exaggeratedly) d'une façon extravagante; **to talk/act e.** dire/faire des folies ou des extravagances

extravaganza [ekstrævə'gænzə] N (lavish show) grand spectacle m

extravasation [ɪkstrævə'seɪʃən] N Med épanchement m

extravert ['ekstrəvɜ:t] ADJ, N = **extrovert**

extreme [ɪks'tri:m] ADJ **1** (heat, difficulty, pleasure etc) extrême; (nationalism) outrancier; (opinions, views) extrême, extrémiste; **to be in e. danger** or **peril** être en (très) grand danger; **to be in e. pain** souffrir à l'extrême; **to behave with e. awkwardness** se conduire avec la dernière gaucherie; **an e. case** un cas exceptionnel; **the question is one of e. delicacy** le problème est délicat entre tous **2** (far) extrême; **the e. opposite** l'extrême opposé; **at the e. end of the quay** tout au bout du quai; Pol **the e. left** l'extrême gauche; **on the e. left of the photograph** à l'extrême gauche de la photo

N extrême *m*; **they were rude in the e.** ils étaient mal polis à l'extrême; **to go from one e. to the other** passer d'un extrême à l'autre; **to go to the e. of calling the police** aller jusqu'à appeler la police; **now he's going to the other e. and …** il est passé d'un extrême à l'autre et maintenant …; **to go to extremes** pousser les choses à l'extrême; **extremes of temperature** extrêmes de température
▸▸ *Cin, TV* **e. close-up** plan *m* très rapproché; *Cin, TV* **e. long shot** plan très éloigné; *Fml* **the e. penalty** le dernier supplice; **e. sports** sports *mpl* extrêmes; *Rel* **e. unction** extrême-onction *f*

extremely [ɪksˈtriːmlɪ] **ADV** extrêmement; **to be e. witty** avoir énormément d'esprit

extremism [ɪksˈtriːmɪz(ə)m] **N** *Pol* extrémisme *m*

extremist [ɪksˈtriːmɪst] **ADJ, N** *Pol* extrémiste *mf*

extremity [ɪksˈtremɪtɪ] **N 1** *(end)* extrémité *f*, point *m* extrême; **the southernmost e. of Europe** l'extrême sud de l'Europe **2 the extremities** *(of the body)* les extrémités *fpl* **3** *(need)* gêne *f*; **how had they arrived at such an e.?** comment étaient-ils parvenus à de telles extrémités?; **to be reduced to the last e.** en être réduit à la dernière extrémité

extricate [ˈekstrɪkeɪt] **VT** dégager, tirer (**sb from a critical position** qn d'un mauvais pas); **to e. oneself from a danger** se tirer d'un danger; **to e. oneself from a conversation** se dégager d'une conversation; **to e. oneself from difficulties** se débrouiller, se tirer d'affaire

extrinsic [eksˈtrɪnsɪk] **ADJ** extrinsèque
▸▸ *Fin* **e. value** valeur *f* extrinsèque

extrovert, extravert [ˈekstrəvɜːt] **N** extraverti, -ie, extroverti, -ie; **a bit (too much) of an e.** un peu (trop) extraverti; **she's much more of an e. than her sister** elle est bien plus extravertie que sa sœur, c'est une extravertie bien plus que sa sœur
ADJ extraverti, extroverti; **to have e. tendencies** être d'un naturel extraverti

extrude [eksˈtruːd] **VT** expulser, faire jaillir (**from** de); *Metal* filer, profiler; *Ind (plastics)* boudiner (à chaud); **extruded section or shape** profilé *m*
VI *Geol (of rock etc)* s'épancher

extrusion [eksˈtruːʒən] **N** expulsion *f*; *(of secretion)* émission *f*; *Geol* épanchement *m*; *Metal* extrusion *f*, filage *m* (à chaud); *Ind (of plastics)* boudinage *m*, extrusion

exuberance [ɪgˈzjuːb(ə)rəns] **N** exubérance *f*, *(of person)* exubérance, gaieté *f* débordante; *(of vegetation)* luxuriance *f*, richesse *f*

exuberant [ɪgˈzjuːb(ə)rənt] **ADJ** *(person)* exubérant, débordant de vie; *(imagination)* exubérant; *(vegetation)* luxuriant, riche; *(health, vitality)* débordant; **she felt e. at the news** la nouvelle la remplit d'une joie exubérante

exuberantly [ɪgˈzjuːb(ə)rəntlɪ] **ADV** avec exubérance; **e. cheerful** d'une gaieté exubérante; **e. healthy** débordant de santé

exude [ɪgˈzjuːd] **VT** exsuder; *Fig* **she exudes health** elle respire la santé; **he exudes (an air of) confidence/well-being/charm** un halo de confiance en soi/de bien-être/de charme se dégage de tout son être
VI exsuder, suinter; *(of sap)* couler, s'écouler

exult [ɪgˈzʌlt] **VI 1** *(rejoice)* exulter, se réjouir (**at, in** de); **they exulted at their enemies' confusion** ils exultaient de voir la confusion dans laquelle se trouvaient leurs ennemis; **to e. in the name of 'Mad Mitch'** porter le nom singulier de 'Mad Mitch' **2** *(triumph)* **to e. over sb** triompher de qn

exultant [ɪgˈzʌltənt] **ADJ** *esp Lit (feeling)* joyeux; *(cry)* de triomphe; **to be e. at sth** *(of person)* exulter de qch

exultantly [ɪgˈzʌltəntlɪ] **ADV** *(to speak etc)* d'un air triomphant

exultation [egzʌlˈteɪʃən] **N** exultation *f*; **to sing in e.** chanter le cœur plein de joie

ex voto [eksˈvəʊtəʊ] **N** *Rel* **e. (offering)** ex-voto *m inv*

ex warehouse **ADV** départ entrepôt

ex works **ADV** départ usine

EYE [aɪ] **N 1** *(of human, animal)* œil *m*, *pl* yeux; **to have blue eyes** avoir les yeux bleus; **a man with green eyes** un homme aux yeux verts; **to have good eyes** avoir de bons yeux; **to open/close one's eyes** ouvrir/fermer les yeux; **to open one's eyes wide** ouvrir les yeux tout grands; **to have the sun/the light in one's eyes** avoir le soleil/la lumière dans les yeux; **I've got something in my e.** j'ai quelque chose dans l'œil; **with tears in one's eyes** les larmes aux yeux; **dry your eyes** essuyez vos larmes; **he could not keep his eyes open** il dormait debout; **at e. level** à la hauteur des yeux; **to maintain e. contact with sb** soutenir le regard de qn; **to make e. contact with sb** regarder qn (droit) dans les yeux; **to try to make e. contact with sb** chercher le regard de qn; **she always avoids e. contact (with me)** elle évite tout le temps mon regard; **to look sb straight in the e.** regarder qn droit dans les yeux; *Zool* **simple e.** œil simple, ocelle *m*; *Zool* **compound e.** œil composé *ou* à facettes

2 *(idioms of observation, awareness etc)* **as far as the e. can see** à perte de vue; **to keep one's eyes and ears open** avoir l'œil et l'oreille aux aguets; **to keep one's eyes open** *or Fam* **peeled** *or Fam* **skinned** avoir *ou* ouvrir l'œil; *Fig* **to open sb's eyes** dessiller les yeux à qn (**to** sur); *Fig* **to do sth with one's eyes open** faire qch en connaissance de cause; **I could do it with my eyes shut** je pourrais le faire les yeux fermés; **to shut** *or* **close one's eyes to sb's faults** fermer les yeux sur les défauts de qn; **to be all eyes** être tout yeux; **all eyes were upon her** elle était au centre de tous les regards, tous les regards étaient posés sur elle; **to strike/catch the e.** frapper/attirer l'œil *ou* les regards; **to catch sb's e.** *(of person, thing)* attirer l'attention de qn; *Parl* **to catch the Speaker's e.** obtenir la parole; **it pleases/delights the e.** cela charme/réjouit les yeux *ou* les regards; **he has eyes in** *or* **at the back of his head** il a des yeux d'Argus; **he has eyes for nobody but her** il n'a d'yeux que pour elle; **to set** *or* **lay eyes on sth** poser les yeux sur qch, apercevoir qch, voir qch; **it was the biggest fish I'd ever laid eyes on** c'était le plus gros poisson que j'aie jamais vu; **to see sth with one's own eyes** voir qch de ses propres yeux; **it took place before my (very) eyes** cela s'est passé sous mes yeux; **to see sth in one's mind's e.** voir qch en imagination *ou* en idée; *Fig* **where are your eyes?** êtes-vous aveugle?; **use your eyes!** ouvre les yeux!; **to run** *or* **cast one's e. over sth** jeter un coup d'œil sur qch; **to look at sth with a critical/experienced e.** regarder qch d'un œil critique/exercé; **with jealous eyes** d'un œil jaloux; **you can see that with half an e.** cela saute aux yeux; **anyone with half an e. can see it's a fake** du premier coup d'œil, n'importe qui verrait que c'est un faux; **with half an e. on the weather** sans quitter le ciel des yeux; **to keep an e. on sb/sth** surveiller qn/qch; **keep your e. on him!** ne le quittez pas des yeux!; **I couldn't keep my eyes off him/it** je ne pouvais pas en détacher mes yeux; **to keep an e. out for sth** être à l'affût de qch; **keep an e. out for anyone trying to sell it** soyez à l'affût au cas où quelqu'un essaierait de le vendre; **keep an e. on the children/potatoes** surveille les enfants/les pommes de terre; **a neighbour is keeping an e. on the house while we're away** un de nos voisins a l'œil sur la maison quand nous sommes absents; **to keep one's e. on the ball** suivre *ou* *Golf* fixer la balle; **keep your eyes on the road** regarde la route; **to have one's e. on sb/sth** *(be watching)* avoir qn/qch à l'œil; *(be thinking of acquiring)* avoir l'œil sur qn/qch; **the police have had their e. on him for some time** cela fait un certain temps que la police l'a à l'œil; **under the (watchful) e. of …** sous la surveillance de …

3 *(point of view, perception)* **everyone is equal in the eye(s) of the law** tout le monde est égal devant la loi; **in the eyes of all, he is guilty** aux yeux de tous, il est coupable; **through sb else's eyes** du point de vue de qn d'autre; **to be very much in the public e.** occuper une position très en vue; **to have an e. for a horse** s'y connaître en chevaux, être bon juge des chevaux; **to have an e. for a bargain** savoir reconnaître une bonne affaire; **with the e. of a painter** d'un œil de peintre; **an e. for detail/colour** l'œil pour le détail/la couleur

4 *(idiomatic expressions)* **to be up to the** *or* **one's eyes in work/debt** avoir du travail/des dettes par-dessus la tête; **to see e. to e. with sb** voir les choses du même œil que qn; **for your eyes only** confidentiel; *Fam* **that's one in the e. for him!** ça lui fait les pieds!; *Old-fashioned Fam* **my e.!** mon œil!; *Bible* **an e. for an e., a tooth for a tooth** œil pour œil, dent pour dent; **to pass through the e. of a needle** passer par le trou d'une aiguille; *Fig* **at the e. of the hurricane** dans un havre de paix, dans un îlot préservé; **to make eyes at sb**, *Fam* **to give sb the (glad) e.** lancer des œillades *ou* faire de l'œil à qn; *Fam* **to make sheep's eyes at sb** lancer des œillades amoureuses à qn; **with an e. to …** en vue de …; **he does everything with an e. for** *or* **on** *or* **to the main chance** il fait tout avec son propre intérêt en vue

5 *(specialist uses) (bud)* œil *m*, *pl* yeux, bourgeon *m*; *(on potato)* germe *m*; *(in grafting)* œilleton *m*; *(hole) (of needle, rigging)* œil, *pl* œils; *(of support, prop)* collet *m*, œillet *m*; *(with screw thread)* piton *m*; *Met (of storm)* œil; *Mil* **eyes right/left!** tête (à) droite/(à) gauche!; *Mil* **eyes front!** fixe!; *Sport* **to get one's e. in** se faire la main; **eyes** *(on peacock's tail)* yeux *mpl*, miroirs *mpl*; **bird's eyes** *(in mahogany etc)* tourbillons *mpl*; *Electron* **electric** *or* **magic e.** cellule *f* photo-électrique

6 *Fam (private detective)* détective *m ou* enquêteur *m* privé

VT (**eyed; eyeing**) *(look at)* regarder, observer (**with suspicion** d'un air soupçonneux); *(weigh up) (person, obstacle etc)* mesurer des yeux; **to e. sb up and down** regarder qn de la tête aux pieds
▸▸ **e. bank** banque *f* des yeux; **e. camera** caméra *f* oculaire; *Fam* **e. candy** beaux mecs/belles nanas; **his latest piece of e. candy** sa dernière nana; **e. contact** croisement *m* des regards; **e. drops** gouttes *fpl* pour les yeux; **e. end** *(of cable)* œil, piton; **e. hospital** centre *m* hospitalier d'ophtalmologie; **e. make-up** maquillage *m* pour les yeux; **e. movement camera** caméra oculaire; **e. shadow** ombre *f* à paupières; **e. socket** orbite *f* de l'œil; **e. test** examen *m* de la vue
▸ **eye up VT SEP** *Fam* **1** *(with sexual interest)* **to e. up the girls/boys** reluquer les filles/les garçons; **he eyed her up** il l'a reluquée
2 *(estimate strength etc of) (opponent etc)* jauger (d'un coup d'œil)

eyeball ['aɪbɔːl] N globe m oculaire; *Fig* **to come e. to e.** *(of two people)* s'affronter; **to come e. to e. with sb** affronter qn; **an e. to e. confrontation** un affrontement direct ▸ VT *Fam* regarder en face

eyebath ['aɪbɑːθ] N *Br Med* **1** œillère f **2** *(liquid)* bain m d'œil

eyebrow ['aɪbraʊ] N sourcil m; *Fig* **he never raised an e.** *(in disapproval, astonishment)* il n'a pas sourcillé; *Fig* **(some) eyebrows were raised at this suggestion** *(in disapproval)* cette proposition a suscité des grimaces de désapprobation; *(in astonishment)* cette proposition a suscité de l'étonnement ▸▸ **e. pencil** crayon m à sourcils; **e. tweezers** pince f à épiler

eye-catching ADJ *(design, dress, title)* accrocheur, -euse; *(advertisement)* tapageur, -euse

eyecup ['aɪkʌp] N *Am* = eyebath 1

-eyed [aɪd] SUFF **blue-e.** aux yeux bleus; **wide-e.** aux grands yeux

eyeful ['aɪfʊl] N **to get an e. of mud/sand/water** recevoir de la boue/du sable/de l'eau plein les yeux; *Fam* **to get an e.** *(look)* se rincer l'œil; *Fam* **she's quite an e.** elle vaut le coup d'œil

eyeglass ['aɪglɑːs] N *(monocle)* monocle m; **watchmaker's e.** loupe f d'horloger

eyeglasses ['aɪglɑːsɪz] NPL *Am (spectacles)* lunettes fpl

eyehole ['aɪhəʊl] N **1** *(in mask)* **eyeholes** ouvertures fpl pour les yeux **2** *(small opening)* petite ouverture f, judas m; *Tech* trou m de regard ou de visite

eyelash ['aɪlæʃ] N cil m ▸▸ **e. curlers** recourbe-cils m inv

eyelet ['aɪlɪt] N œillet m

eyelevel ['aɪlev(ə)l] ADJ qui est à la hauteur des yeux ▸▸ **e. grill** gril m surélevé

eyelid ['aɪlɪd] N paupière f; *Fig* **he didn't bat an e.** il n'a pas sourcillé

eye-line N *TV etc* direction f du regard

eyeliner ['aɪlaɪnər] N eye-liner m, pl eye-liners

eye-opener N **1** **that was an e. for him** cela lui a ouvert les yeux, ça a été une révélation pour lui **2** *Am (drink)* petit verre m du matin

eye-opening ADJ qui ouvre les yeux, révélateur, -trice; **it was very e.** ça a été très révélateur

eyepatch ['aɪpætʃ] N cache m (sur l'œil); **eyepatches** caches (pour les yeux)

eyepiece N ['aɪpiːs] N *Opt (of microscope etc)* oculaire m, viseur m; *(on camera)* œilleton m, oculaire m de visée; *Metal (of furnace)* lunette f de regard; *(of gas mask)* lunette f

eyepopping ['aɪpɒpɪŋ] ADJ *Am Fam* sensationnel

eyeshade ['aɪʃeɪd] N visière f

eyesight ['aɪsaɪt] N vue f; **to lose one's e.** perdre la vue; **to have good e.** avoir une bonne vue ou de bons yeux; **my e. is failing** ma vue baisse

eyesore ['aɪsɔːr] N **the building is an e.** le bâtiment est une horreur ou blesse la vue

eyespot ['aɪspɒt] N *(of butterfly etc)* ocelle m

eyestrain ['aɪstreɪn] N **to suffer from e.** avoir les yeux fatigués; **you'll give yourself e.** tu vas te fatiguer les yeux

eyetooth, pl **eyeteeth** ['aɪtuːθ, -tiːθ] N *(dent f)* canine f; **to cut one's eyeteeth** faire ses canines; *Fam (come to end of childhood)* sortir de sa première enfance; **I'd give my eyeteeth to go with them** je donnerais n'importe quoi pour aller avec eux

eyewash ['aɪwɒʃ] N *Pharm* collyre m; *Fig* **that's a lot** or **load of e.** *(nonsense)* tout ça, c'est du boniment

eyewitness ['aɪwɪtnɪs] N témoin m oculaire (**of** de); **an e. account** le récit d'un témoin oculaire

eyrie ['ɪərɪ] N *(of eagle)* aire f

ezine, e-zine ['iːziːn] N ezine m, e-zine m

F, f [ef] N **1** (letter) F, f m; **two f's** deux f **2** Mus fa m; **in F** en fa **3** Sch **to get an F** être recalé ► ► Br Euph **the F word** ≃ le mot de Cambronne

FA [eˈfeɪ] N **1** Br Ftbl (abbr **Football Association**) = fédération f anglaise de football; **FA Cup** coupe f de la fédération anglaise de football **2** Sl **sweet FA** rien du tout, nib de nib

fa [fɑː] N Mus fa m

fab [fæb] ADJ Br Fam super, génial, -aux ► ► **the f. Four** = surnom des Beatles

Fabian [ˈfeɪbɪən] ADJ Pol fabien, -ienne

fable [ˈfeɪb(ə)l] N fable f, conte m

fabled [ˈfeɪb(ə)ld] ADJ de la fable; Fig légendaire

fabric [ˈfæbrɪk] N **1** Tex etc tissu m, étoffe f; **dress fabrics** tissus pour robes; **silk, woollen and cotton fabrics** soieries fpl, lainages mpl et cotonnades fpl **2** (of building, system) structure f; **the f. of society** l'édifice m social; **the urban f.** le tissu urbain

> Note that the French word **fabrique** is a false friend and is never a translation for the English word **fabric**. Its most common meaning is **factory**.

fabricate [ˈfæbrɪkeɪt] VT (news, story, alibi) forger, fabriquer; (document) contrefaire

fabrication [fæbrɪˈkeɪʃən] N (of news, story, alibi) fabrication f; (of document) contrefaçon f; **it's pure f.** c'est de la pure fabrication; **a pure f.** (lie) une histoire inventée de toutes pièces

fabulous [ˈfæbjʊləs] ADJ **1** (marvellous) prodigieux, fabuleux; (price) fou, f folle; **we had a f. evening** on a passé une soirée merveilleuse ou fabuleuse **2** (fairy story) fabuleux; (character, city) légendaire

fabulously [ˈfæbjʊləslɪ] ADV (rich etc) fabuleusement, prodigieusement

façade [fæˈsɑːd] N Archit, Fig façade f; **they put on a f. of family happiness** ils adoptent une façade de bonheur familial

FACE [feɪs]

N	visage **1** ▪ figure **1** ▪ mine **2** ▪ apparence **3** ▪ surface **5** ▪ face **6** ▪ façade **6**
VT	faire face à **1, 2** ▪ être confronté à **1** ▪ revêtir **3**
VI	être orienté

N **1** (of person) figure f, visage m; Fam **shut your f.!** ferme-la!, la ferme!; **you should have told him to shut his f.** tu aurais dû lui dire de la fermer ou boucler; **to hide one's f. in shame** se cacher le visage de honte; **to set one's f. against sth** s'opposer résolument à qch; **he won't show his f. here again!** il ne remettra pas les pieds ici!; **I told him so to his f.** je le lui ai dit en face; **I shall never be able to look her in the f. again** je ne pourrai jamais plus la regarder en face; Fam **I'm just going to put my f. on** je vais me maquiller; **her f. doesn't fit** (in job, company etc) sa tête ne nous/leur/etc revient pas; Br Sl **to be off one's f.** (drunk) être pété ou bourré; (on drugs) être défoncé; **the f. of Britain is changing** le visage de la Grande-Bretagne est en train de changer; **the unacceptable f. of capitalism** le visage inacceptable du capitalisme; **Communism with a human f.** le communisme à visage humain; **in the f. of danger** devant le danger; **in the f. of an enemy** en face d'un ennemi; **in the f. of this threat, he …** confronté à cette menace, il …; **full-f. portrait** portrait m de face

2 (expression) mine f, physionomie f; **to pull a long f.** tirer une tête longue comme ça, Fam tirer une tête de six pieds de long; **to make** or **pull faces** faire des grimaces (at à); **to keep a straight f.** garder son sérieux; **to put a good f. on it** faire contre mauvaise fortune bon cœur

3 (appearance) (of sth) apparence f, aspect m; **on the f. of it** au premier aspect, à première vue; **to save/lose f.** sauver/perdre la face; **loss of f.** humiliation f

4 Fam (cheek) culot m, front m, toupet m

5 (surface) (of the earth) surface f; **they disappeared from** or **off the f. of the earth** ils ont disparu de la surface du globe; **my keys can't just have disappeared off the f. of the earth!** mes clés n'ont pas pu se volatiliser tout de même!

6 (side) (of coin, cliff, polyhedron, golf club etc) face f; (of material) endroit m; (of document) recto m; (of building) devant m, façade f; (of crystal) facette f, plan m; (of hammer) plat m; (on valve seat) portée f; **bearing f.** (sur)face portante; **the north f. of the Eiger** la face nord de l'Eiger; **f. up/down** face en dessus/en dessous; **the toast landed f. up/down** le toast est tombé du bon/mauvais côté; Min (coal) **f.** front m de taille (du charbon)

7 (of clock, watch) cadran m

8 Typ (of character) œil m; **bold/light f.** (caractère m) gras m/maigre m

VT **1** (confront) (difficulties, enemy) affronter, faire face à; (danger) braver, affronter; **to f. facts** regarder les choses en face; **f. it** sois réaliste; **let's f. it** voyons les choses comme elles sont; **f. it – you've lost/she's not coming back** accepte-le – tu as perdu/elle ne reviendra pas; **the problem that faces us** le problème qui se pose à nous, le problème auquel nous sommes confrontés; **to be faced with a difficulty** se heurter à une difficulté; **to be faced with a decision** être confronté à une décision; **to f.** or **be faced with a crisis/a grim future** être confronté à une crise/un avenir lugubre; **he dared not f. me** il n'a pas osé me rencontrer face à face; Fig **to f. the music** faire front

2 (look towards) faire face à; **to f. the front** regarder devant soi; **sunflowers always f. the sun** le tournesol est toujours tourné vers le soleil; **hotel facing the square** hôtel en façade sur la place; **the picture facing page 10** la gravure en regard de la page 10; **facing each other** l'un en face de l'autre; Rail **seat facing the direction of travel** place f dans le sens de la marche

3 Metal etc (dress) dresser, planer, surfacer; Constr (cover) (wall etc) revêtir (with de)

VI être orienté; **the house faces north** la maison est exposée au nord ou regarde le nord; **terrace facing south** terrasse orientée au sud; **to f. both ways** faire face aux deux côtés; Fig ménager la chèvre et le chou; Mil **right/left f.!** face à droite/à gauche!

► ► **f. card** figure (de jeu de cartes); **f. cloth** ≃ gant m de toilette; **f. cream** crème f pour le visage; Br **f. flannel** ≃ gant de toilette; Sport **f. guard** masque m protecteur; **f. mask** (cosmetic) masque (de beauté); Sport masque; **f. pack** masque (de beauté); **f. powder** poudre f; TV, Cin **f. shot** plan de visage; Am **f. time** (meeting) = rencontre f en face à face entre deux personnes (par opposition aux contacts par téléphone ou courrier électronique); (on TV) temps m de présence à l'écran; **we need some f. time to solve this** il faut qu'on se voie pour régler ça; **f. value** (of bank note, traveller's cheque) valeur f nominale; (of stamp) valeur faciale; **I took him at (his) f. value** je l'ai jugé sur les apparences; **to take what sb says at f. value** prendre ce que qn dit pour argent comptant

► **face about** VI Mil faire demi-tour

► **face down** VT SEP (confront) (enemy, critic) faire face

► **face on to** VT INSEP (garden, street) donner sur

► **face out** VT SEP (deal with, confront) (problems, difficult situation) faire face à; (threat) défier; (oppose, resist) (person) résister à; **to f. it out** ne pas broncher; **to f. out opposition** résister à l'opposition

► **face up to** VT INSEP **1** (confront) (person, danger) affronter; **to f. up to one's fears** faire face à ses craintes; **you have to f. up to him over his treatment of you** il faut que tu lui dises en face que tu n'aimes pas la façon dont il te traite

2 (accept) regarder en face, faire face à; **to f. up to one's responsibilities** faire face à ses responsabilités

► **face with** VT SEP **to f. sb with sth** (confront with) confronter qn à qch; **why don't you f. them with it?** (what they said or did) pourquoi est-ce que tu ne le leur dis pas en face?; **he confessed when faced with the evidence/the dead man's wife** il a avoué lorsqu'il a été confronté aux preuves/à la femme du défunt

faceless [ˈfeɪslɪs] ADJ Fig anonyme

face-lift N **1** lifting m; **to have a f.** se faire faire un lifting **2** Fig (of façade of building) restauration f, *(of flat, house)* rénovation f, retapage m; **Glasgow's had a f.** Glasgow a été remis à neuf

facer ['feɪsər] N *Br Fam* **that's a f.!** quelle tuile!

face-saving ADJ *(agreement, compromise etc)* qui sauve la face

facet ['fæsɪt] N **1** *(of diamond, insect's eye)* facette f **2** *Fig (of situation)* aspect m; **there are several facets to this problem/question** ce problème/cette question a plusieurs facettes
‖ VT **(-tt-,** *Am* **-t-)** *(precious stone)* facetter

facetious [fə'siːʃəs] ADJ *(person, remark)* facétieux, plaisant, bouffon; **I was being f.** je plaisantais; **there's no need to be so f.** il n'y a pas de quoi se moquer

facetiously [fə'siːʃəslɪ] ADV facétieusement; *(to say sth)* d'un ton facétieux; **do you have to behave so f.?** faut-il absolument que tu fasses le bouffon?

facetiousness [fə'siːʃəsnɪs] N caractère m facétieux, bouffonnerie f *(mood)* humeur f facétieuse; **I find his f. a bit tiresome** je trouve ses bouffonneries un peu lassantes; **there's no need for f.** il n'y a pas de quoi se moquer

face-to-face ADJ *(meeting)* face-à-face; **a f. encounter** un face-à-face; **to bring sb f. with sb/the consequences of one's actions** confronter qn avec qn/aux conséquences de ses actions; **to come f. with sb** se trouver face à face avec qn; **to meet sb f.** rencontrer qn face à face

facetted ['fæsɪtɪd] ADJ à facettes

facia ['feɪʃə] N *Br Aut* tableau m de bord

facial ['feɪʃ(ə)l] ADJ *(nerve, tic)* facial, -aux; *(expression, hair)* du visage
‖ N soins mpl du visage; **to have a f.** se faire faire des soins du visage
▸▸ **f. scrub** exfoliant m

facialist ['feɪʃəlɪst] N = esthéticienne f spécialisée dans les soins du visage

facile ['fæsaɪl, -ɪl] ADJ **1** *(simplistic)* simpliste **2** *Old-fashioned Pej* facile; **to be a f. liar** être un menteur habile

facilitate [fə'sɪlɪteɪt] VT *(action)* faciliter

facilitator [fə'sɪlɪteɪtər] N *Mktg* auxiliaire mf

facility [fə'sɪlɪtɪ] N **1** *(ease)* facilité f, **f. in speaking/writing** facilité à parler/écrire; **to do sth with great f.** faire qch avec une grande facilité; **to have a f. at** *or* **for doing sth** avoir de la facilité à *ou* pour faire qch **2** *(means) (usu pl)* **facilities** aménagements mpl; **the building has limited facilities for the handicapped** le bâtiment est doté d'aménagements limités pour les handicapés; **storage/cooking facilities** installations fpl de stockage/cuisine; **transport facilities** moyens mpl de transport; **play/educational facilities** équipements mpl récréatifs/scolaires; **the village has few shopping facilities** le village ne compte pas beaucoup de magasins; **we have no facilities for it** nous ne sommes pas équipés pour cela; **facilities for payment** facilités fpl de paiement; **they are given every f. for improving their French** on leur accorde toutes facilités de se perfectionner en français; *Aviat* **ground facilities** installations au sol; *Euph* **can I use the facilities?** *(toilet)* est-ce que je peux utiliser les toilettes?; *TV etc* **facilities man** technicien m, prestataire m **3** *esp Am (establishment)* établissement m; *(hotel)* hôtel m; **training/research f.** établissement de formation/recherche

facing ['feɪsɪŋ] N **1** *Sewing (material)* revers m; *(on outside)* parement m; *(on inside)* parementure f, *Constr (of wall etc)* revêtement m; *Mil* **regimental facings** = parements mpl (de

la manche ou du col) servant à distinguer les différents corps **2** *(in shop)* frontal m, frontale f
‖ ADJ *(page)* ci-contre
▸▸ *Constr* **f. brick** brique f de parement; **f. pages** pages fpl en regard

facsimile [fæk'sɪmɪlɪ] N **1** *(copy)* fac-similé m, pl fac-similés; *Law (of will etc)* copie f figurée; **to reproduce sth in f., to make a f. of sth** faire un fac-similé de qch; **f. signature** signature f autographiée **2** *Tel* télécopie f
▸▸ **f. machine** télécopieur m

fact [fækt] N fait m; **f. and fiction** le réel et l'imaginaire; **scientific facts** les vérités fpl scientifiques; **to stick to the facts** s'en tenir aux faits; **just give me the facts** donnez-moi simplement les faits; **the f. that you're a woman** le fait que vous soyez une femme; **the f. (of the matter) is that ...** le fait est que ...; **owing to the f. that ...** du fait que ...; **it's a f. that ...** il est de fait que ...; **to know for a f. that ...** savoir pertinemment que ...; **apart from the f. that ...** hormis que ...; **in f.** de fait; **in point of f.** en fait; *Law* **the jury only decides issues of f.** les jurés ne sont juges que du fait; **the facts of life** les choses de la vie; **it's a f. of life** c'est une réalité
▸▸ **f. sheet** fiche f d'informations

fact-finding ADJ *(mission etc)* d'information, d'enquête

faction[1] ['fækʃən] N *(group)* faction f

faction[2] N *Cin, TV* docudrame m

factious ['fækʃəs] ADJ factieux

factitious [fæk'tɪʃəs] ADJ factice, artificiel, -elle

factor ['fæktər] N **1** facteur m; *Math* diviseur m, facteur; *Tech (of drag, amplification etc)* coefficient m; *Math* **the highest common f.** le plus grand commun diviseur; *Econ* **f. of production** facteur de production; **demand f.** facteur de consommation; **f. of safety, safety f.** facteur de sécurité; *Tech* **load f.** coefficient m de charge; **the human f.** le facteur humain **2** *Com (agent)* agent m, dépositaire m; *Scot (of estate)* intendant m **3** *Fin (factoring company)* société f d'affacturage
▸▸ *Math* **f. analysis** analyse f factorielle; *Econ* **f. market** marché m des facteurs de production

factorage ['fæktərɪdʒ] N *Fin* courtage m, commission f (d'affacturage)

factoring ['fæktərɪŋ] N *Com* affacturage m
▸▸ **f. company** société f d'affacturage

factory ['fækt(ə)rɪ] N usine f, **munitions f.** fabrique f de munitions; **biscuit f.** biscuiterie f
▸▸ **f. farm** ferme f industrielle; **f. farming** élevage m industriel; **f. inspection** inspection f du travail; **f. inspector** inspecteur, -trice du travail; **f. manager** directeur, -trice d'usine; **f. overheads** frais mpl généraux de fabrication; **f. price** prix m usine, prix sortie usine; **f. (retail) outlet** magasin m d'usine; **f. ship** navire-usine m, pl navires-usine; **f. shop** magasin d'usine; **f. work** travail m en usine *ou* d'usine; **f. worker** ouvrier, -ère en usine

factotum [fæk'təʊtəm] N factotum m, homme m/femme f à tout faire

factual ['fæktʃʊəl] ADJ *(account, information, description)* factuel, -elle, reposant sur les faits; *(knowledge)* des faits

factually ['fæktʃʊəlɪ] ADV en ce qui concerne les faits; *(to report, describe etc)* objectivement

facultative ['fækəltətɪv] ADJ facultatif, -ive

faculty ['fækəltɪ] N **1** *(of mind, body)* faculté f, pouvoir m; **the f. of speech** le don de la parole; **to be in possession of all one's faculties** jouir de toutes ses facultés **2** *(ability)* facilité f, talent m; **to have a f. for doing sth** avoir

des facilités pour faire qch; **to have the f. of observation** être observateur **3** *Univ (departments)* faculté f, *Am (teaching staff)* professorat m, corps m enseignant

fad [fæd] N lubie f, **it's only a passing f.** ce n'est qu'une toquade, ce n'est qu'un engouement passager; **the f. for macrobiotic food** la lubie pour les aliments macrobiotiques; **to have a f. about sth** se toquer de qch

faddiness ['fædɪnɪs] N **his f.** ses goûts mpl difficiles

faddy ['fædɪ] ADJ capricieux, maniaque; **he's f. about his food, he's a f. eater** il est difficile sur la nourriture

fade [feɪd] VI **1** *(of flowers)* se faner, se flétrir; *(of colours)* passer; *(of material)* se décolorer, déteindre; *(of hope)* s'éteindre; *(of light, sound)* s'affaiblir; **the light is fading** *(daylight)* le jour baisse; *TV, Cin* **to f. to black** faire un fondu au noir; **colours that f. into each other** couleurs qui se fondent; **summer fades into autumn** peu à peu l'automne succède à l'été; **to f. from memory** s'effacer de la mémoire **2** *TV, Cin* faire un fondu; **to f. to black** faire un fondu au noir **3** *Am Fam (leave)* s'esbigner, calter
‖ VT **1** faner, décolorer; **curtains faded by the sun** rideaux décolorés par le soleil **2** *TV, Cin* fondre
‖ N **1** *TV, Cin* fondu m **2** *(of drum brakes)* fading m, évanouissement m
▸ **fade away** VI *(of light, sound)* s'affaiblir; *Fig (of person)* dépérir
▸ **fade in** VI *(of scene in film)* ouvrir en fondu; *(of music)* commencer en fondu sonore
‖ VT SEP *TV, Cin* ouvrir en fondu; *Radio (sound)* monter; **to f. the music in** introduire la musique en fondu sonore
▸ **fade out** VI *(of scene in film)* se terminer en fondu; *(of music)* se terminer en fondu sonore
‖ VT SEP *TV, Cin* fermer en fondu; *(music)* terminer par un fondu sonore

faded ['feɪdɪd] ADJ *(flower, memory)* fané, flétri; *(material)* décoloré; *(beauty, colour)* défraîchi, passé; *(photograph)* jauni

fade-in N *(of scene, music)* ouverture f en fondu

fade-in-fade-out *Cin, Radio, TV* N fondu m enchaîné
‖ VI faire un fondu enchaîné

fade-out N *(of scene, music)* fermeture f en fondu

fader ['feɪdər] N *TV, Cin* potentiomètre m

fading ['feɪdɪŋ] ADJ *(flower)* qui se fane; *(light)* pâlissant
‖ N **1** *(of plant)* flétrissure f, *(of material)* décoloration f **2** *Radio* fading m **3** *Cin* fondu m

faecal, *Am* **fecal** ['fiːk(ə)l] ADJ fécal, -aux
▸▸ **f. matter** matières fpl fécales, déjections fpl

faeces, *Am* **feces** ['fiːsiːz] NPL *Physiol* fèces fpl, matières fpl fécales

faff [fæf] *Br Fam* N *(panic)* panique f, *(effort)* **it's too much of a faff** c'est trop compliqué
‖ VI **1** *(waste time)* glander; **stop faffing!** arrêtez de tourner en rond! **2** *(potter)* s'occuper, bricoler
▸ **faff about, faff around** VI **1** *(waste time)* glander; **stop faffing about!** arrêtez de tourner en rond! **2** *(potter)* s'occuper, bricoler; **stop faffing about with the radio** arrête de tripoter la radio

fag [fæg] N **1** *Br Fam (unpleasant job)* corvée f **2** *Am Pej Sl (homosexual)* pédé m, pédale f **3** *Br Fam (cigarette)* clope m, sèche f **4** *Br Sch (pupil)* = jeune élève m attaché au service d'un grand
‖ VI **(-gg-) 1** *Br Sch* **to f. for a senior** *(of pupil)* faire les corvées d'un grand **2** *Old-fashioned Fam (work hard)* travailler dur, s'échiner

▸▸*Br Fam* **f. end** *(of cigarette)* mégot *m; Fig (remainder)* reste *m; (of material, winter)* bout *m; (of conversation)* dernières bribes *fpl; Sl* **f. hag** fille *f* à pédés
▸ **fag out** VT SEP *Fam (of work etc)* éreinter; **fagged out** épuisé, éreinté

fagged [fægd] *Br Fam* **I can't be f.** ça ne me dit pas; **I could never really be f. about things like that** ces trucs-là ne m'ont jamais trop rien dit; **I don't know how he can be f. doing that** je ne sais pas comment il peut s'embêter à faire ça

faggot ['fægət] N **1** *Am Pej Sl (homosexual)* pédé *m*, pédale *f* **2** *Br Culin* boulette *f* (de viande) **3** *(bundle of wood)* fagot *m*

faggy ['fægɪ] ADJ *Am Pej Sl* qui fait tapette

fah [fɑː] N *Mus* = **fa**

Fahrenheit ['færənhaɪt] ADJ *Phys (scale, thermometer)* Fahrenheit; **ten degrees F.** dix degrés Fahrenheit

faience [faɪ'jɑːns] N *Cer* faïence *f*

FAIL [feɪl]

> N échec **1**
> VI recaler ▪ rater
> VT échouer **1** ▪ baisser **2** ▪ tomber en panne **2** ▪ manquer **2**

N **1** *(in exam)* échec *m;* **she got three passes and two fails** elle a réussi trois examens et en a raté deux; **he had never had a single f. in his life** il n'avait jamais raté un examen de sa vie
2 *Comput (when logging in)* erreur *f*
3 **without f.** sans faute
VI **1** *(not succeed) (of person)* ne pas réussir, échouer, manquer son coup; *(in exam)* échouer; *(of negotiations etc)* ne pas aboutir; *(of play)* faire fiasco; *(of business)* faire faillite; *(of project)* échouer; **he failed in his attempt to ...** il a échoué dans sa tentative de ...; **I f. to see why/how ...** je ne vois pas pourquoi/comment ...; **the discussions have failed to bring any progress** les discussions n'ont pas réussi à produire le moindre progrès; **the high proportions of pupils who are failing** la forte proportion d'élèves qui échouent à leurs examens
2 *(be inadequate)* manquer, faire défaut; *(of health, patient)* décliner; *(of health, light, memory, strength)* baisser; *(of eyesight)* faiblir, baisser; *(of brakes, heart, support)* lâcher; *(of engine)* tomber en panne; **his parachute failed** son parachute ne s'est pas ouvert; **if all else fails** en désespoir de cause; **to f. in one's duty** manquer à son devoir; **to f. to do sth** négliger de faire qch; **she was charged with failing to report an accident** elle a été inculpée pour avoir manqué de signaler un accident; **he failed to mention that ...** il a omis de faire remarquer que ...; **the cheque failed to arrive** le chèque n'est pas arrivé; **the engine failed to start** le moteur a refusé de démarrer; **she never fails to visit me on Sundays** elle ne manque jamais de me rendre visite le dimanche; **it never fails** *(it always happens)* ça ne manque jamais; *(of remedy)* ça ne rate jamais
VT *Sch (candidate)* refuser, recaler; *(exam)* être refusé *ou* recalé à; *(essay)* rater; **to f. a drugs test** être positif au contrôle antidopage; **words f. me** les mots me manquent; **his nerve failed him** le courage lui a fait défaut, il a manqué de courage; **I won't f. you** vous pouvez compter sur moi; **he had failed her before** il lui avait déjà fait faux bond; **his memory/eyesight was beginning to f. him** sa mémoire/vue commençait à lui faire défaut

failed [feɪld] ADJ *(candidate)* refusé, recalé; *Com (company)* en faillite; *(project, scheme)*

qui n'a pas abouti; *(artist, politician)* raté
▸▸*Comput* **f. login** ouverture *f* de session avortée

failing ['feɪlɪŋ] ADJ *(sight, strength etc)* défaillant, baissant; **to be in f. health** avoir une santé défaillante
N *(fault)* faiblesse *f*, défaut *m;* **with all her failings** malgré tous ses défauts
PREP à *ou* au défaut de; **f. a satisfactory reply** faute de réponse satisfaisante; **f. which** faute de quoi; **f. all else** en désespoir de cause; **call me at home or, f. that, at the office** appelle-moi à la maison ou, à défaut, au bureau

failsafe ['feɪlseɪf] ADJ *(system)* protégé contre les incidents; **f. device** dispositif *m* de sécurité positive

failure ['feɪljər] N **1** *(lack of success)* insuccès *m*, non-réussite *f, (in exam, of play)* échec *m; Com* faillite *f;* **the experiment was or proved or turned out a f.** l'expérience n'a pas réussi *ou* a raté; **the expedition ended in f.** l'expédition s'est soldée par un échec; **the team's f. to win the championship was a great surprise** cela a été une grande surprise que l'équipe n'ait pas remporté le championnat; **the f. of his new film** l'échec qu'a rencontré son nouveau film
2 *(person)* raté, -ée; *(play etc)* four *m*, fiasco *m;* **I'm a complete f. as a teacher** comme professeur, je suis complètement nul; *Sch* **there are too many failures** trop de candidats ont été recalés
3 *(neglect)* manque *m;* **f. to keep a promise** manquement *m* à une promesse; **f. to pay a bill** défaut *m* de paiement d'un effet; **your f. to apologise is inexcusable** tu es inexcusable de ne pas avoir demandé pardon; **he was angry at her f. even to write** il était en colère qu'elle n'écrive même pas
4 *(of machine)* panne *f, (of software, hardware)* panne, défaillance *f, (of organ)* insuffisance *f, Elec* **power f.** panne de courant;
▸▸*Am Com* **f. investment** investissement *m* en valeurs de redressement *ou* de retournement; **f. rate** taux *m* de panne

fain [feɪn] ADV *Arch, Lit* volontiers

faint [feɪnt] ADJ **1** *(weak) (hope, light, sound, possibility etc)* faible; *(praise)* tiède; *(colour)* pâle, délavé; *(sound, touch, bruise etc)* léger, -ère; *(idea)* vague, peu précis; *(mark etc)* à peine visible; *(inscription)* indistinct; **to give a f. smile** *(not be amused or pleased)* sourire du bout des lèvres; **I could detect a f. smile on her lips** j'ai décelé un petit sourire sur ses lèvres; **a f. tinge of blue** une légère nuance bleuâtre; **I haven't the faintest (idea)** je n'en ai pas la moindre idée; **the sound of the footsteps grew fainter** le bruit des pas s'affaiblit
2 **to feel** *or* **be f.** se sentir mal; **I was feeling f. with hunger** j'avais tellement faim que la tête me tournait; **to be f. with tiredness** tomber de fatigue
3 *Arch (timid)* timide; *Prov* **f. heart never won fair lady** jamais honteux n'eut belle amie
N *Med* évanouissement *m*, défaillance *f,* **to fall down in a f.** tomber évanoui
VI s'évanouir, défaillir; **she fainted with pain** elle s'évanouit de douleur

faint-hearted [-'hɑːtɪd] ADJ pusillanime

faint-heartedly [-'hɑːtɪdlɪ] ADV avec pusillanimité

faint-heartedness [-'hɑːtɪdnɪs] N pusillanimité *f*

fainting ['feɪntɪŋ] N évanouissement *m*
▸▸ **f. fit** évanouissement

faintly ['feɪntlɪ] ADV *(to hear, shine)* faiblement; *(uneasy, amused, ridiculous)* légèrement; *(to remember, see)* vaguement; **f. visible** à peine visible; **to smile f.** esquisser

un sourire; **it is f. possible that ...** il y a une faible possibilité pour que ...

faintness ['feɪntnɪs] N *(of voice, sound etc)* faiblesse *f, (of breeze etc)* légèreté *f, Med* malaise *f,* **have you been suffering from f.?** avez-vous souffert d'évanouissements?; **it's the f. of the writing that's the problem** le problème c'est que l'écriture est pâle

fair¹ [feər] N foire *f,* **world f.** exposition *f* universelle; *Br (fun)* **f.** fête *f* foraine; **village f.** kermesse *f*

FAIR²

> ADJ juste **1** ▪ équitable **1** ▪ assez bon **2** ▪ favorable **3** ▪ beau **4** ▪ blond **6**
> ADV loyalement **1**

ADJ **1** *(just)* juste, équitable; *(price)* raisonnable; *(wage)* équitable; *(fight)* loyal, -aux; **to get a f. trial** être jugé de façon équitable; **f.'s f.** il faut être juste; **that's only f.** ce n'est que juste; **it's not f.** ce n'est pas juste; **it isn't f. to expect children to ...** ce n'est pas raisonnable de demander à des enfants de ...; **f. enough!** ça va!, d'accord!; **it's all f. and above board** *or* **all f. and square** c'est de bonne guerre; **he is strict but f.** il est sévère mais juste *ou* sans parti pris; **it is only f. to say that ...** il faut dire que ...; **but, to be f.** mais, pour être honnête; **as is only f.** comme il se doit; *Sl* **f. do's** ce n'est que justice; **a f. example** un bon exemple; **a f. exchange** un échange équitable; *Prov* **f. exchange is no robbery** tout le monde est content; **everyone deserves their f. share** chacun mérite d'avoir ce qui lui est dû; **he got more than his f. share!** il a eu plus que ce qui lui revenait!; **he's had more than his f. share of criticism/problems** il a eu largement sa part de critiques/problèmes; **by f. means or foul** d'une manière ou d'une autre; *Prov* **all's f. in love and war** à la guerre comme à la guerre
2 *(quite good)* assez bon; **a f. amount of** pas mal de; **he has a f. chance of success** il a des chances de réussir; **in f. condition** acceptable; **a f. idea** une bonne idée; **a f. number of ...** un nombre respectable de ...; **a f. pace** un bon pas *ou* rythme; **f. to middling** comme ci comme ça; **in a f. way to recovering** en bonne voie de rétablissement
3 *(wind etc)* propice, favorable; **f. weather** beau temps
4 *esp Lit, Arch (attractive)* beau, *f* belle; **the fair(er) sex** le beau sexe; *Hum* **to make sth with one's own f. hands** faire qch de ses propres mains, *Hum* faire qch tout seul comme un grand
5 *(specious)* spécieux; **f. promises/words** de belles promesses/paroles
6 *(light-coloured) (person, hair)* blond; *(skin)* blanc, *f* blanche
7 *Sl (intensive)* **we had a f. old time of it at the party** nous nous sommes drôlement bien amusés à la fête
ADV **1** *(to act)* loyalement; **to play f.** jouer franc jeu; **to fight f.** se battre loyalement; **you can't say fairer than that** il n'y a pas plus équitable
2 *(completely)* complètement; **struck f. (and square) on the chin** frappé en plein menton
▸▸*Br* **f. copy** copie *f* au propre *ou* au net; **f. game** proie *f* légitime; **f. play** fair-play *m inv;* franc-jeu *m inv; Com* **f. trade** commerce *m* équitable

fairground ['feəgraʊnd] N champ *m* de foire

fair-haired ADJ blond, aux cheveux blonds; *Am Fig* **f. boy** chouchou *m*

fairing ['feərɪŋ] N *Aviat, Aut* carénage *m*

fairish ['feərɪʃ] ADJ **1** *(hair)* plutôt blond **2** *(quite good)* assez bon

fairly ['feəlɪ] ADV **1** *(to judge etc)* équitablement, avec justice; **to treat sb f.** traiter qn équitablement *ou* avec impartialité **2** *(to act, play etc)* honnêtement; *(to fight)* loyalement; **to come by sth f. (and squarely)** obtenir qch par des moyens honnêtes; **to win f. and squarely** *(clearly, easily)* remporter une nette victoire; *(without dishonest means)* vaincre honnêtement **3** *(quite) (rich, skilful etc)* assez; **f. good wine** vin passablement *ou* assez bon; **it is f. certain that …** il est à peu près certain que …; **to do sth f. well** faire qch d'une façon acceptable *ou* passable **4** *(well)* bien; **once the ship was f. under way** une fois le navire en bonne route; **we f. raced through the work** nous avons fait notre travail à bonne allure **5** *Fam (completely)* complètement, absolument

fair-minded ADJ équitable, juste

fairness ['feənɪs] N **1** *(of decision)* impartialité *f*, *(of person)* équité *f*, impartialité; *(of law, share)* équité *f*; **in all f.** en toute justice; **in f. to him, he did help us a lot** pour lui rendre justice, il faut dire qu'il nous a beaucoup aidés **2** *Arch, Lit (beauty)* beauté *f* **3** *(of hair)* blondeur *f*; *(of skin)* blancheur *f*

fair-sized ADJ assez grand

fairway ['feəweɪ] N **1** *Golf* fairway *m* **2** *Naut* chenal *m*, passe *f*, passage *m*

fair-weather ADJ *(boat)* qui convient seulement pour le beau temps; **a f. friend** un ami des beaux *ou* bons jours

fairy ['feərɪ] N **1** fée *f*; **the wicked f.** la fée Carabosse **2** *Sl, Pej (homosexual man)* pédé *m*, tapette *f*, tante *f*
ADJ féerique; **f. footsteps** des pas *mpl* légers; **f. voices** des voix *fpl* de fées
▶ **f. godmother** bonne fée *f*, *Fig* marraine *f* gâteau; **f. lights** guirlande *f* électrique; **f. queen** reine *f* des fées; **f. story** conte *m* de fées; *Fig (lie)* histoire à dormir debout; **f. tale** conte de fées; *Fig (lie)* histoire à dormir debout

fairyland ['feərɪlænd] N pays *m ou* royaume *m* des fées; *Fig (imaginary world)* féerie *f*

faith [feɪθ] N **1** *(trust)* foi *f*; **to have (every) f. in sb/sth** avoir (entièrement) confiance en qn/qch; **I don't have much f. in doctors** je ne fais pas beaucoup confiance aux médecins; **to have f. in God** avoir foi en Dieu; **to put one's f. in sb** accorder toute sa confiance à qn; **an act of f.** un acte de foi **2** *(religion)* religion *f*, foi *f*, croyance *f*; **what f. are you?** de quelle religion êtes-vous?; **to be of the Catholic/Jewish f.** être de religion catholique/juive; **the Christian f.** la foi chrétienne; **to lose one's f.** perdre la foi **3** *(loyalty)* **to keep f. with sb** tenir ses engagements envers qn; **to break f. with sb** manquer de foi *ou* de parole à qn; **good f.** bonne foi; **to say sth in good f.** dire qch en toute bonne foi; **to do sth in all good f.** faire qch en tout honneur; **bad f.** perfidie *f*
▶ **f. healer** guérisseur, -euse spirituel(elle); **f. healing** guérison *f* par la foi; **f. school** école *f* religieuse

faithful ['feɪθfʊl] ADJ **1** *(friend etc)* fidèle, loyal, -aux; *(copy)* exact, juste; *(translation, description, account)* fidèle; **to remain f. to sb/one's promises** rester fidèle à qn/ses promesses; **f. in every detail** exact jusqu'au moindre détail **2** *Rel* **the f.** les fidèles *mpl*, *(Islam)* les croyants *mpl*, *Pol* **the party f.** les fidèles du parti

faithfully ['feɪθfʊlɪ] ADV **1** *(loyally)* fidèlement, loyalement; **yours f.** *(in formal letter)* recevez l'expression de mes/nos sentiments distingués; **he promised f. to come tomorrow** il a promis f. de venir demain **2** *(to copy)* exactement; *(to translate, follow instructions)* fidèlement

faithfulness ['feɪθfʊlnɪs] N **1** *(loyalty)* fidé-

lité *f*, loyauté *f* (**to** envers) **2** *(accuracy) (of report etc)* fidélité *f*, exactitude *f*

faithless ['feɪθlɪs] ADJ **1** *Rel (lacking faith)* infidèle, sans foi **2** *(to husband, wife etc)* infidèle (**to** à); *(to party, friend etc)* déloyal, -aux

faithlessness ['feɪθlɪsnɪs] N **1** *(lack of trust)* manque *m* de confiance **2** *(to husband, wife etc)* infidélité *f* (**to** à); *(to party, friend)* déloyauté *f*

fake [feɪk] N *(object)* article *m* faux *ou* truqué; **it's a f.** c'est un faux; **he's a f.** c'est un bluffeur
ADJ faux, *f* fausse
VT *(calculations etc)* truquer; *(signature)* contrefaire; *(illness)* simuler; **faked balance sheet** bilan truqué; **to f. a story** inventer une histoire; **she faked her own death** elle a fait croire à sa propre mort; **it's all faked** *(in cinema etc)* c'est du trucage
VI *(pretend)* faire semblant, jouer la comédie

faker ['feɪkər] N *Fam (who pretends)* comédien, -ienne

faking ['feɪkɪŋ] N **it's just f.** c'est de la comédie

fakir ['feɪkɪər, fə'kɪər] N fakir *m*

falcon ['fɔːlkən] N *(bird)* faucon *m*

falconer ['fɔːlkənər] N fauconnier *m*

falconry ['fɔːlkənrɪ] N fauconnerie *f*

Falkland ['fɔːlklənd] N **the F. Islands, the Falklands** les (îles *fpl*) Malouines *fpl*, les îles Falkland

FALL ['fɔːl]		
N	chute **1, 3, 5, 8, 9** ▪ automne **2** ▪ chutes **3** ▪ baisse **4, 5**	
VI	tomber **1–3, 6–8** ▪ s'écouler **3** ▪ baisser **4, 5**	

N **1** *(of body etc)* chute *f*, *(in wrestling)* tombé *m*; *Theat (of curtain)* baisser *m*; *(of snow, rain)* précipitations *fpl*; **a f. of earth/rock** *(actual earth, rocks)* un éboulis de terre/pierres; **there's been another f.** il y a encore eu un éboulement; **to have a f.** faire une chute; **a bad f.** une mauvaise chute; **there has been a heavy f. of snow** il est tombé beaucoup de neige; *Fig* **to be heading** *or* **riding for a f.** courir à sa perte **2** *Am (autumn)* automne *m* **3** *(waterfall)* *(usu pl)* **falls** chute *f* (d'eau); **Victoria Falls** les chutes Victoria; **Niagara Falls** les chutes du Niagara **4** *(lowering) (of water)* décrue *f*, baisse *f*; *(of tide)* reflux *m*, jusant *m*; *(of voice)* cadence *f* **5** *(decrease) (in weight, number etc)* diminution *f*, *(of barometer, in pressure etc)* chute *f*, *(in temperature, interest, income, frequency)* baisse *f*, *Com, Fin (of prices, shares)* baisse; *(of currency)* dépréciation *f*, **f. in prices** baisse de prix **6** *(slope) (of road etc)* pente *f* **7** *(ruin) (of person)* perte *f*, ruine *f*, **after this f. from grace** après être tombé en disgrâce **8** *(capture) (of city)* chute *f*, *(of empire etc)* chute, déchéance *f*; **the F. of the Roman Empire** la chute de l'Empire romain; **the F. of the Bastille** la prise de la Bastille **9** *Rel* **the F. (of Man)** la chute
VI *(pt* **fell** [fel]*, pp* **fallen** ['fɔːlən]*)* **1** *(from a height)* tomber; *Astron (of star)* filer; **to f. to the ground** tomber à terre; **she fell to her death** elle a fait une chute mortelle; **to f. off a ladder** tomber d'une échelle; **to f. 20 feet** faire une chute de six mètres; **the water falls over 800 m to the valley below** l'eau tombe dans une cascade de plus de 800 m de haut jusque dans la vallée; **the cliff falls sheer to the ocean below** la falaise descend à pic vers l'océan; **to f. out of the window** tomber par la fenêtre; **to f. on one's feet** retomber sur ses pieds; *Fig* avoir de la chance;

to f. short of a target manquer la cible; **to f. short of a past performance** être loin d'une performance passée; **to f. into a trap** tomber *ou* donner dans un piège; **to f. into sb's hands** tomber entre les mains de qn; **night is falling** la nuit tombe; **rain/snow had fallen overnight** il avait plu/neigé pendant la nuit; **his hair fell to his shoulders** *(hung down)* ses cheveux lui descendaient *ou* tombaient jusqu'aux épaules; **his hair keeps falling into his eyes** ses cheveux n'arrêtent pas de lui tomber dans les yeux **2** *(from standing or perpendicular position)* **to f. to the ground** tomber par terre; **to f. on one's knees** tomber à genoux; **to f. (in battle)** tomber au champ d'honneur; *Fig* **the scheme fell flat** le projet est tombé à l'eau **3** *(collapse) (of building)* s'écrouler, s'effondrer; **to f. to pieces** *ou* **bits** tomber en morceaux; **when Liège fell** lorsque Liège capitula; **the government has fallen** le gouvernement a été renversé *ou* est tombé **4** *(diminish) (of price etc)* diminuer, baisser, chuter; *(of exchange etc)* baisser, se déprécier; *(of wind)* tomber; *Fig* **his stock is falling** son crédit est en baisse; **the thermometer/temperature has fallen ten degrees** le thermomètre/la température a baissé *ou* chuté de dix degrés **5** *(become lower) (of ground)* aller en pente, s'incliner; *(of tide etc)* baisser; **her eyes fell** elle a baissé les yeux; **his face fell** sa figure s'allongea; **my spirits fell** j'ai perdu tout courage; **to f. from one's position** déchoir de sa position; **to f. to the bottom of the league/list** tomber en bas du classement/de la liste; **to f. in sb's estimation** baisser dans l'estime de qn **6** *Rel (sin)* tomber, pécher; **to f. from grace** perdre la grâce; *Fig* **to f. from grace with sb** tomber en disgrâce auprès de qn **7** *(alight)* **a shadow fell on the wall** une ombre se projeta sur le mur; **his eye fell on a box/a curious headline** son regard est tombé sur une boîte/un titre curieux **8** *(occur)* tomber; **Christmas falls on a Thursday** Noël tombe un jeudi; **the accent falls on the last syllable** l'accent tombe sur la dernière syllabe; **it fell to me to break the bad news** c'est à moi qu'il est revenu d'annoncer la mauvaise nouvelle; **these facts f. under another category** ces faits entrent dans une autre catégorie; **that falls outside the scope of our investigation** ceci dépasse les limites de notre enquête **9** *(enter into given state)* **to f. under suspicion** *(of person)* devenir l'objet des soupçons, devenir suspect; **the country has fallen on hard times** le pays connaît des jours difficiles; **I soon fell in with their ways** *(became used to their way of doing things)* je me suis vite accoutumé à leur manière de faire; *(learnt routine)* j'ai bientôt appris la routine; **to f. in love with sb/sth** tomber amoureux de qn/qch; **to f. into a habit** contracter une habitude; **to f. into error** être induit en erreur; **to f. into despair** sombrer dans le désespoir; **to f. into line with** s'aligner sur **10** *(become)* **to f. asleep** s'endormir; **to f. ill** *or* **sick** tomber malade; **to f. silent** *(of person, guns)* se taire; **the room fell silent** le silence se fit dans la salle; **to f. vacant** *(of post)* se trouver vacant; **to f. (a) victim to …** être victime de … **11** *(begin)* **they fell to work/discussing (again)** ils se (re)mirent au travail/à discuter
▶ *Fam* **f. guy** *(dupe)* pigeon *m*; *(scapegoat)* bouc *m* émissaire
▶ **fall about** VI *(fall in different directions)* tomber de côté et d'autre; **to f. about (laughing)** se tordre de rire
▶ **fall apart** VI *(fall to pieces)* se désintégrer,

tomber en morceaux; *(of marriage)* se désintégrer, sombrer

► **fall away** vi **1** *(of ground)* s'affaisser

2 *(crumble)* se désintégrer; *(of plaster, paint)* s'écailler

3 *(of attendance)* diminuer; *(of followers etc)* déserter

4 *(of prejudice etc)* disparaître

► **fall back** vi **1** *(fall)* tomber à la renverse *ou* en arrière; **to f. back on the cushions** *(after trying to get up)* retomber sur les coussins; *(sink back)* se basculer en arrière sur les coussins; *(from standing position)* tomber à la renverse sur les coussins

2 *(of troops)* se replier, reculer; **to f. back a pace** reculer d'un pas

3 *StExch, Fin* **to f. back two points** se replier de deux points

► **fall back on** vt insep *(resort to)* avoir recours à; **she fell back on the usual clichés** elle a eu recours aux clichés habituels; **to have some money to f. back on** avoir de l'argent en réserve au cas où; **he knew he could always f. back on his parents** il savait qu'il pouvait compter sur ses parents

► **fall behind** vi *(of runner, political party etc)* être à la traîne, se faire distancer, rester en arrière; **to f. behind with the rent** être en retard pour payer son loyer; **to f. behind with one's work** prendre du retard dans son travail

► **fall down** vi **1** *(fall to ground)* tomber à terre *ou* par terre

2 *(of building etc)* s'écrouler, s'effondrer

3 *(fail)* échouer; **that's where their argument falls down** c'est sur ce point que leurs arguments ne tiennent plus debout; **where the whole thing falls down is …** là où plus rien ne tient debout *ou* où tout s'écroule, c'est …; **I fell down badly on the first question** j'ai complètement raté la première question; **to f. down on the job** ne pas être à la hauteur

► **fall for** vt insep *Fam* **1** *(fall in love with)* *(person)* tomber amoureux de; **I've fallen for that antique chair** j'ai eu le coup de foudre pour cette vieille chaise

2 *(be deceived by)* *(story etc)* se laisser prendre à; **to f. for it** s'y laisser prendre; **I'm not falling for that one!** ça ne prend pas!, à d'autres!

► **fall in** vi **1** *(of building, roof etc)* s'écrouler, s'effondrer; *(of trench etc)* s'ébouler; **I was running along the edge of the pool when I fell in** je courais le long de la piscine quand je suis tombé dedans

2 *Mil (of troops)* former les rangs; **f. in!** rassemblement!

► **fall in with** vt insep **1** *(person)* *(meet up with)* rencontrer par hasard; *(associate with)* fréquenter; **my son fell in with a bad crowd** mon fils s'est mis à avoir de mauvaises fréquentations

2 *(agree with)* *(suggestion)* accepter; *(request)* accéder à; **I fell in with the plans for a picnic** j'ai accepté le projet d'un pique-nique

► **fall off** vi **1** *(fall from something)* tomber; **I picked the violin up and the neck fell off** j'ai pris le violon et le manche est tombé

2 *(of followers etc)* faire défection; *(of profits)* diminuer; *(of speed)* ralentir; *(of wind)* tomber; *(of zeal)* se relâcher; *(of popularity)* baisser

3 *(of skills, standards, quality)* baisser

4 *Naut* abattre sous le vent

► **fall on** vt insep **1** *(of blame, responsibility, suspicion)* retomber sur

2 *(attack)* *(enemy)* attaquer; *(food)* se jeter sur; **they fell on each other in delighted relief** vivement soulagés, ils tombèrent dans les bras l'un de l'autre

► **fall out** vi **1** *(fall from inside sth)* tomber dehors; *(of hair)* tomber

2 *Mil (of troops)* rompre les rangs; **f. out! rompez!**

3 *(quarrel)* se brouiller, se fâcher *(with* avec); **they have fallen out** ils sont fâchés *ou* brouillés

4 *(occur)* se passer, se dérouler; **as things fell out** en fin de compte

► **fall over** vi *(of person)* tomber (par terre); *(of thing)* se renverser, être renversé

vt insep *(stumble on)* trébucher sur; **move that suitcase before someone falls over it** déplace cette valise avant que quelqu'un ne se prenne les pieds dedans; *Fam* **publishers were falling over each other for her new book** les éditeurs se disputaient avec acharnement son nouveau livre; **he was falling over himself to please her** il se mettait en quatre pour lui plaire

► **fall through** vi *(of scheme etc)* ne pas aboutir, échouer, *Fam* tomber à l'eau

► **fall to** vi *Old-fashioned Fam (begin eating)* s'attaquer au repas

► **fall upon** vt insep = **fall on**

fallacious [fə'leɪʃəs] adj erroné

fallacy ['fæləsɪ] n erreur *f*; *(in logic)* sophisme *m*; **it is a f. that …** ce serait une erreur de croire que …; **the f. of this argument is that …** ce qui est faux dans ce raisonnement, c'est que …

fallback ['fɔːlbæk] n solution *f* de remplacement

adj de remplacement, alternatif

fallen ['fɔːlən] adj **1** *(leaf, tree etc)* tombé; *(angel)* déchu; *(idol)* tombé en disgrâce **2** *(immoral)* perdu

npl *Mil, Lit* **in memory of the f.** en mémoire des soldats tombés au combat

► ► *Med* **f. arches** affaissement *m* de la voûte plantaire; *Old-fashioned* **f. woman** femme *f* déchue, fille *f* perdue

fallibility [fælɪ'bɪlɪtɪ] n faillibilité *f*

fallible ['fælɪb(ə)l] adj faillible

falling ['fɔːlɪŋ] adj *(piece of masonry, tile)* qui tombe; *(darkness etc)* tombant; *(temperature, membership, standards)* en baisse; *Com (prices)* qui baisse; *(market)* avec tendance à la baisse

n chute *f*, *(of prices, barometer etc)* baisse *f*

► ► **f. away** *(of support)* affaiblissement *m*; *(of supporters)* défection *f*, désertion *f*; **f. rocks** chute *f* de pierres; *Arch* **f. sickness** épilepsie *f*; **f. star** étoile *f* filante

fall(ing)-off n *(of support)* affaiblissement *m*; *(of supporters)* désertion *f*, défection *f*; *(of figures, rate etc)* diminution *f*, baisse *f*; *(of power, popularity)* déclin *m*; *(of zeal)* relâchement *m*; *(of orders, business)* ralentissement *m*

Fallopian [fə'ləʊpɪən] adj

► ► *Anat* **F. tube** trompe *f* de Fallope

fallout ['fɔːlaʊt] n retombées *fpl* (radioactives); *Fig* **the political f. from the scandal** les retombées politiques du scandale

fallow¹ ['fæləʊ] *Agr* n jachère *f*

adj *(land)* en jachère; **to lie f.** être en jachère; *Fig* **a f. period** une période de régénération

fallow² adj

► ► *Zool* **f. deer** daim *m*

false [fɔːls] adj **1** *(incorrect)* faux, *f* fausse; *(idea)* erroné; **to give sb a f. impression of sth** donner à qn une fausse impression sur qch; **to put a f. interpretation on sb's actions/words** mal interpréter les actions/paroles de qn; **one f. move and he would have killed me** il m'aurait tué, au faux mouvement, il m'avait fait un faux mouvement; **to put sb in a f. position** donner de qn l'image qu'il en tort

2 *(dishonest)* hypocrite; *(unfaithful)* infidèle; *(promise etc)* mensonger; **he turns on the charm for them – it's all so f.!** il veut leur

faire du charme – quelle hypocrisie!; **to be in a f. position** être dans une situation délicate; **under f. pretences** par des moyens frauduleux; *(by lying)* sous des prétextes fallacieux

adv *(not real)* *(beard, nose etc)* faux, *f* fausse, artificiel, -elle, postiche; *(action etc)* feint, prétendu; *(coin, seal, document)* faux, contrefait; **it's a f. economy** ça ne revient pas moins cher

adv *Lit, Old-fashioned* **to play sb f.** trahir qn; **his memory played him f.** sa mémoire l'a trahi *ou* lui a joué des tours

► ► **f. alarm** fausse alerte *f*, *Fam* canard *m*; **f. bottom** *(of box etc)* double fond *m*; **f. claim** *(made for product)* promesse *f* mensongère; **f. dawn** lueurs *fpl* annonciatrices de l'aube; *Acct* **f. entry** fausse écriture *f*, *Ling* **f. friend** faux ami *m*; **f. invoice** fausse facture *f*, *Psy* **f. memory syndrome** syndrome *m* des faux souvenirs; **f. modesty** fausse modestie *f*, **f. name** faux nom *m*; *Mus* **f. note** fausse note *f*, *Fig* **to strike a f. note** créer une fausse note; **f. positive** *(pregnancy etc test)* résultat *m* faussement positif; **f. report** fausse nouvelle *f*, *Sport* **f. start** faux départ *m*; **to get off to a f. start** faire un faux départ; **f. teeth** fausses dents *fpl*, dentier *m*; **f. trade description** description *f* commerciale erronée *ou* mensongère; **f. witness** faux témoin *m*; **to bear f. witness** faire un faux témoignage

false-hearted [-'hɑːtɪd] adj *Lit* fourbe

falsehood ['fɔːlshʊd] n **1** **to distinguish truth from f.** distinguer le vrai du faux **2** *Fml (lie)* mensonge *m*; **to tell a f.** dire un mensonge

falsely ['fɔːlslɪ] adv faussement; **to smile f.** affecter un sourire; *esp Lit* **to act f.** agir déloyalement

falseness ['fɔːlsnɪs] n **1** *(of report, manner etc)* fausseté *f* **2** *Old-fashioned (of lover etc)* infidélité *f*

falsers ['fɔːləz] npl *Br Fam Hum (teeth)* râtelier *m*, dentier *m*

falsetto [fɔːl'setəʊ] *Mus* n **1** *(voice)* voix *f* de fausset; **to sing (in) f.** chanter en fausset **2** *(singer)* fausset *m*

adj *(voice)* de fausset

falsies ['fɔːlsɪz] npl *Fam* **1** *(padding for breasts)* soutien-gorge *m* rembourré **2** *(false breasts)* faux seins *mpl*

falsifiable [fɔːlsɪ'faɪəb(ə)l] adj *Phil* falsifiable

falsification [fɔːlsɪfɪ'keɪʃən] n falsification *f*

falsify ['fɔːlsɪfaɪ] vt (**falsified; falsifying**) **1** *(make false)* *(document)* falsifier; *(balance sheet)* fausser; *(facts etc)* dénaturer **2** *(disprove)* prouver la fausseté de

falsity ['fɔːlsɪtɪ] n = **falseness**

falter ['fɔːltər] vi *(of voice)* hésiter, trembler; *(of person)* chanceler; *(in one's belief, conviction)* vaciller; *(of courage, determination)* défaillir; **his steps faltered as he neared the room** ses pas se firent hésitants tandis qu'il s'approchait de la pièce; **he faltered in his speech** il eut un moment d'hésitation

vt dire d'une voix hésitante; **he faltered his way through his speech** *(nervously)* il a prononcé son discours d'une voix hésitante; *(losing thread)* il n'a pas arrêté de perdre le fil de son discours

► **falter out** vt sep *(excuse etc)* balbutier

faltering ['fɔːltərɪŋ] adj *(voice etc)* hésitant; *(courage, memory etc)* défaillant; *(legs)* chancelant; **to speak in a f. voice** parler d'une voix mal assurée; **to reply in f. Spanish** répondre dans un espagnol mal assuré; **with f. steps** d'un pas mal assuré *ou* chancelant; **a child's first f. steps** les premiers pas hésitants d'un enfant

fame [feɪm] N renom m, renommée f; **to win f.** devenir célèbre; **to rise** or **come to f. as an explorer** atteindre la renommée en tant qu'explorateur; **to seek f. and fortune** rechercher la gloire et la fortune; **house of ill f.** maison mal famée; **not Chandler of Philip Marlowe f.?** le Chandler célèbre pour son Philip Marlowe?

famed [feɪmd] ADJ célèbre, bien connu (**for** pour); **she was f. for her rudeness** elle était bien connue pour son impolitesse

familiar [fəˈmɪlɪər] ADJ **1** (well-known) familier, -ière, bien connu; **a f. face** un visage familier; **she looks f.** je l'ai déjà vue quelque part; **an experience that will be f. to everyone** une expérience bien connue de tous; **it strikes one as f.** (seen before) cela laisse une impression de déjà vu; (heard before) cela laisse une impression de déjà entendu; **to be on f. ground** être sur son terrain; **an all too f. story of drug addiction and homelessness** c'est une histoire malheureusement banale de gens qui se droguent et qui sont à la rue; **his voice sounded f. to me** il me sembla reconnaître sa voix; **there was something f. about him/it** il/cela me disait quelque chose **2** (acquainted) **to be f. with sb/sth** bien connaître qn/qch; **to be f. with the customs** être au courant des usages; **to become more f. with sb/sth** se familiariser avec qn/qch **3** (intimate) familier, intime; Ling familier; **to adopt a f. tone** prendre un ton familier ou d'intimité; **to be on f. terms with sb** bien connaître qn; Old-fashioned **you are rather too f.** vous prenez trop de privautés; **don't let the pupils get too f. (with you)** ne laissez pas les élèves prendre trop de familiarités (avec vous)

N **1** (in witchcraft) (spirit) démon m familier **2** Old-fashioned (friend) familier m, intime m
▶▶ **f. spirit** (in witchcraft) démon m familier

familiarity [fəmɪlɪˈærɪtɪ] N **1** (intimacy) familiarité f; Prov **f. breeds contempt** la familiarité engendre ou fait naître le mépris **2** (acquaintance) connaissance f (**with** de); **her f. with French** sa connaissance du français

familiarization [fəmɪlɪəraɪˈzeɪʃən] N **after a period of f. with ...** après une période de familiarisation avec ...; **greater f. with the details of the proposal** une connaissance plus poussée des détails de la proposition
▶▶ Com **f. trip** voyage m d'études ou de familiarisation

familiarize [fəˈmɪlɪəraɪz] VT **1** (acquaint) **to f. sb with sth** faire connaître qch à qn, familiariser qn avec qch; **to f. oneself with a language/the rules** se familiariser avec une langue/le règlement **2** (make known) rendre familier; **science-fiction had long familiarized us with the idea** la science-fiction nous avait depuis longtemps rendu cette idée familière ou habitués à cette idée

familiarly [fəˈmɪlɪəlɪ] ADV familièrement; **f. known as ...** communément connu comme ...

family [ˈfæmlɪ, -ɪlɪ] N **1** VOIR GRAMMAIRE A11 famille f; **large f.** famille nombreuse; **a friend of the f.**, **a f. friend** un ami de la famille; **they don't want (to have** or **start) a f. yet** ils ne veulent pas encore avoir un enfant ou fonder de famille; **to be one of the f.** être de la maison; Fam **we've got f. coming to stay** nous allons avoir de la famille en visite; Fam **she's like f.** c'est comme si elle était de la famille; **it runs in the f.** cela tient de famille; **disease that runs in the f.** maladie f héréditaire; **the painting has been in the f. for generations** ce tableau est dans la famille depuis des générations; **we will keep it in the f.** (of heirloom, land etc) ça restera dans

la famille; (of scandal) ça ne sortira pas de la famille; **you can see the f. resemblance** or **likeness** on ne peut se ne pas remarquer un air de famille; Fam **she's in the f. way** elle est enceinte; **to get** or **put sb in the f. way** mettre qn enceinte; **f. business** entreprise f familiale; **f. butcher** boucher m du coin; **f. doctor** médecin m de famille; **a f. dinner** un dîner en famille; **a f. celebration** une fête de famille; Fam **f. get-together** réunion f familiale; **f. life** vie f familiale; **f. likeness** air m de famille; **f. portraits** portraits mpl d'ancêtres; **sorry, it's a f. joke** désolé, c'est une plaisanterie qu'on ne peut comprendre que si l'on fait partie de la famille; Com **f.-size(d) jar/packet** pot m/paquet m familial; **f. programme** émission f tout public; **unsuitable for f. viewing** non approprié aux enfants; **I wouldn't call it f. viewing** ce n'est pas exactement un spectacle à conseiller aux enfants; **this film is not f. viewing** ce n'est pas un film tout public **2** Biol, Ling (of plants, words etc) famille f
▶▶ Br Admin Formerly **f. allowance** ≃ allocations fpl familiales; **f. car** familiale f; Br Admin Formerly **f. income supplement** ≃ complément m familial; Fam Hum **f. jewels** (man's genitals) bijoux mpl de famille; **f. man** père m de famille; **f. name** nom m de famille; **f. planning** planning m familial; **f. planning clinic** centre m de planning familial; **f. rate** tarif m famille; **f. room** (in hotel) chambre f familiale; Am (in house) salle f de séjour; Br (in pub) salle réservée aux familles; **f. saloon** berline f familiale; **f. tree** arbre m généalogique

family-run ADJ (hotel, restaurant) géré en famille, familial, -aux

famine [ˈfæmɪn] N (food shortage) famine f; **to die of f.** mourir de faim; **f. prices** prix mpl exorbitants ou faramineux

famished [ˈfæmɪʃt] ADJ affamé; Fam **to be** or **feel f.** (hungry) mourir de faim, être affamé

famous [ˈfeɪməs] ADJ **1** célèbre, renommé (**for** pour, par); **many f. names have stayed here** beaucoup de personnages célèbres ont séjourné ici; **f. in history** célèbre dans l'histoire; **town f. for its monuments** ville célèbre ou renommée pour ou par ses monuments; Iron **f. last words!** c'est cela, oui! **2** Old-fashioned Fam (excellent) parfait, fameux
NPL **the f.** les célébrités fpl

famously [ˈfeɪməslɪ] ADV **1 the castle has often been the scene of important events, most f. when ...** le château a souvent été la scène d'événements importants, le plus célèbre d'entre eux ayant eu lieu quand ... **2** Old-fashioned Fam (very well) fameusement, à merveille; **I get on f. with him** on s'entend à merveille

fan[1] [fæn] N **1** (hand-held) éventail m **2** (mechanical) ventilateur m; Ind soufflet m; Sl **when the shit** or **it hits the f.** quand la merde me/nous/lui/etc tombera dessus; Aut **radiator f.** ventilateur m **3** Agr (winnowing machine) tarare m

VT (**-nn-**) **1** (blow air on) (person) éventer; (fire, embers) souffler sur; Fig (stir up) (passions) attiser, exciter; (quarrel) attiser, envenimer; **these remarks had fanned the flames of nationalist feeling** ces remarques avaient exacerbé le sentiment nationaliste; **to f. the embers of sb's passion** raviver les flammes de la passion de qn; **terraces fanned by cool sea breezes** terrasses rafraîchies par les brises de mer **2** Agr (winnow) (grain) vanner
▶▶ Aut **f. belt** courroie f de ventilateur; **f. heater** radiateur m soufflant; **f. palm** palmier-éventail m, pl palmiers-éventails; Archit **f. vaulting** voûte(s) f(pl) en éventail

▶ **fan out** VI (spread out) se déployer en éventail
VT SEP (spread out) étaler (en éventail)

fan[2] N Fam (enthusiast) (of television, sport etc) fanatique mf, fana mf; (of singer, actor) fan mf; **a f. of sb/sth** un fana de qn/qch; **I'm a big f. (of hers)** je suis un de ses fans les plus fervents; **I'm not a great f. of his** il est loin d'être mon idole; **football f.** fana de football
▶▶ **f. base** public m; **f. club** cercle m ou club m de fans; **f. mail** courrier m des admirateurs

fan(-assisted) oven [(əsɪstɪd)] N four m à chaleur pulsée

fanatic [fəˈnætɪk] ADJ, N fanatique mf

fanatical [fəˈnætɪk(ə)l] ADJ fanatique

fanatically [fəˈnætɪklɪ] ADV fanatiquement

fanaticism [fəˈnætɪsɪz(ə)m] N fanatisme m

fanciable [ˈfænsɪəb(ə)l] ADJ Fam attirant

fancied [ˈfænsɪd] ADJ (imaginary) imaginaire

fancier [ˈfænsɪər] N (of dogs etc) connaisseur, -euse

fanciful [ˈfænsɪfʊl] ADJ **1** (unrealistic) (project, idea etc) chimérique; **he was being rather f.** (being unrealistic) il se faisait des idées, il rêvait; (indulging his imagination) il se laissait porter par son imagination **2** (imaginative) (person) capricieux, fantasque; (work etc) fantaisiste; (portrait) plein de fantaisie

fancifully [ˈfænsɪfʊlɪ] ADV d'une manière fantasque; (decorated) de manière fantaisiste; **somewhat f. described as ...** désigné sous le terme plutôt fantaisiste de ...

fan-cooled [-kuːld] ADJ refroidi par ventilateur

fancy [ˈfænsɪ] N **1** (imagination) imagination f, fantaisie f, (imagined thing) chose f imaginaire; **the realm of f.** le domaine de l'imaginaire ou de l'imagination; **it's only f.!** c'est pure imagination!; **idle fancies** vaines imaginations **2** (whim) fantaisie f, caprice m; **just as the f. takes me** comme l'idée me prend, Fam comme ça me chante **3** (liking) **he took a f. to the house** la maison lui a plu; **to take an immediate f. to sth** s'enticher de qch; **to take a f. to sb** (become fond of) prendre qn en affection; (become sexually attracted to) s'éprendre ou s'enticher de qn; **it took** or **caught my f. at once** cela m'a séduit du premier coup

ADJ (jewels, gadget, hat) de fantaisie; (writing style) recherché; **just a bottle of ordinary wine, nothing f.** juste une bouteille de vin ordinaire, rien de spécial; **f. biscuits** biscuits assortis; **f. footwork** beau jeu de jambes; Fig **I had to do a bit of f. footwork** j'ai dû faire des pieds et des mains; Fam **to cut out the f. stuff** élaguer, faire moins de fantaisies; **f. price** prix excessif ou exorbitant

VT **1** (imagine) s'imaginer, se figurer; Fam **f. now!**, **just f.!**, **f. (that)!** figurez-vous ça!; **f. meeting you!** tiens, toi ici!; **f. him not knowing that!** il ne sait pas ça! incroyable! **2** (have impression) **to f. (that)** croire ou penser que; **I f. I have seen her before** j'ai l'impression de l'avoir déjà vue; **he fancied he heard footsteps** il a cru entendre des pas **3** Br Fam (feel desire for) **to f. sb** être attiré par qn; **he fancies you** tu lui plais; **I like him as a person but I don't f. him** je l'aime bien en tant que personne mais il ne m'attire pas; **he fancies her rotten** elle lui plaît vachement **4** Fam (have good opinion of) **to f. oneself** être infatué de sa petite personne, se gober; **he fancies himself as a speaker** il se croit orateur; **I don't f. their chances of winning** je ne crois pas qu'ils aient des chances de gagner; **they were not fancied to win** personne ne pensait qu'ils gagneraient; *Horse-racing* **strongly fancied horse** cheval très coté

5 *Br Fam* **to f. sth** *(like)* bien aimer qch; *(feel like)* avoir envie de qch; **I don't f. his offer** son offre ne me dit rien; **I f. a bit of chicken** je mangerais volontiers un morceau de poulet, j'ai envie d'un morceau de poulet; **I wouldn't f. being in her shoes** je ne voudrais pas être à sa place; **I don't f. going** ça ne me dit rien d'y aller, je n'ai pas envie d'y aller; **she wasn't sure if she fancied the idea** elle n'était pas sûre que l'idée la tentait; **I didn't really f. the sound of her second novel** son deuxième roman ne m'a trop rien dit
▸▸ *Fam* **F. Dan** *(dandy)* dandy *m*; *(show-off)* frimeur *m*; *Br* **f. dress** déguisement *m*, costume *m*; **f. dress party** fête *f* déguisée; *Br* **f. goods** articles *mpl* de fantaisie; *Fam Pej* **f. man** jules *m*; *Fam Pej* **f. woman** maîtresse *f*, poule *f*

fancy-free ADJ **to be f.** avoir le cœur libre
fancywork ['fænsɪwɜːk] N *Sewing* broderie *f*, *(crochet work)* crochet *m*
fanfare ['fænfeər] N fanfare *f*
fanfold ['fænfəʊld] ADJ
▸▸ *Comput* **f. paper** papier *m* continu plié en accordéon
fang [fæŋ] N *(of dog etc)* croc *m*; *(of viper)* crochet *m*; *(of vampire)* canine *f*
fanlight ['fænlaɪt] N imposte *f*
fanny ['fænɪ] N **1** *Br Vulg (vagina)* chatte *f* **2** *Am Fam (buttocks)* derrière *m*, fesses *fpl* **3** *Br Sl Euph* **sweet f. adams** rien du tout, nib de nib
▸▸ *Am* **f. pack** banane *f (pochette)*
▸ **fanny about, fanny around** VI *Br Sl* perdre son temps à des bricoles, glander
fan-shaped ADJ en éventail
fantabulous [fæn'tæbjʊləs] ADJ *Fam* sensass
fantail ['fænteɪl] N *(bird)* pigeon *m* paon
fantailed ['fænteɪld] ADJ
▸▸ **f. pigeon** pigeon *m* paon
fantasia [fæn'teɪzɪə] N *Mus* fantaisie *f*
fantasize ['fæntəsaɪz] VI fantasmer (**about** sur); **he fantasized about being able to read people's minds** son fantasme était de pouvoir lire les pensées; **she was still fantasizing about making love to Robert Redford when ...** elle fantasmait encore qu'elle faisait l'amour avec Robert Redford quand ...
VT **to f. that ...** imaginer que ...
fantastic [fæn'tæstɪk] ADJ **1** *Fam (excellent)* formidable, fantastique; **we had a f. time** nous nous sommes vraiment bien amusés **2** *(enormous) (price, size etc)* énorme; **a f. sum** une somme faramineuse; *Com* **f. reductions** soldes *mpl* monstres **3** *(unbelievable) (person, thing)* bizarre; *(thing)* fantastique, grotesque; *(animals)* fantastique; *(claim)* grotesque, absurde; **that's the most f. thing I've ever heard** c'est la chose la plus grotesque *ou* absurde que j'aie jamais entendue; **what is absolutely f. about all this is that ...** ce qu'il y a de vraiment fantastique dans toute cette histoire, c'est que ...; **it sounds f., but it's true** *(unbelievable)* ça paraît inouï, mais c'est vrai; **it's f. to suppose/claim that ...** *(absurd)* c'est absurde de penser/de prétendre que ...
fantastically [fæn'tæstɪklɪ] ADV **1** *Fam* **f. beautiful/old/mean** incroyablement beau/vieux/méchant **2** **somewhat f., the story ends with ...** l'histoire se termine d'une manière un peu invraisemblable avec ...
fantasy ['fæntəsɪ, -zɪ] N **1** *(imagined event)* vision *f* bizarre; *(idea)* idée *f* fantasque; *(proposal)* extravagance *f*; **sexual f.** fantasme *m* sexuel; **his f. was to own a house**

in the country son rêve était d'avoir une maison à la campagne **2** *(imagination)* fantaisie *f*; **you live in a f. world!** tu vis dans un monde imaginaire!; **he has a strong sense of f.** il a énormément de fantaisie; **the realm of f.** le domaine de l'imaginaire **3** *(work)* Art œuvre *f* fantastique; *Mus* fantaisie *f*

> Note that the French word **fantaisie** is a false friend.

fanzine ['fænziːn] N fanzine *m*
FAO [efeɪ'əʊ] N *(abbr Food and Agriculture Organization)* FAO *f*
PREP *(abbr for the attention of)* à l'attention de
FAQ [efeɪ'kjuː] N *Comput (abbr frequently asked questions)* FAQ
▸▸ *Comput* **F. file** fichier *m* FAQ

FAR [fɑːr]

| ADV loin **1** ▪ beaucoup **3** |
| ADJ lointain **1** ▪ éloigné **1** ▪ autre **2** ▪ extrême **2** |

VOIR GRAMMAIRE A26 ADV **(farther, farthest** ['fɑːðər, -ɪst], **further, furthest** ['fɜːðər, -ɪst]) **1** *(distance)* loin; **to go f.** aller loin; **how f. did you go?** jusqu'où êtes-vous allé?; **I got as f. as Birmingham** je suis allé jusqu'à Birmingham; *Fig* **this young man will go f.** ce jeune homme ira loin; **a pound does not go very f. nowadays** on ne va pas loin avec une livre de nos jours; **to go so f. as to do sth** aller jusqu'à faire qch; **I'll go so f. as to say that ...** j'irai jusqu'à dire que ...; **things went so f. that ...** les choses sont allées si loin que ...; *Fig* **to go too f.** aller trop loin; **that is going too f.** cela passe la mesure; **to live f. away** *(from here)* habiter loin d'ici; *(from there)* habiter loin; **her thoughts were f. away** sa pensée était ailleurs; **it isn't f. off** ce n'est pas loin; **f. from ...** loin de ...; **not f. from ...** à peu de distance de ...; *Fig* **f. from it** loin de là; *Fig* **not f. from it** peu s'en faut; **f. be it from me to ...** loin de moi l'idée de ...; **f. from admiring him, I loathe him** bien loin de l'admirer, je le déteste; **f. out at sea** au (grand) large; **f. beneath/above us** loin au-dessous/au-dessus de nous; **f. and wide** or **near** de tous côtés; **they searched f. and wide for a suitable site** ils ont cherché partout un emplacement convenable; **the story so f. =** résumé *m* des chapitres précédents; **how f. have you got?** *(with your reading etc)* où en êtes-vous?; **as f. as the eye can see** à perte de vue; **as f. as I know** autant que je sache; **I will help you as f. as I can** or **as f. as possible** je vous aiderai de mon mieux; **as f. as I can judge ...** pour autant que je puisse en juger ...; **as f. as I know** autant que je sache; **in so f. as ...** dans la mesure où ...; **by f.** de loin; **by f. the best** de beaucoup *ou* de loin le meilleur

2 *(time)* **so f.** jusqu'ici; **so f. so good** jusqu'ici tout va bien; **have you seen him? – not so f.** l'avez-vous vu? – pas encore; **as f. back as I can remember** aussi loin que je puisse me rappeler; **as f. back as 1990** déjà en 1990; **she is not f. off sixty** elle n'est pas loin de la soixantaine; **to work f. into the night** travailler fort avant dans la nuit

3 *(much)* beaucoup; **it is f. better** c'est beaucoup mieux; **she's f. too intelligent to do that** elle est bien trop intelligente pour faire ça; **to be f. too many/little/etc** être beaucoup trop nombreux/petit/*etc*; **f. and away the best** de beaucoup *ou* de loin le meilleur; **the night was f. advanced** la nuit était fort avancée

ADV **(farther, farthest** ['fɑːðər, -ɪst], **further, furthest** ['fɜːðər, -ɪst]) **1** *(distant)* lointain, éloigné; **a f. country** un pays lointain; **in the f. distance** tout au loin

2 *(other)* **the f. end** *(of plank etc)* l'autre bout, le bout le plus éloigné; **the f. bank of the river** la rive opposée de la rivière; *Pol* **the f. left/right** l'extrême-gauche/-droite *f*
▸▸ **the F. East** l'Extrême-Orient *m*

farad ['færæd] N *Elec* farad *m*
faraway ['fɑːrəweɪ] ADJ lointain, éloigné; *(country)* lointain; **his eyes had a f. look** il avait le regard perdu dans le vague
farce [fɑːs] N *Theat* farce *f*, knockabout **f.** grosse farce; *Fig* **the trial was a f.** le procès relevait de la farce *ou* était grotesque; **this is an absolute f.!** c'est grotesque!; **the whole thing was a f.** tout a tourné à la farce; **their marriage had been little more than a loveless f.** leur mariage n'avait été qu'une comédie sans amour
farcical ['fɑːsɪk(ə)l] ADJ *Theat* bouffon, burlesque; *Fig (incident, idea, accusation)* absurde, grotesque; **the whole thing is becoming f.** c'est en train de tourner à la farce
farcically ['fɑːsɪklɪ] ADV d'une manière absurde *ou* grotesque
fare[1] [feər] N **1** *Rail, Aviat* prix *m* du voyage; *(in bus)* prix *m*; *(in taxi)* prix *m* de la course; **half f.** demi-place *f*, *pl* demi-places; **single f.** aller *m* *(simple)*; **return f.** aller et retour *m*; **to pay one's f.** payer son billet; *(in taxi)* payer sa course; **fares, please!** *(in bus)* tickets, s'il vous plaît!; **rail/bus fares are going up** les billets de train/les tickets de bus augmentent **2** *(taxi passenger)* client, -ente **3** *esp Fml (food)* chère *f*, **traditional f.** cuisine *f* traditionnelle; **good f.** bonne chère; **prison f.** régime *m* de prison
▸▸ **f. structure** structure *f* tarifaire
fare[2] VI **how is he faring?** comment ça marche pour lui?, comment se débrouille-t-il?; *(after operation etc)* comment va-t-il?; **she fared badly** elle ne s'en est pas bien tirée; **she fared well** elle s'en est bien tirée, elle s'est bien débrouillée; **he went out to see how the lambs were faring** il est sorti pour voir ce que devenaient les agneaux
farewell [feə'wel] INT, N adieu *m*; **to bid sb f.** dire adieu à qn; **to say** or **make one's farewells** faire ses adieux; **a f. dinner** un dîner d'adieu
far-fetched [-fetʃt] ADJ *(idea, example, story)* tiré par les cheveux
far-flung ADJ **1** *(large) (empire etc)* très étendu **2** *(distant) (countries)* lointain; *(villages, places)* éloigné
farinaceous [færɪ'neɪʃəs] ADJ farineux, farinacé; **f. foods** farineux *mpl*, féculents *mpl*
farm [fɑːm] N **1** *Agr* ferme *f*, exploitation *f* agricole; **I work on a f.** je travaille dans une ferme; **dairy f.** ferme laitière; **fish f.** établissement *m* piscicole; **poultry f.** exploitation avicole; **sheep/trout f.** élevage *m* de moutons/truites; **stud f.** haras *m*; *Am Sl* **to buy the f.** *(die)* clamser, calancher **2** *(installation)* **sewage f.** champs *mpl* d'épandage **3** *(centre)* **health f.** établissement *m* de cure
VT *(land)* cultiver, exploiter; **to f. 400 acres** = exploiter 160 hectares; *(animals)* élever
VI être cultivateur
▸▸ **f. animals** animaux *mpl* de ferme; **f. buildings** bâtiments *mpl* de la ferme; *(outhouses)* dépendances *fpl*; **f. hand** ouvrier, -ière agricole; **f. holiday** vacances *fpl* à la ferme; **f. horse** cheval *m* de ferme; **f. labourer** ouvrier, -ière agricole; **f. machinery** machines *fpl* agricoles; **f. tourism** tourisme *m* agricole, agritourisme *m*; **f. worker** ouvrier, -ière agricole
▸ **farm out** VT SEP *Fam (send to other people) (children)* confier à l'extérieur; **she farmed out the children to their aunty** elle a confié les enfants à leur tante; **to f. out work** don-

ner du travail à des collaborateurs extérieurs; *(subcontract)* sous-traiter du travail

farmable ['fɑːməbl] ADJ *(land)* cultivable

farmer ['fɑːmər] N agriculteur, -trice, cultivateur, -trice; **(tenant) f.** fermier, -ière; **sheep f.** éleveur, -euse de moutons; **poultry f.** aviculteur, -trice
▸▸ **farmers' market** marché *m* fermier

farmhouse ['fɑːmhaʊs] N (corps *m* de) ferme *f*

farming ['fɑːmɪŋ] ADJ
N agriculture *f*; **the f. of the land** la culture de la terre; **mixed f.** polyculture *f*; **sheep f.** élevage *m* de moutons; **poultry f.** aviculture *f*
▸▸ **f. communities** communautés *fpl* rurales

farmland ['fɑːmlænd] N terre(s) *f(pl)* arable(s)

farmstead ['fɑːmsted] N ferme *f*

farmyard ['fɑːmjɑːd] N cour *f* de ferme

Faroe ['feərəʊ] N **the F. Islands, the Faroes** les îles *fpl* Féroé

far-off ADJ *(place)* lointain, éloigné; *(country)* lointain; *(time)* reculé; **the day was not f. when** ... le jour était proche où ...

far-out ADJ *Fam (avant-garde)* avant-gardiste; *(fantastic)* super

far-reaching ['fɑːˈriːtʃɪŋ] ADJ de grande envergure, d'une grande portée; **to have a f. influence** avoir une grande portée

farrier ['færɪər] N *Br* maréchal-ferrant *m*, *pl* maréchaux-ferrants

farrow ['færəʊ] N *(piglets)* portée *f* de cochons
VT *(of sow) (piglets)* mettre bas
VI *(of sow)* **to f. (down)** faire des petits, cochonner

far-seeing ADJ clairvoyant; *(providing for the future)* prévoyant; **to be f.** voir loin

far-sighted ADJ **1** *(providing for the future) (person)* prévoyant; *(decision etc)* avisé, sage **2** *(long-sighted)* hypermétrope; *(because of old age)* presbyte

far-sightedness [-ˈsaɪtdnɪs] N **1** *(of government, leader)* prévoyance *f*, perspicacité *f*; *(of decision)* sagesse *f* **2** *(long-sightedness)* hypermétropie *f*; *(because of old age)* presbytie *f*

fart [fɑːt] *Fam* N pet *m*; *Fig* **a boring old f.** un vieux rasoir; **you stupid f.!** espèce de con!
VI péter, lâcher un pet
▸ **fart about, fart around** VI *Fam* **1** *(play the fool)* déconner **2** *(waste time)* glander; **he's been farting about with the car for days** il a passé des journées entières à trifouiller la voiture; **if you hadn't spent so much time farting about with your make-up** si tu n'avais pas autant traîné en te maquillant

farther ['fɑːðər] *(comp of* far*)* VOIR GRAMMAIRE A26 ADV **1** *(place)* plus loin (**than** que); **f. off** plus éloigné, plus loin; **they stopped a little f. on** ils se sont arrêtés un peu plus loin; **f. on in the book** plus loin dans le livre; **I can go no f.** je ne saurais aller plus loin; *(exhausted)* je n'en peux plus; **f. down/west** plus bas/à l'ouest; **before she could get any f. with her story** ... avant qu'elle ne puisse continuer son histoire ... **2** *(time)* **f. (back)** plus en arrière; **f. back than 1500** avant 1500
ADJ plus lointain; **at the f. end of the room** à l'autre bout de la salle

farthest ['fɑːðɪst] *(superl of* far*)* VOIR GRAMMAIRE A26 ADV le plus loin; **this is the f. east they reached** voici le point le plus à l'est qu'ils ont atteint
ADJ **1** *(distant)* **f. (off)** le plus éloigné, le plus reculé **2** *(distance etc)* le plus long

farthing ['fɑːðɪŋ] N *Br Hist (coin)* quart *m* d'un penny; *Fig Fam* **not to have a f.** n'avoir pas le sou; *Old-fashioned Fam* **I don't care a brass f.** je m'en moque éperdument

farthingale ['fɑːðɪŋgeɪl] N *Hist* vertugadin *m*

FAS *Com (abbr* free alongside ship*)* FLQ, FAS, franco quai

fascia, *pl* **fascias** ['feɪʃə, -z] N **1** *Archit* bandelette *f*, bande *f*; *(on shop front)* enseigne *f* en forme d'entablement **2** *(dashboard)* tableau *m* de bord; *(for mobile phone)* coque *f*
▸▸ **f. panel** planche *f* de bord

fascicle ['fæsɪk(ə)l], **fascicule** ['fæsɪkjuːl] N *Typ* fascicule *m*

fascinate ['fæsɪneɪt] VT *(person)* fasciner; **insects f. him** les insectes le fascinent; **to be fascinated by sth** être fasciné par qch

fascinating ['fæsɪneɪtɪŋ] ADJ fascinant

fascination ['fæsɪˈneɪʃən] N fascination *f*, attrait *m*; **I don't understand the f. of tennis** je ne comprends pas l'attrait que peut avoir le tennis; **the sport has** *or* **holds a f. for millions** ce sport fascine des millions de gens; **he has always had a f. for dinosaurs** les dinosaures ont toujours exercé une fascination sur lui, il a toujours été fasciné par les dinosaures; **she watched/listened in f.** elle regardait/écoutait, fascinée

fascism ['fæʃɪz(ə)m] N *Pol* fascisme *m*

fascist ['fæʃɪst] ADJ, N *Pol* fasciste *mf*

fash [fæʃ] VT *Scot (person)* agacer, ennuyer; **dinna f. yersel** ne te fais pas de bile

fashion ['fæʃən] N **1** *(in clothes etc)* mode *f*, vogue *f*; **in f.** à la mode, en vogue; **out of f.** passé de mode, démodé; **in the latest f.** à la dernière mode; **to set the f.** lancer la mode; **to follow f.** suivre la mode; **to become the f., to come into f.** devenir à la mode; **to go out of f.** se démoder; **the Costa del Sol was going out of f. with British holidaymakers** la Costa del Sol n'était plus aussi à la mode pour les vacanciers britanniques; **it's all the f.** c'est la grande vogue; **it's the latest f.** c'est la dernière mode **2** *(manner)* manière *f*; **crabs walk in a peculiar f.** les crabes marchent d'une façon étrange; **we rubbed noses, Eskimo f.** nous nous sommes frotté le nez à la manière des Esquimaux; **after a f.** tant bien que mal; **he loved her, after a f.** il l'aimait à sa façon
VT façonner, former; *(dress etc)* confectionner; **to f. a log into a canoe** façonner un tronc d'arbre en canot
▸▸ **f. designer** modéliste *mf*; **f. editor** rédacteur, -trice de mode; **f. house** maison *f* de (haute) couture; **f. magazine** journal *m* de mode; **f. model** mannequin *m*; *Old-fashioned* **f. parade** défilé *m* de mode; **f. photographer** photographe *mf* de mode; **f. photography** photo *f* de mode; **f. show** présentation *f* des modèles *ou* des collections, défilé *m* de mode; *Hum* **f. victim** esclave *mf* de la mode; **f. writer** chroniqueur, -euse de mode, critique *m* de mode

fashionable ['fæʃənəb(ə)l] ADJ à la mode, en vogue; **a f. film director** un metteur en scène en vogue; **a f. part of town** un quartier très en vogue *ou* à la mode *ou* branché

fashionably ['fæʃənəblɪ] ADV *(dressed)* à la mode; *Hum* **they arrived f. late** ils sont arrivés en retard, comme il se doit

FAST¹ [fɑːst]

ADJ	rapide **1** ▪ en avance **2** ▪ solide **3**
ADV	vite **1** ▪ solidement **2**

ADJ **1** *(rapid)* rapide; *Phot (film)* rapide; **you're a f. walker** vous marchez vite; **he likes f. cars** il aime les voitures qui vont vite; *Sport* **a f. time** *(in race etc)* un bon temps, un

bon chrono; *Fam* **he pulled a f. one on me** il m'a joué un mauvais tour; **he's a f. worker** travaille vite
2 *(clock, watch)* en avance; **my watch is** *or Fam* **I'm five minutes f.** ma montre avance *ou* j'avance de cinq minutes
3 *(secure) (stake etc)* ferme, fixe, solide; *(grip etc)* ferme; *(door, lid etc)* bien fermé; *(colour)* solide, résistant; **these colours are not f.** ces couleurs ne résistent pas au lavage; *Naut* **to make f. (to a buoy)** prendre le corps-mort; **to make f. (alongside)** s'amarrer
4 *(immoral)* **f. living** débauche *f*; **f. woman** femme légère
ADV **1** *(rapidly)* vite, rapidement; **she was walking faster than me** elle marchait plus vite *ou* rapidement que moi; **not so f.!** pas si vite!, doucement!; **bad news travels f.** les mauvaises nouvelles courent vite
2 *(securely)* ferme, solidement; **to hold f.** tenir ferme, tenir bon; **to stick f.** bien tenir; *(stuck)* rester pris, rester collé; **the door was shut f.** la porte était bien fermée; *Tex* **f. dyed** grand teint *inv*; **to be f. asleep** dormir d'un sommeil profond; *Fam* **to play f. and loose** prendre des risques; **to play f. and loose with sb's emotions** se jouer des émotions de qn; **to play f. and loose with the statistics** truquer *ou* falsifier les statistiques
▸▸ **f. food** fast-food *m*, prêt-à-manger *m* *inv*; **f. forward (button)** *(on tape recorder)* avance *f* rapide; *Aut* **f. idle** ralenti *m* accéléré; **the f. lane** *(on motorway)* la voie rapide; *Fig* **life in the f. lane** la vie à cent à l'heure; *Cin, TV* **f. motion** accéléré *m*; *Mktg* **f. mover** *(product)* article *m* à forte rotation; *Br* **f. train** rapide *m*

fast² N jeûne *m*; **to break one's f.** rompre le jeûne; *Rel* **a f. day** un jour de jeûne
VI jeûner; *Med* être à la diète

fastback ['fɑːstbæk] N *Aut* arrière *m* profilé; *(car)* voiture *f* à l'arrière profilé

fasten ['fɑːs(ə)n] VT **1** *(attach)* attacher (**to** à); **to f. papers together with a clip** attacher des papiers (ensemble) avec une agrafe; **to f. one's eyes/attention on sth** fixer le regard/son attention sur qch **2** *(hold)* fixer; **to f. a door with a bolt** fermer une porte au verrou, verrouiller une porte; **to f. one's seatbelt** accrocher *ou* attacher sa ceinture; **to f. one's buttons** se boutonner; **to f. one's coat** boutonner son manteau
VI s'attacher, se fixer; *(of garment)* s'agrafer, se boutonner (**at the back** par derrière); *(of door etc)* se verrouiller; *(of attention, eyes)* se fixer; **door that fastens with a bolt** porte qui se ferme au verrou
▸ **fasten down** VT SEP fixer (en place); *(tent, furniture)* fixer au sol; *(patient)* accrocher
▸ **fasten on, fasten onto** VT INSEP **1** *(seize)* s'accrocher à; *(of eyes)* se fixer sur **2** *(evidence, statement, idea etc)* s'accrocher à; **she fastened on(to) this kiss as evidence of his affection** elle se raccrochait à ce baiser comme à une preuve de son affection; **she quickly fastened on(to) this excuse** elle saisit l'excuse à la volée; **the assessor fastened on(to) the irregularities in the accounts** le contrôleur des impôts s'obstinait sur les irrégularités que contenaient les comptes
▸ **fasten up** VT SEP *(one's dress etc)* agrafer, boutonner
VI **this dress fastens up at the back** cette robe se boutonne *ou* s'agrafe dans le dos
▸ **fasten upon** VT INSEP = **fasten on, fasten onto**

fastener ['fɑːs(ə)nər] N attache *f*, *(of garment) (hook)* agrafe *f*, *(of purse)* fermoir *m*; *(of window etc)* fermeture *f*, *(of French window)* espagnolette *f*, **(snap) f.** (bouton *m* à) pression *f*, **(zip) f.** fermeture à glissière, fermeture Éclair®

fastening ['fɑːs(ə)nɪŋ] N *(device)* = **fastener; fastenings** attaches *fpl*

fast-forward VT *(cassette)* mettre en avance rapide; VI *(of tape)* se dérouler en avance rapide; *(of person)* (faire) avancer; **I'm just waiting for the tape to f.** j'attends que la cassette ait fini de se dérouler

fastidious [fæ'stɪdɪəs] ADJ difficile (**about sth** sur qch); *(about manners, hygiene, details)* pointilleux; *(about appearance)* méticuleux; *(about choice of friends)* exigeant, difficile; **she's always been a very f. eater** elle a toujours été très difficile sur la nourriture

Note that the French word **fastidieux** is a false friend and is never a translation for the English word **fastidious**. It means **tedious**.

fastidiously [fæ'stɪdɪəslɪ] ADV méticuleusement

fastidiousness [fæ'stɪdɪəsnɪs] N *(about appearance, details)* méticulosité *f*; **I was unused to such f. about hygiene** je n'étais pas accoutumé à ce qu'on soit aussi pointilleux sur l'hygiène; **because of his f. about what he eats** parce qu'il est difficile sur la nourriture

fasting ['fɑːstɪŋ] N jeûne *m*; *Med* diète *f* (absolue)

fast-moving ADJ rapide; **f. events** des événements *mpl* rapides
► ► *Mktg* **f. consumer goods** biens *mpl* de consommation à forte rotation

fastness ['fɑːstnɪs] N **1** *(of colour, dye)* solidité *f* **2** *(of moorings etc)* sûreté *f*, fiabilité *f* **3** *Lit (stronghold)* mountain **f.** forteresse *f*

FAT *Comput (abbr* file allocation table*)* Fat *f*

fat [fæt] ADJ (**fatter; fattest**) **1** *(person)* gros, *f* grosse, gras, *f* grasse, corpulent; *(meat)* gras; *(tissue)* adipeux; *Fam (cheque, salary)* gros; **to get f.** engraisser; *Fig* **to grow f. on sth/at the expense of others** s'engraisser de qch/aux dépens d'autrui; *Fam* **a f. lot of good that'll do you!** cela vous fera une belle jambe!; *Fam* **that was a f. lot of good** *or* **use!** on est bien aidé avec ça!; *Fam* **a f. lot of difference that has made!** ça n'a guère avancé les choses!; *Fam* **a f. lot you know about it!** comme si vous en saviez quelque chose!; *Fam* **f. chance he's got!** il est mal barré!; **a f. volume** un gros tome; **a f. wallet** un portefeuille bien garni
2 *(land)* riche, fertile, gras; *(clay, lime etc)* gras
N graisse *f*, *(of meat)* gras *m*; **fats** matières *fpl* grasses; **animal/vegetable f.** graisse animale/végétale; *Fig, Fam* **the f.'s in the fire!** ça va chauffer!; **to live off the f. of the land** vivre comme un coq en pâte
► ► *Fam Fig* **f. cat** *(rich, prosperous)* richard *m*; *(in industry)* = personne *f* touchant un salaire extrêmement élevé de façon injustifiée; **f. content** (teneur *f* en) matières grasses; **f. intake** ration *f* de corps gras

fatal ['feɪt(ə)l] ADJ **1** *(blow, accident, disease)* mortel, -elle; **this condition can prove f.** cela peut être mortel **2** *(action, consequences)* désastreux, catastrophique; *(mistake)* fatal, -als, grave **3** *Lit (ordained by fate)* fatal, -als; **the f. hour** l'heure *f* fatale
► ► **f. accident enquiry** enquête *f* à la suite d'un accident mortel; *Comput* **f. error** erreur *f* fatale

fatalism ['feɪtəlɪz(ə)m] N fatalisme *m*

fatalist ['feɪtəlɪst] N fataliste *mf*

fatalistic [feɪtə'lɪstɪk] ADJ fataliste

fatality [fə'tælɪtɪ] N **1** *(person killed)* mort *m*, victime *f* **2** *(fatal nature)* fatalité *f*

Note that the most common meaning of the French word **fatalité** is **fate**.

fatally ['feɪt(ə)lɪ] ADV *(wounded)* mortellement; **f. ill** condamné; **to be f. damaging to sth, to f. damage sth** causer un tort irréparable à qch; **f. damaged** qui a subi un tort irréparable

Note that the French word **fatalement** is a false friend and is never a translation for the English word **fatally**. It means **inevitably**.

fate [feɪt] N destin *m*, sort *m*; **stroke of f.** coup *m* du destin *ou* du sort; **f. decreed that ...** le sort a voulu que ...; *Myth* **the Fates** les Parques *fpl*; **to leave sb to their f.** abandonner qn à son sort; **to meet one's f.** trouver la mort; **to escape one's f.** échapper à son destin; **to suffer** *or* **share a similar f.** avoir le même sort; **a f. worse than death** un destin pire que la mort

fated ['feɪtɪd] ADJ **1** *(destined)* destiné, condamné (**to do sth** à faire qch); **this was f. to be the last time they would ever meet** le sort a voulu que ce soit la dernière fois qu'ils se voyaient **2** *(doomed)* voué à la destruction

fateful ['feɪtfʊl] ADJ **1** *(words)* fatidique **2** *(day)* fatidique; *(event)* fatal, -als

fathead ['fæthed] N *Fam* imbécile *mf*

fatheaded [fæt'hedɪd] ADJ *Fam* abruti, bête

father ['fɑːðər] N **1** père *m*; **from f. to son** de père en fils; **he's his f.'s son** c'est bien le fils de son père; **on the f.'s side** du côté paternel; **like a f.** paternellement; **he was like a f. to me** il était comme un père pour moi; **like f. like son** tel père tel fils
2 *Lit (ancestor)* **our fathers** nos ancêtres *mpl*, nos aïeux *mpl*
3 *(founder) (of science, art etc)* père *m*, fondateur *m*; **the Fathers of the Church** les Pères de l'Église
4 *Rel (God)* Père *m*; **God the F.** Dieu le Père; **Our F. which** *or* **who art in Heaven** notre Père qui êtes aux cieux
5 *Rel (priest)* père *m*; **the Holy F.** *(Pope)* le Saint-Père; **F. O'Riley** *(in monastic order)* l'abbé O'Riley; *(priest)* le Père O'Riley; **yes, F.** oui, mon Père
6 *(leader) Pol* **the F. of the House** = titre *m* traditionnel donné au doyen (par l'ancienneté) des parlementaires britanniques; **f. of chapel** *(in printing or publishing union)* représentant *m* du personnel
VT *(child)* engendrer; *(steam engine etc)* inventer; *(project, idea)* concevoir
► ► *Br* **F. Christmas** le Père Noël; **f. confessor** directeur *m* de conscience, père spirituel; **F.'s Day** la fête des pères; **f. figure** = personne *f* qui joue le rôle du père; **F. Time** le Temps

fatherhood ['fɑːðəhʊd] N paternité *f*

father-in-law, *pl* **fathers-in-law** N beau-père, *pl* beaux-pères

fatherland ['fɑːðəlænd] N patrie *f*

fatherless ['fɑːðəlɪs] ADJ sans père, orphelin, -ine de père

fatherly ['fɑːðəlɪ] ADJ *(person, tone, manner etc)* paternel, -elle; **to behave in a f. way towards sb** se montrer paternel envers qn

fathom ['fæðəm] N *Naut (measurement)* brasse *f*
VT *Naut* sonder; *Fig (mystery)* pénétrer, sonder; **I can't f. him (out)** je ne le comprends pas; **I can't f. out why he did it at all** je n'arrive pas à me figurer pourquoi il a fait cela

fatigue [fə'tiːg] N **1** *(tiredness)* fatigue *f*; **to be suffering from f.** être épuisé; **mental f.** fatigue cérébrale; **to be dropping with f.**

tomber de fatigue **2** *Tech (in material)* fatigue *f*; **metal f.** fatigue des métaux **3** *Mil (chore)* corvée *f*; **to put sb on f.** mettre qn de corvée; **cookhouse f.** corvée de cuisine(s); **fatigues** treillis *m*
VT **1** *(person)* fatiguer; *(stronger)* épuiser; **to f. oneself doing sth** se fatiguer/s'épuiser à faire qch **2** *Tech (metal etc)* fatiguer
► ► *Mil* **f. dress** treillis *m*; *Mil* **f. duty** corvée; *Mil* **f. party** *(détachement m de)* corvée

fatiguing [fə'tiːgɪŋ] ADJ fatigant; *(stronger)* épuisant

fatness ['fætnɪs] N *(of person)* embonpoint *m*, corpulence *f*; *(of stomach, buttocks)* grosseur *f*; *(of flesh etc)* adiposité *f*

fatso ['fætsəʊ] N *Fam* gros *m*; *(woman)* grosse *(bonne femme)* *f*; *(more insulting)* gros lard *m*; *(woman)* grosse vache *f*

fatted ['fætɪd] ADJ *Prov* **to kill the f. calf** tuer le veau gras

fatten ['fæt(ə)n] VT *(sheep, calves etc)* engraisser
VI engraisser
► **fatten up** VT SEP = **fatten** VT; *Fam (person)* faire grossir, engraisser; **we'll have to f. you up a bit** il va falloir qu'on t'engraisse un peu

fattening ['fæt(ə)nɪŋ] ADJ *(food)* qui fait grossir
N *(of animals)* engraissement *m*, engraissage *m*

fatty ['fætɪ] ADJ graisseux; *(tissue etc)* adipeux; *(meat)* gras, *f* grasse; **avoid f. foods** évitez les matières grasses ou les aliments gras
N *Fam* gros *m*; *(woman)* grosse *(bonne femme)* *f*; **hey, f.!** ohé, mon gros!/ma grosse!; **they always called him f.** ils l'appelaient toujours le gros
► ► *Chem* **f. acid** acide *m* gras

fatuity [fæ'tjuːɪtɪ] N sottise *f*, imbécillité *f*; **the utter f. of his efforts/the enterprise** l'absurdité de ses efforts/de l'entreprise

fatuous ['fætjʊəs] ADJ imbécile, idiot; *(attempt)* ridicule; *(smile)* béat

fatuously ['fætjʊəslɪ] ADV sottement, d'un air imbécile

fatuousness ['fætjʊəsnɪs] N = **fatuity**

faucet ['fɔːsɪt] N *Am* robinet *m*

fault [fɔːlt] N **1** *(flaw)* défaut *m*; **in spite of all his faults** malgré tous ses défauts *ou* travers; **scrupulous to a f.** scrupuleux à l'excès; **to find f. with sb/sth** trouver à redire contre qn/à qch; **she's always finding f.** elle trouve toujours quelque chose à redire
2 *Tech (inherent)* problème *m*, défaut *m*; **a f. has developed on the line** il y a un problème sur la ligne
3 *(guilt)* faute *f*; **to be at f.** être en faute, être coupable; **you were at f. in not warning us** vous avez eu tort de ne pas nous prévenir; **his memory was at f.** sa mémoire lui a fait défaut; **whose f. is it?** à qui la faute?; **I am afraid it was (all) my f.** je crains bien que ce ne soit de ma faute; **it's his own silly f.** c'est de sa faute, à cet imbécile; **through no f. of mine** sans que je sois en cause
4 *Tennis* faute *f*; **double f.** double faute; **foot f.** faute de pied
5 *Geol* faille *f*
VT *(person)* prendre en défaut; *(something)* trouver un défaut dans; **I can't f. her research** je ne trouve aucune erreur dans ses recherches
► ► **f. line** ligne *f* de faille; **f. plane** plan *m* de faille; *Com* **f. tree** arbre *m* de défaillances

Note that the most common meaning of the French word **faute** is **error**.

fault-finder N *(person)* critiqueur, -euse; *(device)* détecteur *m* de fuites

fault-finding ADJ *(critical)* ergoteur, -euse, pinailleur, -euse

N 1 (criticism) disposition f à critiquer; **I'd had enough of her petty f.** j'en avais assez de ses pinailleries **2** Tech localisation f des défauts

faultiness ['fɔːltɪnɪs] N défectuosité f, imperfection f

faultless ['fɔːltlɪs] ADJ (work, performance, craftmanship etc) sans faute, impeccable; (dress, behaviour) impeccable, irréprochable

faultlessly ['fɔːltlɪslɪ] ADV impeccablement

fault-tolerant ADJ Comput quasi insensible aux défaillances, tolérant les pannes

faulty ['fɔːltɪ] ADJ (work, device etc) défectueux; (style etc) incorrect; (reasoning etc) erroné; (logic) défaillant; Gram (construction etc) vicieux; **f. workmanship** mauvaise construction f

faun [fɔːn] N Myth faune m

fauna ['fɔːnə] N (of region, country) faune f

faux pas ['fəʊ'pɑː] N faux pas m, gaffe f

favour, Am **favor** ['feɪvər] N 1 (approval) faveur f, approbation f; **to be in/out of f.** (of person) être bien/mal vu; Fam avoir/ne pas avoir la cote; (of style) être à la mode/démodé; **to look on sb/sth with f.** être favorable à qn/qch, être bien disposé envers qn/qch; **to find f. with sb** trouver grâce aux yeux de qn; (of theory, explanation) être favorablement reçu auprès de qn; **to gain sb's f.** gagner la faveur de qn; **to be restored** or **to return to f.** rentrer en grâce; **to fall out of f. with sb** perdre les bonnes grâces de qn, tomber en défaveur aux yeux de qn; **this method has rather fallen out of f. in recent years** cette méthode a été plus ou moins abandonnée au cours de ces dernières années

2 (service) service m; **to ask sb a f., to ask a f. of sb** solliciter un service ou une faveur de qn; **as a f.** à titre gracieux; **as a personal f.** à titre personnel; **to do sb a f.** faire une faveur à qn, obliger qn; **you could at least do me the f. of listening** tu pourrais au moins me faire la faveur d'écouter; **will you do me a great f.?** voulez-vous me rendre un grand service?; Br Sl **do me a f.!** (you must be joking!) tu rigoles?; Fam **why don't you do everyone a f. and shut up?** tu vas faire plaisir à tout le monde et la fermer, d'accord?; **she's not doing herself any favours by being so arrogant** son arrogance la dessert

3 (preference) partialité f, préférence f; **to show f. towards sb** favoriser qn; **to speak in sb's f.** parler en faveur de qn; **he has everything in his f.** tout lui sourit; **design C has everything in its f.** le projet C a tous les avantages; **in f. of ...** en faveur de ...; **all those in f. raise your hand** (in meeting, debate etc) que tous ceux qui sont pour lèvent la main; **this route was abandoned in f. of a more direct one** cette route a été abandonnée pour une autre qui était plus directe; **to be in f. of sth** être partisan de qch, préconiser qch; **he's in f. of introducing subsidies** il est favorable à ou partisan de la mise en place de subventions; **a point in sb's/sth's f.** un élément en faveur de qn/qch; Fin **balance in your f.** solde en votre faveur

4 Arch (ribbon etc) faveur f, cocarde f

5 Lit, Hum **favours** (of woman) faveurs fpl; **she was rather too free with her favours** elle était un peu trop prodigue de ses faveurs

VT 1 (approve of) (something) approuver, préférer; (project) être pour; (person) accorder une préférence à; **I f. allowing more time for the planning stage** je suis partisan d'accorder plus de temps au stade préparatoire

2 (bestow favour on) (person) favoriser; **to f.**

sb with a smile gratifier qn d'un sourire; Iron **we have not, as yet, been favoured with a reply** on ne nous a pas encore fait la faveur de nous répondre

3 (give advantage to) (person) avantager, montrer de la partialité pour; (something) faciliter; **to be favoured by circumstances** avoir les circonstances en sa faveur; **the town is uniquely favoured as a holiday destination** cette ville est exceptionnellement avantagée en tant que destination de vacances

4 (of fact etc) (theory etc) soutenir

favourable, Am **favorable** ['feɪv(ə)rəb(ə)l] ADJ favorable; (weather, wind etc) propice; (reception etc) bienveillant; (terms etc) bon, f bonne, avantageux; (report etc) bon, rassurant; **in a f. light** sous un jour favorable; Com **on f. terms** à des conditions avantageuses

favourably, Am **favorably** ['feɪv(ə)rəblɪ] ADV favorablement; **to be f. disposed to(wards) sb/sth, to look f. on sb/sth** être favorable à qn/qch, être bien disposé à l'égard de qn/qch; **I hope everything goes f. for you** j'espère que tout ira bien pour toi; **to compare f. with sth** n'avoir rien à envier à qch; **I was f. impressed** j'ai été favorablement impressionné

favoured, Am **favored** ['feɪvəd] ADJ 1 (person) favorisé, avantagé; **he is one of our most f. clients** c'est un de nos clients privilégiés; **most-f. nation status** statut m de nation la plus favorisée; **the f. few** les élus mpl **2** Old-fashioned **ill-f.** laid, de mauvaise mine

favourite, Am **favorite** ['feɪv(ə)rɪt] N favori, f favorite, préféré, -ée; (song) succès m, tube m; Comput **favorites** (websites) favoris mpl; Sport **to back the f.** jouer le favori; **chocolate cake is a firm f. with children** c'est vraiment le gâteau au chocolat que les enfants préfèrent; **it's a great f. of mine** c'est l'un/l'une de mes préféré(e)s; **he's a great f. with the old ladies** les vieilles dames l'affectionnent particulièrement; **roast duck? (that's) my f.!** du canard rôti? c'est mon plat préféré!

ADJ favori, préféré

▸▸ **f. son** (family member) enfant m chéri; Am Pol = candidat m favorisé par les électeurs du même état que lui

favouritism, Am **favoritism** ['feɪv(ə)rɪtɪz(ə)m] N favoritisme m

fawn [fɔːn] N 1 (deer) faon m **2** (colour) fauve m

ADJ fauve

VI **to f. on sb** ramper devant qn

fawning ['fɔːnɪŋ] ADJ (flattering) adulateur, -trice; (servile) servile

N adulation f

fax [fæks] N 1 (machine) télécopieur m, fax m; **to send sth by f.** envoyer qch par fax ou par télécopie **2** (copy, message) fax m; **to send sb a f.** envoyer un fax à qn

VT (document) faxer, envoyer par fax ou télécopie; (person) envoyer un fax ou une télécopie à; **I'll f. the figures to you** je vous faxe les chiffres, je vous envoie les chiffres par fax ou télécopie

▸▸ **f. board** carte f fax, carte de télécopie; Comput **f. card** carte fax; **f. machine** télécopieur, fax; **f. message** fax, télécopie; Comput **f. modem** modem-fax m, pl modems-fax; **f. number** numéro m de fax ou de télécopie; **f. shot** publicité f directe par télécopie; **f. software** logiciel m de télécopie

▸ **fax back** VT SEP (return by fax) renvoyer par fax ou par télécopie (**to** à); **I'll f. you back** je vous réponds par fax

faxable ['fæksəb(ə)l] ADJ (document) faxable, télécopiable

faze [feɪz] VT Fam (person) déconcerter

FBI [efbiː'aɪ] N Am (abbr **Federal Bureau of Investigation**) FBI m, ≃ Police f Judiciaire

▸▸ **F. agent** agent m du FBI

FC [ef'siː] N (abbr **Football Club**) Club m de Football

FCL-FCL Com (abbr **full container load-full container load**) FCL-FCL

FCL-LCL Com (abbr **full container load-less than container load**) FCL-LCL

FD (abbr **floppy disk**) disquette f

FDA [efdiː'eɪ] N Am (abbr **Food and Drug Administration**) = office f du contrôle pharmaceutique et alimentaire

FDD (abbr **floppy disk drive**) unité f de disquette

FDI [efdiː'aɪ] N Econ (abbr **foreign direct investment**) IED m

fealty ['fɪəltɪ] N Hist fidélité f

fear [fɪər] N 1 crainte f, peur f; **my greatest f. was that they would forget** ce que je craignais le plus, c'est qu'ils oublient; **f. seized her** la peur l'envahit; **deadly f.** effroi m; **in f. and trembling** tremblant de peur; **to be overcome by** or **with f.** être en proie à la frayeur; **to be** or **stand** or **go in f. of sb/sth** avoir peur de ou redouter ou craindre qn/qch; **to go in f. of one's life** craindre pour sa vie; **there are fears for her life** sa vie est en danger; **for f. of waking the baby** de crainte de réveiller le bébé; **for f. of making a mistake** de crainte d'erreur; **there is no f. that he will come back** il n'y a pas de danger qu'il revienne; **without f. or favour** sans distinction de personnes; Fam **no f.!** pas de danger!, jamais de la vie!

2 (respect) (of God, the law etc) respect m, crainte f; Fam **to put the f. of God into sb** (reprimand) faire à qn une semonce dont il se souviendra longtemps; (frighten) inspirer une peur bleue à qn

VT 1 (somebody, something) craindre, redouter; (event) appréhender, craindre; **what they most feared** ce qu'ils craignaient le plus; **he fears failure above all else** l'échec est ce qu'il craint ou redoute par-dessus tout; **she is an adversary to be feared** c'est une adversaire redoutable; **it is to be feared that ...** il est à craindre que ...; Fml **I f. it is too late** j'ai peur ou je crains qu'il ne soit trop tard; Fml **I f. he will not come** je crains qu'il ne vienne pas; **I f. so/not** je crains que oui/que non; Fml **I f. he may be out** je crains qu'il ne soit pas là; Fml **I f. I'm late** je crois bien être en retard; **I f. the worst!** je crains ou redoute le pire!

2 (respect) (God etc) craindre

VI avoir peur; **we'll be here tomorrow, never f.** nous serons là demain, ne crains rien; Old-fashioned **f. not** or **never f., help is at hand** n'ayez crainte, l'assistance ne saurait tarder; **to f. for sb/sth** s'inquiéter au sujet de qn/qch; **I was beginning to f. for her sanity** je commençais à m'inquiéter pour son état mental; **we feared for our lives** nous craignions pour nos vies

feared [fɪəd] ADJ (person etc) redouté

fearful ['fɪəfʊl] ADJ 1 (consequences, doubt) affreux, effrayant; (pain, accident) atroce, affreux; esp Old-fashioned Fam (terrible) affreux; **he's a f. bore** il est affreusement rasoir; **a f. mess** un désordre effrayant ou formidable **2** (person) peureux, craintif; **don't look so f.!** n'aie pas l'air aussi apeuré!; **f. of ...** qui craint ou a peur de ...; **f. of what would happen ...** par crainte de ce qui arriverait ...

fearfully ['fɪəfʊlɪ] ADV 1 (frighteningly) affreusement, terriblement **2** esp Old-fashioned Fam (very) affreusement; **f. clever/interesting** terriblement intelligent/intéressant **3** (out of fear) peureusement

fearfulness ['fɪəfʊlnɪs] N **1** (of noise etc) caractère m terrifiant; **the f. of his appearance** son aspect terrifiant **2** (of person) (fear) crainte f, (concern) appréhension f

fearless ['fɪəlɪs] ADJ intrépide, courageux; **f. of ...** sans peur de ...; **he was f. of danger** il ne reculait devant aucun danger

fearlessly ['fɪəlɪslɪ] ADV intrépidement

fearlessness ['fɪəlɪsnɪs] N intrépidité f, courage m

fearsome ['fɪəsəm] ADJ (weapon, opponent) effrayant, redoutable; (bark, growl) effrayant

feasibility [fiːzə'bɪlɪtɪ] N (of plan etc) faisabilité f, **to doubt the f. of a suggestion** douter qu'une suggestion puisse être mise en pratique; **the f. of finding backers** la possibilité de trouver des garants
▸▸ **f. report** rapport m de faisabilité; **f. stage** phase f de faisabilité; **f. study** étude f de faisabilité; **f. test** essai m probatoire

feasible ['fiːzəb(ə)l] ADJ **1** (plan etc) faisable, réalisable, praticable **2** (story etc) vraisemblable

feast [fiːst] N **1** (large meal) festin m, banquet m; Fig **a f. for the eyes/the senses** un plaisir pour les yeux/les sens **2** Rel fête f
VI faire festin, festoyer; **to f. (up)on sth** se régaler de qch
VT Old-fashioned (person) régaler, fêter; **to f. one's eyes on sth** repaître ses yeux de qch
▸▸ **f. day** (jour m de) fête; Rel **F. of Tabernacles** fête des Tabernacles

feasting ['fiːstɪŋ] N Lit festoiement m

feat [fiːt] N **1** (exploit) exploit m; **f. of arms** fait m d'armes **2** (achievement) tour m de force; **a remarkable f. of modern technology** une remarquable prouesse technologique; **feats of engineering** triomphes mpl de l'ingénieur; **f. of skill** tour m d'adresse

feather ['feðər] N **1** plume f, (of tail, wing) penne f, (on arrow) (em)penne f, **as light as a f.** léger comme une plume; **in fine f.** dans une forme éblouissante; Fig **to show the white f.** manquer de courage; **you could have knocked me down with a f.** je n'en revenais pas; Fig **that's a f. in her cap** elle peut en être fière; Fig **to smoothe sb's ruffled feathers** rasséréner qn; Fig **to make the feathers fly** déclencher les hostilités **2** (in rowing) nage f plate
VT **1** (arrow) empenner; Fig **to f. one's nest** faire sa pelote ou son beurre **2** (in rowing) (oar) ramener à plat; **f. your oars!** avirons à plat! **3** Aviat (propeller) mettre en drapeau
VI (in rowing) nager plat
▸▸ **f. bed** lit m de plumes; Fig sinécure f, **f. boa** boa m de plumes; **f. cut** (hairstyle) coupe f en dégradé; **f. duster** plumeau m

featherbed ['feðəbed] VT Econ protéger par des subventionnements excessifs; Fig (children) élever dans du coton

featherbedding ['feðəbedɪŋ] N Econ subventionnement m excessif

featherbrain ['feðəbreɪn] N Fam tête f de linotte; **he's a real f.** c'est une vraie tête de linotte

featherbrained ['feðəbreɪnd] ADJ Fam étourdi; (scheme, idea) insensé

feather-edge N Carp etc biseau m

feather-edged ADJ taillé en biseau, biseauté

feathering ['feðərɪŋ] N **1** (of birds) plumage m **2** (of arrow) empennage m **3** (in rowing) nage f plate **4** Aviat (of propeller) mise f en drapeau

featherstitch ['feðəstɪtʃ] N Sewing point m d'épines

featherweight ['feðəweɪt] N Boxing poids m plume; Fig **he's a bit of a f.** il ne fait pas vraiment le poids

feathery ['feðərɪ] ADJ (snow, wheat etc) plumeux; **it has a light, f. feel to it** c'est doux et léger comme la plume

feature ['fiːtʃər] N **1** (of face) trait m; **prominent features** traits accusés
2 (of landscape, person, car) caractéristique f, (of software) fonction f, **a f. of the course is ...** un des aspects de la formation est ...; **paper that makes a f. of sports** journal qui fait une large place aux sports; **to make a f. of the fact that ...** attirer l'attention sur le fait que ...; **they decided to make a f. of the huge pillar in the dining area** ils ont décidé de mettre en valeur l'énorme pilier qui se trouve dans la salle à manger; **physical features of a country** topographie f d'un pays; **distinguishing f.** trait distinctif; **distinguishing features** (in passport) signes mpl particuliers; **main features** grands traits; **prominent** or **salient f.** trait saillant; **the redeeming f.** (of sth) le bon côté; **special f.** particularité f
3 (film) long métrage m; **double-f. programme** programme m à deux longs métrages
4 Journ (item) article m vedette; (news report etc) grand reportage m
VT **1** Cin (person) représenter; **a film featuring John Wayne** un film avec John Wayne en vedette; **also featuring Mark Williams** avec Mark Williams
2 Journ (news item) mettre en manchette; **the story was featured in all the main newspapers** cette affaire a fait la manchette de tous les grands quotidiens
3 (have as special feature) présenter, comporter; **the new model features four-wheel drive** le nouveau modèle comporte quatre roues motrices
VI **1** Cin (of actor) faire une apparition
2 (appear) figurer
▸▸ Journ **f. article** article de fond; Journ **features department** service m des rubriques; Journ **features editor** rédacteur, -trice de rubrique, journaliste mf responsable d'une rubrique; Cin **f. film** long métrage; Journ **f. story** article de fond; Journ **features writer** grand reporter mf, éditorialiste mf

feature-length Cin ADJ
▸▸ **f. cartoon** film m d'animation; **f. film, f. movie** long métrage m

featureless ['fiːtʃəlɪs] ADJ sans caractéristiques bien marquées

Feb abbr February

febrile ['fiːbraɪl] ADJ Med, Fig fébrile

February ['februərɪ] N VOIR GRAMMAIRE A81; 860 février m; **in F.** au mois de février, en février; (on) **the first/the seventh of F.** le premier/le sept février

fecal, feces Am = faecal, faeces

feckless ['feklɪs] ADJ **1** (irresponsible) (person) étourdi, irréfléchi; (lifestyle) inconscient, irresponsable **2** (ineffectual) (person) propre à rien, incapable; (attempt) inepte

fecklessness ['feklɪsnɪs] N **1** (irresponsibility) étourderie f **2** (of plan) ineptie f

fecund ['fiːkənd] ADJ esp Fml fécond

fecundity [fɪ'kʌndɪtɪ] N fécondité f

Fed [fed] N Am **1** Fin (abbr Federal Reserve Board) banque f centrale (des États-Unis) **2** Fin (abbr Federal Reserve (System)) (système m de) Réserve f fédérale **3** Fam (abbr Federal Agent) agent m du FBI

fed [fed] PT, PP see feed

federal ['fedərəl] ADJ (government etc) fédéral, -aux
N Am Hist fédéral m, nordiste m
▸▸ Am **the F. Reserve** la Réserve fédérale

federalism ['fedərəlɪz(ə)m] N fédéralisme m

federalist ['fedərəlɪst] ADJ, N fédéraliste mf

federalize ['fedərəlaɪz] VT **1** fédéraliser **2** Am (put under federal control) charger le gouvernement fédéral du contrôle de

federate [1] ['fedərət] ADJ (state etc) fédéré

federate [2] ['fedəreɪt] VT fédérer
VI se fédérer

federation [fedə'reɪʃən] N fédération f, **employers' f.** association f patronale

fedora [fɪ'dɔːrə] N feutre m

fed up ADJ Fam **to be f.** en avoir marre, en avoir ras le bol; **she's f. with him** elle en a marre de lui; **she's f. with it** elle en a marre; **to be f. (to the back teeth) with sb/sth** en avoir (vraiment) marre ou ras le bol de qn/qch; **what are you looking so f. about?** pourquoi as-tu l'air aussi écœuré?; **you sound f.** tu as l'air d'en avoir marre ou ras le bol

fee [fiː] N **1** (of physician, lawyer etc) honoraires mpl; (of actor) cachet m; (of company director) jeton m de présence; **for a small f.** moyennant une légère redevance; **is there a f. for joining?** est-ce que l'inscription est payante?; **school fees** frais mpl de scolarité; **boarding-school fees** pension f; **entrance f.** droit m d'entrée; **membership fee(s)** droit d'inscription; **registration f.** (for conference etc) droit d'inscription; (for letter) taxe f de recommandation **2** Law property held in f. **simple** propriété sans conditions ou libre **3** Hist (fief) fief m
▸▸ **f. note** note f d'honoraires

feeb [fiːb] N Am Fam crétin, -ine

feeble ['fiːb(ə)l] ADJ **1** (weak) faible; Fam **that's pretty f.** (as an excuse, attempt) c'est un peu léger; (as a joke) ce n'est pas très drôle **2** Fam (ineffectual) mou, f molle, peu capable; (film) faible, médiocre

feeble-minded ADJ d'esprit faible, arriéré
NPL **the f.** les débiles mpl mentaux

feeble-mindedness [-'maɪndɪdnɪs] N faiblesse f d'esprit, arriération f

feebleness ['fiːb(ə)lnɪs] N (of person) faiblesse f, (of excuse) pauvreté f, faiblesse; (of film, book, play) médiocrité f, faiblesse

feebly ['fiːblɪ] ADV **1** (weakly) faiblement **2** (ineffectually) mollement; **to say sth f.** dire qch d'un ton peu convaincu

feed [fiːd] N **1** (animal food) nourriture f, pâture f, (for horses etc) fourrage m; Fam (meal) repas m; **to have a good f.** bien manger; **the horse is off his f.** le cheval boude sur son avoine; Fam **to be off one's f.** (of baby) bouder sur la nourriture; **it's time for baby's f.** il faut donner à manger au bébé **2** (portion) (of food for animals) mesure f, ration f, **f. of oats** picotin m d'avoine **3** Theat etc (actor) acteur, -trice qui donne la réplique; (of comedian) faire-valoir m inv **4** Tech (of machine etc) (process) alimentation f, (device) appareil m ou système m d'alimentation; (pipe) conduit m d'alimentation
VT (pt, pp fed [fed]) **1** (give food to) (person) nourrir, donner à manger à; (family etc) nourrir; (country etc) approvisionner; (army) ravitailler; (dog etc) faire manger; (livestock) affourager; (breastfeed) allaiter; (of mother bird) (chicks) donner la becquée à; **to f. the birds** donner à manger aux oiseaux, nourrir les oiseaux; **he can f. himself already** il arrive déjà à manger tout seul; **we were well fed** nous étions bien nourris; Fam **to f. one's face** s'en mettre plein la lampe, se goinfrer; **the animals are fed a diet of fruit** les animaux sont nourris de fruits; **we were fed bread and water** on nous donnait de l'eau et du pain; **they were fed to the lions** ils ont été jetés en pâture aux lions; **field that feeds three cows** champ qui nourrit trois vaches; **manure feeds the ground** le fumier nourrit la terre; **to f. the mind/sb's anger/**

sb's **obsession** nourrir l'esprit/la colère de qn/l'obsession de qn
2 *(supply with)* *Tech (machine, fire etc)* alimenter; *(furnace etc)* charger; *Comput (paper)* faire avancer, alimenter; *Comput* **to f. data into a computer** entrer des données dans un ordinateur; **to f. coins into a parking meter** mettre des pièces dans un parcmètre; **to f. sb with false information** fournir de fausses informations à qn; *Ftbl etc* **to f. the forwards** alimenter les avants
3 *Theat (actor)* donner la réplique à
vi manger; *(of cattle, sheep)* paître, brouter; **to f. on sth** se nourrir *ou* vivre de qch
▸▸ **f. belt** *(of machine gun)* bande-chargeur *f* (souple), *pl* bandes-chargeurs; **f. line** *(of comedian)* réplique *f*, *Tech* **f. pipe** tuyau *m* d'alimentation - ; *Tech* **f. pump** pompe *f* d'alimentation -
▸ **feed back** **vt sep** *(information)* envoyer; *(send back again)* retransmettre
vi **to f. back into a system** être incorporé à un système
▸ **feed in** **vt sep** *Comput* introduire en machine *ou* en mémoire; **to f. sth into the computer** entrer qch dans l'ordinateur, mettre qch en mémoire
▸ **feed up** **vt sep** *(animals)* engraisser; **he needs feeding up** *(person)* il a besoin d'engraisser un peu

feedback ['fi:dbæk] **n 1** *Electron etc* réaction *f*, rétroaction *f*, *Fam* feed-back *m inv*; *(in microphone)* effet *m* Larsen **2** *(of information)* retour *m*, remontée *f*; *(reaction)* réactions *fpl*; **we haven't had much f.** nous n'avons pas eu beaucoup d'écho; **positive/ negative f.** réactions positives/négatives

feedbag [fi:bæg] **n 1** *(container)* sac *m* à nourriture; *(containing food)* sac de nourriture **2** *Am (for horse)* musette *f*, mangeoire *f* portative

feeder ['fi:dər] **n 1** *(person)* *(of machine etc)* alimenteur, -euse; *(of furnace etc)* chargeur, -euse; *(eater)* mangeur, -euse; **heavy f.** gros mangeur **2** *(feeding bottle)* biberon *m*; *Br (bib) (for baby)* bavette *f*, bavoir *m* **3** *Geog (of river)* affluent *m*; *Tech* canal *m* d'alimentation *ou* d'amenée; *(road)* route *f* de raccordement; *(air route)* ligne *f* régionale *(regroupant les passagers vers un aéroport principal)*; *Rail* embranchement *m*; *(for gas etc)* canalisation *f*, *Elec* câble *m* *ou* ligne *f* d'alimentation **4** *(device)* dispositif *m* d'alimentation **5** *(for printer, scanner, photocopier)* chargeur *m*
▸▸ **f. airline** compagnie *f* aérienne d'apport; **f. flight** vol *m* d'apport; **f. network** *(for airport)* réseau *m* d'apport; *Br Sch* **f. (primary) school** = école *f* primaire d'où arrivent les élèves d'un collège donné

feeding ['fi:dɪŋ] **n 1** *(of person, machine etc)* alimentation *f*, *(of livestock)* affouragement *m* **2** *Tech* avance *f*, avancement *m*
▸▸ **f. bottle** biberon *m*; *Med* **f. cup** canard *m*; **f. frenzy** *(of sharks)* = frénésie *f* causée par la présence de nourriture; *Fig* **speculators were in a f. frenzy** les spéculateurs se sont déchaînés; *Zool* **f. grounds** = endroit *m* où les animaux viennent trouver leur nourriture; *Ind* **f. mechanism** mécanisme *m* d'avance *ou* d'avancement; *(for liquid)* mécanisme d'alimentation; **f. time** *(for child, animal)* heure *f* des repas

FEEL [fi:l]
┌───┐
n toucher **1, 2**
vt toucher **1** ▪ sentir **2** ▪ ressentir **2** ▪ penser **2**
vi avoir **1** ▪ se sentir **1–3** ▪ avoir envie de **1, 2** ▪ être **3** ▪ chercher **4**
└───┘

n 1 *(act of touching)* toucher *m*; **rough to the f.** rude au toucher; **to have a f. of sth** tou-

cher qch, tâter qch; **to have a f. in a drawer for sth** chercher qch à tâtons dans un tiroir; *Fig* **I don't like the f. of this** ça ne me dit rien qui vaille; *Sl* **to give sb a (quick) f.** tripoter qn
2 *(texture) (of paper etc)* toucher *m*; **it has a nice f. to it** *(fabric)* c'est agréable au toucher; *(place)* il y a une bonne atmosphère; *(name)* ça sonne bien; **there's a funny f. to this gearstick** le levier de vitesses fait un peu drôle; **to recognize sth by the f. of it** reconnaître qch au toucher
3 *(sensation)* sensation *f*; **the f. of silk against your skin** le contact de la soie contre la peau
4 *(knack)* **he has the f. of his car** il a sa voiture bien en main; **you'll soon get the f. of the work** vous allez bientôt vous habituer au travail; **to have a f. for translation** avoir le sens de la traduction; **you need to have a f. for it** il faut l'avoir en soi
vt *(pt, pp* **felt** [felt]*)* **1** *(touch) (sth with one's hand)* toucher; *(pulse, pocket etc)* tâter; *(organ)* palper; **to f. one's way** *(in darkness)* avancer à tâtons; *Fig* **to f. one's way towards sth** avancer vers qch à tâtons; *Fig* **to f. one's way into sth** se faire à qch; **to f. one's way around** essayer de s'y retrouver; **he felt her scalp to see if there was a lump** il tâta son crâne pour voir s'il y avait une bosse
2 | VOIR GRAMMAIRE A41; B35 | *(be conscious of, experience)* sentir; *(bitterness, pain, joy etc)* éprouver, ressentir; **I felt the floor tremble** *or* **trembling** j'ai senti trembler le sol; **she felt his arms around her** elle sentait ses bras l'entourant; **f. the weight of that!** pèse un peu ça!; **to f. the heat** être sensible à la chaleur; **to f. the cold** être sensible au froid, être frileux; **to make one's authority felt** affirmer son autorité, faire sentir son autorité; **she felt nothing, only emptiness** elle ne ressentait rien, seulement un vide; **do you f. anything for her?** est-ce que tu éprouves *ou* ressens quelque chose à son égard?; **I f. it in my bones that I shall succeed** quelque chose en moi me dit que je réussirai; **I felt it necessary to intervene** j'ai jugé nécessaire d'intervenir; **what do you f. about …?** qu'est-ce que vous pensez de …?; **what I f. about it is …** mon sentiment là-dessus, c'est que …; **I felt that he could have tried harder** j'avais le sentiment qu'il aurait pu faire plus d'efforts; **to f. a fool** se sentir bête *ou* stupide; **to f. a new woman/man** se sentir comme neuve/neuf
vi *(of person)* **to f. hot/cold** avoir chaud/froid; **to f. tired** se sentir fatigué; **to f. ill** ne pas se sentir bien; **I f. really stupid** je me sens vraiment stupide; **to f. sick** *Br (about to vomit)* avoir envie de vomir; *Am (ill)* ne pas se sentir bien, se sentir malade; **she felt sick when she thought of …** ça la rendait malade de penser à …; **he felt really bad about leaving her** ça l'ennuyait vraiment de la laisser; **they felt betrayed** ils se sont sentis trahis; **my foot feels better** mon pied va mieux; **how do you f.?, how are you feeling?** comment te sens-tu?; **to f. all the better for it** s'en trouver mieux; **I f. ten years younger** je me sens dix ans de moins; **not to f. oneself** ne pas être dans son assiette; **I f. quite myself again** je me sens tout à fait rétabli; **to f. up to doing sth** *(well enough)* se sentir assez bien pour faire qch; *(competent enough)* se sentir de taille à faire qch; **f. certain/convinced that …** être certain/ convaincu que …; **how would you f. if I were to offer you a job?** qu'est-ce que vous diriez si je vous offrais un emploi?; **how would you f. if she left you?** qu'est-ce que tu ressentirais si elle te quittait?; **how do you think I f.?** *(that's a stupid question)* qu'est-ce que tu crois?; **how would you f.?** *(if sb did that to you)* qu'est-ce que tu ressen-

tirais, toi?; **she feels strongly about it** elle a des idées très arrêtées là-dessus; **I f. as if …** j'ai l'impression que …; **I felt as if I'd seen him before** j'avais l'impression de l'avoir déjà vu; **I felt as if** *or Fam* **like I was wasting my time** j'avais l'impression de perdre mon temps; **to f. like a fool** se sentir bête *ou* stupide; **to f. like a new man/woman** se sentir comme neuf/neuve
2 *(want sth/to do sth)* **to f. like doing sth** se sentir d'humeur à faire qch; **I felt like crying** j'avais envie de pleurer; **if you f. like it** si ça vous dit, si le cœur vous en dit; **I don't f. like it** ça ne me dit rien; **I f. like a cup of tea** j'ai envie d'une tasse de thé
3 *(of things)* **to f. hard/soft** être dur/doux au toucher; **the wall/her forehead felt hot** le mur/son front était chaud au toucher; **his legs/head felt heavy** il se sentait les jambes/la tête lourde(s); **the atmosphere felt tense** on sentait une certaine tension dans l'air; **my hands f. cold** j'ai froid aux mains; **my arm feels as if it's broken** j'ai l'impression que je me suis cassé le bras; **the room feels damp** la pièce (me) paraît humide; **it feels like …** cela donne la sensation de …; **it feels like (it's going to) rain** on dirait qu'il va pleuvoir; **it felt good to be alive** c'était bon d'être en vie; **it feels different/dead now she's gone** c'est différent/mort depuis qu'elle est partie; **what did it f. like when you won?** qu'est-ce que vous avez ressenti en gagnant?
4 *(explore, touch with fingers)* **to f. in one's pockets for sth** chercher qch dans ses poches; **he felt on the ground for his keys** il cherchait ses clefs à tâtons sur le sol
▸ **feel about, feel around** **vi** *(search by touching)* chercher à tâtons; **to f. about** *or* **around for sth** chercher qch à tâtons
▸ **feel for** **vt insep** *(feel sympathy for)* éprouver de la compassion à l'égard de; **I f. for her** elle a toute ma sympathie; **to f. for sb in their sorrow** partager la douleur de qn; **I really felt for you then** je t'ai sincèrement plaint à ce moment
▸ **feel up** **vt sep** *Sl (touch sexually)* peloter

feeler ['fi:lər] **n 1** *Biol (of insect etc)* antenne *f*, *(of snail)* corne *f*, *(of mollusc etc)* tentacule *m* **2** *Fig (tentative enquiry etc)* ballon *m* d'essai; **to put out feelers** lancer un ballon d'essai, tâter le terrain **3** *Tech (gauge)* calibre *m* d'épaisseur (à lames)
▸▸ *Tech* **f. gauge** calibre d'épaisseur (à lames)

feel-good factor **n** sentiment *m* de bien-être

feeling ['fi:lɪŋ] **adj** *(person)* sensible
n 1 *(sense of)* **f.** toucher *m*; **to have no f. in one's arm** avoir le bras mort; **to lose the f. in one's arm/leg** ne plus avoir aucune sensation dans le bras/la jambe
2 *(sensation)* sensation *f*
3 *(emotion)* sentiment *m*; **there is a f. of grief/joy throughout the country** le chagrin/la joie règne dans tout le pays; **a f. of emptiness** une impression de vide; **to hurt sb's feelings** blesser qn; **I don't want anybody to have hurt feelings about it** je ne veux pas que cela blesse qui que soit; **her feelings are hurt** elle est blessée; **she had a f. of elation** elle éprouvait un sentiment d'allégresse; **his feelings towards me** ses sentiments envers moi; **to have no feelings** n'avoir aucun cœur; **I know the f.!** je sais ce que c'est!; **I had a f. I might find you here** je pensais bien vous trouver ici; **I've got a nasty** *or* **unpleasant f. that …** j'ai la désagréable impression que …; **no hard feelings!** sans rancune!; **with f.** *(to speak etc) (emotionally)* avec émotion; *(warmly)* chaleureusement; *(angrily)* avec emportement; *(to sing etc)* avec expression *ou* âme

4 *(opinion)* **what are your feelings about fox-hunting?** qu'est-ce que vous pensez de la chasse au renard?; **I don't have any strong feelings about it** ça m'est plus ou moins égal; **feelings are running very high** les esprits sont très échauffés; **public f. ran high against the proposal** le sentiment populaire s'élevait contre cette proposition; **there is a general f. that …** l'impression règne (dans le public) que …, le sentiment général est que …

5 *(sensitivity)* sensibilité *f*; **to have a f. for music/nature** être sensible à la musique/la nature; **to have a f. for sth** *(do well)* être doué pour qch

feelingly ['fiːlɪŋlɪ] ADV *(to speak)* avec émotion; *(warmly)* chaleureusement; *(to sing, play)* avec expression

feet NPL *see* **foot** N

feign [feɪn] VT *(anger etc)* feindre, simuler; *(surprise)* affecter; **to f. illness** feindre *ou* simuler la maladie; **to f. sleep** faire semblant de dormir

feigned [feɪnd] ADJ *(illness)* simulé; *(surprise)* feint

feint [feɪnt] N *Mil* fausse attaque *f*; *Boxing, Fencing etc* feinte *f*; **his anger is only a f.** sa colère n'est qu'une simulation
VI *Mil* faire une fausse attaque; *Boxing etc* feinter; *Boxing* **to f. with the right** feinter du droit

feint-ruled [-ruːld] ADJ *(paper)* à réglure légère

feistiness ['faɪstɪnɪs] N *esp Am* **1** *(spirit, energy)* fougue *f*, impétuosité *f* **2** *(pugnacity)* attitude *f* contestataire

feisty ['faɪstɪ] ADJ *esp Am* **1** *(full of energy)* impétueux, fougueux **2** *(pugnacious)* contestataire

feldspar ['feldspɑːr] N *Miner* feldspath *m*

felicitous [fɪ'lɪsɪtəs] ADJ *Lit (choice, decision)* heureux; *(word, expression etc)* bien trouvé, à propos

felicity [fɪ'lɪsɪtɪ] N *Lit* **1** *(happiness)* félicité *f*, bonheur *m* **2** *(aptness)* *(of remark, expression etc)* à-propos *m*, bien-trouvé *m*; *(of choice, decision)* caractère *m* heureux

feline ['fiːlaɪn] ADJ félin; **f. grace** grâce *f* féline, grâce de chat
N félin *m*

fell[1] [fel] VT *(opponent etc)* abattre, terrasser; *(tree)* abattre, couper; **felled wood** *or* **timber** abattis *m*, bois *m* gisant, vente *f*

fell[2] PT *see* **fall** VI

fell[3] ADJ **at one f. swoop** d'un seul coup

fell[4] N *Br (hill, mountain)* colline *f*; **the fells** *(high moorland)* les landes *fpl* des plateaux
▸▸ **f. running** course *f* en basse montagne; **f. walking** randonnée *f* en basse montagne

fell[5] N *(animal skin)* peau *f*

fella, feller ['felə, -ər] N *Br Fam* mec *m*, type *m*; *(boyfriend)* copain *m*, mec, *Can* chum *m*

fellatio [fə'leɪʃɪəʊ] N fellation *f*

felling ['felɪŋ] N *(of cow, forest)* abattage *m*; *(of timber)* abattage, coupe *f*

fellow ['feləʊ] N **1** *(comrade)* camarade *mf*, compagnon *m*
2 *(colleague)* semblable *mf*, pareil *m*; *(one of a pair)* pendant *m*; **a vase and its f.** un vase et son pendant
3 *(at university)* *(professor)* = professeur *m* titulaire; *(postgraduate student)* chargé, -ée de cours; *(of learned society)* membre *m*; **F. of the Royal Society** = membre de la Société royale (de Londres)
4 *Br Fam (boyfriend)* copain *m*, mec *m*, *Can* chum *m*
5 *Old-fashioned, Fam (man)* homme *m*, gars *m*; **a good f.** un brave garçon; **a decent f.** un bon gars; **he's a queer f.** c'est un drôle de type; **the poor little f.** le pauvre petit
ADJ **f. being** *or* **creature** semblable *mf*; **f. citizen** concitoyen, -enne; **f. countryman/countrywoman** compatriote *mf*; **f. passenger/sufferer** compagnon de voyage/misère; **f. soldier** compagnon d'armes, camarade de régiment; **f. student** camarade d'études
▸▸ **f. feeling** sympathie *f*; **f. traveller** *(companion on journey)* compagnon, *f* compagne de voyage *ou* de route; *Fig* compagnon *m* de route; *Pol* communisant, -ante

fellowship ['feləʊʃɪp] N **1** *(friendship)* **(good) f.** amitié *f*, camaraderie *f* **2** *(association)* association *f*, corporation *f* **3** *(at university)* bourse *f* universitaire *(avec obligation de faire un cours, des recherches)*; *(of learned society)* titre *m* de membre

felon ['felən] N *Law Arch* criminel, -elle

felonious [fe'ləʊnɪəs] ADJ *Law Arch* criminel, -elle; **f. act** action *f* qui constitue un crime

felony ['felənɪ] N *Law Arch* crime *m*; **to compound a f.** pactiser avec un crime

felspar ['felspɑːr] N = **feldspar**

felt[1] [felt] N *Tex etc* feutre *m*; **tarred f.** feutre bitumé
VT *Tex (wool, hairs)* feutrer; *Constr (roof etc)* couvrir de feutre bitumé

felt[2] PT, PP *see* **feel** VT, VI

felt-tip N *(stylo m)* feutre *m*
▸▸ **f. pen** *(stylo)* feutre

female ['fiːmeɪl] ADJ *(person)* féminin; *(voice etc)* de femme; *(animal, plant etc)* femelle; *Tech* femelle; **the young f. giraffe** la jeune girafe femelle; **f. company** la compagnie féminine *ou* des femmes; **f. executive** femme *f* cadre; *Tech* **f. screw** écrou *m*; *Tech* **male-f. coupling/connection/adapter** accouplement *m*/accordement *m*/adaptateur *m* mâle-femelle
N **1** *(animal, plant)* femelle *f*, *(person)* femme *f* **2** *Pej (woman)* bonne femme *f*, **some f. called for you** il y a une bonne femme qui t'a demandé au téléphone
▸▸ **f. impersonator** travesti *m (dans un spectacle)*

Note that the French word **femelle** is never used to refer to human beings.

feminine ['femɪnɪn] VOIR GRAMMAIRE A16–17; B7–8; B9–10 ADJ féminin; *Gram* **this word is f.** ce mot est féminin
N *Gram* féminin *m*; **in the f.** au féminin

femininity [femɪ'nɪnɪtɪ] N féminité *f*

feminism ['femɪnɪz(ə)m] N féminisme *m*

feminist ['femɪnɪst] ADJ, N féministe *mf*

femoral ['femərəl] ADJ *Anat* fémoral, -aux

femur, *pl* **femurs**, **femora** ['fiːmər, -əz, 'femərə] N *Anat* fémur *m*

fen [fen] N marais *m*, marécage *m*; **the Fens** = les plaines *fpl* marécageuses de l'est de l'Angleterre

fence [fens] N **1** *(for delimiting an area)* clôture *f*, *(more solid, for preventing entry)* barrière *f*, **sunk f.** saut *m* de loup; **to sit on the f.** ménager la chèvre et le chou; **to get** *or* **come off the f.** arrêter de ménager la chèvre et le chou; *Fig* **to be on the other side of the f.** être de l'autre côté de la barricade, avoir une opinion contraire; **I don't often find myself on the same side of the f. as you** je n'ai pas souvent les mêmes opinions que toi; *esp Am Fig* **to mend one's fences** *(of politician)* regagner la confiance des électeurs; *Am Fig* **to mend one's fences with sb** se remettre en bons termes avec qn
2 *Horseriding (in steeplechasing)* obstacle *m*, haie *f*, *(in showjumping)* obstacle, barrière *f*
3 *Tech (of circular saw etc)* guide *m*; *(of machine tool etc)* garde *f*
4 *Sl (receiver of stolen property)* receleur, -euse *(d'objets volés)*
VT *(field)* clôturer
VI **1** *Sport* faire de l'escrime; *Fig* **to f. with a counsel** répondre en éludant les questions d'un avocat; *Fig* **stop fencing!** arrête d'éluder la question! **2** *Sl (receive stolen property)* faire du recel
▸▸ **f. post** piquet *m* de clôture
▸ **fence in** VT SEP *(land etc)* clôturer
▸ **fence off** VT SEP séparer par une clôture

fence-mending N *esp Am Fig* reprise *f* des relations

fencer ['fensər] N *Sport* escrimeur, -euse

fencing ['fensɪŋ] N **1** *(barrier etc)* clôture *f*, barrière *f*, *(material)* matériaux *mpl* pour clôture; **wire f.** treillage *m* en fil de fer **2** *(action)* *(of land etc)* action *f* de clôturer **3** *Sport* escrime *f*, **f. master** maître *m* d'armes; **f. match** assaut *m* d'armes; **f. school** salle *f* d'escrime *ou* d'armes **4** *Sl (receiving)* recel *m*

fend [fend] VI **to f. for oneself** se débrouiller
▸ **fend off** VT SEP *(blow, questions etc)* parer, détourner; *(attack)* parer

fender ['fendər] N *Am Aut* aile *f*, *(protecting wall, door, post etc)* bouteroue *f*, *(for fireplace)* garde-feu *m inv*; *Am Rail (on train engine, tram)* pare-chocs *m inv*, *(for clearing track)* chasse-pierres *m inv*; *Naut* bourrelet *m* de défense

fender-bender N *Am Fam* (petit) accrochage *m*

feng shui [fəŋ'ʃweɪ] N Feng Shui *m*

fenland ['fenlænd] N pays *m* marécageux

fennel ['fen(ə)l] N *Bot, Culin* fenouil *m*

feral ['ferəl] ADJ *Fml (cat, dog etc)* féral, -als, *ou* -aux

ferment ['fɜːment] N **1** *(yeast etc)* ferment *m* **2** *(fermentation)* *(of liquid)* fermentation *f*, *Fig (commotion)* effervescence *f*, agitation *f*, **the whole town was in a (state of) f.** toute la ville était en effervescence *ou* dans un état d'agitation
VI *(of liquids etc)*, *Fig (of sedition)* fermenter; *(of wine)* travailler
VT *(liquid)* laisser fermenter

fermentation [fɜːmen'teɪʃən] N *(of liquid etc)* fermentation *f*, *(of wine)* travail *m*; *Fig* agitation *f*

fern [fɜːn] N *(plant)* fougère *f*, hillside covered with **f.** coteau couvert de fougères

ferocious [fə'rəʊʃəs] ADJ *(animal, person, look etc)* féroce

ferociously [fə'rəʊʃəslɪ] ADV férocement, avec férocité

ferocity, ferociousness [fə'rɒsɪtɪ, fə'rəʊʃəsnɪs] N férocité *f*

ferret ['ferɪt] N *(animal)* furet *m*
VI **(-t-) 1** *(hunt)* chasser au furet **2** *Fam* **to f. (about) in one's pockets** fouiller dans ses poches (**for sth** pour trouver qch); **what are you ferreting for?** qu'est-ce que tu cherches?
VT *(rabbits etc)* chasser au furet
▸ **ferret out** VT SEP *(dislodge)* *(somebody, something)* dénicher; *(secret, the truth)* déterrer

ferreting ['ferɪtɪŋ] N *(hunting)* chasse *f* au furet

ferrety ['ferɪtɪ] ADJ de furet; *Pej* **f. eyes/face** yeux *mpl*/visage *m* de fouine

ferric ['ferɪk] ADJ *Chem* ferrique

Ferris wheel ['ferɪs] N *(at fairground)* grande roue *f*

ferrite ['feraɪt] N ferrite *f*

ferroconcrete ['ferəʊ'kɒŋkriːt] N béton *m* armé

ferromagnetic ['ferəʊmæg'netɪk] ADJ ferromagnétique

ferrous ['ferəs] ADJ *Chem (oxide etc)* ferreux
▸▸ **f. sulphide** pyrite *f* de fer

ferrule ['ferəl, -u:l] N *(of walking stick)* bout *m* ferré, embout *m*

ferry ['ferɪ] N *(boat)* bac *m*, ferry *m*; **to take the f.** prendre le bac *ou* le ferry; **passenger/car f.** bac *ou* ferry à piétons/à voitures; **train f.** bac transbordeur; **air f.** avion *m* transbordeur
VT **to f. sb/a car across a river** passer qn/une voiture en bac *ou* en ferry de l'autre côté de la rivière; **to f. voters to the polls** transporter des électeurs aux urnes; **she ferries her children backwards and forwards to school by car** elle fait la navette pour conduire ses enfants à l'école et les en ramener
▸▸ **f. port** port *m* de ferry; **f. service** ligne *f* de ferry

ferryboat ['ferɪbəʊt] N bac *m*, ferry *m*

ferrying ['ferɪɪŋ] N transport *m* en *ou* par bac *ou* ferry

ferryman, *pl* **ferrymen** ['ferɪmən] N passeur *m*

fertile ['fɜ:taɪl] ADJ *(soil, woman, imagination etc)* fertile, fécond **(in** en); *(man)* fécond; *(egg)* fécondé

fertility [fɜ:'tɪlɪtɪ] N *(of soil, person's imagination, woman etc)* fertilité *f*, fécondité *f*
▸▸ *Med* **f. clinic** centre *m* de traitement de la stérilité; *Med* **f. drug** médicament *m* pour le traitement de la stérilité; **f. symbol** symbole *m* de fertilité; *Med* **f. treatment** traitement *m* de la stérilité

fertilization [fɜ:tɪlaɪ'zeɪʃən] N *(of egg etc)* fertilisation *f*, fécondation *f*; *Biol* **self f.** autofécondation *f*

fertilize ['fɜ:tɪlaɪz] VT **1** *(egg, plant etc)* fertiliser, féconder **2** *Agr (soil)* fertiliser, engraisser

fertilizer ['fɜ:tɪlaɪzər] N *Agr* engrais *m*; **artificial fertilizers** engrais chimiques

fervent ['fɜ:vənt] ADJ *(prayer, supporter, belief)* ardent, fervent; *(wish, desire)* ardent

fervently ['fɜ:vəntlɪ] ADV *(to plead, believe, pray etc)* avec ferveur; *(to wish, support etc)* avec ardeur

fervid ['fɜ:vɪd] ADJ = **fervent**

fervour, *Am* **fervor** ['fɜ:vər] N *(of prayer, speech, belief)* ferveur *f*; *(of wish, supporter)* ardeur *f*

▸ **fess up** [fes] VI *Am Fam (confess)* se mettre à table

fester ['festər] VI *(of wound etc)* suppurer, s'envenimer; *(of conflict, resentment)* s'envenimer; *(of dislike, sense of injustice)* s'aviver

festering ['festərɪŋ] ADJ *(wound etc)* ulcéreux, suppurant; *(conflict, resentment)* qui s'envenime; *(dislike, sense of injustice)* aggravé, de plus en plus vif

festival ['festɪv(ə)l] N *(of music, drama etc)* festival *m*, *pl* -als; *(religious)* fête *f*, *esp Rel* **harvest f.** = office *m* d'action de grâces (célébré après la rentrée des récoltes); **film f.** festival du film; **street f.** fête de quartier

festive ['festɪv] ADJ *(day etc)* de fête; **the f. season** l'époque *f* des fêtes; **to be in (a) f. mood** *(of person)* avoir le cœur en fête

festivity [fes'tɪvɪtɪ] N *(merriness)* gaieté *f*, **an air/atmosphere of f.** un air/une atmosphère de fête; **festivities** *(celebrations)* festivités, réjouissances

festoon [fes'tu:n] N feston *m*, guirlande *f*
VT festonner **(with** de); *(flowers etc)* disposer en festons

feta ['fetə] N feta *f*
▸▸ **f. cheese** feta

---

fetal ['fi:t(ə)l] ADJ = **foetal**

fetch [fetʃ] VT **1** *(go to get)* aller chercher; **to f. water from the river** aller puiser de l'eau dans la rivière; **to f. sb from the airport** aller chercher qn à l'aéroport; **I'll f. you** je viendrai te chercher; **f.!** *(to dog)* va chercher!
2 *Com* rapporter; *(specific price)* atteindre; **it fetched a high price** cela s'est vendu cher; **it fetched £100,000** cela a atteint les 100 000 livres; **I'd be surprised if it fetched that much** cela m'étonnerait que cela rapporte autant *ou* que cela se vende aussi cher
3 *(hit)* **to f. sb a blow** flanquer un coup à qn
4 *Lit (utter) (sigh, moan)* pousser
VI **I'm not going to f. and carry for you!** je ne vais pas être ta bonne à tout faire!
▸ **fetch back** VT SEP *(bring back) (somebody)* ramener; *(something)* rapporter
▸ **fetch up** VI *(reach)* **to f. up at a port** parvenir *ou* arriver à un port; **the kite fetched up in the branches of a tree** le cerf-volant est resté accroché dans les branches d'un arbre; *Fam* **they finally fetched up at our house** ils ont finalement atterri chez nous; *Fam* **the car fetched up against a wall** la voiture s'est (finalement) arrêtée en heurtant un mur
VT SEP **1** *(bring from lower place) (somebody)* faire monter; *(something)* remonter **2** *Fam (vomit)* dégueuler

fetching ['fetʃɪŋ] ADJ *(woman, air)* séduisant, attrayant; *(hat, smile)* ravissant

fête [feɪt] N fête *f*, **village f.** fête communale
VT *(person, event)* fêter; *(person)* faire fête à

Fête

En Grande-Bretagne, les "village fêtes" sont des manifestations en plein air où l'on vend des produits faits maison et où l'on organise des manifestations sportives et des jeux pour enfants; elles sont généralement destinées à réunir des fonds pour une œuvre de charité.

fetid ['fetɪd, 'fi:tɪd] ADJ fétide, puant

fetish ['fetɪʃ] N *(magic object)*, *Psy* fétiche *m*; **he has a f. for black silk** il est obsédé par la soie noire; **to make a f. of sth** être obsédé par qch

fetishism ['fetɪʃɪz(ə)m] N *Psy* fétichisme *m*

fetishist ['fetɪʃɪst] N *Psy* fétichiste *mf*

fetishistic [fetɪ'ʃɪstɪk] ADJ *Psy* fétichiste

fetlock ['fetlɒk] N *(of horse) (part of leg)* partie *f* postérieure du pied; *(joint)* boulet *m*; *(hair)* fanon *m*

fetter ['fetər] N *(usu pl)* **fetters** *(of prisoner etc)* chaînes *fpl*, fers *mpl*, **in fetters** enchaîné, dans les fers; **to put sb in fetters** mettre qn aux fers; *Fig* **to place fetters on sb/on sb's freedom** entraver qn/la liberté de qn; **the fetters of marriage** les chaînes du mariage
VT *(person)* enchaîner; *(horse)* entraver; *Fig (unions etc)* garrotter

fettle ['fet(ə)l] N **to be in fine** *or* **good f.** être en condition *ou* en forme

fetus ['fi:təs] N = **foetus**

feud [fju:d] N *(between families, clans etc)* inimitié *f*, **blood f.** vendetta *f*, **family f.** querelle *f* familiale
VI se quereller **(over** au sujet de); **the feuding parties** les opposants *mpl*, les parties *fpl* en conflit

feudal ['fju:d(ə)l] ADJ *Hist (system, service etc)* féodal, -aux; *Pej (attitude, approach to sth)* moyenâgeux

feudalism ['fju:dəlɪz(ə)m] N le système féodal; **under late f.** pendant les dernières années du système féodal

feudally ['fju:d(ə)lɪ] ADV féodalement

---

fever ['fi:vər] N *Med (high temperature, disease)* fièvre *f*, **high f.** forte fièvre; **she's** *or* **she is running a f.** elle a de la fièvre; *Fig* **to be in a f. of excitement** être animé d'une excitation fébrile *ou* fiévreuse; **expectation had reached f. pitch** l'attente était fiévreuse; **things are at f. pitch** l'atmosphère est enfiévrée; **gold f.** fièvre de l'or

fevered ['fi:vəd] ADJ *(brow)* fiévreux; *Fig (imagination)* enfiévré

feverish ['fi:vərɪʃ] ADJ *Med* fiévreux, fébrile; **to be f.** avoir de la fièvre, être fiévreux *ou* fébrile; **to feel f.** se sentir fiévreux; *Fig* **f. activity** activité fébrile *ou* fiévreuse

feverishly ['fi:vərɪʃlɪ] ADV fiévreusement, fébrilement

feverishness ['fi:vərɪʃnɪs] N *Med* état *m* fébrile; *(of activity)* fébrilité *f*

FEW [fju:] VOIR GRAMMAIRE A6
ADJ peu de **1** ■ quelques **2**
PRON peu **1** ■ quelques-uns **2**

ADJ **1** *(not many) (people, things)* peu de; **to have f. friends** avoir peu d'amis; **very f. opportunities** très peu d'occasions; **with f. exceptions** à de rares exceptions près; **on the f. occasions I've spoken to her** les rares fois où je lui ai parlé; **his visits/tourists are f. and far between** ses visites/les touristes sont rarissimes; **trains every f. minutes** trains toutes les deux ou trois minutes; **every f. days** tous les deux ou trois jours; **too f. points** pas suffisamment de points; **f. in number** peu nombreux; **f. novelists have equalled her** peu de romanciers l'ont égalée
2 *(some)* **a f.** quelques; **I have only a f. pounds** je n'ai que quelques livres; **he had a good f. enemies** il avait pas mal d'ennemis; **in a f. minutes** dans quelques minutes; **quite a f. minutes passed** un bon moment s'est écoulé; **in the next f. days** dans les jours qui suivent/suivaient

PRON **1** *(not many) (people etc)* peu; **there are very/too f. of us** nous sommes très peu/trop peu nombreux; **f. (of them) could speak French** peu parmi eux parlaient français; **there are so f. of them** ils sont tellement peu nombreux
2 *(some)* **a f. of these cakes/oranges** quelques-uns de ces gâteaux/quelques-unes de ces oranges; **a f. of the survivors** quelques-uns des survivants; **I know a f. of them** j'en connais quelques-uns; **a f. of us** quelques-uns d'entre nous; **I've seen/read a f.** j'en ai vu/lu quelques-uns; *Fam* **you've had a f. too many** *(drunk too much)* tu as un peu trop bu; **she only knew a f. (of them)** elle ne connaissait que quelques-uns d'entre eux
NPL **the f.** la minorité; **the fortunate f.** les heureux élus *mpl*, **the f. who came** les rares personnes qui sont venues

fewer ['fju:ər] ADJ *(comp of few)* moins de; **there are f. trees here** il y a moins d'arbres ici; **no f. than thirty** pas moins de trente; **the houses became f.** les maisons devenaient plus rares *ou* moins nombreuses; **f. and f. people** de moins en moins de gens
PRON moins; **there are f. (of them) than I thought** il y en a moins que je n'avais pensé

fewest ['fju:ɪst] ADJ *(superl of few)* le moins de; **the f. people possible** le moins de gens possible; **the area where there are the f. houses** la région où il y a le moins de maisons
PRON **the region where the f. live** la région où vit le moins grand nombre de gens

fey [feɪ] ADJ **1** *(charming)* qui possède un charme éthéré **2** *(silly)* un peu idiot **3** *Scot (foreseeing death)* qui a des pressentiments de mort ou des visions de l'au-delà; *(having second sight)* doué de seconde vue

fez [fez] N *(hat)* fez *m*

fiancé, *f* **fiancée** [fɪ'ɒnseɪ] N fiancé, -ée

fiasco [fɪ'æskəʊ] N fiasco *m;* **to be a f.** faire un four, être un fiasco

fiat ['faɪæt] N *(decree)* décret *m*
▶▶ *Am* **Fin f. money** monnaie *f* fiduciaire

fib [fɪb] *Fam* N petit mensonge *m;* **that's a f.!** ce n'est pas vrai!, c'est des histoires!; **you're telling me fibs** tu me racontes des histoires; **I told them a f. about having to do some work** je leur ai raconté qu'il fallait que je travaille
▶ VI (**-bb-**) *(lie)* raconter des histoires; **you're fibbing to me again** tu es encore en train de me raconter des histoires; **I'm sure he was fibbing about how much he earns** je suis sûr qu'il a menti *ou* raconté des histoires à propos de l'argent qu'il gagne; **I fibbed to them about having to do some work** je leur ai raconté qu'il fallait que je travaille

fibber ['fɪbər] N *Fam* menteur, -euse; **she's a terrible f.** elle raconte tout le temps des histoires; **what a f. you are!** quel menteur tu fais!

fibre, *Am* **fiber** ['faɪbər] N **1** fibre *f, (of cloth, wood)* fibre; **artificial/natural fibres** fibres artificielles/naturelles; *Fig* **moral f.** force *f* morale; *Fig* **to love sb/sth with every f. of one's being** aimer qn/qch de tout son être **2** *(in diet)* fibres *fpl;* **to be high in f.** *(foodstuff)* être riche en fibres; **high-f. diet** régime *m ou* alimentation *f* riche en fibres
▶▶ *Comput* **f. optics** fibre(s) *f(pl)* optique(s)

fibreboard, *Am* **fiberboard** ['faɪbəbɔːd] N panneau *m* de fibres agglomérées

fibreglass, *Am* **fiberglass** ['faɪbəglɑːs] N fibre *f* de verre; **it's (made of) f.** c'est en *ou* la fibre de verre

fibre-optic, *Am* **fiber-optic** ADJ *(technology)* de la fibre optique; *(system)* qui utilise la fibre optique; *(components)* en fibre optique
▶▶ **f. cable** câble *m* optique, câble en fibres optiques

fibrescope, *Am* **fiberscope** ['faɪbəskəʊp] N *Med, Opt* fibroscope *m*

fibrillation [faɪbrɪ'leɪʃən] N fibrillation *f*

fibroid ['faɪbrɔɪd] ADJ *(tumour etc)* fibroïde N *Med* fibrome *m*

fibroma, *pl* **fibromata** [faɪ'brəʊmə, -mətə] N *Med* fibrome *m*

fibrosis [faɪ'brəʊsɪs] N *Med* fibrose *f*

fibrositis [faɪbrəʊ'saɪtɪs] N *Med* fibrosite *f*

fibrous ['faɪbrəs] ADJ *(tissue etc)* fibreux

fibula ['fɪbjʊlə] N *Anat* péroné *m*

fickle ['fɪk(ə)l] ADJ inconstant, capricieux; *(character)* changeant, versatile; *(esp romantically)* volage; *(weather)* capricieux

fickleness ['fɪk(ə)lnɪs] N inconstance *f*, humeur *f* volage; **the f. of luck** les caprices *mpl* de la chance

fiction ['fɪkʃən] N **1** *(creation of imagination)* fiction *f*, création *f* de l'imagination; *Law* **legal f.** fiction légale; **these tales are pure f.** tous ces contes sont totalement imaginaires; *Fig* **his entire statement is a piece of f.** sa déposition est fabriquée de toutes pièces **2** *(in library, bookshop)* romans *mpl*, **light f.** romans de lecture facile; **a piece of f.** une œuvre de fiction; **f. writer** auteur *m* d'ouvrages de fiction

fictional ['fɪkʃən(ə)l] ADJ fictif; **a f. autobiography** une autobiographie romancée

fictionalize ['fɪkʃənəlaɪz] VT romancer

fictitious [fɪk'tɪʃəs] ADJ *(character, events)* fictif; *(account)* inventé; **her statement is entirely f.** sa déposition est fabriquée de toutes pièces

▶▶ *Fin* **f. assets** actif *m* fictif; *Fin* **f. person** personne *f* fictive

fictitiously [fɪk'tɪʃəslɪ] ADV fictivement

fiddle ['fɪd(ə)l] N *Fam* **1** *(violin)* violon *m; (musician)* (joueur, -euse de) violon; **bass f.** contrebasse *f, Fig* **to play second f.** jouer un rôle secondaire (**to sb** auprès de qn) **2** *Br (swindle)* combine *f*, magouille *f*; **to be on the f.** faire du fricotage
▶ VI **1** *(play violin)* jouer du violon; *Pej* racler du violon; *Fig* **to f. while Rome burns** = s'occuper de choses futiles au lieu de lutter contre une calamité
2 *(play, fidget)* **to f. (about** *or* **around) with** jouer avec, tripoter, trifouiller; *(details etc)* chipoter sur, ergoter sur; **to f. with one's watch** jouer avec sa montre; **don't f. with the switch** laisse l'interrupteur tranquille, ne tripote pas l'interrupteur; **she fiddled with a few knobs** elle a manipulé quelques boutons; **stop fiddling about** *or* **around and get down to some work!** arrête de tourner en rond et mets-toi au travail!
3 *Br Fam (swindle)* combiner, fricoter
▶ VT *Br Fam (tamper with) (meter etc)* bricoler; *(obtain dishonestly)* carotter; **to f. the accounts** truquer les comptes; **he fiddled a week's leave** il a carotté huit jours de permission; **he fiddled it** *or* **things so that ...** il s'est arrangé pour que ... + *sub*

fiddlededee [fɪd(ə)ldɪ'diː] INT *Old-fashioned Fam* bah!, turlututu!

fiddle-faddle [-fæd(ə)l] *Old-fashioned Fam* N bagatelles *fpl*, balivernes *fpl*, fadaises *fpl*
INT = **fiddledededee**

fiddler ['fɪdlər] N *Fam* **1** *Mus* joueur, -euse de violon; *Pej* violoneux *m* **2** *Br (swindler)* combinard, -arde

fiddlesticks ['fɪd(ə)lstɪks] INT *Old-fashioned Fam (nonsense)* balivernes!, quelle blague!; *(annoyance)* zut de zut!

fiddling ['fɪdlɪŋ] ADJ *(insignificant)* futile, insignifiant
N **1** *Fam Pej (on violin)* raclage *m* **2** *(fidgeting)* trifouillage *m*, tripotage *m;* **his f. with the details of my reports** la manière qu'il avait de chipoter *ou* d'ergoter sur les détails de mes rapports **3** *Br Fam (dishonest dealing)* combines *fpl*, fricotage *m;* **a lot of f. goes on around here** ça magouille *ou* ça fricote pas mal par ici

fiddly ['fɪdlɪ] ADJ *(work)* délicat, minutieux; *(details)* minutieux; **it was f. getting this nut off** ça a été délicat d'enlever cet écrou

fidelity [fɪ'delɪtɪ] N **1** *(of person, to person)* fidélité *f* **2** *(of translation, sound reproduction)* fidélité *f*, **f. to the original** fidélité à l'original; *Radio etc* **high f.** haute fidélité

fidget ['fɪdʒɪt] N **1** *(usu pl)* **the fidgets** l'agitation *f* nerveuse; **to have the fidgets** ne pas tenir en place **2** *(person)* **he's a f.** il ne tient pas en place; **what a f. you are!** mais tu ne tiens donc pas en place!; **don't be such a f.!** mais tiens-toi donc tranquille!
▶ VI (**-t-**) être agité, ne pas tenir en place; *(become excited)* s'énerver; **to f. around with sth** tripoter qch; **don't f.!** *(to child)* tiens-toi tranquille!

fidgetiness ['fɪdʒɪtɪnɪs] N agitation *f* nerveuse

fidgety ['fɪdʒɪtɪ] ADJ agité, qui ne tient pas en place; *(excited)* nerveux, impatient

fiduciary [fɪ'djuːʃərɪ] *Law, Fin* ADJ fiduciaire
N fiduciaire *m; (trustee)* dépositaire *m*
▶▶ **f. account** compte *m* fiduciaire; **f. issue** émission *f* fiduciaire

fief [fiːf] N *Hist Fig* fief *m*

field [fiːld] N **1** *(land)* champ *m; (under pasture)* pré *m; (of oil, gas, coal, diamonds etc)* gisement *m;* **to work in the fields** travailler

dans les champs; **to cut across the fields** couper à travers champs; **f. of wheat** champ de blé; **strawberry f.** plantation *f* de fraisiers; **in the open f.** en plein champ; *Aviat* **landing f.** terrain *m* d'atterrissage
2 *Mil* **f.** *(of battle)* champ *m* de bataille; **in the f.** en campagne; **to hold the f.** se maintenir sur ses positions; *(of theory etc)* faire autorité; **to take the f.** entrer en campagne; **f. of honour** champ d'honneur
3 *Sport (ground) Ftbl, Cr etc* terrain *m; (for baseball)* champ *m; Cr (bowlers)* chasseurs *mpl*
4 *(in race), Horseracing* **the f.** les partants *mpl,* **big f.** champ *m* fourni; **a strong f.** un bel éventail de concurrents; *Fig* **there are three candidates in the f.** trois candidatures ont été déposées; **well ahead of the rest of the f.** loin devant les autres; **to lead the f.** *Sport* mener le peloton; *Fig (of theory, ideas etc)* faire autorité; **our company leads the f. when it comes to fitted kitchens** notre entreprise est en tête du marché pour ce qui est des cuisines encastrées; *Fam* **to play the f.** *(keep options open)* ne pas s'engager; *(in relationships)* papillonner, avoir de nombreuses aventures amoureuses
5 *(domain) (of operation etc)* théâtre *m*, champ *m; (of science)* domaine *m;* **in the political f.** sur le plan politique; **she is the leading artist in her f.** elle est la plus grande artiste dans son domaine; **they were first in the f. with miniaturized TVs** ils ont été les premiers à commercialiser les télévisions miniaturisées; **that's not my f.** ce n'est pas mon domaine; **to work in the f.** *(not in office etc)* travailler sur le terrain; **to test a product in the f.** essayer un produit sur le terrain
6 *Opt, Phot etc* champ *m;* **f. of view** *or* **of vision** champ visuel; *Phys* **f. of force** champ de force; **magnetic f.** champ magnétique
7 *Her* champ *m*, sol *m; Art (of painting etc)* champ, fond *m; (of medal)* champ
8 *Comput (in database)* champ *m*
▶ VT **1** *Sport (team)* réunir; *Mil etc* **to be able to f. 50,000 men** pouvoir mettre 50 000 hommes en ligne; *Pol* **to f. 500 candidates** présenter 500 candidats **2** *Cr* **to f. a ball** arrêter (et relancer) une balle; **to f. a question (well)** bien répondre à une question
▶ VI *Cr* tenir le champ
▶▶ **f. agent** agent *m* sur le terrain; *Mil* **f. artillery** artillerie *f* de campagne; *Mil* **f. battery** batterie *f* de campagne; *Opt, Phot* **f. coil** bobine *f* d'excitation *ou* d'inducteur, bobine inductrice; **f. day** *Sch* journée *f* en plein air; *Mil* jour *m* des grandes manœuvres; *Fig* **to have a f. day** s'en donner à cœur joie; *Comput* **f. delimiter** délimiteur *m* de champ; **f. engineer** ingénieur *m* de chantier *ou* sur le terrain; *Sport* **f. events** concours *mpl* de saut et de lancer; *Mil* **f. exercise** exercice *m* en campagne, manœuvre *f*, **f. experiment** expérience *f* sur le terrain; **f. glasses** jumelles *fpl, Mil* **f. gun** canon *m; Am* **f. hockey** hockey *m* (sur gazon); *Mil* **f. hospital** antenne *f* chirurgicale, hôpital *m* de campagne; *Mktg* **f. interviewing** sondage *m* sur le terrain; **f. label** *(in dictionary)* rubrique *f*, indicateur *m* de domaine; *Mil* **f. marshal** maréchal *m; Mil* **f. officer** officier *m* supérieur; *Mil* **f. rations** ration *f* de guerre; **f. research** études *fpl* sur le terrain; **f. research executive** responsable *m/f* des études sur le terrain; **f. sales manager** directeur, -trice des ventes sur le terrain; **f. sales personnel** personnel *m* de vente sur le terrain; *Comput* **f. separator** séparateur *m* de champs; *Mil* **f. service** service *m* en campagne; *Comput* **f. size** taille *f* de champ; **f. study** étude *f* sur le terrain; *Mil* **f. telegraph** télégraphe *m* militaire; **f. trials** *(for machine)* essais *mpl* sur le terrain; *Sch, Univ* **f. trip** voyage *m* d'études; *(of one afternoon, one*

day) sortie *f* d'études; **f. work** *(research etc)* travaux *mpl ou* recherches *fpl* sur le terrain *ou* sur les lieux; **f. worker** *(social worker)* travailleur, -euse social(e); *(researcher)* chercheur, -euse de terrain

fielder ['fi:ldər] N *Cr etc* chasseur *m*

fieldmouse, *pl* **fieldmice** ['fi:ldmaʊs, -maɪs] N mulot *m*

fiend [fi:nd] N **1** *(demon)* démon *m*, diable *m* **2** *(evil person)* monstre *m* (de cruauté) **3** *Fam (fanatic)* **fresh-air f.** maniaque *mf ou* fanatique *mf* du plein air; *Old-fashioned* **dope f.** toxicomane *mf*

fiendish ['fi:ndɪʃ] ADJ diabolique, satanique; *Fig* diabolique; *(weather)* atroce, abominable; **to take a f. pleasure in sth** prendre un plaisir diabolique à qch

fiendishly ['fi:ndɪʃlɪ] ADV diaboliquement; **to laugh f.** avoir un rire diabolique; **a f. clever plan/piece of software/virus** un plan/logiciel/virus drôlement malin; **f. complicated/expensive** affreusement compliqué/cher; *Fam* **f. difficult** d'une difficulté infernale; *Fam* **it was f. cold** il faisait un froid de tous les diables

fierce ['fɪəs] ADJ *(person)* redoutable; *(animal)* féroce; *(fire etc)* ardent; *(heat)* torride; *(battle, competition, opposition)* acharné; *(critic, opponent)* ardent; *(wind etc)* furieux, violent; **to give sb a f. look** jeter un regard féroce à qn; **f. encounter** rencontre violente; **there was f. criticism of the policy** la politique a suscité des critiques violentes; **she was f. in her defence of him** elle le défendait avec acharnement; **f. fighting** lutte *f* acharnée; *Aut etc* **f. brake** frein *m* brutal

fiercely ['fɪəslɪ] ADV *(to lash out, criticize)* violemment; *(to glare)* d'un œil féroce; *(to defend, fight)* avec acharnement; **to be f. opposed to sth** être ardemment opposé à qch; **the sun beat down f.** le soleil frappait très fort

fierceness ['fɪəsnɪs] N *(of person, opposition, criticism)* violence *f*, véhémence *f*; *(of animal)* férocité *f*; *(of fire etc)* ardeur *f*; *(of battle)* acharnement *m*; *(of wind etc)* fureur *f*; *Aut etc (of brakes)* brutalité *f*; **the f. of her tone** son ton véhément

fieriness ['faɪərɪnɪs] N **1** *(of sun)* ardeur *f*, **the f. of the seasoning** l'assaisonnement très relevé *ou* épicé **2** *(of character)* ardeur *f*, fougue *f*, impétuosité *f*, emportement *m*

fiery ['faɪrɪ] ADJ **1** brûlant, enflammé; *(alcoholic drink)* extrêmement fort, brûlant; **f. coal(s)** charbons *mpl* ardents; **f. furnace** fournaise *f* ardente; **f. red** rouge *m* ardent, rouge feu; **f. sky** ciel *m* embrasé; **f. taste** saveur *f* très épicée, goût *m* piquant **2** *(person, character)* fougueux, emporté, impétueux; **to make f. speeches against sb** vomir feu et flamme contre qn; **f. temper** tempérament *m* fougueux *ou* emporté

▸▸ *Am* **the f. cross** la croix en flammes *(symbole du Ku Klux Klan)*

FIFA ['fi:fə] N *(abbr* **Fédération Internationale de Football Association)** FIFA *f*

fife [faɪf] N *Mus* fifre *m*

FIFO [fi:fəʊ] *Com (abbr* **first in, first out)** PEPS

fifteen [fɪf'ti:n, 'fɪfti:n] N **1** quinze *m*; **she is f. (years old)** elle a quinze ans; **the plane will land at f. thirty (hours)** l'avion va atterrir à quinze heures trente **2** *Rugby* **the French f.** le quinze de France

fifteenth [fɪf'ti:nθ, 'fɪfti:nθ] ADJ quinzième; **Louis the F.** Louis Quinze; **(on) the f. (of the month)** le quinze du mois

N **1** *(person, thing)* quinzième *mf* **2** *(fraction)* quinzième *m*

fifth [fɪfθ] ADJ cinquième; **Henry the F.** Henri Cinq

N **1** *(of month)* cinq *m*; **on the f.** le cinq **2** *(person, thing)* cinquième *mf* **3** *(fraction)* cinquième *m* **4** *Mus* quinte *f*

▸▸ *Am* **F. Amendment** Cinquième Amendement *m (de la Constitution des États-Unis, permettant à un accusé de ne pas répondre à une question risquant de jouer en sa défaveur)*; *Law, Hum* **to plead the F. Amendment, to take the F. Amendment** = refuser de répondre pour ne pas dire quelque chose pouvant être utilisé contre soi; *Pol* **f. column** cinquième colonne *f*; *Pol* **f. columnist** membre *m* de la cinquième colonne; *Br Sch* **f. form** ≃ classe *f* de seconde; *Aut* **f. gear** cinquième vitesse *f*; *Aut* **f. wheel** *(trailer coupling)* sellette *f*; *(on test car)* cinquième roue *f*, *Am* **to feel like a f. wheel** avoir l'impression d'être la cinquième roue du carrosse

fifth-generation ADJ *Comput* de la cinquième génération

fifthly ['fɪfθlɪ] ADV cinquièmement

fifth-rate ADJ *Fam* médiocre

fiftieth ['fɪftɪəθ] ADJ cinquantième

N **1** *(person, thing)* cinquantième *mf* **2** *(fraction)* cinquantième *m*

fifty ['fɪftɪ] NUM ADJ, N cinquante *m*; **f.-one** cinquante et un; **f.-two** cinquante-deux; **about f. books** une cinquantaine de livres; **the fifties** les années cinquante; **to be f.** avoir cinquante ans; **to be in one's fifties** avoir entre cinquante et soixante ans; **to be over f.** avoir cinquante ans passés, avoir plus de cinquante ans

fifty-fifty ADJ, ADV *(partnership)* à parts égales; **to split the profits f.** partager les bénéfices à parts égales; **to go f. on sth** partager le coût de quelque chose à parts égales; **her chances are f.** *(of surviving)* elle a cinquante pour cent de chances de s'en tirer; *(of winning)* elle a cinquante pour cent de chances de gagner

fig¹ [fɪg] N **1** *(fruit)* figue *f*; **fresh** *or* **green figs** figues fraîches; **dried figs** figues sèches; *Old-fashioned Fam* **he doesn't give** *or* **care a f.** what you think il se fiche éperdument de ce que tu penses **2** *(tree)* figuier *m*

▸▸ **f. leaf** *Bot* feuille *f* de figuier; *(on statue, in painting)* feuille *f* de vigne; *Fig* camouflage *m*; *Fig* **it's just a f. leaf** ce n'est qu'une couverture; **f. tree** figuier

fig² *(abbr* **figure)** *(in book etc)* fig; **see f. 21b** voir fig 21b

fight [faɪt] N *Boxing, Mil etc* combat *m*; *(brawl)* bagarre *f*, *(argument)* dispute *f*, **f. to the death** lutte *f* à mort; **they had a f.** *(in which they hit each other)* ils se sont battus; *(they argued)* ils se sont disputés; **to get into a f. with sb** se battre avec qn; *(argue)* se disputer avec qn; **I don't want us to get into a f. over this, but …** je ne veux pas que nous nous disputions pour ça, mais …; **do you want a f.?** tu veux te battre?; **a fair f.** un combat loyal; **the f. for life** la lutte pour la vie; **her f. against cancer** sa lutte contre le cancer; **to carry on a stubborn f. against sb** soutenir une lutte opiniâtre contre qn; **to show some f.** résister, offrir de la résistance; **I won't give in without a f.** je ne vais pas me laisser faire sans me battre; *Sport* **to put up a good f.** bien se défendre; **there was no f. left in him** il n'avait plus le cœur à se battre; **he still has a lot of f. left in him** il n'a pas dit son dernier mot; **you'll have a f. on your hands** *(it will be difficult)* tu vas avoir du mal; **the f. for the leadership of the party** la lutte pour la tête du parti

VI *(pt, pp* **fought** [fɔːt]*)* *(physically)* se battre; *(struggle)* lutter; *(argue)* se disputer; *Mil* **he fought in Russia** il s'est battu en Russie; **to f. against the enemy** combattre l'ennemi; **to f. against adversity/disease** lutter contre l'adversité/la maladie; **to f. against sleep**

lutter contre le sommeil; **to f. for sb** se battre pour qn; **to f. for sth** *(on behalf of)* se battre pour qch; *(to get sth)* se battre pour obtenir qch; **to f. for breath** avoir beaucoup de mal à respirer; **to f. for one's rights/freedom** se battre *ou* lutter pour ses droits/sa liberté; **she fought to clear her name** elle s'est battue pour prouver son innocence; **to f. on two fronts** se battre sur deux fronts; **two dogs fighting over a bone** deux chiens qui se disputent un os; **to f. fair** se battre loyalement; **they were fighting over some islands/who would sleep where** ils se battaient pour des îles/pour décider qui allait dormir où; **to be fighting for one's life** *(of someone seriously ill, competitor)* lutter pour sa vie; **to f. to the finish** se battre jusqu'au dernier moment; **to go down fighting** se battre jusqu'au bout

VT *(person)* se battre avec *ou* contre; *(enemy, fire, new measure, decision)* combattre; *(illness, temptation)* lutter contre; *(match)* disputer; *Boxing* **to f. the champion** affronter le champion; **I'll f. you in the courts** je vous traînerai en justice; **I'll f. you for custody** je me battrai contre toi pour obtenir la garde des enfants; **to f. a battle** livrer (une) bataille; **to f. a duel** se battre en duel; *Fig* **to f. a losing battle** livrer *ou* mener une bataille perdue d'avance; **to f. a losing battle to do sth** tenter vainement de faire qch; *Rel etc* **to f. the good f.** combattre pour la bonne cause; *Fig* **to f. sb's battles** prendre le parti de qn; **I'm not going to f. your battles for you** c'est à vous de vous débrouiller; **he fought his way through the crowd** il se fraya un chemin à travers la foule; **to f. one's way out** se frayer un passage pour sortir; **to f. one's way to the top** *(of one's profession)* se battre pour atteindre le sommet; **to f. an action (at law)** se défendre dans un procès; **to f. an election** se présenter à une élection; **she will be fighting a popular businessman** *(in election)* elle sera opposée à un homme d'affaires populaire; **to f. an emotion** lutter contre une émotion; **f. it!** résiste!

▸▸ **the f. game** la boxe

▸ **fight back** VT SEP **1** *(suppress) (emotion etc)* lutter contre; *(tears)* refouler **2 to f. one's way back again** remonter le courant

VI *(retaliate)* riposter, résister; **to f. back against an illness** lutter contre une maladie

▸ **fight down** VT SEP *(suppress) (passion, resistance etc)* vaincre; *(impulse, urge)* réprimer

▸ **fight off** VT SEP *(repel) (enemy, attack, sb's advances etc)* repousser; *(illness etc)* combattre; *(inflation)* juguler; **to f. off one's fear** lutter contre *ou* combattre sa peur

▸ **fight out** VT SEP **to f. it out** se mesurer l'un à l'autre; **you'll have to f. that out with him** tu régleras ça avec lui

fighter ['faɪtər] N **1** *(person who fights)* combattant *m*; *(boxer)* boxeur *m*; *Fig* **she's a f.** c'est une battante **2** *Mil, Aviat (plane)* chasseur *m*, avion *m* de chasse

▸▸ *Mil, Aviat* **f. aircraft** chasseur, avion de chasse; *Mktg* **f. model** modèle *m* d'attaque; *Mil, Aviat* **f. pilot** pilote *m* de chasse; *Mil, Aviat* **f. plane** chasseur, avion de chasse; *Mil, Aviat* **f. squadron** escadron *m* de chasse

fighter-bomber N chasseur-bombardier *m*, *pl* chasseurs-bombardiers

fighting ['faɪtɪŋ] ADJ **that's f. talk!** tu cherches la bagarre?/il cherche la bagarre!/*etc*, *Fam* **I still have a f. chance** j'ai encore de bonnes chances; **to be f. fit** être dans une forme éblouissante; **to get f. drunk** se saouler et chercher la bagarre

N *Mil* combat *m*; *Boxing* boxe *f*, **there was a lot of f. at my school** il y avait beaucoup de bagarre dans mon école; **the f. on the eastern front** les combats sur le front est

▸▸ **f. cock** coq *m* de combat; *Mil* **f. forces** effectifs *mpl* sous les armes; *Mil* **f. men** combattants *mpl*; *Mil* **f. unit** unité *f* de combat

figment ['fɪgmənt] **N** a **f. of the imagination** un phénomène imaginaire; **it's a f. of your imagination** tu te fais des idées, c'est le fruit de ton imagination; **is this a f. of my imagination, or …?** est-ce que je me fais des idées, ou bien …?

figurative ['fɪgərətɪv] **ADJ 1** (*language, meaning*) figuré, métaphorique; **in the f. sense** au (sens) figuré **2** (*art*) figuratif

figuratively ['fɪgərətɪvlɪ] **ADV 1** (*to speak, write*) au figuré, métaphoriquement; **f. speaking, …** métaphoriquement parlant, … **2** *Art* figurativement

FIGURE ['fɪgər, *Am* 'fɪgjər]

N	chiffre **1** ▪ figure **2, 6, 7** ▪ silhouette **2** ▪ ligne **2, 3** ▪ personnage **4**
VI	figurer **1** ▪ sembler logique **3**
VT	penser **1** ▪ supposer que **2**

N 1 (*number*) chiffre *m*; **it's difficult to give an exact f.** il est difficile de donner un chiffre exact; **figures** (*for project etc*) détails *mpl* chiffrés; (*involving calculation*) calculs *mpl*; (*statistics*) statistiques *fpl*; **the figures for 2001** les statistiques de 2001; **to find a mistake in the figures** trouver une erreur de calcul; **there must be a mistake in the figures** il doit y avoir une erreur dans les calculs; *Com* **sales figures** chiffres *mpl* de vente; **unemployment figures** le taux de chômage; **in round figures** en chiffres ronds; **to put a f. on sth** (*assess price, cost*) évaluer le prix/ coût de qch; (*assess quantity*) évaluer le nombre de qch; **to be good at figures** être bon en calcul; **to fetch a high f.** se vendre cher; **his score barely managed to get into double figures** son score s'élevait tout juste à un nombre à deux chiffres; **our takings have reached four figures** nous avons décroché les quatre chiffres; **to get inflation down to single figures** réduire l'inflation à un taux inférieur à dix pour cent

2 (*shape*) figure *f*; (*of person*) silhouette *f*; **to have a good f.** être bien fait de sa personne; (*of woman*) avoir une jolie silhouette; **to look after/keep one's f.** soigner/garder sa ligne; **to be f.-conscious** faire attention à sa ligne

3 (*human form*) ligne *f*; **a fine f. of a man** un bel homme; **a fine f. of a woman** une belle femme; *Art* **reclining f.** corps *m* au repos

4 (*person, character*) personnage *m*; **a distinguished f.** une personnalité; **a f. of fun** un objet de ridicule; **a hate f.,** **a f. of hate** un objet de haine; **the central f. of a painting** le personnage principal d'un tableau

5 (*appearance*) apparence *f*, air *m*; **to cut a sorry f.** faire piètre figure; **to cut an elegant f.** être élégant de sa personne; **to cut a pathetic f.** avoir l'air lamentable

6 (*illustration*) illustration *f*; **see f. 21b** (*in book*) voir figure 21b; **geometrical f.** figure *f* géométrique

7 (*pattern*) figure *f*; (*on material*) dessin *m*; **the figures of a dance** les figures d'une danse

8 (*rhetorical*) **f. of speech** façon *f* de parler; **it was just a f. of speech** ce n'était qu'une façon de parler

VI 1 (*appear*) figurer; **his name figures on the list** son nom figure sur la liste

2 (*calculate*) calculer

3 *esp Am Fam* (*make sense*) sembler logique *ou* normal; **that doesn't f.** ce n'est pas logique, ça n'a pas de sens; **that figures** ça colle

4 *esp Am* **go f.!** allez *ou* va comprendre!

VT 1 *esp Am* (*think*) penser; **I figured that**

she might be feeling lonely je me suis dit qu'elle se sentait peut-être seule

2 *esp Am* (*estimate*) **I f. that it will take three years** j'estime que cela prendra trois ans

3 (*put pattern on*) (*silk etc*) brocher, gaufrer; (*cotton etc*) imprimer

4 (*bass*) chiffrer

5 *esp Lit* (*imagine*) (*person, landscape etc*) figurer, représenter; **f. to yourself a happy family** imaginez une famille heureuse

▸▸ **f. of eight** (*shape*) (figure en forme de) huit *m*; *Sport* **to cut figures of eight** (*in skating etc*) faire des huits; **to draw figures of eight** décrire des huits; **f. skater** patineur, -euse artistique; **f. skating** patinage *m* artistique

▸ **figure on** **VT INSEP** *esp Am Fam* s'attendre à; (*plan on*) compter sur; **to f. on doing sth** avoir l'intention de *ou* compter faire qch; **I didn't f. on this happening** je ne m'attendais pas à ce que cela se produise; **he didn't f. on a woman for the position** (*did not consider hiring one*) il ne pensait pas à une femme pour le poste; (*did not think one would get it*) il ne s'attendait pas à ce qu'une femme obtienne le poste

▸ **figure out** *Fam* **VT SEP** (*work out*) (*amount*) calculer; (*problem*) résoudre; **he couldn't f. out what she meant** il n'arrivait pas à comprendre ce qu'elle voulait dire; **we couldn't f. out what to do next** nous n'arrivions pas à décider ce que nous devions faire; **we couldn't f. out where we were** nous n'arrivions pas à découvrir où nous étions; **we figured out that they must have paid more than we did** nous avons réalisé qu'ils avaient dû payer plus que nous; **she can't f. you out at all** elle n'arrive pas du tout à te comprendre

VI *Am* **it will f. out at about $100** cela coûtera une centaine de dollars

▸ **figure up** **VI** *Am* (*amount*) **to f. up to sth** s'élever à qch

Note that when referring to the human body, the French noun **figure** means **face**.

-figure **SUFF** **three/four/etc-f.** à trois/quatre/etc chiffres; **four-f. number** nombre *m* à quatre chiffres

figured ['fɪgəd] **ADJ 1** (*material, velvet etc*) façonné; (*silk etc*) broché **2** *Mus* (*counterpoint*) figuré; (*bass*) chiffré

figurehead ['fɪgəhed] **N** (*on ship*) figure *f* de proue; *Fig, Pej* (*man*) homme *m* de paille; **she's just a f.** elle n'agit qu'en prête-nom

figure-hugging **ADJ** moulant

figurine ['fɪgəriːn] **N** *Art etc* figurine *f*

Fiji ['fiːdʒiː] **N F., the F. Islands** les îles *fpl* Fidji

Fijian [fiːˈdʒiːən] **ADJ** fidjien
N Fidjien, -ienne

filament ['fɪləmənt] **N 1** *Elec* filament *m* **2** *Biol* filament *m*, filet *m*

▸▸ **f. lamp** lampe *f* à incandescence

filbert ['fɪlbət] **N** aveline *f*, (*hazelnut*) grosse noisette *f*

filch [fɪltʃ] **VT** *Fam* faucher, piquer (**sth from sb** qch à qn)

file¹ [faɪl] **N** (*tool*) lime *f*, **nail f.** lime à ongles
VT (*metal etc*) limer; **to f. one's nails** se limer les ongles

file² **N 1** (*folder*) classeur *m*; (*documents*) dossier *m*; **the f. on James Brown, the James Brown f.** le dossier James Brown; **to keep a f. on sb/sth** constituer un dossier sur qn/qch; **have we got anything on f. about it?** y a-t-il quelque chose là-dessus dans les dossiers?; **files** archives *fpl*; **we have placed your report on our files** nous avons classé votre rapport dans nos dossiers; **card-index f.** fichier *m*; **card f.** fichier sur cartes

2 *Comput* fichier *m*

VT 1 (*classify*) (*documents, letters etc*) classer; **it was filed under 'jazz'** c'était classé dans la catégorie 'jazz'; **the books are filed according to author** les livres sont classés par auteur

2 **to f. a petition** (*of court official*) déposer une requête; (*of plaintiff*) enregistrer une requête; **to f. one's petition (in bankruptcy)** déposer son bilan; **to f. a claim for damages** intenter une action en dommages-intérêts; **to f. an insurance claim** faire une déclaration de sinistre; *Am* **to f. one's tax return** remplir sa déclaration d'impôts; **to f. a story** (*of journalist*) boucler un sujet; **to f. copy** (*of journalist*) rapporter une copie

3 *esp Am Admin* (*document, complaint*) déposer (**with sb** auprès de qn)

VI **to f. for divorce** faire une demande de divorce

▸▸ *Comput* **f. allocation table** table *f* des fichiers; *Am* **f. cabinet** classeur *m*; **f. card** fiche *f* (de classeur); *Am* **f. clerk** documentaliste *mf*; *Comput* **f. compression** compression *f* de fichiers; *Comput* **f. conversion** conversion *f* de fichiers; **f. copy** copie *f* à classer; **f. divider** carte-guide *f*, *pl* cartes-guides, guide-classement *m*, *pl* guide-classements; *Comput* **f. extension** extension *f* du nom de fichier; *Comput* **f. format** format *m* de fichier; *Comput* **f. management** gestion *f* ou tenue *f* des fichiers; *Comput* **f. management system** système *m* de gestion de fichiers; *Comput* **f. manager** gestionnaire *m* des fichiers; **f. number** (*of document in file*) cote *f*; *Comput* **f. protection** protection *f* de fichiers; **f. separator** carte-guide, guide-classement; *Comput* **f. server** serveur *m* de fichiers; *Comput* **f. sharing** partage *m* de fichiers; *Comput* **f. structure** structure *f* de fichiers; *Comput* **f. transfer** transfert *m* de fichiers; *Comput* **f. transfer protocol** protocole *m* de transfert de fichiers; **f. trolley** bac *m* roulant; *Comput* **f. viewer** visualiseur *m*

▸ **file away** **VT SEP 1** (*documents etc*) classer, archiver; *Fig* (*mentally*) enregistrer

2 = file down **1**

file³ **N** (*line*) file *f*; **in single** *or* **Indian f.** en file indienne; **to walk in single f.** marcher à la file *ou* en file indienne; *Mil* **in f.** (en rang) par deux

VI *Mil etc* (*walk in line*) marcher à la file *ou* en ligne de file; **to f. off** défiler; **to f. past** défiler; **to f. past sb/sth** défiler devant qn/qch; **to f. in/out** entrer/sortir un à un

▸ **file down** **VT SEP 1** (*remove by filing*) (*rough edge etc*) enlever à la lime, limer

2 (*smooth by filing*) (*surface*) polir à la lime, limer; (*of blacksmith etc*) (*horseshoe*) raboter

▸ **file off** **VT SEP** = file down **1**

file-compatible **ADJ** *Comput* compatible du point de vue des fichiers

filename ['faɪlneɪm] **N** *Comput* nom *m* de fichier

▸▸ **f. extension** extension *f* du nom de fichier

filer ['faɪlər] **N** *Comput* classeur *m*, gestionnaire *m* de fichiers et de répertoires

filial ['fɪlɪəl] **ADJ** *Fml* filial, -aux

filibuster ['fɪlɪbʌstər] **N 1** *Pol* obstruction *f*, **a six-hour f.** un discours obstructionniste de six heures **2** *Hist* (*pirate*) flibustier *m*

VI *Pol* faire de l'obstruction; **filibustering tactics** manœuvres *fpl* ou tactiques *fpl* obstructionnistes

filigree ['fɪlɪgriː] **N** filigrane *m*; **f. work** (travail *m* en) filigrane

filing¹ ['faɪlɪŋ] **N 1** (*of metal etc*) limage *m* **2** (*small pieces of metal etc*) (*usu pl*) **filings** limaille *f*

filing² **N 1** (*of documents, letters etc*) classement *m*; (*for long-term storage*) archivage *m*; **f. by subject** classement *m* par sujet **2** *Law*

(of petition) (by court official) enregistrement *m*; *(of claim) (by plaintiff)* dépôt *m*
► ► **f. cabinet** classeur *m*; **f. clerk** documentaliste *mf*; **f. system** méthode *f* de classement; **f. tray** corbeille *f* pour correspondance à classer

Filipino [fɪlɪ'piːnəʊ] **ADJ** philippin
N Philippin, -ine

FILL [fɪl]

VT remplir **1** ▪ boucher **2** ▪ occuper **3** ▪ répondre à **4**
VI se remplir **1**

N 1 to have had one's f. of sth en avoir assez de qch; **to eat one's f.** manger à sa faim; **the horse ate its f. of straw** le cheval s'est rassasié de paille
2 *Tech* matériau *m* de remplissage; *Constr* remblai *m*; **a f. of tobacco** une pipée de tabac
VT 1 *(jug etc)* remplir, emplir (**with** de); *(pipe)* bourrer; *(cart etc)* charger; **to f. sb's glass** servir à boire à qn; *(to the brim)* verser une rasade à qn; **to f. the air with one's cries** remplir l'air de ses cris; **a smell of cooking filled the house** une odeur de cuisine envahissait la maison; **to f. one's head with useless things** se farcir la tête de choses inutiles; **to be filled with admiration** être rempli d'admiration; **the thought filled him with jealousy** cette pensée le remplissait de jalousie; **to be filled with hope** être plein d'espoir; **to be filled with fear/envy** être dévoré de peur/d'envie
2 *(plug) (opening, gap etc)* combler, boucher; *(tooth)* plomber; *(of employer) (vacancy)* pourvoir à; **to f. the woodwork** *(before painting)* mastiquer les boiseries; **I'm having two teeth filled tomorrow** on va me faire deux plombages demain; **two places remain to be filled** deux postes restent à pourvoir; **the position has already been filled** le poste a déjà été pourvu
3 *(occupy) (time)* occuper; **a position she has filled for some time** un poste qu'elle occupe depuis quelque temps; **to f. sb's shoes** *(take on sb's responsibilities)* prendre les fonctions de qn; **it's going to be difficult to f. his shoes** ça va être difficile de trouver quelqu'un pour le remplacer; **the thoughts that filled his mind** les pensées qui occupaient son esprit; **reading fills my evenings** la lecture remplit mes soirées
4 *(fulfil) (order, prescription)* exécuter; *esp Am* **to f. every requirement** répondre à tous les besoins
5 *(pour)* verser
VI 1 *(of tank, bath, container, hall etc)* se remplir; *(of hole)* se combler; **her eyes filled with tears** ses yeux se sont remplis de larmes
2 *(of sails)* se gonfler
► **fill in** **VT SEP 1** *(make level) (hole)* combler, boucher; *(ditch)* remblayer; *(block off) (door)* condamner
2 *(complete) (form)* remplir; **to f. in a gap in one's knowledge** combler un vide *ou* une lacune dans ses connaissances; **to f. in the blanks** remplir les blancs
3 *(insert) (date etc)* insérer
4 *Fam* **to f. sb in on the details** mettre qn au courant des détails; **she quickly filled us in on what had been happening** elle nous a rapidement mis au courant de ce qui s'était passé
5 *(use up)* **to f. in time** occuper son temps
VI to f. in for sb remplacer qn; **I'm filling in while she's on holiday** je la remplace pendant ses vacances
► **fill out** **VT SEP 1** *(pad out) (speech etc)* étoffer
2 *(complete) (form)* remplir

VI *(of sails)* se gonfler; *(of person)* s'étoffer; *(of adolescent female)* prendre des formes; **her cheeks are filling out** ses joues se remplissent, elle prend des joues
► **fill up** **VT SEP 1** *(with liquid) (glass)* remplir jusqu'au bord; *Aut Fam* **f. her up** (faites) le plein
2 *(plug) (hole with putty etc)* boucher
3 *(complete) (form)* remplir
VI 1 *(become full) (of tank, container etc)* se remplir (**with** de); *(of hole)* se combler, se remplir
2 *(fill tank etc)* **to f. up with petrol/water** faire le plein d'essence/d'eau

filler ['fɪlər] **N 1** *(person)* remplisseur, -euse; *(machine)* remplisseuse *f*; **oil f.** entonnoir *m*; **2** *(substance)* (matière *f* de) remplissage *m*; *(of cigar)* tripe *f*, *(for wood etc)* bouche-pores *m inv*; *(before painting)* mastic *m*; *Fig (between main acts etc)* bouche-trou *m*, *pl* bouche-trous; *(in media)* bouche-trou, passe-partout *m inv* **3** *(word)* mot *m* de remplissage
► ► *Aut* **f. cap** bouchon *m* du réservoir d'essence; *TV* **f. light** éclairage *m* d'appoint; *TV* **f. mike** micro *m* d'appoint; **f. paste** mastic *m* de bouchage; **f. word** mot de remplissage

fillet ['fɪlɪt] **N 1** *Culin (of beef, sole)* filet *m*; *(of veal)* rouelle *f* **2** *(for hair)* ruban *m* **3** *Typ* filet *m*
VT (-t-) *Culin (fish)* détacher les filets de; **filleted sole** filets *mpl* de sole
► ► *Culin* **f. steak** filet de bœuf

filling ['fɪlɪŋ] **ADJ** *(food)* bourratif
N 1 *(of hole)* comblement *m*; *(of tooth)* plombage *m* **2** *(substance)* (matière *f* de) remplissage *m*; *(in dentistry)* plombage *m*; *Carp* mastic *m*; *Constr* remplissage; *(rubble)* blocage *m*; *(liquid)* coulis *m*; *Culin (for pie, sandwich)* garniture *f*, **cake with a chocolate f.** gâteau fourré au chocolat
► ► **f. station** station-service *f*, *pl* stations-service, station d'essence

fillip ['fɪlɪp] **N** *(stimulus)* stimulant *m*, encouragement *m*; **to give a f. to business** stimuler *ou* doper les affaires

fill-up **N** *Aut* plein *m*; **do you want a f.?** *(more to drink)* je te remplis ton verre?

filly ['fɪlɪ] **N 1** *(horse)* pouliche *f* **2** *Old-fashioned Fam (girl)* jeune fille *f*

film [fɪlm] **N 1** *Cin* film *m*; *(celluloid strip)* bande *f*, **the f. of the book** le film tiré du livre; **full-length/short f.** long/court métrage *m*; **news f.** actualités *fpl*; **to shoot** *or* **make a f.** tourner un film; **to be in films** faire du cinéma **2** *Phot* pellicule *f*, film *m*; **I've run out of f.** ma pellicule est finie; **a roll of f.** un rouleau de pellicule, une pellicule; **colour f.** pellicule *ou* film couleur(s) **3** *(layer) (of ice, oil)* pellicule *f*, couche *f*, *(of plastic)* film *m*; *(of mist, smoke etc)* voile *m*; *Med (over eye)* taie *f*, **wrapped in plastic f.** emballé dans un film en plastique
VT *Cin (scene)* filmer, tourner; *(novel)* porter à l'écran; *(person, interview etc)* filmer
VI 1 *Cin, TV* filmer; **we start filming next week** on commence à tourner la semaine prochaine **2** = **film over**
► ► **f. actor** acteur *m* de cinéma; **f. actress** actrice *f* de cinéma; **f. archives** cinémathèque *f*, **f. buff** cinéphile *mf*, **f. camera** caméra *f*, **f. cassette** cartouche *f* de pellicule *ou* de film; **f. clip** séquence *f ou* extrait *m* de film; **f. club** ciné-club *m*, *pl* ciné-clubs; **f. crew** équipe *f* de tournage; **f. critic** critique *m* de cinéma; **f. director** réalisateur, -trice, metteur *m* en scène; **f. editor** monteur, -euse; **f. festival** festival *m* cinématographique *ou* du cinéma; **the f. industry** l'industrie *f* cinématographique *ou* du cinéma; **f. laboratory** laboratoire *m* de film, labo *m*; **f. library** cinémathèque *f*, **f. maker** cinéaste

mf; **f. producer** producteur, -trice de cinéma; **f. projector** appareil *m* de projection; **f. reel** bobine *f* de film; **f. review** critique *f* cinématographique; **f. reviewer** critique *m* de cinéma; **f. rights** droits *mpl* film; **f. scanner** lecteur *m* de télé-cinéma, analyseur *m* de film; **f. script** scénario *m*; **f. set** plateau *m* de tournage; **f. star** vedette *f* de cinéma; **f. stock** pellicule vierge; **f. strip** bande (de film) fixe; **f. studies** filmologie *f*, **f. studio** studio *m* (de cinéma); **f. test** bout *m* d'essai
► **film over** **VI SE** couvrir d'une pellicule; *Med (of eyes)* se couvrir d'une taie

filmgoer ['fɪlmɡəʊər] **N** amateur *m* de cinéma, cinéphile *mf*; **she is a regular f.** elle va régulièrement au cinéma

filmic ['fɪlmɪk] **ADJ** filmique

filming ['fɪlmɪŋ] **N** *Cin* tournage *m*; **to get permission for f.** obtenir l'autorisation de tourner

filmless camera ['fɪlmlɪs] **N** caméra *f* sans film

film-making **N** production *f* cinématographique

filmography [fɪl'mɒɡrəfɪ] **N** filmographie *f*

filmset ['fɪlmset] **VT** *Br Typ* photocomposer

filmsetter ['fɪlmsetər] **N** *Br Typ (machine)* photocomposeuse *f*, *(person)* photocompositeur *m*

filmsetting ['fɪlmsetɪŋ] **N** *Br Typ* photocomposition *f*

filmy ['fɪlmɪ] **ADJ** *(eye)* couvert d'une taie; *(lace, cloud etc)* léger, -ère, diaphane

Filofax® ['faɪləʊfæks] **N** organiseur *m*

filter ['fɪltər] **N 1** filtre *m*; *(for oil etc)* épurateur *m*; *(cigarette)* cigarette *f* à filtre; *Br* **a packet of Regal**® **f.** un paquet de Regal® filtres; **coffee f.** filtre à café **2** *Opt, Phot, Cin* filtre *m*; **colour f.** filtre de couleur, écran *m* filtre **3** *Elec, Electron etc* **frequency** **f.** filtre *m* de fréquences **4** *Br Aut (signal) (on traffic light)* flèche *f* de dégagement
VT *(water etc)* filtrer; *(air etc)* épurer
VI 1 *(of water etc)* filtrer (**through** à travers); *(seep)* suinter **2** *Br Aut etc* changer de file; **to f. to the right/left** prendre la voie de dégagement vers la droite/la gauche **3** *Fam* **to f. into a building** entrer par petits groupes dans un immeuble
► ► *Constr* **f. bed** couche *f* de filtration; **f. circuit** circuit *m* de filtrage; **f. coffee** café *m* filtre, *pl* cafés-filtre; *Aut* **f. element** cartouche *f* filtrante; *Br Aut* **f. lane** voie *f* de dégagement; **f. paper** papier *m* filtre; **f. tip** *(tip)* (bout *m*) filtre; *(cigarette)* cigarette (bout) filtre; *Br Aut* **f. signal** *(on traffic light)* flèche de dégagement
► **filter down** **VI** filtrer; **the information finally filtered down to them** les informations ont fini par filtrer jusqu'à eux
► **filter out** **VT SEP** *(remove with filter) (impurities)* séparer par filtrage; *Fig (in selection procedure etc)* éliminer; **f. out the solids** retenir les solides par filtrage
VI *(leave slowly)* quitter lentement; **information is beginning to f. out that …** des informations commencent à filtrer selon lesquelles …; **to f. out of a building** sortir par petits groupes d'un édifice
► **filter through** **VI** *(pass slowly)* passer lentement; **the news soon filtered through** les nouvelles n'ont pas tardé à filtrer
VT INSEP **the light filtered through the branches** la lumière filtrait à travers les branches

filterable ['fɪltərəb(ə)l] **ADJ** *Med (virus)* filtrant

filtering ['fɪltərɪŋ] **N** filtrage *m*, filtration *f*
► ► *Comput* **f. software** logiciel *m* de filtrage

filth [fɪlθ] **N 1** *(dirt)* immondices *fpl*, *(excreta)* ordure *f*, **to live in f.** vivre dans la saleté **2** *(obscenity)* **to talk f.** dire des obscénités;

what are you reading that f. for? pourquoi est-ce que tu lis ces cochonneries?; **this isn't art, it's f.!** ce n'est pas de l'art, c'est de la pornographie! **3** *Br Sl, Pej* **the f.** *(the police)* les flics *mpl*, les poulets *mpl*

filthy ['fɪlθɪ] **ADJ 1** *(very dirty)* (très) sale; **your hands are f.!** tes mains sont dégoûtantes!; **to get f.** *(of person)* se salir; *(of part of machine)* s'encrasser; **my hands got f.** je me suis sali les mains; **my jacket got f.** j'ai sali ma veste **2** *Fam* **he gave me a f. look** il m'a jeté un sale regard, il m'a regardé d'un sale œil; *Fam* **in a f. temper** d'une humeur massacrante; *esp Br Fam* **f. weather** temps *m* de chien **3** *(obscene) (language, talk etc)* ordurier, obscène; *(suggestion)* obscène, dégoûtant; *(person)* dégoûtant; **you've got a f. mind!** tu as l'esprit mal tourné!; **you f. beast!** espèce de gros dégoûtant!

▸ **ADV** *Fam* **f. dirty** dégoûtant; **f. rich** pourri de fric; **the f. rich** les gros richards *mpl*

filtration [fɪl'treɪʃən] **N** filtration *f*, filtrage *m*

fin [fɪn] **N 1** *(of fish, whale etc)* nageoire *f*; *(of shark)* aileron *m*; **fins** *(for swimmer, diver)* palmes *fpl* **2** *(of boat)* dérive *f*; *(of plane)* empennage *m*; *(of bomb etc)* ailette *f*; *Aut etc (of radiator etc)* ailette; **cooling fins** ailettes de refroidissement; **stabilizer f.** aileron stabilisateur **3** *Am Fam (five-dollar bill)* billet *m* de cinq dollars

finagle [fɪ'neɪg(ə)l] **VT** *Fam* = **wangle VT**

final ['faɪn(ə)l] **ADJ 1** *(last)* final, -als *ou* -aux, dernier, -ière; **f. details/preparations** derniers détails/préparatifs; **to make a f. effort** faire un dernier effort; **to put the f. touches to sth** mettre la dernière main à qch **2** *(definitive)* définitif; **f. text** texte *m* définitif; **the umpire's decision is f.** la décision de l'arbitre est sans appel; **take this as f.** tenez-le-vous pour dit **3** *Gram, Phil (clause, cause)* final, -als *ou* -aux

▸ **N 1** *Sport* **the f.** *or* **finals** la finale; **to be through to the final(s)** être en finale; *Ftbl* **cup f.** finale de coupe **2** *Univ* **to sit** *or* **take one's finals** = passer son dernier examen de licence **3** *Journ* dernière édition *f*; **late f.** dernière édition du soir

▸ **Com f. acceptance** réception *f* définitive; *Cin* **f. cut** final cut *m*; **f. date** date *f* limite; *Com* **f. demand** dernier rappel *m*; *St Exch* **f. dividend** dividende *m* définitif *ou* final; **edition** *(of newspaper)* dernière édition *f*; *Com* **f. handover** réception *f* définitive; **f. instalment** dernier versement *m*, versement de libération; *Law* **f. judgment** jugement *m* définitif *ou* sans appel; **f. offer** dernière proposition *f*; *Fin* **f. settlement** solde *m* de tout compte; **f. warning** dernier avertissement *m*

finale [fɪ'nɑːlɪ] **N** *Mus* finale *m*; *Theat etc* conclusion *f*; **grand f.** apothéose *f*; **there was a grand f. to the match** le match s'est terminé en apothéose

finalist ['faɪnəlɪst] **N** finaliste *mf*

finality [faɪ'nælɪtɪ] **N 1** *(of decision)* caractère *m* définitif, irrévocabilité *f*; **to say sth with f.** dire qch d'un ton irrévocable *ou* sans appel **2** *Phil* finalité *f*

finalization [faɪnəlaɪ'zeɪʃən] **N** *(of details, plans etc)* mise *f* au point

finalize ['faɪnəlaɪz] **VT** *(details, plans etc)* mettre au point; *(deal, arrangement)* conclure; **details of the visit have yet to be finalized** les détails de la visite restent à préciser

finally ['faɪn(ə)lɪ] **ADV 1** *(lastly)* à la fin, en dernier; **and f., I would like to thank Mr Smith** et enfin *ou* et pour finir, j'aimerais remercier M. Smith **2** *(at last)* finalement, enfin **3** *(irrevocably)* définitivement

finance [faɪ'næns, fɪ-] **N 1** finance *f*, *(funding)* finances *fpl*; **high f.** la haute finance **2** *(funds)* fonds *mpl*; **his finances are low** ses fonds sont bas; **what state are your finances in?** comment vont tes finances?; **it's a problem of f.** c'est un problème financier; **where are they going to get the f. from?** où vont-ils trouver les fonds nécessaires?

▸ **VT** *(project)* financer; *(person, company etc)* financer, commanditer; *Acct* **financed from cashflow** autofinancé

▸ ▸ **f. charges** frais *mpl* financiers; **f. company** société *f* financière; **f. costs** frais financiers *ou* de trésorerie; **f. department** service *m* financier; **f. director** directeur, -trice financier(ère); *Br* **f. house** société financière, = société britannique de financement pour les achats à crédit

financial [faɪ'nænʃəl, fɪ-] **ADJ** *(difficulty, planning, scandal etc)* financier, -ière

▸ ▸ **f. accountant** comptable *mf* financier(ère); **f. accounting** comptabilité *f* générale *ou* financière; **f. adviser** conseiller, -ère financier(ère); **f. aid** aide *f* financière; **f. analyst** analyste *mf* financier(ère); **f. appraisal** évaluation *f* financière; **f. assistance** appui *m* financier, aide financière; **f. backing** financement *m*, aide financière; **f. centre** place *f* financière; **f. circles** sphères *fpl* de la finance; **f. consultant** conseiller, -ère financier(ère), conseil *m* financier; **f. control** contrôle *m* financier; **f. controller** contrôleur, -euse financier(ère); **f. correspondent** correspondant, -ante sur les questions financières; *Acct* **f. costs** frais *mpl* financiers; **f. deal** opération *f* financière; **f. department** service *m* financier; **f. director** directeur, -trice financier(ère); **f. engineering** ingénierie *f* financière; *St Exch* **f. future** instrument *m* financier à terme; **f. gearing** effet *m* de levier financier; **f. healthcheck** diagnostic *m* financier; **f. institution** établissement *m* financier; **f. instrument** instrument financier; **f. intermediary** intermédiaire *mf* financier(ère); **f. management** direction *f* ou gestion *f* financière; **f. management accounting** comptabilité-gestion *f* financière; **f. manager** directeur, -trice financier(ère); **f. market** marché *m* financier; **f. marketplace** marché financier; *(centre)* place *f* financière; *Radio, TV* **f. news** chronique *f* financière; **f. ombudsman** arbitre *m* financier; **f. pages** pages *fpl* financières; **f. period** période *f* comptable; **f. position** position *f* ou situation *f* financière; **f. press** presse *f* financière; **f. services** services *mpl* financiers; **f. statement** état *m* financier, déclaration *f* de résultats; **f. statements** document *m* de synthèse; **The F. Times** = quotidien *m* britannique d'information financière; **F. Times-Stock Exchange 100 Share Index** = principal indice *m* boursier du Financial Times basé sur 100 actions cotées à la Bourse de Londres; **f. transaction** opération financière; **f. year** *(in business)* l'exercice *m* financier; *(in politics)* l'année *f* budgétaire

> **Financial Year**
>
> Pour les impôts sur le revenu en Grande-Bretagne, l'année fiscale commence le 5 avril.

financially [faɪ'nænʃəlɪ, fɪ-] **ADV** financièrement; **f. sound** solvable; **f. successful** aux finances prospères

financier [faɪ'nænsɪər, fɪ-] **N** financier *m*

financing [faɪ'nænsɪŋ, fɪ-] **N** *(of project etc)* financement *m*

▸ ▸ **f. gap** déficit *m* de financement; **f. plan** plan *m* de financement; **f. terms** modalités *fpl* de financement

finch [fɪntʃ] **N** *(bird)* fringillidé *m*

FIND [faɪnd]

> **N** découverte ▪ trouvaille
> **VT** trouver **1, 2, 4** ▪ retrouver **1** ▪ chercher **2** ▪ constater **3** ▪ se trouver **4** ▪ déclarer **5**
> **VI** prononcer

N découverte *f*, trouvaille *f*; *(artist, actor etc)* découverte; **he's quite a f.** c'est une perle rare; **it's quite a f.** c'est une fameuse trouvaille

VT *(pt, pp* **found** [faʊnd]*)* **1** *(discover by chance)* trouver, découvrir; **to f. happiness with sb** trouver *ou* rencontrer le bonheur auprès de qn; **to f. sb at home** *or* **in** trouver qn chez lui; **they found him dead** on l'a trouvé mort; **I found her waiting in the hall** je l'ai trouvée qui attendait dans le vestibule; **we must leave everything as we f. it** il faut tout laisser dans l'état où nous l'avons trouvé; **I often f. myself smiling** je me surprends souvent à sourire; **I found myself in London** je me suis retrouvé à Londres; **they found an unexpected supporter in Mr Smith** ils ont trouvé en M. Smith un partisan inattendu

2 *(discover by searching)* **to try to f. sth** chercher qch; **to f. an answer/a solution** trouver une réponse/une solution; **f. some paper** allez chercher du papier; *Comput* **to f. and replace** trouver et remplacer; **I ran to f. a doctor** j'ai couru chercher un médecin; **the (lost) key has been found** la clef a été retrouvée; **she was nowhere to be found** elle était introuvable; **you won't f. a better motorbike at this price** vous ne trouverez pas une meilleure moto à ce prix; **to f. a job for sb** trouver un emploi à qn; **to f. sth for sb** trouver qch à qn; **to f. a leak in a main** localiser une fuite dans une conduite; **the bullet found its mark** la balle a atteint son but; **I can f. no reason for …** je ne vois pas de raison pour …; **he keeps finding excuses** il arrive toujours à trouver des excuses; **to f. it in one's heart to do sth** avoir le cœur de faire qch; **he couldn't f. it in his heart to tell her** il n'avait pas le cœur de le lui dire; **to f. favour with sb** gagner la faveur de qn; **to f. one's balance** trouver son équilibre; **to f. one's way** trouver sa voie; *Fig* **such ideas can easily f. their way into the minds of the young** de telles idées peuvent facilement entrer dans les jeunes esprits; **to f. a way to do sth** trouver moyen de faire qch; **to f. oneself** *(one's true self)* se trouver

3 *(learn, be told)* apprendre; *(come to realize, discover)* constater; **you will f. that I am right** vous verrez que j'ai raison; **I was surprised to f. that …** j'ai été surpris de constater que …; **after his death, his family found that …** après sa mort, sa famille a appris que …

4 *(experience)* **to f. some difficulty in doing sth** éprouver quelque difficulté à faire qch; **they will f. it easy/difficult** cela leur sera facile/difficile; **to f. it impossible/necessary to do sth** se trouver dans l'impossibilité/la nécessité de faire qch; **I found it almost impossible to understand him** j'ai eu un mal fou à le comprendre; **how do you f. this wine?** comment trouvez-vous ce vin?; **how did you f. the meal?** le repas vous a-t-il plu?; **I f. her rather offhand/friendly** je la trouve plutôt désinvolte/aimable

5 *Law* **to f. sb guilty/innocent** déclarer qn coupable/innocent

6 *(provide)* **to f. the money for an undertaking** procurer les capitaux *ou* fournir l'argent pour une entreprise; **to f. half the costs for a project** financer la moitié des coûts d'un projet; **cost £20, all found** prix 20 livres, tout compris

VI *Law* **to f. for/against sb** prononcer *ou* rendre un verdict en faveur de/contre qn
▸▸ *Comput* **f. command** commande *f* de recherche

▸ **find out** VT SEP **1** *(discover) (facts)* se rendre compte de; *(truth)* découvrir; **we found out that she was French** nous avons découvert qu'elle était française; **did you f. anything out?** est-ce que vous avez découvert quoi ce soit?
2 to f. sb out *(learn truth about)* découvrir le vrai caractère de qn; *(catch doing wrong)* prendre qn en défaut; **we've been found out** nous nous sommes fait prendre; **they had found her out for the liar she was** ils avaient découvert quelle menteuse elle était; **she had been found out transferring money into her own account** on avait découvert qu'elle transférait de l'argent sur son propre compte
VI *(discover)* **I'll f. out** je le saurai; **your mother had better not f. out!** j'espère pour toi que ta mère ne l'apprendra pas!; **to f. out about sth** se renseigner sur qch; **I have found out all about it** j'ai tout appris à ce sujet

finder ['faɪndər] N **1** *(of lost item)* **there's a reward for the f.** la personne qui le trouvera recevra une récompense; **well, it's yours then, finders keepers** eh bien, c'est à toi maintenant, puisque tu l'as trouvé **2** *(of telescope)* chercheur *m*

finding ['faɪndɪŋ] N *(usu pl)* **findings** *(of scientist, enquiry, investigation etc)* résultat *m*; *(of tribunal, jury, committee, report)* conclusion *f*; **he published his findings in a scientific journal** il a fait publier les résultats de ses recherches dans un journal scientifique; **his f. is that …** il est arrivé à la conclusion que …

fine[1] [faɪn] *Law* N amende *f*; **to impose a f. on sb** infliger une amende à qn; **to pay a f.** payer une amende; **parking f.** amende pour stationnement illégal
VT condamner à une amende; **to f. sb £20** frapper qn d'une amende de 20 livres

FINE[2]

ADJ excellent **1** ▪ bien **1** ▪ beau **3, 4** ▪ fin **7, 8, 10** ▪ subtil **9**
ADV bien **1**

ADJ **1** *(excellent)* excellent, magnifique; **meat/wine of the finest quality** viande/vin de premier choix; **a f. athlete** un excellent athlète; **that's f.!** c'est parfait!; **that's f. by** *or* **with me** ça me va; **she's/everything is f.** elle/tout va bien; **we had a f. time** nous nous sommes bien amusés; *Iron* **he had a f. time explaining what he was doing there** il a passé un mauvais quart d'heure quand il a fallu qu'il explique ce qu'il faisait là-bas; *Iron* **you're a f. one, you are!** vous êtes joli, vous!; *Iron* **you're a f. one to talk!** vous pouvez bien parler!
2 *Fam (intensive)* **he was in a f. (old) temper!** ce qu'il rageait!; **this is another f. mess you've got us into!** tu nous a encore mis dans un beau pétrin!
3 *(beautiful)* beau, bel, *f* belle; **a f. piece of writing** un bon texte
4 *(weather)* beau, bel, *f* belle; **when the weather is f.** quand il fait beau; **a f. day** une belle journée; **it's turned out f. again** aujourd'hui encore il fait beau
5 *(noble, admirable)* **to appeal to sb's finer feelings** faire appel aux sentiments élevés de qn; **she's a f. woman** c'est une femme admirable
6 *Old-fashioned* **a f. lady** *(elegant)* une dame élégante; *(of high rank)* une grande dame
7 *(texture, hair, rain etc)* fin; *(gravel etc)* menu, fin

8 *(pointed)* effilé; *(writing)* délié, mince; *(needle)* fin; *(blade)* affilé, aigu; *(pen)* pointu; **f. print** petits caractères *mpl*; **to read the f. print** lire ce qui est écrit en petits caractères
9 *(subtle)* subtil; **a f. distinction** une distinction subtile; **she's got washing the car down to a f. art** elle est passée maître dans l'art de laver la voiture; **there's a f. line between eccentricity and madness** il n'y a qu'un pas de l'excentricité à la folie; **not to put too f. a point on it** pour parler franchement
10 *(pure) (metals, oil etc)* fin; **gold twenty-two carats f.** or à vingt-deux carats de fin
INT *(agreed)* bon!, entendu!, d'accord!
ADV **1 to get on** *or* **do f.** *(in new job etc)* se débrouiller très bien; *(be well)* aller bien; **to get on f.** *(of two people)* bien s'entendre
2 to chop meat f. hacher menu la viande; *Fig* **to cut it (a bit) f.** calculer un peu juste; **that's cutting it a bit f.** là tu calcules/il calcule/*etc* un peu juste; *Billiards* **to cut the ball too f.** prendre la bille trop fin *ou* trop fine
▸▸ **f. arts** beaux-arts *mpl*

▸ **fine down** VT SEP **1** *(refine) (beer)* clarifier
2 *(make thinner) (metal, wood)* amincir, désépaissir; *(plans, proposals)* dégrossir

fine-cut ADJ **1** *(features)* finement *ou* délicatement ciselé **2** *(tobacco)* haché fin

fine-drawn ADJ **1** *(features etc)* fin **2** *(distinction)* subtil **3** *(wire)* finement étiré; *(thread)* délié

fine-grained [-greɪnd] ADJ *(wood, leather)* à grain fin

fine-looking ADJ beau, bel, *f* belle

finely ['faɪnlɪ] ADV **1** *(excellently)* magnifiquement **2** *(skilfully)* habilement **3** *(delicately)* délicatement; **f. drawn features** traits *mpl* fins **4** *(in small size)* **f. powdered** finement pulvérisé; **f. chopped** haché fin; **f. ground** moulu très fin

fineness ['faɪnnɪs] N **1** *(excellence)* qualité *f* supérieure, excellence *f* **2** *(splendour) (of dress etc)* splendeur *f*, magnificence *f* **3** *(in texture) (of hair, material etc)* finesse *f* **4** *(purity) (of gold)* titre *m*, aloi *f*

finery ['faɪnərɪ] N parure *f*; **decked out in all his f.** paré de ses plus beaux atours

fine-spun ADJ **1** *Tex* au fil ténu *ou* délié **2** *(reasoning etc)* subtil

finesse [fɪ'nes] N **1** *(skill) (of style etc)* finesse *f*, délicatesse *f* **2** *(ruse)* finesse *f*, ruse *f* **3** *Cards* impasse *f*

fine-tooth ADJ *(comb)* fin; *Fig* **to go through sth with a f. comb** passer qch au peigne fin

fine-tune VT *(radio, engine etc)* régler avec précision; *Fig (plan, proposals)* peaufiner

finger ['fɪŋgər] N **1** *(of hand, glove etc)* doigt *m*; **first** *or* **index f.** index *m*; **middle f.** médius *m*, doigt du milieu; **ring f.** annulaire *m*; **little f.** auriculaire *m*; **to eat sth with one's fingers** manger qch avec les doigts; **to keep one's fingers crossed** croiser les doigts; **they could be counted on the fingers of one hand** on pourrait les compter sur les doigts de la main; *Fig* **he's got them (wrapped) round his little f.** il fait d'eux ce qu'il veut; **the f. (of suspicion) is pointed at him** on le soupçonne; **he has a f. in every pie** il est mêlé à tout; **I've been working my fingers to the bone** je me suis tué à la tâche; **don't you dare lay a f. on him** je vous défends de le toucher; *Fig* **I can't quite put my f. on it** je n'arrive pas à mettre le doigt dessus; **to lay** *or* **put one's f. on the source of the trouble** mettre le doigt sur la source du mal; **she wouldn't lift a f. to help you** elle ne remuerait pas le petit doigt pour vous aider; **he's so lazy, I've never seen him lift a f.** il est si paresseux, je ne l'ai jamais vu faire le moindre effort; *Br Fam* **get** *or* **pull your f. out!** remue-

toi!, *Sl* bouge ton cul!; *Fam* **to put the f. on sb** *(inform on)* balancer qn; **to give sb the f.** *(rude gesture)* faire un doigt d'honneur à qn
2 *(measure etc)* **f. of brandy** doigt *m* de cognac; **f. of cake** petit morceau *m* (rectangulaire) de gâteau
VT **1** *(feel)* toucher, tâter; **stop fingering that food!** arrête de tripoter la nourriture!
2 *Mus (piece of music)* doigter; **to f. the piano** tapoter sur le piano
3 *Sl (inform on)* balancer
▸▸ *Culin* **f. biscuit** biscuit *m* à la cuiller; **f. board** *(of violin etc)* touche *f*; **f. bowl** rince-doigts *m inv*; **f. buffet** = buffet *m* où sont servis des petits sandwiches, des petits fours, des légumes crus, etc; *Mus* **f. exercises** exercices *mpl* de doigté; **f. food** = petits fours, petits sandwiches et légumes crus, etc, servis à un buffet et que l'on mange avec les doigts; *Mus* **f. hole** trou *m*; **f. painting** peinture *f* avec les doigts; **she's being doing f. paintings all afternoon** elle a peint avec ses doigts tout l'après-midi; **f. plate** *(on door etc)* plaque *f* de propreté

fingering ['fɪŋgərɪŋ] N *Mus* doigté *m*

fingermark ['fɪŋgɑːk] N trace *f* de doigt

fingernail ['fɪŋgəneɪl] N ongle *m* (de la main)

fingerprint ['fɪŋgəprɪnt] N empreinte *f* digitale; **to take sb's fingerprints** prendre les empreintes digitales de
VT *(person)* prendre les empreintes digitales de; **the police fingerprinted him** la police a pris ses empreintes digitales
▸▸ **f. expert** spécialiste *mf* en empreintes digitales *ou* en dactyloscopie; **f. identification** dactyloscopie *f*

fingerstall ['fɪŋgəstɔːl] N *Med* doigtier *m*

fingertip ['fɪŋgətɪp] N bout *m* du doigt; **he is a Frenchman to his fingertips** il est français jusqu'au bout des ongles; **to have sth at one's fingertips** savoir qch sur le bout des doigts
▸▸ **f. controls** commandes *fpl* à touches

finial ['fɪnɪəl] N *Archit* fleuron *m*

finicky ['fɪnɪkɪ] ADJ *(person)* méticuleux, *Pej* tatillon, vétilleux; *(style, layout)* alambiqué; *(job, task)* minutieux; *(device, recipe)* compliqué; **to be a very f. eater** être très difficile sur la nourriture; **this is a f. dish to make** c'est un plat très délicat à préparer; **there are all these f. little bits and pieces** il y a toutes ces petites pièces embêtantes à manier

FINISH ['fɪnɪʃ]

N fin **1** ▪ finition **2**
VT finir **1, 3** ▪ terminer **1** ▪ achever **2**
VI se terminer ▪ finir

N **1** *(end)* fin *f*; *Sport (of race)* arrivée *f*; **she was exhausted by the f.** sur la fin elle était épuisée; *Sport* **he has a fast f.** il a un bon finish; *Sport* **it's going to be a close f.** l'arrivée va être serrée; *Fam* **that was the f. (of him)** ce fut le coup de grâce; **to be in at the f.** être là pour voir la fin; *St Exch* **price at the f.** prix *m* de clôture
2 *(workmanship) (of work etc)* fini *m*; *Tech (operation)* finition *f*; *(surface)* apprêt *m*; **paint with a gloss/matt f.** peinture vernie/mate; **paper with a gloss/matt f.** papier glacé/mat; **all the woodwork has been given a pine f.** toutes les boiseries ont été teintées imitation pin; **car with a metallic/silver f.** voiture métallisée/argentée
VT **1** *(end)* finir, terminer, achever; *(cake, food)* finir; *(meal)* finir, terminer; **to f. doing sth** terminer *ou* finir de faire qch; **you can f. telling me tomorrow** tu peux me raconter la fin demain; **to f. what one was saying** finir ce qu'on avait à dire; **when do you f. work?**

à quelle heure est-ce que tu finis?; **f. your soup!** finis ta soupe!

2 *(ruin, kill) (person)* achever; **he's finished!** il est fini *ou* achevé!; **this defeat has finished the team's chances** cette défaite a mis un terme aux chances de l'équipe; **she was finished as a singer** sa carrière de chanteuse était finie; **you're finished here** *(I'm sacking you)* tu es viré

3 *(put finishing touches) (to piece of work etc)* finir, donner du fini à; *Tex (fabric)* apprêter; *Metal (part)* usiner; *Sewing* **to f. a buttonhole** brider une boutonnière; **the wood/paintwork hasn't been very well finished** le bois/la peinture n'a pas un très bon fini

VI se terminer, s'achever; **they finished long before the others** ils ont fini *ou* terminé bien avant les autres; **the meeting finished in a brawl** le meeting se termina par des coups; **when do you f.?** *(leave work)* quand est-ce que tu finis?; **have you finished?** *(eating, shouting etc)* tu as terminé?; **to f. in a point** *(of blade, shape etc)* se terminer en pointe; **the book finishes with him returning to the family house** à la fin du livre, il retourne à la maison familiale; **I'd like to f. on an optimistic note** je voudrais terminer *ou* finir sur une note optimiste; **he finished by calling me a liar** il a fini par me traiter de menteur; *Sport* **to f. fourth** finir *ou* arriver quatrième; *Sport* **where did she f.?** à quelle place est-ce qu'elle a fini?

▸ **finish off VT SEP 1** *(complete) (task)* terminer; *Sewing* **to f. off a buttonhole** brider une boutonnière

2 *(have the last of) (cake, milk etc)* finir

3 *Fam (kill)* achever; *(exhaust)* achever, épuiser; *(ruin) (company, industry)* causer la ruine de; *(hopes)* ruiner, anéantir; **to f. off a wounded animal** donner le coup de grâce à une bête; **this fly killer will soon f. them off!** ce tue-mouches aura bientôt raison d'elles!; **cirrhosis of the liver finally finished him off** une cirrhose du foie a fini par avoir raison de lui

VI *(end)* finir, terminer; **we should be finishing off soon** nous devrions bientôt avoir fini *ou* terminé; **they finished off with some fruit/a song** ils ont fini avec des fruits/une chanson

▸ **finish up VT SEP 1** *(complete)* finir, terminer; **f. up your soup!** finis ta soupe!

2 *(have the last of)* finir; **don't f. up the pie** ne mange pas toute la tourte

VI *(end up)* finir; **we finished up in a ditch** nous avons fini dans un fossé; **I'm going to f. up a nervous wreck!** je vais finir par m'user les nerfs!; **I'm going to f. up hating him** je vais finir par le détester

▸ **finish with VT INSEP 1** *(stop using)* ne plus avoir besoin de; **have you finished with the dictionary/mustard?** est-ce que tu as fini avec le dictionnaire/la moutarde?; **I've finished with it** je n'en ai plus besoin

2 *(stop doing)* en avoir fini avec; **I've finished with acting** j'en ai fini avec le théâtre; **I've finished with trying to help people** plus jamais je n'essaierai d'aider les gens

3 *(finish dealing with)* **I haven't finished with you!** je n'en ai pas fini avec toi!; **wait until I've finished with him!** *(threat)* attendez que je lui aie réglé son compte!

4 *(end relationship with)* rompre avec; **I've finished with you** tout est fini entre nous; **I've finished with men forever!** les hommes et moi, c'est fini!

finished ['fɪnɪʃt] ADJ **1** *(item etc)* fini, apprêté; *(product)* ouvré; **machine f.** apprêté à la machine; **badly f. goods** marchandises mal finies; **beautifully/professionally f.** d'un fini magnifique/professionnel **2** *(appearance etc)* soigné, fini; *(performance)* au

point, parfait **3** *(ruined)* **he's f. as a boxer** sa carrière de boxeur est finie; **if I can't raise the money, I'm f.!** si je n'arrive pas à trouver l'argent, je suis fichu!

finisher ['fɪnɪʃər] N *Ind, Sport (person)* finisseur, -euse; *Sport* **he's a fast f.** c'est un bon finisseur, il a un bon finish

finishing ['fɪnɪʃɪŋ] ADJ dernier, -ière; **f. coat** *(of paint etc)* dernière couche f; **the f. stroke** le coup de grâce
  ◻ **N 1** *(completion) (of task etc)* achèvement m; **2** *Tech* finition f; *(of leather, paper)* apprêtage m
  ▸ ▸ *Br Sport* **f. line** ligne f d'arrivée; **f. school** = école f privée de jeunes filles surtout axée sur l'enseignement des bonnes manières; *Ind* **f. shop** atelier m de finitions; **f. touches** finitions fpl; **to put the f. touches to sth** mettre la dernière main à qch

finite ['faɪnaɪt] ADJ *(universe)* fini, limité; *(resources, means)* limité; *Gram (verb)* à un mode fini; **a f. number of possibilities** un nombre limité de possibilités
  ◻ **N the f. and the infinite** le fini et l'infini

fink [fɪŋk] *Am Fam, Pej* **N 1** *(unpleasant person)* salaud m **2** *(strikebreaker)* jaune m **3** *(informer)* balance f, indic m
  ◻ **VI** moucharder; **to f. on sb** balancer qn

Finland ['fɪnlənd] N Finlande f

Finn [fɪn] N VOIR GRAMMAIRE A19 Finlandais, -aise, Finnois, -oise

finnan ['fɪnən] N
  ▸ ▸ *Scot Culin* **f. haddie** haddock m

Finnish ['fɪnɪʃ] VOIR GRAMMAIRE A19 ADJ finlandais, finnois
  ◻ **N** *Ling* finlandais m, finnois m

fiord [fjɔːd] N *Geog* fjord m, fiord m

fir [fɜːr] N *(tree, wood)* sapin m
  ▸ ▸ *Br* **f. cone** pomme f de pin; **f. tree** sapin m

FIRE ['faɪər]

| **N** feu **1–3** ▪ radiateur **1** ▪ incendie **2** |
| ▪ enthousiasme **5** |
| **VT** enthousiasmer **2** ▪ tirer **6** |
| ▪ décharger **6** ▪ virer **7** |
| **VI** tourner **1** ▪ tirer **2** |

N 1 *(in hearth etc)* feu m; **to make** *or* **light a f.** faire du feu; **to set** *or* **lay a f.** préparer un feu; **wolves are afraid of f.** les loups ont peur du feu; *Fig* **to go through f. and water for sb** subir des épreuves pour qn; *Fig* **to play with f.** jouer avec le feu; *Fig* **to fight f. with f.** combattre le mal par le mal; **gas/electric f.** radiateur m à gaz/électrique; **to throw sth into the f.** jeter qch au feu; **open f.** feu de cheminée; **a roaring f.** une belle flambée; **blacksmith's f.** feu de forge

2 *(large, destructive)* incendie m; **bush f.** feu m de brousse; **to cause** *or* **start a f.** provoquer un incendie; *Br* **to catch f.**, *Am* **to catch on f.** prendre feu; **f.!** au feu!; **on f.** en feu; **to set f. to sth, to set sth on f.** mettre le feu à qch; *Fam* **my singing isn't going to set the world** *or Br* **the Thames on f.** la façon dont je chante n'a rien de fantastique; *Fam* **to get on like a house on f.** *(of work etc)* marcher rondement; *(of two people)* s'entendre à merveille

3 *Mil etc (act)* feu m, tir m; *(shots)* coups mpl de feu; **individual f., f. at will** tir *ou* feu à volonté; **to open f.** ouvrir le feu; **to hold one's f.** *(stop firing)* arrêter de tirer, cesser le feu; *(postpone firing)* ne pas tirer; **to cease f.** cesser le feu; **to return (sb's) f.** riposter (au tir de qn); **under enemy f.** sous le feu de l'ennemi; **we are under f.** on nous tire dessus; **to come under f.** être exposé aux tirs (**from sb** *ou* qn); *Fig* **to be/come under f.** être exposé à de sévères critiques (**from** de la part de); **to draw sb's f.** attirer sur soi les tirs de qn; *Mil, Fig* **between two fires** entre deux feux; *Fig*

to hang f. *(of project etc)* être en attente

4 *(of diamond)* lumière f, éclat m

5 *(enthusiasm)* enthousiasme m; *(ardour)* fougue f; **the f. of youth** l'enthousiasme de la jeunesse; **the speech lacked f.** le discours manquait de mordant; **he lacks the f. of his predecessor** il n'a pas l'ardeur de son prédécesseur

VT 1 *Fml, Lit (set on fire)* mettre le feu à

2 *(fill with enthusiasm)* animer, enthousiasmer; *(the imagination)* exciter; **she was fired with an intense desire to help others** elle était animée d'un désir intense d'aider autrui; **to be fired with enthusiasm for sth** brûler d'enthousiasme pour qch; **the speech had fired them with enthusiasm** le discours les avait remplis d'un enthousiasme ardent

3 *Cer (pottery etc)* cuire

4 *(heat) (locomotive etc)* chauffer; *(boiler)* allumer; **oil-fired/gas-fired central heating** chauffage m central au mazout/au gaz

5 *(fuel mix in engine)* enflammer

6 *Mil etc (shot, salvo)* tirer; *(rifle, pistol)* décharger; *(rocket, torpedo)* lancer; *(cannon)* tirer un coup de; **to f. a gun at sb** tirer un coup de fusil sur qn; **without firing a shot** sans tirer un seul coup de feu; *Fig* **to f. a question at sb** poser une question à qn à brûle-pourpoint

7 *Fam (dismiss) (employee etc)* virer, saquer; **you're fired!** vous êtes viré!

VI 1 *(of spark plug)* s'allumer; *(of engine)* tourner; **to f. on all (four) cylinders** tourner rond; *Fig* **I'm not firing on all (four) cylinders this morning** je ne tourne pas tout à fait rond ce matin

2 *Mil etc (of person)* tirer; *(of shot)* partir; **we could hear the guns firing** on entendait le bruit des canons; **the revolver failed to f.** le revolver a fait long feu; **to f. at** *or* **on sb/sth** tirer sur qn/qch; **to f. at sb with a revolver** tirer un coup de revolver sur qn; **f.! feu!**; **to f. at will** tirer à volonté; **we were fired on** nous avons reçu des coups de feu, on nous a tiré dessus

  ▸ ▸ **f. alarm** alarme f d'incendie; **f. blanket** couverture f pare-flamme; *Br* **f. brigade** brigade f des pompiers *ou* sapeurs-pompiers, *Suisse* service m du feu; *Naut, Aviat* **f. bulkhead** cloison f pare-feu; *Comput* **f. button** *(on joystick)* bouton m feu; **f. chief** capitaine m des pompiers *ou* sapeurs-pompiers; **f. clay** argile f réfractaire; **f. damage** dégâts mpl causés par le feu; *Am* **f. department** brigade f des pompiers *ou* sapeurs-pompiers, *Suisse* service du feu; **f. door** porte f coupe-feu; **f. drill** exercice m de sécurité *(en cas d'incendie)*; **f. engine** voiture f de pompiers; **f. escape** escalier m de secours *ou* d'incendie; **f. fighter** pompier m, sapeur-pompier m *(volontaire)*, *Suisse* homme m du feu; **f. fighting** lutte f contre l'incendie; **f. hazard** risque m d'incendie; **that old gas cooker must be a f. hazard** cette vieille cuisinière à gaz doit présenter un risque d'incendie; **f. hose** tuyau m de pompe à incendie; *Br* **f. hydrant** bouche f d'incendie, *Suisse* hydrant m; **f. insurance** assurance-incendie f; **f. irons** accessoires mpl de cheminée; *Am* **f. marshal** capitaine des pompiers *ou* sapeurs-pompiers; **f. master** capitaine des pompiers; **f. notice** *(in hotel etc)* consignes fpl en cas d'incendie; **f. power** puissance f de tir; **f. raiser** incendiaire mf; **f. regulations** consignes en cas d'incendie; *(posted in hotel room)* consignes d'incendie; **f. safety** sécurité f incendie; **f. sale** = vente f au rabais de marchandises ayant subi de légers dégâts à la suite d'un incendie; **f. screen** écran m de cheminée; **f. station** caserne f de pompiers; **f. tender** voiture de pompiers; *Am* **f. truck** voiture de pompiers; **f. worship** culte m du feu

▸ **fire away VI** *Mil etc* tirer à feu continu (**at**

sur); *Fig* **f. away!** allez-y!, commencez!
▸ **fire off** VT SEP *Mil etc (round etc)* tirer; *Fig (questions)* poser à brûle-pourpoint; **she fired off a letter of complaint** elle a envoyé une lettre de réclamation sur-le-champ

fire-and-brimstone ADJ *(sermon, preacher)* annonçant les feux de l'enfer

firearm ['faɪərɑːm] N arme f à feu; **firearms training** formation f à l'utilisation des armes à feu

fireball ['faɪbɔːl] N **1** *Met* éclair *m* en boule **2** *Astron* bolide *m* **3** *(ball of fire)* boule f de feu; **he heard a loud noise and saw a f. in the sky** il a entendu un grand bruit et il a vu une boule de feu dans le ciel **4** *Fig* **she's a real f.** elle déborde d'énergie

fireboat ['faɪbəʊt] N bateau-pompe *m*, *pl* bateaux-pompes

firebox ['faɪbɒks] N foyer *m*, boîte f à feu

firebrand ['faɪbrænd] N **1** *(burning wood)* tison *m*, brandon *m* **2** *(agitator)* brandon *m* de discorde

firebreak ['faɪbreɪk] N *(in forest etc)* coupe-feu *m inv*

firebrick ['faɪbrɪk] N brique f réfractaire

firebug ['faɪbʌg] N *Fam* incendiaire *mf*, pyromane *mf*

firecracker ['faɪəkrækər] N *Am* pétard *m*

firedamp ['faɪədæmp] N *Min* grisou *m*
▸▸ **f. explosion** coup *m* de grisou

firedog ['faɪədɒg] N *(in fireplace)* chenet *m*

fire-eater N **1** *(at fair etc)* avaleur *m* de feu **2** *Fam (aggressive person)* batailleur, -euse

fire-extinguisher N extincteur *m* (d'incendie)

fire-fighting N lutte f contre les incendies
▸▸ **f. equipment** matériel *m* de lutte contre l'incendie

firefly ['faɪflaɪ] N *(insect)* luciole f

fireguard ['faɪəgɑːd] N **1** *(in front of open fire)* écran *m* pare-étincelles, garde-feu *m inv*, devant *m* de cheminée **2** = **firebreak**

firehouse ['faɪəhaʊs] N *Am* poste *m* d'incendie; *(with living quarters)* caserne f de (sapeurs-)pompiers

firelight ['faɪəlaɪt] N **to read by f.** lire à la lumière du feu; **in the f.** à la lumière du feu

firelighter ['faɪəlaɪtər] N allume-feu *m*, *pl* allume-feux

fireman, *pl* **firemen** ['faɪəmən] N **1** *(firefighter)* (sapeur-)pompier *m* **2** *Rail (of steam engine)* chauffeur *m*

fireman's lift N **to give sb a f.** transporter qn sur l'épaule

fireplace ['faɪəpleɪs] N cheminée f

fireplug ['faɪəplʌg] N *esp Am* bouche f d'incendie

fireproof ['faɪəpruːf] ADJ *(door, safe)* à l'épreuve du feu; *(clothing, toys)* ininflammable; *(dish)* allant au feu
VT rendre ininflammable, ignifuger

fire-retardant ADJ ignifuge

fireside ['faɪəsaɪd] N coin *m* du feu; **sitting by the f.** assis au coin du feu
▸▸ **f. chair** fauteuil *m*; **f. chat** *(by politician)* causerie f au coin du feu

firestorm ['faɪəstɔːm] N tempête f de feu

firetrap ['faɪətræp] N **this building's a real f.** ce bâtiment est un véritable piège (en cas d'incendie)

firewall ['faɪəwɔːl] N **1** *Am Aut* pare-feu *m inv* de moteur **2** *Comput* mur *m* coupe-feu, garde-barrière f

firewarden ['faɪəwɔːdən] N *Am* guetteur, -euse d'incendies

firewatcher ['faɪəwɒtʃər] N *Br* guetteur, -euse d'incendies

firewatching ['faɪəwɒtʃɪŋ] N *Br* surveillance f contre les incendies

firewater ['faɪəwɔːtər] N *Fam* gnole f, gnôle f, gniole f

firewood ['faɪəwʊd] N bois *m* de chauffage; **bundle of f.** fagot *m*; **to go out in search of f.** aller chercher du bois; **to chop sth up for f.** couper qch en morceaux pour en faire du bois de chauffage

firework ['faɪəwɜːk] N **1** *(device)* pièce f d'artifice **2** *(display) (usu pl)* **fireworks** feu *m* d'artifice; *Fig Fam* **there'll be fireworks** il va y avoir du grabuge
▸▸ **f. display** feu d'artifice

firing ['faɪərɪŋ] N **1** *Mil etc (of rocket)* tir *m*; *(shooting)* tir, feu *m*; **heavy f. could be heard** on entendait une vive fusillade; **they could hear the f. of the guns** ils entendaient les coups de feu **2** *(heating) (of oven, locomotive etc)* chauffage *m*, chauffe f; **coal/oil f.** chauffe au charbon/mazout **3** *Cer (of bricks, pottery etc)* cuisson f; **they'll be given a second f.** elles seront cuites une deuxième fois **4** *(of engine)* allumage *m*
▸▸ *Mil* **f. line** ligne f de tir; *Aut* **f. order** *(of cylinders)* ordre *m* d'allumage; **f. party** *(for execution)* peloton *m* d'exécution; *(for ceremonial duties)* = peloton chargé de tirer la salve d'honneur; **f. pin** percuteur *m*; **f. position** *(of weapon)* position f de tir; *(of person)* position du tireur; **f. practice** exercice *m* de tir; **f. range** champ *m* de tir; **within f. range** à portée de fusil; **f. sequence** *(of cylinders)* ordre d'allumage; **f. squad** *(for execution)* peloton d'exécution; *(for ceremonial duties)* = peloton chargé de tirer la salve d'honneur

firm¹ [fɜːm] N VOIR GRAMMAIRE A11 *Com* maison f (de commerce), entreprise f, firme f; **the f.'s giving us a rise** la firme nous accorde une augmentation; **a large f.** une grosse entreprise; **f. of auditors** cabinet *m* comptable; **f. of solicitors** étude f de notaires

firm² ADJ **1** *(flesh, mattress, handshake etc)* ferme; *(post, nail, foundations etc)* solide; **as f. as a rock** inébranlable; **to rule with a f. hand** gouverner d'une main ferme; **to walk with a f. step** *or* **tread** marcher d'un pas assuré; **I'm on firmer ground when it comes to the marketing side** je suis plus à mon affaire pour ce qui touche au marketing
2 *(intention, person etc)* ferme; *(voice)* ferme, assuré; *(friendship)* solide; *(date)* fixe; *(evidence)* convaincant; **a f. favourite for the Derby/with the crowd** un grand favori dans le Derby/auprès de la foule; **there has been no f. news** il n'y a aucune nouvelle certaine; **to be f. about sth** tenir bon sur qch; **she was polite but f.** elle a été polie mais ferme; **to have a f. belief that ...** avoir la ferme conviction que ...; **I'm a f. believer in corporal punishment** je suis résolument partisan du châtiment corporel; **I'm a f. believer in the value of a high fibre diet** je crois fermement à la valeur d'un régime riche en fibres
3 *(offer, sale, order)* ferme; **these shares remain f. at ...** ces actions se maintiennent à ...; **the dollar remained f. against the yen** le dollar est resté fort contre le yen
ADV **to stand f.** tenir bon *ou* ferme; **to stand f. about sth** tenir bon sur qch; **to hold f.** tenir bon, résister; **to hold f. to one's principles/beliefs** être fidèle à ses principes/croyances
VT **to f. the soil** affermir *ou* tasser le sol
VI = **firm up** VI
▸ **firm up** VT SEP *(make firm)* raffermir; *(details)* préciser
VI *(become firm) (of price, muscles etc)* se raffermir

firmament ['fɜːməmənt] N *Lit* firmament *m*; *Fig* **one of the brightest stars in the Holly-**

wood f. l'une des plus grandes stars de l'univers hollywoodien

firmly ['fɜːmlɪ] ADV *(tied, to deny)* fermement; *(to nail down, screw on)* solidement; *(to walk)* d'un pas assuré; *(to say)* d'un ton ferme, fermement; *(to act)* avec fermeté; **I f. believe that ...** j'ai la ferme conviction que ...; **to deal f. with sb** traiter qn fermement *ou* avec fermeté; **she remains f. entrenched in her views** elle demeure fermement retranchée derrière ses opinions

firmness ['fɜːmnɪs] N **1** *(solidity)* fermeté f; *(of character etc)* force f; *(of tread)* assurance f **2** *(of intention, person, voice etc)* fermeté f; *(of friendship)* solidité f; **the f. of her voice** l'assurance qu'il y avait dans sa voix **3** *Com, Fin etc (of shares etc)* stabilité f

firmware ['fɜːmweər] N *Comput* microprogrammation f, microprogrammes *mpl* constructeurs

---

FIRST [fɜːst]

ADJ	premier
N	le premier **1** ▪ première **3**
ADV	d'abord **1** ▪ pour la première fois **2** ▪ plutôt **3** ▪ le premier **4**

ADJ SEE GRAMMAR B59 *(in time, order)* premier, -ière; **the f. (day) of the month** le premier (jour) du mois; **twenty-f.** vingt et unième; **eighty-f.** quatre-vingt-unième; **ninety-f.** quatre-vingt-onzième; **one hundred and f.** cent unième; **the f. of April** le premier avril; **the f. three years** les trois premières années; **Charles the F.** Charles Premier *m*; **to use** *or* **wear sth for the f. time** étrenner qch; **it was my f. flight** c'était mon baptême de l'air; **to be the f. person to do sth** être le premier/la première à faire qch; **English is my f. language** l'anglais est ma langue maternelle; **English is my f. foreign language** l'anglais est ma première langue; **to have news at f. hand** tenir une nouvelle de première main; **to put f. things f.** commencer par le commencement; **f. things f.!** commençons par le commencement!; **f. things f., let's talk about financing** avant tout, parlons du financement; **I don't know the f. thing** *or* **have the f. idea about motorbikes** je ne connais absolument rien aux motos; **f. thing in the morning** *(as soon as I get up)* dès que je me lève; *(as soon as I arrive at the office etc)* dès que j'arrive; *(immediately the shop etc opens)* à l'ouverture; **at the f. attempt** au premier *ou* de prime abord; **at f. light** aux premières lueurs du jour; **at f. sight** à première vue; *Gram* **in the f. person** à la première personne; **in the f. place, I didn't ask for your help** d'abord *ou* pour commencer, je ne t'ai rien demandé; **why didn't you tell me that in the f. place?** pourquoi ne me l'as-tu pas dit dès le début?; **of the f. water** de la plus belle eau; **on the f. floor** *Br* au premier étage; *Am* au rez-de-chaussée; **f. draft** premier jet *m*; *Br* **f. year** *Univ* première année f, *Sch* = sixième f

N **1** *(person, thing)* premier, f première; **we were the very f. to arrive** nous sommes arrivés les tout premiers; **we were the f. to tell him** nous avons été les premiers à le lui dire; **she was the f. to finish** elle a terminé la première; **you'll be the f. to know** vous serez le premier à le savoir; *Sport etc* **to come in an easy f.** arriver bon premier; **to be the f. to do sth** être le premier/la première à faire qch; *Univ* **to get a f.** avoir une licence avec mention très bien; **the inflatable life jacket was a Scottish f.** *(it was invented there)* le gilet de sauvetage gonflable est une invention écossaise; **this is a f. for France** *(the first time it has won the competition)* c'est une première pour la France; **it's the f. I've heard of it!** première nouvelle!

2 *(beginning)* commencement *m*; **from f. to last** depuis le début jusqu'à la fin; **from the f.** dès le commencement *ou* début; **at f.** d'abord

3 *Aut (gear)* première *f* (vitesse); **in f.** en première (vitesse); **to put the car into f.** se mettre en première, passer la première

ADV **1** *(firstly)* d'abord; **I shall f. have to give it careful consideration** il faudra d'abord que j'examine cela soigneusement; **f., make sure the parts are clean** premièrement, assurez-vous que les différentes pièces sont propres; **do this f.** *(before anything else)* commence par ça; **what should I do f.?** par quoi est-ce que je dois commencer?; **f. and foremost** avant toute chose; **f. of all** pour commencer, en premier lieu; *Fam* **f. off, why did you do it?** pour commencer *ou* et d'abord, pourquoi est-ce que tu as fait cela?; **f., forget that …** commencez par oublier que …

2 *(for the first time)* pour la première fois; **when did you f. see him?** quand l'avez-vous vu pour la première fois?

3 *(rather)* plutôt; **I'll see him damned f.** qu'il aille plutôt au diable

4 *(before others)* le premier, la première; **he arrived/left/died f.** il est arrivé/parti/mort le premier; **you go f.!** *(in queue)* passez devant!; **to claim the right to speak f.** réclamer la priorité de parole; **to come f.** passer en premier; **to come f. in an examination** être reçu premier à un examen; **it's a case of f. come f. served** les premiers arrivés sont les premiers servis; **tickets were handed out on a f. come f. served basis** les billets ont été distribués par ordre d'arrivée; **ladies f.!** place aux dames!; **women and children f.!** les femmes et les enfants d'abord!; **to fall head f.** tomber la tête la première; **he was carried out feet f.** on l'a emporté les pieds devant

▸▸**f. aid** secourisme *m*, premiers secours *mpl*; **I've had f. aid training** j'ai une formation de secouriste; **f. aid certificate** brevet *m* de secourisme; **f. aid class** cours *m* de secourisme; **f. aid kit** trousse *f* de secours; **f. aid post** poste *m* de (premiers) secours; **f. aider** secouriste *mf*; **f. cousin** cousin, -ine germain(e); **f. edition** édition *f* originale; *Mktg* **f. entry** premier lancement *m*; *Aut* **f. gear** première (vitesse); **F. Lady** *(in US)* = femme *f* du président des États-Unis; *Fig* **the f. lady of rock/of the detective novel** la grande dame du rock/du roman policier; **f. lieutenant** *Naut* lieutenant *m* de vaisseau; *Am Mil, Aviat* lieutenant; **f. love** premier amour *m*; *Naut* **f. mate** second *m*; *Pol* **F. Minister** *(of Scottish Parliament, Welsh Assembly, Northern Ireland Assembly)* Premier ministre *m*; *Mktg* **f. mover** premier entré *m*; *Mktg* **f. mover advantage** avantage *m* du premier entré; **f. name** prénom *m*; *Theat etc* **f. night** première *f*; *Law* **f. offence** premier délit *m*; *Law* **f. offender** délinquant, -ante primaire; *Naut* **f. officer** second *m*; *Theat etc* **f. performance** première; *Fin* **f. quarter** *(of financial year)* premier trimestre *m*; **f. reading** *(of bill)* première lecture *f*; *Pol* **F. Secretary** premier secrétaire *m*; *Cin* **f. showing** première exclusivité *f*; *Mus* **f. violin** *(person, instrument)* premier violon *m*; **the F. World War** la Première Guerre mondiale

---

first-born ADJ, N *esp Lit (boy)* premier-né *m*, *pl* premiers-nés; *(girl)* première-née *f*, *pl* premières-nées

first(-)class ADJ **1** *(compartment, ticket)* de première (classe); *(item)* de première qualité; *(hotel, player, performance etc)* de premier ordre; **the food was f.** la nourriture était excellente **2** *(letter, stamp)* au tarif normal; **to send a letter by f. mail** envoyer une

lettre au tarif normal **3** *Br Univ* **she got a f. honours degree (in French)** elle a eu mention très bien (en français); **to graduate with f. honours** obtenir son diplôme avec mention très bien

ADV **to travel f.** voyager en première; **to send a letter f.** envoyer une lettre au tarif normal

first-day ADJ
▸▸ *Philat* **f. cover** (enveloppe *f*) premier jour *m* (d'émission)

first-degree ADJ
▸▸ *Med* **f. burn** brûlure *f* au premier degré; *Am Law* **f. murder** meurtre *m* avec préméditation

first-foot *Scot* N = première personne *f* à se rendre chez quelqu'un pour souhaiter la bonne année
VI **to f. sb** = être le premier à se rendre chez qn pour souhaiter la bonne année

first-hand ADJ, ADV *(news)* de première main; **she had the news f.** elle a appris la nouvelle de première main; **to experience sth f.** faire personnellement l'expérience de qch

first-in first-out ADJ *Comput, Ind* premier entré, premier sorti

firstly ['fɜːstlɪ] ADV premièrement, en premier lieu; **f. she rang the office** elle téléphona d'abord au bureau

first-nighter [fɜːst'naɪtər] N *Theat* habitué, -ée des premières

first-notice day N *St Exch* premier jour *m* de notification

first-off N *Mktg* produit *m* vedette

first-past-the-post ADJ *Br Pol (system)* majoritaire à un tour; **the f. electoral system** le scrutin majoritaire à un tour

first-rate ADJ excellent, de première classe; **f. idea** fameuse idée *f*, of **f. quality** de toute première qualité; **I feel f.!** je suis en pleine forme!

first-strike ADJ *(missile, capability etc)* de première frappe

first-time ADJ **f. visitors to the country** les personnes visitant le pays pour la première fois
▸▸ **f. buyer** *(of property)* = personne *f* devenant propriétaire pour la première fois; **f. user** nouvel utilisateur *m*

firth [fɜːθ] N *Scot Geog* estuaire *m*; **the F. of Forth** le golfe du Forth

fiscal ['fɪsk(ə)l] ADJ *Fin (resources, control)* fiscal, -aux; *(policy)* budgétaire
N *Scot* **(procurator) f.** procureur *m* général
▸▸ *Fin* **f. austerity** austérité *f* fiscale; *Fin* **f. balance** équilibre *m* fiscal; *Am Acct* **f. period** période *f* comptable; *Am* **f. year** *Fin* exercice *m* (financier), année fiscale *ou* d'exercice; *Admin* année *f* budgétaire

> **Fiscal Year**
> En Grande-Bretagne, l'année fiscale commence le 1er avril pour les entreprises et le 6 avril pour les particuliers. Aux États-Unis, l'année fiscale correspond à l'année civile pour les particuliers.

fish, *pl* **fishes** *or* **fish** [fɪʃ, 'fɪʃɪz] N **1** VOIR GRAMMAIRE A12 poisson *m*; **I don't like f.** *(as food)* je n'aime pas le poisson; *Br* **f. and chips** poisson frit avec des frites; *Fig Fam* **I've other f. to fry** j'ai d'autres chats à fouetter; *Fig* **there are plenty more f. in the sea** un(e) de perdu(e), dix de retrouvé(e)s; **to feel like a f. out of water** ne pas se sentir dans son élément; **a big f. in a small pond** une gloire locale; **at university, she was a small f. in a big pond** à l'université, elle se sentait complètement perdue dans la masse; *Fig* **neither f.**

nor fowl ni chair ni poisson **2** *Astron* **the Fish** les Poissons *mpl*
VI pêcher; **to f. for trout/pearls** pêcher la truite/des perles; **to go fishing** aller à la pêche; *Fam* **to f. for compliments** chercher des compliments
VT **1** *(salmon etc)* pêcher **2** *(river)* pêcher dans **3** *(remove)* **to f. sb/sth from somewhere** tirer qn/qch de quelque part; **they fished the body from the pond** ils ont repêché le corps de l'étang
▸▸ **f. bone** arête *f* (de poisson); **f. cake** croquette *f* de poisson; **f. course** plat *m* de poisson; **f. dish** plat de poisson; **f. farm** établissement *m* piscicole; **f. farmer** pisciculteur, -trice; **f. farming** pisciculture *f*; *Br* **f. fingers** bâtonnets *mpl* de poisson; **f. fork** fourchette *f* à poisson; **f. kettle** poissonnière *f*, **f. knife** couteau *m* à poisson; **f. market** marché *m* au poisson; **f. meal** farine *f* de poisson; **f. pond** étang *m*; **f. shop** poissonnerie *f*, **f. slice** pelle *f* à poisson; *Am* **f. sticks** bâtonnets de poisson; **f. tank** *(in house)* aquarium *m*; *(on fish farm)* vivier *m*
▸ **fish out** VT SEP *(remove from water)* repêcher; **to f. out a dead body** (re)pêcher un cadavre; **she put her hand in the drawer and fished out a twenty-dollar bill** elle a mis la main dans le tiroir et en a sorti un billet de vingt dollars; **he fished a pencil out of his pocket** il a fouillé dans sa poche et en a tiré un crayon
▸ **fish up** VT SEP *(bring up from water)* repêcher; *(dead body)* (re)pêcher; *(mine)* relever; *(information)* dénicher

fish-and-chip ADJ
▸▸ *Br* **f. shop** = boutique *f* qui vend du poisson frit et des frites

fisherman, *pl* **fishermen** ['fɪʃəmən] N pêcheur *m*
▸▸ **f.'s bend** *(knot)* nœud *m* de grappin

fishery ['fɪʃərɪ] N *(fishing ground)* pêcherie *f*, *(fishing industry)* pêche *f*
▸▸ **f. protection vessel** garde-pêche *m inv*

fisheye *Phot* N *Fam* grand-angle *m*
▸▸ **f. lens** objectif *m* ultra grand angle, objectif fish-eye

fish-hook N hameçon *m*

fishing ['fɪʃɪŋ] N pêche *f*, **there's good f. to be had here** il y a du poisson par ici; **trout f.** pêche à la truite; **pearl f.** pêche des perles; **fly f.** pêche à la mouche
▸▸ **f. boat** bateau *m* de pêche; **f. ground** zone *f* de pêche; **f. line** ligne *f* de pêche; **f. net** filet *m* de pêche; **f. port** port *m* de pêche; **f. rights** droits *mpl* de pêche; **f. rod** canne *f* à pêche, gaule *f*, **f. smack** bateau de pêche; **f. tackle** articles *mpl* de pêche; **f. trip** partie *f* de pêche; **f. vessel** navire *m* de pêche, pêcheur *m*; **f. village** village *m* de pêcheurs

fishmonger ['fɪʃmʌŋgər] N *esp Br (person)* poissonnier, -ière; **f.'s (shop)** poissonnerie *f*

fishnet ['fɪʃnet] N *esp Am Fishing* filet *m* de pêche
▸▸ **f. stockings** bas *mpl* résille; **f. tights** collant *m* résille

fishplate ['fɪʃpleɪt] N *Rail* éclisse *f*

fishpole mike ['fɪʃpəʊl] N micro *m* sur perche

fishwife, *pl* **fishwives** ['fɪʃwaɪf, -waɪvz] N marchande *f* de poisson, poissonnière *f*; **she swears like a f.** elle jure comme un charretier

fishy ['fɪʃɪ] ADJ **1** *(smell, taste)* de poisson **2** *Fam (suspicious) (business etc)* louche; **f. story** histoire qui ne tient pas debout; **there's something f. going on here** il y a quelque chose de louche

fissile ['fɪsaɪl] ADJ fissile

fission ['fɪʃən] N **1** *Phys* fission *f*, **nuclear/**

thermal f. fission nucléaire/thermique **2** *Biol* scissiparité *f*

fissure ['fɪʃər] **N** *(in wall, rock etc)* fissure *f*, fente *f*

VT *(rock etc)* fissurer, fendre

VI *(of rock etc)* se fissurer, se fendre

fist [fɪst] **N** poing *m*; **to clench one's f., to make a f.** serrer le poing; **to shake one's f.** *or* **fists at sb** menacer qn du poing; **he went for them with his fists** il tomba sur eux à coups de poing

fistful ['fɪstfʊl] **N** *(of money etc)* poignée *f*

fisticuffs ['fɪstɪkʌfs] **NPL** *Br Old-fashioned, Hum* coups *mpl* de poing; **if he finds out, there'll be f.!** s'il s'en rend compte il va y avoir de la bagarre *ou* du grabuge

fistula ['fɪstjʊlə] **N** *Med* fistule *f*

fit[1] [fɪt] **N** *(of madness etc)* accès *m*; *(of coughing)* quinte *f*, *(apoplexy)* crise *f* d'apoplexie; **(epileptic) f.** crise d'épilepsie; **to have** *or Fam* **throw a f.** piquer une crise; *Fam* **he'll have a f. when he finds out** il va avoir une attaque quand il apprendra ça; **in a f. of temper** dans un mouvement de colère; **f. of crying** crise de larmes; **f. of laughter** accès de rire; **to be in fits (of laughter)** avoir le fou rire; **to have sb in fits** donner le fou rire à qn; **in a f. of carelessness** dans un moment d'inattention; **to work by fits and starts** travailler par à-coups

FIT[2]

ADJ bon **1**	▪ en forme **4**
VT s'accorder **1**	▪ aller à **2** ▪ adapter, ajuster **3** ▪ assembler **4** ▪ munir, pourvoir **5**
VI aller	

ADJ (**fitter; fittest**) **1** *(appropriate)* bon, propre (**for sth** à qch); **f. to eat** bon à manger, mangeable; **f. to drink** buvable, potable; **I've nothing f. to wear** je n'ai rien à me mettre; **story that is not f. to be repeated** histoire qu'il ne serait pas convenable de répéter; **a meal f. for a king** un repas digne d'un roi; **I'm not f. to be seen** je ne suis pas présentable; **to think f.** *or* **see f. to do sth** trouver bon de faire qch; **do as you see** *or* **think f.** faites comme bon vous semble; **this is no f. way to behave** ce comportement est inacceptable; **this is no f. way to run a company** ce n'est pas comme ça qu'on dirige une entreprise; **he's not f. to polish my boots** il n'est même pas bon à cirer mes chaussures

2 *(capable)* capable; **f. to do sth** capable de faire qch; **that's all he's f. for** il n'est bon qu'à cela; **she's not a f. mother** c'est une mère indigne

3 *(ready)* **I felt f. to drop** je me sentais prêt à tomber (de fatigue); **she worked until she was f. to drop** elle a travaillé jusqu'à tomber de fatigue

4 *(healthy)* en forme; **to get f.** retrouver la forme; **I'm a lot fitter** je suis bien plus en forme; **to be (fighting) f.** être en forme; **to keep f.** se maintenir en forme; **he is not yet f. to go back to work** il n'est pas encore en état de reprendre son travail; **f. for duty** bon pour le service; *Mil* valide; *Fam* **to be as f. as a fiddle** être en parfaite santé, se porter comme un charme

5 *Br Fam (attractive)* bien foutu(e)

N your coat is a perfect/poor f. votre manteau vous va parfaitement/ne vous va pas très bien; **easy/tight f.** coupe *f* confortable/ajustée; **it was a tight f. but everyone squeezed in** il n'y avait pas beaucoup de place mais tout le monde a tenu

VT (**-tt-**) **1** *(be suitable for)* s'accorder avec; **to make the punishment f. the crime** proportionner la peine au délit

2 *(of clothes)* **to f. sb** aller à qn; **it fits/they f. me** elle me va/elles me vont; **it fitted her perfectly** il était exactement à sa taille; **key that fits the lock** clef qui va à la serrure

3 *(install)* adapter, ajuster (**sth to sth** qch à qch); **to f. a nozzle on the end of a pipe** adapter un ajutage à l'extrémité d'un tuyau; **to f. a handle to a broom** emmancher un balai; **to f. one part into another** emboîter une pièce dans une autre; **to f. a carpet** poser une moquette; **I'm going to be fitted for my new dress** je vais faire l'essayage de ma nouvelle robe

4 *(assemble)* **to f. parts together** monter *ou* assembler des pièces; **to f. a machine together** assembler une machine

5 *(equip)* munir, pourvoir (**sth with sth** qch de qch); **fitted with two propellers** pourvu de deux hélices

6 *(insert)* **to f. sb/sth into/onto sth** mettre *ou Fam* caser qn/qch dans/sur qch; **we can f. another two (people) inside** il y a de la place pour deux personnes de plus

VI aller; **the lid doesn't f.** ce n'est pas le bon couvercle; **your dress fits well/badly** votre robe vous va/ne vous va pas bien; **she no longer fits into her dress** elle n'entre plus dans sa robe; **I can't f. into these jeans any more** je n'arrive plus à rentrer dans ce jean; **to f. (together)** s'ajuster, s'adapter; **to f. into sth** *(of piece etc)* s'emboîter dans qch; **all her tools easily fitted into the bag** tous ses outils tenaient largement dans le sac; **we won't all f. into the car** nous ne tiendrons pas tous dans la voiture; **the photos just f. onto the page** les photos tiennent juste sur la page; **the phrase/colour has to f.** l'expression/la couleur doit bien aller avec le reste; *Fam* **his face didn't f.** on n'aimait pas sa gueule

▶ **fit in VT SEP** *(find room, time for)* **I can't f. any more clothes in** je ne peux plus mettre aucun vêtement; **the hairdresser says she can f. me in tomorrow** la coiffeuse dit qu'elle peut s'arranger pour me prendre demain; **I'll check my diary and see if I can f. you in** je vais regarder mon agenda et voir si je trouve un moment pour toi

VI 1 *(go into place)* tenir; **there's no way they'll all f. in** ils ne tiendront jamais tous; **to f. in between two things** s'emboîter entre deux choses

2 *(harmonize)* **to f. in with sth** *(of piece of furniture, building, colour)* être en accord avec qch; **your plans don't f. in with mine** vos projets ne cadrent pas avec les miens; **to f. in with sb's plans** *(of person)* s'adapter aux projets de qn; **he doesn't f. in there** il n'y est pas dans son élément; **you'll have to make more of an effort to f. in** il va falloir que tu fasses plus d'efforts pour t'adapter *ou* t'intégrer

3 *(agree)* correspondre (**with** à); *Fam* coller (**with** avec); **that doesn't f. in with what I was told** ça ne correspond pas à ce qu'on m'a dit; *Fam* **ça ne colle pas avec ce qu'on m'a dit**

▶ **fit out VT SEP** équiper (**sth with sth** qch de qch); *(ship)* armer; *(new ship)* équiper; **to f. sb out** équiper qn (**with clothes/etc** de vêtements/*etc*)

▶ **fit up VT SEP 1** *(provide)* doter, pourvoir, munir (**with** de); **they fitted me up with an artificial leg** ils m'ont mis une jambe artificielle

2 *Fam* **to f. sb up (for a crime)** monter un coup contre qn; **they claim to have been fitted up by the Serious Crimes Squad** ils se prétendent tous victimes d'un coup monté organisé par la Brigade criminelle

fitful ['fɪtfʊl] **ADJ** *(sleep, night)* agité; **to make f. progress** progresser par à-coups

fitfully ['fɪtfəlɪ] **ADV** *(to sleep)* d'un sommeil agité; *(to work)* par à-coups

fitment ['fɪtmənt] **N 1** *Br (piece of furniture)* élément *m* **2** *(of machine)* accessoire *m*

fitness ['fɪtnɪs] **N 1** *(health)* forme *f* (physique) **2** *(suitability)* *(of person)* aptitude *f* (**for a job**/*etc* à un emploi/*etc*); *(of remark)* justesse *f*, à-propos *m*; **her f. for government** *or* **power** son aptitude à gouverner

▶▶ *Br* **f. centre** club *m* de gym; *Fam* **f. freak** fana *mf* d'exercice physique; **f. room** salle *f* de musculation

fitted ['fɪtɪd] **ADJ 1** *(garment)* ajusté **2** *(suitable)* *(of person, thing)* **to be f. for sth** convenir à qch

▶▶ **f. carpet** moquette *f*; **f. cooker** four *m* encastré; **f. kitchen** cuisine *f* intégrée; **f. sheet** drap-housse *m*, *pl* draps-housses; **f. wardrobe** garde-robe *f* encastrée, *pl* garde-robes encastrées

fitter ['fɪtər] **N 1** *Tech, Aut etc* ajusteur *m*, assembleur, -euse; **electrical f.** installateur *m* d'appareils électriques **2** *Sewing* essayeur, -euse

fitting ['fɪtɪŋ] **ADJ** convenable, approprié (**to** à); *(remark)* à propos; **it was a f. tribute to a great athlete** c'était un hommage mérité rendu à un grand athlète; **it was only f. he should score the winning goal** ce n'était que justice qu'il marque le but gagnant; **a f. end for a murderer** une fin appropriée pour un meurtrier

N 1 *(of clothes)* essayage *m*; *Com* **made in three fittings** fabriqué en trois tailles; *(of shoes)* fabriqué en trois largeurs **2** *(usu pl)* **fittings** *(of office etc)* installations *fpl*, *(of bathroom etc)* accessoires *mpl*; **door fittings** ferrures *fpl* de porte; **brass fittings** garnitures *fpl* en cuivre; *Elec* **light f.** appareil *m* d'éclairage; **ceiling f.** plafonnier *m*; **wall f.** applique *f*

▶▶ **f. out** *(of expedition etc)* équipement *m*; *(of ship)* armement *m*; **f. room** salon *m ou* salle *f* d'essayage; *(cubicle)* cabine *f* d'essayage; *Ind* **f. shop** atelier *m* d'ajustage

fittingly ['fɪtɪŋlɪ] **ADV** convenablement, à propos; **f., he was buried in his home town** comme il convenait, il a été enterré dans sa ville natale; **f., he died the sort of violent death he had inflicted on so many others** ce n'est que justice qu'il soit mort de la même mort violente qu'il avait infligée à tant d'autres

five [faɪv] **N 1** *(number, numeral)* cinq *m inv*; **f. times table** table *f* des cinq; **f. and f. are ten** cinq et cinq font dix; *Cards* **the f. of hearts** le cinq de cœur; **to be f.** *(in age)* avoir cinq ans; **it's f. o'clock** il est cinq heures; **it's f. to/past f.** il est cinq heures moins cinq/cinq heures cinq; **come at f.** venez à cinq heures; **to get f. out of ten** avoir cinq sur dix; **a table for f.** une table pour cinq (personnes); *Fam* **to take f.** faire un break de cinq minutes; *Fam* **give me f.!** tope là! *(pour conclure un marché, dire bonjour ou manifester son approbation)* **2** *Sport* **fives** *(game)* = balle *f* au mur

PRON cinq; **f. is not enough** cinq, ce n'est pas assez; **I need f. (of them)** il m'en faut cinq, j'en ai besoin de cinq

NUM ADJ cinq; **f. people** cinq personnes; **on page f.** à (la) page cinq; **they live at number f.** ils habitent au numéro cinq

five-day week N semaine *f* de cinq jours

five-door model N *Aut* (version *f*) cinq portes *f*

five-finger ADJ

▶▶ *Mus* **f. exercises** exercices *mpl* de doigté

fivefold ['faɪvfəʊld] **ADJ** quintuple; **a f. increase/rise** une augmentation au quintuple

ADV au quintuple; **to increase f.** quintupler, augmenter au quintuple

fiver ['faɪvər] **N** *Fam Br* billet *m* de cinq livres, *Am* billet de cinq dollars; *Br* **it'll cost you a f.** ça te coûtera cinq livres

five-seater N *Aut* cinq places f

five-speed gearbox N *Aut* boîte f cinq-vitesses, boîte de vitesses cinq rapports

fivespot ['faɪvspɒt] N *Am Fam* billet m de cinq dollars

five-star ADJ *(hotel)* cinq étoiles, quatre étoiles-luxe; **f. accommodation** héberge-ment m en hôtel cinq étoiles

five-year ADJ quinquennal, -aux

Five-Year Plan N *Econ* Plan m quin-quennal

FIX [fɪks]

| N pétrin **1** ▪ dose **2** |
| VT fixer **1, 2, 6** ▪ arranger **2, 3** |
| ▪ réparer **3** ▪ préparer **3** |

N **1** *Fam (difficulty)* embarras m, difficulté f; **to be in a f.** être dans le pétrin; **to get into a f.** se mettre dans l'embarras *ou* dans le pé-trin; **I'm in a bit of a f. financially** j'ai quel-ques difficultés financières **2** *Sl (of drug)* dose f; *(injection)* piqûre f (de drogue); **to give oneself a f.** se piquer, se shooter; *Fam Fig* **my daily f. of television news** ma dose quotidienne de journaux té-lévisés **3** *Aviat, Naut* position f; **to get a f. on a ship/etc** déterminer la position d'un navire/etc **4** *Fam (set-up)* **the match/quiz was a f.** le match/jeu était truqué; **it's a f.!** c'est de l'ar-naque!

VT **1** *(attach securely)* fixer; *(bait to a line etc)* accrocher; **to f. sth in one's memory** graver qch dans sa mémoire; **to f. one's attention on sth** fixer son attention sur qch; **to f. one's eye(s) on sb** fixer qn (du regard) **2** *(decide) (limits, interest rates etc)* fixer, établir; *(meeting place)* choisir; *(itinerary, date, price etc)* fixer; *(meeting etc)* arranger; **there's nothing fixed yet, nothing is fixed yet** il n'y a encore rien de décidé *ou* de fixé **3** *(repair)* réparer, retaper; *(prepare) (meal etc)* préparer; **to f. sth with sb** arranger qch avec qn; **I've fixed it with her** je me suis ar-rangé avec elle; *Fam* **I'll f. him!** je lui ferai son affaire!; **just wait while I f. my hair** attends que je me coiffe **4** *(set up) (camp)* établir **5** *(bribe)* graisser la patte à; *(rig) (match, jury etc)* truquer **6** *Chem, Phot etc (mercury, dye etc)* fixer **7** *Am Dial* **to be fixing to do sth** envisager de faire qch

▸ **fix on** VT SEP *(attach)* fixer
VT INSEP *(choose, decide) (holiday destina-tion, dress, house etc)* se décider pour; *(date, itinerary, price, time)* fixer

▸ **fix up** VT SEP *Fam* **1** *(assemble, put up) (tent)* monter; **they fixed up a temporary tele-phone** ils ont installé une ligne de téléphone provisoire; **to f. up a room as a study** trans-former une pièce en bureau **2** *(arrange) (business, meeting)* arranger; **it's all fixed up** c'est une affaire réglée, tout est arrangé; **I've already fixed up to go out tonight** j'ai déjà prévu de sortir ce soir **3** *(improve) (car, bike)* réparer, retaper; *(house, apartment)* retaper; **you should f. yourself up a bit** tu devrais t'arranger un peu **4** *(provide)* **to f. sb up with a job/room** trou-ver un travail/une chambre pour *ou* à qn; **I've fixed you up with a date** je t'ai arrangé un rendez-vous; **they've been trying to f. me up with her for weeks** ça fait des semai-nes qu'ils essaient de me monter un plan avec elle

---

fixated [fɪk'seɪtɪd] ADJ **to be f. on** *or* **with sth** être obsédé par qch; **he was still f. by the idea** cette idée l'obsédait encore

fixation [fɪk'seɪʃən] N *Psy* fixation f; **to have a mother f.** faire une fixation sur sa mère

fixative ['fɪksətɪv] ADJ, N *Art* fixatif m

fixed [fɪkst] ADJ **1** fixe; *(rule)* établi, absolu; *(smile)* figé; **of f. length** de longueur cons-tante; **to have f. ideas** avoir des idées (bien) arrêtées; **to have no f. plans** ne pas avoir de projets bien déterminés **2** *Fam* **how are you f. for money/for condoms?** tu as assez d'ar-gent/de capotes?; **how are you f. for time?** tu as du temps libre?; **how are you f. for ac-commodation/transport?** est-ce que tu as un endroit où loger/un moyen de trans-port?; **how are we f. for disks?** on a des dis-quettes? **3** *Chem (oil, salt)* fixe **4** *Fam Pej (rigged)* truqué
▸▸ *Acct, Fin* **f. asset** actif m immobilisé; *Acct, Fin* **f. assets** immobilisations fpl, actif immobilisé; *Cin, TV* **f. camera** caméra f fixe; *Fin* **f. charge** frais mpl fixes; *Fin* **f. cost** charge f fixe, coût m fixe *ou* constant; *Com* **f. depo-sit** dépôt m à terme (fixe) *ou* à échéance fixe; *Comput* **f. disk** disque m fixe; *Fin* **f. ex-change rate** taux m de change fixe; *Fin* **f. in-come** revenu m fixe; *Fin* **f. interest** intérêt m fixe; *Fin* **f. investment** immobilisations f. fixe; *Fin* **f. point** point m fixe, point de repère; *Math* **f. point arithmetic** arithmétique f en virgule fixe; **f. price** prix m fixe *ou* forfaitaire; *Fin* **f. rate** taux m fixe; *Com* **f. salary** salaire m fixe

fixed-income ADJ *Fin* à revenu fixe
▸▸ **f. investment** placement m à revenus fixes; **f. securities** valeurs fpl à revenu fixe

fixed-interest ADJ *Fin* à intérêt fixe
▸▸ **f. market** marché m des obligations; **f. securities** valeurs fpl à intérêt fixe

fixedly ['fɪksɪdlɪ] ADV fixement

fixed-price menu N menu m à prix fixe

fixed-rate ADJ *Fin (loan, mortgage)* à taux fixe; *(investment)* à revenu fixe
▸▸ **f. bond** obligation f à revenu fixe; **f. bor-rowing** emprunts mpl à taux fixe

fixed-term ADJ *Com* à terme fixe
▸▸ *Fin* **f. bill** effet m à date fixe; *Com* **f. contract** contrat m à durée déterminée, CDD m; *Fin* **f. credit** crédit m à durée déter-minée; *Fin* **f. deposit** dépôt m à terme fixe *ou* à échéance fixe

fixer ['fɪksər] N **1** *Fam (person)* combinard m **2** *Art* fixatif m; *Phot* fixateur m

fixing ['fɪksɪŋ] N **1** *(repairing)* réparation f **2** *Com (of prices etc)* établissement m; *St Exch* fixage m **3** *(usu pl) Am* **fixings** *(trimmings)* accessoires mpl; *(food)* accompagnements mpl, garnitures fpl; **roast turkey with all the fixings** dinde rôtie avec tout ce qui s'en-suit
▸▸ *Phot* **f. bath** *(container)* cuvette f de fi-xage; *(solution)* bain m de fixage; *Phot* **f. so-lution** solution f de fixage

fixity ['fɪksɪtɪ] N fixité f; *Fml* **f. of purpose** détermination f

fixture ['fɪkstʃər] N **1** *(installation)* appareil m fixe; **fixtures** *(of house etc)* aménage-ments mpl; *(electrical etc)* appareils m, **fixtures and fittings** agencements mpl, installations fpl fixes; **£3,000 for fixtures and fittings** 3 000 livres de reprise; **bathroom fixtures and fittings** installations et accessoires de salles de bain; *Fam* **he's become a f. here** il fait partie des meubles à présent; **she was something of a f. at his parties** elle appa-raissait inévitablement à chacune de ses soirées; **she was becoming a f.** elle commençait à faire partie des meubles **2** *Br Sport* rencontre f (prévue), match m (prévu)
▸▸ *Sport* **f. list** calendrier m

fizz [fɪz] N **1** *(sound) (of champagne etc)* pétil-lement m; *(of steam)* sifflement m; *(fizziness)* gaz m **2** *Fam (soft drink)* boisson f gazeuse; *(champagne)* champagne m

VI *(of champagne)* pétiller; *(of steam, fire-work)* siffler; **the champagne fizzed out of the bottle** le champagne est sorti de la bou-teille en pétillant; **the Coke® fizzed up and spilled onto the table** le Coca® a moussé et s'est répandu sur la table

fizzle ['fɪz(ə)l] VI *(of wine)* pétiller; *(of gas burner etc)* siffler
▸ **fizzle out** VI *Fam (of plan)* tomber à l'eau; *(of enthusiasm, interest, desire)* tomber; *(of hope)* s'envoler; *(of story, film)* finir en queue de poisson; **the evening fizzled out** la soirée se traîna lamentablement

fizzy ['fɪzɪ] ADJ *(mineral water, drink)* ga-zeux; *(wine)* mousseux

fjord [fjɔːd] N *Geog* fjord m, fiord m

Fla *abbr* Florida

flab [flæb] N *Fam (fat)* graisse f; **he was try-ing to get rid of his f.** il essayait de perdre sa graisse

flabbergast ['flæbəgɑːst] VT *Fam* abasour-dir, ahurir; **I was flabbergasted** j'en étais sidéré

flabbiness ['flæbɪnɪs] N *(of flesh, skin)* flac-cidité f, manque m de fermeté; *(of person)* flaccidité; *(of person's grip)* mollesse f; *(of prose, writing, novel)* prolixité f; *(of argu-ment, idea)* manque de rigueur

flabby ['flæbɪ] ADJ *(muscles etc)* flasque, mou, f molle; *(cheeks)* pendant; *(person)* grassouil-let; *(grip)* mou; *Fig (prose)* prolixe; *(reasoning, ideas, morals)* qui manque de rigueur

flaccid ['flæsɪd] ADJ mou, f molle; *(flesh)* flasque

flag¹ [flæg] N **1** *(cloth, emblem)* drapeau m; *Naut* pavillon m; *Fig* **to fly the f. for one's country** défendre les couleurs de son pays; *also Fig* **to show the f.** faire acte de pré-sence; **black f.** *(of pirate)* pavillon noir; **yel-low f.** pavillon de quarantaine **2** *(of taxi)* drapeau m; **taxi with the f. up** taxi m libre **3** *Comput (marker)* drapeau m, marqueur m **4** *(for file, folder)* papillon m
VT (-gg-) **1** = **flag down 2** *(mark)* marquer; *(error in text etc)* marquer, signaler
VI *(of sail)* battre; *(of plant)* s'étioler, languir; *(of person)* s'alanguir; *(of conversation)* traî-ner, languir; *(of attention, courage, determi-nation)* faiblir; **our spirits were flagging** notre moral faiblissait; **his strength was flagging** ses forces baissaient
▸▸ **f. airline** compagnie f aérienne natio-nale; *Naut* **f. captain** commandant m du na-vire amiral; **f. carrier** *(airline)* compagnie aérienne nationale; *(shipping company)* compagnie maritime nationale; *Naut* **f. of convenience** pavillon de complaisance; *Am* **F. Day** le 14 juin *(fête nationale des États-Unis)*; *Br* **f. day** = jour m de quête d'une œu-vre de charité; *Naut* **f. officer** contre-amiral m, pl contre-amiraux; **f. signals** signalisa-tion f par fanions

▸ **flag down** VT SEP *(stop)* arrêter, stopper
▸ **flag out** VT SEP *Sport (racetrack)* jalonner
▸ **flag up** VT SEP *(mark, indicate)* marquer; *(mistake)* signaler, marquer

flag² N = **flagstone**
VT *Constr (pave)* daller; *(pavement etc)* pa-ver de carreaux

flag³ N *(plant)* iris m

flagellate ['flædʒəleɪt] ADJ, N *Zool* flagellé m
VT flageller, fouetter

flagellation [flædʒə'leɪʃən] N flagellation f

flageolet ['flædʒəlet, flædʒə'let] N *Mus, Culin* flageolet m

flagged [flægd] ADJ *(floor)* dallé

flagging¹ ['flægɪŋ] ADJ *(conversation etc)* languissant; *(courage, determination, atten-tion)* faiblissant; *(strength, health)* baissant; **to revive sb's f. spirits** remonter le moral à qn

flagging[2] N (paving) dallage m

flagon ['flægən] N 1 (large bottle) grosse bouteille f (ventrue), bonbonne f 2 (jug) pot m (à anse)

flagpole ['flægpəʊl] N mât m de drapeau; Fig, Fam **to run sth up the f.** proposer qch pour voir les réactions

flagrant ['fleɪgrənt] ADJ (offence, miscarriage of justice, lie) flagrant; **a f. injustice** une injustice criante; **this f. disobedience** cet acte de désobéissance effronté; **what a f. cheek!** ça alors, quel culot!

flagrante delicto, in flagrante delicto [ɪnfləˈgræntɪdɪˈlɪktəʊ] ADV Law en flagrant délit

flagrantly ['fleɪgrəntlɪ] ADV d'une manière flagrante; **f. dishonest** d'une malhonnêteté flagrante; **f. unfair** d'une injustice criante

flagship ['flægʃɪp] N Naut (navire m) amiral m; Fig **the London store is the f. of the chain** le magasin de Londres est le plus important de la chaîne; **this latest model is the f. of their new range** ce dernier modèle est le produit vedette de leur nouvelle gamme; **the Conservatives' f. council** le conseil municipal qui est le fleuron du parti Conservateur

flagstaff ['flægstɑːf] N mât m de drapeau; Naut mât de pavillon

flagstone ['flægstəʊn] N dalle f
▸▸ **f. pavement** dallage m en pierre

flag-waving N Pej, Fam (patriotic remarks) déclarations fpl cocardières; **f. speech** discours m cocardier

flail [fleɪl] N Agr fléau m
VT 1 Agr battre au fléau 2 **he flailed his fists at me** il balançait les poings dans ma direction; **the animal was flailing its legs in the air** l'animal battait l'air de ses pattes
VI (of rope, cable) se balancer violemment; **I dodged my assailant's flailing arms** j'ai esquivé les coups de mon assaillant
▸ **flail about, flail around** VI (wave wildly) (of arms, legs) s'agiter dans tous les sens; **she was flailing about in the water** elle se débattait des mains et des pieds dans l'eau

flair ['fleər] N (skill) aptitude f (**for** à); (skill in detecting things etc) flair m; (energy etc) dynamisme m; **to have a f. for languages/cooking** avoir le don des langues/pour cuisiner; **to dress/write with f.** (stylishness) s'habiller/écrire avec style; **he had no f. for business** il n'avait pas le sens des affaires; **they have a real f. for making the right choices** ils ont vraiment le don de faire les bons choix

flak [flæk] N 1 (artillery) artillerie f antiaérienne; (fire) tir m contre-avions 2 Fam (criticism) critique f; **she got a lot of f. for this decision** on l'a beaucoup critiquée pour cette décision
▸▸ **f. jacket** gilet m pare-balles

flake [fleɪk] N 1 (of snow, oat, corn) flocon m; (of metal etc) écaille f, éclat m, paillette f; (of paint, plaster) écaille; **soap flakes** savon m en paillettes; **a f. of skin** un petit morceau de peau morte 2 Am Fam (crazy person) barjo mf
VI (of metal, paint etc) s'écailler; (of arms, nose) peler; **my skin was flaking** je pelais
▸ **flake away, flake off** VI (of metal, paint etc) s'écailler; **the skin on my nose is flaking off** mon nez pèle, j'ai le nez qui pèle
▸ **flake out** VI Fam (fall asleep) s'endormir; **I just want to f. out on the sofa** j'ai envie de m'effondrer sur le canapé et roupiller; **she's gone upstairs to f. out** elle est montée roupiller; **to be flaked out** (exhausted) être vidé ou crevé; (asleep) roupiller

flaking ['fleɪkɪŋ] ADJ (paint) qui s'écaille; (skin) qui se détache

flaky ['fleɪkɪ] ADJ 1 (mineral etc) écailleux; (paint) écaillé; **her skin was all dry and f.** elle avait la peau toute sèche qui pelait 2 Fam (crazy) barjo
▸▸ Br Culin **f. pastry** pâte f feuilletée

flamboyance [flæmˈbɔɪəns] N (of personality, manner, clothes, car) extravagance f; (of physical gesture) caractère m magistral

flamboyant [flæmˈbɔɪənt] ADJ (personality, generosity, manner, clothes, car) extravagant; (physical gesture) magistral

flamboyantly [flæmˈbɔɪəntlɪ] ADV (to behave, dress) avec extravagance; (designed) aux lignes extravagantes

flame [fleɪm] N 1 flamme f; **in flames** en flammes, en feu; **to go up in flames** être détruit par le feu; Fig (of hopes, chances) s'envoler, partir en fumée; **to burst into flame(s)** s'enflammer, se mettre à flamber
2 (light) éclat m
3 Lit (passion) passion f, ardeur f; Fam (lover) béguin m; **he is an old f. of mine** c'est un de mes anciens amoureux; **the f. of passion** les feux de la passion; **the f. of enthusiasm** la flamme de l'enthousiasme; **to keep the f. of freedom burning** ne pas laisser s'éteindre la flamme de la liberté
4 Comput message m injurieux
VI 1 (of fire etc) flamber, flamboyer; Lit (of passions etc) brûler; **her cheeks flamed** ses joues s'empourprèrent
2 (of diamond etc) briller
3 Comput rédiger un message injurieux
VT 1 Culin flamber 2 Comput incendier
▸▸ Tech **f. cutter** chalumeau m à découper; Agr **f. gun** agriflamme m; **f. red** rouge m feu; **f. red hair** chevelure f flamboyante; Bot **f. tree** flamboyant m; Comput **f. war** guerre f d'insultes
▸ **flame up** VI (blaze) s'enflammer

flame-coloured ADJ ponceau inv, couleur de feu inv

flamenco [fləˈmeŋkəʊ] N Mus flamenco m

flameproof ['fleɪmpruːf] ADJ ininflammable; (material) ignifugé; Elec antidéflagrant

flamer ['fleɪmər] N Comput auteur m d'un message injurieux

flamethrower ['fleɪmθrəʊər] N Mil etc lance-flammes m inv

flaming ['fleɪmɪŋ] N Comput = échange m d'insultes sur l'Internet
ADJ 1 (fire) flambant, flamboyant 2 (sun) ardent; (sunset) flamboyant; (sky) embrasé; **f. red** rouge feu inv; Fam **in a f. temper** d'une humeur massacrante 3 Br Fam (intensifier) sacré; **you f. idiot!** sacré imbécile!; **a f. cheek** un culot monstre
ADV Br Fam complètement, carrément; **he's so f. stupid** il est complètement stupide; **he's so f. brilliant** il est carrément génial; **it was f. expensive** c'était super cher

flamingo, pl **flamingos, flamingoes** [fləˈmɪŋgəʊ, -əʊz] N (bird) flamant m

flammable ['flæməb(ə)l] ADJ inflammable

flan [flæn] N Culin tarte f, (savoury) quiche f
▸▸ **f. case** fond m de tarte

Flanders ['flɑːndəz] N Flandre f

flange [flændʒ] N (of tube, pipe) bourrelet m, collerette f, (of piece of sheet metal) collet m, rebord m; (of wheel) boudin m, rebord; (of beam) aile f, Rail (of rail) patin m, **cooling f.** ailette f de refroidissement
▸▸ **f. coupling** raccordement m à bride

flanged [flændʒd] ADJ (tube) à bride(s); (wheel) à boudin; (rail) à patin; (beam) à aile; (piece of sheet metal) à bord tombé; Aut (radiator) à ailettes

flank [flæŋk] N 1 (of person, animal) flanc m; Culin (of beef) flanchet m 2 (of mountain etc) côté m, flanc m 3 Mil (of army etc) flanc m;

left/right f. aile f gauche/droite; **to protect one's flanks** se couvrir sur les flancs
VT 1 flanquer; **to f. sth with** or **by sth** flanquer qch de qch; **flanked by two policemen** encadré de deux gendarmes 2 Mil (the enemy) prendre de flanc; (trench) enfiler; **flanking movement** attaque f par le/les flanc(s)
▸▸ Mktg **f. attack** attaque f latérale; **to launch a f. attack** lancer une attaque latérale

flanker ['flæŋkər] N 1 Rugby avant-aile m, pl avant-ailes 2 Mktg produit m de protection latérale
▸▸ Mktg **f. brand** marque f de protection latérale, marque dérivée

flannel ['flæn(ə)l] N 1 Tex (material) flanelle f, **flannels** (trousers) pantalon m de flanelle 2 Br (face) **f.** = gant m de toilette 3 Br Fam (wordy language) blabla(bla) m; (flattery) flatteries fpl
ADJ (trousers etc) de flanelle
VI Br Fam faire du baratin; **stop flannelling** arrête ton baratin

flannelette [flænəˈlet] N pilou m, veloutine f

flap [flæp] N 1 (movement, sound) (of wing) battement m, coup m; (of sail) claquement m 2 (piece of material etc) (of envelope, dustcover for book, tent) rabat m; (of pocket) patte f, (of table) abattant m; (of cellar door) trappe f, (on studio light) volet m; Aviat volet; Tech clapet m (à charnière); **desk with a writing f.** secrétaire m; **a f. of skin** un lambeau de peau 3 Fam (panic) affolement m; **to get into a f.** s'affoler, se mettre dans tous ses états; **to be in a f.** ne plus savoir où donner de la tête; **there's a big f. on** c'est la panique, c'est l'affolement total
VT (-pp-) (wings) battre de; (hands, piece of paper) agiter; **the bird flaps its wings** l'oiseau bat des ailes; **to f. one's arms about** agiter les bras
VI 1 (of sail) battre, claquer; (of wings) battre; **the eagle flapped off/away** l'aigle s'envola/s'éloigna en battant des ailes; **when she started talking to me it really set his ears flapping** quand elle a commencé à me parler il a tendu l'oreille 2 Fam (panic) s'affoler, se mettre dans tous ses états; **once he stopped flapping (about)** une fois son affolement passé
▸▸ Aut **f. valve** (in throttle) valve f papillon, papillon m

flapjack ['flæpdʒæk] N Culin 1 Am (pancake) crêpe f 2 Br (biscuit) biscuit m à l'avoine

flapper ['flæpər] N = jeune femme f (des années 20)

flapping ['flæpɪŋ] N (of wings) battement m; (of sail) claquement m

flare [fleər] N 1 (bright flame) flamboiement m; (of jet engine etc) flammes fpl 2 (signal) feu m de signal; (rocket) fusée f éclairante; 3 (of pipe etc) évasement m; (of skirt) godet m; **(pair of) flares** (trousers) pantalon m (à) pattes d'éléphant
VI 1 (of lamp, light etc) flamboyer 2 (of skirt etc) s'évaser; (of nostrils) se dilater (**with** de) 3 (of temper) s'échauffer; **tempers flared at the council meeting** le ton est monté pendant la réunion du conseil
VT (pipe, skirt etc) évaser; (nostrils) dilater
▸▸ **f. gun** pistolet m de signalisation; Br **f. path** piste f à balises lumineuses; **f. pistol** pistolet de signalisation
▸ **flare up** VI 1 (of candle etc) s'enflammer brusquement 2 (of anger, fighting etc) éclater; (of person) s'emporter; (of medical condition, skin condition) se déclencher; **he flares up at the slightest thing** il monte comme une soupe au lait

flared [fleəd] ADJ (skirt, pipe etc) évasé; **f. trousers** pantalon m à pattes d'éléphant

flare-up N **1** (with flames) flambée f soudaine **2** (outbreak) (of war) déclenchement m; (of anger) éruption f, (renewal of anger, war) recrudescence f, (argument) altercation f, (of person) flambée f ou éclat m de colère; (of violence) explosion f; **there has been a new f. in the Balkans** il y a eu une nouvelle recrudescence des combats dans les Balkans

FLASH [flæʃ]

N	éclat **1** ▪ flash **2, 4** ▪ torche **3**
VI	briller **1** ▪ clignoter **1** ▪ passer comme un éclair **2**
VT	lancer **1** ▪ diriger **1** ▪ montrer rapidement **2** ▪ projeter **2**
ADJ	tape-à-l'œil

N **1** (light) éclair m; (of diamond etc) éclat m; (of firearm) lueur f, éclair; **a f. of lightning** un éclair; **f. of wit** saillie f; **f. of inspiration** éclair de génie; **(as) quick as a f.** vif comme l'éclair; **in a f.** en un rien de temps, en un clin d'œil; **it came to her in a f.** ça lui est venu subitement; Fig **a f. in the pan** un feu de paille

2 Phot flash m, pl flashes; **I took this one with a f.** celle-ci je l'ai prise au flash ou avec le flash

3 Am Fam (torch) torche f (électrique)
4 Journ flash m; **news f.** flash d'information
5 Br Mil (badge) écusson m

VI **1** (of light, diamonds) briller; (of light on police car etc) clignoter; (of eyes) jeter des éclairs; (with enthusiasm) briller; **the light flashed once then went out** la lumière s'est allumée puis s'est éteinte; **his eyes flashed with anger** ses yeux lançaient des éclairs de colère

2 (move fast) **to f. past** passer comme un éclair; **he flashed past me on a skateboard** elle m'a doublé en skateboard à la vitesse de l'éclair; **he flashed through the exercises** il a fait les exercices à toute vitesse; **the days seemed to f. by** les journées ont passé à toute vitesse; **it flashed across my mind that ...** l'idée m'est venue tout d'un coup que ...; **my life flashed before me** ma vie a défilé devant mes yeux; **a look of panic flashed across his face** une expression de panique passa rapidement sur son visage; **a smile flashed across her lips** un sourire se dessina soudain sur ses lèvres

3 Br Fam (expose oneself) s'exhiber (at devant)

VT **1** (smile, look) lancer (**at sb** à qn); **to f. a light in sb's eyes** diriger une lumière dans les yeux de qn; **she flashed her headlights at us** elle nous a fait un appel de phares; **she flashed a mirror to signal for help** elle a fait des signaux avec un miroir pour appeler à l'aide; **he was flashing a fat wad of money** il exhibait un gros paquet de billets; **she flashed a report to head office** elle a envoyé un rapport-éclair au siège social

2 (show quickly) montrer rapidement; (picture etc on screen) projeter; **he flashed a photo in front of me** il m'a passé une photo sous les yeux; **he flashed a £50 note at them** il leur passa un billet de cinquante livres sous le nez

3 Am Fam (expose oneself to) s'exhiber devant

ADJ Br Fam (showy) tape-à-l'œil inv, voyant, extravagant; inv, (spiv) filou m

▸▸**f. burn** brûlure f (causée par un éclat très violent et brûlant, comme celui d'une bombe); **f. flood** crue f subite; Phot **f. gun** flash; Br Fam **f. Harry** frimeur m; Com **f. pack** (discounted) = emballage m portant une réduction de prix; **f. photography** photographie f au flash; **f. point** Tech (of oil etc) point m d'inflammabilité; Fig situation f critique ou explosive; **f. welding** soudure f par étincelage

▸**flash around** VT SEP Fam (show off) montrer, exhiber; **he likes flashing his money around** il aime étaler sa richesse; **don't f. your money around here!** ne montre ou n'exhibe pas ton argent ici!

▸**flash back** VI Cin (of film) revenir en arrière, faire un retour en arrière ou un flashback; (of mind) remonter (dans le passé); **my thoughts flashed back to the last time we had all been together** j'ai soudain repensé à la dernière fois où nous étions tous ensemble

▸**flash forward** VI (of film) faire un saut en avant

flashback ['flæʃbæk] N Cin retour m en arrière, flash-back m; **their story is told in f.** leur histoire est racontée par flash-back ou par retours en arrière; Fig **he had a f. to that fateful day** cette journée fatidique lui revint soudain à l'esprit

flashbulb ['flæʃbʌlb] N Phot ampoule f (de) flash

flashcard ['flæʃkɑːd] N étiquette f

flashcube ['flæʃkjuːb] N Phot flash m cube

flasher ['flæʃər] N **1** Br Fam (man exposing himself) exhibitionniste m **2** Aut Fam (lamp) clignotant m
▸▸Aut **f. unit** centrale f clignotante

flash-forward N Cin, TV projection f en avant

flashily ['flæʃɪlɪ] ADV Fam Pej d'une manière tapageuse ou tape-à-l'œil, tapageusement; **f. dressed** habillé tapageusement

flashing [1] ['flæʃɪŋ] ADJ (signal, light, torch) clignotant; (eyes, gems) étincelant
N (of diamond) éclat m; (of mirror) miroitement m; (of signal) clignotement m

flashing [2] N (on roof) revêtement m

flashlamp ['flæʃlæmp] N torche f (électrique)

flashlight ['flæʃlaɪt] N **1** Phot flash m **2** esp Am (torch) torche f (électrique)
▸▸Phot **f. photography** photographie f au flash

flashover ['flæʃəʊvər] N Elec étincelle f de rupture

flashy ['flæʃɪ] ADJ Pej (clothes, car, jewellery) voyant, tapageur, -euse; (taste) tapageur; **f. young man** jeune homme habillé tapageusement; **you and your f. friends** toi et tes copains aux goûts tapageurs

flask [flɑːsk] N flacon m; Chem fiole f, (spherical) ballon m; **brandy f.** flacon à cognac; **(vacuum) f.** Thermos® m ou f; **a f. of tea** un(e) Thermos® de thé

FLAT [flæt]

ADJ	plat **1** ▪ net **2** ▪ catégorique **2** ▪ terne **3** ▪ éventé **3** ▪ à plat **3** ▪ fixe **4** ▪ en dessous du ton **5**
ADV	à plat **1** ▪ nettement **2** ▪ en dessous du ton **4**
N	plat **1** ▪ appartement **5** ▪ bémol **7** ▪ crevaison **8**

ADJ **1** (countryside, chest, stomach, shoes) plat; (roof) plat, en terrasse; (curve etc) aplati; (surface) plat, uni; (nose) camus; Med (feet) plat; (picture) sans relief; (in painting) (colour) mat; Archit (vault) plat, (arch) déprimé; **to beat sth f.** aplatir qch; **the city had been bombed f.** les bombardements avaient rasé la ville; **as f. as a pancake** plat comme une galette; Fam **to go into a f. spin** (of person) s'affoler

2 (absolute) net, f nette; (denial) formel, absolu; (refusal) net, catégorique; **to give a f. refusal** refuser net; Fam **and that's f.!** voilà qui est net!; **I'm not going, and that's f.** je n'y vais pas, un point c'est tout

3 (existence etc) monotone, ennuyeux;

(style etc) terne; (voice) terne, blanc; (drink) éventé, plat; (battery) à plat; **to go f.** (of drink) s'éventer; **business has been a bit f. lately** les affaires sont calmes ces derniers temps

4 Com (rate, fee) fixe
5 (sound) sourd; Mus bémol; **symphony in D f.** symphonie en ré bémol; **you're f.** (singing) vous chantez en dessous du ton; (playing) vous jouez en dessous du ton; **her voice went a bit f. at the end** elle a fini un peu en dessous du ton

ADV **1** (in level position) à plat; also Fig **to knock sb f.** faire tomber qn à la renverse; **to fall f. on one's face** tomber à plat ventre; Fam (be humiliated) essuyer une humiliation; **to fall f.** (of joke etc) manquer son effet, tomber à plat; (of play etc) faire un four; **stretched out f. on the ground** étendu à plat sur le sol; **to fold f.** se plier; **he pressed himself f. against the wall** il s'est collé au mur

2 (absolutely) nettement, positivement; Fam **he told me f. that ...** il m'a dit carrément que ...; **to turn sb down f.** envoyer qn balader, envoyer qn sur les roses; Fam **to be f. broke** être à sec; **to work f. out** travailler d'arrache-pied; **to go f. out** (run) filer à toute allure; Fig **she was going f. out for the championship** elle mettait tout en jeu pour le championnat; **to lie f. out** être allongé à plat; **to be f. out** (exhausted) être à plat

3 (exactly) **in twenty seconds f.** en vingt secondes pile; **in less than ten seconds f.** en moins de dix secondes

4 Mus (to sing, play etc) en dessous du ton
N **1** (of sword etc) plat m; **the f. of the hand** le plat de la main
2 (land) plaine f, (left exposed at low tide) sèche f
3 on the f. (horizontally) horizontalement; Rail (track) en palier; Sport sur le plat
4 Horseracing **the f.** (season) la saison du plat; (racing) les courses fpl de plat, le plat
5 esp Br (rooms) appartement m; **furnished/unfurnished f.** appartement meublé/non meublé; **service f.** appartement avec service
6 Theat (scenery) panneau m de décor
7 Mus bémol m
8 Fam (puncture) crevaison f, (flat tyre) pneu m à plat; (punctured) pneu crevé
▸▸**f. bed** (of lorry) plateau m; **f. blade screwdriver** tournevis m (à lame) plate; Naut **f. calm** calme m plat; Br **f. cap** casquette f, **f. fare** (on bus etc) tarif m unique; Comput **f. file** fichier m de données non structurées; Comput, TV **f. monitor** écran m plat; Comput **f. panel display** moniteur m à écran plat; Horseracing **f. race** course f de plat; Horseracing **f. racing** (races) plat m; (season) saison f des courses de plat; Comput, TV **f. screen** écran plat; **f. screen television** téléviseur m à écran plat; **f. screen tube** tube m cathodique plat; **f. sheets** (in bookbinding) feuilles fpl à plat; Aut **f. spot** point m mort; **f. swapping** échange m d'appartement; **f. top** (haircut) brosse f, Am Fam (aircraft carrier) porte-avions m inv; **f. tyre** pneu m à plat; (punctured) pneu crevé

flatbed ['flætbed] ADJ
▸▸Br **f. lorry** semi-remorque m à plateau, pl semi-remorques à plateau; Comput **f. plotter** traceur m à plat; Comput **f. scanner** scanneur m à plat; **f. truck** semi-remorque à plateau

flat-bottomed ['-'bɒtəmd] ADJ à fond plat

flatcar ['flætkɑːr] N Am Rail wagon m en plateforme

flat-chested [-'tʃestɪd] ADJ plat

flatfish, pl **flatfishes** or **flatfish** ['flætfɪʃ, -fɪʃɪz] N poisson m plat

flatfoot ['flætfʊt] N **1** Med pied m plat **2** Old-

fashioned Br Fam (policeman) agent *m* de police, *Fam* poulet *m*

flat-footed ADJ **1** *Med* à pied plat, aux pieds plats **2** *Br Fig, Fam (clumsy, inelegant)* maladroit

flatiron ['flætaɪən] N fer *m* à repasser

flat-leaf parsley N *Bot, Culin* persil *m* plat

flatlet ['flætlɪt] N *esp Br* petit appartement *m*, studio *m*

flatline ['flætlaɪn] *Med* N électrocardiogramme *m* plat
▪ VI avoir un électrocardiogramme plat

flatly ['flætlɪ] ADV **1** *(absolutely)* nettement, carrément; *(to refuse)* net; *(to deny)* absolument; *(to say)* sèchement **2** *(monotonously)* d'une façon monotone; **the speaker's voice droned f. on** l'orateur continuait de sa voix lassante et monotone

flatmate ['flætmeɪt] N *Br* colocataire *mf* *(d'un appartement)*; **we used to be flatmates** avant, nous partagions un appartement

flatness ['flætnɪs] N **1** *(of surface etc)* nature *f* plate; *(of countryside)* absence *f* de relief; *(of curve etc)* aplatissement *m* **2** *(of refusal)* netteté *f* **3** *(of existence etc)* monotonie *f*; *(of style etc)* insipidité *f*, platitude *f*; *(of beer etc)* évent *m*; *(of colour)* caractère *m* terne; *(of sound)* caractère sourd; **there was a f. in his voice which suggested that ...** le détachement que l'on décelait dans sa voix suggérait que ...

flat-rate ADJ
▪▪*Comput* **f. connection** *(to Internet)* connexion *f* à tarif forfaitaire; *Comput* **f. monthly charge** *(to Internet)* forfait *m* mensuel

flatten ['flæt(ə)n] (**-n-**) VT **1** aplatir; *(road)* aplanir; *(of wind, rain) (corn etc)* coucher; **to f. oneself against a wall** se plaquer *ou* se coller contre un mur; *Fam* **to f. sb** *(in fight)* mettre la pâtée à qn; *(humiliate)* écraser qn **2** *(make dull)* rendre fade *ou* insipide; *(make less striking)* atténuer **3** *Mus (note)* bémoliser
▪ VI **1** s'aplatir **2** *(become dull)* devenir fade *ou* insipide; *(of colour)* se ternir
▸ **flatten out** VI **1** *Aviat* reprendre le vol horizontal; *(after dive)* se redresser; *(of inflation, unemployment etc)* se stabiliser *(at* à*)* **2** *(of terrain, slope)* s'aplanir

flattened ['flæt(ə)nd] ADJ **1** aplati; *(nose)* épaté **2** *Mus (note)* bémolisé

flatter ['flætər] VT flatter; **the portrait/dress flatters her** ce portrait/cette robe la flatte *ou* l'avantage; **he flatters himself that he will succeed** il est persuadé de sa réussite; **I f. myself on my goulash/my ability to judge people** je me flatte de faire un bon goulasch/de savoir juger les gens; *Fam* **don't f. yourself!** tu rêves!
▪ VI être flatteur

flatterer ['flætərər] N flatteur, -euse; *(who exaggerates)* flagorneur, -euse

flattering ['flætərɪŋ] ADJ *(words, photo etc)* flatteur, -euse; *(exaggerated)* adulatoire; **it is f. to be asked to give this speech** c'est flatteur d'être sollicité pour faire ce discours; **to speak in f. terms of sb, to make f. remarks about sb** parler de qn en termes flatteurs; **I didn't get a very f. impression of the city/ your boss** la ville/ton patron ne m'a pas fait une impression très favorable

flatteringly ['flætərɪŋlɪ] ADV *(to speak)* en termes flatteurs; **the photograph had been f. lit** la photo avait été prise dans une lumière flatteuse

flattery ['flætərɪ] N flatterie *f*; *(exaggerated)* flagornerie *f*; **f. will get you nowhere!** ça ne vous apportera rien de flatter les gens!

flatulence ['flætjʊləns] N *Med* flatulence *f*;

to suffer from f. avoir des vents; **to cause f.** provoquer des flatulences

flatulent ['flætjʊlənt] ADJ **1** *Med (person)* qui souffre de flatulences **2** *Fig (style)* boursouflé

flatware ['flætweər] N *Am* vaisselle *f* plate

flaunt [flɔːnt] VT *(wealth, knowledge)* étaler, afficher, faire parade de; *(jewels)* étaler, arborer; *(bad manners, ignorance)* afficher

Attention: ne pas confondre avec le verbe **to flout**.

flautist ['flɔːtɪst] N *Mus* flûtiste *mf*

flavour, *Am* **flavor** ['fleɪvər] N saveur *f*, goût *m*; *(of tea etc)* arôme *m*; *(of ice cream etc)* parfum *m*; **what f. (of) ice cream did you want?** quel parfum tu voulais?; *Fam* à quoi tu voulais ta glace?; **it comes in six different flavours** il existe en six parfums différents; **her stories have a Mediterranean f.** ses histoires sentent bon la Méditerranée; **there was a f. of regret about his remarks** ses remarques contenaient une pointe de regret; **her book gives the true f. of the Mexican hinterland** son livre fleure bon l'arrière-pays mexicain; *Fam* **I'm not f. of the month** je ne suis pas en odeur de sainteté; **she's definitely f. of the month** décidément, elle a la cote ce mois-ci
▪ VT *(dish etc)* assaisonner, parfumer; **to f. a sauce with garlic** relever une sauce avec de l'ail; **vanilla flavoured** (parfumé) à la vanille
▸▸ **f. enhancer** agent *m* de sapidité

flavouring, *Am* **flavoring** ['fleɪvərɪŋ] N *(savoury)* assaisonnement *m*; *(sweet)* parfum *m*; **artificial f.** arôme *m* artificiel

flavourless, *Am* **flavorless** ['fleɪvəlɪs] ADJ *(food etc)* sans saveur, fade, insipide; *(wine)* plat

flaw [flɔː] N **1** défaut *m*, imperfection *f*; *(in plan)* point *m* faible; **there is one f. in their argument** il y a une faille dans leur argument; **to have a f. in one's character** avoir un défaut **2** *Law (in document etc, making it null and void)* vice *m* de forme
▪ VT *(spoil)* endommager, défigurer; **the plan is flawed by the lack of ...** le point faible de ce plan est le manque de ...

flawed [flɔːd] ADJ *(reasoning)* défectueux; *(novel, film)* qui a des défauts; *(sweater, scarf, fabric)* qui a un/des défaut(s); *(wood)* gercé; *(diamond)* qui a un crapaud *ou* un défaut

flawless ['flɔːlɪs] ADJ sans défaut, parfait; *(technique)* impeccable

flawlessly ['flɔːlɪslɪ] ADV parfaitement

flawlessness ['flɔːlɪsnɪs] N perfection *f*

flax [flæks] N *(plant)* lin *m*
▪▪ **f. field** linière *f*

flaxen ['flæksən] ADJ *(hair)* blond de lin *inv*, blond filasse *inv*

flay [fleɪ] VT **1** *(skin) (animal)* écorcher; **to be flayed alive** être écorché vif **2** *(whip)* fouetter; *Fig* **the critics flayed him** les critiques l'ont éreinté

flea [fliː] N *(insect)* puce *f*; **to have fleas** avoir des puces; *Fig Fam* **she sent him away with a f. in his ear** elle l'a envoyé promener
▪▪ **f. collar** collier *m* antipuces; **f. market** marché *m* aux puces

fleabag ['fliːbæg] N *Sl* **1** *Br (person)* pouilleux, -euse; *(animal)* sac *m* à puces **2** *Am (hotel)* hôtel *m* pouilleux

fleabite ['fliːbaɪt] N **1** morsure *f* de puce **2** *Fig (trifle)* vétille *f*, bagatelle *f*

flea-bitten ADJ *(dog, cat, person)* plein de puces; *(hotel)* pouilleux; *(old jacket)* miteux

fleapit ['fliːpɪt] N *Old-fashioned Br Sl (cinema)* cinéma *m* pouilleux

fleck [flek] N **1** *(mark) (of light etc)* petite tache *f*; *(of colour, paint)* moucheture *f* **2** *(particle) (of dust)* particule *f*

▪ VT tacheter; **flecked with clouds** moucheté de nuages; **hair flecked with grey** cheveux qui grisonnent; **flecked material** tissu moucheté

fled PT, PP *see* **flee**

fledged [fledʒd] ADJ *(bird)* qui a toutes ses plumes; *see* **fully-fledged**

fledgling ['fledʒlɪŋ] N **1** *(young bird)* oisillon *m* **2** *(beginner)* novice *mf*, débutant, -e; **a f. lawyer** un avocat novice; **a f. industry/ state** une industrie/un État jeune

flee [fliː] *(pt, pp fled)* VI *(of person)* s'enfuir, prendre la fuite; *(of time etc)* voler; *(of hope)* s'envoler; **to f. from a place** s'enfuir d'un endroit; **to f. from temptation/persecution** fuir la tentation/les persécutions; **to f. to America** s'enfuir en Amérique
▪ VT *(country etc)* s'enfuir de; *(person, temptation etc)* fuir

fleece N **1** *(of sheep)* toison *f*; *Liter* **the Golden F.** la Toison d'or **2** *Tex (material)* laine *f* polaire; *(garment)* polaire *f*
▪ VT *Fam (cheat, overcharge)* écorcher; **I've been fleeced** je me suis fait estamper

fleece-lined ADJ doublé de laine polaire

fleecing ['fliːsɪŋ] N *Fam (overcharging)* estampage *m*

fleecy ['fliːsɪ] ADJ *(wool)* floconneux; *(material etc)* laineux; *(cloud)* moutonné

fleeing ['fliːɪŋ] ADJ *(army etc)* en fuite

fleet [fliːt] N **1** *Naut* flotte *f*; *(naval unit)* escadre *f*; **the F.** ≃ la Marine nationale; **the Atlantic F.** l'escadre de l'Atlantique; **merchant f.** flotte de commerce; **fishing f.** flottille *f* de pêche **2** *(of cars, taxis)* parc *m*; **air f.** flotte aérienne; **a f. of coaches took the tourists to their hotel** une caravane de cars a amené les touristes à leur hôtel
▪ ADJ *Lit* vite, leste; **f. of foot** au pied léger
▪▪ *Naut* **f. admiral** ≃ amiral *m* de France; *Naut* **the F. Air Arm** = l'aéronavale *f* britannique; **F. Street** = rue *f* de Londres, dont le nom sert à désigner les grands journaux britanniques; **F. Street journalist** journaliste *mf* de la presse nationale

Fleet Street
Traditionnellement, cette rue de la City était celle des journaux. Aujourd'hui, beaucoup de journaux ont établi leur siège dans d'autres quartiers, notamment les Docklands. Cependant, le terme "Fleet Street" est encore employé pour désigner la presse et le monde du journalisme.

fleet-footed ADJ *Lit* au pied léger

fleeting ['fliːtɪŋ] ADJ *(time, moment)* fugitif, fugace; *(beauty)* passager; *(happiness)* éphémère; *(relationship)* de courte durée; **for a f. moment** l'espace d'un instant; **to pay sb a f. visit** faire une courte visite à qn; **to catch a f. glimpse of sth** entrevoir qch; **to give sb a f. glance** lancer un regard fugace à qn

fleetingly ['fliːtɪŋlɪ] ADV *(to glimpse, appear)* un court instant; **she has been f. involved with a number of men** elle a eu un certain nombre d'aventures de courte durée

Fleming ['flemɪŋ] N Flamand, -ande

Flemish ['flemɪʃ] ADJ flamand
▪ N *Ling* flamand *m*

flesh [fleʃ] N **1** *(of person, fruit)* chair *f*; **to put on f.** *(of animal)* prendre chair; *(of person)* grossir, prendre de l'embonpoint; **to put some f. on an idea** étoffer *ou* développer une idée; **there he was in the f.** c'était lui en chair et en os; **to make sb's f. creep** *or* **crawl** donner la chair de poule à qn; **his own f. and blood** la chair de sa chair; **it is more than f. and blood can stand** *or* **bear** c'est plus que la nature humaine ne saurait endurer; **I'm only f. and blood!** je ne suis pas un surhomme!; *Fam* **to press the f.** serrer des mains

2 *(as opposed to spirit) Rel* **to mortify the f.** mortifier sa chair; *Rel, Lit* **to go the way of all f.** payer sa dette à la nature; *Rel, Lit* **the sins of the f.** le péché de la chair; *Rel, Prov* **the spirit is willing but the f. is weak** l'esprit est prompt, mais la chair est faible

3 *Arch (meat)* viande *f*; **f.-eating animals** les animaux *mpl* carnivores; *Rel* **to eat f.** faire gras

▸▸ **f. colour** couleur *f* chair; *Theat* **f. tights** collant *m* chair; *Art* **f. tints** carnations *fpl*; **f. wound** blessure *f* superficielle *ou* légère

▸ **flesh out** **vt sep** *(plan, character, remarks)* étoffer

 vi *(become fatter)* s'étoffer

flesh-coloured **adj** *(tights etc)* (couleur) chair

fleshpots ['fleʃpɒts] **npl** *Lit, Hum* **the f.** les lieux *mpl* de perdition

fleshy ['fleʃɪ] **adj** *(limb, fruit etc)* charnu; *(leaf)* succulent

fleur-de-lis, *pl* fleurs-de-lis ['flɜːdə'liː] **n** *Her* fleur *f* de lis

flew **pt** *see* **fly**[3]

flex [fleks] **vt** *(one's arm, knees etc)* fléchir; *(one's muscles)* faire jouer; *Fig* **he's just flexing his muscles** ce n'est qu'une démonstration d'autorité de sa part

 vi *(of spring)* fléchir

 n *Br Elec* cordon *m*, câble *m*

flexibility [fleksɪ'bɪlɪtɪ] **n** *(of material, plan, person)* flexibilité *f*; *(of character)* souplesse *f*

flexible ['fleksɪb(ə)l] **adj** *(material, plans)* flexible, souple; *(character, principles)* souple; **when would you like the appointment? – I'm f.** quand désirez-vous prendre rendez-vous? – je suis disponible à peu près tout le temps; **f. ticket** billet *m* sans condition; **f. working hours** horaire *m* à la carte *ou* flexibles, *Can* horaire flexible

flexion ['flekʃən] **n** *(of spring etc)* flexion *f*, courbure *f* **2** *(bend)* courbe *f*

flexitime ['fleksɪtaɪm], **flextime** ['flekstaɪm] **n** *Ind etc* horaire *m* à la carte, *Can* horaire flexible; **we're on f.** nous avons des horaires à la carte

flexor ['fleksər] **n** *Anat (muscle)* fléchisseur *m*

flibbertigibbet [flɪbətɪ'dʒɪbɪt] **n** *Fam* écervelé, -ée, évaporé, -ée, hurluberlu *m*

flick [flɪk] **n 1** *(of whip, tail etc)* petit coup *m*; *(with finger)* chiquenaude *f*; **a f. of the wrist** un tour de main; **at the f. of a switch** juste en appuyant sur un bouton **2** *Old-fashioned Br Fam (film)* film *m*; **the flicks** *(cinema)* le ciné, le cinoche; **to go to the flicks** aller au ciné *ou* au cinoche

 vt *(with whip etc)* effleurer; *(with finger)* donner une chiquenaude à; **he had to keep flicking the hair out of his eyes** il n'arrêtait pas de chasser du doigt les cheveux qui lui tombaient dans les yeux; **she was flicking cigarette ash all over the floor** elle faisait tomber la cendre de cigarette partout; **she flicked the dust from her shoulders** du doigt elle fit envoler la poussière qui se trouvait sur ses épaules; **to f. a duster over sth** donner un coup de torchon à qch

 ▸▸ *Br* **f. knife** (couteau *m* à) cran *m* d'arrêt; *Aut* **f. wipe** balayage *m* unique

▸ **flick away** **vt sep** chasser; *(with fingers)* repousser d'une chiquenaude

▸ **flick off** **vt sep** *(with fingers)* enlever d'une chiquenaude; **to f. sth off with a duster** faire envoler qch d'un coup de torchon; **he flicked the dandruff off his collar** il secoua les pellicules qui se trouvaient sur son col

▸ **flick on** **vt sep** **to f. on the lights** allumer; *Aut* allumer les phares

▸ **flick out** **vi** sortir; **the snake's tongue was flicking in and out** la langue du serpent sortait et rentrait à petits coups rapides

▸ **flick through** **vt insep** *(book)* feuilleter; *(photographs)* jeter un œil parmi

flicker ['flɪkər] **n** petit mouvement *m* vacillant; *(of eyelids)* battement *m*; *Cin* scintillement *m*; *(of TV, computer screen)* papillotement *m*; *Fig* mince battement de cil; **a f. of light** une petite lueur tremblotante; **a f. of recognition** une lueur de reconnaissance; **a f. of hope/a smile** l'ombre d'un espoir/d'un sourire; **a f. of interest/annoyance** une pointe d'intérêt/d'énervement

 vi *(of flame etc)* trembloter, vaciller; *(of eyelids)* cligner; *(of light)* clignoter; *(of snake's tongue)* onduler; *(of instrument needle etc)* osciller; *Cin* scintiller; *(of TV, computer screen)* papilloter; **the candle flickered out** la bougie vacilla et s'éteignit; **a smile flickered on his lips** il eut un petit sourire

flicker-free **adj** *(screen)* anti-scintillements

flickering ['flɪkərɪŋ] **adj** *(light)* clignotant; *(shapes, images, candle)* vacillant

 n *Cin* scintillement *m*; *(of TV, computer screen)* papillotement *m*

flier ['flaɪər] **n 1** *(pilot etc)* aviateur, -trice; **I'm not a good f.** *(passenger)* je n'aime pas prendre l'avion

2 *Fam (fall)* **to take a f. over the handlebars** faire un vol plané par-dessus le guidon **3** *(leaflet)* feuille *f* volante, prospectus *m* **4** *(in race) (of sprinter)* départ *m* en flèche **5** **to take a f.** *(financial risk)* prendre un risque financier

flight[1] [flaɪt] **n 1** *(act of flying) (of bird, plane etc)* vol *m*; *(of projectile, star etc)* course *f*; **these birds are not capable of f.** ces oiseaux ne peuvent pas voler; **very graceful in f.** très gracieux en vol; **once we're in f.** quand nous serons à notre altitude de croisière; *Aviat* **level f.** vol horizontal *ou* en palier; *Fig* **f. of fancy** essor *m* de l'imagination

2 *(distance) (of bird etc)* volée *f*, distance *f* parcourue; *(of birds etc)* migration *f*; *(of projectile)* trajectoire *f*; *Aviat* **it's an hour's f. from London** c'est à une heure de vol de Londres

3 *(specific trip)* vol *m*; **f. A200 to Brussels** vol A200 pour Bruxelles; **I don't want to miss my f.** je ne veux pas rater mon avion; **my f. is at 2.15** mon avion est à 2h 15; **how was your f.?** comment s'est passé le vol?; **f. only** vol sec

4 *(group) (of birds etc)* vol *m*, volée *f*; *(of planes)* escadrille *f*; *Fig* **in the top f.** parmi les tout premiers; *Aviat* **the Queen's/King's F.** = avions *mpl* au service de la famille royale

5 f. (of stairs) escalier *m*; **you go up two flights** tu montes de deux étages *ou* de deux volées d'escalier; **they live six flights up from me** ils habitent six étages au-dessus de chez moi; **he lives up four flights (of stairs)** il habite au quatrième; *Sport* **f. of hurdles** *(in obstacle race)* série *f* de haies **6** *(on arrow, dart)* plume *f*

 ▸▸ **f. attendant** *(male)* steward *m*; *(female)* hôtesse *f* de l'air; **f. clearance** autorisation *f* de vol; **f. control** *(action of individual aircraft)* conduite *f*; *(from ground)* contrôle *m* de la navigation aérienne; *Mil* contrôle des missions aériennes; *(place)* contrôle aérien; *(people)* contrôleurs *mpl* aériens; **f. crew** équipage *m* *(d'un avion)*; **f. deck** *(of aircraft)* poste *m* *ou* cabine *f* de pilotage, habitacle *m*; *(of aircraft carrier)* pont *m* d'envol; **f. engineer** mécanicien, -ienne navigant(e) *(d'avion)*, ingénieur *m* de vol; *Orn* **f. feather**

(of bird) penne *f*; **f. formation** formation *f* de vol; **f. lieutenant** = capitaine *m* de l'armée de l'air britannique; **f. log** journal *m* de vol; **f. mechanic** mécanicien, -ienne navigant(e); **f. number** numéro *m* de vol; **f. path** trajectoire *f* de vol; **f. pattern** formation de vol; **f. personnel** personnel *m* navigant; **f. plan** plan *m* de vol; **f. recorder** enregistreur *m* de vol; **f. simulator** simulateur *m* de vol; **f. time** *(duration)* durée *f* de vol; *(take-off time)* heure *f* du vol

flight[2] **n** *(escape)* fuite *f*; **his sudden f. from the room** sa sortie précipitée de la pièce; **in the course of her f. from justice** alors qu'elle fuyait la justice; **to take (to) f.** prendre la fuite; **to put the enemy to f.** mettre l'ennemi en fuite; **in full f.** en pleine déroute; *Fin* **f. of capital** exode *m* *ou* fuite *f* des capitaux

 ▸▸ *Fin* **f. capital** capitaux *mpl* flottants *ou* fébriles

flightiness ['flaɪtɪnɪs] **n** inconstance *f*

flightless ['flaɪtlɪs] **adj** *(bird)* coureur

flighty ['flaɪtɪ] **adj** inconstant; *(emotionally)* volage

flimsily ['flɪmzɪlɪ] **adv** *(built, constructed)* d'une manière peu solide

flimsiness ['flɪmzɪnɪs] **n 1** *(of dress, cloth)* légèreté *f*; *(of building, plane)* manque *m* de solidité; *(of walls, wooden beams)* minceur *f* **2** *(of excuse etc)* faiblesse *f*, pauvreté *f*

flimsy ['flɪmzɪ] **adj 1** fragile, peu solide; *(paper etc)* fin, fragile; *(dress, cloth)* léger **2** *(excuse)* faible, pauvre; *(evidence, alibi)* peu convaincant; *(novel, plot)* faible; **to condemn sb on the flimsiest evidence** condamner qn en s'appuyant sur des preuves très peu convaincantes

 n 1 *(paper)* papier *m* pelure **2** *Journ (copy)* copie *f* *(de reporter)*

flinch [flɪntʃ] **vi 1** *(shy away)* **not to f. from doing sth** ne pas hésiter à faire qch; **she didn't f. from carrying out her duty** elle ne s'est pas dérobée à son devoir **2** *(with pain)* tressaillir (**with** de); **to bear pain without flinching** supporter la douleur sans broncher; **I flinched at the thought of it** ça m'a fait tressaillir d'y penser; **the very thought of telling her about it made him f.** la simple pensée de lui en parler le faisait frémir

fling [flɪŋ] **n 1** *(throw)* jet *m*, coup *m*

2 *Fam (attempt)* **I'll have a f. at it** je vais essayer; **to give sth a f., to have a f. at sth** essayer qch; **to have a f. at doing sth** essayer de faire qch; **he had given French a f. a few years before** il avait essayé de se mettre au français quelques années auparavant

3 *(dance)* **(highland) f.** = pas *m* seul écossais

4 *Fam (impulsive behaviour)* **to have one's f.** faire la fête; **the summer seemed to be having one last f.** l'été semblait avoir un dernier sursaut

5 *Fam (affair)* **to have a f.** avoir une aventure (**with sb** avec qn)

 vt *(pt, pp flung* [flʌŋ]*)* jeter; *(ball etc)* lancer; **to f. sb into prison** jeter qn en prison; **to f. oneself into sb's arms/an armchair** se jeter dans les bras de qn/un fauteuil; **to f. oneself into a task** se lancer dans une tâche; **to f. one's arms around sb** jeter ses bras autour de qn

▸ **fling about** **vt sep** *(objects)* jeter de côté et d'autre; **to f. one's arms about** gesticuler violemment; **to f. one's money about** mener grand train

▸ **fling away** **vt sep** *(throw)* jeter de côté; *(get rid of)* se débarrasser de; **to f. one's money away** gaspiller son argent

▸ **fling back** **vt sep** *(sheets, blanket)* rejeter; **to f. back one's head** rejeter la tête en arrière

▸ **fling down** **vt sep** *(to the ground, floor)* jeter par terre; *(blinds, hatch)* refermer brusquement; *Fig (ultimatum)* imposer; **he flung the books down on the table** il a jeté les livres sur la table; **f. down my keys, will you?** lance-moi mes clés, s'il te plaît

▸ **fling off** VT SEP **1** *(rid oneself of) (impositions, restrictions)* se débarrasser de; *Lit* **to f. off the yoke of tyranny** secouer le joug de la tyrannie **2** *(take off) (one's coat etc)* retirer brusquement

▸ **fling open** VT SEP *(window, door etc)* ouvrir toute grande

▸ **fling out** VT SEP **1** *(throw out)* jeter dehors; *(get rid of) (unwanted object)* jeter, balancer; *(bill, legislation, case)* rejeter; *Fam* **to f. sb out** flanquer qn à la porte; **she flung him out of the house** elle l'a flanqué à la porte, elle l'a viré de chez elle **2** *(extend)* **to f. out one's arm** étendre le bras d'un grand geste; **he flung out a fist and knocked his assailant out** il mit son assaillant K-O d'un coup de poing; **he flung out a foot and turned the ball into the net** il tendit le pied et dévia la balle vers le filet

▸ **fling up** VT SEP **1** *(throw in air)* jeter en l'air; **he flung the bag up to her** il lui a envoyé le sac **2** *Fam (possibility)* entraîner; **what did your investigations f. up?** qu'ont produit vos recherches?

flint [flɪnt] N *Miner* silex *m*; *(for making fire)* pierre *f* à feu; *(for cigarette lighter)* pierre à briquet; *Hist* **f. tools** outils *mpl* en silex taillés
▸▸ **f. glass** flint(-glass) *m*

flinty ['flɪntɪ] ADJ **1** *(of or resembling flint)* de silex **2** *Fig (heart)* de pierre, dur; *(person)* au cœur de pierre; *(expression, manner)* dur; **cold f. eyes** un regard froid et dur

flip[1] [flɪp] N *(flick)* chiquenaude *f*, pichenette *f*
VT (-pp-) **1** *(flick) (pancake, card etc)* retourner vivement; **to f. a coin** *(to decide)* jouer à pile ou face; **she flipped the coin into the air** elle lança la pièce en l'air; **he flipped the leaflet into the bin** il balança le prospectus dans la poubelle; *Fam* **to f. one's lid** *(get very angry)* sortir de ses gonds, piquer une crise; *(go crazy)* perdre la boule; **he absolutely flipped his lid at us** il a piqué une drôle de crise contre nous **2** *Elec (switch)* basculer **3** *Fam (turn over) (record)* retourner
VI *Sl* **1** *(get very angry)* sortir de ses gonds, piquer une crise; *(go crazy)* perdre la boule **2** *(become ecstatic)* flasher, flipper (**over** sur)
▸▸ **f. card** *(as prompt)* aide-mémoire *m inv*; **f. chart** tableau *m* à feuilles; *Fam* **f. side** *(of record)* face *f* B; *Fig (of policy, situation)* face *f* cachée; **there is, of course, a f. side to the expansion of industry** l'expansion de l'industrie a, comme toute médaille, son revers
▸ **flip open** VT SEP ouvrir
▸ **flip out** VI **1** *esp Am Fam (get very angry)* sortir de ses gonds, piquer une crise **2** *(of end of lorry)* déraper
▸ **flip over** VT SEP *(turn over) (record)* retourner; **to f. over the pages of a magazine** feuilleter les pages d'un magazine
VI *(turn over)* se retourner
▸ **flip through** VT INSEP *(book)* feuilleter; *(photos, posters, wallpaper samples etc)* jeter un coup d'œil à

flip[2] ADJ *Fam (flippant)* léger, désinvolte, cavalier

flip-flop N **1** *(sandal) (usu pl)* **flip-flops** tongs *fpl* **2** *(jump)* saut *m* périlleux; *(change of opinion)* volte-face *f inv* **3** *(circuit)* *(circuit m)* basculeur *m* monostable
▸▸ *Electron* **f. circuit** *(circuit)* basculeur monostable

flippancy ['flɪpənsɪ] N légèreté *f*, désinvolture *f*

flippant ['flɪpənt] ADJ désinvolte, cavalier

flippantly ['flɪpəntlɪ] ADV *(to say)* d'un ton *ou* d'une manière désinvolte

flipper ['flɪpər] N *(of whale, seal)* nageoire *f*; *(of scuba diver etc)* palme *f*

flipping ['flɪpɪŋ] *Br Fam* ADJ fichu; **don't be such a f. idiot!** arrête donc de faire l'imbécile!
ADV sacrément; **it's f. hot** il fait sacrément chaud; **he's so f. stupid** il est bête comme ses pieds; **not f. likely!** il n'y a pas de risque!

flip-top ADJ *(carton, pack)* à rabat

flirt [flɜːt] N flirteur, -euse
VI flirter avec (**with sb** à qn); **to f. with danger/Marxism** flirter avec le danger/le Marxisme; **to f. with an idea/death** jouer avec une idée/la mort

flirtation [flɜː'teɪʃən] N flirt *m*; **to have a f. with sb** flirter avec qn; **to have a f. with danger/an idea** jouer avec le danger/une idée

flirtatious [flɜː'teɪʃəs] ADJ *Fam* charmeur; *(look, smile)* enjôleur; **to be f. with sb** faire du charme à qn

flirtatiously [flɜː'teɪʃəslɪ] ADV *(to say sth)* d'un ton charmeur; **she smiled f. at him** elle lui fit un sourire enjôleur

flit [flɪt] N *Br Fam* **to do a (moonlight) f.** déménager à la cloche de bois
VI (-tt-) **1** *(of bird etc)* **to f. by** passer légèrement; **to f. about** aller et venir d'un pas léger; *Fig* **to f. from one thing to another** passer d'une chose à l'autre **2** *Scot, North Eng (move house)* déménager **3** *Br Fam (leave stealthily)* déménager à la cloche de bois

flitch [flɪtʃ] N *(of bacon)* flèche *f*

float [fləʊt] N **1** *(of boiler, carburettor etc)* flotteur *m*
2 *Fishing (on fishing line, net)* flotteur *m*, bouchon *m*
3 *Biol (of aquatic plant)* flotteur *m*; *(of fish)* vessie *f* natatoire
4 *(raft)* radeau *m*; *(floating logs)* train *m* (de bois); *(swimming aid)* flotteur *m*
5 *Theat* **the floats** *(footlights)* la rampe
6 *(vehicle) (in carnival etc)* char *m* de carnaval; *Br* **milk f.** voiture *f* de livraison du lait
7 *Com esp Am (petty cash)* petite caisse *f*; *esp Br (in cash till etc)* fond *m* de caisse; *(advance)* avance *f*; **they gave me a f. of £200 for the trip** *(advance)* ils m'ont donné un viatique de 200 livres, ils m'ont donné 200 livres pour le voyage
8 *esp Am Culin (drink)* = soda *m*, jus *m* de fruit ou milk-shake *m* dans lequel on ajoute une boule de glace
9 *St Exch* flottant *m*; **clean f.** taux *mpl* de change libres ou flottants; **dirty f.** taux de change concertés
VI **1** *(in water)* flotter; *(of boat)* être à flot; *Swimming* faire la planche; **to f. down the stream** descendre le courant
2 *(move as if in water)* **to f. to the surface** revenir à la surface; **to f. in the air** planer dans l'air; **she floated out of the room** elle est sortie de la pièce d'un pas léger; **he seems to just f. through life** *(has no worries)* il semble ne jamais avoir de soucis; *(has no goals)* il semble se laisser porter par les événements
3 *Tech (of part of machine)* avoir du jeu
VT **1** *(timber etc)* flotter; *(launch) (ship)* mettre à flot ou à l'eau; *(refloat) (ship)* renflouer **2** *Com (company etc)* lancer; *Fin (loan)* émettre, lancer; *(idea, rumour)* lancer; *(proposal)* introduire; **to f. sth on the Stock Exchange** introduire qch en Bourse
▸▸ *Am* **f. bowl** *(in engine)* cuve *f*; **f. chamber** *(in engine)* cuve *f*; **f. glass** verre *m* flotté
▸ **float about, float around** VI *(of news etc)* circuler, courir; *(in a daze etc)* flotter; **there were rumours floating about that …** le bruit courait que …; *Fam* **he's floating**

around somewhere il traîne dans les parages; *Fam* **he just floats around all day** il traîne sans rien faire toute la journée
▸ **float off** VI *(of ship etc)* se déséchouer
VT INSEP *(of ship etc)* **the boat floated off the sandbank at high tide** à marée haute, le bateau s'est dégagé du banc de sable
VT SEP *(wrecked ship etc)* renflouer, déséchouer; **they floated the boat off the sandbank** ils ont remis à flot *ou* renfloué le bateau échoué sur un banc de sable

floating ['fləʊtɪŋ] ADJ **1** flottant, à flot; **this ship is, in effect, a f. hotel** en fait, ce bateau est un hôtel flottant **2** *(population)* flottant, fluctuant; *Fin (currency, exchange rate)* flottant; *(capital)* circulant, mobile; *Tech (bearing)* flottant
N *(of ship)* mise *f* à flot; *(of wrecked ship etc)* renflouage *m*; *(of timber)* flottage *m*; *Com (of company etc)* lancement *m*; *(onto stock market)* introduction *f* en Bourse; *Fin (of loan, bonds)* émission *f*
▸▸ *Acct* **f. assets** actif *m* circulant; **f. bridge** pont *m* de bateaux *ou* de radeaux; *Banking* **f. charge** nantissement *m* général; **f. crane** ponton-grue *m*, *pl* pontons-grues; *Fin* **f. debt** dette *f* flottante *ou* non consolidée; *Culin* **f. islands** île *f* flottante; *Med* **f. kidney** rein *m* flottant; **f. off** *(of wrecked ship etc)* renflouage; *Comput* **f. point** virgule *f* flottante; *Fin* **f. rate** taux *m* flottant; *Anat* **f. ribs** côtes *fpl* flottantes; *Pol* **f. vote** *(voters)* indécis *mpl*, électorat *m* flottant; *Pol* **f. voter** électeur, -trice indécis(e); *Comput* **f. window** fenêtre *f* flottante

floating-point ADJ *Comput* à *ou* en virgule flottante
▸▸ **f. arithmetic** arithmétique *f* en virgule flottante; **f. notation** notation *f* en virgule flottante; **f. processor** coprocesseur *m* arithmétique

floating-rate ADJ *Fin* à taux flottant
▸▸ **f. bond** obligation *f* à taux flottant *ou* variable; **f. interest** intérêt *m* à taux flottant; **f. investment** investissement *m* à taux flottant *ou* variable; **f. note** effet *m* à taux flottant; **f. securities** titres *mpl* à taux flottant *ou* variable

flock[1] [flɒk] N *(of sheep, geese)* troupeau *m*; *(of animals)* bande *f*; *(of birds)* volée *f*; **a pastor and his f.** un pasteur et ses ouailles *fpl*; **a f. of visitors** une foule de visiteurs
VI *(gather)* s'attrouper, s'assembler; **everybody is flocking to see the exhibition** tout le monde vient en masse pour voir l'exposition; **in summer people f. to the sea** en été les gens vont en foule au bord de la mer; **people flocked towards the park** les gens se sont dirigés en foule vers le parc; **crowds flocked to the stadium** des foules de gens sont allés au stade

flock[2] N *(material)* bourre *f* (de laine)
▸▸ **f. mattress** matelas *m* en bourre de laine; **f. wallpaper** papier *m* tontisse
▸ **flock together** VI s'assembler

floe [fləʊ] N *(ice)* **f.** masse *f* de glaces flottantes, banquise *f*

flog [flɒg] VT (-gg-) **1** *(person)* flageller, fouetter; *(with stick)* frapper à coups de bâton; **to f. a horse** cravacher un cheval; *Fam Fig* **to f. a dead horse** se dépenser en pure perte; *Fam Fig* **to f. a subject to death** s'étendre indéfiniment sur une question; **we've flogged the subject to death** nous avons épuisé le sujet **2** *Br Fam (sell)* vendre; *(sell off quickly)* bazarder; *(stolen goods etc)* fourguer
▸ **flog off** VT SEP *Br Fam (sell off)* bazarder

flood [flʌd] N inondation *f*; **the river was in f.** la rivière débordait; **the victims of the f.** les inondés *mpl*; *Bible* **the F.** le Déluge; **the floods of the Nile** les crues *fpl* du Nil; **a f. of**

light des flots *mpl* de lumière; **floods of tears/abuse** un torrent de larmes/d'injures **VT** *(land, the bathroom etc)* inonder; *Naut (hold)* noyer; *Agr (for irrigation)* irriguer; *Aut (carburettor)* noyer; *(engine)* étouffer, noyer; **the river flooded its banks** la rivière est sortie de son lit, la rivière a débordé; **to be flooded** *(of ship)* être envahi par l'eau; *(of house)* être inondé; **to f. the market with ...** inonder le marché de ...; **to be flooded with letters/telephone calls** être submergé de lettres/de coups de téléphone; **flooded with light** *(room)* inondé de lumière

VI *(of river etc)* *(overflow)* déborder; *(be in flood)* être en crue; *Fig* **the sun's rays came flooding through the window** les rayons du soleil entraient à flots par la fenêtre; **spectators were flooding into the stadium** les spectateurs affluaient dans le stade

▸▸ **f. plain** plaine *f* d'inondation, lit *m* majeur; **f. tide** flux *m*, marée *f* montante; **f. water** inondation *f*; **the f. waters receded** les inondations ont diminué

▸ **flood back VI** *(return to memory)* revenir (à l'esprit); **it all came flooding back** tout m'est/leur est/*etc* soudain revenu; **all the feelings came flooding back** un flot d'émotions familières m'envahit/l'envahit/*etc*; **it all comes flooding back** tout me/te/*etc* revient, tout à coup

▸ **flood in VI** *(of light, water)* arriver à flots; *(of correspondence, people, thanks)* affluer

▸ **flood out VT SEP** *(force to leave)* forcer à partir; **many families have been flooded out** les inondations ont forcé beaucoup de familles à évacuer leur maison

VI *(of people)* sortir à flots; **light flooded out of the open casement** des flots de lumière s'échappaient de la fenêtre ouverte; **money flooded out of the country** il y eut d'énormes fuites de capitaux

flooded ['flʌdɪd] **ADJ** *(land)* inondé; *(carburettor)* noyé

floodgate ['flʌdgeɪt] **N** vanne *f* (de décharge), porte *f* d'écluse; **to open/close the floodgates** lever/mettre les vannes; *Fig* **to open the floodgates to immigration/immorality/*etc*** ouvrir les vannes de l'immigration/l'immoralité/*etc*

flooding ['flʌdɪŋ] **N** *(of land etc)* inondation *f*; *(of river etc)* débordement *m*; *Agr (for irrigation)* irrigation *f*; *Naut (of hold)* noyage *m*; **road liable to f.** *(road sign)* route inondable; **there has been f. in many parts of the country** il y a eu des inondations dans de nombreuses régions

floodlight ['flʌdlaɪt] **N** projecteur *m*; *Phot* (lampe *f*) flood *f*; **under** *or* **by f.** à la lumière des projecteurs

VT *(pt, pp* **floodlighted** *or* **floodlit)** illuminer aux projecteurs

floodlighting ['flʌdlaɪtɪŋ] **N** illumination *f* aux projecteurs; *(lights)* projecteurs *mpl*

floodlit ['flʌdlɪt] **ADJ** illuminé (aux projecteurs)

floor [flɔ:r] **N 1** sol *m*; *(wooden)* plancher *m*; *(of Stock Exchange, the House)* parquet *m*; *(of studio)* plateau *m*; **parquet f.** parquet *m*; **tiled f.** carrelage *m*; *Fam* **to wipe the f. with sb** battre qn à plate(s) couture(s); **to take the f.** *(at meeting)* prendre la parole; *(at dance)* se joindre aux danseurs; **Mr Taylor has the f.** la parole est à M. Taylor; **questions from the f.** *(at meeting)* questions du public; **to give sb the f.** donner la parole à qn; **dance f.** piste *f* de danse; *Ind* **the factory** *or* **shop f.** l'atelier *m*

2 *(storey)* étage *m*; **house on two floors** maison à deux étages; *Br* **ground f.** rez-de-chaussée *m inv*; **first f.** *Br* premier étage, *Am* rez-de-chaussée; **to live on the fifth f.** *Br* habiter au cinquième, *Am* habiter au qua-

trième; **we live on the same f.** nous habitons sur le même palier, nous sommes voisins de palier; **on the f. above/below** à l'étage du dessus/dessous; **we're ten floors up** nous sommes au dixième étage; **their offices are two floors down** leurs bureaux sont deux étages plus bas

3 *(of ocean)* fond *m*; *Min (of gallery)* sole *f*; **on the ocean f.** au fond de l'océan; **the forest f.** le sol de la forêt

VT 1 *(room)* *(with floorboards)* planchéier; *(with wooden blocks)* parqueter; *(with tiles)* carreler **2** *(knock down) (opponent)* terrasser, envoyer au tapis **3** *Fam (of problem, question)* **to f. sb** réduire qn à quia, clouer le bec à qn

▸▸ *TV* **f. assistant** assistant, -ante de plateau; **f. cleaner** (produit *m*) nettoyant *m* pour sols; **f. clerk** *(in hotel)* responsable *m* d'étage; *TV* **f. crew** personnel *m* de plateau; **f. housekeeper** *(in hotel)* gouvernante *f* d'étage; **f. manager** *(in department store)* chef *m* de rayon; *TV* régisseur, -euse de plateau; **f. plan** plan *m*; **f. polish** encaustique *f*, cire *f*, *Com* **f. price** prix *m* seuil; *Aut* **f. shift** levier *m* (de vitesses) au plancher; **f. show** spectacle *m* de cabaret; **f. tile** carreau *m*; *St Exch* **f. trader** commis *m*; *St Exch* **f. trading** cotation *f* à la corbeille; **f. waiter** *(in hotel)* garçon *m* d'étage

floorboard ['flɔ:bɔ:d] **N** planche *f*

floorcloth ['flɔ:klɒθ] **N** serpillière *f*

flooring ['flɔ:rɪŋ] **N 1** *(action)* *(with floorboards)* planchéiage *m*; *(with wooden blocks)* parquetage *m*; *(with tiles)* carrelage *m*; *(with large slabs)* dallage *m* **2** *(floor)* plancher *m*; *(tiles)* carrelage *m*

floorspace ['flɔ:speɪs] **N** *(of room etc)* surface *f* (couverte), superficie *f*; *(of vehicle)* surface au plancher; **there was barely enough f. for all of them** il y avait tout juste assez d'espace pour eux tous

floorwalker ['flɔ:wɔ:kər] **N** *Am* inspecteur, -trice, surveillant, -ante (de magasin)

floozie, floozy ['flu:zɪ] **N** *Fam* pouffiasse *f*

flop [flɒp] **N** *Fam* **1** *(failure)* four *m*, fiasco *m*, bide *m*; *(novel, product)* bide; *(person) (in life)* raté, -ée; *(in film, play)* nul, *f* nulle; **it was a f.** ça a fait un four *ou* un bide, c'était un fiasco **2** *Am (hotel)* hôtel *m* borgne; *(hostel)* asile *m* de nuit

VI (**-pp-) 1** *(fall)* faire plouf, faire floc; *(of person)* se laisser tomber, s'affaler; *(into water)* tomber; **to f. down on(to) a seat** tomber lourdement sur un siège, se laisser tomber comme un sac sur un siège **2** *Fam (fail)* échouer; *(of play, novel, product etc)* faire un bide; *(of jokes, sketch)* tomber à plat

flophouse ['flɒphaʊs] **N** *Am Sl* asile *m* de nuit

floppy ['flɒpɪ] **ADJ** *(hat)* mou; *(garment)* lâche, trop large; **with f. ears** à oreilles pendantes

N *Comput* disquette *f*, disque *m* souple; **on f.** sur disquette

▸▸ *Comput* **f. disk** disquette; **f. (disk) controller** contrôleur *m* d'unité de disquette; **f. (disk) drive** unité *f* de disquettes

floptical ['flɒptɪk(ə)l] **ADJ** *Comput*

▸▸ **f. disk** *(hard)* disque *m* optique; *(floppy)* disquette *f* optique; **f. drive** *(hard)* unité *f* de disque optique; *(floppy)* unité de disquette optique

flora ['flɔ:rə] **N** *(of country, region)* flore *f*; **the f. and fauna of a region** la flore et la faune d'une région

floral ['flɔ:rəl] **ADJ** floral, -aux; **dress with a bold f. design** robe *f* à grands ramages

▸▸ **f. tribute** bouquet *m ou* gerbe *f* de fleurs; *(funeral wreath)* couronne *f* de fleurs

floret ['flɒrɪt] **N** *Bot* fleuron *m*

florid ['flɒrɪd] **ADJ** *(style etc)* fleuri, orné à l'excès; *(complexion)* coloré

Florida ['flɒrɪdə] **N** Floride *f*

florin ['flɒrɪn] **N** *Br Hist (coin)* pièce *f* de deux shillings

florist ['flɒrɪst] **N** fleuriste *mf*; **f.'s (shop)** magasin *m* de fleurs; **to go to the f.'s** aller chez le fleuriste

floss [flɒs] **N** *(dental)* **f.** fil *m* (de soie) dentaire

VT to f. one's teeth se nettoyer les dents avec du fil dentaire

▸▸ *Tex* **f. silk** bourre *f* de soie

flotation [fləʊ'teɪʃən] **N 1** *Com (of company)* lancement *m*; *(onto Stock Market)* introduction *f* en Bourse **2** *Fin (of loan)* émission *f*; *(of currency)* flottement *m*

flotilla [flə'tɪlə] **N** *Naut* flottille *f*, *(of small boats)* escadrille *f*

flotsam ['flɒtsəm] **N** épave(s) *f(pl)* flottante(s); **f. and jetsam** choses *fpl* refoulées par la mer; **sometimes the f. and jetsam of a wrecked ship would be washed up on the shore** parfois les restes d'une épave, refoulés par la mer, venaient s'échouer sur la rive; *Fig* **the f. of the war/of society** *(people)* les laissés-pour-compte *mpl* de la guerre/de la société

flounce [flaʊns] **N 1** *(of indignation, impatience)* mouvement *m* vif; **with a f. of her long skirt, she marched out of the room** elle sortit de la pièce d'un pas ferme, en faisant voltiger sa longue jupe **2** *Sewing* volant *m*

VI to f. in/out/off entrer/sortir/partir brusquement; **don't you go flouncing off!** ne te sauve pas si vite!

VT *Sewing* garnir de volants; **flounced skirt** jupe *f* à volants

flouncy ['flaʊnsɪ] **ADJ** *(dress, skirt)* froufroutant

flounder[1] ['flaʊndər] **N** *(fish)* flet *m*, carrelet *m*

flounder[2] **VI** *(in water, mud etc)* patauger; **to f. about in the water** se débattre dans l'eau; **to f. along** avancer en trébuchant; **to f. in a speech/course** patauger dans un discours/cours

flour ['flaʊər] **N** farine *f*; **to dust sth with f.** (en)fariner qch; **potato f.** fécule *f* de pommes de terre

VT (en)fariner, saupoudrer de farine

▸▸ **f. dredger** saupoudreuse *f* à farine; **f. mill** minoterie *f*

flourbin ['flaʊəbɪn] **N** farinière *f*, huche *f*, maie *f*

flourish ['flʌrɪʃ] **N 1** *(in writing, style)* fioriture *f*; *(after signature)* parafe *m* **2** *(gesture)* grand geste *m*; *(of sword)* brandissement *m*; **with a f. of his sword/umbrella** en brandissant son épée/parapluie; **to raise one's hat with a f.** saluer d'un grand coup de chapeau; **to carry things off with a f.** faire les choses avec panache **3** *Mus* fioriture(s) *f(pl)*, ornement *m*; *(of trumpets)* fanfare *f*

VI *(of plant)* croître, se développer; *(of person, business etc)* être florissant, prospérer; *(of arts)* fleurir; **to f. in sandy soil** se plaire dans un terrain sablonneux; **trade is flourishing** le commerce est prospère

VT *(sword, stick, newspaper etc)* brandir

flourishing ['flʌrɪʃɪŋ] **ADJ** *(plant, industry etc)* florissant; *(business)* prospère

floury ['flaʊərɪ] **ADJ 1** *(hands etc)* enfariné, couvert de farine **2** *(potatoes, texture etc)* farineux; *(rolls)* saupoudré de farine

flout [flaʊt] **VT** *(person's authority, convention etc)* faire fi de; *(person)* passer outre à la volonté de

Attention: ne pas confondre avec le verbe **to flaunt.**

FLOW [fləʊ] **N 1** *(movement) (of liquid)* coulée *f*, *(of river, blood)* écoulement *m*; *Elec (of current)* passage *m*; *(of air, fuel etc)* passage, arrivée *f*; *(of tide)* flot *m*, flux *m*; *Fin (of capital)* mouvement *m*; *(of information)* circulation *f*; **a steady f. of immigrants** un flot ininterrompu d'immigrés; **a f. of ideas/proposals** un flot d'idées/de propositions; **f. of funds** mouvement de fonds; **f. of money** flux monétaire; **the speaker was interrupted in full f.** l'orateur a été interrompu en plein discours; **to follow the f. of sb's argument** suivre le fil de l'argumentation de qn; **to go with the f.** suivre le mouvement

2 *(volume) (of liquid)* volume *m*; *(of river, pump, electric current)* débit *m*; **the f. of traffic** le flux de la circulation; **there was a heavy f. of traffic** il y avait beaucoup de circulation

3 *(stream)* courant *m*, cours *m* (d'eau); *(of lava)* coulée *f*; *(of blood etc)* flot *m*; *Physiol* **menstrual f.** règles *fpl*

4 *Sewing (of garment)* drapé *m*

VI 1 *(of water, river)* couler, s'écouler; *(of electric current, blood in veins)* circuler; *(of traffic, crowd)* s'écouler; *(of hair etc)* flotter; *(of tide)* monter, remonter; *Fin (of capital, money)* circuler; **to f. into the sea** se verser dans la mer; **lava that flows down the mountain** lave qui s'écoule le long de la montagne; **the tears flowed down her cheeks** les larmes coulaient sur ses joues; **blood flowed from the wound** le sang s'écoulait de la blessure; **blood flowing to the head** sang qui afflue à la tête; *Prov* **land flowing with milk and honey** pays *m* de cocagne, terre *f* d'abondance; **you can feel the energy f.** on sent circuler l'énergie; **the work is flowing nicely** le travail suit bien son cours; **the ideas are really flowing today** les idées affluent aujourd'hui

2 *(of literary style, prose)* couler; **to keep the conversation flowing** entretenir la conversation; **these two paragraphs don't f.** ces deux paragraphes ne s'enchaînent pas bien; **the film flows very nicely** tout s'enchaîne vraiment bien dans le film

3 *(result)* dériver, découler (**from** de); **God from whom all blessings f.** Dieu, de qui découlent toutes les grâces

▸▸ **f. chart** organigramme *m*; **f. diagram** organigramme, graphique *m* d'évolution; *Comput* ordinogramme *m*; *Comput* **f. path** branche *f* de traitement

▸ **flow away VI** *(of liquid)* s'écouler; **the small craft flowed away on the tide** le petit bateau s'éloigna dans le flot de la marée

▸ **flow back VI** *(of water)* refluer; *(in pipe etc)* regorger

▸ **flow in VI** *(of liquid)* entrer; *(of people, money)* affluer; **the stream flowed in to the river** le ruisseau se jetait dans la rivière

▸ **flow out VI** *(of liquid)* sortir, s'écouler; *(of people)* partir; *(of money)* disparaître; **people flew out of the country in their thousands** les gens quittèrent le pays par milliers

flower ['flaʊər] **N 1** fleur *f*; **in f.** *(of plant)* en fleur; **in full f.** en plein épanouissement; **to burst into f.** fleurir; *Fig* **in the (first) f. of youth** dans la première fleur de la jeunesse; **to put flowers on a grave** fleurir une tombe; **no flowers by request** ni fleurs ni couronnes **2** *Chem* **flowers of sulphur** fleurs *fpl* de soufre **3** *Fig (best part) (of an army etc)* fine fleur *f*, crème *f*

VI *(of plant) (action)* fleurir; *(state)* être en fleur; *(of art etc)* fleurir, s'épanouir

▸▸ **f. arrangement** *(art)* art *m* floral; *(example)* composition *f* florale; **f. arranging** art floral; **f. child** hippie *mf* *(surtout des années soixante)*; **f. garden** jardin *m* d'agrément; **f. girl** *(selling flowers)* marchande *f* de fleurs; *(at wedding)* = petite fille *f* qui porte des

fleurs dans un mariage, ≃ demoiselle *f* d'honneur; **f. head** capitule *m*; **f. market** marché *m* aux fleurs; **f. people** hippies *mpl* *(surtout des années soixante)*; **f. power** = pacifisme *m* prôné par les hippies, surtout dans les années soixante; **f. seller** *(in street)* marchand, -ande de fleurs; **f. show** exposition *f* de fleurs; *(outdoors, on a large scale)* floralies *fpl*; **f. vase** vase *m* à fleurs

flowerbed ['flaʊəbed] **N** plate-bande *f*, *pl* plates-bandes; *(round)* corbeille *f*

flowered ['flaʊəd] **ADJ** *(material, wallpaper etc)* à fleurs

-flowered ['flaʊəd] **SUFF** white/yellow/*etc*-f. à fleurs blanches/jaunes/*etc*; **many-f.** multiflore

flowering ['flaʊərɪŋ] **ADJ 1** *(in flower) (garden, plant)* fleuri, en fleur **2** *(that flowers) (shrub)* à fleurs

N *(of plant)* fleuraison *f*; *Fig* **her late f. as an artist** son épanouissement tardif en tant qu'artiste

flowerpot ['flaʊəpɒt] **N** pot *m* de fleurs; *(ornamental)* cache-pot *m inv*

flowery ['flaʊərɪ] **ADJ 1** *(meadow)* fleuri; *(dress, carpet)* à fleurs **2** *(language, speech)* fleuri

flowing ['fləʊɪŋ] **ADJ** *(style etc)* coulant, fluide; *(movement)* fluide; *(hair)* tombant *(dans le cou)*; *(beard)* long; **a fast f. stream** un ruisseau au cours rapide

flowline ['fləʊlaɪn] **N** *(on organization chart)* ligne *f* de jonction de symboles

flowmeter ['fləʊmiːtər] **N** *(for liquid etc)* débitmètre *m*, indicateur *m* d'écoulement *ou* de débit

flown PP *see* **fly³**

flu [fluː] **N** *Med* grippe *f*; **I've got (the) f.** j'ai la grippe, je suis grippé; **a bad dose** *or* **case of (the) f.** une mauvaise grippe

▸▸ **f. epidemic** épidémie *f* de grippe; **f. jab** vaccin *m* contre la grippe; **f. virus** virus *m* de la grippe

flub [flʌb] *Am Fam* **N** gaffe *f*, bourde *f*

VI (-bb-) faire une gaffe, gaffer

VT to f. a question répondre de travers à une question

fluctuate ['flʌktjʊeɪt] **VI 1** fluctuer; *(of pulse, heartbeat)* être irrégulier; *(of conditions etc)* varier; *Fin (of exchange rate, share prices)* fluctuer; **to f. between sth and sth** osciller entre qch et qch **2** *(of person) (in one's opinions etc)* vaciller, balancer

fluctuating ['flʌktjʊeɪtɪŋ] **ADJ** *(temperature etc)* variable; *(rate, prices)* oscillant, fluctuant; *(heartbeat)* irrégulier; *(interest)* variable, fluctuant

fluctuation [flʌktjʊ'eɪʃən] **N** *(of temperature etc)* variations *fpl*; *(of support, interest)* fluctuation(s) *f(pl)*; *Fin* **exchange f.** fluctuation(s) *f(pl)* du change

flue [fluː] **N 1** *Constr* tuyau *m* de cheminée, conduit *m* de fumée **2** *Mus (of organ)* bouche *f* (de tuyau d'orgue)

▸▸ **f. boiler** chaudière *f* à tubes-foyers; **f. brush** hérisson *m inv*; *Mus* **f. pipe** *(of organ)* tuyau à bouche; **f. stop** jeu *m* de flûte

fluency ['fluːənsɪ] **N** *(of speech, style)* facilité *f*; **her f. in French** son aisance à s'exprimer en français

fluent ['fluːənt] **ADJ** *(speech etc)* coulant, facile; **to be a f. speaker** s'exprimer avec aisance; **he is a f. speaker of French, he speaks f. French, he is f. in French** il parle le français couramment

fluently ['fluːəntlɪ] **ADV** *(to speak a language, read a language)* couramment; *(to express oneself)* avec facilité, avec aisance

fluff [flʌf] **N 1** *(of fabric)* duvet *m*; *(of wool)* coton *m*; **a bit of f.** une peluche; *Old-fash-*

ioned Br Fam (girl) une poule; **(pieces of) f.** *(under bed etc)* moutons *mpl* **2** *(of rabbit etc)* fourrure *f* douce; *(of chicks)* duvet *m* **3** *Theat Fam (mistake)* raté *m* **4** *(trifle)* frivolités *fpl*

VT 1 = **fluff out, fluff up 2** *Fam (entrance, line, exam, interview)* rater, louper; *Sport* **to f. a shot** rater un coup

▸ **fluff out, fluff up VT SEP** *(one's hair, cushions)* faire bouffer; **to f. up its feathers** *(of bird)* hérisser ses plumes; **f. up the potatoes with a fork** fouetter la purée avec une fourchette

fluffy ['flʌfɪ] **ADJ** *(sheet)* pelucheux; *(woollen material) (naturally)* duveteux; *(after wear)* pelucheux; *(chick, beard, hair etc)* duveteux; *(clouds)* cotonneux; *(mashed potatoes, cake mixture)* léger et mousseux

▸▸ **f. toy** *(jouet m* en) peluche *f*

fluid ['fluːɪd] **ADJ** *(substance)* fluide, liquide; *Tech (transmission)* fluide; *(style etc)* coulant, facile; *(movement, grace)* fluide, coulant; *(opinions etc)* changeant, inconstant; **industry in a f. state** industrie en voie de transformation rapide

N fluide *m*, liquide *m*; **body fluids** sécrétions *fpl*; *Med* **fluids only** liquides uniquement

▸▸ *Tech* **f. clutch** embrayage *m* hydrodynamique; **f. ounce** *(in UK)* = 0,028 litre; *(in US)* = 0,03 litre

fluidity [fluː'ɪdɪtɪ] **N** *(of style etc)* fluidité *f*, aisance *f*; *(of opinions etc)* caractère *m* changeant *ou* fluctuant

fluke¹ [fluːk] **N 1** *(fish)* flet *m* **2** *(worm) (in liver)* douve *f*

▸▸ **f. worm** *(in liver)* douve

fluke² **N 1** *Naut (of anchor)* patte *f*, aile *f* **2** *(of whale)* **flukes** nageoires *fpl*

fluke³ *Fam* **N** *(coincidence)* hasard *m*; *(stroke of luck)* coup *m* de veine, coup de pot; **it was a pure f.** c'était un véritable coup de veine *ou* de pot; *(just coincidence)* c'était un pur hasard; **his success was due to a f.** c'est un hasard qu'il ait réussi; **by a pure f.** purement par hasard

ADJ that was a f. goal il a marqué ce but complètement par hasard; **it was a f. guess** c'est par hasard qu'il a deviné juste

fluky ['fluːkɪ] **ADJ** *Fam (person)* chanceux; **that was a f. goal** il a marqué ce but complètement par hasard; **it was a f. guess** c'est par hasard qu'il a deviné juste

flume [fluːm] **N 1** *(of watermill)* buse *f* **2** *(for logs etc)* canal *m* d'amenée; *(water chute in amusement park)* toboggan *m* **3** *Am (ravine)* ravin *m*

flummox ['flʌməks] **VT** *Fam* réduire à quia

flung PT, PP *see* **fling**

flunk [flʌŋk] *esp Am Fam* **VI** *(in exam)* se faire recaler, se faire coller

VT 1 *(of teacher) (person in exam)* recaler, coller **2** *(of student) (exam)* rater, se faire coller *ou* recaler à

flunkey ['flʌŋkɪ] **N** *Pej* laquais *m*

fluorescence [flʊə'resəns] **N** fluorescence *f*

fluorescent [flʊə'resənt] **ADJ** fluorescent
▸▸ **f. lighting** éclairage *m* au néon

fluoridation [flʊərɪ'deɪʃən] **N** *Chem* fluoration *f*

fluoride ['flʊəraɪd] **N** *Chem* fluorure *m*
▸▸ **f. toothpaste** dentifrice *m* au fluor

fluorine ['flʊəriːn] **N** *Chem* fluor *m*

fluoroscope ['flʊərəskəʊp] **N** *Med* fluoroscope *m*

flurry ['flʌrɪ] **N 1** *(of snow)* rafale *f* **2** *(agitation)* agitation *f*, bouleversement *m*, émoi *m*; **f. of excitement/protest** vague *f* d'excitation/de protestations

VT to get flurried perdre la tête

flush¹ **N 1** *(of lavatory)* chasse *f* (d'eau); *(of* *drain)* curage *m*; **to pull the f.** tirer la chasse (d'eau) **2** *(of light, beauty etc)* éclat *m*; *(of emotion etc)* accès *m*; *(of enthusiasm)* élan *m*; **in the first f. of victory** dans l'ivresse de la victoire; **in the first f. of youth** dans le premier éclat de la jeunesse **3** *(redness of face)* rougeur *f*, *Med* suffusion *f*; **the words brought a f. to her cheeks** ces mots l'ont fait rougir

VT 1 *(water)* faire jaillir; **to f. a drain** donner une chasse à un égout; **to f. the lavatory** tirer la chasse d'eau; **to f. sth down the lavatory** jeter qch dans les toilettes (et tirer la chasse d'eau) **2** *(redden)* faire rougir; **the exercise had flushed their cheeks** l'exercice leur avait fait monter le sang au visage

VI 1 *(of person)* rougir (**with** de); **he** *or* **his face flushed** il a rougi; **she flushed crimson** elle est devenue écarlate **2** *(in lavatory) (of person)* tirer la chasse d'eau; **the lavatory isn't flushing properly** la chasse d'eau ne fonctionne pas bien

▶ **flush away VT SEP** *(dispose of in lavatory)* jeter dans les toilettes (et tirer la chasse d'eau)

VI it wouldn't f. away ça ne voulait pas partir

flush² N *Cards (in poker)* flush *m*, longue couleur *f*; **straight f.** quinte *f* flush

flush³ ADJ **1** *(surface etc)* de niveau; *(door, lock etc)* encastré; *(screw, nail)* noyé; *(rivet)* à tête noyée *ou* perdue; **to be f. with sth** être à fleur de qch, être de niveau avec qch; **f. mounted** monté à fleur; **f. with the ground** à ras de sol **2** *Fam* **to be f. (with money)** *(of person)* être en fonds

ADV 1 *Typ* **f. left/right** justifié à gauche/droite **2** *(fit, be positioned)* **this piece has to fit f. into the frame** ce morceau doit être de niveau avec la charpente

flush⁴ VT *(in hunting) (partridge etc)* (faire) lever, faire partir

▶ **flush out VT SEP 1** *(force to emerge)* forcer à sortir, faire sortir de force; *(force to reveal oneself)* faire se trahir; **they used tear gas to f. the students out** ils ont utilisé des gaz lacrymogènes pour faire sortir les étudiants **2** *(clean)* rincer par circulation d'eau; **to f. out a drain** donner une chasse à un égout

flushed [flʌʃt] ADJ *(face)* empourpré, congestionné; **f. with anger/joy** rouge de colère/plaisir; **f. with success** exalté par le succès

fluster ['flʌstər] N agitation *f*, trouble *m*; **in a f.** paniqué

VT *(person)* décontenancer; *(cause to panic)* faire perdre la tête à; *(make nervous)* rendre nerveux; **to get flustered** se troubler, perdre contenance

VI he doesn't f. easily il ne se trouble pas facilement, il ne perd pas facilement contenance

flustered ['flʌstəd] ADJ *(look)* paniqué; *(reaction)* de panique; **it was a rather f. Jim that came out of the meeting** Jim était plutôt décontenancé quand il est sorti de la réunion

flute [fluːt] N **1** *Mus* flûte *f* traversière; **transverse f.** flûte traversière; *Theat* **the Magic F.** la Flûte Enchantée **2** *(groove) (of column)* cannelure *f* **3** *(glass)* flûte *f*

▶▶ **f. glass** flûte *f*; **f. player** joueur, -euse de flûte, flûtiste *mf*; **f. stop** *(on organ)* jeu *m* de flûte

fluted ['fluːtɪd] ADJ *(wood etc)* à cannelures; *(column)* cannelé

fluting ['fluːtɪŋ] N *(no pl) (grooves)* cannelures *fpl*

flutist ['fluːtɪst] N *esp Am Mus* flûtiste *mf*

flutter ['flʌtər] N **1** *(of bird)* voltettement *m*; *(of wings, eyelids)* battement *m*; *(of heart)* palpitation *f*; *(of flag)* flottement *m*; *(of*

sound) pulsation *f*; *(on tape)* pompage *m*; **she thinks she can get whatever she wants with a f. of her eyelashes** elle croit pouvoir obtenir tout ce qu'elle veut d'un simple battement de cils

2 *Fig (agitation)* agitation *f*, trouble *m*; **to be in a f. of excitement** *or Fam* **all in a f.** être tout en émoi

3 *Br Fam (bet)* **to have a little f.** faire un ou deux petits paris; *(in gambling house etc)* risquer de petites sommes au jeu; **to have a f. on the horses** risquer de petites sommes au tiercé

VI *(of birds, insects) (fly)* voleter; *(flap wings)* battre des ailes; *(of flag etc)* flotter, s'agiter (au vent); *(of heart)* palpiter; *(of pulse)* battre irrégulièrement; **to make sb's heart f.** faire tressaillir le cœur de qn; **the letter fluttered to the ground** la lettre a volé par terre; **the pigeons fluttered off** *or* **away** les pigeons s'éloignèrent en voletant; **he was fluttering about nervously** il s'agitait nerveusement; **she fluttered happily round the house** elle virevoletait gaiement dans toute la maison

VT to f. its wings *(of bird)* battre des ailes; **she fluttered her eyelashes at him** elle l'a regardé en battant des cils

fluvial ['fluːvɪəl] ADJ fluvial, -aux

flux [flʌks] N **1** *Med (of blood etc)* flux *m* **2** *(constant change)* changement *m* continuel; **to be in a (constant) state of f.** être sujet à des changements fréquents **3** *Phys* flux *m* **4** *Metal* fondant *m*, flux *m*; **gold f.** *(in glassmaking)* aventurine *f*

fluxion ['flʌkʃən] N *Med (of blood etc)* fluxion *f*

fluxmeter ['flʌksmiːtər] N *Phys* fluxmètre *m*

fly¹, *pl* **flies** [flaɪ, -z] N **1** *(insect)* mouche *f*; **they were dying** *or* **dropping like flies** ils tombaient comme des mouches; **he wouldn't hurt a f.** il ne ferait pas de mal à une mouche; *Fam* **a f. in the ointment** os; *Fig* **to catch flies** bayer aux corneilles; *Fam* **there are no flies on her** elle n'est pas bête; **I wish I could be a f. on the wall** *(at that interview, meeting etc)* si je pouvais être une petite souris; *TV* **f.-on-the-wall documentary** documentaire *m* intimiste, documentaire avec caméra cachée

2 *Fishing* mouche *f*; **wet-f.** mouche mouillée *ou* noyée; **wet-/dry-f. fishing** pêche *f* à la mouche noyée/sèche

▶▶ **f. agaric** amanite *f* tue-mouches; **f. orchid** *(plant)* ophrys *m* mouche; **f. spray** bombe *f* insecticide; **f. swat(ter)** tapette *f* tue-mouches; **f. whisk** chasse-mouches *m inv*

fly² N **1** *(often in pl)* **flies, f.** *(of trousers)* braguette *f*; **your flies are** *or* **f. is undone** *or* **open** ta braguette est ouverte **2** *(roof)* double toit *m* **3** *Theat* **the flies** les cintres *mpl*

FLY³ *(pt* **flew** [fluː], *pp* **flown** [fləʊn]) VI **1** *(of bird etc)* voler; **a flock of geese flew across the sky** un troupeau d'oies traversa le ciel à tire d'aile; *Fig, Fam* **the bird has flown** l'oiseau s'est envolé; **to f. high** voler haut; *Fig (of person)* avoir de l'ambition

2 *Aviat (of aircraft, pilot, missile)* voler; *(of passenger)* prendre l'avion, voyager en avion; **I've never flown before** c'est la première fois que je prends l'avion; **it's cheaper to f.** il est moins cher de prendre l'avion; **I've never flown in a 747** je n'ai jamais voyagé en 747; **to f. blind** voler sans visibilité; **to f. over London** survoler Londres; **to f. across the Channel** traverser la Manche en avion; **we flew 400 miles** nous avons parcouru 640 kilomètres en avion; **who did you f. with?** *(which airline)* avec quelle compagnie est-ce que tu as voyagé?; **to f. direct** effectuer un vol direct; **to f. via London** faire escale à

Londres; **we f. to over a dozen destinations** *(of airline)* nous desservons plus d'une douzaine de destinations; **we f. to Berlin four days a week** nous avons des vols pour Berlin quatre jours par semaine; **the airline only flies to Hong Kong via Karachi** tous les vols de la compagnie à destination de Hongkong s'effectuent via Karachi; **they don't f. from Heathrow any more** ils n'ont plus de vols au départ de Heathrow

3 *(of hair etc)* flotter; *(of flag)* flotter, battre; **the American flag flew above the building** le drapeau américain flottait au-dessus du bâtiment

4 *(move quickly etc) (of person etc)* courir *ou* aller à toute vitesse; *(flee)* s'enfuir; *(of time)* filer; *(of cork etc)* voler, sauter en l'air; **the insults were really flying** les insultes fusaient de toutes parts; **to f. to sb's aid** voler au secours de qn; *Fam* **it's late, I must f.** il se fait tard, il faut que je me sauve; *Fam* **I flew home to change** j'ai filé à la maison pour me changer; **time is flying** le temps passe à toute vitesse; **the door flew open** la porte s'ouvrit brusquement; **to f. into a rage** *or Fam* **off the handle** s'emporter, sortir de ses gonds; **to f. into a temper** se mettre en colère; **to f. at sb** *(attack them)* se jeter sur qn; **to let f.** *(lose one's temper)* s'emporter; *(arrow)* décocher; *(string of insults)* lâcher; **to let f. at sb** *(abuse, reprimand)* passer un savon à qn, sonner les cloches à qn; *(hit)* flanquer un coup à qn; *Fam* **to send sb/sth flying** envoyer rouler qn/qch; **to f. (in)to pieces** *or* **to bits** éclater, voler en éclats; *Fig* **to f. in the face of the evidence/current thinking** aller à l'encontre de l'évidence/des idées actuelles; **to f. in the face of reason/logic** défier la raison/toute logique

VT 1 *Aviat (plane)* piloter; *(person, object)* emmener en avion, transporter par avion; **we'll f. it to you tomorrow** nous vous l'enverrons par avion demain; **we were flown to Norway** on nous a emmenés en Norvège en avion; **to f. ABC airlines** voyager avec la compagnie aérienne ABC; **several airlines f. this route** plusieurs compagnies aériennes empruntent cette route; **he had flown three missions** il avait effectué trois missions en vol; **I'd never flown the Atlantic before** je n'avais jamais traversé l'Atlantique en avion auparavant; **her employers flew her to the States** ses employeurs l'ont envoyée aux États-Unis en avion; **we're flying them home on the first flight** nous les rapatrions par le premier vol

2 *Naut (flag)* déployer; **the ship was flying the Italian flag** le bateau arborait le pavillon italien

3 **to f. a kite** faire voler un cerf-volant; *Fig* lancer un ballon d'essai; *esp Am* **go f. a kite!** *(go away)* fiche-moi le camp!; *(I'm not going to do it)* va te faire voir!

4 *(flee)* **to f. the country** s'enfuir du pays; *esp Am* **to f. the coop** disparaître; **to f. the nest** *(of fledgling, child)* quitter le nid

▶ **fly about, fly around VI** *(of bird)* voler çà et là; *(of butterfly)* voltiger; *Fig (of rumours)* courir; **there are lots of figures flying about** *or* **around** on entend tellement de chiffres différents

▶ **fly away VI** *(of bird etc)* s'envoler

▶ **fly by VI 1** *(of time)* passer à toute vitesse; **the time has flown by!** comme le temps a passé!; **as the days flew by** à mesure que les jours s'enfuyaient

2 *Aviat (of aircraft)* passer

▶ **fly in VI 1** *(arrive by aircraft)* arriver en avion

2 *(approach) (of pilot, aircraft)* arriver; **the planes flew in over the coast** les avions sont arrivés en survolant la côte

VT SEP *(transport by aircraft)* amener en avion; **the air force flew in supplies/rein-**

forcements les forces aériennes ont amené des ravitaillements/du renfort

▸**fly off** VI *(of bird, aircraft etc)* s'envoler; *(leave in aircraft)* partir en avion; *(of button, lid etc)* sauter
VT SEP *(transport by aircraft)* envoyer par avion; **they were flown off by helicopter** ils ont été évacués par hélicoptère

▸**fly out** VI **1** *(of bird)* sortir en volant
2 *(leave in aircraft)* partir en avion; **a medical team flew out to the disaster area** une équipe médicale s'est rendue en avion dans la région sinistrée
3 *(be ejected)* être éjecté; **the knife flew out of his hand** le couteau lui a échappé de la main
VT SEP *(transport by aircraft)* emmener en avion; **her husband's employer flew her out to be with him** l'employeur de son mari lui a payé le billet d'avion pur qu'elle aille retrouver celui-ci

▸**fly past** VI **1** *(of bird, aircraft)* passer (en volant); *Mil, Aviat (in formation)* exécuter un défilé aérien; *Fig* **he flew past on a bicycle** il est passé à toute vitesse en bicyclette
2 *(of time)* passer vite

▸**fly up** VI **1** *(of bird etc)* s'envoler; **I flew up from London on Saturday** j'ai pris l'avion depuis Londres samedi
2 *(become vertical) (of arm etc)* s'élever; **the other end of the broom flew up** l'autre extrémité du balai s'est relevée

fly⁴ ADJ **1** *Br Sl* malin, *f* -igne; *(scheme)* rusé, astucieux; **he's very f.** c'est un malin; **on the f.** en douce **2** *Am Sl (excellent)* génial, -aux, géant; *(stylish, attractive)* chouette

flyaway ['flaɪəweɪ] ADJ **1** *(hair)* indiscipliné **2** *(person)* léger, étourdi

flyblown ['flaɪbləʊn] ADJ *(meat)* plein *ou* couvert d'œufs de mouches

flyby ['flaɪbaɪ] N *Mil, Aviat* défilé *m* aérien

fly-by-night *Fam Pej* ADJ *(company etc)* douteux, véreux
N *(dishonest person)* personne *f* qui file à l'anglaise pour éviter de payer; *(who doesn't pay rent)* déménageur *m* à la cloche de bois; *(firm)* entreprise *f* douteuse *ou* véreuse

flycatcher ['flaɪkætʃər] N *(bird)* gobe-mouches *m inv*; *Am* moucherolle *f*; **spotted f.** gobe-mouches gris

fly-drive N formule *f* avion plus voiture
▸▸**f. holiday** formule avion plus voiture

flyer ['flaɪər] N = **flier**

fly-half N *Rugby* demi *m* d'ouverture

flying ['flaɪɪŋ] ADJ **1** *(bird, fish etc)* volant; *(ribbon, hair etc)* volant, léger; **they were hurt by f. glass** ils ont été blessés par des bris de verre; **unidentified f. object** objet *m* volant non identifié
2 *(rapid)* rapide; **to take a f. leap** *or* **jump over sth** franchir qch d'un saut
3 to pass an exam with f. colours réussir un examen haut la main
4 *(school)* d'aviation; *(staff)* navigant
5 *(fleeing)* en fuite
N **1** *(flight)* vol *m*; *(of plane)* pilotage *m*; *Aviat (activity)* aviation *f*; **he loves f.** *(as pilot)* il adore piloter; *(as passenger)* il adore prendre l'avion; **I don't like f.** *(as passenger)* je n'aime pas prendre l'avion; **I haven't done much f.** *(as pilot)* je n'ai pas beaucoup piloté; *(as passenger)* je n'ai pas pris l'avion très souvent; **night f.** vol *m* de nuit
2 *(of flag)* déploiement *m*
▸▸**f. ambulance** avion-ambulance *m, pl* avions-ambulances; **f. boat** hydravion *m*; **f. bomb** bombe *f* volante; *Constr* **f. buttress** arc-boutant *m, pl* arcs-boutants; **f. circus** *(exhibition)* voltige *f* aérienne; *(group)* groupe *m* de voltige aérienne; **f. club** aéro-club *m, pl* aéro-clubs; *Mil* **f. column** colonne *f* mobile, groupement *m* mobile; *Am Aviat* **f.**

corps corps *m* d'armée aérien; **f. doctor** médecin *m* volant; **the F. Dutchman** *(legend)* le Hollandais volant; *Zool* **f. fox** roussette *f*; **f. machine** machine *f* volante; *Ind* **f. picket** piquet *m* de grève volant; **f. saucer** soucoupe *f* volante; **the F. Squad** = brigade *f* de détectives britanniques spécialisés dans la grande criminalité; *Sport* **f. start** départ *m* lancé; **the runner got off to a f. start** le coureur est parti comme une flèche; *Fig* **the campaign got off to a f. start** la campagne a démarré sur les chapeaux de roues; **f. time** heures *fpl* ou temps *m* de vol; **200 hours f. time** 200 heures de vol; **f. visit** visite *f* éclair; **to pay a f. visit to London** faire une visite éclair à Londres

fly-kick N *Rugby* coup *m* de pied à suivre

flyleaf ['flaɪliːf] N *(of book)* page *f* de garde

Flymo® ['flaɪməʊ] N = tondeuse *f* à gazon sur coussin d'air

flyover ['flaɪəʊvər] N **1** *Br (elevated road)* pont *m* routier **2** *Am Aviat* survol *m*; *(ceremonial)* défilé *m* aérien
▸▸*Br* **f. crossing** croisement *m* à niveaux différents

flypaper ['flaɪpeɪpər] N papier *m* tue-mouches

fly-past N *Mil, Aviat* défilé *m* aérien

flypost ['flaɪpəʊst] VI coller illicitement des affiches

flyposting ['flaɪpəʊstɪŋ] N affichage *m* illégal

flysheet ['flaɪʃiːt] N **1** *(on tent)* auvent *m* **2** *(leaflet)* feuille *f* volante

fly-tipping N *Br* dépôt *m* d'ordures illégal

flyweight ['flaɪweɪt] N *Boxing (boxer, category)* poids *m* mouche; **f. champion** champion *m* poids mouche

flywheel ['flaɪwiːl] N *Tech etc* volant *m* (de commande)

FM [e'fem] N *Radio (abbr* **frequency modulation)** FM *f*, **FM radio** *(radio f)* FM; **a station on FM, an FM station** une station FM

f-number N *Phot* échelle *f* d'ouverture

FO [e'fəʊ] N *Br Admin (abbr* **Foreign Office)** ministère *m* des Affaires étrangères

foal [fəʊl] N poulain *m*, pouliche *f*; *(of donkey)* ânon *m*, bourriquet *m*; **mare in** *or* **with f.** jument *f* pleine
VI pouliner
VT *(colt, filly)* mettre bas

foam [fəʊm] N **1** *(on sea)* écume *f*, *(on beer)* mousse *f*, **waves white with f.** vagues moutonneuses; **to break into f.** *(of wave)* déferler; **f.-flecked** moucheté d'écume **2** *(from mouth)* bave *f*, écume *f* **3** *(artificial substance)* mousse *f*, **polystyrene f.** mousse *f* de polystyrène; **f.-backed** doublé de mousse
VI *(of sea etc)* écumer; *(of beer etc)* mousser; **to f. at the mouth** avoir l'écume aux lèvres; *(of dog etc)* baver; *Fam Fig (be furious)* écumer (de rage); **he was foaming at the mouth about the latest price rises** il écumait de rage en évoquant les dernières hausses de prix
▸▸**f. bath** bain *m* moussant; **f. fire extinguisher** extincteur à mousse carbonique; **f. rubber** caoutchouc *m* Mousse®

▸**foam up** VI mousser, faire de la mousse

foaming ['fəʊmɪŋ] ADJ *(sea, horse etc)* écumant; *(sea)* moutonnant; *(blood, saliva)* spumeux; *(beer etc)* moussant
▸▸*Hum* **f. ale** bière *f*

foamy ['fəʊmɪ] ADJ *(sea)* écumant; *(drink)* mousseux

fob [fɒb] N *(chain)* chaîne *f* (de gousset); *(pocket)* gousset *m*; *(watch)* montre *f* de gousset
▸▸**f. pocket** gousset *m*; **f. watch** montre de gousset

▸**fob off** VT SEP **1 to f. sb off** se débarrasser de qn; **they fobbed him off with some excuse** ils lui ont donné la première excuse venue; **she'll try to f. it off on(to) some unsuspecting buyer** elle essaiera de le vendre *ou Fam* fourguer à un acheteur peu soupçonneux **2 to f. sth off as sth** faire passer qch pour qch

f.o.b, FOB [efəʊ'biː] ADJ *Com (abbr* **free on board)** f. à b., FAB, FOB; **F. port of embarkation** FAB port d'embarquement

focal ['fəʊk(ə)l] ADJ **1** *Phys, Opt, Math* focal, -aux **2** *Med (infection)* focal, -aux
▸▸*Opt* **f. distance** distance *f* focale, focale *f*, *Opt* **f. length** distance focale, focale; *Phot* **f. plane shutter** obturateur *m* focal *ou* à rideau; **f. point** *Opt* foyer *m*; *Fig (of room)* point *m* de convergence; *(of discussion etc)* point central

focalization ['fəʊkəlaɪ'zeɪʃn] N focalisation *f*

fo'c'sle ['fəʊks(ə)l] N = **forecastle**

focus N *(pl* **foci, focuses** ['fəʊkəs, 'fəʊsaɪ, 'fəʊkəsɪz]) **1** *Opt, Math etc (of lens etc)* foyer *m*; **in f.** *(of image)* net, au point; *(of instrument)* réglé; **out of f.** *(of image)* flou, pas au point; *(of instrument)* non réglé, déréglé; **to bring sth into f.** *(image)* mettre qch au point; **to bring a problem into f.** mieux définir un problème, clarifier la nature d'un problème; **these unemployment figures bring the economic crisis into an even sharper f.** ces chiffres du chômage mettent la crise économique encore plus en relief; *Phot* **fixed-f. camera** appareil *m* à mise au point fixe
2 *(of discontent, unrest)* foyer *m*; *(of interest, attention)* centre *m*; *Med (of illness)* siège *m*; **she was the f. of attention** elle était le centre d'attention; *Med* **f. of infection** foyer d'infection; **these proposals have been the f. of much concern** ces propositions ont fait l'objet de profondes inquiétudes; **the organization will provide some kind of a f. for opposition to the project** l'organisation fournira un point de ralliement à l'opposition au projet; **this became a f. of people's discontent** le mécontentement s'est concentré là-dessus
VT *(-s-)* **1** *(rays of light etc)* concentrer *(*in dans; on sur*)*; *(rays)* faire converger; *(one's interest, concern)* centrer; *(one's energies)* concentrer; **all eyes were focused on him** il était le point de mire de tous les regards; **to f. one's attention on sth** concentrer son attention sur qch; **to f. attention on sth** attirer l'attention des gens sur qch
2 *(microscope, camera etc)* mettre au point; **to f. a camera on sth** faire la mise au point d'un appareil photo sur qch
VI **1 to f. on sth** *(with eyes)* fixer qch; *(of debate, speaker etc)* se concentrer sur qch; *Phot* **to f. on an object** mettre son point sur un objet
2 *(of light, sound etc)* converger *(*on sur*)*
▸▸*Phot* **f. control** *(on camera)* mise *f* au point; *Mktg, Pol* **f. group** groupe *m* témoin; *Phot* **f. knob** bouton *m* de mise au point; *Phot* **f. puller** responsable *m* point, assistant cameraman *m*

focusing ['fəʊkəsɪŋ] N *(of camera, microscope etc)* mise *f* au point
▸▸**f. screen** loupe *f* de mise au point

fodder ['fɒdər] N fourrage *m*; **green/dry f.** fourrage (en) vert/(en) sec
VT *(animal)* donner le fourrage à

foe [fəʊ] N *Lit* ennemi *m*, adversaire *m*

foetal ['fiːt(ə)l] ADJ *Biol* fœtal, -aux
▸▸**f. heartbeat** rythme *m* cardiaque du fœtus; **f. position** position *f* fœtale; **in a f. position** en position fœtale

foetid ['fiːtɪd] ADJ = **fetid**

foetus, *pl* **foetuses** ['fiːtəs, -əsɪz] N *Biol* fœtus *m*

fog [fɒɡ] N **1** *Met* brouillard *m*; **in the f.** dans le brouillard; *Fig* **I'm in a f.** je ne sais plus où j'en suis; **she was in a complete f. about what she was supposed to be doing** elle ignorait complètement ce qu'elle était censée faire; **he is in a f. on anything related to economics** il est complètement perdu pour tout ce qui touche à l'économie **2** *Phot (on negative)* voile *m*

VT (-gg-) **1** *Fig (ideas)* brouiller; *(person, issue)* embrouiller; **I am a bit fogged** je ne sais plus très bien où j'en suis; **don't be fogged by all the long words he uses** ne vous laissez pas embrouiller par ses grands mots **2** *Phot (negative)* voiler **3** *(mirror etc)* embuer, couvrir de buée

VI **1** = **fog up 2** *Phot (of negative)* se voiler
▸▸ **f. bank** banc *m* de brume; *Aviat etc* **f. dispersal** dénébulation *f*, *Br* **f. lamp** feu *m* de brouillard; **f. light** feu de brouillard; **f. signal** *Naut* signal *m* de brume; *Rail* pétard *m*
▸ **fog up** VI *(of spectacles, windows)* se couvrir de buée, s'embuer

fogbound ['fɒɡbaʊnd] ADJ *(airport)* bloqué par le brouillard

fogey ['fəʊɡɪ] N *Fam* **old f.** vieille baderne *f*, **I'm afraid I'm turning into a bit of an old f.** je crois que je suis en train de m'encroûter; **he dresses like such an old f.** il s'habille tellement vieux jeu; **young f.** pépère *m*

fogginess ['fɒɡɪnɪs] N **1** *(of weather)* temps *m* brumeux **2** *(of person's ideas)* confusion *f*, *Phot* voile *m*

foggy ['fɒɡɪ] ADJ **1** *(weather, climate etc)* brumeux; **on a f. day** par un jour de brouillard; **it's f.** il y a du brouillard; **due to f. conditions** pour cause de brouillard; **the roads are rather f.** il y a du brouillard sur les routes **2** *(photograph etc)* voilé; **to have only a f. idea of sth** n'avoir qu'une vague idée de qch; *Fam* **I haven't the foggiest (idea)!** je n'en ai pas la moindre idée!

foghorn ['fɒɡhɔːn] N *Naut* corne *f* de brume, sirène *f*, *Fam* **voice like a f.** voix *f* de stentor

foible ['fɔɪb(ə)l] N *(idiosyncrasy)* particularité *f*, *(weakness)* point *m* faible

foil[1] [fɔɪl] N **1** *(metal sheet, gold etc)* feuille *f*, **silver f.** feuille d'argent; *Culin* **cooking** *or* **kitchen f.** papier *m* aluminium; **sandwiches wrapped in f.** sandwiches enveloppés dans du papier aluminium **2** *(person, thing)* repoussoir *m*; **to serve as a f. to sb's beauty** servir de repoussoir à la beauté de qn **3** *Aviat, Naut (of hydrofoil)* patin *m*, aile *f* **4** *Archit (of arch etc)* lobe *m*

foil[2] N *Fencing* fleuret *m*; **foils** *(event)* escrime *f* au fleuret

foil[3] VT *(thwart) (attempt etc)* faire échouer; *(plan, plot)* contrecarrer; **to be foiled at all points** *(of person)* échouer sur toute la ligne; **foiled again!** encore raté!; **once again they have been foiled by their own incompetence** une fois encore ils ont échoué à cause de leur propre incompétence

foist [fɔɪst] VT refiler **(sth on sb** qch à qn); **to f. oneself on sb** s'imposer à qn *ou* chez qn; **I try not to f. my opinions/ideas on people** j'essaie de ne pas imposer mes opinions/idées à autrui

fold[1] [fəʊld] N **1** *(crease) (in paper, skirt etc)* pli *m*; **folds of fat** bourrelets *mpl* de graisse **2** *Geol* pli *m*, plissement *m*

VT **1** *(sheet of paper etc)* plier; **to f. sth in two** *or* **in half** plier qch en deux; **to f. sth in paper** envelopper qch dans du papier; **to f. sb in one's arms** enlacer qn, serrer qn dans ses bras; **to f. one's arms** (se) croiser les bras; **with folded arms** les bras croisés; **to f. one's hands** joindre les mains **2** *Culin* **f. the whites**

into the mixture incorporer les blancs dans le mélange

VI **1** *(of screen etc)* se (re)plier **2** *Fam (of business)* cesser ses activités; *Theat* **the play folded after a week** la pièce a été retirée de l'affiche au bout d'une semaine
▸ **fold away** VI *(of table etc)* se replier, être escamotable

VT SEP *(store)* plier et ranger; **f. your clothes away neatly** plie tes affaires et range-les; **I slept on a campbed which I folded away every morning** je dormais sur un lit de camp que je repliais tous les matins
▸ **fold back** VT SEP *(collar etc)* rabattre; *(bedcovers, page)* replier

VI *(of door etc)* se rabattre
▸ **fold down** VT SEP *(bedcovers)* replier

VI *(of seat etc)* se rabattre; *(of sofa)* se déplier
▸ **fold in** VT SEP *Culin* **to f. in the whites of the eggs** incorporer les blancs d'œufs
▸ **fold over** VT SEP plier; **she had folded the top of the paper over** elle avait replié le haut de la feuille par-dessus
▸ **fold under** VT SEP *(edges)* replier en dessous
▸ **fold up** VT SEP *(seat, table)* (re)plier; *(screen)* replier, fermer

VI se (re)plier

fold[2] N **1** *Agr (sheep)* **f.** parc *m* à moutons **2** *Fig (of Church, family)* sein *m*; **to return to the f.** *(of member of family)* rentrer au bercail; *(of politician etc)* rentrer dans les rangs; **to welcome sb back to the f.** accueillir l'enfant prodigue; **they welcomed Paul back to the f.** ils ont accueilli Paul comme l'enfant prodigue

VT *Agr (sheep)* (em)parquer

-fold [fəʊld] SUFF **three/eleven/twenty/etc-f.** *(in three/eleven etc parts)* en trois/onze/vingt/etc parties; *(to increase)* (par) trois/onze/vingt/etc fois

foldaway ['fəʊldəweɪ] ADJ *(bed, table)* pliant, escamotable; *(seat)* pliant, rabattable

foldback ['fəʊldbæk] N *TV etc* ré-injection *f*, retour *m*, play-back *m inv*

folder ['fəʊldər] N **1** *(for papers etc)* chemise *f* **2** *Com (leaflet)* prospectus *m* (plié) **3** *(device)* plioir *m* **4** *Comput (directory)* dossier *m*

folding ['fəʊldɪŋ] ADJ pliant; *(joint, shutter)* brisé; **car with a f. top** voiture *f* décapotable

N **1** *(of material etc)* pliage *m*; *(in bookbinding) (of pages)* pliure *f*, *Geol (of land)* plissement *m* **2** *Br Sl (paper money)* biffetons *mpl*, fafiots *mpl*
▸▸ **f. camera** appareil *m* à soufflet; **f. door** porte *f* (en) accordéon; **f. machine** *(for documents)* machine *f* à plier les documents; *Fam* **f. money** billets *mpl* de banque; **f. screen** paravent *m*; **f. seat** pliant *m*; **f. stool** pliant; **f. table** table *f* pliante *ou* escamotable; *(with extending sections)* table à battants; **f. tray** *(in plane, train)* tablette *f* (qui se relève)

foldout ['fəʊldaʊt] N dépliant *m*

foliage ['fəʊlɪdʒ] N feuillage *m*, frondaison *f*
▸▸ **f. plant** plante *f* cultivée pour son feuillage

foliate ['fəʊlɪeɪt] ADJ *Bot* feuillu

foliation [fəʊlɪ'eɪʃən] N **1** *(of plant)* foliation *f*, feuillaison *f* **2** *Archit (ornementation* f *en)* rinceaux *mpl* **3** *Geol (of rock)* foliation *f* **4** *(of book)* foliotage *m*

folic acid ['fəʊlɪk] N acide *m* folique

folio, *pl* **folios** ['fəʊlɪəʊ, -əʊz] N *(in bookbinding) (sheet)* folio *m*, feuille *f*, *Typ (page number)* numéro *m*; **(book in) f.** (livre *m*) in-folio *m inv*
▸▸ **f. book** livre *m* in-folio, in-folio *m inv*

folk [fəʊk] N *(pl* **folk,** *esp Am* **folks)** VOIR GRAMMAIRE A11 *(people)* gens *mfpl*; *(music)*

folk *m*; **I don't care what f. think** je me moque de ce que les gens pensent; **country f.** campagnards *mpl*; **my f./your f.** les miens, ma famille/les vôtres, votre famille; *esp Am Fam* **hi, folks!** salut, tout le monde!
▸▸ **f. concert** concert *m* de folk; **f. dance** danse *f* folklorique; **f. festival** festival *m* de folk; **f. medicine** remèdes *mpl* de bonne femme; **f. museum** musée *m* folklorique, musée des arts et traditions populaires, musée du folklore; **f. music** *(traditional)* musique *f* folklorique; *(contemporary)* musique folk, folk; **f. singer** *(traditional)* chanteur, -euse *f* de chansons folkloriques; *(contemporary)* chanteur, -euse folk; **f. song** *(traditional)* chanson *f ou* chant *m* folklorique; *(contemporary)* chanson folk; **f. tale** conte *m* folklorique

folklore ['fəʊklɔːr] N folklore *m*

folksy ['fəʊksɪ] ADJ *Fam (friendly)* sociable; *(smile, greeting, cheerfulness)* bon enfant; *(dress)* traditionnel

foll *(abbr* **following)** suiv

follicle ['fɒlɪk(ə)l] N *Anat, Bot etc* follicule *m*

FOLLOW ['fɒləʊ] VT **1** *(person, car, suspect etc)* suivre; **to f. sb about** suivre qn partout; **to f. sb up the stairs/into a room** monter l'escalier/entrer dans une pièce à la suite de qn; *Fam* **to f. one's nose** y aller à l'instinct **2** *(go along) (path, road, itinerary)* suivre; **the road follows the coast** la route longe la côte **3** *(succeed)* succéder à; **the years followed one another and nothing changed** les années passèrent et rien ne changea; **as sure as day follows night** aussi sûr que deux et deux font quatre; **in the months that followed his resignation** dans les mois qui ont suivi sa démission; **George IV was followed by William IV** Guillaume IV a succédé à George IV; **dinner followed by a dance** dîner suivi d'un bal; **how do you expect me to f. that?** comment veux-tu passer après un truc comme ça?; **following our correspondence** (comme) suite à notre échange de lettres **4** *(imitate, adhere to) (person)* être le disciple de; *(the old masters)* imiter; *(person's example, teaching, pattern, fashion)* suivre; *(diet)* s'assujettir à, suivre; **to f. instructions** suivre les consignes **5** *(practise, carry out) (profession)* exercer, suivre; *(career)* poursuivre; **to f. suit** *(do the same)* faire de même; **you're not following the music** vous ne suivez pas la musique **6** *(understand) (explanation etc)* suivre, comprendre; **I don't quite f. you** je ne vous comprends *ou* suis pas très bien; **I didn't f. why they killed him** je n'ai pas compris pourquoi ils l'ont tué **7** *(pay attention to) (speech etc)* prêter attention à; *(events, news, programme)* suivre; **I don't f. the tennis any more** je ne suis plus le tennis **8** *(support)* **to f. a football team** être supporter d'une équipe de foot

VI **1** *(come after) (of person, event)* suivre, venir après; **my husband is following later** mon mari viendra plus tard; **in the days that followed** dans les jours qui ont suivi; **a long silence followed** un long silence s'ensuivit; **roast beef with strawberries to f.** du rosbif, suivi par des fraises; **proceed as follows** procéder comme suit; **our method is as follows** notre méthode est la suivante; **what follows is a brief account** ce qui suit est un bref compte-rendu **2** *(result)* s'ensuivre, résulter **(from** de); **it follows that ...** il s'ensuit que ...; **it does not f. that ...** ça ne veut pas nécessairement dire que ... + *ind*; **it follows from this that ...** il en résulte que ...; **I don't see how that conclusion follows** je ne vois pas comment tu arrives/il arrive/*etc* à cette conclusion; *(in logic etc)* je ne vois pas comment cette conclusion s'ensuit; **that doesn't f.** pas nécessairement, pas forcément

3 *(understand)* suivre; **I don't f.** je ne suis pas ▸▸ *Cin, TV* **f. shot** plan *m* d'accompagnement

▸ **follow on** VI **1** *(come after)* suivre; **you go ahead, we'll f. on** partez en avant, nous vous suivons; **she said she would f. on later** elle a dit qu'elle nous rejoindrait plus tard

2 *(result)* **it follows on from this that ...** il en résulte que ...; **I don't see how that follows on at all** je ne vois pas du tout comment on en arrive là

3 *Cr* = reprendre la garde du guichet au commencement de la seconde partie du match (au lieu d'alterner avec l'autre équipe)

▸ **follow out** VT SEP *(orders)* exécuter; *(instructions)* suivre; *(investigation)* procéder à

▸ **follow through** VT SEP *(execute)* **to f. a project through (to the end)** poursuivre un projet jusqu'à sa conclusion; **she seems incapable of following anything through** on dirait qu'elle est incapable de mener quoi que ce soit à bien
VI *Sport* suivre le coup

▸ **follow up** VT SEP *(take further)* poursuivre; *Com (letter)* faire suivre d'une seconde lettre; *(person)* relancer; *(advantage)* poursuivre; *(enquiry, order etc)* donner suite à; *(opportunity)* saisir; *(success)* exploiter; *(victory etc)* donner suite immédiate à; *(tip-off)* suivre; **to f. up a clue** suivre une piste
VI *(add to previous action)* continuer; *(in selling)* faire de la relance; **he followed up with a right to the jaw** il a continué avec un droit à la mâchoire; **it's up to you now to f. up** c'est à toi d'agir maintenant

follower ['fɒləʊər] N **1** *(supporter)* partisan, -ane, disciple *mf*; *(of football club)* supporter *m*; **as followers of this programme will be aware, ...** comme les personnes qui suivent cette émission le savent, ...; **she had never really been much of a f. of the arts** elle ne s'était jamais beaucoup intéressée à l'art **2** *(servant) (of prince etc)* serviteur *m*; **the King and his followers** le roi et sa suite **3** *Mktg* suiveur *m*

following ['fɒləʊɪŋ] ADJ suivant; **on the f. day** le jour suivant, le jour d'après, le lendemain; **the f. Monday** le lundi suivant; **the f. resolution** la résolution que voici *ou* suivante; **the f. persons** les personnes dont les noms suivent, les personnes suivantes; **two days f.** deux jours de suite
N **1** *Pol etc (of leader)* partisans *mpl*; *(of prince)* suite *f*; **to have a big f.** avoir un grand nombre de partisans *ou* de disciples; **a television programme that commands a wide f.** une émission télévisée très suivie; **a team with a large f.** une équipe qui a beaucoup de supporters **2** *the* **f.** *(things, points)* ce qui suit; *(people)* les personnes suivantes *ou* dont les noms suivent; **the f. is the full list** voici la liste complète
PREP après, à la suite de
▸▸ *TV, Cin* **f. pan** pano *m* de poursuite; *Naut* **f. wind** vent *m* arrière

follow-me product N *Mktg* produit *m* tactique

follow-my-leader N *Br* = sorte *f* de jeu dans lequel les participants se déplacent en file indienne et doivent répéter les gestes de celui qui ouvre la marche

follow-on N *Cr* **to try to avoid** *or* **save the f.** = s'efforcer de marquer le nombre de points requis pour ne pas avoir à reprendre la garde du guichet

follow-the-leader N *Am* = **follow-my-leader**

follow-through N *Sport* fin *f* du coup

follow-up N suite *f*; *Com etc (of advertising etc)* relance *f*; *(of order)* suivi *m*; *Med (appointment)* examen *m* de contrôle
▸▸ **f. action** suite; **to take f. action on sth** donner suite à qch; *Med* **f. care** soins *mpl* post-hospitaliers; **f. interview** *(for job, research)* deuxième entretien *m*; **f. letter** lettre *f* de rappel *ou* de relance; *Mktg* **f. publicity** publicité *f* de rappel; **f. story** suite *f*; **f. system** système *m* de relance; **f. visit** *(medical)* visite *f* de contrôle; *(in selling)* visite de relance

folly ['fɒlɪ] N **1** folie *f*, sottise *f*; **an act of f., a f.** une folie; **it would be the height of f. to ...** ce serait la plus grande folie de ...; **this decision is sheer f. on the part of the government** c'est de la folie furieuse pour le gouvernement d'avoir pris cette décision **2** *Archit* folie *f*

foment [fə'ment] VT **1** *(discord, discontent)* fomenter **2** *Med (wound)* fomenter

fomentation [fəʊmen'teɪʃən] N **1** *(of discord, discontent)* fomentation *f* **2** *Med (of wound)* fomentation *f*

fond [fɒnd] ADJ **1** **to be f. of sb/sth** *(to like)* bien aimer qn/qch; **they are f. of each other** ils s'aiment bien; **I'm f. of you but I don't love you** je t'aime bien mais c'est tout; **he was very f. of me** il me portait beaucoup d'affection; **to become f. of sb** s'attacher à qn; **to be f. of music** être amateur de musique; **f. of sweets** friand de sucreries; **to be passionately f. of reading** adorer la lecture; **he is rather too f. of the sound of his own voice** il aime un peu trop s'écouter parler; **he was f. of the odd whisky** il aimait bien prendre un petit whisky de temps à autre

2 *(loving) (person, embrace)* affectueux, tendre; *(smile)* attendri; *(parent)* indulgent, bon; **with f. regards** *(in letter)* bien amicalement

3 *(memory)* agréable

4 *(foolish)* **in the f. hope of catching a glimpse of my idol** dans le fol espoir d'apercevoir mon idole; **she still retained the f. belief that he would return** elle persistait à croire qu'il reviendrait

fondant ['fɒndənt] N fondant *m*

fondle ['fɒnd(ə)l] VT *(person)* caresser, câliner; *(of lover, mother)* faire des câlins à; *(dog, cat etc)* caresser; **he was fondling her leg under the table** il lui caressait la jambe sous la table

fondly ['fɒndlɪ] ADV **1** *(lovingly) (to smile, stroke etc)* tendrement, affectueusement **2** *(naively) (to hope, believe etc)* naïvement; **I f. believed that ...** j'ai naïvement cru que ...

fondness ['fɒndnɪs] N **1** *(affection)* affection *f*, tendresse *f* (**for** pour, envers) **2** *(liking)* penchant *m*, prédilection *f*, goût *m* (**for sth** pour qch); *(strong liking)* goût profond (**for sth** de qch)

fondue ['fɒnduː] N *Culin* fondue *f*; **beef/cheese f.** fondue bourguignonne/savoyarde

font[1] [fɒnt] N *Rel* fonts *mpl* baptismaux

font[2] N *Typ, Comput* police *f*, fonte *f*
▸▸ **f. cartridge** cartouche *f* de polices; **f. cassette** cassette *f* de polices de caractères, cassette de fontes; **f. size** taille *f* de police

fontanel(le) [fɒntə'nel] N *Anat* fontanelle *f*

food [fuːd] N **1** *(no pl)* nourriture *f*; *(as opposed to drink)* manger *m*; *(for expedition)* vivres *mpl*, *Agr (for animals)* pâture *f*, *(for poultry)* mangeaille *f*, **f. and drink** le boire et le manger; *Com* **f. and non-f.** alimentaire et non-alimentaire; **there's some f. in the fridge** il y a à manger dans le Frigidaire®; **f. is expensive here** la nourriture est chère ici; **take some f. for the journey** prenez de quoi manger pendant le voyage; **a hotel where the f. is good** un hôtel où la cuisine *ou* la table est bonne; **to be off one's f.** ne pas avoir d'appétit; **to hunt** *or* **search for f.** *(of animal)* chercher sa nourriture; **f. for the mind** nourriture de l'esprit; **to give sb f. for thought** donner à penser à qn

2 *(type of food)* aliment *m*; **canned** *or Br* **tinned foods** aliments de conserve (en boîte); **health foods** *(for special diet)* produits *mpl* diététiques; *(natural foods)* produits alimentaires naturels
▸▸ **f. allergy** allergie *f* alimentaire; *Ecol* **f. chain** chaîne *f* alimentaire; **f. combining** combinaisons *fpl* alimentaires; **f. counter** *(in large store)* buffet *m*; **f. critic** critique *mf* gastronomique; **f. hall** rayon *m* d'alimentation; **f. hygiene** hygiène *f* alimentaire; **f. hygiene regulations** réglementation *f* sur l'hygiène alimentaire; **f. industry** industrie *f* alimentaire; **f. manufacturer** fabricant *m* de produits comestibles; **f. mixer** mixeur *m*, **f. packaging** emballage *m* des produits alimentaires; **f. poisoning** intoxication *f* alimentaire; **f. processor** robot *m* ménager *ou* de cuisine; **f. products** produits *mpl* alimentaires; *Am* **f. stamp** bon *m* alimentaire *(accordé aux personnes sans ressources)*; **the F. Standards Agency** = organisme *m* britannique de contrôle de la sécurité alimentaire; **f. value** valeur *f* nutritive

foodie ['fuːdɪ] N *Fam* fin gourmet *m*

foodstore ['fuːdstɔːr] N magasin *m* d'alimentation

foodstuff ['fuːdstʌf] N *(usu pl)* **foodstuffs** produits *mpl* alimentaires *ou* d'alimentation

fool[1] [fuːl] N imbécile *mf*, idiot, -ote; *Hist (jester)* fou *m*; **to play** *or* **act the f.** faire l'idiot; **to make a f. of oneself** se couvrir de ridicule; **no one likes being made a f. of** personne n'aime être ridiculisé; **I felt such a f.** me sentais vraiment idiot; **you'd be a f. to buy it** tu serais bête de l'acheter; **only a f. would pay that much for it** il faudrait être bête pour le payer aussi cher; **what f. was responsible for this decision?** quel est l'idiot *ou* l'imbécile qui a pris cette décision?; *Fam* **silly f.!** espèce d'idiot!; **what a f.!** quel idiot!; **he's no f.** il n'est pas bête; **he's a bigger f. than I thought** il est plus bête que je ne le pensais; **more f. you!** *(for believing them, buying it etc)* ce que tu es bête!; **if you agreed to that, then more f. you** si tu as accepté, c'est que tu es vraiment bête; **like a f., I agreed** comme un idiot, j'ai accepté; **any f. knows that** le premier imbécile venu sait cela; **some f. doctor** un imbécile de docteur; *Prov* **there's no f. like an old f.** il n'y a pire imbécile qu'un vieil imbécile; **to make a f. of sb** *(make look ridiculous)* exposer qn au ridicule, ridiculiser qn; *(tease)* se moquer de qn; **she's nobody's** *or* **no one's f.** c'est une maline *ou* une rusée; **to go on a f.'s errand** y aller pour des prunes *ou* pour le roi de Prusse; **I went on a f.'s errand trying to buy a turkey on Christmas Eve** j'ai essayé de trouver une dinde la veille de Noël mais il n'y a pas eu moyen; **the sales trip promised to be nothing but a f.'s errand** ce voyage d'affaires s'annonçait comme une perte de temps; **to send sb on a f.'s errand** envoyer qn décrocher la lune; **All Fools' Day, April Fools' Day** le premier avril; **they're living in a f.'s paradise** ils rêvent tout éveillés *ou* debout
ADJ *esp Am* stupide; **what a damn f. idea!** quelle idée stupide!
VI **1** *(act foolishly)* faire l'idiot; **stop fooling!** assez de bêtises!; **I'm becoming tired of your fooling** je commence à en avoir assez de tes bêtises **2** *(not be serious)* dire des blagues; **I was only fooling** je plaisantais
VT *(deceive)* duper; *(tease)* faire marcher; **you can't f. me** on ne m'a pas comme ça; **to**

(allow oneself to) be fooled se laisser duper; **to be fooled into doing sth** être amené à faire qch par duperie; **he fooled me into believing it** il me l'a fait croire; **he had tried to f. her into providing him with an alibi** il avait essayé de l'embobiner pour qu'elle lui fournisse un alibi; **they had me completely fooled** ils m'ont bien eu; **you didn't have me fooled for a moment** je n'ai pas été dupe un seul instant; **at that point I knew I had them fooled** à ce moment-là j'ai su qu'ils avaient mordu; *Iron* **her? a socialist? you could've fooled me!** elle? une socialiste? je ne l'aurais pas cru!

▸▸ *Miner* **f.'s gold** pyrite *f* de fer; **f.'s parsley** petite ciguë *f*

▸**fool about, fool around** VI **1** *(act foolishly)* faire l'imbécile; **to f. about** *or* **around with sth** *(with electrical appliance etc)* tripoter qch; *(with gun)* jouer avec qch; **I still enjoy fooling around with my old train set** j'aime encore bien m'amuser avec mon vieux train électrique; **she fooled around with drugs** elle a touché à la drogue **2** *(waste time)* traîner; **this is no time to f. around, young man** ce n'est pas le moment de traîner, jeune homme **3** *(have affair)* avoir *ou* se payer des aventures; **if I thought my husband/wife was fooling around …** si je pensais que mon mari/ ma femme me trompait …; **to f. around with sb** coucher avec qn; **if I found that he'd been fooling around while I was away** si j'apprenais qu'il m'avait fait des infidélités pendant que j'étais en voyage

▸**fool with** VT INSEP *Am (handle or play with carelessly) (electrical appliance etc)* tripoter; *(gun)* jouer avec; **to f. with drugs** toucher à la drogue; **don't f. with me!** ne me cherche pas!; **nobody fools with Mental Mickey** on ne plaisante pas avec Mental Mickey

fool² N *Br Culin* = dessert *m* à base de crème et de fruits; **gooseberry f.** crème *f* de groseilles (à maquereau)

foolery ['fuːlərɪ] N **1** *(stupidity)* **(piece of) f.** sottise *f*, folie *f* **2** *(playing the fool)* bouffonnerie *f*, pitreries *fpl*

foolhardiness ['fuːlhɑːdɪnɪs] N témérité *f*, imprudence *f*

foolhardy ['fuːlhɑːdɪ] ADJ téméraire, imprudent; **he was brave to the point of being f.** son courage frôlait la témérité

foolish ['fuːlɪʃ] ADJ *(stupid)* bête; *(imprudent)* insensé; **don't be so f.!** ne sois pas bête!; **it is f. of him to …** c'est stupide de sa part de …; **a f. hope** un fol espoir; **to do something f.** faire une bêtise; **to look f.** avoir l'air penaud; **to make sb look f.** tourner qn en ridicule, ridiculiser qn; **to feel f.** se sentir idiot

foolishly ['fuːlɪʃlɪ] ADV bêtement; **she looked at him rather f.** elle le regardait d'un air plutôt bête; **f., he decided to invade the country** il prit la folle décision d'envahir le pays

foolishness ['fuːlɪʃnɪs] N *(of person)* bêtise *f*, *(of plan, decision, idea etc)* stupidité *f*, **it is sheer f. to believe that …** il est absolument stupide de croire que …; **they've described the project as nothing but f.** ils ont qualifié le projet d'absurdité; *Old-fashioned* **what f. is this?** qu'est-ce que c'est que ces bêtises?

foolproof ['fuːlpruːf] ADJ *(mechanism)* indéréglable, indétraquable, de sûreté, à toute épreuve; *(scheme)* à toute épreuve, sûr; *(method, system)* infaillible; **it's f.** *(scheme etc)* il n'y a aucun risque, ça marche à tous les coups; **if this plan of yours is so f.** si ton plan est aussi sûr que tu le dis

foolscap ['fuːlskæp] N *esp Br (paper)* papier *m* ministre

FOOT [fʊt] N *(pl* **feet** [fiːt]*)* **1** *(of human, animal with cloven hoof)* pied *m*; *(of dog, cat, bird etc)* patte *f*; **the fore/hind feet** *(of horse)* le bipède antérieur/postérieur; **to put one's feet up** *(have a rest)* se reposer; **she put her feet up on the table** elle a mis les pieds sur la table; **to put one's f. in the door** *(of salesperson etc)* coincer son pied dans la porte; **to set f. on an island** mettre pied sur une île; **I shall never set f. in his house again** jamais je ne remettrai les pieds chez lui; **to rise to one's feet** *(stand)* se lever; *(in debate)* prendre la parole; **he jumped to his feet** d'un bond il fut debout; **to be on one's feet** se tenir debout; **she is on her feet all day** elle est sur ses jambes du matin au soir; **to be on one's feet again** être de nouveau sur pied; **he's constantly getting under my feet** je l'ai toujours dans les pattes; **on f.** à pied; **to go on f.** aller à pied; **under f.** sous les pieds; **to trample** *or* **tread sth under f.** fouler qch aux pieds; **feet first** les pieds devant

2 *(idioms) Fam* **to have/get cold feet** avoir la frousse; **to have one's feet firmly on the ground** avoir les pieds sur terre; **to have one f. in the grave** avoir un pied dans la tombe; **not to put a f. wrong** ne faire aucune erreur; **to catch sb on the wrong f.** prendre qn au dépourvu; *Tennis etc* prendre qn à contrepied; **to start** *or* **get off on the wrong f.** *(of two people)* faire un mauvais départ; **to put one's best f. forward** *(get on with task)* abattre la besogne; *(make rapid progress)* avancer vite *ou* à toute allure; **to put one's f. down** *(be firm)* faire preuve de fermeté; *(stop sth)* mettre le holà; *Aut Fam* mettre le pied au plancher; *Fam* **to put one's f. in it, to put one's f. in one's mouth** faire une gaffe; **to sit at sb's feet** être le disciple de qn; **to set sb on their feet** (re)mettre qn sur pied, (r)établir qn; **to begin to find one's feet** *(in new job, situation etc)* commencer à s'adapter; **to get a f. in the door** établir un premier contact; **it's not much of a job, but it's a f. in the door** ce n'est pas terrible comme travail, mais ça fait un contact; **to have feet of clay** être un colosse aux pieds d'argile; *Fam* **my f.!** mon œil!

3 *(no pl) Mil, Arch (infantry)* fantassins *mpl*, soldats *mpl* d'infanterie; **a regiment of f.** un régiment d'infanterie; **the 42nd F.** le 42ème d'infanterie

4 *(lower part) (of stocking)* pied *m*; *(of table)* bout *m*, pied *m*; *(of bed, tombstone, glass)* pied; *(of lake)* extrémité *f* inférieure; *(of column etc)* base *f*, *(of mountain, ladder)* pied, bas *m*; *Typ (of letter)* pied; **at the f. of the stairs** au bas *ou* en bas de l'escalier; **at the f. of the page/list** au bas de la page/liste

5 *Liter (in poetry)* pied *m*

6 *(measurement)* pied *m* anglais (= 30,48 cm); **square f.** pied carré; **cubic f.** pied cube; **to be five f.** *or* **feet high/thick** avoir cinq pieds de haut(eur)/d'épaisseur; **three f.** *or* **feet six (inches)** trois pieds six pouces; **a f. of water** un pied d'eau; **at 2,000 feet (above sea level)** à 2 000 pieds (au-dessus du niveau de la mer)

VT *Fam* **1** **to f. it** *(walk)* marcher **2** *(pay)* **to f. the bill** payer la note *ou* les dépenses

3 *Am* = **foot up**

▸▸ **f. control** commande *f* au pied; *Tennis* **f. fault** faute *f* de pied; **f. passenger** passager, -ère sans véhicule; *Br Mil* **f. patrol** patrouille *f* à pied; **f. pump** pompe *f* à pied; *Bot, Vet* **f. rot** piétin *m*; **f. scraper** gratte-pieds *m inv*; **f. soldier** *Mil* fantassin *m*; *(of political party)* militant, -ante de base; **f. spa** bain *m* de pieds à remous

▸**foot up** VT SEP *Am Fam (add up) (bill)* additionner

footage ['fʊtɪdʒ] N **1** *(length)* longueur *f* (en

pieds) **2** *Cin (length of film)* métrage *m* **3** *Cin (sequence, film)* séquences *fpl*

foot-and-mouth disease N *Vet* fièvre *f* aphteuse

football ['fʊtbɔːl] N **1** *(soccer)* football *m*; *Fam* foot *m*; *Am* football américain **2** *(ball)* ballon *m* (de football); *Fig* **it has become a political f.** c'est devenu une question que tous les politiciens espèrent utiliser à leur avantage

▸▸ **f. boot** chaussure *f* de football; *Br* **f. club** club *m* de football; **f. fan** supporteur, -trice d'une équipe de football; *Am* **f. field** terrain *m* de football; *Br* **f. ground** terrain *m* de football; **f. hooligan** hooligan *m*; **f. hooliganism** vandalisme *m*, hooliganisme *m*; **the F. League** = association *f* réunissant la majorité des clubs de football professionnels en Angleterre; *Br* **f. pitch** terrain de football; **f. player** *Br* joueur, -euse de football; *Am* joueur, -euse de football américain; *Br* **f. pools** ≃ Loto *m* sportif; **f. season** saison *f* de football; *Br Rail* **f. special** = train *m* mis en service spécialement pour un match de foot; **f. supporter** supporteur, -trice d'une équipe de football

footballer ['fʊtbɔːlər] N *Br* footballeur, -euse; *Am* joueur, -euse de football américain

footbath ['fʊtbɑːθ] N bain *m* de pieds

footbrake ['fʊtbreɪk] N *Aut* frein *m* à pédale *ou* à pied

footbridge ['fʊtbrɪdʒ] N pont *m* pour piétons; *(narrow)* passerelle *f*

footer ['fʊtər] N **1** *Comput* bas *m* de page **2** *Old-fashioned Br Fam (soccer)* foot *m*

footfall ['fʊtfɔːl] N **1** *(sound)* (bruit *m* de) pas *m*; **I heard a light f.** j'ai entendu un pas léger **2** *Mktg (people entering shop, airport etc)* taux *m* de fréquentation

foot-fault *Tennis* VI faire une faute de pied; VT *(of umpire)* **to f. a player** pénaliser un joueur pour faute de pied

footgear ['fʊtgɪər] N *(grosses)* chaussures *fpl*

foothills ['fʊthɪlz] NPL collines *fpl* basses *ou* avancées; *(of mountain range)* avant-monts *mpl*

foothold ['fʊthəʊld] N prise *f* pour le pied; **to get a f.** prendre pied; *Fig* **enemy troops gained a f. on the island** les troupes ennemies ont pris pied sur l'île

footie ['fʊtɪ] N *Br Fam (soccer)* foot *m*

footing ['fʊtɪŋ] N **1** **to lose one's f.** *(in bathing etc)* perdre pied; **to miss one's f.** poser le pied à faux **2** *(situation) (of person)* position *f*, condition *f*; *(of institution etc)* condition, état *m*; **on a war f.** *(of troops)* sur le pied de guerre; *(of country, economy)* en état de guerre; **to be on a sound f.** *(of company, economy)* être sain *ou* ferme *ou* bien établi; **to place two people on the same f.** mettre deux personnes au même niveau; **to be on an equal f.** être de pair *ou* sur un pied d'égalité *(with* avec*)*; **to be on a friendly f. with sb** avoir des rapports amicaux avec qn

▸**footle about, footle around** ['fuːt(ə)l] VI *Fam (waste time)* traînailler; **to f. about** *or* **around with sth** jouer avec qch, tripoter qch

footlights ['fʊtlaɪts] NPL *Theat* rampe *f*

footling ['fuːtlɪŋ] ADJ *Fam* insignifiant

footloose ['fʊtluːs] ADJ *(person)* libre; *(existence)* sans attaches; **to be f. and fancy-free** être libre comme l'air

footman, *pl* **footmen** ['fʊtmən] N valet *m* de pied

footnote ['fʊtnəʊt] N note *f* de bas de page; *Fig* détail *m*; **he is now little more than a f. to the history of the period** il n'a guère plus qu'un rôle d'arrière-plan dans l'histoire de l'époque

footpath ['fʊtpɑːθ] N sentier m (pour piétons); (alongside canal, railway) banquette f, accotement m; (in street) trottoir m

footplate ['fʊtpleɪt] N Rail (of railway engine) plate-forme f, pl plates-formes, tablier m

footplateman, pl **footplatemen** ['fʊtpleɪtmən] N Rail mécanicien m de locomotive

foot-pound N (pl **foot-pounds**) Phys (measurement) pied-livre m, pl pieds-livres

footprint ['fʊtprɪnt] N **1** empreinte f de pas; **footprints in the sand** (empreintes de) pas mpl sur le sable **2** (of object, appliance), Comput encombrement m **3** (of satellite) empreinte f

footrest ['fʊtrest] N (on chair, motorcycle) repose-pied(s) m, pl repose-pieds; Med porte-pieds m inv, repose-pied(s); (on bicycle) cale-pied m, pl cale-pieds

foot-second N (pl **foot-seconds**) Phys (measurement) pied m par seconde

Footsie ['fʊtsɪ] N (abbr **Financial Times-Stock Exchange 100 Index**) = principal indice boursier du Financial Times basé sur la valeur de 100 actions cotées à la Bourse de Londres

footsie N Fam **to play f. with sb** faire du pied à qn

footslog ['fʊtslɒɡ] VI (**-gg-**) marcher, faire la route à pied

footsore ['fʊtsɔːr] ADJ qui a mal aux pieds; **they arrived f. and weary** ils sont arrivés les pieds en compote et épuisés

footstall ['fʊtstɔːl] N Archit socle m

footstep ['fʊtstep] N **1** (sound) pas m; **I hear footsteps** j'entends des pas ou un bruit de pas **2** (footprint) (empreinte f de) pied m ou pas m; Fig **to follow** or **tread** or **walk in sb's footsteps** marcher sur les traces ou pas de qn; Fig **to follow in one's father's footsteps** suivre les traces de son père

footstool ['fʊtstuːl] N tabouret m (pour les pieds)

footwarmer ['fʊtwɔːmər] N chancelière f

footway ['fʊtweɪ] N chemin m (pour piétons)

footwear ['fʊtweər] N chaussures fpl

footwell ['fʊtwel] N Aut place f aux pieds

footwork ['fʊtwɜːk] N (in dancing, sports etc) jeu m de pieds ou de jambes; Fig **it required some rather fancy f. on his part** il a dû faire des pieds et des mains

footy ['fʊtɪ] = **footie**

fop [fɒp] N Pej bellâtre m, dandy m

foppish ['fɒpɪʃ] ADJ (man) qui met trop de recherche à sa toilette; (clothes, manners) d'une élégance affectée; (taste, elegance) bellâtre, de dandy

FOR [efəʊ'ɑːr] Com (abbr **free on rail**) franco wagon

FOR [fɔːr, unstressed fər]

| **PREP** | pour **2–5, 7–13, 16** ■ en raison de **7** ■ de **7** ■ à **9** ■ pendant **10** |
| **CONJ** | car |

PREP 1 (representing) **A f. Andrew** A comme André; **what's the Russian f. 'book'?** comment dit-on 'livre' en russe?

2 (as) **to have sb f. a teacher** avoir qn comme professeur; **f. the first time** pour la première fois

3 (in return for) **you can hire a car f. five pounds a day** on peut louer une voiture pour cinq livres par jour; **to sell sth f. ten euros** vendre qch dix euros; **three f. £5** trois

pour 5 livres; **to be paid f. one's services** recevoir un paiement pour ses services; **oh, f. some peace and quiet!** que ne donnerais-je pas pour un peu de tranquillité!

4 (in favour of) **he is f. free trade** il est partisan du libre-échange, il est pour le libre-échange; **I'm all f. it** je suis tout à fait pour; Law **judgment f. the plaintiff** arrêt m en faveur du demandeur

5 (purpose) **garments f. men** vêtements pour hommes; **can you give me something f. the pain?** est-ce que vous pouvez me donner quelque chose pour ou contre la douleur?; **f. books on gardening, try Jackson's bookshop** pour trouver des livres sur le jardinage, essayez la librairie Jackson

6 (in trouble) Fam **he's f. it!** ['fɔːrɪt], **he's in f. it!** ['ɪnfɔːrɪt] qu'est-ce qu'il va prendre!; **I really thought I was in f. it** j'ai bien crû que mon compte était bon

7 (because of) **to choose sb f. his/her ability** choisir qn en raison de sa compétence; **he's well known f. his views on taxation** il est célèbre pour ses opinions sur l'impôt; **she couldn't sleep f. the pain** elle ne pouvait pas dormir à cause de la douleur; **I feel all the better f. it** je me sens vraiment mieux, ça m'a fait du bien; **I'm a few million poorer and I'm all the better f. it** j'y ai laissé quelques millions et je ne m'en porte que mieux

8 (considering) **f. all the use he is, he might as well go and play** pour ce qu'il fait d'utile, il pourrait aussi bien aller jouer; **f. all the sense it made** pour ce que c'était clair

9 (direction) **ship (bound) f. America** navire à destination de l'Amérique; **the train f. London** le train pour ou à destination de ou en direction de Londres; **I'm leaving f. France** je pars pour la France; **his feelings f. you** ses sentiments envers vous ou à votre égard; **to swim f. sth** nager vers qch

10 (extent) **the road is lined with trees f. two miles** la route est bordée d'arbres pendant deux mil(l)es; **bends f. one mile** (on sign) virages sur un mil(l)e; **I'm going away f. a fortnight** je pars pour quinze jours; **he will be away f. a year** il sera absent pendant un an; **she won't be back f. a month** elle ne sera pas de retour avant un mois; **we have food f. three days** nous avons des vivres pour trois jours; **I lived there f. five years** j'y ai vécu (pendant) cinq ans; **I have not seen him f. three years** il y a trois ans que je ne l'ai pas vu; **I have been here f. three days** il y a trois jours que je suis ici, je suis ici depuis trois jours; **I had known him f. years** je le connaissais depuis des années, il y avait des années que je le connaissais; **f. now, f. the time being** pour l'instant, pour le moment SEE GRAMMAR B31

11 (intention, destination) **this box is f. you** cette boîte est pour vous; **it's f. you** (letter, phone call) c'est pour toi; **your job f. tomorrow** votre travail pour demain; **you are the man f. me/the job** vous êtes l'homme qu'il me faut/qui convient pour ce poste; **that is just the thing f. you** c'est juste ce qu'il vous faut; **there's no time f. that** il n'y a pas de temps pour ça; **it'll do f. temporary accommodation** ça ira comme logement provisoire

12 (to the amount of) **a cheque f. £50** un chèque de 50 livres; **put me down f. £5** inscrivez-moi pour 5 livres

13 (with regard to) **he is big f. his age** il est grand pour son âge; **not bad f. a beginner!** pour un débutant ce n'est pas si mal!; **sheer impudence, his remarks are hard to beat** pour ce genre de l'effronterie, ses commentaires sont imbattables; **as f. him** quant à lui; **as f. that** pour ce qui est de cela; **f. myself, f. my part** pour moi, quant à moi, pour ma part; **this shop is better f. books** ce magasin est mieux pour les livres

14 (in spite of) **f. all that** malgré tout, malgré cela, tout de même; esp Lit **f. all that he wanted to believe them** pour autant qu'il veuille les croire; **she loved him, f. all his faults** elle l'aimait malgré tous ses défauts

15 (owing to) **were it not f. her** or **but f. her, I should have died** sans elle, je serais mort

16 (corresponding to, in opposition to) **they sell twenty red bikes f. every black one** pour chaque vélo noir vendu, il y en a vingt rouges

17 (introducing an infinitive clause) **it is easy/difficult/impossible f. him to come** il lui est facile/difficile/impossible de venir; **it is too late f. us to set off** il est trop tard pour que nous partions; **they made way f. him to pass** on se rangea pour le laisser passer; **I have brought it f. you to see** je l'ai apporté pour que vous le voyiez; **it is not f. me to decide/to criticize him** ce n'est pas à moi de décider/de le critiquer; **it is usual f. the mother to accompany her daughter** il est d'usage que la mère accompagne sa fille; **it's no good f. him to talk** il a beau dire; (because he is similarly guilty etc) il peut parler; **f. that to be done** pour que ça soit fait; **it took an hour f. the taxi to get to the station** le taxi a mis une heure pour aller jusqu'à la gare; **the best plan will be f. you to go away f. a time** le mieux sera que vous vous absentiez pour quelque temps; **it would be a disgrace f. you to back out now** vous retirer maintenant serait honteux

CONJ Lit car; **f. it was too late** car il était trop tard

forage ['fɒrɪdʒ] N (animal food) fourrage(s) m(pl); **to go on the f.** (search for provisions) chercher de la nourriture; **to have a f. for sth** (search for sth) fouiller ou fourrager pour trouver qch
■ VI fourrager; **to f. for sth** fourrager ou fouiller pour trouver qch; **never mind me, I'll f. for myself** ne t'occupe pas de moi, je me débrouillerai
▸▸ Mil **f. cap** calot m
▸ **forage about, forage around** VI (rummage) fourrager, fouiller (in dans)

foray ['fɒreɪ] N razzia f, incursion f, raid m; **she was on one of her forays round the bookshops** elle procédait à l'une de ses expéditions dans les librairies; Fig **to make a brief f. into the business world** faire une courte incursion dans le monde des affaires
■ VI faire des incursions ou des raids

forbear[1] ['fɔːbeər] N = **forebear**

forbear[2] [fɔː'beər] (pt **forbore** [fɔː'bɔːr], pp **forborne** [fɔː'bɔːn]) Lit VT s'abstenir de
■ VI **to f. from doing sth** s'abstenir de ou se garder de faire qch

forbearance [fɔː'beərəns] N **1** patience f, Lit longanimité f; **to show f. towards sb** montrer de l'indulgence envers qn **2** Fml **your f. from doing this** le fait que vous vous soyez abstenu de faire ceci

forbearing [fɔː'beərɪŋ] ADJ patient, indulgent

forbid [fə'bɪd] VT (pt **forbade** [fə'bæd, -'beɪd], pp **forbidden** [fə'bɪd(ə)n]) **1** (prohibit) défendre, interdire; (custom etc) proscrire; Law prohiber; **I f. it!** je l'interdis!; **to f. sb sth** défendre qch à qn; **to f. sb to do sth** défendre ou interdire à qn de faire qch; **I am forbidden (to drink) tea** le thé m'est défendu; **smoking is strictly forbidden** il est formellement interdit de fumer; **to be forbidden from doing sth** ne pas avoir le droit de faire qch; **he was forbidden from seeing her again** on lui a interdit de la revoir
2 (prevent) empêcher; **my condition forbids strenuous exercise** mon état ne me permet pas de me livrer à des exercices violents; **Heaven f. that I should do such a**

thing! Dieu me préserve de faire une telle chose!; **God f.!** à Dieu ne plaise! (**that** que + sub)

forbidden [fə'bɪd(ə)n] ADJ défendu, interdit; **to tread on f. ground** empiéter sur un terrain défendu; Fig toucher à un sujet tabou
▸▸ Bible, Fig f. fruit fruit m défendu

forbidding [fə'bɪdɪŋ] ADJ (face, aspect) sinistre; (character) peu avenant; (sky, weather) sombre; (rock, building) menaçant; (look, stare) sombre, menaçant; **a text of f. density/complexity** un texte d'une densité/complexité rébarbative

forbiddingly [fə'bɪdɪŋlɪ] ADV the castle towered f. over the town le château, menaçant, dominait la ville; **f. difficult/complex** d'une difficulté/complexité rébarbative

FORCE [fɔːs]

N force **1**, **3–5** ▪ autorité **2** ▪ poids **6** ▪ en vigueur (in force) **7**
VT forcer **1**, **2** ▪ arracher **1** ▪ imposer **1**

N **1** (strength, violence) force f; **by sheer or brute f.** de vive force; **by sheer f. of will** à force de volonté; **by f. of circumstance(s)** par la force des choses; **f. of habit** force de l'habitude; **f. of personality** force de personnalité; **to use f. against the strikers** avoir recours à la force contre les grévistes; **armed f.** force armée
2 (authority) influence f, autorité f; **f. of example** influence de l'exemple; **moral f.** force morale
3 (effort) énergie f, (power) (of blow, wind etc) intensité f, (of imagination etc) vigueur f, **a blow with plenty of f. behind it** un coup bien appuyé ou bien asséné; **considerable f. would be needed to break the door down** il faudrait une force considérable pour défoncer la porte; **the full f. of the explosion** toute la force de l'explosion; **the forces of Nature** les forces de la Nature; **a f. for good** une influence positive; **to be a f. for change** être le moteur du changement; **the forces at work here** les forces en jeu ici; **several forces conspired to bring about his downfall** plusieurs facteurs ont conspiré à provoquer sa chute
4 Phys force f, effort m; **f. exerted by an engine** effort d'un moteur; **f. of gravity** (force de la) pesanteur f; Met **f. ten on the Beaufort scale** force dix sur l'échelle de Beaufort
5 Mil etc (group) force f, troupe f, élément(s) m(pl); **a f. of 20,000 men** une troupe de 20 000 hommes; **an armed f.** une force (armée); **the (armed) forces** les forces armées; **he was in the forces** il était dans l'armée; **forces slang** argot m militaire; **the police f., Fam the F.** la Police; **a strong f. of police** un gros détachement de police; **two different police forces** deux forces de police différentes; **we turned out in (full) f.** nous sommes venus en masse
6 (value) (of argument) poids m; (sense) (of word, document) signification f, (of word, expression) valeur f, **I mean it with the full f. of the word** je le dis et je pèse mes mots
7 (of law, rule etc) **to be in f.** être en vigueur; **to put the law into f.** appliquer la loi; **to come into f.** entrer en vigueur
VT **1** (compel) **to f. sb to do sth** or **into doing sth** forcer ou obliger qn à faire qch; **no one's forcing you!** (to go etc) personne ne t'y force ou oblige!; **I am forced to conclude that …** je suis forcé de conclure que …; **to be forced to give way** céder à la force; **that forced me to think** cela m'a obligé à réfléchir; **to f. sb into/out of the room** faire entrer/sortir qn de force; **to f. sth on sb** imposer qch à qn; **to f. drink on sb** contraindre qn à boire; **to**

f. a promise/confession from sb arracher une promesse/confession à qn
2 (obtain, produce etc by effort) (break open) (door, window) forcer, enfoncer; (lock) forcer; **to f. sb's hand** forcer la main à qn; **to f. the issue** précipiter les choses; **to f. the pace** forcer l'allure ou le pas; **she forced a smile** elle s'est forcée à sourire; **to f. (the meaning of) a word** forcer le sens d'un mot; **to f. legislation through Parliament** forcer le Parlement à voter une législation; **to f. a plant** forcer une plante; Aut **to f. the engine** trop pousser le moteur; **to f. a car/sb off the road** faire sortir une voiture/qn de la route; **to f. one's way into a house** pénétrer de force dans une maison; **to f. one's way through the crowd** se frayer un passage à travers la foule; **to f. sth into sth** faire entrer qch de force dans qch; **to f. oneself on sb** s'imposer à qn; **compressed air forces the liquid up the pipe** l'air comprimé fait monter le liquide dans le tuyau
▸ **force back** VT SEP (enemy forces etc) repousser, faire reculer; (air, water, tears etc) refouler; (impulse, laugh) réprimer
▸ **force down** VT SEP faire descendre de force; (suitcase lid) fermer de force; **to f. prices down** faire baisser les prix; Aviat **the plane was forced down** on a forcé l'avion à atterrir; **to f. down food/medicine/etc** avaler un aliment/un médicament/etc à contre-cœur; **to f. food/medicine/etc down sb** faire avaler un aliment/un médicament/etc de force à qn
▸ **force open** VT SEP (door, window) ouvrir de force, forcer; (lock) forcer; **it took all his strength to f. open the dog's jaws** il a dû y aller de toutes ses forces pour réussir à ouvrir la mâchoire du chien
▸ **force out** VT SEP faire sortir de force; (in engine) (exhaust gas) refouler au dehors; **shopkeepers were forced out of the town centre by the rising rents** la hausse des loyers a chassé les petits commerçants du centre-ville; **to be forced out of business** être forcé à fermer boutique; **to f. out a few words of congratulation** féliciter qn du bout des lèvres
▸ **force up** VT SEP faire monter de force; (prices) faire monter

forced [fɔːst] ADJ **1** forcé **2** (smile) forcé, artificiel; **to give a f. laugh** rire du bout des lèvres, avoir un rire forcé **3** (plant, fruit, vegetables) forcé
▸▸ **f. feeding** (of person) alimentation f de force; (of livestock) gavage m; **f. labour** travail m forcé; Aviat **f. landing** atterrissage m forcé; Mil **f. march** marche f forcée; **f. sale** vente f forcée; Fin **f. saving** épargne f forcée

force-feed VT (pt, pp **force-fed** [-fed]) (goose) gaver; (person) nourrir de force

forceful ['fɔːsfʊl] ADJ (personality) énergique; (argument, case) puissant; (language) musclé; (reason) bon

forcefully ['fɔːsfʊlɪ] ADV (to speak, act) énergiquement; (to express oneself, reason, write) avec vigueur; (to argue) énergiquement, avec force; **I was f. struck by it** ça m'a fortement marqué

forcefulness ['fɔːsfʊlnɪs] N vigueur f

force-land VI Aviat faire un atterrissage forcé

forcemeat ['fɔːsmiːt] N Culin farce f

forceps ['fɔːseps] NPL (pair of) f. pince f, Surg forceps m; (in dentistry) davier m;
▸▸ Obst f. **delivery** accouchement m au forceps

forcible ['fɔːsɪb(ə)l] ADJ **1** (by force) de force **2** (argument) vigoureux, plein de force; (reminder) brutal, -aux
▸▸ Law f. **entry** effraction f

forcibly ['fɔːsɪblɪ] ADV **1** (by force) de force; **to detain sb f.** retenir qn de force **2** (convincingly) vigoureusement; **she argued f. for their release** elle a argumenté énergiquement ou avec force en faveur de leur libération; **they put their case very f.** ils se sont défendus avec force ou vigueur; **we were all f. reminded of our own mortality** nous avons été brutalement rappelés à notre condition de mortels

forcing ['fɔːsɪŋ] N **1** (of lock) forcement m; (of door) enfoncement m **2** (in gardening) forçage m, culture f forcée
▸▸ Culin f. **bag** poche f à douille; **f. frame** châssis m; **f. house** (for plants) forcerie f, Fig Fam **it's just an academic f. house** dans cette boîte, tout ce qui compte ce sont les résultats aux examens

ford [fɔːd] N (in river) gué m
VT (river) guéer, traverser à gué

fordable ['fɔːdəb(ə)l] ADJ (river) guéable

fore [fɔːr] ADJ **1** (front) à l'avant, antérieur; **the f. and hind legs** les pattes de devant et de derrière **2** Naut (de l')avant
N Naut avant m; **at the f.** au mât de misaine; Fig **to the f.** (prominent) en vue, en évidence, en vedette; **this question has been very much to the f. in the talks** cette question a été au tout premier plan au cours des discussions; **to come to the f.** (of person) commencer à être connu; **this issue came to the f. during last year's negotiations** ce problème a été mis en évidence lors des négociations de l'an dernier; **to bring to the f.** (aspect, problem, importance of sth) mettre en évidence, souligner; (theory, philosophy) mettre au premier plan
ADV Naut de l'avant; **f. and aft** de l'avant à l'arrière
INT Golf gare devant!
▸▸ Typ f. **edge** petit fond m, gouttière f, Naut f. **hatch** panneau m avant

fore-and-aft ADJ Naut aurique
▸▸ Naut f. **bulkhead** cloison f médiane; Mil f. **cap** calot m; Naut f. **movement** (of engine) déplacement m longitudinal; Naut f. **sail** voile f aurique

forearm¹ ['fɔːrɑːm] N avant-bras m inv

forearm² [fɔːr'ɑːm] VT (person) prémunir; **he came forearmed** il est venu prémuni ou préparé; **she would always ensure that she was forearmed before going** elle prenait toujours soin de se prémunir avant d'y aller

forebear ['fɔːbeər] N aïeul m, pl aïeux, aïeule f, ancêtre mf, Fig ancêtre mf

forebode [fɔː'bəʊd] VT to f. **disaster** présager ou laisser prévoir le désastre

foreboding [fɔː'bəʊdɪŋ] N (intuition) (mauvais) pressentiment m; **she was filled with (a sense of) f.** elle était envahie par un mauvais pressentiment; **to have a f. that …** avoir le pressentiment que …; **she thought with f. of what the future would hold** elle songea avec appréhension à ce que l'avenir lui réservait

forecast ['fɔːkɑːst] N prévision f, **his f. was wrong/right** ses prévisions étaient fausses/exactes; **forecasts of higher interest rates** des prévisions d'augmentation des taux d'intérêts; **racing f.** pronostic m des courses; (weather) f. prévisions météorologiques, Fam météo f, **long-/short-range f.** prévision à longue échéance/sur période courte
VT (pt, pp **forecast(ed)**) (events, storm etc) prévoir; Sport (result) pronostiquer; **I wouldn't like to f. a winner** je ne voudrais pas avoir à prédire qui va gagner;
▸▸ Acct f. **balance sheet** bilan m prévisionnel

forecaster ['fɔːkɑːstər] N pronostiqueur,

-euse; *Econ* expert *m*; **weather f.** météorologiste *mf*

forecasting ['fɔːkɑːstɪŋ] N *(of result etc)* pronostication *f*; *(of weather, economic matters, sports)* prévision *f*
▸▸ **f. firm** société *f* de prévisions; **f. model** modèle *m* de prévisions

forecastle ['fəʊks(ə)l] N *Naut* gaillard *m*; *(in merchant vessel)* poste *m* de l'équipage

foreclose [fɔː'kləʊz] *Law* VT **to f. the mortgage** saisir l'immeuble hypothéqué
VI *(on a mortgage)* saisir l'immeuble hypothéqué; *(on a loan)* récupérer le prêt; **to f. on a loan** interrompre un crédit, rompre un crédit avant son terme; **the bank has foreclosed on us** la banque nous a saisi l'immeuble hypothéqué/a décidé de récupérer le prêt

foreclosure [fɔː'kləʊʒər] N *Law (on a mortgage)* saisie *f* (d'une hypothèque), forclusion *f*

forecourt ['fɔːkɔːt] N avant-cour *f*, *pl* avant-cours; *(of garage, station)* devant *m*; *(of car dealer)* parc *m* d'exposition

foredoomed [fɔː'duːmd] ADJ condamné d'avance (**to** à)

forefather ['fɔːfɑːðər] N *Lit* aïeul *m*, *pl* aïeux; *Fig* ancêtre *m*

forefinger ['fɔːfɪŋgər] N index *m*

forefoot, *pl* **forefeet** ['fɔːfʊt, -fiːt] N *(of dog, cat, bird)* patte *f* de devant; *(animal with cloven hoof)* pied *m* antérieur

forefront ['fɔːfrʌnt] N **to bring sth to the f.** mettre qch au premier plan; **this question is still in the f.** cette question occupe toujours le premier plan

foregather [fɔː'gæðər] VI = **forgather**

forego [fɔː'gəʊ] VT = **forgo**

foregoing [fɔː'gəʊɪŋ] ADJ *esp Fml* précédent, antérieur; *(previously cited)* cité ci-avant; **the f.** ce qui précède

foregone ['fɔːgɒn] ADJ **it was a f. conclusion** c'était couru d'avance

foreground ['fɔːgraʊnd] N *Art, Phot etc* premier plan *m*; **in the f.** au premier plan; **they must be hoping that this issue will fade from the f.** ils doivent espérer que ce problème ne restera pas longtemps au premier plan
VT *Art etc* mettre au premier plan; *Fig* privilégier
▸▸ *TV, Cin* **f. matte** cache *m* d'avant-plan; *Comput* **f. processing** traitement *m* en avant-plan; *Comput* **f. program** programme *m* prioritaire

forehand ['fɔːhænd] N *Tennis* coup *m* droit; **to have a strong/weak f.** avoir un coup droit puissant/faible; **to play a f.** jouer un coup droit; **to serve to one's opponent's f.** servir sur le coup droit adverse
▸▸ **f. drive** drive *m* de coup droit; **f. stroke** coup droit

forehead ['fɒrɪd, 'fɔːhed] N *Anat* front *m*

foreign ['fɒrɪn] ADJ **1** *(from different country, countries)* étranger; **she looked f.** elle paraissait étrangère; **a f.-sounding name** un nom aux consonances étrangères; **f. countries, f. parts** pays *mpl* étrangers, l'étranger *m*; **our relations with f. countries** nos rapports avec l'extérieur; **I don't like f. food** je n'aime pas la cuisine étrangère; **f. investment** investissement *m* à l'étranger; **f. travel** voyages *mpl* à l'étranger **2** *(not belonging)* étranger (**to** à); **such feelings are f. to his nature** de tels sentiments lui sont étrangers; **lying is f. to her nature** ce n'est pas dans sa nature de mentir
▸▸ *Fin* **f. account** compte *m* étranger; **f. affairs** affaires *fpl* étrangères; **f. aid** *(to foreign country)* aide *f* aux pays étrangers; *(from for-*

eign country) aide de l'étranger; *Med* **f. body** corps *m* étranger; *Journ* **f. correspondent** correspondant, -ante à l'étranger; *Fin* **f. currency** devises *fpl* étrangères; *Fin* **f. currency account** compte en devises étrangères; *Fin* **f. currency earnings** apport *m* de devises étrangères; *Fin* **f. currency holding** avoir *m* en devises étrangères; *Fin* **f. currency loan** prêt *m* en devises étrangères; *Fin* **f. currency option** option *f* de change; *Fin* **f. currency reserves** réserves *fpl* de change, réserves en devises; *Fin* **f. debt** dette *f* extérieure; *Econ* **f. direct investment** investissement *m* étranger direct; *Fin* **f. exchange** devises étrangères; *Fin* **f. exchange gain** gain *m* de change; *Fin* **f. exchange loss** perte *f* de change; *Fin* **f. exchange market** marché *m* des changes; *Fin* **f. exchange option** option sur devises; *Fin* **f. exchange rate** cours *m* des devises; *Fin* **f. exchange reserves** réserves de change, réserves en devises; *Fin* **f. exchange risk** risque *m* de change; **f. legion** légion *f* étrangère; **f. market** marché extérieur; *Pol* **f. minister** ministre *m* des affaires étrangères; **the F. Office** le Foreign Office, le ministère britannique des Affaires étrangères; **the F. Secretary** = le ministre britannique des Affaires étrangères; *Am* **f. service** service *m* diplomatique; **f. trade** commerce *m* extérieur

foreign-built ADJ *(car)* de marque étrangère; *(ship)* construit à l'étranger

foreigner ['fɒrɪnər] N étranger, -ère; **I feel like a f. here** je me sens étranger ici

> Attention: ne pas confondre avec **stranger**.

foreignness ['fɒrɪnnɪs] N air *m* étranger; *(of place)* caractère *m* étranger; *(exotic nature)* exotisme *m*; **the f. of the food/their way of life** la nourriture/leur mode de vie bien à part; **given the f. of this concept to our culture** étant donné que ce concept est étranger à notre culture

foreknowledge [fɔː'nɒlɪdʒ] N *esp Fml* connaissance *f* anticipée; **to have f. of sth** avoir connaissance à l'avance de qch

foreland ['fɔːlənd] N cap *m*, promontoire *m*

foreleg ['fɔːleg] N patte *f* de devant; *(of horse)* jambe *f* de devant

forelock ['fɔːlɒk] N *(of person)* mèche *f* (de cheveux) sur le front; **to touch** *or* **tug one's f.** = porter la main à son front (pour saluer qn); *Fig* faire une révérence

foreman, *pl* **foremen** ['fɔːmən] N **1** *Ind etc* contremaître *m*; *Typ* prote *m*; *(of gang of workmen)* chef *m* d'équipe ou de brigade; **works f.** conducteur *m* de travaux **2** *(of jury)* président *m*

foremast ['fɔːmɑːst] N *Naut* mât *m* de misaine

forementioned [fɔː'menʃənd] ADJ *Law, Admin* précité

foremost ['fɔːməʊst] ADJ *(in importance)* le plus important; *(in place)* le plus en avant; **of the f. importance** de la plus haute importance
ADV **to rank f.** se classer parmi les premiers; **I shall only leave this room feet f.** je ne quitterai cette pièce que les pieds devant

forename ['fɔːneɪm] N prénom *m*

forenoon ['fɔːnuːn] N *esp Scot, Irish* matinée *f*; **in the f.** dans *ou* pendant la matinée

forensic [fə'rensɪk, fɒ-] ADJ légal, -aux
▸ *Fam* **forensics** *(department)* service *m* médico-légal; **did forensics come up with anything?** est-ce que le service médico-légal a trouvé quelque chose?
▸▸ **f. evidence** = preuves *fpl* relevées lors d'une expertise criminalistique; **f. laboratory** laboratoire *m* de criminalistique; **f. medi-**

cine médecine *f* légale; **f. science** criminalistique *f*; **f. scientist** expert *m* légiste *ou* en criminalistique

foreordain ['fɔːrɔː'deɪn] VT *Fml* prédestiner (**sb to sth** qn à qch; **sb to do sth** qn à faire qch)

foreplay ['fɔːpleɪ] N *(sexual)* préliminaires *mpl*; **he doesn't go in much for f.** il n'est pas très porté sur les préliminaires

forequarter ['fɔːkwɔːtər] N *(of cow etc)* quartier *m* de devant; **forequarters of a horse** avant-main *m ou* avant-train *m* d'un cheval

forerunner ['fɔːrʌnər] N ancêtre *m*; *(person)* précurseur *m*

foresail ['fɔːseɪl, 'fɔːs(ə)l] N *Naut* (voile *f* de) misaine *f*

foresee [fɔː'siː] VT *(pt* **foresaw** [fɔː'sɔː]*, pp* **foreseen** [fɔː'siːn]*) (misfortune, event, development)* prévoir; **I f. difficult times/a problem** j'entrevois des moments difficiles/un problème; **it was an accident which should have been foreseen** c'était un accident qu'on aurait dû prévoir

foreseeable [fɔː'siːəb(ə)l] ADJ *(future, consequence, result etc)* prévisible; **not in the f. future** pas dans un avenir prévisible

foreshadow [fɔː'ʃædəʊ] VT *(event etc)* annoncer, présager

foreshore ['fɔːʃɔːr] N laisse *f* de mer; *(beach)* plage *f*

foreshorten [fɔː'ʃɔːt(ə)n] VT *Art (object)* dessiner en raccourci *ou* en perspective; **foreshortened figure** figure vue en raccourci; **the distances are foreshortened** les distances sont réduites (par la perspective)

foreshortening ['fɔːʃɔːt(ə)nɪŋ] N *Art* raccourci *m*

foresight ['fɔːsaɪt] N **1** prévoyance *f*; **lack of f.** manque de prévoyance, imprévoyance *f*; **with f. this could all have been avoided** avec un peu de prévoyance tout ceci aurait pu être évité **2** *(on gun)* guidon *m*, bouton *m* de mire

foreskin ['fɔːskɪn] N *Anat* prépuce *m*

forest ['fɒrɪst] N forêt *f*; **deciduous/coniferous f.** forêt à feuilles caduques/de conifères; **f.-covered hills** collines *fpl* boisées; *Fig* **a f. of masts/telegraph poles** une forêt de mâts/poteaux télégraphiques
VT *(region)* boiser (**with** de)
▸▸ **f. fire** incendie *m* de forêt; *Am* **f. ranger** garde *m* forestier

forestall [fɔː'stɔːl] VT *(attempt, criticism)* anticiper, devancer; *(rivals)* devancer

forestay ['fɔːsteɪ] N *Naut* étai *m* de misaine

forested ['fɒrɪstɪd] ADJ boisé (**with** de)

forester ['fɒrɪstər] N (garde *m*) forestier *m*

forestry ['fɒrɪstrɪ] N sylviculture *f*
▸▸ **the F. Commission** = organisme *m* britannique de gestion des forêts domaniales, ≃ les eaux et forêts *fpl*

foretaste ['fɔːteɪst] N avant-goût *m*, *pl* avant-goûts; **to give** *or* **offer sb a f. of sth** donner un avant-goût de qch à qn

foretell [fɔː'tel] VT *(pt, pp* **foretold** [fɔː'təʊld]*) (of person)* prédire

forethought ['fɔːθɔːt] N prévoyance *f*; **to do sth with a lack of f.** manquer de prévoyance en faisant qch; **if you had given it some f.** si tu y avais un peu réfléchi à l'avance

forever [fə'revər] ADV **1** *(until end of time)* pour toujours, à jamais; **a good bike should last f.** un vélo de bonne qualité devrait durer pour toujours; **to live f.** vivre éternellement *ou* pour toujours; **nobody lives f.** personne n'est éternel; **nothing lasts f.** tout a une fin; *(object, possession)* rien n'est éternel; **the**

journey seemed to last f. le voyage a semblé durer une éternité **2** *(ceaselessly)* sans cesse, sans arrêt; **he was f. changing his mind** il changeait sans cesse *ou* sans arrêt d'avis
N *Fam* **to take f. to do sth** prendre *ou* mettre une éternité à faire qch; **it took me f. to persuade him to come** ça m'a pris une éternité pour le persuader de venir

forewarn [fɔː'wɔːn] **VT** prévenir, avertir; **to f. sb of sth** prévenir *ou* avertir qn de qch; *Prov* **forewarned is forearmed** un homme averti en vaut deux

forewoman, *pl* **forewomen** ['fɔːwʊmən, -wɪmɪn] **N 1** *Ind etc* contremaîtresse *f* **2** *Law (of jury)* présidente *f*

foreword ['fɔːwɜːd] **N** *(to book)* avant-propos *m inv*, préface *f*

forex ['fɒreks] **N, ADJ** *Fin (abbr* **foreign exchange)** devises *fpl* étrangères
►►**f. trading** transactions *fpl* en devises étrangères

forfaiting ['fɔːfeɪtɪŋ] **N** *Banking* forfaitage *m*, forfaitisation *f*

forfeit ['fɔːfɪt] **ADJ** *Hist, Law* confisqué; **his lands were f.** on lui a confisqué ses terres
N 1 *Law (fine)* amende *f*; *(for non-performance of contract)* dédit *m*; **to have to pay a f.** être mis à l'amende **2** *(in game)* gage *m*; **to play forfeits** jouer aux gages
VT 1 *(have confiscated) (object)* perdre par confiscation; *(right)* être déchu de **2** *(lose)* perdre; *(give up)* renoncer à, abandonner; **to f. one's life** payer de sa vie; **to f. one's honour** perdre l'honneur; **he had forfeited his independence in return for financial security** il avait sacrifié son indépendance au profit de la sécurité financière; *Fin* **to f. a deposit** perdre les arrhes

forfeiture ['fɔːfɪtʃər] **N 1** *Law (act of having confiscated) (of property)* perte *f* par confiscation; *Law, Fin (of shares, right)* déchéance *f*, forfaiture *f* **2** *esp Fml (loss) (of sb's respect, one's life, honour etc)* perte *f*

forgather, foregather [fɔː'gæðər] **VI** *Fml* se réunir

forge [fɔːdʒ] **N** atelier *m* de forgeron, forge *f*
VT 1 *(of blacksmith etc) (horseshoe etc)* forger; *Metal (iron)* forger, cingler; *Fig* **to f. an alliance/a friendship** forger une alliance/une amitié **2** *(counterfeit) (signature, banknotes, cheque)* contrefaire; *(document, passport)* faire un faux de
►►**f. hammer** marteau-pilon *m*, *pl* marteaux-pilons

> Note that the French verb **forger** never means **to counterfeit**.

►**forge ahead VI 1** *(press forward)* faire des progrès; *(in race, election campaign)* prendre de l'avance; *(in business, undertaking)* aller de l'avant; **to f. ahead with one's plans** aller de l'avant dans ses projets, mener ses projets de l'avant **2** *(outstrip competitors)* dépasser tous ses concurrents; **to f. ahead of one's rivals** prendre de l'avance sur ses rivaux

forged [fɔːdʒd] **ADJ 1** *Metal (iron)* forgé **2** *(document, banknote, signature)* faux, *f* fausse, contrefait; **f. document** faux *m*; *(identity paper)* faux papier

forger ['fɔːdʒər] **N** *(of banknotes)* contrefacteur *m*, faussaire *mf*; *(of signature etc)* faussaire *mf*

forgery ['fɔːdʒərɪ] **N 1** *(activity)* contrefaçon *f*; *(of documents)* falsification *f*; *Law* **to be guilty of f.** être coupable de faux **2** *(thing forged)* faux *m*; **it's a f.** *(of signature)* c'est une fausse signature; **it's a clever/obvious f.** c'est une contrefaçon bien/mal réussie; **it's a f. of my signature** c'est une contrefaçon de ma signature

forget [fə'get] *(pt* **forgot** [fə'gɒt], *pp* **forgotten** [fə'gɒt(ə)n], *prp* **forgetting) VT 1** VOIR GRAMMAIRE A44 *(fact, person, knowledge)* oublier; *(one's French)* désapprendre; **to f. to do sth** oublier *ou* omettre de faire qch; **don't f. to ...** n'oubliez *ou* ne manquez pas de ...; **to f. how to do sth** oublier comment on fait qch, ne plus savoir faire qch; **to f. oneself** s'oublier; **have I forgotten anyone?** est-ce que j'ai oublié quelqu'un?; **to f. sb's birthday** oublier (de souhaiter) l'anniversaire de qn; **to f. one's manners** oublier ses bonnes manières; **have you forgotten your manners?** où sont tes bonnes manières?; *(to child)* veux-tu être poli!; **f. it!** *(in reply to apology, thanks)* il n'y a pas de quoi!; **f. it, it wasn't important** *(what I said)* non, non, ça n'a pas d'importance; **look, f. it, will you?** *(stop talking about it)* écoute, laisse tomber, d'accord?; **they can f. it!** *(they're being unreasonable)* ils peuvent faire une croix dessus *ou* Fam aller se faire voir!; *(they've no chance)* ils peuvent faire une croix sus!, Fam ils sont foutus!; **you can f. the holiday** *(we can't afford it)* tu peux laisser tomber l'idée d'aller en vacances; **he's only ten years old, don't f.** n'oubliez pas qu'il n'a que dix ans; **to be forgotten** tomber dans l'oubli; **he felt that he had been forgotten by his friends** il avait l'impression que ses amis l'avaient oublié; **it's best forgotten** il vaut mieux ne plus en parler; **it's all been forgotten now** tout ça c'est du passé; **things best forgotten** des choses qu'il vaut mieux oublier
2 *(leave by mistake) (handkerchief, gloves etc)* oublier; **I forgot my hat on the train** j'ai oublié mon chapeau dans le train
VI oublier; **before I f.** *(can you do sth?)* avant que j'oublie *ou* que je n'oublie; **to f. about sb/sth** oublier qn/qch; **he warned me of the danger but I forgot (all) about it** il m'a averti du danger mais je n'y ai plus pensé; **and you can f. about going to London!** et ce n'est pas la peine de songer à aller à Londres!

forgetful [fə'getfʊl] **ADJ 1 to be very f.** avoir très mauvaise mémoire **2** *(negligent)* oublieux *(* **of** *de)*; **to be f. of one's duty** être oublieux de *ou* négliger son devoir

forgetfulness [fə'getfʊlnɪs] **N** manque *m* (habituel) de mémoire; **a moment of f.** un moment de distraction

forget-me-not N *(plant)* myosotis *m*

forging ['fɔːdʒɪŋ] **N** *Metal (activity)* travail *m* de forge; *(forged item)* pièce *f* forgée;
►►**f. mill** forge *f*; **f. press** marteau-pilon *m*, *pl* marteaux-pilons

forgivable [fə'gɪvəb(ə)l] **ADJ** excusable, pardonnable

forgivably [fə'gɪvəblɪ] **ADV** de façon excusable *ou* pardonnable; **he was f. angry/surprised** il est compréhensible *ou* naturel qu'il ait été en colère/surpris; **f. so, in my opinion** ce qui est tout à fait compréhensible *ou* naturel, à mon avis

forgive [fə'gɪv] *(pt* **forgave** [fə'geɪv], *pp* **forgiven** [fə'gɪv(ə)n]) **VT 1** *(something)* pardonner; *Rel, Arch (mistake, insult)* remettre; **to f. sb sth** pardonner qch à qn; **to f. sb a debt** faire grâce d'une dette à qn; **if you'll f. the pun** pardonnez-moi ce jeu de mots; **she was not prepared to f. his rudeness** elle n'était pas prête à lui pardonner sa grossièreté
2 to f. sb pardonner à qn; **he asked me to f. him** il m'a demandé pardon, il m'a demandé de le pardonner; **am I forgiven?** est-ce que tu me pardonnes?; **I'll never f. him for what he did** je ne lui pardonnerai jamais ce qu'il a fait; **one might perhaps be forgiven for thinking that ...** il n'est pas interdit de pen-

ser que ...; **f. me for intruding/interrupting** excusez-moi de vous déranger/interrompre
VI pardonner; **f. and forget** il faut oublier et pardonner

forgiveness [fə'gɪvnɪs] **N 1** *(act) (of sins)* rémission *f*, to ask sb's f. demander pardon à qn; **she pleaded for his f.** elle la implora pour qu'il la pardonne **2** *(quality)* indulgence *f*, to show f. faire preuve d'indulgence, se montrer indulgent

forgiving [fə'gɪvɪŋ] **ADJ** indulgent *(* **of** *envers)*

forgo, forego [fɔː'gəʊ] **VT** *(pt* **forwent** [fɔː'went], *pp* **forgone** [fɔː'gɒn])* renoncer à; **to f. doing sth** s'abstenir de faire qch

forgotten [fə'gɒt(ə)n] **ADJ** oublié; **the f. man of Scottish football** le laissé-pour-compte du football écossais

fork [fɔːk] **N 1** *(for food)* fourchette *f*; *Agr* fourche *f*; **garden f.** fourche à bêcher; *Mus* **tuning f.** diapason *m* **2** *(sth with shape of fork) (of water diviner)* baguette *f* divinatoire; *(to support branch etc)* poteau *m* fourchu; **f. of lightning** zigzag *m* (d'éclair); *Cycling* **front f.** fourche *f* avant *ou* de direction **3** *(division) (in road)* bifurcation *f*, jonction *f*; *(of branches)* fourche *f*; **take the left f.** prenez la route/le sentier de gauche
VI *(of tree etc)* fourcher; *(of road)* faire une fourche, bifurquer; **follow the road until it forks** suivez la route jusqu'à la bifurcation *ou* fourche; **f. right for York** *(on sign)* prenez à droite pour York
VT *Agr (earth, hay)* fourcher; **they were forking hay onto the truck** ils chargeaient du foin à la fourche dans le camion
►►**f. lunch** buffet *m*

> When translating **fork**, note that **fourchette** and **fourche** are not interchangeable. **Fourchette** is an item of cutlery, whereas **fourche** is an agricultural implement.

►**fork in VT SEP** *(compost)* enfouir en fourchant
►**fork off VI** *(of road, driver)* bifurquer
►**fork out** *Fam* **VT SEP** *(provide, often unwillingly)* **to f. out for sth** raquer, casquer
VI *(pay out money)* **to f. out for sth** casquer pour qch; **he had to f. out (for it)** il a dû allonger la monnaie, il a dû casquer; **come on, f. out** *(what you owe me)* allez, aboule
►**fork over VT SEP** *(flowerbed)* retourner légèrement à la fourche

forked [fɔːkt] **ADJ** *(branch, pipe)* fourchu, bifurqué, en fourche; *(road)* qui bifurque, à bifurcation; *(tongue)* fourchu; *(lightning)* ramifié

forkful [fɔːkfʊl] **N 1** *(of food etc)* fourchetée *f* **2** *(of hay etc)* fourchée *f*

fork-lift N chariot *m* élévateur à fourche
►►**f. truck** chariot élévateur à fourche

forlorn [fə'lɔːn] **ADJ** *Lit* **1** *(place)* désert, abandonné; *(look)* triste; *Am* **f. of hope** privé de tout espoir; **to look f.** avoir l'air triste; **a f. expression** une expression de tristesse **2** *(desperate) (attempt)* désespéré; **it's a f. hope** c'est un vain espoir; **to do sth in the f. hope that ...** faire qch dans le fol espoir que ...

FORM [fɔːm]

N	forme **1–4, 6, 10**	▪ silhouette **1**
▪ formulaire **5**	▪ classe **8**	
VT	former **1-3**	▪ façonner **1** ▪ se
former **1**	▪ contracter **2**	
▪ constituer **3**		
VI	se former **1**	

N 1 *(shape) (of object)* forme *f*, configuration *f*; *(of person, animal)* silhouette *f*; **to take f.** prendre forme

2 *(manifestation)*, Biol, Gram, Liter, Mus forme *f*; **f. and content** *(of book etc)* la forme et le fond; **work that lacks f.** œuvre qui manque de forme; **tonic taken in the f. of pills** remontant pris sous (la) forme de pilules; **what f. did the lesson take?** quelle forme la leçon a-t-elle prise?; **poverty in every f.** la misère sous toutes ses formes; **it's a f. of disease** c'est une forme spéciale de maladie; **the different forms of worship** les différentes pratiques religieuses

3 *(formality)* formalité *f*; Law etc **in due** or **proper f.** en bonne (et due) forme; **a receipt in due f.** une quittance régulière; **to go through the f. of refusing** faire semblant de refuser; **for f.'s sake** pour la forme; **as a matter of f.** par manière d'acquit; **it is a mere matter of f.** c'est une pure formalité; *Fam* **to know the f.** *(what to do)* savoir ce qu'il faut faire; **it is good f.** c'est de bon ton; **good f. demands that …** la politesse exige que …; **it is not good f., it's bad f.** c'est de mauvais ton, ça fait mauvais genre; **it is bad f. to ask a lady her age** ce n'est pas poli de demander son âge à une dame; **it would have been good f. to at least tell me** la moindre des politesses aurait été de me le dire

4 *(formula)* *(of legal document etc)* formule *f*, forme *f*; **correct f. of words** tournure *f* de phrase correcte; **forms of address** *(when writing)* formules de politesse; *(when speaking)* titres *mpl* de politesse

5 *(printed document with spaces)*, Comput formulaire *m*; **order f.** bulletin *m* de commande

6 *esp Sp* *(condition)* forme *f*, condition *f*; Horseracing *(of horse)* performances *fpl*; *(in newspaper etc)* *(of horses)* tableau *m* des performances; **to be in/out of f.** être/ne pas être en forme; **to be in good f.** *(at a party etc)* être en train ou en forme; **in excellent f.** dans une forme excellente; **he felt in good f.** il se sentait en forme; **on present f.** *(the company will make a profit etc)* si l'on en juge par la situation actuelle; Horseracing **to study (the) f.** étudier les performances des chevaux

7 *Br Sl* **he's got f.** *(a criminal record)* son casier judiciaire n'est pas vierge; **has he got f.?** est-ce qu'il a un casier judiciaire?

8 *Br Sch (class)* classe *f*; **first f.** (classe *f* de) sixième *f*; **sixth f.** (classe de) première *f*

9 *Br Old-fashioned (bench)* banc *m*, banquette *f*

10 *(mould)* Metal forme *f*, moule *m*; Constr etc *(for reinforced concrete)* coffrage *m*, coffre *m*; *Am Typ (frame)* forme

11 *(of hare)* gîte *m*, forme *f*

vt 1 *(shape)* former, faire, façonner; *(the mind)* développer; *(character)* former; *(idea etc)* se former, se faire; *(doubts)* concevoir; **to f. the impression that …** avoir l'impression que …

2 *(habit etc)* contracter; *(relationship)* établir; *(plan)* arrêter; **to f. a friendship** *(of two people)* devenir amis; **to f. a friendship with sb** devenir ami avec qn; **to f. a successful partnership** former une association réussie; **he had formed a plan to …** il avait projeté de …

3 *(constitute)* former, faire; *(government, organisation)* constituer; *(company etc)* former, organiser; *(republic etc)* instituer, établir; *(new word etc)* former, faire; **to f. an obstacle to sth** faire obstacle à qch; **Portugal formed the last remaining obstacle** le Portugal constituait le dernier obstacle; **the walls f. a square** les murs forment un carré; **to f. part of sth** faire partie de qch; **they formed themselves into a committee** ils se constituèrent en comité; **the past tense is formed by the addition of -ed** le passé se forme en ajoutant -ed

vi 1 *(of ideas, opinions)* prendre forme, se former; *(of character, personality)* se former; *(of company)* se constituer; *(of friendship, relationship)* naître

2 Mil **to f. into a line** se mettre en ligne

▸▸ Comput **f. document** document *m* canevas; Comput **f. feed** avancement *m* du papier; Comput **f. field** champ *m* de saisie; **f. letter** lettre *f* circulaire; *Br Sch* **f. master** ≃ professeur *m* principal; *Br Sch* **f. mistress** ≃ professeur principal; *Br Sch* **f. room** salle *f* de classe, classe *f*; *Br Sch* **f. teacher** = ≃ professeur principal; *Br Sch* **f. tutor** = ≃ professeur principal

▸ **form up** vi Mil former des rangs

formal ['fɔːm(ə)l] ADJ **1** *(welcome, reception, occasion etc)* cérémonieux, solennel; *(invitation)* officiel; **a f. dinner** un grand dîner; **is it f.?** *(the party, dance etc)* est-ce que c'est habillé?

2 *esp Pej (person)* compassé, formaliste; *(tone, manner)* guindé; *(language)* soutenu; **f. style** style *m* empesé ou compassé

3 *(procedure, notification)* formel, en règle; *(order, denial, agreement)* formel; *(contract)* en due forme; *(logic, grammar)* formel; *(garden)* à la française; **f. request for payment** mise *f* en demeure de payer; **to give sb a f. warning** avertir qn dans les formes; **a purely f. arrangement** un arrangement purement formel; **a f. similarity** une similarité de forme; **she had no f. schooling** elle n'a pas fait d'études conventionnelles

▸ *N Am (dress)* robe *f* de soirée; *(occasion)* soirée *f* de cérémonie; *(with dancing)* bal *m* de cérémonie

▸▸ **f. demand** mise *f* en demeure; **f. dress** *(for ceremony)* tenue *f* de cérémonie; *(for evening)* tenue de soirée; **f. notice** mise *f* en demeure; **f. religion** religion *f* officielle

formaldehyde [fɔːˈmældɪhaɪd] N Chem formaldéhyde *m*, aldéhyde *m* formique

formalin ['fɔːməlɪn] N Chem formol *m*

formalism ['fɔːməlɪz(ə)m] N formalisme *m*

formality [fɔːˈmælɪtɪ] N **1** *(procedure)* formalité *f*; **legal formalities** formes *fpl* ou formalités juridiques; **a mere f.** une pure formalité; **to dispense with the formalities** se dispenser des formalités **2** *(stiffness)* *(of speech)* compassement *m*; **the f. of the dance** le caractère cérémonieux du bal

formalize ['fɔːməlaɪz] VT *(contract, relations etc)* donner une forme officielle à; Ling, Phil *(grammar, proposition)* formaliser

formally ['fɔːməlɪ] ADV **1** *(with formality)* cérémonieusement; **they greeted her f.** ils l'ont accueillie cérémonieusement; **to dress f.** s'habiller de façon stricte; *(in evening dress)* porter une tenue de soirée

2 *(openly, officially)* officiellement; **the organization f. renounced violence** l'organisation a officiellement renoncé à la violence

3 *(procedurally)* **f. correct** correct quant à la forme, dans les formes; **the institute is f. subordinate to the Department** sur le papier l'institut est subordonné au Département

Note that the French word **formellement** is a false friend. Its most common meaning is **strictly** or **categorically**.

format ['fɔːmæt] N *(of book, disk, TV programme etc)* format *m*; *(of meeting, evening etc)* organisation *f*

▸ VT *(-tt-)* Comput *(disk)* formater; *(page, text)* mettre en forme, formater

formation [fɔːˈmeɪʃən] N **1** *(act of creating)* *(of plural, coal, new policy, character etc)* formation *f*; *(of opinions, child's mind)* développement *m*; *(of company etc)* constitution *f*, formation; *(of republic etc)* établissement *m*

2 Mil etc *(arrangement)* *(of troops)* formation *f*, dispositif *m*; **battle f., Am combat f.** formation de combat; **close f.** ordre *m* serré; **to break f.** décrocher

3 Mil *(unit)* unité *f*, **armoured f.** formation blindée

4 Geol **granite f.** formation *f* granitique

▸▸ **f. dancing** danse *f* en formation; **f. flying** vol *m* en formation

formative ['fɔːmətɪv] ADJ *(experience, influence etc)* formateur, -trice; **the f. years** les années de formation

▸ N Ling élément *m* formateur

formatted ['fɔːmætɪd] ADJ *(disk)* formaté; *(text, page)* mis en forme, formaté

formatting ['fɔːmætɪŋ] N Comput *(of disk)* formatage *m*; *(of page, text)* mise *f* en forme, formatage

▸▸ **f. command** commande *f* de formatage; **f. instructions** instructions *fpl* pour le formatage

forme [fɔːm] N Br Typ forme *f*

former ['fɔːmər] ADJ **1** *(previous)* antérieur, -eure, précédent; *(pupil, servant, colleague etc)* ancien; **my f. pupils** mes anciens élèves; **a f. convict** un repris de justice; **in f. times** autrefois; **in a f. life** dans une vie antérieure; **he is a mere shadow of his f. self** il n'est plus que l'ombre de lui-même

2 VOIR GRAMMAIRE A77 *(as opposed to the latter)* premier; **I prefer the f. alternative to the latter** je préfère la première alternative à la deuxième

PRON VOIR GRAMMAIRE A77 **the f.** celui-là, *f* celle-là, *pl* ceux-là, celles-là; **the f. …, the latter …** le premier …, le second …; **of the two methods I prefer the f.** des deux méthodes je préfère celle-là

-former ['fɔːmər] SUFF Br Sch **first/second/ etc-f.** élève *mf* de sixième/cinquième/etc

formerly ['fɔːməlɪ] ADV autrefois, jadis; **Mr Martin, f. a liberal** M. Martin, autrefois libéral; **Mrs Boyle, f. Miss Reid** Madame Boyle, auparavant Mademoiselle Reid; **f. of London** résidant auparavant à Londres; **Burkina Faso, f. Upper Volta** le Burkina Faso, ancienne Haute-Volta

formic ['fɔːmɪk] ADJ Chem *(acid)* formique

Formica® [fɔːˈmaɪkə] N Formica® *m*; **F. worktop** plan *m* de travail en Formica®

formidable ['fɔːmɪdəb(ə)l] ADJ *(opponent, difficulty, appearance, weapon)* redoutable; *(performance, talent, defence)* formidable

Note that the most common meaning of the French word **formidable** is **fantastic**, **excellent**.

formidably [fɔːˈmɪdəblɪ] ADV *(armed, difficult)* redoutablement; *(talented, thorough, equipped)* formidablement, remarquablement

forming ['fɔːmɪŋ] N **1** *(of company etc)* constitution *f*, formation *f* **2** Metal formage *m*, façonnage *m*

▸▸ Mil **f. up** rassemblement *m*

formless ['fɔːmlɪs] ADJ informe, sans forme; *(desire, idea)* indéfini, flou

Formosa [fɔːˈməʊsə] N Formerly Formose *f*

formula, pl **formulas, formulae** ['fɔːmjʊlə, -əz, -iː] N **1** *(scheme, plan)* formule *f*; **an infallible f. for success/happiness** une recette infaillible pour réussir/trouver le bonheur; **a f. acceptable to all parties** une formule qui soit acceptable à tous les partis; **these romantic novels are all done to the same f.** ces romans à l'eau de rose sont tous écrits selon la même formule **2** *(recipe)*, Chem, Math etc *(pl usu* **formulae***)* formule *f*; **gentle f.** *(shampoo, make-up remover etc)* formule douce **3** *(for feeding baby)* lait *m* en poudre

▸▸ Aut **F. 1** la formule 1; Aut **F. 1 car** voiture *f* formule 1

formulaic [fɔːmjʊˈleɪɪk] ADJ Fml stéréotypé

formulate [ˈfɔːmjʊleɪt] VT **1** (law, doctrine, theory etc) formuler; (plan, strategy, policy) élaborer **2** (one's opinion, objections) formuler, exprimer; (one's response) formuler; **difficult to f. in words** difficile à exprimer en paroles

formulation [fɔːmjʊˈleɪʃən] N **1** (development) (of plan, policy) élaboration f, élaboration f **2** (putting into words, expressing) expression f **3** (wording) formulation f

formwork [ˈfɔːmwɜːk] N (for reinforced concrete) coffrage m

fornicate [ˈfɔːnɪkeɪt] VI forniquer

fornication [fɔːnɪˈkeɪʃən] N fornication f

fornicator [ˈfɔːnɪkeɪtər] N (man) fornicateur m; Fam coureur m de jupons; (woman) coureuse f

forsake [fəˈseɪk] VT (pt forsook [fəˈsʊk], pp forsaken [fəˈseɪk(ə)n]) esp Lit **1** (abandon) (person) abandonner, délaisser; (shelter) abandonner; **his habitual assurance had forsaken him** son assurance habituelle l'avait abandonné **2** (renounce) (belief, career etc) renoncer à, abandonner; (conduct, life of ease) renoncer à

forsooth [fəˈsuːθ] Arch, Lit ADV (in truth) en vérité

INT par exemple!, ma foi!

forswear [fɔːˈsweər] VT (pt forswore [fɔːˈswɔːr], pp forsworn [fɔːˈswɔːn]) Fml **1** renoncer à; Rel abjurer, renier **2** Law **to f. oneself** se parjurer

forsythia [fɔːˈsaɪθɪə] N (shrub) forsythia m

fort [fɔːt] N Mil fort m, forteresse f; Fam **to hold the f.** (look after house etc) garder la maison; (look after office, shop etc) tenir la boutique

forte¹ [fɔːt, ˈfɔːtɪ] N (strong point) fort m

forte² [ˈfɔːtɪ] Mus ADJ, ADV forte inv
N forte m

forth [fɔːθ] ADV **1** (forwards) en avant; **to walk back and f.** marcher de long en large, faire les cent pas; **the ferry goes back and f. between …** le ferry fait la navette entre …; Arch **from this time f.** désormais, dorénavant; **from that/this day f.** à partir de ce jour/d'aujourd'hui **2 and so f.** (etcetera) et ainsi de suite, et cetera

forthcoming [fɔːθˈkʌmɪŋ] ADJ **1** (imminent) prochain, à venir; (book, film) qui va sortir; **the f. session** la prochaine session **2** (available) **to be f.** ne pas se faire attendre; **the money will be f.** on trouvera l'argent nécessaire; **no answer was f.** aucune réponse n'est venue (**from** de); **the promised help was not f.** les secours promis ont fait défaut **3** (person) (sociable) sociable, expansif; (frank) ouvert, franc, f franche; **not (very) f.** réservé, renfermé (**about** au sujet de)

forthright [ˈfɔːθraɪt] ADJ (person, reply) franc, f franche

forthrightness [ˈfɔːθraɪtnɪs] N franchise f (**about** au sujet de)

forthwith [fɔːθˈwɪθ] ADV Fml tout de suite, immédiatement, aussitôt; **the council must be summoned f.** il faut convoquer le conseil d'urgence; **to dispense with sb's services f.** se dispenser sur-le-champ ou immédiatement des services de qn

fortieth [ˈfɔːtɪɪθ] ADJ quarantième
N **1** (person, thing) quarantième mf **2** (fraction) quarantième m

fortification [fɔːtɪfɪˈkeɪʃən] N fortification f

fortified [ˈfɔːtɪfaɪd] ADJ Mil fortifié
▸▸ **f. town** ville f fortifiée, place f forte; Br **f. wine** vin m de liqueur, vin doux naturel

fortify [ˈfɔːtɪfaɪ] VT **1** (ship etc) renforcer,

fortifier; (person) fortifier; Fig (person, person's resolve) affermir, fortifier; **to f. oneself for the coming struggle** rassembler ses forces pour la lutte à venir; **fortified with the rites of the Church** muni des sacrements de l'Église; **to f. oneself against the cold** se prémunir contre le froid **2** (wine) viner; (food) augmenter la valeur nutritive de **3** Mil (place) fortifier

fortifying [ˈfɔːtɪfaɪɪŋ] ADJ fortifiant; (drink etc) remontant

fortissimo [fɔːˈtɪsɪməʊ] Mus ADV fortissimo
N fortissimo m inv

fortitude [ˈfɔːtɪtjuːd] N force f morale

fortnight [ˈfɔːtnaɪt] N esp Br quinzaine f, quinze jours mpl; **today f.** (d')aujourd'hui en quinze; **a f. tomorrow** demain en quinze; **in a f.'s time** dans une quinzaine (de jours); **a f. ago** il y a quinze jours; **to adjourn a case for a f.** remettre une cause à quinzaine; **to take a f.'s holiday** prendre quinze jours de vacances

fortnightly [ˈfɔːtnaɪtlɪ] esp Br ADJ bimensuel, semi-mensuel
ADV (to appear) bimensuellement, tous les quinze jours; (to meet) tous les quinze jours

FORTRAN [ˈfɔːtræn] N Comput FORTRAN m

fortress [ˈfɔːtrɪs] N forteresse f, (town) place f forte; **the place was built like a f.** l'endroit était construit comme une forteresse
▸▸ **f. city** cité f fortifiée

fortuitous [fɔːˈtjuːɪtəs] ADJ esp Fml fortuit, imprévu

fortuitously [fɔːˈtjuːɪtəslɪ] ADV esp Fml fortuitement, par hasard

fortunate [ˈfɔːtʃənət, -tʃ-] ADJ **1** (person etc) **to be f.** avoir de la chance; **to be f. enough to …** avoir la chance de …; **I consider myself f. to know her** j'ai la chance de la connaître; **we've been quite f. in the weather** nous avons eu de la chance pour ce qui est du temps; **we've been quite f. in our choice** nous avons fait un choix très heureux; **the less f. among them** les plus infortunés d'entre eux
2 (occasion etc) propice, favorable, heureux; **a f. choice of words** une tournure heureuse; **it was f. that you remembered** encore heureux que tu t'en sois souvenu; **how f.!** quel bonheur!, quelle chance!

> Note that the French adjective **fortuné** is a false friend. It means **wealthy**.

fortunately [ˈfɔːtʃənətlɪ, -tʃ-] ADV heureusement, par bonheur; **we're quite f. situated as far as the shops are concerned** nous sommes plutôt bien lotis en ce qui concerne les magasins

fortune [ˈfɔːtʃən] N **1** (prosperity) prospérité f, richesse f, (riches) richesses fpl, biens mpl; **a man of f.** un homme riche; **to make a** or **one's f.** faire fortune; **you must be making a f.** tu dois gagner un argent fou; **she has made and lost several fortunes** elle a fait fortune plusieurs fois dans sa vie; **to come into a f.** hériter une fortune; **her jewels are worth a f.** ses bijoux valent une fortune; Fam **it cost me a (small) f.** cela m'a coûté un argent fou ou une fortune ou les yeux de la tête ou la peau des fesses; **to spend a (small) f. on books/decorating the house** dépenser une fortune en livres/pour décorer la maison; **her face is her f.** son visage est son grand atout
2 (luck) fortune f, (chance) hasard m, chance f, (destiny) destinée f, sort m; Myth **le Sort, le Destin; ill f.** malchance f, mauvais sort; **piece of good f.** coup m de chance, bonheur m; **by (sheer) good f.** par bonheur; **f. favours** or **is kind to him** la fortune lui sourit; **the fortunes of war** le sort des armes; **he**

followed the team's changing fortunes il a suivi l'équipe bon an mal an; **despite its changing fortunes over the years, the company …** en dépit des adversités qu'elle a rencontré au fil des ans, la compagnie …; **to tell fortunes** dire la bonne aventure; **to tell sb's f.** dire la bonne aventure à qn; **to tell sb's f. by the cards** tirer les cartes à qn
▸▸ **f. cookie** = biscuit m chinois dans lequel est caché un horoscope; Fin **F. 500** = les cinq cents plus grosses entreprises fpl américaines (dont la liste est établie, chaque année, par le magazine Fortune)

fortune-hunter N (man) coureur m de dot; (woman) croqueuse f de diamants

fortune-teller N diseur, -euse de bonne aventure; (with cards) tireur, -euse de cartes

fortune-telling N la bonne aventure; (with cards) cartomancie f

forty [ˈfɔːtɪ] ADJ, N quarante m; **f.-one** quarante et un; **f.-two** quarante-deux; **about f. guests** une quarantaine d'invités; **to be f. (years old)** avoir quarante ans; Prov **life begins at f.** la vie commence à quarante ans; **the forties** les années quarante; **to be in one's forties** avoir passé la quarantaine; Fam **to have f. winks** piquer ou faire un petit somme

forty-five N Old-fashioned (record) (disque m) quarante-cinq tours m

fortyish [ˈfɔːtɪɪʃ] ADJ d'une quarantaine d'années; **I'd say she was f.** je lui donne la quarantaine ou une quarantaine d'années; **he was balding, f. and plump** il perdait ses cheveux et avait la quarantaine rondouillarde

forum [ˈfɔːrəm] N **1** tribune f libre, forum m; Antiq (square) forum m; **a f. in which workers can put forward their views** un forum permettant aux ouvriers d'exprimer leurs opinions **2** Comput (on Internet) forum m (de discussion)

forward [ˈfɔːwəd, Naut ˈfɔrəd] ADJ **1** (of place) de devant, situé en avant; Naut (de l')avant, sur l'avant; (movement etc) en avant; **f. and backward movement** mouvement m d'avant en arrière
2 (of time) (plants) avancé, précoce; (child) précoce, en avance; **a f. thinking company** une entreprise tournée vers l'avenir
3 (impudent, bold) effronté, hardi; **it would have been thought f. of a woman to …** cela aurait été considéré comme effronté de la part d'une femme de …
4 Fin (price etc) à terme
ADV (occ forwards [ˈfɔːwədz]) **1** (of time) **from this/that day f.** à partir d'aujourd'hui/de ce jour-là
2 (of direction) en avant; **to go** or **move f.** (s')avancer; **to step f.** faire un pas en avant; **f.!** en avant!; Mil **f. march!** en avant, marche!
3 (of position) à l'avant; **the seat is too far f.** la banquette est trop avancée ou trop en avant; **we're sitting too far f.** nous sommes assis trop à l'avant; Naut **f. of the beam** sur l'avant du travers; **the crew's quarters are f.** le logement de l'équipage est à l'avant
4 Com (carried) **f.** report m; Com Com charges **f.** frais mpl à percevoir à la livraison; Com, Fin **to sell f.** vendre à terme
N Sport (player) avant m
VT **1** (send) (letter, e-mail) faire suivre; (goods etc) expédier, envoyer, Spec transiter; **please f.** (on letter) prière de faire suivre, à faire suivre; **to f. sth to sb** faire parvenir qch à qn; **we'll f. your complaint/report to the relevant department** nous transmettrons votre plainte/rapport au service correspondant
2 (promote) (person's interests etc) favoriser
▸▸ Fin **f. account** compte m à terme; Fin **f. buying** achat m à terme; Fin **f. contract**

contrat *m* à terme; *Fin, Com* **f. dealing** opérations *fpl* à terme; *Com* **f. delivery** livraison *f* à terme; *Fin* **f. exchange** change *m* à terme; *Fin* **f. exchange market** marché *m* des changes à terme; *Aut* **f. gears** marches *fpl* avant; *Econ* **f. integration** intégration *f* en aval, intégration descendante; *Mktg* **f. invention** invention *f* de produits totalement nouveaux; *Fin, Com* **f. market** marché à terme; **f. motion** marche *f* (en) avant; *Sport* **f. pass** (*in rugby*) passe *f* en avant; **f. planning** planification *f*; *Mil* **f. positions** premières positions *fpl*; **f. post** avant-poste *m*, *pl* avant-postes; *Fin, Com* **f. purchase** achat à terme; *Fin* **f. rate** cours *m* à terme, taux *m* pour les opérations à terme; *Fin* **F. Rate Agreement** accord *m* de taux à terme; *Com* **f. requirement** commande *f* prévisionnelle; *Com* **f. sale** vente *f* à terme; *Comput* **f. search** recherche *f* avant; *Br Comput* **f. slash** barre *f* oblique; *Fin, Com* **f. trading** opérations *fpl* à terme; *Naut* **f. turret** tourelle *f* avant

forwardation [fɔːwəˈdeɪʃən] N *Fin* report *m*

forwarder [ˈfɔːwədər] N *Com* transitaire *m*; **f. and consolidator** transitaire-groupeur *m*

forwarding [ˈfɔːwədɪŋ] N (*sending*) expédition *f*, envoi *m*;
▸▸ **f. address** adresse *f* pour faire suivre le courrier; *Com* adresse pour l'expédition; *Com* **f. agent** transitaire *m*; *Com* **f. charges** frais *mpl* d'expédition; *Com* **f. instructions** indications *fpl* concernant l'expédition

forward-looking ADJ progressiste

forwardness [ˈfɔːwədnɪs] N **1** (*eagerness*) empressement *m*, ardeur *f* **2** (*boldness*) hardiesse *f*, présomption *f*

forwards [ˈfɔːwədz] ADV *see* **forward** ADV

forwent PT *see* **forgo**

Fosbury flop [ˈfɒzbərɪ] N *Sport* Fosbury *m*

fossil [ˈfɒs(ə)l] N fossile *m*; *Fam Pej* **an old f.** (*person*) un vieux croûton, un vieux fossile
ADJ (*plant, bones etc*) fossile
▸▸ **f. fuel** combustible *m* fossile

fossilization [fɒsɪlaɪˈzeɪʃən] N fossilisation *f*

fossilize [ˈfɒsɪlaɪz] VT fossiliser
VI se fossiliser; *Fig* (*of person*) s'encroûter

fossilized [ˈfɒsɪlaɪzd] ADJ fossilisé; (*ideas, attitudes etc*) fossile

foster [ˈfɒstər] VT **1** (*child*) prendre en famille d'accueil; **to f. a child (out)** mettre un enfant en famille d'accueil **2** (*promote*) (*idea, hope, belief etc*) entretenir, nourrir; (*person's plans, sense of responsibility*) encourager, favoriser; (*the arts etc*) protéger; **to f. friendship between peoples** stimuler l'amitié entre les peuples
▸▸ **f. child** enfant *m* placé dans une famille d'accueil; **f. father** père *m* de la famille d'accueil; **f. home** famille *f* d'accueil; **f. mother** mère *f* de la famille d'accueil; **f. parents** famille d'accueil

fostering [ˈfɒstərɪŋ] N **1** (*of child*) prise *f* en famille d'accueil; (*fostering out*) mise *f* en famille d'accueil **2** (*of the arts etc*) patronage *m*, encouragement *m*

fought PP, PT *see* **fight**

foul [faʊl] ADJ **1** (*disgusting*) (*smell*) infect, nauséabond; (*thoughts*) immonde, impur, corrompu; (*language*) grossier, ordurier; (*water*) croupi; *Fam* **that soup was f.!** cette soupe était infecte!; *Fam* **what f. weather!** quel sale temps!, quel temps infect!; *Naut* **f. weather** gros temps *m*; **to be f. to sb/about sth** être infect *ou* abject avec qn/au sujet de qch; **f. air** air *m* vicié; **f. breath** mauvaise haleine *f*, *esp Lit* **f. deed** infamie *f*; **f.-smelling/-tasting** qui a une odeur/un goût infect(e); *Fam* **I'm in a f. temper today** je suis d'une humeur massacrante aujourd'hui; **she has a f.**

temper elle a un sale caractère; **she's got a f. tongue** elle a une langue de vipère
2 (*gun, spark plug*) encrassé; **f. bottom** (*of anchorage*) mauvais fond *m*; (*of ship*) carène *f* sale
3 *Sport etc* (*unfair*) déloyal, -aux, illicite; (*criminal behaviour*) action criminelle; (*underhand dealings*) intrigue *f*
N *Sport* coup *m* illicite *ou* déloyal; *Ftbl, Rugby* faute *f*
ADV **1** **it smells f.!** ça pue!; **it tastes perfectly f.** c'est infect; **it looks f.** c'est horrible *ou* atroce; *Fam* **to feel f.** ne pas se sentir bien
2 (*unfairly*) irrégulièrement, déloyalement; *Old-fashioned* **to fight f.** se battre déloyalement; *Naut* **to run f. of another ship** (*collide with*) entrer en collision avec *ou* aborder *ou* heurter un autre navire; **to fall** *or* **run f. of the law/sb** avoir des démêlés avec la justice/qn
VT **1** (*dirty*) (*place, reputation etc*) salir, souiller; (*of dog*) (*pavement*) souiller; (*gun barrel, spark plugs*) encrasser
2 (*obstruct, jam*) (*ropes etc*) s'emmêler dans; (*collide with*) (*ship*) entrer en collision avec, (se) heurter contre; **weeds fouled the anchor** l'ancre était prise *ou* coincée dans des algues; **the ropes fouled the propeller** les cordes avaient bloqué l'hélice
3 *Sport* (*another player*) commettre une faute contre
VI **1** (*of gun barrel etc*) s'encrasser; (*of pump*) s'engorger **2** *Naut* (*of anchor, rope etc*) se coincer; (*of anchor*) surjaler; *Tech* (*of moving part*) toucher
▸▸ *Sport* **f. play** jeu *m* irrégulier *ou* déloyal; (*in cards, games*) tricherie *f*; **f. play is not suspected** on ne croit pas à un crime
▸ **foul up** VT SEP **1** (*put out of order*) (*machine*) dérégler **2** *Fam* (*ruin*) (*plan*) gâcher; **it will f. things up if he finds out** ça va tout gâcher s'il l'apprend
VI **1** *Sl* (*of person*) merder; **don't f. up again/this time!** tâche de ne plus merder/ne pas merder cette fois! **2** (*of gun barrel etc*) s'encrasser; (*of pump*) s'engorger

fouler [ˈfaʊlər] N *Sport* **he's a persistent f.** il commet des fautes sans arrêt

fouling [ˈfaʊlɪŋ] N **1** (*of pipes*) engorgement *m*; (*of spark plugs*) encrassement *m* **2** *Sport* **a lot of f.** beaucoup de jeu déloyal

foully [ˈfaʊlɪ] ADV **1** (*to speak etc*) grossièrement **2** (*to behave*) bassement, ignoblement; *Lit* **he was f. murdered** il fut ignoblement assassiné

foul-mouthed [ˈfaʊlˈmaʊðd] ADJ (*person*) au langage ordurier, grossier, -ière; (*reply, tirade*) ordurier, grossier

foulness [ˈfaʊlnɪs] N **1** (*dirtiness*) saleté *f*; (*of air etc*) fétidité *f*; **the f. of the smell** l'odeur infecte, la puanteur **2** (*of language etc*) grossièreté *f*, obscénité *f* **3** (*of a deed, behaviour*) infamie *f*, ignominie *f*

foul-tempered ADJ **to be f.** avoir un sale caractère

foul-up N *Fam* (*mistake*) cafouillage *m*; **there's been a f.** quelque chose a cloché *ou* cafouillé, il y a eu un cafouillage

found¹ [faʊnd] VT **1** (*city, hospital, dynasty*) fonder; (*college, club, organization etc*) fonder, créer; (*company, business etc*) établir, créer; **to f. a fortune** (*lay foundations of fortune*) établir les bases d'une fortune; (*make fortune*) bâtir une fortune (**on** sur) **2** (*suspicions, hope, social order etc*) baser, fonder (**on** sur); **founded on fact** (*of novel etc*) reposant sur des faits véridiques

found² PT, PP *see* **find**
ADV (*with adv prefixed*) (*ship etc*) **well-f.** bien équipé (**in** de)

found³ VT *Metal* (*metals*) fondre; (*casting*) mouler

foundation [faʊnˈdeɪʃən] N **1** (*action*) (*of city etc*) fondation *f*, (*of empire*) établissement *m*, institution *f*, (*of company*) établissement *m*, création *f*; (*of hospital*) fondation et dotation *f*
2 *Constr* (*base*) (*of building*) fondement *m*, fondation *f*, (*of road*) assiette *f*, (*of machine etc*) assise *f*, *Fig* **to lay the foundation(s) of an alliance** jeter les bases d'une alliance; **the foundations of modern society** les assises *ou* fondations de la société moderne; *Constr* **to lay the f. stone** poser la première pierre
3 (*basis*) (*of theory etc*) fondement *m*, base *f*, (*of doubt*) motif *m*, cause *f*, **rumour without f.** bruit dénué de fondement
4 (*institution*) institution *f* dotée, fondation *f*, (*legacy*) capital *m* légué pour œuvres de bienfaisance, fondation; **a charitable f.** une institution charitable; **the Ford f.** la fondation Ford
5 (*in clothing*) **embroidery on a silk f.** broderie *f* sur fond de soie
6 (*make-up*) fond *m* de teint
▸▸ *Br* **f. course** cours *m* introductif; **f. cream** fond de teint; *Old-fashioned* **f. garment** (*girdle*) gaine *f*, (*full-length*) combiné *m*; *Br* **f. hospital** = hôpital *m* dépendant du NHS mais possédant une autonomie importante en ce qui concerne le budget, les salaires et les conditions de travail; **f. scholar** élève *mf* boursier; *Br* **f. school** = école *f* privée qui reçoit une subvention de l'État

founder¹ [ˈfaʊndər] N (*of hospital etc*) fondateur *m*
▸▸ *Br* **f. member** membre *m* fondateur

founder² N *Metal* fondeur *m*

founder³ VI (*of hopes, horse*) s'effondrer; (*of talks, negotiations*) avorter; (*of project, scheme*) péricliter; (*of ship*) sombrer, couler; **to f. on the rocks** s'échouer sur les rochers
VT (*horse*) courbaturer

foundering [ˈfaʊndərɪŋ] N (*of hopes*) effondrement *m*

founding¹ [ˈfaʊndɪŋ] ADJ (*member*) fondateur, -trice
N = **foundation 1**
▸▸ **f. father** père *m* fondateur; *Hist* **the F. Fathers** les pères *mpl* fondateurs (*aux États-Unis*)

founding² N *Metal* fonderie *f*, moulage *m*

foundling [ˈfaʊndlɪŋ] N *Old-fashioned* enfant *mf* trouvé(e)
▸▸ *Hist* **f. hospital** hospice *m* des enfants trouvés

foundry [ˈfaʊndrɪ] N *Metal* (*iron etc*) fonderie *f*
▸▸ **f. iron** fonte *f* de moulage

fount¹ [faʊnt] N *Lit* (*spring*) source *f* (d'eau); *Fig* (*of happiness etc*) source

fount² [faʊnt, fɒnt] N *Typ* fonte *f*

fountain [ˈfaʊntɪn] N (*natural*) fontaine *f*, source *f* (d'eau); (*man-made*) fontaine; (*in park etc*) jet *m* d'eau; **a f. of water shot from the broken pipe** un jet d'eau jaillit du tuyau cassé
▸▸ **f. pen** stylo *m* à encre

fountainhead [ˈfaʊntɪnhed] N *esp Fig* source *f*

four [fɔːr] N **1** (*number, numeral*) quatre *m inv*; **twenty-f.** vingt-quatre; **f. fives are twenty** quatre fois cinq font vingt; **it's f. o'clock** il est quatre heures; **at f. thirty** à quatre heures et demie; **to be f.** (*in age*) avoir quatre ans; **on all fours** à quatre pattes; **to get down on all fours** se mettre à quatre pattes
2 *Sport* (*in rowing*) quatre *m*; **would you like to make up a f.?** (*for a game of bridge*) voudriez-vous vous joindre à nous pour faire une partie à quatre?; *Cr* **to hit a f.** marquer

quatre points; *Golf* **a f.-ball (match)** une partie à quatre joueurs et quatre balles
PRON quatre
ADJ quatre; **the f. corners of the earth** les quatre coins du monde; **open to the f. winds** ouvert à tous les vents *ou* aux quatre vents; **the F. Horsemen of the Apocalypse** les quatre cavaliers de l'Apocalypse

four-colour, *Am* **four-color** ADJ *Typ etc* à quatre couleurs
► ► **f. printing** impression *f* en quadrichromie; **f. work** *(process)* quadrichromie *f*

four-cornered ADJ à quatre coins; *(quadrangular)* quadrangulaire

four-cycle ADJ *Am (engine, cylinder etc)* à quatre temps

four-door ADJ *Aut* à quatre portes; **f. model** quatre portes *f*; **f. saloon** berline *f* à quatre portes

four-engined [-'endʒɪnd] ADJ *(plane)* quadrimoteur

four-eyes [-aɪz] N *Fam* binoclard, -arde

four-figure ADJ *Math (number, sum)* à quatre chiffres; *(logarithm)* à quatre décimales

fourfold ['fɔːfəʊld] ADJ **a f. increase** une augmentation au quadruple
ADV quatre fois autant, au quadruple; **to increase f.** quadrupler

four-footed [-'fʊtɪd] ADJ *(animal)* quadrupède, à quatre pattes; *Fam* **a f. friend** un animal à quatre pattes

four-handed [-'hændɪd] ADJ **1** *Cards (game)* à quatre (personnes) **2** *Mus (piece)* à quatre mains

four-in-hand N *(carriage)* véhicule *m* à quatre chevaux

four-leaf clover N trèfle *m* à quatre feuilles

four-leaved ADJ *(plant)* quadrifolié
► ► **f. clover** trèfle *m* à quatre feuilles

four-legged ADJ *(animal)* quadrupède; *(table)* à quatre pieds; **our f. friends** nos amis les bêtes

four-letter word N *Fam* gros mot *m*, obscénité *f*; **for some people, 'socialism' seems to be a f. w.** pour certains, il semble que le mot 'socialisme' soit tabou

four-part ADJ *Mus* à quatre parties; *(singing)* à quatre voix

four-phase ADJ *Elec (system)* tétraphasé

four-poster N lit *m* à colonnes *ou* à baldaquin
ADJ *(bed)* à colonnes

fourscore [fɔː'skɔːr] ADJ *Arch, Lit* quatre-vingts

four-seater N *Aut* voiture *f* à quatre places

foursome ['fɔːsəm] N *(four people)* groupe *m* de quatre personnes; *(two couples)* deux couples; *Golf (game)* partie *f* (de) double *ou* à deux contre deux; **to go out in a f.** *(of four people)* sortir à quatre; *(of two couples)* sortir à deux couples; **to make up a f.** *(of four people)* former un groupe de quatre personnes; *(of two couples)* former deux couples; *(be the fourth person)* faire le quatrième

four-speed ADJ *Aut* à quatre vitesses

foursquare ['fɔː'skweər] ADJ **1** *(refusal)* carré **2** *(building)* solide
ADV *(to refuse)* carrément; *(to build)* solidement; **to stand f. behind sb** soutenir qn fermement *ou* résolument

four-star N *Br (petrol)* super *m*
► ► **f. hotel** hôtel *m* quatre étoiles *ou* de première catégorie; **f. petrol** super, super-carburant *m*; **f. unleaded** super sans plomb

four-stroke ADJ *(engine)* à quatre temps

fourteen ['fɔː'tiːn] ADJ, N quatorze *m*; **she is f.** elle a quatorze ans; **the plane will arrive at**

f. thirty (hours) l'avion arrivera à quatorze heures trente

fourteenth [fɔː'tiːnθ] ADJ quatorzième; **Louis the F.** Louis Quatorze
N **1** *(of month)* quatorze *m*; **(on) the f. of May** le quatorze mai **2** *(fraction)* quatorzième *m* **3** *(person, thing)* quatorzième *mf*

fourth [fɔːθ] ADJ quatrième; **Henry the F.** Henri Quatre
N **1** *(of month)* quatre *m*; **on the f.** le quatre; **the f. of January, January the f.** le quatre janvier
2 *(fraction)* quart *m*; **three-fourths of the globe** les trois quarts du globe
3 *(in series)* quatrième *mf*
4 *Mus* quarte *f*
5 *Aut* quatrième *f*
6 *Cards* **to make a f.** faire le quatrième
► ► **the f. estate** *(press)* la presse; *Aut* **f. gear** quatrième vitesse *f*; *Am* **F. of July** = anniversaire *m* du jour de l'indépendance *(fête nationale américaine)*; *Pol* **the F. World** le quart-monde; *Br Sch* **f. year** ≃ classe *f* de troisième

fourthly ['fɔːθlɪ] ADV quatrièmement, en quatrième lieu

four-wheel ADJ *(vehicle)* à quatre roues
► ► *Aut* **f. drive** propulsion *f* à quatre roues; **does it have f. drive?** est-ce qu'il a quatre roues motrices?; **it's a f. drive** c'est un quatre-quart; *Aut* **f. steering** quatre roues *fpl* directrices

four-wheeled ADJ à quatre roues

four-wheeler N voiture *f* à quatre roues

fowl [faʊl] N **1** *(domesticated bird)* volaille *f*; **to keep fowl(s)** élever de la volaille *ou* des volailles; *Culin* **boiling f.** poule *f* (au pot) **2** *(wild bird)* *(pl* **fowl**) gibier *m* ailé **3** *Lit (bird)* oiseau *m*
► ► **f. pest** peste *f* aviaire; **f. pox** diphtérie *f* aviaire

fowling ['faʊlɪŋ] N **to go f.** aller à la chasse au gibier ailé
► ► **f. piece** carabine *f*, fusil *m* de chasse léger

fox [fɒks] N renard *m*; **red f.** renard commun; **Arctic f.** renard bleu; **silver f.** renard argenté; *Fam* **an old f.** *(cunning man)* un vieux renard, un vieux madré; *Fam* **a sly f.** un fin renard, un roublard
VT 1 *(mystify)* *(person)* mystifier, tromper; **you've got me foxed** je suis perplexe; **it foxes me why he did it** je n'arrive pas à saisir pourquoi il a fait ça; **she was absolutely foxed by the problem** le problème la laissait complètement perplexe **2** *(trick, deceive)* tromper, duper **3** *(discolour)* *(pages of book)* tacher de roux; *(engraving)* maculer
► ► **f. brush** queue *f* de renard; **f. cub** renardeau *m*; **f. fur** *(peau f* de*)* renard *m*; **a f. fur coat** un manteau *m* en renard

foxglove ['fɒksglʌv] N *(plant)* digitale *f* (pourprée)

foxhole ['fɒkshəʊl] N **1** renardière *f*, terrier *m* de renard **2** *Mil* abri *m* individuel; *(for sniper)* trou *m* de tirailleur

foxhound ['fɒkshaʊnd] N fox-hound *m*, *pl* fox-hounds

foxhunt ['fɒkshʌnt] N chasse *f* au renard

foxhunting ['fɒkshʌntɪŋ] N chasse *f* au renard

foxiness ['fɒksɪnɪs] N **1** *(craftiness)* roublardise *f* **2** *Am Fam (of woman)* air *m* sexy

foxtail ['fɒksteɪl] N **1** *(flower)* queue *f* de renard **2** *(plant)* vulpin *m*
► ► **f. grass** vulpin

fox-terrier N fox-terrier *m*, *pl* fox-terriers, *Fam* fox *m*

foxtrot ['fɒkstrɒt] N *(dance)* fox-trot *m inv*
VI (-tt-) danser le fox-trot

foxy ['fɒksɪ] ADJ **1** *(crafty)* rusé, astucieux, *esp Pej* roublard **2** *Am Fam (woman)* sexy; **a f. lady** une nana sexy

foyer ['fɔɪeɪ, 'fwæjeɪ] N *Theat* foyer *m* du public; *Cin* (hall *m* d')entrée *f*; *(of hotel)* hall (de réception)

FPA [efpiː'eɪ] N *(abbr* **Family Planning Association)** = association *f* pour le planning familial

FPU [efpiː'juː] N *Comput (abbr* **floating-point unit)** FPU *f*, coprocesseur *m* arithmétique

Fr 1 *Rel (abbr* **Father)** Père **2** *abbr* **France 3** *Fin abbr* **franc**

FRA [efɑːr'eɪ] N *Fin (abbr* **Future Rate Agreement, Forward Rate Agreement)** ATF *m*

fracas ['frækɑː] N remue-ménage *m inv*; **to cause a f.** faire du remue-ménage

fractal ['fræktəl] N fractal *m*

fraction ['frækʃən] N **1** VOIR GRAMMAIRE A76; B59 *Math* fraction *f*; **vulgar** *or* **common f.** fraction ordinaire; **compound f.** fraction de fraction; **decimal f.** fraction décimale **2** *(small part)* petite portion *f*, petite partie *f*; **the new method takes only a f. of the time** la nouvelle méthode prend bien moins de temps; **he escaped death by a f. of a second** il a été à deux doigts de la mort; **a f. too small/large** un tout petit peu trop petit/grand; **a f. earlier/too late** un tout petit peu plus tôt/trop tard; **she won by a f.** elle a gagné d'un rien **3** *Fin (of share)* fraction *f*, rompu *m* **4** *Chem (of distillation)* fraction *f* **5** *Pol (of party)* fraction *f*, groupe *m* fractionnaire

fractional ['frækʃən(ə)l] ADJ **1** *Math* fractionnaire; *Fig* **the difference is only f.** la différence est minime **2** *Chem* fractionné
► ► *Chem* **f. distillation** distillation *f* fractionnée

fractionally ['frækʃən(ə)lɪ] ADV légèrement, un tout petit peu

fractionate ['frækʃəneɪt] VT *Chem, Ind (petroleum etc)* fractionner

fractionize ['frækʃənaɪz] VT *Math* fractionner

fractious ['frækʃəs] ADJ de mauvaise humeur; *(tone of voice, expression)* irrité; *(baby)* pleurnicheur; **to be f.** *or* **in a f. mood** être de mauvaise humeur; *(baby)* pleurnicher

fractiousness ['frækʃəsnɪs] N mauvaise humeur *f*; *(of baby)* pleurnicherie *f*, pleurnichage *m*; **the f. of her voice** l'irritation qu'il y avait dans sa voix

fracture ['fræktʃər] N **1** *Med* fracture *f*; **to set a f.** réduire une fracture **2** *(of axle etc)* fracture *f*, rupture *f*; *Geol* cassure *f*, fracture *f*
VT **1** *Med (bone)* fracturer; **fractured skull** crâne fracturé; **fractured ribs** côtes cassées **2** *(break)* casser, briser
VI **1** *Med (of bone, limb)* se fracturer **2** *(break)* se casser, se briser

fragile ['frædʒaɪl] ADJ **1** *(cup, peace)* fragile **2** *(person) (weak)* fragile, faible; *(delicate)* délicat; **she was a f. child** c'était une enfant fragile; **he's become very f. recently** il s'est beaucoup affaibli ces derniers temps; **emotionally f.** fragile sur le plan émotionnel; **he sounded rather f. over the phone** il avait l'air plutôt abattu au téléphone; *Fam* **I'm feeling a bit f. this morning** *(hung over)* j'ai mal aux cheveux ce matin

fragilely ['frædʒaɪllɪ] ADV fragilement

fragility [frə'dʒɪlɪtɪ] N **1** *(of ornament, peace)* fragilité *f* **2** *(of person) (weakness)* fragilité *f*, faiblesse *f*; *(delicateness)* délicatesse *f*; **emotional f.** fragilité émotionnelle

fragment[1] ['frægmənt] N **1** *(of porcelain etc)* fragment *m*, morceau *m*; *(of paper)* morceau; *(of mortar shell)* éclat *m*; *(of story, account)* fragment; **to fly into fragments** voler en morceaux *ou* en éclats **2** *Liter* fragment *m*; *(of book)* extrait *m*; *(of author)* œuvre *f* inachevée

fragment² [fræg'ment] **VI** se fragmenter

VT réduire en fragments, briser en morceaux; **the family structure/the party has been fragmented** la structure familiale/le parti a été fragmenté(e)

fragmentary ['frægmənt(ə)rɪ] **ADJ** fragmentaire

fragmentation [frægmən'teɪʃən] **N** fragmentation *f*
▸▸**f. bomb** bombe *f* à fragmentation

fragrance ['freɪɡrəns] **N** parfum *m*; **bubble bath with the f. of bilberries** bain moussant (parfumé) à la myrtille

fragrant ['freɪɡrənt] **ADJ** parfumé, odorant, fragrant; *(scent)* embaumé; **to be** *or* **smell f.** sentir bon; **woods f. with wild strawberries** bois qui embaument les fraises sauvages

fraidy cat ['freɪdɪ] **N** *Am Fam* poule *f* mouillée

frail [freɪl] **ADJ 1** *(person)* faible, frêle; **a f. old man** un vieil homme frêle *ou* fragile; **to be in f. health** avoir une santé délicate **2** *(object)* peu solide, fragile; *(beauty)* éphémère; *(happiness)* précaire; *(hope)* fragile

frailness ['freɪlnɪs] **N 1** *(of person)* faiblesse *f*, *(of character)* faiblesse morale; **the f. of his health** sa santé délicate **2** *(of glass etc)* fragilité *f*, *(of beauty)* caractère *m* éphémère; *(of happiness)* précarité *f*

frailty ['freɪltɪ] **N 1** = frailness **1 2** *(moral flaw)* faible *m*, défaut *m*; **human f.** faiblesse *f* des hommes

frame [freɪm] **N 1** *(of picture, mirror, web page)* cadre *m*, encadrement *m*; *(of window, door)* chambranle *m*, châssis *m* dormant; *(picture)* TV trame *f* (double); *(of reel of film)* image *f*, *(of comic strip)* case *f* **2** *(framework)* *(of person, animal, wing of plane)* ossature *f*, *(of building, bridge etc)* charpente *f*, *(of bicycle etc)* cadre *m*; *(of railway engine, car)* châssis *m*; *(of machine)* bâti *m*; *(of umbrella)* monture *f*, *(of racket)* armature *f*, *(of bed)* châlit *m*; *(of ship)* membrure *f*, carcasse *f*, *(in gardening)* châssis *m*; **his huge f. filled the doorway** sa large carrure s'encadrait dans la porte; **man of gigantic f.** homme bâti comme un colosse; **(spectacle) frames** monture (de lunettes); **glasses with metal frames** lunettes à monture de métal **3** **f. of mind** état *m ou* disposition *f* d'esprit; **he is in a bad f. of mind** il est mal disposé; **f. of reference, reference f.** *Math* système *m* de coordonnées, référentiel *m*; *Fig* système *m* de référence **4** *(in embroidery)* *(floor-standing)* métier *m* (à broder); *(hand-held)* tambour *m* (à broder) **5** *Sport (in snooker) (wooden device)* triangle *m*; *(game)* partie *f*

VT 1 *(surround) (picture etc)* encadrer; *TV (the picture)* cadrer, centrer; *Phot, TV (subject)* cadrer; **black hair framed her face** des cheveux noirs encadraient son visage **2** *(compose) (poem etc)* composer; *(law)* rédiger; *(one's thoughts)* mettre de l'ordre dans; *(opinion)* formuler; *(answer, reply)* composer, formuler **3** *Fam (falsely incriminate) (person)* monter une accusation *ou* un coup contre; **I've been framed** c'est un coup monté (contre moi); **she was framed by the police for a bank robbery** la police a monté un coup contre elle et l'a accusée d'avoir dévalisé une banque
▸▸*Comput* **f. format** *(of network)* protocole *m*; *Am* **f. house** maison *f* en bois

framer ['freɪmər] **N** *(of pictures)* encadreur *m*

frame-up **N** *Sl (false incrimination)* coup *m* monté

framework ['freɪmwɜːk] **N** *(of building, ship)* charpente *f*, carcasse *f*, *(of novel, play)* charpente; *(of negotiations)* structure *f*; **a political/legal/constitutional f.** un cadre politique/légal/constitutionnel; **it comes within the f. of the UN** cela entre dans le cadre de l'ONU

framing ['freɪmɪŋ] **N 1** *(of picture etc)* encadrement *m*; *Cin, Phot* cadrage *m* **2** *(structuring) (of poem etc)* composition *f* **3** *Fam (false incrimination)* accusation *f* inventée de toutes pièces **4** metal **f.** *(for window)* vitrière *f*

franc [fræŋk] **N 1** *(Swiss currency)* franc *m* **2** *Formerly (French and Belgian currency)* franc *m*

France [frɑːns] **N** France *f*, **in F.** en France

franchise ['fræntʃaɪz] **N 1** *Com (granted by public body)* concession *f*, *(granted by manufacturer)* franchise *f*, *(shop, outlet)* établissement *m* en franchise **2** *Pol* droit *m* de vote
▸▸*Com* **f. agreement** accord *m* de franchise; *Com* **f. holder** franchisé, -ée

franchisee [fræntʃaɪ'ziː] **N** *Com* franchisé, -ée

franchising ['fræntʃaɪzɪŋ] **N** *Com* franchisage *m*

franchisor ['fræntʃaɪzər] **N** *Com* franchiseur, -euse

Franciscan [fræn'sɪskən] **N, ADJ** franciscain *m*

Francis of Assisi ['frɑːnsɪs] **N** saint François d'Assise

franco ['fræŋkəʊ] *Com* **ADJ** franco
ADV franco

francophile ['fræŋkəʊfaɪl] **ADJ, N** francophile *mf*

francophobe ['fræŋkəʊfəʊb] **ADJ, N 2** francophobe *mf*

francophone ['fræŋkəʊfəʊn] **ADJ, N** francophone *mf*

frangible ['frændʒɪb(ə)l] **ADJ** cassant, fragile

frangipane ['frændʒɪpeɪn] **N** frangipane *f*

Franglais [frɒŋ'ɡleɪ] **N** franglais *m*

Frank [fræŋk] **N** *Hist* Franc *m*, Franque *f*

frank¹ [fræŋk] **ADJ** *(person, answer)* franc, *f* franche, sincère; *(speech)* direct, ouvert; *(discussion, exchange of views)* à cœur ouvert; **to be quite f. with you** pour être franc avec vous; **I don't think you're being f. with me** je ne crois pas que tu me dises la vérité

frank² **VT** *(letter)* affranchir *(à la machine)*; *(by post office)* oblitérer

Frankenstein food ['fræŋkənstaɪn] **N** *Fam* = surnom donné aux aliments génétiquement modifiés par leurs détracteurs

Frankfurt ['fræŋkfɜːt] **N** Francfort

frankfurter ['fræŋkfɜːtər] **N** saucisse *f* de Francfort

frankincense ['fræŋkɪnsens] **N** encens *m*

franking ['fræŋkɪŋ] **N** *(of letter)* affranchissement *m (à la machine)*
▸▸**f. machine** machine *f* à affranchir

Frankish ['fræŋkɪʃ] **ADJ** *Hist* franc, *f* franque

Franklin stove ['fræŋklɪn] **N** *Am* poêle *m* à bois

frankly ['fræŋklɪ] **ADV** franchement; **I tell you f. that ...** je vous dis carrément que ...; **(quite) f., no!** franchement, non!; **I'll speak f. to you** je vais vous parler franchement *ou* à cœur ouvert

frankness ['fræŋknɪs] **N** franchise *f*, sincérité *f*, **I admire her f. in telling him** j'admire la franchise *ou* la sincérité avec laquelle elle le lui a dit

frantic ['fræntɪk] **ADJ** *(rush, pace)* fréné-

tique, forcené; **in a f. attempt to ...** dans une folle tentative pour ...; **everyone was quite f. in their efforts to meet the deadline** tout le monde se déchaînait *ou* travaillait comme des fous pour essayer de respecter la date limite; **the last month had been absolutely f.** le mois précédent avait été complètement fou; **f. with pain/worry** fou, *f* folle de douleur/d'inquiétude; **it drives him f.** cela le met hors de lui; **I'm f.** je suis hors de moi; **I was f. when I heard she'd had an accident** j'ai paniqué en apprenant qu'elle avait eu un accident

frantically, *esp Am* **frantically** ['fræntɪklɪ] **ADV 1** *(to work, try)* frénétiquement, avec frénésie; **to rush f. around** courir frénétiquement dans tous les sens; **she was f. trying to help** elle essayait désespérément d'apporter son aide; **f. worried** fou, *f* folle d'inquiétude **2** *Fam* affreusement, terriblement; **I'm f. busy** je ne sais plus où donner de la tête

frat [fræt] **ADJ** *Am Univ Fam* = confrérie *f* d'étudiants
▸▸**f. house** maison *f* communautaire (où résident des étudiants appartenant à une même organisation); **f. rat** = membre *m* d'une confrérie d'étudiants

fraternal [frə'tɜːn(ə)l] **ADJ** fraternel

fraternally [frə'tɜːn(ə)lɪ] **ADV** fraternellement

fraternity [frə'tɜːnɪtɪ] **N 1** *(brotherliness)* fraternité *f* **2** *(group engaged in same activity)* confrérie *f*; **the banking/medical f.** la confrérie des banquiers/des médecins; **the sporting f.** la grande famille du sport **3** *Am Univ* = confrérie *f* d'étudiants
▸▸*Am Univ* **f. house** maison *f* communautaire (où résident des étudiants appartenant à une même confrérie)

fraternization [frætənaɪ'zeɪʃən] **N** fraternisation *f* (**with** avec); **f. with the enemy is forbidden** il est interdit de fraterniser avec l'ennemi

fraternize ['frætənaɪz] **VI** fraterniser (**with** avec); **they tend not to f. with each other** ils ont tendance à ne pas fraterniser

fraud [frɔːd] **N 1** *(deception)* supercherie *f*, tromperie *f*, *Law* fraude *f*, dol *m*; **to obtain sth by f.** obtenir qch frauduleusement *ou* par fraude; **guilty of f.** coupable de manœuvres frauduleuses; **he had carried out a wages f.** il avait fraudé sur les salaires **2** *(person)* imposteur *m*; *(thing, place)* farce *f*, attrape *f*, **this place is a f.** cet endroit ne répond pas à la réputation qu'on lui a faite
▸▸*Br* **the F. Squad** brigade *f* de répression des fraudes

fraudulence ['frɔːdjʊləns] **N** *(of transaction)* caractère *m* frauduleux; *(of concerns, sentiments)* fausseté *f*

fraudulent ['frɔːdjʊlənt] **ADJ** *(false) (sympathy, feelings)* faux, *f* fausse, affecté; *(charge, accusation)* faux; *Law (bankrupt, transaction)* frauduleux
▸▸**f. bankruptcy** faillite *f* frauduleuse

fraudulently ['frɔːdjʊləntlɪ] **ADV** frauduleusement

fraught [frɔːt] **ADJ 1** plein (**with problems** de problèmes); **the voyage was f. with danger** la traversée a été remplie *ou* pleine d'embûches; **an atmosphere f. with emotion/tension** une atmosphère chargée d'émotion/de tension; **things have been rather f.** l'atmosphère est assez tendue; **a f. day** une journée stressante **2** *(distressing)* pénible; **it's a f. subject** c'est un thème ardu **3** *(person) (distressed)* désespéré; *(anxious)* inquiet

fray¹ [freɪ] **N** *(brawl)* bagarre *f*, échauffourée *f*, mêlée *f*; **in the thick of the f.** au plus épais de la mêlée; **to enter the f.** descendre dans l'arène; **to return to the f.** rentrer en lice; **ready for the f.** prêt à entrer dans la mêlée

fray[2] **VT** *(material etc)* érailler, effiler

VI 1 *(of material) (at edges)* s'effilocher, s'effiler; *(at collar, seams)* s'élimer **2** *(of nerves)* être à vif; *(of tempers)* s'échauffer

frayed [freɪd] **ADJ 1** *(cloth, garment etc) (at edges)* effiloché, effrangé; *(at collar, seams)* élimé; *(rope)* usé **2** *(nerves)* à vif; **my nerves are f.** je suis à bout de nerfs; **tempers were getting a little f.** tout le monde commençait à être à bout de nerfs

frazzle ['fræz(ə)l] **N** *Fam* **to be worn to a f.** *(of person)* être complètement éreinté; **a joint cooked** *or* **burnt to a f.** un rôti calciné; **you look burnt to a f.** *(by sun)* tu as l'air d'avoir pris un de ces coups de soleil

frazzled ['fræzəld] **ADJ** *Fam* **1** *(mentally)* à bout de nerfs; **his nerves were still f.** il était encore à bout de nerfs **2** *(burnt)* calciné; **I got f. on the beach** je me suis pris un gros coup de soleil sur la plage

freak [fri:k] **N 1 f.** *(of nature)* monstre *m*, phénomène *m*; **a circus f.** un phénomène de cirque; **what kind of a f. would do something like that?** il faut être taré pour faire un truc pareil!; **people treat me as some kind of f.** *(because of what I think, do etc)* les gens me trouvent anormal; **by some f. (of fortune) he won** par un coup de chance il a gagné **2** *(enthusiast)* fana *mf*, **jazz/film f.** fana de jazz/cinéma

ADJ *(storm)* anormal, -aux; *(accident)* insolite, bizarre; **f. weather conditions** des conditions atmosphériques anormales

VI = freak out 1

► **freak out** *Fam* **VI 1** *(become angry)* piquer une crise (**at** contre; **about** à propos de); *(be shocked, scared)* flipper, avoir les boules; *(become mentally unbalanced)* être déboussolé; *(of drug taker)* se défoncer; **mum'll f. out when she sees that mess** Maman va piquer une crise quand elle verra tout ce désordre; **f. show** exhibition *f* de monstres **2** *(abandon restraint)* s'éclater; **look at him freaking out on the dancefloor!** regarde-le s'éclater sur la piste de danse!

VT SEP *(person) (shock, scare)* mettre les boules à, faire flipper; *(mentally unbalance)* rendre dingue

freaking ['fri:kɪŋ] *Am Sl* **ADJ** *(for emphasis)* sacré, foutu; **where are those f. kids?** mais où sont passés ces foutus gamins?

ADV *(for emphasis)* vachement; **it's f. cold out there** ça pince vachement dehors; **I don't f. know!** j'en sais foutre rien!

freakish ['fri:kɪʃ] **ADJ 1** *(weather etc)* insolite, anormal, -aux **2** *(imagination, idea, appearance, hairdo)* bizarre; *(stronger)* délirant

freaky ['fri:kɪ] **ADJ** *Fam (person, appearance etc)* bizarre; *(stronger)* délirant

freckle ['frek(ə)l] **N** tache *f* de rousseur; **she's got freckles** elle a des taches de rousseur

freckled ['frek(ə)ld], **freckly** ['freklɪ] **ADJ 1** *(person, face, arm etc)* couvert de taches de rousseur **2** *(animal's coat)* tacheté

Frederick the Great ['fred(ə)rɪk] **N** *Hist* Frédéric le Grand

FREE [fri:]

ADJ	libre **1, 2** ▪ gratuit **3** ▪ franco **3** ▪ généreux **4**
ADV	gratuitement **1**
VT	libérer **1** ▪ dégager **2**

ADJ 1 *(unrestricted) (person, animal, movement, translation)* libre; *Chem (gas)* (à l'état) libre, non combiné; **to set f.** *(prisoner, hos-*

tage) relâcher, remettre en liberté; *(slave)* affranchir; *(person) (from relationship, contract)* libérer; *(bird)* laisser s'envoler; **to break f.** *(of bonds)* se dégager (**of** de); *(escape)* s'échapper; **to be allowed to go f.** être mis en liberté, être relâché; **to be (entirely) f. to do sth** être (entièrement) libre de faire qch; **I am f. to do what I please** je suis libre de mes mouvements; **f. from** *or* **of sth** débarrassé de qch; **the area is now f. of** *or* **from contamination** cette zone a été complètement décontaminée; **to remain f. of** *or* **from sth** être préservé de qch; **to be f. of sb** être débarrassé de qn; **to be f. from care** *or* **worry** *or* **anxiety** être sans souci; **she's f. and graceful in all her actions** elle fait tout avec aisance et grâce; **as f. as the air** *or* **a bird** libre comme l'air; *Fig* **it's a f. country** on est en démocratie; **f. end** *(of rope)* extrémité *f* libre; **with his f. hand** avec sa main libre; *Fig* **to have a f. hand** avoir pleine liberté d'action, avoir ses coudées franches (**to do** pour faire); **to give** *or* **allow sb a f. hand** donner carte blanche à qn; **to make a f. choice** décider librement *ou* en toute liberté; **right of f. entry** droit *m* de passer librement les frontières

2 *(unoccupied)* libre; *Tel (line)* libre; **is this table f.?** est-ce que cette table est libre?; **I am f. tomorrow** je suis libre demain; **to have some time f.** avoir du temps libre; **f. time** temps *m* libre, loisir *m*

3 *(without charge) (concert, sample etc)* gratuit; *Theat (ticket)* de faveur; **it came f. with the magazine** c'était en prime pour l'achat du magazine; *Fig* **there's no such thing as a f. lunch** tout se paie; **admission f.** entrée gratuite; *Com* **delivery f.** livré franco *inv*; **post f.** franco de port; **f. in and out** bord à bord; *Com* **f. alongside ship** franco long du quai; **f. overside** franco allège; *Com* **f. at frontier** franco rendu; *Com* **f. at frontier** franco frontière; *Com* **f. carrier** franco transporteur; *Com* **f. destination** franco rendu point de destination; *Com* **f. of average** franc de toute avarie; **f. of customs duty** franco de douane; *Fin* **f. of duty** *(in customs)* exempt de droits d'entrée; **to import sth f. of duty** faire entrer qch en franchise; **f. of packing charges** franco d'emballage; **f. of tax** franc d'impôts; *Fin* **interest f. of tax** intérêts nets *ou* exempts d'impôt; **f. of VAT** en franchise de TVA; **f. on board** franco à bord; *Com* **f. on rail** franco wagon; **f. on truck** franco camion

4 *(generous) (person)* libéral, -aux, généreux; **to be f. with one's time** être généreux de son temps; **to be f. with one's money** être prodigue de son argent; **he was very f. with his advice** il a été très prodigue en conseils

5 *esp Pej (uninhibited)* **you'll like it here, things are f. and easy** tu te plairas ici, on ne fait pas de façons; **things are a bit too f. and easy here** ici on est un peu trop sans gêne *ou* désinvolte; **he's pretty f. and easy as a boss** il est plutôt décontracté comme patron; **to make f. with sth** se servir de qch sans se gêner; **he made very f. with my whisky** il ne se gênait pas pour boire mon whisky; **to be rather f. in one's conversation** tenir des propos peu convenables; *Fam* **feel f.** faites comme chez vous; *Fam* **may I take another? – feel f.** puis-je en reprendre? – je vous en prie; **feel f. to speak your mind** n'hésitez pas à dire ce que vous pensez

ADV 1 *(without charge)* franco, gratuitement; **catalogue sent f. on request** catalogue gratuit sur demande; **the museum is open f. on Saturdays** l'entrée du musée est gratuite le samedi; **for f.,** *Fam* **f. gratis and for nothing** gratis; **to get sth for f.** obtenir qch gratis; **you are allowed to bring in half a litre f.** *(exempt from duty)* il y a une tolérance d'un demi-litre

2 *(followed by a present participle)* **f. flow-**

ing qui coule abondamment; **f. flowering** qui fleurit abondamment

VT **(freed; freeing) 1** *(prisoner, caged animal etc)* libérer, relâcher; *(of rescuer) (hostage, prisoner)* délivrer; *(slave, colony)* affranchir; *(sth stuck, one's foot etc)* dégager; *(funds)* dégager; *(time, space)* libérer; **to f. sb's hands** *(untie)* détacher les mains de qn; **to f. oneself from sb's grasp** se dégager des mains de qn; **to f. sb from an obligation** libérer qn d'une obligation; **to f. oneself from one's commitments** se libérer *ou* se délier de ses engagements; **to f. sb to do sth** libérer qn pour qu'il puisse faire qch; **to f. the pound/franc** libéraliser le cours de la livre/ du franc

2 *(clear obstructions from)* débarrasser (**from, of** de); *(path etc)* dégager; *Tech etc (part)* dégager; *(blocked filter)* désobstruer; *(pump)* dégorger; **to f. a property (from mortgage)** déshypothéquer une propriété

► ► **f. agent** personne *f* libre *ou* indépendante; *(sports player)* joueur, -euse indépendant(e); *Fig* **to be a f. agent** être libre de ses mouvements; *Psy* **f. association** association *f* libre; *Sport* **f. climbing** escalade *f* libre; *Sch* **f. composition** composition *f* libre; **f. copy** *(in publishing)* spécimen *m*; **f. demonstration** démonstration *f* gracieuse; **f. diving** plongée *f* sous-marine autonome; *Econ* **f. enterprise** libre entreprise *f*; **f. fall** chute *f* libre; *Hist* **f. France** la France libre; *Hist* **the F. French** les Français *mpl* libres; *Com* **f. gift** cadeau *m*; *Br* **f. house** = pub *m* libre de ses approvisionnements (et non lié à une brasserie particulière); *St Exch* **f. issue** attribution *f* d'actions gratuites; *Sport* **f. kick** coup *m* franc; **f. love** union *f* libre; *Econ* **f. market** économie *f* de marché; *Law* **f. pardon** grâce *f*, *Customs* **f. port** port *m* franc; **f. press** liberté *f* de la presse; *Med* **f. radical** radical *m* libre; **f. speech** liberté *f* de parole *ou* d'expression; **f. spirit** non-conformiste *mf*, *pl* non-conformistes; *Econ* **f. trade** libre-échange *m*; *Econ* **f. trade area** zone *f* de libre-échange; *Econ* **f. trade policy** politique *f* antiprotectionniste, politique de libre-échange; *Com* **f. trial** essai *m* gratuit; *Com* **f. trial period** période *f* d'essai gratuit; **f. verse** vers *m* libre; **f. vote** vote *m* libre; **f. will** libre arbitre *m*; **of one's own f. will** de (son) plein gré; *Pol* **the F. World** le monde libre; *Com* **f. zone** zone franche

► **free up** **VT SEP** *(funds)* dégager; *(time, space)* libérer; **this will f. up sales people to do more actual selling** cela donnera plus de temps au personnel de vente pour se consacrer à la vente même

-free [fri:] **SUFF** sans; **sugar/gluten/etc-f.** sans sucre/gluten/*etc*

freebie, freebee ['fri:bi:] **N** *Fam (for customer etc)* cadeau *m*; **it was a f. with the magazine** c'était un cadeau offert avec le magazine

freeboard ['fri:bɔ:d] **N** *Naut* (franc-)bord *m*

freeborn ['fri:bɔ:n] **ADJ** libre de naissance, né libre

freedom ['fri:dəm] **N 1** liberté *f*, **in f.** en liberté; **we have less f. now** nous sommes moins libres maintenant; **f. to do sth** liberté de faire qch; **f. to overfly a country without landing** droit *m* de survol d'un État; **f. of action** liberté d'action; **f. of entry** liberté d'entrée; **f. of the press** liberté de la presse

2 *(frankness) (of a conversation etc)* franchise *f*, *Pej (uninhibitedness)* sans-gêne *m*, familiarité *f*; **to speak with complete f.** parler en toute liberté

3 *(exemption)* exemption *f*, franchise *f*, **f. from tax** exemption d'impôts; **with my new f. from worry** désormais libéré de mes inquiétudes

4 *(free use)* **the f. of sth** le libre usage de qch; **the f. of the seas** la liberté de la haute mer; **f. of the air** liberté *f* de l'air; **f. of the city** droit *m* de cité; *(honorary citizenship)* citoyenneté *f* d'honneur d'une ville; **to receive the f. of a city** être nommé citoyen/citoyenne d'honneur d'une ville; **to give sb the f. of one's library** mettre sa bibliothèque à la disposition de qn

▸▸ **f. of expression** liberté d'expression; **f. fighter** guérillero *m*, révolutionnaire *mf*; **f. of information** liberté d'information; **f. of movement** liberté de mouvement; **f. of religion** liberté de culte; **f. of speech** liberté d'expression; **f. of worship** liberté de culte

free-flowing ADJ **1** *(river, stream)* qui coule librement; *(traffic, substance)* fluide **2** *(information)* librement accessible; *Fin (capital)* flottant

Freefone® ['fri:fəʊn] N *Br Tel* appel *m* gratuit, numéro *m* vert; **call F. 123** composez le numéro vert 123

free-for-all N mêlée *f* générale; **when the food arrived, the queue quickly turned into a f.** quand la nourriture est arrivée, la file d'attente s'est transformée en pagaille générale

free-form ADJ *Art* à forme libre
▸▸ *Mus* **f. jazz** free-jazz *m inv*

freehand ['fri:hænd] ADJ, ADV *Art* à main levée

free-handed [-'hændɪd] ADJ généreux

freehold ['fri:həʊld] *Law* ADJ tenu en propriété perpétuelle et libre
N *(property)* propriété *f* foncière perpétuelle et libre; **to buy the f.** acheter en pleine propriété

freeholder ['fri:həʊldər] N propriétaire *m* foncier (à perpétuité)

freeing ['fri:ɪŋ] N *(of prisoner)* libération *f*, *(of slave)* affranchissement *m*; *(of funds, resources)* dégagement *m*

freelance ['fri:lɑːns] N indépendant, -ante, free-lance *mf inv*; *(esp journalist etc)* indépendant, -ante, pigiste *mf*; **to work as a f.** travailler en indépendant *ou* free-lance; *(esp journalist)* travailler comme pigiste *ou* en indépendant, travailler à la pige
ADJ *(contributor, worker)* free-lance, indépendant; *(esp journalist etc)* qui travaille à la pige, free-lance; *(rates)* du travail free-lance
ADV **to work f.** travailler en indépendant *ou* en free-lance; *(esp journalist)* travailler comme pigiste *ou* en indépendant, travailler à la pige
VI travailler en indépendant *ou* en free-lance; *(esp journalist)* faire de la pige, travailler comme pigiste *ou* en indépendant
▸▸ **f. work** travail *m* indépendant *ou* à la pige *ou* (en) free-lance

freelancer ['fri:lɑːnsər] N free-lance *mf*; *(esp journalist)* pigiste *mf*

freeload ['fri:ləʊd] VI *esp Am Fam* parasiter

freeloader ['fri:ləʊdər] N *esp Am Fam* pique-assiette *mf inv*, parasite *m*

freely ['fri:lɪ] ADV **1** *(copiously, abundantly)* librement; **to give f. to sb** faire des libéralités à qn; **to give out advice f.** se répandre en conseils; **the wine was flowing f.** le vin coulait à flots **2** *(without hindrance)* librement; *(to speak, act etc)* en toute liberté; **to speak f. to sb** parler à qn à cœur ouvert; **f. available** *(for sale)* en vente libre; *(easy to get hold of)* qu'on peut se procurer facilement; **I f. admit that …** j'avoue sans peine que …

freeman, *pl* **freemen** ['fri:mən] N **1** *Hist* homme *m* libre **2** *(of city)* citoyen *m* d'honneur; **to be made a f. of the city** être nommé citoyen d'honneur

free-marketeer N libéral, -ale

freemason ['fri:meɪs(ə)n] N franc-maçon *m*, *pl* francs-maçons

freemasonry ['fri:meɪs(ə)nrɪ] N franc-maçonnerie *f*

freenet ['fri:net] N *Comput* libertel *m*

Freepost® ['fri:pəʊst] N *Br* correspondance-réponse *f*

free-range ADJ *(eggs, chicken)* de ferme

freesia ['fri:ʒə] N *(plant)* freesia *m*

free-spoken ADJ *(person)* franc, *f* franche, qui parle ouvertement

freestanding ['fri:stændɪŋ] ADJ *(wall etc)* auto-portant; *Archit (column)* isolé; *(clinic, restaurant, machine)* autonome

freestyle ['fri:staɪl] N *Swimming* nage *f* libre; *(wrestling)* lutte *f* libre

freethinker [fri:'θɪŋkər] N *Old-fashioned* libre penseur, -euse

free-trader N *Econ* libre-échangiste *mf*, *pl* libre-échangistes

freeware ['fri:weər] N *Comput* freeware *m*, logiciel *m* public
▸▸ **f. programs** freewares *mpl*, logiciels *mpl* publics

freeway ['fri:weɪ] N *Am* autoroute *f* *(gratuite)*

freewheel ['fri:wi:l] VI **1** *Cycling* être en roue libre; *Aut* rouler au point mort; **to f. down a hill** descendre une côte en roue libre/au point mort **2** *esp Am (travel in carefree fashion)* se laisser aller, aller sans but précis
N *roue libre*

freewheeling ['fri:wi:lɪŋ] ADJ *Fam (discussion)* libre; **her f. approach to such serious matters** sa façon un peu légère *ou* désinvolte de traiter des questions aussi sérieuses; **to lead a f. existence** mener une existence insouciante

freeze [fri:z] N **1** *Met* gel *m*, gelée *f*; **the big f.** la grande gelée; **we had a big f. last winter** il a gelé très fort l'hiver dernier **2** *(act of fixing)* **price and wage f.** blocage *m ou* gel *m* des prix et des salaires; **to put a f. on further changes/expenditure** bloquer le processus de changement/les dépenses
V IMPERS *(pt* **froze** [frəʊz], *pp* **frozen** ['frəʊz(ə)n]*)* **it's freezing** il gèle
VI **1** *(of liquid, washing on line)* geler; *(of food)* se congeler; **the river has frozen** la rivière est prise *ou* a gelé; **the earth had frozen hard** la terre avait gelé; **the sausages had frozen together** les saucisses s'étaient congelées et ne formaient plus qu'un bloc; **his hand had frozen to the ice axe** le gel avait collé sa main au piolet; **it has frozen solid** *(mud)* elle a gelé; *(food)* ça s'est congelé; *(milk)* il est gelé; **to f. to death** mourir de froid; *Fam* **I'm freezing** je meurs de froid, je gèle; *Fam* **we froze in our thin clothes** on n'était pas assez couvert, on s'est caillé; **the smile froze on his lips** le sourire se figea sur ses lèvres
2 *(of person) (not move)* rester cloué sur place, se figer; *(stiffen)* se raidir, se guinder; *(become speechless)* rester sans voix; **f.!** on ne bouge plus!; **I froze at the sound of his voice** je me suis immobilisé au son de sa voix
3 *Comput (of screen, computer)* se bloquer
VT **1** *(turn to ice)* geler; *(food)* congeler; **to f. the blood (in one's veins)** glacer le sang *ou* le cœur; **she froze them with a look** d'un regard, elle les glaça sur place; **to be frozen to death** mourir de froid
2 *Fin (credit, currency, prices)* geler; *(wages)* bloquer; **to f. assets** immobiliser des actifs
3 *Med* insensibiliser par anesthésie locale
4 **to f. a film** *or* **a frame** faire un arrêt sur image; **f. it!** arrêtez l'image!

▸ **freeze out** VT SEP *Fam (exclude) (person)* évincer; *(rival)* supplanter; **to f. sb out of** the conversation exclure qn de la conversation

▸ **freeze over** VI the pond has/is frozen over l'étang a/est complètement gelé

▸ **freeze up** VI *(become frozen)* geler; *Fig (of person)* rester sans voix; **the river has frozen up** la rivière est prise *ou* gelée; **the radiator froze up** le radiateur a gelé

freeze-dried ADJ lyophilisé(e)

freeze-dry VT lyophiliser

freeze-frame N *Cin* arrêt *m* sur image

freezer ['fri:zər] N congélateur *m*; *(in refrigerator)* freezer *m*; **chest f.** congélateur bahut
▸▸ **f. compartment** compartiment *m* à glace *(d'un réfrigérateur)*, freezer *m*

freeze-up N *Met* gelée *f*

freezing ['fri:zɪŋ] ADJ *(weather, room, temperature etc)* glacial, -als *ou* -aux; **it's f. in here!** ça caille ici!; **I'm f.** je gèle
ADV **the weather's f. cold** il fait un temps glacial; **I'm f. cold** je suis gelé; **a f. cold shower** une douche glacée
N **1** *(becoming frozen)* congélation *f*, gel *m*; **the temperature was below f.** la température était inférieure à zéro **2** *(making frozen) (of liquid etc)* réfrigération *f*; *(of meat)* congélation *f* **3** *Fin (of wages etc)* blocage *m*; *(of credit, prices)* gel *m*
▸▸ **f. compartment** *(in refrigerator)* freezer *m*, compartiment *m* à glace *(d'un réfrigérateur)*; **f. instructions** *(for food)* consignes *fpl* pour la congélation; **f. mixture** mélange *m* réfrigérant; **f. point** point *m* de congélation

freight [freɪt] N **1** *(transport)* fret *m*, transport *m* (de marchandises); **air f.** transport par air **2** *(cargo)* fret *m*, cargaison *f*, chargement *m*; *Rail, Aviat* marchandises *fpl* (transportées) **3** *(price of transport)* fret *m*
VT **1** *(load) (vessel)* charger **2** *(hire) (ship)* (af)fréter; *(of owner)* donner à fret **3** *esp Am (transport)* transporter
▸▸ **f. bill** connaissement *m*; *Am* **f. car** wagon *m* de marchandises, fourgon *m*; **f. charges** fret, frais *mpl* de transport; **f. collect** port *m* avancé; **f. consolidator** groupeur *m*; **f. depot** gare *f* de marchandises; **f. forward** port avancé; **f. forwarder** agent *m* de fret, transitaire *m*; **f. forwarding** transit *m*; **f. insurance** assurance *f* sur fret; **f. plane** avion-cargo *m*, *pl* avions-cargos; avion *m* de fret; **f. price** prix *m* de transport; **f. release** bon *m* à délivrer; **f. shipping** messageries *fpl* maritimes; **f. terminal** terminal *m* de fret; **f. ton** tonne *f* d'affrètement; *Am* **f. train** train *m* de marchandises; **f. vehicle** véhicule *m* de transport de marchandises

freightage ['freɪtɪdʒ] N fret *m*; *(transport)* transport *m*

freighter ['freɪtər] N **1** *(ship)* cargo *m*, navire *m* de charge; *Am Rail* wagon *m* de marchandises; *Aviat* avion-cargo *m*, *pl* avions-cargos, avion *m* de fret **2** *(hirer) (of ship)* affréteur *m* **3** *Am (of goods carried overland)* consignateur, -trice **4** *(operator of transport company)* entrepreneur *m* de transports, exportateur *m*

Freightliner® ['freɪtlaɪnər] N *Rail* train *m* de marchandises en conteneurs, train *m* conteneur

French [frentʃ] ADJ français; *(dish, fashion etc)* à la française; *(class, teacher)* de français; **the F. ambassador** l'ambassadeur, -drice de France; *Fam* **to take F. leave** filer à l'anglaise
N **1** *Ling* français *m*; **to speak F.** parler français; **to learn/know F.** apprendre/savoir parler le français; **say it in F.** dites-le en français; **her F. is excellent** elle parle très bien (le) français; **Canadian F.** français canadien *ou* du Canada; *Hum* **excuse my F.** passez-moi l'expression **2 the F.** *(people)* les Français *mpl* **3** *Sl Old-fashioned (fellatio)* pipe *f*

▶▶**F. bean** haricot *m* vert; **F. bread** baguette *f*, **F. Canada** le Canada français; **F. Canadian** *(person)* Canadien, -ienne français(e); *(language)* français *m* canadien; **F. chalk** craie *f* de tailleur; *Am* **F. doors** porte-fenêtre *f*, *pl* portes-fenêtres; *Culin* **F. dressing** *(in UK)* vinaigrette *f*, *(in US)* = sauce *f* de salade à base de mayonnaise et de ketchup; **F. Foreign Legion** Légion *f* étrangère; **F. fried potatoes** pommes *fpl* frites; **F. fries** frites *fpl*; **F. Guiana** Guyane *f* francaise; **F. horn** cor *m* d'harmonie; **F. kiss** baiser *m* avec la langue, *Fam* patin *m*; *Br Fam* **F. letter** *(condom)* capote *f* anglaise; **F. loaf** baguette *f*; **F. plait** *(hairstyle)* natte *f* africaine; *Br* **F. polish** vernis *m* (à l'alcool); **F. roll** *(hairstyle)* chignon *m* banane; **F. service** *(in restaurant)* service *m* à la française *ou* au guéridon; **F. stick** baguette *f*; **F. Switzerland** la Suisse Romande; **F. toast** pain *m* perdu; **F. West Indies** Antilles *fpl* Françaises; *Br* **F. window** porte-fenêtre *f*

Frenchify ['frentʃɪfaɪ] vT *Pej (one's style etc)* franciser

French-kiss *Fam* vT rouler une pelle *ou* un patin à
vI se rouler une pelle *ou* un patin

Frenchman, *pl* **Frenchmen** ['frentʃmən] N Français *m*

French-polish vT *Br (table etc)* vernir au tampon

French-speaking ADJ *(native speaker)* francophone; *(who can speak French)* qui parle français; **the F. world** la francophonie

Frenchwoman, *pl* **Frenchwomen** ['frentʃwʊmən, -wɪmɪn] N Française *f*

Frenchy ['frentʃɪ] N *Old-fashioned Fam* Français, -aise

frenetic [frə'netɪk] ADJ *(person, action etc)* frénétique

frenetically [frə'netɪklɪ] ADV frénétiquement

frenzied ['frenzɪd] ADJ *(person)* affolé, forcené; *(rage)* fou, *f* folle; *(applause, activity)* frénétique; *(attack, mob)* déchaîné; **f. with worry/rage** fou d'inquiétude/de rage; **there was a f. look in her eye** elle avait un regard halluciné

frenzy ['frenzɪ] N *(of despair etc)* frénésie *f*, folie *f*, **in a f. of excitement/hatred** dans un accès d'excitation/de haine; **to work oneself into a f.** *(get angry, upset)* se mettre dans tous ses états; **the children worked themselves into a f.** *(of excitement)* les enfants se sont mis dans un état de surexcitation folle

frequency ['fri:kwənsɪ] N **1** fréquence *f*, **to recur with increasing f.** se faire de plus en plus fréquent; **the increasing f. of his absences** ses absences de plus en plus fréquentes; *Math* **f. of errors** répartition *f* des erreurs **2** *Phys* fréquence *f*, *Elec* **high/low f.** haute/basse fréquence; *Radio* **very high f.** très haute fréquence
▶▶*Radio* **f. band** bande *f* de fréquences; **f. modulation** modulation *f* de fréquence; **f. range** gamme *f* de fréquences

frequent¹ ['fri:kwənt] ADJ *(visits etc)* fréquent; *(visitor)* assidu; *(customer)* habituel; *(widespread)* très répandu; *(explanation, state of affairs etc)* commun, habituel; **he became a f. visitor to our house** c'est devenu un habitué de la maison; **it is a f. occurrence** cela se produit souvent; **it is a f. sight in the summer months** on en voit souvent pendant les mois d'été; **this bird is a f. visitor to our shores** cet oiseau visite régulièrement nos rivages; **the theatregoers** des gens qui vont souvent au théâtre; **the doctor recommended f. changes of the dressing** le docteur a recommandé que le pansement soit changé souvent; **it's quite a f. practice** c'est une coutume assez répandue

▶▶**f. flyer club** club *m* de fidélité de compagnie aérienne; **f. flyer programme** programme *m* de fidélisation des passagers de compagnies aériennes; *Mktg* **f. user card** carte *f* de fidélité; *Mktg* **f. user programme** programme de fidélisation

frequent² [frɪ'kwent] vT fréquenter; *(theatres, pubs etc)* hanter

frequenter [frɪ'kwentər] N *(of a house etc)* habitué, -ée, familier *m*; **a great f. of public houses** un pilier de bar

frequently ['fri:kwəntlɪ] ADV fréquemment; **I f. can't remember my address** il m'arrive fréquemment de ne pas pouvoir me souvenir de mon adresse; **how f.?** avec quelle fréquence?, *Fam* tous les combien?; **I can't say how f. it happened** je ne saurais pas dire avec quelle fréquence cela se produisait

fresco, *pl* **frescos, frescoes** ['freskəʊ, -əʊz] N *Art* fresque *f*, **to paint in f.** peindre à fresque; **f. painter** fresquiste *mf*

fresh [freʃ] ADJ **1** *(fruit, eggs, fish, colour etc)* frais, *f* fraîche; *(person) (full of vigour)* vigoureux, alerte; *(refreshed) (after sleep, rest)* dispos; *(horse)* fougueux, animé; *(complexion)* frais, fleuri; **as f. as a daisy** frais et dispos; **a f.-faced youth** un jeune homme au teint frais; **I felt fresher after a shower** une douche m'a ragaillardi
  2 *(new)* nouveau, -el, *f* -elle; *(news, blood, footprints)* frais, *f* fraîche; **a f. change of clothes/socks** un habit/chaussettes de rechange; **f. dangers to face** de nouveaux dangers à affronter; **to make a f. start on a problem** reprendre un problème à zéro; **to put f. courage into sb** ranimer le courage de qn; **to put f. water in the fish tank** changer l'eau de l'aquarium; **f. outbreak of fire/disease** reprise *f* du feu/de la maladie; **it is still f. in my mind** je l'ai encore frais à la mémoire; **the wound was f.** la plaie était récente; **f. from London** nouvellement arrivé de Londres; **and now, f. from his tour of the States, we present ...** et maintenant, tout juste rentré de sa tournée aux États-Unis, nous vous présentons ...; **the bread was f. from the oven** le pain sortait du four; **f. paragraph** nouveau paragraphe; **f. troops** troupes fraîches
  3 *(air)* frais, *f* fraîche, pur; *(cool)* frais; **it's f. this morning** il fait frais ce matin; **in the f. air** au grand air, en plein air; **to let f. air into a room** aérer une pièce; *Fam* **f.-air fiend** fanatique *mf* d'air frais; *(outdoor person)* fanatique du grand air; *Naut* **f. breeze** bonne brise; **f. water** eau douce
  4 *esp Am Fam (impudent)* effronté; **to get f. with a girl** prendre des libertés avec une jeune fille; **don't (you) get f. with me!** ne te fiche pas de moi!
  ADV *(arrived, painted etc)* fraîchement, nouvellement, récemment; **f.-cut flowers** fleurs nouvellement cueillies; *esp Am* **to be f. out of sth** ne plus avoir de qch; **f.-frozen** congelé à la fabrication; *(fish)* congelé sur le bateau

freshen ['freʃən] vI *(of temperature)* (se) rafraîchir; *(of wind, weather)* fraîchir
  vT *(air, one's memory etc)* rafraîchir; *esp Am* **can I f. your drink?** est-ce que je vous sers un autre verre?
▶**freshen up** vI *(wash)* faire un brin de toilette
  vT SEP **1** *(renew) (make-up)* retoucher; **to f. up the paint** (r)aviver la couleur; **to f. up one's lipstick** se remettre du rouge à lèvres; **to f. oneself up** faire un brin de toilette **2** *(change air in) (room)* aérer

fresher ['freʃər] N *Br Fam* = **freshman**

freshly ['freʃlɪ] ADV *(with pp only)* fraîchement; **f. baked** sortant du four; **f. picked pea-**

ches des pêches fraîchement cueillies; **f. squeezed orange juice** orange *f* pressée

freshman, *pl* **freshmen** ['freʃmən] N *Univ Fam* étudiant, -ante de première année

freshness ['freʃnɪs] N **1** *(of fruit, fish etc)* fraîcheur *f* **2** *(of event)* caractère *m* récent; *(of impression, approach etc)* fraîcheur *f* **3** *(of wind etc)* fraîcheur *f* **4** *(liveliness)* vigueur *f*, vivacité *f* **5** *esp Am Fam (impudence)* effronterie *f*

freshwater ['freʃwɔːtər] ADJ
▶▶**f. fish** poisson *m* d'eau douce; **f. fishing** pêche *f* en eau douce

fret¹ [fret] N *Fam* **to be in a f.** être dans tous ses états; *(extremely worried)* se faire du mauvais sang *ou* de la bile
  vI (-tt-) *(worry)* s'inquiéter, se tourmenter; **don't f.!** *(don't worry)* ne vous inquiétez pas!; *(don't upset yourself)* ne vous faites pas de bile!, ne vous faites pas de mauvais sang!; **child fretting for his mother** enfant qui réclame sa mère en pleurnichant; **she's fretting because her pony is missing** elle est dans tous ses états parce que son poney a disparu; **children always tend to f. in hospital** les enfants ont toujours tendance à se tourmenter quand ils sont à l'hôpital
  vT **1** *(worry)* **don't f. yourself!** ne te tracasse pas!; **to f. one's life away** passer sa vie à se tracasser *ou* se tourmenter **2** *(wear away)* ronger; **to f. a rope** érailler un cordage

fret² N *Mus (on guitar etc)* touchette *f*, touche *f*

fret³ vT *Carp (wood)* découper
▶▶**f. saw** scie *f* à découper

fretful ['fretfʊl] ADJ *(anxious) (person)* inquiet, qui se fait du mauvais sang; *(voice)* inquiet; *(peevish)* grincheux; **a f. baby** un bébé agité

fretfully ['fretfʊlɪ] ADV *(to speak, complain)* d'un ton grincheux; *(to look at sb)* d'un air chagrin

fretfulness ['fretfʊlnɪs] N irritabilité *f*

fretting ['fretɪŋ] N **1** *(worrying)* inquiétude *f* *(over* à propos de); *(being upset)* agitation *f*, **I wish he'd stop his f.!** si seulement il pouvait arrêter de se faire du mauvais sang! **2** *(of rope etc)* usure *f*

fretwork ['fretwɜːk] N *Carp (technique)* découpage *m*; *(finished work)* travail *m* ajouré, bois *m* découpé *ou* chantourné

Freudian ['frɔɪdɪən] ADJ *Psy* freudien
▶▶**F. slip** lapsus *m*

Freudianism ['frɔɪdɪənɪzm] N freudisme *m*

FRG [efɑː'dʒiː] N *Formerly (abbr* **Federal Republic of Germany)** RFA *f*

Fri *abbr* **Friday**

friable ['fraɪəb(ə)l] ADJ *(soil etc)* friable

friar ['fraɪər] N *Cathol* moine *m*, frère *m*, religieux *m*; **Grey Friars** Franciscains *mpl*; **Black Friars** Dominicains *mpl*; **White Friars** Carmes *mpl*
▶▶*Pharm* **f.'s balsam** baume *m* de benjoin

friary ['fraɪərɪ] N monastère *m*

fricassee [frɪkə'siː] N *Culin* fricassée *f*, *(of rabbit or hare)* gibelotte *f*
  vT fricasser

fricative ['frɪkətɪv] *Ling* ADJ *(consonant)* fricatif
  N fricative *f*

friction ['frɪkʃən] N **1** *Phys* friction *f*, frottement *m*; *(of two bodies)* frottement; *(of scalp etc)* friction *f* **2** *(disagreement)* friction *f*, désaccord *m*; **there's f. between them** il y a du tirage entre eux
▶▶*Aut* **f. clutch** embrayage *m* à friction; *Aut* **f. cylinder** cylindre *m* de friction; *Aut* **f. drive** entraînement *m* par friction; *Comput* **f. feed** avancement *m* par friction; **f. glove** *(for massage)* gant *m* de crin; *Aut* **f. lining** garni-

ture *f* de friction; *Aut* **f. plate** plateau *m* de friction; *Am* **f. tape** chatterton *m*

Friday ['fraɪdɪ] N VOIR GRAMMAIRE A81; B61 vendredi *m*; **F. 26 February** vendredi 26 février; **F. morning/evening** vendredi matin/soir; **it's F. today** nous sommes vendredi aujourd'hui; **she comes on Fridays** elle vient le vendredi; **he's coming on F.** il vient vendredi; **every F.** tous les vendredis; **(Man) F.** *Liter* Vendredi; *Fig* factotum *m*, homme *m* à tout faire; *Fam* **girl F.** aide *f* de bureau

fridge [frɪdʒ] N *Fam* frigo *m*

fridge-freezer N *Fam* frigo *m* avec congélateur

fried [fraɪd] ADJ **1** *(food)* frit; **they eat a lot of f. food** ils mangent beaucoup de friture **2** *Am Fam (drunk)* bourré, pété; *(on drugs)* raide, parti
PT, PP *see* **fry**[1]
▸▸ **f. egg** œuf *m* sur le plat; **f. potatoes** pommes *fpl* de terre sautées

friend [frend] N **1** ami, *f* amie; *(acquaintance)* connaissance *f*; **we're the best of friends** nous sommes les meilleurs amis du monde; **let's be friends again** faisons la paix; **I'm offering you a bargain, my f.** *(to stranger)* cher ami, c'est une affaire que je vous propose; **I am speaking to you as a f.** je vous parle en ami(e); **that's what friends are for** c'est à ça que servent les amis; **she's been a good f. to us** elle a beaucoup fait pour nous; **we're just good friends** nous sommes bons amis, c'est tout; **school f.** ami(e) ou camarade *mf* d'école; **man f.** *(pl* **men friends)** ami homme, *pl* amis hommes; **woman f.** *(pl* **women friends)** amie femme, *pl* amies femmes; *Old-fashioned* **lady f.** petite amie *f*; **to be friends with sb** être ami avec qn; **they've been friends for years** ils sont amis depuis des années; **to be more than friends** être plus qu'amis; **to make friends** *(with others)* se faire des amis; **they made friends** *(with each other)* ils sont devenus amis; **I made friends with them** nous sommes devenus amis, je suis devenu ami avec eux; *Prov* **a f. in need is a f. indeed** c'est dans le besoin que l'on connaît ses amis; **he has been a real f. in need** il ne m'a/t'a/*etc* pas abandonné dans le besoin; **you'd better be** *or* **stay friends with them** vous feriez bien de ne pas vous brouiller avec eux; **let us part friends** séparons-nous (en) bons amis; **he's no f. of mine** *(he's an enemy)* je ne le compte pas parmi mes amis; *(he means me no good)* il ne me veut pas de bien; **Britain is no f. of those who seek to ...** la Grande-Bretagne n'est pas favorable à ceux qui cherchent à ...; *Fig* **to have friends in high places** *or* **at court** avoir des amis influents; *Fig* **a f. at court** un ami en haut lieu *ou* bien placé; **f. or foe?** *(said by sentry)* qui va là?

2 *(supporter) (of law and order etc)* ami, *f* amie, partisan *m*; *(of the arts etc)* patron, -onne; **f. of the poor** bienfaiteur, -trice des pauvres; **she's no f. of trade unionism** elle n'est pas favorable au syndicalisme; **the Friends of Canterbury Cathedral** la Société des Amis *ou* les Amis de la Cathédrale de Cantorbéry

3 *Rel* **F.** *(Quaker)* Quaker, -eresse, Ami, -ie; **the Society of Friends** la Société des Amis

friendless ['frendlɪs] ADJ sans amis; **I am totally f. now** je n'ai plus aucun ami

friendliness ['frendlɪnɪs] N amabilité *f* **(to, towards** envers); **to show great f. towards sb** se montrer très aimable envers qn

friendly ['frendlɪ] ADJ **1** *(people, smile, slap on the back, welcome)* amical, -aux; *(city, neighbours, face)* sympathique; *(well disposed)* favorable, favorablement disposé; *(dog)* gentil; *(quarrel, argument)* entre amis; **you should try to be a bit more f. to people**

tu devrais essayer d'être un peu plus aimable; **why is he so f. all of a sudden?** pourquoi est-il aussi aimable tout à coup?; **to be f. with sb** être ami avec qn; **she's very f. with the boss all of a sudden** elle est très copine avec le patron tout d'un coup; **they became very f.** *(to each other)* ils se sont pris d'amitié l'un pour l'autre; **to get too f. with sb** se montrer trop familier avec qn; **piece of f. advice** avis amical; **someone ought to have a f. word with him and explain that ...** quelqu'un devrait lui expliquer gentiment que ...; **f. gathering** réunion *f* d'amis; **in a f. manner** *or* **way** *(to talk, argue, smile)* amicalement; **to be on f. terms with sb** être en bons termes avec qn; **he gave me a f. wave** il m'a fait un signe amical de la main

2 *(software, layout etc)* convivial, -aux

3 *Mil* **is this aircraft f.?** est-ce que cet avion est des nôtres?; **a f. nation** un pays ami
N *Sport* match *m* amical
▸▸ *Mil* **f. fire** tirs *mpl* amis; **to come under f. fire** tomber sous les tirs des siens; **f. forces** troupes *fpl* amies *ou* alliées; **the F. Islands** Tonga *m*, les îles *fpl* des Amis; *Br Fin* **f. society** société *f* de mutualité; *Fin* **f. takeover bid** OPA *f* amicale

-friendly ['frendlɪ] SUFF **ozone-f.** qui préserve la couche d'ozone; **environment-f.** qui respecte l'environnement

friendship ['frendʃɪp] N amitié *f*, **to form a f. with sb** se lier (d'amitié) avec qn; **to lose sb's f.** perdre l'amitié de qn; **her f. means more to me than anything** notre amitié est ce qu'il y a de plus important pour moi; *esp Fml* **to enjoy the f. of sb** côtoyer qn

fries [fraɪz] NPL *esp Am Fam* **(French) f.** frites *fpl*

Friesian ['friːʒən] ADJ frison
N **1** *(person)* Frison, -onne; *(cow)* frisonne *f* **2** *Ling* frison *m*

frieze [friːz] N **1** *Archit* frise *f* **2** *(of wallpaper)* frise *f*

frig [frɪg] VT *Vulg (have sex with)* baiser avec
VI *Vulg (of woman)* se masturber, se toucher
▸ **frig about, frig around** VI *Sl (waste time)* traînailler, glandouiller; *(play the fool)* déconner
▸ **frig off** VI *Sl* **f. off!** va te faire foutre!

frigate ['frɪgət] N **1** *Naut* frégate *f*, escorteur *m* **2** *(bird)* frégate *f*
▸▸ **f. bird** frégate *f*

frigging ['frɪgɪŋ] *Sl* ADJ foutu; **this f. car** cette foutue bagnole, cette putain de bagnole; **what a f. waste of time!** putain, quelle perte de temps!; **he's a f. nuisance** il est chiant comme pas deux
ADV foutrement; **don't f. lie to me!** ne me mens pas, bordel!

fright [fraɪt] N **1** peur *f*, effroi *m*; **to take f.** s'effrayer (**at** de); **to give sb a f.** faire peur à qn; **to get** *or* **be given the f. of one's life** avoir une peur bleue; *Fam* **I got an awful f.** j'ai eu une sacrée peur **2** *Fam* **what a f. you look!** tu es à faire peur!; **that dress makes you look a real f.!** tu es moche à faire peur dans cette robe!

frighten ['fraɪt(ə)n] VT effrayer, faire peur à; **it frightens him/her** cela lui fait peur; **it frightens me that so many people believe him** ça m'effraie que tant de personnes le croient; **he is easily frightened** il s'effraie pour un rien; **these animals are easily frightened** ces animaux s'effarouchent d'un rien; **to f. sb into doing sth** faire peur à qn pour qu'il fasse qch; **to f. sb out of doing sth** faire peur à qn et le dissuader de faire qch; *Fam* **to f. the life** *or* **the living daylights out of sb** faire mourir qn de peur; *Fam* **to f. sb out of their wits, to f. the wits out of sb** rendre qn fou de peur; **you frightened me to death** vous m'avez fait une peur bleue

VI **I don't f. easily** c'est difficile de me faire peur; **he frightens easily** il s'effraie pour un rien
▸ **frighten away, frighten off** VT SEP *(scare) (animal)* effaroucher; *(person)* faire peur à, faire fuir

frightened ['fraɪt(ə)nd] ADJ *(look, voice etc)* apeuré; **to be** *or* **feel f.** avoir peur **(of** de); **I wasn't as f. as you were** je n'avais pas aussi peur que vous; **he's a very f. man** il a très peur; **I was f. of waking her** j'avais peur de la réveiller; **f. out of one's wits** terrifié; **f. to death** mort de peur

frighteners ['fraɪtnəz] NPL *Br Sl* **to put the f. on sb** menacer qn

frightening ['fraɪt(ə)nɪŋ] ADJ effrayant

frighteningly ['fraɪt(ə)nɪŋlɪ] ADV à faire peur; **they were f. close** ils se rapprochaient dangereusement; **they look f. similar** ils se ressemblent tellement que c'en est effrayant; **f. expensive** terriblement cher, hors de prix

frightful ['fraɪtfʊl] ADJ effroyable, épouvantable, affreux

frightfully ['fraɪtfʊlɪ] ADV affreusement; **he is f. ugly** il est laid à faire peur; **I am f. sorry** je regrette énormément; **f. rich/stupid** incroyablement riche/stupide; **f. expensive** affreusement cher; *Fam Hum* **f. f.** = maniérisme *m* utilisé pour décrire les manières et l'accent de la haute bourgeoisie britannique

frightfulness ['fraɪtfʊlnɪs] N atrocité *f*

frigid ['frɪdʒɪd] ADJ **1** *(sexually)* frigide **2** *Geog etc* glacial, -als *ou* -aux, (très) froid **3** *(style, smile, atmosphere)* glacial, -als *ou* -aux; *(response, silence)* glacé

frigidity [frɪ'dʒɪdɪtɪ] N **1** *(sexual)* frigidité *f* **2** *(of style, response, atmosphere)* froideur *f*

frigidly ['frɪdʒɪdlɪ] ADV *(to answer, reply etc)* d'un ton glacial; **f. polite** d'une politesse glaciale

frill [frɪl] N *(on clothing etc)* volant *m*, ruche *f*, *Culin (on ham etc)* papillote *f*; **shirt f.** jabot *m*; *Fig* **a plain meal without frills** un repas simple sans présentation compliquée

frilled [frɪld] ADJ *(ribbon etc)* froncé, ruché; *(shirt)* à jabots
▸▸ *Zool* **f. lizard** iguane *m* australien

frilly ['frɪlɪ] ADJ *(shirt, sleeves)* froncé, ruché; *(style, language)* fleuri

fringe [frɪndʒ] N **1** *(of tablecloth, scarf etc)* frange *f* **2** *Br (of hair)* frange *f* **3** *(edge)* bordure *f*, bord *m*; **the outer fringe(s) of London** la grande banlieue de Londres; **to live on the f. of society** vivre en marge de la société; **to be on the radical f. of a party** appartenir à la frange radicale d'un parti
VT *(carpet etc)* franger; **eyes fringed with black lashes** yeux bordés de cils noirs
▸▸ **f. benefits** avantages *mpl* annexes *ou* en nature; **f. group** frange *f*; **f. market** marché *m* marginal; *Pol* **f. meeting** réunion *f* parallèle; *Br* **f. theatre** théâtre *m* d'avant-garde *ou* expérimental

frippery ['frɪpərɪ] N *(usu pl)* fripperies *(ornaments)* colifichets *mpl*

Frisbee® ['frɪzbɪ] N Frisbee® *m*; **to play F.** jouer au Frisbee®

Frisco ['frɪskəʊ] N *Am Fam* San Francisco

frisk [frɪsk] N **1** *(search)* fouille *f*; **to give sb a f.** fouiller qn **2** *(movement)* **with a f. of its tail** en donnant un coup de queue
VT **1** *(search) (suspect etc)* fouiller; **to be frisked for weapons/alcohol** être fouillé pour vérifier qu'on ne cache pas d'armes/d'alcool **2** *(of dog etc)* **to f. its tail** remuer la queue
VI *(of lambs etc)* s'ébattre, gambader, folâtrer
▸ **frisk about** VI = frisk VI

friskiness ['frɪskɪnɪs] N vivacité f

frisking ['frɪskɪŋ] N (of suspect, traveller) fouille f; **to get a f. from a policeman, to be given a f. by a policeman** se faire fouiller par un policier

frisky ['frɪskɪ] ADJ vif; (horse) qui fait des cabrioles; **to feel f.** (of person) se sentir plein d'entrain; Fam (sexually) avoir le feu au derrière; Fam **to get f.** s'échauffer; **for an old man, he was still remarkably f.** il avait un tempérament encore très ardent pour son âge

fritillary [frɪ'tɪlərɪ] N **1** (plant) fritillaire f **2** (butterfly) damier m

fritter ['frɪtər] N Culin beignet m; **apple/banana f.** beignet aux pommes/à la banane
▸ **fritter away** VT SEP Fam (fortune) dissiper; (money, time) gaspiller; **to f. away one's money on clothes/jewellery** gaspiller son argent dans des vêtements/des bijoux; **I feel as if I've just frittered away the day** j'ai l'impression d'avoir perdu ma journée

frivolity [frɪ'vɒlɪtɪ] N frivolité f

frivolous ['frɪvələs] ADJ (person etc) frivole; (remark) frivole, futile; (objection, criticism) futile

frivolously ['frɪvələslɪ] ADV (to behave, say sth) frivolement

frivolousness ['frɪvələsnɪs] N (of person) frivolité f; (of objection etc) futilité f

frizz [frɪz] VT (hair) crêper, frisotter
VI (of hair) frisotter

frizziness ['frɪzɪnɪs] N **the f. of my hair** mes cheveux crépus

frizzle ['frɪz(ə)l] VI (of meat etc in frying pan) grésiller
VT Culin (burn) laisser brûler

frizzy ['frɪzɪ] ADJ (hair) crêpelé, crépu

FRN [efɑː'ren] N Banking (abbr floating-rate note) effet m à taux flottant

fro [frəʊ] ADV **to go to and f.** aller et venir

frock [frɒk] N (for child, woman) robe f; (of monk) froc m, bure f
▸ ▸ **f. coat** redingote f

frog¹ [frɒg] N **1** (animal) grenouille f; Fam **to have a f. in one's throat** avoir un chat dans la gorge **2** Br Offensive Sl **F.** (French person) Français, -aise

frog² N Mil etc **1** (for sword) porte-épée m inv; (for bayonet) porte-baïonnette m inv **2** (braid) brandebourg m

frogged [frɒgd] ADJ (uniform, tunic etc) orné de brandebourgs

frogging ['frɒgɪŋ] N (on uniform etc) brandebourgs mpl

Froggy ['frɒgɪ] N Br Offensive Sl (French person) Français, -aise

frogman, pl frogmen ['frɒgmən] N homme-grenouille m, pl hommes-grenouilles

frogmarch ['frɒgmɑːtʃ] VT (person) emmener de force; **they frogmarched her out of the room** ils l'ont fait sortir de la pièce de force

frogspawn ['frɒgspɔːn] N (no pl) œufs mpl de grenouille

frolic ['frɒlɪk] N (of young animal, child etc) ébats mpl; **to have a f. in the fields** s'ébattre ou gambader dans les champs
VI (frolicked) s'ébattre

FROM [frɒm, unstressed frəm]

- de **1, 2, 5, 8, 9** ▪ à partir de **3, 4**
- depuis **4** ▪ d'après **7**

PREP **1** (place) de; **he returned f. London** il est revenu de Londres; **f. Paris to London** de Paris à Londres; **f. town to town** de ville en ville; **f. here** d'ici
2 (origin) to take/remove/steal/etc sth f. sb

prendre/ôter/voler/etc qch à qn; **to take sth f. somewhere** prendre qch quelque part; **to remove sth f. somewhere** enlever qch de quelque part; **where do you come f.?, where are you f.?** d'où viens-tu?; **a train/plane f. Manchester** un train/avion en provenance de Manchester; **wheat f. Russia** blé (venant) de Russie; **a quotation f. Shakespeare** une citation tirée de Shakespeare; **he grabbed a revolver f. the table** il saisit un revolver sur la table; **I have brought it to you f. a friend** je vous l'apporte de la part d'un ami; **tell her that f. me** dites-lui cela de ma part; **f. ... (on parcel)** expéditeur/expéditrice ...
3 (range) à partir de; **potatoes f. 50 pence a kilo** des pommes de terre à partir de 50 pence le kilo; **the bird lays f. four to six eggs** l'oiseau pond de quatre à six œufs; **wine f. four euros a bottle** vins à partir de quatre euros la bouteille; **the price has been increased f. fifty pence to sixty pence** on a augmenté le prix de cinquante pence à soixante pence; **every flavour of ice cream f. vanilla to pistachio** tous les parfums de glace de la vanille à la pistache
4 (time) depuis, dès, à partir de; **f. that day** depuis ce jour, à partir de ce jour; **f. tomorrow on** à partir de demain; **house let f. 1 June** maison louée à compter du 1er juin; **f. his childhood** depuis ou dès son enfance; **she remembered him f. her childhood** elle se souvenait de lui dans son enfance; **he remembered the name f. his time with the BBC** il se souvenait du nom de l'époque où il était à la BBC; **f. morning till night** du matin au soir
5 (distance) **not far f. ...** pas loin de ...; **ten kilometres f. Paris** à dix kilomètres de Paris
6 (change) **f. bad to worse** de mal en pis
7 (because of) **to act f. conviction** agir par conviction; **I know him f. seeing him at the club** je le reconnais pour l'avoir vu au cercle; **f. his looks you might suppose that ...** à le voir on dirait que ...; **f. what I heard ...** d'après ce que j'ai entendu dire ...; **f. what I can see ...** à ce que je vois ...
8 (with adv, prep) **f. above** d'en haut; **I saw him f. a long way off** je l'ai vu de loin; **f. among the trees ...** de parmi les arbres ...; **take one f. among ...** prenez-en un parmi ...
9 (after adv) **to come down f. one's room** descendre de sa chambre; **to move away f. sb** s'éloigner de qn

frond [frɒnd] N (of fern) fronde f; (of palm tree) feuille f

FRONT [frʌnt]

N	devant **1, 5** ▪ avant **1** ▪ façade **1, 3** ▪ front **4** ▪ en avant (in front) **5**
ADJ	de devant
VT	diriger **2**

N **1** devant m; (of building) façade f; (of shop) devanture f; (of car) avant m; (of shirt) devant; **carriage at the f. of the train** voiture en tête du train; **at the f. of the book** au début du livre; **I spilled soup all down my f.** je me suis renversé de la soupe dessus; Theat **out f.** dans la salle; Br **the f.** (promenade at seaside) la promenade; Br **house on the f.** maison faisant face à la mer
2 (first row) premier rang m; **to push one's way to the f.** se frayer un chemin jusqu'au premier rang; Fig **se pousser** (en avant)
3 (outward appearance) **to put on a bold f.** faire bonne contenance; **it's only a f. on his part** (way of behaving etc) ce n'est qu'une façade; **the company was just a f. for their arms dealing operation** la société n'était qu'une couverture pour leur trafic d'armes; Br Fam **to have the f. to do sth** (nerve) avoir l'effronterie ou le front de faire qch
4 Mil, Pol, Met front m; Pol **common f.** front

commun; **popular f.** front populaire; Fig **to make progress on all fronts** faire des progrès sur tous les fronts; Met **warm/cold f.** front chaud/froid
5 in f. devant, en avant; (in race, contest) en tête; **Manchester United are now five points in f.** Manchester United mène par cinq points; **to send sb on in f.** envoyer qn devant; **in f. of, Am f. of** devant; (opposite) en face de; **he was standing right in f. of me** (facing me) il se trouvait juste en face de moi; (in queue, crowd etc) il se trouvait juste devant moi; **it's right in f. of you** (what you are looking for) c'est juste devant vous; **he opened it/talked about it in f. of her** il l'a ouvert/en a parlé devant elle
6 Fam **I want the money up f.** je veux mon argent avant; **to pay up f.** payer d'avance; Fam **he was very up f. about it** il a été franc sur ce point
ADJ (garden, teeth) de devant; **the f. part of the brain** la partie antérieure du cerveau; **f. carriage** (of train) voiture f de tête; Theat **f.-row seat** siège m de premier rang; **to have a f.-row seat** Theat être assis au premier rang; Fig être aux premières loges; Aut **f. wheel** (of car, bicycle) roue f avant
VI **1** (of building) **the house fronts north** la maison est exposée ou orientée au nord
2 Mil faire front; **left f.!** à gauche front!, à gauche, gauche!
VT **1** (building) donner une (nouvelle) façade à
2 (government) diriger; TV (programme) présenter; Mus **to f. a band** (lead it) diriger un orchestre
3 Am Fam (pay in advance) avancer; **the cashier can f. you the money** le caissier peut vous faire une avance ou vous avancer l'argent
4 Am Fam (give, lend money to) filer; **can you f. me five bucks?** tu pourrais pas me filer cinq dollars?
▸ ▸ Journ **f. cover** (of magazine) couverture f, première f de couverture, Fam première de couve; **to appear on the f. cover** faire la une; **f. desk** réception f; **f. door** (of house) porte f d'entrée; (of vehicle) portière f avant; Theat **f. of house** = partie f d'un théâtre où peuvent circuler les spectateurs; **f.-of-house manager** (in hotel) directeur m administratif, directeur de l'hébergement; Theat directeur m administratif; Mil **the f. line** la première ligne; **f. man** prête-nom m, pl prête-noms, homme m de paille; (presenter) présentateur m; **to act as a f. man for sb** servir de prête-nom ou d'homme de paille à qn; Banking **f. office** front-office m, pl front-offices; **f. organization** couverture f, façade f; **f. page** (of newspaper) première page f; Fam **to be f. page news** faire la une; **f. panel** face f avant; Cin **f. projection** projection f frontale; **f. room** (at front of house) = pièce f qui donne sur le devant de la maison; (sitting room) salon m; **f. row** premier rang m; Rugby première ligne f; **in the f. row** ou premier rang; Rugby **f.-row forward** avant m de première ligne; Aut **f. seat** siège m avant; **f. view** vue f de face; Archit élévation f du devant
▸ **front on, front onto** VT INSEP (of building) (be opposite) faire face à; (point towards) être tourné vers; **the river and the houses fronting on it** (overlooking) le fleuve et les maisons qui donnent dessus

frontage ['frʌntɪdʒ] N **1** (of building) longueur f de façade; (of shop) devanture f; **premises with frontages on two streets** local avec façades sur deux rues **2** (of river etc) terrain m en bordure **3** (land at front of building etc) espace m sur le devant d'un immeuble

frontal ['frʌnt(ə)l] N **1** Rel devant m d'autel, fronteau m **2** (of building) façade f

ADJ *Anat* frontal, -aux; *Archit (view etc)* de face

▸▸ **f. attack** *Com* attaque *f* frontale; *Mil* attaque de front; *Aut* **f. impact** choc *m* frontal; *Aut* **f. impact test** test *m* de choc frontal; *Met* **f. system** système *m* de fronts

frontbench [frʌnt'bentʃ] **N** *Br Pol (members of the government)* ministres *mpl*; *(members of the opposition)* ministres du cabinet fantôme; **he's never been on the f.** *(government)* il n'a jamais été ministre; *(opposition)* il n'a jamais été membre du cabinet fantôme; **the frontbenches** *(in Parliament)* = à la Chambre des communes, bancs *mpl* situés à droite et à gauche du Président et occupés respectivement par les ministres du gouvernement en exercice et ceux du gouvernement fantôme

▸▸ **f. MP** *(member of the government)* ministre *m*; *(member of the opposition)* membre *m* du cabinet fantôme; **f. spokesperson** *(of cabinet)* porte-parole *m inv*; *(of shadow cabinet)* porte-parole du cabinet fantôme; **f. team** *(cabinet)* équipe *f* ministérielle; *(shadow cabinet)* cabinet *m* fantôme

frontbencher ['frʌnt'bentʃər] **N** *Br Pol (member of the government)* ministre *m*; *(member of the opposition)* membre *m* du cabinet fantôme

front-end N *Comput* interface *f*

▸▸ *Comput* **f. computer** ordinateur *m* frontal; *Fin* **f. fee** frais *mpl* d'entrée; *Fin* **f. loading** = système *m* de prélèvement des frais sur les premiers versements; *Comput* **f. processor** processeur *m* frontal

frontier ['frʌntɪər] **N** frontière *f*; **natural frontiers** frontières naturelles; **the frontiers of human knowledge** les bornes *fpl* des connaissances humaines

▸▸ **f. guard** garde-frontière *m*, *pl* gardes-frontière; **f. town** = ville *f* de l'Ouest américain, à l'époque des pionniers

frontispiece ['frʌntɪspiːs] **N** *Typ* frontispice *m*

front-line ADJ *Mil (soldiers, troops)* en première ligne

▸▸ *Am Sport* **f. player** avant *m*

front-loader N *(washing machine)* machine *f* à laver avec chargement frontal

front-loading ADJ *(washing machine)* avec chargement frontal

frontrunner ['frʌntrʌnər] **N** *(leader)* coureur/cheval/concurrent *m* de tête; *(in election etc)* favori, -ite

front-wheel drive N traction *f* avant

frosh [frɒʃ] **N** *Am Univ Fam* étudiant, -ante de première année

frost [frɒst] **N** *Met* gelée *f*, gel *m*; **there was a f. last night** il a gelé la nuit dernière; **there was f. on the ground** le sol était gelé; **ground f.** gelée blanche; **heavy/light f.** grosse/petite gelée; **ten degrees of f.** dix degrés au-dessous de zéro

VT 1 *(windows etc)* givrer **2** *esp Am Culin (cake etc)* glacer **3** *(damage by frost) (fruit tree etc)* geler **4** *(in glassmaking) (glass)* dépolir

VI = **frost over, frost up**

▸ **frost over, frost up VI** *(of windscreen etc)* se givrer, se couvrir de givre

frostbite ['frɒstbaɪt] **N** *Med (of feet etc)* gelure *f*; **to have f.** avoir des gelures

frostbitten ['frɒstbɪt(ə)n] **ADJ 1** *(nose etc)* gelé **2** *(plant)* brûlé par le froid, grillé (par la gelée)

frostbound ['frɒstbaʊnd] **ADJ** *(earth)* gelé

frosted ['frɒstɪd] **ADJ 1** *(windscreen)* givré **2** *esp Am Culin (cake)* glacé **3** *(glass)* dépoli

frost-free ADJ *(refrigerator, freezer)* à dégivrage automatique

frostily ['frɒstɪlɪ] **ADV** *(to say)* sur un ton glacial; **to greet sb f.** faire un accueil glacé à qn; **she smiled f.** elle fit un sourire glacial

frostiness ['frɒstɪnɪs] **N 1** *(of the morning etc)* froid *m* glacial **2** *(of person)* manière *f* glaciale; **the f. of her smile/behaviour** son sourire/comportement glacial

frosting ['frɒstɪŋ] **N** *esp Am Culin (on cake)* glaçage *m*; *Fig* **the f. on the cake** la cerise sur le gâteau

frostproof ['frɒstpruːf] **ADJ** résistant à la gelée

frosty ['frɒstɪ] **ADJ 1** *(night, air etc)* glacial, -als *ou* -aux **2** *(answer, smile, greeting)* glacial, -als *ou* -aux **3** *(window)* couvert de givre; *(ground)* gelé

froth [frɒθ] **N 1** *(foam)* écume *f*, *(on beer, fizzy drink etc)* mousse *f* **2** *Pej (empty words)* paroles *fpl* creuses

VI écumer, mousser; *(of beer, fizzy drink etc)* mousser; *(of waves)* moutonner; **he was frothing at the mouth** il avait l'écume aux lèvres; **the frothing water** *(of sea)* les eaux écumantes

▸ **froth up VI** mousser

frothy ['frɒθɪ] **ADJ 1** écumeux, mousseux; *(waves)* moutonneux; *(beer, fizzy drink etc)* mousseux **2** *(speech, play, style)* léger; *Pej* vide, creux

frown [fraʊn] **N** froncement *m* de sourcils; *(disapproving look)* air *m* désapprobateur; *(stern look)* regard *m* sévère; **to say sth with a f.** dire qch en fronçant les sourcils

VI *(of person)* froncer les sourcils, se renfrogner; **she frowned disapprovingly/in annoyance** elle fronça les sourcils d'un air désapprobateur/irrité; **to f. at sb** regarder qn en fronçant les sourcils

▸ **frown on, frown upon VT INSEP** *(disapprove of)* *(suggestion etc)* désapprouver; **such behaviour was frowned upon** un tel comportement était mal vu

frowning ['fraʊnɪŋ] **ADJ** *(expression)* renfrogné

frowsty ['fraʊstɪ] **ADJ** *Br Fam (room)* qui sent le renfermé; *(smell, atmosphere)* de renfermé

frowzy ['fraʊzɪ] **ADJ** *Fam* **1** *(musty) (room)* qui sent le renfermé **2** *(person, clothes etc)* peu soigné

froze PT *see* **freeze**

frozen ['frəʊz(ə)n] **ADJ 1** gelé, glacé; *(meat, peas etc)* congelé, surgelé; *Fam* **my hands are f.** j'ai les mains gelées *ou* glacées **2** *Fin (credit, wages)* gelé, bloqué; *(assets, currency, prices)* gelé; *(account)* bloqué **3** *Comput (screen)* bloqué

PP *see* **freeze**

▸▸ **f. food** *(in refrigerator)* aliments *mpl* congelés; *(industrially frozen)* surgelés *mpl*; **f. food compartment** congélateur *m*; **f. yoghurt** yaourt *m* glacé

fructify ['frʌktɪfaɪ] **VI** fructifier

VT faire fructifier

fructose ['frʌktəʊs] **N** *Chem* fructose *m*

frugal ['fruːg(ə)l] **ADJ** *(person, life)* frugal, -aux; *(meal etc)* frugal, -aux, sobre; *(thrifty)* économe; **to be f. with sth** ménager qch

frugality [fruːˈgælɪtɪ] **N** *(of person, life)* frugalité *f*; *(of meal)* frugalité, sobriété *f*; *(thriftiness)* économie *f*

frugally ['fruːg(ə)lɪ] **ADV** frugalement

fruit [fruːt] **N 1** fruit *m*; **would you like some f.?** prendrez-vous un fruit?; **apples and other fruit(s)** les pommes et autres fruits; **a piece of f.** un fruit; **eat more f.** mangez plus de fruits; *Br* **soft f.**, *Am* **small f.** petits fruits; **to bear f.** *(of tree)* donner des fruits, porter fruit; *Fig (of labour)* porter ses fruits; **my enquiries bore f.** mes recherches furent cou-

ronnées de succès **2** *Fig* fruit *m*; *Lit* **the fruits of the earth** les fruits de la terre; *Lit* **the f. of her womb** le fruit de ses entrailles **3** *Old-fashioned Br Fam* yes, old f. oui, mon vieux **4** *Am Offensive Sl (homosexual)* pédé *m* **VI** *(of tree)* porter des fruits

▸▸ **f. basket** *(for display)* corbeille *f* à fruits; *Zool* **f. bat** chauve-souris *f* frugivore, *pl* chauves-souris frugivores; **f. bowl** coupe *f* à fruits, compotier *m*; **f. bud** bourgeon *m* à fruit; **f. cocktail** macédoine *f ou* salade *f* de fruits; **f. cup** *(dessert)* coupe de fruits; *(drink)* boisson *f* aux fruits *(parfois alcoolisée)*; **f. dish** *(individual)* coupe, coupelle *f*, *(large)* coupe à fruits, compotier; **f. drop** bonbon *m* aux fruits; **f. farmer** producteur, -trice de fruits; **f. farming** arboriculture *f* (fruitière); **f. fly** mouche *f* du vinaigre, drosophile *f*, **f. grower** fruiticulteur, -trice; **f. juice** jus *m* de fruits; **f. knife** couteau *m* à fruit(s); *Br* **f. machine** machine *f* à sous; **f. salad** macédoine *ou* salade de fruits; **f. shop** fruiterie *f*, **f. stall** étalage *m* de fruit; **f. tree** arbre *m* fruitier

fruit-bearing ADJ *(tree etc)* frugifère, fructifère

fruitcake ['fruːtkeɪk] **N 1** *Culin* cake *m* **2** *esp Br Fam (eccentric, mad person)* cinglé, -ée, fou, *f* folle; **he's as nutty as a f.** il est complètement cinglé

fruit-eating ADJ *(animal)* frugivore

fruiterer ['fruːtərər] **N** *esp Br Old-fashioned* fruitier, -ière; **f.'s (shop)** fruiterie *f*

fruitful ['fruːtfʊl] **ADJ 1** *(work, discussion etc)* fructueux **2** *(tree etc)* fructueux, productif; *(soil etc)* fertile, fécond

fruitfully ['fruːtfʊlɪ] **ADV** fructueusement; **they had spent the day f.** la journée avait été fructueuse pour eux

fruitfulness ['fruːtfʊlnɪs] **N 1** *Fig (of work, discussion etc)* caractère *m* fructueux **2** *(of tree etc)* productivité *f*, *(of earth etc)* fertilité *f*

fruiting ['fruːtɪŋ] **ADJ** *(tree etc)* frugifère, fructifère

fruition [fruːˈɪʃən] **N** *(of plan, hope)* réalisation *f*, **to come to f.** porter ses fruits; **to bring sth to f.** mener qch à bien

fruitless ['fruːtlɪs] **ADJ** *(discussions, negotiations)* stérile, infructueux; *(efforts, attempt)* infructueux, vain; **at least the trip won't have been entirely f.** au moins le voyage n'aura pas tout à fait servi à rien

fruity ['fruːtɪ] **ADJ 1** *(taste etc)* de fruit; *(wine)* fruité, fruiteux **2** *Fam* **a f. voice** une voix (trop) étoffée; **a f. laugh** un rire généreux **3** *esp Br Old-fashioned (novel, scandal etc)* corsé **4** *Am Offensive Sl (homosexual)* de pédé **5** *Am (crazy)* toqué, cinglé

frump [frʌmp] **N** femme *f* mal attifée; **she's a f.** elle est ficelée comme l'as de pique

frumpish ['frʌmpɪʃ], **frumpy** ['frʌmpɪ] **ADJ** *(clothes)* tarte, moche; *Fam* **f. woman** femme *f* mal attifée *ou* mal fagotée

frustrate [frʌs'treɪt] **VT 1** *(upset, annoy) (person)* décevoir, frustrer **2** *(thwart) (person)* contrecarrer; *(plan)* faire échouer; **to f. sb's hopes** frustrer qn dans son espoir, frustrer l'espoir de qn

frustrated [frʌs'treɪtɪd] **ADJ** *(writer etc)* frustré; **(sexually)** *f.* frustré

frustrating [frʌs'treɪtɪŋ] **ADJ** *(experience etc)* frustrant

frustration [frʌs'treɪʃən] **N 1** *(emotion)* frustration *f* **2** *(of person's plans)* anéantissement *m*; *(of hopes, ambitions)* frustration *f*

fry [fraɪ] (**fried**) **VT 1** *Culin (fish etc)* (faire) frire; **to f. an egg** faire cuire un œuf sur le plat **2** *esp Am Sl (convict)* faire passer à la chaise électrique

VI 1 *(of food)* frire **2** *esp Am Sl (of convict)* passer à la chaise électrique

fry² N *(no pl)* *(of fish)* frai *m*, fretin *m*, alevin *m*; **small f.** menu fretin; *Fig (insignificant people)* menu fretin, gens *mpl* insignifiants; *(children)* gosses *mpl*; **salmon f.** saumoneaux *mpl* dans la deuxième année

fry³ N *(offal)* issues *fpl*; *(of lamb, pig)* fressure *f*

fryer ['fraɪər] N *Culin* **1** *(person)* = personne *f* qui fait de la friture **2** *(frying pan)* poêle *f* à frire; **(deep) f.** friteuse *f* **3** *(chicken)* poulet *m* à frire

frying ['fraɪɪŋ] N friture *f*
▸ ▸ **f. pan** poêle *f* (à frire); *Prov* **to jump out of the f. pan into the fire** tomber de Charybde en Scylla

fry-pan N *Am* poêle *f* à frire

fry-up N *Br Culin Fam* = bacon, saucisses, tomates etc frits ensemble, généralement consommés au petit déjeuner

FSA [efes'eɪ] N **1** *Fin (abbr* **Financial Services Authority)** = organisme *m* gouvernemental britannique chargé de contrôler les activités du secteur financier **2** *(abbr* **Food Standards Agency)** = organisme *m* britannique de contrôle de la sécurité alimentaire

f-stop N *Phot* ouverture *f* du diaphragme

ft *(abbr* **foot/feet)** p., pd.

FT 100 index [ef'ti:] N *St Exch (abbr* **Financial Times-Stock Exchange 100 Index)** = principal indice *m* boursier du Financial Times basé sur la valeur de 100 actions cotées à la Bourse de Londres

FTP [efti:'pi:] *Comput* N *(abbr* **File Transfer Protocol)** FTP
vt télécharger par FTP
▸ ▸ **F. server** serveur *m* FTP; **F. site** site *m* FTP

FTSE ['fʊtsi] N *St Exch (abbr* **Financial Times Stock Exchange)** = principal indice *m* boursier du Financial Times basé sur la valeur de 100 actions cotées à la Bourse de Londres, ≃ indice *m* CAC 40

fuchsia ['fju:ʃə] N *(plant)* fuchsia *m*

fuck [fʌk] *Vulg* N **1** *(intercourse)* baise *f*; **they had a quick f.** ils ont baisé *ou* tiré un coup en vitesse; **to be a good f.** bien baiser; **to be an easy f.** coucher avec tout le monde
2 *(as intensifier)* **what the f. is that?** qu'est-ce que c'est que ça, bordel de merde?; **I can't really afford it, but what the f.!** c'est un peu cher pour moi, mais je m'en fous!; **who the f. told you about it/did this?** quel est le connard qui t'en a parlé/qui a fait ça?; **as stupid/rich as f.** foutrement con/riche; **he ran like f.** il a couru comme un dératé; **shut the f. up!** ferme ta gueule putain *ou* bordel!; **get the f. out of here!** casse-toi connard!; **for f.'s sake!** bordel!, putain!; **f. knows why I agreed to come!** putain *ou* bordel, pourquoi est-ce que j'ai accepté de venir?; **not to care** *or* **give a f.** n'en avoir rien à foutre (**about sth** de qch); **why should I give a f. about what you think?** qu'est-ce que ça peut me foutre, ce que tu penses?; **she'd like you to apologize – like f. I will!** elle voudrait que tu t'excuses – qu'elle aille se faire foutre!; **did you invite them? – like f. I did!** tu les as invités? – tu déconnes ou quoi?; **like f. I'm going to help that bastard!** qu'il aille se faire foutre, ce connard, je ne l'aiderai pas!; **get to f.!** va te faire foutre!
INT merde!, bordel!
vt 1 *(person)* baiser **2 f. it!** merde!; **f. this!** et puis merde!; **f. you!, go f. yourself!** va te faire foutre!, je t'emmerde!; **f. him!** qu'il aille se faire foutre!; **f. what he thinks/says!** je m'en fous de ce qu'il pense/dit!; **f. me!** putain!; **f. the President!** aux chiottes le Président!; **f. all** que dalle; **she does f. all work** elle en fout pas une rame
vi baiser
▸ **fuck about, fuck around** *Vulg* **vi** *(play the* *fool)* déconner; *(waste time)* glander; **to f. about** *or* **around with sth** *(car, radio)* trifouiller qch; **if you spent less time fucking about** *or* **around with your computer program …!** si tu passais moins de temps sur ton putain de logiciel …!
vt sep *(person) (treat badly)* emmerder; *(waste time of)* faire tourner en bourrique
▸ **fuck off** *Vulg* **vi** *(go away)* se casser; **to tell sb to f. off** dire à qn d'aller se faire foutre, envoyer qn se faire foutre; **f. off!** va te faire foutre!
vt sep *(annoy) (person)* emmerder, faire chier; **she's been feeling really fucked off about work recently** le boulot la fait vraiment chier ces temps-ci
▸ **fuck over vt sep** *Am Vulg* **to f. sb over** *(cheat)* baiser qn, arnaquer qn; **I really got fucked over on that one** là je me suis vraiment fait baiser *ou* arnaquer; **he had been fucked over for a thousand dollars** il s'était fait baiser de mille dollars
▸ **fuck up** *Vulg* **vt sep** *(ruin)* foutre en l'air, niquer; *(person)* foutre en l'air; **I think I've fucked up the exam/the meringue** je crois que j'ai loupé ce putain d'examen/cette putain de meringue; **she was badly fucked up by her parents** ses parents l'ont complètement foutue en l'air; **to be fucked up** *(of person)* être à côté de ses pompes
vi *(bungle sth)* déconner, merder

fucked [fʌkt] ADJ *Vulg (car, stereo etc)* foutu, naze; **I'm f.!** *(exhausted)* je suis mort *ou* crevé!; **his knee/heart/eye is f.** son genou/cœur/œil est naze *ou* niqué; **his chances of winning the race were completely f.!** il n'avait plus une chance de gagner cette putain de course!

fucker ['fʌkər] N *Vulg* **1** *(person)* stupid f. connard *m*; **old f.** vieux con *m* **2** *(thing, object)* saloperie *f*; **I can't get the f. out** je n'arrive pas à retirer cette saloperie

fuckface ['fʌkfeɪs] N *Vulg* tête *f* de con

fucking ['fʌkɪŋ] *Vulg* ADJ foutu; **this f. car** cette voiture de mes deux, cette putain de voiture; **I've cut my f. finger** bordel *ou* putain, je me suis coupé le doigt; **he's a f. idiot!** c'est un connard!; **you're a f. liar!** tu n'es qu'un connard de menteur!; **that's a f. lie!** c'est des conneries!; **you haven't got a f. clue, have you?** tu n'y connais foutrement rien, hein?; **f. hell!** bordel de merde!; **who the f. hell does she think she is?** mais merde, pour qui elle se prend?; **why/when the f. hell did you do that?** pourquoi/quand est-ce que tu as fait ça putain *ou* bordel?
ADV *(cold, expensive, good)* vachement; *(stupid)* foutument; **it's f. cold** putain, il fait vachement froid; **you're f. well out of your mind!** bordel, ça va vraiment pas dans ta tête!; **what did you f. expect?** mais qu'est-ce que tu croyais putain *ou* bordel?
N baise *f*

fuck-up N *Vulg* gâchis *m*; **the whole thing was a complete f.** tout a merdé; **to make a f. of sth** *(task, job)* saloper qch; *(marriage)* foutre qch en l'air; **I made a real f. of the exam/interview** j'ai complètement merdé à l'examen/l'entretien

fuckwit ['fʌkwɪt] N *Vulg* connard *m*, connasse *f*

fuddle ['fʌd(ə)l] vt *(person)* embrouiller; **he had fuddled his brain with drink and drugs** l'alcool et la drogue lui avaient embrouillé le cerveau

fuddled ['fʌd(ə)ld] ADJ *Fam* **1** *(drunk)* soûl; **to get f.** se soûler, s'enivrer; **slightly f.** un peu gris **2** *(confused)* embrouillé

fuddy-duddy ['fʌdɪdʌdɪ] *Fam* N vieil encroûté *m*; **don't be such an old f.!** arrête de t'encroûter comme ça!
ADV vieux jeu *inv*

fudge [fʌdʒ] N **1** *Culin* fondant *m* **2** *Journ (late news)* dernières nouvelles *fpl* **3** *(evasion)* **his answer was a f.** sa réponse n'était qu'une dérobade
vt *Fam (botch) (piece of work etc)* bousiller; *(falsify) (accounts etc)* truquer; **to f. an issue** *(avoid)* éluder une question
vi *Fam* se dérober; **I've had enough of their fudging** j'en ai assez de leurs dérobades

fuel [fjʊəl] N combustible *m*; *(for engine)* carburant *m*; **domestic** *or* **household f.** combustible de ménage; *Fig* **to add f. to the flames** jeter de l'huile sur le feu; *Fig* **to add fresh f. to a quarrel** alimenter une querelle
vt *(-ll-, Am -l-) (furnace etc)* alimenter, charger; *(vehicle, machine etc)* ravitailler *ou* alimenter en carburant; *Fig (speculations)* nourrir; *(doubts, hatred, argument)* alimenter
vi se ravitailler en carburant
▸ ▸ **f. bill** *(of household)* facture *f* de chauffage; *(of region)* dépenses *fpl* énergétiques; **f. consumption** consommation *f* d'énergie; *(of car)* consommation de carburant; **f. costs** *(of household)* coûts *mpl* de chauffage; *(of region)* coûts de l'énergie; **f. element** élément *m* combustible; **f. gauge** jauge *f* d'essence; *Tech* **f. injection** alimentation *f* par injection, injection *f* (de carburant); *Tech* **f. injection system** système *m* d'injection (de combustible); *Tech* **f. injector** injecteur *m* de carburant; **f. level** niveau *m* de carburant; **f. oil** mazout *m*, fuel *m*, fioul *m*; **f. pipe** tuyau *m* d'alimentation en carburant; **f. pressure** pression *f* de carburant; **f. pump** pompe *f* d'alimentation; *Nucl* **f. rod** assemblage *m* d'éléments combustibles; **f. tank** *(in home)* cuve *f* à mazout; *(in car)* réservoir *m* de carburant ou d'essence; *(in ship)* soute *f* à mazout *ou* à fuel; **f. tank shield** bouclier *m* de réservoir de carburant; **f. tax** taxe *f* sur les carburants; **f. temperature gauge** jauge *f* de température du carburant

fuel/air mixture N mélange *m* air/carburant

fuel-injected ['fjʊəlɪndʒektɪd] ADJ *Aut etc* à injection

fuelling, *Am* **fueling** ['fjʊəlɪŋ] N ravitaillement *m* en carburant
▸ ▸ **f. stop** escale *f* de ravitaillement (en carburant)

fug [fʌg] N *esp Br Fam* forte odeur *f* de renfermé; *(in smoke-filled room)* air *m* saturé de fumée de cigarette; **there's a terrible f. in here!** ce que ça pue le renfermé/le tabac là-dedans!

fuggy ['fʌgɪ] ADJ *esp Br Fam (room etc)* qui sent le renfermé; *(atmosphere)* confiné

fugitive ['fju:dʒɪtɪv] N fugitif, -ive, fuyard, -arde; *(refugee)* réfugié, -ée; **f. from justice** fugitif recherché par la justice
ADJ **1** *(prisoner)* fugitif, fuyard **2** *esp Lit (happiness)* fugitif, fugace; *(smile, impression, thought)* fugitif

fugue [fju:g] N *Mus, Psy* fugue *f*

fulcrum, *pl* **fulcra, fulcrums** ['fʌlkrəm, -krə, -krəmz] N *(of lever)* pivot *m*

fulfil, *Am* **fulfill** [fʊl'fɪl] vt *(Br* **fulfils,** *Am* **fulfills;** *Br, Am* **fulfilled, fulfilling)** *(task, prophecy)* accomplir; *(expectations)* répondre à, remplir; *(wish)* satisfaire; *(prayer, plea)* exaucer; *(obligation, duties)* remplir, s'acquitter de; *(conditions, instructions, purpose, contract)* remplir; *(requirements, need, purpose)* répondre à, satisfaire à; *(promise)* exécuter; *(commandment)* obéir à; *(ambition, plan, potential)* réaliser; **to f. oneself** se réaliser, s'épanouir; **administrative work doesn't f. me** le travail de bureau ne me permet pas de me réaliser; **to feel fulfilled** *(of person)* se sentir épanoui

fulfilling [fʊl'fɪlɪŋ] **ADJ** *(work etc)* épanouissant

fulfilment, *Am* **fulfillment** [fʊl'fɪlmənt] **N** *(of prophecy, duty, wish etc)* accomplissement *m*; *(of prayer, plea)* exaucement *m*; *(of plan, contract)* exécution *f*; *Law (of condition)* accomplissement *m*; *(of ambition)* réalisation *f*; *(of promise)* exécution; **to find** *or* **achieve f.** se réaliser; **to have a feeling** *or* **sense of f.** avoir un sentiment de plénitude

FULL [fʊl]

> **ADJ** plein **1, 2, 4, 5** ▪ rempli **1**
> ▪ ample **3** ▪ complet **4** ▪ large **5**
> **N** intégralement
> **ADV** complètement **1** ▪ carrément **2**

ADJ 1 *(receptacle, cupboard)* plein, rempli; *(room)* comble; *(bus etc)* plein; *(day)* chargé; *(sail)* plein, gonflé; *(disk)* saturé; **f. to the brim** rempli jusqu'au bord *ou* à ras bord; **f. to overflowing** plein à ras bord; **don't speak with your mouth f.** ne parle pas la bouche pleine; **to be f. (up)** *(of person)* être repu *ou* rassasié; **on a f. stomach** le ventre plein; **the bus is f. up** l'autobus est au complet; **the sails are f.** les voiles portent bien; **to be f. of sth** être plein de qch; **the (news)papers were f. of it** les journaux ne parlaient que de ça; **to become f.** *(of disk)* arriver à saturation; **to have one's pockets f. of money** avoir les poches pleines d'argent; **her eyes were f. of tears** ses yeux étaient remplis de larmes; **f. of holes** plein de trous

2 look f. of hatred regard chargé de haine; **to be f. of hope** être rempli d'espoir; **to be f. of ideas** être plein d'idées; **to be f. of life/energy/vitality** être plein de vie/d'énergie/de vitalité; **to be f. of praise for sb** ne pas tarir d'éloges sur qn; **to be f. of one's own importance** être pénétré de sa propre importance; *Pej* **f. of oneself** plein de soi-même

3 *(written notes, details etc)* ample, copieux; **she received her f. share of the money** elle a reçu tout l'argent qui lui revenait; **in the fullest detail** dans les plus grand détail; **to ask for fuller information about sth** demander des précisions sur qch

4 *(complete)* complet, entier; **the f. horror of the situation** toute l'horreur de la situation; **roses in f. bloom** roses épanouies; **to be in f. cry** *(of hounds)* donner de la voix; *Fig* **the press was in f. cry after the minister** la presse se déchaînait contre le ministre; **in f. flow** en plein discours; **on f. beam** en feux de route, en pleins phares; *Mil, Fig* **in f. flight/retreat** en pleine déroute/retraite; *Mil, Fig* **at f. strength** au grand complet; **below f. strength** pas au complet; **in f. uniform** en grande tenue; **to be in f. swing** *(of party, sales etc)* battre son plein; **in f. view of the police/the enemy** sous les yeux de la police/de l'ennemi; **to lead a f. life** mener une vie bien remplie; **I waited two f. hours** *or* **a f. two hours** j'ai attendu deux bonnes heures; **we were under f. sail** nous avions toutes voiles dehors; **to give f. scope to sb** donner libre carrière à qn; **to give f. scope to sb's talents** donner libre champ aux talents de qn; **f. amount** somme totale; **at f. blast** à fond; **f. cargo** plein chargement; *Phot* **in f. colour** tout en couleur; *Sch* **f. marks** dix sur dix/vingt sur vingt/*etc*; *Fig* **f. marks for all those who spotted the mistake** bravo à tous ceux qui ont trouvé l'erreur; **f. meal** repas complet; *Com* **f. set of bills of lading** jeu *m* complet de connaissements; **(at) f. speed** à toute vitesse, à fond; *Naut* **f. speed ahead!** en avant toute!; *Fig* **it's f. speed ahead** maintenant on peut y aller

5 *(face)* plein, rond; *(sleeve etc)* large, bouffant; **f. face portrait** portrait de face; **a f. fi-**
gure *(of woman)* une silhouette généreuse; **f. lips** grosses lèvres, lèvres charnues; **f. skirt** jupe *f* bouffante; **f. voice** voix pleine *ou* ronde

N to publish a letter in f. publier une lettre intégralement; **money refunded in f.** *(on notice etc)* on rembourse intégralement l'argent *ou* l'argent en totalité; **to pay in f.** payer intégralement; **name in f.** nom et prénoms; **to write out a word in f.** écrire un mot en toutes lettres; **to the f.** tout à fait; **to live life to the f.** vivre sa vie pleinement; **to indulge one's tastes to the f.** donner libre cours à ses goûts

ADV 1 *(completely)* complètement, entièrement; **to turn a tap f. on** *or* **on f.** ouvrir un robinet en grand; **to turn the radio f. on** *or* **on f.** mettre la radio à fond; **to drive (one's car) f. out** *(at top speed)* conduire à toute vitesse; **to work f. out** travailler à toute vitesse; **I know it f. well** je le sais bien *ou* parfaitement

2 *(right)* carrément; **lying f. in the sun** couché en plein (au) soleil; **hit f. in the face** atteint en pleine figure

▸▸**f. board** pension *f* complète; *Fin* **f. consolidation** intégration *f* globale; *Com* **f. container load** conteneur *m* chargé complètement; *Acct* **f. cost accounting (method)** méthode *f* de capitalisation du coût entier; *Fin* **f. costing** méthode du coût complet; *Fin* **f. discharge** quitus *m*; *Tel* **f. duplex** bidirectionnel *m* simultané, full duplex *m*; *Econ* **f. employment** plein emploi *m*; **f. employment policy** politique *f* de plein emploi; **f. house** *Cards* full *m*; *Theat* salle *f* comble; *Aut* **f. licence** permis *m* tous véhicules; **f. member** membre *m* à part entière; *Fam* **the f. Monty** *(everything)* la totale; **to do a f. Monty** *(strip)* faire un strip-tease intégral; **f. moon** pleine lune *f*, **f. name** *(on form)* nom *m* en toutes lettres; **what is your f. name?** quels sont vos nom et prénoms?; **f. pay** paie *f* entière; **leave on f. pay** congé *m* à solde entière; *Fin* **f. payment** paiement *m* intégral; **to make f. payment for a share** libérer entièrement une action; *Typ* **f. point** *(in punctuation)* point *m*; **f. price** prix *m* fort; **to pay f. price** payer place entière; **to pay the f. price for sth** payer le prix fort pour qch; *Am* **f. professor** professeur *m* d'université *(titulaire d'une chaire)*; *Comput* **f. screen** plein écran *m*; **f. session** *(of a committee etc)* réunion *f* plénière; *TV, Cin* **f. shot** plan *m* d'ensemble, plan général; *Br* **f. stop** *(pause)* arrêt *m* complet; *Gram* point; *Comput* point final; **f. text** texte *m* intégral; **f. time** *(of working week)* temps *m* complet; *Sport* fin *f* de match; **f. warranty** garantie *f* totale; *Com* **f. weight** poids *m* juste

fullback ['fʊlbæk] **N** *Sport* arrière *m*; **at f.** à l'arrière

full-blooded **ADJ 1** *(racially)* de race pure; *(horse)* de sang, pur-sang *inv* **2** *(vigorous)* vigoureux

full-blown **ADJ 1** *(rose etc)* épanoui, en pleine fleur **2** *(crisis)* de la plus grande envergure; **a f. argument** une vraie dispute **3** *Fig (doctor etc)* qualifié; **she is a f. lawyer** elle a (obtenu) tous ses diplômes; **to have f. AIDS** avoir le sida avéré

full-bodied ['fʊl'bɒdɪd] **ADJ** *(wine)* corsé, qui a du corps

full-cost pricing **N** *Mktg* fixation *f* du prix en fonction du coût

full-cream **ADJ**
▸▸**f. milk** lait *m* entier

full-dress **ADJ** *(attire)* en habit de cérémonie
▸▸**f. debate** débat *m* de fond; **f. uniform** tenue *f* de cérémonie, grande tenue

fuller ['fʊlər] **N f.'s earth** terre *f* à foulon

full-faced ['fʊl'feɪst] **ADJ** *(person)* à la figure ronde, au visage plein

full-fledged **ADJ** *Am* = **fully-fledged**

full-frontal **ADJ** *(attack, assault)* de front
N nudité *f* vue de face, nu *m* de face
ADV nu de face
▸▸**f. nudity** *(in show)* nu *m* intégral

full-grown **ADJ** *(tree)* qui a atteint son développement complet; *(person, cow)* adulte

full-length **ADJ** *(portrait)* en pied; *(mirror)* qui permet de se voir en pied; *(evening dress)* long; **a f. novel** un vrai roman
ADV **he was stretched out f. on the floor** il était étendu de tout son long par terre
▸▸*TV, Cin* **f. film** long métrage *m*; *TV, Cin* **f. shot** plan *m* général

ful(l)ness ['fʊlnɪs] **N 1** *(of receptacle)* état *m* plein; **out of the f. of his heart** comme son cœur débordait; **to speak out of the f. of one's grief** parler le cœur débordant de chagrin **2** *(of strength)* plénitude *f*, perfection *f*, totalité *f*; **in the f. of time** avec le temps **3** *(of skirt, report etc)* ampleur *f*, *(of detail)* abondance *f*, *(of figure)* rondeur *f*, *(of style etc)* richesse *f*

full-out **ADJ** *Typ* au fer, sans alinéa

full-page **ADJ** pleine page
▸▸**f. advertisement** annonce *f* pleine page; *Comput* **f. display** écran *m* pleine page

full-scale **ADJ 1** = **full-size(d) 2** *(reform)* complet, intégral, -aux; *(panic, drought, retreat)* total, -aux; *(attack, war)* de grande envergure; *(emergency)* absolu

full-screen **ADJ** *Comput* plein écran
▸▸*Comput* **f. menu** menu *m* plein écran

full-size(d) **ADJ** *(drawing, model etc)* grandeur nature; *(tree)* adulte; *(keyboard, wheel)* aux dimensions standard; *(violin, bicycle)* d'adulte

full-strength **ADJ** de force normale

full-time **ADV** *(work)* à plein temps, à temps complet
ADJ *(work, employee, job)* à temps complet, à plein temps; *Fig* **looking after the baby is a f. job** s'occuper du bébé ne laisse pas une minute de libre
▸▸*Sport* **f. score** score *m* final

fully ['fʊlɪ] **ADV 1** *(completely)* *(involved, occupied in sth, taken up)* entièrement; *(satisfied, justified, convinced)* pleinement, entièrement; *(to understand)* parfaitement; *(to treat subject etc)* à fond; **to be f. aware** *or* **conscious of the fact that ...** être parfaitement conscient du fait que ...; **I f. expect to be back here on Monday** je pense vraiment être de retour lundi; **f. licensed** *(hotel, restaurant etc)* qui a obtenu une licence pour la vente d'alcool; **f. loaded** *(van, plane etc)* en pleine charge; **f. paid** payé intégralement; **f. paid up** *(capital)* intégralement libéré; **this topic is dealt with more f. below** ce thème est traité plus en détail ci-après

2 *(at least)* **it takes f. two hours** cela prend bien *ou* au moins deux heures

fully-fashioned ['fʊlɪ'fæʃənd] **ADJ** *(stockings, sweater)* bien ajusté

fully-fledged **ADJ** *(bird)* qui a toutes ses plumes; *Fam (doctor etc)* qualifié; **now you're a f. actor!** maintenant tu es un vrai acteur!

fulmar ['fʊlmər] **N** *(bird)* pétrel *m* glacial

fulminate ['fʌlmɪneɪt] **VI** fulminer (**against** contre)

fulmination [fʌlmɪ'neɪʃən] **N** malédiction *f*, imprécation *f*

fulsome ['fʊlsəm] **ADJ** *(praise)* enthousiaste; *(excessive)* excessif, exagéré; *(welcome, greeting)* plein d'effusion; **to be f. in one's praise of sb/sth** porter qn/qch aux nues

fulsomely [ˈfʊlsəmlɪ] ADV to praise sb/sth f. porter qn/qch aux nues; 'it's gorgeous!', she said f. 'c'est magnifique!', dit-elle pleine d'enthousiasme

fumarole [ˈfjuːmərəʊl] N Geol fumerolle f

fumble [ˈfʌmb(ə)l] VI (in enclosed space) fouiller (au hasard); (on floor, in dark etc) tâtonner; **to f. (about** or **around) in a drawer for sth** fouiller dans un tiroir pour trouver qch; **to f. (about** or **around) in a dark room for sth** chercher qch à tâtons dans une pièce obscure; **to f. for words** chercher ses mots; **to f. with sth** manier qch maladroitement
VT manier maladroitement; (opportunity) gâcher; **to f. a question** répondre à une question en bafouillant; Sport **to f. the ball** mal attraper la balle

fumbling [ˈfʌmblɪŋ] ADJ maladroit, gauche

fume [fjuːm] N (vapour) vapeur f, (gas) gaz m; **petrol fumes** vapeurs d'essence; Aut **exhaust fumes** gaz d'échappement
VI Fam (be angry) rager; **I was fuming** je rageais (**at** contre), j'étais exaspéré (**at** par)

Note that the French verb **fumer** is a false friend and is never a translation for the English verb **to fume**. It means **to smoke**.

fumigate [ˈfjuːmɪgeɪt] VT (flat etc) désinfecter par fumigation

fumigation [fjuːmɪˈgeɪʃən] N fumigation f

fumigator [ˈfjuːmɪgeɪtər] N (device) appareil m fumigatoire

fumitory [ˈfjuːmɪtərɪ] N (plant) fumeterre f

fun [fʌn] N amusement m, gaieté f, (joking) plaisanterie f, **to have f.** s'amuser, se divertir; **to get a lot of f. out of doing sth** bien s'amuser en faisant qch; **we had lots of** or **great** or **good f.** on s'est bien amusé; **to have f. at sb's expense** s'amuser aux dépens de qn; **there'll be f. and games** ça va chauffer, il va y avoir du grabuge; **it was great f.** c'était très drôle; **he is great f.** or **full of f.** il est très drôle; **she's f. to be with** on s'amuse avec elle; **to make f. of** or **poke f. at sb/sth** se moquer de qn/qch, rire de qn/qch; **to say sth in f.** dire qch en plaisantant; **in f.** (as a joke) par plaisanterie; **for f.** (for enjoyment) pour se distraire; **I did it for the f. of the thing** or **of it** je l'ai fait pour le plaisir; **where's the f. in that?** je ne vois pas ce que ça a d'agréable; **it wasn't much f. walking home in the rain** rentrer à pied sous la pluie n'avait rien d'une partie de plaisir; **it won't be half as much f. without you** ce ne sera pas si drôle sans toi; **all the f.'s gone out of it** ce n'est plus drôle du tout; esp Am Fam **a f. party** une soirée où l'on s'amuse bien; **she's a f. person to be with** on s'amuse bien avec elle; **I don't want to spoil your f.** je ne veux pas vous empêcher de vous amuser; **to take the f. out of sth** rendre qch plus drôle du tout; **to put the f. back into sth** redonner tout son charme à qch; **that's half the f. as far as I'm concerned** c'est là tout le charme de la chose pour moi; **to join in the f.** s'amuser avec tout le monde; Iron **that's when the f. began** (trouble) c'est là que ça a commencé à barder; **all the f. of the fair** toutes les attractions de la foire; **what f.!** comme c'est amusant!; Iron très amusant!; **f.-loving** qui aime s'amuser; **a f.-packed** or **-filled holiday** des vacances pendant lesquelles on n'a pas le temps de s'ennuyer
▸▸ **f. fur** fourrure f synthétique; **f. run** course f à pied pour amateurs (pour collecter des fonds pour des organisations caritatives)

funboard [ˈfʌnbɔːd] N funboard m

function [ˈfʌŋkʃən] N 1 (of body, machine, institution) fonction f, (of person) fonction,

charge f, **in his f. as a magistrate** en sa qualité de magistrat; **he combines the functions of servant and gardener** il tient le double emploi de domestique et de jardinier; **to discharge one's functions** s'acquitter de ses fonctions; **my f. in life** ma raison d'être; **the spring performs the f. of a shock absorber** le ressort joue le rôle d'(un) ou fait fonction d'amortisseur
2 (occasion) (reception) réception f, réunion f, (public ceremony) cérémonie f publique; **society f.** réception mondaine
3 Math etc fonction f, also Fig **to be a f. of sth** être fonction de qch
VI (operate, work) fonctionner; **to f. as sth** (fill a role) faire fonction de qch
▸▸ Comput **f. key** touche f de fonction; **functions manager** (at hotel) responsable m des réceptions; **f. room** salle f de réception

functional [ˈfʌŋkʃən(ə)l] ADJ **1** (furniture etc) fonctionnel, utilitaire **2** (operational) **to be f.** fonctionner; **I'm barely f. before ten o'clock** je ne suis guère opérationnel avant dix heures **3** Math, Med fonctionnel
▸▸ Med **f. disorder** trouble m fonctionnel; **f. illiterate** illettré, -ée

functionality [fʌŋkʃəˈnælɪtɪ] N fonctionnalité f

functionally [ˈfʌŋkʃən(ə)lɪ] ADV **to be f. illiterate** = être illettré au point de ne pas pouvoir faire face aux situations courantes; **to be f. equivalent to sth** avoir la même fonction que qch; **the human appendix is f. unnecessary** l'appendice humain est inutile du point de vue fonctionnel

functionary [ˈfʌŋkʃənərɪ] N often Pej fonctionnaire mf

functioning [ˈfʌŋkʃənɪŋ] N (of machine etc) fonctionnement m

fund [fʌnd] VOIR GRAMMAIRE A10 **1** Fin etc fonds m, caisse f, **to start a f.** lancer une souscription **2 funds** fonds mpl, ressources fpl pécuniaires; (of government) fonds publics; **to be in funds** être en fonds; **funds are low** les fonds sont bas; **to be short of** or **low on funds** être à court d'argent; Banking '**no funds**' 'défaut de provision', 'manque de fonds'; **f.-holder** rentier, -ière **3** (supply) (of wit) fonds m; (of information) source f, **unfailing f. of humour** des ressources d'humour intarissables; **a f. of anecdotes** un stock d'anecdotes
VT Fin (project) financer; (company etc) pourvoir de fonds; (public debt) consolider; **to f. money** placer de l'argent dans les fonds publics; Acct **funded from cashflow** autofinancé
▸▸ Fin **funds flow statement** tableau m des emplois et ressources; **f. of funds** fonds de fonds; **f. management** gestion f de fonds; **f. manager** gestionnaire mf de fonds

fundamental [fʌndəˈment(ə)l] ADJ **1** fondamental, -aux, essentiel; (question) principal, -aux, de fond; **of f. importance** d'une importance capitale; **to be f. to one's understanding/the success of sth** être fondamental ou essentiel à la compréhension/essentiel au succès de qch **2** Mus fondamental
N **1 fundamentals** principe(s) m(pl), (of science) notions fpl fondamentales, fondements mpl, (of system) partie f essentielle; **to reach agreement on fundamentals** réaliser un accord sur les points essentiels; **let's get down to fundamentals** allons à l'essentiel **2** Mus fondamentale f
▸▸ Mus **f. note** note f fondamentale

fundamentalism [fʌndəˈmentəlɪz(ə)m] N Rel fondamentalisme m

fundamentalist [fʌndəˈmentəlɪst] ADJ, N Rel fondamentaliste mf

fundamentally [fʌndəˈmentəlɪ] ADV (honest, incorrect, important) fondamentale-

ment; **f., there's nothing wrong with the idea** l'idée en soi n'est pas mauvaise; **f., it's a question of who's got more money** au fond, ce qui importe c'est qui a le plus d'argent

funded [ˈfʌndɪd] ADJ Fin (assets) en rentes
▸▸ **f. capital** capitaux mpl investis; **f. debt** dette f consolidée; **f. pension scheme** régime m de retraite par capitalisation

fundholder [ˈfʌndhəʊldər] N (person) rentier, -ière

funding [ˈfʌndɪŋ] N **1** (for project) financement m **2** (of debt) consolidation f, (of annuity) assiette f
▸▸ **f. operation** opération f de financement; **f. plan** plan m de financement

fund-raiser N **1** (professional) = personne f employée par une œuvre de bienfaisance pour rassembler des fonds **2** (event) = match m/concert m/etc au profit d'une œuvre de bienfaisance

fund-raising N collecte f de fonds pour une œuvre de bienfaisance; **Nadia is in charge of f.** Nadia est chargée de rassembler les fonds
ADJ (dinner, project, sale) organisé pour collecter des fonds

funeral [ˈfjuːnərəl] N funérailles fpl, obsèques fpl, (including burial) enterrement m; **to attend sb's f.** assister à l'enterrement de qn; Fam **that's your f.!** ça, c'est votre problème!
▸▸ **f. ceremony** cérémonie f funèbre; **f. director** entrepreneur, -euse de pompes funèbres; Am **f. home** établissement m de pompes funèbres; **f. march** marche f funèbre; **f. parlour** établissement m de pompes funèbres; **f. procession** cortège m funèbre; **f. pyre** bûcher m (funéraire); **f. service** service m ou office m funèbre

funereal [fjuːˈnɪərɪəl] ADJ lugubre, funèbre, triste; (voice) lugubre, sépulcral, -aux; (pace) lent; **to proceed at a f. pace** avancer à un pas d'enterrement

funfair [ˈfʌnfeər] N (travelling) fête f foraine, foire f, (fixed) parc m d'attractions

fungal [ˈfʌŋgəl] ADJ fongique
▸▸ Med **f. infection** mycose f

fungible [ˈfʌndʒɪb(ə)l] ADJ St Exch fongible

fungicide [ˈfʌndʒɪsaɪd] N fongicide m

fungicidal [ˈfʌndʒɪˈsaɪdl] ADJ antifongique, fongicide

fungoid [ˈfʌŋgɔɪd] ADJ **1** Bot fongoïde **2** Med fongueux

fungous [ˈfʌŋgəs] ADJ Med fongueux

fungus, pl **funguses, fungi** [ˈfʌŋgəs, -əsiz, -gaɪ, -dʒaɪ] N **1** Bot champignon m; (on walls) moisissure f, Hum **face f.** (moustache) moustache f, bacchantes fpl, (beard) barbe f **2** Med fongus m

funicular [fjuːˈnɪkjʊlər] N, ADJ (railway) funiculaire m

funk¹ [fʌŋk] Old-fashioned esp Br Sl N (fright) frousse f, **to be in a (blue) f.** avoir une peur bleue, avoir une frousse de tous les diables; **to get into a f.** caner
VT **to f. sth/doing sth** avoir peur de qch/de faire qch; **to f. it** caner, se dégonfler
VI caner, se dégonfler
▸▸ Mil Fam **f. hole** abri m, planque f

funk² N Mus funk m; **f. band** groupe m funk

funky [ˈfʌŋkɪ] ADJ **1** Mus funky, funk **2** Am Fam (smelly) puant **3** esp Am Old-fashioned Fam (fashionable) cool, branché **4** esp Br Old-fashioned Sl (cowardly) froussard

funnel [ˈfʌn(ə)l] N **1** (of locomotive, steamship) cheminée f **2** (for filling) entonnoir m; Ind (loading) **f.** trémie f, hotte f **3** (for ventilation) tuyau m ou cheminée f d'aération
VI (-ll-, Am -l-) **the crowd funnelled into a**

narrow passage/through the gates la foule s'est engouffrée dans un passage étroit/entre les grilles

VT *(direct)* canaliser; **to f. a liquid into a bottle** verser un liquide dans une bouteille à l'aide d'un entonnoir; **complaints are funnelled to the head office** les réclamations sont canalisées vers le bureau central

funnelling, *Am* **funneling** ['fʌn(ə)lɪŋ] N *Mktg (in questionnaire construction)* entonnoir *m*

funnily ['fʌnɪlɪ] ADV **1** *(amusingly)* comiquement **2** *(curiously)* curieusement, bizarrement; **f. enough** ... chose curieuse ...

funniness ['fʌnɪnɪs] N **1** *(amusing nature) (of person)* caractère *m* amusant *ou* drôle **2** *(strangeness)* bizarrerie *f*

funny ['fʌnɪ] ADJ **1** *(amusing)* drôle, amusant; **it was really too f.!, it was too f. for words!** c'était vraiment trop drôle!, c'était tordant!; **she's a very f. woman** *(comic, actress)* elle est très drôle; **none of your f. tricks!, don't try to be f.!** pas de blagues!; **the f. thing about it is** ... le comique de la chose, c'est que ...

2 *(strange)* curieux, bizarre; **he is a f. person** c'est un drôle d'homme; **he was f. that way** il était comme ça; **a f. idea** une drôle d'idée; **well, that's f.!** voilà qui est curieux *ou* étrange; **f., I thought I'd locked the door** tiens, c'est drôle, je pensais avoir fermé la porte à clé; **(it's) f. you should say that** c'est drôle que vous disiez cela; **it's a f. thing, but** ... c'est drôle, mais ...; **there's something f. about the entire business** il y a quelque chose de louche dans cette affaire; *Fam* **no f. business!** pas de blagues!, pas de bêtises!; **this butter tastes/smells f.** ce beurre a un drôle de goût/une drôle d'odeur; **it feels f.** ça fait drôle; **the engine sounds f.** le moteur fait un drôle de bruit; **his voice sounded f.** il avait une drôle de voix; *Fam* **I came over all f.** je me suis senti(e) tout(e) drôle; **I've got a f. feeling in my stomach** j'ai un peu mal au cœur; **I had a f. feeling we were going to meet again** j'avais comme l'impression que nous nous reverrions; **he went a bit f. in his old age** il devint un peu bizarre en vieillissant; *Fam* **f. peculiar or f. ha-ha?** comment ça, drôle? bizarre ou rigolo?

NPL *esp Am Fam* **the funnies** *(in magazine)* bandes *fpl* dessinées, pages *fpl* comiques

▸ ▸ *Br Fam* **f. bone** petit juif *m*; *Fam* **f. farm** maison *f* de fous; *Fam* **f. money** des sommes *mpl* mirobolantes *ou* astronomiques

fur [fɜːr] N **1** *Com* fourrure *f*; *Zool* poil *m*; *Fam* **to make the f. fly, to set the f. flying** *(make a scene)* faire une scène violente; *(fight)* se battre avec acharnement; **furs** *(of animals)* peaux *fpl*; **f.-lined boot** bottillon *m* fourré; **f.-lined coat** manteau doublé de fourrure **2** *(deposit) (in kettle, boiler)* tartre *m*; *Med (on tongue)* enduit *m*

▸ ▸ **f. coat** *(manteau m de)* fourrure; **f. farm** élevage *m* d'animaux à fourrure; **f. seal** phoque *m*; **f. skins** peaux *fpl*; **f. trade** commerce *m* de fourrures, pelleterie *f*

▸ **fur up** VI *(of boiler etc)* s'incruster, s'entartrer; *Med (of tongue)* se charger, s'empâter

furbish ['fɜːbɪʃ] VT **1** *(polish) (piece of metal)* fourbir, polir, astiquer **2** *(renovate) (furniture)* remettre à neuf

furious ['fjʊərɪəs] ADJ furieux; *(look)* furibond; *(battle, activity, efforts etc)* acharné, forcené; *(storm, sea, wind)* déchaîné; **to drive at a f. speed** conduire à une allure folle; **to get f.** entrer en fureur; **to be f. with sb/oneself** être furieux contre qn/soi-même

furiously ['fjʊərɪəslɪ] ADV furieusement; *(to work)* avec acharnement; *(to fight)* avec acharnement, avec furie; *(to drive)* à une al-

lure folle; **the fire was blazing f.** l'incendie faisait rage

furl [fɜːl] VT *(umbrella, flag etc)* rouler; *Naut (sail)* serrer, ferler

furlong ['fɜːlɒŋ] N *(measurement)* furlong *m* *(= 201 mètres)*; **a race over seven furlongs** une course de 1 400 mètres

furlough ['fɜːləʊ] N *Mil etc* congé *m*, permission *f*; **to be/go on f.** être/aller en permission

furnace ['fɜːnɪs] N **1** fourneau *m*, four *m*; *Fig* fournaise *f*; **this room is like a f.** cette pièce est une (vraie) fournaise **2 (central-heating) f.** calorifère *m*

furnish ['fɜːnɪʃ] VT **1** *(house, flat etc)* meubler; **to f. one's room/home/flat** se meubler **2** *esp Fml (provide) (information)* fournir, donner; *(funds)* pourvoir; *(reasons)* produire, alléguer; *(opportunity)* offrir, présenter, fournir; *(needs)* pourvoir à; **to f. sb with sth** fournir qch à qn, pourvoir *ou* munir qn de qch; **to f. an army (with provisions)** fournir une armée en provisions

furnished ['fɜːnɪʃt] ADJ **1** *(flat, room)* meublé; **to live in f. rooms** loger en meublé **2** *(provided)* pourvu, fourni, équipé (**with** de); **well f. shop** magasin bien achalandé

furnishing ['fɜːnɪʃɪŋ] N **f. fabrics** tissus *mpl* d'ameublement

furnishings ['fɜːnɪʃɪŋz] NPL *(furniture) (of house)* ameublement *m*; **soft f.** *(fabrics)* tissus *mpl* d'ameublement; *(carpets and curtains)* tapis *mpl* et rideaux *mpl*

furniture ['fɜːnɪtʃər] N **1** *(in house etc)* meubles *mpl*, mobilier *m*; **a piece of f.** un meuble; *Fam* **I feel as if I'm part of the f.** j'ai l'impression de faire partie des meubles; **dining-room f.** mobilier *ou* meubles de salle à manger **2** *(of door, coffin etc)* ferrures *fpl*

▸ ▸ **f. polish** encaustique *f*, cire *f*; **f. remover** déménageur *m*; **f. showroom** magasin *m* de meubles; **f. van** camion *m* de déménagement

Note that the French noun **fourniture** is a false friend. Its most common meaning is **supplies**.

furore [fjʊ'rɔːreɪ], *Am* **furor** ['fjʊərɔːr] N *(uproar)* tumulte *m* (**over** au sujet de); *(enthusiasm)* enthousiasme *m* démesuré; **to cause** *or* **create a f.** *(cause uproar)* provoquer un tumulte; *(be very popular)* faire fureur; **there's been a great f. over those scenes** ces scènes ont provoqué un énorme tumulte

furred [fɜːd] ADJ *(boiler etc)* entartré, encrusté; *(kettle, pipe)* entartré; *(tongue)* pâteux, chargé

furrier ['fʌrɪər] N pelletier, -ière, fourreur *m*

furring ['fɜːrɪŋ] N *(in boiler etc)* tartre *m*

furrow ['fʌrəʊ] N *(in field)*, *Fig (in stone)* sillon *m*; *Fig (on face)* ride *f* profonde, sillon; *Fig* **to plough a lonely f.** *(of inventor, reformer etc)* poursuivre seul une idée; *(keep oneself to oneself)* faire bande à part

VT **1** *(earth)* creuser des sillons dans; *Lit* **the boats furrowed the seas** les bateaux sillonnaient les mers **2** *(forehead etc)* rider profondément; **his brow is furrowed with wrinkles** des rides profondes lui sillonnent le front

furrowed ['fʌrəʊd] ADJ *(forehead, brow)* coupé de rides profondes; **f. with concentration** plissé de concentration

furry ['fɜːrɪ] ADJ **1** *(animal)* à poil; *(tail, ears)* poilu; *(insect)* velu; *(moss etc)* qui ressemble à (de) la fourrure; **the husky has a f. coat** le husky a de longs poils; **a f. little kitten** un chaton tout doux **2** *(boiler, kettle)* entartré; *(tongue)* chargé, pâteux

FURTHER ['fɜːðər] *(comp of* **far***)* VOIR GRAMMAIRE A26

| ADV | plus loin **1** ▪ plus **1** ▪ de plus **2** ▪ suite à *(further to)* **3** |
| ADJ | plus éloigné **1** ▪ additionnel **2** |

ADV **1** *(distance)* plus loin (**than** que); *(extent)* davantage, plus; **to penetrate f. into the country** pénétrer plus avant dans le pays; **I can go no f.** je ne peux pas aller plus loin; *(I'm exhausted)* je n'en peux plus; *Fam* **this mustn't go any f.** ceci ne doit pas se propager; **to move f. away** s'éloigner; **I didn't question him any f.** je ne l'ai pas interrogé davantage; **until you hear f.** jusqu'à nouvel avis; **I've nothing f. to say** je n'ai rien d'autre à dire; **to go no f. into the matter** en rester là; **to add water to the wine to make it go f.** allonger le vin d'eau; **that doesn't get us much f.** cela ne nous avance pas beaucoup; **f. back** *(in time)* à une période plus reculée; **f. back than the last century** antérieurement au siècle dernier

2 *(moreover)* d'ailleurs, de plus; **we would f. add that** ... nous nous permettons d'ajouter en outre que ...

3 *Fml* **f. to** *(following)* suite à

ADJ **1** *(of two)* plus éloigné, plus lointain; **at the f. end of the room** à l'autre bout *ou* au fond de la salle; **the f. bank of the river** la rive opposée de la rivière; **the f. of the two villages** le plus éloigné des deux villages

2 *(additional)* additionnel, supplémentaire; **upon f. consideration** après plus ample(s) réflexion(s); **do you have any f. instructions?** est-ce que vous avez d'autres consignes?; **one or two f. details** encore un ou deux détails; **without f. loss of time** sans perdre plus de temps; **to await f. news** attendre de plus amples nouvelles; **until f. notice** jusqu'à nouvel ordre; **without f. warning** sans plus d'avertissement; *(about au sujet de)*; **f. information** renseignements *mpl* complémentaires; *Com* **I would like to place a f. order** je voudrais passer une nouvelle commande; *esp Mil* **to await f. orders** attendre les ordres

VT *(cause, person's interests)* servir; *(one's attempts, efforts, career)* favoriser

▸ ▸ *Br* **f. education** enseignement *m* postscolaire

furtherance ['fɜːðərəns] N *(of work etc)* avancement *m*; **for the f.** *or* **in f. of sth** pour servir qch

furthermore [fɜːðə'mɔːr] ADV en outre, de plus, par ailleurs

furthermost ['fɜːðəməʊst] ADJ *(place etc)* le plus lointain, le plus reculé, le plus éloigné; *Lit* **to the f. ends of the earth** jusqu'au bout du monde

furthest ['fɜːðɪst] *(superl of* **far***)* VOIR GRAMMAIRE A26 ADV **he went f.** il est allé le plus loin; **when it's f. from the sun** lorsqu'il se trouve le plus éloigné du soleil; **this is the f. north I've ever been** c'est le plus au nord que j'aie jamais été

ADJ **the f. part of the cave** la partie la plus reculée de la caverne

furtive ['fɜːtɪv] ADJ *(manner, person)* sournois, cachottier; *(smile, look etc)* furtif, dérobé

furtively ['fɜːtɪvlɪ] ADV *(behave)* sournoisement; *(smile, look)* furtivement

fury ['fjʊərɪ] N **1** *(of person)* furie *f*, fureur *f*; *(of wind etc)* déchaînement *m*, violence *f*; **to be in a f.** *(of person)* être furieux, être en furie *ou* fureur; **to get into a f.** entrer en furie *ou* fureur, s'emporter; *Fam* **to work like f.** travailler avec acharnement; **to run like f.** courir comme un dératé **2** *Myth* **the Furies** les Furies *fpl*

furze [fɜːz] N (plant) ajonc m

fuse, Am **fuze** [fjuːz] N 1 Mil etc (for shell etc) fusée f; (for bomb) amorce f; Min étoupille f, mèche f; **safety f.** cordeau m (Bickford); **time f.** fusée à retard(ement); **to set a f.** régler une fusée; Fig **the incident which lit the f. of the revolution** l'incident qui a déclenché la révolution; Fig Fam **to have a short f.** démarrer au quart de tour 2 Elec **(safety) f.** fusible m (de sécurité), Fam plomb m; **to blow a f.** faire sauter un plomb; Fig Fam (of person) sortir de ses gonds; **the f. has blown** or Fam **gone** le plomb a sauté
VT 1 (melt) (metal etc) fondre, mettre en fusion; **to f. two pieces together** réunir deux pièces par fusion 2 (join) fusionner, amalgamer 3 Br Elec (circuit) faire sauter les plombs de; **to f. the lights** faire sauter les plombs 4 Mil etc (bomb) amorcer
VI 1 (of metals etc) fondre; **the parts had fused together** les pièces avaient fondu et s'étaient collées les unes aux autres 2 (of parties etc) fusionner 3 Br Elec **the lights have fused** les plombs ont sauté
▸▸ **f. box** boîte f à fusibles, coupe-circuit m inv; Aut porte-fusible m, pl porte-fusibles; **f. wire** fusible m

fused [fjuːzd] ADJ Elec muni d'un fusible

fuselage ['fjuːzəlɑːʒ] N Aviat fuselage m

fusilier [fjuːzɪˈlɪər] N Mil fusilier m

fusillade [fjuːzɪˈleɪd] N Mil **a f. (of shots)** une fusillade; **a f. of criticism/questions** une avalanche de critiques/questions

fusion ['fjuːʒən] N 1 Phys fusion f; (of metal) fonte f; Phys **cold f.** fusion à froid; Nucl, Phys **controlled f.** fusion contrôlée 2 (amalgamation) (of banks etc) fusionnement m; Pol (of parties etc) fusion f
▸▸ Nucl **f. bomb** bombe f thermonucléaire ou à hydrogène; Culin **f. food** = cuisine f qui mêle saveurs d'orient et d'occident

fuss [fʌs] N (exaggeration) histoires fpl; **what's all the f. about?** qu'est-ce que c'est que toutes ces histoires?; (what's wrong) qu'est-ce qui cloche?; **without any f.** (to get married) sans cérémonies; (to get through customs) sans aucun problème; **can you have him ejected from the studio without too much f.?** est-ce que vous pouvez le faire évacuer du studio discrètement?; **I don't want any f. made when I retire** je ne veux pas qu'on fasse tout un cinéma quand je prendrai ma retraite; **a lot of f. about** or over **nothing** beaucoup de bruit pour rien; **if you knew the f. your letter caused** si tu savais le remue-ménage que ta lettre a provoqué; **a great f.** bien des cérémonies; **to make a f.,** Fam **to kick up a f.** (complain loudly) faire un tas d'histoires, faire tout un cinéma; **don't make such a f. about it** ne faites pas tant d'histoires; **I don't see what all the f. is about** (I think it's a harmless, poor-quality film/product etc) je ne vois pas pourquoi on fait un tel cinéma; **to make a f. of** or over **sb** être aux petits soins pour qn; (talk about with excessive admiration) faire grand cas

de qn; **he likes to be made a f. of** or over (of person) il aime qu'on fasse grand cas de lui; (of dog) il aime qu'on le caresse
VI (be active) faire des embarras ou des histoires; **stop fussing!** arrête de faire des histoires!; **she never stops fussing with her hair** elle ne cesse pas d'arranger nerveusement ses cheveux
VT (person) tracasser, agiter; Fam **I'm not fussed** ça ne me fait rien
▸ **fuss about, fuss around** VI (be busy) s'affairer
▸ **fuss over** VT INSEP (person) être aux petits soins pour

fussily ['fʌsɪlɪ] ADV 1 (to arrange things) d'une manière tatillonne; (to say sth) d'un air important 2 (over-ornately) de façon tarabiscotée; **f. dressed** vêtu avec trop de recherche; **the room was rather f. decorated** la décoration de la pièce était surchargée

fussiness ['fʌsɪnɪs] N 1 (of person) (behaviour) tendance f à faire beaucoup d'embarras; (character) esprit m tracassier; **his f. about food is ridiculous** il est si difficile sur la nourriture que c'en est ridicule; **her f. about details** l'attention exagérée qu'elle porte aux détails 2 (of dress, decor etc) manque m de simplicité

fusspot ['fʌspɒt] N Br Fam Pej (finicky person) (about preparing food, cleaning house) tatillon, -onne; (about getting wet, dirty etc) chichiteux, -euse; (worrier) tracassier, -ière; **don't be such a f. about a little bit of rain** ne sois pas aussi chichiteux, ce n'est qu'une petite pluie; **don't be such a f., leave the housework for one day** ne sois pas aussi tatillon, laisse tomber le ménage pour aujourd'hui; **don't be such a f., I'm sure he is safe** ne te tracasse pas comme ça, je suis sûr qu'il est en sécurité

fussy ['fʌsɪ] ADJ 1 (person) (who worries) tracassier, qui fait des histoires; (who is finicky, particular) tatillon, -onne; **I'm not the f. kind** je ne suis pas difficile; **I'm not f.** cela m'est égal; **we can't afford to be too f.** nous ne pouvons pas nous permettre d'être trop difficiles; **to be f. about one's food** être difficile sur la nourriture 2 (dress, decor) surchargé; (style) qui manque de simplicité, surchargé

fustian ['fʌstɪən] N Tex futaine f; Fig Lit (pompousness) grandiloquence f, emphase f

fustiness ['fʌstɪnɪs] N 1 (smell) odeur f de moisi 2 Fig (of theory etc) caractère m démodé

fusty ['fʌstɪ] ADJ 1 (house, clothes) qui sent le renfermé; (smell) de renfermé 2 Fig (ideas etc) suranné, démodé

futile ['fjuːtaɪl] ADJ 1 (vain) inutile; (attempt, protest) vain 2 (trifling) (remark etc) futile

futility [fjuːˈtɪlɪtɪ] N futilité f; (of efforts etc) inutilité f; **an exercise in f.** une vaine entreprise

futon ['fuːtɒn] N futon m

future ['fjuːtʃər] ADJ futur; (events) à venir; **my f. wife** ma future épouse; **at some f. date** dans l'avenir; **for f. reference** à titre d'information; Com **goods for f. delivery** marchandises livrables ultérieurement; Fin **to sell for f. delivery** vendre livrable à terme
N 1 avenir m; **in (the) f., for the f.** à l'avenir; **in the near f.** dans un proche avenir, sous peu; **in the distant f.** dans un avenir lointain; **at some point** or **stage in the f.** un jour; **what does the f. hold for us?** qu'est-ce que l'avenir nous réserve?; **the public transport of the f.** les transports en commun de l'avenir
2 (of person) avenir m; **job with a (good) f.** situation d'avenir; **to ruin one's f.** briser son avenir; **she has a brilliant f. (before her)** elle a un bel avenir devant elle
3 Fin contrat m à terme; **futures** opérations fpl à terme; **futures and options** contrats mpl à terme et options
4 VOIR GRAMMAIRE A50-2; B31 Gram (temps m) futur m; **verb in the f.** verbe au futur
▸▸ Fin **futures contract** contrat à terme; Fin **futures exchange** marché m à terme; Fin **futures market** marché à terme; Fin **futures option** option f sur contrats à terme; Gram **f. perfect** futur antérieur; Gram **f. tense** futur, temps futur VOIR GRAMMAIRE A50-2; B31 ; Fin **futures trading** négociations fpl à terme; Fin **f. value** valeur f capitalisée

future-proof esp Comput ADJ évolutif
VT rendre évolutif

futurism ['fjuːtʃərɪz(ə)m] N Art futurisme m

futurist ['fjuːtʃərɪst] ADJ, N Art futuriste mf

futuristic ['fjuːtʃəˈrɪstɪk] ADJ futuriste

futurologist [fjuːtʃəˈrɒlədʒɪst] N futurologue mf

futurology [fjuːtʃəˈrɒlədʒɪ] N futurologie f

fuze [fjuːz] N, VT Am = **fuse**

fuzz [fʌz] N 1 (on blankets etc) peluches fpl, bourre f 2 (on peach, skin) duvet m
NPL Sl **the f.** (the police) les flics mpl

fuzziness ['fʌzɪnɪs] N 1 (of outline, recording etc) manque m de netteté; (of photo etc) flou m 2 **the f. of my hair** mes cheveux crépus

fuzzy ['fʌzɪ] ADJ 1 (outline etc) sans netteté; (recording) qui manque de netteté; (idea, look) flou, vague; Art, Phot flou; **everything looks f. to me** j'ai une vue confuse de tout; **I feel a bit f.-headed** je n'ai pas les idées très claires 2 (hair) crépu; (cloth etc) floconneux
▸▸ Comput **f. logic** logique f floue

fwd abbr **forward**

FX [efˈeks] NPL Cin effets mpl spéciaux
N Fin (abbr **foreign exchange**) devises fpl étrangères
▸▸ Fin **FX broker** cambiste mf, courtier, -ière en devises; Fin **FX market** marché m des changes; Fin **FX option** option f sur devises

FYI (abbr **for your information**) à titre indicatif

G, g [dʒi:] **N 1** (*letter*) G, g *m*; **two g's** deux g **2** *Mus* sol *m*; **in G minor** en sol mineur **3** *Fam Br* (*thousand pounds*) mille livres *fpl*; *Am* (*thousand dollars*) mille dollars *mpl* **4** *Phys* conductance *f* **5** *Am, Austr Cin* visible par tous **6 G7** G7 *m*, groupe *m* des 7; **G7 summit** sommet *m* du G7; **G8** G8 *m*, groupe des 8

g ² (*abbr* **gramme**) gr.

Ga *abbr* **Georgia**

GAAP [dʒi:eɪeɪ'pi:] **NPL** *Acct* (*abbr* **generally-accepted accounting principles**) PCGR *mpl*

gab [gæb] *Fam* **N** (*chat, talk*) **we had a good g. on the phone** on a taillé une bonne bavette au téléphone; **to have the gift of the g.** avoir la langue bien pendue; (*be convincing talker*) avoir du bagou(t)
VI (**-bb-**) (*chat*) bavarder, *Pej* papoter; (*gossip*) caqueter, jaser

gabardine [gæbə'di:n, 'gæbədi:n] **N** gabardine *f*

gabble ['gæb(ə)l] **N** bredouillement *m* (*de paroles prononcées trop vite*); **to speak in a g.** bredouiller; **to listen to the g. of voices** écouter les bruits des conversations; **there was an incomprehensible g. coming from the garden** on entendait une conversation inintelligible dans le jardin
VI bredouiller, manger ses mots
VT (*speech*) débiter à toute vitesse
▸ **gabble away VI** baragouiner; **two foreigners were gabbling away to each other** deux étrangers baragouinaient dans leur langue
▸ **gabble out VT SEP** = **gabble VT**

gaberdine [gæbə'di:n, 'gæbədi:n] **N** gabardine *f*

gable ['geɪb(ə)l] **N** pignon *m*
▸▸ **g. end** pignon; **g. roof** comble *m* sur pignon(s); **g. window** fenêtre *f* sur pignon

gabled ['geɪb(ə)ld] **ADJ** *Archit* (*house*) à pignon(s); (*wall*) en pignon; (*roof*) sur pignon(s)

Gabon [gæ'bɒn] **N** Gabon *m*

Gabonese [gæbə'ni:z] **ADJ** gabonais
N Gabonais, -aise

▸ **gad about** [gæd] **VI** courir le monde; **he spent a year gadding about Europe** il a passé un an à parcourir l'Europe; **she's been out gadding about (town) all night** elle a passé toute la nuit à faire la fête (en ville)

gadfly ['gædflaɪ] **N** (*insect*) taon *m*; *Fig* casse-pieds *mf inv*

gadget ['gædʒɪt] **N** gadget *m*; **it's just another g.** c'est un gadget de plus; **what's that g. for?** à quoi sert ce truc-là?

gadgetry ['gædʒɪtrɪ] **N** gadgets *mpl*

Gaelic ['geɪlɪk] **ADJ** gaélique
N *Ling* gaélique *m*

gaff ¹ [gæf] **N 1** *Fishing* gaffe *f* **2** *Naut* corne *f*
VT *Fishing* gaffer
▸▸ *Naut* **g. topsail** voile *f* de flèche

gaff ² **N** *Fam* **to blow the g.** vendre la mèche; **to blow the g. on** (*sb's plans*) dévoiler; (*corruption*) dénoncer; **to blow the g. on sb** dénoncer qn, vendre qn

gaff ³ **N** *Br Fam* (*home*) baraque *f*; **he's staying at my g. for the weekend** il crèche chez moi ce week-end

gaffe [gæf] **N** (*blunder*) gaffe *f*, bourde *f*

gaffer ['gæfər] **N 1** *Br Fam* (*foreman*) contremaître *m*, chef *m* d'équipe; (*boss, owner*) patron *m*, singe *m*; *Cin, TV* chef électricien, gaffer *m* **2** *Fam* (*old man*) vieux *m*
▸▸ *Cin, TV* **g. grip** pince *f* pour projecteur; **g. tape** ruban *m* adhésif en toile

gag [gæg] **N 1** (*on mouth*) bâillon *m*; *Surg* ouvre-bouche *m inv*; *Fig* **the law was used as a g. on the freedom of the press** la loi servait à bâillonner la presse **2** *Fam* (*joke*) blague *f*, (*visual*) gag *m*; **to do sth for a g.** faire qch pour rire *ou* pour s'amuser
VT (**-gg-**) (*put a gag on*) (*person, the press*) bâillonner
VI *Fam* (*retch*) avoir des haut-le-cœur; **to make sb g.** donner envie de vomir à qn

gaga ['gɑːgɑː] **ADJ** *Fam* gaga *inv*, gâteux; **to go g.** devenir gaga *ou* gâteux

gage ¹ [geɪdʒ] **N** *Old-fashioned* (*pledge*) gage *m*, garantie *f*

gage ² **N**, **VT** *Am* = **gauge**

gage ³ **N** = **greengage**

gagging ['gægɪŋ] **N** (*of person, press*) bâillonnement *m*
▸▸ *Law* **g. order** = décision *f* de justice visant à interdire à la presse de publier tout article à propos d'une affaire, *Can* ordonnance *f* imposant le secret

gaggle ['gæg(ə)l] **N** (*of geese*) troupeau *m*; *Fig* **a g. of young schoolgirls** un troupeau de jeunes élèves
VI (*of goose*) cacarder

gagman, *pl* **gagmen** ['gægmən] **N** *Am Cin, Theat* auteur *m* de gags, gagman *m*, *pl* gagmen

gaiety ['geɪətɪ] **N 1** (*cheerfulness*) gaieté *f* **2** *Old-fashioned* (*festivities*) (*usu pl*) gaietés réjouissances *fpl*

gaily ['geɪlɪ] **ADV 1** (*happily*) gaiement, allègrement **2** (*with bright colours*) de couleurs gaies; **g. coloured** aux couleurs gaies *ou* vives

gain [geɪn] **N 1** (*profit*) gain *m*, profit *m*, avantage *m*; **to do sth for g.** faire qch par intérêt; **my g. is your loss** le profit de l'un est le dommage de l'autre
2 (*increase*) augmentation *f*, (*in value*) hausse *f*, *Fin* **g. in value** plus-value *f*, **g. in weight** prise *f* de poids; **there has been a net g. in their income** leurs revenus ont nettement augmenté; *St Exch* **there has been a g. of 100 points on the Dow Jones** l'indice Dow Jones a gagné 100 points; *Pol* **Labour made important gains in London** le parti travailliste a beaucoup progressé à Londres
3 *Electron* gain *m*
VT 1 (*acquire*) (*reputation*) acquérir; (*sympathy*) gagner; **you will g. nothing by it** vous n'y gagnerez rien; **to g. permission** obtenir une permission; **to g. sb's affection** gagner l'affection de qn; **to g. experience** acquérir de l'expérience; **to g. entrance** *or* **admission** s'introduire; **to g. the impression that ...** avoir l'impression que ...; **to g. an advantage** obtenir un avantage; **we have not so much lost a daughter as gained a son, we're not losing a daughter, we're gaining a son** nous n'avons pas perdu une fille mais gagné un fils
2 (*acquire more of*) gagner, prendre; (*time*) gagner; (*strength*) (re)prendre; **to g. weight** prendre du poids; **to g. popularity** devenir plus populaire; **he has gained prestige through this action** cette action a rehaussé son prestige; **the party has gained support** le parti a gagné des voix; **to g. ground** (*of racer, pursuer*) gagner du terrain (**on** sur); (*of a custom*) se répandre, se développer; **to g. share** (*of market*) gagner des parts de marché
3 (*win*) **to g. a victory** remporter une victoire; **they gained two points** ils ont gagné deux points; **to g. the upper hand** prendre le dessus
4 (*of clock*) **to g. five minutes a day** avancer de cinq minutes par jour
VI 1 (*benefit*) **to g. by** bénéficier de, être aidé par; **we have all gained by his hard work** nous avons tous bénéficié de son labeur; **we have gained by having her in the team** cela nous a aidés de l'avoir dans l'équipe; **I had a good teacher and I think I gained by that** j'ai eu un bon professeur et je crois que ça m'a servi
2 (*increase*) **to g. in popularity/experience** gagner en popularité/acquérir de l'expérience; **to g. in self-confidence** gagner *ou* prendre de l'assurance; **to g. in number** devenir plus nombreux
3 (*of clock*) avancer
4 (*of racer, pursuer*) gagner du terrain
▸ **gain on VT INSEP** (*adversary, competitor*) gagner du terrain sur

gainer ['geɪnər] **N** gagnant, -ante

gainful ['geɪnfʊl] **ADJ** profitable, rémunérateur, -trice; **to be in g. employment** avoir un emploi rémunéré

gainfully ['geɪnfʊlɪ] **ADV** **to be g. employed** (*doing sth useful*) faire quelque chose d'utile; (*earning money*) avoir un emploi rémunéré

gainsay [geɪn'seɪ] **VT** (*pt, pp* **gainsaid** [geɪn'sed]) *usu Lit* contredire; **there's no gainsaying his honesty/skill** son honnêteté/son adresse est indéniable

gait [geɪt] **N** démarche *f*, (*of horse*) train *m*; **unsteady g.** pas *m* mal assuré

gaiter ['geɪtər] **N 1** (clothing) guêtre f **2** Aut soufflet m

gal¹ abbr **gallon(s)**

gal² [gæl] **N** Old-fashioned Fam (girl) fille f

gala ['gɑːlə] **N** gala m; **swimming g.** grand concours m de natation; **in g. dress** en habit de gala
  ▸▸ **g. evening** soirée f de gala; **g. performance** représentation f de gala

galactic [gə'læktɪk] **ADJ** Astron (pole etc) galactique

Galahad ['gæləhæd] **N** Myth **Sir G.** Galaad m; Fig personne f noble et généreuse, seigneur m

Galapagos [gə'læpəgəs] **N the G. (Islands)** les (îles fpl) Galapagos fpl

galaxy ['gæləksɪ] **N 1** Astron galaxie f; **the G.** (Milky Way) la Voie Lactée **2** Fig (of famous people, filmstars etc) pléiade f

gale [geɪl] **N** grand (coup m de) vent m, vent fort; **the roof was blown off in a g.** un grand coup de vent a emporté le toit; **it's blowing a g.** le vent souffle en tempête; Fig **a g. of laughter** un éclat de rire
  ▸▸ Met **g.-force winds** vents forts; Met **g. warning** avis m de coup de vent, avis de tempête

galena [gə'liːnə] **N** Miner galène f

Galilean [gælɪ'liːən] **N** Bible **ADJ** galiléen **N** galiléen, -éenne

Galilee ['gælɪlɪ] **N** Galilée f; **the Sea of G.** la mer ou le lac de Galilée

Galileo [gælɪ'leɪəʊ] **N** Galilée m

gall¹ abbr **gallon(s)**

gall² [gɔːl] **N 1** Physiol bile f **2** (impudence) effronterie f, culot m, toupet m; **she had the g. to ...** elle a eu le culot ou le toupet de ...
  ▸▸ Anat **g. bladder** vésicule f biliaire

gall³ **N** (sore) (on horse etc) écorchure f; Fig **the criticism was a g. to his pride** la critique l'a piqué au vif
  VT 1 (make sore) écorcher (par frottement) **2** (annoy) irriter, exaspérer

gall⁴ **N** Bot galle f, cécidie f

gallant **ADJ 1** ['gælənt] (brave) brave, vaillant; **the ship and her g. crew** le navire et son valeureux équipage; **g. deed** acte de bravoure **2** [gə'lænt] (with women) galant

gallantly **ADV 1** ['gæləntlɪ] (bravely) bravement, vaillamment **2** [gə'læntlɪ, 'gæləntlɪ] (with women) galamment, en homme galant

gallantry ['gæləntrɪ] **N 1** (bravery) vaillance f, bravoure f; **a medal for g.** une médaille de bravoure **2** (with women) galanterie f

galleon ['gælɪən] **N** Naut, Hist galion m

gallery ['gælərɪ] **N 1** (in hall etc) galerie f; TV régie f; **strangers' or public g.** (in Houses of Parliament) tribune f du public; **press g.** tribune de la presse; Theat **the g.** (seats) la (troisième) galerie, Fam le paradis; Fig **to play to the g.** jouer pour la galerie **2** (private, Com (art)) galerie f, (museum) musée m (d'art) **3** Min galerie f **4** shooting g. stand m de tir **5** Am (balcony) balcon m; (veranda) véranda f

galley ['gælɪ] **N 1** (ancient ship) galère f; (rowing boat) yole f **2** Naut, Aviat (kitchen) cuisine f **3** Typ galée f, (proof) (épreuve f en) placard m
  ▸▸ Typ **g. proof** (épreuve en) placard m; **g. slave** galérien m

Gallic ['gælɪk] **ADJ 1** (French) (flair, charm, sophistication) français; **a G. shrug** un haussement d'épaules (typiquement français) **2** Hist (of Gaul) gaulois; **the G. Wars** la guerre des Gaules

gallicism ['gælɪsɪz(ə)m] **N** Ling gallicisme m

gallicize ['gælɪsaɪz] **VT** franciser **VI** se franciser

galling ['gɔːlɪŋ] **ADJ** irritant, exaspérant; **it was g. to reflect that ...** ça me/la/etc rendait malade de penser que ...

gallium ['gælɪəm] **N** Chem gallium m

▸ **gallivant about, gallivant around** ['gælɪvænt] Fam **VI** partir en vadrouille; **he goes out gallivanting around every night** il part en vadrouille tous les soirs
  VT INSEP (travel around) **I'm fed up with gallivanting about the country** j'en ai marre de toujours être par monts et par vaux; **he's gallivanting around the South of France** il est parti en vadrouille dans le Midi

gallon ['gælən] **N** gallon m (= 4,54 l, Am = 3,78 l); Aut **miles per g.** = consommation f d'essence aux cent kilomètres; Fam **they drink gallons of beer** ils boivent de la bière à tire-larigot

gallop ['gæləp] **N 1** (pace) galop m; **at a g.** au galop (allongé); **(at) full g.** au grand galop **2** (ride) galopade f, **to have** or **go for a g.** faire une galopade
  VI (-p-) (of horse) galoper; (of horse, rider) aller au galop; **to g. away** or **off** partir au galop; **he came galloping down the steps** (of person) il a descendu les escaliers quatre à quatre ou à son grand galop; Fig **to g. through one's work/a task** expédier un travail/une tâche; Fig **to g. through prayers** réciter les prières à toute vitesse
  VT (horse) faire galoper

galloping ['gæləpɪŋ] **ADJ** (horse) au galop; Fig **at a g. pace** à la vitesse grand V
  ▸▸ **g. inflation** inflation f galopante

Gallo-Roman ['gæləʊ'rəʊmən] **ADJ** gallo-romain, pl gallo-romains

gallows ['gæləʊz] **NPL** (often with sing verb) potence f, gibet m
  ▸▸ Old-fashioned **g. bird** gibier m de potence; Br **g. humour** humour m noir; **g. tree** potence, gibet

gallstone ['gɔːlstəʊn] **N** Med calcul m biliaire; **to have gallstones** avoir des calculs

Gallup ['gæləp] **N**
  ▸▸ **G. poll** sondage m Gallup

galore [gə'lɔːr] **ADV** Fam à gogo; **children g.** une flopée d'enfants; **books/money g.** des livres/de l'argent à gogo

galoshes [gə'lɒʃɪz] **NPL** caoutchoucs mpl

galumph [gə'lʌmf] **VI** Fam galoper lourdement (et bruyamment)

galvanic [gæl'vænɪk] **ADJ** galvanique

galvanism ['gælvənɪz(ə)m] **N** galvanisme m

galvanization [gælvənaɪ'zeɪʃən] **N** galvanisation f

galvanize ['gælvənaɪz] **VT** galvaniser; Fig **to g. sb/sth into life** galvaniser qn/qch

galvanized ['gælvənaɪzd] **ADJ** galvanisé
  ▸▸ **g. iron** fer m galvanisé

galvanizing ['gælvənaɪzɪŋ] **ADJ**
  ▸▸ **g. effect** effet m de galvanisation; Fig **the imminent danger had a g. effect on us** la proximité du danger nous a galvanisés

galvanometer [gælvə'nɒmɪtər] **N** galvanomètre m

Gambia ['gæmbɪə] **N the G.** la Gambie; **the G. (River)** la Gambie

Gambian ['gæmbɪən] **N** Gambien, -ienne **ADJ** gambien

gambit ['gæmbɪt] **N** Chess gambit m; Fig tactique f, stratagème m; Fig **opening g.** manœuvre f d'approche; **a g. to get their sympathy** un stratagème pour gagner leur sympathie

gamble ['gæmb(ə)l] **N** (risk) risque m; **I know it's a g. but ...** je sais que c'est risqué mais ...; **to take a g.** prendre un risque; **it's a g. but it may pay off** c'est un risque ou c'est risqué mais ça peut être payant

VI jouer de l'argent; **I don't g.** je ne joue pas pour de l'argent; **to g. on a throw of the dice** miser sur un coup de dé(s); **to g. on the Stock Exchange** jouer en Bourse, spéculer; **to g. on a rise in prices** jouer à la hausse; Fig **they're gambling on there not being an inspector on the train** ils misent sur le fait qu'il n'y aura pas de contrôleur dans le train; Fig **she's gambling on getting home by 8 o'clock** elle compte rentrer avant 8 heures; Fig **Napoleon gambled and lost** Napoléon a joué et perdu
  VT to g. one's money on horses jouer son argent aux courses; Fig **the government has gambled its political future on the plan's success** le gouvernement a joué son avenir sur le succès du projet
▸ **gamble away** **VT SEP** (fortune) perdre au jeu

gambler ['gæmblər] **N** joueur, -euse (de l'argent)

gambling ['gæmblɪŋ] **N** jeu m, jeux mpl d'argent; **g. on the Stock Exchange** la spéculation en Bourse; **my father was a g. man** mon père jouait
  ▸▸ **g. debts** dettes fpl de jeu; Pej **g. den, g. house**, Am **g. joint** tripot m

gambol ['gæmb(ə)l] **N** cabriole f, gambade f
  VI (-ll-, Am -l-) gambader, cabrioler

gambrel ['gæmbrəl] **N** Archit toit m en croupe

game¹ [geɪm] **N 1** (activity, sport) jeu m; **g. of skill/chance** jeu d'adresse/de hasard; **outdoor games** jeux de plein air; Br Sch **games** sports mpl; **games teacher** professeur m d'éducation physique; Br Sch **he's good at games** il est bon en sport, c'est un sportif; **the children were playing a g. of cowboys and Indians** les enfants jouaient aux cowboys et aux Indiens

2 (contest) Sport match m; (friendly) (of cards, chess, golf, snooker etc) partie f, (part of a game of cards) manche f, (in tennis match) jeu m; **how's the g. going?** comment marche la partie?; **we're having a g. of football after work** on va jouer au football après le travail; **anyone for darts/tennis? – I'll give you a g.** quelqu'un veut faire une partie de fléchettes/de tennis? – oui, moi; **you might get a g.** (if someone is absent) tu pourras peut-être jouer; **he played 65 games for England** il a joué 65 fois pour l'Angleterre; **we had a good g.** (played well) nous avons bien joué; **he plays a good g. of cards/billiards** il joue bien aux cartes/au billard; Tennis **g., set and match** jeu, set et match; Chess **opening/middle/end g.** début m/milieu m/fin f de partie

3 Fig **to play the g.** jouer le jeu, jouer selon les règles; **that's not playing the g.** ce n'est pas loyal; **to beat sb at his own g.** battre qn à son propre jeu; **two can play at that g.** on peut jouer à deux à ce petit jeu-là; Fam **what's his g.?** où veut-il en venir?, à quoi joue-t-il?; **I know your (little) g.!** je sais bien où vous voulez en venir!; **so that's your g.!** voilà donc ce que vous manigancez!; **politics is just a g. to him** la politique n'est qu'un jeu pour lui; **it isn't a g.!** (it's serious) ce n'est pas un jeu!; **to play games with sb** jouer avec qn; **let's stop playing games and come to the point** trêve de plaisanteries, passons aux choses sérieuses; **to play a dangerous g.** jouer un jeu dangereux; **he's up to his old games again** voilà qu'il refait des siennes; **the g.'s up** l'affaire est à l'eau; **the g. is not worth the candle** le jeu n'en vaut pas la chandelle; **I've been in this g. a long time** ça fait longtemps que je suis de la partie; Fam **how long have you been in the newspaper g.?** ça fait combien de temps que tu es dans les journaux?; Br Sl **to be on the g.** (be a prostitute) faire le trottoir; **to spoil sb's little**

g. déjouer les plans de qn; **what a g.!** (a lot of trouble) quel cinéma!; **they were just playing a g., pretending to be angry** ils faisaient semblant d'être en colère

4 Culin, (in hunting) gibier m; **small g.** menu gibier; **big g.** les grands fauves mpl; **big-g. hunting** la chasse aux grands fauves

VI jouer (de l'argent)

ADJ Fam (brave) courageux; **to be g. (to do sth)** (willing) être partant (pour faire qch); **I'm g.!** d'accord (j'en suis)!, je suis partant!; **he's g. for anything** il est toujours partant, Pej il est prêt à tout ou capable de tout

▸▸**g. birds** gibier à plumes; **g. licence** permis m de chasse; Culin **g. pie** tourte f au gibier, ≃ pâté m en croûte; Tennis **g. point** balle f de jeu; Comput **games port** port m (de connexion pour) jeux, sortie f jeux; **g. reserve** réserve f (pour animaux sauvages); **games room** salle f de jeux; Math **g. theory** théorie f des jeux

game ² **ADJ** = gammy

gamebag ['geɪmbæg] **N** gibecière f

gamecock ['geɪmkɒk] **N** coq m de combat

gamekeeper ['geɪmkiːpər] **N** garde-chasse m, pl gardes-chasse(s)

gamely ['geɪmlɪ] **ADV** courageusement

gameplan ['geɪmplæn] **N** Chess, Fig stratégie f; Mktg stratégie (de mercatique)

gamer ['geɪmər] **N 1** (who plays computer games) ≃ amateur m de jeux vidéo **2** Am (athlete, sportsperson) ≃ sportif m très compétitif

gameshow ['geɪmʃəʊ] **N** TV jeu m télévisé; Radio jeu radiophonique

gamesmanship ['geɪmzmənʃɪp] **N** astuce f; **this is just g.** ce n'est qu'une astuce pour déstabiliser son adversaire

gamete ['gæmiːt, gæ'miːt] **N** Biol gamète m

gameware ['geɪmweər] **N** Comput ludiciel m

gamey ['geɪmɪ] **ADJ** = gamy

gaming ['geɪmɪŋ] **N 1** (gambling) jeu m **2** (playing of computer games) (pratique f des) jeux mpl électroniques

▸▸**g. house** maison f de jeu; **g. table** table f de jeu

gamma ['gæmə] **N** (in Greek alphabet) gamma m

▸▸**g. ray** rayon m gamma

gamma-ray therapy **N** Med gammathérapie f

gammon ['gæmən] **N** (bacon) quartier m; (ham) jambon m fumé

▸▸Br **g. steak** ≃ épaisse tranche f de jambon fumé

gammy ['gæmɪ] **ADJ** Fam **a g. leg** une patte folle

gamp [gæmp] **N** Br Old-fashioned Fam parapluie m, pépin m

gamut ['gæmət] **N** (of colours), Mus, Fig gamme f; **this character runs the whole g. of emotions** ce personnage passe par toute la gamme des émotions

gamy ['geɪmɪ] **ADJ** faisandé

gander ['gændər] **N 1** (male goose) jars m **2** Br Sl (look) coup m d'œil; **just take a g.!** mate-moi ça!

gang [gæŋ] **N** (of criminals) bande f, gang m; (of children) bande; (of workmen) équipe f; (of prisoners) convoi m; **can I join your g.?** (of children) je peux faire partie de votre bande?; Fam **the whole g.** (of friends, colleagues) toute la bande; Pol, Hist **the G. of Four** la Bande des Quatre VOIR GRAMMAIRE A11

▸▸**g. rape** viol m collectif; **g. war(fare)** guerre f des gangs

▸**gang up** **VI** Fam former un gang; **to g. up with sb** s'allier avec qn; **to g. up on sb** se liguer contre qn

ganga ['gændʒə] **N** = ganja

gangbang ['gæŋbæŋ] **N** Sl **1** (group rape) viol m collectif **2** (group sex) partouse f

ganger ['gæŋər] **N** Br Rail chef m d'équipe

Ganges (the) [ðæ:ndʒi:z] **N** le Gange

gangland ['gæŋlænd] **N** (area) (in big city) territoire m contrôlé par des gangsters; (underworld) le milieu

▸▸**g. boss** chef m de gang; **g. killing** règlement m de compte (entre gangsters); **g. warfare** guerre f des gangs

gangling ['gæŋglɪŋ] **ADJ** dégingandé; **a g. youth** un jeune dégingandé

ganglion, pl **ganglia** ['gæŋglɪən, -ɪə] **N** Anat ganglion m

gangplank ['gæŋplæŋk] **N** Naut passerelle f; **to make sb walk the g.** forcer qn à marcher sur la planche (de telle sorte qu'il tombe dans la mer)

gang-rape **VT** commettre un viol collectif sur; **women who have been gang-raped** les femmes qui ont été victimes de viols collectifs; **they gang-raped her** ils l'ont violée

gangrene ['gæŋgri:n] **N** Med gangrène f, nécrose f; **to have g.** avoir la gangrène

gangrenous ['gæŋgrɪnəs] **ADJ** gangreneux, gangrené; **to go g.** (of wound) se gangrener

gangster ['gæŋstər] **N** gangster m; **g. film** film m de gangsters

▸▸**g. capitalism** ≃ système m économique débridé exclusivement basé sur la recherche du profit

gangsterism ['gæŋstərɪz(ə)m] **N** gangstérisme m

gangway ['gæŋweɪ] **N 1** (passage) passage m; (of bus etc) couloir m central; **when you set the chairs out, leave a g.** laissez un passage entre les chaises quand vous les installerez; **g.!** dégagez, s'il vous plaît! **2** Naut (gangplank) passerelle f de service; Aviat (for plane) passerelle

ganja ['gændʒə] **N** Sl (marijuana) herbe f

gannet ['gænɪt] **N** (bird) fou m (de Bassan); Hum Fig (glutton) goinfre mf

gantry ['gæntrɪ] **N 1** (for travelling crane) pont m roulant; (for rocket) portique m de lancement; Rail **signal g.** portique de signalisation; **travelling g.** portique roulant **2** (for barrel) chantier m

▸▸**g. crane** grue f (à) portique

gaol [dʒeɪl] **N, VT** Br = jail

gaolbird ['dʒeɪlbɜ:d] **N** Br = jailbird

gaolbreak ['dʒeɪlbreɪk] **N** Br évasion f de prison

gaolbreaker ['dʒeɪlbreɪkər] **N** Br évadé, -ée de prison

gaoler ['dʒeɪlər] **N** Br = jailer

gap [gæp] **N 1** (hole, opening) (which needs mending) trou m; (in floorboards) interstice m; (created deliberately) trouée f, ouverture f; (in a wall) brèche f; (in clouds) trou; (in trees) trouée; (of spark plug, points) écartement m; (in piston ring) jeu m à la coupe (des segments); **that fills a g.** (of snack) ça cale bien; **a g. in the bookshelf** un vide sur l'étagère; **the demolition of the house left a g. in the street** la démolition de la maison a laissé un espace vide dans la rue; **a g. of 2 cm** un intervalle de 2 cm; **leave a g. of six centimetres between the chairs** laissez un espace de six centimètres entre les chaises; **there's a g. in the curtains** les rideaux bâillent; **the g. in his teeth** l'écart entre ses dents; **there were gaps in his teeth** il avait les dents écartées; **the shelling had opened great gaps in the ranks** le bombardement avait éclairci les rangs; Aut **(spark) g.** intervalle m d'allumage; Com **g. in the market** créneau m

2 (difference) différence f; **age g.** différence

d'âge; **the g. between us and our competitors** l'écart entre nos concurrents et nous; **to close the g.** réduire l'écart; **there is a vast g. in ability between the two teams** il y a une grande différence de niveau entre les deux équipes; **the g. between rich and poor has widened** le fossé entre les riches et les pauvres s'est élargi

3 (in time) écart m; **there is a g. of two years in the records** il y a un trou de deux ans dans les archives; **after a g. of over twenty years** après un intervalle de plus de vingt ans

4 Fig (in memory etc) trou m, lacune f, vide m; **his death leaves a g. in all of our lives** sa mort laisse un vide dans nos vies; **to fill the gaps in one's education** combler les lacunes de son éducation; **there are a lot of gaps in her account of the event** il y a beaucoup d'omissions dans sa version des événements

5 Geog (opening in hills, mountains) trouée f, esp Am (pass) col m

6 (in recording) blanc m sonore; (in recorded tape) plage f de silence

▸▸Mktg **g. analysis** étude f des créneaux; Mktg **g. level** écart m de performance; Br **g. year** = année f, souvent passée à voyager, que s'accorde un étudiant avant son entrée à l'université ou à la fin de ses études

gape [geɪp] **VI 1** (stare) être ou rester bouche bée; **to g. in admiration/astonishment** être bouche bée d'admiration/d'étonnement; **to g. at sb/sth** regarder qn/qch bouche bée; **what are you gaping at?** qu'est-ce que tu regardes bouche bée?; **stop gaping!** remets-toi! **2 to g. (open)** (of thing) s'ouvrir (tout grand); (of seam etc) bâiller; (of hole) être béant

N I could tell from his astonished g. that ... je savais à son air éberlué que ...; **with a g. of disbelief** la bouche ouverte ou bée en signe d'incrédulité

gaping ['geɪpɪŋ] **ADJ** ATTRIB (hole etc) béant

gappy [gæpɪ] **ADJ** (list etc) incomplet; **g. smile** sourire m édenté; Fam **g. teeth** dents fpl écartées

gap-toothed [-tu:θt] **ADJ** aux dents écartées

garage ['gæra:ʒ, -rɪdʒ] **N** Aut garage m; (multistorey) parking m; **there is g. space for two cars** il y a de la place pour garer deux voitures

VT (car) rentrer; (for longer period) remiser

▸▸**g. attendant** gardien m de parking; **g. mechanic** garagiste mf, mécanicien, -ienne; **g. owner, g. proprietor** garagiste; **g. sale** ≃ vente f d'occasion, ≃ vide-greniers m inv

garb [gɑːb] Lit **N** costume m, habit m; **in clerical g.** en habit ecclésiastique

VT (usu passive) habiller, vêtir (in de); **garbed all in black** tout de noir vêtu

garbage ['gɑːbɪdʒ] **N 1** esp Am (waste) ordures fpl (ménagères); Comput **g. in, g. out** mauvaises données à l'entrée égale mauvais résultats à la sortie **2** Fig Fam (nonsense) bêtises fpl; **he's talking g.** il dit n'importe quoi **3** Fig Fam (worthless things) **their new album is a load of g.** leur dernier album est vraiment nul; **I've been eating too much g. lately** je mange trop de cochonneries en ce moment

▸▸Am **g. can** poubelle f, **g. collector** éboueur m; Am **g. disposal unit** broyeur m d'ordures; Am **g. heap** tas m d'ordures; **g. man** éboueur

garbanzo [gɑː'bænzəʊ] **N** Am pois m chiche

garble ['gɑːb(ə)l] **VT** (news, quotation) fausser; (facts) dénaturer; (text) altérer; **garbled account** compte rendu m trompeur ou mensonger; **garbled message** message m confus

Garda, pl **Gardai** ['gɑːdə, 'gɑːdiː] **N 1** (police force) police f (de la République d'Irlande) **2**

(policeman) policier m (de la République d'Irlande)

garden ['gɑːd(ə)n] **N** jardin m; **back/front g.** jardin de derrière/de devant; **g. of remembrance** = jardin en souvenir des défunts; **public garden(s)** jardin public, parc m; Fig Fam **to lead sb up the g. path** duper qn, faire marcher qn

VI (usu continuous) jardiner, faire du jardinage

▸▸ **g. centre** jardinerie f; **g. chair** chaise f de jardin; **g. city** cité-jardin f, pl cités-jardins; Br **g. flat** rez-de-jardin m inv; **g. furniture** meubles mpl de jardin; **g. hose** tuyau m d'arrosage; Br **g. party** garden-party f, pl garden-parties ou garden-partys; **g. plant** plante f de jardin; **g. produce** produits mpl maraîchers; **g. suburb** banlieue f verte; **g. tools** outils mpl de jardinage

gardener ['gɑːdnər] **N** jardinier, -ière f; **he's a keen g.** c'est un adepte du jardinage

gardenia [gɑːˈdiːnɪə] **N** (flower) gardénia m

gardening ['gɑːdnɪŋ] **N** jardinage m
▸▸ **g. book** livre m de jardinage; **g. expert** spécialiste mf du jardinage; **g. programme** émission f sur le jardinage; **g. tools** outils mpl de jardinage

gargantuan [gɑːˈgæntjʊən] **ADJ** gargantuesque

gargle ['gɑːg(ə)l] Med **N** gargarisme m
VI se gargariser

gargoyle ['gɑːgɔɪl] **N** Archit etc gargouille f

garish ['geərɪʃ] **ADJ 1** (clothes) voyant; (wallpaper) criard; (taste) vulgaire **2** (light, colour) cru

garishly ['geərɪʃlɪ] **ADV** de façon criarde

garishness ['geərɪʃnɪs] **N 1** (of clothes) aspect m voyant ou tapageur; (of wallpaper) aspect criard; (of taste) vulgarité f **2** (of light, colour) crudité f

garland ['gɑːlənd] **N** guirlande f
VT parer de guirlandes, enguirlander; **garlanded with flowers** paré de guirlandes de fleurs

garlic ['gɑːlɪk] **N** ail m, pl ails ou aulx; **clove of g.** gousse f d'ail; **head of g.** bulbe m d'ail
▸▸ **g. bread** = pain m chaud au beurre d'ail; **g. butter** beurre m d'ail; **g. press** presse-ail m inv; **g. sausage** saucisson m à l'ail

garlicky ['gɑːlɪkɪ] **ADJ** qui sent l'ail; (taste) d'ail

garment ['gɑːmənt] **N** Fml vêtement m; **the g. industry** l'industrie f du vêtement

garner ['gɑːnər] **VT** (collect) (information) recueillir

garnet ['gɑːnɪt] **N** Miner grenat m; **g. necklace** collier m de grenat

garnish ['gɑːnɪʃ] **N** garniture f
VT garnir, orner (**with** de); Culin (dish) garnir

garnishee [gɑːnɪˈʃiː] **N**
▸▸ Law **g. order** ordonnance f de saisie-arrêt

garnishing ['gɑːnɪʃɪŋ] **N** garnissage m; Culin garniture f

garret ['gærət] **N** mansarde f; **to live in a g.** habiter sous les combles

garrison ['gærɪs(ə)n] Mil **N** garnison f
VT (station) mettre en garnison; **troops garrisoned at Lille** troupes en garnison à Lille; **to g. a town** (provide with a garrison) mettre une garnison dans une ville
▸▸ **g. duty** service m de place ou de garnison; **g. town** ville f de garnison

garrotte, Am **garrote** [gəˈrɒt] **N 1** (device) garrot m **2** (execution) supplice m du garrot
VT 1 (strangle) étrangler (avec un fil, une corde) **2** (execute) faire subir le supplice du garrot à

garrotting, Am **garroting** [gəˈrɒtɪŋ] **N 1**

(strangling) strangulation f (avec un fil, une corde) **2** (execution) supplice m du garrot

garrulity [gæˈruːlɪtɪ], **garrulousness** ['gærʊləsnɪs] **N** loquacité f

garrulous ['gærʊləs] **ADJ** loquace, bavard

garrulously ['gærʊləslɪ] **ADV** avec volubilité, de façon loquace

garter ['gɑːtər] **N** jarretière f; Am (suspender) (for stockings) jarretelle f, Am (for socks) fixe-chaussette m, pl fixe-chaussettes; Br **Knight of the (Order of the) G.** chevalier m de l'Ordre de la Jarretière
▸▸ Am **g. belt** porte-jarretelles m inv; **g. snake** couleuvre f; Knitting **g. stitch** point m mousse

gas, pl **gases** [gæs, 'gæsɪz] **N 1** gaz m inv; **to pay the g. bill** payer le gaz; **the g. has been cut off** le gaz a été coupé; **to cook with** or **by g.** faire la cuisine au gaz; **to have g.** (as anaesthetic) se faire anesthésier au gaz; **town g.** gaz m de ville
2 Mil gaz m de combat
3 Min grisou m
4 Am (gasoline) essence f; **to fill up with g.** faire le plein d'essence; **to step on the g.** Aut appuyer sur le champignon; Fig (hurry) se presser, Fam se grouiller
5 Fam (worthless talk) bavardage m, verbiage m
6 esp Am **what a g.!** (situation, activity) quelle rigolade!; **we did it for a g.** on l'a fait pour rigoler
VT (-ss-) (person) asphyxier (avec un gaz); (deliberately) gazer; **to g. oneself** (deliberately) se suicider au gaz; (accidentally) être asphyxié
VI Fam (chat) bavarder, jaser
▸▸ **g. attack** attaque f aux gaz; Admin **G. Board** compagnie f du gaz; **g. burner** brûleur m à gaz; **g. chamber** chambre f à gaz; **g. cooker** cuisinière f à gaz; **g. cylinder** bouteille f de gaz; **g. explosion** (in home or street) explosion f due à une fuite de gaz; (in mine) coup m de grisou; **g. field** gisement m de gaz; Br **g. fire** (appareil m de) chauffage m au gaz; **g. fitter** installateur, -trice d'appareils à gaz; **g. furnace** fourneau m à gaz; **g. gangrene** gangrène f gazeuse; Am Fam **g. guzzler** = voiture f qui consomme beaucoup; **g. holder** gazomètre m, réservoir m à gaz; **g. industry** industrie f du gaz; Br **g. lamp** (in street) bec m de gaz; **g. leak** fuite f de gaz; **g. lighter** (for cooker) allume-gaz m inv; (for cigarettes) briquet m à gaz; **g. main** conduite f de gaz; (large) gazoduc m; **g. mantle** manchon m à incandescence; **g. mask** masque m à gaz; **g. meter** compteur m à gaz; **g. oven** (domestic) four m à gaz; (cremation chamber) four m crématoire; **she threatened to put her head in a g. oven** elle a menacé de se suicider; **g. pipe** tuyau m à gaz; Comput **g. plasma screen** écran m à plasma; Br **g. poker** allume-gaz m inv; Br **g. ring** (part of cooker) brûleur m; (small cooker) réchaud m à gaz; Am **g. station** poste m d'essence, station-service f, pl stations-service; **g. stove** cuisinière f à gaz; **g. tank** (domestic) cuve f à gaz; Am Aut (petrol tank) réservoir m à essence; **g. tap** (on cooker) bouton m de cuisinière; (at mains) robinet m de gaz; **g. turbine** turbine f à gaz; **g. turbine engine** moteur m à turbine à gaz; **g. warfare** guerre f chimique

gasbag ['gæsbæg] **N** Fam bavard, -arde; (boaster) vantard, -arde

Gascony ['gæskənɪ] **N** la Gascogne

gas-cooled reactor [-ˈkuːld] **N** réacteur m à refroidissement par gaz

gaseous ['gæsɪəs, 'geɪsɪəs, 'geɪʃɪəs] **ADJ** gazeux

gas-fired [-ˈfaɪəd] **ADJ** au gaz

gash [gæʃ] **N** (on body) coupure f, entaille f,

(on face) balafre f, (in earth's surface etc) fente f; **the iceberg had ripped a great g. in the ship's side** l'iceberg avait fait une grande déchirure sur le côté du bateau
VT (wound) entailler, couper; (face) balafrer; **to g. one's chin** se faire une entaille au menton

gasholder ['gæshəʊldər] **N** réservoir m à gaz

gasify ['gæsɪfaɪ] **VT** gazéifier
VI se gazéifier

gasket ['gæskɪt] **N** Tech (of joint) joint m d'étanchéité, garniture f; Aut (of cylinder head) joint de culasse; **to blow a g.** Aut faire sauter un joint de culasse; Fig Fam se mettre en rage, piquer une colère; Fam **he just about blew a g.** il a pété les plombs

gaslight ['gæslaɪt] **N** lumière f du gaz; **by g.** à la lumière du gaz

gasman, pl **gasmen** ['gæsmæn, -men] **N** Fam contrôleur m ou employé m du gaz, gazier m

gasoline ['gæsəliːn] **N** Am essence f

gasometer [gæˈsɒmɪtər] **N** gazomètre m, réservoir m à gaz

gasp [gɑːsp] **N** (of surprise) hoquet m, sursaut m; **there were gasps of admiration from the audience** il y a eu des sursauts d'admiration dans le public; **..., she said with a g.** ..., dit-elle, le souffle coupé; **to be at one's last g.** agoniser, être à l'agonie; Fig Fam être sur le point de rendre son dernier soupir; **to give one's last g.** rendre le dernier soupir; **to defend sth to the last g.** défendre qch jusqu'à son dernier souffle
VI (with surprise, fright, horror) avoir le souffle coupé (**with** de); **to make sb g.** couper le souffle à qn; **to g. for breath** or **for air** haleter, suffoquer; Fam **I'm gasping (for a drink)** je meurs de soif; Fam **I'm gasping (for a cigarette)** je meurs d'envie de fumer une cigarette
VT dire d'une voix entrecoupée; **she managed to g. her name** elle a réussi à dire son nom d'une voix entrecoupée
▸ **gasp out VT SEP** = **gasp VT**

gasper ['gɑːspər] **N** Fam (cigarette) tige f

gas-permeable **ADJ** (contact lens) semi-rigide

gassed [gæst] **ADJ** Fam (drunk) bourré

gassing ['gæsɪŋ] **N 1** (of person) (deliberate) gazage m **2** Fam (talk) bavardage m

gassy ['gæsɪ] **ADJ** (beer etc) trop gazeux

gastrectomy [gæsˈtrektəmɪ] **N** Med gastrectomie f

gastric ['gæstrɪk] **ADJ** gastrique
▸▸ **g. flu** grippe f intestinale ou gastro-intestinale; **g. juices** sucs mpl gastriques; **g. ulcer** ulcère m de l'estomac, gastrite f ulcéreuse

gastritis [gæsˈtraɪtɪs] **N** Med gastrite f; **to have g.** avoir ou faire une gastrite

gastro-enteritis [gæstrəʊentəˈraɪtɪs] **N** Med gastro-entérite f, pl gastro-entérites

gastroenterology [gæstrəʊentəˈrɒlədʒɪ] **N** Med gastro-entérologie f

gastro-intestinal ['gæstrəʊ-] **ADJ** Anat gastrointestinal, -aux; **the g. tract** les voies f digestives

gastronome ['gæstrənəʊm] **N** gastronome mf

gastronomic(al) [gæstrəˈnɒmɪk, -ɪk(ə)l] **ADJ** gastronomique

gastronomy [gæsˈtrɒnəmɪ] **N** gastronomie f

gastropod ['gæstrəpɒd] **N** (mollusc) gastéropode m

gastropub ['gæstrəʊpʌb] **N** Br pub m gastronomique

gasworks ['gæswɜːks] **NPL** (usu with sing verb) usine f à gaz

gate [geɪt] **N 1** *(of castle, city, factory)* porte *f*, *(of manor house)* portail *m*; **the gate(s) of hell** les portes de l'enfer

2 *(of garden)* portail *m*; *(metal)* grille *f*, *(of field)* barrière *f*, *Ski* porte *f*, *Aviat* g. **15** *(at airport)* porte **15**; *Sport* **(starting) g.** starting-gate *m*, *pl* starting-gates

3 *(at stadium)* entrée *f*, **to pay at the g.** payer à l'entrée; *Sport* **the g.** *(spectators)* le public; *(takings)* la recette, les entrées

4 *Tech (lock)* **g.** vanne *f* (d'écluse)

5 *Aut (for gearstick)* grille *f* (de changement de vitesse)

6 *Electron* porte *f*, **(logic) g.** porte logique

VT *Br Sch, Univ* **to be gated** se faire consigner

▸▸ *Aviat* **g. lounge** salle *f* d'embarquement; *Sport* **g. money** la recette, les entrées; **g. pattern** *(of gearbox)* disposition *f* de grille, type *m* de grille

gâteau [ˈgætəʊ] **N** gros gâteau *m* à la crème

gate-crash **VI** resquiller

VT to g. a party aller à une soirée sans y être invité

gate-crasher [-kræʃər] **N** resquilleur, -euse

gatefold [ˈgeɪtfəʊld] **N** page *f* qui se déplie, dépliant *m* (dans un magazine)

gatehouse [ˈgeɪthaʊs] **N 1** *(of an estate)* loge *f* **2** *(of a castle)* corps-de-garde *m inv*

gatekeeper [ˈgeɪtkiːpər] **N 1** gardien, -ienne **2** *Mktg* contrôleur *m*, relais *m*, filtre *m* **3** *Rail* garde-barrière *mf. pl* gardes-barrière(s)

gate-leg(ged) [-leg(d)] **ADJ** *(table)* à abattants

gatepost [ˈgeɪtpəʊst] **N** montant *m* (de barrière); *Fam* **between you, me and the g.** entre nous soit dit

gateway [ˈgeɪtweɪ] **N 1** porte *f*, entrée *f*, *Fig* **the g. to the Continent** la porte du Continent; **a g. to a successful career** un passeport pour une carrière réussie **2** *Comput* passerelle *f* de connexion

gather [ˈgæðər] **VT 1** *(collect) (people)* assembler, rassembler; *(things)* rassembler; *(flowers)* cueillir; *(information)* recueillir; *(wood, papers)* ramasser; *(strawberries etc)* cueillir, faire la cueillette de; *(one's skirts)* serrer autour de ses jambes; *(in bookbinding) (pages of a book)* rassembler; **to g. the harvest** rentrer la moisson; **to g. honey from the flowers** *(of bees)* butiner les fleurs; **we are gathered here today ...** nous sommes rassemblés ici aujourd'hui ...; **to g. one's thoughts** rassembler ses idées; **to g. all one's strength (in order) to do sth** rassembler toutes ses forces pour faire qch; **to g. one's hair into a bun/a ponytail/bunches** se faire un chignon/une queue de cheval/des couettes; *Lit Euph* **to be gathered to one's fathers** expirer

2 *(accumulate)* **to g. dirt** s'encrasser; **to g. dust** ramasser la poussière; **to g. force** *(of argument)* gagner du terrain; **to g. momentum, to g. speed** prendre de la vitesse; **to g. strength** *(of person)* reprendre des forces

3 *(pull together) Sewing (skirt etc)* froncer; **to g. the blankets round one** se serrer dans les couvertures; **he gathered her in his arms** il l'a serrée dans ses bras

4 *(conclude, understand)* conclure; **so far as I can g.** à ce que je sache; **I g. from the papers that ...** à en croire les journaux ...; **I g. he has been ill** j'ai appris qu'il a été malade; **I g. from the evidence given that ...** je déduis *ou* j'infère de ces témoignages que ...; **as you may/must already have gathered** comme vous l'avez peut-être/sûrement déjà compris; **I had (already) gathered as much** *(it was not news to me)* j'avais déjà compris; **prices have gone up – so I g.** les prix ont augmenté – c'est bien ce qu'il me semble

VI 1 *(of people)* se réunir, s'assembler, se rassembler; **a crowd gathered** une foule se forma **2** *(of objects, dust)* s'accumuler, s'amonceler; **tears were gathering in her eyes** ses yeux se remplissaient de larmes; **the clouds are gathering** les nuages s'amoncellent; **a storm is gathering** un orage se prépare **3** *Med (of abscess)* mûrir, aboutir; **the pus gathers** le pus s'accumule

▸ **gather in VT SEP 1** *(collect) (crops, harvest)* rentrer; *(sheep)* faire rentrer; *(exam papers, questionnaires)* ramasser **2** *Sewing* froncer

▸ **gather round VT INSEP** se rassembler autour de

VI s'approcher; **g. round!** approchez-vous!

▸ **gather together VT SEP** *(collect) (belongings, children etc)* rassembler

VI *(assemble)* se rassembler

▸ **gather up VT SEP** *(collect) (belongings, things)* ramasser; **she gathered up her skirts** elle a serré sa jupe autour de ses jambes; **to g. up one's hair** attacher *ou* relever ses cheveux; **he gathered her up in his arms** il l'a serrée dans ses bras

gathered [ˈgæðəd] **ADJ** *Sewing (flounce etc)* froncé, à fronces

▸▸ **g. pages** *(in bookbinding)* feuilles *fpl* assemblées

gathering [ˈgæðərɪŋ] **N 1** *(people) (in a hall etc)* assemblée *f*, réunion *f*, *(in a street)* rassemblement *m*, attroupement *m*; **the g. of the clans** le rassemblement des clans; **a small g. was listening to him** quelques personnes attroupées l'écoutaient **2** *(of information, data)* collecte *f*, *(of fruit etc)* cueillette *f*, *Sewing (pleats)* fronces *fpl*

ADJ ATTRIB in the g. darkness dans la nuit grandissante; **with g. force** avec une force croissante

gathers [ˈgæðəz] **NPL** *Sewing* fronces *fpl*

gator [ˈgeɪtər] **N** *Am Fam (alligator)* alligator *m*

GATS [gæts] **N** *(abbr **General Agreement on Trade in Services**)* AGCS *m*

GATT [gæt] **N** *(abbr **General Agreement on Tariffs and Trade**)* GATT *m*, AGETAC *m*

gauche [gəʊʃ] **ADJ** gauche, maladroit

gaucheness [ˈgəʊʃnɪs] **N** gaucherie *f*, maladresse *f*

gaudily [ˈgɔːdɪlɪ] **ADV** d'une manière voyante; *(painted)* avec des couleurs criardes

gaudiness [ˈgɔːdɪnɪs] **N** *(of colour etc)* éclat *m* criard

gaudy [ˈgɔːdɪ] **ADJ** *(colour)* voyant, criard; *(display)* de mauvais goût

gauge [geɪdʒ] **N 1** *(size) (of screw etc)* calibre *m*; *Rail (of track)* écartement *m* **2** *(standardization device)* étalon *m*; *(for liquid)* jauge *f*, **wire g.** calibre *m* pour fils métalliques **3** *(control instrument)* indicateur *m*; *Tech* **water-/oil g.** indicateur *ou* jauge *f* de niveau d'eau/d'huile; **pressure g.** manomètre *m*; *Aut (petrol or fuel)* **g.** jauge d'essence; *Fig* **an opinion poll is a useful g. of public opinion** un sondage constitue un indicateur utile de l'opinion

VT *(screw etc)* calibrer; *(oil)* jauger, mesurer; **in order to g. the amount of petrol/water necessary to ...** pour évaluer la quantité d'essence/d'eau nécessaire à ...; *Fig* **to g. a situation** évaluer une situation; **it was difficult to g. how interested they were/their enthusiasm** il était difficile de juger dans quelle mesure ils étaient intéressés/de juger de leur enthousiasme

gauging [ˈgeɪdʒɪŋ] **N**

▸▸ **g. rod, g. stick** jauge *f*

Gaul [gɔːl] **N** *Antiq* **1** *(region)* Gaule *f* **2** *(inhabitant)* Gaulois, -oise

Gaullist [ˈgəʊlɪst] **ADJ, N** *Pol* gaulliste *mf*

gaunt [gɔːnt] **ADJ 1** *(person, face)* maigre, décharné **2** *(place)* désolé

gauntlet[1] [ˈgɔːntlɪt] **N 1** *(part of armour)* gantelet *m*, gant *m*; *Fig* **to throw or fling down the g.** jeter le gant; *Fig* **to take up the g.** relever le gant **2** *(glove)* gant *m* à crispins *ou* à manchette

▸▸ **g. glove** gant à crispins *ou* à manchette

gauntlet[2] **N to run the g.** *Mil* passer par les baguettes; *Naut* courir la bouline; *Fig* soutenir un feu roulant (de critiques adverses); **they had to run the g. of enemy fire** ils ont dû soutenir le feu roulant de l'ennemi; **he had to run the g. of their abuse** il a dû soutenir le feu roulant de leurs injures

gauntness [ˈgɔːntnɪs] **N** *(of person, face)* maigreur *f*, *(of place)* désolation *f*, **the g. of his face** son visage hâve

gauze [gɔːz] **N** gaze *f*, *Med* **(antiseptic) g.** gaze aseptique; **(wire) g.** toile *f* métallique

▸▸ *Med* **g. bandage** bande *f* de gaze

gave **PT** *see* give

gavel [ˈgæv(ə)l] **N** *(of auctioneer, of judge)* marteau *m*

gavotte [gəˈvɒt] **N** *Mus* gavotte *f*

Gawd [gɔːd] **N** *Sl* = **God**

gawk [gɔːk] *Fam* **N** lourdaud, -aude

VI = **gawp**

gawker [ˈgɔːkər] **N** *Am* badaud *m*, curieux, -ieuse

gawkiness [ˈgɔːkɪnɪs] **N** gaucherie *f*, *Fam* air *m* empoté

gawky [ˈgɔːkɪ] **ADJ** gauche, *Fam* empoté

gawp [gɔːp] **VI** *Fam* rester bouche bée, gober les mouches; **to g. at sth** regarder qch d'un air bête; **stop gawping!** ne reste pas planté là à regarder!

gay [geɪ] **ADJ 1** *(homosexual)* homosexuel, gay *inv*; **the g. community** la communauté homosexuelle *ou* gay; **g. club/magazine** boîte de nuit/magazine pour homosexuels **2** *Sl (stupid)* nul **3** *Old-fashioned (happy)* gai, allègre; *(laugh)* enjoué; *(colour)* vif, *f* vive, gai; **to have a g. old time** bien s'amuser

N homosexuel, -elle

gayness [ˈgeɪnɪs] **N** *(homosexuality)* homosexualité *f*

Gaza [ˈgɑːzə] **N** Gaza; **the G. Strip** la Bande de Gaza

gaze [geɪz] **N** regard *m* fixe; **she turned her g. on the dog** elle a tourné son regard vers le chien; **to meet sb's g.** regarder qn dans les yeux; **exposed to the public g.** exposé aux regards inquisiteurs de tous

VI regarder fixement; **they gazed around them** ils ont regardé autour d'eux; **to g. at or on sb/sth** fixer *ou* contempler *ou* considérer qn/qch

gazebo [gəˈziːbəʊ] **N** *(with a view)* belvédère *m*; *(without a view)* kiosque *m*

gazelle [gəˈzel] **N** *(animal)* gazelle *f*

gazette [gəˈzet] **N** *(official journal)* journal *m* officiel; **the Police G.** ≃ la Gazette des tribunaux

VT *(bankruptcy, appointment etc)* annoncer *ou* publier dans un journal officiel

gazetteer [gæzɪˈtɪər] **N** répertoire *m* géographique

gazump [gəˈzʌmp] **VT** *Br Fam* **to g. sb** = revenir sur une promesse de vente faite à qn pour accepter une offre plus élevée; **we were gazumped** le propriétaire est revenu sur la promesse de vente qu'il nous avait faite

gazumping [gəˈzʌmpɪŋ] **N** *Br Fam* = fait de revenir sur une promesse de vente pour accepter une offre plus élevée

GB [ˈdʒiːˈbiː] **N 1** *Aut (abbr **Great Britain**)* **GB plate** plaque *f* GB; **GB sticker** autocollant *m* GB **2** *Comput (abbr **gigabyte**)* Go *m*

GBH [dʒiːbiːˈeɪtʃ] N *Law* (*abbr* **grievous bodily harm**) coups *mpl* et blessures *fpl*

GCE [dʒiːsiːˈiː] *Br Sch Formerly* (*abbr* **General Certificate of Education**) N = certificat *m* britannique de fin d'études secondaire en deux étapes (O level et A level) dont la première est aujourd'hui remplacée par le GCSE

GCHQ [dʒiːsiːeɪtʃˈkjuː] N *Br* (*abbr* **Government Communications Headquarters**) = centre *m* de renseignement du gouvernement britannique

GCSE [dʒiːsiːesˈiː] N *Br Sch* (*abbr* **General Certificate of Secondary Education**) = première partie *f* de l'examen de fin d'études secondaires

---

GCSE

Cet examen a remplacé les "O levels", ou le "GCE O level", et le "CSE". On le passe après cinq ans de scolarité dans l'enseignement secondaire. Chaque élève choisit les matières dans lesquelles il veut se présenter (généralement entre cinq et dix) selon un système d'unités de valeur. Le nombre d'unités et les notes obtenues déterminent le passage dans la classe supérieure. Les élèves qui sont admis au GCSE peuvent ensuite préparer les "**A levels**" (l'équivalent du baccalauréat français). En Écosse, l'examen équivalent au GCSE s'appelle le "Standard Grade".

GDP [dʒiːdiːˈpiː] N *Econ* (*abbr* **gross domestic product**) PIB *m*; **G. per capita** PIB par habitant

GDR [dʒiːdiːˈɑːr] N *Formerly* (*abbr* **German Democratic Republic**) RDA *f*

Gds *abbr* **Gardens**

gear [gɪər] N **1** (*speed*) vitesse *f*; (*mechanism*) appareil *m*, mécanisme *m*; *Tech etc* (*gearwheel*) engrenage *m*; **in g.** (*car*) embrayé, en prise; *Sl* **get your arse in g.!** remue-toi!; **out of g.** (*car*) au point mort; **to throw** *or* **put out of g.** (*car*) débrayer; *Fig* (*plan, process*) perturber; **a ten-g. racing bike** un vélo de course à dix vitesses; *Aut* **neutral g.** point *m* mort; *Aut* **first** *or* **bottom g.** première vitesse; *Aut* **top g.** cinquième/sixième vitesse; *Fig* **we're not operating in top g.** nous ne sommes pas à notre maximum *ou* au top de notre forme; **to change** *or Am* **shift g.** *Aut, Fig* changer de vitesse; *Cycling* changer de vitesse *ou* de braquet **2** (*equipment*) équipement *m*; *Naut* appareaux *mpl*; (*for camping, fishing, photography*) équipement, matériel *m*; *Fig Fam* **he arrived with all his g.** (*belongings*) il est arrivé avec tout son attirail **3** *Fam* (*clothes*) fringues *fpl* **4** *Br Sl* (*drugs*) dope *f* **5** (*harness*) (*of draught horse*) harnais *m*, harnachement *m*

VT **1** *Tech* engrener, embrayer **2** *Fin* (*link*) indexer (**to** à); **salaries are geared to the cost of living** les salaires sont indexés au coût de la vie

▸▸**g. change** changement *m* de vitesse; **g. lever** levier *m* (de changement) de vitesse; **g. ratio** rapport *m* du changement de vitesse

▸**gear down** VI (*of factory etc*) ralentir la production

VT SEP **1** **to g. down production** ralentir la production **2** *Tech* démultiplier

▸**gear to** VT SEP (*intend for*) **to g. sth to sth** adapter qch en fonction de qch; **wages geared to the cost of living** salaires indexés sur le coût de la vie; **this book is geared to the needs of students** ce livre est spécialement adapté aux besoins des étudiants

▸**gear up** VI (*prepare*) se préparer; **the shops are gearing up for Christmas** les magasins se préparent pour Noël

VT SEP **1** (*prepare*) préparer; **businesses were getting geared up for the single European market** les entreprises se préparaient en vue du marché unique européen **2** (*increase*) augmenter; **we must g. up production to meet the demand** il nous faut augmenter la production pour faire face à la demande **3** *Tech* multiplier

gearbox [ˈgɪəbɒks] N *Aut* boîte *f* de vitesses

▸▸**g. ratio** rapport *m* de boîte

gearing [ˈgɪərɪŋ] N **1** *Tech etc* (*gears*) engrenage *m*, embrayage *m*, système *m ou* jeu *m* d'engrenages; (*drive*) transmission *f* **2** *Fin* (*leverage*) effet *m* de levier; (*as percentage*) ratio *m* d'endettement

▸▸*Fin* **g. adjustment** redressement *m* financier; *Tech* **g. down** démultiplication *f*; *Tech* **g. up** multiplication *f*

gearshift [ˈgɪəʃɪft] N *Am Aut* (*lever*) levier *m* de vitesses; (*action*) changement *m* de vitesse; **automatic g.** changement de vitesse automatique

gearstick [ˈgɪəstɪk] N levier *m* de vitesses

gearwheel [ˈgɪəwiːl] N *Tech* engrenage *m*; *Cycling* pignon *m*

gecko, *pl* **geckos, geckoes** [ˈgekəʊ, -əʊz] N gecko *m*

gee [dʒiː] INT **1** (*to horse*) **g. up!** hue! **2** *Am* **g. (whiz(z))!** ça alors!, mince alors!

gee-gee [ˈdʒiːdʒiː] N *Fam* (*horse*) dada *m*

geek [giːk] N *Fam* crétin, -ine, débile *mf*

geeky [ˈgiːkɪ] ADJ *Fam* ringard, débile

geese [giːs] NPL *see* **goose**

geezer [ˈgiːzər] N *Fam* **1** *Br* (*man*) type *m*; **old g.** vieux type; **funny old g.** drôle *m* de bonhomme **2** *Am* (*old person*) vioque *mf*

Geiger counter [ˈgaɪgər] N compteur *m* Geiger

geisha [ˈgeɪʃə] N geisha *f*

gel [dʒel] N *Chem* colloïde *m* (coagulé); (*for hair, eyes*) gel *m*

VI (**-ll-**) se coaguler; *Fig* (*of ideas, plans*) prendre corps *ou* forme; *Fig* **the musicians didn't g.** la cohésion ne s'est pas faite entre les musiciens

gelatine [ˈdʒeɪətiːn] N gélatine *f*

▸▸**g. paper** papier *m* gélatine

gelatinize [dʒɪˈlætɪnaɪz] VT gélatiniser

VI se gélatiniser

gelatinous [dʒɪˈlætɪnəs] ADJ gélatineux

geld [geld] VT (*animal*) châtrer; (*horse*) hongrer

gelding [ˈgeldɪŋ] N (*animal*) animal *m* châtré; (*horse*) (cheval *m*) hongre *m*

gelignite [ˈdʒelɪgnaɪt] N gélignite *f*

gem [dʒem] N **1** (*precious stone*) pierre *f* précieuse **2** *Fig* (*marvellous thing or person*) perle *f*; **he's a g. of a husband** c'est la perle des maris; **the g. of the collection** le joyau de la collection **3** *Typ* diamant *m*

Gemini [ˈdʒemɪnaɪ] NPL *Astrol* Gémeaux *mpl*; **to be (a) G.** être (des) Gémeaux

gemstone [ˈdʒemstəʊn] N pierre *f* gemme

Gen *Mil* (*abbr* **General**) gal

gen [dʒen] N *Br Fam* renseignements *mpl*, tuyaux *mpl* (**on** sth sur qch)

▸**gen up** VT SEP *Br Fam* (*provide with information*) (*person*) rencarder (**on** sur)

▸**gen up on** VT INSEP *Br Fam* se rencarder sur

gender [ˈdʒendər] N **1** *Gram* genre *m*; **to agree in g.** s'accorder en genre (**with** avec) SEE GRAMMAR B5-7 **2** (*sex*) sexe *m*; **the male/female g.** le sexe masculin/féminin; **it is not a question of g.** ce n'est pas une question de sexe

▸▸**g. bias** discrimination *f* sexuelle; **g. reassignment** réassignation *f* sexuelle

gender-bender N *Fam* **1** (*person*) travesti, -ie **2** *Comput* commutateur *m*, changeur *m* de genre

gender-changer N *Comput* commutateur *m*, changeur *m* de genre

gene [dʒiːn] N *Biol* gène *m*; *Fig* **music's in his genes** chez lui la musique, c'est héréditaire; **it's in his genes** c'est inné, il est né comme ça

▸▸**g. pool** patrimoine *m* génétique; **g. therapy** thérapie *f* génique

genealogical [dʒiːnɪəˈlɒdʒɪk(ə)l] ADJ généalogique

▸▸**g. chart, g. tree** arbre *m* généalogique

genealogist [dʒiːnɪˈælədʒɪst] N généalogiste *mf*

genealogy [dʒiːnɪˈælədʒɪ] N généalogie *f*

genera [ˈdʒenərə] NPL *see* **genus**

general [ˈdʒen(ə)r(ə)l] ADJ **1** (*paralysis, improvement etc*) général, -aux; **the rain has been pretty g.** il a plu un peu partout; **the g. tone of her remarks was that ...** ce qui ressortait de ses remarques, c'est que ...; **he made himself a g. nuisance** il a été embêtant à tout point de vue; **I had a g. tidy-up** j'ai fait du rangement un peu partout; **g. effect** effet *m* d'ensemble; **a word in g. use** un mot couramment employé; **to come into g. use** se généraliser; **as a g. rule** en règle générale; **in g. terms** en termes généraux; **speaking in a g. way** d'une manière générale **2** (*in titles*) **inspector g.** inspecteur *m* général *ou* en chef; *Hist* **Estates G.** États *mpl* généraux

N **1 in g.** en général; **what effect will this have in g.?** quel effet général est-ce que cela va avoir?; **to argue from the g. to the particular** aller du général au particulier **2** *Mil* général *m*; (*rank*) général d'armée; *Rel* (*of religious order*) général

▸▸*Banking* **g. account manager** chargé, -ée de clientèle grand public; **g. accounts** comptabilité *f* générale; **G. Agreement on Tariffs and Trade** accord *m* général sur les tarifs douaniers et le commerce; *Med* **g. anaesthetic** anesthésie *f* générale; **G. Assembly** assemblée *f* générale; *Com* **g. business** (*on agenda*) questions *fpl* diverses; *Rel* **g. confession** confession *f* en commun; *Am* **g. delivery** poste *f* restante; **g. election** élections *fpl* législatives; *Acct, Fin* **g. expenses** frais *mpl* généraux; **g. hospital** centre *m* hospitalier; **g. knowledge** culture *f* générale; *Law* **g. lien** privilège *m* général; **g. manager** directeur, -trice général(e); **g. Manager, European Operations** Directeur des Opérations européennes; **g. meeting** assemblée générale; *Fin* **g. obligation bond** emprunt *m* de collectivité locale; **g. officer** général *m* en chef; **g. overheads** frais d'administration générale; *Com* **g. partnership** société *f* commerciale en nom collectif; **g. practice** médecine *f* générale; **g. practitioner** médecin *m* généraliste, omnipraticien, -ienne; **the g. public** le grand public; **g. staff** état-major *m*, *pl* états-majors; **g. strike** grève *f* générale; **g. wholesaler** grossiste *m* généraliste

general-interest ADJ *TV* généraliste

▸▸**g. channel** chaîne *f* généraliste; **g. station** station *f* généraliste

generalissimo [dʒenərəˈlɪsɪməʊ] N *Mil* généralissime *m*

generality [dʒenəˈrælɪtɪ] N **1** (*statement*) **to confine oneself to generalities** s'en tenir aux généralités **2** (*quality*) (*of remarks, opinions*) caractère *m* général **3** *Fml* (*majority*) **the g. of mankind** la plupart des hommes

generalization [dʒen(ə)rəlaɪˈzeɪʃən] N généralisation *f*; **to make generalizations** généraliser

generalize [ˈdʒen(ə)rəlaɪz] VI **1** généraliser,

faire des généralisations; **I don't like generalizing, but** … je n'aime pas faire de généralisations, mais … **2** *Med (of disease)* généraliser
vt 1 *(conclusion, facts etc)* généraliser à partir de **2** *(make widespread) (custom etc)* généraliser; **to become generalized** *(of practice)* se généraliser

generalized ['dʒen(ə)rəlaɪzd] **ADJ** généralisé

generally ['dʒenrəlɪ] **ADV 1** *(widely)* généralement; **the word is g. understood to mean** … le mot veut généralement dire …; **this information is not g. available** le public n'a pas accès à ces informations; **it is not g. known that** … beaucoup de gens ignorent que …
2 *(taken overall)* dans l'ensemble; **to make oneself g. useful** se rendre généralement utile; **she behaved in a g. antisocial manner** d'une manière générale, elle s'est comportée de façon antisociale
3 *(as a general rule)* en règle générale, généralement, en général; **g. speaking** d'une manière générale; **the roads are g. crowded at this time** en général, les routes sont très encombrées à cette heure-ci

general-purpose ADJ universel, à usages multiples

generalship ['dʒen(ə)rəlʃɪp] **N** *Mil (skill)* l'art *m* d'être général; **his g.** la compétence de général dont il a fait preuve

generate ['dʒenəreɪt] **vt** *(result, electric current, heat etc)* produire; *(income)* créer; *(feeling, reaction, response)* provoquer, engendrer; *(interest, ideas)* faire naître; *Comput* créer, générer; *Math* engendrer; *Ling* générer; **tourism generated three million pounds for the region** le tourisme a rapporté trois millions de livres à la région; **environment that generates crime** environnement qui engendre la délinquance

generating ['dʒenəreɪtɪŋ] **ADJ** générateur, -trice
N génération *f*
▸▸ **g. station** centrale *f* électrique

generation [dʒenə'reɪʃən] **N 1** *(period, people, computers etc)* génération *f*; **from g. to g.** de génération en génération, de père en fils; **for generations there had always been a doctor in the family** ils étaient médecins de père en fils; **people of my g. will remember** … les gens de ma génération se souviendront …; **he's my g.** il est de ma génération; **we're a different g.** nous appartenons à des générations différentes; **the younger/older g.** la jeune/l'ancienne génération; **the g. gap** l'écart *m* ou le fossé entre les générations VOIR GRAMMAIRE A11
2 *(production) (of ideas etc)* génération *f*, formation *f*, *Elec, Phys etc (of heat etc)* génération, production *f*, *Math* génération; *Ling* production, génération; *Comput* création *f*, génération

-generation SUFF second-g. immigrant immigrant de la deuxième génération; **third-g. fax machines** télécopieurs de la troisième génération

generative ['dʒenərətɪv] **ADJ** *Ling* génératif
generator ['dʒenəreɪtər] **N** *Elec* génératrice *f*, dynamo *f*, *(backup device)* groupe *m* électrogène; *Comput* (programme *m*) générateur *m*; *Tech (of heat etc)* générateur; **tourism is a major g. of income** le tourisme est une source importante de revenus

generatrix, *pl* **generatrices** ['dʒenəreɪtrɪks, -ɪsiːz] **N** *Math* génératrice *f*

generic [dʒɪ'nerɪk] **ADJ** *(term, noun)* générique
N *Mktg* produit *m* générique
▸▸ *Mktg* **g. advertising** publicité *f* générique; *Com, Mktg* **g. brand** marque *f* géné-

rique; **g. drug** médicament *m* générique, générique *m*; **g. market** marché *m* générique; **g. name** *Biol* nom *m* du genre; *Com, Mktg (of product, drug)* nom générique; *Mktg* **g. product** produit générique

generically [dʒɪ'nerɪklɪ] **ADV** génériquement; **they are g. distinct** ils se distinguent en genre

generosity [dʒenə'rɒsɪtɪ] **N** *(with money, gifts)* générosité *f*, libéralité *f*, *(of spirit)* grandeur *f*, magnanimité *f*; **in a spirit of g.** *(to act)* par générosité; **thanks to the g. of Mr Jones** grâce à la générosité de M. Jones

generous ['dʒenərəs] **ADJ** *(person) (with money, gifts)* généreux; *(remarks, comments)* bienveillant; **he has a g. nature** c'est une âme généreuse; **he's a bit too g. with his advice** il n'est pas avare de conseils; **that's a g. interpretation of his motives** c'est faire preuve de bienveillance que d'interpréter ainsi ses raisons; **to be g. in victory** se montrer magnanime; **to be g. in defeat** être bon perdant; **g. mark** *(for homework etc)* note généreuse; **she's g. with her money** elle n'est pas avare de son argent; **a g. helping of food/measure of whisky** une portion généreuse de nourriture/un bon verre de whisky; **he took a g. helping of the stew** il s'est servi amplement de ragoût; *Fam* **she's built on g. lines** elle a des formes généreuses

generously ['dʒen(ə)rəslɪ] **ADV** *(to give, donate etc)* généreusement; **he g. congratulated her on her victory** bon joueur, il l'a félicitée pour sa victoire; **he helped himself g. to the stew** il s'est servi amplement de ragoût; **she g. offered to help** elle a généreusement proposé son aide; **her g. proportioned figure** ses formes généreuses

genesis ['dʒenɪsɪs] **N** genèse *f*, origine *f*, *Bible* **(the Book of) G.** la Genèse

genetic [dʒɪ'netɪk] **ADJ** *Biol* génétique
▸▸ **g. code** code *m* génétique; **g. engineering** génie *m* génétique; **g. fingerprint** empreinte *f* génétique; **g. fingerprinting** analyse *f* de l'empreinte génétique; **g. modification** modification *f* génétique

genetically [dʒɪ'netɪklɪ] **ADV** *Biol* génétiquement; **g. modified** *(plant, food)* génétiquement modifié; **to g. alter a mouse** faire des manipulations génétiques sur une souris

geneticist [dʒɪ'netɪsɪst] **N** *Biol* généticien, -ienne

genetics [dʒɪ'netɪks] **N** *Biol* génétique *f* VOIR GRAMMAIRE A10

Geneva [dʒɪ'niːvə] **N** Genève *f*; **Lake G.** le lac Léman; *Hist* **the G. Convention** la Convention de Genève

Genghis Khan ['geŋgɪs'kɑːn] **N** Gengis Khan

genial ['dʒiːnɪəl] **ADJ** *(person, tone, manner)* plein de bienveillance, affable, plein de bonne humeur

> Note that the French word **génial** is a false friend and is never a translation for the English word **genial**. It means **brilliant**.

geniality [dʒiːnɪ'ælɪtɪ] **N** bienveillance *f*, bonne humeur *f*

genially ['dʒiːnɪəlɪ] **ADV** affablement, avec affabilité

genie, *pl* **genii** ['dʒiːnɪ, 'dʒiːnɪaɪ] **N** djinn *m*, génie *m*

genital ['dʒenɪt(ə)l] **ADJ** génital, -aux
NPL genitals organes *mpl* génitaux externes
▸▸ *Med* **g. herpes** herpès *m* génital

genitalia [dʒenɪ'teɪlɪə] **NPL** organes *mpl* génitaux externes

genitive ['dʒenɪtɪv] VOIR GRAMMAIRE A15–16

Gram N génitif *m*; **in the g.** au génitif
ADJ génitif
▸▸ **g. case** génitif

genito-urinary [-'jʊərɪnərɪ] **ADJ** *Med* génito-urinaire

genius ['dʒiːnɪəs] **N 1** *(pl* **geniuses** ['dʒiːnɪəsɪz]) *(person)* génie *m*; **she's a mathematical g.** c'est un génie en mathématiques
2 *(no pl) (great talent)* génie *m*; **man/work of g.** homme *m*/œuvre *f* de génie; **to show g.** faire preuve de génie; **that goal was pure g.** ce goal, c'était du génie pur et simple
3 *(no pl) (aptitude)* aptitudes *fpl* naturelles; **to have a g. for business** avoir le sens des affaires; **to have a g. for doing sth** avoir le don de faire qch
4 *Lit (no pl) (of a nation, era)* génie *m*
5 *Lit (pl* **genii** ['dʒiːnɪaɪ]) *(spirit) (of place etc)* génie *m* ou esprit *m* tutélaire; **she is his good/evil g.** c'est son bon/mauvais génie

Genoa ['dʒenəʊə] **N** Gênes *f*

genocidal [dʒenəʊ'saɪd(ə)l] **ADJ** génocide

genocide ['dʒenəsaɪd] **N** génocide *m*

Genoese [dʒenəʊ'iːz] **ADJ** génois
N Génois, -oise

genome ['dʒiːnəʊm] **N** *Biol* génome *m*

genotype ['dʒenəʊtaɪp] **N** *Biol* génotype *m*

genre ['ʒɑːnrə] **N** genre *m*
▸▸ *Cin* **g. film** film *m* de genre; **g. painting** peinture *f* de genre

gent [dʒent] **N** *Br Fam* **1** monsieur *m*; **he's a real g.** c'est un gentleman; **gents' footwear** chaussures pour hommes **2** gents *(toilets)* toilettes *fpl* pour hommes; **where's the gents?** où sont les toilettes?

genteel [dʒen'tiːl] **ADJ 1** *Pej (affected)* maniéré, affecté **2** *(respectable)* comme il faut; **g. poverty** pauvreté *f* digne; **g. society** la bonne société

> Note that the French word **gentil** is a false friend and is never a translation for the English word **genteel**. It means **kind**.

gentian ['dʒenʃɪən] **N** *(plant)* gentiane *f*
▸▸ **g. bitter** (amer *m* de) gentiane; **g. blue** bleu *m* gentiane

Gentile ['dʒentaɪl] **N** Gentil
ADJ des Gentils

gentility [dʒen'tɪlɪtɪ] **N 1** *Pej (affectation)* prétention *f* au bon ton **2** *Old-fashioned (respectability)* respectabilité *f*; **the g.** *(people)* la haute bourgeoisie; **shabby g.** la misère en habit noir

gentle ['dʒent(ə)l] **ADJ** **(gentler, gentlest) 1** *(delicate, kind)* doux, *f* douce; *(reprimand)* peu sévère; *(tap on shoulder etc)* léger; *(exercise)* modéré; *(slope)* doux, faible; **to be g. with sb** être doux avec qn; **g. as a lamb** doux comme un agneau; **the gentle(r) sex** le sexe faible; **a g. breeze** une petite brise; **a g. giant** un bon géant **2** *Old-fashioned (noble)* **of g. birth** bien né

> Note that the French word **gentil** is a false friend and is never a translation for the English word **gentle**. It means **kind**.

gentlefolk ['dʒent(ə)lfəʊk] **NPL** *Old-fashioned* personnes *fpl* de bonne famille

gentleman, *pl* **gentlemen** ['dʒent(ə)lmən] **N 1** *(well-bred man)* homme *m* bien élevé, gentleman *m*; **to act** *or* **behave like a g.** se conduire en gentleman; **he's no g.** il est mal élevé; **thank you, you're a g.** merci, vous êtes un gentleman
2 *(man)* monsieur *m*, homme *m*; **Ladies and Gentlemen!** *(to audience)* mesdames et messieurs!; **there's a g. to see you** il y a un monsieur qui voudrait vous parler; **this young g.'s lost** ce petit jeune homme est perdu; *Old-fashioned* **g. friend** *(of woman)*

ami *m*; **gentlemen** *(on toilet)* messieurs; **g.'s g.** valet *m* de chambre; *Hum* **g. of the road** *(tramp)* clochard *m*
3 *(nobleman etc)* gentilhomme *m, pl* gentilshommes; **g. (of independent means)** rentier *m*; **G. in waiting** gentilhomme de service *(près du roi)*
4 *Sport Old-fashioned* amateur *m*
▸▸**g.'s agreement** gentleman's agreement *m*; **gentlemen's club** club *m* dont l'accès est réservé aux hommes

gentleman-farmer N gentleman-farmer *m, pl* gentlemen-farmers

gentlemanly ['dʒent(ə)lmənlɪ] ADJ bien élevé; **it would have been more g. to say nothing** un homme bien élevé *ou* un gentleman n'aurait rien dit

gentleness ['dʒent(ə)lnɪs] N douceur *f*

gently ['dʒentlɪ] ADV *(to handle etc)* doucement; *(to remind, imply, dissuade)* gentiment; **to speak g.** parler d'un ton doux *ou* avec douceur; **to deal g. with sb** traiter qn avec douceur; **g. (does it)!** allez-y doucement!; **the road slopes g. down to the beach** la route descend en pente douce jusqu'à la plage

gentrification [dʒentrɪfɪ'keɪʃən] N *Br* embourgeoisement *m*

gentrified ['dʒentrɪfaɪd] ADJ *Br (area, street)* qui s'est embourgeoisé

gentry ['dʒentrɪ] N *(no pl)* petite noblesse *f*, **landed g.** aristocratie *f* terrienne

genuflect ['dʒenjʊflekt] VI faire une génuflexion

genuflection, genuflexion ['dʒenjʊ-'flekʃən] N génuflexion *f*

genuine ['dʒenjʊɪn] ADJ **1** *(manuscript etc)* authentique, véritable; *Com (article)* garanti d'origine; *(champagne)* authentique; *(diamond)* véritable **2** *(sincere)* sincère, franc, *f* franche; *(belief)* sincère; *(friend)* loyal, -aux; **I think he's being g.** je crois qu'il est sincère; **she comes across as a g. person** elle donne l'impression d'être une personne sincère; **it was a g. mistake on her part** elle ne l'a pas fait exprès; *Com* **g. buyer** acheteur *m* sérieux; **a g. surprise** une véritable surprise

genuinely ['dʒenjʊɪnlɪ] ADV **1** authentiquement **2** *(to believe, be sorry etc)* sincèrement; **g. surprised** vraiment surpris

genuineness ['dʒenjʊɪnnɪs] N **1** *(of manuscript etc)* authenticité *f* **2** *(sincerity)* sincérité *f*

genus, *pl* **genera** ['dʒiːnəs, 'dʒenərə] N *Biol* genre *m*

geo- ['dʒiːəʊ] PREF géo(-)

geode ['dʒiːəʊd] N *Geol* géode *f*

geodemographic [dʒiːəʊdemə'græfɪk] ADJ *Mktg* géodémographique
▸▸**g. profile** profil *m* géodémographique; **g. segment** segment *m* géodémographique; **g. segmentation** segmentation *f* géodémographique

geodesic [dʒiːəʊ'diːzɪk] ADJ géodésique
▸▸**g. dome** dôme *m* géodésique

geodesy [dʒiː'ɒdɪsɪ] N géodésie *f*

geodynamics [dʒiːəʊdaɪ'næmɪks] N géodynamique *f*

geographer [dʒɪ'ɒgrəfər] N géographe *mf*

geographic(al) [dʒɪə'græfɪk, -ɪk(ə)l] ADJ géographique; **a g. survey** un relevé topographique
▸▸*Mktg* **g. pricing** tarification *f* géographique

geographically [dʒɪə'græfɪklɪ] ADV géographiquement

geography [dʒɪ'ɒgrəfɪ] N géographie *f*, **I haven't quite got a grasp of the g. of the building** je ne m'oriente pas encore très bien

dans le bâtiment; **g. book** livre *m* de géographie

geologic(al) [dʒɪə'lɒdʒɪk, -ɪk(ə)l] ADJ géologique
▸▸**g. survey** relevé *m* géologique

geologically [dʒɪə'lɒdʒɪklɪ] ADV géologiquement

geologist [dʒɪ'ɒlədʒɪst] N géologue *mf*

geology [dʒɪ'ɒlədʒɪ] N géologie *f*

geometer [dʒɪ'ɒmɪtər] N géomètre *mf*

geometric(al) [dʒɪə'metrɪk, -ɪk(ə)l] ADJ géométrique; **g. design** dessin *m* géométrique
▸▸**g. progression** progression *f* géométrique

geometrically [dʒɪə'metrɪklɪ] ADV géométriquement

geometrician [dʒɪɒmɪ'trɪʃən] N géomètre *mf*

geometry [dʒɪ'ɒmɪtrɪ] N géométrie *f*

geomorphologic(al) [dʒɪːɒmɔːfə'lɒdʒɪk, -ɪk(ə)l] ADJ géomorphologique

geomorphology [dʒiːɒmɔː'fɒlədʒɪ] N géomorphologie *f*

geophysical [dʒiːəʊ'fɪzɪk(ə)l] ADJ géophysique

geophysicist [dʒiːəʊ'fɪzɪsɪst] N géophysicien, -ienne

geophysics [dʒiːəʊ'fɪzɪks] N géophysique *f* VOIR GRAMMAIRE A10

geopolitics [dʒɪəʊ'pɒlɪtɪks] N géopolitique *f* VOIR GRAMMAIRE A10

Geordie ['dʒɔːdɪ] *Br Fam* N *(resident)* habitant, -ante de Newcastle-upon-Tyne ou de sa région; *(by birth)* originaire *mf* de Newcastle-upon-Tyne ou de sa région; *(dialect)* dialecte *m* parlé dans la région de Newcastle-upon-Tyne
ADJ *(dialect etc)* de Newcastle-upon-Tyne

George [dʒɔːdʒ] N **1** *Old-fashioned Fam* **by G.!** sapristi! **2** *Aviat Fam (automatic pilot)* George *m*
▸▸**G. Cross** = décoration *f* britannique décernée aux civils pour des actes de bravoure; **G. Medal** = décoration britannique décernée aux civils ou aux militaires pour des actes de bravoure

georgette [dʒɔː'dʒet] N *Tex* crêpe *m* georgette

Georgia ['dʒɔːdʒɪə] N Géorgie *f*

Georgian[1] ['dʒɔːdʒən] ADJ *Br Hist* **1** du règne des quatre rois George; **a G. house** une maison datant de l'époque 1720-1830 **2** *(of George V)* du règne de George V

Georgian[2] *Geog* ADJ géorgien
N Géorgien, -ienne

geoscience [dʒiːəʊ'saɪəns] N sciences *fpl* de la terre

geosphere ['dʒiːəʊsfɪər] N géosphère *f*

geostationary [dʒiːəʊ'steɪʃənərɪ] ADJ géostationnaire
▸▸**g. orbit** orbite *f* géostationnaire; **g. satellite** satellite *m* géostationnaire

geothermal [dʒiːəʊ'θɜːməl] ADJ géothermique

geotropism [dʒɪ'ɒtrəpɪz(ə)m] N géotropisme *m*

geranium [dʒə'reɪnɪəm] N **1** *(plant)* géranium *m* **2** *(colour)* vermeil *m*
▸▸**g. red** vermeil

gerbil ['dʒɜːbɪl] N gerbille *f*

geriatric [dʒerɪ'ætrɪk] *Med* N malade *mf* gériatrique; *Pej (old person)* vieux croulant *m*, vieille croulante *f*
ADJ gériatrique
▸▸**g. medicine** gériatrie *f*; **g. ward** service *m* de gériatrie

geriatrician [dʒerɪə'trɪʃən] N gériatre *mf*

geriatrics [dʒerɪ'ætrɪks] N SING *Med* gériatrie *f* VOIR GRAMMAIRE A10

germ [dʒɜːm] N **1** *Med (of disease)* germe *m*, microbe *m*; **I don't want your germs!** je ne veux pas de tes microbes! **2** *Biol (of organism)* germe *m*; *Fig* **the g. of an idea** le germe d'une idée
▸▸**g. cell** cellule *f* germinale *ou* reproductrice; **g. warfare** guerre *f* bactériologique

German ['dʒɜːmən] ADJ allemand; *Formerly* **West/East G.** ouest-/est-allemand
N **1** Allemand, -ande; *Formerly* **West/East G.** Allemand de l'Ouest/de l'Est **2** *Ling* allemand *m*; **High/Low G.** haut/bas allemand
▸▸*Formerly* **G. Democratic Republic** République *f* démocratique Allemande; **G. measles** rubéole *f*; *esp Am* **G. shepherd** *(dog)* berger *m* allemand

germander [dʒɜː'mændər] N *(plant)* germandrée *f*

germane [dʒɜː'meɪn] ADJ *Fml* se rapportant (**to** à)

germanic [dʒɜː'mænɪk] ADJ germanique

Germanist ['dʒɜːmənɪst] N *Ling* germaniste *mf*

Germanize ['dʒɜːmənaɪz] VT germaniser

Germany ['dʒɜːmənɪ] N Allemagne *f*, *Hist* **West/East G.** l'Allemagne de l'Ouest/de l'Est; **the two Germanies** les deux Allemagnes

germ-free ADJ *(environment)* stérile

germicidal [dʒɜːmɪ'saɪd(ə)l] ADJ germicide

germicide ['dʒɜːmɪsaɪd] N germicide *m*

germinate ['dʒɜːmɪneɪt] VI *(of seed)*, *Fig (of idea)* germer
VT *(seeds)* faire germer

germination [dʒɜːmɪ'neɪʃən] N germination *f*

gerontocracy [dʒerɒn'tɒkrəsɪ] N gérontocratie *f*

gerontologist [dʒerɒn'tɒlədʒɪst] N gérontologue *mf*

gerontology [dʒerɒn'tɒlədʒɪ] N gérontologie *f*

gerrymander ['dʒerɪmændər] *Pol* VT & VI **to g. (constituencies)** faire du tripatouillage électoral
N tripatouillage *m* électoral

gerrymandering ['dʒerɪmændərɪŋ] N *Pol* tripatouillage *m* électoral

gerund ['dʒerənd] N *Gram* gérondif *m*, nom *m* verbal; **in the g.** au gérondif VOIR GRAMMAIRE A43–4

gerundive [dʒɪ'rʌndɪv] *Gram* ADJ du gérondif
N adjectif *m* verbal

gesso ['dʒesəʊ] N *Art (coating) (for frescos)* enduit *m* de plâtre; *(substance)* plâtre *m* de Paris, gypse *m*

gestalt [gə'ʃtælt] N *Psy* gestalt *f*
▸▸**g. therapist** gestalt thérapeute *mf*; **g. therapy** gestalt-thérapie *f*

Gestapo [gəs'tɑːpəʊ] N Gestapo *f*

gestate [dʒes'teɪt] VI être en gestation

gestation [dʒes'teɪʃən] N *Physiol*, *Fig* gestation *f*
▸▸**g. period** période *f* de gestation

gesticulate [dʒes'tɪkjʊleɪt] VI gesticuler

gesticulation [dʒestɪkjʊ'leɪʃən] N gesticulation *f*

gesture ['dʒestʃər] N geste *m*; **to make a g.** faire un geste; **with a sweeping g.** d'un geste large; **g. of defiance** geste de défi; *Fig* **as a g. of friendship** en témoignage d'amitié; **a g. towards peace** un geste indiquant une volonté de paix
VI faire des gestes; **she gestured to them to be silent** elle leur a fait signe de se taire
VT exprimer par gestes; **he gestured us over** il nous a fait signe d'approcher

GET [get] (*pt* **got** [gɒt], *pp* **got**, *Arch, Am also* **gotten** [ˈgɒt(ə)n], *prp* **getting**[ˈgetɪŋ])

VT obtenir **1** ▪ acheter **1** ▪ prendre **1**, **4** ▪ recevoir **2** ▪ gagner **2** ▪ avoir **2, 3**, **17** ▪ attraper **4** ▪ atteindre **5** ▪ comprendre **8** ▪ aller chercher **10** ▪ préparer **11** ▪ faire faire **12, 14–16**
VI aller **1** ▪ devenir **4**

VT 1 (*obtain*) obtenir; **to g. sth for sb** procurer qch à qn; (*buy*) acheter qch pour qn; **where did you g. that?** où avez-vous trouvé/acheté cela?; **where can we g. some information?** où est-ce que nous pouvons obtenir des informations?; **to g. something to eat** (*find*) trouver de quoi manger; (*eat in restaurant etc*) manger quelque chose; **we g. our eggs from the farm next door** nous achetons nos œufs à la ferme d'à-côté; **I got this car cheap** j'ai eu *ou* j'ai acheté cette voiture à un bon prix; **if you're going to buy shoes, g. good ones** si tu achètes des chaussures, prends-en de bonnes; **to g. a job** trouver un travail; **I haven't got the right answer** je n'ai pas trouvé la solution; **to g. sb's permission to do sth** obtenir la permission de qn de faire qch; **to g. one's own way** faire valoir sa volonté; **I'll do it if I g. the time/a moment** je le ferai si j'ai le temps/si je trouve un moment; **I've got six more to g.** (*in collection*) il m'en manque six; **you g. a fine view from here** il y a une vue magnifique d'ici; **you g. a lot of people marrying young here** il y a beaucoup de gens qui se marient jeunes par ici; **we don't g. many accidents here** nous n'avons pas beaucoup d'accidents par ici; **I finally got her on her own** *ou* **alone** j'ai fini par réussir à la voir en tête à tête; **you need to g. (yourself) a good lawyer** il te faut un bon avocat

2 (*receive*) (*present, medal etc*) recevoir; (*prize*) gagner, remporter; **what did you g. for your birthday?** qu'est-ce que tu as eu pour ton anniversaire?; **I got your letter last week** j'ai eu *ou* reçu ta lettre la semaine dernière; **I didn't g. a reply** je n'ai pas eu de réponse; **room that gets no sun** pièce où le soleil ne donne pas; **we g. quite a lot of rain in summer** il pleut beaucoup en été; **he gets his shyness from his mother** il tient sa timidité de sa mère; **I got the idea from a book** j'ai trouvé l'idée dans un livre; **I need all the advice I can g.** j'ai besoin de tous les conseils qu'on peut me donner; **to g. ten years** prendre dix ans de prison; **to g. £15,000 a year** gagner 15 000 livres par an; **to g. 10% interest** recevoir 10% d'intérêt; **to g. a good price for sth** obtenir un bon prix pour qch; **what did you g. for your car?** combien est-ce que tu as vendu ta voiture?; **she got very little from her lessons** elle a très peu appris de ses leçons

3 *Radio, TV* **we can't g. Moscow/Channel 4** nous ne pouvons pas avoir Moscou/Channel 4; **we can only g. three channels here** nous ne pouvons recevoir que trois chaînes ici; **we g. the Guardian** (*newspaper*) nous achetons le Guardian; *Tel* **I had a job getting you** j'ai eu du mal à vous joindre; *Tel* **I couldn't g. her at the office** je n'ai pas pu l'avoir au bureau; *Tel* **g. me Washington 330 330** (*to operator*) appelez-moi Washington 330 330; **could you g. the phone/the door?** (*answer*) est-ce que tu peux décrocher?/ouvrir la porte?

4 (*catch*) prendre, attraper; (*train, bus*) prendre; (*cold, illness*) attraper; (*note down, record*) noter; *Fam* **we'll g. them yet!** on les aura!; **I'll g. you for that** je te revaudrai ça; **you've got me this time** (*caught me*) cette fois-ci vous m'avez eu; (*I don't know the answer*) je donne ma langue au chat; **the piranhas got him in the end** les piranhas ont fini par l'avoir

5 (*hit*) (*with fist, foot*) atteindre; (*with bullet, arrow, stone etc*) toucher; **he got a bullet in his shoulder** il a reçu une balle dans l'épaule

6 *Fam* (*move emotionally*) émouvoir; **the play didn't really g. me** la pièce ne m'a pas fait grand-chose

7 *Fam* (*annoy*) mettre en boule; **that gets me** *or* **gets my goat** ça me met en boule; **what gets me is that …** ce qui me met en boule, c'est que …

8 *Fam* (*understand*) comprendre; **I don't g. your meaning** je ne vous comprends pas; **if you g. my meaning** si tu vois ce que je veux dire; **g. me?** tu y es?, tu piges?; **oh, I g. you!** ah! j'ai pigé!; **I don't g. it** je ne comprends pas; **to g. a joke** comprendre une blague; **g. it?** (*do you understand the joke?*) tu piges?

9 *Sl* (*consider*) **g. a load of this!** (*listen*) écoute un peu ça!; **g. him!** (*he looks outrageous*) regarde-le, celui-là!; (*he made an outrageous remark*) écoute-le, celui-là!; **g. him, riding around in a Rolls when he's on the dole!** tu te rends compte, il roule en Rolls alors qu'il touche le chômage!

10 (*fetch*) aller chercher; **he went and got a book from the library** il est allé chercher un livre à la bibliothèque; **go and g. a doctor** allez chercher un médecin; **g. me the big screwdriver** allez me chercher le gros tournevis; **can I g. you anything?** (*to sb ill etc*) est-ce vous avez besoin de quelque chose?; **g. him a chair, someone** est-ce quelqu'un peut lui apporter une chaise?

11 (*prepare*) faire, préparer; **can I g. you an omelette?** est-ce que je peux vous faire une omelette?; **she got herself some breakfast** elle s'est préparé un petit déjeuner; **to g. lunch** (*ready*) préparer le déjeuner

12 (*move, send*) faire parvenir, faire transporter; **you'll never g. that box through the door** tu n'arriveras jamais à faire passer cette boîte par la porte; **they got her to the airport on time** ils l'ont amenée à l'aéroport à l'heure; **I got a message to them** je leur ai fait parvenir un message; **how can I g. it to you?** comment puis-je vous le faire parvenir?; **how am I to g. this parcel home?** (*by myself*) comment vais-je faire pour transporter ce paquet jusqu'à chez moi?; **to g. the children to bed** coucher les enfants, mettre les enfants au lit; *Fig* **where has all this got us?** (*our hard work, arguing*) où est-ce que tout ça nous a menés?; **this is getting us nowhere** (*of method, argument*) ça ne nous mène nulle part, ça ne nous mène à rien; **to g. sb on(to) a subject** amener qn à parler sur un sujet

13 (*cause to be*) **to g. sth dry/wet** sécher/mouiller qch; **to g. sth clean/dirty** nettoyer/salir qch; **to g. sb angry** mettre qn en colère; **to g. sb nervous** rendre qn nerveux; **I got myself terribly agitated** je me suis rendu malade; **they've got me so I don't know whether I'm coming or going** c'en est à un tel point que je ne sais plus où j'en suis; **I couldn't g. the drawer open** je n'arrivais pas à ouvrir le tiroir; **to g. the answer right** trouver la bonne réponse; **I got his name wrong** j'ai fait erreur sur son nom; **you've got him worried** tu l'as fait s'inquiéter; **to g. people interested (in sth)** intéresser les gens (à qch)

14 (*with pp or inf or prp*) (*cause*) **to g. sth done by sb, to g. sb to do sth** faire faire qch à *ou* par qn; **to g. sth mended** faire réparer qch; **to g. oneself noticed** se faire remarquer; **g. him to read it** faites-le-lui lire; **to g. sb to agree** décider qn à consentir; **you'll never g. him to admit to it** tu ne le lui feras jamais admettre; **we must g. him to come and see us** il faut le persuader de venir nous voir; **I can't g. the door to shut** je n'arrive pas à fermer la porte; **to g. one's work finished** venir à bout de son travail; **to g. one's dress**

torn déchirer sa robe; **to g. sb doing sth** faire faire qch à qn; **if you want to g. him going … (angry)** si tu veux le mettre en colère …; (*cause him to talk a lot*) si tu veux le faire parler …; **once he gets going, there's no stopping him** quand il commence, il n'y a plus moyen de l'arrêter; *Aut* **to g. the engine running** mettre le moteur en marche; **that got him guessing** ça l'a intrigué VOIR GRAMMAIRE A56–7

15 (*do eventually*) **to g. to do sth** finir par faire qch; **you'll g. to like him** vous finirez par l'aimer; **to g. to know sth** apprendre qch; **when you g. to know him** quand on le connaît mieux; **they got to be friends** ils sont devenus amis; **she got to be very rich** elle est devenue très riche

16 (*have opportunity to do*) **to g. to do sth** avoir l'occasion de faire qch; **as a diplomat she got to visit many countries** en tant que diplomate elle a pu visiter *ou* a eu l'occasion de visiter de nombreux pays; **I didn't g. to speak to him in person** je n'ai pas pu lui parler en personne; **I finally got to see the Taj Mahal** j'ai finalement réussi à voir le Taj Mahal

17 (*have*) **to have got** avoir; **have you got any children?** avez-vous des enfants?; **I haven't got any** je n'en ai pas; **have you got a light?** avez-vous du feu?; **what have you got there?** qu'avez-vous là?; **she's (really) got something** elle a (vraiment) quelque chose; **it's got something** (*of play, poem, song etc*) il y a quelque chose là-dedans; **he's got measles** il a la rougeole; **what's that got to do with it?** qu'est-ce que cela a à voir?; *Fam* **you've got it!** vous y êtes!, c'est ça! VOIR GRAMMAIRE A56

18 (*must*) **to have got to do sth** être obligé de *ou* devoir faire qch; **it has got to be done** il faut que cela soit fait; **have you really got to work on Sundays?** est-ce que vous êtes vraiment obligé de travailler le dimanche?; **but that's got to be the right answer!** c'est forcément la bonne réponse! VOIR GRAMMAIRE A60

VI 1 (*reach, make one's way*) arriver, se rendre (**to** à); **how does one g. there?** comment fait-on pour y aller?; **when I got home** quand je suis arrivé à la maison; **how do I g. to the station?** (*asking one's way*) où se trouve la gare?; **to g. there** (*reach a place*) arriver; (*reach a goal*) y arriver, réussir; **we're not getting anywhere, we're getting nowhere** nous n'aboutissons à rien, nous n'arrivons à rien, nous n'allons nulle part; **to g. to the top of a tree/ladder** monter jusqu'en haut d'un arbre/d'une échelle; **where has he got to?** où est-ce qu'il est passé?; **where have you got to?** (*in your work etc*) où en êtes-vous?; **she got to the door and turned round** elle est allée jusqu'à la porte et s'est retournée; **to g. to one's feet** se lever; **to g. to university** aller à l'université; **they only got as far as Marseilles** ils ne sont pas allés plus loin que Marseille; **he got as far as saying …** il a été jusqu'à dire …; **we got onto (the subject of) divorce** nous en sommes venus à parler de divorce; **it got to the point where they weren't speaking to one another** c'en est venu au point qu'ils ne se parlaient plus; **eventually we got to talking about politics** nous avons fini par en venir à parler de politique; *Sl* **it really gets to me** (*annoys me*) ça me met hors de moi; (*thrills me*) ça me fait quelque chose

2 (*move*) **to g. behind a tree** se mettre derrière un arbre; **she got inside the barrel** elle est rentrée dans le tonneau

3 **to g. to work** (*start working*) se mettre au travail; (*reach workplace*) arriver à son (lieu de) travail

4 (*with adj complement*) (*become*) devenir; **to g. old** devenir vieux, vieillir; **I'm getting**

used to it je commence à m'y habituer; **to g. angry** se mettre en colère; **to g. better** *(improve)* s'améliorer; *(after illness)* se remettre

5 *(with pp)* **to g. dressed** s'habiller; **to g. married** se marier; **to g. shaved** *(by self)* se raser; *(by barber)* se faire raser; **to g. killed** se faire tuer; **to g. drowned** se noyer; **to g. caught** *(by police etc)* se faire prendre; *(by rain etc)* être surpris; **he got sacked** il s'est fait renvoyer; **to g. started** commencer **VOIR GRAMMAIRE A54–5**

6 *(with prp)* *(start)* **to g. going** *(leave)* partir, se déplacer en route; *(start work)* se mettre au travail; *(hurry)* se dépêcher; **let's g. going** allons-y!; **to g. talking with sb** entrer en conversation avec qn

▸ **get about** vi **1** *(move around)* circuler; **he gets about a great deal** il se déplace beaucoup; **she can't g. about very easily** *(of invalid)* elle se déplace difficilement; **I don't g. about so much these days** *(of old person)* je ne sors plus tellement ces temps-ci

2 *(of news etc)* se répandre, circuler; **it got about that she was planning to resign** le bruit s'est répandu qu'elle projetait de démissionner

▸ **get across** vi **1** *(succeed in crossing)* traverser

2 *(communicate)* communiquer; **she can't g. across to her audience** elle ne peut pas communiquer avec son public; **our message is not getting across** notre message ne passe pas; *Theat* **the play didn't g. across to the audience** la pièce n'a pas passé la rampe

vt sep **1** *(over water, over street)* *(person)* faire traverser; **we couldn't g. the supplies across** *(across the river)* nous ne pouvions pas faire passer les vivres de l'autre côté; **it was easy to g. the people across** *(across the border)* il était facile de faire passer les gens

2 *Fam (communicate)* **I couldn't g. it across to him** je n'ai pas réussi à le lui faire comprendre; **we're not getting our message across** notre message ne passe pas

▸ **get ahead** vi **1** *(make progress)* avancer; **you'll never g. ahead unless you work hard** tu n'arriveras à rien si tu ne travailles pas dur

2 *(move in front)* prendre la tête

▸ **get along** vi **1** *(leave)* s'en aller, partir; **it's time for me to be getting along, it's time I was getting along** il est temps que je parte; *Fam* **g. along with you!** *(go away)* allez-vous-en!; *(that's silly, not true)* allons donc!, vous plaisantez!

2 *(progress)* **how are you getting along in your new job?** comment ça va, ton nouveau travail?; **how are you getting along in the new house?** comment ça va, dans la nouvelle maison?; **we've got along all right without their help/them** nous nous sommes bien débrouillés sans leur aide/eux

3 *(be on good terms)* (bien) s'entendre (**with** avec); **I wish I got along better with my neighbours** j'aimerais bien m'entendre mieux avec mes voisins

▸ **get around** vi **1** *(be active)* bouger; *(gain experience)* rouler sa bosse; **old people find it hard to g. around** les personnes âgées ont du mal à se déplacer; **she gets around a great deal** *(travels)* elle voyage beaucoup; **you g. around, don't you!** tu sors beaucoup, hein!

2 *(spread)* se répandre; **the word got around that he had some information** on a raconté qu'il avait des informations

vt insep *(avoid, circumvent)* *(difficulties)* couper à, échapper à; **there's no getting around it, we'll have to tell her** il n'y a pas d'autre moyen, il va falloir que nous le lui disions; **there's no getting around the fact that he lied to us** il reste qu'il nous a menti

▸ **get around to** vt insep **to g. around to doing sth** trouver le temps de faire qch; **I'll g.**

around to it one day je trouverai le temps de le faire un de ces jours; **could you g. around to telling me why you're here?** est-ce que tu pourrais enfin me dire pourquoi tu es ici?

▸ **get at** vt insep **1** *(reach, have access to)* *(place, person)* atteindre; **the study is locked and I can't g. at my books** le bureau est fermé à clef et je ne peux pas accéder à mes livres; **it's on the top shelf where the children can't g. at it** c'est sur l'étagère du haut où les enfants ne peuvent pas l'atteindre; **to g. at the truth** découvrir la vérité; *Fam* **just let me g. at him!** si jamais il me tombe sous la main!

2 *(imply)* **what are you getting at?** où voulez-vous en venir?

3 *Fam (suborn)* *(witness)* suborner

4 *Fam (criticize unfairly)* *(person)* attaquer; **she's always getting at her husband** elle est toujours à dénigrer son mari; **you're not being got at, no one's getting at you** on ne s'en prend pas à toi, personne ne s'en prend à toi

▸ **get away** vi *(leave)* partir; *(escape)* s'échapper, se sauver; **to g. away for a few days** s'absenter pendant quelques jours; **g. away!** allez-vous-en!; *Fam* **g. away (with you)!** *(stop joking)* tu plaisantes!, ça ne prend pas!; **car that gets away quickly** voiture qui a une bonne reprise

vt sep *(remove)* *(person)* emmener; *(object)* s'emparer de

▸ **get away from** vt insep *(leave, escape from)* *(place)* quitter; **to g. away early from the office** quitter le bureau de bonne heure; **I couldn't g. away from him** *(he wouldn't stop talking)* je ne pouvais pas m'en défaire; **how wonderful to g. away from it all!** quel plaisir de tout quitter!; *Fig* **there's no getting away from it** il faut bien l'admettre

vt sep *(remove from)* **g. that child away from the road!** éloignez cet enfant de la route!; **g. me away from here!** fais-moi sortir d'ici!; **g. your dog away from my garden!** faites sortir votre chien de mon jardin!; **they managed to g. him away from the TV** ils ont fini par l'arracher de devant la télévision; **to g. sth away from sb** prendre qch à qn

▸ **get away with** vt insep **1** *(escape with)* **the burglars got away with £10,000** les cambrioleurs sont repartis avec *ou* ont raflé 10,000 livres

2 *(be let off with)* s'en tirer avec; **he got away with a small fine** il s'en est tiré avec une petite amende

3 *(not be punished for)* **that child gets away with murder** on lui laisse tout faire à ce gamin; **children who play truant mustn't be allowed to g. away with it** les enfants qui font l'école buissonnière doivent être punis; **she pretended she was a doctor and she got away with it** elle a fait semblant d'être médecin et ça a marché; **her skirt is really short but she gets away with it** sa jupe est vraiment très courte mais elle peut se le permettre

▸ **get back** vi **1** *(return)* revenir, retourner; **when did you g. back?** quand est-ce que tu es rentré?; **I got back from Italy yesterday** je suis rentré d'Italie hier; **to g. back home** rentrer chez soi; **to g. back into bed** se recoucher

2 *(move away, step back)* reculer (**from** de); **g. back or I'll shoot!** reculez ou je tire!

vt sep **1** *(recover)* *(something)* récupérer; *(one's strength)* reprendre; **I'll g. the book back from her tomorrow** je lui demanderai de rendre le livre demain; **to g. one's money back** *(loan returned)* récupérer son argent; *(reimbursed)* se faire rembourser

2 *(return)* *(something)* rendre; **g. the file back to me as soon as possible** *(in person)* rendez-moi le dossier dès que possible; *(by*

post etc) faites en sorte que je récupère le dossier dès que possible

3 *(put back)* *(something)* remettre; **to g. sth back into its box** faire rentrer qch dans sa boîte

▸ **get back at** vt insep *(have revenge on)* se venger de

▸ **get back to** vt insep **1** *(return to)* retourner à; **to g. back to London** rentrer à Londres; **to g. back to work** *(after illness)* reprendre le travail; *(after short break)* se remettre au travail; **to g. back to nature** retourner à la nature

2 *(contact again)* recontacter; **can we g. back to you on that later?** est-ce que nous pouvons vous donner une réponse à ce sujet plus tard?

▸ **get behind** vi *(become delayed)* prendre du retard; **to g. behind with** *or* **in one's work** prendre du retard dans son travail; **to g. behind with the rent** être en retard pour payer son loyer

vt insep **1** *(move to the back of)* se mettre derrière; **g. behind that tree** mets-toi derrière cet arbre

2 *esp Am Fam (support, sympathize with)* appuyer

▸ **get by** vi **1** *(pass)* passer

2 *Fam (manage)* se débrouiller; **we just g. by** on s'en tire, sans plus; **he thinks he'll g. by without studying** il croit qu'il va s'en tirer sans étudier; **you can g. by on a few dollars a day** vous pouvez vous en tirer avec quelques dollars par jour

vt insep **1** *(move past)* **can you g. by the washing machine?** est-ce que vous avez assez de place pour passer à côté de la machine à laver?

2 *(escape attention of)* *(censor, editor)* échapper à

▸ **get down** vi **1** *(from wall, tree etc)* descendre (**from, off** de)

2 *(lower one's body)* **g. down or she'll see us!** baisse-toi sinon elle va nous voir!; **to g. down on one's knees** se mettre à genoux; **g. down!** *(to dog)* couché!

3 *(leave table)* quitter la table, sortir de table; **may I g. down?** est-ce que je peux quitter la table?

vt sep **1** *(bring, fetch down)* *(book from shelf etc)* descendre

2 *(reduce)* *(temperature, inflation etc)* faire baisser; **to g. one's weight down** perdre du poids

3 *(make a note of)* noter (**in writing, on paper** par écrit)

4 *(depress)* déprimer; **this rain is getting me down** cette pluie me déprime

5 *(swallow)* avaler; **try and g. this down (you)** essaye d'avaler ça

▸ **get down to** vt insep *(tackle)* se mettre à; **to g. down to work** se mettre au travail; **to g. down to doing sth** se mettre à faire qch; **we'd better g. down to the facts** il faut en venir aux faits; **we eventually got down to details** nous avons fini par en arriver aux détails; **when you g. down to it, there's very little difference between them** en fin de compte, il y a très peu de différence entre eux

▸ **get in** vi **1** *(gain entrance)* entrer; **how did the thieves g. in?** comment est-ce que les voleurs sont entrés?; **water had got in everywhere** l'eau avait pénétré partout

2 *(arrive)* *(of train etc)* arriver; **when does the London train g. in?** à quelle heure est-ce que le train de Londres arrive?; **we got in at about eleven** *(home)* nous sommes rentrés (chez nous) vers onze heures

3 *Pol (be elected)* être élu; **the Conservatives didn't g. in** les conservateurs n'ont pas été élus

vt insep *(enter)* **g. in the car!** monte dans la voiture!; **the smoke got in our eyes** la fumée nous est venue dans les yeux

VT SEP 1 *(summon)* *(doctor, police etc)* faire venir

2 *(bring in, bring inside)* *(washing, harvest etc)* rentrer; *(dog)* faire rentrer; **shouldn't Jack be in on this meeting? – of course, could you g. him in?** on n'a pas besoin de Jack pour cette réunion? – si, bien sûr, tu peux lui demander de venir?

3 *(plant in the ground)* planter, mettre en terre

4 *(manage to do)* réussir à faire; **she got in some last-minute revision before the exam** elle a réussi à faire des révisions de dernière minute avant l'examen; **I'd like to g. in some golf over the weekend** j'aimerais trouver le temps de faire un peu de golf ce week-end

5 *(insert)* faire pénétrer; **I couldn't g. a word in** je n'ai pas pu placer un mot, je n'ai pas pu en placer une

6 *(stock up with)* *(food, coal etc)* faire provision de; **to g. coal in for the winter** faire une provision de *ou* faire rentrer du charbon pour l'hiver; **to g. in a round of drinks** *(in pub)* payer une tournée; **I'll g. the pints in** je m'occupe des bières

7 *(assure of admission)* permettre d'entrer; **a press card should g. you in** une carte de presse devrait vous permettre d'entrer; **these exam results will g. you in** *(to university)* les notes que vous avez obtenues à l'examen vous permettront d'être admis

8 *(ensure election of)* *(person, party)* assurer l'élection de; **her reputation for integrity got her in** sa réputation d'intégrité a assuré son élection

▸ **get into VT INSEP 1** *(gain entrance to)* *(house etc)* entrer dans; *(car, train etc)* monter dans; **to g. into Parliament** être élu député; **to g. into university** entrer à la faculté

2 *(put on)* *(clothes)* mettre, enfiler; *(overcoat etc)* mettre, enfiler, endosser; **I can't g. into this dress any more** je n'entre plus dans cette robe

3 *(affect)* **I don't know what's got into her** je ne sais pas ce qu'elle a *ou* ce qui lui prend

4 *(become involved in)* **to g. into (a) conversation** entamer une conversation; **to g. into a fight** se bagarrer; **to g. into trouble** s'attirer des ennuis; **I got into trouble at school today** je me suis fait disputer à l'école aujourd'hui; **to g. into debt** s'endetter

5 **to g. into the way of doing sth** prendre l'habitude de faire qch; **the system may seem difficult but you'll soon g. into it** le système peut sembler difficile mais tu t'y feras vite

6 *Fam (become interested in)* *(music etc)* commencer à s'intéresser à; **it's a hard book to g. into** c'est un livre dans lequel il est difficile de rentrer

7 *(phrases)* **to g. into a panic** être pris de panique; **to g. into a rage** se mettre en rage; **to g. into a bad habit** acquérir *ou* prendre une mauvaise habitude

VT SEP 1 *(insert into)* **to g. sth into sth** (faire) (r)entrer qch dans qch; **to g. the key into the lock** mettre *ou* introduire la clef dans la serrure; **to g. an article into a paper** faire accepter un article par un journal; **to g. an idea into one's head** se mettre une idée en tête; **when are you going to g. it into your thick head that that isn't how things work?** quand est-ce que tu te mettras dans la tête que les choses ne se passent pas comme ça?

2 **you got me into this mess** tu m'as mis dans ce pétrin; **to g. sb into a rage** mettre quelqu'un en rage; **to g. sb into a good mood** mettre qn de bonne humeur; *Fam* **he got me into jazz** c'est lui qui m'a fait connaître le jazz

▸ **get in with VT INSEP 1** *(ingratiate oneself with)* s'insinuer dans les bonnes grâces de, se mettre bien avec; **if you want to g. in**

with him ... si tu veux te mettre bien avec lui ...

2 *(associate with)* *(person, group etc)* fréquenter; **he has got in with ...** il fréquente ...; **she got in with the wrong crowd at school** elle avait de mauvaises fréquentations à l'école

▸ **get off VI 1** *(descend from vehicle)* descendre; *Fig* **I told him where to g. off** *(rebuked him)* je lui ai dit ses quatre vérités

2 *(let go of sth)* lâcher; **hey! g. off! that's my book!** hé! laisse ça! c'est mon livre!

3 *(go unpunished)* s'en tirer; **to g. off lightly** s'en tirer à bon compte

4 *(leave, especially referring to work)* quitter, sortir; **I'd like to g. off early tomorrow** j'aimerais bien quitter (le travail) tôt *ou* sortir tôt (du travail) demain

5 to g. off (to sleep) s'endormir

6 to g. off to a late start commencer avec du retard; **to g. off to a good/bad start** bien/mal commencer

VT INSEP 1 *(descend from)* descendre de; **to g. off a bike** descendre d'une bicyclette; **g. off that wall!** descends de ce mur!; **g. off the grass!** ne marche pas sur la pelouse!

2 *(let go of)* **g. off me!** laisse-moi tranquille!, lâche-moi!

3 *(be exempted from)* couper à, échapper à; **he managed to g. off military service** il s'est débrouillé pour couper au service militaire

VT SEP 1 *(remove)* *(lid etc)* enlever; *(stain)* faire partir; **g. your feet off the table!** enlève tes pieds de sur la table!; **g. your hands off me/that cake** ne me touche pas/ne touche pas ce gâteau; **we got his clothes off** nous lui avons enlevé ses vêtements; *Fig* **to g. sth off one's chest** vider son sac

2 *(send)* *(letter)* expédier, envoyer; **to g. the children off to bed** envoyer les enfants au lit; **to g. a baby off (to sleep)** endormir un bébé; *Naut* **to g. a ship off** *(from sandbank etc)* renflouer un bateau, remettre un bateau à flot

3 *(save from punishment)* **to g. sb off** tirer qn d'affaire; *Law (person standing trial)* faire acquitter qn

4 *(have as holiday)* **to g. a day/week off** prendre un jour/une semaine de congé; **can you g. tomorrow afternoon/next week off?** est-ce que tu peux prendre un congé demain après-midi/la semaine prochaine?

5 *Fam (obtain)* **to g. sth off sb** obtenir qch de qn; **I got that story off the woman next door** je tiens cette histoire de la voisine; **I got this cold off the woman next door** la voisine m'a passé son rhume

6 *(free from)* **to g. sb off doing sth** dispenser qn de faire qch; **those burns got him off work** ces brûlures l'ont dispensé d'aller travailler

7 **that got the meeting off to a late start** la réunion a commencé en retard à cause de ça

▸ **get off on VT INSEP** *Fam* prendre son pied avec

▸ **get off with VT INSEP 1** *(a fine etc)* s'en tirer avec; **he got off with it for years before the police caught him** on l'a laissé tranquille pendant des années avant que la police ne l'arrête

2 *Br Fam* **to g. off with sb** *(have sex with)* coucher avec qn; **did you g. off with anybody at the party?** *(meet anybody)* tu as rencontré quelqu'un d'intéressant à la soirée?; **to g. off with each other** *(kiss etc)* se peloter

▸ **get on VI 1** *(board)* monter

2 *(succeed, progress)* réussir, progresser; **to g. on in life** *or* **in the world** arriver dans la vie

3 *(continue with work, journey)* continuer; **right, let's g. on, shall we?** bien, si on continuait?

4 *(cope, manage)* **how are you getting on?** *(how are you)* comment ça va?; *(at work)*

comment va votre travail?; **how did you g. on?** *(in exam, at dentist's)* comment ça s'est passé?; **I was getting on perfectly well without you** je me débrouillais très bien sans vous; **I'll let you know how he's getting on** je vous donnerai de ses nouvelles

5 *(have good relationship)* s'entendre; **to g. on well/badly with sb** bien/mal s'entendre avec qn

6 *(become late)* se faire tard; **time's getting on** l'heure tourne

7 *(age)* **to be getting on (in years)** se faire vieux

VT SEP *(put on)* *(clothing)* mettre, enfiler; **I can't g. these trousers on any more** je n'entre plus dans ce pantalon; **she's just getting her coat on** elle est en train de mettre *ou* d'enfiler son manteau; **I can't g. the lid on** je n'arrive pas à mettre le couvercle

VT INSEP 1 *(board, enter)* *(bus, train, plane etc)* monter dans

2 *(climb onto)* *(chair, ladder)* monter sur; *(with some effort)* grimper sur

3 how did these papers g. on my desk? comment est-ce que ces papiers se sont retrouvés *ou* sont arrivés sur mon bureau?

▸ **get on at VT INSEP** harceler; **he keeps getting on at me to have my hair cut** il est toujours après moi pour que je me fasse couper les cheveux; **you'll have to really g. on at her if you want her to do something** il va falloir que tu sois toujours derrière elle si tu veux qu'elle fasse quelque chose

▸ **get on for VT INSEP** *(approach)* **he must be getting on for forty** il doit approcher de *ou* friser la quarantaine; **it's getting on for midnight** il est presque minuit; **there were getting on for 200 people at the wedding** il y avait près de 200 personnes au mariage

▸ **get onto VT INSEP 1** *(contact)* contacter, se mettre en contact avec, se mettre en rapport avec; **I'll g. onto the bank about it** je vais contacter la banque à ce sujet; **I'll g. onto him to finish the work** je vais le contacter pour lui dire de finir le travail

2 *(locate, find name of)* *(person)* trouver le nom *ou* les coordonnées de; **how did you g. onto me?** comment est-ce que vous avez trouvé mon nom?

3 *(move forward to)* en arriver à; **they eventually got onto (the subject of) money** ils ont fini par en arriver à parler d'argent

4 = get on VT INSEP

▸ **get on with VT INSEP 1** *(have good relationship with)* s'entendre bien avec; **I don't g. on with my parents** je ne m'entends pas avec mes parents

2 *(continue with)* **how are you getting on with the painting?** alors, ça avance la peinture?; **just g. on with what you are supposed to be doing** *(said by teacher etc)* continuez ce que vous avez à faire; **let Dad g. on with his work** laissez Papa travailler en paix; **I wish the press would let me g. on with my life** si la presse pouvait me laisser vivre en paix; **I've got enough work to be getting on with** j'ai assez de travail à faire, j'ai assez de pain sur la planche

▸ **get out VI 1** *(leave)* sortir; *(from car)* descendre; *Fam* **g. out, you bastard!** fiche(-moi) le camp, espèce de salaud!

2 *(be released from prison, hospital)* sortir; **when does she g. out?** quand est-ce qu'elle sort?; **how did the news g. out?** comment la nouvelle s'est-elle répandue?; **the secret got out** le secret a transpiré

3 *(leave one's house, flat)* sortir (de chez soi); **he ought to g. out more** il devrait sortir plus

VT SEP 1 *(bring out)* *(tools, books etc)* sortir; **to g. one's car out** *(from garage)* sortir sa voiture; **to g. a book out from the library** emprunter un livre à la bibliothèque; **he could hardly g. a word out** c'est à peine s'il a pu sortir un mot; **we have to g. this report out by Monday** nous devons sortir ce rapport pour lundi

2 *(free) (hostages etc)* libérer

3 *(remove)* enlever; *(nail etc)* arracher; *(cork)* retirer; *(stain)* faire disparaître

4 *Cr (batsman)* renverser le guichet à

▸ **get out of** VT INSEP **1** *(leave)* sortir de; *(car)* descendre de; **let's g. out of here** partons d'ici; **he managed to g. out of the country** *(of criminal, refugee)* il a réussi à quitter le pays; **to g. out of bed** se lever; **to g. out of prison/the army** sortir de prison/quitter l'armée; **to g. out of sb's way** s'écarter du chemin de qn, faire place à qn; *Sl* **g. the hell out of here!** fiche(-moi) le camp!

2 *(extricate oneself from)* se faire exempter de; **to g. out of doing sth** se faire exempter de faire qch; **he always gets out of doing the washing-up** il arrive toujours à couper à la corvée de vaisselle; **to g. out of a difficulty** se tirer d'une position difficile; **I'd like to see her g. out of this one** j'aimerais bien voir comment elle va s'en tirer cette fois

3 *(become unaccustomed to)* **to g. out of (the habit of) doing sth** perdre l'habitude de faire qch

VT SEP **1** *(bring out of)* sortir de; **g. the phone book out of the drawer** sors l'annuaire du tiroir; **she got the nail out of her shoe** elle a retiré le clou de sa chaussure; **to g. a secret out of sb** arracher un secret à qn; **I can't g. anything out of him** je ne peux rien en tirer; **we finally got the truth out of her** nous avons fini par lui arracher la vérité; **I can't g. the idea out of my mind** je ne peux pas chasser cette idée de mon esprit; **to g. money out of sb** soutirer de l'argent à qn; **I got ten pounds out of it** j'y ai gagné dix livres; **to g. sb out of a difficulty** tirer qn d'affaire; **the firemen got us out of the building** les pompiers nous ont fait sortir du bâtiment; **to g. a stain out of a carpet** enlever une tache d'un tapis

2 *(derive from)* **I didn't g. much out of my lessons** je n'ai pas tiré grand-chose de mes leçons; **he could have got more out of the experience** il aurait pu tirer davantage de l'expérience

▸ **get over** VI **1** *(over road etc)* traverser; **to g. over to France/America** aller en France/Amérique; **to g. over to visit sb** *(in another city, country etc)* aller rendre visite à qn; **we'll try to g. over next weekend** *(to visit)* nous essayerons de venir le week-end prochain; **the wall was low, it was easy to g. over** le mur était bas, il a été facile de le franchir

2 *(communicate)* **to g. over to sb** se faire comprendre de qn

VT INSEP **1** *(cross) (wall etc)* escalader, passer par-dessus; *(road, river etc)* franchir

2 *(recover from) (illness)* se remettre de; *(difficulties)* venir à bout de; *(surprise)* revenir de; **she can't g. over it** *(illness, emotional shock, trauma)* elle ne s'en remet pas; *(surprise, shock etc)* elle n'en revient pas; *(loss)* elle est inconsolable; **it will take her a long time to g. over it** elle s'en ressentira longtemps, ça lui prendra longtemps pour s'en remettre

3 *(overcome) (fear etc)* surmonter

VT SEP **1** *(communicate)* faire passer; **she got her point over very well** elle a très bien fait passer ce qu'elle voulait dire

2 *(to other side of something)* faire passer; **we got the children over the road** nous avons fait traverser la route aux enfants

▸ **get over with** VT SEP *(complete)* terminer, finir; **she got her work over with as quickly as possible** elle a fini son travail aussi vite que possible; **when I g. my exams over with, I'll be able to relax** quand j'aurai terminé mes examens, je pourrai me détendre; **let's**

g. it over with as quickly as possible finissons-en au plus vite

▸ **get round** VI **1** **it would take a day to g. round** *(round the exhibition, museum)* ça prendrait une journée pour en faire le tour

2 **the doctor said she'd g. round as soon as she could** le docteur a dit qu'elle viendrait *ou* passerait dès qu'elle pourrait; **I didn't manage to g. round to each pupil in the class** je n'ai pas réussi à m'occuper de chaque élève de la classe

3 *(of news, rumour)* se répandre; **news gets round pretty quickly in small towns** les nouvelles circulent vite dans les petites villes

VT INSEP **1** *(exhibition, museum)* faire le tour de; *(corner)* passer

2 *(circumvent) (difficulty, regulations etc)* contourner; *(persuade) (person)* embobiner; **there's no getting round it** *(you'll have to own up)* il n'y a pas moyen d'y couper; **will you be able to g. round your dad?** est-ce que tu réussiras à persuader ton père?; **how did they g. round the regulations?** comment est-ce qu'ils ont réussi à contourner les réglementations?

VT SEP **1** *(bring, take)* **I'll g. the books round (to you)** as soon as I can je t'apporterai les livres dès que je le pourrai

2 *(persuade)* **we eventually got him round to our way of thinking** nous avons finalement réussi à le convaincre

▸ **get round to** VT INSEP = **get around to**

▸ **get through** VI **1** *(arrive)* **the road was blocked and no one could g. through** la route était bloquée et personne ne pouvait passer; **the message didn't g. through** le message n'est pas passé; **only a few trains got through to the besieged city** seuls quelques trains sont arrivés jusqu'à la ville assiégée; **the news got through to them** la nouvelle leur est parvenue

2 *Tel* obtenir la communication (**to sb** avec qn); *Fig (communicate)* se faire comprendre (**to sb** de qn); *Fig* **I'm not getting through (to you), am I?** je ne me fais pas bien comprendre, hein?

3 *Am (finish)* finir, terminer; **the class doesn't usually g. through until six o'clock** la leçon ne se termine généralement pas avant six heures

4 *(pass exam)* être reçu

VT INSEP **1** *(pass through) (hole etc)* passer à travers; **I thought I'd never g. through the day** j'ai cru que la journée n'en finirait jamais; **they got through the day without a single argument** ils ne se sont pas disputés une seule fois de toute la journée; **the Government may have difficulty getting through another six months** le gouvernement aura peut-être du mal à tenir encore six mois; **I couldn't g. through another winter in Moscow** je ne pourrais pas passer un hiver de plus à Moscou; **you won't g. through the roadblock** tu n'arriveras pas à franchir le barrage routier

2 *(succeed in) (exam)* être reçu à, réussir

3 *(finish) (work etc)* achever, arriver au bout de; *(food, drink etc)* consommer; **to g. through a lot of work** abattre beaucoup de travail

4 *(use up)* **he gets through eight shirts a week** il salit huit chemises par semaine; **we'll never g. through all this food** nous ne viendrons jamais à bout de toute cette nourriture; **she gets through her wages very quickly** elle dépense son salaire très rapidement

VT SEP **1** *(transport, send successfully)* faire parvenir; **they got the food supplies through** ils ont réussi à faire parvenir les provisions alimentaires (à destination); **to g. sth through customs** (faire) passer qch à la douane; **they got a message through** ils ont fait passer un message; **you'll never g.**

that desk through tu n'arriveras jamais à faire passer ce bureau; *Parl* **to g. a bill through** faire adopter un projet de loi

2 **I finally got it through to him that I wasn't interested** j'ai fini par lui faire comprendre que je n'étais pas intéressé

3 *(cause to succeed)* **it was your essay that got you through (the exam)** c'est grâce à ta dissertation que tu as réussi l'examen

4 *(enable to endure)* **I need four cups of coffee to g. me through the day** il me faut mes quatre tasses de café par jour

▸ **get together** VI *(of people)* se réunir, se rassembler (**to do** pour faire); **the two countries got together to deal with coastal pollution** les deux pays ont collaboré pour s'attaquer au problème de la pollution côtière

VT SEP *(collect) (objects)* rassembler; *(friends etc)* réunir; **g. your things together, we're going** rassemble tes affaires, nous partons; **to g. some money together** réunir une somme d'argent; **let me g. my thoughts together** laissez-moi rassembler mes idées

▸ **get under** VT INSEP *(get into position beneath) (table etc)* se mettre sous; **they got under the fence and escaped** ils sont passés sous la clôture et se sont enfuis

VT SEP *(place beneath)* mettre *ou* placer sous; **I can't g. the carpet under the table** je n'arrive pas à placer le tapis sous la table

▸ **get up** VI **1** *(get out of bed)* se lever; *(stand up)* se lever, se mettre debout; **g. up!** levez-vous!; **to g. up from a chair/the table** se lever de sa chaise/de table

2 *Met* **the wind/a storm was getting up** le vent/une tempête se levait

VT INSEP *(climb) (stairs)* monter; *(ladder)* monter à; *(mountain)* faire l'ascension de

VT SEP **1** **to g. up speed** prendre de la vitesse

2 *(organize) (party etc)* organiser; *Pol* **to g. up a petition** organiser *ou* faire une pétition

3 *(move up)* monter; **how are we going to g. this desk up to the fifth floor?** comment allons-nous monter ce bureau jusqu'au cinquième étage?; **to g. sb up the stairs** *(help climb)* aider qn à monter l'escalier

4 *(rouse)* faire (se) lever; **have you got the children up?** est-ce que tu as fait lever les enfants?

5 **to g. oneself up as sb/sth** *(dress up)* se déguiser en qn/qch

6 *Vulg* **to g. it up** *(achieve an erection)* bander; **he couldn't g. it up** il n'a pas réussi à bander

▸ **get up to** VT INSEP **1** *(reach)* arriver à; **it took ages to g. up to the top of the hill** ça a pris une éternité pour arriver en haut de la colline; **I've got up to chapter 5** j'en suis au chapitre 5; **where have you got up to?** *(in your reading etc)* où en êtes-vous?

2 *(do)* **those children are always getting up to something** *or* **to some mischief** ces enfants sont toujours en train de faire des bêtises; **what have you been getting up to?** qu'est-ce que tu as fabriqué?; **the dog's been getting up to his usual tricks** le chien a encore fait des siennes

getatable, get-at-able [get'ætəb(ə)l] ADJ *Fam* accessible, d'accès facile

getaway ['getəweɪ] N *(of criminal)* fuite *f*; **to make one's g.** s'enfuir

▸▸ **g. car** = voiture *f* utilisée pour s'enfuir

get-go N *Am Fam* **from the g.** *(from the beginning)* dès le début; **he's a crook from the g.** *(completely)* c'est un escroc total, c'est un véritable escroc

Gethsemane [geθ'semənɪ] N Gethsémani *m*

get-rich-quick ADJ *Fam* **a g. scheme** un stratagème pour s'enrichir rapidement

get-together N *Fam* réunion *f*; **I'm having a**

g. with some friends nous faisons une petite soirée entre amis; **you and I must have a little g. one day** il faut qu'on se voie un de ces jours tous les deux

get-up N *Fam* **1** *(clothes)* accoutrement *m*, tenue *f*; *(fancy dress)* déguisement *m*; **what a g.!** quel accoutrement! **2** *Com (of merchandise)* présentation *f*

get-up-and-go N *Fam* allant *m*, entrain *m*; **where's your g.?** allez, remue-toi!

get-well(-soon) card N = carte *f* que l'on envoie à un malade pour lui souhaiter un prompt rétablissement

gewgaw ['gjuːgɔː] N babiole *f*

geyser ['giːzər] N **1** *Geol* geyser *m* **2** *Old-fashioned Br (water heater)* chauffe-eau *m inv* à gaz

G-force N pesanteur *f*

Ghana ['gɑːnə] N Ghana *m*

Ghanaian, Ghanian [gɑːˈneɪən, ˈgɑːnɪən] N Ghanéen, -éenne

ADJ ghanéen

ghastliness ['gɑːstlɪnɪs] N *(of crime)* horreur *f*

ghastly ['gɑːstlɪ] ADJ **1** *(experience)* horrible, affreux, épouvantable; **what a g. weather!** quel temps épouvantable *ou* abominable!; **a g. mistake** une erreur monstrueuse **2** *(pale)* blême; *(pallor)* mortel; *(light)* blafard; **he looked g.** il avait l'air d'un déterré

ghee [giː] N *Culin* beurre *m* clarifié

Ghent [gent] N Gand *m*

gherkin ['gɜːkɪn] N cornichon *m*; **pickled gherkins** cornichons au vinaigre

ghetto ['getəʊ] N ghetto *m*

▸▸ *Fam* **g. blaster** = grand radiocassette *m* portatif

ghillie ['gɪlɪ] N = gillie

ghost [gəʊst] N **1** fantôme *m*, spectre *m*; **to believe in ghosts** croire aux revenants *ou* fantômes; **you look as if you've seen a g.** comme tu es pâle, tu as l'air d'avoir reçu un sacré choc; **to be the mere g. of one's former self** n'être plus que l'ombre de soi-même; **not the g. of a chance** pas la moindre chance; **g. of a smile** esquisse *f* de sourire **2** *Rel* **the Holy G.** l'Esprit *m* Saint, le Saint-Esprit **3** *Arch (soul)* âme *f*; *Fig* **to give up the g.** *(die)* rendre l'âme, expirer; *Fig Fam* **the car finally gave up the g. yesterday** la voiture a finalement rendu l'âme hier **4** *Opt* spectre *m* secondaire, image *f* blanche; *TV* écho *m* **5** *Liter (ghostwriter)* nègre *m*

VI *Liter* servir de nègre (**for an author** à un écrivain)

VT *Liter (sb's speeches)* écrire; **to g. a book** servir de nègre pour l'écriture d'un livre; **ghosted work** ouvrage écrit par un nègre

▸▸ **g. ship** vaisseau *m* fantôme; *Mktg* **g. shopping** achats *mpl* simulés pour audit; **g. story** histoire *f* de revenants; **g. town** ville *f* fantôme

ghosting ['gəʊstɪŋ] N *TV* images *fpl* fantôme

ghostly ['gəʊstlɪ] ADJ spectral, -aux

ghostwrite ['gəʊstraɪt] VT = ghost VT

ghostwriter ['gəʊstraɪtər] N nègre *m*

ghoul [guːl] N **1** *(evil spirit)* goule *f*, *Fig (person)* personne *f* qui a des goûts macabres *ou* morbides; **a crowd of ghouls had gathered at the scene of the accident** une foule d'amateurs de spectacles macabres s'était assemblée sur la scène de l'accident **2** *Old-fashioned (grave robber)* déterreur *m* de cadavre

ghoulish ['guːlɪʃ] ADJ **1** *(humour etc)* macabre **2** *Myth* de goule

GHQ [dʒiːeɪtʃˈkjuː] N *Mil (abbr* **General Headquarters)** QG *m inv*

GHz *(abbr* **gigahertz)** GHz *m*

GI [dʒiːˈaɪ] N *Fam* GI **(Joe)** soldat *m* américain, GI *m inv*; **GI bride** = femme *f* étrangère ayant épousé un GI

giant ['dʒaɪənt] N *Myth, Fig* géant *m*

ADJ *(oak, package)* géant; **with g. strides** à pas de géant

▸▸ *Br Sport* **g. killer** vainqueur *m* surprise

giantess [dʒaɪənˈtes] N géante *f*

Gib [dʒɪb] N *Fam* Gibraltar *m*

gibber ['dʒɪbər] VI *(like a monkey, an idiot)* produire des sons inarticulés; *(of foreigners speaking amongst themselves)* baragouiner; **he was gibbering with rage/fear** il bégayait de rage/frayeur; **it reduced him to a gibbering wreck** il en est devenu bègue; *Fam* **gibbering idiot** espèce de crétin

gibberish ['dʒɪbərɪʃ] N baragouin *m*, charabia *m*; **to talk g.** raconter n'importe quoi

gibbet ['dʒɪbɪt] N gibet *m*, potence *f*

gibbon ['gɪbən] N *(monkey)* gibbon *m*

gibbous ['gɪbəs] ADJ *Astron (moon)* gibbeux

gibe [dʒaɪb] N raillerie *f*, quolibet *m*; **to make a g.** lancer une raillerie *ou* un quolibet (**at** à)

VI **to g. at sb** railler qn, se moquer de qn

giblets ['dʒɪblɪts] NPL *(of poultry)* abats *mpl*, abattis *mpl*

Gibraltar [dʒɪˈbrɔːltər] N Gibraltar *m*

giddily ['gɪdɪlɪ] ADV **1** *(to rise)* de manière vertigineuse **2** *(frivolously)* étourdiment

giddiness ['gɪdɪnɪs] N **1** *(vertigo)* étourdissement *m*, vertige *m*; **fits of g.** des étourdissements, des vertiges **2** *(frivolousness)* frivolité *f*

giddy ['gɪdɪ] ADJ **1** *(dizzy) (person)* étourdi; **to be** *or* **feel g.** avoir le vertige; **I feel g.** la tête me tourne; **it makes me (feel) g.** cela me donne le vertige **2** *(height)* vertigineux, qui donne le vertige **3** *(frivolous)* frivole; **g. round of pleasures** tourbillon *m* de plaisirs; *Br Old-fashioned* **oh my g. aunt!** ciel!

GIF [gɪf] N *Comput (abbr* **Graphic Information Format)** GIF *m*

gift [gɪft] N **1** *(to individual)* cadeau *m*; **it was a g.** c'était un cadeau; *(of bargain)* c'était donné; *Fam (easy victory)* c'était un jeu d'enfants; **I wouldn't have it as a g.** je n'en voudrais pas même si on m'en faisait cadeau; *Prov* **never look a g. horse in the mouth** à cheval donné on ne regarde pas la bouche **2** *(donation)* don *m*; **a g. of £2,000** un don de 2 000 livres; **to make a g. of sth to sb** faire don de qch à qn; *Law* **as a g.** en cadeau; **in the g. of sb** à la discrétion de qn **3** *Com (on presentation of coupons)* prime *f*; **free g.** cadeau *m* **4** *(talent)* don *m*; **to have a g. for mathematics** avoir le don *ou Fam* la bosse des mathématiques

▸▸ **g. shop** boutique *f* de cadeaux; *Fin* **g. tax** impôt *m* sur les donations; **g. token**, *Br* **g. voucher** bon *m* d'achat

gifted ['gɪftɪd] ADJ doué; *(artist)* de talent

giftwrap ['gɪftræp] VT emballer *(et faire un paquet-cadeau)*; **shall I g. it?** je vous fais un paquet-cadeau?

giftwrapped ['gɪftræpt] ADJ *Com (article)* sous paquet-cadeau; **would you like it g.?** c'est pour offrir?, je vous fais un paquet-cadeau?

giftwrapping ['gɪftræpɪŋ] N *(paper, ribbons etc)* emballage-cadeau *m*

gig¹ [gɪg] N **1** *(carriage)* cabriolet *m* **2** *Naut* yole *f*

gig² N *Mus Fam* concert *m*

giga- ['gɪgə] PREF giga-

gigabyte ['gɪgəbaɪt] N *Comput* gigaoctet *m*

gigahertz ['gɪgəhɜːts] N gigahertz *m*

gigantic [dʒaɪˈgæntɪk] ADJ géant, gigantesque; *(building, bridge)* colossal

gigantically [dʒaɪˈgæntɪklɪ] ADV de façon démesurée

giggle ['gɪg(ə)l] N petit rire *m*; *(of young girl)* gloussement *m*, rire *m* bébête; **to have (a fit of) the giggles** avoir le fou rire; **to give a nervous g.** avoir un petit rire nerveux; *Fam* **to do sth for a g.** faire qch pour se marrer *ou* pour rigoler; **the evening was a g. from start to finish** on s'est marré toute la soirée; **she was a real g. as usual** elle était tordante comme d'habitude

VI avoir un petit rire; *(nervously)* rire nerveusement; *(of young girls)* glousser, rire bêtement; **what are you giggling about?** qu'est-ce qui vous fait rire?

giggling ['gɪg(ə)lɪŋ] ADJ qui pousse de petits rires; *(nervously)* qui rit avec nervosité; *(young girl)* qui glousse, qui rit bêtement

N petits rires *mpl*; *(nervous)* petits rires nerveux; *(of young girl)* rires bébêtes, gloussements *mpl*

giggly ['gɪg(ə)lɪ] ADJ qui se met à rire bêtement pour un rien; **to get** *or* **go all g.** se mettre à rire bêtement; **to be in a g. mood** être d'humeur joyeuse

GIGO [dʒiːaɪdʒiːˈəʊ] *Comput Sl abbr* **garbage in, garbage out**

gigolo ['dʒɪgələʊ] N gigolo *m*

gigot ['dʒɪgət] N gigot *m*

gild [gɪld] VT *(pt* **gilded**; *pp* **gilded**, *occ* **gilt** [gɪlt]*)* dorer; *Fig* **to g. the lily** surcharger; *Lit* **gilded youth** la jeunesse dorée; **to be like a bird in a gilded cage** vivre dans une prison dorée

gilding ['gɪldɪŋ] N dorure *f*

gill¹ [gɪl] N *(usu pl)* **1** *(of fish)* **gills** ouïes *fpl*, branchies *fpl* **2** **gills** *(of mushroom)* lamelles *fpl* **3** *Fam* **to be** *or* **look green about the gills** *(look ill)* avoir le teint verdâtre *ou* jaune; *(through disgust, shock etc)* être vert; **he went green about the gills** *(looked ill)* son teint est devenu verdâtre *ou* jaune; *(through disgust, shock etc)* il est devenu vert

gill² [dʒɪl] N *(measure)* quart *m* de pinte *(= 0,142 l)*

gillie ['gɪlɪ] N *Scot* serviteur *m* *(de chasseur, pêcheur etc)*

gillyflower ['dʒɪlɪflaʊər] N **1** *(wallflower)* giroflée *f* jaune *ou* des murailles **2** *(clove)* **g.** œillet *m* giroflée

gilt [gɪlt] PP *see* **gild**

ADJ *(frame etc)* doré

N *(gold)* dorure *f*, doré *m*; *St Exch* **gilts** fonds *mpl* d'État, *Fam* valeurs *fpl* de tout repos *ou* de père de famille; *Fam* **that takes the g. off the gingerbread** voilà qui enlève le charme *ou* l'attrait

gilt-edged ADJ *(book)* doré sur tranche

▸▸ *St Exch* **g. market** marché *m* des valeurs de premier ordre; *St Exch* **g. market maker** teneur *m* de marché des valeurs de premier ordre; *St Exch* **g. stock(s)** fonds *mpl* d'État

gimbals ['dʒɪmb(ə)lz] NPL *Aviat, Naut etc* (suspension *f* à) cardan *m*

gimcrack ['dʒɪmkræk] ADJ *Old-fashioned (furniture)* de pacotille; *(house)* en carton; *(jewellery)* en toc; *(scheme, theory etc)* à la noix

gimlet ['gɪmlɪt] N **1** *Carp (tool)* vrille *f*, foret *m* à bois; *Fig* **g. eyes** yeux *mpl* perçants **2** *(cocktail)* = cocktail *m* à base de gin ou de vodka et de jus de citron vert

gimme ['gɪmɪ] CONTR *Sl* = **give me**

gimmick ['gɪmɪk] N truc *m*, astuce *f*; **advertising g.** astuce *ou* truc publicitaire

gimmickry ['gɪmɪkrɪ] N astuces fpl

gimmicky ['gɪmɪkɪ] ADJ plein d'astuces; **a bit too g.** trop artificiel

gin¹ [dʒɪn] N (drink) gin m; (made in Holland) genièvre m
▸▸ Fam Hum **g. palace** troquet m; Cards **g. rummy** gin-rummy m, gin-rami m

gin² N **1** (trap) piège m **2** Tex (cotton) **g.** égreneuse f de coton

ginger ['dʒɪndʒər] N **1** Bot, Culin gingembre m; **preserved** or **crystallized g.** gingembre confit; **g. biscuit** biscuit m au gingembre **2** Fam (liveliness) énergie f **3** (redhead) **hi, g.!** ohé, poil de carotte! **4** Scot Fam (fizzy drink) boisson f gazeuse
ADJ Fam (hair) roux, f rousse
▸▸ **g. ale** = boisson f gazeuse aux extraits de gingembre pouvant servir à couper un alcool; **g. beer** = limonade f au gingembre; **g. group** = dans une organisation politique ou autre, faction dynamique cherchant à faire bouger les choses en incitant à l'action; **g. snap,** Br **g. nut** biscuit au gingembre; **g. wine** = boisson alcoolisée à base de gingembre
▸ **ginger up** VT SEP Fam (apathetic person) secouer les puces à; (film, text, storyline etc) donner du punch à; **we need something to g. up the party** il nous faut quelque chose pour mettre un peu d'animation dans la soirée

gingerbread ['dʒɪndʒəbred] N Culin pain m d'épice
▸▸ **g. man** bonhomme m en biscuit parfumé au gingembre

gingerly ['dʒɪndʒəlɪ] ADV avec précaution; (trying not to make a noise) doucement; **he stepped g. between the cowpats** il a avancé précautionneusement entre les bouses de vache

gingery ['dʒɪndʒərɪ] ADJ **1** (taste) de gingembre **2** (hair, colour) qui tire sur le roux

gingham ['gɪŋəm] N Tex vichy m; **g. curtains/dress** rideaux/robe en vichy

gingivitis [dʒɪndʒɪ'vaɪtɪs] N Med gingivite f

ginormous [dʒaɪ'nɔːməs] ADJ Fam gigantesque, énorme

ginseng ['dʒɪnseŋ] N ginseng m

gippo ['dʒɪpəʊ] N Br Offensive Sl romanichel, -elle

gippy ['dʒɪpɪ] ADJ Fam **to have a g. tummy** avoir la courante

gipsy ['dʒɪpsɪ] N bohémien, -ienne, Pej romanichel, -elle; (Spanish) gitan, -ane
▸▸ **g. caravan** roulotte f; **g. moth** zigzag m, bombyx m disparate

gipsyish ['dʒɪpsɪɪʃ] ADJ comme un bohémien ou Pej un romanichel; (dark-skinned) brun de peau

giraffe [dʒɪ'ræf, -'rɑːf] N girafe f

gird [gɜːd] VT (pt, pp **girded, girt** [gɜːt]) Arch, Lit **1** (wrap around with a belt) ceindre; **to g. up one's loins** se ceindre les reins; **to g. (on) one's sword** ceindre son épée **2** (surround) ceindre (**with** de)

girder ['gɜːdər] N Constr poutre f (métallique)

girdle¹ ['gɜːd(ə)l] N (corset) gaine f, (belt) ceinture f
VT Lit ceindre, entourer

girdle² N = **griddle**

girl [gɜːl] N fille f, (young woman) jeune fille, jeune femme f, **little g.** petite fille, fillette f, **when I was a g.** quand j'étais petite; **g.'s name** prénom m féminin ou de fille; **girls' school** école f de filles; Br Sch **old g.** ancienne élève f, **a French/an Indian g.** une jeune Française/Indienne; **his g.** (daughter) sa fille; Old-fashioned (girlfriend) sa petite amie; **the Smith(s') g.** la fille (des) Smith;

that's my g.! (well done) bravo!, très bien!; Old-fashioned **my dear g.!** ma chère!; Old-fashioned Fam **the old g.** la vieille femme, Pej la vieille; (wife) ma femme, la bourgeoise; (mother) ma mère; (boss) la patronne; (car) ma vieille voiture ou bagnole; Old-fashioned **hello, old g.!** salut, ma vieille!
▸▸ **g. band** girls band m; **G. Guide** éclaireuse f, **g. power** = slogan m associé au groupe féminin britannique The Spice Girls, revendiquant l'égalité des sexes; **G. Scout** éclaireuse

girlfriend ['gɜːlfrend] N (of boy, man) petite amie f, (of girl, woman) amie, Fam copine f

girlhood ['gɜːlhʊd] N (childhood) enfance f, (young womanhood) jeunesse f, **in my g.** dans ma jeunesse, quand j'étais jeune fille

girlie ['gɜːlɪ] N Fam **1** (effeminate boy) fillette f **2** Br (young woman) (jeune) fille f, **to have a g. chat** bavarder entre filles
▸▸ **g. magazine** magazine m de femmes à poil

girlish ['gɜːlɪʃ] ADJ **1** (behaviour) de fille; (figure) de jeune fille; **g. laughter** un rire de (petite) jeune fille **2** (boy) efféminé; **g. good looks** air enfantin ou de très jeune fille

girlishly ['gɜːlɪʃlɪ] ADV (to behave, dress) comme une petite fille

giro ['dʒaɪrəʊ] N Br **1** (system) = système m de virement interbancaire introduit par la Poste britannique; Banking **National G.** = service m de chèques postaux; **bank g.** virement m bancaire **2** Fam (for unemployed) chèque m d'allocation de chômage; **I haven't had my g. (cheque) yet** (unemployment benefit) mon allocation de chômage ne m'a pas encore été payée
▸▸ **g. account** compte m chèque postal, CCP m; **g. cheque** chèque m postal, chèque de virement; **g. transfer** transfert m par CCP

Girobank ['dʒaɪrəʊbæŋk] N = service m bancaire de la Poste britannique

girt PT, PP see **gird**

-girt [gɜːt] SUFF Lit **sea-g. isle** île f encerclée par les mers

girth [gɜːθ] N **1** (circumference) (of tree etc) circonférence f, (of chest, waist) tour m; **of considerable g.** (of person) d'une belle corpulence **2** (on harness) sangle f, **saddle g.** sangle de selle

gismo ['gɪzməʊ] N = **gizmo**

gist [dʒɪst] N (of conversation) essentiel m; (of question) point m essentiel; **to get the g. (of the matter)** saisir l'essentiel; **could you just give me the g. (of it) now?** pourrais-tu m'en donner l'essentiel?; **I got the g. of what she was saying** j'ai compris l'essentiel de ce qu'elle disait; **the g. of what she was saying was …** elle a dit en substance …

git [gɪt] N Br Sl con, f conne; **stupid g.!** espèce de con/conne!

GIVE (pt **gave** [geɪv], pp **given** ['gɪv(ə)n])

VT donner 1–3, 5, 7, 8	▪ accorder 6
▪ faire 9	▪ rendre 10
VI donner 1	▪ céder 2
N élasticité	

VT **1** (present, bestow, pledge, provide) **to g. sth to sb, to g. sb sth** donner qch à qn; **to g. sb a present** faire ou donner un cadeau à qn; **to g. an example** donner un exemple; **to g. a discount** accorder un escompte; Fml **to g. a dinner** (in honour of sb) donner un dîner; **to g. sb one's hand** (to hold) donner ou tendre la main à qn; **to g. sb a note from sb** remettre à qn un petit mot de qn; **to g. no sign of life** ne donner aucun signe de vie; **to g. sb sth to eat/drink** donner à manger/à boire à qn; **to g. sb six months' imprisonment** condamner qn à six mois de prison; **he was

given life il a été condamné à perpétuité; **to g. a child a name** donner un nom à un enfant; **to g. sb a job to do** assigner une tâche à qn; **g. her my love** embrasse-la pour moi; **to g. sb one's support** prêter son appui à qn; Euph **she gave herself to him** elle s'est donnée à lui; **g. me the good old days!** parlez-moi du bon vieux temps!; **g. me British weather any day!** rien ne vaut le climat de la Grande-Bretagne!
2 (in exchange) donner; **to g. a good price for sth** donner ou payer un bon prix pour qch; **I'll g. you £10 for it** je vous en donnerai 10 livres; **to g. sth in exchange for sth** donner en échange de ou contre qch; **to g. one's life for one's beliefs** donner sa vie pour ses convictions; **I would g. a lot** or **a great deal to know …** je donnerais beaucoup pour savoir …
3 (devote) donner, consacrer; **to g. oneself to one's studies** se consacrer entièrement ou s'adonner à ses études; **to g. one's attention to sth** porter son attention sur qch; **he gave it considerable thought** il y a beaucoup réfléchi; **I've given you six years of my life** je t'ai donné six ans de ma vie; **she gave this job the best years of her life** elle a consacré à ce travail les plus belles années de sa vie
4 (do) **to g. a laugh** rire, laisser échapper un rire; **to g. a sigh** soupirer, pousser un soupir; **to g. sb's hand a squeeze** serrer la main à qn; **to g. sb a smile** faire un sourire à qn; **he gave me an odd look** il m'a lancé un regard singulier; **she gave her hair a comb** elle s'est donnée un coup de peigne; **he gave his face a wash** il s'est lavé le visage; **he gave the table a wipe** il a essuyé la table
5 (reason, explanation, opinion, answer, reference number) donner; **the answer (that) he gave me** la réponse qu'il m'a faite ou donnée; **he gave his age as twenty** il a déclaré avoir vingt ans; **to g. a decision** faire connaître sa décision; Law rendre un arrêt; **don't g. me that!** (don't try to fool me) ne me raconte pas d'histoires!, à d'autres!; **don't g. me that stuff about how hard your life is** épargne-moi le récit de tous tes malheurs
6 (grant) **she gave him her hand (in marriage)** elle lui a accordé sa main; **to g. sb an interview** accorder une interview à qn; **we were given a choice** on nous a fait choisir; **g. me a break!** fais-moi des vacances!, lâche-moi les baskets!; **g. me a chance!** donne-moi une chance!; **I can g. you 10 minutes** je peux te consacrer ou t'accorder 10 minutes; **we'll g. them in two hours, g. or take a few minutes** on fera le trajet en deux heures, à quelques minutes près; **g. us a song!** chante-nous quelque chose!; **aren't you going to g. me a kiss?** tu ne m'embrasses pas?; **married? those two? I'll g. it a year at the outside** mariés? ces deux-là? je leur donne un an au grand maximum; **he's keen, I'll g. you that** il est très enthousiaste, je te l'accorde
7 (perform, execute) (concert etc) donner; **she gave an outstanding performance** (of actress) son interprétation était remarquable; **I g. you our host** (in proposing toast) je bois à la santé de notre hôte
8 (pass on) **he gave me his cold** il m'a donné ou passé son rhume; **that gave me the idea of travelling** cela m'a donné l'idée de voyager; **don't g. him ideas!** ne va pas lui mettre des idées dans la tête!
9 (cause) (embarrassment, pleasure) faire, causer; **to g. oneself trouble** se donner du mal; **to g. sb to believe** or **understand that …** faire croire ou donner à entendre à qn que …
10 (yield) rendre; **investment that gives 10%** placement qui rend ou rapporte 10%; **this lamp gives a poor light** cette lampe é-

claire mal; **to g. an average of ...** donner une moyenne de ...

11 *Fam (hit etc)* **to g. it (to) sb** *(beat up)* rosser qn; *(reprimand)* laver la tête à qn; **g. it to them!** allez-y!; **I gave him what for!** *(reprimanded him)* je lui ai passé un savon!; **caviare on toast? I'll g. him caviare on toast!** *(in annoyance at request)* du caviar et des toasts! je vais lui en donner, moi, du caviar et des toasts!

VI 1 *(give gift etc)* donner, offrir; *Prov* **it is better** *or* **more blessed to g. than to receive** donner vaut mieux que recevoir; **please g. generously** *(to charity collection)* soyez généreux; **to g. generously of one's time** donner beaucoup de son temps; **to g. and take** faire des concessions; **to g. as good as one gets** rendre coup pour coup

2 *(of cloth, elastic)* se détendre; *Fig (of person)* céder; **something's got to g.** ça va exploser; **the springs don't g. enough** les ressorts manquent de souplesse; **the door will g. if you push hard enough** la porte cédera si vous la poussez assez fort

3 *esp Am Fam* **what gives?** *(hi!)* salut!; *(what's going on?)* qu'est-ce qui se passe?; *(what's the news?)* quoi de neuf?

4 *Sl* **g.!** *(tell me etc)* vide ton sac!

N élasticité *f*, *(in mechanism etc)* jeu *m*

▸▸ **g. way sign** signal *m* de priorité

▸ **give away** VT SEP **1** *(give for nothing)* donner, faire cadeau de; **I'm practically giving them away!** *(said by salesman)* c'est pratiquement donné!; **you couldn't g. them away** tu n'arriveras pas à t'en débarrasser (même si tu en faisais cadeau)

2 *(at ceremony)* **to g. away the prizes** distribuer les prix; **to g. the bride away** conduire la mariée à l'autel

3 *(betray, reveal) (of person)* trahir, vendre; *(of accent, clothes etc)* trahir; **to g. oneself away** se trahir; **to g. the game** *or* **show away** vendre la mèche; **I'm not going to g. anything away** *(that might help you)* je ne veux rien vous révéler

▸ **give back** VT SEP *(something)* rendre, restituer (**to sb** à qn); *(echo)* renvoyer; *(image)* refléter; **to g. sb back his liberty** rendre la liberté à qn

▸ **give in** VT SEP *(hand over)* donner, remettre; **I gave the wallet in to the police** j'ai remis le portefeuille à la police; **to g. in one's name** donner son nom; **to g. in one's examination paper** remettre sa copie d'examen

VI *(under pressure)* céder; *(in fight, battle)* se rendre; *(of rebel)* se soumettre; *(not know the answer)* renoncer, abandonner; **to g. in to intimidation** se laisser intimider; **you g. in too easily** tu abandonnes trop facilement; **to g. in to sb** céder à qn

▸ **give off** VT SEP *(emit) (smell)* dégager, émettre; *(heat)* émettre, répandre; *Chem (gas)* dégager

▸ **give onto** VT INSEP *(of window, door etc)* *(garden, street)* donner sur

▸ **give out** VT SEP **1** *(distribute) (supplies, books etc)* distribuer

2 *(emit) (smell)* dégager; *(heat)* répandre; *(sound)* émettre

3 *(make known)* **it was given out that ...** on a annoncé *ou* dit que ...

VI 1 *(become used up)* manquer, faire défaut; *(of supplies)* s'épuiser; **my strength/patience was giving out** j'étais à bout de forces/patience; **my luck has finally given out** finalement, la chance a tourné

2 *(of radio, car etc)* tomber en panne

▸ **give over** VT SEP **1** *(transfer)* remettre (**to sb** entre les mains de qn)

2 *(devote) (afternoon, rest of the evening etc)* consacrer (**to** à)

3 *(usu passive) (abandon)* **given over to despair** abandonné *ou* en proie au désespoir

VI *Fam (stop)* **g. over, will you?** vraiment, ça

suffit!; **g. over kicking your sister** arrête de donner des coups de pieds à ta sœur

▸ **give up** VT SEP **1** *(abandon) (possessions, pretensions)* abandonner; *(plan etc)* renoncer à; **to g. up the idea of doing sth** renoncer à (l'idée de) faire qch; **he gave up all hope of being promoted** il a abandonné tout espoir d'être promu; **to g. up smoking** cesser de fumer; **to g. up one's job** quitter son emploi; **to g. up the game/struggle** abandonner la partie/renoncer à la lutte; **to g. sth up as a bad job** renoncer à qch (en raison du manque de résultats); **to g. sb up (for lost)** considérer qn comme perdu; **the doctors have given him up** les médecins disent qu'il est perdu; **I'd given you up!** *(given up waiting)* je ne vous attendais plus!; **he gave himself up to grief** il s'est laissé aller au désespoir

2 *(surrender) (prisoner)* livrer; **to g. up one's seat to sb** céder sa place à qn; **to g. oneself up** se constituer prisonnier, se rendre; **I want to g. myself up** je veux me rendre; **she gave herself up to her studies** elle s'est consacrée entièrement à ses études; **his mornings were given up to business** ses matinées étaient consacrées aux affaires

VI 1 *(surrender)* se rendre; **I g. up** *(I don't know the answer)* j'abandonne, je donne ma langue au chat

2 *(abandon a course of action, struggle etc)* abandonner, laisser tomber; **you mustn't g. up now** tu ne peux pas abandonner maintenant; **I g. up!** *(you're or it's etc hopeless)* j'abandonne!

▸ **give up on** VT INSEP *(stop having faith in)* **even his mother had given up on him** même sa mère avait perdu tout espoir à son sujet; **don't g. up on me** ne me laisse pas tomber

▸ **give way** VI **1** *(collapse)* s'effondrer; *(of ladder)* se casser, se rompre; *(of cable)* céder, partir; **the ground gave way under our feet** le sol s'est affaissé *ou* s'est dérobé sous nos pieds; **my legs are giving way (under me)** mes jambes fléchissent *ou* mollissent *ou* se dérobent sous moi; **his health is giving way** sa santé s'affaiblit

2 *(yield)* **to g. way to sb** *(in argument)* céder à qn; **to g. way to despair/grief** s'abandonner au désespoir/à la douleur; **g. way** *(on sign)* cédez le passage; **to g. way (to a car)** céder le passage (à une voiture)

3 *(be superseded by)* **her tears gave way to laughter** le rire l'a emporté sur ses larmes; **natural fibres have given way to synthetics** les fibres naturelles ont été remplacées par les synthétiques

---

give-and-take N *(mutual concession)* concessions *fpl* (mutuelles); **there has to be some g.** il faut que chacun fasse des concessions, il faut que chacun y mette du sien

giveaway ['gɪvəweɪ] N *Fam* **1** *(revelation)* révélation *f* involontaire; *(clue)* indice *m*; **her remark about inflation was the g.** sa remarque sur l'inflation l'a trahie; **it was a dead g.** c'était un geste/un mot/*etc* qui en disait long **2** *Com (free gift)* prime *f*, cadeau *m* **3** *Am Radio* jeu *m* radiophonique; *TV* jeu télévisé

▸▸ **g. paper** journal *m* gratuit; **g. price** prix *m* défiant toute concurrence; *Am* **g. program** *Radio* jeu radiophonique; *TV* jeu télévisé

given ['gɪv(ə)n] ADJ **1** *(specific)* donné, déterminé; **in a g. time** dans une période donnée; **at any g. time** à tout moment; **at a g. point** à un point donné **2** *(apt, likely)* **to be g. to forgetfulness** avoir tendance à être distrait; **I'm g. to losing my temper** c'est dans ma nature de me mettre en colère

PREP **g. these facts, explain why ...** à partir de ces données, expliquez pourquoi ...; **g.**

her age *(considering it)* étant donné son âge; **g. a triangle ABC** soit un triangle ABC

▸▸ *Am* **g. name** prénom *m*

giver ['gɪvər] N *(of blood, organ)* donneur, -euse; *(of money)* donateur, -trice

giving ['gɪvɪŋ] ADJ *(person)* généreux, -euse; **of a g. nature** d'une nature généreuse

gizmo ['gɪzməʊ] N *esp Am Fam* machin *m*, truc *m*, bidule *m*

gizzard ['gɪzəd] N gésier *m*; *Fig Fam* **that sticks in my g.** j'ai du mal à le digérer

glacé ['glæseɪ] ADJ

▸▸ *Culin* **g. cherries** cerises *fpl* confites

glacial ['gleɪsɪəl, -ʃəl] ADJ **1** *Geol (erosion, valley etc)* glaciaire **2** *(wind, Fig manner etc)* glacial, -als

glaciation [gleɪsɪ'eɪʃən, -ʃɪ'eɪ-] N glaciation *f*

glacier ['glæsɪər, 'gleɪs-, *Am* 'gleɪʃər] N *Geol* glacier *m*

glad [glæd] ADJ *(gladder, gladdest)* **1** *(person)* heureux, content; **to be g. to hear sth** apprendre qch avec plaisir, être heureux *ou* content d'apprendre qch; **I'm g. you like him** je suis content que vous l'aimiez; **I'm (so) g.** *(to know that you're better etc)* ça me fait plaisir (de l'apprendre); **he is only too g. to help you** il ne demande pas mieux que de vous aider; **they would be g. of your help** ils seraient bien heureux d'avoir votre aide; **to be g. of an opportunity to do sth** se réjouir de l'occasion de faire qch; **it makes my heart g. to hear him** cela me réjouit le cœur de l'entendre

2 *(smile)* de contentement; *(shout)* de plaisir; **g. news,** *Lit* **g. tidings** bonne nouvelle *f*, *Old-fashioned Fam* **to give sb the g. eye** faire de l'œil à qn; *Am* **to give sb the g. hand** faire un accueil chaleureux à qn *(souvent dans un but intéressé)*; *Fam Hum* **to put on one's g. rags** se mettre sur son trente et un

gladden ['glæd(ə)n] VT *(person)* rendre heureux; **it gladdens my heart to see them** cela me réjouit le cœur de les voir

glade [gleɪd] N *esp Lit (in forest)* clairière *f*

glad-hand VT *Am (welcome warmly)* faire un accueil chaleureux à; *(of politician etc)* serrer la main à *(souvent dans un but intéressé)*

gladiator ['glædɪeɪtər] N gladiateur *m*

gladiatorial [glædɪə'tɔ:rɪəl] ADJ *(combats)* de gladiateurs

▸▸ *Fig* **g. politics** = politique *f* qui fait de la confrontation son moyen d'action

gladiolus, *pl* **gladioli** [glædɪ'əʊləs, -laɪ] N glaïeul *m*

gladly ['glædlɪ] ADV *(willingly)* avec plaisir, volontiers; **I accept g.** j'accepte avec grand plaisir

gladness ['glædnɪs] N joie *f*, allégresse *f*

Gladstone bag ['glædstən] N = petit sac *m* de voyage

Glam *abbr* **Glamorganshire**

glam [glæm] ADJ *Fam* = **glamorous**

glamorize ['glæməraɪz] VT rendre séduisant *ou* attrayant; **to g. war** présenter la guerre de telle sorte qu'elle apparaisse attrayante; **a TV programme that glamorizes violence** une émission de télé qui rend la violence attrayante; **an advertising campaign that seeks to g. smoking** une campagne publicitaire qui cherche à redorer l'image des fumeurs

glamorous ['glæmərəs] ADJ *(person)* chic et élégant; *(dress)* habillé; *(job, football club etc)* prestigieux, -ieuse; *(job as model etc)* qui fait rêver; **a g. grandmother** une grand-mère sophistiquée; **working in the film industry is not always g.** il n'y a pas que des métiers de prestige dans le cinéma

glamour, *Am* glamor ['glæmər] N *(of person)* glamour *m*, chic *m* fascinant; *(of name, lifestyle)* prestige *m*; *(of ceremony etc)* éclat *m*; **the false g. of war** la fascination trompeuse qu'exerce la guerre; **g. is back in fashion** le chic revient à la mode

▸▸*Fam* **g. boy** beau gosse *m*; *Fam* **g. girl** pin-up *f inv*; *(model)* mannequin *m*

glam-rock N *Mus* glam-rock *m*

glance [gla:ns] N *(quick look)* regard *m*, coup *m* d'œil; **at a g.** d'un coup d'œil; **at first g.** à première vue, au premier coup d'œil; **to give sth a g., to have a g. at sth** jeter un coup d'œil sur qch

VI *(look quickly)* **to g. at sb/sth** jeter un regard sur qn/qch, lancer un coup d'œil à qn/sur qch; **to g. around** jeter un coup d'œil autour de soi; **to g. through** *or* **over sth** *(examine)* parcourir rapidement qch; **to g. through a book** parcourir *ou* feuilleter un livre; **he glanced up briefly when I came in** il a brièvement levé la tête quand je suis entré

▸ **glance off** VI *(of bullet etc)* ricocher
VT INSEP ricocher sur; *(of light)* se refléter sur; **the blow glanced off his helmet** le coup a ricoché sur son casque

glancing ['gla:nsɪŋ] ADJ *(blow)* oblique; **she caught him with a g. blow** elle lui a donné un coup sur le côté

gland¹ [glænd] N glande *f*

gland² N *Tech* **packing g.** bague *f* de presse-étoupe

glanders ['glændəz] NPL *(with sing verb)* Vet morve *f*

glandular ['glændjʊlər] ADJ *Physiol, Med* glandulaire

▸▸**g. fever** mononucléose *f* (infectieuse)

glans [glænz], *pl* **glandes** ['glændiːz] N *Anat* gland *m*

glare [gleər] N **1** *(angry stare)* regard *m* fixe et furieux **2** *(of sun, headlight etc)* éclat *m*, lumière *f* éblouissante; *Fig* **in the full g. of publicity** sous le feu croisé des médias

VI **1** *(stare angrily)* fixer un regard furieux *ou* furibond (**at sb** *sur* qn) **2** *(of sun etc)* être aveuglant

▸▸*Comput* **g. filter** filtre *m* antireflet; *Comput* **g. screen** écran *m* antireflet

glaring ['gleərɪŋ] ADJ **1** *(eyes)* furieux **2** *(light)* éblouissant, éclatant; *(sun)* aveuglant; *(colour etc)* voyant **3** *Fig (fact etc)* manifeste, patent, qui saute aux yeux; *(error, injustice, omission)* flagrant; *(abuse)* scandaleux, choquant

glaringly ['gleərɪŋlɪ] ADV **it's g. obvious** ça saute aux yeux

glasnost ['glæznɒst] N *Pol* glasnost *f*

glass [gla:s] N **1** *(material)* verre *m*; **g. bottle** bouteille *f* de *ou* en verre; **g. door** porte vitrée, porte *f* de *ou* en verre; **g. partition** cloison *f* de *ou* en verre; **the g. industry** l'industrie *f* du verre; *Prov* **people who live in g. houses shouldn't throw stones** il faut être sans défauts pour critiquer autrui; **to keep/display sth under g.** garder/exposer qch sous verre

2 *(single piece) (of window)* vitre *f*, carreau *m*; *(of car)* glace *f*, vitre *f*; *(of watch, lamp)* verre *m*

3 *(cup)* verre *m*; **wine g.** verre à vin; **g. of wine** verre de vin; **to sell wine by the g.** vendre le vin au verre

4 *(no pl) (glassware)* verrerie *f*

5 *(lens) (of optical instrument)* lentille *f*

6 *(telescope) (field)* **g.** lunette *f* d'approche, longue-vue *f*, *pl* longues-vues

7 *(mirror)* **(looking) g.** glace *f*, miroir *m*

8 *Old-fashioned (barometer)* baromètre *m* (à cadran); **the g. is falling** le baromètre baisse

9 *(in gardening)* **grown under g.** *(in cold*

frame) cultivé sous verre *ou* sous châssis; *(in glasshouse)* cultivé en serre

▸▸**g. case** *(for display)* vitrine *f*; **to keep/display sth in a g. case** garder/exposer qch sous verre; **g. ceiling** = plafond *m* de verre qui désigne métaphoriquement l'ensemble des facteurs qui empêchent les femmes de parvenir aux postes les plus élevés dans le monde professionnel; **g. cutter** *(person)* vitrier *m*; **g. cutting** taille *f* du verre; **g. fibre** fibre(s) *f(pl)* de verre; *Boxing etc Fam* **g. jaw** mâchoire *f* fragile; **g. manufacturer** verrier *m*; **g. roof** verrière *f*; **g. wool** laine *f* de verre

▸ **glass in** VT SEP *(balcony etc)* entourer d'une cloison vitrée

glass-blower N souffleur *m* de verre

glass-blowing N soufflage *m* de verre

glasscloth ['gla:sklɒθ] N torchon *m* (pour essuyer les verres)

glasses ['gla:sɪz] NPL *(spectacles)* lunettes *fpl* VOIR GRAMMAIRE A10

glassful ['gla:sfʊl] N *(of water etc)* (plein) verre *m*

glasshouse ['gla:shaʊs] N **1** *Br (in garden)* serre *f* **2** *Br Mil Fam* prison *f* militaire, *Fam* trou *m* **3** *Am (factory)* verrerie *f*

glasspaper ['gla:speɪpər] N papier *m* de verre

glassware ['gla:sweər] N verres *mpl*, *(stylish)* verrerie *f*

glassworks ['gla:swɜːks] NPL *(usu with sing verb)* verrerie *f*; *(for crystal)* cristallerie *f*

glassy ['gla:sɪ] ADJ *(smooth)* vitreux; **g. look/eye** regard/œil terne

Glaswegian [glæz'wi:dʒən] N *(resident)* habitant, -ante de Glasgow; *(by birth)* originaire *mf* de Glasgow
ADJ de Glasgow

glaucoma [glɔː'kəʊmə] N *Med* glaucome *m*; **to have g.** avoir un glaucome

glaucous ['glɔːkəs] ADJ glauque

glaze [gleɪz] N **1** *Cer* vernis *m* (luisant) **2** *Culin* glaçage *m* **3** *Art* vernis *m* **4** *Am (ice)* verglas *m*

VT **1** *(window, house)* vitrer **2** *Cer (pottery)* vernisser; *(tiles etc)* vitrifier **3** *Culin* glacer **4** *Art (painting)* glacer; *Phot (print)* émailler

▸ **glaze over** VI *(of eyes)* devenir vitreux

glazed [gleɪzd] ADJ **1** *(door)* vitré **2** *Cer* verni; *(brick)* vitrifié **3** *Culin* glacé **4** *(eye, look)* vitreux

glazier ['gleɪzɪər] N vitrier *m*

glazing ['gleɪzɪŋ] N **1** *(fitting of windows etc)* pose *f* des vitres **2** *(no pl) (windows)* vitrerie *f*, *Cer* vernissage *m*

GLC [dʒiːel'siː] N *Formerly (abbr* **Greater London Council)** = anciennement, conseil *m* municipal du grand Londres

gleam [gli:m] N *(of light)* rayon *m*, trait *m*; *(of knife etc)* reflet *m*; **there's a strange g. in his eye** il y a une drôle de lueur dans son regard; *Hum* **when you were just a g. in your father's eye** bien avant ta naissance

VI luire, reluire; *(of water)* miroiter; *(of eyes)* briller; **she polished the silverware until it gleamed** elle a astiqué l'argenterie jusqu'à ce qu'elle reluise

gleaming ['gli:mɪŋ] ADJ luisant; *(surface of water)* miroitant; *(silverware etc)* reluisant; **g. eyes** yeux brillants

glean [gli:n] VT *(corn, information etc)* glaner; **I couldn't g. much from the brochure** je n'ai pas pu tirer grand-chose de la brochure
VI *Agr* faire la glane

gleaner ['gli:nər] N *Agr* glaneur, -euse

gleaning ['gli:nɪŋ] N **gleanings** *(of crops)* glanes *fpl*; *Fig* **gleanings from the newspapers** informations *fpl* glanées dans les journaux

glebe [gli:b] N *Rel* terre *f* assignée à un bénéfice

glee [gli:] N **1** *(delight)* joie *f*, allégresse *f*; *(malicious pleasure)* jubilation *f*; **the children gave shouts of g.** les enfants ont poussé des cris de joie; **she announced it with some g.** elle l'a annoncé avec un malin plaisir **2** *Mus* petit chant *m* à trois ou quatre parties *(pour voix d'hommes)*

▸▸*Am Mus* **g. club** chorale *f*

gleeful ['gli:fʊl] ADJ joyeux, allègre; *(maliciously)* plein d'une joie malicieuse

gleefully ['gli:fʊlɪ] ADV allègrement, plein de joie; *(maliciously)* avec une joie malicieuse

glen [glen] N vallée *f*; *(narrower)* gorge *f*

glengarry (bonnet) [glen'gærɪ] N *Scot* = béret *m* écossais

glib [glɪb] ADJ *(answer)* spécieux; *(speaker)* qui a du bagou(t); **his explanation was a bit too g.** son explication était un peu trop facile

glibly ['glɪblɪ] ADV *(to reply)* spécieusement; *(to speak)* avec aisance

glibness ['glɪbnɪs] N *(of excuse, reply)* spéciosité *f*; *(of person)* bagou(t) *m*

glide [glaɪd] N **1** *(movement)* glissement *m*; *(in dancing)* glissade *f*, glissé *m* **2** *(of glider)* vol *m* plané; *(of aircraft)* descente *f* en (vol) plané **3** *Mus* port *m* de voix **4** *Ling* son *m* transitoire

VI **1** *(slide)* glisser; **to g. (along) over the water** glisser sur l'eau **2** *(of birds)* planer; *(of aircraft)* planer, faire un vol plané; *(in glider)* faire du vol à voile

▸▸**g. path** *(of aircraft)* trajectoire *f* d'atterrissage

glider ['glaɪdər] N *Aviat* planeur *m*

▸▸**g. pilot** pilote *m* de planeur

gliding ['glaɪdɪŋ] N *Aviat* vol *m* plané *m*; *(sport)* vol à voile

glimmer ['glɪmər] N *(of candle etc)* faible lueur *f*; *(of water etc)* reflet *m*; **g. of hope/intelligence** lueur d'espoir/d'intelligence; **not a g. of interest** pas le moindre intérêt
VI jeter une faible lueur; *(of water)* miroiter

glimmering ['glɪmərɪŋ] ADJ *(water)* miroitant; **a g. light** une faible lueur

glimpse [glɪmps] N vision *f* momentanée; **to catch a g. of sb/sth** entrevoir qn/qch; **she had only caught a g. of her assailant** elle n'avait fait qu'entrevoir son assaillant; **a g. of the future** un aperçu de ce que sera le futur

VT entrevoir

glint [glɪnt] N *(of light) (flash)* éclair *m*; *(continuous)* scintillement *m*; *(of knife etc)* reflet *m*; **hair with glints of gold** chevelure à *ou* aux reflets d'or

VI étinceler; *(on water)* miroiter; **the blade glinted in the sunlight** la lame miroita/miroitait au soleil; **his eyes were glinting with fury** ses yeux étincelaient de fureur

glissando [glɪ'sændəʊ] N *Mus* glissando *m*

glisten ['glɪs(ə)n] VI (re)luire, scintiller; *(of sea)* miroiter; **his forehead glistened with sweat** la sueur perlait sur son front

glistening ['glɪs(ə)nɪŋ] ADJ luisant, scintillant; *(sea)* miroitant

glitch [glɪtʃ] N *Fam (problem etc)* pépin *m*; *Comput* défaillance *f* subite

glitter ['glɪtər] N scintillement *m*; *Fig (of occasion etc)* éclat *m*

VI briller, scintiller, (re)luire; **her eyes glittered with excitement** ses yeux brillaient *ou* scintillaient de joie; *Prov* **all that glitters is not gold** tout ce qui brille n'est pas or

glitterati [glɪtə'rɑːtiː] NPL *Fam* **the g.** le beau monde

glittering ['glɪtərɪŋ] ADJ scintillant; *(occa-*

sion) brillant; *Fig* **the g. world of showbusiness** le monde de lumière du show-business

glitz [glɪts] N *Fam (of showbusiness etc)* tape-à-l'œil *m*

glitzy ['glɪtsɪ] ADJ *Fam (party etc)* tape-à-l'œil *inv*

gloaming ['gləʊmɪŋ] N *Lit* crépuscule *m*; **in the g.** au crépuscule

gloat [gləʊt] VI jubiler; **don't g.** ne te réjouis pas; **to g. about sth** se réjouir à l'idée de qch N **to have a g. about sth** se réjouir à l'idée de qch
► **gloat over** VT INSEP **to sit gloating over one's possessions** jubiler à la vue de ses possessions; **to g. over sb's misfortune** se réjouir du malheur de qn; **he was gloating over his victory/success** il jubilait en pensant à sa victoire/son succès

gloating ['gləʊtɪŋ] ADJ *(eye)* avide; *(smile, look)* jubilant

glob [glɒb] N *Fam (of cream etc)* petite boule *f*

global ['gləʊb(ə)l] ADJ **1** *(worldwide)* mondial, -aux, international, -aux; **on a g. scale** à l'échelle mondiale **2** *(comprehensive)* global, -aux
► *Mktg* **g. audience** audience *f* globale; *Fin* **g. banking** banque *f* universelle; *Comput* **g. change** changement *m* global; **g. corporation** multinationale *f*, **g. custody** conservation *f* globale; **g. economy** économie *f* mondiale; *Fin* **g. equities market** marché *m* mondial des actions; **g. finance** la finance internationale; *Com* **g. market** marché global; *Mktg* **g. marketing** marketing *m* global *ou* international; *Com* **g. marketplace** marché global; *Com* **g. player** acteur *m* international; *Comput* **g. search and replace** recherche *f* et remplacement *m* global; **g. village** village *m* planétaire; **g. war(fare)** guerre *f* mondiale; **g. warming** réchauffement *m* de la planète

globalism ['gləʊbəlɪzm] N mondialisme *m*

globalization [gləʊb(ə)laɪ'zeɪʃən] N **1** *(making worldwide)* mondialisation *f* **2** *(generalization)* globalisation *f*

globalize ['gləʊb(ə)laɪz] VT **1** *(make worldwide)* mondialiser **2** *(generalize)* globaliser

globally ['gləʊbəlɪ] ADV **1** *(generally)* globalement **2** *(worldwide)* mondialement; **the problem of over-population must be dealt with g.** on doit résoudre le problème de la surpopulation à l'échelle planétaire

globe [gləʊb] N *(sphere)* sphère *f*, *(with map)* globe *m* terrestre; *(lampshade)* globe *(de lampe)*; *Anat (of eye)* globe; **to go round the g.** faire le tour du globe; *Sl* **globes** *(breasts)* nichons *mpl*, nénés *mpl*
► **g. artichoke** artichaut *m*; **g. lightning** éclair *m* en boule

globe-fish N poisson-globe *m*, *pl* poissons-globes

globetrotter ['gləʊbtrɒtər] N *Fam* globe-trotter *m*, *pl* globe-trotters

globetrotting ['gləʊbtrɒtɪŋ] N *Fam* voyages *mpl* dans le monde entier

globular ['glɒbjʊlər] ADJ *(globe-shaped)* globulaire; *(composed of globules)* globuleux

globule ['glɒbjuːl] N *(of fat etc)* globule *m*; *(of wax, molten metal)* gouttelette *f*

globulin ['glɒbjʊlɪn] N *Biol, Chem* globuline *f*

glockenspiel ['glɒkənʃpiːl] N *Mus* glockenspiel *m*

glomerulus [glɒ'merʊləs] N *Anat* glomérule *m*

gloom [gluːm] N **1** *(darkness)* obscurité *f*, ténèbres *fpl* **2** *(melancholy)* mélancolie *f*, tristesse *f* empreinte de pessimisme; **to cast or**

throw **a g. over** *or* **on the company** jeter une ombre *ou* un voile de tristesse sur l'assemblée; **there is g. in the City** la Bourse de Londres est pessimiste

gloomily ['gluːmɪlɪ] ADV avec mélancolie, mélancoliquement

gloominess ['gluːmɪnɪs] N **1** **the g. of the sky** le ciel gris; **the g. of the weather** ce temps maussade **2** *(melancholy)* tristesse *f*, mélancolie *f*

gloomy ['gluːmɪ] ADJ **1** *(dark)* sombre, *Littér* ténébreux; **the weather is g.** il fait sombre; **to turn g.** s'assombrir **2** *(melancholy)* morne, sombre; *(stronger)* lugubre; *(prediction etc)* sombre; **to become g.** *(of person)* devenir sombre, se rembrunir; **g. thoughts** de noires pensées; *Fig* **to paint a g. picture** faire un tableau plutôt sombre

glorification [glɔːrɪfɪ'keɪʃən] N glorification *f*

glorified ['glɔːrɪfaɪd] ADJ **1** *Rel* glorifié; *(body)* glorieux **2** **it's just a g. motor scooter** ce n'est qu'un scooter amélioré; **in fact he's just a g. janitor** en fait ce n'est qu'un simple concierge

glorify ['glɔːrɪfaɪ] VT glorifier, célébrer; *(God)* rendre gloire à; **the book glorifies war** ce livre glorifie la guerre

glorious ['glɔːrɪəs] ADJ **1** *(reign, martyr)* glorieux; *(victory)* éclatant; *(action)* remarquable; *Br Hist* **the G. Revolution** la (seconde) Révolution d'Angleterre; **the G. Twelfth** = le 12 août, début de la chasse à la grouse **2** *(splendid, beautiful)* resplendissant, radieux; **g. in her youth and beauty** resplendissante de jeunesse et de beauté **3** *(excellent)* magnifique, splendide; **what g. weather!** quel temps superbe!

gloriously ['glɔːrɪəslɪ] ADV glorieusement; *Fam* **g. drunk** ivre bien comme il faut

glory ['glɔːrɪ] N **1** *(honour)* gloire *f*, **the athletes get all the g.** ce sont les athlètes qui remportent toute la gloire; **to give g. to God** rendre gloire à Dieu; **g. be to God!** gloire à Dieu!; *Old-fashioned Fam* **g. be!** oh mon Dieu!; *(thank heavens)* Dieu soit loué! **2** *(thing)* sujet *m* de gloire; **to be the g. of the age** faire la gloire du siècle **3** *(splendour)* *(of spectacle etc)* splendeur *f*, éclat *m*; **in all her g.** parée de ses plus beaux atours; **Spain, in the days of her g.** l'Espagne, au temps de sa splendeur; **the glories of the Irish countryside** les splendeurs de la campagne irlandaise **4** *Rel* gloire *f*; **the saints in g.** les glorieux *mpl* **5** *(halo) (of saint)* gloire *f*
► **g. hole** *Naut (locker)* petit placard *m*; *(storeroom)* soute *f*, *Br Fam (cupboard)* débarras *m*; *(untidy place)* capharnaüm *m*
► **glory in** VT INSEP *(rejoice in)* se glorifier de; **to g. in one's freedom** profiter pleinement de sa liberté; **the dog gloried in the name of Marmaduke** le chien portait le nom ronflant de Marmaduke

Glos *abbr* **Gloucestershire**

gloss[1] [glɒs] N *(shine)* lustre *m*, vernis *m*, brillant *m*; *Tex* cati *m*; *(paint)* peinture *f* brillante; *Fig (veneer) (of legality etc)* vernis *m*; *Fig* **to take the g. off sth** gâcher qch VT *(make shine)* lustrer
► **g. paint** peinture *f* brillante
► **gloss over** VT INSEP **1** *(deal hurriedly with)* ne pas s'étendre sur; *(sb's shortcomings)* glisser *ou* passer sur **2** *(conceal, cover up)* dissimuler

gloss[2] *Liter* N glose *f*
VT *(text)* annoter

glossary ['glɒsərɪ] N glossaire *m*, lexique *m*

glossiness ['glɒsɪnɪs] N lustre *m*, vernis *m*

glossy ['glɒsɪ] ADJ lustré, brillant; *(paper)*

glacé; *(coat) (of dog)* lustré; *Phot (paper)* brillant
N *(pl* **glossies**) *Journ* magazine *m (sur papier glacé)*; *(women's magazine)* magazine féminin de luxe; **the glossies** la presse féminine de luxe
► **g. magazine** magazine *m (sur papier glacé)*; *Phot* **g. print** épreuve *f* sur papier brillant

glottal ['glɒt(ə)l] ADJ *Ling* glottal, -aux; *Anat* glottique
► *Ling* **g. stop** coup *m* de glotte

glottis ['glɒtɪs] N *Anat* glotte *f*

glove [glʌv] N gant *m*; **to put on one's gloves** mettre ses gants, se ganter; **to take off one's gloves** enlever ses gants, se déganter; **it fits like a g.!** ça me/te/lui/*etc* va comme un gant!; *Fig* **the gloves were off** on n'a pas mis de gants, on y est allé carrément
VT ganter
► *Aut* **g. compartment** boîte *f* à gants; **g. counter, g. department** *(in large store)* rayon *m* des gants, ganterie *f*, **g. maker, g. manufacturer** gantier, -ière; *Br* **g. puppet** marionnette *f (à gaine)*

glovebox ['glʌvbɒks] N *Aut* boîte *f* à gants

glover ['glʌvər] N gantier, -ière

glow [gləʊ] N **1** *(light)* lueur *f*, *(of hot metal)* rougeoiement *m*, incandescence *f*; **the g. of the setting sun** l'embrasement *m* du ciel au couchant **2** *(of complexion)* **to have a healthy g. in one's cheeks** avoir les joues bien rouges; **g. of health** bonne mine *f*, **a g. of pleasure** une rougeur de plaisir **3** *Fig (warm feeling)* it gave him a g. of pride cela le faisait rayonner d'orgueil; **he felt a warm g. spread over him as the whisky went down** il sentit une sensation de chaleur dans tout le corps après avoir bu le whisky; **it gives you a warm g.** *(of news, scene etc)* ça vous fait chaud au cœur
VI *(of light, fire, hot metal)* rougeoyer; *(of person, face)* rayonner; **her face was glowing with pleasure** son visage rayonnait de plaisir; **to g. with enthusiasm** brûler d'enthousiasme; **to be glowing with health** être rayonnant de santé; **his cheeks were glowing** il avait les joues en feu

glower ['glaʊər] VI avoir un air renfrogné; **to g. at sb** *(with disapproval or anger)* lancer un/des regard(s) noir(s) à qn

glowering ['glaʊərɪŋ] ADJ *(expression)* renfrogné; **to give sb a g. look** lancer à qn un regard noir

glowing ['gləʊɪŋ] ADJ **1** *(metal)* chauffé au rouge, incandescent, rougeoyant **2** *(coal, embers, cigarette)* rougeoyant; *(eyes)* de braise **3** *(complexion)* rayonnant; *(cheeks)* rouge **4** *(colours, words)* chaleureux; *(description)* en termes chaleureux; *Fig* **to paint sth in g. colours** présenter qch sous un jour des plus favorables; **the reviews were g.** les critiques étaient très élogieuses; **to speak in g. terms of sb** faire les louanges de qn

glow-worm N ver *m* luisant

gloxinia [glɒk'sɪnɪə] N *(plant)* gloxinia *m*

glucose ['gluːkəʊs] N glucose *m*

glue [gluː] N colle *f* (forte), glu *f*, *Fam* **he sticks to me like g.** il me suit partout comme un petit chien
VT *(glued; gluing)* coller (à la colle forte); **to g. sth on** *or* **to sth** coller qch sur qch; **I glued it on** je l'ai collé dessus; **to g. two things together** coller deux choses (ensemble); *Fig* **with her face glued to the window** le visage collé à la fenêtre; *Fig* **they were glued to the television** ils étaient rivés à la télévision; *Fig* **keep your eyes glued to the road** gardez les yeux rivés *ou* fixés sur la route
► *Med* **g. ear** otite *f* séreuse
► **glue down** VT SEP coller

gluepot ['glu:pɒt] N pot m de colle

glue-sniffer N sniffeur, -euse (de colle)

glue-sniffing ['glu:snɪfɪŋ] N inhalation f de colle; **to be into g.** sniffer de la colle

gluey ['glu:ɪ] ADJ gluant, poisseux

glug [glʌg] Fam N **g. (g.)** glouglou m VI **(-gg-)** faire glouglou

glum [glʌm] ADJ (face, expression) renfrogné, maussade; (appearance) morne, maussade

glumly ['glʌmlɪ] ADV d'un air maussade

glumness ['glʌmnɪs] N air m maussade

glut [glʌt] N Com (on market) encombrement m; (of commodity) surabondance f, **g. of money** pléthore f de capitaux VT **(-tt-) 1** Com (market) encombrer, inonder; **the market is glutted with …** le marché regorge de … **2 to g. oneself** se rassasier, se gorger (**on** de)

glutamine ['glu:təmɪn] N glutamine f

gluten ['glu:tən] N gluten m

glutinous ['glu:tɪnəs] ADJ glutineux

glutted ['glʌtɪd] ADJ (market) encombré

glutton ['glʌt(ə)n] N (person) glouton, -onne, goinfre m; **she's a g. for work** c'est un bourreau de travail; **you're a g. for punishment** tu cherches les complications

gluttonous ['glʌtənəs] ADJ glouton

gluttonously ['glʌtənəslɪ] ADV gloutonnement

gluttony ['glʌtənɪ] N gloutonnerie f, goinfrerie f

glycaemia [glaɪˈsiːmɪə] N Med glycémie f

glycerin(e) ['glɪsərɪn, -iːn] N Chem etc glycérine f

glycerol ['glɪsərɒl] N Chem etc glycérol m

glyceryl trinitrate ['glɪsərɪltraɪ'naɪtreɪt] N Pharm trinitrine f

glycol ['glaɪkɒl] N Chem glycol m

GM [dʒi:'em] ADJ **1** abbr **genetically modified 2** abbr **grant maintained**

G-man, pl **G-men** [dʒi:mæn, -men] N Am Fam agent m du FBI

GMC [dʒi:em'si:] N (abbr **general management committee**) comité m de direction

GMO [dʒi:em'əʊ] N (abbr **genetically modified organism**) OMG m

GMT [dʒi:em'ti:] N (abbr **Greenwich Mean Time**) G. M. T. m

gnarled [nɑ:ld] ADJ **1** (tree) (knotty) noueux; (twisted) tordu **2** (hands, fingers) noueux; (old man, woman) fripé

gnarly ['nɑ:lɪ] ADJ Am Fam (excellent, awful) mortel

gnash [næʃ] VT **to g. one's teeth** grincer des dents

gnashing ['næʃɪŋ] N grincement m; Lit, Hum **there was much weeping and g. of teeth** il y eut moult pleurs et grincements de dents

gnat [næt] N (insect) moucheron m

gnaw [nɔ:] VT (pt **gnawed;** pp **gnawed, gnawn**) (of rodent) ronger; **to g. a bone** (of dog) ronger un os; Fig **gnawed by hunger** tenaillé par la faim; **gnawed by remorse** rongé par le remords

▸ **gnaw at, gnaw into, gnaw through** VT INSEP ronger

gnawing ['nɔ:ɪŋ] ADJ (hunger, anxiety) dévorant; **the g. pains of hunger** les tiraillements mpl de la faim

GNE [dʒi:en'i:] N Econ (abbr **gross national expenditure**) DNP f, dépense f nationale brute

gneiss [naɪs] N Geol gneiss m

gnome [nəʊm] N Myth gnome m; (garden) g. = statue f de nain qui décore un jardin; Fam

Pej **the gnomes of Zurich** les banquiers mpl internationaux de Zurich

gnomic ['nəʊmɪk] ADJ Lit gnomique

gnosis ['nəʊsɪs] N gnose f

gnostic ['nɒstɪk] ADJ, N Rel gnostique mf

gnosticism ['nɒstɪsɪz(ə)m] N Rel, Hist gnosticisme m

GNP [dʒi:en'pi:] N Econ (abbr **Gross National Product**) PNB m; **G. per capita** PNB par habitant

gnu [nu:] N (animal) gnou m

GO [gəʊ]

VT aller **1, 3, 15, 16** ▪ marcher **2, 3**	
▪ passer **4** ▪ faire **6** ▪ aller ensemble **7**	
▪ s'en aller **8** ▪ partir **8**	
▪ disparaître **9** ▪ s'user **10** ▪ sauter **10**	
▪ se casser **10** ▪ se vendre **11**	
▪ aller (+ infinitive) **12, 13** ▪ future tense **13** ▪ entrer **14** ▪ contribuer **17**	
▪ s'étendre **18** ▪ devenir **19**	
VI dire **2**	
N allant **2** ▪ coup **3** ▪ essai **3**	
▪ tour **3**	

VI (**he goes;** pt **went** [went], pp **gone** [gɒn]) **1** aller; **to go to a place** aller ou se rendre à un endroit; **to go to Paris/to the country** aller à Paris/à la campagne; **to go to France/Japan** aller en France/au Japon; **to go home** aller ou rentrer chez soi; **to go to church/Mass** aller à l'église/à la messe; **to go to the doctor's** aller chez le médecin; **to go to prison** aller en prison; **to go to the lavatory** aller aux toilettes; **do you need to go?** (to toilet) tu as besoin de faire pipi?; **I went before I came** (to toilet) j'ai fait (pipi) avant de venir; **to go to sb's house** aller chez qn; **to go on foot/by train/by car** aller à pied/par le train/en voiture; **there he goes!** le voilà (qui passe)!; Mil **who goes there?** qui va là?; **the car was going very slowly/fast** la voiture allait très lentement/vite; **to go at 100 km an hour** faire 100 km ou au cent à l'heure; **you go first** (after you) à vous l'honneur, vous d'abord; (you leave first) partez le premier ou devant; **to go up/down/across a street** remonter/descendre/traverser une rue; **which road goes to London?** quelle est la route de Londres?; Fig **where do we go from here?** et maintenant?; **to go one's own way** faire à sa guise; **there you go!** (handing sth to sb) voilà!; **it's expensive, but there you go** (that's how it is) c'est cher, mais c'est comme ça; **there you go again!** vous voilà reparti!; **to go riding** (aller) se promener à cheval; **to go hunting/fishing** aller à la chasse/à la pêche; **to go looking for sth** partir à la recherche de qch

2 (be active, function) marcher; **to set** or **get a piece of machinery going** mettre une machine en marche ou en mouvement; Fam **get going!** file!, vas-y!; **my watch has stopped going** ma montre ne marche plus; **the bell went ten minutes ago** la cloche a sonné il y a dix minutes; **enough timber to keep three sawmills going** assez de bois pour alimenter trois scieries; **to keep the conversation going** entretenir la conversation; **when he gets going, he never stops** quand il est lancé ou une fois lancé, il ne sait pas s'arrêter

3 (progress) **everything's going well** tout marche bien; **things are going badly** cela va mal; **how are things going?, how is it going?** comment ça va?; **if all goes well** si tout va bien; **the rehearsal went well/badly** la répétition a bien/mal marché; **the way things are going** au train où vont les choses; **I forget how the tune goes** l'air m'échappe; **how does the chorus go?** quelles sont les paroles du refrain?; **how does it go?** (of

tune, music) c'est comment?; **as things go today** par les temps qui courent; **that's not dear as things go today** ce n'est pas cher au prix où sont les choses; **which way will the decision go?** que décidera-t-on?; **I don't know how things will go** je ne sais pas comment cela tournera

4 (of time) passer; **there were only five minutes to go before …** il ne restait que cinq minutes avant …; **how's the time going?** combien de temps nous reste-t-il?; **it has just gone eight** il est un peu plus de huit heures

5 (be the rule) **what she says goes** c'est elle qui commande; **anything goes** (do, wear etc whatever you like) on fait ce qu'on veut

6 Fam (make sound, perform action) **to go crack/bang** faire crac/pan; **go like this with your left foot** fais comme ça du pied gauche

7 (match) **these colours don't go** ces couleurs jurent; **these colours go perfectly** ces couleurs vont parfaitement ensemble

8 (leave) partir, s'en aller; **after** or **when I had gone** après mon départ, après que je sois parti; **we must go** or **must be going** il est temps de partir; **let me go** laissez-moi partir; **go!** (go away) allez-vous-en!; Sport (in race etc) partez!; **from the word go** dès le début; **that old chair will have to go** il va falloir se débarrasser de cette vieille chaise; **a hundred employees will have to go** il va falloir mettre cent employés à la porte; Euph **his wife went first** (died) sa femme est partie avant lui; Euph **when I am gone, after I have gone** (died) quand je ne serai plus là

9 (disappear) disparaître; **my hat has gone** mon chapeau a disparu; **it's all gone** il n'y en a plus; **that's the way the money goes** voilà comme l'argent file; **most of my money goes on food** la plus grande partie de mon argent passe dans la nourriture; **her sight is going** elle est en train de perdre la vue

10 (break) (se) casser; **the spring went** le ressort s'est cassé; **the batteries are going** les piles sont presque mortes; Elec **a fuse went** un plomb a sauté; **my dress is going at the seams** ma robe s'use aux coutures

11 (be on sale, available) **they are going for ten euros each** on les vend dix euros pièce; **the lot went for £20** (at auction) le lot fut adjugé à 20 livres; **going! going! gone!** (at auction) une fois! deux fois! adjugé!; **let's see if there's any lunch going** allons voir si le déjeuner est prêt; **there are drinks going in the drawing room** on sert l'apéritif dans le salon; **there's a job going at the factory** il y a une place à l'usine

12 (introducing an action) **to go and do sth** aller faire qch; **to go to dinner with sb** aller dîner avec qn; (at their place) aller dîner chez qn; **to go to** or **and see sb** aller voir qn; **go and see** or esp Am **go see what's happening** va voir ce qui se passe; **to go and look for sth** aller chercher qch; Fam **and then he went and got married** et puis, il a eu l'idée de se marier; Fam **what did you have to go and tell him for?** qu'est-ce qui t'a pris d'aller le lui dire?; Fam **you've gone and done it now!** vraiment, tu as tout gâché!; **he went** (forward) **to help her, but …** il a fait un mouvement pour l'aider, mais …

13 (aux forming future) **I'm going to tell you a story** je vais vous raconter une histoire; **the shortage is not going to last** la disette ne durera pas; **I'm going to have my own way** je vais faire comme je l'entends; **I'm not going to be cheated** je ne me laisserai pas abuser; **I was going to walk** (intention) j'avais l'intention d'y aller à pied; **I'm going to go to France for my holiday** je compte passer mes vacances en France; **he knew it was going to be difficult** il savait que ce serait difficile; **she was going to telephone the police when she was shot** elle s'apprêtait à téléphoner à la police quand la balle l'a frappée VOIR GRAMMAIRE A51

14 (fit) **too big to go into the basket** trop grand pour entrer dans le panier; **the key won't go in(to) the lock** la clef n'entre pas dans la serrure; **the piano won't go through the door** le piano ne passe pas par la porte; *Math* **six into twelve goes twice** douze divisé par six fait deux; **four into three won't go** trois n'est pas divisible par quatre

15 (belong) **where does this book go?** où va ce livre?; **the scissors go in the drawer** les ciseaux vont *ou* se rangent dans le tiroir

16 (be given) **the proceeds will go to charity** les bénéfices iront à des œuvres de charité; **the estate will go to his eldest son** la propriété va revenir à son fils aîné

17 (contribute) **the qualities that go to make a great man** les qualités qui font un grand homme; **ingredients that go to make a good dish** ingrédients qui contribuent à faire un bon plat; **these reforms go some way to(wards) improving the situation** ces réformes contribuent à améliorer la situation; **this money will go to(wards) building a new school** cet argent servira à construire une nouvelle école; **to go to prove sth** servir à prouver qch; **it only goes to show that ...** cela montre bien que ...

18 (extend) s'étendre; **the garden goes down to the river** le jardin s'étend jusqu'à la rivière; **that's true, as far as it goes** c'est vrai jusqu'à un certain point; **her essay's quite good, as far as it goes** malgré ses faiblesses, sa dissertation n'est pas mauvaise

19 (become) devenir; **to go Communist** devenir communiste; **you'll just have to go hungry** il va falloir que tu supportes la faim; **while half the world go hungry** tandis que la moitié du monde n'a rien à manger *ou* connaît la faim; **he went cold all over** son sang s'est glacé; **the tea's gone cold** le thé a refroidi; **to go red** rougir; **to go white** blanchir; **my hair is going grey** mes cheveux grisonnent *ou* deviennent gris; **to go to the bad** mal tourner

VT 1 *Fam* **that's really going it!** (that's fast) ça, c'est de la vitesse!; **to go it alone** agir tout seul; (in business) se lancer tout seul; *Fam* **I could really go a beer** je me paierais bien une bière; **to go 10** (in gambling) risquer 10; *Cards* **to go no/two/three trumps** annoncer sans/deux/trois atout(s); **to go one better** surenchérir (**than sb** sur qn)

2 *Fam* (say) dire; **so she goes, 'you're lying!', and I go, 'no, I'm not!'** alors elle me fait 'tu mens!', et je lui fais 'non, je mens pas!'

N (*pl* **goes**) **1** (activity) **to be always on the go** être toujours à trotter *ou* à courir, *Fam* avoir la bougeotte; **to keep sb on the go** faire trimer qn; **it's all go** on n'a pas une minute à soi, ça n'arrête pas

2 (energy) **to be full of** *or* **have plenty of go** avoir de l'allant

3 (try) coup *m*, essai *m*; **to make a go of it** (succeed) y réussir; **(it's) your go!** (in game) à vous de jouer!; **to have a go (at doing sth)** essayer (de faire qch); **can I have a go?** je peux essayer?; **let's have a go!** tentons le coup!, allons-y!; (let me try) laisse-moi essayer!; **she had a go at me** (abused me verbally) elle s'en est prise à moi; *Fam* **to have a go** (stop or arrest criminal) tenter quelque chose (alors qu'on n'est pas de la police); **(it's) no go!** rien à faire!; **at one go** d'un (seul) coup; **£1 a go** (at fair etc) une livre la partie *ou* le tour; **to have a go on the Dodgems®** faire un tour d'autos tamponneuses; **he wouldn't let me have** *or* **give me a go** (on his bicycle etc) il ne voulait pas me laisser l'essayer; **you've had three goes already** (attempts) tu as déjà essayé trois fois; (on bicycle etc) tu as déjà fait trois tours

4 Old-fashioned **it's all the go** (fashionable) ça fait fureur *ou* rage

ADJ Astronaut **all systems are go** tout est paré et en ordre de marche (pour le départ)

▸ **go about** **VI** (move) circuler; (of rumour) courir; *Naut* (turn) virer de bord; **policemen usually go about in pairs** en général, les policiers circulent par deux; **you can't go about saying things like that!** il ne faut pas raconter des choses pareilles!; **someone has been going about saying that ...** quelqu'un a été raconter que ...; **she's been going about with that Smith boy** on l'a vue traîner avec le fils Smith

VT INSEP 1 (country) parcourir; **to go about the streets** circuler dans les rues

2 (tackle) **how to go about it** comment s'y prendre; **how do I go about getting a licence?** que dois-je faire pour obtenir un permis?

3 (one's work, business) vaquer à

▸ **go across** **VI** traverser; **she's gone across to Mrs McGinty's** elle est en face, chez Mme McGinty

VT INSEP (bridge etc) traverser

▸ **go after** **VT INSEP** (pursue) essayer d'obtenir; (person) courir après; **she really goes after what she wants** elle fait tout pour obtenir ce qu'elle veut

▸ **go against** **VT INSEP** (conflict with, act contrary to) aller contre; **to go against sb's wishes** contrarier les désirs de qn; **this goes against everything I believe in** ceci est contraire à tout ce en quoi je crois; **the judgement/decision went against them** le jugement/la décision leur a été défavorable

▸ **go ahead** **VI 1** (proceed) continuer, poursuivre; **may I say something? – go ahead** puis-je dire quelque chose? – allez-y; **to go ahead with sth** commencer qch; **he went ahead and did it** (without hesitating) il l'a fait sans l'ombre d'une hésitation; (despite warnings) rien ne l'a arrêté; **the building work was finally able to go ahead** la construction a pu commencer; **they went straight a.** ils sont allés droit devant eux; **the project is going a.** (has been approved) le projet a été accepté; **they're going ahead with the project after all** ils ont finalement décidé de mener le projet à bien

2 (go in front) avancer; **you go (on) ahead** (I'll follow later) partez devant; **to go ahead of sb** devancer qn

▸ **go along** **VI 1** (walk, ride, drive etc) avancer; **as we go along** en chemin; **we were going along quite slowly when ...** nous avancions plutôt lentement quand ...

2 (proceed) **I check the figures as I go along** je vérifie les chiffres au fur et à mesure; **you'll have to make it up as you go along** il faudra que tu improvises au fur et à mesure

3 (go to meeting, party etc) aller

▸ **go along with** **VT INSEP** (agree with) (person) coopérer avec; (something) approuver, accepter; **she wouldn't go along with it** elle n'était pas d'accord

▸ **go around** **VI** = **go about** **VI**

▸ **go at** **VT INSEP** (somebody, something) s'attaquer à; **to go at it hard** ne pas y aller de main morte; **he was still going at it when I left** (working hard) il était encore à la tâche quand je suis parti; **they went at the task with a will** ils se sont mis à la tâche avec beaucoup de détermination

▸ **go away** **VI** (leave) s'en aller, partir; **go away!** va-t'en!; **to go away on business/for the weekend** s'absenter pour affaires/pour le week-end; **to go away with sth** emporter qch

▸ **go back** **VI 1** (return) revenir, s'en retourner; (turn back) retourner (en arrière); (move back) reculer; **go back! it's dangerous!** recule! c'est dangereux!; **to go back home** retourner *ou* rentrer chez soi; **to go**

back to Paris retourner à Paris; **he's never gone back** (to that place) il n'y est jamais retourné; **let's go back the way we came** reprenons le même chemin qu'à l'aller; **to go back two paces** faire deux pas en arrière; **to go back to the beginning** reprendre depuis le début; **he went back to his reading** il s'est replongé dans sa lecture; **to go back to sleep** se rendormir; **to go back to one's old ways** retomber dans ses anciennes habitudes; **to go back to doing sth** (resume task, habit) se remettre à faire qch; **he went back to teaching** il est revenu à l'enseignement

2 (date back) remonter (**to** à); **there are records going back to 1700** il y a des récits qui remontent à 1700; **we go back a long way** (our acquaintance) ça fait longtemps qu'on se connaît

3 (extend) **the garden goes back 40 metres behind the house** le jardin s'étend sur 40 mètres derrière la maison

4 **the clocks go back tonight** on retarde les pendules d'une heure cette nuit

▸ **go back on** **VT INSEP** (abandon, alter) (decision, promise) revenir sur

▸ **go before** **VI** précéder; *Euph* **those who have gone before** (the dead) ceux qui nous ont précédés

VT INSEP (tribunal, committee etc) se présenter devant; *Law* comparaître devant; **the case goes before the court/the judge tomorrow** l'affaire passe au tribunal/devant le juge demain; **it goes before the committee tomorrow** elle passe en commission demain

▸ **go below** **VI** *Naut* descendre

▸ **go by** **VI 1** (pass) passer; **to watch people going by** regarder passer les gens; *Fig* **to let an opportunity go by** laisser passer une occasion

2 (elapse) s'écouler; **half an hour went by** une demi-heure s'est écoulée; **as the years go by** à mesure que les années passent

VT INSEP 1 (judge on the basis of) juger d'après; **don't go by what he says/his opinion** ne juge pas d'après ce qu'il dit/ne tiens pas compte de ses opinions; **to go by appearances** juger d'après les apparences

2 (follow) **to go by the rules** suivre *ou* respecter les règles; **promotion goes by seniority** l'avancement se fait à l'ancienneté; **go by your sister's example** suis l'exemple de ta sœur

3 (be known by) **to go by a different/false name** être connu sous un nom différent/un faux nom; **the product goes by the name of 'Bango' in France** ce produit est vendu sous le nom de 'Bango' en France

▸ **go down** **VI 1** (descend) descendre; (of sun) se coucher; (of ship) sombrer; **going down!** (in lift) on descend!, pour descendre!; **go down and answer the door** descends ouvrir; **to go down on one's knees** se mettre à genoux; *Sl* **to go down on sb** (perform oral sex on) sucer qn; *Fam* **to go down with flu** attraper la grippe; **to have gone down in the world** avoir connu des jours meilleurs; **the captain went down with his ship** le capitaine a sombré avec son navire; **I'm not going to go down without a fight** (be defeated) je me battrai jusqu'à la fin

2 (decrease) (of floods, temperature) baisser, s'abaisser; (of wind) baisser, tomber; (of prices, value) baisser; **to go d.** in **sb's estimation** baisser dans l'estime de qn

3 (be received) **to go down well** (of drink) se laisser boire; (of food) se laisser manger; (of entertainment, speech, suggestion) plaire, être bien reçu; **he went down in history as a tyrant** l'histoire a retenu de lui l'image d'un tyran

4 (shrink) (of swelling) désenfler, se dégonfler; (of tyre, balloon) se dégonfler

5 *(extend)* continuer; *(to end of page etc)* aller jusqu'à; **the mineshaft goes down three hundred metres** le puits de mine a trois cents mètres de profondeur

6 *Br Univ (esp Oxford and Cambridge)* **to go down (from university)** *(at end of studies)* quitter l'université; *(at end of term)* partir en vacances

7 *Cards (bridge)* chuter

8 *Am Fam* **what's going down?** *(happening)* qu'est-ce qui se passe?

9 *Comput* tomber en panne; *(of computer network)* planter

VT INSEP *(descend)* *(hill, ladder, street)* descendre; *Sch* **to go down a class/a grade** descendre d'une classe; **some of his food went down the wrong way** il a avalé de travers; **my weight has gone down a few pounds** j'ai perdu quelques kilos; *Fig* **I don't want to go down that road** je ne veux pas m'engager là-dedans

▸ **go for** **VT INSEP 1** *(attack)* *(person)* attaquer, tomber sur; **go for him!** *(to dog)* attaque!; **they went for each other in court** *(physically)* ils se sont empoignés devant le tribunal; *(verbally)* ils se sont disputés *ou Fam* engueulés devant le tribunal

2 *(strive to attain)* essayer d'obtenir; **if you really want the job, go for it!** si tu veux vraiment le poste, mets-y le paquet!; **with his next jump, he's going for the gold** avec son prochain saut, il vise la médaille d'or

3 *(like)* être porté sur, être attiré par; **I don't go for him much** *(don't like him)* je ne l'aime pas tellement; *(don't think him attractive)* il ne m'attire pas spécialement; **tabloid newspapers go for stories like those** la presse à scandales adore ce genre d'histoires

4 *(choose)* prendre; **I'll go for the blue one** je prendrai le bleu

5 **she's got a lot going for her** elle a tout pour elle; **the third proposal has a lot going for it** la troisième proposition a bien des avantages

6 **the same goes for you** ça s'applique à vous aussi

▸ **go forth** **VI** *Rel* **go forth and multiply** croissez et multipliez; *Lit* **the word went forth that …** on a fait savoir que …; *Hum* **the word has gone forth that the boss would like …** le patron a fait savoir qu'il voudrait …

▸ **go forward** **VI** (s')avancer; **the clocks go forward tomorrow** on avance les pendules demain; **if this scheme goes forward …** si ce projet est accepté …

▸ **go in** **VI 1** *(enter)* entrer, rentrer; **let's go in!** entrons!; **it's too big, it won't go in** c'est trop grand, ça ne rentrera pas

2 *(of sun)* se cacher

3 *Cr* prendre son tour au guichet

4 *Mil etc Fam (attack)* attaquer

VT INSEP *(enter)* *(house, room etc)* entrer dans, rentrer dans

▸ **go in for** **VT INSEP 1** *(use, produce, show interest in)* **they don't go in for injections so much nowadays** ils ne sont pas tellement pour les piqûres de nos jours; **why do scientists go in for all that jargon?** pourquoi est-ce que les scientifiques utilisent tout ce jargon?; **this publisher doesn't really go in for fiction** cet éditeur ne fait pas tellement dans le roman; **we don't go in for pop music** nous ne sommes pas très musique pop

2 *(engage in)* s'adonner à, se consacrer à; **he doesn't go in for team sports** il n'est pas très porté sur les sports d'équipe; **to go in for painting** *(as hobby)* faire de la peinture; **to go in for teaching** *(as career)* entrer dans l'enseignement

3 *(enter)* **to go in for an examination** se présenter à un examen; **to go in for a competition** prendre part à un concours

▸ **go into** **VT INSEP 1** *(enter)* entrer dans, rentrer dans; **she's gone into hospital** elle est

(r)entrée à l'hôpital; **to go into fits of laughter** avoir des crises de fou rire; **to go into the army** s'engager (dans l'armée); *(be called up)* partir au régiment; **to go into teaching** *(as career)* entrer dans l'enseignement; **to go into a convent** entrer au couvent

2 *(examine)* *(question)* examiner, étudier; **I shall go into the matter** je vais m'occuper de l'affaire; **to go into the reasons (given) for sth** rechercher les raisons de qch

3 *(explain, provide the reasons for)* expliquer; **to go into details** entrer dans les détails

4 *(embark on)* *(description)* s'embarquer dans, se lancer dans

5 *(collide with)* entrer dans

▸ **go in with** **VT INSEP** *(person in a business etc)* se joindre à

▸ **go off** **VI 1** *(leave)* partir, s'en aller; *Theat* quitter la scène; *Fam* **she's gone off and left him** elle l'a quitté; **he went off with the woman next door** il est parti avec la voisine; **to go off with sth** emporter qch, enlever qch

2 *(deteriorate)* *(of milk)* tourner; *(of butter)* rancir; *(of fish, meat)* se gâter; *(of tennis player etc)* perdre sa forme

3 *(proceed)* **everything went off well** tout a bien marché, tout s'est bien passé; **how did the concert go off?** comment le concert s'est-il passé?

4 *(cease working, be disconnected)* **the power/light went off** l'électricité a été coupée/la lumière s'est éteinte

5 *(of gun)* partir, se décharger; *(of bomb)* éclater; **the pistol didn't go off** le coup n'est pas parti; **the firework went off in my face** la fusée m'a explosé dans la figure; *Fam* **to go off at the deep end** piquer une crise, péter les plombs

6 *(of alarm)* se déclencher; *(of alarm clock)* sonner

7 *(go to sleep)* s'endormir

VT INSEP *(lose liking for)* *(something)* perdre le goût de; **I've gone off cheese** je ne mange plus de fromage; **I've completely gone off him** *(husband, boyfriend)* je me suis complètement détachée de lui; *(actor, singer, writer)* je ne l'aime plus du tout; **funny how you can go off people** c'est drôle comme on se lasse des gens parfois; **I've gone off the idea** cette idée ne me dit plus rien

▸ **go on** **VI 1** *(continue)* continuer (**doing sth** à faire qch); **'and that's not all', he went on** 'et ce n'est pas tout', a-t-il poursuivi; **go on with what you were doing** continuez ce que vous étiez en train de faire; **I must go on with my work** il me faut continuer mon travail; **as time went on, her intentions became clear** à mesure que le temps passait, ses intentions devenaient plus claires; **the lecture went on rather a long time** le cours a duré assez longtemps; **I have enough to be going on with** j'en ai assez pour le moment; **to go on to another question** passer à une autre question; **go on, take one** allez, prends-en un; **go on, try it** allez, essaie-le; **can I? – yes, go on** est-ce que je peux? – oui, vas-y; *Old-fashioned Fam* **go on (with you)!** allons donc!

2 *(talk excessively, unreasonably)* parler à n'en plus finir (**about** de); **how he goes on!** impossible de l'arrêter!; **once he starts, he goes on and on** une fois qu'il est parti, il n'y a plus moyen de l'arrêter; **what are you going on about now?** qu'est-ce que vous racontez?; **she went on a bit** elle s'est un peu étendue sur la question; **he's always going on at me** il est toujours à me faire des remontrances

3 *(happen)* **this has been going on for years** cela fait des années que ça dure; **what's going on here?** qu'est-ce qui se passe ici?

4 *(begin to operate, be connected)* se mettre

en marche; *(of streetlight)* s'allumer

5 *Theat (walk on stage)* entrer en scène; **the band went on at 10 o'clock** le groupe est entré en scène à 10 heures

6 *(fit)* **I can't get the lid to go on** je n'arrive pas à mettre le couvercle; **these shoes won't go on** ces chaussures ne vont pas; **these jeans won't go on any more** je ne rentre plus dans ce jean

VT INSEP 1 *(enter)* *(boat, train)* monter dans

2 *(embark on)* **to go on a journey/a holiday** partir en voyage/en vacances; **to go on a diet** se mettre au régime; **to go on social security** s'inscrire au chômage

3 *(approach)* aller sur; **she's two going on three** elle va sur ses trois ans

4 *(be guided by)* se fonder sur; **the police have nothing to go on** la police n'a rien sur quoi se fonder

▸ **go for** **VT INSEP** *(approach)* approcher de, aller sur; **he's going on for forty** il va sur ses quarante ans

▸ **go out** **VI 1** *(leave house etc)* sortir; **to go out for a meal** aller au restaurant; **she's gone out to get a paper** elle est sortie (pour) acheter un journal; **to go out for a walk** sortir se promener; **we don't go out much in the evenings** nous ne sortons pas beaucoup le soir; **she was dressed to go out** elle était en tenue de ville; **she's decided to go out to work** elle a décidé de travailler à l'extérieur; **what time did he go out to work?** à quelle heure est-il parti travailler?; *Ind* **to go out (on strike)** se mettre en grève; **the magic seemed to have gone out of their marriage** leur mariage semblait avoir perdu de son charme; **her heart went out to them** elle a ressenti de la compassion pour eux; **my heart goes out to you** je partage votre douleur; *Iron* j'en ai les larmes aux yeux

2 *(date)* **they've been going out (together) for a month** ils sortent ensemble depuis un mois; **to go out with sb** sortir avec qn, fréquenter qn; **he went out with her for two years before they got married** il l'a fréquentée pendant deux ans avant de l'épouser

3 *(of fire, light)* s'éteindre; **the lights go out at midnight** on éteint les lumières à minuit; *Fam* **I went out like a light** *(fell asleep)* je me suis endormi tout de suite

4 *(of tide)* baisser, se retirer

5 *(become unfashionable)* passer de mode, se démoder

6 *Sport (be eliminated)* être éliminé, *Fam* se faire sortir; **I bet they go out in the next round** je parie qu'ils vont être éliminés à la prochaine manche; **Henman went out to Agassi** Henman s'est fait sortir par Agassi

7 *(of letter)* être envoyé

8 *TV, Radio (of programme)* être diffusé

▸ **go over** **VI 1** *(cross)* **I went over and tapped him on the shoulder** je suis allé vers lui et je lui ai tapé sur l'épaule

2 *(transfer allegiance)* **to go over to the enemy** passer à l'ennemi; **to go over to the other side** changer de parti; **he's thinking of going over to cigars** il songe à passer aux cigares

3 *(be received)* **to go over well/badly** *(of suggestion, joke)* bien/mal passer; *(of play)* être bien/mal reçu; *Fam* **to go over big** avoir un grand succès

4 *(turn upside down)* se retourner

VT INSEP 1 *(pass across)* **to go over a bridge** passer un pont; **to go over a river** passer par-dessus une rivière; **the ball went over the wall** la balle est passée par-dessus le mur

2 *(examine)* *(accounts, report)* examiner, revoir; *(papers etc)* passer en revue; *(document)* relire; *(lesson)* repasser, revoir; **to go over sth in one's mind** repasser qch dans son esprit

3 *(discuss)* parler de; *Fig* **we are just going**

over the same old ground on ressasse les mêmes choses

4 *(rehearse)* refaire; *(bars of music)* rejouer; *(sing)* rechanter

▸ **go round** VI **1** *(make a detour)* faire un détour

2 *(spin)* tourner; **my head's going round** la tête me tourne

3 *(visit)* **I said I'd go round (and see her)** j'ai dit que j'irais la voir; **he's gone round to a friend's** il est allé chez un ami

4 *(circulate) (of rumour)* circuler, courir; *(of bottle, cold, flu)* circuler

5 *(suffice)* **the food only just went round** il y avait juste assez de nourriture pour tout le monde; **to make the food go round** ménager la nourriture; **there isn't enough to go round** il n'y en a pas assez pour tout le monde

VT INSEP **1** *(make a detour by)* **to go round the long way** faire un long détour

2 *(tour) (museum)* faire le tour de; **I hate going round the shops** j'ai horreur de faire les boutiques; **they went round the neighbourhood looking for their cat** ils ont fait le tour du quartier pour chercher leur chat

3 *(be sufficient for)* suffire pour; **will the soup go round twenty?** est-ce qu'il y aura assez de soupe pour vingt?

▸ **go through** VI **1** *(travel through, penetrate)* passer, traverser; **the gates were open and we went through** les barrières étaient ouvertes et nous sommes passés

2 *(be completed, accepted) (of deal)* être conclu; *(of divorce)* être prononcé; *Parl (of bill)* passer

VT INSEP **1** *(penetrate)* traverser

2 *(suffer) (trials and tribulations)* subir, essuyer; **he went through agony** *(wondering what had happened)* il était au supplice; **in spite of all she had gone through** malgré tout ce qu'elle avait enduré

3 *(complete) (formalities)* remplir

4 *(examine) (documents)* examiner; *(lesson, accounts)* revoir

5 *(search) (suitcases)* fouiller; **to go through sb's pockets** fouiller dans les poches de qn, *Fam* faire les poches à qn

6 *(use up) (money)* dépenser; *(supplies, paper, toner etc)* utiliser; *(food)* consommer; **to go through all one's money** dépenser tout son argent; **have we gone through the salmon already?** est-ce qu'on a déjà fini le saumon?

▸ **go through with** VT INSEP *(carry out)* réaliser, exécuter, aller jusqu'au bout de; **she decided that she couldn't go through with the wedding** elle a décidé qu'elle ne pouvait pas se marier; **I mean to go through with it** j'ai l'intention d'aller jusqu'au bout

▸ **go together** VI **1** *(harmonize)* aller ensemble

2 *(date)* sortir ensemble; **they've been going together for a long time** ils sortent ensemble depuis longtemps

▸ **go under** VI **1** *(of drowning man)* couler, s'enfoncer; *(of ship)* couler, sombrer

2 *(go bankrupt)* faire faillite

3 *(under anaesthetic)* s'endormir

VT INSEP **to go under a false/different name** utiliser *ou* prendre un faux nom/un nom différent; **since the divorce she's been going under her old name** depuis le divorce, elle utilise son nom de jeune fille; **a glue that goes under the name of Stikit** une colle qui s'appelle Stikit

▸ **go up** VI **1** *(climb, rise)* monter; **to go up to bed** monter se coucher; **to go up in a helicopter** monter en hélicoptère; **going up!** *(in lift)* on monte!, pour monter!; *Theat* **before the curtain goes up** avant le lever du rideau; **a shout went up from the crowd** un cri s'éleva de la foule; *Br Univ* **to go up (to Oxford/ etc)** entrer à l'université (d'Oxford/*etc*); **to go**

up in the world faire son chemin

2 *(of prices, temperature etc)* monter; **bread is going up** *(in price)* le pain augmente; **to go up in sb's estimation** monter dans l'estime de qn

3 *(explode, be destroyed)* sauter; **to go up in flames** se mettre à flamber; *Fig* **their plans went up in smoke** leurs projets sont partis en fumée

▸ **go up to** VT INSEP **1** *(approach)* **to go up to sb/sth** se diriger vers qn/qch; **the path goes up to the front door** le chemin mène à la porte d'entrée

2 *(go as far as)* **the book only goes up to the end of the war** le livre ne va que jusqu'à la fin de la guerre; **I will go up to £100** je veux bien aller jusqu'à 100 livres

▸ **go with** VT INSEP **1** *(accompany)* aller de pair avec; **mathematical ability usually goes with skill at chess** des capacités en mathématiques vont souvent de pair avec un don pour les échecs; **a company car goes with the job** ce poste donne droit à une voiture de fonction

2 *(harmonize with)* s'accorder avec, aller avec; *(of colours)* se marier avec; **the carpet doesn't go with the furniture** le tapis n'est pas assorti aux meubles; **this behaviour doesn't go with what I know about her** un tel comportement ne cadre pas avec ce que je sais d'elle

3 *(date) (person)* sortir avec, fréquenter; **is she going with someone?** est-ce qu'elle sort avec quelqu'un?

4 *(have sex with)* coucher avec

▸ **go without** VI *(not have sth)* **I'd rather go without** je préfère m'en passer; **as children, they often went without** lorsqu'ils étaient enfants, ils ont souvent été privés; **they went without so that the children got enough to eat** ils ont dû se priver pour que les enfants aient assez à manger

VT INSEP *(not have)* se passer de; **I went without breakfast so I wouldn't be late** je me suis passé de petit déjeuner pour ne pas être en retard

goad [gəʊd] N *also Fig* aiguillon *m*

VT *(cattle)* aiguillonner, piquer; *(sb's curiosity)* piquer, stimuler; **to g. sb into doing sth** talonner qn jusqu'à ce qu'il fasse qch

▸ **goad on** VT SEP aiguillonner; **don't g. him on!** arrête de l'exciter!

go-ahead *Fam* ADJ *(enterprising)* entreprenant

N **to give sb the g.** donner le feu vert à qn; **to give sth the g.** donner le feu vert pour qch

goal [gəʊl] N **1** *(aim)* but *m*, objectif *m*; **to achieve a g.** atteindre un but, réaliser un objectif; **my g. is in sight** j'approche de mon but *ou* du but **2** *Sport* but *m*; *(structure)* but, cages *fpl*; **Macleod was in g. for Rangers** Macleod était dans les buts des Rangers

▸▸ **g. kick** coup *m* de pied au but, dégagement *m* aux six mètres; **g. line** ligne *f* de but; **g. scorer** buteur *m*; **the leading** *or* **top g. scorer** le meilleur buteur

goalkeeper ['gəʊlkiːpər], *Fam* **goalie** ['gəʊlɪ] N *Ftbl etc* gardien *m* de but, goal *m*

goalless ['gəʊllɪs] ADJ *Ftbl etc* sans but marqué

▸▸ **g. draw** match *m* nul 0-0

goalmouth ['gəʊlmaʊθ] N *Ftbl etc* entrée *f* de but; **there was no shortage of g. incident** il y avait beaucoup d'action devant les cages

goalpost ['gəʊlpəʊst] N *Ftbl etc* montant *m* *ou* poteau *m* (de but); *Fig* **to move** *or* **shift the goalposts** changer les règles du jeu

goat [gəʊt] N **1** chèvre *f*; **she g.** chèvre, *Fam* bique *f*; **he g.** bouc *m*; **g.'s milk** lait *m* de chèvre; **g.'s (milk) cheese** fromage *m* de chèvre; *Fig Fam* **it really gets my g.!** ça me met en boule!, ça me tape sur les nerfs!; *Fig* **to act**

or **play the g.** faire l'idiot **2** *Fam Pej* **old g.** *(lecherous man)* vieux *m* cochon; *Am (old woman)* vieille toupie *f*, *(old man)* vieux schnock *m*

goatee [gəʊ'tiː] N *(beard)* barbiche *f*, bouc *m*

goatherd ['gəʊthɜːd] N chevrier, -ière

goatskin ['gəʊtskɪn] N **1** peau *f* de chèvre *ou* *Fam* de bique **2** *(bottle)* outre *f* (en peau de bouc)

goatsucker ['gəʊtsʌkər] N *Am (bird)* engoulevent *m*

gob [gɒb] N **1** *Br Fam (spittle)* crachat *m*; **a g. of spit** un crachat **2** *esp Br Sl (mouth)* gueule *f*, **shut your g.!** ferme-la!, ta gueule!

VI *Br Sl (spit)* cracher (**at** sur)

gobble ['gɒb(ə)l] VT *Fam (eat)* avaler gloutonnement, dévorer, *Fam* bouffer; **don't g. (your food)!** *(to child)* n'avale pas si vite!

N *(of turkey)* glouglou *m*

VI *(of turkey)* glouglouter

▸ **gobble down** VT SEP *(eat quickly)* avaler gloutonnement, *Fam* bouffer

▸ **gobble up** VT SEP *(eat quickly)* engloutir, engouffrer, *Fam* bouffer; *Fig (money, pay rise)* engloutir; *Fig* **the empire gobbled up these territories** l'empire a absorbé ces territoires

gobbledegook, gobbledygook ['gɒb(ə)ldɪɡuːk] N *Fam* charabia *m*

go-between N intermédiaire *mf*; **to act** *or* **serve as a g.** servir d'intermédiaire (**to** à)

goblet ['gɒblɪt] N verre *m* à pied; *Lit (drinking cup)* coupe *f*

goblin ['gɒblɪn] N lutin *m*

gobo ['gəʊbəʊ] N *(camera matte)* drapeau *m*

gobshite ['gɒbʃaɪt] N *Sl (bastard)* trouduc *m*

gob-smacked [-smækt] ADJ *Br Sl* **I was g.** j'en étais tout estomaqué

gobstopper ['gɒbstɒpər] N *Br* gros bonbon *m* rond

go-by N *Fam* **to give sb the g.** snober qn

GOC [dʒiːəʊ'siː] N *Mil (abbr* general officer commanding*)* général *m* commandant en chef

go-cart N **1** *(child's toy)* petit chariot *m*; *Sport* kart *m* **2** *Am (baby-walker)* trotteur *m*; *(pushchair)* poussette *f*

▸▸ **g. racing** karting *m*

God [gɒd] N Dieu *m*; *Rel* **G. the Father, G. the Son** and **G. the Holy Ghost** Dieu le père, le fils et le Saint-Esprit; **a man of G.** un homme de Dieu; **to play G.** se prendre pour Dieu; **I wish to G. ...** plût à Dieu ...; **in G.'s name, in the name of G.** au nom du Ciel; *Fam* **G. knows** Dieu seul le sait; **G. willing** si Dieu le veut; *Fam* **for G.'s sake!, for the love of G.!** pour l'amour de Dieu!; *Fam* **what in G.'s name are you doing?** que faites-vous là, grand Dieu!; *Fam* **she's G. knows where** elle est Dieu sait où; *Fam* **oh G.!, my G.!** mon Dieu!; **G. forbid!** à Dieu ne plaise!; *Fam* **he thinks he's G.'s gift to women** il croit que toutes les femmes vont tomber à ses pieds; **he's not exactly G.'s gift to women** ce n'est pas vraiment l'homme dont rêvent toutes les femmes; **an act of G.** un cas de force majeure

god [gɒd] N dieu *m*; **the g. of war** le dieu de la guerre; **a river g.** une divinité de la rivière; **to make a g. of money** diviniser l'argent; *Theat Fam* **the gods** *(gallery)* le poulailler

god-awful ADJ *Fam* dégueulasse

god-botherer [-bɒðərər] N *Fam* cul-bénit *m*, *pl* culs-bénits

godchild, *pl* **godchildren** ['gɒdtʃaɪld, -tʃɪldrən] N filleul, -eule

goddammit [gɒd'dæmɪt] INT *Am Sl* bordel!

goddamn ['gɒd'dæm] *esp Am Sl* **INT** nom de Dieu!

ADJ (*also* **god-damned**) fichu, sacré; **don't be such a g. fool!** ne sois donc pas si bête!

goddaughter ['gɒdɔ:tər] **N** filleule *f*

goddess ['gɒdɪs] **N** déesse *f*, *Fig* **a g. of the screen, a screen g.** une idole du grand écran

godfather ['gɒdfɑ:ðər] **N** parrain *m*

god-fearing ['gɒdfɪərɪŋ] **ADJ** (*person*) très religieux; **decent g. folk** les gens croyants bien comme il faut

godforsaken ['gɒdfəseɪk(ə)n] **ADJ** (*place, town*) perdu; **what a g. place!** quel bled!

godhead ['gɒdhed] **N** divinité *f*

godless ['gɒdlɪs] **ADJ** (*person, action etc*) impie

godlike ['gɒdlaɪk] **ADJ** divin, de dieu

godliness ['gɒdlɪnɪs] **N** piété *f*

godly ['gɒdlɪ] **ADJ** dévot, pieux; **to lead a g. life** vivre pieusement

godmother ['gɒdmʌðər] **N** marraine *f*

godparent ['gɒdpeərənt] **N** (*woman*) marraine *f*, (*man*) parrain *m*; **my godparents** mon parrain et ma marraine

godsend ['gɒdsend] **N** aubaine *f*; **this money is a g. to him** cet argent est un don du ciel; **the president's gaffe was a g. to the opposition** la gaffe du président a été une aubaine pour l'opposition

godson ['gɒdsʌn] **N** filleul *m*

godsquad ['gɒdskwɒd] **N** *Fam* bondieusards *mpl*

goer ['gəʊər] **N 1** **to be a good/bad g.** (*of horse*) courir bien/mal; (*of car*) marcher bien/mal **2** *Fam* **she's a real g.!** (*promiscuous*) c'est une femme facile!; (*good in bed*) c'est un bon coup!

-goer ['gəʊər] **SUFF** church/cinema/theatre-**g.** personne qui va souvent à l'église/au cinéma/au théâtre

gofer, gopher ['gəʊfər] **N 1** *esp Am Fam* (*menial assistant*) (*male*) grouillot *m*, homme *m* à tout faire; (*female*) bonne *f* à tout faire **2** *Comput* (*serveur m*) gopher *m*

go-getter [-getər] **N** *Fam* battant, -ante

go-getting [-getɪŋ] **ADJ** *Fam* (*person, approach*) entreprenant, dynamique

goggle ['gɒg(ə)l] **VI** (*of person*) rouler de gros yeux; (*of eyes*) être saillant; **to g. at sb/sth** regarder qn/qch en roulant de gros yeux

gogglebox ['gɒg(ə)lbɒks] **N** *Br Fam* télé *f*

goggle-eyed **ADJ** *Fam* qui a les yeux en boules de loto; **they watched g.** ils regardaient, les yeux en boules de loto

goggles ['gɒg(ə)lz] **NPL** (*for motorcyclist*) lunettes *fpl* protectrices *ou* de moto; (*for skier*) lunettes (de ski); (*for diver, swimmer*) lunettes (de plongée); *Ind* lunettes de travail; (*for welder*) lunettes (protectrices); *Hum* (*spectacles*) carreaux *mpl*

go-go dancer **N** = homme *m* ou femme *f* légèrement vêtu(e) qui danse sur un podium de boîte de nuit

going ['gəʊɪŋ] **ADJ 1** (*functioning*) qui marche; **to start** *or* **set sth g.** mettre qch en marche; **the business is a g. concern** c'est une affaire qui marche; **to be sold as a g. concern** à vendre avec fonds **2** (*current*) **the g. price** *or* **rate** prix courant *ou* actuel

N 1 (*progress*) **that's very good g.!** voilà qui n'est pas mal du tout!; **it was slow g.** (*walking, climbing*) on progressait lentement; (*working, learning*) ça avançait lentement; **it was hard g.** (*walking, climbing*) on progressait difficilement; (*learning, working*) c'était dur; *Typ* **g. to press** mise *f* sous presse **2** (*leaving*) départ *m*

3 g. back (*return*) retour *m*; **g. back on one's word** manque *m* de parole; **there's no g.** **back now** il n'y a pas moyen de revenir en arrière

4 *Horseracing etc* (*condition of ground*) état *m* du sol; **the g. is rough** le chemin est rude; *Horseracing* **good/heavy g.** bon terrain/terrain lourd; *Fig* **heavy g.** (*of film, book etc*) indigeste; *Fig* **it's heavy g. getting him to talk** on a du mal à le faire parler; *Fig* **while the g. is good** tant que c'est favorable; **to get out while the g.'s good** partir tant que les choses vont bien

-going ['gəʊɪŋ] **SUFF 1** theatre/cinema-g. fréquentation *f* des théâtres/des cinémas **2** slow/fast-g. qui marche lentement/vite

going-away **ADJ** **a g. party/present** une soirée/un cadeau d'adieu
▸▸ **g. dress** robe *f* de voyage de noce

going-over **N** *Fam* **to give sb a g.** (*beating*) tabasser qn; (*criticism*) sonner les cloches à qn; **the burglars had given the flat a real g.** les cambrioleurs avaient laissé l'appartement sens dessus dessous; **the auditors gave the accounts a thorough g.** les experts ont soigneusement examiné les comptes

going-rate pricing **N** *Mktg* alignement *m* sur les prix du marché

goings-on ['gəʊɪŋzɒn] **NPL** *Fam* (*events*) événements *mpl*; (*behaviour*) conduite *f*; **the g. of the Royals** les activités *fpl* des membres de la famille royale; **there were strange g.** il se passait de drôles de choses; **what extraordinary g.!** quelles histoires extraordinaires!

goitre, *Am* **goiter** ['gɔɪtər] **N** *Med* goitre *m*

go-kart **N** *Sport* kart *m*
▸▸ **g. racing** karting *m*

gold [gəʊld] **N 1** or *m*; **to pay sb in g.** payer qn en or **2** (*medal*) médaille *f* d'or; **to win g.** gagner la médaille d'or **3** (*colour*) or *m*; **the reds and golds of autumn** les rouges et les ors de l'automne

ADJ (*made of gold*) en or; (*gold-coloured*) doré; **g. brooch/necklace** broche/collier en or; **g. dress** robe couleur d'or *ou* dorée; **g. lamé dress** robe lamée d'or; **g. paint** peinture dorée
▸▸ *Fin* **g. bond** obligation *f* or; **g. braid** galon *m* d'or; **g. bullion** or en barre *ou* en lingots, encaisse *f* or; **the G. Coast** (*in Australia*) = suite *f* de stations balnéaires sur la côte est de l'Australie; *Am* (*expensive area*) les beaux quartiers *mpl*; *Formerly* (*Ghana*) le Ghana; **g. coin** pièce *f* d'or; **g. content** teneur *f* en or; **g. currency** monnaie *f* d'or; **g. dust** poudre *f* d'or; *Fig* **tickets for the game are like g. dust** il est pratiquement impossible de se procurer des billets pour le match; **g. fever** fièvre *f* de l'or; **g. filling** (*in tooth*) obturation *f* à l'or *ou* en or; **g. foil** feuille *f* d'or, or en feuille; **g. ingot** lingot *m* d'or; **g. leaf** feuille d'or, or en feuille; **g. market** marché *m* de l'or; **g. medal** médaille *f* d'or; *also Fig* **g. mine** mine *f* d'or; **g. money** monnaie d'or; **g. plate** (*utensils*) orfèvrerie *f*, vaisselle *f* d'or; (*plating*) plaqué *f* d'or; *Mus* **g. record** disque *m* d'or; *Fin* **g. reserve** réserve *f* d'or; **g. rush** ruée *f* vers l'or; **g. standard** étalon-or *m inv*

goldbrick ['gəʊldbrɪk] *Am Fam* **N 1** **to sell sb a g.** rouler qn **2** (*malingerer*) tire-au-flanc *m*
VT (*swindle*) rouler
VI (*malinger*) tirer au flanc

goldcrest ['gəʊldkrest] **N** (*bird*) roitelet *m* huppé

gold-digger **N** chercheur *m* d'or; *Pej Fig* (*woman*) croqueuse *f* de diamants

golden ['gəʊld(ə)n] **ADJ 1** (*made of gold*) en or; *Bible, Fig* **to worship the g. calf** adorer le veau d'or **2** (*gold-coloured*) d'or; **g. hair** cheveux d'or **3** (*excellent, best*) **a g. opportunity** une occasion en or; **g. boy/girl** enfant *mf* chéri/chérie

▸▸ **the g. age** l'âge *m* d'or; **G. Delicious** (*apple*) golden *f*; **g. eagle** aigle *m* royal; *Myth* **the G. Fleece** la Toison d'or; **the G. Gate Bridge** le Golden Gate; *Cin, TV* **G. Globe** Golden Globe *m*; *Ftbl* **g. goal** but *m* en or; *Fig* **g. goose** poule *f* aux œufs d'or; *Fam* **g. handcuffs** primes *fpl* (*versées à un cadre à intervalles réguliers pour le dissuader de partir*); *Fam* **g. handshake** gratification *f* de fin de service; *Fam* **g. hello** prime *f* d'embauche; **g. jubilee** (*fête f du*) cinquantième anniversaire *m*; **the g. mean** le juste milieu; *Fam* **g. oldie** vieux tube *m*; *Fam* **g. parachute** prime *f* de licenciement (*versé à certains cadres supérieurs en cas de rachat de l'entreprise*); **g. pheasant** faisan *m* doré; **g. rule** règle *f* d'or; *Fin* **g. share** participation *f* majoritaire (*souvent détenue par le gouvernement britannique dans les entreprises privatisées*); **the G. State** = la Californie; *Br* **g. syrup** mélasse *f* raffinée; **g. wedding** noces *fpl* d'or

goldenrod ['gəʊld(ə)nrɒd] **N** *Bot* (*plant*) verge *f* d'or

goldfield ['gəʊldfi:ld] **N** champ *m ou* région *f* aurifère

goldfinch ['gəʊldfɪntʃ] **N** chardonneret *m*

goldfish ['gəʊldfɪʃ] **N** poisson *m* rouge
▸▸ **g. bowl** bocal *m* (à poissons rouges); *Fig* **it's like living in a g. bowl** c'est comme être en vitrine

Goldilocks ['gəʊldɪlɒks] **N** Boucle d'Or *f*

gold-plated **ADJ** plaqué or

gold-rimmed **ADJ** (*glasses*) à monture dorée

goldsmith ['gəʊldsmɪθ] **N** orfèvre *m*

gold-tipped **ADJ** à bout doré

golf [gɒlf] *Sp* **N** golf *m*
VI jouer au golf; **I went golfing yesterday** hier, j'ai fait du golf *ou* j'ai joué au golf
▸▸ **g. ball** (*for golf*) balle *f* de golf; (*for typewriter*) boule *f*, **g. ball typewriter** machine *f* à écrire à boule; **g. club** (*stick*) club *m ou* crosse *f ou* canne *f* de golf; (*building, association*) club de golf; **g. course** terrain *m ou* parcours *m* de golf, golf; **g. links** links *mpl*, **g. umbrella** parapluie *m* de golf

golfer ['gɒlfər] **N** golfeur, -euse, joueur, -euse de golf

golfing ['gɒlfɪŋ] **N** golf *m*
▸▸ **g. holiday** = vacances *fpl* prises pour jouer au golf

Goliath [gə'laɪəθ] **N** *Bible, Fig* Goliath *m*

golliwog ['gɒlɪwɒg] **N** = poupée *f* en étoffe représentant un Noir

golly ['gɒlɪ] **INT** *Old-fashioned Fam* fichtre!, mince (alors)!

N *Br* = **golliwog**

goloshes [gə'lɒʃɪz] **NPL** = **galoshes**

gonad ['gɒnæd, 'gəʊ-] **N** *Biol* gonade *f*

gondola ['gɒndələ] **N 1** (*boat*) gondole *f* **2** *Aviat* (*of airship, balloon*) nacelle *f*, *Am* (*cable car*) nacelle *ou* cabine *f* de téléphérique **3** *Am Rail* wagon *m* plat **4** *Mktg* (*in supermarket etc*) gondole *f*
▸▸ *Am Rail* **g. car** wagon plat; *Mktg* **g. end** tête *f* de gondole

gondolier [gɒndə'lɪər] **N** gondolier *m*

gone [gɒn] **PP** *see* **go**
ADJ 1 **to be g.** (*dead*) être mort, être parti; **when I'm g.** quand je ne serai plus là; *Fam* **oh well, that's that g.!** (*of broken machine etc*) bon, ben c'est foutu!
2 to be pretty far g. (*drunk*) être complètement bourré; (*on drugs*) être complètement camé; (*of dying patient*) être très mal; *Fam* **to be six months g.** (*pregnant*) être enceinte de six mois; **how far g. is she?** (*pregnant*) elle est enceinte de combien?
3 *Fam* **g. on sb** amoureux *ou Fam* toqué de qn

4 *(past)* **it's g. ten o'clock** il est plus de dix heures, il est dix heures passées

goner [ˈgɒnər] N *Fam* mourant, -ante; **I thought she was a g.** je pensais qu'elle allait mourir; **if the engine fails now, we'll all be goners** si le moteur tombe en panne, on va tous crever *ou* on est tous foutus; *Fig* **I'm a g. if she finds out where I've been** je suis fichu *ou* foutu si elle apprend où je suis allé

gong [gɒŋ] N **1** *Mus etc* gong *m*; **to sound the g.** faire retentir le gong **2** *Br Fam (medal)* médaille *f*; **he was wearing all his gongs** il exhibait toute sa batterie de cuisine

gonna [ˈgɒnə] CONTR *Fam* = going to

gonorrhoea, *Am* **gonorrhea** [gɒnəˈrɪə] N *Med* blennorragie *f*; **to have g.** avoir *ou* faire une blennorragie

goo [guː] N *Fam* **1** *(sticky substance)* substance *f* visqueuse **2** *(sentimentality)* mièvrerie *f*

goober [ˈguːbər] N *Am Fam* crétin, -ine

GOOD [gʊd]

> | ADJ | bon **1–7, 10–12, 15, 17** • beau **1** |
> | | • sage **8** • aimable **9** |
> | ADV | bien **1–3** |
> | N | bien **1, 2** • pour de bon *(for good)* **4** |
> | INT | bien |

ADJ (**better, best**) **1** *(of fine quality)* bon, *f* bonne; **a g. wine** un bon vin; **g. handwriting** belle écriture; **to have a g. ear (for music)** avoir de l'oreille; **she was wearing her g. dress** elle portait sa belle robe; **we only use the g. cutlery when we have guests** nous n'utilisons nos beaux couverts que lorsque nous avons des invités; **he has a g. style, but …** son style est agréable, mais …; **g. weather** beau temps; **g. to eat** bon à manger; **the leaves are g. to eat as well as the root** les feuilles, de même que la racine, sont comestibles *ou* bonnes à manger; **this fruit is a bit bashed, but it's still g. to eat** ce fruit est un peu écrasé, mais il est encore bon; **is the meat still g.?** est-ce que la viande est encore bonne?; *Fam* **that's a g. one!** *(of story, joke)* elle est bien bonne, celle-là!; **he's too g. for that job** il mérite une meilleure situation; **I suppose he thinks he's too g. for us** j'imagine qu'il se trouve trop bien pour nous; **if it's g. enough for you, it's g. enough for me** si ça vous va, alors ça me va aussi; **this isn't g. enough!** *(you will have to do better)* c'est insuffisant!; **it's looking g.** ça a l'air de bien se passer; *(is going to succeed)* ça se présente bien; **he's looking g.** *(of boxer, athlete, candidate in election)* il a toutes ses chances; **g. living, the g. life** la belle vie

2 *(appropriate)* bon, *f* bonne; **a g. opportunity** une bonne occasion; **to be in a g. position to do sth** être bien placé pour faire qch; **it is not always g. to …** il n'est pas toujours bon de …

3 *(pleasant, enjoyable)* heureux; **g. news** bonnes *ou* heureuses nouvelles; **to have a g. time** (bien) s'amuser; **to show sb a g. time** faire passer un bon moment à qn; **a g. time was had by all** tout le monde s'est bien amusé; **too g. to be true** trop beau pour être vrai; **it's g. to be alive!** que la vie est belle!; **it's g. to know you've got friends** ça fait plaisir de savoir qu'on a des amis; **it's g. to see you** je suis/nous sommes content(s) de te voir; **it's been g. seeing you again** ça m'a/nous a fait plaisir de vous revoir

4 *(attractive)* bon, beau; **she looks g. in that hat** ce chapeau lui va bien; **that pizza looks g.** cette pizza a l'air bonne; **the vase looks g. there** le vase rend très bien là; **(that) sounds g.!** *(good idea)* bonne idée!; **to have a g. figure** être bien fait

5 *(beneficial)* **this medicine is very g. for coughs** ce remède est très bon pour la toux; **beer is not g. for me** la bière ne me vaut rien; **you'll accept, if you know what's g. for you** tu accepteras, si tu as deux sous de bon sens; **to drink more than is g. for one** boire plus que de raison; **it will be g. for them to have some company** ça leur fera du bien d'avoir de la compagnie; **it isn't g. for people to live alone** il n'est pas bon de vivre seul; **it's g. for your health** c'est bon pour la santé; **he's not g. for her** il a une mauvaise influence sur elle; **to be g. for business** être bon pour les affaires

6 *(skilful, effective etc)* bon, *f* bonne; **to be g. with one's hands** être adroit *ou* habile de ses mains; **to be g. with children** *(of person)* savoir y faire avec les enfants; **to be g. at maths** être bon *ou* fort en math; **to be g. at sport** être bon en sport; **to be g. for doing sth** *(of equipment, medicine, chemical etc)* être bien pour faire qch; **to be g. on French history/contract law** *(of author)* être bon en histoire de France/sur le droit des contrats; **to be g. on sth** *(of book)* être complet sur qch; **to be g. in bed** être un bon/une bonne partenaire sexuel(le); **g. for nothing** bon à rien

7 *(morally good)* bon, *f* bonne; **g. Christian** bon chrétien, bonne chrétienne; **to lead a g. life** vivre en homme de bien, pratiquer le bien; **he proved to be a g. friend** il s'est montré un véritable ami; **g. nature** bon naturel *m*; **they take advantage of his g. nature** ils profitent de son bon caractère

8 *(well-behaved)* sage; **answer would you, there's a g. boy** sois gentil, réponds; **be g.!** *(to child)* sois sage!; **g. dog!** *(encouraging)* oh, le beau chien!; *(congratulating)* c'est bien, le chien!; **he's g. with children** *(of dog, pony etc)* il est très doux avec les enfants; **g. conduct** *or* **behaviour** bonne conduite *f*, **as g. as gold** sage comme une image

9 *(kind)* aimable; **that's very g. of you** c'est bien aimable *ou* gentil de votre part; **he was very g. about it** il s'est montré très compréhensif; **would you be g. enough to …?** auriez-vous l'amabilité *ou* la gentillesse de …?; **she has always been g. to me** elle s'est toujours montrée bonne pour moi; **life has been g. to me** j'ai eu de la chance dans la vie; **he's a g. sort** *or* **chap** c'est un brave type; **to do sb a g. turn** rendre service à qn

10 *(valid)* **a g. reason** une bonne raison, une raison valable; **he** *or* **his credit is g. for £25,000** on peut lui faire jusqu'à 25 000 livres de crédit; **he should be g. for a couple of hundred pounds** on devrait pouvoir en tirer quelques centaines de livres; **how much is he g. for?** de combien dispose-t-il?; **this car ought to be g. for another five years** cette voiture devrait me faire encore cinq ans; **this pass is g. for another six months** cette carte d'abonnement est encore valable six mois; *Fam* **she's g. for another ten years yet** elle en a encore pour une bonne dizaine d'ans

11 *(substantial)* **it makes a g. meal for four** ça fait un bon repas pour quatre; **to earn g. money** bien gagner sa vie; **you've got a g. chance** tu as toutes tes chances; **of a g. size** de bonne taille; **a g. way into the first act** bien après le début du premier acte; **it's a g. distance** *or* **way (from here)** c'est assez loin d'ici; **I was a g. way into the book when I realized that …** j'avais déjà bien avancé dans ma lecture quand je me suis rendu compte que …

12 *(thorough)* bon; **a g. spanking/beating** une bonne fessée/correction; **to have a g. look at sb/sth** bien regarder qn/qch; **to have a g. cry** pleurer un bon coup (**about sth** à propos de qch); **I had a g. sleep last night** j'ai bien dormi la nuit dernière; **we had a g. laugh (about it)** on (en) a ri un bon coup

13 to make g. *(of person)* prospérer, faire son chemin; **an immigrant made g.** un immigrant qui a fait son chemin; **to make g. a loss** remplacer ce qu'on a perdu; **to make g. one's losses** compenser ses pertes; **to make g. a deficiency** pallier une insuffisance; **to make g. an injustice/damage** réparer une injustice/des dégâts; **to make g. one's promise** remplir *ou* tenir sa promesse; **he made g. his escape** il a réussi son évasion

14 *(expressions with 'as')* **it's as g. a way as any other** c'est une façon qui en vaut une autre; **it's as g. a place as any to stay** qu'on séjourne là ou ailleurs, ça ne fait pas de différence; **this is as g. as you can get** c'est ce qui se fait de mieux; **to give as g. as one gets** rendre coup pour coup; **this method is as g., if not better** cette méthode est aussi bonne, pour ne pas dire meilleure; **it's as g. as new** il/elle est comme neuf/neuve; **to make sth as g. as new** remettre qch à neuf; **it's as g. as settled** c'est comme si c'était fait; **are you married? – as g. as** *(I'm living with sb)* tu es marié? – non, mais c'est tout comme; **it is as g. as saying that …** ça revient à dire que …; **he as g. as told me it would be a disaster** il m'a quasiment dit que ce serait un désastre; **he as g. as called me a liar to my face** c'est comme s'il m'avait traité de menteur

15 *(used affectionately)* **g. old Anne, I knew she wouldn't let us down!** cette brave Anne, je savais bien qu'elle ne nous laisserait pas tomber!; **g. old London** le bon vieux Londres; **the g. old days** le bon vieux temps; *Old-fashioned* **his g. lady (wife)** son épouse; **your g. lady** votre dame; *Old-fashioned* **my g. man** mon brave

16 *(greetings, exclamations)* **g. morning/afternoon!** bonjour (monsieur/*etc*)!; *Fml* **g. day** *(hello)* bonjour; *(goodbye)* au revoir; **g. night!** *(when going to bed)* bonne nuit!; *(when leaving)* bonsoir!; **very g.!** *(well done, congratulations etc)* très bien!, parfait!; **very g., sir!** bien, monsieur!; *esp Fml (I'll do as you say)* très bien, je m'en charge!; **g. for you!,** *esp Austr* **g. on you!** tant mieux pour toi!; **g. Lord!** grand Dieu!; **g. heavens!, g. gracious!** bon sang!; **g. grief!** fichtre!

17 *(with quantity, number)* **a g. half** une bonne moitié; **a g. two hours** deux bonnes heures; **a g. while, a g. time** pas mal de temps; **a g. round sum** une somme rondelette; **a g. twenty years ago** il y a bien vingt ans; **a g. deal, a g. many** beaucoup; **a g. few** pas mal; **a g. few people** pas mal de gens; **to come in a g. third** arriver bon troisième

ADV 1 bien; **a g. long break** une pause bien longue; **to have a g. long soak in the bath** rester des heures dans le bain

2 *Fam* **they beat us g. and proper** ils nous ont écrasés; **he was g. and mad** il était absolument furieux; **I'll do it when I'm g. and ready** je le ferai quand ça me chantera; **I like my coffee g. and strong** j'aime le café bien fort; **make sure it's stuck on g. and hard** vérifie que c'est vraiment bien collé; **put the paint on g. and thick** appliquer la peinture en couches bien épaisses

3 *esp Dial Fam (well)* bien; **she sure sings g.** elle chante bien, c'est sûr; **how are you? – g., thanks** comment allez-vous? – bien, merci

N 1 *(morally good behaviour)* bien *m*; **to return g. for evil** rendre le bien pour le mal; **to do g.** faire le bien; **he's up to no g.** il prépare un mauvais coup; **to come to no g.** finir mal; **there is g. and bad everywhere** il y a du bien et du mal partout; **there's g. and bad in everyone** il y a du bon et du mauvais en chacun de nous; **to see the g. in sb/sth** voir le bon côté de qn/qch

2 *(benefit, use)* **I did it for your own g.** je l'ai fait pour votre bien; **for the g. of one's health** pour sa santé; **to act for the common g.** agir dans l'intérêt général; **it will do you g.**

(to spend a week in the country) cela vous fera du bien (de passer une semaine à la campagne); **what g. will that do you?, what g. will it be to you?** à quoi cela vous avancera-t-il?; **that won't be much g.** ça ne servira pas à grand-chose; **for all the g. it will do** pour la différence que cela fera; **what's the g. of (doing) that?** à quoi bon?; **it's no g. talking about it** inutile d'en parler; **that's no g.** (pointless) cela ne sert à rien; (worthless) ça ne vaut rien; **he's no g.** il est nul; **it's no g. complaining** se plaindre ne sert à rien **3** (profit) **to be five pounds to the g.** avoir cinq livres de gagné ou de profit; **it is all to the g.** c'est autant de gagné **4 for g. (and all)** (permanently) pour de bon; **he is gone for g.** il est parti pour de bon; **to settle down for g.** se fixer définitivement **5 the g. and the bad** (pl) (people) les bons et les méchants

INTbien; **g., that's settled then** eh bien, c'est arrangé alors; **I feel better today – g.!** je me sens mieux aujourd'hui – tant mieux!

▸ ▸ **the G. Book** la sainte Bible; **G. Friday** le vendredi saint; **G. Housekeeping seal** label m britannique de bonne qualité; **g. looks** (attractive appearance) beauté f; Bible **the G. Samaritan** le bon Samaritain

---

Good Friday
En Grande-Bretagne, il est traditionnel, le jour du vendredi saint, de manger des "hot cross buns" (petits pains ronds aux fruits secs, marqués d'une croix).

---

goodbye ['gʊd'baɪ] INT, N au revoir m; **g. for now!** à bientôt!; **to say g. to sb** dire au revoir à qn; **she said her goodbyes** elle a dit au revoir; (for good) elle a fait ses adieux; **it was g. to Paris for the time being** il fallait dire au revoir à Paris pour le moment; **that was g. to £5,000** j'ai dû dire adieu à mes 5 000 livres; **he can say g. to any hope of an ambassadorship** il peut dire adieu à ses espoirs de devenir ambassadeur; **to give sb a g. kiss/hug** embrasser qn/serrer qn dans ses bras pour lui dire au revoir

▸ ▸ **g. present** cadeau m d'adieu

good-for-nothing ADJ (person) qui n'est bon à rien; **her g. husband** son bon à rien de mari

N bon m à rien, bonne f à rien, vaurien, -ienne

good-hearted [-'hɑ:tɪd] ADJ qui a bon cœur; (gesture) généreux

good-humoured, Am **good-humored** [-'hju:məd] ADJ (person) d'un caractère agréable, facile à vivre; (on particular occasion) de bonne humeur; (smile, air) bon enfant inv; (answer) plaisant; (joke etc) sans malice; **he is always g.** il a bon caractère; **in that g. way of hers** avec sa bonne humeur habituelle

good-humouredly, Am **good-humoredly** [-'hju:mədlɪ] ADVavec bonhomie; (to laugh) avec bonne humeur

goodish ['gʊdɪʃ] ADJ Fam **1** (quite good) assez bon, passable **2** (number etc) assez grand; **it's a g. step from here** c'est à un bon bout de chemin d'ici; **it's a g. size** c'est assez grand; **add a g. pinch of salt** ajoutez une bonne pincée de sel

good-looker N Fam **he's/she's a g.** il/elle est beau/belle

good-looking ADJ (better-looking, best-looking) beau, f belle; **he's very g.** il est beau garçon; **she's quite g.** elle n'est pas mal; **hey, g.!** (to woman) eh, ma jolie!; (to man) eh, beau gosse!

goodly ['gʊdlɪ] ADJ Old-fashioned, Lit (por-

---

tion etc) large, ample; (number) considérable; **a g. sum (of money)** une belle somme (d'argent)

good-natured [-'neɪtʃəd] ADJ (person) accommodant, d'un caractère agréable; (laugh) jovial

good-naturedly [-'neɪtʃədlɪ] ADV avec bonhomie

goodness ['gʊdnɪs] N **1** (of person) bonté f; Fml **would you have the g. to inform me next time?** auriez-vous la bonté de m'informer la prochaine fois? **2** (of thing) bonne qualité f; **contains all the g. of full cream milk** (in advert) contient toutes les bonnes choses du lait entier; **to extract all the g. out of sth** extraire tout ce qu'il y a de bon de qch; **it's where the g. is** (in fruit etc) c'est ce qu'il y a de plus nutritif **3** (as euphemism) **g. gracious (me)!** bonté divine!, mon Dieu!; **g. (me)!** mon Dieu!, oh là là!; **thank g.!** Dieu merci!; **for g.' sake, be quiet!** taisez-vous, pour l'amour de Dieu!; **I wish to g. he'd shut up!** je prie le ciel qu'il se taise!; **g. (only) knows what I'm going to do** Dieu seul sait ce que je dois faire

goodnight [gʊd'naɪt] N after they had said **their goodnights** (and gone to bed) après qu'ils se furent dit bonne nuit; (and left) après qu'ils se furent dit bonsoir; **to give sb a g. kiss** donner un baiser à qn pour lui dire bonne nuit

goods [gʊdz] NPL **1** Law biens mpl, effets mpl; **g. and chattels** possessions fpl **2** Com, Econ marchandises fpl; **manufactured g.** produits mpl manufacturés; **leather g.** articles mpl en cuir, maroquinerie f; **to deliver the g.** livrer la marchandise ou les marchandises; Fig (keep one's promise) remplir ses engagements, tenir parole; Fig **a computer that can deliver the g.** un ordinateur qui tient ses promesses; Fig **to come up with the g.** faire le nécessaire; Am Fam **to have the g. on sb** avoir la preuve de la culpabilité de qn

▸ ▸ Rail **g. depot** dépôt m de marchandises; Rail **g. station** gare f de marchandises; Rail **g. train** train m de marchandises; Br **g. vehicle** poids m lourd, véhicule m utilitaire

good-tempered ADJ d'un caractère facile, qui a bon caractère; (reply, discussion) aimable

good-till-cancelled order N St Exch ordre m à révocation

good-time ADJ Fam qui ne pense qu'à s'amuser

▸ ▸ **g. girl** fille f rigolote; (sexually) fille facile

goodwill [gʊd'wɪl] N **1** (benevolence) bienveillance f, bon vouloir m (towards pour, envers); **a gesture of g.** un geste de bonne volonté; **a g. tour** un voyage d'amitié; **to retain sb's g.** conserver les bonnes grâces de qn **2** (willingness) bonne volonté f **3** Com fonds m de commerce, actif m incorporel

▸ ▸ **g. mission** mission f de conciliation

goody ['gʊdɪ] Fam N **1** (person) brave type m; (too good) petit saint m; **the goodies and the baddies** les bons mpl et les méchants **2 goodies** (treats) bonnes choses fpl

INT **(g.) g.!** chouette!

goody-goody Fam Pej N petit saint m, petite sainte f

ADJ de petit saint; **she's awfully g.** elle prend toujours des airs de petite sainte

goody-two-shoes N = goody-goody

gooey ['gu:ɪ] ADJ Fam **1** (sticky) gluant, collant **2** (sentimental) à l'eau de rose

goof [gu:f] Fam N **1** (blunder) gaffe f, bourde f **2** (idiot) cave m

VT **1** (blunder) gaffer, faire une gaffe ou une bourde **2** (joke) rigoler; **to g. with sb** (tease)

---

faire enrager qn **3** (stare) **to g. at sb/sth** regarder qn/qch bêtement

▸ ▸ **g. sheet** pense-bête m, pl pense-bêtes

▸ **goof about, goof around** VI Fam (act foolishly) faire l'idiot; (waste time) glander, glandouiller

▸ **goof off** VI Am Fam (evade work, waste time) glander, glandouiller

▸ **goof up** Am Fam VT SEP **to g. sth up** foirer qch

VI merder

goofball ['gu:fbɔ:l] N Am Sl **1** (fool) cave m **2** (drug) somnifère m

goofy ['gu:fɪ] ADJ Fam **1** (stupid) loufoque **2** Br (teeth) en avant

googly ['gu:glɪ] N Cr = balle f lancée avec de l'effet qui prend le batteur à contre-pied alors qu'il pensait l'avoir bien anticipée; Fig **to bowl sb a g.** essayer de tromper qn

gook [gu:k] N Am **1** Offensive Sl (Oriental) Chinetoque mf **2** Fam (muck) saleté f, crasse f

goolies ['gu:lɪz] NPL Br Sl couilles fpl

goon [gu:n] N Fam **1** (stupid person) imbécile mf **2** Am (criminal) gorille m

goosander [gu:'sændər] N (bird) harle m bièvre

goose, pl **geese** [gu:s, gi:s] N **1** (bird) oie f; Fig **you've cooked your g., your g. is cooked** tu es fichu; Fig **to cook sb's g.** couler qn; Fig **to kill the g. that lays the golden egg** tuer la poule aux œufs d'or; Fig **all his geese are swans** à l'entendre, tout ce qu'il fait tient du prodige; **goose('s) egg** œuf m d'oie **2** Old-fashioned Fam (silly person) niais m, niaise f; **I'm not such a g.** je ne suis pas si bête que ça

VT Sl pincer les fesses à

▸ ▸ esp Am **g. bumps** chair f de poule; **to have g. bumps** avoir la chair de poule; **g. fat** graisse f d'oie; Br **g. flesh, g. pimples** chair f de poule; **to get g. flesh** or **pimples** avoir la chair de poule; Mil **g. step** pas m de l'oie

gooseberry ['gʊzb(ə)rɪ] N (fruit) groseille f à maquereau, groseille verte; (bush) groseillier m; Culin **g. fool** crème f de groseilles (à maquereau); Br Fam **to play g.** tenir la chandelle

▸ ▸ **g. bush** groseillier m; **I told her children were found under a g. bush** je lui ai dit que les petites filles naissent dans les roses et les petits garçons dans les choux

goosegog ['gʊzgɒg] N Br Fam groseille f à maquereau

goose-step VI (-pp-) Mil marcher au pas de l'oie

GOP [dʒi:əʊ'pi:] N Am Pol (abbr Grand Old Party) le Parti républicain

gopher ['gəʊfər] N **1** (rodent) (pocket) **g.** géomys m **2** (ground squirrel) spermophile m **3** = gofer

gorblimey ['gɔ:blaɪmɪ] INT Eng Dial nom d'un chien!

Gordian ['gɔ:dɪən] ADJ Fig **to cut the G. knot** trancher le nœud gordien

gore [gɔ:r] N (blood) sang m; **blood and g.** du sang et encore du sang; **there's plenty of g. in this movie** ce film est sanglant à souhait; Lit **he lay in his g.** il baignait dans son sang

VT (of bull) blesser avec les cornes, encorner; **gored to death** tué d'un coup/à coups de corne

gorge¹ [gɔ:dʒ] N **1** Geog gorge f, défilé m **2** Lit (throat) gorge f; **it makes my g. rise** cela me soulève le cœur

gorge² VI se gorger, se repaître, se rassasier, Fam s'empiffrer (on de)

VT (person) rassasier; **to g. oneself** se gaver, Fam s'empiffrer

gorgeous ['gɔːdʒəs] ADJ magnifique; *(weather)* superbe, magnifique; *(meal)* somptueux; *Lit (palaces)* fastueux; *Fam* **hello, g.!** *(usu to young woman)* bonjour, ma beauté!

gorgeously ['gɔːdʒəslɪ] ADV magnifiquement, somptueusement

gorgon ['gɔːgən] N *Myth* gorgone *f*

gorilla [gə'rɪlə] N *(animal), Fam (bodyguard)* gorille *m*

gormless ['gɔːmlɪs] ADJ *Br Fam* idiot, imbécile

gorse [gɔːs] N *Bot (shrub)* ajoncs *mpl*
▸▸ **g. bush** ajonc *m*

gory ['gɔːrɪ] ADJ sanglant, ensanglanté; *(film)* sanglant; **in g. detail** avec les détails les plus sanglants; *Fig* **spare me the g. details** épargne-moi les détails

gosh [gɒʃ] INT *Fam* zut (alors)!, mince (alors)!

goshawk ['gɒshɔːk] N *(bird)* autour *m*

gosling ['gɒzlɪŋ] N oison *m*

go-slow N *Br Ind* grève *f* du zèle

gospel ['gɒsp(ə)l] N évangile *m*; *Mus* gospel *m*; **St Mark's G., the G. according to St Mark** l'Évangile selon saint Marc; *Fig* **to take sth as g.** accepter qch comme parole d'évangile; *Fig* **it's the g. truth** c'est parole d'évangile; *Rel* **the g. for the day** l'évangile du jour; **to preach the g.** prêcher l'évangile; *Fig* **to preach the g. of monetarism** prêcher le monétarisme
▸▸ **g. music** gospel *m*; **g. oath** serment *m* prêté sur l'Évangile; **g. singer** chanteur, -euse de gospels

gospeller ['gɒspələr] N **(hot) g.** évangélisateur, -trice

gossamer ['gɒsəmər] N **1** *(spider's web)* fils *mpl* de la Vierge, filandres *fpl* **2** *Tex* gaze *f* légère
ADJ *(cloth)* très léger, arachnéen
▸▸ **g. thread** filandre *f*

gossip ['gɒsɪp] N **1** *(person)* bavard, -arde; *(ill-natured)* commère *f*, cancanier, -ière **2** *(talk)* bavardage *m*; *(ill-natured)* commérage(s) *m(pl)*, *Fam* cancans *mpl*, potins *mpl*; **to have a good g.** se raconter les derniers potins
VI bavarder; *(ill-naturedly) Fam* cancaner, potiner; **to g. about sb** faire des commérages sur qn
▸▸ **g. column** échos *mpl*, **g. columnist, g. writer** échotier *m*, rédacteur, -trice mondain(e)

gossiping ['gɒsɪpɪŋ] N bavardage *m*; *(ill-natured)* commérage *m*
ADJ ATTRIB cancanier

gossipmonger ['gɒsɪpmʌŋgər] N commère *f*

gossipy ['gɒsɪpɪ] ADJ *(style)* anecdotique; *(person)* cancanier, -ière; **g. letter** lettre pleine de petits potins

got PT, PP *see* get

gotcha ['gɒtʃə] INT *Fam (I understand)* pigé!; *(cry of success)* ça y est (je l'ai)!; *(when catching someone doing something)* je t'y prends!; *(when one has an advantage over someone)* je te tiens!

Gothic ['gɒθɪk] ADJ *Archit, Art, Ling, Typ etc* gothique
N **1** *Art* gothique *m* **2** *Ling* gotique *m*, gothique *m*
▸▸ **G. novel** roman *m* gothique

gotta ['gɒtə] CONTR *Fam* = **got to**

gotten *Am, Arch* PP *see* get

gouache [gʊ'ɑːʃ] N *Art* gouache *f*

gouge [gaʊdʒ] N *Carp, Surg* gouge *f*
VT *Carp (wood)* gouger
▸ **gouge out** VT SEP *(groove, channel etc)* creuser; **to g. sb's eye out** arracher un œil à qn

goulash ['guːlæʃ] N *Culin* goulasch *m*, goulache *m*

gourd [gʊəd] N **1** *(plant)* gourde *f* **2** *(container)* gourde *f*, calebasse *f* **3** *Fam* **out of one's g.** maboul

gourmand ['gʊəmənd] N *(glutton)* glouton, -onne; *(gourmet)* gourmet *m*

gourmet ['gʊəmeɪ] N gourmet *m*, gastronome *mf*; **g. cooking** cuisine *f* gastronomique; **g. restaurant** restaurant *m* gastronomique

gout [gaʊt] N *Med* goutte *f*; **to have g.** avoir la goutte

gouty ['gaʊtɪ] ADJ *(person, joint etc)* goutteux

Gov 1 *abbr* **government 2** *abbr* **governor**

.gov [dɒt'gʌv] *Comput* = abréviation *f* désignant les sites gouvernementaux dans les adresses électroniques

govern ['gʌvən] VT **1** *(rule) (state etc)* gouverner, régir; *(province etc)* administrer **2** *(control) Tech* gouverner; *Gram (the accusative etc)* se construire avec; **laws that g. chemical reactions** lois qui régissent les réactions chimiques **3** *(restrain) (emotions)* maîtriser, contenir
VI *(rule)* gouverner

governance ['gʌvənəns] N *Lit* **1** *(act, manner) (of state etc)* gouvernement *m*; *(of province etc)* administration *f* **2** *(control)* emprise *f*

governess ['gʌvənɪs] N gouvernante *f*

governing ['gʌvənɪŋ] ADJ **1** *Pol etc* gouvernant; **the g. party/coalition** le parti/la coalition au pouvoir **2** *Fig* dominant; **the g. concept of his philosophy** le principe qui sous-tend toute sa philososphie
N gouvernement *m*
▸▸ **g. body** conseil *m* d'administration

government ['gʌv(ə)nmənt] N **1** *Pol* gouvernement *m*; *Mil* **it's g. issue** c'est fourni par le gouvernement VOIR GRAMMAIRE A11 **2** *(cabinet)* ministère *m*; **to form a g.** former un gouvernement *ou* un ministère
▸▸ **g. action** action *f* gouvernementale; **g. advertising** publicité *f* gouvernementale; **g. adviser** conseiller *m* du gouvernement; **g. aid** aide *f* gouvernementale *ou* de l'État; *Fin* **g. bond** obligation *f* du gouvernement; **g. borrowings** emprunts *mpl* de l'État; *Br* **g. broker** agent *m* du Trésor; **g. expenditure** dépenses *fpl* publiques; **g. finance** financement *m* par l'État; **g. grant** subvention *f* d'État; *Br* **G. House** palais *m* du gouverneur; **g. intervention** intervention *f* du gouvernement; **g. loan** emprunt *m* public *ou* d'État; **g. market** marché *m* de l'État; **g. monopoly** monopole *m* d'État; **g. offices** bureaux *mpl* du Gouvernement; **g. organization** collectivité *f* publique; **g. representative** représentant *m* du gouvernement; **g. restraints, g. restrictions** restrictions *fpl* gouvernementales; **g. revenue** recettes *fpl* publiques; **g. sector** secteur *m* public; **g. securities** effets *mpl* publics, fonds *mpl* publics *ou* d'État; **g. spending** dépenses *fpl* publiques; **g. spending review** examen *m* des dépenses publiques; **g. stocks** rentes *fpl* de l'État, bons *mpl* du Trésor

governmental [gʌvən'ment(ə)l] ADJ gouvernemental, aux

government-sponsored [-spɒnsəd] ADJ parrainé par le gouvernement

governor ['gʌv(ə)nər] N **1** *(of colony, bank, US state)* gouverneur *m*; *(of prison, reform school etc)* directeur *m*; *(member of board of governors of a school etc)* membre *m* du conseil d'administration; *Br Fam* **the g.** *(boss)* le patron, le singe; *Fam* **where to, g.?** *(said by a taxi driver)* on va où, patron? **2** *Tech (device)* régulateur *m*; *(of speed)* modérateur *m*
▸▸ **g. general** gouverneur *m* général

governorship ['gʌvənəʃɪp] N *(post)* poste *m* de gouverneur; *(function)* fonctions *fpl* de gouverneur

Govt *abbr* **government**

gown [gaʊn] N **1** *(woman's)* robe *f* **2** *(of magistrate, academic etc)* robe *f*, toge *f*, *(of surgeon)* blouse *f*; *Univ* **town and g.** = les gens *mpl* de la ville et les étudiants *mpl*

goy, *pl* **goys, goyim** [gɔɪ, -z, 'gɔɪɪm] N goy *m*, *pl* goyim

GP [dʒiː'piː] N *Br Med (abbr* **general practitioner***)* (médecin *m*) généraliste *mf*

GPA [dʒiːpiː'eɪ] N *Am (abbr* **grade point average***)* moyenne *f*

GPO [dʒiːpiː'əʊ] N *Br Formerly (abbr* **General Post Office***)* Poste *f* principale

GPRS [dʒiːpiːɑː'res] N *Tel (abbr* **General Packet Radio Service***)* GPRS *m*

GPS [dʒiːpiː'es] N *(abbr* **Global Positioning System** *)* GPS *m (système de navigation par satellite)*

gr *(abbr* **gramme(s))** g.

grab [græb] N **1** *(movement)* **to make a g. at sth** faire un mouvement vif pour saisir qch; *Fam* **to be up for grabs** être à prendre; *(be on market, for sale)* être à vendre; **they're getting rid of all the furniture, so those chairs are up for grabs** ils se débarrassent de tous leurs meubles, alors ces chaises sont à qui veut les prendre; **is that last chocolate up for grabs?** est-ce que je peux prendre le chocolat qui reste?; **you can take it if you like, it's up for grabs** vous pouvez le prendre si vous voulez, il est là pour ça **2** *Constr* benne *f* preneuse *ou* piocheuse **3** *Aut (brakes)* blocage *m*
VT (-bb-) **to g. (hold of) sb/sth** saisir qn/qch (d'un geste brusque), empoigner qn/qch; **he grabbed a revolver from the table** il a saisi un revolver sur la table; **she grabbed the letter from my hands** elle m'a arraché la lettre des mains; **he grabbed me by the lapels** il m'a empoigné par le revers; **to g. a rope** *(to save oneself)* se raccrocher à un cordage; **to g. a chance/an opportunity** saisir une chance/une occasion; **to g. sb's attention** retenir *ou (stronger)* accaparer l'attention de qn; **I'll g. something to eat on the way** j'avalerai quelque chose en chemin; *Fam Fig* **how does that g. you?** *(my suggestion)* ça te dit?; **the idea doesn't g. me** ça ne me dit rien
VI **to g. at sb** s'agripper à qn; **to g. at sth** se saisir de qch, se jeter sur qch; **don't g.!** *(esp to children)* ne m'arrache/ne lui arrache/*etc* pas les choses/la nourriture/*etc* des mains!
▸▸ *Am* **g. bag** *(game)* = jeu *m* consistant à chercher des cadeaux enfouis dans un grand sac; *(assortment)* fourre-tout *m inv*; *Constr* **g. bucket** benne preneuse *ou* piocheuse

grabby ['græbɪ] ADJ *Fam* **don't be so g.** *(don't grab things)* ne te jette pas sur les choses; *(don't grab me)* ne t'agrippe pas à moi; **he's very g.** *(of child picking things up)* il touche à tout

grace [greɪs] N **1** *(of movement, dancer etc)* grâce *f*, *(of language)* élégance *f*
2 *(of manners)* grâce *f*, **to do sth with (a) good/bad g.** faire qch de bonne/mauvaise grâce; **to have the (good) g. to apologize** avoir la bonne grâce de faire des excuses; **the social graces** le savoir-vivre
3 *(favour)* faveur *f*, **to be in/get into sb's good graces** être dans/entrer dans les bonnes grâces de qn; *Rel* **the g. of God** la grâce de Dieu; **there, but for the g. of God, go I**

remercie le ciel de m'avoir épargné; **in a state of g.** en état de grâce; **to fall from g.** perdre la grâce; *Old-fashioned* **in the year of g. 1066** en l'an de grâce 1066

4 *Fin (for payment of a bill)* **days of g.** délai *m*; **to give a creditor seven days' g.** accorder à un créancier sept jours de grâce *ou* de faveur; *Com* **period of g.** jours *mpl* de grâce

5 *(prayer) (before meal)* bénédicité *m*; *(after meal)* grâces *fpl*; **to say g.** réciter le bénédicité

6 *(address)* **His G.** *(the duke)* Monsieur (le duc de …); *(the archbishop)* Monseigneur (l'archevêque de …); **Her G.** *(the duchess)* Madame (la duchesse de …)

7 *Myth* **the Graces** les Grâces *fpl*

8 *Arch (pardon)* grâce *f*, pardon *m*

VT 1 *(honour)* honorer (**with** de); **to g. a meeting with one's presence** honorer une réunion de sa présence **2** *(ornament)* embellir, orner

▶▶ *Comput* **g. log in** connexion *f* de grâce; *Mus* **g. note** note *f* d'agrément, ornement *m*

grace-and-favour ADJ *Br (residence etc)* = prêté gratuitement par le souverain à un sujet qui lui a rendu service

graceful ['greɪsfʊl] ADJ **1** *(person, movement)* gracieux; **g. figure** silhouette élégante; **she is a g. dancer** elle danse avec grâce **2** *(speech)* gracieux, poli, bien tourné

gracefully ['greɪsfʊlɪ] ADV avec grâce, avec élégance

gracefulness ['greɪsfʊlnɪs] N grâce *f*, élégance *f*

graceless ['greɪslɪs] ADJ *(inelegant)* gauche, inélégant; *(rude)* effronté

gracious ['greɪʃəs] ADJ **1** *(kind, polite)* poli, affable; *(generous, noble-minded)* courtois; **to be g. to sb** être affable avec *ou* envers qn; **to be g. in accepting sth** accepter qch avec courtoisie; **our g. King/Queen** notre gracieux souverain **2** *(God)* plein de grâce *ou* de miséricorde (**to** envers) **3** *(living, house etc)* luxueux

INT **g. (me)!, good(ness) g.!** miséricorde!, mon Dieu!; **good g. no!** jamais de la vie!

graciously ['greɪʃəslɪ] ADV *(to accept, allow)* gracieusement, de bonne grâce; *(to reply, behave)* avec politesse; *Fml* **to be g. pleased to do sth** daigner faire qch

graciousness ['greɪʃəsnɪs] N **1** *(kindness)* gentillesse *f*, *(politeness)* courtoisie *f* **2** *(of God)* bonté *f*, miséricorde *f* **3** *(of life, house etc)* luxe *m*

gradate [grə'deɪt] VI se dégrader (**into** en) VT *(colours)* dégrader

gradation [grə'deɪʃən] N **1** *Art (of colours)*, *Phot* gradation *f* **2** *(degree) (on thermometer etc)* degré *m*; **gradations of meaning** nuances *fpl* de sens

grade [greɪd] N **1** *(of hierarchy etc)* grade *m*, rang *m*; *(of administration)* échelon *m*

2 *(quality) (of paper, coffee, flour)* qualité *f*; *(of potato)* calibre *m*; *(of petrol)* grade *m*; *Fig* **to make the g.** se montrer à la hauteur

3 *esp Am (gradient)* pente *f*

4 *esp Am Sch (mark)* note *f*, **to get high grades** avoir de bonnes notes

5 *Am Sch (year at school)* classe *f*, *Am* **the grades** ≃ l'école *f* primaire

6 *Agr* **grades** bétail *m* amélioré par croisement

VT **1** *(classify) (produce, oil, jobs)* classer; *(potatoes)* calibrer; *Am Sch* **to g. essays** noter des dissertations **2** *Am Rail (track)* ménager *ou* régulariser la pente de; *Constr (land)* niveler **3** *Agr (breed etc)* améliorer

▶▶ *Agr* **g. cattle** bétail *m* amélioré par croisement; *Am Rail* **g. crossing** passage *m* à niveau; **g. crossing gate** barrière *f* de passage

à niveau; *Com* **g. label** étiquette *f* de calibrage; *Am* **g. point average** moyenne *f*; *Am* **g. school** école *f* primaire

▶ **grade down** VT SEP *(move to lower category)* classer dans une catégorie inférieure

▶ **grade up** VT SEP **1** *(move to higher category)* classer dans une catégorie supérieure **2** *Agr (breed etc)* améliorer

graded ['greɪdɪd] ADJ calibré; **g. exercises** exercices gradués

▶▶ **g. tax** *(upwards)* impôt *m* progressif; *(downwards)* impôt dégressif

gradient ['greɪdɪənt] N **1** *Constr etc* inclinaison *f*, *(of ground)* dénivellation *f*; **downward g.** pente *f*, déclivité *f*; **upward g.** rampe *f*, montée *f*; **a g. of 1 in 6, a 1 in 6 g.** une dénivellation d'un sixième; **steep/low g.** forte/faible pente **2** *Math, Phys (of temperature etc)* gradient *m*

grading ['greɪdɪŋ] N **1** *(classification) (of oil, tasks, exercises)* classement *m*, gradation *f*; *(of potatoes)* calibrage *m*; *(of ore etc)* triage *m*; *Am Sch (marking)* correction *f* **2** *Am Constr, Rail (of slope)* (a)ménagement *m*

gradual ['grædjʊ(ə)l] ADJ progressif, graduel; **a g. process** un processus graduel; **a g. slope** une pente douce; **a g. transition** une transition progressive (**from … to …** de … à …)

N *Rel* graduel *m*

gradualism ['grædjʊəlɪzm] N gradualisme *m*

gradually ['grædjʊ(ə)lɪ] ADV petit à petit, progressivement; **it happened very g.** ça s'est produit très progressivement; **g. you'll be able to type without looking at the keyboard** graduellement *ou* petit à petit *ou* progressivement, tu seras capable de taper sans regarder le clavier

graduate¹ ['grædjʊət] N diplômé, -ée; *Univ* ≃ licencié, -ée; **biology g.** ≃ licencié, -ée en biologie; *Am Sch* **high school g.** ≃ titulaire *mf* du baccalauréat

▶▶ **g. entry** échelon *m* d'entrée pour les diplômés; *Am Univ* **g. school** = école *f* où l'on poursuit ses études après la licence; *Am Univ* **g. studies** études *fpl* de troisième cycle; **g. training scheme** programme *m* de formation professionnelle pour les diplômés

graduate² ['grædjʊeɪt] VI obtenir son diplôme; *Univ (complete one's degree)* obtenir sa licence; *(receive one's degree certificate)* recevoir son diplôme de licence; **he graduated from Oxford** il a fait ses études à Oxford; **I graduated in 2002** j'ai eu ma licence en 2002; *Am Sch* **to g. from high school** terminer ses études au lycée; *Fig* **to g. from sth to sth** passer de qch à qch; **she learnt on a cheap violin before graduating to a better instrument** elle a appris à jouer avec un violon bon marché avant de passer à un meilleur instrument

VT **1** *(scale, thermometer etc)* graduer; **graduated in centimetres** gradué en centimètres **2** *Am Sch, Univ* remettre un diplôme/un diplôme de licence à

graduated ['grædjʊeɪtɪd] ADJ *(thermometer etc)* gradué; **a g. pay rise/tax increase** une augmentation de salaire/des impôts progressive; **g. income tax** impôt *m* progressif; *Am Fin* **g. payment mortgage** hypothèque *f* à paiements échelonnés

graduation [grædjʊ'eɪʃən] N **1** *Univ* remise *f* des diplômes; *(by student)* réception *f* d'un diplôme; *Fig* **my g. to the post of supervisor** ma promotion au poste de surveillant **2** *(of thermometer etc)* graduation *f*, *(of tax)* progressivité *f*; **graduations** degrés *mpl*, grades *mpl*

▶▶ *Univ* **g. ceremony** cérémonie *f* de remise des diplômes

Graduation

Dans les pays anglo-saxons, la "graduation" est la cérémonie officielle au cours de laquelle les étudiants reçoivent leur diplôme du main du président de l'université. La cérémonie de remise des diplômes est une occasion solennelle – dans certaines universités elle se fait en latin – et les étudiants doivent porter la toge traditionnelle avec capuchon et mortier. Le diplôme ainsi que la photo prise le jour de la cérémonie sont ensuite gardés précieusement par la famille. Aux États-Unis, le terme "graduation" désigne également la cérémonie organisée en l'honneur des élèves qui achèvent leurs études secondaires.

graffiti [græ'fiːtiː] NPL graffiti *mpl*; **a piece of g.** un graffiti; **there's some g. on the wall** il y a des graffiti sur le mur

▶▶ **g. artist** tagueur, -euse

graft¹ [grɑːft] N **1** *(from a plant)* greffon *m*; *(from a tree)* ente *f* **2** *Surg* greffe *f*; **bone/skin g.** greffe osseuse/de peau; **I had to have a skin g.** on a dû me faire une greffe de peau VT *(onto a plant)* greffer; *(onto a tree)* enter; *Surg* greffer (**onto** sur); *Fig* **this piece was grafted onto the symphony later** ce morceau a été rajouté à la symphonie plus tard; **the tower was grafted onto the original edifice** la tour a été ajoutée à l'édifice d'origine

graft² *Fam* N **1** *Am (bribery etc)* pot-de-vin *m*, *pl* pots-de-vin **2** *Br (work)* **to achieve sth by hard g.** réussir qch en bossant dur

VI **1** *Am (engage in bribery etc) (give)* verser des pots-de-vin; *(take)* recevoir des pots-de-vin **2** *Br (work hard)* bosser dur

grafter ['grɑːftər] N *Br Fam (hard worker)* bosseur, -euse

grafting ['grɑːftɪŋ] N *(in horticulture, arboriculture)* greffe *f*, greffage *m*; *Surg* greffe; **skin g.** greffe de peau

Grail [greɪl] N **the G., the Holy G.** le Saint-Graal; *Fig* **the G. of full employment/world peace** la croisade pour parvenir au plein emploi/instaurer la paix mondiale

grain [greɪn] N **1** *(of wheat, pepper, salt, sand etc)* grain *m*; *Fig* **there's not a g. of truth in what he says** il n'y a pas un grain de vérité dans ce qu'il dit; *Fig* **not a g. of common sense** pas un grain *ou* pas deux sous de bon sens, pas une once de bon sens

2 *(no pl) (cereals)* céréales *fpl*; **a shipment of g.** une cargaison de céréales

3 *(measurement)* grain *m* (= 0,0648 g)

4 *(in wood, photo, stone)* grain *m*; *(in meat)* fil *m*; *(in leather)* grain, grenure *f*; **against** or **across the g.** contre le fil, à contre-fil; *Fig* **it goes against the g. for me to do it** ça m'est difficile de le faire, c'est contre ma nature de le faire

▶▶ **g. alcohol** alcool *m* de grains; **g. crop** récolte *f* de céréales, récolte céréalière; **g. elevator** silo *m* à céréales; **g. market** marché *m* céréalier

grainy ['greɪnɪ] ADJ *Phot* granuleux

gram [græm] N gramme *m*

grammage ['græmɪdʒ] N *(of paper)* grammage *m*

grammar ['græmər] N **1** grammaire *f*, **that's not good g.** ce n'est pas grammaticalement correct **2** *(book)* grammaire *f*; **a French g.** une grammaire française

▶▶ **g. book** grammaire; *Comput* **g. checker** correcteur *m* grammatical; **g. school** *(in UK)* = type d'école secondaire; *(in US)* ≃ école *f* primaire

Grammar School

En Grande-Bretagne, ce terme désigne une école secondaire recevant une aide de l'État mais pouvant être privée, réputée dispenser un enseignement de qualité de type traditionnel et préparant aux études supérieures. L'admission se fait sur concours ("eleven-plus") ou sur dossier. Moins de cinq pour cent des élèves britanniques fréquentent ce type d'école, qui existe en Angleterre, au pays de Galles et en Irlande du Nord.

grammarian [grə'meərɪən] **N** grammairien, -ienne

grammatical [grə'mætɪk(ə)l] **ADJ 1** grammatical, -aux; **g. mistake** faute de grammaire **2** *(correct)* grammaticalement correct

grammatically [grə'mætɪklɪ] **ADV** grammaticalement

gramme [græm] **N** gramme *m*

Grammy ['græmɪ] **N** = distinction *f* récompensant les meilleures œuvres musicales américaines de l'année (classique exclu)

Gramophone® ['græməfəʊn] **N** *Old-fashioned Br* gramophone *m*
  ▶▶ **g. record** disque *m*

grampus ['græmpəs] **N** *(killer whale)* épaulard *m*, orque *f*

gran [græn] **N** *esp Br Fam (grandmother)* grand-mère, *pl* grands-mères *(in children's language)* mamie *f*, mémé *f*

granary ['grænərɪ] **N** *Agr* grenier *m*; *Com* entrepôt *m* de grain; **Egypt was the g. of the ancient world** l'Égypte était le grenier de l'antiquité
  ▶▶ *Br* **Granary**®. **bread, Granary**®. **loaf** = pain *m* complet avec des morceaux de blé non moulu

grand [grænd] **ADJ 1** *(imposing)* grandiose, imposant, magnifique; **to do things on a g. scale** faire les choses en grand; **to entertain on a g. scale** recevoir des gens en grande pompe; **to invest on a g. scale** faire de gros investissements; **to build on a g. scale** réaliser de grands projets de construction; **in g. style** en grande pompe; **it was all part of his g. design** tout cela faisait partie de son grand projet; **the g. manner of the aristocracy** le faste de l'aristocratie; **the mayor looked very g. in his robes** le maire avait un air très imposant avec ses vêtements de cérémonie; **the g. old man of trade unionism/ Scottish folk music** le patriarche du syndicalisme/de la musique folklorique écossaise; **a g. lady** une grande dame; **'lexicographer' is just a g. name for someone who writes dictionaries** 'lexicographe' est simplement un mot pompeux pour désigner une personne qui écrit des dictionnaires
  2 *Fam (excellent) (food, accommodation)* excellent; *(weather)* magnifique; **I'm not feeling too g.** je ne suis pas dans mon assiette; **she sounded absolutely g. when I spoke to her on the phone** elle avait l'air en pleine forme quand je l'ai eue au téléphone; **to have a g. time** bien s'amuser; *Iron* **we had a g. old time trying to find the house!** on s'est marré pour trouver la maison!
  N 1 *Fam Am (thousand dollars)* mille dollars *mpl*; *Br (thousand pounds)* mille livres *fpl*; **two g.** *Am* deux mille dollars; *Br* deux mille livres **2** *Mus* piano *m* à queue
  ▶▶ **g. concert** grand concert; **g. duchess** grande-duchesse *f*, *pl* grandes-duchesses; **g. duke** grand-duc *m*, *pl* grands-ducs; **g. finale** apothéose *f*; *Am* **g. jury** jury *m* d'accusation; *Am* **g. larceny** vol *m* qualifié; **G. Master** *(in chess)* grand maître *m*; *(of maso-*

nic lodge) Grand Maître *m*; *Horseracing* **the G. National** = la plus importante course d'obstacles de Grande-Bretagne, qui se déroule à Aintree, dans la banlieue de Liverpool; **g. opera** grand opéra *m*; **g. piano** piano *m* à queue; *Sport, Cards* **g. slam** grand chelem *m*; **g. total** total *m*; **a g. total of £4575** une somme totale de 4575 livres; **the G. Tour** le tour d'Europe *(entrepris jadis par les jeunes aristocrates pour compléter leur éducation)*; *Hum* **would you like a g. tour of the house?** veux-tu que je te fasse visiter la maison?

grandad ['grændæd] **N** *Fam* papi *m*, pépé *m*

grandaddy ['grændædɪ] **N** = **grandad**; *Fig* **the g. of them all** *(of car, locomotive etc)* l'ancêtre *mf*

grandchild, *pl* **grandchildren** ['græntʃaɪld, -tʃɪldrən] **N** *(boy)* petit-fils *m*, *pl* petits-fils; *(girl)* petite-fille *f*, *pl* petites-filles; **that will be something to tell your grandchildren** voilà quelque chose que tu pourras raconter à tes petits-enfants

granddad ['grændæd] **N** *Fam* papi *m*, pépé *m*

granddaughter ['grændɔːtər] **N** petite-fille *f*, *pl* petites-filles

grandee [græn'diː] **N** *Hist* grand *m* *(d'Espagne)*; *Fig* **Tory grandees** = personnes *fpl* influentes du parti conservateur

grandeur ['grændjər] **N 1** *(of person)* grandeur *f*, noblesse *f*, éminence *f* **2** *(of building, surroundings etc)* splendeur *f*, magnificence *f*; **the g. of the landscape** la majesté du paysage; **an air of g.** quelque chose de grandiose; **faded g.** *(of house, furnishings etc)* splendeur passée

grandfather ['grænfɑːðər, 'grænd-] **N** grand-père *m*, *pl* grands-pères
  ▶▶ **g. clock** horloge *f* (de parquet)

grandfatherly ['grænfɑːðəlɪ] **ADJ** de grand-père

grandiloquence [græn'dɪləkwəns] **N** grandiloquence *f*, emphase *f*

grandiloquent [græn'dɪləkwənt] **ADJ** grandiloquent

grandiose ['grændɪəʊs, -əʊz] **ADJ** *(building etc)* grandiose, magnifique; *(term, theory, title etc)* pompeux; *(idea, scheme)* grandiose

grandly ['grændlɪ] **ADV 1** *(impressively)* de façon grandiose *ou* impressionnante **2** *(pompously)* pompeusement

grandma ['grænmɑː, 'grænd-, 'græm-] **N** *Fam* mamie *f*, mémé *f*

grandmother ['grænmʌðər, 'grænd-] **N** grand-mère *f*, *pl* grands-mères

grandnephew ['grænnefjʊ, 'grænd-] **N** petit-neveu *m*, *pl* petits-neveux

grandness ['grændnɪs] **N** grandeur *f*, *Pej* caractère *m* pompeux

grandniece ['grænniːs, 'grænd-] **N** petite-nièce *f*, *pl* petites-nièces

grandpa ['grænpɑː] **N** *Fam* papi *m*, pépé *m*

grandparent ['grænpeərənt, 'grænd-] **N** *(male)* grand-père *m*; *(female)* grand-mère *f*; **grandparents** grands-parents; **children are often looked after by a g.** les enfants sont souvent gardés par un de leurs grands-parents

grandson ['grænsʌn, 'grænd-] **N** petit-fils *m*, *pl* petits-fils

grandstand ['grænstænd, 'grænd-] **N** *Sport* tribune *f* (d'honneur); **to have a g. view of sth** être bien placé pour voir qch
  VI *Fig* faire le mariolle
  ▶▶ **g. finish** *(of race)* arrivée *f* palpitante; *(of match)* fin *f* palpitante

grange [greɪndʒ] **N 1** *Br (country house)* petit manoir *m* **2** *Arch (granary)* grange *f*

granite ['grænɪt] **N** granit(e) *m*; **g. building** édifice en granit(e)

granitic [grə'nɪtɪk] **ADJ** granitique, graniteux

grannie, granny ['grænɪ] **N** *Fam* mamie *f*, mémé *f*; **an old g.** une vieille mémé
  ▶▶ **g. flat** = partie *f* d'une maison aménagée indépendamment pour héberger un parent âgé; **g. knot** nœud *m* de ménagère *ou* de soldat

Granny Smith **N** *(apple)* granny-smith *f inv*

grant [grɑːnt] **N 1** *(financial aid)* subvention *f*, *Univ* bourse *f* d'études; **I can't live on my g.** je n'arrive pas à m'en sortir avec seulement ma bourse d'études; **to make a g. to sb** accorder une subvention/une bourse d'études à qn; **to receive a g.** être subventionné, recevoir une subvention; *Univ* recevoir *ou* se voir accorder une bourse d'études
  2 *(action)*, *Com (of patent)* délivrance *f*, *Law (of property etc)* cession *f*
  VT 1 *(permission)* donner; *(interview, audience, request etc)* accorder; *(authorization, patent)* délivrer; *Law (property etc)* faire cession de; **he was granted permission to ...** il reçut la permission de ...; **the countries that have been granted autonomy** les pays qui se sont vus accorder l'autonomie; **God g. that ...** Dieu veuille que ...; **to take sth for granted** considérer qch comme allant de soi *ou* comme normal; **you take too much for granted** vous présumez trop; **he takes it for granted that he can borrow my books** il se croit permis d'emprunter mes livres; **we take all this for granted** tout cela nous semble aller de soi; **she felt that she was being taken for granted** elle avait le sentiment qu'elle ne comptait pas; **I'm tired of the way everybody just takes me for granted** j'en ai assez que personne ne fasse attention à moi; **the party has been accused of taking its members for granted** on a accusé le parti de ne pas tenir compte de ses membres
  2 *(subsidy)* accorder, allouer (**to** à)
  3 *(admit)* admettre; **it must be granted that ...** il faut reconnaître que ...; **I g. you that he is lazy** il est paresseux, je vous l'accorde; **I'll g. you that** je vous l'accorde

grant-aided **ADJ** subventionné par l'État

grant-in-aid **N** subvention *f*

grant-maintained school **N** *Br Sch* = école *f* privée qui reçoit une subvention de l'État

granular ['grænjʊlər] **ADJ** *(surface, texture)* granulaire, granuleux

granulate ['grænjʊleɪt] **VT** *(powder etc)* granuler, grener, grainer; *(sugar)* cristalliser

granulated sugar ['grænjʊleɪtɪd] **N** sucre *m* cristallisé

granulation [grænjʊ'leɪʃən] **N** granulation *f*

granule ['grænjʊl] **N** grain *m*, granule *m*; **coffee/tea granules** granules de café/thé

grape [greɪp] **N** grain *m* de raisin; **a (variety of) g.** un raisin; **to eat grapes** manger du raisin; **to pick grapes** faire les vendanges, cueillir le raisin
  ▶▶ **g. harvest** vendanges *fpl*; *Bot* **g. hyacinth** muscari *m*; **g. juice** jus *m* de raisin; **g. picker** vendangeur, -euse

> Note that the French word **grappe** is a false friend. It means **bunch** or **cluster**.

grapefruit ['greɪpfruːt] **N** pamplemousse *m*
  ▶▶ **g. juice** jus *m* de pamplemousse; **g. tree** pamplemoussier *m*

grapeshot ['greɪpʃɒt] **N** *(ammunition)* mitraille *f*

grapevine ['greɪpvaɪn] **N 1** vigne *f*, treille *f* **2** *Fig* téléphone *m* arabe; **I heard on the g.**

graph 409 **gravely**

that ... j'ai appris par le téléphone arabe que ...

graph [grɑːf] N graphique *m*, diagramme *m*
VT faire la représentation graphique de
▸▸ **g. paper** papier *m* quadrillé; *(in milli-metres)* papier millimétré

graphic ['græfɪk] ADJ 1 *Math (also* **graphical**) *(representation etc)* graphique 2 *(vivid) (description etc)* très vivant; *(shocking)* cru 3 *Art* graphique
N graphique *m*
▸▸ **g. art** art *m* graphique; **g. artist** graphiste *mf*, **g. design** conception *f* graphique; **g. designer** graphiste, maquettiste *mf*, **g. equalizer** égaliseur *m* graphique; *Comput* **g. interface** interface *f* graphique

> Note that the French adjective **graphique** never means **vivid** or **shocking**.

graphically ['græfɪklɪ] ADV 1 *Math (to solve a problem)* graphiquement 2 *(vividly)* de fa-çon très vivante; *(in a shocking way)* crûment

graphical user interface ['græfɪk(ə)l] N *Comput* interface *f* utilisateur graphique

graphics ['græfɪks] N VOIR GRAMMAIRE A10 1 *(art)* arts *mpl* graphiques 2 *Comput* graphis-mes *mpl*, graphiques *mpl*
▸▸ *Comput* **g. accelerator** accélérateur *m* graphique; *Comput* **g. accelerator card** carte *f* accélérateur graphique; *Comput* **g. capability** aptitude *f* graphique; *Comput* **g. card** carte graphique; **g. designer** concepteur *m* graphiste; **g. digitizer** convertisseur *m* nu-mérique de graphiques; *Comput* **g. display** affichage *m* graphique; **g. generator** géné-rateur *m* graphique; *Comput* **g. mode** mode *m* graphique; *Comput* **g. package** grapheur *m*; **g. resolution** résolution *f* graphique; *Comput* **g. software** logiciel *m* graphique

graphite ['græfaɪt] N graphite *m*, mine *f* de plomb

graphologist [græ'fɒlədʒɪst] N grapholo-gue *mf*

graphology [græ'fɒlədʒɪ] N graphologie *f*

grapnel ['græpnəl] N *Naut* grappin *m*, cro-chet *m*; *Aviat (of balloon)* ancre *f*

grapple ['græp(ə)l] N = **grapnel**
VI *(fight)* lutter corps à corps; *Fig* **to g. with** *(difficulty, problem, computer, machine etc)* se débattre avec; **to g. with inflation** être aux prises avec l'inflation
VT *Am (person)* empoigner; **to g. sb to the floor** mettre qn à terre

grappling ['græp(ə)lɪŋ] N *Naut* **g. iron** *or* **hook** grappin *m*, crochet *m*

grasp [grɑːsp] N 1 *(hold)* prise *f*, **to wrest sth from sb's g.** arracher qch des mains de qn; **to have a strong g.** *(handshake)* avoir de la poigne; *Fig* **to have sth within one's g.** avoir qch à sa portée; *Fig* **it is now within every-one's g.** *(financially etc)* c'est maintenant à la portée de tout le monde; *Fig* **to let an op-portunity slip from one's g.** rater une occa-sion 2 *Fig (understanding)* compréhension *f*, **to have a good g. of modern history** avoir une bonne connaissance de l'histoire mo-derne; **his g. of the problem was poor** il do-minait mal le problème
VT 1 *(hold firmly)* saisir, empoigner; **to g. sb's hand** serrer la main à qn; **I grasped his arm** il m'a agrippé par le bras; *Fig* **to g. the opportunity** saisir l'occasion (**of doing sth** de faire qch) 2 *Fig (understand)* comprendre, saisir; **to g. the importance of sth** saisir l'im-portance de qch
▸ **grasp at** VT INSEP *(attempt to take hold of)* tenter de saisir *ou* d'atteindre; *Fig (seize) (op-portunity, offer)* saisir avidement; *Fig* **to g. at straws** se raccrocher à de faux espoirs

grasping ['grɑːspɪŋ] ADJ *(mean)* avide, cupide

grass [grɑːs] N 1 *(plant)* herbe *f*, *Fig* **she doesn't let the g. grow under her feet** elle ne perd pas son temps
2 *(lawn)* pelouse *f*, gazon *m*; *Tennis* gazon; **keep off the g.** défense de marcher sur le gazon *ou* sur la pelouse, pelouse interdite; *Prov* **the g. is always greener (on the other side of the fence)** c'est toujours mieux ail-leurs; *Tennis* **she plays well on g.** elle joue bien sur gazon
3 *(pasture)* herbage *m*; **to put** *or* **turn a horse out to g.** mettre un cheval en pâture; *Fig* **to put sb out to g.** mettre qn à la retraite; **to be (out) at g.** *(of animal)* être au vert; **to put land under g.** enherber une terre, met-tre une terre en herbe
4 *Fam (marijuana)* herbe *f*
5 *Br Sl (informer)* balance *f*, indicateur *m*
VT 1 *(cover with grass) (field)* mettre en herbe, enherber; *(garden)* gazonner 2 *Sl (in-form on)* **to g. sb** balancer, dénoncer
VI *Br Sl (inform)* parler; **to g. on sb** balancer *ou* dénoncer qn
▸▸ **g. box** *(on lawn mower)* panier *m* à her-bes; *Tex* **g. cloth** toile *f* de) ramie *f*, *Tennis* **g. court** court *m* (en gazon); **the g. roots** *(of political party etc)* la base; **the feeling at the g. roots is that ...** le sentiment à la base est que ...; **g. seed** *(for lawn)* graine *f* pour gazon; *(as feed)* graine fourragère; **g. snake** couleuvre *f* à collier; **g. widow** = femme *f* dont le mari est toujours en déplacement; *(who is divorced or separated)* femme divor-cée/séparée (de son mari); **I'm a g. widow this weekend** je suis célibataire ce week-end
▸ **grass over** VT SEP *(garden)* gazonner; *(field)* mettre en herbe, enherber
▸ **grass up** VT SEP *Br Fam* **to g. sb up** balancer qn, moucharder qn

grass(-)green ADJ *(colour)* vert gazon *inv*

grasshopper ['grɑːshɒpər] N sauterelle *f*

grassland ['grɑːslænd] N prairies *fpl*, prés *mpl*

grass-root(s) ADJ de base, qui émane de la base; **there is no g. support for their policy** il n'y a pas de soutien de la base pour leur politique; **the g. feeling is that ...** le senti-ment à la base est que ...; **at g. level** à la base
▸▸ *Mktg* **g. forecasting** prévision *f* de la base

grassy ['grɑːsɪ] ADJ herbu, herbeux; *(lane)* vert; *(plain)* verdoyant

grate [greɪt] N *(of hearth)* grille *f*, *(fireplace)* foyer *m*, âtre *m*; **a fire in the g.** un feu dans la cheminée
VT 1 *(cheese, carrot, nutmeg)* râper 2 *(scrape)* **to g. sth on sth** frotter qch contre qch (avec un grincement); **to g. one's teeth** grincer des dents
VI 1 *(of machinery)* grincer; *(of chalk on blackboard)* crisser 2 *(irritate)* taper sur les nerfs (**on sb** à qn); **it really grates (on me)** ça me tape vraiment sur les nerfs; **to g. on the ear** *(of music, particular accent)* écorcher l'oreille; *(of noise)* faire mal aux oreilles

G-rated ADJ *Am Cin (movie)* tous publics

grateful ['greɪtfʊl] ADJ reconnaissant (**to sb for sth** à *ou* envers qn de qch); **I'm g. for all you've done** je vous suis reconnaissant de tout ce que vous avez fait, *esp Fml* je vous sais gré de tout ce que vous avez fait; **he gave her a g. smile** il lui a adressé un sourire reconnaissant; **I would be g. if you could let me know as soon as possible** je vous serais reconnaissant de m'informer dès que pos-sible; **I was g. it wasn't me** j'étais bien content que ce ne soit pas moi; **I suppose we should be g. for that** on devrait s'en esti-mer heureux

gratefully ['greɪtfʊlɪ] ADV avec reconnais-

sance; **to smile g.** faire un sourire re-connaissant

grater ['greɪtər] N râpe *f*

gratification [grætɪfɪ'keɪʃən] N satisfac-tion *f*, plaisir *m*; **to do sth for one's own g.** faire qch pour sa propre satisfaction; **she had the g. of knowing that she'd been pro-ved right** elle avait la satisfaction de savoir qu'on lui avait donné raison

gratified ['grætɪfaɪd] ADJ satisfait, content (**with** de); *(smile)* de satisfaction

gratify ['grætɪfaɪ] VT 1 *(please) (person)* faire plaisir à 2 *(satisfy) (passion etc)* satis-faire, contenter; **to g. sb's whims** satisfaire les caprices de qn

gratifying ['grætɪfaɪɪŋ] ADJ satisfaisant

grating[1] ['greɪtɪŋ] ADJ *(noise)* discordant, grinçant; *(voice)* éraillé; **g. laugh** ricane-ment *m*; **g. sound** grincement *m*
N *Culin* râpage *m*

grating[2] N *(bars) (of window)* grille *f*

gratis ['grɑːtɪs] ADJ gratis, gratuit
ADV gratis, gratuitement

gratitude ['grætɪtjuːd] N gratitude *f*, recon-naissance *f* (**to** envers); **to show one's g.** té-moigner de sa reconnaissance

gratuitous [grə'tjuːɪtəs] ADJ *(unnecessary)* gratuit, sans raison; **g. violence** violence *f* gratuite

gratuitously [grə'tjuːɪtəslɪ] ADV gratuite-ment, sans raison

gratuity [grə'tjuːɪtɪ] N *Fml (tip)* pourboire *m*; **no gratuities** pourboires interdits

> Note that the French word **gratuité** is a false friend and is never a translation for the English word **gratuity**. It indicates that something is free of charge.

grave[1] [greɪv] N tombe *f*, tombeau *m*; **(mass) g.** fosse *f* commune; *(in wartime)* charnier *m*; **to be in one's g.** être dans la tombe; **she worked herself into an early g.** elle s'est tuée au travail; **he took his secret with him to the g.** il a emporté son secret dans la tombe; **he drank himself into an early g.** l'alcool l'a pré-maturément tué; **he's drinking himself into an early g.** il se détruit à force de boire; *Fig* **he must have turned in his g.** il a dû se re-tourner dans sa tombe; **it would make her turn in her g.** elle se retournerait dans sa tombe; **someone has just walked over my g.** j'ai eu un frisson; **to be digging one's own g.** creuser sa propre tombe; **to have one foot in the g.** avoir un pied dans la tombe; **from beyond the g.** d'outre-tombe
ADJ *(serious)* grave, sérieux; *(tone)* solennel; *(situation)* grave; *(error)* lourd; **g. news** de graves nouvelles; **to make a g. mistake** se tromper lourdement
▸▸ **g. robber** *(who robs valuables from graves)* = personne *f* qui vole les objets de valeur laissés dans les tombes, pilleur *m* de tombes; *(body snatcher)* déterreur, -euse de cadavres

grave[2] [grɑːv] ADJ grave
N accent *m* grave; **it's spelt with an "e" g.** ça s'écrit avec un "e" accent grave
▸▸ **g. accent** accent grave

gravedigger ['greɪvdɪgər] N fossoyeur *m*

gravel ['græv(ə)l] N gravier *m*
VT (-ll-, *Am* -l-) 1 *(cover with gravel)* couvrir de gravier; **gravelled path** chemin *m* de gra-vier 2 *esp Am Fam (perplex) (person)* embar-rasser
▸▸ **g. path** chemin de gravier; **g. pit** gra-vière *f*, carrière *f* de gravier

gravelly ['græv(ə)lɪ] ADJ *(containing gravel)* graveleux; *(river bed)* pierreux; **g. voice** voix râpeuse

gravely ['greɪvlɪ] ADV *(to say)* gravement,

solennellement; **to be g. mistaken** se tromper lourdement; **g. ill** gravement malade; **g. wounded** grièvement blessé

graven ['greɪvən] ADJ *Arch, Lit* **g. on his memory** gravé dans sa mémoire
▸▸ *Rel* **g. image** idole *f*, image *f*

graveness ['greɪvnɪs] N *(of manner, tone)* gravité *f*

Graves' disease ['greɪvz-] N *Med* maladie *f* de Basedow

graveside ['greɪvsaɪd] N **at the g.** près de la tombe; **his next of kin were there at the g.** ses proches étaient présents à l'enterrement

gravestone ['greɪvstəʊn] N pierre *f* tombale

graveyard ['greɪvjɑːd] N *(for people)*, *Fig (for cars)* cimetière *m*; *Fig* **this town is a g.** cette ville est mortelle; **this department has been the g. of more than one young hopeful's ambitions** ce service a mis fin aux ambitions de plus d'un jeune
▸▸ **g. shift** équipe *f* de nuit; *Radio, TV* **g. slot** tranche *f* nocturne

graving dock ['greɪvɪŋ] N *Naut* bassin *m* de radoub

gravitate ['grævɪteɪt] VI *Phys* graviter (**towards** vers; **round** autour de); *Fig* **most of the guests had gravitated towards the bar/kitchen** la plupart des invités s'étaient rapprochés du bar/de la cuisine; **at a party, she gravitates towards anybody who can help her career** dans les soirées, elle est tout de suite attirée par les personnes qui peuvent l'aider dans sa carrière; **he had gravitated towards a pro-European position** il s'était rallié à la cause européenne

gravitation [grævɪ'teɪʃən] N *Phys* gravitation *f*; *Fig* **there was a general g. towards the bar** tout le monde s'est dirigé vers le bar; *Phys* **law of g.** loi *f* de la gravitation

gravitational [grævɪ'teɪʃən(ə)l] ADJ *Phys* gravitationnel; *(field)* de gravitation
▸▸ **g. pull** gravitation *f*

gravity ['grævɪtɪ] N **1** *Phys* gravité *f*, pesanteur *f*; **law of g.** loi *f* de la pesanteur **2** *(of person)* gravité *f*, sérieux *m*; *(of situation, injury)* gravité *f*
▸▸ *Phys* **g. feed** alimentation *f* par gravité

gravure [grə'vjʊər] N *Typ (process, impression)* gravure *f*, *(plate)* plaque *f* gravée

gravy ['greɪvɪ] N **1** *Culin* jus *m*; *(thickened)* sauce *f* (au jus) **2** *Am Sl (money) (gained easily)* bénef *m*; *(gained illegally)* profit *m* illicite; **to get on the g. train** trouver le filon; **she's been on the g. train for years** elle a eu la vie facile pendant des années; **it's just a g. train for him and his friends** c'est une véritable mine d'or pour lui et ses amis
▸▸ **g. boat** saucière *f*

gray [greɪ] ADJ, N, VI *Am* = **grey**

grayling ['greɪlɪŋ] N **1** *(fish)* ombre *m* (de rivière) **2** *(butterfly)* (papillon *m*) agreste *m*

graze[1] [greɪz] *Agr* VI *(of cattle etc)* paître, brouter; **to g. on grass** brouter l'herbe; **to g. in a field** paître au champ
VT *(of farmer) (herd)* (faire) paître; *(field)* mettre en pâturage; *(of cattle etc) (field)* pâturer; *(grass)* brouter, paître

graze[2] N écorchure *f*, *(slighter)* éraflure *f*
VT **1** *(scrape) (knees etc)* écorcher; *(slighter)* érafler **2** *(brush past)* effleurer; **the bullet grazed his shoulder** la balle lui rasa l'épaule

grazing ['greɪzɪŋ] N *Agr* **1** *(of herd etc)* pâturage *m* **2** *(land)* pâture *f*, pacage *m*
▸▸ **g. ground,** *Am* land pâture, pacage; **g. rights** droit *m* de pâturage *ou* de pacage

grease [griːs] N *Culin, Tech etc* graisse *f*; *Tech (dirty)* cambouis *m*; **g. stain** *(on clothing etc)* tache *f* de gras *ou* de graisse
VT *Tech (machine)* graisser, lubrifier; *Culin*

(cake tin) beurrer; *Fig Fam* **to g. sb's palm** graisser la patte à qn
▸▸ **g. box** boîte *f* à graisse *ou* de graissage; **g. gun** *(pistolet m)* graisseur *m*, pompe *f* à graisse; *Am Fam (submachine gun)* mitraillette *f*, *Fam* **g. monkey** mécano *m*; **g. nipple** graisseur
▸ **grease back** VT SEP **to g. back one's hair** se gominer les cheveux

greased [griːst] ADJ *Fam* **like g. lightning** en quatrième vitesse; **he's like g. lightning** c'est un rapide

greasepaint ['griːspeɪnt] N maquillage *m* (de théâtre); **stick of g.** crayon *m* gras (de maquillage); *Fig* **the smell of g.** le mirage du théâtre

greaseproof ['griːspruːf] ADJ *(paper)* sulfurisé

greaser ['griːsər] N **1** *Br esp Aut Sl (mechanic)* mécano *m* **2** *Old-fashioned Br Sl (motorcyclist)* motard *m* **3** *Am Offensive Sl (Mexican)* Mexicain, -aine

greasiness ['griːsɪnɪs] N **1** état *m* graisseux *ou* gras **2** *Fam (of manner)* onctuosité *f*

greasy ['griːsɪ] ADJ **1** *(containing, covered in grease)* graisseux, huileux; *(sausage etc)* gras; *(grease-stained)* taché de graisse; **his hands felt g.** il avait les mains grasses; **you'll get your jacket all g.** tu vas mettre plein de graisse sur ta veste; **g. complexion** peau grasse; **g. hair** cheveux gras **2** *(slippery) (road etc)* glissant **3** *Fam (manner)* onctueux, mielleux
▸▸ *Sport, Fig* **the g. pole** le mât de cocagne; *Fam* **g. spoon** boui-boui *m*, *pl* bouis-bouis

GREAT [greɪt] ADJ **1** *(large, important)* grand; **a g. crowd** une foule nombreuse *ou* énorme; **a g. deal of time/money** beaucoup de temps/d'argent; **I expect a g. deal from my staff** j'attends beaucoup de mon personnel; **you're expecting a g. deal if you think that ...** tu espères trop si tu crois que ...; **a g. many people** beaucoup de gens *ou* de monde; **the g. majority, the greater part** la plupart, la majeure partie (**of** de); **to a g. extent, in g. part** en grande partie; **to reach a g. age** parvenir à un âge avancé; **his greatest fault** son plus grand défaut, son défaut capital; **to take g. care** prendre grand soin (**of** de); **g. difference** grande *ou* forte différence; **the g. divide between rich and poor/the two communities** le fossé immense qui sépare les riches et les pauvres/les deux communautés; **to take a g. interest in sb/sth** s'intéresser beaucoup à qn/qch; **with g. pleasure/with the greatest of pleasure** avec grand/avec le plus grand plaisir; **it gives me g. pleasure to inform you that ...** j'ai l'immense plaisir de vous informer que ...; **they are g. friends** ce sont de grands amis; **it is no g. matter** ce n'est pas une grosse affaire; **to have no g. opinion of sb** ne pas avoir une haute opinion de qn; **the g. thing is that ...** le grand avantage *ou* ce qui est bien, c'est que ...; **g. artist** grand artiste; **a g. man** un grand homme; *Old-fashioned Fam* **G. Scott!** grands dieux!
2 *(in proper names)* **Alexander the G.** Alexandre le Grand
3 *Fam (very good)* **to have a g. time** bien s'amuser; **(that's) g!** parfait!, (c'est) super!; *Iron* bravo!; **he's a g. guy** c'est un gars super; **a g. idea** une idée géniale; **isn't he g.!** qu'est-ce qu'il est bien!; **to be g. at tennis** être excellent au tennis; **she's g. at making the past come alive** elle arrive merveilleusement bien à faire revivre le passé; **I'm not g. on Roman history** je ne suis pas très fort *ou* calé en histoire romaine; *Iron* **she's a g. one for borrowing things without asking people** elle est spécialiste pour emprunter les choses sans demander l'autorisation

4 *(enthusiastic)* **she's a g. hillwalker** elle fait beaucoup de randonnée; **I'm a g. reader** je lis énormément; **to be a g. believer in sth** croire beaucoup en qch
ADV *Fam* **1** *(well)* très bien; **I feel g.!** je me sens super bien!; **I don't feel g. about what I did** je ne me sens pas très fier de ce que j'ai fait; **you look g. in that suit** il te va vraiment bien ce costume; **you look g.** *(very healthy)* tu as vraiment bonne mine; **he's doing g.** *(in health)* il se porte à merveille
2 *(intensifier)* **a g. big dog** un énorme chien; **be careful with your g. clumsy feet!** fais attention avec tes grands pieds maladroits!; **you g. fat slob!** espèce de gros lard!
N **1** *(person)* grand *m*, grande *f*, **one of the greats of world cinema** un des grands du cinéma mondial
2 the g. and the good les gens influents
▸▸ *Zool* **the g. apes** les grands singes *mpl*; *Astron* **the G. Bear** la Grande Ourse; **G. Britain** Grande-Bretagne *f*, **G. Dane** danois *m*; **the G. Lakes** les Grands Lacs *mpl*; **the G. Plains** les Grandes Plaines *fpl*; *Am* **g. room** séjour *m* cathédrale, *Can* salle *f* de séjour à toit cathédrale; **the G. Wall of China** la Grande Muraille (de Chine); **the G. War** la Grande Guerre, la guerre de 14 *ou* de 14–18

great-aunt N grand-tante *f*, *pl* grands-tantes

greatcoat ['greɪtkəʊt] N **1** pardessus *m* **2** *Mil (worn by cavalry)* manteau *m*; *(worn by infantry)* capote *f*

Greater London [greɪtə] N Londres *m* et son agglomération

Greater Manchester N Manchester *m* et son agglomération

greater-than sign N signe *m* plus grand que, signe supérieur à

greatest ['greɪtɪst] N *Fam* **to be the g.** *(best)* être le meilleur/la meilleure

great-grandchild, *pl* **great-grandchildren** N *(boy)* arrière-petit-fils *m*, *pl* arrière-petits-fils; *(girl)* arrière-petite-fille *f*, *pl* arrière-petites-filles; **great-grandchildren** arrière-petits-enfants *mpl*

great-granddaughter N arrière-petite-fille *f*, *pl* arrière-petites-filles

great-grandfather N arrière-grand-père *m*, *pl* arrière-grands-pères, bisaïeul *m*

great-grandmother N arrière-grand-mère *f*, *pl* arrière-grands-mères, bisaïeule *f*

great-grandparents NPL arrière-grands-parents *mpl*, bisaïeuls *mpl*

great-grandson N arrière-petit-fils *m*, *pl* arrière-petits-fils

great-great-grandfather N arrière-arrière-grand-père *m*, trisaïeul *m*

great-great-grandmother N arrière-arrière-grand-mère *f*, trisaïeule *f*

great-hearted [-'hɑːtɪd] ADJ généreux

greatly ['greɪtlɪ] ADV très; **to be g. influenced/surprised/amused** être très influencé/surpris/amusé; **g. irritated** très *ou* fortement irrité; **the difficulties have been g. exaggerated** on a beaucoup exagéré les difficultés; **he has g. improved since last year** il a fait beaucoup de progrès depuis l'année dernière; **I would g. prefer ...** je préférerais nettement ...; **to contribute g. to a result** largement contribuer à un résultat; **g. though I admired/respected him ...** j'avais beau l'admirer/le respecter beaucoup ...

great-nephew N petit-neveu *m*, *pl* petits-neveux

greatness ['greɪtnɪs] N **1** *(of person, action etc)* grandeur *f*, *(of thought)* élévation *f*, noblesse *f*, **g. of soul** grandeur d'âme **2** *(extent, size)* grandeur *f*, importance *f*

great-niece N petite-nièce f, pl petites-nièces

great-uncle N grand-oncle m, pl grands-oncles

grebe [gri:b] N (bird) grèbe m; **great crested g.** grèbe huppé

Grecian ['gri:ʃən] ADJ grec, f grecque; **in the G. style** à la grecque

Greece [gri:s] N Grèce f

greed [gri:d] N **1** (for material things) avidité f, cupidité f; **g. for fame/power** la recherche avide de célébrité/pouvoir; **it's sheer g.!** c'est de l'avidité pure et simple **2** (gluttony) gourmandise f

greedily ['gri:dɪlɪ] ADV **1** (to hoard, keep for oneself etc) avidement, cupidement **2** (to eat) goulûment; (to look, say) avec gourmandise

greediness ['gri:dɪnɪs] N = greed

greedy ['gri:dɪ] ADJ **1** (for material things) avide, cupide **2** (gluttonous) gourmand
▸▸ Sl **g. guts** goinfre mf

Greek [gri:k] ADJ grec, f grecque; **the G. Church** l'Église grecque
N **1** (person) Grec m, Grecque f; Prov **beware of Greeks bearing gifts** = méfiez-vous des étrangers qui vous veulent du bien **2** Ling grec m; **modern G.** le grec moderne; Fam **it's all G. to me** c'est de l'hébreu pour moi

green [gri:n] ADJ **1** (colour) vert; **to paint sth g.** peindre qch en vert; Lit **to keep sb's memory g.** entretenir la mémoire de qn; **to give sb the g. light** donner le feu vert à qn (**to do sth** pour faire qch); **to go** or **turn g.** (of traffic lights) passer au vert; (of person) verdir, blêmir; (of lawn, fields) verdir; **she has** Br **g. fingers** or Am **a g. thumb** elle a la main verte; **to grow g.** verdir; (of grass) verdoyer; Agr **the g. revolution** la révolution verte; **g. with envy** vert de jalousie, pâle d'envie; **to make sb g. with envy** faire pâlir qn d'envie
2 Fam (young, inexperienced) jeune, inexpérimenté; (naive) naïf, f naïve; **he's not as g. as he looks** il n'est pas si niais qu'il en a l'air; **she's as g. as grass** (person) elle est extrêmement naïve
3 Pol (consumer, policy etc) vert, écologiste
N **1** (colour) vert m
2 (of trees, plants etc) verdure f
3 greens (vegetables) légumes mpl verts
4 (grassy area) pelouse f, gazon m; **village g.** pelouse communale, pré m communal; **the g.** la pelouse; Golf **le green; bowling g.** (terrain m pour) jeu m de boules
5 Pol (person) écologiste mf
▸▸ **g. audit** = rapport m sur l'impact des activités d'une entreprise sur l'environnement; **g. bean** haricot m vert; **g. belt** ceinture f verte; **the G. Berets** les Bérets mpl verts; **g. card** (for insurance) carte f verte (prouvant qu'un véhicule est assuré pour un voyage à l'étranger); (work permit) carte de séjour (temporaire, aux États-Unis); **g. channel** (at customs) file f "rien à déclarer"; **g. keeper** (of bowling green, golf course) préposé, -ée à l'entretien des pelouses; **g. marketing** marketing m vert ou écologique; Br Pol **G. Paper** livre m blanc; **G. Party** (in UK) parti m écologiste; **g. pea** petit pois m; **g. pepper** poivron m vert; Br Econ **g. pound** livre f verte; Mktg **g. product** produit m vert ou écologique; **g. rate** taux m vert; **g. salad** salade f (verte); Fin **g. taxation** fiscalité f écologique; **g. tourism** tourisme m vert; Br Fam **g. wellies** = bottes fpl de caoutchouc vertes (le terme évoque les classes bourgeoises ou aristocratiques habitant à la campagne)

greenback ['gri:nbæk] N Am Fam billet m vert

greenery ['gri:nərɪ] N verdure f

green-eyed ADJ aux yeux verts; Lit **the g. monster** (jealousy) la jalousie

greenfield site ['gri:nfi:ld] N (for factory etc) terrain m non-bâti

greenfinch ['gri:nfɪntʃ] N (bird) verdier m

greenfly ['gri:nflaɪ] N (insect) puceron m; **to have g.** (of plant) avoir des pucerons; **g. spray** produit m à vaporiser contre les pucerons

greengage ['gri:ngeɪdʒ] N reine-claude f, pl reines-claudes

greengrocer ['gri:ngrəʊsər] N esp Br marchand, -ande de fruits et légumes; **g.'s (shop)** magasin m de fruits et légumes

greenhorn ['gri:nhɔ:n] N Fam blanc-bec m, pl blancs-becs; Mil bleu m

greenhouse ['gri:nhaʊs] N serre f
▸▸ **g. effect** effet m de serre; **g. gas** gaz m à effet de serre

greening ['gri:nɪŋ] N **the recent g. of the Labour Party** la récente conversion du Parti travailliste à l'écologie

greenish ['gri:nɪʃ] ADJ verdâtre

Greenland ['gri:nlənd] N Groenland m; **in G.** au Groenland

Greenlander ['gri:nləndər] N Groenlandais, -aise

greenmail ['gri:nmeɪl] N Fin greenmail m

greenness ['gri:nnɪs] N (of fruit etc) immaturité f, (inexperience) inexpérience f, (naivety) naïveté f, simplicité f, (of countryside etc) vert m, verdure f, **the g. of the wood made the fire difficult to light** le feu avait du mal à prendre parce que le bois était vert

greenroom ['gri:nru:m] N TV salle f de détente; Theat foyer m des artistes

greenstick fracture ['gri:nstɪk] N Med fracture f en bois vert

greenstuff ['gri:nstʌf] N **1** Br (vegetables) légumes mpl verts **2** Am Sl (paper money) billets mpl

greensward ['gri:nswɔ:d] N Lit pelouse f, (tapis m de) gazon m

Greenwich [-'grenɪdʒ-] N Greenwich
▸▸ **G. Mean Time** heure f (du méridien) de Greenwich; **G. meridian** méridien m de Greenwich

greenwood ['gri:nwʊd] N Lit bois m, forêt f (en été)

greet [gri:t] VT (person) saluer; (welcome) accueillir avec quelques paroles aimables; **to g. a speech with cheers** acclamer un discours; **the announcement was greeted with cheers** l'annonce a été saluée par des acclamations; **his words were greeted with resentful silence** ses mots ont été accueillis par un silence désapprobateur; **the first thing to g. my ear was ...** la première chose que j'ai entendue a été ...; **to g. the eyes** s'offrir à l'œil
VI Scot (cry) pleurer
N Scot (cry) **to have a g.** pleurer (**about sth** à cause de qch)

greeting ['gri:tɪŋ] N salutation f, salut m; **to send greetings to sb** envoyer ses salutations à qn; **New Year/Christmas greetings** vœux mpl de bonne année/Noël; **greetings card** carte f de vœux

gregarious [grɪ'geərɪəs] ADJ (person) sociable; Zool, Bot grégaire

┌─────────────────────────────────────┐
│ Note that the French adjective **grégaire** is │
│ a false friend. It never means **sociable**. │
└─────────────────────────────────────┘

gregariously [grɪ'geərɪəslɪ] ADV Zool (to live) en groupe; **she was not g. inclined** elle n'avait pas le tempérament grégaire

gregariousness [grɪ'geərɪəsnɪs] N (of person) sociabilité f, Zool, Bot grégarisme m, instinct m grégaire

Gregorian [grɪ'gɔ:rɪən] ADJ Rel (chant, calendar etc) grégorien

gremlin ['gremlɪn] N Fam lutin m; Fig **to get all the gremlins out of the system** se débarrasser de toutes les petites bêtises qui ralentissent le système

Grenada [grə'neɪdə] N la Grenade

grenade [grə'neɪd] N Mil grenade f
▸▸ **g. attack** attaque f à la grenade; **g. launcher** lance-grenade m, pl lance-grenades

grenadier [grenə'dɪər] N Mil grenadier m

grenadine ['grenədi:n] N (syrup) grenadine f

grew PT see **grow**

grey, Am **gray** [greɪ] ADJ **1** gris; **to turn** or **go g.** grisonner; Fig **it's a g. area** c'est une zone d'ombre **2** (complexion) blême; **to turn g.** blêmir **3** (outlook etc) sombre, morne; **a g. dismal morning** un matin gris et triste; **a g. existence** une existence morne
N **1** (colour) gris m; **hair touched with g.** cheveux grisonnants; Comput **shades of g.** niveaux de gris **2** (horse) cheval m gris
VI (of hair) grisonner; **to be greying at the temples** avoir les tempes grisonnantes, grisonner aux tempes
▸▸ **g. import** importation f grise; St Exch **g. knight** chevalier m gris; St Exch, Com **g. market** marché m gris; Anat **g. matter** matière f grise; Hum **to exercise the g. matter** faire marcher sa matière grise; **G. Panthers** = groupe m de pression composé de personnes âgées; **g. power** = pouvoir m économique, social etc des personnes âgées; **g. squirrel** écureuil m gris, petit-gris m, pl petits-gris; **g. wolf** loup m (gris); **g. zone** zone f grise

greybeard ['greɪbɪəd] N esp Lit (old man) vieillard m sage, Pej vieux barbon m

grey-eyed ADJ aux yeux gris

grey-haired, grey-headed ['greɪ'heəd, -'hedɪd] ADJ aux cheveux gris; (greying) grisonnant

greyhound ['greɪhaʊnd] N lévrier m
▸▸ **g. racing** course f de lévriers; **g.(-racing) track** cynodrome m

greying ['greɪɪŋ] ADJ grisonnant; **a g. population** une population vieillissante

greyish ['greɪɪʃ] ADJ grisâtre

greylag ['greɪlæg] N oie f cendrée
▸▸ **g. goose** oie cendrée

greyness ['greɪnɪs] N **1** (colour) teinte f grise; **the g. of London** la grisaille de Londres **2** (depressing quality) caractère m morne ou sombre, tristesse f

greyscale ['greɪskeɪl] N Comput niveau m de gris
▸▸ **g. monitor** moniteur m de niveau de gris

grid [grɪd] N **1** (of bars etc) grille f, grillage m **2** (electrode) grille f, Br **the national g.** le réseau électrique national **3** (on chart) grille f, (lines on map) quadrillage m **4** Sport (of motor racing circuit) **(starting) g.** grille f de départ **5** Comput grille f **6** = **gridiron**
▸▸ **g. layout** (of town) quadrillage, damier m; **g. lines** droites fpl du quadrillage; **g. reference** coordonnées fpl de la grille; **g. system** réseau m de quadrillage

griddle ['grɪd(ə)l] N Culin (iron plate) plaque f en fonte; (on top of stove) plaque chauffante
▸▸ **g. cake** = sorte de galette épaisse

gridiron ['grɪdaɪən] N Am Ftbl (field) terrain m de football; (game) football m américain

gridlock ['grɪdlɒk] N (on road) embouteillage m; Fig impasse f

grief [gri:f] N **1** (pain) chagrin m, douleur f, **to die of g.** mourir de chagrin; **to come to g.** (of person) (in undertaking) échouer; (have an accident) avoir un accident; (of rider)

faire une chute; *(of plan etc)* échouer, mal tourner; **she came to g. in the written exam** elle a échoué à l'écrit; *Fam* **good g.!** mon Dieu! **2** *Fam (trouble, inconvenience)* embêtements *mpl*; **to give sb g.** embêter qn
▸▸*Am* **g. counselor** = conseiller *m* qui propose une assistance psychologique aux personnes qui ont perdu un être cher

> Note that the French word **grief** is a false friend and is never a translation for the English word **grief**. It means **grievance**.

grief-stricken ADJ accablé de douleur *ou* de chagrin

grievance ['gri:vəns] N **1** *(feeling of having been wronged)* grief *m*; **to have a g. against sb** avoir un grief contre qn; **to air** *or* **state one's grievances** conter *ou* exprimer ses doléances **2** *(wrong)* doléance *f*; **to redress a g.** réparer un tort
▸▸**g. procedure** = procédure *f* permettant aux salariés de faire part de leurs revendications

grieve [gri:v] VI se chagriner, s'affliger (**over** *or* **about sth** de qch); **the whole nation grieved at his death** la nation entière pleura sa mort; **he was grieving for his lost daughter** il pleurait sa fille perdue; **she is still grieving** elle a encore de la peine
▪ VT *(person)* chagriner, affliger; **we are grieved to learn ...** nous apprenons avec peine ...; **it grieves me to ...** cela me peine de ...

grieved [gri:vd] ADJ chagriné, affligé (**at** de); **deeply g.** navré (**at** de)

grieving ['gri:vɪŋ] ADJ éploré

grievous ['gri:vəs] ADJ *Fml* **1** *(causing grief)* douloureux, pénible; *(news)* affligeant, douloureux; *(loss)* cruel **2** *(wound etc)* grave
▸▸*Law* **g. bodily harm** coups *mpl* et blessures *fpl*; **to cause g. bodily harm** causer de graves blessures

grievously ['gri:vəslɪ] ADV *(seriously)* gravement; *(wounded)* grièvement

griffin ['grɪfɪn] N *Myth* griffon *m*

griffon ['grɪfən] N **1** *(dog)* griffon *m* **2** *Myth* griffon *m* **3** *(bird)* vautour *m* fauve
▸▸**g. vulture** vautour fauve

grift [grɪft] VT *Am Sl* escroquer

grifter ['grɪftər] N *Am Sl* escroc *m*

grill [grɪl] N *Br Culin* **1** *(food)* grillade *f*; **a mixed g.** un assortiment de grillades **2** *(room in restaurant)* grill-room *m*, *pl* grill-rooms; *(restaurant)* rôtisserie *f* **3** *(device)* gril *m*; **to cook sth under the g.** cuire qch sur le *ou* au gril
▪ VT **1** *Br (cook) (meat etc)* faire griller **2** *Fam (interrogate) (prisoner etc)* cuisiner
▪ VI *Br Culin* griller

grill(e) [grɪl] N *(bars) (of gate)* grille *f*, **(counter) g.** *(in bank etc)* grille de comptoir; *Aut* **(radiator) g.** calandre *f*

grilled [grɪld] ADJ *Br Culin* grillé; **g. meat** viande *f* grillée, grillade *f*

grilling ['grɪlɪŋ] N **1** *Br (of food)* cuisson *f* sur le *ou* au gril **2** *Fam (interrogation)* **to give sb a g.** cuisiner qn

grillroom ['grɪlrʊm] N *(in restaurant)* grill-room *m*, *pl* grill-rooms; *(restaurant)* rôtisserie *f*

grim [grɪm] ADJ *(countryside, surroundings)* sinistre, lugubre; *(news, report)* sombre; *(face)* sévère; *(smile)* sardonique; *(humour)* macabre; **g. determination** volonté inflexible; **to hold on like g. death** se cramponner (**to sb/sth** à qn/qch); **to look g.** *(of person) (serious)* avoir une mine sévère; *(very ill)* avoir très mauvaise mine; **things are looking g.** ça s'annonce mal; **the g. prospect of another famine** la perspective sinistre d'une autre famine; *Fam* **how do you**

feel? – pretty g. comment ça va? – plutôt mal; *Fam* **I thought it was pretty g.** *(not well done, of poor quality)* j'ai trouvé ça plutôt minable
▸▸**the G. Reaper** La Faucheuse

grimace [grɪ'meɪs] N grimace *f*; **to make a g.** faire la grimace
▪ VI grimacer, faire la grimace

grime [graɪm] N saleté *f*, *(dust)* poussière *f* de charbon *ou* de suie

griminess ['graɪmɪnɪs] N saleté *f*, noirceur *f*

grimly ['grɪmlɪ] ADV sinistrement, de façon lugubre; *(to fight, hold on)* avec acharnement

grimness ['grɪmnɪs] N *(of surroundings, landscape)* caractère *m* sinistre *ou* lugubre; *(of face)* sévérité *f*, *(of struggle)* acharnement *m*; **the g. of the situation in the country** la situation désespérée du pays; **the g. of the news from the front** les sombres nouvelles du front

grimy ['graɪmɪ] ADJ sale, encrassé, noirci; *(with soot)* noir (de suie)

grin [grɪn] N **1** *(smile)* large sourire *m*; **to give a broad g.** avoir la bouche fendue jusqu'aux oreilles **2** *(grimace)* grimace *f* (qui découvre les dents)
▪ VI (**-nn-**) **1** *(smile)* sourire; *(broadly)* faire un large sourire; **he grinned broadly** son visage s'est épanoui en un large sourire, il fit un large sourire; *Fig* **to g. and bear it** *(tâcher de)* garder le sourire, *Fam* encaisser (sans broncher) **2** *(grimace)* grimacer en montrant les dents

grind [graɪnd] N **1** *Fam (work)* labeur *m* monotone et continu; **the daily g.** le labeur quotidien; **what a g.!** quelle corvée! **2** *(erotic dance)* déhanchement *m* **3** *(sound)* grincement *m*, crissement *m*
▪ VT (*pt, pp* **ground** [graʊnd]) **1** *(pulverize) (grain, coffee, pepper)* moudre; *Am (meat)* hacher; *also Fig* **to g. sth to dust** pulvériser qch; **to g. sth under one's heel** écraser qch avec le talon; *Fig* écraser qch; *Fig* **to g. the faces of the poor** opprimer les pauvres; **to g. one's teeth** grincer des dents **2** *(polish) (glass)* dépolir; *Opt* **to g. lenses** polir des lentilles **3** *(sharpen)* aiguiser, affûter; *(on grindstone)* passer à la meule **4** **to g. a barrel organ** jouer de l'orgue de Barbarie; **to g. a pepper mill** moudre du poivre
▪ VI **1** *(of wheels)* grincer, crisser; *(of gears)* craquer; **to g. to a halt** *(of vehicle)* s'immobiliser; *(of machine), Fig (production)* stopper; **the whole country ground to a halt** *or* **standstill during the General Strike** le pays a été complètement paralysé pendant la grève générale **2** *Old-fashioned Fam (work hard)* bûcher, turbiner; *Sch* bachoter
▸ **grind away** VI **1** *(working)* progresser laborieusement; **to g. away at sth** travailler laborieusement à qch **2** *Fam (sexually)* s'envoyer en l'air
▸ **grind down** VT SEP **1** *(opposition)* écraser; **a people ground down by poverty** un peuple accablé par une pauvreté extrême; *Fam* **don't let the bastards g. you down!** ne te laisse pas enfoncer par ces salauds! **2** *(pulverize) (grain, coffee)* moudre **3** *(sharpen)* aiguiser, affûter
▪ VI *(of substance)* **it grinds down easily** c'est facile à moudre
▸ **grind on** VI *(proceed relentlessly)* ne pas en finir; *(of negotiations, speech)* traîner en longueur, s'éterniser; **the accordion music ground on in the background** en fond sonore on entendait l'accordéon, intriminable et monotone
▸ **grind out** VT SEP **1** *(produce without originality) (articles, poems)* pondre; **to g. out a tune** jouer un air avec monotonie; **he ground out the same jokes night after night**

il a débité les mêmes plaisanteries soir après soir **2** *(cigarette)* écraser
▸ **grind up** VT SEP *(pulverize)* pulvériser; **to g. sth up small** moudre qch fin

grinder ['graɪndər] N **1** *(device)* appareil *m* broyeur, broyeuse *f*; *(for coffee)* moulin *m* à café; *(for sharpening)* meule *f*; *Fig* **to put sb through the g.** faire passer un mauvais quart d'heure à qn **2** *(person)* broyeur, -euse; *(of knives etc)* rémouleur *m* **3** *(molar)* molaire *f* **4** *Am Fam (sandwich)* gros sandwich *m*

grinding ['graɪndɪŋ] ADJ *(boredom, monotony etc)* mortel; *(worry, insecurity)* accablant; *(of gears)* craquement *m*; **to come to a g. halt** *(of vehicle)* s'immobiliser en grinçant; *(of machine), Fig (production)* stopper; **to bring sth to a g. halt** *(production)* stopper qch; *(country, rail network)* paralyser qch; **g. poverty** extrême pauvreté; **g. sound** *(of machine, car, lift)* grincement *m*
▪ N *(of corn)* mouture *f*; *(sound) (of machine, factory)* grincement *m*; *(of gears)* craquement *m*

grindingly ['graɪndɪŋlɪ] ADV **g. boring/monotonous** ennuyeux/monotone à mourir

grindstone ['graɪndstəʊn] N meule *f*, *Fig Fam* **he keeps our noses to the g.** il ne nous laisse aucun répit; **it's going to be noses to the g.** il va y avoir du boulot

gringo ['grɪŋgəʊ] N *Fam usu Pej (English speaker in Latin America)* gringo *m*

grip [grɪp] N **1** *(hold, grasp)* prise *f*, *(of wheels on road)* adhérence *f*, **to have a strong g.** *(of person)* avoir une bonne poigne; **your g. is wrong** *(on tennis racket, golf club etc)* tu ne tiens pas ta raquette/ton club/*etc*/comme il faut; *Fig* **I can't get to grips with Shakespeare** je n'arrive pas à comprendre Shakespeare; **to come to grips with sb** *(physically)* s'en prendre à qn; **to get a g. on sth** avoir une prise sur qch; *Fig* **to get a g. on the situation** *(bring under control)* prendre la situation en mains; *Fig* **to get** *or* **take** *or* **keep a g. on oneself** se maîtriser; **to have a firm g. on sth** *(physically)* tenir qch bien en main; *Fig* **although he has officially retired, Sir Charles retains a firm g. on financial decisions** bien qu'il soit officiellement à la retraite, Sir Charles est toujours très impliqué dans les décisions financières; *Br Fig Fam* **get a g.!** *(control yourself)* reprends-toi!; *(behave normally, be realistic)* arrête de déconner!; **to lose one's g.** *(on rope etc)* lâcher prise; *Fig (mentally)* baisser; **I must be losing my g.** je vieillis, je baisse; **to lose one's g. on reality** perdre le sens des réalités; **he was beginning to lose his g. on the situation** il commençait à perdre le contrôle de la situation; **in the g. of a disease/despair/pessimism** en proie à une maladie/au désespoir/au pessimisme; *Fig* **the country was in the g. of the worst winter for years** le pays connaissait l'hiver le plus rigoureux qu'il avait connu depuis des années
2 *(handle) (of oar, handlebars)* poignée *f*, *(of pistol)* poignée, crosse *f*; *Tennis (of racket)* manche *m*
3 *Tech etc (device)* pince *f*
4 **(hair) g.** pince *f* (à cheveux)
5 *Old-fashioned Am (bag)* mallette *f*
6 *TV, Cin* **grip(s)** machiniste *m* (de plateau)
▪ VT (**-pp-**) *(seize)* saisir, prendre; *(hold)* empoigner, agripper; **to g. sth in a vice** serrer qch dans un étau; **the tyres g. the road well** les pneus adhèrent bien (à la route); *Fig* **to be gripped by panic** être pris *ou* saisi de panique; **the region has been gripped by cold weather** la région a été saisie par une vague de froid; *Fig* **the play gripped the audience** la pièce a captivé les spectateurs
▪ VI *(of tyre)* adhérer

gripe [graɪp] N **1** *Fam (complaint)* sujet *m* de mécontentement; **what's your g.?** de quoi est-ce que tu te plains?; **they've always got some g.** ils sont toujours en train de râler **2** *(pain)* **gripes** coliques *fpl*
   VI *Fam (complain)* ronchonner, râler (**about sth** à propos de qch)
   ▸▸ **g. water** calmant *m (pour coliques)*

griping ['graɪpɪŋ] ADJ **g. pains** coliques *fpl*
N *Fam (complaining)* plaintes *fpl*

gripping ['grɪpɪŋ] ADJ *(book, film)* passionnant

grisly ['grɪzlɪ] ADJ *(murder, discovery)* macabre, sinistre; *(story, sight)* effrayant, épouvantable

grist [grɪst] N blé *m* à moudre; *Fig* **it's all g. to their mill** cela apporte de l'eau à leur moulin

gristle ['grɪs(ə)l] N *(in meat)* nerfs *mpl*

gristly ['grɪslɪ] ADJ *(meat)* nerveux

grit [grɪt] N **1** *(particles)* grès *m*, sable *m*; *(for icy roads)* sable; *Tech etc* impuretés *fpl* **2** *Fig (courage, determination)* cran *m*, courage *m*; **to have a lot of g.** avoir beaucoup de cran **3** *(stone)* grès *m (dur)*
   VT (-tt-) **1** *(put grit on) (slippery road surface etc)* sabler **2 to g. one's teeth** grincer des dents; *Fig* **you'll just have to g. your teeth** il va falloir que tu prennes ton mal en patience
   VI *(put grit on roads)* sabler (les routes)

grits [grɪts] NPL *Am (dish)* gruau *m* d'avoine

gritstone ['grɪtstəʊn] N grès *m (dur)*

gritter ['grɪtər] N *Br (vehicle)* camion *m* de sablage

gritting ['grɪtɪŋ] N *Br (of roads)* sablage *m*
   ▸▸ **g. lorry** camion *m* de sablage

gritty ['grɪtɪ] ADJ **1** *(soil)* cendreux; *(texture)* graveleux **2** *Fam (brave)* qui a du cran, résolu; **g. determination** détermination farouche **3** *(realistic) (writing etc)* très réaliste; **g. realism** *(of book, film etc)* réalisme cru

grizzle ['grɪz(ə)l] VI *esp Br Fam (complain)* ronchonner, râler; *(whine)* pleurnicher, geindre

grizzled ['grɪz(ə)ld] ADJ *(hair, person)* grisonnant

grizzling ['grɪzlɪŋ] N *esp Br Fam (whining)* pleurnicherie *f*, pleurnichement *m*

grizzly ['grɪzlɪ] ADJ **1** *(hair, person)* grisonnant **2** *Fam (whining)* grognon
   N *(bear)* grizzli *m*, grizzly *m*
   ▸▸ **g. bear** grizzli, grizzly

groan [grəʊn] N *(of pain)* gémissement *m*; *(at boring story, bad joke)* grognement *m* désapprobateur; *(of agreement, dismay)* grognement; *(of tree, timber)* grincement *m*; **to give** or **utter a deep g.** pousser un profond gémissement
   VI *(in pain)* gémir, pousser un gémissement; *(complain)* geindre; *(at bad joke, in dismay)* grogner; *(of tree, timber)* grincer; **to g. inwardly** étouffer une plainte *ou* un gémissement; **to g. under the weight of sth** grincer sous le poids de qch; **the cart is groaning under the load** la charrette grince sous le fardeau
   VT *(say)* gémir

groats [grəʊts] NPL *(of oats, wheat)* gruau *m* d'avoine/de froment

grobag® ['grəʊbæg] N = sac *m* de terreau que l'on perfore et qui sert directement de pépinière

grocer ['grəʊsər] N épicier, -ière *f*; **the g.'s will be closed** l'épicerie sera fermée; **to go to the g.'s** aller à l'épicerie *ou* chez l'épicier

groceries ['grəʊsərɪz] NPL *(articles mpl d')* épicerie *f*

grocery ['grəʊsərɪ] N *(shop)* épicerie *f*; **to be in the g. business** être dans l'épicerie

grog [grɒg] N *(drink)* grog *m*

groggy ['grɒgɪ] ADJ *Fam* chancelant, titubant; *(boxer)* groggy; **to feel g.** avoir les jambes en coton; **I'm feeling a bit g.** je ne suis pas dans mon assiette

grogshop ['grɒgʃɒp] N *Austr Fam* = magasin où l'on vend des boissons alcoolisées

groin [grɔɪn] N **1** *Anat* aine *f*, *Euph* **she kicked him in the g.** elle lui a donné un coup de pied dans les parties; **g. injury** blessure *f* à l'aine **2** *Archit (of vault)* arête *f*

grommet ['grɒmɪt] N *Tech* bague *f* d'étoupe; *Naut* erse *f*, erseau *m*

groom [gru:m] N **1** *(of horse)* palefrenier *m* **2** *(at wedding)* marié *m* **3** *(of King's bedchamber etc)* gentilhomme *m*, valet *m*
   VT **1** *(horse)* panser **2** *Fig (candidate)* préparer, former *(en vue d'un poste ou d'une fonction dans la politique etc)*; **the dictator groomed his successor for power** le dictateur a préparé son successeur au pouvoir

groomed [gru:md] ADJ **well-g.** *(horse)* bien entretenu; *(person)* bien soigné, soigné de sa personne

grooming ['gru:mɪŋ] N **1** *(of horse)* pansage *m* **2** *(of person)* **good g. is very important** il est important d'avoir une bonne présentation **3** *Fig (of candidate)* préparation *f*

groove [gru:v] N **1** *(slot)* rainure *f*; *(of gun etc)* rayure *f*; *(of column etc)* cannelure *f*; *(on record)* sillon *m* sonore; *(for sliding shutter etc)* coulisse *f*, glissière *f* **2** *Fig (routine)* routine *f*; **to get into a g.** s'encroûter, devenir routinier
   VT rainer; *(gun etc)* rayer; *(column)* canneler
   VI *Fam (dance)* danser; **to g. to the beat** danser en rythme

groovy ['gru:vɪ] ADJ *Old-fashioned Fam* sensass

grope [grəʊp] N **1** *(in dark etc)* tâtonnement *m* **2** *Fam (sexual)* pelotage *m*; **they were having a g.** ils se pelotaient
   VI tâtonner; **to g. for sth** chercher qch à tâtons *ou* à l'aveuglette; **to g. for a word** chercher un mot
   VT **1 to g. one's way** avancer à tâtons, se diriger en tâtonnant (**towards sth** vers qch) **2** *Fam (sexually)* peloter

groper ['grəʊpər] N *(fish)* mérou *m*

groping ['grəʊpɪŋ] ADJ tâtonnant
   N **1** *(in dark etc)* tâtonnement *m* **2** *(sexual)* pelotage *m*

grosbeak ['grəʊsbi:k] N *(bird)* gros-bec *m*, *pl* gros-becs

grosgrain ['grəʊgreɪn] N *Tex* gros-grain *m*

gross¹ [grəʊs] N INV *(twelve dozen)* douze douzaines *fpl*, grosse *f* VOIR GRAMMAIRE A12–13

gross² ADJ **1** *(fat)* gras, *f* grasse **2** *(blatant) (error)* grossier; *(ignorance)* crasse; *(injustice, carelessness, idiocy)* flagrant; *(abuse)* choquant **3** *(vulgar) (joke, person)* grossier; *esp Am Fam* **that's g.!** *(repulsive)* c'est dégoûtant! **4** *Com, Fin (profit, income)* brut **5** *Naut (displacement)* global, -aux, total, -aux
   N *(whole amount)* montant *m* brut
   VT *Com etc (of company)* gagner brut; *(of sale)* produire brut; *(of film)* rapporter une recette brute de
   ▸▸ **g. amount** montant *m* brut; **g. assets** actif *m* brut; *Fin* **g. dividend** dividende *m* brut; **g. domestic product** produit *m* intérieur brut; **g. income** *(in accounts)* produit *m* brut; *(of individual)* revenu *m* brut; *Fin* **g. margin** marge *f* brute; **g. national expenditure** dépense *f* nationale brute; **g. national income** revenu national brut; **g. national product** produit national brut; *Law* **g. negligence** faute *f* lourde; *Acct* **g. operating profit** bénéfice *m* *ou* résultat *m* brut d'exploitation; **g. profit** bénéfice brut; *Acct* **g. profit margin** marge commerciale brute; *Acct* **g. receipts** recettes *fpl* brutes; *Acct* **g. redemption yield**

rendement *m* actuariel brut; *Naut* **g. register tonnage** (tonnage *m* de) jauge *f* brute; *Fin* **g. return** rendement brut; *Naut* **g. ton** tonne *f* de jauge; *Naut* **g. tonnage** (tonnage de) jauge brute, tonnage brut; **g. weight** poids *m* brut, brut *m*; *Fin* **g. yield** rendement brut
   ▸ **gross out** VT SEP *Fam* **to g. sb out** répugner qn, dégoûter qn

grossed-up price ['grəʊst-] N prix *m* fort, plein tarif *m*

grossly ['grəʊslɪ] ADV **1** *(vulgarly)* grossièrement **2** *(exaggerated, negligent)* énormément; **to be g. mistaken** se tromper grossièrement; **his skills have been g. overrated** ses capacités ont été vraiment surestimées

grossness ['grəʊsnɪs] N **1** *(obesity)* obésité *f* **2** *(of abuse, stupidity, error etc)* énormité *f* **3** *(vulgarity)* grossièreté *f*

grossout ['grəʊsaʊt] N *Am Fam* = chose *f* ou situation *f* répugnante; **what a g.!** c'est vraiment dégueulasse!

grot [grɒt] N *Fam (muck)* crasse *f*

grotesque [grəʊ'tesk] ADJ *(bizarre)* grotesque
   N *Art* grotesque *m*

grotesquely [grəʊ'tesklɪ] ADV grotesquement

grotto, *pl* **grottoes, grottos** ['grɒtəʊ, -əʊz] N grotte *f*

grotty ['grɒtɪ] N *Br Fam* dégueulasse; *(ill)* vaseux

grouch [graʊtʃ] *Fam* N **1** *(person)* râleur, -euse **2** *(complaint)* plainte *f*, **to have a g. about sth** se plaindre de qch; **to have a g. against sb** en vouloir à qn
   VI râler, ronchonner (**to sb** après qn; **about sth** à propos de qch)

grouchy ['graʊtʃɪ] ADJ *Fam* râleur, ronchonneur

ground¹ [graʊnd] ADJ **1** *(coffee, wheat)* moulu **2** *(steel)* meulé; *(glass)* dépoli
   ▸▸ *Am* **g. beef** bœuf *m* haché; *Am* **g. meat** viande *f* hachée; **g. rice** farine *f* de riz

GROUND²

N	terre **1, 7** • sol **1** • terrain **2** • parc **3** • fond **4, 5** • raison **6** • motif **6**
VT	fonder **1** • former **2** • mettre à la terre **3**

N **1** *(earth etc)* sol *m*, terre *f*, **sitting on the g.** assis par terre; **to pick sth up off the g.** ramasser qch par terre; **to fall to the g.** tomber à *ou* par terre; **above/below g.** sur/sous terre; **curtains down to the g.** rideaux qui pendent jusqu'à terre; **burnt (down) to the g.** brûlé de fond en comble; *Fam* **that suits me** *Br* **down to the g.** *or Am* **from the g. up** *(of arrangement etc)* ça me convient parfaitement; *Fig* **to cut the g. from under sb's feet** couper l'herbe sous le pied à qn; **the plane didn't get off the g.** l'avion n'a pas décollé, l'avion n'a pas quitté le sol; *Fig* **the idea never got off the g.** l'idée n'a jamais abouti à rien; *Fig* **the idea may take a while to get off the g.** l'idée risque de mettre du temps à prendre forme; **when the project eventually did get off the g.** quand le projet a enfin démarré; *Fig* **to work oneself into the g.** se tuer au travail; *Fig* **he's driven this car into the g.** il a usé cette voiture jusqu'au bout; **to go to g.** *(of fox)*, *Fig* se terrer; **to run a fox to g.** traquer un renard jusqu'à son terrier; *Fig* **to run sb to g.** *(criminal, person sought by police)* traquer qn; **I finally ran him to g. in the library** j'ai fini par le trouver à la bibliothèque **2** *(land, for sport)* terrain *m*; *Fig* **to find common g. for negotiations** trouver un terrain d'entente en vue de négocier; *Fig* **to be on firm g.** être sûr de soi; *Fig* **to be on shaky g.** marcher sur des œufs; *Fig* **to change** or **shift one's g.** changer de tactique; *Fig* **to break new** or **fresh g.** faire œuvre de pionnier, innover; **to cover a lot of g.** (*travel a great distance*) faire beaucoup de chemin *ou* de kilomètres; *Fig* (*deal with many subjects*) couvrir de très nombreux domaines; **to cover a lot of g. looking for sb** rechercher qn dans un vaste rayon; **to gain g.** gagner du terrain, progresser; (*of idea*) faire son chemin; **to lose g.** (*of troops, company, government*) perdre du terrain; **we are losing g. to the competition** la concurrence gagne du terrain; **to give g.** (*of troops, company, government*) céder du terrain; **to stand** or **hold one's g.** tenir bon, tenir ferme; *Fig* **to confront/defeat sb on his own g.** affronter/battre qn sur son propre terrain

3 grounds (*of school, hospital, country house*) parc *m*; **the school has extensive grounds** l'école est entourée d'un immense parc; **country house with extensive grounds** château aux vaste domaine

4 (*of sea*) fond *m*; *Naut* **to touch g.** (*of ship*) talonner, heurter le fond

5 (*background*) (*of painting*) fond *m*, champ *m*; **light colour on a dark g.** couleur claire sur un fond sombre

6 grounds (*reasons*) raison *f*, cause *f*, motif *m*; (*of suspicions etc*) base *f*; **g.** or **grounds for complaint** raisons de se plaindre; **she has no g. for complaint** elle n'a aucune raison de se plaindre; **to have (good) g.** or **grounds for doing sth** avoir de bonnes raisons de faire qch; **they had no grounds for treating her like that** ils n'avaient pas le droit de la traiter de cette manière; **... and with good g.** ... et avec raison; **what grounds have you for saying that?** qu'est-ce qui vous permet d'affirmer cela?; **it gives us grounds to suspect that ...** cela nous donne des raisons de suspecter que ...; **on what grounds?** à quel titre?; **on personal/medical/moral grounds** pour des raisons personnelles/médicales/morales; **on grounds of ill-health** pour raisons de santé; *Law* **grounds for divorce** motifs de divorce; *Law* **grounds for appeal** voies *fpl* de recours

7 *Am Elec* terre *f*, masse *f*; **to connect to g.** (*pole*) mettre à la masse, relier à la terre

8 grounds (*of coffee*) marc *m*

VT 1 (*base*) fonder, baser, appuyer (**on** or **in** sth sur qch); (*belief*) asseoir (**on** sur)

2 to g. sb in sth (*give a grounding in*) former qn en qch

3 *Am Elec* (*current*) mettre à la masse *ou* à la terre

4 (*ship*) échouer; (*airplane*) interdire de vol; *Fam* **to be grounded** (*of teenager*) ne pas avoir le droit de sortir; *Mil* **g. arms!** reposez armes!

VI (*of ship*) échouer, s'échouer (**on** sur); (*of balloon*) atterrir

▸▸*Mil* **g. attack** offensive *f* terrestre; *Mus* **g. bass** basse *f* contrainte; *Am Aut* **g. cable** câble *m* de masse; *Aut* **g. clearance** hauteur *f* du châssis au-dessus du sol, garde *f* au sol; *Am Elec* **g. connection** prise *f* de terre; *Aviat* **g. control** contrôle *m* au sol; *Aviat* **g. crew** personnel *m* au sol, personnel non-navigant; *Br* **g. floor** rez-de-chaussée *m inv*; *Mil* **g. forces** armée *f* de terre; **g. frost** gelée *f* blanche; *TV, Cin* **g. lamp** lampe *f* de rampe; **g. level** (*ground floor*) rez-de-chaussée; (*lowest level in organization*) base *f*; *Fishing* **g. line** ligne *f* de fond; **g. note** son *m* fondamental; *Aviat* **g. operator** (*who organizes services, transfers etc*) voyagiste *m ou* agence *f* de réceptif, réceptif *m*; **g. personnel** personnel au sol, personnel non navigant; **g. plan** (*plan of ground floor*) plan *m* au sol; (*plan of action*) plan préparatoire; **g.**

rent redevance *f* foncière (*as source of income*) rente *f* foncière; **g. rule** procédure *f*, règle *f*; **g. staff** *Sport* = personnel responsable de l'entretien d'un terrain de sport; *Br Aviat* personnel au sol, personnel non-navigant; *TV* **g. station** station *f* terrestre; *TV* **g. transmitter** émetteur *m* terrestre; *Mil* **g. zero** hypocentre *m*, point *m* zéro; **G. Zero** (*in New York*) Ground Zero

groundbait ['graʊndbeɪt] **N** *Fishing* amorce *f* de fond

ground-breaking **ADJ** révolutionnaire; **this is g. technology** c'est une véritable percée technologique

grounded ['graʊndɪd] **ADJ 1** (*based*) (*argument, belief etc*) fondé; **well/ill g.** (*belief*) bien/mal fondé **2** *Am Elec* (mis) à la masse, relié à la terre

groundhog ['graʊndhɒg] **N** marmotte *f* d'Amérique

▸▸*Am* **G. Day** = le 2 février, jour où les marmottes sont censées avoir fini leur hibernation et sortir de leur terrier, annonçant l'arrivée prochaine du printemps si elles restent dehors, et le prolongement de l'hiver si elles ne font qu'une brève apparition

grounding ['graʊndɪŋ] **N 1** (*of argument on sth*) fondement *m* **2** *Am Elec* (*of current*) mise *f* à la terre *ou* à la masse **3** (*of ship*) échouage *m*; (*of airplane*) interdiction *f* de vol; (*of balloon*) atterrissage *m* **4 to have a good g. in Latin** avoir de bonnes bases en latin

groundless ['graʊndlɪs] **ADJ** (*suspicion etc*) mal fondé, sans fondement

groundnut ['graʊndnʌt] **N** *Br* arachide *f*

▸▸**g. oil** huile *f* d'arachide

groundsel ['graʊndsəl] **N** (*weed*) séneçon *m*

groundsheet ['graʊndʃiːt] **N** (*of tent*) tapis *m* de sol

groundsman, *pl* **groundsmen** ['graʊndzmən] **N** *Sport* responsable *m* de l'entretien d'un terrain de sport

groundspeed ['graʊndspiːd] **N** *Aviat* vitesse *f* au sol

groundswell ['graʊndswel] **N** *Naut* lame *f* de fond; *Fig* **g. of public opinion** grand mouvement *m* d'opinion publique; **there has been a g. of support for the proposal** il y a eu un raz-de-marée en faveur de la proposition

ground-to-air **ADJ** *Mil* (*missile etc*) sol-air *inv*

ground-to-ground **ADJ** *Mil* (*missile etc*) sol-sol *inv*

groundwork ['graʊndwɜːk] **N** (*initial work*) travail *m* préparatoire; *Fig* **to do** or **lay the g. for a project/economic reform** jeter les fondations d'un projet/de réformes économiques; **I've laid the g., the rest is up to you** j'ai préparé le terrain, le reste dépend de toi

group [gruːp] **N** VOIR GRAMMAIRE A11 **1** (*of people, companies*), *Mus* groupe *m*; (*of things*) groupe, ensemble *m*; **to form a g.** se grouper; **(arranged) in groups of three** répartis en groupes de trois; **g. of accounts** classe *f* de comptes; **political g.** groupe(ment) *m* politique **2** *Mil, Aviat* (*unit*) groupe *m*

VT grouper

VI se grouper (**round** autour de)

▸▸**g. booking** réservation *f* de groupe; **g. captain** colonel *m* de l'armée de l'air; **g. decision** décision *f* collective; **g. discount** remise *f* pour les groupes; *Psy* **g. dynamics** dynamique *f* de groupe; **g. fare** tarif *m* de groupe; **g. insurance** assurance *f* collective; **g. interview** entretien *m* de groupe; **g. leader** (*on package tour*) accompagnateur, -trice; (*for group of children*) moniteur, -trice; **g. manager** chef *m* de groupe; **g. meeting** réunion *f*

de groupe; **g. photograph** photographie *f* de groupe; *Med* **g. practice** cabinet *m* médical; (*of dentists*) cabinet dentaire; **g. product manager** chef *m* de groupe de produits; **g. rate** tarif de groupe; **g. sex** relations *fpl* sexuelles à plusieurs; *Cin, TV* **g. shot** plan *m* de groupe (*de personnages*); **g. subscription** abonnement *m* collectif; **g. therapy** thérapie *f* de groupe; **g. travel** voyages *mpl* en groupe; *Fin* **g. turnover** chiffre *m* d'affaires consolidé *ou* du groupe

groupage ['gruːpɪdʒ] **N** groupage *m*

▸▸*Com* **g. bill** connaissement *m* de groupage

grouped consignment [gruːpt] **N** *Com* envoi *m* groupé

grouper ['gruːpər] **N** (*fish*) mérou *m*

groupie ['gruːpɪ] **N** *Fam* groupie *f*

grouping ['gruːpɪŋ] **N 1** (*putting together*) (*of packages, consignments etc*) groupage *m*; (*of figures etc*) groupement *m* **2** (*group*) groupe *m*; **political g.** groupement *m* politique

groupware ['gruːpweər] **N** *Comput* logiciel *m* de groupe, synergiciel *m*

grouse [graʊs] **N INV** (*bird*) tétras *m*, grouse *f*, **red g.** lagopède *m* (rouge) d'Écosse; **black g.** tétras lyre

▸▸**g. shooting** chasse *f* à la grouse

grouse **N** (*grumble*) grogne *f*, (*complaint*) plainte *f*, **he enjoys a good g.** il aime ronchonner

VI ronchonner, grogner (**at, about** contre)

grouser ['graʊsər] **N** râleur, -euse

grousing ['graʊsɪŋ] **N** ronchonneries *fpl*; **I've had enough of your g.!** j'en ai assez de t'entendre ronchonner!

grout [graʊt] *Constr* **N** coulis *m*, mortier *m* clair *ou* liquide; **cement g.** lait *m ou* laitance *f* de ciment

VT jointoyer

grove [grəʊv] **N** futaie *f*, bosquet *m*; **beech g.** hêtraie *f*, **olive g.** oliveraie *f*, *Lit* **the groves of Academe** les hautes sphères de l'université

grovel ['grɒv(ə)l] **VI** (-ll-, *Am* -l-) être à quatre pattes; **what are you doing grovelling around on the floor?** qu'est-ce que tu fais à quatre pattes?; *Fig* **to g. to** or **before sb** ramper devant qn

grovelling, *Am* **groveling** ['grɒv(ə)lɪŋ] **ADJ** (*humble*) servile; **a g. apology** une excuse obséquieuse

N servilité *f*, (*before sb*) obséquiosité *f*

grow [grəʊ] (*pt* **grew** [gruː], *pp* **grown** [grəʊn]) **VI 1** (*of plants, hair*) pousser; (*of seeds*) germer; **to g. back** (*of plants, hair*) repousser; **she let her hair g. long** elle a laissé pousser ses cheveux, elle s'est laissé pousser les cheveux; **olives do not g. in England** les oliviers ne poussent pas en Angleterre

2 (*of person, animal*) grandir; (*of company*) s'agrandir; **you've grown to us grandi; you've grown really tall** qu'est-ce que tu as grandi; **this variety of tree will g. fairly tall in five years** cette variété d'arbre atteint une taille assez importante en cinq ans; **she has grown 2 inches** elle a grandi de 5 cm

3 (*increase*) augmenter, s'accroître; **the crowd grew** la foule augmenta *ou* grossit; **the economy has grown by 5% in the last two years** la croissance de l'économie a été de 5% au cours des deux dernières années; **his influence grew** son influence a grandi; **support for the strike is growing** la grève est de plus en plus soutenue; **the rumour was growing** la rumeur grandissait; **to g. in wisdom/beauty** grandir en sagesse/beauté

4 (*become*) devenir; **to g. old** vieillir; **to g. younger** rajeunir; **to g. big/bigger** (*of person*) grandir; (*of animal, database, crowd, tumour*) grossir; (*of town, company*) s'agrandir;

(of plant, tree) pousser; (of problem) s'accroître; **to g. smaller** (of person) rapetisser; (of swelling, problem) diminuer; **the noise grew louder** le bruit a augmenté ou s'est amplifié; **to g. alarmed/excited** s'alarmer/s'exciter; **to g. angry** se fâcher; **to g. less** diminuer; **it is growing dark** il commence à faire sombre

5 (reach point) **I have grown to think that ...** j'en suis à penser que ...; **they grew to like the house** ils ont fini par aimer la maison

VT 1 (roses, vegetables) cultiver; **soil that will not g. asparagus** sol peu propice aux asperges

2 (beard) se laisser pousser; **to g. one's hair (long)** se laisser pousser les cheveux, laisser pousser ses cheveux; **the stag grows fresh antlers every year** de nouveaux andouillers poussent au cerf chaque année

3 Com **to g. the business** augmenter le chiffre d'affaires; **to g. a company** développer une entreprise

▸ **grow apart** VI (of people) s'éloigner; **we gradually grew apart as we got older** nous nous sommes progressivement éloignés l'un de l'autre en vieillissant

▸ **grow in** VI (of hair) repousser; (of nail) s'incarner

▸ **grow into** VT INSEP **1** (become) devenir; **she had grown into a woman** elle était devenue femme; **the company grew into a huge organization** l'entreprise est devenue une énorme société **2** (become big enough for) **he has grown into his brother's shirts** les chemises de son frère lui vont maintenant

▸ **grow on** VT INSEP Fam **that picture grows on me** plus je regarde ce tableau plus il me plaît; **this music grows on you** plus on écoute cette musique plus on l'aime; **it's grown on me** je me suis mis à l'aimer petit à petit; **it will g. on you** tu finiras par l'aimer; **the idea was beginning to g. on me** l'idée commençait à me séduire

▸ **grow out** VI **she let the dye g. out** elle a laissé pousser ses cheveux jusqu'à ce que les traces de teinture aient disparu

▸ **grow out of** VT INSEP **1** (become too large for) ne plus rentrer dans; **he's grown out of his shoes** ses chaussures sont maintenant trop petites pour lui **2** (become too old for) **to g. out of doing sth** passer l'âge de faire qch; **she grew out of her dolls** elle a passé l'âge de jouer à la poupée; **it's just a phase, he'll g. out of it** ce n'est qu'une tocade, ça lui passera; **to g. out of one's friends** ne plus avoir grand-chose en commun avec ses amis

▸ **grow up** VI **1** (become adult) grandir; **I want to be a doctor when I g. up** je veux être docteur quand je serai grand; **we didn't have television when I was growing up** nous n'avions pas la télévision quand j'étais petit

2 (behave like adult) **I wish you'd g. up!** j'aimerais bien que tu cesses tes gamineries!; **g. up!** (be realistic) reviens sur terre!

3 (develop) se développer, se faire jour; **a theory has grown up that ...** une théorie s'est fait jour selon laquelle ...; **a custom has grown up** la coutume s'est établie; **a legend grew up around these events** une légende s'est développée autour de ces événements; **the town grew up around the castle** la ville s'est développée autour du château; **a close friendship gradually grew up between them** une étroite amitié s'est développée entre eux petit à petit

grower ['grəʊər] N **1** (person) cultivateur, -trice **2** (plant) **fast/slow g.** plante f qui pousse vite/lentement

growing ['grəʊɪŋ] ADJ **1** (child) en pleine croissance; (town, population etc) en pleine

expansion **2** (increasing) (debt) qui augmente; (opinion, belief) de plus en plus répandu; (discontent, opposition, problem) grandissant; **there was a g. fear that ...** on craignait de plus en plus que ...; **there is g. support for this party** le parti a de plus en plus d'adhérents; **there are g. problems** il y a de plus en plus de problèmes

▸▸ **g. pains** (of children) douleurs fpl de croissance; (of business, project) difficultés fpl de croissance, problèmes mpl de départ

-growing ['grəʊɪŋ] SUFF **wheat/potato-g.** culture f du blé/de la pomme de terre; **a potato-g. region** une région à pommes de terre; **fast/slow-g.** (plant) qui pousse vite/lentement

growl [graʊl] N (of dog, bear, tiger etc) grondement m, grognement m

VT & VI **1** (of dog, lion etc) grogner, gronder (**at** contre) **2** (of person) grogner, grommeler (**at sb** contre qn)

growling ['graʊlɪŋ] N (of dog, bear etc) grognement m, grondement m

grown [grəʊn] ADJ grand; **a g. woman** une femme adulte; **when fully g., these animals can ...** lorsqu'ils ont atteint l'âge adulte, ces animaux peuvent ...

PP see **grow**

grown-up N ['grəʊnʌp] grand m, grande personne f; **the grown-ups** les grands, les grandes personnes

ADJ [grəʊn'ʌp] adulte; **he's very g. for his age** il est très mûr pour son âge

growth [grəʊθ] N **1** (of person, plant) croissance f; Med **(human) g. hormone** hormone f somatotrope ou de croissance, somatotrophine f

2 (increase) accroissement m; (of business) croissance f, (of business, company, population) expansion f; **(economic) g.** croissance économique; **to go for g.** favoriser la croissance; **rate of g.** taux m d'expansion ou de croissance; **the recent g. in the number of small businesses** l'augmentation récente du nombre de petites entreprises

3 (something that has grown) **the entrance was covered by a dense g. of weeds** l'entrée était envahie par les mauvaises herbes; **g. of hair** poussée f de cheveux; **with a week's g. (of beard) on his chin** le menton couvert d'une barbe de huit jours; **yearly g.** (of plant) pousse f annuelle

4 (tumour) grosseur f, excroissance f; **benign/malignant g.** tumeur f bénigne/maligne; **I have a g. on my neck** j'ai une grosseur au cou

▸▸ **g. area** secteur m en expansion; **alternative medicine has really been a g. area in recent years** les médecines parallèles ont connu un boom ces dernières années; Mktg **g. developer** stimulateur m de croissance; **g. industry** industrie f en plein essor ou de pointe; Mktg **g. inhibitor** inhibiteur m de croissance; **g. market** marché m porteur; St Exch **g. shares, g. stock** valeurs fpl d'avenir ou de croissance; **g. strategy** stratégie f de croissance

growth-share matrix N Mktg matrice f croissance-part de marché

groyne [grɔɪn] N brise-lames m inv

grub [grʌb] N **1** (larva) larve f; (maggot) asticot m, Fam ver m (blanc) **2** Sl (food) bouffe f, **g.'s up!** à la bouffe!

▸▸ **G. Street** le monde des plumitifs

▸ **grub about, grub around** VI (search) fouiller, farfouiller; **I was grubbing about in the dirt looking for my key** j'étais en train de farfouiller par terre dans les saletés pour trouver ma clef

▸ **grub out** VT SEP (roots etc) extirper

▸ **grub up** VT SEP (root) extirper; (plant) déraciner; (of bird, animal) déterrer

grubbiness ['grʌbɪnɪs] N (dirtiness) saleté f, malpropreté f, Fig (immorality) bassesse f

grubby ['grʌbɪ] ADJ (dirty) crasseux, malpropre; Fig (immoral) sordide, sale; Fig **I felt g. when I found out he was married** je me suis méprisée quand j'ai appris qu'il était marié; **I don't want him getting his g. hands on these documents** je ne veux pas que cet animal mette la main sur ces documents

grubstake ['grʌbsteɪk] N Am = provisions fpl données à un prospecteur contre un pourcentage de ses profits

grudge [grʌdʒ] N rancune f; **to bear sb a g., to have a g. against sb** tenir rancune à qn, en vouloir à qn; **she's not one to bear a g.** elle n'est pas du genre rancunier

VT **1** (give unwillingly) **to g. sb sth** donner qch à contrecœur à qn; **she grudged them every penny she gave them** elle leur donnait chaque penny à contrecœur; **to g. sb the food they eat** lésiner sur la nourriture de qn **2** (resent) **to g. sb their pleasures** mal supporter que qn passe du bon temps; **she grudges him his success** elle lui en veut à cause de son succès; **I don't g. spending money but ...** je ne répugne pas à dépenser mais ...; **I g. having to get up so early** je supporte très mal d'avoir à me lever si tôt

▸▸ **g. match** règlement m de compte

grudging ['grʌdʒɪŋ] ADJ (praise, gift) fait/donné à contrecœur

grudgingly ['grʌdʒɪŋlɪ] ADV (to do sth) à contrecœur, à regret

gruel ['gruːəl] N gruau m (d'avoine); (thin) brouet m

gruelling, Am **grueling** ['gruːəlɪŋ] ADJ (race, interview) éreintant, épuisant; (match) âprement disputé; **we had a g. time** ça a été très dur

gruesome ['gruːsəm] ADJ horrible, abominable; Hum **the g. twosome** les deux terreurs fpl

gruesomely ['gruːsəmlɪ] ADV horriblement, abominablement

gruff [grʌf] ADJ (tone) bourru, brusque; **a g. voice** une grosse voix

gruffly ['grʌflɪ] ADV d'un ton bourru

gruffness ['grʌfnɪs] N brusquerie f, **the g. of his tone** son ton bourru

grumble ['grʌmb(ə)l] N grommellement m, grognement m; **his letter contained the usual grumbles** sa lettre contenait les plaintes habituelles; **to obey without a g.** obéir sans murmurer; Fam **to have a good old g.** rouspéter un bon coup

VI grommeler, grogner, Fam rouspéter; Fig (of thunder) gronder; **(we) mustn't g.** il ne faut pas se plaindre; **to g. about the food** se plaindre de la nourriture; **to g. at sb** grommeler ou rouspéter contre qn; **my stomach's grumbling** j'ai l'estomac qui gargouille

VT **'I do all the work here', he grumbled,** 'c'est moi qui fait tout ici', a-t-il grommelé

grumbler ['grʌmblər] N grognon m, ronchonneur, -euse, Fam rouspéteur, -euse

grumbling ['grʌmblɪŋ] ADJ grognon; **the g. crowd waited impatiently** la foule attendait avec des ronchonnements d'impatience; **g. noises** des ronchonnements mpl

N Fam rouspétance f

▸▸ Med **g. appendix** appendicite f chronique

grummet ['grʌmɪt] N = **grommet**

grump [grʌmp] N Fam **1** (person) grincheux, -euse **2** Old-fashioned **to have the grumps** être grincheux

grumpily ['grʌmpɪlɪ] ADV (to agree, wonder, say) en ronchonnant; (to look at) d'un air ronchon

grumpiness ['grʌmpɪnɪs] N mauvaise humeur f

grumpy ['grʌmpɪ] ADJ (person) ronchon, grincheux; (attitude, tone) renfrogné; (answer) grincheux; **a g. old man** un vieux grincheux ▪ N **what's wrong, g.?** qu'est-ce qui ne va pas, grincheux?

grundyism ['grʌndɪɪzm] N pudibonderie f

grunge [grʌndʒ] N Fam **1** (dirt) crasse f **2** (fashion, music) grunge m

grungy ['grʌndʒɪ] ADJ Fam (town) nul; (flat, hotel) miteux; (sweater, trainers) crasseux; (mood) désagréable

grunt[1] [grʌnt] N (of pig, person) grognement m; **to give a g.** pousser ou faire entendre un grognement
▪ VI (of pig, person) grogner, pousser un grognement
▪ VT **to g. an answer** grogner une réponse

grunt[2] N Am Mil Sl (private) bidasse m

grunting ['grʌntɪŋ] N grognement(s) m(pl)

gryphon ['grɪfən] N = griffin

GSM [dʒi:es'em] N Tel (abbr global system for mobile communication) GSM m

G-spot N point m G

GST [dʒi:es'ti:] N Can Fin (abbr goods and services tax) TPS f (taxe sur les produits et services)

G-string N **1** Mus corde f de sol **2** (underwear) cache-sexe m inv; string m

G-suit N combinaison f spatiale

gt (abbr great) grand

Guadeloupe [gwa:də'lu:p] N Geog Guadeloupe f

guano ['gwa:nəʊ] N guano m

guarantee [gærən'ti:] N **1** Com (document, promise) garantie f; **a clock with a 12-month g.** une horloge garantie 12 mois; **this camera's still got two months' g. left** cet appareil photo est encore garanti deux mois; **it's still under g.** il est encore sous garantie **2** (security) garantie f, caution f; **to leave sth as a g.** laisser qch en garantie **3** (assurance) garantie f
▪ VT (stand surety for) se porter garant ou caution pour; (debt, product) garantir; **watch guaranteed for two years** montre garantie deux ans; **it's guaranteed not to rust** c'est garanti anti-rouille; **I can't g. that she'll come** je ne garantis pas qu'elle viendra; **to g. sb against loss** garantir qn contre les pertes
▪ ▸ g. **certificate** certificat m de garantie; g. **commission** commission f de garantie; g. **company** société f de sécurité; g. **fund** fonds m de garantie

guaranteed [gærən'ti:d] ADJ (success) garanti, assuré; Fin g. **by** (on document) pour aval, bon pour aval
▪ ▸ Fin g. **bond** obligation f garantie; Fin g. **loan** prêt m garanti

guarantor [gærən'tɔ:r] N garant, -ante, caution f; (of bill) donneur d'aval m, avaliste mf; **to stand as g. for sb** se porter garant ou caution pour qn

guaranty ['gærəntɪ] N = guarantee

guard [ga:d] N **1** (readiness) garde f; **to be on one's g.** être ou se tenir sur ses gardes; **to be on one's g. against sth** être sur ses gardes contre qch; **to put sb on his g.** mettre qn en garde; **to be caught off one's g.** être pris au dépourvu; Fencing, Boxing **on g.!** en garde!
2 (of sentry etc) **to be on g. (duty)** être en ou de faction, être de garde; **to go on g., to mount g.** monter la garde; **to come off g.** descendre de garde; **to keep g.** monter la garde, être de garde; **to keep a prisoner under g.** garder un prisonnier à vue; **he was marched off under g.** il fut emmené sous escorte

3 (no pl) Mil (men) garde f; **one of the old g.** un vieux de la vieille; **g. of honour** garde d'honneur; **to form a g. of honour** faire une haie d'honneur; **to set a g. on a bridge** faire surveiller un pont
4 (person) Mil soldat m de garde; Br Rail chef m de train; Am (prison) g. gardien m de prison; Br Mil **the Guards** les Gardes mpl du corps
5 (device) dispositif m protecteur, protection f; (on machine) protecteur m; Fencing (of foil) garde f, (fire) g. garde-feu m inv
▪ VT **1** (entrance etc) garder; **to g. sb from** or **against a danger** ou protéger qn d'un danger **2** to g. **one's tongue** tenir sa langue **3** Tech (gears etc) protéger
▪ ▸ g. **dog** chien m de garde; Br Mil **Guards officer** un officier de la Garde; Br Rail g.'s **van** wagon m du chef de train; (for luggage etc) fourgon m
▸ **guard against** VT INSEP (be careful to avoid) se garder de; **to g. against colds** se protéger ou se prémunir contre les rhumes; **to g. against an error** prendre garde à ne pas commettre une erreur

guarded ['ga:dɪd] ADJ **1** (speech, reply, comments etc) prudent; **he was very g.** il est resté très prudent **2** (mechanism) protégé **3** (prisoner) gardé à vue; (building) gardé, surveillé

guardedly ['ga:dɪdlɪ] ADV avec circonspection, avec prudence

guardhouse ['ga:dhaʊs] N Mil corps m de garde

guardian ['ga:dɪən] N gardien, -ienne; Law (of minor) tuteur, -trice
▪ ▸ g. **angel** ange m gardien

guardianship ['ga:dɪənʃɪp] N garde f, Law gestion f tutélaire, tutelle f

guardrail ['ga:dreɪl] N garde-fou m, pl garde-fous, parapet m; (on ship) bastingage m

guardroom ['ga:dru:m] N Mil **1** (for guards) corps m de garde **2** (for prisoners) salle f ou poste m de police

guardsman, pl **guardsmen** ['ga:dzmən] N Mil **1** Br (soldier) soldat m de la Garde; (officer) officier m de la Garde **2** Am (National) G. soldat m de la Garde Nationale

Guatemala [gwætɪ'ma:lə] N Geog Guatemala m

Guatemalan [gwætɪ'ma:lən] Geog ADJ guatémaltèque
▪ N Guatémaltèque mf

guava ['gwa:və] N **1** (fruit) goyave f **2** (tree) goyavier m
▪ ▸ g. **tree** goyavier

gubernatorial [gu:bənə'tɔ:rɪəl] ADJ esp Am (residence) du gouverneur; (election) au poste de gouverneur

gudgeon[1] ['gʌdʒən] N (fish) goujon m

gudgeon[2] N Tech goujon m, tourillon m, axe m
▪ ▸ g. **pin** axe de piston, (in machine) tourillon de la crosse

guelder-rose ['geldə'rəʊz] N (shrub) boule-de-neige f, pl boules-de-neige

gueridon ['gerɪdən] N guéridon m

Guernsey ['gɜ:nzɪ] N **1** Geog Guernesey f **2** (sweater) jersey m; (cow) vache f de Guernesey

guer(r)illa [gə'rɪlə] N Mil guérillero m; **band of guer(r)illas** groupe m de guérilleros
▪ ▸ g. **attack** attaque f de guérilleros; g. **leader** chef m de guérilla; g. **warfare** guérilla f

---

Note that the French word **guérilla** is a false friend and is never a translation for the English word **guerrilla**. It means **guerrilla warfare**.

---

guess [ges] N conjecture f, estimation f; **to have** or **make a g.** deviner; **that was a lucky g.!** je suis/tu es/etc tombé juste!; **it was just a lucky g.** c'était un coup de chance; **your g. is as good as mine** j'en sais autant que toi; **it's anybody's g.** qui sait?, Dieu seul le sait; **it's my g. ...** à mon avis, ...; **I give you three guesses** tu as droit à trois essais; **at a g., I'd say he's German** a priori, je dirais qu'il est allemand; **at a rough g., I'd say he's forty** je dirais qu'il a quarante ans; **at a g., there will be 40 people at the party** je pense qu'il y aura environ 40 personnes à la soirée; **40 at a rough g.** environ quarante
▪ VT **1** deviner; (estimate) (the length of sth etc) estimer; **g. who did it!** devine qui a fait ça!; **I guessed him to be twenty-five** je lui ai donné vingt-cinq ans; **to g. sth from sb's manner** deviner qch d'après l'attitude de qn; **g. what! I saw Ian yesterday** tu sais quoi? j'ai vu Ian hier; **g. who!** devine qui!; **you've guessed it!** vous l'avez deviné!
2 esp Am (think) croire, penser; **I g. you're right** tu as raison; **I g. so/not** je crois que oui/non
▪ VI deviner; **to g. right** deviner juste; **to g. wrong** se tromper; **you'll never g.** tu ne devineras jamais; **to keep sb guessing** laisser qn dans l'ignorance; **to g. at sth** (essayer de) deviner qch; **we could only g. at their plans** nous ne pouvions qu'essayer de deviner leurs intentions; **I couldn't begin to g.** je n'en ai pas la moindre idée; Iron **I would never have guessed** je n'aurais jamais deviné

guessing ['gesɪŋ] N estimation f
▪ ▸ g. **game** devinette f

guesstimate ['gestɪmɪt] N Fam calcul m au pif

guesswork ['geswɜ:k] N estimation f, conjecture f; **it's pure** or **sheer g.** c'est de la pure conjecture; **by g.** au jugé; **by sheer** or **pure g.** à vue de nez

guest [gest] N **1** invité, -ée; (at meal) convive mf, also Iron **be my g.!** faites comme chez vous!; **with a g. appearance from ...** avec comme invité, -ée d'honneur ...; **to make a g. appearance in a programme** être invité dans une émission; Cin, TV g. **star ...** (in credits) avec la participation de ...; **our thanks to this week's g. star, Billy Connolly** nous remercions Billy Connolly, qui nous a fait la gentillesse d'être avec nous cette semaine
2 (at hotel) client, -iente; **the landlord and his guests** l'hôtelier et ses hôtes; g. **comments** commentaires mpl clients
▪ VI TV, Radio **to g. on sb's show** faire une apparition dans l'émission de qn; Mus **another guitarist guested on one of the numbers** un autre guitariste a participé à l'un des morceaux
▪ ▸ g. **artist** invité-vedette m, invitée-vedette f, m pl invités-vedettes, f pl invitées-vedettes; g. **book** (in house, hotel), Comput (of Web page) livre m d'or; g. **list** liste f des invités; g. **night** (in club) = soirée f d'un club où les non-membres sont invités; g. **occupancy** taux m d'occupation des lits; g. **room** chambre f d'ami(s); g. **speaker** conférencier, -ière (invité à parler par une organisation, une association)

guesthouse ['gesthaʊs] N **1** (hotel) pension f de famille **2** (of monastery etc) hôtellerie f

guff [gʌf] N Fam bêtises fpl, âneries fpl; **don't talk g.!** ne dis pas d'âneries!; **the film was a load of g.** le film était vraiment débile

guffaw [gʌ'fɔ:] N gros rire m
▪ VI s'esclaffer

GUI ['gu:i] N Comput (abbr graphical user interface) interface f utilisateur graphique

Guiana [gaɪ'a:nə] N (region) Guyane f

guidance ['gaɪdəns] N **1** direction f,

conduite *f*; **under the g. of ...** sous la direction de ...; **sent for your g.** envoyé à titre d'indication **2** *(of missile)* guidage *m*
▸▸ **g. counsellor** conseiller, -ère d'orientation; *Aviat* **g. system** système *m* de guidage

guide [gaɪd] **N 1** *(person)* guide *m*; *Br* **(Girl) G.** guide *f*, éclaireuse *f* **2** *(book)* guide *m*; *(of railways)* indicateur *m*; **g. to Switzerland** guide de la Suisse; **the book is a useful g. to the world of finance** le livre constitue un guide utile du monde de la finance **3** *(indication)* indication *f*, exemple *m*; **as a g.** à titre indicatif
▸ **VT** guider, conduire; **to g. a child's first steps** guider les premiers pas d'un enfant; **I will be guided by your advice** je suivrai vos conseils
▸▸ **g. dog** chien *m* d'aveugle; *Rail* **g. rail** contre-rail *m*, *pl* contre-rails; **g. rope** *(for hoist)* corde *f* de guidage; *(for hot-air balloon)* guiderope *m*

guidebook ['gaɪdbʊk] **N** guide *m*

guided ['gaɪdɪd] **ADJ** *(tour etc)* guidé
▸▸ **g. missile** missile *m* guidé *ou* téléguidé

guideline ['gaɪdlaɪn] **N 1** *(indication)* directive *f* (**on** concernant); **as a general** *or* **rough g.** en règle générale **2** *(line)* ligne *f*

guidepost ['gaɪdpəʊst] **N** poteau *m* indicateur

guiding ['gaɪdɪŋ] **ADJ ATTRIB** *(principle)* directeur, -trice; **without his g. hand** sans ses conseils; *Fig* **g. star** *or* **light** guide *m*

guild [gɪld] **N 1** *Hist* corporation *f*, **merchant g.** guilde *f* de commerçants **2** *(organization)* association *f*, confrérie *f*; **church** *or* **parish g.** cercle *m* paroissial

guilder ['gɪldər] **N** *Formerly (Dutch currency)* florin *m*

guildhall ['gɪldhɔ:l] **N 1** *(of a guild)* salle *f* de réunion d'une guilde **2** *(town hall)* hôtel *m* de ville

guile [gaɪl] **N** ruse *f*; **she is without g.** elle est candide

guileless ['gaɪlləs] **ADJ** *(naive)* candide

guillemot ['gɪlɪmɒt] **N** *(bird)* guillemot *m*

guillotine ['gɪlətɪːn] **N 1** *(for execution)* guillotine *f*; **to be executed by g.** être guillotiné; **to go to the g.** aller à la guillotine, être mené à la guillotine **2** *(for cutting paper)* massicot *m* **3** *Parl* = imposition *f* d'une limite de temps pour les débats parlementaires
▸ **VT 1** *(execute)* guillotiner **2** *(cut) (paper etc)* massicoter **3** *Parl (bill)* imposer une limite de temps pour la discussion de

guilt [gɪlt] **N 1** culpabilité *f* (**for sth** pour qch); **the g. does not lie with him alone** il n'est pas le seul coupable **2** *(feeling)* culpabilité *f*; **to feel g.** ressentir de la culpabilité; **feelings of g.** sentiments *mpl* de culpabilité; **to be on a g. trip** culpabiliser
▸▸ **g. complex** complexe *m* de culpabilité

guiltily ['gɪltɪlɪ] **ADV** coupablement, d'un air coupable; **she looked away g.** elle a détourné les yeux d'un air coupable

guiltless ['gɪltləs] **ADJ** innocent (**of sth** de qch)

guilty ['gɪltɪ] **ADJ 1** coupable (**of** de); **g. person** coupable *mf*; **he is not the only g. party** il n'est pas le seul coupable; *Law* **to plead g./not g.** plaider coupable/non coupable; *Law* **to find sb g./not g.** déclarer qn coupable/non coupable; *Law* **verdict of g./not g.** verdict *m* de culpabilité/d'acquittement
2 *(feeling guilt)* **I feel g. about not telling them** je me sens coupable *ou* je culpabilise de ne pas leur avoir dit; **you're making me feel g.** tu me culpabilises; **she looked very g.** elle avait un air très coupable; **g. conscience** mauvaise conscience *f*; *(more serious)* conscience chargée
3 *(act)* coupable

Guinea ['gɪnɪ] **N** *Geog* Guinée *f*

guinea ['gɪnɪ] **N 1** *Br (money)* guinée *f* (*ancienne monnaie britannique*) **2** *Am Sl Pej (Italian)* Rital, -ale, macaroni *mf*
▸▸ **g. fowl** pintade *f*; **g. pig** cobaye *m*, cochon *m* d'Inde; *Fig* **to be a g. pig** servir de cobaye

Guinea-Bissau [-bɪ'saʊ] **N** la Guinée-Bissau

Guinean [gɪ'neɪən] **N** Guinéen, -enne **ADJ** guinéen

guise [gaɪz] **N** dehors *m*, apparence *f*; **under** *or* **in the g. of friendship** sous l'apparence *ou* sous le masque de l'amitié; **under the g. of religion** sous le manteau *ou* le couvert de la religion; **it's the same idea in a new g.** c'est la même idée présentée sous une autre forme

guitar [gɪ'tɑ:r, *Am* also 'gɪtɑ:r] **N** guitare *f*; **to play the g.** jouer de la guitare
▸▸ **g. player** guitariste *mf*

guitarist [gɪ'tɑ:rɪst] **N** guitariste *mf*

gulch [gʌltʃ] **N** *Am* ravin *m*

gulf [gʌlf] **N 1** *Geog* golfe *m*; **the (Persian) G.** le Golfe **2** *(abyss)* gouffre *m*, abîme *m*; *Fig* **there is a g. between the two ideologies** un abîme sépare les deux idéologies
▸▸ **the G. Stream** le Gulf Stream; **the G. War** la guerre du Golfe; **G. War syndrome** syndrome *m* de la guerre du Golfe

gull¹ [gʌl] **N** *(bird)* mouette *f*; *(bigger)* goéland *m*; *Aut* **g.-wing doors** portes *fpl* papillon

gull² **VT** *Arch, Lit (person)* duper, rouler

gullet ['gʌlɪt] **N** *Anat* œsophage *m*; *Fam (throat)* gosier *m*; *Fam Fig* **it really sticks in my g.** ça me reste en travers du gosier

gulley ['gʌlɪ] **N** = **gully**

gullibility [gʌlɪ'bɪlɪtɪ] **N** crédulité *f*

gullible ['gʌlɪb(ə)l] **ADJ** crédule

gully ['gʌlɪ] **N** *Geol* petit ravin *m*

gulp [gʌlp] **N 1** *(act of gulping)* coup *m* de gosier; **to swallow sth at one g.** avaler qch d'un coup; **he confessed with a g. that ...** il admit, la gorge serrée, que ... **2** *(mouthful)* grosse bouchée *f*, *(of drink)* goulée *f*
▸ **VT 1** *(swallow)* = **gulp down 2** *(say nervously, with shock)* **'me?', she gulped** 'moi', dit-elle, la voix étranglée
▸ **VI** essayer d'avaler; **he gulped** sa gorge se serra; **g.!** *(as in comic strip)* gulp!, glup!
▸ **gulp back VT SEP** *(swallow)* **to g. back one's tears** avaler *ou* refouler ses larmes
▸ **gulp down VT SEP** *(swallow)* avaler à grosses bouchées; *(oyster etc)* avaler; **he gulped it down** *(in one mouthful)* il n'en fit qu'une bouchée; *(drinking)* il n'en fit qu'une gorgée

gum¹ [gʌm] **N 1** *Bot* gomme *f*, *(adhesive)* colle *f*, gomme **2** *(chewing)* chewing-gum *m*; **two sticks of g.** deux chewing-gums; **(wine/fruit/etc) g.** boule *f* de gomme
▸ **VT** **(-mm-)** **1** *(coat with adhesive) (paper)* gommer, encoller **2** *(stick with adhesive) (page in book etc)* coller; **to g. two pages together** coller deux feuilles **3** = **gum up**
▸▸ **g. arabic** gomme *f* arabique; **g. tree** gommier *m*; *Fig Fam* **to be up a g. tree** être dans le pétrin

gum² **N** *Anat* gencive *f*
▸▸ **g. disease** gingivite *f*

gum³ **INT** *Old-fashioned Br Fam* **by g.!** fichtre!, mazette!

▸ **gum up VT SEP** *Tech (piston)* gommer; *(file)* encrasser; *Fam* **to g. up the works** enrayer le mécanisme; *Fig* compliquer les choses

gumboil ['gʌmbɔɪl] **N** abcès *m* à la gencive, *Spec* parulie *f*

gumboot ['gʌmbuːt] **N** botte *f* en *ou* de caoutchouc

gumdrop ['gʌmdrɒp] **N** *(sweet)* boule *f* de gomme

gummed [gʌmd] **ADJ** *(label etc)* gommé

gummy ['gʌmɪ] **ADJ 1** gommeux; *(sticky)* gluant **2** **he gave her a g. smile** il lui sourit, découvrant ses gencives encore sans dents

gumption ['gʌmʃən, 'gʌmp-] **N** *Fam* jugeote *f*, sens *m* pratique; **she's got plenty of g.** c'est une débrouillarde

gumshield ['gʌmʃiːld] **N** *Boxing etc* protège-dents *m inv*

gumshoe ['gʌmʃuː] **N 1** *(rubber overshoe)* caoutchouc *m* **2** *Fam (detective)* privé *m*

gun [gʌn] **N 1** *Mil (artillery)* canon *m*, pièce *f* (d'artillerie); **the guns** l'artillerie *f*, le canon; **the big guns** la grosse artillerie, les grosses pièces; *Fam* **big g.** *(important person)* gros manitou, grosse légume *f*; **do you hear the guns?** entendez-vous le canon?; **21-g. salute** salve de 21 coups de canon; *Fam* **it was blowing great guns** il faisait un vent à décorner les bœufs; *Fam* **to be going great guns** *(of work, sale)* marcher très fort; **to jump the g.** *(in race)* faire un faux départ; *Fig* s'emballer
2 *(rifle)* fusil *m*; *(handgun)* revolver *m*, pistolet *m*; **machine g.** mitrailleuse *f*; *Fig* **to stick to one's guns** rester sur ses positions, tenir bon; **a party of six guns** *(hunters)* une bande de six chasseurs
3 *Tech etc* **(grease) g.** seringue *f*, injecteur *m* (à graisse); **(spray) g.** pistolet *m* (à peinture); *Electron* **(electron) g.** canon *m* à électrons
▸ **VT (-nn-)** *Aut (engine)* (faire) emballer
▸ **VI** *Fam* **to g. along** *(of car, driver)* foncer
▸▸ **g. barrel** *(of rifle)* canon *m* de fusil; *(of revolver)* canon de revolver; **g. carriage** affût *m* de canon; *(at military funeral)* prolonge *f* d'artillerie; **g. dog** chien *m* d'arrêt; **g. licence** permis *m* de port d'armes; **g. mike** micro *m* canon; **g. room** *(in house)* armurerie *f*, *(on warship)* poste *m* des aspirants; **g. turret** tourelle *f*

▸ **gun down VT SEP** *(kill)* abattre

▸ **gun for VT INSEP** *(only in continuous tenses)* **1** *(want to reprimand, punish)* en avoir après; **he's gunning for us** il nous en veut, il en a après nous **2** *(try to get)* pourchasser; **he's gunning for the heavyweight title** il vise le titre poids lourd

gunboat ['gʌnbəʊt] **N** aviso-torpilleur *m*, *pl* avisos-torpilleurs
▸▸ **g. diplomacy** diplomatie *f* imposée par la force, politique *f* de la canonnière

guncotton ['gʌnkɒt(ə)n] **N** fulmicoton *m*

gundeck ['gʌndek] **N** *Naut* batterie *f*

gunfight ['gʌnfaɪt] **N** fusillade *f*, échange *m* de coups de feu

gunfighter ['gʌnfaɪtər] **N** *(in Western film, novel)* bandit *m* armé

gunfire ['gʌnfaɪər] **N** *Mil (of artillery)* canonnade *f*, feu *m* (des pièces); *(of smaller guns)* coups *mpl* de feu; **we heard g.** nous avons entendu des coups de feu

gunge [gʌndʒ] **N** *(no pl) Fam* crasse *f* graisseuse

gung-ho [gʌŋ'həʊ] **ADJ** *(enthusiastic)* tout feu tout flamme; *(ready to fight)* belliqueux

gunk [gʌŋk] **N** *Fam* = **gunge**

gunmaker ['gʌnmeɪkər] **N** armurier *m*

gunman, *pl* **gunmen** ['gʌnmən] **N 1** *(terrorist)* terroriste *m*; *(robber)* bandit *m* armé **2** *Am* = **gunmaker**

gunmetal ['gʌnmet(ə)l] **N 1** *(bronze)* bronze *m* à canon **2** *(colour)* gris métallisé *m inv*; **a car with a g. finish** une voiture gris métallisé
▸▸ **g. grey** gris métallisé

gunnel ['gʌn(ə)l] **N** = **gunwale**

gunner ['gʌnər] **N** artilleur *m*; *Naut (warrant officer)* canonnier *m*; **(machine) g.** mitrailleur *m*

gunnery ['gʌnərɪ] N *Mil (guns)* artillerie *f*
▸▸ **g. officer** officier *m* d'artillerie

gunny ['gʌnɪ] N *esp Am (material)* toile *f* de jute; *(bag)* sac *m* en jute
▸▸ **g. sack** sac en jute

gunplay ['gʌnpleɪ] N *esp Am* coups *mpl* de revolver

gunpoint ['gʌnpɔɪnt] N **at g.** sous la menace d'un pistolet/d'un fusil; **to hold sb at g.** menacer qn d'un pistolet/d'un fusil

gunport ['gʌnpɔːt] N *Naut* sabord *m* de batterie

gunpowder ['gʌnpaʊdər] N poudre *f* (à canon); *Br Hist* **the G. Plot** la Conspiration des Poudres

gunrunner ['gʌnrʌnər] N trafiquant, -ante d'armes

gunrunning ['gʌnrʌnɪŋ] N trafic *m* d'armes

gunship ['gʌnʃɪp] N *(helicopter)* **g.** hélicoptère *m* de combat

gunshot ['gʌnʃɒt] N coup *m* de feu; *(of rifle)* coup de fusil; **within/out of g.** à/hors de portée de fusil
▸▸ **g. wound** blessure *f* par balle; **to receive a g. wound** être blessé par balle

gun-shy ADJ *(dog)* qui a peur des coups de feu

gunslinger ['gʌnslɪŋər] N *Am Fam* bandit *m* armé

gunsmith ['gʌnsmɪθ] N armurier *m*; **g.'s (shop)** armurerie *f*

gunstock ['gʌnstɒk] N fût *m* (de fusil)

gunwale ['gʌn(ə)l] N *Naut* plat-bord *m*, *pl* plats-bords; **full to the gunwales** plein à ras bord

guppy ['gʌpɪ] N *(fish)* guppy *m*

gurgle ['gɜːg(ə)l] N *(of liquid)* glouglou *m*; *(of stream)* murmure *m*; *Fig (of pleasure, delight)* gloussement *m*, roucoulement *m*; **happy gurgles could be heard coming from the baby's cot** on entendait l'enfant gazouiller dans son berceau; *Fig* **gurgles of laughter** des gloussements
VI *(of liquid)* glouglouter, faire glouglou; *(of stream)* murmurer, gargouiller; *(of person)* glousser, roucouler; *(of baby)* gazouiller; **he gurgled with laughter** il eut un rire perlé
VT **she gurgled her delight** elle roucoula de plaisir

gurgling ['gɜːg(ə)lɪŋ] ADJ *(liquid in bottle)* glougloutant, qui fait glouglou; *(stream)* murmurant; **a g. laugh** un rire perlé

Gurkha ['gɜːkə] N Gurkha *m*

gurnard ['gɜːnəd], **gurnet** ['gɜːnɪt] N *(fish)* grondin *m*

gurney ['gɜːnɪ] N *Am* chariot *m* (d'hôpital)

guru ['gʊruː] N *Rel, Fig* gourou *m*

gush [gʌʃ] N *(of spring, fountain)* jaillissement *m*; *(of tears)* torrent *m*; *(of blood)* jet *m*, flot *m*; *Fig* **a g. of words** un flot de paroles; *Fig* **a g. of enthusiasm** un élan d'enthousiasme; **a g. of anger/emotion** une bouffée de colère/d'émotion
VI **1** *(spurt, pour)* jaillir, couler à flots; **tears gushed from her eyes** un torrent de larmes coulait de ses yeux **2** *Pej (talk effusively)* faire de longs discours sentimentaux, *Fam* la faire au sentiment; **she gushed over their baby** elle s'attendrissait sur leur bébé
VT **1 to g. water/oil** lancer des jets d'eau/un jet de pétrole **2** **'how wonderful to see you!',** **she gushed** 'qu'est-ce que ça me fait plaisir de te voir!', s'exclama-t-elle
▸ **gush forth, gush out** VI = **gush** VI

gusher ['gʌʃər] N **1** *Pej (person)* personne *f* trop exubérante **2** *Petr* source *f* (de pétrole) jaillissante, puits *m* jaillissant

gushing ['gʌʃɪŋ] ADJ **1** *(water)* jaillissant; **the car was swept away by a g. torrent of**

water la voiture a été emportée par un véritable torrent d'eau; **a g. stream fed by melting snow** les flots déchaînés d'un ruisseau grossi par la fonte des neiges **2** *Pej (person)* trop exubérant; *(compliments)* très élogieux

gushy ['gʌʃɪ] ADJ *Pej* = **gushing 2**

gusset ['gʌsɪt] N *Sewing* soufflet *m*; *(in sleeve)* gousset *m*

gust [gʌst] N **g. (of wind)** rafale *f*, bourrasque *f*; *Naut* grain *m*; **g. of rain** ondée *f*, giboulée *f*; **a g. of hot air** une bouffée d'air chaud; *Fig* **a g. of anger** une bouffée de colère
VI *(of wind)* souffler par rafales

gustatory [gʌs'teɪtərɪ] ADJ *Fml* gustatif

gusto ['gʌstəʊ] N délectation *f*, goût *m*; **to eat sth with g.** manger qch en savourant; **to do sth with g.** faire qch avec grand plaisir

gusty ['gʌstɪ] ADJ *(weather)* venteux; *(wind)* soufflant en rafales; *(day)* de grand vent

gut [gʌt] N **1** *(intestine) (of animal)* boyau *m*; *(of human)* intestin *m*; *Fig Fam* **to sweat or work one's guts out** se casser les reins; *Fig Fam* **she hates my guts** elle ne peut pas me saquer *ou* m'encadrer; *Fig Fam* **I'll have his guts for garters** je vais le massacrer; *Fig* **it's just a g. feeling** c'est une intuition; **g. reaction** réaction *f* instinctive *ou* viscérale
2 *Fig Fam (courage)* **to have guts** avoir du cran, avoir du cœur au ventre; **I didn't have the guts to tell them** je n'ai pas eu le courage de le leur dire; **he hasn't any guts** il manque de cran
3 *Fam (stomach)* bide *m*; **pull in your g.** rentre ton bide; **to have sore guts** avoir mal au bide; **g. ache** mal *m* de bide
4 *(for violins etc)* corde *f* de boyau
VT *(-tt-)* **1** *(animal)* étriper; *(fish, poultry)* vider **2** **the house had been gutted by the fire** la maison avait été ravagée par l'incendie; **she gutted the house and completely redecorated it** elle a cassé tout l'intérieur de la maison et a tout refait

gutless ['gʌtlɪs] ADJ *Fam (cowardly)* lâche

gutsy ['gʌtsɪ] ADJ *Fam* **1** *(brave)* qui a du cran, courageux **2** *(powerful) (prose etc)* vigoureux **3** *(greedy)* goinfre

gutted ['gʌtɪd] ADJ *Br Fam (disappointed)* dégoûté, hyper déçu

gutter ['gʌtər] N **1** *(in street)* caniveau *m*; *(on roof)* gouttière *f*, chéneau *m*; *Fig* **to end up in the g.** finir sous les ponts; *Fig* **to drag oneself out of the g.** se sortir de la misère; **the language of the g.** la langue de la rue **2** *Typ* gouttière *f*, petits fonds *mpl* (de deux pages en vis-à-vis)
VI *(of candle)* vasciller
▸▸ **g. pipe** tuyau *m* de descente; *Pej* **g. press** presse *f* de bas étage, presse à scandale **g. tile** tuile *f* creuse

guttered ['gʌtəd] ADJ *Br Fam (drunk)* bourré, pété

guttering ['gʌtərɪŋ] N *Constr (on building)* gouttières *fpl*

guttersnipe ['gʌtəsnaɪp] N *Old-fashioned Pej* gamin, -ine des rues

guttural ['gʌtərəl] ADJ guttural, -aux
N *Ling* gutturale *f*

guv [gʌv], **guv'nor** ['gʌvnər] N *Br Sl* **the g.** *(boss)* le patron, le singe; *Old-fashioned (father)* le vieux, le paternel; **all right, g.** d'accord, chef

guy¹ [gaɪ] N **1** *Fam (man)* type *m*, mec *m*; **a great g.** un type *ou* mec super; **a tough g.** un dur; **I didn't like the look of those guys** ces types avaient une sale tête **2** *esp Am Fam (as second person plural)* **hurry up, you guys!** allez, dépêchez-vous!; **what are you guys doing tonight?** vous faites quoi, vous, ce soir?; **ok guys, let's go** OK, les amis, on y va; **do you guys want to go out?** vous voulez sortir?; **hi guys!** salut tout le monde! **3** *Br*

(effigy) = effigie *f* burlesque de Guy Fawkes, le chef de la Conspiration des Poudres (1605)

Guy Fawkes Night
Cette fête se déroule le 5 novembre en plein air autour d'un grand feu de joie sur lequel on est censé brûler une effigie ("the Guy") de Guy Fawkes, l'instigateur de la conspiration des poudres. Des feux d'artifice sont également organisés.

guy² VT *Old-fashioned* se moquer de, *Fam* charrier, mettre en boîte

guy³ N corde *f* de tente
▸▸ **g. rope** corde de tente

Guyana [gaɪ'ænə] N *(country)* Guyana *f*

Guyanese [gaɪə'niːz] ADJ guyanais
N Guyanais, -aise

guzzle ['gʌz(ə)l] *Fam* VT *(food)* bâfrer, bouffer; *(drink)* descendre; *esp Am* **to g. gas** *(of car)* bouffer de l'essence
VI *(of eater)* s'empiffrer, goinfrer; *(of drinker)* boire avidement

guzzler ['gʌzlər] N *Fam (of food)* bâfreur, -euse, goinfre *m*; *(of drink)* soiffard, -arde

gym [dʒɪm] N **1** *(hall, building)* gymnase *m*; *(fitness club)* club *m* de gym **2** *(activity, school subject)* gym *f*, **we have g. today** on a gym aujourd'hui
▸▸ **g. shoes** *(chaussures fpl de)* tennis *mpl*

gymkhana [dʒɪm'kɑːnə] N *Br (for horses)* concours *m* hippique; *esp Am Aut* gymkhana *m*

gymnasium, *pl* **gymnasiums, gymnasia** [dʒɪm'neɪzɪəm, -ɪəmz, -ɪə] N *Sport* gymnase *m*

gymnast ['dʒɪmnæst] N gymnaste *mf*

gymnastic [dʒɪm'næstɪk] ADJ gymnastique

gymnastics [dʒɪm'næstɪks] N gymnastique *f*, **to do g.** faire de la gymnastique; *Fig* **mental/verbal g.** gymnastique intellectuelle/verbale VOIR GRAMMAIRE A10

gymnosperm ['dʒɪmnəʊspɜːm] N gymnosperme *m*

gymslip ['dʒɪmslɪp] N *esp Br Sch* tunique *f*

gynaecologic(al), *Am* **gynecologic, gynecological** [gaɪnɪkə'lɒdʒɪk, -ɪk(ə)l] ADJ gynécologique

gynaecologist, *Am* **gynecologist** [gaɪnɪ'kɒlədʒɪst] N gynécologue *mf*

gynaecology, *Am* **gynecology** [gaɪnɪ'kɒlədʒɪ] N gynécologie *f*

gyp [dʒɪp] N *Br Fam* **to give sb g.** *(of aching tooth etc)* faire souffrir qn

gypsum ['dʒɪpsəm] N *Miner* gypse *m*

gypsy ['dʒɪpsɪ] N = **gipsy**

gyrate [dʒaɪ'reɪt] VI tourner; *(less regularly) (of dancers)* tournoyer

gyration [dʒaɪ'reɪʃən] N giration *f*

gyratory ['dʒaɪrətrɪ, -ərɪ, dʒaɪ'reɪtərɪ] ADJ giratoire; **g. (traffic) system** *(système m de circulation en)* sens *m* giratoire

gyrfalcon ['dʒɜːfɔːlkən] N *(bird)* gerfaut *m*

gyro ['dʒaɪrəʊ] ADJ gyroscopique
N **1** = **gyroscope 2** = **gyrocompass**
▸▸ **g. control** commande *f* gyroscopique

gyrocompass ['dʒaɪrəʊkʌmpəs] N *Naut* gyrocompas *m*, compas *m* gyroscopique

gyromagnetic [dʒaɪrəʊmæg'netɪk] ADJ gyromagnétique

gyropilot ['dʒaɪrəʊpaɪlət] N *Aviat* pilote *m* automatique, gyropilote *m*; *Naut (compass)* gyropilote

gyroplane ['dʒaɪrəplein] N *Aviat* autogyre *m*

gyroscope ['dʒaɪrəskəʊp] N gyroscope *m*, gyro *m*

gyroscopic [dʒaɪrə'skɒpɪk] ADJ gyroscopique

gyrostat ['dʒaɪrəstæt] N gyrostat *m*

H, h [eɪtʃ] N **1** *(letter)* H, h *m*; **two h's** deux h; **to drop one's h's** [ˈeɪtʃɪz] avaler ses h *(et révéler par là ses origines populaires)* **2** *Sl (heroin)* héro f, blanche f
▸▸**H bomb** bombe *f* H

ha [hɑ:] INT ha!, ah!; *Fam* **ha bloody ha!** ha ha ha!, très drôle!

habeas corpus [ˈheɪbɪəsˈkɔːpəs] N *Law* **(writ of) h.** habeas corpus *m*

haberdasher [ˈhæbədæʃər] N *Com Old-fashioned* **1** *Br (for sewing articles)* mercier, -ière **2** *Am (for men's clothes)* chemisier *m*

haberdashery [ˈhæbədæʃərɪ] N *Com Old-fashioned* **1** *Br (sewing articles)* mercerie f **2** *Am (men's clothes)* chemiserie f

habit [ˈhæbɪt] N **1** *(custom, practice)* habitude f, coutume f; *(picking nose, biting nails etc)* habitude; **bad habits** mauvaises habitudes; **to be in the** *or* **make a h. of doing sth** avoir l'habitude de faire qch; **I try not to make a h. of working late** j'essaye de ne pas prendre l'habitude de travailler tard; **don't make a h. of it** ne recommence pas; **it's a h. with him** c'est une habitude chez lui; **to get into the h. of doing sth** prendre l'habitude de faire qch; **to get sb into the h. of doing sth** habituer qn à faire qch; **to get into bad habits** prendre de mauvaises habitudes; **to get out of a h.** perdre une habitude; **from force of h.** poussé par l'habitude; **to do sth by sheer force of h.** faire qch (simplement) par habitude
2 *Fam (addiction)* **to have a (drug) h.** être accro; **to have a cocaine/heroin h.** être accro à la cocaïne/à l'héroïne
3 *(costume) (of monk, nun)* habit *m*; **riding h.** tenue f d'équitation

habitable [ˈhæbɪtəb(ə)l] ADJ habitable; **to make a room h.** rendre une pièce habitable

habitat [ˈhæbɪtæt] N habitat *m*

habitation [hæbɪˈteɪʃən] N **1** *(occupation) (of house)* habitation f; **fit for h.** habitable; **unfit for h.** inhabitable; **there were no signs of h.** l'endroit ne semblait pas habité **2** *(dwelling place)* habitation f, demeure f

habit-forming ADJ *(drug)* qui crée une accoutumance

habitual [həˈbɪtjʊəl] ADJ **1** *(customary)* habituel **2** *(liar, drunk)* invétéré; **h. criminal** *or* **offender** récidiviste *mf*
▸▸*Mktg* **h. buying behaviour** comportement *m* d'achat habituel

habitually [həˈbɪtjʊəlɪ] ADV habituellement, d'habitude

habituate [həˈbɪtjʊeɪt] VT **to h. sb to sth/to doing sth** habituer *ou* accoutumer qn à qch/à faire qch; **to become habituated to sth/to doing sth** s'habituer à qch/à faire qch

Habsburg [ˈhæpsbɜːɡ] N *Hist* Habsbourg

hacienda [hæsɪˈendə] N ranch *m*, hacienda f

hack¹ [hæk] N *(cut)* taillade f, entaille f; *(blow) (with foot, arm)* coup *m*; *Ftbl etc (kick)* coup de pied
VT **1** *(cut)* hacher; **to h. sb/sth to pieces** mettre *ou* tailler qn/qch en pièces; *Fig* **my article has been hacked to pieces** mon article a été massacré; **to h. sb to death** lacérer qn à mort; **to h. one's way through the jungle** se frayer un chemin à coups de machette dans la jungle **2** *Ftbl etc* **to h. sb's shins** donner délibérément un coup de pied dans le tibia à qn; **to h. the ball** donner un petit coup de pied dans le ballon **3** *Fam* **he can't h. it** *(cope)* il ne s'en sort pas, il est complètement dépassé
VI **1** *(cut)* taillader, entailler; **to h. (away) at a tree** entailler un arbre à coups de hache; **to h. at one's meat** taillader son morceau de viande; **to h. away at a text** sabrer un texte *ou* des passages d'un texte **2** *(cough)* émettre une toux sèche **3** *(kick)* **to h. at sb's shins** essayer de donner un coup de pied/des coups de pied dans le tibia à qn
▸ **hack about** VT SEP *(often passive) (body)* mutiler; **the piece of wood had been hacked about** on avait taillé ce morceau de bois; **the article had been hacked about a bit** on avait pas mal remanié l'article
▸ **hack down** VT SEP *(tree)* abattre
▸ **hack into** VT INSEP *Comput* **to h. into a database/system** s'introduire en fraude dans une base de données/un système, *Fam* pirater une base de données/un système
▸ **hack off** VT SEP **1** *(chop off)* trancher **2** *Fam (annoy)* **to h. sb off** prendre la tête à qn; **to be hacked off (with)** en avoir marre (de)
▸ **hack up** VT SEP *(chop up)* mettre en pièces

hack² N **1** *Fam Pej (journalist)* journaleux, -euse, tâcheron *m*; **there were all the usual Labour Party hacks** on y trouvait tous les habitués du parti travailliste; **literary h.** écrivaillon *m* **2** *(horse for hire)* cheval *m*, -aux de louage; *(for riding)* cheval de selle; *Fam (nag)* rosse f **3** *Am Fam (taxi)* taxi *m*; *(taxi driver)* chauffeur *m* de taxi
▸▸*Fam* **h. writer** écrivaillon f; *Fam* **h. writing** travail *m* d'écrivaillon

hack³ VI *Br (ride)* se promener à cheval

hacker [ˈhækər] *Comput Fam* N **1** *(illegal user)* pirate *m* informatique **2** *(expert user)* bidouilleur, -euse

hacking¹ [ˈhækɪŋ] N **1** *Ftbl etc* coups *mpl* de pied (sur le tibia) **2** *Comput Fam (illegal)* piratage *m* informatique
ADJ **h. cough** toux f sèche

hacking² N *Br (riding)* promenade(s) f(pl) à cheval
▸▸**h. jacket** veste f de cheval

hackle [ˈhæk(ə)l] N *(of bird)* plume f du cou; **hackles** camail *m*; **his hackles rose** *(of dog)*, *Fig (of person)* il s'est hérissé; *Fig* **to get one's hackles up** se hérisser, monter sur ses ergots; *Fig* **his hackles are up** il se prépare pour

la bagarre; *Fig* **to make sb's hackles rise** hérisser qn

hackney [ˈhæknɪ] N **1** *(taxi)* **h. cab** *or* **carriage** fiacre *m* **2** *(carriage for hire)* cabriolet *m* de louage **3** *(horse)* cheval *m*, -aux de selle; *(trotter)* trotteur *m*

hackneyed [ˈhæknɪd] ADJ *(language)* rebattu, usé, banal, -als; **a h. argument** un argument éculé; **h. phrase** formule f stéréotypée, cliché *m*

hacksaw [ˈhæksɔː] N scie f à métaux

hackwork [ˈhækwɜːk] N *Fam* **to do h.** *(of writer)* écrire au kilomètre; *(routine work)* c'est du travail alimentaire; **the report was a piece of shoddy h.** ce rapport, c'était du travail d'écrivaillon

had PT, PP *see* **have**

haddock [ˈhædək] N *(fish)* aiglefin *m*, églefin *m*; *Culin* **smoked h.** haddock *m*

Hades [ˈheɪdiːz] N *Myth* les Enfers *mpl*

hadn't [ˈhæd(ə)nt] CONTR = **had not**, *see* **have**

Hadrian's Wall [ˈheɪdrɪənzwɔːl] N le Mur d'Hadrien

haema- [ˈhiːmə] PREF *Med etc* héma-

haematite, *Am* **hematite** [ˈhiːmətaɪt] N hématite f

haemato- [ˈhiːmətɒ, -təʊ] PREF *Med etc* hémato-

haematology, *Am* **hematology** [hiːməˈtɒlədʒɪ] N *Med* hématologie f

haematoma, *Am* **hematoma,** *pl* **haematomas, haematomata** [hiːməˈtəʊmə, -əʊməz, -əʊmətə] N *Med* hématome *m*

haemo- [ˈhiːməʊ, -mə] PREF *Med etc* hémo-

haemoglobin, *Am* **hemoglobin** [hiːməʊˈɡləʊbɪn] N *Med* hémoglobine f

haemophilia, *Am* **hemophilia** [hiːməʊˈfɪlɪə] N *Med* hémophilie f

haemophiliac, *Am* **hemophiliac** [hiːməʊˈfɪlɪæk] N *Med* hémophile *mf*

haemophilic, *Am* **hemophilic** [hiːməʊˈfɪlɪk] ADJ *Med* hémophile

haemorrhage, *Am* **hemorrhage** [ˈhemərɪdʒ] N *Med, Fig* hémorragie f
VI *Med* faire une hémorragie; *Fig (disappear, fade fast) (of support etc)* s'évanouir, se dissiper; **party membership was haemorrhaging badly** les effectifs du parti diminuaient de façon spectaculaire; **foreign capital would h. if …** il y aurait une hémorragie *ou* fuite de capitaux si …

haemorrhoids, *Am* **hemorrhoids** [ˈhemərɔɪdz] NPL *Med* hémorroïdes *fpl*; **to have h.** avoir des hémorroïdes

haemostat, *Am* **hemostat** [ˈhiːməʊstæt] N *Med (instrument)* pince(s) f(pl) hémostatique(s)

haft [hɑːft] N *(of tool etc)* manche *m*, poignée f

hag [hæɡ] N *(witch)* (vieille) sorcière f, *Fam*

(unpleasant old woman) vieille taupe f, vieux chameau m

haggard ['hægəd] ADJ **1** (gaunt) hâve; (face) décharné **2** (wild) (face) égaré, hagard

haggis ['hægɪs] N Scot Culin = panse f de brebis farcie (d'un hachis d'abats et de farine d'avoine très épicé)

haggle ['hægəl] VI marchander, Fam chipoter; **I'm not going to h.** je ne vais pas chipoter; **to h. about** or **over the price of sth** chicaner sur le prix de qch

haggler ['hæglər] N (over details etc) chipoteur, -euse

haggling ['hæg(ə)lɪŋ] N marchandage m

hagiographer [hægɪ'ɒgrəfər] N hagiographe mf

hagiography [hægɪ'ɒgrəfɪ] N hagiographie f

hag-ridden ADJ (by nightmares) tourmenté par des cauchemars; (by an idea etc) obsédé, tourmenté

Hague (the) [ðeheɪg] N La Haye

hah [hɑː] INT ha!, ah!

ha-ha[1] [hɑː'hɑː] INT ha, ha!

ha-ha[2] ['hɑːhɑː] N (ditch) saut-de-loup m, pl sauts-de-loup

haiku ['haɪkuː] N haïku m

hail[1] [heɪl] N Met grêle f; **h. of blows/stones** grêle ou volée f de coups/pierres; **a h. of bullets** une pluie de balles; **a h. of fire** un déluge de feu; **a h. of abuse** une pluie d'injures; **to be met by a h. of insults** être reçu sous ou par une pluie d'insultes
▸ V IMPERS Met grêler; **it's hailing** il grêle
▸ VT **to h. blows on sb** donner une volée de coups à qn; **to h. insults/abuse/obscenities on sb** asséner des insultes/des injures/des obscénités à qn
▸ **hail down** VI (blows/missiles) **hailed down on our heads** nous avons reçu une volée de coups/une pluie de missiles; **criticism hailed down on him** il a subi une avalanche ou un déluge de critiques
▸ VT SEP (throw) **they hailed stones down on us** ils nous ont bombardés de cailloux; **they hailed insults down on the President** ils ont déversé un flot d'insultes à l'intention du président

hail[2] INT Arch, Lit salut!; **h., Caesar!** Avé César!; **h., Mary, full of grace!** je te salue, Marie, pleine de grâce!
▸ N Old-fashioned **within h.** à portée de (la) voix
▸ VT **1** Old-fashioned (greet) (person) saluer **2** (attract attention of) (person, ship, taxi) héler; **within hailing distance** à portée de (la) voix **3** (acclaim) acclamer; **he has been hailed as the new ...** il a été acclamé comme le nouveau ...; **the bridge was hailed as an engineering marvel** le pont a été salué comme une merveille de technicité; **the plan was hailed as the solution to their problems** le projet a été salué comme la solution à tous leurs problèmes
▸ VI **where does he h. from?** d'où vient-il?; **to h. from a port** (of ship) (be based at) venir ou Spec dépendre d'un port; (come from) venir ou arriver d'un port
▸ Rel **H. Mary** (prayer) Je vous salue Marie m inv; Ave (Maria) m inv; **to say two H. Marys** dire deux Ave Maria

hail-fellow-well-met ADJ **to be h. with everyone** être à tu et à toi avec tout le monde

hailstone ['heɪlstəʊn] N grêlon m

hailstorm ['heɪlstɔːm] N averse f de grêle

hair [heər] N **1** (of human head) cheveux mpl; (single) cheveu m; **the h.** les cheveux, la chevelure; **to have fair h.** avoir les cheveux clairs; **woman with short h.** femme aux cheveux courts; **I like your h.** j'aime bien ta

coiffure; **to wash one's h.** se laver la tête; **to have** or **get one's h. cut** se faire couper les cheveux; **to do one's h.** se coiffer; **to have one's h. done** aller chez le coiffeur; **to have one's h. done** aller chez le coiffeur; **if you harm** or **touch a h. on that child's head ...** si tu touches un cheveu de cet enfant ...; **it was enough to make your h. stand on end** c'était à faire dresser les cheveux sur la tête; Fam **keep your h. on!** calmez-vous!; Fam **to get in sb's h.** taper sur les nerfs de qn, enquiquiner qn; **to comb one's h.** se peigner; **h. crack** (in metal) gerçure f

2 (individual hair, of human face and body, animals, plants) poil m; **(body) h.** (of human) poil m; **(facial) h.** (of human) poils mpl du visage; Fig **h. of the dog** (for hangover) antidote m; Fam Hum **this'll put hairs on your chest!** tiens, bois/mange ça, c'est bon pour la santé!

3 (coat) (of animal) poil m, pelage m; (of horse) crin m; (of pig) soie f

4 Opt (of gun sight etc) cheveu m, fil m; **cross hairs** réticule m
▸ **h. conditioner** après-shampooing m; **h. cream** crème f pour les cheveux; **h. drier, h. dryer** (hand-held) sèche-cheveux m inv; (over the head) casque m; **h. gel** gel m pour les cheveux; **h. lacquer** laque f (pour les cheveux); **h. lotion** lotion f capillaire; **h. mattress** matelas m de crin; **h. mousse** mousse f coiffante; **h. oil** huile f capillaire; **h. remover** crème f dépilatoire; Br **h. restorer** produit m pour la repousse des cheveux; **h. shirt** haire f, cilice m; **h. slide** barrette f; Typ **h. space** espace f fine; **h. spray** laque f; **h. straighteners** (appliance) fer m à défriser, défriseur m; **h. tonic** lotion f capillaire; **h. trigger** (in firearm) détente f ou gâchette f sensible

hairball ['heəbɔːl] N (in cat's stomach) boule f de poils

hairband ['heəbænd] N bandeau m

hairbrush ['heəbrʌʃ] N brosse f à cheveux

haircut ['heəkʌt] N **1** (act) coupe f de cheveux; **to have a h.** se faire couper les cheveux **2** (hairstyle) coupe f de cheveux, coiffure f

hairdo ['heəduː] N Fam coiffure f

hairdresser ['heədresər] N coiffeur, -euse; **to go to the h.'s** aller chez le coiffeur

hairdressing ['heədresɪŋ] N coiffure f
▸ **h. salon** salon m de coiffure; **h. school** école f de coiffure

-haired [heəd] SUFF **short/grey/etc-h.** aux cheveux courts/gris/etc

hairgrip ['heəgrɪp] N esp Br pince f à cheveux

hairless ['heəlɪs] ADJ (bald) chauve; (face) glabre, imberbe; (body, animal) sans poils

hairline ['heəlaɪn] N **1** (of person) racine f des cheveux; **his h. is receding** son front commence à se dégarnir, il commence à se dégarnir **2** Typ délié m **3** Tech (in metal) gerçure f **4** Opt (of gun sight etc) cheveu m, fil m; **hairlines** réticule m
▸ **h. crack** fêlure f; Med **h. fracture** fêlure f; Typ **h. space** espace f fine

hairnet ['heənet] N filet m, résille f

hairpiece ['heəpiːs] N mèche f postiche

hairpin ['heəpɪn] N épingle f à cheveux
▸ **h. bend** virage m en épingle à cheveux

hair-raising ADJ effrayant; (adventure) effroyable; (account) à vous faire dresser les cheveux sur la tête

hair's-breadth N épaisseur f d'un cheveu; **he escaped death by a h.** il a été à deux doigts de la mort, il a frisé la mort; **to be within a h. of disaster** être à un cheveu de la ruine

hair-splitting N ergotage m; (dispute) chicane f
▸ ADJ (distinction etc) (trop) subtil

hairspring ['heəsprɪŋ] N (of watch, clock etc) spiral m, pl spiraux

hairstyle ['heəstaɪl] N coiffure f

hairstylist ['heəstaɪlɪst] N coiffeur, -euse

hairy ['heərɪ] ADJ **1** (hands, chest etc) velu, poilu; (person) hirsute **2** Fam (dangerous) périlleux; (frightening) effrayant; **things are getting rather h.** la situation devient assez désespérée

Haiti ['heɪtɪ, 'haɪ-] N Haïti m ou f

Haitian ['heɪʃən, 'heɪtɪən] ADJ haïtien
▸ N Haïtien, -ienne

hake [heɪk] N (fish) merluche f, colin m

halal [hæ'læl] ADJ Muslim Rel hal(l)al inv

halation [hæ'leɪʃən] N Phot halo m, irradiation f

halberd ['hælbəd] N Mil, Hist hallebarde f

halcyon ['hælsɪən] N (kingfisher) halcyon m
▸ Lit **h. days** bon vieux temps m, jours mpl heureux

hale [heɪl] ADJ vigoureux, robuste, encore gaillard; **to be h. and hearty** être frais et gaillard

HALF, pl **halves** [hɑːf, hɑːvz]

| N demi **1–3** • moitié **1** • mi-temps **3** • camp **3** |
| ADJ demi |
| ADV à moitié |

▸ N VOIR GRAMMAIRE A5 **1** moitié f; (of beer, hour) demi m; **to fold/cut sth in h.** or **into halves** plier/couper qch en deux; **three and a h.** trois et demi; **what is h. of twelve?** quelle est la moitié de douze?; **h. a dozen** une demi-douzaine; **a h. of lager** un demi de blonde; Fig **h. the time he isn't there** les trois quarts du temps, il n'est pas là; **h. of them were students** la moitié d'entre eux étaient étudiants; **the first h. of the year** la première moitié de l'année; **she gave each of us h.** elle nous en a donné la moitié à chacun; **I'll be with you in a h. a second** or Br Fam **(give me) h. a tick** je suis à vous dans une seconde; **I've got h. a mind to complain** j'ai bien envie de faire une réclamation; Fam **my better** or **other h.** ma (chère) moitié; Fam **how the other h. lives** comment vivent les autres; **bigger by h.** plus grand de moitié; Fam **she is too clever by h.** elle est beaucoup trop maligne; Fam **you haven't heard the h. of it!** tu n'en sais pas encore le quart!; **but that's h. the fun of it!** mais c'est le plus amusant!; **that was h. the point of going there** c'était tout l'intérêt d'y aller; **they don't do things by halves** ils ne font pas les choses à moitié; **to go halves with sb** partager avec qn; Br **one and two halves** (on bus, train) un tarif normal, deux tarifs enfant; Rail **outward/return h.** (of ticket) coupon m d'aller/de retour; **chicken halves** (portions) demi-poulets mpl

2 (time) **h. an hour** une demi-heure; **h. past twelve** midi/minuit et demi; **it's h. past two** or Fam **h. two** il est deux heures et demi; **I waited for two and a h. hours** j'ai attendu pendant deux heures et demi

3 Sport (player) demi m; **the first/second h. (of the game)** la première/seconde mi-temps; **in our h. (of the pitch)** dans notre camp
▸ ADJ demi; **at h. price** à moitié prix; Br Fam **h. seas over** gris, soûl, ivre
▸ ADV à moitié; **she only h. understands** elle ne comprend qu'à moitié; **he h. opened the door** il entrouvrit la porte; **the bottle was h. full/empty** la bouteille était à moitié ou à demi pleine/vide; **you're h. right** tu n'as pas tout à fait tort; **h. laughing, h. crying** moitié riant, moitié pleurant; **I was h. afraid that you wouldn't come** j'avais quelque crainte que vous ne veniez pas; **h. as big** moitié

moins grand; **h. as big again** plus grand de moitié; **it was not h. as expensive as I thought it would be** c'était bien moins cher que je ne le pensais; **he gets h. as much money as you** il reçoit moitié moins d'argent que vous; *Br Fam* **it isn't h. bad** ce n'est pas mal du tout; *Br Fam* **it isn't h. cold!** il fait rudement froid!; *Br Fam* **he doesn't h. say some stupid things!** il dit vraiment n'importe quoi *ou* des âneries!; *Br Fam* **not h.!** et comment! **PREF h. dressed** à demi vêtu; **h. naked/asleep/dead** à moitié nu/endormi/mort; **h. done** *(work)* fait à moitié; *(cooked meat etc)* à moitié cuit

▸▸ *Tech* **h. bearing** demi-palier *m, pl* demi-paliers; **h. board** demi-pension *f, Admin* **h. day** demi-journée *f, pl* demi-journées; *Comput* **h. duplex** semi-duplex *m inv; Ftbl etc* **h. time** (la) mi-temps; **the h. time score** le score à la mi-temps; *Tennis* **h. volley** demi-volée *f, pl* demi-volées; **h. year** semestre *m*

half-a-crown N *Br Arch* demi-couronne *f*

half-and-half ADJ, ADV moitié l'un moitié l'autre, *Fam* moitié-moitié; **how shall I mix them? – h.** comment faut-il les mélanger? – à doses égales; **how do you like your coffee? – h.** comment prenez-vous le café? – moitié café, moitié lait

N *Am (milk and cream)* = mélange *m* de lait et de crème liquide

half-arsed [hɑːfˈɑːst], *Am* **half-assed** [hɑːfˈæst] ADJ *Sl* foireux

halfback [ˈhɑːfbæk] N **1** *Ftbl Old-fashioned* demi-arrière *m, pl* demi-arrières **2** *(in rugby)* demi *m*

half-baked ADJ *Fam (poorly planned)* nul; *(idea)* qui ne tient pas debout, ridicule

half-binding N demi-reliure *f*

half-blood N = **halfbreed**

halfbreed [ˈhɑːfbriːd] N **1** *Old-fashioned Offensive Sl (person)* métis, -isse **2** *(horse)* cheval *m* demi-sang, *pl* chevaux demi-sang *ou* demi-sangs

half-brother N demi-frère *m, pl* demi-frères; *Law (through mother)* frère utérin; *(through father)* frère consanguin

half-caste ADJ, N *Old-fashioned usu Offensive* métis, -isse

half-circle N demi-cercle *m, pl* demi-cercles; *Naut* **to turn a h.** faire demi-tour

half(-)cock N **at h.** *(rifle etc)* à moitié armé, sur le cran de sûreté; *Fig Fam* **to go off at h.** mal partir, mal démarrer

half-crown N = **half-a-crown**

half-cut ADJ *Br Fam (drunk)* bourré, pété, fait

half-fare ticket N billet *m* demi-tarif

halfhearted [hɑːfˈhɑːtɪd] ADJ sans enthousiasme; *(effort)* timide, hésitant

halfheartedly [hɑːfˈhɑːtɪdlɪ] ADV sans enthousiasme

halfheartedness [hɑːfˈhɑːtɪdnɪs] N tiédeur *f*, manque *m* d'enthousiasme

half-hour N demi-heure *f*, **on the h.** à la demie

half-hourly ADV toutes les demi-heures

ADJ **there is a h. train service** il y a des trains toutes les trente minutes; **he needs his h. break** il lui faut faire une pause toutes les trente minutes; **at h. intervals** toutes les demi-heures, toutes les trente minutes

half-inch VT *Br Sl (pinch)* piquer, faucher; **he got his wallet half-inched** il s'est fait piquer son portefeuille

half-length N **1** *Horseracing* demi-longueur *f, pl* demi-longueurs **2** *(portrait)* en buste

half-life N *Nucl etc (of isotope etc)* demi-vie *f, pl* demi-vies

half-light N demi-jour *m, pl* demi-jours

half-mast N *Br* **at h.** à mi-mât; **flag at h.** pavillon *m* en berne; *Hum* **to be at h.** *(of trousers)* arriver à mi-mollet; *(of socks)* descendre

half-moon N **1** demi-lune *f, pl* demi-lunes **2** *(of fingernail)* lunule *f*

half-nelson N *(in wrestling)* simple prise *f* de tête à terre

half-note N *esp Am Mus* blanche *f*

half-pay N demi-salaire *m; (in civil service)* demi-traitement *m; Mil* demi-solde *f*, **on h.** à mi-salaire/à demi-traitement/en demi-solde

halfpenny [ˈheɪpnɪ, ˈhɑːfpenɪ] N *Br Arch* demi-penny *m*, sou *m; Fam* **it isn't worth a h.** ça ne vaut pas un sou!; **he's down to his last h.** il ne lui reste que quelques sous

half-price ADJ *(ticket)* demi-tarif
ADV (à) demi-tarif; **children get in h.** les enfants payent demi-tarif

half-shaft N demi-arbre *m, pl* demi-arbres

half-sister N demi-sœur *f, pl* demi-sœurs; *Law (through mother)* sœur utérine; *(through father)* sœur consanguine

half-size N *(in dress)* demi-taille *f, pl* demi-tailles; *(in shoes)* demi-pointure *f, pl* demi-pointures; **we don't stock half-sizes of that shoe** nous n'avons pas les demi-pointures de ce modèle en stock

half-staff N *Am* = **half-mast**

half-term N *Br Sch* congé *m* de mi-trimestre

half-timbered ADJ *Archit (house)* à colombages

half-title N *Typ (of book)* faux-titre *m, pl* faux-titres

halftone [hɑːfˈtəʊn] N **1** *Art* demi-teinte *f, pl* demi-teintes; *Phot* similigravure *f* (tramée) **2** *Am Mus* demi-ton *m, pl* demi-tons

half-track N *Aut* (auto) chenille *f*, half-track *m*

half-truth N demi-vérité *f, pl* demi-vérités

halfway [hɑːfˈweɪ] ADV **1** à mi-chemin; *(of piston)* à mi-course; **h. between the two towns** à mi-chemin entre les deux villes; **h. to Paris** à mi-chemin de Paris; **we're h. there** nous avons fait la moitié du chemin; *(in project etc)* nous sommes à mi-chemin; **h. up (the hill)** à mi-côte, à mi-pente; **I was h. up/down the stairs** j'étais à mi-hauteur de l'escalier; **the lift got stuck h. up** l'ascenseur s'est bloqué à mi-hauteur; **h. through the project** à mi-projet; **we're h. through the year and … six** mois ont déjà passé et …; **we're h. through the summer holidays/week** nous sommes à la moitié des grandes vacances/de la semaine; **it happened h. through the holidays** ça s'est passé en plein milieu des vacances; **we're h. through the work** nous avons fait la moitié du travail; **to meet sb h.** *(in distance)* aller à la rencontre de qn à mi-chemin; **let's meet up h. in Bath** disons que chacun fait la moitié du chemin et qu'on se retrouve à Bath; **let's meet h.** *(in distance)* faisons chacun la moitié du chemin; **I'll meet you h.** *(in price)* faisons moitié-moitié, trouvons un compromis; *(in concessions asked for)* faisons un arrangement

2 *(partly)* à peu près; **haven't you got a h. acceptable shirt?** tu n'as pas une chemise à peu près convenable?

▸▸ **h. house** *(on journey)* (auberge *f*) relais *m; (for rehabilitation)* centre *m* de réadaptation *(pour anciens détenus, malades mentaux, drogués etc); Fig (halfway stage)* (stade *m* de) transition *f, (compromise)* compromis *m; Sport* **h. line** ligne *f* médiane

halfwit [ˈhɑːfwɪt] N faible *mf* d'esprit, simple *mf* d'esprit

halfwitted [hɑːfˈwɪtɪd] ADJ faible d'esprit, simple

half-yearly ADJ semestriel; **h. result** demi-résultat *m*, résultat à six mois
ADV une fois par semestre, tous les six mois

halibut [ˈhælɪbət] N *(fish)* flétan *m*

halitosis [hælɪˈtəʊsɪs] N *Med* mauvaise haleine *f*, **to suffer from h.** avoir mauvaise haleine

hall [hɔːl] N **1** *(entrance)* h. *(of house)* entrée *f, (of hotel)* hall *m* **2** *Am (corridor)* couloir *m*, corridor *m* **3** *(room, building)* salle *f*, **(dining) h.** *(of stately home)* salle à manger; *Univ* réfectoire *m; the servants' h.* l'office *m; Br Univ* **h. (of residence)** résidence *f* universitaire, maison *f* d'étudiants; *Br Univ* **to eat in h.** manger au réfectoire *ou* RU; *Br Univ* **to live in h.** loger en résidence universitaire **4** *(manor house)* manoir *m;* **she works up at the h.** elle travaille au château; **Ludgely H.** *(in name)* le château de Ludgely

▸▸ *esp Am* **H. of Fame** ≃ Panthéon *m;* **he's in the baseball h. of fame** il fait partie du panthéon de l'histoire du baseball; **h. porter** *(in hotel)* portier *m;* **h. stand** portemanteau *m*

hallelujah [hælɪˈluːjə] INT, N alléluia *m*

hallmark [ˈhɔːlmɑːk] N *(on silver)* (cachet *m* de) contrôle *m*, poinçon *m; Fig* **the h. of genius** l'empreinte *f* du génie; **to bear all the hallmarks of …** porter l'empreinte de …, avoir tous les signes de …
VT *(silver)* contrôler, poinçonner

hallo [həˈləʊ] INT = **hello**

hallow [ˈhæləʊ] *Rel* N *Old-fashioned* **All Hallows' (Day)** (le jour de) la Toussaint
VT sanctifier, consacrer; **hallowed be Thy name** que Ton nom soit sanctifié

hallowed [ˈhæləʊd] ADJ béni, sanctifié
▸▸ *Rel* **h. ground** terre *f* sainte *ou* bénie; *Fig* lieu *m* de culte

Hallowe'en [hæləʊˈiːn] N = veille *f* de la Toussaint, *Can* halloween *f*

> **Hallowe'en**
> Il s'agit d'une fête d'origine païenne célébrée dans les pays anglo-saxons la veille de la Toussaint, à l'époque de l'année où les morts étaient censés rendre visite aux vivants. Aujourd'hui la tradition demeure: on évide des citrouilles pour les transformer en lanternes en forme de crâne, et les enfants vont de maison en maison déguisés en sorcières ou en fantômes. De nos jours, la coutume britannique a adopté la tradition américaine de "trick or treat", consistant pour les enfants à demander un petit cadeau aux habitants des maisons visitées et à les menacer d'un mauvais tour s'ils refusent.

hallucinate [həˈluːsɪneɪt] VT **he was hallucinating that his skin had turned green** dans ses hallucinations, il se voyait avec la peau verte
VI avoir des hallucinations

hallucination [həluːsɪˈneɪʃən] N hallucination *f*

hallucinatory [həˈluːsɪnət(ə)rɪ] ADJ hallucinatoire

hallucinogen [həˈluːsɪnədʒen] N hallucinogène *m*

hallucinogenic [həluːsɪnəʊˈdʒenɪk] ADJ hallucinogène

hallway [ˈhɔːlweɪ] N **1** vestibule *m*, entrée *f* **2** *Am (corridor)* couloir *m*

halo, *pl* **halos, haloes** [ˈheɪləʊ, -əʊz] N **1** *(of saint)* auréole *f*, nimbe *m; Hum* **your h.'s slipping!** tu te dévergondes! **2** *Astron, Opt, Phot* halo *m; (of moon)* auréole *f*
▸▸ *Mktg* **h. effect** effet *m* de halo

halogen ['hælədʒən] ADJ, N *Chem* halogène *m*; **h. headlights** phares *mpl* halogènes

halt¹ [hɒlt] N 1 *(act of stopping)* arrêt *m*, interruption *f* (momentanée), halte *f*, pause *f*; **a brief h. at an inn** une brève halte dans une auberge; **to bring to a h.** *(process etc)* arrêter; *(movement, action)* provoquer l'interruption momentanée de; *(vehicule, crowd etc)* arrêter, faire stopper; **to come to a h.** marquer un temps d'arrêt, s'interrompre momentanément, s'arrêter, stopper; *(on journey)* faire halte; *(in a speech)* rester sans rien dire; **to call a h.** (demander à) faire une halte; **to call a h. to sth** arrêter qch
2 *Br Rail (small station)* halte *f*

VI faire halte, s'arrêter; **to h. at …** faire un arrêt à …, s'arrêter à …; *Mil* **company h.!** compagnie halte!; *Mil* **h.! who goes there** halte! qui va là?

VT *(person)* faire faire (une) halte à; *(something) (for good)* arrêter, mettre un terme *ou* un point final à; *(temporarily)* interrompre
▸▸ *Aut* **h. sign** stop *m*

halt² *Bible, Arch* ADJ boiteux
NPL **the h. and the lame** les estropiés *mpl*

halter ['hɔːltər] N 1 *(for horse)* licou *m* 2 *(on women's clothing)* bain *m* de soleil; **dress with a h. neck, h.-neck dress** robe *f* dos nu *ou* bain de soleil 3 *(rope) (for hanging person)* corde *f*
▸▸ **h. top** bain *m* de soleil

halting ['hɔːltɪŋ] ADJ *(words, speech etc)* hésitant; *(style)* heurté

haltingly ['hɔːltɪŋlɪ] ADV en hésitant

halve [hɑːv] VT 1 *(cut)* diviser en deux (moitiés), couper en deux (moitiés) 2 *(share)* partager en deux 3 *(reduce) (expenses, costs etc)* réduire de moitié

halves [hɑːvz] NPL *see* **half**

halyard ['hæljəd] N *Naut* drisse *f*

ham [hæm] N 1 *Culin* jambon *m*; **h. sandwich** sandwich *m* au jambon **h. and eggs** œufs *mpl* au jambon 2 *Fam (buttocks)* **the hams** les fesses *fpl*, le derrière 3 *Fam (actor)* cabotin *m* 4 *Radio Fam (enthusiast)* **(radio) h.** radioamateur *m*

VI (-mm-) *Fam* jouer comme un pied
VT *Fam* **he hams all his parts** il charge tous ses rôles, il en fait trop
▸▸ *Fam* **h. acting** cabotinage *m*; *Fam* **h. actor** cabotin *m*
▸ **ham up** VT SEP *Fam* **to h. it up** jouer comme un pied

Hamburg ['hæmbɜːg] N Hambourg

Hamburger ['hæmbɜːgər] N *(person)* Hambourgeois, -oise

hamburger ['hæmbɜːgər] N *Culin* hamburger *m*; *Am (meat)* viande *f* hachée

ham-fisted ['hæm'fɪstɪd] ADJ *Fam* maladroit

Hamitic [hə'mɪtɪk] ADJ chamitique

hamlet ['hæmlɪt] N hameau *m*

hammer ['hæmər] N 1 *(tool)* marteau *m*; *(heavy)* masse *f*; *Pol* **the h. and sickle** la faucille et le marteau; **to go at it h. and tongs** *(work etc energetically)* y aller de bon cœur, ne pas y aller de main morte; *(quarrel)* se quereller; *(fight)* se bagarrer; *Am Fam* **to let the h. down** appuyer sur le champignon, mettre les gaz; *Sport* **throwing the h.** lancement *m* du marteau
2 *(of auctioneer)* marteau *m*; **to come under the h.** être mis aux enchères
3 *(in clock, alarm, piano etc)* marteau *m*
4 *Anat (of inner ear)* marteau *m*
5 *(of firearm)* chien *m*

VT marteler; *Fam (beat) (person)* tabasser; *(of boxer etc) (opponent)* cogner dur sur; *(defeat) (opponent, other side)* battre à plate(s) couture(s), écraser; *(criticize) (person, book*

etc) massacrer, descendre; **to h. a nail into sth** enfoncer un clou dans qch avec un marteau; **to h. into shape** *(pot etc)* façonner à coups de marteau; *Fig Fam (plan etc)* perfectionner; *Fam* **to h. sth into sb** faire entrer qch dans la tête de qn; **I'll h. it into her** je veux lui faire entrer ça dans la tête; **to h. prices** écraser les prix

VI 1 travailler avec un marteau, travailler au marteau; **to h. at** *or* **on the door** frapper à la porte à coups redoublés 2 *Fam* **to h. down the motorway** foncer sur l'autoroute
▸▸ **h. thrower** lanceur, -euse de marteau
▸ **hammer along** VI *Fam (in car)* foncer
▸ **hammer away** VI 1 *(with hammer)* **they've been hammering away all evening** ils ont donné des coups de marteau toute la soirée; **to h. away at sth** marteler qch 2 *(of heart)* battre très fort (dans la poitrine) 3 *Fig* **to h. away at sth** *(at agreement)* travailler d'arrache-pied à qch; **to h. away at the keyboard** frapper de toutes ses forces sur le clavier
▸ **hammer home** VT SEP 1 *(something)* enfoncer (à l'aide d'un marteau); **make sure you h. the nails home** assure-toi que tu as bien enfoncé les clous 2 *Fig (insist on)* **to h. sth home** insister sur qch, répéter cent fois qch
▸ **hammer in** VT SEP *(nail)* enfoncer à coups de marteau
▸ **hammer out** VT SEP 1 *(in metalwork) (gold etc)* étendre sous le marteau; *(copper)* panner; **to h. out a dent in sth** débosseler qch 2 **to h. out a tune (on the piano)** pianoter un air; **to h. out a message on the pipes** tapoter un message sur les conduits 3 *Fig Fam (draw up)* élaborer, mettre au point; **unions and management hammered out an agreement** les syndicats et le patronat sont parvenus à un accord

hammered ['hæməd] ADJ *Fam (drunk)* bourré, beurré, pété

hammerhead ['hæməhed] N 1 *(shark)* requin *m* marteau 2 *(bird)* ombrette *f* (du Sénégal)
▸▸ **h. shark** requin marteau

hammering ['hæmərɪŋ] N *(with hammer)* martelage *m*; *(noise)* martèlement *m*; *(of iron)* battage *m*; *Fam (with fists)* volée *f* de coups; **to give sb a h.** *(hit)* cogner dur sur qn, rouer qn de coups; *(defeat)* battre qn à plate(s) couture(s), écraser qn; *(criticize)* descendre qn; **to give sb a h.** *(criticize)* descendre qch; **our team got a h.** notre équipe a été battue à plate(s) couture(s)

hammertoe ['hæmətəʊ] N *Med* orteil *m* en marteau *ou* en cou de cygne

hammock ['hæmək] N hamac *m*

hammy ['hæmɪ] ADJ *Fam (acting)* outrancier; **h. actor** cabotin *m*, acteur *m* qui en fait trop

hamper¹ ['hæmpər] N panier *m*; *(for oysters etc)* bourriche *f*; **Christmas h.** panier rempli de gourmandises de Noël

hamper² VT *(person)* embarrasser, gêner, entraver; **to h. the progress of business** entraver la marche des affaires; **high winds hampered the rescue work** les sauveteurs ont été gênés dans leur travail par la force des vents; **they were hampered in their efforts (to do sth) by the terrible weather** ils furent gênés dans leurs efforts (pour faire qch) par le mauvais temps; **she was hampered by her long cloak** elle était empêtrée dans son grand manteau

hamster ['hæmstər] N hamster *m*

hamstring ['hæmstrɪŋ] N tendon *m* du jarret; **h. injury** lésion *f* du tendon du jarret
VT *(pt, pp* **hamstringed** *or* **-strung**) 1 *(cut hamstrings of) (person, horse)* couper le(s) jarret(s) à 2 *Fig* paralyser; *(financially) (person)* couper les moyens à; **we are ham-**

strung by a lack of funds nous sommes paralysés par l'absence de fonds suffisants

┌─────────────────────────────────────┐
HAND [hænd]
| N | main **1–9, 12** ▪ ouvrier **10** ▪ écriture **11** ▪ paume **13** ▪ aiguille **14** |
| VT | passer ▪ donner |
└─────────────────────────────────────┘

N 1 *(part of body)* main *f*; **on one's hands and knees** à quatre pattes; **give me your h.** donnez-moi la main; **to hold in one's h.** *(sword, hat)* tenir à la main; *(grain)* tenir dans la main; *(success)* tenir entre les mains; **to hold hands** se tenir (par) la main; **keep your hands to yourself** ne touche pas, enlève *ou* retire tes mains de là; **to lay hands on sth** mettre la main sur qch; **to lay hands on sb** faire violence à qn; **to pass sth from h. to h.** passer qch de main en main; **I can't put my h. on it** je n'arrive pas à mettre la main dessus; **to take sb by the h.** prendre qn par la main; **he writes with his left h.** il écrit de la main gauche; **I only have one pair of hands!** je n'ai que deux mains!; **made/done by h.** fait à la main; **to wash clothes by h.** laver du linge à la main; **by h.** *(on letter etc)* = remise par porteur (sans timbre); **to send/deliver a letter by h.** envoyer/distribuer une lettre par porteur; **sword in h.** sabre au poing; **hands off!** n'y touchez pas!; *(off me)* bas les pattes!; **hands up!** haut les mains!
2 *(responsibility, control, ownership etc)* **to have a h. in sth** être impliqué dans qch, être mêlé à qch; **I had no h. in this crime** je n'ai absolument rien à voir avec ce crime; **the h. of God** le doigt de Dieu; **I see Moriarty's h. in this** je reconnais la griffe de Moriarty dans cette affaire; **to have one's hands full** *(literally)* avoir les mains prises; *Fig (be busy)* avoir du pain sur la planche, être débordé; **I've got my hands full trying to cope as it is** j'ai déjà assez à faire comme ça; **to fall into enemy hands** tomber aux mains *ou* entre les mains de l'ennemi; **in the wrong hands this knowledge could be very dangerous** si elles tombaient aux mains de personnes malintentionnées, ces connaissances pourraient être très dangereuses; **to be in good hands** être en (de) *ou* entre (de) bonnes mains; **to put oneself in sb's hands** se confier à qn; **it's in your own hands what happens next** la suite dépend de vous; **to put a matter in the hands of a lawyer** confier une affaire à un avocat; **the matter's in their hands now** désormais, l'affaire est entre leurs mains; **it's out of my hands** je ne peux (plus) rien y faire; **the case is off our hands** l'affaire ne dépend plus de nous; **to get sth off one's hands** se débarrasser de qch; **to change hands** *(of goods etc)* changer de mains; *(of business etc)* changer de propriétaire
3 *(skill)* **to try one's h. at sth** essayer de faire qch, s'essayer à qch; **to get one's h. in** se faire la main; **to keep one's h. in** garder la main; **she can turn her h. to anything** c'est une femme qui peut tout faire
4 *(idioms)* *Fml* **he asked for her h. (in marriage)** il lui a demandé sa main; *Fam* **he never does a h.'s turn** il ne fait jamais rien de ses dix doigts; *Fam* **to give sb a big h.** *(applaud)* applaudir vivement qn; **to give** *or* **lend sb a (helping) h.** aider qn, donner un coup de main à qn; **to lend a h.** mettre la main à la pâte; *Fig* **to have one's hands tied** avoir les mains liées; **I could beat you at tennis with one h. tied behind my back** je pourrais te battre au tennis même avec une main dans le dos; *Fam* **to put** *or* **dip one's h. in the till** puiser dans la caisse; **to be h. in glove with sb** être d'intelligence *ou* *Péj* de mèche avec qn; *Fam* **to make money h. over fist** s'enrichir rapidement; **to be living from h. to mouth** vivre au jour le jour; *Sport etc* **to win hands down** gagner haut la main; **to**

beat sb hands down battre qn à plate(s) couture(s)

5 (phrases with **at**) **to be (near) at h.** (of object etc) être à portée de la main ou sous la main; (of event etc) approcher, être proche; **the hour is at h.** l'heure est proche; **there is always a doctor at h.** il y a toujours un médecin de service; **to suffer at the hands of ...** souffrir aux mains de ou entre les mains de ...

6 (phrases with **in**) **to walk h. in h. with sb** marcher avec qn la main dans la main; **to work h. in h. with sb** agir de concert avec qn; **to have so much money in h.** avoir tant d'argent disponible; **stock in h.** marchandises en magasin; **I've five minutes in h.** j'ai encore cinq minutes; **the matter in h.** l'affaire en question; **work in h.** travail en cours ou en chantier; **the situation is well in h.** la situation est bien en main; **to take sb in h.** prendre qn en main

7 (phrases with **on**) **work on h.** travail en cours ou à faire; **to have sb/sth on one's hands** avoir qn/qch à sa charge ou Fam sur les bras; **to have an hour on one's hands** avoir une heure à tuer; **to have time on one's hands** avoir du temps libre; **she's got a lot on her hands at the moment** elle est très occupée en ce moment; **I'm on h. if you need me** je suis à votre disposition si vous avez besoin de moi; **on the one h.** d'une part; **on the other h.** d'autre part

8 (phrases with **out of**) **these birds will eat out of your h.** ces oiseaux te mangeront dans la main; Fig **I'll soon have him eating out of my h.** bientôt, il me mangera dans la main; **to do sth out of h.** faire qch sur-le-champ; **to shoot sb out of h.** abattre qn sans autre forme de procès; **to get out of h.** (of situation, inflation etc) échapper à notre/leur/etc contrôle; (of children, class etc) perdre toute discipline

9 (phrases with **to**) **to come to h.** tomber sous la main; **you can use anything that comes to h.** tu peux utiliser tout ce qui te tombe sous la main; **your parcel came to h. this morning** votre paquet m'est parvenu ce matin; **use whatever is to h.** utilisez ce que vous avez sous la main; **the first excuse to h.** le premier prétexte venu

10 (worker) ouvrier, -ière; Naut matelot m; Ind etc **to take on hands** embaucher de la main-d'œuvre; Naut **the (ship's) hands** l'équipage m; **all hands on deck!** tout le monde sur le pont!; **to be lost with all hands** (of ship) périr corps et biens; **an old h. (at sth)** un expert (en/dans qch), un spécialiste (en/de qch); **an old h. at doing sth** un expert ou spécialiste pour ce qui est de faire qch; **he was an old h. at spotting such tricks** c'était un expert dans l'art de reconnaître de telles ruses

11 (handwriting) écriture f; **in one's own h.** (write a letter) de sa propre main; Law, Arch **to set one's h. to a deed** apposer sa signature à un acte

12 Cards (cards received) main f, jeu m; (player) joueur, -euse; (round) partie f, **to have a good h.** avoir un beau jeu, avoir du jeu; **first/fourth h.** (player) premier m/dernier m en cartes; **to show one's h.** faire voir son jeu

13 (measurement) paume f; **horse fifteen hands high** cheval de quinze paumes

14 Typ index m; (of signpost, barometer) indicateur m; (of clock, watch) aiguille f; **the little h. is pointing to three** la petite aiguille est sur les trois

15 (of bananas) régime m

VT passer, remettre, donner (**sth to sb** qch à qn); **he handed her the letter to read** il lui a donné la lettre à lire; Fig **to h. sth to sb on a plate** apporter à qn qch sur un plateau; Fig Fam **to h. it to sb** reconnaître la supériorité

de qn; **you've got to h. it to him** devant lui, chapeau!; **you've got to h. it to these Russians, they know how to dance!** il faut reconnaître que ces Russes savent danser!

▸▸ **h. baggage** bagages mpl à main; Ftbl **h. ball** (foul) (faute f de) main f; **h. basin** lavabo m; **h. controls** commandes fpl manuelles; **h. cream** crème f pour les mains; TV etc **h. cue** signal m de départ de la main; Old-fashioned **h. glass** (for reading) loupe f, (mirror) miroir m de sac; Mil **h. grenade** grenade f à main; **h. lotion** lotion f pour les mains; **h. luggage** bagages à main; **h. microphone** micro m portatif; Theat **h. puppet** marionnette f, **h. signal** signal m de la main

▸ **hand around** VT SEP = hand round

▸ **hand back** VT SEP (return) repasser; **she handed me back the bottle** elle m'a repassé la bouteille; **should Britain h. Gibraltar back to Spain?** est-ce que la Grande-Bretagne devrait rétrocéder Gibraltar à l'Espagne?

▸ **hand down** VT SEP **1** (give) **h. me down that bottle** descends-moi cette bouteille **2** (help down) **to h. sb down** donner la main à qn pour l'aider à descendre **3** (bequeath etc) (necklace, tradition) transmettre (**from** de; **to** en); **all her clothes had been handed down from her older sisters** tous ses vêtements venaient de ses sœurs aînées **4** Law **to h. down a sentence** prononcer une sentence

▸ **hand in** VT SEP remettre, déposer; **to h. in one's resignation** démissionner; **to h. in a piece of homework** rendre un devoir; **to h. in a piece of lost property in (to the police)** remettre un objet trouvé (à la police)

▸ **hand off** VT SEP Rugby (player) raffûter

▸ **hand on** VT SEP (custom) transmettre; (news) passer (**to** à)

▸ **hand out** VT SEP **1** (distribute) (leaflets, biscuits) distribuer **2** (give) donner; **he's always handing out advice** il se permet de donner des conseils, Fam il est sans cesse à donner des conseils; **he's fond of handing it out, but can't take it** (criticism) il se permet de critiquer les autres mais il déteste qu'on le critique

▸ **hand over** VT SEP **1** (give) donner, remettre **2** (deliver) remettre, livrer; **she handed over the documents to a lawyer** elle a remis les documents à un avocat **3** (surrender) (property) céder; **h. over your wallet!** donne ton portefeuille!; **to h. sb over to justice** livrer qn à la justice, remettre qn aux mains de la justice **4** (transfer) (power) transmettre; **we now h. you over to our foreign affairs correspondent** nous passons maintenant la parole au responsable des affaires étrangères; **to h. over the command to ...** remettre le commandement à ...

VI 1 (transfer) **I now h. over to the weatherman** je passe maintenant la parole au présentateur de la météo; **when will she h. over to the new president?** quand va-t-elle laisser la place au nouveau président? **2** Fam (give) **I know you have it, so h. over!** passe-le moi, je sais que tu l'as!

▸ **hand round** VT SEP (circulate) (bottle etc) faire passer, faire circuler; **to h. round a hat** faire passer (à la ronde) un chapeau

hand- [hænd] PREF à la main; **h.-sewn** cousu (à la) main; **h.-operated** à commande manuelle

handbag ['hændbæg] N sac m à main, Can sacoche f

handball ['hændbɔːl] N Sport (game) handball m

handbell ['hændbel] N sonnette f, clochette f

handbill ['hændbɪl] N prospectus m

handbook ['hændbʊk] N **1** (for traveller, tourist) guide m; (for use in museum etc) livret m **2** Sch etc (of science etc) manuel m

handbrake ['hændbreɪk] N frein m à main

handcart ['hændkɑːt] N charrette f à bras

handclap ['hændklæp] N **to give sb a slow h.** ≃ siffler qn

handcuff ['hændkʌf] VT (person) mettre ou passer les menottes à, menotter; **to h. sb to sb** attacher qn à qn d'autre avec des menottes; **to h. sb to sth** attacher qn à qch avec des menottes

handcuffs ['hændkʌfs] NPL menottes fpl

handful ['hændfʊl] N **1** (of sand etc) poignée f **2** (small number) petit nombre m; **there was or were only a h. of people there** il n'y avait là que quelques personnes **3** Fam (difficult person) **that child is a real h.** cet enfant-là me donne du fil à retordre

handgrip ['hændgrɪp] N Cycling etc poignée f

handgun ['hændgʌn] N revolver m, pistolet m

hand-held N Comput ordinateur de poche ▸▸ Cin, TV **h. camera** caméra f portable; Comput **h. computer** ordinateur m de poche; Comput **h. scanner** scanner m ou scanneur m à main

handhold ['hændhəʊld] N prise f

handicap ['hændɪkæp] N **1** (disadvantage) handicap m, désavantage m; Med handicap m; **to have a severe h.** avoir un lourd handicap **2** Sport handicap m; (weight) **h.** (of racehorse) surcharge f, handicap; **time/distance h.** handicap en temps/distance

VT (-pp-) **1** (disadvantage) handicaper, désavantager; **their lack of preparation handicapped them** ils ont été désavantagés par leur manque de préparation **2** Sport handicaper

handicapped ['hændɪkæpt] ADJ handicapé NPL **the (physically/mentally) h.** les handicapés mpl (physiques/mentaux)

handicraft ['hændɪkrɑːft] N (usu pl) **1** (trade) artisanat m, métier m manuel **2** (result) artisanat m, produit m artisanal

handily ['hændɪlɪ] ADV commodément; **h. shaped** d'une forme très pratique; **they h. left their fingerprints** ils ont laissé leurs empreintes, ce qui était bien pratique

handiness ['hændɪnɪs] N **1** (of tool etc) commodité f; **the h. of the house for the shops** l'emplacement très commode de la maison près des magasins **2** (skill with hands) adresse f, dextérité f, habileté f (manuelle)

handing down N (of tradition) transmission f

handing over N (of hostages, keys) remise f (**to** aux mains de); Law (of property) cession f; (of power) transmission f

handiwork ['hændɪwɜːk] N **1** (action) travail m manuel **2** (result) ouvrage m, travail m, œuvre f; **the repair/fruit bowl is Jenny's h.** c'est Jenny qui a fait la réparation/la corbeille à fruits; Iron **is this your h.?** c'est ton œuvre?; **this quarrel (of theirs) is your h.** c'est de ta faute s'ils se disputent

hand-job N Sl **to give sb a h.** branler qn

handkerchief ['hæŋkətʃɪf] N mouchoir m

hand-knit(ted) ADJ (sweater etc) tricoté (à la) main

handle ['hænd(ə)l] N **1** (of broom, knife, tool etc) manche m; (of pump) bras m, balancier m; (of wheelbarrow) bras; (of stretcher) brancard m; (of sword, lever, box, suitcase etc) poignée f; (of tap) clef f; (of frying pan) queue f; (of basket, bucket etc) anse f, **(door) h.** poignée; Fam **to fly off the h.** s'emballer; **to get a h. on a problem** savoir comment s'y prendre pour résoudre un problème

2 *Fam (title)* titre *m*; *(CB radio user's call name)* indicatif *m*, code *m*; **to have a h. to one's name** avoir un nom à rallonge(s)

VT 1 *(touch, hold)* tâter, toucher; **to h. a material** tâter *ou* toucher un tissu; **h. with care** *(on package)* ≃ fragile; **to h. stolen goods** recéler des objets volés; *Ftbl* **to h. the ball** toucher la balle, faire une main

2 *(operate) (object)* manier, manipuler; *(ship, sails etc)* manœuvrer; *(ship)* gouverner; *(car)* conduire; **how to h. a gun** comment se servir d'un fusil

3 *(treat)* traiter; **to h. sb roughly** malmener qn, rudoyer qn; **the author handles the subject well** l'auteur traite bien le sujet

4 *(manage, cope with)* **to h. a situation** prendre en main une situation; **you handled that very well** vous vous en êtes très bien sorti; **to h. a crisis** résoudre une crise; **don't worry, I'll h. this/him** ne vous inquiétez pas, je vais m'en occuper/je vais m'occuper de lui; **to h. oneself (well) in a crisis** bien se comporter *ou* se conduire en cas de crise; *Fam* **I can't h. interviews** je n'arrive pas à affronter les interviews; *Fam* **he can't h. it when people get aggressive** il n'arrive pas à faire face aux gens agressifs; **she can h. would-be Romeos** elle sait comment faire avec ce genre de dragueurs; *Fam* **could you h. another potato?** tu reprendras bien une autre pomme de terre?

5 *(deal with)* **we h. a lot of business for them** nous travaillons beaucoup pour eux; **who handles your business in …?** qui s'occupe de votre entreprise en …?; **we don't h. that sort of business** nous ne nous occcupons pas de ce genre d'affaires; **to h. large orders** s'occuper de grosses commandes; **to h. a lot of money** brasser beaucoup d'argent; **we h. 10,000 passengers a week** 10 000 passagers passent par nos services chaque semaine; **we don't h. that kind of material/product any more** nous ne faisons plus ce genre de matériel/produit; **who handles your products in France?** qui distribue vos produits en France?; **to h. figures/words** manier les chiffres/les mots

VI **to h. well** *(of car, boat)* être agréable à conduire; **how does it h.?** elle/il est comment?

handlebar ['hænd(ə)lbɑːr] N *(usu pl)* **handlebars** guidon *m*
▶▶ **h. moustache** moustache *f* en guidon de vélo

handler ['hændlər] N *Com* manutentionnaire *mf*; *(of spy)* contact *m*; **(dog) h.** maître *m* (de) chien

handling ['hændlɪŋ] N **1** *(touching, holding)* manipulation *f*, action *f* de toucher; *(of stolen goods)* recel *m*

2 *(of tool)* maniement *m*; *(of explosives)* manipulation *f*, *(of a ship)* manœuvre *f*

3 *(of a car)* maniabilité *f*, comportement *m* routier

4 *(treatment) (of person, subject etc)* traitement *m*; **rough h.** traitement brutal

5 *(of crisis, situation)* prise *f* en main; *(of funds)* maniement *m*

6 *Com* manutention *f*, distribution *f*

7 *Ftbl* (faute *f* de) main *f*
▶▶ **h. capacity** capacité *f* de traitement; **h. charges** frais *mpl* de traitement; *(for physically shifting goods)* frais de manutention; **h. fee** frais d'administration

handmade ['hænd'meɪd] ADJ fait *ou* fabriqué à la main, fait main

handmaid ['hændmeɪd], **handmaiden** ['hændmeɪd(ə)n] N *Old-fashioned* servante *f*

hand-me-down N *Fam* **hand-me-downs, h. clothes** vêtements usagés *ou* d'occasion, frusques *fpl*; **I used to wear my brother's hand-me-downs** je récupérais les vêtements usagés de mon frère

hand-out, handout ['hændaʊt] N **1** *Pej (alms)* aumône *f*, *(food)* = nourriture *f* distribuée aux pauvres; **I don't want to live off hand-outs** je ne veux pas vivre de la charité des autres; **state** or **government h.** aumône du gouvernement **2** *Journ* compte rendu *m* communiqué à la presse, communiqué *m*; *Sch, Univ* notes *fpl* (polycopiées), polycopié *m* *(donné aux élèves etc)* **3** *Com (brochure)* prospectus *m*, brochure *f*, tract *m*; *(sample)* cadeau *m* publicitaire

handover ['hændəʊvər] N *(of hostage, ransom)* remise *f*, **h. of power** passation *f* de pouvoirs

hand-pick VT *(fruit etc)* cueillir à la main; **the volunteers have been hand-picked** les volontaires ont été triés sur le volet

hand-picked ['hænd'pɪkt] ADJ *(fruit etc)* cueilli à la main; *(person, team)* trié sur le volet

handrail ['hændreɪl] N *(of staircase etc)* rampe *f*, main *f* courante; *(of bridge etc)* garde-fou *m*, *pl* garde-fous, garde-corps *m inv*; *Naut, Rail* rambarde *f*

handsaw ['hændsɔː] N scie *f* à main

handset ['hændset] N *Tel* **1** *(of telephone)* combiné *m* **2** *(mobile phone)* téléphone *m* portable

hands-free ADJ *Tel (phone, dialling)* mains libres; **phone with h. facility** téléphone *m* avec fonction mains-libres

handshake ['hændʃeɪk] N **1** poignée *f* *ou* serrement *m* de main **2** *Comput* dialogue *m* d'établissement de liaison
▶▶ *Comput* **h. message** message *m* d'établissement de liaison, message de prise de contact

handshaking ['hændʃeɪkɪŋ] N *Comput* établissement *m* d'une liaison

hands-off ADJ *Pol* non-interventionniste; **the director has a h. style of management** le directeur est partisan de laisser de l'autonomie à son personnel, *Pej* le directeur a un sens très large de la délégation de pouvoir

handsome ['hænsəm] ADJ **1** *(good-looking)* beau, *f* belle; **a h. man** un bel homme; **she was a h. woman** c'était une belle femme; **a h. building** une belle construction **2** *(conduct etc)* gracieux, généreux; *(praise, apology)* sincère, sans réserve; **he received very h. treatment** on l'a traité d'une façon très généreuse **3** *(considerable) (price)* bon; *(gift)* généreux; **to make a h. profit** faire *ou* réaliser de beaux bénéfices; **h. fortune** belle fortune; **a h. sum** une coquette somme

handsomely ['hænsəmlɪ] ADV **1** *(dressed, furnished etc)* bien **2** *(to act)* généreusement; *(to treat, praise, apologize)* avec sincérité, sans réserve; *(to pay)* libéralement

handsomeness ['hænsəmnɪs] N **1** *(of person, monument etc)* beauté *f* **2** *(of an action)* générosité *f*, *(of reward)* libéralité *f*, *(of an apology)* sincérité *f*

hands-on ADJ *(experience)* pratique; **h. exhibition** *(at museum)* = exposition *f* où les gens sont encouragés à toucher aux objets; **the director has a h. style of management** le directeur n'a pas peur de mettre la main à la pâte

handspring ['hændsprɪŋ] N *Gym* saut *m* de mains

handstand ['hændstænd] N *Gym* **to do a h.** faire un équilibre sur les mains, faire l'arbre droit

hand-to-hand ADJ *(fighting)* corps-à-corps
▶▶ ADV **to fight h.** se battre au corps-à-corps

hand-to-mouth ADJ, ADV **to live h., to lead a h. existence** tirer le diable par la queue

hand-tooling N **1** *Tech (on a lathe etc)* tra-

vail *m* à la main **2** *(in bookbinding)* dorure *f* à froid faite à la main

handwork ['hændwɜːk] N travail *m* fait à la main, travail manuel

handwriting ['hændraɪtɪŋ] N écriture *f*
▶▶ **h. expert** graphologue *mf*; *Comput* **h. recognition** reconnaissance *f* de l'écriture manuscrite

handwritten ['hændrɪt(ə)n] ADJ *(letter etc)* manuscrit

handy ['hændɪ] ADJ **1** *(useful) (tool etc)* pratique; *(ship)* maniable; **that would come in very h.** ça serait bien utile; **a h. tip** un bon conseil

2 *(convenient)* commode; **the flat's h. for the shops** l'appartement est tout près des commerces

3 *(within reach)* à portée (de la main); **I always keep my tools h.** j'ai toujours mes outils sous la main

4 *(skilful) (with one's hands)* adroit, habile (de ses mains); **he's very h. about the house** *(good at making, repairing things)* c'est un bon bricoleur; **h. at sth/at doing sth** adroit à qch/à faire qch; **to be h. with one's fists** savoir se servir de ses poings

handyman, *pl* **handymen** ['hændɪmæn, -men] N *(employee)* homme *m* à tout faire *ou* à toutes mains; *(DIY expert etc)* bricoleur *m*; *Am* **h.'s special** = maison *f* qui a besoin de beaucoup de travaux

HANG [hæŋ] N **1** *(of clothing)* tombé *m*; *(of material)* drapé *m*

2 *Fam* **to get the h. of sth** *(understand)* comprendre qch, piger qch; **when you've got the h. of it** *(acquired skill)* quand tu auras attrapé le coup; **I haven't got the h. of this new keyboard yet** je ne connais pas encore très bien ce nouveau clavier!; **when you've got the h. of things** *(in new office, job etc)* quand vous serez au courant

3 *Fam* **I don't give** or **care a h.** je m'en moque *ou* m'en fiche

VT *(pt, pp hung* [hʌŋ]*)* **1** *(suspend)* pendre, accrocher, suspendre (**on, from** à); *(door)* monter; **to h. a coat on a hook** pendre *ou* suspendre un manteau à une patère; **to h. sth on the wall** accrocher qch au mur; **they hung banners from their windows** ils ont accroché des bannières à leurs fenêtres; **to h. a picture** suspendre un tableau; *(exhibit)* exposer un tableau *(au Salon etc)*; **to h. wallpaper** poser du papier peint

2 *(droop)* **to h. one's head** baisser la tête

3 *(decorate)* **to h. a room with tapestries** tendre une salle de tapisseries; **hall hung with flags** salle ornée de drapeaux

4 *Culin (meat, game)* faire faisander

5 **to h. fire** *(of troops etc)* suspendre le feu; *Fig (of decision etc)* traîner (en longueur), faire traîner les choses

6 *(pt, pp hanged* [hæŋd]*) (criminal)* pendre; **he hanged himself** il s'est pendu; *Br Pol Fam Pej* **the h. 'em and flog 'em brigade** = les partisans *mpl* de la peine de mort et des châtiments corporels; *Fam* **I'm hanged if I know!** je n'en sais fichtre *ou* foutre rien!; **h. it!** zut!, mince alors!; *Prov* **as well be hanged for a sheep as for a lamb** quitte à avoir des ennuis, autant que ça en vaille la peine; *Hist* **to be hanged, drawn and quartered** être pendu, éventré et écartelé; *Fig* **he was hanged, drawn and quartered by the press** il s'est fait étriper par la presse

VI 1 *(be suspended)* pendre, être suspendu; *Culin (of game)* se faisander; **a picture hanging on the wall** un tableau pendu *ou* accroché au mur; **he was hanging by his arms from the tree** il était suspendu à l'arbre par les bras; **to h. out of the window** *(of person)* se pencher à la fenêtre; *(of object)* pendre à la fenêtre

2 *(of drapery, clothes etc)* tomber, se draper; **to h. loose** *or* **limply** pendiller, *Fam* pendouiller; **his clothes h. loosely on him** il flotte dans ses vêtements; *esp Am Sl* **h. loose!** relax, Max!; *Am Sl* **to h. tough** s'accrocher; *Sl* **how's it hanging?** *(how are you?)* comment ça va?; **this door hangs badly** cette porte est mal suspendue (sur ses gonds); **time hangs heavy (on my hands)** le temps me pèse *ou* me semble long

3 *Am Fam (spend time)* traîner; **he's hanging with his friends** il traîne avec ses copains

4 *(of criminal)* être pendu; **to h. for murder** être pendu pour meurtre; *Fig Fam* **if he doesn't like it he can go h.** si ça ne lui plaît pas, qu'il aille se faire pendre; *Old-fashioned* **you'll h. for this!** tu seras pendu pour ça!

▸ **hang about, hang around** vi *Fam* **1** *(wait)* poireauter; **to keep sb hanging about** faire poireauter qn; **h. about, that's not what I said!** eh, minute! ce n'est pas ce que j'ai dit!

2 *(waste time)* traîner, flâner; **to h. about the house doing nothing** traîner à la maison sans rien faire; **young men hanging about on street corners** jeunes qui traînent dans les rues; **don't h. about or we'll never finish!** ne perds pas de temps ou nous n'aurons jamais fini!; *Fam* **you don't h. about, do you!** vous êtes un/une rapide, vous!; *Fam* **this car doesn't h. about** cette voiture est un vrai bolide

3 *(associate)* **to h. about with sb** traîner avec qn

vt insep *(frequent) (place)* fréquenter, traîner dans

▸ **hang back** vi *(not go forward)* rester en arrière; *(hesitate)* hésiter; **to h. back from doing sth** renâcler à faire qch

▸ **hang down** vi pendre *(from sth de qch)*

▸ **hang in** vi *esp Am Fam (persevere, not lose heart)* tenir bon, persévérer; **just h. in there** courage, tenez bon

▸ **hang on** vi **1** *(hold)* se cramponner, s'accrocher; **h. on tight!** cramponne-toi bien!

2 *Fam (wait)* patienter, attendre; *Tel* **h. on!** ne quittez pas!; **h. on for a moment** attendez un moment, patientez un instant

3 *(survive)* supporter, *Fam* tenir le coup; **to h. on by the skin of one's teeth** s'en sortir de justesse

vt insep **1** *(hold)* **to h. on sb's arm** *(of thing)* pendre au bras de qn; *(of person)* se pendre au bras de qn

2 *(be attentive to)* **to h. on sb's lips** *or* **words** être pendu aux lèvres de qn; **the children hung on his every word** les enfants buvaient ses paroles *ou* étaient suspendus à chacune de ses paroles

3 *(depend on)* dépendre de, tenir à; **everything hangs on his answer** tout dépend de sa réponse

vt sep *Am Sl* **to h. one on** *(get drunk)* prendre une cuite

▸ **hang on to** vt insep **1** *(hold tightly)* se cramponner à, ne pas lâcher; **he hung on to the cliff face** il s'est agrippé à la paroi de la falaise

2 *(keep)* garder; **I'd h. on to those documents if I were you** si j'étais toi, je garderais précieusement ces documents; **he hung on to these outdated ideas** il se raccrochait à ces idées démodées; **to h. on to an opinion** persister dans son opinion; **he hung on to his version of events** il a maintenu sa version des faits

▸ **hang out** vt sep *(suspend) (object)* pendre *ou* mettre au dehors; **to h. out the washing** étendre le linge; **to h. out a flag** arborer un pavillon

vi **1** *(be suspended)* pendre (au dehors); **the rocks h. out over the gully** les rochers surplombent le ravin; **his shirt was hanging out**

sa chemise dépassait; *Sl* **to let it all h. out** se défouler

2 *Fam (spend time)* traîner; **to h. out with one's friends** traîner avec ses amis; **he hangs out at the local bar** c'est un habitué du café du coin

▸ **hang over** vt insep *(hover over)* planer *ou* peser sur; **a thick fog hangs over the town** un épais brouillard plane sur la ville; **a heavy silence hung over the meeting** un lourd silence pesait sur l'assemblée; **to have a threat hanging over one** avoir une menace qui pèse sur soi; **a question mark is hanging over the outcome of the debate** il reste un point d'interrogation quant à l'issue du débat; **I have an appointment with the dentist hanging over me** il y a une visite chez le dentiste qui me pend au nez; **we've got the threat of eviction hanging over us** nous risquons d'être expulsés d'une minute à l'autre

▸ **hang together** vi **1** *(of people)* rester unis **2** *(of statements etc)* s'accorder, *Fam* tenir debout

▸ **hang up** vt sep *(hat, picture etc)* accrocher, pendre, suspendre; *Fig* **to h. up one's boots/racket** *(retire)* raccrocher

vi *Tel* raccrocher (l'appareil); **to h. up on sb** raccrocher au nez de qn

hangar ['hæŋər] N *esp Aviat* hangar *m*

hangdog ['hæŋdɒg] ADJ **h. look** air *m* de chien battu

hanger ['hæŋər] N **(coat** *or* **clothes) h.** cintre *m*

hanger-on, *pl* **hangers-on** N parasite *m*, pique-assiette *m inv*

hang-glide vi faire du deltaplane

hang-glider N *(craft)* deltaplane® *m*; *(person)* libériste *mf*

hang-gliding N (sport *m* du) deltaplane® *m*; **to go h.** faire du deltaplane®

hanging ['hæŋɪŋ] ADJ *(hook etc)* pendant; *Geog (valley)* suspendu

N **1** *(execution)* pendaison *f*, *Fig* **it's not a h. offence** ce n'est pas un crime gravissime **2** *(of picture etc)* suspension *f*, *(of door)* montage *m*, accrochage *m*, *(of wallpaper)* pose *f* **3 (wall)** h. tenture *f*, tapisserie *f*

▸▸ *Art* **h. committee** = comité *m* de réception ou jury d'admission des tableaux; **h. cupboard** armoire *f* murale; **the H. Gardens of Babylon** les jardins *mpl* suspendus de Babylone; *Comput* **h. indent** présentation *f* en sommaire; *Law* **h. judge** juge *m* à la main lourde; **h. paragraph** paragraphe *m* en sommaire; **h. valley** vallée *f* suspendue; **h. wardrobe** penderie *f*

hangman, *pl* **hangmen** ['hæŋmən] N **1** bourreau *m* **2** *(game)* le pendu

hangnail ['hæŋneɪl] N envie *f*

hang-out N *Fam (haunt)* repaire *m*, nid *m*, endroit *m* favori; **this is one of his hang-outs** c'est l'un des endroits où on le trouve le plus souvent; **it's a real student h.** c'est un endroit très fréquenté par les étudiants

hangover ['hæŋəʊvər] N **1** *(from drinking)* **to have a h.** avoir la gueule de bois, *Hum* avoir mal aux cheveux **2** *(practice, belief etc)* reliquat *m*; **a h. from the past** un reliquat du passé

hang-up N *Fam (complex)* complexe *m*; **he's got a h. about driving** il fait un blocage, il ne veut pas conduire; **you've got a lot of hang-ups** tu es très complexé **2** *Comput* arrêt *m* imprévu

hank [hæŋk] N *(of wool etc)* écheveau *m*; *(of thread)* peignée *f*

hanker ['hæŋkər] vi **to h. after** *or* **for sth** avoir bien envie de qch, soupirer après qch, convoiter qch

hankering ['hæŋkərɪŋ] N vif désir *m*, grande

envie *f* **(after, for** de**); to have a h. for sth** avoir grande envie de qch

hankie, hanky ['hæŋkɪ] N *Fam* mouchoir *m*

hanky-panky ['hæŋkɪ'pæŋkɪ] N *Fam* **1** *(sexual activity)* batifolage *m*, galipettes *fpl* **2** *(underhand behaviour)* coup *m* fourré, entourloupette *f*

Hanoverian [hænə'vɪərɪən] ADJ hanovrien N Hanovrien, -ienne

Hansard ['hænsɑːd] N *Br Parl* = compte *m* rendu officiel des débats parlementaires

Hanseatic [hænsɪ'ætɪk] ADJ *Hist* **the H. League** la Ligue hanséatique

hansom ['hænsəm] N *Hist* cab *m*
▸▸ *Hist* **h. cab** cab *m*

Hants [hænts] *abbr* Hampshire

ha'penny, *pl* **ha'pence** ['heɪpənɪ, -pəns] N *Br Fam* = halfpenny

haphazard [hæp'hæzəd] ADJ *(attempt)* au petit bonheur (la chance); *(arrangement)* fortuit; **to choose in a h. way** choisir à l'aveuglette

haphazardly [hæp'hæzədlɪ] ADV au petit bonheur (la chance), à l'aveuglette

hapless ['hæplɪs] ADJ *Arch, Lit* infortuné, malheureux

HAPPEN ['hæp(ə)n] vi *(take place)* arriver, se passer, se produire; **it happened ten years ago** cela s'est passé il y a dix ans; **did anyone see what happened?** *(of accident, incident)* quelqu'un a-t-il vu ce qui s'est passé *ou* est arrivé?; **it happens over and over again** c'est toujours la même chose; **don't let it h. again!** que cela n'arrive plus!, que cela ne se reproduise pas!; **it couldn't h. here** ce n'est pas ici que ça arriverait; **I don't like what's happening in this country** je n'aime pas ce qui se passe dans ce pays; **just as if nothing had happened** comme si de rien n'était; **whatever happens** quoi qu'il arrive; **as it happens** justement, précisément; **as often happens** comme il est fréquent; **what has happened to him?** *(what has occurred?)* qu'est-ce qui lui est arrivé?; *(what has become of him?)* qu'est-ce qu'il est devenu?; **if anything happens to me** *(if I die)* s'il m'arrive quelque chose; **what's happened to my pen?** *(where is it?)* qu'est-ce qu'on a fait de mon stylo?; *(what's wrong with it?)* qu'est-il arrivé à mon stylo?

vt *(chance)* **I happened to pass that way** il se trouve que je passais par là; **a taxi happened to be passing** par hasard un car bonheur, un taxi passait; **I h. to know that ...** il se trouve que je sais que ...; **do you h. to know whether ...?** sauriez-vous par hasard si ...?; **it just so happens that ...** il se trouve justement que ...; **if you h. to find it** s'il arrive que vous le trouviez; **she happens to be my sister** il se trouve qu'elle est ma sœur

▸ **happen along, happen by** vi *(arrive by chance)* arriver par hasard

▸ **happen on, happen upon** vt insep *(come across) (person, object)* tomber sur

happening ['hæp(ə)nɪŋ] N événement *m*; *Theat* happening *m*

ADJ *Fam (fashionable)* branché, dans le coup

happenstance ['hæp(ə)nstæns] N *esp Am* **it was h.** c'était le hasard, c'était le fait d'un heureux hasard

happily ['hæpɪlɪ] ADV **1** heureusement; **they laughed h.** ils rirent de bon cœur; **we were sitting there quite h. watching television** nous étions installés tout tranquillement devant la télévision; **to live h.** vivre heureux; **a h. married couple** un ménage heureux; **they lived h. ever after** *(at end of fairy story)* ≃ ils furent heureux et eurent beaucoup d'enfants; **he'll quite h. say one**

thing and do the opposite ça ne le gêne pas de dire une chose et de faire exactement le contraire **2** *(fortunately)* heureusement

happiness ['hæpɪnɪs] N bonheur *m*, félicité *f*

happy ['hæpɪ] ADJ **1** *(content)* heureux; **to be h. to do sth** être heureux *ou* content de faire qch; **h. to oblige** ravi de rendre service; **to make sb h.** rendre qn heureux; **his money hasn't made him h.** l'argent n'a pas fait son bonheur; **a h. life** une vie heureuse; **a h. ending** une fin heureuse; **to have a h. ending** bien se terminer; **to be as h. as the day is long** être heureux comme un poisson dans l'eau; **as h. as a lark** *or* **a sandboy** gai comme un pinson; **those were h. days** c'était le bon temps; **in happier circumstances** dans des circonstances plus favorables; **in happier times** en des jours meilleurs; **I'm very h. with his work** je suis très satisfait ou content de son travail; **I'm not at all h. about it** cela ne me plaît pas du tout; **if you are h. with these conditions ...** si vous êtes satisfait de ces conditions ...; **give me a good book and I'm h.** un bon livre suffit à me satisfaire; **to keep sb h.** satisfaire qn; **this game keeps the children h. for hours** avec ce jeu, les enfants sont contents pendant des heures; *Fam* **he's not a h. camper** *ou Br* **chappy** *or* **bunny** ça lui pas jouasse; *Old-fashioned Fam* **to be h.** *(drunk)* être un peu gris; **h. birthday!** joyeux *ou* bon anniversaire!; **h. Christmas!** joyeux Noël!; *Fam* **h. days!** *(as toast)* à votre santé!

2 *(wording etc)* bien choisi, à propos; *(coincidence)* heureux

▸▸**h. families** *(card game)* jeu *m* des sept familles; **h. hour** *(in pub, bar)* happy hour *f* (*heure, généralement en début de soirée, pendant laquelle les boissons sont moins chères)*; **h. medium** équilibre *m*, juste milieu *m*

happy-clappy [hæpɪ'klæpɪ] *Br Fam Pej* ADJ *(service, meeting, Christian)* d'une joie exubérante et agaçante

N chrétien, -ienne évangélique

happy-go-lucky ADJ *(person)* sans souci, insouciant; **to do sth in a h. fashion** faire qch au petit bonheur

Hapsburg ['hæpsbɜːg] N *Hist* Habsbourg

harangue [hə'ræŋ] N harangue *f*

VT haranguer; **to h. sb into doing sth** sermonner qn pour qu'il fasse qch

harass ['hærəs, hə'ræs] VT **1** *Mil (enemy forces)* harceler, tenir en alerte **2** *(pester) (person)* tracasser, tourmenter, harceler; *(sexually)* harceler; **to h. sb to do sth** harceler qn pour qu'il fasse qch; **to h. sb into doing sth** harceler qn jusqu'à ce qu'il fasse qch; **he was harassing me for money** il me harcelait pour que je lui donne de l'argent

> Note that the French verb **harasser** is a false friend and is never a translation for the English verb **to harass**. It means **to exhaust**.

harassed [hə'ræst] ADJ stressé

harassment ['hærəsmənt, hə'ræs-] N *(pestering)*, *Mil* harcèlement *m*; **police h.** tracasseries *fpl* policières; **sexual h.** harcèlement sexuel

harbinger ['hɑːbɪndʒər] N *Lit* avant-coureur *m*, *pl* avant-coureurs; **the riot was a h. of things to come** la bagarre annonçait ce qui allait arriver

harbour, *Am* **harbor** ['hɑːbər] N *Naut* port *m*; *(of small port)* lieutenant *m* de port

VT *(person)* héberger, donner asile à; *(criminal)* receler, cacher; *(dirt)* attirer, garder, retenir; *(suspicions)* entretenir, nourrir; **to h. a grudge against sb** garder rancune à qn

▸▸**h. dues** droits *mpl* de port; **h. lights** lumières *fpl* du port; **h. master** capitaine *m* de port; **h. terminal** gare *f* maritime

HARD [hɑːd]

ADJ	dur **1–3** ▪ concret **1** ▪ difficile **2** ▪ rude **4**
ADV	dur **1** ▪ fort **1** ▪ difficilement **2**

ADJ **1** *(substance etc)* dur; *(snow)* durci; **to become** *or* **get h.** *(of cement etc)* durcir; **to become harder** durcir *ou* se durcir davantage; *Fig* **h. fact** fait *m* brut; **the h. facts** la dure réalité; **the h. fact is that there isn't enough money** la vérité, c'est qu'il n'y a pas assez d'argent; **the argument was not backed up by any h. fact** l'argument ne s'appuyait sur rien de concret; **there's no h. evidence** il n'y a pas de preuve tangible; *Br Fam* **h. luck!, h. lines!**; **h. cheese!** pas de chance!, quelle guigne!;

2 *(difficult)* difficile; *(task)* pénible; **to learn the h. way** apprendre à ses dépens; **I learnt it the h. way** j'en ai bavé et maintenant, je le sais; **to do things the h. way** *(through choice)* se compliquer la vie; *(due to circumstances)* en baver; **h. work** *(working hard)* travail *m* assidu; *(hard task)* *(difficult)* tâche *f* difficile; *(strenuous)* travail ingrat; **he's not afraid of h. work** le travail ne lui fait pas peur; **it was h. work to convince him** j'ai eu fort à faire pour le convaincre; **it is h. work for me to ...**, **I find it h. work to ...** j'ai beaucoup de peine *ou* bien du mal à ...; **it was h. work!** (que) c'était dur!; **the hardest part of the job is done** le plus dur est fait; **to play h. to get** jouer les insaisissables; **to be h. to please** être exigeant *ou* difficile à contenter; **to be h. of hearing** être dur d'oreille; **the h. of hearing** les malentendants *mpl*; **the laws make it h. to leave the country** à cause des lois, il est difficile de quitter le pays; **I find it h. to believe that ...** j'ai peine à croire que ... + *subj*; **it is h. to understand** c'est difficile à comprendre; **it's h. to say** c'est difficile à dire; **that book was h. to read** ce livre était difficile à lire; **to have a h. fight** *or* **struggle on one's hands** avoir une lourde tâche devant soi

3 *(severe, harsh)* *(person, manner etc)* dur, sévère *(to, towards* envers*)*; *(master)* sévère, exigeant; *(heart)* dur; *Phot (print)* heurté, contrasté; **a h. man** *(tough)* un dur; **he's h.** *(a hard man)* c'est un dur; **to be h. on sb** être sévère envers qn; **it's hardest on the children** le plus dur, c'est pour les enfants; **it's h. to lose a child** c'est une épreuve de perdre un enfant; **to say h. things to sb** avoir des mots très durs pour qn, dire des choses très dures à qn; **it's a h. blow for him** c'est un coup terrible pour lui; **no h. feelings?** tu ne m'en veux pas?; **a h. life** une vie difficile *ou* dure; **times are h.** les temps sont durs *ou* difficiles; **he's been giving her a h. time** il lui en a fait voir de toutes les couleurs; **to have a h. time of it** en voir de rudes; **to be as h. as nails** ne pas avoir de cœur; *(physically)* être un vrai dur

4 *(intense)* **to try one's hardest** faire tout son possible; **to be a h. worker** travailler dur; **a h. winter** un hiver rude *ou* rigoureux; **a h. frost** une forte gelée; *Com* **to give sth the h. sell** promouvoir qch de façon très agressive

5 h. drinker gros *ou* grand buveur *m*; *Fam* **a drop of the h. stuff** une goutte d'alcool *ou* d'eau-de-vie

6 *Fin (stock, rates)* soutenu, ferme

ADV **1** *(vigorously)* fort; **as h. as one can** de toutes ses forces; **to hit** *or* **strike h.** cogner dur; **to push/pull h.** pousser/tirer fort; **to jam on the brakes h.** serrer les freins à bloc; **to look** *or* **gaze** *or* **stare h. at sb** regarder fixement qn; **we can't find it – well, look**

harder! nous ne le trouvons pas – et bien cherchez mieux!; **you didn't look very h.!** tu n'as pas bien cherché; **to try h.** faire de son mieux; **to try harder** faire plus d'efforts; **to think h.** réfléchir profondément; **to work h. at sth** travailler dur à qch; **she works too h.** elle se surmène; **to be h. at work** être en plein travail; **he works h. and plays h.** il se dépense beaucoup dans son travail et dans ses loisirs; **to play h.** *(roughly)* avoir un jeu (très) physique; **to drink h.** boire beaucoup; **it's raining h.** il pleut à verse; **to turn h. to the left** braquer à gauche, faire un virage très sec vers la gauche; **to swim h. for the shore** nager de toutes ses forces vers le rivage; *Naut* **h. over!** la barre toute!

2 *(with difficulty)* difficilement, avec peine; **you'd be h. pushed** *or* **pressed** *or* **put to find a shop open at this time** tu vas avoir du mal à trouver une boutique ouverte à cette heure-ci; **she took the news h.** elle a très mal pris la nouvelle; *Old-fashioned* **it will go h. with him if ...** cela sera sérieux (pour lui) si ...

3 *(near)* **to follow h.** *(up)***on** *or* **after** *or* **behind sb** suivre qn de près; **his resignation followed h.** *(up)***on this news** sa démission a suivi tout de suite cette nouvelle; *Old-fashioned* **h. by** tout près, tout contre

4 *Fam (harshly)* **to feel h. done by** se sentir traité de façon injuste

▸▸ *Typ, Comput* **h. carriage return** retour *m* chariot obligatoire; **h. cash** *(argent m)* liquide *m*; *Fin* **h. commodities** minerais *mpl*; *Ling* **h. consonant** consonne *f* dure; *Comput* **h. copy** copie *f* sur papier, sortie *f* papier; **h. core** *(nucleus)* noyau *m* dur; *Constr* empierrement *m*; *Mus* hard rock *m inv*; hard *m inv*; *(pornography)* porno *m* hard; *Br Tennis* **h. court** court *m* en ciment; **h. currency** monnaie *f ou* devise *f* forte; *Comput* **h. disk** disque *m* dur; *Comput* **h. drive** unité *f* de disque dur; **h. drug** drogue *f* dure; *Horseriding* **h. gallop** galop *m* vif; **h. hat** *(of construction worker)* casque *m*; *Am Fam (construction worker)* ouvrier *m* du bâtiment; *Typ, Comput* **h. hyphen** césure *f* imposée, trait *m* d'union imposé; **h. labour** travaux *mpl* forcés; *Metal* **h. lead** plomb *m* aigre; *Pol* **the h. left** l'extrême gauche *f*; *Tech* **h. light** lumière *f* crue; **the president takes a h. line on drugs** le président a pris une position très ferme concernant la drogue; **h. liquor** spiritueux *mpl*; *Fin* **h. loan** prêt *m* aux conditions du marché; *Journ* **h. news** nouvelles *fpl* sûres *ou* vérifiées; *Typ, Comput* **h. page break** fin *f* de page obligatoire; *Anat* **h. palate** voûte *f* du palais, palais *m* dur; **h. porn** porno hard; *Comput* **h. reset** réinitialisation *f* totale de la machine; *Typ, Comput* **h. return** saut *m* de ligne manuel; *esp Am Culin* **h. sauce** = sauce *f* au beurre, au sucre et au brandy ou au rhum servie avec le pudding; **h. sell** vente *f* agressive; *Aut* **h. shoulder** bande *f* d'arrêt d'urgence; *Typ* **h. space** espace *m* insécable; *Econ* **h. terms** conditions *fpl* du marché; **h. water** eau *f* calcaire *ou* dure

hard-and-fast ADJ *(rule etc)* absolu

hardback ['hɑːdbæk] N livre *m* cartonné; **the book is only available in h.** ce livre n'est disponible qu'en version cartonnée

ADJ *(book)* cartonné

hard-bitten ADJ *Fam (person)* dur à cuire

hardboard ['hɑːdbɔːd] N *Constr* carton *m* dur, Isorel® *m*

hard-boiled ADJ *Fam (person)* dur à cuire

▸▸ *Culin* **h. egg** œuf *m* dur

hard-core ADJ *(reactionary, supporter)* de la tendance dure

▸▸ *Mktg* **h. loyal** fidèle *mf* absolu(e); *Mktg*

loyalty fidélité *f* absolue; **h. pornography** pornographie *f* hard

hardcover ['hɑːdkʌvər] **N** *esp Am* = hardback

hard-earned **ADJ** *(money etc)* péniblement gagné; *(prize)* bien mérité; **don't waste your h. wages** ne gaspille pas l'argent que tu as péniblement gagné

harden ['hɑːd(ə)n] **VT 1** *(something)* durcir, endurcir; *(steel etc)* tremper; *Med (muscles etc)* scléroser; **to h. oneself** *or* **to become hardened to the cold** s'endurcir *ou* s'aguerrir au froid; **to h. sb's heart** endurcir le cœur à qn (**to sb** à l'égard de qn) **2** *Metal* = **case-harden 3** = **harden off**
VI 1 *(of substance)* (se) durcir, s'endurcir; *(of person, constitution)* s'endurcir, s'aguerrir; **attitudes have hardened** les attitudes se sont durcies; **scientific opinion has hardened to the view that …** de plus en plus, les scientifiques sont d'avis que … **2** *Fin (of shares etc)* se raffermir; **prices are hardening** les prix sont en hausse
▸ **harden off** **VT SEP** **to h. off seedlings** fortifier de jeunes plantes
▸ **harden up** **VI** *Fin (of shares etc)* se raffermir

hardened ['hɑːd(ə)nd] **ADJ** *(substance)* durci, endurci; *(steel, glass)* trempé; *(criminal)* endurci

hardener ['hɑːd(ə)nər] **N** *(for paint, glue)* durcisseur *m*

hardening ['hɑːd(ə)nɪŋ] **N 1** durcissement *m*, endurcissement *m*, affermissement *m*; *Metal (of steel)* trempe *f*, *Med* **h. of the arteries** durcissement *m ou* sclérose *f* des artères; *Fig* **a h. of attitudes** un durcissement des attitudes; *Fin* **a h. of prices** un raffermissement des prix **2** *Metal* = **case-hardening**

hard-faced, **hard-featured** ['hɑːd'feɪst, -'fiːtʃəd] **ADJ** *(person)* aux traits durs *ou* sévères

hard-fought **ADJ** vivement contesté

hard-hat **ADJ** *esp Am* = caractéristique des attitudes conservatrices et des préjugés attribués aux ouvriers de la construction

hard-headed **ADJ 1** *(tough)* dur, réaliste; *(realism)* sans concession; *(attitude)* réaliste; **h. business man** homme d'affaires réaliste **2** *esp Am (stubborn)* obstiné, têtu

hard-hearted ['hɑːd'hɑːtɪd] **ADJ** *(person)* impitoyable, au cœur dur; *(attitude)* impitoyable

hard-hit **ADJ** gravement atteint *ou* touché; **one particularly h. village** un village touché de façon particulièrement dure

hard-hitting ['hɑːd'hɪtɪŋ] **ADJ** *(boxer)* qui frappe dur; *(critic, speech)* très dur; **the speech was a h. attack on this policy** le discours était une attaque directe contre cette politique

hardiness ['hɑːdɪnɪs] **N** robustesse *f*, vigueur *f*

hardline ['hɑːdlaɪn] **ADJ** *Pol etc (Conservative etc)* convaincu; *(policy)* intransigeant

hardliner [hɑːd'laɪnər] **N** *Pol etc* dur *m*, dure *f*

hardly ['hɑːdlɪ] **ADV** *(scarcely)* à peine, ne … guère; **h. anyone/anything** presque personne/rien; **h. ever** presque jamais; **she can h. read** c'est à peine si elle sait lire; **I need h. say …** il va sans dire …; **she would h. set her own house on fire** elle n'aurait sûrement pas mis le feu à sa propre maison; **he could h. have said that** il n'aurait sûrement pas dit cela VOIR GRAMMAIRE A78

hardness ['hɑːdnɪs] **N 1** *(of substance, water)* dureté *f*, *(of steel)* trempe *f*, *(of print, painting)* tons *mpl* heurtés **2** *(of task, problem)* difficulté *f*; *Med* **h. of hearing** surdité *f* partielle **3** *(harshness) (of rule etc)* sévérité *f*, ri-

gueur *f*, *(of person)* caractère *m* insensible, dureté *f*, **h. of heart** sécheresse *f* de cœur **4** *Fin (of market, shares)* raffermissement *m*

hard-nosed ['hɑːdnəʊzd] **ADJ** *esp Am Fam* = hard-headed

hard-on **N** *Sl* **to have a h.** bander, avoir la trique

hard-packed **ADJ** **h. snow** congère *f*

hard-pressed, **hard-pushed** [hɑːd'prest, -'pʊʃt] **ADJ** *(troops, personnel)* très sollicité; *(funds, finances)* qui s'épuisent; *(debtor)* aux abois, fort embarrassé; *(tolerance, patience)* presqu'à bout; **to be h. to do sth** avoir du mal à faire qch; **to be h. for time** manquer de temps; **to be h. for money** être à court d'argent

hard-sectored ['hɑːdsektəd] **ADJ** *(disk)* à secteurs pré-définis

hardship ['hɑːdʃɪp] **N 1** *(circumstance)* privation *f*, (dure) épreuve *f*; **he has suffered great hardship(s)** il en a vu de rudes **2** *(suffering)* souffrance *f*, *(deprivation)* privation *f*, **to live in h.** vivre dans la misère
▸▸ **h. allowance** = aide *f* accordée à un étudiant en cas de graves problèmes financiers

hardtack ['hɑːdtæk] **N** *Naut* biscuit *m* de mer

hardtop ['hɑːdtɒp] **N** *Aut* hard-top *m*

hard-up **ADJ** *Fam* **to be h. (for money)** être fauché *ou* à sec; *Fam* **to be h. for volunteers/suggestions** manquer de bénévoles/suggestions

hardware ['hɑːdweər] **N** *(no pl)* **1** *Com* quincaillerie *f* **2** *Comput* matériel *m*, hardware *m*; **h. problem** problème *m* de matériel **3** *(weapons)* armement *m*; *Sl (gun)* pétard *m*, soufflant *m*
▸▸ **h. dealer** quincaillier, -ière; **h. shop, h. store** quincaillerie

hard-wearing **ADJ** *(garment etc)* de bon usage; *(material)* durable

hard-wired ['hɑːdwaɪəd] **ADJ** *Comput* câblé

hard-won **ADJ** *(trophy, victory)* âprement disputé, remporté de haute lutte

hardwood ['hɑːdwʊd] **N** bois *m* dur

hard-working **ADJ** laborieux, travailleur, -euse, assidu

hardy ['hɑːdɪ] **ADJ 1** *(robust)* robuste; *Bot* résistant; *(shrub)* vivace, *(plant)* de pleine terre **2** *(courageous)* hardi, courageux, audacieux
▸▸ *Bot* **h. annual** plante *f* annuelle

hare [heər] **N** lièvre *m*; **doe h.** hase *f*, *Fig* **to run with the h. and hunt with the hounds** ménager la chèvre et le chou; *(play double game)* jouer double jeu; **to start a h.** *(in hunting)* lever un lièvre; *(in conversation)* donner un nouveau tour à la conversation; *Sport* **h. and hounds** ≃ jeu *m* de piste, rallye *m*
VI *Fam (of person)* courir comme un lièvre *ou* à toutes jambes; **to h. off after sb** s'élancer à la poursuite de qn
▸▸ *Sport* **h. coursing** chasse *f* à courre au lièvre

harebell ['heəbel] **N** *(plant)* campanule *f*

harebrained ['heəbreɪnd] **ADJ** écervelé, étourdi; **h. scheme** projet *m* insensé

harelip ['heəlɪp] **N** *Med* bec-de-lièvre *m*, *pl* becs-de-lièvre

harem [hɑː'riːm, 'heərəm] **N** harem *m*

haricot ['hærɪkəʊ] **N** haricot *m* blanc
▸▸ **h. bean** haricot blanc

hark [hɑːk] **VI** *esp Arch, Lit* prêter l'oreille (**at, to** à); **h.!** écoutez!; *Fam* **h. at him!** comme il y va!
▸ **hark back** **VI** *(recall)* **to h. back (to the past)** ressasser le passé; **to h. back to sth** *(in conversation)* ramener la conversation sur qch

harlequin ['hɑːlɪkwɪn] **N** *Theat* arlequin *m*; **h. coat** habit *m* bigarré

harlot ['hɑːlət] **N** *Arch, Lit* prostituée *f*

harm [hɑːm] **N** mal *m*; *(to reputation etc)* tort *m*; **to do h. to sb** faire du mal/du tort à qn; **what h. has she done you?** quel mal vous a-t-elle fait?; **it will do more h. than good** cela fera plus de mal que de bien; **that won't do any h.** cela ne gâtera rien; **it won't do him any h.** cela ne lui fera pas de mal; **to see no h. in sth** ne pas voir de mal à qch; **you will come to no h.** il ne vous arrivera pas de mal; **out of h.'s way** *(of fragile object etc)* à l'abri du danger, en sûreté; *(of dangerous object etc)* mis dans l'impossibilité de nuire à personne; **they put the china in a cupboard, out of h.'s way** ils ont mis la porcelaine à l'abri dans un placard; **put these chemicals where they'll be out of h.'s way** mets ces produits chimiques en lieu sûr; **there's no h. in saying so** il n'y a pas de mal à le dire; **there's no h. in trying** on peut toujours essayer
VT *(person) (physically)* faire du mal à; *(non-physically)* faire du mal *ou* du tort à, causer du tort à, nuire à; *(reputation)* salir; *(person's interests)* léser; *(health)* nuire à

harmful ['hɑːmfʊl] **ADJ** *(substances)* nocif; *(remarks)* nuisible; *(ideas, influence)* malfaisant, pernicieux; **it's h. to your health** cela nuit à votre santé; **in small doses the drug is not h.** à petites doses, ce médicament n'est pas dangereux; **it had a h. effect on her education** cela a eu des conséquences fâcheuses sur son éducation; **h. side-effects** effets secondaires dangereux

harmfully ['hɑːmfʊlɪ] **ADV** de façon nuisible *ou* dangereuse, dangereusement

harmfulness ['hɑːmfʊlnɪs] **N** nocivité *f*, nature *f* nuisible

harmless ['hɑːmlɪs] **ADJ** *(animal, person)* inoffensif; *(pastime)* innocent; *(drug, sex scenes etc)* anodin; **to render h.** *(explosives)* désamorcer; *(chemical)* neutraliser; **it was just a bit of h. fun** c'était pour rire; **h. gossip** propos inoffensifs

harmlessly ['hɑːmlɪslɪ] **ADV** sans faire de mal; *(to enjoy oneself)* innocemment; *(to tease)* gentiment

harmonic [hɑː'mɒnɪk] **ADJ** harmonique
N 1 *Mus (of root)* harmonique *m*; *(on stringed instrument)* harmonique, son *m* flûté; **harmonics** sons harmoniques; *(science)* harmonie *f* **2** *Math, Phys (of wave motion)* harmonique *m*
▸▸ *Phys* **h. motion** mouvement *m* sinusoïdal; **h. series** *Mus* échelle *f* harmonique; *Math, Phys* série *f* harmonique

harmonica [hɑː'mɒnɪkə] **N** harmonica *m*

harmonious [hɑː'məʊnɪəs] **ADJ 1** *(combination, relationship)* harmonieux **2** *(music)* mélodieux

harmoniously [hɑː'məʊnɪəslɪ] **ADV** harmonieusement; *(to work, live)* en harmonie

harmonium [hɑː'məʊnɪəm] **N** *Mus* harmonium *m*

harmonization [hɑːmənaɪ'zeɪʃən] **N** harmonisation *f*

harmonize ['hɑːmənaɪz] **VT 1** *Mus (melody)* harmoniser **2** *(ideas etc)* harmoniser; *(texts etc)* faire s'accorder; *(colours etc)* allier, harmoniser (**with** avec)
VI 1 *Mus (of singer)* chanter en harmonie; *(of musician)* jouer en harmonie **2** *(of sounds, colours etc)* s'harmoniser; *(of people, ideas etc)* se mettre en harmonie, s'accorder (**with** avec); **colours that h. well (with one another)** couleurs qui vont bien ensemble

harmony ['hɑːmənɪ] **N 1** *Mus* harmonie *f*, **to study h.** étudier l'harmonie; **songs full of h.** chants mélodieux **2** *(of people, ideas etc)* harmonie *f*, accord *m*; *(of voices, instruments)* concert *m*; *(of texts)* concordance *f*; **to live in perfect h. (with sb)** vivre en parfaite intelligence (avec qn); **in h. with ...** en accord avec ...; **to be in h. with sb/sth** être en harmonie avec qn/qch

harness ['hɑːnɪs] N **1** *(of horse)* harnais *m*, harnachement *m*; **draught h.** harnais d'attelage; *Fig* **to get back into h.** *(of person)* reprendre le collier; *Fig* **to die in h.** mourir à la peine *ou* au travail *ou* à la tâche; **to work in h. (with sb)** travailler de concert (avec qn) **2** *Aviat* **(parachute) h.** ceinture *f ou* harnais *m* (de parachutiste); *Ind, Aut etc* **(safety) h.** harnais (de sécurité) **3** *Tex (of loom)* harnais *m*

VT **1** *(horse)* harnacher; **to h. a horse to a cart** atteler un cheval à une charrette; *Fig* **to be harnessed to sth** être étroitement lié à qch **2** *(waterfall etc)* aménager; **to h. atomic energy for industrial purposes** mettre l'énergie nucléaire au service de l'industrie

▶▶ **h. horse** cheval *m* d'attelage; *Sport* **h. race** course *f* attelée; **h. room** sellerie *f*

harnessing ['hɑːnɪsɪŋ] N **1** *(of a horse)* harnachement *m* **2** *(of waterfall etc)* aménagement *m*; *(of energy)* exploitation *f*

harp [hɑːp] N *Mus* harpe *f*

▶ **harp on** VI revenir sans arrêt sur la même chose; **he's always harping on about inflation** il est toujours en train de nous rebattre les oreilles avec l'inflation

harpist ['hɑːpɪst] N *Mus* harpiste *mf*

harpoon [hɑː'puːn] N harpon *m*, lance *f*

VT harponner

▶▶ **h. gun** *(on deck of ship)* canon *m* lance-harpon; *(hand-held)* fusil *m* à harpon

harpsichord ['hɑːpsɪkɔːd] N *Mus* clavecin *m*

harpsichordist ['hɑːpsɪkɔːdɪst] N *Mus* claveciniste *mf*

harpy ['hɑːpɪ] N *Myth* harpie *f*; *Fam* **old h.** vieille mégère *f*

▶▶ **h. eagle** harpie

harridan ['hærɪd(ə)n] N *Lit* vieille sorcière *f*

harrier ['hærɪər] N *(bird)* busard *m*

harrow ['hærəʊ] *Agr* N herse *f*

VT *(soil)* herser; *Fig* **to h. sb's feelings, to h. sb** déchirer le cœur à qn

harrowed ['hærəʊd] ADJ ATTRIB *Fig (appearance)* meurtri

harrowing ['hærəʊɪŋ] ADJ *(story etc)* poignant, navrant; *(cry)* déchirant; *(experience)* très douloureux, cruel

Harry ['hærɪ] N *Old-fashioned Br Fam* **to play old H. with sb** en faire voir des vertes et des pas mûres à qn; **to play old H. with sb's health** ruiner la santé de qn

harry ['hærɪ] VT *(enemy forces)* attaquer, harceler; **he was being harried by his creditors** il était harcelé par ses créanciers

harsh [hɑːʃ] ADJ **1** *(rough to the touch)* dur, rêche, rude; *(taste)* âpre; *(sound)* strident; *(voice)* rude, rauque **2** *(severe, brutal) (character)* bourru; *(treatment)* dur; *(master, answer, climate, winter)* rude; *(punishment)* sévère, rude; *(light)* cru; **to say h. things to sb** dire des choses (très) dures à qn; **she was very h. about them** elle a été très dure à leur égard; **to be h. on sb** être dur avec qn; **h. words** mots *mpl* durs

harshly ['hɑːʃlɪ] ADV *(to answer etc)* durement, rudement; *(to treat sb)* sévèrement

harshness ['hɑːʃnɪs] N **1** *(roughness to the touch)* dureté *f*, rudesse *f*; *(of light)* dureté, crudité *f*; *(of style, voice)* âpreté *f*; *(of climate etc)* rudesse *f*; **the h. of these sounds** ces sons stridents **2** *(severity) (of punishment, law)* sévérité *f*

hart [hɑːt] N cerf *m*; *(in hunting)* cerf âgé de plus de cinq ans

harum-scarum ['heərəm'skeərəm] *Fam* ADJ étourdi, écervelé

ADV étourdiment

N écervelé, -ée

harvest ['hɑːvɪst] N **1** *(of corn)* moisson *f*, *(of fruit)* récolte *f*, cueillette *f*, *(of wine)* vendange *f*, *Fig* récolte; **a good/poor h.** une bonne/mauvaise récolte; **to get in the h.** faire la moisson; **to help with the h.** aider à la moisson; *Fig* **it yielded a rich h. of information** on a récolté beaucoup d'informations **2** *(time of year)* (temps *m ou* époque *f* de la) moisson; **at h. (time)** à l'époque de la moisson

VT *(corn)* moissonner; *(fruit)* récolter, faire la cueillette de; *Fig* récolter; *(market)* exploiter

VI rentrer *ou* faire la moisson

▶▶ *Br* **h. festival** = action *f* de grâce après la rentrée des récoltes; *Br* **h. home** *(festival)* fête *f* de la moisson; *(harvesting)* moisson *f*, **h. moon** pleine lune *f* (de l'équinoxe d'automne); *Zool* **h. mouse** rat *m* des moissons; *Am, Scot* **h. thanksgiving** = action de grâce après la rentrée des récoltes

harvester ['hɑːvɪstər] N **1** *(person)* moissonneur, -euse **2** *(machine)* moissonneuse *f*

harvesting ['hɑːvɪstɪŋ] N (rentrée *f* de la) moisson *f*

has-been N *Fam Pej (person)* ringard, -arde; **he is a has-been** *mf inv*; **he's a h.** il est fini, c'est un ringard

hash [hæʃ] N **1** *Culin* hachis *m* **2** *Fam (mess)* **to make a h.(-up) of sth** faire un beau gâchis de qch; **he made a h. of everything** il a tout bousillé *ou* saboté; **to settle sb's h.** régler son compte à qn **3** *Sl (hashish)* hasch *m* **4** *(symbol)* dièse *m*

VT **1** *Culin* **to h. meat** hacher de la viande (en petits morceaux) **2** *Fam* = **hash up**

▶▶ *Culin* **h. browns** = pommes *fpl* de terre râpées et sautées (présentées parfois sous forme de galette); *Typ* **h. sign** dièse *m*

▶ **hash over** VT SEP *esp Am Fam (discuss sth)* discuter

▶ **hash up** VT SEP *Fam (mess up) (something)* bousiller

hashed index [hæʃt] N *Comput* index *m* de totalisation

hashish ['hæʃiːʃ] N hachisch *m*

hasn't ['hæz(ə)nt] CONTR = **has not**, *see* **have**

hasp [hɑːsp] N *(on door)* loquet *m*; *(on book etc)* fermoir *m*; **(staple) h.** *(for padlocking)* moraillon *m*

hassle ['hæs(ə)l] *Fam* N **1** *(inconvenience)* problème *m*, embêtement *m*; **it's too much h. going by train** c'est trop d'embêtements d'aller par le train; **all the h. of filling out the form** tous les embêtements pour remplir le formulaire **2** *(argument)* dispute *f*; **I don't want any h., right?** pas d'histoires, d'accord?; **the police give us a lot of h.** la police nous fait des tas d'histoires

VT *(person)* ennuyer, embêter; **he keeps hassling me for money** il n'arrête pas de m'embêter pour que je lui donne de l'argent

hassock ['hæsək] N *Rel* agenouilloir *m*

haste [heɪst] N hâte *f*, célérité *f*; **to do sth in h.** faire qch à la hâte; **a note written in h.** un billet écrit à la hâte; *Fml* **to make h.** se hâter, se presser, se dépêcher *(***to do sth** de faire qch)*; *Prov* **more h. less speed** plus on se hâte moins on avance

hasten ['heɪs(ə)n] *esp Lit, Fml* VT *(one's pace etc)* accélérer; *(person's departure)* hâter, presser, avancer; **to h. the hour when ...** hâter l'heure où ...

VI se hâter, se dépêcher, se presser *(***to do sth** de faire qch)*; **I don't agree with him, I h. to add** je m'empresse d'ajouter que je ne suis pas d'accord avec lui

hastily ['heɪstɪlɪ] ADV **1** *(quickly)* à la hâte, précipitamment **2** *(rashly)* de façon irréfléchie; *(to speak)* sans réfléchir; *(to judge sth)* à la légère, trop vite

hastiness ['heɪstɪnɪs] N **1** *(speed)* précipitation *f*, hâte *f* **2** *(rashness)* irréflexion *f*

hasty ['heɪstɪ] ADJ **1** *(departure, farewell)* précipité; *(sketch)* fait à la hâte; *(meal)* sommaire; **I sent him a h. note** je lui ai envoyé un billet écrit à la hâte; **to be too h. in doing sth** mettre trop de hâte à faire qch; **a h. decision** une décision hâtive; **to jump to a h. conclusion** conclure à la légère **2** *(short-tempered)* vif; **to have a h. temper** s'emporter facilement

hat [hæt] N chapeau *m*; **paper h.** chapeau en papier; *Fig* **I'm saying that with my lawyer's h. on** je dis ça en ma qualité de juriste; *Fig* **she wears several different hats in the company** elle remplit plusieurs rôles dans la société; **to put on/take off one's h.** mettre/enlever son chapeau; *Fig* **I take my h. off to him/you/etc!** chapeau!; **hats off!** chapeaux bas!; *Fig* **to hang up one's h.** raccrocher; *Fig* **to pass the h. round** faire passer le chapeau (à la ronde), faire la quête (**for sb/sth** pour qn/qch); *Fig* **to throw one's h. into the ring** se porter candidat; *Old-fashioned Fam* **my h.!** mon Dieu!; *Fam* **to talk through one's h.** parler à tort et à travers; *Fig Fam* **to keep sth under one's h.** garder qch pour soi; *Fam* **if that comes off I'll eat my h.** si ça réussit, je mange mon chapeau; *Fam* **that's old h.** c'est vieux jeu

▶▶ *Br* **h. trick** *(three goals)* hat-trick *m*, *pl* hat-tricks; *(three wins)* trois victoires *fpl* consécutives; *Cr* = mise *f* hors jeu de trois batteurs avec trois balles de suite

hatband ['hætbænd] N ruban *m* de chapeau

hatbox ['hætbɒks] N carton *m* à chapeau

hatch¹ [hætʃ] N **1** *Naut* descente *f*, écoutille *f*, *(cover)* panneau *m* de descente, panneau (d'écoutille); **cargo h.** panneau de chargement *ou* de déchargement; *Fam* **down the h.!** *(when drinking)* cul sec! **2** *(trap door)* trappe *f*, panneau *m* d'accès; **(service or serving) h.** passe-plats *m inv*; *Aviat etc* **(escape) h.** panneau d'évacuation **3** *Tech* vanne *f* d'écluse

▶▶ **h. cover** panneau de descente, panneau (d'écoutille)

hatch² N *Agr* **1** *(of egg, clutch of birds)* éclosion *f* **2** *(clutch of birds)* couvée *f*

VT *(chickens)* faire éclore; *(eggs)* incuber, (faire) couver; *(in fish farming, of fish) (eggs)* incuber; *Fig* **to h. a plot** ourdir *ou* tramer un complot

VI *(of young birds, eggs)* éclore; **newly hatched chickens** poussins qui sortent de la coquille

▶ **hatch out** VI = **hatch²** VI

hatch³ VT *(drawing)* hacher, hachurer

hatchback ['hætʃbæk] N *Aut* **1** *(car)* voiture *f* à hayon (arrière) **2** *(part, door)* hayon *m* (arrière)

hatchery ['hætʃərɪ] N *Agr* couvoir *m*, couveuse *f*; *(in fish farming)* appareil *m* à éclosion

hatchet ['hætʃɪt] N hachette *f*; *Fig* **to bury the h.** enterrer la hache de guerre

▶▶ **h. face** visage *m* en lame de couteau; *Fam* **h. job** démolissage *m*; *Fam* **to do a h. job on sb/sth** démolir qn/qch; *Fam* **h. man** *(killer)* tueur *m* à gages; *Ind, Pol* = personne *f* dont le rôle est de restructurer une entreprise *ou* une organisation, le plus souvent à l'aide de mesures impopulaires

hatching ['hætʃɪŋ] N *(in drawing)* hachure(s) *f(pl)*

hatchway ['hætʃweɪ] N *Naut* descente *f*, écoutille *f*

hate [heɪt] N **1** (*hatred*) haine *f* **2** (*object of dislike*) objet *m* d'aversion; **her pet h.** sa bête noire

VT (*somebody, something*) haïr, détester, exécrer; **I h. him** je le déteste, je le hais; **I h. classical music** je déteste la musique classique; **I h. myself for agreeing to it** je m'en veux d'y avoir consenti; **I h. it when he's in a bad mood** je déteste quand il est de mauvaise humeur; **to h. to do sth** détester (de) faire qch; **to h. doing sth** détester faire qch; **she hates having her hair washed** elle déteste qu'on lui lave les cheveux; **he hates to be contradicted** il ne peut pas souffrir qu'on le contredise; **she hates being kissed** elle a horreur qu'on l'embrasse; **I'd h. anyone to find out** je ne supporterais pas que quelqu'un l'apprenne; *Fam* **I h. to tell you, but I think you've missed your train** je regrette de devoir te le dire mais je pense que tu as raté ton train

▶▶ **h. mail** lettres *fpl* d'injures

hated ['heɪtɪd] ADJ détesté, haï

hateful ['heɪtfʊl] ADJ (*person, thing*) odieux, détestable

hatefully ['heɪtfʊlɪ] ADV odieusement, détestablement

hater ['heɪtər] N ennemi *m* (**of** de); **to be an animal-h.** détester les animaux

hatless ['hætlɪs] ADJ (*person*) sans chapeau, tête nue

hatpeg ['hætpeg] N patère *f*

hatpin ['hætpɪn] N épingle *f* à chapeau

hatrack ['hætræk] N porte-chapeaux *m inv*

hatred ['heɪtrɪd] N haine *f* (**of sb** de *ou* contre qn)

hatshop ['hætʃɒp] N (*for men*) chapellerie *f*, (*for women*) boutique *f* de modiste

hatstand ['hætstænd] N porte-chapeaux *m inv*

hatter ['hætər] N chapelier, -ière; *Prov* **he's as mad as a h.** il a un grain, il travaille du chapeau

haughtily ['hɔːtɪlɪ] ADV hautainement, d'une manière hautaine *ou* arrogante

haughtiness ['hɔːtɪnɪs] N hauteur *f*, arrogance *f*

haughty ['hɔːtɪ] ADJ hautain, arrogant

haul [hɔːl] N **1** (*pull*) **to give a h. on sth** tirer sur qch

2 (*fish caught*) prise *f*, pêche *f*, *Fig* (*of thieves etc*) butin *m*; **drugs h.** saisie *f* de drogue; **to make** *or* **get a good h.** (*of fishermen*) (une) bonne pêche; *Fig* (*of thieves etc*) faire son butin; **you've got a good h.!** (*of presents*) c'est un joli tas de cadeaux que tu viens de recevoir!

3 *Fam* (*distance, journey*) parcours *m*, trajet *m*; *Aviat etc* **short/long h.** étape *f* ou distance *f* courte/longue; **there's still a long h. ahead** il reste un long chemin à parcourir; **it's a long h. from Glasgow to Naples** (*by road*) c'est un long trajet de Glasgow à Naples; **it's a real h.** c'est un sacré trajet

VT **1** (*pull*) tirer; (*load*) traîner; (*boat, train*) remorquer; *Fam* **to h. sb over the coals** réprimander qn, *Fam* passer un savon à qn **2** *Com* (*transport by road*) (*goods*) transporter par camions

VI **1** (*pull*) tirer, traîner; **they all hauled together** ils ont tous tiré ensemble; *Naut* **to h. on a rope** haler sur une manœuvre **2** *Naut* (*sail, move etc*) **to h. alongside** accoster

▶ **haul down** VT SEP (*bring down*) (*something*) descendre; *Naut* (*sails etc*) haler bas, affaler; (*flag*) rentrer

▶ **haul in** VT SEP (*bring in*) (*something*) tirer (à l'intérieur); *Naut* (*sail, nets*) amener; *Fam* (*suspects, people for questioning*) emmener; *Fam* **they hauled in some experts to back up**

their case ils ont amené des experts pour les soutenir

▶ **haul up** VT SEP **1** (*hoist*) (*something*) monter; *Naut* (*flag*) hisser; **to h. up a boat** (*on ship*) rentrer une embarcation; (*on the beach*) haler un bateau à sec **2** (*call to account*) **to h. sb up** demander des comptes à qn (**for sth** de qch); **to be hauled up before the court** être traîné devant les tribunaux; **he was hauled up before the headmaster** il a dû se présenter devant le principal

haulage ['hɔːlɪdʒ] N *Com* **1** (*transportation*) (transport *m* par) roulage *m*, charriage *m*, camionnage *m*; **road h.** transports *mpl* routiers **2** (*costs*) frais *mpl* de roulage *ou* de transport

▶▶ **h. contractor** entrepreneur *m* de transports routiers

haulier ['hɔːlɪər], *Am* **hauler** ['hɔːlər] N *Com* camionneur *m*, entrepreneur *m* de transports, transporteur *m*; (*driver*) routier *m*

hauling ['hɔːlɪŋ] N *Naut* halage *m*

▶▶ **h. rope** câble *m* de halage

haunch [hɔːntʃ] N **1** *Anat* hanche *f*; **haunches** arrière-train *m*; **sitting** *or* **squatting on his haunches** (*person*) accroupi; (*dog*) assis **2** *Culin* (*of venison*) cuissot *m*

haunt [hɔːnt] N retraite *f*, repaire *m*; (*of group of people*) rendez-vous *m inv*; **this pub was one of his haunts** ce pub était l'un de ses repaires; **the h. of existentialists** le lieu de rendez-vous des existentialistes

VT **1** (*of ghost*) (*house etc*) hanter **2** (*of person, animal*) (*place, person*) fréquenter **3** (*of thoughts etc*) (*person*) obséder, poursuivre; (*mind, sleep*) troubler, hanter; **to be haunted by memories** être obsédé par des souvenirs; **a lack of finance haunted the project** le problème du manque de moyens les a hantés tout le long du projet; **these problems have returned to h. us** ces problèmes nous minent une fois de plus

haunted ['hɔːntɪd] ADJ (*castle, room etc*) hanté; **he has a h. look** il a l'air égaré

haunting ['hɔːntɪŋ] ADJ (*melody, memory*) qui vous hante; (*memory etc*) obsédant

Havana [hə'vænə, -'vɑː-] N **1** La Havane **2 a H. (cigar)** un havane

HAVE [hæv]

avoir **1–4, 6, 7, 10–12, 19**		obtenir **3**
prendre **5**	faire faire **14**	
vouloir **15, 16**	mettre **17**	devoir **18**
être **19**		

N *Fam* **the haves and the h.-nots** les riches *mpl* et les pauvres

VT VOIR GRAMMAIRE A55–7 (*pr* **have**; *3rd pers sing* **has** [hæz], *3rd pers pl* **have**; *pr sub sing, pl* **have**; *past, past sub* **had** [hæd], *plural* **had**; *prp* **having**; *pp* **had**; **have not, has not, had not** *are frequently shortened into* **haven't, hasn't, hadn't**; **I have, he has, we have** *etc into* **I've, he's, we've** *etc*; **I had** *etc into* **I'd** *etc*)

1 avoir; **a week has seven days** une semaine a sept jours; **he had no friends** il n'avait pas d'amis; **all I h.** tout ce que je possède *ou* que j'ai; **she has a shop** elle tient *ou* a une boutique; **he has big hands** il a de grosses mains; **my bag has no name on it** ma valise ne porte pas de nom; **she had the pen in her desk** le stylo était dans son bureau; **I h. nothing to do** je n'ai rien à faire; **I h. work to do** j'ai à travailler *ou* du travail; **to h. a right** avoir un droit, jouir d'un droit; **I h. it!** (*solution*) j'y suis!; *Br Fam* **come on!, let's be having you!** (*come forward*) allez, venez par ici!; (*hurry up!*) allez!, dépêche-toi; *Fam* **he had it coming to him** c'est bien fait pour lui, il l'a bien mérité; *Sl* **I'm not having any** (*I don't believe it*) ça ne prend pas avec moi; (*I'm not getting involved*) je ne vais pas m'en mêler

2 (*invite etc*) **we're having visitors tomorrow** nous attendons des invités demain; **to h. friends to dinner** avoir des amis à dîner

3 (*obtain*) **there was no work to be had** on ne pouvait pas obtenir de travail; **they were the cheapest seats to be had** ce sont les places les moins chères qu'on pouvait trouver; **to h. one's wish** obtenir ce que l'on désire

4 (*receive etc*) **to h. news from sb** recevoir des nouvelles de qn; **I h. it on good authority** je l'ai appris de bonne source; **I will let you h. it for £5** je vous le céderai pour cinq livres; **let me h. your keys** donnez-moi vos clefs; **you shall h. it back tomorrow** je vous le rendrai demain; *Fam* **I let him h. it** (*verbally*) je lui ai dit son fait; (*physically*) je lui ai flanqué un coup; *Fam* **I've had it!** (*if sb finds out*) je suis foutu!; (*I'm exhausted*) je suis crevé!; *Fam* **this coat has had it** (*is worn out*) ce manteau est foutu; *Fam* **the car has just about had it** la voiture va bientôt rendre l'âme; *Fam* **he's had it** (*dead, dying*) il a sa dose; *Fam* **I've had it up to here with him** j'en ai jusque-là de ce type-là; *Fam* **I've had it up to here with you** j'en ai marre de toi

5 (*take*) (*meal*) prendre; **to h. tea with sb** prendre le thé avec qn; **what will you h., sir? – I'll h. lasagne, please** que prendra monsieur? – donnez-moi *ou* je prendrai les lasagnes

6 (*in numerous verbal phrases*) **to h. measles** avoir la rougeole, *Fam* faire une rougeole; **to h. a cold** avoir un rhume, être enrhumé; **to h. the choice** avoir le choix; **to h. an idea** avoir une idée; **to h. a dream** faire un rêve; **to h. a game** faire une partie; **to h. a fall** faire une chute; **to h. a lesson** prendre une leçon; **to h. a bath** prendre un bain; **to h. a wash** se laver; **to h. a shave** se raser; **to h. a cigarette** fumer une cigarette

7 (*experience*) **I had a pleasant evening** j'ai passé une soirée agréable; **I didn't h. any trouble in finding it** je n'ai eu aucune peine à le trouver; **we had a rather strange adventure** il nous est arrivé une aventure assez étrange; **to h. fine/wet weather** avoir du beau temps/de la pluie

8 (*claim*) **public opinion has it that he is not telling the truth** on pense généralement qu'il ne dit pas la vérité; **she has it that John has been having an affair** elle prétend que John a une liaison; **rumour has it that …** le bruit court que …; **as Plato has it** comme dit Platon, comme l'a écrit Platon

9 (*hold*) **to h. sb in one's power** avoir qn en son pouvoir; **he had me by the throat** il me tenait à la gorge

10 *Fam* (*outwit*) **to be had** donner dans le panneau, *Fam* donner dedans; **you've been had!** on vous a eu!; (*for a purchase*) on vous a refilé un rossignol; **you h. me there!** là, je donne ma langue au chat!

11 (*give birth to*) avoir; **our cat has had kittens** notre chatte a fait des petits

12 **he had two children by her** il a eu d'elle deux enfants

13 *Sl* (*have sexual intercourse with*) prendre, coucher avec

14 (*causative*) **to h. sth done** faire faire qch; **to h. sb do sth** faire faire qch à qn; **to h. one's hair cut** se faire couper les cheveux; **three houses had their windows shattered** trois maisons ont eu leurs fenêtres brisées; **I had my watch stolen** je me suis fait voler ma montre; **to h. a tooth out** se faire arracher une dent; **I shall h. everything ready** je veillerai à ce que tout soit prêt VOIR GRAMMAIRE A56; B37

15 (*want*) **which one will you h.?** lequel voulez-vous?; **she won't h. him** elle ne veut pas de lui; **as luck would h. it he arrived too late** la malchance voulut qu'il arrivât trop tard; **what would you h. me do?** (*despairing*) que voulez-vous que j'y fasse?;

I'll h. you know that … sachez que …
16 (allow) **I will not h. such conduct** je ne supporterai pas une conduite pareille; **I won't h. you coming in here** je ne veux pas que vous entriez ici; Fam **he wouldn't h. it** (that he was wrong) il n'a pas voulu me/ nous/etc écouter, il ne voulait pas en convenir; Fam **we tried to give the dog a bath but he wasn't having any of it!** nous avons essayé de donner un bain au chien, mais rien n'y a fait; **I'm not having any of your nonsense** pas de bêtises
17 (place) mettre; **I'll h. the television in that corner** (when I get one) je mettrai la télé dans ce coin; (to person holding it) mettez la télé dans ce coin; Horseracing **to h. money on a horse** (a bet) miser (de l'argent) sur un cheval
18 (be compelled) **to h. to do sth** devoir faire qch, être obligé ou forcé de faire qch; **I had to go away** j'ai dû m'en aller; **I don't h. to work** je n'ai pas besoin de travailler; Iron **of course you had to go and tell him!** bien sûr, il a fallu que tu ailles le lui dire!; **the clock will h. to be mended** la pendule a besoin d'une réparation; **I don't like housework but it has to be done** je n'aime pas faire le ménage mais il faut bien que quelqu'un le fasse; **first the potatoes h. to be washed** il faut d'abord laver les pommes de terre
19 (as auxiliary) **to h. been/given/done** avoir été/donné/fait; **to h. come** être arrivé; **to h. hurt oneself** s'être blessé; **I h. lived in London for three years** j'habite Londres depuis trois ans; **well, you h. grown!** ce que tu as grandi!; **you h. forgotten your gloves – so I h.!** vous avez oublié vos gants – en effet! ou tiens, c'est vrai!; **you h. been in prison before – I haven't!** vous avez déjà fait de la prison – c'est faux!; **you've forgotten, haven't you?** vous avez oublié, n'est-ce pas?; **you haven't forgotten, h. you?** vous n'avez pas oublié, n'est-ce pas? VOIR GRAMMAIRE A50; B26–8
20 (with better, sooner) **I had better say nothing** je ferais mieux de ne rien dire; **I'd sooner leave at once** j'aimerais bien mieux partir tout de suite VOIR GRAMMAIRE A41
▸ **have around** VT SEP **1** (keep available) garder ou avoir sous la main; **I h. the documents around somewhere** les documents sont là quelque part, j'ai les documents quelque part; **she's a useful person to h. around** il est bon de l'avoir sous la main; **I don't like having children around** je n'aime pas la compagnie des enfants
2 (invite) inviter; **we must h. them around for dinner** il faudra qu'on les invite à dîner
▸ **have away** VT SEP Br Sl (have sexual intercourse) **to h. it away (with sb)** s'envoyer en l'air (avec qn)
▸ **have back** VT SEP **1** (invite) **we're having them back on Saturday** (in return) nous leur rendons leur invitation samedi prochain; (for second visit) nous les réinvitons samedi prochain
2 (invite after an event) **after the movie we had them back for coffee** après le cinéma, nous les avons invités à venir prendre le café chez nous
▸ **have down** VT SEP (invite from upstairs, the north) inviter; **we're having the neighbours down for dinner tomorrow** nous avons invité nos voisins du dessus à venir dîner demain
▸ **have in** VT SEP **1** (summon) appeler, faire venir; **we had to h. the doctor in** nous avons dû faire venir le médecin; **we're having the painters in next week** les peintres viennent la semaine prochaine
2 (invite) inviter, recevoir; **let's h. him in to discuss it** (ask to come in) demandons-lui de venir nous en parler; **she had friends in for tea** elle a reçu quelques amis pour le thé

3 Fam **to h. it in for sb** (have a grudge against) en avoir après qn, garder à qn un chien de sa chienne; **they had it in for me from the day I arrived** ils en ont eu après moi dès mon arrivée
▸ **have off** VT SEP **1** (remove) retirer; **the barber nearly had my ear off** le coiffeur a failli me couper l'oreille
2 (have removed) faire retirer; **she's having the plaster off next week** on lui retire son plâtre la semaine prochaine
3 Br Sl (have sexual intercourse) **to h. it off (with sb)** s'envoyer en l'air (avec qn)
▸ **have on** VT SEP (wear) porter; **they had nothing on** ils étaient nus; **she had her black dress on** elle avait ou portait sa robe noire
VT SEP **1** Fam (fool) (person) faire marcher; **I was only having you on** c'était juste pour te faire marcher
2 (have arranged) **he has a lot on this week** il est très occupé cette semaine; **I h. something else on tonight** j'ai d'autres projets pour ce soir
3 (install, put on) installer, mettre; **they soon had the roof-rack on** très vite, ils ont installé ou mis la galerie; **she had her coat on in no time** en un clin d'œil, elle a mis son manteau
VT SEP **to h. sth on sb** avoir qch sur qn; **the police h. nothing on him** la police n'a rien sur lui
▸ **have out** VT SEP **1** (remove) (object) retirer; (of dentist) (tooth) extraire, arracher
2 (have extracted) (tooth) se faire arracher
3 (resolve) **to h. it out with sb** mettre les choses au point avec qn; **let's h. this out once and for all** mettons les choses au point une fois pour toutes
▸ **have over, have round** VT SEP = **have around 2**
▸ **have up** VT SEP **1** (usu passive) (bring to court) **to be had up (for vagrancy/etc)** passer devant le tribunal (pour vagabondage/ etc)
2 (erect, install) installer, mettre en place; **they had the decorations up in a few hours** ils ont installé les décorations en quelques heures
3 (invite from downstairs, the south) inviter; **we'd better h. him up for a chat** (ask to come up) on devrait lui demander de venir; **he had them up (to his flat) for tea** il les a invités à venir prendre le thé

haven ['heɪv(ə)n] N (shelter) abri m, asile m, refuge m; Lit (port) havre m, port m; **safe h.** enclave f de protection; **to provide a safe h. for sb** offrir une terre d'asile à qn; (within a war zone) offrir un refuge à qn
have-not N démuni, -ie; **the have-nots of our society** les (plus) démunis de notre société
haven't ['hæv(ə)nt] CONTR = **have not**, see **have**
haversack ['hævəsæk] N havresac m (de camping); Mil musette f
havoc ['hævək] N ravage m, dégâts mpl, dévastation f; **to cause** or **wreak h.** (in a country etc) faire de grands dégâts ou de grands ravages; **to play h. with** (harvest etc) ravager; (person's health etc) déranger, détraquer; (person's plans etc) désorganiser complètement
haw [hɔː] N Bot cenelle f
Hawaii [hə'waɪiː] N Hawaï m, Hawaii m
Hawaiian [hə'waɪən] ADJ hawaïen
N Hawaïen, -ïenne
▸▸ Mus **H. guitar** guitare f hawaiienne ou hawaïenne
hawk [hɔːk] N **1** (bird) faucon m; **he has eyes like a h.** (sharp eyesight) il a des yeux d'aigle ou de lynx; (misses nothing) rien ne lui échappe; **to watch sb/sth like a h.** ne

pas lâcher qn/qch des yeux, ne pas quitter qn/qch du regard **2** Pol faucon m; **hawks and doves** faucons et colombes fpl
VI (hunt) chasser au faucon
▸▸ **h. moth** sphinx m, crépusculaire m, smérinthe m
hawk [hɔːk] VT (sell) (goods) colporter; (rumour etc) répandre; **to h. one's wares** (in market etc) vendre ses marchandises à la criée; (from door to door) faire du porte-à-porte; Hum (of prostitute) offrir ses services
hawk VI (clear throat) se racler la gorge; (spit) cracher
▸ **hawk up** VT SEP expectorer
hawker ['hɔːkər] N (hunter) fauconnier m
hawker N (seller) colporteur m, démarcheur, -euse
hawk-eyed ADJ (sharp-sighted) aux yeux d'aigle; (who misses nothing) à qui rien n'échappe
hawking ['hɔːkɪŋ] N (hunting) chasse f au faucon, fauconnerie f
hawking N (selling) colportage m
hawkish ['hɔːkɪʃ] ADJ Pol etc belliciste; **h. politician** faucon m
hawknosed ['hɔːknəʊzd] ADJ (person) au nez aquilin
hawser ['hɔːzər] N Naut haussière f, aussière f, (for mooring only) amarre f; **steel h.** aussière/amarre en fil d'acier
hawthorn ['hɔːθɔːn] N (shrub) aubépine f
hay [heɪ] N foin m; **to make h.** faire le(s) foin(s), faner; **to make h. while the sun shines** ≃ battre le fer pendant qu'il est chaud; Sl **to hit the h.** se coucher
▸▸ **h. rake** râteau m, fauchet m
haycart ['heɪkɑːt] N fourragère f de foin
haycock ['heɪkɒk] N tas m ou meulette f de foin
hayfever ['heɪfiːvər] N Med rhume m des foins
hayfork ['heɪfɔːk] N fourche f à foin
haying ['heɪɪŋ] N fenaison f
hayloft ['heɪlɒft] N fenil m
haymaker ['heɪmeɪkər] N **1** (person) faneur, -euse; (machine) faneuse f, tourne-foin m inv **2** Fam (punch) uppercut m, swing m
haymaking ['heɪmeɪkɪŋ] N fenaison f
hayrack ['heɪræk] N râtelier m d'écurie
hayrick ['heɪrɪk] N meule f de foin; (square) barge f
hayride ['heɪraɪd] N Am = promenade f dans un chariot rempli de paille; Fig **it was no h.** ça n'a pas été une partie de plaisir
hayseed ['heɪsiːd] N Am Fam (yokel) péquenaud m
haystack ['heɪstæk] N = **hayrick**
haywire ['heɪwaɪər] ADJ Fam confus, embrouillé; **to go h.** (of plan) louper, finir en queue de poisson; (of mechanism etc) se détraquer; **he's gone h.** (crazy) il déménage, il perd la boule
hazard ['hæzəd] N **1** (danger) risque m, danger m, péril m; Aut etc (place) point m dangereux; **ice presents another h. for drivers** le verglas est un danger supplémentaire pour les automobilistes **2** Golf accident m de terrain
VT (one's life, fortune) risquer, hasarder; **to h. an opinion** risquer une opinion; **to h. a guess** tenter de deviner
▸▸ Mktg **h. forecasting** prévision f événementielle; Aut **h. lights** feux mpl de détresse

---

Note that the French word **hasard** is a false friend and is never a translation for the English word **hazard**. It means **chance**.

heatstroke ['hi:tstrəʊk] N *Med* coup *m* de chaleur

heatwave ['hi:tweɪv] N *Met* vague *f* de chaleur, canicule *f*

heave [hi:v] N **1** effort *m*; **with a mighty h.** avec un énorme effort; *Naut* **h. of the sea** houle *f* **2** *(retch)* haut-le-cœur *m inv*
vт (*pt, pp* heaved *or esp Naut* hove [həʊv]) **1** *(lift) (load)* faire un effort pour lever *ou* soulever; *(pull)* faire un effort pour tirer; *(push)* faire un effort pour pousser; *(drag)* faire un effort pour traîner; *(throw)* faire un effort pour lancer; **he heaved the sacks of coal onto the truck** il a hissé les sacs de charbon dans le camion (à grand-peine); **she heaved herself out of her chair** elle s'est soulevée de la chaise avec effort; *Naut* **to h. the anchor** lever l'ancre; **to h. a sigh of relief** pousser un soupir de soulagement
2 *Naut* **to h. the ship ahead/astern** virer le navire de l'avant/de l'arrière
vı **1 h.!** *(push)* poussez!; *(pull)* tirez!; *(lift)* soulevez!; **they heaved on the rope** ils ont tiré très fort sur la corde
2 *(swell)* (se) gonfler, se soulever; *(of sea)* s'agiter, se soulever; *(of ship)* se soulever sur la lame; *(of bosom)* palpiter
3 *(retch) (of person)* avoir des haut-le-cœur; *(of stomach)* se soulever
4 *Naut (of land, ship)* **to h. into sight** paraître (à l'horizon)
▸ **heave to** *Naut* vı se mettre en panne *ou* à la cape; *(in gale)* caranguer
vт sep mettre en panne

heave-ho ınт *Naut* oh hisse!
N *Fam* **to give sb the h.** *(of employer)* sacquer qn, virer qn; *(of boyfriend etc)* plaquer qn; **to get** *or* **be given the h.** se faire jeter

heaven ['hev(ə)n] N ciel *m*, *pl* cieux; **in h.** au ciel; *Fig (overjoyed)* au paradis, aux anges; **to go to h.** aller au ciel *ou* en *ou* au paradis; **this is h.!** c'est merveilleux!; **it's h. on earth** c'est le paradis sur terre; **to move h. and earth to do sth** remuer ciel et terre pour faire qch; **the heavens opened** il s'est mis à pleuvoir à torrents; *Fam* **it stinks to high h.** ça pue; **(good) heavens!, heavens above!** bon Dieu!; **thank h. (for that)!** Dieu merci!; **h. (alone) knows!** Dieu seul le sait!; **h. knows why/when/***etc* ... Dieu seul sait pourquoi/quand/*etc* ...; **for h.'s sake!** pour l'amour de Dieu!, pour l'amour du ciel!; **where in the name of h.** *or* **in h.'s name is he?** où diable est-il?; **h. forbid!** que le ciel nous (en) préserve!

heavenly ['hev(ə)nlı] ADJ **1** *(from God) (gift, mercy etc)* du ciel; *(music etc)* céleste; **our h. Father** notre Père céleste **2** *Fam (wonderful)* divin; **what h. peaches!** quelles pêches délicieuses!; **to have a h. evening** passer une soirée merveilleuse
▸▸ **h. body** corps *m* céleste

heaven-sent ADJ providentiel

heavily ['hevɪlı] ADV **1** *(to fall, lean)* lourdement; *(to walk)* lourdement, d'un pas pesant; **time hangs h. on his hands** le temps lui pèse
2 *(to a considerable extent)* fortement, fort; **h. underlined** souligné d'un gros trait; **to drink/smoke h.** boire/fumer beaucoup; **it was raining h.** il pleuvait fort, il pleuvait beaucoup; **to rely** *or* **depend h. on sth** dépendre beaucoup de qch; **to lose h.** perdre gros; **to be h. defeated** subir une lourde défaite; **h. in debt** fortement endetté; **the secret service was h. involved in training guerillas** les services secrets étaient lourdement impliqués dans la formation des guérilleros; **to be h. hit** *(by financial misfortune etc)* être gravement atteint; **to be h. taxed** être fortement imposé

3 *(deeply) (to sigh, sleep)* profondément
4 *(with difficulty) (to breathe)* péniblement

heaviness ['hevɪnɪs] N **1** *(of body, gait)* lourdeur *f*, pesanteur *f*; *(of burden)* poids *m*; *(of food)* lourdeur **2** *(of limbs)* engourdissement *m*; **h. of heart** serrement *m* de cœur

heaving ['hi:vɪŋ] ADJ *Br Fam (extremely busy)* hyper animé

HEAVY ['hevɪ]

ADJ lourd **1–5, 7** ▪ grave **1** ▪ gros **2, 3, 7** ▪ pénible **5** ▪ chargé **5** ▪ sérieux **6**
ADV lourd
N dur **1**

ADJ **1** *(in weight)* lourd, pesant; *(step)* pesant, lourd, alourdi; *(style)* lourd; *Phys (body)* grave; *Nucl (atom)* lourd; **h. blow** coup violent; **fate had dealt her a h. blow** le destin lui avait porté un coup très rude; **h. meal** repas lourd à digérer; **h. with sleep** lourd de sommeil
2 *(large, thick) (coat, shoes)* gros, *f* grosse; **h. beard** forte barbe; **h. features** gros traits *mpl*; **h. losses** lourdes *ou* fortes pertes; **h. wire** fil *m* (de) grosse épaisseur
3 *(intense)* **h. rain** forte pluie; **a h. shower** une grosse averse; *Med* **a h. cold** un gros rhume; **h. period(s)** règles *fpl* abondantes; **h. sleep** profond sommeil, sommeil de plomb
4 *(oppressive) (smell)* fort; *(smell of perfume)* lourd; *(sky)* sombre, morne; **air h. with scent** air chargé de parfums; **h. responsibility** lourde responsabilité; **h. fine** lourde amende; **to rule with a h. hand** gouverner de façon très autoritaire
5 *(hard) (work)* pénible, difficile, dur; *(breathing)* pénible; *(task)* lourd; *(day)* chargé; *(football pitch, race course)* lourd; *Fam* **to be h. on electricity/petrol** consommer beaucoup d'électricité/d'essence; **she did the h. work** c'est elle qui a fait le gros travail; **this book is h. reading** *or* **going** ce livre est indigeste; **to find it h. going** trouver cela difficile; **h. soil** sol *m* gras; **h. user** gros utilisateur *m*; **he made h. weather of it** il s'est noyé dans un verre d'eau; **to make h. weather of sth** faire une montagne de qch, se compliquer la vie (en ce qui concerne qch); **h. sea** forte mer, grosse mer
6 *(serious) Theat* **h. part** rôle *m* sérieux; *Fam* **to come the h. father** prendre un ton de père autoritaire
7 *(eater, drinker)* gros; **to be a h. sleeper** avoir le sommeil lourd; **to be a h. smoker** fumer beaucoup
8 *Sl (tense, frightening) (situation etc)* difficile, menaçant; **to get h. with sb** devenir agressif avec qn; **things started to get a bit h.** ça a commencé à craindre
ADV **to weigh h.** *(of time, duty etc)* peser lourd; **food that lies h. on the stomach** nourriture lourde *ou* indigeste *ou* qui pèse sur l'estomac
N **1** *Fam (thug)* dur *m*
2 *Theat (serious part)* rôle *m* sérieux; *(role of villain)* rôle de scélérat
3 *Journ Fam* **heavies** journaux *mpl* sérieux
▸▸ *Naut* **h. armament** artillerie *f* lourde; *Mil* **h. fire** feu *m* nourri, feu intense; *Br Transp* **h. goods vehicle** poids *m* lourd; *Am* **h. hitter** *(in baseball)* = joueur *m* qui frappe fort et marque beaucoup de points; *Fig* homme *m* influent, gros bonnet *m*; *Ind* **h. industry** industrie *f* lourde; *St Exch* **h. market** marché *m* lourd; **h. metal** *Phys* métal *m* lourd; *Mus* **heavy metal** *m inv*; *Typ* **h. type** caractères *mpl* gras; *Phys* **h. water** eau *f* lourde

heavy-duty ADJ *(machine)* à grand *ou* fort rendement, de grande puissance; *(clothing)* résistant; *(boots)* solide, robuste; *Aut (tyre)* tout-terrain; **h. oil** huile *f* HD

heavy-eyed ADJ aux yeux battus

heavy-handed ['hevɪ'hændɪd] ADJ **1** *(clumsy)* maladroit, gauche **2** *(harsh)* oppressif, cruel

heavy-hearted [hevɪ'ha:tɪd] ADJ qui a le cœur lourd *ou* gros; **to feel h.** avoir le cœur gros

heavy-laden ADJ **1** lourdement chargé **2** *(with cares)* accablé de soucis

heavyweight ['hevɪweɪt] N **1** *Boxing* poids lourd *m* **2** *(serious, important person)* personne *f* de poids *ou* d'influence; **he is not a literary h.** ce n'est pas un grand de la littérature
ADJ **1** *Boxing* (catégorie (des)) poids lourd(s) **2** *Tex* lourd
▸▸ *Boxing* **h. champion** champion *m* poids lourd *ou* dans la catégorie poids lourd

hebe [hi:b] N *Am Offensive Sl* youpin, -ine

Hebrew ['hi:bru:] ADJ *Bible* hébreu, *f* hébraïque
N **1** *Bible (person)* Hébreu *m* **2** *Ling* hébreu *m*

Hebridean [hebrɪ'di:ən] ADJ des Hébrides

Hebrides (the) [ðe'hebrɪdi:z] N les Hébrides *fpl*

heck [hek] *Fam* ınт sapristi!, zut!
N **what the h. are you doing here?** que diable fais-tu là?; **a h. of a lot** *(quantity)* tout un tas; **not a h. of a lot** *(not greatly)* pas tellement, pas beaucoup, pas des masses; **that's a h. of a lot of money!** c'est une sacrée somme d'argent!; **we saw a h. of a good film** on a vu un vachement bon film; **oh, what the h.!** et puis flûte!

heckle ['hek(ə)l] vт *(at public meetings) (speaker)* interpeller; **he was heckled non-stop** il s'est fait chahuter tout le temps
vı chahuter

heckler ['heklər] N *Pol etc* **there were two hecklers in the audience** il y avait deux membres du public qui faisaient du chahut

heckling ['hek(ə)lɪŋ] N chahut *m*

hectare ['hekteə] N *(measurement)* hectare *m*

hectic ['hektɪk] ADJ **1** *(busy)* agité, fiévreux; *(existence, morning)* mouvementé; **to lead a h. existence** mener une vie trépidante; **it gets very h. in the post office at Christmas** c'est la bousculade à la poste à Noël; **we had a h. time** nous ne savions où donner de la tête **2** *Med (fever)* hectique

hectically ['hektɪklı] ADV fiévreusement

hectolitre, *Am* **hectoliter** ['hektəli:tər] N hectolitre *m*, *Fam* hecto *m*

hector ['hektər] vт *(person)* rudoyer
vı prendre des tons autoritaires

hectoring ['hektərɪŋ] ADJ *(tone etc)* autoritaire, impérieux

hectowatt ['hektəwɒt] N hectowatt *m*

he'd [hi:d] CONTR **1** = he had, *see* have = he would, *see* will

hedge [hedʒ] N **1** haie *f*, *Fig* **to buy sth as a h. against inflation** acheter qch pour se mettre à l'abri de l'inflation **2** *St Exch* couverture *f*
vт *(field)* mettre une haie autour de; *St Exch (position)* protéger, couvrir; **to h. one's bets** *(in betting)* répartir les risques; *Fig (cover oneself)* se couvrir, éviter de se compromettre; **the laws are hedged about with exceptions** les lois sont remplies d'exceptions
vı **1** *(in discussion)* se réserver, éviter de se compromettre **2** *Horseracing* parier pour et contre **3** *St Exch* se couvrir (**against** contre)
▸▸ **h. clippers** taille-haies *m inv*; *St Exch* **h. fund** société *f* d'investissement; *St Exch* **h. ratio** ratio *m* de couverture; **h. shears** taille-haies
▸ **hedge in** vт sep *(surround) (field)* entourer d'une haie; *(person)* entourer; **hedged in with difficulties** entouré de difficultés

▸ **hedge off** VT SEP *(separate with a hedge)* *(field)* séparer par une haie (**from** de)

hedgehog ['hedʒhɒg] N hérisson *m*; *Am (porcupine)* porc-épic *m*, *pl* porcs-épics; **to curl up like a h.** se pelotonner, se recroqueviller (sur soi-même)

hedgehop ['hedʒhɒp] VI (**-pp-**) *Aviat Fam* voler en rase-mottes, faire du rase-mottes

hedgerow ['hedʒrəʊ] N bordure *f* d'arbres *ou* d'arbustes formant une haie; **animals of the hedgerows** animaux qui vivent dans les haies

hedging ['hedʒɪŋ] N **1** *(care of hedges)* entretien *m* des haies; **h. and ditching** entretien des haies et des fossés **2** *(hedges)* bordure *f* **3** *Horseracing* répartition *f* des risques **4** *St Exch* couverture *f* **5** *(in discussion etc)* hésitation *f* à prendre des décisions

hedonism ['hiːdənɪz(ə)m, 'hed-] N hédonisme *m*

hedonist ['hiːdənɪst, 'hed-] N hédoniste *mf*

hedonistic [hiːdə'nɪstɪk, hed-] ADJ hédoniste

heebie-jeebies ['hiːbɪ'jiːbɪz] NPL *Fam* **to have the h.** *(be nervous)* avoir la frousse; **he gives me the h.** *(revolts me)* il me hérisse; *(scares me)* il me donne la chair de poule

heed[1] [hiːd] *esp Lit* N **to give** *or* **pay h. to sth/sb** faire attention à qch/qn; **to take h.** prendre garde; **to take h. of a warning** tenir compte d'un avertissement
▪ VT tenir compte de; **his advice was not heeded** on n'a tenu aucun compte de ses conseils

heedful ['hiːdfʊl] ADJ *Fml* **to be h. of ...** être attentif à ...

heedless ['hiːdlɪs] ADJ **to be h. of** *(what is happening)* être inattentif à; *(the future etc)* être peu soucieux de; **they continued, h. of her warning/the danger** ils ont continué sans se soucier de son avertissement/du danger

heedlessly ['hiːdlɪslɪ] ADV étourdiment, avec insouciance

hee-haw ['hiːhɔː] N hi-han *m*
▪ VI braire, faire hi-han

heel[1] [hiːl] N **1** *(of foot)* talon *m*; **to have the police at one's heels** avoir la police à ses trousses; **to tread on sb's heels** marcher sur les talons de qn; **to follow close on sb's heels** suivre qn de près, emboîter le pas à qn; **to take to one's heels** prendre ses jambes à son cou; *Fam* **to cool** *or* **kick one's heels** poireauter; **to turn on one's h.** tourner les talons; **to be down at h.** *(of shoes)* être éculé; *(of person)* avoir l'air miteux; **to come to h.** *(of dog)* venir au pied; *Fam (of person, state)* se soumettre; **h.!** *(to dog)* au pied!; **to bring sb to h.** rappeler qn à l'ordre; *Aut* **h. and toe** talon-pointe *m*
2 *(of shoe, sock)* talon *m*; **high heels** talons hauts; **she was wearing heels** elle portait des talons
3 *(of bread)* croûton *m*
4 *Sl (contemptible person)* chameau *m*, salaud *m*
5 *Tech etc (of tool)* talon *m*; *Naut (of mast)* pied *m*, caisse *f*, *(of rudder)* talon
6 *(of hoof of horse etc)* derrière *m* du sabot
▪ VT **1** *(shoe) (fit with a heel)* mettre un talon à; *(repair)* réparer le talon de; **to get one's shoes heeled** (faire) refaire le talon des chaussures **2** *Rugby (ball)* talonner
▸ ▸ **h. bar** talon-minute *m*, *pl* talons-minutes, réparations-minute *fpl*

heel[2] *Naut* N *(of ship)* bande *f*, gîte *f*, inclinaison *f*
▪ VI *(of ship)* avoir *ou* donner de la bande, prendre de la gîte
▸ **heel over** VI = **heel**[2] VI

heelpiece ['hiːlpiːs] N *(of shoe)* contrefort *m* du talon

heeltap ['hiːltæp] N *(in shoe)* rondelle *f* en cuir *(pour talon)*

heft [heft] VT *Am Fam, Br Dial* **1** *(lift)* soulever **2** *(guess weight of)* soupeser

hefty ['heftɪ] ADJ *Fam* **1** *(person)* fort, solide, costaud **2** *(heavy)* lourd, pesant; **a h. blow** un coup violent **3** *(substantial)* gros, important; **a h. bill** une note de taille

Hegelian [he'geɪlɪən] ADJ, N hégélien, -ienne

hegemony [hɪ'gemənɪ] N hégémonie *f*

hegira [hɪ'dʒaɪrə] N *Muslim Rel* hégire *f*

heifer ['hefər] N *Agr* génisse *f*

heigh-ho ['heɪ'həʊ] INT eh bien!

height [haɪt] N **1** hauteur *f*, *(of person)* taille *f*, stature *f*; **wall two metres in h.** mur qui a deux mètres de haut; **a h. of 20 metres** une hauteur de 20 mètres; **overall h.** *(of vehicle)* hauteur totale; **what's your h.?, what h. are you?** combien mesurez-vous?; **of average h.** de taille moyenne
2 *(of an arch)* flèche *f*, montée *f*
3 *(altitude)* altitude *f*; **h. above sea level** altitude au-dessus du niveau de la mer; *Aviat* **cruising h.** altitude de croisière; **the plane was gaining/losing h.** l'avion prenait/perdait de l'altitude; **to have a good head for heights** ne pas avoir le vertige; **I'm scared of heights** j'ai le vertige
4 *Fig (highest point)* *(of career, glory etc)* apogée *m*; *(of eloquence)* sommet *m*; **at the h. of his glory** au faîte de la gloire; **it's the h. of madness!** c'est de la folie pure!; **this is the h. of insolence!** c'est de la plus haute insolence!; **at the h. of the storm** au plus fort de l'orage; **an actress at the h. of her career** une actrice à l'apogée de sa carrière; **at the h. of summer** en plein été; **the season is at its h.** la saison bat son plein; **it's the h. of fashion** c'est la dernière mode *ou* le dernier cri
▸ ▸ *Aviat* **h. indicator** altimètre *m*

height-adjustable ADJ réglable en hauteur

heighten ['haɪt(ə)n] VT **1** *(increase etc)* *(pleasure)* accroître, augmenter; *(contrast)* accentuer; *(colour etc)* relever, faire ressortir; *(impression, speculation)* renforcer; **to h. the interest in sth** augmenter l'intérêt pour qch; **to h. public awareness** sensibiliser le public; **the riots have heightened racial tensions in the city** les émeutes ont accentué *ou* aggravé les tensions raciales dans la ville **2** *(increase height of)* *(wall etc)* surélever, rehausser
▪ VI *(of tension)* s'accroître

heightened ['haɪt(ə)nd] ADJ accru; *(sensitivity)* exacerbé; **there is a h. awareness of the dangers of pollution** il y a une prise de conscience accrue des dangers de la pollution

heightening ['haɪt(ə)nɪŋ] N **1** *(increase etc)* *(of pleasure)* accroissement *m*; **there has been a h. of speculation** il y a eu un renforcement de la spéculation **2** *(raising of height) (of wall etc)* surélévation *f*, rehaussement *m*

heights [haɪts] NPL *(area of high ground)* éminence *f*, hauteurs *fpl*

heinous ['heɪnəs] ADJ *Fml (crime)* odieux, atroce, abominable

> Note that the French word **haineux** is a false friend and is never a translation for the English word **heinous**. It means **full of hatred**.

Heinz [haɪnz] N *Fam Hum (dog)* bâtard *m*

heir [eər] N héritier *m*; **to be h. to an estate** être l'héritier d'une propriété; **the h. to the throne** l'héritier du trône

▸ ▸ **h. apparent** *Law* héritier *m* présomptif; *Fig (of political party, company)* dauphin *m*; *Law* **h. presumptive** héritier présomptif *(sauf naissance d'un héritier en ligne directe)*

heir-at-law, *pl* **heirs-at-law** N *Law* héritier *m* légitime

heiress ['eərɪs] N héritière *f*

heirloom ['eəluːm] N héritage *m*; **a family h.** *(furniture)* un meuble de famille; *(jewellery)* un bijou de famille

heist [haɪst] N *esp Am Sl* fric-frac *m*, casse *m*; **to pull a h.** faire un casse

Helen of Troy ['helɪnəv'trɔɪ] N Hélène de Troie

helianthus [hiːlɪ'ænθəs] N *(flower)* hélianthe *m*, tournesol *m*

heliboarding ['helɪbɔːdɪŋ] N héliboarding *m*, snowboard *m* avec dépose en hélicoptère

helical ['helɪk(ə)l] ADJ *Tech (gear etc)* hélicoïdal, -aux; *(spring)* hélicoïde, en hélice; **h. shell** coquille *f* contournée

helicopter ['helɪkɒptər] N *Aviat* hélicoptère *m*
▸ ▸ **h. gunship** hélicoptère *m* de combat; **h. pilot** pilote *mf* d'hélicoptère
▸ **helicopter in** VT SEP *(troops, supplies)* amener en hélicoptère, héliporter
▸ **helicopter out** VT SEP *(people)* emmener en hélicoptère, héliporter

heliograph ['hiːlɪəɡræf] N *(for signalling)* héliographe *m*

heliotrope ['hiːlɪətrəʊp] N *(flower)* héliotrope *m*
▪ ADJ *(colour)* héliotrope *inv*

helipad ['helɪpæd] N *Aviat* zone *f* d'atterrissage pour hélicoptère

heliport ['helɪpɔːt] N *Aviat* héliport *m*

heliskiing ['helɪskiːɪŋ] N héliski *m*, ski *m* avec dépose en hélicoptère

helium ['hiːlɪəm] N *Chem* hélium *m*
▸ ▸ **h. balloon** ballon *m* gonflé à l'hélium

helix, *pl* **helices** ['hiːlɪks, 'hiːlɪsiːz] N **1** *Math* hélice *f*, *Archit etc* spirale *f* **2** *Anat (of the ear)* hélix *m* **3** *(snail)* hélice *f*, colimaçon *m*

hell [hel] N **1** enfer *m*; *Myth* les enfers
2 *Fam (unpleasant state or experience)* **it was h. working in the mine** c'était l'enfer de travailler dans la mine; **it can be h. trying to park here** quelquefois, c'est l'enfer pour se garer ici; **to make sb's life h.** *or* **a h. on earth** faire un enfer de la vie de qn; **I feel like h.** je suis au trente-sixième dessous, je me sens horriblement mal; **to give sb h.** *(tell off)* passer un savon à qn, engueuler qn; *(give a hard time)* faire une vie d'enfer à qn; **these shoes are giving me h.** ces chaussures me font un mal de chien; **it was all h. let loose** c'était infernal; **all h. broke loose** c'était l'horreur; **there'll be h. to pay if your mother finds out** ça va barder si ta mère l'apprend
3 *Fam (idioms)* **go to h.!** va au diable!; *(stronger)* va te faire voir!; **to go to h. and back** connaître des moments très difficiles (mais s'en sortir); **to h. with him!** qu'il aille au diable!; **get the h. out of here!** fichemoi le camp d'ici!; *Br* **it's as cold as h.** il fait un froid de canard; **to run like h.** courir comme un dératé; **to work like h.** travailler comme un malade; **like h. (I will)!, the h. I will!** jamais de la vie!; **(you can wait) till h. freezes over** tu peux attendre jusqu'à la saint-Glinglin; **I wish to h. I could remember** si seulement je pouvais me souvenir; **come h. or high water** quoi qu'il arrive; **to go h. for leather** *(running)* courir ventre à terre; *(driving)* conduire comme un fou; *(working, playing music)* travailler/jouer comme un malade; **to do sth for the h. of it** faire qch sans raison particulière; **I did it for the h. of it** je l'ai fait parce que cela me chantait;

why don't you just do it for the h. of it? et si tu le faisais juste comme ça?; **to play merry h. with sth** foutre qch en l'air; *esp Am* **the whole country's going to h. in a handcart** tout fout le camp dans ce pays

4 *Fam (intensifier)* **a h. of a price** un prix salé *ou* démentiel *ou* ahurissant; **you've got a h. of a nerve!** tu as un culot du diable!; **there was a** *or* **one h. of a fight** il y a eu une bagarre terrible; **he's a h. of a guy** c'est un type formidable *ou* un mec super; **it was a h. of a good film** c'était un sacrément bon film; **we had a h. of a time** *(bad)* on en a bavé; *(good)* on s'est super marrés; **you'll have a h. of a time** *(bad)* tu vas en baver; *(good)* tu vas te marrer; **I had a h. of a time getting here** *(bad)* j'en ai bavé pour arriver jusqu'ici, ça a été l'enfer pour arriver ici; **a h. of a lot of ...** énormément de ...; **not a h. of a lot** pas des masses; **what the h. do you think you're doing?** qu'est-ce que tu fous?; **what the h.'s going on?** qu'est-ce qui se passe, nom de Dieu?; **who the h. are you?** qui diable êtes-vous?; **what the h., you only live once** que diable, on ne vit qu'une fois

INT *Fam* **(oh) h.!** zut alors!; *(stronger)* merde alors!; *Fam* **h.'s bells!, h.'s teeth!, h. and damnation!** *(sacré)* nom de nom!

he'll [hiːl] = **he will,** *see* **will**[2]

hellacious [helˈeɪʃəs] ADJ *Am Fam* **1** *(bad, unpleasant)* infernal, -aux **2** *(excellent)* super, génial, -aux

hellbender [ˈhelbendər] N *Am Fam (drinking bout)* (séance *f* de) beuverie *f*

hellbent [ˈhelbent] ADJ *Fam* **to be h. on doing sth** vouloir à tout prix faire qch; **the human race seems h. on self-destruction** la race humaine semble vouloir s'autodétruire à tout prix

hellcat [ˈhelkæt] N *Fam* sorcière *f*, mégère *f*

hellebore [ˈhelɪbɔːr] N *(plant)* ellébore *m*

Hellene [ˈheliːn] N Hellène *mf*

Hellenic [heˈlenɪk] ADJ *(people)* hellène; *(language, history)* hellénique

hellfire [ˈhelfaɪər] N feu *m* de l'enfer
▸▸ **h. preacher** prédicateur *m* fanatique *(qui est toujours en train de rappeler aux pécheurs qu'ils sont voués à la damnation éternelle)*

hellhole [ˈhelhəʊl] N *Fam (bar, club etc)* bouge *m*, boui-boui *m*

hellish [ˈhelɪʃ] *Fam* ADJ *(unpleasant)* infernal, -aux; **I feel h.** je ne me sens vraiment pas bien
ADV terriblement, vachement

hellishly [ˈhelɪʃlɪ] ADV *Fam* diaboliquement, vachement

hello [heˈləʊ] INT bonjour!, *Fam* salut!; *(in evening)* bonsoir!, *Fam* salut!; *Tel* allô!; **h. there, wake up!** *(calling attention)* holà! réveille-toi!; **h., what's this?** *(indicating surprise)* tiens!, qu'est-ce que c'est que ça?; **to say h.** dire bonjour; **say h. to him for me** dis-lui bonjour de ma part; **she gave them a cheery 'h.'** elle leur a lancé un 'bonjour' joyeux

hell-raiser N *Fam* chahuteur *m*

hell-raising N *Fam* vie *f* de patachon, vie de bâton de chaise; **his h. days** sa vie de patachon

helluva [ˈheləvə] *Fam* = **hell of a,** *see* **hell** N **4**

helm [helm] N *Naut* gouvernail *m*, timon *m*; **the man at the h.** *Naut* l'homme de barre; *Fig* l'homme qui tient le gouvernail *ou* qui dirige l'entreprise; *Naut, Fig* **to be at the h.** être à la barre; *Fig* **to take (over) the h.** prendre la direction des affaires
VT *Naut* gouverner, barrer; *Fig* diriger; *(film)* mettre en scène

helmet [ˈhelmɪt] N *(of soldier, fireman etc)* casque *m*; **(crash) h.** casque protecteur

helmsman, *pl* **helmsmen** [ˈhelmzmən] N *Naut* homme *m* de barre, timonier *m*

HELP [help]

N aide **1–3** ▪ secours **1** ▪ personnel **4**	
VT aider **1** ▪ faciliter **2** ▪ servir **3**	
VI aider **1**	

N **1** aide *f*, assistance *f*, *(when in danger etc)* secours *m*, aide; **with God's h.** avec l'aide de Dieu, grâce à Dieu; **to shout for h.** crier au secours, appeler à l'aide; **he's past h.** *(is dying)* il est perdu; *(is crazy, stupid)* on ne peut rien pour lui; **can I be of (any) h.?** puis-je vous aider?; **to be of h. to sb** être d'un grand secours à qn; **some students need h. to decide which course to take** certains étudiants ont besoin qu'on les aide à choisir leur cursus; **she needs h.** *(from a psychiatrist etc)* il faut qu'elle voie un psychiatre, elle a des problèmes psychologiques; **if you think that's funny, you need h.** si tu trouves ça drôle, c'est que tu dois avoir un problème; **to give h. to sb** aider qn; *(at accident etc)* porter secours à qn; **to provide some financial h.** offrir une aide financière; **the map wasn't much h.** la carte n'a pas servi à grand-chose; **for all the h. you've been** pour ce que tu nous as aidés; **I had h.** *(I didn't do it on my own)* on m'a aidé; *Fam* **a (fat) lot of h. you are** tu parles d'une aide!; **to come to sb's h.** venir au secours de qn

2 to be a h. to sb rendre service à qn; **my daughter's been a great h.** ma fille m'a bien rendu service; **that was a big h. (to me)** ça m'a beaucoup aidé; *Iron* **you're a great h.!** merci pour ton aide!

3 *(helper)* aide *mf*, *esp Br* **daily h.** femme *f* de ménage; *esp Br* **home h.** aide *f* ménagère; **mother's h.** aide *f* familiale

4 *esp Am (pl* **help***) (worker)* **a hired h.** un ouvrier *ou (white collar)* employé intérimaire; **we need more h.** on a besoin de plus de personnel

5 *(alternative)* **there was no h. for it** il n'y avait rien d'autre à faire

VT **1** *(person)* aider; **to h. one another** s'entraider; **can I** *or* **may I h. you?** puis-je vous aider?; *(in shop, restaurant)* que désirez-vous?; *(on telephone)* que puis-je faire pour vous?; *Law* **do you swear to tell the truth, so h. you God?** jurez-vous de dire la vérité, que Dieu vous vienne en aide?; **so h. me God!** *(it's the truth)* c'est la vérité!; *Fam* **so h. me** je jure; **come and h. me** venez m'aider *ou* me donner un coup de main; **he helped me with my homework** il m'a aidé à faire mes devoirs; **to h. sb (to) do sth** aider qn à faire qch; **he helped the old lady up the stairs** il a aidé la vieille dame à monter l'escalier; **to h. sb on/off with their coat** aider qn à mettre/enlever son manteau; **to h. sb out of a difficulty** aider qn à se tirer d'une difficulté; **he helped the ball into the goal** il a donné un petit coup au ballon pour le faire entrer dans les buts; *Prov* **God helps those who h. themselves** aide-toi et le ciel t'aidera; **it helped me knowing that someone was waiting for me** ça m'a aidé de savoir que quelqu'un m'attendait; **a man is helping the police with their enquiries** un homme est interrogé par la police; **it helped to give the impression that ...** cela a contribué à donner l'impression que ..., à cause de cela, on avait l'impression que ...; **h.! I'm late!** *(when in danger etc)* au secours!; **h.!, I'm late!** mon Dieu, je suis en retard! VOIR GRAMMAIRE A41

2 *(improve) (digestion, progress)* faciliter; **that doesn't h. the situation,** that doesn't h.

much cela ne nous avance pas (beaucoup); *Iron* **to h. matters, we had a puncture** pour ne rien arranger, nous avons crevé

3 *(at table) (person)* servir; **to h. sb to soup/ wine** servir du potage/verser du vin à qn; **to h. oneself to sth** *(serve)* se servir en *ou* de qch; *Fam, Iron (steal)* voler *ou* prendre *ou* chiper qch; **h. yourself!** servez-vous!

4 *(prevent) (with negation expressed or implied)* **it can't be helped!** tant pis!, il n'y a rien à faire, on n'y peut rien; **I can't h. laughing** je ne peux pas m'empêcher de rire; **I couldn't h. overhearing** je n'ai pu m'empêcher de surprendre la conversation; **I can't h. wondering** je ne peux pas m'empêcher de poser la question; **I can't h. it** c'est plus fort que moi, je ne peux pas m'en empêcher; *(it can't be helped)* je n'y peux rien; **they can't h. being born there** ils n'ont pas demandé à naître là; **I'm not going back if I can h. it** si j'ai le choix, je n'y retournerai pas

VI **1** aider; **can I h.?** est-ce que je peux faire quelque chose?; **I was only trying to h.!** je voulais seulement vous/les/*etc* aider!; **he offered to h. with the clearing up** il a proposé de nous/les/*etc* aider à ranger; **it helps if you can speak the language** c'est plus facile si on parle la langue; **forgetting the map didn't h. (much)** le fait d'avoir oublié la carte n'a pas arrangé les choses; **it's near the post office if that helps** *(of information)* c'est près du bureau de poste si ça peut vous aider; **every little helps** les petits ruisseaux font les grandes rivières

2 *(avoid)* **don't be away longer than you can h.** tâchez d'être absent le moins de temps possible

▸▸ *Comput* **h. button** case *f* d'aide; **h. desk** service *m* d'assistance téléphonique; *Comput (for computing queries)* service d'assistance; *Comput* **h. file** fichier *m* d'aide; *Comput* **h. function** fonction *f* d'aide; *Comput* **h. key** touche *f* d'aide; *Comput* **h. menu** menu *m* d'aide; *Comput* **h. screen** écran *m* d'aide; *Comput* **h. window** fenêtre *f* d'aide

▸ **help out** VI *(help)* aider; **everyone helped out with the cleaning up** tout le monde a aidé à nettoyer; **I could h. out with the cooking** je pourrais vous/les/*etc* aider à faire les repas
VT SEP *(help)* aider; **I need £20, can you h. me out?** j'ai besoin de 20 livres, est-ce que tu peux me les avancer?; **they helped him out with food and money** ils l'ont aidé en lui donnant de la nourriture et de l'argent, ils lui ont donné de la nourriture et de l'argent pour l'aider

helper [ˈhelpər] N aide *mf*, *(assistant)* assistant, -ante; **voluntary h.** bénévole *mf*

helpful [ˈhelpfʊl] ADJ **1** *(person)* secourable, serviable; **he always tries to be h.** il essaie toujours de rendre service; **he was not being very h.** il n'a pas fait grand-chose pour nous aider; *(wasn't telling us much)* il ne disait pas grand-chose **2** *(book, advice)* utile; **this dictionary is not very h.** ce dictionnaire ne sert pas à grand-chose

helpfully [ˈhelpfʊlɪ] ADV **she very h. offered/lent us ...** elle a eu la gentillesse *ou* l'amabilité de nous offrir/prêter ...; **it's very h. indexed** l'index est très utile; **it's h. explained in the brochure** c'est très bien expliqué dans la brochure; *Iron* **someone had very h. let the battery run down** quelqu'un a eu l'amabilité de décharger la pile

helpfulness [ˈhelpfʊlnɪs] N **1** *(of person)* serviabilité *f* **2** *(of book etc)* utilité

helping [ˈhelpɪŋ] ADJ **to lend a h. hand** aider; **to give sb a h. hand** donner un coup de main à qn
N *(of food)* portion *f*; **two helpings of soup** deux assiettées *fpl* de soupe; **I had two hel-**

pings *or* a second h. j'en ai repris, je me suis resservi

helpless ['helplɪs] **ADJ** *(powerless)* faible, impuissant; *(orphan etc)* sans appui, délaissé; *(handicapped person)* infirme; *(ship)* désemparé; **I am h. in the matter** je n'y puis *ou* peux rien; **a h. onlooker** un spectateur impuissant; **we were h. to prevent what was happening** nous ne pouvions rien faire contre ce qui se passait; **I was h. with laughter** je n'en pouvais plus de rire; *Fam* **he's one of the h. sort** il est incapable de se débrouiller; **carry it yourself, you're not h.** débrouille-toi, tu peux très bien le porter tout seul

helplessly ['helplɪslɪ] **ADV** *(to struggle)* en vain; **to gesture h.** lever les mains en signe d'impuissance; **to watch h.** regarder en spectateur impuissant; **they were h. convulsed with laughter** ils n'en pouvaient plus de rire

helplessness ['helplɪsnɪs] **N** impuissance *f;* **because of his h. around the house** parce qu'il est incapable de se débrouiller tout seul chez lui

helpline ['helplaɪn] **N** *Tel (for information)* ligne *f* d'assistance; *(for battered women)* ≃ SOS femmes battues; *(for victims of child abuse)* ≃ SOS enfants martyrs

Helsinki [hel'sɪŋkɪ] **N** Helsinki

helter-skelter ['heltə'skeltər] **ADV** *(to run, flee)* pêle-mêle, à la débandade
N *Br (at fairground)* toboggan *m*

hem¹ [hem] *Sewing* **N 1** *(of garment)* bord *m;* *(turned over part)* ourlet *m;* **let the h. down** j'ai rallongé ma jupe en en défaisant l'ourlet
2 = **hemline**
VT ourler, faire l'ourlet de
▸ **hem in VT SEP** *(surround) (enemy troops)* entourer, cerner; *(place)* investir; **hemmed in by high mountains** enserré entre de hautes montagnes

hem² **INT** hem!, hum!

hem³ **VI** = **hum¹** **VI 2**

hema- ['hi:mə] **PREF** *Am Med* = **haema-**

he-man, *pl* **he-men** ['hi:mæn, -men] **N** *Fam* homme *m* viril

hemato- [hi:mə'təʊ] **PREF** *Am Med* = **haemato-**

hemicycle ['hemɪsaɪk(ə)l] **N** *Archit* hémicycle *m*

hemiplegia [hemɪ'pli:dʒɪə] **N** *Med* hémiplégie *f*

hemisphere ['hemɪsfɪər] **N** hémisphère *m;* *Geog* **the northern/southern h.** l'hémisphère nord *ou* boréal/sud *ou* austral; **left/right h.** *(of brain)* hémisphère gauche/droit

hemispherical [hemɪ'sferɪk(ə)l] **ADJ** hémisphérique

hemline ['hemlaɪn] **N** *Sewing* bas *m* de l'ourlet; **hemlines are coming down** la mode rallonge; **daring hemlines** des jupes très courtes

hemlock ['hemlɒk] **N** ciguë *f*

hemo- ['hi:məʊ] *pref Am Med* = **haemo-**

hemp [hemp] **N 1** *(plant)* chanvre *m; Tex* chanvre, filasse *f* **2** *Pharm etc* **Indian h.** chanvre indien, hachisch *m*

hemstitch ['hemstɪtʃ] *Sewing* **N** ourlet *m* à jour
VT *(handkerchief etc)* ourler à jour

hen [hen] **N 1** *(chicken)* poule *f* **2** *(female bird)* femelle *f* **3** *Scot Fam (term of address)* ma poule, ma cocotte
▸▸ **h. bird** oiseau *m* femelle; **h. harrier** busard *m* Saint-Martin; *Fam* **h. night, h. party** = soirée *f* où une femme enterre sa vie de jeune fille; **h. pheasant** poule faisane

henbane ['henbeɪn] **N** *(plant)* jusquiame *f,* herbe *f* aux poules

hence [hens] **ADV 1** *(referring to consequence)* de là, d'où, en conséquence; **h. his anger** de là *ou* d'où sa fureur **2** *(referring to time)* dorénavant, désormais, à partir d'aujourd'hui; **five years h.** dans cinq ans **3** *Arch, Lit (referring to place)* **(from)** h. d'ici; **five miles h.** à deux lieues d'ici

henceforth [hens'fɔ:θ], **henceforward** [hens'fɔ:wəd] **ADV** *Fml* désormais, dorénavant, à l'avenir

henchman, *pl* **henchmen** ['hentʃmən] **N** *Pol etc Pej* acolyte *m*

hencoop ['henku:p] **N** cage *f* à poules

henhouse ['henhaʊs] **N** poulailler *m*

henna ['henə] **N** *(shrub, dye)* henné *m*
VT **to h. one's hair** se faire un henné; **hennaed hair** cheveux teints au henné

henpecked ['henpekt] **ADJ** **h. husband** mari mené par le bout du nez; **he's h.** sa femme le mène par le bout du nez

henroost ['henru:st] **N 1** *(perch)* juchoir *m,* perchoir *m* **2** = **henhouse**

Henry the Eighth, **Henry VIII** ['henrɪ ðɪ':eɪtθ] **N** Henri VIII

hep [hep] **ADJ** *Old-fashioned Fam* à la page, dans le vent

heparin ['hepərɪn] **N** *Pharm* héparine *f*

hepatic [he'pætɪk] **ADJ** *Anat etc* hépatique

hepatitis [hepə'taɪtɪs] **N** *Med* hépatite *f;* **h. A/B/C** hépatite A/B/C

hepatology [hepə'tɒlədʒɪ] **N** *Med* hépatologie *f*

heptagon ['heptəgən] **N** *Math* heptagone *m*

her VOIR GRAMMAIRE A27–8; B18–19 *(unstressed* [hər], *stressed* [hɜ:r]*)* **PERS PRON 1** *(unstressed) (direct)* la; *(before a vowel sound)* l'; *(indirect)* lui; *(reflexive, after preposition)* elle; **I hate h.** je la déteste; **have you seen h.?** l'avez-vous vue?; **I shall tell h. so** je le lui dirai; **look at h.** regardez-la; **tell h.** dites-lui; **I am thinking of h.** je pense à elle; **I remember h.** je me souviens d'elle; **she closed the door behind h.** elle referma la porte derrière elle; *Fml* **Poland's friends deserted h.** *(country)* la Pologne a été abandonnée par ses amis; **the enemy sank h.** *(ship)* il a été coulé par l'ennemi; *Fam* **I'll get h. started** *(car etc)* je vais la faire démarrer
2 *(stressed)* elle; *Lit (with dem force)* celle; **I can forgive h.** son but not her je peux pardonner à son fils, mais pas à elle; *Lit* **to h. who should take offence at this I would say …** à celle qui s'en offenserait je dirais …; **who better than h. to break the news?** qui, mieux qu'elle, saurait annoncer la nouvelle?
3 *(complement of verb* **to be***)* **it's h.!** c'est elle!; **that's h.!** la voilà!
POSS ADJ son, *f* sa, *pl* ses; **h. dress/dresses** sa robe/ses robes; **h. hat** son chapeau; **h. father and mother** son père et sa mère; *Admin* **ses père et mère; h. eyes are blue** elle a les yeux bleus; **she has hurt h. hand** elle s'est fait mal à la main; **H. Majesty** sa Majesté; *Fml* **France reassured h. allies** la France rassura ses alliés; **the ship and h. crew** le navire et son équipage VOIR GRAMMAIRE A30; A43; B21–2
N *Fam* **it's a h. not a him** *(of baby)* c'est une fille, pas un garçon; *(of animal)* c'est une femelle, pas un mâle

herald ['herəld] **N 1** héraut *m* **2** *Fig (of spring etc)* présage *m*
VT *Fml, Lit (arrival etc)* annoncer, proclamer; **these negotiations h. a new era for world peace** ces négociations marquent le début d'une ère nouvelle pour la paix mondiale; **to h. the dawn** annoncer l'aube

heraldic [hɪ'rældɪk] **ADJ** héraldique; **h. bearing** armoirie *f,* blason *m*

heraldry ['herəldrɪ] **N** héraldique *f, (coat of arms)* blason *m;* **book of h.** armorial *m,* -aux

herb [hɜ:b, *Am* ɜ:b] **N** *(plant)* herbe *f, Culin* **herbs** (fines) herbes; **herbs and spices** condiments *mpl;* **medicinal herbs** plantes *fpl* médicinales
▸▸ *Hort* **h. garden** jardin *m* d'herbes aromatiques; *Bot* **h. Robert** herbe à Robert, géranium *m* robertin; **h. tea** infusion *f,* tisane *f*

herbaceous [hɜ:'beɪʃəs] **ADJ** *Bot* herbacé
▸▸ **h. border** bordure *f* de plantes herbacées

herbage ['hɜ:bɪdʒ] **N** *(plants)* herbes *fpl,* herbage(s) *m(pl)*

herbal ['hɜ:b(ə)l, *Am* 'ɜ:b(ə)l] **N** *Old-fashioned (book)* herbier *m*
ADJ *(drink)* fait avec des plantes; *(remedy)* à base d'herbes *ou* de plantes
▸▸ **h. cigarettes** cigarettes *fpl* aux plantes; **h. infusion** infusion *f,* tisane *f;* **h. medicine** *(practice)* phytothérapie *f; (medication)* médicament *m* à base de plantes; **h. tea** infusion, tisane

herbalist ['hɜ:bəlɪst, *Am* 'ɜ:bəlɪst] **N** herboriste *mf*

herbarium [hɜ:'beərɪəm, *Am* ɜ:'beərɪəm] **N** herbier *m*

herbicide ['hɜ:bɪsaɪd, *Am* 'ɜ:bɪsaɪd] **N** herbicide *m*

herbivore ['hɜ:bɪvɔ:r] **N** *(animal)* herbivore *m*

herbivorous [hɜ:'bɪvərəs, *Am* ɜ:'bɪvərəs] **ADJ** *(animal)* herbivore

Herculean [hɜ:kjʊ'li:ən] **ADJ** *(effort, strength)* herculéen

Hercules ['hɜ:kjʊli:z] **N** *Myth, Astron* Hercule; *Fig (strong man)* hercule *m*
▸▸ *Comput* **H. monitor** moniteur *m* Hercules

herd [hɜ:d] **N** *(of cattle, elephants etc)* troupeau *m; (of deer)* troupeau *m, Spec* harde *f; (of horses etc)* troupe *f,* bande *f; (of people)* troupeau, foule *f;* **the h. instinct** *(in animals, people)* l'instinct grégaire; **the common h.** le peuple, *Pej* la canaille, la populace
VT *(cattle)* garder, surveiller; *Fam (tourists etc)* diriger; **the cattle were herded into the barn** on a fait entrer le bétail dans la grange; **the candidates were then all herded into the waiting room** on a alors entassé les candidats dans la salle d'attente; **the prisoners were herded onto trucks** on a entassé les prisonniers dans des camions
▸ **herd together VT** *(of animals) (live in herds)* vivre en troupeaux; *(form a herd)* s'assembler en troupeau; *Fam (of people)* se regrouper
VT SEP *(cattle etc)* rassembler en troupeau

herder ['hɜ:dər] **N** *esp Am* = **herdsman**

herdsman, *pl* **herdsmen** ['hɜ:dzmən] **N** *esp Br* gardien *m* de troupeau

HERE ['hɪər] **ADV** VOIR GRAMMAIRE A21 **1** *(this place)* ici; **come h.!** (venez) ici!; **in h., please** par ici, s'il vous plaît; **near h.** près d'ici; **over h.** par ici; **from h. to there** d'ici à là-bas; **Mr Green's not h. today** M. Green n'est pas là aujourd'hui; **over h. in Scotland** ici, en Écosse; **h. and now** immédiatement, tout de suite; **it's h. to stay** *(of fashion)* cela restera; **h. lies …** *(on tombstone)* ci-gît …; *Lit* **h. below** *(on this earth)* ici-bas
2 *(point in time, argument etc)* **I think we could break h. for lunch** je crois que nous pouvons nous arrêter là pour déjeuner; **h. I am referring to taxation** *(at this point)* c'est aux impôts que je fais allusion; **we disagree h.** c'est là que nous ne sommes pas d'accord; **h.'s what you have to do** voilà ce que tu as à faire

3 h.'s your hat! voici *ou* voilà votre chapeau!; **h. you are!** *(on seeing, finding sb)* vous voici!, vous voilà!; *(giving sth)* tenez!; **h. we are!** *(on finding sth)* voilà! j'ai trouvé!; *(on arriving somewhere)* nous y sommes!, nous voilà arrivés! *ou* rendus!; **h. she comes!** la voici (qui vient)!; **h. I am!** me voici!, me voilà!; **h. is** *or* **h. we have a woman who ...** voici une femme qui ...; **my friend h. will tell you** mon ami que voici vous le dira; *Fam* **this h. ... ce...,** *f* **cette ...; h. goes!** allons-y!; **h. we go (again)!** *(said with a sigh)* c'est reparti!; *(annoyed)* encore?

4 *(esp over drink etc)* **h.'s to you!** à votre santé!; **h.'s to the success of your venture!** à votre succès!

5 h. and there partout, ça et là, *Lit* par-ci, par-là; **h., there and everywhere** (un peu) partout; **neither h. nor there** ni ici ni ailleurs; *Fig* **that's neither h. nor there** cela n'a aucun rapport

INT 1 *(at roll call)* présent!

2 *(to attract sb's attention)* **h.! come and look at this** eh! viens voir ça!; **h., take this** tiens, prends ça

3 *(to express annoyance)* **h., that's my chair!** eh, c'est ma chaise!; **h., stop that!** écoute, tu arrêtes un peu!

N the h. and now le présent

hereabout(s) ['hɪərəbaʊt(s)] **ADV** près d'ici, par ici

hereafter [hɪər'ɑ:ftər] **ADV** *Fml* **1** *(of position)* *(in book, writings etc)* ci-après, ci-dessous **2** *esp Jur (of time)* dorénavant, désormais **3** *(after death)* dans l'autre monde
N *Lit* **the h.** l'au-delà *m*; **in the h.** dans l'autre monde, dans l'au-delà

hereby [hɪə'baɪ, 'hɪəbaɪ] **ADV** *Fml* par ceci, par ce moyen, par là; *Law* par la présente *ou* les présentes; **the council h. declares that ...** le conseil déclare par le présent acte que ...

hereditary [hɪ'redɪt(ə)rɪ] **ADJ** *(disease etc)* héréditaire

heredity [hɪ'redɪtɪ] **N** hérédité *f*

herein [hɪər'ɪn] **ADV** *Law, Lit* **1** *(of place, position)* ici, en ce lieu; *(in document)* dans ce document; **the letter enclosed h.** la lettre ci-incluse **2** *(in this matter)* sur ce point

heresy ['herəsɪ] **N** *Rel, Fig* hérésie *f*, **it smacks of h.** *(of opinion)* c'est une hérésie

heretic ['herətɪk] **N** *Rel, Fig* hérétique *mf*

heretical [hɪ'retɪk(ə)l] **ADJ** *Rel, Fig* hérétique

hereto [hɪə'tu:, 'hɪətu:] **ADV** *Law* annexed **h., h. annexed** ci-joint

heretofore ['hɪətʊ'fɔ:r] **ADV** *Arch, Lit* jusqu'ici; **as h.** comme par le passé

hereunder [hɪər'ʌndər] **ADV** *Law etc* ci-dessous

hereupon ['hɪərəppn] **ADV** *Law etc* là-dessus; **h. he left** sur ce *ou* là-dessus, il partit

herewith [hɪə'wɪθ] **ADV 1** = **hereby 2** *Com* **price list h. enclosed** prix-courant ci-inclus *ou* sous ce pli

heritable ['herɪtəb(ə)l] **ADJ 1** *Biol (disease)* héréditaire **2** *Law (right)* héréditaire; *(property)* dont on peut hériter; *(person)* capable d'hériter

heritage ['herɪtɪdʒ] **N** héritage *m*, patrimoine *m*; *(of nation, humanity)* patrimoine
▸▸ **h. site** site *m* patrimoine; **h. tourism** tourisme *m* culturel; **h. trail** = parcours *m* touristique qui va d'un lieu historique à un autre

hermaphrodite [hɜ:'mæfrədaɪt] **ADJ, N** *Zool, Bot* hermaphrodite *m*

hermaphroditic [hɜ:mæfrə'dɪtɪk] **ADJ** hermaphrodite

hermetic [hɜ:'metɪk] **ADJ** hermétique; *Fig*

the university was a h. world l'université était un monde très fermé *ou* hermétique

hermetically [hɜ:'metɪklɪ] **ADV** *(sealed)* hermétiquement

hermit ['hɜ:mɪt] **N** ermite *m*; **to live like a h.** vivre en solitaire *ou* en ermite
▸▸ **h. crab** bernard-l'ermite *m inv*, pagure *m*

hermitage ['hɜ:mɪtɪdʒ] **N** ermitage *m*

hernia ['hɜ:nɪə] **N** *Med* hernie *f*, **to have a h.** avoir une hernie

hero, *pl* **heroes** ['hɪərəʊ, -əʊz] **N** héros *m*; **a sporting h.** un champion sportif; *Fam* **my h.!** mon héros!
▸▸ **h. worship** *(admiration)* adulation *f*, culte *m* (du héros); *Antiq* culte *m* des héros

Herod ['herəd] **N** *Hist* Hérode

heroic [hɪ'rəʊɪk] **ADJ** héroïque; **h. deed** acte *m* d'héroïsme
▸▸ **h. couplet** distique *m* héroïque; *Liter* **h. poem** poème *m* épique; *Liter* **h. verse** vers *m* décasyllabe héroïque

heroically [hɪ'rəʊɪklɪ] **ADV** héroïquement

heroics [hɪ'rəʊɪks] **NPL 1** *Pej (behaviour)* coup *m* d'éclat; *(in opera)* emphase *f* **2** *(heroic efforts)* efforts *mpl* héroïques

heroin ['herəʊɪn] **N** *Chem, Pharm* héroïne *f*
▸▸ **h. addict** héroïnomane *mf*; **h. chic** = apparence *f* cultivée par certains mannequins, inspirée de celle des héroïnomanes *(extrême maigreur, mauvaise mine etc)*

Attention: ne pas confondre avec **heroine**.

heroine ['herəʊɪn] **N** héroïne *f*

Attention: ne pas confondre avec **heroin**.

heroism ['herəʊɪz(ə)m] **N** héroïsme *m*

heron ['herən] **N** *(bird)* héron *m*

hero-worship **VT** *(person)* idolâtrer

herpes ['hɜ:pi:z] **N** *Med* herpès *m*; **to have h.** avoir de l'herpès
▸▸ *Med* **h. simplex** herpès *m*; **h. virus** virus *m* de l'herpès; *Med* **h. zoster** zona *m*

herring ['herɪŋ] **N** *(fish)* hareng *m*
▸▸ **h. boat** harenguier *m*; **h. fleet** flotille *f* de harenguiers

herringbone ['herɪŋbəʊn] **N 1** *(pattern)* dessin *m* à chevrons **2** *Sewing (stitch)* point *m* croisé, point d'épine **3** *Ski* montée *f* en ciseaux *ou* en pas de canard
▸▸ **h. pattern** dessin à chevrons; *Sewing* **h. stitch** point croisé, point d'épine

hers [hɜ:z] **POSS PRON** le sien, la sienne, *pl* les siens, les siennes; **this book is h.** ce livre est à elle *ou* lui appartient; **a friend of h.** un(e) de ses ami(e)s, un(e) ami(e) à elle; **it's no business of h.** ce n'est pas son affaire **VOIR GRAMMAIRE A30; B21**

herself [hɜ:'self] **PERS PRON** **VOIR GRAMMAIRE A29–30 1** *(emphatic)* elle-même; **she did all the work h.** elle a fait tout le travail elle-même *ou* toute seule; **she's looking (quite) h. again** *(after illness)* elle paraît complètement remise; **she's not h. today** elle n'est pas elle-même aujourd'hui, elle n'est pas dans son état normal aujourd'hui
2 *(reflexive)* se; **she hurt h.** elle s'est fait mal **SEE GRAMMAR B28–9**
3 *(after preposition)* elle(-même); **'well, well!' she said to h.** 'eh bien!' se dit-elle; **she isn't being honest with h.** elle n'est pas honnête avec elle-même; **she kept one for h.** elle s'en est gardé un/une pour elle; **she painted a picture of h.** elle a fait son autoportrait; **she was living by h.** elle vivait seule

Herts [hɑ:ts] *abbr* **Hertfordshire**

hertz [hɜ:ts] **N** *Elec* hertz *m*

he's [hi:z] **CONTR 1** = **he is,** *see* **be 2** = **he has,** *see* **have**

hesitancy ['hezɪtənsɪ] **N** hésitation *f*

hesitant ['hezɪtənt] **ADJ** hésitant, irrésolu; **I would be h. to ...** j'hésiterais à ...; **he's a very h. speaker** il hésite beaucoup en parlant

hesitantly ['hezɪtəntlɪ] **ADV** avec hésitation

hesitate ['hezɪteɪt] **VI** *(in speaking, acting)* hésiter; **without hesitating** sans hésiter **VT** **to h. to do sth** hésiter à faire qch

hesitation [hezɪ'teɪʃən] **N** hésitation *f*, **without (the slightest) h.** sans (la moindre) hésitation; **he has no h. about it** il n'a pas le moindre doute à ce sujet

hessian ['hesɪən] **N** *Tex* toile *f* de jute

hetero ['hetərəʊ] **ADJ, N** *Fam* = **heterosexual**

heterodox ['hetərəʊdɒks] **ADJ** hétérodoxe

heterogeneous [hetərə'dʒi:nɪəs] **ADJ** hétérogène

heterosexism [hetərə'seksɪzm] **N** discrimination *f* envers les homosexuels

heterosexual [hetərəʊ'seksjʊəl] **ADJ, N** hétérosexuel, -elle

het up [het'ʌp] **ADJ** *Br Fam (annoyed)* fâché, en rogne; *(upset, tense)* énervé, à cran; **don't get h. up about it** ne t'en fais pas pour cela

heuristic [hjʊ'rɪstɪk] **ADJ** heuristique
N heuristics heuristique *f* **VOIR GRAMMAIRE A10**
▸▸ *Math, Phil* **h. model** modèle *m* heuristique

hew [hju:] **VT** *(pt* **hewed** [hju:d], *pp* **hewed, hewn** [hju:n]) *(with axe, chisel etc)* couper, tailler; *(stone)* tailler, équarrir, dresser; **to h. coal** abattre le charbon
▸ **hew down VT SEP** *(cut down) (tree)* abattre
▸ **hew off VT SEP** *(branch)* abattre
▸ **hew out VT SEP** creuser; **the cavern had been hewn out of the rock** la caverne a été creusée dans la pierre

hewer ['hju:ər] **N** *(of stones)* tailleur *m*

hex¹ [heks] *Am Fam* **N** *(spell)* sortilège *m*, (mauvais) sort *m*; **to put a h. on sb/sth** jeter un sort à qn/qch
VT jeter un sort à

hex² *Comput* **N** notation *f* hexadécimale; **in h.** en hexadécimal
▸▸ **h. code** code *m* hexadécimal, notation hexadécimale; **h. file** fichier *m* hexadécimal

hexadecimal [heksə'desəm(ə)l] **ADJ** *Comput* hexadécimal, -aux

hexagon ['heksəgən] **N** *Math* hexagone *m*

hexagonal [hek'sægən(ə)l] **ADJ** hexagonal, -aux

hexameter [hek'sæmɪtər] **N** *Liter* hexamètre *m*

hey [heɪ] **INT 1** *(to attract attention)* hé!, holà! **2 h. presto!** passez muscade!, le tour est joué!; **h., that's a good idea!** hé, c'est une bonne idée, ça!

heyday ['heɪdeɪ] **N** apogée *m*; **in its h. it was one of the busiest ports in the world** à son heure de gloire, c'était l'un des ports les plus importants du monde; **to be in the h. of youth** être dans *ou* à la fleur de l'âge

HFEA [eɪtʃefiː'eɪ] **N** *Br (abbr* **Human Fertilization and Embryology Authority)** = organisme *m* chargé de réglementer les traitements de la stérilité et la recherche en embryologie

HGH [eɪtʃdʒiː'eɪtʃ] **N** *Biol (abbr* **human growth hormone)** hormone *f* de croissance

HGV [eɪtʃdʒiː'viː] **N** *Br Admin (abbr* **heavy goods vehicle)** poids lourd *m*
▸▸ **H. licence** permis *m* PL

hi [haɪ] **INT 1** *Fam (hello)* salut! **2** *(to attract attention)* hé!, là-bas!, ohé!

hiatus, *pl* **hiatuses** [haɪ'eɪtəs, -əsɪz] **N 1** *Fml (gap in series, text etc)* lacune *f* **2** *Fml (pause in conversation etc)* silence *m*; *(pause in negotiation etc)* interruption *f*, **apart from a h.**

between **1993** and **1995** mis à part une interruption entre 1993 et 1995 **3** *Gram* hiatus *m*
▸ ▸ *Med* **h. hernia** hernie *f* hiatale

hibernate [ˈhaɪbəneɪt] **vi** hiberner

hibernation [haɪbəˈneɪʃən] **N** *also Comput* hibernation *f*; **to go into h.** hiberner

hibiscus [hɪˈbɪskəs] **N** *(plant)* ketmie *f*, hibiscus *m*

hiccup, hiccough [ˈhɪkʌp] **N 1** hoquet *m*; **to have (the) hiccups** avoir le hoquet **2** *Fig (problem)* problème *m*, *Fam* hic *m*; **there's been some sort of h. with the delivery** il y a eu un hic à la livraison
vi hoqueter

hick [hɪk] *Am Fam* **N** paysan *m*, rustaud *m*
ADJ a h. town un bled

hickey [ˈhɪkɪ] **N** *Am Fam* **1** *(spot)* bouton *m*; *(love bite)* suçon *m* **2** *(gadget)* machin *m*, truc *m*

hickory [ˈhɪkərɪ] **N** *(tree or wood)* noyer *m* (blanc) d'Amérique, hickory *m*

hid **pt** *see* **hide**[1]

hidden [ˈhɪd(ə)n] **pp** *see* **hide**[1]
ADJ *(difficulty, treasure etc)* caché; **she has h. talents** elle a des talents cachés
▸ ▸ **h. camera** caméra *f* cachée, caméra invisible; *Fin* **h. cost** coût *m* caché; *Com* **h. defects** défauts *mpl* ou vices *mpl* cachés; *Com* **h. extras** dépenses *fpl* supplémentaires inattendues; **no h. extras** garanti tout compris; *Comput* **h. file** fichier *m* caché; *Fig* **h. hand** influence *f* occulte; *Fin* **h. reserves** réserve *f* latente; **I have h. reserves** j'ai encore des réserves

hide[1] [haɪd] **N** *Br (place for hunter etc)* affût *m*, cachette *f*
vt *(pt* **hid** [hɪd], *pp* **hidden** [ˈhɪd(ə)n]) cacher; *(feelings, emotions)* dissimuler; **to h. sth from sb** cacher qch à qn; *(not divulge information)* taire qch à qn; **I've got nothing to h.** je n'ai rien à cacher; **to h. one's face** se cacher le visage; **where has she hidden herself?** où est-elle allée se cacher *ou Fam* se fourrer?; **they hid him from the police** ils l'ont caché pour que la police ne le trouve pas; **to h. sth from sight** soustraire qch aux regards; **trees h. the house from sight** les arbres cachent la maison; **clouds hid the sun** des nuages voilaient le soleil; *Fig* **to h. one's light under a bushel** cacher son talent; *Fig* **he doesn't exactly h. his light under a bushel** il ne se prend pas pour le quart de la moitié d'un citron, ce n'est pas la modestie qui l'étouffe
vi se cacher *(from sb* de qn); **have you been hiding from me?** tu te caches?; **she was hiding in a corner** *(of shy person)* elle restait dans son coin; **to h. behind an excuse/statistics** prétexter une excuse/les statistiques; *Fig* **to h. behind sb** se réfugier derrière qn
▸ **hide away** **vi** = **hide**[1] **vi**
vt sep = **hide**[1] **vt**
▸ **hide out** **vi** *(be in hiding)* se cacher, se terrer

hide[2] **N** *(skin) (of animal)* peau *f*, dépouille *f*; *Com (leather)* cuir *m*; *Fam* **to save one's h.** sauver sa peau; *Fam* **to tan sb's h.** tanner le cuir à qn; *Fam* **I haven't seen h. nor hair of her** je ne l'ai pas vue du tout

hide-and-seek, *Am* **hide-and-go-seek**
N cache-cache *m*; **to play h.** jouer à cache-cache

hideaway [ˈhaɪdəweɪ] **N** cachette *f*, *Fam* planque *f*

hidebound [ˈhaɪdbaʊnd] **ADJ** *(person)* aux vues étroites, plein de préjugés; *(attitude)* rigide; **the country's h. legal profession** les hommes de loi conservateurs et bornés de ce pays

hideous [ˈhɪdɪəs] **ADJ** *(appearance etc)* hi-

deux, affreux, effroyable; *(crime)* horrible, odieux; **what a h. painting!** quelle peinture abominable!

hideously [ˈhɪdɪəslɪ] **ADV** hideusement, affreusement

hideousness [ˈhɪdɪəsnɪs] **N** laideur *f*; **the h. of his wounds/the crime** ses blessures abominables/le crime abominable

hide-out **N** cachette *f*, *Fam* planque *f*; **so this is your h.!** alors, c'est ici que tu te caches!

hidey-hole [ˈhaɪdɪhəʊl] **N** *Fam* cachette *f*

hiding[1] [ˈhaɪdɪŋ] **N** **to go into h.** se cacher; **to be in h.** se tenir caché, se cacher; **to live in h.** vivre dans la clandestinité; **to come out of h.** sortir de sa cachette; *(stop living in hiding)* sortir de la clandestinité
▸ ▸ **h. place** cachette *f*

hiding[2] **N** *Fam (beating)* raclée *f*, rossée *f*, volée *f*; **to give sb a good h.** donner une raclée à qn; **to be on a h. to nothing** n'avoir aucune chance (de réussir)

hierarchic(al) [haɪəˈrɑːkɪk, -ɪk(ə)l] **ADJ** hiérarchique; **in h. order** par ordre hiérarchique

hierarchy [ˈhaɪərɑːkɪ] **N** hiérarchie *f*

hieroglyph [ˈhaɪərəglɪf] **N** hiéroglyphe *m*

hieroglyphic [haɪərəˈglɪfɪk] **ADJ** hiéroglyphique

hieroglyphics [haɪərəˈglɪfɪks] **N** *(system)* hiéroglyphes *mpl*; *(characters)* signes *mpl* hiéroglyphiques; *Fig Fam (bad handwriting)* hiéroglyphes VOIR GRAMMAIRE A10

hifalutin(g) [haɪfəˈluːtɪn, -tɪŋ] **ADJ** *Fam* = **highfalutin**

hi-fi [ˈhaɪfaɪ] **N** hi-fi *f inv*, *(stereo system)* chaîne *f* (hi-fi)
ADJ hi-fi *inv*
▸ ▸ **h. system** chaîne (hi-fi)

higgledy-piggledy [ˈhɪg(ə)ldɪˈpɪg(ə)ldɪ] **ADV** *Fam* en pagaïe, pêle-mêle

---

HIGH [haɪ]

ADJ haut **1, 3, 7**	▪ élevé **1, 2, 4**
▪ grand **2**	▪ noble **4** ▪ aigu **7**
ADV haut **1**	▪ en haut **1**
N haut **1**	

ADJ 1 haut, élevé; **built on h. ground** construit sur un terrain élevé; **this house is much higher (up) than the village** cette maison est située à beaucoup plus haute altitude que le village; **the highest mountain in the country** la plus haute montagne du pays; **wall two metres h.** mur haut de deux mètres, mur d'une hauteur de deux mètres, mur de deux mètres de hauteur; **at h. water** *or* **tide** à marée haute; **h. neck** *(on garment)* col montant; **h. cheekbones** pommettes saillantes; **with one's head h.** la tête haute

2 *(in number, degree) (price)* élevé; *(percentage)* gros; *(speed)* grand; **to fetch a h. price** se vendre cher; **to pay a h. price** payer le prix fort; **to make a higher bid** faire une offre supérieure, surenchérir; **highest bidder** surenchérisseur *m*; *Cards, Fig* **to play for h. stakes** jouer gros (jeu); **ore with a h. mineral content** minerai à haute teneur; **cheese is h. in calcium** le fromage est riche en calcium; **h. latitudes** hautes latitudes; **to have a h. opinion of sb** avoir une haute opinion de qn, tenir qn en haute estime; **of the highest importance** de première importance; **to be h. farce** tourner à la farce; **h. quality** bonne qualité; *Com* **h. value added** à haute valeur ajoutée; **a h. fever** une forte *ou* grosse fièvre; **h. winds** vents forts

3 *(superior, advanced)* haut; **of h. rank** de haut rang; **she is h. up in the government** elle est haut placée dans le gouvernement; **to be in a h. position** être haut placé; **she's**

acting **all h. and mighty** elle agit avec beaucoup d'arrogance; **higher posts** postes *ou* emplois supérieurs; **higher mathematics** mathématiques *fpl* supérieures

4 *(noble) (principles, character etc)* élevé, noble; **h. ideals** idéaux élevés; **she has very h. moral standards** elle a des principes (de moralité) très élevés

5 *(strong)* **h. colour** couleur *f* vive

6 *(good)* **to be in h. spirits** être plein d'entrain; **our spirits were h.** nous avions le moral; **the h. life** la vie mondaine; **the h. point of the match** le point culminant du match; **one of the h. points of the evening** un des points forts de la soirée

7 *Mus etc* **h. voice** voix élevée *ou* haute; *(thin)* voix grêle; **h. note** note *f* aiguë; *Fig* point *m* culminant

8 **h. summer** plein été; **it's h. time he went to school** il est grand temps qu'il aille à l'école; *Br Com* **the h. season** la haute saison

9 *(meat etc)* avancé; *(bad)* avarié; *(game)* faisandé; **to get h.** *(of game)* se faisander; **to smell h.** avoir une forte odeur

10 *Fam (person)* **to be h.** *(on drugs)* planer; *Fig (euphoric)* être dans un état d'euphorie; **h. on cocaine** défoncé à la cocaïne; *Fig* **they were h. on success** ils ne se sentaient plus après ce succès

11 *Fam (lively)* **to have a h. old time** faire la noce

12 **h. and dry** *(of ship)* échoué au plein; *(pulled up on beach etc)* à sec; *Fam* **to be left h. and dry** *(of person)* être laissé en plan

ADV 1 *(to aim, jump etc)* haut, en haut; **higher (up)** plus haut; **higher and higher** de plus en plus haut; **to rise h. in public esteem** monter très haut dans l'estime du public; **to hunt h. and low for sth** chercher qch partout; **higher up the river** en amont

2 *(in bidding etc)* **to go as h. as £2,000** aller jusqu'à 2 000 livres; *Cards etc* **to play** *or* **stake h.** jouer gros jeu

3 **to run h.** *(of sea)* être grosse *ou* houleuse; *(of prices)* être élevés; **feelings are running h.** les passions s'exacerbent; *(between countries)* la tension monte; **tempers were running h.** les esprits s'échauffaient

4 **to have memory loaded h.** avoir chargé en mémoire haute

N 1 *(high point)* **highs and lows** *(of share prices etc)* hausses *fpl* et baisses *fpl*; *(of career etc)* hauts *mpl* et bas *mpl*; **prices have reached a new h.** les prix ont atteint un nouveau maximum

2 *Met* aire *f* anticyclonique

3 *Fam* **to be on a h.** *(from drugs etc)* planer; *(from success etc)* être sur son petit nuage

4 *Rel* **the Most H.** le Très-Haut, le Tout-Puissant; **on h.** en haut, dans le ciel; *Rel, Fig* **from on h.** d'en haut
▸ ▸ *Rel* **h. altar** maître-autel *m*, *pl* maîtres-autels; **h. beam** *Am Aut* feux *mpl* de route; *(in gym)* poutre *f*; *Med* **h. blood pressure** hypertension *f*; *Br Rel* **H. Church** Haute Église *f*; *Mil* **h. command** haut commandement *m*; **H. Commission** = représentation *f* officielle d'un pays, équivalente à une ambassade; **H. Commissioner** = représentant *m* officiel d'un pays, équivalent à un ambassadeur; *Law* **H. Court** Tribunal *m* de grande instance; *Com, Mktg* **h. end** *(of market)* haut *m*; *Mil* **h. explosive** explosif *m* puissant; **h. fashion** haute couture *f*; **h. fidelity** haute-fidélité *f*; *Electron* **h. frequency** haute fréquence *f*; **H. German** haut allemand *m*; **h. hat** *Mus* cymbales *fpl*; *Old-fashioned Fam (person)* arrogant *m*, snob *mf*; *Cin, TV* petit pied *m* de caméra, pied de sol; **h. heels** talons *mpl* hauts; *Sport* **h. jump** saut *m* en hauteur; *Sport* **h. jumper** sauteur, -euse *(qui fait du saut en hauteur)*; *Rel* **H. Mass** grand-messe *f*, *pl* grand(s)-messe, grande messe *f*; *Comput* **h. memory** mémoire *f* haute; *Comput* **h. me-**

mory area zone *f* de mémoire haute; **h. noon** plein midi *m*; *Rel* **h. priest** grand prêtre *m*; *Fig* **the h. priests of fashion** les grands noms de la mode; *Rel* **h. priestess** grande prêtresse *f*, **h. school** *(in UK)* = établissement *m* d'enseignement secondaire regroupant collège et lycée; *(in US)* lycée *m*; *Naut* **the h. seas** la haute mer; *Br Admin* **H. Sheriff** = dans les comtés anglais et gallois, représentant *m* officiel du monarque; **h. society** haute société *f*, grand monde *m*; *Br* **the h. street** *(street)* la grand-rue, la rue principale; *(shops)* les commerçants *mpl*, le commerce; **the h. table** la table d'honneur; *Sch, Univ* la table des professeurs *(au réfectoire)*; *Br* **h. tea** = repas *m* léger pris en début de soirée et accompagné de thé; **h. tech** haute technologie *f*; **h. treason** haute trahison *f*; *Elec* **h. voltage** haute tension *f*, **h. wire** corde *f* raide *ou* de funambule

high-ability ADJ **h. children** enfants *mpl* surdoués

high-angle shot N *Cin* plan *m* en plongée

highball ['haɪbɔːl] N = whisky-soda *m* avec de la glace servi dans un grand verre

highborn ['haɪbɔːn] ADJ de haute naissance

highboy ['haɪbɔɪ] N *Am (furniture)* commode *f* haute

highbrow ['haɪbraʊ] *Fam* N intello *mf* ADJ intello

highchair ['haɪtʃeər] N *(for baby)* chaise *f* haute

high-class ADJ *(merchandise etc)* de premier ordre, de première qualité; *(hotel)* de grande classe; *(prostitute)* de luxe

high-definition TV N télévision *f* haute définition

high-density ADJ **1** *Comput (disk, graphics, printing)* haute densité; *(in high-rise buildings)* grands ensembles *mpl* **2** *(housing)* à forte concentration de population

high-diving N plongeon *m* de haut vol, haut vol *m*

high-end ADJ *(top-of-the-range)* haut de gamme

Higher ['haɪər] N *Scot* = diplôme *m* de fin d'études secondaires sanctionnant une matière déterminée

higher court N *Law* instance *f* supérieure

higher education N enseignement *m* supérieur

higher-income group N groupe *m* de contribuables à revenus élevés

highfalutin(g) [haɪfə'luːtɪn, -ɪŋ] ADJ *Fam (style, language)* ampoulé, prétentieux, pompeux

high-fibre ADJ *Culin* riche en fibres

high-fidelity ADJ de haute fidélité

high-five N *Fam* = tape *f* amicale donnée dans la paume de quelqu'un, bras levé, en signe de victoire

high-flier, high-flyer N *(successful person)* ambitieux, -euse; *(company)* société *f* qui va de l'avant; **she's a real h.** elle ira loin

high-flown ADJ *(style, language)* ampoulé, pompeux

high-flying ADJ *(successful)* ambitieux, qui ira loin

high-frequency ADJ *Elec (current)* à haute fréquence; *(amplifier)* de haute fréquence

high-grade ADJ *(ore etc)* à haute teneur; *(merchandise)* de première qualité, de (premier) choix; *Aut* **h.** *Br* **petrol** *or Am* **gasoline** supercarburant *m*

high-handed [haɪ'hændɪd] ADJ *(person, behaviour etc)* trop autoritaire, tyrannique; **was there any need to be so h. about it?** était-il nécessaire de te montrer si autoritaire?

high-heeled shoes [haɪ'hiːld] NPL chaussures *fpl* à hauts talons, talons *mpl* hauts

high-income ADJ à haut revenu
▶▶**h. group** groupe *m* des gros salaires, groupe des salaires élevés

high-involvement ADJ *Mktg (purchasing)* à forte participation des consommateurs

highjack, highjacker *etc* = **hijack, hijacker** *etc*

highland ['haɪlənd] N pays *m* montagneux; **the Highlands** *(of Scotland)* les Highlands *mpl* ADJ des montagnes; *(from Scotland)* des Highlands
▶▶**H. cattle** race *f* bovine des Highlands

Highland Games

En Écosse, il s'agit d'une sorte de kermesse locale en plein air où se déroulent simultanément toutes sortes de concours (danse, cornemuse) et d'épreuves sportives (courses, lancer du marteau, mais aussi "tossing the caber", "tug o' war" etc).

highlander ['haɪləndər] N montagnard, -arde; **H.** *(from Scotland)* Highlander *m*, habitant, -ante de la Haute Écosse; *Mil* = soldat *m* d'un régiment écossais

high-level ADJ *(discussion)* à haut niveau; *(official, officer)* de haut niveau
▶▶*Comput* **h. language** langage *m* évolué *or* de haut niveau; *Comput* **h. programming language** langage *m* de programmation évolué

highlight ['haɪlaɪt] N **1** *(important moment)* grand moment *m*; *(of celebration etc)* clou *m*; *(of match etc)* point *m* culminant; *TV* **they didn't show the whole match, just the highlights** ils n'ont pas retransmis tout le match, seulement les meilleurs moments; **the news highlights** les grands titres de l'actualité **2** *Phot* rehaut *m*; **highlights** *(in a painting)* rehauts *mpl*, clairs *mpl* **3** **highlights** *(in hair)* reflets *mpl*, mèches *fpl* **4** *Comput* relief *m* VT **1** *(problem, need)* souligner **2** *(with coloured marker)* surligner **3** *Comput (text block)* sélectionner; **to be highlighted** *(of text)* apparaître en surimpression *ou* en surbrillance

highlighted ['haɪlaɪtɪd] ADJ *Comput* lumineux, contrasté

highlighter ['haɪlaɪtər] N *(pen)* surligneur *m*, stylo *m* surligneur, marqueur *m* surligneur

highly ['haɪlɪ] ADV **1** **h. placed official** haut fonctionnaire *m*; **to be h. placed** être haut placé; **his services are h. paid** on paie très cher ses services; **to think h. of sb** avoir une haute opinion de qn **2** *(extremely)* fort, très, fortement; **h. amusing** très amusant; **h. coloured** *(painting, style)* haut en couleur; *(account, report)* coloré, haut en couleur; **h. displeased** fort mécontent; **h. seasoned** fortement assaisonné; **to be h. sexed** avoir une forte libido; **h. strung** *(person)* très sensible, *Fam* hypersensible

high-margin product N produit *m* à forte marge

high-minded ADJ aux sentiments nobles, généreux; *(action, nature)* magnanime; **to be too h.** avoir trop de principes

high-mindedness ['haɪ'maɪndɪdnɪs] N noblesse *f* de sentiments, grandeur *f* d'âme; *(of action etc)* magnanimité *f*

Highness ['haɪnɪs] N *(title)* Altesse *f*; **His/ Her Royal H.** son Altesse Royale

high-octane ADJ *(fuel)* à indice d'octane élevé

high-performance ADJ *(car, engine)*, *Comput (chip)* (à) haute performance

high-pitched ADJ **1** *(sound)* aigu, -uë; *(voice)* aigu, criard **2** *Constr (roof)* à forte inclinaison, à forte pente

high-powered ADJ *(engine, car, telescope)* très puissant; *(microscope)* à fort grossissement; *Fig (person)* dynamique et compétent; **a h. businessman** un homme d'affaires de poids; **she is something h. in the City** elle a un poste important à la Cité de Londres; **a h. job** un poste très important, *Fam* un super boulot

high-pressure ADJ **1** *Tech (cylinder, machine)* à haute pression, à haute tension; *Met (area)* anticyclonique, de hautes pressions **2** *Pej (salesman)* agressif

high-principled ADJ aux principes élevés

high-profile ADJ *(politician etc)* en vue; *(company)* connu; *(campaign etc)* de grande envergure

high-quality ADJ haut de gamme

high-resolution ADJ *Phot, TV etc (screen, graphics)* à haute résolution

high-rise N tour *f*
▶▶**h. building** tour

high-risk ADJ *(occupation, category etc)* à haut(s) risque(s)

highroad ['haɪrəʊd] N **1** *Old-fashioned* grand-route *f* **2** *Fig* **on the h. to success** sur la route du succès

high-sounding ADJ *(title)* pompeux, ronflant

high-speed ADJ ultra-rapide; *(machine)* à marche rapide; *(engine)*, *Phot* grande vitesse; *Comput* à grande vitesse
▶▶*Comput* **h. access** accès *m* rapide; *Comput* **h. bus** bus *m* rapide; **h. camera** caméra *f* grande vitesse; **h. printer** imprimante *f* rapide; *Rail* **h. train** train *m* à grande vitesse, TGV *m*

high-spirited ADJ plein d'ardeur *ou* de feu; *(horse)* fougueux

high-street ADJ **a h. bank** une banque populaire, une banque de dépôt; **h. shops** commerces *mpl*; **prices in the h. shops** prix dans le commerce

high-strung ADJ *(character, person)* très sensible

hightail ['haɪteɪl] VT *esp Am Fam* **to h. it** se tirer en vitesse; **he hightailed it out of town** il a fichu le camp de la ville; **he hightailed it back to the ranch** il est retourné au ranch en quatrième vitesse

high-tech ['haɪtek] ADJ, N = **hi-tech**

high-tensile steel N acier *m* à haute résistance élastique

high-tension ADJ *Elec (wire, tension, coil)* (à) haute tension

high-up *Fam* N gros bonnet *m*, grosse légume *f*
ADJ *(judge, politician etc)* haut placé

high-viscosity ADJ *(oil)* à haute viscosité

highway ['haɪweɪ] N **1** *esp Am (main road)* route *f* nationale, autoroute *f*; **highways and byways** chemins *mpl* et sentiers *mpl*; *Fam* **that's h. robbery!** c'est du vol! **2** *Br Admin (public road)* voie *f* publique
▶▶*Br Aut* **the H. Code** le code de la route; *Br* **h. engineer** ≃ ingénieur *m* des Ponts et Chaussées; *Am* **h. patrol** police *f* de la route; *Am* **h. patrolman** membre *m* de la police de la route

highwayman, *pl* **highwaymen** ['haɪweɪmən] N *Hist* voleur *m* de grand(s) chemin(s)

high-yield ADJ *Fin (bond, security)* à rendement élevé

hijack ['haɪdʒæk] N détournement *m* VT *(plane in flight)* détourner; *(vehicle)* s'emparer de force de; *Fig* **the government hi-**

jacked the opposition's policy le gouvernement s'est approprié la politique de l'opposition

hijacker ['haɪdʒækər] N (of aircraft) pirate mf de l'air; (of vehicle) pirate de la route; the hijackers of the Israeli Boeing les pirates de l'air du Boeing israélien

hijacking ['haɪdʒækɪŋ] N (of aircraft) (general practice) piraterie f aérienne; (single incident) détournement m; (of vehicle) = vol m à main armée d'un véhicule et de son contenu

hike [haɪk] N 1 (walk) (longue) promenade f à pied, randonnée f; to go on or for a h. faire une (longue) promenade à pied, faire une randonnée; Am Fam he can take a h.! il peut aller se faire voir! 2 (in interest rates etc) augmentation f, hausse f
▸ VI (walk) faire une (longue) promenade à pied, faire une randonnée
▸ hike up VT SEP (trousers, skirt) remonter; (interest rates) augmenter; to h. oneself up on to sth se hisser jusqu'à qch

hiker ['haɪkər] N randonneur, -euse (à pied)

hiking ['haɪkɪŋ] N randonnée f pédestre; to go on a h. holiday partir en vacances faire de la randonnée
▸▸ h. boots chaussures fpl de marche

hilarious [hɪ'leərɪəs] ADJ (very amusing) hilarant, Fam marrant; it was h.! c'était à se tordre (de rire)!

hilariously [hɪ'leərɪəslɪ] ADV (unlikely, old-fashioned looking) à vous faire tordre de rire; (to laugh) aux éclats; it was h. funny c'était à se tordre (de rire)

hilariousness [hɪ'leərɪəsnɪs] N (of scene, joke) caractère m hilarant

hilarity [hɪ'lærɪtɪ] N hilarité f

hill [hɪl] N 1 colline f, (sloping ground) coteau m; up h. and down dale par monts et par vaux; Mil h. 304 la cote 304; Fig Fam to be over the h. commencer à se faire vieux; Am Fam it ain't worth a h. of beans, it doesn't amount to a h. of beans (of opinion etc) ça ne vaut pas tripette; to be as old as the hills (of joke, person etc) dater de ou remonter à Mathusalem 2 (on road) côte f, (uphill) montée f, (downhill) descente f, steep h. (uphill) montée abrupte; (downhill) descente abrupte
▸▸ h. country pays m de collines; Aut h. start démarrage m en côte; h. station (in India) station f de montagne

hillbilly ['hɪlbɪlɪ] N Am Fam Pej villageois, -oise un peu rustaud(e)
▸▸ h. music folk m (des Appalaches) (du sud-est des États-Unis)

hill-climbing N randonnée f (en pays vallonné); (of vehicle) montée f

hillfarm ['hɪlfɑːm] N ferme f à flanc de coteau

hilliness ['hɪlɪnɪs] N vallonnement m

hillock ['hɪlək] N petite colline f, (smaller) butte f, tertre m

hillside ['hɪlsaɪd] N flanc m de coteau, coteau m

hilltop ['hɪltɒp] N sommet m de (la) colline

hill-walker N randonneur, -euse (en pays vallonné)

hill-walking N randonnée f (en pays vallonné)

hilly ['hɪlɪ] ADJ (country) montagneux; (terrain) accidenté; (road) montueux, à fortes pentes

hilt [hɪlt] N (of sword) poignée f, (of dagger, knife etc) manche m; Fig right up to the h. jusqu'au bout; to back or support sb to the h. soutenir qn sans réserve ou à fond; mortgaged up to the h. (person) endetté jusqu'au cou, qui doit rembourser des emprunts énormes; (property) fortement hypothéqué

him [hɪm] PERS PRON 1 (direct) le; (before a vowel sound) l'; I hate h. je le déteste; do you love h.? l'aimez-vous?; have you seen h.? l'avez-vous vu?; I remember h. je me souviens de lui VOIR GRAMMAIRE A27–8; A43
2 (indirect and reflexive, after prepositions) lui; I shall tell h. so je le lui dirai; tell h. I have come dites-lui que je suis là; we are thinking of h. nous pensons à lui; he took his luggage with h. il a pris ses bagages avec lui; he closed the door behind h. il a fermé la porte derrière lui; I object to h. borrowing the car je m'oppose à ce qu'il emprunte la voiture
3 (as complement of verb to be) it's h.! c'est lui!
4 (stressed) lui; Lit (with dem force) celui; we can forgive his parents but not him nous pouvons pardonner à ses parents, mais pas à lui; who better than h. to break the news? qui, mieux que lui, pourrait annoncer la nouvelle?; Lit to h. who should take offence at this I would say … à celui qui s'en offenserait, je dirais …

Himalayan [hɪmə'leɪən] ADJ himalayen, -enne

Himalayas [hɪmə'leɪəz] NPL the H. (les) montagnes fpl de) l'Himalaya m

himbo ['hɪmbəʊ] N Fam beau mec m pas très futé

himself [hɪm'self] PERS PRON VOIR GRAMMAIRE A29–30 1 (emphatic) lui-même; he doesn't want to do it h. il ne veut pas le faire lui-même; he's not (quite) h. again yet (after illness) il n'est pas encore complètement remis; he's not h. today il n'est pas lui-même aujourd'hui, il n'est pas dans son état normal aujourd'hui; I spoke to the author h. j'ai parlé à l'auteur lui-même ou en personne
2 (reflexive) se; he hurt h. il s'est fait mal; he lives by h. il vit seul; 'well, well!', he said to h. 'eh bien!', se dit-il; he kept one for h. il s'en est gardé un/une VOIR GRAMMAIRE B28–9
3 (used impersonally) soi(-même); everyone for h. chacun pour soi

hind¹ [haɪnd] N (female deer) biche f
▸▸ h. calf faon m femelle

hind² ADJ de derrière, postérieur; h. legs/feet pattes fpl de derrière; Fam to get up on one's h. legs (of person) se lever

hinder¹ ['hɪndər] VT 1 (impede) gêner, embarrasser; (movement) entraver; (delay) retarder 2 (prevent) empêcher, retenir (from doing de faire)

hinder² ['haɪndər] ADJ de derrière, postérieur

Hindi ['hɪndɪ] N Ling hindi m

hindmost ['haɪndməʊst] ADJ dernier; Prov devil take the h.! chacun pour soi; it's a case of devil take the h. vu les circonstances, c'est chacun pour soi

hindquarters ['haɪndkwɔːtəz] NPL arrière-train m

hindrance ['hɪndrəns] N empêchement m, obstacle m, entrave f, he is a h. il gêne; they were more of a h. than a help ils nous/les/etc gênaient plus qu'ils ne nous/les/etc aidaient

hindsight ['haɪndsaɪt] N recul m, sagesse f que donne le recul; with (the benefit of) h. après coup, avec le recul; with all the advantages of h. avec tous les avantages que donne le recul

Hindu [hɪn'duː] ADJ hindou N Hindou, -oue

Hinduism ['hɪnduːɪz(ə)m] N hindouisme m

Hindustan [hɪndʊ'stɑːn] N Geog Hindoustan m

Hindustani [hɪndʊ'stɑːnɪ] Ling N hindoustani m
ADJ hindi

hinge [hɪndʒ] N charnière f, (of door) gond m; the door came off its hinges la porte est sortie de ses gonds; (stamp) h. charnière VT (mount on hinges) (door etc) monter sur ses gonds; (put hinges on) (box etc) mettre des charnières à
VI Tech tourner, pivoter (on autour de); to h. forward (of seat etc) basculer vers l'avant
▸ hinge on, hinge upon VT INSEP (depend on) dépendre de; everything hinges on his answer tout dépend de sa réponse

hinged [hɪndʒd] ADJ (door, lid etc) à charnière(s); h. flap (of counter) abattant m; (of aircraft) volet m articulé

hinky ['hɪŋkɪ] ADJ Am Fam (suspect) louche

hint [hɪnt] N 1 (allusion) allusion f (indirecte); broad h. allusion évidente ou claire; gentle h. allusion discrète; to give or drop sb a h. toucher un mot à qn; to know how to take a h. comprendre à demi-mot; we can take a h. nous avons compris l'allusion; he can't take a h. il faut lui mettre les points sur les i
2 (sign) signe m, indication f, suggestion f, not a h. of surprise pas une ombre de surprise; not the slightest h. of … pas le moindre soupçon de …; there was a h. of garlic in the stew il y avait un soupçon d'ail dans le ragoût
3 (piece of advice) petit conseil m; the book is full of useful hints on how to save money le livre est plein de tuyaux pour faire des économies; can you give me some hints? (about how I should proceed) pouvez-vous me donner quelques conseils?; (about the right answer) pouvez-vous me mettre sur la voie?
VT to h. that … insinuer que …; to h. to sb that … laisser entendre à qn que …
▸ hint at VT INSEP faire (une) allusion à

hinterland ['hɪntəlænd] N arrière-pays m

hip¹ [hɪp] N 1 Anat hanche f, to have narrow/wide hips avoir les hanches fines/larges; he stood with his hands on his hips il était debout, les mains sur les hanches; esp Am Fig he shoots from the h. réagir de façon impulsive; 2 Constr arêtier m, arête f
▸▸ Br h. bath bain m de siège; h. flask flasque f, Anat h. joint articulation f de la hanche; h.measurement tour m de hanches; Constr h. piece (of roof) arêtier, arête; Br h. pocket poche f revolver; Constr h. rafter (of roof) arêtier, arête; Med h. replacement (operation) mise f en place d'une prothèse de la hanche; h. size tour m de hanches

hip² N (fruit) cynor(r)hodon m, fruit m du rosier

hip³ ADJ Fam (trendy) branché; to be h. to sth être branché sur qch

hip⁴ INT h.! h.!, hurray! hip! hip! hourra!

hipbone ['hɪpbəʊn] N os m iliaque

hip-huggers ['hɪp'hʌgəz] NPL Am = hipster 2

-hipped [hɪpt] SUFF broad-h. aux hanches fortes; narrow-h. aux hanches fines ou étroites

hippie ['hɪpɪ] ADJ, N hippie mf; Hum ageing h. vieillissant(e) hippie

hippo ['hɪpəʊ] N Fam hippopotame m

Hippocrates [hɪ'pɒkrətiːz] N Hippocrate

Hippocratic [hɪpə'krætɪk] ADJ Med hippocratique
▸▸ H. oath serment m d'Hippocrate

hippodrome ['hɪpədrəʊm] N hippodrome m; (not for racing) arène f

hippopotamus, pl hippopotamuses, hippopotami [hɪpə'pɒtəməs, -məsɪz, -maɪ] N hippopotame m

hippy¹ ['hɪpɪ] ADJ (with large hips) aux hanches larges

hippy² ADJ, N = hippie

hipster ['hɪpstər] N **1** *esp Am Old-fashioned* beatnik *mf* (*des années 40 et 50*) **2** *Br* **hipsters** (*trousers*) pantalon *m* (à) taille basse

hire ['haɪər] N **1** *Br* (*of car, room*) location *f*; **for h.** (*sign on taxi*) libre; **for** *or* **on h.** à louer **2** *Am* (*of labour*) embauche *f*; (*of servant*) louage *m* **3** *Lit* (*wages*) salaire *m*, gages *mpl* ▸ VT **1** *Br* (*car etc*) louer **2** (*take on*) (*lawyer, private detective etc*) s'assurer les services de, engager **3** *Am* (*worker*) embaucher, engager; (*domestic staff*) prendre à son service ▸ VI *esp Am* (*take on workers*) embaucher
▸▸ *Br* **h. car** voiture *f* de location; **h. charges** (frais *mpl ou* prix *m* de) location
▸ **hire out** VT SEP *Br* louer, donner en location (**to sb** à qn)

hired ['haɪəd] ADJ *Br* (*car etc*) de location
▸▸ **h. gun** tueur *m* à gages; **h. hand** ouvrier *m* agricole; **h. killer** tueur à gages; **h. man** *Am* (*servant*) domestique *m*; (*farmworker*) ouvrier agricole

hireling ['haɪəlɪŋ] N *Pej* laquais *m*

hire-purchase N *Br Com* location-vente *f*, **to buy sth on h.** acheter qch en location-vente
▸▸ **h. agreement** contrat *m* de location-vente

hi-res ['haɪrez] ADJ *Comput Fam* (*abbr* **high-resolution**) (à) haute résolution

hiring ['haɪ(ə)rɪŋ] N **1** *Br* (*of a car etc*) location *f* **2** (*of staff etc*) embauche *f*; *Fam* **he does the h. and firing** il est chargé des embauches et des licenciements

hirsute [hɜː'sjuːt] ADJ *Lit* hirsute, velu, poilu

his [hɪz] POSS ADJ son, *f* sa, *pl* ses; **one of h. friends** un de ses amis, un ami à lui; **h. father and mother** son père et sa mère; *Admin* ses père et mère; **h. own son** son propre fils; **he has hurt h. hand** il s'est fait mal à la main; **h. eyes are brown** il a les yeux bruns; **I object to h. borrowing the car** je m'oppose à ce qu'il emprunte la voiture VOIR GRAMMAIRE A30; A43; B21–2

POSS PRON le sien, la sienne, *pl* les siens, les siennes; **he took my pen as well as h.** il a pris mon stylo avec le sien; **this book is h.** ce livre est à lui, c'est son livre à lui; **a friend of h.** un de ses amis, un ami à lui; **it is no business of h.** cela ne le regarde pas; **it's no business of h. to tell me what to do** ce n'est pas à lui de me dire quoi faire VOIR GRAMMAIRE A30; B21–2

Hispanic [hɪs'pænɪk] ADJ hispanique N *Am* Hispano-Américain, -aine

Hispano-American [hɪ'spænəʊə'merɪk(ə)n] ADJ hispano-américain N Hispano-Américain, -aine

hiss [hɪs] N **1** (*sound*) sifflement *m*; *Theat etc* sifflets *mpl*; (*on tape*) bruit *m* parasite, bruit de piste **2** *Ling* sifflante *f*
VT & VI (*of person, steam, geese etc*) siffler; (*of steam, gas*) chuinter; **to h. (at) an actor** siffler un acteur; **to be hissed** être sifflé

hissing ['hɪsɪŋ] ADJ **h. noise** sifflement *m*; (*of gas*) chuintement *m* N sifflement *m*; (*of gas*) chuintement *m*

hissy fit ['hɪsɪ] N *Fam* **to have a h.** faire une crise

histamine ['hɪstəmɪn, -miːn] N *Physiol* histamine *f*

histogram ['hɪstəgræm] N histogramme *m*

historian [hɪs'tɔːrɪən] N historien, -ienne

historic [hɪs'tɒrɪk] ADJ **1** historique; **h. event/moment** événement/moment historique **2** *Gram* past **h.** passé *m* simple VOIR GRAMMAIRE B30
▸▸ **h. building** monument *m* historique

Il faut noter que les adjectifs **historic** et **historical** ne sont pas interchangeables. **Historic** signifie **important d'un point de vue historique** alors que **historical** signifie **qui se rapporte à l'histoire**.

historical [hɪs'tɒrɪk(ə)l] ADJ (*character, event, novel*) historique; **h. background** contexte *m* historique; **of purely h. interest** d'intérêt purement historique; **h. record/account** historique *m*; **h. research** recherche *f* en histoire
▸▸ *Acct* **h. cost accounting** comptabilité *f* par coûts historiques; **h. linguistics** linguistique *f* diachronique

Voir note ci-dessus.

historically [hɪs'tɒrɪklɪ] ADV historiquement

historiographer [hɪstɔːrɪ'ɒgrəfər] N historiographe *mf*

historiography [hɪstɔːrɪ'ɒgrəfɪ] N historiographie *f*

history ['hɪst(ə)rɪ] N **1** (*of country, ship etc*) histoire *f*; **French h.** l'histoire de France; **ancient/modern h.** l'histoire ancienne/moderne; *Fig* **that's h.** c'est du passé; *Fam* **he's h.!** (*in trouble*) il est fini!; (*no longer in my/her/etc life*) avec lui, c'est terminé!; **that's ancient h.** c'est une vieille histoire, c'est l'histoire ancienne; **we're making h.** nous faisons l'histoire, nous entrons dans l'histoire; *Sch* **h. book/teacher/etc** livre *m*/professeur *m*/etc d'histoire; **Shakespeare's h. plays** les pièces *fpl* historiques de Shakespeare **2** (*book*) histoire *f*, (*chronological account*) historique *m* **3** (*tradition*) tradition *f*; **there is a long h. of cultural links between these cities** il existe une longue tradition de liens culturels entre ces villes; **there is a h. of heart disease in her family** il y a des antécédents de maladie cardiaque dans sa famille **4** *Comput* historique *m*
▸▸ *Comput* **h. file** fichier *m* historique; *Comput* **h. list** historique *m*

histrionic [hɪstrɪ'ɒnɪk] ADJ **1** histrionique **2** *Theat, Liter* théâtral, -aux

histrionics [hɪstrɪ'ɒnɪks] NPL *Pej* démonstrations *fpl* affectées (*de colère etc*); **I've had enough of his h.** j'en ai assez de ses simagrées *ou Fam* son cinéma; **it's just h. on her part** elle nous joue la comédie

HIT [hɪt]

N	coup **1, 2** ▪ succès **3** ▪ tube **3** ▪ hit **6**
VT	frapper **1** ▪ heurter **1** ▪ atteindre **1–3** ▪ toucher **2, 3** ▪ arriver à **5** ▪ buter sur **6**
VI	frapper

N **1** (*blow*) coup *m*; *Fig Fam* **that's a h. at you** c'est à vous que s'adresse l'allusion **2** *Fencing* touche *f*, coup *m*; *Billiards* touche; *Baseball* coup de batte; *Hockey* coup de crosse; *Hockey* **free h.** coup franc; **to score a h.** *Fencing* toucher; (*in shooting*) atteindre la cible; *Fig* **to score a h. against sb** marquer des points contre qn; **to score a direct h.** (*of bomber, tank etc*) taper dans le mille; **to score a direct h. on sth** (*of bomber etc*) toucher qch en plein dans le mille; (*of bomb*) tomber en plein dans qch; **built to withstand a direct h.** construit pour résister à une bombe; **the ship suffered two direct hits from missiles** le bateau a été touché par deux missiles **3** *Theat, TV etc* (*success*) succès *m*; (*song, record*) tube *m*; **she had a h. with her song 'Spinning Around'** sa chanson 'Spinning Around' a été un tube; **h. show** spectacle *m* à succès; **Frank Sinatra's greatest hits** les plus grands succès de Frank Sinatra; **to make** *or* **score a h. with sb** faire bonne impression à qn; (*romantically*) avoir une touche avec qn; **one-h. wonder** (*group, singer*)

= groupe *m* ou chanteur *m* qui n'a eu qu'un seul tube **4** *Sl* (*murder*) meurtre *m* **5** *Sl* (*of hard drugs*) fix *m*; (*of joint*) taffe *f*, (*effect of drugs*) effet *m* (*procuré par une drogue*); **you get a good h. off that grass** cette herbe fait rapidement de l'effet **6** *Comput* (*visit to website*) hit *m*, accès *m*; **this website counted 20,000 hits last week** ce site Web a été consulté 20 000 fois la semaine dernière
VT (*pt, pp* **hit**; *prp* **hitting**) **1** (*of person*) frapper; *Comput* (*key*) appuyer sur; (*of bullet*) (*person*) atteindre; (*of car etc*) (*tree, bus*) percuter; **to h. sb in the face** frapper qn au visage; **to h. one's foot against a stone** se cogner le pied contre une pierre; (*and stumble*) buter contre une pierre; **to h. one's head on the ceiling** se cogner la tête contre le plafond; **to h. a reef** (*of ship, boat*) heurter un récif; **the bullet h. her in the arm** la balle l'a touchée au bras; **to h. the target** (*with gun, missile etc*) toucher la cible; *Am Fam* **that really h. the spot** (*is just what was needed*) c'est juste ce qu'il me fallait; *Journ Fam* **to h. the headlines** défrayer la chronique; *Fig* **to h. the nail on the head** tomber juste; *Fig* **to h. the roof** être furieux; *Sl* **to h. the bottle** picoler; *Sl* **to h. the hay** *or* **Am the sack** se pieuter; **it suddenly h. me that …** j'ai réalisé tout d'un coup que …; **he didn't know what had h. him** il se demandait ce qui lui était arrivé **2** (*reach*) atteindre; *Fencing, Billiards* toucher; **to h. the wrong note** (*on the piano etc*), *Fig* faire une fausse note; (*in singing*) chanter faux; **I can't h. those high notes any more** je n'arrive plus à chanter ces notes aiguës; **to h. ninety** (*miles an hour*) faire du 140 km/h; **to h. an all-time low** (*of investment, relationship etc*) être au plus bas; **to h. rock-bottom** atteindre son point le plus bas **3** (*affect*) **to be hard h.** (*by losses etc*) être sérieusement touché; **the strike has h. several factories** la grève a atteint plusieurs usines **4** *Am Fam* (*borrow from*) **he h. his friend for $100** il a tapé son ami de 100 dollars **5** (*arrive at*) (*place, town*) arriver à; **the circus hits town tomorrow night** le cirque arrive en ville demain soir; **to h. the beach** (*of troops*) atteindre la plage; **let's h. the beach!** allons à la plage!; **when it hits the shops** quand il arrivera sur le marché; **to h. the trail** *or* **the road** (*start*) se mettre en route; *Fig* **to h. the ground running** être opérationnel immédiatement **6** (*encounter*) (*problem, difficulty*) buter sur; **the tunnellers h. rock** les ouvriers qui creusaient le tunnel sont tombés sur de la roche; **we h. a terrible snowstorm** nous nous sommes trouvés dans une tempête de neige terrible; **to h. a sticky** *or* **bad patch** rencontrer des difficultés **7** *esp Am Sl* (*murder*) buter
VI frapper; (*collide*) se heurter; **to h. hard** frapper fort, *Fam* cogner fort; *Fig* **the remark h. home** la remarque a eu l'effet escompté
▸▸ *Comput* **h. counter** compteur *m* d'accès; *Fam* **h. list** liste *f* noire; *Fam* **h. man** tueur *m* à gages; *Old-fashioned* **h. parade** hit-parade *m*, *pl* hit-parades; *Mus* **h. record** tube *m*
▸ **hit back** VI **1** (*return blow*) rendre coup pour coup (**at sb** à qn) **2** *Fig* (*answer accusation, criticism etc*) riposter, répondre VT SEP (*return blow to*) **to h. sb back** donner un coup en retour à qn
▸ **hit off** VT SEP **1** (*imitate*) (*in satirical drawing*) caricaturer; (*impersonate*) imiter **2** *Fam* **to h. it off** (*get on well*) bien s'entendre (**with** avec)
▸ **hit on** VT INSEP **1** *Am Fam* **to h. on sb** draguer qn, faire du plat à qn **2** = **hit upon**

▸ **hit out** vi **1** (punch etc) frapper; **she h. out at her attackers** elle a frappé ses agresseurs; **he h. out in all directions** il donnait des coups dans tous les sens

2 (verbally) attaquer (verbalement); **to h. out at sb** s'en prendre à qn

▸ **hit up** vt sep Sl **to h. it up** (inject drugs) se piquer

▸ **hit upon** vt insep (discover) (idea, method etc) trouver

hit-and-run N (accident) accident m avec délit de fuite

▸▸ **h. accident** accident avec délit de fuite; **h. driver** conducteur, -trice coupable de délit de fuite; Mil **h. raid** raid m éclair

hitch [hɪtʃ] N **1** (difficulty) empêchement m, anicroche f, contretemps m; **there's a h. somewhere** il y a quelque chose qui cloche; **there's been a h.** il y a eu un problème; **without a h.** sans anicroches, sans accroc; Radio, TV etc **technical h.** incident m technique **2** (knot) nœud m; **half h.** demi-clef f **3** Am Fam (length of time) **a three-year h. in the army** (une période de) trois ans dans l'armée; **to do a three-year h. in prison** faire trois ans de prison **4** (movement) saccade f, secousse f; (of horse) léger boitement m

vt **1** (attach) accrocher, attacher; Naut amarrer (**to** à); **she hitched her horse to a post** elle a attaché son cheval à un poteau; **they hitched the horses to the cart** ils ont attelé les chevaux à la charrette **2** Fam (hitchhike) **to h. a lift** or **ride** faire du stop, Can faire du pouce; **we hitched a ride to Paris** on nous a pris en stop jusqu'à Paris **3** Fam **to get hitched** (married) se caser

vi **1** Fam =hitchhike **2** (of person) **to h. on to sth** s'accrocher à qch

▸ **hitch up** vt sep **1** (harness) (horse) harnacher **2** (lift) (trousers, skirt) remonter

hitchhike ['hɪtʃhaɪk] vi faire de l'auto-stop ou du stop, Can faire du pouce; **to h. to Paris** aller à Paris en stop

hitchhiker ['hɪtʃhaɪkər] N auto-stoppeur, -euse

hitchhiking ['hɪtʃhaɪkɪŋ] N (auto-)stop m

hi-tech ['haɪtek] ADJ de haute technologie, de pointe; (furniture) hi-tech; **they've adopted a h. approach** ils ont eu recours à la technologie de pointe; **we're very h. here** nous faisons un usage intensif de l'automatisation ou de l'informatique ici

N technologie f de pointe, hi-tech f, Archit hi-tech

hither ['hɪðər] ADV Arch, Lit ici; **h. and thither** çà et là; Hum **to give sb a 'come h.' look** jeter un coup d'œil coquin à qn

hitherto ['hɪðə'tuː] ADV jusqu'ici, jusqu'à présent

hit-or-miss ADJ (method) aléatoire, Fam au pif, au pifomètre; **it was all rather h.** c'était au pifomètre ou au pif; **in a h. sort of way** au pifomètre, au pif; **to reply in a h. sort of way** répondre au hasard ou au petit bonheur; **their method is rather h.** ils font les choses au pif

ADV (to answer) au petit bonheur, Fam au pif

HIV [eɪtʃaɪ'viː] N Med (abbr human immuno-deficiency virus) HIV m, VIH m; **H. case** cas m de séropositivité; **H. deaths** morts liées à la séropositivité **H. patients** patients mpl séropositifs; **to be H. positive** être séropositif; **to be H. negative** être séronégatif

hive [haɪv] N (for bees) ruche f, Fig **a h. of industry** une véritable ruche ou fourmilière

vt (swarm) mettre dans une ruche

vi (of swarm) entrer dans la ruche

▸ **hive off** vt sep (separate) détacher ou séparer (d'un tout); **to h. off work** sous-traiter, donner du travail en sous-traitance; Br Com

part of the industry was hived off to private ownership une partie de cette industrie a été privatisée

vi (split off) se séparer (**from** de)

hives [haɪvz] NPL Med urticaire f, **to have h.** avoir de l'urticaire

hiya ['haɪjə, haɪ'jɑː] INT Fam salut!

HM [eɪtʃ'em] Br abbr **His/Her Majesty**

h'm [hm] INT (expressing doubt) heu!, hum!

HMG [eɪtʃem'dʒiː] Br Admin abbr **His/Her Majesty's Government**

HMI [eɪtʃem'aɪ] Br (abbr **His/Her Majesty's Inspector**) inspecteur m de l'éducation nationale (britannique)

HMS [eɪtʃem'es] Br Naut abbr **His/Her Majesty's Ship**

HMSO [eɪtʃeme'səʊ] N Br (abbr **Her/His Majesty's Stationery Office**) ≃ Imprimerie f nationale

HNC [eɪtʃen'siː] N Br (abbr **Higher National Certificate**) = diplôme m technique préparé en un an

HND [eɪtʃen'diː] N Br (abbr **Higher National Diploma**) = diplôme m technique préparé en deux ans

HO N Br (abbr **Home Office**) = le ministère britannique de l'Intérieur

ho [həʊ] INT Old-fashioned (to attract attention) hé!, ohé!; Naut **land ho!** terre! **2 ho! ho!** (laughter) ha! ha!

hoar [hɔːr] N gelée f blanche

hoard [hɔːd] N amas m; (of provisions, food etc) réserve f, **h. of money** trésor m, Fam magot m; **he has a whole h. of stories** il a une réserve d'histoires assez extraordinaire

vt (corn, information) amasser; (provisions, food etc) mettre ou tenir en réserve; (causing shortage for others) accaparer; (money) thésauriser

▸ **hoard up** vt sep =hoard vt

Attention: ne pas confondre avec le nom anglais **horde**.

hoarder ['hɔːdər] N (animal) animal m prévoyant; **petrol hoarders were arrested** ceux qui accaparaient l'essence ont été arrêtés; **she's a real h.** elle garde absolument tout, elle ne jette absolument rien

hoarding[1] ['hɔːdɪŋ] N (of provisions) mise f en réserve

hoarding[2] N **1** Br (for advertising) panneau m d'affichage **2** (fencing) clôture f en planches; (around worksite etc) palissade f

▸▸ Com **h. site** emplacement m d'affichage

hoarfrost ['hɔːfrɒst] N gelée f blanche

hoarse [hɔːs] ADJ (voice etc) enroué, rauque; **to be h.** être enroué; **to shout oneself h.** s'enrouer à force de crier

hoarsely ['hɔːslɪ] ADV d'une voix rauque ou enrouée

hoarseness ['hɔːsnɪs] N enrouement m

hoary ['hɔːrɪ] ADJ **1** Lit (hair) blanchi, chenu; Bot, Entom (foliage, insect) couvert d'un duvet blanc **2** (old) vieux, f vieille

hoax [həʊks] N canular m, farce f, Journ Fam canular, canard m; (bomb) **h.** fausse alerte f à la bombe; **it turned out to be a h.** finalement, c'était un canular; **to play a h. on sb** faire un canular à qn

vt monter ou faire un canular à

▸▸ Br **h. call** canular m téléphonique; Br **h. caller** mauvais plaisant m (qui donne de fausses informations par téléphone)

hoaxer ['həʊksər] N farceur, -euse; (hoax caller) mauvais plaisant m (qui donne de fausses informations par téléphone)

hob [hɒb] N (on electric cooker) plaque f, (on hearth) plaque de côté

hobble ['hɒb(ə)l] N **1** (limp) boitillement m **2** (for horses etc) entrave f

vi boitiller, clopiner; **to h. along** marcher en boitillant

vt (horse etc) entraver

▸▸ **h. skirt** jupe f entravée

hobby ['hɒbɪ] N passe-temps m inv, hobby m, violon m d'Ingres; **to take up a h.** se trouver un hobby; **to take up sth as a h.** se mettre à qch pendant son temps libre

hobbyhorse ['hɒbɪhɔːs] N (toy) (of merry-go-round) cheval m de bois; (rocking-horse) cheval à bascule; Fig dada m, cheval de bataille; Fig **to get on one's h.** enfourcher son dada ou son cheval de bataille

hobgoblin [hɒb'gɒblɪn] N Myth lutin m

hobnail ['hɒbneɪl] N clou m, fer m (pour les chaussures); **hobnail(ed) boot** chaussure f ferrée

hobnob ['hɒbnɒb] vi (-bb-) Fam **to h. with sb** frayer avec qn

hobo ['həʊbəʊ] N Am **1** (tramp) clochard m **2** (itinerant worker) ouvrier m saisonnier

Hobson ['hɒbsən] N **it's H.'s choice** je n'ai pas/il n'a pas/etc vraiment le choix (se dit d'une situation où le choix n'est qu'apparent)

hock[1] [hɒk] N (of horse) jarret m

hock[2] N (wine) vin m du Rhin

hock[3] Fam N **in h.** (of watch etc) en gage, Fam au clou, Fam chez ma tante; (of person) (in debt) endetté; **to put sth in h.** (pawn) mettre qch en gage; **to be in h. to the bank** devoir de l'argent à la banque

vt (pawn) mettre au clou

hockey ['hɒkɪ] N Sport **1** Br hockey m (sur gazon); **to play h.** jouer au hockey **2** Am (ice hockey) hockey m (sur glace), Can hockey

▸▸ **h. stick** Br crosse f de hockey; Am crosse de hockey sur glace

hockshop ['hɒkʃɒp] N Am Fam crédit m municipal, mont-de-piété m, pl monts-de-piété

hocus-pocus ['həʊkəs'pəʊkəs] N **1** (formula used by conjurers) abracadabra **2** (trickery) tromperie f, supercherie f

hod [hɒd] N **1** (of bricklayer) oiseau m, hotte f **2** (for coal) seau m, caisse f

▸▸ **h. carrier** apprenti m ou aide m maçon

hodgepodge ['hɒdʒpɒdʒ] N esp Am = **hotchpotch**

Hodgkin's disease ['hɒdʒkɪnz] N Med maladie f de Hodgkin

hoe [həʊ] N houe f, binette f, (weeding) **h.** sarcloir m; (Dutch) **h.** griffe-bineuse f, pl griffes-bineuses

vt (hoed; hoeing) (soil) biner; (weeds) sarcler

hoedown ['həʊdaʊn] N esp Am bal m populaire

hog [hɒg] N **1** (castrated pig) porc m châtré; Am (pig) porc, cochon m, pourceau m; Fam **to go the whole h.** aller jusqu'au bout; **they went the whole h. for the party** (didn't stint) ils n'ont pas fait les choses à moitié; Am Fig Fam **to live high on the h.** mener joyeuse vie **2** Fig (glutton) goinfre m, glouton m **3** Am Fam (motorbike) grosse bécane f

vt (-gg-) Fam (take, use etc more than one's fair share of) prendre plus que sa part de; **to h. the television** monopoliser la télé; **to h. the limelight** accaparer la vedette; Aut **to h. the road** prendre toute la place; Aut **to h. the centre lane** monopoliser la voie centrale

Hogmanay [hɒgmə'neɪ] N Scot la Saint-Sylvestre

Hogmanay

Ce mot désigne les fêtes de la veille du nouvel an célébrées en Écosse. Traditionnellement, les Écossais préféraient célébrer la nouvelle année plutôt que Noël et jusqu'au XVIIIème siècle, la tradition était d'offrir des cadeaux le jour de l'an. Les coutumes écossaises sont aussi anciennes que diverses: des coups de canon sont tirés à minuit; à ce moment les gens vont rendre visite à leurs voisins avec un morceau de charbon en guise de cadeau, et tout le monde boit une petite goutte de whisky pour fêter la nouvelle année.

hogshead ['hɒgzhed] N *(barrel)* tonneau *m*, barrique *f*

hogtie ['hɒgtaɪ] VT*Am (animal)* lier les quatre pattes de; *Fig (the economy etc)* entraver

hogwash ['hɒgwɒʃ] N *(swill)* eaux *fpl* grasses *(que l'on donne aux porcs); Fam (nonsense)* foutaise *f*

hogweed ['hɒgwiːd] N *(plant)* berce *f* commune

hoi polloi ['hɔɪpə'lɔɪ] NPL*Pej* the h. la foule *f*, les masses *fpl*

hoist [hɔɪst] N 1 *(act)* levage *m; Fam* **to give sb a h. (up)** aider qn à monter; *(from beneath also)* faire la courte échelle à qn 2 *(device)* appareil *m ou* engin *m* de levage; *(winch)* treuil *m*, grue *f*, palan *m; Min* bourriquet *m; (for goods)* monte-charge *m inv*
VT *(load)* lever, hisser; *Naut (ship's boat, flag)* hisser; **to h. boats in/out** embarquer/débarquer les canots; **h. away!** hissez!; **she hoisted herself on to the wall** elle s'est hissée sur le mur; *Fig* **to be h. with one's own petard** tomber dans son propre piège

hoity-toity ['hɔɪtɪ'tɔɪtɪ] INT ta, ta, ta!, tarata!
ADJ qui se donne des airs, qui fait l'important; **she can get quite h.** elle fait l'importante quelquefois

hokey ['həʊkɪ] ADJ *Am Fam (nonsensical)* absurde; *(sentimental)* à l'eau de rose

hokey-cokey [həʊkɪ'kəʊkɪ] N *Br* = danse *f* et chanson traditionnelles londoniennes

hokum ['həʊkəm] N*Am Fam (in film etc)* niaiseries *fpl, (nonsense)* bêtises *fpl*, âneries *fpl*

HOLD [həʊld]

N	prise **1** ▪ cale **4** ▪ soute **4**
VT	tenir **1, 3, 4, 6, 10, 11** ▪ maintenir **1** ▪ retenir **2, 6, 8** ▪ contenir **5** ▪ stocker **5** ▪ réserver **8** ▪ avoir **9** ▪ détenir **9**
VI	tenir bon **1** ▪ durer **2** ▪ attendre **4**

N 1 *(grip)* prise *f; Boxing* tenu *m; (in wrestling)* prise; **to have h. of sb/sth** tenir qn/qch; **to catch** *or* **get** *or* **take h. of sb/sth** saisir *ou* empoigner qn/qch; **to get h. of sth** *(find)* mettre la main sur qch; **where did you get h. of that?** où vous êtes-vous procuré cela?; **they prevented us from getting h. of the code** ils nous ont empêchés de nous emparer du code; **to get h. of the wrong idea** mal comprendre; **it's difficult to get h. of this book** *(find a copy of it)* ce livre est difficile à trouver; **to relax one's h.** relâcher son étreinte; **to let go one's h.** lâcher prise; **to lose one's h. on reality** perdre le sens des réalités; **to have a h. on** *or* **over sb** avoir prise *ou* de l'emprise sur qn; **to gain a firm h. over sb** acquérir un grand pouvoir sur qn; **no holds barred** tous les coups sont permis; **a no-holds-barred argument/contest** une dispute/compétition où tous les coups sont permis; **a no-holds-barred**

discussion une discussion très franche

2 *(in rockclimbing etc)* point *m* d'appui
3 **on h.** *(of project)* en suspens; **to put sth on h.** mettre qch en suspens; **the road building programme is on h.** la construction de la route est interrompue; *Tel* **to put sb on h.** mettre qn en attente *ou* en parcage; *Tel* **to be on h.** *(of caller)* attendre, être en attente
4 *(of ship)* cale *f, (for luggage on plane)* soute *f*
VT *(pt, pp* **held** [held]) 1 *(grip) (child etc)* tenir; **to h. sth in one's hand** tenir qch à la main; *(something very small)* tenir qch dans la main; **to h. sth/sb tight(ly)** serrer qch/qn, tenir qch/qn serré; **they held (each other's) hands** ils se tenaient (par) la main; **to h. one's sides with laughter** se tenir les côtes de rire; **to h. one's nose** se boucher le nez; **to h. sth in position** tenir *ou* maintenir qch en place; **four screws h. the shelf to the wall** l'étagère est fixée au mur par quatre vis; **the table is held in place by steel bolts** la table est maintenue par des boulons d'acier
2 *(detain etc)Law* **to be held on remand** être incarcéré *(en détention provisoire)*; **to h. sb prisoner** retenir qn prisonnier; **to h. sb (as) hostage** retenir qn en otage; **she was held without trial for six weeks** elle est restée en prison six semaines sans avoir été jugée
3 *(command etc)* **to h. one's ground** tenir bon, ne pas lâcher pied; **to h. one's own** se maintenir, se défendre; *Mil* **to h. a fort** défendre une forteresse; **to h. a position** tenir une position; **to h. the stage** *(of actor)* captiver son auditoire; *Fig (in discussion etc)* occuper le devant de la scène; *Naut etc* **to h. course** tenir la route; **car that holds the road well** voiture qui tient bien la route
4 *(carry)* tenir; **to h. one's head high** garder la tête haute; **to h. oneself straight/well** se tenir droit/bien
5 *(contain)* contenir, renfermer; *Comput* stocker; **barrel that holds twenty litres** tonneau d'une contenance de vingt litres; **how much data will this disk hold?** quelle quantité de données cette disquette peut-elle stocker?; **car that holds six people** voiture à six places; **to h. water** *(of cask etc)* être étanche; *Fig (of theory, story etc)* tenir debout; **the theory doesn't h. water** la théorie ne tient pas (debout); **to be able to h. one's drink** bien supporter l'alcool; **what the future holds for us** ce que l'avenir nous réserve; **sport held no interest for them** pour eux, le sport ne présentait aucun intérêt
6 *(conduct etc) (meeting)* tenir; *(party etc)* donner; **the meeting will be held at 8pm** la réunion aura lieu à 8 heures du soir; **to h. a conversation with sb** s'entretenir avec qn; **the two sides held talks** des discussions ont eu lieu entre les deux parties; **to h. a surgery for one's patients** recevoir ses patients
7 *(restrain)* **to h. one's breath** retenir sa respiration *ou* son souffle; **there's no holding him** (une fois lancé) il n'y a pas moyen de l'arrêter; **h. your tongue!** taisez-vous!; *Fam* **h. it!, h. your horses!** arrêtez!, attendez!, stop!; **h. it!** *(at photographer's)* ne bougez plus!, on ne bouge plus!; *Mil* **to h. the enemy** contenir l'ennemi; **to h. the front page** garder la une
8 *(keep) (airline seat)* réserver; **to h. sb's interest** retenir l'attention de qn; **the film doesn't h. the attention for long** le film ne retient pas l'attention très longtemps; **to h. one's audience** retenir l'attention de son auditoire; **to h. sb to their promise** obliger *ou* contraindre qn à tenir sa promesse; **we can h. a room for you until tomorrow** la chambre vous sera réservée jusqu'à demain, on vous gardera la chambre jusqu'à demain; *Am* **h. the onions** *(in restaurant)* sans oignons
9 *(possess) (title)* avoir, posséder; *(opinion)*

avoir; *(position, post)* occuper; *(record, shares)* détenir; *(passport)* être porteur *ou* détenteur de; **to h. 5% of the shares in a company** détenir 5% du capital d'une société; **she had held (government) office before** elle avait déjà assumé des fonctions au gouvernement; *Com* **to h. sb's commercial bill** détenir un effet sur qn
10 *(consider)* **to h. sth lightly** faire peu de cas de qch, attacher peu d'importance à qch; **to h. sth sacred** tenir qch pour sacré; **to h. sb responsible** tenir qn responsable; **to be held in respect** être respecté de tous; **to h. that ...** soutenir que ...
11 *Mus* **to h. a note** tenir *ou* prolonger une note
12 *Tel* **h. the line!** ne quittez pas!; **h. all my calls** ne me passez aucun appel
VI 1 *(of rope etc)* tenir (bon); **h. tight!** tenez bon!; *Aut* **tyres that h. in the wet** pneus qui tiennent bien la route par temps de pluie
2 *(last) (of agreement etc)* durer, persister; *(of weather)* se maintenir; **if your luck holds** si votre chance dure
3 *(be valid)* **to h. (good** *or* **true)** être vrai *ou* valable; **the same holds true in respect of ...** il en est de même pour ...
4 *Tel* attendre
▶ **hold against** VT SEP *(dislike for)* **to h. sth against sb** tenir rigueur de qch à qn; **I won't h. it against you** je ne t'en voudrai pas
▶ **hold back** VI 1 *(stay in the background)* rester en arrière
2 *(restrain oneself)* se retenir; **to h. back from doing sth** attendre avant de faire qch; *(stronger)* se retenir de faire qch; **buyers are holding back** les acheteurs s'abstiennent
VT SEP 1 *(restrain) (person, anger, tears)* retenir; *(anger, tears, crowd)* contenir
2 *(impede)* freiner, entraver; **lack of investment is holding industry back** l'absence d'investissements freine l'industrie
3 *(withhold) (truth)* cacher, dissimuler; **he's holding something back** il cache quelque chose
▶ **hold down** VT SEP 1 *(restrain) (person)* maintenir à terre; **to h. down interest rates** empêcher l'augmentation des taux d'intérêt
2 **to h. down a job** *(occupy)* avoir un emploi; *(keep)* garder un emploi; **although she is a student, she holds down a full-time job** bien qu'elle étudie, elle occupe un poste à plein temps; **he never holds down a job for more than a week** il ne peut jamais garder un emploi plus d'une semaine
3 *Comput (key, mouse button)* maintenir enfoncé
▶ **hold forth** VI *(speak pompously)* disserter (**on sth** sur qch); **he's always got something to h. forth about** il trouve toujours quelque chose sur quoi disserter
▶ **hold in** VT SEP *(laughter)* réprimer; *(emotion)* maîtriser; *(anger)* contenir; *(horse)* serrer la bride à, contenir; **to h. one's stomach** *or* **oneself in** rentrer son ventre; **to h. oneself in** *(emotionally)* se maîtriser
▶ **hold off** VT SEP 1 *(keep away) (enemy)* tenir à distance; **he held off his assailants** il a tenu ses assaillants en respect; **she held the press off by promising to make a statement** elle a fait attendre les journalistes en leur promettant un communiqué
2 *(refrain from) (decision, choice etc)* remettre à plus tard; **to h. off doing sth** attendre pour faire qch; **they held off buying a new car** ils ont repoussé l'achat d'une nouvelle voiture
VI *(keep away)* se tenir à distance (**from** de); *(refrain from doing sth, from deciding)* différer, surseoir; **the rain is holding off** jusqu'ici il ne pleut pas
▶ **hold off from** VT INSEP *(decision, choice etc)* remettre à plus tard; **to h. off from doing sth** attendre avant de faire qch

▸ **hold on** VI **1** *(endure)* tenir, résister

2 *(wait)* attendre, patienter; **h. on (a minute)!** *(not so fast)* pas si vite!; *Tel* **h. on a moment** ne quittez pas

3 *(keep one's grip)* se tenir; **h. on (tight)!** *(on bus, motorbike etc)* tiens-toi bien!

VT SEP *(keep attached) (piece of wood etc)* fixer; **the tiles are held on with glue** les carreaux sont maintenus en place par de la colle

▸ **hold on to** VT INSEP **1** *(grip) (thing)* s'agripper à; *Fig (idea, hope etc)* se raccrocher à

2 *(keep)* garder; **h. on to that book** *(it may be valuable)* garde ce livre précieusement; **she held on to her money** elle se cramponnait à son argent

▸ **hold out** VT SEP **1** *(stretch out) (one's hand)* tendre

2 *(offer) (hope)* offrir, laisser; **the doctor doesn't h. out much hope** le docteur ne laisse pas beaucoup d'espoir

VI **1** *(resist)* tenir (le coup); **to h. out against an attack** résister à une attaque; **to h. out for a higher price** espérer un prix plus élevé

2 *(of supplies etc)* durer

▸ **hold out on** VT INSEP *(not give information to)* **you've been holding out on me** *(I didn't know you played the piano etc)* tu m'as caché des choses

▸ **hold over** VT SEP **1** *(postpone)* remettre (à plus tard); *(decision)* ajourner; *(payment)* arriérer

2 to h. sth over sb *(threaten with)* menacer qn de qch

▸ **hold to** VT INSEP *(abide by)* s'en tenir à; **to h. to a belief** rester attaché à une croyance; **to h. to one's decision** s'en tenir à *ou* maintenir sa décision

▸ **hold together** VT SEP *(two objects)* maintenir ensemble; *(party, alliance)* maintenir la cohésion de; **the two pieces of wood are held together by nails** les deux morceaux de bois sont cloués ensemble

VI *(of objects)* tenir (ensemble); *(of ideas)* être cohérent; **the story doesn't h. together** l'histoire ne tient pas debout

▸ **hold up** VT SEP **1** *(support)* soutenir; **these ropes h. the tent up** ces cordes maintiennent la tente bien droite

2 *(raise)* lever (en l'air); **to h. one's head up (with pride)** lever la tête (avec fierté); **she held the book up** *(so that everyone could see)* elle brandit le livre; *Fig* **to h. sb up as an example** citer qn comme exemple; **to h. sb up to ridicule** tourner qn en ridicule

3 *(delay) (person)* retenir, retarder; *(train, kick-off etc)* retarder; *(traffic, agreement, decision)* bloquer; **the car was held up at the traffic lights** la voiture a dû s'arrêter au feu rouge; **our departure was held up by bad weather** notre départ a été retardé par le mauvais temps; **the goods were held up at customs** les marchandises ont été retenues à la douane; **financial difficulties are holding the project up** le projet est freiné par des difficultés financières

4 *(in order to rob) (person, bank)* attaquer; *(train)* attaquer à main armée

VI **1** *(stay in place) (of shelf etc)* tenir (en place); *(of good weather)* se maintenir; **the old building is still holding up** le vieux bâtiment est toujours debout; **I hope the good weather holds up** j'espère que le beau temps va durer; **she's holding up well under the pressure** elle supporte bien la pression; **my finances are holding up well** je tiens le coup financièrement

2 *(of theory etc)* tenir debout

▸ **hold with** VT INSEP *(usu neg)* **I don't h. with such behaviour/his opinions** je n'approuve pas une telle conduite/ses opinions

---

holdall ['həʊldɔːl] N *Br* sac *m* de voyage, fourre-tout *m inv*

holder ['həʊldər] N **1** *(person) (of passport, permit etc)* possesseur *m*, détenteur, -trice; *(of ticket)* possesseur; *(of degree, record, shares)* détenteur, -trice; *(of opinion, belief)* tenant *m*; *Fin (of bonds, bill)* porteur, -euse; *(of right, post, account, degree etc)* titulaire *mf*; *(of championship)* tenant; *Sport* **the present h.** *(of the title)* l'actuel tenant du titre **2** *(device)* support *m*; **(drill) h.** porte-foret *m*, *pl* porte-forets; **(soap) h.** porte-savon *m*, *pl* porte-savons; **pot plant h.** cache-pot *m*, *pl* cache-pots; **(cigarette) h.** porte-cigarettes *m inv*

holding ['həʊldɪŋ] N **1** *Agr (property)* terre *f* affermée, ferme *f*; *Fin* effets *mpl* en portefeuille; *(shares in company)* participation *f*; **he has holdings in several companies** il est actionnaire de plusieurs sociétés **2** *(action) (of congress etc)* tenue *f*; *Mus (of note)* tenue; *(lengthening)* prolongation *f* **3** *Aviat (delay)* attente *f*; **h. letter/reply** réponse *f* d'attente

▸▸ *Fin* **h. company** *(société f* en) holding *m*, société à portefeuille; **h. costs** coûts *mpl* de détention; **h. operation** opération *f* de maintien; *Fig* **we need a h. operation** il faut trouver un moyen de retarder les choses; *Aviat* **h. pattern** circuit *m* d'attente

hold-up N **1** *(delay)* arrêt *m*; *(on road)* embouteillage *m*; **there's been a h. on the line** il y a eu des perturbations sur la ligne; **there have been no hold-ups with the project** le projet n'a eu à souffrir d'aucun retard **2** *(armed robbery)* attaque *f* à main armée, hold-up *m*; **this is a h.** c'est un hold-up

hole [həʊl] N **1** *(in the ground)* trou *m*, creux *m*, cavité *f*, *Golf* trou; *(of rabbit)* terrier *m*; *(of fox)* tanière *f*, *(of mouse etc)* trou; **to dig a h.** creuser un trou; **what a h.!** *(of room etc)* quel gourbi!; *(of house)* quel taudis!; *(of town)* quel bled!; *Golf* **h. in one** trou réussi en un coup

2 *(opening)* trou *m*; *(in metal plate etc)* perforation *f*, *(of drive belt etc)* point *m*; *(of flute)* perce *f*, *(in theory etc)* point faible; *Comput* **(punch) h.** perforation *f*, *Med* **h. in the heart** trou dans le cœur; **h. in the wall** restaurant/café/endroit exigu; **to make a h. in** faire un trou dans *ou* à; *(piece of clothing)* trouer; *Fig* **to make a h. in one's savings** *(of expenditure)* faire un (gros) trou dans ses économies; **this jersey is full of holes** ce tricot est tout troué *ou* est plein de trous; **to pick holes in sth** relever des erreurs dans qch; **to pick holes in a theory** relever les points faibles d'une théorie

3 *Fam (difficult situation)* situation *f* difficile; **to be** *or* **find oneself in a h.** être *ou* se trouver dans une situation délicate

VT **1** *(make a hole in)* trouer, faire un trou dans; **the ship was holed below the water line** le navire avait des avaries au-dessous de la ligne de flottaison; **the building had been holed by shellfire** le bâtiment a été endommagé par les obus **2** *(put into a hole)* **to h. the ball** *Golf* envoyer *ou* mettre la balle dans le trou; *Billiards* bloquer; *Fig* **holed in one!** vous avez deviné juste!

VI *(of stockings etc)* se trouer, se percer

▸▸ **h. punch** perforatrice *f*, *Fam* **h. in the wall** *(cashpoint)* guichet *m* automatique; *(restaurant)* petit restaurant *m*; *(shop)* petite boutique *f*, *Am (apartment)* appartement *m* minuscule

▸ **hole out** VI *Golf* mettre la balle dans le trou
▸ **hole up** VI *Fam (hide)* se terrer

hole-and-corner ADJ *Fam* clandestin; *(affair)* un peu louche

holey ['həʊlɪ] ADJ *Fam* (tout) troué, plein de trous

holiday ['hɒlɪdɪ, -deɪ] N **1** *Br* vacances *fpl*; **a month's h.** un mois de vacances; **how much h. do you get?** combien est-ce que tu as de vacances?; **the summer holidays** les gran-

des vacances; **to be on h.** être en vacances; **to take a h.** prendre des vacances; **when are you going on h.?** quand est-ce que vous allez prendre vos vacances?; **where are you going on h.** *or* **for your holidays?** où allez-vous pour vos vacances?; **camping h.** vacances passées à faire du camping; **ski** *or* **skiing h.** vacances de neige

2 *Br (day off)* (jour *m* de) congé *m*; *Sch* **half-day h.** demi-journée *f* de congé; **I'm going to take a h. today** je vais prendre un jour de congé aujourd'hui

3 *(day of festival)* (jour *m* de) fête *f*, jour férié; **public** *or Br* **bank h.** fête légale

VI *Br* passer les vacances

▸▸ **h. brochure** catalogue *m* de vacances; *Br* **h. camp** = centre *m* de vacances familial (avec animations et activités diverses); **h. centre** centre *m* de vacances; *Br* **h. cottage** gîte *m*; **h. entitlement** nombre *m* de jours de vacances auquel un employé a droit, droit *m* aux vacances; *Br* **h. home** maison *f* de vacances, résidence *f* secondaire; **h. market** marché *m* du tourisme; **h. period** période *f* de fêtes; *Br* **h. resort** lieu *m* de vacances *ou* de séjour; *Br* **h. season** saison *f* des vacances; **h. village** village *m* des vacances; **h. worker** vacataire *mf*

holiday-maker N *Br* vacancier, -ière; *(in summer)* estivant, -ante

holier-than-thou ['həʊlɪəðən'ðaʊ] ADJ *(attitude etc)* hypocritement pieux

holiness ['həʊlɪnɪs] N sainteté *f*; **His/Your H.** *(of the Pope)* Sa/Votre Sainteté

holism ['həʊlɪz(ə)m] N *Phil, Med* holisme *m*

holistic [həʊ'lɪstɪk] ADJ *Phil, Med* holistique

Holland ['hɒlənd] N Hollande *f*

holland ['hɒlənd] N *Tex* toile *f* de Hollande, toile bise

holler ['hɒlər] N braillement *m*
VI crier à tue-tête, brailler

hollow ['hɒləʊ] ADJ **1** *(cheek)* creux, rentré; *(eye)* cave; *Fig* **to feel h.** *(emotionally)* se sentir vide *ou* vidé; *(hungry)* avoir le ventre *ou* l'estomac creux; *Fig* **he's got h. legs** *(can eat a lot)* il mange comme quatre, il a le ver solitaire **2** *(sound)* sourd; **in a h. voice** d'une voix caverneuse; **a h. laugh** un ricanement **3** *(insincere) (promise, friendship etc)* faux, *f* fausse, trompeur, -euse; *(worthless)* qui sonne creux; **a h. victory** une victoire sans signification

ADV **1 to sound h.** sonner creux **2** *Br Fam* **to beat sb h.** battre qn à plate(s) couture(s)

N *(of hand, tree, in field etc)* creux *m*; *(larger depression in ground)* dépression *f* (du sol); *Geog (basin)* cuvette *f*

▸▸ *Mil, Hist* **h. square** carré *m*

▸ **hollow out** VT SEP *(carve, scrape out etc)* creuser, évider; **to h. out the ground** *(of water)* raviner le terrain

hollow-cheeked [-'tʃiːkt] ADJ aux joues creuses

hollow-eyed ADJ aux yeux caves

hollowness ['hɒləʊnɪs] N **1** *(of tree etc)* creux *m*, cavité *f* **2** *(of voice)* timbre *m* caverneux **3** *(of promise etc)* manque *m* de sincérité; *(worthlessness) (of victory etc)* absence *f* de signification

holly ['hɒlɪ] N houx *m*

▸▸ **h. berry** baie *f* de houx, cenelle *f*; **h. tree** houx

hollyhock ['hɒlɪhɒk] N *(plant)* rose *f* trémière

Hollywood ['hɒlɪwʊd] N Hollywood
ADJ hollywoodien

holm [həʊm] N *Eng Dial (island)* petite île *f*, îlot *m* (de rivière)

holm [N *(tree)* yeuse *f*, chêne *m* vert

▸▸ **h. oak** yeuse, chêne vert

horizontal [hɒrɪ'zɒnt(ə)l] **ADJ** horizontal, -aux; *Am* **a h. increase in salaries of 10%** une augmentation uniforme de 10% sur toutes les rétributions; *Fam* **I was h. for a few days with the flu** je suis resté couché *ou* au lit pendant quelques jours avec la grippe
▪ **N** horizontale *f*
▸▸*Sport* **h. bar** barre *f* fixe; *Fin* **h. equity** équité *f* horizontale; *Mktg* **h. integration** intégration *f ou* concentration *f* horizontale; *Comput* **h. justification** justification *f* horizontale; **h. market** marché *m* horizontal; *Comput* **h. orientation** (format *m*) paysage *m*; *Fin* **h. spread** écart *m* horizontal

horizontally [hɒrɪ'zɒntəlɪ] **ADV** horizontalement

hormonal [hɔː'məʊn(ə)l] **ADJ** *Physiol* hormonal, -aux

hormone ['hɔːməʊn] **N** *Physiol* hormone *f*
▸▸*Med* **h. replacement therapy** traitement *m* hormonal substitutif

horn [hɔːn] **N 1** (of cattle, ram, snail etc) corne *f*; (of stag beetle) antenne *f*; (of owl) aigrette *f*; **horns** (of deer) bois *mpl*; *Fig* **to draw in one's horns** restreindre son ardeur, rabattre (de) ses prétentions; (economize) se serrer la ceinture, faire des économies, diminuer ses dépenses; **to be (caught) on the horns of a dilemma** être en proie à un dilemme
2 (of moon) corne *f*; (of estuary) branche *f*, **Cape H., the H.** le cap Horn
3 (material) corne *f*; **h. comb** peigne *m* en corne
4 *Mus* cor *m Sl* (brass or woodwind instrument) trompette *f*, **English/French h.** cor anglais/d'harmonie; **to sound** *ou* **blow the h.** sonner du cor; *Am Fig* **to blow one's own h.** se vanter; **the h. section, the horns** les cors
5 *Br Sl* (erection) érection *f*, **to have the h.** avoir la trique *ou* le gourdin; **to give sb the h.** (arouse) exciter qn
6 *Am Fam* (telephone) bigophone *m*; **to get on the h. to sb** passer un coup de fil *ou* de bigophone à qn
7 (on car) klaxon *m*; **to sound one's h.** klaxonner
8 (of loudspeaker) pavillon *m*
▪ **VT** (gore) encorner, donner un coup de corne à
▸▸**the H. of Africa** la corne de l'Afrique; *Mus* **h. player** corniste *mf*; *Lit* **h. of plenty** corne d'abondance
▸ **horn in** **VI** *Am Sl* (interrupt, intrude) intervenir sans façon, ramener sa fraise (**on a conversation** dans une conversation); **I don't want him horning in on this deal** je veux pas qu'il fourre son nez dans cette affaire

hornbeam ['hɔːnbiːm] **N** (tree) charme *m*

hornbill ['hɔːnbɪl] **N** (bird) calao *m*

horned [hɔːnd] **ADJ** à cornes

hornet ['hɔːnɪt] **N** (insect) frelon *m*; *Fig* **to stir up a h.'s nest** mettre le feu au poudre

hornpipe ['hɔːnpaɪp] **N** *Naut, Mus* matelote *f*

horn-rimmed **ADJ** (spectacles) à monture lourde, à grosse monture

horny ['hɔːnɪ] **ADJ 1** (like horn) corné; (beak etc) de corne, en corne; (hand etc) calleux; **to grow h.** se racornir **2** *Sl* **to be h.** (sexually aroused) être tout excité; **to get h.** s'exciter **3** *Br Sl* (sexy) bandant

horology [hɒ'rɒlədʒɪ] **N 1** (clockmaking) horlogerie *f* **2** (measuring time) horométrie *f*

horoscope ['hɒrəskəʊp] **N** horoscope *m*; **to cast sb's h.** dresser l'horoscope de qn; **my h. said that …** (in newspaper etc) d'après mon horoscope …

horrendous [hɒ'rendəs] **ADJ** affreux, horrible

horrendously [hɒ'rendəslɪ] **ADV** *Fam* (expensive etc) affreusement, horriblement

horrible ['hɒrəb(ə)l] **ADJ 1** horrible, affreux, atroce; (noise) épouvantable; (weather) abominable; **how h.!** quelle horreur! **2** (unkind) atroce; **to be h. to sb** être méchant *ou* horrible avec qn; **to say h. things about sb** dire des horreurs *ou* des choses terribles sur qn

horribly ['hɒrɪblɪ] **ADV** horriblement, affreusement; (to behave) de façon abominable

horrid ['hɒrɪd] **ADJ 1** horrible, affreux; **he's such a h. little man!** c'est un affreux petit bonhomme; **h. sight** chose *f* horrible à voir **2** *Fam* (unkind) méchant, ignoble; **to be h. to sb** être ignoble envers qn, être odieux avec qn; **to say h. things about sb** dire des méchancetés de qn

horridly ['hɒrɪdlɪ] **ADV** *Fam* (to behave) méchamment, de façon odieuse *ou* ignoble

horrific [hɒ'rɪfɪk, hə-] **ADJ** horrible; **h. injuries** blessures *fpl* horribles

horrify ['hɒrɪfaɪ] **VT** horrifier

horrifying ['hɒrɪfaɪɪŋ] **ADJ** horrifiant

horror ['hɒrər] **N** (feeling, terrifying thing) horreur *f*; **paralysed with h.** glacé d'horreur; **to my h.** à ma grande horreur; **to have a h. of sth/doing sth** avoir horreur de qch/faire qch; **he had a h. of being seen naked** il avait horreur qu'on le voie nu; *Fam* **it gives me the horrors** cela me donne le frisson; *Fam* **that child's a little h.** cet enfant est un petit monstre
▸▸**h. film, h.movie** film *m* d'horreur; **h. story** histoire *f* d'horreur; *Fig Fam* **h. stories about hotels where nothing worked** des histoires terribles sur des hôtels où rien ne marchait

horror-stricken, horror-struck **ADJ** saisi *ou* glacé *ou* frappé d'horreur

horse [hɔːs] **N 1** cheval *m*, -aux; *Horseracing* **to put some money on the horses** jouer aux courses; **draught h.** cheval de trait; **to fall off one's h.** tomber de cheval; *Fig* **to get up on one's high h.** monter sur ses grands chevaux (**about sth** à propos de qch); *Fam* **to eat like a h.** manger comme quatre; **I could eat a h.!** j'ai une faim de loup!; *Fig* **to hear sth from the h.'s mouth** apprendre qch de source sûre; *Fam* **hold your horses!** ne t'emballe pas!, doucement!, du calme!
2 (in breeding) cheval *m* mâle, cheval entier; **stud h.** étalon *m*; **to take a mare to h.** faire couvrir une jument
3 *Mil, Hist* (pl) cavalerie *f*, troupes *fpl* montées; **regiment of h.** régiment *m* de cavalerie; *Br* **the (Royal) H. Guards** la Garde Royale (à cheval)
4 *Gym* (vaulting) **h.** cheval(-sautoir) *m*; **pommel h.** cheval d'arçons
5 (for sawing) chevalet *m*, tréteau *m*, chèvre *f*
6 *Tech Fam* **=** horsepower
7 *Sl* (heroin) héro *f*, blanche *f*
▸▸*Mil, Hist* **h. artillery** artillerie *f* montée; **h. blanket** couverture *f* de cheval; **h. brass** médaillon *m* de bronze (fixé à une martingale); *Bot* **h. chestnut** (tree) marronnier *m* (d'Inde); (nut) marron *m* (d'Inde); **h. collar** collier *m* de cheval (fixé sur le harnachement du cheval); *Fam* **h. doctor** vétérinaire *mf*; **h. fair** foire *f* aux chevaux; **h. laugh** gros rire *m* bruyant; **h. meat** viande *f* de cheval; *Am Cin, TV Fam* **h. opera** western *m*; **h. racing** courses *fpl* (de chevaux); *Br* **h. riding** équitation *f*, *Fam* **h. sense** (gros) bon sens *m*; **h. show** concours *m* hippique; **h. trader** maquignon *m*; *also Fig* **h. trading** maquignonnage *m*; **h. trailer** van *m* à chevaux
▸ **horse about, horse around** **VI** (play roughly) faire l'imbécile

-horse [hɔːs] **SUFF** **one/two-h.** à un cheval/deux chevaux; *see* one-horse

horseback ['hɔːsbæk] **N** **on h.** à (dos de) cheval; **to ride on h.** aller à cheval

horsebox ['hɔːsbɒks] **N** (trailer) van *m*; *Rail* wagon *m* à chevaux

horsebreaker ['hɔːsbreɪkər] **N** dresseur, -euse de chevaux

horse-drawn **ADJ** tiré par des chevaux
▸▸**h. vehicle** véhicule *m* attelé

horseflesh ['hɔːsfleʃ] **N 1** (horses) chevaux *mpl*; **to be a good judge of h.** bien s'y connaître en chevaux **2** (meat) chair *f ou* viande *f* de cheval

horsefly ['hɔːsflaɪ] **N** taon *m*

horsehair ['hɔːsheər] **N** crin *m* (de cheval); *Tex* tissu *m* de crin; **h. mattress** matelas *m* de crin

horseman, pl horsemen ['hɔːsmən] **N** cavalier *m*, écuyer *m*; **to be a good h.** bien monter à cheval, être bon cavalier; **the four horsemen of the apocalypse** les quatre cavaliers de l'apocalypse

horsemanship ['hɔːsmənʃɪp] **N** équitation *f*, art *m* de monter à cheval; **we admired her h.** nous avons admiré l'art avec lequel elle montait à cheval, nous avons admiré son talent de cavalière

horseplay ['hɔːspleɪ] **N** **they were having a bit of h. in the pool** ils faisaient les imbéciles dans la piscine; **it's just harmless h.** c'est une bagarre pour rire; **no h.!** jeux de mains, jeux de vilains!

horsepower ['hɔːspaʊər] **N** *Tech etc* puissance *f* en chevaux; (measurement) cheval-vapeur *m*, *pl* chevaux-vapeur; **actual h.** puissance effective en chevaux

horseradish ['hɔːsrædɪʃ] **N** (plant) raifort *m*
▸▸*Culin* **h. sauce** sauce *f* au raifort

horseshoe ['hɔːsʃuː] **N** fer *m* à cheval; **h. brooch/table** broche *f*/table *f* en (forme de) fer à cheval

horsewhip ['hɔːswɪp] **N** cravache *f*
▪ **VT** (-pp-) (person) cravacher

horsewoman, pl horsewomen ['hɔːswʊmən, -wɪmɪn] **N** cavalière *f*, amazone *f*, écuyère *f*; **she's a good h.** elle est bonne cavalière, elle monte bien

horsy, horsey ['hɔːsɪ] **ADJ** (appearance) chevalin; (keen on horses) fou/folle de chevaux; **she's terribly h.** elle ne parle que chevaux; **h. face** figure chevaline

horticultural [hɔːtɪ'kʌltʃər(ə)l] **N** (implement) horticole, d'horticulture
▸▸**h. show** exposition *f* horticole *ou* d'horticulture

horticulture ['hɔːtɪkʌltʃər] **N** horticulture *f*

horticulturist [hɔːtɪ'kʌltʃərɪst] **N** horticulteur, -trice

hose [həʊz] **N 1** (pl hoses) (pipe) tuyau *m*; *Tech* **(flexible) h.** tuyau flexible; (in car) durite *f*, **air h.** tuyau d'air flexible; **garden h.** tuyau d'arrosage **2** (no pl) Com (stockings etc) (for women) bas *mpl*; *Hist* (for men) chausses *fpl*; **half h.** chaussettes *fpl* (d'hommes)
▪ **VT 1** (car etc) laver au jet **2** (lawn) arroser (au jet d'eau)
▸▸*Aut* **h. clip** collier *m* de durite; **h. reel** dévidoir *m*
▸ **hose down** **VT SEP** **=** hose **VT**
▸ **hose out** **VT SEP** (clean out) laver au jet

hosepipe ['həʊzpaɪp] **N** tuyau *m*, flexible *m*
▸▸**h. ban** **=** interdiction *f* d'utiliser les tuyaux d'arrosage pendant les périodes de sécheresse

hosier ['həʊzɪər] **N** *Com* bonnetier, -ière

hosiery ['həʊzɪərɪ] **N** *Com* (stockings and socks) bas *mpl* et chaussettes *fpl*; **h. counter** *or* **department** rayon *m* des bas (et chaussettes); **h. trade** bonneterie *f*

hospice ['hɒspɪs] N hospice *m*; *(for terminally ill)* hospice (pour malades en phase terminale); *(part of hospital)* pavillon *m* des incurables

hospitable [hɒs'pɪtəb(ə)l] ADJ *(climate)* hospitalier, accueillant; *(person)* accueillant

hospitably [hɒs'pɪtəblɪ] ADV avec hospitalité

hospital ['hɒspɪt(ə)l] N **1** hôpital *m*, -aux; **to be in h.** être à l'hôpital; **she had to go (in)to** *Br* **h.** *or Am* **the h.** elle a dû aller à l'hôpital; **to send sb to** *Br* **h.** *or Am* **the h.** hospitaliser qn VOIR GRAMMAIRE A7 **2 Chelsea H.** l'hôpital *m* de Chelsea *(pour les vieux soldats)*; **Greenwich H.** l'Hospice *m* de Greenwich *(pour les invalides de la marine)*
▸▸ **h. bed** lit *m* d'hôpital; **h. radio** radio *f* diffusant dans les hôpitaux; **h. ship** navire-hôpital *m*, *pl* navires-hôpitaux; **h. staff** personnel *m* hospitalier; **h. train** train *m* sanitaire; **h. treatment** traitement *m* hospitalier

hospitality [hɒspɪ'tælɪtɪ] N hospitalité *f*; *Old-fashioned Euph* **to enjoy His/Her Majesty's h.** faire de la prison
▸▸ **h. business** hôtellerie *f*; **h. industry** industrie *f* hôtelière; **h. management** gestion *f* hôtelière; **h. tray** plateau *m* de courtoisie

hospitalization [hɒspɪtəlaɪ'zeɪʃən] N hospitalisation *f*

hospitalize ['hɒspɪtəlaɪz] VT *(sick person)* hospitaliser; **a couple of thugs hospitalized him** deux voyous l'ont envoyé à l'hôpital

host[1] [həʊst] N **1** *(in private house)* hôte *m*; *Com (in hotel etc)* hôtelier *m*; *(in inn)* aubergiste *m*; *TV etc (of chat show, gameshow)* animateur, -trice; **he was the perfect h.** il a été un hôte parfait **2** *Biol* hôte *m* **3** *Comput (of website)* hébergeur *m*
VT **1** *(party)* donner; *TV etc (programme)* présenter; *(gameshow)* animer **2** *(website)* héberger
▸▸ *Comput* **h. computer** ordinateur *m* principal; *(in network)* serveur *m*; *Comput* **h. file** fichier *m* serveur; *Biol* **h. organism** hôte *m*; *Comput* **h. system** système *m* serveur *ou* hôte

host[2] N **1** *(great number)* **a (whole) h.** *(of servants etc)* (toute) une armée; **a h. of good restaurants** une quantité de bons restaurants **2** *Arch, Lit (throng)* armée *f*, multitude *f*

host[3] N *Rel (consecrated bread)* hostie *f*

hostage ['hɒstɪdʒ] N otage *m*; **as (a) h.** en otage, pour otage; **to take sb h.** prendre quelqu'un en otage; **she is being held h.** elle est gardée en otage; *Fig* **that's a h. to fortune** c'est la porte ouverte à tous les ennuis
▸▸ **h. taker** preneur, -euse d'otage; **h. taking** prise *f* d'otage(s)

hostel ['hɒstəl] N *(for the homeless, students)* foyer *m*; **youth h.** auberge *f* de jeunesse

hosteller, *Am* **hosteler** ['hɒstələr] N **(youth) h.** ajiste *mf*

hostelling, *Am* **hosteling** ['hɒstəlɪŋ] N **(youth) h.** ajisme *m*

hostelry ['hɒstəlrɪ] N *Arch* hostellerie *f*; *Br Hum* pub *m*; bar *m*

hostess ['həʊstɪs] N **1** *(in private house, night club)* hôtesse *f*; *(hotel-keeper etc)* hôtelière *f*; *TV etc (of chat show etc)* animatrice *f* **2** *Aviat* **(air) h.** hôtesse *f* de l'air

hostile ['hɒstaɪl, *Am* 'hɒst(ə)l] ADJ *(attitude, climate, environment)* hostile; *(act)* d'hostilité; **to be h. to sb/sth** *(opposed)* être hostile à qn/qch
N *Am* ennemi *m*
▸▸ *Mil* **h. forces** forces *fpl* ennemies; *Com* **h. takeover bid** OPA *f* hostile

hostility [hɒs'tɪlɪtɪ] N **1** hostilité *f* (**to** *or* **contre**); **to feel no h. towards sb** n'avoir au-

cune animosité contre qn **2 hostilities** *(war)* hostilités *fpl*

hosting N *Comput (of website)* hébergement *m*

HOT [hɒt]

ADJ	chaud **1, 5**	fort **2**	épicé **2**
	tout frais **3**	violent **5**	super **6**
	intense **7**	recherché **8**	

ADJ *(hotter, hottest)* **1** chaud; *(sun)* ardent; *(fire)* vif; *Nucl* radioactif; **boiling h.** bouillant; **burning h.** brûlant; **to be very h.** *(of person)* avoir très chaud; *(of water, plate etc)* être très chaud; *(of weather)* faire très chaud; **it was a h. day** il faisait chaud; **to get** *or* **become h.** *(of person)* commencer à avoir chaud; *(of water, plate etc)* devenir chaud, chauffer; *(of weather)* commencer à faire chaud; **to keep a dish h.** tenir un plat au chaud; *Fam* **to get all h. and bothered** devenir tout rouge; *Fam* **to get h. under the collar** *(with embarrassment)* être embarrassé; *(with anger)* se mettre en colère; *Fam* **it's all h. air** ce ne sont que des balivernes; *Fam* **he's full of h. air** il ne raconte que des foutaises; **to sell like h. cakes** se vendre comme des petits pains; **a h. meal** un repas chaud; *Fig Fam* **to be in h. water** être dans le pétrin; *Fig Fam* **to get into h. water** s'attirer *ou* se créer des ennuis **2** *Culin (spicy etc) (pepper)* fort; *(mustard)* piquant, fort; *(food)* épicé; **not all Indian food is h.** la cuisine indienne n'est pas nécessairement relevée **3** *(fresh, recent)* tout frais; **news h. from the press** nouvelles de dernière heure; **a book h. from the press** un livre qui sort tout juste de l'imprimerie; **h. gossip/news** les tous derniers cancans/les toutes dernières nouvelles **4** *(close)* **to be h. on the scent** *or* **trail** être sur la bonne piste; **to be in h. pursuit of sb** suivre qn de près; **you're getting h.** *(in guessing game)* tu brûles **5** *(fiery)* violent; **to have a h. temper** s'emporter facilement; **the political climate has become noticeably hotter in recent weeks** le climat politique est devenu sensiblement plus chaud depuis quelques semaines **6** *(intense)* intense, profond **7** *Fam (good)* super; **that record wasn't so h.** ce disque n'était pas super; **that isn't such a h. idea** ce n'est pas terrible *ou* fameux comme idée; **I'm not very h. on history** *(knowledgeable about)* je ne suis pas très calé en histoire; **they're very h. on formal qualifications** *(attach importance to)* ils insistent beaucoup sur les diplômes; **they're not very h. on hygiene** *(fussy about)* ils ne sont pas très portés sur l'hygiène; **to be h. stuff** *(sexy) (of woman)* être canon; *(of man)* être super (bien); **he's h. stuff at tennis** au tennis, c'est un as; **how are you? – not so h.** comment ça va? – pas terrible *ou* fameux **8** *Fam (dangerous, difficult) (stolen goods etc)* recherché par la police; **the place was getting too h. for me** je me trouvais dans un véritable guêpier; **the situation was too h. to handle** la situation était trop délicate pour qu'on s'en mêle; **to make things** *or* **it too h. for sb** rendre la vie infernale à qn; **the presence of the army made things h. for the smugglers** la présence de l'armée a rendu les choses très difficiles pour les contrebandiers

ADV **to blow h. and cold** *(of person)* changer d'avis sans cesse; *(in moods)* être d'humeur changeante; **she's blowing h. and cold over him** un jour, elle l'aime, un jour, elle ne l'aime pas

▸ **hot up** *Fam* VT SEP *Aut (engine)* gonfler; **to h. up the pace** *(increase)* forcer l'allure
VI *(of campaign etc)* s'échauffer; *(of competi-*

tion, love affair, discussion) s'intensifier; *(of race)* s'animer; **things are beginning to h. up** l'affaire se corse
▸▸ *Br* **h. cross bun** = brioche *f* à la canelle; **h. desking** = pratique *f* qui consiste à ne pas assigner de bureaux individuels aux employés, ces derniers étant libres de s'installer à n'importe quel poste de travail inoccupé; *Br Sport* **h. favourite** grand(e) favori, -ite; *Br* **h. flush,** *Am* **h. flash** bouffée *f* de chaleur; *Comput* **h. key** touche *f* personnalisée; *Tel* **h. line** numéro *m* d'urgence; *Pol (between US and Kremlin)* téléphone *m* rouge; *Comput* **h. link** lien *m* hypertexte; *Fam* **h. money** *(stolen)* argent *m* volé; *Fin* capitaux *mpl* flottants *ou* fébriles; *Am* **h. pad** dessous-de-plat *m inv*; **h. pants** mini short *m (très court et moulant)*; *Fam Fig* **h. potato** sujet *m* brûlant et délicat; *Fam* **to drop sb like a h. potato** laisser tomber qn comme une vieille chaussette *ou* savate; *Ir* **h. press** *(airing cupboard)* = placard *m* chauffé où l'on fait sécher le linge; *Am Fam* **h. seat** *(electric chair)* chaise *f* électrique; **to be in the h. seat** *(be responsible)* avoir toute la responsabilité; *(have to answer difficult questions)* être sur la sellette; **the man in the England h. seat** *(manager of football team etc)* l'homme qui a la tâche difficile de diriger l'équipe d'Angleterre; **h. spot** *(dangerous area)* point *m* chaud *ou* névralgique; *Fam (night club)* boîte *f* de nuit; *Tech* point *m* chaud; **h. spring** source *f* chaude; **h. tip** tuyau *m* de première

hot-air balloon N montgolfière *f*, ballon *m* à air chaud

hotbed ['hɒtbed] N **1** *Fig (of rebellion, intrigue etc)* foyer *m* **2** *(in gardening)* couche *f*

hot-blooded ADJ ardent, passionné; **to be h.** avoir le sang chaud; **the Italians are a h. race** les Italiens sont un peuple qui a le sang chaud

hotchpotch ['hɒtʃpɒtʃ] N mélange *m* confus; **this book's a bit of a h.** *(good and bad)* ce livre est de qualité inégale; *(mixture)* ce livre est un patchwork

hotdog ['hɒtdɒg] N *Culin* hot-dog *m*

hot-dog VI *Ski* faire du ski acrobatique

hot-dogging ['hɒtdɒgɪŋ] N *Ski* ski *m* acrobatique

hotel [həʊ'tel] N hôtel *m*; **at** *or* **in my h.** à mon hôtel; **to stay at a h.** descendre dans un hôtel; **private** *or* **residential h.** = pension *f* de famille; **h. and catering industry** industrie *f* de l'hôtellerie et de la restauration
▸▸ **h. accommodation** hébergement *m* en hôtel; **h. administration** gestion *f* hôtelière; **h. bed** lit *m* d'hôtel; **h. bedroom** chambre *f* d'hôtel; **the h. business** l'hôtellerie *f*; **h. chain** chaîne *f* d'hôtels; **h. clerk** employé *m* d'hôtel; **h. group** groupe *m* hôtelier; **the h. industry** l'industrie *f* hôtelière, l'hôtellerie *f*; **h. keeper** hôtelier, -ière; **h. keeping** hôtellerie *f*; **h. lobby** hall *m* d'hôtel, hall d'entrée d'un hôtel; **h. management** *(training)* gestion *f* hôtelière; *(people)* direction *f* (de l'hôtel); **h. manager** gérant, -ante d'hôtel, directeur, -trice d'hôtel; **h. occupancy** taux *m* d'occupation des hôtels; **h. reception** réception *f* d'hôtel; **h. receptionist** réceptionniste *mf* d'hôtel; **h. register** agenda *m* *ou* livre *m* de réservation; **h. school** école *f* hôtelière; **h. tax** taxe *f* sur l'hôtellerie; **h. taxi** taxi *m* d'hôtel; **the h. trade** l'industrie hôtelière, l'hôtellerie *f*; **h. transfer** transfert *m* (de la gare/l'aéroport à l'hôtel)

hotelier [həʊ'telɪeɪ] N hôtelier, -ière

hotfoot ['hɒtfʊt] ADV *(to set off, arrive)* à toute vitesse, en (toute) hâte
VT *Fam* **to h. it** galoper, aller à toute allure

hothead ['hɒthed] N exalté, -ée

hot-headed ADJ *(rash)* exalté, impétueux; *(quick-tempered)* emporté, violent

hothouse ['hɒthaʊs] N serre *f* chaude; *Fig (of new talent etc)* pépinière *f*
▸▸ *Fig* **h. plant** plante *f* de serre (chaude); *Fig (person)* plante de serre

hotlist ['hɒtlɪst] N *Comput* liste *f* de signets

hotly ['hɒtlɪ] ADV **1** *(to reply, protest)* vivement; **h. contested** âprement disputé **2** *(to pursue)* avec acharnement

hotplate ['hɒtpleɪt] N *(for cooking)* plaque *f* chauffante; *(on table)* chauffe-plat *m*, *pl* chauffe-plats

hotpot ['hɒtpɒt] N *esp Br Culin* = ragoût *m* de viande aux pommes de terre cuit à l'étuvée

hotrod ['hɒtrɒd] N *Aut Fam* bolide *m*, voiture *f* gonflée

hots [hɒts] NPL *Sl* **to have the h. for sb** *(of woman)* mouiller pour qn; *(of man)* bander pour qn

hot-shoe N *Phot* sabot-contact *m*

hotshot ['hɒtʃɒt] *Fam* ADJ magnifique, terrible; **a h. chess player** un joueur d'échecs super-doué; **they've hired some h. lawyer** ils ont pris un as du barreau
N *(expert)* as *m*, crack *m*; *Br (VIP)* gros bonnet *m*; *Am Pej (self-important person)* = personne *f* qui a la grosse tête

hot-tempered ADJ colérique, coléreux

Hottentot ['hɒt(ə)ntɒt] ADJ hottentot
N Hottentot, -ote

hottie ['hɒtɪ] N *Am Fam (attractive woman)* canon *m*; *(attractive man)* beau mec *m*

hot-water bottle N bouillotte *f*

hound [haʊnd] N **1** *(in hunting)* chien *m* de meute; *Fam (dog)* chien *m*; **the hounds** *(pack)* la meute *f*; **as if all the hounds of hell were after him** comme s'il avait tous les diables de l'enfer à ses trousses; **to ride to hounds** chasser à courre **2** *Sport (in paper chase)* coureur *m*, poursuivant *m* **3** *Old-fashioned Fam (contemptible person)* canaille *f*
VT *Fig* **she was hounded by the press** elle était traquée *ou* poursuivie par la presse; **hounded from place to place** pourchassé d'un endroit à un autre; **he was hounded out of France** il fut chassé de France
▸ **hound down** VT SEP *(person)* traquer jusqu'à la capture; **wherever you are we'll h. you down** où que vous soyez, on vous aura; **he's been hounded down** il s'est fait prendre

hour ['aʊər] N **1** *(period)* heure *f*; **an h. and a half** une heure et demie; **half an h.,** *esp Am* **a half h.** une demi-heure; **a quarter of an h.** un quart d'heure; **h. by h.** d'heure en heure; **to pay sb by the h.** payer qn à l'heure; **to be paid £5 an h.** être payé 5 livres de l'heure; *Ind etc* **output per h.** rendement *m* à l'heure; **there's a train every h. on the h.** il y a un train toutes les heures (à l'heure juste); **to take hours over sth** mettre des heures à faire qch; *Fam* **we've been waiting (for) hours** ça fait des heures que nous attendons VOIR GRAMMAIRE A80–1; B60
2 *(in timetables)* **office hours** heures *fpl* de bureau; **what are your hours?, what hours do you work?** quels sont vos horaires de travail?; **to keep late hours** rentrer à des heures indues; *(go to bed late)* se coucher très tard; **they keep odd** *or* **unusual hours** ils ont des horaires bizarres; **to work long hours** faire de longues journées (de travail); **after hours** *(of office)* après les heures de travail; *Br (of pub)* après l'heure de la fermeture
3 *(time of day)* **at this h.?!** à cette heure-ci?!; **in the small** *or* **early hours** en pleine nuit; **well on into the small hours** très avant dans la nuit; **people come and go at all hours** les gens vont et viennent à toute heure; **till all hours** jusqu'à des heures impossibles
4 *(moment)* heure *f*, moment *m*; **in the h. of**

need/death à l'heure du besoin/de la mort; **his h. has come** son heure est venue; **I thought my final h. had come** j'ai cru ma dernière heure arrivée; **her last hours** ses dernières heures; **he was the man of the h.** c'était l'homme du moment
▸▸ **h. hand** petite aiguille *f*

-hour ['aʊər] SUFF **one/two/etc-h.** d'une/de deux/*etc* heure(s); **an eight-h. day** une journée de travail de huit heures; **a 30-h. week** une semaine de trente heures; **a three-h. delay** un retard de trois heures; **to put a twenty-four-h. watch/guard on sb/sth** surveiller qn/qch vingt-quatre heures sur vingt-quatre

hourglass ['aʊəglɑːs] N sablier *m*
▸▸ **h. figure** taille *f* de guêpe

hourlong ['aʊəlɒŋ] ADJ *(meeting)* d'une heure

hourly ['aʊəlɪ] ADJ de toutes les heures; *(train service etc)* à chaque heure; *(output, yield, wage)* horaire, à l'heure; **at h. intervals** toutes les heures; **there is an h. train from platform 8** il y a un train toutes les heures sur le quai numéro 8
ADV toutes les heures
▸▸ **h. rate** taux *m* horaire

-hourly ['aʊəlɪ] SUFF **two/three/etc-h.** toutes les deux/trois/*etc* heures

house¹, *pl* **houses** [haʊs, 'haʊzɪz] N **1** maison *f*; **at his h.** chez lui; **we invited him to our h.** nous l'avons invité chez nous; **from h. to h.** de porte en porte; **to keep h. for sb** tenir *ou* diriger la maison de qn; **they keep open h.** on est toujours les bienvenus chez eux; **to set up h.** s'installer; *(of young unmarried couple)* se mettre en ménage; *Fig* **the government should put** *or* **set its own h. in order before criticizing others** le gouvernement devrait balayer devant sa porte avant de critiquer les autres; *Fam* **they get on like a h. on fire** ils se sont immédiatement entendus à merveille; *Fam* **he's progressing like a h. on fire** il a fait des progrès du feu de Dieu; *Fam* **it's coming on like a h. on fire** ça marche du feu de Dieu; *Br Fam* **the bus goes all round the houses** le bus fait tout le tour de la ville; *Fig Fam* **to go all round the houses** *(avoid being direct in talking)* tourner autour du pot; **the son/daughter of the h.** le fils/la fille de la maison; **to move h.** déménager
2 *(institution)* **the h. of God** *(church)* la maison de Dieu; **h. of prayer** *or* **worship** église *f*, *(Protestant)* temple *m*; *Br* **the H.** *(parliament)* le Parlement; *(the Stock Exchange)* la Bourse (de Londres)
3 *Com etc (company)* maison *f*, **banking h.** établissement *m* bancaire; **publishing h.** maison d'édition; **in h.** dans les locaux de la compagnie; *see* **in-house**
4 *(restaurant etc)* **to have a drink on the h.** prendre une consommation aux frais du patron *ou* de la maison
5 *Br Sch* = groupe *m* d'élèves qui rivalise avec un autre pour les activités sportives *etc*
6 *Astrol* maison *f*
7 *(of crane)* cabine *f*; *Naut (on deck)* rouf *m*; *(at helm)* kiosque *m*
8 *(household)* maison *f*, *(dynasty)* famille *f*, maison; **the H. of Stuart/Bourbon** les Stuarts *mpl*/les Bourbons *mpl*; **the whole h. was down with flu** toute la maisonnée avait la grippe
9 *Theat* salle *f*, auditoire *m*, assistance *f*; **is there a doctor in the h.?** y a-t-il un médecin dans la salle?; **a full h.** une salle pleine; **h. full** complet; **to play to an empty h.** jouer devant les banquettes vides, jouer devant une salle vide; **to play to packed houses** jouer devant une salle comble, faire salle comble; **there wasn't a dry eye in the h.** tout le monde pleurait dans la salle; *Cin Old-*

fashioned the first h. la première séance
▸▸ *Br* **h. agent** agent *m* immobilier; *Am Fam* **h. ape** *(child)* môme *mf*, chiard *m*; **h. arrest** assignation *f* à domicile *ou* à résidence; *Fin* **h. bill** double *m* de connaissement, lettre *f* de change creuse; *also Fig* **h. of cards** château *m* de cartes; **the H. of Commons** la Chambre des communes; **h. detective** responsable *m* de la sécurité, détective *m* de l'hôtel; *Naut* **h. flag** pavillon *m* d'armateur *ou* de compagnie (de navigation); **h. guest** invité, -ée; *Theat* **h. lights** lumières *fpl ou* éclairage *m* de la salle; **the H. of Lords** la Chambre des lords; **h. magazine** journal *m* interne, bulletin *m*; *Theat* **h. manager** directeur, -trice de théâtre; *Orn* **h. martin** hirondelle *f* de fenêtre; *Br Parl* **Houses of Parliament** Parlement *m*; **h. party** *(social occasion)* fête *f* de plusieurs jours *(dans une maison de campagne)*; *(guests)* invités *mpl*, **h. phone** *(in hotel)* téléphone *m* intérieur; **h. physician** médecin *m* de garde; **h. plant** *Bot* plante *f* d'intérieur, plante d'appartement; *Parl* **the H. of Representatives** la Chambre des représentants *(aux États-Unis)*; **h. rule** règle *f* de la maison; *(in games)* règle *f* du jeu particulière; **h. special, h. specialty** *(in restaurant)* spécialité *f* (de la) maison; *Br Typ, Journ* **h. style** style *m* maison; *Med* **h. surgeon** chirurgien *m* de garde; *Br* **h. wine** vin *m* de la maison

House of Commons
La Chambre des communes britannique est composée de 659 députés ("MPs") élus pour cinq ans et qui siègent environ 175 jours par an. Les députés du parti majoritaire s'assoient d'un côté de la Chambre (les "government benches"), tandis que les députés de l'opposition s'assoient de l'autre côté (sur les "opposition benches"). Si un projet de loi n'obtient pas l'approbation de la majorité des députés dans la Chambre des communes, il est renvoyé à la Chambre des lords, et doit par ailleurs obtenir l'assentiment du souverain avant de devenir loi.

House of Lords
La Chambre des lords est composée de pairs et d'hommes d'Église. Il s'agit de la plus haute cour du Royaume-Uni (en excluant l'Écosse). Elle a le pouvoir d'amender certains projets de loi qui ont été votés par la Chambre des communes. Le gouvernement travailliste de Tony Blair, élu en 1997, a entrepris des réformes visant à réduire les pouvoirs de la Chambre des lords.

House of Representatives
La Chambre des représentants constitue, avec le Sénat, l'organe législatif américain; ses membres sont élus par le peuple, en proportion de la population de chaque État.

house² [haʊz] VT **1** *(person)* loger, héberger; *(population)* pourvoir au logement de; **a building that can h. ten families** un bâtiment qui peut loger dix familles **2** *(of museum etc) (collection)* contenir; *(locomotive)* mettre à l'abri *ou* à couvert; **the gears are housed in a steel case** l'engrenage est contenu dans un carter d'acier; **this section houses the main engines** dans cette section se trouvent les moteurs principaux

houseboat ['haʊsbəʊt] N house-boat *m*, *pl* house-boats, péniche *f* (aménagée)

housebound ['haʊsbaʊnd] ADJ obligé de rester à la maison; *(invalid)* immobilisé à la maison

housebreaker ['haʊsbreɪkər] N *(burglar)* cambrioleur m

housebreaking ['haʊsbreɪkɪŋ] N *(burglary)* cambriolage m, vol m avec effraction

housecoat ['haʊskəʊt] N *(woman's)* robe f d'intérieur

housefly ['haʊsflaɪ] N mouche f domestique *ou* commune

houseful ['haʊsfʊl] N **to have a h. of guests** avoir sa maison pleine d'invités

household ['haʊshəʊld] N 1 *(people in house)* (membres mpl de la) maison f; *(economically, statistically)* ménage m; **there are five people in this h.** *(in house)* cinq personnes habitent dans cette maison; *(in family)* cette famille compte cinq personnes; **h. chores** *or* **duties** *or* **tasks** tâches fpl ménagères, travaux mpl ménagers; **not for h. use** *(on industrial cleaner etc)* usage industriel uniquement; **she's a h. name** son nom est connu de tous; **to be a h. name** être connu de tous 2 *(servants)* domestiques mfpl 3 Br **the H.** la Maison du souverain; **the H. troops** la Garde
▸▸ **h. appliances** électro-ménager m; **h. articles** articles mpl pour le ménage; **h. budget** budget m du ménage; **h. consumption** consommation f des ménages; **h. expenses** frais mpl de *ou* du ménage; **h. goods** articles mpl pour le ménage, produits mpl ménagers; **h. unit** foyer m

householder ['haʊshəʊldər] N *(owner)* propriétaire mf d'une/de la maison; *(tenant)* locataire mf

househusband ['haʊshʌzbənd] N homme m au foyer

housekeeper ['haʊskiːpər] N femme f de charge; *(of priest etc)* gouvernante f; *(at castle etc)* économe f, intendante f; *(in hotel)* gouvernante; **to be a good h.** *(at home)* être une bonne maîtresse de maison

housekeeping ['haʊskiːpɪŋ] N *(art)* économie f domestique; *(work)* soins mpl du ménage; *Comput (file management)* aménagement m; **h. (allowance** *or* **money)** argent m du *ou* pour le ménage; **she knows nothing about h.** ce n'est pas une femme d'intérieur
▸▸ **h. book** carnet m de dépenses

housemaid ['haʊsmeɪd] N *Old-fashioned* bonne f, femme f de chambre
▸▸ *Med Fam* **h.'s knee** hygroma m du genou

houseman, pl **housemen** ['haʊsmən] N *Br Med (at hospital)* interne m; *(in hotel)* homme m de ménage

housemaster, housemistress ['haʊsmɑːstər, -mɪstrɪs] N *Br Sch (in boarding school)* = professeur m chargé de la surveillance d'un internat; *(in day school)* = professeur chargé d'un groupe d'élèves

house-proud ADJ **she is very h.** c'est une femme d'intérieur méticuleuse, *Pej* c'est une véritable maniaque du ménage

houseroom ['haʊsruːm] N place f *(pour loger qn, qch)*; *Fam* **I wouldn't give it h.** je n'en voudrais pas même si on m'en faisait cadeau

house-sit VI **to h. for sb** s'occuper de la maison de qn pendant son absence

house-sitter N = personne f qui garde une maison en l'absence de ses occupants

house-style book N guide m du style maison; *(for design)* charte f graphique; *(editorial)* charte f rédactionnelle

house-to-house ADJ *(enquiry, selling etc)* à domicile; **the police made a h. search** la police a fait une fouille maison par maison, la police a perquisitionné maison après maison

▸▸ *Mktg* **h. canvassing** porte-à-porte m inv, démarchage m

housetop ['haʊstɒp] N toit m; *Fig* **to shout** *or* **proclaim sth from the housetops** crier qch sur tous les toits

house-train VT *Br (dog etc)* dresser à la propreté; **house-trained** *(dog etc)* propre; *Fam Hum* **she got him (properly) house-trained** *(taught clean habits)* elle lui a appris la propreté; *(taught basic housekeeping)* elle lui a appris à se débrouiller à la maison

house-warming N **to give** *or* **have a h.** pendre la crémaillère
▸▸ **h. party** pendaison f de crémaillère, soirée f pour pendre la crémaillère

housewife, pl **housewives** N 1 ['haʊswaɪf, -waɪvz] femme f au foyer 2 ['hʌzɪf, -vz] *Br Old-fashioned (sewing kit)* trousse f de couture

housewifely ['haʊswaɪflɪ] ADJ de femme au foyer

housewifery ['haʊswɪf(ə)rɪ] N *Old-fashioned* économie f domestique; *(work)* soins mpl du ménage

housework ['haʊswɜːk] N travaux mpl domestiques *ou* de ménage; **to do the h.** faire le ménage

> Attention: ne pas confondre avec **homework**, qui signifie **devoirs à faire à la maison**.

housey-housey ['haʊsɪ'haʊsɪ] N *Br (jeu m de)* loto m

housing ['haʊzɪŋ] N 1 *(of people)* logement m; **the h. problem** *or* **shortage** la crise du logement 2 *(for machine, mechanism etc)* boîtier m; *(bigger)* coffre m; *(of gears, differential)* carter m
▸▸ **h. association** = association f britannique à but non lucratif qui construit ou rénove des logements pour les louer à ses membres; *Br* **h. benefit** *Admin* = allocation f logement versée par l'État aux individus justifiant de revenus faibles; *Br* **h. estate** grand ensemble m, *Pej* cité f; **h. market** marché m de l'immobilier; *Am* **h. project** grand ensemble m, *Pej* cité f; *(plan)* plan m d'aménagement immobilier; *Am* **h. starts** = mise f en chantier de logements; **h. stock** parc m immobilier

hove PT, PP *see* **heave**

hovel ['hɒv(ə)l] N *Pej* taudis m, masure f

hover ['hɒvər] VI 1 *(of bird, insect)* planer, se balancer; *(of helicopter)* effectuer un vol stationnaire; **the helicopter hovered just above us** l'hélicoptère s'immobilisa au-dessus de nos têtes
  2 *Fig (of person)* tourner en rond; *(waiting to pounce, do sth)* guetter; **danger is hovering over him** le danger le menace; **a waitress was hovering near our table** une serveuse tournait autour de notre table; **I don't like him hovering over me** je n'aime pas qu'il soit sur mon dos; **don't just h. in the background** ne reste pas dans ton coin; **to h. between two courses of action** hésiter entre deux possibilités; **a smile hovered on his lips** l'ombre d'un sourire passa sur ses lèvres; **she hovered between life and death** elle oscilla *ou* resta entre la vie et la mort; **he seemed to be hovering on the brink of saying something** il semblait hésiter à dire quelque chose
▸ **hover around** VT INSEP *(move about, near)* **to h. around sb** errer *ou* rôder autour de qn; **prices are hovering around the £3.50 mark** les prix oscillent autour de 3 livres 50
  VI *(move about nearby)* tourner

hovercraft ['hɒvəkrɑːft] N INV aéroglisseur m, *Fam* hovercraft m

hoverport ['hɒvəpɔːt] N hoverport m, gare f des aéroglisseurs

hovertrain ['hɒvətreɪn] N aérotrain m

HOW [haʊ]

> | ADV | comment **1, 3** ▪ comme **4** ▪ que **4, 5** |
> | N | comment |

ADV 1 *(in what manner)* comment; **h. do you spell this word?** comment écrit-on ce mot?; *Fam* **h. the devil …?, h. on earth …?, h. in the world …?** comment diable …?; **h. did they find out?** comment est-ce qu'ils l'ont su *ou* appris?; **tell me h. he did it** dites-moi comment il (l')a fait; **h. was she dressed?** comment est-ce qu'elle était habillée?, qu'est-ce qu'elle portait?; **h. is it that …?** comment se fait-il que …?; **h. so?** comment ça?; *Fam* **h. come?** comment cela se fait-il?, et comment ça se fait?; **h. come she didn't tell you?** comment ça se fait qu'elle ne te l'ait pas dit?; **h.'s that?** *(how can that be?)* comment ça?; *(repeat that)* pardon?; *Cr* = appel m à l'arbitre, pour savoir si le guichet est sauf ou si la balle a été bien attrapée; **suppose I offer you another £500, h.'s that?** et si je t'offre 500 livres en plus, qu'est-ce que tu en dis?; **h.'s that for a sandwich?** qu'est-ce que tu dis de ce sandwich?; **h.'s that for size?** *(of jacket etc)* ça va comme taille?; *Fam* **and h.!** et comment!; **h. could you?** *(shame on you)* vous n'avez pas honte?; **I don't know h. he can say that!** je ne sais pas comment il peut dire une chose pareille!; **to learn h. to do sth** apprendre à faire qch; **h. do you like this wine?** comment trouvez-vous ce vin?; **h. do you like your steak?** comment voulez-vous votre steak?; **here's h.!** *(toast)* santé! VOIR GRAMMAIRE A74–5
  2 *(to what extent)* **h. much/many** combien (de); **h. many times?, h. often?** combien de fois?; **h. many are there of you?** vous êtes combien (de personnes)?; **h. long have you been here?** depuis combien de temps êtes-vous là?; **h. long is the flight?** quelle est la durée du vol?; **you know h. useful he is to me** vous savez à quel point il m'est utile; **you don't know h. right you are** vous ne savez pas combien vous dites vrai, vous ne savez pas à quel point vous avez raison; **h. early would you like to be woken?** à quelle heure voulez-vous qu'on vous réveille?; **h. wide is this room?** quelle est la largeur de cette pièce?; **h. old are you?** quel âge avez-vous?; **h. likely is that to happen?** quelle est la probabilité d'un tel événement?; **h. keen are you on fish?** aimez-vous le poisson?
  3 *(greetings, enquiries after health etc)* **h. are you?** comment allez-vous?, *Fam* comment ça va?; **h. do you do?** *(when being introduced)* enchanté (de faire votre connaissance); *(hello)* bonjour; *Fam* **h. are things?** comment ça va?; *Fam* **h.'s it going?** comment ça se passe?; **h.'s your leg?** et (comment va) ta jambe?; **h.'s business?** comment vont les affaires?; *Fam* **h.'s life?** comment vas-tu?
  4 *(in exclamations)* comme, que; **h. pretty she is!** comme elle est jolie!; **h. disgusting!** quelle horreur!; **h. kind (of you)!** comme *ou* que c'est gentil (de votre part)!; **h. she has changed!** comme elle a changé!; **h. I wish I could!** si seulement je pouvais!; **h. surprised he was when …!** quelle ne fut pas sa surprise lorsque …!
  5 *Fam (introducing indirect statement)* que; **I told him h. there had been a great storm** je lui ai dit qu'il y avait eu un gros orage
  6 **h. about …?** *(making suggestion)* et si …?; **h. about a game of cards/going out for a meal?** et si on faisait une partie de cartes/allait au restaurant?; **h. about you?** et toi?

N **the hows, whys and wherefores** les comment et les pourquoi, tous les détails

illiteracy [ɪ'lɪt(ə)rəsɪ] N analphabétisme m

illiterate [ɪ'lɪt(ə)rət] ADJ **1** (unable to read or write) illettré, analphabète **2** (lacking culture) (person) qui n'a aucune culture; (usage, style) incorrect
▶ N illettré, -ée, analphabète mf

ill-judged [-'dʒʌdʒd] ADJ (action) malavisé, peu sage

ill-mannered ADJ grossier, malappris; **to be i.** être mal élevé

ill-matched ADJ mal assorti

ill-natured [-'neɪtʃəd] ADJ (person) d'un mauvais caractère, désagréable; (remark, criticism etc) désagréable; **to be i.** avoir mauvais caractère

illness ['ɪlnɪs] N maladie f VOIR GRAMMAIRE A7

illogical [ɪ'lɒdʒɪk(ə)l] ADJ illogique

illogicality [ɪlɒdʒɪ'kælɪtɪ] N manque m de logique, illogisme m

illogically [ɪ'lɒdʒɪk(ə)lɪ] ADV sans logique; **the i. ordered universe** l'univers désordonné

ill-prepared ADJ mal préparé

ill-starred ADJ Lit (person) infortuné; (day) malheureux, néfaste

ill-suited [-'suːtɪd] ADJ (couple) mal assorti; **such clothes were i. to a hot climate** ces vêtements n'étaient pas adaptés à un climat chaud; **arts graduates are i. to this job** les diplômés en lettres ne sont pas aptes à ce travail

ill-tempered ADJ (person) (in general) grincheux; (on specific occasion) de mauvaise humeur, grincheux; **to be i.** (in general) avoir mauvais caractère; **why must he always be so i.?** pourquoi faut-il qu'il soit toujours d'aussi mauvaise humeur?

ill-timed [-'taɪmd] ADJ (remark) mal à propos, hors de propos, inopportun; (arrival) inopportun

ill-treat VT (person, dog) maltraiter

ill-treatment N mauvais traitement m

illuminate [ɪ'luːmɪneɪt] VT **1** (room etc) éclairer; (building) illuminer **2** Fig (subject, question) éclairer, élucider **3** Art (manuscript) enluminer

illuminated [ɪ'luːmɪneɪtɪd] ADJ **1** (sign) lumineux **2** Art (manuscript) enluminé

illuminating [ɪ'luːmɪneɪtɪŋ] ADJ (speech, interview) qui éclaire la situation; (comparison, remark, example) éclairant; **the programme was very i.** l'émission m'a appris beaucoup de choses
▶ N **1** (of building) illumination f **2** Art (of manuscript) enluminure f

illumination [ɪluːmɪ'neɪʃən] N **1** (of room etc) éclairage m; (of building) illumination f, esp Br **illuminations** (decorative outdoor lights) illuminations **2** Art (of manuscript) enluminure f **3** Opt (of lens etc) éclat m; Phys (degree of) i. éclairement m **4** Rel etc (enlightenment) illumination f

illuminator [ɪ'luːmɪneɪtər] N Art enlumineur, -euse

illumine [ɪ'luːmɪn] VT Lit illuminer

ill-use [-'juːs] N mauvais traitement m

ill-use[2] [-'juːz] VT **1** (physically) maltraiter **2** (behave badly towards) ne pas bien traiter; **he feels he's been ill-used** il a le sentiment qu'il n'a pas été bien traité

illusion [ɪ'luːʒən] N illusion f; **to be under the i. that …** s'imaginer que …; **I have no illusions or am under no i. on that score** je ne me fais aucune illusion à ce sujet

illusionist [ɪ'luːʒənɪst] N illusionniste mf

illusory [ɪ'luːs(ə)rɪ] ADJ illusoire, trompeur

illustrate ['ɪləstreɪt] VT **1** (book, newspaper) illustrer; **illustrated by Cruikshank** (on title

page etc) illustré par ou illustrations de Cruikshank; **illustrated magazine** (journal m ou magazine m) illustré m **2** (explain, give example of) illustrer; **to i. my point** pour illustrer ce que je veux dire; **the lecture will be illustrated by slides** la conférence sera accompagnée de diapositives

illustration [ɪləs'treɪʃən] N **1** (picture) (in book etc) illustration f, gravure f; **illustrations** (in book) iconographie f **2** (publishing process) illustration f; **he works in i.** il est illustrateur **3** Fig (of principle etc) illustration f, exemple m; **to be an i. of sth** illustrer qch; **by way of i.** à titre d'exemple

illustrative ['ɪləstr(ə)tɪv] ADJ illustratif; **this incident is i. of his state of mind** cet incident reflète bien son état d'esprit

illustrator ['ɪləstreɪtər] N illustrateur, -trice

illustrious [ɪ'lʌstrɪəs] ADJ illustre, célèbre

illustriously [ɪ'lʌstrɪəslɪ] ADV de façon illustre

ILO [aɪel'əʊ] N Ind (abbr International Labour Organization) OIT f

I'm [aɪm] CONTR = I am, see be

image ['ɪmɪdʒ] N **1** (copy) image f; **God created man in his own i.** Dieu créa l'homme à son image; **he's the (very or living or Fam spitting) i. of his father** c'est le portrait de son père, Fam c'est son père tout craché **2** (representation) portrait m; (sculpture) image f (sculptée); (of god etc) représentation f, statue f; (for worship) idole f **3** (mental picture) image f **4** (of politician, party etc) image f, **its i. is that of a dirty industrial city** cette ville a la réputation d'être une ville industrielle sale; **he/it needs a bit of i. building** il a besoin de rehausser un peu son image de marque; **the company is suffering from an i. problem** l'entreprise a un problème d'image **5** Liter image f, métaphore f **6** Comput, Opt image f
▶▶ Comput **i. bank** banque f d'images; Phys **i. converter** convertisseur m d'image(s); Electron, TV **i. distortion** distorsion f d'image; Comput **i. editing** édition f d'images; Comput **i. editing program, i. editor** logiciel m d'édition d'images, éditeur m d'images; Opt, Phot **i. enhancement** correction f de l'image, retouche f d'images; Opt, Phot **i. enhancer** correcteur m d'images; Comput **i. file** fichier m vidéo ou image; Comput **i. format** format m graphique; Comput **i. manipulation** manipulation f d'images; Comput **i. map** image cliquable; Mktg **i. pricing** fixation f de prix en fonction de l'image; Comput **i. processing** traitement m des images; Comput **i. processor** unité f de traitement d'images; **i. refresh rate** taux m de rafraîchissement d'images

image-conscious ADJ qui se soucie de son image

image-maker N Mktg responsable mf des relations publiques

imager ['ɪmɪdʒər] N Comput imageur m

imagery ['ɪmɪdʒ(ə)rɪ] N Liter, Cin images fpl

imagesetter ['ɪmɪdʒsetər] N Typ photocomposeuse f

imaginable [ɪ'mædʒɪnəb(ə)l] ADJ imaginable; **the finest thing i.** la plus belle chose qu'on puisse imaginer

imaginary [ɪ'mædʒɪn(ə)rɪ] ADJ imaginaire

imagination [ɪmædʒɪ'neɪʃən] N imagination f, **to have no i.** n'avoir aucune imagination; **it's your i.!** tu te fais des idées!; **use your i.!** fais preuve d'un peu d'imagination!; **it's all in your i.** tout ça c'est dans ta tête

imaginative [ɪ'mædʒɪnətɪv] ADJ (person, story etc) imaginatif; (solution, excuse, reason) plein d'imagination

imaginativeness [ɪ'mædʒɪnətɪvnɪs] N (of

person) imagination f, esprit m inventif; (of story, solution, reason, excuse etc) caractère m imaginatif

imagine [ɪ'mædʒɪn] VT **1** (picture in one's mind) imaginer; **I can just i. her saying/doing that** je la vois très bien dire/faire ça; **I just can't i. you in that hat** je ne t'imagine ou te vois pas du tout avec ce chapeau; **I can't i. living anywhere else** je n'imagine pas vivre ailleurs; **to be always imagining things** se faire des idées; **I was beginning to i. all sorts of things!** je commençais à m'imaginer des tas de choses; **you're imagining things** tu rêves; **that child is always imagining things** c'est un enfant très imaginatif; **you must have imagined it** tu as dû rêver; **as may (well) be imagined** comme on peut (se) l'imaginer; Fam **i. meeting you here!** ça alors, toi ici!; **just i. my despair** tu imagines à quel point j'étais désespéré; **you can't i. it!** vous n'avez pas idée!; **well, what did you i.?** qu'est-ce que tu croyais?, qu'est-ce que tu t'imaginais?
2 (suppose) imaginer; **I i. them to be fairly rich** j'imagine qu'ils sont assez riches; **don't i. that I'm satisfied** n'allez pas croire que je sois satisfait; **I i. that you must be very tired** j'imagine ou je suppose que vous devez être fatigué
▶ VI **he ate all of it, can you i.?** il a tout mangé, tu t'imagines?; **I can i.** je veux bien le croire!, j'imagine!

imagined [ɪ'mædʒɪnd] ADJ imaginé, imaginaire

imaging device ['ɪmɪdʒɪŋ] N Comput imageur m

imaginings [ɪ'mædʒɪnɪŋz] NPL **the i. of a fevered mind** les élucubrations d'un esprit enfiévré

imam [ɪ'mɑːm] N imam m

IMAX® ['aɪmæks] N (procédé m) Imax m
▶▶ **I. cinema** cinéma m Imax

imbalance [ɪm'bæləns] N déséquilibre m

imbecile [ɪ'mbɪsiːl] N Med, Old-fashioned, Fam imbécile mf
▶ ADJ ATTRIB imbécile

imbecilic [ɪmbɪ'sɪlɪk] ADJ imbécile

imbecility [ɪmbɪ'sɪlɪtɪ] N **1** Fam (stupidity) stupidité f, imbécillité f **2** Med Old-fashioned imbécillité f

imbibe [ɪm'baɪb] VT Fml (of person) (knowledge, ideas) absorber, assimiler; (drink) boire, avaler; **to i. the atmosphere** s'imprégner de l'atmosphère
▶ VI Fam Hum boire trop, Fam picoler

imbroglio [ɪm'brəʊlɪəʊ] N Lit imbroglio m

imbue [ɪm'bjuː] VT Lit (person) imprégner (**with** de); (with an idea d'une idée); **to be imbued with melancholy/hope** (of novel etc) être empreint de mélancolie/d'espoir

IMF [aɪem'ef] N Econ (abbr International Monetary Fund) FMI m

imitable ['ɪmɪtəb(ə)l] ADJ imitable

imitate ['ɪmɪteɪt] VT **1** (copy) (person) imiter, copier; **to i. sb's style** imiter le style de qn **2** (mimic) (person) singer, mimer; (call of bird etc) imiter; **to i. its surroundings** (of insect etc) prendre l'aspect de son milieu

imitation [ɪmɪ'teɪʃən] N **1** (action) imitation f; **in i. of sb/sth** à l'imitation de ou imitant qn/qch; Prov **i. is the sincerest form of flattery** l'imitation est la flatterie la plus sincère qui soit **2** (copy) copie f, imitation f; Com imitation; **beware of imitations** méfiez-vous des contrefaçons; **i. marble/crocodile skin** en imitation marbre/crocodile
▶▶ **i. jewellery** bijoux mpl (de) fantaisie; **i. leather** imitation f cuir, similicuir m; **i. pearls** fausses perles fpl

imitative ['ɪmɪtətɪv] ADJ (sound etc) imitatif; **manner/style i. of sb** manière *f*/style *m* qui imite qn

▸▸*Mktg* **i. product** produit *m* d'imitation

imitator [ˈɪmɪteɪtər] N *(copier)* imitateur, -trice; **the Beatles had their imitators** les Beatles ont eu des imitateurs

immaculate [ɪˈmækjʊlət] ADJ **1** *(dress, desk, room)* impeccable; *Lit (snow, white)* immaculé; *Fig* **her attendance record is i.** elle n'a pas été absente une seule fois **2** *(morally pure) (reputation)* sans tache

▸▸*Rel* **the I. Conception** l'Immaculée Conception *f*

immaculately [ɪˈmækjʊlətlɪ] ADV *(dressed)* impeccablement; **the children behaved i.** les enfants se sont admirablement bien tenus

immanent [ˈɪmənənt] ADJ *Phil* immanent

immaterial [ɪməˈtɪərɪəl] ADJ **1** *(unimportant, irrelevant)* sans importance; **that fact is (quite) i.** cela n'a aucune importance **2** *(ghost etc)* immatériel, incorporel

immature [ɪməˈtjʊər] ADJ **1** *(young, undeveloped) Biol* immature; *(fruit etc)* qui n'est pas mûr **2** *(childish)* immature, qui manque de maturité; **stop being so i.!** arrête de te comporter comme un gamin!; **i. work** œuvre *f* de jeunesse *ou* d'apprenti

immaturity [ɪməˈtjʊərɪtɪ] N **1** *(youth, lack of development) (of person), Biol* immaturité *f* **2** *(childishness)* immaturité *f*, manque *m* de maturité; *(of work of art)* manque de maturité

immeasurable [ɪˈmeʒərəb(ə)l] ADJ *(space, complexity etc)* incommensurable; *(time)* infini; **to have an i. influence on sth** avoir une influence énorme sur qch

immeasurably [ɪˈmeʒərəblɪ] ADV *(difficult, painful, bad)* extrêmement, *Lit* incommensurablement; **she influenced her contemporaries i.** elle a énormément influencé ses contemporains

immediacy [ɪˈmiːdɪəsɪ] N caractère *m* immédiat *(of* de); *(of danger)* imminence *f*, *(of need)* urgence *f*

immediate [ɪˈmiːdɪət] ADJ **1** *(urgent, imminent) (need)* pressant, urgent; *(danger)* imminent; **my i. objective** mon objectif premier; **what are your i. plans?** que proposez-vous de faire d'abord?; **I have no i. plans to retire** je n'ai pas l'intention de prendre ma retraite dans un futur proche **2** *(instant) (answer, delivery etc)* immédiat; **house for sale with i. possession** maison à vendre avec jouissance immédiate **3** *(closest) (neighbour, surroundings)* immédiat, proche; **the i. family** les proches parents; **in the i. future** dans un avenir immédiat

immediately [ɪˈmiːdɪətlɪ] ADV **1** *(without delay)* immédiatement, tout de suite; **he is i. recognizable** on le reconnaît immédiatement *ou* tout de suite; **the distinction isn't i. obvious** la distinction n'est pas évidente tout de suite; **please send ... i.** veuillez (bien) envoyer immédiatement *ou* d'urgence ...; **i. after** aussitôt après **2** *(directly)* immédiatement, directement; **it does not affect me i.** cela ne me touche pas directement **3** *(in space)* juste; **i. after the traffic lights** juste après le feu

CONJ *Br* dès que; **i. I saw her I knew ...** dès que je l'ai vue j'ai su que ...

immemorial [ɪmɪˈmɔːrɪəl] ADJ *Lit* immémorial, -aux; **from time i.** depuis des temps immémoriaux

immense [ɪˈmens] ADJ *(expanse, success, satisfaction etc)* immense; *(quantity)* énorme; **of i. size** de taille immense

immensely [ɪˈmenslɪ] ADV *(large, rich)* immensément; *(to enjoy oneself)* énormément; **to be i. successful** avoir énormément

de succès; **i. entertaining** extrêmement divertissant; **she is i. fat** elle est absolument énorme

immensity [ɪˈmensɪtɪ] N **1** *(of universe, fortune etc)* immensité *f* **2** *(of problem, task)* énormité *f*

immerse [ɪˈmɜːs] VT **1** *(in liquid)* plonger; *Rel* baptiser par immersion **2** **to i. oneself in sth** *(become absorbed by)* se plonger dans qch; **to be immersed in one's work/thoughts** être plongé *ou* absorbé dans son travail/ses pensées

immersion [ɪˈmɜːʃən] N **1** *(in liquid)* immersion *f*, *Rel* baptême *m* par immersion **2** *(mental)* absorption *f* (**in** dans); **to learn a language by i.** apprendre une langue par immersion

▸▸**i. course** cours *m* de langue intensif *(dans lequel seule la langue apprise est utilisée)*; **i. heater** chauffe-eau *m inv* à immersion

immigrant [ˈɪmɪɡrənt] ADJ, N *(in the process of emigrating)* immigrant, -ante; *(who has emigrated)* immigré, -ée; **i. families** familles *fpl* immigrées

▸▸**i. worker** travailleur *m* immigré

immigrate [ˈɪmɪɡreɪt] VI immigrer

immigration [ɪmɪˈɡreɪʃən] N immigration *f*; **to go through i.** *(at port, airport etc)* passer à l'immigration

▸▸**i. control** contrôle *m* de l'immigration; **i. department** service *m* de l'immigration; **i. laws** lois *fpl* sur l'immigration; **i. officer** agent *m* du service de l'immigration; **i. quotas** quotas *mpl* d'immigration

imminence [ˈɪmɪnəns] N imminence *f* (**of** de)

imminent [ˈɪmɪnənt] ADJ *(danger, disaster, arrival etc)* imminent

immobile [ɪˈməʊbaɪl] ADJ immobile

immobility [ɪməˈbɪlɪtɪ] N immobilité *f*

immobilize [ɪˈməʊbɪlaɪz] VT *(wounded limb, traffic etc), Fin* immobiliser

immobilizer [ɪˈməʊbɪlaɪzər] N *(for vehicle)* antidémarrage *m* codé

immoderate [ɪˈmɒd(ə)rət] ADJ *(drinking)* immodéré; *(feeling, attitude, display of grief)* exagéré, excessif; *(behaviour)* excessif; *(thirst)* anormal, -aux; *(gaiety)* exagéré

immoderately [ɪˈmɒd(ə)rətlɪ] ADV immodérément

immodest [ɪˈmɒdɪst] ADJ **1** *(indecent) (person, dress, behaviour)* impudique **2** *(vain)* présomptueux

immodestly [ɪˈmɒdɪstlɪ] ADV **1** *(indecently)* impudiquement **2** *(vainly)* présomptueusement

immolate [ˈɪməʊleɪt] VT *Lit* immoler

immoral [ɪˈmɒrəl] ADJ immoral, -aux; *(novel etc)* contraire à la morale; *Law* **for i. purposes** aux fins de débauche; *Law* **living on i. earnings** *(of pimp)* proxénétisme *m*

immorality [ɪməˈrælɪtɪ] N immoralité *f*, *(sexual)* débauche *f*

immorally [ɪˈmɒrəlɪ] ADV immoralement, de façon immorale

immortal [ɪˈmɔːt(ə)l] ADJ immortel; **the i. memory of ...** le souvenir impérissable de ...

N immortel, -elle

immortality [ɪmɔːˈtælɪtɪ] N immortalité *f*

immortalize [ɪˈmɔːtəlaɪz] VT *(person, author's name, sb's memory etc)* immortaliser

immovable [ɪˈmuːvəb(ə)l] ADJ *(object)* (qui est) impossible à déplacer; *Fig (opposition)* inébranlable; *(person)* inflexible; *Fig* **they were i.** ils sont restés inflexibles

NPL *Law* **immovables** immeubles *mpl*, biens *mpl* immobiliers

▸▸*Rel* **i. feast** fête *f* fixe; *Law* **i. property** biens immeubles *ou* immobiliers

immune [ɪˈmjuːn] ADJ **1** *Med* immunisé (**to** contre) **2** *Fig* **i. to criticism** imperméable à la critique; **no-one was i. from criticism** personne n'a échappé aux critiques; **i. from taxation** exempt d'impôts; **i. from prosecution** à l'abri de poursuites judiciaires

▸▸*Med* **i. deficiency** immunodéficience *f*, *Physiol* **i. system** système *m* immunitaire

immunity [ɪˈmjuːnɪtɪ] N **1** *Med* immunité *f* (**to** contre) **2** *(exemption)* exemption *f* (**from** de); **they were guaranteed i. from prosecution** on leur a assuré qu'ils seraient à l'abri de poursuites judiciaires

immunization [ɪmjʊnaɪˈzeɪʃən] N *Med* immunisation *f* (**against** contre)

immunize [ˈɪmjʊnaɪz] VT *Med* immuniser (**against** contre)

immunodeficiency [ɪmjʊnəʊdɪˈfɪʃənsɪ] N *Med* immunodéficence *f*

immunoglobulin [ɪmjʊnəʊˈɡlɒbjʊlɪn] N *Med* immunoglobuline *f*

immunological [ɪmjʊnəʊˈlɒdʒɪk(ə)l] ADJ *Med* immunologique

immunology [ɪmjʊˈnɒlədʒɪ] N *Med* immunologie *f*

immunosuppressant [ɪmjʊnəʊsəˈpresənt] N *Med* immunosuppresseur *m*

immunosuppression [ɪmjʊnəʊsəˈpreʃən] N *Med* immunosuppression *f*

immunosuppressive [ɪmjʊnəʊsəˈpresɪv] ADJ *Med* immunosuppresseur

immunotherapy [ɪmjʊnəʊˈθerəpɪ] N *Med* immunothérapie *f*

immure [ɪˈmjʊər] VT *Arch, Lit* **1** *(shut away) (person)* enfermer, cloîtrer; **he had immured himself in the library** il s'était enfermé dans la bibliothèque; **immured in silence** cloîtré dans le silence **2** *(wall up) (victim)* emmurer

immutability [ɪmjuːtəˈbɪlɪtɪ] N *Fml* immutabilité *f*, caractère *m* immuable

immutable [ɪˈmjuːtəb(ə)l] ADJ immuable

immutably [ɪˈmjuːtəblɪ] ADV immuablement

imp [ɪmp] N diablotin *m*, lutin *m*; *Fam* **(little) i.** *(boy)* petit garnement *m*, galopin *m*; *(girl)* petite coquine *f*

impact [ˈɪmpækt] N **1** *(shock)* choc *m*; *(of bullet)* impact *m*; **on i.** *(of projectile)* au moment de l'impact **2** *Fig (of speech, play, advertising campaign etc)* impact *m*; **the play has lost none of its i.** la pièce n'a pas du tout perdu de son impact; **he seems to have made quite an i. on you** il semble avoir fait une forte impression sur vous

▸▸*Br* **i. adhesive** colle *f* instantanée; *Aut* **i. bar** barre *f* de renfort; *St Exch* **i. day** = jour *m* où l'on annonce une nouvelle émission d'actions; *Comput* **i. printer** imprimante *f* à impact; *Aut* **i. test** essai *m* au choc

▸ **impact on** VT INSEP *(trade figures, section of population etc)* avoir un impact sur, affecter

impacted [ɪmˈpæktɪd] ADJ *Surg (fracture)* avec impaction *ou* incongruence

▸▸**i. tooth** dent *f* barrée

impair [ɪmˈpeər] VT *(sight, hearing, mental faculties)* affaiblir; *(strength)* faire perdre, diminuer; *(relations, person's authority, chances)* compromettre; **his health has been (seriously) impaired by the expedition** sa santé s'est (gravement) détériorée à la suite de l'expédition

impairment [ɪmˈpeəmənt] N *(of sight, hearing, memory)* affaiblissement *m*; *(of health, relations)* dégradation *f*, *(of strength)* diminution *f*, **without i. of quality** sans perte de qualité

impala [ɪmˈpɑːlə] N *(antelope)* impala *m*

impale [ɪmˈpeɪl] VTempaler; **to be impaled** *(on railings etc)* être empalé, s'empaler

impalpable [ɪmˈpælpəb(ə)l] ADJ **1** *(intangible)* impalpable, intangible **2** *(to the mind)* insaisissable

impanel [ɪmˈpænəl] VT = **empanel**

impart [ɪmˈpɑːt] VT *Fml* **1** *(lend)* *(courage etc)* donner; *(movement)* imprimer, communiquer (**to** à); *(heat, light)* transmettre **2** *(transmit)* *(knowledge)* communiquer; *(news)* faire connaître, annoncer; *(secret)* confier; *(truth)* transmettre (**to** à)

impartial [ɪmˈpɑːʃəl] ADJ *(person, conduct)* impartial, -aux (**towards** envers); **to be i.** être impartial *ou* équitable

impartiality [ɪmpɑːʃɪˈælɪtɪ] N impartialité *f* (**towards** envers)

impartially [ɪmˈpɑːʃəlɪ] ADV impartialement, avec impartialité; *(to judge)* équitablement

impassable [ɪmˈpɑːsəb(ə)l] ADJ *(river, barrier, pass)* infranchissable; *(road)* impraticable

impasse [ˈæmpɑːs] N impasse *f*; **we have reached an i.** nous sommes dans une *ou* l'impasse

impassioned [ɪmˈpæʃənd] ADJ *(orator, speech, defence etc)* passionné; *(style)* chaleureux

impassive [ɪmˈpæsɪv] ADJ *(person, face)* impassible

impassively [ɪmˈpæsɪvlɪ] ADV impassiblement

impatience [ɪmˈpeɪʃəns] N impatience *f* (**to do** de faire); **i. to leave** hâte *f* de partir; **there was a note of i. in his voice** on sentait l'impatience dans sa voix; *Fml* **he was known for his i. of sloppy work** il avait la réputation de mal supporter le travail brouillon

impatient [ɪmˈpeɪʃənt] ADJ *(person, tone)* impatient; *(reply)* vif, emporté; **to get** *ou* **grow i.** s'impatienter; **to get i. with sb** s'impatienter contre qn; **I am getting so i. with this photocopier!** je perds complètement patience avec cette photocopieuse!; **to be i. for change/reform** avoir soif de changement/réforme; **to be i. to do sth** être impatient *ou* brûler de faire qch; *Lit* **he was i. of those less intelligent than himself** il supportait mal ceux qui étaient moins intelligents que lui

impatiently [ɪmˈpeɪʃəntlɪ] ADV *(to wait)* avec impatience; *(to answer)* sur un ton *ou* d'un ton d'impatience

impeach [ɪmˈpiːtʃ] VT **1** *Law (accuse)* accuser (**of** *or* **with a crime** d'un crime); *Br* **to i. sb for high treason** inculper qn pour haute trahison; *Am* **to i. a public official** = mettre un haut fonctionnaire en accusation devant le Congrès **2** *Fml (call into question)* *(truth, sb's integrity)* attaquer, mettre en doute; *Law (witness)* récuser, reprocher; *(evidence)* révoquer

impeachable [ɪmˈpiːtʃəb(ə)l] ADJ *Am Law* = passible d'une mise en accusation devant le Congrès

impeachment [ɪmˈpiːtʃmənt] N *Law (of minister etc)* mise *f* en accusation; *Am* impeachment *m*

impeccable [ɪmˈpekəb(ə)l] ADJ *(house, room etc)* impeccable; *Fig (conduct, management, manners)* irréprochable; **he speaks i. English** il parle un anglais impeccable

impeccably [ɪmˈpekəblɪ] ADV *(to behave)* irréprochablement; *(dressed)* impeccablement

impecunious [ɪmpɪˈkjuːnɪəs] ADJ *Fml* impécunieux

impedance [ɪmˈpiːdəns] N *Elec* impédance *f*

impede [ɪmˈpiːd] VT *(progress, activity, sb's efforts etc)* entraver, gêner; *(traffic)* gêner; **to i. the enemy's movements** gêner les déplacements de l'ennemi; **she was impeded by her skirt** sa jupe entravait ses mouvements

impediment [ɪmˈpedɪmənt] N obstacle *m* (**to** à); **speech i.** défaut *m* de prononciation

impedimenta [ɪmpedɪˈmentə] NPL *Mil, Fig* impedimenta *mpl*

impel [ɪmˈpel] VT (**-ll-**) **1** *(motivate, oblige)* obliger, forcer (**sb to do sth** qn à faire qch) **2** *(push)* projeter (en avant)

impeller [ɪmˈpelər] N *Tech* rotor *m*; *(of water pump)* turbine *f*, *(of converter)* roue *f* pompe

impending [ɪmˈpendɪŋ] ADJ *(danger, arrival, downfall etc)* imminent

impenetrability [ɪmpenɪtrəˈbɪlɪtɪ] N impénétrabilité *f*

impenetrable [ɪmˈpenɪtrəb(ə)l] ADJ *(defences, mystery, mist)* impénétrable; *(jargon)* incompréhensible

impenitence [ɪmˈpenɪtəns] N *Fml* impénitence *f*

impenitent [ɪmˈpenɪtənt] ADJ, N *Fml* impénitent, -ente

impenitently [ɪmˈpenɪtəntlɪ] ADV sans repentir

imperative [ɪmˈperətɪv] ADJ **1** *(need etc)* urgent; **it is i. that he should come** il est impératif qu'il vienne **2** *(tone)* impérieux, péremptoire **3** *Gram (mood)* impératif N *Gram* (mode *m*) impératif *m*; **in the i.** à l'impératif VOIR GRAMMAIRE A40; B34–5

imperceptible [ɪmpəˈseptɪb(ə)l] ADJ *(movement, difference, improvement etc)* imperceptible; *(sound, difference)* insaisissable

imperceptibly [ɪmpəˈseptɪblɪ] ADV imperceptiblement

imperfect [ɪmˈpɜːfɪkt] ADJ **1** *(not perfect)* imparfait; *Com (goods)* qui a un défaut; **it's slightly i.** *(of item for sale)* il a un léger défaut **2** *Gram (tense)* imparfait N *Gram* imparfait *m*; **verb in the i.** verbe *m* à l'imparfait SEE GRAMMAR B30

imperfection [ɪmpəˈfekʃən] N **1** *(flaw)* imperfection *f*, défectuosité *f* **2** *(state of being imperfect)* caractère *m* imparfait

imperfectly [ɪmˈpɜːfɪktlɪ] ADV imparfaitement

imperial [ɪmˈpɪərɪəl] ADJ **1** *(government, crown etc)* impérial, -aux; **His/Her I. Majesty** Sa Majesté Impériale **2** *Br (weights and measures)* = relatif au système de mesure utilisé traditionnellement dans les pays anglo-saxons **3** *(commanding)* majestueux, altier

imperialism [ɪmˈpɪərɪəlɪz(ə)m] N impérialisme *m*

imperialist [ɪmˈpɪərɪəlɪst] ADJ, N impérialiste *mf*

imperialistic [ɪmpɪərɪəˈlɪstɪk] ADJ impérialiste

imperially [ɪmˈpɪərɪəlɪ] ADV **1** *Pol* impérialement **2** *(in a commanding manner)* impérieusement

imperil [ɪmˈperɪl] VT (**-ll-**, *Am* **-l-**) *(sb's life etc)* mettre en danger; *(one's reputation)* compromettre

imperious [ɪmˈpɪərɪəs] ADJ *(person, tone, character)* impérieux, dictatorial, -aux

imperiously [ɪmˈpɪərɪəslɪ] ADV *(to speak, act)* impérieusement

imperishable [ɪmˈperɪʃəb(ə)l] ADJ impérissable

impermanent [ɪmˈpɜːmənənt] ADJ impermanent

impermeable [ɪmˈpɜːmɪəb(ə)l] ADJ imperméable

impersonal [ɪmˈpɜːsən(ə)l] ADJ **1** *(style etc)* impersonnel **2** *Gram (verb)* impersonnel SEE GRAMMAR B29–30
  ▸▸ *Fin* **i. accounts** comptes *mpl* impersonnels

impersonally [ɪmˈpɜːsən(ə)lɪ] ADV impersonnellement, de façon impersonnelle

impersonate [ɪmˈpɜːsəneɪt] VT *(pretend to be)* se faire passer pour; *Theat, TV etc (imitate)* imiter

impersonation [ɪmpɜːsəˈneɪʃən] N *(pretence of being)* usurpation *f* d'identité (**of** de); *Theat, TV etc (imitation)* imitation *f*; **to do an i. of sb** imiter qn

impersonator [ɪmˈpɜːsəneɪtər] N *(imposter)* imposteur *m*; *Theat, TV etc (mimic)* imitateur, -trice

impertinence [ɪmˈpɜːtɪnəns] N impertinence *f*, insolence *f*; **an i., a piece of i.** une impertinence

impertinent [ɪmˈpɜːtɪnənt] ADJ **1** *(person, remark)* impertinent, insolent (**to sb** envers qn) **2** *esp Jur (not relevant)* non pertinent

impertinently [ɪmˈpɜːtɪnəntlɪ] ADV **1** *(to say, look at sb)* de façon impertinente, impertinemment **2** *esp Jur* de façon non pertinente

imperturbable [ɪmpəˈtɜːbəb(ə)l] ADJ imperturbable

impervious [ɪmˈpɜːvɪəs] ADJ **1** insensible (**to criticism** à la critique); **she is i. to reason** on ne peut pas la raisonner **2** *(material etc)* **to be i. to light/water** ne pas laisser passer la lumière/être imperméable

impetigo [ɪmpɪˈtaɪɡəʊ] N *Med* impétigo *m*; **to have i.** avoir un impétigo

impetuosity [ɪmpetjʊˈɒsɪtɪ] N = **impetuousness**

impetuous [ɪmˈpetjʊəs] ADJ *(person, character, action)* impétueux; *(decision)* hâtif

impetuously [ɪmˈpetjʊəslɪ] ADV impétueusement, avec impétuosité

impetuousness [ɪmˈpetjʊəsnɪs] N *(of person, action)* impétuosité *f*

impetus [ˈɪmpɪtəs] N **1** élan *m*; **to give an i. to sth** donner de l'élan à qch; **to gain i.** prendre *ou* gagner de l'importance; **to lose i.** perdre de son élan **2** *Phys* vitesse *f* acquise

impiety [ɪmˈpaɪətɪ] N impiété *f*

▸ **impinge on** [ɪmˈpɪndʒ] VT INSEP **1** *(affect)* affecter; **it impinges in a big way on all our lives** ça affecte énormément notre vie à tous; **to i. on sb's conscious mind** venir à la conscience de qn; **it didn't even i. on his consciousness** il ne s'en est même pas rendu compte; **in so far as it impinges on our department** dans la mesure où cela affecte *ou* a des répercussions sur notre service **2** *(infringe on)* *(sb's rights etc)* empiéter sur

impingement [ɪmˈpɪndʒmənt] N *(on sb's rights etc)* empiètement *m*

impious [ˈɪmpɪəs] ADJ impie

impiously [ˈɪmpɪəslɪ] ADV avec impiété

impish [ˈɪmpɪʃ] ADJ *(laughter, face)* de petit diable, d'espiègle; *(child, remark)* espiègle, malicieux

impishly [ˈɪmpɪʃlɪ] ADV comme un petit diable

impishness [ˈɪmpɪʃnɪs] N espièglerie *f*

implacable [ɪmˈplækəb(ə)l] ADJ implacable (**towards** à, pour, à l'égard de)

implacably [ɪmˈplækəblɪ] ADV implacablement

implant¹ [ˈɪmplɑːnt] N *Surg* implant *m*

implant² [ɪmˈplɑːnt] VT **1** *(insert)*, *Surg* implanter (**in** dans) **2** *Fig (opinion, principle)* inculquer (**in sb** à qn); *(idea)* implanter (**in sb** dans la tête de qn); **from his youth this**

ideal had been implanted in his mind dès sa jeunesse cet idéal lui avait été inculqué

implausible [ɪmˈplɔːzɪb(ə)l] ADJ peu plausible, invraisemblable

implausibly [ɪmˈplɔːzɪblɪ] ADV invraisemblablement; to end i. (of book, film etc) se terminer de façon peu vraisemblable

implement[1] [ˈɪmplɪmənt] N outil m, instrument m; gardening implements outils de jardinage; kitchen implements ustensiles mpl de cuisine

implement[2] [ˈɪmplɪment] VT (treaty, plan, agreement, technique, decision) mettre en application; (promise) exécuter; (change) introduire

implementation [ɪmplɪmenˈteɪʃən] N (of treaty, plan, agreement, technique, decision) mise f en œuvre; (of promise) exécution f; (of change) introduction f
▸▸ Mktg i. stage (of product development) phase f de mise en œuvre

implicate [ˈɪmplɪkeɪt] VT 1 impliquer, mêler (sb in a crime qn dans un crime); without implicating anyone sans compromettre personne 2 Fml (imply) impliquer, renfermer

implication [ɪmplɪˈkeɪʃən] N implication f; by i. implicitement; the full i. of what he said was not lost on us nous avons tout de suite vu ce que ses paroles impliquaient

implicit [ɪmˈplɪsɪt] ADJ 1 (implied) (condition, meaning etc) implicite; (recognition) tacite 2 (absolute) (obedience) absolu; i. faith confiance f aveugle (in dans)

implicitly [ɪmˈplɪsɪtlɪ] ADV 1 implicitement; to i. recognize a country reconnaître un pays de manière tacite 2 (absolutely) (to obey) aveuglément; to trust sb i. faire totalement confiance à qn

implied [ɪmˈplaɪd] ADJ implicite; i. meaning sous-entendu m, pl sous-entendus

implode [ɪmˈpləʊd] VI imploser

implore [ɪmˈplɔːr] VT (person) implorer, supplier (to do sth de faire qch); (forgiveness) implorer

imploring [ɪmˈplɔːrɪŋ] ADJ (look, tone) implorant, suppliant

imploringly [ɪmˈplɔːrɪŋlɪ] ADV (to say) d'un ton suppliant; (to look at sb) d'un air suppliant

implosion [ɪmˈpləʊʒən] N implosion f

imply [ɪmˈplaɪ] VT 1 (of person) sous-entendre; you seem to i. that ... ce que vous dites laisse supposer que ...; are you implying that I stole the money? est-ce que tu sous-entends que j'ai volé l'argent?; your silence implies that you are guilty votre silence laisse à penser que vous êtes coupable 2 (of circumstance) (presuppose) impliquer; the new deadline implies a lot of hard work les nouvelles échéances impliquent qu'il va falloir travailler dur

impolite [ɪmpəˈlaɪt] ADJ impoli (to, towards envers)

impolitely [ɪmpəˈlaɪtlɪ] ADV impoliment

impoliteness [ɪmpəˈlaɪtnɪs] N impolitesse f

impolitic [ɪmˈpɒlɪtɪk] ADJ peu judicieux

imponderability [ɪmpɒndərəˈbɪlɪtɪ] N impondérabilité f

imponderable [ɪmˈpɒndərəb(ə)l] ADJ (reasons, motives) impondérable
N impondérable m

import[1] [ˈɪmpɔːt] N 1 Com (item) article m d'importation, importation f; (activity) importation f; i. and export l'importation et l'exportation f; imports importations f; Fig the art of lacemaking was an i. from France l'art de la (fabrication de la) dentelle nous est venu de France 2 Fml (meaning) (of word)

sens m, signification f; (of document etc) teneur f 3 Fml (importance) (of event, discovery) importance f; (of remark) portée f; a matter of great i. une affaire de première importance
▸▸ i. agent commissionnaire mf importateur(trice), agent m importateur; i. ban interdiction f d'importation; to impose an i. ban on sth interdire qch d'importation; i. bonus prime f d'importation; i. controls contrôles mpl à l'importation; i. duty droit m d'entrée, taxe f d'importation; i. goods marchandises fpl à l'import; i. licence licence f d'importation; i. list liste f des importations; (of prices) tarif m d'entrée; i. permit permis m d'importer, permis d'importation; i. price prix m à l'importation, prix (à l')import; i. quotas contingents mpl d'importation; i. restrictions restrictions fpl à l'importation; i. tariff tarif m import; i. trade commerce m d'importation; i. wholesaler grossiste m importateur

import[2] [ɪmˈpɔːt] VT 1 Com (goods) importer (from de); imported goods marchandises fpl importées ou d'importation 2 Comput importer (from depuis) 3 Fml (mean) signifier, vouloir dire

importance [ɪmˈpɔːtəns] N importance f; to be of i. avoir de l'importance; of vital/strategic i. d'une importance capitale/stratégique; it is of the utmost i. to remember that ... il est absolument essentiel de se rappeler que ...; it is of no great i. cela importe peu; a detail of no i. un détail sans importance; to attach i. to sth mettre ou attacher de l'importance à qch; Pej to be full of one's own i. être imbu de sa personne; Mktg i.-performance analysis analyse f importance-performance

important [ɪmˈpɔːtənt] ADJ important; (difference) considérable; what is more i.? qu'est-ce qui est le plus important?; to become more i. (of issue, nation etc) prendre de l'importance; it is i. to know that ... il est important de savoir que ...; it is i. for you to know that ..., it is i. that you should know that ... il est important que vous sachiez que ...; his children/hobbies are very i. to him ses enfants/passe-temps sont très importants pour lui; Pej he was trying to look i. il essayait de se donner l'air important

importantly [ɪmˈpɔːtəntlɪ] ADV (to look at) d'un air important; (to say) d'un ton important; but, more i. ... mais, ce qui est plus important ...

importation [ɪmpɔːˈteɪʃən] N 1 (of goods) importation f 2 (imported article) importation f, article m d'importation 3 Comput importation f

importer [ɪmˈpɔːtər] N (person) importateur, -trice; (country) pays m importateur; an oil i. un pays importateur de pétrole; Japan is still a net i. of technology le Japon est toujours un importateur net de technologie
▸▸ i. margin marge f de l'importateur

import-export N import-export m
▸▸ i. trade import-export

importing [ˈɪmpɔːtɪŋ] ADJ (country) importateur, -trice
N (of goods) importation f

importunate [ɪmˈpɔːtjʊnɪt] ADJ Fml (creditor, visitor) importun

importune [ɪmˈpɔːtjuːn] VT Fml importuner

importunity [ɪmpɔːˈtjuːnɪtɪ] N Fml importunité f

impose [ɪmˈpəʊz] VT (silence, one's will, restrictions etc) imposer (on sb à qn); his bearing imposes respect il en impose; to i. a ban on sth interdire qch; the EU is in favour of imposing a ban on tobacco advertising l'UE

est en faveur d'interdire la publicité pour le tabac; to i. a tax on sugar taxer le sucre; to i. a fine on sb condamner qn à (payer) une amende; to i. the maximum penalty provided appliquer le maximum de la peine; to i. oneself on a situation/a political party (exert strong influence over) s'imposer dans une situation/un parti politique
VI (take advantage) abuser; I hope I'm not imposing (by staying) j'espère que je ne m'impose pas; to i. on or upon sb abuser de l'amabilité de qn; to i. on or upon sb's kindness abuser de la bonté de qn

imposing [ɪmˈpəʊzɪŋ] ADJ (air, tone) imposant; (spectacle, building) impressionnant

imposition [ɪmpəˈzɪʃən] N 1 (of task, tax) imposition f; (of fine) fait m d'infliger 2 (abuse) I told him I thought it was a bit of an i. asking me to ... je lui ai dit que je trouvais qu'il abusait un peu de ma bonté en me demandant de ... 3 (tax) imposition f, impôt m, taxe f 4 Br Sch Old-fashioned (punishment) punition f

impossibility [ɪmpɒsɪˈbɪlɪtɪ] N impossibilité f; it's a physical i. c'est matériellement impossible

impossible [ɪmˈpɒsɪb(ə)l] ADJ 1 (task, demand) impossible; it is i. for me to do it il m'est impossible de le faire; to make it i. for sb to do sth mettre qn dans l'impossibilité de faire qch; it's not i. that ... il n'est pas impossible que ...; (it's) i. to say or tell c'est impossible à dire 2 (unbelievable) (story, account) invraisemblable 3 Fam (intolerable) (life, person) impossible; you're i.! vous êtes impossible!
N impossible m; to attempt the i. tenter l'impossible

impossibly [ɪmˈpɒsɪblɪ] ADV (long, difficult) incroyablement; he's i. stupid est-il possible d'être aussi stupide!; Fam the children were behaving i. les enfants étaient vraiment impossibles

impostor [ɪmˈpɒstər] N imposteur m

imposture [ɪmˈpɒstʃər] N imposture f, tromperie f

impotence [ˈɪmpətəns] N 1 (powerlessness) impuissance f; (weakness) faiblesse f, impotence f 2 (sexual) impuissance f

impotent [ˈɪmpətənt] ADJ 1 (sexually) impuissant 2 (powerless) impuissant; (weak) faible

> Note that the French word **impotent** is a false friend. It means **infirm**.

impound [ɪmˈpaʊnd] VT 1 Law (confiscate) confisquer, saisir 2 (put in pound) (animal, car etc) mettre en fourrière

impounding [ɪmˈpaʊndɪŋ] N 1 Law (of goods) arrêt m, saisie f 2 (putting in pound) (of animals, cars etc) mise f en fourrière

impoverish [ɪmˈpɒvərɪʃ] VT (person, country, soil) appauvrir

impoverished [ɪmˈpɒvərɪʃt] ADJ appauvri, pauvre

impoverishment [ɪmˈpɒvərɪʃmənt] N appauvrissement m

impracticability [ɪmpræktɪkəˈbɪlɪtɪ] N impraticabilité f

impracticable [ɪmˈpræktɪkəb(ə)l] ADJ infaisable, impraticable

> Attention: ne pas confondre avec **impractical**.

impractical [ɪmˈpræktɪk(ə)l] ADJ (person) qui n'a pas le sens ou l'esprit pratique; (project, suggestion) peu réaliste; he's completely i. il n'a aucun sens pratique

Attention: ne pas confondre avec **impracticable**.

imprecation [ɪmprɪˈkeɪʃən] N imprécation f

imprecise [ɪmprɪˈsaɪs] ADJ imprécis, vague

imprecision [ɪmprɪˈsɪʒən] N imprécision f, manque m de précision

impregnable [ɪmˈpregnəb(ə)l] ADJ **1** (fortress) imprenable; **i. to attack** imprenable **2** Fig (truth, argument) invincible

impregnate [ˈɪmpregneɪt] VT **1** Biol féconder **2** Tech imprégner, imbiber (**sth with sth** qch de qch); **allow the oil to i. the wood** laissez le bois s'imprégner d'huile

impregnation [ɪmpregˈneɪʃən] N **1** Biol fécondation f **2** Tech (of fabric, wood etc) imprégnation f

impresario [ɪmpreˈsɑːrɪəʊ] N impresario m

impress¹ [ˈɪmpres] N Fml, Lit **1** (imprint) empreinte f, impression f **2** Fig (distinctive style etc) marque f distinctive

impress² [ɪmˈpres] VT **1** (create strong impression on) impressionner, faire une impression à; **I was deeply impressed by it** j'ai été très impressionné, cela m'a fait une grande impression; Fam **I'm not impressed!** c'est pas terrible!; **she wasn't impressed by my excuse** mon excuse ne l'a pas vraiment convaincue; **he impressed me favourably** il m'a fait bonne impression; **she impressed me as hard-working** elle m'a fait l'impression d'être travailleuse
2 (make understood) faire bien comprendre (**sth on** or **upon sb** qch à qn); (idea) inculquer (**on** or **upon sb** à qn); **you must i. on him that …** il faut bien lui faire comprendre que …
3 (imprint) **to i. sth on** or **upon sth** imprimer qch sur qch; **to i. sth with a seal** faire une impression sur qch avec un cachet; Fig **to i. sth on the mind** graver qch dans la mémoire; Fig **to i. sb with the idea that …** inculquer à qn l'idée que …
▸ VI (of person, remark) faire impression

impression [ɪmˈpreʃən] N **1** (effect) impression f, **to make an i.** faire impression; **to make a good/bad i.** faire bonne/mauvaise impression (**on** sur); **my argument was making no i.** (having no effect) mon argument ne lui faisait aucun effet
2 (idea, opinion) impression f, **I'm under the i. that I've seen him before** j'ai l'impression de l'avoir déjà vu; **I don't know where she got that i. from** je ne sais pas où elle est allée chercher ça; **I had the i. that you liked her** j'avais l'impression que tu l'aimais bien; **to create** or **give the i. that …** donner ou produire l'impression que …; **my first i. wasn't favourable** ma première impression n'a pas été favorable
3 (imprint) (of seal) empreinte f, impression f, **to take an i. of sth** prendre l'empreinte ou l'impression de qch
4 (reprint) (of book etc) tirage m
5 (imitation) imitation f, **to do impressions** faire des imitations; **this is my i. of you eating** je t'imite en train de manger
▸ ▸ **i. cylinder** cylindre m de rotative

impressionable [ɪmˈpreʃənəb(ə)l] ADJ (person) influençable

Note that the French word **impressionnable** is a false friend. It means **easily upset**.

impressionism [ɪmˈpreʃənɪz(ə)m] N Art impressionnisme m

impressionist [ɪmˈpreʃənɪst] ADJ Art impressionniste
▸ N **1** impressionniste mf **2** (mimic) imitateur, -trice

impressionistic [ɪmpreʃəˈnɪstɪk] ADJ impressionniste

impressive [ɪmˈpresɪv] ADJ (spectacle, language) impressionnant

impressively [ɪmˈpresɪvlɪ] ADV d'une manière impressionnante

imprest [ˈɪmprest] N Fin avance f
▸ ▸ **i. account** compte m d'avances (à montant fixe); **i. fund** fonds m de caisse à montant fixe; **i. system** comptabilité f de prévision

imprimatur [ɪmprɪˈmɑːtər] N imprimatur m

imprint¹ [ˈɪmprɪnt] N **1** (of seal, animal's feet etc) empreinte f, **to take an i. of a credit card** passer une carte de crédit dans la facturette; **the events left their i. on her mind** les événements sont restés gravés dans son esprit **2** (publisher's) **i.** (mark) marque f de l'éditeur; **XYZ books is an i. of JMG Publishers** XYZ fait partie des Éditions JMG; **published under the Pentagon i.** édité chez Pentagon
▸ ▸ **i. page** (of book) page f portant l'adresse bibliographique

imprint² [ɪmˈprɪnt] VT imprimer; **to i. sth with sth** marquer ou empreindre qch de qch; **the shape of an animal's foot was imprinted in the earth** l'empreinte du pied d'un animal était restée dans la terre; **to i. sth on the memory** graver ou fixer qch dans la mémoire

imprinter [ˈɪmprɪntər] N (for credit card payment) pressographe m

imprison [ɪmˈprɪzən] VT emprisonner, mettre en prison; **to keep sb imprisoned** garder qn prisonnier

imprisonment [ɪmˈprɪzənmənt] N emprisonnement m; **ten days' i.** dix jours d'emprisonnement ou de prison

improbability [ɪmprɒbəˈbɪlɪtɪ] N improbabilité f

improbable [ɪmˈprɒbəb(ə)l] ADJ improbable; **it's highly i. that he'll come** il est très improbable ou très peu probable qu'il vienne

improbably [ɪmˈprɒbəblɪ] ADV invraisemblablement; **quite i., he won** contre toute attente, il a gagné; **he was wearing an i. large hat** il portait un chapeau d'une grandeur invraisemblable

impromptu [ɪmˈprɒmptjuː] ADV (to do sth) sans préparation, impromptu
ADJ (poem, speech) impromptu; **to make an i. speech** improviser un discours
N Theat, Mus impromptu m

improper [ɪmˈprɒpər] ADJ **1** (incorrect) (use, purpose) impropre **2** (indecent) (suggestion, remark) indécent, inconvenant **3** (not fitting) (behaviour, dress) déplacé; **it would be i. to refuse** il serait de mauvaise grâce de refuser
▸ ▸ Math **i. fraction** expression f fractionnaire; **i. practices** pratiques fpl irrégulières

improperly [ɪmˈprɒpəlɪ] ADV **1** (incorrectly) (to use a tool, one's power) improprement **2** (indecently) (to behave) d'une manière inconvenante, avec indécence **3** (inappropriately) (to speak, behave) d'une façon déplacée; **to be i. dressed** ne pas porter une tenue convenable

impropriety [ɪmprəˈpraɪətɪ] N **1** (unsuitable expression, gesture etc) inconvenance f, indécence f, **to be guilty of improprieties** avoir commis des inconvenances **2** (incorrectness) (of language etc) impropriété f, (of behaviour) inconvenance f, indécence f

improve [ɪmˈpruːv] VT (one's French, the flavour, translation etc) améliorer; (wine etc) bonifier; (one's knowledge) étendre, élargir; (one's taste) affiner; Agr (soil) bonifier, enri-

chir; **to i. the appearance of sb/sth** embellir qn/qch; esp Hum **to i. one's mind** se cultiver
VI (of situation, sb's health etc) s'améliorer; (of wine etc) s'améliorer, se bonifier; Com (of prices, markets) monter; **business is improving** les affaires reprennent
▸ **improve on, improve upon** VT INSEP (make better) améliorer; Com **to i. on sb's offer** offrir plus que qn

improved [ɪmˈpruːvd] ADJ (situation etc) amélioré; (invention) perfectionné; Com (offer) supérieur

improvement [ɪmˈpruːvmənt] N **1** (in situation, health etc) amélioration f (in de); (of invention) perfectionnement m; **to be an i. on sb/sth** surpasser qn/qch; **the weather is a bit of an i. on what it was yesterday** il fait légèrement meilleur aujourd'hui qu'hier; **we should see something of an i. in the weather tomorrow** le temps devrait s'améliorer demain; **my new car is a great i. on the old one** ma nouvelle voiture est bien supérieure à l'ancienne; **the cakes were an i. on my first attempt** les gâteaux étaient mieux réussis que la première fois; **her new boyfriend's a bit of an i.** son nouveau petit ami est un peu mieux que le(s) précédent(s) **2** (usu pl) Constr etc **improvements** améliorations fpl, embellissements mpl; **we're making some improvements to the house** nous rénovons la maison
▸ ▸ Br **i. grant** = subvention f pour la rénovation d'une maison

improvidence [ɪmˈprɒvɪdəns] N **1** (rashness) imprévoyance f **2** (carelessness with money) prodigalité f

improvident [ɪmˈprɒvɪdənt] ADJ **1** (rash) imprévoyant **2** (careless with money) prodigue

improvidently [ɪmˈprɒvɪdəntlɪ] ADV **1** (rashly) de façon imprévoyante **2** (to spend money) de façon prodigue

improving [ɪmˈpruːvɪŋ] ADJ (book etc) édifiant; (influence, environment) bénéfique

improvisation [ɪmprəvaɪˈzeɪʃən] N improvisation f

improvise [ˈɪmprəvaɪz] VT improviser; **hastily improvised** sommairement organisé; **improvised speech** discours improvisé ou impromptu; **they improvised bandages from bedsheets** ils ont fait des bandages de fortune avec des draps; **improvised raft** radeau m de fortune
VI improviser; **to i. on the piano** improviser au piano; **you will have to i.** (make do) il faudra que vous vous débrouilliez avec ce qu'il y a

improviser [ˈɪmprəvaɪzər] N improvisateur, -trice

imprudence [ɪmˈpruːdəns] N imprudence f, (with money) manque m de prévoyance

imprudent [ɪmˈpruːdənt] ADJ imprudent; **i. with money** imprudent dans ses dépenses; **she's rather i. in her choice of friends** elle choisit mal ses amis

imprudently [ɪmˈpruːdəntlɪ] ADV imprudemment

impudence [ˈɪmpjʊdəns] N impudence f, insolence f

impudent [ˈɪmpjʊdənt] ADJ impudent, insolent; **he's an i. fellow** c'est un insolent

impudently [ˈɪmpjʊdəntlɪ] ADV avec impudence ou insolence

impugn [ɪmˈpjuːn] VT Fml (sb's honour, motives) mettre en doute ou en question; Law (sb's evidence) récuser

impulse [ˈɪmpʌls] N **1** (desire) envie f, Psy (sexual etc) pulsion f, **to feel an i. to do sth** avoir une soudaine envie de faire qch; **a sudden i. made me start running** instinctivement, j'ai commencé à courir; **to act on i.**

agir spontanément *ou* sur le coup d'une impulsion; **I did it on i.** j'ai fait ça sur un coup de tête **2** *(stimulation, force)* impulsion *f*; *Fig* **to give an i. to trade** donner une impulsion au commerce **3** *Phys* quantité *f* de mouvement; *Elec* **electrical impulses** impulsions *fpl* électriques; *Physiol* **nerve i.** signal *m* nerveux
▸▸ *Mktg* **i. buy** achat *m* d'impulsion; **i. buyer** acheteur, -euse impulsif(ive); **i. buying** achats *mpl* d'impulsion; **i. goods** produits *mpl* d'achat impulsif

impulsion [ɪmˈpʌlʃən] N impulsion *f*

impulsive [ɪmˈpʌlsɪv] ADJ **1** *(person, gesture, decision, remark)* impulsif; **i. action** acte *m* impulsif, coup *m* de tête; **i. buy** achat *m* d'impulsion; **i. buyer** acheteur, -euse impulsif(ive) **2** *Tech* impulsif, propulsif
▸▸ *Tech* **i. force** force *f* impulsive *ou* projective

impulsively [ɪmˈpʌlsɪvlɪ] ADV *(to act)* par impulsion, de façon impulsive

impulsiveness [ɪmˈpʌlsɪvnɪs] N caractère *m* impulsif

impunity [ɪmˈpjuːnɪtɪ] N impunité *f*; **to do sth with i.** faire qch impunément *ou* en toute impunité

impure [ɪmˈpjʊər] ADJ impur

impurity [ɪmˈpjʊərɪtɪ] N *(of water etc)*, *Fig* *(of thoughts)* impureté *f*

imputation [ɪmpjuːˈteɪʃən] N imputation *f*

impute [ɪmˈpjuːt] VT *(action etc)* imputer, attribuer (**to sb** à qn)

IN [ɪn]

PREP dans **1, 2, 5, 9, 11** ▪ en **1, 5, 6, 8–10, 13–16, 20** ▪ à **1, 10** ▪ chez **2** ▪ sur **4** ▪ de **5**	
CONJ puisque	
ADV à la maison **1** ▪ à l'intérieur **2** ▪ dedans **2**	
ADJ à la mode **1**	

PREP VOIR GRAMMAIRE A70; B54–7 **1** *(of place)* en, à, dans; **in France** en France; **in Japan** au Japon; **in the United States** aux États-Unis; **in Paris** à Paris; **in the provinces** en province; **to be in town/in the country** être en ville/à la campagne; **in his country** dans son pays; **in prison** en prison; **in church** à l'église; **in bed** au lit; **in the house/city** dans la maison/ville; **in the water** dans l'eau; **the key is in the door** la clef est sur la porte; **in this book** dans ce livre; **in my hand** dans ma main; **with a cigar in his mouth** un cigare à la bouche; **in the distance** au loin; **in your place** à votre place; **wounded in the shoulder** blessé à l'épaule **2** *(among)* **in the crowd** dans la foule; **the temperature was in the nineties** la température était dans les 30 degrés; **this illness is rare in men** cette maladie est rare chez les hommes; **this is a common theme in Shakespeare's work** c'est un thème fréquent dans les œuvres de Shakespeare **3** *(regarding)* **an expert in economics** un expert en économie politique; **two metres in length** long de deux mètres; **in certain respects he was right** à certains égards il avait raison **4** *(of ratio)* **one in ten** un sur dix; **once in ten years** une fois tous les dix ans **5** *(of time, age)* **in 1997** en 1997; **in the thirties** dans les années trente; **in the night** pendant la nuit; **in the afternoon/evening** l'après-midi/le soir; **at four o'clock in the afternoon** à quatre heures de l'après-midi; **the baby usually goes for a sleep in the afternoon** d'habitude le bébé dort (dans) *ou* pendant l'après-midi; **in spring/summer/autumn/winter** au printemps/en été/en automne/en hiver; **in (the month of) April** au mois d'avril, en avril; **in the future** à l'avenir;

never in my life have I met … jamais de ma vie je n'ai rencontré …; **in my time** de mon temps; **he's in his sixties** il a la soixantaine; **to do sth in three hours** *(within)* faire qch en trois heures; **he'll be here in three hours** il sera là dans trois heures; **in a little while** dans un petit moment; **I haven't seen you in years** je ne t'ai pas vu depuis des années, ça fait des années que je ne t'ai pas vu **6** *(introducing a gerund)* en; **in crossing the river** en traversant la rivière; **we had no problem/difficulty in doing it** nous n'avons eu aucun problème/aucune difficulté à le faire **7** *(of condition, state)* **in good health** en bonne santé; **in a good mood** de bonne humeur **8** *(clothed in, surrounded by)* **in his shirt** en chemise; **in slippers** en pantoufles; **dressed in white** habillé de *ou* en blanc; **the man in black** l'homme en noir; **wrapped in paper** enveloppé de papier; *Culin* **beef in a red wine sauce** bœuf dans une sauce au vin rouge; **fish in breadcrumbs** poisson pané **9** *(of weather, light)* en, dans; **to go out in the rain/snow** sortir par la pluie/la neige; **in this warm weather** par ce temps chaud; **to work in the rain** travailler sous la pluie; **in the sun** au soleil; **in the dark** dans l'obscurité **10** *(engaged in)* **in politics** en politique; **to be in politics** être dans la politique; **killed in action** tué au combat; **in the navy** dans la marine; **she's been in a lot of films** elle a joué dans beaucoup de films; **he wasn't in that race** il n'a pas pris part à cette course **11** *(due to)* dans; **in their hurry/panic** dans leur hâte/panique; **the fence blew down in the storm** la barrière est tombée pendant la tempête **12** *(of manner)* **in a gentle voice** d'une voix douce; **in a businesslike manner** d'une façon professionnelle; **in the French style** à la française; **to be in fashion** être à la mode **13** *(of medium)* **to write in French** écrire en français; **in writing** par écrit; **to talk in whispers** parler en chuchotant; **they were paid in gold/cash** ils étaient payés en or/liquide **14** *(of arrangement)* **to stand in a circle** se tenir en cercle; **in alphabetical order** par ordre alphabétique; **line up in twos** mettez-vous par deux **15** *(of form)* **I've nothing in your size** je n'ai rien à *ou* dans votre taille; **do you have it in a 5?** est-ce que vous l'auriez dans le 38?; **in the form of a pill** sous forme de pilule; **she was curled up in a ball** elle était roulée en boule; **do you have it in red/silk?** est-ce que vous l'avez en rouge/soie? **16** *(of degree, extent)* **in large quantities** en grandes quantités; **in part** en partie; **in places** par endroits **17** *(of purpose)* **in reply to …** en réponse à …; **in honour of …** en l'honneur de …; **in search of …** à la recherche de …; **in the cause of humanity** pour la cause de l'humanité **18** *(with reflexive pronoun)* **this product is not a poison in itself** ce produit n'est pas un poison en soi **19** *(of character, ability)* **I didn't think she had it in her** je ne l'en croyais pas capable; **he had it in him to be cruel** il était capable de cruauté; **it's not in her nature to be cruel** ce n'est pas dans sa nature d'être cruelle **20** *Mus* en; **symphony in B minor** symphonie en si mineur

CONJ **in that** parce que, puisque, vu que; **in so far as** dans la mesure où

ADV 1 *(inside building, room, boundary etc)* *(at home)* à la maison, chez soi; *(in one's office etc)* dans son bureau *etc*; **is he in?** est-ce qu'il est là?; **is your mother in?** est-ce que votre mère est à la maison?; **we've got the builders in** nous avons des ouvriers à la mai-

son; *Fam* **what's he in for?** *(in prison)* pourquoi est-ce qu'il fait de la tôle?; *(in hospital)* pourquoi est-ce qu'il est à l'hôpital?; *Agr* **the harvest is in** la moisson est rentrée; **to be in** *(of bus, plane etc)* être arrivé; **the train is in** le train est en gare *ou* est arrivé; *Tennis* **the ball is in** la balle est bonne **2** *(indoors, inside)* à l'intérieur, dedans; **in with you!** *(come in)* allons, rentrez!; *(go in)* allez-y! **3** *(in a situation)* **the Liberals were in** *(in power)* le parti libéral était au pouvoir; **stripes are in this year** *(in fashion)* les rayures sont à la mode cette année; *Fam* **to be (well) in with sb** *(in favour)* être en bons termes avec qn, être dans les petits papiers de qn; **my luck is in** je suis en veine; *Cr* **to be in** battre la balle, *Fam* être à la batte **4** *(phrases)* **I'm in for a thousand pounds** *(have invested etc)* j'ai engagé mille livres; **we're in for a storm** nous aurons sûrement de l'orage; **he's in for a surprise** il va être surpris, il va avoir une surprise; *Fam* **he's in for it** qu'est-ce qu'il va prendre!; *Fam* **to have it in for sb** avoir une dent contre qn; **to be in at the start/finish of sth** assister au début/à la fin de qch; **to be in on a secret** être dans le secret; **I wasn't in on it** je n'étais pas dans le coup; **to go in and out** entrer et sortir; **she and I were always in and out of each other's house** nous étions tout le temps fourrées l'une chez l'autre; **to be all in** *(exhausted)* être complètement crevé

ADJ 1 *(fashionable)* **it's the in thing these days** c'est la mode aujourd'hui; **the in people** or **crowd** les gens à la mode *ou* *Fam* dans le coup **2** *(exclusive)* **an in joke** une plaisanterie de coterie

N 1 *Fam* **to know the ins and outs of a matter** connaître une affaire dans tous ses détails **2** *Am Fam (influence)* **to have an in** avoir de l'influence; **he has an in with the senator** il a ses entrées chez le sénateur **3** *(where film clip begins)* entrée *f*

inability [ɪnəˈbɪlɪtɪ] N incapacité *f* (**to do sth** de faire qch); *(powerlessness)* impuissance *f* (**to do sth** à faire qch)

inaccessibility [ɪnæksesɪˈbɪlɪtɪ] N inaccessibilité *f*

inaccessible [ɪnækˈsesɪb(ə)l] ADJ *(place, poetry, person)* inaccessible (**to** à); **senior civil servants are i. to the public** le public n'a pas accès auprès des hauts fonctionnaires

inaccuracy [ɪnˈækjʊrəsɪ] N *(of rifle, storyteller)* imprécision *f*, manque *m* de précision; *(of report, account)* inexactitude *f*, manque de précision; *(of translation)* infidélité *f*; **full of inaccuracies** *(work)* plein d'inexactitudes

inaccurate [ɪnˈækjʊrət] ADJ *(calculation, idea)* inexact; *(account, translation)* inexact, infidèle

inaccurately [ɪnˈækjʊrətlɪ] ADV *(to calculate, judge, quote, translate etc)* inexactement, de façon inexacte

inaction [ɪnˈækʃən] N inaction *f*

inactive [ɪnˈæktɪv] ADJ *(person, volcano, money, account)* inactif; *(mind)* inerte

inactivity [ɪnækˈtɪvɪtɪ] N inactivité *f*

inadequacy [ɪnˈædɪkwəsɪ] N *(of income)* insuffisance *f*, *(of system etc)* imperfection *f*; *Psy (of person)* complexe *m* d'infériorité; *Fml* **because of his i. to the task** en raison de son incapacité à faire ce travail

inadequate [ɪnˈædɪkwət] ADJ *(not enough)* *(funds, salary, preparations, ventilation etc)* insuffisant; *(unsuitable)* *(diet, precautions)* inadéquat; **that is an i. explanation of his behaviour** cela ne suffit pas à justifier son comportement; **to be i.** *(of thing)* être insuffisant (**for** pour); **she makes me feel i.** elle me donne des complexes; **I feel so i. in a situation like this** dans une situation comme celle-ci je me sens tellement peu à la hauteur

inadequately [ɪn'ædɪkwətlɪ] **ADV** *(ventilated, informed, supplied)* insuffisamment; **they were i. equipped for climbing a mountain** ils n'avaient pas l'équipement adéquat pour faire une ascension; **the vehicle was felt to perform i. on rough terrain** la performance du véhicule sur terrain accidenté a été jugée insuffisante

inadmissible [ɪnəd'mɪsɪb(ə)l] **ADJ** *(theory, claim)* inadmissible; *Law (evidence)* irrecevable

inadvertence [ɪnəd'vɜːtəns] **N** inattention *f*, **through i.** par inadvertance

inadvertent [ɪnəd'vɜːtənt] **ADJ** *(mistake etc)* involontaire

inadvertently [ɪnəd'vɜːtəntlɪ] **ADV** par inadvertance

inadvisability [ɪnədvaɪzə'bɪlɪtɪ] **N** *(of action)* imprudence *f*

inadvisable [ɪnəd'vaɪzəb(ə)l] **ADJ** déconseillé

inalienable [ɪn'eɪlɪənəb(ə)l] **ADJ** *(property, right)* inaliénable

inane [ɪ'neɪn] **ADJ** *(person, action)* inepte, stupide; *(smile)* bête, niais; *(answer)* inepte, saugrenu; **i. remark** ineptie *f*

inanely [ɪ'neɪnlɪ] **ADV** bêtement, stupidement

inanimate [ɪn'ænɪmət] **ADJ** *(body, style etc)* inanimé, sans vie

inanition [ɪnə'nɪʃən] **N** *Med* inanition *f*

inanity [ɪ'nænɪtɪ] **N** *(of remark)* inanité *f*, *(of person)* stupidité *f*

inapplicable [ɪn'æplɪkəb(ə)l] **ADJ** inapplicable (**to** à); **'delete where i.'** 'rayez la mention inutile'

inappropriate [ɪnə'prəʊprɪət] **ADJ** *(behaviour, music)* peu approprié, qui ne convient pas (**to** à); *(word)* impropre; *(speech, joke, remark)* déplacé; **his clothes were i. to the climate** ses vêtements n'étaient guère appropriés au climat; **her dress was i. to this formal occasion** sa robe convenait mal au caractère officiel de l'occasion

inappropriately [ɪnə'prəʊprɪətlɪ] **ADV** *(to behave)* de façon inconvenante; **to be i. dressed** ne pas porter des vêtements appropriés

inapt [ɪn'æpt] **ADJ** *(inappropriate)* peu approprié (**to** à)

inaptitude [ɪn'æptɪtjuːd] **N** *(inability)* incapacité *f*

inarticulate [ɪnɑː'tɪkjʊlɪt] **ADJ 1** *(person)* qui manque de facilité à s'exprimer; *(sound)* inarticulé; *esp Lit (desire)* inexprimé; **he's so i.** il a tellement de mal à s'exprimer; **i. with rage** bégayant de colère; **I was seized by an i. rage** j'ai été pris d'une rage telle que je pouvais à peine m'exprimer **2** *Biol (without joints)* inarticulé

inartistic [ɪnɑː'tɪstɪk] **ADJ** *(production of play, arrangement of flowers etc)* peu artistique; *(person)* dépourvu de sens artistique; **I'm fairly i.** je n'ai pas beaucoup de sens artistique

inasmuch [ɪnəz'mʌtʃ] **CONJ** *Fml* **i. as** dans la mesure où

inattention [ɪnə'tenʃən] **N** inattention *f*, manque *m* d'attention; **i. to detail** inattention aux *ou* manque d'attention pour les détails

inattentive [ɪnə'tentɪv] **ADJ** *(audience, child at school)* inattentif, distrait; *(husband, waiter etc)* peu attentionné, peu prévenant (**to,** towards sb à l'égard de qn), inattentif (**to** sb's needs aux besoins de qn); **to be i. to** *(detail, consequences of one's action, comfort of guests)* ne pas faire attention à

inattentively [ɪnə'tentɪvlɪ] **ADV** sans prêter attention, distraitement

inaudible [ɪn'ɔːdɪb(ə)l] **ADJ** inaudible; *(sound)* imperceptible, inaudible

inaudibly [ɪn'ɔːdɪblɪ] **ADV** de manière inaudible

inaugural [ɪ'nɔːgjʊrəl] **ADJ** *(meeting)* inaugural, -aux; *(speech)* inaugural, -aux, d'inauguration
▪ **N** *Am (speech)* discours *m* inaugural *ou* d'inauguration

inaugurate [ɪ'nɔːgjʊreɪt] **VT** *(building)* inaugurer; *(conference, exhibition)* ouvrir; *Fig (new era)* inaugurer, commencer; *(new system, tradition etc)* instaurer; *(head of state)* faire prêter serment à *(lors de la prise de fonctions)*; **he will be inaugurated today** il prêtera serment aujourd'hui

inauguration [ɪnɔːgjʊ'reɪʃən] **N** *(of building etc)* inauguration *f*, *(of new system etc)* instauration *f*
▸▸ **i. ceremony** *(for building, bridge etc)* cérémonie *f* d'inauguration; **I. Day** = jour *m* de l'investiture du président des États-Unis (le 20 janvier)

inauspicious [ɪnɔː'spɪʃəs] **ADJ** *(circumstances)* défavorable; *(moment)* malencontreux; **an i. sign** un mauvais signe; **the project got off to an i. start** le projet a mal commencé

inauspiciously [ɪnɔː'spɪʃəslɪ] **ADV** de façon peu propice

inauthentic [ɪnɔː'θentɪk] **ADJ** inauthentique

in-between **ADJ** intermédiaire
▪ **N** **but what happens if you're an i.?** et qu'est-ce qu'on fait si on est entre les deux?

inborn ['ɪn'bɔːn] **ADJ** *(instinct, merit)* inné, naturel; *Med* congénital, -aux

inbound ['ɪnbaʊnd] **ADJ** *(flight, passenger)* à l'arrivée
▸▸ **i. tourism** tourisme *m* récepteur *ou* réceptif; **i. travel** tourisme récepteur *ou* réceptif

in-box **N** *Comput (for e-mail)* boîte *f* de réception, corbeille *f* d'arrivée

inbred ['ɪn'bred] **ADJ 1** *(dog, horse etc)* consanguin; **they are so i. that …** la consanguinité chez eux est telle que … **2** *(innate)* inné

inbreed ['ɪn'briːd] **VI** *(pt, pp inbred)* se reproduire entre eux

inbreeding ['ɪn'briːdɪŋ] **N** *(of animals)* accouplement *m* d'animaux consanguins; *(of people)* unions *fpl* consanguines

in-built **ADJ** = built-in

Inc [ɪŋk] *Am Com (abbr Incorporated)* ≃ SARL

Inca ['ɪŋkə] **N** Inca *mf*
▪ **ADJ** inca *inv*

incalculable [ɪn'kælkjʊləb(ə)l] **ADJ** *(consequences, harm)* incalculable; *(loss, help)* inestimable

incalculably [ɪn'kælkjʊləblɪ] **ADV** de façon inestimable

in camera **ADV, ADJ** *Law* à huis clos

incandescence [ɪnkæn'desəns] **N** incandescence *f*

incandescent [ɪnkæn'desənt] **ADJ** incandescent; *(light, light bulb etc)* à incandescence

incantation [ɪnkæn'teɪʃən] **N** incantation *f*

incapability [ɪnkeɪpə'bɪlɪtɪ] **N** incapacité *f*

incapable [ɪn'keɪpəb(ə)l] **ADJ** *(unable)* incapable (**of** de); **I'm not i.!** je ne suis pas impo

tent!; **i. of movement** *(of person)* incapable de bouger; *Fml* **the essay is i. of improvement** *(cannot be improved upon)* cette dissertation ne peut pas être améliorée, tant elle est parfaite; *Law* **declared i. of managing his own affairs** en état d'incapacité légale; *Law* **i. of succeeding to an estate** incapable de prendre la succession d'un domaine

incapacitate [ɪnkə'pæsɪteɪt] **VT 1** rendre incapable (**for work** de travailler); *(vehicle)* mettre hors d'état de marche; **the alcohol had temporarily incapacitated him** l'alcool avait temporairement inhibé ses facultés **2** *Law* frapper d'incapacité

incapacity [ɪnkə'pæsɪtɪ] **N 1** incapacité *f*, incompétence *f* **2** *Law* incapacité *f*

in-car **ADJ** *Aut*
▸▸ **i. listening** = écoute *f* de la radio, de cassettes ou de CD en voiture; *Br* **i. stereo** autoradio *m*

incarcerate [ɪn'kɑːsəreɪt] **VT** *Fml* incarcérer

incarceration [ɪnkɑːsə'reɪʃən] **N** *Fml* incarcération *f*, emprisonnement *m*

incarnate[1] [ɪn'kɑːneɪt] **ADJ** incarné; **the devil i.** le diable incarné; **perfection/wisdom i.** la perfection/la sagesse incarnée

incarnate[2] ['ɪnkɑːneɪt] **VT** incarner

incarnation [ɪnkɑː'neɪʃən] **N** *Rel, Fig (of Christ, an idea)* incarnation *f*, **to be the i. of wisdom** *(of person)* être l'incarnation de la sagesse; **in a previous i.** dans une vie antérieure; *Fig* **in a previous i. he was an MP** à une époque il était député

incautious [ɪn'kɔːʃəs] **ADJ** imprudent; *(remark etc)* inconsidéré; **in an i. moment** dans un moment d'inattention

incautiously [ɪn'kɔːʃəslɪ] **ADV** imprudemment

incendiary [ɪn'sendɪərɪ] **ADJ** *(bomb, device)*, *Fig (remarks, speech)* incendiaire
▪ **N 1** *(arsonist)* incendiaire *mf*, *Fig (agitator)* trublion *m*, agitateur, -trice **2** *(bomb)* bombe *f* incendiaire

incense[1] ['ɪnsens] **N** encens *m*
▸▸ **i. bearer** thuriféraire *m*; **i. burner** encensoir *m*; **i. stick** bâtonnet *m* d'encens

incense[2] [ɪn'sens] **VT** rendre furieux

> Note that the French verb **encenser** is a false friend and is never a translation for the English verb **to incense**. It means **to praise lavishly**.

incensed [ɪn'senst] **ADJ** furieux; **to become** *or* **get i.** être furieux (**with** contre, **about** au sujet de)

incentive [ɪn'sentɪv] **N** encouragement *m*; *Com, Ind (payment)* prime *f*, *Mktg* stimulation *f*, *Fam* stim *f*, *(reduction, freebie)* stimulant *m*, stimulateur *m*; **there is no i. for students here to work hard** il n'y a rien ici qui incite *ou* encourage les étudiants à travailler dur; **i. to buy** incitation *f ou* stimulation à l'achat
▸▸ *Br Com* **i. bonus** prime de rendement *ou* d'encouragement; **i. company** *(in tourism)* agence *f* spécialisée dans le voyage de stimulation; **i. fare** tarif *m* de stimulation; **i. marketing** marketing *m* de stimulation; *Com, Ind* **i. pay** primes de rendement; **i. scheme** *(for buyers)* programme *m* de stimulation; *(for workers)* système *m* de primes; **i. tourism** tourisme *m* de stimulation; **i. travel** voyages *mpl* de motivation *ou* de stimulation; **i. trip** voyage *m* de motivation *ou* de stimulation

inception [ɪn'sepʃən] **N** *Fml (of company, scheme etc)* commencement *m*, début *m*

incessant [ɪn'sesənt] **ADJ** *(noise)* incessant, continuel; *(worry)* éternel

incessantly [ɪn'sesəntlɪ] ADV sans cesse, sans relâche, continuellement

Note that the French word **incessamment** is a false friend. It means **very shortly.**

incest ['ɪnsest] N inceste m

incestuous [ɪn'sestjʊəs] ADJ incestueux; *Fig* the i. world of writers le monde très fermé *ou* en vase clos des écrivains

inch [ɪntʃ] N *(measurement)* pouce m (= 2,54 cm); **he's every i. a** *or* **the soldier** il a tout du militaire; **she won't give (way) an i.** elle ne reculera pas d'une semelle; **by inches, i. by i.** peu à peu, petit à petit; **I know every i. of the neighbourhood** je connais le quartier comme ma poche; **give her an i. and she'll take a mile** tu lui en donnes jusqu'au coude, elle en demande long comme le bras; **to be within an i. of doing** être à deux doigts de faire; **to beat sb to within an i. of their life** battre qn en le laissant pour mort; **I'll beat him to within an i. of his life!** je vais l'étrangler!
▸ **inch along, inch forward** VI avancer tout doucement
VT SEP faire avancer tout doucement; **she inched her way along the window ledge** elle se déplaça tout doucement le long du rebord de la fenêtre

incidence ['ɪnsɪdəns] N **1** *(frequency)* *(of thefts, crime etc)* taux m; *(of disease)* incidence f; **the i. of cancer has increased** les cas de cancer se sont multipliés **2** *Opt, Electron, Aviat etc* **angle of i.** angle m d'incidence

incident ['ɪnsɪdənt] N incident m; **a journey full of incident(s)** un voyage mouvementé
ADJ **1** *Opt, Electron (light beam etc)* incident **2** *Fml (related)* inhérent (**to** à)

incidental [ɪnsɪ'dent(ə)l] ADJ *(minor)* *(event, circumstance, effect)* secondaire; *(extra, supplementary)* *(advantage, benefit)* supplémentaire; **to be i. to sth** être occasionné par *ou* découler de qch; **the disruption i. to the reorganization** le désordre occasionné par la restructuration
N détail m; **incidentals** *(expenses)* faux frais *mpl*
▸▸ **i. costs, i. expenses** faux frais; **i. music** *(for film)* musique f de film; *(for play)* musique de scène

incidentally [ɪnsɪ'dentəlɪ] ADV **1** *(by the way)* soit dit en passant *ou* entre parenthèses; **i., how is he?** au fait, comment va-t-il? **2** *(accidentally, secondarily)* incidemment

Note that the French word **incidemment** only means **accidentally.**

incinerate [ɪn'sɪnəreɪt] VT incinérer

incineration [ɪnsɪnə'reɪʃən] N incinération f

incinerator [ɪn'sɪnəreɪtər] N *Ind etc* incinérateur m; *(in crematorium)* four m crématoire

incipient [ɪn'sɪpɪənt] ADJ naissant, dans ses débuts; **i. madness** folie naissante

incise [ɪn'saɪz] VT *Art etc (inscription etc)* graver

incision [ɪn'sɪʒən] N incision f; **to make an i. in sth** inciser qch, pratiquer une incision dans qch

incisive [ɪn'saɪsɪv] ADJ *(remark, style)* incisif; *(mind)* pénétrant

incisively [ɪn'saɪsɪvlɪ] ADV de façon incisive

incisor [ɪn'saɪzər] N *Anat* incisive f

incite [ɪn'saɪt] VT inciter (**to sth** à qch; **to do sth** à faire qch); **to i. racial hatred** inciter à la haine raciale; **to i. sb to crime/violence** inciter *ou* pousser qn au crime/à la violence

incitement [ɪn'saɪtmənt] N *(of people, actions)* incitation f, encouragement m (**to sth** à qch)

incivility [ɪnsɪ'vɪlɪtɪ] N *Fml* incivilité f

incl 1 *(abbr* **inclusive)** inclus; **from 14th to 23rd November i.** du 14 au 23 novembre inclus; **i. of gas and electricity** gas et électricité compris **2** *(abbr* **including)** avec

inclemency [ɪn'klemənsɪ] N *Fml* inclémence f, rigueur f

inclement [ɪn'klemənt] ADJ *Fml (weather)* inclément

inclination [ɪnklɪ'neɪʃən] N **1** *(desire)* envie f (**for sth** de qch; **to do** de faire); **to have an i. for sth** avoir un penchant pour qch; **she had no i. to help him** elle n'avait pas du tout envie de l'aider; **to have lost all i. for sth** n'avoir plus envie de qch; **to show little i. to do sth** se montrer peu enclin à faire qch; **to follow one's inclinations** faire ce à quoi on est naturellement enclin **2** *(tendency)* tendance f (**towards sth** à qch; **to do** à faire); **my i. would be to ...** j'aurais tendance à ..., je serais porté à ...; **my i. would be to say yes, but ...** je serais enclin à dire oui, mais ...; **she is by i. a cautious person** c'est quelqu'un de très prudent par nature **3** *(angle)* *(of head, body)* inclination f; *Math (of plane)* inclinaison f

incline[1] ['ɪnklaɪn] N pente f

incline[2] [ɪn'klaɪn] VT **1** *(motivate, cause)* inciter; **this inclines me to believe them** ceci me porte *ou* m'encourage à les croire; **her remarks don't i. me to be sympathetic** ses remarques ne m'incitent pas à être compréhensif **2** *(head)* incliner, pencher
VI **1** *(of person)* avoir un penchant (**to sth** pour qch, **to do** à faire), avoir tendance (**to do** à faire); **to i. to the belief that ...** être porté *ou* avoir tendance à croire que ... **2** *(of thing)* s'incliner, pencher (**to** à; **towards** vers)

inclined [ɪn'klaɪnd] ADJ **1** *(person)* *(temporarily)* disposé (**to** à); *(permanently)* enclin (**to** à); **to feel** *or* **be i. to do sth** *(tend to)* avoir tendance à faire qch; *(have desire to)* avoir envie de faire qch; **I am i. to think that he's right** je suis porté *ou* j'ai tendance à croire qu'il a raison; **to be well i. towards sb** être bien disposé envers qn; **if ever you should feel so i.** si jamais l'envie vous en prenait; **prices are i. to fall** les prix ont tendance à baisser; **he's i. to put on weight** il a tendance à grossir; **i. to laziness** *or* **to be lazy** enclin à la paresse; **I'm not musically i.** *(I don't like music)* je ne suis pas très porté sur la musique; *(I have no talent)* je n'ai pas de talent musical; **if you're that way i.** *(if you want to)* si cela vous dit, his house i. tous le biens furent vendus, y compris sa maison; **i. in the price are two excursions** deux excursions sont comprises dans le prix; **ser-**

include [ɪn'kluːd] VT inclure, comprendre; **the speech included several references to Soviet history** le discours comportait plusieurs références à l'histoire de l'Union Soviétique; **the committee includes politicians from all parties** le comité comprend des politiciens de tous les partis; **men over seventy are not included** les hommes de plus de soixante-dix ans ne sont pas compris; **the price does not i. accommodation** le prix ne comprend pas l'hébergement; **if you i. Christmas Day** en comptant le jour de Noël; **to i. sb among one's friends** compter qn parmi *ou* au nombre de ses amis
▸ **include out** VT SEP *Fam Hum* **i. me out** ne compte pas sur moi

included [ɪn'kluːdɪd] ADJ (y) compris; **all his property was sold,** ...

vice i. *(on bill)* service compris; **batteries not i.** les piles ne sont pas comprises

including [ɪn'kluːdɪŋ] PREP y compris; **i. me** moi y compris; **there are five of us, not i. the children** nous sommes cinq, sans compter les enfants; **up to and i. ...** jusqu'à ... inclus

inclusion [ɪn'kluːʒən] N inclusion f

inclusive [ɪn'kluːsɪv] ADJ **1 five i. of the driver** cinq y compris le chauffeur; **from the 4th to the 12th February i.** du 4 au 12 février inclusivement; **i. price** *(at hotel etc)* (prix m) tout compris; **i. of costs** frais inclus; **i. of VAT** toutes taxes comprises, TTC; **i. of VAT** TVA comprise **2** *(all-embracing)* *(policy)* non discriminatoire; **the party needs to be more i.** il faut que le parti adopte une politique moins discriminatoire

inclusively [ɪn'kluːsɪvlɪ] ADV inclusivement

incognito [ɪnkɒg'niːtəʊ] ADJ, ADV **to be/travel i.** être/voyager incognito
N *(name, disguise)* incognito m; **to travel under an i.** voyager incognito

incoherence [ɪnkəʊ'hɪərəns] N incohérence f

incoherent [ɪnkəʊ'hɪərənt] ADJ *(speech, reasoning)* incohérent; *(style)* décousu; **to be i.** *(of person)* tenir des propos incohérents

incoherently [ɪnkəʊ'hɪərəntlɪ] ADV d'une manière incohérente

incombustible [ɪnkəm'bʌstɪb(ə)l] ADJ incombustible

income ['ɪnkʌm] N **1** revenu m, revenus *mpl*; **source of i.** source f de revenu; **their combined i.** leurs revenus additionnels; **i. from investments** revenu(s) provenant de placements; **to have a private i. of £15,000 a year** avoir quinze mille livres de rente; **to be on a low/high i.** avoir un faible revenu/un revenu élevé **2** *Com (receipts)* recettes *fpl*, revenus *mpl*, rentrées *fpl*
▸▸ *Acct* **i. account** compte m de produits; **i. bracket** tranche f de salaire *ou* de revenu; *Econ* **i. elasticity** élasticité f par rapport au revenu; *Acct* **i. and expenditure account** compte de dépenses et recettes; *Acct* **i. from operations** produits *mpl* de gestion courante, produits d'exploitation; **incomes policy** politique f des revenus; **i. smoothing** manipulations *fpl* de revenu; *Am Acct* **i. statement** compte de résultat; *Am St Exch* **i. stocks** valeurs *fpl* de rendement; *Fin* **i. stream** flux m de revenus; *Br Admin* **i. support** ≈ prestation f complémentaire en faveur des personnes justifiant de faibles revenus, ≈ revenu m minimum d'insertion; *Fin* **i. tax** impôt m sur le revenu (des personnes physiques); *Fin* **i. tax allowance** déduction f avant impôt, déduction fiscale; *Fin* **i. tax inspector** inspecteur m des contributions directes *ou* des impôts; *Fin* **i. tax return** déclaration f de revenus, feuille f d'impôt; *Fin* **i. velocity of capital** vitesse f de circulation du capital en revenus; *Fin* **i. velocity of circulation** vitesse de circulation de la monnaie en revenus

incomer ['ɪnkʌmər] N nouvel(le) arrivant, -ante

incoming ['ɪnkʌmɪŋ] ADJ *(government)* nouveau; *(plane, missile)* entrant; *(fax, e-mail)* en entrée; *(tide)* montant; **the i. president** le président élu
NPL *Com, Fin* **incomings** recettes *fpl*, revenus *mpl*, rentrées *fpl*; **incomings and outgoings** dépenses *fpl* et recettes
▸▸ *Tel* **i. call** appel m de l'extérieur; **this telephone takes i. calls only** ce téléphone ne permet que de recevoir des appels; **i. mail** courrier m (du jour); **i. message** message m entrant; **i. tide** marée f montante; **i. tour operator** voyagiste m de réceptif

incommensurable [ɪnkə'menʃərəb(ə)l] ADJ incommensurable (**with** avec); *Math (number)* irrationnel

incommensurate [ɪnkə'menʃərət] ADJ pas en rapport, pas en proportion (**with** avec)

incommode [ɪnkə'məʊd] VT *Fml* incommoder, déranger

incommodious [ɪnkə'məʊdɪəs] ADJ *Fml* incommode

incommunicado [ɪnkəmjuːnɪ'kɑːdəʊ] ADV **to be held i.** être (gardé) au secret

in-company ['ɪnkʌmpənɪ] ADJ **i. training** formation *f* sur le lieu de travail

incomparable [ɪn'kɒmpərəb(ə)l] ADJ incomparable, sans pareil

incomparably [ɪn'kɒmpərəblɪ] ADV incomparablement; **i. beautiful** d'une beauté incomparable

incompatibility [ɪnkəmpætɪ'bɪlɪtɪ] N *(of people, theories, medication etc)* incompatibilité *f* (**with** avec; **between** entre)

incompatible [ɪnkəm'pætɪb(ə)l] ADJ incompatible (**with** avec)

incompetence [ɪn'kɒmpɪtəns] N *also Jur* incompétence *f*

incompetent [ɪn'kɒmpɪtənt] ADJ **1** *(person)* incompétent, incapable **2** *Law (judge, court) (to hear case, carry out act)* incompétent; **I am i. to act** je n'ai pas qualité pour agir ▪ N incompétent, -ente

incomplete [ɪnkəm'pliːt] ADJ *(not complete)* incomplet, ète; *(not finished)* inachevé

incompletely [ɪnkəm'pliːtlɪ] ADV incomplètement

incompleteness [ɪnkəm'pliːtnɪs] N *(of novel, painting etc)* inachèvement *m*; *(of collection of works)* état *m* incomplet

incomprehensible [ɪnkɒmprɪ'hensɪb(ə)l] ADJ *(situation, speech, person)* incompréhensible; *(writing)* indéchiffrable

incomprehensibly [ɪnkɒmprɪ'hensɪblɪ] ADV de manière incompréhensible

incomprehension [ɪnkɒmprɪ'henʃən] N incompréhension *f*

inconceivable [ɪnkən'siːvəb(ə)l] ADJ inconcevable

inconceivably [ɪnkən'siːvəblɪ] ADV inconcevablement

inconclusive [ɪnkən'kluːsɪv] ADJ *(reasoning, evidence)* peu concluant; **it was all very i.** cela n'a donné aucun résultat

inconclusively [ɪnkən'kluːsɪvlɪ] ADV d'une manière peu concluante

incongruity [ɪnkɒŋ'gruːɪtɪ] N incongruité *f*

incongruous [ɪn'kɒŋgrʊəs] ADJ *(behaviour, remark, building)* incongru; *(combination)* bizarre; **the bright red is very i. in this room** le rouge vif détonne fortement dans cette pièce; **they are such an i. couple** ils sont tellement bizarrement assortis

incongruously [ɪn'kɒŋgrʊəslɪ] ADV de manière incongrue, incongrûment

inconsequence [ɪn'kɒnsɪkwəns] N inconséquence *f*

inconsequent [ɪn'kɒnsɪkwənt] ADJ = **inconsequential**

inconsequential [ɪnkɒnsɪ'kwenʃəl] ADJ **1** *(unimportant) (matter, remarks)* sans importance **2** *(not following) (reasoning, ideas)* décousu

inconsiderate [ɪnkən'sɪdərɪt] ADJ *(person)* qui manque d'égards (pour les autres); *(remark, action)* déplacé; **it was most i. of you to do that** tu n'as guère fait preuve de considération en faisant cela; **don't be so i.** pense un peu aux autres

inconsiderately [ɪnkən'sɪdərətlɪ] ADV **to behave i. to sb** manquer d'égards *ou* de

considération envers qn; **he had i. locked the door** il avait fermé la porte à clef sans se soucier des autres

inconsistency [ɪnkən'sɪstənsɪ] N **1** *(lack of logicality) (of person, argument)* incohérence *f* **2** *(inconsistent argument, action)* incohérence *f*; **his book is full of inconsistencies** son livre est bourré d'incohérences **3** *(uneven quality) (of artist's work etc)* irrégularité *f*, manque *m* de régularité

inconsistent [ɪnkən'sɪstənt] ADJ **1** *(remark)* en contradiction, contradictoire (**with** avec); **his words are i. with his conduct** ce qu'il dit est en contradiction *ou* ne cadre pas avec ce qu'il fait **2** *(person)* incohérent; **you're being i.** *(in saying that)* tu te contredis; *(in doing that)* tu n'es pas cohérent; **they're i. in what they say** leurs dires sont contradictoires **3** *(irregular) (work)* irrégulier; **his films are very i. in quality** la qualité de ses films est très irrégulière

> Note that the French word **inconsistant** is a false friend. It means **thin, runny** or **vacuous**, depending on the context.

inconsistently [ɪnkən'sɪstəntlɪ] ADV *(to behave)* de façon incohérente; *(to assert)* de façon contradictoire

inconsolable [ɪnkən'səʊləb(ə)l] ADJ inconsolable

inconspicuously [ɪnkən'spɪkjʊəslɪ] ADV de manière discrète

inconspicuous [ɪnkən'spɪkjʊəs] ADJ *(person)* discret, -ète, qui passe inaperçu; *(error, spot)* qui passe inaperçu; **to remain i.** rester dans l'ombre; **I tried to look i.** j'ai essayé de me faire discret

inconstancy [ɪn'kɒnstənsɪ] N *(of person, character)* inconstance *f*, *(of weather etc)* instabilité *f*, caractère *m* changeant

inconstant [ɪn'kɒnstənt] ADJ *(person, character)* inconstant, volage

incontestable [ɪnkən'testəb(ə)l] ADJ incontestable, indéniable

incontestably [ɪnkən'testəblɪ] ADV incontestablement

incontinence [ɪn'kɒntɪnəns] N *Med* incontinence *f*
  ▸▸ **i. pads** couches *fpl* pour adultes

incontinent [ɪn'kɒntɪnənt] ADJ *Med* incontinent

incontrovertible [ɪnkɒntrə'vɜːtɪb(ə)l] ADJ *(truth)* incontestable; *(evidence)* irrécusable; *(argument)* irréfutable

inconvenience [ɪnkən'viːnjəns] N dérangement *m*; *(more serious)* désagrément *m*; **to cause i. to sb, to be an i. to sb** incommoder qn, déranger qn; **I'm putting you to a great deal of i.** je vous donne beaucoup d'embarras; **without the slightest i.** sans le moindre dérangement; **we apologize for any i.** nous vous prions de nous excuser pour tout désagrément éventuel; **the i. of living so far from town** les inconvénients qu'il y a à vivre si loin de la ville
  ▪ VT déranger, causer du dérangement à

inconvenient [ɪnkən'viːnjənt] ADJ *(time)* inopportun; *(visitor)* gênant; *(house)* incommode, malcommode; **this isn't an i. time, is it?** tu es sûr que je ne te dérange pas?; **it's a bit i. just now, could you call back later?** je n'ai pas vraiment le temps tout de suite, tu pourrais me rappeler plus tard?; **if it is not i. to you** si cela ne vous gêne *ou* dérange pas; **Friday's a bit i.** vendredi ne me convient pas tellement; **it's very i. living so far from town** c'est très incommode d'habiter aussi loin de la ville; **the house is very i. for the shops** la maison est mal située par rapport aux commerces

inconveniently [ɪnkən'viːnjəntlɪ] ADV *(to arrive)* à un moment inopportun; **the announcement was i. timed** le moment de l'annonce a été mal choisi; **i. located** mal situé

inconvertible [ɪnkən'vɜːtɪb(ə)l] ADJ *Fin* inconvertible

incorporate [ɪn'kɔːpəreɪt] VT **1** *(include, add)* inclure, incorporer (**with** à, avec; **in** dans); **to i. a paragraph in(to) a chapter** incorporer un paragraphe dans un chapitre; **her work incorporates all the latest discoveries** ses travaux incluent toutes les découvertes les plus récentes **2** *Com (company)* constituer en société commerciale; *(banks)* réunir en société **3** *(merge)* regrouper pour former un tout; **these organizations were incorporated into a national fire brigade** ces organismes ont été regroupés pour constituer une brigade nationale de pompiers
  ▪ VI **1** s'incorporer **2** *Com* se constituer en société commerciale

incorporated [ɪn'kɔːpəreɪtɪd] ADJ *Am Com* **Sanders I.** ≃ Sanders SARL
  ▸▸ **i. company** association *f* constituée en société commerciale, société *f* par actions

incorporation [ɪnkɔːpə'reɪʃən] N **1** *Com (of company)* constitution *f* en société commerciale **2** *(inclusion)* incorporation *f* (**with** à, avec; **in(to)** dans)

incorrect [ɪnkə'rekt] ADJ **1** *(statement, account etc)* inexact; *(figures)* faux, *f* fausse; *(translation)* incorrect **2** *(style, behaviour etc)* incorrect

incorrectly [ɪnkə'rektlɪ] ADV **1** *(reported, stated)* inexactement; *(to speak)* incorrectement; *(invoiced)* indûment; **i. addressed** *(letter)* mal adressé **2** *(to behave etc)* incorrectement

incorrigible [ɪn'kɒrɪdʒɪb(ə)l] ADJ *(child, laziness etc)* incorrigible

incorruptible [ɪnkə'rʌptɪb(ə)l] ADJ *(metal, judge)* incorruptible

incoterms ['ɪnkəʊtɜːmz] NPL *Com* termes *mpl* commerciaux, incoterms *mpl*

increase¹ ['ɪnkriːs] N **1** *(in price, takings, salary, speed etc)* augmentation *f*, *(in pain, population)* accroissement *m*; *(in zeal, attention)* renouvellement *m*; **i. in the cost of living** augmentation du coût de la vie; **sales have shown an i. over the last six months** les ventes ont progressé ces six derniers mois; **i. in value** *(of property etc)* plus-value *f*; **I've had an i. in salary** j'ai été augmenté; **to be on the i.** être en augmentation *ou* en hausse **2** *Knitting* augmentation *f*

increase² [ɪn'kriːs] VI *(of prices, speed, unemployment etc)* augmenter; *(of noise, dissatisfaction)* grandir, s'agrandir; *(of pain, population)* s'accroître; **to i. in size** s'agrandir; **to i. in price** augmenter; **to i. in value** prendre de la valeur; **his paintings have increased in value fivefold** la valeur de ses tableaux a quintuplé; **to i. in volume** *(of substance)* augmenter de volume; **the volume of traffic increases every year** le volume de la circulation augmente chaque année
  ▪ VT **1** *(speed, production, salaries)* augmenter; *(number, expenses)* grossir, augmenter; *(one's wealth)* accroître, augmenter; *(prices)* majorer, augmenter; *(distance)* allonger, augmenter; *(dissatisfaction)* accentuer, augmenter; **to i. sb's salary** augmenter (le salaire de) qn; **to i. the dose** *(of medicine)* augmenter la dose; **to i. one's efforts** redoubler d'efforts; **increased cost of living** augmentation *f* du coût de la vie; **to i. the size of sth** agrandir qch **2** *Knitting* **i. two in the next row** augmenter de deux mailles au rang suivant

increasing [ɪnˈkriːsɪŋ] ADJ *(numbers, use, difficulty)* croissant; **an i. number of people are opting for …** de plus en plus de gens choisissent …
▸▸*Fin* **i. rate** tarif *m* progressif

increasingly [ɪnˈkriːsɪŋlɪ] ADV*(difficult, big etc)* de plus en plus; **i., people are saying that …** de plus en plus, les gens disent que …

incredible [ɪnˈkredɪb(ə)l] ADJ **1** *(unbelievable)* incroyable; **I find it i. that she didn't know** je n'arrive pas à croire qu'elle n'était pas au courant **2** *Fam (excellent)* incroyable, époustouflant

incredibly [ɪnˈkredɪblɪ] ADV incroyablement; **he's i. stupid** il est d'une sottise incroyable; **i., she agreed** elle a consenti, ce qui est incroyable

incredulity [ɪnkrɪˈdjuːlɪtɪ] Nincrédulité *f*

incredulous [ɪnˈkredjʊləs] ADJ incrédule (**of** à l'égard de); *(smile)* d'incrédulité

incredulously [ɪnˈkredjʊləslɪ] ADV*(to look at sb)* d'un air incrédule; *(to say)* d'un ton incrédule

increment [ˈɪnkrɪmənt] Naugmentation *f*, **to rise in annual increments of £1,000** *(of salary)* augmenter de mille livres par an; **unearned i.** *(of land, shares)* plus-value *f*

incremental [ɪnkrɪˈment(ə)l] ADJ **1** *(increasing)* croissant; **i. increases** augmentations *fpl* régulières **2** *Comput* incrémentiel
▸▸*Fin* **i. cash flow** cashflow *m* marginal; *Comput* **i. compiler** compilateur *m* incrémentiel; *Fin* **i. cost** coût *m* marginal; *Comput* **i. plotter** traceur *m* par pas

incriminate [ɪnˈkrɪmɪneɪt] VT *(implicate)* incriminer, mettre en cause; **I don't want to i. myself** je ne veux rien dire qui me fasse apparaître comme coupable; **you've just incriminated yourself** vous venez de vous compromettre

incriminating [ɪnˈkrɪmɪneɪtɪŋ] ADJ *(circumstance, statement etc)* compromettant

incrimination [ɪnkrɪmɪˈneɪʃən] N mise *f* en cause, incrimination *f*

incriminatory [ɪnˈkrɪmɪnətərɪ] ADJcompromettant

incrustation [ɪnkrʌsˈteɪʃən] N *(action)* entartrage *m*; *(deposit)* tartre *m*, dépôt *m* calcaire

incubate [ˈɪnkjʊbeɪt] VT*(eggs)* couver, incuber
VI *(of eggs)* incuber; *(of disease)* couver

incubation [ɪnkjʊˈbeɪʃən] Nincubation *f*
▸▸**i. period** (période *f* d')incubation

incubator [ˈɪnkjʊbeɪtər] N *(for eggs, bacteria)* incubateur *m*; *(for premature babies)* couveuse *f*

incubus [ˈɪnkjʊbəs] N*Myth* incube *m*; *Fig Lit* cauchemar *m*

in-cue N *TV, Radio* signal *m* de départ

inculcate [ˈɪnkʌlkeɪt] VTinculquer; **to i. sth in sb, to i. sb with sth** inculquer qch à qn

inculcation [ɪnkʌlˈkeɪʃən] Ninculcation *f*

incumbent [ɪnˈkʌmbənt] N**1** *(of administrative position)* titulaire *mf* **2** *Rel* bénéficiaire *m*, titulaire *m (d'une charge)*
ADJ**1** *(necessary)* **to be i. on sb to do sth** incomber *ou* appartenir à qn de faire qch **2** *(official)* en place

incunabulum, *pl* **incunabula** [ɪnkjuːˈnæbjʊləm, -jʊlə] Nincunable *m*

incur [ɪnˈkɜːr] VT (**-rr-**) *(risk)* courir; *(blame)* encourir; *(loss)* subir; *(sb's anger, hatred)* s'attirer; *(debts)* contracter; *(costs, expenses)* engager; **late payments will i. interest of 4%** en cas de retard de paiements, vous serez redevable d'intérêts au taux de 4%

incurable [ɪnˈkjʊərəb(ə)l] ADJ *(disease)* in-curable, inguérissable; *Fig (optimist, bigot)* invétéré, incorrigible; **an i. romantic** un romantique incorrigible

incurably [ɪnˈkjʊərəblɪ] ADVto be **i. ill** avoir une maladie incurable; *Fig* **i. lazy/optimistic** d'une paresse/d'un optimisme incorrigible; **I'm i. romantic** je suis un romantique incorrigible

incurious [ɪnˈkjʊərɪəs] ADJsans curiosité

incursion [ɪnˈkɜːʃən] N incursion *f* (**into** dans)

Ind 1 *(abbr* **Independent***)* indépendant **2** *abbr* **Indiana**

indebted [ɪnˈdetɪd] ADJ **1** *(owing money)* endetté; **to be heavily i. to sb** devoir une forte somme à qn **2** *Fig* redevable (**to sb for sth** à qn de qch); **I am i. to Mr Martin for this information** c'est à M. Martin que je dois ce renseignement

indebtedness [ɪnˈdetɪdnɪs] N endettement *m*; *Fig* dette *f* (**to** envers)

indecency [ɪnˈdiːsənsɪ] Nindécence *f*; *Law* **(public act of) i.** *(assault)* attentat *m* à la pudeur; *(exposure)* outrage *m* public à la pudeur

indecent [ɪnˈdiːsənt] ADJindécent; *Fam Fig (sum of money, salary)* scandaleux; **to do sth with i. haste** faire qch avec une rapidité scandaleuse
▸▸*Law* **i. assault** attentat *m* à la pudeur; **i. behaviour** attentat aux mœurs; **i. exposure** outrage *m* public à la pudeur

indecently [ɪnˈdiːsəntlɪ] ADVde manière indécente; *Fig Fam (rich)* scandaleusement

indecipherable [ɪndɪˈsaɪfərəb(ə)l, -frəb(ə)l] ADJindéchiffrable

indecision [ɪndɪˈsɪʒən] Nindécision *f*

indecisive [ɪndɪˈsaɪsɪv] ADJ **1** *(argument)* peu concluant; *(battle, election)* indécis **2** *(person)* indécis, irrésolu; **she was i. about whether to go or stay** elle ne savait pas si elle devait partir ou rester

indecisiveness [ɪndɪˈsaɪsɪvnɪs] Nindécision *f*

indeclinable [ɪndɪˈklaɪnəb(ə)l] ADJ *Gram* indéclinable

indecorous [ɪnˈdekərəs] ADJ *(person)* inconvenant; *(departure, retreat etc)* peu digne

indecorously [ɪnˈdekərəslɪ] ADV *(to behave)* de manière incorrecte *ou* inconvenante; *(to retreat, leave)* de façon peu digne

indecorum [ɪndɪˈkɔːrəm] N incorrection *f*, inconvenance *f*

indeed [ɪnˈdiːd] ADV **1** *(certainly)* en effet, vraiment; **he was i. a man of genius** c'était vraiment un homme de génie; **I may i. be wrong** il se peut toutefois que j'aie tort
2 *(intensive)* **I am very glad i.** je suis très très content; **thank you very much i.** merci infiniment, merci mille fois
3 *(what is more)* même, à vrai dire; **I think so, i. I am sure of it** je le pense et même j'en suis sûr
4 *(with affirmation or negation)* **you've been to Venice haven't you? – i. I have!** tu es allé à Venise, n'est-ce pas? – oui, j'y suis allé; **you haven't been to Venice – i. I have!** tu n'es jamais allé à Venise – si, j'y suis déjà allé!; **yes i.!** mais certainement!, pour sûr!; **i. not!** certes non!; **it does i.!, i. it does!** *(surprise me, mean that etc)* certainement!
5 *(interrogatively)* **I have lived in Paris – i.?** j'ai vécu à Paris – vraiment?; **have you i.?** *(expressing doubt, lack of interest, mockery)* ah oui?

indefatigable [ɪndɪˈfætɪgəb(ə)l] ADJinfatigable

indefatigably [ɪndɪˈfætɪgəblɪ] ADV infatigablement

indefensible [ɪndɪˈfensɪb(ə)l] ADJ *(theory, argument)* indéfendable; *(behaviour)* inexcusable

indefinable [ɪndɪˈfaɪnəb(ə)l] ADJ *(feeling, quality etc)* indéfinissable

indefinite [ɪnˈdefɪnɪt] ADJ **1** *(period of time, number)* indéterminé; *(leave, strike)* illimité **2** *(ideas, promises etc)* indéfini, vague **3** *Gram (article, pronom)* indéfini VOIR GRAMMAIRE A5–6; B4–5

indefinitely [ɪnˈdefɪnɪtlɪ] ADV*(to postpone sth)* indéfiniment; **I could go on i.** je pourrais continuer à l'infini

indelible [ɪnˈdelɪb(ə)l] ADJ *(ink)* indélébile, ineffaçable; *Fig (mark, memory)* indélébile

indelibly [ɪnˈdelɪblɪ] ADVde façon indélébile; *Fig* **i. printed on her mind** à jamais gravé dans son esprit

indelicacy [ɪnˈdelɪkəsɪ] N*(of person)* indélicatesse *f*, manque *m* de délicatesse; *(of remark, behaviour)* inconvenance *f*

indelicate [ɪnˈdelɪkət] ADJ *(person)* indélicat, qui manque de délicatesse; *(remark, behaviour)* inconvenant

indelicately [ɪnˈdelɪkətlɪ] ADV de façon inconvenante

indemnification [ɪndemnɪfɪˈkeɪʃən] N **1** *(action)* indemnisation *f*, dédommagement *m* (**of sb for sth** de qn de qch) **2** *(money)* indemnité *f*, dédommagement *m*

indemnify [ɪnˈdemnɪfaɪ] VT**1** *(protect)* garantir (**from, against** contre) **2** *(compensate)* indemniser, dédommager (**for a loss** d'une perte)

indemnity [ɪnˈdemnɪtɪ] N **1** *(protection)* *(against loss etc)* garantie *f*, assurance *f* **2** *(compensation)* indemnité *f*, dédommagement *m*

indent[1] [ˈɪndent] N**1** *Typ* alinéa *m* **2** *Br Com Old-fashioned* commande *f* de marchandises **3** *(notch)* entaille *f*, *(in metal)* bosselure *f*

indent[2] [ɪnˈdent] VT**1** *Typ (line)* renfoncer, mettre en retrait *ou* à l'alinéa; **indented line** ligne *f* en alinéa *ou* en retrait; **indented paragraph** paragraphe *m* en retrait **2** *(put notches in)* denteler, entailler; *(surface)* bosseler, bossuer; *Carp (beam)* endenter **3** *Br Com Old-fashioned* **to i. sb for sth** facturer qch à qn
VI *Br Com Old-fashioned* **to i. on sb for sth** commander qch à qn

indentation [ɪndenˈteɪʃən] N **1** *(made in sand by wheels etc)* trace *f*, impression *f* **2** *(action) (of edges of sth)* découpage *m* **3** *(notched, jagged edge)* dentelure *f*, *(notch)* entaille *f* **4** *Typ* alinéa *m*

indenture [ɪnˈdentʃər] *Jur* N contrat *m* synallagmatique, contrat bilatéral; **indentures** *(of apprentice)* contrat d'apprentissage
VT**1** *(bind by contract)* lier par contrat **2** *Arch (of parent or guardian)* mettre en apprentissage (**to sb** chez qn); *(of employer)* engager par un brevet d'apprentissage

independence [ɪndɪˈpendəns] N indépendance *f* (**from** à l'égard de); *(of state)* indépendance, autonomie *f*
▸▸**I. Day** fête *f* nationale de l'Indépendance *(aux États-Unis)*

independent [ɪndɪˈpendənt] ADJ *(person, inquiry, record label, cinema etc)* indépendant; *(state, country)* indépendant, autonome; **to be i. of sb/sth** ne pas dépendre de qn/qch; **person of i. means** rentier, -ière *f*; **an i. thinker** un libre-penseur; **his children are i. now** ses enfants peuvent maintenant pourvoir eux-mêmes à leurs besoins
N*Pol etc*indépendant, -ante
▸▸*Fin* **i. financial adviser** conseiller, -ère financier(ère) indépendant(e); **i. income** revenus *mpl* indépendants, rentes *fpl*; **i. radio** radio *f* privée; **i. retailer** détaillant, -ante in-

dépendant(e); *Br* **i. school** école *f* privée; *Aut* **i. suspension** suspension *f* indépendante

independently [ɪndɪˈpendəntlɪ] ADV **1** *(to behave etc)* avec indépendance; **to live i.** être indépendant **2** *(without being connected)* indépendamment; **i. of that** indépendamment de cela

in-depth ADJ *(study etc)* approfondi, en profondeur; **i. article** article *m* de fond

indescribable [ɪndɪˈskraɪbəb(ə)l] ADJ *(anger, poverty)* indescriptible; *(joy)* indicible

indescribably [ɪndɪˈskraɪbəblɪ] ADV *(angry, painful etc)* atrocement; *(happy)* indiciblement; **it was i. awful** c'était absolument affreux

indestructible [ɪndɪˈstrʌktəb(ə)l] ADJ indestructible

indeterminable [ɪndɪˈtɜːmɪnəb(ə)l] ADJ indéterminable

indeterminate [ɪndɪˈtɜːmɪnət] ADJ *(space etc)*, *Math (quantity)* indéterminé

indeterminately [ɪndɪˈtɜːmɪnətlɪ] ADV *(to continue)* de façon indéterminée; **an i. long period** une période indéterminée; **an i. large number of factors** un nombre de facteurs indéterminé

index [ˈɪndeks], *pl* **indexes, indices** [ˈɪndeksɪz, ˈɪndɪsiːz] N **1** *(pl* **indexes***) (of book)* index *m*, table *f* alphabétique
2 *(pl* **indexes***) (catalogue)* fichier *m*, répertoire *m*
3 *(pl* **indices***) Math etc* indice *m*; *(exponent)* exposant *m*
4 *(pl* **indices***) (finger)* index *m*
5 *(pl* **indices***) Fig (sign)* indice *m*, signe *m* (indicateur)
6 *Typ (pl* **indices***) (cross-reference)* renvoi *m*
VT **1** *(create index of) (book)* dresser l'index de; *Comput (database)* indexer
2 *(put into index) (article etc)* répertorier, classer
3 *(wages, pension)* indexer; **indexed to inflation** indexé sur l'inflation
▶▶ *Am St Exch* **i. arbitrage** arbitrage *m* sur indice; **i. card** fiche *f*; **i. finger** index *m*; *St Exch* **i. fund** fonds *m* à gestion indicielle, fonds indiciel; **i. number** *(in statistics)* indice; *St Exch* **i. option** option *f* sur indice; *Opt* **i. of refraction** indice *m* de réfraction

indexation [ɪndekˈseɪʃən] N indexation *f*
▶▶ *Fin* **i. clause** clause *f* d'indexation

indexing [ˈɪndeksɪŋ] N *Comput* indexation *f*

index-link VT *(wages, pension)* indexer; **to i. a pension to the cost of living** indexer une retraite sur le coût de la vie

index-linked ADJ *(wages, pension)* indexé

index-linking N *(of wages, pension)* indexation *f*

India [ˈɪndɪə] N Inde *f*
▶▶ *Am* **I. ink** encre *f* de Chine; **I. paper** papier *m* bible; *Br* **I. rubber** *(substance)* caoutchouc *m*; *(eraser)* gomme *f*

Indian [ˈɪndɪən] ADJ **1** *(of, from India)* de l'Inde, indien **2** *(of Native Americans) (customs, handicrafts etc)* indien; *Am Pej* **to be an I. giver** = demander la restitution de quelque chose qu'on a donné
N **1** *(inhabitant, native of India)* Indien, -ienne **2** *(Native American)* Indien, -ienne (d'Amérique), Amérindien, -ienne
▶▶ **I. club** massue *f* (pour la gymnastique); *Am Agr* **I. corn** maïs *m*; **I. elephant** éléphant *m* d'Asie; **I. file** file *f* indienne; *Br* **I. hemp** chanvre *m* indien, cannabis *m*; *Br* **I. ink** encre *f* de Chine; **the I. Ocean** l'océan *m* Indien; **I. reserve** réserve *f* indienne; **I. summer** été *m* de la Saint-Martin, été indien; *Fig* vieillesse *f* heureuse

indicate [ˈɪndɪkeɪt] VT **1** *(point to, show)* indiquer, montrer; **to i. sth with one's hand** in-

diquer qch de la main; **at the time indicated** à l'heure dite *ou* indiquée; *Aut* **to i. a left/right turn** mettre son clignotant pour indiquer que l'on va tourner à gauche/droite
2 *(denote)* indiquer, dénoter; **an expression that indicated determination** un visage plein de détermination
3 *(state) (opposition, intention to do sth)* faire connaître; **he has indicated that ...** il a fait savoir que ...
4 *(need) Med* **plenty of rest is indicated** il est recommandé de bien se reposer; **strong measures were clearly indicated** il était évident que la situation exigeait des mesures rigoureuses
VI *Aut* mettre son clignotant

indication [ɪndɪˈkeɪʃən] N **1** *(act of pointing out)* indication *f* **(of sth to sb** de qch à qn)
2 *(sign)* indice *m*, signe *m*, indication *f*; **there is every i. that he was speaking the truth** tout porte à croire qu'il disait vrai; **there is no i. of a struggle** il n'y a aucun signe de lutte; **all the indications are that ...** tout porte à croire que ...; **he gave early indications of his talent** son talent se révéla de bonne heure; **to take sth as an i. that** interpréter qch comme une indication du fait que
3 *(warning, statement)* **to give clear i. of one's intentions** faire connaître clairement ses intentions

indicative [ɪnˈdɪkətɪv] VOIR GRAMMAIRE A40
N *Gram* indicatif *m*; **in the i.** à l'indicatif
ADJ *(suggestive)* révélateur, -trice **(of** de)
▶▶ *Gram* **i. mood** mode *m* indicatif, indicatif

indicator [ˈɪndɪkeɪtər] N **1** *(on instrument, gauge etc)* index *m*, aiguille *f*; *Aut* clignotant *m*; *(LED, on machine)* indicateur *m*; *Naut, Aviat (for speed etc)* indicateur, compteur *m*
2 *(indication, guide)* indicateur *m*, indice *m*
▶▶ *Rail etc* **i. board** tableau *m ou* indicateur *m* des arrivées et des départs; **i. light** signal *m* lumineux; *(on monitor)* voyant *m*

indict [ɪnˈdaɪt] VT *Law* inculper **(for** pour)

indictable [ɪnˈdaɪtəb(ə)l] ADJ *Law (person)* passible de poursuite en justice
▶▶ **i. offence** délit *m*

indictment [ɪnˈdaɪtmənt] N *Law* **1** *(of person)* inculpation *f*, *(by public prosecutor)* réquisitoire *m*; *Fig* **it is an i. of our education system that the illiteracy rate is so high** le taux d'analphabétisme élevé en dit long sur notre système éducatif **2** *(document)* acte *m* d'accusation

indie [ˈɪndɪ] *Fam* N *(music)* indie-rock *m*
ADJ indépendant
▶▶ **i. music** indie-rock

Indies (the) [ðɪˈɪndɪz] NPL *Hist (South and Southeast Asia)* les Indes *fpl*

indifference [ɪnˈdɪfrəns, -fərəns] N **1** *(lack of interest)* indifférence *f* (**to** *or* **towards sth/sb** pour qch/à l'égard de qn); **it's a matter of complete i. to me** cela m'est parfaitement indifférent **2** *(of talent etc)* médiocrité *f*

indifferent [ɪnˈdɪfrənt, -fərənt] ADJ **1** *(not interested)* indifférent (**to** à); **I am** *or* **feel i. about him** il m'est indifférent **2** *(meal, cooking, painter)* médiocre

indifferently [ɪnˈdɪfrəntlɪ] ADV **1** *(disinterestedly)* avec indifférence **2** *(to cook, paint etc)* médiocrement

indigence [ˈɪndɪdʒəns] N *Fml* indigence *f*

indigenous [ɪnˈdɪdʒɪnəs] ADJ *(plant, product, population etc)* indigène (**to** à)

indigent [ˈɪndɪdʒənt] ADJ *Fml* indigent

indigestible [ɪndɪˈdʒestɪb(ə)l] ADJ indigeste

indigestion [ɪndɪˈdʒestʃən] N indigestion *f*; **to have (an attack of) i.** avoir une indigestion

indignant [ɪnˈdɪgnənt] ADJ *(person, air)* in-

digné; *(shout)* d'indignation; **to be** *or* **feel i. at sth** être indigné *ou* s'indigner de qch; **to make sb i.** indigner qn

indignantly [ɪnˈdɪgnəntlɪ] ADV avec indignation; *(to look)* d'un air indigné

indignation [ɪndɪgˈneɪʃən] N indignation *f*

indignity [ɪnˈdɪgnɪtɪ] N indignité *f*; **to suffer indignities** souffrir des affronts; **the i. of it!** quelle honte!

indigo, *pl* **indigo, indigoes** [ˈɪndɪgəʊ, ˈɪndɪgəʊz] N **1** *(dye, colour)* indigo *m* **2** *Bot (plant)* indigotier *m*
ADJ indigo *inv*
▶▶ **i. blue** *(colour)* indigo; *Bot* **i. plant** indigotier

indirect [ɪndɪˈrekt] ADJ *(influence, result, answer)* indirect; *(route, approach, ways)* détourné; *Fin (costs, tax)* indirect
▶▶ *Fin* **i. investment** investissement *m* indirect; *Gram* **i. object** objet *m* indirect; *Mktg* **i. promotional expenditure** coûts *mpl* de promotion indirects; *Mktg* **i. selling** vente *f* indirecte; *Gram* **i. speech** discours *m* indirect
VOIR GRAMMAIRE A21

indirectly [ɪndɪˈrektlɪ] ADV indirectement

indiscernible [ɪndɪˈsɜːnɪb(ə)l] ADJ *(not visible)* indiscernable; *Fig (reason)* obscur; *(difference)* imperceptible

indiscipline [ɪnˈdɪsɪplɪn] N indiscipline *f*

indiscreet [ɪndɪˈskriːt] ADJ indiscret, -ète; **an i. admission** une indiscrétion

indiscreetly [ɪndɪˈskriːtlɪ] ADV indiscrètement; *(to behave)* imprudemment

indiscretion [ɪndɪˈskreʃən] N **1** *(lack of discretion)* manque *m* de discrétion, indiscrétion *f* **2** *(unwise act)* écart *m* de conduite; *(unwise remark)* indiscrétion *f*; **to be guilty of an i.** *(blunder)* commettre une inconséquence; *(sexual)* se compromettre

indiscriminate [ɪndɪˈskrɪmɪnɪt] ADJ *(revenge)* aveugle, qui ne fait pas de distinction; **he's an i. reader** il lit tout ce qui lui tombe sous la main; **he was i. in his praise** il a distribué des compliments sans discernement; **i. slaughter** tuerie *f* générale

indiscriminately [ɪndɪˈskrɪmɪnɪtlɪ] ADV *(to hit, blame, kill)* sans distinction; **he reads i.** il lit tout ce qui lui tombe sous la main; **to fire i. into the crowd** tirer dans la foule sans faire de distinction

indispensable [ɪndɪˈspensəb(ə)l] ADJ *(person, thing)* indispensable

indisposed [ɪndɪˈspəʊzd] ADJ *Fml* **1** *(ill)* indisposé, souffrant; **to be** *or* **feel i.** être indisposé *ou* souffrant **2** *(not inclined)* peu enclin, peu disposé (**to do sth** à faire qch)

indisposition [ɪndɪspəˈzɪʃən] N *Fml* **1** *(illness)* indisposition *f* **2** *(lack of inclination)* peu *m* d'inclination (**to do sth** à faire qch)

indisputable [ɪndɪˈspjuːtəb(ə)l] ADJ incontestable, indiscutable; **it is the i. truth** c'est incontestable

indisputably [ɪndɪˈspjuːtəblɪ] ADV indiscutablement, incontestablement

indissoluble [ɪndɪˈsɒljʊb(ə)l] ADJ *(union, friendship)* indissoluble

indistinct [ɪndɪˈstɪŋkt] ADJ *(object, noise etc)* indistinct, peu distinct; *(sound)* confus; *(memory)* vague

indistinctly [ɪndɪˈstɪŋktlɪ] ADV *(to see, talk)* indistinctement; *(to feel)* vaguement

indistinguishable [ɪndɪˈstɪŋgwɪʃəb(ə)l] ADJ que l'on ne peut distinguer (**from** de), indiscernable; **the forgery was i. from the real thing** le faux et l'original étaient indiscernables, on ne pouvait distinguer le faux de l'original; **the two insects are i.** les deux insectes ne peuvent pas être distingués

individual [ɪndɪˈvɪdjʊəl] ADJ **1** *(for a single*

person or thing) individuel; **his pupils get i. attention** il s'occupe de ses élèves individuellement; **every room has its own i. shower** chaque chambre est équipée de sa propre douche **2** *(taken separately)* **i. animals vary in size** la taille varie selon les individus; **i. cases will be decided on their merits** chaque cas sera étudié individuellement **3** *(unique)* personnel; **she always has a very i. hairstyle** elle est toujours coiffée de façon très personnelle

▸ N individu *m*; **a private i.** un simple particulier

▸▸ *Fin* **i. company accounts** comptes *mpl* sociaux, comptes d'entreprise individuelle; *Am Fin* **i. retirement account** plan *m* d'epargne retraite personnel; *Fin* **i. savings account** plan d'epargne en actions; **i. tuition** cours *mpl* particuliers

individualism [ɪndɪ'vɪdjʊəlɪz(ə)m] N individualisme *m*

individualist [ɪndɪ'vɪdjʊəlɪst] N individualiste *mf*

individualistic [ɪndɪvɪdjʊə'lɪstɪk] ADJ individualiste

individuality [ɪndɪvɪdjʊ'ælɪtɪ] N individualité *f*

individualize [ɪndɪ'vɪdjʊəlaɪz] VT *(to make distinctive)* individualiser; *(adapt to individual needs)* adapter aux besoins de chaque individu

individually [ɪndɪ'vɪdjʊəlɪ] ADV individuellement, séparément; **he spoke to us all i.** il nous a parlé à tous un par un

indivisible [ɪndɪ'vɪzɪb(ə)l] ADJ indivisible

Indochina ['ɪndəʊ'tʃaɪnə] N Indochine *f*

indoctrinate [ɪn'dɒktrɪneɪt] VT endoctriner; **to i. sb with an idea** inculquer une idée à qn

indoctrination [ɪndɒktrɪ'neɪʃən] N endoctrinement *m*

Indo-European ['ɪndəʊ-] ADJ indo-européen
▸ N **1** Indo-Européen, -enne **2** *Ling* indo-européen *m*

indolence ['ɪndələns] N indolence *f*

indolent ['ɪndələnt] ADJ indolent

indolently ['ɪndələntlɪ] ADV indolemment

indomitable [ɪn'dɒmɪtəb(ə)l] ADJ indomptable; *(courage etc)* invincible

Indonesia [ɪndəʊ'niːzɪə, -ʒə] N Indonésie *f*

Indonesian [ɪndəʊ'niːzɪən, -ʒ(ə)n] ADJ indonésien
▸ N **1** Indonésien, -ienne **2** *Ling* indonésien *m*

indoor ['ɪndɔːr] ADJ *(plant)* d'appartement; *(photography)* en intérieur; *(swimming pool, tennis court)* couvert
▸▸ **i. aerial** antenne *f* intérieure; **i. athletics** athlétisme *m* en salle; **i. games** *(sports)* jeux *mpl* pratiqués en salle; *(board games, charades etc)* jeux d'intérieur; *Cin, TV* **i. scene** scène *f* tournée en intérieur; **i. visitor attraction** centre *m* d'intérêt couvert

Attention: ne pas confondre avec l'adverbe **indoors**.

indoors [ɪn'dɔːz] ADV *(inside house)* à la maison; *(inside building)* à l'intérieur; **to go i.** (r)entrer; **to stay i.** rester à l'intérieur; **don't stay i., go out and play!** ne reste donc pas enfermé, va jouer dehors!; **this job's better, at least it's i.** ce poste est mieux, au moins je/tu/il/*etc* travaille(s) à l'intérieur; *Br Sl* **her i.** *(wife)* la bourgeoise

Attention: ne pas confondre avec l'adjectif **indoor**.

indorse [ɪn'dɔːs] VT = **endorse**

indrawn ['ɪndrɔːn] ADJ *(air)* aspiré; **i. breath** aspiration *f*; **he watched with i. breath** il regardait en retenant son souffle

indubitable [ɪn'djuːbɪtəb(ə)l] ADJ indubitable

indubitably [ɪn'djuːbɪtəblɪ] ADV indubitablement

induce [ɪn'djuːs] VT **1** *(persuade)* persuader (**to do** à faire); **nothing will i. him to change his mind** rien ne le fera changer d'idée **2** *(bring about)* *(sleep, vomiting, feeling)* provoquer; *(labour etc)* amorcer, induire; **a drug-induced state** un état provoqué par la drogue **3** *Obst* **to i. labour** provoquer l'accouchement, déclencher le travail; **she's had to be induced** on a dû lui faire une piqûre pour provoquer l'accouchement *ou* déclencher le travail **4** *(in logic), Math* induire

inducement [ɪn'djuːsmənt] N *(incentive)* **the company was offered several inducements to relocate in the area** l'entreprise s'est vu offrir plusieurs avantages pour l'inciter à se relocaliser dans la région; **what inducements were used to persuade him to co-operate?** comment l'a-t-on incité à coopérer?; **fears for his daughter's safety will be enough of an i.** le fait qu'il craint pour la sécurité de sa fille sera une motivation suffisante; **an i. of $10,000** *(bribe)* un pot de vin de 10 000 dollars

induct [ɪn'dʌkt] VT **1** *(install in office)* installer dans sa charge; *Rel (minister)* mettre en possession d'un bénéfice **2** *(initiate)* initier (**into** à); **he was inducted into the Freemasons** il a été initié à la franc-maçonnerie **3** *Am Mil* **to be inducted** *(into the army)* être appelé sous les drapeaux

inducted gas [ɪn'dʌktɪd] N *Aut* gaz *m* aspiré

induction [ɪn'dʌkʃən] N **1** *(of minister, official)* installation *f* **2** *Obst (of labour)* déclenchement *m* **3** *(in logic), Math* induction *f* **4** *Elec* induction *f*
▸▸ *Elec* **i. coil** bobine *f* d'inductance; **i. loop** circuit *m* d'induction

inductive [ɪn'dʌktɪv] ADJ **1** *(reasoning)* inductif, par induction **2** *Elec (current etc)* inducteur, -trice

indulge [ɪn'dʌldʒ] VT **1** *(person)* être trop gentil avec; *(spoil)* gâter; *(hope)* nourrir; *(passion)* se livrer à, donner libre cours à; **they indulged his every whim** ils lui cédaient tous ses caprices; **to i. oneself** se faire plaisir **2** *Com (payer of bill of exchange)* accorder un délai à
▸ VI **to i. in** *(activity)* s'adonner à, se livrer à; **to i. in a cigar** se permettre un cigare; **to i. in a glass of port** s'offrir un verre de porto; **to i. in speculation** se laisser aller à des spéculations (**on, about** sur); **I used to drink a lot but nowadays I rarely i.** je buvais beaucoup mais maintenant c'est rare que je me le permette; *Fam* **thanks, but I don't i.** *(drink, smoke)* merci, mais je ne bois/fume pas

indulgence [ɪn'dʌldʒəns] N **1** *(doting, leniency)* indulgence *f* (**to** envers), *Pej* complaisance *f* (**to** envers) **2** *(act, activity)* **because of his i. in his favourite pastime** parce qu'il s'adonnait *ou* se livrait à son passe-temps préféré; **i. in rich food** excès *mpl* de table **3** *(treat)* **Belgian chocolates are my only i.** les chocolats belges sont mon seul péché mignon; **I allow myself the occasional i.** de temps en temps je me fais plaisir **4** *Cathol* indulgence *f*

indulgent [ɪn'dʌldʒənt] ADJ indulgent (**to** envers, pour); **over-i. father** père *m* trop indulgent

indulgently [ɪn'dʌldʒəntlɪ] ADV avec indulgence

industrial [ɪn'dʌstrɪəl] ADJ *(area, city, activity etc)* industriel; *(conflict)* ouvrier, du travail; **for i. use only** usage industriel uniquement; **in i. quantities** en quantités industrielles
▸▸ **i. accident** accident *m* du travail; **i. accident insurance** assurance *f* contre les accidents du travail; *Br* **i. action** grève(s) *f(pl)*; **i. arbitrator** ≃ prud'homme *m*; *Am Sch* **i. art** = cours *m* technique où l'on apprend le maniement des machines propres à une industrie particulière; **i. bank** banque *f* industrielle; **i. centre** centre *m* industriel; **i. complex** complexe *m* industriel; **i. disease** maladie *f* professionnelle *ou* du travail; **i. espionage** espionnage *m* industriel; *Br* **i. estate** zone *f* industrielle; **i. injuries benefit** indemnité *f* pour accidents du travail; **i. injury** accident *m* du travail; **i. marketer** spécialiste *mf* en marketing; **i. marketing** marketing *m* industriel; **i. medicine** médecine *f* du travail; *Econ* **i. production** production *f* industrielle; **i. relations** relations *fpl* entre le patronat et les travailleurs; *Hist* **the I. Revolution** la révolution industrielle; *St Exch* **i. shares** valeurs *mpl* industrielles; **i. statistics** statistiques *fpl* sur l'industrie; *Br, Austr Law* **i. tribunal** ≃ conseil *m* de prud'hommes; **i. union** syndicat *m* d'industrie; **i. unit** atelier *m*; **i. unrest** agitation *f* ouvrière

Note that the French adjective **industriel** never refers to the relationship between employers and employees.

industrialism [ɪn'dʌstrɪəlɪz(ə)m] N industrialisme *m*

industrialist [ɪn'dʌstrɪəlɪst] N industriel *m*

industrialization [ɪndʌstrɪəlaɪ'zeɪʃən] N industrialisation *f*

industrialize [ɪn'dʌstrɪəlaɪz] VT industrialiser
▸ VI s'industrialiser

industrialized [ɪn'dʌstrɪəlaɪzd] ADJ **i. countries, i. nations** pays *mpl* industrialisés

industrializing [ɪn'dʌstrɪəlaɪzɪŋ] ADJ *(country, economy)* en voie d'industrialisation

industrials [ɪn'dʌstrɪəlz] NPL *St Exch* valeurs *fpl* industrielles *ou* des sociétés industrielles

industrial-strength ADJ *(adhesive, bleach etc)* à usage industriel; *Hum (coffee)* hyper-costaud

industrious [ɪn'dʌstrɪəs] ADJ industrieux, travailleur

industriously [ɪn'dʌstrɪəslɪ] ADV assidûment

industriousness [ɪn'dʌstrɪəsnɪs] N assiduité *f* (au travail), application *f*

industry ['ɪndʌstrɪ] N **1** industrie *f*; **i. has declined in this country** l'industrie a décliné dans ce pays; **heavy/light i.** l'industrie lourde/légère; **2** *(diligence)* assiduité *f* (au travail), application *f*
▸▸ **i. expert** expert *m* de l'industrie; **i. forecast** prévision *f* de l'industrie; **i. sector** secteur *m* industriel *ou* secondaire

industry-standard ADJ normalisé

Indy ['ɪndɪ] ADJ
▸▸ **I. car** = type de voiture de course, aux États-Unis; **the I. 500** = course *f* automobile qui se déroule à Indianapolis, aux États-Unis

inebriate[1] [ɪn'iːbrɪət] *Fml* ADJ ivre; **in his i. state** dans son état d'ébriété *ou* d'ivresse
▸ N ivrogne *mf*

inebriate[2] [ɪn'iːbrɪeɪt] VT enivrer

inebriated [ɪn'iːbrɪeɪtɪd] ADJ ivre

inebriation [ɪniːbrɪ'eɪʃən] N **1** *(act of ma-*

king drunk) enivrement m 2 (drunkenness) ivresse f, ébriété f

inedible [ɪn'edɪb(ə)l] ADJ non comestible; (too disgusting to eat) immangeable

ineducable [ɪn'edjʊkəb(ə)l] ADJ inéducable

ineffable [ɪn'efəb(ə)l] ADJ Fml (joy etc) ineffable, indicible

ineffective [ɪnɪ'fektɪv] ADJ (means, remedy, speech, leader) inefficace; (speaker) terne; (style) plat, terne

ineffectively [ɪnɪ'fektɪvlɪ] ADV (to protest, plead) vainement; (to chair a meeting) de manière inefficace; **the dart bounced i. off the rhino's hide** la flèche a rebondi sur la peau du rhinocéros sans produire aucun effet

ineffectual [ɪnɪ'fektjʊəl] ADJ (effort, reasoning, person) inefficace

inefficacious [ɪnefɪ'keɪʃəs] ADJ Fml inefficace

inefficacy [ɪn'efɪkəsɪ] N inefficacité f

inefficiency [ɪnɪ'fɪʃənsɪ] N (of method, machine, organization, person) manque m d'efficacité, inefficacité f

inefficient [ɪnɪ'fɪʃənt] ADJ (measure, person etc) inefficace

inefficiently [ɪnɪ'fɪʃəntlɪ] ADV inefficacement

inelastic [ɪnɪ'læstɪk] ADJ sans élasticité; Fig rigide, raide

inelegant [ɪn'elɪgənt] ADJ inélégant

inelegantly [ɪn'elɪgəntlɪ] ADV inélégamment

ineligible [ɪn'elɪdʒɪb(ə)l] ADJ (candidate) inéligible; **to be i. for sth** ne pas avoir droit à qch; **he's i. to vote** il n'a pas le droit de voter; **i. for military service** inapte au service militaire

ineluctable [ɪnɪ'lʌktəb(ə)l] ADJ Lit inéluctable

inept [ɪn'ept] ADJ inepte

ineptitude [ɪn'eptɪtjuːd] N ineptie f

ineptly [ɪn'eptlɪ] ADV de façon inepte

inequality [ɪnɪ'kwɒlɪtɪ] N (social, economic) inégalité f

inequitable [ɪn'ekwɪtəb(ə)l] ADJ inéquitable

ineradicable [ɪnɪ'rædɪkəb(ə)l] ADJ indéracinable, inextirpable

inert [ɪ'nɜːt] ADJ inerte; Chem **the i. gases** les gaz mpl inertes

inertia [ɪ'nɜːʃɪə] N Phys, Fam (of person) inertie f
▸ ▸ Br Mktg **i. selling** vente f forcée; Phys **i. switch** contacteur m à inertie

inertia-reel seat-belt N Aut ceinture f (de sécurité) à enrouleur

inescapable [ɪnɪ'skeɪpəb(ə)l] ADJ incontournable

inessential [ɪnɪ'senʃəl] ADJ non essentiel N chose f superflue; **that's one of the inessentials** ça fait partie du superflu

inestimable [ɪn'estɪməb(ə)l] ADJ (value, benefit etc) inestimable

inevitability [ɪnevɪtə'bɪlɪtɪ] N caractère m inévitable

inevitable [ɪn'evɪtəb(ə)l] ADJ (unavoidable) inévitable; (conclusion) incontournable; **his promotion is i.** il va de soi qu'il sera promu; **the i. conclusion** (of a play, novel) le dénouement fatal
N **the i.** l'inévitable m

inevitably [ɪn'evɪtəblɪ] ADV inévitablement; **he's i. late** il est immanquablement en retard

inexact [ɪnɪg'zækt] ADJ (lacking clarity) imprécis; (inaccurate) inexact; **it's an i. science** ce n'est pas une science exacte

inexactitude [ɪnɪg'zæktɪtjuːd] N (inaccuracy) inexactitude f, (lack of clarity) imprécision f

inexactly [ɪnɪg'zæktlɪ] ADV (inaccurately) inexactement; (with a lack of clarity) de façon imprécise

inexactness [ɪnɪg'zæktnɪs] N (inaccuracy) inexactitude f, (lack of clarity) imprécision f

inexcusable [ɪnɪk'skjuːzəb(ə)l] ADJ inexcusable, impardonnable; **that was i. of you** tu es impardonnable

inexcusably [ɪnɪk'skjuːzəblɪ] ADV inexcusablement, impardonnablement; **i. rude/slow** d'une grossièreté/lenteur inexcusable

inexhaustible [ɪneg'zɔːstɪb(ə)l] ADJ inépuisable; (source) intarissable; (patience) inépuisable, sans limite; **she had an i. supply of jokes** elle avait un stock de blagues inépuisable

inexorable [ɪn'eksərəb(ə)l] ADJ inexorable

inexorably [ɪn'eksərəblɪ] ADV inexorablement

inexpedient [ɪnɪk'spiːdɪənt] ADJ inopportun, malavisé

inexpensive [ɪnɪk'spensɪv] ADJ peu coûteux, bon marché inv; **i. to run** (house, car) économique

inexpensively [ɪnɪk'spensɪvlɪ] ADV bon marché, à bas prix; (to live) économiquement, à peu de frais

inexperience [ɪnɪk'spɪərɪəns] N inexpérience f

inexperienced [ɪnɪk'spɪərɪənst] ADJ 1 (person) inexpérimenté, sans expérience; **she is still i.** elle manque encore d'expérience; **he's i. in handling staff** il n'a pas l'habitude de diriger le personnel 2 (eye, ear) inexercé

inexpert [ɪn'ekspɜːt] ADJ inexpert; **he was i. in such matters** il ne connaissait pas grand-chose dans ce domaine; **her i. handling of the situation** la façon maladroite dont elle a géré l'affaire

inexpertly [ɪn'ekspɜːtlɪ] ADV maladroitement, de façon maladroite

inexpiable [ɪn'ekspɪəb(ə)l] ADJ Fml inexpiable

inexplicable [ɪnɪk'splɪkəb(ə)l] ADJ inexplicable

inexplicably [ɪnɪk'splɪkəblɪ] ADV inexplicablement

inexpressible [ɪnɪk'spresɪb(ə)l] ADJ (pleasure) inexprimable

inexpressive [ɪnɪk'spresɪv] ADJ inexpressif, sans expression

inextinguishable [ɪnɪk'stɪŋgwɪʃəb(ə)l] ADJ inextinguible

in extremis [ɪnɪk'striːmɪs] ADV 1 (as a last resort) en dernier recours 2 esp Rel (at the point of death) sur le point de mourir, à l'article de la mort

inextricable [ɪnek'strɪkəb(ə)l] ADJ 1 (situation) inextricable 2 (ties, links) indissoluble

inextricably [ɪnek'strɪkəblɪ] ADV 1 inextricablement 2 (tied, linked) indissolublement

infallibility [ɪnfælɪ'bɪlɪtɪ] N Rel etc infaillibilité f

infallible [ɪn'fælɪb(ə)l] ADJ infaillible, immanquable

infallibly [ɪn'fælɪblɪ] ADV infailliblement, immanquablement

infamous ['ɪnfəməs] ADJ (person) infâme; (behaviour) abominable, infâme; (place) mal famé

infamously ['ɪnfəməslɪ] ADV (to behave) de manière infâme

infamy ['ɪnfəmɪ] N infamie f

infancy ['ɪnfənsɪ] N 1 (early childhood) pe-

tite enfance f, Fig (of an art, industry) débuts mpl; **from i.** dès la plus tendre enfance; Fig **science was in its i.** la science en était à ses balbutiements 2 Law (minority) minorité f

infant ['ɪnfənt] N 1 (until the age of two) nourrisson m; Br (under the age of seven) jeune enfant mf 2 Law (minor) mineur, -eure
ADJ (child) en bas âge; Fig **an i. science** une science naissante
▸ ▸ Br Sch **i. class** classe f enfantine; **i. mortality** mortalité f infantile; **i. mortality rate** taux m de mortalité infantile; **i. prodigy** enfant prodige; Br Sch **i. school** école f maternelle (5–7 ans)

infanticide [ɪn'fæntɪsaɪd] N 1 (crime) infanticide m 2 (person) infanticide mf

infantile ['ɪnfəntaɪl] ADJ 1 (of infants) (mind, imagination) d'enfant; Med (illness) infantile 2 Pej (childish) (reasoning, remark etc) puéril
▸ ▸ Old-fashioned **i. paralysis** paralysie f infantile

infantilism [ɪn'fæntɪlɪz(ə)m] N Fml infantilisme m

infantry ['ɪnfəntrɪ] N Mil infanterie f, (foot soldiers) fantassins mpl

infantryman, pl **infantrymen** ['ɪnfəntrɪmən] N Mil soldat m d'infanterie, fantassin m

infarct ['ɪnfɑːkt] N Med infarctus m

infarction [ɪn'fɑːkʃən] N Med infarctus m

infatuated [ɪn'fætjʊeɪtɪd] ADJ entiché (with sb); **to become i. with sb/sth** s'enticher de qn/de qch

infatuation [ɪnfætjʊ'eɪʃən] N engouement m, Fam toquade f, **to have an i. for sb** s'enticher de qn; **it's just (an) i.** ce n'est qu'une toquade

infect [ɪn'fekt] VT 1 (water supply, area, food), Med (person) contaminer; (wound, limb, disk) infecter; **to i. sb with a disease** (involuntarily) transmettre une maladie à qn; (voluntarily) inoculer une maladie à qn; Fig **to i. sb with one's enthusiasm** communiquer son enthousiasme à qn 2 Fig (corrupt, taint) (air, morals etc) corrompre, vicier

infected [ɪn'fektɪd] ADJ (clothing, food, area) contaminé; (wound, limb, disk) infecté; **to become i.** (of wound) s'infecter

infection [ɪn'fekʃən] N Med (with disease) contamination f, (in part of body) infection f, **source of i.** foyer m d'infection; **to spread/prevent i.** répandre/empêcher l'infection

infectious [ɪn'fekʃəs] ADJ Med (disease) infectieux, contagieux; Fam (person) contagieux; Fig (laughter, optimism, pessimism etc) communicatif

infectiousness [ɪn'fekʃəsnɪs] N 1 Med (of disease) nature f infectieuse 2 Fig (of enthusiasm, hope etc) caractère m communicatif

infelicitous [ɪnfɪ'lɪsɪtəs] ADJ Lit (remark, event) malheureux

infelicity [ɪnfɪ'lɪsɪtɪ] N Lit 1 (remark) expression f malheureuse 2 (unhappiness) malheur m

infer [ɪn'fɜːr] VT (-rr-) 1 inférer, déduire, conclure (sth from sth qch de qch; that que) 2 Fam = **imply**

inference ['ɪnfərəns] N 1 (method) inférence f, **by i.** par déduction 2 (conclusion) déduction f, conclusion f

inferior [ɪn'fɪərɪər] ADJ inférieur; (work) de second ordre; **the expensive screwdriver was i. to the cheap one** le tournevis cher était de moins bonne qualité que celui qui était bon marché; **her second novel is a much i. work** son deuxième roman est bien moins bon; **to be in an i. position** être dans une position inférieure ou subordonnée
N 1 inférieur, -eure; **one's inferiors** les per-

sonnes *fpl* inférieures à soi **2** *Typ* petite lettre f inférieure
▶▶ *Typ* **i. letter** petite lettre inférieure; *Astron* **i. planet** planète f inférieure; **i. quality** qualité f inférieure

inferiority [ɪnfɪərɪ'ɒrɪtɪ] N infériorité f (**to** par rapport à)
▶▶ *Psy* **i. complex** complexe m d'infériorité

infernal [ɪn'fɜːn(ə)l] ADJ **1** *Fam (diabolical)* infernal, -aux, diabolique; **that i. little man!** cet homme infernal *ou* insupportable! **2** *Fam (extreme) (noise, heat etc)* infernal, -aux; **it's an i. nuisance** c'est diablement embêtant **3** *(of hell)* infernal, -aux; **the i. regions** l'enfer m

infernally [ɪn'fɜːn(ə)lɪ] ADV *Fam* diablement; **it's i. hot** il fait une chaleur d'enfer *ou* à crever

inferno, *pl* **infernos** [ɪn'fɜːnəʊ, ɪn'fɜːnəʊz] N **1** *(hell)* enfer m; *Liter* **Dante's I.** l'Enfer de Dante **2** *(fire)* brasier m; **the house was a raging i.** la maison était un véritable brasier

infertile [ɪn'fɜːtaɪl] ADJ *(person, ovum)* stérile; *(land)* stérile, infertile

infertility [ɪnfɜː'tɪlɪtɪ] N *(of person)* stérilité f, *(of soil)* infertilité f, stérilité
▶▶ *Med* **i. clinic** = service m qui s'occupe des problèmes de stérilité dans un établissement hospitalier

infest [ɪn'fest] VT *(of vermin etc)* infester; **to be infested by rats/cockroaches** être infesté de rats/cafards

infestation [ɪnfes'teɪʃən] N *Med* infestation f, *Bot (of plants by parasites etc)* invasion f

-infested [ɪn'festɪd] SUFF **rat-/cockroach-i.** infesté de rats/cafards

infidel ['ɪnfɪdəl] ADJ, N infidèle mf

infidelity [ɪnfɪ'delɪtɪ] N **1** *(of spouse, lover)* infidélité f **2** *(disloyalty) (of servant etc)* infidélité f, déloyauté f

infighting ['ɪnfaɪtɪŋ] N *(within group)* querelles fpl intestines; *Boxing* corps à corps m; **political i.** querelles politiques intestines

infill ['ɪnfɪl] N *Constr* remplissage m

infiltrate ['ɪnfɪltreɪt] VT **1** *Pol etc (of subversives etc) (trade union)* noyauter; *(enemy)* s'infiltrer chez **2** *(cause to enter) (liquid etc)* faire pénétrer (**into** dans); **we've infiltrated someone into the party** l'un des nôtres a réussi à s'infiltrer dans le parti **3** *(of liquid) (substance)* s'infiltrer *ou* pénétrer dans, imprégner
VI *(of fluid, spies etc)* s'infiltrer (**into** dans; **through** à travers)

infiltration [ɪnfɪl'treɪʃən] N **1** *(by spies, troops etc) (trade union)* infiltration f, *Pol* **the i. of the Labour Party by Trotskyists** le noyautage du Parti travailliste par les Trotskistes **2** *(of liquid etc)* infiltration f (**into** dans, **through** à travers)

infiltrator ['ɪnfɪltreɪtər] N *(of political party etc)* agent m qui s'infiltre

infinite ['ɪnfɪnɪt] ADJ infini; **of i. importance** d'une extrême importance; **to go to i. pains to do sth** se donner infiniment de mal pour faire qch; *Rel, Hum* **in his i. wisdom** dans son infinie sagesse
N **the i.** l'infini m

infinitely ['ɪnfɪnɪtlɪ] ADV infiniment

infinitesimal [ɪnfɪnɪ'tesɪməl] ADJ *(quantity)* infinitésimal, -aux; *(majority)* infime
▶▶ **i. calculus** calcul m infinitésimal

infinitive [ɪn'fɪnɪtɪv] N *Gram* infinitif m; **in the i.** à l'infinitif VOIR GRAMMAIRE A40–2; B35–7

infinity [ɪn'fɪnɪtɪ] N **1** *(of space etc)* infinité f **2** *Math etc* infini m; **to i.** à l'infini; *Phot* **to focus on** *or* **for i.** mettre au point sur l'infini

infirm [ɪn'fɜːm] ADJ **1** *(person)* infirme, débile **2** *Fml (mind, judgement)* irrésolu

infirmary [ɪn'fɜːmərɪ] N **1** *(hospital)* hôpital m, -aux **2** *(in school, prison etc)* infirmerie f

infirmity [ɪn'fɜːmɪtɪ] N **1** *(weakness) (of body)* infirmité f **2** *(affliction)* infirmité f, **the infirmities of old age** les infirmités de la vieillesse **3** *(lack of resolve)* **i. of purpose** irrésolution f

in flagrante delicto [ɪnfləˈgræntɪdɪ-ˈlɪktəʊ] ADV *Law* en flagrant délit

inflame [ɪn'fleɪm] VT **1** *(stir up) (desire)* allumer; *(quarrel)* envenimer; *(crowd)* enflammer **2** *Med (wound)* enflammer
VI *Med (of wound, tissue)* s'enflammer

inflamed [ɪn'fleɪmd] ADJ **1** *Med (wound, eye etc)* enflammé; **to become i.** s'enflammer **2** *Fig* enflammé (**with** de); **i. with passion** brûlant d'amour

inflammable [ɪn'flæməb(ə)l] ADJ *(substance etc)* inflammable; *Fig (person, crowd)* prompt à s'échauffer; *Fig* **the situation is highly i.** la situation est explosive

inflammation [ɪnflə'meɪʃən] N *Med* inflammation f

inflammatory [ɪn'flæmətərɪ] ADJ **1** *(speech, leaflet)* incendiaire **2** *Med (disease)* inflammatoire

inflatable [ɪn'fleɪtəb(ə)l] ADJ *(balloon etc)* gonflable; *(raft)* pneumatique
N *(boat)* canot m pneumatique

inflate [ɪn'fleɪt] VT **1** *(fill with air) (balloon, tyre, sail)* gonfler; **to i. the lungs with air** *(one's own)* remplir ses poumons d'air; *(when giving artificial respiration)* souffler dans les poumons **2** *Fin (prices)* faire monter; *Com (account)* grossir, charger; *(expense account, figures)* gonfler; *Econ* **to i. the currency** accroître artificiellement la circulation fiduciaire
VI se gonfler; *Fig* **to i. with pride** se gonfler d'orgueil

inflated [ɪn'fleɪtɪd] ADJ **1** *(balloon, tyre etc)* gonflé; **to become i.** *(with air etc)* se gonfler; *Fig* **i. with pride** bouffi d'orgueil; *Fig* **to have an i. opinion of oneself** avoir une opinion trop flatteuse *ou* surfaite de soi-même **2** *Fin (price)* exagéré **3** *Liter (style)* enflé
▶▶ *Econ* **i. currency** inflation f monétaire

inflation [ɪn'fleɪʃən] N **1** *Econ* inflation f, **rate of i.** taux m d'inflation; **i. now stands at 5%** l'inflation est maintenant à 5%; **i.-proof** *(pension etc)* protégé contre les effets de l'inflation **2** *(of balloon, tyre etc)* gonflage m
▶▶ *Fin* **i. tax** impôt m à la production

inflationary [ɪn'fleɪʃənərɪ] ADJ *Econ* inflationniste
▶▶ **i. spiral** spirale f inflationniste

inflect [ɪn'flekt] VT **1** *Gram (noun, adjective)* décliner; *(verb)* conjuguer **2** *(voice)* moduler; *Mus (note)* altérer **3** *Opt (light beam)* infléchir
VI *Gram* prendre une marque flexionnelle

inflected [ɪn'flektɪd] ADJ *Ling (language)* à flexions, flexionnel; *(vowel)* infléchi

inflection [ɪn'flekʃən] N = **inflexion**

inflexibility [ɪnfleksɪ'bɪlɪtɪ] N *(of person, government etc)* inflexibilité f, *Tech* rigidité f

inflexible [ɪn'fleksɪb(ə)l] ADJ *(person, government etc)* inflexible; *Tech* rigide; **i. code of morals** morale f rigide *ou* inflexible

inflexion [ɪn'flekʃən] N **1** *Gram (of word)* flexion f **2** *(of voice)* inflexion f, *Mus (of note)* altération f **3** *Opt, Math* inflexion f

inflict [ɪn'flɪkt] VT *(suffering, losses), Law (punishment)* infliger (**sth on sb** qch à qn); *(wound)* faire (**on** à); *(unhappiness)* causer, occasionner (**on** à); *Fam Hum* **to i. oneself on sb** s'imposer

infliction [ɪn'flɪkʃən] N *(action)* action f d'infliger; **to take pleasure in the i. of pain** prendre du plaisir à infliger de la douleur

in-flight ADJ *Aviat* en vol
▶▶ **i. catering** restauration f aérienne; **i. entertainment** distractions fpl en vol; **i. magazine** magazine m distribué dans les avions; **i. meal** plateau-repas m, pl plateaux-repas; **i. service** service m à bord (d'un avion)

inflorescence [ɪnflə'resəns] N *Bot* inflorescence f

inflow ['ɪnfləʊ] N *(act of flowing in) (of water)* arrivée f, *(of people, goods, cash)* afflux m; *(of new ideas)* flot m; **i. of capital** afflux de capitaux; **i. of money** rentrée f d'argent;
▶▶ **i. pipe** *(for water)* arrivée d'eau

influence ['ɪnfluəns] N influence f (**upon, on** sur); **to exert** *or* **exercise an i. on sb** exercer une influence sur qn, influencer qn; **to be a good/bad/great i. on sb** avoir une bonne/mauvaise/grande influence sur qn; **to use one's i. with sb** user de son influence auprès de qn; **man of i.** homme m influent; **he owes his position to i.** il doit sa situation à des personnalités influentes; **to have i.** avoir de l'influence; **to have great i. over sb** avoir beaucoup d'influence sur qn; **to be under sb's i.** être sous l'influence de qn; **under the i. of drink,** *Fam* **under the i.** sous l'empire de la boisson
VT influencer; **she's too easily influenced** elle se laisse influencer trop facilement

influencer ['ɪnfluənsər] N *Mktg* préconisateur m

influential [ɪnflu'enʃəl] ADJ influent; **to be i.** *(of person)* avoir de l'influence, *Fam* avoir le bras long; *(of factor etc)* avoir du poids, jouer un rôle; **he was i. in getting her a job** il a fait jouer son influence pour l'aider à obtenir du travail

influenza [ɪnflu'enzə] N *Med* grippe f, influenza f

influx ['ɪnflʌks] N *(of water etc)* arrivée f, *(of people, goods, cash)* afflux m; *(of gas)* afflux; *(of new ideas)* flot m; **a sudden i. of tourists** un soudain afflux de touristes; *Econ* **i. of gold** entrée f *ou* afflux d'or

info ['ɪnfəʊ] N *Fam* renseignements mpl, tuyaux mpl

infobahn ['ɪnfəʊbɑːn] N *Comput* autoroute f de l'information

infohighway [ɪnfəʊ'haɪweɪ] N *Comput* autoroute f de l'information

infomercial [ɪnfəʊ'mɜːʃəl] N *TV* infomercial m

inform [ɪn'fɔːm] VT **1** *(tell)* **to i. sb of sth** informer qn de qch; **to i. sb about sth** *(provide with information)* renseigner qn sur qch; **to keep sb informed of what is happening** tenir qn au courant de ce qui se passe; **why was I not informed (of this)?** pourquoi est-ce que je n'en ai pas été informé?; **to i. the police** avertir la police; **we are writing to i. you of the dispatch of ...** nous vous avisons de l'envoi de ...; **I regret to have to i. you that ...** j'ai le regret de vous annoncer que ...; **we are informed that ...** on nous fait savoir que ... **2** *Lit (pervade) (literary work etc)* imprégner
VI *Law* **to i. against** *or* **on sb** dénoncer qn

informal [ɪn'fɔːməl] ADJ **1** *(person, manner, attitude)* simple, décontracté; *(speech, language, words)* familier; *(clothes)* décontracté; *(reception, dinner)* sans cérémonie; **he's very i. for a prime minister** il est très décontracté pour un premier ministre; **British offices tend to be more i. than German ones** en Grande-Bretagne l'ambiance dans les bureaux tend à être plus décontractée qu'en Allemagne; **dress: i.** *(on invitation)* tenue de ville **2** *(unofficial) (meeting)* non-officiel; *(arrangement)* officieux; **I had an i. chat with the boss** j'ai discuté un peu avec le patron;

the two leaders had **i. talks** les deux dirigeants ont eu des entretiens non-officiels
► ► *Econ* **i. economy** travail *m* au noir

informality [ɪnfɔːˈmælɪtɪ] N *(of person)* simplicité *f*, décontraction *f*; *(of occasion)* absence *f* de formalité *ou* de cérémonie; *(of talks)* caractère *m* non-officiel

informally [ɪnˈfɔːməlɪ] ADV **1** *(to dine)* sans cérémonie, sans formalités; *(to dress)* simplement; **i. known as …** familièrement connu sous le nom de … **2** *(to discuss)* officieusement, à titre non-officiel

informant [ɪnˈfɔːmənt] N informateur, -trice; **I have it from a reliable i.** je le tiens de source sûre

informatics [ɪnfɔːˈmætɪks] N informatique *f* **VOIR GRAMMAIRE A10**

information [ɪnfəˈmeɪʃən] N **1** *(news, facts etc)* renseignement(s) *m(pl)*, information(s) *f(pl)*; **a bit** *or* **piece of i.** un renseignement, une information; **I'm afraid your i. is wrong** je crains qu'on vous ait mal renseigné; **to ask for i. on** *or* **about sb/sth** demander des renseignements sur qn/qch; **for further i. write to …** pour de plus amples informations écrire à …; **why don't you ask at i.?** pourquoi est-ce que tu ne demandes pas aux renseignements?; **for my own i.** pour ma propre information; **I am sending you this brochure for your i.** je vous envoie cette brochure à titre d'information; **for your i., I'm not stupid** sachez que je ne suis pas complètement idiot; **for your i., I've done the dishes for the past week!** je t'apprendrai que j'ai fait la vaisselle toute cette semaine!; **his head is full of useless i.** il encombre sa mémoire de choses inutiles; **I can't retain i. as well as I could** ma mémoire n'est pas aussi bonne qu'avant
2 *Comput* information *f*
3 *Law* dénonciation *f* (**against sb** contre qn), délation *f* (**against sb** de qn); **to lay i. against sb with the police** dénoncer qn à la police, informer contre qn
4 *Am Tel* renseignements *mpl*
► ► *Br* **i. bureau** bureau *m ou* service *m* des renseignements; **i. carrier** support *m* d'information; **i. copy** *(of document)* copie *f* pour information; **i. desk** *(in hotel etc)* bureau des renseignements; *Comput* **i. gathering** collecte *f* d'informations; *Comput* **i. highway** autoroute *f* de l'information, *Can* inforoute *f*; **i. market** marché *m* des informations; **i. overload** surinformation *f*; **i. pack** dossier *m* d'information; *Comput* **i. processing** *(action)* traitement *m* de l'information; *(domain)* informatique *f*; **i. retrieval** recherche *f* documentaire; *Comput* recherche d'information; *Comput* **i. retrieval system** système *m* de recherche documentaire; *Comput* **i. science** science *f* de l'information; *Comput* **i. scientist** informaticien, -ienne; **i. sheet** fiche *f* explicative; *Comput* **i. society** société *f* de l'information; **i. storage** mémorisation *f* des informations; *Comput* **i. system** système *m* informatique; *Comput* **i. technology** technologie *f* de l'information, informatique; **i. theory** théorie *f* de l'information

informative [ɪnˈfɔːmətɪv] ADJ *(programme, book, lecture)* instructif; *(book)* éducatif; **it wasn't very i.** il ne nous a pas appris grand-chose
► ► *Mktg* **i. advertising** publicité *f* informative

informed [ɪnˈfɔːmd] ADJ *(person)* bien renseigné *ou* informé; **the i. opinion is that …** les experts pensent que …; **the i. consumer** le consommateur averti; **an i. estimate/decision** une évaluation faite/une décision prise en connaissance de cause

informer [ɪnˈfɔːmər] N *Pej* indicateur *m*; **to turn i.** dénoncer ses complices

infotainment [ɪnfəʊˈteɪnmənt] N *TV* émissions *fpl* d'information divertissantes

infraction [ɪnˈfrækʃən] N *Fml* = **infringement**

infra dig [ˈɪnfrəˈdɪg] ADJ *Fam* rabaissant; **it would be i. for us to reply** ce serait au-dessous de nous de répondre, ce serait se rabaisser que de répondre

infrared [ɪnfrəˈred] ADJ *Phys* infrarouge
► ► *Comput* **i. keyboard** clavier *m* à infrarouge; *Med* **i. lamp** lampe *f* à rayons infrarouges; *Comput* **i. mouse** souris *f* à infrarouge; **i. radiation, i. rays** radiation *f* infrarouge, infrarouge *m*; **i. remote control** télécommande *f* (à) infrarouge

infrastructure [ˈɪnfrəstrʌktʃər] N infrastructure *f*

infrequency [ɪnˈfriːkwənsɪ] N rareté *f*

infrequent [ɪnˈfriːkwənt] ADJ rare, peu fréquent

infrequently [ɪnˈfriːkwəntlɪ] ADV rarement; **not i.** assez souvent

infringe [ɪnˈfrɪndʒ] VT *(law, rule)* enfreindre, violer, transgresser; **to i. (an author's) copyright** empiéter sur les droits d'un auteur
► **infringe on** VT INSEP *(person's rights)* empiéter sur

infringement [ɪnˈfrɪndʒmənt] N *(of rule)* infraction *f*; *(of law, right)* violation *f*; **i. of sb's rights** infraction *ou* atteinte *f* aux droits de qn; **i. of copyright** non-respect *m* des droits *f* d'auteur

infuriate [ɪnˈfjʊərɪeɪt] VT rendre furieux, enrager

infuriated [ɪnˈfjʊərɪeɪtɪd] ADJ furieux

infuriating [ɪnˈfjʊərɪeɪtɪŋ] ADJ exaspérant; **at times I find him i.** quelquefois il me met hors de moi; **it's i. the way she's always right** ça me met hors de moi qu'elle ait toujours raison

infuriatingly [ɪnˈfjʊərɪeɪtɪŋlɪ] ADV *(to answer)* d'une façon exaspérante; **to be i. slow/difficult** être d'une lenteur/difficulté exaspérante

infuse [ɪnˈfjuːz] VT **1** *(instil)* *(energy, new life, courage)* insuffler (**into sb** à qn) **2** *(soak)* *(tea, herbs)* infuser, faire infuser
VI *(of tea)* infuser

infuser [ɪnˈfjuːzər] N infusoir *m*

infusion [ɪnˈfjuːʒən] N **1** *(liquid)* *(of camomile etc)* tisane *f*, infusion *f*, *Pharm* infusé *m* **2** *(action)* *(of tea, herbs)* infusion *f*; *(of energy, new life etc)* injection *f*

ingenious [ɪnˈdʒiːnɪəs] ADJ *(person, device)* ingénieux

Attention: ne pas confondre avec **ingenuous**.

ingeniously [ɪnˈdʒiːnɪəslɪ] ADV ingénieusement

ingenuity [ɪndʒɪˈnjuːɪtɪ] N *(of person, invention)* ingéniosité *f*

Attention: ne pas confondre avec **ingenuousness**.

ingenuous [ɪnˈdʒenjʊəs] ADJ **1** *(naive)* ingénu, candide, naïf, *f* naïve **2** *(frank)* franc, *f* franche, sincère

Attention: ne pas confondre avec **ingenious**.

ingenuously [ɪnˈdʒenjʊəslɪ] ADV **1** *(naively)* ingénument, naïvement, avec candeur **2** *(frankly)* franchement, sincèrement

ingenuousness [ɪnˈdʒenjʊəsnɪs] N **1** *(naivety)* ingénuité *f*, naïveté *f*, candeur *f* **2** *(frankness)* franchise *f*, sincérité *f*

Attention: ne pas confondre avec **ingenuity**.

ingest [ɪnˈdʒest] VT *Physiol (food)* ingérer

ingestion [ɪnˈdʒestʃən] N *Physiol* ingestion *f*

inglenook [ˈɪŋgəlnʊk] N coin *m* du feu

inglorious [ɪnˈglɔːrɪəs] ADJ *(shameful)* *(defeat etc)* déshonorant, honteux

ingloriously [ɪnˈglɔːrɪəslɪ] ADV *(to retreat)* sans gloire; *(to be defeated)* honteusement

ingot [ˈɪŋgət] N *(of gold, silver)* lingot *m*

ingrained [ɪŋˈgreɪnd] ADJ **1 i. with dirt** encrassé; **i. dirt** crasse *f* **2** *(deep-seated)* *(prejudice, distrust, belief etc)* enraciné; *(habit)* invétéré, enraciné; **certain habits are i. in one's nature** certaines habitudes sont enracinées dans la nature de chacun

ingratiate [ɪnˈgreɪʃɪeɪt] VT **to i. oneself with sb** s'insinuer dans les bonnes grâces de qn

ingratiating [ɪnˈgreɪʃɪeɪtɪŋ] ADJ doucereux; **to act/speak in an i. manner** agir/parler d'une manière doucereuse

ingratiatingly [ɪnˈgreɪʃɪeɪtɪŋlɪ] ADV d'une manière doucereuse

ingratitude [ɪnˈgrætɪtjuːd] N ingratitude *f*

ingredient [ɪnˈgriːdɪənt] N ingrédient *m*; *Fig* **what are the ingredients of her success?** qu'est-ce qui fait son succès?

ingress [ˈɪngres] N *Law* entrée *f*

ingrowing [ˈɪngrəʊɪŋ], **ingrown** [ˈɪngrəʊn] ADJ
► ► *Med* **i. toenail** ongle *m* incarné

inhabit [ɪnˈhæbɪt] VT *(house, town)* habiter, habiter dans; **a fictitious world inhabited by strange people** un monde fictif peuplé de gens étranges

inhabitable [ɪnˈhæbɪtəb(ə)l] ADJ habitable

Note that the French word **inhabitable** is a false friend and is never a translation for the English word **inhabitable**. It means **uninhabitable**.

inhabitant [ɪnˈhæbɪtənt] N habitant, -ante

inhabited [ɪnˈhæbɪtɪd] ADJ habité, peuplé

Note that the French word **inhabité** is a false friend and is never a translation for the English word **inhabited**. It means **uninhabited**.

inhalant [ɪnˈheɪlənt] N *Med* produit *m* à prendre en inhalation

inhalation [ɪnhəˈleɪʃən] N **1** *(of chloroform etc)* inhalation *f* **2** *(of perfume)* aspiration *f*

inhale [ɪnˈheɪl] VT *Med (ether etc)* inhaler; *(perfume)* aspirer, humer; *(cigarette smoke)* respirer, avaler
VI respirer; *(in smoking)* avaler la fumée

inhaler [ɪnˈheɪlər] N **1** *Med (device)* inhalateur *m* **2** *(smoker)* = fumeur *m* qui avale la fumée de sa cigarette

inhaling [ɪnˈheɪlɪŋ] N inhalation *f*

inherent [ɪnˈhɪərənt, -ˈherənt] ADJ inhérent, propre (**in** à); **an i. fault in the design** une anomalie inhérente à la conception; **power i. in an office** pouvoir *m* inhérent à une fonction
► ► **i. stability** *(of plane, ship etc)* stabilité *f* propre; *Com* **i. vice** vice *m* inhérent

inherently [ɪnˈhɪərəntlɪ, -ˈherəntlɪ] ADV fondamentalement; **i. lazy** né paresseux

inherit [ɪnˈherɪt] VT *(house, money etc)*, *Fig (character, looks)* hériter (de); **to i. sth from sb** hériter (de) qch de qn
VI **to i. equally** hériter de parts égales; **to i. jointly** cohériter

inheritance [ɪnˈherɪtəns] N **1** *(act of inheriting)* succession *f*; **the title came to him by right of i.** il a hérité du titre de plein droit; **law of i.** droit *m* successif **2** *(money, jewels etc)*, *Fig* patrimoine *m*, héritage *m*; *Biol (ge-*

netic) patrimoine; **to come into an i.** faire un héritage

▸▸*Fin* **i. tax** droits *mpl* de succession

inherited [ɪnˈherɪtɪd] ADJ *(property, characteristic, taste, wealth)* hérité

inhibit [ɪnˈhɪbɪt] VT **1** *(progress, growth etc)* entraver **2** *Psy (feeling)* inhiber **3** *Med (secretion etc)* inhiber **4** *Law etc* **to i. sb from doing sth** interdire *ou* défendre à qn de faire qch
▸▸*Comput* **i. code** code *m* inhibiteur

inhibited [ɪnˈhɪbɪtɪd] ADJ inhibé; **i. person** inhibé, -ée; **she's not i.** elle n'a pas d'inhibitions

inhibiting [ɪnˈhɪbɪtɪŋ] ADJ *(influence etc)* inhibiteur, -trice

inhibition [ɪn(h)ɪˈbɪʃən] N **1** *Med, Psy* inhibition *f*; **to have no inhibitions** avoir aucune inhibition (**about confessing** pour ce qui est d'avouer) **2** *Law etc* défense *f* expresse, prohibition *f*

inhibitive [ɪnˈhɪbɪtɪv] ADJ *Med* inhibiteur, -trice

inhibitor [ɪnˈhɪbɪtər] N *Mktg, Aut, Med* inhibiteur *m*

inhibitory [ɪnˈhɪbɪt(ə)rɪ] ADJ **1** *(nerve, reflex)* inhibiteur, -trice **2** *(warrant)* prohibitif

in-home placement testing N *Mktg* test *m* à domicile par des consommateurs-témoins

inhospitable [ɪnhɒˈspɪtəb(ə)l, ɪnˈhɒs-] ADJ *(person, climate, region etc)* inhospitalier

inhospitably [ɪnhɒˈspɪtəblɪ] ADV d'une manière inhospitalière

in-house ADJ interne *(à une entreprise)*; **to have an i. accountant** avoir un comptable sur place
ADV **to do sth i.** faire qch sur place; **to keep a job i.** faire un travail sur place
▸▸**i. magazine** revue *f* d'entreprise, magazine *m* interne; **i. newspaper** journal *m* d'entreprise *ou* interne; **i. publication** publication *f* interne; **i. staff** personnel *m* permanent; **i. training** formation *f* interne

inhuman [ɪnˈhjuːmən] ADJ inhumain; *(custom)* barbare

inhumane [ɪnhjuːˈmeɪn] ADJ inhumain, cruel

inhumanity [ɪnhjuːˈmænɪtɪ] N *(of person, action)* inhumanité *f*, cruauté *f*, barbarie *f*; **man's i. to man** la cruauté de l'homme envers son prochain

inimical [ɪˈnɪmɪk(ə)l] ADJ *(people)* ennemi, hostile; *(conditions)* défavorable, contraire (**to** à)

inimitable [ɪˈnɪmɪtəb(ə)l] ADJ inimitable

inimitably [ɪˈnɪmɪtəblɪ] ADV d'une manière inimitable

iniquitous [ɪˈnɪkwɪtəs] ADJ inique

iniquitously [ɪˈnɪkwɪtəslɪ] ADV iniquement

iniquity [ɪˈnɪkwɪtɪ] N iniquité *f*

initial [ɪˈnɪʃəl] ADJ initial, -aux, premier; **her i. delight** son plaisir initial; **the disease is only in the i. stages** la maladie n'en est qu'à son stade initial; **the i. difficulties** les difficultés du début; *Ling* **in i. position** en position initiale
N **1 initials** initiales *f*, *(to alteration of cheque etc)* paraphe *m*; *(of supervisor etc)* visa *m*; *(on garment etc)* monogramme *m* **2** *Typ* lettre *f* initiale, lettrine *f*
VT (**-ll-**, *Am* **-l-**) *(treaty, correction etc)* parapher; *(legal document)* viser, mettre son paraphe au bas de
▸▸**i. letter** initiale *f*, *St Exch* **i. margin** dépôt *m* initial *ou* de marge; *Am St Exch* **i. public offering** introduction *f* en Bourse; *Com* **i. stock** stock *m* de départ; *Fin* **i. value** valeur *f* de départ

initialization [ɪnɪʃəlaɪˈzeɪʃən] N initialisation *f*

initialize [ɪˈnɪʃəlaɪz] VT *Comput* initialiser

initially [ɪˈnɪʃəlɪ] ADV au départ, au début

initiate¹ [ɪˈnɪʃɪeɪt] VT **1** *(begin) (negotiations etc)* commencer, ouvrir; *(project etc)* lancer, amorcer; *(measures etc)* instaurer; *(new policy etc)* inaugurer; *(reform)* être l'initiateur de; *Law* **to i. proceedings against sb** entamer des poursuites contre qn **2** *(induct)* initier; **to i. sb into a secret society** admettre qn dans une société secrète

initiate² [ɪˈnɪʃɪət] N initié, -ée

initiated [ɪˈnɪʃɪeɪtɪd] ADJ initié
NPL **the i.** les initiés *mpl*

initiation [ɪnɪʃɪˈeɪʃən] N **1** *(induction)* initiation *f* (**into** à) **2** *(beginning) (of undertaking)* commencement(s) *m(pl)*, début(s) *m(pl)*
▸▸**i. ceremony** cérémonie *f* d'initiation

initiative [ɪˈnɪʃɪətɪv, ɪˈnɪʃətɪv] N initiative *f*; **to take the i.** prendre l'initiative (**in doing sth** de faire qch); **to do sth on one's own i.** faire qch de sa propre initiative; **to show/lack i.** faire preuve/manquer d'initiative; **use your i.!** fais preuve d'un peu d'initiative!; **we need sb with i.** nous avons besoin de quelqu'un qui a de l'initiative

initiator [ɪˈnɪʃɪeɪtər] N initiateur, -trice

inject [ɪnˈdʒekt] VT *(drug)*, *Fig (capital)* injecter (**into** dans); *(give injection to)* faire une piqûre à (**with sth** de qch); **to i. sb with morphine** faire une piqûre de morphine à qn; **to i. a fluid into a cavity, to i. a cavity with a fluid** injecter un liquide dans une cavité; **to i. drugs** *(of addict)* s'injecter de la drogue, se piquer; *Fig* **to i. new life into sth** donner un nouvel essor à qch; **she tried to i. a little humour into the meeting** elle a essayé d'introduire une note d'humour dans la réunion

injectable [ɪnˈdʒektəb(ə)l] ADJ *(drug)* injectable

injection [ɪnˈdʒekʃən] N *(action)* injection *f*, *Med* **an i.** une injection, une piqûre; **tetanus/polio i.** piqûre *f ou* vaccin *m* antitétanique/antipoliomyélitique; **to give sb an i.** faire une injection *ou* une piqûre à qn; *Fig* **i. of capital into a business** injection *ou* apport *m* de capital dans une entreprise
▸▸*Tech* **i. moulding** moulage *m* par injection; **i. pump** *Constr* pompe *f* à injection; *Aut* pompe d'injection (de carburant)

injector [ɪnˈdʒektər] N *Aut* injecteur *m*

injudicious [ɪndʒuˈdɪʃəs] ADJ peu judicieux, malavisé

injudiciously [ɪndʒuˈdɪʃəslɪ] ADV d'une façon peu judicieuse

Injun [ˈɪndʒən] N *Am Offensive Fam* Indien, -ienne (d'Amérique); **honest I.!** vrai de vrai!, sans blague!

injunction [ɪnˈdʒʌŋkʃən] N **1** *Law* arrêt *m* de suspension, arrêt de sursis; **to take out an i. against sb** faire une demande d'injonction contre qn; **I shall ask for an i.** je vais demander un sursis **2** *(command)* injonction *f*, ordre *m*, recommandation *f*; **to give sb strict injunctions to do sth** enjoindre formellement à qn de faire qch

injure [ˈɪndʒər] VT **1** *(physically)* blesser; **to i. oneself** se blesser, se faire du mal; **she injured her head** elle s'est blessée à la tête; *Fig* **to i. sb's pride** blesser qn dans son amour-propre **2** *(harm) (person)* nuire à, faire tort à, léser; *Law* porter préjudice à; *(sb's reputation)* nuire à, faire du tort à; *(sb's interests)* compromettre; **to i. one's health** s'abîmer la santé

Note that the French verb **injurier** is a false friend and is never a translation for the verb **to injure**. It means **to insult, to abuse**.

injured [ˈɪndʒəd] ADJ **1** *(physically)* blessé; **badly/slightly i.** gravement/légèrement blessé **2** *Fig (offended)* offensé, outragé; *(deceived)* trompé, trahi; **the i. party** l'offensé, -ée; *Law* la partie lésée; **in an i. (tone of) voice** d'une voix offensée; **i. pride** orgueil *m* blessé
NPL **the i.** les blessés *mpl*

injurious [ɪnˈdʒʊərɪəs] ADJ **1** *(harmful)* nuisible, préjudiciable (**to** à); **i. to (the) health** nuisible à la santé **2** *Fml (language)* injurieux, offensant

injury [ˈɪndʒ(ə)rɪ] N **1** *(physical) (to body)* blessure *f*, *Spec* lésion *f*; **to do oneself an i.** se blesser, se faire du mal; **wearing a seat belt can prevent i.** le port de la ceinture de sécurité peut éviter des blessures; **he escaped without i.** il n'a pas été blessé **2** *(wrong)* tort *m*, préjudice *m*; *Law* lésion *f*; **to do sb an i.** faire du tort à qn
▸▸*Sport* **i. time** arrêts *mpl* de jeu

Note that the French word **injure** is a false friend. It means **insult**.

injustice [ɪnˈdʒʌstɪs] N **1** *(of law, system etc)* injustice *f* **2** *(unjust act, remark)* injustice *f*; **you do him an i.** vous êtes injuste envers lui

ink [ɪŋk] N **1** encre *f*; **written in i.** écrit à l'encre; **2** *(of squid, octopus)* noir *m*, encre *f*
VT *Typ (letters, plate)* encrer
▸▸**i. bag** *(of squid, octopus)* glande *f ou* poche *f* du noir; **i. bottle** bouteille *f* d'encre; **i. cartridge** cartouche *f* d'encre; *Comput* **i. channel** *(in printer)* canal *m* encreur; **i. pad** tampon *m* (encreur); **i. pot** encrier *m*; **i. sac** *(of squid, octopus)* glande *ou* poche du noir; **i. stain** tache *f* d'encre
▸ **ink in** VT SEP *Art* **1** *(pencil lines)* tracer à l'encre **2** *(drawing)* mettre à l'encre
▸ **ink out** VT SEP *(word etc)* oblitérer *ou* rayer *ou* biffer à l'encre

inkblot [ˈɪŋkblɒt] N *(on paper)* pâté *m*; *Psy (in Rorschach test)* tache *f* d'encre
▸▸**i. test** test *m* de Rorschach *ou* des taches d'encre

inking [ˈɪŋkɪŋ] N *Typ (of rollers)* encrage *m*

ink-jet, ink-jet printer N imprimante *f* à jet d'encre

inkling [ˈɪŋklɪŋ] N soupçon *m*; **to give sb an i. of sth** faire entrevoir qch à qn; **she gave me no i. of her intentions** elle ne m'a aucunement communiqué ses intentions; **could you give me an i. of what it's about?** est-ce que tu pourrais me donner une idée de ce dont il s'agit?; **he had an i. of the truth** il entrevoyait la vérité; **he has no i. of the matter, he doesn't have an i.** il ne se doute de rien; **she had no i. of what they were up to** elle ne se doutait pas le moins du monde de ce qu'ils préparaient

inkstand [ˈɪŋkstænd] N (grand) encrier *m*

inkwell [ˈɪŋkwel] N encrier *m* (de pupitre)

inky [ˈɪŋkɪ] ADJ **1** *(stained with ink)* taché d'encre; *(blotted with ink)* barbouillé d'encre **2** **i. (black)** noir comme (de) l'encre; **the night was i. black** il faisait nuit noire

inlaid [ɪnˈleɪd] ADJ *(furniture, brooch etc)* incrusté (**with** de); *(with wood)* marqueté; *(floor)* parqueté; **i. work** *(wood)* marqueterie *f*, **i. enamel work** nielle *f*

inland [ˈɪnlænd, ˈɪnlənd] ADJ **1** *(away from sea)* intérieur **2** *Br (mail)* intérieur; **i. postage rates** *(tarif m d')* affranchissement *m* en régime intérieur
ADV vers l'intérieur, dans les terres; **to go i.** pénétrer vers l'intérieur *ou* dans les terres; **the town is situated a few miles i.** la ville est située à quelques kilomètres dans les terres
▸▸**i. clearance depot** dépôt *m* de dédouanement intérieur; **i. freight** fret *m* intérieur;

i. haulage transport *m* routier; **i. navigation** navigation *f* fluviale; *Br* **the I. Revenue** ≃ le fisc, la Direction Générale des Impôts; **i. waterway** voie *f* navigable *ou* fluviale; **i. waterway transport** transport *m* fluvial

in-law N parent *m* par alliance; **in-laws** *(mother and father of spouse)* beaux-parents *mpl*; *(family of spouse)* belle-famille *f*

inlay¹ ['ɪnleɪ] N **1** *(of mother-of-pearl etc)* incrustation *f*, *(piece of marquetry)* marqueterie *f* **2** *(in dentistry)* *(of metal, ceramic etc)* inlay *m*, incrustation *f*

inlay² ['ɪnleɪ, ɪn'leɪ] VT *(pt, pp* **inlaid***)* incruster (**with** de); *(table etc)* *(with wood)* marqueter; **to i. with enamel** nieller; **table inlaid with mother-of-pearl** table incrustée de nacre

inlet ['ɪnlet] N **1** *(in shore etc)* petit bras *m* de mer; *(small bay)* crique *f*, anse *f* **2** *Tech (opening) (for air etc)* orifice *m* d')entrée *f*, *(orifice d')*admission *f*, *(of ventilator etc)* ouïe *f*
▸▸ **i. manifold** conduits *mpl* d'admission, collecteur *m* d'admission; **i. pipe** tuyau *m* d'arrivée; **i. valve** soupape *f* d'admission; *(of fuel pump)* soupape d'alimentation

in-line ADJ
▸▸ *Aut* **i. engine** moteur *m* en ligne; **i. skates** patins *mpl* in-line

inmate ['ɪnmeɪt] N *(in prison)* détenu, -ue; *(in mental hospital)* interné, -ée

in memoriam [ɪnmɪ'mɔːrɪəm] PREP en mémoire de

inmost ['ɪnməʊst] ADJ le plus profond; **our i. thoughts** nos pensées les plus secrètes; **our i. feelings** nos sentiments les plus intimes; **our i. being** le plus profond de nous-mêmes

inn [ɪn] N **1** auberge *f* **2** *Eng Jur* **Inns of Court** = les quatre Écoles de droit de Londres qui seules confèrent le droit d'être avocat

innards ['ɪnədz] NPL *(of person, animal)* entrailles *fpl*, intestins *mpl*, *(of machine)* entrailles

innate [ɪ'neɪt] ADJ inné; **i. common sense** bon sens *m* naturel *ou* foncier; *Phil* **i. ideas** idées *fpl* innées

inner ['ɪnər] ADJ *(chamber, courtyard, calm, lining)* intérieur; *(layer), Anat (ear etc)* interne; **i. suburbs** première couronne *f*; **i. London** Londres intra-muros; **i. conviction** conviction *f* intime; **i. harbour** arrière-port *m*, *pl* arrière-ports;
N *(of target)* = premier cercle *m* autour de la mouche
▸▸ **i. circle** cercle *m* intime (d'amis); *(of political party)* groupe *m* dirigeant; **i. city** = quartier *m* défavorisé dans le centre d'une grande ville; *Rel* **the i. man** *(soul)* l'âme *f*; *Hum* **here's something for the i. man** *(stomach)* voilà de quoi boucher un trou; **i. tube** *(of tyre)* chambre *f* à air

inner-city ADJ **i. children** enfants *mpl* des quartiers pauvres; **i. crime** = crimes *mpl* se produisant dans les quartiers pauvres

innermost ['ɪnəməʊst] ADJ = **inmost**

inning ['ɪnɪŋ] N *Baseball* tour *m* de batte

innings ['ɪnɪŋz] N INV *Cr* tournée *f*, tour *m* de batte *(de chaque équipe ou de chaque membre de l'équipe)*; *Fig* **she had a good i.** elle a vécu longtemps

innit ['ɪnɪt] *Br Fam* ADV **1** *(isn't it)* hein?; **it's great, i.?** c'est super, hein? **2** *(general question tag)* hein?; **that was a kicking night out, i.** on a passé une super soirée, hein?

innkeeper ['ɪnkiːpər] N aubergiste *mf*, hôtelier, -ière

innocence ['ɪnəsəns] N **1** *(of defendant)* innocence *f* **2** *(inexperience, naïveté)* naïveté *f*, innocence *f*; **to lose one's i.** perdre son innocence; **to take advantage of sb's i.** abuser

de l'innocence de qn; **in all i.** en toute innocence

innocent ['ɪnəsənt] ADJ **1** *(not guilty)* innocent; **i. of a crime** innocent d'un crime; **an i. person** un(e) innocent(e); **the bomb killed several i. bystanders** la bombe a tué plusieurs innocents qui se trouvaient là; *Fam* **to act all i.** faire l'innocent
2 *(pure)* innocent; **as i. as a newborn babe** innocent comme l'enfant qui vient de naître
3 *(naive)* naïf, *f* naïve
4 *(harmless) (game, fun)* innocent; *(remark, question etc)* sans malice, innocent
5 *Fml (devoid)* dépourvu (**of** de)
N innocent, -ente; **I was a real i. then** j'étais vraiment innocent à l'époque; **don't come the i. with me** ne fais pas l'innocent avec moi; *Cathol* **Holy Innocents' Day** la fête des saints Innocents

innocently ['ɪnəsəntlɪ] ADV innocemment, en toute innocence

innocuous [ɪ'nɒkjʊəs] ADJ inoffensif; **an i. remark** une remarque anodine

innocuously [ɪ'nɒkjʊəslɪ] ADV *(to remark etc)* de façon inoffensive *ou* anodine

innocuousness [ɪ'nɒkjʊəsnɪs] N *(of remark, joke etc)* caractère *m* anodin; *Med* innocuité *f*

innovate ['ɪnəveɪt] VI innover (**in** à, en, dans)

innovating company N *Mktg* entreprise *f* innovatrice

innovation [ɪnə'veɪʃən] N innovation *f*

innovative ['ɪnəveɪtɪv, -vətɪv] ADJ (in)novateur, -trice

innovator ['ɪnəveɪtər] N (in)novateur, -trice

innuendo, *pl* **innuendos, innuendoes** [ɪnjʊ'endəʊ, -əʊz] N **1** *(insinuation)* insinuation *f*, **to discredit sb by i.** discréditer qn par sous-entendus **2** *(in jokes)* allusion *f* grivoise; **the play is full of i.** la pièce est pleine de sous-entendus **3** *Law* insinuation *f*, mot *m* couvert *(destiné à atteindre qn dans son honneur)*

innumerable [ɪ'njuːmərəb(ə)l] ADJ innombrable, sans nombre; **the successes have been i.** les réussites ne se comptent plus

innumeracy [ɪ'njuːmərəsɪ] N fait *m* de ne pas savoir compter

innumerate [ɪ'njuːmərət] ADJ qui ne sait pas compter

inoculate [ɪ'nɒkjʊleɪt] VT *Med* inoculer, vacciner (**contre** against); **to i. sb with a virus** inoculer un virus à qn

inoculation [ɪnɒkjʊ'leɪʃən] N *Med* inoculation *f*

inoffensive [ɪnə'fensɪv] ADJ **1** *(odour etc)* qui n'a rien de désagréable; *(remark, humour etc)* qui n'a rien d'offensant **2** *(harmless) (animal, person)* inoffensif

inoperable [ɪn'ɒpərəb(ə)l] ADJ **1** *Med* inopérable **2** *(system)* qui ne peut pas être exploité, inexploitable

inoperative [ɪn'ɒpərətɪv] ADJ inopérant

inopportune [ɪn'ɒpətjuːn] ADJ inopportun, intempestif

inopportunely [ɪn'ɒpətjuːnlɪ] ADV inopportunément, mal à propos

inordinate [ɪn'ɔːdɪnət] ADJ démesuré, excessif, immodéré

inordinately [ɪn'ɔːdɪnətlɪ] ADV démesurément, excessivement; **to wait an i. long time** attendre excessivement longtemps

inorganic [ɪnɔː'gænɪk] ADJ inorganique

in-patient N *Med* patient, -ente hospitalisé(e)

in-plant agency N *Am (travel agency)* implant *m*

inpoint ['ɪnpɔɪnt] N *(on tape, film)* point *m* d'entrée

input ['ɪnpʊt] N **1** *(of factory)* besoins *mpl* (en personnel, matières premières etc), *Spec* intrant *m*; *(of machine)* consommation *f*, *Elec, Electron (current etc)* puissance *f* à l'entrée *ou* d'alimentation; *(terminal)* entrée *f*
2 *Comput (of data)* entrée *f*, introduction *f*; *(data)* données *fpl* introduites, données en entrée; **i./output** entrée/sortie *f*
3 *(contribution to discussion etc)* contribution *f*
VT *Comput (data)* entrer
▸▸ *Comput* **i. box** case *f* de saisie; *Comput* **i. buffer** mémoire *f* tampon de saisie; *Comput* **i. data** données introduites, données en entrée; *Comput* **i. device** périphérique *m* d'entrée; *Comput* **i. file** fichier *m* d'entrée; *Comput* **i. mask** masque *m* de saisie; *Comput* **i./output port** port *m* d'entrée/sortie; *Comput* **i. port** port d'entrée; *Comput* **i. program** programme *m* d'introduction; **i. socket** *(for power)* prise *f* d'alimentation; *Fin* **i. tax** TVA *f* récupérée; *Comput* **i. terminal** terminal *m* d'entrée (de données); *Elec* **i. transformer** courant *m* *ou* transformateur *m* d'entrée

inquest ['ɪnkwest] N enquête *f*, *Fig (into reasons for failure of project etc)* analyse *f*

inquire [ɪn'kwaɪər] VT s'informer de (**of sb** auprès de qn); **to i. of sb what is happening** s'informer auprès de qn de ce qui se passe
VI se renseigner (**about** sur); **I'd like to i. about ...** je voudrais des renseignements sur ...; **i. within** s'adresser ici
▸ **inquire after** VT INSEP *(person)* demander des nouvelles de; **to i. after sb's health** s'informer de la santé de qn
▸ **inquire into** VT INSEP faire des recherches sur; *Law (affair)* enquêter *ou* faire une enquête sur; **to i. into the reasons for sth** chercher à connaître les raisons de qch

inquiring [ɪn'kwaɪərɪŋ] ADJ *(mind)* curieux; *(look)* interrogateur, -trice

inquiringly [ɪn'kwaɪərɪŋlɪ] ADV *(to look up, to raise one's eyebrows)* d'un air interrogateur; *(to say)* d'un ton interrogateur; **to look i. at sb** interroger qn du regard

inquiry [ɪn'kwaɪrɪ] N **1** *(official investigation)* recherche *f*, investigation *f*, *(by police)* enquête *f*, **a man is helping the police with their inquiries** la police est en train d'interroger un individu; **to conduct** *or* **hold an i. into sth** procéder à une enquête sur qch
2 *(request for information)* demande *f* de renseignements; **to make inquiries** se renseigner; **to make inquiries about sb** prendre des renseignements sur qn; *(less official)* s'informer *ou* se renseigner sur qn; **to make inquiries after sb** s'enquérir de qn; **to make inquiries into sth** faire des recherches sur qch; **with reference to your i. of 5 May,...** *(in letter)* en réponse à votre demande du 5 mai,...; **as a result of her inquiries** à la suite de ses recherches; **on i.** renseignements pris; *Br* **(private) i. agent** détective *m* (privé); **inquiries** bureau *m* de renseignements
▸▸ **i. desk, i. office** bureau de renseignements

inquisition [ɪnkwɪ'zɪʃən] N *Rel, Hist* **the I.** l'Inquisition *f*; *Fam* **the interview turned into an i.** l'entrevue s'est transformée en inquisition

inquisitive [ɪn'kwɪzɪtɪv] ADJ **1** *(mind, child)* curieux; *(look)* plein de curiosité **2** *Pej (prying)* indiscret; *(gaze)* inquisiteur

inquisitively [ɪn'kwɪzɪtɪvlɪ] ADV *(with curiosity)* avec curiosité; *(to look)* d'un œil inquisiteur; *(to say sth)* sur un ton inquisiteur

inquisitiveness [ɪn'kwɪzɪtɪvnɪs] N curiosité *f*

inquisitor [ɪn'kwɪzɪtər] N **1** *Law* enquêteur, -euse **2** *Rel, Hist, Fig Fam* inquisiteur *m*

inquisitorial [ɪnkwɪzɪ'tɔ:rɪəl] ADJ inquisitorial, -aux

inroad ['ɪnrəʊd] N USU PL **1** to make inroads into (*capital, savings*) entamer, ébrécher; (*opposition's support*) entamer; **they were making inroads into the cheese** ils avaient attaqué le fromage **2** *Mil* (*attack*) incursion *f*

inrush ['ɪnrʌʃ] N (*of water, air etc*) irruption *f*; (*of passengers etc*) afflux *m*

ins 1 (*abbr* **insurance**) asse. **2** (*abbr* **inches**) pouces, ppo.

insalubrious [ɪnsə'lu:brɪəs] ADJ insalubre, malsain

insane [ɪn'seɪn] ADJ **1** (*person*) fou, *f* folle; **to become** *or* **go i.** perdre la raison; **to drive sb i.** rendre qn fou; **to be i. with desire/jealousy** être fou de douleur/jalousie **2** *Fam* (*desire, scheme etc*) insensé, fou, *f* folle; **an i. idea** une idée folle

  NPL the i. les aliénés *mpl*

  ►►*Am* **i. asylum** hospice *m ou* asile *m* d'aliénés

insanely [ɪn'seɪnlɪ] ADV comme un fou/une folle/des fous/*etc*; **he was i. jealous** (*by nature*) il était d'une jalousie maladive; **he became i. jealous every time he saw** ... il devenait fou de jalousie chaque fois qu'il voyait ...

insanitary [ɪn'sænɪt(ə)rɪ] ADJ insalubre, malsain

insanity [ɪn'sænɪtɪ] N **1** *Med* folie *f*, démence *f*, *Fml* aliénation *f* mentale **2** *Fam* (*of course of action etc*) folie *f*; **it's sheer i. doing that** c'est de la folie pure et simple (que) de faire cela

insatiable [ɪn'seɪʃ(ɪ)əb(ə)l] ADJ (*appetite, desire etc*) insatiable

insatiably [ɪn'seɪʃ(ɪ)əblɪ] ADV insatiablement

inscribe [ɪn'skraɪb] VT (*carve*) inscrire, graver (**sth on stone** qch sur la pierre); (*write*) écrire; *Fig* graver (**in sb's memory** dans la mémoire de qn); **to i. a tomb with a name** graver un nom sur un tombeau

inscription [ɪn'skrɪpʃən] N **1** (*of name etc*) inscription *f* **2** (*message*) (*on monument etc*) inscription *f*; (*on coin*) inscription, légende *f*; (*in book etc*) dédicace *f*

inscrutability [ɪnskru:tə'bɪlɪtɪ] N inscrutabilité *f*

inscrutable [ɪn'skru:təb(ə)l] ADJ (*look, face*) impénétrable, énigmatique; (*remark*) énigmatique; **to remain i.** (*of person*) rester impassible

insect ['ɪnsekt] N insecte *m*

  ►►**i. bite** piqûre *f* d'insecte; **i. eater** insectivore *m*; **i. powder** poudre *f* insecticide; **i. repellent** produit *m* insectifuge

insecticide [ɪn'sektɪsaɪd] ADJ, N insecticide *m*

insectivore [ɪn'sektɪvɔ:r] N insectivore *m*

insectivorous [ɪnsek'tɪvərəs] ADJ insectivore

insecure [ɪnsɪ'kjʊər] ADJ **1** (*person*) qui manque d'assurance (sur le plan affectif); **to feel i.** (*because of circumstances*) éprouver un sentiment d'insécurité **2** (*unstable*) (*government*) fragile; (*job, arrangement, future*) précaire; **financially i.** financièrement vulnérable **3** (*place*) exposé **4** (*not solid, tight etc*) (*fastening, border*) peu sûr; (*grip, hold*) lâche

insecurity [ɪnsɪ'kjʊərɪtɪ] N insécurité *f*; (*of job, future*) précarité *f*, *esp Mil* (*of position*) caractère *m* exposé; **to have a feeling of i.** éprouver un manque d'assurance *ou* un sentiment d'insécurité

inseminate [ɪn'semɪneɪt] VT inséminer

insemination [ɪnsemɪ'neɪʃən] N *Biol* insémination *f*

insensate [ɪn'senseɪt] ADJ *Lit* **1** (*insensitive*) insensible **2** (*senseless*) insensé

insensibility [ɪnsensɪ'bɪlɪtɪ] N **1** (*unconsciousness*) inconscience *f* **2** (*indifference*) insensibilité *f* (**to** à), indifférence *f* (**to** pour)

insensible [ɪn'sensɪb(ə)l] ADJ *Fml* **1** (*indifferent*) insensible (**to** à) **2** (*unaware*) inconscient (**of** de); **he was quite i. of the danger he was in** il ne se doutait pas du danger qui le menaçait **3** (*unconscious*) sans connaissance, inconscient; **to become i.** perdre connaissance

insensitive [ɪn'sensɪtɪv] ADJ (*person, approach*) dur, insensible; (*remark*) indélicat; **he can be amazingly i.** il peut manquer de tact *ou* de délicatesse à un point incroyable; **to be i. to sth** être insensible à qch

insensitiveness [ɪn'sensɪtɪvnɪs], **insensitivity** [ɪnsensɪ'tɪvɪtɪ] N insensibilité *f*

inseparable [ɪn'sep(ə)rəb(ə)l] ADJ inséparable (**from** de)

inseparably [ɪn'sep(ə)rəblɪ] ADV inséparablement

insert¹ ['ɪnsɜ:t] N **1** *Cin* scène-raccord *f*, *pl* scènes-raccords; (*in magazine etc*) encart *m* **2** *Typ etc* (*in proofs*) insertion *f* **3** *Comput* insertion *f* **4** *Sewing* incrustation *f*

  ►►*Comput* **i. key** touche *f* d'insertion; *Typ* **i. mark** signe *m* d'insertion; *Comput* **i. mode** mode *m* (d')insertion; *Comput* **i. point** point *m* d'insertion

insert² [ɪn'sɜ:t] VT **1** (*key in lock etc*) introduire, enfoncer; (*page in book, scene in film etc*) insérer; (*clause in contract etc*) insérer, introduire, apposer; **to i. an ad (in the newspaper)** mettre une petite annonce dans le journal **2** *Typ* (*line*) intercaler **3** *Comput* insérer

insertion [ɪn'sɜ:ʃən] N **1** (*act of inserting*) insertion *f*, introduction *f* (**of sth into sth** de qch dans qch); (*of advert in newspaper*) insertion **2** (*thing inserted*) *Typ* insertion *f*, *Sewing* incrustation *f*, (*of lace etc*) entre-deux *m inv*

  ►►*Typ* **i. mark** signe *m* d'insertion; *Typ* **i. point** point *m* d'insertion

inset¹ ['ɪnset] N **1** (*in bookbinding*) (*of four or eight pages*) encart *m*, (*leaf, advertisement*) encartage *m* **2** *Typ* (*map etc*) hors-texte *m inv*, médaillon *m*; *TV, Cin* médaillon **3** *Sewing* incrustation *f*

inset² [ɪn'set] VT (*pt, pp* **inset** *or* **insetted**) **1** (*in bookbinding*) (*leaves, advertisements*) encarter **2** *Typ* insérer en cartouche *ou* en médaillon **3** *Sewing* (*piece of fabric etc*) insérer; (*lace etc*) faire des incrustations de **4** *Typ* (*indent*) (*line, new paragraph*) renfoncer

inshore ['ɪnʃɔ:r] *Naut* ADV près de la côte; (*to head*) vers la côte; **to keep close i.** naviguer près de la côte

  ADJ (*navigation, fishing*) côtier

  ►►**i. waters** eaux *fpl* près de la côte; **i. wind** vent *m* de mer

INSIDE

N	intérieur **1**
ADJ	intérieur **1**
ADV	à l'intérieur **1** ▪ dedans **1**
PREP	à l'intérieur de **1** ▪ dans **1** ▪ en moins de **2**

N ['ɪnsaɪd] **1** (*of garment etc*) (côté *m*) intérieur *m*; (*of house etc*) intérieur *m*; **the door opens from (the) i.** la porte s'ouvre de l'intérieur; **the door had been locked from the i.** la porte était verrouillée de l'intérieur; **on the i.** à l'intérieur; **a scar on the i. of his leg** une cicatrice sur la face interne de sa jambe; **to walk on the i. (of the pavement)** marcher loin de la chaussée; **a motorbike was coming up on the i.** une moto arrivait sur la droite *ou* (*driving on left*) la gauche; *Fam* **to know the i. of an affair** connaître les dessous d'une affaire

  2 *Fam* **insides** (*internal organs*) entrailles *fpl*; **to have pains in one's inside(s)** avoir mal au ventre

  3 i. out (*sweater etc*) à l'envers; **to turn sth i. out** mettre qch à l'envers; *Fig* **to turn everything i. out** mettre tout sens dessus dessous; *Fig* **to know sth i. out** savoir qch à fond; *Fig* **to know Paris i. out** connaître Paris comme sa poche

  ADJ ['ɪnsaɪd] (*wall, door, pocket etc*) intérieur; *Constr* (*measurement, stair etc*) dans œuvre; (*diameter*) interne; *Horseracing* **to be on the i. track** tenir la corde; **it's an i. job** (*of burglary etc*) c'est un coup monté par quelqu'un de la maison; **to have an i. accomplice** avoir un complice à l'intérieur; **I speak with i. knowledge** ce que je dis je le sais de bonne source; **the i. pages** (*of newspaper*) les pages intérieures; **to know the i. story** connaître les dessous de l'histoire

  ADV [ɪn'saɪd] **1** à l'intérieur; **he took the box and looked i.** il a pris la boîte et a regardé dedans *ou* à l'intérieur; **there's nothing i.** il n'y a rien dedans *ou* à l'intérieur; **i. she was angry** intérieurement elle était en colère; **i. and out** au dedans et au dehors, à l'intérieur et à l'extérieur; **to push sb i.** pousser qn à l'intérieur *ou* dedans; **come i.!** entrez!; *Sl* **to put sb/be i.** (*in prison*) mettre qn/être en tôle *ou* taule

  2 (*of time*) (*within*) **i. of three hours** moins de trois heures

  PREP [ɪn'saɪd] **1** (*of place*) (*house etc*) à l'intérieur de, dans; **i. the country/company** au sein du pays/de la société; **the telephone is just i. the door** le téléphone est juste derrière la porte; *Fam* **get this i. you** avale-ça; *Fam* **to get right i. a part** (*of actor*) entrer dans la peau d'un personnage

  2 (*of time*) **i. a week/an hour** en moins d'une semaine/d'une heure

  ►►**i. back cover** troisième *f* de couverture; **i. centre** (*in rugby*) premier centre *m*; **i. front cover** deuxième *f* de couverture; **i. information** renseignements *mpl* privés; **i. lane** (*in athletics*) la corde, le couloir intérieur; (*of road, driving on left*) la voie de gauche; (*driving on right*) la voie de droite; *Ftbl* **i. left** intérieur gauche; **i. leg measurement** entrejambe *m*; *Typ* **i. margin** marge *f* de reliure, (blanc *m* de) petit fond *m*

insider [ɪn'saɪdər] N initié, -ée

  ►►*Fin* **i. dealing**, **i. trading** délit *m ou* opération *f* d'initié

insidious [ɪn'sɪdɪəs] ADJ insidieux

insidiously [ɪn'sɪdɪəslɪ] ADV insidieusement

insight ['ɪnsaɪt] N **1** (*perspicacity*) perspicacité *f*, **i. into character** finesse *f* psychologique; **to have a lot of i.** être très perspicace **2** (*understanding*) aperçu *m*; **to get an i. into sth** avoir un aperçu de qch; **the book offers several valuable insights into** ... le livre donne un bon aperçu de ...

insightful ['ɪnsaɪtfʊl] ADJ perspicace

insignia [ɪn'sɪgnɪə] NPL (*of royal family etc*) insignes *mpl*; *Mil* **i. of rank** insignes du grade

insignificance [ɪnsɪg'nɪfɪkəns] N insignifiance *f*; **my problems fade into i. beside yours** mes problèmes semblent totalement insignifiants à côté des tiens

insignificant [ɪnsɪg'nɪfɪkənt] ADJ insignifiant

insincere [ɪnsɪn'sɪər] ADJ peu sincère, faux, *f* fausse, *Lit* insincère

insincerity [ɪnsɪn'serɪtɪ] N manque m de sincérité, fausseté f

insinuate [ɪn'sɪnjʊeɪt] VT **1** (*suggest indirectly*) insinuer; **are you insinuating that …?** est-ce que vous insinuez que …? **2** Fml (*manoeuvre*) **to i. one's hand/body into an opening** glisser sa main/se glisser dans une ouverture; **to i. oneself into a room** s'introduire dans une pièce; **to i. oneself into sb's favour** s'insinuer dans les bonnes grâces de qn

insinuation [ɪnsɪnjʊ'eɪʃən] N **1** (*indirect suggestion*) insinuation f **2** Fml (*of hand, body*) introduction f

insipid [ɪn'sɪpɪd] ADJ (*food*) insipide, fade; (*style, conversation*) fade, plat, insipide; (*person*) insipide

insipidity [ɪnsɪ'pɪdɪtɪ], **insipidness** [ɪn'sɪpɪdnɪs] N insipidité f, fadeur f

insist [ɪn'sɪst] VI insister (**on doing** pour faire); **to i. on a point** insister ou appuyer sur un point; **I won't i.** je n'insiste pas; **very well, if you i.** très bien, si tu insistes; **he insists on your coming** il insiste pour que vous veniez; **he insisted on paying** il a tenu à payer; **let me pay for the meal, I i. (on it)!** laisse-moi payer l'addition, j'insiste!; **show me what you've got there, I i.!** montre-moi ce que tu as dans les mains, je l'exige!; **to i. upon one's innocence** affirmer son innocence avec insistance; **to i. on one's rights** revendiquer ses droits; **i. on the best** exigez la meilleure qualité

VT **1** (*maintain*) soutenir, maintenir; **people insisted that they had seen him** des gens affirmaient l'avoir vu; **he insisted that it was so** il maintenait qu'il en était ainsi **2 I i. that you let me pay** j'insiste, laisse-moi payer; **I i. that you show me what you have in your hand** j'exige que tu me montres ce que tu as dans la main

insistence [ɪn'sɪstəns] N insistance f; **because of his i. on paying** parce qu'il tenait à payer; **he did it at her i.** il l'a fait parce qu'elle a insisté; **her i. that she was telling the truth didn't convince me** quoi qu'elle ait bien insisté qu'elle disait la vérité, elle ne m'a pas convaincu

insistent [ɪn'sɪstənt] ADJ qui insiste, insistant; (*demands*) instant; (*noise*) incessant; **to be i. about sth** insister sur qch; **to be very i.** insister beaucoup; **don't be too i.** n'insistez pas trop

insistently [ɪn'sɪstəntlɪ] ADV instamment, avec insistance

in situ [ɪn'sɪtjuː] ADV in situ

insofar [ɪnsəʊ'fɑːr] ADV Am **i. as** dans la mesure où

insole ['ɪnsəʊl] N (*of shoe*) (*inner sole*) première semelle f; (*separate piece*) (*of cork, felt etc*) semelle intérieure

insolence ['ɪnsələns] N insolence f (**to** envers)

insolent ['ɪnsələnt] ADJ insolent (**to** envers); **an i. boy** un (jeune) insolent

insolently ['ɪnsələntlɪ] ADV insolemment

insolubility [ɪnsɒljʊ'bɪlɪtɪ] N insolubilité f

insoluble [ɪn'sɒljʊb(ə)l] ADJ **1** (*salt etc*) insoluble **2** (*problem*) insoluble, qu'on ne peut pas résoudre

insolvency [ɪn'sɒlvənsɪ] N insolvabilité f

insolvent [ɪn'sɒlvənt] ADJ (*debtor, company*) insolvable; **to declare oneself i.** se déclarer insolvable; Com déposer son bilan

N (*person*) débiteur m insolvable; (*company*) société f insolvable

insomnia [ɪn'sɒmnɪə] N insomnie f

insomniac [ɪn'sɒmnɪæk] N insomniaque mf

insomuch [ɪnsəʊ'mʌtʃ] ADV = **inasmuch**

inspect [ɪn'spekt] VT **1** (*examine*) examiner,

regarder de près; **my mother inspected our hands (to see if they were clean)** ma mère a regardé si nos mains étaient propres **2** (*carry out official inspection of*) (*school etc*) inspecter; (*accounts of business, machine etc*) contrôler, vérifier **3** Mil (*regiment*) passer en revue; **to be inspected** (*of troops*) être passé en revue

inspecting officer N inspecteur, -trice

inspection [ɪn'spekʃən] N **1** (*of documents etc*) examen m, vérification f; (*of tickets, goods etc*) contrôle m; **on close** or **closer i.** en y regardant de plus près **2** (*of school, factory etc*) (*by official*) (visite f d')inspection f; (*of head, hands etc*) (*by nurse*) inspection; (*of machinery, vehicle*) contrôle m, vérification f; **tour of i.** visite d'inspection; **sanitary i.** contrôle m sanitaire; **medical i.** visite médicale; **3** Mil revue f; **to make** or **hold an i.** passer une revue

► **i. copy** (*in publishing*) spécimen m; Tech **i. hole** orifice m ou trou m ou regard m de visite; Tech **i. panel** panneau m de visite; Aut **i. pit** fosse f (de réparations); Tech **i. port** orifice ou trou ou regard de visite

inspector [ɪn'spektər] N (*of schools, police, mines*) inspecteur, -trice; Br (*on train, bus etc*) contrôleur, -euse

► Br **i. of taxes** ≃ inspecteur, -trice des impôts

inspectorate [ɪn'spektərət] N **1** (*inspectors*) corps m d'inspecteurs **2** (*post*) inspectorat m

inspiration [ɪnspɪ'reɪʃən] N **1** (*stimulus*) inspiration f; **he is the i. of the movement** c'est l'âme du mouvement; **she's an i. to us all** elle est notre modèle à tous; **to lack i.** (*of poet etc*) manquer d'inspiration; **to provide the i. for sth** fournir l'inspiration pour qch; **to have a sudden i.** avoir une inspiration subite **2** Fml (*inhalation*) inspiration f

inspirational [ɪnspɪ'reɪʃənəl] ADJ **1** (*inspiring*) qui inspire, inspirant **2** (*inspired*) inspiré

inspire [ɪn'spaɪər] VT **1** (*stimulate*) inspirer; **to i. a thought/a feeling in sb** inspirer une pensée/un sentiment à qn; **to i. sb with confidence** inspirer (de la) confiance à qn; **to i. sb with hope** donner de l'espoir à qn; **inspired with hope** animé d'espoir; **the programme inspired her to study biology** l'émission l'a poussée à étudier la biologie; **her example inspired us to …** son exemple nous a incités à …; **I don't know what inspired me to turn back** je ne sais pas ce qui m'a poussé à revenir sur mes pas; Iron **what inspired you to do that?** qu'est-ce qui t'a pris de faire ça? **2** Fml (*inhale*) inspirer

inspired [ɪn'spaɪəd] ADJ (*poet, cook etc*) inspiré, plein d'inspiration; (*decision*) inspiré; Fam **no one was (feeling) i.** personne n'était très inspiré; **to make an i. guess** bien tomber, tomber juste; **it was just an i. guess** c'était un coup de chance

inspiring [ɪn'spaɪərɪŋ] ADJ (*speech, example etc*) qui inspire, inspirant; Fam **the menu wasn't very i.** le menu n'avait rien de bien tentant

inst [ɪnst] Com Old-fashioned (abbr **instant**) (*in letter*) **on the 5th i.** le 5 courant

instability [ɪnstə'bɪlɪtɪ] N (*of government, economy etc*) instabilité f; Tech déséquilibre m; Met instabilité (atmosphérique); (*of bridge etc*) manque m de solidité; (*of character*) mobilité f, instabilité

install, Am **instal** [ɪn'stɔːl] VT **1** (*machine, electricity, software*) installer **2** (*settle*) **she installed herself in an armchair/in front of the TV** elle s'est installée dans un fauteuil/devant la télé **3** Rel, Fml (*bishop, person in position*) installer

installation [ɪnstə'leɪʃən] N **1** (*of central heating, machine, bishop, software*) installation f **2** (*thing installed*) installation f

► Comput **i. disk** disquette f d'installation; Comput **i. manual** manuel m d'installation; Comput **i. program** programme m d'installation

installer [ɪn'stɔːlər] N Comput disquette f d'installation

instalment, Am **installment** [ɪn'stɔːlmənt] N **1** Com etc (*part payment*) versement m; **to pay in** or **by instalments** payer par versements, échelonner ou fractionner les paiements; **payable in monthly instalments** payable par mensualités; **final i.** paiement m pour solde **2** (*of work published in parts*) fascicule m, livraison f; (*of work published in periodical*), Radio, TV (*of soap opera etc*) épisode m

► Fin **i. loan** prêt m à tempérament ou à remboursements échelonnés; Am **i. plan** vente f à tempérament; Am **to buy sth on the i. plan** acheter qch à crédit

instance ['ɪnstəns] N **1** (*example*) cas m; **in many instances** dans bien des cas; **in the present i., in this i.** dans le cas présent; **for i.** par exemple **2 in the first i.** en (tout) premier lieu **3** Fml (*urging*) **to do sth at sb's i.** or **at the i. of sb** faire qch à ou sur la demande de qn

VT citer en exemple; **his cruelty is well instanced by …** sa cruauté est bien illustrée par …

> Note that the French noun **instance** is a false friend: it never means **example**.

instant ['ɪnstənt] ADJ **1** (*action, dislike etc*) immédiat; (*solution*) instantané; Fml **this calls for i. remedy** il faut y remédier tout de suite ou sur-le-champ **2** (*quickly prepared*) (*coffee*) instantané; **i. mash** purée f en flocons/en poudre **3** Lit (*urgent*) pressant, urgent **4** Old-fashioned (*in letter*) (*of current month*) courant

N **1** (*moment*) instant m, moment m; **come this i.!** venez immédiatement!; **I just arrived this (very) i.** j'arrive à l'instant; **not an i. too soon** juste à temps; **in an i.** dans un instant; **the i. I saw him** dès que je l'ai vu **2** Fam (*instant coffee*) café m instantané

► Phot **i. camera** appareil m photo à développement instantané; Comput **i. message** message m instantané; Comput **i. messaging** messagerie f instantanée; TV **i. replay** = répétition f immédiate d'une séquence; (*in slow motion*) ralenti m

instant-access ADJ (*bank account*) à accès immédiat

instantaneous [ɪnstən'teɪnɪəs] ADJ instantané

► Mktg **i. audience** audience f instantanée; Phot **i. exposure** pose f instantanée, instantané m

instantaneously [ɪnstən'teɪnɪəslɪ] ADV instantanément

instantly ['ɪnstəntlɪ] ADV tout de suite, immédiatement, sur-le-champ; **she would have died i.** elle serait morte immédiatement; **i. recognizable** immédiatement reconnaissable

instead [ɪn'sted] ADV **1** (*in place of sth*) à la place; (*in sb's place*) à ma/sa/etc place; **if John can't come, take me i.** si Jean ne peut pas venir, emmenez-moi à sa place; **use the hammer i.** utilise le marteau à la place **2 i. of** (*thing*) au lieu de; (*person*) à la place de; **i. of doing sth** au lieu de faire qch

instep ['ɪnstep] N (*of foot*) cou-de-pied m, pl cous-de-pied; (*of shoe*) cambrure f; **to have a high i.** (*of person*) avoir le pied très cambré

instigate ['ɪnstɪgeɪt] VT (*of person*) (*inquiry,*

negotiations, changes, rebellion etc) être à l'origine de; (of event, development etc) (rebellion, change) provoquer; (incite) (person) inciter, pousser (**to do** à faire)

instigation [ɪnstɪ'geɪʃən] N instigation f, incitation f; **at sb's i.** à l'instigation de qn

instigator ['ɪnstɪgeɪtər] N instigateur, -trice

instil, Am **instill** [ɪn'stɪl] VT (Br **instils**, Am **instills**, Br & Am **instilled, instilling**) (courage, pride) inspirer (**in** à); (doubt, jealousy) instiller (**in** à); (idea) inculquer (**into** à)

instinct ['ɪnstɪŋkt] N instinct m; **by** or **from i.** d'instinct, par instinct; **to follow one's instincts** suivre son instinct; **my i. was to run away** mon instinct m'a dit de fuir; **to have an i. for business** avoir le sens des affaires; **she has a strong business i.** elle a vraiment le sens des affaires

instinctive [ɪn'stɪŋktɪv] ADJ instinctif

instinctively [ɪn'stɪŋktɪvlɪ] ADV instinctivement, d'instinct

institute ['ɪnstɪtjuːt] N institut m; **i. for the blind** établissement m pour aveugles
▸ VT **1** (set up) (order, law) instituer, établir; (club etc) fonder, constituer **2** (initiate) (search) lancer; Law (enquiry) ordonner, instituer; **to i. (legal) proceedings against sb** entamer ou engager des poursuites contre qn
▸▸Br **i. of education** école f formant des enseignants; Br **I. for Public Policy Research** = groupe m d'experts de centre gauche à l'origine de plusieurs grandes politiques du gouvernement travailliste

institution [ɪnstɪ'tjuːʃən] N **1** (organization, society) (for education etc) institution f; (public, financial etc) établissement m; (for old people) hospice m; (for mental patients) asile m **2** (action) (of enquiry etc) établissement m; (of law etc) institution f; (of committee) constitution f; (of state) création f; (of search) lancement m **3** (established practice etc) institution f; Fig **to become a national i.** (of person, event etc) devenir une institution nationale; **the i. of marriage is under threat** le mariage est une institution menacée

institutional [ɪnstɪ'tjuːʃən(ə)l] ADJ institutionnel; **he needs i. care** il a besoin d'être hospitalisé; **i. life** la vie en collectivité
▸▸Com **i. advertising** publicité f institutionnelle; Com **i. buying** achats mpl institutionnels; **i. food** nourriture f de cantine; Fin **i. investment** investissement m institutionnel; Com **i. investor** investisseur m institutionnel, Fam zinzin m; Fin **i. savings** épargne f institutionnelle

institutionalize [ɪnstɪ'tjuːʃənəlaɪz] VT **1** (put in a home etc) placer dans un établissement spécialisé **2** (turn into an institution) institutionnaliser

institutionalized [ɪnstɪ'tjuːʃənəlaɪzd] ADJ **1** (person) marqué par la vie en collectivité; **after years in a psychiatric hospital, she had become completely i.** après des années en hôpital psychiatrique, elle était devenue complètement dépendante; **things are less i. in this establishment** cet établissement a un caractère moins institutionnel **2** (practice) établi

in-store ADJ
▸▸Mktg **i. advertising** PLV f, publicité f sur le lieu de vente; Mktg **i. advertising space** espace m de PLV, espace de publicité sur le lieu de vente; **i. demonstration** démonstration f sur le lieu de vente; **i. promotion** promotion f sur le lieu de vente

instruct [ɪn'strʌkt] VT **1** (teach, train) **to i. sb in sth** enseigner qch à qn **2** (command) ordonner (**to do** de faire); **I am instructed by the Board to inform you that ...** la Direction me charge de vous faire savoir que ... **3** Br

Law **to i. a solicitor** donner ses instructions à un avoué; **to i. counsel** constituer avocat **4** Fml (inform) informer (**that** que)

instruction [ɪn'strʌkʃən] N **1** (no pl) (training) instruction f, enseignement m; **we received i. in using the machines** on nous a appris comment utiliser les machines **2** (usu pl) **instructions** (orders) instructions fpl, directives fpl; (to sentry etc) consigne f; (to representative etc) mandat m; Comput (in program) instructions; **instructions (for use)** (for machine, cleaning product etc) mode m ou notice f d'emploi; **to give sb instructions to do sth** ordonner à qn de faire qch; **strict instructions** des instructions formelles, des ordres formels; **I gave strict instructions that I wasn't to be disturbed** j'ai donné l'ordre formel qu'on ne me dérange pas; **to carry out instructions** exécuter des ordres; **to act in accordance with/contrary to instructions** se conformer/ne pas se conformer aux instructions reçues; **our instructions were to arrest him** nous avions reçu l'ordre de l'arrêter; **to follow sb's instructions** suivre les instructions de qn; **to obey sb's instructions** obéir aux ordres de qn; Com **we await your instructions** nous attendons vos instructions; Br Law **to give instructions to a solicitor** donner ses instructions à un avoué
▸▸**i. book, i. booklet** livret m d'instruction(s); Comput **i. code** code m d'instruction; **i. manual** manuel m (d'utilisation et d'entretien); Comput guide m de l'utilisateur; Comput **i. set** jeu m d'instructions

instructive [ɪn'strʌktɪv] ADJ instructif

instructor [ɪn'strʌktər] N enseignant, -ante, professeur m; Am Univ assistant, -ante; Mil instructeur, -trice; Ski, Aut moniteur, -trice; **swimming/judo/riding i.** professeur m de natation/de judo/d'équitation

instructress [ɪn'strʌktrɪs] N maîtresse f, professeur m; Ski, Aut monitrice f

instrument ['ɪnstrəmənt] N **1** Tech, Surg, Mus etc instrument m; **aircraft instruments** instruments de bord; **flying/landing on instruments, i. flying/landing** vol m/atterrissage m aux instruments ou sans visibilité; Aviat, Aut **i. board** or **panel** or **display** tableau m de bord **2** Fml (means, agent) instrument m; **to serve as the i. of sb's vengeance** servir d'instrument à la vengeance de qn **3** Law (legal document) instrument m, acte m juridique; **i. of incorporation** statut m, acte de constitution; Com **i. to order** papier m à ordre
▸ VT **1** Mus (opera etc) orchestrer, instrumenter **2** Tech (workshop etc) équiper ou munir d'outils
▸ VI Law instrumenter

instrumental [ɪnstrʊ'ment(ə)l] ADJ **1** (contributing) **to be i. in doing sth** contribuer à faire qch, jouer un rôle décisif dans qch **2** Tech **by i. means** avec des instruments de mesure **3** Mus instrumental, -aux
▸ N Mus version f instrumentale
▸▸Tech **i. error** erreur f due aux instruments

instrumentalist [ɪnstrʊ'mentəlɪst] N Mus instrumentiste mf

instrumentation [ɪnstrʊmen'teɪʃən] N Mus, Aut instrumentation f

insubordinate [ɪnsə'bɔːdɪnət] ADJ insubordonné, insoumis

insubordination [ɪnsəbɔːdɪ'neɪʃən] N insubordination f, insoumission f

insubstantial [ɪnsəb'stænʃəl] ADJ **1** (thin, flimsy) (reason) qui manque de substance; (argument) vide, creux; (book etc) creux, qui manque de substance; **an i. breakfast** un petit déjeuner frugal **2** (unreal) (fear) imaginaire

insufferable [ɪn'sʌfərəb(ə)l] ADJ insupportable, intolérable

insufferably [ɪn'sʌfərəblɪ] ADV insupportablement, intolérablement

insufficiency [ɪnsə'fɪʃənsɪ] N insuffisance f

insufficient [ɪnsə'fɪʃənt] ADJ (amount, resources, justification etc) insuffisant; (facilities) inadéquat; **the sum is i. to cover our costs** la somme ne suffit pas à couvrir nos frais
▸▸Fin **i. capital** insuffisance f de capitaux; **i. evidence** preuves fpl insuffisantes; Fin **i. funds** provision f insuffisante, insuffisance de provision

insufficiently [ɪnsə'fɪʃəntlɪ] ADV insuffisamment

insular ['ɪnsjʊlər] ADJ **1** (narrow) (mind) étroit, borné; **to be very i. in one's views** être très étroit d'esprit **2** Geog (climate etc) insulaire

Note that the French word **insulaire** is a false friend. It always means **pertaining to an island**.

insularity [ɪnsjʊ'lærɪtɪ] N Pej (of country) manque m d'ouverture sur l'extérieur; **the i. of their views** leur étroitesse d'esprit

insulate ['ɪnsjʊleɪt] VT Elec (wire etc) isoler; (pipe, water tank etc) calorifuger; Radio etc (soundproof) insonoriser; **to i. against vibration** protéger contre les vibrations; Fig **insulated from the outside world** protégé contre le monde extérieur

insulated ['ɪnsjʊleɪtɪd] ADJ Elec isolé; (handle, screwdriver etc) isolant; (against loss of heat) calorifugé; (soundproofed) insonorisé

insulating ['ɪnsjʊleɪtɪŋ] ADJ isolant; (against loss of heat) calorifuge; (soundproofing) insonore
▸▸Elec **i. material** isolant m; **i. properties** propriétés fpl isolantes; **i. tape** ruban m isolant, chatterton m

insulation [ɪnsjʊ'leɪʃən] N **1** (action, state) (of wires etc) isolation f; **heat** or **thermal i.** isolation thermique; **sound i.** (of room etc) insonorisation f **2** (substance) (for wires, against heat loss etc) isolant m

Attention: ne pas confondre avec le terme anglais **isolation**, qui signifie **isolement**.

insulator ['ɪnsjʊleɪtər] N Elec, Constr (substance) isolant m; Elec (device) isolateur m

insulin ['ɪnsjʊlɪn] N Med insuline f
▸▸**i. treatment** insulinothérapie f

insulin-dependent ADJ Med insulinodépendant

insult¹ ['ɪnsʌlt] N (abuse) insulte f, (affront) affront m, insulte; **and to add i. to injury ...** et comme si ça ne suffisait pas ...; **it's an i. to the intelligence** c'est une insulte à l'intelligence

insult² [ɪn'sʌlt] VT (abuse) insulter; (affront) faire affront ou injure à, insulter; **to i. sb's intelligence** (of book, film etc) être une insulte à l'intelligence de qn; (of person) prendre qn pour un/une imbécile; **to feel insulted** se sentir insulté

insulting [ɪn'sʌltɪŋ] ADJ (gesture, expression) insultant, offensant, injurieux; (person) injurieux; **it is i. to suggest that ...** il est insultant de suggérer que ...; **it's i.!** c'est une insulte!; **to use i. language** employer un langage injurieux; **to be guilty of i. behaviour towards sb** s'être conduit insolemment à l'égard de qn; Law (to magistrate, policeman) être coupable d'outrages à qn

insultingly [ɪn'sʌltɪŋlɪ] ADV d'une façon insultante ou offensante

insuperable [ɪn'suːpərəb(ə)l] ADJ *(difficulty, obstacle etc)* insurmontable

insuperably [ɪn'suːpərəblɪ] ADV **i. difficult** impossible

in-supplier N *Mktg* fournisseur *m* agréé

insupportable [ɪnsə'pɔːtəb(ə)l] ADJ insupportable

insurable [ɪn'ʃʊərəb(ə)l, ɪn'ʃɔːr-] ADJ assurable
► ► **i. interest** intérêt *m* pécuniaire

insurance [ɪn'ʃʊərəns, -ʃɔːrəns] N **1** *Com* assurance *f*; **to take out i. on sth** prendre une assurance sur qch; **to take out i. against a risk** prendre une assurance ou s'assurer contre un risque; **he's in i.** il est dans les assurances; **i. against loss of trade** assurance courant d'affaires, assurance perte de l'exploitation **2** *(premium)* prime *f* d'assurance; **to pay the i. on a car** payer l'assurance d'une voiture **3** *Fig (protection)* garantie *f*; **to buy gold as (an) i. against inflation** acheter de l'or pour se prémunir contre l'inflation
► ► **i. adviser** assureur-conseil *m, pl* assureurs-conseils; **i. agent** agent *m* d'assurance(s); **i. banker** bancassureur *m*; **i. broker** courtier, -ière d'assurances; **i. certificate** certificat *m* d'assurance; **i. claim** demande *f* d'indemnité; *(for more serious damage)* déclaration *f* de sinistre; **i. company** société *f* d'assurances; **i. cover** couverture *f* d'assurance; **i. group** groupe *m* d'assurance; **i. inspector** inspecteur, -trice d'une société d'assurances; **i. policy** police *f* d'assurance, contrat *m* d'assurance; **i. portfolio** portefeuille *m* d'assurances; **i. premium** prime d'assurance; **i. value** valeur *f* d'assurance

insure [ɪn'ʃʊər, -ʃɔːr] VT **1** *(of insurance company) (car, valuables etc)* assurer; *(of client) (goods etc)* (faire) assurer; **I'm insured** je suis assuré; **to i. one's life** s'assurer ou se faire assurer sur la vie **2** *esp Am* = **ensure**
► **insure against** VT INSEP *(risk, theft, fire)* s'assurer ou se faire assurer contre; *(danger)* se garantir de; **to i. against loss** couvrir une perte

insured [ɪn'ʃʊəd, -ʃɔːd] ADJ assuré
N **the i.** *(person)* l'assuré, -ée
► ► **i. value** valeur *f* assurée

insurer [ɪn'ʃʊərər, -ʃɔːrər] N assureur *m*

insurgent [ɪn'sɜːdʒənt] ADJ insurgé, révolté
N insurgé, -ée, révolté, -ée

insurmountable [ɪnsə'maʊntəb(ə)l] ADJ *(difficulty, obstacle)* insurmontable

insurrection [ɪnsə'rekʃ(ə)n] N insurrection *f*

insurrectionary [ɪnsə'rekʃənərɪ] ADJ insurrectionnel
N insurgé, -ée

insurrectionist [ɪnsə'rekʃənɪst] N insurgé, -ée

intact [ɪn'tækt] ADJ intact

intaglio [ɪn'tɑːlɪəʊ] N *(gem)* intaille *f*
► ► **i. engraving** gravure *f* en creux

intake ['ɪnteɪk] N **1** *(opening) (for water, electricity)* prise *f*; *(for steam)* arrivée *f*; adduction *f*, admission *f*; *(in engine) (for air)* arrivée, prise; *Min* galerie *f* d'appel d'air; *Tech* aire *f* d'alimentation; **he gave a sharp i. of breath when he heard the news** il a eu le souffle coupé quand il a entendu la nouvelle **2** *(of alcohol, calories etc)* consommation *f* **3** *Sch (of pupils, students)* admission(s) *f(pl)*; *Mil (of recruits)* contingent *m*
► ► *Aut* **i. pipe** conduit *m* d'admission

intangible [ɪn'tændʒɪb(ə)l] ADJ *(benefit)* intangible; *(quality)* indéfinissable
NPL *Acct, Fin* **intangibles** valeurs *fpl* immatérielles, actif *m* incorporel
► ► *Acct, Fin* **i. assets** valeurs immatérielles, actif incorporel; *Acct, Fin* **i. fixed assets** immobilisations *fpl* incorporelles; *Law* **i. property** biens *mpl* incorporels

integer ['ɪntɪdʒər] N *Math* (nombre *m*) entier *m*

integral ['ɪntɪgr(ə)l] ADJ **1** *(essential)* indispensable (**to** pour); **to be** or **form an i. part of sth** faire partie intégrante de qch **2** *Tech (forming a part)* incorporé (**with** à), qui fait partie intégrante (**with** de)
N *Math* intégrale *f*
► ► *Math* **i. calculus** calcul *m* intégral; *Math* **i. number** nombre *m* entier; **i. power supply** accumulateur *m* incorporé

integrate ['ɪntɪgreɪt] VT **1** *(incorporate) (minority)* intégrer (**into** à); *Am* **to i. a school** imposer la déségrégation raciale dans une école **2** *(bring together)* regrouper (**into** en), combiner **3** *Math (function)* intégrer
VI *(social milieu, ethnic group etc)* s'intégrer; *Am (carry out racial integration)* pratiquer la déségrégation raciale

integrated ['ɪntɪgreɪtɪd] ADJ **1** intégré; **an i. transport system** un système de transports cohérent **2** *(school)* qui pratique la déségrégation raciale
► ► *Electron* **i. circuit** circuit *m* intégré; *Electron* **i. circuit card** carte *f* à circuit intégré; *Comput* **i. package** logiciel *m* ou progiciel *m* intégré, intégré *m*; *Comput* **i. software** logiciel intégré

integration [ɪntɪ'greɪʃən] N **1** intégration *f*, **the i. of ethnic minorities** l'intégration des minorités ethniques; **racial i.** déségrégation *f* raciale **2** *Math* **i. by parts** intégration *f* par parties

integrative growth ['ɪntɪgreɪtɪv] N *Com* croissance *f* par intégration

integrator ['ɪntɪgreɪtər] N *Comput* intégrateur *m*

integrity [ɪn'tegrɪtɪ] N **1** *(honesty) (of person)* intégrité *f*, honnêteté *f*, probité *f*; *(of motive)* honnêteté; **woman/man of i.** femme *f*/homme *m* intègre **2** *(wholeness) (of text, computer data)* intégrité *f*

integument [ɪn'tegjʊmənt] N *Biol* tégument *m*

intellect ['ɪntɪlekt] N intelligence *f*, intellect *m*; **a man of i.** un homme intelligent; **he was one of the best intellects of his time** c'était un des plus grands esprits de son époque

intellectual [ɪntɪ'lektjʊəl, -tʃʊəl] ADJ intellectuel
N intellectuel, -elle
► ► *Law* **i. property** propriété *f* intellectuelle

intellectually [ɪntɪ'lektjʊəlɪ, -tʃʊəlɪ] ADV intellectuellement

intelligence [ɪn'telɪdʒəns] N **1** *(mental capacity)* intelligence *f*; *(mind)* esprit *m*; **a person of some i.** une personne assez intelligente; **use your i.!** réfléchis un peu **2** *Mil, Pol (information)* renseignements *mpl*
► ► *Mil, Pol* **i. officer** officier *m* de renseignements; **i. quotient** quotient *m* intellectuel; *Mil, Pol* **i. service** service *m* de renseignements; *Psy* **i. test** test *m* d'aptitude intellectuelle

intelligent [ɪn'telɪdʒənt] ADJ intelligent

intelligently [ɪn'telɪdʒəntlɪ] ADV intelligemment, avec intelligence

intelligentsia [ɪntelɪ'dʒentsɪə] N intelligentsia *f*

intelligibility [ɪntelɪdʒɪ'bɪlɪtɪ] N intelligibilité *f*

intelligible [ɪn'telɪdʒɪb(ə)l] ADJ intelligible; **he was hardly i.** on le comprenait à peine

intelligibly [ɪn'telɪdʒɪblɪ] ADV intelligiblement

intemperance [ɪn'temp(ə)rəns] N intempérance *f*

intemperate [ɪn'temp(ə)rɪt] ADJ *Fml (person)* intempérant; *(climate)* rude; **person of i. habits** personne *f* intempérante; *(exces-*

sive drinker) personne qui s'adonne à la boisson

intend [ɪn'tend] VT **1** *(plan)* **to i. to do sth** avoir l'intention de faire qch, compter faire qch; **was that intended?** était-ce fait à dessein?, était-ce intentionnel?; **the play was intended to shock** la pièce voulait choquer; **that's exactly what I intended** c'était exactement mon intention; **what the author intended and what his readers understood** ce que l'auteur a voulu dire et ce que ses lecteurs ont compris; **I i. to be obeyed** je veux qu'on m'obéisse; **I didn't i. her to see it yet** je ne voulais pas qu'elle le voie déjà; **I intended it as a compliment** mon intention était de vous/lui/etc faire un compliment
2 *(aim, destine)* **a book intended for students** un livre destiné aux étudiants; **this remark is intended for you** cette observation s'adresse à vous

intended [ɪn'tendɪd] ADJ **1** *(hoped-for)* voulu **2** *(intentional)* intentionné
N *Old-fashioned, Hum* **his/her i.** sa fiancée/ son fiancé, sa future/son futur

intense [ɪn'tens] ADJ *(feeling, anxiety)* vif, *f* vive; *(heat, book, colour, activity etc)* intense; *(pain)* vif, intense; *(bombardment, campaign)* intensif; *(hatred)* profond; **i. expression** expression *f* concentrée; **she's too i.** elle est trop sérieuse

intensely [ɪn'tenslɪ] ADV **1** *(greatly) (amusing, entertaining, boring etc)* extrêmement; **it was i. hot** il faisait une chaleur intense; **blue eyes** yeux *mpl* d'un bleu intense **2** *(to look at)* avec intensité, intensément

intensification [ɪntensɪfɪ'keɪʃən] N *(of sound etc)* intensification *f*, *Phot (of negative)* renforcement *m*

intensifier [ɪn'tensɪfaɪər] N *Ling* intensif *m*; *Phot* renforçateur *m*

intensify [ɪn'tensɪfaɪ] VT *(feeling)* intensifier, augmenter, accroître; *(colour)* renforcer
VI s'intensifier, augmenter

intensity [ɪn'tensɪtɪ] N **1** *(of passion, anger)* intensité *f*, *(of pain)* violence *f* **2** *Phys (of sound, current etc)* intensité *f*; *Chem (of reaction)* énergie *f*, *Phot (of negative)* densité *f*

intensive [ɪn'tensɪv] ADJ intensif; *Sch etc* **i. course** cours *m* accéléré
► ► *Med* **i. care** soins *mpl* intensifs; *Med* **to be in i. care** être dans le service de soins intensifs; *Med* **i. care unit** service *m* de soins intensifs; *Mktg* **i. distribution** distribution *f* intensive; *Mktg* **i. distribution strategy** stratégie *f* de distribution intensive; **i. farming** culture *f* intensive

intensively [ɪn'tensɪvlɪ] ADV intensivement

intent [ɪn'tent] N intention *f*, dessein *m*, but *m*; **with good i.** dans une bonne intention; *Law* **with i. to defraud** dans l'intention de frauder; **declaration of i.** déclaration *f* d'intention; **to all intents (and purposes)** quasiment
ADJ **1** **to be i. on doing sth** *(determined)* être résolu ou déterminé à faire qch; **they left i. on murder** ils sont partis, déterminés à commettre un meurtre; **a woman i. on success** une femme déterminée à réussir **2** **to be i. on sth** *(engrossed in)* être tout entier à ou absorbé par qch **3** *(intense) (look)* intense

intention [ɪn'tenʃən] N intention *f*, **I had no i.** or **not the slightest i. of accepting** je n'avais nullement l'intention d'accepter; **to have every i. of doing sth** être résolu à faire qch, avoir la ferme intention de faire qch; **I have every i. of calling her!** *(I won't forget)* j'ai bien l'intention de l'appeler; **was (it) your i. to ...?** est-ce qu'il était de ton intention de ...?; **he acted with the best and most honourable intentions** il a agi en tout bien (et) tout honneur; **her intentions were good** elle avait de bonnes intentions; *Old-fashioned* **his intentions are honourable** *(towards her)* il a l'intention de l'épouser; *Mktg* **i. to buy intention** *f* d'achat; **i.-to-buy scale** échelle *f* des intentions d'achat

intentional [ɪn'tenʃ(ə)l] ADJ intentionnel, voulu; **it wasn't i.** je ne l'ai pas/il ne l'a pas/*etc* fait exprès

intentionally [ɪn'tenʃ(ə)lɪ] ADV intentionnellement; **he didn't do it i.** il ne l'a pas fait exprès *ou* intentionnellement; **I i. didn't invite her** c'est intentionnellement que je ne l'ai pas invitée

intently [ɪn'tentlɪ] ADV *(to listen, look at, study)* attentivement; *(to think)* profondément

inter [ɪn'tɜ:r] VT (-rr-) *Fml (bury)* inhumer, enterrer

interact [ɪntər'ækt] VI *(of chemicals)* interagir; *esp Psy* **to encourage a child to i. with its environment** encourager les échanges d'un enfant avec son environnement; **a situation in which therapist and patient i.** une situation où il y a interaction entre le thérapeute et son patient; **a person who doesn't i. well with others** une personne qui a du mal dans ses rapports avec les autres; **the way the two characters in the novel i.** l'interaction entre les deux personnages dans ce roman

interaction [ɪntər'ækʃən] N interaction *f*

interactive [ɪntər'æktɪv] ADJ interactif
▸▸*Comput* **i. CD** CD-I *m*, disque *m* compact interactif; **i. CD-ROM** CD-ROM *m* interactif; **i. learning** apprentissage *m* interactif; **i. marketing** marketing *m* interactif; **i. television** télévision *f* interactive; *Comput* **i. terminal** terminal *m* (informatique) interactif; **i. video** vidéo *f* interactive

interactiveness, interactivity [ɪntər'æktɪvnɪs, ɪntəræk'tɪvɪtɪ] N interactivité *f*

inter alia ADV *Fml* entre autres

interbank ['ɪntəbæŋk] ADJ ATTRIB interbancaire
▸▸**i. deposit** dépôt *m* interbancaire; **i. loan** prêt *m* de banque à banque *ou* entre banques; **i. market** marché *m* interbancaire; **i. money** argent *m* de gré à gré entre banques; **i. offered rate** taux *m* interbancaire offert; **i. transfer** virement *m* interbancaire

interbreed [ɪntə'bri:d] (*pt, pp* interbred) VT **1** *(breed from same stock)* croiser *(des animaux consanguins)* **2** *(crossbreed)* croiser
VI **1** *(in same family group)* se reproduire entre eux **2** *(crossbreed)* se reproduire par croisement, se croiser

interbreeding [ɪntə'bri:dɪŋ] N **1** *(in same family)* reproduction *f* entre membres d'une même famille; *(of animals)* reproduction par accouplements consanguins **2** *(crossbreeding)* croisement *m*

intercede [ɪntə'si:d] VI intercéder **(with sb** auprès de qn; **for sb, on sb's behalf** en faveur de qn, pour qn)

intercept [ɪntə'sept] VT *(letter, enemy plane, person)*, *Ftbl (pass)* intercepter
VI *Ftbl* intercepter une passe
▸▸*Mktg* **i. interview** entretien *m* spontané

interception [ɪntə'sepʃən] N *(of letter, message etc)*, *Ftbl* interception *f*

interceptor [ɪntə'septər] N **1** *(person) (of message etc)* personne *f* qui intercepte **2** *Aviat, Mil (aircraft)* avion *m* d'interception, intercepteur *m*
▸▸*Aviat, Mil* **i. aircraft** avion d'interception, intercepteur

intercession [ɪntə'seʃən] N intercession *f*

interchange¹ ['ɪntətʃeɪndʒ] N **1** *(of compliments, things, ideas)* échange *m* **2** *Constr (on motorway)* échangeur *m*

interchange² [ɪntə'tʃeɪndʒ] VT *(compliments etc)* échanger (**with** avec); *(two parts of machine etc)* intervertir; **all parts of these machines can be interchanged** toutes les pièces de ces machines sont interchangeables

interchangeable [ɪntə'tʃeɪndʒəb(ə)l] ADJ interchangeable

interchangeably [ɪntə'tʃeɪndʒəblɪ] ADV *(to use)* indifféremment

intercharacter spacing [ɪntə'kærəktə] N *Typ* espacement *m* entre les caractères

inter-city [ɪntə'sɪtɪ] *Br Rail* ADJ *(service, train)* de grandes lignes; **i. travel** déplacements sur les grandes lignes
N *(train)* train *m* de grandes lignes

intercom ['ɪntəkɒm] N *Tel Fam* interphone *m*; **to speak over the i.** parler dans l'interphone

intercommunicate [ɪntəkə'mju:nɪkeɪt] VI *(of rooms etc)* communiquer

intercommunion [ɪntəkə'mju:njən] N *Rel* intercommunion *f*

intercompany [ɪntə'kʌmpənɪ] ADJ interentreprise

interconnect [ɪntəkə'nekt] *Elec, Comput* VT *(circuits, computers)* interconnecter
VI être interconnectés

interconnecting doors [ɪntəkə'nektɪŋ] NPL portes *fpl* de chambres communiquantes

interconnection [ɪntəkə'nekʃən] N *Elec, Comput* interconnexion *f*

intercontinental [ɪntəkɒntɪ'nent(ə)l] ADJ intercontinental, -aux
▸▸*Mil* **i. ballistic missile** missile *m* balistique intercontinental

intercooled ['ɪntəku:ld] ADJ *(engine)* refroidi

intercooler ['ɪntəku:lər] N *Aut* intercooler *m*, refroidisseur *m* intermédiaire

intercostal [ɪntə'kɒst(ə)l] ADJ *Anat* intercostal, -aux

intercourse ['ɪntəkɔ:s] N **1** *(sexual)* **i.** rapports *mpl* sexuels; **to have i. with sb** avoir des rapports sexuels avec qn **2** *Old-fashioned (dealings)* commerce *m*, relations *fpl*, rapports *mpl*; **social i.** la fréquentation du monde

intercut [ɪntə'kʌt] VT *TV, Cin* insérer
▸▸**i. shot** plan *m* de coupe

interdenominational ['ɪntədɪnɒmɪ'neɪʃən(ə)l] ADJ *Rel* interconfessionnel

interdepartmental ['ɪntədɪpɑ:t'ment(ə)l] ADJ *(in company)* entre différents services; *(in university)* entre différents départements

interdependence [ɪntədɪ'pendəns] N interdépendance *f*

interdependent [ɪntədɪ'pendənt] ADJ interdépendant

interdict¹ ['ɪntədɪkt] N **1** *Law* défense *f*, interdiction *f* **2** *Rel* interdit *m*

interdict² [ɪntə'dɪkt] VT **1** *Law* interdire, prohiber **2** *Rel (town)* frapper d'interdit; *(priest)* interdire, frapper d'interdit

interdiction [ɪntə'dɪkʃən] N **1** *(action)* interdiction *f* **2** *(result) Law* interdiction *f*, *Rel* interdit *m*

interdisciplinary [ɪntə'dɪsɪplɪnərɪ] ADJ interdisciplinaire

INTEREST ['ɪnt(ə)rɪst] N **1** *(curiosity)* intérêt *m* (**in** à); **to take/have an i. in sb/sth** s'intéresser à qn/qch; **to show an i. in sth** montrer un intérêt pour qch; **her i. in Latin America** son intérêt pour l'Amérique latine; **to take no further i. in sth, to lose i. in sth** se désintéresser de qch; **two people have shown an i. in (buying) the house** deux personnes sont intéressées par la maison; **there's little**

i. in these old chairs nowadays on ne s'intéresse pas beaucoup à ces vieilles chaises de nos jours
2 *(interesting aspect)* intérêt *m*; **this may be of i. to you** ceci peut vous intéresser; **what he does is of no i. to me** ça ne m'intéresse pas de savoir ce qu'il fait; **there was little of i. on television** il n'y avait pas grand-chose d'intéressant à la télévision; **buildings of historical/architectural i.** bâtiments d'intérêt historique/architectural; **a little garlic will give i. to a stew** l'ail donnera un peu de piquant aux ragoûts
3 *(activity, subject of interest)* **I have many interests** beaucoup de choses m'intéressent; **her interests include skiing and photography** le ski et la photographie font partie de ses centres d'intérêt
4 *(participation)* intérêt *m*, participation *f*; **to have a direct i. in sth** être concerné directement par qch; **I have no financial i. in the business** je ne suis pas intéressé dans cette entreprise; **to have a controlling i. in a company** avoir une participation majoritaire dans une société; **his i. in the company is £10,000** il a une commandite de 10 000 livres
5 *(group)* **the oil/steel interests in the country** l'industrie pétrolière/sidérurgique du pays
6 *(benefit)* intérêt *m*, avantage *m*; **the public i.** l'intérêt public; **it would not be in the public i.** ça ne serait pas dans l'intérêt public; **to act in/against one's (own) interest(s)** agir dans/contre son propre intérêt; **to act in sb's best interest(s)** agir dans l'intérêt de qn; **we look after British interests** nous défendons les intérêts britanniques; **it's in my i. to do it** c'est dans mon intérêt de le faire; **it's not in their i. to offend her** ce n'est pas dans leur intérêt de l'offenser, ils n'ont pas intérêt à l'offenser; **in the interests of justice/peace** dans l'intérêt de la justice/paix; **in the interests of safety/hygiene** par mesure de sécurité/d'hygiène; **in the interests of accuracy** pour être tout à fait précis
7 *Fin* intérêt(s) *m(pl)*; **i. on arrears** intérêt de retard; **i. on capital** rémunération *f* de capital; **to pay i. on a loan** payer des intérêts sur un prêt; **to bear** *or* **yield i.** porter intérêt *ou* des intérêts; **to yield 5% i.** rapporter du 5% *ou* un intérêt de 5%; **i. accrued** fraction *f* d'intérêt; **i. due** intérêts dus *ou* exigibles; **i. due and payable** intérêts exigibles; **i. paid** intérêts versés; **i. payable** intérêt exigible; **i. received** produits financiers, intérêts perçus; *Fig* **to repay an injury with i.** rendre le mal avec usure

VT intéresser; **we couldn't i. her in the idea** nous ne sommes pas parvenus à susciter son intérêt pour cette idée; **we couldn't i. her in a game of cards** nous n'avons pas réussi à la convaincre de venir jouer aux cartes avec nous; **can I i. you in a drink?** puis-je vous proposer un verre?; **it might i. you to learn** *or* **know that …** ça t'intéressera peut-être d'apprendre *ou* de savoir que …
▸▸*Fin* **i. charges** intérêts (à payer); *Banking (on overdraft)* agios *mpl*; *Fin* **i. days** jours *mpl* d'intérêt; *Fin* **i. and dividend income** produits *mpl* financiers; **i. group** groupe *m* d'intérêt; *Fin* **i. payment date** date *f* d'écheance des intérêts; *Fin* **i. rate** taux *m* d'intérêt; *St Exch* **i. rate differential** differentiel *m* de taux; *St Exch* **i. rate swap** échange *m* de taux d'intérêt

interest-bearing ADJ *Banking* productif d'intérêts, qui produit des intérêts
▸▸*Banking* **i. account** compte *m* rémunéré; **i. capital** capital *m* productif d'intérêts; **i. loan** prêt *m* à intérêt; *St Exch* **i. securities** titres *mpl* qui produisent des intérêts

interested ['ɪnt(ə)rɪstɪd] ADJ **1** *(curious)* in-

téressé; **to be i. in painting/music** s'intéresser à la peinture/à la musique; **I am not i.** cela ne m'intéresse pas; **he wasn't i.** *(in the offer, suggestion)* il n'était pas intéressé, ça ne l'intéressait pas; **anyone i.?** il y en a que ça intéresse?, est-ce que quelqu'un est intéressé?; **I should be i. to hear the end of the story** je serais curieux d'apprendre la fin de l'histoire **2** *(involved)* intéressé; **to act from i. motives** agir par calcul
▸▸ *Law* **i. party** ayant droit *m, pl* ayants droit; **the i. parties** les parties *fpl* intéressées

interest-free ADJ *(credit)* gratuit; *(loan)* sans intérêt

interesting ['ɪnt(ə)rɪstɪŋ] ADJ *(book, job etc)* intéressant

interestingly ['ɪnt(ə)rɪstɪŋlɪ] ADV de façon intéressante; **i. enough ...** ce qui est intéressant c'est que ...; **i., a number of her supporters voted against her** il est intéressant de noter qu'un certain nombre de ses partisans ont voté contre elle

interface ['ɪntəfeɪs] N *Comput, Fig* interface *f,* **the patient-doctor i.** les relations médecin-patient; **the extent of the i. between these two subjects** l'étendue des rapports entre ces deux sujets
VI *Comput* avoir une interface (**with** avec); **this device interfaces with most PCs** ce dispositif permet une interface avec la plupart des ordinateurs individuels
VT *Comput (two computers)* mettre en interface, interfacer
▸▸ *Comput* **i. bus** bus *m* d'interface; *Comput* **i. cable** câble *m* de connexion; *Comput* **i. card** carte *f* d'interface; *Comput* **i. switching** *(on laser printer)* commutation *f* d'interface

interfacing ['ɪntəfeɪsɪŋ] N **1** *Comput* interfaçage *m* **2** *Sewing* entoilage *m*

interfere [ɪntə'fɪər] VI **1** *(of person)* s'ingérer, s'immiscer, intervenir (**in a matter** dans une affaire); *(in quarrel)* s'interposer; **to i. in sb's affairs** se mêler des affaires de qn; **don't i. in what doesn't concern you** ne vous mêlez pas de ce qui ne vous regarde pas; **he's always interfering** il fourre son nez partout, il est toujours à se mêler de ce qui ne le regarde pas; **do not i. with the doors** ne pas gêner la fermeture des portes; **someone has interfered with the clock** on a touché à la pendule; *Euph* **was she interfered with?** *(sexually)* est-ce qu'on a abusé d'elle?
2 *(of thing)* **to i. with** *(sb's plans)* gêner, contrarier; *(traffic, person's movements)* gêner, entraver; *(progress of business)* entraver; **pleasure should not be allowed to i. with business** il ne faut pas que les plaisirs empiètent sur les affaires
3 *Phys etc* interférer; *Chem* perturber; *Electron, Radio* **to i. with a signal** brouiller *ou* parasiter un signal

interference [ɪntə'fɪərəns] N **1** *(by person)* intervention *f,* intrusion *f,* ingérence *f* (**in** dans); *Sport (from opponent)* obstruction *f* **2** *Phys* interférence *f,* *Chem* perturbation *f,* *Electron, Radio* interférence(s) *f*, parasite(s) *m(pl)*, brouillage *m*
▸▸ *Opt* **i. figure, i. pattern** figure *f* d'interférence

interfering [ɪntə'fɪərɪŋ] ADJ *(person)* importun, qui se mêle de ce qui ne le regarde pas; **he's so i.** il fourre son nez partout

interferon [ɪntə'fɪərɒn] N *Biol* interféron *m*

interim ['ɪntərɪm] N **in the i.** entre-temps
ADJ *(government, report etc)* intérimaire; **the i. period** l'intérim *m*
▸▸ *Acct* **i. accounts** comptes *mpl* semestriels; *Fin* **i. dividend** dividende *m* intérimaire; *Law* **i. order** avant faire-droit *m inv*; *Acct* **i. profit and loss statement** compte *m* de résultat prévisionnel; **i. report** rapport

m intérimaire; *Acct* **i. statement** bilan *m* intérimaire

interior [ɪn'tɪərɪər] ADJ *(side, trade)* intérieur; *(regions etc)* de l'intérieur; *Math (angle)* interne
N **1** *(of country, region, building)* intérieur *m* **2** *Art* (tableau *m* d')intérieur *m* **3** *Cin, TV* intérieur *m*
▸▸ **i. decoration** décoration *f* (d'intérieurs); **i. decorator** décorateur, -trice (d'intérieurs); *Liter* **i. monologue** monologue *m* intérieur; *TV, Cin* **i. shot** intérieur, scène *f* d'intérieur; *Aut* **i. trim** habillage *m* intérieur

interior-sprung ADJ *(mattress)* à ressorts

interject [ɪntə'dʒekt] VT *(remark etc)* lancer; *(protest)* émettre

interjection [ɪntə'dʒekʃən] N **1** *(action) (of remark etc)* action *f* de lancer; *(of protest)* action d'émettre **2** *(word, phrase)* interjection *f*

interlace [ɪntə'leɪs] VT *(wires, branches)* entrecroiser; *(speech etc)* entremêler (**with** de)
VI s'entrelacer, s'entrecroiser

interlaced [ɪntə'leɪst] ADJ *Comput (display, monitor)* entrelacé

interlard [ɪntə'lɑːd] VT *(speech, story)* entrelarder (**with** de)

interleave [ɪntə'liːv] VT *(book)* interfolier; *(sheets)* intercaler

interlibrary [ɪntə'laɪbrərɪ] ADJ interbibliothèque

interline [ɪntə'laɪn] VT **1** *Typ (document, manuscript)* interligner **2** *Sewing* mettre une doublure intermédiaire à
▸▸ *Typ* **i. spacing** interligne *m*

interlinear [ɪntə'lɪnɪər] ADJ *(text)* interlinéaire

interlining ['ɪntəlaɪnɪŋ] N *Sewing* doublure *f* intermédiaire

interlock [ɪntə'lɒk] VT *(mechanism)* enclencher; *(cogs)* engrener; *(parts of mechanism)* emboîter; *(fingers)* entrelacer
VI *(of mechanism)* s'enclencher; *(of parts)* s'emboîter

interlocking [ɪntə'lɒkɪŋ] ADJ *(parts)* emboîtable; *Tech (gears)* qui s'engrènent *ou* s'enclenchent

interlocutor [ɪntə'lɒkjutər] N *Fml* interlocuteur, -trice

interloper ['ɪntələupər] N intrus, -use

interlude ['ɪntəluːd] N *Theat, Fig* intermède *m*; *TV* interlude *m*; **musical i.** interlude *ou* intermède musical

intermarriage [ɪntə'mærɪdʒ] N *(between families etc)* mariage *m* (entre les membres de différentes familles, castes, races, etc); *(within a family)* mariage consanguin

intermarry [ɪntə'mærɪ] VI *(between families etc)* se marier (entre membres de différentes familles/castes/races/etc); *(within a family)* se marier entre membres d'une même famille; **they began to i.** ils commencèrent à se marier entre eux

intermediary [ɪntə'miːdɪərɪ] N intermédiaire *mf,* **to act as i.** servir d'intermédiaire
ADJ intermédiaire

intermediate [ɪntə'miːdɪət] ADJ *(size etc)* intermédiaire; *Sch (class etc)* (de niveau) moyen;
▸▸ *Fin* **i. broker** intermédiaire *mf,* remisier *m* (en Bourse); *Fin* **i. credit** crédit *m* à moyen terme; *Elec* **i. frequency** fréquence *f* moyenne; **i. goods** biens *mpl* intermédiaires; **i.-range nuclear forces** forces *fpl* nucléaires intermédiaires; **i. stops** *(during journey)* arrêts *mpl* intermédiaires; **i. technology** technologie *f* intermédiaire

interment [ɪn'tɜːmənt] N enterrement *m,* inhumation *f*

intermezzo [ɪntə'metsəʊ] N *Mus, Theat* intermezzo *m*

interminable [ɪn'tɜːmɪnəb(ə)l] ADJ interminable

interminably [ɪn'tɜːmɪnəblɪ] ADV interminablement

intermingle [ɪntə'mɪŋg(ə)l] VT entremêler (**with** de); *(colours)* mélanger
VI se mêler (**with** à), se mélanger (**with** avec)

intermission [ɪntə'mɪʃən] N **1** *Cin, Theat, Mus etc* entracte *m* **2** *(pause)* interruption *f,* pause *f,* *Med (in fever)* intermission *f,* **without i.** sans arrêt

intermittent [ɪntə'mɪtənt] ADJ intermittent;
▸▸ *Aut* **i. facility** *(of wipers)* intermittence *f*

intermittently [ɪntə'mɪtəntlɪ] ADV par intermittence, de façon intermittente

intermodal [ɪntə'məʊdəl] ADJ *Can (transport etc)* intermodal, -aux
▸▸ **i. travel** voyages *mpl* par différents moyens de transport

intern[1] ['ɪntɜːn] N *Am (in hospital)* interne *mf,* *(in company)* stagiaire *mf*

intern[2] [ɪn'tɜːn] VT interner

internal [ɪn'tɜːn(ə)l] ADJ **1** intérieur, interne; *Med (haemorrhage, organ, ear etc)* interne; *(disorder)* organique; **the i. workings of the mind** les opérations *fpl* secrètes de l'esprit **2** *(within a country) (trade)* intérieur; *(legislation)* national, -aux, interne; *(within a company)* interne **3** *(value, proof)* intrinsèque
▸▸ **i. affairs** affaires *fpl* internes; *Fin* **i. audit** audit *m* interne; *Fin* **i. auditor** audit interne, auditeur, -trice interne; *Tel* **i. cable** câble *m* d'immeuble; *Tech* **i. combustion engine** moteur *m* à combustion interne, moteur *m* à explosion; *Comput* **i. command** commande *f* interne; **i. company document** document *m* interne à l'entreprise; *Comput* **i. drive** unité *f* (de disque) interne; *Univ* **i. exam** examen *m* propre à une université; *Univ* **i. examiner** examinateur, -trice *(faisant passer un examen dans son propre établissement)*; *Pol* **i. exile** exil *m*; **i. flight** vol *m* intérieur; **i. injuries** lésions *fpl* internes; **i. mail** courrier *m* interne; **i. marketing** marketing *m* interne; *Comput* **i. modem** modem *m* interne; **i. promotion** promotion *f* interne; *Fin* **i. rate of return** taux *m* de rentabilité interne; *Fin* **i. revenue** recettes *fpl* fiscales; **i. security** sécurité *f* intérieure; **i. student** étudiant, -ante d'une université; **i. telephone** téléphone *m* intérieur; **i. travel** voyages *mpl* à l'intérieur d'un même pays

internalize [ɪn'tɜːnəlaɪz] VT intérioriser

internally [ɪn'tɜːn(ə)lɪ] ADV intérieurement; *Pharm* **not to be taken i.** à usage externe

international [ɪntə'næʃən(ə)l] ADJ international, -aux
N **1** *Sport (player)* (joueur, -euse) international, -ale; *(match)* match *m* international **2** *Pol, Hist* **the I.** l'Internationale *f*
▸▸ **I. Air Transport Association** Association *f* internationale de transport aérien; *Law* **I. Chamber of Commerce** chambre *f* de commerce internationale; **I. Court of Justice** cour *f* internationale de justice; *Law* **I. Criminal Court** Cour *f* pénale internationale; **the I. Date Line** la ligne de changement de date; *Br* **i. dialling code**, *Am* **i. dial code** indicatif *m* du pays; *Ind* **I. Labour Organization** Organisation *f* internationale du travail; *Law* **i. law** droit *m* international; *Fin* **I. Monetary Fund** Fonds *m* monétaire international; *Fin* **i. monetary reserves** réserves *fpl* monétaires internationales; *Fin* **i. money market** marché *m* monétaire international; *Fin* **i. money order** mandat *m* international; **i. reply coupon**

coupon-réponse *m* international, *pl* coupons-réponse internationaux; **i. socialism** socialisme *m* international; **the I. Standards Organization** l'organisation *f* internationale de normalisation; **i. tourism destination** destination *f* touristique internationale; *Am* **I. Trade Commission** = organisme *m* fédéral américain traitant de questions de commerce international; **i. trade fair** foire *f* internationale; **I. Trade Organization** Organisation internationale du commerce; *Com* **i. trading corporation** société *f* de commerce international, SCI *f*

internationalism [ɪntəˈnæʃənəlɪz(ə)m] N internationalisme *m*

internationalize [ɪntəˈnæʃənəlaɪz] VT internationaliser

internationally [ɪntəˈnæʃənəlɪ] ADV internationalement; **an i. recognized qualification** un diplôme reconnu sur le plan international

internaut [ˈɪntənɔːt] N *Comput* internaute *mf*

interne [ˈɪntɜːn] N *Am* = **intern**[1]

internecine [ɪntəˈniːsaɪn] ADJ de destruction réciproque

internee [ɪntɜːˈniː] N interné, -ée

Internet [ˈɪntənɛt] N *Comput* Internet *m*; **on the I.** sur Internet
▸▸ **I. access** accès *m* (à l') Internet; **I. access provider** fournisseur *m* d'accès à l'Internet; **I. account** compte *m* Internet; **I. address** adresse *f* Internet; **I. banking** banque *f* par Internet, services *mpl* bancaires en ligne; **I. café** cybercafé *m*; **I. chat room** site *m* de bavardage, salon *m*; **I. connection** connexion *f* à l'Internet; **I. number** numéro *m* Internet; **I. phone** téléphone *m* Internet; **I. presence provider** = fournisseur d'accès à l'Internet proposant l'hébergement de sites Web; **I. protocol** protocole *m* Internet; **I. relay chat** service *m* de bavardage Internet, canal *m* de dialogue en direct; **I. service provider** fournisseur d'accès à l'Internet; **I. Society** = organisation *f* non gouvernementale chargée de veiller à l'évolution de l'Internet; **I. surfer** internaute *mf*; **I. surfing** navigation *f* sur l'Internet; **I. telephone** téléphone Internet; **I. telephony** téléphonie *f* sur l'Internet; **I. TV** télévision *f* par Internet; **I. user** internaute *mf*

internist [ɪnˈtɜːnɪst] N *esp Am Med* spécialiste *mf* des maladies organiques

internment [ɪnˈtɜːnmənt] N internement *m*
▸▸ **i. camp** camp *m* d'internement

internship [ˈɪntɜːnʃɪp] N *Am Med (position)* internat *m*

interpenetrate [ɪntəˈpɛnɪtreɪt] VI s'interpénétrer

interpenetration [ɪntəpɛnɪˈtreɪʃən] N interpénétration *f*

interpersonal [ɪntəˈpɜːsən(ə)l] ADJ interpersonnel

interplanetary [ɪntəˈplænɪt(ə)rɪ] ADJ interplanétaire

interplay [ˈɪntəpleɪ] N interaction *f*

Interpol [ˈɪntəpɒl] N Interpol *m*

interpolate [ɪnˈtɜːpəleɪt] VT **1** *(insert) (remark, question)* glisser; *(word, passage)* intercaler; **interpolated sheet** *(in bookbinding)* feuille *f* intercalaire **2** *(change) (text)* altérer par interpolation

interpolation [ɪntɜːpəˈleɪʃən] N *(remark)* remarque *f* glissée dans un discours; *(question)* question *f* glissée dans un discours; *(word, passage)* mot *m*/passage *m* intercalé dans un texte; *(intended to change meaning)* interpolation *f*

interpose [ɪntəˈpəʊz] VT interposer; **to i. a remark** *(in conversation)* faire une observation

interpret [ɪnˈtɜːprɪt] VT interpréter; **to i. sb's words as a threat** interpréter les paroles de qn comme une menace
VI faire l'interprète; **can you i. for me?** est-ce que vous pouvez me servir d'interprète?

interpretation [ɪntɜːprɪˈteɪʃən] N interprétation *f*; **to put the wrong i. on sth** donner une fausse interprétation à qch; **she wasn't sure what i. to put on the remarks** elle ne savait pas trop comment elle devait interpréter ces remarques;
▸▸ *Can* **i. centre** *(at historic site etc)* = centre *m* d'accueil et de documentation pour les visiteurs d'un site touristique

interpretative [ɪnˈtɜːprɪtətɪv] ADJ interprétatif

interpreter [ɪnˈtɜːprɪtər] N **1** *(person)* interprète *mf*; **to act as i.** servir d'interprète **2** *Comput (program)* interpréteur *m*

interpreting [ɪnˈtɜːprɪtɪŋ] N *(occupation)* interprétation *f*

interpretive [ɪnˈtɜːprɪtɪv] ADJ interprétatif
▸▸ **i. centre** = centre *m* d'accueil et de documentation pour les visiteurs d'un site touristique

interracial [ɪntəˈreɪʃəl] ADJ *(marriage, conflict etc)* entre des races différentes

interregnum [ɪntəˈrɛgnəm], *pl* **interregnums, interregna** [-əmz, -ə] N interrègne *m*

interrelated [ɪntərɪˈleɪtɪd] ADJ *(facts)* étroitement liés, en corrélation; **i. costs** coûts *mpl* interdépendants; **i. demand** demande *f* en rapport

interrelation [ɪntərɪˈleɪʃən] N corrélation *f*

interrogate [ɪnˈtɛrəgeɪt] VT *(person)* interroger, questionner; *(of police)* faire subir un interrogatoire à; *Comput (database)* interroger

interrogation [ɪntɛrəˈgeɪʃən] N interrogatoire *m*; *Comput (of database)* interrogation *f*; **under i.** en train de subir un interrogatoire;
▸▸ *Mil* **i. centre** *(for prisoners of war)* centre *m* d'interrogatoires; *Gram* **i. mark,** *Am* **i. point** point *m* d'interrogation

Note that the primary sense of **interrogation** in English, as in a police interrogation, is translated by **interrogatoire** and not **interrogation**.

interrogative [ɪntəˈrɒgətɪv] ADJ **1** *(tone, look etc)* interrogateur, -trice **2** *Gram (pronoun etc)* interrogatif
N *Gram (pronoun etc)* interrogatif *m*; *(symbol)* point *m* d'interrogation VOIR GRAMMAIRE A31–2; B16–18

interrogatively [ɪntəˈrɒgətɪvlɪ] ADV interrogativement; d'un air interrogateur

interrogator [ɪnˈtɛrəgeɪtər] N interrogateur, -trice

interrogatory [ɪntəˈrɒgətərɪ] ADJ *(tone, look etc)* interrogateur, -trice

interrupt[1] [ɪntəˈrʌpt] VT **1** *(stop) (action, conversation etc)* interrompre; **am I interrupting something?** est-ce que je vous dérange?; **to i. sb** interrompre qn, couper la parole à qn **2** *(block) (rail etc services)* interrompre; *(communications, supplies)* couper; *(electrical circuit)* interrompre; *(rhythm)* rompre; *(view)* gêner
VI interrompre; **don't i.!** *(when I'm talking)* ne me coupe pas la parole!, ne m'interromps pas!; *(when sb is talking)* ne coupe pas la parole aux gens!, n'interromps pas les gens!; **I'm sorry to i.** *(intrude)* je suis désolé de vous interrompre

interrupt[2] [ˈɪntərʌpt] N *Comput* interruption *f*
▸▸ **i. function** fonction *f* d'interruption

interruption [ɪntəˈrʌpʃən] N interruption *f*, **without i.** sans interruption; **I want no more**

interruptions *(let me finish speaking)* je ne veux plus qu'on m'interrompe; *(leave me in peace)* je ne veux plus être dérangé

interscholastic [ɪntəskəˈlæstɪk] ADJ interscolaire, inter-écoles

intersect [ɪntəˈsɛkt] VT *(of street)* croiser; **Maple Street is intersected by Elm Avenue** Maple Street et Elm Avenue se croisent; **line that intersects another** ligne qui en coupe une autre; **to i. one another** *(of lines, surfaces)* se couper, s'entrecroiser
VI *(of lines)* se couper; *(of streets)* se croiser

intersection [ɪntəˈsɛkʃən] N **1** *Math (of two planes etc)* intersection *f*; **(point of) i.** point *m* d'intersection **2** *esp Am (of roads)* croisement *m*

interspace [ˈɪntəspeɪs] VT *Typ* espacer

intersperse [ɪntəˈspɜːs] VT parsemer *(with* de); **to i. a speech with quotations** émailler un discours de citations; **plain-clothes officers were interspersed in the crowd** des policiers en civil étaient dispersés dans la foule; **carnations are interspersed among the roses** les roses sont parsemées d'œillets; **there will be sunshine interspersed with showers** il y aura une alternance d'averses et d'éclaircies

interstate [ˈɪntəsteɪt] ADJ *(commerce etc) (in United States, Australia etc)* entre États
N *Am Aut* autoroute *f*
▸▸ **i. carrier** transporteur *m* inter-État

interstellar [ɪntəˈstɛlər] ADJ *Astron* interstellaire

interstice [ɪnˈtɜːstɪs] N interstice *m*

intertextual [ɪntəˈtɛkstjʊəl] ADJ intertextuel

intertextuality [ɪntətɛkstjʊˈælətɪ] N intertextualité *f*

intertribal [ɪntəˈtraɪb(ə)l] ADJ entre tribus

intertwine [ɪntəˈtwaɪn] VT entrelacer; **his fate seemed intertwined with hers** son destin semblait lié au sien
VI s'entrelacer; **she found them intertwined** elle les a trouvés enlacés dans les bras l'un de l'autre

interurban [ɪntərˈɜːbən] ADJ interurbain

interval [ˈɪntəvəl] N **1** *(time)* intervalle *m*; *esp Br Theat, Cin* entracte *m*; *Ftbl etc* mi-temps *f inv*, pause *f*; **it rained at intervals** il a plu par intervalles; **I completed the job at intervals over a period of two months** j'ai effectué le travail en plusieurs fois sur une période de deux mois; **I saw him at intervals during my stay** je l'ai vu de temps en temps au cours de mon séjour; **at regular intervals** à intervalles réguliers; **at five-minute intervals, at intervals of five minutes** toutes les cinq minutes; **rainy weather with bright intervals** temps pluvieux avec éclaircies; **after an i. of time** après un certain temps; **an hour's i. between two lectures** une heure de battement entre deux conférences
2 *(space)* écart *m*, espace *m*, intervalle *m*; **at two-metre intervals** à deux mètres d'écart, à un intervalle de deux mètres; **there are trees growing at regular intervals along the road** des arbres jalonnent la route
3 *Mus* intervalle *m*

intervene [ɪntəˈviːn] VI **1** *(take action)* intervenir *(in* dans); **the government intervened to save the company** le gouvernement est intervenu pour sauver l'entreprise **2** *(of event)* survenir; **the war intervened** la guerre est survenue; **ten years intervened** dix ans s'écoulèrent

intervening [ɪntəˈviːnɪŋ] ADJ *(period)* intermédiaire; **during the i. period** entre-temps; **the i. events** les événements qui survinrent entre-temps *ou* dans l'intervalle; **during the i. week** pendant la semaine qui s'écoula entre-temps

intervention [ɪntə'venʃən] N *(by government, individual etc)* intervention *f*
 ►► *Econ* i. price prix *m* d'intervention; *Fin* i. rate taux *m* d'intervention

interventionism [ɪntə'venʃənɪz(ə)m] N interventionnisme *m*

interventionist [ɪntə'venʃənɪst] ADJ interventionniste
 N interventionniste *mf*

interview ['ɪntəvjuː] N **1** *(for job, place at university etc)* entrevue *f*, entretien *m*; *(in survey etc)* entretien; **a job i., an i. for a job** un entretien pour un emploi; **to invite sb to an** *or* **for (an) i.** convoquer qn à un entretien **2** *Journ, TV* interview *f*; **he rarely gives interviews** il donne *ou* accorde rarement des interviews
 VT **1** *(for job, place at university etc)* faire passer un entretien *ou* une entrevue à; *(in survey)* interroger, enquêter; *(criminal, suspect etc)* interroger; **who interviewed you?** qui t'a fait passer l'entretien?; **she's being interviewed tomorrow** elle est convoquée pour un entretien demain **2** *Journ, TV* interviewer
 VI **1** *(of job interviewer etc)* faire passer des entretiens; **he doesn't i. well** *(of job candidate etc)* il n'est pas très bon aux entretiens **2** *Journ, TV* **the new Minister interviews well** le nouveau ministre passe bien aux interviews

interviewee [ɪntəvjuː'iː] N *Journ, TV* personne *f* interviewée; *(for job)* candidat, -ate *(à qui l'on fait passer un entretien)*

interviewer ['ɪntəvjuːər] N *Journ, TV etc* interviewer *m*, intervieweur, -euse; *(for research, in canvassing)* enquêteur, -euse; **her skills as an i.** *(of job applicants)* ses qualités pour faire passer les entretiens *ou* pour examiner les candidats

inter-war ['ɪntə'wɔːr] ADJ **the i. years** *or* **period** l'entre-deux-guerres *m*; **i. politics** la politique de l'entre-deux-guerres

interweave [ɪntə'wiːv] *(pt* **interwove** [ɪntə'wəʊv]*, pp* **interwoven** [ɪntə'wəʊv(ə)n]*)* VT **1** *Tex (gold thread with wool etc)* tisser ensemble; *(branches etc)* entrelacer; **material interwoven with gold threads** tissu broché d'or **2** *Fig (stories)* mêler; **to i. sth into sth** mêler qch à qch; **closely interwoven systems** systèmes étroitement liés l'un à l'autre
 VI *(of branches)* s'entrelacer; *Fig (of stories, narratives)* s'entremêler

interword spacing [ɪntə'wɜːd] N *Typ* espacement *m* entre les mots

intestate [ɪn'testeɪt] *Jur* ADJ intestat *inv*; **she died i.** elle est morte intestat; **i. estate** *or* **succession** succession *f* ab intestat
 N intestat *mf*

intestinal [ɪntes'taɪn(ə)l, ɪn'testɪn(ə)l] ADJ *Anat* intestinal, -aux

intestine [ɪn'testɪn] N *Anat* intestin *m*; **the large i.** le gros intestin; **the small i.** l'intestin grêle

intimacy ['ɪntɪməsɪ] N **1** intimité *f*; **in the i. of the family** dans l'intimité de la famille **2** *(intimate remark etc)* familiarité *f* **3** *Fml (sexual intercourse)* rapports *mpl* sexuels; **evidence that i. took place** preuves *fpl* de relations intimes

intimate¹ ['ɪntɪmɪt] ADJ *(friendship, friend, restaurant etc)* intime; **they're very i.** ils sont très intimes; **a few i. friends** quelques intimes; **the i. nature of their conversation** la nature intime de leur conversation; **to be i. with sb** *(know well)* être intime avec qn; *Fml (have sexual intercourse)* avoir des relations intimes avec qn; **to have an i. knowledge of sth** avoir une connaissance approfondie de qch
 N intime *mf*

intimate² ['ɪntɪmeɪt] VT **1** *(suggest, hint at)* laisser entendre **(sth to sb** qch à qn) **2** *Fml (make known) (order)* intimer; *(one's intentions)* signifier; **to i. sth to sb** notifier qch à qn

intimately ['ɪntɪmətlɪ] ADV intimement; **i. connected** étroitement lié; **to know sb i.** *(well)* connaître qn intimement

intimation [ɪntɪ'meɪʃən] N **1** *Fml (hint)* indication *f*; **she gave me no i. of her intentions** elle ne m'a rien laissé entrevoir de ses intentions; **they had no i. of the difficulties ahead** ils étaient loin de se représenter les difficultés qui les attendaient **2** *Arch (notice)* **an i. of death** un avis de décès

intimidate [ɪn'tɪmɪdeɪt] VT intimider; **I'm not going to be intimidated by her** je ne vais pas me laisser intimider par elle; **to i. sb into doing sth** intimider qn pour qu'il fasse qch

intimidating [ɪn'tɪmɪdeɪtɪŋ] ADJ intimidant

intimidation [ɪntɪmɪ'deɪʃən] N intimidation *f*; *Law* menaces *fpl*

into ['ɪntʊ, 'ɪntə] PREP VOIR GRAMMAIRE A70–1 **1** *(motion, direction)* dans; **to go i. a house** entrer dans une maison; **to fall i. the hands of the enemy** tomber entre les mains de l'ennemi *ou* aux mains de l'ennemi; **the door opens i. the garden** la porte donne sur le jardin; **to come i. a property** *(by inheritance)* hériter d'un bien; **to get i. difficulties** s'attirer des ennuis; **to walk i. a door/sb** rentrer dans une porte/qn; **to cut i. a piece of cheese** couper dans un morceau de fromage; **to speak i. a microphone** parler dans un micro; **I'd like to get i. television** j'aimerais bien rentrer *ou* entrer à la télévision
 2 *(change, result)* en; **to change sth i. sth** changer *ou* transformer qch en qch; **to grow i. a man** devenir un homme; **to divide i. four** diviser en quatre; **to break sth i. pieces** briser qch en morceaux; **to burst i. tears** fondre en larmes; **to go i. a coma** tomber dans le coma; **they cajoled her i. agreeing** ils lui ont arraché son accord à force de cajoleries
 3 *(with time, age etc)* **to work far i. the night** travailler très tard dans la nuit; **he was well i. his sixties before he retired** il avait la soixantaine bien sonnée quand il est parti à la retraite; **it was well i. January before we got any snow** le mois de janvier était bien entamé quand nous avons eu la première neige
 4 *Math* **three i. six goes two** six divisé par trois font deux
 5 *Fam* **to be i. sb/sth** *(like)* bien aimer qn/qch; **he's i. drugs** *(uses)* il se drogue; **he's really i. her/jogging/French cooking** il est fou d'elle/de jogging/de cuisine française; **she's i. the green movement** elle est à fond *ou* elle donne à fond dans le mouvement écolo; **I'm not i. computers/wearing ties** l'informatique/les cravates, ce n'est pas mon truc; **I'm not really i. that sort of thing** ces choses-là, ce n'est pas mon truc; **I'm not i. computers the way you are** je ne suis pas aussi amateur d'informatique que toi; **we're not i. cheating people** *(that's not our style)* nous ne cherchons pas à rouler les gens; **if that's what you're i.!** si c'est ton truc!
 6 *Am (in debt to)* **he's i. them for $5,000** il leur doit cinq mille dollars

intolerable [ɪn'tɒlərəb(ə)l] ADJ intolérable, insupportable

intolerably [ɪn'tɒlərəblɪ] ADV *(boring, vain)* insupportablement; **it was i. hot** il faisait une chaleur intolérable *ou* insupportable; **they are i. rude** ils sont d'une grossièreté intolérable *ou* insupportable

intolerance [ɪn'tɒlərəns] N intolérance *f* *(of, towards* à l'égard de); *Med* **i. of a drug/**foodstuff intolérance à un remède/un aliment

intolerant [ɪn'tɒlərənt] ADJ intolérant *(of* à l'égard de); **to be very i.** être d'une extrême intolérance; *Med* **to be i. of a drug** ne pas tolérer *ou* supporter un médicament

intolerantly [ɪn'tɒlərəntlɪ] ADV avec intolérance, de façon intolérante

intonation [ɪntə'neɪʃən] N intonation *f*

intone [ɪn'təʊn] VT **1** *(speak)* débiter **2** *Rel (litany)* psalmodier

intoxicate [ɪn'tɒksɪkeɪt] VT *(make drunk)* enivrer, rendre ivre; *Fig* griser

intoxicated [ɪn'tɒksɪkeɪtɪd] ADJ *(drunk)* ivre; **to become i.** s'enivrer **(with** de); *Fig* **i. with power** ivre de pouvoir; **i. by their first taste of freedom** grisés par leur première expérience de la liberté

intoxicating [ɪn'tɒksɪkeɪtɪŋ] ADJ *(wine, perfume)* enivrant; *Fig (experience, freedom)* grisant
 ►► **i. liquor** boisson *f* alcoolisée

intoxication [ɪntɒksɪ'keɪʃən] N **1** *(drunkenness)* ivresse *f*; *Fig* griserie *f* **2** *Med* intoxication *f*

intra-Community ['ɪntrəkə'mjuːnɪtɪ] ADJ ATTRIB intracommunautaire
 ►► **i. trade** échange *m* intracommunautaire

intra-company [ɪntrə'kʌmpənɪ] ADJ intra-entreprise

intractability [ɪntræktə'bɪlɪtɪ] N *(of person)* opiniâtreté *f*, inflexibilité *f*; *(of illness, problem)* caractère *m* rebelle

intractable [ɪn'træktəb(ə)l] ADJ *Fml (person) (about specific question)* intraitable; *(child)* insoumis; *(illness)* rebelle; *(problem)* très difficile

intramural [ɪntrə'mjʊərəl] ADJ interne à l'établissement; **i. athletics competition** = épreuves *fpl* d'athlétisme entre membres d'un même établissement scolaire

intramuscular [ɪntrə'mʌskjʊlər] ADJ *(injection)* intramusculaire

Intranet ['ɪntrənet] N *Comput* Intranet *m*

intransigence [ɪn'trænsɪdʒəns] N intransigeance *f*

intransigent [ɪn'trænsɪdʒənt] ADJ, N intransigeant, -ante

intransitive [ɪn'trænsɪtɪv] *Gram* ADJ *(verb)* intransitif
 N intransitif *m*

intransitively [ɪn'trænsɪtɪvlɪ] ADV intransitivement

intra-state carrier [ɪntrə'steɪt] N transporteur *m* intra-État

intrauterine [ɪntrə'juːtəraɪn] ADJ *Anat* intra-utérin
 ►► **i. device** stérilet *m*

intravenous [ɪntrə'viːnəs] ADJ *Med* intraveineux
 ►► **i. drip** perfusion *f* intraveineuse; **i. injection** (injection *f*) intraveineuse *f*

intravenously [ɪntrə'viːnəslɪ] ADV *Med* par voie intraveineuse

in-tray N bac *m* du courrier à traiter *ou* du courrier reçu

intrepid [ɪn'trepɪd] ADJ intrépide

intrepidity [ɪntre'pɪdɪtɪ] N intrépidité *f*

intrepidly [ɪn'trepɪdlɪ] ADV intrépidement

intricacy ['ɪntrɪkəsɪ] N complexité *f*; **the intricacies of the law** les complexités de la loi

intricate ['ɪntrɪkət] ADJ *(mechanism, drawing, design)* compliqué; *(question, plot)* complexe

intricately ['ɪntrɪkətlɪ] ADV d'une manière compliquée; **an i. detailed drawing** un dessin extrêmement détaillé

intrigue¹ ['ɪntriːg] N **1** *(plot, plotting)* intrigue *f* **2** *Old-fashioned (love affair)* aventure *f*

intrigue² [ɪnˈtriːg] vt intriguer; **I'm greatly intrigued by the idea** l'idée m'intrigue énormément

vi intriguer (**against sb** contre qn)

intriguing [ɪnˈtriːgɪŋ] ADJ intrigant; **I find all this very i.** tout cela m'intrigue beaucoup

intrinsic [ɪnˈtrɪnsɪk] ADJ intrinsèque
▸▸*St Exch* **i. value** valeur f intrinsèque

intrinsically [ɪnˈtrɪnsɪklɪ] ADV intrinsèquement

intro [ˈɪntrəʊ] N *Fam* = **introduction 2**

introduce [ɪntrəˈdjuːs] vt **1** *(present)* présenter (**to sb** à qn); **to i. oneself** se présenter; **I don't think we've been introduced** je ne crois pas que nous avons été présentés; **we've introduced ourselves** nous nous sommes déjà présentés; *Cin* **introducing Carlos Bernard** et pour la première fois à l'écran Carlos Bernard; **to be introduced to society** *(of debutante)* faire son entrée dans le monde

2 *(radio or TV programme)* présenter

3 *(initiate)* **to i. sb to sth** faire connaître qch à qn; **he introduced me to Greek** il m'a initié au grec; **they introduced me to drugs/Rabelais** ils m'ont fait connaître la drogue/Rabelais

4 *(put in, bring in) (key into lock, new species, disease)* introduire; **to i. a subject** mettre une question sur le tapis; **to i. sb into sb's presence** introduire qn auprès de qn

5 *(have adopted) (law, usage)* établir, faire adopter; *(fashion, new machinery, methods etc)* introduire; *Parl* **to i. a bill** déposer un projet de loi

6 *Gram (of conjunction, adverb) (phrase)* introduire

7 *Com (product)* lancer; *St Exch (shares)* introduire

introduce-a-friend scheme N *Mktg* offre-ami f, pl offres-ami

introduction [ɪntrəˈdʌkʃən] N **1** *(presentation)* présentation f (**of sb to sb** de qn à qn); **to make the introductions** faire les présentations

2 *(of book)* avant-propos m inv, introduction f; *Mus* introduction f

3 *(book for beginners)* introduction f (**to** à); *(to chemistry, biology etc)* manuel m élémentaire (**to** de), introduction f (**to** à)

4 *(act of initiation)* introduction f, premier contact m (**to sth** avec qch); **this was my i. to Shakespeare** ça a été mon premier contact avec Shakespeare; **this record would be a good i. to her work** ce disque constituerait une bonne introduction à son œuvre

5 *(act of bringing in, putting in) (of new species, disease, key into lock)* introduction f

6 *(of custom etc)* introduction f; **the sport is a recent i. from the United States** ce sport est récemment arrivé des États-Unis

7 *Parl (of bill)* introduction f

8 *Com (of product)* lancement m; *St Exch (of shares)* introduction f au marché hors cote

introductory [ɪntrəˈdʌktərɪ] ADJ (qui sert) d'introduction; *(page, paragraph)* liminaire; **after a few i. words** après quelques mots d'introduction

▸▸**i. music** introduction f musicale, musique f d'ouverture; *Com* **i. offer** offre f de lancement; *Com* **i. price** prix m de lancement

intro-ident N *TV etc* identification f d'intro

introit [ˈɪntrɔɪt] N *Rel* introït m

introspection [ɪntrəˈspekʃən] N introspection f

introspective [ɪntrəˈspektɪv] ADJ introspectif

introversion [ɪntrəˈvɜːʃən] N *Psy* introversion f

introvert [ˈɪntrəvɜːt] ADJ, N introverti, -ie

introverted [ˈɪntrəvɜːtɪd] ADJ introverti; **she's become very i. since the accident** elle est devenue très renfermée depuis l'accident

intrude [ɪnˈtruːd] vi I hope I'm not intruding j'espère que je ne vous dérange pas *ou* que je ne suis pas importun; **to i. on sb's privacy** s'ingérer dans la vie privée de qn; **she didn't want her work to i. on her family life** elle ne voulait pas que son travail empiète sur sa vie de famille; **a supermarket would i. on the character of the village** un supermarché gâcherait le caractère pittoresque du village

vt *(opinion)* imposer; **to i. a note of caution into the discussion** introduire une note de prudence dans la discussion

intruder [ɪnˈtruːdər] N *(on other people)* intrus, -use, importun, -une; *(burglar), Comput* intrus m; **she felt like an i.** elle se sentait de trop

▸▸*Comput* **i. detection** détection f des intrus

intrusion [ɪnˈtruːʒən] N intrusion f; **I hope I am not guilty of an i.** j'espère que je ne suis pas indiscret *ou* que je ne dérange pas

intrusive [ɪnˈtruːsɪv] ADJ *(person)* importun, indiscret; *(noise, presence)* gênant; *Ling* intrusif

intubate [ˈɪntjʊbeɪt] vt *Med* intuber

intuit [ɪnˈtjuːɪt] vt *Fml* deviner intuitivement *ou* par intuition

intuition [ɪntjuːˈɪʃən] N intuition f; **I have an i. that …** j'ai l'intuition que …, mon intuition me dit que …

intuitive [ɪnˈtjuːɪtɪv] ADJ intuitif

intuitively [ɪnˈtjuːɪtɪvlɪ] ADV intuitivement, par intuition

Inuit [ˈɪnjuːɪt] N Inuit m inv
ADJ inuit inv

inundate [ˈɪnʌndeɪt] vt inonder (**with** de); *Fig* **to be inundated with letters** être submergé de lettres; **to be inundated with phone calls** recevoir une quantité énorme de coups de téléphone

inundation [ɪnʌnˈdeɪʃən] N inondation f

inure [ɪˈnjʊər] vt habituer (**to** à)

invade [ɪnˈveɪd] vt *(country), Ftbl (pitch etc)* envahir; **to i. sb's privacy** violer l'intimité de qn

vi envahir

invader [ɪnˈveɪdər] N envahisseur m

invading [ɪnˈveɪdɪŋ] ADJ *(army)* d'invasion

invalid¹ [ɪnˈvælɪd] ADJ *(argument, objection, ticket etc)* non valable; *Law (marriage)* invalide, non valide; *(decision)* nul et non avenu; *Comput* invalide; **your position is morally i.** d'un point de vue moral votre position ne tient pas

▸▸*Comput* **i. character** caractère m invalide; *Comput* **i. file name** nom m de fichier invalide

invalid² [ˈɪnvəlɪd] N *(ill person)* malade mf, *(disabled person)* invalide mf, infirme mf, **I'm not an i.!** je ne suis pas infirme!

ADJ *(chronically ill)* malade; *(disabled)* invalide, infirme; **she has an i. sister** *(disabled)* elle a une sœur infirme; *(in poor health)* elle a une sœur d'une santé délicate

▸▸**i. car** voiture f d'infirme; **i. carriage** véhicule m spécial pour handicapé; **i. chair** fauteuil m roulant

▸ **invalid out** vt sep *esp Br Mil* **to be invalided out (of the army)** être réformé pour raisons médicales

invalidate [ɪnˈvælɪdeɪt] vt **1** *(theory, hypothesis etc)* infirmer **2** *Law (will)* invalider, rendre nul; *(document, contract)* vicier; *(verdict)* casser, infirmer

invalidation [ɪnvælɪˈdeɪʃən] N *(of theory etc), Law (of document, contract)* invalidation f, *Law (of verdict)* infirmation f, cassation f

invalidity [ɪnvəˈlɪdɪtɪ] N **1** *(disability)* invalidité f **2** *(of passport, contract etc)* invalidité f, *(of argument)* manque m de fondement

▸▸*Br Formerly* **i. benefit** prestation f d'invalidité *(aujourd'hui remplacée par l'"incapacity benefit");* *Br* **i. pension** pension f d'invalidité

invaluable [ɪnˈvæljʊəb(ə)l] ADJ extrêmement utile; *(help, assistance)* inestimable; **her help was i. (to us)** elle nous a été d'une aide inestimable *ou* très précieuse

⎡ Attention: ne pas confondre avec l'adjectif **valueless**, qui signifie **sans valeur**. ⎦

invariable [ɪnˈveərɪəb(ə)l] ADJ invariable; *(routine)* immuable

invariably [ɪnˈveərɪəblɪ] ADV invariablement; **he would i. arrive late** il arrivait immanquablement en retard

invariant [ɪnˈveərɪənt] ADJ *Fml* constant

invasion [ɪnˈveɪʒən] N **1** *Mil, Fig (by army, by tourists)* invasion f, **these invasions of my privacy** ces intrusions fpl dans mon intimité **2 i. of sb's rights** violation f des droits de qn

invasive [ɪnˈveɪsɪv] ADJ *Med* invasif

▸▸*Med* **i. surgery** chirurgie f invasive *ou* effractoire

invective [ɪnˈvektɪv] N invective f, **a torrent of i.** un flot d'invectives *ou* d'injures fpl

inveigh [ɪnˈveɪ] vi invectiver (**against** contre)

inveigle [ɪnˈveɪg(ə)l, -viː] vt *(person)* entortiller; **to i. sb into doing sth** entortiller qn pour qu'il fasse qch

invent [ɪnˈvent] vt *(machine, story etc)* inventer; *Fig* **he invented a movie-star mother** il s'est inventé une mère star de cinéma; **recently invented** d'invention récente

invention [ɪnˈvenʃən] N **1** *(something invented)* invention f, *(lie)* invention, mensonge m; **this is pure i.** c'est une pure invention **2** *(ability to invent)* esprit m inventif, inventivité f **3** *(act of inventing) (of machine etc)* invention f, **a story of his own i.** une histoire de son cru

inventive [ɪnˈventɪv] ADJ inventif

inventiveness [ɪnˈventɪvnɪs] N esprit m inventif, inventivité f

inventor [ɪnˈventər] N inventeur, -trice

inventory [ˈɪnvənt(ə)rɪ] N **1** *(list)* inventaire m; **to draw up** *ou* **take an i.** dresser *ou* faire un inventaire **2** *(stock)* stock(s) m(pl)

vt *(property, stock)* inventorier, dresser l'inventaire de

▸▸*Fin* **i. account** compte m de stock; **i. balance** balance f d'inventaire; **i. control** contrôle m des stocks; **i. of fixtures** état m des lieux; **i. level** niveau m des stocks; **i. management** gestion f des stocks; **i. turnaround, i. turnover** rotation f des stocks; **i. turnaround rate, i. turnover rate** vitesse f de rotation des stocks; **i. valuation** valorisation f des stocks; **i. value** valeur f d'inventaire

inverse [ɪnˈvɜːs] ADJ inverse; **in i. order** en sens inverse; **in i. ratio/proportion** en raison/proportion inverse (**to** de)

N inverse m, contraire m (**of** de)

▸▸*Math* **i. function** fonction f inverse

inversely [ɪnˈvɜːslɪ] ADV inversement

inversion [ɪnˈvɜːʃən] N **1** *(of image)* renversement m; *Mus* **i. of a chord** renversement d'un accord; *(result)* accord m dérivé **2** *Gram (of words in phrase), Math (of integral)* inversion f VOIR GRAMMAIRE A78; B62 **3** *Chem (of sugar etc)* inversion f **4** *Psy* **(sexual) i.** inversion f sexuelle

invert[1] ['ɪnvɜːt] ADJ *(sugar)* inverti
N *Psy* inverti, -ie

invert[2] [ɪn'vɜːt] VT **1** *(object) (turn upside down)* renverser, retourner; *Mus (chord)* renverser **2** *(reverse) (order, positions)* invertir, intervertir, renverser; *Gram (subject etc)* inverser **3** *Chem (sugar)* invertir

invertebrate [ɪn'vɜːtɪbrɪt] ADJ, N *Zool* invertébré m

inverted [ɪn'vɜːtɪd] ADJ **1** *(upside down)*, *Mus (chord)* renversé **2** *(reversed) (word order etc)*, *Opt (image)* renversé **3** *Psy (instinct)* inverti
▸▸ *Br* i. **commas** guillemets *mpl*; *Sewing* i. **pleat** pli *m* inverti *ou* creux; **i. snob** = personne *f* qui fait preuve de snobisme à l'envers; **i. snobbery** snobisme *m* à l'envers

invest [ɪn'vest] VT **1** *Fin (money)* placer, investir; *(capital)*, *Fig (time etc)* investir; **to i. money in real estate** faire des placements dans l'immobilier; **capital invested** mise *f* de fonds, capital *m* engagé *ou* investi **2** *Lit (install) (bishop, Pope)* introniser; *(president)* installer
3 *Lit (provide) (person)* investir (**with authority/etc** de l'autorité/etc); **to i. a subject with interest** rendre un sujet intéressant; **his novels i. criminality with too much glamour** ses romans donnent une image trop séduisante du monde du crime
VI investir, faire des placements, placer son argent; **to i. in property** faire des placements dans l'immobilier; **we're going to i. in three new machines** nous allons investir dans trois nouvelles machines; *Fam* **you should i. in a good dictionary** tu devrais t'offrir *ou* te payer un bon dictionnaire

investigate [ɪn'vestɪɡeɪt] VT *(question)* examiner, étudier; *(crime)* faire une enquête sur, enquêter sur
VI **I'll go and i.** je vais voir ce qui se passe

investigating [ɪn'vestɪɡeɪtɪŋ] ADJ
▸▸ i. **committee** commission *f* d'enquête; i. **officer** officier *m* chargé de l'enquête

investigation [ɪnvestɪ'ɡeɪʃən] N investigation *f*, *(by police, tax authority etc)* enquête *f* (**of** sur); **to conduct** *or* **carry out an i.** conduire *ou* effectuer une enquête; **the question is under i.** la question est à l'étude; **on further i.** en poursuivant les recherches; **on further i., the ruins turned out to be …** des recherches plus approfondies ont révélé que les ruines étaient …; **to make investigations** faire des investigations; *(of police)* procéder à une enquête

investigative [ɪn'vestɪɡətɪv] ADJ
▸▸ i. **journalism** journalisme *m* d'investigation *ou* d'enquête; i. **journalist** journaliste *mf* d'investigation; i. **report** reportage *m* d'investigation; i. **reporter** reporter *m* d'investigation; i. **team** équipe *f* d'investigation

investigator [ɪn'vestɪɡeɪtər] N enquêteur, -euse *ou* -trice; **(private) i.** détective *m* privé

investiture [ɪn'vestɪtʃər] N *(installation in office)* investiture *f*, *(of bishop etc)* intronisation *f*

investment [ɪn'vestmənt] N *Fin* placement *m*, investissement *m*; *(money invested)* investissement, mise *f* de fonds; **good** *or* **safe i.** placement sûr; **long-/short-term i.** placement à long/court terme
▸▸ *Banking* i. **account** compte *m* d'investissement; i. **advice** conseil *m* en placements; i. **adviser** conseiller, -ère en placements; i. **analyst** analyste *mf* en placements; i. **bank** banque *f* d'affaires; i. **banker** banquier, -ière d'affaires; i. **banking** banque *f* d'affaires; i. **capital** capital-investissement *m*; i. **company** société *f* de portefeuille *ou* d'investissement; i. **consultancy** société de conseil en investissement; i. **curve** courbe *f* d'investissement; i. **fund** fonds *m* commun de place-

ment, fonds d'investissement; i. **grant** subvention *f* d'investissement; i. **house** société *f* financière; i. **incentives** encouragements *mpl* à l'investissement; i. **income** revenu *m* provenant d'investissements; i. **institution** société d'investissements; i. **instrument** instrument *m* de placement; i. **management** gestion *f* des investissements; i. **plan** plan *m* d'investissement; i. **policy** politique *f* d'investissement; i. **portfolio** portefeuille *m* d'investissements; i. **securities** valeurs *fpl* en portefeuille *ou* de placement; i. **services** services *mpl* d'investissement; i. **stock** valeurs *ou* portefeuille *ou* de placement; i. **subsidy** prime *f* à l'investissement; i. **trust** société de placement, trust *m* de placement

investor [ɪn'vestər] N investisseur *m*; **investors in the company** les personnes qui ont investi dans l'entreprise

inveterate [ɪn'vetərɪt] ADJ *(drunkard, gambler, smoker)* invétéré; *(opponent)* acharné; *(liar)* incorrigible, impénitent

invidious [ɪn'vɪdɪəs] ADJ **1** *(unpleasant)* pénible; *(task)* ingrat, peu agréable; **to be in an i. position** être dans une position peu enviable **2** *(comparison)* inéquitable

invigilate [ɪn'vɪdʒɪleɪt] *Br Sch, Univ* VI surveiller les candidats *(à un examen)*
VT *(exam)* surveiller

invigilator [ɪn'vɪdʒɪleɪtər] N *Br Sch, Univ* surveillant, -ante *(des candidats à un examen)*

invigorate [ɪn'vɪɡəreɪt] VT *(of air, walk, holiday etc)* vivifier; **she invigorates an otherwise lifeless production of Hamlet** elle donne un souffle de vie à un Hamlet plutôt morne

invigorating [ɪn'vɪɡəreɪtɪŋ] ADJ vivifiant

invincibility [ɪnvɪnsɪ'bɪlɪtɪ] N invincibilité *f*, *(of belief, faith)* caractère *m* inébranlable

invincible [ɪn'vɪnsɪb(ə)l] ADJ *(army)* invincible; *(faith, conviction)* inébranlable

inviolability [ɪnvaɪələ'bɪlɪtɪ] N inviolabilité *f*

inviolable [ɪn'vaɪələb(ə)l] ADJ inviolable

inviolably [ɪn'vaɪələblɪ] ADV inviolablement

inviolate [ɪn'vaɪəlɪt] ADJ *Fml* inviolé

invisibility [ɪnvɪzɪ'bɪlɪtɪ] N invisibilité *f*

invisible [ɪn'vɪzɪb(ə)l] ADJ invisible; **i. to the naked eye** invisible à l'œil nu
▸▸ *Fin* i. **earnings** gains *mpl* invisibles; i. **exports** exportations *fpl* invisibles; i. **imports** importations *fpl* invisibles; i. **ink** encre *f* invisible *ou* sympathique; i. **mending** stoppage *m*; i. **trade** commerce *m* de services

invisibly [ɪn'vɪzɪblɪ] ADV invisiblement; **he had it i. mended** *(hole, garment)* il l'avait fait stopper

invitation [ɪnvɪ'teɪʃən] N invitation *f* (**to do sth** à faire qch); *(card)* carte *f* d'invitation; **at sb's i.** sur l'invitation de qn; **an i. to lunch** une invitation à déjeuner; **by i. only** uniquement sur invitation; *Fig* **the speech was an i. to criticism** ce discours ne pouvait pas manquer de provoquer la critique; **that's an i. to burglars** c'est une invitation aux cambrioleurs;
▸▸ i. **card** carte d'invitation

invite[1] [ɪn'vaɪt] VT **1** *(ask to come)* inviter (**to** à); **to i. sb in** inviter qn à entrer; **to i. oneself** s'inviter soi-même; **the invited guests** les invités *mpl* **2** *(request)* inviter (**sb to do sth** qn à faire qch); **to i. bids** *or* **tenders** faire un appel d'offres; **applications are invited for the position** toute personne intéressée est invitée à déposer un dossier de candidature **3** *(arouse) (danger, criticism) (of person)* s'exposer à; *(of action)* provoquer; **to i. trouble** aller au-devant des ennuis

▸ **invite back, invite in, invite round** *etc* =
ask back, ask in, ask round *etc*

invite[2] ['ɪnvaɪt] N *Fam* invitation *f*

inviting [ɪn'vaɪtɪŋ] ADJ attrayant; *(dish)* appétissant; **her eyes were dark and i.** ses yeux étaient sombres et attirants; **not very i.** peu attrayant; **the water looks i.** l'eau donne envie de se baigner

invitingly [ɪn'vaɪtɪŋlɪ] ADV *(arranged, displayed)* d'une manière attrayante; *(to smile, beckon)* en guise d'invitation

in vitro [ɪn'viːtrəʊ] ADJ
▸▸ i. **fertilization** fécondation *f* in vitro

invocation [ɪnvə'keɪʃən] N invocation *f*

invoice ['ɪnvɔɪs] N *Com* facture *f*; **to make out an i.** établir une facture; **to settle an i.** régler une facture; **as per i.** conformément à la facture; **within 30 days of i.** dans les 30 jours après la facturation; **payable against i.** à payer à réception de la facture
VT *(goods, person)* facturer; **who do I i.?** à qui dois-je adresser la facture?; **to i. sb for sth** facturer qch à qn; **invoiced sales** ventes *fpl* facturées
▸▸ *Com* i. **clerk** facturier, -ière; i. **date** date *f* de facturation; i. **of origin** facture originale; i. **price** prix *m* facturé; i. **value** valeur *f* de facture

invoiceable ['ɪnvɔɪsəb(ə)l] ADJ facturable

invoicing ['ɪnvɔɪsɪŋ] N *(of goods etc)* facturation *f*
▸▸ i. **address** adresse *f* de facturation; i. **instructions** instructions *fpl* de facturation; i. **software** logiciel *m* de facturation

invoke [ɪn'vəʊk] VT **1** *(God, sb's memory, law etc)* invoquer; **to i. sb's aid** appeler qn à son secours; **to i. a blessing on an undertaking** demander à Dieu de bénir une entreprise **2** *(summon up) (spirit)* évoquer

involuntarily [ɪn'vɒlənt(ə)rɪlɪ] ADV involontairement

involuntary [ɪn'vɒləntərɪ] ADJ involontaire

involve [ɪn'vɒlv] VT **1** *(in crime, scandal etc)* impliquer (**in** dans); *(in quarrel)* mêler (**in** dans); **he is involved in the plot** il est compromis dans le complot; **over 200 people were involved in planning the event** plus de 200 personnes ont participé à la préparation de l'événement; **he's involved in high finance/language teaching** il est dans la haute finance/l'enseignement des langues; **when I first became involved in teaching** quand j'ai commencé à enseigner; **he's getting involved with the school orchestra** il commence à prendre part aux activités de l'orchestre de l'école; **I'm getting really involved in this job** je commence à trouver ce travail vraiment intéressant; **the novel doesn't really i. the reader** le lecteur ne se sent pas impliqué dans ce roman; **they didn't want to get involved in another war** ils ne voulaient pas s'engager dans un autre conflit; **the police became involved** la police est intervenue; **no one wanted to get involved** personne n'a voulu s'en mêler; **he doesn't want to get involved** il ne veut pas s'engager; **don't get involved!** *(in other people's problems, argument etc)* ne t'en mêle pas!; **I'm too emotionally involved** cela me concerne de trop près *ou* me touche trop; **he got involved with his friend's wife** il a eu une liaison avec la femme de son ami
2 *(include, entail etc)* impliquer, entraîner; **my job involves a lot of travel** je dois beaucoup voyager dans mon travail; **it involves learning new techniques** cela implique l'apprentissage de nouvelles techniques; **what exactly is involved in carrying out a project like this?** qu'est-ce que ça implique exactement la réalisation d'un tel projet?; **it involves getting to London by 5.30 in the**

morning ça veut dire qu'il faut arriver à Londres à 5h 30 le matin; **all it involves is sitting by the phone** tout ce qu'il y a à faire, c'est de rester assis à côté du téléphone

3 *(have to do with)* concerner; **this discussion doesn't i. you** cette discussion ne vous concerne pas; **there's been a theft – how much money is involved?** il y a eu un vol – de combien d'argent s'agit-il?

involved [ɪn'vɒlvd] ADJ *(complicated) (style, discours)* compliqué; *(story, plot)* complexe, compliqué

involvement [ɪn'vɒlvmənt] N **1** *(participation)* participation *f* (**in** à); *(in crime)* implication *f* (**in** dans); **his i. of his sister in the fraud is unforgivable** il est impardonnable qu'il ait impliqué sa sœur dans cette fraude; **I've had no further i. with him since** je n'ai plus jamais eu affaire à lui depuis; **her i. with this man** sa liaison avec cet homme; **our country's i. in this war** la participation de notre pays à cette guerre **2** *(complexity)* complexité *f*

invulnerability [ɪnvʌlnərə'bɪlɪtɪ] N invulnérabilité *f*

invulnerable [ɪn'vʌlnərəb(ə)l] ADJ *(person)* invulnérable; *(position etc)* inattaquable

inward ['ɪnwəd] ADJ **1** *(intimate) (thoughts, feelings etc)* intérieur **2** *(directed to the inside)* (orienté *ou* se dirigeant) vers l'intérieur
  ADV = **inwards**
  ▸▸ *Customs* **i. customs clearance** entrée *f* en douane; *Fin* **i. investment** investissements *mpl* étrangers; *Acct* **i. payment** paiement *m* reçu

inward-looking [-lʊkɪŋ] ADJ introspectif

inwardly ['ɪnwədlɪ] ADV intérieurement; **I was i. pleased** dans mon for intérieur j'étais content

inwards ['ɪnwədz] ADV vers l'intérieur; *Com, Naut* pour l'importation

in-your-face ADJ **1** *(uncompromising) (documentary, film)* sans fard **2** *(aggressive) (attitude, personality)* agressif

I/O ['aɪ'əʊ] N *Comput (abbr* **input/output**) E/S; **I/O port** port *m* d'E/S

IOC [aɪəʊ'siː] N *(abbr* **International Olympic Committee**) CIO *m*

iodine [*Br* 'aɪədiːn, *Am* -daɪn] N *Chem* iode *m*; *Pharm* **(tincture of) i.** teinture *f* d'iode

iodize ['aɪədaɪz] VT *Med, Phot* ioder

iodoform [aɪ'ɒdəfɔːm] N *Chem, Pharm* iodoforme *m*

ion ['aɪən] N *Phys, Chem, Elec* ion *m*; **hydrogen i.** ion d'hydrogène
  ▸▸ **i. beam** faisceau *m* ionique

Ionian [aɪ'əʊnɪən] N **the I. (Sea)** la mer Ionienne

Ionic [aɪ'ɒnɪk] ADJ *Archit, Liter (order, verse)* ionique; *Ling, Mus (dialect, mode)* ionien

ionic [aɪ'ɒnɪk] ADJ *Phys, Chem, Elec* ionique

ionization [aɪənaɪ'zeɪʃən] N **1** *Phys, Elec* ionisation *f* **2** *Med* (traitement *m* par) ionisation *f*

ionize ['aɪənaɪz] *Phys, Elec* VT *(air, gas)* ioniser
  VI *(of acid etc)* s'ioniser

ionosphere [aɪ'ɒnəsfɪər] N ionosphère *f*

iota [aɪ'əʊtə] N **1** *(in Greek alphabet)* iota *m* **2** *(tiny amount)* iota *m*; **she hadn't changed an or one i.** *(looked the same)* elle n'avait pas changé d'un iota; **not an i. of truth** pas un brin de vérité

IOU, *pl* **IOUs** [aɪəʊ'juː, -'juːz] N *(abbr* **I owe you**) reconnaissance *f* (de dette)

IP [aɪ'piː] N *Comput (abbr* **Internet Protocol**) IP **IP address** adresse *f* IP; **IP number** numéro *m* IP

IPA [aɪpiː'eɪ] N *(abbr* **International Phonetic Alphabet**) API *m*

IPO [aɪpiː'əʊ] N *Am StExch (abbr* **initial public offering**) introduction *f* en Bourse

IPPR [aɪpiːpiː'ɑːr] N *(abbr* **Institute for Public Policy Research**) = groupe *m* d'experts de centre gauche à l'origine de plusieurs grandes politiques du gouvernement travailliste britannique

ipso facto ['ɪpsəʊ'fæktəʊ] ADV ipso facto

IQ [aɪ'kjuː] N *(abbr* **intelligence quotient**) QI *m*; **to have an IQ of ...** avoir un QI de ...

IRA [aɪɑː'reɪ] N *(abbr* **Irish Republican Army**) IRA *f*

IRA

L'IRA est une organisation qui lutte pour la réunification de l'Irlande. En 1969, elle s'est scindée en deux factions: la "Provisional IRA", qui a recours à la violence, et la "Official IRA", qui privilégiait un règlement politique du conflit en Irlande du Nord. En 1995, au début du processus de paix qui a abouti à l'accord de 1998 (le "Good Friday Agreement") la "Provisional IRA" a déclaré un cessez-le-feu. Cependant, quelques groupes dissidents, notamment la "Continuity IRA" et la "Real IRA", ont poursuivi les actes terroristes.

Iran [ɪ'rɑːn, ɪ'ræn] N Iran *m*

Iranian [ɪ'reɪnɪən] ADJ iranien
  N **1** Iranien, -ienne **2** *Ling* iranien *m*

Iraq [ɪ'rɑːk, ɪ'ræk] N Irak *m*

Iraqi [ɪ'rɑːkɪ] ADJ irakien, iraquien
  N Irakien, -ienne, Iraquien, -ienne

irascibility [ɪræsɪ'bɪlɪtɪ] N irascibilité *f*

irascible [ɪ'ræsɪb(ə)l] ADJ *(person)* irascible, coléreux; *(temperament)* colérique

irascibly [ɪ'ræsɪblɪ] ADV *(to say etc)* sur un ton irrité

irate [aɪ'reɪt] ADJ *(person, telephone call)* furieux

IRC [aɪɑː'siː] N *Comput (abbr* **Internet relay chat**) IRC *m*, service *m* de bavardage Internet, canal *m* de dialogue en direct
  ▸▸ **I. channel** canal IRC, canal de dialogue en direct

ire [aɪər] N *Lit* courroux *m*, colère *f*

Ireland ['aɪələnd] N Irlande *f*; **Northern I.** l'Irlande du Nord; **the Republic of I.** la République d'Irlande

iridescence [ɪrɪ'desəns] N *Lit (of plumage, fabric etc)* irisation *f*, chatoiement *m*

iridescent [ɪrɪ'desənt] ADJ *Lit* iridescent, chatoyant

iris ['aɪrɪs], *pl* **irides** ['aɪrɪdiːz] *Anat*, *pl* **irises** ['aɪrɪsɪz] *(flower)* N **1** *Anat* iris *m* (de l'œil) **2** *(flower)* iris *m*; **yellow i.** iris jaune *ou* des marais **3** *Myth* **I.** Iris *f* **4** *Phot* iris *m*, diaphragme *m*

Irish ['aɪrɪʃ] ADJ **1** *(people, government, legend etc)* irlandais, d'Irlande **2** *Br Fam (stupid, illogical)* stupide; **that's a bit I.** c'est un peu bête
  N *Ling* irlandais *m*
  NPL **the I.** les Irlandais *mpl*
  ▸▸ **I. American** Américain, -aine d'origine irlandaise; **I. bull** proposition *f* absurde car contradictoire; **I. coffee** Irish coffee *m*, = café *m* noir au whiskey irlandais couronné de crème fraîche; **I. joke** = histoire *f* drôle aux dépens des Irlandais, ≃ histoire belge; **I. Sea** mer *f* d'Irlande; **I. setter** setter *m* irlandais; **I. stew** ragoût *m* à l'irlandaise; **I. wolfhound** lévrier *m* irlandais

Irishism ['aɪrɪʃɪz(ə)m] N expression *f* irlandaise

Irishman, *pl* **Irishmen** ['aɪrɪʃmən] N Irlandais *m*

Irishwoman, *pl* **Irishwomen** ['aɪrɪʃwʊmən, -wɪmɪn] N Irlandaise *f*

irk [ɜːk] VT agacer

irksome ['ɜːksəm] ADJ agaçant

iron ['aɪən] N **1** *(metal)* fer *m*; **(made of) i.** de ou en fer; *Fig* **i. discipline** discipline *f* de fer; **he has an i. constitution** il a une santé de fer; **man of i.** homme dur *ou* sans pitié; **will of i.** volonté *f* de fer; **an i. fist** *or* **hand in a velvet glove** une main de fer dans un gant de velours; **the i. and steel industry** l'industrie *f* sidérurgique, la sidérurgie
  2 *(in diet)* fer *m*
  3 *(device, implement) (for laundry)* fer *m* à repasser; **electric/steam i.** fer (à repasser) électrique/à vapeur; *Fig* **to have several irons in the fire** avoir plusieurs affaires en route; *Fig* **to have too many irons in the fire** courir trop de lièvres à la fois
  4 *Horseriding (of stirrup)* étrier *m*
  5 *Golf (crosse f* en) fer *m*
  6 *Arch (for prisoner)* **irons** fers *mpl*, chaînes *fpl*
  7 *Med* **irons** *(supports)* attelles *fpl*
  VT & VI *(clothes)* repasser; **I've been ironing all morning** j'ai repassé *ou* fait du repassage toute la matinée
  ▸▸ **the I. Age** l'âge *m* du fer; **i. bar** barre *f* de fer; **i. bridge** pont *m* en fer; **the I. Curtain** le rideau de fer; *Med* **i. deficiency** carence *f* en fer; **i. filings** limaille *f* de fer; **i. foundry** fonderie *f (de fonte)*; *Am Hist* **the i. horse** = la locomotive; *Br Pol* **the I. Lady** la Dame de Fer; *Med* **i. lung** poumon *m* d'acier; *Chem* **i. nitride** nitride *m* de fer; *Miner* **i. ore** minerai *m* de fer; *Golf* **i. shot** coup *m* de fer; **i. will** volonté de fer

▸ **iron out** VT SEP *(crease)* faire disparaître au fer *(chaud)*; *Fig (resolve) (problem)* résoudre; **to i. out the difficulties** aplanir les difficultés; **have you ironed out your differences?** est-ce que vous avez résolu vos différends?

ironclad ['aɪənklæd] ADJ **1** *Arch (ship)* cuirassé **2** *Fig (alibi, assurance, guarantee)* à toute épreuve
  N *Naut, Hist* cuirassé *m*

iron-grey ADJ gris (de) fer

ironic(al) [aɪ'rɒnɪk, -ɪk(ə)l] ADJ ironique

ironically [aɪ'rɒnɪklɪ] ADV ironiquement; *(to talk)* avec ironie; **i., the box was empty** l'ironie, c'est que la boîte était vide

ironing ['aɪənɪŋ] N repassage *m*; **I've got a lot of i. to do** j'ai beaucoup de repassage à faire
  ▸▸ **i. board** planche *f ou* table *f* à repasser

ironmonger ['aɪənmʌŋgər] N *Br* quincaillier *m*; **i.'s (shop)** quincaillerie *f*

ironmongery ['aɪənmʌŋgərɪ] N *Br (goods, shop)*, *Hum (medals, jewellery)* quincaillerie *f*

iron-on transfer N transfert *m (appliqué au fer à repasser)*

ironstone ['aɪənstəʊn] N *(clay)* **i.** minerai *m* de fer (argileux)

ironware ['aɪənweər] N ferronnerie *f*

ironwork ['aɪənwɜːk] N **1** *(work in wrought iron)* ferronnerie *f*, *(parts made of iron)* ferrure(s) *f(pl)* **2** *(often with sing verb)* **ironworks** *(for smelting)* fonderie *f* de fonte; *(for casting)* usine *f* sidérurgique, forges *fpl*

irony ['aɪərənɪ] N ironie *f*; **the i. is that ...** l'ironie c'est que ...; **i. of fate** ironie du sort; **in one of life's little ironies** par une ironie du sort

IRR [aɪɑː'rɑː] N *Fin (abbr* **internal rate of return**) taux *m* de rentabilité interne

irradiate [ɪ'reɪdɪeɪt] VT **1** *(of light, heat)* (the

earth etc) irradier; *(of light, rays) (surface)* illuminer **2** *(subject to radiation) (substance etc)* irradier; *Med (patient)* traiter par irradiation; **irradiated food** aliments *mpl* irradiés

irradiation [ɪreɪdɪ'eɪʃən] N **1** *Phys, Opt etc* irradiation *f*, *(of surface by light)* illumination *f* **2** *Nucl* irradiation *f*; *Med* (traitement *m* par) irradiation, radiothérapie *f*

irrational [ɪ'ræʃən(ə)l] ADJ **1** *(person, behaviour, fear)* irrationnel; **don't be so i.!** soyez un peu plus rationnel! **2** *Math (number)* irrationnel
▸ N the **i.** l'irrationnel *m*

irrationally [ɪ'ræʃən(ə)lɪ] ADV *(to behave)* de façon irrationnelle

irreconcilable [ɪrekən'saɪləb(ə)l] ADJ **1** *(enemy)* irréconciliable; *(hatred)* implacable **2** *(belief, idea)* incompatible, inconciliable (**with** avec)

irrecoverable [ɪrɪ'kʌvərəb(ə)l] ADJ *(debt)* irrécouvrable; *(loss)* irrémédiable; *(object)* irrécupérable

irrecoverably [ɪrɪ'kʌvərəblɪ] ADV *(lost)* pour toujours

irredeemable [ɪrɪ'diːməb(ə)l] ADJ **1** *(fault)* irréparable; *(disaster etc)* irrémédiable; *Rel* **no sinner is i.** on peut tous se racheter **2** *Fin (funds)* irremboursable; *(bill)* non convertible

irredeemably [ɪrɪ'diːməblɪ] ADV irrémédiablement

irreducible [ɪrɪ'djuːsɪb(ə)l] ADJ irréductible

irrefutable [ɪrɪ'fjuːtəb(ə)l] ADJ *(evidence)* irréfutable, irrécusable; *(statement)* irréfutable

irregular [ɪ'regjʊlər] ADJ **1** *(not conforming to rule) (behaviour, attendance etc)*, *Gram (plural, verb)* irrégulier; *(life)* déréglé; **this is highly i.** c'est contraire aux règles **2** *(uneven) (outline, shape etc)* irrégulier; *(surface)* irrégulier, inégal, -aux; **i. features** traits *mpl* irréguliers **3** *(pulse, breathing)* irrégulier
▸ N *(usu pl) Mil* **irregulars** troupes *fpl* irrégulières, irréguliers *mpl*
▸▸ *Mil* **i. troops** troupes *fpl* irrégulières, irréguliers *mpl*

irregularity [ɪregjʊ'lærɪtɪ] N irrégularité *f*; *Admin etc* **irregularities** *(in accounts etc)* irrégularités

irregularly [ɪ'regjʊlərlɪ] ADV irrégulièrement, de façon irrégulière

irrelevance [ɪ'reləvəns], **irrelevancy** [ɪ'reləvənsɪ] N **1** *(state of being inapplicable)* inapplicabilité *f* (**to** à); *(inappropriateness)* manque *m* d'à-propos **2** *(remark)* remarque *f* sans rapport avec la question; *(action)* action *f* sans rapport avec la question; **the defence of the frontier has become an i.** la défense de la frontière n'a plus de raison d'être; **irrelevancies** points *mpl* qui n'ont rien à voir avec la question

irrelevant [ɪ'reləvənt] ADJ non pertinent; *(remark etc)* hors de propos; **that is i.** cela n'a aucun rapport *ou* n'a rien à voir avec la question; **the monarchy had become i.** la monarchie n'avait plus de raison d'être, la monarchie avait perdu sa raison d'être; **it's i. now whether he changes his mind or not** maintenant ça ne fait plus rien qu'il change d'avis ou non

irreligious [ɪrɪ'lɪdʒəs] ADJ irréligieux

irremediable [ɪrɪ'miːdɪəb(ə)l] ADJ *(evil, loss etc)* irrémédiable; *(fault)* incorrigible

irremediably [ɪrɪ'miːdɪəblɪ] ADV irrémédiablement

irremovable [ɪrɪ'muːvəb(ə)l] ADJ *(stain)* indélébile; *(official)* inamovible

irreparable [ɪ'repərəb(ə)l] ADJ *(damage)* irréparable; *(loss)* irrémédiable, irrécupérable

irreparably [ɪ'repərəblɪ] ADV *(damaged)* irréparablement; *(lost)* irrémédiablement

irreplaceable [ɪrɪ'pleɪsəb(ə)l] ADJ irremplaçable

irrepressible [ɪrɪ'presɪb(ə)l] ADJ *(urge)* irrésistible, irrépressible; *(yawn)* irrépressible; *(good humour)* que rien n'entame, à toute épreuve; **i. laughter** fou rire *m*; **he's i.** rien ne peut l'abattre

irrepressibly [ɪrɪ'presɪblɪ] ADV **i. optimistic/enthusiastic/good humoured** d'un optimisme/un enthousiasme/une bonne humeur à toute épreuve

irreproachable [ɪrɪ'prəʊtʃəb(ə)l] ADJ irréprochable

irreproachably [ɪrɪ'prəʊtʃəblɪ] ADV irréprochablement, de façon irréprochable

irresistible [ɪrɪ'zɪstɪb(ə)l] ADJ irrésistible

irresistibly [ɪrɪ'zɪstɪblɪ] ADV irrésistiblement

irresolute [ɪ'rezəluːt] ADJ indécis, irrésolu

irresolutely [ɪ'rezəluːtlɪ] ADV d'un air irrésolu

irresoluteness [ɪ'rezəluːtnɪs], **irresolution** [ɪrezə'luːʃən] N indécision *f*, irrésolution *f*

irrespective [ɪrɪ'spektɪv] ADV **i. of sth** indépendamment *ou* sans tenir compte de qch; **we'll go ahead i. of whether you agree or not** nous allons le faire que tu sois d'accord ou non

irresponsibility [ɪrɪspɒnsɪ'bɪlɪtɪ] N irresponsabilité *f*

irresponsible [ɪrɪ'spɒnsɪb(ə)l] ADJ irresponsable; **he was behaving like an i. idiot** il se comportait en irresponsable

irresponsibly [ɪrɪ'spɒnsɪblɪ] ADV de façon irresponsable

irretrievable [ɪrɪ'triːvəb(ə)l] ADJ *(loss)* irrémédiable; *(money)* irrécupérable; *(mistake, situation)* irréparable; **because of the i. breakdown of their marriage** parce que leur mariage était irrémédiablement brisé

irretrievably [ɪrɪ'triːvəblɪ] ADV *(lost)* irrémédiablement, à tout jamais; **to break down i.** *(of marriage)* se briser irrémédiablement

irreverence [ɪ'revərəns] N irrévérence *f* (**towards** envers, pour)

irreverent [ɪ'revərənt] ADJ irrévérencieux

irreverently [ɪ'revərəntlɪ] ADV irrévérencieusement

irreversible [ɪrɪ'vɜːsɪb(ə)l] ADJ **1** *(decision, step etc)* irrévocable **2** *(process)* irréversible

irrevocable [ɪ'revəkəb(ə)l] ADJ irrévocable; **i. letter of credit** lettre *f* de crédit irrévocable, crédit *m* documentaire irrévocable

irrevocably [ɪ'revəkəblɪ] ADV irrévocablement

irrigable [ɪ'rɪgəb(ə)l] ADJ *(land)* irrigable

irrigate [ɪ'rɪgeɪt] VT *Agr, Med (fields, wound)* irriguer

irrigation [ɪrɪ'geɪʃən] N *Agr, Med (of fields, wound)* irrigation *f*; *Agr* **i. canal** *or* **ditch** canal *m* d'irrigation

irritability [ɪrɪtə'bɪlɪtɪ] N irritabilité *f*

irritable [ɪ'rɪtəb(ə)l] ADJ irritable
▸▸ *Med* **i. bowel syndrome** syndrome *m* du côlon irritable

irritably [ɪ'rɪtəblɪ] ADV *(to say, answer)* d'un ton irrité, avec humeur

irritant [ɪ'rɪtənt] ADJ, N *Med* irritant *m*; *Fig* **at least we can be an i.** au moins nous pouvons jouer les empêcheurs de tourner en rond

irritate [ɪ'rɪteɪt] VT **1** *(person)* irriter, agacer; *(animal)* exciter, agacer **2** *Med* irriter

irritating [ɪ'rɪteɪtɪŋ] ADJ **1** irritant, agaçant; **i. little habits** des petites manies agaçantes **2** *Med* irritant

irritatingly [ɪ'rɪteɪtɪŋlɪ] ADV *(to say, behave)* de façon agaçante; **i. slow/jolly** d'une lenteur/bonne humeur exaspérante

irritation [ɪrɪ'teɪʃən] N **1** irritation *f*, **state of nervous i.** état *m* d'énervement **2** *Med (of throat etc)* irritation *f*

IRS [aɪɑːr'es] N *Am (abbr* **Internal Revenue Service)** the **I.** ≃ le fisc

is [ɪz] *see* be

IS [aɪ'es] N *(abbr* **information system)** système *m* informatique

ISA [ˈaɪsə] N *Br (abbr* **individual savings account)** ≃ PEA m, plan m d'épargne en actions

ISBN [aɪesbiː'en] N *(abbr* **International Standard Book Number)** ISBN *m*

ISDN [aɪesdiː'en] *Comput* N *(abbr* **integrated services digital network)** RNIS *m*
▸ VT *Fam* **to I. sth** envoyer qch par RNIS
▸▸ **I. card** carte *f* RNIS; **I. line** ligne *f* RNIS; **I. modem** modem *m* RNIS *ou* Numéris

-ish [ɪʃ] SUFF **1** *(with adjective)* **blueish** bleuâtre; **shortish** plutôt petit **2** *(with noun)* **girlish** de petite fille; **wolfish** de loup **3** *(with time, numbers etc)* **around eightish** vers huit heures, aux environs de huit heures; **he's fortyish** il a la quarantaine

isinglass [ˈaɪzɪŋglɑːs] N *(in wine-making)* ichtyocolle *f*; *Culin* gélatine *f*

Islam [ˈɪzlɑːm] N *(religion)* islam *m*; *(people)* l'Islam, le monde musulman; **to go over to I.** se convertir à l'islam

Islamic [ɪzˈlæmɪk] ADJ islamique

island [ˈaɪlənd] N **1** *Geog* île *f*, *(small)* îlot *m*; **the Pacific Islands** les îles du Pacifique **2** *Fig (in road)* îlot *m*; *(for pedestrians)* refuge *m*; *(of houses etc)* groupe *m*; *(in supermarket)* gondole *f*, **i. of resistance** îlot *m* de résistance; **an i. of calm** un havre de paix
▸▸ *Rail* **i. platform** quai *m* d'entre-voie, quai entre voies

islander [ˈaɪləndər] N *(in general)* insulaire *mf*, *(of specific island)* habitant, -ante de l'île

isle [aɪl] N *(poetic except in certain proper names)* île *f*, **the I. of Man** l'île de Man

islet [ˈaɪlɪt] N îlot *m*

ism [ˈɪz(ə)m] N *Fam usu Pej* doctrine *f*, idéologie *f*

isn't [ˈɪz(ə)nt] CONTR = is not, *see* be

ISO [aɪes'əʊ] N *(abbr* **International Standards Organization)** ISO *f*

isobar [ˈaɪsəʊbɑːr] N *Met, Phys* isobare *f*

ISOC [aɪesəʊ'siː] N *Comput (abbr* **Internet Society)** = organisation *f* non gouvernementale chargée de veiller à l'évolution de l'Internet

isolate [ˈaɪsəleɪt] VT *Med, Pol etc (person)*, *Chem (substance)*, *Biol (culture)* isoler (**from** de, d'avec); **she isolated herself from other people** elle s'est isolée des autres gens

isolated [ˈaɪsəleɪtɪd] ADJ isolé; **i. case** *or* **instance** cas *m* isolé; *Fin* **i. post allowance** prime *f* d'éloignement

isolation [aɪsə'leɪʃən] N **1** *(state, action)* isolement *m*; *Fam* **these problems do not exist in i.** *(from one another)* ces problèmes n'existent pas isolément; **to look at sth in i.** considérer qch isolément **2** *Med (of patient)* isolement *m*
▸▸ *Med* **i. hospital** hôpital *m* d'isolement; *Med* **i. ward** service *m* des contagieux

Attention: ne pas confondre avec le nom anglais **insulation**, qui signifie **isolation**.

isolationism [aɪsə'leɪʃənɪz(ə)m] N isolationnisme *m*

isolationist [aɪsə'leɪʃənɪst] **ADJ, N** isolationniste *mf*

isosceles [aɪ'sɒsɪliːz] **ADJ** *Geom (triangle)*
isocèle

isotherm ['aɪsəʊθɜːm] **N** *Met* isotherme *f*

isotonic [aɪsəʊ'tɒnɪk] **ADJ** isotonique

isotope ['aɪsəʊtəʊp] **N** *Chem, Phys* isotope *m*

ISP [aɪes'piː] **N** *Comput (abbr* **Internet Service
Provider)** fournisseur *m* de services Internet

I-spy **N** *Br* = jeu *m* pour enfants où un des
joueurs donne la première lettre d'un mot
et où les autres doivent deviner l'objet auquel il pense

Israel ['ɪzreɪ(ə)l] **N** Israël *m*

Israeli [ɪz'reɪlɪ] **ADJ** israélien
N Israélien, -ienne

Israelite ['ɪzr(ɪ)əlaɪt] **ADJ** israélite
N Israélite *mf*

ISSUE ['ɪʃ(j)uː]

N	question **1** ▪ émission **2**
	▪ distribution **2** ▪ publication **2**
	▪ délivrance **2** ▪ prêt **2** ▪ numéro **3**
VT	émettre ▪ publier ▪ distribuer
	▪ délivrer ▪ prêter

N 1 *(subject)* problème *m*, question *f*, **an important i.** une question importante; **the issues of the day** les questions du jour; **I
don't want to make an i. of it** je ne veux
pas en faire toute une affaire; **to join i. with
sb** discuter l'opinion de qn (**about sth** au sujet de qch); **the point at i. is the effect it has
on the environment** le problème est l'effet
que cela a sur l'environnement; **to be at i.
with sb** être en désaccord avec qn; **I would
like to take i. with you on that point** je voudrais débattre ce point avec vous; **I would
take i. with that** je ne suis pas d'accord là-
dessus; **that's not the i.** ce n'est pas (là) le
problème; **to evade** *or* **avoid the i.** prendre
la tangente; **to confuse the i.** compliquer
les choses; *Law* **i. (of fact/of law)** *(matter)*
question *ou* point *m* de fait/de droit; *(conclusion)* conclusion *f*

2 *(act of issuing) Admin, Fin (of banknotes,
money orders, stamps etc)* émission *f*; *Admin,
Mil etc (of equipment etc)* distribution *f*; *(of
book)* parution *f*, publication *f*; *Rail etc (of
tickets etc)* délivrance *f*; *(in library) (of
books)* prêt *m*; *Mil etc* **i. boots/shirts** bottes
fpl/chemises *fpl* réglementaires; *Mil* **i. of orders** publication *f* des ordres

3 *(copy) (of magazine)* numéro *m*; **the November i.** le numéro de novembre

4 *Med (of blood, pus)* décharge *f*

5 *Fml (offspring)* descendance *f*, **to die without i.** mourir sans (laisser de) descendance

VI 1 *(of blood, water)* s'écouler (**from** de); *(of
smoke)* s'échapper (**from** de); *(of smell)* se
dégager (**from** de)

2 *Fml (of children)* provenir (**from** de); **the
children issuing from this marriage** les enfants issus de ce mariage

VT *(banknotes etc)* émettre; *(bill)* créer; *(new
edition, prospectus etc)* publier; *Fin (letter of
credit)* fournir; *Mil (order)* publier, donner;
Law (judgement) rendre; *(provisions etc)* distribuer; *(train tickets etc)* délivrer; *(of library)
(books)* prêter; **to i. sb with sth** délivrer qch
à qn; **each man will be issued with two uni-
forms** chaque homme recevra deux unifor-
mes; **no books will be issued after 8 p.m.** le
service de prêt se termine à huit heures; **to i.
a statement** faire une déclaration; *Law* **to i.
a summons** décerner *ou* lancer une citation

▸▸*Fin* **i. premium** prime *f* d'émission; *Fin* **i.
price** prix *m* d'émission, valeur *f* d'émission

Note that the French word **issue** is a false
friend and is never a translation for the
English word **issue**. It means **exit**.

issued ['ɪʃ(j)uːd] **ADJ** *Fin* émis
▸▸**i. capital** capital-action *m* émis; **i. securities** titres *mpl* émis; **i. share capital** capital-
action émis

issueless ['ɪʃ(j)uːlɪs] **ADV** *Fml* **to die i.** mourir sans laisser de descendance

issuer ['ɪʃ(j)uːər] **N** *Fin* **i. of a draft** émetteur
m d'une traite

issuing ['ɪʃ(j)uːɪŋ] **ADJ** *esp Fin* émetteur,
-trice
N *(of loan, banknotes)* émission *f*; *(of provisions)* distribution *f*; *(in library) (of books)*
prêt *m*
▸▸*Br* **i. bank** banque *f* d'émission *ou* émettrice; **i. company** société *f* émettrice; **i.
house** banque d'émission *ou* émettrice

Istanbul [ɪstæn'buːl] **N** Istanbul

isthmus, *pl* **isthmuses** ['ɪsməs, -məsɪz] **N**
Geog isthme *m*

IT [aɪ'tiː] **N** *(abbr* **information technology)**
technologie *f* de l'information; **she's our IT
expert** c'est notre spécialiste en
informatique

IT [ɪt]

| **PERS PRON** | il/elle **1** ▪ le/la **2** ▪ lui **3** |
| | ▪ ce **7, 8** ▪ il **8** ▪ en **10** |

PERS PRON VOIR GRAMMAIRE A27–9; B18–21 *(referring to inanimate objects, animals and children, but in French taking the gender of the
noun for which it stands)* **1** *(subject)* il, elle;
the house is small but it's my own c'est une
petite maison mais elle est à moi; **where is
your hat? – it's in the cupboard** où est votre
chapeau? – il est dans l'armoire SEE GRAMMAR
B66

2 *(direct object)* le, la; *(before vowel)* l'; **I
don't believe it** je ne le crois pas

3 *(indirect object)* lui; **fetch the dog and
give it something to eat** allez chercher le
chien et donnez-lui à manger

4 *Fam (stressed)* **he thinks he's it** il se croit
sorti de la cuisse de Jupiter; **this book is absolutely it!** c'est un livre épatant!; **this is it –
it's now or never!** ça y est, c'est maintenant ou jamais!; **this is it, the
moment we've all been waiting for!** nous y
voilà, c'est le moment que nous attendons
tous!; **that's it, we're in for it now!** ça y est,
on est foutu!; **that's it for today** *(we have no
more time etc)* c'est fini pour aujourd'hui

5 *(as unspecified object of a verb)* **to face it**
faire front; **blast it!** zut!

6 *(as unspecified object of a preposition)*
now for it! et maintenant allons-y!; **there
is nothing for it but to run** il n'y a qu'une
chose à faire, c'est de filer; *Fam* **he's (in) for
it!** qu'est-ce qu'il va prendre!; **to have a bad
time of it** en voir de rudes

7 *(as complement)* **who is it?** qui est-ce?;
that's it c'est bien ça; *(as encouragement)*
c'est bien

8 *(as subject of impersonal verb)* **it frightens
me** cela me fait peur; **it doesn't matter** cela
ne fait rien; **it's raining** il pleut; **it's ten
o'clock** il est dix heures; **it's Monday** c'est
lundi SEE GRAMMAR B29–30

9 **it's nonsense talking like that** c'est *ou* il
est absurde de dire ça; **it's impossible to
work in this heat** c'est *ou* il est impossible
de travailler par cette chaleur; **it says in …**
on lit dans …; **the fog made it difficult to
see** le brouillard réduisait beaucoup la visibilité; **I find it hard to understand why** je
trouve difficile de comprendre pourquoi;
you may rely upon it that he will do his best
vous pouvez être sûr qu'il fera de son mieux
SEE GRAMMAR B66

10 *(with prepositions)* **to consent to it** y
consentir; **above it, over it** au-dessus, dessus; **below it, under(neath) it** au-dessous,

dessous; **as we walked away from it** tandis
que nous nous en éloignions; **he's not bad,
far from it** il n'est pas méchant, loin de là;
give me half of it donnez-m'en la moitié;
think of it pensez-y; **don't tread on it** ne
marchez pas dessus; **the Committee has devoted much care to the task before it** le comité a accordé beaucoup d'attention à la
tâche qui lui incombait; **I cracked his head
with it** je lui ai fendu la tête avec
N *(in children's games)* **you're it!** c'est toi qui
y es *ou* qui t'y colles!

Italian [ɪ'tæljən] **ADJ** italien; *(embassy, ambassador, history)* d'Italie; *(teacher, lesson,
dictionary)* d'italien
N 1 Italien, -ienne **2** *Ling* italien *m*
▸▸**I. Switzerland** Suisse *f* italienne

italic [ɪ'tælɪk] *Typ* **ADJ** *(character)* italique
N italic(s) italique *m*; **to print in italic(s)** imprimer en italique; **the italics are mine** les
italiques sont de moi

italicization [ɪtælɪsaɪ'zeɪʃən] **N** *(putting
into italics)* mise *f* en italique(s)

italicize [ɪ'tælɪsaɪz] **VT** *Typ* imprimer *ou*
mettre en italique; **italicized words** mots
mpl en italique

Italo- [ɪ'tæləʊ] **PREF** italo-; **I. -American** italo-
américain

Italy ['ɪtəlɪ] **N** Italie *f*

ITC [aɪtiː'siː] **N 1** *Br (abbr* **Independent Television Commission)** = commission *f* de surveillance des télévisions britanniques
privées **2** *Am abbr* **International Trade
Commission**

itch [ɪtʃ] **N** démangeaison *f*, **I've got an awful i. on my back** mon dos me démange horriblement; *Fig* **to have an i. for sth/to do sth**
avoir envie de qch/de faire qch; *Fig Fam* **if
you've got an i., scratch it** si ça te dit, vas-y
VI 1 *(of person)* éprouver des démangeaisons; **my hand itches** la main me démange;
where does it i.? où est-ce que cela vous démange?; **these bites really i.** ce que ces piqûres me démangent!; *Fig* **to have an
itching palm** être cupide **2** *Fam* **to be itching
to do sth** brûler d'envie de faire qch; **I was
itching to speak** la langue me démangeait;
she is itching to be off ça la démange de
partir

itching ['ɪtʃɪŋ] **N** démangeaison *f*
▸▸**i. powder** poil *m* à gratter

itchy ['ɪtʃɪ] **ADJ** **I've got an i. hand** j'ai la
main qui me démange; *Fig* **to have i. feet**
brûler d'envie de partir; **I've always had i.
feet** j'ai toujours eu la bougeotte

it'd ['ɪt(ə)d] **CONTR 1** = **it would,** *see* **would 2**
= **it had,** *see* **have**

item ['aɪtəm] **N** *Com* article *m*; *(in bookkeeping)* écriture *f*, article, poste *m*; *Comput (on
menu)* élément *m*; *Journ (very brief)* entrefilet *m*; *(longer)* article; *Radio, TV (news item)*
point *m* *ou* sujet *m* d'actualité; **i. of expenditure** article *ou* chef *m* de dépense; **the second i. of the contract** l'article deux du
contrat; **the items on the agenda** les questions *fpl* à l'ordre du jour; *Theat etc* **the last
i. on the programme** le dernier numéro du
programme; *Journ* **news items** nouvelles
fpl; **there was an i. on the news about it yesterday** ils en ont parlé aux informations
hier; *Fam* **they're an i.** ils sortent ensemble
ADV *Old-fashioned (when listing)* item
▸▸*Am Pol* **i. veto** veto *m* partiel

itemize ['aɪtəmaɪz] **VT** *(bill)* détailler; **itemized billing, itemized invoicing** facturation *f*
détaillée

iterate ['ɪtəreɪt] **VT** réitérer, répéter *(constamment)*; *Comput, Math* itérer

iteration [ɪtə'reɪʃən] **N** itération *f*

iterative ['ɪt(ə)rətɪv] **ADJ** *Comput* itératif

itinerant [ɪˈtɪnərənt, aɪ-] ADJ *(salesman, comedian, musician)* ambulant; *(preacher, worker)* itinérant

itinerary [aɪˈtɪnərəri] N itinéraire *m*

it'll [ˈɪt(ə)l] CONTR = **it will,** *see* **will**[2]

ITN [aɪtiːˈen] N *Br (abbr* **Independent Television News)** = service *m* produisant le journal télévisé d'ITV

ITO [aɪtiːˈəʊ] N *(abbr* **International Trade Organization)** OMC *f*

its [ɪts] VOIR GRAMMAIRE A30; B21–2 POSS ADJ son, sa, *pl* ses; *(in the f before a vowel sound)* son; **i. nose, mouth, and eyes** *(of animal)* son nez, sa bouche, et ses yeux; **the jug has lost its handle** le pichet n'a plus de poignée; **a charm of i. own** un charme qui n'appartient qu'à lui/à elle
POSS PRON le sien, la sienne, *pl* les sien(ne)s

> Attention: ne pas confondre avec **it's,** qui est la forme abrégée de **it is.**

it's CONTR **1** = **it is,** *see* **be 2** = **it has,** *see* **have**

> Attention: ne pas confondre avec l'adjectif et le pronom possessifs **its.**

itself [ɪtˈself] PERS PRON VOIR GRAMMAIRE A29–30

1 *(emphatic)* lui-même, elle-même, soi-même; **it is simplicity i.** c'est tout ce qu'il y a de plus simple; **she is kindness i.** elle est la bonté même **2** *(reflexive)* **the dog hurt i.** le chien s'est fait mal SEE GRAMMAR B28–9 **3** *(after prepositions)* **the child was left by i.** l'enfant était laissé(e) tout(e) seul(e); **the thing in i.** la chose en elle-même; **in i. it's not a bad idea** en soi l'idée n'est pas mauvaise

ITV [aɪtiːˈviː] N *Br (abbr* **Independent Television)** = une des chaînes de télévision privées britanniques

IUD [aɪjuːˈdiː] N *Med (abbr* **intra-uterine device)** stérilet *m*

IV [aɪˈviː] *Med (abbr* **intravenous)** IV

I've [aɪv] CONTR = **I have,** *see* **have**

IVF [aɪviːˈef] N *Med (abbr* **in vitro fertilization)** FIV *f*

ivory [ˈaɪvəri] N **1** *(substance)* ivoire *m*; *(object)* (objet *m* d')ivoire; **a collection of ivories** une collection d'ivoires; *Fig Fam* **ivories** *(teeth)* dents *fpl*; *(piano keys)* touches *fpl* **2** *(colour)* ivoire *m*
ADJ *(made of ivory)* d'ivoire, en ivoire
▶▶ **I. Coast** Côte *f* d'Ivoire; **i. tower** tour *f* d'ivoire; **i. trade** commerce *m* de l'ivoire

ivory-white [ˈaɪvəriˈwaɪt] ADJ *(teeth)* d'une blancheur d'ivoire

ivy [ˈaɪvi] N *(plant)* lierre *m*
▶▶ **the I. League** = groupe *m* des huit universités les plus prestigieuses du nord-est des États-Unis

> ### Ivy League
> On désigne ainsi un groupe de huit universités du nord-est des États-Unis: Brown, Columbia, Cornell, Dartmouth, Harvard, l'Université de Pennsylvanie, Princeton et Yale. Ces universités se caractérisent par une forte proportion d'étudiants de troisième cycle, des moyens financiers importants et la réputation d'excellence de leurs universitaires. Si à l'origine, "Ivy League" servait à promouvoir les rencontres sportives entre les universités qui la composaient, elle est depuis devenue synonyme d'un enseignement prestigieux très compétitif, réservé à l'élite.

IYHF [aɪwaɪeɪtʃˈef] N *(abbr* **International Youth Hostel Federation)** FIAJ *f*

J, j [dʒeɪ] N *(letter)* J, j *m*; **two j's** deux j

jab [dʒæb] N **1** *(with sharp object)* coup *m* (sec); **a j. with an elbow/a knife** un coup de coude/de couteau; **she gave him a sharp j. in the ribs (with her elbow)** elle lui a mis un coup de coude dans les côtes **2** *Br Fam (injection)* injection *f*, piqûre *f*, **to give sb a j.** faire une injection *ou* une piqûre à qn; *(for TB, malaria etc)* vacciner qn; **have you had all the necessary jabs?** est-ce qu'on t'a fait tous les vaccins nécessaires? **3** *Boxing* coup *m* droit, direct *m*

VT (-bb-) **1** *(poke, prick)* **to j. sb/sth** piquer qn/qch (**with sth** avec qch, du bout de qch); **to j. sb with one's elbow/a knife** donner un coup de coude/couteau à qn; **she jabbed him in the eyes with her fingers** elle lui a planté ses doigts dans les yeux **2** *(thrust)* enfoncer, planter (d'un coup sec) (**into** dans); **she jabbed a finger at him to emphasize her point** elle a pointé le doigt dans sa direction pour appuyer ses propos

VI **1** *(poke, prick)* **to j. at sb/sth** piquer qn/qch (**with sth** avec qch, du bout de qch); **to j. at sb with a knife/an umbrella** donner un coup de couteau/de parapluie à qn **2** *Boxing* envoyer un coup droit *ou* un direct (**at** à)

jabber [ˈdʒæbər] *Fam* N **1** *(noise)* brouhaha *m* **2** *(chat)* conversation *f*, *Pej* jacasseries *fpl*; **to have a j.** bavarder, tailler une bavette

VI **1** *(talk fast, unclearly)* baragouiner; **what are you jabbering about?** qu'est-ce que tu baragouines? **2** *(chatter)* bavarder, tailler une bavette, *Pej* jacasser

VT *(excuse, explanation)* bafouiller, bredouiller; **to j. a few words in French**/*etc* baragouiner quelques mots de français/*etc*

▶**jabber away, jabber on** VI baragouiner

▶**jabber out** VT SEP *(excuse, explanation etc)* bafouiller, bredouiller

jabbering [ˈdʒæbərɪŋ] N **1** *(incomprehensible)* baragouinage *m* **2** *(chattering)* bavardage *m*, *Pej* jacasseries *fpl*

jacaranda [dʒækəˈrændə] N *(shrub)* jacaranda *m*

Jack [dʒæk] N **before you could say J. Robinson** sans qu'on ait eu le temps de dire ouf; *Br Fam* **I'm all right, J.** ça marche très bien pour moi (et les autres, je m'en fiche); *Fam* **an 'I'm all right, J.' attitude** une attitude je-m'enfoutiste

▶▶**J. Frost** le Bonhomme Hiver

jack [dʒæk] N **1** *(person)* **every man j. (of them)** absolument tout le monde; **j. of all trades** touche-à-tout *m*; *Prov* **J. of all trades, master of none** propre à tout, propre à rien

2 *(lifting device)* *Aut* cric *m*; *Tech* vérin *m*

3 *Cards* valet *m*; **the j. of spades** le valet de pique

4 jacks *(game)* (jeu *m* d')osselets *mpl*

5 *(in bowling)* cochonnet *m*

6 *Tel* prise *f*, **microphone/headphone j.** prise de microphone/de casque

▶▶*Tech* **j. plug** prise *ou* fiche *f* mâle, jack *m*; *Zool* **j. rabbit** = gros lièvre *m* d'Amérique; *Elec* **j. socket** prise *ou* fiche femelle; *Old-fashioned Fam* **j. tar** matelot *m*

▶**jack around** *Am Sl* VT SEP **to j. sb around** *(treat badly)* se ficher de qn; *(waste time of)* faire perdre son temps à qn

VI *(waste time)* glander, glandouiller

▶**jack in** VT SEP *Br Sl (job, project, girlfriend)* plaquer, laisser tomber

▶**jack off** *Vulg* VT SEP **to j. sb off** branler qn

VI se branler, se paluscher

▶**jack up** VT SEP **1** *Aut, Tech* soulever (avec un cric/un vérin) **2** *Fam (increase) (price, salaries)* relever

VI *Br Sl (inject oneself)* s'injecter, se piquer

jackal [ˈdʒækɔːl, -k(ə)l] N *(animal)* chacal *m*

jackaroo [dʒækəˈruː] N *Austr Fam* = apprenti *m* dans un ranch

jackass [ˈdʒækæs] N **1** *(male donkey)* âne *m*, *Fam* baudet *m* **2** *Fam (person)* idiot, -ote, imbécile *mf* **3 laughing j.** *(bird)* dacélo *m*

jackboot [ˈdʒækbuːt] N *Mil* botte *f* de cavalier; *Fig* **under the j. of a military dictatorship** la vie sous la botte de la dictature militaire

jackdaw [ˈdʒækdɔː] N *(bird)* choucas *m*

jacket [ˈdʒækɪt] N **1** *(man's coat)* veste *f*, veston *m*; *(woman's)* veste, jaquette *f* **2** *Culin* **j. potatoes, potatoes cooked in their jackets** pommes *fpl* de terre en robe des champs *ou* en robe de chambre **3** *(of record, computer diskette)* pochette *f*; *(for documents)* chemise *f*, *Tech (of boiler, pipe)* chemise *f*, *(dust)* jaquette *f* *(of book)* jaquette *f*

VT *Tech (cylinder, boiler etc)* garnir *ou* envelopper d'une chemise, chemiser

jackhammer [ˈdʒækhæmər] N marteau-piqueur *m*

jacking point [ˈdʒækɪŋ-] N point *m* de levage, emplacement *m* prévu pour le cric

jack-in-the-box, *pl* **jack-in-the-boxes** N diable *m* à ressort, boîte *f* à surprise(s); *Fam* **to jump up and down like a j.** ne pas tenir en place; **stop jumping up and down like a j.** arrête de sauter dans tous les sens comme ça

jackknife, *pl* **jackknives** [ˈdʒæknaɪf, -naɪvz] N **1** couteau *m* de poche, canif *m* **2** *Swimming (dive)* saut *m* de carpe

VI **1** *Aut (of articulated vehicle)* se mettre en portefeuille **2** *Swimming* faire un saut de carpe

▶▶*Swimming* **j. dive** saut de carpe

jack-o'-lantern [ˈdʒækəˈlæntən] N *Am (Hallowe'en lantern)* = lanterne *f* faite dans une citrouille sur laquelle on a creusé un visage

jackpot [ˈdʒækpɒt] N **1** *Cards (in poker etc)* pot *m* **2** *(in competition)* gros lot *m*; **to win the j.** gagner le gros lot; *Fig* **to hit the j.** *(be successful) (of person)* gagner le gros lot; *(of book, record etc)* faire un malheur *ou* un tabac

jacksie [ˈdʒæksɪ] N *Br Sl (buttocks)* fesses *fpl*, popotin *m*; *(anus)* troufignon *m*

Jacobean [dʒækəˈbɪən] ADJ de l'époque de Jacques 1ᵉʳ (1603–1625); **the J. period** l'époque *f* de Jacques 1ᵉʳ

Jacobite [ˈdʒækəbaɪt] ADJ, N *Hist* jacobite *m*

Jacuzzi® [dʒəˈkuːzɪ] N *(bath, pool)* jacuzzi *m*

jade [dʒeɪd] N **1** *Miner* jade *m* **2** *(colour)* vert jade *m inv*

ADJ **1** *(made of jade)* de *ou* en jade **2** *(colour)* vert jade *inv*

jaded [ˈdʒeɪdɪd] ADJ *(person) (tired)* las, fatigué; *(performance, piece of writing, cliché)* faiblard; **to be** *ou* **feel j. with sth** être las de qch; **to become j. with sth** se lasser de qch; **I was served a rather j. piece of beef** on m'a servi un morceau de bœuf tout flétri

▶▶**j. palate** palais *m* blasé; *Fig* appétit *m* fatigué

Jag [dʒæg] N *Fam (Jaguar® car)* Jag *f*

jag [dʒæg] N **1** *Sl (drinking bout)* soûlerie *f*; **to go on a (drinking) j.** se soûler, prendre une cuite **2** *Sl* **to have a crying j.** avoir une crise de larmes **3** *Br Fam (injection)* piquouze *f*

jagged [ˈdʒægɪd] ADJ *(coastline, mountain top)* déchiqueté, découpé; *(edge)* déchiqueté, découpé, dentelé; *(line, tear)* irrégulier; *(knife, blade)* entaillé, ébréché; *(rock)* pointu, dentelé; **the j. outline of the coast** les dentelures *fpl* *ou* découpures *fpl* de la côte

jaggy [ˈdʒægɪ] N *(on printed character)* courbe *f* en escalier

jaguar [*Br* ˈdʒægjʊər, *Am* ˈdʒægwɑːr] N *(animal)* jaguar *m*

jail [dʒeɪl] N *(place, imprisonment)* prison *f*, **to be in j.** être en prison; **to put in j., to send to j.** mettre en prison; **to go to j.** aller en prison, faire de la prison; **he was sent to j.** *or* he **went to j. for ten years** il a été condamné à dix ans de prison; **she was in j. for ten years, she went to j. for ten years** elle a fait dix ans de prison; **to break out of j.** s'évader de prison; **open j.** prison ouverte

VT mettre en prison, emprisonner; **to j. sb for theft** condamner qn à la prison pour vol; **he was jailed for ten years** il a été condamné à dix ans de prison

jailbait [ˈdʒeɪlbeɪt] N *Sl (girl)* mineure *f* *(avec qui les relations sexuelles sont interdites)*

jailbird [ˈdʒeɪlbɜːd] N *Fam (actually in prison)* taulard, -arde; *(constantly going to prison)* cheval *m* de retour

jailbreak [ˈdʒeɪlbreɪk] N évasion *f* de prison; **to do a j.** s'évader; **to attempt a j.** essayer de s'évader

jailbreaker [ˈdʒeɪlbreɪkər] N évadé, -ée

jailer [ˈdʒeɪlər] N geôlier, -ière

jailhouse, *pl* **jailhouses** [ˈdʒeɪlhaʊs, -haʊzɪz] N *Am* prison *f*

jailor [ˈdʒeɪlər] N = **jailer**

Jakarta [dʒəˈkɑːtə] N Djakarta

jake [dʒeɪk] N *Br Sl (cannabis cigarette)* joint *m*

jalop(p)y [dʒəˈlɒpɪ] N *Fam* (vieille) bagnole *f*, (vieux) tacot *m*, (vieille) guimbarde *f*

jam¹ [dʒæm] N **1** *Aut (congestion)* bouchon *m*, embouteillage *m*, encombrement *m*
2 *(crowd of people)* **there was a great j. of people outside the theatre** il y avait une foule énorme devant le théâtre
3 *(in pipe, machine etc)* engorgement *m*; *(in printer)* bourrage *m*
4 *Fam (difficult situation)* **to be in/get into a (bit of a) j.** être/se mettre dans le pétrin; **to get out of/get sb out of a j.** se tirer/tirer qn du pétrin
5 *Mus Fam* bœuf *m*, **jam-session**, *pl* jam-sessions
VT (**-mm-**) **1** *(pack, cram)* (en)tasser (**into** dans); *(thrust, put forcefully)* enfoncer, fourrer (**into** dans); **it had been jammed with goodies** il avait été rempli à ras bords de bonnes choses; **to j. one's foot on the brake(s)** écraser le frein *ou* la pédale de frein
2 *(squeeze, wedge)* coincer; **she got her hand jammed** *or* **she jammed her hand in the drawer** elle s'est coincé la main dans le tiroir; **to j. a door open with a book** maintenir une porte ouverte à l'aide d'un livre
3 *(immobilize, stop from working)* *(window, shutter etc)* coincer, bloquer; *(weapon, mechanism)* enrayer, bloquer; *(pipe)* boucher; **the drawer is jammed** le tiroir est coincé *ou* bloqué; **to be jammed in the ice** être bloqué par les glaces
4 *(of people, vehicles)* *(street, corridor etc)* encombrer, bloquer; *(building, town)* envahir; **the hall was jammed (with people), people jammed the hall** la salle était pleine à craquer *ou* bondée
5 *Radio (broadcast, station)* brouiller
6 *Tel (of calls etc) (lines)* encombrer; *(switchboard)* faire sauter; **the switchboard was jammed** le standard était saturé
VI **1** *(of drawer, window, lift etc)* se coincer, se bloquer; *(of gun, machine)* s'enrayer, se bloquer; *(of brake, wheel, paper in printer)* se bloquer **2** *(crowd)* s'entasser (**into** dans)
▸**jam in** VT SEP **1** *(wedge in)* coincer; **the crowd was jamming him in** il était coincé par la foule; **her car was being jammed in by a large truck** un gros camion était en train de le coincer **2** *(pack or press tightly in)* *(passengers etc)* (en)tasser; *(objects)* bourrer; **he had jammed as many quotations as he could find into the essay** il avait farci sa dissertation de toutes les citations qu'il avait trouvées
VI *(crowd in)* s'entasser; **they all jammed in** *(into train)* ils s'y entassèrent tous; **we won't all be able to j. in at once** nous n'allons jamais tous tenir à la fois
▸**jam on** VT SEP **1** *Aut* **to j. on the brakes** écraser le frein *ou* la pédale de frein **2** *(put on forcefully or solidly) (lid, hat etc)* enfoncer
▸▸*Mus Fam* **j. session** bœuf *m*, jam-session *f*, *pl* jam-sessions

jam² N *Culin* confiture *f*, **strawberry j.** confiture de fraises; *Br Fig* **what do you want, j. on it?** ça ne te suffit pas?, que veux-tu de plus?; **jar of j.** pot *m* de confiture(s)
▸▸**j. jar** pot à confiture; *Br Fam Hum* **j. sandwich** *(police car)* voiture *f* de police; **j. tart** tarte *f* à la confiture

Jamaica [dʒəˈmeɪkə] N Jamaïque *f*

Jamaican [dʒəˈmeɪkən] ADJ jamaïquain, jamaïcain, de la Jamaïque
N Jamaïquain, -aine, Jamaïcain, -aine

jamb [dʒæm] N *(side post)* *(of door, window, chimney)* chambranle *m*, jambage *m*, montant *m*

jamboree [dʒæmbəˈriː] N **1** *(scouts' meeting)* jamboree *m* **2** *Fam (celebration, party)* fête *f*, réunion *f*, *(festivities)* réjouissances *fpl* (tapageuses); **village j.** fête *f* de village

jammies [ˈdʒæmɪz] NPL *(in children's language)* pyjama *m*

jamming [ˈdʒæmɪŋ] N **1** *Radio* brouillage *m* (délibéré) **2** *Tel (of lines)* encombrement *m*

jammy [ˈdʒæmɪ] ADJ **1** *(covered with jam)* plein de confiture **2** *Br Fam (lucky)* veinard, verni; **he's a j.** *(easy)* facile; **j. job** filon *m*, bonne planque *f*

jam-packed [ˈdʒæmˈpækt] ADJ *(suitcase, bag etc)* plein à craquer, bourré (**with** de); **j. (with people)** *(hall, bus etc)* plein à craquer, bondé; *(street)* noir de monde, bondé; **this magazine is j. with interesting articles** ce magazine est truffé *ou* regorge d'articles intéressants

jams [dʒæmz] NPL *Am (shorts)* bermuda *m*

Jan *abbr* January

Jane [dʒeɪn] N *Am Sl (woman)* nana *f*
▸▸*Am* **J. Doe** *(average person)* l'Américaine *f* moyenne, ≃ Madame Dupont; *(unidentified woman under arrest)* inconnue *f*; *(corpse)* morte *f* non identifiée

jangle [ˈdʒæŋg(ə)l] N *(of metal objects, keys etc)* cliquetis *m*; *(of bell)* bruit *m* discordant
VI *(of metal objects, keys etc)* cliqueter; *(of bells)* retentir d'un bruit discordant; **it jangled on my nerves** cela me mettait les nerfs en pelote
VT **1** *(keys etc)* faire cliqueter; *(bells)* faire retentir d'un bruit discordant **2** *(upset)* **jangled nerves** nerfs en pelote

jangling [ˈdʒæŋg(ə)lɪŋ] N = **jangle** N

janitor [ˈdʒænɪtər] N *Am, Scot (caretaker)* concierge *mf*

January [ˈdʒænjʊərɪ] N ⟨VOIR GRAMMAIRE A81–2; B60–2⟩ janvier *m*; **in J.** au mois de janvier, en janvier; **(on) the first/the seventh of J.** le premier/le sept janvier

Jap [dʒæp] Offensive Fam N Japonais, -aise
ADJ japonais

Japan [dʒəˈpæn] N Japon *m*

Japanese [dʒæpəˈniːz] ADJ japonais; *(embassy, ambassador, history)* du Japon; *(teacher, lesson, dictionary)* de japonais
N **1** Japonais, -aise; **the J.** les Japonais *mpl* **2** *Ling* japonais *m*
▸▸**J. lantern** lanterne *f* vénitienne

jape [dʒeɪp] N *Old-fashioned* tour *m*, blague *f*; **to play japes on sb** jouer des tours à qn, faire des blagues à qn

japonica [dʒəˈpɒnɪkə] N *Bot* cognassier *m* du Japon

jar¹ [dʒɑːr] N *(jolt, shock)*, *Fig* choc *m*, secousse *f*; **his fall/the news gave him a nasty j.** sa chute/la nouvelle l'a fortement ébranlé *ou* beaucoup secoué; **he gave his wrist a j. when he fell** il s'est cogné le poignet en tombant
VI (**-rr-**) **1** *(make an unpleasant sound)* rendre un son discordant; *Mus (of note)* détonner **2** *(of colours, furniture)* détonner, jurer (**with** avec); *(of ideas, styles, remarks)* détonner, être incompatible, ne pas s'accorder (**with** avec); **to j. (with each other)** *(of colours, ideas)* se heurter, détonner; **to j. on sb's feelings** froisser qn
VT *(window pane, building)* ébranler; *(table, microphone)* faire bouger; *(wrist, ankle etc)* se cogner; *(of news)* ébranler, secouer; **someone jarred my elbow** quelqu'un m'a cogné le coude
▸**jar on, jar upon** VT INSEP *(of noise)* *(the ears)* écorcher; **his voice jars (up)on my nerves** sa voix me tape sur les nerfs *ou* me crispe

jar² N **1** *(container)* pot *m*; *(for storing oil etc)* jarre *f*, **(glass) j.** pot *m*; *(large)* bocal *m* **2** *Br Fam (beer)* pot *m*; **to have a j.** prendre un pot; **we had a few jars** on a pris un pot ou deux

jargon [ˈdʒɑːgən] N *Pej (specialized language)* jargon *m*; **legal j.** jargon juridique, langage *m* du Palais; **to talk (in) j.** parler en jargon, jargonner

jarring [ˈdʒɑːrɪŋ] ADJ *(noise, voice etc)* discordant; *Mus (note)* qui détonne; *Fig (incident, behaviour)* qui produit une sensation désagréable **2** *(blow)* qui ébranle tout le corps

jasmine [ˈdʒæzmɪn, ˈdʒæs-] N *(shrub)* **(common** *or* **white) j.** jasmin *m* (commun *ou* blanc); **winter j.** jasmin d'hiver; **j. perfume** (essence *f* de) jasmin
▸▸**j. tea** thé *m* au jasmin

jaundice [ˈdʒɔːndɪs] N **1** *Med* jaunisse *f*, ictère *m* **2** *Fig (bitterness)* amertume *f*

jaundiced [ˈdʒɔːndɪst] ADJ **1** *Med* ictérique, bilieux **2** *Fig (bitter)* aigri, amer; *(jealous)* jaloux; **to look on the world** *or* **on things with a j. eye** *(bitterly)* voir tout en noir; *(jealously)* tout regarder d'un œil jaloux; **to take a j. view of a situation** voir une situation d'un mauvais œil

jaunt [dʒɔːnt] N (petite) excursion *f*, balade *f*, sortie *f*, **on a j.** en excursion, en balade; **to go on** *or* **for a j.** faire une (petite) excursion *ou* une balade

jauntily [ˈdʒɔːntɪlɪ] ADV *(to remark)* *(casually)* d'une manière désinvolte, avec désinvolture; *(cheerfully)* gaiement, avec entrain, d'un air enjoué; *(to walk)* d'un pas guilleret; *(to wear one's hat)* d'une façon désinvolte; *(of woman, stylishly)* coquettement

jauntiness [ˈdʒɔːntɪnɪs] N *(carefreeness)* désinvolture *f*, insouciance *f*; *(cheerfulness)* enjouement *m*, vivacité *f*; **the j. of his step** son pas guilleret

jaunty [ˈdʒɔːntɪ] ADJ *(carefree)* désinvolte, insouciant, dégagé; *(cheerful, lively)* enjoué; **with a j. air** d'un air dégagé; **j. step** pas *m* guilleret; **he wore his cap at a j. angle** sa casquette était négligemment posée sur sa tête

Java [ˈdʒɑːvə] N **1** *Geog* (île *f* de) Java *f* **2** *Comput* Java® Java® *m*
▸▸*Comput* **J. script** Javascript® *m*, langage *m* Javascript®

java [ˈdʒɑːvə] N *Am Fam (coffee)* caoua *m*, café *m*

Javanese [dʒɑːvəˈniːz] ADJ javanais
N **1** Javanais, -aise; **the J.** les Javanais *mpl* **2** *Ling* javanais *m*

javelin [ˈdʒævlɪn] N *(weapon)*, *Sport* javelot *m*; *Sport* **the j.** *(event)* l'épreuve *f* de javelot
▸▸**j. thrower** lanceur, -euse de javelot; **j. throwing** lancement *m* du javelot

jaw [dʒɔː] N **1** *Anat* mâchoire *f*; **the lion opened its jaws** le lion a ouvert la gueule; *Fig* **her j. dropped** *(in surprise)* elle en est restée bouche bée, les bras lui en sont tombés; *Fig* **to set one's j.** *(show determination)* décider de s'accrocher
2 *Fig* **the jaws of a valley/cave** l'entrée *f* d'une vallée/grotte; **the jaws of a volcano** la bouche d'un volcan; **the jaws of hell** les portes *fpl* de l'enfer; **to snatch sb from the jaws of death/the enemy** arracher qn des griffes de la mort/de l'ennemi
3 *(of pincer, wrench etc)* mâchoire *f*, mors *m*
4 *Fam (moralizing talk)* sermon *m*; **to have a (good) j.** tailler une bavette, bavarder; **he's all j. and no action** il parle beaucoup, mais au moment d'agir …
VI *Fam (chat)* bavarder (**about** de); *(moralize)* prêcher, moraliser; **she's been jawing away on the phone all morning** elle n'a pas

arrêté de papoter au téléphone de toute la matinée

jawbone ['dʒɔːbəʊn] N (os m) maxillaire m, mâchoire f

jawbreaker ['dʒɔːbreɪkər] N **1** Fam (word) mot m imprononçable; (name) nom m à coucher dehors **2** (sweet) bonbon m (très dur)

-jawed [dʒɔːd] SUFF **round/long**/etc-j. à la mâchoire ronde/allongée/etc; Boxing etc Fam **glass-j.** à la mâchoire fragile

jay [dʒeɪ] N (bird) geai m (des chênes); **blue j.** geai bleu

jaywalk ['dʒeɪwɔːk] VI = traverser la rue d'une manière imprudente ou en dehors des passages pour piétons

jaywalker ['dʒeɪwɔːkər] N = piéton m qui traverse en dehors des passages cloutés

jaywalking ['dʒeɪwɔːkɪŋ] N = fait de traverser en dehors des passages cloutés

Jaz® [dʒæz]
▸▸ Comput **J. disk** cartouche f Jaz®; **J. drive** lecteur m Jaz®

jazz [dʒæz] N **1** Mus jazz m; **2** Am Sl (talk) baratin m; **she gave me a lot of j. about it** elle m'a fait tout un baratin là-dessus; **what's (all) this j. about your leaving?** qu'est-ce que c'est que cette histoire comme quoi tu t'en vas? **3** Sl **and all that j.** et tout le tremblement ou bazar
▸▸ **the J. Age** = l'âge m d'or du jazz américain; **j. band** orchestre m de jazz
▸ **jazz up** VT SEP Fam **1** Mus adapter pour le jazz **2** Fig (enliven) (clothes, room, style) égayer; (party) animer, mettre de l'entrain dans; (taste) relever; (building) retaper

jazzy ['dʒæzɪ] ADJ Fam (tune) aux rythmes jazz; Fig (flashy) tapageur, voyant; (nonpejorative sense) sympa

JCB® [dʒeɪsiː'biː] N Br = pelle f hydraulique automotrice

jealous ['dʒeləs] ADJ **1** (fearful of rivals) jaloux, -ouse; **a j. woman** une femme jalouse, une jalouse; **I don't see why you're getting so j.** je ne sais pas pourquoi tu fais une telle crise de jalousie **2** (envious) jaloux (of de); **to be j. of sb** être jaloux de qn, jalouser qn **3** (vigilant, possessive) jaloux (of de); **with a j. eye** d'un œil jaloux; **j. of one's good name** jaloux de sa réputation

jealously ['dʒeləslɪ] ADV **1** (enviously) jalousement, avec jalousie **2** (vigilantly) avec un soin jaloux; **a j. guarded secret** un secret jalousement gardé

jealousy ['dʒeləsɪ] N jalousie f

jeans [dʒiːnz] NPL **(pair of) j.** jean(s) m(pl); **blue j.** blue-jean m

Jeep® [dʒiːp] N Aut jeep® f

jeepers (creepers) ['dʒiːpəz('kriːpəz)] INT Old-fashioned Am Fam ça alors!

jeer [dʒɪər] N raillerie f, moquerie f; **the jeers of the crowd** (boos) les huées fpl de la foule
VI (boo) huer, conspuer; (mock) railler
VT **to j. sb** (boo) huer qn, conspuer qn; (mock) se moquer de qn, railler qn
▸ **jeer at** VT INSEP = **jeer** VT

jeering ['dʒɪərɪŋ] ADJ railleur, moqueur; (laughter) moqueur
N railleries fpl, moqueries fpl; (shouts) cris mpl railleurs ou moqueurs; (of crowd) huées fpl

jeez [dʒiːz] INT Fam mon Dieu!

Jehovah [dʒɪ'həʊvə] N Bible Jéhovah; Rel **J.'s Witness** témoin m de Jéhovah

jejune [dʒɪ'dʒuːn] ADJ Lit naïf, f naïve

jejunum [dʒɪ'dʒuːnəm] N Anat jéjunum m

Jekyll and Hyde [dʒekələnd'haɪd] N **he's a (real) J.** c'est un vrai docteur Jekyll; **to have a J. personality** faire un dédoublement de la personnalité

jell [dʒel] VI **1** (of liquid) se gélifier, prendre (en gelée) **2** Fig (of ideas) prendre corps ou forme; (of plans) prendre tournure ou forme ou corps; (of team, cabinet) parvenir à la cohésion; **they have jelled very well** ils sont parvenus à une excellente cohésion

jellied ['dʒelɪd] ADJ Culin (eel etc) en gelée

jello® ['dʒeləʊ] N Am Culin gelée f

jelly ['dʒelɪ] N **1** gelée f; **my knees were like j.** j'avais les jambes en coton **2** Br Culin (dessert) gelée f **3** Am Culin (aspic) confiture f **4** Br Sl (gelignite) dynamite f
VT Culin gélifier, mettre en gelée
▸▸ Br **j. baby** bonbon m gélifié (en forme de bébé); Am **j. roll** (gâteau m) roulé m

jellybean ['dʒelɪbiːn] N bonbon m mou (couvert de sucre dur et en forme de haricot)

jellyfish, pl **jellyfish** or **jellyfishes** ['dʒelɪfɪʃ] N méduse f

jemmy ['dʒemɪ] Br N (burglar's) j. pince-monseigneur, fpl pinces-monseigneur
VT **to j. a door (open)** forcer une porte à la pince-monseigneur

jenny ['dʒenɪ] N (female bird or animal) j. **wren** roitelet m femelle; **j. donkey** ânesse f

jeopardize ['dʒepədaɪz] VT (health, future, sb's life) compromettre, mettre en danger ou en péril; (chances, career) compromettre; (one's business) laisser péricliter

jeopardy ['dʒepədɪ] N danger m, péril m; **to be in j.** (of person, one's life) être en danger ou en péril; (of one's happiness, career, future etc) être menacé ou compromis; **his business is in j.** son affaire périclite; **to put in j.** (health, future, sb's life) compromettre, mettre en danger ou en péril; (chances, career) compromettre; (one's business) laisser péricliter; **to put sb in j.** mettre qn en danger ou en péril

jerbil ['dʒɜːbɪl] N (rodent) gerbille f

jerk[1] [dʒɜːk] N **1** (sudden pull, push etc) secousse f, saccade f, coup m sec; **she gave the rope a j.** elle a donné une secousse à la corde, elle a tiré un coup sec sur la corde; **to move by jerks** or **in jerks** or **in a series of jerks** (of vehicle etc) avancer par saccades ou par à-coups, cahoter
2 (sudden start, jump) sursaut m; **to wake up with a j.** se réveiller en sursaut
3 Sport (in weightlifting) jeté m
VT (pull, push etc suddenly) donner une secousse ou une saccade à; (repeatedly) donner des secousses ou des saccades à, secouer; (pull) tirer d'un coup sec; **they jerked the washing machine across the floor** ils ont déplacé la machine à laver à travers la pièce par à-coups; **to j. sth out of sb's hands** arracher qch (d'un coup sec) des mains de qn; **to j. forward/back** (of collision etc) (sb's head, body) rejeter en avant/en arrière; **she jerked her head** (in car crash etc) sa tête a été rejetée en arrière
VI **1** (shake) secouer; **to j. (along** or **forward)** (of vehicle) avancer par saccades ou par à-coups, cahoter; **to j. forward/back** (of head, body) être rejeté en avant/en arrière; **she jerked forward then slid back** elle se jeta en avant puis se glissa vers l'arrière; **to j. to a halt** (of vehicle, train) s'arrêter brusquement (avec des secousses)
2 (start, jump) sursauter
3 (of muscle) se contracter, avoir un spasme/des spasmes; Anat avoir un réflexe ou des réflexes
▸ **jerk off** Vulg VT SEP **to j. sb off** branler qn
VI se branler
▸ **jerk out** VT SEP (words, excuses etc) balbutier, dire d'une façon saccadée

jerk[2] N Fam Pej (fool) crétin, -ine, abruti, -ie; (obnoxious person) con(n)ard m; **don't be a j.** ne fais pas le con

jerkily ['dʒɜːkɪlɪ] ADV (to move) par saccades, par à-coups; (to walk) d'un pas saccadé; (to write, speak) d'une manière saccadée ou hâchée

jerky ['dʒɜːkɪ] ADJ (movement) saccadé; (voice, style, speech etc) saccadé, heurté, hâché; **he took his first j. steps at the age of ten months** il a fait ses premiers pas un peu saccadés à l'âge de dix mois; **in j. French** dans un français heurté ou hâché

jerrican ['dʒerɪkæn] N jerrycan m, bidon m

Jerry ['dʒerɪ] N Old-fashioned Fam Pej (soldier) Boche m, Fritz m; (the Germans) les Boches

jerry-built ['dʒerɪbɪlt] ADJ Pej (house) en carton-pâte, construit comme une cabane à lapins

jerry can N = **jerrican**

Jersey ['dʒɜːzɪ] N **1** (island) Jersey f; **in J.** à Jersey **2** (cow) vache f de Jersey ou jersiaise

jersey ['dʒɜːzɪ] N **1** (garment) tricot m (de laine); Sport maillot m **2** (material) jersey m; **j. wool/silk, wool/silk j.** jersey de laine/de soie

Jerusalem [dʒə'ruːsələm] N Jérusalem mf
▸▸ Bot, Culin **J. artichoke** topinambour m

jessie ['dʒesɪ] N Scot Fam (feeble man) mauviette f, **stop pretending you're hurt, you big j.!** arrête de faire semblant d'avoir mal, espèce de mauviette!

jest [dʒest] N (joke) plaisanterie f, (witty remark) mot m d'esprit; **in j.** (to say, speak etc) en plaisantant, pour rire, par plaisanterie; **(only) half in j.** en ne plaisantant qu'à moitié; **to act in j.** plaisanter; Prov **there is) many a true word spoken in j.** on dit souvent la vérité sous le couvert d'une plaisanterie
VI (joke) plaisanter (about sur); (make witty remarks) faire des mots d'esprit; **he's not a person to j. with** on ne plaisante pas ou on ne badine pas avec lui

jester ['dʒestər] N (joker) farceur, -euse; Hist (court) j. bouffon m ou fou m (du roi)

jesting ['dʒestɪŋ] ADJ (remark etc) fait pour plaisanter ou pour rire
N (jokes) plaisanteries fpl; (witty remarks) mots mpl d'esprit

jestingly ['dʒestɪŋlɪ] ADV en plaisantant; **j. known as ...** désigné par le terme farceur de ...

Jesuit ['dʒezjʊɪt] N Rel, Fig Pej jésuite m
ADJ Rel (missionary, theologian) jésuite; (college, seminary) de jésuites

Jesuitical [dʒezjʊ'ɪtɪk(ə)l] ADJ Fig Pej jésuitique

Jesus ['dʒiːzəs] N Jésus m; Rel **J. Christ** Jésus-Christ m
INT Sl **J. (Christ)!** nom de Dieu!; Br **J. wept!** bon sang!; Am **J. Holy Christ** nom de Dieu!
▸▸ Fam **J. freak** chrétien, -ienne hippie

jet[1] [dʒet] N **1** (aircraft) avion m à réaction, jet m; **to travel by j.** voyager en jet ou en avion à réaction; Mil **fighter j.** chasseur m à réaction **2** (of liquid, steam etc) jet m **3** (nozzle) jet m, ajutage m, buse f, (on printer) buse; (of stove) brûleur m; Aut gicleur m; **(water) j.** (in whirlpool, bath etc) gicleur m
VI (-tt-) **1** (of liquid) sortir en jet, gicler **2** Aviat Fam voyager en jet ou en avion à réaction; **she jets round the world** elle parcourt le monde en jet
▸▸ **j. engine** moteur m à réaction; Mil **j. fighter** chasseur à réaction; **j. fuel** kérosène m; **j. lag** = fatigue f due au décalage horaire; **I'm still suffering from j. lag** je suis encore sous le coup du décalage horaire; **j. plane** avion à réaction; **j. propulsion** propulsion f par réaction; Fam **j. set** jet-set m ou f, **j. ski** scooter m des mers, jet-ski m; **j. stream** jet-stream m, pl jet-streams, courant-jet m, pl courants-jets; **j. trail** traînée f de condensation

▶ **jet in** VI arriver par avion
▶ **jet off** VI s'envoler (**to** pour)
jet² N *Miner* jais *m*
  ADJ *(colour)* noir comme (du) jais, (noir) de jais
  ▶▶ **j. black** noir *m* de jais

jetfoil ['dʒetfɔɪl] N hydroglisseur *m*

jet-lagged ['dʒetlægd] ADJ fatigué à cause du décalage horaire; **in my current j. state** fatigué comme je le suis (à cause du décalage horaire)

jet-powered ['dʒet'paʊəd], **jet-propelled** [dʒetprə'peld] ADJ *(engine, aircraft)* à réaction

jetsam ['dʒetsəm] N *(no pl) Naut, Fig* épaves *fpl*

jetsetter ['dʒetsetər] N membre *m* de la jet-set

jet-skiing N scooter *m* des mers, jet-ski *m*

jettison ['dʒetɪs(ə)n] VT *Naut (cargo)* jeter à la mer *ou* par-dessus bord, se délester de; *Aviat (bombs, fuel etc)* larguer; *Fig (hope, plan, tradition etc)* abandonner, renoncer à

jetty ['dʒetɪ] N **1** *(breakwater)* jetée *f*, môle *m* **2** *(for landing)* embarcadère *m*, débarcadère *m*, appontement *m*

Jew [dʒuː] N Juif *m*, Juive *f*; *Mus* **J.'s harp** guimbarde *f*

Jew-baiting ['dʒuːbeɪtɪŋ] N persécution *f* des Juifs

jewel ['dʒuːəl] N **1** *(piece of jewellery)* bijou *m*, joyau *m*; *(gem)* pierre *f* précieuse; *Fig (person)* perle *f*, *(thing of value)* perle, bijou **2** *(of watch)* rubis *m*
  ▶▶ **j. box** coffret *m* à bijoux; **j. case** *(for gems)* coffret à bijoux; *(for compact disc)* coffret

jewelled, *Am* **jeweled** ['dʒuːəld] ADJ *(tiara, brooch)* orné de pierres précieuses; *(watch)* monté sur rubis

jeweller, *Am* **jeweler** ['dʒuːələr] N bijoutier, -ière, joaillier, -ière; **j.'s (shop)** bijouterie *f*, bijouterie-joaillerie *f*

jewellery, *Am* **jewelry** ['dʒuːəlrɪ] N bijoux *mpl*, joyaux *mpl*; **a piece of j.** un bijou

Jewess ['dʒuːes, -ɪs] N Juive *f*

Jewish ['dʒuːɪʃ] ADJ juif, *f* juive

Jewry ['dʒuːərɪ] N la communauté juive, les Juifs *mpl*

JFK [dʒeɪef'keɪ] N **1** *abbr* **John F. Kennedy 2** = aéroport *m* de New York

jib [dʒɪb] N **1** *Naut (sail)* foc *m* **2** *Tech (of crane, derrick)* flèche *f*, bras *m* **3** *Old-fashioned Fig* **I don't like the cut of his j.** son allure ne me plaît guère
  VI (-bb-) **1** *(of person)* se rebiffer, regimber, rechigner (**at sth** devant qch); **to j. at doing** rechigner à faire **2** *(of horse)* regimber, se dérober

jibe¹ [dʒaɪb] N, VI = gibe

jibe² VI *Am (agree)* s'accorder (**with** avec)

jiffy ['dʒɪfɪ] N *Fam* **to do sth in a j.** faire qch en un rien de temps *ou* en moins de deux; **in (half) a j.** en un instant, en un clin d'œil; **I'll be back/there in a j.!** je reviens/j'arrive tout de suite ou dans un instant!
  ▶▶ **J. bag**® enveloppe *f ou* pochette *f* matelassée

jig [dʒɪg] N *(dance, music)* gigue *f*
  VI (-gg-) **1** *(dance)* danser la gigue **2** *(shake)* **to j. (up and down), to j. about** *or* **around** se trémousser (en dansant), sautiller

jigger¹ ['dʒɪgər] N *(measure for whisky)* = 42 ml

jigger² VT *Fam (damage)* esquinter

jiggered ['dʒɪgəd] ADJ *Br* **1** *Old-fashioned Fam (surprised)* étonné; **well I'm j.!**, **well, I'll be j.!** zut alors!; **I'm** *or* **I'll be j. if … (confounded)** que le diable m'emporte si … **2** *Old-fashioned Sl (tired)* crevé, claqué **3** *Fam*

(broken) (TV etc) naze, déglingué, foutu; **my ankle/back is j.** je me suis niqué la cheville/le dos

jiggery-pokery ['dʒɪgərɪ'pəʊkərɪ] N *Br Fam* manigances *fpl*, micmacs *mpl*; **there was some sort of j. going on** il y avait des manigances *ou* des micmacs dans l'air

jiggle ['dʒɪg(ə)l] VT **to j. (about** *or* **around)** remuer légèrement
  VI **to j. (about** *or* **around)** être légèrement secoué; *(of earrings)* se balancer; **try not to let it j. about** fais en sorte qu'il ne soit pas trop secoué; **I can feel something jiggling about** je sens quelque chose qui remue; **her breasts j. when she runs** ses seins ballottent quand elle court; **stop jiggling about!** arrête de gigoter!

jiggy ['dʒɪgɪ] ADJ *esp Am Fam* **to get j. (with it)** *(have sex)* s'envoyer en l'air

jigsaw ['dʒɪgsɔː] N **1** *Carp* scie *f* à chantourner **2** *(game)* puzzle *m*; *Fig* **the pieces of the j. were beginning to fall into place** peu à peu tout devenait clair
  ▶▶ **j. puzzle** puzzle

jihad [dʒɪ'hæd] N *(Muslim holy war)* djihad *m*

jilt [dʒɪlt] VT *(lover, girlfriend etc)* laisser tomber, *Fam* plaquer

jimjams ['dʒɪmdʒæmz] NPL *Fam* **1** pyjama *m* **2** *Hum* **to have the j.** *(fear)* avoir les chocottes; *(revulsion)* avoir la chair de poule; *(anxiety)* avoir les nerfs en pelote

jimmy ['dʒɪmɪ] N, VT *Am* = jemmy

jingle ['dʒɪŋg(ə)l] N **1** *(of bells)* tintement *m*; *(of keys etc)* tintement, cliquetis *m*; *(of spurs)* cliquetis **2** *(catchy tune)* ritournelle *f*, *(for children)* comptine *f*, *Radio, TV (in advertisement)* jingle *m*
  VI *(of bells)* tinter, tintinnabuler; *(of keys, coins etc)* tinter, cliqueter
  VT *(coins, keys etc)* faire tinter *ou* cliqueter; *(bells)* faire tinter *ou* tintinnabuler

jingling ['dʒɪŋglɪŋ] N = jingle N 1
  ADJ **j. sound** *(of bells)* tintement *m*; *(of keys)* cliquetis *m*

jingo ['dʒɪŋgəʊ] N *Old-fashioned Fam* chauvin, -ine; **by j.!** nom d'une pipe!

jingoism ['dʒɪŋgəʊɪz(ə)m] N *Pej* chauvinisme *m*

jingoistic ['dʒɪŋgəʊ'ɪstɪk] ADJ *Pej* chauvin

jinks [dʒɪŋks] NPL *Fam* **high j.** la rigolade; **we had high j.** on a eu une séance de rigolade, on s'est bien marrés; **stop the high j.!** fini de rigolade!; **that's enough high j. for today** assez rigolé pour aujourd'hui; *Iron* **there'll be high j. when my parents find out** ça va barder *ou* chauffer quand mes parents vont l'apprendront

jinx [dʒɪŋks] *Fam* N *(person, object)* porte-malheur *m inv*, porte-guigne *m inv*; *(spell, curse)* maléfice *m*, (mauvais) sort *m*; *(bad luck)* guigne *f*; **to have a j.** avoir la guigne; **to put a j. on** porter la guigne à; **to break the j.** échapper à la guigne
  VT *Fam (usually passive) (person, project etc)* porter la guigne à; **to be jinxed** avoir la guigne

JIT [dʒeɪaɪ'tiː] ADJ *Com (abbr* **just-in-time)** juste à temps, JAT
  ▶▶ **J. distribution** distribution *f* JAT; **J. manufacturing** production *f* JAT; **J. production** production JAT; **J. purchasing** achat *m* JAT

jitterbug ['dʒɪtəbʌg] N *(dance)* jitterbug *m*
  VI (-gg-) danser le jitterbug

jitters ['dʒɪtəz] NPL *Fam* **the j.** *(anxiety)* la frousse, la trouille; **to have** *or* **get the j.** avoir la frousse (**about** de); **she's got the j. about her exam** elle a la trouille à cause de son examen; **it gives me the j.** ça me fiche la trouille *ou* la frousse

jittery ['dʒɪtərɪ] ADJ *Fam (anxious)* (très)

nerveux; **to be j., to get j.** avoir la frousse, être (très) nerveux

jiujitsu [dʒuː'dʒɪtsuː] N jiu-jitsu *m*

jive [dʒaɪv] N **1** *(music, dance)* swing *m* **2** *Am Sl (deceiving talk)* baratin *m*; *(foolish talk)* foutaises *fpl* **3** *(slang)* **j. (talk)** = argot *m* des musiciens de jazz noirs américains de Harlem dans les années trente
  VI **1** *(dance)* danser le swing **2** *Am Sl (talk nonsense)* déconner
  VT *Am Sl (mislead)* baratiner

jive-ass ADJ *Am Sl* à la noix

Jnr *(abbr* **junior)** Jr

Joan [dʒəʊn] N Jeanne *f*; **J. of Arc** Jeanne d'Arc

joanna [dʒəʊ'ænə] N *Br Sl* piano *m*

Job [dʒəʊb] N Job *m*; **to have the patience of J.** avoir la patience d'un ange; **you're a J.'s comforter** vous n'êtes pas d'un grand réconfort

JOB [dʒɒb]

| **N** travail **1–3, 6** ▪ tâche **1** ▪ emploi **3** ▪ mal **4** |
| **VI** faire des petits travaux **1** ▪ travailler à la tâche **2** |

N **1** *(piece of work, task)* travail *m*, tâche *f*; **to do its j.** *(of medicine, alcohol etc)* faire son effet; **to do the j.** faire l'affaire; **if that ointment doesn't do the j.** si cette pommade n'a pas d'effet; **the garage/hairdresser did a good j. on her** le garage/coiffeur a fait un bon travail; **to make a good** *or* **successful j. of sth** bien réussir qch; **it's quite a (difficult) j.** c'est tout un travail (**to do** sth que de faire qch); *Fig* **to lie down** *or* **fall down on the j.** *(avoid working)* tirer au flanc; **on a j.** en déplacement; *Fam* **to be on the j.** *(sexually)* faire une partie de jambes en l'air; **this shelf isn't strong** *or* **good enough for the j.** cette étagère ne tiendra pas le coup; **to do odd jobs** faire des petits travaux, bricoler à droite et à gauche; *Ind* **a j. of precision** c'est un travail de précision; *Fam* **the car has had a paint j.** la bagnole a été repeinte; **he's done a good j. of work** il a fait du bon boulot
  2 *(responsibility, duty)* travail *m*; **they are only doing their j.** ils ne font que leur travail; **I was given the j. of breaking the bad news** c'est à moi que la tâche est revenue *ou* c'est moi qui ai été chargé d'annoncer la mauvaise nouvelle; **it's my j. to …** je suis chargé de …, c'est mon travail de …; **it's my j. to remind her** c'est à moi de le lui rappeler; **that's not your j.** ce n'est pas votre travail, ce n'est pas à vous de faire ça; **I make it my j. to …** je me charge de …; **I'll have the j. of clearing it all up later** c'est moi qui serai obligé de ranger *ou* qui devrai ranger tout ça plus tard; **this muscle has the j. of …** le rôle de ce muscle est de …; **that's not part of his j.** ça n'entre pas dans ses fonctions, ça ne fait pas partie de son travail *ou* de ses attributions
  3 *(employment, post)* emploi *m*, travail *m*, *Fam* boulot *m*, *Fam* job *m*; **to create (new) jobs** créer des emplois, créer de nouveaux emplois; **she knows her j.** elle connaît son travail *ou* son affaire *ou* son métier *ou Fam* son boulot; **to give up one's j., to resign from one's j.** démissionner; *Ind etc* **500 jobs were lost** *or* **axed** il y a eu 500 suppressions d'emplois, 500 emplois *ou* postes ont été supprimés; **it's more than my j. is worth** ça serait risquer de perdre mon emploi, ça ne vaut pas la peine de perdre mon emploi pour ça; **on-the-j. training** formation *f* sur le tas; **to be out of a j.** être sans travail; *Br Fam* **to give jobs to the boys** placer ses copains; **it's jobs for the boys** les boulots vont directement aux copains
  4 *(difficulty, trouble)* **to have (quite) a j.** *or* **a**

difficult j. doing *or* **to do sth** avoir du mal à faire qch; **it was quite a j. getting her to come at all** ça a déjà été difficile de la convaincre de venir; *Fam* **she had the devil** *or Sl* **a hell of a j. doing it** elle a eu tout le mal du monde *ou* un mal de tous les diables *ou* un mal fou à faire cela; *Fam* **they've got a real j. on their hands with that baby** ils ont du pain sur la planche avec ce bébé; **it's a j. and a half** c'est un sacré boulot (**doing** pour faire)

5 *Sl (crime)* coup *m*; **to do a j.** monter un coup; **they did that bank j.** ils ont monté le coup de la banque

6 *Comput* travail *m*; **j. control** gestion *f* des travaux

7 *Fam (manufactured object)* **that TV is a really nice j.** cette télé, c'est du beau travail; **his car is the red j. parked on the corner** sa voiture, c'est le bel engin rouge qui est garé au coin; **a souped-up j.** *(car or motorcycle)* une bagnole/une moto au moteur gonflé

8 *Br Fam (excrement)* caca *m*; **the baby has done a big j.** le bébé a fait un gros caca

9 *Fig (phrases) Br* **it's** *or* **what a good j. (that)** …! heureusement que … + *ind*, c'est heureux que … + *subj*; *Br Fam* **he got what he deserved, (and) a good j. too!** il a eu ce qu'il méritait, et c'est tant mieux *ou* c'est bien fait pour lui *ou* j'en suis très heureux!; **that's just the j.** c'est exactement ce qu'il faut; *Fam* **to do a j. on a car** *(wreck)* bousiller une voiture; *Fam* **to do a j. on sb** *(beat up)* tabasser qn; **that journalist did a real j. on him** ce journaliste l'a descendu en flammes *ou* vraiment soigné; **the make-up department did a good j. (on him)** les maquilleurs se sont surpassés

VI (-bb-) 1 *(do small jobs)* faire des petits travaux, bricoler

2 *(do piecework)* travailler à la tâche *ou* à la pièce

▸▸ **j. creation** création *f* d'emplois; **j. creation scheme** programme *m* de création d'emplois; *Admin* **j. evaluation** analyse *f* des postes; **j. hunter** demandeur, -euse d'emploi; **j. hunting** recherche *f* d'un emploi; **to go j. hunting** aller à la recherche d'un emploi; **j. losses** suppressions *fpl* d'emplois; *Br Com* **j. lot** lot *m*; **a j. lot of books** des livres en vrac, un lot de livres; **to buy/sell sth as a j. lot** acheter/vendre qch en lot *ou* en vrac; **j. offer** offre *f* d'emploi; **j. opportunities** perspectives *fpl* d'emploi, débouchés *mpl*; **j. satisfaction** satisfaction *f* professionnelle; **j. security** sécurité *f* de l'emploi; **j. seeker** demandeur, -euse d'emploi; **j. sharing** partage *m* d'emploi; **j. title** titre *m* (de fonction)

jobbery ['dʒɒbərɪ] N *Br Fam* micmacs *mpl*, trafics *mpl*

jobbing ['dʒɒbɪŋ] *Br* ADJ *(worker)* (qui travaille) à la tâche *ou* à la pièce; **j. gardener** jardinier, -ière à la journée
N **1** *(piecework)* travail *m* à la tâche *ou* à la pièce **2** *(odd jobs)* bricolage *m*

Jobcentre ['dʒɒbsentər] N *Br* ≃ agence *f* nationale pour l'emploi, ANPE *f*

jobless ['dʒɒblɪs] ADJ sans travail, au chômage
NPL **the j.** les chômeurs *mpl*, les demandeurs *mpl* d'emploi; **the j. figures** le nombre des chômeurs *ou* des demandeurs d'emploi

job-share N partage *m* du travail; **we could do it as a j.** nous pourrions nous partager le travail; **they applied for the post as a j.** ils se sont présentés pour le poste en proposant de se partager le travail
VI partager le travail; **we could apply to j.** nous pourrions nous présenter en proposant de nous partager le travail

job-shop specialist N *Mktg* spécialiste *m* de production à la commande

jobsworth ['dʒɒbzwɜːθ] N petit chef *m* qui ne veut pas se mouiller ni se fatiguer

Jock [dʒɒk] N *Sl (Scot)* Écossais; **hello, J.!** salut, l'Écossais!

jock [dʒɒk] N *Am Univ Fam (sportsman)* sportif *m*

jockey ['dʒɒkɪ] N *Horseracing (man)* jockey *m*; *(woman)* femme *f* jockey; **amateur j.** jockey amateur, gentleman(-rider) *m*
VI *(scheme)* manœuvrer, intriguer **(for a job/etc** pour obtenir *ou* se faire donner un poste/etc); **to j. for position** manœuvrer *ou* intriguer pour se placer avantageusement
VT *(persuade forcefully, deceive)* **to j. sb into doing sth** emberlificoter qn pour qu'il fasse qch; **to j. sb out of a job** évincer *ou* chasser qn d'un poste
▸▸ **j. cap** casquette *f* de jockey; **Jockey® shorts** caleçon *m*

jockstrap ['dʒɒkstræp] N slip *m* à coquille

jocose [dʒə'kəʊs] ADJ facétieux

jocular ['dʒɒkjʊlər] ADJ *(humorous)* facétieux, amusant, jovial, -als *ou* -aux; *(jolly)* enjoué; **in (a) j. vein** *(to say, reply etc)* d'un ton facétieux *ou* amusant *ou* rieur

jocularity [dʒɒkjʊ'lærɪtɪ] N *(humour)* humour *m*; *(jollity)* jovialité *f*, **an atmosphere of j.** une atmosphère joviale

jocularly ['dʒɒkjʊlərlɪ] ADV *(humorously)* facétieusement; *(with jollity)* jovialement; **he was j. known as 'the Walrus' by his pupils** ses élèves lui donnaient le surnom facétieux du 'Morse'

jocund ['dʒɒkənd] ADJ *Lit* jovial, -als *ou* aux, enjoué

jodhpurs ['dʒɒdpəz] NPL pantalon *m ou* culotte *f* de cheval, jodhpurs *mpl*

Joe [dʒəʊ] N *Am Fam (man, fellow)* mec *m*, type *m*; **he's an ordinary J.** c'est un mec comme les autres
▸▸ *Br* **J. Bloggs** Monsieur *m* Tout-le-monde, ≃ Monsieur Dupont; *Am, Austr* **J. Blow** Monsieur Tout-le-monde, ≃ Monsieur Dupont; **J. Public** Monsieur Tout-le-monde, ≃ Monsieur Dupont,

joey ['dʒəʊɪ] N *Austr Fam (kangaroo)* petit kangourou *m*

jog [dʒɒg] N **1** *(push)* poussée *f*, coup *m* sec; *(shake)* secousse *f*, *(with elbow)* coup de coude; *Fig* **to give sb's memory a j.** rafraîchir la mémoire de *ou* à qn **2** *(slow run)* jogging *m*; *Horseriding* petit trot *m*; **at a j.** au petit trot; **to break into a j.** *(of person, horse)* se mettre à trotter; *Sport* **to go for a j.** aller faire un jogging
VT **(-gg-)** *(push)* pousser (d'un coup sec); *(shake)* secouer; **she jogged my elbow** elle m'a poussé le coude; *Fig* **to j. sb's memory** rafraîchir la mémoire *ou* à qn; *Fig* **to j. sb into action** inciter qn à l'action; **to j. sb out of it** secouer qn; **to j. sb out of their complacency** tirer qn de sa complaisance
VI *Sport* faire du jogging; **to go jogging** aller faire un jogging
▸▸ **j. trot** petit trot; **at a j. trot** au petit trot
▸ **jog along** VI *(of vehicle etc)* cahoter; *(of person)* trotter; *Fig (of person, factory, country etc)* aller tant bien que mal; *Fig* **I'm jogging along quite happily** je vais mon petit bonhomme de chemin

jogger ['dʒɒgər] N *Sport* **1** *(person)* jogger *m*, joggeur, -euse; *Med Fam* **j.'s nipple** irritation *f* des tétons due au frottement contre les vêtements **2** *(shoe)* chaussure *f* de jogging

jogging ['dʒɒgɪŋ] N *Sport* jogging *m*; **to like j.** aimer faire du jogging, aimer le jogging
▸▸ **j. bottoms** pantalon *m* de jogging *ou Fam* de survêt; **j. shoes** chaussures *fpl* de jogging; **j. suit** tenue *f* de jogging, jogging *m*

joggle ['dʒɒg(ə)l] N légère secousse *f*
VT secouer légèrement; **to j. sth around** re-

muer qch; **he joggled his daughter on his knee** il faisait sauter sa fille sur ses genoux
VI *(shake)* être secoué; **they joggled up and down in the back** ils étaient secoués *ou* bringuebalés à l'arrière

jog-trot VI **(-tt-)** *(of horse)*, *Fig (of person)* aller au petit trot

Johannesburg [dʒəʊ'hænɪzbɜːg] N Johannesburg

John [dʒɒn] N **1** Jean *m*; *(Saint)* **J. the Baptist** saint *m* Jean-Baptiste **2** *Br Fam (term of address)* **got a light, J.?** t'as du feu, chef?
▸▸ **J. Bull** John Bull *(personnification de la nation anglaise, du peuple anglais)*; *Am* **J. Doe** *(average person)* l'Américain *m* moyen, ≃ Monsieur *m* Dupont; *Fam (unidentified man) (under arrest)* inconnu *m*; *(corpse)* mort *m* non identifié; **J. Dory** saint-pierre *m inv*; *Am Fam* **J. Hancock, J. Henry** sa signature, son gribouillis; *Am Fam* **J. Q. Public** Monsieur Tout-le-Monde; *Fam* **J. Thomas** *(penis)* zizi *m*, zob *m*

john [dʒɒn] N **1** *Am Fam* **the j.** *(lavatory)* le petit coin, les cabinets *mpl* **2** *Am Sl (prostitute's client)* micheton *m*

johnny ['dʒɒnɪ] *Fam* N **1** *Old-fashioned (man)* gars *m* **2** *(condom) (rubber)* **j.** capote *f*, ▸▸ *Hum* **J. Foreigner** étranger, -ère; *Hist* **J. Reb** soldat *m* confédéré

Johnny-come-lately N *Fam (new arrival)* nouveau venu *m*; *Pej (upstart)* parvenu *m*

JOIN [dʒɔɪn]

N	raccord **1** ▪ joint **1** ▪ couture **1**
VT	joindre **1** ▪ unir **1** ▪ relier **1**
	▪ raccorder **1** ▪ rejoindre **2–4** ▪ se joindre à **2** ▪ s'inscrire à **5** ▪ entrer dans **5** ▪ adhérer à **5** ▪ s'engager dans **5**
VI	se joindre **1** ▪ se raccorder **1** ▪ se rejoindre **3** ▪ devenir membre **4**

N *(in wallpaper, masonry, tape etc)* raccord *m*; *Tech (junction between elements)* joint *m*; *(in fabric)* couture *f*
VT **1** *(unite) (planks, pieces of material etc)* joindre, unir; *(connect, link) (towns, words, points etc)* relier; *(edges of a wound etc)* rapprocher, réunir; *(pipes, electric wires)* raccorder; **to j. two things end to end** joindre deux choses bout à bout; **the Siamese twins are joined at the thigh** les frères siamois sont rattachés (l'un à l'autre) par la cuisse; **to j. in marriage** *or* **in matrimony** unir par le mariage; *Mil, Fig* **to j. battle** engager le combat (**with** avec); *Fig* **we shall j. forces** nous unirons nos forces; *Fig* **to j. forces** *or* **hands (with sb) to do** *or* **in doing** se joindre *ou* s'unir (à qn) pour faire; **we joined hands** nous nous sommes pris par la main, nous nous sommes donné la main

2 *(catch up with, meet) (person)* rejoindre, retrouver; *(associate oneself with) (person)* se joindre à (**in doing** pour faire); *(take part in) (game)* prendre part à; **to j. a discussion** se joindre à *ou* prendre part à une discussion; **to j. sb in** *or* **for a drink** prendre un verre avec qn, se joindre à qn pour prendre un verre; **will you j. us?** voulez-vous vous joindre à nous?; **may I j. you?** puis-je me joindre à vous?; **why don't you j. (us at) our table?** venez donc vous asseoir à notre table!; **we are joined in the studio by … …** vient nous rejoindre *ou* vient se joindre à nous dans notre studio

3 *(go to, return to)* rejoindre; *Mil, Naut* **to j. one's regiment/ship** rejoindre son régiment/son bâtiment; **we shall soon j. the motorway** nous rejoindrons bientôt l'autoroute

4 *(intersect with, flow into)* rejoindre; **to j. the sea** *(of river)* rejoindre la mer, se jeter dans la mer

5 *(become a member of)* *(club, political party)* s'inscrire à, entrer dans, adhérer à; *(class, course)* s'inscrire pour *ou* à; *(company, group, religious order)* entrer dans; *(the army, navy, police)* s'engager dans, s'enrôler dans, entrer dans; **to j. a religious order/the newspaper** entrer dans les ordres/au journal; **to j. the queue** se mettre à la queue; **I'm looking for a well-paid and interesting job – j. the queue!** je cherche un travail bien payé et intéressant – bienvenue au club!

VI 1 *(of pieces of fabric, planks etc)* se toucher, se joindre; *(of pipes, wires)* se raccorder

2 to j. with sb *(associate oneself with)* se joindre à qn, s'associer à qn *(in doing pour faire)*; **we j. with you in your sorrow** nous compatissons à votre douleur

3 *(of roads, lines, rivers)* se rejoindre

4 *(enrol in club, political party etc)* s'inscrire, devenir membre

▸ **join in** VI *(take part)* se mettre de la partie, participer, prendre part; **I'll sing first and then you (all) j. in** je chanterai d'abord et ensuite vous vous joindrez à moi

VT INSEP *(take part in)* *(game, activity)* prendre part à, participer à; *(discussion)* prendre part à, se joindre à, participer à; **to j. in the protest(s)** s'associer aux protestations, joindre sa voix aux protestations; **to j. in the singing** chanter; **you'll all j. in the chorus** vous chanterez tous le refrain en chœur

▸ **join on** VT SEP *(fasten)* attacher *(to* à*)*; *(add)* ajouter *(to* à*)*

VI *(fasten)* s'attacher *(to* à*)*; **the paragraph joins on here** le paragraphe vient s'ajouter ici; **they joined on at the end of the parade** ils se sont mis à la queue du défilé

▸ **join together** VT SEP = **join** VT **1**

VI = **join** VI **1, 2**

▸ **join up** VI **1** *Mil* s'engager; *(for class etc)* s'inscrire

2 *(of pieces of fabric etc)* se toucher, se joindre; *(of pipes, wires)* se raccorder

3 to j. up with sb *(catch up with, meet)* rejoindre qn, retrouver qn; **the three friends always j. up over Christmas** les trois amis se retrouvent toujours à Noël; **to j. up with the motorway** rejoindre l'autoroute

VT SEP *(planks, pieces of material etc)* joindre, assembler; *(pipes, electric cables)* raccorder; *(two machines)* accoupler

joined-up [dʒɔɪnd-] ADJ **can you do j. writing yet?** tu sais lier les lettres?

joiner ['dʒɔɪnər] N **1** *Br (carpenter)* menuisier *m* **2** *Fam (person who likes joining clubs etc)* = personne *f* qui aime participer à des activités et s'inscrire à des clubs

joinery ['dʒɔɪnərɪ] N *Br* menuiserie *f*, **piece of j.** article *m ou* pièce *f* de menuiserie

joint [dʒɔɪnt] N **1** *Anat* articulation *f*, jointure *f*, **out of j.** déboîté; **to put one's arm/shoulder out of j.** se démettre *ou* se disloquer *ou* se déboîter le bras/l'épaule; *Br Fig* **to put sb's nose out of j.** *(make envious)* dépiter qn

2 *Tech* joint *m*, jointure *f*; *Carp* assemblage *m*; **(soldered *or* welded) j.** soudure *f*

3 *Br Culin* rôti *m*; **j. of beef** rôti de bœuf; **j. of lamb** *(leg)* gigot *m* d'agneau; *(shoulder)* épaule *f* d'agneau

4 *Fam Pej (nightclub)* boîte *f*, *(restaurant)* restau *m*, gargote *f*, *(place)* endroit *m*; **(gambling) j.** tripot *m*

5 *Sl (cannabis cigarette)* joint *m*

VT *Culin (chicken etc)* découper aux jointures

ADJ **1** *(united, combined)* conjugué, commun; **to take j. action** mener une action commune; **thanks to their j. efforts...** grâce à leurs efforts conjugués...

2 *(shared, collective)* joint, commun; *(contract)* *(between two parties)* bilatéral, -aux; *(between more than two parties)* collectif

▸▸*Banking* **j. account** compte *m* joint, compte conjoint; **j. author** coauteur *m*; *Fin* **j. beneficiary** bénéficiaire *mf* conjoint(e); *Mil* **the J. Chiefs of Staff** = organe *m* consultatif du ministère américain de la Défense, composé des chefs d'état-major des trois armées; **j. commission** commission *f* mixte; **j. committee** commission mixte; *Ind* comité *m* paritaire; *Law* **j. custody** garde *f* conjointe; *Fin* **j. debtor** codébiteur, -trice; **j. enterprise** entreprise *f* en participation; **j. fare** tarif *m* commun; *Fin* **j. financing** financement *m* conjoint; **j. heir** cohéritier *m*; **j. holder** *(of record, trophy etc)* codétenteur, -trice; **j. management** cogestion *f*; *Br* **j. owner** *(of property)* copropriétaire *mf*; *Br* **j. ownership** copropriété *f*; **j. partnership** coassociation *f*, **j. passport** passeport *m* conjoint; **j. policy** police *f* conjointe; **j. production** coproduction *f*, **j. purchase** coacquisition *f*, **j. report** rapport *m* collectif; *Fin* **j. and several debtor** débiteur *m* solidaire; *Fin* **j. and several guarantor** garant *m* solidaire; *Fin* **j. and several liability** responsabilité *f* solidaire et indivise; **j. signature** signature *f* collective; *Fin* **j. stock** capital *m* social; **j. tenancy** location *f* commune; **j. undertaking, j. venture** entreprise commune; *(company)* coentreprise *f*, société *f* en participation; **j. venture agreement** accord *m* de partenariat

jointed ['dʒɔɪntɪd] ADJ *(puppet, limb etc)* articulé; **a j. chicken** un poulet découpé

jointing tape ['dʒɪntɪŋ] N *TV etc* bande *f* de collure

jointly ['dʒɔɪntlɪ] ADV conjointement *(with* avec*)*; *Law* **j. liable** *or* **responsible** *(debtors etc)* solidaire; *Law* **to act j.** *(of several parties)* agir solidairement; **j. and severally** conjointement et solidairement; **to own/manage j.** coposséder/cogérer

joint-stock ADJ

▸▸*Br Fin* **j. bank** banque *f* de dépôt; **j. company** société *f* (anonyme) par actions

joist [dʒɔɪst] N *Constr* solive *f*

jojoba [həʊ'həʊbə] N *Bot* jojoba *m*

joke [dʒəʊk] N **1** *(remark)* plaisanterie *f*, *Fam* blague *f*, **to make** *or* **tell** *or* **crack a j.** faire une plaisanterie *(about sth* de qch, à propos de qch*)*; **a dirty j.** une histoire cochonne; **to say/do sth for a j.** dire/faire qch histoire de rire *ou* pour rire; **he's always ready with a j.** il a toujours le mot pour rire; **the j. is on me** je suis le dindon de la farce; **she can't take a j.** elle ne comprend pas la plaisanterie; **he didn't see the j.** *(didn't appreciate something funny)* il n'a pas trouvé ça drôle; *(didn't understand somebody's joke)* il n'a pas compris la plaisanterie; **to make a j. about** *(laugh at)* se moquer de; **to make a j. of everything** prendre tout à la plaisanterie *ou Fam* à la blague *ou* à la rigolade; **he tried to make a j. of it** il a essayé d'en rire; **to make jokes about sth** faire des blagues sur *ou* à propos de qch; **the j. is that ...** le comique de l'histoire, c'est que ...; **what a j.!** *(how ridiculous)* quelle blague!; *(how funny)* ce que c'est amusant *ou* drôle!; *Fam* **that's** *or* **it's no j.!** *(not easy)* ce n'est pas de la tarte!; *(serious)* ce n'est pas de la blague!; **it's no j. waiting for hours** ce n'est pas amusant *ou* drôle d'attendre des heures; **it's getting beyond a j.** ça commence à ne plus être drôle, ça dépasse le stade de la plaisanterie

2 *(prank, trick)* **(practical) j.** farce *f*, plaisanterie *f*, tour *m*, *Fam* blague *f*; **to play a (practical) j. on sb** faire une farce *ou* une plaisanterie *ou Fam* une blague à qn, jouer un tour à qn

3 *Fam (person or thing inspiring ridicule)* plaisanterie *f*, **to be a j.** *(of novel, so-called planning, festival etc)* être lamentable; **their economic policy is nothing more than a j.**

leur politique économique n'est qu'une vaste plaisanterie; **to regard sb as a j.** considérer qn comme un objet de risée; **he treats the rules as a j.** il se moque du règlement; **this is turning into a j.** *(is getting annoying)* c'est en train de tourner à la farce

VI plaisanter, *Fam* blaguer *(about* sur, à propos de*)*; **to j. about** *(laugh at)* se moquer de; **we were able to j. about it afterwards** après nous avons pu en rire; **to j. with sb** plaisanter avec qn; **I was only joking** ce n'était qu'une plaisanterie, je plaisantais; **you're joking!, you must be** *or* **you've got to be joking!** vous voulez rire!, sans blague!; **I'm not joking!** je ne plaisante pas!

joker ['dʒəʊkər] N **1** *(making or playing jokes)* farceur, -euse, *Fam* blagueur, -euse, *Pej* plaisantin *m* **2** *Fam Pej (person)* type *m*, individu *m*; *(stupid person)* abruti *m* **3** *Cards* joker *m*; *Fig* **that's the j. in the pack** c'est la grande inconnue; *Fig* **she's the j. in the pack** avec elle, c'est la grande inconnue

jokey ['dʒəʊkɪ] ADJ = **joky**

jokily ['dʒəʊkɪlɪ] ADV en plaisantant

joking ['dʒəʊkɪŋ] ADJ *(tone)* moqueur, de plaisanterie; *(comment, response)* moqueur

N *(no pl)* plaisanteries *fpl*, *Fam* blagues *fpl*, **the j. must stop** assez plaisanté *ou Fam* blagué; **j. apart** *or* **aside** toute plaisanterie mise à part, *Fam* blague à part

jokingly ['dʒəʊkɪŋlɪ] ADV en plaisantant

joky ['dʒəʊkɪ] ADJ *(person)* qui aime raconter des plaisanteries; *(mood, conversation etc)* jovial, -als *ou* -aux; *(remark)* moqueur; *(present etc)* farfelu

jollies ['dʒɒlɪz] NPL *Am Fam* **to get one's j. (from)** **doing sth** *(get pleasure from)* prendre son pied à faire qch

jollification [dʒɒlɪfɪ'keɪʃən] N *Fam (merrymaking)* réjouissances *fpl*

jolliness ['dʒɒlɪnɪs], **jollity** ['dʒɒlɪtɪ] N *(cheerfulness)* jovialité *f*, gaieté *f*; *(merrymaking)* réjouissances *fpl*

jolly ['dʒɒlɪ] *Fam* ADJ *(cheerful)* jovial, -als *ou* -aux, gai, joyeux; *(pleasant)* agréable; **j. hockey sticks** = expression qui se réfère à une jeune fille *ou* à une femme éduquée dans le privé, adorant le sport, terriblement boute-en-train mais peu intellectuelle

ADV *Br Old-fashioned (very)* drôlement, rudement; **it serves him j. well right!** c'est drôlement *ou* rudement bien fait pour lui!; **yes, I j. well did do it!** oui, je l'ai bel et bien fait!; **j. good!** formidable!; **and a j. good job too!** et c'est tant mieux!

VT amadouer, enjôler; **I jollied him into accepting** je l'ai amadoué *ou* enjôlé tant et si bien qu'il a fini par accepter

▸▸**J. Roger** pavillon *m* noir, drapeau *m* de pirate

> Note that the French word **joli** is a false friend and is never a translation for the English word **jolly**. It means **pretty**.

▸ **jolly along** VT SEP = **jolly** VT

jolt [dʒəʊlt] N **1** *(shake)* secousse *f*, *(of vehicle)* cahot *m*, secousse, à-coup *m*, *pl* à-coups; *(of engine)* à-coup, secousse; **to wake up with a j.** se réveiller en sursaut **2** *Fig (shock, surprise)* choc *m*; **it gave me a bit of a j.** ça m'a fait un choc *ou* un coup

VI *(shake)* secouer; **to j. along** *(of vehicle)* cahoter, tressauter, avancer en cahotant *ou* par à-coups; **to j. forward** *(of vehicle, train)* s'ébranler avec une secousse; **his head jolted forward/back** *(on impact)* sa tête a été rejetée en avant/en arrière; **to j. to a stop** *(of vehicle, train)* s'arrêter en cahotant *ou* avec des à-coups

VT **1** *(shake)* secouer; *(of vehicle)* *(passengers)* cahoter, secouer; **to j. forward/back** *(of collision etc) (sb's head)* rejeter en avant/en arrière; *(passenger, suitcase)* projeter en avant/en arrière; **to j. sth off the roof** faire tomber qch du toit **2** *Fig (shock, surprise)* secouer, donner un choc à; *Fig* **to j. sb into action** secouer (les puces à) qn; *Fig* **the nation was jolted into action by the news** cette nouvelle a poussé le pays à entrer en action; *Fig* **to j. sb out of a depression** faire sortir qn de son état dépressif d'un seul coup; *Fig* **that jolted him out of his smugness!** ça lui a fait perdre sa belle suffisance d'un seul coup!

jolting ['dʒɒltɪŋ] N *(of vehicle)* cahots *mpl*; *(of plane)* secousses *fpl*

Jonah ['dʒəʊnə] N *Bible* Jonas; *Fig (jinx)* porte-malheur *m inv*

jonquil ['dʒɒŋkwɪl] N *(flower)* jonquille *f*

Jordan ['dʒɔːd(ə)n] N *(country)* Jordanie *f*; **the J.** *(river)* le Jourdain

Jordanian [dʒɔː'deɪnɪən] ADJ jordanien; *(embassy, ambassador)* de Jordanie
N Jordanien, -ienne

josh [dʒɒʃ] *Fam* N *(joke)* blague *f*
VT *(tease)* chambrer, vanner (**about** sur), mettre en boîte (**about** à cause de)
VI *(joke)* blaguer; **only joshing!** je blaguais!

joss [dʒɒs] N
► ► **j. stick** bâton *m* d'encens

jostle ['dʒɒs(ə)l] N *(push)* bousculade *f*
VI *(push each other)* se bousculer; *(use one's elbows)* jouer des coudes (**for sth** pour obtenir qch); **to j. against sb** bousculer qn; *Fig* **to j. for jobs** jouer des coudes pour décrocher un emploi; *Fig* **to j. for position** essayer de bien se placer
VT bousculer; **to be jostled, to get (oneself) jostled** se faire bousculer (**by** par); **to j. sb out of the way** écarter qn à coups de coudes *ou* en jouant des coudes; **to j. one's way (through)** se frayer un chemin à coups de coude

jostling ['dʒɒs(ə)lɪŋ] N *(of crowd)* bousculade(s) *f(pl)*

jot [dʒɒt] N *(in negatives)* **he doesn't care a j.** il n'en a rien à faire, il ne s'en soucie pas du tout; **there isn't a j. of truth in what you say** il n'y a pas la moindre parcelle de vérité dans ce que vous dites
► **jot down** VT SEP noter, prendre note de, prendre en note; **to j. down (some) notes** prendre des notes

jotter ['dʒɒtər] N *(notepad)* bloc-notes *m*, *pl* blocs-notes; *Sch (exercise book)* cahier *m*

jottings ['dʒɒtɪŋz] NPL notes *fpl* (prises à la hâte); **she made a few j. of ideas** elle a noté quelques idées à la hâte

joule [dʒuːl] N *Phys* joule *m*
► ► **J. effect** effet *m* Joule

journal ['dʒɜːn(ə)l] N **1** *(periodical)* revue *f*, journal *m* **2** *(record of events)* journal *m*; *Com (for transactions)* livre *m* de comptes **3** *Tech (bearing)* palier *m* (de tourillon)
► ► *Tech* **j. bearing** palier *m* (de tourillon); *Com* **j. entry** écriture *f* comptable, contre-passation *f*, *pl* contre-passations

Note that the most common meaning of the French word **journal** is **newspaper**.

journalese [dʒɜːnə'liːz] N *Pej Fam* style *m ou* jargon *m* journalistique

journalism ['dʒɜːnəlɪz(ə)m] N journalisme *m*

journalist ['dʒɜːnəlɪst] N journaliste *mf*

journalistic [dʒɜːnə'lɪstɪk] ADJ journalistique

journey ['dʒɜːnɪ] N voyage *m*; *(of short distance)* trajet *m*; **it was quite a j. to get here** ça a été toute une épopée pour arriver jusqu'ici; **it is a two-day j. by car** c'est à deux journées de route en voiture; **Bradford is on-**

ly a short **j. away (from here)** Bradford est tout près d'ici; **to make a j.** faire un voyage; **to set off** *or* **out on a j.** partir en voyage; **it's not wise to set out on such a j. at this time of year** ce n'est pas prudent d'entreprendre un tel voyage en cette période de l'année; **to go (away) on a j.** partir en voyage; **to get to** *or* **reach the end of one's j.** arriver à destination, arriver à la fin de son voyage *ou* trajet; **have a good j.!** bon voyage!; **to have an hour's j. to work** avoir une heure de trajet pour se rendre à son travail; **to go on a train j.** prendre le train, voyager par le train; **the return j., the j. home** *or* **back** le voyage de retour, le retour; *(from work)* le trajet de retour; **the outward j.** le voyage d'aller, l'aller *m*
VI *Lit* voyager; **to j. on** continuer son voyage
► ► **j. time** durée *f* du voyage; *(shorter distance)* durée du trajet

Note that the French word **journée** is a false friend and is never a translation for the English word **journey**. It means **day**.

journeyman, *pl* **journeymen** ['dʒɜːnɪmən] N *(craftsman)* compagnon *m*, ouvrier *m*; **j. baker** ouvrier boulanger; **j. carpenter** compagnon charpentier

journo ['dʒɜːnəʊ] N *Fam* journaliste *mf*

joust [dʒaʊst] *Hist, Fig* N joute *f*
VI *Hist* jouter (**with** contre); *Fig* batailler

jousting ['dʒaʊstɪŋ] N *Hist, Fig* joutes *fpl*; **a j. match** une bataille

jovial ['dʒəʊvɪəl] ADJ jovial, -als *ou* -aux, enjoué; **she's in a j. mood** elle est d'humeur joviale; **to feel j.** être enjoué

joviality [dʒəʊvɪ'ælɪtɪ] N jovialité *f*, enjouement *m*

jovially ['dʒəʊvɪəlɪ] ADV jovialement

jowl [dʒaʊl] N **1** *(jaw)* mâchoire *f* **2** *(hanging flesh on cheek)* bajoue *f*; **he had heavy jowls** il avait de grosses bajoues

-jowled [dʒaʊld] SUFF **long/square/etc-j.** à la mâchoire allongée/carrée/etc; **a heavy-j. face** un visage aux grosses bajoues

joy [dʒɔɪ] N **1** *(happiness)* joie *f*; **to jump** *or* **leap/weep** *or* **cry for j.** sauter *ou* bondir/pleurer de joie; **wild with j., beside oneself with j.** fou *ou* ivre de joie; **to our great j.** à notre grande joie; **I wish you (great) j.** je vous souhaite beaucoup de bonheur; *Iron* **I wish you j. (of it)!** je vous souhaite bien du plaisir!, vous m'en voyez fort aise!
  2 *(pleasure)* plaisir *m*; **the joys of marriage/of spring** les joies *ou* plaisirs du mariage/du printemps; **full of the joys of spring** au comble du bonheur; **the joys of having children** les joies qu'apportent les enfants; **the joys of having a car** les joies d'avoir une voiture; **her style is a j. to watch** son style est un plaisir pour les yeux; **he's a j. to work for** c'est un plaisir de travailler pour lui; **our new car is a j. to drive** avec notre nouveau modèle la conduite est un plaisir; **she's a j. to be with, it's a j. to be with her** c'est un plaisir que d'être à ses côtés; **our grandchildren are an absolute j.** nos petits-enfants sont très mignons
  3 *Br Fam (no pl) (success)* succès *m*; **(did you have** *or* **get) any j.?** ça a marché?, tu as réussi?; **no j.!** ça n'a rien donné!, ça n'a pas marché!; **you won't get any j. from him** tu n'arriveras à rien avec lui

joyful ['dʒɔɪfʊl] ADJ *(person, face, news etc)* joyeux

joyfully ['dʒɔɪfəlɪ] ADV joyeusement, avec joie; *(to celebrate, be reunited)* dans la joie

joyfulness ['dʒɔɪfʊlnɪs] N (grande) joie *f*, allégresse *f*

joyless ['dʒɔɪlɪs] ADJ triste, sans joie; *(face, grin)* triste

joylessly ['dʒɔɪlɪslɪ] ADV tristement, sans joie

joyous ['dʒɔɪəs] ADJ *esp Lit (occasion, person etc)* joyeux; *(news)* heureux

joyously ['dʒɔɪəslɪ] ADV *esp Lit* joyeusement, avec joie; *(to celebrate)* dans la joie

joypad ['dʒɔɪpæd] N *Comput* joypad *m*

joyride ['dʒɔɪraɪd] N *(in stolen car)* virée *f* (dans une voiture volée); **to go for a** *or* **on a j.** faire une virée (dans une voiture volée); *Fig* **it's no j. working with him** travailler avec lui, ce n'est pas une partie de plaisir
VI *(pt* **joyrode** [-rəʊd], *pp* **joyridden** [-rɪd(ə)n]*)* faire une virée (dans une voiture volée); **to go joyriding** faire une virée (dans une voiture volée)

joyrider ['dʒɔɪraɪdər] N voleur, -euse *(qui prend une voiture pour faire une virée)*

joystick ['dʒɔɪstɪk] N *Aviat* manche *m* à balai; *Comput* manette *f* (de jeu), manche à balai

JP [dʒeɪ'piː] N *Br Law (abbr* **justice of the peace)** juge *m* de paix

JPEG ['dʒeɪpeg] N *Comput (abbr* **Joint Photographic Experts Group)** *(format m)* JPEG *m*

Jr *(abbr* **Junior)** Thomas Smith, **Jr** Thomas Smith fils

jubilant ['dʒuːbɪlənt] ADJ *(shouts)* de joie; *(expression)* épanoui, radieux; *(crowd)* exultant; *(party, celebration)* joyeux; **to be j.** *(of person)* déborder de joie, jubiler, exulter; **to be j. at** *or* **about** *or* **over the news** être transporté de joie par la nouvelle

jubilantly ['dʒuːbɪləntlɪ] ADV avec jubilation

jubilation [dʒuːbɪ'leɪʃən] N *(of person)* (grande) joie *f*, exultation *f*, jubilation *f*; **to be a cause for (great) j.** être l'occasion de (grandes) réjouissances; **scenes of j.** scènes de réjouissances

jubilee ['dʒuːbɪliː] N **(golden) j.** jubilé *m*, (fête *f* du) cinquantième anniversaire *m* (de mariage etc); **silver/diamond j.** (fête du) vingt-cinquième/soixantième anniversaire

Judaea [dʒuː'diːə] N Judée *f*

Judaic [dʒuː'deɪɪk] ADJ judaïque

Judaism ['dʒuːdeɪɪz(ə)m] N *Rel* judaïsme *m*

Judas ['dʒuːdəs] N **1** *Bible* Judas; **J. Iscariot** Judas Iscariote **2** *(traitor)* judas *m*
► ► **J. kiss** baiser *m* de Judas; **J. tree** arbre *m* de Judée, gainier *m*

judas ['dʒuːdəs] N *(peephole)* judas *m*
► ► **j. hole** judas; **j. window** judas

judder ['dʒʌdər] *Br* N vibrations *fpl*; *(of brakes)* trépidation *f*; *(of clutch, tool)* broutage *m*, broutement *m*
VI vibrer; *(of brakes)* trépider; *(of clutch, tool)* brouter; **to j. to a halt** *(of train, vehicle)* s'arrêter avec de violentes secousses

judge [dʒʌdʒ] N **1** *Law, Sport etc* juge *m*; *(of contest)* juge, membre *m* du jury; *Law* **the judges** *(the bench)* la magistrature assise; *Bible* **(the Book of) Judges** le livre des Juges
  2 *Fig* juge *m*, connaisseur *m*; **good j.** *(of cars, horses, wine)* spécialiste *mf* (**of** en); **she fancies herself as a good j. of men** elle croit savoir juger les hommes; **I'm not sure he's the best j. of such things** je ne suis pas sûr qu'il soit très bon juge en la matière; **to be a good** *or* **keen j. of character** être bon ou fin psychologue; **I'll let you be the j. of that** je vous en fais juge, je vous laisse juge; **I will be the j. of that** c'est moi qui jugerai de cela
VT **1** *Law, Sport etc (try, give decision about)* juger; *Law* **to j. a case** juger une affaire
  2 *(assess critically) (person, situation, text etc)* juger; *(estimate, evaluate) (distance, speed, weight, price etc)* estimer, évaluer; **her latest novel has been judged a failure by the critics** les critiques ont estimé que

son dernier roman était mauvais; **to j. sb by** *or* **on sth** juger qn sur *ou* d'après qch; **to j. people by appearances** juger d'après les apparences; **to j. sth at its true** *or* **proper value/on its merits** juger *ou* apprécier qch à sa juste valeur/selon ses mérites

3 (*think, consider*) juger (**that** que; **if, whether** si); **to j. it necessary to …** juger nécessaire de …

VI (*assess, estimate, pass judgement*), *Law, Rel* juger; **to j. by appearances** juger d'après les apparences; **as far as I can j.** autant que je puisse en juger; **to j. for oneself** (en) juger par soi-même; **judging by** *or* **from his letter/my first impressions** à en juger par *ou* d'après sa lettre/mes premières impressions; **who will be judging?** (*in competition*) qui va faire fonction de juge?

judg(e)ment, *Am* **judgment** ['dʒʌdʒmənt] **N 1** *Law, Rel, Fig* jugement *m*; *Law* **to pass** *or* **give** *or* **deliver j.** prononcer *ou* rendre un jugement (**on** sur); *Law* **to sit in j.** (*of court*) siéger; *Fig* **to sit in j. on** *or* **over sb, to pass j. on sb** porter un jugement sur qn, juger qn; *Fig* **to sit in j., to pass j.** porter des jugements, juger (les gens); *Rel* **the Last J.** le Jugement dernier

2 (*no pl*) (*discernment*) jugement *m*; **political/financial j.** discernement *m* en matière de politique/finances; **to have/lack (good** *or* **sound) j.** avoir du/manquer de jugement; **to have very sound j.** avoir une grande sûreté de jugement, avoir un jugement très sûr; **this decision shows good j.** cette décision montre du discernement; **to trust sb's j.** s'en remettre au jugement de qn

3 (*opinion*) avis *m*, opinion *f*; **to give one's j. on** donner *ou* exprimer son avis sur; **to form a j.** se faire une opinion; **in my j.** à mon sens; **against my better j.** tout en sachant que je me trompe/trompais sans doute

▸▸ *Rel* **J. Day** le Jugement dernier; *Mktg* **j. sample** échantillon *m* discrétionnaire; *Mktg* **j. sampling** échantillonnage *m* discrétionnaire

judg(e)mental, *Am* **judgmental** [dʒʌdʒ'ment(ə)l] **ADJ** (*person, book etc*) critique; **I don't want to seem j. but …** je ne veux pas avoir l'air de critiquer mais …

▸▸ *Mktg* **j. forecasting** prévision *f* par estimation; *Mktg* **j. method** méthode *f* estimative

judicature ['dʒuːdɪkətʃər] **N** *Law* (*administration of justice*) justice *f*; (*system*) organisation *f* judiciaire; (*judges*) magistrature *f*

judicial [dʒuː'dɪʃ(ə)l] **ADJ** *Law* (*inquiry, power, proceedings*) judiciaire

▸▸ **j. inquiry** enquête *f* judiciaire; **j. murder** assassinat *m* légal *ou* juridique; *Am* **j. review** (*of ruling*) examen *m* d'une décision de justice (*par une juridiction supérieure*); (*of law*) examen de la constitutionnalité d'une loi; **j. separation** séparation *f* de corps

judicially [dʒuː'dɪʃəlɪ] **ADV** *Law* judiciairement

judiciary [dʒuː'dɪʃɪərɪ] *Law* **ADJ** judiciaire **N** (*judges*) magistrature *f*; (*branch of government*) pouvoir *m* judiciaire; (*system of courts*) organisation *f* judiciaire

judicious [dʒuː'dɪʃəs] **ADJ** (*person, mind, thought etc*) judicieux

judiciously [dʒuː'dɪʃəslɪ] **ADV** judicieusement

judiciousness [dʒuː'dɪʃəsnɪs] **N** (*of person, mind*) discernement *m*, bon sens *m*; (*of thought, remark*) bon sens

judo ['dʒuːdəʊ] **N** judo *m*

judy, Judy ['dʒuːdɪ] **N** *Old-fashioned Br Sl* (*girl, woman*) nana *f*

jug [dʒʌg] **N 1** *Br* (*for cream, milk, water*) pot *m*; (*for wine*) pichet *m*; **coffee j.** cafetière *f*;

Fam Hum **his ears are like j. handles** il a les oreilles décollées **2** *Old-fashioned Sl* (*prison*) taule *f*, tôle *f*, **in (the) j.** au trou, en taule *ou* tôle **3** *Sl* **jugs** (*breasts*) nichons *mpl*, lolos *mpl*

▸▸ **j. kettle** = bouilloire *f* électrique haute; *Am* **j. wine** vin *m* ordinaire

jugful ['dʒʌgfʊl] **N** (*of cream, milk, water*) (plein) pot *m*; (*of wine*) (plein) pichet *m*

jugged [dʒʌgd] **ADJ**

▸▸ *Culin* **j. hare** civet *m* de lièvre

juggernaut ['dʒʌgənɔːt] **N 1** *Br* (*lorry*) (gros) poids *m* lourd, *Fam* mastodonte *m* **2** *Fig* (*destructive force*) vague *f* de fond, vague déferlante, raz-de-marée *m* inv

juggins ['dʒʌgɪnz] **N** *Old-fashioned Br Fam* (*simpleton*) nigaud, -aude, cruche *f*

juggle ['dʒʌg(ə)l] **VI** (*with balls, figures*) jongler

VT (*balls, figures*) jongler avec

juggler ['dʒʌglər] **N** jongleur, -euse

juggling ['dʒʌglɪŋ] **N** jonglerie *f*, art *m* du jongleur; (*trickery*) fourberie *f*

Jugoslav ['juːgəʊslɑːv] **ADJ, N** = **Yugoslav**

Jugoslavia [juːgəʊ'slɑːvɪə] **N** = **Yugoslavia**

Jugoslavian [juːgəʊ'slɑːvɪən] **ADJ, N** = **Yugoslavian**

jugular ['dʒʌgjʊlər] *Anat* **ADJ** jugulaire

N (*veine f*) jugulaire *f*, *Fig* **to go for the j.** attaquer toutes griffes dehors *ou* tous azimuts

juice [dʒuːs] **N 1** (*of fruit, vegetables, meat*) jus *m*; (*of plant*) suc *m*; *Physiol* **gastric** *or* **digestive juices** sucs gastriques *ou* digestifs **2** *Fam* (*electricity*) jus *m*, courant *m*; (*gas*) gaz *m*; (*petrol*) essence *f* **3** *Am Fam* (*popularity, recognition*) succès *m*; **to have a lot of j.** faire un tabac

VT (*apple, orange etc*) extraire le jus de

▸▸ **j. bar** = bar *m* où l'on sert des jus de fruit; *Br* **j. extractor** centrifugeuse *f* (*pour faire des jus de fruit*)

▸ **juice up VT SEP** *Am Sl* **1** (*liven up*) (*party*) mettre de l'animation *ou* de l'ambiance dans; (*add power to*) (*engine*) gonfler **2** **to get juiced up** (*drunk*) se soûler

juiced [dʒuːst] **ADJ** *Am Fam* (*drunk*) pété, bourré

juicer ['dʒuːsər] **N 1** (*for fruit*) centrifugeuse *f* (*électrique*) **2** *Am Fam* (*alcoholic*) alcolo *mf*, poivrot, -ote

juiciness ['dʒuːsɪnɪs] **N** (*of meat*) juteux *m*; *Fig* (*of story, detail*) piquant *m*, (*côté m*) croustillant *m*; **the j. of these melons** ces melons bien juteux

juicy ['dʒuːsɪ] **ADJ** (*fruit*) juteux; (*meat*) plein de jus, qui rend du jus; *Fig* (*story, detail*) croustillant, piquant; **the j. part of the story** le plus croustillant de l'histoire; *Fam* **a j. deal** (*lucrative*) une affaire juteuse; **a nice j. morsel** (*of meat etc*) un morceau de choix bien succulent; *Fig* **a juicy scandal** un scandale bien juteux; *Br Sl* **she's a j. bit** (*sexy*) elle est très excitante, c'est une sacrée allumeuse

jujitsu [dʒuː'dʒɪtsuː] **N** jiu-jitsu *m*

juju ['dʒuːdʒuː] **N** (*charm, fetish*) gri(s)-gri(s) *m*

jukebox ['dʒuːkbɒks] **N** juke-box *m*, *pl* juke-boxes

Jul *abbr* **July**

julep ['dʒuːlɪp] **N** (*drink*) **(mint) j.** bourbon *m* frappé à la menthe

Julian ['dʒuːlɪən] **ADJ** (*calendar etc*) julien

Julius Caesar ['dʒuːlɪəs] **N** Jules César

July [dʒuː'laɪ, dʒʊ'laɪ] **N** VOIR GRAMMAIRE A81–2; B60–2 juillet *m*; **in J.** au mois de juillet, en juillet; **on the first/the seventh of J.** le premier/le cinq juillet

jumble ['dʒʌmb(ə)l] **N 1** (*disorder*) fouillis *m*, pagaïe *f*, méli-mélo *m*, *Fig* (*of ideas etc*) méli-

---

mélo, fouillis, fatras *m*; (*of words*) fatras; **in a j.** (*papers etc*) en pagaïe, en fouillis; *Fig* (*ideas etc*) (em)brouillé **2** *Br* (*unwanted articles*) bric-à-brac *m* inv

VT (*documents, toys, books etc*) mélanger, mettre la pagaïe dans; (*clothes, shoes etc*) mélanger; *Fig* (*ideas, details, words etc*) (em)brouiller, mélanger; **the pages got all jumbled** les pages se sont complètement mélangées; **the clothes lay jumbled on the floor** les vêtements gisaient pêle-mêle sur le sol; **everything was jumbled** tout était mélangé; **he jumbled the details** il s'est emmêlé *ou* embrouillé dans les détails

▸▸ *Br* **j. sale** = vente *f* de charité où sont vendus des articles d'occasion et des produits faits maison

▸ **jumble together, jumble up VT SEP** = **jumble VT**

jumbo ['dʒʌmbəʊ] *Fam* **ADJ 1** (*giant-sized*) géant, énorme **2** *Am Fin* (*loan*) géant

N (*pl* **jumbos**) **1** (*person, animal, thing*) mastodonte *m*; *Aviat* jumbo-jet *m*, *pl* jumbo-jets, (*avion m*) gros porteur *m* **2** (*elephant*) = surnom typique donné aux éléphants

▸▸ *Aviat* **j. jet** (*avion*) gros porteur; *St Exch* **j. trade** opération *f* jumbo

JUMP [dʒʌmp]

N	saut **1, 5** ▪ bond **1** ▪ obstacle **2**
	▪ hausse **3** ▪ sursaut **4**
VI	sauter **1, 2, 4** ▪ faire un bond **3, 4**
	▪ sursauter **4**
VT	sauter **1, 3** ▪ faire sauter **2**

N 1 (*leap*) saut *m*, bond *m*; (*by parachute*) saut (en parachute); **to take** *or* **make a j.** faire un saut *ou* un bond, sauter; **in** *or* **at one j.** d'un (seul) bond; *Fam* **go take a j.!** va te faire voir (ailleurs)!, va te faire cuire un œuf!; *Fig* **to be one j. ahead of** avoir une longueur d'avance sur; *Fam* **to have the j. on sb** (*have a head start*) avoir pris une longueur d'avance sur qn dès le départ

2 (*on racecourse*) obstacle *m*; **to put a horse over a j.** faire sauter un obstacle à un cheval

3 (*in temperature, unemployment etc*) hausse *f* (soudaine) (**in** de); **the j. in prices** la flambée des prix, la hausse (soudaine) des prix; **to take a (sudden) j.** faire un bond

4 (*sudden movement, start*) sursaut *m*; **that gave me a j.** cela m'a fait sursauter *ou* tressauter

5 *Comput* saut *m*, branchement *m*

VI 1 (*leap*) (*of person, animal etc*) sauter; (*from aircraft*) sauter (en parachute); **j.!** (*to child, dog*) allez, hop!, saute!; **to j. to one's feet** se (re)lever d'un bond; **to j. to the ground** sauter à terre; **to j. for joy** (*feel elated, leap in the air*) sauter de joie; **to j. (down) from a wall/tree** sauter (du haut) d'un mur/arbre; **to j. from a train/vehicle** sauter d'un train/d'un véhicule; **to j. across a ditch** franchir un fossé d'un bond, sauter un fossé

2 (*go directly*) sauter; **to j. from one subject to another** *or* **to the next** sauter d'un sujet à l'autre; **I jumped to the third chapter** je suis passé directement au troisième chapitre; **the film then jumps to the present** puis le film fait un saut jusqu'au présent; **to j. from the bottom to the top of the list** remonter toute la liste d'un seul coup

3 (*of profit, temperature etc*) faire un bond; (*of price*) flamber, faire un bond

4 (*make a sudden movement*) (*of person*) sursauter, tressauter; (*of heart*) faire un bond, bondir; (*of record player needle, chisel, drill*) sauter; **we nearly jumped out of our skins** (*from surprise*) nous avons failli sauter au plafond; (*from fear, shock*) ça nous a fait *ou Fam* fichu un de ces coups; **the sight of her (nearly) made me j. out of my skin** ça m'a fait *ou Fam* fichu un de ces coups de la voir

5 *Fig (phrases)* **to j. at an offer/a chance/a suggestion** sauter sur une offre/une occasion/une proposition; **you should j. at it** vous devriez sauter dessus; **to j. to conclusions** tirer des conclusions prématurées *ou* hâtives; **to j. to the conclusion that ...** conclure prématurément que ...; **and j. to it!** et que ça saute!; **let's wait and see which way she jumps** attendons de voir sa réaction, attendons de voir comment elle va réagir; *Fam* **to j. down sb's throat** *(reply sharply to)* rabrouer qn, rembarrer qn, envoyer qn paître *ou* promener; *(criticize)* engueuler qn; *Am Fam* **to j. all over sb** *(scold, criticize)* passer un savon à qn, engueuler qn

6 *Fam* **to be (really) jumping** *(of party, nightclub)* être très animé

VT 1 *(hedge, ditch etc)* franchir d'un bond, sauter *(par-dessus)*; *Fig (skip) (paragraph, word, page etc)* sauter; *Sch* **to j. a class** sauter une classe; **to j. a or the groove** *(of record player needle)* sauter

2 *(cause to jump) (horse)* faire sauter; *Sport* **to j. a horse over a hurdle** faire sauter une haie à un cheval

3 *Am* **to j. rope** sauter à la corde

4 *(escape from, pass, leave illegally etc) Law* **to j. bail** se dérober à la justice *(alors qu'on jouit de la liberté provisoire)*; *Aut* **to j. the lights** griller *ou* brûler le feu rouge *ou* les feux; *Br* **to j. the queue** passer avant son tour, resquiller; **to j. the rails** *(of train)* dérailler; *Naut* **to j. ship** *(of sailor)* déserter (le navire)

5 *Rail Fam* **to j. a train** *(get on)* sauter dans un train *(to à destination de)*; *(without paying)* voyager sans billet

6 *Fam (attack, ambush, take over)* **to j. sb** sauter *ou* tomber sur (le paletot de) qn; **to j. a train** *(of bandits etc)* attaquer un train; *Am* **to j. a claim** s'emparer illégalement d'une concession

▸▸ *Cin* **j. cut** faux *m* raccord, saut *m* de montage; *Br Aviat* **j. jet** avion *m* à décollage vertical; *Br* **j. leads** câbles *mpl* de démarrage; *Am* **j. rope** corde *f* à sauter; *Br* **j. seat** strapontin *m*; **j. suit** *(clothing)* combinaison-pantalon *f*, *pl* combinaisons-pantalons; *(for baby)* grenouillère *f*

▸ **jump about, jump around** VI sautiller; *Fig (of story, film etc)* partir dans toutes les directions

▸ **jump back** VI *(of person, vehicle)* faire un bond en arrière, reculer d'un bond; **the story then jumps back twenty years** à ce moment-là l'histoire fait un saut de vingt ans en arrière

▸ **jump down** VI *(from wall etc)* sauter (à terre); **to j. down from a wall/tree** sauter (du haut) d'un mur/arbre

▸ **jump forward** VI *(of person, vehicle)* faire un bond en avant; **at this point the film jumps forward two years** à ce moment-là le film fait un saut de deux années en avant; **if I can briefly j. forward to ...** si je peux anticiper brièvement sur ...

▸ **jump in** VI *(into pool, river etc)* sauter (dedans); *(into vehicle, train)* monter (vite); *(into conversation)* intervenir; *Aut* **j. in!** montez!; *Fig* **to j. in at the deep end** se jeter tête baissée dans les problèmes

     VT INSEP = **jump into**

▸ **jump into** VT INSEP *(river, ditch etc)* sauter dans; *(car etc)* sauter *ou* monter dans; **to j. into bed with sb** coucher avec qn

▸ **jump off** VI **1** *(from wall, train etc)* sauter *(from de)*

     2 *Horseriding* faire un barrage

     VT INSEP *(bicycle, train etc)* sauter de; **to j. off a wall/etc** sauter (du haut) d'un mur/etc

▸ **jump on** VI *(on to vehicle, train)* monter; *(on to bicycle)* sauter dessus

     VT INSEP **1** *(bus, train etc)* monter *ou* sauter dans; *(bicycle)* sauter sur

     2 *Fam* **to j. on sb** *(reprimand)* passer un savon à qn; **you should j. on that kind of thing at once** tu devrais couper court à ce genre de choses

▸ **jump out** VI *(from vehicle, train etc)* sauter *(of, from* de); **I'll j. out at the traffic lights** je vais descendre au feu rouge; **to j. out of bed** sauter (à bas) du lit; **to j. out of the window** sauter par la fenêtre; **to j. out of the bushes/one's hiding place** bondir d'entre les buissons/de sa cachette; *Fig* **to j. out at sb** *(of mistake etc)* sauter aux yeux de qn

▸ **jump over** VT INSEP *(hedge, ditch etc)* franchir d'un bond, sauter (par-dessus)

     VI sauter (par-dessus)

▸ **jump up** VI **1** *(to one's feet)* se (re)lever d'un bond; **up she jumped** d'un bond, elle se (re)leva *ou* elle fut debout; **to j. up and down** sautiller

     2 *Fam (increase suddenly)* = **jump** VI **3**

jumped-up [dʒʌmp'tʌp] ADJ *Br Fam Pej (recently promoted, arrogant)* récemment promu (et qui a la grosse tête); *(upstart)* parvenu; **some j. little salesman/civil servant** un petit péteux de vendeur/fonctionnaire

jumper¹ [ˈdʒʌmpər] N **1** *Br (sweater)* pull(-over) *m* **2** *Am (sleeveless dress)* robe *f* chasuble

jumper² N **1** *(horse, athlete)* sauteur, -euse; **to be a good j.** être bon sauteur, bien sauter **2** *Am Aut* jumpers câbles *mpl* de démarrage **3** *Comput (pin)* cavalier *m*

     ▸▸ *Am Aut* **j. cables** câbles de démarrage

jumpily [ˈdʒʌmpɪlɪ] ADV *(nervously)* nerveusement

jumpiness [ˈdʒʌmpɪnɪs] N *(of person)* nervosité *f*, *St Exch (of markets)* nervosité, fébrilité *f*

jumping [ˈdʒʌmpɪŋ] ADJ **1** *(insect)* sauteur **2** *Fam (party, nightclub)* hyper animé

     N *(leaps)* sauts *mpl*; *Horseriding (show jumping)* jumping *m*, concours *m* hippique

     ▸▸ *Bot* **j. bean** pois *m* sauteur; **j. jack** *(firework)* pétard *m* mitraillette; *(puppet)* pantin *m*

jumping-off N **j. place** or **point** *(for journey)* point *m* de départ *(for pour)*; *Fig (for talks, in one's career)* tremplin *m*, point de départ

jumpmaster [ˈdʒʌmpmæstər] N *Am Mil* moniteur, -trice de parachutisme

jump-off N *Horseriding* barrage *m*

jump-start N **to give a j. to** = **jump-start** VT

     VT *(car) (push)* faire démarrer en poussant; *(with jump leads)* faire démarrer au moyen de câbles de démarrage; *Fig* **to j. the economy** relancer l'économie

jumpy [ˈdʒʌmpɪ] ADJ **1** *(nervous) (person, gestures etc)* nerveux; *St Exch (market)* nerveux, fébrile **2** *(fitful, jerky) (style, gestures etc)* saccadé

Jun *abbr* **June**

junction [ˈdʒʌŋkʃən] N **1** *(in roads, railway lines)* embranchement *m*, bifurcation *f*, jonction *f*, *(between two roads)* jonction; *(in rivers)* confluent *m*; *(in pipes)* embranchement, jonction, raccordement *m*; *(crossroads)* carrefour *m*; *(station)* gare *f* de jonction *ou* de raccordement; *(weld)* soudure *f*, *Elec* connexion *f*, *Elec (of wires)* branchement *m*; *Br* **5** *(on motorway) (exit)* la sortie *f5*; *(entrance)* l'entrée *f5*

     2 *Fml (no pl) (joining)* jonction *f*

     ▸▸ *Br Elec* **j. box** boîte *f* de dérivation

     Attention: ne pas confondre avec **juncture**.

juncture [ˈdʒʌŋktʃər] N *esp Fml* **1** *(critical point in time)* **at this j.** en ce moment même, dans ces circonstances; *(in past)* à ce moment même; **we have reached a critical j.** nous sommes dans une situation critique **2** *Anat* jonction *f*

     Attention: ne pas confondre avec **junction**.

June [dʒuːn] N   VOIR GRAMMAIRE A81–2; B60–2
juin *m*; **in J.** au mois de juin, en juin; **(on) the first/the seventh of J.** le premier/le sept juin

     ▸▸ **J. beetle, J. bug** hanneton *m*

jungle [ˈdʒʌŋg(ə)l] N *(forest)*, *Fig (competitive environment)* jungle *f*; **a j. animal/plant** une bête/plante de la jungle; *Fig* **a j. of red tape** une montagne de paperasseries

     ▸▸ *Old-fashioned Offensive Sl* **j. bunny** nègre, *f* négresse; **j. fever** paludisme *m*; *Am* **j. gym** cage *f* à poules *(jeu)*; *Br Fam* **j. juice** gnôle *f*, **j. warfare** combat *m* de jungle

junior [ˈdʒuːnjər] ADJ **1** *(younger person)* cadet, plus jeune; **to be j. to sb** être plus jeune que qn; **she's three years j. to me, she's j. to me by three years** elle a trois ans de moins que moi; **Hudson J.** *or* **Jnr** *or* **Jr** *or* **Jun** *(the son)* Hudson fils *ou* junior *ou* Jr; *(one of two or more brothers)* Hudson junior *ou* Jr

     2 *(in rank)* subalterne; **to be j. to sb** être au-dessous de qn

     3 *(small)* petit; **j. portions available** *(in restaurant)* menu enfant

     N **1** *(younger person)* cadet, -ette; *esp Am Fam* **where's j.?** où est le petit/la petite?; **to be sb's j.** être le cadet de qn, être plus jeune que qn; **she's three years my j., she's my j. by three years** elle est ma cadette de trois ans, elle est plus jeune que moi de trois ans

     2 *(subordinate)* (employé, -ée) subalterne *mf*, *Fam Pej* sous-fifre *m*; **he's our office j.** *(performing general duties)* c'est notre factotum

     3 *Br Sch (between 7 and 11)* élève *mf* du cours élémentaire *ou* du cours moyen; *Am Sch, Univ* élève/étudiant, -ante d'avant-dernière année; *Br* **to go to the juniors, to attend the juniors** *(junior school)* aller à l'école primaire

     4 *Sport (between 13 and 15)* minime *mf*, *(between 15 and 17)* cadet, -ette; *(between 17 and 21)* junior *mf*

     ▸▸ *Br Sch* **j. classes** petites classes *fpl*, **j. clerk** commis *m* ordinaire, jeune employé, -ée, employé, -ée subalterne; *Am Univ* **j. college** = institut *m* universitaire du premier cycle; *Br Univ* **j. common room** salle *f* des étudiants; *Br Law* **j. counsel** jeune avocat, -ate; **j. executive** jeune cadre *m*; *Am* **j. high school** ≃ collège *m* d'enseignement secondaire; **j. minister** sous-secrétaire *m* d'État, *pl* sous-secrétaires d'État **(in à)**; **j. miss** *(clothes size)* fillette *f*, **j. partner** associé, -ée adjoint(e); *Br* **j. school** école *f* élémentaire *(pour les enfants de 7 à 11 ans)*; *Com* **j. sizes** petites tailles *fpl*, **j. teacher** jeune professeur *m*; *Am Sch, Univ* **j. year** avant-dernière année *f*

juniper [ˈdʒuːnɪpər] N *(tree)* genévrier *m*, genièvre *m*

     ▸▸ **j. berries** baies *fpl ou* grains *mpl* de genièvre; **j. oil** essence *f* de genièvre **j. tree** genévrier, genièvre

junk¹ [dʒʌŋk] N *(no pl)* **1** *(unwanted objects)* bric-à-brac *m inv*; *(outdated objects)* vieilleries *fpl*; *(old iron)* ferraille *f*, *(inferior goods)* camelote *f*, pacotille *f*, *Fam* cochonnerie(s) *f(pl)*, saleté(s) *f(pl)*; **clear your j. off the table** retire tout ton bazar de la table

     2 *Fig Fam (bad-quality book, play etc)* navet

m, foutaise *f*; *Sl (nonsense)* foutaises *fpl*; **she eats nothing but j.** elle mange que des saloperies

3 *Sl (heroin etc)* came *f*; **to be on j.** se camer **VT** *Fam (get rid of, discard) (old furniture, documents etc)* balancer, mettre à la poubelle; *(ideas, plan)* laisser tomber, balancer

► ► *StExch* **j. bond** junk bond *m (obligation à haut rendement mais à haut risque)*; **j. dealer** brocanteur, -euse; *Comput* **j. e-mail** messages *mpl* publicitaires; *Fam* **j. food** nourriture *f* de mauvaise qualité; **j. heap** dépotoir *m*; *(in garden etc)* tas *m* de détritus; *(old car)* tas *m* de ferraille; *Fig* **to throw sth/sb on the j. heap** mettre qch/qn au rebut; *Fig* **young people who end up on the j. heap** les jeunes qui finissent sous les ponts; *Am* **j. jewelry** bijoux *mpl* (de) fantaisie; **j. mail** courrier *m* publicitaire; **j. room** pièce *f* de débarras; **j. shop** magasin *m* de brocante

junk² N *(Chinese boat)* jonque *f*

junker ['dʒʌŋkə(r)] N *Am Fam (old car)* vieille bagnole *f*

junket ['dʒʌŋkɪt] N **1** *Culin* lait *m* caillé *(souvent parfumé)* **2** *Fam (feast)* festin *m*, banquet *m* **3** *(pleasure trip)* plaisir *m*, voyage *m* d'agrément; *Pej (by public official)* voyage (d'agrément) aux frais de la princesse *ou* du contribuable

▸ **VI 1** *(feast)* banqueter, festoyer **2** *Am (travel)* faire un voyage d'agrément; *Pej (of public official)* voyager aux frais de la princesse *ou* du contribuable

junketing ['dʒʌŋkɪtɪŋ] N voyages *mpl* aux frais de la princesse *ou* du contribuable

junkie ['dʒʌŋkɪ] N *Sl (drug addict)* drogué, -ée, camé, -ée; *Fig* **a chocolate/sugar j.** un fou/une folle de chocolat/sucre, un(e) accro du chocolat/sucre; *Fig* **a football/chess j.** un(e) fana de football/d'échecs

junkman, *pl* **junkmen** ['dʒʌŋkmæn, -men] N *Am* chiffonnier *m*, brocanteur *m*

junky ['dʒʌŋkɪ] ADJ *Fam (goods)* de camelote; *(novel, film etc)* nul, à la manque
▸ N *Sl* = **junkie**

junkyard ['dʒʌŋkjɑːd] N *(for metal)* dépôt *m* de ferrailleur; *(for rags, discarded objects)* dépôt de chiffonnier; *Fig* **their garden is a real j.** leur jardin est un véritable dépotoir

Juno ['dʒuːnəʊ] N *Myth, Astron* Junon *f*; *Fig* déesse *f*

Junoesque [dʒuːnəʊ'esk] ADJ d'une grâce souveraine

junta ['dʒʌntə] N *Mil, Pol usu Pej* junte *f*

Jupiter ['dʒuːpɪtər] N *Myth* Jupiter *m*; *Astron* Jupiter *f*

Jurassic [dʒuː'ræsɪk] ADJ, N *Geol* jurassique *m*

juridical [dʒʊ'rɪdɪk(ə)l] ADJ juridique

jurisdiction [dʒʊərɪs'dɪkʃən] N **1** *Law* juridiction *f*; **area within** *or* **under the j. of …** territoire soumis à l'autorité judiciaire *ou* à la juridiction de …; **to come** *or* **fall within** *or* **under the j. of a court** *(of question etc)* tomber sous *ou* relever de *ou* rentrer dans la juridiction d'une cour; **to recognize the j. of the Court** reconnaître l'autorité judiciaire du tribunal

2 *(general authority)* autorité *f*; **to have j. over sb** avoir autorité sur qn; **he has no j. over his brother's activities** il n'a aucune emprise *ou* aucun pouvoir sur ce que fait son frère

3 *Fig (field of activity)* compétence *f*, ressort *m*; **this matter does not come within** *or* **is not in** *or* **falls outside our j.** cette affaire ne relève pas de notre compétence, cette affaire n'est pas de notre compétence *ou* de notre ressort

jurisprudence [dʒʊərɪs'pruːdəns] N jurisprudence *f*

jurist ['dʒʊərɪst] N *Fml (expert)* juriste *mf*, légiste *m*; *(writer)* juriste; *Am (lawyer)* avocat, -ate; *(student)* étudiant, -ante en droit

juror ['dʒʊərər] N **1** *Law* juré, -ée *f* **2** *(in competition etc)* membre *m* du jury

jury ['dʒʊərɪ] ▨ VOIR GRAMMAIRE A11 **1** *Law* jury *m*; **to be** *or* **serve** *or* **sit on the j.** faire partie *ou* être membre du jury, *Fam* être du jury; **to pack** *or* **rig** *or* **stack a** *or* **the j.** composer un jury partisan; **foreman of the j.** président *m* du jury; **ladies and gentlemen of the j.!** mesdames et messieurs les jurés!; **the j. is out** le jury est en délibération; *Fig Fam* **the j. is still out on that (one)** *(final decision has not been made)* rien de définitif n'a été décidé; *Am Law* **(federal) grand j.** = tribunal *m* (fédéral) se prononçant sur la mise en accusation; **special j.** jury spécial

2 *(for examination, competition)* jury *m*
▸ ▸ *Law* **j. box** sièges *mpl* des jurés; **j. duty** devoir *m* de participation au jury; **to do (one's) j. duty** s'acquitter de son devoir de participation au jury; **to be called (up) for j. duty** être convoqué comme juré; *Br Sl* **j. nobbling** corruption *f* de jurés; **j. rigging** = composition *f* d'un jury partisan; **j. service** devoir *m* de participation au jury; **to do (one's) j. service** s'acquitter de son devoir de participation au jury; **to be called (up) for j. service** être convoqué comme juré

juryman, *pl* **jurymen** ['dʒʊərɪmən] N juré *m*

jurywoman, *pl* **jurywomen** ['dʒʊərɪwʊmən, -wɪmɪn] N femme *f* juré, jurée *f*

just¹ [dʒʌst] ADJ **1** *(fair) (person, criticism etc)* juste (**to, towards** envers, à l'égard de)

2 *(legitimate) (cause, anger, claim)* juste, légitime; *(reward, punishment, law, peace, war)* juste; **to get one's j. deserts** avoir ce qu'on mérite; **it's only j. that …** ce n'est que justice que … + *sub*; **it's only j. to ask such questions** il est bien normal de poser de telles questions; **as (it) is only j.** comme de juste; **to show j. cause for concern, to have j. cause to be concerned** avoir de bonnes raisons de s'inquiéter

3 *(observation, account etc)* juste
▸ NPL **the j.** les justes *mpl*; *Lit* **to sleep the sleep of the j.** dormir du sommeil du juste

JUST²

juste **1–3, 6, 7, 10**	▪ exactement **1**
▪ seulement **6**	▪ simplement **8**
▪ absolument **11**	

ADV **1** *(exactly, precisely)* juste, justement, exactement, précisément; **he's j. the man you are looking for** c'est juste *ou* exactement *ou* tout à fait l'homme qu'il vous faut; **that's j. what happened** c'est justement *ou* exactement *ou* bien ce qui est arrivé; **j. how many are there?** combien y en a-t-il au juste *ou* exactement?; **j. why does she do it?** pour quelles raisons exactement le fait-elle?, pourquoi exactement le fait-elle?; **that's j. why she did it** c'est précisément *ou* exactement pour cela qu'elle l'a fait, c'est justement pourquoi elle l'a fait; **j. as you wish** (c'est) comme tu veux; **I left the books j. as they were** *or* **the way they were** j'ai laissé les livres exactement comme *ou* tels que je les ai trouvés, j'ai laissé les livres tels quels; **that's j. it** *or* **j. the point!** précisément!, justement!, voilà!; **j. so** *(like this)* exactement comme ça!; *Br (that's right)* exactement!, précisément!, voilà!; **he set the vase down j. so** *(carefully)* il a posé le vase avec soin; *Fam usu Pej* **her house is always j. so** sa maison est toujours architecturée impeccable; **it's** *or* **that's j. like him!** *(typical of him)* c'est bien de lui!; **isn't that j. my luck!** c'est bien ma chance!; **I have j. the same problem** j'ai exactement le même problème; **j.**

the same *(nevertheless)* cela n'empêche, tout de même

2 *(with place)* juste; **j. here** juste ici, ici même

3 *(with time: exactly)* juste; **j. then, j. at that moment** juste à ce moment, à ce moment précis; **it's j. ten o'clock** *or Br* **j. on ten o'clock** il est dix heures juste(s) *ou* pile, il est tout juste dix heures; **j. when** *or* **as the door was opening** au moment même où la porte s'ouvrait; **j. as** *or* **when I was leaving** juste comme *ou* juste quand *ou* au moment même où je partais; **she's j. in time for a drink** elle arrive pile pour *ou* elle arrive juste à temps pour prendre un verre

4 *(with time: at this moment)* **he's busy j. now** il est occupé en ce moment *ou* pour l'instant; **I'm not ready j. now** *or* **j. yet** je ne suis pas encore prêt, je ne suis pas prêt pour le moment; **she's j. leaving, she's leaving j. now** elle part (tout de suite *ou* à l'instant); **she's not leaving j. now** *or* **j. yet** elle ne part pas encore, elle ne part pas tout de suite; **to be j. about to do sth** être sur le point de faire qch; **(I'm) j. coming!, I'm coming j. now!** j'arrive!; **my hair is j. turning grey** *or* **is j. beginning to turn grey** mes cheveux commencent juste à grisonner

5 *(with time: a short while ago, recently)* **to have j. arrived/woken up/written a letter** venir d'arriver/de se réveiller/d'écrire une lettre; **I've only j. seen him and I haven't had time yet to …** je viens seulement de le voir et je n'ai pas encore eu le temps de …; **I've (only) j. seen him going downstairs** je viens de le voir à l'instant qui descendait; **I saw him j. now, I've j. (now) seen him** je l'ai vu à l'instant, je viens de le voir; **I've only j. this minute seen him** je viens de le voir à l'instant, je l'ai vu à l'instant; **I saw him j. yesterday, I j. saw him yesterday** je l'ai vu pas plus tard qu'hier; **he has j. (now) left school** il sort du lycée; **'j. picked/cooked'** *(newly)* 'cueilli/cuit du jour'; **'j. arrived'** 'fraîchement arrivé' VOIR GRAMMAIRE B31

6 *(only, no more than)* seulement, juste; **I have come j. to see you** je viens seulement *ou* juste *ou* uniquement pour vous voir; **we have j. a few copies left** il nous (en) reste quelques exemplaires seulement *ou* juste quelques exemplaires; **I've got j. one left** il ne m'en reste qu'un; **she's j. a baby** ce n'est qu'un bébé; **it costs j. ten dollars** ça ne coûte que dix dollars, ça coûte dix dollars seulement; **it's j. ten o'clock** il est seulement dix heures, il n'est que dix heures; **(wait) j. a moment!** *(attendez)* un petit instant!, un instant!; **j. a minute, aren't you supposed to be somewhere else?** une seconde, tu n'es pas censé être ailleurs?; **give me j. a tiny bit** donnez-m'en (juste) un petit peu

7 *(only a little, slightly)* juste, (un) peu; **j. a little more/less/better** juste un peu plus/moins/mieux; **j. in front/behind/above/below** juste devant/derrière/au-dessus/au-dessous; **j. over/under fifty pounds** un tout petit peu plus de/moins de cinquante livres; **it's j. before ten (o'clock)** il est presque dix heures; **we go to bed j. before ten (o'clock)** nous nous couchons juste avant *ou* peu avant dix heures; **j. after my birthday** juste après *ou* peu après mon anniversaire

8 *(merely, simply)* simplement; **tell him j. to wait** dites-lui qu'il n'a qu'à attendre; *Fam* **I'll j. pop in** je ne ferai qu'entrer et sortir; **j. ask if you need money** vous n'avez qu'à demander si vous avez besoin d'argent; **they won't accept j. to please me** ils n'accepteront pas uniquement pour *ou* rien que pour me faire plaisir à moi; **we j. can't understand it** nous n'arrivons vraiment pas à comprendre; **why not? – because I j. don't** pourquoi pas? – parce que c'est comme ça; **I j. don't want to** je ne veux pas, un point c'est tout

9 *(easily)* **I can j. see him as a doctor** je le vois très bien médecin; **I can j. smell the sea air, looking at these photos** rien qu'en regardant ces photos je sens l'air de la mer
10 *(by a narrow margin, barely)* **(only) j.** de justesse; **he (only) j. (about) managed to catch the train** il a eu le train de justesse, c'est tout juste s'il a eu le train; **they (only) j. missed the train** ils ont manqué le train de peu; **I have (only) j. enough** *or* **j. about enough to live on** j'ai tout juste de quoi vivre; **she caught the train but (only) j.** elle a eu le train mais de justesse; **you're (only) j. in time** vous arrivez à temps, mais c'est de justesse
11 *(utterly, completely)* absolument; **it was j. splendid!** c'était absolument merveilleux!, c'était merveilleux, ni plus ni moins!; **it was j. a nightmare** c'était un véritable cauchemar; *Br* **do you remember? – don't I j.!** vous vous en souvenez? – et comment (que je m'en souviens) *ou* vous pensez (si je m'en souviens)!
12 *(in comparisons)* **j. as, j. about as** tout aussi; **that's j. (about) as good** c'est tout aussi bien, c'est tout comme; **that will do j. as well** ça fera aussi bien l'affaire
13 *(in threats, orders, exhortations)* **j. (you) try!** essaie donc un peu!; **j. (you) wait!** tu n'as qu'à attendre!; *(threat)* attends, tu vas voir!, tu ne perds rien pour attendre!; **j. (you) read this!** lisez donc cela!; **j. think** réfléchis donc un peu; **j. be quiet, will you!** veux-tu bien te taire!; **j. who do you think you are?** pour qui vous prenez-vous, au juste?
14 j. about *(approximately)* plus ou moins, à peu près; *(almost)* quasiment; **it's j. about ten (o'clock)** il est plus ou moins *ou* à peu près dix heures; **j. about!** plus ou moins!, à peu près!; *Fam* **that j. about does it** *(I'm leaving)* ça suffit comme ça *ou* amplement *ou* largement; **I've j. about had enough of this** j'en ai vraiment par dessus la tête de ça
15 *(indicating preference)* **I would j. as soon stay here** j'aimerais tout autant rester ici; **he would j. as soon that …** il aimerait tout autant que … + *sub*
16 it's j. as well (that) … *(fortunate)* heureusement que …; **and (it was) j. as well et**

c'était une chance, et tant mieux; **I might j. as well have remained silent** j'aurais (tout) aussi bien fait de garder le silence; **they could j. as well do without it** ils feraient (tout) aussi bien de s'en passer

justice ['dʒʌstɪs] **N 1** *(no pl)* *(power of law)* justice *f*; **to administer** *or* **dispense/exercise j.** rendre/exercer la justice; **to demand/obtain j.** demander/obtenir justice; **to bring sb to j.** traduire qn en justice
2 *(no pl)* *(fairness)* *(of cause, claim, decision etc)* légitimité *f*, *(of reward, punishment)* justice *f*, **in all j.** en toute justice; **in (all) j. to her, we should say …** pour être juste envers elle *ou* pour lui rendre justice, on devrait dire …; **to do sb j., to do j. to sb** *(of photo, garment, hairstyle etc)* avantager qn, mettre qn en valeur; **to do j. to a meal** faire honneur à un repas; **to do oneself j.** se mettre en valeur, se montrer sous son meilleur jour; *Fml* **with j.** *(with good reason)* avec juste raison, à juste titre
3 *(judge in Supreme Court)* juge *m*; **Mr J. Long** *(title)* Monsieur le juge Long; **Mrs J. Long** Madame le juge Long
▸▸ *Am* **the J. Department** ≃ le ministère de la Justice; **J. of the Peace** juge de paix

justifiable ['dʒʌstɪfaɪəb(ə)l] **ADJ** justifié, légitime
▸▸ *Law* **j. homicide** *(killing in self-defence)* homicide *m* justifiable; *(state execution)* application *f* de la peine de mort

justifiably ['dʒʌstɪfaɪəblɪ] **ADV** légitimement, à juste titre; **they acted quite j.** ils ont agi en toute légitimité

justification [dʒʌstɪfɪ'keɪʃən] **N 1** justification *f* (**for** de, pour); **in j. of** comme justification de; **there's no j. for behaviour like that!** rien ne peut justifier un tel comportement!; **what's her j. for this?** comment justifie-t-elle ceci?; **with some j., I might add** à juste titre, ajouterais-je; **that's no j.!** ce n'est pas une raison! **2** *Typ, Comput* justification *f*, **left/right j.** justification à gauche/droite

justify ['dʒʌstɪfaɪ] **VT 1** *(person, decision, action, sb's behaviour etc)* justifier; **to j. oneself in the eyes of sb** se justifier aux yeux de qn; **that does not j. your voting for my rival** cela

n'est pas une raison suffisante pour que vous votiez pour mon rival; **to be justified in doing sth** *(have a good reason to)* avoir de bonnes raisons pour faire qch, être fondé à faire qch; **a fully justified decison/fear** une décision/une crainte bien fondée *ou* qui se justifie; **am I justified in thinking that …?** ai-je raison de croire que …?
2 *Typ, Comput* justifier; **left/right justified** justifié à gauche/droite

just-in-time **ADJ** *Com* juste à temps
▸▸ **j. distribution** distribution *f* juste à temps; **j. manufacturing** production *f* juste à temps; **j. production** production juste à temps; **j. purchasing** achat *m* juste à temps

justly ['dʒʌstlɪ] **ADV 1** *(fairly, rightly)* avec justice, justement **2** *(accurately, deservedly)* à juste titre; **j. famous** célèbre à juste titre

justness ['dʒʌstnɪs] **N 1** *(of cause, demand)* légitimité *f* **2** *(accuracy)* *(of idea, remark etc)* justesse *f*

▸ **jut out** [dʒʌt] (**-tt-**) **VI** *(of balcony, rock etc)* faire saillie, être en saillie; **to j. out over sth** *(overhang)* surplomber qch, avancer sur qch; **the headland juts (out) into the sea** le cap avance (en saillie) dans la mer; **something is jutting out of your pocket** quelque chose dépasse de votre poche; **his chin juts out** il a un menton en galoche
VT SEP *(chin)* avancer

jute [dʒuːt] **N** *(plant, fibre)* jute *m*

juvenile ['dʒuːvɪnaɪl, *Am* -'n(ə)l] **ADJ 1** *Pej (childish)* *(behaviour, ideas etc)* puéril; **don't be so j.!** ne sois pas si puéril *ou* gamin! **2** *(for young people)* *(books, games etc)* pour enfants, pour la jeunesse; *(hobbies, activities)* d'enfant(s); *Fml (youthful)* juvénile
N *Fml* jeune *mf*, adolescent, -ente
▸▸ **j. court** tribunal *m* pour enfants *(10-16 ans)*; **j. delinquency** délinquance *f* juvénile; **j. delinquent** jeune délinquant, -ante, mineur, -e délinquant(e); **j. offender** accusé, -ée mineur(e)

juvenilia [dʒuːvɪ'nɪlɪə] **NPL** œuvres *fpl* de jeunesse; **a piece of Mozart j.** une œuvre de jeunesse de Mozart

juxtapose [dʒʌkstə'pəʊz] **VT** juxtaposer

juxtaposition [dʒʌkstəpə'zɪʃən] **N** juxtaposition *f*, **to be in j.** se juxtaposer

K, k [keɪ] **N 1** *(letter)* K, k *m*;**two k's** deux k **2** *Comput (abbr* **kilobyte)** K, Ko; **how many k are left?** combien de Ko reste-t-il?; **720k diskette** disquette *f* de 720 Ko **3** *(abbr* **thousand)** K **4** *Fam (abbr* **thousand pounds)** he earns 30K il gagne 30 000 livres **5** *Fam (abbr* **kilometre(s))** kilomètre(s) *m(pl)*; **a 10K race** une course de dix kilomètres

kabuki [kəˈbuːkɪ] **N** kabuki *m*

Kabul [ˈkɑːbʊl] **N** Kaboul

kaffeeklatsch [ˈkæfeɪˈklætʃ] **N** *Am* = réunion *f* de femmes qui bavardent en prenant le café

Kaffir [ˈkæfər] **ADJ 1** *(pertaining to the ethnic group)* caf(f)re *mf* **2** *Offensive Sl* nègre **N 1** *(member of the ethnic group)* Caf(f)re *mf* **2** *Offensive Sl* nègre *m*, négresse *f*

Kafkaesque [kæfkəˈesk] **ADJ** kafkaïen

kaftan [ˈkæftæn] **N** kaftan *m*

kalashnikov [kəˈlæʃnɪkɒv] **N** kalachnikov *m*

kale, kail [keɪl] **N** *(cabbage)* **(curly) k.** chou *m* frisé

kaleidoscope [kəˈlaɪdəskəʊp] **N** kaléidoscope *m*

kaleidoscopic [kəlaɪdəˈskɒpɪk] **ADJ** kaléidoscopique

kamikaze [kæmɪˈkɑːzɪ] **ADJ, N** kamikaze *m*

Kampuchea [kæmpʊˈtʃɪə] **N** *Formerly* Kampuchéa *m*

kangaroo [kæŋgəˈruː] **N 1** *(animal)* kangourou *m* **2** *St Exch Fam* valeur *f* australienne
▸▸ **k. court** tribunal *m* illégal; *(held by strikers, prisoners etc)* ≃ tribunal populaire

Kan(s) *abbr* Kansas

kaolin [ˈkeɪəlɪn] **N** kaolin *m*

kapok [ˈkeɪpɒk] **N** kapok *m*
▸▸ **k. tree** kapokier *m*

Kaposi's sarcoma [kæˈpəʊsɪzsɑːˈkəʊmə] **N** *Med* sarcome *m* de Kaposi

kaput [kəˈpʊt] **ADJ** *Fam* fichu, foutu

karakul [ˈkærəkʊl] **N** *(sheep, fur)* karakul *m*, caracul *m*

karaoke [kærəˈəʊkeɪ] **N** *Mus* karaoké *m*
▸▸ **k. machine** karaoké

karate [kəˈrɑːtɪ] **N** *Sport* karaté *m*
▸▸ **k. chop** coup *m* de karaté *(donné avec le tranchant de la main)*

karma [ˈkɑːmə] **N** *Hindu Rel* karma *m*

kart [kɑːt] **N** kart *m*
▸▸ **k. racing** karting *m*

karting [ˈkɑːtɪŋ] **N** karting *m*; **to go k.** faire du karting

kasbah [ˈkæzbɑː] **N** casbah *m*

Kashmir [kæʃˈmɪər] **N** *Geog* Cachemire *m*

Kashmiri [kæʃˈmɪərɪ] **N 1** *(person)* Cachemirien, -enne **2** *Ling* kashmiri *m*
ADJ cachemirien

Katmandu [kætmænˈduː] **N** Katmandou

kayak [ˈkaɪæk] **N** *(canoe)* kayac *m*, kayak *m*

Kazak(h)stan [kæzækˈstɑːn] **N** Kazakhstan *m*

kazoo [kəˈzuː] **N 1** *(instrument)* mirliton *m* **2** *Am Fam (buttocks)* derrière *m*, arrière-train *m*; *Fig* **to have problems/debts up the k.** avoir des problèmes/des dettes jusqu'au cou

KB [keɪˈbiː] **N** *Comput (abbr* **kilobyte)** Ko *m*

KBE [keɪbiːˈiː] **N** *Br (abbr* **Knight (Commander of the Order) of the British Empire)** Chevalier *m* de l'Ordre de l'Empire britannique

Kbps [keɪbiːpiːˈes] *Comput (abbr* **kilobytes per second)** ko/s

KCB [keɪsiːˈbiː] **N** *Br (abbr* **Knight Commander (of the Order) of the Bath)** Chevalier *m* Commandeur de l'Ordre du Bain

kebab [kəˈbæb] **N** *Culin* brochette *f*; **shish k.** chiche-kébab *m*

kecks [keks] **NPL** *Br Fam (trousers)* fute *m*, falzar *m*

kedge [kedʒ] *Naut* **N** ancre *f* à jet
VT *(boat)* haler, touer sur une ancre à jet
VI se touer sur une ancre à jet
▸▸ **k. anchor** ancre *f* à jet

kedgeree [kedʒəˈriː] **N** *Culin* = mets *m* de riz accommodé avec du beurre, des œufs durs et du poisson fumé

keel [kiːl] **N 1** *Naut, Aviat* quille *f*; **on an even k.** *Naut* sans différence de tirant d'eau *ou* de calaison; *Fig* stable; **to be back on an even k.** *(of situation etc)* être de nouveau stable, s'être stabilisé; *(of person)* avoir retrouvé son égalité d'âme; **to put a company/the economy (back) on an even k.** (re)mettre une entreprise/l'économie d'aplomb **2** *Bot (of leaf, petal etc)* carène *f*
VT *(boat)* mettre en carène
▸ **keel over VI** *(of boat)* chavirer; *Fam (of person)* *(unconscious)* tomber dans les pommes; *(dead)* tomber raide mort; *(of structure, hut etc)* se renverser; **to k. over backwards** tomber à la renverse
VT SEP *(boat)* faire chavirer

keelhaul [ˈkiːlhɔːl] **VT 1** *Naut, Hist (sailor)* faire passer sous la quille **2** *(rebuke)* réprimander sévèrement; *Fam* passer un savon à

keen¹ [kiːn] **ADJ 1** *(enthusiastic)* *(yachtsman, follower)* ardent, assidu; *(reader)* passionné; *(at school, work)* zélé; **as a k. reader of your articles, I …** lecteur assidu de vos articles, je …; **I'll come with you, but I'm not k.** j'y vais avec toi, mais je n'en brûle pas d'envie; **look, I'm really not k.** écoute, je n'en ai vraiment pas envie *ou* je n'y tiens vraiment pas; **she's very k. for us to do it** elle tient beaucoup à ce que nous le fassions; **he seemed very k. at first** *(on idea, proposal etc)* au départ il avait l'air très enthousiaste; **to be as k. as mustard** déborder d'enthousiasme, brûler d'ardeur; **to be k. on doing sth** avoir très envie de faire qch; **to be k. on sth** *(on golf, politics, novel)* adorer qch; *(idea, proposal)* être plein d'enthousiasme pour qch; **he wasn't k. on the idea** l'idée ne l'emballait pas; **she's k. on him** il lui plaît; **she's k. on sport** le sport la

passionne, elle adore le sport; **to take a k. interest in sth** suivre qch avec un intérêt vif; **a k. desire for peace** un désir ardent de paix; **k. competition** concurrence *f* acharnée *ou* âpre; **there is a k. demand for these stocks** ces fonds sont activement recherchés; *Br Com* **k. prices** prix *mpl* au plus bas, prix étudiés; **k. golfer** mordu *m* *ou* passionné de golf; **k. sportsman** ardent sportif *m*; **a k. advocate of …** un partisan fervent de …
2 *(perceptive)* *(eye, look)* perçant, pénétrant, vif; *(mind)* fin, pénétrant, vif; **to have a k. eye for a bargain** être prompt à reconnaître une bonne affaire; **to have a k. ear** avoir l'oreille *ou* l'ouïe fine; **to have a k. ear for a tune/for accents** reconnaître facilement les mélodies/les accents; **a k. sense of smell** un odorat très développé; **to have a k. awareness of a problem** être profondément conscient d'un problème
3 *(intense)* *(sorrow)* aigu, *f* aiguë; *(regret)* poignant; *(remorse)* cuisant; **k. appetite** rude appétit *m*; **to have a k. appetite for success** avoir un appétit de succès dévorant; **k. pleasure** vif plaisir *m*
4 *(cold)* *(wind, air)* vif, piquant
5 *(sharp)* *(knife, blade)* affilé, aiguisé; *Fig (sound)* aigu; **k. edge** fil *m* tranchant; **k. edged** bien affilé, aiguisé, tranchant
6 *Am Sl (very good)* génial, -aux

keen² **VI** *(at funeral)* chanter une mélopée *(en veillant un corps)*

keenly [ˈkiːnlɪ] **ADV 1** *(enthusiastically)* avec enthousiasme; **to be k. interested in …** s'intéresser vivement à …; **a k. contested competition/election/etc** une compétition/des élections/etc âprement disputée(s) **2** *(intensely)* profondément; *(to regret)* amèrement; **to feel sth k.** être profondément affecté par qch **3** **the wind was blowing k.** il faisait un vent âpre

keenness [ˈkiːnnɪs] **N 1** *(of person)* enthousiasme *m*; *(at school, work)* zèle *m*; *(of troops)* mordant *m*; **k. on doing sth** grand désir *m* de faire qch
2 *(of sight)* acuité *f*; *(of hearing, sense of smell)* finesse *f*; *(of mind)* pénétration *f*, finesse *f*
3 *(of feeling, emotion etc)* intensité *f*; *(of grief, sense of remorse)* acuité *f*
4 *(of blade)* tranchant *m*
5 *(of the cold)* âpreté *f*, rigueur *f*

KEEP [kiːp]

VT garder **1-3, 5, 7** ▪ retenir **1**
▪ maintenir **3** ▪ entretenir **5** ▪ tenir **6**, **8, 9** ▪ élever **6** ▪ observer **8**
VI rester **1** ▪ se tenir **1** ▪ aller **1**
▪ continuer **2** ▪ se conserver **3**

N 1 *(food)* nourriture *f*; *(money)* frais *mpl* de subsistance; **to pay for one's k.** payer sa pension; **do you give your parents any money for your k.?** est-ce que tu donnes de l'argent à tes parents pour payer ta pension?; **she can only just afford to pay for her k.** elle arrive tout juste à se nourrir et à se loger; **to earn one's k.** *(earn a living)* subvenir à ses besoins; *(pay one's way) (of employee)* mériter son salaire; *(of lodger etc)* rendre de menus services pour payer sa pension; **to earn its k.** *(of equipment)* être rentable; **the van may be old but it still earns its k.** la camionnette est vieille mais elle nous rend encore bien service

2 *(of castle)* donjon *m*

3 *Fam* **for keeps** pour de bon

VT (*pt & pp* **kept** [kept]) **1** *(retain) (something)* garder; *(sb's attention)* retenir; **you can k. the book I lent you** vous pouvez garder le livre que je vous ai prêté; **to k. sth for sb** garder qch pour qn; **I asked them to k. it for me** je leur ai demandé de me le garder; **to k. sth from sb** *(not inform of)* ne pas révéler qch à qn; **to k. sth for later** garder *ou* conserver *ou* réserver qch pour plus tard; **to k. the best for** *or* **until last** garder le meilleur pour la fin; **to k. sth in reserve** *or* **in store** tenir qch en réserve; **to k. a seat for sb** garder une place à qn; **to k. one's figure** garder la ligne; **to k. its shape/colour** *(of garment)* conserver sa forme/couleur; **to k. one's job** garder *ou* conserver son emploi

2 *(store) (provisions, letters etc)* garder; **the cupboard where I k. the crockery** l'armoire où je mets la vaisselle; **k. medicines out of the reach of children** ranger les médicaments hors de la portée des enfants

3 *(maintain) (order)* maintenir; *(silence, secret)* garder; **to k. one's composure** garder son sang-froid; **to k. one's course** continuer *ou* poursuivre son chemin; **he keeps himself to himself** il est très réservé; **he prefers to k. himself to himself** il évite les contacts; **they k. themselves to themselves** ils font bande à part

4 *(maintain in a condition)* **to k. sth clean/secret** tenir qch propre/secret; **k. dry** craint l'humidité; *Fam* **k. it clean!** *(no vulgarity)* pas de grossièretés!; **to k. oneself warm** *(by staying in the warmth)* se tenir au chaud; *(by dressing warmly)* s'habiller chaudement; **to k. the door open/shut** garder *ou* laisser la porte ouverte/fermée; **the noise kept me awake** le bruit m'a empêché de dormir; **to k. sb wondering** laisser qn se poser des questions; **to k. sb waiting** faire attendre qn; **troops were kept on the alert** les soldats ont été maintenus en état d'alerte; **to k. one's hands in one's pockets** garder les mains dans ses poches

5 *(look after, tend) (sheep, herds)* garder; *(garden etc)* entretenir; *(person)* subvenir aux besoins de; *(mistress)* entretenir; **well/badly kept road** route bien/mal entretenue; **he doesn't earn enough to k. himself** il ne gagne pas de quoi vivre; **he has his parents to k.** il a ses parents à (sa) charge; **I've got a family to k.** j'ai une famille à nourrir

6 *(possess) (bees, poultry etc)* élever; *(shop)* tenir

7 *(detain) (at home, in hospital, prison)* garder; **the doctor kept him in bed** le médecin l'a obligé à garder le lit; **there was nothing to k. me in England/with that firm** rien ne me retenait en Angleterre/dans cette entreprise; **what kept you?** qu'est-ce qui t'a retardé?; *Iron* comment tu as fait pour aller si vite?; **don't let me k. you** *(from your work etc)* je ne veux pas te retenir

8 *(observe) (the law, a rule)* observer, suivre; *(promise)* tenir, remplir; *(vow)* rester fidèle à; *(treaty)* respecter, observer; *(date, appointment)* ne pas manquer à; **to k. late hours** se coucher tard; **to k. one's word** tenir (sa) parole; *Rel* **to k. the commandments** observer les commandements; **if you cannot**

k. the appointment si vous ne pouvez pas être présent au rendez-vous

9 *(diary, accounts)*, *Com (the books)* tenir; **to k. a record of events** prendre les événements en note; **to k. a note of sth** noter qch

10 *(protect)* préserver (**sb from evil** qn du mal); **God k. (you)!** Dieu vous garde!; **God k. his soul!** (que) Dieu ait son âme!; *Sport* **to k. goal** être gardien de but; *Cr* **to k. wicket** garder le guichet

11 *(celebrate) (festival, feast day)* célébrer

VI 1 *(remain, stay)* rester, se tenir; **to k. well** *(stay)* rester en bonne santé; **are you keeping well?** vous vous portez bien?; **she doesn't k. well** elle ne jouit pas d'une bonne santé; **how are you keeping?** comment allez-vous?; **to k. quiet** se tenir *ou* rester tranquille; **to k. awake/calm** rester éveillé/calme; **the weather is keeping cool/fine** le temps reste frais/se maintient au beau

2 *(continue)* continuer; **to k. straight on** continuer tout droit; **k. (to the) left/right** serrez à gauche/droite; **to k. doing sth** ne pas cesser *ou* ne pas arrêter de faire qch; **to k. working** continuer de travailler; **to k. smiling** garder le sourire; **don't k. asking questions** ne posez pas tout le temps des questions; **I wish you wouldn't k. saying that** j'aimerais bien que tu arrêtes de répéter cela; **I don't know how she keeps going on so little sleep** je ne sais pas comment elle arrive à tenir le coup en dormant si peu; **it's amazing the firm has kept going for so long** c'est incroyable que l'entreprise soit parvenue à se maintenir aussi longtemps

3 *(of food etc)* se garder, se conserver; **the story will k.** *(you can tell it to me later)* l'histoire n'y perdra rien; **what I've got to tell you won't k. till tomorrow** ce que j'ai à te dire n'attendra pas jusqu'à demain; **will it k. till later?** *(news etc)* est-ce que ça peut attendre?

▸**keep at VT INSEP 1** *(continue to work at) (one's homework etc)* travailler; **to k. hard at it** travailler sans relâche

2 *(nag)* **to k. at sb to do sth** harceler qn *ou Fam* être toujours sur le dos de qn pour qu'il fasse qch

VT SEP to k. sb at it *(working)* faire travailler qn

▸**keep away VI** ne pas approcher (**from** de); **she told the children to k. away from the river** elle a dit aux enfants de ne pas s'approcher de la rivière; **k. away (from me)!** n'approchez pas!; **I can't k. away from chocolates** je ne peux pas résister quand je vois des chocolats; **to k. away from drugs/alcohol** ne pas toucher à la drogue/à l'alcool

VT SEP k. that dog away (from me)! tenez ce chien loin de moi!; **the wind will k. the rain away** le vent empêchera la pluie; **to k. matches away from the children** tenir les allumettes hors de la portée des enfants; **the rain kept a lot of spectators away** la pluie a dissuadé bien des spectateurs de venir

▸**keep back VI** ne pas approcher; **k. back!** n'approche pas!

VT SEP 1 *(crowd)* contenir, retenir; *(tears)* refouler, retenir; **he tried desperately to k. back his laughter** il s'efforça désespérément de se retenir *ou* s'empêcher de rire

2 *(withhold)* **to k. a sum back from sb's wages** retenir une somme sur le salaire de qn; **you're keeping something back from me** tu me caches quelque chose

3 *Sch (pupil)* garder en retenue; *(oblige to repeat a year)* faire redoubler; **to be kept back a year** redoubler

4 *(delay)* retenir; *(of strong wind etc)* retarder

5 *(prevent from making progress) (of lack of qualifications etc)* handicaper

▸**keep down VI** se baisser

VT SEP 1 *(head, voice)* baisser; **to k. the noise (level) down** faire moins de bruit; *Fig* **to k. one's head down** garder un profil bas; **I can't**

k. my food down je rejette tout ce que je mange

2 *(repress)* garder le contrôle sur, avoir la mainmise sur; *(prices)* empêcher d'augmenter; **they were kept down by a repressive government** ils étaient contrôlés par un gouvernement répressif; *Prov* **you can't k. a good man down** les hommes de bien sont toujours récompensés

▸**keep from VT SEP 1** *(conceal)* **to k. sth from sb** cacher qch à qn

2 *(prevent)* **to k. sb from doing sth** empêcher qn de faire qch

3 *(distract)* **to k. sb from his/her work** empêcher qn de travailler

VT INSEP *(refrain)* **to k. from doing sth** se retenir de faire qch

▸**keep in VT SEP** *(person)* empêcher de sortir; *Sch (pupil)* garder en retenue; *(fire)* entretenir; **the police/the doctor kept him in overnight** la police/le docteur l'a gardé pour la nuit; *Fig* **to k. one's hand in** garder la main

VT SEP *(keep supplied with)* **to k. sb in sth** *(of person)* approvisionner qn en qch; **to k. sb in clothes/food** fournir de l'habillement/de la nourriture à qn; **to k. sb in beer/cigarettes** payer sa bière/ses cigarettes à qn; **to k. sb in luxury** permettre à qn de vivre dans le luxe; **his pocket money just about kept him in beer** son argent de poche lui servait tout juste à payer sa bière; **the grant barely keeps me in food** ma bourse me permet tout juste de me payer de quoi manger

▸**keep in with VT INSEP** *Fam* **k. in with sb** cultiver qn, rester en bons termes avec qn

▸**keep off VI** *(stay away)* ne pas approcher

VT INSEP k. off the grass! défense de marcher sur le gazon!; **would you please k. off those flower beds** s'il vous plaît, ne marchez pas sur ces parterres de fleurs; **if you don't k. off my property …** si vous pénétrez dans ma propriété …

VT SEP 1 k. your hands off that! n'y touchez pas!; **k. your hands off me** bas les mains *ou Fam* les pattes!

2 to k. one's coat off rester sans (son) manteau; **the wind will k. the rain off** le vent empêchera la pluie

▸**keep on VI 1** continuer; **to k. on doing sth** continuer à faire qch, ne pas cesser de faire qch; **don't k. on asking questions** ne posez pas tout le temps des questions

2 *(annoyingly, naggingly)* **don't k. on so!** arrête!; **I can't stand the way he keeps on about it** je ne supporte pas qu'il insiste tout le temps là-dessus; **he just keeps on and on about it** il n'arrête pas d'en parler

VT SEP 1 *(continue to wear) (coat etc)* garder

2 *(not turn off)* **to k. the central heating on** maintenir le chauffage central; **to k. the lights/TV on** laisser les lumières/la télé allumée(s)

3 *(continue to employ)* garder; **he was kept on by the firm** l'entreprise l'a gardé

▸**keep on at VT INSEP** *Fam* **k. on at sb (to do sth)** harceler qn *ou Fam* être toujours sur le dos de qn (pour qu'il fasse qch)

▸**keep out VI** *(avoid, stay away from)* ne pas entrer (**of** dans); **to k. out of danger** rester à l'abri du danger; **try to k. out of trouble** essaie de ne pas t'attirer d'ennuis; **to k. out of an argument** rester en dehors d'une dispute; **k. out** *(sign)* défense d'entrer; **k. out of this!** mêlez-vous de ce qui vous regarde!

VT SEP *(prevent from entering)* empêcher d'entrer

▸**keep to VT INSEP 1** *(adhere to) (promise)* tenir; **to k. to a subject** s'en tenir à un sujet; **to k. to the script** *(of actors)* s'en tenir au script

2 *(remain in, on)* rester dans; *(the left, the right)* tenir; **to k. to one's bed** garder le lit; **to k. to main roads** rester sur les grandes routes

VT SEP 1 *(hold)* **to k. sb to a promise** faire tenir une promesse à qn; **to k. delays/costs to**

a minimum minimiser les délais/les coûts
2 *(not reveal)* **to k. sth to oneself** garder qch pour soi, taire qch; **to k. one's impressions/opinions to oneself** garder ses impressions/opinions pour soi; **you can k. your remarks to yourself!** tes remarques, tu peux te les garder!; **k. your hands to yourself!** bas les mains *ou Fam* les pattes!
▸ **keep up** VI **1** *(of rain, snow etc)* continuer
2 *(remain level, go at same speed)* tenir le rythme
VT SEP **1** *(maintain) (building, road etc)* entretenir
2 *(continue) (custom)* conserver; *(correspondence, one's French etc)* entretenir; **we must k. it up** il nous faut continuer nos efforts; **k. it up!** continuez!; **k. up the good work!** continuez à bien travailler!
3 *(stop from falling or waning) (building, interest etc)* soutenir; *(courage)* soutenir, maintenir; **to k. up appearances** garder *ou* sauver les apparences
4 *(stop from going to bed)* empêcher d'aller se coucher; *(stop from sleeping)* empêcher de dormir; **worry had kept her up all night** l'inquiétude l'avait tenue éveillée toute la nuit
▸ **keep up with** VT INSEP **1** *(remain level with, go at same speed as)* **to k. up with sb** aller à la même allure que qn; **I can't k. up with you** vous marchez/parlez/*etc* trop vite pour moi; **he couldn't k. up with the rest of the children in his class** il n'arrivait pas à suivre dans sa classe; **I can barely k. up with her** *(she changes so much)* ça change tellement vite avec elle que j'ai du mal à suivre; *Fam* **to k. up with the Joneses** rivaliser de standing avec ses voisins; **to k. up with events** suivre les événements; **to k. up with the times** être à la page
2 *(remain in contact)* **to k. up with sb** rester en contact avec qn

keeper ['kiːpər] N *(person)* garde *m*; *(in zoo, of park, lighthouse)* gardien, -ienne; *(of museum etc)* conservateur, -trice; *(of herds)* gardien, -ienne, gardeur, -euse; *(gamekeeper)* garde-chasse *m, pl* gardes-chasse(s); *Ftbl Fam* goal *m*, gardien, -ienne de but; **I'm not my brother's k.** je ne suis pas responsable de mon frère

keep-fit N culture *f* physique, gymnastique *f* (d'entretien); **to do k.** faire de la gymnastique
▸ ▸ **k. class** cours *m* de gymnastique

keeping ['kiːpɪŋ] N *(of rule, promise)* observation *f*, *(of feast day)* célébration *f*; **to have sb/sth in one's k.** avoir qn/qch en garde *ou* sous sa garde; **in God's k.** à la garde de Dieu; **in k. with …** en accord avec …; **in k. with their commitment** conformément à leur engagement; **it is in k. with his principles** c'est conforme à *ou* en accord avec ses principes; **it's in k. with everything I have been told about her** cela concorde avec tout ce qu'on m'a dit sur elle; **out of k. with …** en désaccord avec …; **it was rather out of k. with the spirit of the occasion** cela détonnait avec l'esprit de l'occasion; **good k. qualities** *(of food)* bonnes qualités de conservation

keepsake ['kiːpseɪk] N souvenir *m*; **as a k. of his visit** en souvenir de sa visite

keg [keg] N **1** *(of beer)* barillet *m*; *(of water)* tonnelet *m*; *(of herring)* caque *f* **2** *(beer)* bière *f* pression
▸ ▸ **k. beer** bière pression

keister ['kiːstər] N *Am Fam (buttocks)* fesses *fpl*, derrière *m*

kelp [kelp] N *(seaweed)* varech *m*

Ken *abbr* Kentucky

ken [ken] N *Lit* **within sb's k.** dans les connaissances *ou* la compétence de qn; **beyond sb's k.** hors de la compétence de qn
VT *Scot, Dial* = **know** VT, VI

kennel ['ken(ə)l] N **1** *(of guard dog etc)* niche *f*, *(of hunting dog)* chenil *m*; **kennels** établissement *m* d'élevage de chiens; **to put a dog into kennels** mettre un chien en pension **2** **the k.** *(hounds)* la meute **3** *(of fox)* terrier *m*

kennelmaid ['ken(ə)lmeɪd] N employée *f* d'éleveur de chiens *ou* de chenil

Kenya ['kenjə, 'kiːn-] N Kenya *m*

Kenyan ['kenjən] ADJ kenyan
N Kenyan, -ane

kept [kept] ADJ *Old-fashioned, Hum* **a k. woman** une femme entretenue
PT, PP *see* **keep** VT, VI

keratosis [kerə'təʊsɪs] N kératose *f*

kerb [kɜːb] N **1** *Br (on pavement)* bordure *f ou* bord *m* de trottoir; **to draw up at the k.** s'arrêter le long du trottoir; **2** *St Exch Fam* **to buy/sell on the k.** acheter/vendre après la clôture officielle de la Bourse; **business done on the k.** opérations effectuées en coulisse, après clôture de Bourse
▸ ▸ *St Exch Fam* **k. broker** coulissier *m*, courtier, -ière hors Bourse; **k. drill** précautions *fpl* pour traverser la rue; *St Exch Fam* **k. market** marché *m* hors cote; **k. weight** poids *m* à vide

kerbcrawl ['kɜːbkrɔːl] VI = longer le trottoir en voiture à la recherche d'une prostituée

kerbcrawler ['kɜːbkrɔːlər] N = personne *f* qui longe le trottoir en voiture à la recherche d'une prostituée

kerbcrawling ['kɜːbkrɔːlɪŋ] N = recherche *f* d'une prostituée en voiture

kerbstone ['kɜːbstəʊn] N **1** *Br (of pavement)* pierre *f* de bordure
▸ ▸ *St Exch Fam* **k. market** marché *m* hors cote, coulisse *f*

kerchief ['kɜːtʃɪf] N *Old-fashioned (for head)* mouchoir *m* de tête; *(for neck)* fichu *m*

kerfuffle [kə'fʌf(ə)l] N *esp Br Fam* remueménage *m*, tohu-bohu *m*

kern [kɜːn] VT *Typ* créner, rapprocher

kernel ['kɜːn(ə)l] N **1** *(of nut)* intérieur *m*; *(in stone)* amande *f* *(of pine cone)* pignon *m*; *(of cereal)* grain *m* **2** *Fig (of problem etc)* fond *m*, essentiel *m*; **a k. of truth** un fond de vérité

kerning ['kɜːnɪŋ] N *Typ* crénage *m*, rapprochement *m* de caractères

kerosene ['kerəsiːn] N **1** *Aviat* kérosène *m* **2** *Am (paraffin)* pétrole *m* lampant
▸ ▸ **k. lamp** lampe *f* à pétrole

kestrel ['kestrəl] N *(bird)* (faucon *m*) crécerelle *f*

ketch [ketʃ] N *Naut* ketch *m*, dundee *m*, dindet *m*

ketchup ['ketʃəp] N *(tomato)* **k.** ketchup *m*

kettle ['ket(ə)l] N *(for boiling water)* bouilloire *f*, *(for cooking)* chaudron *m*; **a k. of water** mettre une bouilloire d'eau à bouillir; **has the k. boiled?** est-ce que l'eau a bouilli?; **I'll put the k. on** je mets l'eau à chauffer pour le thé *etc*; *Fam* **here's a pretty k. of fish!** nous voilà dans de beaux draps!; *Fam* **that's quite a different k. of fish** ça c'est une autre affaire

kettledrum ['ket(ə)ldrʌm] N *Mus* timbale *f*

key [kiː] N **1** *(of lock, door etc)* clef *f*, clé *f*; **to turn the k. (in the door)** donner un tour de clef (à la porte); *Old-fashioned Fig* **to have the k. of the door** *(have reached one's majority)* avoir atteint sa majorité
2 *Fig* **the k. to happiness/economic success** la clé du bonheur/de la réussite économique; **the k. to good health** les secrets *mpl* d'une bonne santé; *Fig* **it was the k. to his success** cela lui a ouvert les portes du succès; *Fig* **the k. to understanding sth** la clé permettant de comprendre qch; *Fig* **education is the k. to the nation's progress** l'éducation est la clé du progrès de la nation

3 *(answers) (to mystery, code etc)* clef *f*, *(of map etc)* légende *f*; *Sch* corrigé *m*; *(to exercises)* solutions *fpl*; *Comput (of sort, identification etc)* indicatif *m*, critère *m*
4 *Mus* ton *m*; **major/minor k.** ton majeur/mineur; **the k. of C** le ton d'ut; **to be off** *or* **out of k.** chanter/jouer faux
5 *Art etc (of painting)* caractéristique *f* de luminosité; **picture painted in a low k.** tableau peint dans des tons sombres
6 *(button etc) (of piano, organ, typewriter, computer, telephone etc)* touche *f*, *Elec* manette *f*, *Mus (of wind instrument)* clef *f*
7 *(turning device)* clef *f*, carotte *f*, *(of clock, mechanical toy etc)* remontoir *m*
8 *Constr (roughness of surface)* rappointis *m*
ADJ ATTRIB *(most important)* clé, clef; **k. factor** facteur clé; **remaining competitive is k. to our success** le maintien de la compétitivité est essentiel à notre succès; **one of the k. issues in the election** un des enjeux fondamentaux de ces élections; **k. person** *(in organization)* cheville *f* ouvrière, pilier *m*, pivot *m* (in de)
VT *Comput* taper; *(data, text)* taper, saisir; **to k. to disk** saisir
▸ ▸ **k. bar** *(in shop)* stand *m* de clef-minute; **k. card** *(for hotel room)* carte-clé *f*, *pl* cartesclés; **k. case** porte-clés *m inv*, *Am* **k. club** = club *m* privé dont les membres possèdent chacun une clef; *Comput* **k. combination** combinaison *f* de touches; *Cin* **k. grip** technicien, -ienne en chef *(chargé(e) de l'installation des décors et des rails de caméra au cinéma)*; **k. industries** industries *fpl* clés, industries-clés *fpl*; **k. money** pas *m* de porte; **k. numbers** *(on squared map)* numéros *mpl* de repérage; *Comput* **k. punch** perforatrice *f* à clavier; **k. rack** *(in hotel etc)* tableau *m* (des clés); **k. ring** porte-clés *m inv*; *Mus* **k. signature** armature *f*, armure *f*; *Br Sch* **k. stage** étape *f* clé de la scolarité
▸ **key in** VT SEP *Comput etc* = **key** VT
▸ **key up** VT SEP **1** *(usu passive) (make tense)* **the crowd was keyed up for the match** la foule était tendue dans l'attente du match; **to be all keyed up** être crispé *ou* tendu **2** *Comput* = **key** VT

key-account N *Mktg* compte-clé *m*
▸ ▸ **k. management** gestion *f* de comptesclés; **k. sales** ventes *fpl* aux comptes-clés

keyboard ['kiːbɔːd] N **1** *(of piano, typewriter, computer)* clavier *m* **2** *Mus* **keyboards** claviers *mpl*; **on k.** aux claviers
VT *Comput (text, data)* taper, saisir
VI *Comput* introduire des données par clavier
▸ ▸ *Comput* **k. buffer** mémoire *f* tampon de clavier; **k. instrument** instrument *m* à clavier; *Comput* **k. layout** disposition *f* de clavier; *Comput* **k. map** schéma *m* de clavier; *Comput* **k. operator** claviste *mf*, *Mus* **k. player** joueur, -euse de synthétiseur/piano; *Comput* **k. shortcut** raccourci *m* clavier; *Comput* **k. skills** compétences *fpl* de claviste; *Comput* **k. template** réglette *f* de clavier

keyboarder ['kiːbɔːdər] N *Comput* claviste *mf*, opérateur, -trice de saisie

keyboarding ['kiːbɔːdɪŋ] N *Comput (of data)* frappe *f*, saisie *f*
▸ ▸ **k. accuracy** précision *f* de frappe; **k. error** faute *f* de frappe; **k. problems** problèmes *mpl* au niveau de la frappe; **k. skills** compétences *fpl* de claviste; **k. speed** vitesse *f* de frappe

keyboardless computer ['kiːbɔːdlɪs] N ordinateur *m* sans clavier

keyhole ['kiːhəʊl] N trou *m* de serrure; **to look through the k.** regarder par le trou de la serrure
▸ ▸ *Carp* **k. saw** scie *f* à guichet; *Med* **k. surgery** chirurgie *f* endoscopique

keying ['kiːɪŋ] N **1** *Comput (of data)* frappe *f*, saisie *f* **2** *Mus (of piano)* accordage *m*

►► *Comput* **k. error** faute *f* de frappe; *Comput* **k. speed** vitesse *f* de frappe

keyless entry ['ki:lɪs] N *(to room)* ouverture *f* sans clé

Keynesian ['keɪnzɪən] ADJ keynésien

keynote ['ki:nəʊt] N *Mus* tonique *f*; *(of speech, approach)* idée *f* dominante; *(of policy)* mot *m* d'ordre
▪ VT mettre l'accent sur
►► **k. speaker** orateur *m* qui prononce le discours d'ouverture; **k. speech** discours *m* introductif *ou* liminaire

keynoter ['ki:nəʊtər] N *Am* orateur *m* qui prononce le discours d'ouverture

keypad ['ki:pæd] N *Comput* pavé *m*

keystone ['ki:stəʊn] N *Archit* clef *f* de voûte; *Fig (of policy)* clef de voûte, pivot *m*

keystroke ['ki:strəʊk] N *Comput* frappe *f* (de touche); **keystrokes per minute/hour** vitesse *f* de frappe à la minute/à l'heure

keyword ['ki:wɜːd] N *also Comput* mot-clé *m*, *pl* mot-clés, mot-clef *m*, *pl* mots-clefs

KG [keɪˈdʒiː] N *Br abbr* **Knight of the Order of the Garter**

kg *(abbr* **kilogram***)* kg

KGB [keɪdʒiːˈbiː] N *Formerly* KGB *m*
►► **K. agent** agent *m* du KGB; **K. officer** officier *m* du KGB

khaki ['kɑːkɪ] N *(colour, fabric)* kaki *m*
▪ ADJ kaki *inv*

Khartoum [kɑːˈtuːm] N Khartoum

kHz *(abbr* **kilohertz***)* kHz

kibbutz, *pl* **kibbutzim** [kɪˈbʊts, kɪˈbʊtsiːm] N *Agr* kibboutz *m*, *pl* kibboutzim

kibitz ['kɪbɪts] VI *Am Fam* donner des conseils non sollicités, ramener son grain de sel

kibitzer ['kɪbɪtsər] N *Am Cards etc Fam* celui/celle qui donne des conseils non sollicités, donneur, -euse d'avis; *(meddler)* mouche *f* du coche

kibosh ['kaɪbɒʃ] N *Sl* **to put the k. on** *(hopes, plans)* réduire en poussière; *(holidays, new car etc)* faire tomber à l'eau

KICK [kɪk] N **1** *(with foot)* coup *m* de pied; *(of horse etc)* ruade *f*; **to give sb/sth a k.** donner un coup de pied à qn/qch; **to have a powerful k.** *(of footballer, horse)* avoir un coup de pied puissant; *(of swimmer)* avoir un battement de pied puissant; *Fam* **she just needs a k. up the backside** *or* **in the pants** elle a juste besoin d'un coup de pied au derrière
2 *Fam (vigour)* vigueur *f*, énergie *f*, **a drink with a k. in it** une boisson qui donne un coup de fouet; **to get a k. out of sth/doing sth** prendre plaisir à qch/à faire qch; **to do sth for kicks** faire qch pour s'amuser; **to get one's kicks doing sth** prendre son pied à faire qch; *Sl* **he's on a jazz/tennis k. at the moment** son truc en ce moment c'est le jazz/tennis
3 *(recoil) (of gun)* recul *m*, réaction *f*; *(of mechanism etc)* cahot *m*, secousse *f*
4 *(of engine)* retour *m* en arrière
▪ VI **1** *(once)* donner un coup de pied; *(several times)* donner des coups de pied; *(of animal)* ruer; *Sport (of athlete)* démarrer; *(of gun)* reculer, repousser
2 *Am Fam (die)* calancher, passer l'arme à gauche
▪ VT *(once)* donner un coup de pied à; *(several times)* donner des coups de pied à; *(push with foot)* pousser du pied; *(of horse etc)* détacher un coup de pied à; *Ftbl (ball)* botter; *(goal)* marquer; **to get kicked** *(once)* recevoir un coup de pied; *(several times)* recevoir des coups de pied; *Fig Fam* **to get kicked in the teeth** recevoir un coup en vache; *Fam* **to k. sb's behind** flanquer à qn un coup de pied au derrière; *Sl* **to k. the bucket** casser sa pipe, crever; *Fig* **to k. a man when he's**

down donner le coup de pied de l'âne à qn; *Fig* **to k. sb upstairs** = donner une promotion à qn dont on veut se débarrasser; **I could have kicked myself** je me serais donné des gifles; **I could k. myself!** quel imbécile je fais!; **to k. a bad habit** se défaire d'une mauvaise habitude; **to k. the habit** *(of smoker)* arrêter (de fumer); *(of drug addict)* décrocher, arrêter (la drogue)
►► **k. boxer** tireur, -euse, personne *f* pratiquant la boxe française; **k. boxing** boxe *f* française; **k. pleat** *(in skirt)* pli *m* d'aisance; **k. turn** *(in skiing, skateboarding)* conversion *f*

▸ **kick about, kick around** VI *Fam (hang around)* traîner; *(travel around)* rouler sa bosse; **there are plenty of people like that kicking around** des gens comme ça, ce n'est pas ça qui manque; **you don't find many of these kicking around nowadays** des comme ça, ça ne court pas les rues de nos jours
▪ VT SEP **1** *(play with) (ball)* taper dans; *Fam (idea etc)* tester
2 *(mistreat)* traiter sans ménagements; **you shouldn't let yourself be kicked around like that** tu ne devrais pas te laisser traiter comme ça
▪ VT INSEP *Fam (spend time in)* **to k. around the world/Africa** rouler sa bosse *ou* traîner ses guêtres autour du monde/en Afrique; *Br* **is my purse kicking around the kitchen somewhere?** est-ce que mon porte-monnaie traîne quelque part dans la cuisine?

▸ **kick against** VT INSEP *Fam (rebel against)* regimber contre; *Fig* **to k. against the pricks** *(against fate)* s'en prendre au destin

▸ **kick aside** VT SEP *(ball, piece of paper)* écarter d'un coup de pied; *(pieces of paper)* écarter à coups de pied

▸ **kick away** VT SEP repousser du pied

▸ **kick away at** VT INSEP *(door)* mettre des coups de pied dans

▸ **kick back** VI *(recoil) (of engine)* donner des retours en arrière; *(of gun)* reculer, repousser
▪ VT SEP **1** *(return by kicking) (ball)* relancer
2 *(person)* rendre un coup de pied à; **I immediately kicked him back** je lui ai tout de suite rendu son coup de pied

▸ **kick in** VT SEP *(break open) (door etc)* enfoncer à coups de pied; *Fam* **to get one's head kicked in** se faire casser la tête

▸ **kick off** VT SEP *(shoes)* enlever d'un coup de pied
▪ VI **1** *Ftbl* donner le coup d'envoi; *Fig Fam (start)* démarrer, débuter
2 *Br Fam (become violent)* **it's going to k. off** ça va bastonner

▸ **kick out** VT SEP *(person)* chasser à coups de pied; *Fam (of job, house, pub etc)* mettre à la porte; *Ftbl (ball)* renvoyer; **to be kicked out** *(of job, house, pub etc)* être mis à la porte
▪ VI **1** *(of horse etc)* ruer; *(of person) (once)* donner un coup de pied; *(several times)* donner des coups de pied; **she would k. out at anyone who came near** elle donnait des coups de pied à tous ceux qui s'approchaient
2 *(swim vigorously)* s'élancer avec des battements vigoureux

▸ **kick over** VT SEP *(overturn)* renverser d'un coup de pied; **to k. over the traces** secouer le joug

▸ **kick up** VT SEP *Fam (cause)* **to k. up a fuss** faire des histoires; **to k. up a row** *or* **a racket** faire du tapage *ou* du boucan

kickback ['kɪkbæk] N *Fam Pej (payment)* dessous-de-table *m inv*, pot-de-vin *m*, *pl* pots-de-vin

kicker ['kɪkər] N **1** *Rugby* botteur *m*
2 *(horse, mule)* cheval *m*/mulet *m* qui rue
3 *TV (light)* projecteur *m* de décrochement, contre-jour *m*, *pl* contre-jours
4 *Am Fam (hidden drawback)* os *m*, hic *m*

5 *Am Fam (worst part of situation)* **the work's tough and the k. is the pay's lousy** le travail est dur, et en plus de ça, c'est payé avec un lance-pierres
►► *TV* **k. light** projecteur de décrochement, contre-jour, *pl* contre-jours

kicking ['kɪkɪŋ] *Br Fam* N **to give sb a k.** tabasser qn à coups de latte; **to get a k.** se faire tabasser à coups de latte
▪ ADJ *(party, nightclub)* hyper animé

kickoff ['kɪkɒf] N *Ftbl* coup *m* d'envoi; *Fig Fam* démarrage *m*; *Ftbl* **k. at two o'clock** la partie commence *ou* le coup d'envoi sera donné à deux heures; *Fam* **for a k.** pour commencer

kickstand ['kɪkstænd] N *(of bicycle)* béquille *f*

kick-start N *(on motorbike)* démarreur *m* au pied, kick *m*
▪ VT *(motorbike, engine)* démarrer au kick; *Fig (economy)* relancer, donner un sérieux coup de pouce à

kick-starter N *(on motorbike)* démarreur *m* au pied, kick *m*

kid [kɪd] N **1** *Fam (child)* gamin, -ine, gosse *mf*; *Am say* **k.!** dis-moi, mon petit/ma petite; **my k. brother** mon petit frère; **it's k.'s stuff** *(easy)* c'est facile à faire; *(childish)* c'est (bon) pour les gosses **2** *(animal)* chevreau *m*, chevrette *f*, *(skin)* (peau *f* de) chevreau, cabron *m*
▪ VT *Fam* en conter à, faire marcher; **you're kidding us** tout ça c'est des blagues, tu veux nous faire marcher; **who do you think you're trying to k.?** et tu crois que je vais avaler ça?; **to k. sb that ...** faire croire à qn que ...; **to k. oneself** se faire des illusions; **I k. you not** je ne plaisante pas; **she's just kidding that she's hurt** elle fait semblant d'avoir mal
▪ VI *Fam* **(I was) only kidding** je plaisantais; **daddy's not really hurt, he's just kidding** papa n'est pas blessé pour de vrai, il fait semblant; **no kidding!** sans blague!; **are you kidding?** *(that's a ridiculous suggestion)* tu plaisantes?
►► **k. gloves** gants *mpl* de chevreau

▸ **kid on** VT SEP, VI = **kid** VT, VI

kiddie, kiddy ['kɪdɪ] N *Fam* petit(e) gosse *mf*

kiddo ['kɪdəʊ] N *Fam* **are you ready, k.?** tu es prêt(e), mon grand/ma grande?

kidglove ['kɪdglʌv] ADJ **to give sb the k. treatment** ménager qn, traiter qn avec ménagement

kidnap ['kɪdnæp] VT *(-pp-)* kidnapper

kidnapper ['kɪdnæpər] N kidnappeur, -euse, ravisseur, -euse

kidnapping ['kɪdnæpɪŋ] N *Law* kidnapping *m*, enlèvement *m*, rapt *m*

kidney ['kɪdnɪ] N **1** *Anat* rein *m* **2** *Culin* rognon *m* **3** *Br Lit (temperament)* nature *f*, caractère *f*; *Old-fashioned* **people of that k.** les gens de cette espèce
►► **k. bean** *(red)* haricot *m* rouge; *(white)* haricot de Soissons; **k. donor** donneur, -euse de rein; **k. failure** insuffisance *f* rénale; **k. machine** rein artificiel; **k. stone** calcul *m* rénal; *Med* **k. tray** cuvette *f* à pansements réniforme; *Bot* **k. vetch** (anthyllide *f*) vulnéraire *f*

kidney-shaped ADJ *(bean etc)* en forme de haricot, réniforme

kidology [kɪˈdɒlədʒɪ] N *Br Fam* **it's all k.** ce ne sont que des histoires

kill [kɪl] N **1** *(in hunting) (of fox, deer etc)* mise *f* à mort; *(animals killed)* gibier *m* tué, tableau *m* de chasse; **to be in at the k.** assister à la mise à mort; *Fig* assister au dénouement de qch (et en tirer profit)
2 *Mil (of enemy aircraft)* descente *f*, *(of enemy warship)* coulée *f*

vt1 *(person, animal, microbes)* tuer; *(plant)* faire mourir; *Mil (enemy)* détruire; *(partridge)* tuer, descendre; *(of butcher) (cow etc)* abattre, tuer; *(nerve of tooth)* tuer; *(in hunting) (animal)* servir; **to be killed by gunshots/in an accident** être tué à coups de fusil/dans un accident; **to be killed by the radiation/a mysterious illness** mourir des radiations/d'une maladie mystérieuse; **to k. oneself** se suicider; *Fam (overexert oneself)* se tuer (**doing** à faire); *Fam (with laughing)* être mort de rire; *Iron* **don't k. yourself, will you** surtout, ne te surmène pas *ou* ne te fatigue pas trop!; **to k. oneself with work** se tuer à (force de) travailler; **the shock would k. her** le choc la tuerait; *Fam* **I'll k. you!** *(if you do that again etc)* je t'étrangle!; *Fam* **this one'll k. you** *(of joke)* ça va te faire mourir de rire; **this superstition will be hard to k.** cette superstition aura la vie dure; *Prov* **to k. two birds with one stone** faire d'une pierre deux coups, faire coup double; **to k. sb with kindness** faire du mal à qn par excès de bonté; *Fam* **my feet/these shoes are killing me** mes pieds/ces chaussures me font atrocement souffrir; *Fam* **the heat is killing me!** j'étouffe!, je meurs de chaud!

2 *Fig (time)* tuer; *(ambition)* éteindre; *(love, sense of humanity etc)* détruire, étouffer; *Pol (bill)* couler; *Journ etc (passage, story)* supprimer; *(file)* effacer; *(printer)* arrêter; *(pain)* atténuer; *(smells)* neutraliser; *Tech (sound)* amortir; **to k. time** tuer le temps; **k. that light!** éteignez-moi ça tout de suite!

3 *Ftbl (ball)* bloquer; *Tennis (balle)* tuer, massacrer

vt tuer; **k. or cure remedy** remède *m* de cheval; **k. or be killed** tuer ou se faire tuer; *Fam* **I'd k. for a beer** je me damnerais pour une bière

▸ **kill off** **vt sep** tuer; *(whole population)* exterminer; *(hope)* anéantir; *(small businesses)* faire disparaître; **to k. off a character** *(of author etc)* faire mourir un personnage

killer ['kɪlər] **N1** *(person)* tueur, -euse; *(murderer)* meurtrier, -ière **2** *Fam (difficult question)* colle *f*; **the exam was a real k.** cet examen n'était pas piqué des hannetons; **that dance was a k.!** cette danse m'a tué!; **that walk was a k.!** cette promenade était vraiment crevante; **the real k. is that …** le comble c'est que …; **this one's a k.** *(joke)* celle-là est à mourir de rire

▸▸ *Comput Fam* **k. app** application *f* phare, killer app *f*; **k. disease** maladie *f* meurtrière; *Fig* **k. instinct** agressivité *f*; **he lacks the k. instinct** il manque d'agressivité *ou* de combativité, il a trop de scrupules; *Zool* **k. whale** épaulard *m*, orque *f*

killing ['kɪlɪŋ] **ADJ1** *(blow)* meurtrier, assassin **2** *Fam (exhausting) (work, dance)* tuant, crevant **3** *Fam (very amusing)* crevant; **it's too k. for words** c'est à mourir de rire, c'est à se tordre

N *(of animal for meat)* abattage *m*; *(of person)* meurtre *m*; *Mil (of enemy)* destruction *f*; **the k. of 500 seal pups** le massacre de 500 bébés phoques; *Fam* **to make a k.** *(on Stock Exchange etc)* faire un bénéfice énorme *ou* une affaire à tout casser

-killing ['kɪlɪŋ] **SUFF** -icide; **germ-k.** bactéricide

killingly ['kɪlɪŋlɪ] **ADV** **it's k. funny** c'est à mourir de rire

killjoy ['kɪldʒɔɪ] **N** rabat-joie *m inv*

kiln [kɪln] **N** four *m* (céramique); *(for drying)* séchoir *m*, sécherie *f*, étuve *f*; **k. drying** *or* **seasoning** séchage *m* au four, étuvage *m*; *(in brewing)* touraillage *m*

kilo ['kiːləʊ] **N** kilo *m*

kilobaud ['kɪləbɔːd] **N** kilobaud *m*

kilobit ['kɪləbɪt] **N** *Comput* kilobit *m*

kilobyte ['kɪləbaɪt] **N** *Comput* kilo-octet *m*

kilocalorie ['kɪləʊkælərɪ] **N** *Phys* kilocalorie *f*

kilocycle ['kɪləsaɪk(ə)l] **N** *Phys, Elec* kilocycle *m*

kilogram(me) ['kɪləgræm] **N** kilogramme *m*

kilohertz ['kɪləhɜːts] **N** kilohertz *m*

kilometre, *Am* **kilometer** ['kɪləmiːtər, kɪˈlɒmɪtər] **N** kilomètre *m*; **distance in kilometres** distance *f* kilométrique

kilometric [kɪləˈmetrɪk] **ADJ** kilométrique

kilovolt ['kɪləvəʊlt] **N** *Elec* kilovolt *m*

kilowatt ['kɪləwɒt] **N** *Elec* kilowatt *m*

kilowatt-hour **N** *Elec* kilowatt-heure *m*, *pl* kilowatt-heures

kilt [kɪlt] **N** kilt *m* (écossais)

kilted ['kɪltɪd] **ADJ 1** *(person)* en kilt **2** *(pleated)* **k. skirt** kilt *m*

kilter ['kɪltər] **N** *Fam* **out of k.** *(of machine part)* détraqué; *(out of balance) (of schedule, budget etc)* déséquilibré; **this is running out of k. with the rest of the machine** c'est en décalage par rapport au reste de la machine

kimono [kɪˈməʊnəʊ] **N** kimono *m*

kin [kɪn] **N** *Fml* parents *mpl*; **his k.** ses parents, sa parenté; **to be k. to sb** être parent de qn, être apparenté avec qn; **he's no k. of mine** il n'est pas de ma famille

KIND¹ [kaɪnd] **N1** *(class, sort)* genre *m*, espèce *f*, sorte *f*; **what k. is it?** de quelle sorte *ou* de quel genre (est-ce)?; **what k. of tree is this?** quelle sorte *ou* quel genre d'arbre est-ce?; **what k. of woman is she?** quel genre *ou* quelle sorte de femme est-ce?; **people of all kinds** des gens de toutes sortes; **the worst k. of people** des gens de la pire espèce; **it's a k. of fish** c'est une espèce de poisson; **they have so many different kinds of bread** ils ont tellement de sortes de pain différentes; **they did have some flour, but it wasn't the right k.** ils avaient bien de la farine, mais ce n'était pas la bonne; **something of the k.** quelque chose de ce genre; **nothing of the k.** rien de la sorte; **she's terribly boring – she's nothing of the k.!** elle est terriblement ennuyeuse – pas du tout! loin de là!; **in a k. of a way** en quelque façon; **this k. of woman,** *Fam* **these k. of women** ce genre de femmes; **he's not the understanding k.** il n'est pas du genre compréhensif; **I know your k.!** je connais les gens de ton espèce!; **she's more the stay-at-home k.** elle est plus du genre à rester à la maison; **well, it's beer of a k., I suppose** oui, on peut appeler ça de la bière, je suppose; **he speaks French – of a k.** il parle français – plus ou moins; **we're two of a k.** nous sommes de la même espèce *ou* race; **it's the only one of its k.** c'est le seul en son genre; **what k. of person do you think I am!** pour quel genre de personne me prends-tu?; **he's that k. of person** il est comme ça; **this is my k. of party** c'est le genre de soirée que j'aime; **you're my k. of girl** tu es mon type de femme, tu es le type de femme que j'aime; **I'm not that k. of girl** ce n'est pas mon genre; **is this the k. of thing you're looking for?** est-ce que c'est quelque chose de ce genre que vous cherchez?; **that's not the k. of thing I meant** ce n'est pas exactement ce que je voulais; **this is not the k. of thing you can do overnight** ce n'est pas le genre de chose qu'on fait du jour au lendemain; *Fam* **it was a k. of saucer-shaped thing** c'était une espèce de truc en forme de soucoupe; *Fam* **there's a k. of bump just here** il y a comme une bosse ici; *Fam* **I heard a k. of thump** j'ai entendu une espèce de cognement *ou* comme un cognement **VOIR GRAMMAIRE A13**

2 *(nature, character)* **difference in k.** différence *f* spécifique; **payment in k.** paiement

m en nature; **to repay sb in k.** *(as opposed to cash)* rembourser qn en nature; *(for an injury, disservice)* rendre à qn la monnaie de sa pièce

3 *Fam* **k. of** *(with adjectives and verbs)* un peu, plutôt; **you look k. of tired** tu as l'air un peu *ou* plutôt fatigué; **it's k. of late** il est un peu tard; **I'm k. of worried** je suis un peu inquiet; **I've k. of changed my mind** je crois bien que j'ai changé d'avis; **I k. of expected it** je m'y attendais un peu; **I k. of like it** *(like it a little)* j'aime plus ou moins ça; *(quite a bit)* j'aime bien ça; **do you like it? – k. of** tu aimes ça? – plus ou moins, ça va, couci-couça; **do you agree? – k. of** tu es d'accord? – plus ou moins

kind² **ADJ** gentil; **to be k. to sb** se montrer gentil avec qn, se montrer bon pour *ou* envers qn; **it's very k. of you to …** c'est bien aimable de votre part *ou* à vous de …; *Fml* **(would you) be k. enough to** *or* **so k. as to …** ayez la bonté de …, veuillez (bien) …; **you are really too k.** vous êtes vraiment trop aimable; **k. to the skin** *(of detergents etc)* qui n'irrite pas la peau; **by k. permission of …** avec l'aimable autorisation de …; **give him my k. regards** faites-lui mes amitiés; **k. words** paroles *fpl* bienveillantes

kinda ['kaɪndə] *Fam* **= kind of,** *see* **kind¹ 3**

kindergarten ['kɪndəgɑːt(ə)n] **N** *Sch* école *f* maternelle

kind-hearted ['kaɪnd'hɑːtɪd] **ADJ** *(person)* qui a bon cœur; *(action, response)* bienveillant; **that was very k. of you** c'était très gentil de votre part; **he's very k.** il a très bon cœur, il a le cœur sur la main

kindle ['kɪnd(ə)l] **vt1** *(flame, fire)* allumer; *(coal, wood)* enflammer, embraser **2** *(hatred)* allumer; *(emotions, passions)* faire naître, susciter; *(desires)* enflammer; *(suspicions, sorrow)* aviver; *(enthusiasm)* exciter

vi *(of fire, wood, passions etc)* s'allumer, s'enflammer

kindliness ['kaɪndlɪnɪs] **N** gentillesse *f*, bonté *f*

kindling ['kɪndlɪŋ] **N** bois *m* d'allumage, petit bois

▸▸ **k. wood** bois d'allumage, petit bois

kindly ['kaɪndlɪ] **ADV** gentiment, avec bonté; **she spoke very k. of you** elle a dit des choses très aimables *ou* gentilles à votre égard; **to be k. disposed towards sb/sth** être bien disposé envers qn/qch; **the council k. agreed to let us use the town hall** le conseil nous a aimablement autorisés à utiliser l'hôtel de ville; **(will you) k. close the window** voudriez-vous avoir la bonté *ou* la gentillesse de fermer la fenêtre?; *Com* **k. remit by cheque** prière de nous couvrir par chèque; **not to take k. to sb/sth** ne pas aimer qn/qch

ADJ *(person)* gentil, bon; *(tone, advice)* bienveillant

kindness ['kaɪndnɪs] **N1** gentillesse *f*, amabilité *f* (**towards sb** envers qn), bonté *f* (**towards sb** pour qn); **thanks for your k.** merci de votre gentillesse *ou* amabilité; **to repay sb's k.** payer qn de sa gentillesse; **to show k. to sb** témoigner de la bonté à qn; *Fml* **would you have the k. to …?** voulez-vous avoir la bonté *ou* gentillesse de …?; **to do sth out of the k. of one's heart** faire qch par gentillesse; *Iron* **and I suppose it was out of the k. of your heart that you did that?** et je suppose que c'est ton bon cœur qui t'a poussé à faire ça?

2 **a k.** un service (rendu); **to do sb a k.** rendre service à qn; **would you at least do me the k. of listening to my proposal?** me ferez-vous au moins l'amabilité d'écouter ma proposition?

kindred ['kɪndrɪd] **N** *Old-fashioned (relationship)* parenté *f*; *(family)* famille *f*, parents *mpl*

ADJ *(related)* apparenté; *(similar)* similaire, analogue
▸▸ **k. spirits** âmes *fpl* sœurs

kinematic [kɪnə'mætɪk, kaɪn-] **ADJ** *Phys* cinématique

kinematics [kɪnə'mætɪks, kaɪn-] **N** *Phys* cinématique *f* VOIR GRAMMAIRE A10

kinetic [kɪ'netɪk, kaɪ-] **ADJ** *Phys, Art* cinétique

kinetics [kɪ'netɪks] **N** *Phys* cinétique *f* VOIR GRAMMAIRE A10

kinfolk ['kɪnfəʊk] **NPL** *Am* parents *mpl* et alliés *mpl*

king [kɪŋ] **N 1** *(person)* roi *m*; *Ind etc* magnat *m*; **the kings and queens of England** les souverains *mpl* d'Angleterre; *Fig* **the k. of (the) beasts** le roi des animaux; *Fig* **the fast-food k.** le roi *ou* magnat de la restauration rapide; *Bible* **K. of Kings** Roi des rois; *Bible* **the three Kings** les Rois *mpl* Mages; *Bible* **(the Book of) Kings** le livre des Rois; **a k.'s ransom** une fortune **2** *Chess, Cards* roi *m*; *(in draughts)* dame *f*
▸▸ *Zool* **k. cobra** cobra *m* royal, hamadryade *f*; *Zool* **k. crab** limule *f*, crabe *m* des Moluques; *Bot, Culin* **K. Edward** *(potato)* (pomme *f* de terre) King Edward *f*; *Orn* **k. penguin** manchot *m* royal; *Br Zool* **k. prawn** (grosse) crevette *f*

kingcup ['kɪŋkʌp] **N** *Bot* **1** *(buttercup)* bouton *m* d'or **2** *(marsh marigold)* populage *m*, souci *m* d'eau

kingdom ['kɪŋdəm] **N 1** royaume *m*; **the k. of heaven** le royaume des cieux **2** *(animal)* règne *m*; **in the animal k.** chez les animaux **3** *Rel* règne *m*; **Thy k. come** que Ton règne vienne; *Fam* **k. come** le paradis; *Fam* **to send sb to k. come** expédier qn dans l'autre monde; *Fam* **until k. come** jusqu'à la fin des temps

kingfisher ['kɪŋfɪʃər] **N** martin-pêcheur *m*, *pl* martins-pêcheurs

kingly ['kɪŋlɪ] **ADJ** *Lit* de roi; *(royal)* royal, -aux

kingpin ['kɪŋpɪn] **N 1** *Aut* axe *m* de rotule *ou* de fusée, pivot *m* de fusée; *Fig* *(of organization, company)* cheville *f* ouvrière **2** *(in ten-pin bowling)* quille *f* du milieu

kingship ['kɪŋʃɪp] **N** royauté *f*

king-size(d) ['kɪŋsaɪz, -d] **ADJ** *(bed, mattress)* (très) grand format; *(cigarette)* long (longue); *(packet, container)* géant; *Fam Fig* **I've got a k. hangover** j'ai une gueule de bois carabinée
▸▸ **k. bed** lit *m* king size

kink [kɪŋk] **N 1** vrillage *m*; *(in felt)* grigne *f*, *(of hair)* crêpelure *f*; *Tex* vrille *f*, boucle *f*; **the rope's got a k. in it** il y a un vrillage dans la corde **2** *(in character)* déséquilibre *m*, aberration *f*; **it's one of her little kinks** c'est l'une de ses petites manies
VI *(of rope)* se nouer, se tortiller; *(of thread)* vriller

kinkiness ['kɪŋkɪnɪs] **N** *(sexual) (tastes)* goûts *mpl* bizarres; **no k.!** pas de trucs bizarres!

kinky ['kɪŋkɪ] **ADJ 1** *(hair)* crêpelé, crépu **2** *Sl (person) (sexually)* qui a des goûts sexuels excentriques; *Fam (eccentric)* extravagant; *Fam (clothes etc) (strange)* bizarre, extravagant; *(erotic, pornographic)* pervers

kinsfolk ['kɪnzfəʊk] **NPL** = kinfolk

kinship ['kɪnʃɪp] **N** parenté *f*

kinsman, *pl* **kinsmen** ['kɪnzmən] **N** *Lit* parent *m*

kinswoman, *pl* **kinswomen** ['kɪnzwʊmən, -wɪmɪn] **N** *Lit* parente *f*

kiosk ['ki:ɒsk] **N** kiosque *m*

kip [kɪp] *Br Fam* **N 1** *(sleep)* **to have a k.** piquer un roupillon; **to get some k.** roupiller; **an hour's k.** un roupillon d'une heure **2** *(bed)* pieu *m*, plumard *m*; **to be still in one's k.** être encore au plumard

VI *(-pp-)* *(sleep)* roupiller
▸ **kip down** **VI** *Br Fam* pieuter

kipper ['kɪpər] *Culin* **N** hareng *m* légèrement salé et fumé, kipper *m*
VT *(herring)* saler et fumer; **kippered herring** hareng *m* légèrement salé et fumé; *Fig Fam* **to k. one's lungs** s'enfumer les poumons

kir [kɪər] **N** *(drink)* kir *m*, blanc *m* cassis
▸▸ **k. royale** kir *m* royal

kirby-grip ['kɜːbɪ-] **N** *Br* pince *f* à cheveux

Kirg(h)izia [kɜː'giːzɪə], **Kirg(h)izstan** [kɜːgɪz'stæn] **N** le Kirghizistan

kirk [kɜːk] **N** *Scot* église *f*; **the K.** l'Église (presbytérienne) d'Écosse

kiss [kɪs] **N** baiser *m*; **to give/blow sb a k.** donner/envoyer un baiser à qn; **give mummy a k.!** *(to child)* fais une bise à maman!; *Med* **to give sb the k. of life** faire le bouche-à-bouche à qn; *Fig* **to be the k. of death for sb/sth** *(of act, decision)* être fatal pour qn/qch
VT 1 *(person)* donner un baiser à, embrasser; *(forehead or hand, holy object)* baiser; *(ceremonially) (person)* donner l'accolade à; **to k. sb on the cheek/lips** embrasser qn sur la joue/les lèvres; **they kissed each other** ils se sont embrassés; **mummy will k. it better** maman va te faire un bisou et tu n'auras plus mal; **to k. the book** baiser la Bible (pour prêter serment); *Lit* **to k. the dust** mordre la poussière; **to k. sb goodbye** dire au revoir à qn en l'embrassant; *Fam* **you can k. that promotion goodbye** tu peux dire au revoir à cet avancement; *Br Vulg* **(you can) k. my arse!** va te faire foutre!
2 *(touch lightly)* frôler; *Billiards (of ball)* frapper par contrecoup
VI 1 *(of two people)* s'embrasser; **to k. and make up** se réconcilier; **he's the k. and tell type** il est du genre à aller le crier sur tous les toits quand il a une aventure; **how much did she get for her k. and tell story?** combien on l'a payée pour raconter les détails de son aventure avec lui?
2 *(of two objects)* se frôler; *Billiards (of balls)* se frapper par contrecoup
▸▸ *Br* **k. curl** accroche-cœur *m*, *pl* accroche-cœurs
▸ **kiss away** **VT SEP** **to k. away sb's tears** sécher les larmes de qn en l'embrassant
▸ **kiss off** *Am Fam* **VT SEP 1** *(dismiss)* envoyer promener **2** *(kill)* descendre, buter **3** *(give up hope of)* faire une croix sur, dire adieu à; **you can k. off your promotion!** tu peux faire une croix sur *ou* dire adieu à ta promotion!
VI k. off! va te faire voir!

kisser ['kɪsər] **N 1** *(person)* embrasseur, -euse; **to be a great k.** bien embrasser **2** *Sl (mouth)* gueule *f*

kiss-off ['kɪsɒf] **N** *Am Fam* **to give sb the k.** *(of girlfriend etc)* plaquer qn; *(of employer)* virer qn

kissogram ['kɪsəgræm] **N** = message *m* délivré par une personne déguisée et accompagné d'un baiser; **a k. girl** = une fille qui délivre des messages et est chargée d'embrasser le destinataire

kit [kɪt] **N 1** *(equipment)* matériel *m*, équipement *m*; *Mil etc* petit équipement **2** *Sport (clothes)* tenue *f*; *Fam* **to get one's k. off** se déshabiller **3** *(set of parts)* **to buy sth in k. form** acheter qch en prêt-à-monter *ou* en pièces détachées; **to make sth from a k.** faire qch à partir de pièces détachées
VT *(-tt-)* = **kit out, kit up**
▸▸ **k. inspection** revue *f* de détail
▸ **kit out, kit up** **VT SEP** *esp Br (soldier etc)* équiper, fournir son équipement à; **(all) kitted out** complètement équipé; *Mil* **to be kitted out** toucher son paquetage

kitbag ['kɪtbæg] **N** sac *m* (de) marin; *Mil* sac à paquetage, sac de grande monture

kitchen ['kɪtʃɪn] **N** cuisine *f*
▸▸ **k. cabinet** *(furniture)* buffet *m* (de cuisine); *Br Pol* = conseillers *mpl* proches du chef du gouvernement; **k. foil** aluminium *m* ménager, papier *m* d'aluminium *ou* d'alu; **k. hand** aide *mf* de cuisine; **k. knife** couteau *m* de cuisine; **k. paper** essuie-tout *m inv*; **k. roll** essuie-tout; **k. sink** évier *m*; **k. sink drama** = théâtre *m* et cinéma *m* réalistes des années 50–60 dépeignant l'ennui et la misère des gens ordinaires; **k. stove** cuisinière *f*; **k. unit** élément *m* (de cuisine); **k. utensils** batterie *f* de cuisine

kitchenette [kɪtʃɪ'net] **N** coin-cuisine *m*, *pl* coins-cuisines, cuisinette *f*

kitchenware ['kɪtʃɪnweər] **N** vaisselle *f* de cuisine

kite [kaɪt] **N 1** *(toy)* cerf-volant *m*, *pl* cerfs-volants; *Fam* **as high as a k.** *(drunk)* ivre, soûl; *(drugged)* drogué, camé; *(very excited)* tout fou, *f* toute folle **2** *Fin Fam* traite *f* en l'air, billet *m* de complaisance; **to fly** *or* **to send up a k.** tirer en l'air *ou* à découvert **3** *Br Fam (aeroplane)* avion *m*, taxi *m* **4** *(bird)* milan *m*
▸▸ **k. balloon** ballon *m* observateur

kith [kɪθ] **N** **our k. and kin** nos parents et amis; **to have neither k. nor kin** être seul sur la terre

kiting ['kaɪtɪŋ] **N** *Fin Fam* tirage *m* en l'air, tirage à découvert

kitsch [kɪtʃ] **N** kitsch *m*; **a piece of k.** du kitsch
ADJ kitsch *inv*

kitschy ['kɪtʃɪ] **ADJ** kitsch *inv*; **it's k.** c'est du kitsch

kitten ['kɪt(ə)n] **N** *(young cat)* chaton *m*, petit(e) chat(te); *(term of endearment)* ma petite, ma mignonne; **a cat and her kittens** une chatte et ses petits; *Br Fam* **he'll have kittens** *(of person)* il va se mettre dans tous ses états; **to be having kittens** *(of person)* être dans tous ses états
▸▸ **k. heels** talons *mpl* bobine

kittenish ['kɪtənɪʃ] **ADJ** *(playful)* enjoué; *(flirtatious)* coquet

kittiwake ['kɪtɪweɪk] **N** *(bird)* mouette *f* tridactyle

kitty[1] ['kɪtɪ] **N** *Fam (cat)* minou *m*, minet *m*; *(kitten)* chaton *m*; **here k., k.** minou, minou, viens

kitty[2] **N 1** *Cards etc* cagnotte *f*, *(of group)* cagnotte, caisse *f* commune **2** *(at bowls)* cochonnet *m*

kiwi ['kiːwiː] **N 1** *(bird)* aptéryx *m*, kiwi *m* **2** *Fam (New Zealander)* **K.** Néo-Zélandais, -aise **3** *(fruit)* kiwi *m*
▸▸ **k. fruit** kiwi

KKK [keɪkeɪ'keɪ] **N** *abbr* **Ku Klux Klan**

kleptomania [kleptə'meɪnɪə] **N** kleptomanie *f*

kleptomaniac [kleptə'meɪnɪæk] **ADJ, N** kleptomane *mf*

klieg light [kliːg] **N** *Am Cin* lampe *f* à arc

klutz [klʌts] **N** *Am Fam* brise-tout *m inv*

km *(abbr* **kilometre**) km

km/h *(abbr* **kilometres per hour**) km/h

knack [næk] **N** talent *m*, chic *m*; *(esp physical)* tour *m* de main; **to have the k. of** *or* **a k. for doing sth** avoir le talent de *ou* le chic pour faire qch; *(esp physically)* avoir le coup *ou* le tour de main pour faire qch; **to have lost the k. of sth** n'avoir plus l'habitude de qch; **there's a k. to it** il y a un truc; **there's a k. to opening this door** il y a un truc pour ouvrir la porte; **you have a k. for telephoning me at exactly the wrong moment** tu as le chic pour me téléphoner précisément au mauvais moment

knacker ['nækər] *Br* **N 1** *(of horses)* équarrisseur *m*; **k.'s yard** chantier *m* d'équarrissage, équarrissoir *m* **2** *(of buildings)* entrepreneur *m* de démolitions; *(of ships)* démolisseur *m*

de vieux navires **3** *Vulg* **knackers** *(testicles)* couilles *fpl*
▶ **VT** *Fam (person)* crever, tuer; *(machine etc)* bousiller

knackered ['nækəd] **ADJ** *Br Fam (tired) (person)* crevé, mort; *(broken) (machine etc)* foutu, naze

knackering ['nækərɪŋ] **ADJ** *Br Fam* crevant

knapsack ['næpsæk] **N** *Old-fashioned* havresac *m*, sac *m* à dos; *Mil* sac d'ordonnance, havresac

knave [neɪv] **N 1** *Cards* valet *m*; **k. of clubs** valet de trèfle **2** *Old-fashioned (scoundrel)* fripon *m*, coquin *m*

knavery ['neɪvərɪ] **N** *Old-fashioned* friponnerie *f*, coquinerie *f*

knead [niːd] **VT 1** *(dough, clay)* pétrir, malaxer, travailler **2** *Med (muscles)* masser, pétrir

knee [niː] **N 1** *knee m*, -oux; **these trousers are out at the k.** ce pantalon est troué au genou; **to sit on sb's k.** *or* **knees** s'asseoir sur les genoux de qn; **to put sb over one's k.** *(spank)* donner une fessée à qn; **she put him over her k. and spanked him** elle l'a attrapé sur ses genoux et lui a donné une fessée; **he learnt the song at his mother's k.** il a appris la chanson sur les genoux de sa mère; **to fall** *or* **drop to one's knees** tomber à genoux; **on your knees!** à genoux!; **to go down on one's knees** s'agenouiller; *Fig* se mettre à genoux; *Lit* **to bend** *or* **bow the k. to** *or* **before sb** fléchir le genou devant qn, s'incliner devant qn; *Fig* **to ask for sth on one's (bended) knees** *or* **on bended k.** demander qch à genoux; *Fig* **to bring sb to his knees** obliger qn à capituler; *Fig* **the crisis brought the government to its knees** la crise a mis le gouvernement à genoux; **the famine has brought the country to its knees** la famine a entraîné le pays au bord de la ruine; *Vet* **broken knees** *(of horse)* couronnement *m* **2** *Tech, Constr* raccord *m* coudé, coude *m*; *(in naval architecture)* courbe *f* (de consolidation)
▶ **VT** *(hit)* donner un coup de genou à; **she kneed him in the groin** elle lui a donné un coup de genou dans les parties; **she kneed the door open** *(push)* elle poussa la porte du genou; **he kneed the box out of the way** il écarta la boîte du genou
▶▶ *Tech* **k. bracket** console-équerre *f*, *pl* consoles-équerres; **k. jerk** réflexe *m* patellaire *ou* rotulien; **k. plate** gousset *m* (de charpente); **k. reflex** réflexe patellaire *ou* rotulien; *Carp* **k. timber** bois *m* courbant *ou* coudé

kneecap ['niːkæp] **N** *Anat* rotule *f*
▶ **VT** **to k. sb** tirer dans les rotules de qn

kneecapping ['niːkæpɪŋ] **N** **it was the third k. that week** c'était la troisième fois de la semaine que quelqu'un se faisait tirer dans les rotules

knee-deep **ADJ** *(mud, water)* jusqu'aux genoux; **to be k. in mud** être enfoncé dans la boue jusqu'aux genoux; *Fig* **to be k. in paperwork** être dans la paperasse jusqu'au cou

knee-high **ADJ, ADV** à hauteur du genou; **the snow/water was k.** la neige/l'eau arrivait à hauteur du genou; **to go k. into the water** entrer dans l'eau jusqu'aux genoux; *Fam* **when I was k. to a grasshopper** quand j'étais haut comme trois pommes

kneejerk ['niːdʒɜːk] **ADJ** *(reflex)* automatique
▶▶ *Fig Pej* **k. reaction** réflexe *m*, automatisme *m*; *Pol* **k. support** soutien *m* systématique *ou* inconditionnel

kneel [niːl] **VI** *(pt, pp* **knelt** [nelt], *occ* **kneeled)** s'agenouiller, se mettre à genoux; *Fig Lit*, **to k. to sb** se mettre à genoux devant qn

knee-length **ADJ** *(dress)* qui descend jus-

qu'aux genoux; *(boot, socks)* qui monte jusqu'aux genoux

kneeler ['niːlər] **N** *(cushion) (in church)* agenouilloir *m*

kneeling ['niːlɪŋ] **ADJ** agenouillé, à genoux
▶ **N** agenouillement *m*

kneepad ['niːpæd] **N** genouillère *f*

kneeroom ['niːrʊm] **N** espace *m* aux genoux

knees-up ['niːzʌp] **N** *Br Fam* java *f*; **to have a k.** faire la java; **there was a bit of a k. in the pub** on a un peu fait la java au pub

knee-trembler [tremblər] **N** *Br Fam Hum* **to have a k.** faire l'amour debout

knell [nel] **N** glas *m*; **to toll the (death) k.** sonner le glas; *Fig* **this news/refusal rang the death k. of her hopes** cette nouvelle/ce refus sonnait le glas de ses espérances

knelt **PT, PP** *see* **kneel**

knew **PT** *see* **know**

knickerbocker glory ['nɪkəbɒkər] **N** *Culin* coupe *f* de glace avec fruits et crème Chantilly

knickerbockers ['nɪkəbɒkəz] **NPL** culotte *f* (bouffante), knickerbockers *mpl*

knickers ['nɪkəz] **NPL** VOIR GRAMMAIRE A10 **1** (petite) culotte *f* (de femme); *Old-fashioned Fam* **k.!** *(nonsense)* balivernes!; *Vulg* **to get into sb's k.** s'envoyer qn, culbuter qn; *Br Fam* **to get one's k. in a twist** paniquer *(about* à cause de) **2** *Am (breeches)* = **knickerbockers**

knick-knack ['nɪknæk] **N** *Fam* colifichet *m*, babiole *f*, bibelot *m*

knife, *pl* **knives** [naɪf, naɪvz] **N 1** couteau *m*; *Surg (with narrow blade)* bistouri *m*; **k. and fork** couverts *mpl*; *Old-fashioned Fam* **before you could say k.** en un rien de temps, en moins de deux; **to go through sth like a k. through butter** entrer dans qch comme dans du beurre; **this k. wouldn't cut butter** ce couteau ne coupe que ce qu'il voit *or* ne coupe rien; *Fig* **it was an atmosphere you could have cut with a k.** l'atmosphère était extrêmement tendue; *Fig* **to get** *or* **have one's k. into sb** en vouloir à qn; *Fig* **the knives are out for him** on ne donne pas cher de sa peau; **it was war to the k. between them** ils étaient à couteaux tirés; *Med Fam* **to go under the k.** passer sur le billard; *Med Fam* **he was under the k. for two hours** *(in operation)* il a passé deux heures sur le billard **2** *(blade) (on machine)* lame *f*, *(of guillotine)* couperet *m*
▶ **VT** *(stab)* donner un coup de couteau à, poignarder; **he's been knifed** il a reçu un coup de couteau, il a été poignardé
▶▶ **k. attack** attaque *f* à coups de couteau; **k. grinder** *(person)* rémouleur *m*, repasseur *m* de couteaux; *(instrument)* meule *f* à aiguiser; *Tech* **k. sharpener** aiguisoir *m* (pour couteaux); **k. wound** blessure *f* à coups de couteau

knife-edge **N** *Fig* **he had been on a k. all day** *(nervous)* il avait été sur les nerfs toute la journée; *Fig* **the situation/game/etc was balanced on a k.** la situation/la partie/etc ne tenait qu'à un fil
▶ **ADJ** **trousers with a k. crease** pantalon au pli cassant

knife-point **N** pointe *f* de couteau; **to be robbed at k.** se faire voler sous la menace d'un couteau

knife-rest **N** porte-couteau *m*, *pl* porte-couteaux

knifing ['naɪfɪŋ] **N** attaque *f* au couteau

knight [naɪt] **N 1** chevalier *m* **2** *Chess* cavalier *m*
▶ **VT** faire *ou* créer chevalier
▶▶ **k. errant** chevalier errant, paladin *m*; *Br* **K. of (the Order of) the Garter** chevalier de

l'Ordre de la Jarretière; *Liter* **the Knights of the Round Table** les Chevaliers de la Table Ronde; *Hist* **k. service** service *m* de haubert

knighthood ['naɪthʊd] **N** *(title)* **he has just been given a k.** il vient d'être fait *ou* créé chevalier

knightly ['naɪtlɪ] **ADJ** *(conduct etc)* chevaleresque, de chevalier

knit [nɪt] *(pt, pp* **knitted** *or* **knit)** **VT 1** *(sweater etc)* tricoter; **k. two, purl two** deux à l'endroit, deux à l'envers **2** **to k. one's brows** froncer les sourcils
▶ **VI 1** tricoter, faire du tricot; *(as opposed to purl)* tricoter à l'endroit **2** *Med (of bones)* se souder
▶ **knit together** **VI** *Med (of bones)* se souder
▶ **VT SEP** *(join)* **them together; their experience k. them together more tightly than ever** l'expérience qu'ils ont vécue les a liés plus que jamais
▶ **knit up** **VT SEP** assembler (en le tricotant)

knitted ['nɪtɪd] **ADJ 1** tricoté, de *ou* en tricot; *(lace)* au tricot; **a k. jumper** un tricot **2** **k. eyebrows** sourcils *mpl* froncés
▶▶ **k. fabric** tricot *m*; **k. goods** tricots *mpl*, articles *mpl* en tricot

knitter ['nɪtər] **N** tricoteur, -euse

knitting ['nɪtɪŋ] **N 1** *(activity)* tricotage *m*; *(work)* tricot *m*; **to do some k.** tricoter; **I've brought my k.** j'ai apporté mon tricot **2** *(of bones)* soudure *f*
▶▶ **k. machine** machine *f* à tricoter; **k. needle** aiguille *f* à tricoter; **k. pattern** modèle *m* de tricot; **k. wool** laine *f* à tricoter

knitwear ['nɪtweə(r)] **N** lainages *mpl*

knob [nɒb] **N 1** *(on cane, bannisters)* pomme *f*, *(on door, drawer etc)* bouton *m*, poignée *f*, *(on radio etc)* bouton; *(on surface, forehead etc)* bosse *f*, protubérance *f*, *Br Fam* **it comes with all the knobs on** *(with all refinements etc)* il est équipé de tous les accessoires possibles et imaginables; *Br Fam* **the same to you with knobs on!** c'est celui qui le dit qui l'est! **2** *(piece)* **a k. of butter** une noix de beurre **3** *Br Vulg (penis)* bite *f*, *(man)* trou *m* du cul

knobbed [nɒbd] **ADJ** *(stick)* à pommeau

knobbly ['nɒblɪ] **ADJ** couvert de bosses; *(tree)* noueux; **k. knees** genoux *mpl* bossués

KNOCK [nɒk]

N	coup **1, 2** ▪ cognement **3**
VT	frapper **1** ▪ heurter **1** ▪ cogner **1**
VI	frapper **1** ▪ cogner **2**

N 1 *(blow)* coup *m*; **to give sb a k. on the head** porter à qn un coup à la tête; *(and make unconscious)* assommer qn d'un coup sur la tête; **to get a nasty k.** prendre un vilain coup; *Fam* **his pride took a bit of a k.** sa fierté en a pris un coup; **to give sb's chances/hopes a k.** miner les chances/espoirs de qn; **to be brought up in the school of hard knocks** être élevé à la dure; *Fam* **he's had a few knocks** *(in business, life)* il en a vu de dures; **k.-for-k. insurance** = assurance *f* entraînant le remboursement séparé des clients par leurs compagnies respectives **2 k. at the door** coup *m* à la porte; **to hear a k.** entendre frapper; **to give a loud k.** frapper très fort; **k., k.!** toc, toc!; **a k., k. joke** = blague *f* dont la première ligne du dialogue est 'toc, toc!' **3** *Tech etc (sound)* cognement *m*, cliquetis *m*; *(of fuel in engine)* détonation *f*
▶ **VT 1** *(hit)* frapper, heurter, cogner; **to k. sb on the head** frapper qn sur la tête; **to k. sb unconscious** assommer qn; **to k. sb flying** envoyer valdinguer qn; **to k. one's head against sth** se cogner la tête contre qch; **to k. a nail into a wall** enfoncer un clou dans un mur; **to k. a hole in** *or* **through sth** faire un trou dans qch

2 *Fig (phrases)* **to k. holes in an argument** démolir un argument; **to k. an idea/a scheme on the head** abandonner *ou* laisser tomber une idée/un projet; **our plans have been knocked on the head** nos projets sont tombés à l'eau; *Br Fam* **k. it on the head, will you!** c'est pas bientôt fini?; **to k. some sense into sb** apprendre à vivre à qn; **that'll k. a bit of sense into her!** ça lui apprendra!; **to k. sb into shape** mettre qn au pas; **the army soon knocked his enthusiasm out of him** l'armée a eu tôt fait de tuer en lui toute trace d'enthousiasme; **to k. sb sideways** *or* **for six** *(amaze)* abasourdir *ou* stupéfier qn; **to k. sb dead** *(impress)* en mettre plein la vue à qn; **Kylie knocked them dead last night** hier soir, Kylie a fait un tabac

3 *Fam (criticize)* débiner; **don't k. it until you've tried it** ne crache pas dessus avant d'avoir essayé

vi 1 frapper (**at** à); **to k. at the door** frapper à la porte; **to k. against sth** se donner un coup *ou* se cogner contre qch; **she knocked against him** elle s'est cognée contre lui; **he felt his foot k. against a hard object** il a senti son pied cogner contre *ou* rencontrer quelque chose de dur; **his knees were knocking** ses genoux s'entrechoquaient

2 *(of engine)* cogner, cliqueter; *(of bearings)* tambouriner

▸ **knock about, knock around VT SEP 1** *(mistreat) (person)* bousculer, maltraiter, malmener; **he knocks his wife about** il bat sa femme; **the furniture has been badly knocked about** les meubles ont été fort maltraités

2 *Fam (discuss) (idea, suggestion)* débattre

vi *Fam* **1 to k. about with sb** fréquenter qn; **they knocked about together at school** ils se fréquentaient à l'école

2 *(hang around)* traîner; **has anyone seen my keys knocking about?** quelqu'un a vu traîner mes clés dans un coin?; **that's what I wear to k. about in** ce sont mes vêtements d'intérieur; **he's knocked about quite a bit** il a pas mal roulé sa bosse

VT INSEP *Fam* **to k. about the world/countryside** rouler sa bosse; **she's been knocking about Glasgow for years** ça fait des années qu'elle traîne à Glasgow; **your keys are knocking about the kitchen somewhere** tes clés traînent dans un coin de la cuisine

▸ **knock back VT SEP** *Fam* **1** *(drink)* **to k. back a drink** s'enfiler *ou* s'envoyer un verre

2 *(cost)* coûter; **it knocked me back £200** ça m'a coûté 200 livres

3 *(reject) (idea, proposal)* rejeter; *(candidate)* refuser

4 *(surprise)* abasourdir, sidérer

▸ **knock down VT SEP 1** renverser; *(person)* mettre à terre; *(wall, building etc)* abattre; **he was knocked down by a car** il a été renversé par une voiture

2 *(at auction)* adjuger, vendre; **to k. sth down to sb** adjuger qch à qn

3 *Fam (reduce) (price)* baisser; *(reduce price of)* solder; **it's been knocked down to £50** ça a été soldé à 50 livres; **she wanted £15 but I knocked her down to 10** elle demandait 15 livres mais j'ai réussi à la faire descendre jusqu'à 10

▸ **knock off VT SEP 1** *(cause to fall off)* faire tomber; **he was knocked off his bike by a car** une voiture l'a fait tomber de son vélo; **to k. a book off the table** faire tomber un livre de la table; *Fam* **to k. sb's head** *or* **block off** casser la tête à qn; *Fig* **to k. sb off their pedestal** *or* **perch** faire tomber qn de son piédestal; *Fig* **I managed to get something knocked off the price** j'ai réussi à faire baisser un peu le prix

2 *Fam (steal)* piquer, faucher; **to k. off a bank** se faire une banque

3 *Fam (kill)* zigouiller

4 *Fam* **k. it off!** *(stop it)* arrêtez!, ça suffit!

5 *Fam (produce quickly) (letter, report, song etc)* expédier

vi *(at end of day)* finir; **let's k. off for a coffee** arrêtons-nous pour prendre un café

▸ **knock out VT SEP 1** *(remove)* retirer, enlever; *Fam* **to k. sb's brains/teeth out** casser la tête/les dents à qn

2 *(make unconscious)* assommer raide; *Boxing* mettre knock-out

3 *Sport (in tournament etc)* **to be knocked out** être éliminé

4 *Mil (tank etc)* détruire

5 *Am Fam* **to k. oneself out** *(indulge oneself)* se faire plaisir; **there's plenty of food left, k. yourself out!** il reste plein de nourriture, sers-toi autant que tu veux!

▸ **knock over VT SEP 1** *(cause to fall)* faire tomber; *(overturn)* renverser

2 *Am Fam (rob)* braquer

▸ **knock together VT SEP 1** *(make hastily) (shelter, raft etc)* assembler en vitesse; **we knocked together a rough shelter** on s'est fabriqué une espèce d'abri

2 *(hit together)* entrechoquer; *Fig* **they should have their heads knocked together** il faudrait les secouer un bon coup

vi *(of knees, two objects)* s'entrechoquer

▸ **knock up VT SEP 1** *(make hastily) (shed etc)* construire en vitesse; *(meal)* improviser; **I'll k. us up some spaghetti** je vais nous préparer des spaghetti en vitesse

2 *Br (wake)* réveiller

3 *Cr* **to k. up a century** faire cent points

4 *Sl (make pregnant)* mettre en cloque; **to get knocked up** se faire mettre en cloque

vi *Tennis* faire des balles *(avant la partie, pour se faire la main)*

knockabout ['nɒkəbaʊt] **ADJ** *(game etc)* pour rire; **a k. comedian** un bateleur, bouffon; **a k. comedy** une (grosse) farce

N 1 *(game)* partie *f* pour rire **2** *Naut* petit voilier *m*

knockback ['nɒkbæk] **N** *Br Fam (rejection)* veste *f*; **to get a k.** prendre une veste

knockdown ['nɒkdaʊn] **ADJ 1** *(forceful)* **a k. blow** un coup à assommer un bœuf; **a k. argument** un argument massue **2** *(easy to dismantle)* démontable; **sold in k. form** vendu en kit

▸▸ *Br Fam* **k. price** *(at auction)* prix *m* minimum; *Br* **for sale at k. prices** *(reduced)* en vente à des prix imbattables *ou* défiant toute concurrence; **I got it for a k. price** je l'ai eu pour trois fois rien

knocker ['nɒkər] **N 1** *(door)* **k.** marteau *m* (de porte), heurtoir *m* **2** *Sl* **knockers** *(breasts)* nichons *mpl* **3** *Fam (critic)* critiqueur *m*

knocking ['nɒkɪŋ] **N 1** *(noise)* bruit *m* de coups, cognement *m* **2** *(of engine)* cognement *m*

▸▸ **k. copy** publicité *f* comparative

knocking-off time N *Fam* heure *f* de sortie

knocking-shop N *Br Sl* bordel *m*

knock-kneed [-'niːd] **ADJ** *(person)* cagneux

knock-knees [-niːz] **NPL** genoux *mpl* cagneux

knock-on effect N répercussions *fpl*, businesses are feeling the k. of a strong pound les entreprises subissent le contrecoup d'une livre forte

knockout ['nɒkaʊt] **N 1** *Boxing* knock-out *m inv*, K-O *m*; *Fig* coup *m* de grâce; **to win by a k.** gagner par K-O **2** *Fam (sensation)* **to be a k.** être sensationnel *ou* génial; **she's a k.!** *(beautiful)* elle est canon! **3** *(at auction)* entente *f* *(entre concurrents pour baisser les prix)* **4** *Sport* tournoi *m* *(par élimination directe)*

▸▸ *Boxing* **k. blow** coup *m* qui met K-O; *Fig* coup *m* de grâce; **to deliver the k. blow** *Boxing* mettre K-O; *Fig* donner le coup de grâce;

Fam **k. drops** soporifique *m*, somnifère *m* *(surtout ajouté à une boisson)*

knock-up N *Tennis* **to have a k.** faire quelques balles *(avant la partie, pour se faire la main)*

knoll [nəʊl] **N** tertre *m*, monticule *m*, butte *f*, mamelon *m*

knot [nɒt] **N 1** *(with rope, string)* nœud *m*; **to tie/untie a k.** faire/défaire un nœud; **k. of hair** chignon *m*; *Fam Fig* **to tie the k.** *(get married)* se marier; *Fam Fig* **to tie oneself in knots** s'embrouiller

2 *(in wood)* nœud *m*

3 *Naut (unit of speed)* nœud *m*; **to make 10 knots** *(of ship)* filer 10 nœuds; *Fam* **at a rate of knots** à toute vitesse; *Fig Fam* **she was spending her money at a rate of knots** elle jetait l'argent par les fenêtres

4 *(group) (of people)* groupe *m*; *(of trees)* bouquet *m*

5 *(in muscle)* raideur *f*; **to have a k. in one's stomach** avoir l'estomac noué

VT *(-tt-)* *(piece of string) (make one knot)* faire un nœud à; *(make several knots)* faire des nœuds à; **k. the end of the string around the door handle** nouez le bout de la corde à la poignée de la porte; *Br Fam* **get knotted!** va te faire voir!

vi *(of string)* se nouer, faire des nœuds; **her stomach knotted with fear** la peur lui nouait l'estomac

▸ **knot together VT SEP k. them together** noue-les ensemble

knotty ['nɒtɪ] **ADJ 1** *(rope, hair etc)* plein de nœuds **2** *(problem etc)* épineux, embrouillé; *(question)* difficile, épineux **3** *(wood etc)* noueux, raboteux; *(hands)* noueux

---

KNOW [nəʊ]

VT	connaître 1, 4	▪ savoir 1, 2, 4
	▪ reconnaître 3	▪ distinguer 3
VI	savoir	

N *Fam* **to be in the k.** être au courant (de l'affaire); *Sport etc (have inside information)* avoir des tuyaux; **those in the k.** les initiés *mpl*

VT *(pt* knew [njuː], *pp* known [nəʊn]) **1** *(be acquainted with) (person, place)* connaître; *(poverty, happiness etc)* savoir ce que c'est que; **to get** *or* **come to k. sb** faire la connaissance de qn; **when I first knew her** quand j'ai fait sa connaissance; **to have known happiness/poverty** avoir connu le bonheur/la pauvreté; **I've never known anything like it** je n'ai jamais rien vu de semblable; **I don't k. her to speak to** je ne la connais que de vue; **I k. him to say hello to** nous nous saluons; **I'd like to get to k. him better** j'aimerais bien le connaître mieux; **knowing him, he'll probably want to** que je le connais, il voudra certainement; **he is well known to the police** il est bien connu de la police

2 *(to have knowledge of)* savoir; **I k. that** ça je le sais; **to get to k. sth** apprendre qch; **to k. sth by heart** savoir qch par cœur; **how was I to k. you were saving it?** comment est-ce que je pouvais savoir que tu l'avais mis de côté?; **to k. more than one is telling** en savoir plus long qu'on n'en dit; **the end of civilisation as we k. it** la fin de la civilisation en tant que telle; **well, what do you k.!** sans blague!, tiens, tiens!; **she thinks she knows all the answers** elle croit tout savoir; *Fig Fam* **to k. a thing or two, to k. one's way about** *or* **around** être malin *ou* roublard; **he knows his own mind** il sait ce qu'il veut; **I'll have you k. that …** sachez que …; **everyone knows that …** personne n'ignore que …; **I knew (that) she had talent** je lui connaissais du talent; **how do you k. (that) he will come?** qui vous dit qu'il viendra?; **do you k. when …/why …?** savez-vous quand …/pourquoi …?; **heaven** *or* **God (only) knows when I shall**

get back Dieu (seul) sait quand je serai de retour; **she didn't quite k. what to say** elle ne savait trop que dire; **I don't k. that I do** (agree etc) je n'en suis pas sûr; **I k. him to be a liar** je sais que c'est un menteur; **she is known to be a keen photographer** on sait qu'elle aime beaucoup la photographie; **please let us k. whether …** veuillez nous faire savoir si …; **I don't want it known/widely known** je ne veux pas que cela se sache/que tout le monde l'apprenne; **he let it be known that he was available** il a fait savoir qu'il était disponible; **it has been known (to happen)** c'est une chose qu'on a vue se produire, ça c'est vu; **I have never known him tell a lie** à ce que je sache, il n'a jamais menti; **I've never known him (to) be this late** je ne l'ai jamais vu être aussi en retard; **she doesn't k. what fear is** elle ne sait pas ce que c'est que d'avoir peur; **to k. what it's like to be happy/poor** savoir ce que c'est que d'être heureux/pauvre; **nobody knows anything about it** personne n'en sait rien; **to k. all about cars** être très calé sur les voitures; **we k. all about her!** si nous la connaissons? et comment!; **we knew nothing about or of it** nous l'ignorions; **I'll be back before you k. it** je serai bientôt de retour; **it'll be Christmas before we k. it** le temps va passer vite jusqu'à Noël

3 (recognize) reconnaître; (distinguish) distinguer (**from** de, d'avec); Fam **he doesn't k. one end of a car from another** il n'y connaît absolument rien en voitures; **don't you k. me?** vous ne me reconnaissez pas?; **I'd k. him anywhere** je le reconnaîtrais n'importe où; **I knew her by her walk** je l'ai reconnue à son allure ou à sa démarche; **I knew him for a troublemaker** j'ai deviné que c'était un agitateur; **to k. good from evil** distinguer le bien du mal; **I didn't k. the one from the other** je ne pouvais pas les distinguer l'un de l'autre

4 (understand) savoir; (subject) connaître; **I don't k. much about it** je ne sais pas grand-chose là-dessus; **she knows German** elle sait parler allemand; **do you k. anything about physics?** est-ce que tu connais quelque chose en physique?; **what do you k.?** qu'est-ce que tu en sais?; **to k. what one is talking about** savoir de quoi on parle; **to k. how to read/swim/do sth** savoir lire/nager/faire qch; **to k. how to behave** savoir se conduire

5 Fam **don't I k. it!** à qui le dites-vous!; **wouldn't you k. it!** comme par hasard!; **not if I k. Jean-Luc!** tel que je connais Jean-Luc, sûrement pas!; **she is pretty and doesn't she k. it!** elle est jolie et elle le sait bien!

6 to k. better than to … bien se garder de …; **I k. better (than that)** je m'y connais mieux que ça; (I won't be caught out) on ne m'y prendra pas, Fam pas si bête!; **he is old enough to k. better** à son âge il devrait être plus raisonnable; **you can't blame him, he doesn't k. any better** on ne peut pas lui en vouloir, il ne se rend pas compte; **you k. best** vous en êtes le meilleur juge; **you k. best what should be done** vous savez mieux que personne ce qu'il faut faire

7 Bible (sexually) connaître

vi savoir; **had I known** si j'avais su; **as far as I k.,** for all **I k.** autant que je sache; **I don't want to k.** je ne veux pas le savoir; **when I mentioned that he just didn't want to k.** quand j'ai mentionné ça il n'a rien voulu savoir; Fam **I wouldn't k.** (I don't know) je ne saurais dire; Fam **you k.** (sentence filler) vous voyez; **k. what I mean?** tu vois ce que je veux dire?; **as everyone knows** comme tout le monde le sait; **who knows?** qui sait?; **to k. about sth** être informé de qch, être au courant de qch; **I don't k. about that** (I'm not certain) je n'en suis pas sûr; **to k. of sb** avoir

entendu parler de qn; **to get to k. of sth** apprendre qch; Fam **not that I k. of, not as far as I k.** pas que je sache

know-all N Fam je-sais-tout mf inv; **he's/she's a bit of a k.** c'est un peu monsieur/madame je-sais-tout

know-how N Fam savoir-faire m; (technical) connaissances fpl techniques

knowing ['nəʊɪŋ] ADJ (intelligent, educated) intelligent, instruit; (cunning) fin, malin, rusé; (smile) entendu

N **there's no k.** c'est impossible à dire; **there's no k. what will happen** on ne peut pas savoir ce qui va se passer

knowingly ['nəʊɪŋlɪ] ADV (with knowledge of the facts) sciemment, en connaissance de cause; (cunningly) finement, d'un air rusé; (to smile) d'un air entendu; Com **never k. undersold** si vous trouvez moins cher, avertissez-nous

know-it-all N esp Am Fam je-sais-tout mf inv

knowledge ['nɒlɪdʒ] N **1** (of fact) connaissance f; **it has come to my k. that …** il est venu ou parvenu à ma connaissance que …, j'ai appris que …; **I had no k. of it** je ne le savais pas, je l'ignorais; **lack of k.** ignorance f (**of** de); **it is (a matter of) common k. that …** c'est un fait notoire que …; **to (the best of) my k.** à ma connaissance, (autant) que je sache; **not to my k.** pas que je sache; **without my k.** à mon insu; **to speak with full k. (of the facts)** parler en connaissance de cause ou en pleine connaissance des faits

2 (learning) savoir m, connaissance(s) f(pl); **to have a k. of several languages** savoir parler plusieurs langues; **he has a little k. or a working k. of Latin** il a quelques connaissances en latin; **her k. is immense** ses connaissances sont très étendues; **k. of the world** connaissance du monde; Prov **k. is power** savoir c'est pouvoir; **to show off one's k.** étaler sa science

3 carnal **k.** connaissance f charnelle

▸▸ Comput **k. base** base f de connaissances; **k. economy** économie f de la connaissance; Comput **k. engineer** cogniticien, -ienne

knowledgeable ['nɒlɪdʒəb(ə)l] ADJ (about situation) bien informé; **she's very k. about cars** elle s'y connaît en voitures

knowledge-based system N Comput système m basé sur les connaissances

known [nəʊn] PP see **know**

ADJ **1** (notorious) connu; notoire; **he's a k. drugs dealer** c'est un revendeur de drogue notoire **2** (recognized) reconnu; **she's a k. expert in the field** c'est un expert reconnu ou qui fait autorité dans ce domaine; **it's a k. fact** c'est un fait établi; **to make oneself k.** se faire connaître; **to let it be k.** faire savoir

knuckle ['nʌk(ə)l] N **1** (of human) articulation f ou jointure f (du doigt); (of animal) première phalange f; **I grazed my knuckles on the wall** je me suis écorché les doigts contre le mur; Fam **that was a bit near the k.** (joke, remark) c'était assez limite **2** Culin (joint of meat) jarret m

▸▸ Fam **k. sandwich** coup m de poing; **he'll get a k. sandwich if he's not careful** il va se prendre un coup de poing dans la tronche s'il ne fait pas gaffe

▸ **knuckle down** VI Fam (begin working hard) s'y mettre sérieusement; **to k. down to sth** se mettre à qch

▸ **knuckle under** VI Fam (give in) mettre les pouces

knuckle-duster N coup-de-poing m (américain), pl coups-de-poing

knurl [nɜːl] N **1** (in wood) nœud m **2** (in metalworking) moletage m; (tool) molette f, godronnoir m

VT (in metalworking) molet(t)er, godronner

KO, pl **KO's** ['keɪ'əʊ, 'keɪ'əʊz] Boxing etc Fam ➚ K-O m

VT (3rd person pr **KO's** ['keɪ'əʊz], prp **KO'ing;** pp, pt **KO'd**) mettre K-O

koala [kəʊ'ɑːlə] N Zool koala m

▸▸ **k. bear** koala

Koch's bacillus [kɒksbə'sɪləs] N Med bacille de Koch m

kohlrabi [kəʊl'rɑːbɪ] N chou-rave m, pl choux-raves, turnep(s) m

kola ['kəʊlə] N (plant) cola m, kola m;

▸▸ **k. nut** noix f de cola ou de kola; **k. tree** kolatier m

kook [kʊk] N Am Fam drôle m d'oiseau

kookaburra ['kʊkəbʌrə] N dacélo m

kopeck ['kəʊpek] N kopeck m

Koran (the) [ðəkɔ:'rɑːn] N Rel le Koran, le Coran

Koranic [kɔ:'rænɪk] ADJ Rel coranique

Korea [kə'rɪə] N Corée f; **North/South K.** Corée du Nord/du Sud

Korean [kə'rɪən] ADJ coréen

N **1** Coréen, -enne **2** Ling coréen m

korma ['kɔːmə] N Culin chicken/prawn **k.** poulet m/crevettes fpl korma

kosher ['kəʊʃər] ADJ Rel cascher inv, kascher inv; Fam (legitimate) légitime, comme il faut, impec

kowtow [kaʊ'taʊ] VI **1** Fam (act obsequiously) **to k. to sb** faire des courbettes devant qn **2** (bow) se prosterner (**to** devant)

KP ['keɪ'piː] N Am Mil Sl (abbr kitchen police) **to do KP (duty)** être de corvée de patates

kph [keɪpiː'eɪtʃ] (abbr kilometres per hour) km/h

kraft [krɑːft] N papier m d'emballage fort, papier Kraft

Krakow ['krɑːkɒf] N Cracovie f

Kraut [kraʊt] N Offensive Sl boche mf

Kremlin (the) [ðə'kremlɪn] N le Kremlin; Fam **K. watcher** spécialiste mf du Kremlin, kremlinologiste mf

Kremlinologist [kremlɪ'nɒlədʒɪst] N kremlinologiste mf

krill [krɪl] N krill m

krona ['krəʊnə] N Fin (Swedish currency) couronne f

krone ['krəʊnə], pl **kroner** ['krəʊnə(r)] N Fin (Danish, Norwegian currency) couronne f

Kt abbr knight

kudos ['kjuːdɒs] N (prestige) prestige m; (fame) célébrité f; **to get the k. for sth** recevoir toute la gloire pour qch; **to receive k.** être acclamé

Ku Klux Klan ['kuː'klʌks'klæn] N Ku Klux Klan m

kumquat ['kʌmkwɒt] N kumquat m

kung fu ['kʌŋ'fuː] N kung-fu m; **a k. expert** un expert en kung-fu

Kurd [kɜːd] N kurde

N Kurde mf

Kurdish ['kɜːdɪʃ] ADJ kurde

N Ling kurde m

Kurdistan [kɜːdɪ'stɑːn] N Kurdistan m

Kuwait [kʊ'weɪt, kjuː-] N Koweït m

Kuwaiti [kʊ'weɪtɪ, kjuː-] ADJ koweïtien

N Koweïtien, -ienne

kV (abbr kilovolt) kV

kvetch [kvetʃ] VI Am Fam geindre, se plaindre

kW (abbr kilowatt) kW

kWh (abbr kilowatt-hour) kWh

Ky abbr Kentucky

Kyrie ['kɪrɪeɪ] N Rel **K. (eleison)** Kyrie (eleryson) m inv

L, l [el] N *(letter)* L, l *m;* **two l's** deux l

l [el] **1** *(abbr* **litre)** l. **2** *(abbr* **length)** longueur, long. **3** *(abbr* **line)** ligne **4** *(abbr* **left)** gauche

LA [el'eɪ] N *abbr* Los Angeles

La *abbr* **Louisiana**

la [lɑː] N *Mus* la *m;* **sing it to 'la'** chante-le en la

laager ['lɑːgər] N *Pol (esp in South Africa)* camp *m*

Lab *Br Pol (abbr* **Labour)** *see* **labour** N **3**

lab [læb] N *Fam (abbr* **laboratory)** labo *m*

labcoat ['læbkəʊt] N blouse *f* de laboratoire

label ['leɪb(ə)l] N **1** *(on parcel, bottle etc)* étiquette *f,* **sticky l.** étiquette gommée
 2 *Com (indication of brand)* label *m,* étiquette *f,* **to record on the Motown l.** *(of singer, musician etc)* enregistrer sous le label Motown; **designer l.** *(on clothes)* marque *f,* griffe *f*
 3 *Comput (of tape, file)* label *m*
 4 *Fig (of person)* étiquette *f;* **the l. 'reactionary' stayed with him all his life** l'étiquette de réactionnaire lui est restée toute sa vie
 5 *Chem* marque *f*
 VT (**-ll-,** *Am* **-l-) 1** *(tie label to)* étiqueter; *(stick label on)* coller une étiquette sur; **a bottle labelled poison** une bouteille marquée poison; **all luggage must be clearly labelled** tous les bagages doivent être clairement étiquetés
 2 to l. sb a liar *etc* qualifier qn de menteur *etc*
 3 *Chem* marquer

labelling ['leɪb(ə)lɪŋ] N étiquetage *m*

labellum, *pl* **labella** [lə'beləm, -ə] N *Bot* labelle *m*

labial ['leɪbɪəl] ADJ labial, -aux
 N *Ling* labiale *f*
 ▶▶ *Ling* **l. consonant** consonne *f* labiale

labialize ['leɪbɪəlaɪz] VT *Ling* labialiser

labiate ['leɪbɪeɪt] *Bot* ADJ labié
 N labiée *f*

labiodental [leɪbɪəʊ'dent(ə)l] ADJ *Ling* labiodental

labium, *pl* **labia** ['leɪbɪəm, -ə] N *Anat* labia *(of vulva)* labia *mpl,* lèvres *fpl*

labor, labored *etc Am* = **labour, laboured** *etc*

laboratory [lə'bɒrətrɪ, *esp Am* 'læbrətɔːri] N laboratoire *m;* **dental l.** laboratoire de prothèse dentaire
 ▶▶ **l. assistant** laborantin, -ine; **l. equipment** matériel *m* de laboratoire; **l. experiment** expérience *f* en laboratoire

laboratory-tested ADJ testé en laboratoire

laborious [lə'bɔːrɪəs] ADJ **1** pénible, fatigant; *(task)* laborieux **2** *(style)* laborieux

laboriously [lə'bɔːrɪəslɪ] ADV péniblement

laboriousness [lə'bɔːrɪəsnɪs] N **1** *(of task, ascent etc)* pénibilité *f* **2** *(of literary style)* caractère *m* laborieux

labour, *Am* **labor** ['leɪbər] N **1** *(work)* travail *m,* labeur *m;* **manual l.** travail manuel; **division of l.** division *f* du travail
 2 *(workers)* main-d'œuvre *f,* **male/female l.** main-d'œuvre masculine/féminine; **cost of l.** prix *m* de la main-d'œuvre; **capital and l.** le capital et la main-d'œuvre; *Br Formerly* **Minister of L.** ministre *m* du Travail
 3 *Pol* **L.** les travaillistes *mpl*
 4 *(task)* **the twelve labours of Hercules** les douze travaux *mpl* d'Hercule; **I'm not doing this as a l. of love** je ne fais pas ça pour le plaisir
 5 *Obst* travail *m;* **premature l.** accouchement *m* avant terme; **woman in l.** femme en couches; **to be in l.** être en train d'accoucher; **she went into l. at 3 o'clock** le travail a commencé à 3 heures; **to induce l.** provoquer l'accouchement; **it was a difficult l.** ça a été un accouchement difficile
 VI **1** *(of person)* travailler, peiner; **to l. for sth** se donner de la peine pour obtenir qch; **he laboured all his life for peace** il a travaillé toute sa vie pour la paix; **to l. at** *or* **over sth** peiner *ou* trimer sur qch; **to l. up a hill** gravir péniblement une côte; **to l. under great difficulties** être aux prises avec de grandes difficultés; **to l. under a sense of injustice** nourrir un sentiment d'injustice; **to l. under a misapprehension** être dans l'erreur, être (la) victime d'une erreur
 2 *(of engine)* fatiguer, peiner; *(of ship)* bourlinguer, fatiguer; **to l. uphill** *(of car)* peiner dans les côtes
 VT **I won't l. the point** je ne m'étendrai pas là-dessus
 ▶▶ **l. camp** camp *m* de travail; *Am* **l. contract** contrat *m* de travail; *Am* **L. Day** fête *f* du travail; **l. dispute** conflit *m* du travail; *Br, Can Formerly* **l. exchange** agence *f* pour l'emploi; **l. force** *(in country)* population *f* active; *(in company)* main-d'œuvre *f;* **l. laws** législation *f* du travail; *Pol* **L. leader** dirigeant, -ante (du parti) travailliste; **l. market** marché *m* du travail; **L. Member (of Parliament)** député *m* travailliste; *Obst* **l. pains** douleurs *fpl* de l'accouchement; **the L. Party** le parti travailliste; *Ind* **l. relations** relations *fpl* sociales; **l. shortage** pénurie *f ou* crise *f* de main-d'œuvre; **l. supply** main-d'œuvre disponible; **l. turnover** rotation *f* du personnel; *Am* **l. union** syndicat *m* (ouvrier); **l. unrest** agitation *f* ouvrière; *Obst* **l. ward** salle *f* d'accouchement

laboured, *Am* **labored** ['leɪbəd] ADJ **1** *(breathing)* laborieux **2** *(style etc)* trop travaillé, trop élaboré; *(joke)* laborieux

labourer, *Am* **laborer** ['leɪbərər] N travailleur *m; Ind* manœuvre *m; Prov* **the l. is worthy of his hire** toute peine *ou* tout travail mérite salaire; **unskilled l.** ouvrier *m* non spécialisé; **agricultural l.** ouvrier agricole

labouring, *Am* **laboring** ['leɪbərɪŋ] ADJ **the l. class** la classe ouvrière; **a l. job** un travail manuel

labour-intensive, *Am* **labor-intensive** ADJ qui demande une main-d'œuvre importante

Labourite, *Am* **Laborite** ['leɪbəraɪt] N *Pol* travailliste *mf*

labour-saving, *Am* **labor-saving** ADJ *(device, invention)* qui simplifie la tâche; **l. device** *(in household)* appareil *m* ménager; **computers are not always l. devices** les ordinateurs ne font pas toujours gagner du temps

Labrador ['læbrədɔːr] N **1** *Geog* Labrador *m* **2** *(dog)* labrador *m*

laburnum [lə'bɜːnəm] N *(tree)* cytise *m* (à grappes)

labyrinth ['læbərɪnθ] N **1** *Archit etc* labyrinthe *m,* dédale *m* **2** *Anat (of the ear)* labyrinthe *m*

labyrinthine [læbə'rɪnθaɪn] ADJ *Archit* en labyrinthe; *Fig (procedures, structure)* extrêmement compliqué, labyrinthique

lac [læk] N gomme *f* laque, laque *f*

lace [leɪs] N **1** *Tex* dentelle *f,* **bobbin** *or* **pillow l.** dentelle aux fuseaux *ou* au coussin; **l. curtain** rideau *m* en *ou* de dentelle **2** *(of shoe)* lacet *m* **3** *(braid)* **gold/silver l.** galon *m* d'or/ d'argent
 VT **1** *(shoes)* lacer; **to l. sth with sth** entrelacer qch de *ou* avec qch **2** *Fam* **l. a drink** ajouter de l'alcool à une boisson; **milk laced with rum** lait au rhum; **she laced his cup of tea with poison** elle ajouta du poison à sa tasse de thé; *Fig* **he laced his story with salacious details** il ajoutait des détails salaces à son histoire; **her account was laced with scandalous lies** son récit était plein de mensonges effrontés
 VI *(of boots etc)* se lacer
 ▶ **lace into** VT INSEP *Fam (attack)* s'en prendre à; *(physically)* rosser, s'en prendre à
 ▶ **lace up** VT SEP *(shoes)* lacer
 VI **shoes that l. up** chaussures à lacets; **they l. up at the sides** elles se lacent *ou* s'attachent sur le côté

lacemaker ['leɪsmeɪkər] N fabricant, -ante de dentelles; *(woman only)* dentellière *f*

lacemaking ['leɪsmeɪkɪŋ] N dentellerie *f*

lacerate ['læsəreɪt] VT lacérer, déchirer

lacerated ['læsəreɪtəd] ADJ *(hand, skin)* lacéré; **to be l. by pain** être transpercé par la douleur; **l. feelings** sentiments profondément blessés

laceration [læsə'reɪʃən] N **1** *(action)* lacération *f,* déchirement *m* **2** *(tear)* déchirure *f*

lace-up N *(shoe)* chaussure *f* à lacets
 ADJ *(shoe)* à lacets

lacewing ['leɪswɪŋ] N *Entom* hémérobe *m*
 ▶▶ **l. fly** hémérobe

lacework ['leɪswɜːk] N *(art)* dentellerie f
▸▸ **l. objects** objets *mpl* en dentelle

lachrymal ['lækrɪm(ə)l] ADJ *Anat* lacrymal, -aux
▸▸ **l. duct** conduit *m* lacrymal; **l. gland** glande f lacrymale

lachrymose ['lækrɪməʊs] ADJ larmoyant

lacing ['leɪsɪŋ] N **1** milk with a l. of rum lait avec un petit goût de rhum **2** *(on uniform)* galon *m*

lack [læk] N manque *m* (of de); **l. of judgment/time** manque de jugement/temps; **l. of money** pénurie f d'argent; **she was tired from l. of sleep** elle était fatiguée de n'avoir pas assez dormi; **for l. of …** faute de …
VT *(experience, skill, humour etc)* manquer de; **what the country lacks in modern tourist amenities it more than makes up for in natural beauty** la beauté naturelle du paysage compense largement le manque de structures touristiques; **we l. nothing** nous ne manquons de rien, il ne nous manque rien
VI *(of time)* manquer; **time was lacking** on manquait de temps; **he's lacking in purpose** il lui manque un but; **to be lacking in confidence/experience** manquer de confiance/d'expérience; **they l. for nothing** ils ne manquent de rien; *Fam* **to be lacking** *(mentally)* être (un peu) simplet

lackadaisical [lækə'deɪzɪk(ə)l] ADJ *(person, manner etc)* apathique, *Fam* je-m'en-foutiste; **to take a l. approach to one's work** prendre son travail avec désinvolture

lackey ['lækɪ] N *Pej* larbin *m*

lacklustre, *Am* **lackluster** ['læklʌstər] ADJ *(eyes, gaze)* terne, sans brillant; *(performance)* médiocre

laconic [lə'kɒnɪk] ADJ *(person, answer etc)* laconique

laconically [lə'kɒnɪklɪ] ADV laconiquement

lacquer ['lækər] N *(for wood, hair etc)* laque f, *(coloured)* peinture f laquée; **a red l. screen** un écran recouvert de laque rouge
VT laquer; **a lacquered box** une boîte en laque

lacquerwork ['lækəwɜːk] N laque(s) *m(pl)*

lacrimal ['lækrɪm(ə)l] ADJ = **lachrymal**

lacrosse [lə'krɒs] N *Sport* lacrosse *m*

lacrymal ['lækrɪm(ə)l] ADJ = **lachrymal**

lactate [læk'teɪt] VI produire du lait

lactation [læk'teɪʃən] N lactation f

lacteal ['læktɪəl] ADJ lactaire

lactic ['læktɪk] ADJ *Chem* lactique
▸▸ **l. acid** acide *m* lactique

lactose ['læktəʊz] N *Chem* lactose *m*

lacuna, *pl* **lacunae, lacunas** [læ'kju:nə, -iː, -əz] N *(in knowledge, manuscript)* lacune f

lacustrine [lə'kʌstraɪn] ADJ *(plant etc)* lacustre

lacy ['leɪsɪ] ADJ *(made of lace)* de dentelle; *(resembling lace)* fin comme de la dentelle

lad [læd] N **1** *Fam (young man)* jeune gars *m*; *(boy)* garçon *m*; **he's only a l.** ce n'est qu'un gosse; **the doctor's l.** *(son)* le fils du docteur; **come on, lads!** allons, les gars!; **he's a bit of a l.** *or* **quite a l.** c'est un gaillard; **one of the lads** un des gars; **listen, my l.** écoute, mon petit gars **2** *Br Horseracing* **(stable) l.** lad *m*
▸▸ *Fam* **l. mag** = magazine *m* destiné à un public d'hommes jeunes

ladder ['lædər] N **1** échelle f; **it's unlucky to walk under a l.** ça porte malheur de passer sous une échelle; *Fig* **the social l.** l'échelle sociale; *Fig* **to get one's foot on the l.** mettre un pied dans le circuit; *Fig* **to reach the top of the l.** atteindre le sommet de l'échelle; **fish** *or* **salmon l.** échelle à saumons **2** *esp Br*

(in stocking) échelle f; **I've got a l.** j'ai une échelle à mon collant, mon collant est filé
VT *esp Br (of stocking)* filer
VI *esp Br (of stocking)* se démailler, filer

ladder-proof ADJ *esp Br (stockings)* qui ne filent pas

laddie ['lædɪ] N *Scot Fam* garçon *m*; *(term of endearment)* mon petit gars

laddish ['lædɪʃ] ADJ *Br Fam* = typique d'un style de vie caractérisé par de fréquentes sorties entre copains, généralement copieusement arrosées, un comportement arrogant et macho et un goût prononcé pour le sport et les activités de groupe

laden ['leɪd(ə)n] ADJ chargé (**with** de); **I was l. with shopping** j'avais les bras chargés de commissions; **fully l. ship** navire en pleine charge; **heavily l. tree** arbre chargé de fruits

ladette [læ'det] N *Br Fam* jeune femme f délurée *(qui se revendique l'égale des hommes pour ce qui est des sorties, de la vulgarité, etc)*

la-di-da, **la-de-da** ['lɑːdɪ'dɑː] ADJ *Fam (air, voice)* affecté, maniéré

ladies ['leɪdɪz] N toilettes *fpl* (des dames); *(as sign)* dames; **can you tell me where the l. is?** pouvez-vous m'indiquer où sont les toilettes?

lading ['leɪdɪŋ] N **1** *(action) (of ship)* chargement *m*; *(of merchandise)* mise f à bord **2** *(cargo)* chargement *m*

ladle ['leɪd(ə)l] N **1** *(soup)* **l.** louche f **2** *Ind* puisoir *m*; *Metal* **foundry l.** poche f de fonderie
VT **to l. (out) the soup** servir le potage (avec une louche); *Fam* **to l. out advice** prodiguer des conseils

ladleful ['leɪd(ə)lfl] N pleine louche f (**of** de)

lady, *pl* **ladies** ['leɪdɪ, -ɪz] N **1** dame f; **l. doctor** femme f médecin; **she's a real l.** c'est une femme très comme il faut; **she's no l.** ce n'est pas une femme comme il faut; **a l. and a gentleman** une dame et un monsieur; **a young l.** une jeune fille; *(married)* une jeune dame; **an old l.** une vieille dame; **how are you, young l.?** *(to child)* comment allez-vous, jeune fille?; **listen to me, young l.** écoute un peu, jeune fille; **ladies and gentlemen!** *(at meeting etc)* mesdames, mesdemoiselles, messieurs!; **come in, ladies!** entrez donc, mesdames!; **he's a ladies' man** c'est un homme à femmes; **the l. of the house** la maîtresse de maison; **painted l.** *(butterfly)* belle-dame f, *pl* belles-dames; **ladies' tailor** tailleur *m* pour dames; **l.'s watch** montre pour dames
2 *Rel* **Our L.** Notre-Dame f, la sainte Vierge
3 *(title)* **L. Browne** lady Browne; **the l. of the manor** la châtelaine; *Fam* **stop behaving like L. Muck** arrête de jouer les grandes dames
4 *Old-fashioned (wife)* femme f, épouse f; **how's your good l.?** comment va votre dame?; **this is my l. wife** voici mon épouse; **my young l.** *(fiancée)* ma fiancée, ma future
▸▸ **l. of the bedchamber** *(at court)* dame d'atours; *Pej* **L. Bountiful** = dame patronnesse; **L. Chapel** chapelle f de la Sainte Vierge; **L. Day** *(fête f de)* l'Annonciation f *(le 25 mars)*; **ladies' fingers** *(vegetable)* gombo(s) *m(pl)*; **l.'s maid** femme de chambre; **ladies' night** *(in bar)* = soirée f où les femmes ont droit à des réductions; *Am* **ladies' room** toilettes *fpl* des dames

ladybird, *Am* **ladybug** ['leɪdɪbɜːd, -bʌg] N *Entom* coccinelle f, *Fam* bête f à bon Dieu

ladyfinger ['leɪdɪfɪŋgər] N *Culin* boudoir *m*

lady-in-waiting N *(at court)* dame f d'honneur

lady-killer N *Fam* bourreau *m* des cœurs, don Juan *m*

ladylike ['leɪdɪlaɪk] ADJ *(woman)* comme il

faut, bien élevée; *(air, behaviour)* distingué; **climbing trees isn't very l.** les vraies demoiselles ne grimpent pas aux arbres; **it's not a l. thing to say** ce n'est pas beau dans la bouche d'une jeune fille

ladyship ['leɪdɪʃɪp] N **her l., your l.** madame (la comtesse *etc*); *Iron* **her l. doesn't feel like it** madame n'en a pas envie

lady's-slipper [leɪdɪz'slɪpər] N *(orchid)* sabot *m* de Vénus

lag¹ [læg] N *(delay)*, *Elec* retard *m*; *Ind etc* **time l.** décalage *m*
VI (-gg-) être à la traîne
▸ **lag behind** VI *(of people, walkers, company industry)* être à la traîne; **don't l. behind** ne reste pas à la traîne; **salaries are still lagging behind** les salaires sont restés à un niveau inférieur; **she always lags behind on the way to school** sur le chemin de l'école elle est toujours à la traîne
VT INSEP **to l. behind the others** être à la traîne par rapport aux autres

lag² N *esp Br Sl* **an old l.** *(jailbird)* un repris de justice, un récidiviste

lag³ VT *(boiler etc)* calorifuger, isoler

lager ['lɑːgər] N bière f blonde
▸▸ *Br Fam* **l. lout** = jeune *m* qui, sous l'influence de l'alcool, cherche la bagarre ou commet des actes de vandalisme

lagered (up) ['lɑːgəd] ADJ *Br Fam* bourré à la bière; **he gets l. with his mates every Friday night** il se bourre la gueule à la bière avec ses potes tous les vendredi soir

laggard ['lægəd] N **1** *(in race)* traînard, -arde; **the laggards in the class** ceux qui apprennent plus lentement que les autres **2** *Mktg (product)* innovateur *m* tardif

lagging ['lægɪŋ] N **1** *(action) (of boiler)* garnissage *m*, calorifugeage *m* **2** *(material) (for boiler)* revêtement *m* calorifuge

lagoon [lə'gu:n] N *Geog* **1** *(of atoll)* lagon *m* **2** *(with sand, shingle etc)* lagune f

lah [lɑː] N *Mus* = **la**

lah-di-dah ['lɑːdɪ'dɑː] ADJ = **la-di-da**

laid PT, PP *see* **lay¹** VT

laid-back [leɪd-] ADJ *Fam (person, atmosphere)* relax, décontracté

lain PP *see* **lie²** VI

lair [leər] N *(of big cat)* tanière f, repaire *m*, *esp Litt* antre *m*; *Fig (room etc)* antre; **brigands' l.** repaire de brigands

laird [leəd] N *Scot* propriétaire *m* (foncier)

lairy ['leərɪ] ADJ *Br Fam* culotté

laissez-faire, **laissez-faire** [leseɪ'feər] N *esp Econ* laisser-faire *m*
▸▸ **l. policy** politique f du laisser-faire

laity ['leɪtɪ] N **the l.** les laïques *mpl*

lake¹ [leɪk] N lac *m*; **salt l.** lac salé; **ornamental l.** bassin *m*, pièce f d'eau décorative; **the Great Lakes** les Grands Lacs; **the Lakes** le Lake District, la région des lacs *(dans le nord-ouest de l'Angleterre)*; *Fig* **wine l.** surplus *m* de vin; *Sl* **go jump in the l.** va te faire voir; **l. front** bord *m* de lac; **they live on the l. front** ils habitent au bord du lac
▸▸ **the L. District** le Lake District, la région des lacs *(dans le nord-ouest de l'Angleterre)*; **l. dwelling** habitation f lacustre; **L. Geneva** le lac Léman, le lac de Genève; **the L. poets** les *(poètes mpl)* lakistes *mpl*

lake² N *(pigment)* laque f; **crimson l.** laque carminée

Lakeland ['leɪklənd] N la région des lacs *(au nord-ouest de l'Angleterre)*

lakeshore ['leɪkʃɔː], **lakeside** ['leɪksaɪd] N rive f d'un lac; **they live on the l.** ils habitent au bord du lac
ADJ au bord du lac

lam¹ [læm] N *Am Sl (flight)* fuite f; **to be on**

the l. être en cavale; **to take it on the l.** partir en cavale

lam² vi (-mm-) *Fam* **to l. into sb** (*hit*) rosser qn, étriller qn; (*verbally*) étriller qn

lama ['lɑːmə] N *Rel* lama *m*; **the Dalai** *or* **Grand L.** le dalaï-lama

lamb [læm] N agneau *m*; **ewe l.** agnelle *f*, **ewe with l.** brebis *f* pleine; *Rel* **L. (of God)** Agneau (de Dieu); *Fam* **to be a l.** (*of person*) être gentil comme tout; **she accepted my decision like a l.** elle a accepté ma décision sans broncher; *Fam* **my l.** (*term of endearment*) mon petit; **poor l.** (*person*) pauvre petit(e); *Prov* **to go like lambs to the slaughter** être comme du bétail que l'on mène à l'abattoir; *Culin* **l. cutlet** *or* **chop** côtelette *f* d'agneau; *Bot* **l.'s lettuce** mâche *f*, *Fam* **l.'s tails** (*of hazel tree*) chatons *mpl*
vi (*of ewe*) agneler, mettre bas

lambada [læm'bɑːdə] N lambada *f*

lambast [læm'bæst], **lambaste** [læm'beɪst] vt (*person*) réprimander, *Lit* fustiger

lambing ['læmɪŋ] N agnelage *m*; **the l. season** l'agnelage

lambskin ['læmskɪn] N peau *f* d'agneau; (*fur*) agnelin *m*

lambswool ['læmswʊl] N laine *f* d'agneau, lambswool *m*
ADJ en laine d'agneau, en lambswool

lame [leɪm] ADJ **1** (*person, horse*) boiteux; (*through accident etc*) estropié; **l. leg** jambe boiteuse; **to be l.** boiter; **to be l. in one leg** boiter d'une jambe; **to be completely l.** être handicapé des deux jambes; **to go l.** se mettre à boiter; *Fig* **l. excuse** excuse boiteuse; **l. argument** argument boiteux *ou* qui ne tient pas debout; *Liter* **l. verses** vers boiteux *ou* qui boitent **2** *Am Fam* (*conventional*) vieux jeu *inv*; (*stupid*) cloche, nouille
vt (*person, horse*) estropier; **to be lamed by an accident/illness** rester boiteux à la suite d'un accident/d'une maladie; **she had been lamed by polio** elle est restée boiteuse à cause de la polio
▸▸ *Fig* **l. duck** canard *m* boiteux; *Am Pol* = candidat *m* sortant non réélu qui attend l'arrivée de son successeur

lamé ['lɑːmeɪ] N *Tex* lamé *m*; **gold/silver l.** lamé d'or/d'argent; **a gold l. dress** une robe en lamé d'or

lamebrain ['leɪmbreɪn] N *Fam* idiot, -ote, abruti, -ie

lamely ['leɪmlɪ] ADV (*to apologize*) faiblement

lameness ['leɪmnɪs] N claudication *f*, (*of horse*) boiterie *f*, *Fig* (*of excuse etc*) faiblesse *f*

lament [lə'ment] N **1** lamentation *f* **2** *Mus* complainte *f*
vt se lamenter sur, pleurer; (*person*) pleurer; **I was lamenting my lost youth** je pleurais ma jeunesse perdue; **the nation did not l. the death of the dictator** le pays n'a pas pleuré la mort du dictateur; **it's to be lamented** c'est à regretter
vi se lamenter (**over sth** sur qch), pleurer (**over sb/sth** qn/qch)

lamentable [lə'mɛntəb(ə)l] ADJ (*loss, failure*) déplorable; (*pathetic*) (*performance etc*) lamentable; **it's l.!** c'est déplorable!

lamentably [lə'mɛntəblɪ] ADJ déplorablement; (*pathetically*) lamentablement

lamentation [læmən'teɪʃən] N lamentation *f*, *Bible* **the Lamentations of Jeremiah** les Lamentations de Jérémie

lamented [lə'mɛntɪd] ADJ **the late l. Mr Jones** le regretté M. Jones

laminate ['læmɪneɪt] N stratifié *m*
vt **1** (*bond*) laminer, lamifier; (*glass*) feuilleter; (*plastic*) stratifier; (*wood*) contreplaquer **2** (*split*) diviser en lamelles **3** (*cover*) (*paper etc*) plastifier

vi **1** (*bond*) se laminer **2** (*split*) se diviser en lamelles

laminated ['læmɪneɪtəd] ADJ **1** (*glass*) feuilleté; (*wood*) contreplaqué **2** (*paper etc*) plastifié
▸▸ **l. jacket** (*of book*) jaquette *f* plastifiée; *Ind* **l. plastics** plastique *m* stratifié; **l. plate glass** verre *m* (de sécurité) feuilleté; **l. spring** ressort *m* à lames (superposées)

Lammas ['læməs] N le premier août
▸▸ **L. Day** le premier août

lammergeier ['læməgaɪər] N (*bird*) gypaète *m* barbu

lamp [læmp] N **1** lampe *f*, **bicycle l.** (*fixed*) phare *m* de bicyclette; (*detachable*) lampe de bicyclette; **portable l., inspection l.** (*in garage etc*) baladeuse *f*; **street l.** réverbère *m*; **hanging l.** suspension *f* **2** neon l. lampe au néon; **ultraviolet l.** lampe à ultra-violets

lampblack ['læmpblæk] N noir *m* de fumée

lamplight ['læmplaɪt] N lumière *f* de la lampe; **to work by l.** travailler à la lampe

lamplit ['læmplɪt] ADJ éclairé

lampoon [læm'puːn] N pamphlet *m*, libelle *m*
vt (*person*) brocarder, railler

lampoonist [læm'puːnɪst] N satiriste *m*, pamphlétaire *m*

lamppost ['læmppəʊst] N (*in street*) réverbère *m*

lamprey, *pl* **lampreys** ['læmprɪ, -ɪz] N (*eel*) lamproie *f*

lampshade ['læmpʃeɪd] N abat-jour *m inv*

lampstand ['læmpstænd] N pied *m* de lampe

LAN [læn] N *Comput abbr* **local area network**

lance [lɑːns] N (*weapon*) lance *f*, *Arch*, *Lit* **to break a l. with sb** rompre une lance avec qn
vt *Med* (*abscess*) percer, inciser
▸▸ *Br* **l. corporal** ≃ caporal *m*, *Suisse* ≃ appointé *m*

lanceolate(d) ['lɑːnsɪəleɪt(ɪd)] ADJ *Bot* lancéolé

lancer ['lɑːnsər] N **1** *Mil* lancier *m* **2** (*dance*) **lancers** (quadrille *m* des) lanciers *mpl*

lancet ['lɑːnsɪt] N **1** *Med* lancette *f* **2** *Archit* (*arch*) lancette *f*
▸▸ *Archit* **l. arch** lancette *f*; **l. window** fenêtre *f* en ogive

Lancs *abbr* **Lancashire**

LAND [lænd] N **1** (*as opposed to sea*) terre *f*, **on l.** sur terre; **to travel by l.** voyager par voie de terre; *Naut* **to make l.** reconnaître la terre; *Fig* **to see how the l. lies** tâter le terrain; *Mil etc* **(to attack) by l., sea and air** (attaquer) par terre, par mer et par air
2 (*earth, soil*) terre *f*, sol *m*; **arable l.** terre arable; **man lives off the l.** c'est la terre qui nourrit les hommes; **to live off the l.** (*of farmers*) vivre en autarcie; (*of army*) subsister sans ravitaillement
3 (*country*) pays *m*, terre *f*, **the best in the l.** le meilleur du pays; **to be still in the l. of the living** être encore de ce monde; *Prov* **a l. flowing with milk and honey** un pays où coulent le lait et le miel; **a l. of opportunity** un pays où tout est possible; **the l. of dreams/Nod** le pays des rêves/de Morphée
4 (*property*) terre(s) *f(pl)*; **private l.** terrain privé; **a piece of l.** un terrain; **the farmer wouldn't allow campers on his l.** le fermier n'acceptait pas de campeurs sur ses terres; **to buy l.** acheter des terres
vt **1** (*put on land*) (*from ship, plane*) débarquer; *Com* (*merchandise*) décharger
2 *Aviat* (*bring down to land*) (*plane*) faire atterrir; **they landed him on the deck of the ferry** ils l'ont fait atterrir sur le pont du ferry; **to l. a man on the moon** faire alunir un homme
3 *Zool* (*fish*) amener à terre

4 *Fam* (*win, obtain*) se dégoter; **they landed all the prizes** ils ont raflé tous les prix; **he's just landed a good job** il vient juste de dégoter un bon boulot
5 *Fam* (*in phrases*) **that will l. you in prison** tu vas te retrouver en prison; **you've landed us in a nice mess!** vous nous avez mis dans de beaux draps!; **to be landed with sth** rester avec qch sur les bras; **I've been landed with the job of telling him** c'est à moi qu'il est revenu de le lui dire
vi **1** (*from ship, plane*) débarquer; (*of aircraft, pilot*) atterrir; (*on deck of aircraft carrier*) apponter; **to l. on the moon** alunir; **to l. on the sea** amerrir; *Aviat* **when do we l.?** quand est-ce que nous atterrissons?
2 (*jumping off wall etc*) se recevoir; (*from great height, parachutist*) atterrir; **he slipped and landed in a puddle** il a glissé et a atterri dans une flaque d'eau; **to l. flat on one's back** se retrouver les quatre fers en l'air; **to l. on one's feet** retomber sur ses pieds; (*of cat*) retomber sur ses pattes; *Fig Fam* **he always manages to l. on his feet** il arrive toujours à retomber sur ses pattes
3 *Sport* (*after jumping*) (*of gymnast, ski-jumper, horse*) se réceptionner
▸▸ *Law* **l. act** loi *f* agraire; **l. agent** (*administrator*) régisseur *m*, intendant, -ante; *Br* (*estate agent*) agent *m* immobilier; **l. army** armée *f* de terre; **l. bank** crédit *m* foncier; **l. breeze** brise *f* de terre; **l. bridge** isthme *m*; *Acct* **l. charge** dette *f* foncière; **L.'s End** la pointe des Cornouailles; **l. forces** armée *f* de terre; *Br* **l. girl** fille *f* de ferme (*pendant la Deuxième Guerre mondiale*); *Tel* **l. line** ligne *f* terrestre; **the l. of the midnight sun** le pays du soleil de minuit; **l. mine** mine *f* terrestre; **l. reform** réforme *f* agraire; **l. register** cadastre *m*; **l. route** voie *f* de terre; **l. tax** impôt *m* foncier, contribution *f* foncière; **l. warfare** guerre *f* sur terre
▸ **land up** vi *Fam* (*in a ditch, hospital, jail etc*) se retrouver; **I landed up having to dance with him** il a fallu que je danse avec lui; **I always landed up with the worst jobs** je me retrouvais toujours avec les tâches les plus ingrates à faire

landau ['lændɔː] N (*carriage*) landau *m*, *pl* landaus

landed ['lændɪd] ADJ ATTRIB foncier
▸▸ *Fin* **l. costs** coûts *mpl* fonciers; **l. estate** propriété *f* foncière; **the l. gentry** la petite noblesse; **l. immigrant** résident, -ente permanent(e); **l. property** propriété foncière *ou* territoriale; **l. proprietor** propriétaire *mf* terrien(ienne)

landfall ['lændfɔːl] N *Naut* (*arrival*) atterrissage *m*; (*sight of land*) arrivée *f* en vue de terre; **to make (a) l.** (*arrive*) atterrir; (*sight land*) arriver en vue de terre

landfill ['lændfɪl] N remblai *m*; **to use sth as l.** utiliser qch pour remblayer *ou* comme remblai
▸▸ **l. site** décharge *f* publique

landing ['lændɪŋ] N **1** *Naut* débarquement *m*; *Com* déchargement *m*
2 *Aviat* (*of aircraft*) (*on land*) atterrissage *m*; (*on sea*) amerrissage *m*; (*on deck of ship*) appontage *m*; *Aviat* **blind/instrument l.** atterrissage sans visibilité/aux instruments; **visual l.** atterrissage à vue; **forced** *or* **emergency l.** atterrissage forcé
3 *Constr* (*of staircase*) palier *m*; (*corridor*) couloir *m*
4 (*of fish*) prise *f*
5 (*of gymnast, ski-jumper*) réception *f*
▸▸ **l. card** carte *f* de débarquement; **l. certificate** certificat *m* de déchargement; **l. craft** navire *m* de débarquement; **l. field** terrain *m* d'atterrissage; **l. flap** volet *m* d'atterrissage; *Mil*, *Naut* **l. force** troupes *fpl* de débarquement; *Aviat* **l. gear** train *m* d'atterrissage; **l.**

lights (on plane) phares mpl d'atterrissage; (at airport) balises fpl (d'atterrissage); **l. net** épuisette f (filet); Naut **l. operation** opération f de débarquement; Naut **l. order** permis m de débarquement; Mil, Naut **l. party** compagnie f de débarquement; Com **l. and port charges** frais mpl de débarquement et de port; **l. stage** débarcadère m; **l. strip** piste f d'atterrissage; **l. wheels** train d'atterrissage; Mil, Aviat **l. zone** zone f d'atterrissage (des troupes aéroportées)

landlady [ˈlændleɪdɪ] N **1** (from whom one rents accommodation) (owner) propriétaire f, (living on premises) logeuse f **2** Br (of pub) (owner) propriétaire f, (manageress) gérante f **3** (of small hotel) aubergiste f, hôtelière f, seaside. propriétaire f d'une auberge au bord de la mer

landlegs [ˈlændlegz] NPL Fam (of sailor) **to get one's l.** se familiariser de nouveau avec la terre

landless [ˈlændlɪs] ADJ sans terre; **l. peasants** paysans qui ne sont pas propriétaires

landlocked [ˈlændlɒkt] ADJ (country) sans accès à la mer; (port etc) entouré de terre; **l. sea** mer f intérieure

landlord [ˈlændlɔːd] N **1** (of property) bailleur m; (from whom one rents accommodation) (owner) propriétaire m; (living on premises) logeur m **2** Br (of pub) (owner) propriétaire m; (manager) gérant m; (form of address) patron **3** (landowner) propriétaire m (foncier)

landlubber [ˈlændlʌbər] N Naut Fam Hum marin m d'eau douce

landmark [ˈlændmɑːk] N **1** (building, statue etc) (point m de) repère m; Aviat repère, point de repérage (au sol); Naut amer m, indice m (à terre), point à terre; **that clump of trees is a natural l.** ce groupe d'arbres est un repère naturel **2** (important event) point m décisif, événement m marquant; **to be a l.** (of event) faire date **3** (boundary marker) borne f limite
▸▸**l. building** bâtiment m reconnaissable; **l. decision** décision f qui fait date

landmass [ˈlændmæs] N Geog masse f de terre

landowner [ˈlændəʊnər] N propriétaire m foncier

landowning [ˈlændəʊnɪŋ] ADJ **the l. classes** la classe des propriétaires fonciers

landscape [ˈlændskeɪp] N (land, painting) paysage m; **to print sth in l.** Comput imprimer qch en (mode) paysage; Typ imprimer qch à l'italienne
ADV (to print) Comput en paysage; Typ à l'italienne
VT (area) aménager en parc; **they had their garden landscaped** ils ont employé un jardinier paysagiste pour aménager leur propriété
▸▸**l. architect** architecte mf paysagiste; **l. architecture** architecture f de paysage; **l. designer** paysagiste mf; **l. gardener** jardinier, -ière paysagiste; **l. gardening** paysagisme m; Comput **l. mode** mode m paysage; Art **l. painter** (peintre m) paysagiste

landscaping [ˈlændskeɪpɪŋ] N paysagisme m

landslide [ˈlændslaɪd] N **1** éboulement m, affaissement m, glissement m (de terrain) **2** Pol raz-de-marée m inv électoral; **to win the elections by a l.** gagner les élections avec une écrasante majorité
▸▸**l. majority** majorité f écrasante; **l. victory** victoire f écrasante

landslip [ˈlændslɪp] N = **landslide 1**

landward [ˈlændwəd] ADV (to) l. du côté de la terre, vers la terre

ADJ on the l. side vers l'intérieur, du côté de la terre

lane [leɪn] N **1** (in country) petite route f de campagne; (in town) ruelle f, passage m **2** Naut route f de navigation **3** Aut etc (traffic) l. voie f; **four-l. road** route à quatre voies (de circulation); **don't change lanes** ne change pas de voie; **traffic is reduced to two lanes** la circulation ne se fait plus que sur deux files; **stay in l.** restez dans votre file; **get in(to) l.** mettez-vous sur la bonne file **4** Sport (for runner, swimmer) couloir m
▸▸**l. markings** (on road) signalisation f au sol ou horizontale des voies; Sport (on track) lignes fpl de marquage des couloirs; (in swimming pool) lignes d'eau

langlauf [ˈlænlaʊf] N ski m de fond
▸▸**l. skier** skieur, -euse de fond

language [ˈlæŋgwɪdʒ] N **1** (of a people) langue f; **the English l.** la langue anglaise; **foreign languages** langues étrangères; **I never learned to speak the l.** je n'ai jamais appris à parler la langue; Fig **we don't talk the same l.** nous ne parlons pas le même langage VOIR GRAMMAIRE A8; B4 **2** (vocabulary) langage m; **the l. of flowers** le langage des fleurs; **bad l.** langage grossier, grossièretés fpl; **to use bad/foul l.** parler grossièrement; **(mind your) l.!** surveillez votre langage!; **code l.** langage convenu, code m; **business l.** langage ou langue f des affaires; Comput **computer l., machine l.** langage machine
▸▸**l. course** cours m de langues; **l. exchange holiday** échange m linguistique; **l. laboratory** laboratoire m de langues; **l. learning** apprentissage m de langues; **l. studies** études fpl de langues; **l. teaching** enseignement m de langues

When translating **language**, note that **langue** and **langage** are not interchangeable. **Langue** is used when talking about a specific language used in a country or region, while **langage** refers to the concept of language in general or to a set of vocabulary or terminology.

languid [ˈlæŋgwɪd] ADJ languissant, langoureux

languidly [ˈlæŋgwɪdlɪ] ADV (to move) languissament, langoureusement; (to say) d'une voix langoureuse

languidness [ˈlæŋgwɪdnɪs] N langueur f

languish [ˈlæŋgwɪʃ] VI languir; (of plant) dépérir; **to l. for sb/sth** languir après ou pour qn/qch; Fam **it languished in my intray for a week** c'est resté dans ma corbeille à courrier pendant une semaine; **to l. in prison** moisir en prison; **she spends her day languishing on the sofa** elle passe ses journées langoureusement allongée sur le canapé

languishing [ˈlæŋgwɪʃɪŋ] ADJ languissant, langoureux

languor [ˈlæŋgər] N langueur f

languorous [ˈlæŋgərəs] ADJ langoureux

languorously [ˈlæŋgərəslɪ] ADV langoureusement

lank [læŋk] ADJ **l. hair** cheveux plats

lankness [ˈlæŋknɪs] N (of hair) aspect m terne et sans vigueur

lanky [ˈlæŋkɪ] ADJ (person) grand et filiforme, dégingandé

lanolin(e) [ˈlænəlɪn] N Chem, Pharm lanoline f
▸▸**l. shampoo** shampooing m à la lanoline

lantern [ˈlæntən] N **1** lanterne f, falot m; Naut fanal m, -aux; **Chinese l.** lanterne vénitienne; Hist **magic l.** lanterne magique **2** Archit (of dome) lanterne f, lanternau m
▸▸**l. jaws** joues fpl creuses; **l. slides** plaques fpl de lanterne magique

lantern-jawed [ˈlæntənˈdʒɔːd] ADJ aux joues creuses

lanyard [ˈlænjɑːd, -jəd] N Naut aiguillette f, (for rigging) ride f, (of knife etc) amarrage m

Laos [laʊs] N Laos m

Laotian [ˈlaʊʃɪən] ADJ laotien
N Laotien, -ienne

lap¹ [læp] N (of seated person) genoux mpl, Lit giron m; **to sit on sb's l.** s'asseoir sur les genoux de qn; **it's in the l. of the gods** c'est entre les mains des dieux; **it's not going to fall into your l.** (you'll have to work for it) ça ne va pas te tomber tout cuit (dans le bec); **it dropped in(to) my l.** c'est tombé du ciel; **to live in the l. of luxury** vivre dans le luxe; Fig **to drop sth in sb's l.** coller qch à qn
▸▸ Aut **l. belt** ceinture f ventrale; **l. dancing** = type m de danse exécutée par une entraîneuse nue pour un client; Aut **l. and shoulder belt** ceinture trois points

lap² N **1** Sport (of track, circuit) tour m; **to do three laps** faire trois tours de circuit; **they're on the third l.** ils en sont au troisième tour; Fig **to be on the last l.** en être à la dernière étape; **l. of honour** tour d'honneur **2** Tech recouvrement m; Constr (of tiles, slates) chevauchement m, recouvrement **3** (of wire around cylinder etc) tour m
VT (-pp-) **1** Sport **to l. an opponent** prendre un tour d'avance sur un concurrent; **runners being lapped should move to the outside** les coureurs qui ont un tour de retard doivent s'écarter; **to l. the course** faire un tour de circuit **2** (wrap) **to l. sth round sth** enrouler qch autour de qch **3** Constr (planks) enchevaucher, poser à recouvrement; (tiles) donner du recouvrement à; **to l. a joint with sheet metal** chaperonner un assemblage
VI **1** Sport (of runner) faire le tour du stade; (of car) faire le tour du circuit **2** **to l. over sth** dépasser ou recouvrir qch; (of tiles etc) chevaucher qch
▸▸ Tech **l. joint** enchevauchure f, assemblage m par recouvrement; **l. weld, l. welding** soudure f à recouvrement

lap³ N (of waves) clapotement m, clapotis m
VT (of animal) (milk) laper
VI (of waves) clapoter
▸ **lap up** VT SEP **1** (milk) laper **2** Fig Fam (book) dévorer; **he laps up everything she says** il boit toutes ses paroles; **it was sheer flattery but he lapped it all up** c'était de la flatterie pure et simple mais il a tout gobé ou avalé

laparoscope [ˈlæpərəskəʊp] N Med laparoscope m

laparoscopy [læpəˈrɒskəpɪ] N Med laparoscopie f

laparotomy [læpəˈrɒtəmɪ] N Surg laparotomie f

lapdog [ˈlæpdɒg] N chien m d'appartement; Fig marionnette f

lapel [ləˈpel] N (on jacket) revers m

lapidary [ˈlæpɪd(ə)rɪ] ADJ, N lapidaire m

lapis lazuli [ˈlæpɪsˈlæzʊlɪ] N (stone, colour) lapis(-lazuli) m inv

Lapland [ˈlæplænd] N Laponie f

Laplander [ˈlæplændər] N Lapon, -one

Lapp [læp] ADJ lapon
N **1** Lapon, -one **2** Ling lapon m

lapping [ˈlæpɪŋ] N (of waves) clapotement m, clapotis m

lapse [læps] N **1** (mistake) erreur f, faute f, (fault) faute, défaillance f, (in behaviour) écart m de conduite; (in standards etc) baisse *f* (in de); *(in security)* défaillance; **l. of memory** défaillance *ou* absence *f* de mémoire, oubli *m*; **it was a l. in good manners** il/elle/*etc* a temporairement oublié ses bonnes manières; **a l. in (good) taste** une faute de goût; **a l. in concentration/vigilance** un écart de concentration/vigilance; **it was just a temporary l.** ce n'était qu'une défaillance temporaire; **moral l.** faux pas *m*; *(sexual infidelity)* écart *m*

2 *(passage) (of time)* cours *m*, marche *f*; **a time l.** un laps de temps; **after a l. of three months** après un laps de temps de trois mois **3** *(expiry)* expiration *f*

VI 1 *(make mistake, err)* **he only lapsed once** il n'a fait qu'une seule erreur; **his concentration lapsed for a split second** il a relâché sa concentration pendant une fraction de seconde; **if standards of education are allowed to l.** si on laisse baisser les niveaux scolaires

2 *(fall, go)* **to l. into silence** se taire; **to l. into unconsciousness** sombrer dans l'inconscience; **he's lapsing back into his old ways** il retombe dans ses vieilles habitudes; **it's too easy to l. back into English** c'est trop facile de revenir à l'anglais

3 *(morally)* être coupable d'un écart de conduite; *(more serious)* manquer à ses devoirs; **he tried to give up drinking but he would all too often l.** il essayait d'arrêter de boire mais trop souvent retombait dans son travers

4 *Law (of right, passport etc)* périmer, se périmer; *(of estate)* devenir disponible; *(of legacy)* devenir caduc; *(of law)* tomber en désuétude; *(of insurance policy etc)* cesser d'être en vigueur; *Rel (of person)* cesser de pratiquer; **to allow a right to l.** laisser périmer *ou* laisser tomber un droit; **my club membership has lapsed** ma carte de membre du club a expiré

lapsed [læpst] **ADJ 1** *Rel* déchu **2** *(postal order etc, right)* périmé; *(inheritance)* tombé en dévolu; *(contract, inheritance)* caduc, *f* caduque; *(insurance policy, membership)* expiré

laptop ['læptɒp] **N** *Comput* portable *m*

lapwing ['læpwɪŋ] **N** *(bird)* vanneau *m* (huppé)

larceny ['lɑːsənɪ] **N** *Law* vol *m*; **petty l.** vol simple, vol minime; *Am* **grand l.** vol qualifié

larch [lɑːtʃ] **N** *(tree)* mélèze *m*

lard [lɑːd] **N** saindoux *m*; *esp Am Fam* **he's a tub of l.** c'est un sac de graisse
VT *Culin (meat)* larder, barder; *Fam Pej* **to l. one's writings with quotations** larder ses écrits de citations

Note that the French word **lard** is a false friend. Its most common meaning is **bacon**.

lardarse ['lɑːdɑːs], *Am* **lardass** ['lɑːdæs] **N** *Sl Pej (man)* gros *m* plein de soupe; *(woman)* grosse vache *f*

larder ['lɑːdər] **N** garde-manger *m inv*

lardy ['lɑːdɪ] **ADJ** *Fam Pej* gros, *f* grosse

large [lɑːdʒ] **ADJ 1** *(physical size)* grand; *(bulky) (package, meal, portion)* gros, *f* grosse; *(person) (tall)* grand; *(fat)* gros; **l. audience** public *m* nombreux; **a l. company** une grosse entreprise; **to grow** *or* **get larger** *(of town, deficit)* s'agrandir; *(of person, amount)* grossir; **to make sth larger** agrandir qch; **there she is, as l. as life** la voilà, en chair et en os; **larger than life** hors pair; **the l. size** *(packet etc)* la grande taille; **have you this dress in a l. size?** avez-vous cette robe en grande taille?; **to have a l. following** avoir un public nombreux; **a l. family** une famille nombreuse; **a l. parcel** un gros paquet, un paquet volumineux; **a l. sum** une grosse *ou*

forte somme; **l. town** grande ville; **l. whisky** double whisky *m*

2 *(extensive, significant)* **to a l. extent, in l. part** en grande partie; **a l. part of my time/job/day** une grande partie de mon temps/mon travail/ma journée; **in l. measure** dans une large mesure; **to take a larger part in sth** prendre une plus grande part à qch; **to trade on a l. scale** faire les affaires en grand; **l. powers** *(comprehensive)* pouvoirs larges *ou* étendus; **l. views** *(liberal)* idées larges

ADV 1 by and l. en gros; **by and l. they vote Conservative** ils votent conservateur pour la plupart **2** *Br Fam (to a large extent)* **Arsenal got thrashed l.** Arsenal s'est fait ratatiner *ou* s'est fait battre à plates coutures; **we got drunk l. last night** on s'est pris une cuite maison hier soir

N to set a prisoner at l. élargir *ou* relaxer un prisonnier; **to be at l.** être libre *ou* en liberté; **the murderer is still at l.** l'assassin court toujours; **he was acting as the UN's ambassador at l.** il a joué le rôle de médiateur auprès des Nations Unies; **people at l.** *(in general)* le grand public, la grande masse du public; **teachers at l.** la masse des professeurs; **at l.** *(in detail)* tout au long, en détail; **to talk at l.** parler au hasard
▸▸Fin l. denominations grosses coupures *fpl*; *Anat* **the l. intestine** le gros intestin

Note that the most common meaning of the French adjective **large** is **wide, broad**.

large-handed [lɑːdʒ'hændɪd] **ADJ** généreux

large-hearted [lɑːdʒ'hɑːtɪd] **ADJ** au grand cœur

largely ['lɑːdʒlɪ] **ADV** en grande partie, pour une large part; **his job is l. administrative** son travail est surtout administratif; **it's l. the case that people ...** dans la plupart des cas les gens ...; **it's l. a case of finding the right people** il s'agit surtout de trouver les gens qu'il faut

Note that the French word **largement** is a false friend. It means **widely** or **generously**, depending on the context.

large-minded **ADJ** aux idées larges, à l'esprit large

largeness ['lɑːdʒnɪs] **N** *(of body)* grosseur *f*, *(of profits, majority etc)* grandeur *f*, importance *f*, *(of power)* étendue *f*, *(of ideas)* largeur *f*, *(of soul)* grandeur *f*

large-print **ADJ** **l. book** livre *m* en gros caractères

large-scale **ADJ** *(undertaking, farmer)* gros; *(map)* à grande échelle; **l. disaster** grande catastrophe *f*
▸▸ *Comput* **l. integration** intégration *f* à grande échelle

largess(e) [lɑː'ʒes] **N** largesse *f*

largish ['lɑːdʒɪʃ] **ADJ** assez grand, assez gros

largo, *pl* **largs** ['lɑːgəʊ, -z] **ADV, N** *Mus* largo *m inv*

lariat ['lærɪət] **N 1** *Am* lasso *m* **2** *(for tethering animals)* corde *f* à piquet

lark¹ [lɑːk] **N** *(bird)* alouette *f*; **to rise** *or* **get up** *or* **be up with the l.** se lever au chant du coq; **she sings like a l.** elle chante comme un rossignol

lark² **N** *Fam (joke etc)* farce *f*, rigolade *f*, blague *f*; **to do sth for a l.** faire qch histoire de rire *ou* de rigoler; **what a l.!** quelle farce!; **I'd like to know what his little l. is** je me demande ce qu'il mijote; **I don't want any more of the 'I lost my homework' l.** ne me faites plus le coup du 'j'ai perdu mes devoirs'; **I don't like this fancy dress l.** je n'aime pas du tout cette histoire de bal masqué?; **are**

you still at the teaching l.? tu fais toujours ce foutu métier de prof?
▸ lark about, lark around **VI** *Fam (play jokes)* faire des farces; *(have good time)* rigoler; **some children were larking around with an old tyre** des enfants s'amusaient avec un vieux pneu

larkspur ['lɑːkspɜːr] **N** *(plant)* pied-d'alouette *m*, *pl* pieds-d'alouette

larva, *pl* **larvae** ['lɑːvə, -viː] **N** *Entom* larve *f*

larval ['lɑːv(ə)l] **ADJ** *Entom* larvaire

laryngitis [lærɪn'dʒaɪtɪs] **N** *Med* laryngite *f*, **to have l.** avoir une laryngite

laryngoscope [lə'rɪŋgəskəʊp] **N** laryngoscope *m*

larynx ['lærɪŋks] **N** *Anat* larynx *m*

lasagne [lə'sænjə] **N** *Culin* lasagnes *fpl*

lascivious [lə'sɪvɪəs] **ADJ** lascif

lasciviously [lə'sɪvɪəslɪ] **ADV** lascivement

lasciviousness [lə'sɪvɪəsnɪs] **N** lasciveté *f*

laser ['leɪzər] **N** laser *m*
▸▸ l. beam rayon *m ou* faisceau *m* laser; **l. checkout** *(in supermarket)* caisse *f* munie de lecteurs laser; **l. disk** disque *m* laser; **l. pointer** pointeur *m* laser; **l. printer** imprimante *f* (à) laser; **l. printing** impression *f* laser; **l. printout** imprimé *m* laser, copie *f* laser; *Comput* **l. quality** qualité *f* laser; **l. surgery** chirurgie *f* (au) laser

laser-guided **ADJ** guidé au laser

lash¹ [læʃ] **N 1** *(blow with whip)* coup *m* de fouet; *(end of whip)* lanière *f* (de fouet); **the l.** *(punishment)* le (supplice du) fouet; **to receive ten lashes** recevoir dix coups de fouet; **he felt the l. of the Prime Minister's tongue** il a été durement critiqué par le Premier ministre
2 *Anat* cil *m*
VT 1 *(with whip) (horse etc)* fouetter, cingler; *(person)* fouetter, flageller; *(of rain) (windows, sb's face)* fouetter; *(of waves) (shore)* battre, fouetter; **the wind/storm lashed the sea into a fury** le vent/l'orage s'abattit sur la mer qui se déchaîna; **he lashed the crowd into a frenzy** il a soulevé la foule jusqu'à l'hystérie
2 *(verbally)* cingler; **to l. sb with one's tongue** adresser à qn des paroles cinglantes
3 *(move from side to side)* **to l. its tail** *(of cat, lion etc)* fouetter l'air de la queue
VI to l. against the windows *(of rain)* fouetter les vitres; **the rain** *or* **it was lashing down** il pleuvait dru; **to l. against the shore** *(of waves)* battre *ou* fouetter le rivage; **the rain lashed down on the tent** la pluie fouettait la tente
▸ lash about **VI** *(in pain)* se débattre (de douleur)
▸ lash back **VI** *(reply strongly)* répondre violemment
▸ lash out **VI 1 to l. out at sb** *(physically)* envoyer un coup à qn; *(verbally)* s'en prendre violemment à qn; **he lashed out at me with his fists/feet** il m'a envoyé des coups de poing/coups de pied
2 *Fam (spend extravagantly)* faire une folie *ou* des folies; **I'm going to l. out on a new coat** je vais faire des folies et me payer un nouveau manteau; **they really lashed out on their daughter's wedding** ils ont dépensé une fortune pour le mariage de leur fille
VT SEP *Fam* **I lashed out £10 on a bottle of wine** j'ai claqué 10 livres sur une bouteille de vin

lash² **VT** *(tie)* lier, attacher; *Naut* amarrer; **to l. down a load on a trailer** lier une charge sur une remorque

lashing¹ ['læʃɪŋ] **ADJ** *(rain)* cinglant
N 1 *(with whip)* coups *mpl* de fouet **2** *Old-fashioned (tongue)* **l.** verte réprimande *f*, **to**

give sb a tongue l. réprimander qn sévèrement **3** *Br Fam* **lashings of** sth des tas de qch; **apple pie with lashings of cream** de la tarte aux pommes avec une tonne de crème

lashing [2] **N** *(rope)* câble *m*

lass [læs] **N** *esp Scot, North Eng* jeune fille *f*; **country l.** jeune campagnarde *f*

Lassa ['lɑːsə] **N** *Med* **L. fever** fièvre *f* de Lhassa

lassie ['læsɪ] **N** *esp Scot* fillette *f*; **a wee l.** une petite fille

lassitude ['læsɪtjuːd] **N** lassitude *f*

lasso [læ'suː] **N** lasso *m*
VT prendre au lasso

LAST [1] [lɑːst] **ADJ 1** *(final)* dernier; **the l. guest to arrive** le dernier des invités à arriver; **the l. but one** l'avant-dernier, *pl* les avant-derniers; **the l. syllable but one** l'avant-dernière syllabe; **the l. but three** le troisième à partir de la fin; **this is your l. chance** c'est votre dernière chance; **in the l. resort, as a l. resort** en dernière ressource, en dernier recours; **you are my l. hope** vous êtes mon dernier espoir; **in the l. place** enfin, pour finir; **in the l. analysis** au bout du compte; **to have the l. word** *(come after other speakers)* parler le dernier; *(in argument)* avoir le dernier mot; **the l. word in comfort/luxury** *(hotel etc)* le summum du confort/luxe; **this model is the l. word in car design** ce modèle est le dernier cri de la conception automobile; **I'm down to my l. pound** il ne me reste plus qu'une livre; **every l. scrap of bread had been eaten** on avait mangé jusqu'à la dernière miette; **at the l. moment** *or* **minute** au dernier moment; **the l. day of the month** le dernier jour du mois; **to do sth l. thing at night** faire qch juste avant d'aller se coucher VOIR GRAMMAIRE A26

2 *(most recent)* **l. Tuesday, Tuesday l.** mardi dernier; **l. January** en janvier dernier; **the l. time I saw him** la dernière fois que je l'ai vu; **l. week** la semaine dernière, la semaine passée; **l. night** *(during the night)* la nuit dernière; *(in the evening)* hier (au) soir; **I slept badly l. night** j'ai mal dormi cette nuit; **I haven't been to church for the l. few weeks** je ne suis pas allé à l'église ces dernières semaines; **in the l. fifty years** pendant les cinquante dernières années; **this day l. week** il y a huit jours aujourd'hui; **this day l. year** l'an dernier à la même date; **l. financial year** exercice *m* écoulé

3 *(least likely)* **you're the l. one to criticize** tu es vraiment mal placé pour critiquer; **you're the l. person I expected to see here** tu es bien la dernière personne que je pensais rencontrer ici; **he's the l. person I'd ask to help me** c'est (bien) la dernière personne à qui je demanderais de l'aide; **that's the l. thing that's worrying me** ça c'est le cadet de mes soucis; **that's the l. thing I'd do in your position** c'est (bien) la dernière chose que je ferais si j'étais à ta place

N 1 *(person)* **the l.** le dernier, la dernière; *am* **I the l.?** *(to arrive)* suis-je le dernier?; *Ind* **l. in, first out** dernier entré, premier sorti; *Bible* **the l. shall be first** les derniers seront les premiers

2 *(end)* **we'll never hear the l. of it** on n'a pas fini d'en entendre parler; **we haven't heard the l. of this problem** tôt ou tard ce problème va refaire surface; **I think we've heard the l. of him** je pense qu'on n'en entendra plus parler; **that's the l. I saw of him** je ne l'ai pas revu depuis; **that's the l. of the wine** *(that's all there is left)* c'est tout ce qui reste comme vin; *(that's the last drop gone)* il n'y a plus de vin maintenant; **to** *or* **till the l.** jusqu'au bout, jusqu'à la fin; **faithful to the l.** fidèle jusqu'au bout; **at l., at long l.** enfin; **now at l. I understand** enfin, je comprends;

Lit **to look one's l. on sth** voir qch pour la dernière fois; *Lit* **to breathe one's l.** rendre le dernier soupir; *Lit* **to be near one's l.** *(death)* être proche de sa fin; **towards the l.** vers la fin de sa vie

ADV 1 *(in time)* **when I l. saw him, when I saw him l.** la dernière fois que je l'ai vu; **I can't remember when I l. ate** je ne sais pas depuis quand je n'ai pas mangé

2 *(in order)* **he spoke l.** il a parlé le dernier; **she came** *or* **finished l.** *(in exam)* elle a été dernière; *(in race)* elle est arrivée dernière

3 l., I would like to say … et pour finir, je voudrais dire …; **l. but not least** enfin et surtout; **l. but not least on the list we have Mr …** et enfin sur la liste, je ne voudrais pas oublier M …

VI durer, se maintenir; **it's too good to l.** c'est trop beau pour durer; **if the good weather lasts** si le beau temps se maintient; **cream doesn't l. long** *(deteriorates quickly)* la crème fraîche ne se conserve pas longtemps; **cakes never l. long in this house** *(they get eaten quickly)* les gâteaux ne durent jamais très longtemps *ou Fam* ne font jamais long feu dans cette maison; **the supplies will not l. two months** les vivres ne feront pas deux mois; **their friendship won't l. long** leur amitié ne durera pas; **he won't l. long in that job** il ne tiendra pas très longtemps à ce poste, *Fam* il ne fera pas long feu à ce poste

VT it will l. me a lifetime j'en ai pour la vie; **it has lasted him well** ça lui a fait de l'usage; **she couldn't l. the pace** elle n'a pas pu tenir le rythme

▸▸ **the L. Judgment** le Jugement dernier; **l. name** nom *m* de famille; **l. rites** derniers sacrements *mpl*; *St Exch* **l. trading day** dernier jour *m* de cotation

▸ **last out VT SEP to l. sb out** *(of person)* survivre à qn; **he'll l. us all out** il nous survivra tous; **to l. the year out** *(of person)* survivre jusqu'à la fin de l'année; *(of supplies etc)* suffire pour l'année; **my overcoat will l. the winter out** mon pardessus fera encore l'hiver; **I don't know if I'll be able to l. out the afternoon without any coffee** je ne sais pas si j'arriverai à tenir tout l'après-midi sans café; **the doctor doubted whether she would l. out the night** le docteur n'était pas sûr qu'elle passerait la nuit

VI *(of person)* tenir le coup

last [2] **N** *(for shoe)* forme *f* (à chaussure)

last-ditch **ADJ** ultime; **a l. effort** un ultime effort

lasting ['lɑːstɪŋ] **ADJ** durable; *(material etc)* résistant; **l. peace** paix durable

lastly ['lɑːstlɪ] **ADV** pour finir, en dernier lieu

last-minute **ADJ** *(decision)* de dernière minute

lat *(abbr* **latitude)** latitude, lat.

latch [lætʃ] **N 1** loquet *m*; *(small, for shutters etc)* loqueteau *m*; *(of vehicle door etc)* pêne *m*, gâche *f*; **to leave the door on the l.** fermer la porte sans la verrouiller **2** *Tech (of lever, moving mechanical part)* verrou *m*
VT 1 *(door)* fermer au loquet **2** *Tech (lever, moving part)* verrouiller, bloquer

▸ **latch on VI** *Fam* **1** *(attach oneself)* **to l. on to sb/sth** s'accrocher à qn/qch **2** *(understand)* piger; **to l. on to sth** piger qch; **it took him a while to l. on** il a mis un moment pour piger

latchkey ['lætʃkiː] **N** clef *f* de maison, clef de porte d'entrée; **l. child** *or Fam* **kid** = enfant *mf* dont les parents travaillent et qui doit rentrer seul après l'école

late [leɪt] **ADJ 1** *(after the appointed time)* en retard; *(delayed)* retardé; **to be l. (for sth)** être en retard (pour qch); **she was too l. to help** elle est arrivée trop tard pour apporter son aide; **it was too l. to do anything about it** il était trop tard pour faire quoi que ce soit;

am I too l. to register? est-il trop tard pour que je m'inscrive?; **it's never too l.** il n'est jamais trop tard; **the train is l./is ten minutes l.** le train a du retard/a dix minutes de retard; **we apologize for the l. running of the train** veuillez nous excuser pour ce retard; **her baby was five days l.** son bébé est né avec cinq jours de retard

2 *(far on in the day etc)* tard; **it is l.** il est tard; **it is getting l.** il se fait tard; **it is too l.** il est trop tard; **I was l. going to bed** je me suis couché tard; **to keep l. hours** être un couche-tard; **at this l. hour** à l'heure qu'il est

3 *(towards the end of a period of time)* **why have they left it to this l. hour before informing us?** pourquoi ont-ils attendu la dernière minute pour nous en informer?; **in the l. afternoon** tard dans l'après-midi; **in l. summer** vers la fin de l'été; *Fig* **it's a bit l. in the day (to start making changes)** il est un peu tard (pour commencer à faire des modifications); **to be in one's l. thirties** avoir entre trente-cinq et quarante ans, *Fam* avoir la trentaine bien tassée; **in the l. (nineteen) nineties** vers la fin des années 1990; **a l. marriage** un mariage sur le tard

4 *(fruit etc)* tardif

5 *Fml (deceased)* feu, défunt, décédé; **my l. father** feu mon père; **the l. queen** feu la reine, la feue reine

ADV 1 *(after the appointed time)* en retard; **to arrive too l.** arriver trop tard; *Prov* **better l. than never** mieux vaut tard que jamais

2 *(far on in the day etc)* tard; **he came home very l.** il est rentré fort tard; **to work l.** travailler tard; **to go to bed l.** se coucher tard; **to sleep** *or* **stay in bed l.** faire la grasse matinée; **l. into the night** jusqu'à une heure avancée de la nuit; **l. in the year** vers la fin de l'année; **l. in life** sur le tard; **to marry l. in life** se marier tard *ou* sur le tard

3 *(recently)* **as l. as last week** pas plus tard que la semaine dernière

4 *(formerly)* *esp Fml* **l. of this address** dernièrement domicilié à cette adresse; **Sir Geoffrey, l. of the Diplomatic Corps** Sir Geoffrey, qui fut anciennement membre du Corps diplomatique

5 *Lit* **= lately**

N of l. récemment; **as events of l. have shown …** comme les récents événements l'ont montré …

▸▸ *Mktg* **l. adopter** utilisateur *m* tardif; **l. arrival** *(at hotel)* arrivée *f* tardive; **he will be a l. arrival** il arrivera tard; **l. availability** *(of holiday, seat)* disponibilité *f* de dernière minute; **l. cancellation** *(of flight)* annulation *f* de dernière minute; **l. edition** *(of a newspaper)* dernière édition *f*, *Mktg* **l. entrant** concurrent, -ente tardif(-ive); **l. entry** *(in competition)* inscription *f* de dernière minute; *Mktg* **l. entry** lancement *m* tardif; **Denmark only came into the tournament as a l. entry** le Danemark s'est inscrit au tournoi en toute dernière minute; **l. frosts** gelées tardives *ou* printanières; *Mktg* **l. majority** majorité *f* conservatrice; *Fin* **l. payment** retard *m* de paiement; *Fin* **l. payment penalty** pénalité *f* de retard; *Journ* **l. story** nouvelle *f* de dernière minute; **l. tackle** *(in rugby)* plaquage *m* à retardement; *(in football)* tacle *m* à retardement; *St Exch* **l. trading** opérations *fpl* de clôture

latecomer ['leɪtkʌmər] **N** retardataire *mf*; *Fig* **to be a l. to business/politics** arriver tardivement dans les affaires/en politique

lately ['leɪtlɪ] **ADV** dernièrement, récemment, ces derniers temps; **what have you been doing l.?** qu'avez-vous fait ces derniers temps?; **it is only l. that the matter has become known** la chose n'a été sue que ces jours-ci

latency ['leɪtənsɪ] **N** latence *f*, état *m* latent
▸▸ **l. period** temps *m* de latence

lateness ['leɪtnɪs] **N 1** *(of fruit etc)* tardiveté *f, (of person)* retard *m*; **I will not tolerate l.** je ne tolérerai aucun retard **2 the l. of the hour** l'heure avancée

late-night ADJ **a l. bar/disco** un bar/une discothèque qui ferme très tard; **a l. party** une soirée qui commence tard; **l. showing** *(of film)* séance *f* de minuit

latent ['leɪtənt] ADJ *(disease, homosexuality, possibility)* latent
▸▸ *Bot* **l. bud** œil *m* dormant; **l. defect** vice *m* caché; **l. heat** chaleur *f* latente; **l. period** *Med* incubation *f*, *Psy* latence *f*, état *m* latent, temps *m* de latence

later ['leɪtər] *(comp of* late*)* ADJ ultérieur; *(of two variants) (edition, version, model etc)* dernier; **I caught a l. train** j'ai pris un autre train plus tard; **l. events proved that …** la suite des événements a démontré que …; **at a l. meeting** dans une séance ultérieure; **l. investigations revealed that …** les enquêtes ultérieures *ou* qui ont suivi ont révélé que …; **his l. novels** *(of dead person)* les romans qu'il a écrits vers la fin de sa carrière; *(of living person)* ses romans les plus récents; **in l. life she …** plus tard dans sa vie, elle … VOIR GRAMMAIRE A25
ADV plus tard; **l. (on) we went to the cinema** plus tard nous sommes allés au cinéma; **sooner or l.** tôt ou tard; **no l. than tomorrow** demain au plus tard; **a moment l.** l'instant d'après; **this happened l. (on)** cela est arrivé après *ou* plus tard *ou* ultérieurement; **a few days l.** quelques jours plus tard, *Lit* à quelques jours de là; **three pages l.** trois pages plus loin; **as we shall see l.** comme nous le verrons plus tard *ou* par la suite; *Fam* **see you l.!** à plus tard!

lateral ['lætərəl] ADJ latéral, -aux; **he's good at l. thinking** il sait trouver des approches originales
▸▸ *Tech* **l. motion** mouvement *m* latéral; *Tech* **l. play** jeu *m* latéral

laterally ['lætərəlɪ] ADV latéralement

latest ['leɪtɪst] ADJ *(superl of* late*)* dernier; **this author's l. work** le dernier ouvrage de cet auteur; **his l. views on the subject** ses vues les plus récentes sur ce sujet; **the very l. improvements** les tout derniers perfectionnements; **the very l. news** les informations de toute dernière heure; **the l. edition** la dernière édition; **l. date** *(deadline)* date *f* limite; *Com, Law* terme *m* de rigueur, délai *m* de rigueur; **the l. fashions** la dernière mode; *Com* **l. novelties** dernières nouveautés *fpl* VOIR GRAMMAIRE A25
N have you heard the l.? savez-vous la dernière?; **the l. I can come would be four o'clock** je ne pourrai pas venir après quatre heures; **the l. she could leave the decision until was this evening** elle ne pouvait pas remettre la décision à plus tard que ce soir; **at the l.** au plus tard; **Wednesday at the l.** mercredi au plus tard

latex ['leɪteks] N latex *m*

lath [læθ] **N 1** *Constr* latte *f*, **l.-and-plaster partition** cloison lattée et plâtrée **2** *(of Venetian blind)* lame *f*

lathe [leɪð] **N** tour *m*; **precision l.** tour de précision; **capstan** *or* **turret l.** tour (à) revolver; **polishing l.** touret *m* à polir *ou* de polisseur
▸▸ **l. bed** banc *m ou* bâti *m* de tour

lather ['lɑːðər] **N 1** mousse *f* de savon; **to make l.** *(of soap)* mousser **2** *(on horse)* écume *f*, **horse all in a l.** cheval couvert d'écume; *Fam* **to work oneself** *or* **get into a l.** se mettre dans tous ses états (**about sth** à propos de qch); **don't get into such a l.** ne t'en fais pas la peine de te mettre dans tous tes états
VT 1 savonner (**sb's chin** le menton à qn); **to l. one's face** se savonner le visage; *(in order*

to shave) se mettre du savon à barbe sur le visage **2** *Old-fashioned Fam (thrash)* rosser
VI *(of soap)* mousser

lathe-turned ['leɪðtɜːnd] ADJ fait au tour, tourné

Latin ['lætɪn] ADJ latin; **the L. races** les races latines
N 1 *(Southern European)* Latin, -ine **2** *Ling* latin *m*; **written in L.** écrit en latin
▸▸ **L. America** Amérique *f* latine; **L. American** latino-américain, *pl* latino-américains; **the L. Quarter** *(in Paris)* le Quartier latin

latinize ['lætɪnaɪz] VT latiniser

Latino [læˈtiːnəʊ] N *Am* latino *mf*

latish ['leɪtɪʃ] ADJ **1** *(after the appointed time)* un peu en retard **2** *(far on in the day etc)* un peu tardif; **at a l. hour** à une heure assez avancée
ADV *(see adj)* **1** un peu en retard **2** un peu tard

latitude ['lætɪtjuːd] **N 1** *Geog* latitude *f*, **in northern/southern latitudes** dans les latitudes boréales/australes; **at a l. of 30° north** par 30° (de) latitude nord; **in these latitudes** sous ces latitudes **2** *(freedom)* **to allow sb the greatest l.** laisser à qn la plus grande latitude *ou* la plus grande liberté d'action; **it doesn't give us much l.** *(of deadline, budget etc)* cela ne nous donne pas une grande marge de manœuvre; **they are given a lot of l.** on leur donne beaucoup de liberté

latrine [ləˈtriːn] N *esp Mil* latrines *fpl*

latte ['lɑːteɪ] N café *m* au lait

latter ['lætər] ADJ **1** *(of two)* dernier VOIR GRAMMAIRE A77 **2** *(belonging to the end)* dernier; **the l. years of her life** les dernières années de sa vie; **the l. half** *or* **part of June** la deuxième moitié de juin VOIR GRAMMAIRE A25
N the l. *(of two)* le dernier, la dernière, *pl* les derniers, les dernières VOIR GRAMMAIRE A77

latter-day ADJ **1** moderne, d'aujourd'hui **2** *Rel* **the L. Saints** les Mormons *mpl*

latterly ['lætəlɪ] ADV **1** *(recently)* récemment **2** *(towards the end of a period)* vers la fin

lattice ['lætɪs] N treillis *m*, treillage *m*
▸▸ *Constr etc* **l. beam, l. girder** poutre *f* en treillis *ou* à croisillons; **l. window** fenêtre *f* à croisillons

latticed ['lætɪst] ADJ treillissé, treillagé; *Fig (branches)* entrecroisé

latticework ['lætɪswɜːk] N treillage *m*, treillis *m*

Latvia ['lætvɪə] N Lettonie *f*

Latvian ['lætvɪən] ADJ letton
N 1 Letton, -one **2** *Ling* letton *m*

laud [lɔːd] VT *Lit* louer

laudable ['lɔːdəb(ə)l] ADJ louable, digne de louanges

laudably ['lɔːdəblɪ] ADV louablement; **she was l. restrained** sa retenue était digne de louanges

laudanum ['lɔːd(ə)nəm] N *Pharm* laudanum *m*

laudatory ['lɔːdət(ə)rɪ] ADJ *(speech, remarks etc)* élogieux, louangeur, -euse

LAUGH [lɑːf] **N** rire *m*; **to burst into a (loud) l.** éclater de rire, partir d'un éclat de rire; **to give a short l.** avoir un petit rire; **with a l.** en riant; **he likes a (good) l.** il aime bien rire; **to have the last l.** avoir sa vengeance; **to raise a l.** faire rire; **look outside if you want a l.** regarde dehors si tu veux rigoler; *Fam* **to do sth for a l.** faire qch pour rire; **what a l.!** quelle rigolade!; *Iron* **that's a l.!** quelle blague!, la bonne blague!; **the l.'s on us** on a été refaits; **these old films are usually good for a l.** ces vieux films sont généralement drôles
VI rire; **to l. at** *or* **over** *or* **about sth** rire de

qch; **there's nothing to l. about** il n'y a pas de quoi rire; **to l. at sb** se moquer de qn; **to l. to oneself** rire tout seul; **to l. and cry at the same time** pleurer et rire en même temps; **I didn't know whether to l. or cry** je ne savais pas si je devais rire ou pleurer; **to l. till one cries** *or* **till the tears come** rire (jusqu')aux larmes; **to l. up one's sleeve** rire dans sa barbe; **to l. in sb's face** rire au nez de qn; *Fam* **if I get that job I'll be laughing** si j'obtenais ce travail ça serait génial; *Fam* **if you've already done this before, you're laughing** si tu as déjà fait ça c'est un jeu d'enfant; *Fam* **when his granny dies, he'll be laughing** quand sa grand-mère mourra, il vivra comme un prince *ou* il pourra mettre les doigts de pied en éventail; *Fam* **you've already got your visa, you're laughing** toi, tu as déjà ton visa, tu n'as pas de problèmes; *Fam* **don't make me l.** laissez-moi rire!; *Fam* **I soon made him l. on the other side of his face** je lui ai bientôt fait passer son envie de rire; *Fam* **you'll l. on the other side of your face one of these days** un de ces jours tu vas rire jaune; *Fam* **to l. all the way to the bank** s'en mettre plein les poches; *Prov* **he who laughs last laughs longest, he laughs best who laughs last** rira bien qui rira le dernier
VT he laughed a bitter l. il eut un rire amer; **to l. oneself silly** rire comme un bossu *ou* une baleine; **his suggestion was laughed out of court** sa suggestion fut rejetée catégoriquement; **I'd be laughed out of court** je me couvrirais de ridicule
▸ **laugh down** VT SEP *(proposal)* tourner en ridicule
▸ **laugh off** VT SEP **he laughed the matter off** il tourna la chose en plaisanterie; *Fam* **to l. one's head off** être mort de rire

laughable ['lɑːfəb(ə)l] ADJ risible, ridicule

laughably ['lɑːfəblɪ] ADV risiblement; *(easy)* ridiculement

laughing ['lɑːfɪŋ] ADJ *(face)* riant; *(eyes, expression)* rieur; **it's no l. matter** il n'y a pas de quoi rire; **I'm in no l. mood** je n'ai pas envie de rire
N rires *mpl*; **we could hear the sound of l.** nous entendions des rires
▸▸ **l. gas** gaz *m* hilarant; *Br Fam* **l. gear** bouche *f*, clapet *m*; **l. hyena** hyène *f* tachetée; *Orn* **l. jackass** martin-chasseur *m (d'Australie)*, *pl* martins-chasseurs, kookaburra *m*; **l. stock** risée *f*, **to make a l. stock of oneself** se couvrir de ridicule; **to be a l. stock** être la risée de tous; **to make sb a l. stock** couvrir qn de ridicule; **to make sb the l. stock of the village** faire de qn la risée du village

laughingly ['lɑːfɪŋlɪ] ADV **1** *(to say)* en riant **2 that's l. called art** on a le culot d'appeler ça de l'art

laughter ['lɑːftər] N rire(s) *m(pl)*; **to cause l.** provoquer les rires *ou* l'hilarité; **there was l. at her words** ce qu'elle dit provoqua des rires; **to receive a proposal with l.** accueillir une proposition par des rires; **everything I say is received with l.** on rit de tout ce que je dis

launch [lɔːntʃ] **N 1** *(boat, of warship)* chaloupe *f*, *(of warship)* vedette *f* **2** *(of ship, rocket, missile, new product etc)* lancement *m*
VT *(ship, torpedo, rocket)* lancer; *(ship's boats)* mettre à l'eau; *(person, business, enquiry, new product)* lancer; *Mil (offensive)* déclencher; **to l. sb on a career** lancer qn dans une carrière; **once he is launched on the subject** une fois lancé sur le sujet
▸▸ *Astron* **l. pad** rampe *f ou* plate-forme *f* de lancement, *pl* plates-formes de lancement; **l. party** réception *f (pour le lancement d'un produit, d'un livre etc)*; *Astron* **l. site** base *f* de lancement; *Astron* **l. vehicle** fusée *f* de lancement

▶ **launch into** VT INSEP to l. into abuse of sb se répandre en invectives contre qn; **to l. into a story** se lancer dans une histoire; **to l. into a complaint** se mettre à se plaindre

▶ **launch out** VI to l. out into a new market se lancer sur un nouveau marché; **to l. out on one's own** (in business) faire cavalier seul

launcher ['lɔːntʃər] N (vehicle) lanceur m; (launching pad) rampe f ou plate-forme f de lancement; (for planes) catapulte f de lancement; Mil **grenade l.** lance-grenades m inv (à fusil)

launching ['lɔːntʃɪŋ] N (of ship) lancement m; (of small boat, ship's barge etc) mise f à l'eau; (of torpedo, projectile, rocket) lancement; Com, Fin (of product, loan) lancement m; Mil (of attack, offensive) déclenchement m, lancement
▶▶ Aviat **l. catapult** catapulte f de lancement; Mil, Astron **l. pad, l. platform** (for rockets, missiles) plate-forme f de lancement, pl plates-formes de lancement; Aviat **l. ramp** rampe f de lancement; Astron **l. site** base f de lancement

launder ['lɔːndər] VT (clothes) blanchir; Fig **to l. money** blanchir de l'argent

launderette [lɔːndə'ret] N Br laverie f automatique

laundering ['lɔːndərɪŋ] N (of clothes) blanchissage m; Fig (of money) blanchiment m

laundress ['lɔːndres] N blanchisseuse f

laundrette [lɔːn'dret] N Br laverie f automatique

Laundromat® ['lɔːndrəʊmæt] N Am laverie f automatique

laundry ['lɔːndrɪ] N 1 (place) blanchisserie f, (in house) buanderie f, **to send sth to the l.** envoyer qch à la blanchisserie 2 (clothes) lessive f, (clean) linge m propre; (dirty) linge sale; **to do the l.** faire la lessive
▶▶ **l. bag** sac m de blanchisserie; **l. basket** panier m à linge; **l. list** liste f de blanchissage; **l. room** buanderie f; **l. service** service m de blanchissage

laureate ['lɔːrɪət] ADJ lauréat; Br Poet **L.**, pl **Poets Laureate** poète m lauréat (dignité conférée par la Couronne)
N lauréat, -ate

laurel ['lɒrəl] N (tree) laurier m; Fig **to win laurels** se couvrir de lauriers; Fig **to rest on one's laurels** se reposer sur ses lauriers; Fig **he must look to his laurels** il est en passe d'être éclipsé
▶▶ **l. wreath** couronne f de lauriers

LAUTRO ['laʊtrəʊ] N Formerly (abbr Life Assurance and Unit Trust Regulatory Organization) = organisme m britannique chargé d'établir des codes de conduite à l'usage des compagnies d'assurance-vie et des sociétés d'investissement, et de veiller à leur respect

lav [læv] N Br Fam (abbr lavatory) petit coin m, cabinets mpl

lava ['lɑːvə] N lave f, **l. stream** or **flow** coulée f de lave

lavabo pl lavabos [lə'veɪbəʊ, -əʊz] N Rel lavabo m

lavalier [læ'vælje] N (clip mike) micro m cravate

lavatorial [lævə'tɔːrɪəl] ADJ (humour) scatologique

lavatory ['lævətrɪ] N (room, object) W.-C. mpl, toilettes fpl; **public l.** W.-C. publics, toilettes publiques
▶▶ Br **l. humour** humour m scatologique; **l. pan** cuvette f de W.-C.; Br **l. paper** papier m hygiénique

lavender ['lævɪndər] N (shrub) lavande f
ADJ (colour) lavande inv
▶▶ **l. water** eau f de lavande

lavish ['lævɪʃ] ADJ 1 (person) prodigue; **to be l. with one's money** dépenser sans compter; **to be l. with the cream/sugar** ne pas pleurer la crème/le sucre; **to be l. in one's praise** être prodigue d'éloges 2 (gift, house etc) somptueux; (praise) dithyrambique; (meal) plantureux; (spending) extravagant; **to live in a l. style** mener la grande vie
VT **to l. money on sb** dépenser des fortunes pour qn; **to l. praise on sb** se répandre en éloges sur qn; **to l. care on sb** prodiguer des soins à qn; **to l. care on sth** être extrêmement soigneux avec qch

lavishly ['lævɪʃlɪ] ADV 1 avec prodigalité; **to spend l.** dépenser de l'argent sans compter; **to praise sb l.** se répandre en éloges sur qn; **we were l. entertained by them** ils se sont royalement occupés de nous 2 (to furnish) somptueusement

lavishness ['lævɪʃnɪs] N 1 (of person) prodigalité f 2 (of furnishings etc) somptuosité f

law [lɔː] N 1 (rule) loi f, Phil principe m; Parl **to pass/repeal a l.** voter/abroger une loi; **there's no l. against it** aucune loi ne l'interdit; Phys **the laws of gravity** les lois de la pesanteur; Econ **l. of diminishing returns** loi des rendements décroissants; **l. of supply and demand** loi de l'offre et de la demande; **by the l. of averages** par la loi des probabilités
2 (set of rules) **the l.** la loi; Sport **the off-side l.** les règles ou le règlement du hors-jeu; **it's the l.** c'est la loi; **it's against the l.** c'est contre la loi (**to do sth** de faire qch); **to carry out the l.** appliquer la loi; **to keep/break the l.** respecter ou observer/enfreindre la loi; **l. and order** ordre m public; **to have the force of l.** avoir force de loi; **his word is l.** sa parole a force de loi; **he thinks he's above the l.** il se croit tout permis; **no-one is above the l.** personne n'est au-dessus des lois; **to be a l. unto oneself** n'en faire qu'à sa tête; **there's one l. for the rich and another for the poor** il y a une loi pour les riches et une pour les pauvres; Rel **the L., the l. of Moses** la loi mosaïque
3 Law (system of justice) droit m; **civil l.** ≃ droit civil; **common l.** (as opposed to statute law) droit coutumier; (of general application) droit civil; **criminal l.** droit pénal ou criminel, législation f criminelle; **l. of contract** ≃ droit des obligations; **Roman l.** droit romain; **judgment quashed on a point of l.** arrêt cassé pour vice de forme; **Bachelor/Doctor of Laws** ≃ licencié(e)/docteur en droit; **to read** or **study l.** étudier le droit, faire son droit; **to practise l.** exercer la profession d'avocat; **to go to l.** avoir recours à ou recourir à la justice; **to hand sb over to the l.** remettre qn à la justice; **to be at l.** être en procès; **to take the l. into one's own hands** faire justice soi-même; Fam **the l.** (police) la police; Fam **run! here's the l.!** barre-toi! voilà les flics; Fam **I'll have the l. on you if you don't stop that!** si vous n'arrêtez pas tout de suite, j'appelle les flics; Prov **the long arm of the l.** le bras de la justice
▶▶ **l. costs** frais mpl de procédure; **l. enforcement** application f de la loi; **l. enforcement agency** organisme m chargé de faire respecter la loi; **l. enforcement officer** agent m de police; **l. firm** cabinet m d'avocats, cabinet juridique; Br **l. lord** membre m juriste de la Chambre des Lords; **l. officer** conseiller, -ère juridique; **l. reports** rubrique f juridique (donnant des détails juridiques sur des procès d'un intérêt particulier) ; **l. school** faculté f de droit; **l. student** étudiant, -ante en droit

law-abiding ADJ respectueux des lois, qui observe la loi; **l. people** gens qui respectent les lois

lawbreaker ['lɔːbreɪkər] N transgresseur m de la loi

lawbreaking ['lɔːbreɪkɪŋ] N infraction f à la loi

lawcourt ['lɔːkɔːt] N cour f de justice, tribunal m

lawful ['lɔːfʊl] ADJ (owner, activities) légal, -aux; (right, wife, child etc) légitime; (contract) valide; (claim etc) juste; **to go about one's l. business** vaquer à ses occupations; **l. trade** commerce m licite

lawfully ['lɔːfʊlɪ] ADV légalement, légitimement

lawgiver ['lɔːgɪvər] N Lit législateur m

lawless ['lɔːlɪs] ADJ (country, society) sans loi; (times) d'anarchie; **l. behaviour** comportement débridé

lawlessness ['lɔːlɪsnɪs] N (of times) anarchie f, (of conduct) caractère m débridé; **the town was in a state of utter l.** la ville était plongée dans l'anarchie la plus totale

lawmaker ['lɔːmeɪkər] N législateur m

lawn¹ [lɔːn] N Tex linon m

lawn² N (grass) pelouse f, (parterre m de) gazon m; **do not walk on the l.** ne pas marcher sur la pelouse; **to mow** or **cut the l.** tondre le gazon
▶▶ **l. fertilizer, l. food** engrais m à gazon; **l. sprinkler** arrosoir m de pelouse; (spinning) tourniquet m arroseur; **l. tennis** tennis m sur gazon

lawnmower ['lɔːnməʊər] N tondeuse f (à gazon)

Lawrence of Arabia ['lɒrəns] N Lawrence d'Arabie

lawsuit ['lɔːs(j)uːt] N procès m, action f judiciaire; **to bring a l. against sb** intenter un procès à qn

lawyer ['lɔːjər] N (provides advice, appears in court) avocat, -e; (authenticates documents) notaire m; (in company) conseiller, -ère juridique; **we'll have to see a l.** il nous faudra consulter un avocat

lax [læks] ADJ 1 (conduct, principles) relâché; (person) laxiste; (discipline) lâche; **l. morals** morale laxiste; **to be l. in (carrying out) one's duties** ne pas toujours observer ses devoirs 2 (vague, imprecise) vague; **l. use of the term 'paranoid'** emploi peu précis du mot 'paranoïaque' 3 Med **l. bowels** intestins relâchés

laxative ['læksətɪv] ADJ, N Med laxatif m

laxity ['læksɪtɪ], **laxness** ['læksnɪs] N (of morals, security) relâchement m; (of discipline) laxisme m; **l. in performing one's duties** laxisme dans l'accomplissement de ses devoirs

LAY¹ [leɪ]

VT	coucher 1 ▪ poser 2, 8 ▪ mettre 2
	▪ pondre 4 ▪ miser 5 ▪ soumettre 6
	▪ porter 6 ▪ imposer 7 ▪ tendre 8
	▪ préparer 8
VI	pondre 2

N 1 **l. of the land** configuration f du pays ou du terrain; Fig **to find out the l. of the land** tâter le terrain
2 Sl **she's an easy l.** c'est une fille facile; **he's a good l.** il baise bien
VT (pt, pp laid [leɪd]) 1 (make horizontal) coucher; (of wind, rain) (corn) coucher, abattre; **to l. sb/sth flat** coucher ou étendre qn/qch (par terre); **to l. sb flat** (with punch) terrasser qn, abattre qn; **laid low by sickness** terrassé par la maladie
2 (place) mettre, placer, poser (**sth on sth** qch sur qch); **to l. a book on the table** poser un livre sur la table; **to l. one's hand on sb's shoulder** mettre la main sur l'épaule de qn;

to l. the blame (for sth) on sb faire porter la responsabilité (de qch) à qn; **he laid particular emphasis** *or* **stress on the importance of security** il a particulièrement insisté sur la sécurité; **if you l. a finger on her** si tu touches à un cheveu de sa tête; **to have nowhere to l. one's head** ne pas avoir où reposer la tête; *Fam* **to l. eyes on sb/sth** voir qn/qch; *Fam* **to l. one on sb** en mettre une à qn; **to l. sb to rest** enterrer qn; **to l. sth bare** *(one's feelings, sb's motives)* mettre qch à nu; **to l. oneself open to criticism/the charge that …** s'exposer à la critique/l'accusation selon laquelle …

3 *(cause to subside)* *(dust etc)* fixer; *(ghost)* exorciser, conjurer; **to l. sb's fears to rest** ôter toutes les inquiétudes de qn

4 *(of hen etc)* *(egg)* pondre; *Fig* **he nearly laid an egg** *(in surprise)* il a failli en faire une jaunisse

5 *Sport (bet)* faire; *(sum of money)* parier, miser

6 *esp Fml (present)* *(question, request)* soumettre (**before sb** devant qn); **he laid all the facts before me** il me présenta tous les faits; *Law* **to l. a complaint** déposer une plainte, porter plainte; **to l. a matter before the court** saisir le tribunal d'une affaire; *Law* **to l. information** présenter une information; **to l. claim to sth** prétendre à qch; **the town lays claim to being the place where golf was invented** les gens de cette ville prétendent que c'est ici que le golf fut inventé

7 *(impose)* *(penalty)* imposer (**upon sb** à qn); *(fine etc)* infliger (**on sb** à qn); **to l. a curse on sb/sth** jeter un sort à qn/qch

8 *(dispose, arrange)* *(foundations)* poser, jeter, asseoir; *(bricks)* ranger; *(railway, cable)* poser; *(concrete)* couler; *(carpet)* poser, tendre; *(fire)* préparer; *Naut (mine)* poser, mouiller; *(trap)* dresser, tendre; *(ambush)* tendre; **they laid plans to evacuate the city** ils ont prévu un plan d'évacuation de la ville; **they had laid plans to send their money abroad** ils avaient pris toutes les dispositions nécessaires pour envoyer leur argent à l'étranger; *Br* **to l. the table** *ou* dresser la table; **to l. the table for three** mettre la table pour trois personnes, mettre trois couverts

9 *Sl (have sex with)* **to l. a girl** s'envoyer une fille; **to get laid** s'envoyer en l'air

VI 1 *Sl (incorrectly used for* **lie**) **to l. in bed** rester couché

2 *(of bird)* pondre

3 *Sl* **to l. about one** *(hit out)* frapper de tous côtés

▸▸ *Com* **l. day** jour *m* de planche; **l. days** jours *mpl* de planche, estarie *f*

Attention: ne pas confondre avec le verbe **to lie**, qui signifie **être couché** ou **être posé à plat**.

▸ **lay aside VT SEP** *(prejudices, reservation)* mettre de côté, oublier; *(work, document, money)* mettre de côté; **it's best to have something laid aside for emergencies** il est préférable d'avoir de l'argent de côté en cas de pépins

▸ **lay away VT SEP** *(money etc)* mettre de côté

▸ **lay back VT SEP** *(of horse)* *(ears)* rabattre, coucher

▸ **lay by VT SEP** mettre de côté

▸ **lay down VT SEP 1** *(deposit)* déposer, poser; **to l. down one's arms** rendre *ou* déposer les armes

2 *(place horizontally)* *(person)* coucher, étendre; **to l. oneself down** se coucher

3 *(abandon)* *(one's duties, one's responsibilities for sth)* quitter, se démettre de; **to l. down one's life** sacrifier sa vie, faire le sacrifice de sa vie (**for** pour)

4 *Naut (ship)* mettre en chantier *ou* sur cale

5 *(establish)* *(principle, rule)* poser, imposer, établir; *(conditions)* fixer; *(duties)* spécifier; *(rule of behaviour)* indiquer, prescrire; **to l. down that …** stipuler que …; **to l. down the law** dicter sa loi (**to sb** à qn; **about** sur)

6 *(store)* *(wine)* mettre en cave *ou* sur chantier

VI *Sl* = **lie down**

▸ **lay in VT SEP** faire provision de, s'approvisionner en; **to l. in provisions** faire des provisions; **we've laid in plenty of food for the weekend** nous avons prévu beaucoup de nourriture pour le week-end; *Com* **to l. in goods** *or* **stock** faire provision de marchandises

▸ **lay into VT INSEP** *Fam* **to l. into sb** *(hit)* rosser qn; *(verbally)* passer un savon à qn

▸ **lay off VT SEP 1** *(workers)* licencier; *(temporarily)* mettre en chômage technique

2 *(in insurance)* **to l. off a risk** effectuer une réassurance; *Horseracing etc* **to l. off a bet** faire la contrepartie d'un pari

3 *Sport* **to l. the ball off for sb** placer le ballon en bonne position pour qn

VT INSEP 1 *Fam (abstain from)* s'abstenir de; **to l. off the drink** arrêter de boire; **l. off it, will you!** laisse tomber, tu veux!

2 *Sl* **to l. off sb** *(leave alone)* ficher la paix à qn; **I told her to l. off my husband** je lui ai dit de laisser mon mari tranquille

VI *Sl* **l. off!** *(leave me alone)* fiche-moi la paix!

▸ **lay on VT SEP 1** *Br (install)* *(gas, electricity, water)* installer

2 *Fam (organize)* *(party, entertainment etc)* organiser; **I'll l. on the drinks/food** je m'occuperai de la boisson/la nourriture; **I'll l. on a car for you at the station** j'enverrai une voiture vous chercher à la gare

3 *(apply)* *(coat of plaster etc)* étendre, coucher, appliquer; *Art* **to l. on the paint** peindre dans la pâte *ou* en pleine pâte; *Fam* **to l. it on (thick)** *or* **with a trowel** *(flatter)* flatter grossièrement; *(exaggerate)* exagérer, y aller un peu fort

▸ **lay out VT SEP 1** *(arrange, display)* *(objects)* arranger, disposer; *(merchandise)* étaler, déployer; *(meal)* servir; **to l. out one's reasons** exposer ses raisons

2 *(dead body)* faire la toilette de

3 *Fam (knock down)* *(person)* étendre d'un coup, coucher par terre *ou* sur le carreau; *Boxing* envoyer au tapis

4 **to l. out money** dépenser *ou* débourser de l'argent; **to l. oneself out to help sb** se mettre en quatre pour aider qn; **he's not going to l. himself out** il ne fera pas d'effort, *Fam* il ne va pas se fouler

5 *(plan, design)* *(gardens etc)* tracer; *(physically)* disposer; *Typ (text)* mettre en page

▸ **lay over VI** *Am (during journey)* faire (une) halte

▸ **lay up VT SEP 1** *(store)* mettre en réserve; *(supplies)* accumuler, amasser; **you're laying up a lot of trouble for yourself** tu vas t'attirer beaucoup d'ennuis

2 *(take out of service)* *(ship)* désarmer, déséquiper, mettre en rade; *(car)* mettre sur cales

3 **to be laid up** *(with illness)* être alité, être obligé de garder le lit

lay² **ADJ 1** *(non-clerical)* laïque **2** *(not professional)* profane, non spécialiste; **to the l. mind it seems complicated** aux yeux du profane cela semble compliqué

▸▸ *Rel* **l. brother** frère *m* lai; *Art* **l. figure** mannequin *m*; *Rel* **l. preacher, l. reader** prédicateur *m* laïque; *Rel* **l. sister** sœur *f* converse

lay³ **N** *Arch (song, poem)* lai *m*

lay⁴ **PT** *see* **lie²** **VI**

layabout ['leɪəbaʊt] **N** *Fam* paresseux, -euse

lay-away plan **N** *Am Com* vente *f* réservée *ou* à terme

lay-by **N** *Br (on road)* espace *m* de stationnement *(sur le bas-côté de la route)*; *(on motorway)* aire *f* de stationnement

layer ['leɪər] **N 1** *(of paint, chocolate, clouds, clothes etc)* couche *f*, *(of dung)* lit *m*; *Constr (of cement, bricks etc)* assise *f*, lit; *Geol (of rocks etc)* couche, strate *f*; **the upper layers of the atmosphere** les couches supérieures de l'atmosphère **2** *(hen etc)* **good l.** bonne pondeuse *f* **3** *(of plant)* marcotte *f*

VT 1 poser *ou* disposer en couches; *(hair)* dégrader; **I'd like my hair layered** j'aimerais un dégradé; **a layered cut** une coupe en dégradé **2** *(rosebush etc)* marcotter

▸▸ **l. cake** génoise *f* *(à la crème)*; **l. cut** *(haircut)* coupe *f* en dégradé

layette [leɪ'et] **N** layette *f*

laying ['leɪɪŋ] **N 1** *(of rails, pipes, cables, carpet etc)* pose *f*, *(of foundations)* assise *f*, *(of underwater cable)* immersion *f*, *(of mines)* mouillage *m* **2** *(of eggs)* ponte *f*

▸▸ **l. down** *(of principle, rule etc)* établissement *m*; *(of sewage system, cable)* pose *f*, *(of ship)* mise en chantier *ou* sur cale; *(of arms)* dépôt *m*; **l. hen** poule *f* pondeuse; **l. off** *(of workers)* licenciement *m*; *Rel* **l. on of hands** imposition *f* des mains; **l. out** *(of dead body)* toilette *f*

layman, *pl* **laymen** ['leɪmən] **N 1** *Rel* laïque *m* **2** *Fig* personne *f* non initiée, profane *m*

lay-off **N 1** *Ind (action)* licenciement *m*; *(temporary)* mise *f* en chômage *m* technique **2** *Ftbl* petite passe *f* de côté

▸▸ *Am* **l. pay** indemnité *f* de licenciement

layout ['leɪaʊt] **N 1** *(plan)* *(of building, town)* tracé *m*; *(of gardens)* dessin *m* **2** *(arrangement)* *(of house, building etc)* plan *m*, agencement *m*; *(of piece of machinery)* agencement *ou* disposition *f* des pièces **3** *Typ (of text etc)* mise *f* en page, disposition *f*

▸▸ *Typ* **l. artist** maquettiste *mf*; *Typ* **l. card** *(for pages)* plan de maquette; *Typ* **l. compositor** maquettiste; *Typ* **l. sheet** *(for pages)* maquette *f*, trame *f* de maquette

layover ['leɪəʊvər] **N** *Am* escale *f*

layperson ['leɪpɜːsən] = **layman, laywoman**

laywoman, *pl* **laywomen** ['leɪwʊmən, -wɪmɪn] **N 1** *Rel* laïque *f* **2** *Fig* personne *f* non initiée, profane *f*

Lazarus ['læzərəs] **N** *Bible* Lazare *m*

laze [leɪz] **VI** **to l.** **(about** *or* **around)** paresser, fainéanter; **you've spent the whole morning lazing around** tu as passé la matinée entière à traînasser; **to l. on the beach** faire le lézard sur la plage; **to l. in bed** traînasser au lit, faire la grasse matinée; **to l. away a couple of hours in the sun** passer quelques heures à paresser au soleil

lazily ['leɪzɪlɪ] **ADV** paresseusement

laziness ['leɪzɪnɪs] **N** paresse *f*, fainéantise *f*

lazy ['leɪzɪ] **ADJ 1** *(person)* paresseux, fainéant; **a l. person** un paresseux, une paresseuse; **a l. smile** un sourire nonchalant; **I feel too l. to do it** je n'ai pas l'énergie de le faire; **to have a l. eye** avoir un œil paresseux **2** *(moments)* de paresse; **we spent a l. afternoon in the garden** nous avons passé l'après-midi à paresser dans le jardin; **these l. summer days** ces journées d'été où l'on ne fait rien; **to go for a l. sail around the islands** faire une croisière relax autour des îles

▸▸ **l. Susan** *(on table)* plateau *m* tournant

lazybones ['leɪzɪbəʊnz] **N** *Fam* paresseux, -euse, fainéant, -ante

lb *(abbr* **libra)** livre, lb

LBO [elbiː'əʊ] **N** *Fin (abbr* **leveraged buy-out)** OPA *f* à crédit

L/C N *Com* (*abbr* **letter of credit**) l/c *f*

LCD [elsi:'di:] N *Comput* (*abbr* **liquid crystal display**) affichage *m* à cristaux liquides, LCD *m*
▸ ▸ **L. screen** écran *m* LCD

LCL *Com* (*abbr* **less than container load**) conteneur *m* chargé en partie

LEA [eli:'eɪ] N *Br Admin* (*abbr* **Local Education Authority**) = organisme *m* chargé de l'enseignement au niveau régional

lea [li:] N *Lit* prairie *f*, pâturage *m*

leach [li:tʃ] VT (*liquid*) filtrer; (*ore*) lessiver; **to l. away** *or* **out salts** extraire des sels par lessivage
VI (*of liquid*) filtrer (**through** à travers); **fertilizers have been leaching into the water supply** des engrais ont infiltré la réserve d'eau

LEAD¹ [li:d]

| N tête **1** ▪ exemple **2** ▪ indice **3** ▪ rôle principal **5** ▪ laisse **6** ▪ fil **7** ▪ gros titre **8** ▪ mener **1, 3, 5** ▪ amener **2, 7** ▪ diriger **4** |
| VI mener **1, 2** |

N **1 to take the l., to go** *or* **move into the l.** prendre la tête, prendre la première place; **to take the l. over sb** prendre le pas *ou* les devants sur qn; **to have a l. of 10 metres** avoir une avance de 10 mètres; **she's hanging on to the l.** (*in race*) elle conserve la tête de la course; (*in points table etc*) elle conserve la tête du classement; **she's hanging on to her l.** (*in race*) elle conserve son avance; (*in points table etc*) elle conserve son avance au classement; **he's opened up a tremendous l.** il a pris une avance considérable; **to be in the l.** être en tête; **to lose one's l.** ne plus être en tête; **the company has lost its l. in portables** la société n'est plus le premier producteur de portables
2 (*example*) **to follow sb's l.** suivre l'exemple de qn; **to give a l. (to sb)** donner l'exemple (à qn)
3 (*clue*) indice *m*; **the police have no leads** la police n'a aucune piste; **to give sb a l.** mettre qn sur la voie; **to be following up an important l.** être sur une piste importante
4 *Cards* **to have the l.** jouer le premier; **your l.!** à vous de jouer!; **is it my l.?** c'est mon tour?, c'est à moi de jouer?; **to follow the l.** in clubs fournir à trèfle
5 *Theat, Cin* (*role*) rôle *m* principal; (*actor*) premier rôle masculin; (*actress*) premier rôle féminin; **juvenile l.** jeune premier, jeune première; **to sing the l.** chanter le rôle principal; **to play the l.** jouer le premier rôle
6 (*for dog etc*) laisse *f*; **dogs must be kept on a l.** les chiens doivent être tenus en laisse
7 *Elec* fil *m* électrique, câble *m ou* branchement *m* de canalisation, amenée *f* de courant
8 *Journ* (*main story*) gros titre *m*; **it'll be** *or* **make the l. in tomorrow's papers** ce sera à la une des journaux demain; **the Telegraph has a l. on the Middle East crisis** le Telegraph consacre sa une à la crise au Proche-Orient
VT (*pt, pp* **led** [led]) **1** (*guide*) mener, conduire, guider (**sb to a place** qn à un endroit); (*blind person etc*) conduire, guider par la main; **to l. the conversation round to the subject of ...** amener la conversation sur le sujet de ...; **to l. sb into error** induire qn en erreur; **that leads me to another point I wanted to make** ceci m'amène à un autre point que je voulais soulever; (*horse*) mener par la bride; (*dog*) tenir en laisse; *Prov* **you can l. a horse to water (but you cannot make it drink)** on ne fait pas boire un âne qui n'a pas soif; *Law* **to l. a witness** poser des questions tendancieuses à un témoin; **to l. the way** marcher le premier *ou* en tête;

to l. a team to victory mener une équipe à la victoire; **to l. the conversation back to a subject** ramener la conversation sur un sujet; *Fig* **he is easily led** il est très influençable; **she led them to safety** elle les a conduits en lieu sûr; *Rel* **l. us not into temptation** ne nous soumets pas à la tentation
2 (*cause*) amener, porter (**sb to do sth** qn à faire qch); **that leads me to believe that ...** cela m'amène à croire que ...; **I was led to the conclusion that ...** je fus amené à la conclusion que ...; **what led you to apply for this job?** qu'est-ce qui vous a conduit *ou* amené à postuler?
3 (*happy life, sad life*) mener; **to l. sb a dog's life** faire une vie de chien à qn
4 (*be the leader of*) (*team, government*) diriger; (*army*) commander; **leading his troops** à la tête de ses troupes; **to l. a party** être chef de parti; **to l. an orchestra** diriger un orchestre; **to l. the congregation in prayer** diriger la congrégation à la prière
5 (*be ahead of*) **to l. the field** mener; *Fig* **to l. the field in ...** être au premier rang en matière de ...; **to l. sb by eight points** avoir une avance sur qn de huit points; **she leads the class in maths** elle est la première de sa classe en maths; **we l. the world in ...** nous sommes les leaders mondiaux de ...
6 *Cards* **to l. clubs** jouer trèfle
7 *Tech* (*water to a place*) amener; (*actually install*) installer; (*rope through a pulley*) faire passer
VI **1** (*of road*) mener, conduire (**to** à); **road that leads to the town** route qui mène *ou* va à la ville; **door that leads into the garden** porte qui communique avec le jardin *ou* qui donne accès au jardin; **to l. to a good result** aboutir à un bon résultat, produire un heureux effet; **to l. to a discovery** conduire *ou* aboutir à une découverte; **drinking too much can l. to violence** l'excès d'alcool peut conduire à la violence; **one thing leads to another** une chose en amène une autre; **to l. to nothing** n'aboutir *ou* ne mener à rien; **to l. to a misunderstanding** conduire à un malentendu; **action which led to criticism** action qui a motivé des critiques; **this led to several of them losing their jobs** à cause de cela, plusieurs d'entre eux ont perdu leur emploi
2 (*go first*) (*in competition, race, dance etc*) mener; **you l. and I'll follow** vas-y, je te suis; *Boxing, Cards* ouvrir le jeu, jouer le premier, entamer; **he leads with the left** il est gaucher; **he led with a left** il a donné un coup du gauche; **to l. with** (*of newspaper*) titrer en première page, faire ses gros titres *ou* sa première page sur
3 (*of barrister*) être l'avocat principal; **he led for the prosecution** avocat principal, il dirigea l'accusation
▸ ▸ *Journ* **l. article** article *m* de tête; *Banking, St Exch* **l. manager** chef *m* de file; **l. reins** (*of horse*) grandes guides *fpl*; **l. time** *Ind* délai *m* de préparation; *Com* délai *m* de livraison; *Mktg* **l. user** utilisateur, -trice pilote
▸ **lead away** VT SEP (*prisoner etc*) emmener
▸ **lead back** VT SEP ramener
VI ramener
▸ **lead off** VI **1** (*begin*) commencer, débuter (**with** par); (*in debate*) entamer les débats; (*in game*) jouer le premier; *Billiards* donner l'acquit; (*at dance*) ouvrir le bal
2 several doors/corridors l. off the hall il y a plusieurs portes/couloirs qui donnent dans le hall
VT SEP **1** (*discussion*) amorcer; (*attack*) lancer
2 (*prisoner etc*) emmener
▸ **lead on** VT SEP **to l. sb on to talk (about)** encourager qn à parler (de); **try and l. him on to the subject of football** essaie de l'aiguiller sur le sujet du football *ou Fam* le

brancher sur le football; *Fam* **to l. sb on** (*deceive*) tromper qn, duper qn
VI **l. on!** en avant!
▸ **lead up** VI **l. up to a subject** amener un sujet; **I was just leading up to that** j'allais justement y venir; **I couldn't see what he was leading up to** je ne voyais pas où il voulait en venir; **the chords that l. up to the final movement** les accords qui introduisent le dernier mouvement; **the period leading up to the war** la période précédant la guerre; **there's a path leading up to the ski lift** il y a un chemin qui mène au téléski
VT SEP (*troops, class etc*) faire avancer; **he led us up (a staircase)** il nous a fait monter (un escalier)

lead² [led] N **1** (*metal*) plomb *m*; *Fam* **to go down like a l. balloon** tomber à plat; *Sl* **they pumped him full of l.** ils l'ont truffé *ou* farci de plomb
2 *Br Constr* **roof leads** plombs *mpl* de couverture; **window leads** plombs de vitrail *ou* de vitraux
3 (*for pencil*) mine *f*
4 *Naut* (plomb *m* de) sonde *f*; *Fam* **to swing the l.** tirer au flanc
5 *Fishing* plomb *m*
6 *Typ* réglette *f*
VT (*pt, pp* **leaded** ['ledɪd], *cont* **leading** ['ledɪŋ]) **1** *Constr* (*roof*) plomber; (*windows*) enchâsser dans les plombs
2 *Fishing* (*line, net*) plomber
3 *Typ* (*lines of type*) interligner
▸ ▸ **l. content** (*of fuel*) indice *m* de plomb; **l. crystal** verre *m* de *ou* au plomb; **l. ore** minerai *m* de plomb; **l. paint** peinture *f* à base de plomb; **l. pencil** crayon *m* noir *ou* à papier *ou* à mine de plomb; **l. pipe** tuyau *m* de plomb; **l. poisoning** *Med* intoxication *f* par le plomb, saturnisme *m*; *Am Fam* (*death*) mort *f* par balle(s); (*injury*) blessure *f* par balle(s); **l. shot** grenaille *f* de plomb
▸ **lead out** VT SEP *Typ* (*lines of text*) augmenter l'interlignage de

leaded ['ledɪd] ADJ
▸ ▸ **l. petrol** essence *f* au plomb; **l. window** fenêtre *f* avec verre cathédrale

leaden ['led(ə)n] ADJ (*made of lead*) de plomb; (*complexion*) plombé; **l.-eyed** aux yeux ternes; **l.-footed** à la démarche pesante; **l. limbs** membres inertes; **a l. sky** un ciel de plomb; **the l. calm of the sea** la mer grise et immobile

leader ['li:dər] N **1** (*of expedition, group, organization etc*) chef *m*; *Mil* (*of unit*) commandant *m*; (*of riot*) meneur *m*; *Br Mus* premier violon *m*; *Am Mus* chef *m* d'orchestre; *Br Law* avocat *m* principal; **to be a born l.** être fait pour donner des ordres *ou* commander; *Sport* **team l.** chef d'équipe; **a major group, a l. in its field** un groupe important, un leader dans sa branche
2 (*in race*) **he's still the l.** il mène toujours; **the three leaders** les trois premiers
3 (*in horse team*) cheval *m* de tête; (*in dog team*) chien *m* de tête; **the leaders** l'attelage *m* de devant
4 (*of tape, film*) (bande) amorce *f*
5 *Journ* (*main item*) article *m* principal; (*article*) article de fond; *Br* (*editorial*) éditorial *m*, -aux
6 *Am Com* (*loss leader*) produit *m* d'appel
7 *Mktg* (*product*) numéro un *m* (sur le marché); (*company*) chef *m* de file, leader *m*
▸ ▸ *Br* **L. of the House of Commons** chef de la majorité à la Chambre des Communes; *Br Journ* **l. writer** éditorialiste *mf*

leaderboard ['li:dəbɔːd] N (*in golf*) leaderboard *m*; *Fig* **to be top of the l.** être en tête du classement

leadership ['li:dəʃɪp] N **1** (*qualities shown*) qualités *fpl* de chef; **no one showed any l.**

personne n'a montré des qualités de chef; **the organization lacks l.** l'organisation manque d'un vrai chef; **to be under sb's l.** être sous la conduite de qn **2** *(position) (of party, union etc)* direction *f; (duties as leader)* fonctions *fpl* de chef; *Mil* commandement *m* **3** *(leaders)* dirigeants *mpl*

▸▸ **l. battle, l. contest** bataille *f* pour la direction; *Pol* **l. election** élections *fpl* pour la position de leader; **l. potential** qualités *fpl* de chef

lead-free [led'fri:] ADJ *(petrol, paint)* sans plomb

N *(petrol)* essence *f* sans plomb

lead-in ['li:dɪn] N **1** *(introduction), Mus* introduction *f; Elec, Tel etc (of cable)* entrée *f* **2** *Radio etc (to aerial)* descente *f* d'antenne

▸▸ **l. groove** *(on record)* sillon *m* initial

leading ¹ ['li:dɪŋ] ADJ **1** *(chief)* premier, principal, -aux; **a l. authority in the field** un grand spécialiste du domaine; **the l. statesmen of Europe** les hommes d'État dirigeants de l'Europe; **a l. shareholder** un des principaux actionnaires; **he's one of Britain's l. novelists** c'est l'un des plus grands romanciers contemporains de Grande-Bretagne; **she's a l. light in local politics** c'est une personnalité très influente de la politique locale **2** *(in front) (car)* de tête

N *(of horses etc)* conduite *f,* menage *m*

▸▸ *Journ* **l. article** *Br* éditorial *m; Am* article *m* leader *ou* de tête; **l. axle** *(of vehicle)* essieu *m* porteur d'avant; *Cards* **l. card** première carte *f, Elec* **l. current** courant *m* déphasé en avant; *Aviat* **l. edge** *(of wing)* bord *m* d'attaque; **to be on the l. edge of technology** être à la pointe de la technologie; **l. edge technology** technologie *f* de pointe; *Cin, Theat* **l. lady** premier rôle *m* (féminin); *Cin, Theat* **l. man** premier rôle (masculin); *Cin, Theat* **l. part** premier rôle *m; Mil* **l. patrol** patrouille *f* de tête; **l. question** question *f* orientée; *Law* = question posée au témoin de manière à suggérer la réponse; **l. rein** *(for horse)* longe *f, Br* **l. reins** *(for child)* harnais *m; Cin, Theat* **l. role** premier rôle *m;* **to play a l. role in a matter** jouer un rôle prépondérant dans une affaire; **l. shoot** *(of plant)* pousse *f* principale; *Am* **l. strings** harnais *(pour enfant); Comput* **l. zeroes** zéros *mpl* à gauche

leading ² ['ledɪŋ] N *Typ* interligne *f*

lead-out N *Elec, Tel (of wire etc)* sortie *f*

▸▸ **l. groove** *(of record)* sillon *m* de sortie

lead-up N veille *f;* **in the l. to independence** dans la période qui a précédé l'indépendance

leadwork ['ledwɜːk] N *Archit (of window)* plombs *mpl*

leaf, *pl* **leaves** [li:f, li:vz] N **1** *(of plant, tree)* feuille *f;* **to put out leaves, to come into l.** feuiller; **the trees have already started coming into l.** les arbres commencent déjà à avoir des feuilles; **in l.** couvert de feuilles, en feuilles; **to shake like a l.** trembler comme une feuille

2 *(of book)* feuillet *m;* **single l.** *(in bookbinding)* carton *m* de deux pages; *Fig* **to turn over a new l.** *(of person)* changer de conduite; *Fig* **to take a l. out of sb's book** prendre exemple *ou* modèle sur qn

3 *(of gold, silver etc)* feuille *f*

4 *(of door)* battant *m,* vantail *m, pl* -aux; *(of shutter)* battant; *(of spring)* lame *f,* feuille *f,* feuillet *m; (of table) (inserted)* rallonge *f (de table); (hinged)* battant

▸▸ **l. bud** bourgeon *m* à feuille; **l. green** vert prairie *m inv;* **l. insect** phyllie *f;* **l. mould** terreau *m* de feuilles; **l. tobacco** tabac *m* en feuilles

▸ **leaf through** VT INSEP *(book)* feuilleter

leaflet ['li:flɪt] N *Com etc* prospectus *m; Pol* tract *m;* **instruction l.** mode *m* d'emploi

VT **to l. an area** distribuer des prospectus dans un quartier

▸▸ **l. drop** distribution *f* de prospectus

leafstalk ['li:fstɔːk] N *Bot* pétiole *m*

leafy ['li:fɪ] ADJ *(tree)* feuillu; **a l. lane** *or* **street** une rue bordée d'arbres; **a l. suburb** une banlieue verte; **a l. canopy** un dais de feuillage *ou* de verdure

league ¹ [li:g] N **1** *(association)* ligue *f,* **everyone is in l. against them** tout le monde est ligué contre eux; **to be in l. with sb** être de connivence avec qn; *Fam* être de mèche avec qn **2** *Fig* **I'm not in your l., I'm not in the same l. as you** je ne suis pas de votre niveau; **they're not in the same l.** ils ne sont pas du même niveau; **I thought I was good but he's in another l.** je pensais que j'étais bon mais il est bien meilleur que moi

▸▸ *Sport* **l. champions** champion *m; Sport* **l. leaders** leader *m* du championnat; *Sport* **l. match** match *m* de championnat; *Hist* **the L. of Nations** la Société des Nations; *Br Sport* **l. table** (classement *m* du) championnat *m*

▸ **league together** VI faire alliance (**with** avec); **to l. together against sb/sth** se liguer contre qn/qch

league ² N *Hist (measurement)* lieue *f*

leak [li:k] N **1** *(of liquid, gas, secrets)* fuite *f* **2** *(entry) (of water etc)* infiltration *f,* rentrée *f, Naut* voie *f* d'eau; **to spring a l.** *(of ship)* faire eau, avoir une voie d'eau; *(of shoes)* prendre l'eau **3** *Sl* **to take** *or* **have a l.** *(urinate)* pisser un coup

VI **1** *(of tank etc)* avoir une fuite, fuir; *(of ship etc)* faire eau, avoir une voie d'eau; **roof that leaks** toit qui laisse entrer la pluie; **my shoes l.** mes chaussures prennent l'eau **2** *(of liquid)* fuir, couler; *(of gas)* fuir; *(of truth, news etc)* s'ébruiter, transpirer

VT **1** **the bucket/pipe was leaking water** l'eau coulait du seau/du tuyau; **the pipe had been leaking gas** le tuyau de gaz avait une fuite; **the radiator had been leaking water everywhere** le radiateur avait fui et il y avait de l'eau partout **2** *Fam (information etc)* divulguer

▸ **leak out** VI *(of water, gas etc)* fuir; *Fig (of truth, information etc)* filtrer; **the acid was leaking out of the battery** de l'acide fuyait de la batterie

leakage ['li:kɪdʒ] N **1** *(of water, gas, official secrets)* fuites *fpl* **2** *(loss of stock) (in a business)* coulage *m*

leaky ['li:kɪ] ADJ *(barrel)* qui coule, qui fuit; *(boat)* qui fait eau; *(shoes)* qui prennent l'eau; *(tap, roof)* qui fuit; *Fig Fam* **this department is very l.** il y a plein de fuites dans ce service

lean ¹ [li:n] ADJ **1** *(person, dog)* svelte; *(face)* mince; *(too thin) (animal)* efflanqué; *Fig* **the company is now fitter and leaner than it was before** l'entreprise se porte mieux depuis que sa structure a été allégée

2 *(meat)* maigre

3 **a l. year/period** une année/une période de vaches maigres; **we had a l. time** nous avons eu une période de vaches maigres; **a l. harvest** une mauvaise *ou* maigre récolte

4 *(fuel, mixture)* pauvre

N *(on meat)* maigre *m*

lean ² N *(inclined position)* inclinaison *f*

VI *(pt, pp* **leaned** [li:nd] *or* **leant** [lent]) *(of person)* s'appuyer (**against** contre, à; **on** sur, à); **to l. on one's elbow(s)** s'accouder; **leaning against a wall** appuyé à *ou* contre un mur; **to l. back in one's chair** s'appuyer contre le dossier de sa chaise; *Fig* **to l. on sb** *(for support)* se reposer sur qn; *Fam (to pay money etc)* faire pression sur qn; **she still leans on her father for advice** elle a toujours recours aux conseils de son père; **to l. forward/out of the window** se pencher en

avant/à la fenêtre; **to l. over/towards sth** se pencher sur/vers qch; **that wall is leaning towards the right** ce mur penche vers la droite; **to l. towards a theory** être plutôt partisan d'une théorie; **I think I'm leaning towards the opinion that you were right after all** je commence à penser qu'en fin de compte tu avais raison; **to l. towards socialism** pencher vers le socialisme; *Fam* **to l. over backwards to do sth** se mettre en quatre pour faire qch

VT *(ladder etc)* appuyer (**against** contre); **to l. sth against sth** adosser qch à *ou* contre qch

lean-burn engine N moteur *m* Lean Burn

leaning ['li:nɪŋ] ADJ penché; *(wall)* qui penche

N *(tendency)* inclination *f* (**towards** pour), penchant *m* (**towards** pour, vers), tendance *f* (**towards** à); **to have leanings towards communism** être de tendance communiste, pencher vers le communisme; **to have artistic leanings** avoir des dispositions artistiques

▸▸ **the L. Tower of Pisa** la tour de Pise

leanness ['li:nnɪs] N maigreur *f*

leant PT, PP *see* **lean** ² VI, VT

lean-to N appentis *m*

▸▸ **l. garage** = garage *m* attenant à la maison, avec un toit incliné; **l. roof** comble *m* en appentis

leap [li:p] N *(jump)* saut *m,* bond *m; Fig* **to take a l. in the dark** faire un saut dans l'inconnu; **a l. of faith** un acte de foi; **his heart gave a l.** son cœur bondit, son cœur fit un bond; *Fig* **to advance by leaps and bounds** avancer à pas de géant; **his French had improved by leaps and bounds** il avait fait des progrès phénoménaux en français; **with one l. she cleared the ditch** d'un saut *ou* d'un bond elle franchit le fossé; **the company has taken a great l. forward** la société a fait un grand bond en avant

VI *(pt, pp* **leaped** [li:pt] *or* **leapt** [lept]) **1** sauter, bondir; **to l. to one's feet** se lever brusquement; **to l. over a ditch** sauter un fossé; **to l. at the opportunity** sauter sur l'occasion; **to l. for joy** sauter *ou* bondir de joie; **her heart leapt for joy** elle bondit de joie; **she nearly leapt out of her skin** elle a sauté au plafond **2** *(of flame etc)* jaillir

VT **1** *(ditch)* sauter, franchir d'un saut **2** *(cause to leap)* **to l. a horse over a ditch** faire sauter *ou* faire franchir un fossé à un cheval

▸▸ **l. day** jour *m* intercalaire; **l. year** année *f* bissextile

▸ **leap up** VI **1** *(of person)* bondir (**to do** pour faire); *(get to one's feet)* se lever brusquement; **their dog leapt up at me** leur chien m'a sauté dessus **2** *(of flame)* jaillir

leapfrog ['li:pfrɒg] N **to play l.** jouer à saute-mouton

VT (-gg-) **1** **to l. sth** sauter par-dessus qch à saute-mouton **2** *Fig (stage in process)* sauter; **he leapfrogged several of his more senior colleagues to get the post** il a obtenu le poste en passant devant plusieurs de ses collègues d'un échelon supérieur

leapt PT, PP *see* **leap** VI, VT

learn [lɜːn] *(pt, pp* **learnt** [lɜːnt], *occ* **learned** [lɜːnd]) VT **1** *(French, maths etc)* apprendre; **to l. to read/drive** apprendre à lire/conduire; **she's learning the violin** elle étudie le violon, elle apprend à jouer du violon; *Fig* **he has learnt his lesson** ça lui servira de leçon; **when will she l. her lesson?** quand est-ce qu'elle comprendra? **2** *(hear about) (news, test results etc)* apprendre; **we are sorry to l. that …** nous sommes désolés d'apprendre que … **3** *Arch, Sl (teach)* **to l. sb sth** apprendre qch à qn; *Sl* **that'll l. him!** ça lui apprendra!

VI apprendre; **they're learning about Victorian times** ils étudient l'époque Victorienne;

to **l. from one's mistakes** tirer un enseigne-ment de ses erreurs; **it is never too late to l.** on apprend à tout âge
▸ **learn of** vt insep apprendre

learned ['lɜːnɪd] ADJ *(person)* savant, éru-dit; *(style)* savant; *Law* **my l. friend** mon émi-nent confrère; **l. journal** journal savant; **l. profession** profession f intellectuelle; **l. treatise** traité savant

learner ['lɜːnər] N **1** apprenant, -ante; **lear-ners of English** les apprenants d'anglais, les gens qui apprennent l'anglais; **advanced l.** personne f d'un bon niveau; **intermediate l.** personne d'un niveau intermédiaire; **to be a quick/good l.** apprendre vite/facilement; **she's a slow/bad l.** elle n'apprend pas vite/facilement **2** *(beginner)* élève mf, débutant, -ante; *Aut (driver)* apprenti m conducteur
▸▸ *Aut* **l. driver** apprenti conducteur

learning ['lɜːnɪŋ] N **1** *(act of learning)* ap-prentissage m; *Am* **to be l. disabled** avoir des difficultés scolaires **2** *(knowledge)* ins-truction f, savoir m, connaissances fpl; **seat** or **centre of l.** centre m intellectuel; **a man of great l.** un homme de grand savoir
▸▸ **l. capacity** capacités fpl d'apprentis-sage; **l. curve** courbe f d'assimilation; **l. dis-ability** difficultés fpl d'apprentissage

learnt PT, PP *see* **learn**

lease [liːs] N *Law* bail m, pl baux; *(of equip-ment)* location f, *(of house to let)* bail (à loyer); *(of farming land)* bail à ferme; *(docu-ment)* (contrat m de) bail; **to sign a l.** signer un bail; **long l.** bail à long terme ou à longue échéance; **to take on a new l., to renew the l. of a house** renouveler le bail d'une mai-son; *Fig* **to take on a new l. of life** *(of person)* renaître à la vie; *(of industry, town, football club)* retrouver un nouveau souffle; **meeting Sarah has given him a new l. of life** sa ren-contre avec Sarah lui a redonné goût à la vie; **it's like a new l. of life** on se sent renaî-tre; **cleaning the engine will give the car a new l. of life** ça va retaper la voiture de net-toyer le moteur
vt **1** *(of owner)* **to l. (out)** *(house)* louer, don-ner à bail; *(land)* affermer **2** *(of tenant)* *(house)* louer, prendre à bail; *(of person)* *(equipment, vehicle)* louer; *(land)* affermer
▸▸ **l. charges** charges fpl locatives; **l. contract** *(for property)* contrat de bail; *(for equipment)* contrat en location; *Fin* **l. finan-cing** leasing m, location avec option d'achat; *Acct* **l. revenue** loyers mpl
▸ **lease back** vt sep louer dans le cadre d'une cession-bail

leaseback ['liːsbæk] N cession-bail f

leased line [liːst] N *Comput* ligne f louée

leasehold ['liːshəʊld] N **1** tenure f à bail *(en particulier tenure en vertu d'un bail emphy-téotique)* **2** *(property)* propriété f ou im-meuble m loué(e) à bail
ADJ tenu à bail

leaseholder ['liːshəʊldər] N locataire mf

lease-purchase N crédit-bail m
▸▸ **l. contract** contrat m de crédit-bail

leash [liːʃ] N laisse f; **to put a dog on the l.** mettre une laisse à un chien; *Fig* **to keep sb on a tight l.** tenir la bride haute à qn; **to keep one's emotions on a tight l.** avoir étroite-ment en mains les rênes de ses émotions

leasing ['liːsɪŋ] N *(of house)* location f à bail; *(of land)* affermage m; *Ind, Com (of equip-ment etc)* location; *(on lease-purchase)* loca-tion-bail f, *(system)* location avec option d'achat, LOA f, crédit-bail m

LEAST [liːst]

ADJ	le moindre ▪ le moins de
N	le moins **1** ▪ au moins **2**
ADV	le moins

ADJ *(smallest)* **(the) l.** (le ou la) moindre, (le ou la) plus petit(e); **to get upset at the l. thing** se fâcher pour un rien; **the govern-ment clamps down on the l. sign of opposi-tion** le gouvernement serre la vis au moindre signe d'opposition; **the l. mention of religion was absolutely forbidden** la moindre référence à la religion était inter-dite; **I'm not the l. bit musical** je ne suis pas musicien pour un sou; **I'm not the l. bit tired** je ne suis pas du tout fatigué; **she has the l. money out of all of us** c'est elle qui a le moins d'argent d'entre nous tous

N **1 (the) l.** (le) moins; **to say the l. (of it)** le moins qu'on puisse dire; **she was not very polite, to say the l.** le moins qu'on puisse dire, c'est qu'elle n'a pas été très polie; **it's the l. I can do** c'est la moindre des choses; **that's the l. of my worries** c'est le dernier de mes soucis

2 at l. *(tout)* au moins; **at l. as old/expensive as …** au moins aussi vieux/cher que …; **I can at l. try** je peux toujours essayer; **it cost at l. £1,000** cela lui a coûté 1 000 livres au bas mot; **she's at l. seventy** elle a au moins soixante-dix ans; **at the very l. they should pay your expenses** ce serait vraiment la moindre des choses qu'ils remboursent tes dépenses

3 not in the l. pas du tout, *Fml* aucunement, nullement; **it doesn't matter in the l.** cela n'a pas la moindre importance; **I'm not in the l. upset** je ne suis fâché en aucune manière
ADV **(the) l.** (le) moins; **the l. unhappy** le moins malheureux; **he deserves it l. of all** il le mérite moins que personne; **we didn't ex-pect to win any prizes, l. of all this one** nous ne nous attendions pas à gagner un prix, et en tout cas, certainement pas celui-là; **it al-ways happens when you are l. expecting it** ça arrive toujours au moment où tu t'y at-tends le moins

leastways, *Am* **leastwise** ['liːstweɪz, -waɪz] ADV *Fam* ou (tout) du moins …

leather ['leðər] N **1** cuir m; **l. shoes** chaussu-res fpl en cuir; **fancy l. goods** maroquinerie f **2** *Br Fam (clothes)* **leathers** cuir m **3** *(of pump, valve etc)* cuir m; **stirrup l.** étrivière f
vt *Fam (person)* tanner le cuir à

leather-bound ADJ *(book)* relié (en) cuir

leathercloth ['leðəklɒθ] N toile f cuir

Leatherette® ['leðə'ret] N *Old-fashioned* si-milicuir m

leathering ['leðərɪŋ] N *Fam* **to give sb a l.** tanner le cuir à qn

leatherjacket ['leðədʒækɪt] N *Entom* larve f de la tipule

leatherneck ['leðənek] N *Am Fam* soldat m de l'infanterie de marine

leatherwork ['leðəwɜːk] N **1** *(activity)* tra-vail m du cuir **2** *(products)* articles mpl de cuir; **fancy l.** maroquinerie f

leathery ['leðərɪ] ADJ *(skin)* tanné; *(food)* coriace

LEAVE [liːv]

N	permission **1** ▪ congé **2, 3**
VT	quitter **1** ▪ laisser **2–4** ▪ oublier **2**
	▪ léguer **4**

N **1** *(permission)* permission f, autorisation f; **to ask l. to do sth** demander la permission de faire qch; **to grant** or **give sb l. to do sth** donner ou accorder à qn la permission de faire qch; *Arch, Fml* **by** or **with your l.** avec votre permission; **without so much as a by your l.** sans même en demander la permission **2** *Admin, Mil etc (holiday)* congé m; *(in civil service etc)* congé exceptionnel; **to be on l.** être en congé; **to take two weeks' l.** prendre deux semaines de congé

3 *(farewell)* adieux mpl, congé m; **to take one's l.** prendre congé; **to take (one's) l. of sb** faire ses adieux à qn; **to take l. of one's senses** perdre l'esprit
VT *(pt, pp* **left** [left]*)* **1** *(depart from)* *(place, person)* quitter; *(room)* quitter, sortir de; **he has left London** il est parti de Londres, il a quitté Londres; **he left Oxford without finishing his studies** il a quitté Oxford sans avoir terminé ses études; **she left school at 16** elle a quitté l'école à 16 ans; **she never leaves the house** elle ne sort jamais de la maison; *Sch* **may I l. the room?** puis-je sor-tir?; **his eyes never left her** il ne la quittait pas des yeux; **to l. the table** se lever de table; **to l. one's job** quitter son emploi; *Mil etc* **to l. the service** quitter le service; *Naut* **to l. harbour** sortir du port; **to l. one's wife** quitter sa femme; **to be left behind** or **stand-ing** être dépassé ou distancé (par ses concurrents); **to l. the rails** *(of train)* dérail-ler; **the car left the road** la voiture a quitté la route

2 *(put, deposit)* **to l. sth somewhere** *(delib-erately)* laisser qch quelque part; *(by mis-take)* oublier ou laisser qch quelque part; **to l. things (lying) about** laisser traîner des choses; *Fam* **take it or l. it** c'est à prendre ou à laisser; **to l. a message for sb** laisser un mot ou un message ou un billet pour qn

3 *(allow to remain)* laisser; **to l. the door open** laisser la porte ouverte; **to l. sth unfi-nished** laisser qch inachevé; **he left his sup-per untouched** il ne toucha pas à son dîner; **to l. a page blank** laisser une page en blanc; **l. me alone!** laissez-moi tranquille!; **left to oneself** livré à soi-même; **his work/attitude leaves much to be desired** son travail/atti-tude laisse beaucoup à désirer; **it leaves me cold** ça me laisse froid; **nothing was left to chance** on avait paré à toutes les éventuali-tés; **to l. hold** or **go of sth** lâcher qch; **to l. sb for dead** laisser qn pour mort; *Fig (in race etc)* clouer qn sur place; **to l. sb to do sth** laisser qn faire qch, laisser à qn le soin de faire qch; **to l. sb in charge of sth** confier la responsabilité de qch à qn; **he was left in charge of cooking the food** c'est lui qui s'est occupé de faire à manger; **let's l. it at that, we'll l. it at that** *(not do any more work)* arrêtons-nous là; *(not argue any more)* n'en parlons plus; **to l. sth with sb** confier qch à qn; *Fig* **I'll l. it with you** *(let you make deci-sion etc)* je te laisse t'en occuper; **l. it with me** laisse-moi m'en occuper; **I'll l. it to you** je m'en remets à vous; **l l. it to you to decide** je vous laisse le soin de décider; **l. it to me** laisse-moi faire, je m'en occupe

4 *(after dying)* **to l. a wife and three chil-dren** laisser une femme et trois enfants; **to l. one's money to sb** laisser ou léguer sa for-tune à qn; **she had been left a widow at thir-ty** elle s'était retrouvée veuve à l'âge de trente ans

5 to be left *(remain)* rester; **there are no strawberries left** il ne reste plus de fraises; **how many are there left?** combien est-ce qu'il en reste?

6 *Math* **three from seven leaves four** sept moins trois égale quatre
VI partir; **we l. tomorrow** nous partons de-main; **we are leaving for Paris** nous partons pour Paris; **I was just leaving when …** j'étais sur le point de partir lorsque …
▸▸ **l. of absence** congé (exceptionnel); *(without pay)* congé sans solde; *Mil* permis-sion exceptionnelle
▸ **leave behind** vt sep **1** *(forget)* *(one's hat etc)* oublier

2 *(leave in a place)* laisser; **he left his family behind in Manchester and …** il a laissé sa famille à Manchester et …; **they left me be-hind** ils sont partis sans moi

3 *(in race etc)* **he's left the other runners**

(well) behind il a pris beaucoup d'avance sur les autres concurrents, *Fam* il a largué tous les autres concurrents; **she left the other pupils behind** elle est passée première devant tous les autres élèves
► **leave in** VT SEP *(section of text etc)* inclure, retenir
► **leave off** VT INSEP *Fam* **to l. off doing sth** cesser de faire qch; **to l. off work** cesser le travail; **why can't you l. off the subject for a day?** et si tu arrêtais de parler de ça pendant une journée?; *Fam* **l. off pestering me!** arrête de m'embêter!
VT SEP **1** *(not replace) (lid etc)* ne pas (re)mettre; **to l. sb off a list** *(accidentally)* oublier qn dans une liste; *(deliberately)* exclure qn d'une liste
2 l. the light off n'allume pas; **l. the telly off for a bit** éteins la télé un petit moment; **I left the heating off** je n'ai pas mis le chauffage
VI s'arrêter; **where did we l. off?** *(in reading etc)* où en sommes-nous restés?; *Sl* **l. off!** ça suffit comme ça!, arrête!
► **leave on** VT SEP *(coat, gloves etc)* garder; **to l. the light/TV on** laisser la lumière/la télé allumée
► **leave out** VT SEP **1** *(omit) (a line etc)* omettre **2** *(not involve)* **l. her out of this!** laissez-la en dehors de ça!; **to l. sb out of one's plans** exclure qn de ses projets; **to feel left out** se sentir de trop
3 *(leave ready, available)* **I'll l. your dinner out on the table for you** je te laisse ton dîner sur la table; **l. the disks out where I can see them** laisse les disquettes en évidence
4 *(not put away)* **we l. the car out on the street** nous laissons la voiture dehors dans la rue; **who left the milk out overnight?** qui a oublié de mettre le lait au frigo hier soir?
5 *Sl* **l. it out!** *(stop it)* arrête!
► **leave over** VT SEP **1 what's left over?** qu'est-ce qui reste?; **you can keep what is left over** vous pouvez garder le surplus
2 *(postpone)* remettre à plus tard

leaved [li:vd] ADJ feuillé, feuillu
-leaved [li:vd] SUFF **three-l.** *(screen etc)* à trois panneaux; **broad-l. tree** arbre à larges feuilles; **ivy-l.** à feuilles de lierre
leaven ['lev(ə)n] N *Culin, Fig* levain *m*
VT *(bread, dough)* faire lever; *Fig* **her account is leavened with interesting anecdotes** elle a agrémenté son récit d'anecdotes intéressantes
leavening ['levənɪŋ] N = **leaven**
leaver ['li:vər] N *(school)* **leavers** élèves *mpl* sortants
leave-taking N adieux *mpl*
leaving ['li:vɪŋ] N départ *m*
leavings ['li:vɪŋz] NPL *(from meal)* restes *mpl*
Lebanese [lebə'ni:z] ADJ libanais
N Libanais, -aise
Lebanon ['lebənən] N Liban *m*
► **lech after** [letʃ] VT INSEP *Fam* reluquer
lecher ['letʃər] N débauché *m*, *Fam* coureur *m* de jupons
lecherous ['letʃərəs] ADJ *(person)* lubrique, débauché; *(look, smile)* lubrique
lecherously ['letʃərəslɪ] ADV lubriquement
lechery ['letʃərɪ] N lubricité *f*
lecithin ['lesɪθɪn] N lécithine *f*
lectern ['lektən] N *(in church etc)* lutrin *m*; *(in library)* pupitre *m*
lector ['lektɔ:r] N *Univ (for foreign languages)* lecteur, -trice
lecture ['lektʃər] N **1** conférence *f*, *Univ* cours *m* magistral (**on** sur); **to give/attend a l.** *(public)* donner/assister à une conférence; *(university)* donner/assister à un cours magistral; **history l.** cours *m* d'his-

toire; **l. on Napoleon** cours sur Napoléon **2** *Fam (reprimand)* sermon *m*, semonce *f*; **to give or read sb a l.** faire la morale à qn; *(for wrongdoing)* semoncer qn, sermonner qn
VI donner une conférence *ou* des conférences; *Univ* donner un cours magistral (**on** sur); **he lectured on Eastern affairs** il a donné une conférence sur l'Orient; **she lectures in Economics** elle donne des cours d'économie à l'université, elle est maître-assistant en économie; **he lectures at Stirling** il est maître-assistant à l'université de Stirling
VT *(person)* faire la morale à; *(for wrongdoing)* sermonner, semoncer
►► **l. hall, l. theatre** salle *f* de cours, amphithéâtre *m*

> Note that the French word **lecture** is a false friend and is never a translation for the English word **lecture**. It means **reading**.

lecturer ['lektʃərər] N **1** conférencier, -ière **2** *Univ* **(junior** *or* **assistant) l.** ≃ maître-assistant *m*; **(senior) l.** ≃ maître *m* de conférences; **to be a maths l.** être assistant *m* en maths; **is she a good l.?** est-ce qu'elle est bon professeur?
lectureship ['lektʃəʃɪp] N *Univ* poste *m* de maître-assistant; **she got a l.** elle a été nommée maître-assistante
LED [eli:'di:] N *Comput (abbr* **light-emitting diode)** DEL *f* LED *f*
►► **L. display** affichage *m* (par) LED
led PT, PP *see* **lead**[1] VT, VI
ledge [ledʒ] N **1** rebord *m*, saillie *f*, *(on wall, building)* corniche *f* **2** *Geol* **l. of rock** plateforme *f* rocheuse; *(awash or under water)* banc *m* de rochers
ledger ['ledʒər] N *(in bookkeeping)* grand livre *m*
►► *Mus* **l. line** ligne *f* supplémentaire *(à la portée)*
lee [li:] N **1** *Naut (side)* côté *m* sous le vent **2** *(shelter)* **in** *or* **under the l. of a rock** abrité par un rocher
►► **l. shore** terre *f* sous le vent
leeboard ['li:bɔ:d] N *Naut* aile *f ou* semelle *f* de dérive
leech [li:tʃ] N **1** *(animal)* sangsue *f* **2** *Fam Pej (person)* sangsue *f*, crampon *m*; **to cling or stick to sb like a l.** se cramponner à qn comme une sangsue
► **leech onto** VT INSEP *Fam* se cramponner à
leek [li:k] N *(vegetable)* poireau *m*
leer [lɪər] N *(sexual)* regard *m* lubrique; *(cruel)* regard sadique
VI **to l. at sb** *(sexually)* regarder *ou Fam* reluquer qn d'un air lubrique; *(cruelly)* regarder qn d'un air sadique
leering ['lɪərɪŋ] ADJ *(sexual)* concupiscent, lubrique; *(cruel)* sadique
leery ['lɪərɪ] ADJ *Fam* **to be l. of sb/sth** se méfier de qn/qch; **why are you so l. of showing your emotions?** pourquoi as-tu si peur de montrer tes émotions?
lees [li:z] NPL *(in wine)* lie *f*
leeward ['li:wəd] *Naut* ADJ, ADV sous le vent
N côté *m* sous le vent; **to pass to l. of a ship** passer sous le vent d'un navire
►► **L. Islands** *(in South Pacific or West Indies)* les îles *fpl* sous le Vent
leeway ['li:weɪ] N **1** *(freedom)* liberté *f* d'action; *(safety margin)* marge *f* de sécurité **2** *Naut* dérive *f*; **to make l.** dériver (à la voile); *Fig Fam* **he has a lot of l. to make up** il a un fort retard à rattraper
left[1] [left] ADJ gauche; **on my l. hand** à ma gauche; *Fam* **to have two l. feet** s'emmêler les pinceaux; *esp Am Fam* **to be way out in**

l. field être complètement excentrique; *esp Am Fam* **to come out of l. field** surgir de l'ombre
ADV *(to turn etc)* à gauche; *Typ* **l. justified** justifié à gauche; *Mil* **l. turn!** à gauche, gauche!; **eyes l.!** tête (à) gauche!
N gauche *f*, *Boxing* gauche *m*; **on the l., to the l.** à gauche; *Aut etc* **to keep (to the) l.** tenir la gauche; *Pol* **the L.** la gauche
►► *Comput* **l. arrow** flèche *f* vers la gauche; *Comput* **l. arrow key** touche *f* de déplacement vers la gauche; **l. margin** marge *f* de gauche; *TV, Cin* **l. pan** panoramique *m* horizontal DG; **l. wing** *Pol, Mil* gauche *f*; *Sport (position)* aile *f* gauche; *(player)* ailier *m* gauche; *Sport* **to play on the l. wing** être ailier gauche
left[2] PT, PP *see* **leave** VT, VI
►► *Br* **l. luggage** *(cases)* bagages *mpl* en consigne; *(office)* consigne *f*, **l. luggage lockers** consigne automatique; **l. luggage office** consigne
left-click *Comput* VT cliquer avec le bouton gauche de la souris sur
VI cliquer avec le bouton gauche de la souris (**on** sur)
left-hand ADJ **1** *(pocket, margin etc)* de gauche; **on the l. side** à gauche; **l. turn** virage *m* à gauche **2** *Tech (lock, screw, drill)* à gauche
►► *Aut* **l. drive** conduite *f* à gauche; **to have l. drive** avoir le volant à gauche; *Tech* **l. thread** filetage *m* à gauche
left-handed ['left'hændɪd] ADJ **1** *(person)* gaucher, -ère; *(golf club etc)* pour gaucher; **l. blow** coup *m* de la main gauche **2** *Tech* = **left-hand 2**
ADV **to play tennis l.** jouer au tennis de la main gauche
►► *Fam* **l. compliment** compliment *m* peu flatteur
left-hander ['left'hændər] N *(person)* gaucher, -ère; *Boxing* coup *m* du gauche
leftie ['leftɪ] N *Pol Fam* gauchiste *mf*
leftist ['leftɪst] *Pol* N gauchiste *mf*
ADJ gauchiste; *(person)* de gauche
leftover ['leftəʊvər] ADJ **there was some l. chicken** il restait du poulet; **I made a curry with the l. chicken** j'ai fait un curry avec le reste du poulet; **you could use the l. paint/ wallpaper** tu pourrais utiliser la peinture/le papier peint qu'il reste
N **1** *Com, Culin* **leftovers** restes *mpl* **2** *(from the past)* survivance *f* (**from** de)
►► *Com* **l. stock** restes *mpl*
left-wing ADJ *Pol* de gauche; **they are very l.** ils sont très à gauche; **he has slightly l. ideas** il a des idées gauchisantes
left-winger N **1** *Pol (in party, union)* homme/femme de gauche; *(in Parliament)* député *m* de la gauche; **the left-wingers** la gauche **2** *Sport* ailier *m* gauche
leg [leg] N **1** *(of person, horse)* jambe *f*, *(of dog, bird, insect, reptile)* patte *f*, **wooden l.** jambe de bois; *Fig* **you don't have a l. to stand on** vos arguments ne tiennent pas debout; **you won't have a l. to stand on if they find this letter** s'ils trouvent cette lettre, vous êtes fichu; *Fig* **to be on one's last legs** *(to be tired)* ne plus pouvoir mettre un pied devant l'autre; *(to be dying)* avoir un pied dans la tombe; **the business is on its last legs** la société est au bord de la faillite *ou* mal en point; **after 10 miles we were on our last legs** après 10 mil(l)es nous n'en pouvions plus; **the government is on its last legs** le gouvernement est mal en point; **the car/ TV is on its last legs** la voiture/la télé a fait son temps; *Fam* **to have legs** *(last a long time) (of rumour, theory)* avoir la vie dure; *(of film, play)* qui marche beaucoup mieux que prévu; **to give sb a l. up** *(over a wall, fence etc)* faire la courte échelle à qn; *(into*

the saddle) aider qn à monter en selle; *Fam (in job etc)* donner un coup de pouce à qn; *Fam* **to pull sb's l.** faire marcher qn; *Fam* **show** *or* **shake a l.!** *(it's time to get up)* debout!; *Sl* **to get one's l. over** *(have sex)* s'envoyer en l'air

2 *Culin (of chicken)* cuisse *f*, *(of veal)* cuisseau *m*; **roast l. of pork** cuissot *m* de porc rôti; **l. of lamb** gigot *m*; **frogs' legs** cuisses de grenouille

3 *(of trousers)* jambe *f*, *(of stocking etc)* tige *f*; **these trousers are a bit short in the l.** ce pantalon est un peu court au niveau des jambes

4 *(of table, chair)* pied *m*; *(of tripod etc)* jambe *f*, *(of trestle)* montant *m*

5 *Cr (when the batsman is right-handed)* côté *m* gauche du terrain; *(when the batsman is left-handed)* côté droit du terrain

6 *(of journey, race)* étape *f*, *(in relay race)* relais *m*

vt (-gg-) *Fam* **to l. it** *(walk)* faire la route à pied; *(hurry)* marcher *ou* courir vite
▶▶ *Med* **l. iron** appareil *m* orthopédique; **l. rest** appui-jambes *m inv*; *Med* étrier *m*; *Fam* **l. show** revue *f* légère; *Cr* **l. side** *(when the batsman is right-handed)* côté *m* gauche du terrain; *(when the batsman is left-handed)* côté droit du terrain

legacy ['legəsɪ] **N** *Law* legs *m*; **to come into a l.** faire un héritage; **to leave sb a l.** laisser un héritage *ou* quelque chose en héritage à qn; *Fig* **this desk is a l. from my predecessor** j'ai hérité ce bureau de mon prédécesseur; **the l. of the war was a divided Europe** l'héritage de la guerre fut une Europe divisée; **the crisis left a l. of bitterness** la crise a créé un climat d'amertume

legal ['li:g(ə)l] **ADJ 1** *(lawful)* légal, -aux; *(commerce)* licite; **to be l. currency** *or* **tender** avoir cours (légal)

2 *(error)* judiciaire; *(mind, affairs)* juridique; **by l. process** par voies légales, par voies de droit; **to go into the l. profession** faire une carrière juridique; **to take l. advice** ≃ consulter un avocat; **to have a l. claim to sth** avoir légalement droit à qch

3 *Comput (character etc)* autorisé

4 *Am (paper format)* légal, -aux
▶▶ **l. action** action *f* en justice; **to take l. action against sb** intenter une action contre qn; **l. adviser** conseil *m* juridique; **l. aid** aide *f* juridique; **l. charges** frais *mpl* judiciaires; **l. department** *(in bank, company)* (service *m* du) contentieux *m*; **l. dispute** litige *m*; **l. document** acte *m* authentique; **l. entity** personne *f* morale; **l. expert** expert *m* juridique, avocat *m* conseil; *Am* **l. holiday** jour *m* férié, fête *f* légale; **l. limit** *(of alcohol)* taux *m* d'alcoolémie autorisé; **l. manager** responsable *mf* juridique; **l. owner** propriétaire *mf* légitime; *Am* **l. pad** bloc-notes *m*, *pl* blocs-notes; **l. proceedings** poursuites *fpl* judiciaires; **to initiate l. proceedings against sb** engager des poursuites judiciaires contre qn; **l. recourse** recours *m* contentieux; **l. redress** recours *m* à la justice; **l. reserve** réserve *f* légale; **l. security** caution *f* judiciaire; **l. separation** séparation *f* de corps; **l. status** statut *m* légal, statut juridique; **l. technicality** vice *m* de forme; **l. year** année *f* civile

legalese [li:gə'li:z] **N** *Fam* jargon *m* juridique

legalism ['li:gəlɪz(ə)m] **N** légalisme *m*

legalistic [li:gə'lɪstɪk] **ADJ** formaliste

legality [lɪ'gælɪtɪ] **N** légalité *f*

legalization [li:gəlaɪ'zeɪʃən] **N** légalisation *f*

legalize ['li:gəlaɪz] **VT** *(drug, document)* légaliser; *(deed)* rendre légal, autoriser

legally ['li:gəlɪ] **ADV** légalement; **l. respon-**

sible responsable en droit; **l. binding contract** contrat qui engage les personnes devant la loi

legate ['legɪt] **N** *Rel, Antiq* légat *m*

legatee [legə'ti:] **N** légataire *mf*

legation [lɪ'geɪʃən] **N** légation *f*

legato [lɪ'gɑːtəʊ] **ADV** *Mus* legato

legend ['ledʒənd] **N** *(story, inscription etc)* légende *f*; **to be/become a l. in one's own lifetime** être/devenir une légende vivante

legendary ['ledʒənd(ə)rɪ] **ADJ** légendaire

legerdemain [ledʒədə'meɪn] **N** *Lit Fig* tour *m* de passe-passe

-legged ['legɪd, legd] **SUFF** **short-/bare-/etc-l.** aux jambes courtes/nues *etc*; **two-l.** *(person)* à deux jambes; *(animal)* à deux pattes

leggings ['legɪŋz] **NPL** *(for dancers)* jambières *fpl*, *(for women)* caleçon *m*

leggy ['legɪ] **ADJ** *(person)* aux longues jambes; *(plant)* étiolé; **a l. girl** une fille tout en jambes

Leghorn ['leghɔːn] **N** *Geog* Livourne

legibility [ledʒɪ'bɪlɪtɪ] **N** *(of handwriting)* lisibilité *f*

legible ['ledʒɪb(ə)l] **ADJ** *(handwriting)* lisible, net

legibly ['ledʒɪblɪ] **ADV** *(to write)* lisiblement

legion ['li:dʒ(ə)n] **N** légion *f*; **the Foreign L.** la Légion étrangère; **the L. of honour** la Légion d'honneur
ADJ *Lit (many)* **their name is l.** ils sont légion; **the difficulties were l.** les difficultés étaient innombrables

legionary ['li:dʒənərɪ] **ADJ** de la légion
N légionnaire *m*

legionnaire [li:dʒə'neər] **N** légionnaire *m*; **l.'s disease** maladie *f* du légionnaire

legislate ['ledʒɪsleɪt] **VI** faire des *ou* les lois, légiférer; **we can't l. for all possible situations** nous ne pouvons pas prévoir des lois pour tous les cas de figure possibles; **to l. against sth** instaurer une loi contre qch; **child labour had been legislated out of existence by 1900** grâce à la législation, le travail des enfants fut interdit à partir de 1900

legislation [ledʒɪs'leɪʃən] **N** *(laws)* législation *f*, *(action)* élaboration *f* des lois; **further l. may be needed** il faudrait renforcer la législation; **to bring in l. to** ... créer une loi *ou* des lois pour ...; **piece of l.** loi *f*

legislative ['ledʒɪslətɪv] **ADJ** législatif
▶▶ **the L. Assembly** l'Assemblée *f* législative; **l. power** pouvoir *m* législatif

legislator ['ledʒɪsleɪtər] **N** législateur, -trice

legislature ['ledʒɪslətʃər] **N** corps *m* législatif

legit [lɪ'dʒɪt] **ADJ** *Fam* réglo; **this deal is strictly l.** cette affaire est parfaitement réglementaire

legitimacy [lɪ'dʒɪtɪməsɪ] **N** *(of child, opinion etc)* légitimité *f*

legitimate[1] [lɪ'dʒɪtɪmət] **ADJ** *(child, authority, reason, government etc)* légitime; **l. expenditure** dépenses *fpl* justifiées; **it's l. to assume that** ... on peut légitimement penser que ..., il est légitime de penser que ...; **the l. stage** le théâtre traditionnel

legitimate[2] [lɪ'dʒɪtɪmeɪt] **VT** *(child)* légitimer

legitimately [lɪ'dʒɪtɪmətlɪ] **ADV** légitimement

legitimatize [lɪ'dʒɪtɪmətaɪz], **legitimize** [lɪ'dʒɪtɪmaɪz] **VT** légitimer

legless ['leglɪs] **ADJ 1 l. cripple** cul-de-jatte *m*, *pl* culs-de-jatte **2** *Br Fam (drunk)* bourré, beurré

legman, *pl* **legmen** ['legmæn, -mən] **N** *Am* **1**

Journ = reporter *m* qui fait la chronique des chiens écrasés **2** *(errand boy etc)* garçon *m* de courses, coursier *m*

leg-of-mutton **ADJ** **l. sleeves** manches *fpl* gigot

leg-pull **N** *Fam* blague *f*

leg-puller [-pʊlər] **N** *Fam* blagueur, -euse, farceur, -euse

legroom ['legrʊm] **N** place *f* pour les jambes; **these little cars don't give you any l.** dans ces petites voitures, on n'a aucune place pour les jambes

legume ['legjuːm] **N** *(vegetable)* légumineuse *f*, **legumes** *(plants)* légumineuses *fpl*

leguminous [lɪ'gjuːmɪnəs] **ADJ** *Bot* légumineux; **l. plant** légumineuse *f*

legwarmer ['legwɔːmər] **N** *(usu pl)* **legwarmers** jambières *fpl*

legwork ['legwɜːk] **N** *Fam* **there's a lot of l. in this job** c'est un travail où l'on marche beaucoup; **I'm the one that gets all the l.** c'est toujours moi qui me déplace ici

Leics *abbr* Leicestershire

leisure ['leʒər, *Am* 'liːʒər] **N** loisir(s) *m(pl)*; **to have enough l. for reading** avoir le loisir *ou* le temps de lire; **to do sth at one's l.** faire qch à loisir *ou* dans ses moments de loisir
▶▶ **l. activities** activités *fpl* de loisir; **l. break** court séjour *m* de détente; **l. centre** centre *m* de loisirs; **l. club** club *m* de loisirs; **l. hours** heures *fpl* de loisir; **l. industry** industrie *f* des loisirs; **l. market** marché *m* des loisirs; **l. time** temps *m* libre; **l. tourism** tourisme *m* de loisir, tourisme *m* ludique; **l. wear** vêtements *mpl* sport

leisured ['leʒəd] **ADJ 1** *(life etc)* de loisir **2** *(person)* qui a des loisirs; **the l. classes** les rentiers *mpl*

leisureliness ['leʒəlɪnɪs] **N** *(of pace)* caractère *m* mesuré; *(of weekend)* caractère détendu; **the l. of sea travel** la détente apportée par une croisière

leisurely ['leʒəlɪ] **ADJ** *(person)* qui n'est jamais pressé; *(pace)* tranquille; *(weekend)* détendu, relax; *(journey)* par petites étapes; **progress had been all too l.** nous progressions/ils progressaient beaucoup trop lentement; **they moved with a l. grace** ils se déplaçaient avec grâce et lenteur; **to go for a l. stroll** aller se promener tranquillement; **we had a l. time of it at the beach** nous nous sommes bien reposés à la plage; **to do sth in a l. fashion** faire qch sans se presser
ADV *(without haste)* sans se presser

lemming ['lemɪŋ] **N** lemming *m*; **to follow sb like lemmings** suivre qn comme des moutons (de Panurge)

lemon ['lemən] **N 1** *(fruit, colour)* citron *m*; *Fam* **they squeezed him like a l.** ils l'ont pressé comme un citron **2** *Fam (awkward person)* idiot, -ote; **what a l.!** quelle cruche!; *Fam* **I felt like a real l.** j'ai eu l'air vraiment malin **3** *Fam (useless object)* **it's a l.** c'est de la camelote; **she got sold a l.** elle s'est fait rouler
ADJ **l.(-coloured)** *(jaune)* citron *inv*
▶▶ *Bot* **l. balm** mélisse *f*, citronnelle *f*, *Culin* **l. curd** pâte *f* à tartiner au citron; **l. grass** citronnelle *f*, lemon-grass *m*; **l. juice** jus *m* de citron; *(squash)* sirop *m* de citron; *(freshly squeezed drink)* citron *m* pressé; **l. meringue pie** tarte *f* au citron meringuée; **l. sole** limande-sole *f*; *Br* **l. squeezer** presse-citron *m*, *pl* presse-citrons; **l. tea** thé *m* au citron; **l. tree** citronnier *m*; **l. verbena** verveine *f* citronnelle

lemonade [lemə'neɪd] **N** *(carbonated)* limonade *f*, *(freshly sqeezed)* citronnade *f*

lemony ['lemənɪ] **ADJ** *(smell, taste)* citronné

lemur ['liːmər] **N** maki *m*

lend [lend] *(pt, pp* **lent** [lent]) **VT 1** prêter **(sth**

to sb, sb sth qch à qn); **to l. money at interest** prêter de l'argent à intérêt

2 *(give)* **to l. sb a (helping) hand** donner un coup de main à qn; **to l. an ear** *or* **one's ear to …** prêter l'oreille à …; **to l. one's name to a project** donner son nom à un projet; **to l. dignity to an occasion** rehausser le prestige d'un événement; **to l. weight to an argument** donner du poids à un argument; **to l. credibility/drama to a story** rendre une histoire crédible/dramatique; **the bloodstains on his trousers lent support to his story** les taches de sang sur son pantalon accréditèrent son histoire; **distance lends enchantment to the view** tout paraît beau (vu) de loin; **to l. oneself** *or* **itself to sth** se prêter à qch; **the story doesn't l. itself to dramatization** l'histoire ne se prête pas à une dramatisation

vi *Fin* **to l. against securities** prêter sur titres; **to l. at 12%** prêter à 12%

▸ **lend out vt sep** prêter

lender ['lendər] N *(person)* prêteur, -euse; *Fin (institution)* organisme *m* de crédit

lending ['lendɪŋ] N *(of money, item)* prêt *m*
▸▸ *Fin* **l. bank** banque *f* de crédit; **l. country** pays *m* créancier; **l. library** bibliothèque *f* de prêt; *Fin* **l. limit** plafond *m* de crédit; **l. policy** *(of bank, country)* politique *f* de prêt; *Fin* **l. rate** taux *m* de prêt

lend-lease N *(no pl)* *Econ, Hist* prêt-bail *m*

length [leŋθ] N **1** *(in space)*, *Swimming* longueur *f*; **to swim a few lengths** faire quelques longueurs; **it's 4.50m in l.** ça fait 4,50m de long; **to win by a l./half a l.** *(in race)* gagner d'une longueur/d'une demi-longueur; **to wander the l. and breadth of the country** errer dans tout le pays; **I fell full l. on the ground** je suis tombé de tout mon long

2 *(in time)* durée *f*; *(of book, journey etc)* longueur *f*; **about 300 pages/30,000 words in l.** *(book)* d'une longueur d'environ 300 pages/30 000 mots; **his essay was a bit under l.** sa dissertation était un peu trop courte; **l. of service** *(in post)* ancienneté *f*; **the l. of time required to do sth** le temps qu'il faut pour faire qch; **at (great) l.** *(to talk)* longuement; *(to explain sth)* en détail

3 **to go to the l. of doing sth** aller jusqu'à faire qch; **to go to great lengths to do sth** se donner beaucoup de mal à *ou* pour faire qch; **he would go to any lengths (to do sth)** il ne reculerait devant rien (pour faire qch); **I never dreamed that they would go to such lengths** je n'aurais jamais imaginé qu'ils iraient si loin

4 *(of vowel, syllable)* longueur *f*

5 *Tennis, Cr* longueur *f* de balle

6 *(of string etc)* morceau *m*, bout *m*; *(of material)* pièce *f*, coupon *m*; *(of wood)* morceau *m*; *(of pipe)* tronçon *m*; *Sewing* **dress/trouser l.** coupon de robe/pantalon; *Sewing* **what l. do I need for …?** quel métrage faut-il pour …?

lengthen ['leŋθən] **vt** *(skirt, chain etc)* allonger, rallonger; *(interval)* prolonger; *(vowel, account)* allonger
vi *(of days etc)* allonger, rallonger; *(of intervals etc)* augmenter; *(of shadows)* s'allonger

lengthening ['leŋθənɪŋ] N allongement *m*

lengthily ['leŋθɪlɪ] ADV longuement

lengthways, *Am* **lengthwise** ['leŋθweɪz, -waɪz] ADV dans le sens de la longueur, longitudinalement

lengthy ['leŋθɪ] ADJ *(speech, report)* long, *f* longue, plein de longueurs; *(process, description)* long

leniency ['liːnɪənsɪ] N indulgence *f* (**to, towards** envers)

lenient ['liːnɪənt] ADJ indulgent (**to, towards** envers); *(punishment)* peu sévère; *Law* **a l. sentence** un jugement clément

leniently ['liːnɪəntlɪ] ADV *(to judge)* avec clémence; *(to mark, treat etc)* avec indulgence

Lenin ['lenɪn] N Lénine *m*

Leningrad ['lenɪŋgræd] N *Hist* Léningrad

Leninism ['lenɪnɪz(ə)m] N *Pol* léninisme *m*

Leninist ['lenɪnɪst] ADJ, N *Pol* léniniste *mf*

lenitive ['lenɪtɪv] ADJ, N *Med* lénitif *m*

lens [lenz] N **1** *Opt* lentille *f*, *(of spectacles)* verre *m*; **converging/diverging l.** lentille *f* convergente/divergente; **concave/convex l.** lentille concave/convexe **2** *Phot* objectif *m* (photographique); *Electron* **electron l.** lentille *f* électronique; **mirror l.** objectif à lentille spéculaire **3** *Anat* **(crystalline) l.** *(of the eye)* cristallin *m*
▸▸ *Phot* **l. attachment** accessoire *m* d'objectif; *Phot* **l. cap** bouchon *m* d'objectif; **l. cleaning fluid** produit *m* de nettoyage pour lentilles; *Phot* **l. holder** étui *m* à objectif; *Phot* **l. hood** pare-soleil *m inv*

Lent [lent] N *Rel* Carême *m*; **to keep L.** faire carême; **to give up sth for L.** renoncer à qch pour le Carême

lent [lent] PT, PP *see* **lend**

lentil ['lentɪl] N *Bot, Culin* lentille *f*; **l. soup** soupe *f* aux lentilles

Leo ['liːəʊ] N *Astrol* Lion *m*; **to be (a) L.** être (du) Lion

leonine ['liːənaɪn] ADJ *Lit* léonin

leopard ['lepəd] N léopard *m*; *Fig Fam* **a l. cannot change its spots** on ne se refait pas
▸▸ **l. skin** peau *f* de léopard; **a l.-skin coat** un manteau en léopard

leotard ['liːətɑːd] N maillot *m* (de danseur), justaucorps *m*

leper ['lepər] N *Med, Fig* lépreux, -euse; **l. hospital** *or* **colony** léproserie *f*

lepidopteran [lepɪ'dɒptərən] ADJ, N *Entom* lépidoptère *m*

leprechaun ['leprəkɔːn, -hɔːn] N *Myth* farfadet *m*, lutin *m*

leprosy ['leprəsɪ] N *Med* lèpre *f*; **to have l.** avoir la lèpre

leprous ['leprəs] ADJ *Med* lépreux

lesbian ['lezbɪən] ADJ lesbien
N lesbienne *f*

lesbianism ['lezbɪənɪz(ə)m] N lesb(ian)isme *m*

lesbo ['lezbəʊ] N *Sl Pej (lesbian)* gouine *f*

lesion ['liːʒən] N *Law, Med* lésion *f*

Lesotho [lɪ'suːtuː] N le Lesotho

LESS [les]

ADJ	moins de **1**
PREP	moins
PRON	moins
ADV	moins **1** ▪ de moins en moins **1**
	▪ encore moins **1** ▪ rien de moins **2**
	▪ pas moins de **2** ▪ moins que **2**

ADJ *(comp* **lesser**) **1** *(not so much)* moins de; **we have l. time/money than we thought** nous avons moins de temps/d'argent que nous ne pensions; **l. trouble/difficulty** moins de peine/difficulté; **it's l. than a week's work** cela représente moins d'une semaine de travail; **he has even l. idea about cars than I do** il s'y connaît encore moins que moi en matière de voiture; **he is l. than thirty** il a moins de trente ans; **l. than (sign)** *(signe m)* inférieur à, signe plus petit que VOIR GRAMMAIRE A25-6

2 *(smaller)* **the distance is l. than I thought** la distance est moindre que je ne le pensais

PREP moins; **a year l. two days** une année moins deux jours; **I've £50, l. what I spent on records** j'ai 50 livres, moins ce que j'ai dépensé en disques

PRON moins; **the l. you know the better** le moins tu en sais, le mieux c'est; **I don't think any (the) l. of you** tu n'as pas baissé dans mon estime; **I see l. of her nowadays** je la vois moins ces temps-ci; **in l. than an hour** en moins d'une heure; **in l. than no time** en un rien de temps; **I can't sell it at l. than cost price** je ne peux pas le vendre à moins du prix de revient; **the l. said about it the better** moins on en parle mieux cela vaut; *Fam* **l. of that!** ça suffit!

ADV VOIR GRAMMAIRE A76; B13 **1** moins; **l. (well) known** moins (bien) connu; **she is l. musical than her sister** elle est moins musicienne que sa sœur; **I'm l. happy with that** ça me satisfait *ou* plaît moins; **one person l.** une personne de moins; **one mouth l. to feed** une bouche de moins à nourrir; **not a penny l.** pas un sou de moins; **l. and l.** de moins en moins; **no more, no l.** ni plus ni moins; **still l., even l.** encore moins

2 *(in negative constructions)* **nothing l. than** *(at the very least)* rien (de) moins que; **I want nothing l.** je ne veux rien de moins; **there's nothing I want l. than to hurt him** je ne veux surtout pas le blesser; **he was nothing l. than overjoyed at the news** il fut absolument ravi de la nouvelle; **it's nothing l. than monstrous!** c'est absolument monstrueux!; **this wall is no l. than a metre thick** ce mur n'a pas moins d'un mètre d'épaisseur; **he eats less than he used to** il mange moins qu'avant; **no l. a person than the headmistress** *(came to see me etc)* la directrice en personne; *(had signed the letter etc)* la directrice elle-même; **the letter was signed by Vincent, no l.** la lettre était signée de Vincent, lui-même et en personne; **she was driving a Rolls, no l.** elle conduisait une Rolls, tu te rends compte!; **I expected no l. from you** je ne m'attendais pas à moins de vous; **they don't own a fridge, much l. a freezer** ils n'ont pas de réfrigérateur, et encore moins de congélateur; **the news of his death came as no l. of a shock for being expected** on n'avait beau s'y attendre, la nouvelle de sa mort n'en fut pas moins un choc

-less [lɪs] SUFF sans; **roofless** sans toit; **penniless** sans le sou; **sleeveless** sans manches

lessee [le'siː] N *Law (of premises etc)* locataire *mf* (à bail); *(of casino etc)* tenancier, -ière; *(of farm)* fermier *m*

lessen ['les(ə)n] VI s'amoindrir, diminuer; *(of symptoms etc)* s'atténuer
VT *(costs etc)* diminuer; *(importance, severity of sth)* amoindrir; *(noise)* atténuer; *(activity)* ralentir; *(fervour, enthusiasm)* calmer

lessening ['les(ə)nɪŋ] N amoindrissement *m*, diminution *f*

lesser ['lesər] ADJ VOIR GRAMMAIRE A26 **1** *(in size)* petit **2** *(in importance)* moindre; *Prov* **to choose the l. of two evils** de deux maux choisir le moindre; **to a l. extent** *or* **degree** dans une moindre mesure, à un degré moindre

lesson ['les(ə)n] N **1** *(instruction)* leçon *f*, *Sch* cours *m*; *(in primary school)* leçon; **Spanish l.** cours d'espagnol; **swimming l.** cours de natation; **to be an object l. to sb** servir d'exemple à qn; **to learn a l. from sth** tirer une leçon de qch; **he has learnt his l.** il a compris; **let that be a l. to you!** que cela vous serve de leçon!; **it'll teach him a l.** ça lui servira de leçon **2** *Rel (reading from Bible)* lecture *f* de l'Écriture sainte
▸▸ **l. plan** plan *m* de cours

lessor [le'sɔːr] N *Law* bailleur, -eresse

lest [lest] CONJ **1** *esp Lit* de peur *ou* de crainte que … (ne) + sub; **l. we forget** pour ne pas oublier VOIR GRAMMAIRE A75 **2** *Arch (after verbs of fearing)* **I feared l. he should fall** je craignais qu'il (ne) tombât

LET¹ [let] **VT** (*pt, pp* **let**; *prp* **letting**) **1** VOIR GRAMMAIRE A41; B35 *(allow)* permettre, laisser; **to l. sb do sth** laisser qn faire qch, permettre à qn de faire qch; **the police would not l. anyone pass** la police ne laissait passer personne *ou* ne permettait à personne de passer; **to l. oneself be guided** se laisser guider; **l. me tell you that ...** permettez-moi de vous dire que ...; **it wasn't easy, l. me tell you!** ça n'a pas été facile, crois-moi!; **to l. sth fall** laisser échapper qch; **l. me go with them** laissez-moi partir avec eux; **he l. go the rope** il a lâché la corde; **someone has l. the dog loose** quelqu'un a lâché le chien; **to l. sb know sth** faire savoir qch à qn, faire part de qch à qn; **l. me know when ...** faites-moi savoir quand ...; **l. me know if ...** préviens-moi si ...; **I will l. him know you are here** je vais le prévenir que vous êtes ici; **l. me hear the story** racontez-moi l'histoire; **to l. sth pass** passer sur qch; **we couldn't l. it pass any longer** nous n'avons pas pu laisser passer ça; **to l. sth get one down** se laisser abattre à cause de qch; **to l. sth get to one** se laisser affecter par qch; **to l. things get on top of you** se laisser submerger **2** *Br (house etc)* louer; **(house) to l.** maison à louer **3** *Med Arch* **to l. blood** pratiquer une saignée

V AUX *(supplying 1st & 3rd person of imperative)* **l.'s hurry!** dépêchons-nous!; **l.'s not have an argument about it!** on ne va pas se disputer pour ça!; **why don't we go to the beach on Saturday? – oh yes, l.'s!** et si on allait à la plage samedi? – oh oui! oui!; **l. us pray** prions; **l. there be light** que la lumière soit; **don't l.'s leave yet** ne partons pas tout de suite; **now, don't l.'s have any nonsense!** allons, pas de bêtises!; *Fml* **l. him do it at once!** qu'il le fasse tout de suite!; *Math* **l. AB be equal to CD** supposons que AB soit égal à CD; **l. me see!** voyons un peu!; **l. them all come!** qu'ils viennent tous!; **don't l. me see you here again!** que je ne vous retrouve plus ici! VOIR GRAMMAIRE A40; B34–5

N *Br (of property)* location *f*; **short l.** location de courte durée

▸ **let by** **VT SEP l. sb by** laisser passer qn

▸ **let down** **VT SEP 1** *(blinds etc)* baisser; **to l. one's hair down** laisser tomber ses cheveux; *Fig* se détendre, se laisser aller **2** *Sewing (dress etc)* rallonger **3** *Fam (disappoint) (person)* décevoir; **to l. sb down gently** ménager qn; **I won't l. you down** vous pouvez compter sur moi; **he has been badly l. down** il a été gravement déçu; **the car l. us down again** la voiture nous a encore lâchés; **you've l. everyone down, most of all yourself** tu as fait du tort à tout le monde, à commencer par toi-même; **I've been l. down by the babysitter** la babysitter m'a laissé tomber; **to l. the side down** manquer à ses obligations **4** *(tyre etc)* dégonfler

▸ **let in** **VT SEP 1** *(person)* laisser entrer; *(air, rain, draught)* laisser entrer; **to l. in the light** laisser entrer *ou* passer la lumière; **he's got a key, so he can l. himself in** puisqu'il a une clef, il peut entrer; **my shoes l. in water** mes chaussures prennent l'eau **2** **to l. sb in on a secret** dire un secret à qn; **to l. sb in on a plan** mettre qn au courant d'un projet **3** *Sewing etc (section)* ajouter, introduire **4** *Fam* **I didn't know what I was letting myself in for** je ne savais pas à quoi je m'exposais; **we're letting ourselves in for a lot of work** nous allons avoir beaucoup de travail; **to l. oneself in for a lot of problems** s'exposer à beaucoup de problèmes

▸ **let into** **VT SEP 1** *(person to house etc)* laisser *ou* faire entrer dans

2 **to l. sb into a secret** dévoiler un secret à qn, mettre qn dans le secret **3** *Sewing etc* **to l. a piece into a skirt** mettre *ou* ajouter une pièce à une jupe

▸ **let off** **VT SEP 1** *(explode, fire) (explosive device)* faire partir; *(firework)* tirer, faire partir **2** *(release) (steam)* lâcher, laisser échapper; *Fig* **to l. off steam** se défouler **3** *(excuse)* **to l. sb off from sth/doing sth** dispenser qn de faire qch; **to l. sb off lightly** ne pas être sévère avec qn; **you l. him off too easily** vous n'avez pas été assez sévère avec lui; **I'll l. you off this time** je ferme les yeux pour cette fois; **to be l. off with a fine** en être quitte pour une amende **4** *(permit to leave) (from school, work)* laisser partir **5** *(from vehicle)* laisser (descendre) **VI** *Fam (fart)* péter

▸ **let on** **VI** *Fam* **1** *(tell)* dire; **don't l. on that I was there** n'allez pas dire que j'y étais; **he didn't l. on that he saw her** *(didn't tell anyone)* il n'a pas dit qu'il l'avait vue; *(didn't acknowledge her)* il a fait semblant de ne pas la voir; **don't l. on!** pas un mot! **2** *(claim)* **he wasn't as ill as he l. on** il n'était pas aussi malade qu'il voulait bien le faire croire

▸ **let out** **VT SEP 1** *(release) (person)* laisser sortir; *(bird)* laisser échapper; *(prisoner)* élargir; *(secret)* révéler, divulguer; **the porter l. me out** le gardien m'a ouvert la porte; **I'll l. myself out** ce n'est pas la peine de me raccompagner; **can you l. yourself out?** faut-il vous raccompagner *ou* reconduire?; *Fig* **that lets me out** *(it couldn't have been me)* me voilà soulagé; *(I can't do it)* je suis tranquille; **to l. out the air from** laisser échapper l'air de; *(balloon etc)* dégonfler; **to l. out the bath water** vider la baignoire; **to l. a yell** laisser échapper un cri **2** *(expand) (jacket, trousers etc)* élargir, agrandir; *(sail)* larguer **3** *(fire etc)* **who l. the fire out?** qui a laissé le feu s'éteindre? **4** *Br (rent out)* louer

▸ **let through** **VT SEP** *(person, water, light)* laisser passer

▸ **let up** **VI** *(of rain, pressure of business etc)* se calmer; **once he's started he never lets up** une fois lancé il ne s'arrête plus; **the arguing never lets up** ils n'arrêtent pas de se disputer **VT SEP l. him up** *(from the ground)* laisse-le se relever

let² **CONJ l. alone** sans parler de, encore moins; **we haven't been to England, l. alone Scotland** nous n'avons pas été en Angleterre, pas plus qu'en Écosse

let³ **N** *Tennis f* balle let; **l.!** let!; **to play a l.** remettre une balle let
▸ *Tennis* **l. ball** balle let

let⁴ **N** *Law* **without l. or hindrance** en toute liberté

let-down **N** *Fam* déception *f*

lethal ['li:θ(ə)l] **ADJ** mortel; *Fam* **that vodka's l.!** cette vodka est mortelle!; **l. injury** blessure *f* mortelle
▸ **l. dose** dose *f* mortelle *ou* létale; **l. weapon** arme *f* meurtrière

lethally ['li:θəlɪ] **ADV** **the knife glinted l. in the sun** la lame assassine brillait au soleil; **a l. effective sub-machine gun** une mitraillette d'une efficacité redoutable; **a l. effective debater** un argumentateur d'une efficacité redoutable; **a l. biting wit** un humour mordant redoutable

lethargic [lɪ'θɑ:dʒɪk] **ADJ** *(person)* léthargique; *(movement, attempt, voice)* mou, *f* molle

lethargically [lɪ'θɑ:dʒɪklɪ] **ADV** d'une manière léthargique; **to move l.** se déplacer mollement

lethargy ['leθədʒɪ] **N** léthargie *f*

let-out **N** *Fam (excuse)* excuse *f*
▸ **l. clause** échappatoire *f*

letter ['letər] **N 1** *(communication)* lettre *f*; **I've had a l. from him** j'ai reçu une lettre de lui; **are there any letters for me?** y a-t-il du courrier pour moi?; **to notify sb by l.** informer qn par lettre; **your l. of ...** votre lettre en date du ...; **business l.** lettre d'affaires; **rejection l.** lettre de refus; **letters to the editor** courrier *m* des lecteurs **2** *(of alphabet)* lettre *f*; *Typ* lettre, caractère *m*; **to have letters after one's name** avoir des titres; **according to the l. of the law** selon la lettre de la loi; **to obey to the l.** obéir à la lettre **3** *Am (paper size)* lettre *f* **4** *Lit* **letters** (belles-)lettres *fpl*, littérature *f*; **man of letters** homme *m* de lettres **VT** marquer avec des lettres; *(engrave)* graver des lettres sur
▸ **l. of acknowledgement** accusé *m* de réception; **l. of advice** lettre d'avis; *St Exch* **l. of allotment** avis *m* d'attribution *ou* de répartition, lettre d'allocation; **l. of apology** lettre d'excuse; **l. of application** *(for job)* lettre de demande d'emploi; *St Exch (for shares)* lettre de souscription; **l. bomb** lettre piégée; **l. box** boîte *f* à *ou* aux lettres; **l. card**, *pl* cartes-lettres; *Journ* **letters column** rubrique *f* courrier des lecteurs; **l. of complaint** lettre de réclamation; **l. of confirmation** lettre de confirmation; *Com* **l. of credit** lettre de crédit *ou* de créance; **l. of dismissal** lettre de licenciement; *Com* **l. of exchange** lettre de change; **l. of guarantee** lettre de garantie; *Fin* **l. of guaranty** lettre d'aval; *Fin* **l. of indemnity** cautionnement *m*, lettre de garantie (d'indemnité); *Fin* **l. of intent** lettre d'intention; **l. opener** coupe-papier *m inv*; **letters patent** lettres *fpl* patentes; **l. rate** tarif *m* lettres; **l. of reference** lettre de recommandation; **l. scales** pèse-lettre *m*, *pl* pèse-lettres; **l. tray** corbeille *f ou* panier *m* à courrier

lettered ['letəd] **ADJ 1** *Fml (person)* lettré **2** *(object)* marqué avec des lettres; **a briefcase l. with my initials** une mallette gravée à mes initiales

letterhead ['letəhed] **N** en-tête *m inv*; *(paper)* papier *m* à en-tête

lettering ['letərɪŋ] **N 1** *(action)* lettrage *m* **2** *(result)* caractères *mpl*

letterpress ['letəpres] **N 1** *Typ (method)* impression *f* typographique **2** *(text)* texte *m* *(accompagnant une illustration)*
▸ **l. printing** typographie *f*

letter-quality **N** *Comput* qualité *f* courrier
▸ **l. printer** imprimante *f* qualité courrier

letting ['letɪŋ] **N** *Br (renting out) (of house etc)* location *f*
▸ **l. agency** agence *f* de location

lettuce ['letɪs] **N** laitue *f*

let-up **N** *Fam (in conflict etc)* trêve *f*; *(in pressure)* diminution *f* (**in** de); *(in weather)* accalmie *f*; *(in efforts, fighting)* relâchement *m*; **to work fifteen hours without a l.** travailler quinze heures d'affilée; **there's been no l. in the rain since this morning** il n'a pas arrêté de pleuvoir depuis ce matin

leucocyte ['lu:kəsaɪt] **N** *Med* leucocyte *m*

leucocytosis [lu:kəsaɪ'təʊsɪs] **N** leucocytose *f*

leukaemia, *Am* **leukemia** [lu:'ki:mɪə] **N** *Med* leucémie *f*; **to have l.** avoir une leucémie

leukaemic, *Am* **leukemic** [lu:'ki:mɪk] **ADJ** *Med* leucémique

leukocyte ['lu:kəsaɪt] **N** *Med* leucocyte *m*

Levant [lɪ'vænt] **N the L.** le Levant

Levantine [lə'væntaɪn] **ADJ** levantin
N Levantin, -ine

levee ['levɪ] N *Am Constr (of river)* levée *f*, digue *f*

LEVEL ['lev(ə)l]

| N niveau **1** ▪ taux **1** ▪ hauteur **1** |
| ADJ horizontal **1** ▪ de/à niveau **1** |
| ▪ plat **1** ▪ à la hauteur de **2** ▪ égal **3** |
| ADV à l'horizontale |
| VT niveler **1** ▪ aplanir **1** |

N 1 *(height) (of prices, the sea etc)* niveau *m*; *(in surveying)*, *Geog* altitude *f*, niveau; *(quantity) (of alcohol etc)* taux *m*; **at eye l.** à (la) hauteur des yeux; **to maintain prices at a high l.** maintenir les prix à un niveau élevé; **to be on a l. with sb** être du même niveau que qn, être sur un pied d'égalité avec qn; **on a l. with sth** au niveau *ou* à la hauteur de qch, de niveau avec qch; **her ambition is on a l. with mine** son ambition est du même ordre que la mienne; **to come down to sb's l.** se mettre au niveau *ou* à la portée de qn; **to sink to** *or* **be brought down to sb's l.** tomber au niveau *ou* de qn; *Comput* **l. of access** niveau d'accès; *Phys etc* **energy l.** niveau énergétique; **at ministerial l.** à l'échelon ministériel; **noise l.** *(of engine etc)* niveau de bruit; *Tech* **oil l.** niveau d'huile; **radiation l.** niveau de radiation

2 *(flat ground)* terrain *m* de niveau; **to be dead l.** être parfaitement de niveau; **on the l.** *(built etc)* sur un terrain plat; *Fam (person)* honnête; *Fam* **is he on the l.?** est-ce qu'on peut lui faire confiance?; *Fam* **it's completely on the l.** c'est tout à fait légal

3 *Carp (tool)* niveau *m*; *(rule)* latte *f ou* règle *f* de niveau

ADJ 1 *(not sloping)* horizontal, -aux; *(ground)* de niveau, à niveau; *(road, pitch etc) (flat)* plat; *Fig* **to create a l. playing field** créer une situation qui soit juste pour tout le monde *ou* qui ne défavorise personne

2 l. with ... au niveau de ..., à (la) hauteur de ...; **l. with the ground** au ras du sol, à ras de terre; **they are about l. in ability** leurs compétences se valent; **to do one's l. best** faire tout son possible, faire de son mieux; **it's l. pegging** *(between the two)* il y a égalité; **they're l. pegging** ils sont à égalité; **a l. spoonful** une cuillerée rase

3 *(steady) (tone etc)* égal, -aux; **to keep a l. head** garder son sang-froid

ADV à l'horizontale; **hold the tray l.** tenez le plateau à l'horizontale ou bien à plat; *Aviat* **to fly l.** voler en palier; *Sport, Fig* **to draw l. with ...** arriver à la hauteur de ...; *(in rowing)* venir bord à bord avec ...

VT (-ll-, *Am* -l-) **1** *(surface)* niveler, aplanir; *(land etc)* araser; **to l. a town (to the ground)** raser une ville

2 *(aim) (rifle)* pointer; *(canon)* braquer; *(telescope)* diriger (**at** sur); **to l. one's gun at sb** ajuster *ou* viser qn avec son fusil, mettre qn en joue; **to l. criticism at sb** émettre des critiques sur qn; **to l. accusations at sb** lancer des accusations contre qn; **to l. a blow at sb** porter un coup à qn

3 *(in surveying) (region)* effectuer des opérations de nivellement dans, niveler

VI *Fam* **to l. with sb** parler franchement à qn

▸▸ *Br, Can* **l. crossing** passage *m* à niveau; *Aviat* **l. flight** vol *m* horizontal; *Carp* **l. rule** latte *f ou* règle *f* de niveau

▸ **level down** VT SEP *esp Pol* niveler par le bas

▸ **level off, level out** VT SEP *(ground, surface)* aplanir

VI 1 *(of prices etc)* se stabiliser, plafonner; **demand levels off at this time of year** la demande se stabilise à cette époque de l'année

2 *Aviat* attaquer le palier, voler en palier

▸ **level up** VT SEP *esp Pol* accroître le niveau moyen

level-headed ADJ pondéré

leveller, *Am* **leveler** ['lev(ə)lər] N *Pol* égalitaire *mf*; **death is a great l.** tous les hommes sont égaux devant la mort

lever ['liːvər, *Am* 'levər] N levier *m*; *Tech* levier, manette *f*

VT to l. sth open ouvrir qch avec un levier; **he levered the box open with a piece of wood** il a ouvert la caisse avec un morceau de bois; *Fig* **he has levered himself into a very strong position** il s'est hissé à un poste très important

▸ **lever off** VT SEP *(lid, top, tyre)* enlever (avec un levier); *(padlock)* faire sauter

▸ **lever out** VT SEP *(object)* extraire; *Fig (person)* évincer; **he has been levered out of his job** on l'a évincé de son emploi

▸ **lever up** VT SEP *(lid etc)* soulever (avec un levier); **he levered himself up onto his elbow** il s'est soulevé en s'aidant de son coude

leverage ['liːvərɪdʒ] N **1** *Tech (power)* force *f ou* puissance *f ou* effet *m* de levier; **to bring l. to bear on sth** *(on door etc)* faire pression sur qch **2** *Fig* influence *f*, *(through manœuvre)* effet *m* de levier; **to exert some l. on sb** exercer de l'influence sur qn; **we have no l. we could bring to bear on him** nous n'avons pas de prise sur lui

VT *Com* tirer profit de

leveraged ['liːvərɪdʒd] ADJ *Com* **the company is highly l.** la société est fortement endettée

▸▸ **l. buy-out** rachat *m* d'entreprise financé par l'endettement; **l. management buy-out** rachat d'entreprise par les salariés

lever-arch file N classeur *m* à levier

leveret ['levərɪt] N levraut *m*

leviathan [lɪ'vaɪəθ(ə)n] N **1** *Bible* L. Léviathan *m* **2** *esp Lit (something huge)* monstre *m*

Levis® ['liːvaɪz] NPL Levis® *m*; **a pair of L.** un Levis

levitate ['levɪteɪt] VI se soulever (par lévitation)

VT soulever (par lévitation)

levitation [levɪ'teɪʃən] N lévitation *f*

levity ['levɪtɪ] N légèreté *f*

levy ['levɪ] N **1** *(tax)* impôt *m*, contribution *f*, **to impose a l. on sugar imports** taxer les importations de sucre; **capital l.** prélèvement *m* sur le capital; **import l.** taxe *f* à l'importation **2** *(action) (of tax, troops)* levée *f*

VT 1 *(tax)* lever, percevoir; *(fine)* infliger; **to l. a duty on goods** imposer des marchandises; **to l. a fine on sb** frapper qn d'une amende **2** *Mil (troops)* lever

levying of taxes ['levɪɪŋ] N levée *f* des impôts

lewd [luːd] ADJ *(behaviour, gesture, joke)* obscène; *(smile, look)* lubrique

lewdly ['luːdlɪ] ADV de façon obscène, lubriquement

lewdness ['luːdnɪs] N *(of joke, behaviour, gesture)* obscénité *f*, *(of smile, look)* lubricité *f*

lexical ['leksɪk(ə)l] ADJ lexical, -aux

lexicalize ['leksɪkəlaɪz] VT lexicaliser

lexicographer [leksɪ'kɒgrəfər] N lexicographe *mf*

lexicographical [leksɪkə'græfɪk(ə)l] ADJ lexicographique

lexicography [leksɪ'kɒgrəfɪ] N lexicographie *f*

lexicology [leksɪ'kɒlədʒɪ] N lexicologie *f*

lexicon ['leksɪkən] N lexique *m*

lexis ['leksɪs] N lexique *m*

lez [lez], **lezzy** ['lezɪ] N *Sl Pej (lesbian)* gouine *f*

lh [el'eɪtʃ] *Mus etc (abbr* **left hand***)* main gauche

liabilities [laɪə'bɪlɪtɪz] NPL *Com, Fin* passif *m*; *(in bankruptcy)* masse *f* passive; **assets and l.** actif *m* et passif; **to meet one's l.** faire face à ses engagements

liability [laɪə'bɪlɪtɪ] N **1** *Law (responsibility)* responsabilité *f*, **employer's l.** *(for accidents at work)* responsabilité patronale; **civil l.** responsabilité civile; **limited l. company** société *f* à responsabilité limitée; **her firm wouldn't accept l. for the accident** son entreprise refusa d'endosser la responsabilité de l'accident

2 *(disadvantage)* désavantage *m*, handicap *m*; **your brother is a l. to us** ton frère ne nous attire que des problèmes

3 *(likelihood)* disposition *f*, tendance *f* (**to sth** à qch; **to do sth** à faire qch); **l. to a fine** risque *m* d'amende; **l. for military service obligations** *fpl* militaires; **l. to explode** *(of product etc)* danger *m* d'explosion

4 *Acct* dette *f*

5 *Com (on bills of exchange)* encours *m*

liable ['laɪəb(ə)l] ADJ **1** *Law (responsible)* responsable (**for** de); **you are l. for the damage** vous êtes responsable du dommage; **l. party** responsable *mf*

2 *(subject)* assujetti, tenu, astreint (**to** à); **l. to a tax** assujetti à un impôt, redevable d'un impôt; **l. to tax** passible de taxe *ou* d'impôts; **person l. to tax** assujetti *m*; **l. to a fine** passible d'une amende; **l. to customs duty** passible de droits de douane; **l. to military service** astreint au service militaire

3 *(likely)* **to be l. to do sth** *(of person, thing)* risquer de faire qch; **she's l. to make mistakes** elle est susceptible de faire des fautes; **when he gets angry he is l. to do anything** quand il se met en colère, il est capable de tout

liaise [liː'eɪz] VI **to l. with sb about sth** *(be in contact with)* être en contact avec qn à propos de qch; *(work together with)* collaborer avec qn; **the two parties have agreed to l.** les deux parties ont accepté de collaborer; **the successful applicant will be required to l. with head office** le candidat retenu sera en contact direct avec le siège

liaison [lɪ'eɪzɒn] N **1** *(cooperation)* coopération *f* **2** *(love affair)* liaison *f* (amoureuse)

▸▸ *Mil etc* **l. agent** agent *m* de liaison; **l. officer** officier *m* de liaison

liana [lɪ'ɑːnə] N *Bot* liane *f*

liar ['laɪər] N menteur, -euse; **you l.!** espèce de menteur!

Lib [lɪb] *Pol (abbr* **Liberal***)* libéral

lib [lɪb] N *Fam* = **liberation**; = **women's l.** MLF *m*

libation [laɪ'beɪʃən] N libation *f*

Lib Dem = **Liberal Democrat**

libel ['laɪb(ə)l] N diffamation *f*, *Law* diffamation (par écrit), écrit *m* diffamatoire; **to utter a l. against sb** publier un article *ou* un écrit diffamant qn; **action for l.** procès *m* en diffamation; **to sue sb for l.** poursuivre qn en justice pour diffamation; **that's l.!** c'est une calomnie *ou* de la diffamation!

VT (-ll-, *Am* -l-) *(person)* calomnier; *Law* diffamer par écrit

▸▸ **l. action, l. case** procès *m* en diffamation; **l. laws** législation *f* en matière de diffamation

libellous, *Am* **libelous** ['laɪbələs] ADJ *(document etc)* diffamatoire

liberal ['lɪb(ə)rəl] ADJ **1** *(idea etc)* libéral, -aux; *(person)* d'esprit large; **a l. education** une éducation libérale

2 *(generous)* libéral, -aux, généreux; **l. with one's money** prodigue de son argent

3 *(abundant)* ample; **a l. supply of food** une nourriture abondante; **a l. helping** une portion généreuse

4 *Pol* centriste; **L.** libéral, -aux

N *Pol* centriste *mf*; **L.** libéral, -ale
▸▸ *Br Pol* **L. Democrat** *(party member)* = membre *m* du parti libéral démocrate

liberalism ['lɪb(ə)rəlɪz(ə)m] N libéralisme *m*

liberality [lɪbə'rælɪtɪ] N **1** *(of views)* libéralisme *m* **2** *(with money etc)* libéralité *f*, générosité *f*

liberalize ['lɪb(ə)rəlaɪz] VT libéraliser

liberally ['lɪb(ə)rəlɪ] ADV libéralement, généreusement

liberal-minded ADJ large d'esprit

liberate ['lɪbəreɪt] VT **1** libérer **2** *Chem (gas)* libérer, dégager **3** *Fin* **to l. capital** libérer des capitaux

liberated ['lɪbəreɪtɪd] ADJ *(person)* libéré; *(ideas, views, opinions)* progressiste; **a l. woman** une femme libérée; **these are l. times** on vit à une époque libérée; **her ideas aren't l.** elle n'est pas libérée

liberating ['lɪbəreɪtɪŋ] ADJ libérateur

liberation [lɪbə'reɪʃən] N **1** libération *f*; *Hist* **after the l.** après la Libération; **she doesn't believe in women's l.** elle ne croit pas à la libération de la femme **2** *Chem, Phys (of gas, heat)* dégagement *m* **3** *Fin* **l. of capital** mobilisation *f* de capitaux
▸▸ **l. movement** mouvement *m* de libération

liberator ['lɪbəreɪtər] N libérateur, -trice

Liberia [laɪ'bɪərɪə] N Liberia *m*

Liberian [laɪ'bɪərɪən] ADJ libérien
N Libérien, -ienne

libertarian [lɪbə'teərɪən] N libertaire *mf*
ADJ *(philosophy, idea, tendency etc)* libertaire

libertine ['lɪbətiːn] ADJ, N libertin, -ine

liberty ['lɪbətɪ] N liberté *f*; **l. of conscience** liberté de conscience; **at l.** *(free)* libre; **to be at l. to do sth** être libre de faire qch; **Statue of L.** statue *f* de la Liberté; **to take the l. of doing** *or* **to do sth** se permettre *ou* prendre la liberté de faire qch; *Fam* **what a l.!** quel culot!; **civil liberties** droits civiques; **to take liberties with sb** prendre *ou* se permettre des libertés avec qn; **the government is taking liberties** le gouvernement se fiche du monde; **to take liberties with a translation** se permettre des libertés dans une traduction; *Fam Pej* **it's l. hall in this house** chacun fait ce qui lui plaît *ou* c'est la pétaudière dans cette maison
▸▸ **l. bodice** chemise *f* américaine; *Naut* **l. ticket** permission *f* de terre *ou* d'aller à terre

libidinous [lɪ'bɪdɪnəs] ADJ libidineux

libido [lɪ'biːdəʊ, -'baɪ-] *Psy* libido *f*

LIBOR ['laɪbɔːr] N *Br Fin (abbr* London Inter-Bank Offer Rate) ≃ TIOP *m*

Libra ['liːbrə] N *Astrol* Balance *f*; **to be (a) L.** être (de la) Balance

librarian [laɪ'breərɪən] N bibliothécaire *mf*

> Note that the French word **libraire** is a false friend and is never a translation for the English word **librarian**. It means **bookseller**.

librarianship [laɪ'breərɪənʃɪp] N *(subject)* bibliothéconomie *f*

library ['laɪbrərɪ] N *(of books)*, *Comput (of programs)* bibliothèque *f*; *(of tapes, CDs)* discothèque *f*; *(series of films, videos)* collection *f*; *Br* **mobile l.** bibliobus *m*; **photographic l.** photothèque *f*; **film l.** cinémathèque *f*; **music l.** discothèque *f*; **record l.** discothèque; *Fam* **he's a walking l.** c'est une encyclopédie vivante
▸▸ **l. book** livre *m* de bibliothèque; **l. card** carte *f* de bibliothèque; **l. film** film *m* d'archi-

ves; **l. footage** images *fpl* d'archives; **l. science** bibliothéconomie *f*; **l. steps** *(stepladder)* escabeau *m* de bibliothèque; **l. ticket** carte *f* de bibliothèque

> Note that the French word **librairie** is a false friend and is never a translation for the English word **library**. It means **bookshop**.

librettist [lɪ'bretɪst] N *Theat* librettiste *mf*

libretto, *pl* **libretti, librettos** [lɪ'bretəʊ, -iː, -əʊz] N libretto *mpl* librettos, livret *m* *(d'opéra)*

Libya ['lɪbɪə] N Libye *f*

Libyan ['lɪbɪən] ADJ libyen; **the L. Desert** le désert de Libye
N Libyen, -yenne

lice *see* **louse**

licence, *Am* **license** ['laɪsəns] N **1** permis *m*, autorisation *f*, *Com (to manufacture, sell)* licence *f*; **under l. from the inventor** avec l'autorisation de l'inventeur; **l. to sell alcohol** licence des débits de boissons; **made/manufactured under l.** construit/fabriqué sous licence; **dog l.** taxe *f* sur les chiens; *Br* **(driving) l.,** *Am* **driver's l.** permis de conduire; **gun l.** permis de port d'arme(s); **import/export l.** licence d'importation/d'exportation; *Am* **liquor l.** licence des débits de boissons; **manufacturing l.** brevet *m ou* licence de fabrication; **marriage l.,** *Br* **special l.** = dispense *f* de bans; *Br* **they were married by special l.** ils se sont mariés avec dispense de bans; *Aviat* **pilot's l.** brevet de pilote; **shooting l.** permis de chasse; *Br* **television l.** *(fee)* redevance *f* télévisuelle; **trading l.** carte *f* de commerce
2 *esp Pej (freedom)* licence *f*
▸▸ *Comput* **l. agreement** licence *f*; *Br* **l. fee** *(for television)* redevance *f* télévisuelle; **l. holder** licencié, -ée *m*; **l. number** *(on vehicle)* numéro *m* d'immatriculation; *(on driving licence)* numéro de permis de conduire; **l. plate** plaque *f* minéralogique *ou* d'immatriculation

> Note that the French noun **licence** also means **bachelor's degree**.

license ['laɪsəns] VT **to l. sth to sb** accorder une licence à qn pour qch; **to l. sb to sell drink/practise medicine** autoriser qn à tenir un débit de boissons/exercer la médecine; *Com* **to l. sb to manufacture/sell** accorder une licence à qn pour fabriquer/vendre; **to l. a car** *(of owner)* acheter une vignette pour une voiture; **licensed to sell beer, wines and spirits** autorisé à vendre de l'alcool, *Can* licencié à vendre des boissons alcooliques; **to be licensed to carry a gun** avoir un permis de port d'arme(s)
N *Am* = **licence**

licensed ['laɪsənst] ADJ *(produit)* sous licence; *Admin* autorisé, patenté; *Aviat (pilot)* breveté
▸▸ **l. brand name** nom *m* de marque sous licence; **l. hotel** hôtel *m* ayant la licence des débits de boissons; **l. house, l. premises** débit *m* de boissons; **l. restaurant** restaurant *m* ayant la licence des débits de boissons; *Fml* **l. victualler** débitant *m* de boissons

licensee [laɪs(ə)n'siː] N concessionnaire *mf*, détenteur, -trice d'une patente *ou* d'un permis; *(for manufacturing)* détenteur d'une licence; *(of pub etc)* gérant, -ante, propriétaire *mf*

licensing ['laɪsənsɪŋ] N
▸▸ **l. agreement** accord *m* de licence; **l. hours** *(in UK)* = heures *fpl* d'ouverture des pubs; **l. laws** *(in UK)* = lois *fpl* réglementant la vente d'alcools

licensor N concédant *m*

licentiate [laɪ'senʃɪət] N *Univ* diplômé, -ée

licentious [laɪ'senʃəs] ADJ licencieux

licentiousness [laɪ'senʃəsnɪs] N licence *f*

lichen ['laɪkən, 'lɪtʃən] N lichen *m*

lichgate ['lɪtʃgeɪt] N = porche *m* d'entrée de cimetière surmonté d'un petit toit

licit ['lɪsɪt] ADJ licite

licitly ['lɪsɪtlɪ] ADV licitement

lick [lɪk] N **1** coup *m* de langue; **to give sth/sb a l.** lécher qch/qn; **give me a l. of your ice cream** laisse-moi goûter ta glace; *Old-fashioned Fam* **a l. and a promise** *(wash)* un brin de toilette
2 *Fam (small amount)* **a l. of paint** un petit coup de peinture; **a few licks of paint** deux ou trois coups de pinceau; **l. (of hair)** mèche *f*
3 *Fam (speed)* **at (a) great l., at full l.** à toute allure, à toute vitesse
4 **salt l.** *(provided for cattle)* pain *m* de sel; *(place)* terrain *m* salifère *(où les bêtes viennent lécher le sol)*
VT **1** lécher; *Fig* **to l. one's lips** *or Fam* **one's chops** se lécher *ou* se pourlécher les babines; *Fig* **to l. one's wounds** panser ses blessures; *Fam* **to l. sb's boots** lécher les bottes à qn; *Vulg* **to l. sb's arse** lécher le cul de qn; *Fam* **to l. sb into shape** dresser qn; **to l. sth up** *(of animal)* laper qch; *Fig Fam* **to l. the plate clean** ne pas laisser une miette dans son assiette
2 *Fam (defeat) (opponent)* mettre une raclée à; *(beat physically) (person)* battre, rosser; **he's got them licked** *(is certain to beat)* il va les écraser; **when it comes to marketing, they've got us licked** pour ce qui est du marketing, on ne leur arrive pas à la cheville; **I've got the problem licked** j'ai surmonté le problème; **this one has got me licked** *(of problem)* ça me dépasse

lickety-split ['lɪkɪtɪ'splɪt] ADV *Am Fam* à toute vitesse, *Fam* à toute berzingue

licking ['lɪkɪŋ] N *Fam (of opponent)* raclée *f*, *(physical beating)* raclée *f*, rossée *f*; **they gave the other team a l.** ils ont mis une raclée à l'autre équipe

lickspittle ['lɪkspɪt(ə)l] N *Old-fashioned* lèche-bottes *m inv*

licorice ['lɪkərɪs] N *Am* = **liquorice**

lid [lɪd] N **1** *(of box, pan etc)* couvercle *m*; *Br Fig* **that puts the (tin) l. on it!** ça c'est le comble!; **this put the l. on her hopes of winning** cela a anéanti ses espoirs de gagner; **to take the l. off sth** ôter le couvercle de qch; *Fig* mettre qch au grand jour; *Fam* **to keep the l. on a piece of information** garder une information pour soi **2** *(eyelid)* paupière *f*

lidded ['lɪdɪd] ADJ *(box etc)* à couvercle

lidless ['lɪdlɪs] ADJ *(eyes)* sans paupières

lido ['liːdəʊ] N *Br (swimming pool)* piscine *f* en plein air

lie¹ [laɪ] N *(untruth)* mensonge *m*; **it's all lies** *or* **a pack of lies!** c'est un tissu de mensonges!; **to tell a l.** dire un mensonge; *Fam* **in 2001, no, I tell a l., it was 2002** en 2001, non, je dis une bêtise, c'était en 2002; *Prov* **there are lies, damned lies and statistics** on fait dire ce que l'on veut aux chiffres; **to give the l. to sb** donner tort à qn; **to give the l. to an argument** démentir un argument

VI *(pt, pp* **lied** [laɪd], *prp* **lying** ['laɪɪŋ]) *(tell untruth)* mentir (**to sb** à qn); **to l. about one's age** mentir sur son âge; **to l. through one's teeth** mentir effrontément

VT **she lied her way into the building** elle a pénétré dans l'immeuble grâce à quelques mensonges; **he always lies his way out of difficulties** il se sort toujours des difficultés en mentant

▸▸**l. detector** détecteur *m* de mensonges; **to take a l. detector test** passer au détecteur de mensonges

LIE² N **1** *(of land)* disposition *f*; **l. of the land** configuration *f* ou disposition du terrain, topographie *f*; *Fig* **to find out the l. of the land** tâter le terrain

2 *Golf (of ball)* position *f*, assiette *f*

VI *(pt* **lay** [leɪ], *pp* **lain** [leɪn], *prp* **lying** ['laɪɪŋ]) **1** *(of person, animal) (be in lying position)* être couché (à plat); *(go into lying position)* s'allonger; **he was lying down on the floor** il était allongé *ou* couché par terre; **to l. on one's back/side** être couché sur le dos/côté; **to be lying ill in bed** être (malade et) alité; **we found him lying dead** nous l'avons trouvé mort; **here lies …** *(on gravestone)* ci-gît …; **to l. in bed** rester au lit; **I lay awake all night** je n'ai pas pu dormir de la nuit; **I lay awake until 5.30** je suis resté sans pouvoir dormir jusqu'à 5h30; **to l. hidden** rester caché; **to l. in wait for sb** guetter l'arrivée de qn; **the gamekeeper lay in wait all night for the poacher** le garde-chasse est resté tapi toute la nuit à attendre le braconnier

2 *(of object)* être, se trouver; **the papers lay on the table** les papiers étaient sur la table; **all her clothes were lying on the floor** tous ses vêtements étaient étalés par terre; **town lying in a valley** ville située dans une vallée; **a vast plain lay before us** une vaste plaine s'étendait devant nous; **our way lies through the woods** notre chemin passe par les bois; **to l. in ruins** *(of building)* être en ruines; *(of career etc)* être détruit; **the obstacles that l. in our way** les obstacles qui bloquent notre chemin; **these hills l. between us and the sea** ces collines sont entre nous et la mer; *Naut* **ship lying at her berth** navire mouillé *ou* amarré à son poste; **the money is just lying in the bank doing nothing** l'argent dort à la banque; **the snow did not l.** la neige n'a pas tenu; **to l. dormant** *(of volcano)* être en sommeil *ou* au repos; **to l. (heavy) on one's stomach** *(of food)* peser sur l'estomac

3 *(of abstract thing)* **sins that l. heavy on the conscience** péchés qui pèsent sur la conscience; **the onus of proof lies with them** c'est à eux qu'incombe la charge de la preuve; **the responsibility lies with the author** la responsabilité incombe à l'auteur; **to know where one's interests l.** savoir où se trouvent ses intérêts; **the difference lies in this, that …** la différence réside dans le fait que …; **the fault lies with you** c'est de votre faute; **a brilliant future lies before her** un brillant avenir s'ouvre devant elle; **what lies behind this uncharacteristic generosity?** qu'y a-t-il derrière cette générosité inhabituelle?; **my talents do not l. in that direction**

je n'ai pas de dispositions *ou* de talent pour cela

4 *Law (of action, appeal)* être recevable

> Attention: ne pas confondre avec le verbe **to lay**, qui signifie **poser à plat**.

▸ **lie about** VI *(of thing, person)* traîner; **to leave one's papers lying about** laisser traîner ses papiers

▸ **lie back** VI se coucher sur le dos; *(in armchair)* se renverser; **just l. back and relax** *(literally)* allongez-vous et détendez-vous; **when you've finished you can l. back and take things easy** quand tu auras fini tu pourras te reposer

▸ **lie down** VI se coucher, s'étendre; **go and l. down** va t'allonger; **to l. down on one's bed** s'allonger sur son lit; **to l. down on the ground** se coucher *ou* s'allonger par terre; **l. down!** *(to dog)* couché!; *Fig* **to take an insult lying down** ne pas relever une insulte; *Fig* **he won't take it lying down** il ne se laissera pas faire

▸ **lie in** VI faire la grasse matinée

▸ **lie off** VI *(of ship)* rester au large

▸ **lie over** VI *(of thing)* être remis à plus tard; **to let a bill l. over** différer l'échéance d'un effet

▸ **lie to** VI *(of ship)* être à la cape, tenir la cape

▸ **lie up** VI **1** *(because of illness)* garder le lit, garder la chambre; *(hide)* se cacher **2** *(of car)* être en panne; *(of ship)* désarmer

Liechtenstein ['lɪktənstaɪn] N le Liechtenstein

lie-down N **to have a l.** faire une sieste *ou* un petit somme

lief [liːf] ADV *Arch* **I would as l. …** j'aimerais autant …

liege [liːdʒ] N *Hist* suzerain *m*; **my l.!** sire!

lie-in N **to have a l.** faire la grasse matinée

lien [liː(ə)n] N *Law (on property)* privilège *m*, droit *m* de rétention; **to have a l. on a cargo** avoir un recours sur un chargement; *Fin* **l. on shares** nantissement *m* d'actions

lieu [ljuː, luː] N *Fml* **in l. of …** au lieu de …; **to stand in l. of …** tenir lieu de …; **I'll take something else in l.** je prendrai quelque chose d'autre à la place; **two weeks salary in l. of notice** deux semaines de salaire en guise de préavis; **time off in l.** repos *m* compensateur

Lieut *Mil (abbr* **Lieutenant)** Lieut, Lt.

Lieut-Col *Mil (abbr* **Lieutenant-Colonel)** Lieut.-Col.

lieutenant [lef'tenənt, *esp Am* luː'tenənt] N *Mil, Fig* lieutenant *m*; *Naut* lieutenant de vaisseau

▸▸**l. colonel** lieutenant-colonel *m*, *pl* lieutenants-colonels; **l. commander** capitaine *m* de corvette; **l. general** *(in army)* général *m* de corps d'armée; *(in US airforce)* général de corps aérien; **l. governor** *(in Canada)* lieutenant, -ante gouverneur(e); *(in US)* gouverneur, -eure adjoint(e)

LIFE, *pl* **lives** [laɪf, laɪvz] N **1** *(existence)* vie *f*; **to take sb's l.** tuer qn; **to take one's own l.** se suicider; **to give l. to sb** donner la vie à qn; **to come to l. again** revenir à la vie; **it is a matter of l. and death** c'est une question de vie ou de mort; **to be hovering between l. and death** être entre la vie et la mort; **to believe in l. after death** croire à la vie après la mort; **to risk one's l., to risk l. and limb** risquer sa peau; **to escape with one's l.** avoir la vie sauve; **to lose one's l.** perdre la vie, périr; **no lives were lost** il n'y a eu aucune victime, on ne déplore aucune victime; **100 lives were lost** il y a eu 100 morts; **run for your lives!** sauve qui peut!; **a cat has nine lives** un chat a neuf vies; *Fam* **get a l.!** t'as rien de

mieux à faire de ton temps?; *Br Fam* **my l.!** c'est pas vrai!; *Fam* **not on your l.!** jamais de la vie!; **he was rowing for dear l.** il ramait de toutes ses forces; **she can't sing to save her l.** elle est totalement incapable de chanter; *Fam* **I couldn't for the l. of me think what he wanted** je ne pouvais absolument pas imaginer ce qu'il voulait; *Art* **to draw from l.** dessiner d'après nature; **characters taken from l.** caractères pris sur le vif; **that's her to the l.** *(in that portrait, play etc)* c'est elle toute crachée; **animal/vegetable l.** la vie animale/végétale; **bird l.** la vie des oiseaux

2 *(period of existence) (of person)* vie *f*; **a l. of Tolstoy** une biographie de Tolstoï; **(useful) l.** *(of machine)* vie *ou* durée *f* utile; **to work all one's l.** travailler durant toute sa vie; **never in (all) my l.** jamais de la vie; **in his early l.** quand il était jeune; **to be given a l. sentence,** *Fam* **to get l.** être condamné à vie; **appointed for l.** nommé à vie; *Fam* **to be in for l.** *(in prison)* en avoir pris pour la vie; **to mate for l.** *(of animal, bird)* s'unir pour la vie; *Nucl* **average** *or* **mean l.** *(of atom, isotope)* vie moyenne

3 *(mode of existence)* vie *f*; *Fam* **to live** *or* **lead the l. of Riley** se la couler douce; **to make a new l. for oneself** refaire sa vie; **to depart this l.** quitter ce monde; **the man/woman in one's l.** l'homme/la femme de sa vie; **way of l.** manière *f* de vivre, *(train m de)* vie; **the American way of l.** le style de vie américain; **dieting has become a way of l. with some people** certaines personnes passent leur vie à faire des régimes; **to see l.** se frotter à la vie, partir à l'aventure; **he has seen l.** il sait ce que c'est que la vie; **you really see l. as a cop** quand on est flic, on en voit de toutes les couleurs; **he makes her l. a misery** il lui rend la vie impossible; **to make l. worth living** donner un sens à l'existence; **l. is worth living when I'm with her** avec elle la vie vaut la peine d'être vécu; *Fam* **how's l.?** comment ça va?; **what a l.!** quelle vie!; **such is** *or* **that's l.!** c'est la vie!; **this is the l.!** voilà ce que j'appelle vivre!; **the good l.** la belle vie; **he led** *or* **lived a good l.** il a eu une vie exemplaire

4 *(liveliness)* **to come to l.** *(of person, place, play etc)* s'animer; **to bring a party to l.** *(of person)* animer une fête; **to bring sb to l.** *(of play, book etc)* faire vivre qn; **full of l.** *(person)* plein de vie *ou* d'entrain; *(street etc)* plein de mouvement *ou* d'animation; **to put new l. into** *(person, company etc)* ranimer; **the l. and soul of the party** le boute-en-train de la soirée; **there's no l. in this place** ça manque d'entrain ici; **he may be 80 but there's l. in the old dog yet** il a peut-être 80 ans mais il est encore vif; **the critics say I'm finished but there's l. in the old dog yet** les critiques disent que je suis fini mais je n'ai pas dit mon dernier mot; **there's l. in the old car yet** elle marche toujours, la vieille bagnole

▸▸**l. annuity** pension *f* viagère; *Br* **l. assurance** assurance-vie *f*, *pl* assurances-vie; **l. belt** bouée *f* de sauvetage; **l. buoy** bouée de sauvetage; *Fin* **l. capitalization** capitalisation *f* viagère; **l. class** cours *m* de dessin avec modèle nu; **l. cycle** cycle *m* de vie; **l. expectancy** *(of human, animal)* espérance *f* de vie; *(of machine, product)* durée *f* (utile) de vie; **l. force** élan *m* vital; **l. form** forme *f* de vie; **the L. Guards** = régiment *m* de cavalerie de la garde royale britannique; **l. imprisonment** prison *f* à vie; **l. insurance** assurance-vie *f*; **l. interest** usufruit *m*; *(of possession)* viager *m*; **l. jacket** gilet *m* de sauvetage; **l. member** membre *m* à vie; **l. membership** adhésion *f* à vie; *Br* **l. peer** pair *m* à vie; **l. pension** rente *f* viagère; *Am* **l. preserver** *(life belt)* bouée *f* de sauvetage; *(life jacket)* gilet de sauvetage; **l. raft** radeau *m* de sauvetage; **the l. sciences** les sciences *fpl* de la vie; **l. span** *(of human, animal)* espérance de vie; *(of machine, product)* durée de vie; **l. story** biographie *f*, **l. subscription** abonnement *m* à vie

life-and-death ADJ **a l. situation** une question de vie ou de mort; **a l. struggle** une lutte désespérée; *(literally)* une guerre à mort

lifeblood ['laɪfblʌd] N *(of company etc)* âme *f*, *Lit (of person)* sang *m*; **the government are draining the l. from small businesses** le gouvernement est en train de saigner les petites entreprises; **the l. of the economy** le pivot de l'économie

lifeboat ['laɪfbəʊt] N **1** *(launched from coast)* canot *m* de sauvetage **2 (ship's) l.** embarcation *f* de sauvetage
▸▸ **l. station** poste *m* de sauvetage

lifeboatman, *pl* **lifeboatmen** ['laɪfbəʊtmən] N sauveteur *m*

life-cycle chart N *Mktg (of product)* courbe *f* du cycle de vie

life-giving ADJ vivifiant; *(sun, water)* nourricier

lifeguard ['laɪfgɑːd] N *(at the seaside)* surveillant, -ante de baignade; *(at swimming pool)* maître *m* nageur; **to be on l. duty** surveiller la baignade

lifeless ['laɪflɪs] ADJ sans vie; *(style, gestures, acting etc)* mou, *f* molle; *(expression)* vide; *(performance)* mort; **she fell l. to the floor** elle est tombée raide sur le sol

lifelessly ['laɪflɪslɪ] ADV sans vie

lifelessness ['laɪflɪsnɪs] N *(of party etc)* manque *m* d'animation; *(of gestures)* mollesse *f*, *(of paintings)* froideur *f*

lifelike ['laɪflaɪk] ADJ *(portrait etc)* vivant, qui a de la vie; **it's very l.** c'est très réaliste

lifeline ['laɪflaɪn] N **1** *Naut* ligne *f* de sauvetage; *(aboard ship)* garde-corps *m inv*, attrape *f*, sauvegarde *f*, *(of diver)* corde *f* de communication; *Fig* **to throw sb a l.** venir à l'aide de qn; *Fig* **for us it was a financial l.** cet argent a permis notre survie **2** *(in palmistry)* ligne *f* de vie

lifelong ['laɪflɒŋ] ADJ ATTRIB *(friendship etc)* de toute la vie; **a l. friend** un ami de toujours; **a l. ambition** une ambition de toujours
▸▸ **l. learning** éducation *f* permanente

lifer ['laɪfər] N *Fam* condamné, -ée à perpétuité

life-saver N **1** *(person)* sauveteur *m* **2** *Fig* planche *f* de salut; **that cup of tea was a l.!** cette tasse de thé m'a redonné vie; **you're a l.** tu me sauves la vie!

life-saving N **l. apparatus** appareils *mpl* ou engins *mpl* de sauvetage; **l. vaccine** vaccin *m* qui sauve la vie

life-size(d) ADJ *(portrait etc)* grandeur nature

lifestyle ['laɪfstaɪl] N style *m* de vie, mode *m* de vie
▸▸ *Mktg* **l. analysis** analyse *f* du style de vie; *Mktg* **l. data** données *fpl* de style de vie; *Mktg* **l. group** sociostyle *m*; *Mktg* **l. segmentation** segmentation *f* par styles de vie

life-support ADJ
▸▸ *Med* **l. machine** respirateur *m*; **l. system** *Med* respirateur; *Astron* équipement *m* de survie; *Med* **to be on a l. system** or **machine** être sous assistance respiratoire; *Med* **to switch off the l. system** or **machine** arrêter le respirateur ou la respiration artificielle

life-threatening ADJ *(disease)* qui peut être mortel; **it's not l.** ce n'est pas mortel; **in a l. situation, the fish ...** quand il se sent en danger de mort, le poisson ...

lifetime ['laɪftaɪm] N *(of person)* vie *f*, *(of lamp, machine, Fin of option)* durée *f*, vie;

Nucl (of atom, isotope) durée de vie, longévité *f*, *St Exch (of an option)* durée de vie; **in** or **during one's l.** de son vivant; **such a bill is unlikely within the l. of this parliament** un tel projet de loi est peu probable tant que ce parlement est en place; **a l. of happiness** toute une vie de bonheur; **it's the chance** or **opportunity of a l.** cette chance n'arrive qu'une fois dans la vie; **the holiday of a l.** des vacances sensationnelles; **a l. supply** une réserve pour la vie; **he's bought enough envelopes to last him a l.** il a acheté suffisamment d'enveloppes pour tenir jusqu'à la fin de ses jours

LIFFE [laɪf, 'lɪfɪ] N *(abbr* **London International Financial Futures Exchange)** = marché *m* à terme d'instruments financiers, MATIF *m*

LIFO ['liːfəʊ] *Com (abbr* **last in, first out)** DEPS

lift [lɪft] N **1** *(raising device) Br* ascenseur *m*; *Br* **(goods) l.** monte-charge *m inv*, élévateur *m*; **ski l.** remontée *f* mécanique
2 *esp Br (car ride)* **to give sb a l.** prendre ou emmener qn en voiture; **could you give me a l. to the station?** *(it's on your way)* est-ce que tu peux me déposer à la gare?; *(make special trip)* est-ce que tu peux m'emmener à la gare?; **can I give you a l.?** est-ce que je peux vous conduire ou déposer quelque part?; **I'll try to arrange a l. for anyone who hasn't got a car** je ferai en sorte que tout le monde ait une place dans une voiture; **we've been waiting over two hours for a l.** cela fait deux heures que nous attendons que quelqu'un veuille bien nous prendre; **we got a great l. yesterday, all the way to Lyons** on a eu de la chance hier, il y a quelqu'un qui nous a emmenés jusqu'à Lyon
3 *Fam* **to give sb a l.** *(cheer up)* remonter le moral à qn
4 *(extent of rise) (of crane etc)* hauteur *f* de levage; *(of pump)* hauteur d'élévation; *Tech (of valve, cam)* levée *f*, *(of millrace)* (hauteur de) chute *f*, *(between bearings etc)* différence *f* de niveau
5 *(raising power) (of balloon, gas)* force *f* ascensionnelle; *Aviat* portance *f*, poussée *f* (aérodynamique), sustentation *f*
VT **1** *(weight)* lever, soulever; *(one's head)* lever, dresser; *(one's eyes, arm)* lever; **to l. weights** *(as exercise)* faire des haltères; **he never lifts a finger to help** il ne lève ou bouge jamais le petit doigt pour aider; **she has only to l. a finger and everyone comes running** elle n'a qu'à lever le petit doigt et tout le monde accourt; **to l. sth (up) again** soulever qch, relever qch; **to l. sb (up)** *(who has fallen)* aider qn à se relever; **to l. a child up** *(take in one's arms)* prendre un enfant dans ses bras; *Lit* **to l. (up) one's voice in prayer** adresser une prière au ciel; **to l. sth down** *(from a shelf etc)* descendre qch; **the wind lifted him off his feet** il a été soulevé par le vent
2 *(potatoes, bulbs etc)* arracher; *Com (goods)* enlever
3 *Cr, Golf (ball)* donner de l'essor à; *Tennis (shot)* lifter
4 *Fam (take, steal)* voler, *Fam* piquer; **he had his wallet lifted** il s'est fait piquer son portefeuille; **to l. a passage from an author/a book** piquer un passage chez un auteur/dans un livre
5 *Br Fam (arrest)* agrafer, alpaguer
6 *(remove) (embargo)* lever; *(mortgage)* déshypothéquer
VI **1** *(of valve etc)* se lever, se soulever; *(of floor) (as a result of damp etc)* se soulever **2** *(disperse) (of fog)* se lever, se dissiper; *Am (of rain)* cesser **3** *Naut (of vessel)* s'élever à la lame
▸▸ *Br* **l. attendant** liftier *m*; *Ski* **l. pass** forfait

m de remontées mécaniques; *Br* **l. shaft** cage *f* d'ascenseur
▸ **lift off** VI *(of aircraft, rocket)* décoller
VT SEP *(lid etc)* soulever
▸ **lift out** VT SEP *(from box etc)* sortir (**from** de); *Mil (troops)* évacuer (par avion ou hélicoptère)
▸ **lift up** VT SEP = **lift** VT

liftboy ['lɪftbɔɪ] N *Br* liftier *m*

liftgate ['lɪftgeɪt] N *Am Aut* hayon *m* arrière

lifting ['lɪftɪŋ] N **1** *(of potatoes, bulbs)* arrachage *m* **2** *(of embargo)* levée *f*, *(of mortgage, ban)* mainlevée *f*
▸▸ **l. capacity** puissance *f* de levage; *Aviat* **l. force** force *f* de sustentation, puissance ascensionnelle; *Aut* **l. platform** pont *m* élévateur; *Aviat* **l. power** force de sustentation, puissance ascensionnelle; *Aut* **l. ramp** pont élévateur

liftoff ['lɪftɒf] N *(of rocket)* décollage *m*; **we have l.** lancement réussi

lift-operator N *Br* liftier *m*

ligament ['lɪgəmənt] N *Anat* ligament *m*; **to tear a l.** se déchirer un ligament

ligature ['lɪgətʃər] N **1** *Surg* ligature *f* **2** *Typ* ligature **3** *Mus* liaison *f*
VT **1** *Surg (vein)* ligaturer, barrer **2** *Typ (two vowels)* ligaturer; **o e ligatured** e dans l'o

LIGHT¹ [laɪt]

N lumière **1, 3, 7** ▪ jour **1** ▪ feu **3, 5** ▪ phare **4** ▪ fenêtre **6**	
VT allumer **1** ▪ éclairer **2**	
ADJ clair **1, 2**	

N **1** lumière *f*, **artificial/electric l.** lumière artificielle/électrique; **by the l. of the moon** au clair ou à la clarté de la lune; **the l. of day** la lumière du jour, le jour; **things will look different in the cold l. of day** demain tu verras les choses sous un autre aspect; **it's getting l.** le jour se lève; **to bring sth to l.** *(of investigations)* mettre qch en évidence, révéler qch; **to come to l.** *(of crime etc)* être découvert; **to see the l.** *(realise the truth)* être convaincu ou converti; **to (first) see the l. of day** *(of person)* naître, voir le jour; **to be in sb's l.** faire de l'ombre à qn; *Phys* **infrared/ultraviolet l.** lumière infrarouge/ultraviolette; **source of l.** source *f* lumineuse; **against the l., with one's back to the l.** à contre-jour; **good/bad l.** bon/mauvais éclairage *m*; **to act according to one's lights** agir conformément à ses idées
2 *(figurative senses)* **in a bad l.** sous un mauvais angle; **in a positive/favourable l.** sous un angle positif/favorable; **in a poor l. he could pass for 40** dans la pénombre on pourrait penser qu'il a 40 ans; **in a good l. he could pass for 40** avec un bon éclairage on pourrait penser qu'il a 40 ans; **to throw** or **shed** or **cast l. on sth** faire la lumière sur qch, éclaircir qch; **to see sb/sth in a new l./ in their/its true l.** voir qn/qch sous un jour nouveau/sous son vrai jour; **to see sth in a different l.** voir qch sous un jour différent ou sous un autre angle; **the question should be considered in the l. of these facts** on devrait considérer la question à la lumière de ces faits; **in the l. of ...** *(considering)* prenant en considération ou en compte ...
3 *(object) (in room etc)* lumière *f*, *(on car, train, ship etc)* feu *m*; *Cin, TV* projecteur *m*; **lights out** l'extinction *f* des feux; **to put** or **turn on the l.** allumer; **to put** or **turn off the l.** éteindre (la lumière); *Fam* **to go out like a l.** *(fall asleep quickly)* s'endormir aussitôt couché; *(faint, become unconscious)* s'évanouir; *Fam Hum* **the lights are on but there's nobody home** c'est pas une lumière; **(traffic) lights** feux *mpl* de circulation ou de signalisation routière, *Fam* feu rouge; **turn**

right at the (traffic) lights tournez à droite au feu rouge; *Aut* **dip your lights** roulez en code; **she was showing no lights** *(of ship)* il naviguait *ou* faisait route tous feux éteints; *Tech* **control** *or* **warning l.** voyant *m* lumineux

4 *(lighthouse)* phare *m*

5 *(flame)* feu *m*; **to set l. to sth** mettre le feu à qch; **could I have a l.?** est-ce que tu peux me donner du feu?; **have you got a l.?** vous avez du feu, s'il vous plaît?

6 *Archit (window)* fenêtre *f*, *(small round)* lucarne *f*, *(of mullioned window)* jour *m*; *(of greenhouse)* carreau *m*

7 *Art, Phot* lumière *f*, clair *m*; **l. and shade** les ombres et la lumière

vt *(pt, pp* **lit** [lɪt], *occ* **lighted)** **1** *(lamp, fire etc)* allumer; **to l. a fire** allumer un feu; *Fig* **to l. sb's fire** exciter qn

2 *(room, street)* éclairer, illuminer; **to l. the way for sb** éclairer qn

ADJ 1 *(room etc)* clair, (bien) éclairé; **it is/will soon be l.** il fait/fera bientôt jour

2 *(hair, complexion)* blond; *(colour)* clair; **painted in l. tones** peint en tons clairs *ou* lumineux; **l. blue** bleu clair *inv*

▸▸ **l. beam** faisceau *m* lumineux; **l. box** table *f* lumineuse; **l. bulb** ampoule *f* (électrique); *TV* **l. cue** signal *m* lumineux; **l. effects** effets *mpl ou* jeux *mpl* de lumière; **l. flare** fusée *f* éclairante; **l. meter** posemètre *m*; *Comput* **l. pen** crayon *m* optique; **l. ray** rayon *m* lumineux; **l. source** source *f* lumineuse; **l. switch** interrupteur *m*; **l. table** *(for viewing negatives, film)* table *f* lumineuse; **l. wave** onde *f* lumineuse; *Astron* **l. year** année-lumière *f, pl* années-lumière; *Fig* **they are l. years ahead** ils ont des années-lumière d'avance

▸ **light into** VT INSEP *Fam (attack verbally or physically)* tomber dessus, rentrer dedans; **she really lit into him** elle lui est carrément tombée dessus *ou* rentrée dedans

▸ **light on** VT INSEP *(find) (solution, correct method, cure etc)* trouver; **his eyes lighted on the picture** ses yeux se posèrent sur le tableau

▸ **light out** VI *Am Fam* décamper

▸ **light up** VI *(put lights on)* allumer, mettre la lumière; *Fam (of smoker)* allumer sa cigarette/sa pipe/etc; **his eyes lit up** ses yeux se sont animés; **the whole sky lit up** le ciel entier s'illumina

vt SEP 1 *(room)* éclairer; *(cigarette, pipe)* allumer; **the house was lit up** la maison était illuminée; **a smile lit up her face** un sourire a illuminé son visage

2 *Br Sl* **to be lit up** *(drunk)* être éméché

LIGHT² ADJ **1** *(load, blow etc)* léger; *(soil)* meuble; *(deficient) (weight)* faible; **with a l. step** d'un pas léger; **l. touch** *(of painter, author, film director)* finesse *f*; **she's got a very l. touch with pastry** les pâtisseries qu'elle fait sont très légères; **to be l. on one's feet** avoir le pas léger; **as l. as a feather** léger comme une plume; **to have a l. meal** prendre un repas léger; **to be a l. sleeper** avoir le sommeil léger; **l. showers** ondées *fpl*

2 *(not of full weight, size etc) (aircraft, engine)* léger; *(not fully loaded) (ship)* lège; *Typ (type)* maigre; **l. crop** faible récolte *f*

3 *(not strenuous) (job)* facile; **a little l. housework** un petit peu de ménage mais sans vous forcer; **l. punishment** peine *f* légère; **l. work** petits travaux *mpl*, travail peu fatigant

4 *(not serious) (comedy, style, music etc)* léger; **to make l. of sth** traiter qch à la légère; *(of accusation)* attacher peu d'importance à qch; **l. talk** propos *mpl* frivoles *ou* légers

ADV légèrement; **to travel l.** voyager léger

▸▸ **l. aircraft** avion *m* de tourisme; **l. artillery** artillerie *f* légère *ou* de petit calibre; **l.**

beer bière *f* légère; **l. breeze** petite brise *f*, brise légère; *(on Beaufort scale)* légère brise; *Metal* **l. castings** petites pièces *fpl* de fonderie; *Mil* **l. duty** service *m* réduit; **l. entertainment** variétés *fpl*; **it's not exactly l. entertainment** *(of job)* ce n'est pas ce qu'on fait de plus divertissant; *(of music, play etc)* ce n'est pas ce qu'il y a de plus léger; **l. infantry** infanterie *f* légère; **l. reading** lecture(s) *f(pl)* récréative(s) *ou* délassante(s); *Mktg* **l. user** faible utilisateur, -trice; **l. van** fourgonnette *f*; **l. verse** poésie *f* facile

light-coloured, *Am* **light-colored** ADJ clair

light-emitting diode [laɪtɪmɪtɪŋ] N diode *f* électroluminescente

lighten¹ ['laɪt(ə)n] VT **1** *(light up) (darkness, face)* éclairer; *(house etc)* rendre plus clair **2** *(colour, sky)* éclaircir

vi s'éclairer, s'illuminer; **her face lightened** son visage s'éclaira

lighten² VT *(reduce weight of)* alléger; *(ship)* délester; *Fig* **to l. sb's load** *(make work or life easier)* décharger qn

vi my heart lightened j'ai été soulagé

▸ **lighten up** VI *esp Am Fam* se dérider; **come on, l. up!** tu ne peux pas parler de choses moins sérieuses?

lighter¹ ['laɪtər] N allume-gaz *m inv*, *(for cigarettes)* briquet *m*; *(in car)* allume-cigare *m, pl* allume-cigares

▸▸ **l. flint** pierre *f* à briquet; **l. fluid**, **l. fuel** essence *f* à briquet

lighter² N *Naut* allège *f*, gabare *f*

lighterage ['laɪtərɪdʒ] N *Naut (unloading)* déchargement *m* par allèges *ou* par gabares, gabarage *m*; *(fee)* droits *mpl ou* frais *mpl* d'allège *ou* de gabarage

lighter-than-air ADJ *(aircraft)* plus léger que l'air

light-face *Typ* N (caractère *m*) maigre *m* **ADJ** maigre

light-fingered [laɪt'fɪŋɡəd] ADJ *Fam* **he's l.** c'est un voleur; *Fam* il a la main leste

light-footed ADJ agile, leste, au pied léger

light-headed ADJ **1** *(dizzy)* **to feel l.** *(through lack of food etc)* se sentir un peu étourdi **2** *(frivolous)* écervelé; *(excited)* excité; **the realization that she had won made her feel quite l.** elle était tout excitée de réaliser qu'elle avait gagné

light-hearted ['laɪthɑːtɪd] ADJ *(person)* allègre; *(remark, discussion)* léger

lighthouse ['laɪthaʊs] N phare *m*

▸▸ **l. keeper** gardien *m* de phare

lighting ['laɪtɪŋ] N **1** *(of stage set etc)* éclairage *m*; *(lights themselves)* lumières *fpl* **2** *(of painting)* éclairage *m*, exposition *f*

▸▸ **l. angle** angle *m* d'éclairage; **l. board** pupitre *m* d'éclairage; *Theat, Cin* **l. cameraman** directeur, -trice de la photographie, chef opérateur *m* cadreur; **l. effects** effets *mpl* d'éclairage *ou* de lumière; **l. engineer** éclairagiste *mf*; **l. technician** éclairagiste *mf*, éclairo *m*; *Br Admin* **l. up time** heure *f* d'éclairage

lightly ['laɪtlɪ] ADV **1** légèrement; *(to walk)* d'un pas léger; **to sleep l.** *(generally)* avoir le sommeil léger; *(on one occasion)* dormir d'un sommeil léger; **to cook sth l.** faire cuire qch légèrement; **her responsibilities sit l. on her** ses responsabilités ne lui pèsent pas; **to get off l.** s'en tirer à bon compte **2** *(to say)* d'un ton léger; **to speak l. of sth** parler de qch à la légère; **to take a decision l.** prendre une décision à la légère

lightness¹ ['laɪtnɪs] N *(brightness)* clarté *f*

lightness² N *(in weight etc)* légèreté *f*; **l. of foot** agilité *f*; **l. of heart** gaieté *f* de cœur; **l. of touch** *(of pianist, tennis player)* légèreté;

(of artist) légèreté *f* de pinceau; *(of writer)* légèreté de style

lightning ['laɪtnɪŋ] N éclairs *mpl*, foudre *f*; **a flash of l.** un éclair; **struck by l.** frappé par la foudre; **as quick as l., with l. speed,** *Fam* **like greased l.** rapide comme l'éclair; *Prov* **l. never strikes twice in the same place** la foudre ne frappe jamais deux fois au même endroit

▸▸ **l. attack** attaque *f* éclair; *Am* **l. bug** luciole *f*, **l. conductor,** *Am* **l. rod** paratonnerre *m*; **l. strike** *(by workers)* grève *f* surprise *(inv)*; **l. visit** visite *f* éclair

lightproof ['laɪtpruːf] ADJ opaque

lights [laɪts] NPL *Culin (of cow etc)* mou *m*

light-sensitive ADJ *Phys* photosensible

lightship ['laɪtʃɪp] N *Naut* bateau-feu *m, pl* bateaux-feux, bateau-phare *m, pl* bateaux-phares

lightweight ['laɪtweɪt] N *Boxing* poids *m* léger; *Pej (unimpressive person)* personne *f* qui manque d'envergure; **intellectual/political l.** personne qui manque d'envergure intellectuelle/politique

ADJ *(garment etc)* léger

lignite ['lɪɡnaɪt] N *Miner* lignite *m*

likable ['laɪkəb(ə)l] = **likeable**

LIKE [laɪk] ADJ semblable, pareil; **they are of l. temperament** ils ont le même tempérament; **they are as l. as two peas (in a pod)** ils se ressemblent comme deux gouttes d'eau

PREP 1 *(similar to)* **to be l. sb/sth** être semblable à qn/à qch, ressembler à qn/à qch; **we're l. sisters** nous sommes comme des sœurs; **to taste l. sth** avoir le même goût que qch; **to look l. sth/sb** ressembler à qch/qn; **I want to find one l. it** je veux trouver le/la même; **people l. you** des gens comme vous; **what's the weather l.?** quel temps fait-il?; **you know what she's l.** vous savez comme elle est; **he was l. a father to me** il a été comme un père pour moi; **when I hear things l. that** quand j'entends des choses pareilles; **I know plenty of people l. that** je connais pas mal de gens comme ça; **something very much l. it** quelque chose qui y ressemble beaucoup; **it costs something l. £10** cela coûte environ 10 livres; **it will cost more l. £20** ça coûtera plutôt dans les 20 livres; **that's more l. it** voilà qui est mieux; **we don't have anything l. as many people as we need** on est loin d'avoir tout le monde qu'il nous faut; **it's just l. (at) home** c'est comme à la maison; *Fam* **that's something l. it!** voilà qui est réussi!; **there's nothing l. it** il n'y a rien de mieux; **she is nothing l. as intelligent as you** elle est loin d'être aussi intelligente que vous; **that's not l. him** *(not his way of behaving etc)* ça ne lui ressemble pas; **that's just l. him!** c'est bien de lui!; **that's just l. a woman/a man!** c'est typiquement féminin/masculin!; **l. father l. son** tel père, tel fils

2 *(in the manner of)* comme; **I think l. you** je pense comme vous; **just l. anybody else** comme tout le monde; **to speak French l. a native** parler français comme un natif; *Fam* **to run l. blazes** *or* **hell** *or* **mad** courir comme un dératé; *Fam* **be l. that then!** puisque c'est ça, fais comme tu veux!; **don't be l. that about it,** he didn't mean what he said ne le prends pas mal, ce n'est pas ce qu'il voulait dire; **l. this?** *(am I doing it correctly?)* comme ça?; **whisk the egg whites gently, l. this** battez les blancs délicatement, comme ceci; **don't talk l. that** ne parlez pas comme ça; **I'm sorry to keep bothering you l. this** je suis désolé de vous déranger continuellement comme ça

3 *(such as)* tel que; **take more exercise, l. jogging** fais plus d'exercice, du jogging par exemple

ADV *Fam* **l. enough, (as) l. as not** probablement, vraisemblablement; *Sl* **he looked**

angry, **l.** il était comme en colère; **Sl he just came up behind me, l.** il est arrivé derrière moi, comme ça

conj Fam **1** (= as) comme; **do l. I do** faites comme moi; **l. I said** comme je l'ai dit

2 (= as if) **he behaved l. he was scared** il s'est conduit comme s'il avait peur; **he looked l. he'd seen a ghost** on aurait dit qu'il avait vu un fantôme

N (person) semblable mf, pareil, -eille; **he and his l.** lui et ses semblables; **it's too good for the likes of me** c'est trop bien pour des gens comme moi; **the likes of you** des gens comme toi, Pej des gens de ton acabit; **music, painting and the l.** la musique, la peinture, et autres choses du même genre; **musicians, painters and the l.** musiciens, peintres et compagnie; **I've never seen the l. (of it)** or **its l.** je n'ai jamais vu une chose pareille; **it was music, the l. of which I had never heard** c'était de la musique comme je n'en avais jamais entendue

NPL likes (tastes) goûts mpl, préférences fpl; **likes and dislikes** préférences fpl; **I don't think she has any very strong likes or dislikes** je ne pense pas qu'elle ait des préférences très marquées

VT 1 (person) aimer bien; **I l. him** je l'aime bien, il me plaît bien; **I don't l. him** je ne l'aime pas, il ne me plaît pas; **how do you l. him?** comment le trouvez-vous?; **she is well liked** elle est très appréciée

2 (enjoy) aimer (bien); **he likes school** il aime l'école; **do you l. tea?** aimez-vous le thé?; **I don't l. it at all** (situation etc) cela ne me plaît pas du tout; **if he doesn't l. it he can go elsewhere** si ça ne lui plaît pas il peut aller ailleurs; **whether she likes it or not** que cela lui plaise ou non; **these plants don't l. the damp** ces plantes craignent l'humidité; **I l. to see them now and again** j'aime les voir de temps à autre; Fam Iron **(well) I l. that!** en voilà une bonne!, elle est bien bonne, celle-là!

3 (to want) aimer (**to do** (à) faire); **he doesn't l. people to talk about it** il n'aime pas qu'on en parle; **I would very much l. to go** j'aimerais beaucoup y aller; **would you l. me to go with you?** voulez-vous que je vous accompagne?; **I would l. to know whether ...** je voudrais bien savoir si ...; **I would l. time to consider it** j'aimerais avoir le temps d'y réfléchir; **I would l. some tea** je prendrais bien une tasse de thé; **would you l. a cigarette?** voulez-vous une cigarette?; **I would l. nothing better** je ne demande pas mieux; **I would l. nothing better than a hot bath** il n'y a rien qui me ferait autant plaisir qu'un bon bain chaud; **as you l.** comme vous voudrez; **to do just as one likes** n'en faire qu'à sa tête; **I can do as I l. with it** j'en fais ce que je veux; **he thinks he can do anything he likes** il se croit tout permis; **she is free to do as she likes** elle est libre d'agir à sa guise ou de faire comme il lui plaira; **if you l.** si vous voulez; **when you l.** quand il vous plaira; **as much as you l.** tant que vous voudrez; **I didn't l. to mention it** j'ai préféré ne pas le mentionner; **I wanted to ring you but I didn't l. to** (I would have disturbed you, upset you etc) je voulais te téléphoner mais j'ai préféré ne pas le faire

▸▸ Elec **l. poles** pôles mpl semblables ou de même nom; Math **l. quantities** quantités fpl semblables; Math **l. terms** termes mpl semblables

likeable ['laɪkəb(ə)l] ADJ (person) agréable, sympathique

likeableness ['laɪkəb(ə)lnɪs] N (of person) amabilité f

likelihood ['laɪklɪhʊd] N vraisemblance f, probabilité f, apparence f; **there is little l. of his succeeding** il y a peu de chances qu'il

réussisse; **there's a strong l. that ...** il y a une forte probabilité pour que ... + sub; **there is every l. that ...** il y a toutes les chances que ... + sub; **in all l.** selon toute probabilité, selon toute vraisemblance

likely ['laɪklɪ] ADJ **1** (probable) vraisemblable, probable; **it's not a very l. scenario** ce scénario n'est pas très vraisemblable; **the pub is a l. place to find him** le pub est probablement l'endroit où le trouver; Fam Iron **that's a l. story!** la belle histoire!, en voilà une bonne!; **it's more than l.** c'est plus que probable; **it's not very l.** c'est peu probable; **it's l. to rain** il y a des chances pour qu'il pleuve; **she is quite l. to do it** il y a des chances qu'elle le fasse; **books l. to interest young people** ouvrages susceptibles d'intéresser les jeunes; **this plan is most l. to succeed** ce projet a beaucoup de chances de réussir; **are the neighbours l. to object?** y a-t-il des chances que les voisins s'y opposent?

2 (promising) prometteur; BrDial **a l. lad** un gars qui promet; **a l. candidate/horse** un candidat/cheval susceptible ou qui a des chances de gagner; **this looked a l. spot to find what they were looking for** l'endroit semblait tout indiqué pour trouver ce qu'ils cherchaient

ADV most l., very l., Am Fam **l.** vraisemblablement, très probablement; **as l. as not** vraisemblablement; Fam **not l.!** jamais de la vie!

like-minded ADJ du même avis; (having same tastes) qui ont les mêmes goûts

liken ['laɪk(ə)n] VT comparer (**to** à)

likeness ['laɪknɪs] N **1** (similarity) ressemblance f (**between** entre; **to** à); **God created man in his own l.** Dieu a créé l'homme à son image; **a close l.** une ressemblance étroite; **family l.** air m de famille **2** (image) portrait m, image f; **the portrait is a good l.** le portrait est très ressemblant

likewise ['laɪkwaɪz] ADV (similarly) de même, aussi; **to do l.** faire de même, en faire autant; **pleased to meet you – l.!** ravi de vous rencontrer – moi de même!

liking ['laɪkɪŋ] N goût m, penchant m; **to one's l.** au goût de qn; **is it to your l.?** cela est-il à votre goût?, est-ce que cela vous plaît?; **to have a l. for sth** avoir du goût pour qch, aimer qch; **I have taken a l. to her** elle m'est devenue sympathique; **to acquire a l. for sth** se mettre à aimer qch

lilac ['laɪlək] N (flower, tree, colour) lilas m

ADJ **l.(-coloured)** lilas inv

Lilliputian [lɪlɪ'pjuːʃən] ADJ Lit lilliputien

Lilo® ['laɪləʊ] N matelas m pneumatique

lilt [lɪlt] N **1** (of verse) rythme m, cadence f; **a song with a l.** une chanson au rythme entraînant; **to speak with a Welsh l.** parler avec des intonations galloises **2** Arch, Scot chant m, air m

lilting ['lɪltɪŋ] ADJ (rhythme) musical, -aux; (tune) cadencé, scandé

lily ['lɪlɪ] N (flower) lis m; **l. of the valley** muguet m

▸▸ **l. pad** feuille f de nénuphar

lily-livered ['lɪlɪlɪvəd] ADJ couard

lily-white ADJ blanc, f blanche comme le lis, d'une blancheur de lis; Fam (character) blanc comme neige

lima bean ['liːmə'biːn] N haricot m de Lima

limb [lɪm] N **1** (of body) membre m; **the lower limbs** les membres inférieurs; **to tear an animal l. from l.** mettre un animal en pièces **2** (of tree) (grosse) branche f, (of cross) bras m; Fam **to be out on a l.** (be alone) être en plan; (be in dangerous position) être dans une situation délicate; Fam **his refusal to compromise left him out on a l.** son refus

d'accepter un compromis l'a mis dans une situation délicate; Fam **to go out on a l.** prendre des risques

-limbed [lɪmd] SUFF **loose-l.** souple; **strong-l.** aux membres solides, solide

limber¹ ['lɪmbər] N Mil (of gun carriage) avant-train m, pl avant-trains

▸ **vt to l. a gun** attacher une pièce de canon à l'avant-train

limber² ADJ souple

▸ **limber up** VI Sport s'échauffer

vt sep Sport (muscles) se chauffer; **to l. up one's fingers** (of pianist etc) s'échauffer les doigts

limbering-up exercises [lɪmbərɪŋ'ʌp] NPL exercices mpl d'assouplissement

limbless ['lɪmlɪs] ADJ (person) à qui il manque un membre/plusieurs membres; (with no arms or legs) sans membres; **l. ex-servicemen** grands mutilés mpl de guerre

limbo ['lɪmbəʊ] N **1** Rel les limbes mpl; Rel, Fig **to be in l.** être dans les limbes **2** (dance) limbo m

▸▸ **l. dancer** danseur, -euse de limbo

lime¹ [laɪm] N (fruit) lime f, citron m vert; (fruit tree) limettier m

▸▸ **l. green** vert m jaune; **a l.-green coat** un manteau vert vif; **l. juice** jus m de citron vert

lime² N (linden tree) tilleul m

lime³ N **1** (substance) chaux f **2** (for catching birds) glu f

vt 1 Agr (soil) chauler **2** (twigs) **to l. birds** prendre des oiseaux à la glu ou au gluau

▸▸ **l. pit** (quarry) fosse f à chaux; (in tanning) pelain m; **l. twig** gluau m

limeade ['laɪmeɪd] N = jus m de citron vert additionné de sucre et d'eau gazeuse

limekiln ['laɪmkɪln] N four m à chaux

limelight ['laɪmlaɪt] N **in the l.** sous les feux de la rampe, très en vue; **she doesn't like the l.** elle n'aime pas sentir les projecteurs braqués sur elle; **an actor who's never out of the l.** un acteur très en vue; **to seek the l.** rechercher la vedette; **to steal the l.** voler la vedette

limerick ['lɪmərɪk] N limerick m, = poème m en cinq vers, burlesque et grivois

limestone ['laɪmstəʊn] N Geol calcaire m

limey ['laɪmɪ] Am, Austr Sl N Anglais m

ADJ anglais

limit ['lɪmɪt] N **1** (boundary) limite f, borne f, Tech (of elasticity etc) limite; (in insurance) plein m; **to fix** or **set a l.** or **limits** fixer ou mettre une limite ou des limites (**to** à); **within a ten kilometre l.** dans un rayon de dix kilomètres; **within limits** dans une certaine mesure; **I like jazz but within limits** j'aime le jazz mais jusqu'à un certain point; **the limits of decency** les limites de la décence; **time l.** (for speaker etc) limite de temps; (for payment etc) délai m; (on special privilege etc) durée f; **to be over the (legal) l.** (of drunken driver) avoir bu plus qu'il n'est permis au volant; Fin **credit l.** limite ou plafond m du crédit; **what is the l. on this road?** (speed) quelle est la limitation de vitesse sur cette route?; **to fix a l.** (in insurance) fixer les pleins; **there's a l. to everything!** il y a une limite à tout!; **there's no l. to her ambition** son ambition est sans limites; **to know no limits** ne connaître aucune limite; **his arrogance knows no limits** son arrogance ne connaît pas de limites; **that's the l.!** ça c'est le comble!; **he's the l.!** il est impossible!; **off limits** (place) inaccessible; Mil consigné à la troupe; **to be off limits to sb** (of place) être inaccessible à qn; Mil **to put a bar off limits** consigner un bar

2 Tech (tolerance) tolérance f

vt (somebody, something) limiter, borner, restreindre; **I have to l. my calorie intake** je dois limiter ma consommation de calories; **to l. oneself to ...** *(in speaking)* se borner à ...; **to l. oneself to the bare necessities** se restreindre au strict nécessaire; **to l. oneself to two whiskies** se limiter à deux whiskies; **I will l. myself to observing that ...** je me bornerai à observer que ...

▶▶**l. gauge** *(device)* calibre *m* de tolérance; *(external)* bague *f* à tolérance; *(internal)* bouchon *m* à tolérance

limitation [lɪmɪ'teɪʃən] N limitation *f*; **to know one's limitations** connaître ses limites

limited ['lɪmɪtəd] ADJ *(number, intelligence, skills etc)* limité, restreint; *Com (market)* étroit, restreint

▶▶**l. circulation** circulation *f* restreinte; **l. company** ≃ société *f* à responsabilité limitée, SARL *f*; **l. edition** édition *f* à tirage limité; **l. liability** responsabilité *f* limitée; *Fin* **l. partner** commanditaire *m*; *Fin* **l. partnership** société *f* en commandite (simple); **l. stop bus** bus *m* à nombre d'arrêts limité; **l. stop train** train *m* à nombre d'arrêts limité

limiter ['lɪmɪtər] N *Radio, TV* limiteur *m*

limitless ['lɪmɪtlɪs] ADJ sans bornes, illimité

limousine [lɪmə'ziːn], *Fam* **limo** ['lɪməʊ] N *Aut* limousine *f*

limp[1] [lɪmp] N boitement *m*, *Lit* claudication *f*; **to walk with a l., to have a l.** boiter ▸ VI boiter, *Lit* claudiquer; **to l. home** *Sport* terminer la course tant bien que mal; *Fig* rentrer tant bien que mal; **to l. along** aller en boitant *ou Fam* clopin-clopant; *(of ship etc)* avancer péniblement; **she limped along the corridor** elle remonta le couloir en boitant

limp[2] ADJ mou, *f* molle, flasque; **to go l.** *(of person)* s'affaisser; **let your arm go l.** relâche ton bras; **to feel l.** *(of person)* se sentir mou *ou* sans énergie; **l. with the heat** abattu par la chaleur; **the heat makes me feel l.** je suis abattu par la chaleur

▶▶**l. binding** *(of book)* cartonnage *m* souple

limpet ['lɪmpɪt] N patelle *f*, arapède *m*; *Fam (person)* crampon *m*; **to stick to sb like a l.** ne pas lâcher *ou* cramponner qn

▶▶**l. mine** mine-ventouse *f*, *pl* mines-ventouses

limpid ['lɪmpɪd] ADJ *Fml (water, style)* limpide

limply ['lɪmplɪ] ADV *(without firmness)* mollement, flasquement; *(without energy)* mollement, sans énergie

limpness ['lɪmpnɪs] N mollesse *f*, manque *m* d'énergie

limp-wristed ['lɪmp'rɪstəd] ADJ *Fam* efféminé

linage ['laɪnɪdʒ] N *(for newspaper ad)* lignage *m*

linchpin ['lɪntʃpɪn] N esse *f*, cheville *f* d'essieu; *Fig (of organization etc)* cheville ouvrière

Lincs *Br abbr* **Lincolnshire**

linctus ['lɪŋktəs] N *Pharm* sirop *m*

linden ['lɪndən] N tilleul *m*
▶▶**l. tree** tilleul

LINE[1] [laɪn]

N	ligne **1, 2, 4–8, 10, 12, 13** ▪ trait **1** ▪ ride **1** ▪ rang **2** ▪ file **2** ▪ queue **2** ▪ chaîne **3** ▪ corde **4** ▪ voie **7** ▪ vers **8** ▪ mot **8** ▪ lignée **10** ▪ branche **11**
VT	border **2**

N **1** *(mark)* ligne *f*, trait *m*; *(of shore, face)* contours *mpl*; *(of car etc)* lignes; *Geog Fam* **the L.** *(equator)* la Ligne (de l'Équateur);

straight l. (ligne) droite *f*, **broken/wavy l.** trait discontinu; **to put a l. through sth** barrer qch; *Tennis* **on the l.** sur la ligne; *Aut* **white l.,** *Am* **yellow l.** *(in centre of road)* ≃ ligne blanche, bande *f* médiane; **the lines of the hand** les lignes de la main; **the lines on one's forehead** les rides *fpl* de son front; **his face was covered with lines** son visage était plein de rides; **the hard lines of his face** ses traits durs; **to draw a l. under sth** *(underline it)* souligner qch; *Fig* **you have to draw the l. somewhere** il y a une limite à tout; **he doesn't know where to draw the l.** il ne sait pas où s'arrêter; **that's where I draw the l.** pour moi c'est la limite à ne pas dépasser; *(warning another person etc)* ça va trop loin; **I draw the l. at lying** je refuse de mentir; *(referring to other people)* je ne tolère pas le mensonge

2 *(row of people or things) (side by side)* ligne *f*, rangée *f*; *(one behind the other)* file *f*, *Am (queue)* queue *f*; **twenty cars in a l.** *(one behind the other)* vingt voitures à la file; **l. of traffic** colonne *f* de véhicules; **to put objects in a l.** aligner des objets; **to stand in a l.** *(of person in a queue)* faire la queue; *(of children)* être en rang; *Am* **to stand in l.** faire la queue; **to fall** *or* **get into l., to form a l.** *(of people)* se mettre en ligne; *(of children)* se mettre en rang; *(of soldiers)* former les rangs; **out of l.** désaligné; **to be out of l. with sb** *(in opinions)* être en désaccord avec qn; **to be out of l. with** *(policy etc)* ne pas être conforme avec; *Fig* **to be out of l.** *(in what one does, says)* dépasser les bornes; **to get out of l.** se désaligner; *Fig (of political group)* se désolidariser; *(of individual)* faire cavalier seul; **your decision is not in l.** *or* **is out of l. with government policy** votre décision n'est pas conforme à *ou* n'est pas en accord avec la politique du gouvernement; **in l. with my decision** conformément à ma décision; **he's in l. for promotion** il est sur la liste des promotions (futures); **to overstep the l.** dépasser la mesure; **to fall into l. with sb's ideas** se conformer aux idées de qn; **to be on the l.** *(of one's job, reputation etc)* être en jeu; **to put one's job/reputation on the l.** mettre son travail/sa réputation en jeu; **to lay one's reputation/life on the l.** *(for sb/ sth)* mettre sa réputation/vie en jeu (pour qn/qch); **to lay it on the l.** mettre les choses au point; **to lay it on the l. to sb** parler franchement à qn

3 *Ind (assembly)* **l.** chaîne *f* de montage; **(production) l.** chaîne de production

4 *(cord etc), Naut* ligne *f*, corde *f*, cordage *m*; *(for mooring)* amarre *f*, *(for clothes)* corde *ou* fil *m* à linge; *Fishing* ligne (de pêche); *(in surveying), Constr* cordeau *m*; *Elec* **high-tension l.** ligne à haute tension; *Elec, Tel* **overhead/underground l.** ligne aérienne/souterraine; **your clothes are out on the l.** tes vêtements sont sur le fil

5 *Tel* ligne *f*, **shared** *or* **party l.** ligne partagée; **hold the l. please** restez en ligne s'il vous plaît, ne quittez pas; **the l.'s very bad** la communication est mauvaise; **I have Bill on the l.** j'ai Bill en ligne *ou Fam* au bout du fil; **she's on the other l.** elle est sur l'autre ligne; **all the lines to London are busy** toutes les lignes pour Londres sont occupées; *TV, Radio* **the lines are open from 8 o'clock** *(for viewers and listeners to express their views)* les standards sont ouverts à partir de 8 heures

6 *Mil etc* ligne *f*, **lines** lignes *(de fortification etc)*; **the front/rear lines** le front/l'arrière *m*; **to be in the front l.** *Mil* être au front; *Fig* être en première ligne; *Mil etc* **fighting l., l. of battle** ligne de combat *ou* de bataille; **l. of conduct** ligne de conduite; **to be killed in the l. of duty** *(of policeman)* mourir dans l'exercice de ses fonctions; *(of soldier)* mou-

rir au champ d'honneur; *Fig* **to win all along the l.** gagner sur toute la ligne

7 *(direction) (of march, communication, route)* ligne *f*, *(of communication)* Rail *(track)* voie *f*, *Mil etc* **l. of advance** direction *f* de marche; **l. of argument** raisonnement *m*; **l. of attack** ligne d'attaque; **l. of fire** *(of gun)* ligne de tir; **l. of sight** ligne de visée; *(on rifle)* ligne de mire; **l. of thought** raisonnement *m*; **l. of vision** ligne de mire; **to work on the same lines as sb** travailler dans la même direction que qn; **to be working on the right lines** être en bonne voie; **what l. are you going to take?** quel parti allez-vous prendre?; **we must take a firm l. with such people** il nous faut être ferme avec des gens comme ça; **along the lines of** dans le genre *ou* style de

8 *(of text)* ligne *f*, *(of poetry)* vers *m*; **first l. of a paragraph** alinéa *m*; **new l.** *(in dictating)* à la ligne; **opening/closing lines of a play** premières/dernières répliques d'une pièce; *Theat* **not to know one's lines** ne pas savoir son rôle; **to learn one's lines** apprendre son rôle; **to forget one's lines** oublier son texte, *Fam* avoir un trou; *Fam* **just a l. to tell you ...** deux mots pour vous dire ...; *Fam* **I'll drop you a l.** je vous enverrai un petit mot; **to read between the lines** lire entre les lignes

9 *(information) Fam* **to get a l. on sb** se renseigner sur qn; **I wish I could get a l. on him** j'aimerais avoir des renseignements sur lui; *Fam* **to get a l. on sth** obtenir des tuyaux sur qch; *Fam* **to give sb a l. on sth** tuyauter qn sur qch; *Fam* **don't hand me that l.!** à d'autres!

10 *(family)* lignée *f*, ligne *f*, **male/female l.** ligne masculine/féminine; **long l. of ancestors** longue suite d'ancêtres; **he comes from a long l. of politicians** il descend d'une longue lignée d'hommes politiques; **in (a) direct l.** en ligne directe; **to be descended in (a) direct l. from sb** descendre en droite ligne de qn

11 *Fam (job etc)* métier *m*; **l. of business** genre *m* d'affaires, branche *f*; **what l. (of business) are you in?** dans quelle branche est-ce que tu travailles?; **that's not my l.** ce n'est pas mon rayon; **that's more (in) my l.** *(what I'm good at)* cela est plus dans mes compétences *ou Fam* mes cordes; *(what I like)* je préfère cela, *Fam* c'est plus mon truc

12 *Com (of goods)* ligne *f*, **a new l. in menswear** une nouvelle ligne pour hommes; **they've brought out a new l. in perfume** ils ont sorti une nouvelle ligne de parfum; *Fam* **a rice pudding or something in that l.** un gâteau de riz ou quelque chose dans ce genre(-là)

13 *(company) (of steamers etc)* ligne *f*, compagnie *f*

VT **1** *(piece of paper)* faire des lignes sur; **to become lined** *(of forehead, face)* se rider

2 *(border)* border; **to l. the roads with troops** aligner des troupes sur les routes; **the crowd lined the street** la foule s'alignait le long du trottoir; **lined with trees** bordé d'arbres

▶▶*Mktg* **l. addition** ajout *m* à la ligne; *Comput* **l. break** saut *m* de ligne; **l. caption** légende *f*, *Comput* **l. command** ligne de commande; *Fin* **l. of credit** ligne de crédit, ligne de découvert; **l. dancing** = danse *f* de style country effectuée en rangs; *Mktg* **l. differentiation** différenciation *f* de ligne; **l. drawing** dessin *m* au trait; *Typ, Comput* **l. end** fin *f* de ligne; *Typ, Comput* **l. end hyphen** tiret *m* de fin de ligne; **l. engraving** gravure *f* au trait; *Mktg* **l. extension** extension *f* de ligne; *Comput* **l. feed** changement *m* de ligne; **to do a l. feed** aller à la ligne; *Mktg* **l. filling** consolidation *f* de ligne; **l. fishing** pêche *f* à la ligne; *Com* **l. management** organisation *f* hiérarchique; *Com* **l. manager** chef *m* hiérarchique; **l. noise** parasites *mpl*, *Comput* **l.**

printer imprimante *f* ligne à ligne; *Comput* **l. printout** imprimé *m* ligne à ligne; *Theat* **l. rehearsal** lecture *f* collective; *Tel* **l. rental** abonnement *m*; *Typ, Comput* **l. space** interligne *m*; *Typ, Comput* **l. spacing** interlignage *m*, espacement *m* de lignes; *Typ, Comput* **l. width** longueur *f* de ligne

▶ **line up** VT SEP **1** (*people, objects*) aligner, mettre en ligne

2 *Fam* (*plan*) prévoir, avoir en vue; **have you got anyone lined up for the job?** avez-vous quelqu'un en vue pour le poste?; **what have you got lined up for us?** qu'est-ce que vous nous préparez?

VI (*of people*) s'aligner, se mettre en ligne, se ranger; (*form queue*) faire la queue

line² VT **1** *Sewing etc* (*coat, jacket etc*) doubler (**with** de); **fur-lined gloves** gants fourrés; *Fig Fam* **to l. one's own pockets** se servir, se remplir les poches; **to l. a box with paper** tapisser une boîte de papier; **you need something to l. your stomach** tu dois avaler quelque chose avant; *Culin* **to l. a tin with pastry** foncer un moule de pâte; **nest lined with moss** nid garni de mousse; **the walls were lined with books** les murs étaient couverts de livres

2 *Tech* (*bearing*) garnir, recouvrir; (*wall, furnace*) revêtir, incruster (**with** de); (*well*) cuveler; **to l. a shaft with metal** blinder un puits

lineage¹ ['lɪnɪɪdʒ] N lignée *f*, lignage *m*; **to boast an ancient l.** se vanter d'une longue généalogie; **to trace one's l.** retracer sa généalogie

lineage² ['laɪnɪdʒ] N (*for newspaper ad*) lignage *m*

lineal ['lɪnɪəl] ADJ linéal, -aux; (*descendant, succession*) en ligne directe

lineaments ['lɪnɪəmənts] NPL *Lit* traits *mpl*, linéaments *mpl*

linear ['lɪnɪər] ADJ linéaire
▶▶ **l. equation** équation *f* linéaire; *Phys* **l. expansion** dilatation *f* linéaire; **l. measure** mesure *f* linéaire, mesure de longueur; **l. metre** mètre *m* linéaire; *Comput* **l. programming** programmation *f* linéaire

lined¹ [laɪnd] ADJ (*paper*) réglé, rayé; **deeply l. forehead** front creusé de rides

lined² ADJ **1** (*coat*) doublé; (*glove*) fourré; *Fig Fam* **well l. purse** bourse bien garnie **2** *Aut* (*brake*) garni; **steel-l.** (*cylinder*) chemisé d'acier

linen ['lɪnɪn] N **1** linge *m*; *Old-fashioned* (*underwear*) petit linge; **dirty l.** linge sale; *Fig Fam* **don't wash your dirty l. in public** il faut laver son linge sale en famille **2** *Tex* toile *f* (de lin); **l. dress** robe en lin; **l. industry** l'industrie *f* linière *ou* toilière; **l. sheets** draps fil
▶▶ **l. basket** corbeille *f* à linge; **l. cupboard** armoire *f* à linge; **l. paper** papier *m* toilé; **l. room, l. store** lingerie *f*

line-oriented ADJ *Comput* orienté ligne

line-out N *Rugby* touche *f*, remise *f* en jeu

liner¹ ['laɪnər] N *Naut* (*paquebot m*) transatlantique *m*

liner² N (*of cylinder*) fourreau *m*

linesman, *pl* **linesmen** ['laɪnzmən] N *Tennis* juge *m* de lignes; *Ftbl* juge *m* de touche

line-up N **1** *Am* (*queue*) queue *f* (de personnes); (*for identity parade*) rangée *f* de personnes (*assemblées par la police pour l'identification d'un suspect*) **2** *Sport* formation *f* (d'une équipe sur le terrain); *Radio, TV etc* **this evening's l.** (*of guests, stars*) nos invités ce soir

linework ['laɪnwɜːk] N *Art* dessin *m* au trait

ling¹ [lɪŋ] N (*fish*) lingue *f*

ling² N *Bot* bruyère *f* commune

linger ['lɪŋɡər] VI **1** (*of person*) s'attarder, traîner (**over** sur); (*of custom, memory*) subsister; **to l. over a meal** s'attarder sur un repas; **a doubt still lingered** un doute subsistait encore dans mon *ou* son *etc* esprit **2** (*of invalid*) **to l. (on)** languir, traîner

lingerie ['læⁿʒərɪ] N lingerie *f*

lingering ['lɪŋɡərɪŋ] ADJ **1** (*look*) prolongé; (*doubt*) qui subsiste encore; **I had l. doubts/regrets** je gardais un doute/des regrets; **there was a l. hope that ...** on conservait un vague espoir que ... **2** (*illness*) qui traîne, chronique; (*death*) lent; **she died a l. death** la mort l'a emportée lentement

lingo, *pl* **lingoes** ['lɪŋɡəʊ, -əʊz] N *Fam* **the l. of the country** (*its language*) la langue du pays; **technical/scientific l.** jargon *m* technique/scientifique

lingua franca ['lɪŋɡwə'fræŋkə] N langue *f* de communication, langue véhiculaire

linguist ['lɪŋɡwɪst] N (*student of linguistics*) linguiste *mf*; **to be a good/no l.** être/ne pas être doué pour les langues

linguistic [lɪŋ'ɡwɪstɪk] ADJ linguistique
▶▶ **l. atlas** atlas *m* linguistique

linguistically [lɪŋ'ɡwɪstɪklɪ] ADV linguistiquement

linguistics [lɪŋ'ɡwɪstɪks] N linguistique *f*
VOIR GRAMMAIRE A10

liniment ['lɪnɪmənt] N liniment *m*

lining ['laɪnɪŋ] N (*of coat, jacket, dress*) doublure *f*; (*of hat*) coiffe *f*; *Tech* (*of brakes, bearing*) garniture *f*, fourrure *f*; (*of furnace, pump*) chemise *f*; (*of well*) cuvelage *m*; (*of tunnel*) paroi *f*; (*of stomach*) paroi
▶▶ **l. paper** (*for drawer*) papier *m* pour tiroirs; (*for shelves*) papier pour recouvrir les étagères

link [lɪŋk] N **1** (*of chain*) chaînon *m*, maillon *m*, maille *f*; *Naut* (*of chain*) paillon *m*

2 *Fig* (*connection*) lien *m*, liaison *f* (**between** entre); *Comput* lien *m*; **there's a l. between your health and your job** il y a un lien entre votre santé et votre travail; **air/radio l.** liaison *f* aérienne/radiophonique; **he is a l. between the old world and the new** il sert de trait d'union entre le vieux monde et le nouveau; **he was an unwitting l. in a chain of events which ...** sans le savoir, il était le maillon d'une chaîne d'événements qui ...; **this l. in the chain of events** cet épisode de la série d'événements; **the weak l.** le maillon faible

3 *Tech etc* pièce *f* de liaison, tige *f* d'assemblage

VT (*two machines, two cities, two river banks etc*) relier; **a tunnel linking Britain and France** un tunnel reliant la Grande-Bretagne à la France; **the two companies are in no way linked** il n'y a aucun lien entre les deux sociétés; **closely linked** (*of companies, theories etc*) étroitement lié; **to l. negotiations to a discussion of Palestine** lier des négociations à une discussion sur la Palestine; **I always l. him with my stay in ...** je l'associe toujours dans mon esprit à mon séjour à ...; **his name has been linked with several well-known actresses** son nom a été associé à plusieurs actrices bien connues; **it's all linked together** tout cela se tient; **wages linked to the cost of living** salaires indexés sur le coût de la vie; **to l. hands/arms** se donner la main/le bras

VI **to l. on to sth** s'attacher à qch; *Comput* **to l. to sth** (*of device*) être relié à qch
▶▶ *TV etc* **l. man** speaker *m*; *Comput* **l. program** programme *m* éditeur de liens; **l. road** route *f* de jonction

▶ **link up** VI (*of motorways, spaceships, travellers*) se rejoindre (**with** à); (*of cables*) se raccorder (**with** à); (*of TV stations*) établir une liaison; (*of two companies*) s'associer;

(*of climbers*) (*with rope*) s'attacher (**with** à); **we'll l. up with you in Paris** nous vous rejoindrons à Paris; **that links up with what we were saying earlier about ...** cela rejoint ce que nous disions précédemment à propos de ...; **the space rocket will l. up with the orbiting satellite** la navette spatiale rencontrera le satellite en orbite; *TV* **we'll be linking up with Germany at 10 o'clock** nous serons en liaison directe avec l'Allemagne à 10 heures; **we'll be linking up with a French company for this project** nous serons associés à une entreprise française pour ce projet
VT SEP (*to network, cabling system etc*) rattacher (**to** à); (*two computers, broadcasting stations*) relier; **the computers are all linked up** les ordinateurs sont tous rattachés les uns aux autres; **they haven't been linked up to the network yet** ils n'ont pas encore été reliés au réseau; **it's all linked up with what's happening at ...** ça a un lien avec ce qui se passe à ...

linkage ['lɪŋkɪdʒ] N lien *m*

linked [lɪŋkt] ADJ lié

linking ['lɪŋkɪŋ] N enchaînement *m*, liaison *f*

links [lɪŋks] NPL (*usu with sing verb*) (**golf**) **l.** terrain *m* *ou* parcours *m* de golf

link(-)up N lien *m*, liaison *f* (**between** entre); **a satellite l.** une liaison satellite

linnet ['lɪnɪt] N linotte *f* (mélodieuse)

linoleum [lɪ'nəʊlɪəm], *Fam* **lino** ['laɪnəʊ] N linoléum *m*

Linotype® ['laɪnəʊtaɪp] N *Typ* Linotype® *f*

linseed ['lɪnsiːd] N graine *f* de lin
▶▶ **l. oil** huile *f* de lin

lint [lɪnt] N **1** *Med* pansement *m* ouatiné **2** (*of cotton, duster*) peluche *f*

lintel ['lɪnt(ə)l] N *Constr* (*of door, window*) linteau *m*

lint-free ADJ (*cloth*) sans peluches

lion ['laɪən] N **1** (*animal*) lion *m*; *Fig* **the l.'s share** la part du lion; *Fig* **to put one's head into the l.'s mouth** se fourrer dans la gueule du loup **2** *Old-fashioned* (*famous person*) personnage *m* en vue; **a literary l.** sommité *f* littéraire; **the l. of the day** la célébrité du jour
▶▶ **l. cub** lionceau *m*; **l.'s den, lions' den** antre *m* du lion; **l. house** (*at zoo*) fauverie *f*, **l. hunter** chasseur *m* de lions; **l. tamer** dompteur, -euse (de lions)

lioness ['laɪənes] N (*animal*) lionne *f*

lionheart ['laɪənhɑːt] N *Hist* (**Richard**) **the L.** Richard Cœur de Lion

lion-hearted ['laɪənhɑːtɪd] ADJ au cœur de lion

lionize ['laɪənaɪz] VT (*person*) porter aux nues

lip [lɪp] N **1** (*of person*) lèvre *f*, (*of animal*) babine *f*; **to do** *or* **pay l. service to sth** faire semblant de s'intéresser à qch; **the company is paying l. service to the need for a crèche** l'entreprise prétend s'intéresser à la nécessité d'une crèche; *Fam* **to keep one's l. buttoned** (**up**) ne pas souffler mot; **button your l.!** pas un mot!; **to smack** *or* **lick one's lips** se lécher les babines; **no complaint ever passes his lips** il ne se plaint jamais; **to read sb's lips** lire sur les lèvres de qn; *Fam* **read my lips** (*believe what I say*) écoutez-moi bien

2 *Fam* (*impudence*) effronterie *f*, insolence *f*; **none of your l.!, don't give me any of your l.!** ne fais pas l'insolent

3 *Med* (*of wound*), *Bot* lèvre *f*, (*of orchid*) labelle *m*

4 (*rim*) (*of cup, cavity*) bord *m*, rebord *m*; (*of well*) margelle *f*, (*of crater*) bord; (*projection*) rebord, saillie *f*; **pouring l.** (*of jug*) bec *m*
▶▶ **l. gloss** brillant *m* à lèvres; **l. salve** pommade *f ou* baume *m* pour les lèvres

lip-flap N *(in dubbing)* lèvres *fpl* non-synchro

lipid ['lɪpɪd] N *Med* lipide *m*

lipoma [lɪ'pəʊmə] N lipome *m*

lipoprotein [lɪpəʊ'prəʊti:n] N lipoprotéine *f*

liposuction ['laɪpəʊsʌkʃən] N liposuccion *f*

-lipped [lɪpt] SUFF red-l. aux lèvres rouges

lippy ['lɪpɪ] *Fam* N *Br (lipstick)* rouge *m* à lèvres
ADJ effronté; **don't get l. with me!** il faudrait voir à changer de ton!

lip-read VI lire sur les lèvres
VT **she can l. what you're saying** elle peut lire sur vos lèvres

lip-reader N **to be a good l.** bien savoir lire sur les lèvres

lip-reading N lecture *f* sur les lèvres

lipstick ['lɪpstɪk] N rouge *m* à lèvres

lip-sync(h) ['lɪpsɪŋk] N play-back *m*
VT *(song)* chanter en play-back
VI *(of singer)* chanter en play-back

liquefaction [lɪkwɪ'fækʃən] N liquéfaction *f*

liquefied ['lɪkwɪfaɪd] ADJ **l. natural/petroleum gas** gaz *m* naturel/de pétrole liquéfié

liquefy ['lɪkwɪfaɪ] VT *(gas etc)* liquéfier
VI *(of gas etc)* se liquéfier

liqueur [li:'kɜ:r, lɪ'kjʊər] N **1** liqueur *f* (de dessert) **2** *(in winemaking)* liqueur *f* d'expédition
▸▸ **l. brandy** fine *f*; **l. chocolates** bonbons *mpl* à la liqueur; **l. glass** verre *m* à liqueur

liquid ['lɪkwɪd] ADJ **1** liquide; *(sound)* doux, *f* douce, clair; *Hum* **to have a l. lunch** boire de l'alcool en guise de déjeuner **2** *Fin* liquide, disponible **3** *Ling (consonant)* liquide
N **1** liquide *m* **2** *Ling* (consonne *f*) liquide *f*
▸▸ *Acct* **l. assets** actif *m* liquide, disponibilités *fpl*, liquidités *fpl*; **l. crystal** cristal *m* liquide; **l. crystal display** affichage *m* à cristaux liquides; **l. diet** régime *m* ne comprenant que des liquides, *Spec* diète *f* hydrique; **l. measure** mesure *f* de capacité pour les liquides; **l. oxygen** oxygène *m* liquide; **L. paper**® correcteur *m* liquide; **l. paraffin** huile *f* de paraffine; **l. securities** valeurs *fpl* liquides

liquidate ['lɪkwɪdeɪt] VT **1** *Fin (company, debt)* liquider; *(capital)* mobiliser; *St Exch* **l. a position** liquider une position **2** *(kill)* liquider

liquidation [lɪkwɪ'deɪʃən] N *Fin (of company, debt)* liquidation *f*, *(of capital)* mobilisation *f*; **to go into l.** *(of company)* entrer en liquidation

liquidator ['lɪkwɪdeɪtər] N *(of company in liquidation)* liquidateur, -trice

liquidity [lɪ'kwɪdɪtɪ] N **1** *(of substance)* liquidité *f* **2** *Fin* liquidité *f*
▸▸ *Fin* **l. ratio** ratio *m* de liquidité, coefficient *m* de liquidité

liquidize ['lɪkwɪdaɪz] VT **1** liquéfier **2** *Culin* passer au mixeur

liquidizer ['lɪkwɪdaɪzər] N *Culin* mixeur *m*

liquor ['lɪkər] N **1** *Am* alcool *m*; **he can't hold** *or* **take his l.** il ne supporte pas l'alcool; **to be the worse for l.** être ivre **2** *Culin Old-fashioned (of roast)* jus *m*; *(of oysters)* eau *f*
▸▸ *Am* **l. store** magasin *m* de vins et spiritueux

▸ **liquor up** *Am Sl* VI se soûler
VT SEP soûler; **to be all liquored up** être soûl

liquorice, *Am* **licorice** ['lɪkərɪs] N réglisse *f*

lira ['lɪrə] *(pl* **lire** ['lɪrə]*)* N **1** *(Turkish currency)* lire *f* **2** *Formerly (Italian currency)* lire *f*

LISA [elaɪes'eɪ] N *Br Fin (abbr* **long-term individual savings account***)* plan *m* de retraite en actions

Lisbon ['lɪzbən] N Lisbonne *f*

lisle [laɪl] N *Tex (thread)* fil *m* d'Écosse
▸▸ **l. stockings** bas *mpl* de fil; **l. thread** fil d'Écosse

lisp [lɪsp] N zézaiement *m*; **to have a l., to speak with a l.** zézayer, avoir un cheveu sur la langue
VT dire en zézayant
VI zézayer, parler avec un cheveu sur la langue

lissom ['lɪsəm] ADJ *Lit* souple, agile, leste

list¹ [lɪst] N liste *f*; *Admin etc* bordereau *m*; **l. of names** liste nominative; *Fig* **it's (at the) top of my l.** *(I'll do it first)* c'est la première chose que je doive faire; **a fridge is top of my l.** *(to buy)* la première chose que je doive acheter, c'est un frigidaire; **a diamond necklace is top of my l.** *(as gift)* le cadeau que je préférerais avoir est un collier de diamants; **top of the l. for the government is the appointment of ...** ce qui figure en tête des priorités du gouvernement c'est de nommer ...; *Fig* **it's (at the) bottom of the l.** *(least important)* ce n'est pas à faire en priorité; **you're/your name's not on the l.** vous ne figurez pas sur la liste; **to make out** *or* **draw up a l.** établir *ou* dresser une liste; **to enter sth on a l.** porter qch sur une liste
VT **1** *(enter in list)* enregistrer; *(names etc)* inscrire *ou* porter sur une liste; **his phone number isn't listed (in the directory)** son numéro de téléphone ne figure pas dans l'annuaire; **to l. on the Stock Exchange** introduire en Bourse; **to be listed on the Stock Exchange** être coté en Bourse
2 *(display as list)* **to l. names in alphabetical order** faire une liste des noms par ordre alphabétique; **you can l. the data in various ways** on peut faire apparaître les données de différentes manières
3 *(recite, enumerate)* énumérer; **the striking workers listed their demands** les ouvriers en grève énumérèrent leurs revendications
▸▸ *Fin* **l. of investments** (bordereau *m* de) portefeuille *m*; *St Exch* **l. of quotations** bulletin *m* des cours; *Com* **l. price** prix *m* du catalogue

list² *Naut* N *(leaning)* bande *f*, gîte *f*; **to have a l.** donner de la bande, prendre de la gîte; **l. to starboard** gîte à tribord
VI donner de la bande (**to starboard** à tribord), prendre de la gîte

list³ N *Hist* **lists** *(for tournament)* lice *f*, *Fig* **to enter the lists** entrer en lice (**against sb** contre qn)

listed ['lɪstɪd] ADJ **l. on the Stock Exchange** coté en Bourse
▸▸ *Br* **l. building** bâtiment *m* classé; *Br St Exch* **l. company** société *f* cotée en Bourse; *Br* **l. monument** monument *m* classé; *St Exch* **l. securities**, **l. stock** valeurs *fpl* admises *ou* inscrites à la cote (officielle)

listen ['lɪs(ə)n] VI **1** écouter; **to l. to sb/sth** écouter qn/qch; **to l. with half an ear** n'écouter que d'une oreille; **you're not listening to a word I'm saying!** tu n'écoutes pas un traître mot de ce que je dis!; **we listened to their daughter singing** nous avons écouté chanter leur fille; **I listened to her singing** je l'ai écoutée chanter
2 *(pay attention)* faire attention, écouter; **he wouldn't l.** il n'a rien voulu savoir; **to l. to reason** écouter la voix de la raison; **don't l. to him, make up your own mind** n'écoute pas ce qu'il te dit, prends la décision toi-même; **l.! I've got an idea** écoutez, j'ai une idée
3 **will you l. (out) for the phone?** peux-tu surveiller le téléphone?; **to l. out for the postman/doctor** tendre l'oreille pour entendre l'arrivée du facteur/docteur; **will you l. out for the baby?** si le bébé pleure est-ce que tu peux aller voir?; **he listened for the**

sound of the car driving off il tendit l'oreille pour être sûr d'entendre la voiture quand elle partirait; **she tapped on the wall, listening for a hollow sound** elle cherchait à quel endroit le mur était creux en tapant avec ses doigts
▸ **listen in** VI *Radio* écouter la radio; **to l. in to other people's conversations** écouter les conversations d'autrui; **I'd like to l. in on the discussion** j'aimerais assister à cette discussion

listener ['lɪsnər] N **1 to be a good l.** savoir écouter **2** *Radio* auditeur, -trice

listening ['lɪsnɪŋ] N écoute *f*, *(in language learning)* compréhension *f* orale
▸▸ **l. post** poste *m* d'écoute; **l. time** heure *f* d'écoute; *(length of time)* durée *f* d'écoute

listeriosis [lɪstɪərɪ'əʊsɪs] N *Med* listériose *f*

listing ['lɪstɪŋ] N *(action)* listage *m*; *(position)* classement *m*; *Comput* listing *m*; **the listings** *(in newspapers)* la rubrique des spectacles; *TV* le programme télévisé; *Am Tel* **do you have a l. for J. Smith?** est-ce que vous avez un J. Smith dans vos fichiers?
▸▸ **listings magazine** magazine *m* de spectacles; **l. paper** papier *m* continu, papier listing

listless ['lɪstlɪs] ADJ apathique, sans énergie

listlessly ['lɪstlɪslɪ] ADV sans énergie; **to stare l. into space** regarder dans le vague; **he watched l. as they took away his furniture** il assistait à la saisie de ses meubles le regard vide

listlessness ['lɪstlɪsnɪs] N apathie *f*

lit PT, PP *see* **light¹** VT

litany ['lɪtənɪ] N *Rel* litanies *fpl*, *Fig (of complaints etc)* litanie

litchi ['li:tʃi:, 'laɪ-] N = **lychee**

liter ['li:tər] N *Am* = **litre**

literacy ['lɪtərəsɪ] N alphabétisation *f*; **there's a l. problem in this country** il y a dans ce pays un problème d'alphabétisation; **we want to achieve 90% l. before ...** nous nous fixons comme objectif un taux d'alphabétisation de 90% avant ...; **adult l. classes** cours *m* d'alphabétisation pour adultes
▸▸ **l. campaign** campagne *f* d'alphabétisation; **l. level** degré *m* d'instruction *ou* d'alphabétisation; **l. test** test *m* pour mesurer le niveau d'alphabétisation

literal ['lɪtərəl] ADJ **1** *(translation)* littéral, -aux, mot à mot; **he's very l.-minded** il prend tout au pied de la lettre; **in the l. sense of the word** au sens propre du mot; **to take sth in a l. sense** prendre qch au pied de la lettre; **it meant l. starvation for thousands of farmers** cela signifiait que des milliers de fermiers allaient littéralement mourir de faim **2** *Math (coefficient)* littéral, -aux
N *Typ* coquille *f*
▸▸ *Typ* **l. error** coquille

literally ['lɪtərəlɪ] ADV **1** *(to translate)* littéralement, mot à mot; **l. speaking** à proprement parler; **to take sth l.** prendre qch au pied de la lettre **2** *Fam (as intensifier)* littéralement

literary ['lɪtərərɪ] ADJ *(work, agent, criticism etc)* littéraire; **l. man** homme *m* de lettres

literate ['lɪtərɪt] ADJ **1** qui sait lire et écrire; **computer l.** qui sait utiliser l'informatique **2** *(educated)* lettré

literature ['lɪtərɪtʃər] N **1** littérature *f*, **French l.** la littérature française **2** *(giving information)* documentation *f*, *Com etc* prospectus *mpl*, brochures *fpl*; **the l. of a subject** la littérature publiée sur une question

lithe [laɪð] ADJ agile

lithium ['lɪθɪəm] N *Chem* lithium *m*

lithograph ['lɪθəgrɑːf] N lithographie f
VT lithographier

lithographer [lɪ'θɒgrəfə(r)] N lithographe
mf

lithographic [lɪθə'græfɪk] ADJ lithographique

lithography [lɪ'θɒgrəfɪ] N lithographie f,
procédés mpl lithographiques

Lithuania [lɪθjʊ'eɪnɪə] N Lituanie f

Lithuanian [lɪθjʊ'eɪnɪən] ADJ lituanien
N 1 Lituanien, -ienne 2 Ling lituanien m

litigant ['lɪtɪgənt] Law ADJ l. parties parties
fpl plaidantes ou en litige
N plaideur, -euse

litigate ['lɪtɪgeɪt] Law VI plaider
VT (matter, property) contester, mettre en
litige

litigation [lɪtɪ'geɪʃən] N Law litige m; in l.
en litige; to go to l. (of person) aller en justice; (of matter) être porté en justice

litigious [lɪ'tɪdʒəs] ADJ 1 Law litigieux 2 Fml
Pej (person) chicanier

litmus ['lɪtməs] N Chem tournesol m
▸▸ l. paper papier m de tournesol; l. test
réaction f au tournesol; Fig test m décisif;
this will be a l. test of the government's will
ce sera un test décisif pour juger de la détermination du gouvernement

litre, Am **liter** ['liːtər] N litre m

litter ['lɪtər] N 1 (in public place) détritus
mpl, immondices fpl; (from people eating)
papiers mpl gras; please clear up your l. (in
park) veuillez nettoyer vos ordures; dropping l. is forbidden, no l. (on sign) défense
de déposer des ordures
2 (of animal) portée f, five young at a l. or in
one l. cinq petits d'une portée
3 (for carrying wounded) civière f, Hist (conveyance) litière f, to be carried in a l. être
porté en litière
4 Agr (of straw etc) litière f, (of stable etc) fumier m; (for cat) litière
VT 1 (of person) (streets etc) couvrir de détritus ou d'immondices; (room etc) mettre en
désordre; (of objects) couvrir, joncher; he lit-
ters his room with dirty socks il parsème sa
chambre de chaussettes sales; the streets
were littered with bottles les rues étaient
couvertes ou pleines de bouteilles vides;
table littered with papers table encombrée
de papiers; her works are littered with allusions to the classics ses écrits sont encom-
brés d'allusions aux auteurs classiques; the
pages of the book are littered with obscenities le livre est un tissu d'obscénités; Fig beaches littered with tourists des plages
jonchées de touristes
2 to l. (down) a horse faire la litière à un
cheval; to l. (down) a stable étendre de la
paille dans une écurie
VI (of animal) mettre bas, avoir une portée
▸▸ l. basket (in street) poubelle f, boîte f à
ordures; Br l. bin poubelle, boîte à ordures;
throw it in the l. bin jette-le à la poubelle; Br
Fam l. lout = personne f qui jette des papiers
ou des détritus par terre

litterbug ['lɪtəbʌg] N Fam personne f qui
jette des papiers ou des détritus par terre

LITTLE ['lɪt(ə)l]

ADJ	petit 1 ▪ peu de 2
N	pas grand chose 1 ▪ peu à peu 1
	▪ un peu 2
ADV	peu 1

ADJ 1 (comp **smaller**, Fam **littler**, superl **smallest**, Fam **littlest**) (small) petit; l. girl petite
fille f, fillette f; l. things like that matter les
petits détails comme cela ont leur importance; poor l. girl! pauvre petite!; Fam a tiny
l. house une toute petite maison; wait a l.

while! attendez un petit moment!; a l.
something (gift) une babiole; (to eat) un petit quelque chose **VOIR GRAMMAIRE A17**
2 (comp **less**, superl **least**) (not much) peu
de; l. money peu d'argent; a l. money un
peu d'argent; I could do with a l. lunch je
mangerais bien un petit quelque chose
pour déjeuner; to gain l. advantage from
sth ne tirer que peu d'avantages de qch;
there is l. point in complaining ça ne vaut
pas vraiment la peine de porter plainte; it
makes l. sense ça n'a pas beaucoup de sens;
we're only a l. way into the discussion nous
venons juste d'entamer la discussion; Fam
be it ever so l. si peu que ce soit; with what
l. French I knew avec le peu de français que
je connaissais
3 Pej (mind) mesquin; Prov l. things please
l. minds à petits esprits, peu n'en faut
N 1 (comp **less**; superl **least**) peu m; to eat l.
or nothing manger peu ou pas du tout; he
knows very l. il ne sait pas grand-chose; he
has done l. for us il n'a pas fait grand-chose
pour nous; I see very l. of her je ne la vois
guère; given the l. that I know about this
subject étant donné le peu de connaissances que j'ai dans ce domaine; to think l. of
sb ne pas avoir une haute opinion de qn; to
make or think l. of sth faire peu de cas de
qch; Prov every l. helps les petits ruisseaux
font les grandes rivières; I can only give you
half an hour – every l. helps je ne peux t'accorder qu'une demi-heure – c'est mieux que
rien; l. by l. peu à peu, petit à petit
2 a l. more encore un peu; a l. more and he
would have died il est passé à deux doigts
de la mort; a l. hot un peu chaud; for/after
a l. (time) pendant/après un certain temps;
he helped him a l. il l'a aidé un peu; I was
not a l. afraid j'avais très peur; Prov a l. of
what you fancy does you good il n'y a pas
de mal à se faire du bien; wait a l.! attendez
un peu!
ADV 1 (comp **less**; superl **least**) (hardly) peu;
l. known peu connu; l. more than an hour
ago il y a à peine une heure; that's l. less
than bribery ça frise la corruption; l. short
of disgusting/outrageous quand même un
peu dégoûtant/scandaleux; he studied too
l. il a étudié trop peu, il n'a pas assez étudié;
l. as it matters ... même si ça n'a pas d'important ...; I realized how l. I knew him je
me suis rendu compte à quel point je le
connaissais peu; if you think how l. money
they actually have quand on pense au peu
d'argent dont ils disposent; how l. it really
matters in the end! tout cela est tellement
peu important au bout du compte
2 he l. knows or thinks or suspects ... il ne
se doute guère ...; l. did I think that ... je ne
pensais pas du tout que ...; l l. expected him
to come je ne m'attendais guère à ce qu'il
vienne **VOIR GRAMMAIRE A78**
3 l. enough assez peu; you eat l. enough as
it is tu manges déjà assez peu comme ça
▸▸ l. Englander Hist isolationniste mf (hostile à l'expansion de l'empire britannique);
(chauvinistic) = anglais m chauvin et xénophobe; l. finger petit doigt m; Fam he has
you (twisted) round his l. finger il fait ce
qu'il veut de toi; l. hand (of clock) petite aiguille f, the l. man (the average person) les
petites gens fpl; l. ones (children) enfants
mpl; (of animal) petits mpl; Fam esp Irish the
l. people les lutins mpl; l. toe petit orteil m,
doigt m de pied; Br Hum the l. woman ma/sa
bourgeoise; I'm fed up with the l. woman
role j'en ai marre d'être la petite femme
soumise

littoral ['lɪtərəl] Geog ADJ littoral, -aux
N littoral m

liturgical [lɪ'tɜːdʒɪk(ə)l] ADJ liturgique

liturgy ['lɪtədʒɪ] N liturgie f

livable ['lɪvəb(ə)l] ADJ = liveable

live¹ [laɪv] ADJ 1 (animal, person) vivant, en
vie; (coal) ardent; a l. issue un sujet brûlant;
a restaurant where you order your fish l. un
restaurant où on choisit son poisson vivant;
Fam a real l. filmstar une vedette de cinéma
en chair et en os
2 TV, Radio (broadcast, commentary) en direct; TV recorded before a l. audience enregistré en public; a l. performance un
spectacle (en direct); I never saw a l. performance by the Beatles je n'ai jamais vu les
Beatles en concert; Sinatra l. at the Palladium Sinatra en concert au Palladium
3 Mil (ammunition) actif; (bomb) actif,
amorcé, armé; (cartridge) à balle, réel
4 Tech (load) roulant, mobile
ADV TV, Radio to be broadcast l. être diffusé
en direct; to play/perform l. (of band, comedian) faire de la scène; the band hasn't performed l. for nearly ten years le groupe n'a
pas fait de scène depuis presque dix ans;
the show comes l. from New York City le
spectacle nous arrive en direct de New York;
an astronaut speaking l. from the moon un
astronaute parlant en direct de la lune
▸▸ Tech l. axle essieu m moteur, pont m; l.
bait appât m vivant, vif m; l. birth enfant m
né vivant; Comput l. cam caméra f Internet;
l. end (of studio) salle f de direct; l. entertainment spectacle m; (broadcast) spectacles
mpl en direct; nobody goes to see l. entertainment any more plus personne ne va au
spectacle de nos jours; the theatre and
other forms of l. entertainment le théâtre
et autres formes de divertissement; l. music
musique f live; l. weight (of animal for
slaughter) poids m vif ou vivant; Elec l. wire
fil m sous tension; Fam she's a l. wire elle est
très énergique, Fam elle pète la forme

LIVE² [lɪv] VI 1 (exist, be alive) vivre; as long
as my father lived there was no question of
selling tant que mon père était vivant il
n'était pas question de vendre; she lived in
the 20th century elle vécut au 20ème siècle;
we l. in interesting times nous vivons une
époque intéressante; she'll l. to be 100 elle
vivra jusqu'à 100 ans, elle sera centenaire;
she has only a few months to l. il ne lui reste
plus que quelques mois à vivre; long l. the
king! vive le roi!; as long or so long as l. tant
que je vivrai; Fam you'll l.! tu survivras!;
Prov you l. and learn on apprend à tout âge;
Prov l. and let l. il faut que tout le monde vive; this is what l call living! c'est ce que
j'appelle vivre!; if you've never been to Venice, you haven't lived si tu n'es jamais allé à
Venise tu n'as pas vraiment vécu; I want to l.
a little je veux profiter de la vie; his name
will l. son nom restera ou sera immortalisé;
this day will l. in history ce jour fera date
dans l'histoire; he lives by his writing il vit
de sa plume; he lives by buying and selling
antiques il vit en faisant du commerce d'antiquités; to l. by one's wits (of smuggler etc)
vivre d'expédients; (of people in hardship) se
débrouiller pour survivre; to l. by one's beliefs vivre selon ses croyances; to l. well vivre bien; to l. like a king or a lord vivre
comme un prince; to l. in style mener grand
train; to l. in poverty/fear vivre dans la
pauvreté/peur; she lived only for her husband elle n'a vécu que pour son mari; we're
living for the day we emigrate nous vivons
dans l'attente du jour où ous émigrerons;
she was living for the chance of revenge la
perspective de vengeance était sa raison de
vivre; you'll always l. with the guilt la culpabilité vous poursuivra toute la vie; you'll
just have to l. with the idea! il faudra que tu
te fasses à cette idée!, il faudra que t'y
fasses; it's not ideal but I can l. with it ce
n'est pas l'idéal mais je m'y ferai

2 *(reside)* habiter, vivre; **to l. in Paris** habiter (à) Paris, vivre à Paris; **to l. in France** vivre en France; **to l. in a flat/house** vivre en appartement/dans une maison; **she lives in a fifth floor flat** elle vit dans un appartement au cinquième étage; **to l. at Number 10** habiter au numéro 10; **to l. in the country** habiter *ou* vivre à la campagne; **where do you l.?** où est-ce que vous habitez?; **fish l. in water** les poissons vivent dans l'eau; **the house doesn't seem to be lived in** la maison ne paraît pas habitée; **to l. with** *(boyfriend, parents)* vivre avec; *(friend, parents)* habiter avec; **he lives with his wife and daughter** il vit avec sa femme et sa fille; **he's difficult/easy to l. with** il est difficile/facile à vivre

vt to l. a happy life mener une vie heureuse; **to l. a life of luxury** mener la grande vie; **life is not worth living** la vie ne vaut pas d'être vécue; **it makes life worth living** cela donne une raison de vivre; **to l. a lie** vivre sur un mensonge; *Theat* **to l. a part** entrer dans la peau d'un personnage

▶ **live down vt sep to l. down one's past** faire oublier son passé; **this is awful, I'll never l. it down!** c'est terrible, je n'arriverai jamais à faire oublier ça!

▶ **live in vi 1** *(of student)* **I'll be living in next year** je serai interne l'année prochaine **2** *(of housekeeper etc)* habiter sur place

▶ **live off vt insep to l. off sth** vivre de qch; **to l. off sb** vivre aux crochets de qn

▶ **live on vi** *(continue to live)* continuer à vivre; **he lived on for another three years** il vécut encore trois ans; **his memory will l. on** sa mémoire lui survivra

vt insep *(depend on)* **to l. on vegetables** se nourrir de légumes; **to l. on one's capital** vivre sur son capital; **it's not enough to l. on** ce n'est pas suffisant pour vivre; **to earn enough to l. on** gagner de quoi vivre; **they lived on her salary** ils ont vécu sur son salaire

▶ **live out vi** *(of student)* être externe; *(of servant)* ne pas coucher au domicile de ses patrons

vt sep *(period, one's life)* passer; **they lived out their lives in poverty** ils vécurent toute leur vie dans la pauvreté; **he won't l. out the year** il ne passera pas l'année; **to l. out one's dreams/fantasies** vivre ses rêves/fantasmes

▶ **live through vt insep** *(war, hard times etc)* vivre; *(survive)* *(war, drought)* survivre à; **anyone who has lived through times like these will know that …** quiconque a vécu cette époque sait que …; **he's unlikely to l. through the winter** il est peu vraisemblable qu'il passe l'hiver

▶ **live together vi** vivre ensemble, être en ménage

▶ **live up vt sep** *Fam* **to l. it up** faire la fête

▶ **live up to vt insep to l. up to expectations** *(of person, party, film etc)* tenir ses promesses; **his brother has given him a lot to l. up to** son frère a placé la barre très haut; **it's too much for me to l. up to** on m'en demande trop; **to l. up to one's principles** vivre selon ses principes; **to l. up to one's reputation** ne pas faillir à sa réputation; **to l. up to one's promise** tenir sa promesse

liveable ['lɪvəb(ə)l] ADJ **1** *(life)* supportable **2 l. in** *(house, room)* *(habitable)* habitable; *(acceptable)* vivable **3 l. with** *(person)* avec qui on peut vivre; **he's l. with** c'est quelqu'un avec qui on peut vivre

lived-in ['lɪvdɪn] ADJ *(house, flat)* accueillant; *Fam (face)* mûr; **to have a l. feel (to it)** être accueillant

live-in ADJ *(chauffeur, nanny etc)* logé et nourri

▶▶ **l. accommodation** *(for staff)* logement *m* à demeure; *Hum* **l. lover** compagnon *m*/compagne *f* (avec qui l'on vit)

livelihood ['laɪvlɪhʊd] N moyens *mpl* d'existence, gagne-pain *m inv*; **to earn** *or* **gain one's l.** gagner sa vie *ou* son pain; **tourism is our l.** le tourisme est notre gagne-pain; **to lose one's l.** perdre ses moyens de subsistance

liveliness ['laɪvlɪnɪs] N vivacité *f*; *Fin (of market)* animation *f*

livelong ['lɪvlɒŋ] ADJ *Lit* **the l. day** toute la journée, tout le long du jour; **the l. night** toute la nuit

lively ['laɪvlɪ] ADJ **1** *(person)* vivant, plein de vie; *(cheerful)* gai; *(colour)* vif; *(music)* gai; *(performance)* vivant; *(imagination)* fertile; *(town, description, party, conversation)* animé; **you're very l. today** tu es en forme aujourd'hui; *Fam* **to make it** *or* **things l. for sb** rendre la vie dure à qn; **things are getting l.** *(in discussion, meeting etc)* ça chauffe; **to take a l. interest in sth** s'intéresser vivement à qch **2** *(car, engine)* nerveux; *(horse)* fougueux; *(boat)* rapide; **that's quite a l. clutch** c'est un embrayage plutôt sensible

ADV *Fam* **look l.!** grouille-toi!

▶ **liven up** ['laɪv(ə)n] VT SEP *(person, meeting etc)* animer, égayer; *(proceedings)* activer; **to l. up the conversation** ranimer la conversation; **you need to l. up your style** vous devriez mettre plus de dynamisme dans votre style; **some pictures would l. up the text a bit** quelques photos égaieraient un peu le texte

vi s'animer, s'activer, *Fam* se décoincer

liver[1] ['lɪvər] N *Anat, Culin* foie *m*

▶▶ *Culin* **l. pâté** pâté *m* de foie

liver[2] N *(person)* **fast l.** viveur, -euse, noceur, -euse; **loose l.** libertin *m*, débauché *m*

liveried ['lɪvərɪd] ADJ en livrée

liverish ['lɪvərɪʃ] ADJ *Fig Fam (irritable)* irritable; **to be** *or* **feel l.** avoir une crise de foie

Liverpudlian [lɪvə'pʌdlɪən] ADJ de Liverpool

N personne *f* originaire de Liverpool; *(inhabitant)* habitant, -ante de Liverpool

liverwurst ['lɪvəwɜːst] N *Am* saucisse *f* de foie

livery ['lɪvərɪ] N *(uniform)* livrée *f*; **full l.** grande livrée; **in l.** en livrée

▶▶ *Br* **l. company** confrérie *f* (de la cité de Londres); **l. horse** cheval *m* de louage; **l. stables** *fpl* écuries *fpl* de chevaux de louage

livestock ['laɪvstɒk] N bétail *m* VOIR GRAMMAIRE A11

livid ['lɪvɪd] ADJ **1** *(angry)* furieux; **to be l. with anger,** *Fam* **to be absolutely l.** être fou de rage; **it makes me l.!** ça me met en rage! **2** *(complexion)* livide, blême; *(sky)* plombé; **a l. bruise** un bleu très marqué

living ['lɪvɪŋ] ADJ *(person)* vivant; **did she have any l. relatives?** avait-elle encore de la famille?; **she is our finest l. artist** c'est notre meilleure artiste contemporaine; **while she was l.** de son vivant; **there is not a l. soul to be seen** on ne rencontre pas âme qui vive *ou Fam* pas un chat; **he has done more for them than any man l.** il a fait plus pour eux que n'importe qui; **a l. death** une vie pire que la mort; **to make sb's life a l. hell** faire de la vie de qn un enfer; **within l. memory** de mémoire d'homme; **the sculpture had been carved out of the l. rock** la sculpture avait été taillée à même le roc

N 1 *(way of life)* vie *f*; **l. in the country** la vie à la campagne; **to be fond of good l.** être un bon vivant; **fast l. will do him no good** ça ne lui vaut rien de mener une vie débridée **2** *(livelihood)* vie *f*; **to earn one's l.** gagner sa vie; **to work for one's** *or* **a l.** travailler pour gagner sa vie; **to write for a l.** vivre de sa plume; **what does he do for a l.?** qu'est-ce qu'il fait?, quel est son métier?; **to make a l.**

gagner sa vie; **she makes a l. out of it** elle en vit

3 the l. *(pl)* les vivants *mpl*; **still in the land of the l.** encore vivant *ou* de ce monde

4 *Br Rel* bénéfice *m*, cure *f*

▶▶ **l. allowance** indemnité *f* de séjour; **l. conditions** conditions *fpl* de vie; **l.-flame gas fire** = chauffage *m* au gaz à flammes réelles, imitant une feu de charbon; **l. fossil** espèce *f* fossile; *Fig (person)* vieux fossile *m*; **l. language** langue *f* vivante; **l. proof** preuve *f* vivante; **l. quarters** *(for servants)* logements *mpl*; *(on ship)* partie *f* habitée; **l. room** *(salle f de)* séjour *m*; **l. space** espace *m* vital; **l. standards** niveau *m* de vie; **l. wage** minimum *m* vital; **l. will** = testament *m* dans lequel le testateur exprime sa volonté de ne pas être maintenu en vie artificiellement s'il sombre dans un état végétatif irréversible à la suite d'une maladie ou d'un accident

Livy ['lɪvɪ] N Tite-Live *m*

lizard ['lɪzəd] N lézard *m*; **l. (skin) handbag** sac *m* à main en lézard

llama ['lɑːmə] N lama *m*

LLB [elel'biː] N *(abbr Legum Baccalaureus)* ≃ Bachelier en Droit

LLD [elel'diː] N *(abbr Legum Doctor)* ≃ Docteur en Droit

Lloyd's name [lɔɪdz-] N *Br* = membre *m* du syndicat d'assurances Lloyds

LMBO [elembiː'əʊ] N *Fin (abbr leveraged management buy-out)* = rachat *m* d'entreprise par les salariés

LNG [elen'dʒiː] N *(abbr liquefied natural gas)* GNL *m*

lo [ləʊ] INT *Arch, Lit* voici, voilà; *Hum* **lo and behold, there he was** et voilà qu'il était là

loach [ləʊtʃ] N loche *f*

load [ləʊd] N **1** *(burden)* fardeau *m*; *(of lorry, ship etc)* charge *f*, chargement *m*; *(contents of vehicle)* *(of gravel etc)* camion *m*, tombereau *m*; *(of wood)* charge *f*; **useful l.** charge utile; **that's a l. off my mind!** cela m'enlève un poids!; **to share** *or* **spread the l.** *(of the work)* répartir le travail; **to shed its l. on the motorway** *(of lorry)* répandre son chargement sur l'autoroute

2 *Fam (a lot)* **it's a l. of rubbish** *or* **nonsense** *(novel, theory etc)* c'est n'importe quoi; *Sl* **it's a l. of crap** *or* **bullshit** c'est des conneries; *Fam* **get a l. of that!** *(look)* vise un peu!; *(listen)* écoute un peu ça!; *Fam* **he's got loads of them** il en a des quantités *ou* des tas; *Fam* **loads of money** plein de fric; *Fam* **we've done it loads of times** on l'a fait plein de fois; *Fam* **we've got loads of time** nous avons largement le temps

3 *Tech, Elec* charge *f*, **safe l.** charge de sécurité; **machine working at full l.** machine qui fonctionne *ou* travaille à pleine charge; **under l.** en charge; *Elec* **to shed the l.** délester

vt 1 *(lorry, ship, camera, gun, film, shell, program)* charger; **to l. passengers** *(of bus)* prendre des voyageurs; **to l. a washing machine/dishwasher** mettre du linge dans le lave-linge/de la vaisselle dans le lave-vaisselle, remplir le lave-linge/lave-vaisselle; **to l. a program into a computer** entrer un programme dans un ordinateur; **he was loaded with shopping** il avait les bras chargés de courses; **loaded with cares** accablé de soucis; **I'm going to l. some more work onto you** je vais vous confier encore un peu de travail; **I don't think it's fair to l. all the work onto one person** je trouve que ce n'est pas juste de donner tout le travail à une seule personne

2 *Tech (spring)* serrer, bander

3 *(dice)* piper; *Fig* **the dice were loaded in our favour** la situation nous a été favorable

4 *(in insurance)* *(premium)* majorer

vi *Comput (of software etc)* se charger; *(of*

lorry) prendre un chargement; *(of ship)* prendre une cargaison; *Aut* **no loading or unloading between 9am and 4pm** *(on sign)* chargement ou déchargement interdits entre 9h et 16h

▸▸ **l. bed** *(of truck)* plateau *m* de chargement; **l. box** *(on vehicle)* soute *f*; **l. factor** *(of plane)* coefficient *m* de remplissage; *Elec* facteur *m* ou coefficient de charge; *Tech* facteur de charge; *Naut* **l. line** ligne *f* de charge; **l. restraint mesh** filet *m* de retenu de charge; *Elec* **l. shedding** délestage *m* ; **l. space** coffre *m*; *(of lorry)* plancher *m* de chargement; **l. unit** unité *f* de chargement

▸ **load down** VT SEP **to l. sb down with** *(packages, work, responsibility)* surcharger qn de; **to be loaded down with worry** être accablé de soucis; **to be loaded down with anxiety** être rongé d'anxiété

▸ **load up** VT SEP *(lorry etc)*, *Comput* charger VI *(of ship)* prendre une cargaison; *(of lorry etc)* prendre un chargement

loadable ['ləʊdəb(ə)l] ADJ *(software etc)* qui peut se charger, chargeable

loaded ['ləʊdɪd] ADJ **1** *(lorry, ship, camera, gun etc)* chargé **2** *(dice)* pipé; **the situation was l. against me** la situation m'a été défavorable; **a l. question** une question insidieuse; **a l. word** un mot trop connoté **3** *Sl (person) (wealthy)* richissime; *(drunk)* soûl; *(on drugs)* drogué, camé; **to get l.** *(drunk)* se soûler; *(on drugs)* se camer

loader ['ləʊdər] N **1** *(person)* chargeur *m* **2** *(device)* chargeuse *f*; *Constr* chargeur *m*

loading ['ləʊdɪŋ] N *(of lorry, ship, plane, camera, gun)* chargement *m*; *(on ship)* délai d'embarquement

▸▸ **l. bay** aire *f* de chargement; **l. charges** coût *m* d'affrètement; **l. procedure** procédure *f* de chargement; **l. ramp** rampe *f* de chargement; **l. time** délai *m* de chargement; *(on ship)* délai d'embarquement

loaf, *pl* **loaves** [ləʊf, ləʊvz] N **1** *Culin* pain *m*; **a l. of bread** un pain; *Prov* **half a l. is better than none** *or* **than no bread** faute de grives on mange des merles **2** *Fam (head)* **to use one's l.** faire marcher son ciboulot; **use your l.** fais un peu marcher ton ciboulot

▸ **loaf about, loaf around** VI traîner

loafer ['ləʊfər] N **1** *(person)* fainéant, -ante **2** *(shoe)* mocassin *m*

loam [ləʊm] N *Agr, Geol* terreau *m*

loamy ['ləʊmɪ] ADJ *(soil)* riche en terreau

loan [ləʊn] N *(money, object) (from borrower's point of view)* emprunt *m*; *(from lender's point of view)* prêt *m*; **l. of money** prêt ou avance *f* d'argent; **it was very generous of you to give me a l. of that money** c'était très généreux de ta part de me prêter cet argent; **it's a l., you can have it as a l.** je vous le prête; **can I have the l. of …?** puis-je emprunter …?; **to give sb a l. of sth** prêter qch à qn; **on l. from the Louvre** prêt du Louvre; **to have sth on permanent l.** disposer de qch en prêt permanent; **she's on l. from Head Office** elle est détachée du bureau central; **the video you want is out on l.** la vidéo que vous voulez est sortie; **to raise a l. on an estate** emprunter de l'argent sur une terre; **to take out a l.** faire un emprunt; **to apply for a l.** demander un prêt; **to repay a l.** rembourser un emprunt; **long/short-term l.** prêt/emprunt à long/court terme; **secured l.** prêt/emprunt gagé *ou* garanti; **unsecured l., l. without security** prêt/emprunt à découvert; *Fin* **l. at call, l. repayable on demand** prêt remboursable sur demande; *Fin* **l. at notice** prêt à terme; *Fin* **l. on overdraft** prêt à découvert; **l. to value** = rapport *m* entre le capital restant dû et la valeur du bien

financé; *Acct* **loans and advances to customers** créances *fpl* clients

VT prêter *(* **sth to sb** qch à qn*)*; **loaned by the Louvre** prêt *m* du Louvre

▸▸ *Banking* **l. account** compte *m* de prêt; *Fin* **l. agreement** contrat *m* de prêt; *Fin* **l.-back facility** *(in insurance)* possibilité *f* d'emprunt sur le montant de son assurance-vie; *Fin* **l. capital** capital *m* sur prêt *ou* d'emprunt; *Fin* **l. certificate** titre *m* de prêt; *Fin* **l. company** société *f* de crédit, maison *f* de prêt; *Fin* **l. insurance** assurance *f* crédit; *Fin* **l. maturity** échéance *f* emprunt; *Fin* **l. note** titre d'obligation, titre de créance; *Fin* **l. office** organisme *m* de crédit, maison de prêt; *Acct* **loans outstanding** encours *m*; *Fin* **l. risk cover** couverture *f* du risque de crédit; *Fam Pej* **l. shark** usurier, -ière; *Fin* **l. stock** emprunt *m* obligataire; *Ling* **l. word** mot *m* d'emprunt

loath [ləʊθ] ADJ **to be l. to do sth** hésiter à faire qch; *esp Lit* **nothing l.** sans hésiter

loathe [ləʊð] VT détester, exécrer; **I l. milk** j'ai horreur du lait, je déteste le lait; **to l. doing sth** détester faire qch

loathing ['ləʊðɪŋ] N dégoût *m*, répugnance *f* (**for** pour); **to feel l. for sb** éprouver du dégoût pour qn; **to fill sb with l.** remplir qn de dégoût, dégoûter qn; **to have a l. for milk** avoir horreur du lait

loathsome ['ləʊðsəm] ADJ *(person)* répugnant; *(habit)* détestable; *(smell)* nauséabond; **that was a l. thing to do/say!** c'était vraiment dégoûtant de faire/dire ça!

loathsomeness ['ləʊðsəmnɪs] N nature *f* repoussante *ou* dégoûtante

lob [lɒb] N *Sport* lob *m*, chandelle *f* VT **1** *Tennis, Ftbl* lober **2** *Fam (throw)* balancer; **l. that over!** balance-moi ça!

lobby ['lɒbɪ] N **1** *(corridor)* couloir *m*, antichambre *f*, vestibule *m*; *(of court)* promenoir *m*; *(of theatre)* entrée *f*; *(of hotel)* hall *m* **2 the l. of the House** *(in Parliament)* = la salle des pas perdus; *Parl* **division lobbies** = vestibules *mpl* où passent les députés lorsqu'ils se divisent pour voter **3** *Pol etc (pressure group)* lobby *m*, groupe *m* de pression; **the anti-abortion l.** le groupe de pression contre l'avortement

VI *(of pressure group)* faire pression *(* **in favour of/against** en faveur de/contre*)*; **they're lobbying for tax reform** ils font pression pour obtenir une réforme fiscale

VT *esp Pol (person)* faire pression sur

▸▸ *Br Pol* **l. correspondent** journaliste *mf* parlementaire

lobbying ['lɒbɪɪŋ] N *Pol etc* lobbying *m*, lobbysme *m*

lobbyist ['lɒbɪɪst] N *Pol etc* lobbyiste *mf*, membre *m* d'un groupe de pression

lobe [ləʊb] N **1** *Anat (of ear etc)* lobe *m* **2** *Bot* lobe *m*

lobelia [ləʊ'biːlɪə] N *Bot* lobélie *f*

lobotomize [lə'bɒtəmaɪz] VT *Surg* lobotomiser

lobotomy [lə'bɒtəmɪ] N *Surg* lobotomie *f*

lobster ['lɒbstər] N homard *m*; **spiny l.** langouste *f*

▸▸ **l. boat** homardier *m*; *(for spiny lobster)* langoustier *m*; **l. pot** casier *m* à homards; *(for spiny lobster)* casier à langoustes

local ['ləʊk(ə)l] ADJ local, -aux; **the l. doctor** le médecin du quartier; **a matter of l. politics** une question de politique locale; **they voted for the l. man** ils ont voté pour le candidat local

N **1 the locals** *(people)* les gens *mpl* ou les habitants *mpl* du coin **2** *Med, Fam (anaesthetic)* anesthésie *f* locale **3** *Fam* **the l.** *(pub)* le bar du coin; **this is my l.** c'est le bar où je vais régulièrement **4** *Am Journ (item)* nouvelle *f* locale

▸▸ *Med* **l. anaesthetic** anesthésie *f* locale; **to give sb a l. anaesthetic** faire une anesthésie locale à qn; *Comput* **l. area network** réseau *m* local; *Pol* **l. authorities** autorités *fpl* locales *ou* régionales; *Fin, Com* **l. bill** effet *m* sur place; *Comput* **l. bus** bus *m* local; *Comput* **l. bus card** carte *f* de bus local; *Comput* **l. bus disk** disque *m* connecté au bus local; *Tel* **l. call** communication *f* locale; **l. channel** canal *m* local, chaîne *f* locale; **l. colour** couleur *f* locale; **l. currency** monnaie *f* locale; **l. edition** édition *f* locale; **l. government** administration *f* municipale; **l. news** informations *fpl* régionales; **l. paper** journal *m* local; **l. radio** radio *f* locale; **l. radio station** station *f* de radio locale; **l. showers** averses *fpl* éparses; *Am Fin* **l. taxes** impôts *mpl* locaux; **l. television** télévision *f* locale; **l. time** heure *f* locale; **6am l. time** 6 heures du matin heure locale; **l. train** *(train m)* omnibus *m*; **l. wine** vin *m* du pays

locale [ləʊ'kɑːl] N *(of events)* lieu *m*; **the l. for a film** le lieu de tournage d'un film

locality [ləʊ'kælɪtɪ] N *(neighbourhood)* endroit *m*, lieu *m*; **in our l.** *(part of town)* dans notre quartier; *(out of town)* dans notre région; **in the general l. of the incident** sur les lieux de l'incident; **a man was seen in the l. at around 8 o'clock** un homme a été vu dans les environs vers 8 heures

localize ['ləʊkəlaɪz] VT *(epidemic etc)* localiser; **to become localized** *(of disease, pain)* se localiser *(* **in** dans*)*

localized ['ləʊkəlaɪzd] ADJ localisé

locally ['ləʊkəlɪ] ADV localement; *(to live, be well known, work etc)* dans le quartier; **l. produced wine** vin du pays; **we get them printed l.** nous les faisons imprimer sur place; **l prefer to shop l.** je préfère faire mes courses dans le quartier; **he set up in business l.** il a monté une affaire sur place

locate [ləʊ'keɪt] VT **1** *(to find)* localiser, situer; *Elec (fault etc)* repérer, localiser; **to l. sth on a map** situer qch sur une carte; *Naut* **to l. a ship** déterminer la position d'un navire *(en mer)* **2** *(to situate)* situer; **the new shopping centre is located in the old market square** le nouveau centre commercial est situé sur la place du vieux marché

VI *(of company etc)* s'installer

location [ləʊ'keɪʃ(ə)n] N **1** *(site, place)* emplacement *m* **2** *Cin* lieu *m* de tournage; **to be on l.** tourner en extérieur; **filmed on l.** filmé en extérieur **3** *(finding)* localisation *f*; *Elec (of fault etc)* repérage *m* **4** *Comput* adresse *f* URL

▸▸ *Comput* **l. box** zone *f* d'adresse; *Cin* **l. marks** *(in studio)* points *mpl* de repère au sol; *Mktg* **l. pricing** fixation *f* des prix selon l'endroit; *Cin* **l. shot** plan *m* en extérieur; **l. shots** extérieurs *mpl*

> Note that the French word **location** is a false friend and is never a translation for the English word **location**. It means **renting**.

locative ['lɒkətɪv] ADJ, N *Gram* locatif *m*

loch [lɒx] N *Scot* lac *m*; **sea l.** bras *m* de mer, fjord *m*

LOCK¹ [lɒk]

N	serrure **1** ▪ verrouillage **1**
	▪ verrou **2** ▪ clef **4** ▪ braquage **5**
	▪ écluse **6**
VT	fermer à clef **1** ▪ verrouiller **1, 2**
	▪ enfermer **1** ▪ bloquer **2**
VI	se bloquer **1**

N 1 *(on door etc)* serrure *f*; *(padlock)* cadenas *m*; *Comput (in network)* verrouillage *m*, blockage *m*; **under l. and key** sous clef; *(of person)* sous les verrous

2 *Tech* verrou *m*, *pl* -ous

3 *(on gun)* platine *f*; **we sold it l. stock and barrel** nous avons tout vendu sans exception; **we bought the whole estate l. stock and barrel** nous avons acheté toute la propriété; **he swallowed the story l. stock and barrel** il a tout avalé; **the motion was rejected l. stock and barrel** la motion a été rejetée en bloc

4 *(in wrestling)* étreinte *f*, clef *f*; **arm l.** clef de bras

5 *Aut etc* (rayon *m*) de braquage; **on full l.** braqué au maximum

6 *(on canal)* écluse *f*

7 *Rugby* avant *m* de deuxième ligne

VT 1 fermer à clef, verrouiller; **behind locked doors** à huis clos; **to l. sb in a room** enfermer qn dans une chambre; **to l. sth (away) in a drawer** enfermer qch dans un tiroir; **to l. valuables (away) in a safe** mettre des objets de valeur dans un coffre

2 *(steering wheel) (disable)* bloquer; *(put on full lock)* braquer à fond; *(machine parts)* enclencher; *(computer, keyboard, files)* verrouiller; *(mobile phone)* bloquer; **his jaws were tightly locked** il avait les dents serrées; **to be locked in each other's arms** se tenir étroitement enlacés; **to be locked in a passionate embrace** être passionnément enlacés; *Fig* **to be locked in sb's deadly embrace** être pris dans les griffes de qn; **to be locked (together) in a struggle** *(of people)* être engagés corps à corps dans une lutte; **to be locked in negotiation/dispute** être enfermé dans une négociation/un conflit; *Fig* **to l. horns with the enemy** livrer bataille avec l'ennemi; *Fig* **they have locked horns** *(of people)* ils sont en désaccord

VI 1 *(of wheels etc)* se bloquer; **the door locks on the inside** la porte se ferme de l'intérieur; **the door locks automatically** la porte se verrouille automatiquement; **the parts l. into each other** les parties s'enclenchent l'une dans l'autre

2 *Aut* **to l. left/right** braquer à gauche/à droite

▸▸**l. chamber** *(on canal)* sas *m* (d'écluse); *Rugby* **l. forward** avant *m* de deuxième ligne; **l. gate** *(on canal)* porte *f* d'écluse; *Comput* **l. inhibit** contre-verrou *m*, *pl* contre-verrous; *Br Aut* **l. ring** jonc *m* d'arrêt

▸**lock in** VT SEP **1** *(person)* enfermer à clef, mettre sous clef; **to get locked in** se faire enfermer; **to l. oneself in** s'enfermer

2 to be locked in *(to pension scheme etc)* ne pas avoir la possibilité de changer; *(to contract)* être lié; **to be locked into a company** *(as a source of supply etc)* être totalement dépendant d'une société; *St Exch, Fin* **to l. in a hedge** immobiliser une couverture

▸**lock off** VT SEP *Typ, Comput* débloquer; *(bad sector)* interdire l'accès à; **this key locks the caps on and off** cette touche bloque et débloque les majuscules

▸**lock on** VT SEP *Typ, Comput* bloquer, verrouiller; **l. the caps on before you start typing** bloque les majuscules avant de commencer à taper

▸**lock on to** VT INSEP *(of radar etc)*, *Fig* s'accrocher à

▸**lock out** VT SEP **1 to l. sb out** enfermer qn dehors; **I found myself locked out** en rentrant j'ai trouvé la porte fermée (à clef); **I've locked myself out (of my room)** je me suis enfermé dehors

2 *Ind (workforce)* lock-outer

▸**lock up** VT SEP **1** *(something)* mettre sous clef; *(somebody, something)* enfermer; *(in jail)* mettre sous les verrous; *(house)* fermer à clef; **to l. a house up for the winter** barricader une maison pour l'hiver; **he should be locked up!** il faudrait l'enfermer!

2 *Fin (capital)* immobiliser, bloquer, engager

VI it's time to l. up c'est l'heure de fermer; **to**

l. up for the night fermer le soir jusqu'au lendemain

lock² N *(of hair)* mèche *f*, boucle *f*; *Arch, Lit* **locks** cheveux *mpl*, chevelure *f*

locked-in syndrome ['lɒkt] N *Med* locked-in syndrome *m*, syndrome *m* d'enfermement

locker ['lɒkər] N *(for luggage, in school)* casier *m*; *Naut* coffre *m*; *Aviat* **overhead l.** coffre à bagage

▸▸*Am* **l. room** vestiaire *m* *(avec casiers)*; **l.-room jokes** plaisanteries grossières; **l.-room language** langage grossier

locket ['lɒkɪt] N médaillon *m*

locking ['lɒkɪŋ] **ADJ ATTRIB**

▸▸*Aut* **l. bar** barre *f* antivol; *Comput* **l. connector** connecteur *m* autobloquant; *Comput, Tech etc* **l. device** dispositif *m* de verrouillage; *Tech etc* **l. mechanism** mécanisme *m* de verrouillage; *Electron* **l. on** *(of radar etc)* accrochage *m*; **l. up** mise *f* sous clef; *(of house, room)* fermeture *f*; *Fin (of capital)* immobilisation *f*

lockjaw ['lɒkdʒɔ:] N tétanos *m*; **to have l.** avoir le tétanos

lock-keeper N *(on canal)* gardien *m* d'écluse, éclusier *m*

locknut ['lɒknʌt] N contre-écrou *m*, *pl* contre-écrous

lock-out N lock-out *m inv*

locksmith ['lɒksmɪθ] N serrurier *m*

lock-to-lock ADV *Aut* de butée à butée

lockup ['lɒkʌp] N **1** *Br (for storage)* remise *f*, *(garage)* box *m* **2** *Fam (police cells)* violon *m*, bloc *m* **3** *Aut (of wheel)* lock-up *m*; *(gear)* rapport *m* bloqué

▸▸*Aut* **l. clutch** embrayage *m* de prise directe; **l. garage** box

loco¹ ['ləʊkəʊ] N *Fam (train)* loco *f*

loco² ADJ *Am Fam (mad)* fou, *f* folle, *Fam* dingue

loco³ ADV *Com* loco; **the prices are l.** Hull les prix incluent le transport jusqu'à Hull

locomotion [ləʊkə'məʊʃən] N locomotion *f*

locomotive [ləʊkə'məʊtɪv] ADJ locomotif; *Anat* locomoteur, -trice

N *Rail* locomotive *f*

locum ['ləʊkəm] N *Br (for doctor, cleric)* remplaçant, -ante; **to take a l. job** faire un remplacement, prendre un emploi de remplaçant; **she's working as a l. in a hospital in London** elle fait un remplacement dans un hôpital de Londres

▸▸*Br* **l. tenens** *(for doctor, cleric)* remplaçant, -ante

locus, *pl* **loci** ['ləʊkəs, 'ləʊsaɪ, 'ləʊsi:] N **1** *Math* lieu *m* géométrique **2** *Biol (of gene)* locus *m*

locust ['ləʊkəst] N **1** *Entom* locuste *f*, sauterelle *f* **2** *(carob tree)* caroubier *m*; *(false acacia)* robinier *m*

▸▸**l. bean** caroube *f*; **l. tree** *(carob tree)* caroubier *m*; *(false acacia)* robinier *m*

locution [ləʊ'kju:ʃən] N locution *f*

lode [ləʊd] N *Geol, Min* filon *m*, veine *f*

lodestar ['ləʊdstɑ:r] N **1** étoile *f* directrice; **the l.** l'étoile polaire **2** *Fig* référence *f*

lodestone ['ləʊdstəʊn] N *Miner* aimant *m* naturel

lodge [lɒdʒ] N **1** *(for concierge etc)* loge *f*; **keeper's l.** maison *f* de garde-chasse; **(gate) l.** *(to estate)* pavillon *m* d'entrée, pavillon du garde; *Univ* **master's l.** résidence *f* du directeur du collège; **shooting l.** pavillon *m* de chasse **2** *(freemasons')* loge *f*, atelier *m*; *(meeting)* tenue *f*; **the Grand L. of France** le Grand Orient (de France) **3** *(of otter)* terrier *m*; *(of beaver)* hutte *f* **4** *(of Native Americans)* hutte *f*, wigwam *m*

VT 1 *(accommodate)* loger, héberger **2** *(de-*

posit) déposer, remettre; *(money)* consigner, déposer (**with sb** chez qn); *(bonds)* déposer (**with a bank** dans une banque); **securities lodged as collateral** titres déposés *ou* remis en nantissement; *Law* **to l. an appeal** interjeter appel, faire appel; **to l. a complaint** déposer une plainte; **to l. a complaint against sb** porter plainte contre qn

VI 1 *(of person)* loger; **to l. with sb** *(rent room from)* louer une chambre *ou* des chambres chez qn; *(have meals provided)* être en pension chez qn **2** *(of thing)* rester, se loger; **a fishbone lodged in his throat** il s'est coincé une arête dans le gosier; **a bullet lodged close to his spine** il a reçu une balle qui est allée se loger près de sa colonne vertébrale; **the words had lodged in her memory** les mots étaient gravés dans sa mémoire

▸▸**l. keeper** portier *m*; **l. meeting** *(of freemasons)* tenue *f*

lodger ['lɒdʒər] N locataire *mf* *(en meublé)*, *(who has meals provided)* pensionnaire *mf*; **to take (in) lodgers** louer des chambres; *(provide meals too)* prendre des pensionnaires

lodging ['lɒdʒɪŋ] N **1** *(room etc)* logement *m*; **to find a night's l.** trouver où coucher pour la nuit **2** *(usu pl)* **lodgings** logement *m*, appartement *m* meublé, *Arch* logis *m*; **to live or be in lodgings** loger *ou* habiter en garni *ou* en (hôtel) meublé **3** *(of money, securities etc)* dépôt *m*, consignation *f*, remise *f*; *Law (of complaint)* déposition *f*; *(of appeal)* interjection *f*

▸▸**l. house** garni *m*; *Am* **l. industry** industrie *f* hôtelière

loft [lɒft] N *(attic)* grenier *m*, soupente *f*, *(in church, hall etc)* galerie *f*, tribune *f*

VT *(ball)* donner de la hauteur à

▸▸**l. conversion** combles *mpl* aménagés, loft *m*; **we're thinking of doing a l. conversion** nous avons l'intention d'aménager le grenier

loftily ['lɒftɪlɪ] ADV **1** *(situated)* en hauteur **2** *Pej (to reply)* de manière hautaine

loftiness ['lɒftɪnɪs] N **1** *(of mountain etc)* hauteur *f* **2** *Pej (of person)* arrogance *f*, hauteur *f*

lofty ['lɒftɪ] ADJ **1** *(mountain, tree, building etc)* haut, élevé **2** *Pej (person, manner)* hautain **3** *(aim, desire etc)* noble; *(style)* relevé, soutenu; **the l. words in which the argument is expressed** le style relevé de l'argumentation

N *Fam (tall person)* hello, l.! salut, mon grand!

log¹ [lɒg] N **1** *(of wood)* bûche *f*; *(esp for building)* rondin *m*; *Fig* **to sleep like a l.** dormir comme une souche **2** *(record)* carnet *m* de route *ou* de bord; *Naut* journal *m*, *pl*-aux; *Aviat* carnet de vol; **ship's l.** journal de bord; **to write up the l.** noter les détails du voyage **3** *Naut (for measuring speed)* loch *m*

VT 1 *(order, in accounts)* enregistrer; *Naut etc* porter au journal; *(results etc)* noter sur un registre; *(of computer)* enregistrer; **the ship's arrival at Southampton was logged at 0800 hours** l'arrivée du bateau à Southampton a été portée au journal à 0800 heures; *Aviat* **to l. (up) 1,000 hours** inscrire 1 000 heures de vol **2** *(wood)* tronçonner, débiter en bûches **3 the ship logged 15 knots** le navire filait à 15 nœuds

▸▸**l. cabin** cabane *f* en rondins; *Comput* **l. file** fichier *m* compte-rendu; **l. fire** feu *m* de bois; **l. hut** hutte *f* en rondins, cabane en bois; **l. jam** *(in river)* embâcle *m* de bûches; *Fig (deadlock)* impasse *f*; *Naut* **l. line** ligne *f* de loch; **l. running** flottage *m* du bois; **l. transporter** fardier *m*

▶**log in** VI, VT SEP *Comput* = **log on**

▶**log off** VI *Comput (of user)* sortir, se déconnecter

  VT SEP faire sortir

▶**log on** VI *Comput (of user)* entrer, ouvrir une session; *(to remote system)* entrer en communication; **to l. to a system** se connecter à un système; **to l. on to a data base** entrer dans une base de données

  VT SEP faire entrer

▶**log out** VI, VT SEP *Comput* = **log off**

log² N *Math Fam* logarithme *m*

  ▶▶**l. table** table *f* de logarithmes

loganberry ['ləʊɡənberɪ] N *(fruit)* ronce-framboise *f*, *pl* ronces-framboises

logarithm ['lɒɡərɪð(ə)m] N logarithme *m*

logarithmic [lɒɡə'rɪðmɪk] ADJ *(curve)* logarithmique; *(paper)* à divisions logarithmiques

  ▶▶**l. table** table *f* de logarithmes

logbook ['lɒɡbʊk] N **1** *(record)* registre *m*; *Aviat* carnet *m* de vol; *Aut (personal record)* carnet de route; *Naut* journal *m* de bord; *(of machine)* journal de travail; *Radio* carnet d'écoute **2** *Br Aut (official documents)* ≃ carte *f* grise

logger ['lɒɡər] N bûcheron *m*

loggerheads ['lɒɡəhedz] N *Fam* **to be at l. with sb** avoir un différend avec qn (**about** au sujet de); **they were constantly at l.** ils se disputaient tout le temps; **his views were at l. with …** ses opinions étaient en contradiction avec …

loggia ['lɒdʒɪə] N *Archit* loge *f*, loggia *f*

logging ['lɒɡɪŋ] N **1** *(of details, events)* inscription *f* dans un journal; *Comput* enregistrement *m*; **l. of an order** enregistrement *m* d'une commande **2** *(felling timber etc)* exploitation *f* forestière

  ▶▶**l. camp** camp *m* forestier

logic ['lɒdʒɪk] N logique *f*; **I don't see the l. of it** je ne vois pas la logique (dans tout cela)

  ▶▶*Comput* **l. analyser** analyseur *m* logique; *Comput* **l. board** carte *f* logique; *Comput* **l. bomb** bombe *f* logique *ou* à retardement; *Comput* **l. card** carte *f* logique; *Comput* **l. chip** puce *f* logique; *Comput* **l. circuit** circuit *m* logique; *Comput* **l. gate** porte *f* logique; *Comput* **l. operator** opérateur *m* logique; *Comput* **l. seeking** recherche *f* logique

logical ['lɒdʒɪk(ə)l] ADJ *(conclusion, person)*, *Comput* logique; **do be l.!** essaie d'être logique!

  ▶▶*Comput* **l. access control** contrôle *m* d'accès logique; *Comput* **l. access protection** protection *f* d'accès logique; *Comput* **l. drive** unité *f* logique; *Comput* **l. file** fichier *m* logique; *Comput* **l. log** journal *m* logique; *Comput* **l. operator** opérateur *m* logique

logically ['lɒdʒɪklɪ] ADV logiquement

logic-chopper N ergoteur, -euse

logic-chopping N ergotage *m*

login ['lɒɡɪn] N *Comput* ouverture *f* de session

  ▶▶**l. name** nom *m* d'utilisateur, nom de login

logistic [lɒ'dʒɪstɪk], **logistical** [lɒ'dʒɪstɪk(ə)l] ADJ logistique

logistics [lɒ'dʒɪstɪks] N *Mil* logistique *f*, **l. of the situation** les données logistiques de la situation VOIR GRAMMAIRE A10

logo ['ləʊɡəʊ] N sigle *m*, logo *m*

  ▶▶**l. page** *(of software package)* page *f* d'accueil; **l. screen** *(of software package)* écran *m* d'accueil

logoff ['lɒɡɒf] N **l. timed at …** fin de session enregistrée à …

logon ['lɒɡɒn] N ouverture *f* de session; **l. timed at …** ouverture de session prévue à …

---

logrolling ['lɒɡrəʊlɪŋ] N **1** transport *m* des billes à la rivière **2** *Am Pol* alliance *f* politique dans un but intéressé

logwood ['lɒɡwʊd] N *(wood)* (bois *m* de) campêche *m*; *(tree)* campêcher *m*

loin [lɔɪn] N **1** *Anat, Lit* **loins** reins *mpl*; *Lit* **sprung from the loins of …** sorti des reins de … **2** *Culin (of mutton, veal)* filet *m*; *(of veal)* longe *f*; *(of mutton)* carré *m*; *(of beef)* aloyau *m* et faux-filet; *(of pork)* échine *f*, filet

  ▶▶**l. chop** côtes *fpl* premières

loincloth ['lɔɪnklɒθ] N pagne *m*

loiter ['lɔɪtər] VI *(suspiciously)* rôder; *(delay)* s'attarder (en route); **stop loitering and hurry up** arrête de flâner, dépêche-toi; *Law* **to l. (with intent)** rôder (d'une manière suspecte dans un endroit fréquenté)

loitering ['lɔɪtərɪŋ] N *Law* **l. with intent** délit *m* d'intention

LOL *Comput (abbr* **laughing out loud***)* MDR

loll [lɒl] VI **1** *(of person)* être étendu (paresseusement); **lolling back in an armchair** affalé dans un fauteuil **2** *(of tongue)* **to l. (out)** pendre

▶**loll about, loll around** VI *(of person)* paresser, fainéanter

lollipop ['lɒlɪpɒp] N *(candy)* sucette *f*, *(ice)* glace *f* à l'eau; *(chocolate)* esquimau® *m*

  ▶▶*Br Fam* **l. lady** = contractuelle *f* qui aide les écoliers à traverser la rue; *Br Fam* **l. man** = contractuel *m* qui aide les écoliers à traverser la rue

lollop ['lɒləp] VI *esp Br Fam* **to l. along** courir lourdement; **the rabbit lolloped off** le lapin s'éloigna en bondissant

lolly ['lɒlɪ] N **1** *Fam (candy)* sucette *f*, *(ice)* glace *f* à l'eau; *(chocolate)* esquimau® *m* **2** *Austr Fam (sweet)* bonbon *m* **3** *Br Sl (money)* fric *m*, flouze *m*

Lombard rate ['lɒmbɑːd] N *Banking* taux *f* Lombard

London ['lʌndən] N Londres; **a L. street** une rue de Londres; **a L. bus/taxi** un bus/taxi londonien

  ▶▶*Bot* **L. pride** saxifrage *f* ombreuse; *Br* **L. weighting** = indemnité *f* de vie chère venant compléter certains salaires londoniens

Londoner ['lʌndənər] N Londonien, -ienne; **a L. born and bred** un Londonien pure souche

lone [ləʊn] ADJ *esp Lit (person, thing)* solitaire, seul; *(place)* isolé, désert; **a l. parent** un parent isolé; *Fig* **to play a l. hand** agir tout seul, être seul contre tous

  ▶▶**the L. Star State** = surnom *m* donné au Texas; *Fig* **l. wolf** solitaire *mf*; **to be a bit of a l. wolf** être un peu solitaire

loneliness ['ləʊnlɪnɪs] N *(of house, person, village, political position)* isolement *m*; *(feeling)* solitude *f*; **with only the l. of old age to look forward to** avec la seule perspective de vieillir dans la solitude

lonely ['ləʊnlɪ] ADJ *(person)* seul; *(life, job)* solitaire; *(place, farmhouse)* isolé; **a l. figure** une silhouette; *Fig (politician etc)* une figure isolée; *Fig* **to travel a l. road** avoir un parcours solitaire; **to feel very l.** se sentir bien seul; **are you feeling l.?** vous vous sentez seul?; **life is very l. since the children left home** la vie est bien morne depuis que les enfants ont quitté la maison

  ▶▶**l. hearts club** club *m* de rencontres; **l. hearts column** rubrique *f* rencontres *(des petites annonces)*

loner ['ləʊnər] N solitaire *mf*

lonesome ['ləʊnsəm] ADJ *Am* solitaire, seul; **to feel l.** se sentir seul

  N *Fam* **to be on one's l.** être seul avec soi-même; **to do sth all on one's l.** faire qch tout seul

---

LONG¹ [lɒŋ] (**longer** ['lɒŋɡər], **longest** ['lɒŋɡɪst]) ADJ *(in size)* long, *f* longue; **how l. is the table?** quelle est la longueur de la table?; **to make sth longer** allonger qch, rallonger qch; **to be six metres l.** faire six mètres de long; **a 20 foot l. swimming pool** une piscine de 6 mètres de long; *Fam* **to be l. on charm/good ideas** *etc* être plein de charme/bonnes idées *etc*; **l. in the leg** aux longues jambes; *Fam* **l. in the tooth** *(old)* vieux, *f* vieille; **to go the l. way round** *(to a place)* prendre le chemin le plus long; *Fig* **the best by a l. way** de loin le meilleur; **a l. face** un visage allongé; *Fig* **to have a l. face, to pull a l. face** faire la tête, faire une tête de six pieds de long; **patience is not my l. suit** la patience n'est pas mon fort

2 *(in time)* long, *f* longue; **it will take a l. time** cela prendra longtemps, ce sera long; **a l. time ago** il y a (bien) longtemps; **it's a l. time since I was (last) in Paris** ça fait longtemps que je ne suis pas allé à Paris; **I've been wanting to go for a l. time** ça fait longtemps que j'ai envie d'y aller; **to wait for a l. time** attendre longtemps; **it's been a l. night** la nuit a été longue; **we've all had a l. day** nous avons tous eu une longue journée; **we're going away for a l. weekend** nous partons pour un week-end prolongé *ou* long *ou* grand week-end; **the days are getting longer** les jours rallongent; **three days at the longest** trois jours (tout) au plus; **it was a l. haul** *(of journey)* le voyage a été long; *Fig (to complete this project, make a full recovery from illness etc)* c'était un travail de longue haleine; **it looks like being a l. job** cela va prendre du temps; **to take the l. view of sth** voir qch à long terme; **in the l. term** *or* **run** à long terme, à longue échéance; **it'll be all right in the l. run** tout s'arrangera avec le temps; **to have a l. memory** avoir (une) bonne mémoire; **to have a l. talk with sb** parler longuement avec qn; **he took a l. drink from the flask** il but une longue gorgée à la bouteille; **to take a l. hard look at sth** fixer longuement qch

  N **1 the l. and the short of the matter is that …** le fin mot de l'affaire c'est que …; **that's the l. and the short of it!** un point c'est tout! **2** *St Exch (bill)* effet *m* à longue échéance

  ADV **1** *(for a long period)* longtemps; **I didn't wait l.** je n'ai pas attendu longtemps; **l. live the King/Queen!** vive le roi/la reine!; **as l. as** *(for the same length of time as)* aussi longtemps que; *(during the time that)* tant que; *(provided that)* du moment que; *(since, seeing that)* puisque; **I followed him for as l. as I could** je l'ai suivi aussi longtemps que j'ai pu; **as l. as I am alive** tant que je vivrai; **I'll never forget that day for as l. as I live** jamais de ma vie je n'oublierai ce jour; **as l. as you're happy** *(provided that)* du moment que tu es heureux; **you can take my car so l. as you're careful** tu peux prendre ma voiture du moment que tu es prudent; **to look at sb/sth l. and hard** fixer qn/qch longuement; *Fig* **to look at sth l. and hard** se pencher longuement sur qch; **I've thought l. and hard about this and …** j'y ai longuement réfléchi et …; **he was not l. in coming** il n'a pas tardé à venir; **before l.** avant peu, sous peu; **for l.** pendant longtemps; **I won't stay for l.** je ne resterai pas longtemps; **it won't take l.** cela ne prendra pas longtemps, cela ne sera pas long; **she won't be l.** *(will be here soon)* elle ne tardera pas; *(will soon have finished)* elle a bientôt fini; **is he going to be l.?** *(in arriving, finishing)* il en a pour longtemps?; **are you going to be much longer?** tu en as encore pour longtemps?; *Fam* **so l.!** au revoir!, à bientôt! VOIR GRAMMAIRE B31-2

2 *(since sometime in the past)* depuis longtemps; **I have l. been convinced of it** j'en suis convaincu depuis longtemps; **they have l.**

since left England ça fait longtemps qu'ils ont quitté l'Angleterre

3 how l.? combien de temps?; **how much longer will he be?** *(until ready etc)* il en a encore pour longtemps?; *(until he arrives)* dans combien de temps sera-t-il là?; **how l. have you known her?** depuis combien de temps est-ce que tu la connais?

4 l. before/after longtemps avant/après; **not l. before/after** peu de temps avant/après; **l. before I met you** longtemps avant que je te rencontre; **l. ago** il y a longtemps; **not (very) l. ago** il n'y a pas longtemps; **in the days of l. ago** autrefois, *Lit* jadis

5 *(for the duration of)* **all day/night l.** tout le long du jour/de la nuit, pendant toute la journée/la nuit; **all winter l.** tout au long de l'hiver

6 I could no longer hear him je ne l'entendais plus; **she no longer lives here** elle n'habite plus ici; **I couldn't wait any longer** je ne pouvais plus attendre; **five minutes longer** cinq minutes de plus; **I'll wait five minutes but no longer** je veux bien attendre cinq minutes mais pas plus

▸▸*Fin* **l. credit** crédit *m* à long terme; *Typ* **l. dash** trait *m*; *Math* **l. division** division *f* posée; **l. drink** long drink *m*; *(non-alcoholic)* = grand verre *m* de jus de fruits, de limonade etc; *Com* **l. dozen** treize; *Com* **l. hundred** cent vingt; *Fam* **l. johns** caleçon *m* long, caleçons *mpl* longs; *Sport* **l. jump** saut *m* en longueur; *Sport* **l. jumper** sauteur, -euse en longueur; *Old-fashioned* **l. lease** bail *m* emphytéotique; *Old-fashioned* **l. player** *(record)* longue durée *f*, *St Exch* **l. position** position *f* acheteur *ou* longue; **to take a l. position** acheter à la hausse, prendre une position longue; **l. service award** prime *f* d'ancienneté; **l. shot** *(competitor, racehorse etc)* outsider *m*; *(bet)* pari *m* risqué; *Cin* plan *m* éloigné; *Fig* entreprise *f* hasardeuse; **it's a bit of a l. shot but ...** il n'y a pas de grandes chances que ça marche mais...; **not by a l. shot** loin de là; *Med* **l. stay** (lit *m* de) long séjour *m*; **l. trousers** pantalon *m* long; *Univ* **the l. vacation** les grandes vacances *fpl*; *Radio* **l. wave** grandes ondes *fpl*

long² *vi* **to l. to do sth** avoir bien envie de faire qch, être impatient de faire qch, rêver de faire qch; **to l. for sth** désirer qch fortement *ou* ardemment; **he longed to be free** il avait hâte d'être libre; **I'm longing for the weekend/the holidays** j'ai hâte d'être en week-end/vacances; **I l. for you** tu me manques beaucoup; **I'm longing for home** *(native land)* mon pays me manque; *(my house)* ma maison me manque; **to l. for sb's return** attendre impatiemment le retour de qn; **we're longing for them to leave** nous avons hâte qu'ils partent; **a much longed-for baby** un bébé très désiré; **a longed-for holiday** des vacances très attendues

long³ [lɒŋ] *Geog (abbr* **longitude)** long

long-awaited ['lɒŋəweɪtɪd] ADJ *(event, birth etc)* très attendu

longboat ['lɒŋbəʊt] N *Naut* chaloupe *f*, *(of Vikings)* drakkar *m*

longbow ['lɒŋbəʊ] N *Mil, Hist* arc *m* (d'homme d'armes)

long-dated ADJ *Fin* à longue échéance
▸▸**l. securities** titres *mpl* longs, obligations *fpl* longues

long-distance ADJ *Tel* longue distance; *Tel Fam* **is it l.?** est-ce que c'est un appel longue distance?
ADV **to telephone l.** faire un appel longue distance
▸▸**l. call** communication *f* hors circonscription; **l. footpath** sentier *m* de grande randonnée; *Br* **l. lorry driver** conducteur, -trice de poids lourd; *Sport* **l. race** course *f* de fond; *Sport* **l. runner** coureur, -euse de fond

long-drawn-out ADJ *(sigh etc)* prolongé; *(story, explanation etc)* interminable; **l. tale** récit *m* prolongé *ou* à n'en plus finir; **a l. scream** un cri prolongé

long-established ADJ établi depuis longtemps

longevity [lɒnˈdʒevɪtɪ] N longévité *f*

long-forgotten ADJ oublié depuis longtemps

longhair ['lɒŋheər] *Am* ADJ **1** *(cat, dog)* à poil(s) long(s) **2** *Old-fashioned Fam (for intellectuals)* pour les intellos
N *Fam* **1** *Old-fashioned (intellectual)* intello *mf* **2** *(hippie)* chevelu *m*

longhaired ['lɒŋheəd] ADJ **1** *(cat, dog etc)* à poil(s) long(s); *(person)* aux cheveux longs **2** *Am Fam* = **longhair**

longhand ['lɒŋhænd] N écriture *f* ordinaire *ou* courante *ou* non abrégée; **in l.** *(written)* en clair, écrit à la main

long-haul ADJ *Aviat* long-courrier, *pl* longs-courriers; **a l. carrier** un long-courrier

longing ['lɒŋɪŋ] N désir *m*, grande envie *f* (**for** de); **to be filled with l. to do sth** être plein d'un ardent désir de faire qch
ADJ **to cast l. looks at sth** jeter des regards pleins d'envie à qch

longingly ['lɒŋɪŋlɪ] ADV avec envie; **to look l. at sth** couver qch des yeux; **she was looking l. out of the window** elle regardait languissamment par la fenêtre

longish ['lɒŋɪʃ] ADJ assez long, plutôt long

longitude ['lɒndʒɪtjuːd] N *Geog* longitude *f*

longitudinal [ˌlɒndʒɪˈtjuːdɪn(ə)l] ADJ longitudinal, -aux
▸▸*Constr* **l. beam** longeron *m*

longitudinally [ˌlɒndʒɪˈtjuːdɪn(ə)lɪ] ADV longitudinalement

long-legged ['lɒŋˈlegɪd] ADJ *(person)* aux jambes longues; *(horse)* haut sur pattes; *(bird)* à longues pattes

long-life ADJ *(battery)* longue durée; *(milk, juice)* longue conservation

long-lived ['lɒŋˈlɪvd] ADJ *(person)* qui vit longtemps; **we're a very l. family** dans la famille on vit très vieux
▸▸*Acct* **l. assets** actifs *mpl* à long terme, actifs à longue durée de vie

long-lost ADJ *(manuscript, painting etc)* perdu depuis longtemps; **she has been reunited with her l. brother** elle a retrouvé son frère dont elle avait été séparée depuis très longtemps; **I'm seeking some l. cousins** je suis à la recherche de cousins que j'ai perdu de vue depuis longtemps; **he welcomed me like a l. friend** il m'a accueilli comme si on avait été des amis qui ne s'étaient pas vus depuis des années

long-playing ADJ
▸▸**l. record** disque *m* (de) longue durée, *(disque)* microsillon *m*

long-range ADJ *(plane)* long-courrier; *(gun, radar)* à longue portée
▸▸**l. camera** appareil *m* de photo longue portée; *Met* **l. forecast** prévisions *fpl* météorologiques à long terme; *Mil* **l. missile** missile *m* longue portée

long-running ADJ *(film, play)* qui tient l'affiche; *(TV/radio programme)* qui est diffusé depuis longtemps

long-service ADJ
▸▸*Mil* **l. men** engagés *mpl* à long terme

longship ['lɒŋʃɪp] N *(of Vikings)* drakkar *m*

longshoreman, *pl* **longshoremen** ['lɒŋ-ʃɔːmən] N *Am Naut* débardeur *m*

long-sighted ADJ **1** *Opt* hypermétrope; *(in old age)* presbyte **2** *Fig (policy, decision)* prévoyant

long-sightedness [ˌlɒŋˈsaɪtɪdnɪs] N **1** hy-

permétropie *f*, *(in old age)* presbytie *f* **2** *Fig (of policy, decision)* prévoyance *f*

long-sleeved ADJ *(dress, pullover)* à manches longues

long-standing ADJ *(arrangement, friendship etc)* de longue date
▸▸*Fin* **l. accounts** vieux comptes *mpl*

long-stay ADJ
▸▸*Med* **l. bed** lit *m* (de) long séjour; **l. car park** parking *m* longue durée

long-suffering ADJ patient, endurant; *(tolerant)* indulgent

long-term ADJ **1** *(detainee, prisoner)* qui subit un emprisonnement de longue durée; **the l. unemployed** les chômeurs de longue durée **2** *Fin (loan, policy etc)* à long terme
▸▸*Fin* **l. bond** obligation *f* à long terme; *Acct* **l. borrowings** emprunts *mpl* à long terme; *Acct* **l. capital** capitaux *mpl* permanents; *Fin* **l. credit** crédit *m* (à) long terme; *Fin* **l. debt** dette *f* à long terme; *Br Fin* **l. individual savings account** plan *m* de retraite en actions; *Fin* **l. investments** placements *mpl* à long terme; *(on balance sheet)* immobilisations *fpl* financières; *Fin* **l. liabilities** dettes *fpl ou* passif *m* à long terme; **l. planning** planification *f* à long terme; **l. unemployment** chômage *m* de longue durée

longways ['lɒŋweɪz] ADV = **lengthways**

long-winded [lɒŋˈwɪndɪd] ADJ *Pej (story)* interminable; *(speaker, speech)* verbeux

loo [luː] N *Br Fam* **the l.** les toilettes *fpl*, les cabinets *mpl*; **to go to the l.** aller aux toilettes; **in the l.** aux toilettes, aux cabinets
▸▸*Br Fam* **l. paper** papier *m* hygiénique; *Br Fam* **l. seat** siège *m* des toilettes *ou* des W.-C.

loofah ['luːfə] N *(for washing)*, *Bot* loofa(h) *m*, luffa *m*

LOOK [lʊk]

N	coup d'œil **1** ▪ regard **2** ▪ air **4** ▪ mode **4** ▪ beauté **5**
VI	regarder **1** ▪ chercher **2** ▪ avoir l'air **3** ▪ écouter **4** ▪ chercher à **5**
VT	regarder

N 1 to have *or* **take a l. at sth** regarder qch; *(quickly)* jeter un coup d'œil sur qch; *Fam* **let's have a l.** *(show me)* fais voir; **to take a good l. at sb/sth** bien examiner qn/qch; **I didn't get a good l. at him** je n'ai pas bien vu comment il était; **did you get a good l. at him?** vous l'avez vu clairement?; **to have a l. round the town** faire un tour dans la ville; **to have a l. through some magazines** jeter un coup d'œil à des magazines

2 *(with eyes)* regard *m*; **a suspicious/nasty/angry l.** un regard soupçonneux/mauvais/méchant; **he shot me a poisonous l.** il m'a lancé un regard foudroyant; **he has a strange l. in his eyes** il a un drôle de regard dans les yeux; **we were getting some very odd looks** nous attirions des regards très étonnés; *Prov* **if looks could kill ...** si ses yeux étaient des revolvers ...

3 *(search)* **to have a l. for sth** chercher qch; **have you had a good l. for it?** est-ce que tu as bien cherché?; **let's have a quick l. for it** on va jeter un coup d'œil pour essayer de le trouver

4 *(appearance) (of object)* aspect *m*, air *m*, apparence *f*; *(of person)* tête *f*; **she has the l. of a troublemaker** elle a une tête à faire des histoires; **it has the l. of a successful marriage** cela a l'air d'un mariage heureux; **I don't like the l. of this at all!** cela ne me plaît pas du tout; **the business has a suspicious l. about it** l'affaire paraît suspecte *ou* louche; **I like the l. of him** il me plaît; **I don't like the l. of him** *(he seems suspicious)* sa tête ne me revient pas; **I don't like the l. of the weather** le temps a l'air inquiétant; **she has the l. of**

her grandfather about her elle a des airs de son grand-père; **the New L.** (fashion) le new-look; **this year's new l.** la nouvelle mode de cette année; **the new-l. format/Ford Fiesta®** le format/la Ford Fiesta® nouvelle version

5 good looks beauté f; **to lose one's looks** perdre ses charmes; **looks don't matter** l'apparence ne compte pas; **she's got her mother's looks** elle a la beauté de sa mère

vi 1 regarder; **to l. through** or **out of the window** regarder par la fenêtre; **to l. down a list** parcourir une liste du regard; **to l. the other way** (avert one's gaze) détourner les yeux; Fig fermer les yeux; **to l. into sb's eyes** regarder qn dans les yeux; **I'm just looking, thank you** (to shop assistant) je ne fais que regarder, merci; Prov **l. before you leap** il faut réfléchir avant d'agir; **to l. on the bright side** voir les choses du bon côté; **the house looks south** la maison est exposée au sud; **to l. to** or **towards the future** penser à l'avenir

2 (search) chercher; **we've looked everywhere** nous avons cherché partout

3 (seem, appear) avoir l'air, paraître, sembler; **to l. old** avoir l'air ou faire vieux; **to l. ill** avoir l'air malade, avoir mauvaise mine; **to l. well** (of person) avoir bonne mine; **that dress looks well on you** cette robe vous va bien; **she looks tired** elle a l'air fatigué(e); **she's not as stupid as she looks** elle est moins bête qu'elle n'en a l'air; **he doesn't l. his age** on ne lui donnerait pas son âge; **to l. like sb** ressembler à qn; **what does she l. like?** comment est-elle?; **it looks like an elephant** on dirait un éléphant; **things are looking bad** or **black** les choses prennent une mauvaise tournure; **things are looking good** ça a l'air d'aller ou de bien se passer; **the crops l. promising** la récolte s'annonce bien; **you l. as if you've slept badly** vous avez l'air d'avoir mal dormi; **it looks as if he didn't want to go** il semble qu'il ne veuille pas y aller; **he looks the part** il est fait pour ce rôle; **she looks like winning, it looks like she'll win** on dirait qu'elle va gagner; **it looks like rain** on dirait qu'il va pleuvoir

4 (expressing annoyance, desiring attention etc) **l. here!** écoutez donc!, dites donc!; (now) **l.** écoute; Fam **l. sharp!** fais gaffe!

5 (intend) chercher à; **to be looking to do sth** chercher à faire qch; **she'll be looking to improve on her previous best time** elle cherchera à améliorer son meilleur temps; **I'm not looking to cause any trouble** je ne veux pas causer de problème; **they're looking to appoint a new headmaster** ils envisagent d'engager un nouveau directeur

vt to l. sb (full or straight) **in the face** regarder qn (bien) en face ou dans les yeux; **I can never l. her in the face again** je ne pourrai plus jamais la regarder en face; **to l. sb up and down** regarder qn de haut en bas, toiser qn; **l. what you've done!** regarde ce que tu as fait!; **l. where you're going!** fais attention où tu vas!

▶ **look about** = **look around**

▶ **look after** vt insep (a sick person etc) veiller sur, soigner; (possessions, an object) faire attention à; (one's health, teeth etc) surveiller, faire attention à; (one's interests) prendre soin de; **can you l. after the house for us?** peux-tu garder ou faire attention à la maison?; **could you l. after my things while I go to …?** pourriez-vous surveiller mes affaires pendant que je vais à …?; **granny's looking after the children this weekend** mamie garde les enfants ce week-end; **he needs a lot of looking after** il a bien besoin qu'on s'occupe de lui; **l. after yourself!** prends bien soin de toi!; **you're well looked after** on s'occupe bien de vous; **he can l. after himself** (at home etc) il peut se débrouil-

ler (tout seul); (in fight etc) il sait se débrouiller (tout seul); **the garden needs a lot of looking after** c'est un jardin qui a besoin d'être entretenu; **the car has been well looked after** la voiture est bien entretenue

▶ **look around** vi **1** (turn head around) regarder derrière soi

2 (have a look) regarder autour de soi; (in town, museum etc) faire un tour; **can I just l. around?** (in shop) puis-je jeter un coup d'œil?

3 (search) regarder partout; **to l. around for sth** chercher qch; **I'll go upstairs and l. around** je monte jeter un coup d'œil

vt insep to l. around the house (out of interest) jeter un coup d'œil dans la maison; (search) chercher partout dans la maison; **to l. around town** (have a look) faire un tour en ville; **to l. around the shops** faire le tour des boutiques

▶ **look at** vt insep **1** regarder; **what are you looking at?** qu'est-ce que vous regardez?; **just l. at that!** regardez-moi ça!; Fam **she won't l. at a man** les hommes, elle ne leur jette même pas un regard; **I haven't looked at another woman in the last forty years** en quarante ans, je n'ai pas regardé une autre femme; **they won't l. at our offer** ils ne font aucun cas de notre offre; **what's he like to l. at?** de quoi a-t-il l'air?; **she's not much to l. at** ce n'est pas une beauté; **he's not much to l. at** il n'est pas très beau; **if you l. at the result** si vous considérez le résultat; **I don't like his way of looking at things** je n'aime pas la manière dont il voit les choses; **I don't l. at it that way at all** je ne le vois pas de cet œil-là; **just l. at the mess we're in!** regarde les ennuis qu'on a!; **just l. at you!** (you look awful, a mess etc) mais regarde-toi donc!

2 (examine) (brakes, tooth etc) regarder, jeter un coup d'œil sur

▶ **look away** vi tourner la tête

▶ **look back** vi regarder en arrière; **to l. back on the past** se retourner sur le passé; Fig **he has never looked back since that day** depuis ce jour sa situation n'a cessé de s'améliorer

▶ **look down** vi (from a height) regarder en ou vers le bas; (lower one's eyes) baisser les yeux; **don't l. down!** ne regarde pas en bas!; **she looked down on the town below her** elle regarda la ville en bas; **the chalet looks down on the valley** le chalet donne sur la vallée

▶ **look down on** vt insep (think little of, despise) mépriser

▶ **look for** vt insep chercher; **go and l. for him** allez le chercher; **he's looking for trouble** il cherche les ennuis

▶ **look forward** vi (to the future) regarder vers l'avenir

▶ **look forward to** vt insep attendre avec plaisir; **I'm looking forward to seeing her again** il me tarde de la revoir; **I'm looking forward to the weekend** vivement le weekend!; **he hasn't got much to l. forward to in life** il n'a pas grand-chose à attendre de la vie; **they don't exactly l. forward to a visit to the dentist** ils appréhendent d'aller chez le dentiste; **I'm not exactly looking forward to going** je n'ai pas vraiment envie d'y aller; **I'm so looking forward to seeing you all again** j'aimerais tellement tous vous revoir; **I'm not looking forward to it at all** je n'y tiens pas du tout; **I l. forward to hearing from you** (at end of letter) dans l'attente de vous lire

▶ **look in** vi **1** (at window etc) regarder (à l'intérieur), jeter un coup d'œil (à l'intérieur)

2 (visit) entrer en passant; **I'll l. in again tomorrow** je repasserai demain; **to l. in on sb** aller ou passer voir qn

▶ **look into** vt insep (investigate) examiner, étudier; (allegations) prendre en considération; **it needs a bit of looking into** il faut étudier la question

▶ **look on** vi regarder, être spectateur; **while a crowd looked on** sous les regards de la foule

vt insep (consider) considérer, envisager; **I l. on him as a friend** je le considère comme un ami

▶ **look onto** vt insep (of room) (garden, street etc) donner sur

▶ **look out** vi **1** (through window etc) regarder (à l'extérieur), jeter un coup d'œil (à l'extérieur)

2 (be careful) prendre garde, être sur ses gardes; **l. out!** attention!, prenez garde!

vt sep trouver, Fam dénicher

▶ **look out for** vt insep **1** (look for) guetter (l'arrivée de)

2 (be on guard for) (person, pickpockets, errors etc) faire attention à

3 esp Am (take care of) prendre soin de

▶ **look out onto** vt insep (of room) (garden, street etc) donner sur

▶ **look over** vt insep (have a look at) jeter un coup d'œil sur; (papers) parcourir; (house for sale) visiter

▶ **look round** vi, vt insep = **look around**

▶ **look through** vt insep **1** (papers etc) parcourir, examiner rapidement

2 (not see) **she just looked straight through me** (deliberately) elle m'a ignoré; (not deliberately) elle m'a regardé sans me voir

vi (at window, lock etc) regarder par la fenêtre/la serrure etc

▶ **look to** vt insep **1** (rely on) compter sur; **we're looking to you to help us** or **for help** nous comptons sur vous pour nous aider; **you can't always l. to your parents for money** on ne peut pas toujours s'en remettre à ses parents pour l'argent

2 (ensure) **l. to it that you …** faites en sorte de …; **l. to it that he …** faites en sorte qu'il … + sub; Old-fashioned **l. to your daughter** faites attention à ou surveillez votre fille

▶ **look up** vt sep **1** (word in a dictionary etc) chercher

2 (go to visit) (person) aller voir, passer chez; **l. me up** venez me voir

vi 1 (from below) regarder en haut; (raise one's eyes) lever les yeux; **if you could all l. up at this picture here** si vous regardez tous le tableau du haut

2 Fig **to be looking up** (of business) reprendre; (of shares) remonter; **things are looking up** la situation s'améliore; **things are looking up for her** sa situation s'améliore

▶ **look upon** vt insep = **look on** vt insep

▶ **look up to** vt insep (respect) respecter, estimer

lookalike ['lʊkəlaɪk] N (person) sosie m; **she's a Princess Diana l.** c'est un sosie de la Princesse Diana; **it's just another Renault l.** c'est la copie conforme de la Renault

looker ['lʊkər] N Fam (good) **l.** (of a woman) belle femme f; (younger) beau brin m de fille; (of a man) bel homme m

looker-on, pl **lookers-on** N spectateur, -trice (**at** de), Pej badaud m

look-in N Fam (chance) **he won't have** or **get a l.** il n'a pas la moindre chance; **everyone gets a l.** tout le monde a sa chance

looking-glass ['lʊkɪŋɡlɑːs] N Old-fashioned miroir m, glace f

looking room N TV salle f de visionnage

lookout ['lʊkaʊt] N **1** (post) poste m d'observation ou de vigie

2 (person), Mil guetteur m; Naut homme m de veille ou de vigie

3 (action) surveillance f, observation f; Naut veille f; **to keep a l.** être aux aguets; Naut veiller, être en ou de vigie; **to be on the l. for** (person) guetter; (something) être à la recherche de; **to be on l. duty** être de guet

4 Fam **that's a poor l. for him** c'est de mauvais augure pour lui; **that's your l.!** ça c'est ton affaire *ou Fam* tes oignons!

▸▸ **l. post** poste *m* d'observation *ou* de vigie

lookover ['lʊkəʊvər] **N to give sth a (quick) l.** jeter un coup d'œil sur qch

look-see **N** *Fam* **to go and have** *or* **take a l.** aller jeter un coup d'œil

look-up table **N** *Comput* table *f* de recherche *ou* de référence

loom[1] [luːm] **N** *Tex* métier *m* à tisser

loom[2] **VI** apparaître indistinctement *(comme une menace)*; **dangers looming ahead** dangers qui menacent; **to l. (large)** *(of event etc)* paraître imminent, être tout proche; **it looms large in his view of things** cela joue un rôle important dans sa manière de voir les choses

▸ **loom up** **VI** *(of ship, person in authority etc)* surgir

loon [luːn] **N 1** *(bird) Am* plongeon *m*, *Can* huart *m* **2** *Fam (fool)* imbécile *mf*, *(crazy)* fada *m*

loony ['luːnɪ] *Fam* **N** dingue *mf*

ADJ dingue, timbré

▸▸ *Hum* **l. bin** maison *f* de fous; *Br Pej* **the l. left** les gauchos

loop [luːp] **N 1** *(of ribbon, film etc)* boucle *f*, *(of fingerprint)* anse *f*, *(of river)* méandre *m*, boucle; *(in skating)* croisé *m*; *(of spiral, spool)* tour *m*; *(contraceptive coil)* stérilet *m*; *Aviat* boucle, looping *m*; *Rail (line)* voie *f* d'évitement, voie de raccordement; *(at terminus)* boucle d'évitement; *Am Fam* **to knock** *or* **throw sb for a l.** abasourdir qn; *Am Fam* **to be out of the l.** ne pas être dans le coup; *Fam* **to cut sb out of the l.** mettre qn aux oubliettes **2** *Elec* boucle *f*, bouclage *m*; *Nucl (of reactor)* boucle, circuit *m*; *Comput* boucle d'itération; *Tel* circuit (branché), ligne *f* dérivée

VT 1 *(piece of string etc)* faire une boucle *ou* des boucles à; **to l. sth around sth** enrouler qch autour de qch **2** *Aviat* **to l. the l.** faire un looping, boucler la boucle **3** *Elec* boucler

VI 1 faire une boucle **2** *Comput* tourner sur une boucle

▸▸ *Electron* **l. aerial**, **l. antenna** cadre *m* d'antenne; *Elec* **l. circuit** circuit *m* bouclé; *Elec* **l. current** courant *m* circulant dans un circuit bouclé; *Rail* **l. line** voie *f* d'évitement, voie de raccordement; *(at terminus)* boucle d'évitement; *Sewing* **l. stitch** point *m* de bouclette

▸ **loop back** **VI** *(of river etc)* faire une boucle; *Comput (of program)* faire une boucle pour retourner *(to* à)

VT SEP *(curtain)* retenir avec une embrasse

loophole ['luːphəʊl] **N 1** *(in law, regulations etc)* point *m* faible; **to find a l.** trouver une échappatoire; **a legal l.** un vide juridique **2** *(gap)* trou *m*, ouverture *f*, *(in fortified wall)* meurtrière *f*

looping ['luːpɪŋ] **N** *Aviat* **l. the loop** looping *m*

loopy ['luːpɪ] **ADJ** *Fam (crazy)* toqué, timbré, maboul

LOOSE [luːs] **ADJ 1** *(not fastened or attached) (screw, nail, brick, part)* qui se détache *ou* se défait; *(page)* détaché; *(knot)* défait, délié; *(floorboard)* désajusté; *(tooth)* qui bouge; *Elec (connection)* desserré; *(cable)* volant; *Com (goods)* en vrac; **to come l.**, **to get l.** se dégager, se détacher; *(of knot)* se défaire, se délier; *(of screw)* se desserrer; *(of iron bar etc)* se desceller; **to work l.** *(of machine parts)* se desserrer, prendre du jeu; *(of tooth)* se déchausser; *(of hair in bun etc)* se dénouer; **to let the riot police l. on the crowd** lâcher les CRS sur la foule; **I'm dying to be let l. on the garden** je crève d'envie de pouvoir m'en donner à cœur joie dans le jardin;

to let a dog l. lâcher un chien; **they let their dog run l. in the fields** ils ont laissé leur chien courir en liberté dans les champs; **to let l. a torrent of abuse** lâcher un torrent d'injures; *Fig* **to be at a l. end** se trouver désœuvré, n'avoir rien à faire; *Fig* **to tie up the l. ends** régler les derniers détails

2 *(slack)* détendu; *(cable)* mou, *f* molle; *(knot)* lâche; *(skin)* flasque; *(piece of clothing)* ample; *(coat)* flottant; **this skirt is much too l. at the waist** cette jupe est bien trop large à la taille; **to have l. bowels** avoir la diarrhée

3 *(in structure, arrangement) Tex (weave)* lâche, à claire-voie; *Mil (order)* dispersé

4 *(imprecise)* vague, peu exact; *(style)* lâche, décousu; *(translation)* approximatif

5 *(immoral)* dissolu, débauché; *(woman)* de mauvaise vie

N to be on the l. *(of prisoner)* être en cavale; *(of escaped tiger etc)* être en liberté; **there's a horde of louts on the l. in town** il y a une horde de voyous en vadrouille dans la ville; *Hum* **her husband's on the l. tonight** son mari est en vadrouille ce soir

ADV to hang l. *(of rope etc)* pendre, flotter; *esp Am Fig Fam (relax)* se relaxer, se détendre; *(not panic)* rester calme

VT 1 *(set free)* délier, détacher; **to l. one's hold** lâcher prise

2 *(untie) (knot etc)* délier, dénouer, défaire; *(hair)* dénouer, détacher; *Naut (mooring rope)* larguer; *(sail)* déferler

3 *(fire) (arrow)* décocher

▸▸ **l. ball** *Cr* balle *f* mal lancée; *Tennis* balle qui traîne; **l. cannon** personne *f* incontrôlable; **l. cash**, **l. change** menue monnaie *f*, **l. chippings** gravillons *mpl*; *Med* **l. cough** toux *f* grasse; *Br* **l. cover** *(for armchair, sofa)* housse *f*; **l. end** *(of a rope)* bout *m* qui pend; *Sport* **l. horse** cheval *m* sauvage; **l. insert** *(in newspaper, magazine)* encart *m* libre; **l. living** débauche *f*, vie *f* dissolue; **l. morals** mœurs *fpl* relâchées; **l. talk** des propos *mpl* lestes

▸ **loose off** **VI** *Mil Fam (with machine gun etc)* tirer (**at** sur); *Fig Fam* **to l. off at sb** *(tell off)* engueuler qn

VT SEP *(fire) (a few rounds)* tirer, lâcher

loose-fitting **ADJ** *(item of clothing)* ample, large

loose-leaf **ADJ** *(album)* à feuilles mobiles, à feuillets rechargeables

▸▸ **l. binder** classeur *m* (à feuilles mobiles); **l. paper** feuillets *mpl* mobiles

loose-limbed **ADJ** souple

loosely ['luːslɪ] **ADV 1** *(to hold sth)* sans serrer; **to be l. fixed** être mal serré *ou* mal ajusté, avoir du jeu; **her dress hung l. on her body** elle flottait dans sa robe **2** *(to speak)* sans précision; **l. translated** traduit approximativement; **the word is often used l.** le mot est souvent employé de façon imprécise; **l. connected** *or* **related** vaguement lié

loosen ['luːs(ə)n] **VT** *(slacken) (knot)* défaire, délier, relâcher; *(nut)* desserrer, dégager, décoller; *(rope)* relâcher, détendre; *(necktie, item of clothing)* desserrer; *(restrictions)* assouplir; **to l. sb's bonds** desserrer les liens de qn; **to l. one's grip** relâcher son étreinte; **to l. sb's tongue** délier *ou* dénouer la langue à qn; *Med* **to l. the bowels** avoir un effet laxatif

VI *(of knot etc)* se délier, se défaire; *(of screw etc)* se desserrer; *(of rope)* se relâcher

▸ **loosen up** **VI** *(of person) (relax)* se mettre à l'aise; *(of athlete etc)* s'assouplir; **he always loosens up after a few drinks** il est toujours plus décontracté après un verre ou deux; **she loosens up once you get to know her** elle perd de sa froideur une fois qu'on la connaît

VT SEP *(muscles)* relâcher

looseness ['luːsnɪs] **N 1** *(of tooth, stone etc)* déchaussement *m*; *(of pin, bolt etc)* jeu *m*; *(of skin)* flaccidité *f*; *(of rope)* relâchement *m*; *(of piece of clothing)* ampleur *f* **2** *(of terminology)* imprécision *f* **3** *(of discipline, morals etc)* relâchement *m*

loosestrife ['luːsstraɪf] **N** *(plant)* **(purple) l.** salicaire *f* commune

loot [luːt] **N 1** *(goods)* butin *m*; **soldiers on the l.** soldats qui se livrent à des pillages **2** *Fam (money)* flouze *m*, fric *m*

VT *(city etc)* piller, mettre à sac; *(shops)* piller; *(goods)* voler

VI se livrer au pillage

looter ['luːtər] **N** pilleur, -euse, pillard, -arde

looting ['luːtɪŋ] **N** pillage *m*

lop [lɒp] **VT** (-pp-) *(tree)* élaguer, ébrancher

▸ **lop off** **VT SEP** *(branch)* couper, élaguer

▸ **lope along** [ləʊp] **VI** *(of person)* avancer à grandes enjambées; *(of leopard etc)* courir tout en puissance; *(of hare)* avancer en bondissant

▸ **lope off** **VI** *(of person)* partir d'une démarche élastique; **the tiger loped off into the jungle** le tigre pénétra dans la jungle de sa démarche souple

lop-eared ['lɒpɪəd] **ADJ** *(rabbit, dog etc)* aux oreilles pendantes

lopsided [lɒp'saɪdɪd] **ADJ** qui manque de symétrie, asymétrique; *(picture)* de guingois, de travers; **a l. grin** un sourire en coin; **a l. group with twice as many women as men** un groupe déséquilibré comptant deux fois plus de femmes que d'hommes; **a l. account of the conflict** une description partiale du conflit

loquacious [lɒ'kweɪʃəs] **ADJ** loquace

loquaciousness [lɒ'kweɪʃəsnɪs], **loquacity** [lɒ'kwæsɪtɪ] **N** loquacité *f*

lord [lɔːd] **N 1** seigneur *m*; **l. of the manor** châtelain *m*; **our sovereign l. the king** notre seigneur souverain, le roi; *(in Middle Ages etc)*, *Hum* **her l. and master** son seigneur et maître **2** *Rel* **the L.** le Seigneur; **in the year of our L.** ... en l'an de grâce ...; *Fam* **(good) L.!**, **O L.!** mon Dieu!; *Fam* **L. knows if** ... Dieu sait si ... **3** *Br (title)* lord *m*; **L. Hailsham said that** ... Lord Hailsham a dit que ...; *Pol* **the House of Lords**, **the Lords** la Chambre des Lords

VI *Fam* **to l. it** mener la grande vie; **to l. it over sb** traiter qn de haut

▸▸ **L.'s Day Observance Society** = Société *f* pour l'Observance du Jour du Seigneur; **L. God Almighty** Seigneur Dieu Tout-puissant; **lords and ladies** *(flower)* arum *m* maculé, pied-de-veau *m*, *pl* pieds-de-veau; **the L. Mayor** le Lord Maire; **the L.'s Prayer** le Pater

lordly ['lɔːdlɪ] **ADJ 1** noble, de grand seigneur **2** *Pej (arrogant)* hautain; **his l. airs** ses airs de grand seigneur; **in a l. manner** avec hauteur

lordship ['lɔːdʃɪp] **N 1** *(authority)* suzeraineté *f* **2** *Your L.* *also Hum* votre Seigneurie; *(to nobleman)* monsieur le comte *etc*; *(to judge)* votre honneur

lordy ['lɔːdɪ] **INT** *esp Am Fam* Seigneur!

lore [lɔːr] **N** science *f*, savoir *m*; **country l.** connaissance *f* des choses de la campagne

lorgnette [lɔː'njet] **N** *(spectacles)* face-à-main *m*, *pl* faces-à-main; *(opera glasses)* jumelles *fpl* (de théâtre) à manche

lorry ['lɒrɪ] **N** *Br* camion *m*; *Euph Hum* **it fell off the back of a l.** *(is stolen)* je l'ai trouvé

▸▸ **l. driver** camionneur, -euse

LOSE [luːz] (*pt, pp* **lost** [lɒst], *prp* **losing** ['luːzɪŋ])

| **VT** perdre **1–4** ▪ coûter **6** |
| **VI** perdre **1** ▪ retarder **2** |

vt 1 *(money, right etc)* perdre; *(mislay)* perdre, égarer; *(through death, injury) (one's father, baby, arm, voice etc)* perdre; **you will l. nothing by waiting** vous ne perdrez rien à attendre; **to have nothing to l.** n'avoir rien à perdre; **the expression loses something in translation** l'expression perd quelque chose à la traduction; **to l. one's heart to sb** tomber amoureux de qn; **to l. one's reason** perdre la raison; **to l. one's reputation** se perdre de réputation; **to l. one's nerve** ne pas avoir le courage; **he had lost interest in his work** son travail ne l'intéressait plus; **the patient is losing strength** le malade s'affaiblit; **many lives were lost in the disaster** la catastrophe a coûté la vie à de nombreuses personnes; **to be lost at sea** périr en mer; **to l. one's way, to get lost** perdre son chemin, se perdre, s'égarer; *Sl* **get lost!** fiche-moi le camp!; **to l. one's balance** perdre l'équilibre; **to l. share** *(of market)* perdre des parts de marché; **to l. sight of sb** perdre qn de vue; **to l. sight of the reason for doing sth** perdre de vue la raison pour laquelle on fait/a fait qch; *Fig Fam* **I'm lost!, you've lost me!** je suis largué, je ne vous suis plus; *Fam Fig* **you lost me when you started using technical terms** j'ai perdu le fil quand tu as commencé à employer des termes techniques; *Fam* **to l. one's head** perdre la tête; *Fam* **to l. it** *(go mad)* perdre la boule; *(lose one's temper)* piquer une crise, péter les plombs; *Br Fam* **to l. the plot** perdre la boule
2 *(deliberately)* **to l. weight** perdre du poids; **I've lost 10 kilos** j'ai perdu 10 kilos, j'ai maigri de 10 kilos; **to l. oneself in the crowd** se perdre dans/se mêler à la foule; **to l. one's pursuers** *(of sb being chased)* larguer ses poursuivants; **to l. oneself in a book** se plonger dans un livre
3 *(fail to win) (match, race, battle, trial)* perdre; **the motion was lost** *(in debate)* la motion a été rejetée
4 *(waste) (time)* gaspiller, perdre; **the joke was lost on him** la plaisanterie lui est passée au-dessus de la tête; **American humour is lost on us** nous ne comprenons rien à l'humour américain
5 clock that loses five minutes a day pendule qui retarde de cinq minutes par jour
6 *(bring about loss of)* **the decision will l. us our jobs** la décision nous coûtera nos emplois; **that mistake lost him the match** cette faute lui coûta la partie
vi 1 perdre; **to l. heavily** *(in betting)* perdre une grosse somme; *(by a large margin)* se faire écraser; **both armies lost heavily** les deux armées ont subi de lourdes pertes; **to l. in value** perdre de sa valeur; **our team was losing at half-time** notre équipe perdait à la mi-temps; **we've lost on the sale of the house** nous avons perdu sur la vente de la maison; **it loses in translation** on perd un peu à la traduction
2 *(of clock, watch)* retarder
▸ **lose out vi** être (le/la) perdant(e); **British industry is losing out to the Japanese** les Britanniques sont victimes de la concurrence japonaise
▸ **lose out on vt insep** *Fam* **to l. out on a deal** faire les frais d'une affaire; **to l. out on a contract** *(not get)* laisser échapper un contrat; **they lost out on it** ils ont été perdants

loser ['luːzər] **N** *Sport etc* perdant, -ante; **the winners and the losers** les gagnants et les perdants, les vainqueurs et les vaincus; **to be a good/bad l.** être bon/mauvais joueur; **to back a l.** miser sur un perdant; **you'll be a l.** c'est toi qui y perdras; **he's a born l.** il est toujours perdant, il n'arrive jamais à rien

losing ['luːzɪŋ] **ADJ** perdant; **to fight a l. battle** se livrer à une bataille perdue

d'avance; **the l. side** les vaincus *mpl; Sport* l'équipe *f* perdante

loss [lɒs] **N 1** perte *f*; **there have been heavy government losses in the Midlands** *(in election)* le gouvernement a perdu beaucoup de sièges dans les Midlands; **the catastrophe resulted in great l. of life** la catastrophe a fait beaucoup de victimes; *Mil etc* **to sustain** *or* **suffer heavy losses** subir de grosses pertes; **she has never recovered from the l. of her mother** elle ne s'est jamais remise d'avoir perdu sa mère; **he is a great l. to the British theatre** c'est une grande perte pour le théâtre britannique; **it's no great l. that they're leaving** leur départ n'est pas une grosse perte; **to feel a sense of l.** ressentir un vide; **without l. of face** sans perdre la face; **l. of sight** perte de la vue
2 *Fin, Com (financial)* déficit *m; (in insurance)* sinistre *m; (of product being manufactured or transported)* freinte *f*, déperdition *f*; **to make a l.** perdre de l'argent; **to sell at a l.** vendre à perte; **to run at a l.** *(of business)* tourner à perte; **to cut one's losses** faire la part du feu; **l. in transit** freinte *ou* déchet *m* de route; **total l.** perte *f* totale
3 *Fig* **to be at a l.** ne savoir que faire; *(not know what to say)* ne savoir que dire; *(not know what to answer)* ne savoir que répondre; **to be at a (total) l. to explain …** être (totalement) incapable d'expliquer …; **to be at a l. (to know) what to do/say** ne savoir que faire/dire; **she's never at a l. for an answer** elle a *ou* trouve toujours réponse à tout; **he's never at a l. for something to say** il n'est jamais à court (de mots)
▸ ▸ *Br* **l. adjuster** *Ins* expert *m; Naut* dispatcheur *m*; **l. assessment** fixation *f* des dommages; *Law* **l. of civil rights** perte des droits civiques, dégradation *f* civique; **l. of earnings** manque *m* à gagner; *Rel* **l. of grace** amission *f* de la grâce; *Mktg* **l. leader** produit *m* d'appel; **l. leader price** prix *m* d'appel

loss-making ADJ *Com* qui tourne à perte, déficitaire

lost [lɒst] **PT, PP** *see* **lose**
ADJ perdu; **the child was l.** l'enfant s'était perdu; **to give sb/sth up for l.** abandonner tout espoir de retrouver qn/qch; **30 people were reported l. at sea** 30 personnes auraient péri en mer; **to seem** *or* **look l.** avoir l'air dépaysé; *(at party, in lesson)* avoir l'air perdu; **she's l. to the world** le monde n'existe plus pour elle; **she's completely l. in her book** elle est complètement absorbée dans sa lecture; **to be l. in thought** être perdu dans ses pensées; **the joke was l. on them** ils n'ont rien compris à la plaisanterie; **it's all l. on me** ça me passe au dessus de la tête, je n'y comprends rien; *Fam* **when they talk shop I'm quite l.** quand ils parlent boutique, je suis complètement largué; **to wander (about) like a l. soul** errer comme une âme en peine; **he looks like a l. sheep without his wife** sans sa femme, il a l'air complètement perdu
▸ ▸ **l. cause** cause *f* perdue; **l. and found** objets *mpl* trouvés; *Am* **l. and found department** (bureau *m* des) objets trouvés; **l. property** objets trouvés; *Br* **l. property office** (bureau des) objets trouvés; *Am* **l. river** rivière *f* souterraine; **l. soul** âme *f* perdue, âme damnée

LOT [lɒt]

N beaucoup **1** ▪ tirage au sort **2** ▪ sort **3** ▪ terrain **4** ▪ studio **4** ▪ lot **5** ▪ paquet **5** ▪ le tout **7**
ADV beaucoup

N 1 a l. (of) beaucoup (de); **what a l. of people!** que de monde!; **such a l. of people** tant de monde; **quite a l. (of sth)** une quantité

considérable (de qch), *Fam* pas mal (de qch); **I saw quite a l. of her in Paris** je l'ai vue assez souvent pendant mon séjour à Paris; **not a l.** pas beaucoup; **what did you think of his speech? – not a l.!** qu'as-tu pensé de son discours? – pas grand-chose!; **a l. of explaining to do** beaucoup d'explications à donner; **we had a l. of fun** nous nous sommes bien amusés; **I would have given a l. to …** j'aurais donné gros pour …; **I've got a l. to do before bedtime** j'ai beaucoup à faire avant ce soir; **I've got a whole l. of things to do** j'ai un tas de choses à faire
2 *(selection)* sort *m*, tirage *m* au sort; **drawn by l.** tiré au sort; **to draw** *or* **cast lots for sth** tirer qch au sort, tirer au sort pour qch
3 *(destiny)* sort *m*, part *f*, partage *m*, destin *m*, destinée *f*; **to be happy/content with one's l.** être content de son sort; **it fell to my l. to decide** c'était à moi de décider; **the poor man's l.** la condition du pauvre; **to throw** *or* **cast in one's l. with sb** partager le sort *ou* la fortune de qn
4 *(land)* (lot *m* de) terrain *m; Cin* **(studio) l.** studio *m* (de cinéma); *Am* **parking l.** parking *m*
5 *(at auction) (of merchandise)* lot *m; Fin (of bonds, shares)* paquet *m*; **in lots** par lots; **to buy/sell in one l.** acheter/vendre en bloc
6 *(referring to person/people)* **a bad l.** un mauvais sujet, un vaurien; **a nice l. of people** des gens très agréables; *Iron* **you're a nice l., you are!** vous êtes incroyables, vous!; *Fam Pej* **that l. next door** la bande d'à côté; *Fam* **listen, you l.!** écoutez tous; *Fam* **you arrange to get your l. there in time** arrangez-vous pour que votre groupe soit là à l'heure; **the l.** tous, tout le monde; **the whole l. of you** vous tous; **you rotten l.!** espèces de voyous!; **the whole l. of them** toute la bande
7 the l. *(everything)* le tout; **I bought the l.** j'ai acheté le tout; *Fam* **the whole damn l.** tout le bazar
ADV a l. beaucoup; **a l. bigger** beaucoup *ou* bien plus gros; **such a l.** tellement; **times have changed a l.** les temps ont bien changé; **he thought a l. before deciding** il a beaucoup réfléchi avant de se décider; **thanks a l.** merci beaucoup
▸ ▸ *Fin, St Exch* **l. size** unité *f* de transaction

loth [ləʊθ] **ADJ** = **loath**

lotion ['ləʊʃən] **N** lotion *f*

lots [lɒts] *Fam* **NPL l. (of)** beaucoup (de); **I've got l. of things to do** j'ai beaucoup de *ou* un tas de choses à faire; **he has l. and l. of money** il a énormément d'argent; **he's l. of fun to be with** il est très amusant
ADV *Fam* beaucoup

lottery ['lɒtərɪ] **N** loterie *f, Fig* **it's a bit of a l.** c'est une loterie
▸ ▸ *Br* **l. funding** = fonds *mpl* provenant de la loterie nationale; *Fin* **l. loan** emprunt *m* à lots; *Fin* **l. loan bond** titre *m* à lots

lotto ['lɒtəʊ] **N** *(game)* loto *m*

lotus, pl lotuses ['ləʊtəs, -əsɪz] **N** lotus *m*
▸ ▸ **l. position** position *f* du lotus

lotus-eater N *Myth* mangeur *m* de lotus, lotophage *m*

loud [laʊd] **ADJ 1** bruyant, retentissant; *(noise, shout)* grand; *(explosion)* violent; *(laugh)* gros; *(voice)* fort; *(person, behaviour)* bruyant; **to be l. in one's praise of sb/sth** se répandre en louanges sur qn/qch; **to be l. in one's condemnation of sb/sth** condamner qn/qch avec force; **you're too l.!** tu fais trop de bruit!; **in a l. voice** à haute voix; **l. applause** applaudissements vifs; **l. protests** protestations vives; **l. sobs** gros sanglots
2 *(colour etc)* criard, voyant; *(clothes)* voyant; **he wore a l. checked suit** il portait un costume voyant à carreaux

ADV *(to speak)* haut, à haute voix; *(to shout)* fort; **to talk out l.** parler à haute voix; *(in loud voice)* parler (très) fort; **to think out l.** penser tout haut; **to turn the radio/TV up l.** mettre la radio/TV plus fort; **louder!** parlez plus fort!; *Radio* **I hear you l. and clear** je te reçois cinq sur cinq; *Fam (I understand)* j'ai compris

loudhailer ['laʊd'heɪlər] N *Br* porte-voix *m inv*

loudly ['laʊdlɪ] ADV *(to shout)* haut, fort, à voix haute; *(to laugh)* bruyamment; *(to knock at the door)* rudement; **you're not speaking l. enough** vous ne parlez pas assez fort; **he has always dressed rather l.** il a toujours porté des vêtements assez voyants

loudmouth ['laʊdmaʊθ] N *Fam Pej* **to be a l.** être *ou* avoir une grande gueule; *(not be discreet)* avoir une grande langue

loudmouthed ['laʊdmaʊðd] ADJ *Fam Pej (who speaks loudly)* gueulard; *(who can't keep a secret)* qui ne sait pas tenir sa langue

loudness ['laʊdnɪs] N **1** *(of engine, traffic, radio etc)* bruit *m*; **the l. of her voice** sa voix forte **2** **the l. of his ties** ses cravates voyantes; **the l. of his behaviour** sa conduite tapageuse

loudspeaker [laʊd'spiːkər] N haut-parleur *m, pl* haut-parleurs

▸▸**l. van** camionnette *f* munie d'un haut-parleur

lough [lɒx] N *(in Ireland)* lac *m*

Louis ['luːɪ] N **L. the Fourteenth** Louis XIV

Louisiana [luːiːzɪ'ænə] N Louisiane *f*

lounge [laʊndʒ] N **1** *(in house, hotel)* salon *m* **2** *Am (sofa)* canapé *m*

VI *(on sofa etc)* s'étendre paresseusement; **I've been lounging in an armchair all afternoon** j'ai passé l'après-midi affalé dans un fauteuil

▸▸*Br* **l. bar** = salon *m* dans un pub (souvent plus confortable et plus cher que le 'public bar'); *Am Rail* **l. car** voiture-salon *f, pl* voitures-salons; *Am* **l. chair** fauteuil *m*; *Old-fashioned Fam* **l. lizard** salonnard *m*; *Br* **l. suit** costume *m* de ville; *(on invitation)* tenue *f* de ville

▸**lounge about, lounge around** VI *usu Pej* flâner

▸**lounge away** VT SEP **to l. away the time** passer le temps à flâner

lounger ['laʊndʒər] N **1** *(person)* flemmard, -arde **2** **(sun) l.** chaise *f* longue **3** *Am (settee)* canapé *m*

louse [laʊs] N **1** *(insect) (pl* **lice**) pou *m, pl* poux **2** *Sl (person) (pl* **louses**) fripouille *f*, salaud *m*

▸**louse up** VT SEP *Sl (ruin, spoil)* bousiller, ficher en l'air

lousewort ['laʊswɜːt] N *(plant)* herbe *f* aux poux

lousiness ['laʊzɪnɪs] N *Fam (of weather etc)* caractère *m* horrible; *(of service in restaurant etc)* mauvaise qualité *f*

lousy ['laʊzɪ] ADJ **1** *(full of lice)* pouilleux, plein de poux; *Fig Fam* **this place is l. with ... ça** grouille de ...; *Fam* **to be l. with money** être un gros richard

2 *Fam* affreux; *(headache, cold, day, week)* sale, mauvais; *(weather)* sale, de chien; *(hotel, colour etc)* moche; *(holiday, party, meal, book, essay)* minable, nul; *(quality, workmanship)* mauvais; *(computer, car)* qui ne vaut rien, nul; *(raincoat, pen)* qui ne vaut rien; **that's a l. thing to do** *or* **say** c'est dégueulasse *ou* moche de faire *ou* dire une chose pareille; **he's l. to his wife** il est dégueulasse avec sa femme; **a l. trick** un sale tour; **don't buy them, they're l.** n'achetez pas ça, c'est de la camelote; **they made a l. job of it** ils ont salopé le travail; **he's in a l.**

mood il est d'une humeur de chien; **we had a l. time on holiday** nous avons passé des vacances nulles *ou* dégueulasses; **all for a l. £5** tout ça à cause de 5 malheureuses livres; **to feel/look l.** se sentir horriblement mal/avoir l'air horrible; **I'm l. at science** je suis nul en sciences

lout [laʊt] N *(oaf)* lourdaud *m*, rustre *m*; *(hooligan)* voyou *m*; **you clumsy l.!** espèce de lourdaud!

loutish ['laʊtɪʃ] ADJ rustre, lourdaud; **l. manners** des manières de rustre

louv(e)red ['luːvəd] ADJ *(door)* à persiennes; *Naut* muni d'un louvre *ou* de louvres; *Aut, Aviat (car bonnet, air inlet)* à persiennes, à volet; *Archit (belfry)* à abat-sons

louvre, *Am* **louver** ['luːvər] N **1** *Archit (board)* abat-vent *m inv*, abat-son *m, pl* abat-sons *(de clocher)* **2** *(in door, window)* persienne *f, Naut* louvre *m*; *Aut, Aviat (of ventilation inlet, car bonnet)* persienne, volet *m*; *Tech (of air intake)* ouïe *f*

▸▸*Archit* **l. board** abat-vent *m inv*; abat-son, *pl* abat-sons *(de clocher)*; **l. door** porte *f* à persiennes

lovable ['lʌvəb(ə)l] ADJ *(character, person)* sympathique; *(baby)* adorable; **l. rogue** petit coquin *m*

lovage ['lʌvɪdʒ] N *Bot, Culin* ache *f* de(s) montagne(s)

LOVE [lʌv] N **1** amour *m*; **l. of** *or* **for sb** amour de *ou* pour *ou* envers qn; **l. of** *or* **for sth** amour de qch; **he has a great l. for Scotland** il adore l'Écosse; **there's no l. lost between them** ils ne peuvent pas se sentir; **a teacher with little l. for his pupils** un professeur qui n'a pas beaucoup de sympathie pour ses élèves; **for the l. of God** pour l'amour de Dieu; **give my l. to your parents** faites mes amitiés *fpl* à vos parents; **with l. from ...** *(at end of letter)* affectueuses pensées *fpl* de ...; **Bill sends his l.** Bill vous fait ses amitiés; **give my l. to ...** faites mes amitiés à ...; **I wouldn't do it for l. or money** je ne le ferais pour rien au monde; **to do sth for l.** faire qch pour le plaisir

2 *(between lovers)* amour *m*; **to be/fall in l. with sb** être/tomber amoureux de qn; **head over heels in l.** amoureux fou, éperdument amoureux; **to make l. to sb** faire l'amour avec qn; *Old-fashioned (to court)* faire la cour à qn; **to marry for l.** faire un mariage d'amour; **she's the l. of my life** c'est la femme *ou* l'amour de ma vie; **it was l. at first sight** ce fut le coup de foudre; **his first l.** son premier amour, *Lit* ses premières amours

3 *(term of endearment)* **(my) l.** mon amour; *esp Eng Fam* **more coffee, l.?** tu prends encore du café, mon petit/ma petite?; *esp Eng Fam* **there you are, l.!** voilà, ma petite dame/ mon (petit) gars/mon petit monsieur!

4 *Tennis etc* zéro *m*, rien *m*; **l. fifteen/fifteen l.** rien à quinze/quinze à rien; **two sets to l.** deux sets à rien *ou* à zéro

VT **1** *(person)* aimer; **to l. one another** s'aimer; *Prov* **l. me, l. my dog** qui m'aime aime mon chien

2 *(something)* aimer (passionnément); *(music etc)* adorer; **they l. animals** ils aiment les animaux; **to l. to do sth, to l. doing sth** aimer (à) faire qch; **will you come with me?** – **I'd l. to** voulez-vous m'accompagner? – avec (le plus grand) plaisir; **she'd l. to see you again** elle serait enchantée *ou* ravie de vous revoir; **I'd l. to come** j'aimerais beaucoup venir

▸▸**l. affair** liaison *f* (amoureuse); *Fig* passion *f*; **l. child** enfant *mf* de l'amour; *Tennis* **l. game** jeu *m* blanc; *Fam Hum* **l. handles** poignées *fpl* d'amour; **l. letter** lettre *f* d'amour, billet *m* doux; **l. life** vie *f* sentimentale; **l. match** mariage *m* d'amour; **l. nest** nid *m*

d'amour; **l. seat** canapé *m* deux places, causeuse *f*; **l. song** chanson *f* d'amour; **l. story** histoire *f* d'amour; **l. triangle** ménage *m* à trois

lovebird ['lʌvbɜːd] N *(bird)* perruche *f* inséparable; *Fam Hum* **lovebirds** *(people)* tourtereaux *mpl*

lovebite ['lʌvbaɪt] N suçon *m*

loved-up [lʌv'ʌp] ADJ *Fam* **1** *(on drugs)* tout gentil *(sous l'effet de l'ecstasy)* **2** *(in love)* amoureux

love-hate relationship N relation *f* qui va de l'amour à la haine

love-in-a-mist N *(plant)* nigelle *f* (de Damas), cheveux *mpl* de Vénus

loveless ['lʌvlɪs] ADJ sans amour

love-lies-bleeding ['lʌvlaɪz'bliːdɪŋ] N *(plant)* amarante *f* à fleurs en queue

loveliness ['lʌvlɪnɪs] N beauté *f*, *(of woman, countryside etc)* charme *m*

lovelorn ['lʌvlɔːn] ADJ languissant

lovely ['lʌvlɪ] ADJ **1** *(attractive, fine)* beau, *f* belle; *(food, smell, idea)* bon, *f* bonne; *(day, weather etc)* beau; **what a l. woman!** quelle femme charmante!; **have a l. time** amusez-vous bien; **it's been l. seeing you again** ça a été charmant de vous revoir; *Fam* **it's l. and warm** il fait une chaleur agréable; **I've made a copy for you** – **oh! l.!** j'en ai fait une copie pour vous – comme c'est gentil! **2** *(kind, friendly)* très aimable

lovemaking ['lʌvmeɪkɪŋ] N rapports *mpl* sexuels; *Old-fashioned (courting)* cour *f* (amoureuse); **his l.** la façon dont il fait l'amour

lover ['lʌvər] N **1** amant, -ante; *Old-fashioned (suitor)* amoureux *m*, prétendant *m*; **they were lovers** ils étaient amants; **to take a l.** *(of woman)* prendre un amant; *(of man)* prendre une maîtresse **2** *(of nature etc)* amoureux, -euse, fou, *f* folle

loverboy ['lʌvəbɔɪ] N *Fam Iron* **1** grand séducteur *m*, le chéri de ces dames; **morning, l.!** *(said by a woman)* bonjour, chéri! **2** *(non-romantic sense)* **we're still waiting for l.!** on attend toujours le petit coco!

lovesick ['lʌvsɪk] ADJ qui languit d'amour

lovesickness ['lʌvsɪknɪs] N mal *m* d'amour

lovey-dovey ['lʌvɪdʌvɪ] ADJ *Sl (talk)* mièvre, à la guimauve; **to get l.** *(of person) (get sexy)* s'exciter; **they've gone all l.** ils sont comme deux tourtereaux

loving ['lʌvɪŋ] ADJ affectueux; **a l. husband and father** un mari et un père aimant; *Lit* **l. kindness** bonté *f*; **your l. mother** *(at end of letter)* ta mère qui t'aime

▸▸**l. cup** coupe *f* de l'amitié

-loving ['lʌvɪŋ] SUFF adventure-/danger-l. qui aime l'aventure/le danger; **home-l.** casanier, -ière; **fun-l.** qui aime s'amuser

lovingly ['lʌvɪŋlɪ] ADV affectueusement, tendrement

LOW [ləʊ] ADJ **1** *(not high)* bas, *f* basse; **to cook sth over a l. heat** *or* **a l. fire** faire cuire qch à feu doux; **my stocks are rather l.** mes stocks sont un peu dégarnis; **our water supply is getting l.** notre réserve d'eau baisse; **a dress with a l. neckline** une robe décolletée; **to make sb a l. bow** saluer qn très bas; *Cards* **a l. spade** un petit pique; **a l. blow** un coup bas; **l. price** bas prix; **the lowest price** le prix le plus bas; **l. sales** ventes *fpl* faibles; **l. temperature** basse température *f*; **l. tension** basse tension *f*, **l. wages** salaires *mpl* peu élevés

2 *(inferior)* bas, *f* basse, peu élevé; **all the people, high and l.** tous, du haut comme du bas de l'échelle sociale; **to have a l. opinion of sb** avoir une mauvaise opinion de qn; **the lowest of the l.** le dernier des derniers;

that's a l. trick! ça, c'est un sale coup!; **that was rather a l. thing to do** ce n'était pas très joli de faire une chose pareille; **l. company** mauvaise compagnie; **l. cunning** ruse *f* et bassesse *f*

3 to be very l. *or* **in a very l. state** *(of invalid)* être bien bas; **to feel l., to be in l. spirits** *(depressed)* se sentir déprimé, *Fam* avoir le cafard; *Med* **l. physical condition** mauvaise condition *f* physique

4 *(not loud)* bas, *f* basse; *Mus* **l. note** note *f* basse; **l. murmur** faible murmure *m*; **in a l. voice** à voix basse, à mi-voix

ADV 1 *(to hang, aim)* bas; **to bow l.** saluer très bas; **dress cut l. in the back** robe *f* décolletée dans le dos; *Boxing* **to hit l.** frapper bas; **to fly l.** *(of bird, aircraft)* voler bas; **to bring sb l.** humilier qn, abaisser qn; **to lie l.** se tapir, rester tapi

2 the lowest paid employees les employés les moins payés

3 *(to speak)* à voix basse; **turn the music down l.** baisse la musique; *Mus* **to set lower** *(song etc)* baisser d'une ou de deux octaves; **I can't sing that l.** je ne peux pas chanter aussi bas; **we're (running) l. on fuel/food** nous n'avons presque plus de carburant/ nourriture; **the fire is burning l.** le feu baisse; **light turned l.** lumière en veilleuse

N 1 *Met* zone *f* de basse pression

2 to reach a new l. descendre encore plus bas; **a record l.** le point le plus bas jamais atteint; **sterling has reached an all-time l.** la livre a atteint son niveau le plus bas, la livre n'avait jamais atteint un niveau aussi bas

▸▸ **l. birth** basse naissance *f*; *Cards* **the l. cards** les basses cartes *fpl*; **the L. Countries** les Pays-Bas *mpl*; *Met* **l. front** front *m* de basses pressions; **l. gear** rapport *m* inférieur; *(on automatic gearbox)* conduite *f* lente; *Ling* **l. German** bas allemand *m*; *Rel* **L. Mass** messe *f* basse; *Art* **l. relief** bas-relief *m*; **L. Sunday** Pâques *fpl* closes, dimanche *m* de Quasimodo; **l. technology** technologie *f* de base; **l. tide** marée *f* basse

low² **VI** *(of cattle)* meugler

low-alcohol **ADJ** *(drink)* peu alcoolisé

low-angle shot **N** *TV, Cin* contre-plongée *f*

lowboy ['ləʊbɔɪ] **N** *Am* commode *f*

lowbrow ['ləʊbraʊ] *Pej* **ADJ** peu intellectuel **N** personne *f* peu intellectuelle

low-budget **ADJ** *(film, holiday etc)* à petit budget

low-calorie **ADJ** *(food, diet)* (à) basses calories; *(diet)* hypocalorique

low-class **ADJ** *(lower-class)* populaire

low-cost **ADJ** à bas prix; *(housing, accommodation)* à loyer modéré

low-cut **ADJ** *(dress)* décolleté

low-density **ADJ**
▸▸ **l. housing** zones *fpl* d'habitation peu peuplées

low-down *Fam* **ADJ** *esp Am (mean)* ignoble; **that's a l. trick** ça, c'est un coup rosse
N to give sb the l. tuyauter qn (**on** sur); **to get the l.** se rencarder (**on** sur)

low-end **ADJ** *Mktg* bas de gamme

lower¹ ['ləʊər] **ADJ** *(less high)* inférieur; *(shelves, rungs)* du bas; **l. part** *(of ladder etc)* bas *m*
VT 1 *(head, eyes, window, blinds)* baisser; *(veil)* abaisser, rabattre; *Theat* **to l. the curtain** baisser le rideau; *Aut* **to l. the hood** décapoter
2 *(reduce)* *(light, one's voice, key)* baisser; *(pressure)* réduire; *(price)* baisser, rabaisser; *(temperature)* abaisser; *(enemy's morale)* déprimer; **to l. one's expectations** viser plus bas; **to l. the quality of sth** nuire à la qualité

de qch; *Med* **to l. sb's resistance** *(of tiredness etc)* diminuer la résistance de qn; **to l. standards** devenir moins exigeant; **to l. oneself** *(degrade)* s'abaisser, se ravaler (**to** à)
3 *(reduce in height)* *(object)* diminuer la hauteur de; *(ceiling)* abaisser
4 *(let down)* *(trunk from attic, stretcher into boat)* descendre; **to l. oneself (into/onto sth)** se laisser tomber (dans/sur qch); *Naut (mast)* amener, caler; *(ship's boat)* mettre à la mer; **l. away!** laissez aller!; **to l. sb on a rope** (faire) descendre qn au bout d'une corde; *Boxing* **to l. one's guard** baisser sa garde; *Fig* relâcher son attention
▸▸ **the l. Alps** les basses Alpes *fpl*; **the l. animals** les animaux *mpl* inférieurs; *Comput* **l. ASCII** ASCII *m* inférieur; *Anat* **l. back** reins *mpl*; **to have l. back pain** avoir mal aux reins; **the l. classes** *(in society)* le bas peuple; *(in school)* les petites classes *fpl*; **the l. forms** *(in school)* les petites classes; **l. jaw** mâchoire *f* inférieure; *Med* **l. leg** jambe *f*; **the l. ranks** *(in army etc)* les rangs *mpl* inférieurs; **the l. school** les petites classes

lower² ['laʊər] **VI 1** *(of person)* se renfrogner; **to l. at sb** regarder qn d'un mauvais œil, menacer qn du regard **2** *(of sky)* se couvrir; *(of storm)* menacer

lower-case **ADJ** *Typ* minuscule
▸▸ **l. letter** minuscule *f*

lower-class **ADJ** *(accent)* populaire; **l. people** prolétaires *mpl*

lower-income group **N** groupe *m* de contribuables à revenus moyens

lowering¹ ['ləʊərɪŋ] **N 1** abaissement *m* **2** *(of prices)* abaissement *m*, diminution *f*; *(of pressure)* réduction *f* **3** *(reducing in height)* diminution *f* de la hauteur; *(of ceiling)* abaissement *m* **4** *(letting down)* *(of ladder etc)* descente *f*; *Naut (of mast)* calage *m*; *(of ship's boat)* mise *f* à la mer

lowering² ['laʊərɪŋ] **ADJ** *(look, sky)* menaçant

lowest ['ləʊɪst] **ADJ**
▸▸ **l. bidder** moins-disant *m*; **l. common denominator** plus petit dénominateur *m* commun

low-flying **ADJ** *(airplane)* volant à basse altitude

low-grade **ADJ 1** *(coal etc)* de qualité inférieure **2** *(official)* de grade inférieur

low-heeled ['ləʊhiːld] **ADJ** *(shoe)* à talon plat

low-income **ADJ** *(family)* à faible revenu

lowing ['ləʊɪŋ] **N** meuglement *m*

low-interest **ADJ** *(credit, loan)* à taux réduit

low-key **ADJ** *(approach, debate, discussion)* modéré; *(film)* au style dépouillé; *(person)* réservé; *(lighting)* de faible intensité; **to keep sth l.** contenir qch, modérer qch

lowland ['ləʊlənd] **N** plaine *f* (basse); **the Lowlands** *(in Scotland)* les Lowlands *fpl*

low-level **ADJ 1** *(radioactivity)* faible **2** *(discussion)* à la base
▸▸ *Med* **l. infection** infection *f* bénigne; *Comput* **l. language** langage *m* non évolué *ou* de bas niveau

lowlife ['ləʊlaɪf] **N** *Sl* crapule *f*; **his l. friends** ses amis pas très recommandables

lowlight ['ləʊlaɪt] **N 1** *(in hair)* reflet *m* coloré **2** *Hum* moment *m* décevant

lowliness ['ləʊlɪnɪs] **N** humilité *f*, modestie *f*

low-loader **N** camion *m* à plate-forme surbaissée

lowly ['ləʊlɪ] **ADJ** humble, modeste

low-lying **ADJ** situé à basse altitude; *(land)* bas, enfoncé

low-maintenance battery **N** batterie *f* à entretien réduit

low-necked ['ləʊnekt] **ADJ** *(dress)* décolleté

lowness ['ləʊnɪs] **N 1** *(of wall etc)* faible hauteur *f*; *(of island, hills)* faible altitude *f*
2 *(of note)* gravité *f*
3 *(of behaviour)* bassesse *f*
4 l. (of spirits) abattement *m*, découragement *m*

low-octane fuel **N** carburant *m* à faible indice d'octane

low-pitched ['ləʊpɪtʃt] **ADJ 1** *(sound, voice)* grave; *(piano)* accordé à un diapason bas **2** *(roof)* à faible pente

low-pressure **ADJ 1** *Met (zone)* de basse pression **2** *(cylinder, machine)* à basse pression *ou* tension

low-profile **ADJ** *(politician, company etc)* discret, qui adopte *ou* garde un profil bas
▸▸ *Aut* **l. tyre** pneu *m* à profil bas

low-radiation monitor **N** moniteur *m* basse radiation

low-rent **ADJ 1** *(housing)* à loyer modéré **2** *Fam Pej (low-quality)* bas de gamme

low-resolution **ADJ** à basse résolution

low-rise **N** immeuble *m* bas
▸▸ **l. building** immeuble *m* peu élevé *ou* bas

low-speed **ADJ** *(machine)* à petite vitesse

low-spirited **ADJ** abattu, déprimé

low-tar **ADJ** *(cigarette)* à taux de goudron faible

low-tech ['ləʊtek] **ADJ** rudimentaire, *Fam* pas très évolué; **as regards text-processing they're very l.** en matière de traitement de texte, ils ne sont pas très à la page

low-tension circuit **N** circuit *m* basse tension

low-voltage **ADJ** à faible voltage, à faible tension

low-wage **ADJ**
▸▸ **l. economy** économie *f* où les salaires sont bas

loyal ['lɔɪəl] **ADJ 1** *(friend etc)* fidèle, dévoué (**to** à), loyal, -aux (**to** envers); *Mktg* **l. -customer discount** remise *f* de fidelité au client fidèle **2** *(to sovereign)* fidèle au souverain; **to drink the l. toast** porter le toast au souverain

loyalist ['lɔɪəlɪst] **ADJ, N** loyaliste *mf*

Loyalist

Dans le contexte britannique, le mot "Loyalist" désigne un protestant d'Irlande du Nord souhaitant rester au sein du Royaume-Uni.

loyally ['lɔɪəlɪ] **ADV** fidèlement, loyalement

loyalty ['lɔɪəltɪ] **N** loyalisme *m*; *(to friends, employer etc)* loyauté *f* (**to** envers); **you'll have to decide where your loyalties lie** il faudra que tu décides de quel côté tu es; **to have divided loyalties** être partagé; **to create customer l.** fidéliser la clientèle
▸▸ *Mktg* **l. card** carte *f* de fidélité; *Mktg* **l. discount** remise *f* de fidélité; *Mktg* **l. magazine** = magazine *m* publié par une chaîne de magasins, une banque etc, pour ses clients

lozenge ['lɒzɪndʒ] **N 1** *Pharm* pastille *f* **2** *Math, Her* losange *m*

Note that the French word **losange** never refers to a medicated tablet.

LP [el'piː] **N** *(abbr* **long player***)* 33 tours *m*

L-plate **N** *Br* = plaque *f* apposée sur une voiture et signalant un apprenti conducteur

L-plate
En Grande-Bretagne, la lettre "L" apposée sur l'arrière d'un véhicule indique que le conducteur n'a pas encore son permis mais qu'il est en conduite accompagnée.

LQ [el'kju:] (*abbr* **letter quality**) qualité *f* courrier
▸▸ **LQ printer** imprimante *f* de qualité courrier

LSD [eles'di:] **N 1** (*abbr* **lysergic acid diethylamide**) LSD *m* **2** *Br Formerly abbr* **pounds, shillings and pence**

LSE [eles'i:] **N 1** *Br Univ abbr* **London School of Economics 2** *St Exch abbr* **London Stock Exchange**

L-shaped **ADJ** en (forme de) L

LSI [ele'saɪ] **N** *Comput abbr* **large-scale integration**

Lt *Mil* (*abbr* **Lieutenant**) Lt

lt *abbr* **low tension**

LTA [elti:'eɪ] *abbr* **Lawn Tennis Association**

Ltd *Br Com* (*abbr* **limited**) ≃ SARL

lube [lu:b] **N** lubrifiant *m*
VT lubrifier

lubricant ['lu:brɪkənt] **ADJ** lubrifiant
N lubrifiant *m*

lubricate ['lu:brɪkeɪt] **VT** lubrifier, graisser; **lubricated condom** préservatif *m* lubrifié; *Fig Fam* **we were all well lubricated** (*drunk*) nous étions tous bien imbibés

lubricating ['lu:brɪkeɪtɪŋ] **N** lubrification *f*
▸▸ **l. oil** huile *f* de graissage

lubrication [lu:brɪ'keɪʃən] **N** lubrification *f*, graissage *m*; *Fam Hum* (*alcohol*) gnôle *f*
▸▸ **l. nipple** graisseur *m*; **l. oil** huile *f* de lubrification; **l. system** circuit *m* de lubrification

lubricator ['lu:brɪkeɪtər] **N** (*device*) graisseur *m*, appareil *m* de graissage; **gravity-feed l.** graisseur par gravité

lubricity [lu:'brɪsɪtɪ] **N** *Lit* (*lewdness*) lubricité *f*

Lucerne [lu:'sɜ:n] **N** *Geog* Lucerne; **(the) Lake (of) L.** le lac des Quatre-Cantons

lucerne [lu:'sɜ:n] **N** *Br Bot, Agr* luzerne *f*

lucid ['lu:sɪd] **ADJ** (*mind, style*) lucide; (*explanation*) clair; *Med* **l. interval** intervalle *m* lucide *ou* de lucidité

lucidity [lu:'sɪdɪtɪ] **N** lucidité *f*

lucidly ['lu:sɪdlɪ] **ADV** lucidement; (*explained, outlined etc*) avec clarté

Lucifer ['lu:sɪfər] **N** Lucifer *m*

luck [lʌk] **N** (*chance*) chance *f*; **good l.** bonne chance, bonheur *m*; **bad l.** malchance *f*, mauvaise fortune *f*, *Fam* déveine *f*; **piece** *or* **stroke of l.** coup *m* de chance, aubaine *f*, *Fam* coup de bol; **to bring sb bad/good l.** porter malheur/bonheur à qn; **to keep sth for l.** garder qch comme porte-bonheur; **good l. (to you)!** bonne chance!; **good l. with the exams/for Friday** bonne chance pour les examens/pour vendredi; *Iron* **good l. to him!** qu'il le fasse si ça lui chante!; **to wish sb l.** souhaiter bonne chance à qn; **better l. next time** ça ira mieux la prochaine fois; **to be in l.** avoir de la chance *ou Fam* de la veine; **to be out of l.** ne pas avoir de chance; **to be down on one's l.** avoir la guigne; **to try one's l.** tenter sa chance; **don't trust to l.** n'y compte pas trop; (*when you can do something about it*) ne laisse rien au hasard; **her l. has changed** sa chance a tourné; **he has all the l.** *Fam* c'est un veinard; **to have the l. of the devil** avoir une chance de tous les diables; **just my l.!** c'est bien ma chance!; **with my l. it won't work** avec ma

chance habituelle, ça ne marchera pas; **no such l.!** je n'ai pas (eu) cette chance!, *Fam* **tu parles!**; **hard l.!** pas de chance!; **I've got to work, worst l.** il faut que je travaille, pas de chance!; **by good l.** par bonheur; **as l. would have it** par bonheur; **as l. would have it, I was there** le hasard a voulu que je sois là; **it's the l. of the draw** c'est le hasard
▸ **luck into** **VT INSEP** *Fam* **to l. into sth** dégoter qch
▸ **luck out** **VI** *Am Fam* avoir du pot

luckily ['lʌkɪlɪ] **ADV** heureusement, par bonheur; **l. for her** par chance pour elle

luckless ['lʌklɪs] **ADJ** *Fml* **1** (*person*) malheureux, malchanceux **2** (*day*) de malchance

lucky ['lʌkɪ] **ADJ** (*person*) chanceux; (*time, moment*) propice; **to be l.** (*of person*) avoir de la chance; **you're a very l. person** vous avez beaucoup de chance; **who's the l. man?** (*she's going to marry*) qui est l'heureux élu?; *Fam* (**you**) **l. devil!**, **l. beggar!** veinard!; *Iron* **you'll be l.!** tu peux toujours courir!; **to be born l.** être né coiffé; **to have a l. break** avoir un coup de chance *ou* de pot; **to get l.** avoir de la chance; *Sl* (*find sexual partner*) emballer; **l. in love/at cards** heureux en amour/au jeu; **it's l. you came when you did** c'est une chance que tu sois arrivé à ce moment-là; **she's l. to be alive** elle a de la chance d'être en vie; **l. shot** coup *m* de bol *ou* de veine; **my l. number** mon chiffre porte-bonheur; **to make a l. guess** tomber juste; **it's not my l. day** ce n'est pas mon jour de chance; **that was l.** ça a été un coup de chance; **it's l.** (*of thing*) ça porte bonheur
▸▸ **l. charm** porte-bonheur *m inv*; *Br* **l. dip** jeu *m* consistant à chercher des cadeaux enfouis dans une caisse remplie de sciure ou dans un sac

Lucozade® ['lu:kəzeɪd] **N** = boisson *f* gazeuse à base de glucose

lucrative ['lu:krətɪv] **ADJ** lucratif

lucre ['lu:kər] **N** *Pej Hum* lucre *m*; **to do sth for (filthy) l.** agir par amour du gain *ou* du lucre

ludicrous ['lu:dɪkrəs] **ADJ** risible, comique, ridicule; **it's l. to ...** c'est ridicule de ...; **he looked faintly l.** il avait l'air assez grotesque

ludicrously ['lu:dɪkrəslɪ] **ADV** ridiculement

ludo ['lu:dəʊ] **N** *Br* (*game*) jeu *m* des petits chevaux

luff [lʌf] *Naut* **N 1** (*of sail*) lof *m*, ralingue *f* du vent, chute *f* avant **2** (*of bow*) épaule *f*
VI lof(f)er, faire une aulof(f)ée
VT **to l. the boat (up)** faire loffer la barque

lug¹ [lʌg] (**-gg-**) **VT** (*sth heavy*) traîner, tirer; **to l. sth along** *or* **away** entraîner qch; **to l. sth about with one** promener *ou* trimbaler qch avec soi

lug² **N 1** *Tech* oreille *f* **2** *Fam* (*ear*) esgourde *f*

lug³ **N** *Naut* = **lugsail**

lug⁴ **N** *Zool* = **lugworm**

luge [lu:ʒ] **N** *Sport* luge *f*

luggage ['lʌgɪdʒ] **N** bagage(s) *m(pl)*; **a piece of l.** un bagage
▸▸ *Aviat* **l. bay**, **l. compartment** soute *f* à bagages; *Naut* **l. hold** soute à bagages; **l. label** étiquette *f* à bagages; **l. locker** consigne *f* automatique; *Br* **l. rack** *Rail* (*shelf*) porte-bagages *m inv*; (*net*) filet *m* (à bagages); *Aut* galerie *f* (de toit); *Naut* **l. room** soute à bagages; **l. trolley** chariot *m* à bagages; *Br Rail* **l. van** fourgon *m* (à bagages)

lugger ['lʌgər] **N** *Naut* lougre *m*

lughole ['lʌghəʊl] **N** *Br Fam* oreille *f*, *Fam* esgourde *f*; **are your lugholes blocked?** est-ce que tu as les portugaises ensablées?

lugsail ['lʌgseɪl, 'lʌgs(ə)l] **N** *Naut* voile *f* à bourcet

lugubrious [lʊ'gu:brɪəs] **ADJ** lugubre

lugubriously [lʊ'gu:brɪəslɪ] **ADV** lugubrement

lugworm ['lʌgwɜ:m] **N** *Zool* arénicole *f*

Luke [lu:k] **N** Luc *m*; **Saint L.** saint Luc

lukewarm ['lu:kwɔ:m] **ADJ** (*water, friendship etc*) tiède; **the critics gave the play a l. reception** les critiques ont accueilli la pièce avec tiédeur; **to become l.** tiédir

lull [lʌl] **N** moment *m* de calme; (*in fighting*) répit *m*; *Naut* accalmie *f*; **the l. before the storm** le calme avant la tempête; **there was a l. in the conversation** la conversation tomba
VT (*person*) (*send to sleep*) bercer, endormir; (*fears*) endormir; **to l. a child to sleep** endormir un enfant en le berçant; **to l. sb into a false sense of security** endormir la vigilance de qn

lullaby ['lʌləbaɪ] **N** *Mus* berceuse *f*

lumbago [lʌm'beɪgəʊ] **N** *Med* lumbago *m*; **to have l.** avoir un lumbago

lumbar ['lʌmbər] **ADJ** *Anat* lombaire
▸▸ **l. adjustable seat** siège *m* à réglage lombaire; *Med* **l. puncture** ponction *f* lombaire, rachicentèse *f*

lumber¹ ['lʌmbər] **N 1** *Br* (*useless objects*) objets *mpl* encombrants **2** *Am* (*wood*) bois *m* de charpente *ou* de construction
▸▸ *Br* **l. room** débarras *m*

lumber² **VT 1** (*place*) encombrer, embarrasser; **to l. a room with furniture** encombrer une pièce de meubles; *Fam* **to get lumbered with a task** se taper *ou* se coltiner un travail; **to l. sb with sth** flanquer qch à qn; **they've lumbered me with the cooking** c'est moi qui me suis tapé tous les repas; **I was lumbered with him for the whole evening** je l'ai eu sur le dos pendant toute la soirée **2** *Am* (*trees*) abattre; (*wood*) débiter
VI avancer d'un pas pesant
▸ **lumber about** **VI** se trimbaler çà et là
▸ **lumber along** **VI** (*of person*) avancer à pas pesants *ou* d'un pas lourd

lumbering ['lʌmbərɪŋ] **ADJ** lourd, pesant

lumberjack ['lʌmbədʒæk] **N** *esp Am* bûcheron *m*

lumberjacket ['lʌmbədʒækɪt] **N** blouson *m*; (*longer*) canadienne *f*

lumberman, *pl* **lumbermen** ['lʌmbəmən] **N** *Am* bûcheron *m*

lumberyard ['lʌmbəja:d] **N** *Am* chantier *m* de bois

luminary ['lu:mɪnərɪ] **N** (*person*) lumière *f*; (*of science etc*) sommité *f*

luminescence [lu:mɪ'nesəns] **N** *Phys* luminescence *f*

luminescent [lu:mɪ'nesənt] **ADJ** *Phys* luminescent

luminosity [lu:mɪ'nɒsɪtɪ] **N** luminosité *f*

luminous ['lu:mɪnəs] **ADJ** lumineux; (*socks, strip on clothing, roadsign, colours*) fluorescent

lumme, lummy ['lʌmɪ] **INT** *Br Old-fashioned Fam* nom de Dieu!, mince alors!

lummox ['lʌməks] **N** *Old-fashioned Fam* lourdaud, -aude

lump¹ [lʌmp] **N 1** (*of stone*) gros morceau *m*, bloc *m*; (*of earth, clay*) motte *f*; (*of sugar, cheese etc*) morceau; (*of lead etc*) masse *f*; (*in porridge etc*) grumeau *m*; *Med* (*internal*) grosseur *f*; (*external*) excroissance *f*; (*caused by knock etc*) bosse *f*, *Fig* **to have a l. in one's throat** avoir la gorge serrée; **to pay in a l.** payer en une seule fois; **Parisians, taken in the l., are ...** en général, les Parisiens sont ... **2** *Fam Pej* (*person*) empoté *m*; **great l. of a girl** grosse dondon *f* **3** *Br Fam* **the l.** (*casual workers*) ouvriers *mpl* indépendants (non déclarés)

vt mettre en bloc *ou* en masse *ou* en tas
► **l. sum** somme *f* forfaitaire, montant *m* forfaitaire

► **lump together** vt sep *(things)* rassembler, mettre ensemble; **to l. people together** considérer des personnes en bloc, *Pej* mettre tout le monde dans le même sac

lump² vt *Fam* **if he doesn't like it, he can l. it, he can like it or l. it** que ça lui plaise ou pas, c'est le même prix; **you'll have to l. it!** il faudra que tu fasses avec!, il faudra en passer par là!

lumpectomy [lʌm'pektəmɪ] n *Surg* ablation *f* de tumeur mammaire

lumpen [ˈlʌmpən] adj grossier; **the l. proletariat** le sous-prolétariat

lumpfish [ˈlʌmpfɪʃ] n lompe *m*, lump *m*

lumpish [ˈlʌmpɪʃ] adj **1** *(clumsy)* balourd, pataud; **great l. man** lourdaud *m* **2** *(stupid)* stupide

lumpy [ˈlʌmpɪ] adj *(sauce)* grumeleux; *(surface, mattress)* bosselé; *(forehead etc)* couvert de bosses

lunacy [ˈluːnəsɪ] n **1** *Fam (action, idea)* action *f*/idée *f* folle; **it's sheer l.** c'est de la folie (pure et simple) **2** *Med* aliénation *f* mentale, folie *f*, *Law* démence *f*

lunar [ˈluːnər] adj *(cycle, module, orbit etc)* lunaire
► **l. eclipse** éclipse *f* de lune; **l. landing** alunissage *m*

lunaria [luːˈneərɪə] n *Bot* lunaire *f*

lunatic [ˈluːnətɪk] adj fou, *f* folle
n fou, *f* folle; *Med Old-fashioned* aliéné, -ée
► **l. asylum** asile *m* d'aliénés; **the l. fringe** les extrémistes *mpl*

> Note that the French adjective **lunatique** is a false friend and is never a translation for the English word **lunatic**. It means **moody**.

lunch [lʌntʃ] n déjeuner *m*, *Can, Belg* dîner *m*; *Am (snack) (eaten at any time)* petit repas *m*, casse-croûte *m inv*; **to have l.** prendre son déjeuner, déjeuner; **they have l. at one o'clock** ils déjeunent à une heure; **what time** *or* **when is l.?** à quelle heure déjeune-t-on?; **what's for l.?** qu'y a-t-il pour le déjeuner?; **we're having trout for l.** il y a de la truite au déjeuner; **let's go out for l.** allons déjeuner dehors; **how long do you get for l.?** combien de temps tu as pour déjeuner?; **what are you doing for l.?** que fais-tu à midi?; **we're having people to l.** nous avons du monde à déjeuner; **she's at l.** *or* **has gone to l.** elle est sortie déjeuner; *esp Am Sl* **to be out to l.** *(be crazy)* débloquer un peu, avoir une case de vide VOIR GRAMMAIRE A7
vi *Fml* déjeuner, *Can, Belg* dîner; **we lunched on sandwiches** nous avons déjeuné de sandwichs
vt *Fml (entertain to lunch)* inviter à déjeuner
► **l. break** *(in course of working day)* pause *f* du déjeuner; *Am* **l. counter** *(in store)* bar *m* de restauration rapide; **l. hour** heure *f* du déjeuner; **to go shopping during one's l. hour** aller faire des courses à l'heure du déjeuner; **l. menu** menu *m* déjeuner; **l. time** *(noon, one o'clock etc)* moment *m* du déjeuner

lunchbox [ˈlʌntʃbɒks] n **1** *(for carrying lunch)* panier-repas *m*, *pl* paniers-repas **2** *Br Fam Hum (man's genitals)* service *m* trois pièces, bijoux *mpl* de famille

lunchbucket [ˈlʌntʃbʌkɪt] n *Am* panier-repas *m*, *pl* paniers-repas

luncheon [ˈlʌntʃ(ə)n] n *Fml* déjeuner *m*
► **l. meat** = bloc *m* de viande de porc en conserve; *Br* **l. voucher** Ticket-Restaurant® *m inv*

luncheonette [lʌntʃəˈnet] n *Am* petit restaurant *m*, café-restaurant *m*

lunchpail [ˈlʌntʃpeɪl] n *Am* panier-repas *m*, *pl* paniers-repas

lunchroom [ˈlʌntʃrʊm] n *Am* = pièce *f* où l'on peut manger ses sandwichs etc à l'heure du déjeuner

lung [lʌŋ] n poumon *m*; **to shout at the top of one's lungs** crier à tue-tête
► **l. cancer** cancer *m* du poumon; **l. transplant** greffe *f* du poumon

lunge [lʌndʒ] n **1** mouvement *m* (brusque) en avant; **she made a l. for the ball** elle s'est jetée sur la balle **2** *Fencing* botte *f*
vi *Fencing* se fendre; **to l. at sb** se jeter sur qn; *Fencing* porter *ou* pousser une botte à l'adversaire
► **lunge forward** vi se jeter en avant

lupin, *Am* **lupine** [ˈluːpɪn] n *(plant)* lupin *m*

lupine [ˈluːpaɪn] adj de loup

lupus [ˈluːpəs] n lupus *m*

lurch¹ [lɜːtʃ] n **to leave sb in the l.** *(in danger, difficulty etc)* laisser qn dans le pétrin; *(to desert)* planter là qn

lurch² n *(of ship)* embardée *f*, coup *m* de roulis; *(of car)* embardée *f*; **with a drunken l.** *(to stagger etc)* en titubant; *(to reach out)* d'un geste d'homme/de femme ivre; **to give a l.** *(of ship, car etc)* faire une embardée; **with a l., the train was off again** le train est reparti avec un à-coup; **a l. to the left/right** un virage à gauche/droite
vi **1** *(of ship, car etc)* faire une embardée **2** *(of person)* tituber
► **lurch along** vi *(of person)* marcher en titubant; *(of economy)* progresser tant bien que mal

lurcher [ˈlɜːtʃər] n *(dog)* lévrier *m* bâtard

lure [lʊər] n **1** *(attraction)* attrait *m*; **the l. of the sea** l'attrait de la mer **2** *(in hunting) (decoy)* leurre *m*; *Fig* appât *m*; *(wooden duck)* appât factice
vt **1** *(person)* attirer, séduire; **to be lured into a trap** être attiré dans un piège; **he was lured into it by his friends** il s'y est laissé entraîner par ses amis **2** *(fish, falcon etc)* leurrer

lurid [ˈlʊərɪd] adj **1** *(sensational) (account, language)* corsé, à sensation; **she gave us a l. description of her operation** elle nous a fait une description de son opération avec force détails; **l. details** détails *mpl* effroyables **2** *(fiery)* cuivré; *(flames)* rougeoyant; *Pej (colour)* criard; **a l. sunset** un coucher de soleil flamboyant **3** *Lit (pale) (light)* blafard; *(complexion)* livide

luridly [ˈlʊərɪdlɪ] adv **1** *(to describe)* de façon sensationnelle **2** *(to glow)* en rougeoyant **3** *Lit (with a pale light)* avec une lueur blafarde

lurk [lɜːk] vi se cacher; **there's a man lurking in the alleyway** il y a un homme qui se cache dans la ruelle; **I'll just l. in the background** je me fondrai dans les décors

lurking [ˈlɜːkɪŋ] adj *(feeling, suspicion etc)* vague; **I have one l. doubt** j'ai encore un léger doute; **if you have any l. doubts** s'il vous reste des doutes; **l. errors in the text** des erreurs qui sont passées inaperçues dans le texte

luscious [ˈlʌʃəs] adj succulent; *(fruit)* fondant, succulent; **a l. blonde** une blonde appétissante

lush [lʌʃ] adj **1** *(grass, plant)* plein de sève, luxuriant **2** *(luxurious)* **l. surroundings** environnement *m* luxueux; **a l. sound** un son riche
n *Sl (alcoholic)* poivrot, -ote

lushness [ˈlʌʃnɪs] n *(of grass etc)* luxuriance *f*

lust [lʌst] n *(sexual)* désir *m* (charnel *ou* sexuel), *Pej* luxure *f*; **l. for power** soif *f* de pouvoir

► **lust after** vt insep *(person)* désirer; *(thing)* convoiter

► **lust for** vt insep *(object)* convoiter; **to l. for power/revenge** avoir soif de pouvoir/de revanche

luster, lusterless etc *Am* = **lustre, lustreless** etc

lustful [ˈlʌstfʊl] adj lascif, libidineux

lustfully [ˈlʌstfʊlɪ] adv lascivement

lustily [ˈlʌstɪlɪ] adv *(to sing, shout)* à pleine gorge

lustre, *Am* **luster** [ˈlʌstər] n **1** *(shine)* éclat *m*, lustre *m*; *(of cloth)* cati *m*, lustre **2** *(of chandelier)* pendeloque *f* **3** *(fabric)* **(cotton) l.** lustrine *f*

lustreless, *Am* **lusterless** [ˈlʌstəlɪs] adj terne; *(eyes, hair)* sans éclat

lustreware, *Am* **lusterware** [ˈlʌstəweər] n *Cer* poterie *f* à reflets métalliques, poterie lustrée

lustrous [ˈlʌstrəs] adj *(hair, eyes)* brillant; *(fabric)* lustré

lusty [ˈlʌstɪ] adj vigoureux, fort, robuste; **l. voices** voix puissantes

lute [luːt] n *Mus* luth *m*
► **l. maker** luthier *m*; **l. player** joueur, -euse de luth, luthiste *mf*

Lutheran [ˈluːθərən] adj, n *Rel, Hist* luthérien, -ienne

luv [lʌv] n *Fam* = **love** n 3

luvvie [ˈlʌvɪ] n *Fam (actor, actress)* comédien, -ienne

luxation [lʌkˈseɪʃən] n *Med* luxation *f*

Luxemb(o)urg [ˈlʌksəmbɜːg] n **the Grand Duchy of L.** le Grand-duché de Luxembourg

luxuriance [lʌgˈzjʊərɪəns, lʌkˈs-] n *(of vegetation, style etc)* exubérance *f*, luxuriance *f*

luxuriant [lʌgˈzjʊərɪənt, lʌkˈs-] adj exubérant, luxuriant; **l. (growth of) hair** chevelure *f* abondante; **l. beard** barbe *f* drue

> Attention: ne pas confondre avec **luxurious**.

luxuriantly [lʌgˈzjʊərɪəntlɪ, lʌkˈs-] adv avec exubérance, en abondance

luxuriate [lʌgˈzjʊərɪeɪt, lʌkˈs-] vi **to l. in a hot bath** se prélasser dans un bain chaud

luxurious [lʌgˈzjʊərəs, lʌkˈs-] adj *(apartment, lifestyle)* luxueux, somptueux; *(tastes)* de luxe

> Attention: ne pas confondre avec **luxuriant**.

luxuriously [lʌgˈzjʊərɪəslɪ, lʌkˈs-] adv **1** *(furnished)* luxueusement, avec luxe **2** *(to stretch)* avec volupté

luxuriousness [lʌgˈzjʊərɪəsnɪs, lʌkˈs-] n luxe *m*

luxury [ˈlʌkʃərɪ] n **1** luxe *m*; **to live in (the lap of) l.** vivre dans le luxe **2** *(object)* objet *m* de luxe; **one of life's little luxuries** un des petits plaisirs de l'existence; **to indulge in the l. of a cigar** se payer le luxe d'un cigare; **it's a l. not to have to cook** c'est un luxe de ne pas avoir à faire la cuisine
adj attrib *(car, apartment etc)* de luxe
► **l. brand** marque *f* de luxe; **l. goods** articles *mpl* de luxe; **l. liner** paquebot *m* de luxe; **l. market** marché *m* du luxe; *Fin* **l. tax** taxe *f* (sur les produits) de luxe

> Note that the French word **luxure** is a false friend and is never a translation for the English word **luxury**. It means **lust**.

LV [elˈviː] *Br abbr* luncheon voucher

LW [elˈdʌb(ə)ljuː] *abbr Radio* **(long wave)** LW

lychee [laɪ'tʃiː] N *(fruit)* litchi *m*
lychgate ['lɪtʃgeɪt] N = **lichgate**
lye [laɪ] N *(of soda, potassium)* lessive *f*
lying ['laɪɪŋ] ADJ *(false) (person)* menteur, -euse; *(account)* mensonger
   N *(falsehoods)* mensonges *mpl*
lying-in N *Med Old-fashioned* couches *fpl*
lymph [lɪmf] N *Physiol* lymphe *f*; **l. node** or *Old-fashioned* **gland** glande *f* ou ganglion *m* lymphatique
lymphangitis [lɪmfæn'dʒaɪtɪs] N lymphangite *f*
lymphatic [lɪm'fætɪk] *Physiol* ADJ lymphatique; **l. node** or *Old-fashioned* **gland** glande *f* ou ganglion *m* lymphatique
   N *(vessel)* lymphatique *m*

lymphocyte ['lɪmfəʊsaɪt] N *Med* lymphocyte *m*
lymphoma [lɪm'fəʊmə] N lymphome *m*
lynch [lɪntʃ] VT lyncher
   ▶▶ **l. law** loi *f* de Lynch; **l. mob** lyncheurs *mpl*
lynching ['lɪntʃɪŋ] N lynchage *m*
lynx [lɪŋks] N *(animal)* lynx *m*
lynx-eyed ADJ aux yeux de lynx
Lyons [liːɒn] N Lyon
lyre ['laɪər] N *Mus* lyre *f*
lyrebird ['laɪəbɜːd] N oiseau-lyre *m*, *pl* oiseaux-lyres, ménure *m*
lyric ['lɪrɪk] ADJ *(poet, drama)* lyrique
   N **1** *(poem)* poème *m* lyrique **2** lyrics

(of song) paroles *fpl*
   ▶▶ **l. writer** parolier *m*
lyrical ['lɪrɪk(ə)l] ADJ **1** *(poetry etc)* lyrique **2** *(expressively formulated)* dit ou écrit sur un ton lyrique; *Fam* **she got positively l. about it** elle y a montré un enthousiasme fou; **to wax l. about sth** déborder d'enthousiasme pour qch
lyrically ['lɪrɪklɪ] ADV **1** *Liter* avec lyrisme, lyriquement **2** *(to speak)* avec enthousiasme
lyricism ['lɪrɪsɪz(ə)m] N lyrisme *m*
lyricist ['lɪrɪsɪst] N **1** *(of musical etc)* parolier *m* **2** *(poet)* poète *m* lyrique
lysergic [lɪ'sɜːdʒɪk, laɪ-] ADJ *(acid)* lysergique

M, m¹ [em] **N** *(letter)* M, m *mf;* **two m's** deux m

m² *(abbr* **metre(s)**) m

MA [eˈmeɪ] **N 1** *Univ (abbr* **Master of Arts)** *(degree) Eng* maîtrise *f* de *ou* ès lettres; *Scot* licence *f* de *ou* ès lettres; *(person)* titulaire *mf* d'une maîtrise/licence de *ou* ès lettres; **to have an MA in Russian** avoir une maîtrise/licence de russe; **Susan Long, MA** Susan Long, Maîtrise de lettres/licenciée ès lettres **2** *abbr* **Massachusetts**

ma [mɑ:] **N** *Fam* maman *f*

ma'am [mɑ:m] **N** madame *f*

Mac [mæk] **N** *Comput* Mac *m;* **available for the M.** disponible en version Mac
▸▸ **M. disk** disquette *f* pour Mac; **M. OS** Mac-OS *m*

mac¹ [mæk] **N** *Br Fam (raincoat)* imper *m*

mac² **N** *Am Fam* **hey, m.!** hé, mon vieux *ou* mon pote!

macabre [məˈkɑ:brə] **ADJ** macabre; **a taste for the m.** le goût du macabre

macadam [məˈkædəm] **N** *Constr* macadam *m*

macadamize [məˈkædəmaɪz] **VT** *Constr (road)* macadamiser

macaque [məˈkɑ:k] **N** macaque *m*

macaroni [mækəˈrəʊnɪ] **N** *Culin* macaroni(s) *m(pl)* VOIR GRAMMAIRE A14
▸▸ **m. cheese** macaroni(s) au gratin

macaroon [mækəˈru:n] **N** *Culin* macaron *m*

macaw [məˈkɔ:] **N** *(bird)* ara *m*

Mace® [meɪs] **N** *(gas)* gaz *m* lacrymogène *ou* incapacitant
VT **to m. sb** asperger qn de gaz lacrymogène *ou* incapacitant

mace¹ [meɪs] **N** *(weapon, symbol of office)* masse *f*

mace² **N** *Bot, Culin* macis *m*

macebearer [ˈmeɪsbeərər] **N** massier *m*

Macedonia [mæsɪˈdəʊnɪə] **N** Macédoine *f*

Macedonian [mæsɪˈdəʊnɪən] **ADJ** macédonien
N 1 *(person)* Macédonien, -ienne **2** *Ling* macédonien *m*

macerate [ˈmæsəreɪt] **VT & VI** macérer

Mach [mæk] **N** *Phys* Mach *m;* **at M. 3** à Mach 3
▸▸ **M. number** nombre *m* de Mach

machete [məˈʃetɪ] **N** machette *f*

Machiavellian [mækɪəˈvelɪən] **ADJ** machiavélique

machination [mækɪˈneɪʃən] **N** machination *f,* manœuvre *f*

machine [məˈʃi:n] **N 1** machine *f,* **(vending) m.** distributeur *m* (automatique); **m. made** fait à la machine **2** *Fig Pej (person)* automate *m,* robot *m,* machine *f* **3** *Fig (organization)* **propaganda m.** appareil *m* de propagande; **the organization runs like a m.** l'organisation fonctionne très efficacement

VT 1 *Ind (part)* usiner, façonner, travailler à la machine **2** *Sewing* coudre *ou* piquer à la machine
▸▸ *Comput* **m. code** code *m* machine; *Comput* **m. code instruction** instruction *f* de code machine; **m. gun** mitrailleuse *f, Mil* **m. gunner** mitrailleur *m; Comput* **m. language** langage *m* machine; **m. shop** atelier *m* d'usinage; **m. time** temps-machine *m;* **m. tool** machine-outil *f, pl* machines-outils; *Comput* **m. translation** traduction *f* assistée par ordinateur
▸ **machine down VT SEP** *Ind (metal)* amincir

machine-gun VT mitrailler

machine-gunning [-gʌnɪŋ] **N** *Mil* mitraillage *m*

machine-hour N heure-machine *f, pl* heures-machine

machine-readable ADJ *Comput (data)* lisible par ordinateur; **in m. format** dans un format lisible par ordinateur

machinery [məˈʃi:nərɪ] **N 1** *(parts)* mécanisme(s) *m(pl); (machines)* machines *fpl,* machinerie *f* **2** *(of organization)* **the m. of government** les rouages *mpl* du gouvernement; **administrative m.** appareil *m* administratif

machine-time intensive ADJ qui nécessite beaucoup de temps-machine

machinist [məˈʃi:nɪst] **N 1** *Ind (operator)* opérateur, -trice **2** *Sewing* mécanicien, -ienne

machismo [mæˈkɪzməʊ, -ˈtʃɪz-] **N** *Fam* machisme *m;* **I'm getting a bit tired of his m.** il commence à m'agacer avec son côté macho

macho [ˈmætʃəʊ] **ADJ** *Fam* macho *inv;* **a m. type** un macho

macintosh [ˈmækɪntɒʃ] **N =** **mackintosh**

mack [mæk] **N** *Am Sl* **1** *(pimp)* maquereau *m,* mac *m* **2** *(expert seducer)* tombeur *m*
▸ **mack on VT INSEP** *Am Fam* **to m. on sb** draguer qn

mackerel [ˈmækrəl] **N** *(pl* **mackerel** *or occ* **mackerels)** *(fish)* maquereau *m*
▸▸ **m. sky** ciel *m* pommelé

mackintosh [ˈmækɪntɒʃ] **N** imperméable *m*

mackle [ˈmæk(ə)l] *Typ* **N** maculage *m*
VT mâchurer

mackled [ˈmæk(ə)ld] **ADJ** *Typ* bavocheux

macramé [məˈkrɑ:mɪ] **N** macramé *m*

macro [ˈmækrəʊ] **N** *Comput* macro *m,* macrocommande *f*
▸▸ **m. command** macrocommande; **m. language** macrolangage *m;* **m. virus** virus *m* de macro

macrobiotics [mækrəʊbaɪˈɒtɪks] **N** macrobiotique *f* VOIR GRAMMAIRE A10

macrocomputing [ˈmækrəʊkəmˈpju:tɪŋ] **N** *Comput* macro-informatique *f*

macrocosm [ˈmækrəkɒzəm] **N** macrocosme *m*

macroeconomic [mækrəʊi:kəˈnɒmɪk] **ADJ** macroéconomique

macroeconomics [mækrəʊi:kəˈnɒmɪks] **N** macroéconomie *f* VOIR GRAMMAIRE A10

macromarketing [mækrəʊˈmɑ:kɪtɪŋ] **N** macromercatique *f,* macro-marketing *m*

macron [ˈmækrɒn] **N** *Typ* macron *m*

macroscopic [mækrəˈskɒpɪk] **ADJ** macroscopique

MACRS [emeɪsi:ɑ:ˈres] **N** *Am Acct (abbr* **modified accelerated cost recovery system)** méthode *f* d'amortissement accéléré

mad [mæd] **ADJ** **(madder, maddest) 1** *(insane)* fou, *f* folle, *m before vowel or h mute* fol, dément; *Med* aliéné; *(idea, plan)* insensé; *Fam* **as m. as a hatter** *or* **as a March hare** fou à lier; **she's very nice but as m. as a hatter!** elle est très gentille mais elle a un grain!; **it is enough to drive you m.** il y a de quoi devenir fou, c'est à vous rendre fou; **to go m.** devenir fou; **nationalism gone m.** nationalisme forcené; **m. with fear** mort de peur; **m. with desire/envy/etc** fou de désir/jalousie/*etc*
2 *(enthusiastic)* **to be m. about sb/sth** *(like very much)* être fou de qn/qch; **I'm not m. on Indian food** je ne raffole pas de la cuisine indienne; **to be m. about** *or* **on sport/climbing** être un passionné *ou* mordu de sport/d'escalade, avoir la passion du sport/de l'escalade; **I'm not m. about the idea** ce n'est pas une idée qui m'emballe; **m. for revenge** assoiffé de revanche; *Br* **to be m. for it** *(raring to go)* être prêt à s'éclater
3 *Fam (angry)* furieux, furibond; **that kind of attitude makes me m.** ce genre d'attitude me met hors de moi; **to be m. with** *or* **at sb** être furieux contre qn; **m. bull** taureau furieux *ou* enragé; *Vet* **m. dog** chien *m* enragé
4 *(frantic)* **there was a m. rush for the door** on s'est précipité à la porte; *Fam* **to run/shout/work like m.** courir/crier/travailler comme un fou
ADV *Fam* **m. keen on sb/sth** fou de qn/qch; **to be m. keen on an idea** être emballé par une idée; **I'm not m. keen on Indian food/reggae** je raffole pas de la cuisine indienne/de reggae
▸▸ *Vet* **m. cow disease** maladie *f* de la vache folle

Madagascan [mædəˈgæskən] **ADJ** malgache
N Malgache *mf*

Madagascar [mædəˈgæskər] **N** Madagascar *m;* **they live in M.** ils vivent à Madagascar; **M. is an island** Madagascar est une île

madam [ˈmædəm] **N 1** *(as form of address)* madame *f,* **M. Chairman** Madame la Présidente; **Dear M.** *(in letter)* Madame; *Fam* **that's enough of your cheek, m.!** ça suffit comme ça, petite insolente! **2** *(pl* **madams)** *(in brothel)* tenancière *f* de bordel, maquerelle *f* **3** *Br Fam Pej* **she's a bit of a m.** elle est un peu pimbêche; **she's a proper little m.** c'est une vraie petite pimbêche

madcap ['mædkæp] ADJ *(scheme, idea)* insensé
  N insensé, -ée

madden ['mæd(ə)n] VT *(make angry)* exaspérer, rendre fou

maddening ['mæd(ə)nɪŋ] ADJ *(exasperating)* exaspérant; **the really m. thing is that we could so easily have won** ce qui est rageant c'est qu'on aurait facilement pu gagner

maddeningly ['mæd(ə)nɪŋlɪ] ADV **a m. long wait** une attente interminable; **he's m. slow/ stupid** il est d'une lenteur/bêtise exaspérante; **he was m. calm about the whole thing** il est resté d'un calme horripilant

madder ['mædər] N **1** *Bot* garance *f* **2** *(in dyeing)* teinture *f* de garance
  ▸▸ *Bot* **m. root** alizari *m*

madding ['mædɪŋ] ADJ *Arch, Lit* furieux, déchaîné; **far from the m. crowd** loin de la foule et du bruit

made [meɪd] PT, PP *see* **make**
  ADJ fait, fabriqué; **m. in France** fabriqué en France; *Fam* **he's a m. man** son avenir est assuré, sa fortune est faite; **she's m., she's got it m.** son avenir est assuré

made-for-TV movie N téléfilm *m*

Madeira [mə'dɪərə] N **1** *Geog* Madère *f*, **to go to M.** aller à Madère **2** *(wine)* vin *m* de Madère, madère *m*
  ▸▸ **M. cake** ≃ quatre-quarts *m inv*

made-up ADJ **1** *(not true)* faux, *f* fausse; *(intended to deceive)* inventé de toutes pièces **2** *Sewing (garment)* tout fait **3** *(wearing make-up)* maquillé; **heavily m.** très maquillée **4** *Br Fam (thrilled, very happy)* hyper content

madhouse ['mædhaʊs] N *Arch (lunatic asylum)* maison *f* de fous; *Fig* **this place is a m.!** c'est une véritable maison de fous ici!

madly ['mædlɪ] ADV **1** *(to behave)* comme un fou/une folle **2** *Fam (very)* follement; *(to love)* à la folie, éperdument, follement; **m. in love** follement *ou* éperdument amoureux; **I can't say I'm m. interested in it** je ne peux pas dire que ça m'intéresse follement **3** *(desperately) (to work, rush, struggle etc)* comme un fou/une folle; **people rushed m. in every direction** les gens couraient comme des fous dans tous les sens

madman, *pl* **madmen** ['mædmən] N fou *m*, aliéné *m*, dément *m*; **he's a complete m.!** il est complètement fou!; **like a m.** *(to fight)* comme un forcené, désespérément; *(to shout)* comme un perdu; *(to drive)* comme un fou

madness ['mædnɪs] N folie *f*, démence *f*, **in a fit of m.** dans un accès *ou* dans un moment de folie; **it's sheer m.** c'est insensé, c'est de la folie; **it would be m. to …** ce serait de la folie de …

Madonna [mə'dɒnə] N *Rel (Mary)* Madone *f*, **M., m.** *(statue, picture)* madone *f*

madras curry N curry *m* de Madras

madrigal ['mædrɪg(ə)l] N *Mus* madrigal *m*

madwoman, *pl* **madwomen** ['mædwʊmən, -wɪmɪn] N folle *f*, aliénée *f*, démente *f*

maelstrom ['meɪlstrəʊm] N *(whirlpool)* tourbillon *m*; *Fig* **the m. of modern life** le tourbillon de la vie moderne

maestro, *pl* **maestros, maestri** ['maɪstrəʊ, -trəʊz, -tri:] N *Mus* maestro *m*, *pl* maestros

Mae West ['meɪ'west] N *Old-fashioned Fam (lifejacket)* gilet *m* de sauvetage

MAFF [mæf] N *Br Formerly (abbr* **Ministry of Agriculture, Fisheries and Food)** = ministère *m* de l'Agriculture, de la Pêche et de l'Alimentation

Mafia ['mæfɪə] N Mafia *f*

mafioso [mæfɪ'əʊsəʊ] N mafioso *m*

mag [mæg] N *Fam* = **magazine 1**

mag² ADJ *(abbr* **magnetic)**
  ▸▸ **m. tape** bande *f* magnétique; **m. tape cassette** cassette *f* à bande magnétique; **m. tape reader** lecteur *m* de bandes magnétiques

magalogue ['mægəlɒg] N magalogue *m*

magazine [mægə'zi:n] N **1** *(publication)* magazine *m*, revue *f*; **illustrated m.** revue illustrée, magazine; **sports m.** magazine sportif; **men's/women's magazines** la presse masculine/féminine **2** *Radio, TV (programme)* magazine *m* (télévisé), émission *f* magazine **3** *(for cartridges)* chargeur *m*, magasin *m*; *Phot* magasin *m*, dépôt *m*; *Mil (store) (of arms etc)* magasin *m*, dépôt *m*; **powder m.** *Mil* magasin à poudre, poudrière *f*, dépôt d'explosifs; *Naut* soute *f* aux poudres *ou* à poudre
  ▸▸ *Radio, TV* **m. programme** magazine (télévisé), émission magazine; **m. rack** porte-revues *m inv*; **m. rifle** fusil *m* à répétition *ou* à chargeur

magenta [mə'dʒentə] N *(colour)* magenta *m*
  ADJ *(colour)* magenta *inv*

maggot ['mægət] N ver *m*, asticot *m*

maggoty ['mægətɪ] ADJ véreux, plein de vers *ou* d'asticots

Magi ['meɪdʒaɪ] NPL *Bible* **the (Three) M.** les (trois) rois mages *mpl*

magic ['mædʒɪk] N magie *f*, enchantement *m*; **like m., as if by m.** comme par enchantement; *Fig* **the m. had gone out of their marriage** leur vie conjugale avait perdu tout son charme; **black/white m.** magie noire/blanche
  ADJ **1** magique; **to say the m. word** *(say please)* dire s'il vous plaît **2** *Br Fam (excellent)* génial, -aux, super
  ▸▸ **m. carpet** tapis *m* volant; **m. lantern** lanterne *f* magique; *Fam* **m. mushrooms** champignons *mpl* (hallucinogènes); **m. square** carré *m* magique; **m. wand** baguette *f* magique

▸ **magic away** VT SEP *(pt, pp* **magicked)** faire disparaître comme par magie *ou* par enchantement

magical ['mædʒɪkəl] ADJ magique

magically ['mædʒɪklɪ] ADV magiquement; *Fig (to disappear)* (comme) par magie *ou* par enchantement

magician [mə'dʒɪʃən] N magicien, -ienne

magisterial [mædʒɪs'tɪərɪəl] ADJ **1** *(tone, air)* magistral, -aux; *Pej* doctoral, -aux **2** *Law* de magistrat

magistrate ['mædʒɪstreɪt] N magistrat *m*, juge *m*; *Eng* **magistrates' court** ≃ tribunal *m* d'instance

magma ['mægmə] N *Geol* magma *m*

Magna Carta ['mægnə'kɑːtə] N *Hist* la Grande Charte *(de l'année 1215)*

magnanimity [mægnə'nɪmɪtɪ] N magnanimité *f*, *(nobility)* grandeur *f* d'âme

magnanimous [mæg'nænɪməs] ADJ magnanime; **to be m.** se montrer magnanime

magnanimously [mæg'nænɪməslɪ] ADV magnanimement, avec magnanimité

magnate ['mægneɪt] N *(of industry etc)* magnat *m*

magnesia [mæg'niːʃə] N **1** *Chem* magnésie *f* **2** *Pharm* magnésie *f* blanche

magnesium [mæg'niːzɪəm] N *Chem* magnésium *m*

magnet ['mægnɪt] N **1** aimant *m* **2** *Fig (for tourists etc)* pôle *m* d'attraction; *Fam Hum* **his new car's a babe** *or* **chick m.** sa nouvelle voiture est super pour emballer les gonzesses

magnetic [mæg'netɪk] ADJ **1** *(attraction, field, pole etc)* magnétique **2** *Fig (personality)* magnétique
  ▸▸ *Comput* **m. card** carte *f* magnétique; *Comput* **m. card reader** lecteur *m* de cartes magnétiques; *Comput* **m. character reader** lecteur de caractères magnétiques; *Comput* **m. disk** disque *m* magnétique; *(floppy)* disquette *f* magnétique; *Comput* **m. drive** dérouleur *m* de bande magnétique, unité *f* de bande magnétique; **m. lock** serrure *f* magnétique; **m. media** supports *mpl* magnétiques; **m. needle** aiguille *f* aimantée; **m. north** nord *m* magnétique; *Comput* **m. random access memory** mémoire *f* vive magnétique; *Med* **m. resonance imaging** imagerie *f* par résonance magnétique; **m. soundtrack** bande *f* son magnétique; **m. stripe** piste *f* magnétique; **m. stripe card** carte à piste magnétique; **m. stripe reader** lecteur de pistes magnétiques; **m. tape** bande magnétique; *Comput* **m. tape unit** dérouleur de bande magnétique, unité de bande magnétique

magnetically [mæg'netɪklɪ] ADV magnétiquement

magnetism ['mægnɪtɪz(ə)m] N *Phys, Fig* magnétisme *m*

magnetization [mægnɪtaɪ'zeɪʃən] N aimantation *f*, magnétisation *f*

magnetize ['mægnɪtaɪz] VT **1** *(needle etc)* aimanter **2** *Fig (person)* magnétiser, attirer *(par magnétisme personnel)*; **he was magnetized by her good looks** il était fasciné par sa beauté
  VI *(of iron etc)* s'aimanter

magnetizing ['mægnɪtaɪzɪŋ] ADJ *(current, field etc)* magnétisant

magneto [mæg'niːtəʊ] N *Elec* magnéto *f*

magneto-electric ADJ *Phys* magnéto-électrique

magneto-optical ADJ *Comput* magnéto-optique

magnificat [mæg'nɪfɪkæt] N *Rel* magnificat *m inv*

magnification [mægnɪfɪ'keɪʃən] N *Opt etc* grossissement *m*; *(of sound)* amplification *f*, *Opt* **high m.** fort grossissement

magnificence [mæg'nɪfɪsəns] N magnificence *f*

magnificent [mæg'nɪfɪsənt] ADJ magnifique; *(meal, wine)* excellent

magnificently [mæg'nɪfɪsntlɪ] ADV magnifiquement

magnifier ['mægnɪfaɪər] N verre *m* grossissant

magnify ['mægnɪfaɪ] VT **1** *(image)* grossir, agrandir; *(sound)* amplifier; *Fig (importance)* grossir, exagérer; **to m. sth out of all proportion** beaucoup exagérer l'importance de qch **2** *Rel, Arch (the Lord)* magnifier

magnifying ['mægnɪfaɪɪŋ] ADJ
  ▸▸ **m. glass** loupe *f*, *Opt* **m. power** *(of lens, microscope)* grossissement *m*

magnitude ['mægnɪtjuːd] N importance *f*, *Astron* magnitude *f*, *Math* grandeur *f*, valeur *f*, *Astron* **star of the first m.** étoile *f* de première magnitude; *Fig* **of the first m.** de premier ordre; *(mistake)* gravissime

magnolia [mæg'nəʊlɪə] N *Bot* magnolia *m*, magnolier *m*; *(colour)* rose *m* pâle
  ▸▸ **m. tree** magnolia, magnolier

magnum, *pl* **magnums** ['mægnəm, -əmz] N *(of champagne etc)* magnum *m*

magnum opus N *Liter etc* chef-d'œuvre *m*, *pl* chefs-d'œuvre

magpie ['mægpaɪ] N *(bird)* pie *f*, *Fig Fam (hoarder)* thésauriseur, -euse

Magyar ['mægjɑːr] ADJ magyar
  N Magyar, -are

maharajah [mɑːhəˈrɑːdʒə] N maharajah m
maharani [mɑːhəˈrɑːniː] N maharani f
maharishi [mɑːhəˈriːʃɪ] N Rel maharishi m
mahogany [məˈhɒgənɪ] N (tree, wood, colour) acajou m; **m. table** table f en acajou
Mahometan [məˈhɒmətən] ADJ, N Old-fashioned mahométan, -ane

MAI [emeɪˈaɪ] N Fin (abbr **multilateral agreement on investment**) AMI m

maid [meɪd] N **1** (servant) bonne f, domestique f; **lady's m.** femme f de chambre **2** Arch, Lit (girl) jeune fille f; (virgin) vierge f ▸▸ **m. of all work** bonne à tout faire; **m. of honour** (to queen) demoiselle f d'honneur; (at wedding) première demoiselle d'honneur; Br Culin (cake) petit gâteau m aux amandes; Hist **the M. of Orleans** la Pucelle (d'Orléans); **m. service** (at self-catering apartment) service m de femme de ménage

maiden [ˈmeɪd(ə)n] N **1** Lit (girl) jeune fille f; (virgin) vierge f **2** Cr = série f de six balles pendant laquelle aucun point n'est marqué
ADJ ATTRIB (first) premier, -ère
▸▸ **m. aunt** tante f célibataire; **m. flight** premier vol m, vol inaugural; **m. name** nom m de jeune fille; Cr **m. over** = série de six balles pendant laquelle aucun point n'est marqué; Br **m. speech** = premier discours m prononcé par un parlementaire nouvellement élu; **m. voyage** voyage m inaugural

maidenhair [ˈmeɪd(ə)nheər] N (fern) adiante m, cheveu m de Vénus
▸▸ **m. fern** adiante, cheveu de Vénus

maidenly [ˈmeɪdənlɪ] ADJ virginal, -aux
maidservant [ˈmeɪdsɜːvənt] N Arch domestique f

mail¹ [meɪl] N **1** (letters, parcels) courrier m; **it came in the m.** c'est arrivé au courrier; **was there anything in the m. for me?** est-ce qu'il y avait du courrier pour moi?; **has the m. been yet?** est-ce que le facteur est passé? **2** (postal service) poste f, courrier m **3** Comput courrier m électronique **4** Hist (coach) malle f, malle-poste, pl malles-poste
VT (letters, parcels) (send) envoyer par la poste, expédier; (put in mailbox) mettre à la poste, poster
▸▸ Comput **m. address** adresse f électronique; **m. bomb** (letter) lettre f piégée; (parcel) colis m piégé; **m. bomber** = personne qui envoie une lettre ou un colis piégé; Am **m. carrier** facteur, -trice; Hist **m. coach** malle-poste, pl malles-poste; Am **m. drop** boîte f à ou aux lettres; Comput **m. forwarding** réexpédition f du courrier électronique; Comput **m. gateway** passerelle f (de courrier électronique); **m. order** vente f par correspondance; Comput **m. reader** logiciel m de courrier électronique, client m de messagerie électronique; **m. room** service m du courrier; **m. server** serveur m de courrier; **m. train** train m postal; **m. transfer** virement m par courrier; **m. van** Rail wagon-poste m, pl wagons-poste; Aut voiture f ou fourgon m des postes

mail² N (armour) mailles fpl; **coat of m.** cotte f de mailles

mailbag [ˈmeɪlbæg] N sac m postal
mailbot [ˈmeɪlbɒt] N Comput fonction f de réponse automatique
mailbox [ˈmeɪlbɒks] N Am boîte f aux lettres; Comput **(electronic) m.** boîte aux lettres électronique
mailing [ˈmeɪlɪŋ] N (mailshot) publipostage m, mailing m
▸▸ Mktg **m. card** carte f de publicité; **m. list** Mktg liste f de publipostage; Comput liste de diffusion; Mktg **m. shot** mailing, publipostage m
mailman, pl **mailmen** [ˈmeɪlmæn, -men] N Am facteur m

mailmerge [ˈmeɪlmɜːdʒ] N Comput publipostage m
▸▸ **m. letter** lettre f envoyée par publipostage; **m. program** programme m de publipostage
mail-order ADJ Com de vente par correspondance, de VPC
▸▸ **m. bride** = nom m donné aux jeunes femmes originaires de pays pauvres cherchant à épouser des occidentaux par le biais d'agences matrimoniales spécialisées; **m. catalogue** catalogue m de vente par correspondance; **m. company, m. firm** maison f de vente par correspondance; **m. goods** marchandises fpl vendues ou achetées par correspondance; **m. organization** vépéciste m; **m. retailing, m. selling** vente f par correspondance; **m. specialist** vépéciste m
mailroom [ˈmeɪlruːm] N service m du courrier
mailshot [ˈmeɪlʃɒt] N mailing m, publipostage m
VT envoyer un mailing ou un publipostage à
maim [meɪm] VT (person) estropier, mutiler
main [meɪn] N **1** (pipe) canalisation f ou conduite f maîtresse ou principale; Elec câble m de distribution **2 in the m.** (on the whole) en général, en gros, en somme, généralement (parlant) **3** Arch, Lit **the m.** (ocean) le grand large, l'océan m
ADJ principal, -aux; **the m. body of ...** le gros de ...; **our m. concern** notre préoccupation majeure; **m. idea** (of book, film etc) idée f mère ou maîtresse ou directrice; **m. line of business** activité f principale exercée, APE f; **the m. point** or **thing** l'essentiel, le principal; ▸▸ Comput **m. board** carte f principale; Gram **m. clause** proposition f principale; **m. course** plat m principal ou de résistance; Agr **m. crop** culture f principale; Naut **m. deck** pont m principal; **m. dish** plat principal ou de résistance; Am Fam **m. drag** rue f principale, grande rue; **m. entrance** entrée f principale; Rail etc **m. line** voie f principale, grande ligne f; Sl **m. man** (friend) pote m; Br Sl **when it comes to scoring goals, Michael Owen's the m. man** pour ce qui est de marquer des buts, Michael Owen est champion; Naut **m. masts** mâts mpl majeurs; Comput **m. memory** mémoire f principale; Br **m. road** grande route f, route à grande circulation; ≃ nationale f; **m. sewer** égout m collecteur; Fam **m. squeeze** (boyfriend) mec m, jules m; (girlfriend) nana f, gonzesse f; **m. street** rue principale, grande rue
mainbrace [ˈmeɪnbreɪs] N Naut grand bras m de vergue
mainframe [ˈmeɪnfreɪm] N (computer) ordinateur m central
▸▸ **m. computer** ordinateur central
mainland [ˈmeɪnlænd] N (continental land mass) continent m; **you can see the Scottish m.** on voit la côte écossaise; **we live on the m.** (not on island) nous n'habitons pas dans les îles; **the French m., the m. of France** la France continentale
mainline [ˈmeɪnlaɪn] Sl VI se shooter, se piquer
VT se faire un shoot de; (habitually) se shooter à
mainliner [ˈmeɪnlaɪnər] N Sl (drug addict) junkie mf, shooté, -ée
mainly [ˈmeɪnlɪ] ADV principalement, surtout; **the passengers were m. old men** la plupart des passagers étaient des vieux messieurs; **a m. Spanish-speaking population** une population à majorité ou principalement ou surtout hispanophone; **their diet consists m. of insects** ils se nourrissent essentiellement ou principalement ou surtout d'insectes; **she was m. to blame** c'est elle la

principale responsable, c'est surtout de sa faute
mainmast [ˈmeɪnmɑːst, -məst] N Naut grand mât m
mains [meɪnz] NPL secteur m; **the house hasn't been connected to the m.** la maison n'a pas été raccordée au secteur; **electric m.** (cables) canalisations fpl d'électricité; **gas m.** conduites fpl de gaz; **water m.** canalisations ou conduites d'eau
▸▸ **m. adaptor** adaptateur m secteur; **m. electricity** courant m secteur; Radio **m. set** poste m secteur; **m. water** eau f courante
mainsail [ˈmeɪnseɪl, ˈmeɪns(ə)l] N Naut grand-voile f, pl grand(s)-voiles
mainsheet [ˈmeɪnʃiːt] N Naut grand-écoute f, pl grand-écoutes
mains-powered ADJ fonctionnant sur secteur
mainspring [ˈmeɪnsprɪŋ] N **1** Tech grand ressort m; (of clock etc) ressort moteur **2** Fig (force behind sth) moteur m
mainstay [ˈmeɪnsteɪ] N **1** Naut étai m de grand mât **2** (of economy, philosophy, policy) base f, pilier m; (of family) soutien m principal
mainstream [ˈmeɪnstriːm] N courant m principal; **he belongs to the m. of French tradition** il fait partie de la grande tradition française; **a writer who has moved away from the m.** un auteur qui est sorti des sentiers battus
ADJ **m. Hollywood movies** films mpl dans la grande tradition hollywoodienne; **m. politics** courants mpl politiques dominants; **their second album was much more m.** leur deuxième album était beaucoup plus classique
▸▸ Mus **m. jazz** = style m de jazz qui se situe entre le traditionnel et le moderne
maintain [meɪnˈteɪn] VT **1** (keep in good condition) (road, machine, car) entretenir **2** (support) (family etc) entretenir, subvenir aux besoins de, nourrir; (army) entretenir **3** (order, discipline) maintenir; (conversation etc) soutenir; (relations etc) entretenir; (health, advantage, lead) garder, conserver; (attitude, one's silence) garder; (one's rights) défendre; **to m. speed** conserver l'allure **4** (assert) (opinion, fact) soutenir; **to m. that ...** maintenir ou soutenir que ... + ind
maintenance [ˈmeɪntɪnəns] N **1** (of car), Rail, Tel (of lines) entretien m; (of equipment, roads etc) entretien, maintenance f **2** (of law and order) maintien m **3** (of family, troops etc) entretien m **4** Law (alimony) pension f alimentaire **5** (of one's rights) défense f
▸▸ **m. contract** contract m de maintenance ou d'entretien; **m. costs** frais mpl d'entretien; **m. department** service m de maintenance ou d'entretien; **m. engineer** technicien, -ienne de maintenance; **m. grant** (to student) bourse f d'études; **m. handbook** manuel m d'entretien; **m. kit** trousse f d'entretien; **m. man** ouvrier m chargé de l'entretien ou de la maintenance; **m. manual** manuel d'entretien; Law **m. order** obligation f alimentaire; **m. staff** personnel m d'entretien; **m. vehicle** camion-atelier m, pl camions-ateliers
maintenance-free ADJ qui ne nécessite aucun entretien; **m. battery** batterie f sans entretien
maison(n)ette [meɪzəˈnet] N (appartement m) duplex m
maître d' [metrəˈdiː] N esp Am maître m d'hôtel
maize [meɪz] N esp Br maïs m
Maj Mil abbr **major**
majestic [məˈdʒestɪk] ADJ majestueux; (bearing) majestueux, plein de majesté; (scenery) grandiose

majestically [mə'dʒestɪklɪ] ADV majestueusement

majesty ['mædʒəstɪ] N majesté f, **God in all His m.** Dieu dans toute sa majesté; **His M. (the King)** Sa Majesté le Roi; **Her M. (the Queen)** Sa Majesté la Reine; **Your M.** Votre Majesté; *Br* **on His/Her M.'s Service** (pour le) service de Sa Majesté (≃ service de l'État); *(on envelope)* ≃ en franchise; **Her M.'s Prison Service** *Br* = système *m* pénitentiaire britannique; **Her M.'s Stationery Office** *Br* = maison *f* d'édition publiant les ouvrages ou documents approuvés par le Parlement, les ministères et autres organismes officiels, ≃ l'Imprimerie *f* nationale

Maj Gen *Mil abbr* **major general**

major ['meɪdʒər] ADJ **1** *(big)* grand; *(main)* le plus grand; *(company)* de première importance, de premier ordre; *(distinction, improvement, changes, difficulties)* de taille, grand; *(problem, cause, concern, interest, new novel, discovery, Mus* majeur; *(accident, disaster)* grand; **the m. brands** les marques les plus importantes; **it's a m. brand** c'est une des marques les plus importantes; **the m. teams** les plus grandes équipes; **it's of m. importance** c'est de la plus haute importance; **the significance of this event is quite m.** c'est un événement de toute première importance; **the party was a m. disaster** la fête a été une catastrophe absolue; **any problems? – nothing m.** des problèmes? – rien d'important; **he's our m. programmer** c'est notre programmeur principal; **we invested in a m. way** nous avons investi de manière considérable; **he's taken up Spanish in a m. way** il s'est mis à fond à l'espagnol; **he's fallen for Susie in a m. way** il est tombé follement amoureux de Susie; **the m. portion** la majeure partie, la plus grande partie; **m. decision** décision *f* capitale; **m. illness** maladie *f* grave; *Med etc* **m. operation** grosse opération *f*; **m. repairs** grosses réparations *fpl*; **to undergo m. surgery** subir une intervention chirurgicale importante
2 *Br Sch Old-fashioned* **Martin m.** Martin aîné, l'aîné des deux Martin
N **1** *Mil (in infantry)* chef *m* de bataillon; *(in cavalry etc)* chef d'escadron
2 *Law (person)* majeur, -eure
3 *Am Univ (area of study)* matière *f* principale; **physics m.** *(student)* étudiant, -ante en physique
4 *Cin* **the Majors** *(film companies)* = les sociétés *fpl* de production les plus importantes à Hollywood
VI *Am Univ* **to m. in a subject** se spécialiser dans une matière
▸▸ *Mil* **m. general** général *m* de division; *Mus* **m. key** ton *m* ou mode *m* majeur; *Am Sport* **m. league** première division *f*, *(in baseball)* = une des deux principales divisions de baseball professionnel aux États-Unis et au Canada; *Mil* **m. offensive** vaste offensive *f*, *Phil* **m. premise** majeure *f*, **m. prophets** grands prophètes *mpl*; **m. road** route *f* principale *ou* à grande circulation, ≃ nationale *f*, *Fin* **m. shareholder** actionnaire *mf* de référence; *Am Univ* **m. subject** matière principale

Majorca [mə'jɔːkə] N Majorque *f*

Majorcan [mə'jɔːkən] ADJ majorquin
N Majorquin, -ine

major-domo, *pl* **major-domos** [meɪdʒə-'dəʊməʊ, -əʊz] N majordome *m*

majorette [meɪdʒə'ret] N *Am* **(drum) m.** majorette *f*

majority [mə'dʒɒrɪtɪ] N **1** *(of votes)* majorité *f*, **the m.** *(of people etc)* la plus grande partie, le plus grand nombre; **a two-thirds m.** une majorité des deux tiers; **to have a m.** avoir la majorité; **to be in a** *or* **the m.** être majori-

taire; **elected by a m.** élu à la majorité; **in the m. of cases** dans la majorité des cas ▐VOIR GRAMMAIRE A11▌ **2** *Law (age)* majorité *f*, **to attain** *or* **reach one's m.** atteindre sa majorité, devenir majeur
▸▸ **m. decision** décision *f* prise à la majorité; **m. government** gouvernement *m* majoritaire; **system of m. government** gouvernement à la majorité absolue, système *m* majoritaire; *Fin* **m. holding** participation *f* majoritaire; **m. party** parti *m* majoritaire; **m. rule** gouvernement à la majorité absolue, système majoritaire; **m. shareholder** actionnaire *mf* majoritaire; **m. verdict** verdict *m* majoritaire; **m. vote** majorité *f*; **m. world** tiers-monde *m*, *pl* tiers-mondes

▐**MAKE**▌ [meɪk]

> N marque **1**
> VT faire **1–3, 7, 10** ▪ fabriquer **1**
> ▪ établir **2** ▪ gagner **3** ▪ faire la fortune de **4** ▪ arriver à **8**

N **1** *Com, Ind (of product)* marque *f*, **cars of all makes** voitures de toutes marques; **what m. is it?** c'est quelle marque?
2 *(construction)* façon *f*, fabrication *f*, construction *f*, **of French m.** de fabrication française
3 *Fam* **to be on the m.** *(financially)* chercher à s'enrichir; *(sexually)* draguer
VT *(pt, pp* made [meɪd]) **1** *(construct, produce, prepare etc)* (bread, tea, meal, bed, hole etc) faire; *(machine etc)* construire, fabriquer; *(paper, box, chair etc)* fabriquer, faire; *(payment, transaction)* effectuer, faire; *(a change)* opérer, faire, effectuer; *(mistake)* commettre, faire; *(speech, excuses, promise etc)* faire; **bread is made (out) of flour** on fait le pain avec de la farine; **the chair is made (out) of wood** la chaise est en bois; **what is it made (out) of?** en quoi est-ce fait?, *Fam* c'est en quoi?; **to show what one is made of** donner sa mesure, montrer de quoi on est capable; **just let them try to cause trouble and we'll show them what we're made of!** qu'ils essaient de faire des histoires et ils verront de quel bois on se chauffe!; **I'm not made of money** je ne suis pas millionnaire; **do you want to m. something of it?** ça te dérange?; **to m. something of oneself** faire quelque chose de sa vie; **the army will m. a man of him** l'armée fera de lui un homme; **God made man** Dieu a créé l'homme; **the water had made a hole in the rock** l'eau avait percé la roche; **they seem made for each other** ils semblent faits l'un pour l'autre; **to m. trouble** provoquer le désordre; *(cause problems)* causer des ennuis (**for sb** à qn); **they made room for one more on the sofa** ils se sont poussés pour (lui) faire une place sur le canapé; **could you m. room for some pudding?** est-ce que tu as encore une petite place pour le dessert?; **to m. time to do sth** trouver le temps de faire qch; **to m. a noise** faire du bruit; **I m. the rules around here** ici, c'est moi qui dirige; **to m. an attempt to do sth** essayer de faire qch; **it makes all the difference** ça change tout; **to m. love/war** faire l'amour/la guerre; **to m. one's escape** s'échapper, se sauver; *Knitting* **to m. one/two** faire un jeté simple/double
2 *(form)* établir, assurer (**a connection between ...** le raccordement de ...); *Elec (of contact points) (circuit)* fermer; **two and two m. four** deux et deux font quatre; **that makes (it) the third time he's been late** c'est *ou* ça fait la troisième fois qu'il arrive en retard; **they m. a handsome couple** ils font un beau couple
3 *(gain) (money)* faire; **to m. £400 a week** gagner *ou Fam* se faire 400 livres par semaine; **to m. one's fortune** faire fortune; **to**

m. a fortune *(on a sale etc)* gagner une fortune; *Fam* **to m. a bit on the side** faire de la gratte; **to m. a name for oneself** se faire un nom; **to m. an enemy of sb** se faire un ennemi de qn
4 *(cause to be successful) (person)* faire la fortune de; **this book made her** *or* **her name** ce livre l'a rendue célèbre; **this will m. him or break him** cela sera *ou* son succès ou sa ruine; **it made my day** ça m'a fait très plaisir; *Iron* **you've made my day** tu m'as fait gagner ma journée
5 *(cause to be)* **to m. sb happy/rich/sad** rendre qn heureux/riche/triste; **to m. sb hungry/sleepy** donner faim/sommeil à qn; **to m. sb angry** mettre qn en colère, fâcher qn; **he made her a star** il a fait d'elle une star; **to m. sb one's heir** constituer qn son héritier; **to m. sth known** faire connaître qch; **to m. oneself heard** se faire entendre; **to m. oneself ill** se rendre malade; **to m. oneself tired** se fatiguer; **to m. oneself useful** se rendre utile; **to m. oneself comfortable** se mettre à l'aise
6 *(cause or compel to do)* **to m. sb speak/sleep** faire parler/dormir qn; *(stronger)* forcer *ou* obliger *ou* contraindre qn à parler/dormir; **what makes you say/believe that?** qu'est-ce qui te fait dire/croire ça?; **I made him stop** je l'ai forcé à s'arrêter; **don't m. me laugh!** tu me fais rire!; **her remarks made me feel more cheerful** ses remarques m'ont remonté le moral; **m. them see how important it is** montrez-leur combien c'est important; **he makes playing the violin look easy** à le regarder, on dirait qu'il est facile de jouer du violon; **to m. sb look stupid** faire passer qn pour un idiot; **what made you say that?** qu'est-ce qui vous a fait dire cela?; **you can't m. me!** tu ne peux pas me forcer!; **you made me!** tu m'y as obligé *ou* forcé!; **it makes my eyes water** ça me fait pleurer ▐VOIR GRAMMAIRE A41▌
7 *(estimate, calculate)* **what time do you m. it?** quelle heure avez-vous?; **I make the answer 127** d'après moi, ça fait 127; **I make it $56 each** si je compte bien, ça fait 56 dollars par personne
8 *(reach) (station, port etc)* arriver à; *(catch) (train, flight)* avoir; **will we m. the airport in time?** est-ce que nous arriverons à temps à l'aéroport?; **we'll m. Newport before lunch** nous serons à Newport avant le déjeuner; **he'll be lucky to m. 50** il a de la chance s'il atteint 50 ans; **to m. twenty knots** *(of ship)* faire vingt nœuds
9 *Fam (manage to attend on, at) (show, meeting etc)* assister à; **I can m. 2 o'clock** je peux être là à deux heures; **can you m. Friday?** est-ce que tu es libre vendredi?; **can you m. lunch on Friday?** peux-tu te libérer pour le déjeuner vendredi?
10 *Fam (establish as)* **let's m. it a day everyone can come** autant s'arranger pour que ce soit un jour où tout le monde puisse venir; **if we made it a Wednesday ...** si on faisait ça un mercredi ...; **can we m. it your place?** est-ce qu'on peut faire ça chez toi?; **better m. it** *or* **that two whiskies** mettez-moi un deuxième whisky
11 *(become, be)* être; **she'd m. a good diver/singer** elle ferait une bonne plongeuse/chanteuse; **to m. sb a present of sth** faire cadeau de qch à qn; **you'll never m. a diver/singer** tu ne seras jamais plongeur/chanteur
12 *Sl (have sexual intercourse with)* se faire
13 *Fam* **to m. it** *(arrive in time)* arriver à temps; *(finish in time)* finir à temps; *(manage to attend)* se libérer; *(be successful)* réussir; **you've got it made** tu n'as plus de soucis à te faire pour ton avenir; **to m. it with sb** *(have sexual intercourse)* se faire qn; **we'll never m. it** *(by that time)* nous n'y arriverons jamais; **I made it home for lunch** je suis ar-

rivé à la maison (à temps) pour le déjeuner; **to m. it in politics** réussir en politique

  vi 1 to m. as if or **as though to do sth** (get ready to) s'apprêter à faire qch; (pretend) faire semblant ou mine de faire qch; **he made as if to speak** il a eu l'air de vouloir parler; **she made (as if) to get up** elle a fait mine de se lever

  2 to m. do (cope) se débrouiller; **we'll just have to m. do** (with what we have) il va falloir faire avec; **we could m. do with ten** (though we should have more) nous pourrions nous débrouiller avec dix; **we'll have to m. the milk do** il faut nous contenter du peu de lait que nous avons; **I'll just have to m. that do** il va falloir que je fasse avec

  3 they're just making believe (in playing) ils font comme si; **let's m. believe that …** (in playing) on dirait que …

  4 to m. sure or **certain of sth** s'assurer de qch; **have you made sure?** tu t'en es assuré?

  5 Fam **to m. like** (pretend) faire semblant ou mine de; **he makes like he's the boss** il se conduit comme si c'était lui le patron; **m. like you don't know anything** fais comme si tu savais pas; **m. like you're asleep!** fais semblant de dormir!

▸ **make after vt insep** se lancer à la poursuite de

▸ **make away vi** = make off

▸ **make away with vt insep** Fam **1** (steal) partir avec, voler

  2 (kill) tuer, supprimer; **to m. away with oneself** se suicider

▸ **make for vt insep 1** (head towards) (place, the door) se diriger vers; Naut faire route sur, mettre le cap sur; **where are you making for?** où allez-vous?; **ship making for Hull** navire à destination de Hull

  2 (contribute to) (happiness, wellbeing etc) contribuer à; **these agreements m. for peace** ces accords favorisent la paix; **it doesn't m. for easy reading** c'est difficile à lire

▸ **make into vt sep** you could **m. this room into an office** tu pourrais transformer cette pièce en bureau, tu pourrais faire de cette pièce un bureau

▸ **make of vt sep 1** (understand) **I don't know what to m. of that remark** je ne sais pas comment interpréter cette remarque; **what do you m. of her?** qu'est-ce que tu penses d'elle?; **we couldn't m. much of what he said** nous n'avons pas compris grand-chose à ce qu'il a dit

  2 (attach importance to) attacher de l'importance à; **you're making too much of this** tu y attaches trop d'importance; **the press has made a lot of this visit** la presse a fait beaucoup de bruit autour de cette visite; **the prosecution made much of this fact** l'accusation a fait grand cas de ce fait; **to m. much** or **a lot of** (be attentive to) (person) être aux petits soins pour; (child etc) câliner, choyer; (flatter) flatter

▸ **make off vi** Fam (leave) prendre la fuite, s'enfuir, décamper, filer; **the thieves made off in a van** les bandits se sont enfuis dans une camionnette

▸ **make off with vt insep** Fam (steal) **to m. off with the cash** filer avec l'argent; **somebody's made off with my overcoat** on m'a volé ou chipé mon pardessus

▸ **make out vt sep 1** (write) (list etc) faire, établir, dresser; (bill) établir, dresser, relever; (cheque) faire, établir (**to sb** à l'ordre de qn); **to m. out an invoice** libeller une facture; **who do I m. it out to?** (the cheque) je le mets à quel ordre?

  2 Fam (claim) **she made out she knew them personally** elle a fait croire qu'elle les connaissait personnellement; **to m. sb out to be richer than he is** faire qn plus riche qu'il ne l'est; **she's not such a fool as people**

m. out elle n'est pas aussi bête qu'on le dit; **he made me out to be a miser** il m'a fait passer pour un avare

  3 (usu with neg) (understand, decipher) (riddle, problem) comprendre; (person's reasons, meaning of sth) démêler; (handwriting) déchiffrer; (business, matter) débrouiller; **I can't m. out the address** je n'arrive pas à lire ou déchiffrer l'adresse; **I can't m. this guy out** ce type est une énigme pour moi; **I can't m. it out** (situation, mystery) je ne m'y retrouve pas, je n'y comprends rien

  4 (discern) distinguer, discerner; **I can never m. out whether she's being serious or not** je n'arrive jamais à savoir si elle est sérieuse ou non

  5 (conclude) **how do you m. that out?** comment arrivez-vous à ce résultat ou à cette conclusion?

  vi 1 Fam (succeed) se débrouiller; **how is she making out at her new school?** comment ça marche dans sa nouvelle école?; **he's making out very well** ça marche très bien pour lui

  2 Am Sl (kiss, fondle) se peloter; (have sexual intercourse) faire l'amour

▸ **make over vt sep** (transfer) céder, transférer (**sth to sb** qch à qn); **she has made the estate over to her granddaughter** elle a cédé la propriété à sa petite-fille

▸ **make towards vt insep** (head for) se diriger vers; **he made towards the bar** il s'est dirigé vers le bar

▸ **make up vt sep 1** (invent) (story, excuses) inventer; **he's making the whole thing up** ce qu'il dit est inventé de toutes pièces, il raconte des histoires; **I'm making it up as I go along** j'improvise au fur et à mesure

  2 (compensate for) (deficit, loss) combler; **we made up the time** nous avons rattrapé notre retard; **to m. up lost ground** rattraper; **we've got a lot of ground to m. up** on a beaucoup à rattraper; **I'll m. it up to you** (for forgetting your birthday etc) je me rattraperai, je me ferai pardonner; (for helping me) je te rendrai ça

  3 (complete) (amount) compléter; **we need two more players to m. up the team** il nous faut deux joueurs de plus pour compléter l'équipe; **another two players would m. it up to eleven** avec deux joueurs de plus, on arriverait à onze; **I was only invited to m. up the numbers** (in team, for meal etc) je n'ai été invité que pour compléter l'équipe/la table/etc; **to m. up the difference** parfaire la somme; **I'll m. your savings up to the price of a new bike** je compléterai tes économies pour que tu puisses acheter un nouveau vélo

  4 (form) constituer; **all the elements that go to m. up a happy marriage** tout ce qui contribue à faire un bon mariage; **the community is made up primarily of old people** cette communauté est constituée essentiellement de personnes âgées

  5 (prepare, put together) (list) dresser; (parcel, bed) faire; Com (clothes) faire, confectionner; Com **to m. up orders** préparer des commandes; **customer's own material made up** on travaille à façon; Pharm **to m. up a prescription** préparer les médicaments prescrits sur une ordonnance; **to m. up the fire** préparer le feu; (add fuel) alimenter le feu

  6 (in bookkeeping) (account) régler, établir, arrêter; (the books) régler, balancer; **to m. up one's accounts** faire ses comptes

  7 (apply make-up to) maquiller; **to m. one's face** or **oneself up** se maquiller; **the actors are being made up** les acteurs se font maquiller

  8 to m. it up (settle quarrel) se réconcilier (**with sb** avec qn)

  9 Typ mettre en pages

  vi 1 (end quarrel) se réconcilier

  2 (catch up) **he's making up on the leaders** il rattrape ceux qui sont en tête

  3 (apply make-up) se maquiller

▸ **make up for vt insep** (losses) compenser; (lost time) rattraper; **that makes up for it** c'est une compensation; **to m. up for the lack of sth** suppléer au manque de qch; **how can I m. up for forgetting your birthday?** comment puis-je me faire pardonner d'avoir oublié ton anniversaire?; **what she lacks in skill she makes up for in enthusiasm** son manque de savoir-faire est compensé par son enthousiasme

▸ **make up to vt insep** (ingratiate oneself with) **to m. up to sb** essayer de se faire bien voir de qn

▸ **make with vt insep** Am Fam **1** (produce) faire; **to m. with the music** faire de la musique; **m. with the French fries** (to waiter etc) dépêche-toi de servir les frites; (to cook) dépêche-toi de faire les frites

  2 (use) se servir de; **he made with the food mixer** il s'est servi du mixeur

make-believe n you shouldn't indulge in m. tu ne devrais pas te complaire dans des chimères; **what is real and what is m.?** qu'est-ce qui est du domaine du réel et qu'est-ce qui est du domaine de l'invention?; **that's all m.** tout cela est (de la) pure fantaisie; **to live in the land of m.** se faire des illusions, ne pas avoir le sens des réalités ▸ **adj** a m. **world** un monde imaginaire

make-or-break adj attrib it's m. time! maintenant, ça passe ou ça casse!; **it was one of those m. moments** c'était un moment décisif

makeover ['meɪkəʊvər] **n** (of person) changement m de look; (of building) transformation f

maker ['meɪkər] **n 1** (person) faiseur, -euse; Com, Ind fabricant m; (of machinery, planes, cars etc) constructeur m; **m.'s price** prix m de fabrique; **m.'s trademark** cachet m de fabrique **2** Rel **our M.** le Créateur; **he's gone to meet his M.** il est monté au ciel; **that's between you and your M.** c'est entre toi et le Seigneur

make-ready n Typ mise f en train

makeshift ['meɪkʃɪft] **adj** de fortune; **a m. shelter** un abri de fortune; **m. equipment** installation f de fortune; **it looks a bit m.** ça a l'air un peu rudimentaire; **it's only meant to be m.** ce n'est qu'une solution temporaire ▸ **n** (solution etc) pis-aller m inv, expédient m; (object) pis-aller, moyen m de fortune

make-up n 1 (cosmetics) maquillage m; Theat maquillage, fard m; TV etc (department) (service m) maquillage; **she wears far too much m.** elle se maquille beaucoup trop; **she wears m.** elle se maquille; **I'm not wearing any m.** je ne suis pas maquillée; **to put m. on** se maquiller **2** (composition) composition f; (of person) caractère m; **it's not in his m. to apologize** ce n'est pas dans son caractère de s'excuser **3** Typ mise f en pages, imposition f **4** Am Sch (exam) examen m de rattrapage **5** (putting together, assembly) fabrication f, (of clothes) confection f ▸▸ **m. artist** maquilleur, -euse; **m. bag** trousse f de maquillage; **m. box** boîte f à maquillage; Am Sch **m. classes** cours mpl de rattrapage; Banking **m. date** date f de situation; TV etc **m. department** (service m) maquillage; Theat etc **m. girl** maquilleuse f; Theat etc **m. man** maquilleur m; **m. remover** démaquillant m; TV **m. room** salle f de maquillage

makeweight ['meɪkweɪt] **n** complément m; (stopgap) bouche-trou m, pl bouche-trous; **they only asked me to join the team as a m.** ils ne m'ont demandé d'entrer dans l'équipe que pour leur servir de bouche-trou

making ['meɪkɪŋ] N fabrication f; (of clothes) confection f, façon f; (of bridge, machine) construction f; (of film) tournage m; **this ordeal was the m. of him** cette épreuve lui a forgé le caractère; **history in the m.** l'histoire en train de se faire; **a musician/ poet in the m.** un musicien/poète en herbe; **the film was three years in the m.** le tournage du film a duré trois ans; **problems of one's own m.** des problèmes qu'on s'est créé soi-même; Elec **m. and breaking** (of circuit) fermeture f et ouverture f

makings ['meɪkɪŋz] NPL **to have the m. of** ... avoir tout ce qu'il faut pour devenir ...; **it has the m. of a good film, but it'll need a lot of work** avec beaucoup de travail, ça pourrait faire un bon film; **he has the m. of a statesman** il a l'étoffe d'un homme d'État

malachite ['mæləkaɪt] N Miner malachite f

maladjusted [mælə'dʒʌstɪd] ADJ Psy inadapté, -ée

maladjustment [mælə'dʒʌstmənt] N Psy inadaptation f; **emotional m.** déséquilibre m émotif

maladministration [mælədmɪnɪs'treɪʃən] N mauvaise administration f, mauvaise gestion f

maladroit [mælə'drɔɪt] ADJ maladroit

maladroitly [mælə'drɔɪtlɪ] ADV maladroitement

malady ['mælədɪ] N Fml mal m, maladie f

Malagasy [mælə'gɑːzɪ] N (person) Malgache mf; Ling malgache m
ADJ malgache

malaise [mæ'leɪz] N malaise m

malapropism ['mæləprɒpɪz(ə)m] N pataquès m

malaria [mə'leərɪə] N Med malaria f, paludisme m; **to have m.** avoir la malaria ou le paludisme

malarial [mə'leərɪəl] ADJ paludéen, palustre
▸▸**m. fever** fièvre f paludéenne

malark(e)y [mə'lɑːkɪ] N Fam ânerie f

Malawi [mə'lɑːwɪ] N Malawi m

Malay [mə'leɪ] ADJ malais; **the M. Peninsula** la presqu'île malaise
N 1 Malais, -aise 2 Ling malais m

Malaya [mə'leɪə] N Malaisie f

Malayan [mə'leɪən] ADJ malais
N Malais, -aise

Malaysia [mə'leɪzɪə] N Malaisie f, Malaysia f

Malaysian [mə'leɪzɪən] N Malais, -aise
ADJ malais

malcontent ['mælkəntent] ADJ, N mécontent, -ente

male [meɪl] ADJ (child, hormone, flower) mâle; (sex, attitude, public) masculin; **a m. friend** un ami; **m. line (of descent)** ligne f masculine; **m. plug** fiche f, prise f mâle; **m. socket** prise f mâle; Comput **m. to female adaptor** adaptateur mâle/femelle m
N Biol, Bot mâle m; esp Fam (man) homme m, Fam mec m; **the average French m.** le Français moyen
▸▸**m. bonding** amitié f virile; **m. chauvinism** phallocratie f; **m. chauvinist** phallocrate m; **m. chauvinist pig** sale phallocrate; **m. menopause** andropause f; **m. nurse** infirmier m

Note that the French word **mâle** is a not always a translation for the English word **male**.

malediction [mælɪ'dɪkʃən] N Fml malédiction f

malefactor ['mælɪfæktər] N Fml malfaiteur, -trice

malevolence [mə'levələns] N malveillance f (**towards** envers)

malevolent [mə'levələnt] ADJ malveillant

malevolently [mə'levələntlɪ] ADV avec malveillance; (to look at sb) d'un œil malveillant

malformation [mælfɔː'meɪʃən] N Med etc malformation f, difformité f

malformed [mæl'fɔːmd] ADJ difforme

malfunction [mæl'fʌŋkʃən] N fonctionnement m défectueux, mauvais fonctionnement; Med (of organ) dysfonctionnement m
VI mal fonctionner

Mali ['mɑːlɪ] N Mali m

Malian ['mɑːlɪən] ADJ malien
N Malien, -ienne

malice ['mælɪs] N 1 méchanceté f, malveillance f; **out of m.** par méchanceté ou malveillance; **to bear m. to** or **towards sb, to bear sb m.** en vouloir à qn 2 Law intention f criminelle ou délictueuse; **with m. aforethought** avec intention criminelle, avec préméditation

Note that the French word **malice** is a false friend and is never a translation for the English word **malice**. Its most common meaning is **mischief**.

malicious [mə'lɪʃəs] ADJ 1 méchant, malveillant 2 Law fait avec intention criminelle ou délictueuse, criminel
▸▸Law **m. intent** intention f de nuire ou criminelle

Note that the French word **malicieux** is a false friend and is never a translation for the English word **malicious**. It means **mischievous**.

maliciously [mə'lɪʃəslɪ] ADV 1 (to say, do) méchamment, avec malveillance 2 Law avec intention criminelle, avec préméditation

malign [mə'laɪn] ADJ pernicieux, nuisible
VT calomnier, diffamer; **much maligned man** homme calomnié

malignancy [mə'lɪgnənsɪ] N 1 (of person) malignité f, méchanceté f 2 Med (of disease) malignité f, virulence f; (of tumour) malignité f

malignant [mə'lɪgnənt] ADJ 1 (person) malveillant, méchant 2 Med (tumour etc) malin, f maligne

malignantly [mə'lɪgnəntlɪ] ADV avec malveillance, méchamment

malinger [mə'lɪŋgər] VI faire semblant d'être malade, Fam tirer au flanc

malingerer [mə'lɪŋgərər] N simulateur, -trice, faux malade, f fausse malade; **she's just a m.** c'est une tire-au-flanc

malingering [mə'lɪŋgərɪŋ] N simulation f (de maladie)

mall [mɔːl] N esp Am Com (shopping) **m.** centre m commercial

mallard ['mælɑːd] N (duck) colvert m

malleability [mælɪə'bɪlɪtɪ] N (of person, metal) malléabilité f

malleable ['mælɪəb(ə)l] ADJ (person, metal) malléable

mallet ['mælɪt] N 1 (hammer) (small) maillet m; (large) mailloche f 2 Sport (in croquet, polo) maillet m

mallow ['mæləʊ] N (plant) mauve f

malnourished ['mælnʌrɪʃt] ADJ sousalimenté

malnutrition [mælnjuː'trɪʃən] N malnutrition f, (lack of food) sous-alimentation f

malodorous [mæ'ləʊdərəs] ADJ Fml malodorant

malpractice [mæl'præktɪs] N (in profes-

sional life) faute f professionnelle; (of doctor) négligence f, incurie f
▸▸Law **m. insurance** = assurance f souscrite pour parer à des poursuites judiciaires pour négligence; Am Law **m. suit** = procès m pour faute ou négligence professionnelle

malt [mɔːlt] N malt m; (whisky) whisky m de malt
VT (in brewing) (barley) malter; **malted milk** lait m malté
▸▸**m. extract** extrait m de malt; Am **m. liquor** = boisson f alcoolisée tirée du malt; **m. vinegar** vinaigre m de malt; **m. whisky** whisky de malt

Malta ['mɔːltə] N Malte f

Maltese [mɔːl'tiːz] ADJ maltais
N 1 (person) Maltais, -aise 2 Ling maltais m
▸▸**M. Cross** croix f de Malte

maltreat [mæl'triːt] VT (person, animal) maltraiter, malmener

maltreatment [mæl'triːtmənt] N mauvais traitement(s) m(pl)

mam [mæm] N Dial maman f

mam(m)a N 1 ['mæmə, Old-fashioned mə'mɑː] (mother) maman f 2 ['mæmə] Am Sl (woman) nana f, **big m.** (object) mastodonte m

mammal ['mæməl] N mammifère m

mammalian [mæ'meɪlɪən] ADJ, N mammifère m

mammary ['mæmərɪ] ADJ Anat mammaire
▸▸**m. glands** glandes fpl mammaires

mammogram ['mæməgræm] N Med mammographie f

mammography [mæ'mɒgrəfɪ] N Med mammographie f

Mammon ['mæmən] N Bible Mammon m; Fig **the worship of M.** l'adoration f de l'argent

mammoth ['mæməθ] N mammouth m
ADJ énorme, gigantesque, colossal, -aux

mammy ['mæmɪ] N 1 Fam (mother) maman f 2 Am Old-fashioned (black nurse) bonne f d'enfants noire

Man [mæn] N **the Isle of M.** l'île f de Man

MAN, pl **men** [mæn, men] N 1 (adult male) homme m; **men and women** les hommes et les femmes; **m. and wife** mari et femme; **to live as m. and wife** vivre maritalement; **men** (on public convenience) hommes; **an old m.** un vieillard, un vieil homme; **an ambitious m.** un ambitieux; **a dead m.** un mort; **good m.!** bravo, mon gars!; **I've known him m. and boy** je le connais depuis toujours; **a m.'s jacket/bicycle** une veste/bicyclette d'homme; **men's clothes/trousers** vêtements/pantalon pour homme; Com **men's department** rayon m hommes; **soap for men** savon pour homme; **to make a m. of sb** faire un homme de qn; **the army made a m. of him** l'armée a fait de lui un homme; **he took it like a m.** il a pris ça courageusement; **a game that sorts the men from the boys** un jeu qui distingue les hommes des gamins; **he isn't m. enough to tell me** il n'est pas assez courageux pour me le dire; **to talk to sb m. to m.** parler à qn d'homme à homme; **tell me, m. to m.** dis-moi, entre nous; **he's just the m. for me** c'est l'homme qu'il me faut; **he's just the m. for the job** c'est l'homme de la situation; **to be one's own m.** être son maître, ne dépendre de personne; **he's a m.'s m.** il préfère la compagnie des hommes; **a m. about town** un mondain; **the m. in the street** l'homme de la rue; **what does the m. in the street think?** que pense l'homme de la rue?; **the m. in the moon** = visage m que l'on peut s'imaginer distinguer lors de la pleine lune; **m. of God** homme m d'église; **a m. of learning** un érudit; **a m. of peace** un homme de paix;

Sport **the m. of the match** le héros du match; **our m. in Rome** *Journ* notre correspondant à Rome; *Com* notre représentant à Rome; *(spy)* notre agent à Rome; *(diplomat)* notre envoyé à Rome; **they took on 200 men** ils ont embauché 200 ouvriers; *Mil* **officers and men** officiers *mpl* et hommes de troupe; *Hum* **a m.'s got to do what a m.'s got to do** (il) faut ce qu'il faut! VOIR GRAMMAIRE A13

2 *(individual, person)* homme *m*; **any m.** n'importe qui; **few men** peu de gens; **they replied as one m.** ils répondirent d'une seule voix; **they rose as one m.** ils se levèrent comme un seul homme; **they were patriots/communists to a m.** ils étaient tous patriotes/communistes; **every m. jack** tous sans exception

3 *(humanity)* l'homme *m*; **iron age m.** l'homme de l'âge de fer; *Prov* **m. proposes, God disposes** l'homme propose et Dieu dispose; **m. does not** or **cannot live by bread alone** on ne se nourrit pas que de pain

4 *Br Fam (husband, boyfriend)* mec *m*; **she's got a new m.** elle a un nouveau mec

5 *(type of person)*, *Univ* **an Oxford/a Cambridge m.** un diplômé d'Oxford/de Cambridge; **I'm a whisky m. myself** moi, c'est le whisky que je préfère; **he's a six-pints-a-day m.** il boit ses six pintes par jour

6 *Old-fashioned (manservant)* domestique *m*, valet *m*; *Hist (vassal)* homme *m*

7 *Sport (player)* joueur *m*

8 *(in chess)* pièce *f*, *(in draughts)* pion *m*

9 *esp Am SI* **hey m.!** *(hello)* salut mon pote!; *(as interjection)* eh! mec!; **m., am I tired!** bon sang, qu'est-ce que je suis crevé!; **you should have seen it, m.!** bon sang tu aurais dû voir ça!

10 *(black American slang)* **the M.** *(whites)* les Blancs *mpl*; *(police)* les flics *mpl*; *(drug peddler)* le dealer

VT (-nn-) **1** *(work at)* **who's manning reception today?** qui assure la réception aujourd'hui?; **reception wasn't manned at the time** personne n'assurait ou n'était à la réception à ce moment-là; **someone has to be there to m. the phone** quelqu'un doit être là pour répondre au téléphone; **the campaign office was manned by volunteers** la permanence de la campagne était assurée par des volontaires

2 *(operate) (machine)* assurer le fonctionnement de; *(plane, boat etc)* être membre de l'équipage de; *Mil* **to m. a gun** servir ou manœuvrer une pièce d'artillerie; **to m. the barricades** défendre les barricades; **the fort was manned by a handful of legionnaires** le fort était tenu par une poignée de légionnaires; **m. the pumps!** armez les pompes!; **m. the boats!** mettez les canots (de sauvetage) à la mer!; **the bomber was manned by a crew of five men** le bombardier avait un équipage de cinq hommes; **the plane is manned by a pilot and a navigator** l'équipage de l'avion consiste en un pilote et un navigateur; **was the spaceship manned?** y avait-il des hommes à bord du vaisseau spatial?; **the machines had to be manned all the time** il fallait quelqu'un continuellement pour assurer le fonctionnement des machines

▸▸**m. Friday** *(servant)* fidèle serviteur *m*; *(office worker)* = employé *m* de bureau affecté à des tâches diverses

---

Note that the French expression **homme du monde** doesn't mean **man of the world**; it means a man who belongs to high society.

-man [mæn] **SUFF** **two-m. toboggan** luge *f* à deux places; **five-m. crew** équipage *m* de cinq hommes

manacle ['mænək(ə)l] **N** *(usu pl)* **manacles** menottes *fpl*

VT mettre ou passer les menottes à; **manacled to the wall** attaché au mur par des menottes

manage ['mænɪdʒ] **VT 1** *(run) (company, factory, project, bank etc)* diriger; *(estate)* diriger, gérer; *(the economy, one's money, resources, account)* gérer; **to m. sb's affairs** gérer les affaires de qn; **to m. a pop singer/football team** être (le) manager d'un chanteur de pop/d'une équipe de football

2 *(deal with) (situation)* gérer; **to know how to m. sb** savoir prendre qn; **she finds it difficult to m. her pupils** elle a du mal à tenir ses élèves

3 *(be able to)* **to m. to do sth** *(succeed)* réussir ou arriver ou parvenir à faire qch; *Iron (contrive)* s'arranger pour faire qch, réussir à faire qch; **we managed to persuade her** nous avons réussi à la persuader; **I think I can m. it** je crois que je peux le faire ou que je peux y arriver; **I shall never m. to learn it** jamais je n'arriverai à l'apprendre; **how do you m. not to dirty your hands?** comment faites-vous pour ne pas vous salir les mains?; **I hope she'll m. to be there** j'espère qu'elle pourra venir

4 *(be able to produce, consume, carry etc)* **£100 is the most that I can m.** je ne peux pas aller au-delà de 100 livres; **can you m. some more pudding?** vous reprendrez bien encore du dessert?; **I can't m. Friday** *(I'm not free)* je ne peux pas me libérer vendredi; **can you m. dinner on Thursday?** est-ce que vous pouvez venir dîner jeudi?; **I can't m. three suitcases** je ne peux pas porter trois valises; **can you m. the stairs?** *(carrying so much, being elderly etc)* est-ce que tu arrives à monter les escaliers?

VI se débrouiller; **she manages well** elle se débrouille bien; **can you m.?** *(with all those suitcases etc)* tu y arriveras?; **we shall m. better next time** nous nous débrouillerons mieux la prochaine fois; **he'll m. all right** il se débrouillera; **we could just m.** *(financially)* on avait juste de quoi vivre; **I don't know how I would have managed without you** je ne sais pas comment j'aurais fait sans toi

manageable ['mænɪdʒəb(ə)l] **ADJ 1** *(thing, vehicle)* maniable; *(hair)* facile à coiffer; **the smaller suitcase is a more m. size** la plus petite valise est plus maniable **2** *(person, child)* facile, docile **3** *(undertaking)* faisable **4** *(company)* gérable

managed ['mænɪdʒd] **ADJ**
▸▸*Fin* **m. currency** devise *f* contrôlée, monnaie *f* dirigée; *Fin* **m. fund** *(in insurance)* fonds *m* géré

management ['mænɪdʒmənt] **N 1** *(action)* *(of company, factory, project etc)* gestion *f*, direction *f*, *(of economy, money, resources)* gestion *f*; **business m.** gestion des affaires; **bad m.** mauvaise gestion; *Com* **under new m.** *(change of ownership)* changement *m* de propriétaire; *(change of manager)* nouvelle direction; **m. by exception** direction par exceptions; **m. by objectives** gestion par objectifs **2** *(with sing or pl verb)* *(managers, employers)* administration *f*, direction *f*, senior **m.** les cadres *mpl* supérieurs, la Direction; **representatives of m. and unions** les représentants du patronat et des syndicats

▸▸**m. accountant** contrôleur, -euse de gestion; **m. accounts** comptes *mpl* de gestion; *Fin* **m. buy-in** apport *m* de gestion; *Br Fin* **m. buy-out** rachat *m* d'une société par la direction; **m. committee** comité *m* de direction; **m. consultancy** *(activity)* conseil *m* en gestion d'entreprise; *(firm)* cabinet *m* (de) conseil; **m. consultant** conseiller, -ère en ou de gestion (d'entreprise); **m. contract** contrat *m* de gestion; **m. fee** honoraires *mpl* d'un consultant; **m. function** fonction *f* d'encadrement; **m. information system** système *m* intégré de gestion; **m. report** rapport *m* de gestion; *(accounts statistics)* tableau *m* de bord; **m. skills** qualités *fpl* de gestionnaire; **m. studies** études *fpl* de gestion; **m. style** mode *m* de gestion; **m. summary** résumé *m* managérial; **m. team** équipe *f* dirigeante; **m. technique** méthode *f* de gestion; **m. tool** outil *m* de gestion

manager ['mænɪdʒər] **N 1** *(of bank, company, factory, project)* directeur *m*; *(of café, bar, store)* gérant *m*, patron *m*; *(of department in large store)* chef *m*; *(of funds, money)* gestionnaire *m*; *(of assets)* administrateur *m*; *(of estate)* régisseur *m*; *(of entertainer, rock band, football team etc)* manager *m*; *Pol (of political party)* chef, dirigeant *m*; **I want to see the m.!** je veux voir le responsable!; **she's a good m.** *(of home etc)* elle est bonne ménagère **2** *Comput (of disk etc)* gestionnaire *m*

manageress [mænɪdʒə'res] **N** *(of bank, company, factory, project)* directrice *f*, *(of café, bar, shop)* gérante *f*, patronne *f*

managerial [mænɪ'dʒɪərɪəl] **ADJ** directorial, -aux; *(position)* de commande; **m. experience** expérience *f* de la direction; **at m. level** au niveau de la direction
▸▸**m. skills** qualités *fpl* de gestionnaire; **m. staff** cadres *mpl*, encadrement *m*

managing ['mænɪdʒɪŋ] **ADJ** directeur, -trice
▸▸**m. director** directeur, -trice général(e), P-DG *m*; **m. editor** rédacteur, -trice en chef

manatee [mænə'ti:] **N** *Zool* lamantin *m*

man-bites-dog story [mænbaɪts'dɒg] **N** *Journ Hum* = article *m* dont le contenu va à l'encontre des idées reçues

Manc [mæŋk] **N** *Br Fam (Mancunian)* = natif *m* de la ville de Manchester

Manchuria [mæn'tʃʊərɪə] **N** Mandchourie *f*

Manchurian [mæn'tʃʊərɪən] **ADJ** mandchou
N Mandchou, -oue

Mancunian [mæn'kju:nɪən] **N** habitant, -ante de Manchester; *(by birth)* originaire *mf* de Manchester
ADJ de Manchester

M&A [emən'eɪ] **N** *Fin (abbr* **mergers and acquisitions)** fusions et acquisitions *fpl*

Mandarin ['mændərɪn] **N** *Ling* mandarin *m*
▸▸**M. Chinese** mandarin

mandarin ['mændərɪn] **N 1** *(in Chinese history)*, *Fig* mandarin *m* **2** *(fruit)* mandarine *f*, *(tree)* mandarinier *m* **3** *(colour)* mandarine *f inv*
▸▸**m. collar** col *m* Mao; *Orn* **m. duck** *(canard m)* mandarin

mandate ['mændeɪt] **N 1** *(instructions)*, *Pol* mandat *m*; **the government has a m. to ...** le gouvernement est mandaté pour ...; **his superior had given him a m. to ...** son supérieur lui a donné mandat pour ... **2** *(territory)* pays *m* sous mandat
▸▸*Fin* **m. form** lettre *f* de signatures autorisées

mandatory ['mændətərɪ] **ADJ** *(obligatory)* obligatoire; *Law* mandataire
▸▸**m. writ** mandement *m*

mandible ['mændɪb(ə)l] **N 1** *(of insect)* mandibule *f* **2** *(of vertebrate)* mâchoire *f* inférieure

mandolin(e) [mændə'lɪn] **N** *Mus* mandoline *f*

mandrake ['mændreɪk] **N** *(plant)* mandragore *f*

mandrel, mandril ['mændrəl] **N** *Tech* mandrin *m*, arbre *m* (de tour)

mandrill ['mændrɪl] **N** *(ape)* mandrill *m*

mane [meɪn] **N** *(of horse, lion etc)*, *Fig* crinière *f*

man-eater, *pl* man-eaters N **1** *(animal)* mangeur *m* d'hommes **2** *Fig (woman)* mangeuse *f* d'hommes

man-eating ADJ **1** *(animal)* mangeur d'hommes **2** *(tribe etc)* anthropophage, cannibale
▶▶m. shark requin *m* mangeur d'hommes

maneuver, maneuverable *etc Am* = **manoeuvre etc, manoeuvrable** *etc*

manful ['mænfʊl] ADJ vaillant, courageux

manfully ['mænfʊlɪ] ADV vaillamment, courageusement; **he was struggling m. with the suitcases/his second steak** il se démenait vaillamment avec les valises/son deuxième steak

manganese [mæŋgə'niːz] N *Miner, Chem* manganèse *m*
▶▶m. steel acier *m* au manganèse

mange [meɪndʒ] N *Vet* gale *f*

mangel-wurzel ['mæŋg(ə)l'wɜːz(ə)l] N betterave *f* fourragère

manger ['meɪndʒər] N *Agr* mangeoire *f*, auge *f* d'écurie; *Bible* crèche *f*

mangle[1] ['mæŋg(ə)l] N *(for clothes)* essoreuse *f* (à rouleaux)
VT *(clothes)* essorer *(dans une essoreuse à rouleaux)*

mangle[2] VT **1** *(mutilate) (person, body)* mutiler; *(piece of meat)* charcuter, massacrer; **their bodies were horribly mangled** leurs corps ont été atrocement mutilés **2** *Fig (quotation)* estropier; *(text)* mutiler, dénaturer

mango, *pl* mangoes ['mæŋgəʊ, -əʊz] N *(fruit)* mangue *f*, *(tree)* manguier *m*
▶▶m. chutney = condiment *m* à la mangue

mangrove ['mæŋgrəʊv] N manglier *m*, palétuvier *m*
▶▶m. swamp mangrove *f*, **m. tree** manglier, palétuvier

mangy ['meɪndʒɪ] ADJ **1** *(dog)* galeux **2** *Fam (furniture etc)* minable, miteux

manhandle ['mænhænd(ə)l] VT **1** *(treat roughly) (person)* brutaliser, malmener **2** *(move by hand) (object)* transporter à la force des bras; *(goods etc)* manutentionner; **they manhandled the piano into position** ils ont poussé le piano pour le mettre à sa place

manhole ['mænhəʊl] N *(for drain)* trou *m* de visite, regard *m*; *(for boiler)* trou d'homme
▶▶m. cover, m. lid plaque *f* d'égout

manhood ['mænhʊd] N **1** *(maturity)* âge *m* d'homme, âge viril; **to reach m.** devenir un homme; **he had barely reached m.** il avait à peine atteint l'âge adulte **2** *(masculinity)* virilité *f*; **he felt he had to prove his m.** il pensait devoir prouver sa virilité **3** *(men)* les hommes *mpl*; **British m.** les hommes britanniques **4** *Hum Fam (genitals)* bijoux *mpl* de famille

man-hour N *Ind etc* heure *f* de travail, *Spec* heure-homme *f*, *pl* heures-hommes

manhunt ['mænhʌnt] N chasse *f* à l'homme

mania ['meɪnɪə] N **1** *(passion)* passion *f*, folie *f*, *Pej* manie *f* (**for sth** de qch); **to have a m. for sth** avoir une passion pour qch, avoir la passion *ou* la folie/la manie de qch; **to have a m. for stamp-collecting** avoir la folie des timbres **2** *Psy* manie *f*, **suicidal m.** folie *f* du suicide

maniac ['meɪnɪæk] N *Psy* maniaque *mf*, *Fam (wild person)* fou, *f* folle, cinglé, -ée; *Fam* **a m. driver** un fou du volant; **to drive like a m.** conduire comme un fou; *Fam* **a soccer m.** un fou de football

Note that the French word **maniaque** is most commonly used to describe someone who is obsessive about order and tidiness.

maniacal [mə'naɪək(ə)l] ADJ *(laughter etc)* dément

manic ['mænɪk] ADJ *Psy (wish etc)* qui tient de la folie; *Fig* **she made m. gestures** elle faisait des gestes désordonnés; **at a m. speed** à une vitesse folle
▶▶m. depression psychose *f* maniaco-dépressive

manic-depressive ADJ, N *Psy* maniaco-dépressif, -ive

manicure ['mænɪkjʊər] N soin *m* des mains; **to have a m.** se faire faire les mains et les ongles; **to give sb a m.** faire les mains et les ongles de qn; **how much is a m.?** combien coûte un soin des mains et des ongles?
VT *(person)* soigner les mains de, faire les mains et les ongles à; **to m. one's nails** se faire les ongles; **manicured hands** des mains très soignées
▶▶m. set trousse *f* de manucure

manicurist ['mænɪkjʊərɪst] N manucure *mf*

manifest ['mænɪfest] ADJ manifeste, évident; **to make sth m.** rendre qch évident; **this makes it m. that ...** cela prouve que ...
N *Naut, Aviat (document)* manifeste *m*
VT **1** *(display)* manifester, témoigner; **to m. itself** *(of symptom, talent etc)* se manifester, se révéler **2** *Naut (goods)* faire figurer sur le manifeste

manifestation [mænɪfes'teɪʃən] N manifestation *f*

Note that the French word **manifestation** also means **demonstration**.

manifestly ['mænɪfestlɪ] ADV manifestement

manifesto [mænɪ'festəʊ] N *Pol etc* manifeste *m*

manifold ['mænɪfəʊld] ADJ *(numerous)* multiple, nombreux
N *Tech* tubulure *f*, collecteur *m*

manikin ['mænɪkɪn] N = **mannikin**

Manila [mə'nɪlə] N Manille

manil(l)a [mə'nɪlə] ADJ
▶▶m. envelope enveloppe *f* en papier kraft; **m. paper** papier *m* kraft; **m. rope** (cordage en) manille *f*

manioc ['mænɪɒk] N **1** *Bot* manioc *m* **2** *Culin* cassave *f*

manipulate [mə'nɪpjʊleɪt] VT **1** *(handle, operate etc) (object)* manipuler; *(mechanical device)* manœuvrer, actionner; *(lever, pedal)* actionner; *Med* **to m. bones** faire des manipulations **2** *Pej (person)* manipuler; *(accounts)* truquer

manipulation [mənɪpjʊ'leɪʃən] N **1** *(of object)* manipulation *f* **2** *Pej (of person)* manipulation *f*, *(of accounts)* trucage *m*

manipulative [mə'nɪpjʊlətɪv] ADJ manipulateur, -trice

manipulator [mə'nɪpjʊleɪtər] N **1** *Pej* tripoteur, -euse, manipulateur, -trice **2** *(of machine etc)* manipulateur, -trice

Man(it) *abbr* Manitoba

Manitoba [mænɪ'təʊbə] N Manitoba *m*

mankind [mæn'kaɪnd] N **1** *(the human race)* le genre humain, l'humanité *f*, l'espèce *f* humaine **2** *(men)* les hommes *mpl*

manky ['mæŋkɪ] ADJ *Br Fam* cradingue

manlike ['mænlaɪk] ADJ *(resembling a human)* humain; *(resembling a man)* masculin; *(of woman)* masculin, *Pej* hommasse

manliness ['mænlɪnɪs] N virilité *f*, caractère *m* viril

manly ['mænlɪ] ADJ *(sport, activity)* d'homme, masculin; *(behaviour, character)* mâle, viril

man-made ADJ *(fibre, fabric, product)* synthétique; *(lake, beach)* artificiel; **m. attrac-**

tion *(in tourism)* centre *m* d'intérêt 'non-naturel'; **m. desert** désert *m* créé par l'homme; **m. laws** lois *fpl* faites par l'homme

manna ['mænə] N **1** *Bible etc* manne *f*, *Prov* **was m. from heaven** c'était un don du ciel **2** *Bot, Pharm etc* manne *f* du frêne

manned [mænd] ADJ *(spacecraft, flight)* habité; *see also* **man** VT

mannequin ['mænɪkɪn] N *(person, dummy), Art* mannequin *m*

manner ['mænər] N **1** *(way, method, style)* manière *f*, façon *f* (**of doing sth** de faire qch); **the m. in which ...** la manière dont ...; **in a m. of speaking** en quelque sorte, dans un certain sens; *Gram* **adverb of m.** adverbe *m* de manière; **he does it (as if or as) to the m. born** il le fait comme s'il avait fait ça toute sa vie ‖VOIR GRAMMAIRE A21–2; B12‖
2 *(etiquette)* **manners** manières *fpl*, **(good) manners** bonnes manières, savoir-vivre *m*, politesse *f*, **bad manners** mauvaises manières, manque *m* de savoir-vivre, manque d'éducation; **it's bad manners to stare** il est mal élevé de dévisager les gens; **she has bad table manners** elle ne sait pas se tenir à table; *Fig* **I'll teach you some manners, young man!** *(punish for rudeness)* je vais vous apprendre la politesse, jeune homme!; **where are your manners?** *(to child)* en voilà des manières!; **he's got no manners** il est très mal élevé; **I'm forgetting my manners, would you like some tea?** mais où avais-je la tête?, je ne vous ai pas proposé de thé!
3 *(variety)* espèce *f*, sorte *f*; **all m. of people/things** toutes sortes de gens/choses; *Lit* **what m. of person is she?** quel genre de femme est-ce?; **by no m. of means, not by any m. of means** absolument pas; **they're not rich by any m. of means** ils ne sont absolument pas riches
4 *(attitude, behaviour)* façon *f* d'être; **I do not like his m.** je n'aime pas sa façon d'être; **she's got a very abrasive m.** elle est très acerbe
5 *Lit* **manners** *(customs of a people)* mœurs *fpl*, usages *mpl*

mannered ['mænəd] ADJ *Art, Liter* maniéré *m*; *Pej (person)* maniéré, affecté; *(style)* recherché, précieux

mannerism ['mænərɪz(ə)m] N *Pej (of person)* maniérisme *m*, affectation *f*, *(habit) (of writer etc)* tic *m*; *Art, Liter* maniérisme

mannerly ['mænəlɪ] ADJ poli, courtois

mannikin ['mænɪkɪn] N **1** *(small man)* petit homme *m*; *(dwarf)* nabot *m* **2** *Art, Med, Surg* mannequin *m*

mannish ['mænɪʃ] ADJ *(woman)* hommasse; **she has a m. voice** elle a une voix d'homme; **she looks m.** on dirait un homme

manoeuvrability, *Am* maneuverability [mænuːvrə'bɪlɪtɪ] N maniabilité *f*

manoeuvrable, *Am* maneuverable [mə'nuːvrəb(ə)l] ADJ *(plane, car etc)* manœuvrable, maniable

manoeuvre, *Am* maneuver [mə'nuːvər] N **1** *Mil, Naut etc (action)* manœuvre *f*, **manoeuvres** *(exercise)* manœuvres *fpl*, **troops on manoeuvres** troupes en manœuvres **2** *(action, remark)* manœuvre *f*, **a clever m.** une manœuvre habile; **there wasn't much room for m.** *(between cars etc)* il n'y avait pas beaucoup de place pour manœuvrer *ou* faire une manœuvre; *Fig* il y avait peu de marge de manœuvre; *Pej* **manoeuvres** *(plotting)* menées *fpl*, intrigues *fpl*
VT *Mil, Naut (army, fleet of ships)* manœuvrer, faire manœuvrer; **we manoeuvred the piano through the door** nous avons fait passer le piano par la porte; **she manoeuvred her car into the space** elle a garé sa voiture dans l'emplacement (en manœuvrant); *Fig*

to m. sb into a corner prendre qn au piège, *Fam* coincer qn

vi *Mil, Fig (of troops, politician etc)* manœuvrer; *Naut (of ship)* évoluer

manoeuvring, *Am* **maneuvering** [mə'nuːvrɪŋ] **N** *Mil* manœuvres *fpl*; *Pej (plotting)* menées *fpl*, intrigues *fpl*

man-of-war, *pl* **men-of-war N 1** *Naut Arch* vaisseau *m ou* bâtiment *m* de guerre **2** *(Portuguese)* **m.** *(jellyfish)* physalie *f*, galère *f*

manometer [mæ'nɒmɪtər] **N** manomètre *m*

manor ['mænər] **N 1** *Hist (estate)* seigneurie *f*, *(house)* manoir *m*; **the lord of the m.** le châtelain; **the lady of the m.** la châtelaine **2** *Br Sl (of police, criminal)* territoire *m*
▸▸ **m. house** manoir *m*

manorial [mə'nɔːrɪəl] **ADJ** *Hist* seigneurial, -aux

manpower ['mænpaʊər] **N** *Ind etc (labour)* main-d'œuvre *f*, *Mil* effectifs *mpl*
▸▸ **m. planning** planification *f* de la main-d'œuvre; **m. shortage** manque *m* de main-d'œuvre

manqué ['mɒŋkeɪ] **ADJ** *(placed after noun)* manqué

mansard ['mænsɑːd] **N** *Archit (roof)* toit *m* en mansarde
▸▸ **m. roof** toit en mansarde

manse [mæns] **N** *esp Scot Rel* presbytère *m*

manservant, *pl* **menservants** ['mænsɜːvənt, 'mensɜːvənts] **N** domestique *m*; *(personal)* valet *m* (de chambre)

mansion ['mænʃən] **N** *(in country)* château *m*, manoir *m*; *(in town)* hôtel *m* (particulier)
▸▸ **m. house** *(in country)* château, manoir; *(in town)* hôtel (particulier); **the M. House** = la résidence officielle du maire de Londres

mansize(d) ['mænsaɪz(d)] **ADJ** de la grandeur d'un homme; *Fig (handkerchief etc)* pour homme; *(helping of food)* gros, copieux

manslaughter ['mænslɔːtər] **N** *Law (through negligence)* homicide *m* involontaire *ou* par imprudence

mantel ['mænt(ə)l] **N = mantelpiece**

mantelpiece ['mænt(ə)lpiːs] **N** *(shelf)* dessus *m ou* tablette *f* de cheminée; **on the m.** sur la cheminée

mantilla [mæn'tɪlə] **N** *(clothing)* mantille *f*

mantis ['mæntɪs] **N** *(insect)* mante *f*

mantle ['mænt(ə)l] **N** *(covering) (of lava, snow)* manteau *m*; *(of gas lamp)* manchon *m*; *Arch (cloak) (of woman)* mante *f*, pèlerine *f*, *Fig* **to take on the m. of office** assumer les responsabilités qui incombent au poste

man-to-man **ADJ, ADV** *(talk)* d'homme à homme
▸▸ *Ftbl etc* **m. marking** marquage *m* individuel

mantrap ['mæntræp] **N** piège *m* à hommes

manual ['mænjʊəl] **ADJ** *(work, worker etc)* manuel
N 1 *(handbook)* manuel *m* **2** *(car)* voiture *f* à embrayage manuel **3** *(mode of operation)* **to be on m.** être sur commande manuelle **4** *Mus (of organ)* clavier *m*
▸▸ **m. dexterity** dextérité *f*, habileté *f* manuelle; *Aut* **m. gearbox, m. gears** boîte *f* de vitesses mécanique, boîte manuelle *ou* mécanique; *Aut* **m. transmission** transmission *f* mécanique; **m. typewriter** machine *f* à écrire mécanique

manually ['mænjʊəlɪ] **ADV** manuellement, à la main

manufacture [mænjʊ'fæktʃər] **N 1** *(of industrial product)* fabrication *f*, *(of cars, computers)* construction *f*, *(of clothing)* confection *f*, *of Italian m.* de fabrication italienne **2 manufactures** *(products)* produits *mpl* manufacturés

VT 1 *(industrial product)* fabriquer; *(car, aircraft, computer)* construire; *(clothing etc)* confectionner; **manufactured product** produit *m* manufacturé **2** *Fig (invent)* inventer (de toutes pièces); **to m. an opportunity to do sth** inventer une occasion de faire qch

manufacturer [mænjʊ'fæktʃərər] **N** fabricant, -ante; *(of cars, aircraft, computers)* constructeur *m*; **send it back to the manufacturers** renvoyez-le au fabricant
▸▸ **m.'s agent** agent *m* exclusif; *Mktg* **m. brand** marque *f* de fabricant; **m.'s instructions** notice *f* du constructeur; **m.'s liability** responsabilité *f* du fabricant; **m.'s recommended price** prix *m* conseillé par le fabricant

manufacturing [mænjʊ'fæktʃərɪŋ] **ADJ** industriel; **the country's m. industry** le secteur industriel du pays
N fabrication *f*; **the decline of m.** le déclin de l'industrie manufacturière
▸▸ **m. company** entreprise *f* industrielle; **m. costs** frais *mpl* de fabrication; **m. defect** vice *m ou* défaut *m* de fabrication; **m. licence** licence *f* de fabrication; **m. plant** usine *f* de fabrication; **m. rights** droits *mpl* de fabrication

manure [mə'njʊər] *Agr* **N** engrais *m*; **farmyard m.** fumier *m* (d'étable); **chemical m.** engrais chimique; **liquid m.** purin *m*
VT *(soil)* engraisser; *(with farmyard manure)* fumer
▸▸ **m. heap** tas *m* de fumier

manuscript ['mænjʊskrɪpt] **N** manuscrit *m*; **in m.** *(book)* sous forme de manuscrit
ADJ manuscrit, écrit à la main

Manx [mæŋks] **ADJ** de l'île de Man
N *Ling* mannois *m*
NPL the M. *(people)* les habitants *mpl* de l'île de Man
▸▸ **M. cat** chat *m* (sans queue) de l'île de Man

many ['menɪ] **ADJ** *(comp* **more,** *superl* **most)** un grand nombre de, beaucoup de, de nombreux, bien des; **m. people** beaucoup *ou* un grand nombre de gens; **m. times** bien des fois, de nombreuses fois; **in m. cases** dans bien des cas, dans de nombreux cas; **in m. ways** de bien des façons; **for m. years** pendant de longues années *ou* de nombreuses années; **m. and varied** nombreux et très variés; **one of his m. acquaintances** une de ses nombreuses relations; **like so m. others** comme tant d'autres; **he told me in so m. words that …** il m'a fait comprendre que …; **too m. people** trop de monde; **a few** *(drinks)* **too m.** quelques verres de trop; **how m. times?** combien de fois?; **I have as m. books as you** j'ai autant de livres que vous; **four accidents in as m. days** quatre accidents en quatre jours; **a good m. things** pas mal de choses; **m. a night** *or* **m.'s the night I've done that** j'ai fait ça maintes nuits; **there are only so m. ways you can cook chicken** il n'y a pas une infinité de façons de préparer le poulet; *Prov* **m. hands make light work** à plusieurs, l'ouvrage avance vite **VOIR GRAMMAIRE A5**
PRON beaucoup, un grand nombre; **not (very)** pas beaucoup; **m. of us** beaucoup *ou* un grand nombre d'entre nous; **how m.?** combien?; **as m. as you like** autant que vous voulez; **they tried to bring back as m. as possible** ils ont essayé d'en rapporter le plus possible; **as m. again, as m. more, twice as m.** deux fois plus; **too m.** trop; **there are too m.** il y en a trop; **so m.** tant
NPL the m. la foule, la masse; **the sacrifices made by the few for the m.** les sacrifices faits par la minorité pour la masse

many-coloured **ADJ** multicolore

man-year N année-personne *f*, *pl* années-personnes

many-sided **ADJ 1** *(figure)* à plusieurs côtés **2** *(problem)* complexe, compliqué **3** *(person)* aux talents variés

Maoist ['maʊɪst] **ADJ, N** *Pol* maoïste *mf*

Maori ['maʊrɪ] **ADJ** maori
N 1 Maori, -ie **2** *Ling* maori *m*

map [mæp] **N 1** *(plan)* carte *f* (géographique); *(of town, underground, building)* plan *m*; *(of keyboard)* schéma *m*; *Fig* **it's off the m.** c'est à l'autre bout du monde; *Fig* **to put a town on the m.** mettre une ville en vedette, faire parler d'une ville; *Fig* **this will put us on the m.** ça va nous faire de la publicité; **the village was wiped off the m.** le village a été rayé de la carte; **he's a good m. reader** il sait bien lire les cartes *ou* les plans **2** *Am Sl (face)* tronche *f*, trombine *f*
VT (-pp-) 1 *(region etc)* dresser une carte de **2** *Math* faire un graphique de **3** *Fig (plot) (progress etc)* consigner
▸▸ **m. maker** cartographe *mf*, *Aut* **m. pocket** vide-poche *m*, *pl* vide-poches, bac *m* à cartes; **m. reading** lecture *f* de carte; **m. reference** référence *f* topographique, coordonnées *fpl*
▸ **map out VT SEP** *(route)* tracer; *(programme)* dresser, élaborer; **his life had already been mapped out for him** sa vie était déjà toute tracée

maple ['meɪp(ə)l] **N 1** *(tree)* érable *m* **2** *(wood)* (bois *m* d')érable *m*
▸▸ **m. leaf** feuille *f* d'érable; **m. sugar** sucre *m* d'érable; **m. syrup** sirop *m* d'érable; **m. tree** érable

mapping ['mæpɪŋ] **N 1** *(of region)* établissement *m* d'une carte **2** *Comput (in network)* unité *f* logique **3** *Mktg* mapping *m*

Mar *abbr* **March**

mar [mɑːr] **VT (-rr-)** *(pleasure, performance)* gâter, gâcher; *(joy)* troubler; *(beauty of landscape, scenery)* gâcher, gâter, déparer; *(person's beauty)* déparer, gâcher; **to make** *or* **m. sb** faire la fortune ou la ruine de qn

marabou ['mærəbuː] **N** *(bird)* marabout *m*

maraca [mə'rækə] **N** *Mus* maraca *f*

maraschino [mærəs'kiːnəʊ] **N** marasquin *m*
▸▸ **m. cherry** cerise *f* au marasquin

marathon ['mærəθən] **N** *(race)* marathon *m*; *Fig* **m. meeting** conférence-marathon *f*, **m. speech** marathon oratoire
▸▸ **m. race** marathon; **m. runner** coureur, -euse de marathon, marathonien, -ienne

maraud [mə'rɔːd] **VI** marauder, être en maraude; **to go marauding** partir en maraude

marauder [mə'rɔːdər] **N** maraudeur, -euse

marauding [mə'rɔːdɪŋ] **ADJ** maraudeur, -euse; **m. hordes of looters** des hordes de pillards en maraude

marble ['mɑːb(ə)l] **N 1** *(rock)* marbre *m*; **m. floor** sol *m* de *ou* en marbre; **m. statue** statue *f* de marbre **2** *(glass ball)* bille *f*, **to play marbles** jouer aux billes; *Fig Fam* **she's still got all her marbles** elle a encore toute sa tête; *Fig Fam* **to lose one's marbles** perdre la boule **3** *Art (object)* marbre *m*
VT *Tech (in bookbinding)* marbrer, raciner
▸▸ **m. cake** gâteau *m* marbré; **m. cutter** *(person)* marbrier *m*; **m. quarry** marbrière *f*, carrière *f* de marbre

marbled ['mɑːb(ə)ld] **ADJ** marbré

marbling ['mɑːblɪŋ] **N** marbrure(s) *f(pl)*

March [mɑːtʃ] **N** **VOIR GRAMMAIRE A81–2; B60–2** mars *m*; **in M.** en mars, au mois de mars; **(on) the first/the seventh of M.** le premier/le sept mars

march [mɑːtʃ] **N 1** *(by soldiers etc)* marche *f*, **m. in step** marche au pas; **on the m.** en marche; *Fig* **the middle classes are on the m.** la classe moyenne s'est mobilisée; **it is two days' m. from here** c'est à deux jours de marche d'ici **2** *(pace)* pas *m*, allure *f*; **quick m.** pas cadencé; **slow m.** pas de parade **3** *(demonstration)* marche *f*, manifestation *f*; **to go on a m.** participer à une marche **4** *(progress) (of time etc)* marche *f*, progrès *m*; **to be overtaken by the m. of events** être dépassé par les événements **5** *Mus* marche *f*

VI *Mil etc* marcher; **to m. off** se mettre en marche; **he marched off in a rage** il est parti, fou de rage; **to m. by** *or* **past (sb)** défiler (devant qn); **quick m.!** en avant, marche!; **they marched to the town hall to protest** ils ont manifesté jusqu'à la mairie; **time marches on** *(I ought to go)* l'heure tourne; **she marched into his office** elle est entrée dans son bureau d'un pas décidé

VT *(troops)* faire marcher au pas; **he was marched off to prison** il a été emmené en prison

▸▸ **m. past** défilé *m*

marcher ['mɑːtʃər] **N** *(demonstrator)* manifestant, -ante *f*; **peace m.** manifestant, -ante pour la paix

marching ['mɑːtʃɪŋ] **N** *Mil etc* marche *f*; **in m. order** en tenue de campagne; *(in formation)* en formation de marche;
▸▸ *Mil* **m. orders** feuille *f* de route; *Fig Fam* **to give sb his/her m. orders** mettre qn à la porte

marchioness ['mɑːʃənes] **N** marquise *f*

mare¹ [meər] **N 1** *(animal)* jument *f* **2** *Br Fam Pej (woman)* grognasse *f*; **you silly m!** espèce d'andouille!
▸▸ **m.'s nest** illusion *f*

mare² **N** *Br Fam (nightmare)* cauchemar *m*; **it was a total m.!** c'était un vrai cauchemar!

margarine [mɑːdʒəˈriːn] **N** margarine *f*

margarita [mɑːɡəˈriːtə] **N** *(drink)* margarita *f*

marge [mɑːdʒ] **N** *Br Fam* margarine *f*

margin ['mɑːdʒɪn] **N 1** *(on paper, page etc)* marge *f*; **to write sth in the m.** écrire qch dans la marge; **there were some notes in the m.** il y avait quelques notes dans la marge; **to set the margins** marger; *(action)* pose *f* de marges
2 *(edge)* bord *m*; *(of forest)* lisière *f*; *(of lake etc)* bord, rive *f*; **on the margin(s) of society** en marge de la société
3 *Com, Fin* marge *f*; *St Exch* acompte *m* *(versé à un courtier)*; *Com* **the margins are very tight** les marges sont très réduites; *Com* **to have a low/high m.** avoir une faible/forte marge; *Com* **we make a 10% m.** nous faisons 10% de marge; **to win by a narrow m.** *(in race etc)* gagner de justesse; **to beat sb by a m. of 20 seconds** battre qn de 20 secondes; **to win by an enormous m.** gagner haut la main; **the election was won by a wide m.** ils ont remporté les élections avec une majorité confortable; **she won the election by a m. of 26 votes** elle a gagné les élections à 26 voix près; **a m. of error** une marge d'erreur; **there is little m. for error** la marge d'erreur est très faible
▸▸ *St Exch* **m. call** appel *m* de couverture *ou* de marge *ou* de garantie; *St Exch* **m. default** défaut *m* de couverture; *Typ* **m. release** déclenche-marge *m inv*; *St Exch* **m. requirement** niveau *m* de dépôt requis, couverture *f* (boursière) obligatoire; *Typ* **m. setting** marge; *(action)* pose *f* de marges; *Typ* **m. stop** margeur *m*

marginal ['mɑːdʒɪn(ə)l] **ADJ 1** *(role, activity)* marginal, -aux; **m. case** cas *m* limite **2** *(note)* marginal, -aux, en marge **3** *(slight) (improvement, increase etc)* léger; **of m. interest/importance** d'un intérêt/d'une importance limité(e); **of m. use** d'un usage restreint **4** *Br Pol (seat, constituency)* à majorité précaire
N *Br Pol* siège *m ou* circonscription *f* à majorité précaire

▸▸ *Econ* **m. analysis** analyse *f* marginale; **m. land(s)** terre(s) *f(pl)* pauvre(s); **m. utility** utilité *f* marginale

marginalization [mɑːdʒɪnəlaɪˈzeɪʃən] **N** marginalisation *f*

marginalize ['mɑːdʒɪnəlaɪz] **VT** marginaliser

marginally ['mɑːdʒɪn(ə)lɪ] **ADV** *(slightly)* légèrement

marguerite [mɑːɡəˈriːt] **N** *(plant)* grande marguerite *f*, marguerite des champs

marigold ['mærɪɡəʊld] **N** *(plant)* souci *m*; **African m.** rose *f* d'Inde; **French m.** œillet *m* d'Inde

marihuana, marijuana [mærɪˈhwɑːnə] **N** marijuana *f*

marina [məˈriːnə] **N** port *m* de plaisance, marina *f*

marinade¹ [mærɪˈneɪd] **N** *Culin* marinade *f*

marinade², marinate ['mærɪneɪd, -eɪt] **VT** *Culin* (faire) mariner

marine [məˈriːn] **ADJ** *(life, biology)* marin
N 1 *Mil, Naut (soldier)* ≃ fusilier *m* marin; *Br* **the Royal Marines,** *Am* **the Am M. Corps** ≃ les fusiliers marins; *Fam* **(go) tell it to the marines!** allez raconter ça ailleurs *ou* à d'autres! **2** *Am* **merchant** *or* **mercantile m.** marine *f* marchande
▸▸ **m. architect** ingénieur *m* des constructions navales; **m. artist** peintre *m* de marines; **m. bill of lading** connaissement *m* maritime; **m. engineering** génie *m* maritime; **m. insurance** assurance *f* maritime; **m. insurance policy** police *f* d'assurance maritime; **m. risk** risque *m* maritime

mariner ['mærɪnər] **N** *Naut, Old-fashioned, Lit* marin *m*

marionette [mærɪəˈnet] **N** marionnette *f* à fils

marital ['mærɪt(ə)l] **ADJ** *(relating to marriage)* conjugal, -aux, matrimonial, -aux
▸▸ *Admin* **m. obligations** obligations *fpl* conjugales; **m. status** situation *f* de famille

maritime ['mærɪtaɪm] **ADJ** *(nation, law)* maritime
▸▸ **m. climate** climat *m* maritime

marjoram ['mɑːdʒərəm] **N** *Bot, Culin* marjolaine *f*

Mark [mɑːk] **N** Marc *m*

MARK¹ [mɑːk]

N marque **1, 2, 4** ▪ trace **1, 2** ▪ signe **3** ▪ but **5** ▪ cible **5** ▪ note **6** ▪ série **8**	
VT marquer **1, 4–6** ▪ corriger **3** ▪ célébrer **5**	

N 1 *(scratch, stain etc)* marque *f*, trace *f*
2 *(trace) (of suffering etc)* trace *f*, marque *f*; **to make one's m.** *(succeed)* se faire un nom *ou* une réputation; **he made his m.** *(because he couldn't write)* il a fait une croix; **years of imprisonment had left their m. on him** ses années de captivité avaient laissé des traces
3 *(sign, proof)* signe *m*; **as a m. of respect** en signe de respect
4 *(reference on instrument etc)* marque *f*, repère *m*; *Fam* **he's not up to the m.** *(good enough)* il n'est pas à la hauteur; *Br Fam* **I'm not feeling up to the m.** je ne suis pas dans mon assiette
5 *(target for shooting etc)* cible *f*; *(objective)* but *m*; **unemployment has passed the three million m.** le nombre des chômeurs a passé la barre des trois millions; *Fam* **an easy m.** *(person)* une dupe; *Fig* **to hit the m.** toucher en plein dans le mille; *Fig* **to miss the m.** mettre à côté
6 *Sch (out of twenty etc)* point *m*; *(overall grade)* note *f*; **to give sb/sth marks out of**

ten/twenty noter qn/qch sur dix/vingt; **to get good marks** avoir de bonnes notes; **she got the highest m.** *or* **marks in the class** c'est elle qui a eu la *ou* les meilleure(s) note(s) de la classe; **full marks** *(in a specific subject)* note maximale; **full marks for effort!** bravo d'avoir essayé!; **bad m.** *or* **marks** mauvais point; **(you get) no marks for guessing who did it** tu n'auras aucun mal à deviner qui a fait ça
7 *Sport (starting line)* ligne *f* de départ; **on your marks! get set! go!** à vos marques! prêts! partez!; **to be quick off the m.** *(in race)* démarrer vite; *(to understand)* avoir l'esprit vif; **you were quick off the m.** *(in doing sth)* tu n'as pas perdu de temps; **to be slow off the m.** *(in race)* prendre un mauvais départ; *(to understand)* être long à la détente; **you were too slow off the m.** *(in doing sth)* tu as mis trop de temps
8 *Ind, Mil (of machine etc)* série *f*; **m. II/III** série II/III
9 *(assay)* **m.** *(on gold, silver)* poinçon *m* de garantie
10 *Culin (gas)* **m. 4** thermostat *m* 4
11 *Sl (victim, target)* pigeon *f*, poire *f*
VT 1 *(put mark on)* (linen, silverware, cards etc) marquer; *(goods)* estampiller; *Tech (jewellery etc)* signer; **her towels were marked with her initials** ses serviettes de bain portaient ses initiales; **face marked by** *or* **with smallpox** visage marqué par la petite vérole; **his face was marked with suffering** son visage était marqué par la souffrance
2 *Com* **to m. (the price of) an article** mettre le prix à un article; *St Exch* **to m. stock** coter des valeurs; *St Exch* **to m. to market** comptabiliser au prix de marché
3 *Sch (homework)* corriger, noter; **to m. sth right/wrong** compter qch comme juste/faux; **to m. exam papers** noter *ou* corriger des copies (d'examen); **marked out of 10** noté sur 10
4 *(indicate)* marquer, indiquer; **to m. a place on the map** indiquer un lieu sur la carte; **stream that marks the boundary of the estate** ruisseau qui marque la limite de la propriété; **X marks the spot** X indique l'endroit; **this decision marks a change in policy** cette décision marque un changement de politique
5 *(show) (one's approval, dissatisfaction)* témoigner, montrer; *(the beat)* accentuer; **to m. time** *Mil* marquer le pas; *Fig* piétiner, faire du sur place, ne pas avancer; **to m. an era** faire époque; **to m. an anniversary** célébrer un anniversaire
6 *Sport, Ftbl etc (opponent)* marquer
7 *(characterize)* caractériser
8 *(pay attention to) (person, thing)* faire attention à; **..., m. you** ..., remarque; **m. what I say** faites bien attention à ce que je dis; **m. my words** c'est moi qui vous le dis
▸ **mark down VT SEP 1** *(write down)* relever
2 they had marked him down as a troublemaker ils l'avaient catalogué comme fauteur de troubles; **he was marked down for the post of ...** il avait été pressenti pour le poste de ...
3 *Com (goods)* baisser le prix de, *Spec* démarquer; **everything has been marked down to half price** tout a été réduit à moitié prix
4 *Sch (homework)* baisser la note de
▸ **mark in VT SEP** noter; *(area on map etc)* hachurer
▸ **mark off VT SEP 1** *(in surveying) (line, road)* jalonner; **to m. off a distance on the map** *(measure)* indiquer une distance sur la carte; **the route was marked off in 1 km sections** le trajet était divisé en tronçons d'un kilomètre
2 *(separate with fence etc) (area)* délimiter

3 *(distinguish)* **to m. sb off from sb** distinguer qn de qn
4 *(with a tick etc)* cocher
▸ **mark out** VT SEP **1** *(distinguish)* distinguer (**from** de); **he was marked out for promotion from ...** il était destiné à occuper un poste important dès ...
2 *(mark with lines) (cricket ground etc)* tracer les lignes de
▸ **mark up** VT SEP **1** *(write up)* noter, inscrire
2 *Com (goods)* augmenter le prix de, *Spec* majorer
3 *Sch (essay)* majorer la note de
4 *(text)* préparer, corriger

mark² N **1** *Formerly (German and Finnish currency)* mark *m* **2 convertible m.** *(Bosnian currency)* mark *m* convertible

markdown ['mɑːkdaʊn] N *Com* réduction *f*

marked [mɑːkt] ADJ **1 badly m. face** *(after accident)* visage balafré **2** *(difference, improvement etc)* marqué, *(très)* net *f* nette, *(très)* sensible; *(accent)* prononcé; **the change is becoming more m.** le changement s'accentue
▸▸ **m. card** carte *f* marquée; **m. man** homme *m* marqué; **he's a m. man** il est repéré; *(he's going to be killed)* c'est un homme mort; *Mktg* **m. price** prix *m* marqué

marked-down ADJ *Com* démarqué

markedly ['mɑːkɪdlɪ] ADV de façon marquée *ou* très nette *ou* très sensible; **m. better** nettement meilleur; **m. different** nettement *ou* sensiblement différent

marked-up ADJ *Com* majoré

marker ['mɑːkər] N **1** *Sch* correcteur, -trice; **he's a hard m.** il note sévèrement **2** *(pen)* marqueur *m*; *Ind, Tech (marking device)* marqueur; *(tool)* marquoir *m* **3** *(indicator)* jalon *m*, repère *m*; *(flag)* fanion *m*; *(stick)* piquet *m* d'alignement *ou* de jalonnement; *(for debt)* reconnaissance *f* de dettes; *(biological, genetic)* marqueur *m*; *Aviat etc* (radio)phare *m*, (radio)balise *f* **4** *Ftbl etc* marqueur, -euse
▸▸ *Aviat* **m. beacon** radiobalise *f*, *Naut* **m. buoy** bouée *f* de balisage; **m. pen** marqueur

market ['mɑːkɪt] N **1** *(collection of stalls)* marché *m*; *(large)* foire *f*; **cattle m.** foire aux bestiaux; **fish m.** marché aux poissons **2** *Com, Econ, St Exch* marché; **cotton m.** marché du coton; **to put one's flat on the m.** mettre son appartement en vente; **the most economical car on the m.** la voiture la plus économique du marché; **to come onto the m.** arriver sur le marché; **to take sth off the m.** retirer qch du marché; **to be in the m. for sth** *(of person)* être acheteur de qch; **to find a m. for sth** trouver un débouché *ou* des acheteurs pour qch; **there's no m. for these products** il n'y a pas de marché *ou* de demande pour ces produits, ces produits ne se vendent pas
VT *(-t-)* commercialiser
▸▸ **m. analysis** analyse *f* de marché; **m. analyst** analyste *mf* du marché; **m. appeal** attrait *m* commercial; **m. appraisal** évaluation *f* du marché; **m. behaviour** comportement *m* du marché; *St Exch* **m. capitalization** capitalisation *f* boursière; **m. challenger** challengeur *m*; **m. choice** choix *m* sur le marché; *(product preferred by market)* choix du marché; *St Exch* **m. commentator** chroniqueur *m* boursier; **m. competition** concurrence *f* du marché; **m. conditions** conditions *fpl* du marché; *St Exch* **m. crisis** choc *m* boursier; **m. day** jour *m* de marché; **m. demand** demande *f* du marché; **m. development** développement *m* du marché; **m. economy** économie *f* de marché *ou* libérale; **m. entry** lancement *m* sur le marché; **m. expansion** extension *f* de marché; **m. exploration** prospection *f* sur le marché; **m. exposure** exposition *f* sur le marché; **m. failure** défaillance *f* du marché; **m. fluctuation** mouvement *m* du

marché; **m. follower** suiveur *m* (sur le marché); **m. forces** les forces *fpl* du marché; **m. forecast** prévisions *fpl* du marché, pronostic *m* du marché; **m. gap** manque *m* sur le marché; *Br* **m. garden** jardin *m* maraîcher; *Br* **m. gardener** maraîcher, -ère; *Br* **m. gardening** culture *f* maraîchère; **m. growth** croissance *f* du marché; **m. indicator** indicateur *m* de marché; **m. intelligence** intelligence *f* marketing, information *f* commerciale; **m. leader** *(product)* premier produit *m* sur le marché; *(firm)* leader *m* du marché; *St Exch* **m. maker** mainteneur *m* ou teneur *m* du marché, intermédiaire *mf*; **m. mechanism** mécanisme *m* du marché; **m. minimum** *(base sales)* ventes *fpl* de base; *St Exch* **m. order** ordre *m* au mieux; **m. orientation** orientation *f* marché; **m. participant** intervenant, -ante *ou* acteur *m* sur le marché; **m. penetration** pénétration *f* du marché; **m. penetration pricing** tarification *f* de pénétration du marché; **m. pioneer** pionnier *m*; **m. place** *(market square)* place *f* du marché; *Econ* marché; **the products in the m. place** les produits sur le marché; **m. player** acteur de marché; **m. positioning** positionnement *m* sur le marché; **m. potential** *(of product)* potentiel *m* sur le marché; *(of market)* potentiel du marché; **m. power** pouvoir *m* d'un acheteur sur le marché; **m. price** *Com* prix *m* courant; *St Exch* cours *m* de (la) Bourse; *St Exch* **m. price list** mercuriale *f*; **m. prospects** perspectives *fpl* commerciales; *St Exch* **m. quotation** cotation *f* au cours du marché; *St Exch* **m. rating** cours en Bourse; **m. report** étude *f* de marché, rapport *m* ou bilan *m* commercial; **m. research** recherche *f* commerciale; étude *f* ou études *fpl* de marché; **m. research company** société *f* d'études de marché; **m. researcher** chargé, -ée d'étude de marché; **m. risk** risque *m* du marché; **m. rollout** élargissement *m* du marché; **m. segment** segment *m* de marché; **m. segmentation** segmentation *f* du marché; **m. share** part de marché; **to lose m. share** voir sa part du marché diminuer; **m. size** *(of product)* part de marché; *(of market)* taille *f* du marché; *St Exch* taille boursière; **m. society** société *f* de marché; *Br* **m. square** place du marché; **m. stall** étalage *m*, éventaire *m*; **m. structure** structure *f* du marché; **m. study** étude de marché; **m. survey** enquête *f* de marché; **m. test** marché-test *m*, *pl* marchés-tests, test *m* de marché, test de vente; **m. thrust** percée *f* commerciale; **m. town** bourg *m*; *Br* **m. trader** vendeur, -euse qui fait les marchés; *St Exch* **m. trend** conjoncture *f* boursière; **m. value** *Com (of object, product)* valeur *f* marchande; *St Exch (of share)* valeur boursière *ou* en bourse

marketability [mɑːkɪtə'bɪlɪtɪ] N possibilité *f* d'être commercialisé; **we are doubtful about the m. of these machines** nous doutons que ces machines soient commercialisables

marketable ['mɑːkɪtəb(ə)l] ADJ *(goods)* vendable, commercialisable
▸▸ *Fin* **m. securities** valeurs *fpl* de placement, valeurs réalisables

market-driven ADJ déterminé par les contraintes du marché
▸▸ **m. economy** économie *f* de marché

marketeer [mɑːkɪ'tɪər] N **1** *Br Pol* **(pro-)M.** partisan, -ane du Marché commun **2** *Mktg* mercaticien, -ienne

marketer ['mɑːkɪtər] N *Mktg* mercaticien, -ienne

market-garden ADJ *esp Br* **m. produce** produits *mpl* maraîchers

marketing ['mɑːkɪtɪŋ] N **1** *(of new product)* commercialisation *f*, marketing *m* **2** *(study)* marketing *m*, mercatique *f*

▸▸ **m. agreement** accord *m* de commercialisation; **m. analyst** analyste *mf* mercaticien(ienne); **m. approach** démarche *f* marketing; **m. audit** audit *m* marketing; **m. auditor** audit marketing, auditeur, -trice marketing; **m. campaign** campagne *f* de marketing; **m. channel** circuit *m* de commercialisation *ou* distribution; **m. company** entreprise *f* de marketing; **m. concept** concept *f* de marketing; **m. consultancy** *(service, activity)* conseil *m* en marketing; **m. consultancy firm** société *f* de conseil en marketing; **m. consultant** conseiller, -ère commercial(e), mercaticien, -ienne; **m. costs** frais *mpl* de commercialisation; **m. department** service *m* du marketing; **m. director** directeur, -trice du marketing, dirco *m*, directeur, -trice commercial(e); **m. engineering** marketing informatisé; **m. environment** environnement *m* commercial, environnement marketing; **m. executive** responsable *mf* du marketing, cadre *m* en marketing; **m. expert** mercaticien, -ienne; **m. fit** ajustement *m* stratégique; **m. information system** système *m* d'information marketing; **m. intelligence** intelligence *f* marketing; **m. manager** directeur, -trice du marketing, responsable *mf* du marketing; **m. mix** marchéage *m*, marketing mix *m*, logistique *f* commerciale; **m. network** réseau *m* ou circuit de commercialisation; **m. orientation** optique *f* marketing; **m. plan** plan *m* marketing; **m. planner** responsable de planification mercatique; **m. planning** planification *f* mercatique; **m. policy** politique *f* de commercialisation; **m. questionnaire** questionnaire *m* d'étude de marché; **m. spectrum** marchéage *m*; **m. strategy** stratégie *f* marketing; **m. study** étude *f* commerciale, étude marketing; **m. team** équipe *f* commerciale; **m. technique** technique *f* commerciale

marketization [mɑːkɪtaɪ'zeɪʃən] N marchéisation *f*

marketize ['mɑːkɪtaɪz] VT convertir à l'économie de marché

marking ['mɑːkɪŋ] N **1** *(of linen, cattle etc)* marquage *m* **2 markings** *(distinctive marks)* marques *fpl*; *(on animal) (spots)* taches *fpl*; *(stripes)* rayures *fpl*; *Aviat* insignes *mpl* **3** *Sch (of homework)* correction *f*, *(work to be marked)* copies *fpl* (à corriger) **4** *Ftbl etc* marquage *m* **5** *St Exch (of shares)* cotation *f*; **m. to market** comptabilisation *f* au prix de marché
▸▸ **m. ink** encre *f* à marquer; *Sch* **m. scheme** barème *m*

markka ['mɑːkə] N mark *m* finlandais

marksman, *pl* **marksmen** ['mɑːksmən] N tireur *m* d'élite

marksmanship ['mɑːksmənʃɪp] N adresse *f* ou habileté *f* au tir

markswoman, *pl* **markswomen** ['mɑːkswʊmən, -wɪmɪn] N tireuse *f* d'élite

mark-up N *Com* majoration *f*; **we operate a 2.5 times m.** nous appliquons une marge de 2,5

marl [mɑːl] N *Agr* marne *f*
▸▸ **m. pit** marnière *f*

marlin ['mɑːlɪn] N *(fish)* poisson *m* épieu

marlin(e)spike ['mɑːlɪnspaɪk] N *Naut* épissoir *m*

marly ['mɑːlɪ] ADJ *(soil)* marneux

marmalade ['mɑːməleɪd] N *Culin* **(orange) m.** confiture *f* d'oranges

marmoset ['mɑːməzet] N *(animal)* ouistiti *m*, marmouset *m*

marmot ['mɑːmɒt] N *(animal)* marmotte *f*

maroon¹ [mə'ruːn] N **1** *(colour)* rouge *m* inv foncé, bordeaux *m* inv **2** *(firework)* fusée *f* de détresse

Note that the French word **marron** is a false friend. When referring to a colour, it means **brown**.

maroon² VT abandonner (sur une île déserte)

marooned [mə'ru:nd] ADJ Fig isolé

marquee [mɑ:'ki:] N (tent) grande tente f

marquess, marquis ['mɑ:kwɪs] N marquis m

marquetry ['mɑ:kɪtrɪ] N marqueterie f

marram ['mærəm] N Bot gourbet m
▸▸m. grass gourbet

marriage ['mærɪdʒ] N 1 mariage m; a happy m. un ménage heureux; Fml to take sb in m. épouser qn; Fml to give sb in m. donner qn en mariage; uncle by m. oncle par alliance 2 Fig mariage m, alliance f (entre les choses); a m. of minds une union des esprits
▸▸m. bed lit m conjugal; m. broker agent m matrimonial; Br m. bureau agence f matrimoniale; m. ceremony cérémonie f de mariage; m. certificate extrait m d'acte de mariage; Journ marriages column carnet m blanc; m. of convenience mariage de raison; m. guidance conseil m conjugal; m. guidance counsellor conseiller, -ère conjugal(e); Old-fashioned Br Fam m. lines extrait m d'acte de mariage; m. settlement (dowry) dot f; (between couple) ≃ contrat m de mariage, ≃ régime m matrimonial; m. vows vœux mpl de mariage

marriageable ['mærɪdʒəb(ə)l] ADJ (daughter) mariable, à marier; of m. age en âge de se marier

married ['mærɪd] ADJ marié
▸▸m. couple couple m marié; the young/newly m. couple les jeunes/nouveaux mariés mpl; m. life vie f conjugale; m. name nom m de femme mariée; Br m. quarters logements mpl pour familles

marrow ['mærəʊ] N 1 (in bone) moelle f; to be frozen to the m. être transi de froid, être glacé jusqu'à la moelle 2 Lit (essence) essence f 3 Br (vegetable) m. courge f

marrowbone ['mærəʊbəʊn] N os m à moelle

marrowfat ['mærəʊfæt] N pois m carré
▸▸m. pea pois carré

marry ['mærɪ] (pt, pp married ['mærɪd]) VT 1 (get married to) se marier avec, épouser; they've been married for nearly twenty years cela fait presque vingt ans qu'ils sont mariés; they're happily married ils forment un ménage heureux; will you m. me? veux-tu m'épouser?; to get married se marier; Fig he's married to his job son travail passe avant tout, il n'y a que son travail qui compte 2 (of priest, parent) marier, unir 3 Fig (combine) allier, marier
VI se marier; she never married elle ne s'est jamais mariée; to m. beneath oneself se mésallier; to m. for money faire un mariage d'argent; to m. into money épouser quelqu'un issu d'une famille riche; she married into the Smith family/the aristocracy elle a épousé un membre de la famille Smith/de l'aristocratie; to m. again or a second time se remarier; he isn't the marrying kind il n'est pas du genre à se marier; Prov m. in haste, repent at leisure tel se marie à la hâte qui s'en repent à loisir; Fig the flavours m. well les parfums se marient bien
▸ **marry off** VT SEP (dispose of by marriage) marier; they were desperate to m. her off ils voulaient à tout prix la marier
▸ **marry up** VT SEP (bring together) (two parts) joindre; (colours) marier
VI (line up, fit) coïncider, concorder; (of colours) aller bien ensemble, se marier; check that the two parts m. up vérifier que les deux parties coïncident

Mars [mɑ:z] N Astron Mars f; Myth Mars m

marsh [mɑ:ʃ] N marais m, marécage m
▸▸m. fever fièvre f des marais, paludisme m; m. gas gaz m des marais, méthane m; Bot m. marigold souci m d'eau, populage m

marshal ['mɑ:ʃəl] N 1 Br Mil, Aviat M. of the RAF ≃ Commandant m en Chef des Forces aériennes; Air Chief Marshal = général m d'armée aérienne; M. of the Diplomatic Corps ≃ Chef m du Protocole 2 (at race, demonstration, march) membre m du service d'ordre 3 Am Law = fonctionnaire m ayant les attributions d'un shérif; (police officer) officier m de la police fédérale
VT (-ll-, Am -l-) (people, troops) rassembler (et mettre en ordre/en rang); (arguments) passer en revue; (thoughts) rassembler; Rail (trucks, wagons) trier, manœuvrer; the children were marshalled into a line on a fait mettre les enfants en ligne; he marshalled the children out of the room il a dirigé les enfants vers la sortie; to m. facts rassembler des faits et les mettre en ordre; we need to m. more support for the project il nous faut mobiliser plus de monde pour le projet

marshalling yard ['mɑ:ʃəlɪŋ] N Rail gare f de triage

marshland ['mɑ:ʃlænd] N terres fpl marécageuses, marécages mpl

marshmallow [mɑ:ʃ'mæləʊ] N 1 Culin (pâte f de) guimauve f 2 (plant) guimauve f, althée f

marshy ['mɑ:ʃɪ] ADJ (ground) marécageux

marsupial [mɑ:'su:pɪəl] ADJ, N marsupial m, -aux

mart [mɑ:t] N centre m commercial, marché m; (auction) m. salle f des ventes

marten ['mɑ:tɪn] N (animal) mart(r)e f

martial ['mɑ:ʃəl] ADJ martial, -aux, guerrier
▸▸m. arts arts mpl martiaux; m. law loi f martiale; to declare m. law proclamer l'état de siège

Martian ['mɑ:ʃən] N Martien, -ienne

martin ['mɑ:tɪn] N (bird) (house) m. martinet m

martinet [mɑ:tɪnet] N Mil officier m à cheval sur la discipline; to be a m. être autoritaire

martingale ['mɑ:tɪŋgeɪl] N 1 (part of harness) martingale f 2 Naut m. (guy or stay) martingale f du beaupré

Martini® [mɑ:'ti:nɪ] N Martini® m

Martinican [mɑ:tɪ'ni:kən] ADJ martiniquais
N Martiniquais, -aise

Martinmas ['mɑ:tɪnməs] N la Saint-Martin

martyr ['mɑ:tər] N martyr, -yre; to die a m. in or to a cause mourir martyr d'une cause; he is a m. to rheumatism ses rhumatismes lui font souffrir le martyre; Fam my brother's such a m. mon frère se prend pour un vrai martyr; Fam stop making such a m. of yourself! arrête de jouer les martyrs!
VT (person) martyriser; a martyred people un peuple martyr

martyrdom ['mɑ:tədəm] N Rel, Fig martyre m

martyrize ['mɑ:təraɪz] VT martyriser

marvel ['mɑ:v(ə)l] N merveille f; the marvels of science/the world les merveilles de la science/du monde; it would be a m. if she won ce serait un miracle ou un prodige si elle gagnait; to work marvels faire des merveilles; (of treatment etc) faire merveille; we're not expecting anybody to work marvels nous n'attendons de personne de miracle de personne; Fam you're a m.! tu es un as!; Iron (you idiot) espèce d'andouille!
VI (-ll-, Am -l-) (at splendour, beauty) s'émerveiller (at de); (at cost) s'étonner (at de)
VT I m. that you are always so calm ton

calme m'impressionne; I m. that you can be so calm at a time like this je me demande comment tu peux être aussi calme à un moment pareil; she marvelled that he had agreed elle s'est étonnée qu'il ait consenti

marvellous, Am **marvelous** ['mɑ:v(ə)ləs] ADJ merveilleux; it would be m. if ... ce serait merveilleux si ...; Iron (isn't it) m.! ça c'est le bouquet ou le comble!

marvellously, Am **marvelously** ['mɑ:v(ə)ləslɪ] ADV merveilleusement

Marxian ['mɑ:ksɪən] ADJ Phil marxien, -ienne

Marxism ['mɑ:ksɪz(ə)m] N Pol marxisme m

Marxism-Leninism N Pol marxisme-léninisme m

Marxist ['mɑ:ksɪst] ADJ, N Pol marxiste mf

Marxist-Leninist ADJ, N Pol marxiste-léniniste mf

Mary Magdalene [meərɪ'mægdəli:n] N Marie-Madeleine f

Mary Queen of Scots N Marie Stuart f

Mary Stuart ['stjʊət] N Marie Stuart f

marzipan ['mɑ:zɪpæn] N Culin massepain m, pâte f d'amandes; m. fruits fruits mpl en pâte d'amandes

mascara [mæs'kɑ:rə] N mascara m
VT she had heavily mascaraed eyes elle avait les cils très maquillés

mascot ['mæskət] N mascotte f; (on car bonnet) enjoliveur m de capot

masculine ['mæskjʊlɪn] ADJ 1 masculin, mâle; (woman) masculine; Fam Pej hommasse 2 Gram masculin
N Gram masculin m; in the m. au masculin
SEE GRAMMAR B5–7

masculinity [mæskjʊ'lɪnɪtɪ] N masculinité f

maser ['meɪzər] N Nucl maser m

MASH [mæʃ] N Am Mil (abbr Mobile Army Surgical Hospital) hôpital m de campagne

mash [mæʃ] N 1 (pulp) to reduce to a m. (paper etc) réduire en pâte ou en bouillie 2 Br Fam (mashed potato) purée f de pommes de terre 3 Agr (for pigs, poultry) pâtée f 4 (in brewing) fardeau m (de malt et d'eau chaude)
VT 1 to m. (up) broyer, écraser; Culin faire une purée de 2 (in brewing) brasser, mélanger

mashed [mæʃt] ADJ
▸▸m. potato, m. potatoes purée f (de pommes de terre)

masher ['mæʃər] N Tech (device) broyeur m, écraseur m; mélangeur m; Culin (potato) m. presse-purée m inv

mashie, mashy ['mæʃɪ] N Golf mashie m

mask [mɑ:sk] N 1 masque m; (silk or velvet, for eyes) loup m; to put on a m. mettre un masque, se masquer; with the m. off à visage découvert; Fig a m. of happiness/confidence une apparence de bonheur/confiance trompeuse; Fig the m. had slipped le masque était tombé; Fig to throw off or drop the m. lever le masque, se démasquer 2 (moulded likeness) (of face) moulage m, masque m 3 Phot cache m, masque m
VT 1 (person) masquer 2 (conceal) (one's feelings, thoughts) cacher, dissimuler, déguiser; (taste, smell) dissimuler, masquer; an apparent cheerfulness masked her deep pessimism une gaieté apparente masquait son profond pessimisme 3 Mil etc (battery, beam of light etc) masquer 4 Phot cacher, masquer

masked [mɑ:skt] ADJ (man, robber, ball) masqué
▸▸Mil m. battery batterie f masquée; Comput m. ROM mémoire f morte masquée

masking ['mɑ:skɪŋ] N
▶▶**m. tape** ruban *m* adhésif *(utilisé pour masquer une surface que l'on ne veut pas peindre)*

masochism ['mæsəkɪz(ə)m] N masochisme *m*

masochist ['mæsəkɪst] N, ADJ masochiste *mf*

masochistic [mæsə'kɪstɪk] ADJ masochiste

mason ['meɪs(ə)n] N **1** maçon *m* **2** M. *(freemason)* franc-maçon *m, pl* francs-maçons

Masonic [mə'sɒnɪk] ADJ (franc-)maçonnique, des francs-maçons, de la franc-maçonnerie
▶▶**M. lodge** loge *f* maçonnique

masonry ['meɪsənrɪ] N **1** maçonnerie *f* **2** M. *(freemasonry)* franc-maçonnerie *f*
▶▶**m. drill** foret *m* de maçonnerie

masquerade [mæskə'reɪd] N mascarade *f*
VI **to m. as sb** se faire passer pour qn; **dictatorship masquerading as democracy** dictature qui essaie de se faire passer pour une démocratie

Mass¹ [mæs] N *Rel, Mus* messe *f*; **M. for the dead** messe de requiem, messe des morts; **to celebrate/say M.** célébrer/dire la messe; **to go to M.** aller à la messe

Mass² *abbr* **Massachusetts**

mass [mæs] N **1** *(large number) (of people)* foule *f*, multitude *f*, *Fam* masse *f*; *(of objects, letters)* grande quantité *f*, multitude, *Fam* masse; *Fam* **I've masses (of things) to do** j'ai un tas *ou* des masses de choses à faire; **we've masses of room** nous avons beaucoup de place; **he was a m. of bruises** il était entièrement couvert de bleus; **the (great) m. of the people** la plus grande partie *ou* la majorité de la population; **the masses** les masses *fpl*, le grand public **2** *(body) Phys* masse *f*
VT *(troops etc)* rassembler
VI *(of troops)* se masser; *(of clouds)* s'amonceler
▶▶**m. circulation** grande diffusion *f*, diffusion de masse; **m. communication** communication *f* de masse; **m. consumption** consommation *f* de masse; **m. culture** culture *f* de masse; **m. distribution** distribution *f* de masse, grande distribution; **m. grave** charnier *m*; **m. hysteria** hystérie *f* collective; **m. market** marché *m* de masse; **m. marketing** marketing *m* de grande consommation, marketing de masse; **m. media** mass media *mpl*; **m. meeting** grand rassemblement *m*; **m. murder** tuerie *f*; **m. murderer** *(serial killer)* tueur, -euse en série; *(tyrant, dictator)* boucher *m*; *Chem* **m. number** nombre *m* de masse; **m. production** fabrication *f ou* production *f* en série; **it goes into m. production next week** la production en série commence la semaine prochaine; **m. protest** protestation *f* en masse; *Comput* **m. storage** mémoire *f* de masse; **m. tourism** tourisme *m* de masse; **m. unemployment** chômage *m* sur une grande échelle

massacre ['mæsəkər] N massacre *m*, tuerie *f*, *Sport etc Fam* **it was a m.** cela a été un massacre *ou* une hécatombe
VT *also Fig* massacrer; *Sport etc Fam* **they were massacred** ils se sont fait massacrer *ou* démolir

massage ['mæsɑ:ʒɑm] N massage *m*
VT **1** *(body, scalp)* masser **2** *Fig (manipulate)* **to m. the figures** manipuler *ou* trafiquer les chiffres
▶▶**m. oil** huile *f* de massage; **m. parlour** salon *m* de massage

masseur [mæ'sɜːr] N masseur *m*

masseuse [mæ'sɜːz] N masseuse *f*

massif ['mæsi:f] N *Geog* massif *m*

massive ['mæsɪv] ADJ énorme; *(heart attack, stroke)* foudroyant; **invasion on a m. scale** invasion massive; **the m. scale of the Mafia's operations** l'échelle massive sur laquelle la Mafia opère; *Pharm etc* **m. dose** dose massive
N *Br Sl (gang)* bande *f*; **the Brighton m.** la bande de Brighton

massively ['mæsɪvlɪ] ADV massivement; *(strong, fat)* extrêmement; **to invest m. in sth** investir massivement dans qch

mass-market ADJ *(products)* de grande consommation

mass-produce VT *Ind* fabriquer en série

mass-produced [-prə'dju:st] ADJ *Ind* produit en série

mast [mɑ:st] N **1** *Naut* mât *m*; **the masts** les mâts, la mâture; **to sail before the m.** servir comme simple matelot **2** *Radio, TV, Tel* pylône *m*

mastectomy [mæs'tektəmɪ] N *Surg* mastectomie *f*

-masted ['mɑ:stɪd] SUFF *Naut* **three/four/etc-m.** à trois/quatre/*etc* mâts

master ['mɑ:stər] N **1** *(man in charge, employer, owner of pet)* maître *m*; *Naut (of merchant ship)* capitaine *m*, commandant *m*; *Univ (esp at Oxford and Cambridge)* directeur *m*, principal *m (de certains collèges universitaires)*; **the m. of the house** le maître de (la) maison; **to be m. in one's own house** être maître chez soi; **to be one's own m.** être son (propre) maître; **to be m. of the situation** être maître de la situation; *Prov* **like m. like man** tel maître, tel valet
2 *(skilled person)* maître *m*; **to be a m. of one's art** posséder son art en maître; **she was a m. of the sharp one-liner** elle avait le don de la petite phrase qui tue; **to be a m. of one's brief** connaître son sujet à fond; *Art* **old m.** *(painter)* maître; *(painting)* tableau *m* de maître; **m. carpenter/mason** maître charpentier/maçon
3 *(instructor)* maître *m*; **fencing/dancing m.** maître d'escrime/de danse
4 *esp Br Sch (in primary school)* maître *m*, instituteur *m*; *(in secondary school)* professeur *m*; **French/Geography m.** professeur de français/géographie
5 *Old-fashioned (form of address to small boys)* **M. David Thomas** Monsieur David Thomas; **M. David** *(said by servant)* Monsieur David
6 *Mus (record)* *(disque m)* original *m*
VT *(person)* se rendre maître/maîtresse de; *(horse, emotions, situation, subject)* maîtriser; *(difficulty)* surmonter, triompher de; **to have mastered a subject** posséder un sujet à fond; **I never really mastered the language** je n'ai jamais eu une maîtrise parfaite de la langue; **to have mastered the violin** être un/une violoniste accompli(e); **to m. one's brief** dominer son sujet
▶▶*Univ* **M. of Arts** ≃ maître ès lettres; **m. bedroom** chambre *f* principale; **m. of ceremonies** *(at reception)* maître des cérémonies; *(on TV show)* présentateur *m*; **m. class** cours *m* de maître; *Mus* master class *m*; *Radio, TV* **m. control room** régie *f* centrale; **m. copy** original *m*; *Comput* **m. disk** disque *m* maître; *Comput* **m. file** fichier *m* principal *ou* maître; **M. of hounds** maître d'équipage, grand veneur *m*; **m. key** passe-partout *m inv*; *Naut* **m. mariner** capitaine; *TV* **m. monitor** récepteur *m* de contrôle final; **m. plan** stratégie *f* globale; **m. race** race *f* supérieure; *Mus* **m. record** *(disque m)* original *m*; *Univ* **M. of Science** ≃ maître ès sciences; *Am Mil* **m. sergeant** ≃ sergent-chef *m, pl* sergents-chefs; *Cin, TV* **m. shot** plan *m* de coupe; **m. soundtrack** mixage *m* magnétique final; *Elec* **m. switch** commutateur *m ou* disjoncteur *m* principal; **m. tape** bande *f* originale;

TV cassette *f* prête à diffuser; *Com* **m. of works** maître d'œuvre

-master ['mɑ:stər] SUFF *Naut* **three/four/etc-m.** à trois/quatre-mâts/*etc*

masterbrand ['mɑ:stəbrænd] N *Mktg* marque *f* vedette

Mastercard® ['mɑ:stəkɑ:d] N carte *f* Mastercard®

masterful ['mɑ:stəfʊl] ADJ *(tone, voice, performance)* magistral, -aux; **she was wrapped in his m. arms** il l'enveloppait de ses bras puissants; **you're so m.!** quel homme/quelle femme!

masterfully ['mɑ:stəfʊlɪ] ADV *(to perform)* magistralement; **he said m.** dit-il d'un ton magistral

masterly ['mɑ:stəlɪ] ADJ magistral, -aux, de maître; **m. stroke** coup *m* de maître; **in a m. manner** de main de maître

mastermind ['mɑ:stəmaɪnd] N esprit *m* supérieur; *(of undertaking etc)* cerveau *m*; **she was the m. behind the robbery** c'était elle le cerveau du vol
VT *(project etc)* diriger, organiser; *(plot etc)* tramer

masterpiece ['mɑ:stəpi:s] N chef-d'œuvre *m, pl* chefs-d'œuvre

master/slave system N système *m* maître/esclave

masterstroke ['mɑ:stəstrəʊk] N coup *m* de maître

mastery ['mɑ:stərɪ] N **1** *(control)* contrôle *m* (**of** de), domination *f* (**over** sur) **2** *(knowledge) (of subject)* maîtrise *f*

masthead ['mɑ:sthed] N *Naut* tête *f ou* ton *m* de mât, haut *m* du mât; *(of newspaper)* ours *m*
▶▶*Naut* **m. light** feu *m* de tête de mât

mastic ['mæstɪk] N *(resin, cement)* mastic *m*

masticate ['mæstɪkeɪt] VT **1** *(food)* mâcher, mastiquer **2** *Ind (rubber etc)* triturer, malaxer

mastiff ['mæstɪf] N *(dog)* mastiff *m*

mastitis [mæs'taɪtɪs] N *Med* mastite *f*

mastodon ['mæstədɒn] N mastodonte *m*

mastoid ['mæstɔɪd] N *Anat (process)* mastoïde *f*; *Med Fam* **mastoids** mastoïdite *f*
▶▶*Anat* **m. process** apophyse *f* mastoïde

masturbate ['mæstəbeɪt] VI se masturber
VT masturber

masturbation [mæstə'beɪʃən] N masturbation *f, esp Med* onanisme *m*

masturbatory [mæstə'beɪtərɪ] ADJ masturbatoire, onaniste

mat¹ [mæt] N *(on floor etc) (of straw, rushes)* natte *f, (of wool etc)* (petit) tapis *m*, carpette *f, (at entrance)* paillasson *m*, essuie-pieds *m inv*; *Sport (in wrestling)* tapis; **(table) m.** *(for hot dish)* dessous-de-plat *m inv*; *(for vase, ornament)* napperon *m*; **(table or place) m.** *(for plates)* set *m* de table; *Fig Fam* **to be on the m.** *(be in trouble)* être sur la sellette
VT *(-tt-)* *(hair etc)* emmêler
VI *(of hair, fibres etc)* s'emmêler, se coller ensemble

mat² ADJ *(colour, paint, paper)* mat

matador ['mætədɔ:r] N matador *m*

[mætʃ] N **1** *(of person)* égal, -ale; **to meet one's m.** trouver son maître; **to be more than a m. for sb** être trop fort pour qn; **they were no m. for the other team** ils n'étaient pas à la hauteur de l'autre équipe; **you're no m. for her** tu n'es pas à sa hauteur; **to be a bad/good m.** *(of things)* aller mal/bien ensemble, être mal/bien assortis; **to find a m. for a wallpaper** *(find curtains etc in suitable colour)* assortir un papier peint; *(find the same)* réassortir un papier peint; **perfect m. of colours** assortiment parfait de couleurs

2 *Sport (of football, rugby, cricket, baseball)* match *m*; *(of golf)* partie *f*, *(of tennis)* match, partie; *(swimming)* compétition *f*
3 *(marriage)* mariage *m*; **to make a good m.** faire un bon mariage; **he's a good m.** c'est un bon *ou* un excellent parti
VT *(person)* égaler, être l'égal de, rivaliser avec; *(colours, gloves, stockings)* assortir; **his jacket doesn't m. his trousers** sa veste ne va pas avec son pantalon; **the music didn't m. her mood** la musique ne correspondait pas à son humeur; **we can't m. their prices** nous ne pouvons pas rivaliser avec leurs prix; **will their deeds m. their words?** est-ce que leurs actes seront à la hauteur de leurs paroles?; **there's nobody to m. him** il n'a pas son pareil; **to m. sb against sb** opposer qn à qn; *Sport* **Scotland has been matched against Brazil** l'Écosse rencontrera le Brésil; **evenly matched** de force égale, bien assortis; **we will try to m. this material for you** *(find something similar to)* nous essayerons de trouver un tissu assorti; **a well-matched couple** un couple bien assorti; **I need a new hat to m. my suit** j'ai besoin d'un nouveau chapeau qui aille avec mon tailleur; **m. the names to the faces** *(in competition)* trouvez les noms correspondant aux visages
VI *(of colours etc) (go well together)* aller (bien) ensemble, être bien assortis; *(be exactly the same)* être exactement les mêmes; *(of fingerprints, descriptions etc)* correspondre; **the carpet doesn't m.** la moquette n'est pas assortie au reste; **I need some shoes to m.** il me faut des chaussures assorties *ou* pour aller avec
▶▶ *Golf* **m. play** match-play *m*, *pl* match-plays, partie *f* par trous; *Tennis* **m. point** balle *f* de match
▶ **match up VT SEP** *(combine)* faire correspondre; **to m. up the names with the faces** faire correspondre les noms et les visages; **to m. up two colours** harmoniser *ou* assortir deux couleurs; **I want to m. up this colour** *(find exact match)* j'aimerais trouver exactement la même couleur
VI *(of fingerprints etc)* correspondre; *(of colours etc) (go well together)* aller (bien) ensemble, être bien assortis; *(be exactly the same)* être exactement les mêmes; **the descriptions didn't m. up** les descriptions ne correspondaient pas; **the suit jacket and trousers don't m. up** la veste et le pantalon ne vont pas ensemble
▶ **match up to VT INSEP** **to m. up to sb's expectations** répondre aux espérances *ou* à l'attente de qn

match² **N** *(for lighting)* allumette *f*; **to put a m. to sth** mettre (le) feu à qch

matchbox ['mætʃbɒks] **N** boîte *f* d'allumettes

matched [mætʃt] **ADJ**
▶▶ *St Exch* **m. bargain** mariage *m*

matching ['mætʃɪŋ] **ADJ** *(hat, colours etc)* assorti; **these pictures are a m. pair** ces tableaux se font pendant

matchless ['mætʃlɪs] **ADJ** incomparable, sans égal, -aux, sans pareil

matchmaker ['mætʃmeɪkər] **N** faiseur, -euse de mariages, marieur, -euse

matchmaking ['mætʃmeɪkɪŋ] **N** entremise *f*

matchstick ['mætʃstɪk] **N** allumette *f*; **to have m. legs** avoir des jambes comme des allumettes; **m. man** *ou* **figure** *(drawing)* bonhomme *m* dessiné avec des bâtons

matchwood ['mætʃwʊd] **N** bois *m* d'allumettes; **smashed** *or* **reduced to m.** réduit en miettes

mate¹ [meɪt] **N 1** *(sexual partner) (animal) (male)* mâle *m*; *(female)* femelle *f*; *Fam Hum (husband)* mari *m*; *(wife)* femme *f* **2** *Br Fam (friend) (male)* copain *m*, pote *m*; *(female)* copine *f*; **thanks, m.** *(to friend)* merci, mon pote; *(to stranger)* merci, m'sieur; **watch where you're going, m.!** eh mec, regarde où tu vas! **3** *(assistant)* assistant, -ante, aide *mf*; **plumber's m.** aide plombier **4** *Naut (on merchant vessel)* officier *m*; **first** *or* **chief m.** second *m*; **second m.** lieutenant *m* **5** *Tech (part)* pièce *f* qui s'accouple *(avec une autre)*; pièce qui s'emboîte *(dans une autre)*
VT *(animals, birds)* accoupler; *Old-fashioned* marier, unir (**sb with sb** qn à qn)
VI *(of birds, animals)* s'accoupler

mate² *Chess* **N** mat *m*
VT *(king)* mettre échec et mat, mater

mater ['meɪtər] **N** *Old-fashioned Br Fam* **(the) m.** ma mère, maman *f*

material [mə'tɪərɪəl] **N 1** *(substance)* matière *f*, substance *f*; *(for building)* matériau *m*; **raw material(s)** matière(s) première(s); **glass is a brittle m.** le verre est un matériau cassant; **he isn't officer m.** il n'a pas l'étoffe *ou* l'envergure d'un officier **2** *(equipment for specific activity)* matériel *m*; **photographic materials** matériel de photographie **3** *(cloth)* tissu *m*, étoffe *f*; **dress m.** tissu pour robes **4** *(information for a book etc)* matériaux *mpl*; **the m. for a play** les matériaux d'une pièce **5** *(produced by writer, singer etc)* **this singer writes her own m.** cette chanteuse écrit ses propres textes
ADJ 1 *(point of view etc)* matérialiste; *(comfort, interests)*, *Phil, Phys, Rel* matériel; **to have enough for one's m. comfort** *or* **needs** avoir de quoi vivre matériellement **2** *(important)* important, essentiel (**to** pour) **3** *Law (fact, testimony)* pertinent
▶▶ **m. possessions** biens *mpl* matériels; *Law* **m. witness** témoin *m* de fait

materialism [mə'tɪərɪəlɪz(ə)m] **N** matérialisme *m*

materialist [mə'tɪərɪəlɪst] **ADJ, N** matérialiste *mf*

materialistic [mətɪərɪə'lɪstɪk] **ADJ** matérialiste; *(pleasures, mind etc)* matériel

materialize [mə'tɪərɪəlaɪz] **VI** *(of event)* se réaliser; *(of plans)* aboutir, se réaliser; *(of psychic ectoplasm)* apparaître, prendre forme; **the promised computers never materialized** les ordinateurs promis ne se sont jamais matérialisés; **the job he promised me never materialized** le travail qu'il m'avait promis ne s'est jamais matérialisé; **the project failed to m.** le projet n'a jamais abouti; **she promised to lend me a thousand pounds but the money never materialized** elle avait promis de me prêter mille livres mais je n'en ai jamais vu la couleur

materially [mə'tɪərɪəlɪ] **ADV 1** *Phil, Phys, Rel* matériellement; **to benefit m. from sth** bénéficier matériellement de qch **2** *(appreciably)* sensiblement, d'une manière appréciable; **m. different/better** sensiblement différent/meilleur

materiel, matériel [mətɪərɪ'el] **N** *Mil* matériel *m*

maternal [mə'tɜːn(ə)l] **ADJ** maternel

maternally [mə'tɜːn(ə)lɪ] **ADV** maternellement

maternity [mə'tɜːnɪtɪ] **N** maternité *f*
▶▶ **m. benefit** ≃ allocations *fpl* de maternité; **m. dress** robe *f* de grossesse; **m. hospital** maternité; **m. leave** congé *m* (de) maternité; **m. ward** maternité

matey ['meɪtɪ] **ADJ** *Br Fam* copain-copain; **to be m.** *(of people)* être à tu et à toi, être copains; **she's very m. all of a sudden** elle est bien aimable tout d'un coup

math [mæθ] **N** *Am Fam* = **maths**

mathematical [mæθ(ə)'mætɪk(ə)l] **ADJ** *(science, calculation)* mathématique; *(know-ledge)* en mathématiques; **he's a m. genius** c'est un mathématicien de génie; **victory for the party is now a m. impossibility** mathématiquement, le parti ne peut pas gagner; **I haven't got a m. mind** je n'ai pas l'esprit mathématique

mathematically [mæθ(ə)'mætɪklɪ] **ADV** mathématiquement

mathematician [mæθ(ə)mə'tɪʃən] **N** mathématicien, -ienne

mathematics [mæθ(ə)'mætɪks] **N** VOIR GRAMMAIRE A10 **1** *(subject)* mathématiques *fpl*; **pure/applied m.** mathématiques pures/appliquées; **m. lesson/teacher** cours *m*/professeur *m* de mathématiques **2** *(calculations)* calculs *mpl*

maths [mæθs] **NPL** *Br Fam* math *fpl*; **m. lesson/teacher** cours *m*/professeur *m* de maths
▶▶ *Comput* **m. co-processor** coprocesseur *m* mathématique *ou* arithmétique

matinée ['mætɪneɪ] **N** *Theat, Cin* matinée *f*
▶▶ *Br* **m. coat** veste *f* (de bébé); *Cin Old-fashioned* **m. idol** = acteur *m* idolâtré par les femmes surtout dans les années 30 *ou* 40; *Theat, Cin* **m. performance** matinée

matiness ['meɪtɪnɪs] **N** *Br Fam* camaraderie *f*

mating ['meɪtɪŋ] **N** *(of animals, birds)* accouplement *m*
▶▶ **m. call** appel *m* du mâle/de la femelle; **m. instinct** instinct *m* sexuel; **m. ritual** parade *f* nuptiale; **the m. season** la saison des amours

matins ['mætɪnz] **NPL** *Cathol* matines *fpl*; *(in Church of England)* office *m* du matin

matriarch ['meɪtrɪɑːk] **N** femme *f* chef de tribu *ou* de famille

matriarchal ['meɪtrɪɑːk(ə)l] **ADJ** matriarcal, -aux

matriarchy ['meɪtrɪɑːkɪ] **N** matriarcat *m*

matric [mə'trɪk] **N** *Arch Br Fam* = **matriculation**

matricide ['meɪtrɪsaɪd, 'mæ-] **N 1** *(person)* matricide *mf* **2** *(crime)* matricide *m*

matriculate [mə'trɪkjʊleɪt] **VI 1** *(of student)* s'inscrire, se faire inscrire **2** *Br Formerly (pass exam etc)* être reçu à l'examen d'entrée à l'université

matriculation [mətrɪkjʊ'leɪʃən] **N** *Sch* **1** *(enrolment)* inscription *f (comme étudiant)*; *Br Formerly (exam)* examen *m* de fin d'études *(pour entrer à l'université)*
▶▶ **m. fee** frais *mpl* d'inscription

matrimonial [mætrɪ'məʊnɪəl] **ADJ** *esp Fml* matrimonial, -aux

matrimony ['mætrɪmənɪ] **N** *esp Fml* mariage *m*; *Rel* **joined in holy m.** unis par les liens sacrés du mariage

matrix, *pl* **matrixes, matrices** ['meɪtrɪks, -ɪksɪz, -ɪsiːz] **N 1** *Math etc* matrice *f*; *Fig (of forces, relations etc)* configuration *f* **2** *Geol, Miner* matrice *f*, gangue *f*, gaine *f* **3** *Metal, Typ etc* matrice *f*, moule *m*; *Art, Cer (of plaster moulds etc)* mère *f*
▶▶ *Comput* **m. printer** imprimante *f* matricielle

matron ['meɪtrən] **N 1** *(woman)* matrone *f* **2** *(of institution, boarding school)* intendante *f*; *Old-fashioned (of hospital)* infirmière *f* en chef
▶▶ **m. of honour** *(at wedding)* dame *f* d'honneur

matronly ['meɪtrənlɪ] **ADJ** de matrone

matt [mæt] **ADJ** = **mat²**

matte [mæt] **N** *Cin, TV* cache *m*

matted ['mætɪd] **ADJ** *(cloth)* feutré; *(hair)* emmêlé; **his hair was m. with blood** il avait du sang séché dans les cheveux

---

MATTER ['mætər]

> **N** matière **1, 7** ▪ affaire **2, 3**
> ▪ question **2** ▪ importer **5**
> **VI** importer

N 1 *(substance)* matière *f*; *Phil etc* **form and m.** la forme et la matière; **organic/inorganic m.** la matière organique/inorganique

2 *(affair)* affaire *f*, chose *f*; **it's a m. of the utmost importance** c'est une affaire de la plus haute importance; **the m. is closed** le dossier est clos; **let's come back to the m. in hand** revenons à ce qui nous occupe *ou Fam* à nos moutons; **it's an easy/no easy m.** c'est/ce n'est pas facile; **it's no great m.** ce n'est pas grand-chose; **it's no laughing m.** il n'y a pas de quoi rire; **it is a m. for regret** c'est regrettable; **it's a m. for congratulations** cela mérite des félicitations; **that's quite another m.** cela, c'est tout autre chose; **to do sth as a m. of course** faire qch systématiquement; **that's a m. of opinion/taste** c'est une question d'opinion/de goût; **that is a m. for the courts to decide** sur ce point, c'est à la justice de trancher; **it's simply a m. of time** *(is inevitable)* cela arrivera tôt ou tard; *(is a question of time only)* c'est une simple question de temps; **it'll only be a m. of days before they find out** ce n'est qu'une question de jours avant qu'ils découvrent la vérité; **it's just a m. of knowing which button to press** il s'agit juste de savoir sur quel bouton appuyer; **it's just a m. of replacing a few worn-out parts** il suffit de remplacer quelques pièces usées; **it's just a m. of £100** c'est l'affaire de 100 livres; *Iron* **there's the small m. of that money you owe me** il y a cette question de la petite somme que vous me devez; **within a m. of hours** en quelques heures; **for that m.** d'ailleurs; **and so am I for that m.** moi aussi d'ailleurs; **he isn't very well known in London or anywhere else for that m.** il n'est pas très connu à Londres, et nulle part ailleurs en fait; **it's a m. of fact** c'est un fait; **as a m. of fact** en fait

3 as matters stand au point où en sont les choses; **her remarks made matters worse** ses remarques n'ont fait qu'aggraver les choses; **to make matters worse, it had started to rain** pour tout arranger, il s'était mis à pleuvoir; **matters of the heart** affaires *fpl* de cœur *ou* sentimentales; **in matters of religion** en ce qui concerne la religion; **business matters** affaires; **money matters** affaires d'argent

4 *(problem)* **what's the m.?** qu'est-ce qu'il y a?, qu'y a-t-il?; **what's the m. with you?** qu'est-ce que vous avez?, qu'avez-vous?; **what's the m. with the TV?** qu'est-ce qu'il y a, la télé?; **what's the m. with asking her out to the movies?** je ne vois pas ce qu'il y a de mal à lui demander si elle veut aller au cinéma; **I don't know what's the m. with me** je ne sais pas ce que j'ai; **there's something the m.** il y a quelque chose (qui ne va pas), il se passe quelque chose; **there's something the m. with his throat** il a quelque chose à la gorge; **there's nothing the m. with you/the TV** tu n'as/la télé n'a rien; **he went on talking as if nothing was the m.** il continua de parler comme si de rien n'était

5 no m.! n'importe!, peu importe!; **no m. what he does/says** quoi qu'il fasse/dise; **no m. how** par n'importe quel moyen; **no m. how hard I pushed against the door, it wouldn't open** j'avais beau pousser la porte de toutes mes forces, elle ne s'ouvrait pas; **no m. what** quoi qu'il arrive; **no m. when** à n'importe quel moment; **no m. when you ...** peu importe quand tu ...; **no m. who** qui que ce soit; **no m. who gave it to you** peu importe qui te l'a donné; **no m. where** où que ce soit

6 *Med (pus)* pus *m*

7 *Typ* matière *f*, copie *f*

VI avoir de l'importance, être important (**to** pour), *Fml* importer (**to** à); **nothing matters much to him any more since his wife died** plus rien n'a d'importance pour lui depuis la mort de sa femme; **what really matters is that ...** ce qui est vraiment important, c'est que ...; **that is what matters most** c'est le plus important; **it doesn't m.** ce n'est pas important, cela ne fait rien, peu importe; **it doesn't m. how much it costs** peu importe le prix; **it doesn't m. – perhaps not to you, but it matters to me** ce n'est pas important – pour toi, peut-être, mais pour moi, c'est important; **it doesn't m. a bit** cela n'a pas la moindre importance; **it doesn't m. to her what people think** elle se moque de ce que pensent les gens; **what does it m. to you?** qu'est-ce que cela peut bien vous faire?; **nothing else matters** tout le reste est sans importance; **these things m.** ces choses-là comptent; **you need to identify the people who m. in the company** il faut que tu saches qui compte dans l'entreprise

Matterhorn (the) [ðə'mætəhɔːn] **N** le (Mont) Cervin

matter-of-fact **ADJ** *(person, manner, statement etc)* terre-à-terre, prosaïque; **to say sth in a m. tone** dire qch sur un ton neutre

Matthew ['mæθjuː] **N** Mat(t)hieu *m*

matting ['mætɪŋ] **N** *(material)* natte(s) *f(pl)*, paillassons *mpl*

mattins ['mætɪnz] **NPL** = matins

mattock ['mætək] **N** *Agr (tool)* hoyau *m*, pioche *f*

mattress ['mætrɪs] **N** matelas *m*; **inflatable** *or* **air m.** matelas pneumatique

maturation [mætjʊ'reɪʃən] **N** *(of fruit, abscess etc)* maturation *f*, *(of wine, whisky)* vieillissement *m*; *(of intelligence etc)* développement *m*

mature [mə'tjʊər] **ADJ 1** *(person, fruit)* mûr; *(animal)* adulte; *Psy (intelligence)* qui dénote beaucoup de maturité; **the more m. trees are slower to come into leaf** les arbres les plus vieux ont des feuilles plus tard que les autres; **to be m. for one's age** *or* **years** être mûr pour son âge; **of m. years** *(person)* d'âge mûr; *Br* **would suit a m. person** *(in job advertisement)* conviendrait à une personne d'âge mûr; **after m. consideration** après mûre réflexion; **m. cheese** fromage *m* fait **2** *Fin (bill)* échu

VT the cheese/wine is matured for five years before it's sold le fromage/vin vieillit pendant cinq ans avant d'être vendu

VI 1 *(of plant)* mûrir; *(of wine)* vieillir; *(of person)* devenir plus mûr, acquérir de la maturité; **she had matured into a sophisticated young woman** elle était devenue une jeune femme sophistiquée; **to let a plan m.** laisser mûrir un projet; **his plans had not yet matured** ses projets n'étaient pas encore mûris *ou* mûrs **2** *Fin (of bill)* échoir, arriver à échéance

> ► ► *Fin* **m. economy** économie *f* en pleine maturité; *Br Univ* **m. student** = étudiant *m* plus âgé que la moyenne ou qui entreprend des études sur le tard, *Can* étudiant, -ante adulte

maturely [mə'tjʊəlɪ] **ADV** *(to decide)* de façon raisonnable; **to behave m.** se comporter en adulte

maturity [mə'tjʊərɪtɪ] **N 1** *(of fruit, wine, cheese etc)* maturité *f*; **to come to** *or* **reach m.** arriver à maturité; **the years of m.** *(of person)* l'âge *m* mûr; **the novels of her m.** les romans qu'elle a écrits à l'âge mûr **2** *Fin* **(date of) m.** *(of bill)* échéance *f*; **payable at m.** payable à l'échéance

> ► ► *Fin* **m. date** date *f* d'échéance; *Fin* **m. value** valeur *f* à l'échéance

maudlin ['mɔːdlɪn] **ADJ** larmoyant, pleurard; *(drunk)* dans un état d'ivresse larmoyante; **m. sentimentality** sentimentalité larmoyante; **to become m.** se mettre à larmoyer *ou* à pleurnicher

maul [mɔːl] **N** *Rugby* maul *m*

VT 1 *(of lion etc)* blesser; *(more seriously)* mutiler; *Fig (author, book, play)* éreinter, tailler en pièces **2** *(grope) (woman)* tripoter

mauling ['mɔːlɪŋ] **N to get a m.** *(from a lion etc)* être blessé; *(more seriously)* être mutilé; *Fam (by enemy troops, opposing team)* être battu à plates coutures, recevoir une raclée; *(from critics)* se faire éreinter

maunder ['mɔːndər] **VI 1** *(in speech)* **to m. (on)** radoter, rabâcher **2** *(dawdle)* **to m. (along)** traîner, errer

Maundy ['mɔːndɪ] **N**

> ► ► *Br* **M. money** = pièces *fpl* de monnaie spéciales offertes par le souverain britannique à certaines personnes âgées le jour du jeudi saint; *Rel* **M. Thursday** jeudi *m* saint

Mauritania [mɒrɪ'teɪnɪə] **N** Mauritanie *f*

Mauritanian [mɒrɪ'teɪnɪən] **N** Mauritanien, -ienne

ADJ mauritanien

Mauritian [mə'rɪʃən] **ADJ** mauricien

N Mauricien, -ienne

Mauritius [mə'rɪʃəs] **N** l'île *f* Maurice

mausoleum [mɔːsə'liːəm] **N** mausolée *m*

mauve [məʊv] **ADJ, N** *(colour)* mauve *m*

maverick ['mævərɪk] **N 1** *(unorthodox person)* non-conformiste *mf*, franc-tireur *m*, pl francs-tireurs; **m. MP/salesman** député/vendeur qui fait les choses à sa façon **2** *Am (stray steer)* bouvillon *m* errant sans marque de propriétaire

maw [mɔː] **N 1** *(stomach) (of ruminant)* quatrième poche *f* de l'estomac; *(of bird)* jabot *m*; *Fam (of person)* panse *f* **2** *(mouth) (of animal, fish)* gueule *f*

mawkish ['mɔːkɪʃ] **ADJ** *Pej (person)* d'une sensiblerie outrée, mièvre; *(novel etc)* d'une sentimentalité exagérée, mièvre

mawkishness ['mɔːkɪʃnɪs] **N** *Pej (of person)* sensiblerie *f* outrée, mièvrerie *f*, *(of novel etc)* sentimentalité *f* exagérée, mièvrerie

max [mæks] **N** *(abbr* **maximum)** max *m*; *Am Fam* **to the m.** *(totally)* un max; **did you have a good time? – to the m.!** tu t'es bien amusé? – vachement bien!, un max!

ADV *Fam (at the most)* maxi; **it'll take three days m.** ça prendra trois jours maxi

VT *Am Fam* **to m. an exam** = obtenir le maximum de points à un examen

► **max out** **VI** *Fam Am* **to m. out on chocolate** se gaver de chocolat; **to m. out on booze** picoler un max

VT SEP *Am Fam* **to m. out one's credit card** dépenser le maximum autorisé avec sa carte de crédit

maxed [mækst] **ADJ** *Am Fam* **1** *(extremely drunk)* bourré comme un coing, pété à mort **2 to be m. out on one's credit card** avoir dépensé le maximum autorisé avec sa carte de crédit; **to be m. out on chocolate/sci-fi movies** avoir fait une overdose de chocolat/de films de science-fiction

maxi ['mæksɪ] **ADJ** *(skirt, coat)* maxi *inv*

N *(skirt)* maxi *f*, *(coat)* maxi *m*

maxim ['mæksɪm] **N** maxime *f*

maximal ['mæksɪməl] **ADJ** *Fml* maximal, -aux

maximization [mæksɪmaɪ'zeɪʃən] **N** maximalisation *f*, maximisation *f*

maximize ['mæksɪmaɪz] **VT** maximiser, maximaliser

maximum, *pl* **maxima** ['mæksɪməm, -ə] **N** maximum *m*, -ums, -a; **to the m.** au maximum; **at the m.** au (grand) maximum; **to reach one's m.** plafonner

ADJ maximum, maximal, -aux; **we guarantee m. security** nous garantissons une sécurité maximum

▸▸**m. load** charge *f* maximale *ou* limite; **m. security prison** prison *f* de haute sécurité; **m. security unit** quartier *m* de haute sécurité; **m. speed** *(highest possible)* vitesse *f* maximale *ou* maximum; *(highest permitted)* vitesse limite; **m. temperatures** températures *fpl* maximales

May [meɪ] **N** VOIR GRAMMAIRE A81–2; B60–2 mai *m*; **in M.** en mai, au mois de mai; **(on) the first/the seventh of M.** le premier/le sept mai

▸▸*Entom* **M. beetle, M. bug** hanneton *m*; **M. Day** le Premier mai; **M. Day parade** défilé *m* du Premier mai; **M. queen** = reine *f* des festivités du Premier mai

MAY¹ [meɪ] **V AUX** VOIR GRAMMAIRE A59–60; B39–40 *(3rd person sing* **may**; *pt, cond* **might** [maɪt], *no pres or past participle)* **1** *(expressing possibility)* **he m.** *or* **might return at any moment** il peut *ou* pourrait revenir d'un moment à l'autre; **she m.** *or* **might not be hungry** elle n'a peut-être pas faim, il se peut qu'elle n'ait pas faim; **we m. remind ourselves at this point that …** il n'est pas inutile de rappeler ici que …; **that m.** *or* **m. not be true** cela est peut-être vrai ou peut-être pas; **he m.** *or* **might have lost it** peut-être qu'il l'a perdu, il se peut qu'il l'ait perdu; **Queen Anne m. have stayed here** il se peut que la reine Anne ait séjourné ici; **you m.** *or* **might see her if you stay another hour** vous la verrez peut-être si vous restez encore une heure; **something I said m.** *or* **might have offended him** j'ai peut-être dit quelque chose qui l'a blessé; **it m.** *or* **might not be the fastest car in the world, but …** ce n'est peut-être pas la voiture la plus rapide du monde, mais …; **it m.** *or* **might be that …** il se peut *ou* se pourrait bien que + *sub* …; **you m.** *or* **might be wondering why I'm doing that** vous vous demandez peut-être pourquoi je fais cela; **you m.** *or* **might well ask!** je me le demande!; **you m. find it funny now, but wait till it's your turn!** tu trouves peut-être ça drôle maintenant mais tu verras quand ce sera ton tour!; **be that as it m.** quoi qu'il en soit; **that's as m. be, but we can't afford it** peut-être, mais nous ne pouvons pas nous le permettre; **but that's as m. be, it's all history now** enfin, tout ça, c'est du passé; **whatever faults he m.** *or* **might have** he is never dull quels que soient ses défauts, il n'est jamais ennuyeux; **we m.** *or* **might as well stay where we are** autant rester où nous sommes **2** *(asking or giving permission)* **m. I come in?** est-ce que je peux entrer?; **m. I write to you? – of course you m.** pourrais-je vous écrire? – je vous en prie; **you m. go** vous pouvez partir; *(at end of interview)* vous pouvez disposer; **if I m.** *or* **might be allowed to express an opinion** si je puis me permettre; **if I m.** *or* **might say so** si j'ose dire; **m. I?** vous permettez?

3 *esp Fml (be allowed to)* **passengers m. take only one item of hand luggage** les passagers ne peuvent prendre *ou* ne sont autorisés à prendre qu'un bagage à main; **candidates m. consult a dictionary** l'utilisation d'un dictionnaire est autorisée pendant l'examen

4 *Fml (in clauses expressing purpose, fear etc)* **I only hope it m. last!** pourvu que cela *ou* ça dure!; **I fear you m. be right** j'ai bien peur que tu aies raison; **I pray that you m. be mistaken** j'espère que tu te trompes; **so that others m. sleep in peace** pour que les autres puissent dormir en paix

5 *(expressing a wish)* **m. she rest in peace!** qu'elle repose en paix!; **m. the best man win!** que le meilleur gagne!; **much good m. it do you!** grand bien vous fasse!

may² **N** *(blossom)* fleurs *fpl* d'aubépine

▸▸**m. blossom** fleurs d'aubépine; **m. tree** aubépine *f*

Maya ['maɪə] **N1** Maya *mf* **2** *Ling* maya *m*

Mayan ['maɪən] **ADJ** maya

N1 Maya *mf* **2** *Ling* maya *m*

maybe ['meɪbi:] **ADV** peut-être; **m. so, but …** peut-être mais …; **m. not, but …** peut-être (pas) mais …; **m. yes, m. no** peut-être bien que oui, peut-être bien que non; **m. she won't accept** peut-être qu'elle n'acceptera pas, elle n'acceptera peut-être pas

N *Fam* **I don't want any maybes** c'est oui ou non!

Mayday ['meɪdeɪ] **N** *(signal)* mayday *m*, SOS *m* **INT** *(distress signal)* mayday!

▸▸**M. signal** mayday, SOS

mayfly ['meɪflaɪ] **N** *Entom* éphémère *m* vulgaire

mayhem ['meɪhem] **N1** *(chaos)* confusion *f* totale, chaos *m*; *(violent behaviour)* grabuge *m*; **it was m.** c'était le chaos; **to create** *or* **cause m.** *(to cause chaos)* semer la pagaille; *(to behave violently)* faire du grabuge **2** *Law (maiming)* mutilation *f*; *Am* **to commit m. on sb** se livrer à des voies de fait contre qn

mayn't ['meɪənt] **CONTR** = **may not** *see* **may¹**

mayo ['meɪəʊ] **N** *esp Am Fam* mayo *f*

mayonnaise [meɪə'neɪz] **N** mayonnaise *f*

mayor [meər] **N** maire *m*

mayoress ['meərəs] **N1** *(mayor)* maire *m*, *Old-fashioned* mairesse *f* **2** *esp Br (mayor's wife)* mairesse *f*

maypole ['meɪpəʊl] **N** mât *m*

maze [meɪz] **N** labyrinthe *m*, dédale *m*; *Fig (of streets, regulations etc)* dédale

MB *Comput (abbr* **megabyte)** Mo

Mb *Comput (abbr* **megabit)** Mb

MBA [embiː'eɪ] **N** *Univ (abbr* **Master of Business Administration)** MBA *m*

MBE [embiː'iː] **N** *Br (abbr* **Member of the Order of the British Empire)** *(award)* Ordre *m* de l'Empire britannique; *(person)* membre *m* de l'Ordre de l'Empire britannique

MBI [embiː'aɪ] **N** *Com (abbr* **management buy-in)** apport *m* de gestion

MBO [embiː'əʊ] **N** *Com* **1** *(abbr* **management buy-out)** rachat *m* d'une entreprise par la direction **2** *(abbr* **management by objectives)** gestion *f* selon objectifs

MBS [embiː'es] **N** *Fin (abbr* **mortgage-backed security)** titre *m* garanti par des créances hypothécaires

MC [em'siː] **N** *(abbr* **Master of Ceremonies)** *(at formal event)* maître *m* des cérémonies; *TV etc* animateur *m*, présentateur *m*

m-commerce **N** m-commerce *m*

MCP [emsiː'piː] **N** *Fam (abbr* **male chauvinist pig)** phallocrate *m*, macho *m*

MD [em'diː] **N1** *Med (abbr* **Doctor of Medicine)** docteur *m* en médecine **2** *Com (abbr* **Managing Director)** PDG *m* **3** *(abbr* **Mini-Disc®)** MiniDisc® *m*

Md *abbr* **Maryland**

MDF [emdiː'ef] **N** *(abbr* **medium-density fibreboard)** MDF *m*, panneaux *mpl* de fibres de moyenne densité

ME [em'iː] **N** *Med (abbr* **myalgic encephalomyelitis)** encéphalo-myélite *f* myalgique

Me *abbr* **Maine**

me [*unstressed* mɪ, *stressed* miː] **PERS PRON** VOIR GRAMMAIRE A27; B18–19 **1** *(unstressed)* me; *(before vowel sound)* m'; *(with preposition)* moi; **he**

knows me il me connaît; **he told me so** il me l'a dit; **listen to me** écoutez-moi; **lend it (to) me** prêtez-le-moi; **she wrote me a letter** elle m'a écrit une lettre; **I'll take it with me** je le prendrai avec moi; **he's younger than me** il est plus jeune que moi; **no-one knows the real me** personne ne sait vraiment qui je suis VOIR GRAMMAIRE A43

2 *(stressed)* **you and me** vous et moi; **he was thinking of me** il pensait à moi; **that's for me** ça, c'est pour moi SEE GRAMMAR B20–1

3 *(complement of verb* **to be)** **it's me!** c'est moi!; **is it just me or is there a smell of gas in here?** est-ce que je me fais des idées ou est-ce que ça sent le gaz?; **this jacket isn't really me** cette veste n'est pas vraiment mon style

4 *(in int)* **silly me! I've forgotten the address** ce que je peux être bête! j'ai oublié l'adresse; **clumsy me! I've spilled my drink!** ce que je peux être maladroit! j'ai renversé mon verre!

mead [miːd] **N** *(drink)* hydromel *m*

meadow ['medəʊ] **N** pré *m*, prairie *f*

▸▸*Bot* **m. grass** pâturin *m*; *Orn* **m. pipit** pipit *m* des prés, farlouse *f*; *Br Bot* **m. saffron** safran *m* des prés, colchique *m* d'automne

meadowland ['medəʊlænd] **N** prairie(s) *f(pl)*

meadowsweet ['medəʊswiːt] **N** *(plant)* (spirée *f*) ulmaire *f*, reine *f* des prés

meagre, *Am* **meager** ['miːgər] **ADJ** maigre

meagrely, *Am* **meagerly** ['miːgəlɪ] **ADV** maigrement, piètrement; **they exist m.** ils arrivent tout juste à subsister

meal¹ [miːl] **N** repas *m*; **I've had a huge m.** j'ai mangé comme quatre; **to eat between meals** manger entre les repas; **would you like some wine with your m.?** est-ce que vous prendrez du vin (avec votre repas)?; **in Spain the evening m. is later** en Espagne, on dîne plus tard; **to invite sb round for a m.** inviter qn à dîner; **enjoy your m.!** *(waiter etc to customers)* bon appétit!; *Fig Fam* **don't make a m. of it!** n'en fais pas toute une histoire!; **she always makes a m. of everything** il faut toujours qu'elle complique tout; *Fam* **the job is just a m. ticket** ce travail n'est qu'un gagne-pain; *Fam* **he's just a m. ticket to her** elle n'est avec lui que pour son argent

▸▸**m. tray** plateau *m* repas

meal² **N** *(of oats, rye, corn etc)* farine *f*

meals-on-wheels [miːlzɒn'wiːlz] **N** *Br Admin* = service *m* de repas (servis) à domicile pour personnes âgées ou handicapées; **she gets m.** on lui livre ses repas à domicile

mealtime ['miːltaɪm] **N** heure *f* du repas; **they only see each other at mealtimes** ils ne se voient qu'aux heures des repas

mealworm ['miːlwɜːm] **N** *Entom* ver *m* de farine

mealy ['miːlɪ] **ADJ1** *(in consistency)* farineux **2** *(covered in meal)* saupoudré de farine, poudreux **3** **m. complexion** teint *m* blême

mealy-mouthed [-'maʊðd] **ADJ** *Pej* doucereux, mielleux, patelin

mean¹ [miːn] **N1** *(middle)* (juste) milieu *m*, moyen terme *m*; **the golden** *or* **happy m.** le juste milieu, **2** *Math* moyenne *f*

ADJ *(medium, average)* moyen

▸▸*Comput* **m. time between failures** moyenne de temps entre deux pannes

mean² **ADJ1** *esp Br (with money)* avare, *Fam* radin; **to be m. with one's praise** *or* **compliments** être avare de compliments; **he's very m. about tipping** il n'aime pas donner de pourboires **2** *(low, ignoble)* *(person, character, action)* bas, méprisable, mesquin; *(wretched)* misérable, pauvre; **even to the meanest intelligence** même pour les esprits les plus obtus; **he has a m. streak** il peut être méchant quand il veut; **a m. trick** un vilain tour, *Fam* un sale coup; **that's m. of her** ce n'est pas chic de sa part; *Fam* **I feel very m. about not going** j'ai honte de ne pas y aller **3** *esp Am Fam (vicious, tough)* méchant, vicieux **(with no) no m. …** un très bon …/ une très bonne …; **he's no m. scholar** c'est un grand érudit; **it was no m. feat** ce n'était pas une mince affaire; **it's no m. task (to do sth)** ce n'est pas une mince affaire *ou* ce n'est pas rien (de faire qch) **5** *Fam (excellent)* formidable; **he plays a m. guitar** c'est un guitariste formidable **6** *Am Fam (poorly)* **to feel m.** se sentir mal en train

MEAN³ VT *(pt, pp meant [ment])* **1** *(have intention)* **to m. to do sth** avoir (bien) l'intention de faire qch, (bien) compter faire qch, vouloir faire qch; **what do you m. to do?** que comptez-vous faire?, qu'est-ce que vous avez l'intention de faire?; **I never meant to go** je n'ai jamais eu l'intention d'y aller; **I m. him no harm** je ne lui veux pas de mal; **she didn't m. (to do) it** elle ne l'a pas fait exprès; **without meaning it** sans le vouloir; **I meant to!** *(do what I did)* c'était bien mon intention!; **to m. well by sb** avoir de bonnes intentions à l'égard de qn; **she means well** elle a de bonnes intentions; **I m. to be obeyed** j'entends qu'on m'obéisse; **I m. to succeed** je veux réussir; **I m. to see justice done** je veux que justice soit faite
2 *(intend)* **I meant this book for you** je vous destinais ce livre; **the remark was meant for you** la remarque s'adressait à vous *ou* vous était destinée; **the remark wasn't meant to be overheard** cette remarque n'était pas censée être entendue; **it was meant as a joke/compliment/insult** c'était censé être une blague/un compliment/une insulte; **you weren't meant to open the presents until tomorrow** tu n'étais pas censé ouvrir les cadeaux avant demain; **I have a feeling this was meant to be** *or* **happen** j'ai le sentiment que ça devait arriver; **do you m. him?** est-ce de lui que vous parlez?, est-ce lui à qui vous faites allusion?; **this portrait is meant to be the duke** ce portrait est censé représenter le duc; **we were meant for each other** nous sommes faits l'un pour l'autre
3 *(signify) (of person)* vouloir dire; *(of word, phrase, event etc)* vouloir dire, signifier; **what does that word m.?** que signifie ce mot?; **the name means nothing to me** ce nom ne me dit rien; **what is meant by …?** que veut dire …?; **all this means nothing** tout cela ne rime à rien; **it doesn't m. anything** *(what you saw, heard)* cela ne prouve rien; **this means war/the end of our relationship** c'est la guerre/la fin de notre amitié; **what do you m.?** que voulez-vous dire?; **what do you m. by that?** qu'entendez-vous par là?; **I know what you m.!** *(I quite agree)* et comment!; **what, me?, I don't know what you m.!** qui moi?, je ne vois pas ce que vous voulez dire!; **she knew what it meant to be hungry** elle savait ce que c'était que d'avoir faim
4 *(speak sincerely)* **do you think he meant what he said?** pensez-vous qu'il l'ait dit sérieusement?, est-ce que tu crois qu'il parlait sérieusement?; **I didn't m. that** ce n'est pas ce que je voulais dire; **you don't m. it!** vous voulez rire!, vous plaisantez!; **I m. it** je parle sérieusement; **you're my best friend – do you m. that?** tu es mon meilleur ami – tu le penses vraiment?; **when I say no, I m. no** quand je dis non, c'est non; **do you m. to tell me …?** est-ce que tu es en train de me dire …?; **I m. (to say)!** je veux dire!
5 *(be of importance)* **the price means nothing to him** le prix importe peu pour lui; **doesn't your daughter's education m.**

---

anything to you? est-ce que l'éducation de ta fille ne t'intéresse pas?; **I cannot tell you what he has meant to me** je ne saurais vous dire tout ce qu'il a été pour moi; **my Sundays m./independence means a lot to me** le dimanche/mon indépendance est sacré(e) pour moi
6 *(imply, involve)* signifier, impliquer; **it would m. the children having to change school again** cela signifierait que les enfants devraient changer d'école une fois de plus; **just because you've been to university doesn't m. you know everything** ce n'est pas parce que tu es allé à l'université que tu sais tout; **it doesn't m. we have to stop seeing each other** ça ne veut pas dire que nous devons cesser de nous voir

meander [mɪˈændər] N *Geog* méandre *m*
VI **1** *(of person)* errer çà et là, flâner; *(in speaking)* divaguer **2** *(of river)* serpenter, faire des méandres

meandering [mɪˈændərɪŋ] ADJ **1** *(speech etc)* sans plan, sans suite **2** *(river)* qui serpente *ou* fait des méandres

meanie [ˈmiːnɪ] N *Fam* **1** *esp Br (miserly person)* rapiat, -ate, pingre *mf* **2** *esp Am (nasty person)* **what a m.!** quel chameau!, qu'il est vache!

meaning [ˈmiːnɪŋ] N signification *f*, sens *m*; *Ling (of term etc)* acception *f*; **what is the m. of this word?** que signifie *ou* que veut dire ce mot?; **what's the m. of this?** *(expressing indignation)* qu'est-ce que cela signifie?; *Fig Fam* **loyalty? you don't know the m. of the word!** tu ne sais pas ce que c'est que la loyauté!; **life had no m. for him** la vie n'avait plus aucun sens pour lui; **to understand sb's m.** comprendre ce que qn veut dire; *Fam* **if you get my m.** si tu vois ce que je veux dire; **a look full of m.** un regard significatif
ADJ *(look, smile)* significatif, qui en dit long

meaningful [ˈmiːnɪŋfʊl] ADJ *(full of meaning)* significatif, éloquent; *(expressive) (look, smile)* significatif, qui en dit long; *esp Pol* **m. talks** conversations *fpl* constructives; **a m. relationship** une relation sérieuse

meaningfully [ˈmiːnɪŋfʊlɪ] ADV *(to sing)* de façon expressive; **he smiled m. at her** le sourire qu'il lui fit en disait long

meaningless [ˈmiːnɪŋlɪs] ADJ dénué *ou* vide de sens, qui ne signifie rien; **a m. act/ remark** un non-sens

meanly [ˈmiːnlɪ] ADV **1** *esp Br (in miserly fashion)* en lésinant, chichement **2** *(ignobly) (to act, behave)* peu loyalement, indignement **3** *(wretchedly)* misérablement, pauvrement

meanness [ˈmiːnnɪs] N **1** *esp Br (with money)* avarice *f*, *Fam* radinerie *f* **2** *(nastiness)* mesquinerie *f*, méchanceté *f* **3** *(baseness)* bassesse *f*, petitesse *f*; **the m. of vision expressed in his speech …** l'étroitesse d'esprit que reflétait son discours … **4** *(poor quality, poverty)* médiocrité *f*, pauvreté *f*

means [miːnz] NPL *(often with sing verb)* **1** *(method)* moyen(s) *m(pl)*; **to use every possible m. to do sth** employer tous les moyens pour faire qch; **there is no m. of escape** il n'y a pas d'issue; **by all m.** *(by every possible method)* par tous les moyens (possibles); *(certainly)* mais certainement!, mais oui!; **may I come in? – by all m.!** puis-je entrer? – je vous en prie!; **by no m.** en aucune façon, nullement; **she is not stupid by any (manner of) m.** elle est loin d'être stupide; **by some m. or other** d'une manière ou d'une autre; **by m. of sth** au moyen *ou* à l'aide de qch; **they escaped by m. of a secret passage** il se sont enfuis par un passage secret; **she succeeded by m. of her own hard work** elle a réussi grâce à son travail acharné; **a m. to an end** un moyen d'arriver à ses fins; *Econ* **m. of pro-**

---

duction moyens *mpl* de production; **m. of transport** moyen *m* de transport
2 *(income)* moyens *mpl*, ressources *fpl*; *(wealth)* fortune *f*; **according to our m.** selon nos moyens; **to live beyond/within one's m.** vivre au-dessus de/selon ses moyens; **private m.** ressources personnelles; **a man of m.** un homme dont les revenus sont élevés; **to be without m.** *(without resources)* être sans ressources; *(without wealth)* être sans fortune; **they are without the m. to deal with the problem** ils n'ont pas les moyens de résoudre le problème
▸▸ *Admin* **m. test** enquête *f* sur les revenus *(d'une personne désirant bénéficier d'une allocation d'État)*

means-test VT *Admin* **to m. sb** = faire une enquête sur les ressources de qn avant de lui accorder une aide sociale

meant PT, PP *see* **mean³**

meantime, meanwhile [ˈmiːntaɪm, -waɪl] N, ADV **(in the) meantime, meanwhile** dans l'intervalle, pendant ce temps-là, en attendant

measles [ˈmiːz(ə)lz] NPL *(usu with sing verb)* *Med* rougeole *f*; **to have (the) m.** avoir la rougeole; **German m.** rubéole *f*

measly [ˈmiːzlɪ] ADJ *Fam* insignifiant, minable; **keep your m. money!** garde ton sale argent!; **all I got was one m. bar of chocolate** je n'ai eu qu'une misérable tablette de chocolat!

measurable [ˈmeʒərəb(ə)l] ADJ **1** mesurable; **a m. difference** *(in sb's performance etc)* une différence sensible **2** *Chem etc (constituent)* dosable

measure [ˈmeʒər] N **1** *(measurement)* mesure *f*; *Fig* **to get the m. of sb** prendre la mesure de qn, jauger qn; **to have the m. of sb** savoir comment s'y prendre avec qn
2 *(instrument) (for grain, milk etc)* mesure *f*
3 *(quantity)* dose *f*, mesure *f*; **a m. of whisky** une dose de whisky; **to give sb short m.** donner moins que la mesure à qn; **half m.** demi-mesure *f*, *pl* demi-mesures; *Fig* **there are no half measures with her** avec elle, il n'y a pas de demi-mesure; *Fig* **then she insulted the other man for good m.** elle a aussi insulté l'autre pour ne pas faire de jaloux; **he gave him a couple of kicks for good m.** il lui a donné quelques coups de pied en prime
4 *(degree)* **in some m.** dans une certaine mesure; **she was in great m. to blame for what happened** elle est en grande partie responsable de ce qui s'est passé; **a m. of independence** une certaine indépendance
5 *(limit)* mesure *f*, limite *f*; **beyond m.** outre mesure
6 *(action, step)* mesure *f*, démarche *f*; **to take measures** prendre des mesures; **to take extreme measures** employer les grands moyens
7 *Parl (bill)* projet *m* de loi
8 *(in poetry)* mesure *f*
9 *esp Am Mus* mesure *f*
VT *(distance, time, person etc)* mesurer; *(wall etc)* métrer, mesurer; *(piece of land)* arpenter; *(person for clothes)* mesurer, prendre les mesures de; *Fig* **to m. one's length (on the ground)** *(fall)* s'étaler par terre, tomber de tout son long; *Fig* **to m. one's strength** *or* **oneself with sb** mesurer ses forces avec qn, se mesurer avec *ou* contre qn; *Fig* **to m. one's words** mesurer *ou* peser ses paroles
VI mesurer; **column measuring 10 metres** colonne qui mesure 10 mètres
▸ **measure off** VT SEP *(material etc)* mesurer
▸ **measure out** VT SEP *(corn etc)* mesurer; *(distribute)* répartir, attribuer; **the barman measured out a double whisky** le barman versa un double whisky; **m. out two cups of flour** préparez deux mesures de farine

▶ **measure up** VT SEP (wood) mesurer; **to m. sb up for a suit** prendre les mesures de qn pour un costume; **to get measured up for a new suit** se faire prendre ses mesures pour un nouveau costume; Fig **they measured each other up** (before fight etc) ils se sont jaugés

VI (of employee etc) faire le poids, être à la hauteur

▶ **measure up to** VT INSEP **to m. up to one's job** se montrer à la hauteur de sa tâche; **to m. up to sb/sth** être à la mesure de qn/qch; **to m. up to sb's expectations** répondre aux attentes de qn; **the holiday didn't m. up to their expectations** leurs vacances n'ont pas été à la mesure de leurs espérances; **the meal didn't m. up to her usual standards** le repas qu'elle nous a préparé n'était pas aussi bon que d'habitude

measured ['meʒəd] ADJ **1** (time, distance etc) mesuré, déterminé **2** (deliberate) (movement, step) cadencé; **with m. steps** à pas mesurés ou comptés; **m. tread** marche f scandée **3** (language) modéré; **to speak in m. tones** parler sur un ton modéré **4** (in poetry) (verse etc) mesuré

measurement ['meʒəmənt] N (quantity, length etc) mesure f, (action) mesure, mesurage m; **the measurements of a room/an object** les dimensions fpl d'une pièce/d'un objet; **bust/waist/hip m.** (of person) tour m de poitrine/taille/hanches; **to take a customer's measurements** prendre les mesures d'un client SEE GRAMMAR B59

▶ ▶ **m. ton** tonne f d'encombrement

measuring ['meʒərɪŋ] N

▶ ▶ **m. chain** (in surveying) chaîne f d'arpenteur ou d'arpentage; **m. cup** mesure f, **m. glass** verre m gradué ou doseur; **m. jug** mesure; **m. spoon** cuillère f à doser; **m. tape** mètre m (à) ruban

meat [mi:t] N **1** viande f, Old-fashioned **m. and drink** le manger et le boire; Fig **it was m. and drink to them** c'était une véritable aubaine pour eux; Prov **one man's m. is another man's poison** on ne discute pas des goûts et des couleurs, ce qui guérit l'un tue l'autre **2** Fig (substantial content) (of book, film, article etc) substance f

▶ ▶ **m. broth** bouillon m gras; **m. diet** régime m carné; **m. hook** crochet m de boucherie; **m. loaf** pain m de viande; Br Fam Pej **m. market** (nightclub) = boîte f réputée pour être un lieu de drague; Am Fam **m. wagon** (ambulance) ambulance f

meatball ['mi:tbɔ:l] N **1** Culin boulette f (de viande) **2** Am Fam (person) crétin, -ine, imbécile mf

meathead ['mi:thed] N Am Fam crétin, -ine, imbécile mf

meatpacking ['mi:tpækɪŋ] N Am abattage m et boucherie f

meaty ['mi:tɪ] ADJ **1** (sausage etc) riche en viande; (smell etc) de viande; Fig (book etc) riche **2** (fleshy) charnu

Mecca ['mekə] N la Mecque; Fig **a M. for antique lovers** un paradis pour les passionnés d'objets anciens

mechanic [mɪ'kænɪk] N mécanicien, -ienne; **I'm not much of a m.** je ne suis pas très mécanicien

> Note that the French word **mécanique** is a false friend and is never a translation for the English word **mechanic**. It means **mechanics**.

mechanical [mɪ'kænɪk(ə)l] ADJ **1** Tech mécanique; **he has no m. skill** il n'a aucune compétence en mécanique **2** Fig (reply, smile etc) machinal, -aux, automatique, mécanique; **to give a m. response** répondre

machinalement; **a m. gesture** un geste machinal; **her playing is very m.** (of pianist etc) elle joue d'une façon très mécanique

▶ ▶ **m. breakdown insurance** assurance f panne mécanique; **m. digger** pelleteuse f mécanique; **m. drawing** dessin m aux instruments; **m. efficiency** rendement m mécanique; **m. engineer** ingénieur m mécanicien; **m. engineering** génie m mécanique; **m. failure** défaillance f mécanique, panne f mécanique; **m. wear** usure f mécanique

mechanically [mɪ'kænɪklɪ] ADV **1** Tech mécaniquement; **m. driven** actionné mécaniquement; **I'm not very m. minded** je ne suis pas très doué pour tout ce qui est mécanique **2** Fig (to reply, smile etc) machinalement

mechanics [mɪ'kænɪks] N VOIR GRAMMAIRE A10 **1** (science) mécanique f **2** (working parts) mécanisme m

mechanism ['mekənɪz(ə)m] N (device, working parts), Phil, Psy etc mécanisme m

mechanistic [mekə'nɪstɪk] ADJ (view of universe, explanation) mécaniste

mechanization [mekənaɪ'zeɪʃən] N mécanisation f

mechanize ['mekənaɪz] VT mécaniser; (troops) motoriser

mechanized ['mekənaɪzd] ADJ **m. industry** industrie mécanisée; Mil **m. troops** troupes motorisées

Med (the) [ðə'med] N Fam la Méditerranée

MEd [e'med] N (abbr **Master of Education**) ≃ CAPES m

medal ['med(ə)l] N médaille f, **to award a m. to sb** décerner une médaille ou une décoration à qn; **to be awarded a m. for bravery** être décoré pour sa bravoure

▶ ▶ Am Mil **M. of Honor** = la plus haute distinction américaine donnée en récompense à un soldat

medallion [mɪ'dæljən] N médaillon m

▶ ▶ Br Fam Hum **m. man** = individu m entre deux âges à l'allure machiste et vulgaire, qui essaie de passer pour plus jeune qu'il n'est

medallist, Am **medalist** ['medəlɪst] N Sport etc médaillé, -ée; **gold/silver m.** titulaire mf d'une ou de la médaille d'or/d'argent

meddle ['med(ə)l] VI (interfere) se mêler (**in** de); (tamper) toucher (**with** à); **to m. in other people's affairs** se mêler des affaires d'autrui

meddler ['medlər] N **he's a terrible m.** il met son nez partout

meddlesome ['med(ə)lsəm] ADJ qui se mêle de tout

meddling ['medlɪŋ] ADJ = **meddlesome**
N (action) ingérence f (**in** dans)

media ['mi:dɪə] NPL **the (mass) m.** les médias mpl; **the m. were waiting for her when she flew in** les journalistes l'attendaient à sa descente d'avion VOIR GRAMMAIRE A11

▶ ▶ **m. advertising** publicité f média; **m. analysis** analyse f des médias; **m. analyst** analyste mf des médias; **m. buyer** acheteur, -euse d'espaces (publicitaires); **m. circus** cirque m médiatique; **m. consultant** conseil m en communication; **m. coverage** couverture f médiatique, médiatisation f, **to get too much m. coverage** être surmédiatisé; **m. event** événement m médiatique; **m. exposure** (coverage) couverture médiatique, médiatisation; (of product) exposition f dans les médias; **m. group** groupe m de médias; **m. hype** battage m médiatique; **m. library** médiathèque f, **m. mix** mix m média; **m. mogul** magnat m des médias; **m. overkill** surmédiatisation f, médiatisation f excessive; **m. person** (man) homme m de communication; (woman) femme f de communication; **m. planner** médiaplaneur m, média

planner m; **m. planning** média planning m; **m. release** communiqué m; **m. research** médialogie f, **m. scrum** ruée f de journalistes; **m. studies** = études fpl en communication et journalisme

media-conscious ADJ (politician etc) médiatique

mediaeval, mediaevalist = **medieval, medievalist**

media-friendly ADJ médiatique

mediagenic [mi:dɪə'dʒenɪk] ADJ médiatique

medial ['mi:dɪəl] ADJ intermédiaire (**to** entre); (letter) médial, -aux
N Ling médiale f

median ['mi:dɪən] ADJ médian
N **1** Anat (nerve) nerf m médian; (vein) veine f médiane **2** (in statistics), Math médiane f
▶ ▶ Am Aut **m. strip** terre-plein m central, pl terre-pleins centraux, Belg, Suisse berme f centrale

mediant ['mi:dɪənt] N Mus médiante f

media-shy ADJ qui fuit les médias

mediate ['mi:dɪeɪt] VI (of person) agir en ou servir de médiateur (**between** entre)
VT **to m. a peace** intervenir en qualité de médiateur pour amener la paix

mediation [mi:dɪ'eɪʃən] N médiation f, **to go to m.** recourir à une médiation

mediator ['mi:dɪeɪtər] N médiateur, -trice

medic ['medɪk] N Fam (student) étudiant, -ante en médecine, carabin m; (doctor) toubib m

Medicaid ['medɪkeɪd] N Am = assistance f médicale pour les défavorisés

medical ['medɪk(ə)l] ADJ médical, -aux; (book etc) de médecine; (student) en médecine; **you need m. attention** il faut vous faire soigner par un médecin
N visite f médicale; **to have a m.** passer une visite médicale; **he failed the m.** il n'a pas été accepté pour raisons de santé
▶ ▶ **m. certificate** certificat m médical; **m. examination** visite f médicale; Am **m. examiner** médecin m légiste; **m. history** (patient's file) dossier m médical; (previous problems) antécédents mpl médicaux; **m. jurisprudence** médecine f légale; **M. Officer of Health** directeur, -trice de la santé publique; **m. practitioner** (médecin) généraliste mf; **the m. profession** (people) le corps médical; (activity) la profession médicale; **m. record** dossier médical

medically ['medɪklɪ] ADV médicalement; **to be m. examined** subir un examen médical

medicament [me'dɪkəmənt] N médicament m

Medicare ['medɪkeər] N **1** Am = assistance f médicale pour les personnes âgées et les handicapés **2** Can assurance-maladie f

medicate ['medɪkeɪt] VT (patient) faire suivre un traitement à

medicated ['medɪkeɪtɪd] ADJ (shampoo) médical, -aux, traitant; (soap) médical, -aux

medication [medɪ'keɪʃən] N (medicine, drugs) médicaments mpl; **to take one's m.** prendre ses médicaments; **to be on m.** suivre un traitement

medicinal [me'dɪsɪn(ə)l] ADJ médicinal, -aux, médicamenteux; Hum **it's just for m. purposes** (having a whisky etc) c'est mon médicament
▶ ▶ **m. plants** plantes fpl médicinales; **m. properties** vertus fpl curatives

medicinally [me'dɪsɪn(ə)lɪ] ADV (to use a herb, substance) médicalement, comme médicament; (to treat) médicalement

medicine ['medsɪn] N **1** (practice, science)

médecine f, **to practise m.** exercer la médecine; **to study m.** faire des études de médecine, étudier la médecine **2** *(remedy)* médicament m; *Fig* **to give sb a taste of his/her own m.** rendre la pareille à qn; *Fig* **to take one's m.** avaler la pilule, supporter les conséquences (de son action)

▸▸ **m. ball** medicine-ball m, pl medicine-balls, médecine-ball m, pl médecine-balls; **m. cabinet, m. chest** (armoire f à) pharmacie f, **m. man** sorcier m, medicine-man m

Note that the French word **médecine** never means **remedy**.

medico ['medɪkəʊ] N *Fam* = medic

medieval [medɪ'iːvəl] ADJ du moyen âge, médiéval, -aux; *Fig (attitudes, person)* rétrograde; **it's m. here** c'est le moyen âge ici

medievalist [medɪ'iːvəlɪst] N médiéviste mf

mediocre [miːdɪ'əʊkər] ADJ médiocre

mediocrity [miːdɪ'ɒkrɪtɪ] N *(quality)* médiocrité f, **a m.** *(person)* un/une médiocre

meditate ['medɪteɪt] VI **1** *(reflect)* méditer (**on, upon** sur), réfléchir (**on, upon** sur, à) **2** *(be in or enter into a state of meditation)* méditer; *esp Rel* se recueillir
VT *(project, undertaking)* méditer

meditation [medɪ'teɪʃən] N **1** *(thinking)* méditation f (**upon** sur) **2** *(state)* recueillement m **3** *Liter* **meditations** méditations fpl

meditative ['medɪtətɪv] ADJ méditatif, recueilli

meditatively ['medɪtətɪvlɪ] ADV d'un air méditatif

Mediterranean [medɪtə'reɪnɪən] ADJ méditerranéen; **the M. Sea** la mer Méditerranée
N **the M.** la Méditerranée

medium, pl **-a, -ums** ['miːdɪəm, -ə, -əmz] N
VOIR GRAMMAIRE A13 **1** *(mid-point)* milieu m, moyen terme m (**between** entre) **2** *Art (for working in)* matériau m; *(for advertising)* support m, médium m; **marble is her favourite m.** elle préfère travailler le marbre; **opera is his preferred m.** l'opéra est son moyen d'expression favori; **television is a powerful m.** la télévision est un média ou un moyen de communication ou un moyen de diffusion puissant; **through the m. of the press** par l'intermédiaire de la presse, par voie de presse; **French was the m. through which they communicated** ils communiquaient en français, le français était la langue dans laquelle ils communiquaient; **advertising m.** support publicitaire **3** *Phys* milieu m, véhicule m; *Biol* culture f, bouillon m de culture **4** *(in spiritualism)* médium mf
ADJ moyen; **of m. height** de taille moyenne; **cook in a m. oven** cuire à four moyen; **m. sized** de grandeur moyenne, de taille moyenne; **in the m. term** à moyen terme; **m. dry wine** vin m demi-sec, pl vins demi-secs
N *(something of medium size)* **this teeshirt's a m.** ce tee-shirt est une taille moyenne ou un deux; **available in small, m. and large** disponible en petit, moyen et grand
▸▸ *Cin* **m. close-up** plan m rapproché; *Am Radio* **m. frequency** ondes fpl moyennes; *Cin, TV* **m. long shot** plan de demi-ensemble; *Cin, TV* **m. shot** plan moyen; *Radio* **m. wave** ondes moyennes; **on m. wave** sur ondes moyennes

medium-haul ADJ *(flight, route)* moyen-courrier

medium-range N
▸▸ **m. ballistic missile** missile m balistique de moyenne portée

medium-rare ADJ à point

medium-term ADJ *(financing, forecast)* à

moyen terme; **m. financial assistance** aide f financière à moyen terme
▸▸ **m. credit** crédit m (à) moyen terme; **m. liabilities** dettes fpl à moyen terme; **m. note** billet m à moyen terme (négociable)

medlar ['medlər] N *(fruit)* nèfle f, *(tree)* néflier m
▸▸ **m. tree** néflier

medley ['medlɪ] N *(of people, objects)* mélange m, méli-mélo m, pl mélis-mélos; *Mus* pot-pourri m, pl pots-pourris; *Swimming* **400 metres m. (race)** 4 x 100 mètres quatre nages

medulla [me'dʌlə] N **1** *Bot* médulle f, moelle f **2** *Anat (of bone)* moelle f

meek [miːk] ADJ doux, f douce, docile; **m. and mild** doux comme un agneau

meekly ['miːklɪ] ADV avec soumission, docilement

meekness ['miːknɪs] N douceur f de caractère, soumission f, docilité f

meerschaum ['mɪəʃəm] N **1** *Miner* écume f (de mer) **2** *(pipe)* pipe f en écume (de mer)
▸▸ **m. pipe** pipe en écume (de mer)

MEET¹ [miːt]

| VT rencontrer **1, 3, 5, 8** ▪ croiser **1**
▪ rejoindre **2** ▪ retrouver **2** ▪ aller chercher **2** ▪ faire la connaissance de **3** ▪ satisfaire **7** |

N **1** *(in hunting)* rassemblement m de la meute
2 *Sport* meeting m
3 *esp Am (meeting)* réunion f
VT *(pt, pp* **met** [met]*)* **1** *(by accident) (person)* rencontrer; **to m. sb on the stairs** croiser qn dans l'escalier; **to m. another car** croiser une autre voiture
2 *(by arrangement) (person)* rejoindre, retrouver; **to go to m. sb** aller au-devant de qn, aller à la rencontre de qn; **to m. sb at the station** aller chercher qn à la gare; **the bus meets the train** il y a une correspondance entre le train et l'autobus; **I arranged to m. him at three o'clock** j'ai pris rendez-vous avec lui pour trois heures; **I'll m. you at the crossroads** je te retrouve au croisement
3 *(become acquainted with)* rencontrer, faire la connaissance de; **I met her at the Martins'** je l'ai rencontrée chez les Martin; **pleased to m. you** ravi de faire votre connaissance; **have you met my husband?** vous connaissez mon mari?; **I get to m. a lot of people in my job** mon travail m'amène à rencontrer beaucoup de gens; **I like meeting people** j'aime rencontrer des gens; **she's the nicest person I've ever met** c'est la personne la plus gentille que j'ai jamais rencontrée; **m. Mr Thomas** je vous présente M. Thomas
4 *(join)* **the stream meets the river** le ruisseau se jette dans la rivière; **where East meets West** où l'est et l'ouest se rencontrent; **here the road meets the railway** c'est ici que la route rejoint ou croise le chemin de fer
5 *(come into contact with)* **his eyes met mine** nos regards se sont croisés; **he was afraid to m. her eye** il avait peur de croiser son regard; **her mouth met his** leurs bouches se rencontrèrent; **her car met an oncoming lorry and ...** sa voiture a percuté un camion qui arrivait en sens inverse et ...
6 *(be perceived by)* **a strange sound met our ears** nous avons entendu un bruit étrange; **a remarkable sight met our eyes** nous avons été témoins d'un spectacle incroyable; **there's more to this than meets the eye** on ne connaît pas les dessous de cette affaire; **there's more to him than meets the eye** c'est quelqu'un de plus complexe qu'il n'y paraît au premier abord

7 *(satisfy) (a need)* satisfaire, répondre à; *(demands)* satisfaire; *(condition, requirement)* satisfaire à; *(objection, criticism)* répondre à; *(cheque)* honorer; *Com (order)* satisfaire, assurer; *Com (bill of exchange)* honorer, faire honneur à; **to m. sb's wishes** combler les désirs de qn; **to m. sb's expectations** répondre à l'attente de qn; **to m. one's commitments** remplir ses engagements; *Com* **to m. demand** répondre à la demande; **to m. expenses** supporter les dépenses, subvenir aux frais; **the cost will be met by the company** les frais seront pris en charge par la compagnie
8 *(face) (danger)* affronter; *(the enemy)* rencontrer, affronter; *(difficulty)* se heurter à; **she met her death in an air crash** elle a trouvé la mort ou péri dans un accident d'avion; *Sport* **he will m. the champion in June** il rencontrera ou affrontera le champion en juin
VI **1** *(by accident) (of people)* se rencontrer *(par hasard)*
2 *(by arrangement) (of people)* se retrouver; **let's m. for lunch** on se retrouve pour le déjeuner?; **where shall we m.?** où se retrouve-t-on?; **when shall we m. again?** quand nous reverrons-nous?; **we should m. more often** on devrait se voir plus souvent
3 *(become acquainted)* se rencontrer, se connaître; **they met in 1999** ils se sont rencontrés ou connus en 1999
4 *(of society, assembly)* se réunir; **the club meets every other Tuesday** le cercle se réunit un mardi sur deux
5 *(join)* se rencontrer, se rejoindre; *(of rivers)* confluer, se rejoindre; **a country where East and West m.** un pays où se rencontrent l'est et l'ouest; **his eyebrows m.** ses sourcils se touchent
6 *(come into contact)* se rencontrer; **the two cars met head on** les deux voitures se sont heurtées de plein fouet; **our eyes met** nos regards se sont croisés; **their hands met** leurs mains se rencontrèrent
▸ **meet up** VI se rencontrer; **we'll have to m. up next time I'm in Paris** il faudra qu'on se voie la prochaine fois que je passerai à Paris; **we met up with an Australian** nous avons rencontré un Australien
▸ **meet with** VT INSEP **1** **to m. with a refusal** essuyer un refus; **to m. with difficulties** rencontrer des difficultés; **to m. with failure** échouer; **the proposal has met with fierce opposition** la proposition s'est heurtée à une opposition très vive; **the expedition met with disaster** l'expédition a tourné au désastre; **he has met with an accident** il lui est arrivé un accident; **the plan didn't m. with her approval** le projet n'a pas reçu son accord
2 *esp Am (meet) (for discussion)* rencontrer, retrouver; *(for lunch etc)* retrouver

meet² ADJ *Arch, Lit* convenable, séant; **it is m. that ...** il convient que ...

meet-and-greet VT *(guests)* accueillir

meeting ['miːtɪŋ] N **1** *(encounter)* rencontre f, **during my first m. with him** lors de notre première rencontre; *Lit* **m. of minds** communion f de pensée **2** *(of society, assembly etc)* réunion f, séance f, *(in business, discussion)* réunion, conférence f, **he's in a m.** il est en conférence ou réunion; **at our last m.** lors de notre dernière réunion; **to hold a m.** tenir une réunion; **to call a m. of the shareholders** convoquer les actionnaires; **to open the m.** déclarer la séance ouverte; **to address the m.** prendre la parole **3** *Sport* meeting m; *Horseracing* (réunion f de) courses fpl **4** *Rel (of Quakers)* **to go to m.** aller au temple
▸▸ *Rel* **m. house** temple m; **m. place** *(for gatherings)* lieu m de réunion; *(for rendez-vous)* (lieu de) rendez-vous m; **m. point** *(of*

lines, things) point *m* de jonction; *Math* point de rencontre; *(for people)* lieu de rendez-vous; **meetings secretary** secrétaire *mf* de séance

meg [meg] N *Comput Sl* méga *m*

mega ['megə] ADJ *Fam (tremendous)* super, génial, -aux; *(big)* énorme

mega- ['megə] PREF *Fam* **m.-rich/famous/intelligent** hyper riche/célèbre/intelligent

megabit N *Comput* mégabit *m*

megabucks ['megəbʌks] N *Sl* un fric fou, une fortune; **her job pays m.** elle gagne une fortune dans son travail

megabyte ['megəbaɪt] N *Comput* méga-octet *m, pl* méga-octets, *Fam* méga *m*; **20 m. memory** mémoire *f* de 20 méga-octets

megacycle ['megəsaɪk(ə)l] N *Elec* mégacycle *m*

megadeath ['megədeθ] N mort *f* d'un million de personnes

megaflop ['megəflɒp] N *Comput* mégaflop *m*

megagroup ['megəgruːp] N *Mus* super-groupe *m*

megahertz ['megəhɜːts] N *Elec* mégahertz *m*

megalith ['megəlɪθ] N mégalithe *m*

megalithic [megə'lɪθɪk] ADJ mégalithique

megalomania [megələʊ'meɪnɪə] N mégalomanie *f*

megalomaniac [megələʊ'meɪnɪæk] ADJ, N mégalomane *mf*

megamerger ['megəmɜːdʒər] N *Com* méga-fusion *f*

megaphone ['megəfəʊn] N mégaphone *m*

megapixel ['megəpɪksəl] N mégapixel *m*

megaplex ['megəpleks] N *Am Cin* complexe *m* multisalles, cinéma *m* multisalle *(de plus de 16 salles)*

mega-resort N mégastation *f*, station *f* très importante

megastar ['megəstɑːr] N superstar *f*

megaton ['megətʌn] N mégatonne *f*

megavolt ['megəvɒlt] N *Elec* mégavolt *m*

megawatt ['megəwɒt] N *Elec* mégawatt *m*

megilla [mə'gɪlə] N *Am Fam* **the whole m.** tout le tremblement; **I don't need the whole m., just give me the main points** t'as pas besoin de tout me raconter en détail *ou* par le menu, dis-moi le principal

meiosis [maɪ'əʊsɪs] N **1** *(in rhetoric)* litote *f* **2** *Biol* méiose *f*

melaena [me'liːnə] N *Med* melæna *m*, méléna *m*

melancholia [melən'kəʊlɪə] N mélancolie *f*

melancholic [melən'kɒlɪk] ADJ mélanco-lique

melancholy ['melənkəlɪ] N mélancolie *f*; **a bout of m.** un accès de mélancolie
ADJ *(person)* mélancolique; *(news)* triste, attristant

melee ['meleɪ] N mêlée *f*

mellifluous [me'lɪflʊəs] ADJ *(words etc)* mélodieux

mellow ['meləʊ] ADJ **1** *(flavour, taste)* doux, *f* douce; *(wine)* moelleux, velouté; *(fruit)* fondant, mûr; *(voice, sound)* moelleux, doux; *(colour, light)* chaud, doux, velouté; **m. tobacco** tabac doux **2** *(person)* détendu; *Fam (pleasantly drunk)* un peu gris; **to grow m.** *(of person)* s'adoucir
VI **1** *(of flavour, taste, light)* s'adoucir; *(of wine)* mûrir, prendre du moelleux *ou* du ve-louté; *(of voice, sound)* devenir plus chaud *ou* plus riche *ou* moelleux, s'adoucir **2** *(of character)* s'adoucir; **to m. with age** s'adoucir *ou* devenir plus accommodant *ou* plus tolérant avec l'âge

VT **1** *(flavour, taste)* rendre plus doux; *(wine)* donner du moelleux *ou* du velouté à **2** *(person's character)* adoucir; **age has mellowed her** l'âge a adouci son caractère

▸ **mellow out** VI *Fam* s'adoucir; **why don't you m. out a bit?** pourquoi est-ce que tu n'essayes pas de te détendre un peu?

mellowing ['meləʊɪŋ] N *(of wine)* matura-tion *f*, *(of character)* adoucissement *m*

mellowness ['meləʊnɪs] N *(of flavour, light, colour, character)* douceur *f*; *(of wine)* moel-leux *m*, velouté *m*; *(of voice, sound)* velouté, moelleux

melodic [mɪ'lɒdɪk] ADJ *Mus* mélodique

melodious [mɪ'ləʊdɪəs] ADJ mélodieux

melodiously [mɪ'ləʊdɪəslɪ] ADV mélodieu-sement

melodrama ['melədrɑːmə] N mélodrame *m*

melodramatic [melədrə'mætɪk] ADJ mélo-dramatique

melodramatically [melədrə'mætɪklɪ] ADV d'un air *ou* d'une manière mélodramatique

melody ['melədɪ] N mélodie *f*

melon ['melən] N **1** *(fruit)* melon *m*; **m. seeds** pépins *mpl* de melon **2** *Am Fam (profits, money)* gros bénéfices *mpl* (à distribuer); **to carve** *or* **cut up the m.** distribuer les bénéfi-ces **3** *Sl* **melons** *(breasts)* nichons *mpl*, ro-berts *mpl*

melt [melt] *(pt, pp* **melted;** *pp adj* **molten** ['məʊlt(ə)n])* VI fondre; *(of solid in liquid)* fon-dre, se dissoudre; **to m. in the mouth** fondre dans la bouche; **to m. into ...** *(of colour etc)* se fondre dans ...; *Fig* **my heart** *or* **I melted** j'ai été attendri; **she melted (inside) at his touch** elle fondait sous ses caresses; **to m. into thin air** disparaître
VT *(ice, metal)* (faire) fondre; *(salt etc)* (faire) fondre, (faire) dissoudre; **to m. sb's heart** at-tendrir qn; **m. the butter in a pan** faire fon-dre le beurre dans une casserole; *Fig Fam* **I'm absolutely melted** *(very hot)* je cuis; **melted snow** neige fondue
N *(sandwich)* **bacon/tuna m.** sandwich *m* au bacon/au thon recouvert de fromage fon-du

▸ **melt away** VI **1** *(of snow)* fondre complète-ment **2** *(of clouds, vapour)* se dissiper; *(of crowd)* se disperser; *(of anger, objections, re-sistance etc)* se dissiper, s'évanouir

▸ **melt down** VT SEP *(scrap metal etc)* fondre

meltdown ['meltdaʊn] N **1** *Nucl* fusion *f* **2** *Fig* désintégration *f*; *(of Stock Exchange)* dégrin-golade *f*

melting ['meltɪŋ] ADJ *(wax, neige)* qui fond; *Fig (voice, words etc)* attendrissant
N *(act of melting) (of metal)* fonte *f*, fusion *f*; *(of snow)* fonte
▸▸ **m. point** point *m* de fusion; **m. pot** creu-set *m*; *Fig* melting-pot *m*, creuset; *Fig* **every-thing's in the m. pot** tout est à refaire; *Fig* **the United States is a m. pot** les États-Unis sont un creuset *ou* un melting-pot; **m. tempera-ture** température *f* de fusion

member ['membər] N **1** *(of family, club etc)* membre *m*; *(of party)* adhérent, -ente; **to be a m. of the family** faire partie de la famille; **a m. of the audience** un spectateur, une spec-tatrice; **a m. of the opposite sex** une per-sonne du sexe opposé **2** *(limb)* membre *m*; **(male)** membre (viril) **3** *Math* élément *m*
▸▸ **M. of Congress** membre du Congrès; **m. country** pays *m* membre; **M. of the Euro-pean Parliament** député *m* européen; *St Exch* **m. firm** société *f* membre; **M. of the House of Representatives** membre de la Chambre des représentants; **M. of the Nor-thern Ireland Assembly** membre de l'Assem-blée législative d'Irlande du Nord; **M. of Parliament** membre de la Chambre des communes, ≃ député *m*; **the M. of Parliament**

for Newcastle le député de Newcastle; **M. of the Scottish Parliament** député du parle-ment écossais; **m. state** État *m* membre; **M. of the Welsh Assembly** membre de l'Assem-blée du pays de Galles

membership ['membəʃɪp] N **1** *(state of being a member)* appartenance *f*; **m. of any political party is incompatible with this post** le titulaire de ce poste ne peut adhérer à aucun parti politique; **she resigned her m. of the party** elle a rendu sa carte du parti; **to pay one's m. (fee)** payer sa cotisation; **to re-new one's m.** se réinscrire **2** *(members)* membres *mpl*, adhérents *mpl*; *(number of members) (of society etc)* nombre *m* des membres *ou* des adhérents, effectif *m*; **club with a m. of a thousand** club de mille mem-bres; **the majority of our m.** la majorité de nos membres
▸▸ **m. card** carte *f* d'adhérent *ou* de mem-bre; **m. list** liste *f* des membres; **m. number** numéro *m* d'adhérent

membrane ['membreɪn] N *Biol etc* mem-brane *f*

membranous ['membrənəs] ADJ membra-neux

memento, *pl* **mementoes, mementos** [mɪ'mentəʊ, -əʊz] N souvenir *m*

memo ['meməʊ] N note *f* de service
▸▸ *Comput* **m. field** champ *m* mémo; **m. pad** bloc-notes *m, pl* blocs-notes

memoir ['memwɑːr] N *(essay) (scientific etc)* étude *f*, monographie *f*, *(biography)* notice *f* biographique; **memoirs** mémoires *fpl*

> Attention: ne pas confondre avec le nom anglais **memory**.

memorable ['memərəb(ə)l] ADJ *(speech, oc-casion)* mémorable; **a film m. largely for its sex and violence** un film surtout remarqué pour ses scènes de sexe et de violence

memorably ['memərəblɪ] ADV mémorable-ment, de façon mémorable

memorandum, *pl* **memoranda, memo-randums** [memə'rændəm, -də, -dəmz] N **1** *Ad-min (within office etc)* note *f* de service **2** *(reminder)* note *f* **3** *(in diplomacy)* mémoran-dum *m* **4** *Law (of sale etc)* mémoire *m*; *(of contract)* mémoire, sommaire *m* des arti-cles; **m. and articles of association** statuts *mpl* de société
▸▸ **m. of association** charte *f* constitutive d'une société à responsabilité limitée, acte *m* de société; **m. book** carnet *m*, calepin *m*, agenda *m*

memorial [mɪ'mɔːrɪəl] ADJ *(statue, festival, tablet, plaque etc)* commémoratif
N **1** *(monument)* monument *m* (commémo-ratif) **2** *(prize etc)* prix *m* commémoratif
▸▸ **m. service** commémoration *f*

memorize ['meməraɪz] VT apprendre par cœur

memory ['memərɪ] N **1** *(faculty)* mémoire *f*; **to have a good/bad m.** avoir (une) bonne/ mauvaise mémoire; **to have a good m. for faces/names** avoir la mémoire des visages/ des noms; **to have a bad m. for faces/names** ne pas avoir la mémoire des visages/des noms; *Fam* **m. like a sieve** mémoire de lièvre, très mauvaise mémoire; **loss of m.** perte *f* de mémoire; **if my m. serves me right** si j'ai bonne mémoire; **in** *or* **within living m.** de mémoire d'homme; **from m.** *(to play, recite, paint sth)* de mémoire; **to commit sth to m.** apprendre qch par cœur
2 *(something remembered) (of somebody, something)* souvenir *m*; **I have no m. of you saying any such thing** je ne me souviens pas que tu aies dit cela; **childhood memories** souvenirs *mpl* d'enfance; **I have very pleas-ant memories of your friend** je garde un

excellent souvenir de votre ami; **her earliest memories are of music** ses plus anciens souvenirs sont des airs de musique; **to take a trip down m. lane** *(visit place)* aller sur les lieux de son passé; **it's a real trip down m. lane** hearing that song cette chanson me rappelle ma jeunesse; **this television programme will take viewers on a trip down m. lane** cette émission rappellera de vieux souvenirs aux téléspectateurs; **to keep sb's m. alive** garder le souvenir de qn; **in m. of …** à la mémoire de …, en souvenir de … **3** *Comput* mémoire *f*

▸▸*Comput* **m. address** adresse *f* de mémoire; *Comput* **m. bank** bloc *m* de mémoire; *Comput* **m. buffer** zone *f* de mémoire tampon; *Comput* **m. capacity** capacité *f* de mémoire; *Comput* **m. card** carte *f* mémoire; *Comput* **m. cell** cellule *f* mémoire; *Comput* **m. chip** puce *f* mémoire; *Comput* **m. expansion card** carte d'extension de mémoire; **m. loss** perte de mémoire; *Comput* **m. management** gestion *f* de mémoire; *Comput* **m. manager** gestionnaire *m* de mémoire; *Comput* **m. mapping** adresses *fpl* mémoire; *Aut* **m. seat** siège *m* à positions mémorisables; **m. typewriter** machine *f* à écrire à mémoire; *Comput* **m. upgrade** ajout *m* de mémoire

> Attention: ne pas confondre avec le nom anglais **memoir**.

memory-intensive ADJ *Comput (application)* qui prend beaucoup de place en mémoire

memory-loadable ADJ *Comput* chargeable en résident

memory-resident ADJ *Comput* résident en mémoire

men [men] *see* **man**

menace ['menɪs] N **1** menace *f*; **there was m. in his voice** il parlait d'un ton menaçant; **to demand money with menaces** réclamer de l'argent en usant de menaces **2** *Fam* **that kid's a m.** cet enfant est une véritable plaie; **he's a m. behind the wheel of a car** c'est un vrai danger au volant; **that carpet's a m.** ce tapis est dangereux
VT menacer

menacing ['menəsɪŋ] ADJ menaçant; **in a m. voice** d'une voix menaçante

menacingly ['menəsɪŋlɪ] ADV *(to look)* d'un air menaçant; *(to say)* d'un ton menaçant

menagerie [mɪ'nædʒərɪ] N ménagerie *f*

mend [mend] N **1** *Fam* **to be on the m.** *(of person)* être en voie de guérison; *(of situation)* s'arranger, s'améliorer **2** *(in fabric etc)* raccommodage *m*; *(darn)* reprise *f*; **the socks have a m. in the heel** les chaussettes ont été raccommodées au talon
VT **1** *(repair) (item of clothing etc)* raccommoder; *(darn) (item of clothing, socks)* repriser; *(fishing net)* rem(m)ailler; *(tool, road, shoes etc)* réparer **2** *(put right)* rectifier, corriger; **to m. one's ways** s'amender, se corriger; **to m. one's manners** s'amender; *Prov* **least said soonest mended** moins on parle, mieux cela vaut
VI *(of broken bones)* se ressouder; *Fam* **you'll/it'll soon m.** tu t'en remettras; **we'll have to make do and m.** il va falloir faire avec

mendacious [men'deɪʃəs] ADJ *Fml (person)* menteur, -euse; *(report)* mensonger

mendacity [men'dæsɪtɪ] N *Fml (characteristic)* propension *f* au mensonge

Mendelian [men'diːlɪən] ADJ *Biol* mendélien

mendicant ['mendɪkənt] ADJ *Lit* mendiant, de mendiant
N **1** *Lit* mendiant, -ante **2** *Rel* moine *m* mendiant

▸▸*Rel* **m. friar** moine mendiant; *Rel* **m. order** ordre *m* mendiant

mending ['mendɪŋ] N **1** *(of clothes etc)* raccommodage *m* **2** *(clothes)* vêtements *mpl* à raccommoder

menfolk ['menfəʊk] NPL **the m.** *(in contrast to women)* les hommes *mpl*; **the women worked alongside their** *or* **the m.** les femmes travaillaient aux côtés des hommes

menial ['miːnɪəl] ADJ *(task)* ingrat; *(job)* subalterne
N *usu Pej* laquais *m*; *(in household)* domestique *mf*

meningitis [menɪn'dʒaɪtɪs] N *Med* méningite *f*; **to have m.** avoir *ou* faire une méningite

meniscus, *pl* **menisci, meniscuses** [mɪ'nɪskəs, -saɪ, -skəsəz] N ménisque *m*

menopausal ['menəpɔːzəl] ADJ ménopausique; *(woman)* à la ménopause

menopause ['menəpɔːz] N *Physiol* ménopause *f*; **to be going through the m.** être en ménopause

mensch [menʃ] N *Am Fam (man)* chic type *m*; *(woman)* brave femme *f*

menses ['mensiːz] NPL *Physiol* menstrues *fpl*

menstrual ['menstrʊəl] ADJ *Physiol (cycle)* menstruel

menstruate ['menstrʊeɪt] VI *Physiol* avoir ses règles

menstruation [menstrʊ'eɪʃən] N *Physiol* menstruation *f*

mensuration [mensə'reɪʃən] N **1** *Fml (act of measuring)* mesurage *m*, mesure *f* **2** *Math* mensuration *f*

menswear ['menzweər] N *Com* vêtements *mpl* pour hommes; *(department)* rayon *m* homme

▸▸ **m. department** rayon homme

mental ['mentəl] ADJ **1** *(state, age etc)* mental, -aux; **I made a m. note to speak to her about it** je me suis dit qu'il ne fallait pas oublier de lui en parler; **I've made a m. note of it** j'y pense **2** *Sl (mad)* cinglé, dingue; **to go m.** *(go mad)* devenir dingue *ou* cinglé, perdre la boule; *(lose one's temper)* péter les plombs, péter une durite, piquer une crise; *Br* **it was a m. party!** c'était une fête vraiment démente *ou* dingue!

▸▸ **m. arithmetic** calcul *m* mental; **m. block** blocage *m* psychologique; **m. breakdown** dépression *f*; **m. cruelty** cruauté *f* mentale; **m. defective** handicapé, -e mental(e); **m. deficiency** déficience *f* *ou* débilité *f* mentale; **m. health** santé *f* mentale; **m. home, m. hospital** hôpital *m* *ou* clinique *f* psychiatrique; **m. illness** maladie *f* mentale; **m. reservation** doute *m*

mentality [men'tælɪtɪ] N *(of person)* mentalité *f*

mentally ['mentəlɪ] ADV mentalement; **m. deficient** *or* **defective** débile mental; **m. ill/handicapped** malade/handicapé mental; **to be m. ill** être un malade mental; **the m. ill/handicapped** les malades/handicapés mentaux

menthol ['menθɒl] N menthol *m*

▸▸ **m. cigarettes** cigarettes *fpl* au menthol

mentholated ['menθəleɪtɪd] ADJ *Pharm* mentholé

mention ['menʃən] N *(reference)* référence *f*, mention *f*; **m. was made of …** on a parlé de …, on a fait allusion à …; **I never heard m. of her name again** je n'entendis plus jamais prononcer son nom; **to make no m. of sth** passer qch sous silence, ne pas faire mention de qch; **there is no m. of this extra charge in the brochure** la brochure ne mentionne pas ce supplément; **at the m. of food** quand on parle/a parlé de manger; **at the m.**

of her name he turned white quand il entendit son nom il pâlit; **he gets a brief m. in her autobiography** elle le mentionne brièvement dans son autobiographie; *Mil* **m. in dispatches** citation *f* à l'ordre du jour
VT *(somebody, something)* parler de; *(fact, detail)* relever, mentionner; **the sum mentioned** la somme indiquée; **I had forgotten to m. that …** j'avais oublié de vous dire que …; **she mentioned that she had lived in Bristol** elle mentionna qu'elle avait vécu à Bristol; **I shall m. it to him** je lui en parlerai, je lui en toucherai un mot; **too numerous to m.** trop nombreux pour les citer; **I have no money worth mentioning** je n'ai pour ainsi dire pas d'argent; **I didn't think it was worth mentioning** je ne pensais pas que c'était la peine d'en parler; **as mentioned above** comme mentionné ci-dessus; **not to m. …** sans parler de …; **I heard my name mentioned** j'ai entendu prononcer mon nom; **did she m. my name?** est-ce qu'elle a parlé de moi?; **to m. sb in one's will** coucher qn sur testament; *Fam* **don't m. it!** *(after being thanked)* il n'y a pas de quoi!; *(drop the subject)* ne m'en parlez pas!, n'en parlez pas!; *Mil* **to be mentioned in dispatches** être cité à l'ordre du jour

mentor ['mentɔːr] N mentor *m*, guide *m*

menu ['menjuː] N **1** *Culin* menu *m*; **today's m.** la carte du jour **2** *Comput* menu *m*

▸▸*Comput* **m. bar** barre *f* de menu; *Comput* **m. builder** générateur *m* de menus; *Comput* **m. item** élément *m* de menu; *Comput* **m. option** option *f* de menu

menu-controlled ADJ *Comput* contrôlé par menu

menu-driven ADJ *Comput* contrôlé *ou* piloté par menu(s)

MEP [emiː'piː] N *Br (abbr* **Member of the European Parliament)** député *m* du Parlement européen

Merc [mɜːk] N *Fam (abbr* **Mercedes)** Mercedes *f*

mercantile ['mɜːkəntaɪl] ADJ commercial, -iaux, commerçant

▸▸ **m. agency** agence *f* commerciale; **m. agent** agent *m* commercial; **m. bank** banque *f* de commerce; **m. law** droit *m* commercial; **m. marine** marine *f* marchande; **m. nation** nation *f* commerçante; **m. operations** opérations *fpl* mercantiles

mercantilism ['mɜːkəntɪlɪz(ə)m] N mercantilisme *m*

mercantilist ['mɜːkəntɪlɪst] ADJ, N mercantiliste *m*

mercenary ['mɜːsɪn(ə)rɪ] ADJ *Pej (person)* intéressé; **for purely m. reasons** uniquement pour l'argent; **must you be so m.?** tu ne penses qu'à l'argent!
N *(soldier)* mercenaire *m*

mercerized ['mɜːsəraɪzd] ADJ *Ind (cotton)* mercerisé

merchandise ['mɜːtʃəndaɪz] N marchandise(s) *f(pl)*
VI faire du commerce *ou* du négoce

merchandiser ['mɜːtʃəndaɪzər] N marchandiseur *m*

merchandising ['mɜːtʃəndaɪzɪŋ] N marchandisage *m*

merchant ['mɜːtʃənt] N **1** *Com esp Old-fashioned (dealer)* négociant, -ante, marchand, -ande; **wine m.** négociant en vins **2** *Fam* **speed m.** chauffard *m*; **gloom m.** pessimiste *mf*; *Br Fam* **rip-off** *or* **con m.** arnaqueur, -euse **3** *Am Com (shopkeeper)* marchand, -ande, boutiquier, -ière
ADJ marchand, de commerce

▸▸ **m. bank** banque *f* d'affaires, banque d'investissement; **m. banker** banquier, -ière d'affaires; **m. marine, m. navy** marine *f* marchande; **m. seaman** marin *m* de la marine marchande; **m. ship, m. vessel** navire *m* marchand

merchantman, *pl* **merchantmen** ['mɜ:-tʃəntmən] **N** *(ship)* navire *m* marchand, navire de commerce

merciful ['mɜ:sɪfʊl] **ADJ** *(God)* miséricordieux (**to** pour); *(judge)* clément (**to** envers); **m. heavens!** grands Dieux!; **death was a m. release from his suffering** la mort fut une délivrance pour lui

mercifully ['mɜ:sɪfʊlɪ] **ADV 1** *(showing mercy)* avec clémence **2** *(fortunately)* heureusement

merciless ['mɜ:sɪlɪs] **ADJ** impitoyable, sans pitié, sans merci

mercilessly ['mɜ:sɪlɪslɪ] **ADV** impitoyablement, sans pitié; **the rain beat down m.** la pluie tombait sans répit

Mercosur ['mɜ:kəʊsʊər] **N** *Econ* Mercosur *m*

mercurial [mɜ:'kjʊərɪəl] **ADJ 1** *(lively)* *(temperament, character, person)* vif, *f* vive, éveillé **2** *(changeable)* inconstant, d'humeur changeante **3** *Med, Pharm (product)* mercuriel

Mercury ['mɜ:kjʊrɪ] **N** *Myth* Mercure *m*; *Astron* Mercure *f*

mercury ['mɜ:kjʊrɪ] **N** *Chem* mercure *m*
▸▸ **m. poisoning** empoisonnement *m* au mercure

mercy ['mɜ:sɪ] **N** pitié *f*, *Rel* miséricorde *f*, *Rel* **Lord have m.!** Seigneur prends pitié!; **to show m. to sb** faire preuve de pitié envers qn; **to have m. on sb** avoir *ou* prendre pitié de qn; **to be without m.** être sans pitié *ou* sans pitié; **to call** *or* **beg for m.** demander grâce; **to throw oneself on sb's m.** s'abandonner à la merci de qn; *Old-fashioned* **m.!** grâce!; **at the m. of sb/sth** à la merci de qn/qch; **to be thankful** *or* **grateful for small mercies** être reconnaissant des moindres bienfaits; **what a m.!** quel bonheur!, quelle chance!; **works of m.** œuvres *fpl* de charité
▸▸ **m. flight** vol *m* de secours; **m. killing** *(euthanasia)* euthanasie *f*, *(individual death)* acte *m* d'euthanasie

mere [mɪər] **ADJ** simple; **a m. coincidence** une coïncidence pure et simple; **it's a m. formality** ce n'est qu'une simple formalité; **it was only by the merest chance that …** ce n'est que par le plus grand des hasards que …; **I shudder at the m. thought of it** je frissonne rien que d'y penser; **he's a m. child** ce n'est qu'un enfant; **he clearly hadn't the merest notion of who I was** il était clair qu'il n'avait pas la moindre idée de mon identité

merely ['mɪəlɪ] **ADV** simplement, seulement; **he m. smiled** il se contenta de sourire; **I mention this m. to draw attention to …** je n'ai dit cela que pour attirer l'attention sur …

meretricious [merɪ'trɪʃəs] **ADJ** *Fml (style etc)* factice

merge [mɜ:dʒ] **VT** *(two systems, classes)* fusionner, amalgamer; *Comput (files)* fusionner; **to m. sth in** *or* **into sth** fondre qch dans qch, amalgamer qch avec qch; **the two regiments were merged (into one)** les deux régiments ont été regroupés
VI *Com, Fin (of companies, banks etc)* s'amalgamer, fusionner; *Aut (of lanes, roads etc)* se rencontrer; **the sea and sky merged** le ciel et la mer se confondaient; **the colours/shapes/voices merged (into each other)** les couleurs/formes/voix se mêlaient; **to m. into the background** *(of building, person)* se fondre dans le décor; **to m. into the shadows** disparaître dans l'ombre
N *Comput (of files)* fusion *f*

merger ['mɜ:dʒər] **N** *Com, Fin (of several companies)* fusion *f*, fusionnement *m*
▸▸ **m. accounting** = bases *fpl* de prépara-

tion des comptes consolidés où deux sociétés se sont unifiées; **m. talks** discussions *fpl* en vue d'une fusion

meridian [mə'rɪdɪən] **N 1** *Geog* méridien *m* **2** *Astron (of star)* méridien *m*, point *m* culminant
ADJ *Astron (altitude, angle etc)* méridien
▸▸ **m. line** (ligne *f*) méridienne *f*

meridional [mə'rɪdɪən(ə)l] **ADJ** méridional, -aux
N Méridional, -ale

meringue [mə'ræŋ] **N** *Culin* meringue *f*

merino [mə'ri:nəʊ] **N** *(sheep, wool)* mérinos *m*

merit ['merɪt] **N 1** *(deserving aspect)* mérite *m*; **according to one's merits** *(to be rewarded)* selon ses mérites; *Law* **the merits of a case** le bien-fondé d'une cause; **to judge a proposal on its merits** juger une proposition pour ce qu'elle vaut; **to stand on its own merits** avoir une valeur en soi; *Rel* **to acquire m.** gagner du mérite; **her remarks had the m. of being frank** au moins, ses remarques avaient le mérite d'être franches **2** *(worth)* valeur *f*, mérite *m*; **in order of m.** par ordre de mérite; **these paintings have no m. at all** ces tableaux n'ont aucune valeur artistique
VT *(reward, punishment etc)* mériter
▸▸ **m. increase** augmentation *f* au mérite; *Am Admin* **m. system** système *m* d'avancement fondé sur le mérite

meritocracy [merɪ'tɒkrəsɪ] **N** méritocratie *f*

meritocratic [merɪtə'krætɪk] **ADJ** méritocratique

meritorious [merɪ'tɔ:rɪəs] **ADJ** *Fml (deed, conduct)* méritoire, louable

merlin ['mɜ:lɪn] **N** *(bird)* (faucon *m*) émerillon *m*

mermaid ['mɜ:meɪd] **N** *Myth* sirène *f*

merman, *pl* **mermen** ['mɜ:mæn, -men] **N** *Myth* triton *m*

Merovingian [merəʊ'vɪndʒɪən] *Hist* **ADJ** mérovingien
N Mérovingien, -ienne

merrily ['merɪlɪ] **ADV** gaiement, gaîment, joyeusement

merriment ['merɪmənt] **N** gaieté *f*, gaîté *f*, **there was much m. at the thought of this** l'idée fit beaucoup rire; **sounds of m.** des rires

merry ['merɪ] **ADJ** *(comp* **merrier;** *superl* **merriest) 1** *(happy)* joyeux, gai; **to make m.** se divertir, s'amuser, s'égayer; **M. Christmas!** joyeux Noël!; *Fam* **the weather is playing m. hell with the rail timetables** le mauvais temps a complètement chamboulé l'horaire des trains; *Fam* **my back is giving me m. hell** mon dos me fait souffrir atrocement; *Prov* **the more the merrier** plus on est de fous, plus on rit; **the m. month of May** le gentil mois de mai; **Robin Hood and his m. men** Robin des Bois et ses joyeux *ou* gais lurons **2** *Fam (slightly drunk)* gai, éméché, un peu gris
▸▸ *Arch, Lit* **M. England** l'aimable Angleterre *f*

merry-go-round **N** manège *m*, *Belg, Suisse* carrousel *m*

merrymaking ['merɪmeɪkɪŋ] **N** réjouissances *fpl*

mescalin(e) ['meskəlɪn] **N** *Pharm* mescaline *f*

mesh [meʃ] **N 1** *(of net, sieve etc)* maille *f* **2** *Tech* prise *f*, engrènement *m*, engrenage *m*; **in m.** en prise
VI 1 *(coordinate)* concorder **2** *Tech (of teeth, wheels)* engrener, s'engrener; *(be in mesh)* être en prise (**with** avec); *(engage)* se mettre en prise (**with** avec)

VT *Tech (of cogwheels)* endenter, engrener
▸▸ **m. stockings** bas *mpl* filet

mesmeric [mez'merɪk] **ADJ** *Fml* magnétique, hypnotique

mesmerize ['mezməraɪz] **VT** *Old-fashioned* hypnotiser; *Fig* fasciner

mesmerizing ['mezməraɪzɪŋ] **ADJ** fascinant

meson ['mi:zɒn] **N** *Nucl* méson *m*

Mesopotamia [mesəpə'teɪmɪə] **N** Mésopotamie *f*

mess [mes] **N 1** *(disorder)* désordre *m*, *Fam* pagaïe *f*, pagaille *f*, *(bungled job etc)* gâchis *m*; **the kitchen's a m.** la cuisine est en désordre, *Fam* la cuisine est un vrai foutoir; **you're** *or* **you look a m.!** tu es dans un triste état!; **my hair's a m.** mes cheveux sont dans un triste état; **to be in a m.** *(of person)* être dans le pétrin *ou* dans de beaux draps; **everything's in a m.** tout est en désordre; **to make a m. of** *(job, translation, repair etc)* gâcher, saboter, *Fam* saloper; **the dentist made a real m. of it** le dentiste a vraiment salopé le travail; **to make a m. of things** tout gâcher; *Fam* **after the fight his face was a terrible m.** après la bagarre il avait le visage tout amoché; *Fam* **he's a m.** *(has complexes)* il est bourré de complexes; *(because of drugs etc)* il est dans un piteux état
2 *(dirt)* saleté *f*, **to make a m. of the tablecloth** salir la nappe; **dog's m.** crotte *f* de chien; **the dog's done a m. on the carpet** le chien a fait ses besoins sur le tapis
3 *Mil (food) (for officers)* popote *f*, *(for men)* ordinaire *m*; *(room) (for officers)* mess *m*; *(for men)* réfectoire *m*
4 *Bible (food)* **m. of pottage** plat *m* de lentilles
VT *(make dirty)* salir, souiller
VI 1 *Mil etc* manger en commun; **to m. together** manger à la même table
2 *Sl (exaggerate)* **no messing!** sans blagues!; **there were two hundred of them, no messing!** ils étaient deux cents et je n'exagère pas!
3 *Fam (defecate) (of dog, cat)* faire *ou* ses saletés
▸▸ *Naut* **m. deck** poste *m* d'équipage; **m. jacket** *Mil* veston *m* de tenue de soirée; *(civilian)* veste *f* courte; **m. kit** *Mil (eating equipment)* gamelle *f*, *Br Fam (clothes)* tenue *f* de soirée; *Br* **m. tin** gamelle
▸ **mess about, mess around** **VI 1** *(play the fool)* faire l'imbécile; *(waste time)* traîner, glandouiller
2 *(tinker)* tripoter; **don't m. around with something that doesn't belong to you** ne touche pas à ce qui ne t'appartient pas
3 *(sexually)* **to m. around with sb** s'amuser avec qn; **stop messing around with my sister!** laisse ma sœur tranquille!
VT SEP 1 *(treat badly)* traiter de façon inconsidérée; **I wish you'd stop messing me about and make up your mind** j'aimerais bien que tu arrêtes de te moquer de moi et que tu te décides
2 *(alter)* chambouler
▸ **mess up** **VT SEP 1** *(put in disorder)* *(room, clothes etc)* mettre en désordre, semer la pagaïe dans; **you'll m. up my hair!** tu vas me décoiffer!
2 *(ruin)* *(job)* gâcher, *Fam* saloper; **he's messed everything up** il a tout gâché; **you've messed up all our plans** tu as chamboulé tous nos projets
VI *Am Fam (at work, university etc)* tout rater; **to m. up on an exam** merdouiller dans *ou* à un examen
▸ **mess with** **VT INSEP** *Fam (meddle with)* **don't m. with me!** ne me cherche pas!; **you shouldn't m. with people like that** *(get involved with)* tu ne devrais pas fréquenter des gens comme ça; *(get on wrong side of)* tu ne devrais pas mécontenter ces gens-là;

that's what happens when you m. with drugs! voilà ce qui arrive quand on touche à la drogue!

message ['mesɪdʒ] N **1** message m; **to send a m. to sb** envoyer un message à qn; **to leave a m. for sb** laisser un message ou un mot à qn; *(when telephoning)* laisser un message à qn; *Comput* laisser un message à qn; *Fam* **have you got the m.?, is the m. getting across?** tu as bien compris?, tu as pigé?; *Fam* **people seem to be getting the m., the m. seems to be getting across** les gens ont l'air de commencer à comprendre; *Comput* **you get the screen m. …** l'écran affiche … **2** *(meaning) (of a book etc)* message m; **the film's m. is clear** le message qui ressort du film est clair **3** *Scot (errand)* commission f, course f
▶▶ **m. board** tableau m d'affichage; **m. boy** garçon m de courses; **m. form** fiche-message f, pl fiches-messages; *Comput* **m. handling** messagerie f (électronique); *Comput* **m. switching** commutation f de messages

messenger ['mesɪndʒər] N messager, -ère; *(in large offices etc)* coursier, -ière; *Mil* coureur m; *Admin (in diplomacy)* courrier m (diplomatique); *Com* commissionnaire m; *Br* **King's/Queen's m.** ≃ courrier m d'État; **by m.** par porteur
▶▶ **m. boy** coursier m, garçon m de courses

Messiah [mɪ'saɪə] N *Rel, Mus, Fig* Messie m

messianic [mesɪ'ænɪk] ADJ messianique

messily ['mesɪlɪ] ADV *(to eat)* salement; *Fig* **his first marriage ended rather m.** son premier mariage s'est mal terminé

messmate ['mesmeɪt] N *Mil etc* camarade mf de table; *Naut* camarade de plat

Messrs ['mesəz] NPL *(abbr Messieurs)* MM

mess-up N *Fam* gâchis m, pagaïe f

messy ['mesɪ] ADJ **1** *(dirty)* sale; *(untidy) (room, hair, appearance)* en désordre; *(handwriting)* illisible; **to have a m. appearance** avoir l'air peu soigné; **m. eater** personne qui mange salement, cochon m; **oranges are a m. fruit (to eat)** les oranges sont difficiles à manger proprement; **it's a m. job** c'est salissant; **this room's so m.** cette pièce est dans un tel désordre! **2** *(unpleasantly complex)* confus, embrouillé; **a m. business** *(criminal etc)* une sale histoire; **the official story is getting messier and messier** l'histoire officielle s'embrouille de plus en plus; **it's a rather m. solution** c'est une solution assez compliquée; **his m. private life** sa vie privée troublée

mestiza [me'stiːzə] N métisse f

mestizo, *pl* **mestizos** [me'stiːzəʊ, -əʊz] N métis m

met¹ [met] PT, PP *see* **meet¹**

met² ADJ *Br Fam (abbr* **meteorological)** météo
▶▶ **the M. Office** les services mpl météorologiques britanniques

metabolic [metə'bɒlɪk] ADJ *Biol* métabolique
▶▶ **m. rate** taux m métabolique

metabolism [mɪ'tæbəlɪz(ə)m] N *Biol* métabolisme m

metabolize [mɪ'tæbəlaɪz] VT transformer par métabolisme

metacarpal [metə'kɑːp(ə)l] ADJ, N *Anat* métacarpien m

metacarpus [metə'kɑːpəs] N *Anat* métacarpe m

metal ['met(ə)l] N **1** métal m **2** *Typ* caractères mpl, métal m, plomb m **3** *(stones) Rail* ballast m (de voie ferrée); **(road) m.** cailloutis m, pierraille f **4** *(in glassmaking)* verre m en fusion
ADJ *(made of metal)* métallique, en métal

VT (**-ll-,** *Am* **-l-)** *Br Constr (road)* empierrer; **metalled road** route f empierrée
▶▶ **m. detector** détecteur m de métaux; **m. engraver** graveur, -euse sur métaux; **m. polish** produit m pour faire briller les métaux

metalanguage ['metəlæŋgwɪdʒ] N métalangage m

metallic [mɪ'tælɪk] ADJ *(sound, voice),* *Chem, Elec etc* métallique; *(taste)* de métal; **m. sheen** éclat m métallique; **a m. blue/green** un bleu/vert métallique
▶▶ **m. paint** peinture f métallisée

metallurgical [metə'lɜːdʒɪk(ə)l] ADJ métallurgique

metallurgy [me'tælədʒɪ] N métallurgie f

metalwork ['met(ə)lwɜːk] N **1** *(practice, technique)* travail m des métaux; *Br Sch* **m. teacher/lesson** professeur m/cours m de travail des métaux **2** *(articles)* métal m ouvré; *Art* ferronnerie f, **piece of m.** pièce f en métal ouvré; *Art* objet m en ferronnerie

metalworker ['met(ə)lwɜːkər] N *Ind* (ouvrier m) métallurgiste mf; **art m.** ferronnier m ou serrurier m d'art

metamorphic [metə'mɔːfɪk] ADJ *Geol* métamorphique; *Biol* métamorphosique

metamorphose [metə'mɔːfəʊz] VT métamorphoser, transformer **(into** en)
VI se métamorphoser **(into** en)

metamorphosis, *pl* **metamorphoses** [metə'mɔːfəsɪs, -əsiːz] N métamorphose f

metaphor ['metəfər] N métaphore f, image f **(for** symbolisant); **mixed m.** métaphore multiple

metaphoric(al) [metə'fɒrɪk, -ɪk(ə)l] ADJ métaphorique

metaphorically [metə'fɒrɪklɪ] ADV métaphoriquement

metaphysical [metə'fɪzɪk(ə)l] ADJ métaphysique

metaphysics [metə'fɪzɪks] N métaphysique f VOIR GRAMMAIRE A10

metatarsal [metə'tɑːs(ə)l] ADJ, N *Anat* métatarsien m

metatarsus [metə'tɑːsəs] N *Anat* métatarse m

▶ **mete out** [miːt] VT SEP *(punishment)* distribuer, infliger; *(reward)* distribuer, décerner; **to m. out justice** faire justice

metempsychosis ['metəmsaɪ'kəʊsɪs] N métempsychose f

meteor ['miːtɪər] N météore m
▶▶ **m. shower** pluie f d'étoiles filantes, averse f météorique

meteoric [miːtɪ'ɒrɪk] ADJ *Astron* météorique; *Fig* **m. rise** ascension f fulgurante

meteorite ['miːtɪəraɪt] N météorite f, aérolit(h)e m

meteorological [miːtɪərə'lɒdʒɪk(ə)l] ADJ météorologique

meteorologist [miːtɪə'rɒlədʒɪst] N météorologiste mf, météorologue mf

meteorology [miːtɪə'rɒlədʒɪ] N météorologie f

meter¹ ['miːtər] N *(device)* compteur m; *Aut* parcmètre m, *Can* compteur de stationnement; *Aut Fam* **I'm on a m.** je suis garé à un parcmètre
▶▶ *Am Fam* **m. maid** contractuelle f, pervenche f, *Can* préposée f au stationnement; **m. reader** *(person)* releveur, -euse de(s) compteur(s); **m. reading** relevé m (de(s) compteur(s))

meter² N *Am* = **metre**

methadone ['meθədəʊn] N *Med* méthadone f, **to be on m.** *(of drug addict)* prendre de la méthadone

methane ['miːθeɪn] N *Chem* méthane m

methinks [mɪ'θɪŋks] V IMPERS *(pt* **methought** [mɪ'θɔːt])* *Arch, Lit, Hum* il me semble; **you are sad, m.** il me semble que vous êtes triste

method ['meθəd] N *(in research, science)* méthode f; **the m. of doing sth** la manière de faire qch; *Admin* **methods of payment** modalités fpl de paiement; **to work without m.** travailler sans méthode; **to lack m.** manquer de méthode, ne pas être méthodique; *Prov* **there's m. in his madness** il n'est pas aussi fou qu'il en a l'air
▶▶ *Cin, Theat* **M. acting** la méthode Stanislavski; *Cin, Theat* **M. actor** acteur m adepte de la méthode de Stanislavski; *Cin, Theat* **M. actress** actrice f adepte de la méthode de Stanislavski; *Ind* **methods engineer** ingénieur m des méthodes; *Ind* **methods engineering** étude f des méthodes

methodical [mɪ'θɒdɪk(ə)l] ADJ méthodique

methodically [mɪ'θɒdɪklɪ] ADV méthodiquement, avec méthode

Methodism ['meθədɪz(ə)m] N *Rel* méthodisme m

Methodist ['meθədɪst] ADJ, N *Rel* méthodiste mf

methodology [meθə'dɒlədʒɪ] N méthodologie f

meths [meθs] N *Br Fam* alcool m à brûler

Methuselah [mə'θjuːzələ] N *Bible* Mathusalem m; *Fig* **as old as M.** vieux comme Hérode

methyl ['meθɪl] N *Chem* méthyle m
▶▶ **m. alcohol** méthanol m, alcool m méthylique

methylated ['meθɪleɪtɪd] ADJ
▶▶ **m. spirits** alcool m dénaturé, alcool à brûler

methylene ['meθɪliːn] N *Chem* méthylène m

meticulous [mɪ'tɪkjʊləs] ADJ méticuleux, minutieux; **with m. attention to detail** avec une attention méticuleuse ou minutieuse pour les détails

meticulously [mɪ'tɪkjʊləslɪ] ADV méticuleusement, minutieusement; *(to describe)* dans le détail; **to be m. dressed** être tiré à quatre épingles

meticulousness [mɪ'tɪkjʊləsnɪs] N méticulosité f, minutie f

metonymic [metə'nɪmɪk] ADJ métonymique

metonymy [mɪ'tɒnɪmɪ] N métonymie f

me-too product N *Mktg* produit m tactique

metre,¹ *Am* **meter** ['miːtər] N *Liter (in poetry)* mètre m, mesure f, **in m.** en vers

metre,² *Am* **meter** N *(measurement)* mètre m

metric ['metrɪk] ADJ *(system)* métrique; **to go m.** adopter le système métrique
▶▶ **m. area** métrage m; **m. ton** tonne f, **m. volume** métrage m

metrical ['metrɪk(ə)l] ADJ métrique

metrication [metrɪ'keɪʃən] N adoption f ou introduction f du système métrique

metrics ['metrɪks] N *(in poetry)* métrique f VOIR GRAMMAIRE A10

metro ['metrəʊ] N métro m

metronome ['metrənəʊm] N *Mus* métronome m

metropolis [mɪ'trɒpəlɪs] N *(city)* métropole f

metropolitan [metrə'pɒlɪtən] ADJ *(area etc)* urbain; *Am* **France M.** France f métropolitaine
N *(inhabitant)* habitant, -ante de la métropole ou de la capitale; *Rel (bishop)* métropolitain m
▶▶ **M. Police** *Br* police f londonienne; *Am* police urbaine

mettle ['met(ə)l] N *(courage) (of person)* courage *m*, force *f* d'âme; *(of horse)* fougue *f*; **to be on one's m.** être prêt à donner le meilleur de soi-même; **to show one's m.** montrer de quoi on est capable

mettlesome ['met(ə)lsəm] ADJ *Old-fashioned (person)* plein de courage; *(horse)* fougueux

mew [mjuː] N *(of cat)* miaulement *m*
VI *(of cat)* miauler

mewing ['mjuːɪŋ] N miaulement *m*

mews [mjuːz] NPL *Br* **1** *(street)* ruelle *f (sur laquelle donnaient des écuries)*; **m. cottage, m. house** = maison *f* assez luxueuse aménagée dans une ancienne écurie **2** *Arch (stables)* écuries *fpl*

Mex [meks] *Am Fam Offensive* N Mexicain, -aine
ADJ mexicain

Mexican ['meksɪkən] ADJ mexicain
N Mexicain, -aine

Mexico ['meksɪkəʊ] N Mexique *m*
▸▸ **M. City** Mexico

mezzanine ['metsəniː] N **1** *Archit* mezzanine *f*, entresol *m* **2** *Theat Am* corbeille *f*, *Br* premier dessous *m (de la scène)*
▸▸ *Fin* **m. debt** dette *f* subordonnée *ou* mezzanine; **m. finance** = méthode *f* de financement d'une partie du capital nécessaire pour acheter une entreprise *(utilisée principalement par ses employés)*; *Archit* **m. floor** mezzanine, entresol

mezzo ['metsəʊ] *Mus* ADV mezzo
N = mezzo-soprano
▸▸ **m. forte** mezzo forte

mezzo-soprano N *Mus (voice)* mezzo-soprano *m*, *pl* mezzo-sopranos, -ni; *(singer)* mezzo-soprano *f*

mezzotint ['metsəʊtɪnt] N mezzo-tinto *m inv*

mfd *Com (abbr* **manufactured***)* fabriqué

mg *(abbr* **milligram(s)***)* mg

Mgr *Rel (abbr* **monsignor***)* Mgr

MHz *Elec (abbr* **megahertz***)* Mhz

MI [eˈmaɪ] N *Comput (abbr* **machine intelligence***)* IA *f*

mi [miː] N *Mus* mi *m*

MI5 [emaɪˈfaɪv] N *Br (abbr* **Military Intelligence Section 5***)* MI5 *m*, ≃ DST *f (contre-espionnage)*

MI6 [emaɪˈsɪks] N *Br (abbr* **Military Intelligence Section 6***)* MI6 *m*, ≃ DGSE *f (espionnage)*

MIA [emaɪˈeɪ] ADJ, N *Am Mil (abbr* **missing in action***)* porté disparu

miaow [mɪˈaʊ] N *(of cat)* miaulement *m*, miaou *m*
INT miaou
VI *(of cat)* miauler

mic [mɪk] N *TV, Radio* micro *m*

mica ['maɪkə] N *Miner* mica *m*

mice *see* **mouse**[1]

Mich *abbr* **Michigan**

Michael ['maɪk(ə)l] N Michel *m*; *Br Fam* **to take the M. out of sb** se payer la tête de qn; **are you taking the M.?** tu te payes ma/sa tête?

Michaelmas ['mɪkəlməs] N la Saint-Michel
▸▸ *Bot* **M. daisy** aster *m* (d'automne); *Br Univ* **M. term** premier trimestre *m (de l'année scolaire dans certaines universités)*; *Law* session *f* de la Saint-Michel

Michelangelo [maɪkəˈlæn(d)ʒələʊ] N *Art* Michel-Ange *m*

Michelin man ['mɪtʃlɪn-] N **the M.** le bonhomme Michelin

Mick [mɪk] N *Offensive Sl (Irishman)* Irlandais *m*

Mickey ['mɪkɪ] N *Sl (drugged drink)* = boisson *f* alcoolisée dans laquelle on a versé un sédatif
▸▸ *Sl* **M. Finn** = boisson alcoolisée dans laquelle on a versé un sédatif; **M. Mouse** Mickey *m*

mickey ['mɪkɪ] N *Br Fam* **to take the m. out of sb** se payer la tête de qn; **are you taking the m.?** tu te payes ma/sa tête?

micro ['maɪkrəʊ] N *Comput* micro *m*

micro- ['maɪkrəʊ] PREF micro-

microanalysis [maɪkrəʊəˈnæləsɪs] N *Chem* microanalyse *f*

microbe ['maɪkrəʊb] N microbe *m*

microbial [maɪˈkrəʊbɪəl], **microbic** [maɪˈkrəʊbɪk] ADJ microbien

microbiology [maɪkrəʊbaɪˈɒlədʒɪ] N microbiologie *f*

microbrewery [maɪkrəʊˈbrʊərɪ] N microbrasserie *f*

microcamera [maɪkrəʊˈkæmərə] N appareil *m* de micro-photographie

microchannel architecture [maɪkrəʊˈtʃæn(ə)l] N *Comput* architecture *f* à microcanaux

microchip ['maɪkrəʊtʃɪp] N *Comput* puce *f* (électronique)

microcircuit ['maɪkrəʊsɜːkɪt] N *Comput* microcircuit *m*

microcircuitry ['maɪkrəʊsɜːkɪtrɪ] N *Comput* microcircuits *mpl*

microclimate ['maɪkrəʊklaɪmɪt] N *Met* microclimat *m*

micrococcus [maɪkrəʊˈkɒkəs] N *Biol* micrococque *m*, micrococcus *m*

microcode [maɪkrəʊˈkəʊd] N *Comput* microcode *m*

microcomputer ['maɪkrəʊkəmˌpjuːtər] N micro-ordinateur *m*, *pl* micro-ordinateurs

microcosm ['maɪkrəʊkɒz(ə)m] N microcosme *m*

microdot ['maɪkrəʊdɒt] N micropoint *m*

microeconomic [maɪkrəʊiːkəˈnɒmɪk] ADJ microéconomique

microeconomics [maɪkrəʊiːkəˈnɒmɪks] N microéconomie *f* VOIR GRAMMAIRE A10

microeconomy [maɪkrəʊiːˈkɒnəmɪ] N microéconomie *f*

microelectronics [maɪkrəʊelekˈtrɒnɪks] N micro-électronique *f* VOIR GRAMMAIRE A10

microfibre, *Am* **microfiber** ['maɪkrəʊfaɪbə(r)] N microfibre *m*

microfiche ['maɪkrəʊfiːʃ] N microfiche *f*

microfilm ['maɪkrəʊfɪlm] N microfilm *m*
VT microfilmer

microfloppy ['maɪkrəʊflɒpɪ] N microdisquette *f*

microgroove ['maɪkrəʊgruːv] N microsillon *m*

microlight ['maɪkrəʊlaɪt] N *Aviat* ULM *m*

micromarketing [maɪkrəʊˈmɑːkɪtɪŋ] N micromarketing *m*

micromesh ['maɪkrəʊmeʃ] ADJ *(stocking)* à mailles très fines

micrometer [maɪˈkrɒmɪtər] N micromètre *m*

micron ['maɪkrɒn] N *(measurement)* micron *m*

Micronesia [maɪkrəʊˈniːzɪə] N Micronésie *f*

microorganism [maɪkrəʊˈɔːgənɪz(ə)m] N micro-organisme *m*, *pl* micro-organismes

micropayment [maɪkrəʊˈpeɪmənt] N *Comput* micropaiement *m*

microphone ['maɪkrəfəʊn] N microphone *m*, micro *m*; **speak into the m.** parlez dans le micro; **a good m. voice** une voix qui passe bien à la radio/à l'enregistrement

microphysics [maɪkrəʊˈfɪsɪks] N microphysique *f* VOIR GRAMMAIRE A10

microprocessor ['maɪkrəʊˈprəʊsesər] N *Comput* microprocesseur *m*

microreader ['maɪkrəʊriːdər] N microliseuse *f*

microscooter ['maɪkrəʊskuːtər] N trottinette *f ou* patinette *f* à moteur

microscope ['maɪkrəskəʊp] N microscope *m*; **under the m.** au microscope; *Fig* **to put sth under the m.** examiner qch à la loupe

microscopic [maɪkrəˈskɒpɪk] ADJ **1** *(very small)* microscopique **2** *(examination etc)* au microscope, microscopique

microscopy [maɪˈkrɒskəpɪ] N microscopie *f*

microsecond ['maɪkrəʊsekənd] N microseconde *f*

microsegment ['maɪkrəʊsegmənt] N *Mktg* microsegment *m*

microsegmentation [maɪkrəʊsegmənˈteɪʃən] N *Mktg* microsegmentation *f*

microspacing ['maɪkrəʊspeɪsɪŋ] N *Comput* micro-espacement *m*

microsurgery [maɪkrəʊˈsɜːdʒərɪ] N microchirurgie *f*

microtechnology [maɪkrəʊtekˈnɒlədʒɪ] N microtechnologie *f*

microwave ['maɪkrəʊweɪv] N **1** *(oven)* (four *m* à) micro-ondes *m inv* **2** *Electron, Radio* micro-onde *f*, *pl* micro-ondes
VT **to m. sth** faire cuire qch au (four à) micro-ondes; **microwaved food** nourriture *f* cuite au (four à) micro-ondes
▸▸ **m. oven** (four à) micro-ondes

micturition [mɪktjʊˈrɪʃən] N *Med* miction *f*

mid [mɪd] ADJ in **m. ocean** en plein océan, en pleine mer; **from m. June to m. August** de la mi-juin à la mi-août; **m. season** demi-saison *f*, *pl* demi-saisons; **he stopped in m. sentence** il s'est interrompu au milieu de sa phrase; **m. Wales** le centre du pays de Galles; **the m. 1960s** le milieu des années soixante

midafternoon [mɪdɑːftəˈnuːn] N milieu *m* de l'après-midi; **we had a m. break** on a fait une pause en milieu de l'après-midi

midair [mɪdˈeər] ADJ *(collision)* en plein ciel
N **in m.** en plein ciel

Midas ['maɪdəs] N Midas *m*; *Prov* **to have the M. touch** transformer tout ce qu'on touche en or

mid-Atlantic ADJ **m. accent** accent mi-américain mi-britannique

midday ['mɪd'deɪ] N midi *m*; **at m.** à midi
▸▸ **m. meal** repas *m* de midi

midden ['mɪd(ə)n] N *Br (dunghill)* (tas *m* de) fumier *m*; *Scot Fam* **this room is like a m.** cette pièce est une vraie porcherie

middle ['mɪd(ə)l] ADJ du milieu; *(in between)* intermédiaire; **the m. house/sister** la maison/la sœur du milieu; *Fig* **to steer a m. course** adopter une solution intermédiaire; **in the m. distance** au second plan
N **1** milieu *m*; **in the m. of …** au milieu de …; **in the m. of nowhere** dans un coin perdu; **in the m. of the summer** en plein été; **about the m. of August** à la mi-août; **in the m. of the night** en pleine nuit; **I was in the m. of reading/of watching a programme** j'étais en train de lire/de regarder une émission; **he was driving down the m. of the road** il roulait au (beau) milieu de la route; *Fam* **they split the money down the m.** ils ont partagé l'argent en deux parties égales **2** *Fam (waist)* taille *f*, ceinture *f*, **round one's m.** autour de sa taille; **the water came up to his m.** l'eau lui arrivait à la taille
▸▸ **m. age** l'âge *m* mûr; **man of m. age** un homme d'âge mûr; **in m. age** vers la cin-

quantaine; **in early m. age he ...** vers la cinquantaine il ... ; **the M. Ages** le Moyen Âge m; **M. America** Geog Amérique f centrale; Fig (American middle class) l'Amérique moyenne; Pej l'Amérique bien pensante; Mus **m. C** do m inv du milieu du clavier; **m. classes** bourgeoisie f, Anat **m. ear** oreille f moyenne; **the M. East** le Moyen-Orient; **M. Eastern** moyen-oriental; **M. England** l'Angleterre f moyenne (aux tendances conservatrices); Pej **M. Englander** Anglais, -aise moyen(enne); Ling **M. English** le moyen anglais; **m. finger** majeur m, médius m; Br Fam **m. finger salute** doigt m d'honneur; **to give sb the m. finger salute** faire un doigt d'honneur à qn; **m. ground** (in picture) second plan m; Fig terrain m neutre; Fig **to occupy the m. ground** (in political spectrum) adopter une position intermédiaire; **m. management** cadres mpl moyens; **m. manager** cadre m moyen; **m. name** deuxième prénom m; Fig **procrastination is your m. name!** tu remets toujours tout au lendemain; **honesty is her m. name** c'est l'honnêteté même; **laziness is his m. name** c'est un incorrigible paresseux; **generosity isn't exactly his m. name!** on ne peut pas dire qu'il soit particulièrement généreux; **m. neck** (of beef) côtes fpl découvertes; St Exch **m. price** cours m moyen; **m. school** Br = école f pour enfants de 8 ou 9 à 13 ans; Am = école pour enfants de 10 à 13 ans, ≃ collège m; Am Geog **the M. West** le Midwest

middle-aged ADJ (person) entre deux âges, d'un certain âge
▸▸ **m. spread** bourrelets mpl (qui viennent avec l'âge)

middlebrow ['mɪd(ə)braʊ] ADJ qui ne demande pas trop d'efforts intellectuels

middle-class ADJ bourgeois

middle-income ADJ
▸▸ Mktg **m. group** groupe m de contribuables à revenus moyens

middleman, pl **middlemen** ['mɪd(ə)lmæn, -men] N Com intermédiaire m; **m.'s market** marché m des intermédiaires

middlemost ['mɪd(ə)lməʊst] ADJ le plus proche du milieu

middle-of-the-road ADJ (policy) modéré; Mus Pej grand public

middle-roader [-rəʊdər] N Am Pol modéré, -ée

middle-sized ADJ de taille moyenne

middleweight ['mɪd(ə)lweɪt] N (boxer) poids m moyen; **m. champion** champion m poids moyen

middling ['mɪdlɪŋ] ADJ (mediocre) médiocre; (fairly good) passable, assez bon; Fam **how are you? –** comment allez-vous? – comme ci comme ça

middy ['mɪdɪ] N Naut Fam midship m

Mideast [mɪd'iːst] N esp Am **the M.** le Moyen-Orient

midfield [mɪd'fiːld] N Ftbl etc milieu m de terrain; **to play in m.** jouer au milieu du terrain
▸▸ **m. player** (joueur m du) milieu de terrain

midfielder [mɪd'fiːldər] N Ftbl etc milieu m de terrain

midge [mɪdʒ] N (insect) moucheron m

midget ['mɪdʒɪt] N (small person) nain, f naine, nabot, -ote
ADJ miniature

MIDI ['mɪdɪ] N Comput (abbr musical instrument digital interface) MIDI

midi ['mɪdɪ] ADJ (skirt, coat etc) de longueur moyenne, midi inv
N (skirt, coat etc) jupe f/manteau m/etc de longueur moyenne
▸▸ **m. system** (stereo) chaîne f midi

midland ['mɪdlənd] ADJ (plain etc) du centre (d'un pays)

Midlands (the) [ðə'mɪdləndz] NPL les Midlands fpl (comtés du centre de l'Angleterre); **a M. accent** un accent des Midlands

midlife ['mɪdlaɪf] N quarantaine f
▸▸ **m. crisis** (in professional etc life) crise f à l'abord de la quarantaine; (in sex life also) démon m de midi; **to be going through a m. crisis** traverser la crise de la quarantaine

midmorning [mɪd'mɔ:nɪŋ] N milieu m de la matinée; **m. coffee break** pause-café f au milieu de la matinée

midnight ['mɪdnaɪt] N minuit m; **at m.** à minuit; **to burn the m. oil** travailler tard dans la nuit; **a m. snack** un casse-croûte en plein milieu de la nuit
▸▸ **m. blue** bleu nuit m inv; **m. feast** = petit repas m pris en cachette la nuit par des enfants, à l'insu de leurs parents; **m. Mass** messe f de minuit; **m. sun** soleil m de minuit; **the land of the m. sun** le pays du soleil de minuit

mid-range ADJ Com (computer, car) de milieu de gamme

midriff ['mɪdrɪf] N Anat (diaphragm) diaphragme m; (stomach) ventre m; **bare m.** ventre m nu, taille f nue

midshipman, pl **midshipmen** ['mɪdʃɪpmən] N Naut aspirant m (de marine), Fam midship m

midships ['mɪdʃɪps] ADV Naut au milieu du navire, par le travers

midst [mɪdst] N **in the m. of sth** au milieu de qch; **in the m. of winter** au milieu ou au cœur de l'hiver, en plein hiver; **in the m. of all this** (these events) sur ces entrefaites; **in the m. of the celebration** en plein milieu de la fête; **in our/your/their m.** parmi nous/vous/eux; **there are traitors in our m.** il y a des traîtres parmi nous

midstream [mɪd'striːm] N **in m.** au milieu du courant; Fig **she stopped in m.** (of speaker) elle s'est arrêtée en plein milieu de son récit

midsummer ['mɪdsʌmər] N (middle of summer) milieu m de l'été, cœur m de l'été; (solstice) solstice m d'été; **in m.** au milieu ou au cœur de l'été, en plein été
▸▸ **M. Day** la Saint-Jean; **m. madness** folie f estivale; Liter **A M. Night's Dream** le Songe d'une Nuit d'Été

midterm ['mɪdtɜ:m] N **1** Pol Am milieu m du mandat présidentiel, Br milieu du mandat du Premier Ministre **2** Sch, Univ milieu m du trimestre
▸▸ Sch, Univ **m. break** vacances fpl de milieu de trimestre; Pol **m. elections** = aux États-Unis, élections fpl législatives qui ont lieu au milieu du mandat présidentiel; Sch, Univ **m. exams** examens mpl du milieu du trimestre

midway ['mɪdweɪ] ADV à mi-chemin, à mi-distance; **m. up the hill** à mi-côte; **m. between ... and ...** à mi-distance ou à mi-chemin entre ... et ...; **a style m. between John's and Paul's** un style intermédiaire entre celui de John et celui de Paul

midweek [mɪd'wiːk] N milieu m de la semaine; **I'll see you m.** je te verrai vers le milieu de la semaine; **m. show** spectacle m de milieu de semaine

Midwest [mɪd'west] N Midwest m

Midwestern [mɪd'westən] ADJ du Midwest m

midwife, pl **midwives** ['mɪdwaɪf, -waɪvz] N sage-femme f, pl sages-femmes, accoucheuse f

midwifery ['mɪdwɪfərɪ] N **1** (profession) profession f de sage-femme **2** (obstetrics) obstétrique f

midwinter ['mɪd'wɪntər] N (middle of winter) milieu m de l'hiver, cœur m de l'hiver; (solstice) solstice m d'hiver

mien [miːn] N Lit mine f, air m, contenance f

miffed [mɪft] ADJ Fam froissé, piqué, fâché

MIG [mɪg] N Fin (abbr minimum income guarantee) = revenu m minimum assuré par l'État britannique aux plus de 60 ans

might[1] [maɪt] N (strength) puissance f, force(s) f(pl); **with all one's m.** (to work, push etc) de toute sa force, de toutes ses forces; Lit **with m. and main** de toutes mes/ses/etc forces; **she strove with m. and main to prevent it** elle a fait tout ce qu'elle a pu pour empêcher cela; Prov **m. is right** la raison du plus fort est toujours la meilleure

MIGHT[2] V AUX see may[1] **are you coming? – I m.** tu viens? – peut-être; **she refused, as well she m.** rien d'étonnant à ce qu'elle ait refusé; **when I mentioned his name she blushed, as well she m.** quand j'ai prononcé son nom, elle a rougi, et cela n'a rien d'étonnant; **and who m. you be?** qui êtes-vous, sans indiscrétion?; **and what m. you be doing here?** peut-on savoir ce que vous faites là?; **I wonder what I m. have done to offend him** je me demande ce que j'ai bien pu faire pour le fâcher; **he m. have arrived in time if ... il** aurait pu arriver à temps si ...; **you m. shut the door** vous pourriez fermer la porte!; **all the same, you m. have made less noise!** tout de même vous auriez pu faire moins de bruit!; **I was afraid he m. have done it** j'avais peur qu'il ne l'ait ou Fml l'eût fait VOIR GRAMMAIRE A59–60

might-have-been N Fam (person) raté, -ée

mightily ['maɪtɪlɪ] ADV **1** (powerfully) puissamment, fortement **2** Fam (extremely) extrêmement; **to be m. relieved** être vraiment soulagé

mighty ['maɪtɪ] ADJ (comp **mightier**; superl **mightiest**) **1** (powerful) (nation, army etc) puissant; (blow) grand **2** (large, imposing) grandiose, majestueux **3** esp Am Fam (considerable) grand; **you're in a m. hurry** vous êtes diablement pressé
ADV esp Am Fam rudement; **you're making a m. big mistake** vous commettez là une erreur colossale; **she looked m. pleased with herself** elle avait l'air très contente d'elle

mignonette [mɪnjə'net] N Bot réséda m

migraine ['miːgreɪn, 'maɪ-] N Med migraine f; **to suffer from m.** souffrir de migraines; **a bad m.** une forte migraine; **m. sufferer** migraineux, -euse

migrant ['maɪgrənt] ADJ = migratory
N (person, bird etc) migrateur, -trice
▸▸ **m. worker** (seasonal) (travailleur, -euse) saisonnier, -ière; (foreign) travailleur, -euse immigré(e)

migrate [maɪ'greɪt] VI (of bird) migrer; (of person) émigrer; **to m. south** migrer vers le sud; **people who had migrated from eastern Europe** les gens qui avaient émigré d'Europe de l'est

migration [maɪ'greɪʃən] N (of birds) migration f, (of people) émigration f

migratory ['maɪgrətrɪ, maɪ'greɪtərɪ] ADJ (bird) migrateur, -trice; (movement) migratoire

Mike [maɪk] N Fam **for the love of M.** pour l'amour du ciel

mike [maɪk] N Fam (abbr **microphone**) micro m

milch [mɪltʃ] ADJ
▸▸ **m. cow** vache f laitière; Fig vache à lait

mild [maɪld] ADJ **1** (person, remark) doux, f douce; (answer) conciliant; (criticism) léger, anodin **2** (punishment) peu sévère, léger **3**

(climate) doux, *f* douce, tempéré; *(winter)* doux, clément; **the weather is getting milder** le temps s'adoucit **4** *(dish)* peu épicé; *(cigar, tobacco, soap)* doux, *f* douce; *(sedative, medicine)* léger; **m. cheddar** cheddar *m* doux; **a m. curry** un curry peu épicé **5** *Med (illness, infection)* bénin, *f* bénigne; **a m. form of measles** une forme bénigne de rougeole **6** *(slight) (astonishment)* léger; **the joke caused some m. amusement** la plaisanterie a fait sourire; **the play caused a m. sensation** la pièce a fait un peu de bruit; **the play was a m. success** la pièce a obtenu un succès modéré

N *Br (beer)* bière *f* brune

▶▶ **m. steel** acier *m* doux

mildew ['mɪldjuː] N **1** *(fungus) (on wheat etc)* rouille *f, (on vines etc)* mildiou *m* **2** *(stains) (on fabric, leather etc)* moisissure *f,* moisi *m,* piqûres *fpl*

mildewy ['mɪldjuːɪ] ADJ *(bread)* moisi; *(wallpaper etc)* piqué par l'humidité, moisi; **m. smell** odeur de moisi; **to go m.** *(of plant)* se rouiller, *(of bread)* moisir; *(of vine)* être atteint par le mildiou; *(of paper etc)* se piquer

mildly ['maɪldlɪ] ADV **1** *(to say)* doucement, avec douceur **2** *(moderately)* modérément; **it has a m. laxative effect** ça a un léger effet laxatif; **to be m. successful** *(of play)* obtenir un succès modéré; **to put it m.** pour ne pas dire plus; **he's a bastard, and that's putting it m.!** c'est un salaud, et c'est peu dire

mild-mannered ADJ placide, imperturbable

mildness ['maɪldnɪs] N **1** *(of person, weather)* douceur *f, (of criticism)* caractère *m* anodin; *(of punishment)* légèreté *f* **2** *Med (of disease)* bénignité *f*

mile [maɪl] N *(distance)* mil(l)e *m;* **five miles** cinq mil(l)es; *Sport* **four-minute m.** mil(l)e couru en quatre minutes; **a 200-m. journey** un voyage de 200 mil(l)es; **miles per hour** mil(l)es par heure; **smaller cars do more miles to the or per gallon** les petites voitures consomment moins; **you don't see anyone for miles and miles** on parcourt des kilomètres sans voir personne; **m. after m. of sandy beaches** des plages de sable sur des kilomètres et des kilomètres; **people came from miles around** les gens sont venus de kilomètres à la ronde; **it's miles from anywhere** c'est à des kilomètres de tout; **he lives miles away** il habite très loin d'ici; **you'll recognize him a m. off** tu ne risques pas de le rater; **you can smell the factory a m. off** on sent les fumées de l'usine à des kilomètres; **you can tell she's Italian a m. off** elle a vraiment le type italien; *Fam* **to be miles away** *(be daydreaming)* être dans la lune; **someone not a thousand or million miles from us** une certaine personne qui ne se trouve pas très loin de nous; *Fam* **I feel miles better** je me sens vachement mieux; *Fam* **he's miles better than the others** il est vachement meilleur que les autres; *Fam* **it's miles more interesting** c'est vachement plus intéressant; *Fam* **it sticks out a m.** ça vous crève les yeux, ça se voit comme le nez au milieu de la figure; *Fam* **I can see you coming a m. off!** *(I know what you want)* je te vois venir (avec tes gros sabots)!; *Fam* **he'd run a m.** *(if that happened)* il prendrait ses jambes à son cou; *Fig* **to go the extra m.** faire un petit effort supplémentaire

mileage ['maɪlɪdʒ] N **1** *(distance travelled)* distance *f* en mil(l)es, *Can* millage *m,* ≃ kilométrage *m; Admin, Com etc (allowance)* indemnité *f* kilométrique; **car with a very low or small m.** voiture qui a très peu roulé **2** *(per gallon)* ≃ consommation *f* aux cent kilomètres; **what m. do you get?** combien est-ce que la voiture consomme aux cent?; **you**

can improve the m. by keeping the engine clean on consomme moins avec un moteur propre; *Fig Fam* **the opposition got a lot of m. out of the scandal** l'opposition a largement profité de ce scandale, ce scandale a largement profité à l'opposition; *Fig Fam* **there's no m. in it** *(in idea etc)* ça ne nous mènera nulle part, on ne peut rien en tirer

▶▶ *Admin, Com etc* **m. allowance** indemnité *f* kilométrique

milestone ['maɪlstəʊn] N borne *f* routière, ≃ borne kilométrique; *Fig* événement *m* important; **this discovery is a m. in medical research** cette découverte marque une étape importante dans la recherche médicale

milieu ['miːljɜː] N *Fml* milieu *m*

militancy ['mɪlɪtənsɪ] N militantisme *m*

militant ['mɪlɪtənt] ADJ militant; *Old-fashioned* **the Church m.** l'Église *f* militante

N *Pol etc* militant, -ante

militarily ['mɪlɪtərɪlɪ] ADV militairement

militarism ['mɪlɪtərɪz(ə)m] N militarisme *m*

militarist ['mɪlɪtərɪst] N militariste *mf*

militaristic [mɪlɪtə'rɪstɪk] ADJ militariste

militarize ['mɪlɪtəraɪz] VT militariser

military ['mɪlɪtərɪ] ADJ *(aircraft, base etc)* militaire; **a strong m. presence** une forte présence militaire

NPL **the m.** les militaires *mpl,* l'armée *f;* **the m. were called in** on a fait venir l'armée

▶▶ **m. academy** école *f* militaire; **m. attaché** attaché, -ée militaire; **m. court** tribunal *m* militaire; **m. government** gouvernement *m* militaire; **the m.-industrial complex** le complexe militaro-industriel; *Br* **m. man** militaire *m;* **m. police** police *f* militaire; **m. rule** régime *m* militaire; **m. service** service *m* militaire; **m. tribunal** tribunal militaire

militate ['mɪlɪteɪt] VI *(of fact, reason etc)* militer (**against** contre)

militia [mɪ'lɪʃə] N milice *f, Am* ≃ garde *f* nationale

militiaman, *pl* **militiamen** [mɪ'lɪʃəmən] N milicien *m,* soldat *m* de la milice, *Am* ≃ garde *m* national

milk [mɪlk] N **1** lait *m; Culin* **with m.** au lait; *Lit* **land of m. and honey** pays *m* de cocagne; *Prov* **to be full of the m. of human kindness** être la bonté même; **he's not exactly overflowing with the m. of human kindness** *(kind-hearted)* ce n'est pas un tendre; *(generous)* ce n'est pas quelqu'un de particulièrement généreux **2** *(in plant, coconut)* lait *m; Prov* **there's no point in crying over spilt m.** ce qui est fait est fait

VT **1** *(cow etc)* traire **2** *Fam Pej (exploit) (person)* dépouiller; *(country, colony)* exploiter; **the newspapers milked the story for all it was worth** les journaux ont tiré tout ce qu'ils ont pu de l'histoire; **they just milked all his ideas** ils se sont approprié toutes ses idées

▶▶ **m. bar** milk-bar *m, pl* milk-bars; **m. bottle** bouteille *f* de lait; *Bot* **m. cap** *(fungus)* lactaire *m;* **m. chocolate** chocolat *m* au lait; **m. churn** bidon *m* à lait; **m. diet** régime *m* lacté; **m. duct** canal *m* galactophore; *Br* **m. float** camionnette *f* du laitier; **m. gland** glande *f* lactéale *ou* galactophore; **m. jug** pot *m* à ou au lait; *Pharm* **m. of magnesia** magnésie *f* hydratée; **m. powder** lait *m* en poudre; *Br* **m. pudding** entremets *m* au lait; *Br* **m. round** *(for milk delivery)* tournée *f* du laitier; *Univ* = tournée des universités par les employeurs pour recruter des étudiants en fin d'études; *Fam* **m. run** *Aviat* vol *m* sans histoire, partie *f* de rigolade; *(regular journey)* trajet *m* habituel, tournée habituelle; **m. tooth** dent *f* de lait; **m. train** premier train *m* (du matin)

milk-and-water ADJ insipide

milker ['mɪlkər] N *(cow etc)* **good/bad m.** bonne/mauvaise laitière *f*

milkiness ['mɪlkɪnɪs] N *(of liquid etc)* couleur *f* laiteuse, aspect *m* laiteux

milking ['mɪlkɪŋ] N *(of cow)* traite *f*

▶▶ **m. machine** machine *f* à traire, trayeuse *f;* **m. pail** seau *m* à traire; **m. parlour** salle *f* de traite

milkmaid ['mɪlkmeɪd] N trayeuse *f,* fille *f* de laiterie

milkman, *pl* **milkmen** ['mɪlkmən] N *(delivery man)* laitier *m*

milk-shake N milk-shake *m, pl* milk-shakes

milksop ['mɪlksɒp] N *Old-fashioned Fam Pej* poule *f* mouillée

milkweed ['mɪlkwiːd] N *Bot* laiteron *m,* lait *m* d'âne

milk-white ADJ d'une blancheur laiteuse

milky ['mɪlkɪ] ADJ **1** *(containing milk)* qui contient du lait; **I like my coffee m.** *(with lots of milk)* j'aime mon café avec beaucoup de lait **2** *(colour)* laiteux, *Lit* lactescent; *(gem)* laiteux; **m. white** blanc laiteux

▶▶ *Astron* **the M. Way** la Voie lactée

mill [mɪl] N **1 (flour)** moulin *m* (à farine); *(large)* minoterie *f; Fam* **he's been through the m.** il en a bavé; **to put sb through the m.** en faire baver à qn; **coffee/pepper m.** moulin à café/à poivre; **(crushing) m.** broyeur *m,* concasseur *m* **2** *Metal (rolling)* **m.** laminoir *m,* train *m* (de laminage) **3** *(factory)* usine *f,* **cotton m.** filature *f* de coton; **steel m.** aciérie *f*

VT *(wheat, flour)* moudre; *Tech (crush)* broyer; *Tech (gears)* fraiser, tailler; *(screw)* moleter; *(coin)* créneler

▶▶ *Old-fashioned* **m. hand** ouvrier, -ière (d'usine); **m. owner** industriel *m*

▶ **mill about, mill around** VI *(of crowd)* grouiller

millboard ['mɪlbɔːd] N carton-pâte *m inv*

milled [mɪld] ADJ *(grain etc)* moulu

▶▶ **m. edge** *(on coin)* crénelage *m,* grènetis *m*

millennial [mɪ'lenɪəl] ADJ **m. celebrations** = festivités *fpl* organisées pour marquer l'arrivée du nouveau millénaire

millennium [mɪ'lenɪəm] N **1** *(thousand years)* millénaire *m,* mille ans *mpl* **2** *Rel, Hist* millénium *m*

▶▶ *Comput* **M. bug** bogue *m* de l'an deux mille; **the M. Dome** = centre *m* d'expositions en forme de dôme construit à Londres à l'occasion de l'an 2000

millepede ['mɪlɪpiːd] N mille-pattes *m inv*

miller ['mɪlər] N meunier *m; (on large scale)* minotier *m*

millet ['mɪlɪt] N *Bot, Culin* millet *m,* mil *m;* **Indian m.** sorgho *m,* millet d'Inde

millibar ['mɪlɪbɑːr] N *Met* millibar *m*

milligram(me) ['mɪlɪgræm] N milligramme *m*

millilitre, *Am* **milliliter** ['mɪlɪliːtər] N millilitre *m*

millimetre, *Am* **millimeter** ['mɪlɪmiːtər] N millimètre *m;* **a 10-m. gap** un espace de 10 millimètres

milliner ['mɪlɪnər] N modiste *f,* chapelier, -ière

millinery ['mɪlɪnərɪ] N *Old-fashioned (articles mpl de)* modes *fpl;* **m. department** *(in shop)* rayon *m* des chapeaux

milling ['mɪlɪŋ] N **1** *(grinding) (of grain)* mouture *f,* moulage *m* **2** *Metal* fraisage *m; (of screw etc)* moletage *m; (of coin)* cordonnage *m* **3** *(on coin)* cordon *m,* grènetis *m,* tranche *f* cannelée

▶▶ **m. cutter** fraise *f,* fraiseuse *f,* **m. machine** fraiseuse

million ['mɪljən] N million m; **two m. men** deux millions d'hommes; **half a m.** un demi-million; **worth millions** (person) riche à millions; **an actor who gave pleasure to millions** un acteur qui a diverti des millions de gens; Fam **I've told him a m. times** je le lui ai dit mille fois; Fam **she's one in a m.** elle est unique; Fam **thanks a m.!** merci mille fois!; Iron **eh bien, merci!**; Fam **I feel like a m. dollars** je me sens en pleine forme; **to look like a m. dollars** être superbe VOIR GRAMMAIRE A12–13

millionaire [mɪljə'neər] N millionnaire mf, milliardaire mf; **to be a m. twice/three times over** être deux/trois fois millionnaire; **I've got a m. uncle** j'ai un oncle millionnaire ou milliardaire

millionairess [mɪljə'neəres] N millionnaire f

millionth ['mɪljənθ] ADJ millionième N 1 (person, thing) millionième mf 2 (fraction) millionième m

millipede ['mɪlɪpiːd] N mille-pattes m inv

millisecond ['mɪlɪsekənd] N milliseconde f

millpond ['mɪlpɒnd] N réservoir m ou retenue f de moulin; **sea as calm or smooth as a m.** mer f d'huile

millrace ['mɪlreɪs] N (channel) bief m de moulin; (water) courant m du bief

millstone ['mɪlstəʊn] N meule f (de moulin); Fig **a m. round my neck** un boulet que je traîne

millstream ['mɪlstriːm] N courant m du bief

millwheel ['mɪlwiːl] N roue f de moulin

millwright ['mɪlraɪt] N constructeur m de moulins

milometer [maɪ'lɒmɪtər] N Aut etc compteur m de mil(l)es, ≃ compteur kilométrique

milt [mɪlt] N (of fish) laitance f, laite f

MIME [maɪm] N Comput (abbr Multipurpose Internet Mail Extensions) (protocole m) MIME m

mime [maɪm] Theat N (performance) mime m; (actor) mime mf; **a version of Hamlet in m.** une version d'Hamlet en mime VT (scene) mimer; (song) chanter en play-back VI mimer; (of singer) faire du play-back; **to m. to a song** chanter en play-back ►► **m. artist** mime mf

mimeo(graph)® ['mɪmɪəʊ(grɑːf)] N 1 (machine) machine f à ronéotyper 2 (document) polycopie f VT ronéotyper

mimic ['mɪmɪk] N imitateur, -trice VT (pt, pp mimicked [mɪmɪkt]) (imitate) (person) imiter, mimer, Fam singer; (voice, walk, behaviour, nature etc) imiter

mimicry ['mɪmɪkrɪ] N 1 imitation f 2 Biol mimétisme m

mimosa [mɪ'məʊzə] N (shrub) mimosa m

min 1 (abbr minute(s)) min. 2 (abbr minimum) min

minaret [mɪnə'ret] N minaret m

mince [mɪns] N Br Culin viande f hachée VT 1 (chop up) (meat etc) hacher; **minced meat** viande f hachée 2 (always in negative) **not to m. one's words** (speak plainly) ne pas mâcher ses mots, parler net; **not to m. matters** pour parler net VI 1 (walk in affected manner) marcher à petits pas affectés ou efféminés 2 (talk in affected manner) parler avec une élégance affectée ou minaudière ►► **m. pie** = tartelette f fourrée avec un mélange de fruits secs et d'épices que l'on sert à Noël en Grande-Bretagne

mincemeat ['mɪnsmiːt] N Culin = préparation f de raisins secs, écorce d'oranges et

graisse de bœuf pour tartelettes; Fam **to make m. of sb** (in fist fight, boxing match) réduire qn en bouillie, démolir qn; (in football, tennis match) écraser qn; (in debate, argument) démolir qn; **the lawyer made m. of his testimony** l'avocat a démoli son témoignage

mincer ['mɪnsər] N Culin (device) hachoir m

mincing ['mɪnsɪŋ] ADJ (manner, tone) affecté, minaudier; (steps, gait) efféminé

MIND [maɪnd]

N esprit 1, 6, 8 ■ mémoire 2 ■ avis 3 ■ attention 5 ■ raison 7
VT faire attention à 1, 2 ■ garder 4

N 1 (thoughts) esprit m; **such a thought had never entered his m.** une telle pensée ne lui était jamais venue à l'esprit; **to have sth on one's m.** avoir qch qui vous préoccupe; **it's all in your m.!** tu te fais des idées!; **it's all in the m.** tout ça, c'est dans la tête; **in the m.'s eye** dans l'imagination; **in her m.'s eye she could see them staring at her** elle se les imaginait la fixant; **to put or set sb's m. at rest** rassurer qn; **to be easy/uneasy in one's m.** avoir/ne pas avoir l'esprit tranquille; **I couldn't get it off my m.** je ne pouvais pas m'empêcher d'y penser; **a walk will take my m. off it** une promenade me changera les idées; **it's a problem that is always on my m.** c'est un problème auquel je n'arrête pas de penser; **she couldn't get their faces out of her m.** elle ne pouvait oublier leurs visages; **put it out of your m.** n'y pensez plus

2 (memory) mémoire f; **to have a m. like a sieve** avoir (une) très mauvaise mémoire; **to bear or keep sth in m.** (think about) songer à qch; (take into account) tenir compte de qch; (not forget) ne pas oublier qch, garder qch à l'esprit; **we must bear in m. that she is only a child** il ne faut pas oublier que ce n'est qu'une enfant; **I'll bear it in m.** (what you suggested) je m'en souviendrai; **to call sth to m.** se souvenir de qch; **it brings or calls to m. Beethoven's Fifth** cela rappelle la cinquième de Beethoven; **to put sb in m. of sb/sth** rappeler qn/qch à qn; **it went (completely or clean) out of my m.** cela m'est (complètement) sorti de l'esprit

3 (opinion) avis m, idée f; **to change one's m.** changer d'avis ou d'idée, se raviser; **I've changed my m. about him** j'ai changé d'avis ou d'idée à son égard; **I've changed my m. about moving to London** (don't want to) j'ai changé d'avis, je ne veux plus aller vivre à Londres; (want to) j'ai changé d'avis, je veux maintenant aller vivre à Londres; **I gave him a piece of my m.** je lui ai dit son fait ou ses quatre vérités; **to be of one m., to be of the same m.** être du même avis, être d'accord; **to my m.** selon moi, à mon avis; **to speak one's m.** dire ce qu'on pense; **to keep an open m. about sth** réserver son opinion sur qch

4 (will, wants) **to know one's own m.** savoir ce qu'on veut; **you've got a m. of your own** tu peux décider toi-même; **the car seemed to have a m. of its own** la voiture semblait faire ce que bon lui semblait; **make up your m.!** décidez-vous!; **to make up one's m.** se décider; **I can't make up your m. for you** je ne peux pas décider à ta place; **to be in two minds about sth** être indécis sur qch; **I'm in two minds about going** je ne sais pas si je vais y aller; **I've a good m. to do it** je suis bien tenté de le faire; **I've half a m. to tell his parents** j'ai presqu'envie de le dire à ses parents; **to set one's m. on sth** vouloir absolument avoir qch, se mettre la tête d'avoir qch; **to set one's m. on doing sth** vouloir absolument faire qch, se mettre en tête de faire

qch; **to have sth in m.** avoir qch en vue; **what kind of party did you have in m.?** à quelle sorte de soirée est-ce que tu pensais?; **I had in m. something smaller** je pensais à quelque chose de plus petit; **the person I have in m.** la personne à laquelle je pense; **who did you have in m. for the job?** à qui pensiez-vous pour le poste?

5 (attention) **to give one's whole m. to sth** accorder toute son attention à qch; **to keep one's m. on sth** se concentrer sur qch; **your m. is not on the job** tu n'as pas la tête à ce que tu fais; **I'm sure if you put your m. to it you could do it** je suis sûr que si tu essayais vraiment, tu pourrais le faire

6 (way of thinking) **attitude of m.** manière f de penser; **to have a good m.** être intelligent, avoir la tête bien faite; **to have the m. of a three-year-old** avoir l'esprit ou l'intelligence d'un enfant de trois ans; **I haven't got a scientific m.** je n'ai pas l'esprit scientifique; **you've got a dirty m.!** tu as l'esprit mal placé!; **you've got a nasty m.** tu vois le mal partout; **it's probably just my suspicious m. but I don't trust him** c'est probablement que je suis trop suspicieux, mais je n'ai pas confiance en lui

7 (reason) raison f; **to be out of one's m.** avoir perdu la raison ou la tête; Fam (drunk, from drugs) être parti; **are you out of your m.?, you must be out of your m.!** est-ce que tu as perdu la tête?; Fam **he was out of his m. with boredom** ou **bored out of his m.** il s'ennuyait à mourir; **to be in one's right m.** avoir toute sa raison ou toutes ses facultés

8 (person) esprit m; **one of the most brilliant minds of this century** l'un des esprits les plus brillants de ce siècle; Prov **great minds think alike, (fools seldom differ)** les grands esprits se rencontrent; Hum **how about a drink? – great minds think alike!** si on prenait un verre? – les grands esprits se rencontrent!

VT 1 (pay attention to) (somebody, something) faire attention à, prêter attention à; (concern oneself with) (something) s'occuper de; **never m. the car** ne t'en fais pas ou ne t'inquiète pas pour la voiture; **don't m. him, he's always like that** ne fais pas attention à lui, il est toujours comme ça; Iron **don't m. me, I only live here!** je t'en prie, fais comme chez toi!; **don't m. them** ne faites pas attention à eux; **m. you, I've always thought that ...** remarquez, j'ai toujours pensé que ...; **but, m. you, it was late** mais, voyez-vous, il était tard; **m. what you're doing!** faites attention à ce que vous faites!

2 (take care) **m. you're not late!** faites en sorte de ne pas être en retard!; **m. you write to him!** n'oubliez pas de lui écrire!; **m. you don't fall!** faites attention de ne pas tomber!; **m. the step!** attention à la marche!; **would you m. where you're putting your feet, please?** est-ce que tu peux faire attention où tu mets les pieds, s'il te plaît?; **m. your backs (please)!** attention devant!; **to m. one's language** surveiller son langage; Br Fam **m. how you go!** fais attention à toi!; Fam **don't be late, m.!** surtout, ne sois pas en retard!

3 (object to) **what I m. is ...** ce qui me gêne, c'est que ...; **I don't m. the cold** le froid ne me gêne pas; **I don't m. trying** je veux bien essayer; **do you m. my asking ...?** puis-je vous demander sans indiscrétion ...?; **how much do you earn, if you don't m. my or me asking?** combien est-ce que vous gagnez, sans indiscrétion?; **I wouldn't m. a cup of tea** je prendrais volontiers une tasse de thé; **I wouldn't m. having his salary** ça ne me dérangerait pas de gagner autant que lui

4 (look after) (children) garder, surveiller; (animals etc) garder; (house) garder, veiller sur; **to m. the shop** s'occuper du magasin

5 *Arch, Dial (remember)* se souvenir de, se rappeler

VI 1 *(object)* **would you m. if …?** est-ce que cela vous gênerait *ou* dérangerait si …?; **do you m.!** *(how dare you)* dites donc!; **if you don't m.** si cela ne vous dérange pas; **I don't m.** *(it doesn't matter to me)* cela m'est égal; *(go ahead)* je veux bien; **if nobody minds** si personne n'y voit d'inconvénient; **do you m. if I smoke?** cela ne vous dérange *ou* gêne pas que je fume?; *Fam* **another drop of wine? – I don't m. if I do** encore un peu de vin? – ce n'est pas de refus **2** *(trouble oneself)* **never m.!** *(it doesn't matter)* ça ne fait rien!, tant pis!; *(don't worry)* ne vous inquiétez pas!; *Fam* **never you m.!** *(don't be nosy)* ça, c'est mon affaire!, ça ne te regarde pas!; *(don't get upset)* ne t'en fais pas

▸▸ *Mktg* **m. share** part *f* de notoriété

▸ **mind out** *VI Br* faire attention (**for** à)

mind-blowing ADJ *Sl (drug)* hallucinant; *(experience)* ahurissant, époustouflant

mind-boggling [-bɒglɪŋ] ADJ *Fam* époustouflant

minded ['maɪndɪd] ADJ disposé, enclin (**to do sth** à faire qch); **if you were so m.** si vous le vouliez; **commercially m.** qui a le sens du commerce, commerçant; **to be mechanically m.** être bon mécanicien; **she isn't very money-m.** *(money isn't important to her)* elle n'est pas très préoccupée par les questions d'argent

minder ['maɪndər] N *(bodyguard)* garde *m*; **(child** *or* **baby) m.** gardienne *f, Fam* nounou *f, Ind* **(machine) m.** surveillant *m*

mindful ['maɪndfʊl] ADJ *esp Fml (keeping in mind)* **to be m. of sth** se souvenir de qch, ne pas oublier qch; **m. of this warning …** se souvenant de cet avertissement …; **m. of the danger to her health** soucieuse de sa santé; **he is always m. of others** il pense toujours aux autres

mindless ['maɪndlɪs] ADJ *(senseless)* *(destruction, violence)* gratuit; *(task, job)* stupide, abrutissant

mind-numbing ADJ abêtissant

mind-reader N voyant, -ante; **I'm not a m.!** je ne peux pas lire dans *ou* deviner tes/ses/ etc pensées, je ne suis pas devin

mindset ['maɪndset] N façon *f* de penser

mine¹ [maɪn] N **1** *(for coal etc)* mine *f*; **he went down the m. at 16** il est descendu dans la mine à 16 ans; *Fig* **a m. of information** une mine d'informations **2** *Mil, Naut* mine *f*, **(land) m.** mine terrestre; **to lay a m.** *(on land)* poser une mine; *(at sea)* mouiller une mine

VT 1 *(coal seam)* exploiter; *(coal, gold)* extraire **2** *Mil, Naut* miner; **mined area** zone *f* minée

VI *Min* **to m. for coal/gold** extraire du charbon/de l'or

▸▸ **m. detector** détecteur *m* de mines; **m. shaft** puits *m* de mine; **m. workings** chantiers *mpl* d'exploitation minière

mine² POSS PRON le mien, la mienne, *pl* les miens, les miennes; **this letter is m.** cette lettre est à moi; **this signature is not m.** cette signature n'est pas de moi; **I took her hands in m.** je pris ses mains dans les miennes; **a friend of m.** un(e) de mes ami(e)s, un(e) ami(e) à moi; **it is no business of m.** ce n'est pas mon affaire, ça ne me regarde pas; **everything of m. had been ripped to shreds** toutes mes affaires avaient été réduites en lambeaux; *Fml* **m. was a difficult/thankless task** c'était une tâche difficile/ingrate que la mienne; **what's m. is yours** ce qui est à moi est à toi; **so much money and it's (m.,) all m.!** tant d'argent, et c'est à moi, rien qu'à moi!;

Fam **m.'s a beer** *(in pub)* pour moi, ce sera une bière VOIR GRAMMAIRE A30; B21–2

POSS ADJ *Arch, Lit* mon, ma, *pl* mes; *Hum* **m. host** l'aubergiste *m*

minefield ['maɪnfiːld] N *Mil, Naut* champ *m* de mines; *Fig* terrain *m* miné

minehunter ['maɪnhʌntər] N *Naut* chasseur *m* de mines

minelayer ['maɪnleɪər] N *Naut* mouilleur *m* de mines

minelaying ['maɪnleɪɪŋ] N *Mil* pose *f* de mines; *Naut* mouillage *m* de mines

miner ['maɪnər] N *Min* mineur *m*; **m.'s lamp** lampe *f* de mineur

mineral ['mɪn(ə)rəl] ADJ *(oil etc)* minéral, -aux

N **1** minéral *m*; **the m. resources of a country** les ressources *fpl* minières d'un pays **2** *Old-fashioned Br* **minerals** *(drinks)* boissons *fpl* gazeuses

▸▸ *Min* **m. deposits** gisements *mpl* miniers *ou* minéraux; **the m. kingdom** le monde minéral; **m. spring** source *f* d'eau minérale; **m. water** eau *f* minérale

mineralogist [mɪnə'rælədʒɪst] N minéralogiste *mf*

mineralogy [mɪnə'rælədʒɪ] N minéralogie *f*

minestrone [mɪnə'strəʊnɪ] N minestrone *m*

minesweeper ['maɪnswiːpər] N *Naut* dragueur *m* de mines

minesweeping ['maɪnswiːpɪŋ] N *Naut* dragage *m* des mines

ming [mɪŋ] *VI Br Fam* puer, schlinguer; **it mings in here!** ça schlingue ici!

minger ['mɪŋər] N *Br Fam (unattractive person)* mocheté *f*

minging ['mɪŋɪŋ] ADJ *Br Fam (unattractive)* moche; *(of poor quality)* merdique; **that wine is absolutely m.!** ce vin est vraiment dégueulasse!; **is she going out with him? he's m.!** elle sort avec lui? il est moche comme un pou!

mingle ['mɪŋg(ə)l] VT *(usu passive)* mélanger (**with** avec); **her tears were mingled with laughter** elle pleurait et riait à la fois; **joy mingled with sadness** joie mêlée de tristesse

VI *(of things)* se mélanger; *(of person) (at party)* circuler; **to m. with the crowd** se mêler à la foule

▸ **mingle together** VI se mélanger

mingy ['mɪndʒɪ] ADJ *Br Fam (mean) (person)* mesquin, *Fam* radin; *(salary, gift)* minable; *(amount of money)* ridicule; **a m. helping** une portion minuscule; **a m. five pounds** cinq malheureuses livres

mini ['mɪnɪ] N *Fam (dress etc)* mini *f*, *(style)* mini *m*

▸▸ **m. system** *(hi-fi)* minichaîne *f*, *Comput* **m. tower** mini-tour *f, pl* mini-tours

mini- PREF mini(-); **minibiography** mini-biographie *f*, **minirecording studio** mini-studio *m* d'enregistrement

miniature ['mɪnɪtʃər] N *(figure, bottle, painting)* miniature *f*; **to paint in m.** peindre en miniature; **Paris in m.** *(model)* Paris en miniature

ADJ en miniature; *(garden, bottle etc)* miniature; *(book etc)* minuscule; *Phot (camera)* (de) petit format

▸▸ **m. golf** golf *m* miniature, minigolf *m*; **m. painter** miniaturiste *mf*; **m. poodle** caniche *m* nain

miniaturist ['mɪnɪtʃərɪst] N *Art* miniaturiste *mf*

miniaturize ['mɪnɪtʃəraɪz] VT miniaturiser

minibar ['mɪnɪbɑːr] N minibar *m*

mini-break N *(holiday)* mini-séjour *m, pl* mini-séjours

minibudget ['mɪnɪbʌdʒɪt] N budget *m* auxiliaire *ou* exceptionnel

minibus ['mɪnɪbʌs] N minibus *m*; **m. service** service *m* de minibus

minicab ['mɪnɪkæb] N *Br* radio-taxi *m, pl* radio-taxis; **m. firm** société *f* de radio-taxis

minicomputer [mɪnɪkəm'pjuːtər] N mini-ordinateur *m, pl* mini-ordinateurs

mini-cruise N mini-croisière *f, pl* mini-croisières

MiniDisc® ['mɪnɪdɪsk] N MiniDisc® *m*

▸▸ **M. player** lecteur *m* de MiniDiscs

minidish ['mɪnɪdɪʃ] N mini antenne *f* parabolique

minidisk ['mɪnɪdɪsk] N mini-disquette *f, pl* mini-disquettes

mini-floppy N mini-disquette *f, pl* mini-disquettes

minigolf ['mɪnɪgɒlf] N minigolf *m*

minim ['mɪnɪm] N *Br Mus* blanche *f*

▸▸ **m. rest** demi-pause *f, pl* demi-pauses

minimal ['mɪnɪm(ə)l] ADJ **1** *(very small)* minime **2** *(minimum)* minimal, -aux, minimum

▸▸ **m. value** valeur *f* minimale

minimalism ['mɪnɪməlɪz(ə)m] N minimalisme *m*

minimalist ['mɪnɪməlɪst] N, ADJ minimaliste *mf*

minimization [mɪnɪmaɪ'zeɪʃən] N minimisation *f*

minimize ['mɪnɪmaɪz] VT *(something, importance of something)* minimiser; *(noise, friction etc)* réduire *ou* limiter au minimum; *Comput (window)* réduire

minimum, *pl* **minima** ['mɪnɪməm, -ə] N minimum *m, pl* minimums, minima; **a m. of two years' experience** un minimum de deux ans d'expérience; **as a m.** au minimum; **to reduce sth to a m.** réduire qch au minimum; **keep the questions to a m.** essayez de poser le moins de questions possible; **in order to keep mistakes to a m.** de façon à avoir le minimum d'erreurs; **in order to reduce delays to a m.** de façon à réduire l'attente au maximum

ADJ minimum, minimal, -aux

▸▸ **m. charge** charge *f ou* tarif *m* minimum; **m. connecting time** *(when travelling)* temps *m* minimal de correspondance; *Fin* **m. income guarantee** = revenu *m* minimum assuré par l'État britannique aux plus de 60 ans; *Br Fin Formerly* **m. lending rate** taux *m* de base, taux officiel d'escompte; **m. rates** taux *mpl* minima; **m. speed** vitesse *f* minimum *ou* minimale; *Com* **m. stock level** stock *m* d'alerte; **m. wage** salaire *m* minimum *(légal)*, ≃ SMIC *m*

mining ['maɪnɪŋ] N **1** *Min* exploitation *f* minière; **m. area/town** région *f* /ville *f* minière; **the m. industry** l'industrie *f* minière **2** *Mil, Naut* pose *f* de mines (**of an area** dans une zone), minage *m*

▸▸ **m. engineer** ingénieur *m* des mines

minion ['mɪnjən] N *Pej (lackey)* larbin *m*; *Fam Iron (subordinate)* subordonné, -ée; **the minions of the law** les laquais *mpl* de l'ordre établi

minipill ['mɪnɪpɪl] N mini-pilule *f, pl* mini-pilules

mini-roundabout N mini rond-point *m, pl* mini-ronds-points

miniseries ['mɪnɪsɪəriːz] N *TV* mini-feuilleton *m, pl* mini-feuilletons, mini-série *f, pl* mini-séries

miniskirt ['mɪnɪskɜːt] N minijupe *f*

minister ['mɪnɪstər] N **1** *Pol* ministre *m* (d'État); *Br* **M. of State** ministre d'État; *Br* **M. of Defence** ministre de la Défense; **M. for Tourism** ministre du Tourisme **2** *Rel (Pro-*

testant) pasteur *m*, ministre *m*; *(Jesuit)* ministre

vi to m. to sb soigner qn, s'occuper de qn; **to m. to sb's needs** pourvoir *ou* subvenir aux besoins de qn; *Rel* **to m. to a parish** desservir une paroisse

▸▸*Rel* **m. general** ministre général; **M. Plenipotentiary** ministre plénipotentiaire

ministerial [mɪnɪˈstɪərɪəl] **ADJ 1** *Pol* ministériel **2** *Rel* sacerdotal, -aux **3** *Law* exécutif; **m. functions** fonctions *fpl* exécutives

ministering [ˈmɪnɪstərɪŋ] **ADJ**
▸▸ **m. angel** ange *m* de bonté

ministration [mɪnɪˈstreɪʃən] **N 1** *Fml (assistance)* soins *mpl* **2** *Rel* sacerdoce *m*; **to receive the ministrations of a priest** être administré par un prêtre

ministry [ˈmɪnɪstrɪ] **N 1** *Pol (department)* ministère *m*; *(government)* ministère, gouvernement *m*; *Br* **the M. of Defence** le ministère de la Défense; **M. of Transport** ministère des Transports **2** *Rel* **the m.** le sacerdoce; **he was intended for the m.** il fut destiné à l'Église

mink [mɪŋk] **N 1** *(animal)* **(American) m.** vison *m* **2** *(fur)* vison *m*; *(coat)* (manteau *m* de) vison *m*
▸▸ **m. coat** (manteau de) vison; **m. farm** visonnière *f*, **m. oil** huile *f* de vison; **m. ranch** visonnière

Minn *abbr* **Minnesota**

minnow [ˈmɪnəʊ] **N** *(fish)* vairon *m*; *(any small fish)* fretin *m*; *Fig* menu fretin

Minoan [mɪˈnəʊən] **ADJ** minoen

minor [ˈmaɪnər] **ADJ 1** *(lesser)* secondaire, mineur; *(unimportant)* petit, peu important; *(detail, repair)* mineur, petit; **the film is a m. classic** le film est un petit chef-d'œuvre; **of m. importance** sans grande importance; **to play a m. part** *or* **role** *Cin, Theat etc* avoir un petit rôle; *Fig* jouer un rôle mineur *ou* accessoire; *Med* **m. operation** petite opération *f*, opération sans gravité **2** *Br Sch Old-fashioned* **Martin m.** Martin junior

N 1 *Law* mineur, -eure **2** *Am Univ* matière *f* secondaire

vi *Am Univ* **to m. in physics** étudier la physique comme matière secondaire
▸▸ *Mus* **m. key** ton *m ou* mode *m* mineur; *Rel* **m. orders** ordres *mpl* mineurs; **m. road** route *f* secondaire; *Fin* **m. shareholder** actionnaire *mf* minoritaire; *Am Univ* **m. subject** matière secondaire

Minorca [mɪˈnɔːkə] **N** Minorque *f*

Minorcan [mɪˈnɔːkən] **ADJ** minorquin
N Minorquin, -ine

minority [mɪˈnɒrɪtɪ, maɪ-] **N 1** *(of total number)* minorité *f*; **to be in a** *or* **the m.** être en minorité; **to be in a m. of one** être seul de son opinion VOIR GRAMMAIRE A11 **2** *Law (age)* minorité *f*
▸▸ **m. government** gouvernement *m* minoritaire; *Fin* **m. holding, m. interest** participation *f* minoritaire; **m. opinion** opinion *f* d'une minorité; **m. opinion must be respected** on doit respecter l'opinion de la minorité; *Pol* **m. party** parti *m* minoritaire; **m. report** contre-rapport *m*, *pl* contre-rapports *(soumis par une minorité)*; **m. shareholder** actionnaire *mf* minoritaire

Minotaur [ˈmaɪnətɔːr] **N** *Myth* **the M.** le Minotaure

minster [ˈmɪnstər] **N** *Br* cathédrale *f*, *(attached to abbey)* église *f* abbatiale; **York M.** la cathédrale d'York

minstrel [ˈmɪnstrəl] **N 1** *(in Middle Ages)* ménestrel *m* **2** *Lit (poet)* poète *m*; *(musician)* musicien *m*; *(singer)* chanteur *m* **3** *(actor/singer with blackened face)* acteur *m*/musicien *m* blanc maquillé en noir
▸▸ **m. show** = spectacle *m* de music-hall avec des acteurs blancs déguisés en Noirs

mint¹ [mɪnt] **N** *(plant)* menthe *f*, *(sweet)* bonbon *m* à la menthe; **m. chocolate** chocolat *m* à la menthe
▸▸ **m. julep** cocktail *m* au bourbon et à la menthe; **m. sauce** sauce *f* à la menthe; **m. tea** *(tea with mint)* thé *m* à la menthe; *(herbal tea)* infusion *f* de menthe

mint² **N** *Fin* **the (Royal) M.** ≃ (l'hôtel *m* de) la Monnaie; *Fam* **to be worth a m.** *(of person)* rouler sur l'or; *(of thing)* valoir une somme fabuleuse *ou* une fortune; *Fam* **to make a m.** gagner une fortune; **to be in m. condition** être comme neuf *ou* à l'état neuf; *Philat* **m. stamp** timbre non oblitéré *ou* neuf **VT 1** *(coins)* frapper; *Fig Fam* **he must be minting it** il doit rouler sur l'or; **the company was minting it with their latest model** l'entreprise ramassait l'argent à la pelle grâce au nouveau modèle **2** *Lit (word, expression)* inventer, forger, créer

minted [ˈmɪntɪd] **ADJ** *Br Fam* plein aux as, bourré de fric

minuet [mɪnjʊˈet] **N** *Mus* menuet *m*

minus [ˈmaɪnəs] **PREP** moins; **ten m. eight leaves two** dix moins huit égale(nt) deux; **he managed to escape, but m. his luggage** il a réussi à s'échapper, mais sans (ses) bagages; **it's m. twelve degrees** il fait moins douze degrés
ADJ *Math (quantity, number)* négatif; *Sch* **B m.** B moins; **but, on the m. side, the pay is low** mais le revers de la médaille, c'est que c'est mal payé; **the m. side of a situation** les désavantages d'une situation
N *Math (sign)* moins *m*
▸▸ **m. sign** signe *m* moins, moins

minuscule [ˈmɪnəskjuːl] **ADJ** minuscule; *Fam (salary)* dérisoire

minute¹ [ˈmɪnɪt] **N 1** *(measurement of time)* minute *f*, **it's ten minutes to** *or Am* **of three** il est trois heures moins dix; **ten minutes past** *or Am* **after three** trois heures dix; **to observe a m.'s silence** observer une minute de silence; **at five-m. intervals, at intervals of five minutes** toutes les cinq minutes; **it's five minutes from here** c'est à cinq minutes d'ici; **the town centre is a ten-m. walk/drive from here** le centre-ville est à dix minutes d'ici à pied/en voiture; **a m.'s rest** un moment de repos; **wait a m.!** attendez une minute *ou* un instant!; **go downstairs this m.!** descends immédiatement!; **just a m.** (attendez) un instant *ou* une minute; **he's come in this (very) m.** il vient de rentrer à l'instant, il vient juste de rentrer; **the m. my back was turned she …** j'avais à peine le dos tourné qu'elle …; **he'll be here any m.** il va arriver d'une minute à l'autre; **it'll be ready in a m.** ça sera prêt dans une minute *ou* un instant; **in a few minutes** dans quelques minutes; **I've just popped in for a m.** je ne fais qu'entrer et sortir, je ne fais que passer; **until the last m.** jusqu'à la dernière minute; **at the last m.** à la dernière minute VOIR GRAMMAIRE A80–1; B60 **2** *Math, Astron* minute *f* **3** *(note)* note *f* (de service); **minutes** *(of meeting)* compte rendu *m*, procès-verbal *m*; **to take the minutes of a meeting** faire le compte rendu d'une réunion
VT *(facts, remarks etc)* prendre note de; *(meeting)* dresser le procès-verbal *ou* le compte rendu de
▸▸ **minutes book** registre *m* des procès-verbaux; **m. hand** grande aiguille *f*, aiguille des minutes; **m. steak** entrecôte *f* minute; **m. timer** minuterie *f*

minute² [maɪˈnjuːt] **ADJ 1** *(small)* tout petit, minuscule; **the minutest details** les moindres détails; **he told us about his holiday in m. detail** il nous a raconté ses vacances par le menu **2** *(detailed) (examination etc)* minutieux

minutely [maɪˈnjuːtlɪ] **ADV** *(to examine etc)* minutieusement, en détail

minutiae [maɪˈnjuːʃiiː] **NPL** petits détails *mpl* infimes

minx [mɪŋks] **N** *Fam* friponne *f*, coquine *f*; **you little m.!** petite espiègle!, petite polissonne!

MIPS [mɪps] **N** *Comput (abbr* **million instructions per second)** MIPS *m*

miracle [ˈmɪrək(ə)l] **N** *Rel* miracle *m*; *Fig* miracle, prodige *m*; **by a m.** par miracle; **I can't perform miracles** je ne peux pas faire de miracles; **it sounds like a m.** cela tient du miracle; **it's a m. that …** c'est (un) miracle que … + *sub*
▸▸ *Fig* **m. cure** remède *m* miracle; *Pharm* **m. drug** remède *m* miracle; **m. play** miracle *(drame)*; **m. worker** faiseur, -euse de miracles

miraculous [mɪˈrækjʊləs] **ADJ** *Rel, Fig* miraculeux; **to have a m. escape** s'en sortir indemne comme par miracle; *Iron* **she made a m. recovery as soon as the weekend arrived** comme par miracle, son état de santé s'est amélioré juste avant le week-end

miraculously [mɪˈrækjʊləslɪ] **ADV** miraculeusement, (comme) par miracle; **m. low prices** des prix incroyablement bas

mirage [mɪˈrɑːʒ] **N** mirage *m*

MIRAS [ˈmaɪræs] **N** *Formerly (abbr* **Mortgage Interest Relief at Source**) = système *m* par lequel les intérêts dus à une société de crédit immobilier sont déductibles des impôts

mire [maɪər] **N** *(bog)* bourbier *m*; *(mud)* boue *f*, bourbe *f*, *Lit* fange *f*, *Fig* **to drag sb through the m.** traîner qn dans la boue
VT 1 *Lit (in debt, difficulty)* empêtrer **2** *(in mud)* embourber

mirror [ˈmɪrər] **N** glace *f*, miroir *m*; *Aut* **in my/the m.** dans mon/le rétroviseur; *Fig* **to hold a m. to society** refléter l'image d'une société; *Fig* **the press is the m. of public opinion** la presse est le miroir de l'opinion publique
VT *also Fig* refléter; **the steeple is mirrored in the lake** le clocher se reflète *ou* se mire dans le lac; *Fig* **his experience exactly mirrors my own** nous avons eu des expériences identiques
▸▸ **m. finish** fini *m* spéculaire; **m. image** image *f* en miroir, image spéculaire; *Fig* copie *f* conforme; **m. polish** polissage *m* spéculaire; *Comput* **m. site** *(on Internet)* site *m* miroir; **m. writing** écriture *f* spéculaire *ou* en miroir

mirrorball [ˈmɪrɔːbl] **N** sphère *f* à facettes de verre

mirth [mɜːθ] **N** gaieté *f*, allégresse *f*

mirthful [ˈmɜːθfʊl] **ADJ** *(amused)* gai, joyeux; *(amusing)* amusant

mirthless [ˈmɜːθlɪs] **ADJ** sans gaieté, peu réjouissant; *(laugh)* forcé, sans joie

MIRV [mɜːv] **N** *Mil (abbr* **multiple independently targeted re-entry vehicle)** MIRV *m*

miry [ˈmaɪrɪ] **ADJ** fangeux, bourbeux

MIS [emaɪˈes] **N 1** *Comput (abbr* **management information system)** système *m* intégré de gestion **2** *Mktg (abbr* **marketing information system)** système *m* d'information marketing

misadventure [mɪsədˈventʃər] **N** mésaventure *f*, *(less serious)* contretemps *m*; *Law* **a verdict of death by m.** un verdict de mort accidentelle

misalliance [mɪsəˈlaɪəns] **N** mésalliance *f*

misanthrope [ˈmɪzənθrəʊp] **N** misanthrope *mf*

misanthropic [mɪzənˈθrɒpɪk] **ADJ** *(person)* misanthrope; *(mood etc)* misanthropique

misanthropist [mɪˈzænθrəpɪst] N misanthrope mf

misanthropy [mɪˈzænθrəpɪ] N misanthropie f

misapply [mɪsəˈplaɪ] VT **1** mal employer **2** Fin = **misappropriate**

misapprehend [mɪsæprɪˈhend] VT Fml (somebody, something) mal comprendre; (person's words) mal comprendre, se méprendre sur

misapprehension [mɪsæprɪˈhenʃən] N malentendu m, méprise f; **to be** or **labour under a m.** se méprendre, se tromper; **the Government appears to be (labouring) under the m. that ...** le gouvernement semble s'imaginer que ...

misappropriate [mɪsəˈprəʊprɪeɪt] VT (funds) détourner

misappropriation [ˈmɪsəprəʊprɪˈeɪʃən] N (of funds) détournement m

misbegotten [mɪsbɪˈɡɒt(ə)n] ADJ **1** Old-fashioned Fam (badly thought out) mal conçu, Fam biscornu **2** Arch (child) illégitime, bâtard

misbehave [mɪsbɪˈheɪv] VI se conduire mal; (of child) se tenir mal; **he has been misbehaving at school** il n'a pas été sage à l'école

misbehaviour, Am **misbehavior** [mɪsbɪˈheɪvjər] N (bad behaviour) mauvaise conduite f; (more serious) inconduite f

misc (abbr **miscellaneous**) divers

miscalculate [mɪsˈkælkjʊleɪt] VT (amount, distance etc) mal calculer; (sb's response etc) se tromper sur
VI mal calculer; Fig se tromper

miscalculation [mɪskælkjʊˈleɪʃən] N erreur f de calcul; Fig mauvais calcul m

miscarriage [mɪsˈkærɪdʒ] N **1** Obst fausse couche f, Spec interruption f de grossesse spontanée; **to have a m.** faire une fausse couche **2** (failure) (of project) échec m, insuccès m **3** (in post) (of letter, package) égarement m, perte f
▸▸ Law **m. of justice** erreur f judiciaire

miscarry [mɪsˈkærɪ] VI **1** Obst faire une fausse couche, Spec avorter **2** (of scheme, enterprise) échouer, avorter, ne pas réussir **3** (of letter, parcel) s'égarer, se perdre; (reach wrong address) parvenir à une fausse adresse

miscast [mɪsˈkɑːst] VT (pt, pp miscast) Theat, Cin etc **to m. an actor/actress** donner à un acteur/une actrice un rôle qui ne lui convient pas; **he was m. in the part** ce n'était pas un rôle qui lui convenait; **the play/film was m.** les acteurs de la pièce/du film étaient mal choisis

miscegenation [mɪsɪdʒɪˈneɪʃ(ə)n] N Fml métissage m

miscellaneous [mɪsəˈleɪnɪəs] ADJ varié, divers; **the file marked 'm.'** le dossier 'Divers'
▸▸ Journ **m. news** faits mpl divers

miscellany [mɪˈselənɪ] N **1** (of objects etc) mélange m, collection f **2** Liter recueil m, anthologie f

mischance [mɪsˈtʃɑːns] N mésaventure f; **by m.** par malchance

mischief [ˈmɪstʃɪf] N **1** (naughtiness) bêtises fpl; (esp of very small children) bêtises, sottises fpl; **out of sheer m.** par pure espièglerie; **he's full of m.** il est très espiègle; **to keep sb out of m.** empêcher qn de faire des sottises ou des bêtises; **that'll keep her out of m.** ça l'occupera, pendant ce temps-là elle ne fera pas de bêtises; **I wonder what m. he's up to** je me demande ce qu'il trame ou fricote **2** (trouble) **to make m. (for sb)** créer des problèmes (à qn), faire du tort (à qn); **to make m. between people** semer la

discorde entre les gens **3** Fam (child) fripon, -onne; **little m.** petit(e) espiègle, petit(e) coquin, -ine **4** Fam (injury) **to do oneself a m.** se faire mal, s'esquinter

mischiefmaker [ˈmɪstʃɪfmeɪkər] N brandon m de discorde; (gossip) mauvaise langue f

mischievous [ˈmɪstʃɪvəs] ADJ **1** (naughty) (child) espiègle, malicieux, coquin; **m. trick** or **prank** espièglerie f; **to play a m. trick on sb** jouer un tour ou faire une farce à qn; **as m. as a monkey** malin comme un singe; **a m. grin/wink** un sourire/clin d'œil malicieux **2** (malicious) (person) méchant, malveillant, malfaisant; (remark) malveillant

mischievously [ˈmɪstʃɪvəslɪ] ADV **1** (naughtily) par espièglerie; (to grin, wink, smile) malicieusement **2** (maliciously) méchamment

mischievousness [ˈmɪstʃɪvəsnɪs] N **1** (naughtiness) (of child) malice f, espièglerie f **2** (malice) méchanceté f

misconceive [mɪskənˈsiːv] VT Fml se méprendre sur

misconceived [mɪskənˈsiːvd] ADJ (idea, scheme) mal conçu

misconception [mɪskənˈsepʃən] N (false idea) conception f erronée, idée f fausse; **a popular** or **common m.** une idée fausse très répandue

misconduct[1] [mɪsˈkɒndʌkt] N mauvaise conduite f, Law (sexual) adultère m; **professional m.** faute f professionnelle

misconduct[2] [mɪskənˈdʌkt] VT (matter, business) mal diriger, mal gérer; **to m. oneself** mal se conduire

misconstruction [mɪskənˈstrʌkʃən] N Fml fausse interprétation f

misconstrue [mɪskənˈstruː] VT mal interpréter

miscount[1] [ˈmɪskaʊnt] N (miscalculation) erreur f de calcul; (mistake in addition) erreur d'addition; Pol (of votes) erreur dans le dépouillement du scrutin

miscount[2] [mɪsˈkaʊnt] VT & VI mal compter

miscreant [ˈmɪskrɪənt] ADJ, N Lit scélérat, -ate, misérable mf

Note that the French word **mécréant** is a false friend and is never a translation for the English word **miscreant**. It means **unbeliever**.

misdeal [mɪsˈdiːl] Cards N maldonne f
VT & VI (pt, pp misdealt [mɪsˈdelt]) **to m. (the cards)** faire maldonne

misdeed [mɪsˈdiːd] N méfait m, mauvaise action f, Law crime m, délit m

misdemeanour, Am **misdemeanor** [mɪsdɪˈmiːnər] N **1** Law délit m **2** (minor act of misbehaviour) écart m de conduite; (more serious) méfait m

misdiagnose [mɪsˈdaɪəɡnəʊz] VT Med **to m. the symptoms/illness/**etc faire une erreur de diagnostic; Fig **to m. the situation** faire une mauvaise analyse de la situation

misdiagnosis [mɪsdaɪəɡˈnəʊsɪs] N Med erreur f de diagnostic; Fig **his m. of the situation** sa mauvaise analyse de la situation

misdirect [mɪsdɪˈrekt] VT **1** (person) envoyer au mauvais endroit **2** (letter) envoyer à la mauvaise adresse **3** (blow) mal diriger **4** **to m. the jury** mal instruire le jury

misdirected [mɪsdɪˈrektɪd] ADJ **1** (letter, parcel etc) envoyé à la mauvaise adresse **2** (blow) frappé à faux **3** (zeal) mal employé

misdirection [mɪsdɪˈrekʃən] N **1** (on letter) erreur f d'adresse **2** (of resources, talents) mauvais emploi m, mauvais usage m

miser [ˈmaɪzər] N avare mf

miserable [ˈmɪzər(ə)b(ə)l] ADJ **1** (unhappy) malheureux, triste; **I feel m.** j'ai le cafard; **don't look so m.!** remets-toi!; **to make sb's life m.** rendre la vie impossible à qn **2** (unpleasant) (condition) misérable, déplorable; (journey) pénible, affreux; **if only I didn't have this m. cold!** si je n'avais pas cet affreux rhume!; **what a m. day** quelle journée épouvantable; **what m. weather!** quel temps épouvantable! **3** (poor, wretched) misérable, pitoyable; (wage, amount) dérisoire; **I've only got a m. £70** je n'ai que 70 malheureuses livres; **a m. failure** (plan etc) un ratage complet ou lamentable; (person) un raté

Note that the French adjective **misérable** never means **unhappy**.

miserably [ˈmɪz(ə)rəblɪ] ADV **1** (unhappily) (to look) d'un air malheureux; (to say) d'un ton malheureux **2** (in poverty) pauvrement; **to live m.** vivre dans la misère **3** (very badly) (to perform) lamentablement; **to be m. paid** avoir un salaire de misère; **to fail m.** échouer lamentablement

Miserere [mɪzəˈrɪərɪ] N Rel **1** (psalm) miséréré m, miserere m **2 m. (seat)** = **misericord 2**

misericord [mɪˈzerɪkɔːd] N Rel **1** (in monastery) miséricorde f **2** (seat) miséricorde f, patience f (de stalle)

miserliness [ˈmaɪzəlɪnɪs] N avarice f, pingrerie f

miserly [ˈmaɪzəlɪ] ADJ (person) avare, pingre

misery [ˈmɪzərɪ] N **1** (unhappiness) détresse f, tristesse f; (suffering) souffrance(s) f(pl); (stronger) supplice m; **to make sb's life a m.** rendre la vie impossible à qn; **to put an animal out of its m.** donner le coup de grâce à un animal; Hum **to put sb out of their m.** mettre fin aux souffrances ou au supplice de qn **2** Br Fam (person) geignard, -arde, grincheux, -euse

Note that the French word **misère** is a false friend and is never a translation for the English word **misery**. Its most common meaning is **extreme poverty**.

misery-guts [-ɡʌts] N Fam rabat-joie m inv, empêcheur, -euse de tourner en rond

misfire [mɪsˈfaɪər] N (of rifle) raté m (de percussion); (of missile, car) raté d'allumage
VI (of firearm) rater, faire long feu; (of rocket) avoir un raté d'allumage; (of engine) avoir un raté/des ratés; Fig (of joke) manquer son effet, Fam foirer; (of plan) rater, Fam foirer

misfit [ˈmɪsfɪt] N (person) inadapté, -ée; **a social m.** un inadapté social

misfortune [mɪsˈfɔːtʃən] N malheur m, malchance f; **I had the m. to ...** j'ai eu la malheur ou la malchance de ...

misgiving [mɪsˈɡɪvɪŋ] N doute m (about sth sur qch); **not without misgivings** non sans hésitation; **to have misgivings** avoir des doutes (about sb à l'égard de qn; about sth au sujet de qch); **to be filled with m.** être en proie au doute; **she had misgivings about allowing them to go** elle hésitait à les laisser y aller

misgovern [mɪsˈɡʌvən] VT mal gouverner

misgovernment [mɪsˈɡʌvənmənt] N mauvais gouvernement m, mauvaise administration f

misguided [mɪsˈɡaɪdɪd] ADJ (person) malavisé; (missionary, reformer, politician) mal inspiré; (attempt) malencontreux; (energy, idealism) mal placé; **you would be m. to trust him** vous seriez mal avisé ou inspiré de lui faire confiance; **in the m. belief that ...** croyant à tort que ...

misguidedly [mɪsˈgaɪdɪdlɪ] **ADV** de façon peu judicieuse, malencontreusement

mishandle [mɪsˈhænd(ə)l] **VT 1** *(machine, appliance)* mal se servir de; *(substance, product)* manipuler sans prendre les précautions nécessaires **2** *(manage badly) (situation etc)* mal gérer; *(person)* mécontenter; **if you m. the staff** si vous ne traitez pas le personnel avec considération

mishandling [mɪsˈhændlɪŋ] **N** *(of situation, staff etc)* mauvaise gestion *f*

mishap [ˈmɪshæp] **N** incident *m*, mésaventure *f*; **after many mishaps** après bien des incidents *ou* des mésaventures *ou* des péripéties

mishear [mɪsˈhɪər] **VT & VI** *(pt, pp* **misheard** [mɪsˈhɜːd]) mal entendre

mishmash [ˈmɪʃmæʃ] **N** *Fam* méli-mélo *m*, *pl* mélis-mélos

misinform [mɪsɪnˈfɔːm] **VT** mal informer; **to be misinformed** être mal informé

misinformation [mɪsɪnfəˈmeɪʃən] **N** fausse information *f*

misinterpret [mɪsɪnˈtɜːprɪt] **VT** *(person's words)* mal interpréter; *(person)* mal interpréter les paroles de; **this decision should not be misinterpreted as …** cette décision ne doit pas être interprétée comme …

misinterpretation [mɪsɪntɜːprɪˈteɪʃən] **N** mauvaise *ou* fausse interprétation *f*; **open to m.** *(of rules, statement etc)* susceptible d'être mal interprété

misjudge [mɪsˈdʒʌdʒ] **VT** *(somebody)* mal juger, se tromper sur le compte de; *(something)* mal juger (de), se méprendre sur; *(distance)* mal évaluer; **it appears I misjudged you** il semblerait que je vous aie mal jugé

misjudg(e)ment [mɪsˈdʒʌdʒmənt] **N** jugement *m* erroné, erreur *f* de jugement; *(of distance)* mauvaise évaluation *f ou* estimation *f*

miskey¹ [ˈmɪskiː] **N** faute *f* de frappe

miskey² [mɪsˈkiː] **VT** ne pas taper correctement

mislay [mɪsˈleɪ] **VT** *(pt, pp* **mislaid** [mɪsˈleɪd]) *(one's umbrella etc)* égarer; **I've just mislaid it somewhere** je l'ai juste mis quelque part, mais je ne me souviens plus où

mislead [mɪsˈliːd] **VT** *(pt, pp* **misled** [mɪsˈled]) *(deceive) (person)* induire en erreur, tromper *(as to* quant à); **to m. sb into thinking sth** faire croire qch à qn; **her behaviour misled him into thinking her feelings were stronger** sa conduite lui a laissé croire que ses sentiments étaient plus profonds, mais il n'en était rien

misleading [mɪsˈliːdɪŋ] **ADJ** *(advertisement etc)* trompeur; **the description she gave was deliberately m.** elle a fait exprès de donner une fausse description

mismanage [mɪsˈmænɪdʒ] **VT** *(matter, business)* mal administrer, mal diriger, mal gérer

mismanagement [mɪsˈmænɪdʒmənt] **N** mauvaise administration *f*, mauvaise gestion *f*

mismatch [ˈmɪsmætʃ] **N** *Comput* différence *f*, *(between two sets of data)* décalage *m*; **they're a m.** *(of two people)* ils sont mal assortis

misnomer [mɪsˈnəʊmər] **N** terme *m* qui ne convient pas, terme mal approprié; **changes which, by a great m., are called progress** changements auxquels on donne fort mal à propos le nom de progrès

misogynist [mɪˈsɒdʒɪnɪst, maɪ-] **N** misogyne *mf*

misogynistic [mɪsɒdʒɪˈnɪstɪk, maɪ-] **ADJ** misogyne

misogyny [mɪˈsɒdʒɪnɪ, maɪ-] **N** misogynie *f*

misplace [mɪsˈpleɪs] **VT 1** *(one's affections etc)* mal placer; **misplaced remark** remarque déplacée *ou* hors de propos; **misplaced trust** confiance mal placée **2** *(lose temporarily) (book etc)* égarer **3** *Ling (tonic accent etc)* placer à faux

misprint¹ [ˈmɪsprɪnt] **N** *Typ* erreur *f* typographique, faute *f* d'impression, *Fam* coquille *f*

misprint² [mɪsˈprɪnt] **VT** imprimer incorrectement; **my name was misprinted in the newspaper** il y a eu une coquille dans mon nom sur le journal

mispronounce [mɪsprəˈnaʊns] **VT** mal prononcer

mispronunciation [mɪsprənʌnsɪˈeɪʃən] **N** *(act)* prononciation *f* incorrecte; *(instance)* faute *f* de prononciation

misquotation [mɪskwəʊˈteɪʃən] **N** citation *f* inexacte

misquote [mɪsˈkwəʊt] **VT** *(something, author)* citer incorrectement *ou* inexactement; **I've been misquoted** *(by the press etc)* on a déformé mes propos

misread [mɪsˈriːd] **VT** *(pt, pp* **misread** [mɪsˈred]) *(text etc)* mal lire, mal interpréter; *Comput* ne pas lire correctement; *Fig* **to m. the situation** mal interpréter la situation; **I m. her remarks** j'ai mal interprété ses remarques

misrepresent [mɪsreprɪˈzent] **VT** *(the facts)* dénaturer, présenter sous un faux jour; **I have been misrepresented in the press as …** j'ai été représenté à tort dans la presse comme …

misrepresentation [mɪsreprɪzenˈteɪʃən] **N** *(of the facts etc)* présentation *f* erronée, dénaturation *f*, travestissement *m*; *Law* fausse déclaration *f*

misrule [mɪsˈruːl] **N 1** *(inefficient rule)* mauvais gouvernement *m*, mauvaise administration *f* **2** *(disorder)* désordre *m*, confusion *f*

Miss *abbr* **Mississippi**

MISS¹ [mɪs]

| **VT** | manquer **1, 5, 6** ▪ rater **1** ▪ faillir **1** |
| **VI** | manquer **1, 2** |

N *(shot, stroke etc)* coup *m* manqué; *Billiards* manque *m* de touche; *Fam* **I think I'll give that film/the party a m.** je ne pense pas que j'irai voir ce film/que j'irai à cette soirée; **I'll give the soup a m.** je ne prendrai pas de soupe; **thanks, but I think I'll give it a m.** merci, pas cette fois; *Prov* **a m. is as good as a mile** rater de près ou de loin, c'est toujours rater

VT 1 *(fail to hit, find, attend, catch etc)* manquer, rater; *(opportunity)* manquer, laisser échapper, rater; *(appointment)* manquer; *(meal) (accidentally)* rater; *(skip)* sauter; **to m. one's entrance** *(of actor)* rater son entrée; **to m. one's cue** *(of actor)* manquer sa réplique; **to m. one's way** s'égarer; *Fig Fam* **to m. the boat** *or* **the bus** rater le coche; **I missed him (by two minutes)** je l'ai manqué *ou* raté (de deux minutes); **an opportunity not to be missed** une occasion à ne pas manquer ou laisser passer; **a life of missed opportunities** une vie d'occasions manquées; **I've missed my turn** j'ai perdu mon tour; **I missed the first five minutes of the programme** j'ai raté les cinq premières minutes de l'émission; *Fam* **you haven't missed much!** vous n'avez pas perdu *ou* raté grandchose!; **you don't m. much!** rien ne t'échappe!; *Fam* **you don't know what you're missing** tu ne sais pas ce que tu rates; **he never misses a chance to put other people down** il ne manque jamais une occasion de rabaisser les autres; **he narrowly** *or* **just missed being killed** il a failli se faire tuer; **the boss doesn't m. a thing** rien n'échappe au

patron; **you can't m. the house** vous ne pouvez pas manquer de reconnaître la maison, vous ne pouvez pas rater la maison

2 *(not hear) (question, remark etc)* ne pas entendre; *(not understand) (joke)* ne pas saisir; **you m. a lot if you read this novel in translation** on perd beaucoup à ne pas lire ce roman dans le texte; **you've missed the point** vous n'avez pas compris; *(in your answer)* vous avez répondu à côté

3 *(omit) (word, line)* omettre, sauter; **to m. one's stop** *(of passenger etc)* rater son arrêt

4 *(notice absence of)* **I missed him at the meeting** j'ai remarqué qu'il n'était pas à la réunion; **we are sure to be missed** on va sûrement remarquer notre absence; **they won't m. a few biscuits** quelques biscuits de plus ou de moins, quelle est la différence?

5 *(feel lack of)* **I m. you** tu me manques; **don't you m. your family?** est-ce que ta famille ne te manque pas?; **I m. the countryside/my piano** la campagne/mon piano me manque; **I m. being able to do what I like** ça me manque de ne pas pouvoir faire ce que je veux; **I missed my umbrella** mon parapluie m'aurait été bien utile; **I m. the older version** j'aimais mieux l'ancien modèle; **you can't m. what you've never had** ce que l'on n'a jamais eu ne nous manque pas; **I'm not allowed cigarettes, but I don't m. them** on me défend de fumer, mais ça ne me manque pas

6 *(lack) (always in continuous form)* **the table's missing one of its legs** il manque un pied à la table

VI 1 *(miss target)* manquer *ou* rater son coup; **missed!** manqué!, *Fam* raté!

2 *(be absent) (always in continuous form)* manquer; **how many members are missing tonight?** combien avons-nous de membres absents *ou* d'absents ce soir?, combien y a-t-il d'absents ce soir?; **nothing is missing** il ne manque rien

▶ **miss out** **VI** *(not benefit)* **you missed out there** vous avez raté quelque chose

VT SEP *(omit) (accidentally)* oublier; *(page, paragraph, passage)* sauter, oublier; *(intentionally)* omettre; **this film/book misses out …** il manque … à ce film/livre; **they decided to m. out the pudding** ils ont préféré de se passer de dessert

▶ **miss out on** **VT INSEP** *(good film, great party etc)* rater; **a lot of people are missing out on state benefits they are entitled to** bien des gens ne profitent pas des allocations auxquelles ils ont droit

---

miss² **N 1 M. Martin** Mademoiselle *f* Martin; *(on envelope)* Mademoiselle *ou* Mlle Martin; *Old-fashioned* **the M. Martins, the Misses Martin** les demoiselles *fpl* Martin; **thank you, M. Martin** merci Mademoiselle; **M.!** *(to waitress etc)* Mademoiselle!, s'il vous plaît!; *(to older woman)* Madame!, s'il vous plaît! **2** *Br Sch Fam* la maîtresse; *(in secondary school)* la prof; **yes M.** *(to woman teacher)* oui, madame **3** *Fam Hum (girl)* **(young) m.** jeune demoiselle *f*

▸ ▸ **M. World** Miss *f* Monde

missal [ˈmɪs(ə)l] **N** *Rel* missel *m*

misshapen [mɪsˈʃeɪpən] **ADJ** *(person, limb etc)* difforme; *(hat)* déformé

missile [ˈmɪsaɪl, *Am* ˈmɪs(ə)l] **N 1** *(projectile)* projectile *m* **2** *Mil* missile *m*

▸ ▸ **m. base** base *f* de missiles; **m. launcher** lance-missiles *m inv*

missing [ˈmɪsɪŋ] **ADJ** *(person etc) (not present)* absent; *(object)* égaré, disparu; *(money) (stolen)* disparu; *(lacking)* qui manque; **there are two cups m.** il manque deux tasses, il y a deux tasses qui manquent; **here's the m. part** voilà la pièce qui manquait *ou* qui était perdue *ou* qui avait disparu; **one climber is m.** on est sans nouvelles d'un des alpinistes; *Mil etc* **to report sb m.** porter qn disparu; *Mil* **m. in action** porté disparu au combat; **to go m.** disparaître ►► *also Fig Hum* **m. link** chaînon *m* manquant; **m. person** personne *f* disparue; *Mil* disparu, -ue; **m. persons bureau** service *m* qui s'occupe des personnes disparues

mission ['mɪʃən] N **1** *(task)* mission *f*; **to charge** *or* **entrust sb with a m.** charger qn d'une mission, confier une mission à qn; **m. accomplished** mission accomplie; **minister on a special m.** ministre en mission spéciale; **she thinks her m. is to …** elle croit avoir pour mission de …; **reconnaissance m.** mission de reconnaissance **2** *(body of persons)* mission *f*; *Am (permanent)* représentation *f* diplomatique; **military/trade m.** mission *f* militaire/commerciale **3** *Rel* **foreign/home missions** missions *fpl* étrangères/métropolitaines **4** *Rel (place)* mission *f* ►► **m. control** centre *m* de contrôle; **m. statement** ordre *m* de mission; *Rel* **m. station** mission

missionary ['mɪʃənərɪ] N missionnaire *mf* ADJ *(priest, work)* missionnaire; *(vocation)* de missionnaire ►► **m. position** position *f* du missionnaire; *Mktg* **m. selling** ventes *fpl* de prospection; *also Fig* **m. zeal** prosélytisme *m*

missis ['mɪsɪz] N *Sl* = **missus**

missive ['mɪsɪv] N *Fml* missive *f*

misspell ['mɪs'spel] VT *(pt, pp* **misspelt** ['mɪs'spelt]) mal orthographier

misspelling ['mɪs'spelɪŋ] N faute *f* d'orthographe; **the frequent m. of this word** le fait que ce mot soit fréquemment mal orthographié

misspend ['mɪs'spend] VT *(pt, pp* **misspent** ['mɪs'spent]) *(money, time)* mal employer, gaspiller; **a misspent youth** une jeunesse dissipée

missus ['mɪsɪs, 'mɪsɪz] N *Fam* **1** *(wife)* **the** *or* **my/his/your m.** la patronne **2** *(woman)* **m.!** M'dame!

mist [mɪst] N *Met* brume *f*; *(on mirror etc)* buée *f*; **to see things through a m.** voir trouble; *Fig* **lost in the mists of time** perdu dans la nuit des temps ► **mist over** VI **1** *(of landscape)* disparaître dans la brume **2** *(of mirror)* se couvrir de buée, s'embuer; *(of eyes)* se voiler, s'embuer ► **mist up** VT & VI = **mist over 2**

mistakable [mɪs'teɪkəb(ə)l] ADJ **easily m.** facile à confondre (**for** avec)

mistake [mɪs'teɪk] N erreur *f*, faute *f*; **m. in calculation/in the date** erreur de calcul/de date; **grammatical mistakes** fautes de grammaire; **it would be a m. to imagine that …** ce serait une erreur d'imaginer que …; **to make a m.** faire *ou* commettre une faute *ou* une erreur, se tromper (**about, over** sur, au sujet de, quant à); **you're making a big m.** tu es en train de commettre une grosse erreur; **to make the m. of doing sth** faire *ou* commettre l'erreur de faire qch; **it's an easy m. to make** c'est une erreur qu'il est facile de faire; **make no m.** que l'on ne s'y trompe pas; **by m.** *(to do sth)* par erreur, par méprise; **there is** *or* **can be no m. about that** il n'y a pas à s'y tromper; **there must be some m.** il doit y avoir une erreur; *Fam* **This is hard work and no m.!** c'est vraiment très dur; **(sorry,) my m.!** je suis désolé, je me suis trompé *ou* j'ai fait erreur!; **my m.** c'est moi qui me suis trompé VT *(pt* **mistook** [mɪs'tʊk], *pp* **mistaken** [mɪs'teɪkən]) *(person's words, intentions)* se méprendre sur; *(confuse) (person, object)* confondre (**for sb/sth** avec qn/qch); *(house etc)* se tromper de; **there's no mistaking it** il

n'y a pas à s'y méprendre; **I mistook him for someone else** je l'ai pris pour quelqu'un d'autre, je l'ai confondu avec quelqu'un d'autre

mistaken [mɪs'teɪkən] PP *see* **mistake** VT ADJ *(opinion)* erroné; *(idea)* faux, *f* fausse; **I must be m.** je dois faire erreur; **if I'm not m.** si je ne me trompe (pas); **in the m. belief that …, under the m. impression that …** croyant, à tort, que …; **it was (a case of) m. identity** il y a eu erreur sur la personne

mistakenly [mɪs'teɪkənlɪ] ADV par erreur, par méprise; **it was m. believed to be …** on croyait à tort que c'était …

misted-up [mɪstɪd-] ADJ *(windscreen)* embué

mister ['mɪstər] N *Fam* m'sieur *m*

mistime [mɪs'taɪm] VT *(counterattack, announcement)* faire au mauvais moment; *(entrance on stage)* rater; **to m. a punch/smash/pass** ne pas frapper/smasher/faire une passe au moment opportun; **the launch of the new product had been badly mistimed** le nouveau produit n'avait pas été lancé au moment propice; **he badly mistimed it** il a vraiment choisi le mauvais moment, il a fait une grosse erreur de timing; **she mistimed her entrance/intervention/***etc* elle est entrée/intervenue/*etc* au mauvais moment, elle a mal choisi son moment pour entrer/intervenir/*etc*

mistimed [mɪs'taɪmd] ADJ *(remark, intervention etc)* inopportun, mal à propos; *(blow)* mal calculé

mistiness ['mɪstɪnɪs] N *(mist)* brouillard *m*, brume *f*

mistlethrush ['mɪs(ə)lθrʌʃ] N *(bird)* (grive *f*) draine *f*

mistletoe ['mɪs(ə)ltəʊ] N *Bot* gui *m*

mistook PT *see* **mistake** VT

mistranslate [mɪstræns'leɪt] VT mal traduire; **it's often mistranslated as …** c'est souvent traduit à tort par …

mistranslation [mɪstræns'leɪʃən] N mauvaise traduction *f*; *(mistake in translation)* erreur *f* de traduction

mistreat [mɪs'tri:t] VT *(somebody, something)* maltraiter

mistreatment [mɪs'tri:tmənt] N mauvais traitement *m*

mistress ['mɪstrɪs] N **1** *(woman in charge)* maîtresse *f*; **to be one's own m.** être indépendante, être sa propre maîtresse; **to be m. of oneself** *or* **of one's emotions** être maîtresse de soi(-même); **she was the m. of the situation** elle était maîtresse de la situation; *Old-fashioned* **the m. of the house** la maîtresse de maison **2** *(owner of pet)* maîtresse *f* **3** *esp Br Sch (woman teacher) (in primary school)* maîtresse *f* (d'école), institutrice *f*, *(in secondary school)* professeur *m*; **the French m.** le professeur de français **4** *(lover)* maîtresse *f* **5** *Arch* **M.** *(in titles)* Madame *f*

mistrial [mɪs'traɪəl] N *Law* jugement *m* entaché d'un vice de procédure; *Am (because jury cannot agree)* = procès *m* ajourné, l'unanimité n'ayant pas été atteinte parmi le jury

mistrust [mɪs'trʌst] N méfiance *f* (**of** à l'égard de), défiance *f* (**of** à l'égard de); manque *m* de confiance (**of** en) VT se méfier de, se défier de, ne pas avoir confiance en

mistrustful [mɪs'trʌstfʊl] ADJ méfiant, défiant (**of sth** à l'égard de qch; **of sb** à l'égard de qn, envers qn)

mistrustfully [mɪs'trʌstfʊlɪ] ADV avec méfiance, avec défiance

misty ['mɪstɪ] ADJ *(place etc)* brumeux, embrumé; *(weather)* brumeux; *(form)* flou,

voilé, estompé; *(memory)* vague, confus; **m. eyes** yeux embués; **m. blue** bleu gris; **it's m.** le temps est brumeux; **the windscreen is all m.** le pare-brise est tout couvert de buée

misunderstand [mɪsʌndə'stænd] VT *(pt, pp* **misunderstood** [mɪsʌndə'stʊd]) *(misinterpret) (somebody, something)* mal comprendre; *(misjudge) (somebody)* méconnaître, se méprendre sur le compte de; *(action etc)* mal comprendre, mal interpréter, se méprendre sur; **we misunderstood each other** il y a eu un malentendu entre nous; **don't m. me, I'm as opposed to this plan as you are** comprends-moi bien, je suis aussi opposé à ce projet que toi VI mal comprendre; **if I have not misunderstood** si j'ai bien compris

misunderstanding [mɪsʌndə'stændɪŋ] N **1** *(misconception)* erreur *f*, *(mistake)* malentendu *m*, méprise *f*, *(confusion of two objects)* quiproquo *m*; **I think there's been a m.** je crois qu'il y a eu un malentendu *ou* (une) méprise **2** *(disagreement)* malentendu *m*, désaccord *m*, différend *m*

misuse¹ [mɪs'ju:s] N *(of something)* mauvais usage *m ou* emploi *m*; *(of authority)* abus *m*; *(of word)* emploi abusif; *Law* **fraudulent m. of funds** détournement *m* de fonds

misuse² [mɪs'ju:z] VT *(something)* faire (un) mauvais usage *ou* (un) mauvais emploi de; *(one's authority)* abuser de; *(word)* employer à tort *ou* abusivement

mite [maɪt] N **1** *Arch, Lit (sum of money)* **the widow's m.** le denier de la veuve **2** *(small amount) Fam* **it's a m. expensive** c'est un peu cher **3** *Fam (child)* petit(e) gosse *mf*, mioche *mf*, *(animal)* petite bête *f*, **poor little m.!** pauvre petit! **4** *Entom* acarien *m*

miter ['maɪtər] N, VT *Am* = **mitre**

mitigate ['mɪtɪgeɪt] VT *(sb's anger)* adoucir; *(suffering, grief etc)* adoucir, atténuer; *(pain)* apaiser; *(punishment, effects), Law (crime)* atténuer

mitigating ['mɪtɪgeɪtɪŋ] ADJ ►► *Law* **m. circumstances** circonstances *fpl* atténuantes

mitigation [mɪtɪ'geɪʃən] N *Fml (of pain)* adoucissement *m*; *(of punishment)* atténuation *f*, **if you have anything to say in m. of this offence** si vous avez quelque chose à dire pour votre défense; **in m. of this, it should be noted that …** il faut noter que … et ceci constitue une circonstance atténuante; **in m. of the accused's crime …** à la décharge de l'accusé …

mitral ['maɪtrəl] ADJ ►► *Anat* **m. valve** valvule *f* mitrale

mitre¹, *Am* **miter** ['maɪtər] N *(headdress)* mitre *f*

mitre², *Am* **miter** *Carp* N *(joint)* onglet *m* VT **1** *(shape) (part)* tailler à onglet **2** *(join) (two parts)* assembler à onglet ►► **m. box** boîte *f* à onglet(s); **m. joint** *(assemblage m* à) onglet; **m. square** équerre *f* à onglet

mitt [mɪt] N **1** = **mitten**; *(in baseball)* gant *m* **2** *Fam (hand)* patte *f*, **keep your mitts off my lunch!** touche pas à mon déjeuner!; **get your mitts off me!** bas les pattes!

mitten ['mɪt(ə)n] N *(glove without separate fingers)* moufle *f*, *Can* mitaine *f*, *(glove with no fingers)* mitaine; *Boxing Fam* **mittens** gants *mpl*

MIX [mɪks] N **1** *(of mortar, plaster)* mélange *m*; **(cake) m.** préparation *f* pour gâteaux; **there was a good m. of people at the party** il y avait un mélange intéressant de personnes à la soirée; *Com* **product m.** assortiment *m* de produits, *Spec* mix *m* **2** *Cin, Mus* mixage *m*; **the 12-inch m.** *(record)* le trente centimètres

VT 1 mêler, mélanger (**several things together** plusieurs choses ensemble; **sth with sth** qch à *ou* avec qch); *(drink)* préparer; *(mortar, plaster)* gâcher; *Culin (salad)* retourner; *Am (cards)* battre, mélanger; **to m. business with pleasure** mélanger le travail et les loisirs; **you should never m. your drinks** il ne faut jamais mélanger les alcools; **to m. one's metaphors** confondre deux expressions; *Fam* **to m. it** *(fight)* se bagarrer (**with sb** avec qn); **do you want to m. it?** tu veux te battre?
2 *Cin, Mus* mixer
VI *(of things)* se mélanger (**with** avec, à); **sport and drug-taking don't m.** le sport et l'utilisation de drogue ne font pas bon ménage; **to m. with people** *(of person)* fréquenter des gens; **I don't m. much** je ne fréquente pas beaucoup de gens; **to m. with the crowd** se mêler à la foule; **to m. with the guests** circuler parmi les invités
▸ **mix up VT SEP 1** *(prepare)* *(drink, medication)* préparer
2 *(put in disorder)* *(one's papers etc)* mettre le désordre dans; **everything got mixed up** tout avait été mélangé
3 *(confuse)* confondre (**with** avec); **I was mixing you up with your brother** je vous confondais avec votre frère; **I was getting all mixed up** je ne savais plus où j'en étais
4 *(involve)* **to be mixed up in an affair** être mêlé à une affaire, être compromis *ou* impliqué dans une affaire; **mixed up in something dishonest** impliqué dans quelque chose de malhonnête
5 *esp Am Sl* **to m. it up** *(fight)* en venir aux coups

mix-down N *TV etc* mixage *m* avec réduction de pistes
mixed ['mɪkst] **ADJ** mélangé; **person of m. blood/race** sang-mêlé *mf inv*; *Fam* **they were a m. bag** *(of people or things)* il y avait de tout; **her resignation was a m. blessing** sa démission avait du bon et du mauvais; **to meet with a m. reception** recevoir un accueil mitigé; **in m. company** en présence de personnes des deux sexes; **m. feelings** sentiments *mpl* contradictoires; **it was with m. feelings that I took up the position** j'ai accepté le poste malgré mes réserves
▸▸ *Sport* **m. doubles** double *m* mixte; **m. economy** économie *f* mixte; **m. farming** agriculture *f* mixte; *Culin* **m. grill** assortiment *m* de grillades, mixed grill *m*; **m. marriage** mariage *m* mixte; **m. metaphor** mélange *m* de métaphores; *Br* **m. school** école *f* mixte; *Pol* **m. system** *(of voting)* scrutin *m* mixte; **m. vegetables** jardinière *f* de légumes
mixed-ability **ADJ** *USU ATTRIB (classes)* qui regroupe des élèves de niveaux différents
mixed-media **ADJ** multimédia
mixed-up **ADJ** *Fam (person)* déboussolé, qui ne sait plus où il en est; **a crazy m. kid** un pauvre gosse un peu paumé
mixer ['mɪksər] N **1** *(machine)*, *Ind etc* mélangeuse *f*, agitateur *m*; *TV etc* mixeur *m*, mélangeur *m*; *(tap)* mélangeur; *(tap with single control)* mitigeur *m*; *Culin* **(food) m.** mixeur, mixer *m* **2 to be a good m.** *(socially)* être très sociable **3** *(drink)* = boisson *f* non-alcoolisée que l'on utilise pour allonger certains alcools **4** *esp Am Univ Fam (party)* = soirée *f* pour permettre aux étudiants de faire connaissance
▸▸ *Br* **m. tap** mélangeur; *(with single control)* mitigeur
mixing ['mɪksɪŋ] N **1** mélange *m* **2** *TV etc* mixage *m*, mélange *m* sonore
▸▸ **m. bowl** *(big)* saladier *m*; *(smaller)* bol *m*; **m. chamber** *(in engine)* chambre *f* de mélange *ou* de carburation; **m. console, m. desk**

table *f* de mixage; **m. drum** mélangeur *m* (à tambour); *TV* **m. room** régie *f*
mixture ['mɪkstʃər] N **1** *(of objects, people, styles, fuel)* mélange *m*; **their music is a m. of traditional and modern** leur musique est un mélange de moderne et de traditionnel; **(cake) m.** préparation *f* pour gâteaux; **he's an odd m.** c'est un type difficile à cerner, c'est un drôle de type; *Aut* **m. adjusting screw** vis *f* de richesse **2** *Pharm* mixtion *f*, mixture *f*
mix-up N *(confusion)* confusion *f*; *(misunderstanding)* malentendu *m*; *Fam (mess)* pagaïe *f*, pagaille *f*; **there's been a m. with the reservations** ils se sont embrouillés dans les réservations
mizzen ['mɪz(ə)n] N *Naut* artimon *m*
▸▸ **m. sail** artimon
mizzenmast ['mɪz(ə)nmɑːst] N *Naut* mât *m* d'artimon
ml *(abbr* **millilitre(s))** ml
MLM [emel'em] N *Mktg (abbr* **multi-level marketing)** VRC *f*
MLR [eme'lɑːr] N *Br Fin Formerly (abbr* **minimum lending rate)** taux *m* de base
mm *(abbr* **millimetre(s))** mm
MMC N *Com (abbr* **Monopolies and Mergers Commission)** = commission *f* britannique veillant au respect de la législation antitrust
MMFs [eme'mefs] **NPL** *St Exch (abbr* **money market funds)** = SICAV *fpl* monétaires
MMS [emem'es] N *Tel (abbr* **multimedia messaging service)** MMS *m*
MNA [eme'neɪ] N *Can (in Quebec) (abbr* **Member of the National Assembly)** MAN *m*
mnemonic [nɪ'mɒnɪk] **ADJ** mnémonique
N moyen *m* mnémotechnique
MO [e'məʊ] N **1** *Mil etc abbr* **medical officer 2** *(abbr* **modus operandi)** *(of criminal)* façon *f* d'agir **3** *(abbr* **money order)** mandat-poste *m*, *pl* mandats-poste
mo [məʊ] N *Br Fam* instant *m*, minute *f*; **half a mo!** une petite seconde!
moan [məʊn] N **1** *(sound)* gémissement *m*, plainte *f* **2** *Fam (complaint)* plainte *f*, jérémiades *fpl*; **to have a (good) m.** râler un bon coup
VI 1 *(make sound)* gémir, pousser des gémissements; *(of wind)* mugir, gémir **2** *Fam (complain)* geindre, gémir, *Fam* râler, ronchonner; **to m. about sth** se plaindre de qch; **he's always moaning (and groaning)** il est toujours à gémir *ou* à geindre *ou Fam* à ronchonner; **what are they moaning about now?** de quoi se plaignent-ils maintenant?
VT *(something)* dire en gémissant
moaner ['məʊnər] N *Fam* ronchonneur, -euse, râleur, -euse
moaning ['məʊnɪŋ] N **1** *(sound)* gémissement(s) *m(pl)* **2** *Fam (complaining)* jérémiades *fpl*; **he's a real m. Minnie** c'est un vrai geignard
moat [məʊt] N fossé(s) *m(pl)*, douves *fpl*
mob [mɒb] N **1** *Pej* **the m.** *(the masses)* la populace, *Fam* le populo **2** *(crowd)* foule *f* (agitée); *(gang)* bande *f*, troupe *f*, *(of reporters etc)* meute *f*; **mobs of drunken hooligans** des hordes de hooligans ivres **3** *Fam (gang)* bande *f*, clique *f*; **the M.** *(Mafia)* la Mafia; **which m. were you in?** *(in forces)* dans quel régiment étais-tu?
VT *(-bb-)* *(of angry crowd) (person)* assaillir, attaquer; *(of fans, reporters etc) (person)* assiéger, se presser autour de; *(place)* prendre d'assaut, assiéger; **the crowds mobbing the entrance** la foule qui se pressait à l'entrée
▸▸ **m. rule** règne *m* de la populace
mobbed [mɒbd] **ADJ** *Fam (crowded)* bondé
mobile ['məʊbaɪl] **ADJ** mobile; **the patient is m.** le patient peut se déplacer; *Fam* **are you**

m.? *(do you have a car with you?)* vous êtes motorisé?; **he wants to stay professionally m.** il veut être libre de ses mouvements dans son métier; **m. features** physionomie *f* changeante
N **1** *Art* mobile *m* **2** *(phone)* (téléphone *m*) portable *m*, *Belg* GSM *m*, *Suisse* Natel® *m inv*, *Can* cellulaire *m*
▸▸ *TV etc* **m. control room** régie *f* mobile; *Mil* **m. defence** troupes *fpl* mobiles; **m. home** *(caravan)* camping-car *m*, *pl* camping-cars; *(house)* = maison *f* sans fondations qui peut être déplacée; **the m. Internet** l'Internet *m* mobile; *Mil* **m. kitchen** cuisine *f* roulante; **m. library** bibliobus *m*; **m. phone** (téléphone) portable, *Belg* GSM, *Suisse* Natel®, *Can* cellulaire; **m. shop** commerce *m* ambulant; *TV* **m. studio** studio *m* mobile; **m. telephony** téléphonie *f* mobile; *Radio, TV* **m. unit** car *m* régie, car de reportage; **m. warfare** guerre *f* de mouvement
mobility [məʊ'bɪlɪtɪ] N mobilité *f*; **she has very little m. in her right arm** elle peut à peine bouger son bras droit; **he values his professional m.** il tient à conserver sa liberté de mouvement dans son métier
▸▸ **m. allowance** indemnité *f* de déplacement *(versée aux personnes handicapées)*
mobilization [məʊbɪlaɪ'zeɪʃən] N *(of troops, capital, support etc)* mobilisation *f*
▸▸ *Mil* **m. order** appel *m* de mobilisation; *(to individual recruit)* ordre *m* de mobilisation
mobilize ['məʊbɪlaɪz] **VT** *(troops, capital, public opinion)* mobiliser
VI *Mil, Fig* se mobiliser
mobster ['mɒbstər] N *esp Am* gangster *m*
moby ['məʊbɪ] N *Br Fam (mobile phone)* mobile *m*
moccasin ['mɒkəsɪn] N *(footwear)* mocassin *m*
mocha ['mɒkə] N **1** *(coffee)* moka *m* **2** *(coffee and chocolate flavour)* parfum *m* chocolat-café
▸▸ **m. coffee** *(café m)* moka
mock [mɒk] N *Br Sch, Univ* examen *m* blanc; **to make a m. of sb/sth** se moquer de qn/qch
ADJ *(imitation)* simulé; **m. fight** simulacre *m* de combat; **to indulge in m. heroics** jouer au *ou* se prendre pour un héros; **m. tortoiseshell** *(rims, frame etc)* en imitation écaille; **m. trial/elections** simulacre *m* de procès/d'élections
VT *(ridicule)* *(person)* se moquer de, *Lit* railler; *(imitate)* *(person)* imiter en se moquant, ridiculiser
VI to m. at se moquer de, *Lit* railler
▸▸ *Br Sch, Univ* **m. examination** examen blanc; *Bot* **m. orange** seringa *m*; **m. turtle soup** consommé *m* à la tête de veau
▸ **mock up VT SEP** *Br* faire une maquette de
mocker ['mɒkər] N **1** *(person)* moqueur, -euse, railleur, -euse **2** *Br Fam* **to put the mockers on sth** *(spoil)* foutre qch en l'air
mockery ['mɒkərɪ] N **1** *(action)* moquerie *f*, raillerie *f* **2** *(person, thing)* sujet *m ou* objet *m* de moquerie *ou* de raillerie, objet de risée; **to make a m. of sb** ridiculiser qn; **to make a m. of oneself** se ridiculiser; **to make a m. of sth** faire perdre toute crédibilité à qch **3** *(pretence)* parodie *f*, simulacre *m* (**of** de); **the trial was a mere m.** le procès n'a été qu'un simulacre
mocking ['mɒkɪŋ] **ADJ** moqueur, railleur
N moquerie *f*, raillerie *f*; **she couldn't put up with their m. any more** elle ne pouvait plus supporter leurs railleries
mockingbird ['mɒkɪŋbɜːd] N moqueur *m*
mockingly ['mɒkɪŋlɪ] **ADV** *(to say)* d'un ton moqueur *ou* railleur; *(to smile)* d'un air moqueur
Mockney ['mɒknɪ] *Br Fam* N = personne *f*

issue d'un milieu aisé qui affecte l'accent cockney

ADJ = caractéristique des personnes issues d'un milieu aisé qui affectent l'accent cockney

mockumentary [mɒkjʊ'ment(ə)rɪ] **N** *TV* faux documentaire *m*

mock-up N maquette *f*

MOD [emǝʊ'di:] **N** *Br* (*abbr* **Ministry of Defence**) ministère *m* de la Défense; **M. property** propriété *f* du ministère de la Défense

Mod [mɒd] **N** *Scot Mus* = festival *m* de musique et de littérature dans les Highlands

mod [mɒd] **N** *Br Fam* **mods** = adolescents *mpl* à l'apparence soignée opposés aux rockers pendant les années soixante

▸▸*Fam* **m. cons** confort *m* moderne; **the car comes equipped with the latest m. cons** la voiture dispose de toutes les options

modal ['mǝʊd(ǝ)l] VOIR GRAMMAIRE A57–61; B39–40 *Gram* **ADJ** modal, -aux

N verbe *m* modal

modality [mǝʊ'dælɪtɪ] **N** modalité *f*

mode [mǝʊd] **N 1** (*manner*) mode *m*, façon *f* (**of** de); **m. of transport** mode de transport **2** (*fashion*) mode *f* **3** *Mus, Phil, Comput* mode *m*

model ['mɒd(ǝ)l] **N 1** (*small version*) (built as a hobby) modèle *m* (réduit), maquette *f*; *Com, Ind* maquette; (*in naval architecture etc*) gabarit *m*; (*in surveying*) plan *m* en relief **2** (*example*), *Com* modèle *m*; **this is our latest m.** c'est notre dernier modèle; *Com, Ind* **there are several different models** il y a plusieurs modèles différents; **Paris models** (*clothing*) modèles de la haute couture parisienne **3** *Econ etc* modèle *m* **4** (*perfect example*) **to take sb as one's m.** prendre modèle sur qn, prendre qn pour modèle; **to be a m. of virtue** être un modèle *ou* un exemple de vertu; **m. pupil** écolier, -ière modèle **5** (*person*), *Art* modèle *m*; (**fashion**) **m.** mannequin *m*, modèle

VT (**-ll-,** *Am* **-l-**) **1** *Art* (*figure, group*) modeler (**after,** up(on) **sur**); *Fig* **to m. oneself on sb** prendre exemple sur qn, se modeler sur qn **2** (*of fashion model*) (*dress etc*) présenter **3** *Comput* modéliser

VI (*of artist's model*) poser (comme modèle); (*of fashion model*) travailler comme mannequin *ou* modèle

▸▸**m. aircraft** (*toy*) modèle (réduit) *ou* maquette d'avion; *Ind* maquette d'avion; **m. kit** modèle en pièces détachées; **m. maker** (*as hobby*) modéliste *mf*, *Ind* maquettiste *mf*

modeller, *Am* **modeler** ['mɒdǝlǝr] **N** modeleur, -euse

modelling, *Am* **modeling** ['mɒdǝlɪŋ] **N 1** (*occupation*) métier *m* de mannequin; **to get a career in m.** faire une carrière de mannequin **2** (*of dress etc*) présentation *f* **3** *Art* modelage *m* **4** *Comput* modélisation *f*

▸▸**m. clay** pâte *f* à modeler

modem ['mǝʊdem] *Comput* **N** modem *m*

VT envoyer par modem; **to m. sth to sb** envoyer qch à qn par modem

▸▸**m. cable** câble *m* du modem; **m. card** carte *f* modem; **m. link** liaison *f* par modem; **m. port** port *m* modem; **m. transmission** transmission *f* par modem

moderate¹ ['mɒdǝrɪt] **ADJ** modéré; (*drinker*) tempéré; (*language*) mesuré; (*price*) modéré, modique, moyen; (*income, size*) moyen; **to express oneself in m. language** s'exprimer en termes modérés; **a m. breeze** une légère brise

N *Pol etc* (*person*) modéré, -ée

moderate² ['mɒdǝreɪt] **VT 1** (*one's demands, wishes, one's zeal*) modérer; **to be a moderating influence on sb** exercer une influence modératrice sur qn **2** *Fml* (*meeting*) présider; (*discussion*) arbitrer

VI 1 (*of storm*) s'apaiser, se calmer **2** *Fml* (*at meeting*) présider

moderately ['mɒdǝrɪtlɪ] **ADV** (*to eat, drink, like*) modérément; (*fast, well-off*) assez, moyennement; **m. priced** à prix moyen

moderation [mɒdǝ'reɪʃǝn] **N 1** modération *f*, mesure *f*; (*of language*) sobriété *f*; **in m.** avec modération, modérément; **taken in m. alcohol is not harmful** consommé avec modération, l'alcool n'est pas nocif **2** *Univ* (*at Oxford University*) **Moderations** = premier examen *m* pour le grade de Bachelor of Arts

moderator ['mɒdǝreɪtǝr] **N 1** (*at meeting*) président, -ente **2** *Univ* (*of exam*) = examinateur *m* qui assure l'harmonisation de la notation **3** *Phys* (*of reactor etc*) modérateur *m*, ralentisseur *m*

▸▸*Scot Rel* **M. of the General Assembly** modérateur *m ou* président *m* du synode (de l'Église d'Écosse)

modern ['mɒdǝn] **ADJ** moderne

N 1 (*person*) moderne *mf* **2** *Typ* didot *m*

▸▸**m. art** art *m* moderne; **m. Greek** grec *m* moderne; **m. languages** langues *fpl* vivantes; *Sport* **m. pentathlon** pentathlon *m* moderne; **m. times** les temps *mpl* modernes

modernism ['mɒdǝnɪz(ǝ)m] **N 1** modernisme *m* **2** *Ling* néologisme *m*

modernist ['mɒdǝnɪst] **N, ADJ** moderniste *mf*

modernity [mɒ'dɜ:nɪtɪ] **N** modernité *f*

modernization [mɒdǝnaɪ'zeɪʃǝn] **N** modernisation *f*

modernize ['mɒdǝnaɪz] **VT** moderniser

VI se moderniser

modernizer ['mɒdǝnaɪzǝr] **N** *Pol* modernisateur, -trice

modest ['mɒdɪst] **ADJ 1** (*not boastful*) modeste; **to be m. about one's achievements** ne pas se vanter de ses réussites **2** (*moderate*) (*request*) modeste, modéré; (*fortune*) modeste; **to be m. in one's requirements** être peu exigeant; **a m. house** une maison sans prétentions *ou* à l'aspect modeste **3** *Old-fashioned* (*chaste*) pudique

modestly ['mɒdɪstlɪ] **ADV 1** (*not boastfully*) modestement, avec modestie **2** (*moderately*) modérément **3** (*in sexual sense*) modestement, pudiquement

modesty ['mɒdɪstɪ] **N 1** (*of person*) modestie *f*, **in all m.** en toute modestie **2** (*of request*) modération *f*, (*of expense*) modicité *f* **3** *Old-fashioned* (*chasteness*) pudeur *f*

modicum ['mɒdɪkǝm] **N a m. of …** un minimum de …, un petit peu de …, un brin de …; **a m. of truth** une petite part de vérité; **she doesn't have even a m. of taste** elle n'a aucun goût

modification [mɒdɪfɪ'keɪʃǝn] **N** modification *f*, **to make modifications to sth** apporter des modifications à qch

modifier ['mɒdɪfaɪǝ(r)] **N** *Gram* modificateur *m*

▸▸*Comput* **m. key** touche *f* de modification

modify ['mɒdɪfaɪ] **VT 1** (*alter*) modifier; (*reduce*) (*punishment*) mitiger, atténuer; **she modified her opinion of him in the light of this information** elle a changé d'avis à son égard lorsqu'elle a appris cela **2** *Gram, Ling* (*verb, vowel etc*) modifier

modish ['mǝʊdɪʃ] **ADJ** (*hat etc*) à la mode

modishly ['mǝʊdɪʃlɪ] **ADV** (*dressed*) à la mode

modiste [mǝʊ'di:st] **N** modiste *f*

Mods [mɒdz] **NPL** *Univ Fam* (*at Oxford University*) = premier examen *m* pour le grade de Bachelor of Arts

modular ['mɒdjʊlǝr] **ADJ** *Archit, Math etc* modulaire; (*furniture*) modulaire, à éléments (composables)

modulate ['mɒdjʊleɪt] **VT** (*one's voice, sound*), *Phys* (*amplitude etc*) moduler; **modulating frequency** fréquence *f* de modulation

VI *Mus* moduler

modulation [mɒdjʊ'leɪʃǝn] **N** (*of voice*) modulation *f*, inflexion *f*; *Mus, Elec, Electron* modulation

modulator ['mɒdjʊleɪtǝr] **N** *Elec, Electron* modulateur *m*

module ['mɒdju:l] **N** *Archit, Astronaut, Constr etc* module *m*; *Univ* module, unité *f* de valeur; *Comput* (*of RAM chips*) barrette *f*

modulus, *pl* **moduli** ['mɒdjʊlǝs, -aɪ] **N** *Math, Phys* module *m*, coefficient *m*

modus operandi ['mǝʊdǝsɒpǝ'rændaɪ, -di:] **N** façon *f* de procéder

modus vivendi ['mǝʊdǝsvɪ'vendaɪ, -di:] **N** modus *m* vivendi

mofo ['mǝʊfǝʊ] **N** *Am Vulg* (*abbr* **motherfucker**) enfoiré *m*

moggy ['mɒgɪ] **N** *Br Fam* (*cat*) minou *m*; (*esp male*) matou *m*

Mogul ['mǝʊgǝl] **N** *Hist* mogol *m*

mogul¹ ['mǝʊgǝl] **N** *Fam* (*powerful person*) gros bonnet *m*, grand manitou *m*, nabab *m*; **movie m.** grand manitou du cinéma

mogul² **N** *Ski* bosse *f*

mohair ['mǝʊheǝr] **N** mohair *m*; **m. sweater** pull *m* en mohair

Mohammed [mǝʊ'hæmɪd] **N** *Rel* Mahomet *m*, Mohammed *m*

Mohammedan [mǝʊ'hæmɪd(ǝ)n] **ADJ** mahométan, -ane

Mohawk ['mǝʊhɔ:k] **N** (*native American*) Mohawk *mf*

mohawk ['mǝʊhɔ:k] **N** *Am* (*hairstyle*) iroquoise *f*

Mohican [mǝʊ'hi:kǝn] **N** (*native American*) Mohican *mf*

mohican [mǝʊ'hi:kǝn] **N** *Br* (*hairstyle*) iroquoise *f*

moiré ['mwɑ:reɪ] **ADJ, N** *Tex* moiré *m*

moist [mɔɪst] **ADJ** humide; (*skin, hand*) moite; (*heat*) moite, humide; (*cake*) moelleux; **eyes m. with tears** yeux mouillés de larmes, yeux embués; **to grow m.** se mouiller, s'humecter

moisten ['mɔɪs(ǝ)n] **VT** mouiller, humecter; **to m. a cloth with sth** imbiber un chiffon de qch

VI (*of eyes*) se mouiller

moistness ['mɔɪstnɪs] **N** humidité *f*, (*of skin, palms*) moiteur *f*

moisture ['mɔɪstʃǝr] **N** humidité *f*, (*on mirror etc*) buée *f*

moisturize ['mɔɪstʃǝraɪz] **VT** humidifier; (*skin*) hydrater

moisturizer ['mɔɪstʃǝraɪzǝr] **N** (*for skin*) crème *f ou* lotion *f* hydratante, (lait *m*) hydratant *m*

molar ['mǝʊlǝr] **N** molaire *f*

ADJ molaire

molasses [mǝ'læsɪz] **NPL** (*with sing verb*) mélasse *f*, *Am Fam* **to be as slow as m.** (**in winter**) être d'une lenteur de limace *ou* d'escargot *ou* de tortue

mold, molder *etc Am* = **mould, moulder** *etc*

Moldavia [mɒl'deɪvɪǝ], **Moldova** [mɒl'dǝʊvǝ] **N** Moldavie *f*

Moldavian [mɒl'deɪvɪǝn], **Moldovan** [mɒl'dǝʊvǝn] **N** Moldave *mf*

ADJ moldave

mole¹ [mǝʊl] **N** (*birthmark*) grain *m* de beauté

mole² **N 1** (*animal*) taupe *f* **2** *Fig* (*spy*) espion *m*, taupe *f*

▸▸**m. catcher** taupier *m*; **m. trap** taupière *f*

mortician [mɔː'tɪʃən] N *Am* entrepreneur *m* de pompes funèbres

mortification [mɔːtɪfɪ'keɪʃən] N **1** (*humiliation*) humiliation *f*, *Lit* mortification *f*; **to my (eternal) m.** à ma (grande) honte **2** *Rel* (*of the flesh*) mortification *f* **3** *Med* nécrose *f*

mortify ['mɔːtɪfaɪ] VT **1** (*humiliate*) humilier, *Lit* mortifier; *Fam* **I was mortified** j'étais mort de honte **2** *Rel* (*the flesh*) mortifier VI *Med* se gangrener, se nécroser

mortifying ['mɔːtɪfaɪɪŋ] ADJ (*experience etc*) humiliant, *Lit* mortifiant

mortise ['mɔːtɪs] *Carp* N mortaise *f* VT (*cut mortise in*) mortaiser; **to m. two beams (together)** emmortaiser *ou* emboîter deux poutres
▸▸ **m. lock** serrure *f* encastrée

mortuary ['mɔːtjʊərɪ] N morgue *f* ADJ mortuaire

Mosaic [məʊ'zeɪɪk] ADJ *Bible* (*law etc*) mosaïque, de Moïse

mosaic [məʊ'zeɪɪk] N *Art etc* mosaïque *f*; **m. floor** dallage *m* en mosaïque

Moscow ['mɒskəʊ] N Moscou

Moses ['məʊzɪz] N *Bible* Moïse *m* INT *Old-fashioned Fam* **Holy M.!** grand Dieu!
▸▸ **M. basket** couffin *m*

▸ **mosey along** ['məʊzɪ] VI *esp Am Fam* flâner, se promener sans se presser; **I'll just m. along to the bar** je vais faire un tour au bar; **I'll be moseying along now** (*leaving*) je vais y aller

Moslem ['mɒzləm] ADJ, N musulman, -ane

mosque [mɒsk] N mosquée *f*

mosquito [mɒs'kiːtəʊ] *pl* **mosquitoes** [-əʊz] N moustique *m*
▸▸ **m. bite** piqûre *f* de moustique; **m. net** moustiquaire *f*; **m. repellent** produit *m* antimoustique

moss [mɒs] N *Bot* mousse *f*
▸▸ *Miner* **m. agate** agate *f* mousseuse; *Bot* **m. rose** rose *f* mousseuse *ou* mousseuse; *Sewing* **m. stitch** point *m* de riz

mossy ['mɒsɪ] ADJ moussu

MOST [məʊst] (*superl of* **many, much**)

ADJ	le plus de ▪ la plupart de
N, INDEF PRON	le plus **1** ▪ au plus **1** ▪ la plupart **2** ▪ la plus grande partie **2**
ADV	le plus **1, 3** ▪ bien **2**

ADJ (*cows, milk etc*) le plus de; **you have made (the) m. mistakes** c'est vous qui avez fait le plus de fautes; **m. women** la plupart des femmes; **in m. cases** dans la majorité *ou* la plupart des cas; **for the m. part** (*in greatest number of cases*) pour la plupart; (*most often*) le plus souvent *ou* la plupart du temps

N, INDEF PRON **1** (*greatest amount*) **the m.** le plus, le maximum; **do the m. you can** faites le plus que vous pourrez; **at the (very) m.** au (grand) maximum, (tout) au plus; **to make the m. of a situation** tirer le meilleur parti d'une situation; **to make the m. of one's talents** tirer le meilleur parti de ses capacités; **she made the m. of her time in Mexico** elle a profité au maximum du temps qu'elle a passé au Mexique; **the opposition made the m. of the scandal** l'opposition a tiré tout ce qu'elle pouvait du scandale; **make the m. of it** profitez-en au maximum

2 (*majority*) **m. of the women/cars** la plupart *ou* la majorité des femmes/des voitures; **m. of the work** la plus grande *ou* la majeure partie du travail; **m. of the time** la plupart du temps; **he is more reliable than m.** on peut compter sur lui plus que sur bien des gens

ADV **1** (*to form superl*) le plus; **the m. beautiful woman** la plus belle femme; **they bought**

the m. expensive (ones) ils ont acheté les plus chers/chères; **those who have answered m. accurately** ceux qui ont répondu le plus exactement VOIR GRAMMAIRE A25–6; B11; B13

2 (*very*) très, bien; **m. unhappy** bien malheureux; **m. likely** *or* **probably** très probablement; **he has been m. rude** il a été ou ne peut plus impoli

3 (*to drink, talk etc*) le plus; **what I want m.** ce que je désire par-dessus tout; **that's what worries me (the) m.** c'est ce qui m'inquiète le plus VOIR GRAMMAIRE A26

mostly ['məʊstlɪ] ADV **1** (*in the main*) surtout, principalement; **they come m. from Scotland** ils viennent surtout d'Écosse; **a m. young audience** un public composé pour une large part de jeunes, un public composé en majorité de jeunes; **they're m. working-class** ils sont issus de la classe ouvrière pour la plupart **2** (*most often*) le plus souvent, la plupart du temps

MOT [eməʊ'tiː] N *Br Admin* **1** *Formerly abbr* Ministry of Transport **2** *Aut* (*test*) = contrôle *m* technique **3** *Aut* (*certificate*) = certificat *m* de contrôle technique; **six months' M.** (*in advertisement*) = certificat *m* de contrôle technique valable pendant six mois

mote [məʊt] N *Lit* grain *m* de poussière; *Bible* **the m. in thy brother's eye** la paille dans l'œil du voisin

motel [məʊ'tel] N motel *m*

motet [məʊ'tet] N *Mus* motet *m*

moth [mɒθ] N (*insect*) papillon *m* nocturne *ou* de nuit; (*clothes*) **m.** mite *f*; *Fam* **the moths have been at my fur coat** mon manteau de fourrure est tout mangé par les mites

mothball ['mɒθbɔːl] N boule *f* de naphtaline; *Fig* **to put a project in mothballs** remettre un projet à plus tard; **to take a project out of mothballs** déterrer un projet; *Fig* **to put a ship in mothballs** retirer un navire du service actif et le couvrir de bâches VT *Fig* (*ship*) retirer du service actif et couvrir de bâches; (*plan*) remettre à plus tard; (*piece of equipment*) entretenir en vue d'une utilisation future

moth-eaten ADJ **1** mangé des *ou* par les mites, mité **2** *Fam* (*in poor condition*) miteux, misérable; (*hotel*) miteux

mother ['mʌðər] N **1** mère *f*; *Admin, Law* mère de famille; **yes, m.!** oui, maman!; **m. of six** mère de six enfants; *Br Fam* **shall I be m.?** (*pour out tea*) je fais le service?; *Fig Fam* **I've got the m. and father of all headaches** j'ai un mal de tête épouvantable; *Fig Fam* **we had the m. and father of a row!** nous avons eu une de ces empoignades!; **every m.'s son was there!** tout le monde était là, il ne manquait personne; *Rel* **reverend m.** (*sœur f*) supérieure *f*; (*form of address*) ma mère **2** *Am Vulg* salaud *m*, fumier *m*, ordure *f* VT materner, dorloter
▸▸ **m.'s boy** garçon *m* à sa maman; **m. church** église *f* mère; **m. country** (mère) patrie *f*; (*of colony*) métropole *f*; **M.'s Day** la fête des Mères; **m. hen** mère poule; **m.'s little helper** (*helpful child*) = enfant *mf* qui aide sa mère dans les tâches ménagères; *Fig Hum* = alcool *m* ou médicament *m* consommé pour oublier ses soucis; **M. Nature** la Nature; *Geol* **m. rock** roche *f* mère; *Fig Hum* **m.'s ruin** (*gin*) gin *m*; *Mil* **m. ship** ravitailleur *m*; *Rel* **M. Superior** Mère *f* supérieure; **m.-to-be** future maman *f*; **m. tongue** langue *f* maternelle; *Chem* **m. of vinegar** mère de vinaigre; **m. wit** bon sens *m*

motherboard ['mʌðəbɔːd] N *Comput* carte *f* mère

motherfucker ['mʌðəfʌkər] N *Vulg* salaud *m*, fumier *m*, ordure *f*; **the m. won't start** cette saloperie ne veut pas démarrer

motherfucking ['mʌðəfʌkɪŋ] ADJ ATTRIB *Vulg* putain de

motherhood ['mʌðəhʊd] N maternité *f*

mothering ['mʌðərɪŋ] N soins *mpl* maternels
▸▸ **m. skills** capacité *f* à s'occuper d'un petit; *Br* **M. Sunday** la fête des Mères

mother-in-law *pl* **mothers-in-law** N belle-mère *f*, *pl* belles-mères
▸▸ *Fam* **m.'s tongue** (*plant*) sansevière *f*

motherland ['mʌðəlænd] N patrie *f*, pays *m* natal

motherless ['mʌðəlɪs] ADJ sans mère, orphelin (de mère)

motherly ['mʌðəlɪ] ADJ maternel, de mère

mother-of-pearl N nacre *f*; **m. decoration** décoration *f* en nacre

moth-hole N trou *m* de mite

mothproof ['mɒθpruːf] ADJ traité à l'antimite VT traiter à l'antimite

motif [məʊ'tiːf] N *Art, Mus etc* motif *m*

motion ['məʊʃən] N **1** *Phys etc* mouvement *m*; (*of vehicle, apparatus*) marche *f*, mouvement; *Phys* **body in m.** corps *m* en mouvement; **car in m.** voiture en marche; **to put** *or* **set a machine in m.** mettre une machine en marche; *Fig* **to put** *or* **set a process in m.** mettre un processus en branle; *Fig* **I'll set things** *or* **the wheels in m.** je vais mettre les choses en route

2 (*of arm etc*) mouvement *m*; (*sign*) geste *m*; **to go through the motions** agir machinalement; **he's just going through the motions** il fait juste semblant; **you could at least go through the motions** tu devrais au moins le faire pour la forme

3 (*in meeting, debate*) motion *f*, proposition *f*; **to propose a m.** faire une proposition; **to put the m.** mettre la motion *ou* la proposition aux voix; **the m. was carried** la motion fut adoptée

4 *Law* (*application*) demande *f*, requête *f*

5 *Br* (*bowel evacuation*) évacuation *f*; **motion(s)** (*faeces*) selles *fpl*

VT **to m. sb to do sth** faire signe à qn de faire qch; **to m. sb away/in** faire signe à qn de s'éloigner/d'entrer

VI **to m. to sb to do sth** faire signe à qn de faire qch
▸▸ *Am Cin* **m. picture** film *m*; **the m. picture industry** l'industrie *f* du cinéma; *Tech* **m. study** analyse *f* du mouvement, chronophotographie *f*

motionless ['məʊʃənlɪs] ADJ immobile; **to remain m.** ne pas bouger, rester immobile

motivate ['məʊtɪveɪt] VT (*decision, employees*) motiver; **to m. sb to do sth** pousser *ou* inciter qn à faire qch; **they were motivated by a desire to help others** ils étaient poussés par un désir d'aider les autres

motivated ['məʊtɪveɪtɪd] ADJ motivé; **to be highly m.** être très motivé

motivating ['məʊtɪveɪtɪŋ] ADJ motivant

motivation [məʊtɪ'veɪʃən] N motivation *f*; **he lacked the m. to succeed** il n'était pas assez motivé pour réussir
▸▸ *Mktg* **m. research** recherche *f* de motivation; *Mktg* **m. study** étude *f* de motivation

motivational [məʊtɪ'veɪʃənəl] ADJ motivationnel
▸▸ *Mktg* **m. research** recherche *f* de motivation; *Mktg* **m. study** étude *f* de motivation

motivator ['məʊtɪveɪtər] N **he's a good m.** il sait motiver les gens

motive ['məʊtɪv] N **1** (*reason*) motif *m*, raison *f*; (*for a crime*) mobile *m*; **interest is a powerful m.** l'intérêt est un puissant ressort; **I wonder what his m. is** je me demande pourquoi *ou* pour quelle raison il fait cela; **I**

don't understand what her m. is for refusing to ... je ne comprends pas pourquoi *ou* pour quelle raison elle refuse de ... **2** *Art (of painting etc)* motif *m*
ADJ moteur, -trice
▸▸**m. power** force *f* motrice

motley ['mɒtlɪ] **ADJ 1** *(diverse)* varié, hétéroclite; **m. crew** *or* **crowd** bande *f ou* mélange *m* hétéroclite **2** *(of different colours)* bariolé, bigarré
N 1 *(mixture)* mélange *m* hétéroclite **2** *Hist (jester's costume)* costume *m* de bouffon de cour

motocross ['məʊtəʊkrɒs] **N** *Sport* motocross *m*

motor ['məʊtər] **N 1** *(engine)* moteur *m* **2** *Br Fam (car)* bagnole *f*
ADJ *Anat (muscle, nerve)* moteur, -trice
VI 1 *Old-fashioned (travel by car)* voyager en auto *ou* en voiture; **we motored across France** nous avons traversé la France en voiture **2** *Br Fam* **to be motoring** *(going fast)* foncer; *Fig* **now we're motoring!** cette fois on y vient!
▸▸**m. caravan** camping-car *m*, *pl* camping-cars; *Rail* **m. carriage** *(voiture f)* motrice *f*, **m. engineer** ingénieur *m* en automobile, motoriste *mf*; **m. fuel** carburant *m*; **m. industry** industrie *f* automobile; **m. insurance** assurance *f* automobile; **m. launch** vedette *f*, *Am* **m. lodge** motel *m*; **m. manufacturer** constructeur *m* automobile; **m. mechanic** mécanicien, -ienne; *Med* **m. neurone disease** maladie *f* de Charcot; *Med* **m. paralysis** paralysie *f* des centres moteurs; **m. race** course *f* automobile; **m. racing** courses *fpl* automobiles; **m. rally** rallye *m* automobile; **m. scooter** scooter *m*; **m. show** salon *m* de l'auto(mobile); **m. sport** sport *m* automobile; *Tech* **m. torque** couple *m* moteur; **the m. trade** l'automobile *f*, **m. vehicle** véhicule *m* automobile; *Naut* **m. vessel** bateau *m* à moteur

motorail ['məʊtəreɪl] **N** *Rail* train(s) *m(pl)* auto-couchettes; **m. service** train(s) auto-couchettes

motor-assisted [-ə'sɪstɪd] **ADJ**
▸▸**m. bicycle** cyclomoteur *m*

motorbike ['məʊtəbaɪk] **N** moto *f*

motorboat ['məʊtəbəʊt] **N** canot *m* à moteur; *(fast)* vedette *f*

motorcade ['məʊtəkeɪd] **N** cortège *m* de voitures

motorcar ['məʊtəkɑːr] **N** *Br* automobile *f*, voiture *f*

motorcycle ['məʊtəsaɪk(ə)l] **N** motocyclette *f*, moto *f*; **m. wheel** roue *f* de moto
▸▸**m. accident** accident *m* de moto; **m. combination** moto et sidecar *m*; **m. courier** coursier, -ière, porteur, -euse; **m. gang** bande *f* de motards; **m. policeman** agent *m* motocycliste, motard *m*; **m. rider** motocycliste *mf*, motard

motorcycling ['məʊtəsaɪklɪŋ] **N** motocyclisme *m*

motorcyclist ['məʊtəsaɪklɪst] **N** motocycliste *mf*

motor-driven **ADJ** à moteur; *(device)* actionné *ou* commandé par un moteur

motor-home **N** *Am* auto-caravane *f*, *pl* auto-caravanes, camping-car *m*, *pl* camping-cars

motoring ['məʊtərɪŋ] **N** conduite *f* (automobile); **school of m.** auto-école *f*, *pl* auto-écoles
▸▸**m. correspondent** chroniqueur, -euse automobile; *Old-fashioned* **m. holiday** virée *f* en voiture; **m. offence** infraction *f* au code de la route; **m. organization** association *f* d'automobilistes

motorist ['məʊtərɪst] **N** automobiliste *mf*

motorization [məʊtəraɪ'zeɪʃən] **N** motorisation *f*

motorize ['məʊtəraɪz] **VT** motoriser; **motorized** motorisé; **motorized bicycle** vélomoteur *m*

motorman, *pl* **motormen** ['məʊtəmæn, -men] **N** *Am (on tram)* wattman *m*; *(on subway)* conducteur *m*

motormouth ['məʊtəˈmaʊθ] **N** *Fam* **he's a bit of a m.** c'est un véritable moulin à paroles

motorway ['məʊtəweɪ] **N** *Br* autoroute *f*
▸▸**m. accident** accident *m* sur autoroute; **m. driving** conduite *f* sur autoroute; **m. exit** sortie *f* d'autoroute; **m. madness** la folie de l'autoroute; **m. network** réseau *m* autoroutier; **m. police** police *f* de l'autoroute; **m. restaurant** restauroute *m*, restoroute *m*; **m. services** services *mpl* autoroutiers

Motown® ['məʊtaʊn] **N 1** *Am Fam* = surnom de la ville de Détroit **2** *Mus* style *m* Motown

mottled ['mɒt(ə)ld] **ADJ** *(fabric)* tacheté, moucheté; *(skin)* marbré; *(wood)* madré

motto, *pl* **mottoes** ['mɒtəʊ, -əʊz] **N 1** devise *f*, **that's my m.** voilà ma devise **2** *Her* devise *f* **3** *Typ* épigraphe *f* **4** *Mus* motif *m* **5** *Br (in Christmas cracker) (riddle)* devinette *f*, *(funny saying)* phrase *f* amusante

mould¹, *Am* **mold** [məʊld] **N** *(fungus)* moisi *m*, moisissure *f*

mould², *Am* **mold** **N 1** *Art, Cer etc* moule *m*; *Typ (of character)* matrice *f*, *Culin* **(jelly) m.** moule *m* à gelée; *Lit* **to be cast in a heroic m.** être de la trempe des héros; **he is cast in his father's m.** il est fait dans le même moule que son père; **people cast in the same m.** des gens sortis du même moule; **a star in the John Wayne m.** une star du style John Wayne; *Fig* **to break the m.** rompre avec la tradition **2** *(template), Constr etc* calibre *m*, profil *m*; *Naut, Aviat* gabarit *m* **3** *Culin* **rice m.** gâteau *m* de riz **4** *Archit* moulure *f*
VT 1 *(make from a mould)* mouler; **the bucket is moulded in plastic** le seau est moulé dans du plastique **2** *(shape)* mouler; *(person's character)* façonner, former; **to m. clay/etc into sth** façonner l'argile/etc pour en faire qch; *Fig* **she moulded them into a team** elle a fait d'eux une équipe; *Fig* **public opinion has been moulded by the media** l'opinion publique a été façonnée par les médias **3** *(adhere closely to)* **the dress moulded her figure** la robe moulait ses formes

mould³, *Am* **mold** **N** *(earth)* terre *f* meuble; **vegetable m.** terreau *m*, humus *m*

moulded, *Am* **molded** ['məʊldɪd] **ADJ** *(plastic)* moulé

moulder, *Am* **molder** ['məʊldər] **VI** *(of wood)* tomber en poussière, s'effriter; *(of food)* moisir; *(of building etc)* se désagréger; *Fig (of person)* moisir
▸**moulder away,** *Am* **molder away** **VI** = **moulder**

moulding, *Am* **molding** ['məʊldɪŋ] **N 1** *Metal etc* moulage *m* **2** *Fig (of character, public opinion)* formation *f*, façonnement *m* **3** *Archit (ornament)* moulure *f*, *(edging strip)* baguette *f*, **drip** *or* **weather m.** *(on window, door)* jet *m* d'eau; *(on wall)* larmier *m*; **plain m.** listeau *m*, listel *m*; **grooved m.** moulure à gorge

mouldy, *Am* **moldy** ['məʊldɪ] **ADJ** moisi; **to smell m.** sentir le moisi

moult, *Am* **molt** [məʊlt] **N** mue *f*
VI *(of cat, dog)* perdre ses poils; *(of bird, reptile)* muer; *Hum* **I must be moulting!** je perds mes poils!

moulting, *Am* **molting** ['məʊltɪŋ] **ADJ** en mue
N mue *f*

mound [maʊnd] **N** *(artificial)* tertre *m*, monticule *m*, butte *f*, *Constr etc* remblai *m*; *(of stones etc)* monceau *m*, tas *m*; *(natural)* monticule

mount¹ [maʊnt] **N 1** *(mountain)* mont *m* **2** *(in palmistry)* mont *m*
▸▸**M. Sinai** le mont Sinaï

mount² **N 1** *(support), Tech* montage *m*, support *m*; *Mil etc* affût *m*, trépied *m*; *(of lens, prism)* monture *f*
2 *Art etc (of painting etc)* carton *m* de montage
3 *(horse)* cheval *m*, monture *f*, *Horseracing (ride)* monte *f*
VT 1 *(climb onto) (bicycle, horse)* monter sur, enfourcher; **to m. the scaffold** monter sur l'échafaud; **to m. the throne** monter sur le trône; **to m. the pavement** *(of car etc)* monter sur le trottoir
2 *(mate with)* couvrir, monter
3 *(climb) (stairs, hill)* monter, gravir; *(ladder)* monter à
4 *(set on)* **to m. sb** *(on a horse)* hisser qn sur un cheval; **to m. a squadron of cavalry** monter un escadron de cavalerie; **they were mounted on grey horses** ils chevauchaient des chevaux gris
5 *Tech* installer; *(precious stone)* monter, sertir; *Art, Phot, Cin (painting, photograph, film reel)* monter; *Mil etc (cannon)* mettre sur (son) affût; *(machine, engine etc)* monter, installer
6 *(prepare)* **to m. a play/an exhibition** monter une pièce/une exposition; *Mil* **to m. an offensive** lancer une offensive; *Mil* **to m. guard** monter la garde
VI 1 *Horseriding* se mettre en selle
2 *(rise, climb)* monter; **the blood mounted to his head** le sang lui est monté à la tête; **the cost was mounting** le coût augmentait
▸**mount up** **VI** monter, augmenter; **the bill was mounting up** la facture augmentait; **her savings soon mounted up** ses économies augmentèrent rapidement; **it all mounts up** ça finit par chiffrer

mountain ['maʊntɪn] **N** montagne *f*, **range of mountains** chaîne *f* de montagnes; **to spend one's holidays in the mountains** passer ses vacances à la montagne; *Fig* **a m. of work** un travail monstre; *Fig* **a m. of evidence** des quantités de preuves; *Fig* **mountains of papers to mark** des tas de copies à corriger; **butter/beef m.** *(surplus)* montagne de beurre/bœuf; *Fig* **to make a m. out of a molehill** faire une montagne d'un rien; **m. scenery/stream** paysage *m*/ruisseau *m* de montagne
▸▸**m. ash** *(rowan)* sorbier *m* des oiseleurs *ou* des oiseaux; *(eucalyptus)* eucalyptus *m*; **m. bike** VTT, vélo *m* tout-terrain; **m. biking** VTT, vélo tout-terrain; **m. chain** chaîne de montagnes; **m. climbing** alpinisme *m*; **m. lion** puma *m*, cougouar *m*; **m. pass** col *m*, défilé *m*; **m. pine** pin *m* de montagne; **m. range** chaîne de montagnes; **m. rescue** secours *m* en montagne; **m. rescue service** service *m* de secours en montagne; **m. resort** station *f* de montagne, station montagnarde; **m. sickness** mal des montagnes; **m. side** flanc *m ou* versant *m* de montagne; *Am* **M. Standard Time** heure *f* normale des montagnes Rocheuses; **m. top** sommet *m* de montagne; **m. tribe** tribu *f* montagnarde; **m. troops** chasseurs *mpl* alpins

mountaineer [maʊntɪ'nɪər] **N** alpiniste *mf*
VI faire de l'alpinisme

mountaineering [maʊntɪ'nɪərɪŋ] **N** alpinisme *m*

mountainous ['maʊntɪnəs] **ADJ** *(country etc)* montagneux; *Fig* **m. seas** vagues gigantesques

mountebank ['maʊntɪbæŋk] **N** *Lit* charlatan *m*

mounted ['maʊntɪd] **ADJ**

▸▸ **the m. police** la police montée; **m. policeman** policier *m* à cheval

Mountie ['maʊntɪ] N *Fam* = membre *m* de la Gendarmerie Royale du Canada

mounting ['maʊntɪŋ] N *(support), Tech* support *m; Tech (of machine, engine)* bâti *m*, socle *m; (of rifle etc)* monture *f*, garniture *f; (of precious stone)* monture, sertissage *m; Mil (of machine gun)* affût *m*, trépied *m; Tech* **engine mountings** pièces *fpl* d'assemblage de moteur

▪ ADJ **m. costs/death toll** coût/nombre des morts en augmentation; **there is m. evidence against her** il y a de plus en plus de preuves contre elle

▸▸ **m. bracket** support de montage; **m. point** *(for seatbelt)* point *m* d'ancrage

mounting-block N *Horseriding* montoir *m*

mourn [mɔːn] VT *(somebody, something, sb's death)* pleurer; **there's no point mourning what might have been** cela ne sert à rien de se lamenter sur ce qui aurait pu se passer
▪ VI être en deuil

▸ **mourn for** VT INSEP **to m. for sb** pleurer (la mort de) qn; **to m. for sth** pleurer qch, déplorer qch

▸ **mourn over** VT INSEP = **mourn for**

mourner ['mɔːnər] N **1** *(at funeral)* personne *f* qui suit le cortège funèbre; **the mourners** le convoi, le cortège funèbre **2** *(person grieving)* personne *f* endeuillée, personne qui porte le deuil

mournful ['mɔːnfʊl] ADJ triste, mélancolique

mournfully ['mɔːnfʊlɪ] ADV tristement

mourning ['mɔːnɪŋ] N deuil *m; (clothing)* (vêtements *mpl* ou habits *mpl* de) deuil; **to be in m.** être en deuil; **to wear m.** porter le deuil; **to go into m.** se mettre en deuil, prendre le deuil; **house of m.** maison *f* endeuillée

mouse¹, *pl* **mice** [maʊs, maɪs] N **1** *(animal)* souris *f*; **young m.** souriceau *m*; **m. grey, m. colour(ed)** gris *m* souris *f Fam (timid person)* timide *mf*; **are you a man or a m.?** t'es un homme ou quoi? **3** *Comput* souris *f*
▸▸ *Comput* **m. ball** boule *f* de la souris; *Comput* **m. button** bouton *m* de souris; *Comput* **m. click** clic *m* de souris; *Comput* **m. driver** programme *m* de commande de la souris; **m. hole** trou *m* de souris; *Comput* **m. keys** touches *fpl* souris; *Comput* **m. mat, m. pad** tapis *m* de souris; *Comput* **m. port** port *m* souris

mouse² [maʊz] VI *(of cat etc)* chasser les souris

mouser ['maʊzər] N *(cat etc)* souricier *m*; **she's a good m.** elle attrape bien les souris

mousetrap ['maʊstræp] N souricière *f*, tapette *f; Fam (cheese)* fromage *m* ordinaire, *Can* fromage à souris
▸▸ *Fam* **m. cheese** fromage ordinaire, *Can* fromage à souris

moussaka [mʊ'saːkə] N moussaka *f*

mousse [muːs] N *(for hair), Culin* mousse *f*, **chocolate m.** mousse au chocolat

moustache [məs'taːʃ], *Am* **mustache** ['mʌstæʃ] N moustache(s) *f(pl)*; **short m., clipped m.** moustache courte *ou* en brosse

mousy ['maʊsɪ] ADJ **1** *(colour)* gris sale; *Fam (hair)* châtain terne *inv* **2** *(timid)* timide **3** *(smell etc)* de souris

mouth¹ [maʊθ] N *(pl* **mouths** [maʊðz]*)* **1** *(of person, horse)* bouche *f; (of other animal)* gueule *f*, **to have one's m. full** avoir la bouche pleine; **don't speak with your m. full** ne parle pas (avec) la bouche pleine; **seven mouths to feed** avoir sept bouches à nourrir; *Fig* **big m.** *(person)* gueulard *m*, grande gueule *f*; **to be** *or* **have a big m.** être *ou* avoir une grande gueule; **you had to**

open your big m., didn't you! il a fallu que tu ouvres ta grande gueule!; **me and my big m.!** pourquoi faut-il toujours que je l'ouvre!; *Fam* **he's all m.** parler, c'est tout ce qu'il sait faire; *Fam* **keep your m. shut about this** garde ça pour toi; **to put words into sb's m.** *(misquote)* faire dire à qn ce qu'il n'a dit pas; **I don't want to put words into your m. but …** dites-moi si je me trompe mais …; *Fig Fam* **to be all mouth and (no) trousers** être une grande gueule **2** *(opening etc) (of tunnel, cave)* ouverture *f*, entrée *f; (of river)* embouchure *f*
▸▸ **m. organ** harmonica *m*; **m. ulcer** aphte *m*

mouth² [maʊð] VT **1** *(say without sincerity)* dire de façon mécanique, dire mécaniquement **2** *(say silently) (words)* former; **she mouthed something to me** elle a essayé de me dire quelque chose en remuant les lèvres silencieusement
▪ VI *esp Am (grimace)* grimacer, faire des grimaces

▸ **mouth off** VI *Fam (brag)* se vanter, crâner; *(talk impudently)* la ramener; *(talk indiscreetly)* parler à tort et à travers

mouthful ['maʊθfʊl] N **1** bouchée *f*, *(of soup, wine etc)* gorgée *f*, **to swallow sth in** *or* **at one m., to make one m. of sth** ne faire qu'une bouchée de qch; *(soup, wine)* avaler qch d'une seule gorgée; **I swallowed** *or* **got a m. (of water)** *(when swimming etc)* j'ai bu la *ou* une tasse; *esp Am Fam* **you said a m.** *(were right)* tu as bien parlé; *Br Fam* **to give sb a m.** *(insult)* traiter qn de tous les noms **2** *Fam (long word, phrase)* mot *m*/phrase *f* difficile à prononcer; *(person's name)* nom *m* à coucher dehors; **cerebral thrombosis is quite a m.** thrombose cérébrale est vraiment difficile à prononcer

mouthpiece ['maʊθpiːs] N **1** *(of loudhailer)* embout *m; (of pipe)* tuyau *m*, bout *m; Mus (of clarinet etc)* bec *m; Mus (of horn etc)* embouchure *f; Tel* microphone *m* **2** *(person, magazine) (of party etc)* porte-parole *m inv; Am Sl (lawyer)* avocat *m* (au criminel)

mouth-to-mouth ADJ
▸▸ **m. resuscitation** bouche-à-bouche *m inv*; **to give sb m. resuscitation** faire du bouche-à-bouche à qn

mouthwash ['maʊθwɒʃ] N *Pharm* bain *m* de bouche; *(for teeth)* eau *f* dentifrice

mouthwatering ['maʊθwɔːtərɪŋ] ADJ alléchant, qui fait venir l'eau à la bouche

mouthy ['maʊðɪ] ADJ *Fam* gueulard, grande gueule

movable ['muːvəb(ə)l] ADJ **1** mobile **2** *Law* mobilier, meuble
▪ NPL *Law* **movables** biens *mpl* meubles
▸▸ *Rel* **m. feast** fête *f* mobile; *Law* **m. property** biens *mpl* meubles

MOVE [muːv]

N	mouvement **1** ▪ démarche **2**
	▪ déménagement **3** ▪ coup **4**
VT	déplacer **1** ▪ déménager **1**
	▪ bouger **2** ▪ pousser **3** ▪ émouvoir **4**
	▪ proposer **5**
VI	se déplacer **1** ▪ bouger **1, 2**
	▪ avancer **3** ▪ agir **4** ▪ déménager **5**
	▪ jouer **7**

N 1 *(motion)* mouvement *m*; **to make a m. towards sth** faire un mouvement vers qch; **there was a general m. towards** *or* **for the door** tout le monde s'est dirigé vers la porte; *Fam* **to make a m.** *(leave)* y aller, bouger; *Fam* **it's late, I ought to be making a m.** il se fait tard, il faut que j'y aille *ou* que je parte; **don't make a m.!** *(or I'll shoot, they'll see us etc)* ne bouge pas!; **the police were watching her every m.** la police surveillait ses

moindres gestes; **on the m.** en marche; **to be always on the m.** ne jamais rester en place; *Fam* **to get a m. on** se grouiller, se manier *ou* magner (le train)

2 *Fig (action, step)* démarche *f*, action *f*, manœuvre *f*; **smart m.** manœuvre habile; **at one time there was a m. to …** à un moment, on avait envisagé de …; **what's the next m.?** qu'est-ce qu'il faut faire maintenant?; *Fam* **to make a m. on sb** faire des avances à qn; **to make the first m.** faire le premier pas; **don't make a m. without contacting me** *(don't do anything)* ne fais rien sans me contacter; **when would the enemy make his m.?** quand l'ennemi allait-il se décider à agir?; **the Government has made moves towards resolving …** le gouvernement a pris des mesures pour résoudre …

3 *(from home, office etc)* déménagement *m*; **after ten years in the job she needed a m.** après dix ans passés à faire le même travail, elle avait besoin de changement

4 *Chess etc* coup *m*; **mate in four moves** (échec etc) mat en quatre coups; **to have first m.** commencer la partie; **to make a m.** jouer; **(it's) your m.** à vous de jouer, c'est votre tour; **to learn the moves** apprendre comment les pièces se déplacent

5 *Comput (of text block etc)* déplacement *m*
▪ VT **1** *(shift) (furniture, troops etc)* déplacer, changer de place; *(employee)* muter (**to** à); *(drive) (wheels etc)* entraîner; *Chess etc (piece)* jouer; *Comput (text block etc)* déplacer; *Com* vendre; **to m. sth from its place** changer qch de place; **could you m. your feet/bag (out of the way) please?** est-ce que tu peux pousser tes pieds/ton sac s'il te plaît?; **to m. one's position** changer de place; **to m. one's chair near the fire** approcher son fauteuil du feu; **he was moved to London** on l'a muté à Londres; **to m. house/ premises** déménager; **to m. heaven and earth** remuer ciel et terre; **come on, m. yourself! we're going to be late!** allez, remuetoi! on va être en retard!

2 *(stir) (one's head etc)* remuer, bouger; *(of wind etc) (branches etc)* agiter, remuer; *(set in motion)* mouvoir, animer, mettre en mouvement; *Med* **to m. one's bowels** aller à la selle

3 *Fig (sway)* ébranler la résolution de; **you won't m. me** tu ne me feras pas changer d'avis; **I won't be moved** je ne changerai pas d'avis; **nothing will m. him** il est inflexible; **to m. sb to do sth** pousser *ou* inciter qn à faire qch

4 *(affect emotionally) (somebody)* émouvoir, toucher; **easily moved** émotif; **to m. sb to anger** provoquer la colère de qn; **to m. sb to tears** émouvoir qn (jusqu')aux larmes; **to m. sb to pity** exciter la pitié de qn

5 *(in debate etc) (resolution)* proposer; **to m. that …** proposer que … + *sub*

6 *Com (sell)* écouler, vendre; **we must m. these goods quickly** nous devons vendre ces marchandises rapidement
▪ VI **1** *(stir)* bouger; *(change one's position)* se déplacer; **they won't m. on the question of compensation** ils ne fléchiront pas sur la question des compensations; **to m. to another seat** changer de place; **to m. in high society** fréquenter la haute société; **don't m.!** ne bougez pas!; **I'm stuck, I can't m.** je suis coincé, je ne peux pas bouger; **I can't get it to m.** je n'arrive pas à le/la faire bouger; **could you m. so that we can get in?** pourriez-vous vous pousser que nous puissions entrer?; **the way the dancers m.** la façon de se mouvoir *ou* de bouger des danseurs; **she moves like a model** elle marche comme un mannequin; **I saw the curtains m.** j'ai vu les rideaux bouger; **something moved in the bushes** quelque chose a bougé dans les buissons; *Fam* **come**

on, m.! *(hurry)* allez, magne-toi le train *ou* remue-toi!; **wait till the car stops moving** attends que la voiture soit arrêtée

2 *(of machine parts etc)* bouger; **this part is meant to m.** cette partie est censée bouger; **what makes it m.?** qu'est-ce qui le fait tourner/avancer/descendre/*etc*?; **to m. upwards** monter; **to m. downwards** descendre; **to m. freely** *(of part)* jouer librement; *(of dissident, prisoner)* se déplacer librement

3 *(progress, advance)* avancer; **the earth moves round the sun** la terre tourne autour du soleil; **it moves in an elliptical orbit** il/elle décrit une ellipse; **to m. towards a place** se diriger *ou* s'avancer vers un endroit; **the traffic was only just moving** les voitures avançaient à peine; **things are moving slowly** les choses avancent lentement; **that's really moving!** *(that's fast)* ça fonce!; *(referring to work)* ça avance!, ça progresse!; **it's time we were moving, we must be moving** il est temps de partir

4 *(act)* agir; **it is for him to m. first in the matter** c'est à lui d'agir le premier dans cette affaire

5 *(to new home, office etc)* déménager; **we have moved to new premises** nous avons déménagé dans de nouveaux locaux; **to m. to the country** aller s'installer à la campagne

6 *Com (sell)* se vendre, s'écouler; **this product's not moving** *(not selling)* ce produit ne se vend pas

7 *Chess etc* jouer

▸ **move about, move around** VI bouger, remuer; *(travel and move house)* bouger; **I heard someone moving about** j'ai entendu quelqu'un se déplacer; **he finds it difficult to m. about** il a du mal à se déplacer; **he moves around a lot** *(in job etc)* il est toujours en déplacement

VT SEP *(furniture etc)* déplacer, changer de place; **they keep moving her around from one department to another** ils n'arrêtent pas de la faire passer d'un service à l'autre

▸ **move along** VT SEP *(of police officer)* *(onlookers, beggars etc)* faire circuler

VI **1** *(to make room)* se déplacer, se pousser; **m. along and let the old lady sit down** poussez-vous un peu pour laisser la vieille dame s'asseoir

2 *(leave)* partir, s'en aller; **I ought to be moving along** il faut que je m'en aille; **the policeman told us to m. along** le policier nous a dit de circuler; **m. along (please)!** circulez, s'il vous plaît!

3 *(continue)* **moving along to my next question** pour passer à ma question suivante

▸ **move away** VT SEP *(something)* écarter, éloigner (**from** de)

VI **1** *(go away)* s'éloigner, s'écarter, s'en aller

2 *(go to new home etc)* déménager; **they've moved away from here** ils ont déménagé

▸ **move back** VT SEP **1** *(to more distant position)* *(people)* (faire) reculer; *(things)* mettre en retrait; **could you m. your car back?** pourriez-vous reculer?

2 *(to former position)* remettre en place

VI **1** *(retreat)* (se) reculer

2 *(to former position)* retourner, revenir

3 *(to former home etc)* retourner; **they have moved back to London** *(come)* ils sont revenus habiter à Londres; *(gone)* ils sont repartis habiter à Londres; **to m. back to one's old job** reprendre son ancien travail

▸ **move down** VT SEP **1** *(change position of)* *(something)* descendre; *Typ etc* **m. this section down** mettez cette section plus bas

2 *(demote)* rétrograder; **to m. sb down three places** rétrograder qn de trois places; *Sch* **to be moved down (a class)** descendre de classe

VI *(be demoted)* descendre; **the team**

moved down to the fourth division l'équipe est descendue en quatrième division

▸ **move forward** VT SEP *(object, date etc)* avancer; *(troops)* faire avancer

VI (s')avancer

▸ **move in** VT SEP **1** *(send)* *(troops)* envoyer; **troops were moved in by helicopter** les troupes ont été transportées par hélicoptère

2 *(install)* *(furniture)* installer

VI **1** *(take up residence)* emménager; **he has moved in with his girlfriend** il est allé s'installer chez sa petite amie

2 *(enter situation)* entrer en scène, faire son apparition; **the market changed when the multinationals moved in** le marché a changé quand les multinationales ont fait leur apparition

3 *(advance)* s'avancer; **troops moved in to quell the riots** les troupes sont intervenues pour réprimer les émeutes

▸ **move into** VT INSEP *(diversify into)* se reconvertir dans

▸ **move off** VI **1** *(go away)* s'éloigner, s'en aller, partir

2 *(start journey)* *(of train, army etc)* se mettre en marche; *(of car etc)* démarrer

▸ **move on** VT SEP *(crowd etc)* faire circuler

VI **1** *(go further on journey etc)* avancer, continuer son chemin; **can we m. on to the next item on the agenda?** pouvons-nous passer à la question suivante de l'ordre du jour?; **time's moving on** il se fait tard; **it's time we were moving on** il est temps que nous partions

2 *(make progress)* *(of science)* faire des progrès, évoluer; **women have moved on** les femmes ont évolué *ou* changé

▸ **move out** VT SEP *(remove)* *(something)* sortir; *(somebody)* faire sortir; **the troops will be moved out** les troupes se retireront; **people were moved out (of their homes) to make way for the new road** les gens ont dû quitter leur maison pour permettre la construction de la nouvelle route

VI **1** *(leave home etc)* déménager

2 *Mil (withdraw)* se retirer

▸ **move over** VI se ranger, se pousser; **m. over!** pousse-toi!; **they moved over to a market economy** ils sont passés à une économie de marché

▸ **move up** VT SEP **1** *(change position of)* *(object)* monter; *Typ etc* **m. this section up** tez cette section plus haut; **the regiment was moved up to the front** on a envoyé le régiment au front

2 *(promote)* promouvoir; **they've moved her up to be assistant manager** ils l'ont promue directrice-adjointe; *Sch* **to be moved up (a class)** passer dans la classe supérieure

VI **1** *(advance)* s'avancer, avancer

2 *(be promoted)* être promu; *Sch* passer dans la classe supérieure; *St Exch (of shares)* se relever; **shares moved up three points today** les actions ont gagné trois points aujourd'hui; **he has moved up in my estimation** il est monté dans mon estime

3 *(to make room)* se pousser; **m. up so I can sit down** pousse-toi (un peu) que je m'assoie

moveable ['muːvəb(ə)l] ADJ = **movable**

movement ['muːvmənt] N **1** *(change of place)* mouvement *m*; *(on stock exchange)* activité *f*; *(of vehicles, goods, capital)* mouvement, circulation *f*; *Mil etc* mouvement, manœuvre *f*; *(of prices etc)* mouvement; **there was a general m. towards the door** tout le monde s'est dirigé vers la porte; **to watch sb's movements** *(of police etc)* surveiller les faits et gestes *ou* les allées et venues de qn; *Fig* **there had been little m. in the negotiations** les négociations n'avaient pas beaucoup avancé; **free m. of labour** libre

circulation de la main-d'œuvre **2** *(motion)* *(of one's arm etc)* mouvement *m*, geste *m* **3** *(group, tendency)* *(political, literary, artistic etc)* mouvement *m* **4** *(mechanism of clock)* mouvement *m* **5** *Mus (of symphony etc)* mouvement *m* **6** *Physiol* **to have a (bowel) m.** aller à la selle

mover ['muːvər] N **1** *(in debate)* auteur *m* d'une motion, motionnaire *mf* **2** *Am (removal firm, person)* déménageur *m* **3** **he's a beautiful** *or* **lovely m.** *(footballer etc)* il a une démarche superbe; *(dancer)* il est superbe quand il danse **4** *Fam* **movers and shakers** les grands pontes *mpl*

movie ['muːvɪ] N *esp Am* film *m*; **the movies** *(cinema)* le cinéma; **to go to the movies** aller au cinéma; **she's in the movies** elle travaille dans le cinéma

▸▸ **m. actor** acteur *m* de cinéma; **m. actress** actrice *f* de cinéma; **m. archives** archives *fpl* cinématographiques; **m. buff** cinéphile *mf*; **m. camera** caméra *f*; **m. channel** chaîne *f* de cinéma; **m. clip** extrait *m* de film; **m. critic** critique *mf* de cinéma; **m. director** metteur *m* en scène; *Am* **m. house** (salle *f* de) cinéma *m*; **the m. industry** l'industrie *f* cinématographique *ou* du cinéma; **m. library** cinémathèque *f*; **m. premiere** première *f*; **m. producer** producteur, -trice de cinéma; **m. review** critique *f* cinématographique; **m. reviewer** critique *mf* de cinéma; **m. star** vedette *f* de cinéma; *Am* **m. theater** cinéma *m*

moviegoer ['muːvɪɡəʊər] N *esp Am* cinéphile *mf*, amateur *m* de cinéma

movie-maker N *esp Am* cinéaste *mf*

moving ['muːvɪŋ] ADJ **1** *(in motion)* en mouvement, mouvant; *(train, vehicle)* en marche; *(part etc)* mobile **2** *(force etc)* moteur, -trice; **the m. spirit** *(in a venture)* l'âme *f* **3** *(touching)* *(scene, story etc)* émouvant, touchant

N mouvement *m*; *(being moved)* déplacement *m*; *(from house etc)* déménagement *m*

▸▸ *Phys* **m. body** corps *m* en mouvement; **m. in** *(into house, premises)* emménagement *m*; **m. out** *(from house etc)* déménagement *m*; **m. pavement** trottoir *m* roulant; *Old-fashioned* **m. picture** film *m*; *Am* **m. sidewalk** trottoir roulant; **m. staircase** escalier *m* roulant, escalator *m*; *Mil* **m. target** cible *f* mobile; *Am* **m. van** camion *m* de déménagement

movingly ['muːvɪŋlɪ] ADV d'une manière émouvante *ou* touchante

mow [məʊ] VT & VI *(pt* **mowed** [məʊd], *pp* **mown** [məʊn])* **1** *(lawn)* tondre **2** *Agr (corn, field)* faucher

▸ **mow down** VT SEP *(slaughter)* faucher

mower ['məʊər] N **1** *(machine)*, *Agr* faucheuse *f*, **(lawn) m.** tondeuse *f* (à gazon) **2** *Agr (person)* faucheur, -euse

mowing ['məʊɪŋ] N **1** *(of lawn)* tonte *f* **2** *Agr (of hay etc)* fauchage *m*

mown PP *see* **mow**

Mozambican [məʊzæm'biːkən] N Mozambicain, -aine

ADJ mozambicain

Mozambique [məʊzæm'biːk] N Mozambique *m*

MP [em'piː] N **1** *Br Parl (abbr* **Member of Parliament**) député *m* **2** *Mil (abbr* **Military Police**) police *f* militaire; *(abbr* **Military Policeman**) membre *m* de la police militaire

MP3 [empiː'θriː] N *Comput (abbr* **MPEG1 Audio Layer**) (format *m*) MPEG *m*; **MP3 file** fichier *m* MP3; **MP3 player** lecteur *m* de MP3

MPC [empiː'siː] N *Br Fin (abbr* **monetary policy committee**) = comité *m* formé de quatre membres de la Banque d'Angleterre et de quatre économistes nommés par le gouvernement, dont l'un des rôles est de fixer les taux d'intérêt

MPEG ['empeg] N *Comput* (*abbr* **Moving Pictures Expert Group**) (*format m*) MPEG *m*

mpg [empi:'dʒi:] N (*abbr* **miles per gallon**) mil(l)es au gallon; **what sort of m. do you get?** combien faites-vous au cent?

mph [empi:'eɪtʃ] N (*abbr* **miles per hour**) mil(l)es à l'heure, ≃ kilomètres à l'heure

MPhil [em'fɪl] N (*abbr* **Master of Philosophy**) ≃ DEA *m*

MPV [empi:'vi:] N *Aut* (*abbr* **multi-purpose vehicle**) véhicule *m* multifonction, véhicule à usages multiples

Mr ['mɪstər] N (*form of address, not used without name*) **Mr Thomas** Monsieur Thomas; (*on envelope*) Monsieur ou M. Thomas; **Mr President** Monsieur le Président
▸▸*Fam* **Mr Big** le cerveau de l'affaire; *Fam* **Mr Right** l'homme *m* idéal

MRAM [em'ræm] N *Comput* (*abbr* **magnetic random access memory**) MRAM *f*

MRC [ema:'si:] N *Br* (*abbr* **Medical Research Council**) Comité *m* pour la recherche médicale

MRI [ema:'raɪ] N *Med* (*abbr* **magnetic resonance imaging**) IRM *f*

mrp [ema:'pi:] N *Com* (*abbr* **manufacturer's recommended price**) prix *m* conseillé par le fabricant

Mrs ['mɪsɪz] N (*form of address, not used without name*) **M. Long** Madame Long; (*on envelope*) Madame ou Mme Long

MS,[1] **ms,** *pl* **MSS, mss** (*abbr* **manuscript**) manuscrit *m*

MS[2] [em'es] N (*abbr* **multiple sclerosis**) sclérose *f* en plaques

Ms [mɪz] N (*form of address, not used without name*) **Ms Martin** (*unmarried*) Mademoiselle Martin; (*married*) Madame Martin; (*on envelope*) Madame ou Mme Martin

MSc [emes'si:] N (*abbr* **Master of Science**) (*degree*) maîtrise *f* de ou ès sciences; (*person*) titulaire *mf* d'une maîtrise

MS-DOS [emes'dɒs] N *Comput* (*abbr* **Microsoft Disk Operating System**) MS-DOS *m*

MSG [emes'dʒi:] N (*abbr* **monosodium glutamate**) glutamate *m* de sodium

MSP [emes'pi:] N (*abbr* **Member of the Scottish Parliament**) député *m* du parlement écossais

MST [emes'ti:] N *abbr* **Mountain Standard Time**

Mt (*abbr* **Mount**) Mt

MTBF [emti:bi:'ef] N *Comput* (*abbr* **mean time between failures**) moyenne *f* de temps entre deux pannes

MUCH [mʌtʃ]

ADJ	beaucoup de ▪ combien (de) ▪ tant de
ADV	beaucoup
PRON	beaucoup ▪ autant de

ADJ (*usu only with neg and interr*) beaucoup de; *Fml* **m. care** beaucoup de soin; *Iron* **m. good may it do you!** grand bien vous fasse!; **how m. money?** combien d'argent?; **too m. money** trop d'argent; **so m. money** tellement ou tant d'argent; **as m. money as** autant d'argent que
ADV beaucoup; **I don't like them m., I don't m. like them** je ne les aime pas beaucoup; **(very) m. better** beaucoup mieux; **m. worse** bien pire; **it doesn't matter m.** cela n'a pas beaucoup d'importance; **m. more/less pleasant** beaucoup plus/moins agréable; **m. the largest** de beaucoup le plus grand, le plus grand de beaucoup; **m. too small** beaucoup trop petit; **we are m. obliged to you for …** nous vous sommes très obligés de ou pour …; **thank you very m. (for …)** merci beau-

coup (de ou pour …); **it's (pretty or very) m. the same thing** c'est à peu près la même chose; **he's m. the same** (*of somebody ill*) son état n'a pas changé; **that's m. how I felt** c'est à peu près ce que j'ai ressenti, moi aussi; **m. to my astonishment** à mon grand étonnement; *Fam Iron* **he doesn't like beer, does he? – not m. he doesn't!** il n'aime pas la bière, non? – et comment, il aime ça! VOIR GRAMMAIRE A22–3
PRON **1** beaucoup; **m. remains to be done** il reste beaucoup à faire; **m. has happened while you have been away** il s'est passé bien des choses pendant votre absence; **there is not m. of it** il n'y en a pas beaucoup; **it's not worth m.** or *Fam* **not up to m.** cela ne vaut pas grand-chose; **to make m. of sth** accorder beaucoup d'importance à qch; **I'll say this m. for him** je dirai ceci en sa faveur; **there's not (all) that m.** il n'y en a pas tellement ou tant que ça; **I don't think m. of it** je n'aime pas beaucoup ça; **it wasn't m. of a surprise** ce n'était pas une grande surprise; **she isn't m. of a singer** comme chanteuse, elle n'est pas terrible; **it wasn't m. of a joke** ce n'était pas terrible comme plaisanterie
2 (*phrases*) **m. as I'd like to** (*I can't accept, be there etc*) bien que je le veuille; **m. as I'd like to, I can't come** je voudrais bien, mais je ne peux pas venir; **m. as I like him** quelle que soit mon affection pour lui; **m. as I try, I can't succeed** j'ai beau essayer, je n'y arrive pas; **the result was m. as I expected** le résultat correspondait bien à ce que j'attendais; **as m. autant**; **as m. again** encore autant; **twice as m.** deux fois autant; **I expected as m.** je m'y attendais; **I suspected** or **guessed** or **thought as m.** je m'en doutais; **as m. as possible** autant que possible; **quite as m. as …** tout autant que …; **not quite as m. as …** pas tout à fait autant que …; **it is as m. your fault as (it is) mine** c'est autant de votre faute que de la mienne; **it is as m. as he can do to read** c'est tout juste s'il sait lire; **it was as m. as we could do to stand upright** nous avions le plus grand mal à nous tenir debout; **he looked at me as m. as to say …** il me regarda avec l'air de (vouloir) dire …; **as m. as that?** (au)tant que cela?; **do you love her as m. as that?** vous l'aimez donc tant ou à ce point-là?; **he went away without so m. as saying goodbye** il est parti sans même dire au revoir; **I would not so m. as raise a finger to help him** je ne lèverais pas même le petit doigt pour l'aider; **so m. tant**, tellement; **he has drunk so m. that …** il a tellement bu que …; **so m. the better** tant mieux; **so m. so that …** au point que …, à tel point que …; **not so m. a …, more a …** pas vraiment un …, mais plutôt un …; **so m. for his friendship!** et voilà ce qu'il appelle l'amitié!; **so m. per cent** tant pour cent; **so m. a kilo** tant le kilo; **too m.** trop; **m. too m.** beaucoup trop; **£10 too m.** 10 livres de trop; **to cost too m.** coûter trop cher; **this is (really) too m.!** c'est vraiment trop fort!; *Fam* **that's a bit m.!** c'est un peu fort!; **you can't have too m. of a good thing** abondance de biens ne nuit pas

muchness ['mʌtʃnɪs] N *Fam* **they're much of a m.** (*of pictures, books, people etc*) ils se ressemblent beaucoup; (*of two candidates*) ils se valent; **it's (all) much of a m.** (*doesn't really matter*) ça revient au même

muck [mʌk] N **1** (*dung*) fumier *m* **2** (*dirt*) saleté *f*; (*from the streets*) saletés **3** *Br Fam* (*rubbish, unhealthy food, obscene book etc*) cochonnerie *f*, (*unappetizing food*) saloperie *f*, (*worthless objects*) camelote *f* **4** *Br Fam* (*mess*) **to make a m. of sth** saloper qch
▸▸*Agr* **m. spreader** épandeur *m*
▸ **muck about, muck around** VI, VT SEP *Br Fam* = **mess about, mess around**

▸ **muck in** VI *Br Fam* **to m. in with sb** (*share room*) crécher avec qn; (*join in*) partager le boulot avec qn; **everyone mucked in** (*helped out*) tout le monde s'y est mis
▸ **muck out** VT SEP (*stables etc*) nettoyer VI nettoyer l'écurie/les écuries/etc
▸ **muck up** VT SEP *Br Fam* **1** (*make dirty*) saloper **2** (*make a mess of*) ficher en l'air; (*job*) bousiller; (*plans*) flanquer par terre

mucker ['mʌkə(r)] N *Br Fam* **1** (*friend*) pote *m* **2** (*term of address*) vieux *m*; **alright, me old m.!** salut vieux!, salut mon pote!

muckheap ['mʌkhi:p] N tas *m* de fumier ou d'ordures

muckraker ['mʌkreɪkər] N *Fam* journaliste *mf* à l'affût des scandales, *Sl* fouille-merde *m inv*

muckraking ['mʌkreɪkɪŋ] N *Fam* révélation *f* de scandales

mucky ['mʌki] ADJ *Br Fam* sale; **m. books** (*obscene*) des livres cochons; **you're a m. pup!** que tu es sale!

mucous ['mju:kəs] ADJ muqueux
▸▸*Anat* **m. membrane** muqueuse *f*

mucus ['mju:kəs] N **1** *Physiol* mucus *m*, mucosité *f* **2** *Bot* mucosité *f*

mud [mʌd] N boue *f*, gadoue *f*, (*in swamp*) bourbe *f*; (*river*) **m.** vase *f*; **to get stuck** or **to sink in the m.** s'embourber; (*of ship*) s'envaser; *Fig* **to drag sb's name in the m.** traîner qn dans la boue; *Fig* **to fling** or **sling** or **throw m. at sb** couvrir qn de boue; *Fam* **his name is m.** il est mal vu; *Old-fashioned Fam* **here's m. in your eye!** à votre santé!, à la vôtre!; *Fam* **as clear as m.** clair comme du jus de boudin
▸▸*Med* **m. bath** bain *m* de boue; **m. hut** case *f* en pisé ou en terre; **m. pie** (*made of mud*) pâté *m* (de sable); (*cake*) = sorte de gâteau au chocolat; **m. wrestling** catch *m* dans la boue

mudbank ['mʌdbæŋk] N (*in river*) banc *m* de vase

muddle ['mʌd(ə)l] N confusion *f*, *Fam* embrouillamini *m*; **to be in a m.** (*of things*) être en désordre ou en pagaille ou en pagaïe; (*of person*) ne plus savoir où l'on en est; **to get into a m.** s'embrouiller (**about sth** au sujet de qch); **to make a m. of sth** faire qch de travers
VT **1** (*put in disorder*) (*story*) embrouiller, brouiller; (*matter, affair*) gâcher **2** (*bewilder*) (*person*) embrouiller; **to get muddled** s'embrouiller
▸ **muddle along** VI (*cope haphazardly*) faire son chemin ou se débrouiller tant bien que mal
▸ **muddle through** VI (*get through haphazardly*) se débrouiller ou *Fam* se dépatouiller ou s'en tirer tant bien que mal
VT INSEP **to m. through a crisis** traverser une crise tant bien que mal; **to m. through an exam** passer un examen tant bien que mal
▸ **muddle up** VT SEP **1** (*mix up*) mélanger; **I've muddled the dates up** j'ai mélangé les dates **2** (*bewilder*) (*somebody*) embrouiller

muddled ['mʌd(ə)ld] ADJ **1** (*objects*) en désordre, *Fam* en pagaille ou pagaïe **2** (*person, ideas*) confus, embrouillé

muddleheaded [mʌd(ə)l'hedɪd] ADJ (*person*) à l'esprit confus, brouillon, -onne; **m. ideas** idées confuses ou embrouillées

muddler ['mʌdlər] N brouillon, -onne, esprit *m* brouillon

muddy ['mʌdi] ADJ **1** (*path*) boueux, bourbeux; (*stream*) bourbeux, vaseux; (*jacket etc*) crotté, couvert de boue; **to taste m.** avoir un goût de vase **2** (*liquid, wine etc*) trouble; (*colour*) sale; (*complexion*) brouillé, terreux; **m. brown** couleur (de) terre
VT **1** (*one's clothes etc*) crotter **2** (*water*) trou-

bler; *Fig* **to m. the waters** semer la confusion

mudflap ['mʌdflæp] N pare-boue *m inv*

mudflat ['mʌdflæt] N banc *m* de boue

mudguard ['mʌdgɑːd] N *Br* garde-boue *m inv*

mudlark ['mʌdlɑːk] N *Old-fashioned Fam* gamin, -ine des rues

mudpack ['mʌdpæk] N masque *m* à l'argile

mudskipper ['mʌdskɪpər] N *(fish)* gobie *m* des marais

mudslinger ['mʌdslɪŋər] N *Fam* calomniateur, -trice

mudslinging ['mʌdslɪŋɪŋ] *Fam* N calomnies *fpl*
ADJ diffamatoire

mud-stained ADJ taché de boue

muesli ['mjuːzlɪ] N muesli *m*

muezzin [muːˈezɪn] N muezzin *m*

muff¹ [mʌf] VT *Br Fam (bungle)* rater, louper; *Golf etc (stroke)* manquer, rater

muff² N 1 *(for hands)* manchon *m* 2 *Vulg (female sex organs)* touffe *f*, chatte *f*; **m.-diving** descente *f* au barbu

muffin ['mʌfɪn] N *Culin* muffin *m*

muffle ['mʌf(ə)l] VT 1 *(deaden sound of) (oars, bell etc)* assourdir, étouffer; *Mus (drum)* assourdir 2 *(wrap)* emmitoufler; **to m. oneself up** s'emmitoufler

muffled ['mʌf(ə)ld] ADJ 1 *(sound, footstep)* étouffé, assourdi; *(oar)* assourdi; *(voice)* étouffé; *Mus* **m. drums** tambours voilés 2 *(wrapped)* **m. (up)** emmitouflé

muffler ['mʌflər] N 1 *(scarf)* cache-nez *m inv*, cache-col *m*, *pl* cache-col(s) 2 *Am Aut* silencieux *m*; *Tech* **(exhaust) m.** gueule-de-loup *f*, *pl* gueules-de-loup 3 *Mus (on piano)* étouffoir *m*

Mufti ['mʌftɪ] N *Rel* mufti *m*, muphti *m*

mufti ['mʌftɪ] N *Mil etc Sl* tenue *f* civile; **in m.** en civil

mug [mʌg] N 1 *(for beer)* chope *f*, pot *m*; *(for tea etc)* grande tasse *f*, *(made of metal)* quart *m* 2 *Fam (face)* gueule *f*, trombine *f*, bouille *f*, *esp Am (photo of criminal)* photo *f* (d'un criminel); **ugly m.** sale gueule, gueule d'empeigne; **shut your (ugly) m.!** ferme ta sale gueule! 3 *Br Fam (gullible person)* poire *f*, andouille *f*; **it's a m.'s game** c'est bon pour les poires; **the lottery's a m.'s game** le loto, c'est un attrape-couillons
VT *Fam (attack) (person)* attaquer, agresser
VI faire des grimaces
▶ *esp Am* **m. shot** photo *(d'un criminel)*
▶ **mug up** *Br Sch Fam* VI *(study, revise)* plancher, bûcher; **to m. up on sth** plancher sur qch
VT SEP *(subject)* potasser

mugful ['mʌgfʊl] N *(of beer)* chope *f*, pot *m*; *(of coffee, tea)* grande tasse *f*

mugger ['mʌgər] N *Fam* agresseur *m*

mugging ['mʌgɪŋ] N *Fam* agression *f*

muggins ['mʌgɪnz] N *Br Fam* idiot, -ote, nouille *f*, *(oneself)* mézigue, ma pomme; **I suppose m. will have to do it!** je suppose que c'est ma pomme qui va s'y coller!; **m. (here) paid the bill as usual** comme d'habitude c'est mézigue qui a payé l'addition

muggy ['mʌgɪ] ADJ *(weather)* lourd

mugwump ['mʌgwʌmp] N *Am Pol Fam (independent)* non-inscrit, -ite; *(neutral)* neutre *mf*

mulatto [mjuːˈlætəʊ] *Old-fashioned* ADJ mulâtre
N mulâtre *mf*, mulâtresse *f*

mulberry ['mʌlbərɪ] N *(fruit)* mûre *f*, **m. (bush or tree)** mûrier *m*

mulch [mʌltʃ] N paillis *m*
VT pailler

mulct [mʌlkt] VT 1 *Law* frapper d'une amende 2 *(cheat)* **to m. sb of sth** extorquer qch à qn

mule¹ [mjuːl] N 1 *(he)* m. mulet *m*; *(she)* m., **m. mare** mule *f*; **as stubborn as a m.** têtu comme une mule 2 *Fam (stubborn person)* tête *f* de mule 3 *Sl (drug smuggler)* mule *f* 4 *Tex* renvideur *m*
▶ ▶ **m. driver** muletier *m*; *Tex* **m. jenny** renvideur; **m. path** chemin *m* ou sentier *m* muletier; *Am Fam* **m. skinner** muletier; **m. train** caravane *f* de mules

mule² N *(slipper)* mule *f*

muleteer [mjuːlɪˈtɪər] N muletier *m*

mulish ['mjuːlɪʃ] ADJ entêté, têtu (comme une mule)

mulishness ['mjuːlɪʃnɪs] N entêtement *m*

mull [mʌl] VT *(wine, beer)* chauffer avec des épices
▶ **mull over** VT SEP *(consider) (idea)* ruminer, retourner dans sa tête; **I've been mulling it over** j'y ai réfléchi

mulled [mʌld] ADJ
▶ ▶ **m. wine** vin *m* chaud épicé

mullered ['mʊləd] ADJ *Br Fam (drunk)* bourré, pété

mullet ['mʌlɪt] N 1 *(fish)* **grey m.** muge *m* *(capiton)*, mulet *m*; **red m.** rouget(-barbet) *m* 2 *Fam (hairstyle)* = coupe *f* de cheveux longue sur la nuque, courte sur les côtés et en brosse longue sur le dessus

mulligatawny [mʌlɪgəˈtɔːnɪ] N **m. (soup)** potage *m* au curry

mullion ['mʌlɪən] N *Archit* meneau *m* *(vertical)*

mullioned ['mʌlɪənd] ADJ *Archit (window)* à meneau(x)

multi- ['mʌltɪ] PREF multi-

multiaccess [mʌltɪˈækses] ADJ *Comput* à accès multiple

multiangle ['mʌltɪæŋgəl] ADJ multiangle

multibrand ['mʌltɪbrænd] N *Mktg* marque *f* multiple, multimarque *f*
▶ ▶ **m. store** point *m* de vente multimarque

multicast ['mʌltɪkɑːst] N *Comput* multi-diffusion *f*

multi-centre holiday N vacances *fpl* en circuit

multichannel [mʌltɪˈtʃæn(ə)l] ADJ multicanal, -aux

multicoloured ['mʌltɪkʌləd] ADJ multicolore

multicriterion sorting [mʌltɪkraɪˈtɪərɪən] N *Comput* classement *m* multicritère

multicultural [mʌltɪˈkʌltʃər(ə)l] ADJ multiculturel

multicurrency [mʌltɪˈkʌrənsɪ] ADJ multidevise

multidirectional [mʌltɪdɪˈrekʃ(ə)l] ADJ multidirectionnel

multifaceted [mʌltɪˈfæsɪtɪd] ADJ qui a plusieurs facettes

multifarious [mʌltɪˈfeərɪəs] ADJ *Fml* varié, divers

multiform ['mʌltɪfɔːm] ADJ multiforme

multi-fuel engine N moteur *m* polycarburant

multi-functional ADJ *Comput* multifonction(s)
▶ ▶ **m. key** touche *f* multifonction(s); **m. keyboard** clavier *m* multifonction(s)

multi-function display N affichage *m* multifonction(s)

multi-grade oil N huile *f* multigrade

multilateral [mʌltɪˈlæt(ə)rəl] ADJ multilatéral, -aux; **m. diplomacy** diplomatie *f* multilatérale

multilevel [mʌltɪˈlev(ə)l] ADJ *Comput* multiniveaux
▶ ▶ *Mktg* **m. marketing** marketing *m* de réseau, vente *f* par réseau coopté

multilingual [mʌltɪˈlɪŋgwəl] ADJ *(person)* polyglotte; *(country)* plurilingue

multimedia [mʌltɪˈmiːdɪə] ADJ multimédia
N multimédia *m*
▶ ▶ **m. computer** ordinateur *m* multimédia; **m. group** groupe *m* multimédia

multimillionaire [mʌltɪmɪlɪəˈneər] ADJ, N multimillionnaire *mf*

multimodal operator [mʌltɪˈməʊd(ə)l] N opérateur *m* de transport multimodal, OTM *m*

multinational [mʌltɪˈnæʃən(ə)l] ADJ multinational, -aux
N multinationale *f*
▶ ▶ **m. company** entreprise *f* multinationale; **m. corporation** société *f* multinationale; **m. marketing** marketing *m* multinational

multi-ownership N multipropriété *f*

multi-part stationery N papier *m* multiple

multiparty [mʌltɪˈpɑːtɪ] ADJ *Pol (state)* pluripartite

multi-plate clutch N embrayage *m* à disques multiples

multiple ['mʌltɪp(ə)l] ADJ multiple; *Elec* **batteries in m.** accumulateurs *mpl* en parallèle
N 1 *Math* multiple *m*; **lowest** or **least common m.** plus petit commun multiple 2 *Tel* multiplage *m* 3 *Com (chain store)* magasin *m* à succursales (multiples)
▶ ▶ *Tel* **m. circuit** accumulateurs *mpl* en parallèle; *Cin* **m. image** image *f* multiple; **m. injuries** blessures *fpl* multiples; **m. occupancy** *(by tenants)* colocation *f*, *(by owners)* copropriété *f*; **m. ownership** multipropriété *f*, *Psy* **m. personality** personnalité *f* multiple; *Elec*, *Radio* **m. reception** réception *f* multiple; *Med* **m. sclerosis** sclérose *f* en plaques; **m. store** magasin *m* à succursales (multiples); *Tel* **m. switchboard** multiple *m* téléphonique)

multiple-choice ADJ *(question, exam)* à choix multiple

multiplex ['mʌltɪpleks] N 1 *(cinema)* complexe *m* multisalles 2 *Radio, Tel, TV* multiplex *m*
VT multiplexer
▶ ▶ **m. broadcast** transmission *f* en multiplex; **m. cinema** complexe multisalles

multiplexer ['mʌltɪpleksər] N *Radio, Tel, TV* multiplexeur *m*

multiplexing ['mʌltɪpleksɪŋ] N *Radio, Tel, TV* multiplexage *m*

multiplication [mʌltɪplɪˈkeɪʃən] N *Math etc* multiplication *f* VOIR GRAMMAIRE A77; B59
▶ ▶ **m. table** table *f* de multiplication

multiplicity [mʌltɪˈplɪsɪtɪ] N multiplicité *f*

multiplier ['mʌltɪplaɪər] N *Math, Comput, Elec* multiplicateur *m*

multiply ['mʌltɪplaɪ] VT *Math, Fig* multiplier; **to m. 2 by 6** multiplier 2 par 6
VI 1 *(of species, difficulties etc)* se multiplier 2 *Math* multiplier, faire une/des multiplication(s)

multi-point fuel-injected engine N moteur *m* à injection multipoint

multiprocessing ['mʌltɪprəʊsesɪŋ] N *Comput* multitraitement *m*

multiprocessor [mʌltɪˈprəʊsesər] N *Comput* multiprocesseur *m*

multipurpose [mʌltɪˈpɜːpəs] ADJ *(tool, vehicle)* à usages multiples, polyvalent

multiracial [mʌltɪˈreɪʃəl] ADJ multiracial, -aux

multiscan monitor [ˈmʌltɪskæn] N moniteur m à balayage multiple

multiscreen [ˈmʌltɪskriːn] N **1** *(cinema)* complexe m multisalles, cinéma m multisalle **2** *TV* écran-mosaïque m, pl écrans-mosaïques, multi-écran m, pl multi-écrans
▸▸*TV* **m. channel** canal m mosaïque; **m. cinema** complexe multisalles, cinéma multisalle

multisector [ˈmʌltɪsektər] ADJ multisectoriel
▸▸**m. journey** voyage m multi-secteur; **m. ticketing** délivrance f de billets multisecteurs

multi-spreadsheet N *Comput* multifeuille f

multistage [ˈmʌltɪsteɪdʒ] ADJ *Elec, Tech (amplifier, compressor)* à plusieurs étages
▸▸*Aut* **m. converter** convertisseur m multiétagé; *Astronaut* **m. rocket** fusée f composite à étages multiples

multi-station ADJ *Comput* multipostes

multistorey, *Am* **multistory** [mʌltɪˈstɔːrɪ] ADJ *(building)* à plusieurs étages
N *(car park)* parc m de stationnement *ou* parking m à plusieurs niveaux
▸▸**m. car park** parc de stationnement *ou* parking à plusieurs niveaux

multisyllabic [mʌltɪsɪˈlæbɪk] ADJ polysyllabique

multi-talented ADJ aux talents multiples

multitasking [mʌltɪˈtɑːskɪŋ] N **1** = capacité f à mener plusieurs tâches de front **2** *Comput* multitâche m

multitrack [mʌltɪˈtræk] ADJ *(recording)* multipiste

multitracking [mʌltɪˈtrækɪŋ] N *(in recording)* enregistrement m multipiste

multitude [ˈmʌltɪtjuːd] N **1** *(large number) (of reasons etc)* multitude f, multiplicité f, *Fig* **to cover** *or* **hide a m. of sins** *(of carpet, woodwork etc)* ça cache des horreurs invraisemblables; *esp Hum (of job title, definition)* ça englobe des tas de choses **2** *Fml, Lit (crowd)* multitude f, foule f

multitudinous [mʌltɪˈtjuːdɪnəs] ADJ *Fml* nombreux, innombrable

multi-user ADJ *Comput* pour utilisateurs multiples
▸▸**m. software** logiciel m multi-utilisateur; **m. system** système m multi-utilisateur

multi-valve ADJ multisoupape

multivision [ˈmʌltɪvɪʒən] N multivision f

multivitamin [ˈmʌltɪvɪtəmɪn, *Am* ˈmʌltɪvaɪtəmɪn] N multivitamine f

mum [mʌm] N *Br Fam (mother)* maman f

mum N *Fam* **m.'s the word!** motus (et bouche cousue)!
ADJ **to keep m.** ne pas souffler mot (**about sth** de qch)

mumble [ˈmʌmb(ə)l] N marmonnement m, marmottement m; **to say in a m.** dire en marmonnant
VT marmonner, marmotter; **he mumbled a few words** il a marmonné quelques mots
VI marmonner, parler entre ses dents *ou* dans sa barbe, manger ses mots

mumbo jumbo [ˈmʌmbəʊdʒʌmbəʊ] N *Fam (nonsense)* âneries fpl, *(words etc)* charabia m; *(ritual phrases etc)* bla-bla m; **astrology is just a load of m.** l'astrologie, c'est du pipeau

mummer [ˈmʌmər] N *Theat* mime mf

mummery [ˈmʌmərɪ] N *Theat* momerie f

mummification [mʌmɪfɪˈkeɪʃən] N momification f

mummify [ˈmʌmɪfaɪ] VT momifier
VI se momifier

mummy [ˈmʌmɪ] N *(embalmed body)* momie f

mummy N *Br Fam (mother)* maman f, *Pej* **m.'s boy** fils m à maman

mumps [mʌmps] NPL *(usu with sing verb) Med* oreillons mpl; **to have m.** avoir les oreillons

munch [mʌntʃ] VT mâcher, mâchonner
▸ **munch at** VT INSEP mastiquer
▸ **munch away** VI mastiquer; **he was munching away at an apple** il mastiquait (bruyamment) une pomme
▸ **munch on** VT INSEP = munch at
▸ **munch out** VI *Am Fam* se goinfrer, s'empiffrer

Munchausen [ˈmʌntʃaʊzən] N *Med*
▸▸**M. by proxy** syndrome m de Münchhausen par procuration; **M. Syndrome** syndrome de Münchhausen

munchies [ˈmʌntʃɪz] NPL *Fam (snacks)* petites choses fpl à grignoter; **to have the m., to have an attack of the m.** *(desire to eat)* avoir la fringale

mundane [mʌnˈdeɪn] ADJ banal, -als, ordinaire

Note that the French adjective **mondain** is a false friend and is never a translation for the English word **mundane**. It refers to people or events in high society.

municipal [mjuːˈnɪsɪp(ə)l] ADJ municipal, -aux
▸▸*Am Fin* **m. bond** obligation f de collectivité locale; **m. buildings** ≃ mairie f, *(in large town)* ≃ hôtel m de ville; *Can, Austr* **m. district** ≃ municipalité f

municipality [mjuːnɪsɪˈpælɪtɪ] N municipalité f

munificence [mjuːˈnɪfɪsəns] N munificence f

munificent [mjuːˈnɪfɪsənt] ADJ munificent, généreux

munitions [mjuːˈnɪʃənz] NPL munitions fpl
▸▸**m. dump** dépôt m de munitions; **m. factory** fabrique f de munitions; **m. worker** = personne f qui travaille dans une usine de munitions

muppet [ˈmʌpɪt] N *Br Fam* andouille f

mural [ˈmjʊərəl] *Art* ADJ mural, -aux; **m. paintings** peintures fpl murales
N peinture f murale

murder [ˈmɜːdər] N meurtre m; *Law* homicide m volontaire; *Law* premeditated m., *Am* **m. in the first degree** assassinat m; **to commit (a) m.** commettre un meurtre/assassinat; **the m. weapon** l'arme f du crime; *Fig* **it's (sheer** *or* **downright) m. in the rush hour** c'est (absolument) cauchemardesque *ou* infernal aux heures de pointe; **it's m. trying to park in the town centre** c'est cauchemardesque *ou* infernal d'essayer de se garer dans le centre-ville; *Fig* **he gets away with m.** il peut tout se permettre, personne ne lui dit quoi que ce soit; **their kids get away with m.** leurs gosses font absolument tout ce qu'ils veulent
VT **1** *(kill)* assassiner; *Fig Fam* **I'll m. you (for that)!** je vais te tuer! **2** *Fig Fam (destroy) (song, tune etc)* massacrer, saboter **3** *Fig Fam (defeat heavily)* battre à plates coutures **4** *Br Fig Fam (drink, eat)* **I could m. a beer/pizza** je me taperais bien une bière/une pizza
VI commettre un meurtre
▸▸**m. case** affaire f de meurtre; **m. trial** procès m pour meurtre; **m. weapon** arme f du crime

murderer [ˈmɜːdərər] N meurtrier m, assassin m

murderess [ˈmɜːdəres] N meurtrière f

murderous [ˈmɜːdərəs] ADJ meurtrier, assassin; **with m. intent** dans une intention homicide; **a m.-looking knife** un couteau à l'apparence particulièrement menaçante; **to give sb a m. look** lancer un regard meurtrier à qn

murk [mɜːk] N obscurité f, ténèbres fpl

murky [ˈmɜːkɪ] ADJ obscur, ténébreux; *(sky)* brouillé; *(details)* sordide; **m. past** passé m obscur *ou* ténébreux

murmur [ˈmɜːmər] N **1** *(of voices, waves)* murmure m; *Med* **heart m.** souffle m (au cœur) **2** *(of approval, discontent etc)* murmure m; **without a m.** *(to do something)* sans murmurer, sans broncher; **in a m.** à voix basse
VI murmurer, susurrer; *(complain)* murmurer (**against** contre)
VT *(something)* murmurer, dire à voix basse

murmuring [ˈmɜːmərɪŋ] N murmure m; **murmurings** *(complaints)* murmures (**against** contre)

Murphy [ˈmɜːfɪ] N
▸▸*Am* **M. bed** lit m escamotable; *Fam* **M.'s Law** loi f de l'emmerdement maximum

muscatel [mʌskəˈtel] N muscat m

muscle [ˈmʌs(ə)l] N **1** *Anat* muscle m; **she didn't move a m.** elle n'a pas bronché; **he has plenty of m.** il est bien musclé **2** *Fig (political, financial)* pouvoir m; **it would give our campaign more m.** cela donnerait plus de force à notre campagne
▸▸**m. fibre** fibres fpl musculaires; *Med* **m. strain** élongation f
▸ **muscle in** VI *Fam (force one's way in)* s'immiscer, s'imposer (**on sth** dans qch); **a lot of big companies are muscling in** de nombreuses grosses sociétés arrivent en force; **to m. in on sb's territory** marcher sur les plates-bandes de qn; **we don't want them muscling in** nous ne voulons pas qu'ils marchent sur nos plates-bandes

musclebound [ˈmʌs(ə)lbaʊnd] ADJ très musclé

muscleman, pl **musclemen** [ˈmʌs(ə)lmæn, -men] N *(strongman)* Monsieur m Muscle

muscovado (sugar) [mʌskəˈvɑːdəʊ] N cassonade f

Muscovite [ˈmʌskəvaɪt] ADJ moscovite
N Moscovite mf

muscular [ˈmʌskjʊlər] ADJ **1** *Anat (system, tissue, action)* musculaire **2** *(man)* musclé
▸▸*Med* **m. dystrophy** myopathie f

musculature [ˈmʌskjʊlətʃər] N *Anat* musculature f

Muse [mjuːz] N **1** *Myth* Muse f; **the (nine) Muses** les Muses **2** *(of poet)* **the m.** les muses fpl

muse [mjuːz] VI songer, rêver
VT **that's queer, he mused** voilà qui est bien étrange, songea- t-il
▸ **muse on** VT INSEP songer à

museum [mjuːˈzɪəm] N musée m
▸▸**m. piece** pièce f de musée; *Fig Hum* **his car's a m. piece** sa voiture est une pièce de musée

mush [mʌʃ] N **1** *Fam (pulp)* bouillie f, purée f **2** *esp Am Culin* bouillie f de farine de maïs **3** *Fam (sentimentality)* sentimentalité f (à l'eau de rose)

mushroom [ˈmʌʃrʊm] N **1** *(fungus)* champignon m; **cultivated** *or* **button mushrooms** champignons de couche *ou* de Paris; **m. soup** potage m aux champignons **2** *Sewing* boule f à repriser
VI **1** *(gather mushrooms)* faire la cueillette des champignons; **to go mushrooming** aller aux champignons **2** *(grow rapidly)* pousser comme un champignon/des champignons; *(proliferate)* se multiplier, proliférer; **profits/costs have mushroomed in the past year** les profits/coûts ont considérablement augmenté durant l'année passée
▸▸**m. cloud** champignon m atomique; **m.**

farm champignonnière f; **m. grower** champignonniste mf; **m. town** ville f champignon

mushrooming ['mʌʃrʊmɪŋ] N 1 (gathering of mushrooms) cueillette f des champignons 2 (rapid growth) croissance f rapide; (proliferation) multiplication f rapide, prolifération f

mushy ['mʌʃɪ] ADJ 1 (food etc) en bouillie; (ground etc) détrempé; (pear etc) blet, f blette 2 Fam (sentimental) sentimental, -aux, à l'eau de rose, à la guimauve; **m. sentimentality** sentimentalité f à l'eau de rose ou à la guimauve
▸▸ **m. peas** purée f de petits pois

music ['mjuːzɪk] N musique f; **to set words to m.** mettre des paroles en musique; (sheet) **m.** partition f; **I can't play without m.** je ne peux pas jouer sans partition; Fig **those words were m. to his ears** il était ravi d'entendre ces mots, ces mots le remplirent d'aise
▸▸ **m. box** boîte f à musique; **m. case** portemusique m inv; Old-fashioned **m. centre** chaîne f (midi); TV **m. channel** chaîne musicale; **m. critic** critique m musical; esp Br **m. hall** music-hall m, pl music-halls; **m. lover** mélomane mf; **m. paper** papier m à musique; **m. piracy** piratage m musical; **m. press** presse f musicale; **m. publishing** édition f musicale; **m. stand** pupitre m (à musique); **m. station** station f musicale; **m. video** clip m (vidéo)

musical ['mjuːzɪk(ə)l] ADJ 1 musical, -aux; **to be m.** (of person) être (bon) musicien/(bonne) musicienne 2 (sound, voice) harmonieux, mélodieux
N Cin, Theat comédie f musicale
▸▸ Br **m. box** boîte f à musique; **m. chairs** chaises fpl musicales; also Fig **to play m. chairs** jouer aux chaises musicales; **m. comedy** comédie f musicale, musical m; **m. evening** soirée f musicale; **m. instrument** instrument m de musique

musician [mjuːˈzɪʃən] N musicien, -ienne

musicianship [mjuːˈzɪʃənʃɪp] N qualités fpl de musicien/musicienne

musicologist [mjuːzɪˈkɒlədʒɪst] N musicologue mf

musicology [mjuːzɪˈkɒlədʒɪ] N musicologie f

musing ['mjuːzɪŋ] ADJ songeur, pensif, rêveur
N **musings** rêverie(s) f(pl)

musk [mʌsk] N (substance, smell, plant) musc m
▸▸ Zool **m. cat** civette f; Zool **m. deer** portemusc m, pl porte-muscs; Zool **m. ox** bœuf m musqué, ovibos m; **m. plant** musc; Bot **m. rose** (flower) rose f musquée; (bush) rosier m musqué

musket ['mʌskɪt] N Mil, Hist mousquet m

musketeer [mʌskɪˈtɪər] N Mil, Hist mousquetaire m; **the Three Musketeers** Les Trois Mousquetaires

musketry ['mʌskɪtrɪ] N Mil tir m au fusil

muskrat ['mʌskræt] N 1 (North American) rat m musqué, ondatra m 2 (European) desman m musqué

musky ['mʌskɪ] ADJ musqué, de musc

Muslim ['mʌzlɪm] ADJ, N = Moslem

muslin ['mʌzlɪn] N Tex mousseline f, Am calicot m

muso ['mjuːzəʊ] N Br Fam (musician) musico m

musquash ['mʌskwɒʃ] N 1 (animal) rat m musqué, ondatra m 2 (fur) rat m musqué

muss [mʌs] VT Am Fam = **muss up**
▸ **muss up** VT SEP Am Fam (hair) déranger; (dress) froisser, chiffonner

mussel ['mʌs(ə)l] N moule f; **m. bank** or **bed** banc m de moules; (man-made) moulière f

---

MUST¹ [mʌst] N Fam 1 (necessity) nécessité f, chose f indispensable; **the ability to speak Russian is a m.** il est indispensable de savoir parler russe, une bonne connaissance du russe est un must; **sunglasses are a m.** les lunettes de soleil sont indispensables
2 (thing not to be missed, that must be done) chose f à ne pas manquer/à faire à tout prix; **this film's a m.** c'est un film à ne pas manquer

MODAL AUX V INV VOIR GRAMMAIRE A60; B39
(must not is often contracted into mustn't) 1 (expressing obligation) **you m. be ready at four o'clock** vous devez ou devrez être prêt à quatre heures, il faut ou faudra que vous soyez prêt à quatre heures; **you m. hurry up** il faut vous dépêcher; **you mustn't tell anyone** vous ne devez le dire à personne, il ne faut le dire à personne; **you mustn't touch it!** il ne faut pas y toucher!; **we mustn't be late** il ne faut pas que nous soyons en retard; **they mustn't find out** il ne faut pas qu'ils le sachent; **plant that m. have continual attention** plante qui demande des soins continuels; **I simply m. see him** il faut absolument que je le voie; **he is stupid, I m. say** il est stupide, je dois l'avouer; **I m. say I thought it was rather good** je dois dire que c'était très bien; Iron **very clever, I m. say!** je dois dire que c'est très astucieux!; **if you m. know** si c'est vraiment nécessaire; **m. you be so silly?** qu'est-ce que tu peux être bête!; **why m. you always be so unhelpful?** pourquoi faut-il toujours que tu sois si peu serviable?; **if you m. drink so much, what do you expect?** si tu t'entêtes à boire autant, il ne faut pas t'étonner!
2 (suggesting, inviting) **you m. come and visit us** il faut que vous veniez nous voir; **we m. go out for a drink** il faut que nous allions boire un verre
3 (expressing probability) **you m. be hungry after your walk** vous devez avoir faim après votre promenade; **it m. be interesting working there** ça doit être intéressant de travailler là; **you m. be joking** tu plaisantes!; Fam **she mustn't be very happy** elle ne doit pas être très heureuse; **I m. have made a mistake** j'ai dû me tromper; **she m. have been talking about somebody else** elle devait parler de quelqu'un d'autre; **if he says so it m. be true** s'il le dit c'est que c'est vrai; **was it her?** – **it m. have been** est-ce que c'était elle? – oui, je pense; **I saw that he m. have suspected something** j'ai bien vu qu'il avait dû se douter de quelque chose

must² N (in winemaking) moût m

must³ N (mould) moisi m, moisissure f

mustache ['mʌstæʃ] N Am = **moustache**

mustang ['mʌstæŋ] N (horse) mustang m

mustard ['mʌstəd] N Bot, Culin moutarde f; **French m.** ≃ moutarde de Dijon; Am Fig Sl **to cut the m.** se montrer à la hauteur
▸▸ **m. bath** bain m sinapisé; **m. and cress** moutarde blanche et cresson m alénois; **m. gas** gaz m moutarde, ypérite f; **m. plaster** sinapisme m; **m. pot** moutardier m, pot m à moutarde; **m. powder** farine f de moutarde; **m. seed** graine f de moutarde

muster ['mʌstər] N (action of gathering) rassemblement m; (meeting) assemblée f, réunion f; (roll call), Naut etc appel m; Mil contrôles mpl; Fig **to pass m.** passer, être passable, être acceptable
VT 1 (supporters, funds) rassembler; **society that musters a hundred members** association qui compte cent membres; **she mustered all her strength** elle a rassemblé toutes ses forces; **to m. one's courage** rassembler son courage, prendre son courage à deux mains; **we need all the help we can m.** nous avons besoin de toute l'aide que

nous pouvons trouver 2 Naut (men) faire l'appel de; (crew) assembler
VI s'assembler, se rassembler
▸▸ **m. roll** feuille f d'appel
▸ **muster up** VT SEP = **muster** VT 1

musty ['mʌstɪ] ADJ (taste, smell) de moisi; (books, room) qui sent le moisi; **to smell m.** sentir le moisi; (of room etc) sentir le renfermé

mutability [mjuːtəˈbɪlɪtɪ] N mutabilité f

mutable ['mjuːtəb(ə)l] ADJ 1 variable, mutable 2 Ling sujet à mutation

mutant ['mjuːtənt] ADJ, N mutant m

mutate [mjuːˈteɪt] VI subir une mutation; **to m. into sth** se transformer en qch
VT faire subir une mutation à

mutation [mjuːˈteɪʃən] N altération f, changement m; Biol mutation f; **m. of type** métatypie f

mute [mjuːt] ADJ 1 (person, appeal etc) muet, -ette; **she stood m. with wonder** elle restait muette d'étonnement 2 Ling muet, -ette; (consonant) sourd
N 1 (dumb person) muet, -ette 2 Mus sourdine f
VT 1 (muffle) amortir, étouffer, assourdir 2 Mus mettre une sourdine à, assourdir

muted ['mjuːtɪd] ADJ (sound, voice etc) assourdi, sourd; (colour) sourd; (protest, criticism etc) voilé; Mus (trumpet etc) en sourdine; **to discuss in m. tones** discuter à voix basse

mutely ['mjuːtlɪ] ADV silencieusement, en silence

mutilate ['mjuːtɪleɪt] VT (person) mutiler, estropier; (statue, play) mutiler; Fig (passage, quotation) tronquer

mutilation [mjuːtɪˈleɪʃən] N mutilation f

mutineer [mjuːtɪˈnɪər] N mutiné m, mutin m

mutinous ['mjuːtɪnəs] ADJ rebelle, mutiné, mutin; (crew) mutiné, insurgé

mutiny ['mjuːtɪnɪ] N révolte f, mutinerie f
VI se révolter, se mutiner (**against** contre)

mutism ['mjuːtɪz(ə)m] N mutisme m

mutt [mʌt] N Fam 1 (dog) clebs m, clébard m 2 (idiot) idiot, -ote, andouille f; **poor m.!** pauvre mec!

mutter ['mʌtər] N murmure m; **a m. of discontent** un murmure de mécontentement
VT marmonner, marmotter; (say unclearly) dire dans sa barbe; **a muttered protest** un marmottement de protestation; **he muttered something to himself** (angrily) il a murmuré quelque chose entre ses dents
VI marmonner, marmotter; (speak unclearly) parler dans sa barbe; (complain) murmurer

muttering ['mʌtərɪŋ] N marmottement m, grommellement m; **mutterings** (complaints) murmures mpl de mécontentement

mutton ['mʌt(ə)n] N Culin mouton m; **leg of m.** gigot m; **m. chop** or **cutlet** côtelette f de mouton; Fam **m.-chop whiskers** favoris mpl en côtelette; Fig **m. dressed as lamb** = femme f qui essaie de faire plus jeune que son âge

muttonchops ['mʌt(ə)ntʃɒps] NPL (whiskers) favoris mpl en côtelette

muttonhead ['mʌt(ə)nhed] N Fam andouille f, cornichon m

mutual ['mjuːtʃʊəl] ADJ 1 (reciprocal) (feelings etc) mutuel, réciproque; Elec (attraction) mutuel; **the feeling is m.** c'est réciproque 2 (shared) commun; **a m. friend** un ami commun
▸▸ Fin **m. benefit society** société f de secours mutuel; Fin **m. fund** fonds m commun de placement, FCP m; Fin **m. insurance** (assurance f) mutuelle f, Fin **m. insurance company** société de crédit mutuel, société de

mutualité; *Fin* **m. investment fund** fonds commun de placement, FCP

mutually ['mjuːtʃʊəlɪ] **ADV** mutuellement, réciproquement; **to be m. exclusive** s'exclure l'un(e) l'autre

Muzak® ['mjuːzæk] **N** musiquette *f*

muzzle ['mʌz(ə)l] **N 1** *(mouth of animal)* museau *m* **2** *(device) (for dog etc)* muselière *f*; *(for horse)* bâillon *m* **3** *(of gun)* bouche *f*, gueule *f*
▶ **VT** *(dog)* museler; *Fig (press etc)* museler, bâillonner
▶▶ **m. velocity** vitesse *f* initiale

muzzle-loader **N** *Mil* pièce *f* se chargeant par la bouche

muzzy ['mʌzɪ] **ADJ** *Fam (ideas)* confus; *(outline, picture)* flou, estompé; **I feel m.** *(slightly unwell)* je me sens tout drôle; **my head feels a bit m.** j'ai la tête qui tourne; **she was m. about what it really meant** elle ne comprenait pas bien ce que tout cela signifiait

MV [em'viː] **1** *Elec (abbr* megavolt(s)) MV **2** *Naut (abbr* motor vessel) bateau *m* à moteur

MW [em'dʌb(ə)ljuː] **1** *Radio (abbr* **Medium Wave**) PO *fpl* **2** *Elec (abbr* megawatt(s)) MW

my [maɪ] **POSS ADJ** mon, ma, *pl* mes; *(in the f sing before a vowel sound)* mon; **my hat and gloves** mon chapeau et mes gants; **in my opinion** à mon avis; **one of my friends** un de mes amis, un ami à moi; **my own son** mon propre fils; **my hair is grey** j'ai les cheveux gris; **if you don't mind my asking** si je peux me permettre de vous le demander; **my idea would be to ...** mon idée à moi serait de ...; **my turn!** à moi! VOIR GRAMMAIRE A30; A43; B21
▶ **INT** *Fam* **my! how you've changed!** mon Dieu, comme vous avez changé!; **my! my! aren't we touchy!** oh là là! que vous êtes susceptible!; **(oh) my!** ça par exemple!

myalgic encephalomyelitis [maɪˌældʒɪ-kensefələʊmaɪə'laɪtɪs] **N** *Med* encéphalomyélite *f* myalgique

mycology [maɪ'kɒlədʒɪ] **N** *Bot* mycologie *f*

myelin ['maɪəlɪn] **N** myéline *f*

myelitis [maɪə'laɪtɪs] **N** *Med* myélite *f*

myeloma [maɪə'ləʊmə] **N** *Med* myélome *m*

myna(h) ['maɪnə] **N** *Orn* mainate *m*
▶▶ **m. bird** mainate

myocardial [maɪəʊ'kɑːdɪəl] **N**
▶▶ *Med* **m. infarct, m. infarction** infarctus *m* du myocarde

myopia [maɪ'əʊpɪə] **N** myopie *f*, *Fig* manque *m* de perspicacité

myopic [maɪ'ɒpɪk] **ADJ** *(person, eyes, look)* myope; *Fig* qui manque de perspicacité

myriad ['mɪrɪəd] **N** myriade *f*
▶ **ADJ** *Lit* innombrable

myriapod ['mɪrɪəpɒd] **ADJ, N** *Biol* myriapode *m*

myrmidon ['mɜːmɪd(ə)n] **N** *Pej Hum* homme *m* de main

myrrh [mɜːr] **N** myrrhe *f*

myrtle ['mɜːt(ə)l] **N** *(shrub)* myrte *m*; *Am (periwinkle)* pervenche *f* grimpante

myself [maɪ'self] **PERS PRON** VOIR GRAMMAIRE A29 **1** *(emphatic)* moi(-même); **I did it m.** je l'ai fait moi-même; *Fam* **I'm not quite m.** je ne suis pas dans mon assiette; **I m. believe that ...** (quant à) moi *ou* pour ma part, je crois que ... **2** *(reflexive)* me; *(before vowel sound)* m'; **I've hurt m.** je me suis fait mal; **I was enjoying m. very much** je m'amusais beaucoup SEE GRAMMAR B28–9 **3** *(after preposition)* **I live by m.** je vis tout seul; **I was laughing to m.** je riais tout seul; **I'll keep it for m.** je le garderai pour moi

mysterious [mɪs'tɪərɪəs] **ADJ** mystérieux
▶ **N** *(no pl)* **the m.** le mystérieux

mysteriously [mɪs'tɪərɪəslɪ] **ADV** mystérieusement, de façon mystérieuse

mysteriousness [mɪs'tɪərɪəsnɪs] **N** caractère *m* mystérieux, mystère *m* (**of** de)

mystery ['mɪstərɪ] **N 1** mystère *m*; **to make a m. of sth** faire (un) mystère de qch; **why make such a m. out of it?** pourquoi (faire) tant de mystères?; **it's a m. to me** pour moi, c'est un mystère; **there's no great m. about it** ça n'a rien de mystérieux; *(it's not a secret)* ce n'est un secret pour personne; **the key to the m.** la clef du mystère **2** *Theat (play)* mystère *m*
▶ **ADJ** *(guest, prize)* surprise; **m. man** mystérieux individu *m*; **who was the m. benefactor?** qui était le mystérieux bienfaiteur?
▶▶ **m. novel** roman *m* à énigmes; *Theat* **m. play** mystère *m*; *Mktg* **m. shopper** client, -ente mystère; *Mktg* **m. shopping** pseudo-achat *m*; **m. tour** = excursion *f* dont la destination est inconnue des participants

mystic ['mɪstɪk] **ADJ** *Rel* mystique; *(rites, arts)* ésotérique; *(power)* occulte
▶ **N** mystique *mf*

mystical ['mɪstɪk(ə)l] **ADJ** mystique

mysticism ['mɪstɪsɪz(ə)m] **N** mysticisme *m*

mystification [mɪstɪfɪ'keɪʃən] **N** *(action, result)* mystification *f*; **to our (great) m.** à notre grande perplexité

mystify ['mɪstɪfaɪ] **VT** *(bewilder) (person)* laisser perplexe, déconcerter; **mystified by ...** intrigué par ...; **I was mystified** j'étais perplexe

> Note that the French verb **mystifier** is a false friend. It means **to fool, to take in**.

mystique [mɪs'tiːk] **N** mystique *f*

myth [mɪθ] **N** mythe *m*

mythical ['mɪθɪk(ə)l] **ADJ** mythique

mythological [mɪθə'lɒdʒɪk(ə)l] **ADJ** mythologique

mythology [mɪ'θɒlədʒɪ] **N** mythologie *f*

myxomatosis [mɪksəmə'təʊsɪs] **N** myxomatose *f*

N¹, **n** [en] N *(letter)* N, n *m*; **two n's** deux n

N² **1** *(abbr* **North***)* N **2** *Phys (abbr* **Newton***)* N

n/a, N/A *Admin abbr* **not applicable**

NAACP [eneıeısiːˈpiː] N *Am (abbr* **National Association for the Advancement of Colored People***)* = association *f* nationale pour la promotion des personnes de couleur

NAAFI [ˈnæftə] N *Br Mil (abbr* **Navy, Army and Air Force Institutes***)* *(organization, canteen, shop)* = coopérative *f* militaire

nab [næb] VT *(-bb-)* Sl **1** *(steal)* faucher **2** *(catch doing sth, arrest)* pincer, choper; **to get nabbed** se faire pincer *ou* choper

nabob [ˈneɪbɒb] N nabab *m*

nacelle [næˈsel] N **1** *(of aircraft)* carlingue *f*, habitacle *m*; **(engine) n.** fuseau-moteur *m*, *pl* fuseaux-moteur **2** *(of airship, balloon)* nacelle *f*

nacre [ˈneɪkər] N nacre *f*

nadir [ˈneɪdɪər] N nadir *m*; *Fig* point *m* le plus bas

nads [nædz] NPL *Br Sl (testicles)* couilles *fpl*

naevus, *Am* **nevus,** *pl* **naevi** [ˈniːvəs, -aɪ] N *Med* nævus *m*, *pl* nævi

naff [næf] ADJ *Br Sl* **1** *(tasteless)* ringard **2** *(stupid)* nul, *f* nulle; **it was pretty n. of me to do that** j'ai été carrément nul d'avoir fait ça **3 n. all** que dalle; **I've got n. all money** j'ai que dalle comme argent
▸ **naff off** VI *Br Sl* **n. off!** *(go away)* casse-toi!; *(expressing contempt, disagreement)* va te faire voir!

naffing [ˈnæfɪŋ] *Br Sl* ADJ *(for emphasis)* foutu, sacré; **shut your n. mouth!** ferme-la!, ferme ton clapet!
ADV *(for emphasis)* vachement; **you're so n. stupid!** t'es vraiment débile!

NAFTA [ˈnæftə] N *(abbr* **North American Free Trade Agreement***)* ALENA *m*

nag¹ [næg] N *Fam (horse)* bidet *m*, bourrin *m*

nag² N *(person)* enquiquineur, -euse *(woman also)* chipie *f*; **she's a terrible n.** elle n'arrête pas de nous/le/*etc* harceler
VI *(-gg-)* he's always nagging il n'arrête pas de me/te/*etc* casser les pieds *ou* harceler
VT *(person)* casser les pieds à, harceler; *(of doubt)* harceler; *(of conscience)* ne pas laisser en paix, tourmenter; **she's always nagging (at) him to get it fixed** elle n'arrête pas de lui casser les pieds *ou* Fam de l'asticoter pour qu'il le fasse réparer; **he nags her to death** il la harcèle sans pitié; **why do I always have to n. you into doing everything?** pourquoi faut-il que je sois toujours après toi pour que tu fasses quoi que ce soit?
▸ **nag at** VT INSEP = **nag**² VT, **her conscience was nagging at her to go to the police** sa conscience l'exhortait sans répit à se rendre à la police

nagger [ˈnægər] N = **nag**²

nagging [ˈnægɪŋ] ADJ *(pain)* tenace; *(worry, fear, uncertainty)* tenace, qui persiste; **I've got a n. doubt that ...** je n'arrête pas de me demander si ...; **I've still got this n. doubt about him** je n'arrête pas de me poser des questions à son sujet; **I've got this n. feeling that ...** j'ai cette impression persistante que ...; **he has a n. wife** sa femme est une enquiquineuse
N harcèlement *m*; **I've had enough of your n.!** j'en ai assez que tu me harcèles *ou* Fam m'enquiquines!

naiad, *pl* **naiads, naiades** [ˈnaɪæd, -ædz, -ədiːz] N *Myth* naïade *f*

nail [neɪl] N **1** *(for fixing)* clou *m*; *Fig* **another n. in sb's coffin/the coffin of sth** un autre coup funeste à qn/qch; *Fig Fam* **to hit the n. (right) on the head** mettre le doigt dessus
2 *(on finger, toe)* ongle *m*
3 *Fam* **to pay on the n.** payer rubis sur l'ongle; **she demanded cash on the n.** elle a exigé qu'on la paie en argent comptant
VT **1** *(fasten)* clouer *(onto* à); **to n. sth shut** clouer qch; **she nailed the plank into place** elle a fixé la planche à l'aide de clous; *Fig* **he stood nailed to the spot** il est resté cloué au sol *(in fear/astonishment* de peur/surprise*)*
2 *(shoes, door etc)* clouter
3 *Fam (catch) (person)* attraper, coincer; *Fam* **to n. a lie** exposer un mensonge; **we should n. the lie that unemployment is falling** nous devrions démontrer que la soi-disant baisse du chômage n'est qu'un tissu de mensonges
▸▸ **n. bar** salon *m* de manucure; **n. bomb** bombe *f* à fragmentation *(bourrée de clous)*; *Am* **n. enamel** vernis *m* à ongles; **n. polish** vernis à ongles; **n. punch** chasse-clou *m*, *pl* chasse-clous; **n. scissors** ciseaux *mpl* à ongles; *Tech* **n. set** chasse-clou *m*, *pl* chasse-clous, chasse-pointe *m*, *pl* chasse-pointes; **n. varnish** vernis à ongles
▸ **nail down** VT SEP **1** *(fasten)* *(lid of a box)* clouer; *(furniture)* fixer à l'aide de clous; *Fig Fam* **you'd better n. that table down or it'll walk** tu ferais bien de cadenasser cette table au sol sinon elle va disparaître **2** *Fam* **we couldn't n. him down to anything definite** nous n'avons pu obtenir aucun engagement précis de sa part; **to n. sb down on a date** obtenir de qn qu'il fixe une date
▸ **nail up** VT SEP *(crate, box)* clouer; *(door, window)* condamner

nail-biter N **1** *(person)* personne *f* qui se ronge les ongles **2** *Fam (situation)* situation *f* au suspense insoutenable

nail-biting ADJ *Fam (finish, excitement etc)* palpitant; *(film, story)* à suspense
N habitude *f* de se ronger les ongles

nailbrush [ˈneɪlbrʌʃ] N brosse *f* à ongles

nailfile [ˈneɪlfaɪl] N lime *f* à ongles

naïve, naive [naɪˈiːv] ADJ *(person, manner etc)* naïf, -ïve; *(ingenuous)* ingénu
▸▸ *Art* **n. art** l'art *m* naïf

naïvely, naively [naɪˈiːvlɪ] ADV naïvement

naïveté, naivety [naɪˈiːvtɪ] N naïveté *f*

naked [ˈneɪkɪd] ADJ **1** *(person)* nu, *Fam* à poil; *(arm, back etc)* découvert, nu; *(wall etc)* nu, dégarni; *(countryside, tree)* dénudé, nu; *Biol (stalk, tail etc)* nu; **stark n.** tout nu, *Fam* nu comme un ver; **to strip (oneself) n.** se mettre nu *ou Fam* à poil **2** *Fig (sword, flame, lightbulb)* nu; *(aggression, exploitation) (not concealed)* non dissimulé; *(outright)* flagrant; **n. facts** faits bruts; **visible to the n. eye** visible à l'œil nu; **the n. truth** la pure vérité, la vérité toute nue
▸▸ *Bot* **n. lady** colchique *m* d'automne; *St Exch* **n. option** option *f* d'achat vendue à découvert; **n. sale** vente *f* nue

nakedness [ˈneɪkɪdnɪs] N nudité *f*

NALGO [ˈnælgəʊ] N *Br Formerly (abbr* **National and Local Government Officers' Association***)* = association *f* des fonctionnaires nationaux et régionaux

Nam [nɑːm] N *Am Fam (Vietnam)* le Viêt-Nam

namby-pamby [ˈnæmbɪˈpæmbɪ] N *(ineffectual person)* mollasson, -onne
ADJ *(spineless) (person)* ramolli, gnangnan *inv*; gnian-gnian *inv*; *(remark, attitude)* faiblard

NAME [neɪm] N **1** *(of person, object, plant etc)* nom *m*; *(of ship)* devise *f*, nom; *Com (of company, business)* raison *f* sociale; *(of account)* intitulé *m*; *(of play, novel etc)* titre *m*; **full n.** nom et prénoms *mpl*; **what's your n.?** quel est votre nom?, comment vous appelez-vous?; **my n. is ...** je m'appelle ...; **a man by the n. of Blenkinsop** un nommé Blenkinsop; **to go by *or* under the n. of ...** être connu sous le nom de ...; **he answers to his n.** *(of dog etc)* il répond quand on l'appelle; **to know sb by n.** connaître qn de nom; **to know sb by another *or* a different n.** connaître qn sous un autre nom; **to mention sb/sth by n.** nommer qn/qch; **you were mentioned by n.** on a cité votre nom, on vous a nommé; **to put a n. to sth** donner un nom à qch, mettre un nom sur qch; **to put a n. to a face** mettre un nom sur un visage; **to take sb's n.** *(of police etc)* prendre le nom de qn; *Ftbl* donner un carton jaune à qn; *Ftbl* **to have one's n. taken** recevoir un carton jaune; **he took his idol's n.** il a pris le nom de son idole; **I'm sorry, I didn't catch *or* get your n.** désolé, je n'ai pas bien entendu votre nom; **what n. shall I say?** *(to caller)* qui dois-je annoncer?; **famous n. (person)** célébrité *f*; **Pentagon is a huge n. in the publishing business** Pentagon est une entreprise très importante dans le monde de l'édition; **a big n. in the theatre** un nom bien connu dans le monde du théâtre; **to send in one's n.** *(for competition etc)* se faire inscrire; *(have oneself announced)* se faire annoncer; **to put one's n. down** *(in election)* poser sa candidature; *(on list)* s'inscrire *(for sth* pour qch*)*;

list of names liste nominative; **in the n. of ...** au nom de …; **in the n. of the law/the king** au nom de la loi/du roi; **in the n. of God** or **Heaven, in God's** or **Heaven's n.** pour l'amour de Dieu; *Fam* **what in the n. of God** or **Heaven** or **goodness are you doing?** que diable faites-vous là?; **to be master/prime minister in n. only** n'être maître/premier ministre que de nom; **they are married in n. only** *(marriage hasn't been consummated)* leur mariage est un mariage blanc; *(without love)* ils ne sont mariés que pour la forme; **the PSF is a socialist party in n. only** le PSF n'a de socialiste que le nom; **she was President in all but n.** elle avait tout du Président sauf le nom; **they are married in all but n.** c'est comme s'ils étaient mariés; **to call sb names** insulter qn; **she called me a rude n.** elle m'a insulté; **that's the n. of the game** c'est ce qui compte; **not to have a penny/a decent pair of shoes to one's n.** ne pas avoir un centime/une paire de chaussures convenable à soi; **to have several books to one's n.** être l'auteur de plusieurs livres; **to have several victories/trophies to one's n.** avoir remporté plusieurs victoires/trophées

2 *(reputation)* réputation *f*, renommée *f*; **she has a good/bad n.** elle a (une) bonne/(une) mauvaise réputation; **to get a bad n.** se faire une mauvaise réputation; **she has a n. for honesty** elle est connue ou réputée pour son honnêteté; **the firm has established a n. for quality** l'entreprise s'est bâtie une réputation de qualité; **to have a n. for prompt and efficient service** être réputé pour ses services rapides et efficaces; **to make a n. for oneself** se faire un nom ou une réputation **(as** de)

VT 1 *(give name to) (person, thing)* nommer, donner un nom à; *(ship)* baptiser; **he was named Peter** on lui a donné le nom de Peter, on l'a appelé ou nommé Peter; **someone named Thompson** un nommé Thompson; **to n. sb after sb** or *Am* **for sb** donner à qn le nom de qn; **they named her Cathy after the heroine of Wuthering Heights** ils l'ont appelée Cathy, comme l'héroïne des Hauts du Hurlevent

2 *(appoint)* nommer; **he was named (as) President** il a été nommé président; **she was named (as) best supporting actress** elle a été élue pour le meilleur second rôle féminin

3 *(designate, identify by name)* désigner (par son nom); *(example, fact)* citer; *(reveal name of)* révéler le nom de, nommer; **n. the kings of England/these species of birds** donnez les noms des rois d'Angleterre/de ces espèces d'oiseaux; *Law* **to n. sb as a beneficiary** *(in one's will etc)* désigner qn comme bénéficiaire; *Law* **to n. sb as a witness** citer qn comme témoin; *Br Parl* **to n. a member** *(of the Speaker, in House of Commons)* signaler à la Chambre l'indiscipline d'un membre; **to n. names** donner des noms; **naming no names** sans nommer personne; **to n. and shame** dénoncer publiquement les responsables; *Fam* **you n. it, she's done it/got it** tout ce qu'on peut imaginer, elle l'a fait/le possède

4 *(set) (day, amount)* fixer; **n. your price** donnez-moi un prix

▸▸ *Com* **n. brand** marque *f*; **n. day** *(of person)* fête *f*; *St Exch* deuxième jour *m* de liquidation; **n. label** étiquette *f* de nom; *Mktg* **n. licensing** cession *f* de licence de nom; *Br Cin, Theat* **n. part** vrai rôle *m*; *(title role)* = rôle qui donne son titre à la pièce ou au film; *Com* **n. product** marque

name-calling N insultes *fpl*

named [neɪmd] ADJ nommé; **on the n. day** le jour fixé

name-dropper N she's a terrible n. elle ne manque jamais de glisser des noms de personnalités (supposées connues d'elle) dans la conversation

name-dropping N there was a lot of n. in his speech il n'a pas arrêté de glisser des noms de personnalités (supposées connues de lui) dans son discours

nameless ['neɪmlɪs] ADJ **1** *(unknown) (person)* inconnu, obscur; *(anonymous) (writer, grave etc)* anonyme; **someone who shall be** or **remain n.** quelqu'un dont je tairai le nom **2** *(dread, grief etc)* indéfinissable, indicible, inexprimable; *(vice etc)* abominable

namely ['neɪmlɪ] ADV c'est-à-dire, à savoir

nameplate ['neɪmpleɪt] N écusson *m*, médaillon *m* *(portant un nom)*; *(on door etc)* plaque *f*; **manufacturer's n.** *(on machine etc)* plaque du constructeur

namesake ['neɪmseɪk] N homonyme *mf*; **my famous n.** la célébrité qui porte le même nom que moi

nametape ['neɪmteɪp] N marque *f* à linge

Namibia [nə'mɪbɪə] N Namibie *f*

Namibian [nə'mɪbɪən] N Namibien, -ienne *mf*; ADJ namibien

naming ['neɪmɪŋ] N **1** *(giving name)* attribution *f* d'un nom; *(of ship)* baptême *m*; **n. of a product** attribution *f* d'un nom à un produit **2** *(choosing) (of official)* nomination *f* **3** *(fixing) (of day, amount)* fixation *f*

nan¹, nana ['næn, 'nænə] N *Fam (grandmother)* mamie *f*, grand-maman *f*, mémé *f*

nan² [naːn] N *Culin* pain *m* nan
▸▸ **n. bread** pain nan

nancy ['nænsɪ] *Old-fashioned Pej Sl* N *(effeminate man)* homme *m* efféminé, chochotte *f*; *(homosexual)* tapette *f*
ADJ *(behaviour, ways etc)* de chochotte, de tapette
▸▸ **n. boy** *(effeminate man)* homme efféminé, chochotte; *(homosexual)* tapette

nandrolone ['nændrɪləʊn] N *Pharm* nandrolone *f*

nanny ['nænɪ] N **1** *(nursemaid)* bonne *f* d'enfant, nurse *f*; *(in children's language)* nounou *f* **2** *Fam (grandmother)* mamie *f*, mémé *f* **3** *(goat)* chèvre *f*, *Fam* biquette *f*
▸▸ **n. goat** chèvre, *Fam* biquette; **the n. state** l'État *m* paternaliste

nanoengineering [nænəʊendʒɪ'nɪərɪŋ] N nano-ingénierie *f*

nanosecond ['nænəʊsekənd] N nanoseconde *f*

nanotechnology ['nænəʊtek'nɒlədʒɪ] N nanotechnologie *f*

nap¹ [næp] N *(sleep)* petit somme *m*; **afternoon n.** sieste *f*; **to take** or **have a n.** faire un petit somme; *(after lunch)* faire la sieste
VI **(-pp-)** faire un petit somme; *(doze)* sommeiller; *Fig* **to be caught napping** *(off guard)* être pris au dépourvu

nap² *Tex* N *(of cloth, velvet, felt)* poil *m*; **cloth with raised n.** étoffe molletonnée ou tirée à poil ou garnie; **against the n.** à rebrousse-poil, à rebours
VT *(cloth)* garnir, gratter, lainer; *(wool, cotton)* molletonner

nap³ N **1** *Cards* **to go n.** demander les cinq levées; *Old-fashioned Fig* **to go n. on sth** être sûr et certain de qch; *Old-fashioned Fig* **to hold a n. hand** avoir en main toutes les cartes pour réussir **2** *Horseracing* tuyau *m* sûr
VT *Horseracing Fam* **to n. a winner** donner un tuyau sûr

napalm ['neɪpaːm] N napalm *m*
VT bombarder au napalm
▸▸ **n. bomb** bombe *f* au napalm

nape [neɪp] N **n. (of the neck)** nuque *f*

naphtha ['næfθə] N *Ind* naphte *m*

naphthalene ['næfθəliːn] N *Chem, Com* naphtaline *f*, naphtalène *m*

napkin ['næpkɪn] N **1** *(table)* n. serviette *f* *(de table)* **2** *Br Fml (baby's)* n. couche *f* *(de bébé)* **3** *Am (sanitary)* n. serviette *f* hygiénique
▸▸ **n. ring** rond *m* de serviette

Napoleon [nə'pəʊlɪən] N Napoléon *m*

Napoleonic [nəpəʊlɪ'ɒnɪk] ADJ napoléonien

nappy ['næpɪ] N *Br* couche *f* *(pour bébé)*
▸▸ **n. rash** érythème *m* fessier

narc [naːk] N *Am Sl* = agent *m* de la brigade des stups

narcissism ['naːsɪsɪz(ə)m] N narcissisme *m*

narcissistic [naːsɪ'sɪstɪk] ADJ narcissique

narcissus [naː'sɪsəs], *pl* **narcissi, narcissuses** [naː'sɪsaɪ, -'sɪsaɪz] N *(plant)* narcisse *m*

narcosis [naː'kəʊsɪs] N *Med* narcose *f*

narcotic [naː'kɒtɪk] ADJ narcotique, stupéfiant
N narcotique *m*, stupéfiant *m*; *Am* **narcotics agent** agent *m* de la brigade des stupéfiants; *Am* **narcotics (branch)** *(of police force)* brigade *f* des stupéfiants

nark¹ [naːk] *Sl* N *(informer)* indic *m*, mouchard *m*
VI *(inform)* moucharder; **to n. on sb** balancer qn

nark² VT *Br Fam (annoy)* taper sur les nerfs de, énerver; **to get narked** s'énerver, s'exciter; **she's really narked about it** ça l'énerve vraiment

narky ['naːkɪ] ADJ *Br Fam* de mauvais poil; **to get n.** se mettre en pétard

narrate [nə'reɪt] VT *(of person)* raconter, relater, narrer; *(of story, book)* raconter, relater; *TV, Cin (film, documentary)* lire ou dire le commentaire de; *Radio (play)* narrer

narration [nə'reɪʃən] N **1** *(of story etc)* narration *f*; *TV, Cin (of film, documentary)* (lecture *f* du) commentaire *m*; *Radio (of play)* narration **2** *(account)* récit *m*, narration *f*

narrative ['nærətɪv] N **1** *(story)* récit *m*; *Liter* **the n.** la narration **2** *(art)* (l'art *m* de) la narration
ADJ *(style, poem)* narratif
▸▸ **n. writer** narrateur, -trice

narrator [nə'reɪtər] N narrateur, -trice; *Mus* récitant, -ante

narrow ['nærəʊ] ADJ *(path etc)* étroit; *(body, waist, face)* mince; *(valley etc)* resserré; *(passage, channel)* étranglé; *Ling (vowel)* tendu; *(mind)* étroit, borné; *(existence)* limité, circonscrit; **to grow** or **become n.** se rétrécir; **to have n. shoulders** ne pas être large d'épaules, avoir les épaules étroites; **within n. bounds** dans des limites étroites; **to have a n. escape** or *Fam* **squeak** l'échapper belle; **n. bodied aircraft** avion *m* petit porteur; **a n. interpretation** *(of rules etc)* une interprétation au pied de la lettre; **a n. majority** une faible majorité; **by a n. margin** *(to win, lose)* de peu; **they won by the n. margin of two points** ils ont gagné de deux petits points; **to win/lose by the narrowest of margins** gagner/perdre de très peu; **in the narrowest sense** dans le sens le plus strict; **to suffer a n. defeat** être vaincu de peu; **it was another n. victory for the French side** l'équipe française l'a encore emporté de justesse; **to take a n. view of sth** adopter un point de vue étroit sur qch
NPL **narrows** *(of river)* étranglement *m*
VT *(road etc)* resserrer, rétrécir; *(space, choice, possibilities, chances)* restreindre, limiter; *(gap)* réduire, resserrer; *(ideas)* rétrécir; **to n. a margin of victory/defeat** réduire l'ampleur d'une victoire/défaite; **narrowed eyes** paupières mi-closes

VI *(of road, path)* devenir plus étroit, se rétrécir; **the gap between rich and poor has narrowed** l'écart entre les riches et les pauvres s'est resserré

▸▸ *Rail* **n. gauge** voie *f* étroite; *St Exch* **n. market** marché *m* étroit; *Fin* **n. money** = ensemble *m* des billets et pièces de monnaie en circulation

▸ **narrow down VT SEP** *(limit)* limiter; *(possibilities)* restreindre, réduire; *(candidates)* réduire le nombre de; **that narrows it down to two suspects** cela nous laisse avec *ou* nous ramène à deux suspects

narrow-boat N péniche *f*

narrowcast ['nærəʊkɑːst] *Radio, TV* **VT** diffuser localement

VI = diffuser des émissions destinées à un public spécialisé

narrowing ['nærəʊɪŋ] N *Med (of artery etc)* rétrécissement *m*

narrowly ['nærəʊlɪ] **ADV 1** *(to interpret)* étroitement, strictement, au pied de la lettre **2** *(only just)* de peu; **he n. missed being run over** il a failli se faire écraser; **they n. escaped being caught** ils ont failli se faire prendre; **the missile just n. missed them** le missile les a ratés de peu

narrow-minded ADJ *(person)* (d'un esprit) borné, à l'esprit étroit; *(views, opinions)* borné; *(approach, outlook)* étroit, limité; **to be n. about politics/sex** être borné en ce qui concerne la politique/le sexe

narrow-mindedness [-maɪndɪdnɪs] N *(of person)* étroitesse *f ou* petitesse *f* d'esprit; *(of views, outlook)* caractère *m* borné

narrowness ['nærəʊnɪs] N *(of path, shoulders, passage etc)* étroitesse *f*; *(of sb's waist)* minceur *f*; *(of space etc)* petitesse *f*, exiguïté *f*; *(of gap, difference)* caractère *m* limité; *(of existence, intelligence etc)* limitations *f pl*; **n. of mind** étroitesse d'esprit

narw(h)al, narwhale ['nɑːwəl] N narval *m*, *pl* narvals

NASA ['næsə] N *Astronaut (abbr* **National Aeronautics and Space Administration)** NASA *f*

nasal ['neɪz(ə)l] ADJ *Anat, Ling etc* nasal, -aux; **the n. cavities** les fosses *f pl* nasales; **to have a n. voice** parler du nez

N *Ling* nasale *f*

nasalize ['neɪzəlaɪz] **VT** *(syllable etc)* nasaliser

nasally ['neɪzəlɪ] **ADV** par le nez; **to speak n.** parler du nez, nasiller

nascent ['neɪsənt, 'næs-] ADJ *Fml (talent, discontent, suspicion etc)* naissant; *Chem (body, element)* à l'état naissant

NASDAQ® ['næzdæk] N *St Exch (abbr* **National Association of Securities Dealers Automated Quotation)** Nasdaq *m (Bourse américaine des valeurs technologiques)*

nastily ['nɑːstɪlɪ] **ADV 1** *(unpleasantly)* désagréablement **2** *(maliciously)* méchamment **3** *(indecently)* indécemment

nastiness ['nɑːstɪnɪs] N **1** *(of smell, taste)* caractère *m* désagréable; *(of surroundings, building)* caractère répugnant; **the n. of the weather** le mauvais temps **2** *(of person)* méchanceté *f*; *(of remark)* méchanceté, malveillance *f*; **the n. of his behaviour** son comportement malveillant **3** *(of book, film etc)* ignominie *f*, bassesse *f*, *(of crime, rape)* atrocité *f*, abjection *f*

nasturtium [nə'stɜːʃ(ə)m] N *(plant)* capucine *f*

nasty ['nɑːstɪ] ADJ **1** *(unpleasant, bad)* désagréable; **his behaviour left (me with) a n. taste in the mouth** sa conduite m'a laissé un arrière-goût désagréable; **to give sb a n. fright** faire une sale peur à qn; **he had a n. surprise** il a eu une mauvaise surprise; **n. corner** tournant dangereux; **n. accident** ac-

cident *m* grave; **n. cold/rash** méchant(e) rhume/éruption; **it gave her a n. shock** ça lui a donné un sale coup; **n. wound** vilaine blessure; **she's had a n. attack of bronchitis** elle a fait une mauvaise bronchite; **he's had quite a n. blow to the head** il a pris un mauvais coup sur la tête; **n. weather** sale *ou* mauvais temps; **the weather turned n.** le temps s'est dégradé

2 *(malicious) (person)* méchant, mauvais, déplaisant, *Fam* rosse; **to turn n.** devenir méchant; **to be n. to sb** être méchant envers qn; **that was a really n. thing to do** c'est vraiment méchant d'avoir fait ça; **n. trick** vilain tour, *Fam* sale tour; **what a n. little mind you've got!** que tu es méchant *ou* horrible!; *Fam* **he's a n. piece of work** c'est un sale individu *ou* un sale type

3 *(indecent) (book, film etc)* ignoble; *(crime, rape)* ignoble, atroce; **n. word** vilain mot

4 *Am Fam (excellent)* super, génial, -aux; **she makes a n. pizza** elle fait super bien la pizza

natal ['neɪt(ə)l] ADJ natal, -als, de naissance

natality [nə'tælɪtɪ] N *esp Am (birth rate)* natalité *f*

natch [nætʃ] **INT** *Fam* sûr

nation ['neɪʃən] N **1** *(state)* nation *f*, *Pol* **United Nations (Organization)** (Organisation *f* des) Nations *f pl* Unies **2** *(people)* pays *m*; **the whole n. rose in arms** tout le pays se souleva; **the Prime Minister addressed the n.** le Premier Ministre s'est adressé à la nation; **to serve the n.** servir l'État

national ['næʃ(ə)nəl] ADJ national, -aux; *(custom)* du pays; *Journ* **the n. dailies** les quotidiens nationaux

N **1** ressortissant, -ante *(d'un pays)*; **a French n.** un(e) Français(e); **foreign nationals** ressortissants de pays étrangers **2** *(newspaper)* journal *m ou* quotidien *m* national

▸▸ **n. anthem** hymne *m* national; *Br* **the N. Audit Office** ≃ la Cour des comptes; *Tel* **n. call** appel *m* national; *Fin* **n. debt** dette *f* publique, dette de l'État; *Econ* **n. demand** demande *f* intérieure; **n. grid** *Br Elec* réseau *m* national d'électricité; *Geog* **n. réseau**; *Br* **N. Health Service** ≃ Sécurité *f* sociale; **to get treatment on the N. Health (Service)** se faire soigner sous le régime de la Sécurité sociale; *Horseracing* **n. hunt** courses *f pl* d'obstacles; *Br* **N. Insurance** = système *m* britannique de sécurité sociale (maladie, retraite) et d'assurance chômage; **n. insurance contributions** cotisations *f pl* à la Sécurité sociale; **n. interest** intérêt *m* national; **N. Missile Defence** projet *m* NMD *(programme de défense antimissiles américain)*; **n. newspaper** journal à diffusion nationale; **n. park** parc *m* national; *Fin* **n. product** produit *m* national; **n. readership survey** étude *f* nationale sur le lectorat; **n. scenic area** = zone *f* protégée pour la beauté de son paysage; *Br* **n. service** service *m* militaire; *Econ* **n. treatment** traitement *m* national; *Br* **the N. Trust** = organisme *m* non gouvernemental britannique assurant la conservation de certains paysages et monuments historiques

National Health Service

Le National Health Service ou NHS fut créé par le gouvernement travailliste en 1948, donnant accès à chacun aux soins médicaux gratuits. Cependant, suite notamment aux coupes budgétaires réalisées dans les années 80, le système de santé britannique est aujourd'hui en crise. Au cours des dernières années, la polémique autour du National Health Service s'est intensifiée et est devenue un enjeu majeur lors des élections en Grande-Bretagne.

nationalism ['næʃənəlɪz(ə)m] N nationalisme *m*

nationalist ['næʃənəlɪst] N nationaliste *mf*

ADJ nationaliste; **N. China** la Chine nationaliste

nationalistic [næʃənə'lɪstɪk] ADJ nationaliste

nationality [næʃə'nælɪtɪ] N nationalité *f*; **what n. are you?** de quelle nationalité êtes-vous?, quelle est votre nationalité?; **to take** *or* **adopt British n.** prendre la nationalité britannique VOIR GRAMMAIRE A18–19; B11–12

nationalization [næʃənəlaɪ'zeɪʃən] N **1** *(of industry etc)* nationalisation *f* **2** *(of foreigner)* naturalisation *f*

nationalize ['næʃənəlaɪz] **VT 1** *(industry etc)* nationaliser **2** *(foreigner)* naturaliser

nationalized ['næʃənəlaɪzd] ADJ *(industry etc)* nationalisé

nationally ['næʃənəlɪ] **ADV** nationalement; **to be n. renowned** avoir une renommée nationale

nation-state N *Pol* état-nation *m*, *pl* états-nations

nationwide ['neɪʃənwaɪd] ADJ *(opinion)* répandu dans tout le pays; *(campaign, survey)* au niveau national

ADV *(to advertise etc)* au niveau national; *(to be known)* dans tout le pays

native ['neɪtɪv] N **1** *(person)* *(of country, town)* originaire *mf*; *(in colonial sense)* indigène *mf*; **she was a n. of Scotland** elle était originaire d'Écosse; **n. of Australia** Australien, -ienne de naissance; **she speaks English like a n.** elle parle anglais comme une Anglaise; **to go n.** adopter la manière de vivre des habitants, *Hum* adopter les mœurs des indigènes **2** *(plant, animal)* indigène *mf*; **the koala is a n. of Australia** le koala est originaire d'Australie

ADJ **1** *(country etc)* natal, -als, de naissance; **he returned to his n. London** il est revenu à Londres, sa ville natale **2** *(plant, inhabitant etc)* indigène *(*to, de, à*)* **3** *(qualities etc)* naturel, inné **4** *(metals, minerals)* (à l'état) natif

▸▸ **N. American** Indien, -ienne d'Amérique, Amérindien, -ienne; **n. costume** costume *m* national; **n. labour** main d'œuvre *f* indigène; **n. land** pays *m* natal; **n. language** langue *f* maternelle; *Ling* **n. speaker** locuteur, -trice natif(ive); **n. wit** esprit *m* naturel

native-born ADJ indigène, natif; **a n. German** un(e) Allemand(e) de naissance

nativism ['neɪtɪvɪz(ə)m] N *esp Am Pol* exclusivisme *m* en faveur des autochtones

nativist ['neɪtɪvɪst] *esp Am Pol* N = partisan *m* de l'exclusivisme en faveur des autochtones

ADJ qui favorise les autochtones

Nativity [nə'tɪvɪtɪ] N *Rel* nativité *f*; **the (festival of the) N.** la Nativité

▸▸ **N. play** = pièce *f* jouée par des enfants et représentant l'histoire de la Nativité; **N. scene** crèche *f*, *Art* nativité

Nato, NATO ['neɪtəʊ] N *(abbr* **North Atlantic Treaty Organisation)** OTAN *f*

▸▸ **N. forces** les forces *f pl* de l'Otan

natter ['nætər] *esp Br Fam* N causerie *f*, causette *f*; **to have a n.** bavarder, jacter

VI bavarder, jacter; **what were you two nattering about?** de quoi étiez-vous en train de bavarder, tous les deux?

natty ['nætɪ] ADJ *Fam* **1** *(person, dress etc)* chic *inv* **2** *(gadget etc)* astucieux

natural ['nætʃərəl] ADJ **1** *(colour, taste)* naturel; **the n. world** le monde physique; **the n. order (of things)** l'ordre *m* des choses; **death from n. causes** mort *f* naturelle; **a n. blonde** une vraie blonde; **in the n. state** à l'état naturel *ou* primitif; **for the rest of one's n. life**

or Fam **one's n.** pour le reste de sa vie; **n. gift** *or* **talent (for sth/doing sth)** don *m* naturel (pour qch/faire qch); **and that brings us to a n. break** et ceci nous amène tout naturellement à une pause; **n. rate of unemployment** taux *m* de chômage naturel

2 *(normal, to be expected)* naturel, normal, -aux; **it is n. for a woman to …** il est dans *ou* de la nature de la femme de …; **it's n. (enough) (that) …** il est (bien) naturel que … + *subj*; **it's only n. that …** il est *ou* c'est tout à fait normal que … + *subj*; **as is (only) n.** comme de raison; **n. consequence** conséquence *f* naturelle; **n. inclination** penchant *m* naturel, inclination *f* naturelle; **my n. inclination would be to …** j'inclinerais naturellement à …; **one's** *or* **the n. reaction is to …** la réaction instinctive est de …; **I'm sure there's a perfectly n. explanation for it** je suis sûr qu'on peut l'expliquer de façon tout à fait naturelle; **to be a n. dancer/orator/leader** être un danseur/orateur/dirigeant né

3 *(unaffected)* naturel; **be** *or* **act n.!** soyez naturel!; **that'll look more n.** ça fera plus naturel

4 *Arch (illegitimate) (child)* naturel

N 1 **as an actor, he's a n.** c'est un acteur né; **she's a n. for the part** elle est faite pour ce rôle **2** *Mus (note)* (note) *f* naturelle *f*, *(sign)* bécarre *m*

▸▸ **n. childbirth** accouchement *m* naturel; **n. disaster** catastrophe *f* naturelle; *Phys, Elec* **n. frequency** fréquence *f* propre; **n. gas** gaz *m* naturel; **n. history** histoire *f* naturelle; **n. justice** droits *mpl* naturels; **n. language** langage *m* naturel, langue *f* naturelle; **n. law** loi *f* naturelle; **n. medicine** médecine *f* douce *ou* naturelle, phytothérapie *f*, *Econ* **n. monopoly** monopole *m* naturel; **n. mother** mère *f* naturelle; *Mus* **n. note** (note) naturelle; *Phys Old-fashioned* **n. philosophy** physique *f*, **n. resources** ressources *fpl* naturelles; *Mus* **n. scale** gamme *f* naturelle; **n. sciences** sciences *fpl* naturelles; **n. selection** sélection *f* naturelle; **n. size** grandeur *f* nature; *Radio, TV* **n. sound** son *m* naturel; *Econ, Ind* **n. wastage** départs *mpl* volontaires *ou* en retraite; **n. wavelength** longueur *f* d'onde propre

natural-born ADJ *(singer, leader etc)* né; **n. Frenchwoman** Française de naissance

naturalism ['nætʃərəlɪz(ə)m] N *Liter, Phil* naturalisme *m*

naturalist ['nætʃərəlɪst] ADJ, N *Bot, Zool* naturaliste *mf*

naturalistic [nætʃərə'lɪstɪk] ADJ *Liter etc* naturaliste

naturalization [nætʃərəlaɪ'zeɪʃən] N **1** *(of alien, foreign word)* naturalisation *f* **2** *(of plant, animal)* acclimatation *f*

naturalize ['nætʃərəlaɪz] VT **1** *(alien, word)* naturaliser; **to become naturalized** *(of person)* se faire naturaliser **2** *(plant, animal)* acclimater

VI *(of plant etc)* s'acclimater

naturally ['nætʃərəlɪ] ADV **1** naturellement; *(to speak)* naturellement, sans affectation; *(to behave)* avec naturel; *(to die)* de mort naturelle; **n. occurring** naturel; **n. curly hair** cheveux qui frisent naturellement; **he's n. shy/funny/cheerful** il est timide/drôle/enjoué de nature; **she has a n. optimistic disposition** elle est d'un naturel optimiste; **it comes n. to him** c'est un don chez lui; **it comes n. to him to …** il a une facilité innée pour …; **although it didn't come n., he forced himself to ask questions** bien que cela ne lui vienne pas naturellement, il se forçait à poser des questions **2 n. (enough)** *(of course)* naturellement, bien entendu

naturalness ['nætʃərəlnɪs] N **1** *(of acting)* caractère *m* naturel **2** *(of person)* naturel *m*

nature ['neɪtʃər] N **1** *(character) (of thing)* nature *f*, caractère *m*; *(of person)* nature, naturel *m*, tempérament *m*; **it is in the n. of things that …** il est dans l'ordre *ou* la nature des choses que …; **a jealous n.** un naturel *ou* caractère jaloux; **to have a** *or* **to be of a happy n.** être d'un heureux naturel; **it's not in her n.** ce n'est pas dans sa nature (**to do de** faire); **by n.** par tempérament, de (sa) nature, naturellement; **shy by n.** timide de nature, d'un naturel timide

2 *(sort)* genre *m*, sorte *f*, **things of this n.** les choses de ce genre; **something in the n. of a …** une espèce *ou* une sorte de …; **something of that n., anyway** quelque chose dans le genre *ou* de cette espèce, en tout cas; **that was in the n. of being a compliment, coming from him** c'était plutôt un compliment, venant de lui; *Fml* **what is the n. of your complaint?** quelle est la nature de votre réclamation?; *Admin* **n. of contents** désignation *f* du contenu

3 *(the natural world)* nature *f*, **to let n. take its course** laisser faire la nature; **the n. versus nurture debate** le débat nature/culture; *Hum Fam* **to answer a call of n.** satisfaire un besoin naturel; **to draw/paint from n.** dessiner/peindre d'après nature; **to go against n.** aller contre la nature; **return to n.** retour à l'état de nature

▸▸ **n. lover** amoureux, -euse de la nature; **n. reserve** réserve *f* naturelle; *Sch* **n. study** sciences *fpl* naturelles, histoire *f* naturelle; **n. trail** sentier *m* écologique

naturism ['neɪtʃərɪz(ə)m] N naturisme *m*

naturist ['neɪtʃərɪst] N naturiste *mf*

naught [nɔːt] N **1** *Arch, Lit (nothing)* rien *m*; **to come to n.** *(of plans etc)* échouer, n'aboutir à rien; **to bring to n., to set at n.** anéantir **2** *Am Math* zéro *m*

naughtily ['nɔːtɪlɪ] ADV **to behave n.** se conduire mal, ne pas être sage, être vilain; **rather n., I spread rumours about her private life** j'ai fait courir des rumeurs sur sa vie privée, ce qui est un peu vilain

naughtiness ['nɔːtɪnɪs] N **1** *(of child etc)* mauvaise conduite *f* **2** *(mild indecency)* grivoiserie(s) *f(pl)*

naughty ['nɔːtɪ] ADJ **1** *(child)* vilain, méchant; **it was very n. of you** c'était très vilain de ta part; **you n. child!** petit vilain!; **he's been a n. boy** *or* **n.** il a été vilain *ou* méchant, il n'a pas été sage **2** *Fam (indecent) (story)* grivois, cochon; *(song)* gaillard, paillard; *(book, picture, person)* cochon

▸▸ *Br Euph* **n. bits** parties *fpl* honteuses

nausea ['nɔːsɪə] N **1** *Med* nausée *f*, envie *f* de vomir; **to be overcome with n.** avoir mal au cœur, avoir des nausées **2** *(disgust)* dégoût *m*, nausée *f*, écœurement *m*

nauseate ['nɔːsɪeɪt] VT **1** *Med* donner des nausées à, donner mal au cœur à **2** *(disgust)* donner la nausée à, écœurer, dégoûter

nauseating ['nɔːsɪeɪtɪŋ] ADJ **1** *Med* nauséeux **2** *(disgusting)* dégoûtant, écœurant; **I find him n.** il m'écœure, il me dégoûte; **in n. detail** avec des détails écœurants *ou* à donner la nausée

nauseatingly ['nɔːsɪeɪtɪŋlɪ] ADV d'une façon dégoûtante *ou* écœurante; **he made it look so n. easy** il l'a fait avec une facilité écœurante; **he's n. clever/good-looking** il est tellement intelligent/beau que c'en est écœurant

nauseous ['nɔːsɪəs, *Am* 'nɔːʃəs] ADJ **1** *Med* nauséeux; **to feel n.** avoir mal au cœur, avoir des nausées **2** *(disgusting)* nauséabond, écœurant

nautical ['nɔːtɪk(ə)l] ADJ nautique, marin; *(term, expression)* de navigation, de marine; **he had a n. air/bearing** il avait l'air/l'allure

d'un marin; **he comes from a n. background** il vient d'une famille de marins

▸▸ **n. almanac** éphémérides *fpl* nautiques; **n. club** club *m* nautique; **n. mile** mille *m* marin

nautilus, *pl* **nautiluses, nautili** ['nɔːtɪləs, -əsɪz, -aɪ] N *(mollusc)* nautile *m*

NAV [enei'viː] N *Fin (abbr* **net asset value)** = valeur *f* d'actif net

naval ['neɪv(ə)l] ADJ *(attaché, base, battle etc)* naval, pl -als; *(power)* maritime

▸▸ **n. architect** architecte *mf* naval(e); *(for warships)* ingénieur *m* du génie maritime *ou* en construction navale; **n. architecture** construction *f* navale; **n. college** école *f* navale; **n. dockyard** arsenal *m* maritime; **n. hospital** hôpital *m* naval; **n. officer** officier *m* de marine; **n. station** base *f* navale; **n. stores** *(depot)* entrepôts *mpl* maritimes; *(supplies)* approvisionnement *mpl* ou matériel *m* ou fournitures *fpl* de navires; **n. vessel** navire *m*

nave¹ [neɪv] N *(of wheel)* moyeu *m*

nave² N *Archit (of church)* nef *f*

navel ['neɪv(ə)l] N *Anat* nombril *m*, ombilic *m*; *Fig* **to contemplate one's n.** se regarder le nombril, faire du nombrilisme

▸▸ **n. orange** navel *f*

navel-gazing [-'geɪzɪŋ] N nombrilisme *m*

navigability [nævɪgə'bɪlɪtɪ] N *(of river, vessel)* navigabilité *f*, *(of balloon)* dirigeabilité *f*

navigable ['nævɪgəb(ə)l] ADJ *(river, vessel)* navigable; *(balloon)* dirigeable; **ship in n. condition** vaisseau en état de prendre la mer *ou* de naviguer

navigate ['nævɪgeɪt] VI **1** *(find one's way)* naviguer; *Aut* **I'll drive if you n.** je conduis si vous me dirigez **2** *Comput* naviguer

VT **1** *(seas)* naviguer dans *ou* sur; **this river is difficult to n.** la navigation est difficile sur ce fleuve; **to n. a ship** *(steer)* gouverner *ou* diriger un navire; *(plot path of)* naviguer; *Fam* **to n. one's way to the door** *(through crowd)* se frayer un chemin jusqu'à la porte; **the drunk navigated his way to the door** le soûlard a réussi à trouver son chemin jusqu'à la porte **2** *Comput* naviguer sur; **to n. the Net** naviguer sur Internet

navigating officer ['nævɪgeɪtɪŋ] N officier *m* de navigation, officier navigateur

navigation [nævɪ'geɪʃən] N **1** navigation *f*, *(of ship, balloon)* conduite *f* **2** *Comput (on the Internet)* navigation *f*

▸▸ **n. aids** aides *fpl* à la navigation; **n. bar** barre *f* de navigation; **n. button** bouton *m* de navigation; **n. lights** *Aviat* feux *mpl* de position; *Naut* fanaux *mpl*, feux de bord *ou* de route; **n. officer** officier *m* de navigation, officier navigateur

navigational [nævɪ'geɪʃənəl] ADJ *(instrument etc)* de navigation; *(aids)* à la navigation

navigator ['nævɪgeɪtər] N **1** *Naut, Aviat* (officier *m*) navigateur *m*; *Aut* navigateur *m* **2** *Hist (explorer)* navigateur *m*

navvy ['nævɪ] N *Br (worker)* terrassier *m*

navy ['neɪvɪ] N **1** *(service)* marine *f*, **to serve in the n.** servir dans la marine *ou* sur mer; **2** *(warships collectively)* marine *f* de guerre; *(fleet)* flotte *f*

ADJ de la marine

▸▸ **N. Cut®** tabac *m* haché fin; **n. yard** arsenal *m* maritime

navy, navy blue N bleu *m* marine *inv*

ADJ bleu marine *inv*

nay [neɪ] ADV *Arch, Lit, Dial* non; *Lit (introducing a more emphatic statement)* (et) même, qui plus est, voire; **I am astounded, n., disgusted** j'en suis ahuri, voire révolté

N *Arch, Lit* non *m*; **ayes and nays** (*in voting*) voix *fpl* pour et contre; **I was one of the n.-sayers** j'étais un de ceux qui ont voté contre

Nazarene ['næzəriːn] ADJ, N *Bible* nazaréen, -éenne; **the N.** le Nazaréen

Nazi ['nɑːtsɪ] ADJ nazi; (*persecution, seizure of power*) par les nazis
N nazi, -ie

Nazism ['nɑːtsɪz(ə)m] N nazisme *m*

NB [en'biː] **1** (*abbr* **nota bene**) NB **2** (*abbr* **New Brunswick**) NB

NBC [enbiː'siː] N *TV* (*abbr* **National Broadcasting Company**) = chaîne *f* de télévision américaine

NBG, nbg [enbiː'dʒiː] ADJ *Fam* (*abbr* **no bloody good**) (*person*) nul, bon à rien; (*book etc*) nul

NBV [enbiː'viː] N *Fin* (*abbr* **net book value**) valeur *f* comptable nette

NC *abbr* **North Carolina**

NC-17 *Am Cin* = indique qu'un film est interdit aux moins de 17 ans

NCB [ensiː'biː] N *Br Formerly* (*abbr* **National Coal Board**) = direction *f* des charbonnages britanniques

NCO [ensiː'əʊ] N *Mil* (*abbr* **noncommissioned officer**) sous-officier *m, pl* sous-officiers

ND *abbr* **North Dakota**

NDP [endiː'piː] N *Econ* (*abbr* **net domestic product**) produit *m* intérieur net

Neandert(h)al [nɪ'ændətɑːl] ADJ **1** (*during Stone Age*) néandertalien **2** *Fig Pej* (*attitude etc*) primaire
N *Fig Pej* (*uncultured man*) primate *m*
▸▸ **N. man** (*in anthropology*) l'homme *m* de Néanderthal

neap [niːp] ADJ faible
N morte-eau *f, pl* mortes-eaux
▸▸ **n. tide** marée *f* de morte-eau

Neapolitan [nɪə'pɒlɪt(ə)n] ADJ napolitain
N Napolitain, -aine
▸▸ **N. ice cream** tranche *f* napolitaine

▄▄▄▄ **NEAR** [nɪər] ▄▄▄▄

ADV	près **1** ▪ proche **1**
PREP	près de **1, 3, 4** ▪ sur le point de **3** ▪ proche de **4**
ADJ	proche **1, 3**
VT	approcher de

ADV **1** (*in space or time*) près; (*closely connected by kinship or intimacy*) proche; **she lives quite n.** elle habite tout près; **to come** *or* **draw n.** (s')approcher (**to sb/sth** de qn/qch); **come nearer** venez plus près, approchez-vous; **the time is drawing n.** l'heure approche; **to bring sth nearer** rapprocher qch (**to** de); **nearer and nearer** de plus en plus près; **n. at hand** (*of thing*) tout près, à proximité; (*of event*) tout proche; **keep** *or* **stay n. to me** restez près de moi; **he was standing n. to the table** il se tenait près de la table; **those n. and dear to him** ceux qui le touchent de près, ses proches; **no, it took nearer to three days** non, ça a pris plutôt trois jours

2 (*in extent*) **as n. as I can remember** autant que je puisse m'en souvenir; **they came n. to blows/to splitting up** ils en sont presque venus aux coups/à se séparer; **they were n. to giving up** ils étaient sur le point d'abandonner; **I came n. to crying** j'ai été sur le point de pleurer; **he's nowhere n. so** *or* **as strong as you** il est loin d'être aussi fort que vous; **she's nowhere n. finished** elle est loin d'avoir fini; **as n. as makes no difference** à peu de chose près; **50 or n. enough, 50 or as n. as makes no difference** 50 ou peu s'en faut, à peu de chose près 50; **a n. total failure** un échec presque total

3 *Arch, Lit* presque, à peu près

PREP **1** (*in space*) près de; **n. the village** près du village; **bring your chair near(er) the fire** (r)approchez votre chaise du feu; **to come** *or* **draw n. (to) sb/sth** (s')approcher de qn/qch

2 (*in time*) **it is n. Christmas** Noël approche, on approche de Noël; **we're getting n. that stage** on approche *ou* se rapproche de cette phase; **it was n. the time when he had his accident** c'était à l'époque de son accident

3 (*in extent*) près de, sur le point de; **n. death** sur le point de mourir; **he came n. (to) being run over** il a failli être écrasé; **n. to tears/despair** au bord des larmes/du désespoir

4 (*in resemblance*) **to be** *or* **to come n. sb/sth** ressembler à qn/qch; **language that is nearer Latin than Italian** langue qui est plus près *ou* proche du latin que de l'italien; **nobody can come anywhere n. her** il n'y a personne à son niveau; **he's nowhere n. it!** (*with guess etc*) il n'y est pas du tout!; **perhaps your definition comes n. it** *or* **the mark** votre définition s'approche peut-être de la vérité

ADJ **1** (*relative*) proche; **I felt very n. to her when she said that** je me suis senti très proche d'elle quand elle a dit cela; **we grew n. to one another** nous sommes devenus intimes; **our n. relations** nos proches (parents)

2 (*referring to side*) **n. foreleg** (*of horse etc*) pied *m* du montoir

3 (*place, time, event*) proche; **go to the nearest chemist's** allez à la pharmacie la plus proche; **in the n. future** dans un proche avenir; **give the measurements to the nearest metre** donnez les mesures au *ou* à un mètre près

4 it was a n. thing (*we only just escaped, attempt nearly succeeded*) il s'en est fallu de peu; (*nearly hit target*) il ne manquait pas grand-chose; **this is the nearest thing we have to a conference room** c'est ce que nous avons qui ressemble le plus à une salle de conférence; **it's the nearest you'll get to a bookshop in these parts** c'est ce que vous trouverez de mieux en matière de librairie par ici; **the nearest equivalent** l'équivalent le plus proche; **it's quite n. the original** (*of translation*) c'est assez proche de l'original

NPL *often Hum* **one's nearest and dearest** ses plus proches parents

VT (s')approcher de; **as we were nearing Oxford** comme nous approchions d'Oxford; **the road is nearing completion** la route est près d'être achevée; **we are nearing our goal** nous touchons au but; **he seemed to be nearing a breakdown/a crisis/a turning point** il semblait au bord de la dépression/d'une crise/d'un tournant; *Lit* **he's nearing his end** il approche de la fin
▸▸ **the N. East** le Proche-Orient; *Comput* **n. letter quality** qualité *f* courrier; **n. letter quality printer** imprimante *f* de qualité courrier; **n. miss** coup *m* qui a raté de peu; (*between planes, vehicles etc*) collision *f* évitée de justesse; **it was a n. miss** (*answer*) la réponse était presque bonne; (*accident*) on a frôlé l'accident; **that was a n. miss!** (*escape*) on l'a échappé belle!; **n. money** quasi-monnaie *f, pl* quasi-monnaies; *St Exch* **n. month** échéance *f* proche

near- [nɪər] PREF **n.-perfect** presque parfait; **a n.-disaster** un désastre évité de peu

nearby ADV [nɪə'baɪ] tout près; **is it n.?** est-ce que c'est près d'ici?; **to live n.** habiter dans les parages; **in a house n.** dans une maison voisine; **they stood n., watching** ils se tenaient à proximité et regardaient
ADJ ['nɪəbaɪ] proche; **a n. house** une maison voisine *ou* avoisinante

near-death experience N expérience *f* aux frontières de la mort

nearly ['nɪəlɪ] ADV **1** (*almost*) presque; **it's n.**

midnight il est presque *ou* bientôt minuit; **we're n. there** nous y sommes presque; **I've got n. all of them** je les ai presque *ou* à peu près tous; **I'm n. forty** j'ai près de *ou* presque quarante ans; **it cost n. ten pounds** cela a coûté près de *ou* presque dix livres; **very n.** peu s'en faut; **I very n. resigned on the spot** il s'en est fallu de peu pour que je ne démissionne sur le champ; **I very n. fell/burst out laughing** j'ai bien failli tomber/éclater de rire; **he very n. died** il a frôlé la mort; **she's not n. as old as me** elle est loin d'être aussi âgée que moi **2** (*closely*) (de) près
▸▸ *Fam* **n. man** ≃ éternel second *m*

nearly-new ADJ presque neuf

nearness ['nɪənɪs] N (*of time, place*) proximité *f*, (*of place*) voisinage *m*; (*of friends*) intimité *f*; **their growing n. to one another** leur intimité grandissante

nearside ['nɪəsaɪd] *Br* N (*of horse*) côté *m* gauche; *Aut* (*when driving on left*) (*of road*) gauche *f*, (*of vehicle*) côté gauche; (*when driving on right*) (*of road*) droite *f*, (*of vehicle*) côté droit
ADJ *Aut* (*when driving on left*) gauche; (*when driving on right*) droit; **keep to the n. lane** serrez (*when driving on left*) à gauche *ou* (*when driving on right*) à droite

near-sighted ADJ myope; *Fig* (*policy, government etc*) obtus

near-sightedness [-saɪtɪdnɪs] N myopie *f*, *Fig* imprévoyance *f*

neat [niːt] ADJ **1** (*tidy*) (*person*) ordonné, qui a de l'ordre; (*in one's appearance*) soigné, net, *f* nette; (*room, drawer etc*) bien rangé, en ordre; (*exercise book etc*) bien tenu, propre; (*garden*) bien tenu, *Fam* propret, -ette; (*way of dressing, handwriting*) soigné; **he's a n. worker** son travail est très soigné; **his clothes are always very n.** ses vêtements sont toujours très nets

2 (*elegant, well-formed*) (*turn of phrase, answer etc*) bien tourné, adroit; (*idea, solution*) ingénieux; **she is small and n.** elle est petite et bien faite; *esp Am* **a n. plan** un plan bien pensé; **a n. little gadget** un petit gadget bien conçu; **that's a n. trick** c'est malin; **a n. manoeuvre** une manœuvre adroite; **a n. piece of work** un ouvrage bien exécuté; **she made a n. job of it** elle a fait du bon travail; **the surgeon made a n. job of those stitches** le chirurgien a bien soigné ces points de suture

3 (*tight*) étroit; **it's rather n. across the shoulders/around the waist** c'est un peu étroit au niveau des épaules/à la taille

4 (*undiluted*) pur, sans eau; **to take** *or* **drink one's whisky n.** boire son whisky sec

5 *Am Fam* (*good*) super; **that's really n.** c'est vraiment super

neaten ['niːt(ə)n] VT = **neaten up**
▸ **neaten up** VT SEP (*clothes*) ajuster; (*hair, garden*) arranger; (*hair, by trimming etc*) rafraîchir; (*room*) ranger; (*presentation*) fignoler, peaufiner; **go and n. yourself up a bit** va t'arranger un peu

neatly ['niːtlɪ] ADV **1** (*to put away etc*) d'une manière soignée *ou* ordonnée, avec ordre; **n. written** écrit soigneusement; **n. set out** disposé avec soin; **everything is n. in its place** tout est soigneusement rangé à sa place **2** (*cleverly etc*) adroitement; **n. phrased** bien tourné; **that is n. put** c'est joliment dit; **that brings us n. back to my opening question** cela nous ramène justement à ma question de départ

neatness ['niːtnɪs] N **1** (*of handwriting, clothes*) netteté *f*, (*of garden*) apparence *f* soignée; (*of room etc*) bon ordre *m*; (*of exercise book etc*) propreté *f*; **the n. of her appearance** son allure *ou* apparence soignée; **personal n. is essential** il est essentiel d'avoir une apparence soignée **2** (*skill, cleverness*) adresse f, habileté f, (of solution, idea) ingéniosité f, (of phrase) tournure f adroite

nebula, pl **nebulæ** or **nebulas** ['nebjʊlə, -iː] N Astron nébuleuse f

nebulous ['nebjʊləs] ADJ (vague), Astron nébuleux

necessaries ['nesɪsərɪz] NPL **the n.** (food, money etc) ce qu'il faut pour vivre; Law (means to live) le nécessaire; **we haven't got enough for the n.** nous n'avons pas assez pour nous payer le strict nécessaire

necessarily [nesɪ'serəlɪ] ADV 1 nécessairement; **it's not n. the case** ce n'est pas nécessairement ou forcément vrai 2 (inevitably) inévitablement, forcément

necessary ['nesɪsərɪ] ADJ 1 (indispensable) nécessaire (**to** or **for sb/sth** à qn/qch); **the time/space/resources n.** le temps/l'espace/les ressources nécessaire(s); **everything n.** tout ce qui est nécessaire; **it is n. to do something** il est nécessaire de faire quelque chose, il faut faire quelque chose; **it is n. for him to return** il faut qu'il revienne; **I find it n. to ...** je juge nécessaire de ...; **it is n. that ...** il est nécessaire ou il faut que ... + sub; **it's not n. to be rude** ce n'est pas la peine d'être impoli; **to make all n. arrangements** prendre toutes les dispositions utiles ou nécessaires; **to make it n. for sb to do sth** mettre qn dans l'obligation de faire qch; **if n.** si cela est nécessaire, s'il le faut, le cas échéant, au besoin; **whenever n.** chaque fois qu'il le faudra; **as and when n.** quand c'est/ce sera nécessaire; **to do what is n.** faire le nécessaire; **not to do more than is absolutely n.** ne faire que le strict nécessaire ou l'essentiel

2 (inevitable) (result, conclusion, etc) nécessaire, inévitable; **a n. evil** un mal nécessaire N Fam **the n.** (things, action required) le nécessaire; (money) les fonds mpl; **his father will provide the n.** (money) son père fournira les fonds; **to do the n.** faire le nécessaire

necessitate [nɪ'sesɪteɪt] VT nécessiter, rendre nécessaire

necessitous [nɪ'sesɪtəs] ADJ Fml nécessiteux, dans le besoin; **their present n. state** leur indigence actuelle

necessity [nɪ'sesɪtɪ] N 1 (abstract need) nécessité f, **by** or **from** or **out of n.** par nécessité, par la force des choses; **of n.** nécessairement, forcément; Prov **n. is the mother of invention** en cas de besoin on trouve toujours une solution

2 (specific need) nécessité f, besoin m (**of doing sth** de faire qch); **the n. for sth** le besoin de qch; **if the n. arose** or **should arise** si le besoin s'en faisait sentir; **in case of n.** au besoin, en cas de besoin; **case of absolute n.** cas m de force majeure; **there's no n. to be rude** ce n'est pas la peine d'être impoli; **is there any real n. for such haste?** une telle hâte est-elle nécessaire ou indispensable?

3 (usu pl) **necessities** (things needed) le nécessaire; **the bare necessities** le strict nécessaire; **the necessities of life** les nécessités fpl de la vie; **a car is not one of life's necessities** une voiture n'est pas indispensable; **a washing machine is a n.** une machine à laver est indispensable

4 Fml (poverty) dénuement m; **the family live in dire n.** la famille vit dans le dénuement le plus complet

neck [nek] N 1 (of person, animal) cou m; **to throw** or **fling one's arms round sb's n.** sauter ou se jeter au cou de qn; Fig **to be up to one's n. in work** avoir du travail par-dessus la tête, être débordé de travail; Fam Fig **he's in it up to his n.** il y en est jusqu'au cou; Fig **to stick one's n. out** prendre des risques; (and say sb will win etc) s'engager; Fam Fig **to risk/save one's n.** risquer/sauver sa peau;

Fam **to get it in the n.** en prendre pour son grade; Horseracing **to win by a n.** gagner d'une encolure; **to finish n. and n.** arriver à égalité; **it's n. or nothing** il faut risquer ou jouer le tout pour le tout; Fam **what are you doing in this n. of the woods?** qu'est-ce que tu fais dans le coin?

2 Br Sl (cheek) culot m; **to have a (brass) n.** avoir du culot; **to have the (brass) n. to do sth** avoir le culot de faire qch

3 (of dress, shirt) encolure f, **square/round n.** encolure carrée/ronde; **V-n.** encolure en pointe ou en V; **high n.** col m montant; **low n.** décolleté m

4 Culin (of lamb) collier m, collet m; (of beef) collier

5 (of bottle) goulot m, col m; (of vase) col; (of pipe) rétrécissement m, étranglement m; Anat (of uterus, bone) col; (of land) langue f, (of string instrument) manche m, collet m VI Sl (of couple) se bécoter; **he was necking with her** ils se bécotaient

▸▸**n. microphone** micro m cravate

neckband ['nekbænd] N (ribbon etc) tour m de cou; (on shirt) col m

neckerchief ['nekətʃɪf] N Old-fashioned foulard m, tour m de cou

necklace ['neklɪs] N collier m

necklet ['neklɪt] N collier m (de fourrure etc)

neckline ['neklaɪn] N encolure f, **dress with a plunging n.** robe au décolleté plongeant

necktie ['nektaɪ] N Am cravate f

neckwear ['nekweər] N Com cols mpl, cravates fpl et foulards mpl

necrology [ne'krɒlədʒɪ] N Fml 1 (list of deaths) nécrologie f, Rel nécrologe m 2 (obituary) nécrologie f

necromancer ['nekrəʊmænsər] N nécromancien, -ienne

necromancy ['nekrəʊmænsɪ] N nécromancie f

necrophilia [nekrəʊ'fɪlɪə] N nécrophilie f

necrophobia [nekrəʊ'fəʊbɪə] N nécrophobie f

necropolis [ne'krɒpəlɪs] N nécropole f

necrosis [ne'krəʊsɪs] N Med nécrose f

nectar ['nektər] N 1 Myth, Bot nectar m 2 (fruit juice) nectar m

nectarine ['nektəriːn] N brugnon m, nectarine f

▸▸**n. tree** brugnonier m

ned [ned] N esp Scot Fam casseur m; **he's a bit of a n.** il est du genre casseur

NEDC [eniːdiːˈsiː] N Br Admin Formerly (abbr **National Economic Development Council**) = agence f nationale pour le développement économique

Neddy ['nedɪ] N Br Admin Formerly Fam = NEDC

née [neɪ] ADJ née; **MrsThomas, n. Long** Mme Thomas, née Long

NEED [niːd] N 1 (requirement) besoin m; **to feel/satisfy a n.** éprouver/satisfaire un besoin; **if need(s) be, in case of n.** en cas de besoin, au besoin, s'il (en) est besoin, si besoin (en) est; **n. for sth/sb** besoin de qch/qn; **there is no n. to ...** il n'est pas nécessaire de ..., ce n'est pas la peine de ...; (there's) no n. to wait (il est) inutile d'attendre, ce n'est pas la peine d'attendre; **without the n. for sth** sans nécessiter qch; **the information will be made available on a n.-to-know basis** les informations ne seront fournies qu'à ceux qui en ont besoin; **the boss works on a n.-to-know basis** le patron ne dit que ce qu'on a besoin de savoir; **to be in n.** or **have n. of sth** avoir besoin de qch; **to be badly in n. of repair** avoir bien ou grand besoin d'être réparé; **she is in n. of a rest** elle a besoin de se reposer ou de repos; **to attend to sb's needs**

pourvoir aux besoins de qn; **that will meet my needs** cela fera mon affaire; **my most pressing n. is (for) a ...** ce dont j'ai le plus besoin dans l'immédiat est de ...; **whenever/wherever there's a n. for it** chaque fois que/partout où c'est nécessaire

2 (difficulty) adversité f, difficulté f, (financial difficulty) besoin m, indigence f, **in times** or **in the hour of n.** dans les moments difficiles; **in my hour of n.** au moment où j'en ai eu besoin; **to be in n.** être dans la nécessité ou dans le besoin; **their n. is greater than mine** ils en ont plus besoin que moi

3 Mktg **needs analysis** analyse f des besoins; **needs assessment** estimation f des besoins; **needs-based market** marché m fondé sur les besoins; **needs-based segmentation** segmentation f fondée sur les besoins; **needs study** étude f des besoins; **needs-and-wants exploration** exploration f des besoins et des désirs

VT VOIR GRAMMAIRE A61 (3rd person sing pr ind needs; pt, pp needed) (of person) avoir besoin de; (of thing) exiger, nécessiter, demander; **my bike needs a few repairs** mon vélo a besoin de quelques réparations; **his hair needs cutting** il a besoin de se faire couper les cheveux; **they n. to be oiled/covered in plastic** il faut les graisser/couvrir d'un plastique; **this soup needs more salt/pepper** cette soupe manque de sel/poivre; **to n. rest** avoir besoin de repos; **I work because I n. the money** je travaille par besoin d'argent; **these facts n. no (further) comment** ces faits se passent de commentaire; **a much needed lesson** une leçon dont on avait grand besoin; **what he needs is a thrashing** ce dont il a besoin, c'est d'une bonne raclée, ce qu'il lui faudrait c'est une bonne raclée; **you'll n. to take more money** il va falloir que tu prennes plus d'argent; **the baby needs changing** il faut changer le bébé; **he needs to do more work on it/to see a doctor** il faut qu'il y travaille davantage/qu'il voie un docteur; **they n. to be told everything** il faut qu'on leur dise tout; **I didn't n. to be reminded of it** je n'avais pas besoin qu'on me le rappelle; **he didn't n. to be told twice** il ne se l'est pas fait dire deux fois; **you only needed to ask** vous n'aviez qu'à demander; Iron **that's all I n.!** j'avais bien besoin de ça!; **the last thing we n. is someone like him snooping about the place** la dernière chose qu'il nous faut, c'est bien que quelqu'un comme lui vienne fouiner par ici; **who needs two cars anyway?** comme si on avait besoin d'avoir deux voitures!; **it needs a great deal of skill to do it properly** il faut beaucoup d'habileté pour le faire correctement; **it needs more patience than I have** cela exige ou requiert plus de patience que je n'en ai

MODAL AUX V VOIR GRAMMAIRE A41 (3rd person sing pr ind **need**; pt **need**; no prp; no pp) **adults only n. apply** seuls les adultes peuvent postuler; **you needn't trouble yourself** (vous n'avez) pas besoin de vous déranger; **we needn't have bothered after all** nous n'aurions pas dû nous déranger après tout; **you needn't bother!** ne prends pas cette peine!; **n. you go yet?** est-ce qu'il faut que tu partes déjà?; **n. I go on?** faut-il que je continue?; **you needn't wait** il est inutile que vous attendiez, inutile (pour vous) d'attendre; **I n. hardly tell you how grateful I am** il n'est pas besoin de vous dire combien je vous suis reconnaissant; **it n. not necessarily be true** ce n'est pas nécessairement vrai

▸▸Mktg **n. identification** identification f des besoins; Mktg **n. level** niveau m des besoins; Mktg **n. market** marché des besoins; Mktg **n. recognition** reconnaissance f des besoins; Mktg **n. set** ensemble m de besoins

needful ['niːdfʊl] ADJ *Old-fashioned* nécessaire (**to** à; **for** pour)

N *Fam* **to do the n.** faire le nécessaire; *(pay, provide money)* casquer

neediness ['niːdɪnɪs] N indigence *f*

needle ['niːd(ə)l] N **1** *(for sewing etc)* aiguille *f*; *Bot* (pine) n. aiguille *f* de pin; **it's like looking for a n. in a haystack** c'est comme chercher une aiguille dans une botte de foin; **hypodermic n.** aiguille pour injections hypodermiques; *Fam* **I hate needles!** j'ai horreur des piqûres!; *Sl* **to be on the n.** *(take drugs)* se shooter, se piquer

2 *Br Fam* **to give sb the n.** *(irritate)* taper sur les nerfs à qn, agacer qn; *(deliberately)* faire enrager qn; *(anger)* mettre qn en rogne; **she's got the n.** elle est en rogne (**with** contre); **a bit of n. has crept into the match** les joueurs commencent à s'énerver *ou* disputent le match avec plus d'âpreté

3 *Tech (of record player, compass, speedometer etc)* aiguille *f*; *Aut (in float)* pointeau *m*; *(of scales)* aiguille, langue *f*, languette *f*, **compass n.** aiguille aimantée; *Art* **engraving n.** pointe *f* pour taille douce, pointe sèche

4 *Archit* obélisque *m*; *Geol, Geog* aiguille *f* (rocheuse); *Chem, Miner* **crystalline needles** aiguilles cristallines

VT *Fam (irritate)* agacer, taper sur les nerfs à; *(deliberately)* faire enrager; *(anger)* mettre en rogne; **to n. sb about not having a girlfriend** narguer qn parce qu'il n'a pas de petite amie; **to n. sb about his/her exam results** narguer qn à propos de ses résultats à un examen

VI *Sl (inject drugs)* se shooter, se piquer

▸ ▸ *Br* **n. bank** distributeur-échangeur *m* de seringues, *pl* distributeurs-échangeurs de seringues; **n. exchange scheme** programme *m* d'échange de seringues; *Br Fam* **n. match** match *m* âprement disputé; **n. noise** *(on record player)* bruit *m* d'aiguille; **n. scratch** *(on record player)* bruit *m* d'aiguille; *Sewing* **n. threader** filfilère *m*, enfile-aiguilles *m inv*; **n. valve** soupape *f* à pointeau

needlecord ['niːd(ə)lkɔːd] N *Tex* velours *m* mille-raies

needlecraft ['niːd(ə)lkrɑːft] N travail *m* à l'aiguille, travaux d'aiguille

needle-nosed pliers N pince *f* à bec fin

needlepoint ['niːd(ə)lpɔint] N *(embroidery)* tapisserie *f* à l'aiguille

needless ['niːdlɪs] ADJ inutile; *(remark)* déplacé; **n. to say, we shall refund the money** il va de soi que nous rembourserons l'argent

needlessly ['niːdlɪslɪ] ADV *(to be rude, pedantic, to worry)* inutilement; *(to die, suffer, work)* pour rien

needletime N *(for broadcasting records)* durée *f* de passage à l'antenne

needlewoman, *pl* **needlewomen** ['niːd(ə)lwʊmən, -wɪmɪn] N *(seamstress)* couturière *f*, **I'm no n.** je ne sais pas coudre

needlework ['niːd(ə)lwɜːk] N travaux *mpl* d'aiguille; *(school subject)* couture *f*, **she's good at n.** elle coud bien

needs [niːdz] ADV *Old-fashioned (used only with* must) de toute nécessité; **if n. must ...** s'il le faut absolument...; **ah well! n. must!** ah! il le faut bien; *Prov* **n. must when the devil drives** nécessité fait loi

need-to-know ADJ **information is given on a n. basis** les renseignements ne sont donnés qu'aux personnes concernées

needy ['niːdɪ] ADJ *(person)* nécessiteux, indigent; **to be emotionally n.** manquer d'affection

NPL **the n.** les nécessiteux *mpl*

ne'er [neər] ADV *Lit* (ne ...) jamais; **n. the less** néanmoins

ne'er-do-well N, ADJ propre *mf* à rien

nefarious [nɪ'feərɪəs] ADJ *(person, purpose etc)* infâme, scélérat

nefariously [nɪ'feərɪəslɪ] ADV d'une manière infâme

nefariousness [nɪ'feərɪəsnɪs] N *(of deed, crime, behaviour)* infâmie *f*, *(of person)* scélératesse *f*

neg [neg] N, ADJ *(abbr* **negative)** négatif *m*

negate [nɪ'geɪt] VT **1** *esp Fml (deny)* nier **2** *(nullify) (effect)* annuler; *(efforts, work)* anéantir; *(law etc)* annuler **3** *Gram* mettre au négatif

negation [nɪ'geɪʃən] N **1** *(denial) (of fact, proposition etc)* négation *f* **2** *(nullification) (of sb's work, efforts)* anéantissement *m*

negative ['negətɪv] ADJ *(reply, result, virtue etc)*, *Math, Elec, Phot* négatif; **don't be so n.** ne sois pas aussi négatif; **he's a very n. sort of person** il est très négatif

N **1** *(reply)* négative *f*, *Gram* négation *f*, *Math* valeur *f ou* quantité *f* négative; **to answer in the n.** répondre négativement *ou* par la négative; *Math* **two negatives make a positive** moins moins égale plus; *Gram* **to put a statement into the n.** mettre une affirmation à la forme négative VOIR GRAMMAIRE A47–8; B62–3 **2** *Phot (cliché m)* négatif *m*; *Elec (of battery)* plaque *f* négative

ADV *(in answer to a question)* non

VT **1** *(plan, project)* s'opposer à, rejeter **2** *(hypothesis, theory)* réfuter; *(report)* contredire, nier

▸ ▸ *Fin* **n. amortization** amortissement *m* négatif; *Phot* **n. cutter** monteur *m* négatif; *Fin* **n. equity** plus-value *f* immobilière négative, = situation *f* où l'acquéreur d'un bien immobilier reste redevable de l'emprunt contracté alors que son logement enregistre une moins-value; **n. (income) tax** impôt *m* négatif; *Fin* **n. interest** intérêt *m* négatif; **n. sign** signe *m* moins *ou* négatif

negatively ['negətɪvlɪ] ADV négativement

negativism ['negətɪvɪz(ə)m] N négativisme *m*

negativity [negə'tɪvɪtɪ] N négativité *f*, **because of the n. of his attitude** à cause de son attitude négative; **to feel a lot of n. towards sb** avoir beaucoup de sentiments négatifs contre qn

neglect [nɪ'glekt] N *(of person)* négligence *f*, *(of machine, property etc)* mauvais entretien *m*; **n. of one's duties/responsibilities** manquement *m* à ses devoirs/responsabilités; **out of** *or* **from** *or* **through n.** par négligence; **his n. of his children led to a court case** le fait qu'il néglige ses enfants a donné lieu à un procès; **to die in total n.** mourir complètement abandonné *ou* dans l'abandon le plus total; **to die of n.** mourir à cause d'un manque de soins; **to suffer n.** souffrir d'un manque de soins; **the equipment was allowed to fall into n.** le matériel n'a pas été entretenu

VT **1** *(not look after) (children, health etc)* négliger; **to n. oneself** négliger sa personne, se négliger; **the garden looks neglected** le jardin est mal tenu *ou* à l'abandon; **are you feeling neglected?** est-ce que vous avez l'impression qu'on vous néglige?

2 *(ignore) (duties)* négliger, oublier; *(one's responsibilities)* manquer à; *(one's post)* délaisser, abandonner; **to n. to do sth** omettre de faire qch; **he chooses to n. my advice** il choisit de ne pas tenir compte de mon conseil

neglectful [nɪ'glektfʊl] ADJ négligent; **to be n. of sth/sb** négliger qch/qn; **n. of one's duty** oublieux de son devoir; **to be n. of one's responsibilities/obligations** manquer à ses responsabilités/obligations

negligé, negligée ['neglɪʒeɪ] N négligé *m*, déshabillé *m*

negligence ['neglɪdʒəns] N *(lack of care)*, *Law* négligence *f*, **through n.** par négligence; **n. of one's duties/responsibilities** manquement *m* à ses devoirs/responsabilités

negligent ['neglɪdʒənt] ADJ **1** *(neglectful)* négligent; **to be n. of sth** négliger qch; *(of one's duties, responsibilities etc)* être oublieux de qch, manquer à qch **2** *(casual) (air, tone)* nonchalant, insouciant

negligently ['neglɪdʒəntlɪ] ADV **1** *(neglectfully)* avec négligence; **to fail n. to do sth** avoir la négligence de faire qch **2** *(casually)* négligemment, nonchalamment

negligible ['neglɪdʒɪb(ə)l] ADJ *(amount)* négligeable

negotiability [nɪgəʊʃə'bɪlɪtɪ] ADJ *Fin* négociabilité *f*

negotiable [nɪ'gəʊʃəb(ə)l] ADJ **1** *Fin etc (bill, document, demands, fee etc)* négociable; **not n.** non-négociable; *(on cheque)* non à ordre **2** *(barrier, obstacle etc)* franchissable; *(path etc)* praticable; **the path was not easily n.** le chemin n'était guère praticable

▸ ▸ *Fin* **n. instrument** instrument *m* négociable; *Fin* **n. paper** papier *m* négociable; *Fin* **n. stock** titres *mpl* négociables

negotiate [nɪ'gəʊʃɪeɪt] VT **1** *(business deal, marriage)* négocier, traiter; *(loan, treaty, fee)* négocier; *(peace)* traiter; *Fin (bill, document)* négocier, trafiquer; **price to be negotiated** prix *m* à débattre **2** *(obstacle etc)* franchir; *Fig (difficulty)* surmonter; *Aut (bend)* négocier, prendre; *(minefield)* traverser; *(rapids)* passer

VI négocier; **to be negotiating with sb for sth** être en traité *ou* en marché avec qn pour qch; **to n. for peace** entreprendre des pourparlers de paix; **to n. about sth** négocier qch

negotiating table [nɪ'gəʊʃɪeɪtɪŋ] N table *f* des négociations; **to sit round the n.** s'asseoir à la table des négociations

negotiation [nɪgəʊʃɪ'eɪʃən] N **1** *(of treaty, loan etc)* négociation *f*, **under n.** en négociation; **to be in n. with sb** être en pourparler(s) avec qn; **to break off/resume negotiations** rompre/reprendre les négociations; **pay/redundancy negotiations** négociations sur les salaires/les licenciements; **peace negotiations** pourparlers *mpl* de paix **2** *(of obstacle)* franchissement *m*; *(of corner)* prise *f*

negotiator [nɪ'gəʊʃɪeɪtər] N négociateur, -trice

Negress ['niːgrɪs] N Noire *f*, *(in anthropology)*, *Pej* négresse *f*

Negro, *pl* **Negroes** ['niːgrəʊ, -z] ADJ noir, nègre; **the N. race** la race noire *ou* nègre

N Noir *m*; *(in anthropology)*, *Pej* nègre *m*

▸ ▸ **N. spiritual** (negro) spiritual *m*

Negroid ['niːgrɔɪd] ADJ, N *(in anthropology)* négroïde *mf*

neigh [neɪ] N hennissement *m*

VI hennir

neighbour, *Am* **neighbor** ['neɪbər] N **1** *(person, country)* voisin, -ine; **to be a good n.** être bon voisin **2** *Bible etc (fellow human being)* prochain *m*; **love thy n. as thyself** aime ton prochain comme toi-même

▸ **neighbour on,** *Am* **neighbor on** VT INSEP *(adjoin)* avoisiner, être contigu à; *(of country)* être limitrophe à

neighbourhood, *Am* **neighborhood** ['neɪbəhʊd] N **1** *(vicinity)* **in the n. of** *(place)* aux alentours de, dans les environs de; **to live in the (immediate) n. of ...** demeurer à proximité de ...; **anyone in the n. of the crime should contact the police** quiconque se trouvait à proximité du lieu du crime doit contacter la police; **in the n. of 10** environ 10, dans les 10; **a figure in the n. of £2000**

un chiffre avoisinant les 2 000 livres **2** *(district)* voisinage *m*, quartier *m*; **I was in the n.** j'étais dans le coin *ou* dans le quartier *ou* dans le voisinage; **the whole n. is talking about it** tout le voisinage *ou* le quartier en parle; **a very friendly n.** un quartier très sympa; **a good/bad n.** un bon/mauvais quartier; **she's the n. gossip** c'est la commère du quartier *ou* du voisinage

▸▸ *Br* **n. watch** = système *m* par lequel les habitants d'un quartier s'entraident pour en assurer la surveillance et la sécurité

neighbouring, *Am* **neighboring** ['neɪbərɪŋ] ADJ avoisinant, voisin

neighbourliness, *Am* **neighborliness** ['neɪbəlɪnɪs] N (relations *fpl* de) bon voisinage *m*, bons rapports *mpl* entre voisins; **an act of n.** un acte de bon voisinage; **to show a little n.** se montrer bon voisin; **the n. of the family next door** l'obligeance *f* de la famille d'à-côté

neighbourly, *Am* **neighborly** ['neɪbəlɪ] ADJ *(person)* obligeant, bon voisin; *(action, behaviour etc)* de bon voisin; *(visit)* de bon voisinage; **it was very n. of them** c'était très obligeant de leur part; **to be n. with sb** entretenir des rapports de bon voisinage avec qn; **people used to be more n.** autrefois les gens entretenaient de meilleurs rapports avec leurs voisins

neighing ['neɪɪŋ] N hennissement(s) *m(pl)*

neither ['naɪðər, 'niːðər] VOIR GRAMMAIRE A37 ADV **n. ... nor ...** ni ... ni ...; **he will n. eat nor drink** il ne veut ni manger ni boire; **n. (the) one nor the other** ni l'un ni l'autre; **that's n. here nor there** *(irrelevant)* ça n'a rien à voir CONJ non plus; **n. do I** (ni) moi non plus; **if you don't go n. will I** si vous n'y allez pas je n'irai pas non plus; **I haven't read it, n. do I intend to** je ne l'ai pas lu et d'ailleurs je n'en ai pas l'intention; **the funding wasn't available and n. was the necessary expertise** ni les fonds ni les compétences nécessaires n'étaient disponibles VOIR GRAMMAIRE A73–4 ADJ **n. driver was injured** ni l'un ni l'autre des conducteurs n'a été blessé; **on n. side** ni d'un côté ni de l'autre PRON **which do you want? – n.** lequel voulez-vous? – ni l'un(e) ni l'autre; **n. of my two brothers can come** aucun de mes deux frères ne peut venir; **n. of us is satisfied** nous ne sommes satisfaits ni l'un ni l'autre

nelly ['nelɪ] N *Br Sl* **not on your n.!** jamais de la vie!

nelson ['nels(ə)n] N *(in wrestling)* nelson *m*; **double** *or* **full n.** double nelson

nematode ['nemətəʊd] N nématode *m*

Nemesis ['nemɪsɪs] N *Myth* Némésis *f*, *Fig* **this/he was my n.** cela/il a été ma ruine

neo- ['niːəʊ] PREF néo-

neoclassic(al) [niːəʊ'klæsɪk, -ɪk(ə)l] ADJ néoclassique; **neoclassical economics** économie *f* néoclassique

neoclassicism [niːəʊ'klæsɪsɪz(ə)m] N néoclassicisme *m*

neocolonialism [niːəʊkə'ləʊnɪəlɪz(ə)m] N néocolonialisme *m*

neofascism [niːəʊ'fæʃɪz(ə)m] N néofascisme *m*

neofascist [niːəʊ'fæʃɪst] ADJ, N néofasciste *mf*

neogothic [niːəʊ'gɒθɪk] ADJ, N *Archit* néogothique *m*

neolithic [niːəʊ'lɪθɪk] ADJ néolithique; **the N. age** l'âge *m* de la pierre polie, le néolithique

neologism [nɪ'ɒlədʒɪz(ə)m] N néologisme *m*

neon ['niːɒn] N *Chem* néon *m*
▸▸ *Elec* **n. light** lumière *f* au néon; **n. sign**

enseigne *f* lumineuse (au néon); **n. tube** tube *m* fluorescent *ou* au néon

neonatal [niːəʊ'neɪt(ə)l] ADJ néonatal, -als

neonazi [niːəʊ'nɑːtsɪ] ADJ, N néonazi, -ie

neophyte ['niːəʊfaɪt] N *Rel etc* néophyte *mf*

neoplasm ['niːəʊplæz(ə)m] N *Med* néoplasme *m*

neorealism [niːəʊ'rɪəlɪz(ə)m] N *Cin* néoréalisme *m*

Nepal [nɪ'pɔːl] N Népal *m*

Nepalese [nepə'liːz], **Nepali** [ne'pɔːlɪ] ADJ népalais
N **1** Népalais, -aise **2** *Ling* népalais *m*

nephew ['nefjuː] N neveu *m*

nephrite ['nefraɪt] N *Miner* néphrite *f*

nephritic [ne'frɪtɪk] ADJ *Med* néphrétique

nephritis [ne'fraɪtɪs] N *Med* néphrite *f*, **to have n.** avoir une néphrite

nephron ['nefrɒn] N *Anat* néphron *m*

nepotism ['nepətɪz(ə)m, 'niː-] N népotisme *m*

Neptune ['neptjuːn] N *Astron* Neptune *f*, *Myth* Neptune *m*

nerd [nɜːd] N *Pej Fam* ringard, -arde

nerdy ['nɜːdɪ] ADJ *Pej Fam* ringard

Nereid ['nɪərɪɪd] N *Myth* Néréide *f*

Nero ['nɪərəʊ] N *Antiq* Néron *m*

nerve [nɜːv] N **1** *Anat* nerf *m*; **to take the n. out of a tooth** *(of dentist)* dévitaliser une dent; **to be in a state of nerves** être sur les nerfs; **we're living on our nerves** nous vivons sur les nerfs; **it's her nerves** c'est les nerfs; **my nerves won't stand it** mes nerfs vont lâcher; **to get on sb's nerves** taper sur les nerfs à qn, énerver qn; **she's got nerves of steel** elle a des nerfs d'acier; **war of nerves** guerre des nerfs

2 *(courage)* courage *m*; *(coolness)* sang-froid *m*; **his n. failed him, he lost his n.** le courage lui a manqué; **a pilot who has lost his n.** un pilote qui n'est plus mentalement en état de voler; **he never regained his n.** il n'a jamais retrouvé son courage

3 *Fam (cheek)* culot *m*; **to have the n. to do sth** avoir le toupet *ou* le culot de faire qch; **what a n.!** quel culot!; **you've got a n.!** tu es gonflé!

4 *Bot, Entom, Archit* nervure *f*
VT **to n. oneself to do sth** s'armer de courage pour faire qch; **to n. sb for sth** encourager qn pour qch, donner du courage à qn pour qch

▸▸ **n. cell** cellule *f* nerveuse; **n. centre** *Anat* centre *m* nerveux; *Fig (headquarters)* centre névralgique; **n. ending** terminaison *f* nerveuse; **n. fibre** fibre *f* nerveuse; **n. gas** gaz *m* neurotoxique; **n. impulse** influx *m* nerveux; *Med* **n. specialist** neurologue *mf*

nerveless ['nɜːvlɪs] ADJ **1** *(calm) (person)* calme, plein de sang-froid; *(courage, bravery)* imperturbable **2** *(lacking strength) (person, limb etc)* inerte; *(style etc)* sans vigueur, languissant; **the cup fell from her n. fingers** la tasse a échappé à ses doigts engourdis

nerve-racking, nerve-wracking [-rækɪŋ] ADJ *(experience)* éprouvant; *(wait, suspense)* angoissant

nerviness ['nɜːvɪnɪs] N **1** *Br Fam (tension)* nervosité *f* **2** *Am Fam (cheek)* culot *m*

nervous ['nɜːvəs] ADJ **1** nerveux; *(timid)* craintif; **to be n.** *(before a performance, an exam etc)* avoir le trac; *(before going to the dentist etc)* avoir peur; **to be n. about sth** s'inquiéter à propos de qch; **are you n. about the exams?** est-ce que tu appréhendes les examens?; **he's n. about flying** il appréhende *ou* a peur de voyager en avion; **to be n. about doing sth** avoir peur *ou* appré-

hender de faire qch; **I was a bit n. about lending him the car** j'avais un peu d'appréhension à l'idée de lui prêter ma voiture; **the bank was n. about making the loan** la banque hésitait à accorder le prêt; **I'm still a little n. about taking on this contract** j'hésite encore un peu à accepter ce contrat; **if you're n. about offering him the job** *(are worried)* si vous craignez de lui proposer l'emploi; *(are uncertain)* si vous hésitez à lui proposer l'emploi; **he gets terribly n. every time he has to make a speech** chaque fois qu'il doit faire un discours il a un trac terrible *ou* il devient terriblement nerveux *ou* anxieux; **I feel** *or* **am n. in his presence** sa présence me rend nerveux; **airports make me n.** les aéroports me rendent nerveux; **he makes me n.** *(is intimidating)* il m'intimide; **don't hold your glass like that, you're making me n.** ne tiens pas ton verre comme ça, tu me rends nerveux *ou* tu me fais peur **2** *Anat (exhaustion etc)* nerveux

▸▸ **n. breakdown** dépression *f* nerveuse; **to have a n. breakdown** faire une dépression nerveuse; **n. disorder** maladie *f* nerveuse; **n. energy** énergie *f* nerveuse; **the n. system** le système nerveux

nervously ['nɜːvəslɪ] ADV nerveusement; **he wondered n. if ...** il se demanda, avec une certaine nervosité, si ...

nervousness ['nɜːvəsnɪs] N **1** *(timidity)* timidité *f*; *(before performance)* trac *m* **2** *(tension, anxiety)* nervosité *f*

nervy ['nɜːvɪ] ADJ **1** *Br Fam (tense)* nerveux; **to feel n.** avoir les nerfs en pelote **2** *Am Fam (cheeky)* qui a du culot

nest [nest] N *(of bird, wasps etc)* nid *m*; *(nestful) (of fledglings)* nichée *f*, couvée *f*, *(of eggs)* couvée; *Fig (of bandits, machine guns etc)* repaire *m*, nid; *Fig* **the children have all left** *or* **flown the n.** les enfants ont tous quitté le nid; **n. of tables** tables *fpl* gigognes
VI *(of bird etc)* (se) nicher, faire son nid; *(of tables etc)* s'emboîter
VT **1** *(pipes etc)* emboîter **2** *Comput, Typ* imbriquer

▸▸ **n. box** *(in henhouse)* pondoir *m*; *(in birdhouse)* nichoir *m*; **n. egg** économies *fpl*, bas *m* de laine, pécule *m*

nested ['nestɪd] ADJ *Comput, Typ* imbriqué

nestful ['nestfʊl] N *(of fledglings)* nichée *f*, couvée *f*, *(of eggs)* couvée

nesting ['nestɪŋ] ADJ *(bird)* nicheur; *(time, instinct)* de (la) nidification
N **1** *(building nests)* nidification *f*, **to go (bird) n.** aller dénicher des œufs/des oisillons **2** *Comput, Typ* imbrication *f*

▸▸ **n. box** *(in henhouse)* pondoir *m*; *(in birdhouse)* nichoir *m*; **n. time** saison *f* de la ponte

nestle ['nes(ə)l] VI se pelotonner, se blottir; *(of house, tree)* être blotti; **to n. (up) close to sb** se pelotonner *ou* se blottir *ou* se serrer contre qn; **to n. (up) against sb's shoulder** se blottir contre l'épaule de qn; **village nestling in a valley** village blotti *ou* tapi dans une vallée
VT **to n. one's face against sb's shoulder** se blottir contre l'épaule de qn

nestling ['neslɪŋ] N oisillon *m*

Net [net] N *Comput* **the N.** le Net, l'Internet *m*
▸▸ **N. user** internaute *mf*, utilisateur, -trice du Net

net¹ [net] N **1** filet *m*; **to haul in a n.** relever un filet; *Fig* **to be caught in the n.** être pris au piège *ou* au filet; *Fig* **to slip through the n.** passer à travers les mailles du filet; *Ftbl* **to put the ball in the n.** envoyer la balle dans le filet **2** *Tex* tulle *m* **3** *Tel, TV (national)* réseau *m*; *(channel)* chaîne *f*
VT (-tt-) **1** *(capture) (fish, hares)*, *Fig (criminals etc)* prendre au filet; *Fig (tax evaders, drugs)* mettre la main sur; *Fig* **the charity ap-**

peal **netted several large donations** l'appel caritatif a rapporté plusieurs dons importants **2** *(river)* tendre des filets dans **3** *Ftbl* **he netted the ball twice** *(scored two goals)* il a marqué deux buts **4** *(in gardening) (peas etc)* protéger avec un filet

▸▸**n. curtain** rideau *m* (de tulle *ou* en filet), voilage *m*; *Sport* **n. play** jeu *m* au filet

net² ADJ *(weight, price)* net, *f* nette; **n. proceeds of a sale** (produit *m*) net *m* d'une vente; **terms strictly n.** sans déduction

N *(income, profit, weight)* net *m*

ADV **n. of tax** net d'impôt; **n. of VAT** hors TVA

VT *Fin (sum of money) (of person)* toucher net, gagner net; *(of enterprise etc)* rapporter net; **we netted over \$10,000** nous avons réalisé un bénéfice net de plus de 10 000 dollars; **he nets £20,000 a year** il gagne 20 000 livres net par an

▸▸*Fin* **n. amount** somme *f* nette, montant *m* net; *Fin* **n. assets** actif *m* net; *Br Formerly* **the N. Book Agreement** = accord *m* entre maisons d'édition et libraires stipulant que ces derniers n'ont le droit de vendre aucun ouvrage à un prix inférieur à celui fixé par l'éditeur; *Fin* **n. book value** valeur *f* comptable nette; *Fin* **n. capital expenditure** mise *f* de fonds nette, dépenses *fpl* nettes d'investissement; *Fin* **n. cash flow** cash-flow *m* net, *pl* cash-flows nets; *Fin* **n. cost** prix *m* de revient; *Fin* **n. current assets** actif circulant net; *Fin* **n. dividend** dividende *m* net; *Fin* **n. domestic product** produit intérieur net; *Fin* **n. earnings** *(of company)* bénéfices *mpl* nets; *(of worker)* salaire *m* net; *Fin* **n. income** *(in accounts)* produit net; *(of individual)* revenu *m* net; *Fin* **n. interest income** net financier; *Fin* **n. loss** perte *f* nette; *Fin* **n. margin** marge *f* nette; *Fin* **n. national income** revenu national net; *Fin* **n. national product** produit national net; *Fin* **n. operating profit** rentabilité *f* nette d'exploitation; **n. payable** net à payer; *Fin* **n. present value** valeur actuelle nette; *Fin* **n. present value rate** taux *m* d'actualisation; *Fin* **n. profit** bénéfice *m* net, net commercial; *Fin* **n. profit margin** marge commerciale nette; *Fin* **n. profit ratio** ratio *m* de rentabilité nette, taux de profit net; *Fin* **n. realizable value** valeur réalisable nette; *Fin* **n. receipts** recettes *fpl* nettes; *Fin* **n. result** résultat *m* final; *Fin* **n. return** rendement *m* net, résultat net; *Fin* **n. salary** salaire net; *Comput* **n. storage capacity** capacité *f* nette de stockage; *Fin* **n. tangible assets** actif corporel net; *Fin* **n. tonnage** *(of ship)* tonnage *m* net; *Fin* **n. total** montant net; *Fin* **n. variance** écart *m* net; *Fin* **n. working capital** fonds *m* de roulement net; *Fin* **n. worth** situation *f* nette, valeur nette

.net [dɒt'net] *Comput* = abréviation *f* désignant les organismes officiels de l'Internet dans les adresses électroniques

netball ['netbɔːl] N *Sport* netball *m*

nethead ['nethed] N *Comput Fam* accro *mf* de l'Internet

nether ['neðər] ADJ inférieur, bas, *f* basse; **the n. regions** *Lit* l'enfer *m*, les régions *mpl* infernales; *Hum (of body)* les parties *fpl* basses; **the n. regions of the rue St. Denis** le bas de la rue St. Denis

Netherlands ['neðələndz] NPL **the N.** les Pays-Bas *mpl*; **in the N.** dans les *ou* aux Pays-Bas

netiquette ['netɪket] N *Comput Fam* netiquette *f*

netizen ['netɪzən] N *Comput* internaute *mf*

netspeak ['netspiːk] N *Comput* langage *m* du Net, cyberjargon *m*

nett [net] ADJ, N, ADV, VT = **net²**

netting ['netɪŋ] N *(nets) (for protection, camouflage)* filet(s) *m(pl)*; *(around tennis court*

etc) grillage *m*; *Tex* tulle *m*

nettle ['net(ə)l] N *(weed)* ortie *f*, *Fig* **to grasp the n.** prendre le taureau par les cornes; **to grasp the n. of reorganisation** s'attaquer au problème épineux de la réorganisation

VT *(irritate)* irriter, énerver

▸▸**n. rash** urticaire *f*

NetWare® loadable module ['netweər] N *Comput* module *m* logiciel téléchargeable

network ['netwɜːk] N **1** *(of canals, streets, contacts, users etc)* réseau *m*; **electricity n.** réseau électrique **2** *Comput, TV, Radio* réseau *m*; *TV (channel)* chaîne *f*

VT **1** *(to cover)* parcourir; **the country was networked with canals** le pays était parcouru de canaux; **to n. the country with railway lines/motorways** construire un réseau ferroviaire/autoroutier à travers le pays **2** *TV, Radio* diffuser sur l'ensemble du réseau; **networked programmes** émissions *fpl* diffusées en réseau **3** *Comput* mettre en réseau; **networked systems** systèmes *mpl* en réseau

VI *(establish contacts)* établir un réseau de contacts

▸▸*Comput* **n. access** accès *m* au réseau; *Comput* **n. access costs** coûts *mpl* d'accès au réseau; *Comput* **n. adaptor** carte *f* réseau; *Comput* **n. adaptor card** carte-adaptateur *f* réseau, *pl* cartes-adaptateurs réseau; *Comput* **n. administrator** administrateur, -trice de réseau; *Comput* **n. architecture** architecture *f ou* topologie *f* de réseau; *Comput* **n. card** carte réseau; *Comput* **n. computer** ordinateur *m* de réseau; *TV* **n. controller** contrôleur *m* de réseau, directeur *m* d'antenne *ou* de chaîne; *Comput* **n. driver** gestionnaire *m* de réseau; **n. management** administration *f* de réseau; **n. manager** gestionnaire de réseau; *Comput* **n. operating system** système *m* d'exploitation réseau; *Comput* **n. server** serveur *m* de réseau; *Comput* **n. software** logiciel *m* de réseau; **n. station** station *f* réseau; **n. supervisor** superviseur *m* de réseau; **n. television** réseau (de télévision) national; *Comput* **n. traffic** trafic *m* de réseau

networking ['netwɜːkɪŋ] N **1** *Comput* travail *m* en réseau; *(connecting as network)* mise en réseau; **to have n. capabilities** *(of terminal)* offrir la possibilité d'intégration à un réseau **2** *(establishing contacts)* établissement *m* d'un réseau de contacts

neural ['njʊərəl] ADJ *Anat* neural, -aux

▸▸**n. network** réseau *m* neuronal

neuralgia [njʊˈrældʒə] N *Med* névralgie *f*, **to have n.** avoir une névralgie

neuralgic [njʊˈrældʒɪk] ADJ *Med* névralgique

neurasthenia [njʊərəsˈθiːnɪə] N *Med* neurasthénie *f*

neurasthenic [njʊərəsˈθenɪk] ADJ, N *Med* neurasthénique *mf*

neuritis [njʊˈraɪtɪs] N *Med* névrite *f*

neurobiology [njʊərəbaɪˈɒlədʒɪ] N neurobiologie *f*

neurochemistry [njʊərəˈkemɪstrɪ] N neurochimie *f*

neurological [njʊərəˈlɒdʒɪk(ə)l] ADJ neurologique

neurologist [njʊəˈrɒlədʒɪst] N neurologue *mf*

neurology [njʊəˈrɒlədʒɪ] N neurologie *f*

neuromuscular [njʊərəʊˈmʌskjuːlər] ADJ neuromusculaire

neuron ['njʊərɒn] N *Physiol* neurone *m*

neurone ['njʊərəʊn] N *Biol* neurone *m*

neuropathology [njʊərəʊpəˈθɒlədʒɪ] N neuropathologie *f*

neuropsychiatrist [njʊərəʊsaɪˈkaɪətrɪst] N neuropsychiatre *mf*

neuropsychologist [njʊərəʊsaɪˈkɒlədʒɪst] N

neuropsychologue *mf*

neuroscience ['njʊərəʊsaɪəns] N neuroscience *f*

neurosis, pl **neuroses** [njʊˈrəʊsɪs, -siːz] N névrose *f*

neurosurgeon [njʊərəʊˈsɜːdʒən] N neurochirurgien, -ienne

neurosurgery [njʊərəʊˈsɜːdʒərɪ] N neurochirurgie *f*

neurosurgical [njʊərəʊˈsɜːdʒɪk(ə)l] ADJ neurochirurgical, -aux

neurotic [njʊˈrɒtɪk] ADJ **1** *(person)* névrosé; *Fig Fam* **he's positively n. about it** c'est une obsession chez lui; **to be n. about losing one's keys** avoir une peur obsessionnelle de perdre ses clés; **she gets very n. if everything isn't exactly as she left it** elle pique des crises folles si elle ne trouve pas tout exactement comme elle l'a laissé; **I think I'm getting a bit n. about it** je crois que je suis en train d'en faire une obsession **2** *(relating to a neurosis)* névrotique

N névrosé, -ée

neurotically [njʊˈrɒtɪklɪ] ADV de façon obsessionnelle; **to be n. obsessed with sth** avoir une obsession névrotique de qch

neuroticism [njʊˈrɒtɪsɪz(ə)m] N névrose *f*

neurotransmitter [njʊərəʊtrænzˈmɪtər] N *Biol* neurotransmetteur *m*

neuter ['njuːtər] ADJ **1** *Gram* neutre **2** *Biol* neutre, asexué

N **1** *Gram* neutre *m*; **in the n.** au neutre **2** *(animal)* animal *m* châtré; *(bee)* abeille *f* asexuée *ou* ouvrière

VT *Vet (cat etc)* châtrer

neutraceutical [njuːtrəˈsjuːtɪk(ə)l] N alicament *m*

neutral ['njuːtr(ə)l] ADJ *(colour)*, *Pol etc* neutre; **to remain n.** rester neutre; *Pol* rester neutre, garder la neutralité

N **1** *(nation)* (État *m ou* pays *m*) neutre *m*; *(person)* ressortissant, -ante d'un État neutre **2** *(person) (in an argument, politics etc)* personne *f* neutre **3** *Aut* point *m* mort; **in n.** au point mort

neutralism ['njuːtrəlɪz(ə)m] N neutralisme *m*

neutralist ['njuːtrəlɪst] ADJ, N neutraliste *mf*

neutrality [njuːˈtrælɪtɪ] N *Pol etc* neutralité *f*, *Chem (of salt)* neutralité, indifférence *f*

neutralization [njuːtrəlaɪˈzeɪʃən] N neutralisation *f*

neutralize ['njuːtrəlaɪz] VT *(opposition, country)* neutraliser; **to n. one another** *(of chemical agents)* se neutraliser; *(of forces)* se neutraliser, s'annuler

neutrino [njʊˈtriːnəʊ] N *Phys* neutrino *m*

neutron ['njuːtrɒn] N *Nucl* neutron *m*;

▸▸**n. bomb** bombe *f* à neutrons; **n. star** étoile *f* à neutrons

Nev *abbr* Nevada

never ['nevər] ADV **1** (ne ...) jamais; **I n. go there** je n'y vais jamais; **n. again!** plus jamais!; **I'll n. go there again, n. again will I go there** je n'irai plus jamais; **he n. came back** il n'est jamais revenu; **he's n. yet been beaten** il n'a encore jamais été battu; **I've n. yet understood why** je n'ai jamais compris pourquoi; **n. in (all) my life, in all my born days** jamais de la vie; **that n.-to-be-forgotten day** ce jour inoubliable; **n. say die!** accroche-toi!; **n. fear!** n'aie pas peur!, ne t'en fais pas! VOIR GRAMMAIRE A21; A78 **2** *(emphatic neg)* **I n. expected him to come** je ne m'attendais pas du tout à ce qu'il vienne; **she n. said a word** elle n'a pas dit un mot; **this will n. do!** c'est inacceptable!; **n. ever do that again!** je refais jamais cela!; **they n. even wrote back** ils n'ont même pas répondu; **n. a one** pas un seul; *Fam* **you n. left him all alone!** ne me dites pas que vous l'avez laissé tout seul! **3** *Lit* **be he** n. **so brave** quelque courageux qu'il soit, si courageux soit-il

INT *Br Fam* n.**!** *(incredulity)* pas possible!; **he** n. **did!** ça alors!; *esp Old-fashioned,* **well I** n.**!** ça par exemple!

never-ending ADJ perpétuel, éternel, sans fin; *(complaints, noise)* incessant; *(job, sermon, evening)* interminable; **my problems seem to be** n. mes problèmes semblent ne pas en finir; **a** n. **supply of funny stories** un stock inépuisable d'histoires drôles; **housework is** n. le ménage n'est jamais fini

never-failing ADJ inépuisable, intarissable

nevermore [nevə'mɔːr] ADV *Lit* (ne …) plus jamais, (ne …) jamais plus; **n.!** jamais plus!, plus jamais!

never-never N *Br Fam (hire purchase)* **to buy sth on the** n. acheter qch à crédit *ou* à tempérament
  ADJ imaginaire, chimérique
  ▸▸ n. **land** pays *m* de cocagne; **you're living in** n. **land if you believe that …** tu rêves si tu crois que …

nevertheless [nevəðə'les] ADV néanmoins, cependant; **I love him** n. je l'aime quand même *ou* malgré tout

nevus ['niːvəs] N *Am* = **naevus**

NEW [njuː] ADJ nouveau, -elle; *(before masculine noun beginning with vowel or silent h)* nouvel; *(not used)* neuf, f neuve; **I need a** n. **car** *(different)* il me faut une nouvelle voiture; **I'd prefer a new car** *or* **a car that's** n. *(which has not been used)* je préférerais une voiture neuve *ou* qui soit neuve; **we visited a** n. **country** *(one we did not know)* nous avons visité un nouveau pays; **America was a** n. **country** *(just developing)* l'Amérique était un pays neuf; **I felt a** n. **man** je me sentais un homme nouveau *ou* neuf; **she's got a** n. **man** elle a un nouveau mec; **it's made a** n. **man of him** cela a fait de lui un autre homme *ou* un homme neuf *ou* un nouvel homme; **would you like a** n. **glass?** *(for a different wine)* désirez-vous un autre verre?; **what's** n.**?** quoi de neuf *ou* de nouveau?; **that's nothing** n.**!** rien de nouveau à cela!; **it's quite** n. **to me** c'est tout nouveau *ou* neuf pour moi; *Fam* **that's a** n. **one on me!** c'est la première fois que j'entends/je vois cela!; **she's** n. **to this work** elle débute dans ce travail; **I'm** n. **to this town** je suis nouveau dans cette ville; **to be wearing** n. **clothes** être habillé de neuf; *Com* **in** n. **condition, as** n. à l'état (de) neuf; **to do sth up like** n. remettre qch à neuf; n. **ideas** *(modern ideas)* idées neuves; **a completely** n. **idea** une idée tout à fait nouvelle *ou* neuve; **the subject is quite** n. le sujet n'a pas encore été traité; *Sch* **the** n. **boys** les nouveaux; *Mktg* n. **and improved** nouveau et meilleur; n. **business** nouvelles affaires *fpl, (new company)* nouvelle entreprise *f*; **to look for** n. **business** faire de la prospection
  ADV *(used to form compound adj)* nouvellement; n. **blown** *(flower)* fraîchement *ou Lit* frais épanoui; n.**-cut grass** herbe fraîchement coupée; n.**-found** *(confidence, happiness)* tout neuf; *(friend etc)* nouveau; n.**-laid egg** œuf fraîchement pondu; n.**-made** *or* n.**-baked bread** pain frais; n. **mown hay** foin fraîchement *ou Lit* frais coupé
  ▸▸ n. **account manager** responsable *mf* des nouveaux comptes-clients; **N. Age** new age *m*, nouvel âge *m*; *Fam* n. **blood** sang *m* neuf; **N. Brunswick** le Nouveau-Brunswick; *Mktg* n. **buy situation** situation *f* de nouvel achat; **N. Caledonia** Nouvelle-Calédonie *f*; n. **classical economics** nouvelle économie *f* classique; **N. England** Nouvelle-Angleterre *f*; *Mil* **the** n. **guard** la garde montante; **N. Guinea**

Nouvelle-Guinée *f*; *St Exch* n. **issue** nouvelle émission *f*; *St Exch* n. **issue market** marché *m* des nouvelles émissions, marché primaire; **N. Labour** = nouveau nom *m* donné au parti travailliste britannique vers le milieu des années 90 dans le souci d'en moderniser l'image; *Pol* **the N. Left** la nouvelle gauche; **N. Man** homme *m* moderne *(qui participe équitablement à l'éducation des enfants et aux tâches ménagères)*; n. **maths** maths *fpl* modernes; **the** n. **media** les nouveaux médias *mpl*; **N. Mexico** le Nouveau-Mexique; n. **moon** nouvelle lune *f*; **N. Orleans** La Nouvelle-Orléans; n. **potatoes** pommes *fpl* de terre nouvelles; *Com, Mktg* n. **product** nouveau produit *m*; *Com, Mktg* n. **product development** développement *m* de nouveaux produits; *Com, Mktg* n. **product marketing** marketing *m* de nouveaux produits; **the** n. **rich** les nouveaux riches *mpl*; *Pol* **the N. Right** la nouvelle droite; *Fin* n. **shares** actions *fpl* nouvelles; n. **technology** nouvelle technologie *f*, technologie de pointe; *Bible* **N. Testament** Nouveau Testament *m*; *Br* n. **town** ville *f* nouvelle; *Med* n. **variant CJD** nouveau variant *m* de la maladie de Creutzfeld-Jacob; n. **wave** *(in cinema)* nouvelle vague *f*, *(in pop music)* new wave *f*, n. **wine** vin *m* primeur; **the N. World** le Nouveau Monde; **N. Year** Nouvel An *m*; **N. Year's Day** jour *m* de l'an; **N. Year's Eve** Saint Sylvestre *f*, **N. York** New York; **N. Yorker** New-Yorkais, -aise; **N. Zealand** Nouvelle-Zélande *f*, **N. Zealander** Néo-Zélandais, -aise

newbie ['njuːbɪ] N *Comput Fam* internaute *mf* novice

newborn ['njuːbɔːn] ADJ nouveau-né, f nouveau-née
  ▸▸ n. **baby** nouveau-né, -née, *pl* nouveau-nés, -nées

newcomer ['njuːkʌmər] N nouveau venu *m*, nouvelle venue *f* (**to** dans)

newel ['njuːəl] N *Constr etc* **1** *(of spiral staircase)* noyau *m* (d'escalier) **2** *(of bannister)* pilastre *m*
  ▸▸ n. **post** pilastre *m*

newfangled ['njuːfæŋ(ə)ld] ADJ *Pej* nouveau genre *inv, (word, idea etc)* moderne; n. **gadgets** gadgets *mpl* à la dernière mode

Newfie ['njuːfɪ] N *Can Fam* Terre-Neuvien, -ienne
  ▸▸ **N. joke** = plaisanterie *f* sur les Terre-Neuviens, ≃ histoire *f* belge

Newfoundland ['njuːfəndlænd, -lənd, -'faundlənd] N **1** *Geog* Terre-Neuve *f* **2** *(dog)* terre-neuve *m inv*
  ADJ terre-neuvien
  ▸▸ **N. dog** terre-neuve

Newfoundlander ['njuːfəndlændər, njuː'faundləndər] N *(native)* Terre-Neuvien, -ienne; *(inhabitant)* habitant, -ante de Terre-Neuve

newish ['njuːɪʃ] ADJ *Fam (car, dress etc)* assez neuf, f assez neuve

newly ['njuːlɪ] ADV *(usu hyphenated in conjunction with attributive adj before n)* récemment, nouvellement, fraîchement; n.**-dug** fraîchement creusé; n.**-formed** récemment formé; n.**-discovered/returned** qui vient d'être découvert/de rentrer; n.**-elected MPs** députés nouvellement élus; n.**-painted wall** mur qui vient d'être peint
  ▸▸ n.**-industrialized country** nouveau pays *m* industrialisé; n.**-industrialized economy** économie *f* nouvellement industrialisée; n.**-industrializing country** pays en voie d'industrialisation

newlyweds ['njuːlɪwedz] NPL jeunes mariés *mpl*

newness ['njuːnɪs] N *(of idea etc)* nouveauté *f*,

(of piece of clothing etc) état *m* neuf; *(of bread etc)* fraîcheur *f*, *(of wine)* jeunesse *f*, **her** n. **to** *or* **in the job** le fait qu'elle soit nouvelle à ce poste

news [njuːz] NPL *(usu with sing verb)* **1** nouvelle(s) *f(pl)*; **what's the** n.**?** quelles nouvelles?, quoi de nouveau *ou* de neuf?; **there's been no** n. **so far** on n'a pas encore de nouvelles; **I've got some** n. **for you** j'ai une nouvelle à vous annoncer; **have you heard the** n.**?** est-ce que vous avez appris la nouvelle?; **a sad piece of** n., **sad** n. une triste nouvelle; **good/bad** n. bonne/mauvaise nouvelle; *Prov* **no** n. **is good** n. pas de nouvelles, bonnes nouvelles; *Prov* **bad** n. **travels fast** les mauvaises nouvelles vont vite; **I've got some good** n. **and some bad** n. j'ai deux nouvelles, une bonne et une mauvaise; **have I got** n. **for you!** j'ai quelque chose à vous annoncer!; **that's** n. **to me!** première nouvelle! **2 the** n. *Radio, TV* les informations *fpl*, *TV (bulletin)* le (télé)journal; **to be in the** n. faire parler de soi dans la presse, *esp Pej* défrayer la chronique; **a city that is in the** n. **a lot these days** une ville dont on parle beaucoup ces jours-ci; **he's always in the** n. on parle toujours de lui dans la presse; **I heard it on the** n. je l'ai entendu aux informations; **financial** n. chronique financière; **sports** n. chronique des sports; **local/national/world** n. informations locales/nationales/internationales; n. **in brief** faits *mpl* divers **3** *(person, event etc)* sujet *m* propre au reportage; **to make** n. faire sensation; **she's no longer** n. on ne parle plus d'elle; **the fact that she's leaving is bad** n. **for the company** son départ est mauvais pour la société; *Fam* **he's bad** n. *(is unpopular etc)* c'est un enquiquineur
  ▸▸ n. **agency** agence *f* de presse; *Am Radio, TV* n. **analyst** commentateur, -trice; n. **blackout** black-out *m inv* sur l'actualité, censure *f* de l'actualité; **to impose a** n. **blackout on sth** empêcher la divulgation de qch; **the government has imposed a** n. **blackout** le gouvernement a fait le blackout; n. **broadcasting** diffusion *f* des informations; n. **bulletin** bulletin *m* d'informations; n. **centre** salle *f* de rédaction télévision; n. **channel** chaîne *f* d'information continue; n. **conference** conférence *f* de presse; n. **content** contenu *m* d'informations; n. **coverage** reportage *m* d'actualités; n. **desk** (salle *f* de) rédaction *f*, n. **editor** rédacteur, -trice en chef des actualités; n. **gathering** collecte *f* de l'information; n. **headlines** titres *mpl* de l'actualité; n. **item** nouvelle, information *f*, n. **magazine** news magazine *m*; n. **programme** magazine *m* d'actualités; n. **report** bulletin *m* d'informations; n. **reporter** reporter *m*; n. **satellite** satellite *m* d'informations; *Am* n. **service** = agence de presse qui publie ses informations par le biais d'un syndicat de distribution; n. **sheet** bulletin d'information; n. **short** brève *f*, n. **stand** kiosque *m* à journaux; n. **story** sujet *m*; n. **value** intérêt *m* médiatique; n. **vendor** marchand, -ande de journaux; n. **writer** rédacteur, -trice d'actualités

newsagent ['njuːzeɪdʒənt] N *Br* marchand, -ande de journaux; *(shopkeeper also selling papers)* dépositaire *mf* de journaux; n.**'s (shop)** maison *f* de la presse

newscast ['njuːzkɑːst] N *Radio, TV* informations *fpl*

newscaster ['njuːzkɑːstər] N *Radio, TV* présentateur, -trice du journal

newscasting ['njuːzkɑːstɪŋ] N *Radio, TV* présentation *f* du journal

newsdealer ['njuːzdiːlər] N *Am* = **newsagent**

newsfilm ['njuːzfɪlm] N film *m* d'actualités

newsflash ['nju:zflæʃ] N *Radio, TV* flash m d'information(s)

newsgroup ['nju:zgru:p] N *Comput* newsgroup m, forum m *ou* groupe m de discussion

newshawk, newshound ['nju:zhɔ:k, -haʊnd] N *Fam* reporter m, chasseur m de copie

newsie ['nju:zɪ] N *Am Fam (newspaper vendor)* vendeur, -euse de journaux; *(journalist)* journaleux, -euse

newsletter ['nju:zletər] N bulletin m (d'informations), circulaire f

newsman, pl **newsmen** ['nju:zmən] N journaliste m

newspaper ['nju:zpeɪpər] N journal m; **daily n.** (journal) quotidien m; **weekly n.** (journal) hebdomadaire m; **to work for** *or* **on a n.** travailler dans *ou* pour un journal; **to wrap sth in/line a drawer with n.** emballer qch dans/tapisser un tiroir de (papier) journal
▸▸**n. ads** petites annonces fpl des journaux; **n. advertisement** publicité f presse; **n. advertising** publicité presse; **n. article** article m de presse *ou* journal; **n. artist** *(for layout)* maquettiste mf; **n. clippings** coupures fpl de journaux; **n. cuttings** coupures de journaux; **n. editor** rédacteur, -trice m de journal; **n. group** groupe m de presse; **n. kiosk** kiosque m à journaux; **n. office** bureau m de la presse; **n. photographer** photographe mf de presse; **n. publisher** éditeur m de presse; **n. rack** porte-journaux m *inv*; **n. report** reportage m; **n. reporter** reporter m (de la presse écrite); **n. stand** kiosque à journaux

newspaperman, pl **newspapermen** ['nju:zpeɪpəmən] N **1** *Journ (reporter)* journaliste m; *(proprietor)* propriétaire m de journal **2** *Br (vendor)* marchand de journaux

newspaperwoman, pl **newspaperwomen** ['nju:zpeɪpəwʊmən, -wɪmɪn] N **1** *Journ (reporter)* journaliste f, *(proprietor)* propriétaire f de journal **2** *Br (vendor)* marchande f de journaux

newsprint ['nju:zprɪnt] N papier m (de) journal; **I got my hands covered in n.** *(ink)* je me suis mis de l'encre plein les mains

newsreader ['nju:zri:dər] N *Radio, TV* présentateur, -trice du journal

newsreel ['nju:zri:l] N *Cin* actualités fpl

newsroom ['nju:zru:m] N *Journ, TV* salle f de rédaction des informations

newswoman, pl **newswomen** ['nju:zwʊmən, -wɪmɪn] N journaliste f

newsworthiness ['nju:zwɜ:ðɪnɪs] N intérêt m médiatique

newsworthy ['nju:zwɜ:ðɪ] ADJ d'un intérêt médiatique

newsy ['nju:zɪ] ADJ *Fam (letter)* plein de nouvelles

newt [nju:t] N triton m; *Br Sl* **pissed as a n.** soûl comme une bourrique, beurré comme un petit lu

new-to-the-company product N *Mktg* produit m nouveau dans la compagnie

new-to-the-world product N *Mktg* produit m nouveau dans le monde

NEXT [nekst]

ADJ d'à côté **1**	▪ prochain **2, 3**
▪ suivant **2**	
ADV après **1, 3**	▪ ensuite **1** ▪ la
prochaine fois **2**	▪ à côté de **3**
▪ presque **3**	

ADJ 1 *(in location)* d'à côté; **the n. room** la pièce voisine *ou* d'à côté; **it's the n. house** c'est la maison voisine *ou* d'à côté; **the girl (from) n. door** la jeune fille d'à côté; **he lives**

n. door (to us) il habite à côté (de chez nous); **he's the boy-n.-door type** c'est un bon petit gars; **n.-door neighbours** voisins mpl d'à côté *ou* immédiats; **we are n.-door neighbours** nous sommes voisins; *Fig* **it's n. door to madness** cela confine à la folie; **this has left us n. door to the poorhouse** cela nous a mis quasiment sur la paille
2 *(in time) (in future)* prochain; *(in past or in listing events)* suivant; **I leave n. month** je pars le mois prochain; *Fam* **see you n. week** à la semaine prochaine; **the n. thing I remember is ...** la première chose dont je me rappelle après ça c'est ...; **the n. week it rained** la semaine d'après *ou* suivante il a plu; **the n. month was awful** le mois suivant fut terrible; **in the n. few weeks we will discover ...** dans les semaines à venir *ou* qui vont venir nous allons découvrir ...; **in the n. four weeks we were to discover that ...** dans les quatre semaines suivantes *ou* qui suivirent nous devions découvrir que ...; **this time n. year** d'ici un an; **n. Friday, (on) Friday n.** vendredi prochain; **the n. day** le lendemain, le jour d'après; **the n. day but one** le surlendemain; **(the) n. morning** le lendemain matin; **n. Easter** à Pâques prochain; **n. summer** l'été prochain; **the week/year after n.** dans deux semaines/ans; **from one moment to the n.** d'un instant à l'autre
3 *(in order)* prochain; **it's the n. station** c'est la prochaine gare; **the n. turning on the right** le prochain tournant à droite; **the n. chapter/page** le chapitre/la page suivant(e); **(the) n. time I see him** la prochaine fois que je le verrai; **ask the n. person you meet** demandez à la première personne que vous rencontrerez; **the n. thing is to ...** maintenant il s'agit de ...; **your name is n. on the list** votre nom est le suivant *ou* prochain sur la liste; **n. (person) please** au suivant, s'il vous plaît; **who's n.?, whose turn is it n.?** à qui le tour?, c'est à qui?; **you're n.** après c'est ton tour; **(the) n. to speak is ...** la parole est maintenant à ...; **(the) n. to arrive was Penelope** Penelope est arrivée à la suite; **your train is the n. but one** ton train n'est pas le prochain, mais celui d'après; **the n. size up/down** la taille au-dessus/au-dessous
ADV **1** *(afterwards)* ensuite, après; **what shall we do n.?** qu'est-ce que nous allons faire maintenant?; **what did you do n.?** qu'avez-vous fait après *ou* ensuite?; *Fam* **you'll be asking me to give up my job (for you)** n.! tu n'as qu'à me demander de laisser tomber mon travail pendant que tu y es!; *Fam* **whatever n.!** par exemple!, et quoi encore!; *Fam* **what (ever) will they think of n.!** que ne vont-ils pas inventer!; *Fam* **what will he do n.!** qu'est-ce qu'il va bien pouvoir faire maintenant?
2 *(again)* la prochaine fois; **when I n. saw him, when n. I saw him** quand je l'ai revu; **when shall we meet n.?** quand nous reverrons-nous?; **we had no idea when we would n. meet** nous ignorions complètement quand nous allions nous revoir
3 n. to à côté de; **her room is n. to mine** sa chambre est à côté de la mienne; **I can't bear wool n. to my skin** je ne supporte pas la laine à même la peau; **I got the n. to last loaf** j'ai eu l'avant-dernière baguette; **n. to my dog I like my sister best** après mon chien, c'est ma sœur que je préfère; **I got it for n. to nothing** je l'ai eu pour presque rien *ou* pour une bouchée de pain; **there's n. to nothing left** il ne reste presque rien; **there is n. to no evidence** il n'y a pour ainsi dire pas de preuves; **in n. to no time** en un rien de temps; *Am Fam* **to get n. to sb** *(friendly with)* se mettre bien avec qn; *(emotionally involved with)* se lier avec qn; *(have sex with)* coucher avec qn
4 *(with superlatives)* **the n. best thing**

would be to ... à défaut, le mieux serait de ...; **the n. fastest after the Ferrari was ...** la voiture la plus rapide après la Ferrari était ...; **the n. highest building in the world is** ... le deuxième immeuble dans le monde pour la hauteur, c'est ...; **Mark is the n. oldest/youngest** *(second oldest/youngest of all of them)* Mark est le second par ordre d'âge; **who is the n. oldest/youngest after Mark?** qui est le suivant *ou* le prochain par ordre d'âge après Mark?

next-day delivery N *Com* livraison f lendemain

next-of-kin N *(relative)* parent m le plus proche; *(used as pl)* famille f; **to inform the n.** prévenir la famille

NGO [endʒi:'əʊ] N *(abbr* **non-governmental organization***)* ONG f

NG take [en'dʒi:] N *TV, Cin* mauvaise prise f

NH *abbr* New Hampshire

NHI [eneɪtʃ'aɪ] N *Br (abbr* **National Health Insurance***)* ≃ Sécurité f sociale

NHS [eneɪtʃ'es] N *Br (abbr* **National Health Service***)* ≃ Sécurité f Sociale

NI [e'naɪ] N *Br (abbr* **National Insurance***)* ≃ système m britannique de sécurité sociale (maladie, retraite) et d'assurance chômage

Niagara [naɪ'æg(ə)rə] N Niagara m
▸▸**N. Falls** les chutes fpl du Niagara

nib [nɪb] N **1** *(of fountain pen)* (bec m de) plume f; **broad n.** grosse plume, plume à gros bec; **fine n.** plume fine, plume à bec fin **2** *Tech (of tool etc)* pointe f

nibble ['nɪb(ə)l] N **1** *(action)* grignotement m; **to have a n. at the cake** grignoter le gâteau **2** *Fishing* touche f; **I didn't get** *or* **have a n. all day** le poisson n'a pas mordu *ou* je n'ai pas fait une seule touche de toute la journée **3** *(of biscuit etc)* petit morceau m; **to have a n.** grignoter quelque chose; **I feel like a n. of something** j'ai envie de grignoter un petit morceau; *Fam* **nibbles** amuse-gueules mpl
VT grignoter; **to n. sb's ear** mordiller l'oreille à qn
VI *(of fish), Fam (of person)* mordre à l'hameçon
▸**nibble at** VT INSEP *(biscuit etc)* grignoter; **she was nibbling at his ear** elle lui mordillait l'oreille; **to n. at the bait** *(of fish), Fam (of person)* mordre à l'hameçon; **they're nibbling at our offer** notre offre les séduit
▸**nibble away** VT SEP *(remove)* grignoter entièrement
▸**nibble away at** VT INSEP *(biscuit, carrot)* grignoter; *Fig (value of money etc)* écorner, entamer
▸**nibble on** VT INSEP *(biscuit etc)* grignoter

nibbler ['nɪblər] N grignoteur, -euse; **he's a compulsive n.** il n'arrête pas de grignoter

nibs [nɪbz] N *Fam Iron* **his/her n.** son altesse

NIC [enaɪ'si:] N **1** *(abbr* **newly-industrialized country***)* NPI m **2** *(abbr* **newly-industrializing country***)* pays m en voie d'industrialisation **3** *(abbr* **national insurance contribution***)* cotisation f à la Sécurité sociale **4** *Comput (abbr* **network interface card***)* carte f (d')interface réseau

NiCad battery [nɪ'kæd] N accumulateur m au cadmium nickel

NICAM, Nicam ['naɪkæm] N *(abbr* **near-instantaneous companded audio multiplex***)* Nicam m

Nicaragua [nɪkə'ræɡjʊə] N Nicaragua m

Nicaraguan [nɪkə'ræɡjʊən] ADJ nicaraguayen
N Nicaraguayen, -enne

nice [naɪs] ADJ **1** *(pleasant) (person)* gentil, f gentille, agréable, aimable; *(car, house, shirt, park, trip etc)* joli, beau, f belle; *(meal, idea, hotel etc)* bon, f bonne; *(view)* beau;

(evening, smell, taste) bon, agréable; *(place)* agréable; **it's n. here** c'est bien, ici; **to have a n. time** bien s'amuser; **sending flowers was a n. gesture** c'était gentil d'envoyer des fleurs; **to be n. to sb** se montrer gentil *ou* aimable envers qn; **it is n. of you to ...** c'est gentil de votre part de ..., vous êtes bien aimable de ...; **it's not n. of you to make fun of him** ce n'est pas gentil *ou* bien de vous moquer de lui; **it's not n. thing to happen to anyone** ce n'est pas agréable quand ça arrive; **he's a n. chap** il est gentil, c'est un gentil garçon; **have a n. day!** bonne journée!; **it's turned out n. again** il fait encore beau; **the garden is beginning to look n.** le jardin commence à être joli; *Fam* **n. one!** bien joué!, bravo!

2 *(intensive)* **n. and handy** bien commode; **it's n. and cool** il fait bien frais; **it's n. and easy** c'est très facile; **a n. cold drink** une boisson bien fraîche; **to have a n. long chat** faire une bonne petite causette

3 *(respectable)* **n. people** des gens bien; **he's such a n. boy** il est tellement bien, ce garçon; **it's not n.** ce n'est pas bien; **it's not a n. story** c'est une histoire peu édifiante

4 *Iron* **we are in a n. mess!** nous voilà dans de beaux draps!; **that's a n. way to behave!** en voilà des manières!; **that's a n. way to talk to your mother/father/sister!** en voilà une manière de parler à ta mère/ton père/ta sœur!; **you're a n. one to talk about being punctual!** tu peux bien parler d'être ponctuel!

5 *Fml (delicate, subtle) (question etc)* délicat; *(taste etc)* subtil, fin, recherché; *(distinction)* subtil; **it's a n. point** c'est délicat

6 *Old-fashioned (scrupulous)* scrupuleux

nice-looking [-lʊkɪŋ] **ADJ** beau, *f* belle, joli

nicely ['naɪslɪ] **ADV 1** *(pleasantly, kindly)* gentiment; *(well)* bien; **ask n.!** demande poliment!; **sit n., Jessica!** tiens-toi bien, Jessica!; **to be coming along** *or* **doing n.** *(of roast, cake etc)* être bien en train de cuire; *(of garden)* commencer à prendre tournure; *(of investments)* bien se porter; *(of invalid, pupil)* faire de bons progrès; **to do n.** *(for oneself)* bien s'en sortir; **everything was n. done** tout était bien fait; **those will do (very) n.** ceux-là feront très bien l'affaire; **he spoke very n. about you** il m'a parlé de vous en très bons termes **2** *(accurately) (judged)* exactement, avec justesse; *(scrupulously)* minutieusement, scrupuleusement; **a n. turned phrase** une phrase bien tournée; **that's n. put** voilà qui est bien dit **3** *(respectably)* **n. brought up** bien élevé

niceness ['naɪsnɪs] **N 1** *(pleasantness) (of person)* gentillesse *f*, amabilité *f*; *(of house, hotel etc)* caractère *m* agréable; **the n. of the weather** le temps agréable **2** *Fml (delicacy, subtlety) (of question)* délicatesse *f*; *(of taste, distinction)* subtilité *f*

nicety ['naɪsɪtɪ] **N 1** *(of calculation etc)* exactitude *f*, précision *f*; *(of judgement)* finesse *f*; *(of question)* subtilité *f*, délicatesse *f*; **to a n.** exactement, à la perfection **2 niceties** *(subtleties)* subtilités *fpl*; **social niceties** règles *fpl* de la politesse

niche [niːʃ] **N** *(recess)* niche *f*; *(in market)* créneau *m*; *Fig* **to find one's n.** trouver sa voie; *Fig* **to carve out** *or* **make a n. for oneself** (trouver à) se caser
▸▸ **n. broadcasting** = diffusion *f* d'émissions destinées à un public restreint; *Com, Mktg* **n. market** niche, créneau spécialisé; *Com, Mktg* **n. marketing** marketing *m* de créneau, marketing ciblé; *Com, Mktg* **n. player** acteur *m* sur un segment de marché; *Com, Mktg* **n. product** produit *m* ciblé; *TV* **n. programming** = programmation *f* d'émissions destinées à un public restreint; **n. publish-**

ing = publication *f* d'ouvrages destinés à un public restreint

nicher ['niːʃər] **N** *Mktg* spécialiste *mf* dans une niche

niching ['niːʃɪŋ] **N** *Mktg* segmentation *f* en niches

Nick [nɪk] **N** *Fam* **Old N.** le diable

nick [nɪk] **N 1** *(in wood)* entaille *f*, encoche *f*; *(in blade)* brèche *f*; *(on chin, in finger etc)* entaille, coupure *f*; **to give oneself a n.** se couper **2 in the n. of time** juste à temps; **you've come just in the n. of time** vous tombez bien **3** *Br Fam (condition)* état *m*; **in good/bad n.** en bon/mauvais état; **he's in pretty good n. for his age** il est en bonne forme pour son âge **4** *Br Sl (prison)* taule *f*; *(police station)* poste *m* (de police)
VT 1 *(stick etc)* entailler, encocher; *(blade)* ébrécher; *(cards)* biseauter; **to n. oneself** se couper; **to n. one's finger/chin** s'entailler *ou* se couper le doigt/le menton **2** *esp Br Sl (arrest)* pincer, choper, épingler; **to get nicked** se faire pincer *ou* choper *ou* épingler; **you're nicked!** tu es fait! **3** *esp Br Sl (steal)* piquer, faucher; **it was nicked last week** quelqu'un l'a piqué *ou* fauché la semaine dernière **4** *Am Sl (overcharge)* **they've nicked me for 50 dollars** je me suis fait avoir de 50 dollars; **how much did they n. you for that?** combien ils t'ont fait payer ça?

nickel ['nɪk(ə)l] **N 1** *Metal* nickel *m* **2** *Am (coin)* pièce *f* de cinq cents; *Fam* **it's not worth a plugged n.** ça vaut pas un clou
VT (**-ll-,** *Am* **-l-**) nickeler
▸▸ **n. plating** nickelage *m*

nickel-and-dime **ADJ** *esp Am (business operation)* de quatre sous

nickel-cadmium battery **N** batterie *f* au nickel-cadmium

nickel-plate **VT** nickeler

nicker ['nɪkər] **N** *(no pl)* *Br Sl* livre *f* (sterling); **five n.** cinq livres

nickname ['nɪkneɪm] **N** surnom *m*
VT surnommer

nicotine ['nɪkətiːn] **N** nicotine *f*; **n.-stained** *(fingers, teeth)* jaune de nicotine
▸▸ **n. addict** accro *mf* à la nicotine; **n. addiction** tabagisme *m*; **n. patch** patch *m ou* timbre *m* anti-tabac; **n. poisoning** tabagisme, intoxication *f* nicotinique

nicotinism ['nɪkətiːnɪz(ə)m] **N** *Med* nicotinisme *m*, tabagisme *m*

niece [niːs] **N** nièce *f*

Nielsen ['niːlsən] **N**
▸▸ *Am TV* **N. Ratings** ≃ l'Audimat® *m*

niff [nɪf] *Br Sl* **N** puanteur *f*; **there's a bit of a n. in here** ça pue là-dedans
VI puer

niffy ['nɪfɪ] **ADJ** *Br Sl* puant, qui pue; **it's a bit n. in here** ça pue là-dedans

nifty ['nɪftɪ] **ADJ** *Fam* **1** *(clever) (person)* adroit, débrouillard; *(thing)* commode; **he's pretty n.** il se débrouille bien; **that was a n. piece of driving** ça c'est de la conduite!; **a n. piece of footwork** un beau jeu de jambes; **a n. idea** une idée géniale; **it's a very n. little car** c'est une petite voiture très commode *ou* pratique **2** *Am (attractive) (dress etc)* coquet, pimpant

Niger [niː'ʒeər] **N 1** *(river)* Niger *m* **2** *(country)* (République *f* du) Niger *m*

Nigeria [naɪ'dʒɪərɪə] **N** Nigeria *m*

Nigerian [naɪ'dʒɪərɪən] **ADJ** nigérian
N Nigérian, -ane

niggard ['nɪgəd] **N** *Old-fashioned* pingre *mf*, avare *mf*

niggardliness ['nɪgədlɪnɪs] **N** *(of person)* avarice *f*, pingrerie *f*; *(of sum, salary)* maigreur *f*

niggardly ['nɪgədlɪ] **ADJ** *(person)* avare, pingre, mesquin; *(sum, portion)* maigre; *(budget)* étroit; *(acknowledgement)* mesquin; **don't be so n. with the wine/caviare!** ne sois pas aussi regardant sur le vin/caviar!; **she's quite n. with her compliments/thanks** elle est assez avare de compliments/de remerciements

nigger ['nɪgər] **N** *Offensive Sl* nègre *m*, négresse *f*; *Old-fashioned Fam* **there's a n. in the woodpile** il y a anguille sous roche; *Old-fashioned Fam* **he's the n. in the woodpile** le problème, c'est lui

niggle ['nɪg(ə)l] **VI** *(be overfussy)* couper les cheveux en quatre; **he always has something to n. about** *(complain)* il a toujours quelque chose à redire; **don't n. about details** ne chipote pas sur les détails; **he's been niggling on at** *or* **away at me all week** il m'a cassé les pieds toute la semaine (**about** à propos de)
VT *(of doubt etc)* triturer l'esprit à, tracasser; *(annoy)* embêter; **he keeps niggling me to get it done** il n'arrête pas de m'embêter *ou* de me casser les pieds pour que je le fasse
N 1 *(minor criticism)* petit reproche *m*; **I've just one or two little niggles about ...** il y a juste une ou deux petites choses à revoir au niveau de ... **2** *(worry)* tracasserie *f*, doute *m* **3** *(complaint)* protestation *f*; **to have a little n. about sth** ronchonner à propos de qch

niggler ['nɪglər] **N** *(who annoys people)* enquiquineur, -euse; *(who worries about details)* coupeur, -euse de cheveux en quatre

niggling ['nɪg(ə)lɪŋ] **ADJ** *(details etc)* insignifiant; *(pain)* persistant; *(doubt, worry)* insinuant; **I've got a n. feeling that I left the light on** je n'arrête pas de me demander si je n'ai pas laissé la lumière allumée

nigh [naɪ] *Arch, Lit, Dial* **ADV** près, proche; **n. unto death** près de mourir; **the end is n.!** la fin est proche!
PREP près de

night [naɪt] **N 1** *(hours of darkness)* nuit *f*; *(evening)* soir *m*; **at n.** (à) la nuit; *(in the evening)* le soir; **in the n.** (pendant) la nuit; **last n.** la nuit dernière; *(in the evening)* hier soir; **the n. before** la veille (au soir); **I saw him on Thursday n.** je l'ai vu jeudi soir; **ten o'clock at n.** dix heures du soir; **it was a warm n.** la nuit était douce; **all n.** toute la nuit; **good n.!** *(when going to bed)* bonne nuit!; *(when leaving)* bonsoir!; **to have a good/bad n.** bien/mal dormir; **to have a late/an early n.** se coucher tard/tôt; **too many late nights can be bad for you** se coucher tard trop souvent peut nuire à la santé; **to work day and n.** *or* **n. and day** travailler nuit et jour; **to have a n. off** avoir une soirée libre; **to travel by n.** *or* **at n.** voyager de nuit *ou* la nuit; **we stayed the n. (there)** nous y avons passé la nuit; **to spend the n. together/with sb** passer la nuit ensemble/avec qn; **the n. sky, the sky at n.** le ciel nocturne; **n. is falling** la nuit tombe, il commence à faire nuit; **n. boat/train/flight** bateau *m*/train *m*/vol *m* de nuit

2 *(evening's entertainment)* soirée *f*; **to have a n. out** sortir; **that was a great n. last n.** on a passé une super soirée hier; **to make a n. of it** faire la fête toute la nuit; *Theat etc* **first n.** première *f*; **Wagner n.** soirée Wagner
▸▸ **n. bird** *Orn* oiseau *m* nocturne *ou* de nuit; *Fig (person)* noctambule *mf*, oiseau de nuit; **n. blindness** héméralopie *f*; **n. clerk** *(in hotel)* réceptionniste *mf* de nuit; **n. clothes** vêtements *mpl* de nuit; **n. driving** conduite *f* de nuit; **n. editor** rédacteur, -trice de nuit *(dans un journal)*; *Mil, Aviat* **n. fighter** chasseur *m* de nuit; *Cin* **n. filter** filtre *m* pour effet de nuit; **n. light** lampe *f* veilleuse, veilleuse *f*, **n. manager** directeur, -trice de nuit; **n. nurse** infirmier, -ière de nuit; *Fam* **n. owl** couche-tard *mf inv*, oiseau de nuit; **n. porter**

portier, -ère de nuit; *Fin* **n. rate** tarif *m* de nuit; *Banking* **n. safe** coffre(-fort) *m* de nuit, *pl* coffres(-forts) de nuit; **n. school** cours *mpl* du soir; **n. shift** *(work force)* équipe *f* de nuit; *(period of duty)* poste *m* de nuit; **n. soil** fumier *m (d'excréments humains)*; *Am* **n. stick** *(of policeman)* matraque *f*, **n. storage heater** radiateur *m* à accumulation; *Am* **n. table** table *f* de chevet; **n. watch** *(period, guards)* garde *f* de nuit; *Naut* quart *m* de nuit; **n. watchman** veilleur *m* de nuit; **n. work** travail *m* de nuit

nightcap ['naɪtkæp] N **1** *(drink)* = boisson *f* prise avant de se coucher; **would you like a n.?** prendrez-vous quelque chose avant de vous coucher? **2** *(hat)* bonnet *m* de nuit

nightclub ['naɪtklʌb] N boîte *f* de nuit

nightclubbing ['naɪtklʌbɪŋ] N **to go n.** sortir en boîte

nightdress ['naɪtdres] N chemise *f* de nuit

nightfall ['naɪtfɔːl] N tombée *f* du jour *ou* de la nuit; **at n.** à la nuit tombante

nightgown ['naɪtgaʊn] N chemise *f* de nuit

nighthawk ['naɪthɔːk] N *Am Fam (person)* noctambule *mf*, *Hum* oiseau *m* de nuit

nightie ['naɪtɪ] N *Fam* = **nightdress**

nightingale ['naɪtɪŋgeɪl] N rossignol *m*

nightjar ['naɪtdʒɑːr] N *(bird)* engoulevent *m* (d'Europe)

nightlife ['naɪtlaɪf] N vie *f* nocturne; **what's the n. like?** qu'est-ce qu'on peut faire le soir?; **there's not much n.** il n'y a pas grand-chose à faire le soir

night-light N veilleuse *f*

nightlong ['naɪtlɒŋ] ADJ *(party, wake etc)* qui dure toute la nuit

nightly ['naɪtlɪ] ADJ de toutes les nuits; *(in the evening)* de tous les soirs; **it's a n. occurrence** c'est comme ça toutes les nuits/tous les soirs; **there are n. flights** il y a des vols toutes les nuits; **he would take his n. stroll** il faisait sa promenade nocturne

ADV toutes les nuits; *(in the evening)* tous les soirs; **performances n.** représentations tous les soirs

▸▸ **n. performance** *(sign)* représentation tous les soirs

nightmare ['naɪtmeər] N *also Fig* cauchemar *m*; **to give sb nightmares** donner des cauchemars à qn; **getting to work was an absolute n.** se rendre au travail était un véritable cauchemar; **the journey/experience was a n.** ça a été un voyage/une expérience cauchemardesque

nightmarish ['naɪtmeərɪʃ] ADJ cauchemardesque

night-night INT *Fam* bonne nuit

nightrobe ['naɪtrəʊb] N *Am* chemise *f* de nuit

nights [naɪts] ADV *(to work)* de nuit

nightshade ['naɪtʃeɪd] N *Bot* **(black) n.** morelle *f* noire

nightshirt ['naɪtʃɜːt] N chemise *f* de nuit

nightstand ['naɪtstænd] N *Am* table *f* de nuit

night-time N nuit *f*, **at n.** la nuit

ADJ nocturne; **n. television** télévision *f* de nuit

nightwear ['naɪtweər] N vêtements *mpl* de nuit

nihilism ['naɪ(h)ɪlɪz(ə)m] N nihilisme *m*

nihilist ['naɪ(h)ɪlɪst] N nihiliste *mf*

nihilistic [naɪ(h)ɪ'lɪstɪk] ADJ nihiliste

Nikkei index ['nɪkeɪ] N indice *m* Nikkei

nil [nɪl] N rien *m*; *(on report sheet etc)* néant *m*; *Sport* zéro *m*; *Fin* **the balance is n.** le solde est nul; **they won three n.** ils ont gagné par trois à zéro VOIR GRAMMAIRE A77

Nile [naɪl] N Nil *m*

nimble ['nɪmb(ə)l] ADJ *(person, fingers etc)* agile, souple; *(leap, movement)* leste, agile; *(mind, thinking etc)* vif, *f* vive; **n.-fingered** aux doigts agiles *ou* souples *ou* de fée; **n.-footed** aux pieds agiles *ou* légers

nimbleness ['nɪmb(ə)lnɪs] N *(of person, limbs etc)* agilité *f*, souplesse *f*; *(of movement, leap)* agilité *f*; *(of mind etc)* vivacité *f*

nimbly ['nɪmb(ə)lɪ] ADV *(to move, leap)* agilement, avec légèreté; **she n. unpicked the knot** elle a défait le nœud de ses doigts agiles *ou* souples

nimbus, *pl* **nimbi, nimbuses** ['nɪmbəs, -aɪ, -əsiz] N **1** *Met* nimbus *m* **2** *(of saint) (cloud)* nuage *m* lumineux; *(halo)* halo *m* **3** *Art* nimbe *m*, auréole *f*

NIMBY, nimby ['nɪmbɪ] N *Fam (abbr* **not in my back yard)** = personne *f* qui est favorable à un projet (construction d'autoroute, offre d'asile etc) à condition qu'il ne soit pas mis en œuvre près de chez elle

nimrod ['nɪmrɒd] N *Am Fam (fool)* crétin, -ine, andouille *f*

nincompoop ['nɪŋkəmpuːp] N *Fam* nigaud, -aude, andouille *f*; **you stupid n.!** bougre d'andouille!

nine [naɪn] N neuf *m*; **n. and four are thirteen** neuf et quatre font treize; **it's n. o'clock** il est neuf heures; **to be n.** *(in age)* avoir neuf ans; *Cards* **the n. of diamonds** le neuf de carreau; *Fam* **dressed up to the nines** sur son trente et un; **to work n. to five** travailler de 9 à 5; **I couldn't stand a n.-to-five job** je ne supporterais pas de travailler de 9 à 5; **9/11** *(11 September 2001)* le 11 septembre; **there must never be another 9/11** les événements du 11 septembre ne doivent plus jamais se reproduire

PRON neuf; **I need n. (of them)** il m'en faut neuf, j'en ai besoin de neuf

NUM ADJ neuf; **n. times out of ten** neuf fois sur dix; **to have n. lives** *(of cat)* avoir neuf vies; *(of person)* avoir l'âme chevillée au corps; **to dial** *Br* **999** or *Am* **911** appeler les urgences

ninefold ['naɪnfəʊld] ADJ **there's been a n. increase in …** … a été multiplié par neuf

ADV **to increase n.** (se) multiplier par neuf

ninepin ['naɪnpɪn] N **1 ninepins** *(game)* (jeu *m* de) quilles *fpl* **2** *(pin)* quille *f*, *Fam* **to go down like ninepins** tomber comme des mouches

nineteen [naɪn'tiːn] NUM ADJ, N dix-neuf *m*; **she is n.** elle a dix-neuf ans; *Br Fam* **to talk n. to the dozen** bavarder comme une pie

nineteenth [naɪn'tiːnθ] ADJ dix-neuvième

N **1** *(person, thing)* dix-neuvième *mf* **2** *(fraction)* dix-neuvième *m*

▸▸ *Hum* **the n. hole** *(of golf course)* le bar du golf

1922 Committee [naɪnti:ntwentɪ'tuː] N *Br Pol* = comité *m* rassemblant les députés de base du parti conservateur

ninetieth ['naɪntɪθ] ADJ quatre-vingt-dixième

N **1** *(person, thing)* quatre-vingt-dixième *mf* **2** *(fraction)* quatre-vingt-dixième *m*

ninety ['naɪntɪ] NUM, ADJ, N quatre-vingt-dix *m*, *Belg, Suisse* nonante; **n.-one/n.-nine** quatre-vingt-onze/quatre-vingt-dix-neuf, *Belg, Suisse* nonante-et-un/nonante-neuf; **the nineties** *(decade)* les années quatre-vingt-dix; **temperatures in the nineties** des températures autour de trente-cinq degrés; **she's in her nineties** elle est nonagénaire; *Law* **n.-nine years' lease** bail *m* emphytéotique de quatre-vingt-dix-neuf ans

ninny ['nɪnɪ] N *Old-fashioned Fam* niais, -aise, nigaud, -aude

ninth [naɪnθ] ADJ neuvième

N **1** *(person, thing)* neuvième *mf* **2** *(fraction)* neuvième *m* **3** *Mus* neuvième *f*

Nip [nɪp] N *Br Offensive Sl (Japanese)* jap *mf*

nip¹ [nɪp] N **1** *(pinch)* pincement *m*; **to give sb a n.** pincer qn **2** *(of frost, cold)* morsure *f*, *(frost)* coup *m* de gelée; **the n. of the early morning air** le froid *ou* le piquant du petit jour; *Fam* **there's a n. in the air** ça pince, l'air est piquant

VT **(-pp-) 1** *(pinch)* pincer; **to n. one's finger** se pincer le doigt **2** *(remove) (buds etc)* pincer, éborgner; *Fig Fam* **to n. sth in the bud** écraser *ou* étouffer qch dans l'œuf **3** *(of cold, frost) (face, fingers etc)* pincer, piquer; *(buds etc)* brûler; *Bot* **nipped by the frost** brûlé par la gelée

VI *Br Fam (go quickly)* **just n. across** *or* **along** *or* **down to the baker's** cours vite chez le boulanger, fais donc un saut chez le boulanger; **he nipped back to see if she was alright** il est repassé pour voir si elle allait bien; **to n. in and out of the traffic** se faufiler adroitement parmi les voitures; **I'll n. through to Glasgow next week** je ferai un saut à Glasgow la semaine prochaine

▸ **nip in** VI *Br Fam* **I just nipped in to see him** je suis entré juste un instant pour le voir; **if you're passing, do n. in and see us** si vous passez par ici, rendez-nous donc une petite visite; **she saw a parking place and quickly nipped in** elle a vu une place libre et elle s'est empressée de la prendre; **could I just n. in in front of you?** *(in queue etc)* pourrais-je passer devant vous?; **he always nips into the pub on the way home** il fait toujours un petit détour par le pub en rentrant chez lui; **he nipped into the doorway** il s'engouffra dans l'entrée

▸ **nip off** VI *Br Fam* filer; *(to avoid sb/sth)* s'esquiver

VT SEP **to n. sth off** enlever *ou* couper qch (en le pinçant)

▸ **nip out** VI *Br Fam* sortir; **he's just nipped out for a second** *(from house, office etc)* il est sorti un instant; **I'll n. out and buy a paper** je sors acheter un journal

nip² N *Fam (drink) (of brandy etc)* goutte *f*, petit verre *m*, doigt *m*; **to have** *or* **take a n.** boire *ou* prendre une goutte

nipper ['nɪpər] N **1** *Br Fam (child)* gamin, -ine, gosse *mf*, **I've lived here since I was a n.** j'habite ici depuis que je suis tout(e) gamin(e) *ou* gosse **2** *(of lobster etc)* pince *f* **3** **(pair of) nippers** *(tool)* pince(s) *f(pl)*; *(de serrage)* tenaille(s) *f(pl)*

nipple ['nɪp(ə)l] N **1** *Anat* mamelon *m*, bout *m* de sein; *(of feeding bottle)* tétine *f* **2** *Geog* mamelon *m* **3** *(grease)* n. graisseur *m*

nippy ['nɪpɪ] ADJ *Fam* **1** *Br (nimble)* vif, *f* vive; *(quick)* rapide; **look n.!** grouille-toi!; **a n. little car** une petite voiture nerveuse **2** *(wind etc)* froid, piquant; **it's a bit n. today** il fait un froid/un vent vif *ou* mordant aujourd'hui **3** *(flavour)* fort

nirvana [nɪə'vɑːnə] N *Rel* nirvana *m*

nisi ['naɪsaɪ] ADJ *Law (decree, order)* provisoire; *(decision)* rendu sous condition

Nissen ['nɪs(ə)n] N

▸▸ *Br Mil* **N. hut** abri *m* (en tôle ondulée)

nit [nɪt] N **1** *Entom* lente *f*, **to have nits** avoir des poux **2** *Br Fam (person)* nigaud, -aude, andouille *f*, **you silly n.!** andouille!; **don't be such a n.!** ne sois pas aussi bête!

niter ['naɪtər] N *Am* = **nitre**

nitery ['naɪtərɪ] N *Am Fam* boîte *f* de nuit

nit-pick VI *Fam* chercher la petite bête, ergoter, chinoiser

nit-picker N *Fam* chipoteur, -euse

nit-picking *Fam* N chipotage *m*, chinoiserie *f*, ADJ *(attitude etc)* chipoteur, chicanier; **I'm tired of his n. criticisms of everything I do** j'en ai assez qu'il critique tout ce que je fais avec autant de chicanerie

nitrate ['naɪtreɪt] N *Chem (of silver etc)* nitrate *m*; **potassium n.** nitrate de potassium, salpêtre *m*; *Agr* **n. fertilizers, nitrates** engrais *mpl* azotés

nitre ['naɪtər] N salpêtre *m*

nitric ['naɪtrɪk] ADJ *Chem*
▸▸ **n. acid** acide *m* nitrique; **n. oxide** oxyde *m* nitrique

nitro ['naɪtrəʊ] N *Sl* = **nitroglycerin(e)**

nitrogen ['naɪtrədʒən] N *Chem* azote *m*; **to fix n.** *(of plant)* fixer l'azote
▸▸ **n. dioxide** dioxyde *m* d'azote

nitroglycerin(e) [naɪtrəʊ'glɪsəri:n] N nitroglycérine *f*

nitrous ['naɪtrəs] ADJ *(oxide etc)* nitreux, d'azote

nitty-gritty ['nɪtɪ'grɪtɪ] N *Fam (of a matter)* aspects *mpl* pratiques; **when you get down to the n.** quand on considère les aspects pratiques de la chose

nitwit ['nɪtwɪt] N *Fam* idiot, -ote, imbécile *mf*; **don't be such a n.!** arrête de faire l'idiot ou l'imbécile!

nix [nɪks] *Am Fam* N *(nothing)* rien *m* (du tout), *Sl* que dalle
INT rien à faire!
VT *(project, proposal)* refuser, rejeter

NJ *abbr* New Jersey

NLM [enel'em] N *Comput (abbr* **netware loadable module)** module *m* logiciel téléchargeable

NLQ N *Comput (abbr* **near letter quality)** qualité *f* courrier

NM *abbr* New Mexico

NMD [enem'di:] N *(abbr* **National Missile Defense)** projet *m* NMD *(programme de défense antimissiles américain)*

NMR [enem'ɑ:r] N *Med (abbr* **nuclear magnetic resonance)** RMN *f*

NNTP [enenti:'pi:] N *Comput (abbr* **Network News Transfer Protocol)** NNTP *m*

NO [nəʊ]

ADJ	pas de **1** ▪ ne… pas **2**
ADV	ne… pas **1** ▪ ne… plus **1** ▪ non **2**
N	non

ADJ VOIR GRAMMAIRE A35; B62–3 **1** *(not any)* pas de, aucun, -une *(with* **ne** *expressed or understood)*; **he has no bread** il n'a pas de pain; **this fact is of no importance whatever** ce fait n'a aucune importance; **I have no intention of doing it** je n'ai aucune intention de le faire; **it's no distance** ce n'est pas loin; **I am in no way surprised** je n'en suis aucunement étonné; **no nonsense!** pas de bêtises!; **no smoking** défense de fumer; *esp Lit* **no father was ever more indulgent** jamais père ne fut plus indulgent
2 *(not at all)* ne … pas (du tout); **it's no easy job** ce n'est pas une tâche facile; **he's no artist** ce n'est pas un artiste, il n'est pas artiste; **he's no friend of mine** il ne fait pas partie de mes amis, tant s'en faut; *Cr* **no ball** balle nulle; *Fam* **no way!** pas question!; *Fam* **no way am I going to work on Saturday** il n'est pas question que je travaille samedi; **no way can I get him to admit he was wrong** il n'y a pas moyen de lui faire admettre qu'il a eu tort
3 *(with gerund)* **there's no pleasing him** il n'y a pas moyen de le satisfaire; **there's no getting out of it** impossible de s'en tirer
ADV **1** *(with comparatives)* ne … plus, ne … pas; **I'm no taller than he (is)** je ne suis pas plus grand que lui; **how is she? – no better** comment va-t-elle? – pas mieux; **no less than £100** pas moins de 100 livres; **he's no longer here** il n'est plus ici
2 *(answer)* non; **no, no, you're wrong!** mais

non, mais non, vous vous trompez!; **to say no** dire non; *(deny)* dire que non SEE GRAMMAR B63
3 *Arch, Lit, Scot (not)* pleasant or no, it's true agréable ou non ou pas, c'est vrai; **whether or no** que cela soit ou non
4 *Scot Fam (not)* **it's no bad** c'est pas mal!; **I'm no going** j'y vais pas
N *(pl* **noes)** non *m inv*; **she won't take no for an answer** elle n'acceptera pas de refus; **ayes and noes** *(in voting)* voix *fpl* pour et contre; **the noes have it** c'est le non qui l'emporte

No., no *(abbr* **number)** No, no

Noah ['nəʊə] N *Bible* Noé *m*
▸▸ *Bible* **N.'s ark** l'arche *f* de Noé

nob¹ [nɒb] N *Sl (head)* caboche *f*

nob² N *esp Br Sl (upper-class person)* aristo *mf*; **the nobs** les rupins *mpl*, les aristos *mpl*

nobble ['nɒb(ə)l] VT *Br Fam* **1** *Horseracing* doper *(avant la course)*; *Fig* **to n. sb's chances of doing sth** bousiller ou saboter les chances qn a de faire qch **2** *(bribe) (witness etc)* soudoyer, acheter **3** *(steal)* faucher, piquer **4** *(grab) (thief)* pincer, choper, épingler; *(person)* attraper (au passage); **a journalist nobbled him in the corridor** un journaliste l'a coincé dans le couloir

Nobel [nəʊ'bel] ADJ
▸▸ **N. laureate** lauréat, -ate du prix Nobel; **N. Peace Prize** prix *m* Nobel de la paix; **N. prize** prix Nobel; **N. prize for Literature** prix Nobel de littérature; **N. prizewinner** lauréat, -ate du prix Nobel

nobility [nəʊ'bɪlɪtɪ] N **1** *(of rank, heart etc)* noblesse *f* **2** **the n.** *(nobles)* la noblesse

noble ['nəʊb(ə)l] ADJ **1** *(birth, person)* noble; **to be of n. descent** or **birth** être de naissance noble **2** *(sentiment etc)* noble; *Fam Hum* **I'll be n. and let you have the last piece of cake** je vais me montrer grand seigneur et te laisser le dernier morceau de gâteau; *Fam Hum* **that's very n. of you** c'est très généreux ou charitable de ta part; **to have a n. soul** avoir de la grandeur d'âme **3** *(building, proportions, sight etc)* majestueux; *(mountain)* altier, imposant; **4** *Chem (gas, metal)* noble
N noble *mf*, aristocrate *mf*
▸▸ *Chem* **n. gas** gaz *m* rare; **n. rot** pourriture *f* noble; **n. savage** bon sauvage *m*; **n. soul** grande âme *f*, **n. wine** vin *m* noble, grand vin

nobleman, *pl* **noblemen** ['nəʊb(ə)lmən] N noble *m*, aristocrate *m*

nobleminded [nəʊb(ə)l'maɪndɪd] ADJ *(person)* magnanime, aux nobles sentiments; *(sentiment, action, commitment)* noble

nobleness ['nəʊb(ə)lnɪs] N **1** *(of birth etc)* noblesse *f* **2** *(of mind, action etc)* noblesse *f*, *(of soul)* grandeur *f* **3** *(of statue, horse etc)* proportions *fpl* superbes ou magnifiques; *(of building etc)* aspect *m* majestueux

noblewoman, *pl* **noblewomen** ['nəʊb(ə)lwʊmən, -wɪmɪn] N *(femme f)* noble *f*, aristocrate *f*

nobly ['nəʊb(ə)lɪ] ADV **1** noblement; **n. born** noble de naissance; *Fam Hum* **he n. gave up his weekends** il a magnanimement renoncé à ses week-ends; **she n. offered him the last piece of cake** elle s'est montrée grand seigneur et lui a offert le dernier morceau de gâteau **2** *(splendidly) (proportioned etc)* magnifiquement, superbement

nobody ['nəʊbədɪ] PRON personne *(with* **ne** *expressed or understood)*; **n. spoke to me** personne ne m'a parlé; **who's there? – n.** qui est là? – personne; **n. knows it** personne ne le sait; **n.'s perfect** nul ou personne n'est parfait; **n. was more surprised than me** or **than I (was)** personne n'a été plus étonné que moi; **n. who was there heard anything** aucun de ceux ou personne parmi tous ceux

qui étaient là n'a entendu quoi que ce soit; **there was n. there** or **about** il n'y avait personne; **n. else** personne d'autre; *Fam* **like n.'s business** comme personne, comme pas un; *Fam* **the dogs were barking like n.'s business** les chiens aboyaient à vous rompre les tympans; **she's n.'s fool** elle n'est pas folle; **when he was n.** alors qu'il était encore inconnu; **as far as they're concerned, if you don't have money, you're n.** pour eux si tu n'as pas d'argent tu es un zéro ou un moins que rien SEE GRAMMAR B62–3
N *(person)* nullité *f*, zéro *m*; **they're (mere) nobodies** ce sont des gens de rien; **some n. of a journalist** un journaliste à la manque

no-brainer [-breɪnər] N *Am Fam (person)* crétin, -ine; *(question, problem)* jeu *m* d'enfant

no-claim(s) ADJ
▸▸ **n. bonus** *(in car insurance)* bonus *m*

nocturnal [nɒk'tɜ:n(ə)l] ADJ nocturne *m*

nocturne ['nɒktɜ:n] N **1** *Mus* nocturne *m* **2** *Art* effet *m* de nuit

nod [nɒd] N **1** inclination *f* de la tête; *(of consent)* signe *m* d'assentiment, signe de tête affirmatif; *(greeting)* signe de la tête; **to answer with a n.** répondre d'un signe de tête; **she gave me a n.** elle m'a fait un petit signe de la tête; *Fig* **to give sb the n.** donner le feu vert à qn; *Fam* **on the n.** sans débats; **a n. in sb's direction** un signe de tête à l'intention de qn; **these terms are a n. in the direction of Marxist scholars** ces termes sont des renvois ou références aux intellectuels marxistes; *Prov* **a n. is as good as a wink** = pas besoin d'en dire davantage ou plus (on a compris) **2** **the land of N.** le pays des songes; *Hum* **to be in the land of N.** être dans les bras de Morphée
VT *(-dd-)* **to n. one's head** faire un signe de tête (de haut en bas); **she nodded her head in agreement** elle a fait un signe de tête affirmatif; **he nodded his head in agreement at the proposal** il accepta la proposition d'un signe de tête; **to n. one's agreement/approval** consentir/approuver d'un signe de tête
VI **1** **to n. (in agreement/approval)** consentir/approuver d'un signe de tête; **to n. to sb** *(in greeting)* faire un signe de tête à qn **2** *(in sleep)* dodeliner (de) la tête **3** *(of plumes etc)* ballotter, danser
▸ **nod off** VI *Fam* s'endormir

nodal ['nəʊd(ə)l] ADJ *Opt, Phys* nodal, -aux

nodding ['nɒdɪŋ] N **I'm on n. terms with my neighbours** mes voisins et moi, nous nous saluons; **we are on n. terms, we have a n. acquaintance** nous nous saluons; **we still only have a n. acquaintance** nous nous saluons et c'est tout; *Fig* **she had only a n. acquaintance with the town's history** elle n'avait qu'une vague connaissance de l'histoire de la ville

noddle ['nɒd(ə)l] N *esp Br Fam (head, intelligence)* caboche *f*, **use your n.!** fais marcher ta caboche ou ton ciboulot!

node [nəʊd] N *Astron, Math, Phys (of orbit, curve etc)* nœud *m*, point *m* nodal; *Bot (of tree trunk etc)* nœud *m*; *Med* nœud, nodosité *f*; *Comput* noyau *m*

nodular ['nɒdjʊlər] ADJ *Geol, Med etc* nodulaire

nodule ['nɒdju:l] N *Geol, Med, Bot* nodule *m*

Noël [nəʊ'el] N **1** *(Christmas)* Noël *m* **2** *Arch (carol)* Noël *m*

no-fly zone N zone *f* d'exclusion aérienne

no-frills ADJ *(airline, travel)* sans prestation de services; *(insurance policy etc)* de base; *(car, bicycle etc)* sans gadgets; *(service, wedding)* sans chichis, tout simple

noggin ['nɒgɪn] N **1** *(container)* (petit) pot

m; **to have a n.** *(drink)* prendre un verre **2** *Fam (head)* caboche *f*

no-go ADJ
▶▶**n. area** zone *f* interdite; **this neighbourhood is a n. area for the police** la police n'ose pas s'aventurer dans ce quartier

no-good *esp Am Fam* ADJ bon, *f* bonne à rien
N bon *m* à rien, bonne *f* à rien

no-hoper [-'həʊpər] N tocard *m*

nohow ['nəʊhaʊ] ADV *Am Sl* pas question

noise [nɔɪz] N **1** bruit *m*; **a loud n.** un gros bruit; **to make a n.** faire du bruit; *Fig (complain, make a fuss)* protester (**about sth** au sujet de qch); **he made a lot of n. about improving working conditions** *(talked about it)* il a fait beaucoup de bruit au sujet d'une éventuelle amélioration des conditions de travail; *Fam* **the big n.** *(in company etc)* le grand manitou; *Fam* **she's a big n. in publishing** c'est quelqu'un d'important dans le monde de l'édition; *Fam* **shut** *or* **hold your n.!** ferme-la!
2 *(sound)* bruit *m*, son *m*; *Radio, Electron etc* bruit, parasite(s) *m(pl)*; **she's making noises about retiring** elle donne à entendre qu'elle va prendre sa retraite; **to make encouraging noises** dire des choses encourageantes; **to make the right noises** se montrer compréhensif; **clicking n.** cliquetis *m*; **tinkling n.** tintement *m*
▶▶**n. abatement** lutte *f* contre le bruit; **n. abatement campaign** campagne *f ou* lutte contre le bruit; **n. insulation** insonorisation *f*, **n. level** niveau *m* de bruit

noise-absorbing ADJ insonorisé

noiseless ['nɔɪzlɪs] ADJ *(machine, movement etc)* silencieux; **with n. tread** à pas feutrés

noiselessly ['nɔɪzlɪslɪ] ADV sans bruit, silencieusement

noiselessness ['nɔɪzlɪsnɪs] N silence *f*

noisily ['nɔɪzɪlɪ] ADV bruyamment, à grand bruit

noisiness ['nɔɪzɪnɪs] N caractère *m* bruyant; **because of the n. of the street** à cause du bruit qu'il y a dans la rue; **I can't stand their n.** je ne peux pas supporter le bruit qu'ils font

noisome ['nɔɪsəm] ADJ *Fml* **1** *(offensive)* *(smell)* fétide; *(sight, behaviour, person)* répugnant **2** *(harmful)* *(plant, germ)* nocif, nuisible

noisy ['nɔɪzɪ] ADJ bruyant; **to be n.** *(of person)* faire du bruit; **the TV is a bit n.** la télé est un peu forte

no-load fund N *St Exch* fonds *m* sans frais d'acquisition, fonds qui ne prélève pas une commission

nomad ['nəʊmæd] ADJ, N nomade *mf*

nomadic [nəʊ'mædɪk] ADJ nomade

no-maintenance battery N batterie *f* sans entretien

no man's land N terrains *mpl* vagues; *Mil, Fig* no man's land *m*, zone *f* neutre; *Fig (intellectual, psychological etc)* zone floue

no-mark N *Fam (pathetic person)* *(male)* nul *m*, pauvre type *m*; *(female)* nulle *f*

nom de plume, *pl* noms de plume ['nɒmdə'pluːm] N pseudonyme *m* (d'un auteur)

nomenclature [nəʊ'menklətʃər] N nomenclature *f*

nominal ['nɒmɪn(ə)l] ADJ **1** *(in name only)* *(owner, leader)* de nom *(seulement)*; nominal, -aux; *(ownership, leadership)* nominal; **to be the n. head** n'être chef que de nom **2** *(negligible)* insignifiant, nominal, -aux; **a n. amount** une somme insignifiante **3** *(token)* symbolique; **a n. contribution of one pound**

a year une contribution symbolique d'une livre par an
▶▶*Acct* **n. account** compte *m* d'exploitation générale; *Fin* **n. capital** capital *m* nominal; *Law* **n. damages** dommages-intérêts *mpl* symboliques; *Fin* **n. interest rate** taux *m* d'intérêt nominal; *Acct* **n. ledger** grand-livre *m* général, *pl* grands-livres généraux; *Fin* **n. partner** associé, -ée fictif(ive); *Fin* **n. price** prix *m* nominal; **n. rent** loyer *m* insignifiant; *Fin* **n. value** valeur *f* nominale; *Fin* **n. wages** salaire *m* nominal; *Fin* **n. yield** taux *m* nominal

nominally ['nɒmɪn(ə)lɪ] ADV *(in name)* nominalement

nominate ['nɒmɪneɪt] VT *(appoint)* nommer, désigner; *(propose)* proposer, présenter la candidature de; *(for award)* sélectionner, nominer; **to n. sb to a post** nommer *ou* désigner qn à un poste; **to n. sb for a post** proposer qn pour un poste; **to n. sb as president** nommer qn président; **the film was nominated for an Oscar** le film a été sélectionné *ou* nominé pour un oscar

nomination [nɒmɪ'neɪʃən] N **1** *(proposal)* *(of candidate etc)* proposition *f*; *(for an award)* nomination *f*; **the three nominations for best actor are …** les trois nominés pour le prix du meilleur acteur sont …; **the film got three Oscar nominations** le film a obtenu trois nominations aux oscars **2** *(appointment)* *(of candidate)* nomination *f*, *(of president, judge etc)* investiture *f*
▶▶*Pol* **n. papers** dossier *m* de candidature

nominative ['nɒmɪnətɪv] *Gram* N nominatif *m*; **in the n.** au nominatif
ADJ nominatif

nominator ['nɒmɪneɪtər] N **his nominators** ceux qui ont proposé sa nomination

nominee [nɒmɪ'niː] N **1** *(proposed)* candidat, -ate **2** *(appointed)* personne *f* désignée; **the government nominees on the commission** les membres de la commission nommés par le gouvernement
▶▶*St Exch* **n. account** compte *m* d'intermédiaire; **n. company** prête-nom *m*, *pl* prête-noms; *Fin* **n. name** nom *m* de l'intermédiaire; *St Exch* **n. shareholding** actionnariat *m* intermédiaire

non- [nɒn] PREF non-

nonabsorbent [nɒnəb'zɔːbənt] ADJ non absorbant

nonacceptance [nɒnək'septəns] N *(of bill, treaty)* refus *m* d'acceptation

non-adopter N *Mktg* = consommateur *m* qui n'essaie jamais de nouveaux produits

nonagenarian [nəʊnədʒɪ'neərɪən] ADJ, N nonagénaire *mf*

nonaggression [nɒnə'greʃən] N *Pol* non-agression *f*
▶▶**n. pact** pacte *m* de non-agression

nonalcoholic [nɒnælkə'hɒlɪk] ADJ *(drink)* non-alcoolisé

nonaligned [nɒnə'laɪnd] ADJ *Pol (country)* non aligné

nonalignment [nɒnə'laɪnmənt] N *Pol* non-alignement *m*

no-name product N *Mktg* produit *m* sans nom

nonappearance [nɒnə'pɪərəns] N *(of person)*, *Law* non-comparution *f*; **I put his n. down to the fact that …** j'ai pensé qu'il n'était pas venu parce que …

nonarrival [nɒnə'raɪv(ə)l] N non-arrivée *f*

non-ASCII character N *Comput* caractère *m* non ASCII

nonattendance [nɒnə'tendəns] N absence *f* (**at** à)

non-bank ADJ non-banque

non-business marketing N marketing *m* non-commercial

nonce[1] [nɒns] N *Old-fashioned* **for the n.** pour la circonstance, pour l'occasion
▶▶*Ling* **n. word** mot *m* créé pour l'occasion

nonce[2] N *Br Sl (sex offender)* délinquant *m* sexuel *(s'attaquant en particulier aux enfants)*

nonchalance ['nɒnʃələns] N nonchalance *f*

nonchalant ['nɒnʃələnt] ADJ nonchalant

nonchalantly ['nɒnʃələntlɪ] ADV nonchalamment

noncombatant [nɒn'kɒmbətənt] ADJ, N *Mil* non-combattant *m*, *pl* non-combattants

noncommissioned ['nɒnkə'mɪʃənd] ADJ *Mil* sans brevet
▶▶**n. officer** sous-officier *m*, *pl* sous-officiers

noncommittal [nɒnkə'mɪt(ə)l] ADJ *(answer etc)* qui n'engage à rien; **to be n.** *(when answering)* ne pas s'engager; **why are you being so n.?** pourquoi est-ce que tu ne veux pas t'engager?

non-competition clause N clause *f* de non-concurrence

noncompletion [nɒnkəm'pliːʃən] N *(of job)* non-achèvement *m*; *(of contract)* non-exécution *f*

noncompliance [nɒnkəm'plaɪəns] N refus *m* (de consentement); **n. with an order** refus d'obéissance à un ordre

nonconductor [nɒnkən'dʌktər] N *Phys* non-conducteur *m*, *pl* non-conducteurs, mauvais conducteur *m*; *Elec* isolant *m*

nonconformism [nɒnkən'fɔːmɪz(ə)m] N non-conformisme *m*

nonconformist [nɒnkən'fɔːmɪst] ADJ, N non-conformiste *mf*, *pl* non-conformistes

nonconformity [nɒnkən'fɔːmɪtɪ] N non-conformité *f*

noncontributory [nɒnkən'trɪbjʊt(ə)rɪ] ADJ *(pension scheme)* sans versements de la part des bénéficiaires

nonconvertible [nɒnkən'vɜːtəb(ə)l] ADJ inconvertible

non-cumulative ADJ *Fin* non cumulatif

non-current liabilities NPL *Acct* passif *m* non exigible

noncustodial [nɒnkʌs'təʊdɪəl] ADJ *(sentence)* n'entraînant pas l'emprisonnement

nondescript ['nɒndɪskrɪpt] ADJ *(person, object)* quelconque; *(colour)* neutre, *Pej* fade; **a very n. looking person** une personne d'apparence très quelconque

nondestructive [nɒndɪ'strʌktɪv] ADJ *(test)* non destructif

nondetachable [nɒndɪ'tætʃəb(ə)l] ADJ inamovible

nondirectional [nɒndə'rekʃən(ə)l, -dɪ-] ADJ *Electron, Radio* non directionnel

non-DOS disk N *Comput* disque *m* à format incompatible avec DOS

non-drip ADJ *(paint)* qui ne coule pas

non-dutiable N *Com* exempt de droits de douane

NONE [nʌn] PRON VOIR GRAMMAIRE A35; B62–3 **1** *(not any)* aucun, -une; **n. of you can tell me** aucun d'entre vous *ou* personne ne peut me le dire; **n. of this concerns me** rien de ceci ne me regarde; **any news today? – n.** pas de nouvelles aujourd'hui? – aucune(s); **n. at all** pas un(e) seul(e); **n. of these books are** *or esp Fml* **is worth keeping** tous ces livres sont bons à jeter; **n. of the milk was fresh** tout le lait avait tourné; **how much of the wood did you use? – n. of it** quelle quantité du bois avez-vous utilisée? – pas un seul morceau; **n. of the money/the water was left** il ne restait rien de l'argent/de l'eau; **n. of your impudence!** pas d'insolences!; *Fam* **n. of that!** pas de ça!; *Arch, Hum* **answer came**

there n. de réponse il n'en arriva point

2 (*no-one*) personne, nul; **the visitor was n. other than the king** le visiteur n'était (nul) autre que le roi; **she is aware, n. better, that ...** elle sait mieux que personne que ...

3 *Admin* (*in schedules etc*) néant

ADV 1 I like him n. the better/worse for that je ne l'en aime pas plus/moins

2 he is n. too bright il est loin d'être brillant; **she was n. too happy about it** elle n'en était pas trop contente; **his position is n. too secure** sa position est loin d'être assurée

non-equity share N *St Exch* action *f* sans privilège de participation

non-EU country N pays *m* hors Union européenne

nonentity [nɒˈnentɪtɪ] N (*person*) personne *f* insignifiante; **she's a bit of a n.** elle est plutôt insignifiante

non-erasable memory N *Comput* mémoire *f* non-effaçable

nonessential [nɒnɪˈsenʃəl] **ADJ** non essentiel

N (*usu pl*) **nonessentials** superflu *m*, accessoire *m*; **if you're travelling light forget the nonessentials** si tu voyages avec peu de bagages, n'emporte rien de superflu

nonetheless [nʌnðəˈles] **ADV** = **nevertheless**

nonevent [nɒnɪˈvent] N *Fam* bide *m*; **the press conference was pretty much a n.** la conférence de presse ne valait pas le déplacement

nonexecutive [nɒnɪgˈzekjʊtɪv] N

▸▸ **n. director** administrateur *m* consultant

nonexistence [nɒnɪgˈzɪstəns] N non-existence *f*

nonexistent [nɒnɪgˈzɪstənt] **ADJ** non existant, inexistant

nonferrous [nɒnˈferəs] **ADJ** non ferreux

non-fiction N ouvrages *mpl* généraux

▸▸ **n. section** (*of bookshop*) rayon *m* des ouvrages généraux

non-floating exchange rate N *Econ* taux *m* de change fixe

non-fulfilment, *Am* **non-fulfillment** N (*of contract*) non-exécution *f*

non-governmental organization N organisation *f* non gouvernmentale

non-impact printer N imprimante *f* sans impact

non(in)flammable [nɒn(ɪn)ˈflæməb(ə)l] **ADJ** ininflammable

non-interlaced display N *Comput* affichage *m* non entrelacé

nonintervention [nɒnɪntəˈvenʃən] N *Pol* non-intervention *f*

noninterventionist [nɒnɪntəˈvenʃənɪst] *Pol* N non-interventionniste *mf*, *pl* non-interventionnistes

ADJ (*policy*) non-interventionniste, de non-intervention

non-iron **ADJ** (*clothing*) lavé-repassé *inv*

non-judgmental **ADJ** objectif; **to try to be n.** s'efforcer de ne pas porter de jugements

non-linear **ADJ** non linéaire

nonmalignant [nɒnməˈlɪgnənt] **ADJ** *Med* bénin, *f* bénigne

non-member N (*at club etc*) invité, -ée; **open to non-members** ouvert au public; **non-members of the EU** pays *mpl* non membres de l'UE

non-negotiable **ADJ** (*bill, demands etc*) non négociable

non-nuclear **ADJ** (*country*) non nucléarisé; (*war, defence, policy*) non nucléaire

no-no N *Fam* **that's a n.** c'est défendu; **that subject is a n.** ce sujet est tabou; **criticizing** his cooking is a n. critiquer sa cuisine est fortement déconseillé

non-observance N (*of laws, Lent etc*) inobservance *f*

no-nonsense **ADJ** (*approach*) direct; **she's a very n. kind of person** c'est quelqu'un qui ne plaisante pas; **she told him so in her usual n. way** elle le lui a dit très directement, comme à son habitude; **his n. handling of the unrest** la fermeté avec laquelle il a fait face aux troubles

nonpareil [nɒnpəˈreɪl] *Old-fashioned, Lit* N (*person*) prodige *m*; (*object*) chose *f* sans pareille

ADJ incomparable, sans égal, -aux

non-participating **ADJ** *St Exch* (*share*) sans droit de participation

non-partisan **ADJ** neutre, impartial, -aux

non-payment N non-paiement *m*; **for n.** faute de paiement

non-performance N (*of contract*) non-exécution *f*, inexécution *f*

non-performing loan N *Banking* prêt *m* en souffrance

non-person N *Pol* proscrit, -ite; *Fam* **I felt like a n.** je me suis senti une non-valeur

nonplus [nɒnˈplʌs] **VT** (**-ss-**) interloquer

non-poisonous **ADJ** non toxique; (*snake*) non venimeux; (*mushroom*) non vénéneux

nonpolluting [nɒnpəˈluːtɪŋ] **ADJ** non polluant, propre

non-printable character N caractère *m* non imprimable

non-probability method N *Mktg* (*of sampling*) méthode *f* non probabiliste

non-probability sample N *Mktg* échantillon *m* non probabiliste

non-probability sampling N *Mktg* échantillonnage *m* non probabiliste

non-procedural language N *Comput* langage *m* non procédural

non-productive N (*capital*) improductif

non-profit-making, *Am* **nonprofit** [nɒnˈprɒfɪt] **ADJ** (*association*) sans but lucratif; **on a n. basis** sur une base non lucrative

non-proliferation N *Mil* non-prolifération *f*

▸▸ **n. treaty** traité *m* de non-prolifération

non-racist **ADJ** non raciste

non-random **ADJ**

▸▸ *Mktg* **n. sample** échantillon *m* empirique; *Mktg* **n. sampling** échantillonnage *m* empirique

non-recoverable N *Comput* (*file, data*) non récupérable

nonrecurring [nɒnrɪˈkɜːrɪŋ] **ADJ** exceptionnel, extraordinaire

▸▸ **n. expenditure** frais *mpl* ou dépenses *fpl* extraordinaires

non-reflecting **ADJ** anti-reflet

non-refundable packaging N *Com* emballage *m* perdu

nonresident [nɒnˈrezɪdənt] N non-résident, -ente; *Sch* externe *mf*; (*in hotel*) client, -ente de passage; **open to nonresidents** (*hotel*) ouvert aux hôtes de passage

ADJ non résident

nonreturnable [nɒnrɪˈtɜːnəb(ə)l] **ADJ** (*bottle*) non consigné; (*deposit for holiday etc*) non remboursable; *Com* sans réserve de retour

non-return valve N *Tech* clapet *m* anti-retour

nonscheduled [nɒnˈʃedjuːld] **ADJ** (*flight*) spécial, -aux

▸▸ **n. stop** étape *f* non prévue

nonsectarian [nɒnsekˈteərɪən] **ADJ** non sectaire

nonsense [ˈnɒns(ə)ns] N bêtises *fpl*, idioties *fpl*; **a piece of n.** une bêtise, une absurdité; **to talk (a lot of) n.** dire des bêtises ou des idioties; **I don't think we'll get any more n. from them** je pense qu'ils vont arrêter leurs bêtises; **I've translated all the words, but the result is just n.** j'ai traduit tous les mots, mais le résultat est complètement absurde; **it's n. to think that ...** il est absurde de penser que ...; **to make a n. of sth** (*undo, go against etc*) ôter tout sens à qch; **I won't stand for any n.** je ne supporterai aucune imbécillité; **there's no n. about her** elle ne plaisante pas

INT n.! n'importe quoi!

▸▸ **n. verse** vers *mpl* amphigouriques; **n. word** mot *m* qui ne veut rien dire, non-sens *m*

nonsensical [nɒnˈsensɪk(ə)l] **ADJ** (*speech, reason etc*) absurde, qui n'a pas de sens

nonsensically [nɒnˈsensɪklɪ] **ADV** absurdement

non sequitur [nɒnˈsekwɪtər] N **his conversation was full of non sequiturs** il n'y avait pas de suite dans sa conversation; **that's a n.** ça manque de suite

non-sexist **ADJ** non sexiste

N personne *f* non sexiste

nonshrink [nɒnˈʃrɪŋk] **ADJ** irrétrécissable

nonskid [nɒnˈskɪd] **ADJ** antidérapant

▸▸ **n. tyre** (*pneu m*) antidérapant *m*

non-smoker N **1** non-fumeur, -euse; **she's been a n. all her life** elle n'a jamais fumé de sa vie **2** *Rail* (*compartment*) compartiment *m* non-fumeurs

non-smoking **ADJ** (*carriage, area*) non-fumeurs; (*seat*) non-fumeur

non-speaking part N *Cin, TV* rôle *m* muet

non-specialist N non-spécialiste *mf*, *pl* non-spécialistes

ADJ non spécialisé

nonstandard [nɒnˈstændəd] **ADJ** (*size etc*) spécial, -aux; *Ling* d'usage non général; **it's a n. usage** ce n'est pas un usage général

nonstarter [nɒnˈstɑːtər] N *Sport, Horseracing etc* non-partant *m*, *pl* non-partants; *Fam* **the project's a n.** le projet est fichu d'avance

nonstick [ˈnɒnˈstɪk] **ADJ** (*frying pan etc*) avec revêtement anti-adhésif, qui n'attache pas; (*surface*) anti-adhésif

non-stop **ADJ** *Rail* (*train*) direct; (*journey*) sans arrêt; *Aviat* (*flight*) sans escale; *Cin* (*show*) permanent; (*films, cartoons*) en continu; **n. music programme** programme *m* musical en continu

ADV (*to talk*) sans arrêt; (*to work*) sans interruption; **we flew to Sydney n.** nous avons fait un vol sans escale jusqu'à Sydney

non-synchronous **ADJ** *Cin, TV* non-synchrone

nontaxable [nɒnˈtæksəb(ə)l] **ADJ** non imposable

nontransferability [nɒntrænsfərəˈbɪlɪtɪ] N (*of property, right*) incessibilité *f*

nontransferable [nɒnˈtrænsfərəb(ə)l] **ADJ** (*property, right*) incessible; (*share*) nominatif

non-U **ADJ** *Old-fashioned Br Fam* = pas classe

non-union **ADJ** (*labour*) non syndiqué; (*company, firm*) qui ne reconnaît pas de syndicat en son sein

▸▸ **n. worker** non-syndiqué *m*, *pl* non-syndiqués

non-user N non utilisateur *m*

nonverbal [nɒnˈvɜːb(ə)l] **ADJ** non verbal, -aux

nonvintage [nɒnˈvɪntɪdʒ] **ADJ** (*wine*) non millésimé

nonviolence [nɒnˈvaɪələns] N non-violence f

nonviolent [nɒnˈvaɪələnt] ADJ non violent

nonvoting [nɒnˈvəʊtɪŋ] ADJ Fin (share) sans droit de vote

non-wasting ADJ (asset) indéfectible

non-White ADJ (in South Africa) de couleur N personne f de couleur

noodle [ˈnuːd(ə)l] N 1 Culin (usu pl) **noodles** nouilles fpl 2 Old-fashioned Fam (simpleton) nouille f, nigaud, -aude 3 Fam (head) caboche f

nook [nʊk] N (corner) coin m, recoin m; (in room) renfoncement m; (retreat) refuge m; **nooks and crannies** coins et recoins

nooky, nookie [ˈnʊkɪ] N Sl Hum (sex) crac-crac m; **he wants his n.** il veut s'envoyer en l'air

noon [nuːn] N midi m; **it is twelve n.** il est midi; **about n.** vers midi; **the n. train** le train de midi

noonday [ˈnuːndeɪ], Old-fashioned **noontide** [ˈnuːntaɪd] N Lit midi m; **the n. sun** le soleil de midi

no-one [ˈnəʊwʌn] PRON = nobody

noose [nuːs] N nœud m coulant; (for trapping animals) lacet m, lacs m, collet m; (lasso) lasso m; Fig **to put one's head in a n.** signer son arrêt de mort; (hangman's) **n.** corde f (de potence)

nope [nəʊp] ADV Fam non

nor [nɔːr] CONJ VOIR GRAMMAIRE A73 1 (continuing the force of a negative) ni; **he has neither father n. mother** il n'a ni père ni mère, il n'a pas de père ni de mère; **he neither drinks n. smokes** il ne boit ni ne fume; **neither she n. her mother is at home** ni sa mère ni elle ne sont chez elles
2 (and not) **I do not know, n. can I guess** je n'en sais rien et je ne peux pas le deviner; **n. was this all** et ce n'était pas tout; **I haven't read it, n. do I intend to** je ne l'ai pas lu et d'ailleurs je n'en ai pas l'intention; **he hasn't any, n. have I** il n'en a pas, ni moi non plus ou et moi non plus; **n. do I/does his wife** moi/sa femme non plus VOIR GRAMMAIRE A78

Norah [ˈnɔːrə] N Br Fam flaming N.! punaise!, purée!; bloody N.! putain!

Nordic [ˈnɔːdɪk] Geog ADJ nordique, scandinave
N Nordique mf, Scandinave mf

nordic [ˈnɔːdɪk] ADJ Ski nordique

nor'east [nɔːˈriːst] Naut = northeast

nor'easterly [nɔːˈriːstəlɪ] Naut = northeasterly

nor'eastern [nɔːˈriːstən] Naut = northeastern

nork [nɔːk] N Br, Austr Sl (breast) nichon m

norm [nɔːm] N norme f; **according to the n.** selon la norme; **to deviate from the n.** sortir de la norme; **it's the n.** c'est la règle

normal [ˈnɔːm(ə)l] ADJ (person, situation, behaviour, development, result) normal, -aux; Math (line etc) normal (**to** à); Chem (solution etc) normal, titré; **it's n. to react/feel like that** c'est normal de réagir/se sentir comme ça; **he arrived at the n. time** il est arrivé à l'heure habituelle; **any n. person would have …** toute personne normalement constituée aurait …; **n. temperature** température f moyenne ou normale; **n. working** or **running** (of engine etc) régime m normal
N 1 état m normal, condition f normale; Math normale f, perpendiculaire f; **temperature above n.** température f au-dessus de la normale; **things quickly got back to n. after the strike** les choses rentrèrent rapidement dans l'ordre après la grève; **he'll soon be back to n.** tout rentrera bientôt dans l'ordre
2 Geom normale f

▸▸ **n. distribution** distribution f normale; **n. distribution curve** courbe f de distribution normale

normal-angle lens N Phot objectif m à focale fixe

normality [nɔːˈmælɪtɪ], Am **normalcy** [ˈnɔːməlsɪ] N normalité f; **a return to n.** un retour à la normale; **to return to n.** redevenir normal

normalization [nɔːməlaɪˈzeɪʃən] N normalisation f

normalize [ˈnɔːməlaɪz] VT normaliser
VI se normaliser, redevenir normal

normally [ˈnɔːməlɪ] ADV normalement; **n. I would have offered you a lift, but …** je vous aurais bien proposé de vous emmener, mais …; **I wouldn't n. ask you, but everyone else is away** cela m'ennuie de vous le demander, mais tous les autres sont partis

Norman [ˈnɔːmən] ADJ 1 Geog, Hist normand 2 Archit roman (anglais)
N 1 (person) Normand, -ande 2 Ling normand m
▸▸ Hist **the N. Conquest** la conquête normande (de l'Angleterre); Ling **N. French** normand m

Normandy [ˈnɔːməndɪ] N Normandie f; **in N.** en Normandie
▸▸ Hist **the N. landings** le débarquement

normative economics [ˈnɔːmətɪv] N économie f normative

nor'nor'east [nɔːnɔːˈriːst] Naut = northnortheast

nor'nor'west [nɔːnɔːˈwest] Naut = northnorthwest

Norse [nɔːs] ADJ (Scandinavian) scandinave, nordique; (Norwegian) norvégien
N 1 Hist **the N.** (Norwegians) les Norvégiens mpl; (Vikings) les Vikings mpl 2 Ling nordique m, norrois m; **Old N.** vieux norrois
▸▸ **N. legends** légendes fpl scandinaves; **N. mythology** mythologie f scandinave

Norseman, pl **Norsemen** [ˈnɔːsmən] N Hist Scandinave m

north [nɔːθ] N nord m; **the house faces n.** la maison est exposée au nord; **in the n.** au nord, dans le nord (**of** de); **to live in the n. of England** habiter dans le nord de l'Angleterre; **true n.** nord vrai ou géographique; **magnetic n.** nord magnétique; Hist **the N.** (in American Civil War) = les États mpl anti-esclavagistes du nord des États-Unis; (affluent countries) l'hémisphère m nord; **the (Canadian) Far N.** le Grand Nord Canadien; **the N.-South divide** la division nord-sud
ADV au nord; **to travel n.** voyager vers le nord; **it's n. of here** c'est au nord d'ici; **I'm going up n.** (to northern part of country) je vais dans le nord; **n. by east/by west** nord-quart-nord-est/nord-quart-nord-ouest
ADJ (wind) du nord; (wall, window) exposé au nord; **n. side** côté m nord; **on the n. side** du côté nord; **the n. coast** la côte nord
▸▸ **N. Africa** Afrique f du Nord; **N. African** nord-africain, -aine; **N. America** Amérique f du Nord; **N. American** nord-américain, -aine; Econ **N. American Free Trade Agreement** Accord m de libre-échange nord-américain; **N. Carolina** la Caroline du Nord; **the N. Country** (in England) l'Angleterre f du Nord; (in America) = l'Alaska f, le Yukon et les Territoires du Nord-Ouest; **he has a strong N. Country accent** il a un accent du nord prononcé; **N. Island** l'île f du Nord; **N. Korea** Corée f du Nord; **the N. Pole** le pôle Nord; **the N. Sea** la mer du Nord; **the N. Star** l'étoile f Polaire; **n. transept** (in church) transept m septentrional; **N. Vietnam** le Viêt-Nam du Nord

Northants abbr **Northamptonshire**

northbound [ˈnɔːθbaʊnd] ADJ (traffic) en direction du nord; (lane, carriageway) du nord; (road) vers le nord; **n. traffic is subject to delays** la circulation est ralentie dans le sens nord; **there's a jam on the n. carriageway** il y a un bouchon en direction du nord

northeast [nɔːθˈiːst] N nord-est m; Naut nordé m
ADJ 1 Geog nord-est inv, du nord-est; **in n. Scotland** dans le nord-est de l'Écosse 2 (wind) de nord-est; (to travel) vers le nord-est; **it's 20 miles n. of Birmingham** c'est à 32 kilomètres au nord-est de Birmingham

northeaster [nɔːθˈiːstər] N (wind) vent m du nord-est

northeasterly [nɔːθˈiːstəlɪ] ADJ 1 Geog nord-est inv, du nord-est; **to travel in a n. direction** aller vers le nord-est; Naut **to steer a n. course** faire route vers le nord-est; (when setting out) mettre le cap au nord-est 2 (wind) de nord-est, du nord-est
ADV vers le nord-est
N vent m de ou du nord-est; Naut nordé m, nordet m

northeastern [nɔːθˈiːstən] ADJ nord-est inv, du nord-est; (wind) de nord-est; **the n. suburbs** la banlieue nord-est

northerly [ˈnɔːðəlɪ] ADJ 1 Geog nord inv, du nord; **to travel in a n. direction** aller vers le nord; **n. point** point situé au nord ou vers le nord; **a room with a n. aspect** une pièce exposée au nord; Naut **to steer a n. course** faire route vers le nord; (when setting out) mettre le cap au nord 2 (wind) de nord, du nord
ADV vers le nord

northern [ˈnɔːðən] ADJ 1 Geog nord inv, du nord; **she has a n. accent** elle a un accent du nord; **the n. wing of the castle** l'aile nord du château; **in n. Mexico** dans le nord du Mexique; **the n. migration of swallows in spring** la migration printanière des hirondelles vers le nord 2 (wind) de nord, du nord 3 Hist (in American Civil War) nordiste
▸▸ **n. hemisphere** l'hémisphère m nord ou boréal; **N. Ireland** Irlande f du Nord; **n. lights** aurore f boréale

---

Northern Ireland

L'Irlande du Nord désigne la partie de l'Irlande à majorité protestante restée rattachée à la Grande-Bretagne lors de la partition du pays, en 1921. Les émeutes sanglantes qui ont éclaté en 1969 à la suite de manifestations revendiquant l'égalité des droits pour la minorité catholique ont marqué le début de trente ans de conflit entre catholiques et protestants. Ce conflit vit s'affronter les nationalistes de l'IRA, favorables à un rattachement avec la République d'Irlande, différents groupes paramilitaires protestants anti-catholiques, et l'armée et la police, sous contrôle britannique. Le processus de paix, amorcé en 1994 et qui aboutit au "Good Friday Agreement" de 1998 marqua une nouvelle étape dans l'histoire de l'Irlande du Nord.

---

northerner [ˈnɔːðənər] N 1 habitant, -ante du nord; **he's a n.** il vient du nord 2 Hist (in American Civil War) nordiste mf

north-facing ADJ (house, wall) (exposé) au nord

north-north-east N nord-nord-est m inv
ADJ nord-nord-est inv
ADV au nord-nord-est; (to travel) vers le nord-nord-est

north-north-west N nord-nord-ouest m inv
ADJ nord-nord-ouest inv
ADV au nord-nord-ouest; (to travel) vers le nord-nord-ouest

North-Sea gas N gaz *m* de la mer du Nord

Northumb *abbr* Northumberland

northward ['nɔːθwəd] ADJ vers le nord, en direction du nord
N nord *m*
ADV = **northwards**

northwards ['nɔːθwədz] ADV vers le nord, en direction du nord

northwest [nɔːθ'west] N nord-ouest *m*
ADJ **1** *Geog* nord-ouest *inv*, du nord-ouest **2** *(wind)* de nord-ouest, du nord-ouest
ADV au nord-ouest; *(to travel)* vers le nord-ouest; **n. by west** nord-ouest-quart-ouest; **n. by north** nord-ouest-quart-nord

northwester [nɔːθ'westər] N *(wind)* vent *m* de *ou* du nord-ouest; *Naut* noroît *m*

northwesterly [nɔːθ'westəlɪ] ADJ **1** *Geog* nord-ouest *inv*, du nord-ouest; **to travel in a n. direction** aller vers le nord-ouest; *Naut* **to steer a n. course** faire route vers le nord-ouest; *(when setting out)* mettre le cap au nord-ouest **2** *(wind)* de nord-ouest, du nord-ouest
ADV vers le nord-ouest
N = **northwester**

northwestern [nɔːθ'westən] ADJ nord-ouest *inv*, du nord-ouest

Norway ['nɔːweɪ] N Norvège *f*
▸▸ **N. lobster** langoustine *f*

Norwegian [nɔː'wiːdʒən] ADJ norvégien
N **1** Norvégien, -ienne **2** *Ling* norvégien *m*

nor'west [nɔː'west] *Naut* = **northwest**

nor'westerly [nɔː'westəlɪ] *Naut* = **northwesterly**

nor'western [nɔː'westən] *Naut* = **northwestern**

nose [nəʊz] N **1** *(of person, animal)* nez *m*; **her n. is bleeding** elle saigne du nez; **to blow one's n.** se moucher; **to hold one's n.** se boucher le nez; **to speak through one's n.** parler du nez, nasiller; **to have one's n. in a book** avoir le nez dans un livre; **the parson's** *or* **pope's n.** *(of fowl)* le croupion; *Fig* **he can't see any further than the end of his n.** il ne voit pas plus loin que le bout de son nez; **it's under your n.** vous l'avez sous le nez; **I did it under his very n.** *or* **right under his n.** je l'ai fait sous son nez; **to poke one's n. into other people's business** fourrer *ou* mettre son nez dans les affaires des autres; **to turn up one's n. at sth** dédaigner qch; **to look down one's n. at sb** regarder qn de haut en bas; *Fig (despise)* mépriser qn; **she walked by with her n. in the air** elle passa avec un air dédaigneux *ou* supérieur; *Prov* **to cut off one's n. to spite one's face** se punir soi-même; **that's cutting off your n. to spite your face** c'est toi le perdant; **to lead sb by the n.** mener qn par le bout du nez; *Fam* **to pay through the n. for sth** payer qch une fortune ou les yeux de la tête; **to win by a n.** gagner d'un nez; *Fam* **to rub sb's n. in it** retourner le couteau dans la plaie; *Fam* **to have a n. (a)round** faire un tour d'inspection; **to get up sb's n.** *(of person)* taper sur les nerfs de qn; **it really gets up my n. that …** ça me met en boule que …; *Fig* **to keep one's n. clean** se tenir à carreau **2** *(of wine etc)* bouquet *m*; **to have a good n.** *(of person)* avoir bon nez *ou* le nez fin *ou* l'odorat fin; *Fig* **to have a n. for sth** *(of person)* avoir du flair pour qch **3** *Tech (of vehicle, plane etc)* nez *m*, avant *m*; *(of engine)* nez; *(of tool)* bec *m*, nez; *(of bullet, missile)* pointe *f*, ogive *f*; *Naut (of torpedo)* cône *m* de choc
VT **the ship nosed her way through the fog** le navire avançait à l'aveuglette à travers le brouillard; **the car nosed its way forward/out of the garage** la voiture avança prudemment/sortit prudemment du garage

VI **the ship nosed through the fog** le navire avançait à l'aveuglette à travers le brouillard
▸▸ **n. cone** *(of missile)* ogive *f*, *(of aircraft)* nez *m*; *Aviat* **n. dive** *(vol m)* piqué *m*; *Fam* **to take a n. dive** *(of prices)* faire un plongeon, piquer du nez; **n. drops** gouttes *fpl* nasales *ou* pour le nez; *Fam* **n. job** = intervention *f* esthétique de chirurgie sur le nez; **to have a n. job** se faire refaire le nez; **n. ring** *(of bull)* anneau *m* nasal, nasière *f*, *(of person)* anneau de nez

▸ **nose about, nose around** VI fureter, fouiner; **what are you nosing around here for?** pourquoi est-ce que tu fouines par ici?
VT INSEP *(office, room, garden)* fureter dans, fouiner dans; **a policeman was nosing around the car/dustbin** un agent de police fouinait *ou* furetait autour de la voiture/poubelle

▸ **nose out** VT SEP **1** *(of dog) (game)* flairer **2** *Fam (secret)* découvrir, éventer; *(person)* dépister, dénicher; *(good restaurant, bargain)* dénicher
VI *(of car, driver)* sortir prudemment; **the car nosed out into the traffic** la voiture s'est prudemment faufilée entre les autres; **the van nosed through the crowds/up the ramp** la camionnette a traversé la foule/monté la rampe prudemment *ou* tout doucement

▸ **nose through** VT INSEP *(papers etc)* fouiller dans

nosebag ['nəʊzbæg] N musette *f* (mangeoire)

noseband ['nəʊzbænd] N *(on harness)* muserolle *f*

nosebleed ['nəʊzbliːd] N saignement *m* de nez; **to have a n.** saigner du nez

nose-dive VI *Aviat* piquer du nez, descendre en piqué; *Fam (of prices)* faire un plongeon, piquer du nez

nosegay ['nəʊzgeɪ] N petit bouquet *m* (de fleurs)

nose-to-tail ADJ *(traffic)* pare-choc(s) contre pare-choc(s)

nosey ['nəʊzɪ] ADJ *Fam* = **nosy**

nosh [nɒʃ] *Sl* N *(food)* bouffe *f*; **time for some n.!** c'est l'heure de bouffer *ou* de la bouffe!
VI *(eat)* bouffer

no-show N *(at airport, for travel)* désistement *m*, défection *f*, no-show *m*, *pl* no-shows

nosh-up N *Br Sl (meal)* boustifaille *f*

nosily ['nəʊzɪlɪ] ADV *Fam* indiscrètement

nosiness ['nəʊzɪnəs] N *Fam* indiscrétion *f*, curiosité *f*

no-smoking ADJ *(carriage, area)* non-fumeurs; *(seat)* non-fumeur

nostalgia [nɒs'tældʒɪə] N nostalgie *f*

nostalgic [nɒs'tældʒɪk] ADJ nostalgique; **a n. moment** un moment de nostalgie

nostalgically [nɒs'tældʒɪklɪ] ADV avec nostalgie, nostalgiquement

nostril ['nɒstrɪl] N *(of person)* narine *f*, *(of horse, ox etc)* naseau *m*

nostrum ['nɒstrəm] N *Old-fashioned usu Pej, Fig* panacée *f*, *(quack medicine)* remède *m* de charlatan

nosy ['nəʊzɪ] ADJ *Fam* curieux, fouinard; *(questions)* indiscret, -ète; **don't be so n.!** ne soyez pas si curieux!; **I don't mean to be n. but …** je ne veux pas me mêler de ce qui ne me regarde pas mais …
▸▸ *Br Fam Pej* **n. parker** fouine *f*

NOT [nɒt]

ADV	ne… pas **1, 3** ▪ non **2, 7** ▪ pas **2, 4, 5**

ADV VOIR GRAMMAIRE A23–4 **1** *(following the aux verb informally affixed as* **n't**) ne … pas;
I don't *or* **do n. know** je ne sais pas; **he won't** *or* **will n. come** il ne viendra pas; **is she coming? – no, she isn't** *or* **she's n.** est-ce qu'elle vient? – non, (elle ne vient pas); **don't move** ne bougez pas; **I'm n. in the least surprised** je ne suis nullement étonné; **you understand, don't you?** vous comprenez, n'est-ce pas?; **she would n. wear a hat!** *(stressed)* un chapeau, elle n'en porterait pas! VOIR GRAMMAIRE A47–8

2 *(elliptically in answers etc)* **n. at all, n. a bit (of it)** pas du tout; **n. in any way, n. in the least** pas le moins du monde; **thank you so much! – n. at all!** merci beaucoup! – je vous en prie; **n. if I've got anything to do with it** pas si j'ai mon mot à dire; **n. likely!** jamais de la vie!; **whether he likes it or n.** que cela lui plaise ou non; **little or n. at all** peu ou pas, peu ou point; **I think/hope n.** je crois/j'espère que non; **n. always** pas toujours; **n. any more** *or* **longer** plus maintenant; **n. even in France** (non) pas même en France; **n. just** *or* **simply** pas seulement; **n. so** pas du tout; **n. yet** pas encore

3 *(with a non-finite verb)* **n. wishing to be seen, I drew the curtain** comme je ne désirais pas être vu, j'ai tiré le rideau; **n. including …** sans compter …; **n. to mention …** pour ne pas parler de …; *Fam* **n. to worry!** ne vous en faites pas!; **she asked me n. to do it** elle m'a demandé de ne pas le faire VOIR GRAMMAIRE A47–8

4 *(in contrasts)* **she's n. my mother but my aunt** ce n'est pas ma mère, c'est ma tante; **he is respected but n. loved** il est respecté mais (non) pas aimé; **n. only … but also …** non seulement … mais encore …

5 *(with pronoun or noun)* **n. I** pas moi; **n. one replied** pas un(e) n'a répondu; *Old-fashioned* **he'll never pay, n. he!** il ne paiera jamais, c'est sûr!; **n. everyone was so enthusiastic** tout le monde n'était pas aussi enthousiaste; **n. a word was spoken** on n'a pas dit un mot; **who will believe it? – n. a soul** qui le croira? – personne

6 *(understatement)* **I wasn't sorry to go** j'étais bien content de partir; **a n. inconsiderable sum of money** une somme non négligeable; **n. without reason/regret** non sans raison/regrets; **they were annoyed, n. to say furious** ils étaient ennuyés, pour ne pas dire furieux; *Fam* **n. half!** et comment!, tu parles!

7 *(with adverb or adjective)* non; **n. far from the town** non loin de la ville; **n. guilty** non coupable; **n. negotiable** non négociable

8 *Arch, Lit (following the verb)* **I know n.** je ne sais point; **fear n.!** n'ayez crainte!

9 *Sl* **the party was fantastic, n.!** la fête ne cassait rien du tout; **he's really gorgeous, n.!** c'est pas exactement un Apollon!

CONJ **n. that …** ce n'est pas que … + *sub*, non (pas) que … + *sub*; **n. that I can remember** pas autant que je m'en souvienne
▸▸ **n. equals sign** signe *m* différent de

notability [nəʊtə'bɪlɪtɪ] N *Old-fashioned (person)* notabilité *f*, notable *m*; *(state)* prééminence *f*

notable ['nəʊtəb(ə)l] ADJ *(person, thing)* notable, insigne, remarquable; *(person)* éminent; **with a few n. exceptions** avec quelques exceptions et non des moindres; **in a speech n. only for its length** dans un discours qui n'avait de remarquable que sa longueur; **the town is chiefly n. for …** la ville se distingue essentiellement par …
N *Fml* notable *m*

notably ['nəʊtəblɪ] ADV *(particularly)* notamment, particulièrement

notarize ['nəʊtəraɪz] VT authentifier; **notarized contract/deed** contrat *m*/acte *m* notarié

notary ['nəʊtərɪ] N *Law* notaire *m*; **signed in**

the presence of a n. signé par-devant notaire

▸▸**n. public** notaire

notation [nəʊ'teɪʃən] N *Mus etc* notation *f*, *Math* numération *f*

notch [nɒtʃ] N **1** (*in wood*) entaille *f*, encoche *f*; (*in belt, rack*) cran *m*; (*of toothed wheel*) cran, dent *f*; (*in blade etc*) brèche *f*, *Sewing* cran; (*in diskette*) encoche; **to cut a n.** faire une entaille *ou* une encoche; **to take one's belt in a n.** resserrer sa ceinture d'un cran; *Fig* se serrer la ceinture; *Fig* **a n. on the bedpost** une conquête **2** *Fig* (*grade, level*) **to be a n. above the rest** être dans la catégorie supérieure; **it raised their spirits a n. or two but …** cela leur a quelque peu remonté le moral mais … **3** *Am* (*in mountain*) défilé *m*, gorge *f*

VT (*stick etc*) entailler, encocher; (*wheel*) denteler, créneler; (*blade*) ébrécher

▸ **notch up** VT SEP (*point*) marquer; (*victory*) remporter

note [nəʊt] N **1** (*in writing*) note *f*; (*on a text*) note, annotation *f*, remarque *f*; (*letter*) mot *m*; *Univ* **lecture notes** notes (de cours); **to make notes, to take (down) notes** prendre des notes; **to take** *or* **make a n. of sth** prendre note de qch; **I must make a n. of it** il faut que je m'en souvienne; **they have no n. of any such meeting** ils n'ont aucune trace de cette réunion; **without notes** (*to speak, lecture*) sans notes; **to speak from notes** parler d'après des notes; **to write** *or* **make notes on a text** annoter un texte; **diplomatic n.** note *f* diplomatique, mémorandum *m*; *Acct* **notes to the accounts** annexes *fpl*

2 *Mus* note *f*; (*of piano etc*) touche *f*; **to sing** *or* **play a false n.** faire une fausse note; **there was a n. of impatience in her voice** il y avait une pointe d'impatience dans sa voix; **to introduce a n. of discord/optimism** introduire une note discordante/optimiste; **speech that strikes the right n.** discours dans la note voulue; **to end on a more serious/a lighter n. …** pour conclure sur une note plus sérieuse/gaie, …

3 *Fin, Com* billet *m*; (*money*) billet (de banque); **n. of hand** reconnaissance *f* (de dette), billet simple; **credit/debit n.** note *f ou* bordereau *m* de crédit/de débit; **hundred-euro notes** billets *ou* coupures *fpl* de cent euros

4 (*distinction*) distinction *f*, marque *f*, renom *m*; **a man of n.** un homme de qualité *ou* de marque; **nothing of n.** rien d'extraordinaire *ou* de spécial

5 **to take n. of sth** noter qch

VT (*notice*) noter, remarquer; (*error*) relever; (*fact*) constater; **it should be noted that …** il est à noter que …; **we duly n. that …** nous prenons bonne note (de ce) que …; *Law* **which fact is hereby duly noted** dont acte

▸ **note down** VT SEP prendre note de

notebook ['nəʊtbʊk] N carnet *m*, calepin *m*; (*larger*) cahier *m*; (*for shorthand etc*) bloc-notes *m, pl* blocs-notes, notebook *m*; (*computer*) notebook *m*, ordinateur *m* bloc-notes

▸▸ **n. computer** notebook, ordinateur bloc-notes

notecase ['nəʊtkeɪs] N *Br Old-fashioned* portefeuille *m*

noted ['nəʊtɪd] ADJ (*person*) distingué, éminent; (*thing*) fameux (**for sth** pour qch), remarquable (**for sth** par qch); **the area is n. for its cheese** la région est célèbre *ou* fameuse pour son fromage

notelet ['nəʊtlət] N carte-lettre *f, pl* cartes-lettres

notepad ['nəʊtpæd] N (*for notes*) bloc-notes *m, pl* blocs-notes; (*for letters*) bloc *m* de papier à lettres

▸▸ **n. computer** ardoise *f* électronique

notepaper ['nəʊtpeɪpər] N papier *m* à lettres

note-taking N prise *f* de notes

noteworthy ['nəʊtwɜːðɪ] ADJ (*fact etc*) remarquable; **it is n. that …** il convient de noter que …

not-for-profit ADJ *Am* = **non-profit-making**

NOTHING ['nʌθɪŋ] PRON rien; **n. at all** rien du tout; **he does n.** il ne fait rien; **I saw n.** je n'ai rien vu; **what are you doing? – n.** que faites-vous? – rien; **it's better than n.** c'est mieux que rien; **n. can beat French cooking** il n'y a rien de mieux que la cuisine française; **a cheese sandwich is better than n.** un sandwich au fromage, c'est mieux que rien *ou* c'est toujours ça; **n. could be simpler** rien de plus simple, c'est tout ce qu'il y a de plus simple; **you can't live on n.** on ne peut pas vivre de rien; **he let me have it for almost** *or* **next to n.** il me l'a cédé pour presque rien *ou* pour une bouchée de pain; **they pay him next to n.** ils le paient trois fois rien; **it looks like n. on earth** c'est ridicule; **as if n. had happened** comme si de rien n'était; **say n. about it** n'en dites rien; **to say n. of …** sans parler de …; **she gets angry about n.** elle se fâche pour un rien; **there's n. in these rumours** ces bruits sont sans fondement; *Fam* **there's n. to it** (*it's easy*) c'est simple comme bonjour; **there's n. in it** (*no difference*) il n'y a aucune différence; (*in choosing between two candidates etc*) ils se valent, il n'y a aucune différence entre eux; (*in race*) ils sont à égalité; **he was n. if not discreet** il était surtout discret, il était discret avant tout; **n. new/remarkable** rien de nouveau/de remarquable; **that's n. new** ce n'est pas nouveau; **that's n. unusual** cela n'a rien d'anormal; **n. much** pas grand-chose; **there is n. more to be said** il n'y a plus rien à dire; **I have n. to do** je n'ai rien à faire; **to have n. to do with sb/sth** n'avoir rien à voir avec qn/qch; **that's n. to do with you** ce n'est pas votre affaire, cela ne vous regarde pas; **these people will stop at n.** ces gens ne reculent devant rien; **there's n. to cry/worry about** il n'y a pas de quoi pleurer/s'inquiéter; **to have n. on** (*no engagement*) être libre; (*no clothes*) être tout nu; **as a pianist he has n. on his brother** comme pianiste il n'arrive pas à la cheville de son frère; **he has n. of his father in him** il n'a rien de son père; **n. but …** rien que …; **n. but the best will satisfy her** seul ce qu'il y a de meilleur la satisfait; **n. but the truth** rien que la vérité; **n. else** rien d'autre; **n. else matters** tout le reste n'est rien, rien d'autre n'a d'importance; **there's n. else for it** c'est inévitable; **there's n. like a cold bath in the mornings** il n'y a rien de tel qu'un bain froid le matin; **to do sth for n.** (*in vain*) faire qch pour rien; (*free of charge*) faire qch gratuitement; **it's not for n. that …** ce n'est pas pour rien *ou* sans raison que …; **to come to n.** ne pas aboutir; (*of hopes etc*) s'anéantir; (*of scheme etc*) s'effondrer; **all my efforts came to n.** tous mes efforts se sont révélés inutiles; **to count for n.** ne compter pour rien; **he is n. to her** (*she doesn't care for him*) il lui est indifférent; (*she is much better than he is*) elle est bien meilleure que lui; **£1000 is n. to her** 1000 livres ne sont rien pour elle; **that's n. to what mum will say** ce n'est rien par rapport à ce que Maman va dire; **in those days it was n. to see …** en ce temps-là on voyait facilement …; **it's n. to me either way** cela m'est égal; **to think n. of doing sth** (*not hesitate to do*) ne pas hésiter à faire qch; **she thinks n. of walking 10 km** pour elle 10 km à pied, ce n'est rien; **to think n. of sb** avoir peu d'estime pour qn; **I can make n. of it** je n'y comprends rien du tout; *Fam* **n. doing** rien à faire, pas question; *Fam*

to do sth in n. flat faire qch en deux temps trois mouvements; *Prov* **n. ventured, n. gained** qui ne risque rien n'a rien SEE GRAMMAR B62–3

N **1** (*nonexistence*) néant *m*, rien *m*

2 (*trifle*) bagatelle *f*, rien *m*; (*person*) zéro *m*, nullité *f*; **a hundred euros? – a mere n.!** cent euros? – une bagatelle!; **to whisper sweet nothings to sb/in sb's ear** chuchoter des mots doux à qn/à l'oreille de qn

3 *Math* zéro *m*

ADV **n. like** *or* **near so** *or* **as big** loin d'être aussi grand; **London is n. like as near as that** Londres est loin d'être aussi près que ça; **she looks n. like her sister** elle ne ressemble pas du tout *ou* en rien à sa sœur; **it's n. less than** *or* **short of madness** c'est de la folie ni plus ni moins; **it's n. less than scandalous that …** c'est ni plus ni moins un scandale que …

nothingness ['nʌθɪŋnɪs] N néant *m*; **a feeling** *or* **sense of n.** un sentiment de vide

NOTICE ['nəʊtɪs]

N avis **1** ▪ préavis **1** ▪ congé **1** ▪ démission **1** ▪ affiche **2** ▪ pancarte **2** ▪ critique **3** ▪ annonce **3** ▪ attention **4**		
VT remarquer		
VI remarquer		

N **1** (*notification*) avis *m*, notification *f*; (*warning*) préavis *m*, avertissement *m*; (*served by bailiff*) exploit *m* (d'huissier); **to give sb n. of sth** prévenir *ou* avertir qn de qch; **to give official n. that …** donner acte que …; **n. is hereby given that …** le public est avisé que …; **without (prior) n.** sans préavis; **until further n.** jusqu'à nouvel ordre *ou* nouvel avis; **public n.** avis au public; **important n.** avis important; *Rel* **the weekly notices** les annonces *fpl* de la semaine; *Com* **n. of claim** déclaration *f* de sinistre; **n. of a/ the meeting** convocation *f*; **n. to pay** avertissement *m*; **at short n.** dans un bref délai; **to give sb short n.** prendre qn de court; **that's rather short n.** c'est un peu court comme délai; **at a moment's** *or* **a minute's n.** sur-le-champ; **without a moment's n.** sans crier gare; **to require three months' n.** exiger un préavis de trois mois; **deposit at seven days' n.** dépôt *m* à sept jours de préavis; **next time give me a bit more n.** la prochaine fois prévenez-moi un peu plus à l'avance; **n. (to quit)** (*avis de*) congé *m*; **to be under n. to quit** avoir reçu son congé; **what n. do you require?** quel est le terme du congé?; **to give sb n.** (*of landlord, employer*) congédier qn, donner son congé à qn; (*of employer*) licencier qn; **to give sb a week's n.** donner ses huit jours à qn; **to give n., to give** *or* **hand in one's n.** (*of tenant, employee*) donner *ou* demander (son) congé; (*of employee*) donner sa démission, démissionner

2 (*poster*) affiche *f*, placard *m*; (*sign, card etc*) écriteau *m*, pancarte *f*

3 (*in newspaper etc*) annonce *f*; (*review*) (*of play, work etc*) critique *f*; **they put a birth n. in the local paper** ils ont passé un faire-part de naissance dans le quotidien régional; **the play got good notices** la pièce a eu de bonnes critiques

4 (*attention*) **to take n. of** faire attention *ou* prêter attention à; (*warning*) tenir compte de; **to take not the slightest n. of sth** ne pas prêter la moindre attention à qch; **nobody took any n. of me** personne n'a fait attention à moi; **I warned him but he took no n.** (*of me*) je l'ai prévenu mais il n'a pas prêté la moindre attention à ce que je lui ai dit; **I should take no n.** *or* **I shouldn't take any n. of it if I were you** je n'y ferais pas attention à ta place; **it has come to my n. that …** il est venu à ma connaissance que …; **to attract**

n. *(of author etc)* commencer à être connu *ou* à percer; *(of performance, publication etc)* être remarqué; **to avoid n.** se dérober aux regards; **the fact escaped everyone's n.** ce fait a échappé à tout le monde; **to bring** *or* **call sth to sb's n.** appeler *ou* porter *ou* attirer l'attention de qn sur qch/qn; **the baby is beginning to take n.** le bébé commence à avoir conscience des choses

VT remarquer, s'apercevoir de; *(errors)* relever; **didn't anybody n. him leaving?** est-ce que personne n'a remarqué qu'il partait?; **without his noticing it** sans qu'il s'en aperçoive; **she's beginning to get herself noticed** elle commence à être connu *ou* à percer; **to be noticed** *or* **to get oneself noticed by sb** attirer l'attention de qn (sur soi)

VI remarquer; **nobody will ever n.** personne ne s'en apercevra *ou* ne le remarquera jamais; **what happened? – I don't know, I didn't n.** qu'est-ce qui s'est passé? – je ne sais pas, je ne m'en suis pas rendu compte

▸▸ *Law* **n. of appeal** intimation *f* d'appel; *Com* **n. period** période *f* de préavis; *Com* **n. of receipt** accusé *m* de réception; *Banking, Fin* **n. of withdrawal** avis *m* de retrait de fonds

---

Note that the French word **notice** is a false friend and is never a translation for the English word **notice**. Its most common meaning is **directions (for use)**.

---

noticeable ['nəʊtɪsəb(ə)l] **ADJ** *(perceptible)* perceptible; *(difference, improvement, change)* sensible; **it was very n. that she didn't speak to her husband** on ne pouvait pas ne pas remarquer qu'elle ne parlait pas à son mari

noticeably ['nəʊtɪsəblɪ] **ADV** sensiblement

noticeboard ['nəʊtɪsbɔːd] **N** panneau *m* d'affichage; *(in schools, clubs etc)* tableau *m* d'affichage; *(on house for sale etc)* écriteau *m*

notifiable [nəʊtɪ'faɪəb(ə)l] **ADJ** *(disease)* dont la déclaration aux autorités est obligatoire

notification [nəʊtɪfɪ'keɪʃən] **N** *(of fact etc)* avis *m*, notification *f*; *(of birth etc)* déclaration *f*; **letter of n.** lettre *f* notificative

notify ['nəʊtɪfaɪ] **VT** annoncer, notifier; *(birth)* déclarer; **to n. sb of sth** avertir *ou* aviser qn de qch; **to n. the authorities of a fact** saisir l'administration d'un fait; **to n. the police of sth** signaler qch à la police; **have you notified the police?** avez vous prévenu la police?; **to be notified of sth** recevoir notification de qch, être avisé de qch; *Com* **to send sth n.** expédier qch 'notify'

notion ['nəʊʃən] **N 1** *(idea)* notion *f*, idée *f*; **to have no n. of sth** ne pas avoir la moindre notion de qch; **to have no n. of time** n'avoir pas la notion *ou* le sens de l'heure; **I haven't the first n. about it** je n'en ai pas la moindre idée; **I haven't the first n. about physics/French** je n'y connais absolument rien en physique/français; **I have a n. that ...** j'ai dans l'idée que ...; **she has some pretty strange notions** elle a de drôles d'idées **2** *(whim)* caprice *m*; **as the n. takes him** comme il en a envie; **to have a n. to do sth** avoir envie de faire qch **3** *Phil (concept)* notion *f*, concept *m* **4** *Am* **notions** *(ribbons, needles etc)* (articles *mpl* de) mercerie *f*

notional ['nəʊʃən(ə)l] **ADJ** *(abstract)* hypothétique; *(income)* fictif; *Phil* spéculatif; *(imaginary) (things, relations etc)* imaginaire

notoriety [nəʊtə'raɪətɪ] **N** notoriété *f*; **to seek n.** chercher à se faire remarquer; **this action gained** *or* **earned him some n.** cette action lui a valu une certaine notoriété

notorious [nəʊ'tɔːrɪəs] **ADJ** d'une triste notoriété; *(criminal, thief)* notoire; *(place)* mal

famé; *(liar)* fieffé; **Mexico City is n. for being one of the world's most polluted cities** Mexico est réputée pour être *ou* a la triste notoriété d'être l'une des villes les plus polluées du monde; **to be n. for being late/one's lack of tact** être réputé pour arriver en retard/son manque de tact

notoriously [nəʊ'tɔːrɪəslɪ] **ADV** notoirement; **n. cruel** connu pour sa cruauté; **to be n. difficult/dangerous** être bien connu pour sa difficulté/ses dangers

Notts *abbr* **Nottinghamshire**

notwithstanding [nɒtwɪθ'stændɪŋ] **PREP** malgré, en dépit de; *Fml* nonobstant

ADV quand même, tout de même, néanmoins

nougat ['nuːgɑː] **N** nougat *m*

nought [nɔːt] **N 1** *Math* zéro *m*; *Br* **noughts and crosses** *(game)* ≃ morpion *m* VOIR GRAMMAIRE A77 **2** = **naught 1**

noun [naʊn] **N** *Gram* substantif *m*, nom *m*; **common/proper n.** nom commun/propre VOIR GRAMMAIRE A9–17; B5–8

▸▸ **n. clause** proposition *f*; **n. phrase** groupe *m ou* syntagme *m* nominal

nourish ['nʌrɪʃ] **VT 1** *(person, plant, wood, leather)* nourrir; **to n. sb on** *or* **with sth** nourrir qn de qch; **to be well nourished** être bien nourri **2** *Old-fashioned (feeling, hope etc)* nourrir, entretenir

nourishing ['nʌrɪʃɪŋ] **ADJ** nourrissant, nutritif

nourishment ['nʌrɪʃmənt] **N 1** *(food)* nourriture *f*, aliments *mpl*; *(nourishing quality)* richesse *f* nutritive; **to take (some) n.** se nourrir, s'alimenter; **you're not getting enough n.** tu ne t'alimentes pas bien; **to receive n.** être nourri; *(of plants)* trouver sa nourriture; **it's full of n.** c'est très nourrissant *ou* nutritif **2** *(action)* alimentation *f*

nous [naʊs] **N** *Br Sl* bon sens *m*; *(know-how)* savoir-faire *m*; **she's got a lot of n.** elle a beaucoup de bon sens, elle est très sensée; **anyone with any n.** n'importe qui doté d'un minimum de bon sens

Nov *abbr* **November**

nova, *pl* **novae** *or* **novas** ['nəʊvə, -iː] **N** *Astron* nova *f*, *pl* novae

▸▸ **N. Scotia** Nouvelle-Écosse *f*

novel¹ ['nɒv(ə)l] **N** roman *m*

Note that the French noun **nouvelle** is a false friend. It means **short story**.

---

novel² **ADJ** nouveau, *f* nouvelle, original, -aux; **that's a n. idea!** voilà qui est original!

novelette [nɒvə'let] **N** *(short novel)* nouvelle *f*; *(sentimental story)* petit roman *m* à l'eau de rose

novelist ['nɒvəlɪst] **N** romancier, -ière

novelization [nɒvəlaɪ'zeɪʃən] **N** *(of film)* novélisation *f*

novella [nɒ'velə] **N** nouvelle *f*

novelty ['nɒvəltɪ] **N 1** *(quality)* nouveauté *f*; **the n. will soon wear off** l'attrait de la nouveauté ne tardera pas à s'estomper; **there was no n. in it any more** cela n'avait plus rien de nouveau; **the n. of this scheme is that ...** ce que ce programme a de nouveau *ou* d'innovateur c'est que ... **2** *(thing)* nouveauté *f*, *Com* (article *m* de) nouveauté, fantaisie *f*; **such ideas are a n.** ces idées sont complètement nouvelles; **as the only Chinese child, he was something of a n.** seul enfant chinois, il faisait figure de nouveauté; **to have n. value** avoir l'attrait de la nouveauté

November [nəʊ'vembər] **N** VOIR GRAMMAIRE A81–2; B60–2 novembre *m*; **in N.** au mois de novembre, en novembre; **(on) the first/the seventh of N.** le premier/le sept novembre

novena [nəʊ'viːnə] **N** *Cathol* neuvaine *f*

novice ['nɒvɪs] **N** apprenti, -ie, débutant, -ante; *Rel* novice *mf*; **to be a n. in** *or* **at sth** être novice en qch; **I'm still a bit of a n. at this** je suis encore un peu novice; **he was something of a sexual n.** il était pour ainsi dire novice en matière de sexe

noviciate, novitiate [nəʊ'vɪʃɪət] **N** *Rel* **1** *(state, period)* noviciat *m* **2** *(living quarters)* noviciat *m*, maison *f* des novices

NOW [naʊ]

ADV	maintenant **1** ▪ alors **1** ▪ or **2**
CONJ	maintenant que

ADV 1 *(this instant)* maintenant *(at present)* maintenant, à présent; *(nowadays)* actuellement, à l'heure actuelle; *(in narrative)* alors, à ce moment-là; **what shall we do n.?** qu'est-ce que nous allons faire maintenant?; *Fam* **it's (a case of) n. or never** c'est le moment ou jamais; **n. or never!, n. for it!** allons-y!; **goodbye for n.!** à bientôt!; **that'll do for n.** ça suffit pour le moment; **it's two years n. since his mother died** ça fait maintenant deux ans que sa mère est morte; **he won't be long n.** il ne va pas tarder; **even n., I don't understand** même maintenant je ne comprends pas; **and n. I must go** sur ce je vous quitte; **n. is the time to ...** c'est le bon moment pour ...; **right n.** *(immediately)* tout de suite; **I'm not in a position right n. to decide** je ne peux rien décider pour le moment; **all was n. ready** tout était prêt; **he was even n. on his way** il était déjà en route; **just n.** *(past)* il y a un instant; *(present)* en ce moment; **she left just n.** elle vient de partir; **(every) n. and then, (every) n. and again** de temps en temps, de temps à autre; **n. one thing, n.** *or* **then another** tantôt une chose, tantôt l'autre; **n. here n. there** tantôt ici tantôt là; **up to n.** jusqu'ici; **from n. on** à partir de maintenant, dorénavant; **it should be finished in three days from n.** cela devrait être fini d'ici trois jours; **I'm leaving in three days from n.** je pars dans trois jours; **he ought to be here by n., he ought to have been here before n.** il devrait déjà être arrivé; **until n.** jusqu'ici; **and n. for some music** et maintenant, un peu de musique VOIR GRAMMAIRE A19; A21

2 *(without temporal significance) (explanatory or in development of an argument)* or; **n. to come back to what we were saying** pour revenir à ce que nous disions; **n. it happened that ...** *(in story)* or il advint que ...; **n. what's the matter with you?** qu'avez-vous donc?; **come n.!** voyons!; **n., n.! stop quarrelling!** voyons, voyons! assez de querelles!; **well n.!** eh bien!; **n. then, stop fighting** allons, arrêtez de vous battre; **n. then, listen to what I have to say!** allons *ou* bon, écoutez ce que j'ai à vous dire!; **n. then, what's all the noise about?** eh bien alors, qu'est-ce que c'est que tout ce bruit?

CONJ maintenant que, à présent que; **n. (that) I'm older I think differently** maintenant que je suis plus âgé je pense autrement

ADJ *Fam* **1** *(current)* actuel; **the n. president** le président actuel **2** *(fashionable)* branché

nowadays ['naʊədeɪz] **ADV** aujourd'hui, de nos jours, à l'heure actuelle; **where's she working n.?** où travaille-t-elle actuellement?

nowhere ['nəʊweər] **ADV** nulle part; **she was n. to be found** on ne la trouvait nulle part, elle était introuvable; **we're getting n. fast** nous n'avançons pas d'un poil; **that kind of attitude will get you n. fast** ce genre d'attitude ne t'avancera *ou* ne te servira à rien du tout; **qualifications alone will get you n.** les diplômes seuls ne suffisent pas; **it's n. near the shopping centre** ce n'est pas du tout dans les parages du centre commercial; **it's n. near enough** c'est loin d'être suffisant; **he's n. near as intelligent as his sister** il est loin d'être aussi intelligent que sa sœur; **we're n. near ready** on est loin d'être prêt; **the rest are n.** (in race, sales etc) les autres ne sont plus dans le coup; **she finished n.** elle a fini loin derrière VOIR GRAMMAIRE A62–3

▸ **n a small place in the middle of n.** un petit trou perdu; **he seemed to come from n.** il est apparu tout d'un coup; **the money won't just come from n.** l'argent ne va pas tomber du ciel; **he came from n. to win the race** il a fait une remontée spectaculaire et a gagné la course; **the Greens came from n. to win nearly 15% of the vote** les Verts sont partis de rien et ont remporté près de 15% des votes

nowt [naʊt] **PRON, N** Eng Dial (ne …) rien m; **I don't do owt for n.** je ne fais rien pour rien

noxious ['nɒkʃəs] **ADJ** nocif; (gas, fumes) délétère, nocif

nozzle ['nɒz(ə)l] **N** Tech (of pipe) ajutage m, jet m; (of fire hose etc) lance f, (of syringe) canule f, (of bellows) bec m, tuyau m, buse f, (of vacuum cleaner) suceur m; (of injector, turbine) tuyère f, ajutage; (for icing) douille f, (of petrol pump) pistolet m

NPD [enpi:'di:] **N** Mktg (abbr **new product development**) développement m de nouveaux produits

NPV [enpi:'vi:] **N** Acct (abbr **net present value**) VAN f, valeur f actuelle nette
▸ ▸ **N. rate** taux m d'actualisation

NRS [ena:r'es] **N** (abbr **national readership survey**) étude f nationale sur le lectorat

NS abbr **Nova Scotia**

ns (abbr **nanosecond**) ns

NSPCC [enespi:si:'si:] **N** Br (abbr **National Society for the Prevention of Cruelty to Children**) = comité m national pour la prévention des mauvais traitements envers les enfants

nth [enθ] **ADJ 1** Fam énième; **to the n. degree** au énième degré; **for the n. time** pour la énième fois **2** Math **to the n. power** à la puissance n

nuance ['nju:ɒns] **N** nuance f, **a n. of meaning** une nuance; **I detected a n. of uncertainty in his voice** j'ai décelé une note d'incertitude dans sa voix

nuanced ['nju:ɒnst] **ADJ** nuancé; **finely n.** subtilement nuancé

nub [nʌb] **N 1** (protuberance) bosse f, protubérance f **2 the n. of the matter** or **issue** le cœur du sujet

nubile ['nju:baɪl] **ADJ 1** (sexually attractive) désirable **2** Fml (marriageable) nubile

nuclear ['nju:klɪər] **ADJ 1** Phys, Mil nucléaire **2** Biol nucléaire
▸ ▸ **n. bomb** bombe f atomique; **n. energy** énergie f nucléaire; **n. family** famille f nucléaire; **n. fission** fission f nucléaire; **n. fusion** fusion f nucléaire; **n. magnetic resonance** résonance f magnétique nucléaire; **n. magnetic resonance scanner** scanner m de résonance magnétique nucléaire; **n. physics** physique f nucléaire; **n. power** nucléaire m, énergie f nucléaire; **n. power plant** centrale f nucléaire; **n. powers** puissances fpl nucléaires; **n. power station** centrale f nucléaire; **n. war(fare)** guerre f nucléaire; Mil **n. weapon** arme f nucléaire; **n. winter** hiver m nucléaire

nuclear-free ADJ
▸ ▸ **n. zone** zone f anti-nucléaire

nucleic [nju:'kli:ɪk] **ADJ** Chem (acid) nucléique

nucleus, pl **nuclei** ['nju:klɪəs, -ɪaɪ] **N 1** Phys,

Biol, Astron noyau m **2** Fig (of organization etc) noyau m; (of argument etc) cœur m; **the n. of a library** (beginnings) un commencement de bibliothèque; **the n. of a fine sales team** les premiers éléments d'une bonne équipe de vente

nuddy ['nʌdɪ] **N** Br Fam Hum **in the n.** tout nu, à poil

nude [nju:d] **ADJ** (person) nu
▸ **N 1** Art **a n.** un nu; **the n.** (genre) le nu; **to draw/paint from the n.** dessiner/peindre des nus ou des académies **2 in the n.** tout nu

nudge [nʌdʒ] **N** coup m de coude; Fam **he didn't come home last night, n. n., wink wink** il n'est pas rentré hier soir, si tu vois ce que je veux dire
▸ **VT** pousser du coude, donner un coup de coude à; **to n. one's way through a crowd** jouer des coudes pour se frayer un chemin à travers la foule; **we nudged the sofa forward a few inches** nous avons avancé le sofa de quelques centimètres
▸ ▸ Aut **n. bar** barre f de calandre

nudie ['nju:dɪ] **ADJ** Fam porno
▸ ▸ **n. book** magazine m porno

nudism ['nju:dɪz(ə)m] **N** nudisme m, naturisme m

nudist ['nju:dɪst] **N** nudiste mf, naturiste mf
▸ ▸ **n. camp** camp m de nudistes; **n. colony** camp de nudistes

nudity ['nju:dɪtɪ] **N** nudité f

nugatory ['nju:gətərɪ] **ADJ** Lit, Fml sans valeur

nugget ['nʌgɪt] **N** (of gold) pépite f, Fig **a n. (of useful information)** une information très utile; **a n. (of wisdom)** une perle; **chicken nuggets, nuggets of chicken** morceaux mpl de poulet

nuisance ['nju:səns] **N 1** (person) casse-pieds mf inv; **go away, you('re a) n.!** va-t'en, tu m'embêtes ou tu me casses les pieds!; **she's a bit of a n.** elle est un peu casse-pieds; **he's being a n.** (of child, drunk) il m'embête/l'embête/etc; **to make a n. of oneself** embêter le monde; **the TV won't work – it's a real n.** la télé ne marche pas – c'est vraiment embêtant; **long skirts are a n.** les jupes longues sont gênantes; **this keyboard/pen is a n.** ce clavier/stylo est embêtant; **it's a n. for me to have to …** cela me gêne ou Fam m'embête de devoir …; **what a n.!, that's a n.!** que c'est embêtant ou agaçant!; **at least we won't have the n. of going through customs** au moins nous ne serons pas embêtés à devoir passer à la douane; **to have n. value** être un élément gênant **2** Law dommage m; (to public at large) atteinte f portée aux droits du public; (to individual) atteinte portée aux droits privés des voisins
▸ ▸ Tel **n. call** appel m anonyme; Tel **n. caller** auteur m d'appels anonymes

NUJ [enju:'dʒeɪ] **N** Br (abbr **National Union of Journalists**) = syndicat m national des journalistes

nuke [nju:k] Fam **N** (bomb) bombe f nucléaire
▸ **VT 1** (bomb) atomiser **2** (microwave) faire cuire au four à micro-ondes **3** (defeat) ratatiner, battre à plates coutures

null [nʌl] **ADJ** Law etc (decree, act etc) nul, f nulle; (legacy) caduc, f caduque; **n. and void** nul et non avenu; **to render n.** (decree, will) annuler, infirmer, invalider
▸ ▸ Comput **n. modem cable** câble m de connexion sans modem; **n. set** ensemble m vide; Comput **n. string** chaîne f vide

nullification [nʌlɪfɪ'keɪʃən] **N** annulation f, invalidation f

nullify ['nʌlɪfaɪ] **VT** (contract, result) annuler, rendre nul; (act) infirmer; (decree) invalider; **his marriage was nullified** son mariage a été déclaré nul

nullity ['nʌlɪtɪ] **N** Law (of marriage) nullité f, invalidité f, (of inheritance) caducité f
▸ ▸ **n. suit** demande f en nullité de mariage

NUM [enju:'em] **N** Br (abbr **National Union of Mineworkers**) = syndicat m national des mineurs

numb [nʌm] **ADJ** (limb) engourdi, gourd; (mind) engourdi; **to go n.** s'engourdir; **hands n. with cold** mains engourdies par le froid; **to be n. with shock/grief** être hébété par le choc/la douleur; **n. with terror** glacé d'horreur; **to become n. to sth** devenir insensible à qch
▸ **VT** (limbs, mind etc) engourdir; **she was numbed by her father's death** elle était sous le choc après la mort de son père, la mort de son père l'a laissée sous le choc

NUMBER ['nʌmbər]

N nombre **1, 3, 4, 6**	▪ chiffre **2**
▪ numéro **5**	
VT numéroter **1**	▪ compter **2, 3**

N 1 (quantity), Math nombre m; **three-figure n.** nombre de trois chiffres; **even/odd/prime n.** nombre pair/impair/premier; **the n. of people present** le nombre des présents; **we were in equal numbers** or **equal in n.** nous étions en nombre égal; **they are few in n.** ils sont peu nombreux; Fml **without n.** sans nombre, innombrable; **a n. of …** un certain nombre de …; **she is one of a n. of people who …** elle figure parmi les personnes qui …; **a large n. of men were killed** un grand nombre d'hommes a été tué ou ont été tués; **any n. of …** un grand nombre de …, bon nombre de …; **to be present in small numbers/in (great) numbers** être présents en petit nombre/en grand nombre; **they are coming in ever-increasing numbers** ils sont de plus en plus nombreux à venir; **one of their n.** (l')un d'entre eux; Bible **(the Book of) Numbers** le Livre des Nombres, les Nombres VOIR GRAMMAIRE A76–7; B58–60
2 (symbol) chiffre m; **the n. eight** le chiffre huit
3 (of house, page, telephone etc) numéro m; (of soldier etc) (numéro) matricule m; **I live at n. 40** j'habite au (numéro) 40; Fam **to do a n. one** (in children's language) faire pipi, faire la petite commission; Fam **to do a n. two** (in children's language) faire la grosse commission; Fam **to look after n. one** tirer la couverture à soi; **he's only interested in n. one** tout ce qui l'intéresse c'est sa pomme; **my n. one priority** la première de mes priorités; Fam **to be at n. one** (of record) être (le) numéro un; Fam **he's my n. two** c'est mon adjoint; Aut **registration n.** numéro d'immatriculation; Fig Fam **I've got your n.!** je sais ce que tu es en tête!; **to draw a lucky n.** (at lottery etc) tirer un bon numéro; Fam **his n.'s up** il a son compte, il est fichu
4 Gram nombre m
5 Theat numéro m; **for my next n. I'd like to sing …** j'aimerais vous chanter maintenant …; **instrumental n.** morceau m instrumental
6 Journ (of newspaper etc) numéro m; (of work appearing in editions) livraison f, fascicule m; **current n.** numéro du jour/de la semaine/du mois, dernier numéro; **back n.** vieux numéro
7 Fam (thing, person) **she's a good-looking n.** c'est une jolie nénette; **that car/dress is a nice little n.** elle est pas mal, cette voiture/robe
8 Fam **a cushy n.** (job) une bonne planque; **she's got a nice little n. there** (situation) elle s'est dégoté un bon plan
▸ **VT 1** (give number to) numéroter
2 (count) compter; **his days are numbered**

ses jours sont comptés; **to n. sb among one's friends** compter qn au nombre de *ou* parmi ses amis

3 *(amount to)* **they numbered no more than twenty** ils n'étaient pas plus de vingt; **the town/the army numbers thirty thousand** la ville/l'armée compte trente mille habitants/trente mille hommes

▸▸*Comput* **n. crunching** calculs *mpl* (rapides); *Comput* **n. key** touche *f* numérique; *Comput* **n. lock** verrouillage *m* du clavier numérique;*Comput* **n. lock key** touche de verrouillage du clavier numérique; **n. plate** plaque *f* minéralogique *ou* d'immatriculation; **N. Ten Downing Street** = résidence *f* officielle du Premier ministre britannique

▸**number off** vi *Mil* se numéroter

number-coded ADJcodé en chiffres

number-crunch vt *Comput Fam* faire subir des calculs rapides à

number-cruncher [-krʌntʃər] N *Comput* super-ordinateur *m*, *pl* super-ordinateurs

numbering ['nʌmbərɪŋ] N*(of houses, pages etc)* numérotage *m*

▸▸**n. machine** numéroteur *m*; **n. system** système *m* de numérotation

numberless ['nʌmbəlɪs] ADJ innombrable, sans nombre

number-one ADJ numéro un

numberplate ['nʌmbəpleɪt] N *Br Aut* plaque *f* minéralogique *ou* d'immatriculation

numbly ['nʌmlɪ] ADV *(to react, say)* mollement; *(to look, stare)* d'un air engourdi

numbness ['nʌmnɪs] N *(of fingers etc)* engourdissement *m*; *(of emotions etc)* torpeur *f*

numbskull ['nʌmskʌl] N *Fam* nigaud *m*, -aude, bêta, -asse; **stop behaving like such a n.!** arrête de faire le nigaud comme ça!

numeracy ['nju:m(ə)rəsɪ] N degré *m* d'aptitude en calcul

numeral ['nju:m(ə)r(ə)l] N chiffre *m*, nombre *m*; **Roman numerals** chiffres romains; **the cardinal numerals** les numéraux *mpl* cardinaux

ADJ *(word, letter etc)* numéral, -aux

numerate ['nju:mərət] ADJ qui a le sens de l'arithmétique; **applicants should be highly n.** les candidats doivent avoir des compétences élevées en calcul; **to be barely n.** savoir à peine compter

numeration [nju:mə'reɪʃən] N *Math* numération *f*; **binary n.** numération binaire

numerator ['nju:məreɪtər] N *Math* numérateur *m*

numeric [nju:'merɪk] *Comput* ADJ numérique

NPL **numerics** chiffres *mpl ou* caractères *mpl* numériques

▸▸**n. coding** codage *m* numérique; **n. field** champ *m* numérique; **n. keypad** pavé *m* numérique

numerical [nju:'merɪk(ə)l] ADJ *(value, superiority, order etc)* numérique; **to have a n. advantage** avoir l'avantage du nombre

▸▸**n. control** contrôle *m* numérique; **n. data** données *fpl* numériques; *Mktg* **n. distribution** distribution *f* numérique; *Comput* **n. keypad** pavé *m* numérique

numerically [nju:'merɪklɪ] ADV numériquement

numerous ['nju:m(ə)rəs] ADJ nombreux; **to grow more n.** devenir de plus en plus nombreux

numismatic [nju:mɪz'mætɪk] ADJ numismatique

numismatics [nju:mɪz'mætɪks] N numismatique *f* VOIR GRAMMAIRE A10

numismatist [nju:'mɪz(ə)mətɪst] N numismate *mf*

num lock *Comput* (*abbr* **numbers lock**) verr num; **the n. is on** le pavé numérique est verrouillé

▸▸**n. key** touche *f* de verrouillage du pavé numérique

numpty ['nʌmptɪ] N *Scot Fam (idiot)* crétin, -ine, andouille *f*

numskull ['nʌmskʌl] N *Fam* = **numbskull**

nun [nʌn] N *Rel* religieuse *f*, *Fam* bonne sœur; **to become a n.** se faire religieuse, prendre le voile, entrer en religion

nuncio, *pl* **nuncios** ['nʌnʃɪəʊ, -z] N*Rel* nonce *m*

nunnery ['nʌnərɪ] N *Old-fashioned* couvent *m* de religieuses

nuptial ['nʌpʃəl] *Lit* ADJ nuptial, -aux; **their n. day** le jour de leurs noces

NPL **nuptials** noces *fpl*

NUR [enju:'ɑ:r] N *Br Formerly* (*abbr* **National Union of Railwaymen**) = syndicat *m* national des employés des chemins de fer

nurse [nɜ:s] N **1** *(in hospital)* infirmier, -ière; *(privately employed)* infirmier, -ière, garde-malade *mf*, *pl* gardes-malades; **thank you, n.** merci mademoiselle/madame; **n. will take out the stitches** l'infirmière retirera les points de suture; **(male) n.** infirmier *m*

2 *(looking after children)* nurse *f*, bonne *f* d'enfant; **(wet) n.** nourrice *f*

3 *Entom (of bees, ants)* ouvrière *f*

VT **1** *(sick person)*, *Fam (a cold)* soigner; **she nursed him back to health** elle lui a fait recouvrer la santé grâce à ses soins

2 *(suckle) (baby)* nourrir (de son lait), allaiter

3 *Fig (plants etc)* soigner; *(horse, team etc)* ménager en vue du dernier effort à donner; *(feeling, hope etc)* nourrir, entretenir; *(project)* mitonner, mijoter; **he nursed the damaged plane back to base** il a réussi à ramener l'avion endommagé jusqu'à la base; **they nursed the family business through the worst of the recession** ils ont maintenu l'entreprise familiale qui a pu pire de la récession; *Br Pol* **to n. one's constituency** chauffer ses électeurs; **to n. an old grievance** entretenir un grief

4 *(clasp) (child)* bercer, dorloter; *(whisky, drink)* siroter; **to n. one's knee** tenir son genou dans ses mains

VI **1** *(as profession)* être infirmier, -ière; **she spent a few years nursing** elle a travaillé pendant quelques années comme infirmière **2** *(of baby)* téter

nursemaid ['nɜ:smeɪd] N bonne *f* d'enfants, nurse *f*, *Fig* **I'm not your n.!** je ne suis pas votre bonne!

nursery ['nɜ:s(ə)rɪ] N **1** *(room) (in house)* chambre *f* des enfants *ou* d'enfants; *(in hospital)* pouponnière *f* **2** *(establishment) (school)* (école *f*) maternelle *f*, **(day) n.** crèche *f*, garderie *f* **3** *(for plants, trees)*, *Fig* pépinière *f*

▸▸**n. education** enseignement *m* de l'école maternelle; **n. garden** pépinière *f*; **n. gardener** pépiniériste *mf*; **n. nurse** puéricultrice *f*; **n. rhyme** comptine *f*; **n. school** (école) maternelle; **n. school teacher** instituteur, -trice de maternelle; *Br* **n. slopes** pistes *fpl* pour débutants

nurseryman, *pl* **nurserymen** ['nɜ:s(ə)rɪmən] N pépiniériste *m*

nursing ['nɜ:sɪŋ] ADJ **1** *Med* d'infirmier; **the n. staff** le personnel soignant **2** *(suckling)* allaitant

N **1** *(suckling) (of baby)* allaitement *m* **2** *(care given by a nurse)* soins *mpl* **3** *(profession)* profession *f* d'infirmier/d'infirmière; **to go into n.** devenir infirmier/infirmière

▸▸**n. auxiliary** aide-soignant, *pl* aide-soignants, *f* aide-soignante, *pl* aide-soignan-

tes; **n. home** *(for aged)* maison *f* de retraite; *(for convalescents)* maison de repos; *(for mentally ill)* maison de santé; *Br (private clinic)* hôpital *m* privé, clinique *f* privée; **n. mother** mère *f* qui allaite; *Br* **n. officer** infirmier, -ière en chef; **n. staff** *(in hospital)* personnel *m* soignant, infirmiers, -ières

nurture ['nɜ:tʃər] N éducation *f*, *(of plant)* soins *mpl*

VT **1** *(feed) (children, plants etc)* nourrir; *(feelings etc)* nourrir, entretenir; *(plan, scheme)* préparer, élaborer **2** *(bring up)* élever, faire l'éducation de

nurturing ['nɜ:tʃərɪŋ] ADJ attentionné, maternel

NUS [enju:'es] N *Br* (*abbr* **National Union of Students**) = syndicat *m* étudiant, ≃ UNEF *f*

NUT [enju:'ti:] N *Br* (*abbr* **National Union of Teachers**) = syndicat *m* d'enseignants, ≃ FEN *f*

nut [nʌt] N **1** = terme générique pour les amandes, noisettes, noix etc; **a bag of nuts and raisins** un sachet de fruits secs mélangés; **fruit and n. (chocolate)** chocolat *m* aux fruits et aux noisettes/amandes/*etc*; *Fam* **tough** *or* **hard n. to crack** *(problem)* problème *m* difficile à résoudre; **a hard** *or* **tough n.** *(person)* personne *f* difficile *ou* peu commode

2 *Fam (head)* caboche *f*; **to be off one's n.** être timbré *ou* toqué, avoir perdu la boule; **to go off one's n.** *(go mad)* perdre la boule; *(become angry)* piquer une crise; *Br* **to do one's n.** péter les plombs, piquer une crise

3 *Fam (mad person)* dingue *mf*, barjo *mf*; **don't be a n.** arrête de dérailler *ou* débloquer; **a jazz/tennis n.** un(e) dingue *ou* fana de jazz/de tennis

4 *Tech* écrou *m*; **butterfly** *or* **wing n.** écrou à oreilles, écrou (à) papillon; *Fig* **the nuts and bolts of the problem** les détails pratiques du problème; *Fig* **the nuts and bolts of a language** les éléments de base d'une langue

5 *Br Com, Min* **n. coal, nuts** gailletin *m*, têtes *fpl* de moineau

6 *Sl* **nuts** *(testicles)* couilles *fpl*

▸▸**n. cutlet** côtelette *f* végétarienne *(à base de noix, noisettes etc)*; **n. roast** rôti *m* végétarien

nutball ['nʌtbɔ:l] N *Am Fam* dingue *mf*, cinglé, -ée

nut-brown ADJ *(couleur)* noisette *inv*; *(hair)* châtain; *(skin)* brun

nutcase ['nʌtkeɪs] N *Fam* dingue *mf*, cinglé, -ée; **he's a complete n.** il est complètement dingue *ou* cinglé *ou* timbré

nutcracker ['nʌtkrækər] N **(pair of) nutcrackers** casse-noisette(s) *m inv*; casse-noix *m inv*

nuthatch ['nʌthætʃ] N *(bird)* sittelle *f*

nuthouse ['nʌthaʊs] N *Fam* maison *f* de fous

nutmeg ['nʌtmeg] N *(nut)* (noix *f* de) muscade *f*, *(tree)* muscadier *m*

▸▸**n. grater** râpe *f* à muscade; **n. tree** muscadier

nutrient ['nju:trɪənt] ADJ nutritif

N substance *f* nutritive

nutriment ['nju:trɪmənt] N *Fml* nourriture *f*

nutrition [nju:'trɪʃən] N nutrition *f*

nutritional [nju:'trɪʃənəl] ADJ *(science, research)* nutritionnel; *(value, disorder, process)* nutritif

▸▸*Com* **n. labelling** étiquetage *m* de l'apport nutritionnel

nutritionist [nju:'trɪʃənɪst] N nutritionniste *mf*

nutritious [nju:'trɪʃəs] ADJ nutritif, nourrissant

nutritive ['nju:trɪtɪv] ADJ = **nutritional**

nuts [nʌts] *Fam* ADJ *(mad)* cinglé; **to go n.** *(go mad)* perdre la boule; *(get angry)* péter les plombs, piquer une crise; **that noise is driving me n.** ce bruit me rend dingue; **to be n. about sb/sth** être fou/folle de qn/qch, raffoler de qn/qch

INT *esp Am* zut!; **n. to that!** plutôt crever!

nutshell ['nʌtʃel] N coquille *f* de noix/de noisette/*etc*, *Fig* **that's the whole thing in a n.** voilà toute l'affaire (résumée) en un mot *ou* en deux mots; *Fig* **(to put it) in a n. ...** pour résumer ..., bref ...

nutso ['nʌtsəʊ] ADJ *Am Fam* **to go n.** *(go mad)* perdre la boule; *(get angry)* péter les plombs, piquer une crise; **that noise is driving me n.** ce bruit me rend dingue; **to be n. about sb/sth** être fou/folle de qn/qch, raffoler de qn/qch

nutter ['nʌtər] N *Br Fam* dingue *mf*, toqué, -ée

nutty ['nʌtɪ] ADJ **1** *(in taste)* au goût de noisette; *(taste, flavour)* de noisette; *(containing nuts)* aux noisettes/noix/*etc* **2** *Fam (mad)* dingue; **as n. as a fruitcake** complètement dingue; **to be n. about sb/sth** raffoler de qn/qch

nuzzle ['nʌz(ə)l] VT & VI **to n. (against) sb's shoulder** *(of dog, horse)* fourrer son nez sur l'épaule de qn; *(of person)* se blottir dans le creux de l'épaule de qn; **to n. sb's hand** fourrer son nez dans la paume de la main de qn; **he nuzzled her neck** il lui caressait le cou de ses lèvres; **the dog nuzzled up to my leg** le chien me reniflait la jambe

NY *abbr* **New York**

NYC *abbr* **New York City**

nylon ['naɪlɒn] N *Tex* nylon® *m*; **n. sheets** draps *mpl* en nylon; **n. stockings** bas *mpl* nylon; **n. thread** fil *m* de nylon

NYMEX [enwaɪemi:'eks] N *St Exch* (*abbr* **New York Mercantile Exchange**) = marché *m* à terme des produits pétroliers de New York

nymph [nɪmf] N **1** *Myth* nymphe *f*; **tree** *or* **wood n.** hamadryade *f*; **sea n.** néréide *f*; **water n.** naïade *f* **2** *Entom* nymphe *f*

nymphet ['nɪmfɪt] N nymphette *f*

nympho, *pl* **nymphos** ['nɪmfəʊ, -z] ADJ, N *Fam* = **nymphomaniac**

nymphomania [nɪmfəʊ'meɪnɪə] N *Med* nymphomanie *f*

nymphomaniac [nɪmfəʊ'meɪnɪæk] ADJ, N nymphomane *f*

NYSE [enwaɪes'i:] N *abbr* **New York Stock Exchange**

NZ *abbr* **New Zealand**

O¹, o [əʊ] **N 1** *(letter)* O, o *m*; **two o's** deux o **2** *Tel etc* zéro *m* VOIR GRAMMAIRE A77

O² **INT** *(vocative)* O, ô

O³ *abbr* **Ohio**

oaf, *pl* **oafs** [əʊf, -əʊfs] **N** rustre *m*; **you clumsy o.!** espèce de gros empoté!

oafish ['əʊfɪʃ] **ADJ** rustre

oak [əʊk] **N 1** *(tree)* chêne *m* **2** *(wood)* (bois *m* de) chêne *m*; **o. furniture** meubles *mpl* de *ou* en chêne; **dark o. (colour)** couleur *f* vieux chêne **3** *Br Univ Old-fashioned* = porte *f* extérieure d'un appartement dans les universités d'Oxford et Cambridge; **to sport one's o.** fermer sa porte aux visiteurs
▸▸ **o. apple** noix *f* de galle; **o. grove** chênaie *f*; **o. leaf** feuille *f* de chêne; **o. tree** chêne; **o. wood** *(material)* (bois de) chêne; *(forest)* bois de chênes, chênaie

oaken ['əʊk(ə)n] **ADJ** de *ou* en chêne

oakum ['əʊkəm] **N** étoupe *f* (noire), filasse *f*; **to pick o.** démêler *ou* tirer l'étoupe

OAP [əʊeɪ'piː] **N** *Br* (*abbr* **old age pensioner**) retraité, -ée

oar [ɔːr] **N** aviron *m*, rame *f*, *(as opposed to scull)* aviron de nage; *Fig Fam* **to put** *or* **stick one's o. in** mettre son grain de sel; **good o.** *(rower)* bon rameur, bonne rameuse

oarlock ['ɔːlɒk] **N** *Am* tolet *m*

oarsman, *pl* **oarsmen** ['ɔːzmən] **N** rameur *m*

oarswoman, *pl* **oarswomen** ['ɔːzwʊmən, -wɪmɪn] **N** rameuse *f*

OAS [əʊeɪ'es] **N** (*abbr* **Organization of American States**) OEA *f*

oasis, *pl* **oases** [əʊ'eɪsɪs, -iːz] **N** oasis *f*, *Fig* **an o. of calm** une oasis de calme

oast [əʊst] **N** séchoir *m* (à houblon)

oasthouse ['əʊsthaʊs] **N** sécherie *f* (de houblon)

oat [əʊt] **N** *(plant)* avoine *f* (commune); **oats** *(food)* avoine; **(porridge) oats** flocons *mpl* d'avoine; *Br Sl* **to get one's oats** *(have sex)* baiser, prendre son pied; *Fam* **to sow one's wild oats** faire des fredaines, jeter sa gourme; *Fam* **to be off one's oats** avoir perdu l'appétit; *(be off form)* être patraque; *Fam* **to be feeling one's oats** *(be self-important)* ne plus se sentir; *(be cheerful)* avoir la pêche

oatcake ['əʊtkeɪk] **N** *Culin* galette *f* d'avoine

oath, *pl* **oaths** [əʊθ, əʊðz] **N 1** *(pledge)* serment *m*; **o. of allegiance** serment d'allégeance; **to take an o.,** *Law* **to take the o.** prêter serment; **he took** *or* **swore an o. to avenge his father's death** il a juré de venger la mort de son père; *Law* **to be on** *or* **under o.** être sous serment, être assermenté; *Law* **to put sb on** *or* **under o.** faire prêter serment à qn; **she swore on her o. that …** elle a juré sous serment que … **2** *(swearword)* juron *m*, gros mot *m*

oatmeal ['əʊtmiːl] **N** farine *f* d'avoine; *(col-*

our) beige *m*; *Culin* **o. porridge,** *Am* **o.** bouillie *f* d'avoine, porridge *m*

OAU [əʊeɪ'juː] **N** *Formerly* (*abbr* **Organization of African Unity**) OUA *f*

OB [əʊ'biː] **N** *Br TV* (*abbr* **outside broadcast**) émission *f* en extérieur; **OB unit** car *m* régie, unité *f* mobile; **OB van** car de reportage

obduracy ['ɒbdjʊrəsɪ] **N** entêtement *m*, obstination *f*

obdurate ['ɒbdjʊrɪt] **ADJ** *(stubborn) (person)* entêté, obstiné, têtu; *(refusal, attitude etc)* inflexible; **to remain o.** ne pas fléchir, rester inflexible; **to be o. in the face of pressure** ne pas fléchir sous la pression; **an o. sinner** un pécheur impénitent

obdurately ['ɒbdjʊrɪtlɪ] **ADV** *(stubbornly)* avec entêtement; *(to resist)* inflexiblement; **to remain o. silent** garder un silence obstiné *ou* têtu; **to refuse o.** refuser obstinément, s'entêter à refuser

OBE [əʊbiː'iː] **N** *Br abbr* **Officer of the Order of the British Empire**

obedience [ə'biːdɪəns] **N 1** obéissance *f* (**to** sb à qn; **to the law** à la loi); **to show o. to sb** se montrer obéissant envers qn **2** *Rel* **the Roman o.** l'obéissance *f* de Rome

> Note that the French word **obédience** is a false friend and is not normally used to translate the English word **obedience**.

obedient [ə'biːdɪənt] **ADJ** obéissant; *(animal, child)* obéissant, docile; **to be o. to sb** être obéissant envers qn; *Arch* **Your o. servant** *(in letter)* votre serviteur dévoué

obediently [ə'biːdɪəntlɪ] **ADV** docilement; **she had o. done everything which had been asked of her** elle s'était docilement exécutée

obelisk ['ɒbəlɪsk] **N 1** *Archit* obélisque *m* **2** *Typ* croix *f*, obèle *m*; **double o.** diésis *m*

obese [əʊ'biːs] **ADJ** obèse

obeseness [əʊ'biːsnɪs] **N** obésité *f*

obesity [əʊ'biːsɪtɪ] **N** obésité *f*

obey [ə'beɪ] **VT** *(person, order)* obéir à; **to o. the law** obéir à la loi; **his legs refused to o. him** ses jambes refusaient d'obéir
VI obéir

obfuscate ['ɒbfʌskeɪt] **VT** obscurcir

obfuscation [ɒbfʌ'skeɪʃən] **N** obscurcissement *m*

obituary [ə'bɪtjʊərɪ] **N** nécrologie *f*, notice *f* nécrologique; *Journ* **the obituaries** la nécrologie, la rubrique nécrologique
▸▸ *Journ* **o. column** nécrologie, rubrique *f* nécrologique; **o. list** registre *m* des morts, nécrologe *m*; **o. notice** notice nécrologique

object¹ ['ɒbdʒɪkt] **N 1** *(thing)* objet *m*
2 *(subject etc)* objet *m*; **o. of pity/contempt** objet de pitié/mépris; **to be an o. of ridicule** être en butte au ridicule; **she was the o. of his desires** elle était l'objet de ses désirs; **o. of a contract** objet d'un contrat

3 *(purpose)* but *m*, objectif *m*, fin *f*; **to have sth for** *or* **as an o.** avoir qch pour objectif *ou* pour but; **with this o. (in view)** dans cette intention, à cette fin; **with the sole o. of doing sth** à seule fin de faire qch; **what's the o. of the exercise** *or* **all this?** ça sert à quoi?, quel est le but de tout ceci?; **what is the o. of all this noise?** pourquoi tout ce bruit?; **to defeat one's o.** manquer son but; **the o. of the exercise** le but de l'exercice; **to succeed in** *or* **attain one's o.** atteindre son but
4 *(obstacle)* **expense is no o.** peu importe le prix, le prix n'est pas un obstacle; **distance is no o.** la distance importe peu
5 *Gram* **direct/indirect o.** complément *m* d'objet direct/indirect VOIR GRAMMAIRE A78–9; B52–3
▸▸ *Comput* **o. code** code *m* objet; **o. finder** *(of microscope)* chercheur *m* d'objet; **o. lesson** *(example)* démonstration *f*, illustration *f* (d'un principe); *Sch* leçon *f* de choses; *Comput* **o. linking and embedding** incorporation *f* d'objets liés

object² [əb'dʒekt] **VI** faire une/des objection(s); **to o. to sth** faire objection à qch; *(of demonstrators etc)* protester contre qch; **he objected to being asked to help** il a protesté parce qu'on lui a demandé d'aider; **I o. to being treated like a child** je n'aime pas qu'on me prenne pour un gamin; **to o. to doing sth** se refuser à faire qch; **I o. to the fact that …** ce qui me dérange (vraiment), c'est que …; **to o. to sb** avoir des objections à faire contre qn; **I don't o. to his** *or* **him coming here but …** je ne vois pas d'objection à ce qu'il vienne ici mais …; **he objects (to it)** il s'y oppose; **I o.!** je ne suis pas d'accord!, je proteste!; **if no one objects** si personne n'y voit d'objection(s); *Law* **to o. to a witness** récuser un témoin

objectify [əb'dʒektɪfaɪ] **VT** objectiver

objection [əb'dʒekʃən] **N 1** *(protest)* objection *f*, **no objections were raised at the time** cela n'avait soulevé aucune objection à l'époque; **to make no o. to** *or* **against sth** ne pas voir d'objection à qch; **I have no o. to her doing so** je n'ai pas d'objection à ce qu'elle le fasse; **I have no o. to him** je n'ai rien contre lui; **if you have no o.** si vous n'y voyez pas d'inconvénient; **to raise an o.** soulever une objection; *Law* **o. to a witness** récusation *f* de témoin; **does anyone have any objection(s)?** est-ce que quelqu'un a une objection *ou Fam* quelque chose contre?; **does anyone have any objections if I open the window?** est-ce que quelqu'un verrait un inconvénient à ce que j'ouvre la fenêtre? **2** *(reason for objecting)* inconvénient *m*; **the chief o. to your plan is its cost** le plus grand inconvénient de votre projet, c'est son coût; **I see no o. (to it)** je n'y vois pas d'inconvénient

objectionable [əb'dʒekʃənəb(ə)l] **ADJ** *(unpleasant)* désagréable; *(person)* insupportable; *(view, state of affairs)* inacceptable; *(language etc)* choquant

objective [əbˈdʒektɪv] ADJ**1**objectif; **let's be o.** soyons objectifs; **it is an o. fact that …** le fait est que … **2** Gram (case) accusatif
N1 (aim, goal) objectif m, but m; **to achieve one's objectives** atteindre ses objectifs; **the committee has set out its objectives** le comité a fixé ses objectifs; **our o. for this year is to increase sales by 10%** nous avons pour objectif d'augmenter nos ventes de 10% au cours de l'année prochaine **2** Opt objectif m **3** Gram cas m régime, cas accusatif

objectively [əbˈdʒektɪvlɪ] ADV objectivement, d'une manière objective

objectivism [əbˈdʒektɪvɪz(ə)m] N objectivisme m

objectivity [ɒbdʒekˈtɪvɪtɪ] N objectivité f

objector [əbˈdʒektər] N Pol etc opposant m, personne f qui émet des objections; **the objectors to the plan** les personnes qui s'opposent au projet

object-orientated [-ˈɔːrɪənteɪtɪd] ADJ Comput orienté objet
▸▸ **o. language** langage m à objets; **o. programming** programmation f par objets

oblate [ˈɒbleɪt] ADJ Math etc aplati (aux pôles), raccourci

obligate [ˈɒblɪgeɪt] VT **to o. sb to do sth** mettre qn dans l'obligation de faire qch; **to feel obligated to help** se sentir dans l'obligation d'aider; **to be obligated to do sth** avoir l'obligation de faire qch; **to feel obligated to sb** se sentir redevable envers qn

obligation [ɒblɪˈgeɪʃən] N obligation f, **to put sb/to feel under an o. to …** mettre qn/ se sentir dans l'obligation de …; **moral o.** obligation morale; **to be under an o. to do sth** être dans l'obligation de faire qch; **I am under no o. to go with them** rien ne m'oblige à les accompagner; Com **without o.** sans engagement; **to do sth out of (a sense of) o.** faire qch parce que l'on s'y sent obligé; **to be under an o. to sb** avoir une dette de reconnaissance envers qn; **I am under a great o. to him** je lui suis redevable de beaucoup; Com **to meet one's obligations** faire face à ses engagements VOIR GRAMMAIRE A60–1; B39

obligatory [ɒˈblɪgət(ə)rɪ] ADJ obligatoire; **after the o. exchange of greetings** après les salutations de rigueur; **ties are o.** la cravate est obligatoire

oblige [əˈblaɪdʒ] VT **1** (compel) obliger, astreindre (**sb to do sth** qn à faire qch); **to be obliged to do sth** être obligé ou tenu de faire qch; Admin être astreint à faire qch; **I feel obliged to tell him** je me vois contraint de lui dire **2** (do a favour for) rendre service à, Fml obliger; **he did it to o. us** il l'a fait pour nous rendre service ou par complaisance **3** (make indebted) (usu passive) **to be obliged to sb** être reconnaissant à qn (**for sth** pour qch); Fam **much obliged** merci beaucoup; **I would be obliged if you would …** je vous serais reconnaissant de bien vouloir …
VI **he did it to o.** il l'a fait pour rendre service ou par complaisance; **to be always willing to o.** être très obligeant ou toujours prêt à rendre service; **anything to o.** tout ce que vous voudrez pour vous faire plaisir; **I'm sorry, I can't o.** je suis désolé, je ne peux pas

obliging [əˈblaɪdʒɪŋ] ADJ obligeant, serviable; **that's very o. of you** c'est très aimable de votre part

obligingly [əˈblaɪdʒɪŋlɪ] ADV obligeamment, complaisamment, complaisamment; also Iron **they had very o. left the door open** ils avaient été assez aimables pour laisser la porte ouverte

oblique [əˈbliːk] ADJ (line, angle) oblique (**to** à); (indirect) (reference, hint etc) indirect; **o. glance** regard m en biais

N (line) (ligne f) oblique f, Geom (figure) figure f oblique; Anat (muscle m) oblique m; Typ barre f transversale ou oblique
▸▸ Gram **o. case** cas m indirect ou oblique

obliquely [əˈbliːklɪ] ADV obliquement, de biais, obliquement; (indirectly) (to refer) d'une façon indirecte; (to glance) de ou en biais

obliqueness [əˈbliːknɪs], **obliquity** [əˈblɪkwɪtɪ] N also Geom obliquité f, (indirectness) caractère m indirect

obliterate [əˈblɪtəreɪt] VT (erase) (figures, footprints, traces etc) effacer; (the past, a culture) annihiler; (a stamp) oblitérer; (destroy) (buildings, town, evidence etc) détruire; **the town had been all but obliterated during the war** la ville avait été quasiment rayée de la carte pendant la guerre

obliteration [əblɪtəˈreɪʃən] N (erasing) (of figures, footprints, traces etc) effacement m; (of the past, a culture etc) anéantissement m; (destruction) (of buildings, town, evidence etc) destruction f

oblivion [əˈblɪvɪən] N oubli m; **to fall or sink into o.** tomber dans l'oubli; **to consign to o.** condamner à l'oubli

oblivious [əˈblɪvɪəs] ADJ oublieux (**of, to** de); **I was o. of or to what was going on** je n'étais pas conscient ou je n'avais pas conscience de ce qui se passait; **he was o. to danger** il était inconscient du danger

obliviously [əˈblɪvɪəslɪ] ADV (to carry on etc) en toute inconscience

oblong [ˈɒblɒŋ] ADJ oblong, -ongue; (face etc) allongé
N rectangle m

obloquy [ˈɒbləkwɪ] N Fml opprobre m

obnoxious [əbˈnɒkʃəs] ADJ (person, action etc) odieux; (smell etc) repoussant

oboe [ˈəʊbəʊ] N Mus hautbois m; **o. player** hautboïste mf

oboist [ˈəʊbəʊɪst] N Mus hautboïste mf

obscene [əbˈsiːn] ADJ (indecent) (song, telephone call, word etc) obscène; Fig (profits, prices, demands etc) scandaleux; **it's o. that they are so rich when people are starving** il est scandaleux ou révoltant qu'ils soient aussi riches alors qu'il y a des gens qui meurent de faim

obscenely [əbˈsiːnlɪ] ADV d'une manière obscène; **o. rich** scandaleusement riche

obscenity [əbˈsenɪtɪ] N obscénité f, **disgusted by the o. of such profits/salaries** dégoûté par ces bénéfices/salaires scandaleux; **the o. of people earning millions while others starve** le caractère scandaleux ou révoltant d'une situation où certains gagnent des millions tandis que d'autres meurent de faim
▸▸ **o. laws** lois fpl concernant les outrages à la pudeur

obscurantism [ɒbskjʊˈræntɪz(ə)m] N obscurantisme m

obscurantist [ɒbskjʊˈræntɪst] ADJ, N obscurantiste mf

obscure [əbˈskjʊər] ADJ **1** (unclear) (speech, book etc) obscur; **for some o. reason he thought it would help** il pensait, pour d'obscures raisons, que ça serait utile **2** (little known) (birth, background) obscur; (author, book) inconnu, peu obscur; (village etc) inconnu, ignoré **3** (vague) (feeling) vague, obscur **4** (dark) obscur, sombre, ténébreux; **to grow or become o.** s'obscurcir, s'assombrir
VT1 (hide from view) cacher; **to o. sth from sb's view** cacher qch à qn **2** (make unclear) (argument, facts, truth) obscurcir **3** (overshadow) éclipser, voiler **4** (darken) obscurcir, assombrir

obscurely [əbˈskjʊəlɪ] ADV **1** (to speak) de façon obscure ou mystérieuse **2** (to feel, see) vaguement, obscurément

obscurity [əbˈskjʊərɪtɪ] N obscurité f, Fig **to sink back into o.** retomber dans l'oubli

obsequies [ˈɒbsɪkwɪz] NPL obsèques fpl, funérailles fpl

obsequious [əbˈsiːkwɪəs] ADJ obséquieux

obsequiously [əbˈsiːkwɪəslɪ] ADV obséquieusement

obsequiousness [əbˈsiːkwɪəsnɪs] N obséquiosité f

observable [əbˈzɜːvəb(ə)l] ADJ observable; (change, difference, improvement) perceptible; **it was o. that …** on a pu observer que …

observance [əbˈzɜːvəns] N **1** (of law, custom etc) observation f, observance f **2** (practice) **religious observances** pratiques fpl religieuses

observant [əbˈzɜːvənt] ADJ observateur, -trice (**of** de); **that's very o. of you** tu es bien observateur

observation [ɒbzəˈveɪʃən] N **1** observation f, Mil (of terrain, enemy) surveillance f, **to put/keep under o.** (house, premises) mettre/tenir en observation; (person) mettre/tenir sous surveillance; **this fact has not escaped his o.** ce fait n'a pas échappé à sa vigilance; Med **to keep sb in hospital for o.** garder qn en observation à l'hôpital; **to take an o.** (in surveying), Astron faire une observation; Naut faire le point **2** (remark) observation f, remarque f, **to make an o.** faire une observation ou une remarque (**about sb/ sth** sur qn/qch)
▸▸ **o. aircraft** avion m de reconnaissance; Rail **o.car, o. coach** voiture f panoramique; **o. deck** terrasse f panoramique; **o. point** point m d'observation; Mil **o. post** poste m d'observation; **o. satellite** satellite m d'observation; Med **o. ward** salle f d'observation

observational research [ɒbzəˈveɪʃ(ə)l] N étude f par observation

observatory [əbˈzɜːvət(ə)rɪ] N observatoire m

observe [əbˈzɜːv] VT **1** (stars etc) observer; **to o. the enemy's movements** surveiller les mouvements ennemis **2** (notice) (fact etc) remarquer, noter; **he didn't o. her leaving** il ne l'a pas vue partir **3** (say) **to o. that …** observer ou faire remarquer que … **4** (respect, follow) (the law, the proprieties, a fast) observer; (the Sabbath) respecter, observer; (order) se conformer à; **to o. silence** observer le silence; **a two minutes' silence was observed** on observa/ils observèrent/etc deux minutes de silence

observer [əbˈzɜːvər] N **1** (watcher) observateur, -trice; **to be a close o. of sth** observer qch de près; **to be a keen o. of sth** suivre qch attentivement **2** (strict o. of protocol une personne qui respecte ou observe le protocole à la lettre **3** (expert) expert m, spécialiste mf (**of** de); **political observers** experts ou spécialistes en politique

obsess [əbˈses] VT obséder; **to be obsessed with or by an idea** être obsédé ou hanté par une idée; **to be obsessed with sb** être obsédé par qn

obsession [əbˈseʃən] N obsession f (**with** de); **to have an o. with sb/an idea** être obsédé par qn/une idée; **it's becoming a bit of an o.** ça tourne à l'obsession; **cleanliness is an o. with her** c'est une maniaque de la propreté

obsessional [əbˈseʃən(ə)l] ADJ obsessionnel; **to be o. about sth/sb** être obsédé par qch/ qn

obsessive [əbˈsesɪv] ADJ (person) à tendances obsessionnelles; (behaviour, hatred, *fear)* obsessionnel; *(idea, image)* obsédant; **he was becoming quite o. about it** ça devenait une obsession chez lui; **she never struck me as the o. type** elle ne m'a jamais semblé être du genre obsessionnel

N **he's a bit of an o.** il est du genre obsessionnel; **our boss is a real o. when it comes to punctuality** la ponctualité est une véritable obsession chez notre patron; **you're turning into an o.** ça tourne à l'obsession chez toi

▸▸ *Psy* **o. compulsive disorder** névrose *f* obsessionnelle

obsessively [əb'sesɪvlɪ] ADV de manière obsessionnelle; **he's so. concerned with his appearance** il est obsédé par son apparence; **to be o. afraid of sth** avoir une peur maladive de qch; **he is o. tidy** c'est un maniaque de la propreté; **she is almost o. interested in birds/politics** son intérêt pour les oiseaux/la politique frise l'obsession

obsolescence [ɒbsə'les(ə)ns] N *(of law, ideas)* caractère *m* désuet; *(of word, term)* vieillissement *m*; *Ind etc (of equipment)* obsolescence *f*; **to fall into o.** tomber en désuétude; *Ind* **planned o.** obsolescence prévue; *Ind, Com* **built-in o.** obsolescence programmée

obsolescent [ɒbsə'les(ə)nt] ADJ *(equipment)* obsolescent; *(falling into disuse)* qui tombe en désuétude; *(word, term)* qui vieillit, qui a vieilli

obsolete ['ɒbsəliːt] ADJ *(word, idea, law)* désuet, -ète, tombé en désuétude; *(design etc)* démodé, dépassé; *(technique, equipment)* obsolète, périmé; *(ship)* déclassé; *(institution)* caduc, -ucque

obstacle ['ɒbstək(ə)l] N obstacle *m*; **to be an o. to sth** faire obstacle à qch; **to put obstacles in sb's way** faire obstacle à qn

▸▸ **o. course** parcours *m* d'obstacles; *Fig* parcours du combattant; **it's only one part of the o. course of finding a job** ce n'est qu'un bout du parcours du combattant qu'il faut suivre pour trouver un emploi; **o. race** course *f* d'obstacles

obstetric(al) [ɒb'stetrɪk, -ɪk(ə)l] ADJ obstétrical, -aux

obstetrician [ɒbste'trɪʃən] N médecin *m* accoucheur, obstétricien, -ienne

obstetrics [ɒb'stetrɪks] N obstétrique *f* VOIR GRAMMAIRE A10

obstinacy ['ɒbstɪnəsɪ] N *(of person)* obstination *f*, entêtement *m*; *(of resistance)* ténacité *f*; *Med (of disease)* persistance *f*

obstinate ['ɒbstɪnɪt] ADJ **1** *(person, refusal)* obstiné (**in doing sth** à faire qch); *(resistance etc)* tenace; **to be o.** s'entêter, s'obstiner **2** *(illness, cold, spot)* tenace, coriace; *(stain, grease)* rebelle

obstinately ['ɒbstɪnɪtlɪ] ADV obstinément; *(to resist)* avec acharnement; **to behave o.** se montrer obstiné

obstreperous [əb'strepərəs] ADJ *(rebellious)* rebelle; *(noisy)* bruyant, tapageur; **don't get o. with me!** ne me faites pas d'histoires!; **to get o. about sth** faire un scandale de qch

obstreperously [əb'strepərəslɪ] ADV *(rebelliously)* *Fam* en rouspétant; *(noisily)* bruyamment, tapageusement; **to behave o.** faire des histoires

obstreperousness [əb'strepərəsnɪs] N *(of crowd, children)* caractère *m* tapageur; *(of sb's tone)* agressivité *f*; **I won't put up with your o. any longer** j'en ai assez de tes caprices et de ton agressivité

obstruct [əb'strʌkt] VT **1** *(block) (road etc)* obstruer, encombrer; *(pipe etc)* boucher; *Med (intestine)* oblitérer, obstruer; *(view)* boucher, cacher; **her view was obstructed**

by a tall man un homme de haute taille lui bouchait *ou* cachait la vue **2** *(hinder progress) (person's movements, attempts)* gêner, entraver; *(traffic, shipping)* entraver; *(reforms, inquiry, investigation)* faire obstruction à; **to o. sb's path** barrer le chemin à qn; *Law* **to o. the course of justice** entraver le cours de la justice; **to o. sb in the execution of his duty** gêner qn dans l'exercice de ses fonctions; *Sport* **to o. another player** faire obstruction; *Parl* **to o. a bill** faire obstruction

VI *Sport* faire obstruction

obstruction [əb'strʌkʃən] N **1** *(action) (of road etc)* obstruction *f*, *(of pipe etc)* engorgement *m*; *Med (of intestine)* obstruction, oblitération *f*, *(of traffic, person in their affairs etc)* entravement *m*; *Sport, Pol* obstruction **2** *(blockage) (in road)* encombrement *m*; *(to shipping)* entrave *f*, *(in pipe)* engorgement *m*; **to cause an o.** *(on road)* entraver la circulation; *Rail* **an o. on the line** un obstacle sur la voie

obstructionism [əb'strʌkʃənɪz(ə)m] N *Pol* obstructionnisme *m*

obstructionist [əb'strʌkʃənɪst] ADJ, N *Pol* obstructionniste *mf*

obstructive [əb'strʌktɪv] ADJ *(person)* qui fait de l'obstruction, qui met des bâtons dans les roues; *(tactic, attitude)* d'obstruction; *Med* obstructif, obstruant; *Parl etc* **to be o.** faire de l'obstruction, être obstructionniste

obtain [əb'teɪn] VT *(information, money etc)* obtenir; **to o. sugar from beet** extraire du sucre de la betterave; **I obtained permission to see him** j'ai obtenu la permission de le voir

VI *Fml (of practice etc)* avoir cours; *(of rules)* être en vigueur

obtainable [əb'teɪnəb(ə)l] ADJ **easily o.** facile à obtenir; **this model is only o. in America** on ne peut se procurer ce modèle qu'en Amérique

obtrude [əb'truːd] *Fml* VT mettre en avant; **to o. one's opinions on others** imposer ses opinions à; **to o. oneself** s'imposer

VI **1** *(of person)* s'imposer **2** *(of object)* dépasser (**from** de)

obtrusion [əb'truːʒən] N intrusion *f*

obtrusive [əb'truːsɪv] ADJ **1** *(person, behaviour, question)* importun, indiscret, -ète **2** *(smell etc)* pénétrant

obtrusively [əb'truːsɪvlɪ] ADV importunément; *(to behave)* indiscrètement; **the lights were o. bright** l'éclairage ôtait tout sentiment d'intimité

obtrusiveness [əb'truːsɪvnɪs] N **1** *(of behaviour, presence)* importunité *f* **2** *(of smell)* caractère *m* pénétrant

obtuse [əb'tjuːs] ADJ **1** *(person, mind)* obtus; *(behaviour, remark)* stupide; **you're being deliberately o.** tu fais exprès de ne pas comprendre **2** *(blunt-ended)* obtus, émoussé

▸▸ *Geom* **o. angle** angle *m* obtus

obtuseness [əb'tjuːsnɪs] N *(of person, behaviour, remark)* stupidité *f*

obverse ['ɒbvɜːs] N *(of medal)* avers *m*, face *f*, *(of truth etc)* opposé *m*

▸▸ **o. side** *(of medal)* avers, face

obviate ['ɒbvɪeɪt] VT *(difficulty etc)* parer à, obvier à; *(objection)* répondre à; **this obviates the need to …** ceci pare à la nécessité de …

obvious ['ɒbvɪəs] ADJ évident, clair, manifeste; *(lie, displeasure)* manifeste; *(feature)* frappant; **it's quite o. that she is lying** il est évident *ou* clair *ou* manifeste qu'elle ment, elle ment, cela saute aux yeux; **you were too o.** *(unsubtle)* tu n'as pas été très subtil; **it was the o. thing to do** c'était tout indiqué,

cela s'imposait; **an o. comparison would be with the French Revolution** la première comparaison qui vient à l'esprit est la révolution française; **his patriotism is a little (too) o.** son patriotisme sonne faux; **there was a very o. stain in the middle** il y avait une tache bien visible en plein milieu; **there are several o. objections to the plan** ce projet présente plusieurs inconvénients on ne peut plus évidents

N **to state the o.** enfoncer une porte ouverte; **it would be stating the o. to say that we were surprised by the news** il va sans dire que ces nouvelles nous ont surpris; **to miss the o.** passer à côté de l'essentiel

▸▸ *Com* **o. defect** vice *m* apparent

obviously ['ɒbvɪəslɪ] ADV **1** *(in an obvious way)* manifestement; **he's so o. English** il est si manifestement anglais; **he did it so o.** il l'a fait si ostensiblement; **they are different, but not o.** ils sont différents, mais ça ne saute pas aux yeux; **he wasn't o. the right choice but …** au premier abord il n'était pas évident que c'était le bon choix mais … **2** *(of course)* évidemment; **do you prefer this? – o.** préférez-vous cela? – bien sûr; **o. not!** bien sûr que non!, évidemment non!; **I'll o. have to turn the offer down** il va sans dire que je vais devoir refuser l'offre

obviousness ['ɒbvɪəsnɪs] N évidence *f*, clarté *f*, *(of lie)* caractère *m* manifeste; **the o. of his displeasure** son mécontentement manifeste

OC [əʊ'siː] N *Mil (abbr* **Officer Commanding***)* chef *m* de corps

ocarina [ɒkə'riːnə] N *Mus* ocarina *m*

occasion [ə'keɪʒən] N **1** *(time)* occasion *f*, **on this o.** en cette occasion; **this is not the o. to discuss such matters** les circonstances sont peu appropriées pour parler de ces choses; *Fml* **on the o. of his daughter's marriage** à l'occasion du mariage de sa fille; **I am prepared to overlook it on this o., but …** je veux bien fermer les yeux cette fois-ci, mais …; **on one o.** une fois; **on another o.** une autre fois; **on several occasions** à plusieurs reprises; **on rare occasions** rarement; **on such an o.** en pareille occasion; **on great occasions** dans les grandes occasions; **words appropriate to the o.** paroles de circonstance; **to dress to suit the o.** mettre la tenue appropriée; **she could have dressed to suit the o.** elle aurait pu faire l'effort de s'habiller un peu mieux

2 **on o.** *(occasionally)* parfois, de temps en temps

3 *(event)* événement *m*; **her wedding was quite an o.** son mariage a été un grand événement *ou* n'a pas été une petite affaire; **an o. to remember** un événement mémorable; **we'll make this an o. to remember** nous allons fêter ça dans les règles; **there was a real sense of o.** il y avait une vraie atmosphère de célébration; **he has no sense of o.** *(for celebration)* il n'a pas le sens de la fête; *(for serious event)* il n'a pas le sens des convenances

4 *(opportunity)* occasion *f*, **I'll speak to him on the first o.** je lui parlerai à la première occasion; **should the o. arise** si l'occasion se présente, s'il y a lieu, le cas échéant

5 *Fml (cause)* sujet *m*, cause *f*, **to have o. to suspect sb/to be angry** avoir lieu de soupçonner qn/d'être en colère; **there's** *or* **you have no o. to be alarmed** il n'y a pas lieu de vous inquiéter; **this action was the o. of great suffering** cette action a donné lieu à de grandes souffrances

VT *Fml (fear, inconvenience, surprise etc)* causer; *(response)* susciter, provoquer

occasional [ə'keɪʒ(ə)nəl] ADJ **1** *(visit)* espacé, occasionnel; *(incident)* qui se produit de temps en temps, occasionnel; **o. sho-**

wers averses *fpl* éparses *ou* occasionnelles; **I still get the o. twinge in my back** mon dos m'élance toujours un peu de temps en temps; **I have the o. cigarette/glass of wine** il m'arrive de fumer une cigarette/de boire un verre de vin; **he is an o. smoker** il ne fume qu'occasionnellement **2** *(play, verse etc)* de circonstance

▸▸ **o. chair** chaise *f* volante; *Br* **o. table** table *f* d'appoint

occasionally [ə'keɪʒən(ə)lɪ] ADV de temps en temps, parfois, occasionnellement; **we only see them very o. nowadays** nous ne les voyons que très occasionnellement *ou* de loin en loin ces temps-ci

occident ['ɒksɪdənt] N occident *m*, couchant *m*; *Pol etc* **the O.** l'Occident

occidental [ɒksɪ'dent(ə)l] ADJ occidental, -aux

occipital [ɒk'sɪpɪt(ə)l] ADJ, N *Anat* occipital *m*

occiput ['ɒksɪpʌt] N *Anat* occiput *m*

occlude [ə'kluːd] VT *Fml (opening etc)* occlure, fermer, boucher; *(eyelids)*, *Chem (gas)* occlure

occlusion [ə'kluːʒən] N **1** *(of pipe etc.)*, *Chem (of gas)* occlusion *f* **2** *(of tooth)* occlusion *f* *(molaire/etc)*

occlusive [ə'kluːsɪv] N *Ling* (consonne *f*) occlusive *f*

▸▸ **o. consonant** consonne occlusive

occult [ɒ'kʌlt, 'ɒkʌlt] ADJ occulte, secret, -ète; **the o. sciences** les sciences *fpl* occultes N the o. l'occulte *m*

occultism ['ɒkʌltɪz(ə)m] N occultisme *m*

occupancy ['ɒkjʊpənsɪ] N **1** *Law* possession *f* à titre de premier occupant **2** *(of building)* occupation *f*, habitation *f*

▸▸ **o. forecast** *(in hotels)* prévision *f* du taux d'occupation; **o. level** *(in hotel)* niveau *m* d'occupation

occupant ['ɒkjʊpənt] N *(of house etc)* occupant, -ante; *Law* premier occupant; *(of car etc)* occupant *m*; *(of job)* titulaire *mf*; *(of seat on board, of position)* détenteur, -trice

occupation [ɒkjʊ'peɪʃən] N **1** *(activity)* occupation *f*, *(profession)* métier *m*, profession *f*, *(on form)* qualité *f*; **a leisure o.** un loisir SEE GRAMMAR B5 **2** *(of house, land)* occupation *f*, **to be in o. of a house** occuper une maison; **how long have they been in o.?** cela fait combien de temps qu'ils occupent les lieux?; **fit for o.** *(house)* habitable; **army/troops of o.** armée *f*/troupes *fpl* d'occupation; **they decided to organize an o. of the Embassy** ils ont décidé d'organiser l'occupation de l'Ambassade; *Hist* **the Roman o. of Britain** l'occupation de la Grande-Bretagne par les Romains; *Hist* **the O.** *(of France)* l'Occupation *f*

occupational [ɒkjʊ'peɪʃən(ə)l] ADJ

▸▸ **o. disease** maladie *f* professionnelle; **o. hazard** risque *m* professionnel *ou* du métier; **o. illness** maladie professionnelle; **o. medicine** médecine *f* du travail; **o. therapist** ergothérapeute *mf*; **o. therapy** ergothérapie *f*

occupied ['ɒkjʊpaɪd] ADJ **1** *(house)*, *Mil (territory)* occupé; **this seat is o.** cette place est prise; **in o. France** dans la France occupée *ou* de l'Occupation **2** *(busy)* **to be o. in** *or* **with doing sth** être occupé à faire qch; **he was o. with thoughts of …** il était occupé à penser à …; **to keep sb o.** occuper qn; **to keep one's mind o.** s'occuper l'esprit

occupier ['ɒkjʊpaɪər] N *(tenant)* locataire *mf*; *(of house)* occupant, -ante, habitant, -ante; **to the o.** *(on letter)* à l'attention de l'occupant

occupy ['ɒkjʊpaɪ] VT **1** *(house etc)* occuper, habiter; *(land)* occuper; *(position)* occuper, remplir; *Mil (enemy country)* occuper; *(stra-*

tegic point) s'emparer de; **the workers have occupied the building** les ouvriers ont occupé le bâtiment **2** *(room, space, attention)* occuper; **to o. one's time (in** *or* **with)** doing **sth** occuper son temps à faire qch; **her work occupies all her time** son travail occupe tout son temps; **it occupied two hours of the afternoon** cela a pris deux heures dans l'après-midi; **to o. one's mind** s'occuper l'esprit

occur [ə'kɜːr] VI (-rr-) **1** *(happen)* *(of event etc)* avoir lieu, arriver, se produire; *(of opportunity, vacancy)* se présenter; *(of accident)* avoir lieu, se produire; **this seldom occurs** cela arrive rarement; **I hope it will not o. again** j'espère que cela ne se répétera pas **2** *(be present)* *(of objects, types etc)* se rencontrer, se trouver, se présenter; **this word occurs twice in the letter** on trouve *ou* on rencontre ce mot deux fois dans la lettre **3** *(of idea etc)* venir à l'esprit; **this thought has occurred to me** cela m'est déjà venu à l'esprit; **it didn't o. to them that she might be lying** il ne leur est pas venu à l'esprit que peut-être elle mentait

occurrence [ə'kʌrəns] N **1 two hours before its o.** deux heures avant que cela eût lieu; *Fml* **to be of frequent o.** arriver *ou* se produire fréquemment; **the o. of two murders on the same day** le fait que deux meurtres aient été commis le même jour; **the o. of leukaemia in this community is twice …** le nombre des cas de leucémie dans cette communauté est le double de …; **the o. of storms** *(frequency)* la fréquence des tempêtes; **to prevent the o. of violence** combattre (le phénomène de) la violence **2** *(event)* fait *m*, événement *m*; **an everyday o.** un fait quotidien; **a singular o.** un fait étrange; **this was the first o. of its kind** c'était la première fois qu'un événement de cette espèce se produisait

OCD [əʊsiː'diː] N *Psy (abbr obsessive compulsive disorder)* névrose *f* obsessionnelle

ocean ['əʊʃən] N océan *m*; **the Atlantic O.** l'océan Atlantique; *Fig* **an o. of sand** une mer de sable; *Fig* **we've got oceans of time** nous avons énormément de temps

▸▸ **o. current** courant *m* océanique; **o. floor** fond *m* de l'océan; **o. freight** fret *m* maritime; **o. liner** paquebot *m*

ocean-going ADJ *(ship)* au long cours, de haute mer

Oceania [əʊʃɪ'eɪnɪə] N Océanie *f*

oceanic [əʊʃɪ'ænɪk] ADJ *(voyage, climate)* océanique

oceanographer [əʊʃə'nɒɡrəfər] N océanographe *mf*

oceanography [əʊʃə'nɒɡrəfɪ] N océanographie *f*

ocelot ['ɒsəlɒt] N ocelot *m*

ochre, *Am* **ocher** ['əʊkər] N *Miner* ocre *f*, **red o.** ocre rouge; **yellow o.** jaune *m* d'ocre, ocre jaune

ADJ **o.(-coloured)** ocre *inv*

ocker ['ɒkər] *Austr Fam* N *(boor)* beauf *m*

ADJ *(boorish)* beauf

o'clock [ə'klɒk] ADV **one o.** une heure; **two/three o.** deux/trois heures; **at four o.** à quatre heures; **the seven o. train** le train de sept heures VOIR GRAMMAIRE A80; B60

OCR [əʊsiː'ɑːr] N *Comput* **1** *(abbr optical character reader)* lecteur *m* (à reconnaissance) optique de caractères, lecteur OCR **2** *(abbr optical character recognition)* reconnaissance *f* optique des caractères

▸▸ **O. font** fonte *f* reconnue optiquement; **O. software** logiciel *m* d'OCR

Oct *abbr* **October**

octagon ['ɒktəɡən] N *Geom* octogone *m*

octagonal [ɒk'tæɡən(ə)l] ADJ *Geom* octogonal, -aux

octahedral [ɒktə'hiːdrəl, -'hed-] ADJ *Geom* octaédrique

octahedron, *pl* **octahedrons**, **octahedra** ['ɒktə'hiːdrən, -'hed-, -ɒnz, -ə] N *Geom* octaèdre *m*

octane ['ɒkteɪn] N *Chem* octane *m*; **o. number** *or* **rating** indice *m* d'octane

octave ['ɒktɪv] N *Rel*, *Mus*, *Fencing* octave *f*, *(in poetry)* huitain *m*; *Mus* **an o. apart** à une octave de différence

octavo [ɒk'teɪvəʊ] N *Typ* in-octavo *m inv*

octet [ɒk'tet] N **1** *Mus* octuor *m* **2** *(in poetry)* huitain *m* **3** *Chem* octet *m*

October [ɒk'təʊbər] N VOIR GRAMMAIRE A81–2; B60–2 octobre *m*; **in O.** au mois d'octobre, en octobre; **(on) the first/seventh of O.** le premier/sept octobre

octogenarian [ɒktədʒɪ'neərɪən] ADJ, N octogénaire *mf*

octopod ['ɒktəpɒd] ADJ, N octopode *m*

octopus ['ɒktəpəs] N poulpe *m*, pieuvre *f*

octosyllabic [ɒktəsɪ'læbɪk] ADJ *(verse, word)* octosyllabe, octo-syllabique

octuple ['ɒktjuːp(ə)l] ADJ, N octuple *m*

ocular ['ɒkjʊlər] ADJ *(nerve etc)* oculaire N *Opt (of microscope etc)* oculaire *m*

oculist ['ɒkjʊlɪst] N oculiste *mf*

OD [əʊ'diː] N **1** *Fam (abbr overdose)* overdose *f* **2** *(abbr overdraft)* découvert *m* VI *(pt, pp* **OD'd)** *Fam (abbr overdose)* prendre une overdose (**on** de); *Fig Sl* **I think I've rather OD'd on pizzas** je crois que j'ai un peu forcé sur les pizzas; **they OD'd on soap operas** ils se sont pris une overdose de séries télévisées

ODA [əʊdiː'eɪ] N *(abbr Official Development Assistance)* aide *f* publique au développement

odalisk, **odalisque** ['əʊdəlɪsk] N odalisque *f*

odd [ɒd] ADJ **1** *(strange)* bizarre; **the o. thing about it is that …** le curieux de l'affaire *ou* ce qui est bizarre c'est que …; **it's o. your not knowing about it** c'est drôle *ou* bizarre que vous n'en sachiez rien; **it would look o. to refuse** ça ferait drôle si tu refusais/on refusait/*etc*; **how o. that he should have forgotten it!** comme c'est drôle *ou* bizarre qu'il l'ait oublié!; **(well,) that's o.!** voilà qui est bizarre *ou* singulier!, c'est curieux!; **an o. way of saying sorry** une drôle de manière *ou* une curieuse manière de s'excuser; *Com* **o. size** taille *f* peu courante

2 *Math etc (number)* impair

3 *(one of a set)* dépareillé; *(one of a pair)* déparié, dépareillé; **o. socks** chaussettes dépareillées; **to be the o. man out** être en trop; *Fig* être à part; **she was the o. woman out, not being German** n'étant pas allemande, elle faisait figure d'exception; **which of these books is the o. one out?** lequel de ces livres n'a rien à voir avec les autres?, trouvez l'intrus

4 *(occasional)* **they got the o. tin of food** on leur servait des boîtes de conserve de temps en temps *ou* par-ci par-là; **he scores the o. goal** il marque un but de temps en temps *ou* par-ci par-là; **at o. times** par-ci par-là; **at o. moments** dans mes/ses/*etc* moments perdus; **we get the o. visitor** nous avons de la visite de temps en temps **nobody, apart from the o. anthropologist …** personne, à part quelques (rares) anthropologues …

5 *(odd uses)* **a hundred o. sheep** cent et quelques moutons; **twenty o. pounds** un peu plus de vingt livres; **a few o. things to do** quelques petites choses à faire; **an** *or* **any o. piece of cloth** un bout d'étoffe quelconque; **o. jobs about the house** petits travaux dans la maison

▸▸**o. lot** *Com* lot *m* dépareillé; *St Exch (of shares)* lot de moins de cent actions; *Comput* **o. parity** parité *f* impaire

oddball ['ɒdbɔːl] *Fam* N allumé, -ée, farfelu, -ue
  ADJ *(ideas, friends)* farfelu, loufoque

oddbod ['ɒdbɒd] N *Fam* original, -ale

odd-even ADJ
▸▸**o. check** contrôle *m* de parité; *Mktg* **o. price** prix *m* magique; *Mktg* **o. pricing** fixation *f* des prix magiques

oddity ['ɒdɪtɪ] N **1** *(strangeness)* singularité *f*, bizarrerie *f*; **he has some little oddities** il a quelques petits travers **2** *(thing)* chose *f* bizarre, curiosité *f*; **she's a bit of an o.** *(odd)* elle est un peu bizarre; *(sticks out)* c'est un cas à part; **I'm sick of people treating me like an o.** j'en ai marre qu'on me traite comme si j'étais anormal; **this movie is an o.** *(weird)* c'est un film bizarre; *(unusual)* c'est un film à part

odd-job man, odd-jobber ['ɒd'dʒɒbmæn, -ɒbər] N homme *m* à tout faire

odd-looking ADJ *(à l'apparence)* bizarre

oddly ['ɒdlɪ] ADV bizarrement, étrangement; **o. enough nobody knew anything about it** chose curieuse, personne n'en savait rien; **an o. shaped face** un visage aux contours bizarrement irréguliers; **I find her o. attractive** je la trouve étrangement attirante

oddment ['ɒdmənt] N *(one of a set)* article *m* dépareillé; *(sale item)* fin *f* de série; *(piece of material)* coupon *m* d'étoffe; **remnants and oddments** soldes *mpl* et occasions *fpl*

oddness ['ɒdnɪs] N étrangeté *f*, bizarrerie *f*

odds [ɒdz] NPL **1** *(probability)* chances *fpl*; **what are the o. on his getting the job?** quelles chances a-t-il d'avoir le poste?; **the o. are that she was lying** il y a de grandes chances pour qu'elle ait menti; **the o. are against him/in his favour** il y a peu de chance(s)/de grosses chances qu'il réussisse; **the o. are that he'll succeed** il y a gros à parier qu'il réussira; **it's against all the o.** c'est fort peu probable; **they fought** *or* **struggled against great o. to win the election** bien que les chances de succès étaient extrêmement minces, ils ont réussi à remporter l'élection; **we're always fighting against enormous o.** nous nous battons toujours contre des montagnes; **what are the o. that she'll remember?** quelles chances y a-t-il qu'elle s'en souvienne?; *Br Fam* **what's the o.?** *(what does it matter?)* qu'est-ce que ça fait?; *Br Fam* **it makes no o.** ça ne fait rien, cela n'a pas d'importance; **it makes no o. what she says** ce qu'elle dit n'a pas d'importance
2 *Horseracing etc* cote *f*, **o. on** *or* **against a horse** cote d'un cheval; **short/long o.** faible/forte cote; **the o. are (at) ten to one** la cote est à dix contre un; *Sport* **to give sb o. of ten to one** proposer à qn un pari à dix contre un
3 to be at o. with sb *(be in disagreement)* ne pas être d'accord avec qn; *(be on bad terms)* être brouillé avec qn *(over* à propos de)*; **his latest statement is at o. with his earlier account** sa dernière déposition ne concorde pas avec son premier récit des faits
4 o. and ends *or Br Fam* **sods** *(miscellaneous articles)* bricoles *fpl*; *(of cloth)* bouts *mpl*; **I've still a few o. and ends to do** j'ai encore quelques bricoles *ou* petites choses à faire

odds-on ADJ **it's o. that he won't notice** il y a gros à parier qu'il ne le remarquera pas
▸▸**o. bet** pari *m* inégal; **o. favourite** grand favori *m*

ode [əʊd] N *Liter* ode *f*

odious ['əʊdɪəs] ADJ odieux (**to** à)

odiously ['əʊdɪəslɪ] ADV odieusement

odiousness ['əʊdɪəsnɪs] N caractère *m* odieux, abjection *f*

odium ['əʊdɪəm] N haine *f*; **to bring** *or* **cast o. upon sb** rendre qn odieux (aux yeux des autres)

odometer [əʊ'dɒmɪtər] N *Am* compteur *m* (kilométrique)

odontology [ɒdɒn'tɒlədʒɪ] N odontologie *f*

odor ['əʊdər] N *Am* = **odour**

odorless ['əʊdəlɪs] ADJ *Am* = **odourless**

odorous ['əʊdərəs] ADJ **1** odorant, qui exhale une odeur (agréable) **2** *Fam (bad-smelling)* malodorant

odour, *Am* **odor** ['əʊdər] N odeur *f*, *(pleasant smell)* odeur (agréable), parfum *m*; *Fam (bad smell)* mauvaise odeur; *Fig Fml* **to be in good/bad o. with sb** être bien/mal vu de qn; **you're not in good o. with the boss** tu n'es pas en odeur de sainteté auprès du patron; *Rel* **o. of sanctity** odeur de sainteté

odourless, *Am* **odorless** ['əʊdəlɪs] ADJ inodore, sans odeur

Odyssey ['ɒdɪsɪ] N *Myth* **the O.** l'Odyssée *f*; *Fig* **a spiritual odyssey** une odyssée spirituelle

OECD [əʊiːsiː'diː] N *(abbr* **Organization for Economic Co-operation and Development)** OCDE *f*

oedema, *Am* **edema** [ɪ'diːmə] N œdème *m*

Oedipal ['iːdɪpəl] ADJ *Psy* Œdipien, -ienne

Oedipus ['iːdɪpəs] N *Myth* Œdipe *m*
▸▸**O. complex** complexe *m* d'Œdipe

OEM [əʊiː'em] N *Comput (abbr* **original equipment manufacturer)** constructeur *m* de systèmes originaux

o'er [ɔːr, 'əʊər] PREP, ADV *Lit* = **over**

oesophagus, *Am* **esophagus,** *pl* **esophagi, esophaguses** [iː'sɒfəgəs, -gaɪ, -gəsɪz] N *Anat* œsophage *m*

oestrogen, *Am* **estrogen** ['iːstrədʒən] N *Biol, Chem* œstrogène *m*

oestrous, *Am* **estrous** ['iːstrəs] ADJ *Biol (cycle etc)* œstral, -aux

oestrus, *Am* **estrus** ['iːstrəs] N *Biol* œstrus *m*

OF [ɒv, *unstressed* əv] PREP **1** *(belonging to)* de; **the name of the country/city** le nom du pays/de la ville; **the names of the districts** le nom des régions; **citizen of London** citoyen, -enne de Londres; **he is a friend of mine** c'est un de mes amis VOIR GRAMMAIRE A15–16
2 *(indicating separation, origin, cause)* de; **south of** au sud de; **within a mile of** à moins d'un mil(l)e de; **free of** libre de; **of noble birth** de naissance noble; **works of Shakespeare** œuvres de Shakespeare; **to ask a favour of sb** demander une faveur à qn; **of my own choice** de mon propre choix; **she died of grief** elle mourut de chagrin; **proud of sth** fier de qch; **I'm sick of it** j'en ai assez
3 *(indicating agency)* de; **it is very good** *or* **kind of you** c'est bien aimable de votre part, c'est très gentil à vous; **how clever of her** comme c'est intelligent de sa part; *Arch* **beloved of all** aimé de tout le monde
4 *(indicating material)* de, en; **made of wood** fait de *ou* en bois; **wall of stone** mur en *ou* de pierre; **full of water** plein d'eau
5 *(concerning, in respect of)* **to think of sb** penser à qn; **what do you think of him?** que pensez-vous de lui?; **to warn sb of sth** avertir qn de qch; **of President Taylor it was said that ...** il a été dit du Président Taylor que ...; **guilty of** coupable de; **doctor of medicine** docteur en médecine; **well, what of it?** et bien?, et après?
6 *(in description)* **the city of Rome** la ville de Rome; **man of genius** homme de génie; **people of foreign appearance** gens à l'air étranger; **child of ten** enfant (âgé(e)) de dix ans; **his wife of twenty years** la femme avec qui il est marié depuis vingt ans; **that fool of a sergeant** cet imbécile de sergent; **all of a tremble** tout tremblant
7 *(with grammatical subject)* de; **the love of a mother** l'amour d'une mère
8 *(with grammatical object)* de; **the fear of God** la crainte de Dieu; **great drinker of whisky** grand buveur de whisky
9 *(partitive)* **three quarters of the crowd** trois quarts de la foule; *Fam* **no more of that!** plus de ça!; **how much of it do you want?** combien en voulez-vous?; **many/several of us** beaucoup/plusieurs d'entre nous; **there were two/several of us** nous étions deux/plusieurs; **she is one of us** elle est des nôtres; **one of the best** un des meilleurs; **the best of men** le meilleur des hommes; **the bravest of the brave** le brave des braves; **he, of all men** *or* **people** lui entre tous; **this day of all days** ce jour entre tous; **you, of all people, should know ...** toi, plus que tout le monde, devrais savoir que ...
10 *(with expressions of time)* **of late years** *(pendant)* ces dernières années; **of late** dernièrement, récemment; *Fam* **of an evening** le soir

ofay [əʊ'feɪ] N *Am Fam Offensive* sale Blanc *m*, sale Blanche *f*

Ofcom ['ɒfkɒm] N *Br* = organisme *m* chargé de réglementer le secteur des communications

OFF [ɒf] ADV **1** *(away)* **house a mile o.** maison à un mil(l)e de distance; **some way o.** à quelque distance; **far o.** au loin, dans le lointain; **to go** *or* **be o.** *(leave)* s'en aller, partir; **isn't it time you were o. to bed?** n'est-il pas l'heure que tu ailles te coucher?; **I'm o. to London** je pars pour Londres; **I must be o.** (il faut que) je me sauve, il faut que je m'en aille; **be o. with you!** sauve-toi!, va-t-en!; **o. you go, you'll be late!** sauve-toi *ou* vas-y, tu vas être en retard!; **they're o.!** *(of racers, racehorses etc)* ils sont partis!, ils ont pris le départ!; **to go o. (to sleep)** s'endormir; *Theat* **to speak o.** parler depuis les coulisses; **he's o. again!** *(complaining etc)* le voilà qui remet ça!; **o. we go again!** nous voilà repartis!
2 *(indicating separation, removal)* **to take o. one's coat** retirer *ou* ôter son manteau; **with his jacket/trousers o.** sans sa veste/son pantalon; **a button has come o.** un bouton a sauté; **could you take two centimetres o.?** *(off sleeves etc)* est-ce que vous pourriez enlever deux centimètres?; **to cut sb's head o.** couper *ou* trancher la tête à qn, décapiter qn; **o. with her head!** qu'on lui coupe la tête!; **o. with those wet clothes!** retire(-moi) *ou* enlève(-moi) ces vêtements humides!; **hands o.!** bas les pattes!
3 *(not functioning, turned off)* **the light/radio is o.** la lumière/radio est éteinte; **the gas/electricity/water is o.** le gaz/l'électricité/l'eau est coupé(e); **the ignition is o.** l'allumage est coupé
4 *(in price)* **20%/£5 o.** 20%/5 livres de réduction *ou* de remise, réduction *f ou* remise *f* de 20%/5 livres
5 *(indicating completion)* **to finish o. a piece of work** finir *ou* terminer un travail
6 *(away from work etc)* **have you any time o. during the week?** avez-vous des heures libres pendant la semaine?; **he's o. today** il ne travaille pas aujourd'hui; **to take some time o.** se libérer; **day o.** jour de congé; **to give the staff a day o.** donner un jour de congé à son personnel; **to arrange to take two days o.** prendre deux jours de congé; **I get two hours o. for lunch** j'ai deux heures de libres pour le déjeuner
7 *(in phrases)* **o. and on, on and o.** par intervalles; *(from time to time)* de temps en temps; *Fam* **right** *or* **straight o.** immédiatement, sur-le-champ, tout de suite

PREP 1 *(from)* de; **to fall o. sth** tomber de qch; **to take a ring o. one's finger** ôter une bague de son doigt; **to cut a slice o. sth** couper une tranche de qch; **we dined o. a leg of lamb** nous avons dîné d'une tranche de gigot; *Elec* **to work o. the mains** se brancher sur secteur; **get that knife o. him!** prends-lui son couteau!; *Fam* **to borrow money/buy sth o. sb** emprunter de l'argent/ acheter qch à qn; *Fam* **I caught a cold o. my brother** mon frère m'a passé son rhume; **o. the top of one's head** *(to say, answer etc)* comme ça; **o. the cuff** *(to make a speech)* au pied levé; **(get) o.!** enlevez-vous de là!; **o. the sofa!** *(don't stand on it)* descends du canapé!; *(don't sit on it)* lève-toi du canapé!

2 *(indicating reduction in price etc)* **a third o.** everything rabais d'un tiers sur toute la marchandise; *Com* **10%/£20 o. a price** 10%/ 20 livres de réduction *ou* de remise sur un prix; **that's 2 seconds o. the record** c'est 2 secondes de moins que le record

3 *(away from, outside of)* **street o. the main road** écarté de, éloigné de; **village o. the beaten track** village dans un coin reculé; **street o. the main road** rue qui donne sur la grande route; **it's just o. Regent Street** c'est tout près de Regent Street

4 *(on vacation)* **to have time o. work** avoir du temps (de) libre; *see also* **off** ADV **6**

5 *(not liking)* **to be o. one's food** ne pas avoir d'appétit; **I'm o. coffee at the moment** ces temps-ci je n'ai pas envie de boire de café; *(because of doctor's orders)* en ce moment, je n'ai plus le droit au café; **he's o. drugs/drink** il ne se drogue/boit plus; *Fam* **I'm o. her** je ne l'aime plus

6 *Naut* **o. the Cape** au large du Cap; *(at latitude of)* à la hauteur du Cap; **o. the coast of Spain** au large de la côte espagnole; **to sail o. the wind** naviguer vent largue

ADJ 1 *(not functioning)* **o. position** position *f* arrêt, *(of lever)* position de repos; *(on scale)* position 'zéro'; *(of brakes)* position de desserrage; **o. switch** bouton *m* d'arrêt

2 *(on vacation, not working)* en congé, en vacances; **to be o. sick** être absent parce qu'on est malade, être malade; **he's o. today** il n'est pas là aujourd'hui; **are you o. tomorrow?** tu travailles demain?; *(no school)* tu (n')as pas d(')école demain?; *(no college)* tu (n')as pas (pas) cours demain?; **when are you o. this afternoon?** à quelle heure tu finis cet après-midi?; **I'm o. from 3 to 5** je ne travaille pas entre 3 et 5 heures

3 *(cancelled, finished)* *(marriage, trip, meeting)* annulé; *(engagement)* rompu; **it's all** *or* **the whole thing is o.** *(of relationship)* tout est fini; *(of deal)* la transaction est annulée *ou* ne se fera pas, *Fam* l'affaire est tombée à l'eau; **the lamb is o.** *(in restaurant)* il n'y a plus d'agneau

4 *(not fresh)* **to be o.** *(of food)* ne plus être frais; *(of meat)* être avarié; *(of milk, orange juice etc)* être tourné; **this beer's o.** cette bière est éventée

5 *(inaccurate, unsuccessful)* **his timing was a bit o.** *(when he asked for a rise etc)* il n'a pas choisi un très bon moment; **an o. day** un jour où l'on n'est pas en forme *ou* en train; *(with bad luck)* un jour sans

6 *Fam* **that's a bit o.!** *(improper, unfair)* c'est pas un truc à faire!; *(not nice)* ça c'est pas sympa!

7 **to be well/badly o.** *(financially)* être à l'aise/dans le besoin *ou* la gêne; **to be badly o. for sth** être à court de qch; **how are we o. for money/time?** combien d'argent/de temps avons-nous?; **how are we o. for coffee/bread?** est-ce qu'il y a encore du café/ pain?; **he is better o. where he is** il est bien mieux où il est; **you'd be better o. accepting their offer** tu ferais mieux d'accepter leur offre

N *Horseracing* **the o.** le départ; **to be ready for the o.** être prêt pour le départ

VT *Sl (kill)* descendre, zigouiller

▸▸ *Horseriding* **o. leg** jambe *f* de dehors; *Cr* **o. side** *(when the batsman is right-handed)* côté *m* droit du terrain; *(when the batsman is left-handed)* côté gauche du terrain

off-air ADJ, ADV hors antenne

offal ['ɒf(ə)l] N *(of animal) (edible)* abats *mpl*

off-balance sheet ADJ hors bilan

▸▸ **o. item** poste *m ou* élément *m* hors bilan; **o. transactions** opérations *fpl* de hors bilan

offbeat ['ɒfbiːt] N *Mus* temps *m* faible

ADJ *Fam (person, clothes, music)* original, -aux, excentrique

off-Broadway [-brɔːdweɪ] ADJ *Am Theat (production)* en dehors de Broadway

off-camera ADJ, ADV hors caméra

off-centre, off-centred, *Am* **off-center, off-centered** [ɒf'sentər, -təd] ADJ décentré, décalé; *Cin* décadré; *Fig (analysis, description)* légèrement inexact, pas tout à fait exact; *(humour, style)* excentrique, saugrenu

off-chance N on the o. à tout hasard; **I went on the o. that they would be there** j'y suis allé au cas peu probable où ils y seraient; **they had waited for hours on the o. of meeting their hero** ils avaient attendu pendant des heures dans l'espoir de rencontrer leur héros

off-colour, *Am* **off-color** ADJ **1** *Br (unwell)* **to be** *or* **feel o.** ne pas se sentir dans son assiette; **to look o.** ne pas avoir l'air dans son assiette **2** *Old-fashioned (joke)* d'un goût douteux

off-course ADJ *(bet)* effectué hors des champs de course

offcut ['ɒfkʌt] N *(from wooden plank, cloth, carpet)* chute *f*, *(for animals)* rognures *fpl*, **offcuts** *(of meat)* restes *mpl* du découpage

off-duty ADJ qui n'est pas de service

offence, *Am* **offense** [ə'fens] N **1** *Law etc (minor)* infraction *f*, *(more serious)* délit *m*; **petty** *or* **minor o.** contravention *f* (de simple police); **second o.** récidive *f* **2** *(no pl) (annoyance, displeasure)* blessure *f* faite à la susceptibilité de qn; **to take o.** s'offenser, se froisser (**at sth** de qch); **to take o. at the slightest thing** s'offenser d'un rien; **to cause** *or* **to give o. to sb** *(of person, personal remarks)* offenser *ou* blesser *ou* froisser qn; *(of film, book, programme)* heurter la sensibilité de qn; **I meant no o., I didn't mean to cause o.** je ne voulais offenser personne; **his speech caused a great deal of o. to the Catholic church** son discours a profondément déplu à l'église catholique; **it's an o. to the eye** cela choque la vue *ou* les regards **3** *Mil (attack)* attaque *f*, agression *f* **4** ['ɒfens] *Am Sport* attaque *f*

offend [ə'fend] VT *(person)* offenser, blesser, froisser; *(the Lord, Islam etc)* offenser; **to be offended at** *or* **by sth** se froisser *ou* s'offenser de qch; **to be easily offended** être très susceptible, se froisser facilement; **I hope you won't be offended if I …** j'espère que vous ne vous froisserez pas si je …; **to o. the eye** choquer les regards *ou* la vue; **harsh sound that offends the ear** son dur qui écorche *ou* heurte l'oreille

VI 1 *(cause offence)* **I didn't mean to o.** *(give offence to the general public)* je ne voulais offenser personne; *(give offence to you)* je ne voulais pas t'offenser *ou* te froisser **2** *Law (commit a crime)* commettre une infraction; *(more serious)* commettre un délit; **to o. a second time** récidiver

▸ **offend against** VT INSEP *(law, principle)* violer, enfreindre; *(common sense)* choquer;

(good taste) heurter; **his behaviour offends against good manners** son comportement est un outrage aux bonnes manières

offended [ə'fendɪd] ADJ **1** *(insulted)* blessé, offensé, froissé; **in an o. tone of voice** d'une voix offensée **2** *Law* **the o. party** l'offensé, -ée

offender [ə'fendər] N malfaiteur *m*; *Law* délinquant, -ante; *Law* **first o.** délinquant, -ante primaire

offending [ə'fendɪŋ] ADJ fautif

offense [ə'fens] N *Am* = offence

offensive [ə'fensɪv] ADJ **1** *(word, action)* blessant, offensant, choquant; *(spectacle)* choquant, repoussant; *(smell)* repoussant, nauséabond; **morally o. book** livre moralement choquant; **these remarks were o. to many people** ces remarques ont choqué de nombreuses personnes; **to be o. to sb** *(of person)* se montrer blessant envers qn; **in an o. tone** d'un ton injurieux **2** *Mil etc* offensif

N *Mil, Sport, Fig* offensive *f*, **to take the o.** prendre l'offensive; **to be on the o.** être sur l'offensive

offensively [ə'fensɪvlɪ] ADV **1** *(shockingly)* d'une manière blessante *ou* choquante; *(to say)* d'un ton injurieux **2** *Mil, Sport* offensivement

offensiveness [ə'fensɪvnɪs] N *(of sight, behaviour)* nature *f* offensante *ou* choquante; *(of smell)* nature nauséabonde; *(of remark etc)* nature injurieuse; **the o. of her tone** son ton injurieux

offer ['ɒfər] N offre *f*, proposition *f*, **I had several offers of help** plusieurs personnes m'ont proposé de m'aider; **we need somebody to help, any offers?** nous avons besoin de quelqu'un pour nous aider, est-ce qu'il y a des volontaires?; **I've had the o. of a job** on m'a fait une offre d'emploi, on m'a offert un emploi; **I've had the o. of a car for the weekend** on m'a proposé une voiture pour le week-end; *Com* **to make an o. for sth** faire une offre pour qch; *Com* **on o.** *(on sale)* en vente; **what is on o. in the negotiations?** qu'est-ce qui est proposé dans les négociations?; **£500 or nearest o.** = prix *m* à débattre autour de 500 livres; *Com* **special o.** promotion *f*, **on special o.** en promotion; **job offers** offres d'emploi; **o. of marriage** demande *f* en mariage; **to make sb an o.** faire une offre *ou* une proposition à qn; *esp Hum* **to make sb an o. they can't refuse** faire à qn une proposition à laquelle il est impossible de dire non; *St Exch* **o. by prospectus** offre publique de vente; *Fin* **o. to purchase** offre publique d'achat; *Fin* **o. for sale** mise *f* sur le marché

VT *(something, one's services)* offrir; *(excuses)* présenter; *(one's hand)* tendre; *(remark, criticism, description)* faire; *(opinion)* avancer; *(advice, chance, explanation)* donner; *(definition)* proposer; *(of scheme etc) (difficulties, advantages)* présenter; **to o. sth sth** offrir qch à qn; **he was offered a job** on lui a offert un emploi; **he offered her his car for the weekend** il lui a proposé (de lui prêter) sa voiture pour le week-end; **house offered for sale** maison mise en vente; **the conditions that we are able to o. you** les conditions que nous sommes à même de vous faire; **they're offering two weeks' skiing for £200** ils proposent deux semaines aux sports d'hiver pour 200 livres; **to o. to do sth** offrir de faire qch; **this offers a glimpse of things to come** ceci donne une petite idée de ce qui va suivre; *Law* **to o. a plea** exciper d'une excuse; **to o. resistance** offrir de la résistance

VI **if occasion offers** si une belle occasion se présente

▶▶**o. price** *St Exch* cours *m ou* prix vendeur; *Mktg* prix vendeur, prix offert

▶**offer up** VT SEP *(prayers, thanks to God)* offrir

offering ['ɒfərɪŋ] N **1** *(thing offered)* offre *f; Rel* offrande *f;* this year's offerings from Hollywood ce qu'Hollywood nous propose cette année; his latest o. is a poem entitled ... sa dernière production est un poème intitulé ...; let's hope this essay is better than your last o. espérons que cette dissertation sera meilleure que votre dernier chef-d'œuvre; and this, I believe, was your o., Smith et voici votre torchon, Smith **2** *(action)* offre *f;* the o. of thanks/congratulations les remerciements/félicitations

offertory ['ɒfət(ə)rɪ] N *Rel* **1** *(of mass)* offertoire *m* **2** *(of collection)* quête *f, (amount collected)* montant *m* de la quête

▶▶**o. box** tronc *m*

off-exchange ADJ *St Exch (transaction, contract, market)* hors Bourse, hors cote

offhand [ɒf'hænd] ADV *(immediately)* I don't know o. comme ça de but en blanc, je ne le sais pas; nonsense! o. I can think of six n'importe quoi! je peux en nommer six sur-le-champ

ADJ *(casual)* cavalier, -ière, désinvolte; *(brusque)* brusque; to be o. with sb se montrer désinvolte *ou* cavalier à l'égard de qn; to treat sb in an o. manner traiter qn cavalièrement *ou* avec désinvolture

offhanded [ɒf'hændɪd] ADJ = **offhand** ADJ

offhandedly [ɒf'hændɪdlɪ] ADV *(casually)* avec désinvolture; I didn't like the way she o. assumed that ... je n'ai pas aimé la désinvolture avec laquelle elle a supposé que ...

offhandedness [ɒf'hændɪdnɪs] N *(casualness)* désinvolture *f, (brusqueness)* brusquerie *f*

off-highway ADJ, ADV tout-terrain, hors-route

off-hook, offhook [ɒf'hʊk] ADJ

▶▶*Comput* o. signal signal *m* de réponse *ou* de décrochage

office ['ɒfɪs] N **1** bureau *m; (of solicitor)* étude *f, (of lawyer)* cabinet *m; Am (of doctor, dentist)* cabinet *(de consultation);* to work in an o., to have an o. job avoir un emploi de bureau; to stay late at the o. rester tard au bureau; the whole o. knows tout le monde le sait au bureau, tout le bureau le sait; for o. use only *(on form)* (cadre) réservé à l'administration

2 *Pol etc (position)* charge *f,* fonctions *fpl;* the o. of Prime Minister la fonction de premier ministre; high o. fonctions hautes; public o. fonction publique; to be in o., to hold o. être en fonction; *(of government, politician)* être au pouvoir; he has never held high o. il n'a jamais occupé de poste élevé; to be out of o. ne plus être au pouvoir; to take o., to come into o. entrer en fonctions; *(of government)* arriver au pouvoir; to seek o. chercher à se faire élire

3 *Fml (service)* through *or* owing to the good offices of a friend grâce aux bons offices *ou* par les bons soins d'un ami; to offer one's good offices to sb proposer ses bons offices à qn

4 *Rel* o. of the day office *m* du jour; o. for the dead office des morts; last offices *(for the dead)* derniers devoirs *mpl; (funeral)* obsèques *fpl*

5 *Fml* offices *(of a house)* communs *mpl* et dépendances *fpl*

▶▶*Fin* o. account compte *m* commercial; o. address adresse *f* au bureau; o. automation bureautique *f,* o. block immeuble *m* de bureaux; *Old-fashioned* o. boy garçon *m* de bureau; o. building immeuble de bureaux; *Br* O. of the Deputy Prime Minister = service

m du vice-Premier ministre; o. equipment matériel *m* de bureau; o. expenses frais *mpl* de bureau; the O. of Fair Trading = organisme *m* britannique de défense des consommateurs et de régulation des pratiques commerciales; o. furniture mobilier *m* de bureau; o. hours heures *fpl* de bureau; *Comput* o. IT bureautique *f,* o. manager chef *m* de bureau; *Br* O. for National Statistics ≃ INSEE *m;* o. party = réception *f* organisée dans un bureau à l'occasion des fêtes de fin d'année; o. politics = jeux *mpl* d'alliances, antipathies etc au sein d'une entreprise; o. romance liaison *f* au bureau; o. staff personnel *m* de bureau; o. work travail *m* de bureau; o. worker employé, -ée de bureau

officeholder ['ɒfɪshəʊldər] N employé, -ée de l'État, fonctionnaire *mf*

officer ['ɒfɪsər] N **1** *(official)* fonctionnaire *mf;* municipal o. officier *m* municipal; *Admin* clerical o. secrétaire *mf* d'administration; administrative o. ≃ administrateur, -trice civil(e); customs o. douanier, -ière; police o., *Am* o. agent *m ou* officier de police; *Am* O. Smith officier Smith; yes, o. oui, monsieur/madame l'agent **2** *Mil etc* officier *m; (in Salvation Army)* officier, -ière **3** high o. *(of an order)* grand dignitaire *m*

▶▶*Mil* o. of the day officier *m* de permanence

official [ə'fɪʃəl] ADJ *(statement, visit, strike etc)* officiel; *(language) (officially recognized)* officiel; *(bureaucratic)* administratif; to act in one's o. capacity agir dans l'exercice de ses fonctions; she was speaking in her o. capacity as General Secretary elle parlait en sa qualité de Secrétaire général; the o. organist le/la titulaire de l'orgue

N responsable *mf; (of government)* fonctionnaire *mf, Pej* bureaucrate *mf; (at sports meeting etc)* commissaire *mf, Am Sport (referee)* arbitre *m;* minor officials petits fonctionnaires

▶▶*Fin* o. exchange rate cours *m* officiel; o. letter pli *m* officiel *ou* de service; *St Exch* O. List cote *f* officielle; *Fin* o. market marché *m* officiel; o. opening *(of new factory, museum etc)* inauguration *f; St Exch* o. quotation cours officiel; *Banking* o. rate taux *m* officiel d'escompte; *Br* o. receiver administrateur, -trice judiciaire; *Br* o. receivership liquidation *f* judiciaire; *Sport* o. record record *m* homologué; the O. Secrets Act = loi britannique sur le secret Défense

officialdom [ə'fɪʃəldəm] N *(no pl) (officials)* administration *f, Pej (bureaucracy)* bureaucratie *f,* fonctionnarisme *m*

officialese [əfɪʃə'liːz] N *Fam* jargon *m* administratif

officially [ə'fɪʃəlɪ] ADV officiellement

officiate [ə'fɪʃɪeɪt] VI *Rel* to o. at a service officier à un office; to o. at a church desservir une église; officiating minister (pasteur *m*) officiant *m*

officious [ə'fɪʃəs] ADJ trop zélé

officiously [ə'fɪʃəslɪ] ADV avec trop de zèle; to behave o. towards sb faire l'empressé auprès de qn

offie ['ɒfɪ] N *Br Fam (abbr* off-licence) magasin *m* de vins et spiritueux

offing ['ɒfɪŋ] N in the o. en perspective, en vue; there is an election in the o. une élection est en perspective *ou* en vue; there could be some changes in the o. il se pourrait qu'il y ait des changements en perspective; there's a dispute in the o. il y a de la dispute dans l'air; Christmas is in the o. Noël se profile à l'horizon

off-key ADV *Mus* faux

ADJ **1** *Mus* he/the lead trumpet was o. il/la première trompette n'était pas dans le ton **2**

Fig (remark, comment etc) inopportun, déplacé

off-licence N *Br* **1** *(premises)* = magasin *m* de vins et spiritueux **2** *(licence)* = licence *f* permettant la vente de boissons alcoolisées à emporter

off-line ADJ *Comput* non connecté; *(processing)* en différé; *(printer)* déconnecté; to be o. ne pas être connecté; to go o. se déconnecter

▶▶o. backup sauvegarde *f* externe; *Aviat* o. connection *(changing plane with different airline)* correspondance *f* avec changement de compagnie aérienne; *TV* o. editing montage *m* 'off-line'; *TV* o. editor monteur *m* 'off-line'; o. mode mode *m* autonome; o. operation opération *f* autonome *ou* indépendante; o. reader lecteur *m* non connecté

offload [ɒf'ləʊd] VT **1** *(unload)* décharger; *(from boat)* débarquer **2** *Fig (get rid of)* fourguer *(onto* à); he offloads most of his work on(to) his colleagues il se décharge de la plus grande partie de son travail sur ses collègues; we offloaded the kids onto my parents for the weekend nous avons fourgué les gosses à mes parents pour le week-end; to o. the blame/responsibility onto sb rejeter le blâme/la responsabilité sur qn; he tried to o. the blame for these decisions on to his civil servants il a essayé de mettre ces décisions sur le dos de ses fonctionnaires

offloading [ɒf'ləʊdɪŋ] N *(unloading)* déchargement *m*

off-message ADJ qui ne respecte pas scrupuleusement la ligne du parti

off-peak ADJ *(holidays, accommodation etc)* en basse saison

▶▶*Mktg* o. buying achats *mpl* aux heures creuses; o. electricity électricité *f* consommée pendant les heures creuses; *Rail etc* o. fare = tarif *m* réduit valable en dehors des heures de pointe; o. hours heures *fpl* creuses; *Elec* o. rate tarif *m* de nuit

off-piste ADJ, ADV *Ski* hors-piste

offprint ['ɒfprɪnt] N *Phot* tirage *m* à part, tiré *m* à part

off-putting ADJ *Br Fam (person)* peu engageant; *(smell)* répugnant; *(appearance, manner, prospect)* rébarbatif; *(experience)* démoralisant

off-ramp N *(from motorway)* bretelle *f* de sortie

off-road ADJ

▶▶*Aut* o. driving conduite *f* tout-terrain; o. vehicle véhicule *m* tout-terrain

off-roader [-'rəʊdər] N *Aut* tout-terrain *m inv*

off-sales NPL *Br* = vente *f* de boissons alcoolisées à emporter

offscreen ['ɒfskriːn] *Cin* ADV **1** *(out of sight)* hors champ, off **2** o., he's really charming dans la vie de tous les jours c'est un homme tout à fait charmant

ADJ **1** *(out of sight)* hors champ, off; o. narration commentaire *m* en voix off **2** *(life)* privé; their o. relationship mirrored their love affair in the film la liaison qu'ils entretenaient dans la vie reflétait celle du film

off-season ADJ *(rate etc)* hors-saison *inv,* de basse saison; to go on an o. holiday partir en vacances hors saison *ou* en basse saison

offset ['ɒfset] N **1** *Fin (compensation)* compensation *f* **2** *Tech (of wheel)* désaxage *m,* décentrement *m,* déport *m* **3** *Typ (process)* offset *m;* printed in o. tiré en offset **4** *Bot (of plant)* rejeton *m*

VT *(pt, pp* offset; *prp* offsetting) **1** *Fin (compensate for) (losses, increasing cost etc)* compenser; to o. one thing against another compenser quelque chose par quelque

chose d'autre; **to o. losses against tax** déduire le montant de ses pertes de ses impôts **2** *Tech (wheel)* désaxer, décentrer; *(part)* déporter, décaler **3** *Typ (print) (book)* imprimer en offset
▸▸ *Fin* o. **agreement** accord *m* de compensation; *Typ* o. **lithography** lithographie *f* offset; *Typ* o. **plate** plaque *f* offset

offshoot ['ɒfʃuːt] N *(of tree)* rejeton *m*; *Fig (of family)* branche *f*, *(of language)* dérivé *m*; *(of political party, artistic movement etc)* ramification *f*

offshore ['ɒfʃɔːr] ADV *Petr (to live, drill etc)* en mer, au large
ADJ *(near coast)* côtier, -ière, littoral, -aux; *(far from coast)* éloigné de la côte; *Petr (exploration, drilling)* en mer, off-shore; *Banking, Fin* offshore
▸▸ *Banking* o. **banking** opérations *fpl* bancaires offshore; o. **company** société *f* offshore; o. **fishing** pêche *f* côtière; *Banking, Fin* o. **fund** fonds *m* offshore; *Petr* o. **installations** installations *fpl* pétrolières marines *ou* off-shore; *Banking, Fin* o. **investment** placement *m* offshore; *Petr* o. **oilfield** champ *m* (pétrolifère) en mer *ou* offshore; o. **wind** vent *m* de terre *ou* d'aval

off-shot ADJ, ADV *TV, Cin* hors plan

offside ['ɒf'saɪd] N *Aut (when driving on left)* côté *m* droit; *(when driving on right)* côté gauche
ADJ **1** *Sport* hors jeu **2** *Aut (when driving on left)* du côté droit; *(when driving on right)* du côté gauche
ADV *Sport* hors jeu
▸▸ *Sport* **the o. rule** la règle du hors-jeu

offspring ['ɒfsprɪŋ] N *(no pl) (of animal)*, *Hum (children)* progéniture *f*, **none of her o. were there** sa progéniture n'était pas là; **bring the o.** amenez votre progéniture

offstage [ɒf'steɪdʒ] *Theat* ADV *(to hear voices etc)* derrière la toile; **his life o.** *(of actor)* sa vie privée; **o., he is really charming** dans la vie de tous les jours c'est un homme tout à fait charmant
ADJ *(life)* privé; *(noises)* derrière la toile

off-street ADJ
▸▸ o. **parking** place *f* de parking *(située ailleurs que dans la rue)*

off-the-cuff ADJ *(remark, opinion)* impromptu; *(speech)* improvisé

off-the-peg, *Am* **off-the-rack** ADJ *(clothes)* de prêt-à-porter

off-the-record ADJ *(comment, briefing)* officieux; **on the understanding that it is strictly o.** à titre strictement officieux

off-the-shelf ADJ *Com (goods)* prêt à l'usage

off-the-wall ADJ *Fam* bizarroïde

off-topic ADJ *Comput* hors sujet

off-white ADJ blanc cassé *inv*
N blanc *m* cassé

OFGAS ['ɒfgæs] N *Br Formerly (abbr Office of Gas Supply)* = organisme *m* chargé de contrôler les activités des sociétés de distribution de gaz en Grande-Bretagne

Ofgem ['ɒfdʒem] N *Br (abbr Office of Gas and Electricity Markets)* = organisme *m* chargé de réglementer les secteurs de la fourniture de gaz et d'électricité en Grande-Bretagne

OFSTED ['ɒfsted] N *Br (abbr Office for Standards in Education)* = organisme *m* chargé de veiller au maintien du niveau des élèves dans l'enseignement public en Grande-Bretagne

oft [ɒft] ADV *Arch, Lit* souvent; **many a time and o.** maintes et maintes fois

oft- [ɒft] PREF *Arch, Lit* **o.-visited/-quoted** souvent visité/cité

OFTEL ['ɒftel] N *Br (abbr Office of Telecommunications)* = organisme *m* chargé de contrôler les activités des sociétés de télécommunications en Grande-Bretagne

often ['ɒf(ə)n, 'ɒft(ə)n] ADV souvent, fréquemment; **I don't see her very o. now** je ne la vois plus très souvent; **how o.?** *(how many times)* combien de fois?; *(at what intervals)* tous les combien?; **how o. have I told you!** combien de fois ne vous l'ai-je pas dit!; **I visited her as o. as I could** je lui rendais visite aussi souvent que je le pouvais; **as o. as not** assez souvent; **more o. than not** le plus souvent; **every so o.** de temps en temps, de temps à autre; **it cannot be repeated too o.** on ne saurait trop le répéter; **once too o.** une fois de trop VOIR GRAMMAIRE A21

OFWAT ['ɒfwɒt] N *Br Com (abbr Office of Water Services)* = organisme *m* chargé de contrôler les activités des sociétés de distribution d'eau en Grande-Bretagne

ogle ['əʊg(ə)l] VT lorgner, guigner, reluquer

O-grade N *Sch Formerly Scot* ≃ BEPC *m*

ogre ['əʊgər] N ogre *m*

ogress ['əʊgrɪs] N ogresse *f*

oh [əʊ] INT oh; *(expressing doubt)* ah?; **oh, what a surprise!** oh, quelle surprise!; **oh no!** oh non!; **oh yes you will!** mais si!; **oh really?** ah oui?; **oh damn!** et merde!, oh merde!, et zut!

ohc [əʊtʃ'siː] N *(abbr overhead camshaft)*
▸▸ o. **engine** moteur *m* ACT

ohm [əʊm] N *Elec* ohm *m*

OHMS [əʊəʊɪtʃem'es] *Br (abbr On His/Her Majesty's Service)* = tampon *m* apposé sur le courrier administratif britannique

oho [əʊ'həʊ] INT *(expressing triumph)* ah ah!

OHP [əʊeɪtʃ'piː] N *(abbr overhead projector)* rétroprojecteur *m*

oi [ɔɪ] INT *Fam* hé!

OID [əʊaɪ'diː] N *Fin (abbr original issue discount bond)* obligation *f* à prime d'émission

oik [ɔɪk] N *Br Sl* prolo *mf*

oil [ɔɪl] N **1** *(in general)* huile *f*, **to cook sth in oil** (faire) cuire qch à l'huile; **fried in o.** frit à l'huile; **to paint in oils** peindre à l'huile; *Fig* **to pour o. on troubled waters** apaiser les esprits **2** *Ind (petroleum)* pétrole *m*; *(for lubricating etc)* huile *f* (de graissage); *Aut* huile; *Aut* **to check the o.** vérifier le niveau d'huile; *StExch* o. **shares** valeurs *fpl* pétrolières **3** *essential* o. essence *f*, huile *f* essentielle
VT *(machine)* huiler, graisser, lubrifier; **to o. one's skin** s'enduire la peau d'huile; **to o. the wheels** graisser les roues; *Fig* faciliter les choses
▸▸ o. **cake** tourteau *m* (pour bétail); o. **change** vidange *f*, **to have an o. change** faire faire la vidange; o. **company** compagnie *f* pétrolière; o. **cooling** refroidissement *m* par huile; o. **crisis** choc *m* pétrolier; o. **drain hole** orifice *m* d'écoulement d'huile; o. **drain plug** bouchon *m* de vidange; o. **drum** bidon *m* à pétrole; o. **filter** filtre *m* à huile; o. **gauge** *(for measuring level)* jauge *f* ou indicateur *m* de niveau d'huile; *(for measuring pressure)* indicateur de pression d'huile; o. **gland** glande *f* uropygienne; o. **heating** chauffage *m* au mazout; o. **industry** industrie *f* pétrolière; o. **lamp** *(burning oil)* lampe *f* à huile; *(burning paraffin)* lampe à pétrole; o. **paint** peinture *f* à l'huile *(substance)*; o. **painting** peinture à l'huile; o. **pressure** pression *f* d'huile; o. **prices** prix *mpl* pétroliers; o. **pump** pompe *f* à huile; o. **refinery** raffinerie *f* de pétrole; o. **rig** *(onshore)* derrick *m*; *(offshore)* plate-forme *f* pétrolière, *pl* plates-formes pétrolières; *Fin* o. **royalty** redevance *f* pétrolière; o. **seal** joint *m* d'huile; o. **slick** *(on sea)* nappe *f* de pétrole; *(on beach)* ma-

rée *f* noire; o. **sump** carter *m* d'huile; o. **tanker** *(ship)* pétrolier *m*, tanker *m*; *(lorry)* camion-citerne *m*, *pl* camions-citernes *(pour l'essence)*; o. **temperature gauge** indicateur de température d'huile; o. **well** puits *m* de pétrole

oil-bearing ADJ *Geol* pétrolifère

oilcan ['ɔɪlkæn] N *(for applying oil)* burette *f*, *(large container)* bidon *m* à huile

oilcloth ['ɔɪlklɒθ] N toile *f* cirée

oil-cooled [-kuːld] ADJ refroidi par huile

oiled [ɔɪld] ADJ huilé; *Fig Fam* **to be well o.** *(drunk)* être soûl; **to get well o.** se soûler
▸▸ o. **silk** taffetas *m* imperméable

oiler ['ɔɪlər] N *Naut (tanker)* pétrolier *m*

oilfield ['ɔɪlfiːld] N gisement *m* ou champ *m* pétrolifère

oil-fired [-faɪəd] ADJ
▸▸ o. **central heating** chauffage *m* central au mazout

oiliness ['ɔɪlɪnɪs] N **1** *(of clothes, rags etc)* aspect *m* graisseux; *(of dish, sauce)* caractère *m* huileux **2** *Pej (of person)* onctuosité *f*

oilpaper ['ɔɪlpeɪpər] N papier huilé

oil-producing ADJ **1** *(shale etc)* pétrolifère; *(country)* producteur, -trice de pétrole **2** *(plant)* oléifère; *(substance etc)* oléifiant

oilrich ['ɔɪlrɪtʃ] ADJ *(countries)* enrichi par le pétrole

oilskin ['ɔɪlskɪn] N *(fabric)* toile *f* cirée; *(garment)* ciré *m*

oilstone ['ɔɪlstəʊn] N *(for sharpening)* pierre *f* à huile

oily ['ɔɪlɪ] ADJ **1** *(hands, rag)* graisseux; *(food)* huileux **2** *Pej (manner etc)* onctueux; *(voice)* gras, *f* grasse

oink [ɔɪŋk] VI *(of pig)* grogner
N *(of pig)* grognement *m*

ointment ['ɔɪntmənt] N onguent *m*, pommade *f*

OK, okay ['əʊ'keɪ] *Fam* INT OK! OK!, bon!, d'accord!; OK? OK?, d'accord?; **OK, if I could have your attention for a moment ...** bon, si je pouvais avoir votre attention pour un instant ...; **OK, it wasn't a great movie but I've seen worse** bon, d'accord, ce n'était pas un film super mais j'ai vu pire
ADJ **1** *(in order, fine)* correct, exact; **everything's OK** tout est en règle *ou* OK; **to be OK** *(unhurt)* aller bien; **are you OK?, did I hurt you/are you upset?** ça va?, je ne t'ai pas fait mal/tu es fâché?; **I'll be OK when I get home** ça ira une fois que je serai à la maison; **but is the car OK?** mais est-ce que la voiture n'a rien?; **that's OK by** *or* **with me** d'accord!; **is that OK by** *or* **with your mother** est-ce que ta mère est d'accord?; **is it OK to bring my friend?** est-ce que ça vous dérange si je viens avec mon ami?; **no, it is not OK** pas question; **clothes like that are OK for a party** des vêtements comme ça, ça va bien pour aller à une soirée
2 *(acceptable) (meal, film etc)* pas mal; *(candidate, singer etc)* pas mauvais, pas mal; **how are things? – OK** comment ça va? – ça peut aller; **the meal/her performance was more than OK** le repas/sa prestation était au-dessus de la moyenne; **was I OK?** comment j'étais?; **an OK computer** un ordinateur pas mal
3 *(understanding)* **she was OK about it** elle n'a pas fait d'histoires; **are you sure he'll be OK about letting us use the car?** tu es sûr qu'il ne fera pas d'histoires pour nous laisser la voiture?
4 *(likeable etc) (person)* **he's an OK sort of guy** c'est un type plutôt bien; **she's OK but ...** elle est assez sympa mais ...
5 to be OK for work/money *(have enough of)* avoir assez de travail/d'argent; **is every-**

ness, war) début *m*, commencement *m*; **the o. of a disease** la première attaque d'une maladie **2** *(attack)* assaut *m*, attaque *f*

onshore ['ɒnʃɔːr] ADJ **1** *(wind etc)* du large **2** *(oil rig etc)* à terre

on-site ADJ, ADV *(supervision, maintenance)* sur site

onslaught ['ɒnslɔːt] N assaut *m*, attaque *f*; *(of policies etc)* attaque

on switch N bouton *m* de marche

Ont *abbr* Ontario

on-target earnings NPL *Com* salaire *m* de base plus commissions

on-the-job ADJ *(training, experience)* sur le tas

on-the-spot fine N amende *f* immédiate

onto ['ɒntʊ, *unstressed* 'ɒntə] PREP = **on to**, *see* **on**

ontological [ɒntə'lɒdʒɪk(ə)l] ADJ *Phil* ontologique

ontology [ɒn'tɒlədʒɪ] N *Phil* ontologie *f*

onus ['əʊnəs] N responsabilité *f*, obligation *f*; **the o. is on the government to compensate the victims** il incombe au gouvernement d'indemniser les sinistrés; **the o. is now on United to attack** United se doit maintenant d'attaquer; **the o. is on you to lodge a complaint** il tient à toi de déposer une plainte; *Law* **o. of proof** charge *f* de la preuve; **the o. of proof lies with you** c'est à vous qu'il incombe d'en apporter la preuve

onward ['ɒnwəd] ADV = **onwards**

ADJ *(motion etc)* en avant; **we wish you a pleasant o. journey** nous vous souhaitons une bonne continuation pour votre voyage
▶ ▶ **o. connection** correspondance *f*; **o. flight** correspondance

onwards ['ɒnwədz] ADV en avant, plus loin; **from tomorrow/then o.** à partir de demain/de ce moment-là; **from this time o.** désormais, dorénavant

onyx ['ɒnɪks] N *Miner* onyx *m*

oodles ['uːd(ə)lz] NPL *Fam* **there's o. of it** il y en a un tas *ou* des tas *ou* une tapée; **to have o. of money** avoir un paquet *ou* une tonne de fric; **o. of cream** des tonnes de crème; **o. of time/space** plein de temps/d'espace

ooh [uː] INT *(expressing surprise, awe, pleasure)* oh!

oolite ['əʊəlaɪt] N *(rock)* oolithe *m*

oomph [ʊmf] N *Fam* **1** *(energy)* énergie *f*; **to have plenty of o.** *(person)* avoir la pêche, avoir du punch; *(song, plot etc)* avoir du punch; **their new album lacks the o. of the last one** leur nouvel album n'a pas la pêche du précédent **2** *(sex appeal)* sex-appeal *m*

oops [uːps] INT **1** *(to child who has fallen down)* houp-là! **2** *(after sb has made a mistake)* oh là là!

oops-a-daisy INT = **oops**

ooze [uːz] N **1** *(mud)* vase *f*, limon *m* **2** *(flow) (of liquid)* suintement *m*

VI suinter (**from** de); **the wound was oozing with pus/blood** du pus/sang suintait de la plaie; **water that oozes out from the rock** eau qui sourd du rocher; **the walls were oozing with water** les murs suintaient, l'eau suintait des murs; **the mud oozed up between her toes** la boue sourdait lentement entre ses orteils; *Fig* **to o. with confidence** déborder d'assurance

VT **the wound was oozing pus/blood** du pus/sang suintait de la plaie; *Fig* **to o. confidence** déborder d'assurance; **to o. charm** déborder de charme; *Fig* **this place just oozes wealth** cet endroit sue l'opulence

op[1] [ɒp] N *Surg, Mil Fam (abbr* **operation**) opération *f*

op[2] ADJ *Art* **op art** op art *m*

opacity [əʊ'pæsɪtɪ] N opacité *f*; *Fig (of writing etc)* caractère *m* obscur, obscurité *f*

opal ['əʊp(ə)l] N **1** *(mineral)* opale *f*; **o. necklace** collier *m* d'opale **2** *(colour)* opale *m inv* **3** *(glass)* verre *f* opale, opaline *f*
▶ ▶ **o. glass** verre opale, opaline

opalescence [əʊpə'lesəns] N opalescence *f*

opalescent [əʊpə'lesənt] ADJ opalescent; *(hue)* opale *inv; (haze etc)* opalisé

opaline ['əʊpəlaɪn] ADJ opalin
N *(glass)* opaline *f*

opaque [əʊ'peɪk] ADJ **1** opaque; **to become o.** s'opacifier **2** *Fig (words, comments, style)* obscur

opaqueness [əʊ'peɪknɪs] N = **opacity**

OPEC ['əʊpek] N *(abbr* **Organization of Petroleum-Exporting Countries**) OPEP *f*; **O. countries/prices** *mpl/pl* de l'OPEP

op-ed ['ɒped] N *Journ (in newspaper)* page *f* face éditoriale; **an o. piece** un article d'opinion *(situé sur la page faisant face à l'éditorial)*

OPEIC [əʊpiːiːaɪ'siː] N *Fin (abbr* **open-ended investment company**) SICAV *f*, société *f* d'investissement à capital variable

OPEN ['əʊp(ə)n]

ADJ	ouvert **1, 3–5, 7** ▪ découvert **2**
	▪ franc **3** ▪ libre **5** ▪ non résolu **6**
VT	ouvrir **1** ▪ déboucher **1**
	▪ commencer **3** ▪ engager **3**
VI	s'ouvrir **1, 3, 4** ▪ ouvrir **2**
	▪ commencer **4**

ADJ **1** *(box, door, book, shop etc)* ouvert; *Fig* **my door is always o.** ma porte t'est/vous est/*etc* toujours ouverte; **half o.** *(door, window)* entrebâillé, entrebâillé; **o. to the public** *(museum etc)* ouvert *ou* accessible au public; **o. late** ouvert en nocturne; *Law* **in o. court** en plein tribunal; **career o. to very few** carrière accessible à très peu de gens *ou* très fermée **2** *(not enclosed)* découvert, non couvert; *(coast, position)* exposé (**to** à); **o. country** *(not offering protection)* terrain *m* découvert; **in (the) o. country** *(not wooded)* en pleine *ou* rase campagne; **in the o.** *countryside* en pleine campagne, en rase campagne; **there's a lot of o. countryside** c'est la pleine campagne; **to work in the o. fields** travailler dans les champs; **in the o. air** au grand air, à ciel ouvert; **to sleep in the o. air** coucher à la belle étoile; **the o. sea** la haute mer, le large; **the city was designed with lots of o. spaces** la ville a été conçue de manière très aérée; **the wide o. spaces** les grands espaces; **o. view** vue *f* dégagée; **o. to the elements/to the winds** exposé aux intempéries/aux quatre vents; **o. to doubt** douteux; **o. to ridicule** qui prête au ridicule; **o. to criticism** critiquable; **o. to question** contestable; **she is still o. to persuasion on the issue** on peut encore lui faire changer d'avis sur la question; **the Government has left itself o. to the criticism that …** le gouvernement a prêté le flanc à la critique de …; **o. to any reasonable offer** disposé à considérer toute offre raisonnable; **to be o. to suggestions** être ouvert à toute suggestion; *Ftbl* **to leave the goal o.** dégarnir ses buts **3** *(frank) (person, personality)* ouvert, franc, *f* franche; *(conflict, disagreement)* ouvert; *(preference, favouritism)* manifeste, public, *f* -ique; **to be o. in one's affection** témoigner ouvertement son affection; **to be o. with sb** parler franchement à qn, être franc avec qn; **he is o. about his homosexuality** il ne cache pas son homosexualité; **her o. dislike** son aversion déclarée; **they are in o. revolt** ils sont en révolte ouverte

4 *(flower, lips, hand)* ouvert; **o. at the neck** *(of dress)* échancré; **his shirt was o. at the neck** le col de sa chemise était ouvert; **with eyes o. wide** les yeux écarquillés; **to welcome with o. arms** *(person)* accueillir à bras ouverts; *(proposal, development etc)* accueillir avec enthousiasme

5 *(clear, unobstructed)* libre, non obstrué; **road o. to traffic** route ouverte à la circulation; **to keep one's bowels o.** aller à la selle régulièrement; *(of diet)* faciliter le transit intestinal; **to keep a day o. for sb** réserver un jour pour qn; **the job is still o.** la place est toujours vacante; **membership o. to anyone over 18** inscription ouverte à toute personne de plus de 18 ans; **two courses/choices are o. to us** deux moyens/choix s'offrent à nous; **an o. border** une frontière ouverte

6 *(unresolved)* non résolu; *(question, case)* pendant; **to keep an o. mind on sth** réserver son opinion sur qch; **to leave the matter o.** ne pas prendre de décision *ou* ne pas trancher sur la question; **I want to leave the return date o.** *(on ticket)* je ne veux pas réserver le retour tout de suite

7 *Sport (play) (free-flowing)* ouvert, dégagé

N **1 in the o.** *(outdoors)* dehors; *(to go for a stroll, work etc)* au grand air, dehors; *(not hidden)* au grand jour; **to sleep in the o.** dormir à la belle étoile; *Fig* **to bring sth out into the o.** mettre qch au grand jour; **their mutual dislike was out in the o.** ils affichaient ouvertement l'antipathie qu'ils avaient l'un pour l'autre; *Fig* **let's get all this out in the o.** jouons cartes sur table; **to come out into the o. about sth** révéler qch

2 *Sport* open *m*

ADV **to fling the door wide o.** ouvrir la porte toute grande; **the door flew o.** la porte s'ouvrit brusquement; **to cut o.** couper, ouvrir; **to force sth o.** forcer qch; **to smash/lever sth o.** ouvrir qch en le fracassant/à l'aide d'un levier

VT **1** *(door, book, parcel, hand, eyes etc)* ouvrir; *(bottle)* ouvrir, déboucher; *(letter)* ouvrir, décacheter; *(post)* ouvrir, dépouiller; *(institution, establishment)* inaugurer; *(legs etc)* écarter; **to o. the door wide** ouvrir la porte toute grande; *Med* **to o. the bowels** aller à la selle; **to o. one's shop** *(in morning etc)* ouvrir son magasin; **to o. a new shop** *ou* monter un nouveau magasin; **to o. a park to the public/a road (to traffic)** ouvrir un parc au public/une route à la circulation; **to o. one's heart** ouvrir son cœur, s'ouvrir (**to sb** à qn); **that opens new prospects for me** cela m'ouvre de nouveaux horizons; **to o. Parliament** ouvrir la session du Parlement **2** *(make) (tunnel)* creuser; *(hole)* faire **3** *(begin)* commencer; *(negotiations, conversation, debate)* entamer, engager; *(performance)* ouvrir; *(fire, hostilities)* ouvrir; **to o. an account in sb's name** ouvrir un compte à qn; **to o. a line of credit** ouvrir un crédit; *Law* **to o. the case** exposer les faits

VI **1** s'ouvrir; **to half o.** *(of door etc)* s'entrebâiller, s'entrouvrir; **door that opens into the garden** porte qui donne sur le jardin; **o. wide!** *(said by doctor, dentist etc)* ouvrez grand la bouche! **2** *(of shop, museum)* ouvrir; **to o. late** *(of shop)* ouvrir en nocturne; **as soon as the season opens** dès l'ouverture de la saison **3** *(of view, prospects)* s'étendre; *(of flower)* s'épanouir, s'ouvrir **4** *(begin)* commencer; **the play opens with a death scene** la pièce s'ouvre sur une scène de mort; *Cin* **the film opens next week** le film sort la semaine prochaine; *St Exch* **the FTSE opened at 1083** l'indice FT a ouvert à 1083
▶ ▶ *Banking* **o. account** compte *m* ouvert; **o. carriage** voiture *f* découverte; *Golf, Tennis* **o.**

championship championnat *m* open *inv ou* ouvert; *Banking* **o. cheque** chèque *m* ouvert *ou* non barré; *St Exch* **o. contract** position *f* ouverte; *Fin* **o. credit** crédit *m* à découvert; **o. enemy** ennemi *m* déclaré; **o. hostilities** guerre *f* ouverte; **o. inquiry** enquête *f* publique; **o. invitation** invitation *f* permanente; **it's an o. invitation to tax-dodgers/thieves** c'est une invitation à la fraude fiscale/aux voleurs; **o. letter** lettre *f* ouverte; **o. market** marché *m* libre; *St Exch* **o. outcry system** système *m* de criée; *St Exch* **o. position** position ouverte; **o. prison** prison *f* ouverte; **o. sandwich** tartine *f*; *Br* **o. season** saison *f*; *Br* **o. secret** secret *m* de Polichinelle; *Ind* **o. shop** *Br (open to non-union members)* = entreprise *f* ne pratiquant pas le monopole d'embauche; *Am (with no union)* établissement *m* sans syndicat; **o. side** *(in rugby)* grand côté *m*, côté ouvert; **o. space** *(park)* espace *m* vert; *Mus* **o. string** corde *f* à vide; **o. ticket** billet *m* open; *Sport* **o. tournament** *(tournoi m)* open *m*; *Br* **O. University** = enseignement *m* universitaire par correspondance doublé d'émissions de télévision ou de radio; *Law* **o. verdict** verdict *m* de décès sans cause déterminée; *Ling* **o. vowel** voyelle ouverte; **o. wound** *(gaping)* plaie *f* béante; *(not healed)* plaie non cicatrisée

▸ **open out** VI **1** *(of flower)* s'ouvrir; *(of wings)* se déployer; *(of view, prospects)* s'ouvrir, s'étendre

2 *(become wider)* s'élargir *(**into** pour donner dans)*

3 *Fig (of person)* s'ouvrir

VT SEP **1** *(unfold) (sheet of paper, map)* ouvrir, déplier

2 *(develop) (company)* développer

3 *(widen) (hole)* élargir, agrandir; *(mouth of pipe)* évaser

▸ **open up** VI **1** *(of flower)* s'ouvrir

2 *(of view, prospects)* s'ouvrir, s'étendre; **new markets are opening up** de nouveaux marchés sont en train de s'ouvrir

3 *(of shopkeeper etc)* ouvrir; **this is the police, o. up!** police! ouvrez!

4 *(of new shop etc)* ouvrir

5 *Fig (of person)* s'ouvrir *(**to sb** à qn)*

6 *Mil* ouvrir le feu

VT SEP **1** *(letter, parcel, box, newspaper)* ouvrir

2 *(make accessible) (a country to trade, mine)* ouvrir; *(path)* ouvrir, frayer, rendre praticable; **this remote area is being opened up for development** cette région reculée commence à être exploitée

3 *(possibility of something)* ouvrir; **to o. up opportunities** donner des chances

4 *(start)* **to o. up a business, to o. up shop** ouvrir *ou* monter une affaire

open-air ADJ *(restaurant, market, cinema, life etc)* en plein air; *(swimming pool)* découvert

open-and-shut ADJ **it was an o. case** tout était clair comme de l'eau de roche; **this may not be such an o. case as it first appears** ce n'est peut-être pas aussi simple que cela paraît au premier abord

opencast ['əʊpənkɑːst] ADJ *Br (mining)* à ciel ouvert, au jour

open-date ticket N billet *m* open *inv ou* ouvert

open-door ADJ

▸▸ **o. policy** *(for immigrants)* politique *f* d'ouverture des frontières; *(of university etc)* politique d'ouverture

open-ended [-'endɪd] ADJ *(credit, contract)* à durée indéterminée; *(question)* ouvert; **it's a bit too o.** c'est un peu trop vague; **can we leave it o. for the time being?** est-ce nous pouvons ne pas tout fixer tout de suite?; **avoid o. commitments** évite de t'engager sans fixer de limites; **o. discussion** libre discussion *f*; **could we keep the arrangement o.?** pourrions-nous garder une certaine flexibilité au niveau de notre arrangement?

▸▸ *Fin* **o. investment company, o. investment trust** SICAV *f*, société *f* d'investissement à capital variable; **o. spanner** clé *f* ouverte

opener ['əʊpənər] N **1** *Theat (item on programme)* premier numéro *m*; *Fam* **for openers** pour commencer **2** *(device) (bottle)* **o.** décapsuleur *m*; *(can or tin)* **o.** ouvre-boîtes *m inv* **3** *Cr* premier batteur *m*

open-eyed ADJ qui a les yeux ouverts; **to look at sb in o. astonishment** regarder qn les yeux écarquillés de surprise

open-handed [-'hændɪd] ADJ généreux; **to be o.** être généreux, avoir la main sur le cœur

open-heart ADJ *(surgery)* à cœur ouvert

open-hearted [-'hɑːtɪd] ADJ *(kind)* charitable

open-hearth ADJ

▸▸ *Metal* **o. furnace** four *m* Martin

opening ['əʊpənɪŋ] N **1** *(of door, shop, account, one's heart etc)* ouverture *f*; **formal o.** inauguration *f*; **the o. of Parliament** l'ouverture du Parlement; *Com* **late o. Friday** ≃ nocturne le vendredi **2** *(beginning) (of play, new era)* commencement *m*, début *m*; *(of negotiations)* ouverture *f*; *(start of letter)* formule *f* de début; *Law (speech by lawyer)* exposition *f* des faits **3** *(open space) (in wall)* ouverture *f*, trou *m*; *(for door, window)* embrasure *f*, baie *f*; *(in forest)* clairière *f*, *(manmade also)* percée *f*; *(between the trees)* échappée *f* **4** *(mouth, entrance) (of cave, tunnel)* entrée *f*, *(of sack)* ouverture *f* **5** *(opportunity)* occasion *f* favorable; *(job)* poste *m*, place *f* (**as** de); *Com (for goods)* débouché *m*; **we have exploited an o. in the market** nous avons exploité une ouverture sur le marché; **this could be your big o.** ça pourrait être la chance de ta vie

ADJ **o. address** *or* **speech** discours *m* d'ouverture; *Theat* **the o. lines** les premières lignes; *Cin, Theat* **the o. scene** la scène d'ouverture

▸▸ *Acct* **o. balance** solde *m* d'ouverture; *Acct* **o. balance sheet** bilan *m* d'ouverture; *Cr* **o. batsman** premier batteur *m*; *Cards* **o. bid** annonce *f* d'entrée *ou* d'indication; **o. bracket** parenthèse *f* ouvrante; **o. ceremony** cérémonie *f* d'inauguration; *Cin, TV* **o. credits** générique *m* de début; *St Exch* **o. day** jour *m* d'ouverture; *Acct* **o. entry** écriture *f* d'ouverture; *Com* **o. hours** heures *fpl* d'ouverture; *Theat* **o. night** première *f*; *St Exch* **o. price** *(at start of trading)* cours *m* d'ouverture, premier cours; *(of new shares)* cours d'introduction; **o. quotation marks** guillemets *mpl* ouvrants; *Fin* **o. session** séance *f* d'ouverture; *Fin* **o. stock** stock *m* initial *ou* d'ouverture; *Com* **o. time** heure *f* d'ouverture; *Cin* **o. weekend** premier week-end *m* d'exploitation

openly ['əʊpənlɪ] ADV ouvertement; *(publicly)* publiquement; *(in front of everyone)* au vu (et au su) de tous; *(to speak)* sans réticence; **to be o. critical of sb** critiquer qn ouvertement; **to act o.** agir à découvert *ou* cartes sur table, jouer franc jeu

open-minded ADJ qui a l'esprit ouvert; **to be o. on** *or* **about sth** ne pas avoir de parti pris *ou* d'idée préconçue sur qch; **her parents are very o.** ses parents sont des gens très ouverts

open-mouthed [-'maʊðd] ADJ **to stand o.** *or* **in o. astonishment** rester bouche bée

openness ['əʊpənnɪs] N **1** *(frankness)* franchise *f*; **I was surprised by the o. with which they expressed their criticism** cela m'a sur-

pris qu'ils expriment leurs critiques aussi ouvertement **2** *(of mind)* largeur *f*, ouverture *f* **3** *(of coastline etc)* situation *f* exposée; *(of terrain)* aspect *m* découvert; **the o. of the countryside** les grands horizons

open-plan ADJ *(office)* paysager; *(flat)* sans cloison; **we've gone o.** nous avons maintenant un bureau paysager

open-top ADJ décapotable

open-topped bus N autobus *m* à impériale

openwork ['əʊpənwɜːk] N *(piece of embroidery)* ouvrage *m* ajouré *ou* à jour; *(holes)* jours *mpl*, ajours *mpl*

▸▸ **o. stockings** bas *mpl* ajourés *ou* à jour

opera ['ɒp(ə)rə] N opéra *m*; *(company)* (compagnie *f* d')opéra; **comic o.** opéra bouffe *ou* comique

▸▸ **o. bouffe** opéra bouffe *ou* comique; **o. glasses** jumelles *fpl* de théâtre; **o. goer** amateur *m* d'opéra; **o. house** opéra *m*; **o. singer** chanteur, -euse d'opéra

operable ['ɒp(ə)rəb(ə)l] ADJ **1** *Surg (disease, tumour)* opérable **2** *(system etc)* utilisable

operand ['ɒpərænd] N opérande *m*

operate ['ɒpəreɪt] VI **1** *(of machine)* fonctionner; *(of burglar, company etc)* opérer, travailler; **the wage increase will o. from the first of January** l'augmentation des salaires prendra effet à partir du premier janvier **2** *Surg* opérer; **to o. (on sb) for appendicitis** opérer (qn) de l'appendicite; **to be operated on** subir une opération *ou* une intervention chirurgicale, se faire opérer

VT **1** *(of person) (machine)* manœuvrer; *(brakes)* actionner; *(of part of machine)* commander, actionner; **operated by electricity** actionné par l'électricité **2** *Com (rail or bus service, business)* exploiter

operatic [ɒpə'rætɪk] ADJ d'opéra

NPL **operatics** *(amateur)* opéra *m* d'amateurs

▸▸ **o. society** groupe *m* d'opéra d'amateurs

operating ['ɒpəreɪtɪŋ] ADJ ATTRIB

▸▸ *Am Fin* **o. account** compte *m* d'exploitation; *Acct* **o. assets** actif *m* d'exploitation; *Acct* **o. budget** budget *m* d'exploitation, budget *m* de fonctionnement; *Am* **o. capital** capital *m* d'exploitation, capital de roulement; *Acct* **o. cash flow** cash-flow *m* disponible, *pl* cash-flows disponibles; **o. cost** charge *f* opérationnelle; *Acct* **o. costs** frais *mpl ou* coûts *mpl* d'exploitation; *Fin* **o. deficit** déficit *m* d'exploitation; *Acct* **o. expenses** frais d'exploitation; **o. income** produits *mpl* d'exploitation; **o. instructions** mode *m* d'emploi; *Fin* **o. leverage** levier *m* d'exploitation; *Acct, Fin* **o. loss** perte *f* d'exploitation; *Acct, Fin* **o. margin** marge *f* (nette) d'exploitation; *Acct, Fin* **o. profit** bénéfice *m* d'exploitation; *Acct* **o. ratio** coefficient *m ou* ratio *m* d'exploitation; *Am* **o. room** salle *f* d'opération, bloc *m* opératoire; *Comput* **o. speed** vitesse *f* d'exécution; *Fin* **o. statement** compte *ou* rapport *m* d'exploitation; *Comput* **o. system** système *m* d'exploitation; *Comput* **o. system command** commande *f* du système d'exploitation; **o. table** table *f* d'opération; *Br* **o. theatre** salle d'opération, bloc opératoire

operation [ɒpə'reɪʃən] N **1** *(functioning) (of appliance, machine)* fonctionnement *m*, marche *f*; *(of mechanism)* jeu *m*; **in o.** *(machine)* en marche, en fonctionnement; *(law)* en application, en vigueur; **to come into o.** *(of machine)* commencer à fonctionner; *(of law)* entrer en application *ou* en vigueur; *(of curfew, rationing)* être imposé **2** *(controlling) (of machine etc)* manœuvre *f*, commande *f*; *(of reactor, ship, transport system, business)* exploitation *f*

3 *(process)* opération *f*, *(element) (of manu-*

facture etc) unité f; **it's a tricky o.** c'est une opération délicate; **(mathematical) o.** opération (mathématique); *Comput* **(computer) o.** opération (machine); **a firm's operations** les activités fpl d'une entreprise; **the company is moving its soft drinks o.** la société déménage sa branche de boissons non alcoolisées

4 *Mil etc* opération f; **O. Snow** opération Neige

5 *Surg* opération f, intervention f (chirurgicale); **an o. to have one's appendix out** une opération de l'appendicite; **to perform an o. on sb** opérer qn (**for** de); **to undergo** or **have an o.** se faire opérer, subir une opération ou une intervention chirurgicale (**for** de); **a throat o.** une opération de la gorge

▸▸**operations manager** directeur, -trice des exploitations; **operations research** recherche f opérationnelle; **operations room** salle f d'opérations (d'un état-major)

operational [ɒpə'reɪʃən(ə)l] ADJ **1** *Mil etc* opérationnel **2** *(machine)* opérationnel, en état de marche ou de fonctionnement; **the new power station should be o. next year** la nouvelle centrale électrique devrait être opérationnelle l'an prochain **3** *Com (costs, requirements)* d'exploitation

▸▸*Acct* **o. audit** audit m opérationnel; *Acct* **o. cost accounting** comptabilité f analytique d'exploitation; *Acct* **o. cost centre** centre m d'analyse opérationnel; **o. marketing** marketing m opérationnel; *Com* **o. planning** planification f des opérations; *Mktg* **o. research** recherche f opérationnelle; *Mil* **o. training** instruction f tactique, entraînement m au combat

operative ['ɒpərətɪv] ADJ **1** *(law, rule etc)* en vigueur; **to become o.** *(of law)* entrer en vigueur, prendre effet; **the o. word** le mot clé **2** *Surg (method)* opératoire

N **1** *(worker)* ouvrier, -ière; *(of machine etc)* opérateur, -trice **2** *Am (detective)* détective m **3** *(secret agent)* agent m secret

operator ['ɒpəreɪtər] N **1** *(person) (of machine)* opérateur, -trice; *(of business)* exploitant, -ante; **the o. of the service, British Airways …** la compagnie qui assure le service, British Airways …; **(tour) o.** tour opérateur m, voyagiste m; *Fam* **he's a pretty slick o.** c'est un petit débrouillard, il se débrouille plutôt bien; **he's a pretty quick o.** il va vite en besogne **2** *Tel* téléphoniste mf, *Com (in hotel etc)* standardiste mf; **radio** or **wireless o.** (opérateur, -trice de) radio m; *Tel* **switchboard o.** standardiste **3** *Math (of logarithm, logical)* opérateur m **4** *St Exch* opérateur m

operetta [ɒpə'retə] N *Mus* opérette f

ophthalmic [ɒf'θælmɪk] ADJ *(nerve, complaint)* ophtalmique; *(hospital)* ophtalmologique

▸▸**o. optician** opticien, -ienne (optométriste)

ophthalmologist [ɒfθæl'mɒlədʒɪst] N *Med* ophtalmologiste mf, ophtalmologue mf

ophthalmology [ɒfθæl'mɒlədʒɪ] N *Med* ophtalmologie f

opiate ['əʊpɪɪt] N *Pharm* opiacé m; *Fig Pej* **the o. of television** la télévision, cette drogue abrutissante

opine [əʊ'paɪn] VT *Am Old-fashioned, Lit (be of opinion)* être d'avis (**that** que + *sub*); *(state opinion)* exprimer l'avis (**that** que + *ind*)

opinion [ə'pɪnjən] N opinion f; **in my o.** à mon avis, à mon sens; **in the o. of experts** de l'avis ou au dire des experts, suivant ou selon l'opinion des experts; **to be of the o. that …** être d'avis ou estimer que …; **to be of the same o. as sb** être du même avis que qn, avoir la même opinion que qn; **to have a high/low o. of sb** avoir une bonne/mauvaise opinion

de qn; **to express** or **put forward an o.** exprimer une opinion; **to ask sb's o.** demander l'avis de qn, consulter qn; **I'd like your o.** j'aimerais avoir ton opinion ou savoir ce que tu en penses; **that's my o., for what it's worth** c'est mon humble avis; **to form an o. of sb/sth** se faire une opinion sur ou de qn/qch; **I have no strong opinion(s) on the matter** je n'ai pas d'opinion très arrêtée sur la question; **what is your o. of him/on the situation?** que pensez-vous de lui/de la situation?; **opinions differ** les avis sont partagés; **o. is divided on the subject** les avis divergent sur le sujet; **that's a matter of o.** chacun ses opinions; **it's a matter of o.** c'est discutable; **it is the o. of the court that …** la cour est d'avis que …; **you ought to have a second o.** *Med* vous devriez consulter un autre médecin; *(generally)* vous devriez consulter quelqu'un d'autre

▸▸*Mktg* **o. former,** or **o. leader** leader m d'opinion; *Mktg* **o. measurement** sondage m d'opinion; *Mktg* **o. measurement technique** technique f de sondage d'opinion; *Mktg* **o. poll** sondage (d'opinion), enquête f (d'opinion); *Mktg* **o. pollster** sondeur, -euse (d'opinion); *Mktg* **o. survey** sondage d'opinion (publique), enquête (d'opinion)

opinionated [ə'pɪnjəneɪtɪd] ADJ *Pej (tone)* dogmatique; *(person)* qui a des idées très arrêtées; **he can be quite o. on the subject** il a des idées très arrêtées sur le sujet

opium ['əʊpɪəm] N opium m

▸▸**o. addict** opiomane mf; **o. den** fumerie f d'opium; **o. poppy** pavot m (somnifère)

Oporto [ə'pɔːtəʊ] N Porto

opossum [ə'pɒsəm] N *(animal)* opossum m

opp *(abbr* **opposite)** en face

opponent [ə'pəʊnənt] N *(of reform, deregulation, in argument, match)* adversaire mf; *(of government)* opposant, -ante (**of** à)

opportune ['ɒpətjuːn] ADJ *(time)* opportun; *(action)* à propos; **you have come at an o. moment** vous arrivez à propos, vous tombez bien

opportunely [ɒpə'tjuːnlɪ] ADV opportunément; *(to arrive)* opportunément, en temps opportun

opportunism [ɒpə'tjuːnɪz(ə)m] N opportunisme m

opportunist [ɒpə'tjuːnɪst] ADJ, N opportuniste mf

opportunistic [ɒpətjuː'nɪstɪk] ADJ *(person, policy, disease)* opportuniste

opportunity [ɒpə'tjuːnɪtɪ] N occasion f **(for** or **of doing sth, to do sth** de faire qch); **at every o.** à la moindre occasion; **at the first** or **earliest o.** à la première occasion; **I would go if I were you, it's the o. of a life-time** à ta place j'irais, c'est la chance de ta vie; **if I get an o.** si l'occasion se présente, si j'en ai l'occasion; **to miss an o.** laisser passer une occasion; **I'd like to take this o. to thank everyone** j'aimerais profiter de cette occasion pour remercier tout le monde; **a job with opportunities** un emploi qui offre des perspectives; *Mktg* **o. and issue analysis** analyse f des attraits et des atouts; *Mktg* **o. and threat analysis** analyse des opportunités et des menaces; *Mktg* **o. to hear** occasion d'entendre; *Mktg* **o. to see** occasion de voir

oppose [ə'pəʊz] VT **1** *(resist) (person)* s'opposer à, résister à; *(reform, act etc)* faire obstacle ou opposition à; **to be opposed to sth** être opposé à qch; *Law* **to o. an action/a marriage** s'opposer à un acte/un mariage **2** *(contrast)* opposer; *(two colours etc)* mettre en opposition ou en contraste

opposed [ə'pəʊzd] ADJ opposé; **as o. to** par opposition à; **I'd say he was 'robust' as o. to**

simply **'fat'** je dirais qu'il était 'costaud' plutôt que simplement 'gros'

opposing [ə'pəʊzɪŋ] ADJ *(armies, characters, viewpoints)* opposé; *(party)* opposant; **o. team** équipe f adverse

opposite ['ɒpəzɪt] ADJ *(characters)* opposé; *(opinion)* contraire; *(end of room etc)* autre; *(wall)* d'en face, opposé; **to be of the o. opinion** être d'opinion contraire ou d'un avis contraire; **in the o. direction** en sens inverse, dans le sens opposé; **they went in o. directions** ils prirent des directions opposées; **the diagram on the o. page** la figure ci-contre

N contraire m; **the exact o.** exactement le contraire

ADV en face; **the house o.** la maison (d')en face; **the page o.** la page ci-contre

PREP en face de, vis-à-vis (de); **to stand/sit o. sb** être (debout)/être assis en face de qn, faire vis-à-vis à qn; **a house o. the church** une maison en face de l'église ou qui fait face à l'église; **we live o. them** nous habitons en face de chez eux; *Theat, Cin* **she played o. many famous stars** elle a eu beaucoup de grandes vedettes comme partenaires

▸▸*Aut* **o. lock** contre-braquage m, pl contre-braquages; **to apply o. lock** contrebraquer; **o. number** homologue mf; **the o. sex** l'autre sexe m

opposition [ɒpə'zɪʃən] N opposition f, résistance f, *Com (competitors)* concurrence f, **to act in o. to public opinion** agir contrairement à l'opinion publique; **to meet with fierce o.** rencontrer une farouche opposition; **to break down all o.** vaincre toutes les résistances; **the o.** le camp adverse; *Br Pol* **the O.** l'opposition; *Pol* **to be in o.** être dans l'opposition; *Astron* **in o.** en opposition

oppress [ə'pres] VT *(conquered race, poor etc)* opprimer; *(the mind)* oppresser, opprimer

oppressed [ə'prest] ADJ *(people)* opprimé

NPL **the o.** les opprimés mpl

oppression [ə'preʃən] N oppression f

oppressive [ə'presɪv] ADJ **1** *(law, régime)* oppressif, opprimant **2** *(atmosphere)* lourd, étouffant; *(heat)* oppressant, accablant, étouffant **3** *(mental burden, excessive attentiveness, affection)* oppressant

oppressively [ə'presɪvlɪ] ADV **1** *(to rule)* d'une manière oppressive **2** **it was o. hot** il faisait une chaleur accablante ou étouffante **3** *(with excessive affection)* d'une manière oppressante ou étouffante

oppressiveness [ə'presɪvnɪs] N **1** *(of law, regime)* caractère m oppressif **2** *(of weather)* lourdeur f, **the o. of the heat** la chaleur accablante ou étouffante **3** *(emotional)* caractère m oppressant

oppressor [ə'presər] N oppresseur m

opprobrious [ə'prəʊbrɪəs] ADJ *Fml* injurieux, outrageant

opprobrium [ə'prəʊbrɪəm] N *Fml* opprobre m; **to incur sb's o.** s'attirer le mépris de qn

opt [ɒpt] VI opter (**for** pour; **between** entre); **to o. to do sth** choisir de faire qch

▸ **opt in** VI *(join)* choisir de participer

▸ **opt into** VT INSEP *(join)* **to o. into an association/the European Union/etc** entrer dans une association/l'Union européenne/etc

▸ **opt out** VI choisir de ne plus participer (**of** à); **to o. out of one's responsibilities/an agreement** se désengager de ses responsabilités/d'un accord; *Br* **to o. out (of local authority control)** *(of school, hospital etc)* devenir autonome; **to o. out of society** se mettre en marge de la société; **I'm opting out** pour moi, c'est terminé

optative ['ɒptətɪv] ADJ, N *Gram* optatif m

optic ['ɒptɪk] ADJ optique

N Br Optic® = mesure f transparente (utilisée dans les bars)

▸▸ Comput o. **drive** lecteur m optique; Anat o. **nerve** nerf m optique; Comput o. **scanner** scanneur m optique

optical ['ɒptɪk(ə)l] ADJ optique; (instrument) d'optique

▸▸ o. **axis** (of lens) axe m optique; o. **centre** (of lens) centre m optique; Comput o. **character reader** lecteur m optique de caractères; Comput o. **character recognition** reconnaissance f optique de caractères; Comput o. **disk** disque m optique; Comput o. **drive** lecteur m optique; o. **fibre** fibre f optique; o. **fibre cable** câble m à fibre optique; o. **fibre technology** fibre optique; o. **illusion** illusion f ou effet m d'optique; Comput o. **mouse** souris f optique; Comput o. **scanner** scanneur m optique

optician [ɒp'tɪʃən] N opticien, -ienne

optics ['ɒptɪks] N optique f VOIR GRAMMAIRE A10

optimal ['ɒptɪm(ə)l] ADJ optimal, -aux

▸▸ Mktg o. **price** prix m optimum; Mktg o. **pricing** fixation f du prix optimal; Mktg o. **psychological price** prix psychologique optimum

optimism ['ɒptɪmɪz(ə)m] N optimisme m

optimist ['ɒptɪmɪst] N optimiste mf; **ever the o.** l'éternel optimiste

optimistic [ɒptɪ'mɪstɪk] ADJ optimiste; **things are looking quite o.** les choses se présentent plutôt bien

optimistically [ɒptɪ'mɪstɪklɪ] ADV d'une manière optimiste, avec optimisme; **they o. predicted record profits** ils se sont montrés optimistes et ont prédit des bénéfices record

optimize ['ɒptɪmaɪz] VT Comput optimiser

optimizer ['ɒptɪmaɪzər] N Comput optimiseur m

optimum, pl **optima** ['ɒptɪməm, -ɪmə] N optimum m

ADJ o. **conditions** conditions fpl optimums ou optima

option ['ɒpʃən] N 1 (choice) option f, choix m; **I can see no other o.** je ne vois pas d'autre solution; **the military o.** l'option militaire; **to have the o. of doing sth** avoir la possibilité ou le choix de faire qch; **we have the o. of staying here** nous avons la possibilité de rester ici; **to give** or **allow sb the o. of doing sth** donner à qn la possibilité de faire qch; **he didn't give me much o.** il ne m'a pas vraiment donné le choix; **we have no o. but to agree** nous ne pouvons rien faire d'autre que donner notre accord; **I haven't got any o., I've got no o.** je n'ai pas le choix; **do I have any o.?** est-ce que j'ai le choix?; **you leave me no o. but to phone the police** vous ne me laissez pas d'autre choix que celui d'appeler la police; Law **imprisonment without the o. of a fine** emprisonnement sans substitution d'amende; **which of them is the best o.?** lequel est le meilleur choix?; **there was no soft o.** il n'y avait pas de solution facile; **it's no soft o.** ce n'est pas une partie de plaisir; **they always go for the soft o.** ils choisissent toujours la solution de facilité; **it's best to leave** or **keep your options open** il est préférable d'envisager toutes les possibilités; **to consider** or **review one's options** considérer toutes les lignes d'action possibles 2 Com, St Exch etc option f, (marché m à) prime f; o. **on shares** option sur actions; o. **to double** option du double; o. **to buy** option d'achat; o. **to sell** option de vente; **to take an o. on sth** prendre une option sur qch; St Exch **buyer's/seller's o.** prime acheteur/vendeur; St Exch **to take up an o.** lever une prime

VT Cin (book) prendre une option sur les droits de

▸▸ Comput o. **box** case f d'option; Comput o. **button** case d'option; St Exch o. **date** jour m d'option; St Exch o. **day** (jour de la) réponse f des primes; St Exch **options desk** desk m d'options; Comput o. **key** touche f Option; St Exch **options market** marché à options ou à primes; St Exch o. **money** (montant m de la) prime; St Exch o. **price** prix m de l'option; St Exch o. **spread** écart m de prime; St Exch **options trading** négociations fpl à prime

optional ['ɒpʃən(ə)l] ADJ facultatif; **evening dress is o.** la tenue de soirée n'est pas de rigueur; o. **retirement at sixty** préretraite f à soixante ans

▸▸ o. **extras** accessoires mpl en option; Mktg o.-**feature pricing** fixation f du prix en fonction des options; Sch o. **subjects** (one must be chosen) matières fpl à option ou optionnelles; (possible to choose none) matières facultatives

optionee [ɒpʃə'niː] N St Exch bénéficiaire mf d'options

optomagnetic [ɒptəmæg'netɪk] ADJ magnéto-optique

optometrist [ɒp'tɒmɪtrɪst] N optométriste mf

opt-out ADJ ATTRIB (clause, provisions) de désengagement
N désengagement m

opulence ['ɒpjʊləns] N (wealth) opulence f, richesse f

opulent ['ɒpjʊlənt] ADJ 1 (wealthy) opulent 2 (plentiful) généreux, opulent

opulently ['ɒpjʊləntlɪ] ADV (to dress, decorate, dine etc) avec opulence; (to live) dans l'opulence

opus, pl **opuses** or **opera** ['əʊpəs, 'ɒp-, -əsɪz, 'ɒpərə] N opus m

or [ɔːr, unstressed ər] CONJ ou; (with neg) ni; **do you want beef or ham?** voulez-vous du bœuf ou du jambon?; **either one or the other** soit l'un soit l'autre, l'un ou l'autre; **either come in or (else) go out** entrez ou (bien) sortez; **don't move or (else) I'll shoot** pas un geste ou je tire; **either you or he has done it** c'est vous ou (c'est) lui qui l'a fait; **without money or luggage** sans argent ni bagages; **in a day or two** dans un ou deux jours; **a mile or so** environ un mil(l)e; **did she do it or not?** est-ce qu'elle l'a fait ou pas?; **we could go to the beach or we could go to the zoo** nous pourrions aller soit à la plage soit au zoo; Fam **do it now or else** fais-le tout de suite ou sinon … (ça va aller mal)

VOIR GRAMMAIRE A74

oracle ['ɒrək(ə)l] N oracle m; (priest, priestess) oracle; **the Delphic o.** l'oracle de Delphes; **to consult the o.** consulter les oracles

oracular [ɒ'rækjʊlər] ADJ 1 (relating to an oracle) oraculaire 2 Fig (wise) prophétique; (mysterious) sibyllin

oracy ['ɒrəsɪ] N Fml facultés fpl orales

oral ['ɔːrəl] ADJ (agreement, tradition, contraceptive) oral, -aux; (vaccine) buccal, -aux; (administration of medication) par la bouche, par voie orale

N Sch (examen m) oral m

▸▸ Anat o. **cavity** cavité f orale ou buccale; Sch o. **examination** (examen) oral; o. **sex** rapports mpl bucco-génitaux; (fellatio) fellation f, (cunnilingus) cunnilingus m

Attention : ne pas confondre avec **aural**.

orally ['ɔːrəlɪ] ADV oralement, de vive voix; Pharm par la bouche, par voie orale

Orange ['ɒrɪndʒ] N 1 Geog **the O. (River)** l'Orange m 2 Hist **the Prince of O.** le prince d'Orange; **William of O.** Guillaume d'Orange

orange ['ɒrɪndʒ] N 1 (fruit) orange f 2 (tree) oranger m 3 (colour) orange m, orangé m
ADJ (colour) orangé, orange inv

▸▸ o. **blossom** fleur f ou fleurs fpl d'oranger; o. **flower water** eau f de fleur d'oranger; O. **Free State** l'État m libre d'Orange; o. **grove** orangeraie f; o. **juice** jus m d'orange; o. **marmalade** marmelade f d'orange, confiture f d'orange ou d'oranges; O. **Order** ordre m des Orangistes; o. **peel** écorce f ou peau f d'orange; Fig (cellulite) peau d'orange; o. **red** rouge m orangé; o. **segment** quartier m d'orange; o. **squash** boisson f à l'orange; o. **stick** bâtonnet m (de) manucure; O. **Walk** = défilé m des Orangistes, le 12 juillet; o. **tree** oranger m

Orange marches

Depuis des siècles, les Orangistes défilent dans les villes d'Irlande du Nord pour commémorer les dates clés de l'histoire du protestantisme en Irlande. L'événement le plus important fut la bataille de la Boyne en 1690 où le protestant Guillaume d'Orange l'emporta sur Jacques II, roi catholique déposé. Les Orangistes sont farouchement attachés à la Couronne britannique et s'opposent à tout rapprochement avec la République d'Irlande. Leurs défilés annuels donnent souvent lieu à de violents affrontements, notamment quand ils traversent les quartiers catholiques.

orangeade [ɒrɪn'dʒeɪd] N (fizzy) soda m (à l')orange, boisson f gazeuse à l'orange

Orangeman, pl **Orangemen** ['ɒrɪndʒmən] N Br = Orangiste m (du parti protestant de l'Irlande du Nord)

orangery ['ɒrɪndʒərɪ] N orangerie f

orang-outang, orang-utan [ɔːræŋ̩uː'tæŋ, -'tæn] N (ape) orang-outan(g) m, pl orangs-outan(g)s

oration [ɔː'reɪʃən] N allocution f, discours m; **funeral o.** oraison f funèbre

orator ['ɒrətər] N orateur, -trice

oratorical [ɒrə'tɒrɪk(ə)l] ADJ (style, talent) oratoire; o. **emphasis** accent m oratoire

oratorio [ɒrə'tɔːrɪəʊ] N Mus oratorio m

oratory[1] ['ɒrət(ə)rɪ] N (art) art m oratoire; (speaking skill) éloquence f, powers of o. facultés fpl oratoires; **a brilliant piece of o.** un brillant spécimen d'art oratoire; **flight of o.** envolée f éloquente

oratory[2] N Rel oratoire m

orb [ɔːb] N globe m, sphère f, (of regalia) globe; Arch, Lit (planet etc) orbe m; **the o. of the sun** le globe du soleil; **the o. and the sceptre** l'orbe et le sceptre

orbit ['ɔːbɪt] N 1 (of planet, space vehicle), Fig (of country) orbite f, **in o.** en orbite; **to enter** or **go into o.** se mettre ou se placer en orbite; **to send a satellite into o.** lancer un satellite en orbite, mettre un satellite sur orbite; Fig **the family o.** le cercle familial; Fam **to go into o.** (get angry) entrer en furie 2 Anat (of eye) orbite f 3 Fig (scope) domaine m; **such matters don't come within the o. of my department** ces affaires-là ne sont pas du domaine de mon service ou ne relèvent pas de mon service

VT **to o. the sun** décrire une orbite ou orbiter autour du soleil

VI (of satellite etc) être en orbite, décrire une orbite

orbital ['ɔːbɪt(ə)l] ADJ 1 Astron etc orbital, -aux 2 Anat (cavity etc) orbitaire
N Br (road) périphérique m
▸▸ Br o. **road** périphérique

Orcadian [ɔː'keɪdɪən] N habitant, -ante des

îles Orcades; *(native)* originaire *mf* des îles Orcades ▪ **ADJ** des îles Orcades

orchard [ˈɔːtʃəd] **N** verger *m*; **apple o.** pommeraie *f*

orchestra [ˈɔːkɪstrə] **N** *Mus* orchestre *m*; *Am Theat* **the o.** les fauteuils *mpl* d'orchestre
VOIR GRAMMAIRE A11
▸▸ **o. pit** fosse *f* d'orchestre; **o. stalls** fauteuils *pl* d'orchestre

orchestral [ɔːˈkestr(ə)l] **ADJ** orchestral, -aux

orchestrate [ˈɔːkɪstreɪt] **VT** *(symphony etc)*, *Fig (press campaign etc)* orchestrer

orchestration [ɔːkɪsˈtreɪʃən] **N** orchestration *f*

orchid [ˈɔːkɪd] **N** *(plant)* orchidée *f*, *(wild)* orchis *m*

orchis [ˈɔːkɪs] **N** *(plant)* orchis *m*

ordain [ɔːˈdeɪn] **VT 1** *(decree)* ordonner, fixer; *(measure)* décréter; **fate ordained** *or* **it was ordained that we should meet** il était écrit que nous nous rencontrerions, le sort a voulu que nous nous rencontrions **2** *Rel (priest)* ordonner; **to be ordained** être ordonné, recevoir les ordres

ordeal [ɔːˈdiːl] **N 1** épreuve *f*; **to go through a terrible o.** subir *ou* passer par une terrible épreuve; **it is an o. for me to make a speech** je suis au supplice quand je dois faire un discours; **they spoke of their o.** ils ont évoqué le supplice *ou* l'épreuve qu'ils ont vécu(e) **2** *Law, Hist* épreuve *f* judiciaire, ordalie *f*, **o. by fire** épreuve du feu

ORDER [ˈɔːdər]

N	ordre **1, 3, 4, 7–10** ▪ commande **2**
▪ mandat **3** ▪ état **5** ▪ classe **10**	
VT	ordonner **1, 4** ▪ commander **2**
▪ classer **3**	
VI	commander

N 1 *(instruction)* ordre *m*; *Mil* ordre, consigne *f*; **I have orders to remain here** j'ai ordre de rester ici; **to give orders/an o.** donner des ordres/un ordre; **he gave orders for the trunks to be packed** il donna l'ordre de boucler les malles; **to obey** *or* **follow orders** obéir aux ordres, suivre la consigne; **our orders are to …** nous avons l'ordre de …; **to be under orders from the President** tenir ses ordres du Président; **and that's an o.!** c'est un ordre!; **orders are orders** les ordres sont les ordres; *Fig* **I don't take (my) orders from him** je ne suis pas à ses ordres; **until further orders** jusqu'à nouvel avis *ou* ordre; **by o. of the King** par ordre du roi, de par le roi **2** *(in restaurant)*, *Com* commande *f*; **to place an o. with sb, to give sb an o.** passer une commande à qn, commander qch à qn; **to fill an o.** exécuter une commande; **to deliver an o.** livrer une commande; **your o. has now arrived** votre commande est arrivée; **as per o.** conformément à votre commande; **another firm got the o.** ils ont passé la commande auprès d'une autre compagnie; **it's on o.** c'est commandé; **made to o.** fabriqué sur commande; *(suit)* fait sur mesure; **I can't do it to o.** ça ne se commande pas; **have you given your o.?** *(in restaurant)* est-ce que vous avez commandé?; **have they taken your o.?** est-ce qu'on a pris votre commande?; *Am* **an o. of French fries** une portion de frites **3** *(document)* ordre *m*; *Com*, *Admin* bon *m*; *Fin* mandat *m*; **deportation o.** arrêté *m* d'expulsion; *Fin* **pay to the o. of J. Martin** payez à l'ordre de J. Martin; **pay J. Martin or o.** payez à J. Martin ou à son ordre; **by o. and for account of J. Martin** d'ordre et pour compte de J. Martin; **cheque to o.** chèque *m* à ordre **4** *(peace, harmony)* ordre *m*; **to keep** *or*

maintain o. in a town assurer *ou* maintenir l'ordre dans une ville; *Sch* **to keep o. in class** maintenir la discipline dans une classe; **to establish/restore o.** mettre de/rétablir l'ordre **5** *(condition)* **machine in (good) working o.** machine *f* en (bon) état de fonctionnement *ou* de marche; **out of o.** *(mechanism)* détraqué, dérangé; *(telephone)* en dérangement; *(lift, machine)* en panne **6** *(in meeting etc)* **to rule a question out of o.** statuer qu'une interpellation n'est pas dans les règles; *Br Fam* **you're out of o.!** tu as dépassé les bornes!; **to call sb to o.** rappeler qn à l'ordre; *Parl* **o.! o.!** de l'ordre!; *Law* **o. in court!** silence dans la salle! **7** *(tidiness, organization)* ordre *m*; **in o.** *(as it should be)* en ordre; *(document)* en règle, conforme à la règle; **to put things in o.** mettre les choses en ordre; **to put** *or* **set one's affairs in o.** mettre ses affaires en ordre, régler ses affaires; *Fig* **to set one's house in o.** remettre de l'ordre dans ses affaires **8** *(system)* ordre *m*; **the old o. is changing** l'ancien ordre des choses devient caduc; **it's not in the natural o. of things** ce n'est pas dans l'ordre des choses; **I think a celebration is in o.** je pense que ça mérite d'être fêté; **it's perfectly in o. for them to ask for your papers** ils ont parfaitement le droit de vous demander vos papiers **9** *(sequence)* ordre *m*; **in the correct** *or* **right/wrong o.** dans le bon ordre/le désordre; **in alphabetical/chronological o.** en *ou* par ordre alphabétique/chronologique; **in o. of age** par rang d'âge; *Theat*, *Cin* **in o. of appearance** par ordre d'apparition; **o. of battle** ordre de bataille **10** *(class)* classe *f*, *Biol* ordre *m*; **the higher/lower orders (of society)** les classes supérieures/inférieures; **workmanship of the highest o.** travail *m* de premier ordre; **population of** *or* **in** *or* *Am* **on the o. of 100,000** population *f* de l'ordre de 100 000 habitants; **o. of magnitude** ordre de grandeur; **a disaster/a project/investment of this o. (of magnitude)** un désastre/un projet/des investissements de cette envergure; *Archit* **Ionic/Doric o.** ordre ionique/dorique; *Rel* **to take holy orders** entrer dans les ordres; **to be in (holy) orders** être prêtre/moine/religieuse; **monastic o.** ordre monastique; **o. of knighthood** ordre de chevalerie **11 in o. to do** sth afin de *ou* pour faire qch; **in o. that they understand** afin *ou* pour qu'ils comprennent VOIR GRAMMAIRE A75
VT 1 to o. sb to do sth ordonner à qn de faire qch; **she ordered them into her office/off the premises** elle leur a ordonné d'entrer dans son bureau/de quitter les lieux; **he's been ordered to report tomorrow** il a reçu l'ordre de se présenter demain; **he ordered them into battle** il leur a donné l'ordre de livrer bataille; *Law* **to be ordered to pay costs** être condamné aux dépens **2** *(in restaurant)*, *Com* commander; **to o. goods from Paris** commander des marchandises à Paris; **we can o. it for you** nous pouvons vous le commander; **to o. a taxi** (faire) appeler un taxi; **what have you ordered for dessert?** qu'est-ce que vous avez commandé comme dessert? **3** *(arrange) (furniture etc)* arranger; *(papers, books etc)* classer, ranger; *(one's life)* ordonner, agencer; *(one's thoughts)* mettre de l'ordre dans; **to o. sth according to author/size** classer *ou* ranger qch par auteur/taille; **to o. one's affairs** mettre ses affaires en ordre; *Mil* **o. arms!** reposez armes! **4** *Med (treatment)* prescrire, ordonner; *Fig* **that's just what the doctor ordered** c'est exactement ce qu'il me fallait
VI *(in restaurant)* commander
▸▸ *Com* **o. book** carnet *m* de commandes;

o. in council = décret *m* du gouvernement, arrêté ministériel; *(statutory order)* décret-loi *m*, *pl* décrets-lois; *Law* **o. of the court** injonction *f* de la cour; *Com* **o. cycle time** durée *f* du cycle de commande; *Mil*, *(in meeting etc)* **o. of the day** ordre du jour; *Fig* **simplicity/optimism was the o. of the day** la simplicité/l'optimisme était de rigueur; **promiscuity/extravagance was the o. of the day in Ancient Rome** la promiscuité sexuelle/un faste somptuaire était monnaie courante dans la Rome antique; *Com* **o. department** service *m* des commandes; **o. form** bon de commande; **the O. of the Garter** l'ordre de la Jarretière; **the O. of Merit** l'ordre du Mérite; *Com* **o. number** numéro *m* de commande; *Pol* **o. paper** (feuille *f* de l') ordre du jour; **o. to pay, o. for payment** ordonnance *f* de paiement; *Com* **o. processing** traitement *m* des commandes; *Com* **o. to remittance cycle** cycle *m* commande-livraison-facturation; **o. to sell** ordre de vente; *Rel* **o. of service** office *m*; *Com* **o. taking** prise *f* de commande; **o. to view** permis *m* de visiter *(une maison à vendre)*

▸ **order about, order around VT SEP** *(person)* commander; **he likes ordering people about** il aime commander les autres; **you can't o. me about!** je n'ai pas d'ordres à recevoir de toi

▸ **order in VT SEP** *(supplies, food)* commander; *(police, troops)* faire venir

▸ **order off VT SEP** *Sport (player)* expulser (du terrain)

▸ **order out VT SEP** *(from room etc)* mettre dehors

▸ **order up VT SEP 1** *(troops, air support etc)* faire monter
2 *(stationery supplies, round of drinks etc)* commander

order-driven ADJ *St Exch (market)* dirigé par les ordres

ordered [ˈɔːdəd] **ADJ** ordonné; *(in good order)* en bon ordre; **an o. life** une vie régulière *ou* réglée

orderer [ˈɔːdərər] **N** acheteur *m*

orderliness [ˈɔːdəlɪnɪs] **N 1** *(methodical nature)* méthode *f*, *(of existence)* caractère *m* rangé *ou* réglé; **the o. of her records/room/papers/etc** le bon ordre dans lequel se trouvaient ses disques/sa chambre/ses papiers/etc **2** *(discipline) (of crowd, football supporters etc)* discipline *f*, *(of pupils)* bonne conduite *f*

orderly [ˈɔːdəlɪ] **ADJ 1** *(arrangement)* ordonné, méthodique; *(room etc)* en ordre, ordonné, rangé; *(life)* réglé, rangé, régulier; *(mind)* méthodique; **to be very o.** *(of person)* avoir beaucoup de méthode; **to do sth in an o. way** *or* **manner** faire qch avec beaucoup de méthode **2** *(crowd)* discipliné; **leave the building in an o. fashion** quittez l'immeuble dans l'ordre et avec calme; **an o. retreat/withdrawal** une retraite/un repli ordonné(ée)
N 1 *Mil* planton *m*; **to be on o. duty** être de planton **2 hospital o., medical o.** aide-infirmier, -ière, *pl* aides-infirmiers, -ières; *Mil* infirmier *m*, ambulancier *m*
▸▸ *Br Mil* **o. officer** officier *m* de permanence; *Mil* **o. room** salle *f* des rapports

ordinal [ˈɔːdɪn(ə)l] **ADJ** *(number)* ordinal, -aux VOIR GRAMMAIRE A76; B59
N *(number)* nombre *m* ordinal

ordinance [ˈɔːdɪnəns] **N** *Fml (decree)* ordonnance *f*, règlement *m*

ordinand [ˈɔːdɪnænd] **N** *Rel* ordinand *m*

ordinarily [ˈɔːdɪn(ə)rɪlɪ, *Am* ɔːdɪˈnerɪlɪ] **ADV 1** *(in an everyday manner)* normalement; **he was quite o. dressed** il était habillé de façon tout à fait banale; **a more than o. gifted/stupid child** un enfant d'une intelligence/stupidité supérieure à la normale; **a more than o. attractive woman** une femme d'une beauté exceptionnelle **2** (usually) d'habitude, ordinairement, d'ordinaire; **did he seem nervous? – not more than he o. is** est-ce qu'il avait l'air nerveux? – pas plus que d'habitude ou qu'à l'ordinaire

ordinary ['ɔ:dɪn(ə)rɪ] ADJ ordinaire; **she was just an o. tourist** c'était une touriste comme une autre; **this is no o. house/car** ce n'est pas une maison/voiture ordinaire; **in the o. course of events, in the o. run of things** d'ordinaire; Pej **a very o. kind of man** un homme tout à fait ordinaire ou quelconque; **an o. Englishman** un Anglais moyen ou typique

N **1** ordinaire m; **out of the o.** exceptionnel, qui sort de l'ordinaire; **nothing out of the o. happened** il n'est rien arrivé d'inhabituel ou d'exceptionnel **2** Rel **the O. (of the Mass)** l'Ordinaire m (de la messe)

▸▸**o. activities** Com activités fpl ordinaires; Acct (balance sheet item) opérations fpl courantes; Fin **o. creditor** créancier, -ière ordinaire; Br Sch Formerly **O.-level**, Scot **O.-grade** = examen m qui sanctionnait autrefois la fin des études au niveau de la seconde, ≃ BEPC m; **o. seaman** matelot m breveté; Br St Exch **o. share** action f ordinaire; Br St Exch **o. share capital** capital m en actions ordinaires

ordinate ['ɔ:dɪnɪt] N Math ordonnée f

ordination [ɔ:dɪ'neɪʃən] N Rel ordination f

ordnance ['ɔ:dnəns] N **1** Mil (unit) (service m du) matériel m; Br **Royal Army O. Corps** Service m du Matériel; **o. and supplies** les ravitaillements mpl **2** Mil (artillery) artillerie f, **piece of o.** bouche f à feu, pièce f d'artillerie

▸▸**o. factory** usine f d'artillerie; Am **O. Service** Service du Matériel; Br **O. Survey** service m national de cartographie, ≃ IGN m

ordure ['ɔ:djʊər] N Lit ordure f

ore [ɔ:r] N minerai m; **iron/aluminium o.** minerai de fer/d'aluminium; **rich** or **high-grade o.** minerai à ou de haute teneur

▸▸**o. deposit** gisement m de minerai

Ore(g) abbr Oregon

oregano [ɒrɪ'gɑ:nəʊ] N Bot, Culin origan m

.org [dɒt'ɔ:g] Comput = abréviation f désignant les organisations à but non lucratif dans les adresses électroniques

organ ['ɔ:gən] N **1** Mus orgue m; Rel orgues fpl; **grand o.** grand orgue, grandes orgues; **choir o.** orgue du chœur; **American o.** orgue de salon; **street o.** orgue de Barbarie **2** Anat (of human body, plant) organe m; Euph (penis) membre m; **o. of hearing** organe de l'ouïe; **the vocal organs** l'appareil m vocal **3** Fig (instrument) (of government) organe m; (newspaper) (of government, party) organe, porte-parole m inv; **an efficient o. of propaganda** un organe de propagande efficace; **the official o.** l'organe officiel

▸▸**o. builder** facteur m d'orgues; **o. gallery, o. loft** tribune f d'orgue; **o. pipe** tuyau m d'orgue; **o. stop** jeu m d'orgue; **o. transplant** transplantation f d'organe

organdie ['ɔ:gəndɪ] N Tex organdi m; **o. dress** robe f d'organdi

organ-grinder N joueur, -euse d'orgue de Barbarie; Fig **I want to speak to the o., not the monkey** je veux parler au responsable, pas au sous-fifre

organic [ɔ:'gænɪk] ADJ **1** organique; (fertilizer) organique, biologique; Ecol (food, farming, gardening etc) biologique **2** (structural) organique; (fundamental) organique, fondamental, -aux; **an o. whole** un ensemble systématique, un tout intégré; **o. growth/change** croissance f/changement m natu-

rel(elle) ou spontané(ée); **an o. part** une partie intégrante

▸▸**o. chemist** organicien, -ienne; **o. chemistry** chimie f organique

> Note that the French word **organique** is never used in relation to food or farming.

organically [ɔ:'gænɪklɪ] ADV **1** organiquement; (to farm, garden) avec un engrais organique; **o. grown foods** produits mpl biologiques **2** Fig **to change/grow o.** changer/grandir naturellement ou spontanément; Fig **to be o. linked** être fondamentalement lié

organigram [ɔ:'gænɪgræm] N organigramme m

organism ['ɔ:gænɪz(ə)m] N organisme m

organist ['ɔ:gənɪst] N organiste mf

organization [ɔ:gənaɪ'zeɪʃən] N **1** (action) organisation f; Ind **o. and methods** organisation f scientifique du travail; Ind **o. and methods department** bureau m des méthodes **2** (association) organisation f, organisme m; **charity o.** organisation charitable, œuvre f de charité; **youth o.** mouvement m de jeunesse **3** Ind (of labour) syndicalisation f

▸▸**o. chart** organigramme m; **o. tree** organigramme m en arborescence

organizational [ɔ:gənaɪ'zeɪʃən(ə)l] ADJ (defect, skills etc) d'organisation, de structure, organisationnel

▸▸**o. buyer** acheteur, -euse (pour une organisation); **o. marketer** mercaticien, -ienne au sein d'une organisation

organizationally [ɔ:gənaɪ'zeɪʃən(ə)lɪ] ADV du point de vue de l'organisation; **he doesn't get involved o. in the project** il n'est pas impliqué au niveau de l'organisation du projet

organize ['ɔ:gənaɪz] VT **1** (sort out, put into groups etc) organiser; **to o. people into work groups** répartir les gens dans des groupes de travail

2 (arrange, bring about) (concert, party etc) organiser; (transport, food, accommodation) s'occuper de; (money) s'occuper de trouver; (one's time) organiser, aménager; Fam (a day off etc) se faire accorder; **she organized it so that we got in free** elle s'est arrangée pour que nous puissions entrer sans payer; **I'll just go and o. something to eat** (do it myself) je vais préparer quelque chose à manger; **don't worry, it's all organized** ne t'inquiète pas, tout est organisé

3 Ind (workers) syndiquer

VI **1** s'organiser **2** Ind (of workers) se syndiquer

organized ['ɔ:gənaɪzd] ADJ (society, person, files) organisé

▸▸**o. crime** le crime organisé; Sch **o. games** jeux mpl dirigés; **o. labour** main-d'œuvre f syndiquée, pl mains-d'œuvre syndiquées; **o. religion** religion f organisée

organizer ['ɔ:gənaɪzər] N (person) organisateur, -trice; (diary etc) organiseur m; (electronic) agenda m (électronique); (software) organiseur m; **she's a born o.** elle a le sens de l'organisation, c'est une organisatrice née

organizing ['ɔ:gənaɪzɪŋ] ADJ ATTRIB (ability, committee) d'organisation

orgasm ['ɔ:gæz(ə)m] N Physiol orgasme m; **to have an o.** avoir un orgasme, jouir; Fig Sl **they were having orgasms** ça les faisait bander, ils ont trouvé ça jouissif ou bandant

orgasmic [ɔ:'gæzmɪk] ADJ Physiol orgastique; Sl (pleasure, experience etc) jouissif

orgiastic [ɔ:dʒɪ'æstɪk] ADJ orgiaque

orgy ['ɔ:dʒɪ] N (sexual), Fig (of colour) orgie f; (of violence) déchaînement m; **orgies** (in an-

cient Greece, Rome) orgies, bacchanales fpl; **drunken o.** beuverie f, Fam soûlerie f

oriel ['ɔ:rɪəl] N Archit oriel m

▸▸**o. window** oriel

orient [1] ['ɔ:rɪənt] N orient m; **the O.** l'Orient

orient [2] ['ɔ:rɪənt] VT = **orientate**

oriental [ɔ:rɪ'ent(ə)l] ADJ oriental, -aux

N **O.** (person) Oriental, -ale

▸▸**o. rug** tapis m d'Orient

orientalist [ɔ:rɪ'entəlɪst] N orientaliste mf

orientate ['ɔ:rɪənteɪt] VT (map) orienter; **to o. oneself** (physically, psychologically) s'orienter

orientation [ɔ:rɪən'teɪʃən] N orientation f

▸▸esp Am **o. course** cours m d'introduction

oriented ['ɔ:rɪentɪd] ADJ orienté

-oriented ['ɔ:rɪentɪd] SUFF profit-o. axé sur le profit; **youth-o.** qui s'adresse à la jeunesse; Comput **computer-o. language** langage orienté machine; **export-o.** (company, industry) tourné vers l'exportation

orienteering [ɔ:rɪən'tɪərɪŋ] N Sport course f d'orientation

orifice ['ɒrɪfɪs] N orifice m

origami [ɒrɪ'gɑ:mɪ] N (art m du) pliage m, origami m

origin ['ɒrɪdʒɪn] N **1** origine f; **to trace an event back to its o.** remonter à l'origine d'un événement; **to have its origins in ...** tirer son origine de ...; **the custom has its o. or origins in ...** l'origine de cette coutume est ...; Archit **point of o.** (of curve etc) point m d'origine; **word/woman of Greek o.** mot m/femme f d'origine grecque; **a man of humble o.** un homme d'humble origine ou extraction; Com **country of o.** pays m d'origine; Com **certificate of o.** certificat m d'origine **2** Anat (of muscle) attache f

▸▸Com **o. of goods label** marque f d'origine

original [ə'rɪdʒ(ə)l] ADJ **1** (first) (suggestion, idea etc) premier, initial, -aux; (manuscript, painting) original, -aux; **the o. colour** la couleur d'origine; **the o. members of the band** les premiers membres du groupe; TV etc **based on an o. idea by ...** d'après une idée originale de ...; **the o. meaning of a word** le sens premier d'un mot; **in the o. Chinese** dans le texte original en chinois/dans le texte chinois d'origine; **to translate from the o. German** traduire d'après le texte allemand original **2** (innovative) (writer, style, idea, approach etc) original, -aux

N **1** (of painting, invoice etc) original m; Fin (of bill of exchange) primata m; **to copy sth from the o.** copier qch sur l'original; **to read the classics in the o.** lire les classiques dans le texte **2** Fam (person) original, -ale

▸▸Fin **o. capital** capital m d'origine; Fin **o. cost** coût m initial; Com **o. defect** vice m originaire; Acct **o. document** pièce f comptable; **o. edition** édition f originale; **o. guarantee** garantie f d'origine; Fin, Com **o. invoice** facture f originale; Com **o. packaging, o. packing** emballage m d'origine; Rel **o. sin** péché m originel; Fin **o. value** valeur f initiale ou d'origine; Cin **o. version** version f originale, VO f

> When translating **original**, note that the French words **originel** and **original** are not interchangeable.

originality [ərɪdʒɪ'nælɪtɪ] N originalité f

originally [ə'rɪdʒɪn(ə)lɪ] ADV **1** (initially, to begin with) à l'origine, au départ; **the building was o. used as a warehouse** à l'origine ou au départ, l'immeuble servait d'entrepôt; **o. we come from Hampshire** nous sommes originaires du Hampshire; **where do you come from o.?** d'où êtes-vous originaire?; **that's what I o. thought** c'est ce que je pensais au début *ou* au départ; **I o. heard about it in Spain** c'est en Espagne que j'en ai entendu parler pour la première fois **2** *(in an innovative way)* d'une façon originale, avec originalité

originate [ə'rɪdʒɪneɪt] **VI** *(of person)* être originaire (**from** de); *(of language)* dériver, provenir (**from** de); *(of river)* prendre sa source (**in** dans); **the fire originated under the floor** le feu a pris naissance sous le plancher; **the scheme originated with me** je suis à l'origine de ce projet, je suis l'auteur *ou* l'initiateur de ce projet; **the custom originated in France** cette coutume est née en France; **originating airline** compagnie *f* aérienne de départ
VT donner naissance à, être l'auteur de; *(proposal)* être l'auteur de; *(reform, project etc)* être à l'origine de, être l'auteur *ou* l'initiateur, -trice de

originator [ə'rɪdʒɪneɪtər] **N** créateur, -trice; *(of proposal)* auteur *m*; *(of scheme)* auteur, initiateur, -trice

oriole ['ɔːrɪəʊl] **N** *(bird)* loriot *m*, *Can* oriole *m*; **golden o.** loriot (jaune d'Europe)

Orkneys (the) [ðiː'ɔːknɪz] **NPL** les Orcades *fpl*

ormolu ['ɔːməluː] **N** similor *m*

ornament[1] ['ɔːnəmənt] **N 1** *(vase etc)* ornement *m* **2** *(no pl)* *(decoration)* *(of style, architecture etc)* ornements *mpl*; *(on dress etc)* garniture *f*; **by way of o.** pour ornement **3** *Mus* ornement *m*

ornament[2] ['ɔːnəmənt] **VT** *(room etc)* orner, ornementer (**with** de); *(dress etc)* agrémenter, embellir (**with** de); *(one's style)* orner (**with** de)

ornamental [ɔːnə'ment(ə)l] **ADJ** décoratif, ornemental, -aux; **o. tree/plant** arbre *m*/plante *f* d'ornement; **o. lake** *or* **pond** pièce *f* d'eau

ornamentation [ɔːnəmen'teɪʃən] **N** ornementation *f*

ornate [ɔː'neɪt] **ADJ** orné, ornementé, *Pej* chargé; **o. style** style *m* imagé *ou* fleuri

ornately [ɔː'neɪtlɪ] **ADV** de façon très ornementée, *Pej* avec une surabondance d'ornements; *(written)* dans un style très fleuri

ornery ['ɔːnərɪ] **ADJ** *Am Fam (unpleasant)* désagréable; *(bad-tempered)* rouspéteur, -euse; *(stubborn)* têtu

ornithological [ɔːnɪθə'lɒdʒɪk(ə)l] **ADJ** ornithologique

ornithologist [ɔːnɪ'θɒlədʒɪst] **N** ornithologue *mf*, ornithologiste *m*

ornithology [ɔːnɪ'θɒlədʒɪ] **N** ornithologie *f*

orotund ['ɒrəʊtʌnd] **ADJ** *esp Lit (sound)* plein, riche; *(writing)* *(pompous)* emphatique, pompeux

orphan ['ɔːfən] **N 1** orphelin, -ine; **to be left an o.** devenir orphelin; **war o.** pupille *mf* de la Nation **2** *Typ* orpheline *f*
ADJ **an o. child** un orphelin, une orpheline
VT **he had been orphaned at the age of six** il est devenu orphelin à l'âge de six ans; **they were orphaned by the war** ils ont perdu leurs parents pendant la guerre
▸▸ *Pharm* **o. drug** médicament *m* orphelin

orphanage ['ɔːf(ə)nɪdʒ] **N** orphelinat *m*

Orpheus ['ɔːfjuːs] **N** *Myth* Orphée *m*

orthodontics [ɔːθəʊ'dɒntɪks] **N** orthodontie *f* VOIR GRAMMAIRE A10

orthodontist [ɔːθəʊ'dɒntɪst] **N** orthodontiste *mf*

orthodox ['ɔːθədɒks] **ADJ 1** *Rel* orthodoxe; **the O. Church** l'Église *f* orthodoxe **2** *(historian etc)* traditionaliste, orthodoxe; *(method, opinion etc)* orthodoxe
NPL *Rel* **the o.** *(people)* les orthodoxes *mpl*

orthodoxy ['ɔːθədɒksɪ] **N 1** *(of doctrine, person's opinions)* orthodoxie *f* **2** *(in Jewish religion)* judaïsme *m* rabbinique

orthogonal [ɔː'θɒgən(ə)l] **ADJ** *Math* orthogonal, -aux

orthographic(al) [ɔːθə'græfɪk, -ɪk(ə)l] **ADJ** orthographique

orthographically [ɔːθə'græfɪklɪ] **ADV** orthographiquement

orthography [ɔː'θɒgrəfɪ] **N 1** *(spelling)* orthographe *f* **2** *Math* projection *f* orthogonale

orthopaedic, *Am* **orthopedic** [ɔːθə'piːdɪk] **ADJ** *Med (treatment, device)* orthopédique
▸▸ **o. surgeon** (chirurgien, -ienne) orthopédiste *mf*; **o. surgery** chirurgie *f* des os

orthopaedics, *Am* **orthopedics** [ɔːθə'piːdɪks] **N** *Med* orthopédie *f* VOIR GRAMMAIRE A10

orthopaedist, *Am* **orthopedist** [ɔːθə'piːdɪst] **N** *Med* orthopédiste *mf*

orthoptist [ɔː'θɒptɪst] **N** orthoptiste *mf*

ortolan ['ɔːtələn] **N** ortolan *m*
▸▸ **o. bunting** ortolan

Orwellian [ɔː'welɪən] **ADJ** orwellien

oryx ['ɒrɪks] **N** *(antelope)* oryx *m*

OS [əʊ'es] **N** *Comput (abbr operating system)* système *m* d'exploitation

Oscar ['ɒskər] **N** *Cin* oscar *m*; **the Oscars, O. night** *(ceremony)* la cérémonie des oscars, les oscars; **O.-winning film** film *m* primé aux oscars; **in her O.-winning role** dans le rôle qui lui a valu l'oscar

OSCE [əʊessiː'iː] **N** *(abbr* **Organization for Security and Cooperation in Europe***)* OSCE *f*

oscillate ['ɒsɪleɪt] **VI** *Phys, Radio* osciller; *Fig* **to o. between two opinions** osciller *ou* balancer *ou* hésiter entre deux opinions

oscillating ['ɒsɪleɪtɪŋ] **ADJ** *(electron)* oscillateur, -trice

oscillation [ɒsɪ'leɪʃən] **N** *(of pendulum etc)* oscillation *f*

oscillator ['ɒsɪleɪtər] **N** oscillateur *m*; **o. valve** *or* **tube** lampe *f* oscillatrice

oscillatory ['ɒsɪleɪt(ə)rɪ] **ADJ** oscillant, oscillatoire

oscillogram [ɒ'sɪləgræm] **N** oscillogramme *m*

oscillograph [ɒ'sɪləgræf] **N** oscillographe *m*

oscilloscope [ɒ'sɪləskəʊp] **N** *Elec* oscilloscope *m*

osculate ['ɒskjʊleɪt] **VI 1** *Fml, Hum (kiss)* s'embrasser **2** *Geom* **curve that osculates with a line** courbe osculatrice à une ligne (**at a point** en un point)

osculation [ɒskjʊ'leɪʃən] **N** *Geom* osculation *f*; **point of o.** point *m* d'attouchement

osier ['əʊzɪər, 'əʊʒər] **N** osier *m*; **o. basket** panier *m* d'osier
▸▸ **o. bed** oseraie *f*

osmosis [ɒz'məʊsɪs] **N** *Chem, Physiol, Fig* osmose *f*

osmotic [ɒz'mɒtɪk] **ADJ** *Chem, Physiol* osmotique

osprey ['ɒspreɪ] **N 1** *(bird)* balbuzard *m* pêcheur *ou* fluviatile, *Can* aigle *m* pêcheur **2** *(feather)* aigrette *f*

ossicle ['ɒsɪk(ə)l] **N** *Anat (of ear)* osselet *m*

ossification [ɒsɪfɪ'keɪʃən] **N** ossification *f*

ossified ['ɒsɪfaɪd] **ADJ** *(cartilage)* ossifié; *Fig (mind, ideas, social system)* sclérosé; *(person)* à l'esprit sclérosé; **the o. old fools who run this country** les vieux fossiles abrutis qui dirigent ce pays

ossify ['ɒsɪfaɪ] **VI** *(of cartilage)* s'ossifier; *Fig (of person)* se fossiliser; *(of government, mind)* se scléroser

VT *(cartilage)* ossifier; *Fig* amener *ou* entraîner la sclérose de

ossuary ['ɒsjʊərɪ] **N** ossuaire *m*

Ostend [ɒs'tend] **N** Ostende

ostensible [ɒs'tensɪb(ə)l] **ADJ** prétendu; **the o. justification for their action was ...** la raison qu'ils ont avancée pour justifier leur acte était ...

> Note that the French adjective **ostensible** is a false friend and is never a translation for the English adjective **ostensible**. It means **conspicuous**.

ostensibly [ɒ'stensɪblɪ] **ADV** en apparence, prétendument; **while the Confederation is o. a single state, ...** alors qu'en apparence *ou* qu'officiellement la Confédération est un état unique, ...; **he went out o. to buy some tobacco** il sortit sous prétexte d'acheter du tabac *ou* soi-disant pour acheter du tabac; **he married her o. for love** il l'a soi-disant épousée par amour

> Note that the French adverb **ostensiblement** is a false friend and is never a translation for the English adverb **ostensibly**. It means **conspicuously**.

ostentation [ɒsten'teɪʃən] **N** ostentation *f*

ostentatious [ɒsten'teɪʃəs] **ADJ** plein d'ostentation; *(person, attitude)* prétentieux, ostentatoire

ostentatiously [ɒsten'teɪʃəslɪ] **ADV** avec ostentation, d'une manière ostentatoire; **to display sth o.** faire ostentation de qch; **to be o. rich** faire ostentation de sa richesse

ostentatiousness [ɒsten'teɪʃəsnɪs] **N** = **ostentation**

osteoarthritis [ɒstɪəʊɑː'θraɪtɪs] **N** *Med* arthrose *f*; **to have o.** avoir de l'arthrose

osteomyelitis [ɒstɪəʊmaɪə'laɪtɪs] **N** *Med* ostéomyélite *f*

osteopath ['ɒstɪəpæθ], *Am* also **osteopathist** [ɒstɪ'ɒpəθɪst] **N** *Med* (médecin *m*) ostéopathe *mf*

osteopathy [ɒstɪ'ɒpəθɪ] **N** *Med* ostéopathie *f*

osteoplasty ['ɒstɪəʊplæstɪ] **N** ostéoplastie *f*

osteoporosis [ɒstɪəʊpɔː'rəʊsɪs] **N** *Med* ostéoporose *f*

ostler ['ɒslər] **N** *Hist* valet *m* d'écurie, garçon *m* d'écurie

ostracism ['ɒstrəsɪz(ə)m] **N** ostracisme *m*; **to suffer the o. of the press** être frappé d'ostracisme par la presse

ostracize ['ɒstrəsaɪz] **VT** frapper d'ostracisme, mettre au ban de la société; *(country, company)* frapper d'ostracisme; **she's been ostracized at work** on l'a mise en quarantaine au travail

ostrich ['ɒstrɪtʃ] **N** autruche *f*; *Fig* **o. policy** politique *f* de l'autruche

OT [əʊ'tiː] **1** *(abbr* **Old Testament***)* AT *m* **2** *abbr* **occupational therapy; occupational therapist**

OTC [əʊtiː'siː] **N 1** *Br Sch (abbr* **Officers' Training Corps***)* corps *m* de formation des officiers **2** *St Exch (abbr* **over-the-counter***)* hors cote
▸▸ *St Exch* **O. market** marché *m* hors cote

OTE [əʊtiː'iː] **NPL** *Com (abbr* **on-target earnings***)* salaire *m* de base plus commissions

OTH [əʊtiː'eɪtʃ] *Mktg (abbr* **opportunity to hear***)* ODE *f*

OTHER ['ʌðər] **ADJ** autre; **the o. one** l'autre *mf*; **every o. day/week** un jour/une semaine sur deux, tous les deux jours/toutes les deux semaines; **the o. day** l'autre jour; **the o. four** les quatre autres; **potatoes and o. ve-**

getables pommes de terre et autres légumes; **o. people have seen it** d'autres l'ont vu; **o. people's property** le bien d'autrui; **any o. book** tout autre livre; *Acct* **o. debtors** (*item on balance sheet*) créances *fpl* diverses; *Br Mil* **o. ranks** = ensemble *m* des militaires non gradés; **no one o. than he knows it** nul autre que lui ne le sait, il n'y a que lui qui le sache; **somebody o. than me/you/her/***etc* quelqu'un d'autre; **all verbs o. than those in -er** tous les verbes autres que ceux en -er; **some woman or o.** une femme quelconque; **the o. woman/man** (*in relationship*) l'autre VOIR GRAMMAIRE A36–7; B15

PRON autre *mf*; **one after the o.** l'un après l'autre; **the others** les autres; **all the others are there** tous les autres sont là; **some ... others ...** les uns ... les autres ...; **have you got any others?** (*any more*) en avez-vous encore?; (*any different ones*) en avez-vous d'autres?; **I have no o.** je n'en ai pas d'autre; **for this reason, if for no o.** pour cette raison, à défaut d'une autre; **no o. none o. than the great actress Greta Garbo** nulle autre que la grande Greta Garbo; **one o. of us will see to it** l'un de nous y veillera; **others** (*other people*) les autres; (*not as grammatical subject*) autrui *m*; **to see oneself as others see one** se voir comme les autres vous voient; **they prefer you to all others** ils vous préfèrent à tout autre; **the property of others** le bien d'autrui; **someone or o. said ...** quelqu'un a dit ...; **something or o. I said** quelque chose que j'ai dû dire; **somehow or o.** d'une façon ou d'une autre; **to be somewhere or o.** être dans les parages VOIR GRAMMAIRE A36–7; B16

ADV autrement; **to see things o. than as they are** voir les choses autrement qu'elles ne le sont; **o. than that everything is fine** à part ça *ou* autrement, tout va bien; **she never speaks of them o. than admiringly** c'est toujours avec admiration qu'elle parle d'eux

N *Hum* **your significant o.** l'homme/la femme de ta vie; **to talk about this, that and the o.** parler de ci et ça; *Br Fam Hum* **to have a bit of the o.** (*sex*) s'envoyer en l'air

otherwise ['ʌðəwaɪz] ADV **1** (*differently*) autrement (**than** que); **he could not do o.** il n'a pas pu faire autrement; **to think o.** penser différemment *ou* autrement; **if she's not o. engaged** si elle n'est pas occupée à autre chose; (*socially*) si elle n'a pas d'autres obligations; **except where o. stated** sauf indication contraire; **all people rich or o.** tout le monde, riches et pauvres **2** (*apart from that*) à part cela *ou* ça, autrement; **o. he is quite sane** à part cela il est complètement sain d'esprit

ADJ **the facts were o.** les faits étaient différents *ou* autres; *Fml* **should it be o.** s'il en était autrement

CONJ autrement, sans quoi, sans cela; **do what I tell you, o. everything will go wrong** faites ce que je vous dis, autrement *ou* sans quoi *ou* sans cela tout ira de travers

otherworldly [ʌðə'wɜːldlɪ] ADJ détaché de ce monde

otic ['əʊtɪk] ADJ *Anat* otique

otitis [əʊ'taɪtɪs] N *Med* otite *f*

OTS [əʊtiː'es] *Mktg* (*abbr* **opportunity to see**) ODV *f*

OTT [əʊti'tiː] ADJ *esp Br Sl* (*abbr* **over the top**) exagéré; **there was no need to be quite so O. about it** ce n'était pas la peine d'en faire toute une histoire; **the house is nice, but the decor's a bit O.** la maison est bien, mais la décoration est un peu lourdingue

otter ['ɒtər] N (*animal*) loutre *f*; **sea o.** loutre de mer *ou* marine

▸▸**o. hound** chien *m* pour la chasse aux loutres

Ottoman ['ɒtəmən] *Hist* ADJ ottoman
N Ottoman, -ane

ottoman ['ɒtəmən] N (*furniture*) ottomane *f*

OU [əʊ'juː] N *Br Univ* (*abbr* **Open University**) = organisme *m* d'enseignement universitaire par correspondance doublé d'émissions de télévision et de radio éducatives

ouch [aʊtʃ] INT (*expressing pain*) aïe!, ouille!

ought¹ [ɔːt] V AUX VOIR GRAMMAIREA60–1; B39 (*with present and past meaning; inv; ought not is frequently abbreviated to oughtn't*) **1** (*obligation*) **this o. to have been done before** on aurait dû *ou* il aurait fallu le faire avant; **to behave as one o.** se conduire comme il convient; **to drink more than one o.** boire plus que de raison; **I thought I o. to let you know about it** j'ai cru devoir vous en faire part; **one o. never to be unkind** il ne faut *ou* on ne doit jamais être malveillant

2 (*desirability*) **you o. to go and see it** vous devriez aller le voir; **you o. not to have waited** vous n'auriez pas dû attendre; **I o. to be going** il me faut partir; **you o. to have seen it!** tu aurais dû *ou* il fallait voir ça!

3 (*probability*) **they o. to be in Paris by now** ils doivent être à Paris maintenant; **you o. to be able to get £50 for it** tu devrais pouvoir en tirer 50 livres; **your horse o. to win** votre cheval devrait gagner; **you o. to know** vous êtes bien placé pour le savoir, vous devriez le savoir

ought² N *Arch, Lit* = **aught**

Ouija® ['wiːdʒə] N **O. (board)** oui-ja *m*

ounce¹ [aʊns] N (*measurement*) once *f*, = 28, 35g.; (**troy**) **o.** (*of gold, silver*) = 31,1035g.; *Fig* **an o. of intelligence/humanity/***etc* une once *ou* un tant soit peu d'intelligence/d'humanité/etc; **if you had an o. of sense** si tu avais un gramme de bon sens; *Fig* **he hasn't an o. of courage** il n'a pas un sou de courage, il n'est pas courageux pour deux sous

ounce² N (*animal*) once *f*, panthère *f* des neiges

our ['aʊər] POSS ADJ VOIR GRAMMAIRE A30; A43; B21 notre, *pl* nos; **o. father and mother** notre père et notre mère, nos père et mère; **o. friends** nos ami(e)s; **o. two** les deux nôtres; *Com* **o. Mr Martin** M. Martin de notre maison

ours ['aʊəz] POSS PRON VOIR GRAMMAIRE A30; B21–2 le nôtre, la nôtre, *pl* les nôtres; **your house is larger than o.** votre maison est plus grande que la nôtre; **this is o.** ceci est à nous, ceci nous appartient; **o. is a nation of travellers** nous sommes une nation de voyageurs; **a friend of o.** un(e) de nos ami(e)s, un(e) ami(e) à nous; **it's no business of o.** cela ne nous regarde pas

ourself [aʊə'self] PERS PRON (*said by monarch, editor etc*) nous-même

ourselves [aʊə'selvz] PERS PRON PL VOIR GRAMMAIRE P. 29-30 **1** (*emphatic*) nous-mêmes; **we o. do not believe it** nous, pour notre part, ne le croyons pas **2** (*reflexive*) nous; **we are enjoying o. very much** nous nous amusons bien SEE GRAMMAR B28 **3** (*after preposition*) nous, nous-mêmes; **we say to o.** nous nous disons; **we shouldn't talk about o.** on ne doit pas parler de soi; **instead of fighting among o.** au lieu de nous battre entre nous

ousel ['uːz(ə)l] N = **ouzel**

oust [aʊst] VT **1** évincer; **the ousted ruler** le dirigeant évincé; **to o. sb from his post** déloger qn de son poste **2** *Law* (*deprive*) déposséder, évincer (**of** de)

OUT [aʊt] ADV **1** (*outside*) dehors; **to go** *or* **walk o.** sortir; **to run/stagger o.** sortir en courant/chancelant; **it's colder inside than o.** il fait plus froid à l'intérieur qu'à l'extérieur; **what's it** *or* **the weather like o.?** quel temps fait-il dehors?; **where are you going? – o. où allez-vous? –** dehors; **o. you go!** sortez!, hors d'ici!, allez, hop!; **voyage o.** voyage *m* d'aller

2 (*not in, not at home, released*) **I was only o. for a minute** je ne suis sorti qu'une minute; **my father is o.** mon père est sorti; **she's o. a lot in the daytime** elle est souvent absente pendant la journée; **we've been o. a lot recently** (*to theatres, restaurants etc*) nous sommes beaucoup sortis ces temps-ci; (*not been at home*) nous avons été beaucoup absents ces temps-ci; **he's o. in September** (*of prisoner*) il sort en septembre; **he is o. and about again** il est de nouveau sur pied; **she loves getting o. and about in her pushchair** elle aime beaucoup qu'on la promène en poussette; **she's o. picking mushrooms** elle est sortie (pour aller) cueillir des champignons; **the men are o.** (*on strike*) les ouvriers sont en grève; **to bring the workforce o.** appeler le personnel à la grève; **you'll have everybody o. if you're not careful** tu vas provoquer une grève générale si tu ne fais pas attention; **the jury was o. for two hours** le jury s'est retiré pendant deux heures pour délibérer; **the tide is o.** la marée est basse

3 (*distant*) **a long way o.** loin, éloigné; **o. at sea** en mer, au large; **four days o. from Rio** à quatre jours de Rio; **o. there** là-bas; **she does not live far o.** (*of the town*) elle n'habite pas loin de la ville; **o. in the country** dans la campagne

4 (*uncovered, in the open*) découvert, exposé; (*secret*) connu; (*flower*) épanoui; **he's been o. for years** (*openly homosexual*) cela fait des années qu'il ne cache plus son homosexualité; **he's not o.** il n'a pas révélé son homosexualité; **the tulips are o. early this year** les tulipes ont fleuri de bonne heure cette année; **the cherry tree is o.** le cerisier est en fleur; **the sun is o.** il fait soleil; **the moon is/the stars are o.** on voit la lune/les étoiles; *Fam* **the best game o.** le meilleur jeu qui soit; **the book is o.** (*published*) le livre est paru; (*borrowed*) le livre est en prêt; **to be o. at the elbows** (*of garment*) être troué *ou* percé aux coudes; **to whip o. a revolver** tirer *ou* sortir vivement un revolver; **o. loud** tout haut, à haute voix; **to say sth straight** *or* **right o.** dire qch carrément *ou* sans détours; *Fam* **o. with it!** allons, dites-le!, expliquez-vous!; **truth will o.** tôt ou tard la vérité se saura

5 (*indicating aim*) **he's simply o. for money** tout ce qui l'intéresse c'est l'argent; **she was o. for a good time** elle cherchait à s'amuser; **he's only o. for what he can get** il ne cherche qu'à servir ses propres intérêts; (*sexually*) tout ce qu'il veut, c'est s'envoyer en l'air; **to be o. to get sb** en avoir après qn; **I am not o. to reform the world** je n'ai pas entrepris de réformer le monde; **I'm o. for big results** je vise (à) de grands résultats

6 (*not in place*) **I've put my shoulder o.** (*of joint*) je me suis luxé l'épaule; *Pol* **the party that's o.** (*of power*) le parti qui n'est pas au pouvoir; **long skirts are o. this year** les jupes longues ne sont plus à la mode cette année; **the players who are o.** (*of the game*) les joueurs qui sont hors jeu *ou* ont été éliminés; *Cr* **not o.** = encore au guichet (*à la fin de l'innings, de la journée*); **to be o. for ten** avoir marqué dix

7 (*inaccurate*) **to be o.** être dans l'erreur; **I was £25 o.** je m'étais trompé de 25 livres; **to be o. in one's calculations** s'être trompé dans ses calculs; **I was not far o.** je ne me trompais pas de beaucoup; **the shot was only a centimetre o.** le coup n'a manqué le but que d'un centimètre; *Fam* **he was miles o.** il était totalement à côté

8 (*not functioning*) **the fire/gas is o.** le feu/

gaz est éteint; **the light was o.** la lumière était éteinte

9 *(indicating completion)* **before the week is o.** avant la fin de la semaine; *Radio* **o.!** terminé!

10 *(unconscious)* **to be o. cold** être K-O; **to be o. for seven seconds** *(of boxer)* rester au plancher pendant sept secondes; *Fam* **to be o. on one's feet** tomber de fatigue; **I went** *or* **was o. like a light** *(fell asleep)* je me suis endormi comme une bûche

11 o. of *(outside)* hors de, en dehors de; **o. of danger** hors de danger; **o. of sight** hors de vue; **to be o. of the country** être à l'étranger; **o. of doors = outdoors** *ADV*; **hardly were the words o. of my mouth** à peine avais-je prononcé ces mots; **I'm glad I'm o. of the whole business** je suis content de ne plus rien avoir à faire avec ça; **to feel o. of it** se sentir de trop; **to go o. of the house** sortir de la maison; *Fam* **I'm o. of here** je me casse; *Fam* **let's get o. of here** allez, on se casse; **is there a way o. of it?** y a-t-il (un) moyen d'en sortir?; **to throw sth/to jump o. of the window** jeter qch/sauter par la fenêtre; **from o. of the open window came bursts of laughter** par la fenêtre ouverte arrivaient des éclats de rire; **Gladiator by Monarch o. of Gladia** *(in breeding)* Gladiateur par *ou* issu de Monarch et Gladia; **to drink o. of a glass** boire dans un verre; **to drink o. of the bottle** boire à (même) la bouteille; **to copy sth o. of a book** copier qch dans un livre; **the firemen are paid o. of the rates** on paie les pompiers sur le budget de la ville; **she paid them o. of her own pocket** elle les a payés de sa poche; **choose one o. of these ten** choisissez-en un parmi les dix; **three days o. of four** trois jours sur quatre; **one o. of every three** un sur trois; **hut made o. of a few old planks** cabane faite de quelques vieilles planches; **o. of friendship/curiosity** par amitié/curiosité; **to act o. of fear** *(habitually)* agir sous l'emprise de la peur; *(on precise occasion)* agir sous le coup de la peur; **to be o. of tea/ideas** être à court de thé/d'idées; **o. of cash** démuni d'argent; *Com* **I'm o. of this item** je n'ai plus cet article pour le moment

INT 1 o. (with you)! sortez!, hors d'ici!
2 *Tennis* out!

ADJ *(outward)* **the o. door** la (porte de) sortie

N 1 *esp Am Fam (from difficult situation)* échappatoire *f*, **always leave yourself an o.** garde-toi toujours une porte de sortie *ou* une échappatoire
2 *Tennis* balle *f* (qui tombe) en dehors des limites
3 *TV, Cin (point where clip ends)* sortie *f*

PREP to go o. the door sortir par la porte; **to look o. the window** regarder par la fenêtre

VT to o. sb *(reveal to be homosexual)* révéler que qn est homosexuel

▸▸ *Comput* **o. box, o.tray** *(for e-mail)* corbeille *f* de départ; *TV, Radio* **o. words** mots *mpl* en trop (dans une séquence)

---

out- *PREF* **the government is attempting to out-Tory the Tories** le gouvernement essaie d'être plus conservateur que les conservateurs eux-mêmes

outage [ˈaʊtɪdʒ] **N 1** *Com (amount lost)* perte(s) *f(pl)*; quantité *f* perdue; **stock o.** rupture *f* de stock **2** *Elec* coupure *f*, *(of machine)* panne *f*

out-and-out *ADJ (liar, villain)* fieffé, achevé; *(republican etc)* convaincu; *(disaster, failure)* total, -aux; *(scandal, disgrace)* véritable; *(success, triumph)* éclatant

outasight [aʊtəˈsaɪt] *ADJ, INT esp Am Sl* fantastique

outback *Austr* **N** [ˈaʊtbæk] **the o.** l'intérieur *m*
ADV [aʊtˈbæk] à l'intérieur

outbid [aʊtˈbɪd] **VT** *(pt* **outbid**; *pp* **outbid, -bidden** [-ˈbɪdən]) *(at auction)* **to o. sb** enchérir sur qn et emporter la vente; **they were easily o. by the Getty Museum** le musée Getty n'a eu aucun mal à surenchérir et emporter la vente

outboard [ˈaʊtbɔːd] *Naut* **N** *(motor)* moteur *m* hors-bord
▸▸ **o. motor** moteur hors-bord

outbound [ˈaʊtbaʊnd] *ADJ* en partance
▸▸ **o. tourism** tourisme *m* émetteur

outbox [ˈaʊtbɒks] **VT** boxer mieux que; **he was completely outboxed** il a été complètement dominé

outbreak [ˈaʊtbreɪk] **N** *(of hostilities)* déclenchement *m*, début *m*, commencement *m*; *(of violence)* déclenchement; **there's been an o. of flu** il y a eu de nombreux cas de grippe; **there has been another o. of cholera** de nouveaux cas de choléra ont été enregistrés; **precautions against an o. of typhus** précautions contre une épidémie de typhus; **in order to prevent another o.** *(epidemic)* pour empêcher une autre épidémie; **o. of fire** incendie *m*; **at the o. of war** quand la guerre a éclaté

outbuilding [ˈaʊtbɪldɪŋ] **N** bâtiment *m* extérieur; **outbuildings** dépendances *fpl*

outburst [ˈaʊtbɜːst] **N** éclat *m*; *(of generosity)* élan *m*; *(of hatred etc)* déchaînement *m*, éruption *f*, *(of energy)* accès *m*; *(of activity, enthusiasm)* débordement *m*; *(of violence, gunfire)* explosion *f*; **an o. of laughter** un grand éclat de rire; **o. of temper** accès *ou* éclat de colère; **she apologized for her o.** elle s'est excusée de l'éclat qu'elle venait de faire

outcast [ˈaʊtkɑːst] **N** banni, -ie, proscrit, -ite; **an o. of society, a social o.** un paria

outclass [aʊtˈklɑːs] **VT** *(competitor)* surclasser

outcome [ˈaʊtkʌm] **N** résultat *m*, issue *f*; **the o. of our labours** le fruit de nos travaux; **I don't know what the o. will be** je ne sais pas ce qui en résultera

outcrop [ˈaʊtkrɒp] **N 1** *Geol* affleurement *m*, pointement *m* **2** *(projecting part)* saillie *f*

outcry [ˈaʊtkraɪ] **N** *(protest)* protestations *fpl*, tollé *m*; **there was a public o. when the hospital was closed** un tollé général s'est élevé contre la fermeture de l'hôpital; **to raise an o. against sb/sth** crier haro sur qn/qch; *StExch* **by open o.** à la criée

out-cue N *TV, Cin* signal *m* de sortie; *(video)* point *m* de sortie

outdated [aʊtˈdeɪtɪd] *ADJ (clothes, furniture)* démodé; *(custom, beliefs)* désuet, -uète, démodé; *(word, expression)* vieilli, démodé; *(textbook, theory)* démodé, périmé

outdistance [aʊtˈdɪstəns] **VT** distancer, dépasser

outdo [aʊtˈduː] **VT** *(pt* **outdid** [aʊtˈdɪd], *pp* **outdone** [aʊtˈdʌn])* l'emporter *ou* renchérir sur, surpasser *(sb in sth* qn en qch)*; **we don't want to be outdone when it comes to quality** nous ne voulons surtout pas être surpassés en ce qui concerne la qualité; **they are all anxious to o. each other** c'est à qui fera le mieux; **not to be outdone** pour ne pas être en reste *(in* de)*

outdoor [ˈaʊtdɔːr] *ADJ (life)* au grand air, en plein air, de plein air; *(swimming pool)* en plein air, découvert; *(games, activities)* de plein air; **she's an o. person** c'est une personne qui aime le grand air *ou* qui aime être dehors; **he's not an o. person** il n'aime pas spécialement le grand air
▸▸ **o. advertising** publicité *f* extérieure; **o. aerial** antenne *f* extérieure; **o. clothes** *(warm)* vêtements *mpl* chauds; *(waterproof)* vêtements de pluie; *Mktg* **o. network** réseau *m* d'affichage; *Cin, TV* **o. scene** extérieur *m*; *Cin* **o. set** décor *m* en extérieur; **o. shoes** *(warm)* grosses chaussures *fpl*, *(waterproof)* chaussures imperméables; *(for walking)* chaussures de marche; **leave your o. shoes at the door** laissez vos chaussures à la porte; *Cin, TV* **o. shot** extérieur *m*; **o. work** travail *m* (à l')extérieur *ou* en plein air

> Attention: ne pas confondre avec l'adverbe **outdoors**.

outdoors [aʊtˈdɔːz] *ADV* dehors; *(in open air)* en plein air; **to sleep o.** coucher à la belle étoile; **to sow o.** *(in gardening)* semer en pleine terre
N the o. la vie au grand air *ou* en plein air; **the great o.** la nature à l'état sauvage; **she's an o. person** c'est une personne qui aime le grand air *ou* qui aime être dehors

> Attention: ne pas confondre avec l'adjectif **outdoor**.

outer [ˈaʊtər] *ADJ ATTRIB (walls, covering)* extérieur; *(surface)* externe, extérieur; **the secretary in the o. office** la secrétaire qui se trouve dans le bureau à l'extérieur; **just within the o. limits of what is acceptable** tout juste à la limite de l'acceptable
▸▸ *Archit* **o. door** avant-portail *m, pl* avant-portails; **o. garments** vêtements *mpl* de dessus; **O. Mongolia** Mongolie-Extérieure *f*, **o. space** espace *m* intersidéral, cosmos *m*

outermost [ˈaʊtəməʊst] *ADJ* **1** *(closest to outside)* le plus à l'extérieur; **the o. layer was waterproofed** la première couche était imperméable; **make sure the coloured side is o.** assure-toi que le côté coloré se trouve à l'extérieur **2** *(most remote)* le plus reculé *ou* écarté; **to the o. parts of the earth** jusqu'aux extrémités de la terre

outfall [ˈaʊtfɔːl] **N** *(of pipe)* embouchure *f*

outfit [ˈaʊtfɪt] **N 1** *(clothes)* ensemble *m*; *Mil* tenue *f*, *(for child to play with)* panoplie *f* **2** *(equipment)* équipement *m* **3** *Fam (organization, company etc)* boîte *f*, *(of workers)* équipe *f* d'ouvriers; *Mil (unit)* unité *f*, *(rock band etc)* groupe *m*
VT *(person, expedition, ship)* équiper (**with** de)

outfitter [ˈaʊtfɪtər] **N 1** *esp Br (for clothes)* spécialiste *mf* de la confection **2** *Am (for hunting etc equipment)* fournisseur *m*

outflank [aʊtˈflæŋk] **VT 1** *Mil (enemy position)* déborder, tourner; **outflanking movement** mouvement *m* débordant *ou* tournant **2** *Fig (person)* circonvenir

outflow [ˈaʊtfləʊ] **N** *(of liquid)* écoulement *m*; *(of lava)* coulée *f*, *(from sewer)* décharge *f*, *Fin (of gold, currency)* sortie *f*

outfox [aʊtˈfɒks] **VT** *(person)* se montrer plus rusé que; *(security system)* déjouer

outgoing [ˈaʊtgəʊɪŋ] *ADJ* **1** *(departing)* *(tenant, official)* sortant; *(minister)* sortant; *(resigning)* démissionnaire; *(train, boat, plane)* en partance; *Tel (call)* sortant **2** *(sociable)* sociable; *(extrovert)* extraverti
NPL outgoings *Fin* dépenses *fpl*, débours *mpl*, sorties *fpl* de fonds
▸▸ *Com* **o. inventory** inventaire *m* de sortie; **o. mail** courrier *m* à expédier; *Ind* **o. shift** équipe *f* sortante *ou* relevée; **o. tide** marée *f* descendante

outgrow [aʊtˈgrəʊ] **VT** *(pt* **outgrew** [aʊtˈgruː], *pp* **outgrown** [aʊtˈgrəʊn])* **1** *(one's clothes etc)* devenir trop grand pour **2** *(habit)* perdre avec le temps *ou* en vieillissant; **I would have thought he'd have outgrown all that by now** j'aurais pensé qu'il aurait dépassé tout ça à présent; **to have outgrown one's friends** ne plus avoir grand-chose en commun avec ses amis **3** *(grow larger than)* *(person, thing)* croître plus vite que, devenir plus grand que

outgrowth ['aʊtgrəʊθ] N excroissance f

outguess [aʊt'ges] VT *(person)* déjouer les intentions de

outgun [aʊt'gʌn] VT avoir une puissance de feu supérieure à

out-Herod VT *Lit* to o. Herod se montrer plus cruel qu'Hérode

outhouse ['aʊthaʊs] N bâtiment m extérieur, dépendance f, *Am (outside lavatory)* toilettes fpl extérieures

outing ['aʊtɪŋ] N 1 *(excursion)* excursion f, sortie f; *(drive)* sortie, excursion, promenade f en voiture; *(walk)* promenade; *Sport (of footballer etc)* match m; **his first o. this season** *(of horse)* son premier concours de la saison; **day's o.** *(in a car etc)* sortie pour la journée; **school o.** sortie scolaire 2 *(of homosexual person)* révélation f de l'homosexualité

outlandish [aʊt'lændɪʃ] ADJ incongru, bizarre

outlast [aʊt'lɑːst] VT *(object)* durer plus longtemps que; *(person)* survivre à; **it has outlasted ten centuries of war, weather and vandalism** cela a résisté à dix siècles de guerres, d'intempéries et de vandalisme; **the theory has outlasted all its critics** cette théorie a résisté à l'assaut de tous les critiques

outlaw ['aʊtlɔː] N hors-la-loi m inv; **to declare sb an o.** déclarer qn hors la loi
▸ VT 1 *Hist (person)* mettre hors la loi, proscrire 2 *(custom etc)* proscrire, bannir

outlay ['aʊtleɪ] N frais mpl, dépenses fpl, débours mpl; **to get back** or **recover one's o.** rentrer dans ses fonds; **without any great o.** *(by company)* sans grande mise de fonds; *(by individual)* à peu de frais

outlet ['aʊtlet] N 1 *Tech* orifice m *(d'émission)*; *(for air, gas)* sortie f, *(for steam)* échappement m; *(of pipe)* débouché m 2 *Fig* exutoire m; **an o. for one's energy** un exutoire pour son trop-plein d'énergie 3 *Com (for goods)* débouché m; **(retail) o.** point m de vente 4 *esp Am Elec* prise f de courant
▸ *Tech* **o. drain, o. pipe** tuyau m d'écoulement; *Com* **o. village** = centre m commercial spécialisé dans les marques à prix réduit

outline ['aʊtlaɪn] N 1 *(form)* **outline(s)** *(of hill, building, boat etc)* contour(s) m(pl), profil m; *(of person, building)* silhouette f, *(of car)* ligne f 2 *(drawing)* dessin m au trait, tracé m; *(in text processing)* plan m de document; *Fig (of play, novel)* argument m, canevas m; *(of plan, policy etc)* grandes lignes fpl, grands traits mpl; **drawn in o.** dessiné au trait; **in o.** en gros, dans les grandes lignes; **rough o.** premier jet m; **main** or **general** or **broad outlines** *(of project)* ébauche f; **a fairly detailed o. of the plan** une description assez détaillée du projet; **could you give us a quick o. of your plans?** pourriez-vous nous décrire les grandes lignes de votre projet?; **an o. of French history** un résumé de l'histoire de France; **outlines of astronomy** éléments mpl d'astronomie
▸ VT 1 *(the shape of sth)* silhouetter 2 *(plot of a novel etc)* esquisser; *(plan, project)* esquisser, tracer les grandes lignes de; *(plan of action)* ébaucher, indiquer; **I briefly outlined my objections/what needed to be done** j'ai donné un bref aperçu de mes objections/de ce qui devait être fait
▸ **o. agreement** protocole m d'accord; **o. drawing** dessin au trait; *Comput* **o. font** police f vectorielle; **o. plan** plan schématique *ou* d'ensemble; *Cin, TV* **o. script** scénario m indicatif

outliner ['aʊtlaɪnər] N *Comput* outliner m

outlive [aʊt'lɪv] VT *(person)* survivre à; **he will o. us all** il nous enterrera tous; **to have outlived its usefulness** *(of machine, theory etc)* ne plus servir (à rien); **he had outlived the era which had need of him** l'époque qui avait besoin de lui était maintenant révolue

outlook ['aʊtlʊk] N 1 *(view)* vue f, perspective f; **the political/economic o.** l'horizon m politique/économique; **the o. is gloomy** *(for industry, economy, weather etc)* les perspectives ne sont pas réjouissantes 2 *(attitude)* façon f de voir les choses; **we need a fresh o. on the matter** nous avons besoin d'un nouveau regard sur le sujet; **o. on life** conception f de la vie 3 **to be on the o. for sth** être à l'affût de qch

outlying ['aʊtlaɪɪŋ] ADJ ATTRIB éloigné, isolé; **o. areas** régions fpl périphériques

outmanoeuvre, *Am* **outmaneuver** [aʊtmə'nuːvər] VT *Mil (the enemy)* l'emporter sur en tactique; *Fig (person)* déjouer les tactiques de; **we've been outmanoeuvred** nos tactiques ont été déjouées

outmatch [aʊt'mætʃ] VT surclasser, dominer

outmoded [aʊt'məʊdɪd] ADJ *(custom, beliefs)* désuet, -uète, démodé; *(furniture, theory, word)* démodé

outnumber [aʊt'nʌmbər] VT *(the enemy etc)* l'emporter en nombre sur; **we were heavily outnumbered** nous étions très minoritaires; **they outnumbered us three to one** ils étaient en majorité de trois à un par rapport à nous

out-of-body experience N expérience f hors du corps, EHC f, autoscopie f

out-of-court ADJ *(settlement)* à l'amiable

out-of-doors ADV = **outdoors** ADV

out-of-focus ADJ flou

out-of-phase ADJ *TV, Cin* déphasé

out-of-pocket ADJ
▸ **o. expenses** menues dépenses fpl, frais mpl

out-of-shot ADJ *TV, Cin* en dehors du champ

out-of-sync ADJ désynchronisé, hors synchronisation

out-of-the-way ADJ 1 *(place etc)* écarté, loin de tout et de tous 2 *(unusual)* peu ordinaire, peu commun, insolite; **it was nothing o.** cela n'avait rien d'extraordinaire

out-of-town ADJ *(shopping centre, retail park)* situé en dehors du centre-ville

out-of-towner [-'taʊnər] N *Am Fam* étranger, -ère à la ville; **he's an o.** il n'est pas d'ici

outpace [aʊt'peɪs] VT *(competitor etc)* dépasser, distancer; **demand has outpaced production** la demande a dépassé la production

outpatient ['aʊtpeɪʃənt] N malade mf qui vient consulter à l'hôpital; **he was being treated as an o.** il était traité en consultation externe
▸ **outpatients' clinic, outpatients' department** service m des consultations externes; **o. treatment** traitement m ambulatoire

outplacement ['aʊtpleɪsmənt] N = licenciement m accompagné d'aide et de conseils fournis par l'employeur pour trouver un autre emploi

outplay [aʊt'pleɪ] VT *(person)* jouer mieux que; **she was outplayed** son adversaire a joué mieux qu'elle

outpoint [aʊt'pɔɪnt] N *(on tape, film)* point m de sortie

outpost ['aʊtpəʊst] N *Mil* poste m avancé; **the last o. of civilization** le dernier bastion de la civilisation

outpouring ['aʊtpɔːrɪŋ] N *(of feelings)* épanchement m, effusion f, *(of ideas, literary creativity)* déluge m, flux m; **outpourings of the heart** épanchements, effusions

output ['aʊtpʊt] N 1 *(of factory, worker)* production f, rendement m; *(of machine)* débit m, rendement; **o. of an author** production littéraire d'un auteur; **he kept up a phenomenal o. throughout his writing career** il a produit à un rythme phénoménal tout au long de sa carrière littéraire; **our o. is not keeping pace with demand** notre production est insuffisante pour répondre à la demande 2 *Tech etc (of engine)* puissance f, rendement m; *Elec (of generator)* débit m; *Elec* **power o.** puissance débitée *ou* de sortie 3 *Comput (of data, information)* sortie f, *(of data processing operation)* résultat(s) m
▸ VT *(pt, pp output)* 1 *(of factory etc)* produire 2 *Comput (data)* sortir (**to** sur)
▸ *Comput* **o. buffer** mémoire f tampon de sortie; *Comput* **o. card** carte f sortie, carte résultat; *Comput* **o. device** périphérique m de sortie; *Comput* **o. file** fichier m de sortie; *Comput* **o. formatting** mise f en forme de sortie; *Econ* **o. gap** écart m de production; *Comput* **o. port** port m de sortie; *Tech* **o. shaft** arbre m de sortie; *Acct* **o. tax** TVA f encaissée, impôt m à la consommation; *Tech* **o. torque** couple m en sortie; *Elec* **o. voltage** tension f de sortie

outrage ['aʊtreɪdʒ] N 1 *(vicious act)* atrocité f, *(violation of decency)* scandale m; **to commit an o. on** or **against sb** commettre une atrocité sur qn; **$200 a ticket?!, it's an o.!** 200 dollars un billet?!, c'est un scandale!; **o. against humanity/society** crime m contre l'humanité/la société *ou* de lèse-humanité/ de lèse-société; **bomb o.** *(in headline)* attentat m à la bombe 2 *(indignation)* indignation f *(at* contre)
▸ VT 1 *(public decency, feelings etc)* outrager, faire outrage à 2 *(make indignant) (person)* scandaliser, outrer; **she's easy to o.** elle se scandalise facilement; **I am outraged** je suis scandalisé *ou* outré

outrageous [aʊt'reɪdʒəs] ADJ *(cruelty)* atroce; *(price, conduct)* scandaleux; *(statement, accusation)* outrageant; **it's/he's o.!** cela/il dépasse toutes les bornes!; **he enjoys being o.** il aime scandaliser; *Fam* **an o. get-up** une tenue extravagante

outrageously [aʊt'reɪdʒəslɪ] ADV *(cruel)* atrocement; *(expensive)* scandaleusement; *(to behave)* d'une façon scandaleuse; *(to dress)* de façon extravagante

outrageousness [aʊt'reɪdʒəsnɪs] N *(of behaviour)* caractère m scandaleux; *(of clothes, hairstyle)* extravagance f, **the o. of the prices** les prix scandaleux

outrank [aʊt'ræŋk] VT 1 *(be of higher rank than)* être supérieur en grade à; **he was outranked by most of those present** la plupart des personnes présentes avaient un grade supérieur au sien 2 *(take precedence over)* avoir *ou* prendre le pas sur; **to be outranked by** donner *ou* céder le pas à

outreach ['aʊtriːtʃ] N *Admin* = activité f visant à encourager les gens à profiter des avantages sociaux
▸ **o. worker** = employé, ée dans un bureau d'aide sociale

outrider ['aʊtraɪdər] N *(on horseback)* cavalier m d'escorte; **(motor-cycle) o.** motard m d'escorte

outrigger ['aʊtrɪgər] N 1 *(in rowing)* portenage m inv en dehors; *(boat)* outrigger m 2 *(on canoe)* balancier m

outright ADV [aʊt'raɪt] 1 *(completely)* complètement; *(immediately)* du premier coup, sur le coup; **to buy sth o.** acheter qch (au) comptant; **he was killed o.** il fut tué sur le coup *ou* net 2 *(bluntly)* sans ménagement;

(frankly) franchement, carrément; *(to deny)* carrément; **to refuse o.** refuser tout net

ADJ ATTRIB ['aʊtraɪt] *(failure)* total, -aux; *(refusal)* net; **it's o. wickedness** c'est de la pure méchanceté; **an o. disaster** un vrai désastre; **the o. winner** le vainqueur incontesté

▸▸**o. gift** don *m* pur et simple; **o. payment** somme *f* forfaitaire; **o. sale** vente *f* au comptant

outrival [aʊt'raɪv(ə)l] VT (**-ll-**, *Am* **-l-**) *(person)* surpasser, l'emporter sur

outrun [aʊt'rʌn] VT *(pt* outran [aʊt'ræn], *pp* outrun; *prp* outrunning) **1** *(go faster than)* **to o. sb** gagner qn de vitesse; **he can o. the rest of the team** il court plus vite que le reste de l'équipe **2** *(exceed)* **his zeal outruns his discretion** son ardeur l'emporte sur son jugement

outs [aʊts] NPL *Am Fam* **to be on the o. with sb** être brouillé avec qn; **they're on the o.** ils sont brouillés

outsell [aʊt'sel] VT *(pt, pp* outsold [aʊt'səʊld]) *(object)* se vendre mieux que; *(competitors)* vendre plus que; **we are being outsold by the competition** nos concurrents vendent plus que nous

outset ['aʊtset] N commencement *m*; **at the o.** au départ, au début; **from the o.** dès le début

outshine [aʊt'ʃaɪn] VT *(pt, pp* outshone [aʊt'ʃɒn]) **1** *(shine brighter than)* briller plus que **2** *Fig (surpass)* surpasser, éclipser; **I don't like being outshone** je n'aime pas qu'on m'éclipse *ou* me surpasse

OUTSIDE

| N extérieur ▪ dehors |
| ADJ extérieur **1** ▪ maximum **2** |
| ADV dehors |
| PREP à l'extérieur de **1** ▪ devant **1** ▪ en dehors de **3** |

N [aʊt'saɪd] *(of book, building etc)* extérieur *m*; **on the o.** à l'extérieur de qch; **from the o.** de l'extérieur, du dehors; **the fruit is yellow on the o.** le fruit est jaune à l'extérieur; **friends on the o.** *(of prisoner)* des amis dehors; **to open a door from the o.** ouvrir une porte du dehors *ou* de l'extérieur; **at the o.** *(at most)* tout au plus, au maximum; **to come up on the o.** *(in race)* arriver sur l'extérieur

ADJ [aʊt'saɪd] **1** *(influence)* extérieur; *(help)* de l'extérieur; **the o. world** le monde extérieur

2 *(price, odds, amount etc)* maximum; **there's an o. chance** *(remote)* ce n'est pas exclu (**of** … que … + *sub*); **I think we have an o. possibility** je pense que nous avons une toute petite chance

ADV [aʊt'saɪd] dehors, à l'extérieur, au dehors; **to go o.** sortir, aller dehors; **to run/dash/etc o.** sortir en courant/à toute vitesse/etc; **the taxi is o.** le taxi vous attend dehors; **seen from o.** vu de dehors *ou* de l'extérieur; *Fam* **o. of** à l'extérieur de, en dehors de; *Fam* **o. of a few friends nobody knows anything about it** sauf *ou* à part quelques amis, personne n'en sait rien

PREP [aʊt'saɪd] **1** *(in space)* en dehors de, hors de, à l'extérieur de; **o. my bedroom** *(at the door)* à la porte de ma chambre; *(below the windows)* sous les fenêtres de ma chambre; **I'll meet you o. the cinema** je vous retrouverai devant le cinéma; **o. the town** en dehors de la ville

2 *(not part of)* **o. working hours** en dehors des heures de travail; **he's o. the family** il n'appartient pas à la famille; **that's o. our agreement** ça ne fait pas partie de notre accord; **that's o. our terms of reference** cela n'entre pas dans nos attributions; **it's o. our**

range (of gun, tank etc) c'est hors de (notre) portée; *(of aircraft)* ce n'est pas dans notre rayon d'action; *(too expensive)* ce n'est pas dans nos prix

3 *(apart from)* en dehors de; **o. a few friends** en dehors de quelques amis

▸▸**o. aerial** antenne *f* extérieure; *TV* **o. broadcast** émission *f* réalisée en dehors des studios; *TV* **o. broadcasting** émissions réalisées en dehors des studios; *TV* **o. broadcasting vehicle** car *m* régie, unité *f* mobile de tournage; *St Exch* **o. broker** courtier, -ière marron *ou* libre; *Rugby* **o. centre** deuxième centre *m*; **o. diameter** diamètre *m* extérieur; *Rugby* **o. half** demi *m* d'ouverture; **o. interests** intérêts *mpl* en dehors de son travail/de sa famille; **o. lane** *(driving on left)* file *f ou* voie *f* de droite; *(driving on right)* file *ou* voie de gauche; *Sport* couloir *m* extérieur; *Sport* **o. left** ailier *m* gauche; *Tel* **o. line** ligne *f* extérieure; *St Exch* **o. market** marché *m* hors cote *ou* en coulisse; *Constr* **o. measurements** dimensions *fpl* hors d'œuvre; *Sport* **o. right** ailier droit; **o. work** travail *m* extérieur *ou* à l'extérieur; *(in open air)* travail au grand air *ou* en plein air; **o. worker** *(at home)* ouvrier, -ière à domicile

outsider [aʊt'saɪdər] N **1** *(socially)* étranger, -ère; **he had always been a bit of an o.** il avait toujours été un peu à l'écart **2** *(in election), Horseracing, Sport etc* outsider *m* **3** *St Exch* coulissier *m*

outsize ['aʊtsaɪz] N *Com (large size)* très grande taille *f*, *(in men's clothes)* très grand patron *m*

outsize(d) ['aʊtsaɪz(d)] ADJ USU ATTRIB **1** **o. dress** robe en très grande taille **2** *(packet etc)* géant; *(appetite, ego)* démesuré

outskirts ['aʊtskɜːts] NPL limites *fpl*, (a)bords *mpl*; *(of forest)* orée *f*, lisière *f*, *(of town)* faubourgs *mpl*; *(of city)* banlieue *f*, périphérie *f*

outsmart [aʊt'smɑːt] VT *Fam (person)* surpasser en finesse; **they had been outsmarted once again** une fois de plus ils avaient trouvé plus malin qu'eux

outsource [aʊt'sɔːs] VT externaliser; **computer maintenance has been outsourced to another company** l'entretien du matériel informatique a été externalisé

outsourcing ['aʊtsɔːsɪŋ] N externalisation *f*

outspend [aʊt'spend] VT dépenser plus que

outspoken [aʊt'spəʊkən] ADJ *(person)* franc, *f* franche, carré; **to be o.** parler franc, ne pas mâcher ses mots; **o. criticism** critique *f* franche

outspokenly [aʊt'spəʊkənlɪ] ADV franchement, carrément, rondement

outspokenness [aʊt'spəʊkənnɪs] N franchise *f*, franc-parler *m, pl* francs-parlers

outspread [aʊt'spred] ADJ étendu, étalé, déployé; **with wings o., with o.** ['aʊtspred] **wings** les ailes déployées; **with o. arms, with arms o.** les bras grand ouverts

outstanding [aʊt'stændɪŋ] ADJ **1** *(remarkable)* remarquable, exceptionnel, hors du commun; **a man of o. talents/merits/intelligence** un homme aux talents/mérites exceptionnels/à l'intelligence exceptionnelle; **a matter of o. importance** une affaire de première importance; **she plays o. tennis** c'est une joueuse de tennis exceptionnelle *ou* remarquable **2** *(main, prominent)* *(feature)* marquant **3** *(unresolved)* *(business)* en suspens, en cours de règlement; *(problem)* pas encore résolu **4** *Fin (amount, account)* impayé, à recouvrer, à percevoir; *(payment)* arriéré, en retard; *(invoice)* en souffrance; *(interest)* échu, arriéré

▸▸*Fin* **o. balance** solde *m* à découvert;

Banking **o. cheques** chèques *mpl* en circulation; *Fin* **o. debts** créances *fpl* à recouvrer, recouvrements *mpl*

outstandingly [aʊt'stændɪŋlɪ] ADV éminemment, exceptionnellement

outstay [aʊt'steɪ] VT *(person)* rester plus longtemps que; **I hope I haven't outstayed my welcome** j'espère ne pas avoir abusé de votre hospitalité

outstretched ['aʊtstretʃt] ADJ *(wing)* déployé; *(leg, arm)* tendu; **with arms o., with o. arms** *(to welcome sb)* les bras grand ouverts; **to lie o.** être allongé de tout son long

outstrip [aʊt'strɪp] VT (**-pp-**) *(person when running)* devancer, dépasser; *Sport (competitor)* distancer; *Fig (expectations, budget)* dépasser; *(surpass)* surpasser (**sb in sth** qn en qch)

out-supplier N *Com* fournisseur *m* potentiel

outta ['aʊtə] PREP *Fam (out of)* **let's get o. here!** allez, on se casse!; **you must be o. your mind!** mais t'es complètement dingue!; *Am* **o. sight** *(excellent)* dingue, dément

outtake ['aʊteɪk] N *Cin, TV* coupure *f*, prise *f* non-utilisée, coupe *f*

outvote [aʊt'vəʊt] VT *(usu in pass) (person, government)* mettre en minorité; *(proposal)* rejeter à la majorité des voix; **we were outvoted** nous avons été mis en minorité, la majorité des voix a été contre nous

outward ['aʊtwəd] ADJ **1 in an o. direction** vers l'extérieur; **o. journey** voyage *m* aller **2** *(appearance)* extérieur; **o. form** extérieur *m*, dehors *m*

ADV = **outwards**; *Naut* **o.-bound** *(ship)* en partance; *(for foreign destination)* en route pour l'étranger; **O.-Bound®** course école *f* d'endurance (en plein air)

▸▸**o. half** *(of ticket)* billet *m* aller; *Econ* **o. investment** investissement *m* à l'étranger

outwardly ['aʊtwədlɪ] ADV en apparence; **she was o. calm** en apparence elle était calme

outwards ['aʊtwədz] ADV vers l'extérieur; **to turn one's feet o.** tourner les pieds en dehors

outwear [aʊt'weər] VT *(pt* outwore [aʊt'wɔːr], *pp* outworn [aʊt'wɔːn]) **the system has outworn its usefulness** le système est désormais périmé

outweigh [aʊt'weɪ] VT **1** *(be more important than)* l'emporter sur; **these arguments were outweighed by considerations of security** les questions de sécurité l'ont emporté sur ces arguments **2** *(weigh more than)* peser plus que

outwit [aʊt'wɪt] VT (**-tt-**) *(person)* se montrer plus malin que; *(thwart plans of)* déjouer les intentions *ou* les menées de; **once again he had been outwitted** une fois de plus il avait trouvé plus malin que lui

outwith [aʊt'wɪθ] PREP *Scot* = **outside 3**

outworn ['aʊtwɔːn] ADJ *(custom, idea)* périmé

ouzel ['uːz(ə)l] N *(bird)* **ring o.** merle *m* à plastron *ou* à collier; **water o.** cincle *m* plongeur, merle d'eau

oval ['əʊv(ə)l] ADJ (en) ovale; *Am Pol* **the O. Office** = le bureau du Président des États-Unis; **he has decided to make a bid for the O. Office** il a décidé de se présenter à la Maison-Blanche

N ovale *m*

ovarian [əʊ'veərɪən] ADJ *Anat, Bot* ovarien

ovariectomy [əʊvərɪ'ektəmɪ] N *Surg* ovariectomie *f*

ovary ['əʊvərɪ] N *Anat, Bot* ovaire *m*

ovate ['əʊveɪt] ADJ *Biol* ové, ovale

ovation [əʊˈveɪʃən] N ovation f; **to give sb an o.** faire une ovation ou un triomphe à qn; **to give sb a standing o.** se lever pour applaudir qn; **the performers received a standing o.** tout le monde s'est levé pour applaudir les acteurs

oven [ˈʌv(ə)n] N four m; Ind four, étuve f; **electric/gas o.** four électrique/à gaz; **to put sth in the o.** mettre qch au four; **to cook sth in a slow/quick o.** cuire qch à four doux/vif; **it's like an o. in here** on se croirait dans un four ici; **to put one's head in the o.** se suicider (au gaz); **o. gloves** or **mitts** gants mpl isolants

oven-proof ADJ (dish) allant au four

oven-ready ADJ (meal, dish) prêt à mettre au four; (chicken, meat) prêt à rôtir

ovenware [ˈʌv(ə)nweər] N vaisselle f allant au four

OVER [ˈəʊvər]

| **PREP** sur **1, 2** ▪ par-dessus **1** ▪ au-dessus de **2** ▪ à propos de **3** ▪ plus de **5** |
| **ADV** encore **2** ▪ plus **7** |
| **ADJ** fini |

PREP 1 (on surface of, on top of) sur; **to spill ink o. the table** répandre de l'encre sur la table; **to spread a cloth o. sth** étendre une toile sur ou par-dessus qch; **all o. the north of England** sur tout le nord de l'Angleterre; **to search all o. Paris** chercher dans tout Paris; **famous all o. the world** célèbre dans le monde entier; **to glance o. sth** parcourir qch des yeux ou du regard; **length o. all** longueur totale ou hors tout; Fam **to be all o. sb** (be excessively polite) faire l'empressé auprès de qn; (be excessively physical) accaparer qn; **o. (the top of) sth** par-dessus qch; **to throw sth o. the wall** jeter qch par-dessus le mur; **to read o. sb's shoulder** lire par-dessus l'épaule de qn; **with his coat o. his shoulder** le manteau sur l'épaule; **he wore an old coat o. his uniform** il portait un vieux manteau par-dessus son uniforme; **to stumble** or **trip o. sth** buter contre qch

2 (above) directly **o. our heads** juste au-dessus de nos têtes; **bending o. his work** courbé sur son travail; **to have a chat o. a glass of wine** bavarder tout en prenant un verre de vin; **to discuss sth o. lunch** discuter de qch pendant le déjeuner; **I couldn't hear her o. the noise of the machine** je ne pouvais pas l'entendre à cause du bruit de la machine; **with his hat o. his eyes** le chapeau enfoncé jusqu'aux yeux; Math **12 o. 3** 12 divisé par 3; **to have an advantage o. sb** avoir un avantage sur qn; **to reign/govern o. a country** régner sur/gouverner un pays VOIR GRAMMAIR A72

3 (about) à propos de; **to laugh o. sth** rire (à propos) de qch; **to cry o. sb/sth** pleurer qn/qch; **we had trouble o. the tickets** nous avons eu des ennuis à propos de ou au sujet des billets; **to fight o. sth** se battre à cause de ou au sujet de qch; (in order to obtain it) se battre pour (obtenir) qch

4 (across) **to cross o. the road** traverser la rue; **the house o. the way** la maison d'en face; **o. the border** de l'autre côté ou au-delà de la frontière; **to live o. the river** habiter de l'autre côté de la rivière; **from o. the seas** de par delà les mers; **the bridge o. the river** le pont qui enjambe la rivière VOIR GRAMMAIRE A72

5 (in excess of) **numbers o. a hundred** numéros au-dessus de cent; **o. ten pounds** plus de dix livres; **not o. 250 grams** (in post office) jusqu'à 250 grammes; **to be o. the limit** dépasser la limite; (of drunk driver) avoir dépassé le taux légal d'alcoolémie; **children o. five (years of age), the o. fives** les enfants au-dessus de ou de plus de cinq

ans; **he's o. fifty** il a (dé)passé la cinquantaine; **he spoke for o. an hour** il a parlé pendant plus d'une heure; **he receives tips o. and above his wages** il reçoit des pourboires en sus de son salaire

6 (in the course of) **o. the last three years** au cours des trois dernières années; **o. Christmas** pendant la période de Noël ou des fêtes; **I'll do it o. the weekend** je le ferai pendant le week-end; **o. a period of several weeks** pendant plusieurs semaines; **let's spread it o. a period of weeks** étalons-le sur une période de plusieurs semaines

7 (recovered from the effects of) **I'm/you're/she's/etc o. the worst** le plus mauvais moment est passé; **to be o. a cold** être guéri d'un rhume; **she's o. the disappointment** elle est remise de sa déception; **don't worry, you'll be o. her soon** ne t'en fais pas, bientôt tu n'y penseras plus

ADV 1 (everywhere) **famous the world o.** célèbre dans le monde entier; **to ache all o.** avoir mal partout; **that's him all o.** c'est tout lui

2 (indicating repetition) encore; **I've had to do it all o. again** j'ai dû tout refaire, j'ai dû le faire de ou à nouveau; **ten times o.** dix fois de suite; **twice o.** à deux reprises; **o. and o. (again)** à de nombreuses reprises, esp Lit maintes et maintes fois, esp Lit à maintes reprises; **he did it o. and o. (again) until …** il a recommencé des dizaines de fois jusqu'à ce que …

3 (over the top of sth) par-dessus, dessus; **throw it o.!** (over the wall etc) lance-le par-dessus!; Fam (throw it to me) lance-le moi!; **Concorde flew o.** le Concorde est passé

4 (down) **to knock sth o.** renverser qch; **and o. I went** et me voilà par terre

5 (to other side) **please turn o.!** voir au dos!, tournez s'il vous plaît!; **to turn sth o. and o.** tourner et retourner qch; **to bend sth o.** plier qch

6 (across) **he led me o. to the window** il m'a conduit à la fenêtre; **to cross o.** (street etc) traverser; (the Channel etc) faire la traversée; **o. here** ici, de ce côté; **o. there** là-bas; **ask him o.** demandez-lui de venir (chez nous); **our friends are coming o. tomorrow** nos amis vont venir nous voir demain; **to deliver sth o. to sb** remettre qch à qn; **to hand sth o. to sb** remettre qch entre les mains de qn; Radio **o. to you**; Radio **o. and out** à vous, terminé; **o. to you** (it's your turn) c'est votre tour, c'est à vous; **now o. to our Cardiff studio** nous passons maintenant l'antenne à nos studios de Cardiff

7 (with specific figure or amount) plus; **articles costing £100 or o.** les articles de 100 livres et plus

8 (in excess) en plus, en excès; **allow five minutes o.** ajoutez-y cinq minutes; **children of fourteen and o.** les enfants de quatorze ans et plus; **three into seven goes twice and one o.** sept divisé par trois donne deux, et il reste un; **you will keep what is (left) o.** vous garderez l'excédent ou le surplus; **I have one card left o.** il me reste une carte

9 (excessively) (easy, difficult, expensive) trop; **we're not o. busy** nous n'avons pas trop à faire; **he didn't look o. cheerful** il n'était pas d'une gaieté folle

10 (until later) **to hold o.** (decision) remettre (à plus tard)

ADJ (finished) fini, terminé; **the danger is o.** le danger est passé; **the rain is o.** la pluie s'est arrêtée ou a cessé; **the game is o.** la partie est finie; **the war was just o.** la guerre venait de finir ou de s'achever; **when the strike is o.** quand la grève sera finie; **it is (all) o.** c'est fini; **it is all o. with me** c'en est fait de moi; **it's all o. between us** tout est fini entre nous; **that's o. and done with** voilà qui est fini et bien fini

N **1** Com **shorts and overs** déficits mpl et excédents mpl; **overs** (in publishing) exemplaires mpl de passe

2 Cr série f de six balles

overabundance [əʊvərəˈbʌndəns] N surabondance f

overabundant [əʊvərəˈbʌndənt] ADJ surabondant

overachieve [əʊvərəˈtʃiːv] VI (exceed expectations) faire mieux que prévu; **parents shouldn't push their children to o.** les parents ne devraient pas pousser leurs enfants à en faire trop

overachiever [əʊvərəˈtʃiːvər] N esp Sch personne f qui en fait trop; (successful person) surdoué, -ée

overact [əʊvəˈrækt] VI (of actor) forcer son jeu

overactive [əʊvərˈæktɪv] ADJ trop actif; Med **to have an o. thyroid** faire de l'hyperthyroïdie

overaffectionate [əʊvərəˈfekʃənət] ADJ affectueux à l'excès

over-age ADJ au-dessus de l'âge limite

overall ADJ [ˈəʊvərɔːl] **1** (from one end to the other) total, -aux, hors tout **2** (taken as a whole) général, -aux

ADV [əʊvərˈɔːl] dans l'ensemble, globalement; **England came third o.** au classement général l'Angleterre a fini troisième; **yacht measuring … o.** yacht dont la longueur totale ou hors tout est de …

N [ˈəʊvərɔːl] (garment) blouse f, (child's) tablier m, blouse; **overalls** combinaison f (de travail), salopette f, Fam bleus mpl (de travail)

▸▸ **o. budget** budget m global; **o. consumption** consommation f totale; **o. demand** demande f globale; **o. efficiency** (total efficiency) rendement m total; (efficiency in general) rendement global

overanxious [əʊvərˈæŋkʃəs] ADJ **1** (excessively worried) trop inquiet; **you're being o. about her** tu t'inquiètes beaucoup trop pour elle; **he is o. about getting us to follow the regulations** sa grande préoccupation c'est de nous faire suivre le règlement **2** (excessively eager) **o. to please** trop soucieux de plaire

overarm [ˈəʊvərɑːm] ADV **to serve o.** (in tennis, badminton) servir par en dessus; Cr **to bowl o.** servir par en dessus

▸▸ Cr **o. bowling** service m au-dessus de la tête; **o. service** (in tennis, badminton) service au-dessus de la tête; Swimming **o. stroke** brasse f indienne, nage f (à l')indienne

overassess [əʊvərəˈses] VT Fin (for tax) surimposer

overassessment [əʊvərəˈsesmənt] N Fin (for tax) surimposition f

overawe [əʊvərˈɔː] VT intimider; (of prospect, difficulty, surroundings) impressionner; **don't be overawed by him** ne te laisse pas intimider par lui, ne sois pas intimidé par lui

overbalance [əʊvəˈbæləns] VI (of person) perdre l'équilibre; (of thing) se renverser
VT (knock over) renverser

overbearing [əʊvəˈbeərɪŋ] ADJ autoritaire; **in an o. manner** autoritairement

overblown [əʊvəˈbləʊn] ADJ (flower) trop épanoui ou ouvert; (style, book) ampoulé; (praise) excessif

overboard [ˈəʊvəbɔːd] ADV Naut par-dessus bord; **to be washed o.** être enlevé par une lame; **to throw sb/sth o.** (into water) jeter qn/qch par-dessus bord ou à la mer; Fig **to throw sb/sth o.** se débarrasser de qn/abandonner qch; **to fall o.** tomber à la mer; **man o.!** un homme à la mer!; Fam **to go o.** (be enthusiastic) s'emballer (**for sb/sth** pour qn/qch)

overbook [əʊvəˈbʊk] VT & VI *(of airline etc)* surréserver, surbooker; **this flight was over-booked** il y a eu surréservation sur ce vol

overbooking [əʊvəˈbʊkɪŋ] N surréservation *f*, surbook(ing) *m*, surlocation *f*

overboot [ˈəʊvəbuːt] N couvre-chaussure *m*, *pl* couvre-chaussures

overborrow [əʊvəˈbɒrəʊ] VI *Fin (of company)* emprunter de façon excessive

overborrowing [əʊvəˈbɒrəʊɪŋ] N *Fin (of company)* surendettement *m*

overbought [əʊvəˈbɔːt] ADJ *St Exch (market)* surévalué, suracheté

overburden [əʊvəˈbɜːd(ə)n] VT *(with work, responsibility)* surcharger, accabler (**with** de); **he is not overburdened with principles** ce ne sont pas les principes qui l'étouffent

overcapacity [ˈəʊvəkəˈpæsɪti] N *Ind* surcapacité *f*

overcapitalization [əʊvəkæpɪtəlaɪˈzeɪʃən] N *Fin* surcapitalisation *f*

overcapitalize [əʊvəˈkæpɪtəlaɪz] VT *Fin* surcapitaliser

overcast [ˈəʊvəkɑːst] ADJ *(sky, weather)* couvert, nuageux; *(day)* nuageux; *Fig (face)* assombri; *(expression, look)* sombre; **it will become o. later** cela se couvrira plus tard; **it's looking a bit o.** ça a l'air un peu couvert

overcautious [əʊvəˈkɔːʃəs] ADJ trop prudent (**about** à propos de)

overcautiously [əʊvəˈkɔːʃəslɪ] ADV avec trop de prudence, avec une prudence excessive

overcharge [əʊvəˈtʃɑːdʒ] VT **1** *Com* faire payer trop cher à; **to o. sb for** *or* **on sth** faire payer qch trop cher à qn; **he overcharged me by a pound** il m'a fait payer une livre en trop **2** *Fig (overload) (battery)* surcharger ▸ VI *(of shopkeeper etc)* faire payer trop cher

overcoat [ˈəʊvəkəʊt] N pardessus *m*

overcome [əʊvəˈkʌm] VT *(pt* **overcame** [əʊvəˈkeɪm]*, pp* **overcome**) **1** *(one's opponents etc)* triompher de, vaincre; *(difficulty, problem)* venir à bout de, avoir raison de; *(one's reluctance, fears etc)* dominer, maîtriser; *(obstacle)* surmonter, vaincre; **to o. a disability** surmonter un handicap **2 to be o. with** *or* **by** *(grief)* être accablé de; *(sleep, tears)* être gagné par; *(emotion, heat)* succomber à; *(fumes)* être asphyxié par; **I was quite o.** j'ai été bouleversé

overcompensate [əʊvəˈkɒmpenseɪt] VI surcompenser; **to o. for sth** surcompenser qch

overcomplicated [əʊvəˈkɒmplɪkeɪtɪd] ADJ trop *ou* excessivement compliqué

overconfidence [əʊvəˈkɒnfɪdəns] N confiance *f* exagérée (**in** en); **to be guilty of o.** faire preuve d'une confiance exagérée

overconfident [əʊvəˈkɒnfɪdənt] ADJ **1** *(about winning, finding a job etc)* trop confiant; **you're being o. about her reaction/the exam** tu présumes un peu trop de sa réaction/de ta réussite à l'examen **2** *(self-important)* présomptueux

overcook [əʊvəˈkʊk] VT (faire) trop cuire

over-correction N *(of air/fuel ratio etc)* sur-correction *f*

overcritical [əʊvəˈkrɪtɪk(ə)l] ADJ trop critique

overcrowd [əʊvəˈkraʊd] VT *(bus etc)* trop remplir, surcharger; *(city, region etc)* surpeupler

overcrowded [əʊvəˈkraʊdɪd] ADJ trop rempli (**with** de); *(with people)* surchargé, bondé; *(city, region etc)* surpeuplé; *(classroom)* surchargé

overcrowding [əʊvəˈkraʊdɪŋ] N *(of bus)* remplissage *m* excessif; *(of room etc)* en-combrement *m*; *(of city)* surpeuplement *m*; **o. is a problem in our schools** les sureffectifs sont un problème dans nos écoles

overdemand [əʊvədɪˈmɑːnd] N demande *f* excédentaire

overdeveloped [əʊvədɪˈveləpt] ADJ *Phot etc* trop développé

overdo [əʊvəˈduː] VT *(pt* **overdid** [əʊvəˈdɪd]*, pp* **overdone** [əʊvəˈdʌn]) **1** *(exaggerate) (welcome, praise)* exagérer; **to o. one's enthusiasm** manifester un enthousiasme un peu forcé; **he overdoes the charm** il fait un peu trop le charmeur

2 *(do or have too much of)* forcer *ou* exagérer sur; **don't o. the chocolates** ne te gave pas de chocolats; **you've overdone the salt/cream** tu as un peu forcé sur le sel/la crème; **she overdoes the jogging** elle force un peu trop sur le jogging; **to o. the telly-watching** trop regarder la télé; *Fam* **to o. it** *or* **things** *(work too hard)* en faire trop, se surmener; **you've been overdoing it** *or* **things** *(you need a rest)* tu en as trop fait; *Iron* **don't o. it!** surtout ne te surmènes pas! **3** *Culin* trop cuire

overdose [ˈəʊvədəʊs] N dose *f* excessive, surdose *f*, overdose *f*; **to take an o.** prendre une dose excessive *ou* une surdose *ou* une overdose de drogue; *(commit suicide)* prendre une dose massive de barbituriques/*etc*; **to die of an o.** mourir d'overdose ▸ VI **he overdosed on heroin** *(took too much)* il a pris une overdose *ou* surdose d'héroïne; *(died)* il est mort d'une overdose *ou* surdose d'héroïne; *Fig* **to o. on chocolate** exagérer sur le chocolat; **to o. on TV** se prendre une overdose de télé

overdraft [ˈəʊvədrɑːft] N *Banking* découvert *m*, solde *m* débiteur; **to have an o.** avoir un découvert; **to allow** *or* **give sb an o.** accorder à qn un découvert; **to pay off an/one's o.** rembourser un/son découvert ▸▸ **o. facility** autorisation *f* de découvert, facilités *fpl* de caisse; **o. limit** plafond *m* de découvert; **o. loan** prêt *m* à découvert

overdraw [əʊvəˈdrɔː] *(pt* **overdrew** [əʊvəˈdruː]*, pp* **overdrawn** [əʊvəˈdrɔːn]) *Banking* VT **to o. one's account** mettre son compte à découvert; **overdrawn account** compte *m* à découvert *ou* désapprovisionné, compte débiteur; **to be overdrawn** être à découvert; **your account is overdrawn** votre compte est débiteur; **to be £100 overdrawn** avoir un découvert de 100 livres; **to go overdrawn** passer en découvert ▸ VI tirer à découvert

overdress [əʊvəˈdres] VI *(dress too elegantly)* s'habiller de façon trop élégante; *(wear too many clothes)* trop se couvrir; **to be overdressed** être habillé de façon trop élégante/être trop couvert

overdrive [ˈəʊvədraɪv] N *Aut* vitesse *f* surmultipliée, overdrive *m*; **in o.** en surmultipliée; *Fig* **to go into/be in o.** passer/être passé (à) la vitesse supérieure

overdub [əʊvəˈdʌb] VT *(sound)* doubler

overdubbing [əʊvəˈdʌbɪŋ] N doublage *m*, voice over *m*

overdue [əʊvəˈdjuː] ADJ *(amount, account)* en souffrance; *(interest)* qui n'a pas été payé à l'échéance; *(person, train, library book)* en retard; *(reform, law, improvement etc)* qui fait défaut; **to be long o.** *(of law, reform etc)* faire défaut depuis longtemps; **changes to the law on divorce were long o.** ça faisait longtemps qu'on aurait dû apporter des modifications à la loi sur les divorces; **the baby was two weeks o.** le bébé avait deux semaines de retard; **she's o.** *(of pregnant woman)* elle a dépassé le terme

overeat [əʊvəˈriːt] VI *(pt* **overate** [əʊvəˈret]*,*

pp **overeaten** [əʊvəˈriːt(ə)n]) trop manger, manger avec excès

overeating [əʊvəˈriːtɪŋ] N excès *mpl* alimentaires *ou* de table

overelaborate [əʊvərɪˈlæbərət] ADJ *(style, ideas, design)* trop recherché; *(proposal)* trop compliqué

overemphasis [əʊvəˈremfəsɪs] N accentuation *f* excessive

overemphasize [əʊvəˈremfəsaɪz] VT trop accentuer; **it would be impossible to o. it** on ne saurait en exagérer l'importance

overemployment [əʊvərɪmˈplɔɪmənt] N suremploi *m*

overenthusiastic [əʊvərɪnθjuːzɪˈæstɪk] ADJ (par) trop enthousiaste

overestimate [əʊvəˈrestɪmeɪt] VT *(cost, person's talent, difficulty)* surestimer, surévaluer; *(danger)* exagérer; *(one's strength)* trop présumer de; *Com (assets)* majorer; **to o. one's own importance** surestimer sa propre importance

overexcite [əʊvərekˈsaɪt] VT surexciter

overexcited [əʊvəreˈksaɪtɪd] ADJ surexcité

overexcitement [əʊvərekˈsaɪtmənt] N surexcitation *f*

overexert [əʊvəregˈzɜːt] VT **to o. oneself** trop se fatiguer, se surmener

overexertion [əʊvəregˈzɜːʃən] N surmenage *m*

overexpose [əʊvəreksˈpəʊz] VT *Phot* surexposer

overexposed [əʊvəreksˈpəʊzd] ADJ **1** *Phot* surexposé **2** *Pej (person)* trop présent dans les médias

overexposure [əʊvəreksˈpəʊʒər] N *Phot* surexposition *f*; *Fig (on the media)* surmédiatisation *f*; **to suffer from o.** faire trop parler de soi; **because of people's o. to advertising** parce que les gens sont bombardés de publicité

overextend [əʊvəreksˈtend] VT *Fin* **to o. oneself** s'engager au-dessus de ses moyens

overfamiliar [əʊvəfəˈmɪliər] ADJ **to be o. with sb** *(too friendly etc)* se montrer trop familier *ou* prendre des libertés excessives avec qn; **I'm not o. with the rules** les règlements ne me sont pas tellement familiers; **I'm not o. with what's been going on here** je ne suis pas très au courant de ce qui s'est passé ici

overfeed [əʊvəˈfiːd] VT suralimenter; **to be overfed** être suralimenté ▸ VI se suralimenter, trop manger

overfishing [əʊvə(r)ˈfɪʃɪŋ] N surpêche *f*

overflow[1] [ˈəʊvəfləʊ] N **1** *(action)* débordement *m* **2** *(excess liquid)* débordement *m*; *Comput* dépassement *m* de capacité; *Fig (of population)* surplus *m* **3** *(outlet)* trop-plein *m*, *pl* trop-pleins ▸▸ **o. pipe** *(from sink, cistern)* trop-plein; *(large-scale)* déversoir *m*

overflow[2] [əʊvəˈfləʊ] VI *(of liquid, cup, heart)* déborder; *(of gutter, stream)* déborder, dégorger; **a room overflowing with people** une salle qui regorge de monde; **the guests overflowed into the other rooms** les invités se sont répandus dans les autres pièces; *Fig esp Lit* **her heart overflowed with joy** son cœur débordait de joie ▸ VT **to o. its banks** *(of river)* sortir de son lit

overflowing [əʊvəˈfləʊɪŋ] ADJ *(water, river etc)* qui déborde; *(container)* plein à déborder; *(joy, gratitude)* débordant ▸ N **full to o.** plein à déborder

overfly [əʊvəˈflaɪ] VT *(pt* **overflew** [əʊvəˈfluː]*, pp* **overflown** [əʊvəˈfləʊn]) survoler

overfond [ˈəʊvəfɒnd] ADJ trop attaché (**of**

à); **I'm not o. of oranges** je ne raffole pas des oranges

overfull [əʊvə'fʊl] **ADJ** trop plein (**of, with** de); **to be o.** (after eating too much) être gavé

overgear [əʊvə'gɪər] **VT** Fin (company) surendetter; **to be overgeared** être surendetté

overgearing [əʊvə'gɪərɪŋ] **N** Fin surendettement m

overgrown [əʊvə'grəʊn] **ADJ 1** (re)couvert (**with sth** de qch); **o. with weeds** (re)couvert de ou envahi par les mauvaises herbes; **o. with ivy** (re)couvert de ou tapissé de ou envahi de lierre **2 he's like an o. schoolboy** il est resté très gamin; **you great big o. baby you!** espèce de grand bébé!

overhang¹ ['əʊvəhæŋ] **N** surplomb m; Constr **to have an o.** porter à faux; **a balcony with an o. of three feet** un balcon avec une saillie d'un mètre

overhang² [əʊvə'hæŋ] (pt, pp **overhung** [əʊvə'hʌŋ]) **VT** (of balcony, rocks etc) surplomber, faire saillie au-dessus de

VI (of balcony, rocks etc) surplomber, être en surplomb, faire saillie; (of wall) être en surplomb, déverser

overhanging [əʊvə'hæŋɪŋ] **ADJ** (rocks, balcony) en surplomb; (wall) en surplomb, déversé

overhaul¹ ['əʊvəhɔːl] **N 1** (examination) (of machine etc) révision f, vérification f; **complete o.** révision complète **2** (repairs) (of vehicle, machine) révision f, remise f en état; Fig (of organization, theory, schedule) remaniement m

overhaul² [əʊvə'hɔːl] **VT 1** (examine) (machine) réviser, vérifier **2** (repair) (machine) remettre en état; Fig (organization, theory, schedule) remanier **3** (overtake) dépasser

overhead **ADV** [əʊvə'hed] au-dessus; **the stars are o.** les étoiles dans le ciel

ADJ ['əʊvəhed] (cable etc) aérien

N ['əʊvəhed] Com charge f opérationnelle; Am **o.**, Br **overheads** frais mpl généraux; **to reduce overheads** réduire les frais généraux ▸▸ Fin **o. budget** budget m des charges; Tech **o. camshaft** arbre m à cames en tête; Com **o. charges** frais généraux; Constr, Rail **o. crossing** croisement m supérieur; Com **o. expenses** frais généraux; **o. lighting** éclairage f vertical; **o. projector** rétroprojecteur m; **o. railway** chemin m de fer aérien; Cin, TV **o. shot** plan m en plongée; **o. valve** soupape f en dessus ou en tête; Tennis **o. volley** volée f rattrapée au-dessus de la tête

overhead-valve engine **N** moteur m à soupapes en tête

overhear [əʊvə'hɪər] (pt, pp **overheard** [əʊvə'hɜːd]) **VT** (conversation etc) surprendre, entendre (par hasard); **they were overheard discussing it** ils ont été surpris en train d'en parler; **I couldn't help overhearing what you were saying** je n'ai pas pu m'empêcher d'entendre ce que vous disiez

VI I couldn't help overhearing je n'ai pas pu m'empêcher d'entendre ce que vous disiez/ ce qu'il disait/etc

overheat [əʊvə'hiːt] **VT** (oven etc) surchauffer, trop chauffer; (economy) provoquer la surchauffe de

VI (of engine etc) chauffer; (of economy) entrer en surchauffe

overheated [əʊvə'hiːtɪd] **ADJ** (engine, room) surchauffé; (economy) en surchauffe; **to get o.** (of engine, brakes etc) chauffer; (of economy) entrer en surchauffe; Fig (of person) (become agitated) (trop) s'échauffer

overheating [əʊvə'hiːtɪŋ] **N** surchauffe f; Tech échauffement m (anormal)

overhype [əʊvə'haɪp] **VT** faire tout un tabac sur; (counter-productively) faire trop de battage sur

overindulge [əʊvərɪn'dʌldʒ] **VT** (person) montrer trop d'indulgence envers; (spoil) gâter; (own predilections etc) accorder une place excessive à; **to o. oneself** se faire plaisir; (eating, drinking) exagérer (sur la nourriture/la boisson), faire des excès (de table); **she tends to o. her taste for fine food** elle aime la bonne chère et elle ne se prive pas

VI (to eat, drink too much) faire des excès (de table); **to o. in chocolate/champagne** forcer sur le chocolat/le champagne

overindulgence [əʊvərɪn'dʌldʒəns] **N 1** indulgence f excessive (**of sb** envers qn) **2** (in food, drink) excès mpl, abus m

overinvest [əʊvərɪn'vest] Fin **VT** trop investir

VI trop investir, surinvestir (**in** dans)

overinvestment [əʊvərɪn'vestmənt] **N** Fin surinvestissement m

overjoyed [əʊvə'dʒɔɪd] **ADJ** ravi, enchanté (**at** de), transporté de joie (**at** par); **he was o. to meet her** il était ravi ou enchanté de la rencontrer

overkeen [əʊvə'kiːn] **ADJ** empressé (**to do** de faire); **he wasn't o. on her/the idea** elle/ l'idée ne lui plaisait pas outre mesure

overkill ['əʊvəkɪl] **N** Mil surcapacité f de tuer; Fig **it's o.** c'est exagéré, c'est trop; **don't you think we could be accused of o.?** ne croyez-vous pas qu'on pourrait nous accuser d'exagérer?; **so many police for such a demonstration was o.** le nombre d'agents de police était complètement disproportionné face à une telle manifestation; **media o.** médiatisation f excessive, surmédiatisation f

overladen [əʊvə'leɪd(ə)n] **ADJ** surchargé (**with** de)

overland **ADV** [əʊvə'lænd] par voie de terre; **ADJ** ['əʊvəlænd] par voie de terre; **o. journey** voyage m par voie de terre; **o. route** voie f de terre; Aviat trajet m survolant la terre

overlap¹ ['əʊvəlæp] **N 1** (act, state of overlapping) recouvrement m; Constr (of tiles etc) chevauchement m; **an o. of two inches** un chevauchement de 5 cm; **there is some o. between philosophy and religion** il y a des points communs entre la philosophie et la religion; **the o. between two departments** les activités communes à deux départements **2** (overlapping part) partie f chevauchante

overlap² [əʊvə'læp] **VT & VI** (-pp-) recouvrir (partiellement); (of categories etc) avoir un domaine commun; (in time) coïncider; (of theories, evidence) avoir des points communs; **to o.** (one another) (of tiles, slates) se chevaucher; **our holidays will o. by a week** nos vacances vont coïncider pendant une semaine

overlapping [əʊvə'læpɪŋ] **ADJ** (tiles, planks etc) qui se chevauchent; (responsibilities) qui se recoupent; (holidays) qui coïncident

overlay¹ ['əʊvəleɪ] **N 1** (of paint, varnish) couche f **2** Comput recouvrement m
▸▸ Comput **o. program** programme m à recouvrement

overlay² [əʊvə'leɪ] **VT** (pt, pp **overlaid** [əʊvə'leɪd]) **1** recouvrir, couvrir (**with** de) **2** TV, Cin incruster, superposer

overleaf [əʊvə'liːf] **ADV** au dos (de la page); **see o.** voir au verso ou au dos

overlie [əʊvə'laɪ] **VT** (pt **overlay** [əʊvə'leɪ], pp **overlain** [əʊvə'leɪn]) recouvrir, couvrir

overload¹ ['əʊvələʊd] **N 1** Elec surcharge f, surélévation f d'intensité; (of engine) excès m d'injection; **o. running** marche f en surcharge **2** (of vehicle) (excess weight) (poids m en) surcharge f

overload² [əʊvə'ləʊd] **VT** (lorry, machine, market) surcharger; (person) surmener; **to**

o. sb with work/responsibility surcharger qn de travail/responsabilités

overlong [əʊvə'lɒŋ] **ADV** trop longtemps **ADJ** trop long, trop longue

overlook [əʊvə'lʊk] **VT 1** (look out over) avoir vue sur, donner sur; **the castle/hill overlooks the town** le château/la colline surplombe la ville; **the window overlooks the street** la fenêtre donne sur la rue; **we are overlooked by our neighbours** nos voisins ont vue sur nous **2** (fail to notice) (detail, fact) négliger; (opportunity) négliger, laisser échapper; **I overlooked the fact** ce fait m'a échappé **3** (disregard) (contribution, project) ne pas prendre en compte; (breaches of procedure) fermer les yeux sur; (mistake) laisser passer; **I cannot o. this insolence** je ne peux pas laisser passer cette insolence; **he had been overlooked for promotion once again** une fois de plus quelqu'un d'autre avait été promu à sa place

overlord ['əʊvəlɔːd] **N** Hist suzerain m

overly ['əʊvəlɪ] **ADV** trop, excessivement; **not o.** pas trop

overlying [əʊvə'laɪɪŋ] **ADJ** superposé; (stratum) surjacent

overmanned [əʊvə'mænd] **ADJ** **to be o.** avoir un personnel trop nombreux; Ind avoir un surplus de main-d'œuvre

overmanning [əʊvə'mænɪŋ] **N** surplus m de personnel ou Ind de main-d'œuvre

overmuch [əʊvə'mʌtʃ] **ADV** (par) trop, outre mesure; **she didn't seem to mind o.** ça ne semblait pas trop la déranger, ça ne semblait pas la déranger outre mesure

overnight **ADV** [əʊvə'naɪt] (pendant) la nuit; (to change etc) du jour au lendemain; **to stay o.** passer la nuit; **leave to soak o.** laisser tremper toute la nuit; **he became famous/rich o.** il est devenu célèbre/riche du jour au lendemain

ADJ ['əʊvənaɪt] d'une nuit; **to be an o. success** devenir célèbre du jour au lendemain
▸▸ **o. bag** sac m ou nécessaire m de voyage; **o. case** mallette f; **o. guest** ami, -ie qui passe la nuit (chez qn); (in hotel) client, -ente qui passe la nuit; Sport **o. leader** leader m du jour; Fin **o. loan** prêt m du jour au lendemain; Fin **o. rate** taux m de l'argent au jour le jour; **o. stay** séjour m d'une nuit; (in hotel) nuitée f; **o. stop** arrêt m pour la nuit

overoptimism [əʊvə'rɒptɪmɪz(ə)m] **N** optimisme m exagéré; **to suffer from** or **be guilty of o.** être excessivement ou par trop optimiste

overoptimistic [əʊvərɒptɪ'mɪstɪk] **ADJ** excessivement ou par trop optimiste (**about** quant à); **I am not o. about their chances** je ne crois pas qu'ils aient de grandes chances

over-packaging **N** Mktg suremballage m

overpaid [əʊvə'peɪd] **ADJ** surpayé, trop payé

overparticular [əʊvəpə'tɪkjələr] **ADJ** (par) trop exigeant; **he's not o. about these things** il se moque pas mal de ces choses-là

overpass ['əʊvəpɑːs] **N** (for pedestrians) passerelle f surélevée; (road) autopont m, pont m autoroutier

overpay [əʊvə'peɪ] **VT** (pt, pp **overpaid** [əʊvə'peɪd]) (person) surpayer, trop payer

overpayment [əʊvə'peɪmənt] **N 1** (of taxes, on bill) trop-perçu m, pl trop-perçus **2** (of employee) rémunération f excessive

overplay [əʊvə'pleɪ] **VT** **to o. one's hand** Cards annoncer au-dessus de ses moyens; Fig présumer de ses chances (de réussite)

overpolite [əʊvəpə'laɪt] **ADJ** trop poli

overpopulated [əʊvə'pɒpjʊleɪtɪd] **ADJ** surpeuplé

overpopulation [əʊvəpɒpjʊ'leɪʃən] **N** surpeuplement m, surpopulation f

overposition [əʊvəpəˈzɪʃən] **VT** *Mktg* surpositionner

overpositioning [əʊvəpəˈzɪʃənɪŋ] **N** *Mktg* surpositionnement *m*

overpower [əʊvəˈpaʊər] **VT** *(person)* maîtriser; **to be overpowered by superior numbers** succomber sous *ou* être écrasé par le nombre

overpowering [əʊvəˈpaʊərɪŋ] **ADJ** *(grief, heat etc)* accablant; *(smell, taste)* *(unpleasant)* effroyable; *(much stronger than others)* prédominant; *(desire etc)* irrésistible; **I find him o.** je le trouve par trop imposant

overprice [əʊvəˈpraɪs] **VT** demander un prix excessif pour

overpriced [əʊvəˈpraɪst] **ADJ** trop cher, d'un prix excessif

overpricing [əʊvəˈpraɪsɪŋ] **N** fixation *f* d'un prix trop élevé

overprint [ˈəʊvəprɪnt] **N 1** *Typ* impression *f* en surcharge; *(on postage stamp etc)* surcharge *f*; *Phot* surimpression *f* **2** *(postage stamp)* timbre-poste *m* surchargé, *pl* timbres-poste surchargés

overprint [əʊvəˈprɪnt] **VT** *Typ* *(correction)* imprimer en surcharge; *Comput* surimprimer; *(postage stamp)* surcharger; *Phot* tirer en surimpression
▸ **VI** *Comput* surimprimer

overprinting [əʊvəˈprɪntɪŋ] **N** *Typ* impression *f* en surcharge; *Comput* surimpression *f*, *Phot* *(tirage m en)* surimpression

overproduce [əʊvəprəˈdjuːs] **VT & VI** surproduire

overproduction [əʊvəprəˈdʌkʃən] **N** surproduction *f*

overrate [əʊvəˈreɪt] **VT** *(person's abilities, person)* surévaluer, surestimer; *(restaurant, film)* surfaire; **I think he's overrated as an actor** j'estime que sa réputation en tant qu'acteur est surfaite; **sex is overrated** le sexe, ce n'est pas aussi formidable qu'on le dit

overrated [əʊvəˈreɪtɪd] **ADJ** *(film, book)* surfait; *(actor)* à la réputation surfaite

overreach [əʊvəˈriːtʃ] **VT to o. oneself** trop présumer de ses forces
▸ **VI** *(of horse)* (s')attraper

overreact [əʊvərɪˈækt] **VI** réagir de façon excessive (**to** à; **against** contre); **I don't want to o. but I do think something has to be done** sans vouloir dramatiser je crois vraiment qu'on devrait faire quelque chose

overreaction [əʊvərɪˈækʃən] **N** réaction *f* trop forte *ou* excessive; **to accuse sb of o.** accuser qn de réagir de façon excessive

override [əʊvəˈraɪd] **N** *Tech* forçage *m* en mode manuel; **manual o.** *(on automatic camera, lift etc)* commande *f* de passage en mode manuel
▸ **VT** *(pt* **overrode** [əʊvəˈrəʊd]*, pp* **overridden** [əʊvəˈrɪd(ə)n]*)* **1** *(disregard)* *(objections, protest, decision)* passer outre à **2** *(take precedence over)* avoir plus d'importance que, avoir la priorité sur; **decision that overrides a former decision** décision qui annule une décision antérieure; **this duty overrode all her other commitments** cette tâche a pris la priorité sur tous ses autres engagements **3** *(automated process)* annuler **4** *(horse)* surmener

overriding [əʊvəˈraɪdɪŋ] **ADJ** *(ambition, factor)* principal, -aux; *(importance)* capital, -aux; *(objection)* majeur; *(principle)* premier; **it was not an o. factor** ce n'a pas été un facteur décisif; **to have an o. desire to do sth** être en proie à un irrésistible désir de faire qch; **but there are o. reasons** mais il y a des raisons d'ordre majeur

overripe [əʊvəˈraɪp] **ADJ** trop mûr; *(cheese)* trop fait

overrule [əʊvəˈruːl] **VT** *(proposal, advice)* rejeter; *Law* *(decision)* annuler, casser; *Law* *(claim, objection)* rejeter; **she was overruled by her boss** son patron a rejeté ce qu'elle avait proposé; *Am Law* **objection overruled** objection rejetée

overrun [ˈəʊvərʌn] **N 1** *Typ* *(at end of line)* chasse *f*, *(at end of page)* report *m*, ligne(s) *f(pl)* à reporter **2** *Com* **(cost) overruns** dépassement *m* du coût estimé
▸ ▸ *Comput* **o. error** perte *f* d'informations par engorgement; *Aut* **o. valve** limiteur *m* de régime

overrun [əʊvəˈrʌn] *(pt* **overran** [əʊvəˈræn]*, pp* **overrun**; *prp* **overrunning**) **VT 1** *(of invaders)* *(country)* envahir; **a garden o. with weeds** un jardin envahi par les mauvaises herbes; **a house o. with mice** une maison infestée de souris **2** *(allotted time)* dépasser; *Rail* *(signal)* brûler; **to o. a budget** dépasser un budget **3** *Typ* *(word)* reporter à la ligne/à la page suivante; **words that o. the line** mots qui chassent
▸ **VI** *TV, Radio* déborder; **words that o. (into the margin)** mots qui chassent; **the TV programme/the speech overran** le programme télévisé/le discours a duré plus longtemps que prévu; **you mustn't o.** vous ne devez pas dépasser le temps qui vous est imparti; **the project has o. by three weeks** le projet a dépassé la date limite de trois mois

oversale [ˈəʊvəseɪl] **N** *Am* surlocation *f*

overseas **ADJ** [ˈəʊvəsiːz] *(colony, trade)* d'outre-mer; *(branch, office of business)* à l'étranger; *(market)* étranger
▸ **ADV** [əʊvəˈsiːz] à l'étranger, *Lit* par delà les mers; **from o.** d'outre-mer
▸ ▸ **o. investment** investissement *m* extérieur

oversee [əʊvəˈsiː] **VT** *(pt* **oversaw** [əʊvəˈsɔː]*, pp* **overseen** [əʊvəˈsiːn]*)* *(workshop, site etc)* surveiller

overseer [ˈəʊvəsɪər] **N** surveillant, -ante; *Ind* contremaître, -esse; *Constr* chef *m* de chantier

oversell [ˈəʊvəsel] **VT** *(pt, pp* **oversold** [əʊvəˈsəʊld]*)* **1** *(praise too highly)* exagérer les mérites de **2** *Com (sell too much of)* vendre trop de; **the flight/concert had been oversold** trop de billets avaient été vendus par rapport au nombre de places pour le vol/concert

oversensitive [əʊvəˈsensɪtɪv] **ADJ** hypersensible; **you're just being o.** tu es trop susceptible; **to be a bit o. about criticism** être un peu trop sensible aux critiques

oversew [ˈəʊvəsəʊ] **VT** *(pt* **oversewed** [ˈəʊvəsəʊd]*, pp* **oversewn** [ˈəʊvəsəʊn]*)* *Sewing* surjeter; *(edge)* surfiler

oversexed [əʊvəˈsekst] **ADJ** qui a une libido démesurée; **you're o.** tu es un obsédé sexuel, tu ne penses qu'à ça

overshadow [əʊvəˈʃædəʊ] **VT 1** *(spread shadow over)* ombrager, couvrir de son ombre **2** *Fig (of atmosphere)* planer sur; **the negotiations were overshadowed by gloom** une atmosphère morose planait sur les négociations; **his success had been overshadowed by his father's death** sa réussite avait été assombrie par la mort de son père **3** *Fig (eclipse)* éclipser; **he had always been overshadowed by his brother** son frère l'avait toujours éclipsé

overshoe [ˈəʊvəʃuː] **N** couvre-chaussure *m*, *pl* couvre-chaussures; *(with wooden soles)* galoche *f*, **rubber overshoes** caoutchoucs *mpl*

overshoot [əʊvəˈʃuːt] *(pr, pp* **overshot** [əʊvəˈʃɒt]*)* **VT** dépasser; *(of shot, gun)* porter au delà de; **to o. the mark** dépasser le but; *Fig* dépasser les bornes; *Aviat* **to o. the run-**

way dépasser la piste; *(deliberately)* survoler la piste; **to o. a production target** dépasser *ou* excéder un objectif de production
▸ **VI** *(of plane, pilot)* dépasser la piste

overshot [ˈəʊvəʃɒt] **ADJ** *Tech (wheel)* mû par en dessus

oversight [ˈəʊvəsaɪt] **N 1** *(omission)* oubli *m*, omission *f*; **through** *or* **by an o.** par mégarde, par inadvertance, par oubli **2** *(supervision)* surveillance *f*

oversimplification [əʊvəsɪmplɪfɪˈkeɪʃən] **N** simplification *f* excessive

oversimplify [əʊvəˈsɪmplɪfaɪ] **VT & VI** simplifier à outrance

oversized [ˈəʊvəsaɪzd] **ADJ** trop grand; *(class)* surchargé; *Fam (very big)* énorme; **you great o. oaf!** espèce de grosse brute!

oversleep [əʊvəˈsliːp] **VI** *(pt, pp* **overslept** [əʊvəˈslept]*)* ne pas se réveiller à temps, *Fam* avoir une panne d'oreiller; **in order to stop him from oversleeping** pour qu'il se réveille à temps, *Fam* pour qu'il n'ait plus de pannes d'oreiller

oversleeve [ˈəʊvəsliːv] **N** manchette *f*

oversold [əʊvəˈsəʊld] **ADJ** *St Exch (market)* sous-évalué

overspend [əʊvəˈspend] *(pt, pp* **overspent** [əʊvəˈspent]*)* **VI** dépenser trop; **to o. by ...** dépenser ... de trop
▸ **VT** *(budget)* dépasser

overspending [əʊvəˈspendɪŋ] **N** dépense *f* excessive; *Fin* dépassement *m* budgétaire

overspill [ˈəʊvəspɪl] **N** *(population)* surplus *m* *ou* déversement *m* de population
▸ ▸ **o. population** surplus *ou* déversement de population; **o. town** = ville *f* servant à décongestionner une agglomération surpeuplée

overstaffed [əʊvəˈstɑːft] **ADJ** qui a un excédent de personnel

overstaffing [əʊvəˈstɑːfɪŋ] **N** excédents *mpl* de personnel, sureffectifs *mpl*

overstate [əʊvəˈsteɪt] **VT** *(facts etc)* exagérer; **I am neither overstating nor understating the case** je n'exagère ni dans un sens ni dans l'autre; **it would not be overstating the problem to say that ...** on pourrait dire sans exagérer que ...

overstay [əʊvəˈsteɪ] **VT to o. one's welcome** abuser de l'hospitalité de ses hôtes; *Mil* **to o. one's leave** dépasser la durée de sa permission

oversteer [ˈəʊvəstɪər] **N** *Aut* comportement *m* survireur, survirage *m*

oversteer [əʊvəˈstɪər] **VI** *Aut* survirer; **a car which oversteers** une voiture survireuse

overstep [əʊvəˈstep] **VT** (**-pp-**) *(limit, boundary, one's powers)* outrepasser; *Fig* **to o. the mark** dépasser les bornes

overstock [əʊvəˈstɒk] **VT** *(outlet)* munir de stocks excessifs; *(market)* encombrer; *(farm)* mettre trop de bétail dans; *(pond)* mettre trop de poissons dans; **to be overstocked** *(of shop)* avoir des stocks excessifs

overstocking [əʊvəˈstɒkɪŋ] **N** *Com* stockage *m* excessif

overstrike [ˈəʊvəstraɪk] **N** *(in printing)* surimpression *f*

oversubscribe [əʊvəsəbˈskraɪb] **VT** *Fin (share issue)* sursouscrire

oversubscribed [əʊvəsəbˈskraɪbd] **ADJ** *Fin* sursouscrit

oversubscription [əʊvəsəbˈskrɪpʃən] **N** *Fin (of share issue)* sursouscription *f*

overt [əʊˈvɜːt] **ADJ** évident, manifeste; **do you have to be quite so o. about it?** dois-tu absolument le montrer aussi clairement?
▸ ▸ *Law* **o. act** acte *m* manifeste

overtake [əʊvəˈteɪk] **VT** *(pt* **overtook**

[əʊvə'tʊk], pp **overtaken** [əʊvə'teɪk(ə)n]) **1** esp Br (go past) (competitor, car) doubler, dépasser; (previous level) dépasser; **demand has overtaken supply** la demande a dépassé l'offre **2** (of fate etc) s'abattre sur; **their plans/we were overtaken by fate** le sort s'est joué de leurs projets/nous; **overtaken by events** dépassé ou devancé par les événements; **darkness overtook us** la nuit nous surprit

overtaking [əʊvə'teɪkɪŋ] N esp Br Aut dépassement m; **no o.** défense de doubler
  ▸ ▸ **o. lane** (when driving on right) voie f de gauche; (when driving on left) voie de droite

overtax [əʊvə'tæks] VT **1** Fin (nation) accabler sous les impôts; (individual) surtaxer, surimposer **2** (overburden) (person) surmener; (resources) peser lourdement sur; **to o. one's strength** se surmener, abuser de ses forces; **to o. sb's patience** abuser de la patience de qn

over-the-counter ADJ (sales) au comptant; (medication) vendu sans ordonnance
  ▸ ▸ St Exch **o. market** marché m hors cote, marché des transactions hors séance

overthrow[1] ['əʊvəθrəʊ] N (of empire, government) renversement m, (of person) chute f

overthrow[2] [əʊvə'θrəʊ] VT (pt **overthrew** [əʊvə'θruː], pp **overthrown** [əʊvə'θrəʊn]) (person) défaire, vaincre; (empire) renverser, abattre; (government, established order) renverser

overtime ['əʊvətaɪm] N **1** Ind heures fpl supplémentaires; **to do o.** faire des heures supplémentaires; **to get o. (pay)** être payé pour les heures supplémentaires que l'on fait **2** Am Sport temps m supplémentaire
  ADV Ind **to work o.** faire des heures supplémentaires; Fig **my imagination was working o.** mon imagination galopait ou s'emballait
  ▸ ▸ Ind **o. ban** refus m de faire des heures supplémentaires; Ind **o. pay** paiement m des heures supplémentaires; Ind **o. rate** tarif m des heures supplémentaires

overtire [əʊvə'taɪər] VT (person) surmener; **to o. oneself, to get overtired** se surmener, trop se fatiguer; **to be overtired** (of child) être trop fatigué

overtiredness [əʊvə'taɪədnɪs] N Med surmenage m

overtly [əʊ'vɜːtlɪ] ADV ouvertement

overtness [əʊ'vɜːtnɪs] N franchise f

overtone ['əʊvətəʊn] N **1** (suggestion) (of sadness, bitterness) nuance f, soupçon m; **there are overtones of racism in her books** il y a des relents de racisme dans ses livres; **the phrase has an o. of disparagement** l'expression comporte un soupçon ou un rien de dénigrement; **an o. of criticism** une note critique **2** Mus harmonique m

overtrade [əʊvə'treɪd] VI avoir une marge d'exploitation trop étroite

overture ['əʊvətjʊər] N Mus ouverture f, Fig **to make overtures to sb** (sexually) faire des avances à qn; (for business purposes) faire des propositions à qn; **peace overtures** propositions fpl de paix

overturn [əʊvə'tɜːn] VT (table, government, status quo) renverser; (car) faire verser; (boat) faire chavirer; (theory) démonter; **the bill was overturned in the Senate** le projet de loi a été rejeté par le Sénat
  VI se renverser; (of vehicle) verser, capoter; (of boat) chavirer; (of plane) capoter

overuse[1] [əʊvə'juːs] N emploi m excessif (of de); **the phrase has been made meaningless by o.** l'expression a perdu tout son sens à force d'être trop employée

overuse[2] [əʊvə'juːz] VT trop employer

overvaluation [əʊvəvælju:'eɪʃən] N surévaluation f

overvalue [əʊvə'vælju:] VT **1** Com (assets) surestimer, majorer; (object) surestimer, surévaluer **2** Fig (person's abilities etc) surestimer, surévaluer, exagérer

overview ['əʊvəvju:] N (of situation etc) vue f d'ensemble

overvoltage protection [əʊvəvəʊltɪdʒ] N protection f contre la surtension

overwater [əʊvə'wɔːtər] VT (plant) trop arroser

overwatering [əʊvə'wɔːtərɪŋ] N (of plant) arrosage m excessif

overweening [əʊvə'wiːnɪŋ] ADJ (person, attitude) outrecuidant, présomptueux; (ambition, vanity) sans bornes

overweight ADJ [əʊvə'weɪt] (person) trop gros; (luggage) en excédent; **he's a few kilos o.** il a quelques kilos en trop
  N ['əʊvəweɪt] (excess weight) surpoids m, poids m en excès

overwhelm [əʊvə'welm] VT (the enemy) écraser, accabler; (with kindness) combler; (with shame) confondre; **overwhelmed with work** débordé de travail; **overwhelmed with phone calls** submergé d'appels; **I am overwhelmed (by your kindness)** je suis confus (de votre gentillesse); **overwhelmed with joy/grief/despair** au comble de la joie/du malheur/du désespoir; **to be overwhelmed with relief** être profondément soulagé

overwhelming [əʊvə'welmɪŋ] ADJ (need, desire etc) irrésistible; (joy, happiness) débordant; (grief, sense of guilt) accablant; (heat, pressure) écrasant, accablant; (defeat, majority) écrasant; **to have an o. desire to do sth** éprouver le besoin irrésistible de faire qch

overwhelmingly [əʊvə'welmɪŋlɪ] ADV (beaten, defeated) d'une manière écrasante; **it is o. sad** c'est affreusement triste

overwind [əʊvə'waɪnd] VT (pt, pp **overwound** [əʊvə'waʊnd]) (watch etc) trop remonter

overwork [əʊvə'wɜːk] N surmenage m; **suffering from o.** surmené
  VT (person) surmener, surcharger de travail; (muscle, heart) surmener; (idea, metaphor etc) utiliser à outrance; **to o. oneself** se surmener
  VI se surmener

overworking [əʊvə'wɜːkɪŋ] N surmenage m

overwrite[1] ['əʊvəraɪt] N
  ▸ ▸ Comput **o. mode** mode m de superposition

overwrite[2] [əʊvə'raɪt] VT Comput (data) superposer

overwrought [əʊvə'rɔːt] ADJ (with grief) accablé; **to be o.** (nervous and upset) avoir les nerfs à vif, être angoissé; **the child was o.** l'enfant était à bout; **to become o.** s'affliger, se tourmenter

overzealous [əʊvə'zeləs] ADJ trop zélé

Ovid ['ɒvɪd] N Ovide m

oviduct ['əʊvɪdʌkt] N Biol oviducte m

ovine ['əʊvaɪn] ADJ (animal etc) ovin

oviparous [əʊ'vɪpərəs] ADJ Biol ovipare

ovoid ['əʊvɔɪd] ADJ ovoïde
  N figure f ovoïde

ovulate ['ɒvjʊleɪt] VI Biol ovuler

ovulation [ɒvjʊ'leɪʃən] N Biol ovulation f

ovule ['ɒvju:l] N Biol ovule m

ovum, pl **ova** ['əʊvəm, 'əʊvə] N Biol ovule m

ow [aʊ] INT aïe!, ouille!

owe [əʊ] (pp, pt **owed** [əʊd]) VT **1** (money) devoir; **to o. sb sth, to o. sth to sb** devoir qch à qn; **the sum owed (to) her by her brother** la somme que son frère lui doit ou qui lui est due par son frère; **I still o. you for**

the petrol je vous dois encore l'essence; **what or how much do I o. you?** qu'est-ce que je te dois?, combien est-ce que je te dois?
  2 Fig (respect, obedience etc) devoir; **I o. you an apology/an explanation** je vous dois des excuses/une explication; **you o. it to yourself to do your best** vous vous devez à vous-même de faire de votre mieux; **I o. my life to you** je vous dois la vie; **to o. sb a favour** être redevable d'un service à qn; **to what do I o. this honour?** qu'est-ce qui me vaut cet honneur?; **he owes his success to his parents' influence** il doit son succès à l'influence de ses parents

owing ['əʊɪŋ] ADJ **1** there is £5 o. 5 livres restent dues; **all the money o. to me** tout l'argent qui m'est dû **2** o. to (because of) en raison de, à cause de; **o. to a recent bereavement** en raison d'un deuil récent; **o. to the force of circumstances** par la force des choses

owl [aʊl] N hibou m, pl -oux, chouette f, Fig a **wise old o.** (person) un vieux sage; Fam **o. glasses** lunettes fpl (parfaitement) rondes

owlet ['aʊlɪt] N jeune hibou m, jeune chouette f

owlish ['aʊlɪʃ] ADJ de hibou; **o. look** air m de sage

OWN [əʊn]

VT	posséder **1**
ADJ	propre
PRON	le mien/le sien/etc **1** ▪ seul **2**

VT **1** (land, house, car etc) posséder, être propriétaire de; (washing machine, stereo, dog etc) avoir, posséder; **who owns this land?** qui est le propriétaire de cette terre?; **who owns this stereo?** à qui appartient cette chaîne stéréo?; **he behaves as if he owned the place** il se conduit comme en pays conquis; **you don't o. me!** je ne t'appartiens pas!; **company owned by the state** compagnie qui appartient à l'État

2 Fml (admit) **I o. that I was wrong** je reconnais que j'ai eu tort, j'ai eu tort, je l'avoue ou je le reconnais; **to o. oneself beaten** s'avouer vaincu; esp Jur **to o. a child** (recognize as one's own) reconnaître un enfant; Fam **I won't o. you!** je ne te connais plus!
  VI **to o. to a mistake** reconnaître ou avouer une erreur; **he owns to being forty** (admits he is) il admet qu'il a quarante ans

ADJ propre; **her o. money** son propre argent; **I saw it with my o. eyes** je l'ai vu de mes propres yeux; **I had my o. table** j'avais ma table à moi; **I do my o. cooking** je fais la cuisine moi-même, je fais ma propre cuisine; **the supermarket does its o. baking** le supermarché cuit son propre pain; **to roll one's o. cigarettes** rouler ses cigarettes; **to score an o. goal** Ftbl marquer un but pour l'équipe adverse; Fig apporter de l'eau au moulin de l'adversaire; **to be one's o. man/woman** vivre à sa façon ou à son idée
  PRON **1** my/his/etc **o.** le mien/le sien/etc; **one's o.** le sien; **they are my o.** ce sont les miens, ils sont à moi, ils m'appartiennent; **to look after one's o.** (property) soigner son bien; (friends, relatives) s'occuper des siens; **I have money of my o.** j'ai de l'argent à moi; **a child of his o.** un enfant à lui; **the house is my o.** la maison est à moi ou m'appartient; **to make sth one's o.** s'approprier qch; **she took the song and made it her o.** elle s'est appropriée la chanson; **she has a copy of her o.** elle a un exemplaire à elle ou en propre; **for reasons of his o.** pour des raisons qui le regardent; **his ideas are his o.** ses idées lui sont propres; **a style of one's o. or all one's o.** un style original ou propre ou spécifique; Fam **to roll one's o.** rouler ses ci-

garettes; **the landscape has a wild beauty of its o.** le paysage a une beauté sauvage qui lui est propre; **may I have it for my (very) o.?** est-ce que je peux l'avoir pour moi seul?; **there's not a thing here that I can call my o.** il n'y a pas ici un objet qui m'appartienne en propre; **my time is my o.** mon temps est à moi *ou* m'appartient, je suis libre de mon temps

2 to do sth on one's o. *(without company)* faire qch tout seul; *(on one's own initiative)* faire qch de sa propre initiative *ou* de son propre chef; **to be** *or* **work on one's o.** travailler tout seul; *(be in business alone)* être établi à son propre compte; **I am (all) on my o.** je suis seul; **you're on your o.!** c'est à toi de te débrouiller!

3 to come into one's o. *(develop fully)* s'épanouir; **to get one's o. back** se venger; **to hold one's o.** *(of patient, in argument, fight etc)* se maintenir

▸ **own up** VI *(confess)* avouer; **to o. up to a crime/to having done sth** avouer un crime/avoir fait qch

own-brand *Mktg* ADJ **our o. butter** du beurre sous notre propre marque
N marque *f* de distributeur
▸▸ **o. label** marque de distributeur; **o. product** produit *m* à marque de distributeur

own-branding N *Mktg* apposition *f* de sa propre marque

owner ['əʊnər] N *(of house, land, car)* propriétaire *mf*; *(of business)* patron, -onne, propriétaire; *(of dog etc)* propriétaire, maître, -esse; **the o. of this stereo** la personne à qui cette chaîne stéréo appartient; **cars parked here at (the) owners' risk** les voitures garées ici le sont aux risques de leurs propriétaires; *Naut* **the owners** *(of ship)* les armateurs *mpl*, l'armement *m*
▸ *Acct* **o.'s capital account** compte *m* de l'exploitant; *Aut* **o. driver** conducteur, -trice propriétaire

ownerless ['əʊnəlɪs] ADJ sans propriétaire; *(dog)* sans maître

owner-occupancy N fait *m* d'être propriétaire du logement qu'on occupe; **o. has increased** de plus en plus de gens sont propriétaires de leurs logements

owner-occupier N propriétaire-occupant *m*, *pl* propriétaires-occupants

ownership ['əʊnəʃɪp] N possession *f*, *(right)* (droit *m* de) propriété *f*; **to have o. of sth** être en possession de qch; **she wants o. of the car** elle veut être propriétaire de la voiture; **the o. of the house is contested** les droits de propriété sont contestés; **change**

of o. *Com* changement *m* de propriétaire; *Law* mutation *f*; **under new o.** *(notice in shop, restaurant etc)* nouveau propriétaire; **during her o. of the property** pendant qu'elle possédait la propriété; **the bus company is now in private o.** la compagnie de bus est maintenant aux mains du secteur privé

own-label ADJ = **own-brand**

owt [aʊt] PRON *Eng Dial* = **anything**

ox, *pl* **oxen** [ɒks, 'ɒks(ə)n] N bœuf *m*; **ox cart** char *m* à bœufs; *Culin* **ox heart/tongue** cœur *m*/langue *f* de bœuf

oxalic [ɒk'sælɪk] ADJ *Chem* oxalique

oxblood ['ɒksblʌd] N *(colour)* rouge *m* sang
ADJ rouge sang *inv*

oxbow ['ɒksbəʊ] N *Geog* bras *m* mort *(d'un cours d'eau)*
▸▸ **o. lake** bras mort

Oxbridge ['ɒksbrɪdʒ] N les universités *fpl* d'Oxford et de Cambridge
ADJ *(graduate etc)* de l'université d'Oxford ou de Cambridge

---

Oxbridge

Oxbridge désigne conjointement les universités d'Oxford et de Cambridge, les plus anciennes et les plus prestigieuses d'Angleterre. Oxford et Cambridge se distinguent des autres établissements d'enseignement supérieur, notamment par leur structure collégiale et leurs conditions d'admission très rigoureuses. De nos jours, Oxbridge est toujours synonyme d'élitisme en dépit des efforts entrepris pour élargir le recrutement des deux universités. Jusqu'à une époque très récente, un diplôme d'Oxbridge était considéré comme indispensable pour accéder à des postes importants dans le monde de la politique ou de la diplomatie.

---

oxen *see* **ox**

oxeye ['ɒksaɪ] N **o. daisy, white o.** *(flower)* marguerite *f* des champs

Oxfam ['ɒksfæm] N *Br* = œuvre *f* de bienfaisance travaillant pour le tiers-monde
▸▸ **O. shop** = magasin *m* où l'œuvre de bienfaisance Oxfam vend des articles d'occasion et d'artisanat au profit du tiers-monde

Oxford ['ɒksfəd] N
▸▸ **O. bags** *(trousers)* pantalon *m* très large; **O. blue** *(colour)* bleu *m* foncé; *(sportsperson)*

= sportif *m* qui porte ou a porté les couleurs de l'université d'Oxford; **O. shoes** oxfords *mpl*, souliers *mpl* richelieu

oxherd ['ɒkshɜːd] N bouvier, -ière

oxhide ['ɒkshaɪd] N cuir *m* de bœuf

oxidation [ɒksɪ'deɪʃən] N *Chem* oxydation *f*

oxide ['ɒksaɪd] N *Chem* oxyde *m*

oxidization [ɒksɪdaɪ'zeɪʃən] N *Chem* oxydation *f*

oxidize ['ɒksɪdaɪz] *Chem* VT oxyder
VI s'oxyder

Oxonian [ɒk'səʊnɪən] ADJ oxfordien, -ienne, oxonien, -ienne
N *Univ* membre *m* de l'université d'Oxford

oxtail ['ɒksteɪl] N *Culin* queue *f* de bœuf
▸▸ **o. soup** soupe *f* de queue de bœuf

oxyacetylene [ɒksɪə'setɪliːn] N
▸▸ **o. burner** chalumeau *m* oxyacétylénique de découpage; **o. cutting** découpage *m* au chalumeau; **o. torch** chalumeau oxyacétylénique de découpage

oxygen ['ɒksɪdʒən] N *Chem* oxygène *m*
▸▸ **o. bottle, o. cylinder** bouteille *f* d'oxygène; **o. mask** masque *m* à oxygène; **o. tent** tente *f* à oxygène

oxygenate ['ɒksɪdʒɪneɪt, ɒk'sɪ-] VT oxygéner

oxygenation [ɒksɪdʒɪ'neɪʃən] N oxygénation *f*

oxygenize ['ɒksɪdʒɪnaɪz] VT oxygéner

oxymoron [ɒksɪ'mɒrɒn] N oxymoron *m*, oxymore *m*

oyez [əʊ'jeɪ, əʊ'jez] INT **o.! o.!** oyez!

oyster ['ɔɪstər] N huître *f*; **pearl o.** (huître) perlière *f*; *Fig* **the world is your o.** le monde t'appartient
▸▸ **o. bank, o. bed** huîtrière *f*, banc *m* d'huîtres; **o. breeder** ostréiculteur, -trice; **o. farm** parc *m* à huîtres; **o. farmer** ostréiculteur, -trice; **o. knife** couteau *m* à huîtres; **o. mushroom** pleurote *f*; **o. park** parc à huîtres; **o. shell** écaille *f* d'huître

oystercatcher ['ɔɪstəkætʃər] N *(bird)* huîtrier *m*

Oz [ɒz] N *Sl* Australie *f*

oz *abbr* **ounce(s)**

ozone ['əʊzəʊn] N *Chem* ozone *m*; *(bracing air)* bon air *m* frais
▸▸ **o. depletion** diminution *f* de l'ozone; **o. layer** couche *f* d'ozone; *Met* ozonosphère *f*

ozone-friendly ADJ *(product, aerosol)* qui préserve la couche d'ozone

Ozzie ['ɒzɪ] N *Sl* Australien, -ienne

P, p [piː] **N 1** (*letter*) P, p *m*; **two p's** deux p; *Mktg* **the four P's** les quatre P, le marketing mix; *Fam* **to mind one's P's and Q's** (*be polite*) se surveiller **2** *Br* (*abbr* **penny, pence**) penny *m*, *pl* pence; **a 20p stamp** un timbre à 20 pence

p. (*abbr* **page**) p.

P45 [piːfɔːtɪˈfaɪv] **N** *Br* = document *m* administratif donné à tout employé lorsqu'il quitte un emploi et devant être présenté à tout nouvel employeur, où figurent le total des rémunérations versées par l'employeur ainsi que les sommes payées par l'employé en impôts et cotisations sociales; *Fig* **to be handed one's P45** se faire licencier

PA [piːˈeɪ] **N 1** (*abbr* **public address**) **PA (system)** (système *m* de) sonorisation *f*, système *m* de haut-parleurs, *Fam* sono *f*; **an announcement over the PA** une annonce par haut-parleurs

2 (*abbr* **personal appearance**) **to do a PA** venir en personne; **a PA has been scheduled to promote their new album** ils vont venir faire la promotion de leur nouvel album en personne

3 (*abbr* **personal assistant**) (*of executive*) assistant, -ante; (*with secretarial duties*) secrétaire *mf* (de direction)

4 (*abbr* **Press Association**) agence *f* de presse britannique

5 (*abbr* **production assistant**) assistant, -ante de production

Pa *abbr* **Pennsylvania**

pa [paː] **N** *Fam* papa *m*

p.a. [piːˈeɪ] (*abbr* **per annum**) par an; **£16,000 p.a.** 16 000 livres par an

pace¹ [peɪs] **N 1** (*step*) pas *m*; **ten paces off** à dix pas de distance; *Mil etc* **one p. forward!** un pas en avant!

2 (*gait*) allure *f*, (*of horse etc*) amble *m*; **to put a horse through its paces** faire passer un cheval à la montre; **to put a car/machine through its paces** mettre une voiture/une machine à l'épreuve; **to put sb through his/her paces** mettre qn à l'épreuve

3 (*speed*) vitesse *f*, train *m*, allure *f*; **there was a lot of p. on the ball** la balle filait à toute allure; **at a smart p.** à vive allure; **at a slow p.** à petite allure; **at walking p.** au pas; **to keep pace with sb** marcher du même pas que qn, aller à la même allure que qn; *Fig* (*in activity*) suivre le rythme de qn; **I can't keep p. with today's teenagers** avec les adolescents d'aujourd'hui, je n'arrive pas à suivre; **supply is keeping p. with demand** l'offre suit la demande; **our incomes haven't kept p. with inflation** nos revenus n'ont pas augmenté au même rythme que l'inflation; **the company did not keep p. with developments in the industry** la société n'a pas suivi le rythme des développements dans l'industrie; **it's all happened so fast I can barely keep p. with it** tout est arrivé si vite que j'ai

du mal à suivre le rythme; **to force the p.** forcer le pas *ou* l'allure; **the p. has slackened** l'allure s'est ralentie; **to set the p.** donner le pas; *Sport* donner *ou* régler l'allure; (*of company etc*) mener le train; **to stand the p.** tenir le rythme; **he can't stand the p.** il ne tient pas le rythme

VI marcher à pas mesurés; (*of horse etc*) aller à l'amble; **to p. about** *or* **up and down** faire les cent pas

VT (*room, street*) arpenter; *Sport* (*runner*) tirer; **to p. oneself** (*when running, drinking*) trouver son rythme; (*when eating*) garder de la place pour la suite

▸▸ **p. bowler** (*in cricket*) lanceur *m* rapide *ou* puissant

▸ **pace off, pace out** **VT SEP** (*distance*) mesurer au pas

pace² [ˈpɑːtʃeɪ] **PREP** *Fml* n'en déplaise à

pacemaker [ˈpeɪsmeɪkər] **N 1** *Sport* (*of runner*) meneur, -euse de train **2** *Med* (*device*) stimulateur *m* (cardiaque), pacemaker *m* **3** *Anat* nœud *m* sinusal cardiaque

pacesetter [ˈpeɪssetər] **N** *Sport* meneur, -euse de train; *Fig* **to be a p.** mener le train

pacey [ˈpeɪsɪ] **ADJ** = **pacy**

pachyderm [ˈpækɪdɑːm] **N** (*animal*) pachyderme *m*

pacific [pəˈsɪfɪk] **ADJ 1** *Geog* **the P. (Ocean)** l'océan *m* Pacifique, le Pacifique **2** *Fml* (*not aggressive*) pacifique; (*peaceful*) paisible

pacifically [pəˈsɪfɪklɪ] **ADV** pacifiquement

pacification [pæsɪfɪˈkeɪʃən] **N** *Pol* (*of country etc*) pacification *f*, (*of person*) apaisement *m*

pacifier [ˈpæsɪfaɪər] **N 1** *esp Am* (*for babies*) sucette *f*, tétine *f* **2** (*person*) pacificateur, -trice

pacifism [ˈpæsɪfɪz(ə)m] **N** pacifisme *m*

pacifist [ˈpæsɪfɪst] **N, ADJ** pacifiste *mf*

pacify [ˈpæsɪfaɪ] **VT** (*crowd, country etc*) pacifier; (*person, sb's anger*) apaiser, calmer; (*sb's demands*) apaiser; **she refused to be pacified** elle n'a jamais voulu se calmer

---

PACK [pæk]

N	paquet 1	▪ sac à dos 1	▪ bande 2
	▪ meute 2		
VT	empaqueter 1	▪ entasser 2	
	▪ remplir 3	▪ bourrer 3	
VI	faire sa valise 1	▪ s'entasser 2	

N 1 (*bundle etc*) (*of goods*) paquet *m*, ballot *m*; (*backpack*) sac *m* à dos; (*of beast of burden*) bât *m*; *esp Am* (*of cigarettes*) paquet; **an economy p. of washing powder** un paquet de lessive de taille économique; **a four-/six-p. of beer** un pack de quatre/six; **a p. of lies** un tissu de mensonges; *Med* **wet/cold p.** enveloppement *m* humide/froid

2 (*group*) (*of people, thieves*) groupe *m*, bande *f*, (*of wolves, foxhounds*) meute *f*, (*of

staghounds*) équipage *m*; (*of cub scouts, Brownies*) meute; **wolves hunt in packs** les loups chassent en meutes; **p. of fools** bande *ou* tas *m* d'imbéciles; *Rugby* **the p.** le pack

3 (*set*) (*of playing cards*) jeu *m*

4 *Geog* (*ice*) **p.** banquise *f*

VT 1 (*put into box, carton etc*) emballer, empaqueter; (*put into suitcase etc*) mettre dans sa valise/son sac/sa malle/*etc*; (*in cotton wool, newspaper etc*) emballer, envelopper; *Com* emballer, conditionner; **did you p. any towels?** est-ce que tu as mis des serviettes dans les bagages?; *esp Am* **shall I p. these for you?** (*in supermarket*) je vous emballe vos achats?

2 (*cram*) (*passengers into a train etc*) entasser; (*earth into a hole etc*) tasser; **we were packed in like sardines** nous étions serrés comme des harengs (en caque) *ou* comme des sardines; *Naut* **to p. on all sail** mettre toutes voiles dehors

3 (*fill*) remplir, bourrer (**sth with sth** qch de qch); *Constr, Min etc* (*trench*) remblayer; **to p. one's case/one's bags** faire sa valise/ses bagages; *Fig* **to p. one's bags** (*leave*) plier bagages; **we're not packed** nous n'avons pas fait nos bagages; *Theat* **the show packed the house** le spectacle a fait salle comble, le spectacle s'est joué à guichets fermés

4 *esp Am* (*carry in a backpack*) transporter dans un sac à dos; **to p. a pistol** porter un revolver; *Fam* **to p. a punch** (*of person*) cogner dur; (*of drink*) donner un coup de fouet

5 *Tech* (*packing box*) garnir, étouper

6 (*rig*) **to p. a jury** se composer un jury favorable; **to p. a meeting** s'assurer un nombre prépondérant de partisans à une réunion; *Cards* **to p. the cards** apprêter les cartes

7 *Comput* (*database*) condenser, compacter

VI 1 (*prepare luggage*) faire sa/ses valise(s) *ou* ses bagages; **a tent that packs easily** une tente facile à emballer; *Fam* **to send sb packing** envoyer promener qn

2 (*crush*) (*of person, animal*) s'entasser (**into** dans)

3 *Rugby* former le pack

▸▸ **p. animal** bête *f* de somme; *Mil* **p. drill** exercice *m* avec paquetage (*à titre de punition*); **p. ice** pack *m*, banquise *f*; *TV, Cin* **p. shot** pack shot *m*; **p. train** convoi *m* de bêtes de somme

▸ **pack away** **VT SEP 1** (*store*) ranger; (*bed*) replier

2 *Fam* **I've never seen anyone p. it away like him/p. away the beer like he does** je n'ai jamais vu personne engouffrer de la nourriture comme lui/avaler autant de bière que lui; **she can really p. away the food when she gets going** ce qu'elle peut engouffrer quand elle s'y met

VI (*of bed*) se replier; **this tent packs away easily** cette tente se replie *ou* se range facilement

▸ **pack down** VT SEP *(earth, snow etc)* tasser
VI **1** *(be compacted)* **to p. down hard** *(of snow etc)* se tasser
2 *Rugby* former la mêlée

▸ **pack in** VT SEP **1** *(cram in)* entasser; **I couldn't p. anything more in** je ne pouvais pas en faire rentrer plus; **they packed a lot of sightseeing into their short trip** ils ont visité énormément d'endroits pendant leur bref séjour; **one more thing to be packed into the Christmas period** une chose de plus pour laquelle il va falloir trouver du temps pendant la période de Noël; *Fam* **this movie is packing them in** ce film attire les foules; **we were packed in like sardines** nous étions serrés comme des harengs (en caque) *ou* comme des sardines
2 *Br Fam (stop, give up)* arrêter; *(job)* laisser tomber, plaquer; **to p. in smoking** arrêter de fumer; **to p. in jogging** laisser tomber le jogging; **p. it in!** arrête!, ça suffit!
3 *Fam (finish relationship with)* larguer, plaquer
4 *Am (bring in)* **if you p. it in, p. it out** = remenez vos ordures
VI **1** *(crowd in)* entrer en foule *ou* en masse
2 *Fam (stop working) (of machine etc)* tomber en panne; *(of person)* arrêter; **the photocopier's just packed in on me** la photocopieuse vient de me lâcher

▸ **pack off** VT SEP *Fam (send)* expédier; **to p. the kids off to school/bed** expédier *ou* envoyer les enfants à l'école/au lit; **his father packed him off to America/to boarding school** son père l'a expédié en Amérique/en pension

▸ **pack out** VT SEP *Fam (fill completely) (room)* remplir à craquer; **the pub was packed out** le bar était plein à craquer *ou* comble *ou* bondé; **the theatre had been packed out for weeks** le théâtre faisait salle comble depuis des semaines; **the event was completely packed out** il n'y avait plus un seul billet pour ce spectacle

▸ **pack up** VT SEP *(suitcase)* faire; *(belongings)* emballer; *(at end of class, work etc) (books, tools)* ranger
VI **1** *(before moving house)* emballer ses affaires **2** *(store things away at end of class, work etc)* ranger ses affaires, *Fam* remballer **3** *Fam (stop working) (of machine etc)* tomber en panne; **my car's packed up** ma voiture m'a lâché; **her heart has packed up** son cœur a lâché *ou* cédé

package ['pækɪdʒ] N **1** *(parcel)* paquet *m*, colis *m* **2** *Comput (software)* logiciel *m* **3** *Com (offer)* offre *f*; **the employment p. includes ...** les avantages accompagnant ce poste sont ...; **the p. includes a company car** l'offre comprend une voiture de société; **I didn't know this would be extra, I thought we were buying a p.** je ne savais pas que ce serait en supplément, je pensais que tout était compris; **you get all these services in a complete p.** tous ces services sont inclus dans le contrat **4** *TV (of channels)* bouquet *m*
VT *Com etc* emballer, conditionner; *Fam* **to p. sb** *(pop star, candidate etc)* créer l'image de marque de qn; **she has packaged herself as a sex symbol** elle s'est créé *ou* fabriqué une image de sex-symbol
▸▸ **p. deal** transaction *f* globale, accord *m* global; **p. holiday** vacances *fpl* à prix forfaitaire; *Am* **p. store** = magasin *m* qui vend des boissons alcoolisées (à emporter); **p. tour** voyage *m* à prix forfaitaire; **p. tourism** tourisme *m* organisé

packager ['pækɪdʒər] N *(in publishing)* packager *m*

packaging ['pækɪdʒɪŋ] N *(action)* emballage *m*, conditionnement *m*; *(materials)* emballage; *Fam (of pop star, candidate etc)*

image *f (fabriquée autour d'une personnalité publique)*; **the p. of the project is all wrong** la façon dont on a présenté le projet ne marche pas du tout; **p. charges** *or* **costs** frais *mpl* d'emballage

packed [pækt] ADJ **p. (with people)** *(bus, train etc)* bondé; *(hall etc)* plein à craquer, comble, bondé; **p. with tourists** plein de touristes; **the book was p. with information** le livre était truffé *ou* bourré de renseignements; *Theat etc* **to play to a p. house** faire salle comble
▸▸ **p. lunch** panier-repas *m, pl* paniers-repas, casse-croûte *m inv*

packer ['pækər] N **1** *Com etc (person)* emballeur, -euse, empaqueteur, -euse; **fruit p.** emballeur, -euse de fruits **2** *(device)* machine *f* à emballer *ou* à empaqueter; *(for tamping down)* bourroir *m*

packet ['pækɪt] N **1** *(of tea, cigarettes etc)* paquet *m*; *Comput (of data)* paquet; **I made the sauce from a p.** j'ai fait la sauce à partir d'un sachet; **pay p.** *(envelope)* enveloppe *f* de paie; *(money)* paie *f*; **wage p.** *(envelope)* enveloppe de salaire; *(money)* salaire *m*; **(postal) p.** colis *m* (postal), paquet poste; *Sl* **to make** *or* **earn a p.** gagner un fric fou; *Sl* **that'll cost a p.** ça va coûter les yeux de la tête **2** *Old-fashioned (boat)* paquebot *m* **3** *Sl (male genitals)* = contour *m* des parties génitales masculines moulées dans un pantalon; **what a p.!** quel entrejambe!
▸▸ *Old-fashioned* **p. boat** paquebot *m*; **p. soup** soupe *f* en sachet; *Comput* **p. switching** commutation *f* de paquets; *Comput* **p.-switching network** réseau *m* à commutation de paquets

packhorse ['pækhɔːs] N cheval *m* de somme; *Fam* **I'm not your p.!** je ne suis pas ton porteur

packing ['pækɪŋ] N **1** *Com etc (material, act)* emballage *m*; **postage and p.** frais *mpl* d'emballage et d'envoi **2** *(for holiday etc)* **to do one's p.** faire sa/ses valise(s), faire ses bagages; **there isn't much p. (to do)** il n'y a pas beaucoup de bagages à faire **3** *(material, object added or inserted)*, *Constr (for trench etc)* remblai *m*
▸▸ *Tech* **p. box** presse-étoupe *m, pl* presse-étoupe(s); **p. case** caisse *f* d'emballage; **p. charges, p. costs** frais d'emballage; **p. list** liste *f* de colisage; **p. materials** matériaux *mpl* d'emballage; **p. paper** papier *m* d'emballage; *Tech* **p. ring** *(of cylinder)* rondelle *f ou* bague *f* de garniture; *(of piston)* segment *m*, bague, garniture *f*; *Com* **p. slip** bon *m* de livraison

packsaddle ['pæksæd(ə)l] N bât *m*

pact [pækt] N pacte *m*; **to make a p. with sb** faire un pacte avec qn, pactiser avec qn (**to do sth** pour faire qch)

pacy ['peɪsɪ] ADJ *(film, novel)* mouvementé, vivant; *(sportsperson)* rapide

pad [pæd] N **1** *(for protection, to prevent chafing etc)* coussinet *m*; *(for brake)* plaquette *f*; *(keypad)* bloc *m*; *Sport* **shin pads**, *Cr* **pads** jambières *fpl*; **shoulder p.** *(in dress, jacket)* épaulette *f*
2 *Med* tampon *m*, compresse *f*; *(for feminine hygiene)* serviette *f* hygiénique
3 *(on body) (of finger, toe)* pulpe *f*; *(of dog, fox, hare etc)* coussinet *m*
4 *(writing paper)* bloc *m*; *(on desktop)* sous-main *m inv*; *(inking)* tampon *m* encreur
5 *Aviat etc (for helicopters)* aire *f* de décollage et d'atterrissage; **launching p.** aire *ou* plate-forme *f* de lancement
6 *Sl (home)* baraque *f*, casbah *f*; **let's go to my p.** allons chez moi; **you can crash at my p.** tu peux pieuter chez moi
7 *(sound) (of animal)* pas *mpl* sourds; *(of person)* pas feutrés; **the p. of his footsteps**

ses pas feutrés; **she heard the p. of feet in the corridor** elle a entendu quelqu'un qui marchait à pas feutrés dans le couloir
VT (**-dd-**) **1** *(armchair, door, wall)* capitonner
2 = **pad out**
VI **to p. (along)** *(of dog etc)* trotter; **to p. about** *(of person)* aller et venir à pas feutrés; **he padded downstairs in his slippers** il descendit l'escalier en pantoufles; **stop padding about in your bare feet** ne marche pas pieds nus
▸ **pad out** VT SEP *(fill out) (speech, essay etc)* étoffer; **they included two old songs to p. the album out** ils ont inclu deux vieilles chansons pour étoffer l'album; **they padded out the meal with some rice** ils ont complété le repas avec du riz

padded ['pædɪd] ADJ *(door, wall etc)* capitonné; *(garment)* matelassé, ouatiné; *(envelope)* rembourré
▸▸ **p. bra** soutien-gorge *m* à bonnets renforcés, *pl* soutiens-gorge; **p. cell** cellule *f* capitonnée; **p. shoulders** *(of dress, jacket)* épaulettes *fpl*

padding ['pædɪŋ] N **1** *(material) (for cushion etc)* bourre *f*, rembourrage *m*; *(for seat, jacket etc)* rembourrage; *(on walls, door)* capitonnage *m* **2** *(in speech, essay etc)* délayage *m*

paddle ['pæd(ə)l] N **1** *(for canoe)* pagaie *f*, **double p.** pagaie à double pale
2 *(blade) (of paddleboat, waterwheel)* aube *f*, pale *f*, palette *f*
3 *(of turtle, penguin, cetacean)* nageoire *f*, *(of duck)* patte *f*
4 *(table-tennis bat)* raquette *f* de ping-pong
5 *(walk in water)* **to go for a p.** aller patauger dans l'eau
VT **1** **to p. a/the/one's canoe** pagayer; *Prov* **to p. one's own canoe** *(get by on one's own)* se débrouiller (tout seul), arriver par soi-même **2** *Am Fam (hit)* donner une fessée à
VI **1** *(in canoe)* pagayer; *(in rowing boat)* tirer en douce; *(of duck)* nager **2** *(walk in water)* patauger; *(in mud etc)* patauger, patouiller
▸▸ **p. boat** bateau *m* à aubes *ou* à roues; **p. steamer** bateau à aubes *ou* à roues; *Naut* **p. wheel** roue *f* à aubes

paddling pool ['pædlɪŋ] N pataugeoire *f*

paddock ['pædək] N *(field for horse)*, *Horse-racing* paddock *m*; *Austr (field)* champ *m*

Paddy ['pædɪ] N *Fam (Irishman)* Irlandais *m*; **hey, P.!** hé, l'Irlandais

paddy ['pædɪ] N **1** *Com (rice)* paddy *m* **2** *Br Fam* **to be/get in a p.** être/se mettre en rogne (**about** pour)
▸▸ **p. field** rizière *f*, *Am Fam* **p. wagon** panier *m* à salade

padlock ['pædlɒk] N cadenas *m*
VT *(door)* cadenasser, fermer au cadenas; **he padlocked his bike to the fence** il a cadenassé son vélo à la grille

padre ['pɑːdreɪ] N *Rel* prêtre *m*; *Mil* aumônier *m* (militaire)

paean ['piːən] N *Fml* péan *m*, pæan *m*

paediatric, *Am* **pediatric** [piːdɪ'ætrɪk] ADJ *(hospital, care etc)* de pédiatrie; *(specialist)* en pédiatrie
▸▸ **p. surgery** chirurgie *f* pédiatrique

paediatrician, *Am* **pediatrician** [piːdɪə-'trɪʃən] N pédiatre *mf*

paediatrics, *Am* **pediatrics** [piːdɪ'ætrɪks] N pédiatrie *f*

paedology, *Am* **pedology** [piː'ɒlədʒɪ] N pédologie *f*

paedophile, *Am* **pedophile** ['piːdəʊfaɪl] N pédophile *mf*

paedophilia, *Am* **pedophilia** [piːdəʊ'fɪlɪə] N pédophilie *f*

pagan ['peɪgən] ADJ, N païen, -ïenne

paganism ['peɪgənɪz(ə)m] N paganisme m

page¹ [peɪdʒ] N page f; **on p. 6** à la page 6; **continued on p. 6/on back p.** suite f (en) page 6/en dernière page; **the sports/business pages** (in newspaper) la section sport/économie; Fig **a glorious p. in our history** une page glorieuse de l'histoire de notre pays
VT (book) paginer
▸▸ Comput **p. break** saut m de page; Comput **p. break character** caractère m de changement de page; Typ **p. bromide** bromure m de page; Typ **p. depth** hauteur f de page; Comput **p. description language** langage m de description de page; Typ, Comput **p. design** mise f en page; Comput **p. down key** touche f page suivante; Comput **p. down key** touche f page suivante; Typ, Comput **p. format** format m de page; Comput **p. layout** mise en page; Typ **p. length** longueur f de page; Typ **p. make-up** mise en pages; **p. number** numéro m de page; Typ **p. numbering** numérotage m des pages, pagination f, Journ **p. one** la une; Typ **p. plan** plan m de mise en page, chemin m de fer; Comput **p. preview** aperçu m avant l'impression; Comput **p. printer** imprimante f page par page, imprimante par pages; Comput **p. printer language** langage d'imprimante par pages; Typ **p. proofs** épreuves fpl en pages; Comput **p. scanner** lecteur m de pages; Comput **p. setup** format de page; Journ **p. three** = page sur laquelle une femme pose seins nus dans certains quotidiens de la presse populaire britannique; Journ **p. three girl** = jeune femme f posant seins nus dans certains quotidiens de la presse populaire britannique; Comput **p. up** page précédente; Comput **p. up key** touche page précédente
▸ **page down** VI Comput feuilleter en avant
▸ **page off** VT SEP Typ paginer
▸ **page up** VI Comput feuilleter en arrière

page² N (at hotel) jeune chasseur m; (at wedding) page m (d'honneur); (attending person of rank) page
VT (call) **to p. sb** (of pageboy) appeler qn; (by loudspeaker) appeler qn par haut-parleur; (by sending messenger) envoyer chercher qn au chasseur; (by paging device) biper qn; **I'm having her paged** je la fais appeler; **paging Mr Wilson** on demande M. Wilson

pageant ['pædʒənt] N (display) spectacle m grandiose ou majestueux; (of historical events) cortège m historique; Fig **the rich p. of our country's history** la riche galerie de tableaux de l'histoire de notre pays

pageantry ['pædʒəntrɪ] N apparat m, pompe f

pageboy ['peɪdʒbɔɪ] N **1** (hairstyle) coiffure f à la Jeanne d'Arc **2** = **page**² N
▸▸ **p. style** (hairstyle) coiffure à la Jeanne d'Arc

pager ['peɪdʒər] N Tel récepteur m d'appel ou de poche

page-turner N Fam (book) livre m passionnant ou captivant

paginate ['pædʒɪneɪt] VT (make into pages) mettre en pages; (number pages in) paginer

pagination [pædʒɪ'neɪʃən] N (page make-up) mise f en pages; (numbering) pagination f

pagoda [pə'gəʊdə] N Archit pagode f

pah [pɑː] INT pouah!

paid [peɪd] PT, PP see pay VT, VI
ADJ **1** (person, work) rétribué, rémunéré; **to get p. sick/maternity leave** avoir droit aux congés de maladie/de maternité **2** Com (goods, bill) payé; **p. (on bill)** pour acquit **3 to put p. to sb's chances/hopes** réduire les chances/espoirs de qn à néant; **well,**

that's **put p. to that!** et voilà, tout tombe à l'eau!
▸▸ **p. holidays** congés mpl payés

paid-out ADJ ATTRIB
▸▸ **p. form** bon m de décaissement; **p. voucher** bon de débours

paid-up ADJ **1** (fully) **p. member** (of party) membre m qui a payé sa cotisation **2** Fin (capital) versé; (shares) libéré; **fully p. policy** police f d'assurance dont les primes sont à jour; **to make a life assurance policy p.** cesser de cotiser à une assurance-vie (sans l'annuler)
▸▸ Fin **p. share capital** capital m appelé et libéré

pail [peɪl] N (bucket) seau m

pailful ['peɪlfʊl] N plein seau m

pain [peɪn] N **1** (physical) douleur f; (mental) peine f, douleur; **I have a p. in my leg** j'ai une douleur à la jambe; **there was a lot of p. in his right arm** son bras droit lui faisait très mal ou le faisait terriblement souffrir; **to cause sb p.** (physical) faire mal à qn, faire souffrir qn; (mental) faire de la peine à qn; **to be in great p.** souffrir beaucoup; **he was carried from the field in great p.** il souffrait beaucoup quand on l'a transporté hors du terrain; **the p. was unbearable** la douleur était insupportable; **to put a wounded animal out of its p.** achever un animal blessé; **shooting pains** élancements mpl, douleurs lancinantes; **labour pains** douleurs de l'accouchement
2 Fam (nuisance) **he's a p. (in the neck** or Vulg **arse)** il est casse-pieds ou emmerdant ou chiant; **working can be a p. sometimes** il y a des fois où c'est vraiment casse-pieds d'avoir à travailler
3 (trouble) (usu pl) **pains** peine f, **to take pains** or **be at great pains** or **go to great pains to do sth** se donner de la peine ou du mal pour faire qch; **as she was at pains to explain** ce qu'elle se donnait du mal à expliquer; **to take pains over sth** se donner du mal pour qch; **to have nothing for one's pains** en être pour sa peine
4 Fml **on** or **under p. of death** sous peine de mort
VT **1** (mentally) faire de la peine à, peiner, attrister; **it pained her to see them quarrel** ça lui faisait de la peine ou ça la peinait de les voir se disputer; **it pains me to have to tell you that …** je regrette infiniment d'avoir à vous dire que …
2 Old-fashioned (physically) faire souffrir, faire mal à; **the wound still pained her** la blessure la faisait encore souffrir ou lui faisait encore mal
▸▸ **p. barrier** seuil m de douleur; **p. relief** soulagement m; **aspirin for fast p. relief** aspirine pour soulager rapidement la douleur

pained [peɪnd] ADJ **p. expression** air m affligé ou peiné; **to look p.** avoir l'air affligé ou peiné

painful ['peɪnfʊl] ADJ **1** (wound, part of the body) douloureux; **I find walking p.** j'ai mal quand je marche; **to become p.** (of limb etc) devenir douloureux, s'endolorir; **that looked p.!** ça a dû faire mal!
2 (unpleasant) (spectacle, effort, subject) pénible; **a p. memory** un souvenir désagréable; **it was p. to see (it)** c'était pénible à voir; **the expensive shops were a p. reminder of their poverty** les boutiques chères leur rappelaient péniblement leur pauvreté
3 (difficult) (task) laborieux, pénible
4 Fam (bad) (performance, singing) atroce

painfully ['peɪnfʊlɪ] ADV **1** (with physical pain) douloureusement; **her head throbbed p.** elle sentait une douleur lancinante à la tête; **she fell p.** elle s'est fait mal en tombant
2 (shy, embarrassing) atrocement, pénible-

ment; **it was p. obvious** c'était tellement évident que c'en était embarrassant **3** (with difficulty etc) laborieusement

painkiller ['peɪnkɪlər] N calmant m, analgésique m

painkilling ['peɪnkɪlɪŋ] ADJ calmant, analgésique

painless ['peɪnlɪs] ADJ indolore, sans douleur; Fam Fig **replacing the fan belt was fairly p.** remplacer la courroie de ventilateur n'a pas posé trop de problèmes; **the p. way to pay your bills** la manière commode de payer vos factures

painlessly ['peɪnlɪslɪ] ADV (without pain) sans douleur; Fam Fig (effortlessly) sans effort, sans problème

painstaking ['peɪnzteɪkɪŋ] ADJ (person) soigneux, appliqué, assidu; (labour) soigné; (investigation) poussé; (accuracy, attention to detail) extrême

painstakingly ['peɪnzteɪkɪŋlɪ] ADV avec (grand) soin; **to be p. accurate/detailed in one's work** faire preuve d'une extrême précision/attention aux détails dans son travail

paint [peɪnt] N peinture f, Art couleur f, Med badigeon m; **p. (face make-up)** fard m; **wet p.!** (on sign) attention, peinture fraîche!; **box of paints** boîte f de couleurs; **tube of p.** tube m de peinture ou de couleur
VT **1** Art peindre; **to p. a portrait in oils** peindre un portrait à l'huile; **to p. a picture** peindre un tableau; **to p. (a picture of) sb** faire le portrait de qn
2 (coat with paint) (room, door etc) peindre (**green** en vert); Med (throat) badigeonner; **the kitchen needs painting** la cuisine a besoin d'être repeinte; Theat **to p. the scenery for a play** brosser les décors d'une pièce; **to p. one's nails** se vernir les ongles; Fam **to p. one's face** (put on make-up) se maquiller, se farder; Fig **to p. the town red** faire la noce ou la bringue
3 (depict) dépeindre; **to p. a favourable/an unfavourable picture of a situation** brosser un tableau favorable/défavorable de la situation; **to p. everything in rosy colours** peindre tout en rose
VI Art faire de la peinture; **to p. in watercolours/in oils** faire de l'aquarelle/de la peinture à l'huile; **I've always wanted to p.** j'ai toujours voulu faire de la peinture; **I wish I could p. like that!** si seulement je pouvais peindre comme cela!
▸▸ **p. gun** pistolet m à peinture; Br **p. pot** pot m de peinture; Comput **p. program** programme m de dessin bitmap; **p. roller** rouleau m à peinture; **p. shop** magasin m de couleurs; (in factory etc) atelier m de peinture; **p. stick** palette f de bois (utilisée pour mélanger la peinture)

paintball ['peɪntbɔːl] N paintball m

paintbox ['peɪntbɒks] N boîte f de couleurs

paintbrush ['peɪntbrʌʃ] N pinceau m

painter¹ ['peɪntər] N **1** Art peintre m; (of toys etc) coloriste mf; **landscape/portrait p.** paysagiste mf/portraitiste mf **2** (house) **p.** peintre m (en bâtiments); **J. Smith, painters and decorators** J. Smith, peintre et décorateur

painter² N Naut (rope) bosse f; **to cut the p.** couper l'amarre

painting ['peɪntɪŋ] N **1** (picture) tableau m, peinture f **2** (of house, picture etc) peinture f, **to study p.** étudier la peinture; **landscape/portrait p.** peinture de paysages/portraits; **(house) p.** peinture en bâtiment

paintwork ['peɪntwɜːk] N peinture(s) f(pl); (on car etc) peinture f

pair [peər] N **1** (of shoes, scissors, vases, legs etc) paire f, (of horses) attelage m; (man and woman, male and female animal) couple m; (in rowing) deux m; **in pairs** deux par deux;

the p. of you vous deux; **they can go to bed without their supper, the p. of them!** qu'ils aillent au lit sans manger tous les deux!; **what a p.!** (of two people) quelle paire!; **a p. of trousers** un pantalon; Old-fashioned **a p. of scales** une balance; **p. of step(ladder)s** escabeau m; **these two pictures are a p.** (match) ces deux tableaux se font pendant; **socks that are not a p.** chaussettes dépareillées; **where is the p. of this glove?** où se trouve l'autre gant de cette paire?; **a p. of aces/tens** une paire d'as/de dix VOIR GRAMMAIRE A10

2 Br Parl (two MPs from opposing parties) = deux membres mpl de partis adverses qui se sont associés (pour un vote); (MP from opposing party) = membre du parti adverse avec qui on peut s'associer

vi faire la paire (**with sb/sth** avec qn/qch); (of birds etc) s'accoupler, s'apparier (**with** avec); Br Parl s'associer (**with sb** avec qn)

vt (socks etc) appareiller, assortir; (birds etc) accoupler, apparier; Mktg **paired comparison** comparaison f par paire

▸▸ Cards **p. royal** brelan m

▸ **pair off** vi (of people) former un/des couple(s)

vt sep (objects) arranger deux par deux; (people) mettre deux par deux; **they were paired off by their hostess** leur hôtesse les a mis ensemble; **he's trying to get them paired off** (in a relationship) il essaie de les mettre ensemble

▸ **pair up** vi s'associer, se mettre ensemble; **to p. up with sb** s'associer avec qn, se mettre avec qn

paisley ['peɪzlɪ] N **p. scarf** foulard m à dessin cachemire

▸▸ Tex **p. pattern** (dessin m) cachemire m

pajamas [pə'dʒɑːməz] NPL Am = **pyjamas** VOIR GRAMMAIRE A10

Paki ['pækɪ] N, ADJ Br Offensive Sl pakistanais, -aise mf; (corner shop) épicerie f tenue par un/des Pakistanais

Paki-basher [-bæʃər] N Br Offensive Sl = raciste mf qui attaque les gens issus du sous-continent indien

Paki-bashing N Br Offensive Sl = persécution f des gens issus du sous-continent indien

Pakistan [pɑːkɪ'stɑːn] N Pakistan m

Pakistani [pɑːkɪ'stɑːnɪ] ADJ pakistanais
N Pakistanais, -aise

pakora [pə'kɔːrə] NPL Culin = beignets mpl de légumes/poisson/etc

pal [pæl] N Fam copain m, copine f; **be a p. and make me a coffee!** sois gentil, tu voudrais bien me faire un café?; **watch where you're going p.!** regarde où tu vas mon vieux ou (more aggressively) mon coco!

▸ **pal about, pal around** vi Fam **to p. about** or **around with sb** copiner avec qn, être pote avec qn; **they're about together** ils sont toujours fourrés ensemble

▸ **pal up** vi Fam (become friends) (of two people) devenir copains/copines; **to p. up with sb** devenir copain/copine avec qn

palace ['pælɪs] N **1** palais m; **bishop's/archbishop's p.** palais épiscopal/archiépiscopal **2** Br **the P., Buckingham P.** (royal entourage) Buckingham m; **the P. raised no objections to the visit** Buckingham n'a élevé aucune objection concernant la visite; **a P. spokesperson** un porte-parole de Buckingham

▸▸ **p. guard** (person) garde m du palais; (all guards) garde f du palais; **p. revolution** révolution f de palais

Note that the French word **palace** is a false friend and is never a translation for the English word **palace**. It means **luxury hotel**.

paladin ['pælədɪn] N Hist, Lit paladin m

palaeographer [pælɪ'ɒgrəfər] N paléographe mf

palaeography [pælɪ'ɒgrəfɪ] N paléographie f

Palaeolithic [pælɪəʊ'lɪθɪk] ADJ paléolithique; **the P. age** le paléolithique, l'âge m de la pierre taillée

palaeontologist [pælɪɒn'tɒlədʒɪst] N paléontologiste mf, paléontologue mf

palaeontology [pælɪɒn'tɒlədʒɪ] N paléontologie f

palatable ['pælətəb(ə)l] ADJ (meal) d'un goût agréable, agréable au palais; (wine) qui se laisse boire; Fig (doctrine, suggestion etc) acceptable (**to** aux yeux de)

palatal ['pælət(ə)l] ADJ Anat, Ling palatal, -aux
N Ling palatale f

palatalize ['pælətəlaɪz] vt Ling palataliser, mouiller

palate ['pælɪt] N Anat palais m; **hard p.** palais (dur), voûte f du palais, voûte palatine; **soft p.** voile m du palais; **to have a good p.** avoir le palais fin

palatial [pə'leɪʃəl] ADJ (building) magnifique, grandiose; (dimensions, scale) monumental, -aux

palatinate [pə'lætɪnɪt] N Hist palatinat m; **the Rhineland p.** le palatinat du Rhin

palaver [pə'lɑːvər] N **1** Fam (fuss) histoires fpl; **what's all the p. about?** qu'est-ce qui cloche? **2** Old-fashioned (discussion) palabre m ou f; **after a long p.** après de longs ou longues palabres

pale¹ [peɪl] ADJ pâle; (because ill, angry, afraid etc) blême, pâle; (colour) pâle, clair; **a p. blue dress** une robe bleu pâle; **p. as death, deathly p.** pâle comme un mort, d'une pâleur mortelle; **to grow** or **become p.** pâlir; **to turn p. with fright** pâlir de terreur; **by the p. light of the moon** à la lumière blafarde de la lune; Fig **a p. reflection/imitation of sth** un pâle reflet/une pâle copie de qch
vi (of person) pâlir, blêmir; Fig **my adventures p. beside yours** mes aventures semblent bien pâles auprès des vôtres; Fig **to p. into insignificance** devenir insignifiant

▸▸ **p. ale** pale-ale f, pl pale-ales, bière f blonde légère

pale² N **1** (of fence) pieu m **2 beyond the p.** (behaviour, remarks) inacceptable; (of person) pas fréquentable

paleface ['peɪlfeɪs] N visage m pâle

pale-faced ['peɪlfeɪst] ADJ au visage ou au teint pâle; **they looked p.** leurs visages étaient pâles

paleness ['peɪlnɪs] N pâleur f

Palestine ['pælɪstaɪn] N Palestine f; **the P. Liberation Organization** l'Organisation f de libération de la Palestine

Palestinian [pælɪ'stɪnɪən] ADJ palestinien
N Palestinien, -ienne

palette ['pælɪt] N Art palette f
▸▸ **p. knife** Art couteau m (à palette); Culin spatule f

palimony ['pælɪmənɪ] N Fam = pension f alimentaire versée au concubin/à la concubine

palimpsest ['pælɪmpsest] ADJ, N palimpseste m

palindrome ['pælɪndrəʊm] N palindrome m

paling ['peɪlɪŋ] N (fence) palissade f, palis m; (stake) pieu m

palisade [pælɪ'seɪd] N **1** palissade f **2** Am **palisades** (cliffs) falaises fpl abruptes

pall¹ [pɔːl] N **1** (over coffin) poêle m **2** Fig (of smoke etc) voile m; (of snow, darkness, gloom etc) manteau m

pall² vi (become uninteresting) perdre son attrait (**on sb** pour qn); **it never palls on** on ne s'en lasse pas

pallbearer ['pɔːlbeərər] N porteur m (du cercueil)

pallet¹ ['pælɪt] N (straw mattress) paillasse f; Lit (poor bed) grabat m

pallet² N **1** Com palette f **2** Art = **palette**
▸▸ **p. truck** chariot m élévateur, transpalette m

palletizable [pælɪ'taɪzɪb(ə)l] ADJ Com palettisable

palletization [pælɪtaɪ'zeɪʃən] N Com palettisation f

palletize ['pælɪtaɪz] vt Com palettiser

palletizer ['pælɪtaɪzər] N Com palettiseur m

palliasse ['pælɪæs] N paillasse f

palliate ['pælɪeɪt] vt Fml (make less severe) pallier; (illness) lénifier; (fears) apaiser; (offence) pallier, atténuer; **her words had a palliating effect** ses paroles ont eu un effet lénifiant

palliative ['pælɪətɪv] ADJ, N palliatif m; **to have a p. effect** (of medicine) avoir un effet palliatif ou lénifiant; (of words) avoir un effet lénifiant; **p. care** soins mpl palliatifs

pallid ['pælɪd] ADJ (person, face, complexion etc) pâle, blême, blafard; (skin, hands) pâle; (light, moon) blafard; Fig (performance) fade, insipide; **a p. reflection/imitation of sth** un pâle reflet/une pâle copie de qch

pallidness ['pælɪdnɪs], **pallor** ['pælər] N pâleur f

pally ['pælɪ] ADJ Fam **to be p. with sb** être copain/f copine avec qn

palm [pɑːm] N **1** (of hand) paume f; (of glove) empaumure f; **to read sb's p.** lire les lignes de la main à qn; Fam **to grease sb's p.** graisser la patte à qn; Fam **to have** or **hold sb in the p. of one's hand** avoir qn dans sa poche **2** (tree) palmier m **3** (branch) palme f, Rel rameau m, buis m (bénit); Fig **to bear** or **win** or **carry off the p.** remporter la palme
vt (conceal) (coin, brooch, card etc) escamoter; **to p. a card** (in conjuring) filer une carte
▸▸ Br **p. court orchestra** = petit orchestre m jouant dans le salon d'un hôtel (décoré de palmiers); **p. grove** palmeraie f; **p. leaf** feuille f de palmier; **p. oil** huile f de palme; **p. plantation** palmeraie f; Rel **P. Sunday** le dimanche des Rameaux, les Rameaux mpl; **p. tree** palmier m; **p. wine** vin m de palme

▸ **palm off** vt sep **1** (dispose of something unwanted) faire passer, Fam refiler (**sth on sb** qch à qn); **they're palming the children off on us for the weekend** ils vont nous refiler les enfants pour le week-end **2** (give something worthless to) **when I complained, they palmed me off with a standard letter** quand je me suis plaint, ils se sont contentés de me refiler une lettre toute faite; **she tried to p. me off with some ridiculous excuse** elle a essayé de me faire avaler une excuse ridicule

palmist ['pɑːmɪst] N chiromancien, -ienne

palmistry ['pɑːmɪstrɪ] N chiromancie f

palmtop ['pɑːmtɒp] N (computer) ordinateur m de poche
▸▸ **p. computer** ordinateur de poche

palmy ['pɑːmɪ] ADJ **p. days** (of country etc) époque f florissante; **in his p. days** dans ses beaux jours

palpable ['pælpəb(ə)l] ADJ (tangible) palpable, que l'on peut toucher; Fig (obvious) (lack of enthusiasm, interest) manifeste; (lie) évident; (difference) sensible, manifeste

palpably ['pælpəblɪ] ADV manifestement

palpate ['pælpeɪt] vt Med palper

palpation [pæl'peɪʃən] N Med palpation f, palper m

palpitate ['pælpɪteɪt] VI palpiter

palpitating ['pælpɪteɪtɪŋ] ADJ palpitant

palpitation [pælpɪ'teɪʃən] N palpitation f, **to get** or **have palpitations** avoir des palpitations

palsied ['pɔːlzɪd] ADJ Med paralysé; Lit (step, grip) tremblant

palsy ['pɔːlzɪ] N Med Old-fashioned paralysie f

palsy-walsy ['pælzɪ'wælzɪ] ADJ Fam **to be p. with sb** être comme cul et chemise avec qn, être à tu et à toi avec qn; **they're very p. all of a sudden** ils sont très potes ou copain-copain tout d'un coup

paltry ['pɔːltrɪ] ADJ (amount, sum) misérable, dérisoire; **p. excuses** piètres excuses fpl

pampas ['pæmpəz] N Geog **the P.** la Pampa
  ▸▸ **p. grass** herbe f de la pampa

pamper ['pæmpər] VT (person) choyer, dorloter; **a hotel where you will be pampered** un hôtel où l'on sera à vos petits soins; **to p. oneself** se faire plaisir; **pampered tastes** goûts mpl difficiles

pamphlet ['pæmflɪt] N brochure f, (literary, scientific) opuscule m; (libellous, scurrilous) pamphlet m

Note that the French word **pamphlet** always refers to a satirical tract.

pamphleteer [pæmflɪ'tɪər] N auteur m de brochures; (scurrilous) pamphlétaire mf

Pan [pæn] N Myth Pan

pan [pæn] N 1 (for cooking) casserole f 2 (of scales) plateau m; Min (for gold) batée f, (toilet) **p.** cuvette f (de W.-C.); Fam **to go down the p.** s'en aller en fumée; **that's six months' work down the p.!** voilà six mois de travail qui s'en vont en fumée! 3 Geol etc cuvette f, bassin m de déposition ou de sédimentation; **salt p.** marais m salant, saline f, salin m 4 TV, Cin panoramique m
VT (-nn-) 1 Min (gravel etc) laver à la batée 2 **to p. the camera** faire un panoramique, panoramiquer; **to p. the camera across the room** prendre la salle en panoramique, faire un panoramique de la salle 3 Fam (criticize adversely) (film, play etc) éreinter, esquinter
VI 1 Min laver le gravier/etc à la batée; **to p. for gold** laver le gravier/etc à la batée pour en extraire l'or 2 TV, Cin panoramiquer; **the camera pans around the bay** la caméra prend la baie en panoramique ou fait un panoramique de la baie; **to p. across the room** prendre la salle en panoramique, faire un panoramique de la salle; **a panning shot** une prise panoramique, un panoramique
  ▸▸ TV, Cin **p. down** panoramique vers le bas; Scot **p. loaf** pain m de mie; **p. scourer** éponge f à récurer les casseroles; TV, Cin **p. up** panoramique vertical
  ▸ **pan down** VI TV, Cin faire un panoramique vers le bas
  ▸ **pan out** VI Fam (turn out) **it didn't p. out (well)** cela n'a pas marché; **it depends how things p. out** ça dépend de comment les choses vont s'arranger
VT SEP Min (wash) laver à la batée
  ▸ **pan up** VI TV, Cin faire un panoramique vers le haut

panacea [pænə'sɪə] N panacée f

panache [pə'næʃ] N (style) panache m

Pan-African ADJ panafricain

Pan-Africanism [-'æfrɪkənɪz(ə)m] N panafricanisme m

Panama ['pænəmɑː] N 1 (country) Panama m; **the P. Canal** le canal de Panama 2 **p.** (hat) panama m
  ▸▸ **p. hat** panama

Panamanian [pænə'meɪnɪən] ADJ panaméen
  N Panaméen, -enne

Pan-American ADJ panaméricain; **the P. Highway** la route panaméricaine

Pan-Americanism N panaméricanisme m

panatella [pænə'telə] N panatel(l)a m
  ▸▸ **p. cigar** panatel(l)a

panavision ['pænəvɪʒən] N panavision f

pancake ['pænkeɪk] N 1 Culin crêpe f 2 Aviat atterrissage m brutal 3 (make-up) fond m de teint
  VI Aviat faire un atterrissage brutal
  ▸▸ Br **P. Day** mardi m gras; Aviat **p. landing** atterrissage brutal; **p. make-up** fond de teint; Br **P. Tuesday** mardi gras

panchromatic [pænkrəʊ'mætɪk] ADJ Phot panchromatique

pancreas ['pæŋkrɪəs] N Anat pancréas m

pancreatic [pæŋkrɪ'ætɪk] ADJ pancréatique

pancreatitis [pæŋkrɪə'taɪtəs] N pancréatite f

panda ['pændə] N panda m; **giant p.** panda géant
  ▸▸ Br **p. car** voiture f de police

pandemic [pæn'demɪk] Med ADJ pandémique
  N pandémie f

pandemonium [pændɪ'məʊnɪəm] N **it's p.** c'est la confusion la plus totale, c'est un désordre indescriptible; **their entire household was in p.** c'était un véritable cirque chez eux quand je suis arrivé

pander ['pændər] VI **these films p. to our worst instincts** ces films font appel à nos pires instincts; **to p. to sb** encourager qn; **to p. to a vice** encourager un vice; **to p. to sb's whims** se prêter aux exigences de qn

Pandora [pæn'dɔːrə] N Myth Pandore; **P.'s box** boîte f de Pandore

pane [peɪn] N (of window) vitre f, carreau m; (of computer screen) panneau m; **a p. of glass** un carreau, une vitre

panegyric [pænɪ'dʒaɪrɪk] ADJ, N Fml panégyrique m

panel ['pæn(ə)l] N 1 (on wall, of door) panneau m; (in ceiling) caisson m; (of altarpiece) panneau; (of cartoon strip) case f, Sewing panneau; Archit, Constr entre-deux m inv 2 (list of jury members) tableau m ou liste f du jury; (of committee members) liste des membres d'un comité ou d'une commission; (group) (of enquiry etc) comité m, commission f, (working party) groupe m de travail; (round table) table f ronde; **the p.** Radio, TV les invités mpl; Scot Law (the accused) l'accusé, -ée, pl les accusé(e)s; **p. of experts** comité ou commission d'experts; Mktg (for market research) panel m; Mktg **p. of expert opinion** panel de spécialistes 3 Radio, TV (mixing desk, console) pupitre m
  VT (-ll-, Am -l-) recouvrir de panneaux; (wall) lambrisser; (surface) plaquer
  ▸▸ Br Aut **p. beater** carrossier m, tôlier m; **p. discussion** débat m, table ronde; Br **p. game** Radio jeu m radiophonique; TV jeu télévisé; **p. light** lampe f ou éclairage m de tableau de bord; **p. member** (jury member) juré, -ée; (in radio or TV quiz) invité, -ée; (in public debate) panéliste mf; (of committee) membre m du comité; Br **p. pin** pointe f à tête d'homme, clou m à panneau; **p. research** recherches fpl par panel; Am Aut **p. truck** camionnette f, fourgonnette f

panelled, Am **paneled** ['pæn(ə)ld] ADJ (room, wall) recouvert ou revêtu de boiseries, lambrissé

panelling, Am **paneling** ['pæn(ə)lɪŋ] N 1 (wall covering) lambris m, boiseries fpl, placage m; **oak p.** lambris mpl de chêne 2 (material) panneaux mpl

panellist, Am **panelist** ['pæn(ə)lɪst] N (jury member) juré, -ée; (of committee) membre m du comité; (of working party) membre du groupe de travail; (in radio or TV quiz) invité, -ée

pang [pæŋ] N **pangs of jealousy** tourments mpl de la jalousie; **to feel a p.** sentir un pincement au cœur; **a p. of conscience** un soubresaut de conscience; **to feel** or **have pangs of remorse** être tiraillé par les remords; **pangs of hunger** tiraillements mpl d'estomac

panhandle ['pænhænd(ə)l] Am N 1 Geog langue f de terre; **the Texas p.** = langue de terre correspondant à la partie nord-ouest du Texas 2 TV, Cin manche m (de tête de caméra)
  VI Fam mendier
  VT Fam essayer de taper

panhandler ['pænhændlər] N Am Fam mendiant, -ante

panic¹ ['pænɪk] N panique f, Fam **there's no p.** il n'y a pas le feu; **to create** or **cause (a) p.** causer un mouvement de panique; **to throw the crowd/the stockmarkets into a p.** affoler la foule/les marchés; **in a p.** paniqué, affolé; **to get into a p. over** or **about sth** s'affoler à cause de qch; Fam **it was p. stations** c'était la panique totale ou l'affolement général
  VT (pt, pp panicked) (person, crowd etc) remplir de panique, paniquer, affoler; (horse) affoler; **the news panicked the government into action** la panique provoquée par cette nouvelle a poussé le gouvernement à l'action; **she was panicked into resigning** sous le coup de la panique, elle a démissionné
  VI être pris de panique, s'affoler, paniquer (about à propos de); **don't p.!** ne t'affole pas!, ne panique pas!
  ▸▸ **p. attack** crise f de panique; **p. button** signal m d'alarme; Fam Fig **to hit the p. button** paniquer; **p. buying** = achats mpl massifs provoqués par la crainte de la pénurie; St Exch achats de précaution; **p. measures** mesures fpl dictées par la panique; **p. reaction** réaction f de panique

panic² N Bot panic m (d'Italie)
  ▸▸ **p. grass** panic (d'Italie)

panicky ['pænɪkɪ] ADJ Fam (feelings) panique; (person) sujet à la panique; (reaction, response) affolé; (market etc) enclin à la panique; **a p. decision** une décision prise sous le coup de la panique; **don't get p.!** ne paniquez pas!, ne vous affolez pas!

panic-stricken ADJ pris de panique, affolé; (reaction, response, look) affolé

panjandrum [pæn'dʒændrəm] N Lit gros bonnet m

pannier ['pænɪər] N (basket) panier m; (on motorbike or bicycle) sacoche f, (of beast of burden) panier de bât

panning ['pænɪŋ] N TV, Cin panoramique m
  ▸▸ TV, Cin **p. handle** poignée f de panoramique; TV, Cin **p. shot** prise f panoramique

panoply ['pænəplɪ] N panoplie f

panorama [pænə'rɑːmə] N panorama m

panoramic [pænə'ræmɪk] ADJ (view etc) panoramique
  ▸▸ Cin **p. screen** écran m panoramique

panpipes ['pænpaɪps] NPL Mus flûte f de Pan

pansy ['pænzɪ] N 1 (flower) pensée f 2 Offensive Sl (male homosexual) pédale f, tante f

pant [pænt] **N** souffle *m* pantelant *ou* haletant

VI 1 *(gasp)* haleter; *(of animal)* battre du flanc; **to p. for breath** chercher à reprendre haleine; **she panted up the hill** elle a monté la côte en haletant *ou* soufflant **2** *Fam (be eager)* **he's panting to do it** il a tellement envie de le faire

VT listen to me, she panted écoute-moi, dit-elle d'une voix haletante

▸ **pant out VT SEP** *(say)* dire en haletant

pantechnicon [pæn'teknɪkən] **N** *Br Old-fashioned (van)* camion *m* de déménagement

pantheism ['pænθiːɪz(ə)m] **N** panthéisme *m*

pantheist ['pænθiːɪst] **ADJ, N** panthéiste *mf*

pantheistic [pænθiːˈɪstɪk] **ADJ** panthéiste

pantheon ['pænθiːən] **N** panthéon *m*

panther ['pænθər] **N** panthère *f*; *Am (puma)* couguar *m*, puma *m*; *Am Pol* **Black P.** Panthère *f* noire; **the (Black) Panthers** = mouvement *m* politique fondé par des militants noirs américains dans les années soixante

panties ['pæntɪz] **NPL** culotte *f*, slip *m (de femme)*

pantihose ['pæntɪhəʊz] **NPL** *Am* collant *m*

panting ['pæntɪŋ] **N** halètement *m*

panto ['pæntəʊ] **N** *Br Theat Fam* = **pantomime 1**

pantograph ['pæntəɡrɑːf] **N 1** *Art* pantographe *m*, singe *m* **2** *Elec (of electric train)* pantographe *m*

pantomime ['pæntəmaɪm] **N 1** *Br Theat (traditional winter show)* = revue-féerie *f* à grand spectacle (présentée aux environs de Noël) **2** *(dumb show)* pantomime *f* **3** *Br Fam (ridiculous situation)* cirque *m*, sérénade *f*; **there was a bit of a p. over who should pay** ça a été une sérénade pour savoir qui devait payer

Note that the French word **pantomime** is a false friend and is never a translation for the English word **pantomime**. It means **mime**.

Pantomime

Le genre typiquement britannique de la "pantomime" est très conventionnel; certains personnages-types ("pantomime dame", "principal boy") et certaines rengaines ("Behind you!", "Oh yes he is! – Oh no he isn't!") apparaissent dans toutes les pièces. Ces pièces, qui se jouent au moment des fêtes de fin d'année, sont généralement inspirées d'un conte de fées.

pantry ['pæntrɪ] **N** *(cupboard)* (grand) placard *m* à provisions, dépense *f*

pants [pænts] **NPL** VOIR GRAMMAIRE A10 **1** *Br (underwear)* slip *m*; *(boxer shorts)* caleçon *m* **2** *esp Am (trousers)* pantalon *m*; *Fam* **to give sb a kick in the p.** donner un coup de pied au derrière à qn; *Fam* **to beat the p. off sb** mettre une sacrée volée à qn; *Fam* **to scare the p. off sb** faire une peur *ou* trouille bleue à qn; *Fam* **to bore the p. off sb** barber qn comme ce n'est pas permis; *Fam* **to be caught with one's p. down** être pris dans une situation des plus embarrassantes; *Fam* **to wear the p.** porter la culotte; *Fam* **it's clear who wears the p. around here** il n'y a pas de doute sur qui porte la culotte ici

ADJ *Br Fam (of poor quality)* nul

INT *Br Fam* zut!, mince!

panty ['pæntɪ] **N**

▸▸ **p. girdle** gaine-culotte *f*, *pl* gaines-culottes; **p. liner** protège-slip *m*, *pl* protège-slips

pantyhose ['pæntɪhəʊz] **NPL** *Am* collant *m*

panzer ['pænzər] **N** panzer *m*; **a p. division** une division blindée

Pap [pæp] **N** *Med* **P. test** *or* **smear** frottis *m* vaginal

pap [pæp] **N** *(baby food)* bouillie *f*; *Pej (non-sense)* idioties *fpl*, stupidités *fpl*

papa [pə'pɑː] **N** *Old-fashioned* papa *m*

papacy ['peɪpəsɪ] **N** papauté *f*

papadum ['pæpədəm] **N** = **poppadom**

papal ['peɪp(ə)l] **ADJ** papal, -aux

▸▸ **p. bull** bulle *f* papale; **p. interdict** interdit *m* papal; **p. nuncio** nonce *m* du Pape; **p. throne** trône *m* pontifical

paparazzi [pæpə'rætsɪ] **NPL** *Journ, Phot Pej* paparazzi *mpl*

papaw [pə'pɔː] **N** *Bot* **1** *(asimina triloba) (fruit)* asimine *f*; *(tree)* asiminier *m* **2** = **papaya**

papaya [pə'paɪə] **N** *(carica papaya)* papaye *f*; *(tree)* papayer *m*

paper ['peɪpər] **N 1** papier *m*; *(for wall)* papier peint; **a sheet/a piece of p.** une feuille/un morceau de papier; **a pile of p.** une pile de papier; **to put sth down on p.** mettre qch par écrit; **on p. it is an army of 300,000** sur le papier *ou* en théorie, c'est une armée de 300 000 hommes; **it's a good plan on p.** ce projet est excellent en théorie; **the p. industry** l'industrie *f* papetière, la papeterie **2** *(document)* écrit *m*, document *m*; *Fin etc* papier *m* valeur; *(banknotes)* billets *mpl* de banque; **private** *or* **personal papers** papiers personnels; **(identity) papers** papiers (d'identité); *Fin* **long/short p.** papier à long/court terme **3** *Sch* **(examination) p.** épreuve *f* écrite; *(questions)* questions *fpl* d'examen; *(answer)* copie *f*; **the Shakespeare/history p.** l'épreuve (écrite) sur Shakespeare/d'histoire **4** *(scholarly study, report)* article *m*; **to read** *or* **give a p.** faire un exposé **5** *(newspaper)* journal *m*, -aux; *Am Fam* **go peddle your papers!** va voir ailleurs si j'y suis!

VT *(room)* tapisser

▸▸ **p. advance** *(of printer)* entraînement *m* du papier; **p. aeroplane** avion *m* en papier; **p. bag** sac *m* en papier; **p. bin** *(of printer)* bac *m* à papier; **p. blockage** *(of printer)* bourrage *m* de papier; **p. chase** rallye-papier *m*, ≃ jeu *m* de piste; *Fig* **education has become an academic p. chase** l'éducation est devenue une véritable course aux diplômes; *Fin* **p. company** société *f* d'investissement; **p. cup** gobelet *m* en carton, **p. currency** papier-monnaie *m*, *pl* papiers-monnaies; **p. dart** avion *m* en papier; *Comput, Typ* **p. feed** alimentation *f* du papier; **p. folding machine** machine *f* à plier les documents; *Comput, Typ* **p. format** format *m* de papier; **p. guide** *(of printer)* guide-papier *m*, *pl* guides-papier; **p. handkerchief** mouchoir *m* en papier; **p. handling** *(of printer)* gestion *f* du papier; *Fam* **p. hankie** mouchoir en papier; **p. input** *(of printer)* entrée *f* de papier; **p. jam** *(of printer)* bourrage de papier; *Fin* **p. loss** moins-value *f*, *pl* moins-values; **p. mill** usine *f* à papier; *(on small scale)* fabrique *f* de papier; *Fin* **p. money** papier-monnaie *m*, *pl* papiers-monnaies, monnaie *f* fiduciaire; **p. out indicator** *(of printer)* indicateur *m* de fin du papier; **p. out light** *(of printer)* voyant *m* de fin du papier; **p. out warning** *(of printer)* avertissement *m* de fin du papier; **p. park function** *(of printer)* fonction *f* de parcage de l'imprimante; **p. path** *(of printer)* chemin *m* du papier; **p. plate** assiette *f* en carton; **p. profits** profits *mpl* fictifs; **p. release arm** *(of printer)* levier *m* de dégagement du papier; **p. round** livraison *f* de journaux; **to have** *or* **do a p. round** distribuer les journaux; *Fin* **p.**

securities titres *mpl* fiduciaires, papiers valeurs; *Br* **p. shop** marchand *m* de journaux; *Comput* **p. tape** bande *f* perforée; *Comput* **p. tape reader** lecteur *m* de bandes de papier; **p. tiger** tigre *m* de papier; **p. tissue** mouchoir en papier; **p. towel** serviette *f* en papier; **p. transaction** jeu *m* d'écritures; **p. tray** *(of printer)* bac à feuilles

▸ **paper over VT SEP** **to p. sth over** *(with wallpaper)* masquer qch en le tapissant; *Fig* **to p. over the cracks** *(disguise faults)* masquer les défauts; *(disguise disagreements)* masquer les mésententes

paperback ['peɪpəbæk] **N** livre *m* de poche; **available in p.** disponible en livre de poche; **p. sales** ventes *fpl* de livres de poche

ADJ **p. book/edition** livre *m*/édition *f* de poche

paperboard ['peɪpəbɔːd] **N** carton *m*

paperboy ['peɪpəbɔɪ] **N** *(deliverer)* livreur *m* de journaux; *(seller)* vendeur *m* de journaux

paperclip ['peɪpəklɪp] **N** trombone *m*

papergirl ['peɪpəɡɜːl] **N** *(deliverer)* livreuse *f* de journaux; *(seller)* vendeuse *f* de journaux

paperhanger ['peɪpəhæŋər] **N 1** *(decorator)* peintre *m* décorateur **2** *Am Sl (counterfeiter)* faux-monnayeur *m*, *pl* faux-monnayeurs

paperknife ['peɪpənaɪf] **N** coupe-papier *m inv*

paperless ['peɪpəlɪs] **ADJ**

▸▸ **p. office** bureau *m* entièrement informatisé; *StExch* **p. trading** marché *m ou* cotation *f* électronique

paperweight ['peɪpəweɪt] **N** presse-papiers *m inv*

paperwork ['peɪpəwɜːk] **N** paperasseries *fpl*; *(official documents)* papiers *mpl*; **to do the p.** s'occuper du travail de bureau; **I'm drowning in p.** je suis dans la paperasserie jusqu'au cou

papery ['peɪpərɪ] **ADJ** qui ressemble à du papier; *(thin)* mince comme du papier; **p. skin** peau *f* parcheminée

papier-mâché ['pæpjeɪ'mæʃeɪ] **N** carton-pâte *m*, *pl* cartons-pâtes

papilloma [pæpɪ'ləʊmə] **N** *Med* papilloma *m*

papist ['peɪpɪst] **N, ADJ** *Pej* papiste *mf*

papistry ['peɪpɪstrɪ] **N** *Pej* papisme *m*

paprika [pə'priːkə] **N** paprika *m*

Papua ['pæpjʊə] **N** *Hist* Papouasie *f*

▸▸ **P. New Guinea** Papouasie-Nouvelle-Guinée *f*

Papuan ['pæpjʊən] **ADJ** papou

N Papou, -oue

papyrus, *pl* **papyri** [pə'paɪrəs, -raɪ] **N** papyrus *m*

par [pɑːr] **N 1** *(equality)* pair *m*, égalité *f*; **to be on a p. with sb/sth** être au niveau de qn/qch; **they're on a p.** ils sont au même niveau **2** *above/below p.* au-dessus/au-dessous du pair; **at p.** au pair; **to issue shares at p.** émettre des actions au pair; **close to p.** au voisinage de la parité **3** *(average)* moyenne *f*; **above/below p.** au-dessus/au-dessous de la moyenne; *Fam* **to feel below p., not to feel up to p.** ne pas être dans son assiette; **the film wasn't really up to p.** le film n'est pas aussi bon qu'on aurait pu s'y attendre **4** *Golf* par *m*; **to be under/over p.** être en dessous/au-dessus du par; **a p.-three (hole)** un par trois; *Fam Fig* **that's about p. for the course** c'est ce à quoi il faut s'attendre; **his behaviour was about p. for the course** son comportement n'a rien eu de vraiment surprenant

▸▸ *Fin, StExch* **p. bond** obligation *f* émise au pair; *Fin, St Exch* **p. of exchange** pair du change; *Fin, St Exch* **p. value** valeur *f* au pair *ou* nominale

para ['pærə] **N 1** (*abbr* **paragraph**) par. **2** *Mil Fam* (*abbr* **paratrooper**) para *m*

parable ['pærəb(ə)l] **N** parabole *f*; **teaching in parables** enseignement *m* en paraboles

parabola [pə'ræbələ] **N** *Math* parabole *f*

parabolic [pærə'bɒlɪk] **ADJ** *Math etc* (*curve, mirror*) parabolique
▸▸ *TV* **p. dish** antenne *f* parabolique, parabole *f*

paracetamol [pærə'siːtəmɒl] **N** paracétamol *m*; **take two p.** *or* **paracetamols** prenez deux cachets de paracétamol

parachute ['pærəʃuːt] **N** parachute *m*; **to drop sb/sth by p.** larguer qn/qch par parachute, parachuter qn/qch; **brake** *or* **tail p.** parachute de freinage (à l'atterrissage) **VI** sauter en parachute
VT (*person, supplies*) parachuter, larguer par parachute
▸▸ **p. descent** descente *f* en parachute; **p. flare** fusée *f* (éclairante) à parachute; **p. harness** ceinture *f ou* harnais *m* de parachute; **p. jump** saut *m* en parachute; **to make a p. jump** sauter en parachute; **p. pack** (*parachute*) parachute (plié et prêt à servir); (*container*) enveloppe *f ou* sac *m* de parachute
▸ **parachute in VT SEP** (*troops, supplies etc*) parachuter, envoyer par parachute; *Fig* (*new manager, candidate etc*) parachuter
VI être parachuté; **I'll p. in** je vais me faire parachuter, je vais descendre en parachute

parachuting ['pærəʃuːtɪŋ] **N** (*activity*) parachutisme *m*; (*of person, supplies*) parachutage *m*

parachutist ['pærəʃuːtɪst] **N** parachutiste *mf*

parade [pə'reɪd] **N 1** *Mil* (*exercise*) exercice *m*; **church p.** (*of battalion etc*) rassemblement *m* pour assister à l'office du dimanche; **on p.** à l'exercice
2 (*procession*) défilé *m*; *Rel* procession *f*; **fashion p.** défilé de mannequins; *Mil* **to go on p.** défiler
3 (*display*) parade *f*; *Pej* **to make a p. of one's knowledge/feelings** étaler sa culture/ses sentiments; **a street where you'll see all the new fashions on p.** une rue où l'on arbore toutes les dernières créations de la mode; **all the world leaders were on p.** il y avait tout une panoplie de chefs d'états
4 (*along beach*) boulevard *m*; **a p. of shops** une rangée de magasins
5 *Fencing* parade *f*
VT 1 *Mil* (*troops*) faire parader, faire défiler; (*assemble*) (*battalion*) rassembler **2** (*riches*) faire parade *ou* étalage de; (*knowledge, feelings, opinions*) afficher, faire étalage de; **to p. one's dislike of sb** montrer clairement son antipathie à l'égard de qn
VI 1 *Mil* (*for exercise, inspection*) parader; **to p. through the streets** défiler dans les rues **2** *Fig* (*show off*) se pavaner; **young people parading up and down the beach with next to nothing on!** des jeunes gens qui se pavanent sur la plage avec presque rien sur le dos!
▸▸ *Mil* **p. ground** terrain *m* d'exercices *ou* de manœuvres

paradigm ['pærədaɪm] **N** paradigme *m*

paradigmatic [pærədɪg'mætɪk] **ADJ** paradigmatique

paradise ['pærədaɪs] **N** *Rel, Fig* paradis *m*; **an earthly p.** un paradis sur terre; **to go to p.** aller au paradis; **bird of p.** paradisier *m*, oiseau *m* de paradis

paradisiac [pærə'dɪzɪæk], **paradisiacal** [pærədɪ'zaɪək(ə)l] **ADJ** paradisiaque

paradox ['pærədɒks] **N** paradoxe *m*

paradoxical [pærə'dɒksɪk(ə)l] **ADJ** paradoxal, -aux

paradoxically [pærə'dɒksɪklɪ] **ADV** paradoxalement

paraffin ['pærəfɪn] **N** paraffine *f*, (*fuel*) pétrole *m* (lampant), kérosène *m*; *Pharm* **liquid p.** huile *f* de paraffine; **to coat with p.** paraffiner
▸▸ **p. lamp** lampe *f* à pétrole; **p. oil** (*fuel*) pétrole (lampant), kérosène; **p. wax** paraffine

paragliding ['pærəglaɪdɪŋ] **N** *Sport* parapente *m*

paragon ['pærəgən] **N** (*of virtue, beauty*) modèle *m*

paragraph ['pærəgrɑːf] **N** paragraphe *m*, alinéa *m*; *Journ* (*short article*) entrefilet *m*; *Typ* (*mark*) pied *m* de mouche; **new p.** (*when dictating*) à la ligne; **to start a new p.** aller à la ligne
VT (*piece of writing*) diviser en paragraphes
▸▸ **p. indent** alinéa; *Typ* **p. mark** pied de mouche

Paraguay ['pærəgwaɪ] **N** Paraguay *m*

Paraguayan [pærə'gwaɪən] **ADJ** paraguayen **N** Paraguayen, -enne

parakeet ['pærəkiːt] **N** (*bird*) perruche *f*

parallel ['pærəlel] **ADJ 1** *Math etc* parallèle (**to** *or* **with sth** à qch); **to be** *or* **run p. to sth** être parallèle à qch **2** (*analogous*) pareil, semblable; (*case, situation*) analogue (**to** *or* **with sth** à qch); **the two cases are exactly p.** les deux cas sont analogues
N 1 *Math* (*ligne f*) parallèle *f*, *Geog, Astron* parallèle *m*; *Mil* (*trench*) (tranchée *f*) parallèle *f*, *Typ* **parallels** barres *fpl* **2** *Elec* **in p.** (*connected*) en parallèle, en dérivation; **out of p.** (*of dynamo*) déphasé, hors de phase, hors de synchronisme **3** (*analogy*) parallèle *m*, comparaison *f*; **to draw a p. between two things** établir un parallèle *ou* une comparaison entre deux choses; **without p.** sans pareil
VT (-**l**-) **1** (*be similar to*) être analogue à **2** (*be equal to*) égaler; **the victory has not been paralleled** cette victoire est restée sans égal
▸▸ *Gym* **p. bars** barres parallèles; *Elec* **p. circuits** circuits *mpl* parallèles; *Elec* **p. connection** couplage *m ou* montage *m* en parallèle *ou* en dérivation; **p. importing** importations *fpl* parallèles; *Comput* **p. input** entrée *f* parallèle; *Comput* **p. interface** interface *f* parallèle; **p. lines** lignes *fpl* parallèles; *Comput* **p. output** sortie *f* parallèle; **p. parking** stationnement *m* en créneau; *Comput* **p. port** port *m* parallèle; *Comput* **p. printer** imprimante *f* en parallèle; *Comput* **p. printer cable** câble *m* d'imprimante parallèle; *Comput* **p. printer port** port d'imprimante parallèle; *Comput* **p. processing** traitement *m* en parallèle *ou* en simultanéité; *Fin* **p. rate of exchange** cours *m* parallèle; **p. rule, p. ruler** règle *f* à (tracer des) parallèles, parallèle *m*; *Mktg* **p. selling** vente *f* parallèle; *Comput* **p.-to-serial converter** convertisseur *m* parallèle-série; *Ski* **p. turn** virage *m* en parallèle

parallelism ['pærəlelɪz(ə)m] **N** parallélisme *m*

parallelogram [pærə'leləgræm] **N** parallélogramme *m*

paralyse, *Am* **paralyze** ['pærəlaɪz] **VT** *Med, Fig* paralyser; **paralysed in one leg** paralysé d'une jambe; *Fig* **laws that p. industry** lois qui paralysent l'industrie; **paralysed with fear** paralysé par l'effroi, glacé d'effroi

paralysing, *Am* **paralyzing** ['pærəlaɪzɪŋ] **ADJ** *Med, Fig* (*poison, fear etc*) paralysant

paralysis [pə'ræləsɪs] **N** *Med, Fig* paralysie *f*

paralytic [pærə'lɪtɪk] **ADJ 1** *Med* paralytique **2** *Br Fam* (*very drunk*) ivre mort
N *Med* paralytique *mf*
▸▸ *Med* **p. stroke** attaque *f* de paralysie

paralytically [pærə'lɪtɪklɪ] **ADV** *Br Fam* **p. drunk** ivre mort

paralyze, paralyzing *Am* = **paralyse, paralysing**

paramedic [pærə'medɪk] **N** auxiliaire *mf* médical(e)
ADJ (*skills, qualification*) paramédical, -aux

parameter [pə'ræmɪtər] **N** *Math, Comput etc* paramètre *m*; **to set the parameters of** paramétrer; *Fig* **within the parameters of the enquiry** dans les limites fixées par les paramètres de l'enquête

paramilitary [pærə'mɪlɪtrɪ] **ADJ** paramilitaire
N membre *m* d'une formation paramilitaire

paramount ['pærəmaʊnt] **ADJ** (*chief, leader*) suprême; (*necessity, consideration, interest*) primordial, -aux; **it is of p. importance** c'est d'une importance primordiale; **it is p. that we do this** il est primordial que nous fassions ceci

paramour ['pærəmʊər] **N** *Old-fashioned, Lit* amant, -ante

paranoia [pærə'nɔɪə] **N** paranoïa *f*; *Fam Fig* **you're suffering from p.** tu es parano

paranoiac [pærə'nɔɪɪk] **N** paranoïaque *mf*; **he's an absolute p.** il est complètement paranoïaque

paranoid ['pærənɔɪd] **ADJ** paranoïaque; (*delirium, madness*) paranoïde; *Fig* **he's p. about being cheated** il est obsédé par l'idée qu'on cherche à l'avoir; **you're being p.** tu es parano; **I know it'll sound p., but …** je suis sûr que tu vas me trouver parano mais …

paranormal [pærə'nɔːməl] **ADJ** (*experience, phenomenon etc*) paranormal, -aux
N the p. le paranormal

parapet ['pærəpet] **N 1** *Mil* (*in fortress*) parapet *m*; (*of trench*) berge *f* **2** (*wall*) parapet *m*; (*railing*) garde-fou *m*, *pl* garde-fous; (*of bridge*) garde-corps *m inv*

paraphernalia [pærəfə'neɪlɪə] **NPL** (*things*) affaires *fpl*; (*equipment*) attirail *m*; **and all the other p.** et tout le bazar

paraphrase ['pærəfreɪz] **N** paraphrase *f*
VT paraphraser

paraplegia [pærə'pliːdʒə] **N** *Med* paraplégie *f*

paraplegic [pærə'pliːdʒɪk] **ADJ, N** *Med* paraplégique *mf*

parapsychology [pærəsaɪ'kɒlədʒɪ] **N** parapsychologie *f*, métapsychique *f*

parasite ['pærəsaɪt] **N** (*animal, plant*), *Fig* parasite *m*; **to be a p. on society** (*of person*) parasiter la société

parasitic [pærə'sɪtɪk] **ADJ** (*insect, plant, person*) parasite (**on** de); (*existence*) de parasite; **to be p. on an organism/on society** parasiter un organisme/la société
▸▸ *Electron etc* **p. noise** (bruit *m*) parasite *m*

parasitism ['pærəsaɪtɪz(ə)m] **N** parasitisme *m*

parasitize ['pærəsɪtaɪz] **VT** parasiter

parasitology [pærəsaɪ'tɒlədʒɪ] **N** parasitologie *f*

parasol ['pærəsɒl] **N** (*over table etc*) parasol *m*; (*ladies'*) ombrelle *f*
▸▸ *Bot* **p. mushroom** coulemelle *f*, lépiote *f*; **p. pine** pin *m* parasol

paratrooper ['pærətruːpər] **N** *Mil* parachutiste *m*

paratroops ['pærətruːps] **NPL** *Mil* parachutistes *mpl*

paratyphoid [pærə'taɪfɔɪd] **N** *Med* paratyphoïde *f*

parboil ['pɑːbɔɪl] **VT** *Culin* faire cuire à demi (dans l'eau)

parcel ['pɑːs(ə)l] **N 1** (*bundle, packet*) paquet *m*, colis *m* **2** (*of land*) parcelle *f* **3** *St Exch* (*of bonds*) paquet *m*; *Com* (*batch*) lot *m*
VT (-**ll**-, *Am* -**l**-) emballer, empaqueter

▸▸**parcel(s) office** bureau *m* des messageries, messageries *fpl*; **p. post** service *m* de colis postaux; **parcels service** *(courier)* messagerie *f*; *Aut* **p. shelf** tablette *f*

▸**parcel out** VT SEP *(distribute) (inheritance)* parceller, partager; *(land)* lotir, morceler; *(provisions, books)* répartir

▸**parcel up** VT SEP *(wrap)* empaqueter, emballer

parch [pɑːtʃ] VT *(of sun) (grass, earth etc)* dessécher; *(cereal crops)* rôtir, griller, sécher

parched [pɑːtʃt] ADJ *(earth, grass etc)* desséché; *(lips, throat etc)* sec, *f* sèche; *Fam* **to be** or **feel p.** *(be thirsty)* mourir de soif

parchment ['pɑːtʃmənt] N parchemin *m*
▸▸**p. paper** papier *m* parchemin ou parcheminé

pardon ['pɑːd(ə)n] N **1** (**I beg your) p.?** *(asking sb to repeat sth)* pardon?, comment?; **I beg your p.!** *(in disapproval, shock etc)* je vous demande pardon!, *Fam* pardon?, hein?
2 *Law* grâce *f*, *(document)* lettre *f* de grâce; **free p.** grâce; **to grant sb a free p.** *(of monarch)* faire grâce à qn; **to receive the King's/Queen's p.** être gracié; **general p.** amnistie *f*
VT **1** *(fault etc)* pardonner, excuser; **p. my contradicting you, p. me for contradicting you** pardonnez (-moi) si je vous contredis
2 to p. sb pardonner à qn; **to p. sb for sth** pardonner qch à qn; **you could be pardoned for thinking so** il est facile de croire cela; **p. me!** *(in apology)* je vous demande pardon!; *Am* **p. me?** *(asking sb to repeat sth)* pardon?; *Iron* **p. me for speaking!** hou là là, excuse-moi d'avoir osé m'exprimer!; **p. me for breathing!** hou là là, excuse-moi d'exister!
3 *Law* gracier, amnistier; *Rel* **to p. sb sth** absoudre qn de qch

pardonable ['pɑːdənəb(ə)l] ADJ **1** pardonnable, excusable **2** *Law* graciable

pardonably ['pɑːdənəblɪ] ADV de façon bien pardonnable ou excusable; **he was p. late** il est bien pardonnable ou excusable qu'il soit arrivé en retard

pare [peər] VT *(vegetable etc)* éplucher; *(finger nails)* rogner; *(horseshoe)* parer; **expenses have been pared to the bone** les frais généraux ont été réduits ou ramenés au strict minimum
▸**pare down** VT SEP *(expenditure etc)* réduire; **the budget has been pared down to the bone** le budget a été réduit ou ramené au strict minimum

parent ['peərənt] N père *m*, mère *f*, *pl* parents *mpl*; **when you first become a p.** quand on devient père/mère; **the p.-child relationship** la relation parents-enfant; **each p. should ...** le père et la mère devraient ...; **if neither p. can ...** si ni le père ni la mère ne peuvent ...
ADJ **the p. plant** la plante mère; **the p. tree** l'arbre d'origine; **the p. birds feed their young** les parents nourrissent leurs oisillons
▸▸*Com* **p. company** société *f* ou maison *f* mère; *Sch* **p. power** pouvoir *m* de décision des parents d'élèves; *Sch* **p.-teacher association** = association *f* regroupant parents d'élèves et enseignants

parentage ['peərəntɪdʒ] N origine *f*, **of unknown p.** de parents inconnus

parental [pə'rent(ə)l] ADJ *(authority etc)* des parents, parental, -aux

parenthesis, *pl* **parentheses** [pə'renθəsɪs, -iːz] N parenthèse *f*; **in parentheses** entre parenthèses

parenthesize [pə'renθəsaɪz] VT *(words)* mettre entre parenthèses

parenthetical [pærən'θetɪk(ə)l] ADJ entre parenthèses
▸▸*Gram* **p. clause** incidente *f*

parenthetically [pærən'θetɪklɪ] ADV entre

parenthèses, par parenthèse; **could I just say p. ...** je voudrais dire entre parenthèses que ...

parenthood ['peərənthʊd] N *(fatherhood)* paternité *f*, *(motherhood)* maternité *f*

parenting ['peərəntɪŋ] N *(art)* art *m* d'être parent; *(activity)* métier *m* de parent; **to benefit from good p.** bénéficier d'une bonne éducation parentale
▸▸**p. skills** capacités *fpl* à élever des enfants

pariah [pə'raɪə] N paria *m*
▸▸**p. dog** *(chien m)* paria

paring ['peərɪŋ] N *(usu pl)* parings *(of vegetables etc)* épluchures *fpl*, *(of nails)* rognures *fpl*, *(of metal)* cisaille *f*
▸▸**p. knife** couteau *m* à légumes

pari passu [pærɪ'pæsʊ] ADV **1** *Lit* **to go p. with ...** marcher de pair avec ... **2** *Fin, St Exch* pari passu (**with** avec)

Paris ['pærɪs] N Paris *m*; **the P. basin** le bassin parisien

parish ['pærɪʃ] N *Rel* paroisse *f*, *Br Admin* **(civil) p.** commune *f*
▸▸**p. boundary** limites *fpl* de la paroisse; **p. church** église *f* paroissiale; **p. council** ≃ conseil *m* municipal *(d'une petite commune, en Angleterre)*; **p. hall** salle *f* paroissiale; **p. priest** *(Catholic)* curé *m*; *(Protestant)* pasteur *m*; **p.-pump issue** histoire *f* de clocher; **p.-pump politics** politique *f* d'intérêts de clocher; **p. register** registre *m* paroissial; **p. school** école *f* communale

parishioner [pə'rɪʃənər] N paroissien, -ienne

Parisian [pə'rɪzɪən] ADJ parisien
N Parisien, -ienne

parity ['pærɪtɪ] N **1** *(equality) (of status, rank etc)* égalité *f*, *(of pay)* égalité, parité *f*; **to achieve p. of productivity with Japan** atteindre le niveau de productivité du Japon; **ambulance staff want p. with firemen** les ambulanciers veulent obtenir l'égalité de statut avec les pompiers
2 *Fin* parité *f*; **the two currencies were at p.** les deux monnaies étaient à parité; **euro-dollar p.** parité euro-dollar
3 *Comput* parité *f*; **odd p./even p./no p.** parité impaire/parité paire/pas de parité
4 p. of reasoning raisonnement *m* analogue
▸▸*Comput* **p. bit** bit *m* de parité; *Comput* **p. check** contrôle *m* de parité; *Comput* **p. error** erreur *f* de parité; *Econ, Fin* **p. of exchange** parité de change; **p. ratio** rapport *m* de parité; **p. table** table *f* des parités; *Fin* **p. value** valeur *f* au pair

park [pɑːk] N **1** parc *m*; *(in hunting)* réserve *f*, **(public) p.** jardin *m* public, parc; **deer p.** parc *(clôturé)* réservé aux cerfs; **national p.** parc national; *Ind, Com* **business/industrial p.** zone *f* commerciale/industrielle; *Br* **car p.** parc de stationnement, parking *m*
2 *Aut (gear)* stationnement *m*
VT **1** *(car)* garer, parquer; **to be double parked** *(of car, driver)* être garé en double file; *Fam* **she parked her bags in the hall** elle a laissé ses sacs dans l'entrée; *Fam* **to p. one-self beside sb/on sth/etc** se poser ou poser ses fesses à côté de qn/sur qch/etc
2 *(sheep)* parquer
3 *Mil (artillery etc)* mettre en parc
4 *Comput (hard disk)* parquer; **to be parked** être en parquage **5** *St Exch* mettre en attente
VI *(of car, driver, aircraft etc)* stationner, se garer
▸▸*Br* **p. keeper** *(of large park)* gardien, -ienne de parc; *(of smaller park)* gardien de jardin public; **p. officer** gardien de parc

parka ['pɑːkə] N *(coat)* parka *m* ou *f*

park-and-ride N = système *m* de contrôle

de la circulation qui consiste à garer les voitures à l'extérieur des agglomérations dans des parkings prévus à cet effet, puis à prendre un autobus vers le centre-ville

parked [pɑːkt] ADJ *(car, plane etc)* en stationnement, garé

parker ['pɑːkər] N **she's a good p.** elle sait très bien faire les créneaux

parking ['pɑːkɪŋ] N **1** *(of cars, planes etc)* stationnement *m*; **p. is a problem in town** il est difficile de se garer ou de stationner en ville; **no p.** défense de stationner; **p. prohibited** stationnement interdit; **p. in double file; to get a p. ticket** avoir une contravention pour stationnement illégal **2** *St Exch* mise *f* en attente
▸▸**p. area** aire *f* de stationnement, parking *m*; **p. attendant** *(in car park)* gardien, -ienne; *(at hotel)* voiturier *m*; **p. bay** aire de stationnement; *Am* **p. brake** frein *m* à main; **p. fees** tarif *m* de stationnement; **p. fine** amende *f* de stationnement; **p. lights** feux *mpl* de position; **p. lock** *(on automatic gearbox)* position *f* parking; *Am* **p. lot** parking, parc *m* de stationnement; **p. meter** parcmètre *m*, parcomètre *m*, *Can* compteur *m* de stationnement; *Astronaut* **p. orbit** orbite *f* d'attente; **p. place** *(for one vehicle) (in street, car park)* place *f* de parking; **p. space** *(for one vehicle) (in street, car park)* place de parking; **there's more p. space behind the restaurant** il y a encore des places de parking derrière le restaurant

Parkinson ['pɑːkɪnsən] N **1** *Med* **P.'s disease** maladie *f* de Parkinson; **to have P.'s disease** avoir la maladie de Parkinson ou un parkinson **2** *Hum* **P.'s law** = plus on a de temps pour accomplir une tâche plus on prend de temps pour l'accomplir

parkland ['pɑːklænd] N espace *m* vert

parkway ['pɑːkweɪ] N *Am Aut* = grande voie *f* de communication

parky ['pɑːkɪ] ADJ *Br Fam (weather)* frisquet

parlance ['pɑːləns] N langage *m*, parler *m*; **in common p.** dans la langue de tous les jours, en langage courant; **in legal/civil service/football p.** en termes juridiques ou de pratique/administratifs/de football; **in the p. of the EU** dans le langage de l'UE

parley ['pɑːlɪ] N conférence *f*, *Mil (with enemy)* pourparlers *mpl*; **to hold a p.** parlementer (**with** avec)
VI être en pourparlers, parlementer (**with the enemy** avec l'ennemi); *(begin discussions)* entrer en pourparlers, parlementer

parliament ['pɑːləmənt] N parlement *m*; **P.** le Parlement; **in P.** au Parlement VOIR GRAMMAIRE A11

parliamentarian [pɑːləmen'teərɪən] N *(member of parliament)* parlementaire *mf*, membre *m* du Parlement; *(expert in parliamentary procedures)* expert *m* en procédures parlementaires

parliamentary [pɑːlə'ment(ə)rɪ] ADJ *(government, rule)* parlementaire
▸▸**p. candidate** candidat *m* aux *(élections)* législatives; *Br* **p. committee** commission *f* parlementaire; **p. election** élection *f* législative; **p. majority** majorité *f* parlementaire; **p. private secretary** = en Grande-Bretagne, député *m* qui assure la liaison entre un ministre et la Chambre des communes; **p. privilege** immunité *f* parlementaire; *Br* **p. question** = question *f* posée au cours d'un débat parlementaire; **p. reporter** journaliste *mf* parlementaire; *Br* **p. secretary** ≃ sous-secrétaire *m* d'État, *pl* sous-secrétaires; *Br* **p. sovereignty** souveraineté *f* parlementaire

parlour, *Am* **parlor** ['pɑːlər] N *Old-fashioned (living room)* salon *m*; *(of convent)* parloir *m*; **beauty p.** salon de beauté; *Am* **beer p.**

bar *m* (où l'on sert de la bière); **funeral p.** entreprise *f* de pompes funèbres; *Am* **ice-cream p.** salon de dégustation de glaces

▸▸ **p. games** petits jeux *mpl* de salon *ou* de société

parlourmaid ['pɑːləmeɪd] N bonne *f (affectée au service de table)*

parlous ['pɑːləs] ADJ *Lit, Hum (state)* précaire; *(situation)* périlleux

Parma ['pɑːmə] N Parme

▸▸ **P. ham** jambon *m* de Parme

Parmesan [pɑːmɪ'zæn] N *(cheese)* parmesan *m*

▸▸ **P. cheese** parmesan

Parnassus [pɑː'næsəs] N Parnasse *m*

parochial [pə'rəʊkɪəl] ADJ *Rel* paroissial, -aux; *Fig Pej* provincial, -aux; **p. outlook** esprit *m* de clocher

▸▸ *Am* **p. school** école *f* religieuse

parochialism [pə'rəʊkɪəlɪz(ə)m] N *Pej* esprit *m* de clocher; *(of approach, attitude)* provincialisme *m*

parodist ['pærədɪst] N parodiste *mf*

parody ['pærədɪ] N parodie *f*, pastiche *m*; *(of justice)* parodie; *(of truth)* travestissement *m*
VT parodier, pasticher

parole [pə'rəʊl] N *Law (from jail)* libération *f* conditionnelle; **prisoner on p.** prisonnier, -ière *(de droit commun)* libéré(e) conditionnellement; *Mil* prisonnier sur parole; **to be put on p.** être mis en liberté conditionnelle, être libéré conditionnellement; **to break one's p.** manquer à sa parole; **day p.** libération conditionnelle de jour
VT *Law* libérer conditionnellement, mettre en liberté conditionnelle; *Mil* libérer sur parole; **paroled inmate** prisonnier, -ière libéré(e) conditionnellement, libéré, -ée conditionnel(elle)

▸▸ **p. supervisor** surveillant, -ante de liberté conditionnelle

parolee [pərəʊ'liː] N *Am* prisonnier, -ière en liberté conditionnelle

paroxysm ['pærəksɪz(ə)m] N *Med (of fever)* paroxysme *m*; *(of anger, guilt)* accès *m*; *(of jealousy, grief)* crise *f*; **to be in paroxysms of laughter** avoir le fou rire; **to send sb into paroxysms of laughter** donner le fou rire à qn; **to be in a p. of delight** être absolument ravi

parquet ['pɑːkeɪ] N **1** *(floor)* parquet *m* **2** *Am Theat* premiers rangs *mpl* du parterre

▸▸ **p. floor** parquet; **p. flooring** parquet

parricide ['pærɪsaɪd] N **1** *(person)* parricide *mf* **2** *(crime)* parricide *m*

parrot ['pærət] N *(bird)*, *Fig (person)* perroquet *m*; *Fam* **I was as sick as a p.** ça m'a rendu malade
VT répéter comme un perroquet

parrot-fashion ADV *Fam* **to repeat sth p.** répéter qch comme un perroquet; **to learn sth p.** *(by repetition)* apprendre qch en le répétant; **he learnt it p.** *(by mimicking sounds)* il est capable de le répéter comme un perroquet

parrotfish ['pærətfɪʃ] N perroquet *m* de mer

parry ['pærɪ] N *Fencing, Boxing* parade *f*
VT *Fencing, Boxing etc (blow)* parer; *Fig (question)* se dérober à, éluder
VI *Fencing* **to p. and thrust** parer et tirer

parse [pɑːz] VT **1** *Gram (word)* faire l'analyse (grammaticale) de; *(sentence)* faire l'analyse logique de **2** *Comput* analyser

▸▸ *Comput* **p. error** erreur *f* d'analyse (syntaxique)

Parsee ['pɑːsiː, pɑː'siː] ADJ, N parsi, -ie

parser ['pɑːzər] N *Comput* analyseur *m* syntaxique

parsimonious [pɑːsɪ'məʊnɪəs] ADJ parci-

monieux; **to be p. with one's money** dépenser son argent avec parcimonie

parsimoniously [pɑːsɪ'məʊnɪəslɪ] ADV parcimonieusement

parsimony ['pɑːsɪmənɪ] N *esp Fml* parcimonie *f*; **this is not a time for p.** ce n'est guère l'occasion de se montrer parcimonieux

parsing ['pɑːzɪŋ] N **1** *Gram (of word)* analyse *f* grammaticale; *(of sentence)* analyse logique **2** *Comput* analyse *f* syntaxique

parsley ['pɑːslɪ] N *Bot* persil *m*

▸▸ *Culin* **p. sauce** sauce *f* au persil

parsnip ['pɑːsnɪp] N *Bot, Culin* panais *m*

parson ['pɑːs(ə)n] N *(clergyman)* ecclésiastique *m*; *(Protestant priest)* pasteur *m*; **the p.'s nose** *(of chicken etc)* le croupion

parsonage ['pɑːsənɪdʒ] N *Old-fashioned* ≃ presbytère *m*, cure *f*

PART [pɑːt]

N partie **1, 3, 5** ▪ pièce **1** ▪ rôle **2** ▪ épisode **6**	
VT séparer ▪ entrouvrir	
VI s'entrouvrir ▪ se quitter ▪ céder	

N 1 *(portion, component)* partie *f*, *Ind etc* pièce *f*; **(a) p. of the house is to let** une partie de la maison est à louer; **good in parts** bon en partie; **it's not bad in parts** il y a des parties qui ne sont pas mal; **the funny/odd p. about it is that ...** ce qu'il y a de comique/d'étrange c'est que ...; **the best/worst p. was when he started laughing** le mieux/le pire ça a été quand il s'est mis à rire; **the hard p. is remembering** le plus dur c'est de se souvenir; **that was the easy p.** ça c'était le plus facile; **in the early p. of the week** au début *ou* dans les premiers jours de la semaine; **for the best** *or* **greater p. of five years** *(to wait, last etc)* presque cinq ans; **the greater p. of the population** la plus grande partie de la population; **(one) p. of her wanted to agree with them** une partie d'elle-même voulait être d'accord avec eux; **to be** *or* **form p. of sth** faire partie de qch; **it's become (a) p. of our daily routine** ça fait maintenant partie de notre routine quotidienne; **it's all p. of growing up** c'est ce qui se passe quand on grandit; **it is p. and parcel of ...** c'est une partie intégrante *ou* essentielle de ...; **to contribute in p. to the expenses** contribuer pour partie aux frais; **this is due in p. to inflation** c'est en partie dû à l'inflation; **for the most p.** pour la plupart; *Culin etc* **ten parts of water to one of milk** dix mesures d'eau pour une mesure de lait; **the parts of the body** les parties du corps SEE GRAMMAR B21; **(spare) parts** pièces détachées *ou* de rechange

2 *(active role)* part *f*; *Theat, Cin etc* rôle *m*; **to play a p.** *Theat* avoir un rôle; *Fig (act, pretend)* jouer la comédie; *Theat etc* **small p.** petit rôle; **then she took** *or* **played the p. of Esmeralda** elle a joué le rôle d'Esmeralda; **to play a p. in sth** *(be involved in, contribute to)* jouer un rôle dans qch; **to have** *or* **play a large/small p. in sth** avoir *ou* jouer un rôle important/peu important dans qch; **she played a large p. in persuading the company to relocate** c'est surtout elle qui a persuadé l'entreprise de se relocaliser; **to take p. in sth** prendre part à qch, participer à qch; **to take p. in the conversation** prendre part à *ou* se mêler à la conversation; **she takes an active p. in decision-making** elle participe activement au processus de prise de décision; *TV etc* **those taking p. were ...** avec le concours de ...; **to take no p. in sth** ne pas prendre part à qch, ne pas participer à qch; **I had no p. in it** je n'y suis pour rien; **I want no p. of** *or* **in it** *(I don't want to be involved)* je ne

veux rien avoir à faire là-dedans; **to dress/look the p.** mettre une tenue de circonstance/avoir la tête de l'emploi

3 *Mus (for specific instrument or voice)* partie *f*; *(of song, fugue)* voix *f*; *(written score)* partition *f*; **a two-p. song** une mélodie à deux voix

4 *(side)* parti *m*; **to take sb's p.** prendre parti pour qn, prendre fait et cause pour qn; **an indiscretion on the p. of ...** une indiscrétion de la part de ...; **for my p.** pour ma part; **to keep one's p. of the agreement** respecter sa part de l'accord

5 *(region)* **in that p. of the world** dans cette partie du monde; **in those parts** dans cette région-là, *Fam* dans ce coin-là; **they are not from our p. of the world** ils ne sont pas de chez nous; **in these parts** par ici; **what are you doing in these parts?** qu'est-ce que vous faites ici *ou* dans ces parages?

6 *(in publishing, of part work)* fascicule *m*, livraison *f*; **p. two** *(of book, TV programme)* deuxième partie *f*; *Radio, TV* **a serial in four parts** un feuilleton en quatre épisodes

7 **to take sth in good/bad p.** prendre qch en bonne/mauvaise part, prendre qch du bon/mauvais côté

8 *Fml (usu pl)* **parts** *(abilities)* moyens *mpl*, facultés *fpl*; **a man of many parts** un homme à facettes

9 *Am (parting in hair)* raie *f*

ADV partiellement, en partie; **I'm p. Spanish** je suis en partie espagnol; **p. silk, p. cotton** mi-soie mi-coton; **a mythical creature, p. woman, p. fish** une créature mythique mi-femme, mi-poisson; **p. one and p. the other** moitié l'un moitié l'autre; **will you take it in p. exchange?** voulez-vous le reprendre?

VT séparer (**sth from sth** qch de qch); *(rock etc)* séparer en deux; *(curtains)* entrouvrir; *(two people)* séparer; *(of bodyguard) (crowd)* ouvrir un passage dans; **to p. one's hair** se faire une raie (dans les cheveux); **to p. one's hair in the middle/at the side** se faire la raie au milieu/sur le côté; **his hair was parted on the left/in the middle** il avait la raie à gauche/au milieu; **they can't bear to be parted** ils ne supportent pas d'être séparés; **to p. company** *(of associates, friends)* se séparer; *(become detached) (of one object from another)* se détacher (**from** de); *Hum* **to p. company with one's horse/bike** *(fall off)* tomber de son cheval/vélo; **this is where we p. company** *(I'm going in the opposite direction)* c'est ici que nous nous quittons; *(where I begin to disagree with you)* c'est là que nos points de vue divergent, c'est là que je ne suis plus d'accord

VI *(of crowd etc)* se diviser; *(of two people)* se quitter, se séparer; *(of roads)* diverger; *(of cable etc)* rompre, céder; **her lips parted in a smile** ses lèvres s'entrouvrirent dans un sourire; **the curtains parted** les rideaux s'entrouvrirent; **to p. good friends** se quitter bons amis; **let us p. (as) friends** séparons-nous (en) bons amis; **to p. from sb** quitter qn; *(separate)* se séparer de *ou* d'avec qn; **to p. with sth** *(get rid of)* se débarrasser *ou* se défaire de qch; *(give up)* céder qch; *Law (right, possession)* aliéner qch; **he hates to p. with (his) money** il n'aime pas débourser

▸▸ *Com* **p. consignment** expédition *f* partielle; **parts and labour warranty** garantie *f* pièces et main-d'œuvre; **parts list** nomenclature *f*; *Com* **p. load** chargement *m* partiel; **p. music** musique *f* d'ensemble; **p. owner** copropriétaire *mf*; **p. ownership** copropriété *f*; *Com* **p. shipment** expédition *f* partielle; **p. singing** chant *m* polyphonique *ou* à plusieurs voix; **p. song** chant polyphonique *ou* à plusieurs voix; *Gram* **parts of speech** parties du discours; *Br* **p. work** ouvrage *m* à fascicules

partake [pɑ:'teɪk] VI (*pt* **partook** [pɑ:'tʊk], *pp* **partaken** [pɑ:'teɪkən]) *Fml* **to p. in sth** participer à qch (**with sb** avec qn); **to p. of the nature of sth** relever de qch; **it partakes of a certain grandeur** c'est empreint d'une certaine grandeur; *Old-fashioned* **to p. of a meal** prendre un repas; *Old-fashioned, Hum* **do you p.?** (*would you like a drink?*) vous prendrez bien un petit verre?; **I no longer p.** (*don't drink*) je ne bois plus; *Rel* **to p. of the Sacrament** s'approcher des sacrements

parterre [pɑ:'teə(r)] N *Am* (*in theatre*) parterre *m*

parthenogenesis [pɑ:θənəʊ'dʒenɪsɪs] N *Biol* parthénogénèse *f*

Parthian ['pɑ:θɪən] ADJ
▸▸**P. shot** flèche *f* du Parthe

partial ['pɑ:ʃəl] ADJ **1** (*biased*) partial, -aux (**towards sb** envers qn); (*unjust*) injuste **2** *Fam* **to be p. to sb/sth** (*like*) avoir un faible *ou* une prédilection pour qn/qch; **I am rather p. to a spot of whisky after dinner** je bois volontiers un petit verre de whisky après dîner **3** (*in part*) partiel
▸▸**p. disability** incapacité *f* partielle; **p. eclipse** éclipse *f* partielle; *Ins* **p. loss** perte *f* partielle, sinistre *m* partiel; *Fin* **p. payment** paiement *m* partiel

> When translating the English word **partial**, note that the French words **partial** and **partiel** are not interchangeable. **Partial** means **biased** and **partiel** is the opposite of **complete**.

partiality [pɑ:ʃɪ'ælɪtɪ] N **1** (*bias*) partialité *f* (**towards** envers, en faveur de); (*favouritism*) favoritisme *m* **2** (*liking*) prédilection *f*, penchant *m*, faible *m* (**for** pour)

partially ['pɑ:ʃəlɪ] ADV **1** (*with bias*) avec partialité **2** (*partly, in part*) partiellement, en partie; **p. sighted** malvoyant; **the p. sighted** (*npl*) les malvoyants *mpl*

participant [pɑ:'tɪsɪpənt] ADJ, N participant, -ante (**in** à)

participate [pɑ:'tɪsɪpeɪt] VI (*of person*) prendre part, participer (**in sth** à qch); *Lit* **to p. in sb's joy** s'associer à la joie de qn

participating [pɑ:'tɪsɪpeɪtɪŋ] ADJ participant
▸▸*Fin* **p. interest** intérêt *m* de participation; **to hold a p. interest in a company** avoir un intérêt de participation dans une société

participation [pɑ:tɪsɪ'peɪʃən] N participation *f* (**in sth** à qch); **thank you for your p.** merci d'avoir participé
▸▸*St Exch* **p. certificate** titre *m ou* bon *m* de participation; *St Exch* **p. rate** taux *m* d'activité

participial [pɑ:tɪ'sɪpɪəl] ADJ *Gram* participial, -aux

participle ['pɑ:tɪsɪp(ə)l] N *Gram* participe *m*; **present/past p.** participe présent/passé
VOIR GRAMMAIRE A44–6; B37–9

particle ['pɑ:tɪk(ə)l] N **1** (*of matter*) particule *f*, (*of metal*) paillette *f*, (*of sand*) grain *m*; *Nucl* particule, corpuscule *m*; **there's not a p. of truth in the story** il n'y a pas une ombre de vérité dans ce récit **2** *Gram* particule *f*
▸▸*Phys* **p. accelerator** accélérateur *m* de particules; *Constr* **p. board** panneau *m* d'aggloméré, panneau de particules; **p. physics** physique *f* des particules

parti-coloured, *Am* **parti-colored** ['pɑ:tɪ-] ADJ *esp Lit* bigarré, bariolé

particular [pə'tɪkjʊlər] ADJ **1** (*specific*) particulier; **that p. book** ce livre-là, ce livre en particulier; **is there any p. time you'd like to come?** y a-t-il une heure qui vous convienne en particulier?; **they didn't have this p. brand** ils n'avaient pas cette marque-

là; **which p. thing/person did you have in mind?** à quoi/qui pensiez-vous en particulier?; **this one is a p. favourite of mine** j'affectionne tout particulièrement celui-ci; **he is a p. friend of mine** c'est l'un de mes meilleurs amis; **why did you insist on this p. one?** pourquoi as-tu insisté sur celui-là en particulier?; **in my p. field (of study/research)** dans ma spécialité; **my own p. feelings** mes sentiments personnels; **to take p. care over doing sth** faire qch avec un soin (tout) particulier; **to take p. care to do sth** mettre un soin (tout) particulier à faire qch; **to do sth for no p. reason** faire qch sans raison précise; **I didn't notice anything (in) p.** je n'ai rien remarqué de particulier; **in p.** en particulier

2 *Old-fashioned, Fml* (*detailed*) (*account etc*) détaillé, circonstancié

3 (*person*) (*exacting*) méticuleux, minutieux, soigneux; (*about rules etc*) pointilleux; (*about choice of friends, methods used etc*) difficile, exigeant; **I have to be quite p. about what I eat** je dois faire très attention à ce que je mange; **it had to be pure silk, he was most p. about it** il fallait que ce soit de la soie pure, il a insisté; **to be p. about one's food** (*demanding*) être exigeant pour la nourriture; (*difficult*) être difficile pour la nourriture; **to be p. about one's dress** soigner sa mise *ou* sa tenue; *Fam* **I'm not p. (about it)** (*I don't care*) je n'y tiens pas plus que ça; **he's not p. about where the goods come from** l'origine des marchandises lui importe peu
N détail *m*; **alike in every p.** semblables en tout point; **they differ in several particulars** ils diffèrent en plusieurs points; **to go into particulars** entrer dans les détails; **to give particulars of sth** donner les détails de qch; **to ask for fuller particulars about sth** demander des précisions *ou* des détails supplémentaires sur qch; **to take down sb's particulars** prendre les coordonnées de qn; **for further particulars apply to ...** pour plus amples détails *ou* renseignements s'adresser à ...
▸▸*Fin* **p. lien** privilège *m* spécial

particularity [pətɪkjʊ'lærɪtɪ] N **1** (*special quality*) particularité *f* **2** (*exacting nature*) méticulosité *f*, (*detailed nature*) (*of description etc*) minutie *f*

particularize [pə'tɪkjʊləraɪz] *Fml* VT spécifier
VI entrer dans les détails, préciser

particularly [pə'tɪkjʊləlɪ] ADV particulièrement, en particulier; **it's cold here, p. at night** il fait froid ici, particulièrement *ou* spécialement la nuit; **note p. that ...** notez en particulier que ...; **be p. careful** faites particulièrement attention *ou* spécialement; **not p.** pas particulièrement *ou* spécialement; **she's not p. rich** elle n'est pas tellement riche

particulate emissions [pɑ:'tɪkjʊlɪt] NPL émission *f* de particules

parting ['pɑ:tɪŋ] N **1** (*division*) séparation *f*, (*of the waters*) partage *m*; *Fig* **to be at** *or* **to have come to the p. of the ways** être à la croisée des chemins **2** (*leave-taking*) séparation *f*, **it was a painful p.** la séparation a été douloureuse; **p. kiss** baiser *m* d'adieu; **p. words** mots *mpl* d'adieu **3** *Br* (*in hair*) raie *f*, **centre/side p.** raie au milieu/sur le côté
▸▸*Fig* **p. shot** flèche *f* du Parthe

partisan [pɑ:tɪ'zæn] N (*supporter, resistance fighter*) partisan *m*
ADJ **1** partisan; **to act in a p. spirit** (*of politician etc*) faire preuve d'esprit de parti; (*be prejudiced*) faire preuve de parti pris **2** *Mil* partisan

partisanship [pɑ:tɪ'zænʃɪp] N partialité *f*, (*of politician etc*) esprit *m* de parti

partition [pɑ:'tɪʃən] N **1** (*dividing*) division *f*, découpage *m*; (*of conquered country, inheritance etc*) (*division*) partition *f*, (*sharing out*) partage *m* **2** (*screen*) séparation *f*, cloisonnage *m*; (*wall*) cloison *f*, (*of ship's hold etc*) compartiment *m*; *Constr* **internal p., p. wall** cloison **3** *Comput* partition *f*
VT **1** (*divide*) diviser; (*inheritance etc*) partager; (*conquered country*) démembrer, partager **2** = **partition off 3** *Comput* (*hard disk*) découper
▸ **partition off** VT SEP (*room*) cloisonner; (*part of a room*) séparer par une cloison

> Note that the French word **partition** never means **wall**.

partitive ['pɑ:tɪtɪv] ADJ, N *Gram* partitif *m*
SEE GRAMMAR B5

partly ['pɑ:tlɪ] ADV partiellement, en partie; **wholly or p.** en tout ou en partie; **p. by force, p. by persuasion** moitié par la force, moitié par la persuasion; **a p. eaten sandwich** un sandwich à moitié mangé; **she was only p. convinced** elle n'était qu'à moitié convaincue
▸▸*Fin* **p. paid-up capital** capital *m* non entièrement versé; *St Exch* **p. paid-up shares** actions *fpl* non entièrement libérées; *Fin* **p. secured creditor** créancier, -ière partiellement nanti(e)

partner ['pɑ:tnər] N *Com etc* associé, -ée (**with sb in sth** de qn dans qch); (*in tennis, driving etc*) partenaire *mf*; (*in dancing*) cavalier, -ière, partenaire; (*of cowboy, bank robber etc*) acolyte *m*; (*person one lives with*) compagnon *m*, compagne *f*, (*boyfriend, girlfriend*) ami *m*, amie *f*; **our European partners** nos partenaires européens; **partners should consider each other's moods** chacun au sein du couple doit prendre les humeurs de l'autre en considération; **they became partners** ils se sont associés; **to be sb's p. in a crime** être associé à qn dans un crime; *Cards* **to cut** *or* **draw for partners** = faire les rois
VT *Com etc* (*be partner of*) être associé à *ou* avec; (*become partner of*) s'associer à *ou* avec; (*in games*) être le/la partenaire de; (*in dancing*) être le cavalier/la cavalière de

partnership ['pɑ:tnəʃɪp] N **1** association *f* (**in sth with sb** avec qn dans qch); **p. in crime** association dans le crime; *Com etc* **to enter** *or* **go into p. with sb** s'associer avec qn; **to take sb into p.** prendre qn comme associé(e) **2** *Com etc* (*company*) = société *f* en nom collectif
▸▸**p. agreement** accord *m* de partenariat; *EU* **P. and Cooperation Agreements** Accords *mpl* de partenariat et de coopération; **p. marketing** marketing *m* de partenariat; *St Exch* **p. share** part *f* d'association; **p. sponsoring** parrainage-partenariat *m*

partridge ['pɑ:trɪdʒ] N (*pl* **partridges, partridge**) perdrix *f*, *Culin* perdreau *m*

part-time ADJ (*job, work*) à temps partiel, à mi-temps; **on a p. basis** à temps partiel, à mi-temps; **p. worker/employee** ouvrier, -ière/ employé, -ée qui travaille à temps partiel *ou* à mi-temps; **p. contract** contrat *m* à temps partiel
ADV (*to work*) à temps partiel, à mi-temps

parturition [pɑ:tjʊ'rɪʃən] N *Med* parturition *f*

partway ['pɑ:tweɪ] ADV **they were p. through the rehearsal** ils avaient commencé à répéter depuis déjà un moment; **I'm only p. through it** (*the book, the task*) je ne l'ai pas encore fini; **they had gone p. towards an agreement** ils s'acheminaient vers un accord; **we were p. there** (*in project etc*) nous en avions fait une bonne partie; **this will go p. towards covering the costs** cela couvrira une bonne partie des coûts

party ['pɑːtɪ] N **1** *Pol* parti *m*; **a p. member, a member of the p.** un membre du parti; **p. quarrels** querelles *fpl* partisanes; **p. spirit** esprit *m* de parti; **he's just making a p. political point** son argument ne relève que de la politique politicienne; **to follow** *or* **toe the p. line** obéir aux directives du parti

2 *(gathering)* fête *f*, *(evening celebration)* soirée *f*, *(reception)* réception *f*; **dinner p.** dîner *m*; *Fam* **he's caught the p. spirit** il s'est abandonné aux joies de la fête

3 *(group) (of tourists etc)* groupe *m*, bande *f*; *Min (of miners, workers etc)* brigade *f*, équipe *f*, groupe; *Mil etc* détachement *m*; **the official p.** le groupe des officiels, les officiels *mpl*; **will you join our p.?** voulez-vous être des nôtres?; **we're a small p.** nous sommes peu nombreux; **I was one of the p.** j'étais de la partie; **the wedding/funeral p.** les invités au mariage/le cortège funéraire

4 *(participant), Law (to a suit, to a dispute)* partie *f*; **the parties to the case** les parties en cause; **to be p. to a suit** être en cause; *Com etc* **parties to a bill of exchange** intéressé(e)s à une lettre de change; **to be/become (a) p. to a crime** être/se rendre complice d'un crime; **I would never be (a) p. to such a thing** je ne me ferais jamais complice d'une chose pareille, je ne m'associerais jamais à une chose pareille

5 *Fam (person)* individu *m*, type *m*

VI *Fam* faire la bringue, faire la fête; **let's p.!** faisons la bringue *ou* la fête!; **to p. the night away** faire la bringue *ou* la fête toute la nuit

▸▸ *Fam* **p. animal** fêtard, -arde; **she's a real p. animal** elle adore faire la fête; **p. convention** Congrès *m* du parti; **p. dress** robe *f* habillée; **p. games** = jeux *mpl* auxquels on joue dans les soirées ou les fêtes; **p. leader** chef *m* de parti; **p. line** *Tel* ligne *f* commune *(à plusieurs abonnés)*; *Pol* ligne du parti; *Pol* **p. machine** machine *f* du parti; *Pol* **p. man** homme *m* de parti; *Br Fam* **p. piece** numéro *m* *(à l'occasion d'une fête)*; *Iron* **that's his p. piece** c'est son numéro habituel; *TV, Radio* **p. political broadcast** émission *f* reservée à un parti politique; **that was a p. political broadcast on behalf of the Labour P.** vous venez de voir/d'entendre une émission du parti travailliste; **p. politics** politique *f* politicienne; *Fam* **p. pooper** rabat-joie *m inv*; **p. system** système *m* des partis; *Constr* **p. wall** mur *m* mitoyen

partygoer ['pɑːtɪɡəʊər] N habitué, -ée des soirées; *(on one occasion)* invité, -ée; **the streets were full of partygoers** les rues étaient pleines de gens se rendant à des soirées

party-list system N *Pol (of voting)* scrutin *m* de liste

PASCAL [pæ'skæl] N *Comput* PASCAL *m*

paschal ['pæsk(ə)l] ADJ pascal, -aux

pashmina [pæʃ'miːnə] N *(wool, garment)* pashmina *m*

PASS [pɑːs]

N col **1**	▪ laissez-passer **2**
▪ moyenne **3**	▪ passe **4**
VT passer devant **1**	▪ dépasser **1**
▪ passer **1, 4–6, 9**	▪ être reçu à **2**
▪ voter **4**	
VI passer **1, 3, 4, 6**	▪ se passer **2, 5**
▪ être adopté **8**	

N **1** *(in mountains)* col *m*

2 *(permit)* permis *m*, laissez-passer *m inv*; *Mil* permission *f*; **(free) p.** *Rail etc* titre *m ou* carte *f* de circulation; *Theat etc (free ticket)* billet *m* gratuit *ou* de faveur

3 *Sch, Univ (in examination)* moyenne *f*, mention *f* passable; **to obtain** *or* **get a p.** être reçu

4 *(movement) (of footballer, magician etc)*

passe *f*; *Fencing* passe, passade *f*, botte *f*; **the aircraft made two low passes over the village** l'avion a effectué deux passages à basse altitude au-dessus du village; *Fam* **to make a p. at sb** draguer qn, faire des propositions à qn

5 *(in data analysis)* examen *m* (**through** de); *(of read head)* passage *m*; **to make a p. over sth** passer sur qch

6 *Old-fashioned Fam (situation)* **things have come to a pretty p.!** voilà donc où en sont les choses!; **things came to such a p. that ...** les choses en vinrent à ce point *ou* à tel point que ...

VT **1** *(go past) (window, building etc)* passer devant; *(person)* croiser; *(destination)* dépasser; *(frontier)* passer, franchir; *Naut (headland)* dépasser, doubler; *(overtake) (person, another ship)* dépasser, rattraper; *(another car, runner)* doubler, dépasser; *(in league table)* passer devant; **not a word about it had passed her lips** elle n'en avait pas dit un mot; *Lit* **to p. understanding** dépasser l'entendement

2 *(succeed in) (exam)* être reçu *ou* admis à; **to p. a test** *(of vehicle, product)* subir une épreuve avec succès; *(of person)* réussir une épreuve, subir une épreuve avec succès

3 *(be accepted by)* **bill that has passed the House of Commons** projet de loi qui a été voté par la Chambre des communes; **to p. the censor/the customs** être accepté par la censure/la douane

4 *(approve) (invoice)* approuver, admettre, apurer; *(expenditure)* allouer; *Parl etc (bill, resolution)* passer, voter, adopter; **to p. a bill through Parliament** faire adopter une loi par le Parlement; **to p. a dividend of 5%** *(of company)* approuver un dividende de 5%; **the censor has passed the play/the film** le censeur a accordé le visa; **to p. for press** donner le bon à tirer; *Sch* **to p. a candidate** recevoir un candidat, admettre un candidat; *Mil etc* **to be passed fit** être reconnu apte

5 *(give, transfer)* (faire) passer; *(counterfeit banknote etc)* (faire) passer, écouler, *Fam* refiler; **to p. sth from hand to hand** passer qch de main en main; **p. me the salt, please** passez-moi le sel, s'il vous plaît; *Ftbl etc* **to p. the ball** passer le ballon

6 *(put)* passer; **to p. one's hand between the bars** passer *ou* glisser sa main à travers les barreaux; **to p. a rope round sth** passer une corde autour de qch; **to p. a sponge over sth** passer l'éponge sur qch; **to p. one's hand over one's brow** se passer la main sur le front

7 *Mil* **to p. troops in review** passer des troupes en revue

8 *Fin* **to p. a dividend** conclure un exercice sans payer de dividende

9 to p. the time *(of person)* passer le temps; **it passes the time** cela fait passer le temps

10 *(utter)* **to p. criticism on sth** faire la critique de qch; **to p. remarks** faire des commentaires *ou* des observations (**on sth** sur qch); *Law* **to p. sentence** prononcer le jugement; **to p. judgement on sb** porter un jugement sur qn, juger qn

11 *Physiol* **to p. water** uriner; *Med* **to p. blood** avoir du sang dans les urines; **has he passed anything?** est-ce qu'il a uriné ou été à la selle?

VI **1** *(go past)* passer; *Aut (overtake)* doubler, dépasser; *Cards* passer, renoncer, passer parole; *(at dominoes)* bouder; **we p. on the stairs every morning** nous nous croisons tous les matins dans l'escalier; **the tourists passed into the dining hall** les touristes sont passés dans le réfectoire; **words passed between them** ils ont eu une altercation; **to p. along a street** passer par une rue; **the procession passed slowly** le cortège passa *ou*

défila lentement; **everyone smiles as he passes** tout le monde sourit à son passage; **the motorway passes close to the village** l'autoroute passe tout près du village; **to let sb p.** *or* **allow sb to p.** laisser passer qn; **they shall not p.!** ils ne passeront pas!; *Rail etc* **p. along** *or* **down the car!** avancez!, dégagez la portière!; **to p. unobserved** passer inaperçu; **I can't allow such a mistake to p. unremarked** je ne peux pas permettre qu'une telle erreur ne soit pas relevée; **let it p.!** passe pour cela!, *Fam* laisse courir!; **I'd like to say in passing** soit dit en passant; *Aut* **no passing** défense de doubler; *Cards, Fig* **p.!** je passe!; *Fig* **I think I'll p. on the onions** je le voudrais sans les oignons; **can I p. on the mountain climbing this afternoon?** est-ce que je peux être dispensé d'escalade cet après-midi?

2 *(of time)* (se) passer, s'écouler; **when five minutes had passed** au bout de cinq minutes; **it seemed like no time at all had passed since I had last seen her** on aurait dit que pas une minute ne s'était écoulée depuis la dernière fois que je l'avais vue; **how time passes!** comme le temps passe (vite)!; **to let the opportunity p.** laisser passer l'occasion

3 *(be transferred)* **water passes from a liquid to a solid state when it freezes** l'eau passe de l'état de liquide à celui de solide quand il gèle; **the expression has passed into the language** l'expression est passée dans la langue; **his fortune passed to his brother** sa fortune est revenue à son frère

4 *(go away)* passer; *(of clouds etc)* s'en aller; **I was about to say something witty, but the moment passed** j'allais dire quelque chose de spirituel, mais j'ai laissé passer l'occasion

5 *Old-fashioned (take place)* avoir lieu, se passer; **I don't know what passed between them** je ne sais pas ce qui s'est passé entre eux; *Arch, Lit* **to come to p.** arriver, avoir lieu; *Arch, Lit* **it came to p. that ...** or il arriva *ou* advint que ...

6 *(be accepted)* **it would p. in certain circles** cela passerait dans certains milieux; *Fam* **you'd p. in a crowd!** tu n'es pas si mal que ça!; **she could p. for an Italian** elle pourrait passer pour une Italienne

7 *(succeed in examination)* être reçu

8 *Pol* **to p. through Parliament** *(of bill)* être adopté par le Parlement

▸▸ *Banking* **p. book** livret *m* de banque; **p. laws** = lois *fpl* qui anciennement restreignaient la liberté de mouvement de la population noire en Afrique du Sud; *Br Sch* **p. mark** moyenne; **to get a p. mark** avoir la moyenne

▸ **pass away** VI **1** *Euph (die)* s'éteindre **2** *(disappear)* disparaître

▸ **pass by** VI **1** *(go past)* passer; *(carry on without stopping)* continuer son chemin; **luckily a taxi was passing by** heureusement un taxi passait par là **2** *(of time)* passer
VT INSEP *(go past) (house etc)* passer devant
VT SEP *(ignore)* ignorer; **life is passing me by** je n'ai pas l'impression de vivre une vie épanouissante; **life has passed her by** elle n'a pas vraiment vécu; **whenever a chance comes, don't let it p. you by** quand une occasion se présente, ne la laissez pas échapper

▸ **pass down** VT SEP **1** *(hand down)* passer; **p. me down that cup** passez-moi cette tasse **2** *(knowledge, story etc)* transmettre; *(clothing etc)* passer (**from ... to** de ... en)

▸ **pass off** VI **1** *(take place)* **everything passed off well** tout s'est bien passé **2** *(end) (of pain)* passer, disparaître; **is the nausea passing off?** est-ce que la nausée se passe?
VT SEP **1** *(pretend to be)* **to p. oneself off as an artist** se faire passer pour (un) artiste; **she passed him off as a duke** elle l'a fait passer pour un duc; **to p. sth off as sth** faire passer qch pour qch **2** *(dismiss)* **to p. sth off as a**

joke *(accept a~ ~ joke)* prendre qch en riant ou comm~ ~ une plaisanterie; *(claim to be a i~t~)* dire qu'on a fait/dit qch pour rire
▸ **pass on** VI **1** *Euph (die)* décéder, s'éteindre **2** *(proceed) (on journey)* continuer son chemin *ou* sa route; **to p. to another subject** passer à un autre sujet; **passing on to the question of cost, …** si nous passons maintenant à la question du coût, …
VT SEP *(tell or give to other people)* faire circuler; *(give to other people)* (faire) passer; **read this and p. it on** lisez ceci et faites circuler; **these price increases have been passed on to the consumer** ces hausses de coûts ont été répercutées sur le consommateur; **these cost reductions have been passed on to the consumer** le consommateur a bénéficié de ces réductions des coûts
▸ **pass out** VI **1** *(faint)* s'évanouir **2** *(leave)* sortir *(of* de*)*; **don't let this document p. out of your hands** gardez soigneusement ce document **3** *Sch etc (after final examination)* sortir; **cadets passing out** élèves sortants; **passing-out list** classement *m* de sortie
VT SEP *(distribute)* distribuer
▸ **pass over** VT SEP **1** **to p. sb over** *(for promotion)* passer par-dessus le dos à qn; **he's been passed over again** on lui a encore passé par-dessus le dos **2** **to p. one's eye over sth** jeter un coup d'œil à qch
VT INSEP **1** *(cross) (river etc)* traverser, franchir; *(obstacle)* franchir, passer sur **2** *(ignore)* passer sous silence; *(difficulty etc)* passer sur, glisser sur; **they passed over the subject in silence** ils ont passé la question sous silence
VI **1** *(end) (of storm)* se dissiper, finir **2** **to p. over to the enemy** passer à l'ennemi
▸ **pass round** VT SEP faire passer; **p. the cakes round** faites passer les gâteaux; *Fig* **to p. round the hat** faire une quête
▸ **pass through** VI *(travel through)* passer; **I was just passing through** je ne faisais que passer; **the bullet passed right through** la balle a traversé; **the bus doesn't stop in Hull, it just passes through** le bus ne s'arrête pas à Hull, il ne fait que traverser la ville
VT INSEP **1** *(travel through) (country etc)* traverser; **he was only passing through Paris** il n'était que de passage à Paris **2** *(experience) (crisis)* traverser
▸ **pass up** VT SEP **1** *Fam (not take) (offer of a job etc)* refuser; *(chance)* laisser passer **2** *(hand up)* passer; **p. (me) up that hammer** passe-moi ce marteau

> Note that the French expression **passer un examen** does not mean **to pass an exam**. It means **to sit an exam**.

passable ['pɑːsəb(ə)l] ADJ **1** *(of acceptable quality)* passable, assez bon; **it's p.** ce n'est pas trop mal; **a very p. soufflé** un soufflé plutôt bien réussi **2** *(river, forest etc)* traversable, franchissable; *(road)* praticable

passably ['pɑːsəblɪ] ADV passablement, assez; **to perform p.** offrir une performance passable

passage ['pæsɪdʒ] N **1** *(act of passing) (journey)* passage *m*; *esp Naut* traversée *f*; *Pol (of bill)* adoption *f*; **with the p. of time** avec le temps; **bird of p.** oiseau *m* de passage; *Naut* **to have a bad** *or* **rough p.** avoir *ou* faire une mauvaise traversée; *Naut* **to work one's p.** gagner son passage (en travaillant à bord); **to force a p.** se forcer un passage; *Law* **right of p.** droit *m* de passage **2** *(corridor)* couloir *m*, corridor *m*; *(alley, at end of street)* passage *m*, ruelle *f*; **underground p.** passage souterrain; *Geog* **the North-West/North-East p.** le passage Nord-Ouest/Nord-Est

3 *Tech* canalisation *f*, conduit *m*, conduite *f*; **air p.** conduit d'aérage, conduit(e) d'air; *Anat* **air passages** voies *fpl* aérifères; *Anat* **the back p.** le rectum
4 *(from book, piece of music etc)* passage *m*; **selected passages** morceaux *mpl* choisis

passageway ['pæsɪdʒweɪ] N **1** *(space)* passage *m*; **to leave a p.** laisser le passage libre **2** *(alley)* passage *m*, ruelle *f*; *(corridor)* couloir *m*, corridor *m*

passé ['pæseɪ] ADJ *(outdated)* qui n'est plus à la mode, dépassé

passel ['pæs(ə)l] N *Am Fam (of people etc)* tas *m*

passenger ['pæsəndʒər] N **1** *(on train)* voyageur, -euse; *(on ship, aircraft, in car)* passager, -ère **2** *esp Br Fam (non-contributing member)* non-valeur *f*, pl non-valeurs, poids *m* mort; **we can't carry passengers** on ne peut pas traîner de poids morts
▸▸ *Rail* **p. car** voiture *f ou* wagon *m* de voyageurs; **p. and cargo plane** avion *m* mixte; **p. and cargo ship** bateau *m* mixte; *Rail* **p. carriage** voiture *ou* wagon de voyageurs; **p. compartment** *(of car)* habitacle *m*; **p. kilometre** kilomètre-passager *m*, pl kilomètres-passagers; **p. load factor** *(in transport)* taux *m* d'occupation des places; *Aut* **p. safety cage** habitacle de sécurité; *Aut* **p. survival cell** cellule *f* de survie; *Aut* **p. wagon** voiture familiale

passe-partout [pæspɑːˈtuː] N **1** *(key)* (clef *f*) passe-partout *m inv* **2** *Art, Phot (method of framing)* encadrement *m* sous verre; *(gummed paper)* bande *f* de papier de bordure

passer-by ['pɑːsəbaɪ], *pl* **passers-by** ['pɑːsəzbaɪ] N passant, -ante

passim ['pæsɪm] ADV passim

passing ['pɑːsɪŋ] ADJ *(hour, minute etc)* qui passe/passait; *(remark)* en passant; *(whim, fancy)* passager, éphémère; **he is growing stronger with each p. day** il devient de plus en plus fort avec chaque jour qui passe; **flag down a p. car** fais signe à une voiture de s'arrêter; **she flagged down a p. car** elle a fait signe à une voiture qui passait de s'arrêter; *Lit* **the p. hour** l'heure *f* fugitive
N **1** *(going past) (of train, birds etc)* passage *m*; *(overtaking) (of another car)* dépassement *m*, doublement *m*; *Com (of dividend)* passation *f*, **in p.** *(incidentally)* en passant **2** *(of time)* écoulement *m*, *(of sb's beauty)* disparition *f*, *esp Fml (death)* mort *f* **3** *(approval) Pol etc (of resolution)* adoption *f*, *(of law)* vote *m*; *Fin, Com (of accounts)* approbation *f* **4** *(giving) (of message etc)* transmission *f*, *Law (of judgement)* prononcé *m*; *Ftbl etc (of the ball)* passes *fpl*
ADV *Arch, Lit* **p. fair** de toute beauté
▸▸ *Literary* **p. bell** glas *m*; **p. customer** client, -ente de passage; **p. place** *Aut (on narrow road)* aire *f* de croisement; *(in general)* endroit *m* pour doubler; *Rail* voie *f* d'évitement *ou* de dédoublement; **p. shot** *Tennis* passing-shot *m*, *pl* passing-shots; *Cin, TV* **p. shot** plan *m* avec déplacement d'un personnage ou d'un objet devant la caméra fixe ou vice versa; *Com* **p. trade** clients *mpl ou* clientèle *f* de passage

passion ['pæʃən] N **1** passion *f*, **to have a p. for sb** aimer qn passionnément; *Fig* **to have a p. for music/painting/cars** avoir la passion de la musique/de la peinture/des voitures; **to have a p. for Chinese cooking** adorer la cuisine chinoise; *Law* **crime of p.** crime *m* passionnel
2 *(anger)* colère *f*, emportement *m*; **a fit of p.** un accès de colère; **to be in a p. about sth** être fou de colère à cause de qch; **to fly into a p.** s'emporter

3 *(strong emotion)* passion *f*, **passions are running high on this issue** ce sujet déchaîne les passions; **to sing/speak with great p.** chanter/parler avec passion; **imagine getting into such a p. about a football match!** se mettre dans un tel état à propos d'un match de foot!; **to hate sb/sth with a p.** avoir horreur de qn/qch
4 *Rel* **the P. (of Christ)** la Passion (de Jésus-Christ)
▸▸ **p. fruit** fruit *m* de la Passion; *Rel* **p. play** mystère *m* de la Passion; *Rel* **P. Sunday** le dimanche de la Passion; *Rel* **P. week** la semaine de la Passion

passionate ['pæʃənɪt] ADJ **1** *(speech)* véhément; *(advocate, believer)* fervent, ardent; **a p. plea for justice** un véhément appel à la justice **2** *(love, lover)* passionné, ardent; *(embrace, kiss)* passionné; *(relationship)* passionnel; **to make p. love** faire l'amour avec passion; **a p. weekend** un week-end de passion

passionately ['pæʃənɪtlɪ] ADV *(to love, defend sth)* passionnément, ardemment, avec passion; *(to believe, be committed to)* ardemment, avec ferveur; *(to speak)* avec passion, avec véhémence; *(to sing)* avec passion; **to be p. in love with sb** aimer qn passionnément; **to be p. fond of sth/doing sth** adorer qch/faire qch

passionflower ['pæʃənflaʊər] N *(plant)* passiflore *f*

passionless ['pæʃənlɪs] ADJ sans passion

passive ['pæsɪv] VOIR GRAMMAIRE A54–5; B39
ADJ **1** passif; *Metal, Elec (iron, electrode etc)* passif **2** *Gram* passif; **the p. voice** la voix passive **3** *Com (debts)* ne portant pas d'intérêt
N *Gram* **the p.** la voix passive, le passif; **in the p.** au passif
▸▸ *Psy* **p. aggressivity** comportement *m* passif-agressif; *Comput* **p. matrix screen** écran *m* à matrice passive; **p. resistance** résistance *f* passive; **p. smoking** tabagisme *m* passif

passive-aggressive ADJ *Psy* passif-agressif

passively ['pæsɪvlɪ] ADV **1** passivement **2** *Gram* au passif, à la forme passive

passiveness ['pæsɪvnɪs], **passivity** [pæ'sɪvɪtɪ] N *(of mind, metal etc)* passivité *f*

passkey ['pɑːskiː] N (clef *f*) passe-partout *m inv*

Passover ['pɑːsəʊvər] N *Rel* la Pâque

passport ['pɑːspɔːt] N passeport *m*; **ship's p.** permis *m* de navigation; *Fig* **this job was her p. to fame** ce travail a été son passeport pour la célébrité; **money is a p. to anything** l'argent ouvre toutes les portes
▸▸ **p. control** contrôle *m* des passeports; **p. number** numéro *m* de passeport

passport-sized photograph N photo *f* d'identité

password ['pɑːswɜːd] N *Mil, Comput etc* mot *m* de passe
▸▸ *Comput* **p. protection** protection *f* par mot de passe

password-protected ADJ *Comput* protégé par mot de passe

past [pɑːst] ADJ passé; **the time for negotiating is p.** l'heure n'est plus à la négociation; **those days are p.** ces temps sont révolus; **in p. times., in times p.** autrefois, *Lit* au temps jadis; **p. chairmen** *(former chairmen)* anciens présidents; **she's a p. master at it** elle est experte en la matière; **she's a p. master at doing it** elle est passée maître dans l'art de le faire; **the p. week** la semaine dernière *ou* passée; **the p. two months** les deux derniers mois; **for some time p.** depuis quelque temps; *Gram* **in the p. tense** au passé
N **1** **the p.** le passé; **in the p.** autrefois; **it is a**

thing of the p. *(no longer exists) (of institution, custom)* ça n'existe plus; *(of relationship)* c'est du passé; *(is old-fashioned)* c'est périmé; **those days are a thing of the p.** cette époque est révolue; **to live in the p.** vivre dans le passé **2** *(background) (of person)* passé *m*; **woman with a p.** femme *f* qui a vécu *ou* qui a un passé; **town with a p.** ville *f* historique; **our country's glorious p.** le glorieux passé de notre pays **3** *Gram* passé *m*; **in the p.** au passé VOIR GRAMMAIRE A49–50; B30
PREP *(beyond)* au delà de; **a little p. the bridge** un peu plus loin que le pont, un peu au delà du pont; **to walk p. the house** passer devant la maison; **it is p. four (o'clock)** il est quatre heures passées; **half/a quarter p. four** quatre heures et demie/et quart; *Br* **ten (minutes) p. four** quatre heures dix; **it is half p.** il est la demie; **this bread is p. its sell-by date** ce pain a dépassé sa date limite de vente; **to be p. all understanding** dépasser toute compréhension; **p. endurance** insupportable; **that's p. all belief** c'est incroyable; **I'm p. work** *(too old)* je ne suis plus d'âge à travailler; *(too ill)* je ne peux plus travailler; **I'm p. caring** *(what happens, what you or they have done etc)* je n'en ai plus rien à faire; *Fam* **to be p. it** *(of person)* être trop vieux *(pour travailler, pour jouer au tennis etc)*; *(of car, machine)* avoir son compte; *Fam* **I wouldn't put it p. her** elle en est bien capable; **I wouldn't put anything p. this government** ce gouvernement est capable de tout *ou* du pire
ADV **to walk/go p.** passer; **to run p.** passer en courant
▸▸ *Gram* **p. historic** passé simple; *Gram* **p. participle** participe *m* passé; *Gram* **p. perfect** plus-que-parfait *m*, *pl* plus-que-parfaits

pasta ['pæstə] N *Culin* pâtes *fpl* (alimentaires)
paste [peɪst] N **1** *(malleable substance)* pâte *f*, *Cer* **hard/soft p.** pâte dure/tendre **2** *(glue)* colle *f* **3** *Culin (for pastry)* pâte *f* (à pâtisserie); **fish p.** = mousse *f* de poisson; **liver p.** = sorte de pâté de foie; **meat p.** = sorte de pâté **4** *(jewellery)* stras(s) *m*; **it's only p.** ce n'est que du stras(s); **p. jewellery** bijoux *mpl* en stras(s)
VT **1** *(glue) (poster, picture etc)* coller (**on** sur; **in** dans); *(wallpaper)* encoller; *Comput* coller (**into/onto** dans) **2** *Fam (beat up)* rosser, casser la figure à; *(defeat heavily)* mettre la pâtée à
▸▸ **p. pot** pot *m* de colle
▸ **paste up** VT SEP **1** *(notice)* afficher; *(bill, advert)* coller, monter **2** *Typ (page)* monter
pasteboard ['peɪstbɔːd] N carton *m*
pastel ['pæst(ə)l] N *Art (crayon)* (crayon *m*) pastel *m*; *(drawing)* pastel; **drawing in p.** *(dessin m au)* pastel; **p. blue** bleu pastel *m inv*
▸▸ **p. drawing** *(dessin au)* pastel; **p. shades** tons *mpl* pastel
pastern ['pæstən] N pâturon *m*, paturon *m*
paste-up N *(in publishing)* maquette *f*
pasteurization [pæstʃəraɪ'zeɪʃən] N pasteurisation *f*
pasteurize ['pæstʃəraɪz] VT pasteuriser; **pasteurized milk** lait *m* pasteurisé
pastiche [pæ'stiːʃ] N pastiche *m*
pastille ['pæstɪl] N **1** pastille *f*, **fruit pastilles** = pâtes *fpl* de fruits **2** *(for fumigating the air)* pastille *f* à brûler
pastime ['pɑːstaɪm] N passe-temps *m inv*
pastiness ['peɪstɪnɪs] N **1** *(of face)* teint *m* terreux **2** *(of bread etc)* consistance *f* pâteuse
pasting ['peɪstɪŋ] N **1** *(gluing) (of poster etc)* collage *m*; *(of wallpaper)* encollage *m* **2** *Fam (beating)* rossée *f*, raclée *f*; **to give sb a p.**

mettre une raclée à qn, rosser qn; *Sport* **to get a p.** être battu à plate(s) couture(s); *Sport* **to give sb a p.** mettre la pâtée à qn
pastor ['pɑːstər] N *Rel* pasteur *m*
pastoral ['pɑːstərəl] ADJ **1** *(rural)* pastoral, -aux; **a p. people** un peuple de bergers **2** *Rel* pastoral, -aux **3** *Sch (care)* qui concerne la santé physique et spirituelle des élèves
▸ N **1** *Liter, Mus, Art, Theat* pastorale *f* **2** *Rel* (lettre *f*) pastorale *f*
▸▸ **p. land** pâturages *mpl*; *Rel* **p. letter** (lettre) pastorale
pastrami [pə'strɑːmɪ] N *Culin* = bœuf *m* fumé et épicé
pastry ['peɪstrɪ] N pâte *f*, *(cake)* pâtisserie *f*, **short(-crust) p.** pâte brisée; **flaky** *or* **puff p.** pâte feuilletée
▸▸ **p. board** planche *f* à pâtisserie; **p. brush** pinceau *m* (à pâtisserie); **p. case** croûte *f*; **p. cutter** emporte-pièce *m inv*
pastrycook ['peɪstrɪkʊk] N pâtissier, -ière
pasturage ['pɑːstʃərɪdʒ] N **1** *(right)* (droit *m* de) pâturage *m ou* pacage *m* **2** *(land)* = **pasture** N
pasture ['pɑːstʃər] N *(land)* (lieu *m* de) pâture *f*, pâturage *m*, herbage *m*; **to be put out to p.** *Agr* être mis au pré *ou* au pâturage; *Fig* être mis à la retraite *ou* au vert; *Fig* **to move on to pastures new** *or* **greener pastures** aller vers de nouveaux horizons
▸ VI paître, pâturer, pacager
▸ VT *(of shepherd) (animals)* (faire) paître; *(of animals) (field)* pâturer
▸▸ **p. land** (lieu de) pâture, pâturage, herbage
pasty[1] ['peɪstɪ] ADJ **1** *(face, complexion)* terreux; *(person)* qui a le teint terreux; **p.-faced** au teint terreux **2** *(texture)* pâteux
pasty[2] ['pæstɪ] N *Br Culin* = (petit) pâté *m* en croûte *(cuit sans moule)*; **Cornish p.** = pâté (en croûte) qui contient du bœuf, des pommes de terre et autres légumes
pat[1] [pæt] VT (-**tt**-) *(tap)* tapoter; *(animal)* caresser, flatter (de la main); **to p. one's hair** se tapoter les cheveux; **she patted the little boy's head** elle a tapoté la tête du petit garçon; **to p. sb on the back** donner une tape dans le dos à qn; *Fig (congratulate)* féliciter qn; *Fig* **to p. oneself on the back** se féliciter
▸ N **1** *(tap)* petite tape *f*, *(on animal)* petite tape, caresse *f*; **to give sb a p. on the back** donner une tape dans le dos à qn; *Fig (congratulate)* féliciter qn; *Fig* **to give oneself a p. on the back** se féliciter **2** *(lump) (of butter)* rondelle *f*, médaillon *m*; **cow p.** bouse *f* de vache
▸ ADJ *(answer, solution)* facile; *(explanation)* simple
▸ ADV **his answer came p.** il a répondu du tac au tac; **to know** *or* **have sth off p.** savoir qch par cœur; **he had his explanation off p.** il avait une explication toute prête; **to stand p.** *Cards* jouer d'autorité; *esp Am (not give in)* refuser de bouger
▸ **pat down** VT SEP *(soil, cement etc)* tasser (doucement)
pat[2] **1** *(abbr patent)* brev. **2** *(abbr patented)* breveté
Patagonia [pætə'gəʊnɪə] N Patagonie *f*
patch [pætʃ] N **1** *(of cloth)* pièce *f* (pour raccommoder un vêtement); *(on garment)* pièce (rapportée); *(on sail)* placard *m*; *(for bromide corrections)* cache *m*; *Med (nicotine, drug treatment)* timbre *m*, patch *m*; *Comput (correction)* correction *f*, *Aut etc* **(rubber) p.** *(for inner tube)* rustine *f*; **to put a p. on a garment** mettre une pièce à *ou* rapiécer un vêtement; *Fam* **his last novel isn't a p. on the others** son dernier roman est loin de valoir les autres; **(eye) p.** couvre-œil *m*, *pl* couvre-œils

2 *(of colour, light)* tache *f*, *(of fog, mist)* nappe *f*, *(of oil)* flaque *f*, *(of ice)* plaque *f*, **p. of blue sky** pan *m ou* coin *m ou* échappée de ciel bleu; **rough patches** *(on wood, metal etc)* aspérités *fpl*; **the book was good in patches** le livre contient de bons passages; *Fam* **to be going through** *or* **to have struck a bad p.** traverser une mauvaise période
3 *(of land)* lopin *m*, parcelle *f*, *(of vegetables)* carré *m*; *Fam (of prostitute, salesperson, police officer)* secteur *m*; *Fam* **keep off my p.** *(territory)* ne mets pas les pieds sur mon territoire!
▸ VT *(piece of clothing)* mettre une pièce à, rapiécer; *(inner tube)* poser une rustine à; *Naut (sail)* placarder
▸▸ *Tel* **p. board** tableau *m* de raccordement; *Elec, Tel* **p. cord** cordon *m* de commutation; *Sewing* **p. pocket** poche *f* plaquée
▸ **patch together** VT SEP *Fam (temporary shelter, something broken)* assembler; *(business plan, team, government)* mettre sur pied; **they patched together a documentary** ils ont monté un documentaire tant bien que mal; **we are beginning to p. together an understanding of …** petit à petit nous commençons à nous faire une idée de …; *Pej* **the whole thing is a bit patched together** tout ça est un peu mal fichu
▸ **patch up** VT SEP *Fam (repair temporarily) (object)*, *Fig (marriage)* rafistoler; *Med Fam (person)* retaper; **I managed to p. the car up** j'ai réussi à retaper la voiture; **we've patched things up** *(after quarrel, argument)* nous avons réussi à arranger les choses; **they patched up their differences** ils ont réglé leurs différends
patching ['pætʃɪŋ] N *(of piece of clothing)* rapiéçage *m*, rapiècement *m*; **we can use that old jacket for p.** nous pouvons utiliser cette vieille veste pour faire du rapiécement *ou* rapiéçage
patchwork ['pætʃwɜːk] N *Sewing, Fig* patchwork *m*; *Fig* **a p. team** une équipe disparate *ou* hétéroclite; **a p. of measures** un ensemble de mesures hétéroclites; *Fig* **a p. of fields** une campagne bigarrée
▸▸ **p. quilt** couverture *f* en patchwork
patchy ['pætʃɪ] ADJ *(paintwork etc)*, *Fig novel etc)* inégal, -aux
pate [peɪt] N *Arch, Hum (head)* caboche *f*, **bald p.** crâne *m* chauve
pâté ['pæteɪ] N *Culin* pâté *m*; **liver p.** pâté de foie; **p. sandwich** sandwich *m* au pâté
patella, *pl* **patellae, patellas** [pə'telə, -iː, -əz] N *Anat* rotule *f*
paten ['pæt(ə)n] N *Rel* patène *f*
patent ['peɪtənt, 'pætənt] ADJ **1** *(protected by patent)* breveté **2** *Law* **letters p.** lettres *fpl* patentes *ou* de noblesse; *(of inventor)* lettres patentes, brevet *m* d'invention *ou* d'inventeur **3** *(evident) (lack of concern, disrespect)* manifeste; *(fact)* évident; **that's a p. lie!** c'est un mensonge éhonté!
▸ N **1** *(right)* brevet d'invention; *(invention)* invention *f*/fabrication *f* brevetée; **to take out a p. for an invention** faire breveter une invention; **p. applied for, p. pending** demande de brevet déposée; **infringement of a p.** contrefaçon *f* **2** *(grant of nobility)* lettres *fpl* patentes; **p. of nobility** lettres d'anoblissement *ou* de noblesse
▸ VT *(invention) (of authorities)* protéger par un brevet, breveter; *(of inventor)* faire breveter, prendre un brevet pour; **patented** breveté
▸▸ **p. agent** agent *m* en brevets; **p. application** demande *f ou* dépôt *m* de brevet; *Am* **p. attorney** conseil *m* en matière de brevets; **p. goods** articles *mpl* brevetés; **p. leather** cuir *m* verni, vernis *m*; **p.-leather shoes** chaussures *fpl* vernies; **p. medicine** médicament *m*

vendu sans ordonnance; *Pej (cure-all)* élixir *m* universel, remède *m* de charlatan; **P. Office** ≃ Institut *m* national de la propriété industrielle; **p. rights** propriété *f* industrielle

patentable ['peɪtəntəb(ə)l] **ADJ** brevetable

patentee [peɪtən'tiː] **N** détenteur, -trice d'un/du brevet

patently ['peɪtəntlɪ] **ADV** manifestement; **he was p. lying** il était manifeste qu'il mentait; **it was p. obvious that …** il était absolument évident que …

patentor ['peɪtəntər] **N** organisme *m* délivrant un brevet

pater ['peɪtər] **N** *Old-fashioned Br Fam* **(the) p.** le paternel

paterfamilias [peɪtəfə'mɪlɪæs] **N** *Fml* chef *m* de famille

paternal [pə'tɜːnəl] **ADJ** *(love, attention)* paternel; *(role, responsibilities)* de père; *Lit* **under the p. roof** dans la maison paternelle
▶▶**p. grandparents** grands-parents *mpl* paternels

paternalism [pə'tɜːnəlɪz(ə)m] **N** paternalisme *m*

paternalist [pə'tɜːnəlɪst] **ADJ** paternaliste
N personne *f* à tendances paternalistes

paternalistic [pətɜːnə'lɪstɪk] **ADJ** paternaliste

paternalistically [pətɜːnə'lɪstɪklɪ] **ADV** *(to govern)* avec paternalisme; *(to say)* d'un ton paternaliste; *(to smile)* d'un air paternaliste

paternally [pə'tɜːnəlɪ] **ADV** paternellement

paternity [pə'tɜːnɪtɪ] **N** paternité *f*; **there are doubts about his p.** on n'est pas sûr de l'identité de son père
▶▶**p. leave** congé *m* de paternité; *Law* **p. suit** action *f* en recherche de paternité

path, *pl* **paths** [pɑːθ, pɑːðz] **N 1** *(through forest etc)* chemin *m*, sentier *m*; *(in garden)* allée *f*, *Fig (in research etc)* voie *f*; *(of inquiry, investigation)* ligne *f*; *Comput (of paper in printer)* chemin; *Comput (of directory structure)* chemin (d'accès); *Fig* **the p. of glory** le chemin de la gloire; **this was a certain p. to disaster** cela menait tout droit au désastre
2 *(course) (of moving body)* trajet *m*, course *f*, *(of projectile, particle, planet)* trajectoire *f*, *(of ray of light)* passage *m*, trajet; *(of sun)* route *f*; **p. of a bullet** *(through the air)* trajectoire d'une balle; *(through the body)* trajet ou sillon *m* d'une balle; **he killed everyone in his p.** il a tué tout le monde sur son chemin *ou* passage; **in the p. of a vehicle** sur le chemin *ou* passage d'un véhicule; **a tree blocked his p.** un arbre lui bloquait le passage *ou* chemin; **their paths had crossed before** leurs chemins s'étaient déjà croisés

pathetic [pə'θetɪk] **ADJ 1** *(touching) (sight etc)* touchant, attendrissant; **she looked rather p.** elle était touchante **2** *Fam (weak, poor, useless) (excuse, game, person etc)* lamentable, pitoyable; **you're p.!** tu es lamentable!; **how p.!, it's p.!, isn't it p.?** c'est (vraiment) lamentable! **3** *Liter* **the p. fallacy** l'attribution *f* des caractéristiques humaines à la nature

Note that the French word **pathétique** never means **appalling**.

pathetically [pə'θetɪklɪ] **ADV 1** *(touchingly)* pitoyablement; **they wept p.** ils pleuraient d'une façon pitoyable; **she looked at him p.** elle lui jeta un regard pitoyable **2** *Fam (atrociously)* lamentablement; **p. bad** *(performance, speech etc)* lamentable; **p. easy** si facile que c'en est ridicule; **that's a p. weak excuse** c'est une excuse lamentable; **they performed p.** ils ont offert une performance lamentable *ou* pitoyable; **he's so p. arrogant** il est si arrogant que c'en est ridicule

pathfinder ['pɑːθfaɪndər] **N 1** *(scout)* éclaireur, -euse; *(pioneer)* pionnier, -ière **2** *(aircraft)* avion *m* éclaireur

pathname ['pɑːθneɪm] **N** *Comput* chemin *m* d'accès

pathological [pæθə'lɒdʒɪk(ə)l] **ADJ** *(hatred, liar etc)* pathologique

pathologically [pæθə'lɒdʒɪklɪ] **ADV** pathologiquement; **to be p. afraid of sth** avoir une peur pathologique de qch

pathologist [pə'θɒlədʒɪst] **N** pathologiste *mf*, **(forensic) p.** médecin *m* légiste

pathology [pə'θɒlədʒɪ] **N** pathologie *f*

pathos ['peɪθɒs] **N** pathétique *m*

pathway ['pɑːθweɪ] **N** sentier *m*

patience ['peɪʃəns] **N 1** patience *f*; **to try or tax sb's p.** éprouver la patience de qn; **my p. is exhausted or is at an end** ma patience est à bout, je suis à bout de patience; **you've exhausted my p.** tu as abusé de ma patience; **(have) p.!** *(prenez)* patience!; **to lose p.** perdre patience; **I've no p. with him** il m'énerve, il m'agace **2** *Br Cards* réussite *f*; **to play p.** faire des réussites

patient ['peɪʃənt] **ADJ** patient; **to be p.** *(naturally)* être patient, avoir de la patience; *(on specific occasion)* être patient, patienter, prendre patience; **you will have to be p.** il vous faudra être patient
N malade *mf*, patient, -ente; *(after operation)* opéré, -ée; **a doctor and his patients** un médecin et ses clients *ou* patients
▶▶**p. care** soins *mpl* administrés aux patients

patiently ['peɪʃəntlɪ] **ADV** patiemment; **a long illness, p. borne** une longue maladie, endurée avec patience

patina ['pætɪnə] **N** patine *f*; **to take on a p.** *(of bronze)* se patiner

patio ['pætɪəʊ] **N** patio *m*
▶▶**p. doors** porte-fenêtre *f*, *pl* portes-fenêtres

patriarch ['peɪtrɪɑːk] **N** *Rel etc* patriarche *m*

patriarchal [peɪtrɪ'ɑːk(ə)l] **ADJ** patriarcal, -aux

patriarchy ['peɪtrɪɑːkɪ] **N** patriarcat *m*, système *m* patriarcal

patrician [pə'trɪʃən] **ADJ, N** *Antiq etc* patricien, -ienne

patricide ['pætrɪsaɪd] **N 1** *(person)* parricide *mf* **2** *(crime)* parricide *m*

patrimony ['pætrɪmənɪ] **N 1** *(inheritance)* patrimoine *m* **2** *(of church)* biens-fonds *mpl*, revenu *m*

patriot ['peɪtrɪət, 'pæ-] **N** patriote *mf*

patriotic [peɪtrɪ'ɒtɪk, pæ-] **ADJ** *(person)* patriote; *(speech, feeling etc)* patriotique

patriotically [peɪtrɪ'ɒtɪklɪ, pæ-] **ADV** patriotiquement, avec patriotisme

patriotism ['peɪtrɪətɪz(ə)m, 'pæ-] **N** patriotisme *m*

patrol [pə'trəʊl] **N** patrouille *f*, *(of police)* patrouille (de surveillance); *(of nightwatchman, police officer on foot)* ronde *f*; **to be on p.** être en patrouille, patrouiller
VI (**-ll-**) patrouiller, être en patrouille
VT *(area etc)* patrouiller dans, faire une patrouille dans; *(border)* patrouiller à; **the border is heavily patrolled** de nombreuses patrouilles surveillent la frontière
▶▶**p. bomber** patrouilleur *m* de bombardement, bombardier *m* patrouilleur; **p. car** voiture *f* de police; *Naut* **p. craft** patrouilleur, vedette *f* de surveillance; **p. leader** chef *m* de patrouille; *Naut* **p. vessel** patrouilleur, vedette de surveillance

patrolman, *pl* **patrolmen** [pə'trəʊlmən] **N 1** *Br (employee of AA, RAC etc)* patrouilleur *m* **2**

Am (policeman) agent *m* de police (en service de ronde)

patrolwoman, *pl* **patrolwomen** [pə'trəʊlwʊmən, -wɪmɪn] **N** *Am* femme *f* agent de police (en service de ronde)

patron ['peɪtrən] **N 1** *(of artists, the arts etc)* protecteur, -trice, mécène *m*; *(of charity)* patron, -onne; *Rel, Hist (of living)* patron *m*, collateur *m* **2** *Com (of shop)* client, -ente; *(regular)* habitué, -ée
▶▶**p. saint** (saint) patron, (sainte) patronne

Note that the French word **patron** is a false friend and is never a translation for the English word **patron**. It means **boss**.

patronage ['pætrənɪdʒ] **N 1** *(support etc)* patronage *m*, protection *f*, *(of arts)* mécénat *m*; *(of charity)* patronage; *Pej (condescension) (towards sb)* attitude *f* condescendante (of envers); **concert under the p. of …** concert patronné par … **2** *(of hotel etc)* clientèle *f* **3** *Church of Eng* droit *m* de présentation (à un bénéfice) **4** *Pol* népotisme *m*; **yet another p. appointment** encore une nomination qui tient du népotisme

patroness ['peɪtrənɪs] **N** *Old-fashioned (of the arts etc)* protectrice *f*, *(of charity)* (dame *f*) patronnesse *f*

patronize ['pætrənaɪz] **VT 1** *(artist etc)* patronner; *(art)* encourager; *(hospital etc)* subventionner; *(charitable institution)* souscrire à **2** *Pej (treat in a patronizing way)* traiter avec condescendance; **don't p. me!** je n'ai pas besoin de ta condescendance! **3** *Com (company, shop)* accorder sa clientèle à; *(cinema, restaurant etc)* être un(e) habitué(e) de, fréquenter; **a restaurant patronized by the famous** un restaurant fréquenté par des gens célèbres

patronizing ['pætrənaɪzɪŋ] **ADJ** *(person, tone etc)* condescendant; **to be p. towards sb** se montrer condescendant envers qn, traiter qn avec condescendance

patronizingly ['pætrənaɪzɪŋlɪ] **ADV** *(to look)* d'un air condescendant; *(to say)* d'un ton condescendant; *(to treat sb)* avec condescendance

patronymic [pætrə'nɪmɪk] **ADJ** patronymique
N patronyme *m*, nom *m* patronymique

patsy ['pætsɪ] **N** *Am Sl (dupe)* gobeur *m*, jobard *m*

patten ['pæt(ə)n] **N** socque *m* *(pour protéger les chaussures de la boue)*

patter[1] ['pætər] **N** *(of footsteps)* petit bruit *m*; *(of mice)* trottinement *m*; *(of rain)* crépitement *m*; *(gentler)* tambourinement *m*; *Hum* **soon we'll be hearing the p. of tiny feet** la famille s'élargira bientôt
VI *(walk)* trottiner, marcher à petits pas rapides; *(of rain)* crépiter; *(more gently)* tambouriner
▶ **patter about** **VI** *(walk, run)* trottiner çà et là

patter[2] **N** *(of sales person)* baratin *m*, boniment *m*; *(of comedian)* bagout *m*; *(chatter)* bavardage *m*
VI *(chatter)* bavarder sans arrêt, caqueter
▶▶*Fam* **p. merchant** baratineur *m*

pattern ['pæt(ə)n] **N 1** *(design) (on wallpaper, fabric etc)* motif *m*; *(of hit marks on a target, on the ground etc)* groupement *m*; *Comput (of perforations)* combinaison *f*; **streets arranged in an orderly p.** rues établies suivant un plan ordonné
2 *(of events, behaviour etc)* **the normal p. of trade** la tendance normale du marché; **some clear patterns emerge from the statistics** des tendances nettes ressortent des statistiques; **the evening followed the usual p.** la soirée s'est déroulée selon le schéma habi-

tuel; **a typical p. of events** une suite d'événements type; **patterns of behaviour** comportements *mpl* types; **there was a certain p. in his behaviour** son comportement suivait un certain schéma

3 *(model)* modèle *m*, dessin *m*; *Sewing etc (paper cutout)* patron *m*; *Knitting* modèle; *Metal* modèle, gabarit *m*, calibre *m*; **machines all built to one p.** machines construites *ou* fabriquées toutes sur le même modèle; *Sewing* **to cut out a shirt from a p.** tailler une chemise sur un patron

4 *(example)* modèle *m*, exemple *m*; **to set a p.** créer un modèle; **this opening debate set the p. for …** ce débat d'ouverture a donné le ton *ou* la note de …

5 *Com (sample)* échantillon *m*

VT 1 *(draw patterns on)* tracer des motifs sur; *(decorate with patterns)* orner de motifs **2** *(model)* **to p. sth after** *or* **(up)on sth** modeler qch sur qch

▶▶ *Mil* **p. bombing** bombardement *m* systématique; *Com* **p. book** livre *m* d'échantillons; *Com* **p. card** carte *f* d'échantillons; *Ind* **p. designer** dessinateur, -trice de patrons; *Sch* **p. drill** exercice *m* d'apprentissage des structures grammaticales; **p. maker** modeleur, -euse; *Comput* **p. recognition** reconnaissance *f* de formes

patterned ['pætənd] **ADJ** à dessins, à motifs

patty ['pætɪ] **N** *Culin* pâté *m* (en croûte)

paucity ['pɔːsɪtɪ] **N** *(of information, proof etc)* manque *m*; *(of money, food, materials, talent etc)* manque, pénurie *f*

paunch [pɔːntʃ] **N** *(of person)* ventre *m*, *Fam* bide *m*, bedaine *f*, *(of ruminant)* panse *f*, rumen *m*; **to develop a p.** prendre du ventre *ou Fam* du bide

paunchy ['pɔːntʃɪ] **ADJ** *Fam* ventru, pansu

pauper ['pɔːpər] **N** indigent, -ente; **to die a p.** mourir dans l'indigence; **p.'s grave** fosse *f* commune

pause [pɔːz] **N 1** pause *f*, arrêt *m*; *(on recording)* blanc *m* sonore; *(in conversation etc)* silence *m*; **to have a p.** faire une pause **2** *(in poetry)* repos *m*; *(caesura)* césure *f* **3** *Mus* point *m* d'orgue; *(over a rest)* point d'arrêt **4** *esp Lit* **to give sb p.** faire hésiter qn; *(make sb think)* donner à réfléchir à qn

VI 1 *(stop) (when working)* faire une pause; *(when speaking)* s'interrompre, faire une pause; *(when leaving etc)* marquer un temps d'arrêt, s'arrêter; **to p. for breath/thought** faire une pause pour reprendre son souffle/réfléchir **2** *(hesitate)* hésiter; **to make sb p.** faire hésiter qn; *(make sb think)* donner à réfléchir à qn **3** **to p. on a word** s'arrêter sur un mot; *Mus* **to p. on a note** tenir une note

▶▶ *Comput* **p. key** touche *f* pause

pave [peɪv] **VT** *(road etc)* paver; *Fig* **to p. the way** préparer le terrain (**for sth** pour qch); **the streets here aren't paved with gold** on ne roule pas sur l'or ici

pavement ['peɪvmənt] **N 1** *esp Br (path beside street)* trottoir *m* **2** *Am (roadway)* chaussée *f* **3** *(material)* pavé *m*

▶▶ *Br* **p. artist** artiste *mf* de rue *(qui dessine sur les trottoirs)*; **p. café** café *m*, terrasse *f* d'un café

pavilion [pə'vɪlɪən] **N** *Br Sport, Archit etc* pavillon *m*

paving ['peɪvɪŋ] **N 1** *(action)* pavage *m*; *(with tiles)* carrelage *m*; *(with slabs)* dallage *m* **2** *(surface)* pavé *m*; *(made of bigger slabs)* dalles *fpl*

▶▶ **p. stone** pavé *m*; **p. tile** carreau *m* (de pavage); *(bigger)* dalle *f* (de pavage)

Pavlova ['pævˈləʊvə] **N** *Culin* vacherin *m*; **raspberry P.** vacherin à la framboise

Pavlovian [pævˈləʊvɪən] **ADJ** *Psy (treatment, reaction, response)* pavlovien

paw [pɔː] **N** *(of animal), Fam (of person)* patte *f*, *Fam* **paws off!** bas les pattes!; *Fam* **you're not getting your dirty** *or* **sweaty paws on my new bike!** il n'est pas question que tu touches à mon nouveau vélo!

VT 1 *(of animal)* donner un/des coup(s) de patte à; **to p. the ground** *(of horse)* gratter (la terre) du pied **2** *Fam (of person)* tripoter, peloter

pawky ['pɔːkɪ] **ADJ** *Scot (witty)* pince-sans-rire

pawl [pɔːl] **N** *Tech etc (of catch)* cliquet *m*; **p. and ratchet wheel** roue *f ou* encliquetage *m* à rochet

pawn¹ [pɔːn] **N 1** *(object pawned)* gage *m*, nantissement *m* **2** **in p.** en gage; **to put one's watch in p.** mettre sa montre en gage *ou* au mont-de-piété *ou Fam* au clou; **to get sth out of p.** dégager qch (du mont-de-piété)

VT mettre en gage *ou* au mont-de-piété *ou Fam* au clou, engager; *Fig (one's life, honour)* engager

▶▶ **p. ticket** reconnaissance *f* du mont-de-piété

pawn² **N** *Chess* pion *m*; *Fig* **to be sb's p.** être le jouet de qn

pawnbroker ['pɔːnˌbrəʊkər] **N** prêteur, -euse sur gage(s)

pawnbroking ['pɔːnˌbrəʊkɪŋ] **N** prêt *m* sur gage(s)

pawnshop ['pɔːnʃɒp] **N** bureau *m* de prêt sur gage(s), mont-de-piété *m*, *pl* monts-de-piété

pawpaw ['pɔːpɔː] **N** = **papaw**

pax [pæks] **INT** *Br Sl (truce)* pouce!

PAY [peɪ]

N	salaire ▪ paie ▪ traitement
VT	payer **1, 2** ▪ régler **1**
VI	payer **1, 2** ▪ régler **1**

N salaire *m*, paie *f*, paye *f*, *(of domestic staff)* gages *mpl*, *(of civil servant)* traitement *m*, salaire; *(of member of parliament)* indemnité *f*, *Mil* solde *f*, **to get an extra £10 a week in one's p.** toucher 10 livres de salaire en plus par semaine; **the p.'s good/terrible** ça paie bien/mal; *Pej* **to be in sb's p.** être à la solde *ou* aux gages de qn

VT *(pt, pp* **paid** [peɪd]*)* **1** *(account, invoice)* payer, régler; *(fine)* payer; *(dividend)* distribuer; *(debt)* payer, liquider, régler, acquitter; *(creditor)* rembourser; *(money)* verser; *(premium)* verser, acquitter; **to p. sb £100** payer 100 livres à qn; **how much do you p. for tea?** combien est-ce que vous payez le thé?; **I paid £5 for it** je l'ai payé cinq livres; **I expect to p. my way** je m'attends à payer mon écot; **to be paid in four instalments** payable en quatre versements; **to p. cash (down)** *or* **ready money** payer (argent) comptant, payer au comptant; **p. self, p. cash** *(on cheque)* payez (à l'ordre de) moi-même; **to p. money into an account** alimenter un compte, approvisionner un compte; **to p. money into sb's account** verser de l'argent au compte de qn; **to p. something on account** verser une somme à titre de provision; *Fam* **to make sb p. through the nose** écorcher qn; *Fig* **they paid a heavy price for this mistake** cette erreur leur a coûté cher

2 *(employees)* payer; **to be paid by the hour/the week** être payé à l'heure/la semaine; **badly paid job** travail *m* mal payé; **to p. sb to do sth** payer qn pour faire qch; **I wouldn't do it if you paid me** je ne le ferais pas même si on me payait

3 *(give)* **to p. tribute** *or* **homage to sb** rendre hommage à qn; **to p. one's respects to sb** présenter ses respects à qn; **to p. one's (last) respects to sb** rendre les derniers devoirs à qn; **to p. a visit to sb** rendre visite à

qn; **we paid a visit to the Louvre** nous avons visité le Louvre; **p. attention to what you are doing** faites attention à ce que vous faites

4 *(profit)* **it will p. you to do it** c'est dans votre intérêt de le faire

VI 1 payer; **who's paying?** qui paie?; **p. at the gate** *or* **door** entrée payante; *Admin Br* **p. as you earn**, *Am* **p. as you go** retenue *f* (de l'impôt sur le revenu) à la base *ou* à la source; **how would you like to p.?** comment souhaitez-vous régler?; **to p. by cheque** payer *ou* régler par chèque

2 *Com, Fin etc* **to p. in advance** payer d'avance; **to p. on delivery** payer à la livraison; **to p. in full** payer intégralement *ou* en totalité; **to p. on demand** payer à vue *ou* à présentation; **p. to the order of …** payez à l'ordre de …; *Fin* **p. to bearer** payez au porteur

3 *(be profitable)* **business that doesn't p.** affaire qui ne rapporte pas *ou* qui n'est pas rentable; **it wouldn't p.** cela ne serait pas rentable; **it pays to advertise** la publicité rapporte; **it pays to be honest** l'honnêteté est toujours récompensée; **it doesn't always p. to tell the truth** on n'a pas toujours intérêt à dire la vérité

▶▶ **p. award** augmentation *f* de salaire; *Br* **p. bed** lit *m* payant; *Mil* **p. book** livret *m* de solde; *TV* **p. channel** chaîne *f* à péage *ou* payante; **p. cheque**, *Am* **p. check** chèque *m* de règlement de traitement *ou* de salaire; **p. deductions** retenues salariales; **p. desk** caisse *f*, **p. dirt** *(earth)* gisement *m*; *Fam (discovery)* trouvaille *f*, *Fam* **to hit p. dirt** trouver un bon filon; **p. and display** *(car park)* parking *m* à horodateur; **p. dispute** conflit *m* salarial; **p. formula** formule *f* de paie; **p. freeze** gel *m ou* blocage *m* des salaires; **p. increase** augmentation *f* de salaire; **p. ledger** livre *m* de paie; *Br* **p. packet** *(envelope)* enveloppe *f* contenant le salaire; *(money)* paie, salaire; **p. phone** téléphone *m* public; *(enclosed)* cabine *f* téléphonique; **p. rise** augmentation de salaire; **p. slip** bulletin *m* de paie; **p. television, p. TV** télévision *f* à péage, télévision payante

▶ **pay back VT SEP 1** *(loan, person)* rembourser

2 *Fig (have revenge on)* **to p. sb back in his own coin** rendre la pareille à qn; **I'll p. you back for this!** je te le revaudrai!, tu me le paieras!

▶ **pay for VT INSEP** *(something)* payer; **his uncle paid for his schooling** son oncle a payé ses études; *Fig Fam* **he'll p. for this!, I'll make him p. for this!** il me le payera!; *Fig Fam* **you'll p. for this tomorrow** *(for drinking too much etc)* tu vas en subir les conséquences demain; **it's all paid for** *(someone has paid for everything)* tout a été réglé; *(I've paid for everything)* c'est à mes frais; **a free holiday with everything paid for** des vacances gratuites tout compris

▶ **pay in VT SEP** *(cheque, money)* verser sur son compte; **to p. in a cheque** déposer un chèque, *esp Fml* remettre un chèque à l'encaissement

VI faire un versement

▶ **pay off VT SEP 1** *(finish paying) (debt etc)* liquider, régler; *(creditor)* rembourser; *(mortgage)* purger; **to p. sth off over three years** acheter *ou* payer qch en trois ans; **I'm still paying it off** je n'ai pas encore fini de le payer

2 *(dismiss) (worker, troops)* licencier; *(sailors)* débarquer; *(servant)* congédier

3 *Fam (bribe)* soudoyer, donner des pots de vin à

VI *(of deal etc)* être payant *ou* rentable *ou* fructueux; *(of efforts etc)* porter ses *ou* des fruits; **all these years of work have paid off at last** nous sommes enfin récompensés

après toutes ces années de travail; **it paid off** ça a valu la peine
▸ **pay out** VT SEP **1** (spend) payer, débourser; **I've had to p. out a lot on car repairs this year** j'ai eu beaucoup à débourser pour les réparations de voiture cette année
2 (salaries) payer
3 (pt, pp **payed**) Naut (cable) (laisser) filer VI payer
▸ **pay up** VI (pay debt) payer, Fam s'exécuter; **I finally made him p. up** j'ai finalement réussi à le faire payer ou débourser; **p. up!** allez, l'argent!, Sl aboule!
VT SEP (pay) payer

payable ['peɪəb(ə)l] ADJ **1** payable; **rates by the tenant** = impôts à la charge du locataire; Com **p. at sight/to order/to bearer** payable à vue/à ordre/au porteur; Com **p. at thirty days** exigible: trente jours; **p. in cash** payable comptant; **p. on delivery/with order** payable à la livraison/à la commande; **to make a bill p. to sb** faire un billet à l'ordre de qn; **cheque p. to bearer** chèque m au porteur; **please make your cheque p. to Miss Johnston** veuillez libeller votre chèque à l'ordre de Miss Johnston; **bonds made p. in euros** bons libellés en euros **2** Min (seam etc) exploitable
NPL **payables** Am factures fpl à payer
pay-as-you-earn N Br prélèvement m de l'impôt à la source
pay-as-you-go N facturation f à la durée; Tel paiement m par carte prépayée
pay-as-you-view TV N télévision f à la carte
payback ['peɪbæk] N **1** Fin récupération f du capital investi **2** esp Am (revenge) revanche f, **it's p. time** c'est le moment de la revanche
▸▸ **p. period** délai m de récupération, période f de remboursement
payday ['peɪdeɪ] N jour m de paie, paie f, Mil jour de solde; St Exch jour de liquidation ou de règlement
PAYE [piːeɪwaɪ'iː] N Br (abbr **pay as you earn**) retenue f (de l'impôt sur le revenu) à la base ou à la source; **P. and NIC return** déclaration f sociale
payee [peɪ'iː] N (of postal order, cheque etc) bénéficiaire mf; Com (of bill) porteur m, preneur m
payer ['peɪər] N payeur, -euse; **they're slow payers** ils ne payent pas vite
paying ['peɪɪŋ] N paiement m; Fin **p. up of a share** libération f d'une action
ADJ **1** (student etc) payant **2** (business etc) rémunérateur, -trice, profitable, qui rapporte; **it's not a p. proposition** ce n'est pas une proposition intéressante
▸▸ Com **p. agent** domiciliataire m; **p. agent for commercial bills** domiciliation f d'effets de commerce; **p. back** (of loan) remboursement m; Fin **p. bank** domiciliataire, établissement m payeur, domiciliation bancaire; **p. guest** hôte m payant, pensionnaire mf, **p. in** (of money, cheque etc) (into one's account) versement m, encaissement m; **p.-in book** carnet m de versements; **p.-in date** date f d'encaissement; **p.-in slip** bordereau m de versement ou de remise; **p. off** (of debt) liquidation f, règlement m; (dismissal) (of workers) licenciement m; (of sailors) débarquement m; (of servants) congédiement m
payload ['peɪləʊd] N (of vehicle) charge f payante ou utile; (of missile) charge utile; Aviat poids m utile
paymaster ['peɪmɑːstər] N intendant m, caissier m, payeur m; Mil trésorier m; Naut commissaire m; **the terrorists' p.** le commanditaire des terroristes
▸▸ **the P. General** le Trésorier-payeur-général britannique

payment ['peɪmənt] N **1** (act or fact of paying) (of money) paiement m, versement m; (of debt) paiement, liquidation f, règlement m, acquittement m; (of fine) paiement; (of invoice) paiement, règlement; (of creditor) remboursement m; **to make a p.** effectuer un versement; **to stop p. on a cheque** faire opposition sur un chèque; **(hire purchase) p.** paiement par traites; **I'm behind on the payments** je suis en retard dans les paiements; **non p.** défaut m de paiement; **to present a bill for p.** présenter un effet au paiement ou à l'encaissement; **on p. of £100** contre paiement de 100 livres; **p. against documents** paiement contre documents; **p. by cheque** paiement par chèque; **p. by electronic transfer** paiement électronique; **p. on account** acompte m; **to make a p. on account** donner un acompte; **p. in advance** paiement anticipé ou par anticipation ou d'avance; **p. in arrears** paiement arriéré; **p. in cash** paiement comptant, règlement au comptant; **p. on delivery** livraison f contre remboursement; **p. in full** paiement intégral; **p. by instalments** paiement par acomptes; **p. of a dividend** passation f ou distribution f d'un dividende; **p. in kind** paiement ou avantages mpl en nature; **p. at maturity** paiement à échéance; **p. at sight** paiement à vue
2 (remuneration) paiement m, rémunération f, **as (a) p. for your services** en rémunération de vos services; **they offered their services without p.** ils ont offert leurs services à titre gracieux; **she would not accept p.** elle n'a pas voulu accepter de paiement; **you can expect little but gratitude in p. for your efforts** ne vous attendez pas à beaucoup plus que de la gratitude en retour de vos efforts; **p. received** (stamped on invoice) pour acquit
▸▸ **p. advice** avis m de paiement; **p. card** carte f de paiement; **p. day** jour m de paiement, jour de règlement; **p. facilities** facilités fpl de paiement; **p. method** mode m de paiement; **p. order** ordre m de paiement; **p. period** délai m de paiement; **p. schedule** échéancier m de paiement; **p. term** délai de paiement
payoff ['peɪɒf] N **1** (final payment) règlement m; Fin rentabilité f **2** Fam (bribe) pot-de-vin m, pl pots-de-vin **3** Fam (ending) dénouement m **4** (reward) récompense f
payola [peɪ'əʊlə] N Fam (bribe) pot-de-vin m, pl pots-de-vin
pay-per-view TV N système m de télévision à la carte ou à la séance
ADV (channel) à péage; (film, programme) à la carte, à la séance
payroll ['peɪrəʊl] N **1** (list of employees) liste f du personnel; Mil feuille f ou état m de solde; **to be on the p.** être salarié; **how many do you have on the p.?** combien d'employés avez-vous?; **she's been on our p. for over twenty years** elle fait partie de notre personnel depuis plus de vingt ans; Pej **he's on our p.** (we're bribing him) on l'a acheté
2 (money paid) masse f salariale
▸▸ Fin **p. ledger** journal m ou livre m de paie; Fin **p. tax** impôt m sur la masse salariale
PBX [piːbiː'eks] N Tel (abbr **private branch exchange**) autocommutateur m privé
PC ['piː'siː] N **1** Br (abbr **Police Constable**) = agent m de police **2** (abbr **personal computer**) PC m, ordinateur m individuel; **P. disk** disquette f pour PC
ADJ (abbr **politically correct**) politiquement correct
pc ['piː'siː] N (abbr **postcard**) carte f postale
PCB [piːsiː'biː] N **1** Chem (abbr **polychlorinated biphenyl**) PCB m **2** Electron (abbr **printed circuit board**) carte f à ou de circuits imprimés

PC-compatible ADJ compatible PC
PCI [piːsiː'aɪ] N Comput (abbr **peripheral component interface**) PCI m
PCMCIA [piːsiː'emsiːaɪ'eɪ] N Comput (abbr **PC memory card international association**) PCMCIA
PD ['piː'diː] Am (abbr **Police Department**) service m de police
PDA [piːdiː'eɪ] N Comput (abbr **personal digital assistant**) agenda m électronique de poche, assistant m numérique de poche
PDF [piːdiː'ef] N Comput (abbr **portable document format**) (format m) PDF m
pdq [piːdiː'kjuː] ADV Fam (abbr **pretty damn(ed) quick**) illico presto, rapido
N (abbr **processes data quickly**) (machine) terminal m électronique de paiement, TEP m
PDSA [piːdiːes'eɪ] N Br (abbr **People's Dispensary for Sick Animals**) ≃ SPA f
PE ['piː'iː] N Sch (abbr **physical education**) EPS f, **PE lesson/teacher** cours m/professeur m d'EPS
pea [piː] N pois m; Culin (green or garden) **peas** petits pois; **like two peas in a pod** comme deux gouttes d'eau; **p. soup** soupe f aux pois; (thick) purée f de pois (cassés)
▸▸ **p. green** vert pomme m inv; **p. jacket** caban m; **p. pod** cosse f de pois
peace [piːs] N **1** (absence of war, conflict) paix f, (treaty) traité m de paix; **at p.** en paix (**with** avec); **to live in p. with one's neighbours** (of person, tribe, country) vivre en paix ou en harmonie avec ses voisins; **in time of p.** en temps de paix; **to make (one's) p. with sb** faire la paix ou se réconcilier avec qn; **we come in p.** nous venons en amis; Hist **the P. of Amiens** la Paix d'Amiens
2 (public order) **to keep the p.** (of citizen) ne pas troubler l'ordre public; (of police, troops) veiller à l'ordre public; **to break or disturb the p.** troubler ou violer l'ordre public; (at night) faire du tapage nocturne
3 (tranquillity) (of soul, night etc) tranquillité f, **for the sake of p. and quiet** pour avoir la paix; **to leave sb in p.** laisser qn tranquille ou en paix; **he gave me no p. until I agreed** il ne m'a pas laissé tranquille ou en paix tant que je n'ai pas accepté; esp Rel **go in p.!** allez en paix!; **p. of mind** tranquillité d'esprit; **it will give you p. of mind** ça te tranquillisera; **to be at p.** (of dead person) reposer en paix; **to hold or keep one's p.** se taire
▸▸ Br **p. campaigner** militant, -ante pour la paix; **P. Corps** = américaine de coopération avec les pays en voie de développement; **p. dividends** dividendes mpl de la paix; **p. formula** formule f de paix; **p. initiative** initiative f de paix; **p. movement** mouvement m pour la paix; **p. negotiations** négociations fpl pour la paix; **p. offering** offrande f de paix; **p. pipe** calumet m (de la paix); **p. plan** plan m de paix; **p. process** processus m de paix; **p. studies** = discipline f universitaire consistant à étudier les rapports stratégiques entre pays, le rôle de l'armée et la promotion de la paix dans le monde; **p. talks** pourparlers mpl de paix; **p. treaty** traité m de paix
peaceable ['piːsəb(ə)l] ADJ pacifique, qui aime la paix; **a p. man** un homme de paix; **p. means** moyens pacifiques
peaceably ['piːsəblɪ] ADV pacifiquement
peaceful ['piːsfʊl] ADJ **1** (calm) paisible, calme, tranquille; (death) paisible; (colour) doux, f douce **2** (not warlike or aggressive) pacifique; **p. settlement of a dispute** règlement m pacifique d'un litige
peacefully ['piːsfʊlɪ] ADV (to sleep, die) paisiblement, tranquillement; (to demonstrate, resolve differences) pacifiquement; **p. situ-**

ated situé dans un lieu paisible; **p., at home** *(in death notice)* mort dans son lit

peacefulness ['pi:sfʊlnɪs] N tranquillité *f*, paix *f*; **the organizers have guaranteed the p. of the demonstration** les organisateurs ont garanti que la manifestation se déroulerait dans le calme

peacekeeping ['pi:ski:pɪŋ] N maintien *m* de la paix
▸▸ *Mil* **p. force** force *f* de maintien de la paix

peace-loving ADJ pacifique

peacenik ['pi:snɪk] N *Fam Pej* pacifiste *mf*

peacetime ['pi:staɪm] N temps *m* de paix; **in p.** en temps de paix

peach [pi:tʃ] N pêche *f*; *(tree)* pêcher *m*; **p. (colour)** pêche *f inv*; **a peaches and cream complexion** un teint de pêche; *Fam* **she's a p.** c'est une jolie fille; *Fam* **it's a p.** c'est magnifique; **a p. of a goal/dress** un but/une robe magnifique
▸ VI *Old-fashioned Sl* **to p. on sb** *(inform on)* moucharder qn
▸▸ **p. melba** pêche melba; **p. tree** pêcher

peachy, peachy keen ['pi:tʃɪ(ki:n)] ADJ *Am Fam* super, génial, -aux, grand

peacock ['pi:kɒk] N *(bird)* paon *m*; *(colour)* bleu canard *m inv*
▸▸ **p. blue** bleu canard; **p. butterfly** paon de jour

peahen ['pi:hen] N paonne *f*

peak [pi:k] N **1** *(of mountain)* pic *m*, cime *f*, sommet *m*; *(mountain)* pic; **the highest peaks** les plus hauts sommets; *Culin* **whisk the egg white until it forms stiff peaks** battre les blancs en neige jusqu'à ce qu'ils forment des becs **2** *(maximum point)* maximum *m*; *(of graph, load)* pointe *f*; *Med (of fever)* pointe, poussée *f*; *Phys (of wave)* crête *f*; **prosperity was at its p.** la prospérité était à son apogée *ou* à son maximum; **in p. condition** dans une forme excellente **3** *(of cap)* visière *f*; *(of bicycle saddle, anchor etc)* bec *m*; *(of roof)* pointe *f*
▸ VI *(of curve etc)* passer par son apogée; **inflation peaked at 10%** l'inflation a fait une pointe à 10%; *Sport* **she peaked in time for the Olympics** *(of athlete)* elle a atteint le maximum de sa forme juste à temps pour les Jeux olympiques
▸▸ **p. demand** demande *f* maximum; **p. hours** *(for traffic)* heures *fpl* de pointe; *(in shop etc)* heures d'affluence; **p. load** charge *f* maximum; *(of generator)* débit *m* maximum; **p. period** *(for traffic)* heures de pointe; *(in shop etc)* heures d'affluence; *St Exch* **p. price** prix *m* maximum; **p. rate** tarif *m* heures pleines; **p. sales** ventes *fpl* maximales; *Br TV* **p. time** heures de grande écoute, prime time *m*; *Br TV* **p. time advertisement** publicité *f* aux heures de grande écoute *ou* en prime time; *Br TV* **p. time advertising** publicité aux heures de grande écoute *ou* en prime time; *Br TV* **p. viewing hours** heures de grande écoute; *Br TV* **p. viewing time** heure *f* de grande écoute
▸ **peak out** VI *(reach top limit)* atteindre son maximum

peaked [pi:kt] ADJ *(cap)* à visière

peaky ['pi:kɪ] ADJ *Fam* **to look p.** ne pas avoir l'air dans son assiette; **to feel p.** ne pas se sentir dans son assiette

peal [pi:l] N *(bells)* carillon *m*; *(noise)* carillon, carillonnement *m*; *(of organ)* grondement *m*; *(of thunder)* coup *m*, grondement; **to ring a p.** sonner un carillon, carillonner; **peals of laughter** éclats *mpl* de rire; **to go** *ou* **break into peals of laughter** lancer de grands éclats de rire
▸ VI *(of bells)* *(chime)* carillonner; *(ring out loudly)* sonner à toute volée; *(of thunder, of the organ)* retentir, gronder; *(of laughter)* ré-

sonner; **to p. with laughter** éclater de rire
▸ VT *(bells)* sonner à toute volée; *(tune)* carillonner
▸ **peal out** VI = peal VI

peanut ['pi:nʌt] N cacahuète *f*; *Fam* **they pay us peanuts** *(small sum of money)* ils nous paient trois fois rien; **that's peanuts to him** pour lui, c'est rien
▸▸ **p. butter** beurre *m* de cacahuètes; *Am Fam* **p. gallery** *(in theatre)* poulailler *m*; **p. oil** huile *f* d'arachide

pear [peər] N poire *f*; *(tree)* poirier *m*
▸▸ **p. tree** poirier

peardrop ['peədrɒp] N bonbon *m* parfumé à la poire

pearl[1] [pɜ:l] N **1** perle *f*, *(cultured)* perle de culture; *Prov* **to cast pearls before swine** jeter des perles aux cochons *ou* aux pourceaux; **he comes out with some real pearls** *(amusing comments etc)* il sort de vraies perles; **pearls of dew** perles de rosée; **pearls of wisdom** perles de sagesse; *Iron* inepties *fpl*; **p. button** bouton *m* de nacre; **p. necklace** collier *m* de perles
▸ VI **1** *(of moisture etc)* perler, former des gouttelettes **2** *(dive for pearls)* pêcher des perles
▸▸ **p. barley** orge *m* perlé; **p. diver** pêcheur, -euse de perles; **p. grey** gris perle *m inv*; **p. lightbulb** ampoule *f* opale; **p. oyster** huître *f* perlière

pearl[2] N, VT *Knitting* = purl

pearly ['pɜ:lɪ] ADJ perlé; **p. (white) teeth** dents *fpl* perlées *ou* de perle
▸▸ *Fam* **the P. Gates** les portes *fpl* du paradis; **p. king** = marchand *m* des quatre saisons de Londres portant une tenue traditionnelle couverte de boutons de nacre; *Zool* **p. nautilus** *(mollusc)* nautile *m*, nautilus *m*; **p. queen** = marchande *f* des quatre saisons de Londres portant une tenue traditionnelle couverte de boutons de nacre

pear-shaped ADJ en forme de poire; *(female figure)* qui s'épaissit au niveau des hanches; *Br Fam* **to go p.** *(go wrong)* partir en eau de boudin

peasant ['pezənt] N paysan, -anne, *Pej* péquenaud, -aude, rustre *mf*; **p. ways** mœurs *fpl* paysannes

peasantry ['pezəntrɪ] N *(people)* paysannerie *f*, paysans *mpl*

pease [pi:z] N
▸▸ *Culin* **p. pudding** = purée *f* de pois au jambon

peashooter ['pi:ʃu:tər] N petite sarbacane *f*

peasouper ['pi:'su:pər] N *esp Br Fam (fog)* purée *f* de pois

peat [pi:t] N tourbe *f*; turf *or* sod *or* block of p. motte *f* de tourbe; **to cut** *or* **dig p.** tourber
▸▸ **p. bog** tourbière *f*; **p. cutter** tourbier, -ière; **p. cutting, p. digging** tourbage *m*; *Bot* **p. moss** sphaigne *f*

peaty ['pi:tɪ] ADJ *(soil)* tourbeux; *(taste)* de fumée de tourbe

pebble ['peb(ə)l] N **1** caillou *m*, -oux; *(big, smooth and rounded)* galet *m*; *Fam* **you're not the only p. on the beach** il n'y a pas que toi au monde; **p. beach** plage *f* de galets **2** *Opt (crystal)* cristal *m* de roche; *(lens)* lentille *f* en cristal de roche
▸▸ *Constr* **p. dash** crépi *m* (moucheté); **p.-dash finish** crépi

pebble-dash VT *Constr (wall)* crépir

pebbly ['peblɪ] ADJ caillouteux; *(beach)* de galets

pecan ['pi:kən, pɪ'kæn] N *(nut)* noix *f* de pecan, *Can* pacane *f*; *(tree)* pacanier *m*
▸▸ **p. nut** noix de pecan, *Can* pacane; *Culin* **p. pie** tourte *f* aux noix de pecans *ou Can* aux pacanes; **p. tree** pacanier

peccadillo [pekə'dɪləʊ] N peccadille *f*

peccary ['pekərɪ] N *(animal)* pécari *m*

peck[1] [pek] N **1** *(of bird)* coup *m* de bec; **to have a p. at sth** picoter qch **2** *Fam (kiss)* bise *f*, bécot *m*; **to give sb a p.** faire une bise à qn
▸ VT **1** *(of bird)* *(something)* picoter, becqueter; *(person)* donner un coup de bec à **2** *Fam (to kiss)* faire une bise à
▸ VI **to p. (at sth)** *(of bird)* picoter (qch), donner des coups de bec (à qch)

peck[2] N *(measure)* *(of oats etc)* picotin *m*

pecker ['pekər] N **1** *Fam (bird)* pic *m* vert **2** *Br Sl* **keep your p. up!** (du) courage! **3** *esp Am Vulg (penis)* bite *f*

peckerwood ['pekəwʊd] N *Am Sl* **to be a p.** être génial *ou* super

pecking ['pekɪŋ] N
▸▸ **p. order** *(among birds)* hiérarchie *f* du becquetage; *Fig* hiérarchie sociale; *(in business etc)* hiérarchie

peckish ['pekɪʃ] ADJ *Fam* **to be** *or* **feel p.** avoir un creux

pecs [peks] NPL *Fam (pectorals)* pectoraux *mpl*

pectin ['pektɪn] N *Chem* pectine *f*

pectoral ['pektər(ə)l] ADJ *Anat, Med etc* pectoral, -aux
▸ N **1** *Rel, Hist* pectoral *m* **2** *Anat (muscle m)* pectoral *m*
▸▸ **p. cross** *(of bishop)* croix *f* pectorale; **p. fin** *(of fish)* nageoire *f* pectorale

peculate ['pekjʊleɪt] VI détourner des fonds
▸ VT *(funds)* détourner

peculation [pekjʊ'leɪʃən] N malversation *f*

peculiar [pɪ'kju:lɪər] ADJ **1** *(strange)* bizarre, curieux; *(eccentric)* original, -aux; **well, that's p.** tiens, c'est bizarre *ou* curieux!, voilà qui est singulier!; **he/she is a little p.** il/elle est un peu bizarre **2** *(characteristic)* particulier; **her singing style is p. to her** son style de chant lui est particulier; **this species is p. to Scandinavia** cette espèce n'existe qu'en Scandinavie **3** *(special)* spécial, -aux, particulier; **of p. interest** d'un intérêt tout particulier

peculiarity [pɪkju:lɪ'ærɪtɪ] N **1** *(strangeness)* bizarrerie *f*, singularité *f*; *(eccentricity)* originalité *f*; **one of her little peculiarities** une de ses petites manies **2** *(distinctive feature)* particularité *f*

peculiarly [pɪ'kju:lɪəlɪ] ADV **1** *(strangely)* singulièrement **2** *(specially)* particulièrement

pecuniary [pɪ'kju:nɪərɪ] ADJ *Fml* pécuniaire; **p. difficulties** embarras *mpl* pécuniaires *ou* financiers, ennuis *mpl* d'argent

pedagogic(al) [pedə'gɒdʒɪk, -ɪk(ə)l] ADJ pédagogique

pedagogue ['pedəgɒg] N pédagogue *m*, *Pej* pédant, -ante

pedagogy ['pedəgɒdʒɪ] N pédagogie *f*

pedal ['ped(ə)l] N *(of bicycle, car, machine, musical instrument etc)* pédale *f*; *Mus (note)* (note *f* de) pédale; **soft p.** *(of piano)* pédale douce, sourdine *f*; **loud p.** *(of piano)* pédale forte
▸ ADJ *Anat (relating to foot)* pédieux
▸ VI *(-ll-, Am -l-)* **1** *Cycling etc* pédaler; **she had pedalled around France when she was a teenager** adolescente, elle avait parcouru la France à vélo; **he pedalled off** il est parti (à vélo) **2** *Mus (in playing organ)* jouer sur le pédalier; *(in playing piano)* mettre la pédale
▸ VT *(bicycle)* appuyer sur les pédales de; **to p. a bicycle around Europe** parcourir l'Europe à vélo *ou* à bicyclette; **he pedalled his bike up the hill** il a pédalé jusqu'en haut de la côte sur son vélo
▸▸ *Br* **p. bin** poubelle *f* à pédale; **p. boat** pédalo® *m*; **p. car** voiture *f* à pédales; **p. keyboard** *(of organ)* pédalier *m*; *Mus* **p. note**

(note de) pédale; *Aut* **p. pressure** pression *f* sur la pédale; **p. pushers** (pantalon *m*) corsaire *m*

pedalo, *pl* **pedalos, pedaloes** ['pedələʊ, -əʊz] **N** pédalo® *m*

pedal-operated [-ɒpəreɪtɪd] **ADJ** *Tech etc* commandé par pédale(s)

pedant ['pedənt] **N** *Pej* pédant, -ante; **don't be such a p.!** ne sois pas aussi pédant!

pedantic [pɪ'dæntɪk] **ADJ** pédant

pedantically [pɪ'dæntɪklɪ] **ADV** avec pédantisme; *(to say)* d'un ton pédant

pedantry ['pedəntrɪ] **N** pédantisme *m*, pédanterie *f*

peddle ['ped(ə)l] **VI** faire du colportage; *(with drugs)* faire du trafic de drogues ▪ **VT** *(goods)*, *Fig* ideas, theories) colporter; **to p. drugs** faire du trafic de drogues

peddler ['pedlər] **N 1 (drug) p.** trafiquant, -ante de drogues **2** *Am* = pedlar

pederast ['pedəræst, 'piː-] **N** pédéraste *m*

pederasty ['pedəræstɪ, 'piː-] **N** pédérastie *f*

pedestal ['pedɪst(ə)l] **N** *Archit, Art etc* piédestal *m*, socle *m*; *Fig* **to put sb on a p.** mettre qn sur un piédestal
▸▸**p. table** guéridon *m*; **p. washbasin** lavabo-colonne *m*, *pl* lavabos-colonnes

pedestrian [pɪ'destrɪən] **ADJ** *(on foot)* pédestre; *Fig (style etc)* prosaïque, terre à terre *inv*; *(pace, rhythm)* lourd ▪ **N** piéton, -onne
▸▸*Br* **p. crossing** passage *m* clouté *ou* piétons; **p. precinct** zone *f* piétonnière

pedestrian-controlled crossing N passage *m* piéton à bouton d'appel

pedestrianization [pɪdestrɪənaɪ'zeɪʃən] **N** *(of area)* aménagement *m* en zone piétonnière; **in favour of p.** en faveur de l'aménagement de zones piétonnières

pedestrianize [pɪ'destrɪənaɪz] **VT** *(road)* aménager en zone piétonnière

pediatric, pediatrician *etc Am* = **paediatric, paediatrician** *etc*

pedicure ['pedɪkjʊər] **N 1** *(activity)* soins *mpl* des pieds, *Spec* pédicurie *f*; **to have a p.** se faire soigner les pieds, aller chez le/la pédicure **2** *(person)* pédicure *mf* ▪ **VT** *(feet)* soigner

pedigree ['pedɪgriː] **N 1** *(of dog etc)* pedigree *m*; **to have a p.** *(of dog)* être un chien de race, avoir un pedigree **2** *(background)* passé *m*, antécédents *mpl*; **she had an impeccable political p.** ses antécédents politiques étaient irréprochables **3** *(person's ancestry)* ascendance *f*, généalogie *f* **4** *(genealogical table)* arbre *m* généalogique ▪ **ADJ** *(dog etc)* de (pure) race; *(person)* de bonne lignée

pediment ['pedɪmənt] **N** *Archit* fronton *m*

pedlar ['pedlər] **N** colporteur *m*, marchand *m* ambulant

pedology **N** *Am* = **paedology**

pedometer [pɪ'dɒmɪtər] **N** podomètre *m*

pedophile, pedophilia *Am* = **paedophile, paedophilia**

pee [piː] **N** *Fam* pipi *m*; **to go and have a p.** aller faire pipi; **he was desperate for a p.** il avait énormément envie de faire pipi; **cat's p.** pipi de chat ▪ **VI** *Fam* faire pipi; **it's peeing down** *(raining)* il pleut comme vache qui pisse
▸ **pee off VT SEP** *Sl (annoy)* **to p. sb off** faire chier qn; **to be peed off** être fumasse *ou* furibard; **to be peed off at sb/about sth** être en pétard contre qn/à cause de qch; **to be peed off with sb/sth** *(have had enough of)* en avoir ras le bol de qn/qch

peek [piːk] **N** regard *m* furtif, coup *m* d'œil (furtif); **to take** *or* **have a p. (at sth/sb)** jeter

un coup d'œil (furtif) (à *ou* sur qch/qn) ▪ **VI** jeter un regard *ou* un coup d'œil furtif (**at** sur), risquer un coup d'œil; **no peeking!** on ne regarde pas!

peekaboo ['piːkəbuː] **INT** coucou! ▪ **ADJ** *Am (blouse etc) (see-through)* transparent; *(with holes)* avec *ou* en broderie(s) ajourée(s)

peel [piːl] **N** *(of apple etc)* pelure *f*, épluchure *f*, *(of potato etc)* épluchure; *(of orange, lemon)* écorce *f*, *Culin* zeste *m* ▪ **VT** *(fruit)* peler, éplucher; *(potatoes etc)* éplucher; *(oak, almonds)* décortiquer; **to p. the bark/skin** enlever l'écorce/la peau; **to keep one's eyes peeled** ouvrir l'œil; **we were all keeping our eyes peeled for a pub** nous guettions tous un pub, nous étions tous à l'affût d'un pub ▪ **VI** *(of paint etc)* s'écailler; *(of nose, back etc)* peler; *Med* se desquamer; *(of bark)* se détacher; *(of wall)* se décrépir; **you're peeling** tu pèles; **the skin on his back was starting to p.** son dos commençait à peler
▸ **peel off VT SEP** *(rind, skin, shirt, vest)* enlever; **to p. off one's clothes** se déshabiller ▪ **VI 1** *(become detached) (of paint, nail varnish etc)* s'écailler; *(of skin)* se détacher; *Med* se desquamer; *Aviat* se détacher de la formation; **the skin on my nose is peeling off** mon nez pèle **2** *Fam (undress)* se déshabiller

peeler ['piːlər] **N 1** *Culin (device)* éplucheur *m*; **potato p.** économe *m* **2** *Br Arch (policeman)* agent *m* de police

peeling ['piːlɪŋ] **N 1** *Med (of skin)* desquamation *f* **2 peelings** *(of potato etc)* épluchures *fpl* ▪ **ADJ** *(nose, back etc)* qui pèle/pelait

peep[1] [piːp] **N 1** *(furtive glance)* coup *m* d'œil furtif; **to have** *or* **take a p. at sth** jeter un regard furtif sur qch; **to get a p. at sth** entrevoir qch **2** *(of light)* rayon *m* ▪ **VI** *(glance furtively)* jeter un coup d'œil; **to p. at sb/sth** regarder qn/qch à la dérobée, jeter un coup d'œil furtif sur qn/qch; **to p. through the door** jeter un coup d'œil (furtif) par la porte; **I saw you peeping through the keyhole** je vous ai vu regarder par le trou de la serrure; **someone was peeping at her from behind the curtains** quelqu'un l'observait, caché derrière les rideaux; **no peeping!** on ne regarde pas!; **a Peeping Tom** un voyeur
▸ **peep out VI** *(be visible)* se laisser entrevoir, se montrer; *(of flower)* percer, pointer; **his feet were peeping out from beneath the curtains** ses pieds dépassaient de derrière les rideaux; **her big toe was peeping out through a hole in her sock** son gros doigt de pied pointait par un trou de sa chaussette

peep[2] **N** *(sound) (of bird)* pépiement *m*, piaulement *m*; *(of mouse)* cri *m*; *Fam* **if I hear so much as a p. out of you** si tu fais le moindre bruit; *Fam* **we haven't heard a p. from him for months** ça fait des mois qu'il n'a pas donné le moindre signe de vie ▪ **VI** *(of bird)* pépier, piauler; *(of mouse)* crier

peep-bo [-bəʊ] **INT** coucou! ▪ **N** **to play (at) p.** jouer à cache-cache *(avec un enfant)*

peepers ['piːpəz] **N** *Sl (eyes)* mirettes *fpl*

peephole ['piːphəʊl] **N 1** *(in door)* judas *m* **2** *Tech etc (trou m de)* regard *m*

peepshow ['piːpʃəʊ] **N** *(pictures)* vues *fpl* stéréoscopiques; *(erotic, with live model)* peepshow *m*

peer[1] [pɪər] **N 1** *(equal)* pair *m*; **you will not find his p.** vous ne trouverez pas son pareil; **he is without p.** il n'a pas son pareil; **she does not have many peers** peu l'égalent; *Law* **a jury of one's peers** un jury de ses pairs **2** *(noble)* pair *m*; *Br* **p. of the realm** pair du Royaume-Uni; *Br* **life p.** pair à vie

▸▸ **p. group** pairs; **p. pressure** influence *f* des pairs *ou* du groupe

peer[2] **VI** **to p. at sb/sth** scruter qn/qch du regard; **he peered at the writing** il fixa son regard sur ce qui était écrit; **he peered (out) into the night** il cherchait à percer l'obscurité; **to p. round the corner** risquer un coup d'œil au coin de la rue; **he was peering through the curtains** il guettait entre les rideaux; **he was peering into the bottom of his glass** il scrutait le fond de son verre; **several pairs of eyes were peering at her** plusieurs paires d'yeux étaient braquées sur elle

peerage ['pɪərɪdʒ] **N 1** *(noble title, rank)* pairie *f*, life *f*, pairie à vie; **to confer a p. on sb, to raise sb to the p.** élever qn à la pairie **2** *(no pl)* **the p.** *(peers)* les pairs *mpl* **3** *(book)* (almanach *m*) nobiliaire *m*

peeress ['pɪərɪs] **N** pairesse *f*

peerless ['pɪəlɪs] **ADJ** *Lit* sans pareil, sans égal, hors pair

peer-to-peer **ADJ** peer-to-peer

peeve [piːv] **VT** *Fam* mettre en boule, irriter; **to be peeved** être fâché *ou* irrité; **to be peeved at sb for not doing sth** être fâché contre qn parce qu'il n'a pas fait qch; **I was peeved at his behaviour/the decision** son comportement/cette décision m'a mis en boule *ou* m'a irrité

peevish ['piːvɪʃ] **ADJ** maussade, irritable; *(response)* maussade; *(child)* grognon

peevishly ['piːvɪʃlɪ] **ADV** *(to say)* avec mauvaise humeur, d'un ton irrité; *(to respond)* d'un air maussade

peevishness ['piːvɪʃnɪs] **N** *(of person)* maussaderie *f*, mauvaise humeur *f*, *(of response, behaviour)* maussaderie

peewit ['piːwɪt] **N** *(bird)* vanneau *m* (huppé)

peg [peg] **N 1** *(pin, bolt) (wooden)* cheville *f*, *(metal)* fiche *f*, *(of barrel)* fausset *m*, fosset *m*; *Tech* clavette *f*, goupille *f*, *(for tent)* piquet *m*; *Mus (on violin)* cheville; *Br (clothes)* **p.** pince *f* à linge; **(hat** *or* **coat) p.** patère *f*, *esp Br Com* **a suit off the p.** un costume de confection; **off the p. clothing** prêt-à-porter *m*, *pl* prêts-à-porter; *Fig* **to take sb down a p. (or two)** remettre qn à sa place; **that's a p. to hang a grievance on** ce n'est pas qu'un prétexte pour se plaindre; **we can use this as a p. to hang our story on** nous pouvons centrer notre article là-dessus **2** *Br (of whisky etc)* doigt *m*
▪ **VT** *(-gg-)* **1** *(structure, joint)* cheviller; **to p. sth in place** cheviller qch; **to p. clothes on the line** accrocher du linge sur la corde *(avec des pinces à linge)* **2** *St Exch, Fin (prices) (fix)* fixer; *(stabilize)* stabiliser; **to p. sth to the rate of inflation** indexer qch sur le taux de l'inflation; **oil was pegged at $20 a barrel** le prix du pétrole était fixé à 20 dollars le baril; **export earnings are pegged to the exchange rate** le revenu des exportations varie en fonction du taux de change
▸▸*Fam* **p. leg** *(wooden leg)* jambe *f* de bois, pilon *m*; *(artificial leg)* jambe artificielle; *(person)* = personne *f* qui a une jambe de bois ou une jambe artificielle
▸ **peg away VI** *Fam (work hard)* bosser (**at** sth à qch); **to p. away at one's algebra** piocher *ou* bûcher son algèbre
▸ **peg down VT SEP** *(fix) (net etc)* fixer avec des piquets; *Fig* **to p. sb down to a price** obliger qn à s'engager sur un prix
▸ **peg out VT SEP 1** *(mark with pegs) (plot of land)* piqueter, jalonner, borner; *(line)* jalonner **2** *(hang)* **to p. out clothes on the line** accrocher du linge sur la corde *(avec des pinces à linge)*
▪ **VI 1** *Sl (die)* casser sa pipe **2** *(in croquet)* toucher le piquet final (et se retirer de la partie)

pegboard ['pegbɔːd] N **1** *(for hanging things)* panneau *m* alvéolé **2** *(for game)* table *f* à trous

pegging ['pegɪŋ] N **1** *St Exch, Fin (of prices etc) (fixing)* fixation *f*; *(stabilizing)* stabilisation *f*; *(to rate of inflation etc)* indexation *f* **2** *Br Sport, Fig* **it's level p.** ils sont à égalité

PEI [piːiːˈaɪ] N *Geog (abbr* **Prince Edward Island)** IPE *f*

pejorative [pɪˈdʒɒrətɪv] ADJ péjoratif N *(mot m)* péjoratif *m*

pejoratively [pɪˈdʒɒrətɪvlɪ] ADV péjorativement

peke [piːk] N *Fam (chien m)* pékinois *m*

Pekinese [piːkɪˈniːz] ADJ pékinois N **1** *(person)* Pékinois, -oise **2** *(dog)* (chien *m)* pékinois *m*

Peking [piːˈkɪŋ] N Pékin

Pekingese [piːkɪŋˈiːz] ADJ, N = **Pekinese**

pelagic [pɪˈlædʒɪk] ADJ pélagique

pelargonium [peləˈgəʊnɪəm] N *(plant)* pélargonium *m*

pelican ['pelɪkən] N *(bird)* pélican *m*
▸▸ *Br* **p. crossing** = passage *m* piétons à commande manuelle

pellagra [peˈlægrə, -ˈleɪ-] N *Med* pellagre *f*

pellet ['pelɪt] N *(of paper, bread, clay etc)* boulette *f*; *(of dung)* bille *f*; *(in shotgun cartridge)* grain *m* de plomb; *Pharm* pilule *f*, grain; *Orn (regurgitated food of owl etc)* boulette (d'aliments regurgités), bol *m* alimentaire; *Metal, Chem* boulette

pell-mell ['pel'mel] ADV pêle-mêle; *(to run)* à la débandade

pellucid [peˈluːsɪd] ADJ *Lit* pellucide, transparent; *Fig (mind etc)* lucide; *(style)* clair, limpide

pelmet ['pelmɪt] N lambrequin *m*

Peloponnese (the) [ðəpeləpəˈniːs] N le Péloponnèse

Peloponnesian [peləpəˈniːsɪən] ADJ péloponnésien, du Péloponnèse

pelota [pəˈlɒtə] N *(game)* pelote *f* basque

pelt¹ [pelt] N **1** *(skin) (of sheep, goat)* peau *f*, fourrure *f* **2** *(in tanning) (with hair on)* peau *f* verte; *(without hair)* peau in tripe

pelt² VT **to p. sb with stones/snowballs** bombarder qn de pierres/boules de neige; **he pelted abuse at them** il les a criblés d'injures; **to p. sb with criticism** mitrailler *ou* accabler qn de critiques
VI **1** *(of rain etc)* tomber à verse; **it was pelting with rain** la pluie tombait à verse, il pleuvait à verse; **pelting rain** pluie *f* battante **2** *(go fast)* aller à toute vitesse *ou* à toute allure, *Fam* foncer; **he came pelting round the corner** il a débouché du coin à toute allure; **the kids pelted off down the street** les gosses ont descendu la rue à toute allure *ou* ventre à terre; **he pelted upstairs** il est monté comme une flèche *ou* ventre à terre; **she's really pelting through her work** elle abat son travail à toute allure; **he pelted through the exam** il a passé l'examen à toute allure *ou* à toute vitesse
N **(at) full p.** *(to run, flee)* à toute vitesse, ventre à terre
▸ **pelt down** VI *(of rain etc)* tomber à verse; **the rain** *or* **it was pelting down** la pluie tombait à verse, il pleuvait à verse

pelvic ['pelvɪk] ADJ *Anat* pelvien
▸▸ **p. bone** ilion *m*; **p. fins** *(of fish)* pelviennes *fpl*; **p. floor** plancher *m* pelvien; **p. girdle** ceinture *f* pelvienne; **p. inflammatory disease** syndrome *m* inflammatoire pelvien

pelvis ['pelvɪs] N *Anat* **1** bassin *m*, pelvis *m* **2** *(of kidney)* bassinet *m*

pen¹ [pen] N stylo *m*; **fountain p.** stylo à plume, stylo-plume *m*, *pl* stylos-plumes;

ball(point) p. stylo à bille, stylo-bille *m*, *pl* stylos-billes; **felt(-tip) p.** *(crayon m ou* stylo) feutre *m*; **drawing** *or* **mapping p.** plume *f* à dessin; **stroke of the p.** trait *m* de plume; **to put p. to paper** prendre la plume; **to live by one's p.** vivre de sa plume; *Prov* **the p. is mightier than the sword** la plume blesse souvent plus que l'épée
VT (-nn-) *(letter, article etc)* écrire, rédiger
▸▸ **p. drawing** dessin *m* à la plume *ou* à l'encre; *Br* **p. friend** correspondant, -ante *(épistolaire)*; **p.-and-ink drawing** dessin à la plume *ou* à l'encre; **p. name** nom *m* de plume, pseudonyme *m*; *Fam* **p. pal** correspondant *(épistolaire)*; *Comput* **p. plotter** traceur *m* à plumes

pen² N **1** *(for sheep etc)* parc *m*, enclos *m*; *(for bulls)* toril *m*; *(for pigs)* porcherie *f* **2** *Naut (for submarine)* abri *m* **3** *Am Sl (penitentiary)* tôle *f*, taule *f*, trou *m*; **in the p.** en tôle *ou* taule, au trou; **he spent ten years in the p.** il a fait dix ans de tôle *ou* taule
VT (-nn-, *Lit* pent) *(sheep etc)* parquer
▸ **pen in, pen up** VT SEP *(sheep etc)* parquer; **we were penned up in the room for weeks** nous sommes restés parqués dans la pièce pendant des semaines; **we spent the week penned up in a caravan** nous avons passé toute la semaine enfermés dans une caravane

pen³ N *(female swan)* cygne *m* femelle

penal ['piːn(ə)l] ADJ *Law (laws, code)* pénal, -aux; *(offence)* qui comporte *ou* entraîne une pénalité
▸▸ **p. colony** colonie *f* pénitentiaire; *Fin* **p. rate** taux *m* d'usure; **p. servitude** travaux *mpl* forcés, bagne *m*; **p. settlement** colonie pénitentiaire

penalization [piːnəlaɪˈzeɪʃən] N infliction *f* d'une peine (**of sb** à qn); *Sport* pénalisation *f*

penalize ['piːnəlaɪz] VT **1** *(impose a penalty on) (person)* sanctionner; *Sport (competitor, player)* pénaliser **2** *(attach a penalty to) (crime)* attacher une peine à **3** *(disadvantage)* désavantager, pénaliser; **to p. sb for doing sth** désavantager *ou* pénaliser qn parce qu'il a fait qch; **this penalizes those living in the country** ceci défavorise *ou* désavantage les gens qui habitent à la campagne

penalty ['penəltɪ] N **1** *(punishment)* peine *f*, pénalité *f*, *Com (for late delivery etc)* amende *f*, *Admin* sanction *f* (pénale); **to impose penalties** prendre des sanctions; **on** *or* **upon** *or* **under p. of death** sous peine de mort; **the p. for this is death/excommunication** la peine encourue pour ce crime est la mort/l'excommunication; **to pay the p. of one's foolishness** subir les conséquences *ou* être puni de sa sottise; **one of the penalties of fame/wealth** un des désavantages dont la gloire/la richesse s'accompagne; **to pay the p. of fame** payer la rançon de la gloire **2** *Sport* pénalisation *f*, pénalité *f*, *(kick) (in football)* penalty *m*, *pl* penalties; *(in rugby)* pénalité
▸▸ *Ftbl* **p. area** surface *f* de réparation; **p. box** *Ftbl* surface de réparation; *(in ice hockey)* banc *m* de pénalité; *Law* **p. clause** clause *f* pénale; *Fin* **p. interest** pénalité de retard, intérêts *mpl* moratoires; **p. kick** *(in football)* penalty; *(in rugby)* (coup *m* de pied de) pénalité; *Ftbl* **p. shootout** épreuve *f* des penalties; *Ftbl* **p. spot** point *m* de réparation; *Golf* **p. stroke** coup *m* d'amende; *Sport* **p. throw** penalty

penance ['penəns] N *Rel* pénitence *f*; **to do p.** faire pénitence (**for** de, pour); **to do sth as a p.** faire qch par pénitence

pence [pens] *see* **penny**

pencil ['pens(ə)l] N **1** crayon *m*; **to mark/**

write sth in p. *or* **with a p.** marquer/écrire qch au crayon; **drawing in p.** *(dessin m au)* crayon, crayonnage *m* **2** *Geom (of curves etc)* faisceau *m*; *Opt* **p. of light rays** faisceau de lumière
VT (-ll-, *Am* -l-) *(mark with a pencil)* marquer au crayon; *(draw, sketch in pencil)* dessiner/esquisser au crayon, crayonner; *(write) (note)* écrire au crayon, crayonner; **to p. one's eyebrows** se faire les sourcils (au crayon); **pencilled eyebrows** sourcils *mpl* dessinés au crayon
▸▸ **p. case** trousse *f*; **p. drawing** *(dessin au)* crayon, crayonnage; **p. lead** mine *f* de crayon; **p. mark** trait *m ou* marque *f* de *ou* au crayon; **p. sharpener** taille-crayon *m*, *pl* taille-crayon(s); **p. sketch** croquis *m* au crayon
▸ **pencil in** VT SEP *(write)* écrire au crayon; **the date has been pencilled in** on a fixé provisoirement la date; **p. me in for Friday** inscrivez-moi provisoirement pour vendredi; *Fig* en principe, vous pouvez compter sur moi vendredi

pendant ['pendənt] N **1** *(necklace)* pendentif *m* **2** *(ornamental piece) (of necklace)* pendentif *m*; *(on bracelet)* breloque *f*; *(of chandelier)* pendeloque *f*

pending ['pendɪŋ] ADJ *(trial)* pendant, en instance; *(negotiations)* en cours; *Admin, Com (documents)* en souffrance, en attente
PREP en attendant
▸▸ *Br* **p. tray** corbeille *f* des dossiers en attente

pendulous ['pendjʊləs] ADJ *(breasts, lip, ear etc)* pendant

pendulum ['pendjʊləm] N *Phys* pendule *m*; *(in clockmaking)* balancier *m*, pendule
▸▸ **p. ball, p. bob** lentille *f* de pendule *ou* de balancier; **p. clock** horloge *f* à pendule *ou* à balancier

penetrable ['penɪtrəb(ə)l] ADJ **1** *(material, defences)* pénétrable; **easily p.** facile à pénétrer **2** *(prose etc)* **barely p.** difficilement compréhensible

penetrate ['penɪtreɪt] VT pénétrer; **darkness that the eye could not p.** ténèbres que l'œil ne pouvait percer; **to p. sb's mind** voir clair dans l'esprit de qn
VI pénétrer; *(of ideas, beliefs)* s'implanter; **the water is penetrating everywhere** l'eau pénètre *ou* s'introduit partout; **to p. through sth** passer à travers qch; **to p. into a forest** pénétrer dans une forêt; **the custom has not penetrated to this part of the country** cette coutume n'est pas parvenue jusqu'à cette partie du pays; **it hasn't penetrated** *(hasn't been understood)* ça n'a pas fait le tour, ça n'est pas rentré

penetrating ['penɪtreɪtɪŋ] ADJ *(wind, cold)* pénétrant; *(sound, voice, scream)* perçant; *(bullet, shell)* perforant; *(mind, analysis)* pénétrant; **to have a p. eye** avoir des yeux perçants; **a p. stare** un regard pénétrant *ou* perçant
▸▸ **p. oil** dégrippant *m*

penetration [penɪˈtreɪʃən] N pénétration *f*
▸▸ *Mktg* **p. price** prix *m* de pénétration

penetrative ['penɪtrətɪv] ADJ *(sex)* avec pénétration; *(questioning)* approfondi

penguin ['peŋgwɪn] N manchot *m*, gorfou *m*, *Fam* pingouin *m*
▸▸ *Br Fam Hum* **p. suit** costard *m* chic

penholder ['penhəʊldər] N porte-plume *m inv*

penicillin [penɪˈsɪlɪn] N pénicilline *f*

peninsula [pɪˈnɪnsjʊlə] N péninsule *f*, presqu'île *f*

peninsular [pɪˈnɪnsjʊlər] ADJ péninsulaire

penis, *pl* **penes** ['piːnɪs, -niːz] N *Anat* pénis *m*, verge *f*
▸▸ *Psy* **p. envy** envie *f* du pénis

penitence ['penɪtəns] N pénitence f, repentir m; **to perform p.** faire pénitence; **to show (one's) p. for one's actions** se repentir ou faire pénitence de ses actions; **to be without p.** ne pas se repentir

penitent ['penɪtənt] ADJ pénitent, repentant; **to be** or **feel p.** se repentir, faire pénitence
N pénitent, -ente

penitential [penɪ'tenʃəl] ADJ pénitentiel
N (book) pénitentiel m

penitentiary [penɪ'tenʃərɪ] N **1** Am (prison) pénitencier m **2** Cathol (person) pénitencier m; (tribunal) pénitencerie f
ADJ Am (crime) puni de réclusion dans un pénitencier ou une centrale

penitently ['penɪtəntlɪ] ADV d'un air contrit; (to say etc) d'un ton contrit; (to act, behave) avec contrition

penknife ['pennaɪf] N canif m

penmanship ['penmənʃɪp] N (calligraphy) calligraphie f

Penn(a) abbr Pennsylvania

pennant ['penənt] N flamme f, banderole f; Naut flamme, guidon m

penniless ['penɪlɪs] ADJ sans le sou; **to be p.** être sans le sou, ne pas avoir le sou; **to leave sb p.** laisser qn sans le sou

Pennines (the) [ðə'penaɪnz] NPL la chaîne Pennine, les Pennines fpl

pennon ['penən] N flamme f, banderole f

Pennsylvania [pensɪl'veɪnɪə] N Pennsylvanie f

penny ['penɪ] N VOIR GRAMMAIRE A13 **1** Br (coin) (pl usu **pennies**) penny m, pl pennies; **they haven't a p. (to their name** or Old-fashioned **to bless themselves with)** ils sont sans le sou ou sans un sou vaillant; **pennies from heaven** une aubaine; Prov **take care of the pennies and the pounds will take care of themselves** les petits ruisseaux font les grandes rivières; **to count every p.** compter ses sous; **it was worth every p.** je n'ai/nous n'avons/etc pas regretté le prix que je l'ai/nous l'avons/etc payé; **you'd better start saving (up) your pennies** tu ferais mieux de commencer à mettre de l'argent de côté; **not a p. more** pas un sou de plus; Fam **the p.'s dropped** (I understand now) j'y suis, ça y est; (I've understood) il y est, ça y est
2 Br (value) (pl **pence** [pens]) penny m, pl pence; **I paid 60 pence for it** je l'ai payé 60 pence; **a ten/fifty pence piece** une pièce de dix/cinquante pence; **to buy ten pence worth of sweets** acheter pour dix pence de bonbons; **(new) p.** = nouveau penny; **(old) p.** (before 1971) = ancien penny; Fig **they're two** or **ten a p. nowadays** c'est monnaie courante à l'heure actuelle; **a p. for your thoughts** or **for them** à quoi rêvez-vous ou pensez-vous?; Prov **in for a p. in for a pound** quand le vin est tiré il faut le boire; esp Br Fam **a bad p.** (rogue, worthless person) bon m à rien, bonne f à rien; **it didn't cost them a p.** ça ne leur a pas coûté un centime; **that'll cost a p. or two** cela va coûter de l'argent; **to earn** or **turn an honest p.** gagner honnêtement sa vie
3 Am, Can (cent) cent m
▸▸ Philat **p. black** = premier timbre-poste m britannique; **p. farthing** (bicycle) vélocipède m; Br St Exch **p. shares** actions fpl d'une valeur de moins d'une livre sterling; Fin, St Exch **p. stock** = actions d'une valeur de moins d'un dollar; **p. whistle** pipeau m

penny-dreadful N Old-fashioned Fam roman m à deux sous ou à sensation

penny-in-the-slot ADJ Old-fashioned (machine) à sous

penny-pincher [-pɪntʃər] N pingre mf, radin, -ine

penny-pinching [-pɪntʃɪŋ] ADJ (person) radin, pingre, qui fait des économies de bouts de chandelle; (action, step) mesquin; (lifestyle, measures) de lésine, d'économie de bouts de chandelle
N pingrerie f (with, on sur)

penny-wise ADJ Prov **to be p. and pound-foolish** chipoter sur les petites dépenses sans regarder aux grandes

pennyworth ['penɪwɜ:θ] N **to buy a p. of sweets** acheter pour un penny de bonbons; Fig **not a p.** rien du tout

penology [pi:'nɒlədʒɪ] N pénologie f

penpusher ['penpʊʃər] N Fam Pej gratte-papier m inv, scribouillard, -arde

penpushing ['penpʊʃɪŋ] Fam Pej ADJ (job etc) de gratte-papier
N paperasse f, paperasserie f

pension N **1** ['penʃən] (payment) retraite f, pension f, **government** or Br **state p.** pension sur l'État; **to be on a p.** (of elderly person) vivre de sa retraite ou d'une pension; **to retire on a p.** prendre sa retraite; **(retirement** or **old age) p.** (pension de) retraite **2** ['pɒnsɪɒn] (hotel) pension f de famille; **en p.** (at hotel) en pension
▸▸ Br **p. book** ≃ titre m de pension (carnet permettant de retirer sa pension de retraite); **p. contribution** cotisation f vieillesse; **p. fund** caisse f de retraite, fonds m de pension; **p. plan** plan m de retraite; **p. scheme** caisse de retraite
▸ **pension off** VT SEP mettre à la retraite; Fam (something) mettre au rebut

pensionable ['penʃənəb(ə)l] ADJ (person) qui a droit à une pension ou à sa retraite; (injury, job etc) qui donne droit à une pension
▸▸ **p. age** âge m de la mise à la retraite

pensioner ['penʃənər] N pensionné, -ée; **(old-age) p.** retraité, -ée

Note that the French term **pensionnaire** is never a translation for the English word **pensioner**.

pensive ['pensɪv] ADJ pensif; (music, silence) méditatif

pensively ['pensɪvlɪ] ADV pensivement, d'un air pensif

pent [pent] PT, PP see pen² VT

pentagon ['pentəgən] N Geom pentagone m; Am Mil **the P.** le Pentagone

pentagonal [pen'tægən(ə)l] ADJ pentagonal, -aux

pentameter [pen'tæmɪtər] N (in poetry) pentamètre m

Pentateuch (the) [ðə'pentətju:k] N Bible le Pentateuque

pentathlete [pen'tæθli:t] N Sport pentathlonien, -ienne

pentathlon [pen'tæθlən] N Sport pentathlon m

Pentecost ['pentɪkɒst] N Rel Pentecôte f

pentecostal [pentɪ'kɒst(ə)l] ADJ Rel de la Pentecôte; **the P. Church** l'église pentecôtiste

penthouse ['penthaʊs] N **1** (apartment) = appartement m de standing au dernier étage d'un immeuble **2** (shed) appentis m
▸▸ **p. suite** (in hotel) suite f avec terrasse

Pentium® ['pentɪəm] N Comput Pentium® m

pent-up ADJ (emotion, frustation, desire) refoulé; (energy, rage) contenu

penultimate [pe'nʌltɪmɪt] ADJ pénultième, avant-dernier

penumbra [pe'nʌmbrə] N pénombre f

penurious [pe'njʊərɪəs] ADJ Fml (poor) indigent; **reduced to a p. condition** réduit à l'indigence

penury ['penjʊrɪ] N **1** (poverty) indigence f **2** (dearth) manque m (**of** de)

peony ['pi:ənɪ] N (plant) pivoine f

PEOPLE ['pi:p(ə)l]

| N gens **1** ▪ personnes **1** ▪ peuple **2–4** ▪ nation **2** |
| VT peupler |

N VOIR GRAMMAIRE A11 (with pl verb) **1** gens mpl; **there were five p. in the room** il y avait cinq personnes dans la pièce; **young p.** les jeunes gens; **old p.** les personnes fpl âgées, Fam les vieux mpl; **old p.'s home** maison f de retraite pour personnes âgées; **there were not many p.** il n'y avait pas beaucoup de gens ou de monde; **most p.** la plupart des gens; **rich p.** les (gens) riches; **homeless p.** les sans-abris mpl; **blind/deaf p.** les aveugles mpl/les sourds mpl; **stop annoying p.** arrête d'embêter le monde; **he's one of those p. who …** il est de ceux qui …, c'est un homme qui …; **you of all p. should know better!** tu devrais bien être le dernier/la dernière à faire pareille erreur!; **I met Janet of all p. at the theatre** Janet était bien la dernière personne que je m'attendais à rencontrer au théâtre; **it's a question of knowing the right p.** il faut avoir des relations; **we're having p. to dinner tonight** nous avons des invités ou du monde à dîner ce soir; **p. don't like being told they're wrong** les gens n'aiment pas qu'on leur dise qu'ils ont tort; **p. say that …** on dit que …; **she's a p. person** elle est très sociable
2 (nation) peuple m, nation f; **the French p.** les Français mpl; **the Sikhs/Russians are a proud p.** les Sikhs/les Russes sont un peuple fier; **English-speaking peoples** peuples ou nations de langue anglaise
3 (citizens) peuple m, citoyens mpl (d'un État); **the common p.** le peuple, Pej la populace; **a man of the p.** un homme sorti du peuple; **a king and his p.** un roi et ses sujets ou son peuple; **to go to the p.** (call an election) en appeler au peuple
4 (population) peuple m, habitants mpl; **the p. of Paris** les habitants de Paris; **town p.** gens mpl de la ville, citadins mpl; **country p.** gens de la campagne, campagnards mpl
5 (employees) employés, -ées; (workers) ouvriers, -ières; **I'll get one of my p. to do it** un de mes employés/ouvriers le fera; **our p. in Moscow** (representatives) nos représentants à Moscou; (compatriots) nos compatriotes installés à Moscou; **the p. in accounts** les gens de la comptabilité
6 Old-fashioned Fam (family) famille f; **how are your p.?** comment va votre famille?
VT peupler (**with** de); **a country peopled by many different races** un pays multiracial
▸▸ **p. carrier** (car) monospace m; **p. meter** (for viewing figures) audimètre m; **p. mover** (car) monospace; **p. power** pouvoir m populaire; **p.'s republic** république f populaire

PEP [pep] N Formerly (abbr personal equity plan) PEA m

pep [pep] N Fam entrain m, allant m, fougue f; **full of p.** plein d'entrain ou d'allant
▸▸ **p. pill** stimulant m, excitant m; **p. talk** discours m d'encouragement
▸ **pep up** VT SEP (-pp-) Fam (person) ragaillardir, revigorer; (dish, punch etc) relever; (presentation, style) égayer; (plant) revigorer; **to pep up a business** dynamiser une entreprise

pepper ['pepər] N **1** (spice) poivre m; (plant) poivrier m; **black/white p.** poivre noir ou gris/blanc **2** (vegetable) **(sweet) p.** piment m doux, poivron m; **green/red/yellow p.** poivron vert/rouge/jaune
VT **1** (meat etc) poivrer **2** Fig **to p. with bullets** cribler de balles; **peppered with swear-**

words pimentée de jurons; **peppered with spelling mistakes** parsemé de fautes d'orthographe

▸▸**p. mill** moulin *m* à poivre; **p. plant** poivrier; **p. pot** poivrier, poivrière *f*; *Br Culin* **p. steak** steak *m* au poivre

pepper-and-salt ADJ *(hair)* poivre et sel; *(jacket etc)* marengo

peppercorn ['pepǝkɔ:n] N grain *m* de poivre
▸▸*Br* **p. rent** loyer *m* modique

peppermint ['pepǝmɪnt] N **1** *(plant)* menthe *f* poivrée; *(flavour)* menthe poivrée; peppermint m **2** *(sweet)* bonbon *m* à la menthe, pastille *f* de menthe

peppery ['pepǝrɪ] ADJ **1** *(dish etc)* poivré **2** *(person)* irascible, coléreux, colérique

peppy ['pepɪ] ADJ *Fam (person)* plein d'entrain *ou* d'allant

pepsin ['pepsɪn] N *Chem, Physiol* pepsine *f*

peptic ['peptɪk] ADJ *Physiol* peptique
▸▸**p. ulcer** ulcère *m* gastro-duodénal *ou* de l'estomac

peptide ['peptaɪd] N *Biol, Chem* peptide *m*

peptone ['peptǝʊn] N *Biol, Chem* peptone *f*

Péquiste [peɪ'ki:st] N *Can (member, supporter of Parti québécois)* péquiste *mf*

per [pɜ:r] PREP *Com etc* par; **sent p. carrier** envoyé par messagerie; **p. day** par jour; **100 km p. hour** cent kilomètres à l'heure; **ten euros p. kilo** dix euros le kilo; **as p. invoice** suivant facture; **as p. your instructions** conformément à vos instructions; **as p. sample** conformément à l'échantillon; *Fam* **as p. usual** comme d'habitude
▸▸**p. annum** ['ænǝm] par an; **p. capita** ['kæpɪtǝ] par personne; **p. capita consumption** consommation *f* par tête; **the highest p. capita income in Europe** le revenu par habitant le plus élevé d'Europe; **p. cent = percent**; **p. pro signature** signature *f* par procuration; **p. se** [seɪ] en soi; **it is not a bad idea p. se** en soi, ce n'est pas une mauvaise idée

peradventure [pɜ:rǝd'ventʃǝr] ADV *Arch (by chance)* par aventure, par hasard

perambulate [pǝ'ræmbjʊleɪt] VT *Fml (one's garden etc)* parcourir, se promener dans

perambulator [pǝ'ræmbjʊleɪtǝr] N *Arch, Fml* landau *m*

p/e ratio [pi:'i:] N *Acct (abbr price/earnings ratio)* ratio *m* cours-bénéfice

perceive [pǝ'si:v] VT **1** *(notice) (sound, light, smell)* percevoir; *(person)* apercevoir; *(difference)* percevoir, distinguer; *(become aware of)* s'apercevoir de; **he perceived that he was being watched** il s'aperçut qu'on l'observait **2** *(understand) (the truth etc)* percevoir **3** *Mktg (product, brand)* percevoir

perceived [pǝ'si:vd] ADJ
▸▸*Mktg* **p. performance** résultats *mpl* perçus; *Mktg* **p. quality** qualité *f* perçue; **p. risk** risque *m* perçu; *Mktg* **p. service** service *m* perçu; *Mktg* **p. value** valeur *f* perçue; *Mktg* **p. value pricing** tarification *f* en fonction de la valeur perçue

percent [pǝ'sent] N pourcentage *m*; **10 p.** 10 pour cent; **what p. of people ...?** combien de personnes ...?; *(speaking statistically)* quel pourcentage de personnes ...?; **50 p. of the staff** la moitié du personnel; *(speaking statistically)* 50 pour cent du personnel
ADJ **a 5 p. increase** une augmentation de 5 pour cent; **thirty p. solution** solution à trente pour cent
ADV **a hundred p. efficient** cent pour cent efficace; **I'm ninety p. sure** je suis sûr à quatre-vingt dix pour cent
▸▸**p. sign** signe *m* pour cent

percentage [pǝ'sentɪdʒ] N **1** *(proportion)* pourcentage *m*; **p. of acid/alcohol** teneur *f*

en acide/en alcool; **to express sth as a p.** exprimer qch en pourcentage; **what p. of tenants own a car?** combien de locataires ont une voiture?; *(speaking statistically)* quelle est la proportion de locataires qui ont une voiture?; **in a high/tiny p. of cases** dans une vaste/petite proportion des cas **2** *Com* pourcentage *m*; **to allow a p. on all transactions** allouer un pourcentage *ou* un tantième sur toutes les opérations; *Fam* **what's my p.?** quel pourcentage est-ce que je touche?; *Fig Fam* **there's no p. in it** il n'y a rien à gagner

percentile [pǝ'sentaɪl] N centile *m*

perceptibility [pǝseptɪ'bɪlɪtɪ] N perceptibilité *f*

perceptible [pǝ'septɪb(ǝ)l] ADJ perceptible; *Phil* cognoscible; *(difference)* sensible; **p. to the eye** visible; **p. to the ear** perceptible à l'oreille, audible

perceptibly [pǝ'septɪblɪ] ADV sensiblement

perception [pǝ'sepʃǝn] N **1** *(act of perceiving)* perception *f*; **organs of p.** organes *mpl* percepteurs **2** *(ability to perceive)* sensibilité *f*; **powers of p.** facultés *fpl* perceptives **3** *(understanding)* perception *f*; **the public's p. of the government's role** la façon dont l'opinion publique perçoit le rôle de l'État; **to have different perceptions of a situation** percevoir une situation différemment

perceptive [pǝ'septɪv] ADJ **1** *(perspicacious) (person, remark)* perspicace; *(analysis, article)* qui témoigne de clairvoyance **2** *(able to perceive)* perceptif; **p. faculties** facultés *mpl* perceptives

perceptively [pǝ'septɪvlɪ] ADV *(to write, comment)* avec perspicacité

perceptiveness [pǝ'septɪvnɪs] N *(perspicacity)* perspicacité *f*

perceptoscope [pǝ'septǝskǝʊp] N *Mktg Old-fashioned* perceptoscope *m*

perceptual [pǝ'septjʊǝl] ADJ **1** *(organ)* percepteur **2** *Mktg* perceptuel
▸▸*Mktg* **p. map** carte *f* perceptuelle

perch¹ [pɜ:tʃ] N **1** *(for bird)* perchoir *m*; *Fam* **to knock sb off his/her p.** *(depose)* détrôner qn; *(force to abandon pretensions)* rabattre son caquet à qn **2** *Arch (measurement)* perche *f*
VI *(of bird)* se percher *(on* sur*)*; *(of person)* se percher, se jucher; *Orn* **perching bird** oiseau *m* percheur
VTA **castle perched on a hill** un château perché sur *(le sommet d')*une colline; **with his glasses perched on the end of his nose** avec ses lunettes perchées sur le bout du nez; **to p. oneself on sth** se percher *ou* se jucher sur qch

perch² N *(fish)* perche *f*

perchance [pǝ'tʃɑ:ns] ADV *Arch, Lit (perhaps)* peut-être

percipient [pǝ'sɪpɪǝnt] ADJ *Fml (faculty)* percepteur, -trice; *(person)* perspicace

percolate ['pɜ:kǝleɪt] VI *(of liquid)* s'infiltrer; *(of coffee etc)* filtrer, passer; *Fig (of information, news)* filtrer
VT *(of liquid) (sand etc)* filtrer à travers, s'infiltrer dans; *(of person, with filter etc) (liquid)* filtrer; *(coffee)* passer

percolator ['pɜ:kǝleɪtǝr] N cafetière *f* à pression; *(for large quantities)* percolateur *m*

percussion [pǝ'kʌʃǝn] N **1** *Mus (section)* percussions *fpl* **2** *(in firearm)* percussion *f*
▸▸**p. drill** perceuse *f* à percussion; **p. gun** fusil *m* à percussion; *Mus* **p. instruments** instruments *mpl* de *ou* à percussion; *Mil* **p. pin** rugueux *m* (de fusée); *Mus* **p. player** percussionniste *mf*; *Mus* **p. section** percussions

percussionist [pǝ'kʌʃǝnɪst] N percussionniste *mf*

percussive [pǝ'kʌsɪv] ADJ percutant

perdition [pǝ'dɪʃǝn] N *Lit* perte *f*, ruine *f*; *Rel* perdition *f*

peregrination [perɪgrɪ'neɪʃǝn] N *Lit* pérégrination *f*

peregrine falcon ['perɪgrɪn] N faucon *m* pèlerin

peremptorily [pǝ'remptǝrɪlɪ] ADV *(to order etc)* péremptoirement, de façon péremptoire

peremptory [pǝ'remptǝrɪ] ADJ péremptoire; *(refusal)* absolu, sans appel; *(tone, person)* péremptoire, impérieux
▸▸*Br Law* **p. writ** assignation *f* à comparaître en personne

perennial [pǝ'renɪǝl] ADJ *(problems, worries)* continuel, perpétuel; *(beauty, hope)* perpétuel, éternel; *(interest)* continuel; *(plant)* vivace
N plante *f* vivace

perennially [pǝ'renɪǝlɪ] ADV *(worried, dissatisfied etc)* continuellement, perpétuellement; *(beautiful)* éternellement

perestroika [perǝ'strɔɪkǝ] N perestroïka *f*

perfect¹ ['pɜ:fɪkt] ADJ **1** parfait; **a p. example of ...** un parfait exemple de ...; **a p. piece of work** un travail impeccable *ou* parfait; **her behaviour was far from p.** son comportement a beaucoup laissé à désirer; **to be in p. condition** *(of thing)* être impeccable; *(of person)* être en excellente forme; **her English is p.** son anglais est impeccable *ou* parfait; **no one's p.** personne n'est parfait; **p.!** parfait!; **the p. gift** le cadeau idéal; **the p. opportunity** l'occasion idéale *ou* rêvée; **a wine that is the p. accompaniment for fish** un vin qui accompagne parfaitement le poisson; **it was a p. day** *(weather)* il faisait un temps magnifique; *(activities)* nous avons passé une excellente journée **2** *(complete)* **he's a p. stranger to me** il m'est tout à fait inconnu; **I have a p. right to be here** j'ai parfaitement le droit d'être ici; **it makes p. sense (to me)** cela me semble être une excellente idée; *Fam* **he's a p. idiot** c'est un parfait imbécile; **he's being a p. nuisance** il est carrément empoisonnant **3** *Math (number, square)* parfait; *Mus (interval)* juste; *(chord)* parfait; **to have p. pitch** avoir l'oreille absolue
N *Gram* **the p.** le passé composé, le parfait; **a verb in the p.** un verbe au passé composé *ou* au parfait VOIR GRAMMAIRE A50; B30
▸▸**p. binding** *(in bookbinding)* reliure *f* sans couture; *Mus* **p. cadence** cadence *f* parfaite; *Gram* **the p. tense** le passé composé, le parfait

perfect² [pǝ'fekt] VT *(make perfect) (method)* perfectionner, parfaire; *(invention, design)* mettre au point

perfectibility [pǝfektɪ'bɪlɪtɪ] N perfectibilité *f*

perfectible [pǝ'fektɪb(ǝ)l] ADJ perfectible

perfection [pǝ'fekʃǝn] N **1** *(state)* perfection *f*; **it was sheer p.** c'était absolument parfait; **p. itself** la perfection même; **to attain p.** toucher *ou* arriver à la perfection; **to do sth to p.** faire qch à la perfection **2** *(action) (of job etc)* perfectionnement *m*

perfectionism [pǝ'fekʃǝnɪz(ǝ)m] N perfectionnisme *m*

perfectionist [pǝ'fekʃǝnɪst] N perfectionniste *mf*; **she's such a p.** elle est tellement perfectionniste
ADJ perfectionniste

perfective [pǝ'fektɪv] *Gram* ADJ perfectif
N aspect *m* perfectif

perfectly ['pɜ:fɪktlɪ] ADV *(symmetrical, flat, harmless)* parfaitement; *(idiotic, meaningless, useless)* complètement; *(to know sth)* à fond; *(to do sth)* à la perfection; **she's p. right**

elle a parfaitement raison; **to be p. honest / frank with you** pour être tout à fait honnête/ franc avec vous; **I'm p. capable of doing it** je suis tout à fait ou parfaitement capable de le faire; **you know p. well** (what I mean) tu le sais parfaitement bien ou très bien; **it would be p. pointless** cela ne servirait à rien du tout

perfecto [pɜːˈfektəʊ] N Am (cigar) = cigare m effilé aux deux bouts

perfidious [pəˈfɪdɪəs] ADJ Lit perfide
▸▸ **p. Albion** la perfide Albion

perfidiously [pəˈfɪdɪəslɪ] ADV Lit perfidement

perfidiousness [pəˈfɪdɪəsnɪs], **perfidy** [ˈpɜːfɪdɪ] N Lit perfidie f

perforate [ˈpɜːfəreɪt] VT (pierce) perforer, percer, transpercer; (metal sheet, ticket) poinçonner; Tech (paper) (with line of holes) perforer en pointillé
VI Med (of ulcer) [pɜːfəreɪtɪd] déterminer une perforation

perforated [ˈpɜːfəreɪtɪd] ADJ perforé; (stamps) dentelé; Med (eardrum) crevé; **tear along the p. line** détachez suivant le(s) pointillé(s)
▸▸ Comput **p. paper** papier m à bandes perforées; Comput **p. tape** bande f perforée; Med **p. ulcer** perforation f ulcéreuse

perforation [pɜːfəˈreɪʃən] N 1 (action) perforage m, perçage m; (of stamps) perforage 2 (hole) perforation f, (petit) trou m; Med perforation; (for counterfoils etc) (perforation(s) en) pointillé m; (of postage stamp) denteleure f, **tear along the perforations** déchirer selon le(s) pointillé(s)
▸▸ Philat **p. gauge** adontomètre m; Comput **p. skip** saut m de perforation

perforce [pəˈfɔːs] ADV Lit forcément

perform [pəˈfɔːm] VT 1 (ritual) célébrer; (miracle) faire; (one's duty) remplir; (actions) effectuer, réaliser; (task) accomplir; **to p. a contract** exécuter un contrat; Surg **to p. an operation on sb** opérer qn 2 Theat etc (play) jouer, représenter; (dance) exécuter; (piece of music) exécuter, jouer; Fig (rôle) tenir, remplir
VI 1 (of machine) marcher, fonctionner; **it performs well in all conditions** (of vehicle, machine etc) elle donne de bonnes performances en toutes conditions; **to p. well/ badly** (of student etc) avoir de bons/mauvais résultats; **how are your shares performing?** comment vos actions se tiennent-elle?; **the Miami branch is not performing well** les résultats de la succursale de Miami ne sont pas très satisfaisants; **how did the company p. in the first quarter?** comment la société a-t-elle fonctionné au premier trimestre?; **how does he p. in bed?** comment est-il au lit?; **I couldn't p.** (sexually) je n'ai pas pu 2 Theat etc (of theatre company) donner une/des représentation(s), jouer; (of actor, instrumentalist, orchestra) jouer; (of singer) chanter; (of dancer) danser; (of mime artist etc) exécuter un/des numéro(s); **to p. in a play** tenir un rôle ou jouer dans une pièce; **he performed well in the role of Claudius** il a bien joué ou interprété le rôle de Claudius; **to p. on the flute** jouer de la flûte

performance [pəˈfɔːməns] N 1 (action) (of contract) exécution f, (of task, duty) accomplissement m; (of rite) célébration f
2 (quality, ability), Sport etc performance f, (of actor) interprétation f, (of musician) exécution f, interprétation; (of dancer) exécution; (of pupil, economy, exports) résultats mpl, performances; (in bed) performance sexuelle; (of employee, plane, engine, piece of equipment) rendement m, performance; (of shares) rendement; (at work) productivité f, Ind cadence f (de travail); Tech (of machine) fonctionnement m, marche f, (of

material) comportement m, tenue f, **to put up a good p.** (of team etc) accomplir une bonne performance; (in exam, interview, court case) bien s'en tirer; **a good/poor p. in exams** de bons/mauvais résultats à des examens; Theat, Mus **she gave a superb p.** son interprétation était fantastique
3 (event), Theat etc (of play etc) représentation f, (at cinema) séance f, **first p.** première f, **there is no p. tonight** il y a relâche ce soir; Fig **he made such a p. about having to wash his hair** il a fait toute une histoire parce qu'il devait se laver les cheveux; Fig **what a p.!** quel spectacle!; Fig **it's such a p. cooking Christmas dinner!** c'est toute une histoire de préparer un dîner de Noël!
▸▸ **p. appraisal** (system) système m d'évaluation; (individual) évaluation f, **p. art** performance, action f, **p. artist** = artiste mf spécialisé(e) dans la performance; **p. bonus** prime f de rendement ou de performance; Aut **p. car** voiture f puissante, voiture haute performance; **p. indicator** indice m de performance; Fin **p. ratio** coefficient m ou ratio m d'exploitation; **p. statistics** statistiques fpl de performance

> Note that the French word **performance** never means show.

performance-enhancing [-en'hɑːnsɪŋ] ADJ (drug) qui améliore les performances

performance-related ADJ (pay) au rendement

performative [pəˈfɔːmətɪv] ADJ, N Ling performatif m

performer [pəˈfɔːmər] N Mus exécutant, -ante, artiste mf, interprète mf, Theat acteur, -trice, artiste mf, **he has been a consistent p.** (in sport) il a toujours été régulier; **an accomplished p. on the flute** un joueur de flûte accompli; **a good/bad p.** (student) un bon/ mauvais élève; (car) une voiture performante/peu performante

performing [pəˈfɔːmɪŋ] ADJ (dog, seal) savant
N (of symphony etc) exécution f, interprétation f
▸▸ **p. arts** arts mpl du spectacle; **p. rights** Theat droits mpl de représentation; Mus droits d'exécution

perfume[1] [ˈpɜːfjuːm, Am pəˈfjuːm] N parfum m
▸▸ **p. counter** (in shop) rayon m parfumerie

perfume[2] [pəˈfjuːm] VT parfumer; **to p. the air** embaumer l'air

perfumed [ˈpɜːfjuːmd] ADJ (soap etc) parfumé

perfumery [pəˈfjuːmərɪ] N parfumerie f

perfunctorily [pəˈfʌŋktrɪlɪ] ADV (to examine) superficiellement; (to order, instruct) sommairement; (to read) mécaniquement; (to greet sb) négligemment

perfunctory [pəˈfʌŋkt(ə)rɪ] ADJ (examination, glance) rapide; (smile) mécanique; (letter, style, instructions) sommaire; **it was just a p. enquiry** il/elle/etc m'a juste demandé pour la forme; **her p. manner** ses manières négligentes; **he greeted me with a p. nod** il m'a salué de façon automatique d'un petit signe de la tête

pergola [ˈpɜːgələ] N pergola f

perhaps [pəˈhæps, præps] ADV peut-être; **p. (so)/not** peut-être (bien) que oui/que non; **p. he's forgotten** peut-être qu'il a oublié; **p. we shall come back tomorrow** peut-être reviendrons-nous demain; **p. you would like to try it** on voulez-vous l'essayer?

perigee [ˈperɪdʒiː] N Astron périgée m

perihelion [perɪˈhiːlɪən] N Astron périhélie m

peril [ˈperɪl] N péril m, danger m; **in p.** en danger, en péril; **in p. of one's life** en danger de mort; **to do sth at one's (own) p.** faire qch à ses risques et périls; **peril(s) of the sea** (in marine insurance) fortune(s) f(pl) de mer

perilous [ˈperɪləs] ADJ périlleux, dangereux

perilously [ˈperɪləslɪ] ADV dangereusement; **p. close to the edge of the cliff** dangereusement proche du bord de la falaise; **he came p. close to getting himself sacked** il a bien failli se faire mettre à la porte

perimeter [pəˈrɪmɪtər] N périmètre m
▸▸ Mktg **p. advertising** publicité f périphérique; **p. alarm** alarme f périmétrique; Mktg **p. board** panneau m publicitaire (autour d'un terrain de sport); **p. fence** grillage m

perinatal [perɪˈneɪt(ə)l] ADJ Med (treatment, care, death) périnatal, -als ou -aux

perineum [perɪˈniːəm] N Anat périnée m

period [ˈpɪərɪəd] N 1 période f, (stage) moment m, époque f, stade m; Astron cycle m, période; Phys période; **for a p. of three months** pendant une période de trois mois; **during or for the p. of their stay here** pendant (la durée de) leur séjour ici; **a long p. of illness** de longs ennuis de santé; **p. of notice** délai-congé m, pl délais-congés; **within the agreed p.** dans les délais convenus; Banking **deposit for a fixed p.** dépôt m à terme fixe; Met **clear periods** éclaircies fpl, **sunny periods** intervalles mpl ensoleillés
2 Sch heure f de cours; **a French/maths p.** un cours de français/maths; **a free p.** une heure de libre
3 (menstruation) (monthly) period(s) règles fpl, **I've got my p.** j'ai mes règles; **when you have your first p.** la première fois que tu auras tes règles
4 (age) époque f, (era) ère f, **p. play/novel/ drama** comédie f/roman m/drame m historique
5 esp Am Gram, Typ (full stop) point m; Am Fam **he's no good at math! - he's no good, p.!** il est nul en math! - il est nul tout court!; Am Fam **you're not going to the party, p.!** tu n'iras pas à cette soirée, un point c'est tout!
6 Liter (sentence) phrase f, Mus phrase complète
▸▸ Fin **p. bill** effet m à terme; **p. costume** toilette f d'époque; **p. detail** détail m historique; **p. dress** (costume) costume(s) m(pl) de l'époque; (woman's garment) robe f de style; **p. furniture** meubles mpl de style ou d'époque; Fin **p. of grace** délai m de grâce; Banking **p. money** dépôts à terme; **p. pains** règles douloureuses; **p. piece** (object, antique) objet m d'époque; (film) film m historique; (play) pièce f historique

periodic [pɪərɪˈɒdɪk] ADJ périodique
▸▸ Fin **p. inventory** inventaire m périodique; Chem **p. table** classification f périodique (des éléments), tableau m de Mendeleïev

periodical [pɪərɪˈɒdɪk(ə)l] ADJ périodique
N (publication f) périodique m; **the p. room** la salle des périodiques

periodically [pɪərɪˈɒdɪklɪ] ADV périodiquement

periodontal [perɪəˈdɒnt(ə)l] ADJ parodontal, -aux

peripatetic [perɪpəˈtetɪk] ADJ ambulant, itinérant; (teacher) en poste sur plusieurs établissements

peripheral [pəˈrɪfərəl] ADJ 1 (area, vision etc) périphérique; **of purely p. importance** d'une importance purement accessoire; **this issue is p. to the central debate** ce problème est accessoire au débat principal 2 Comput périphérique
N Comput périphérique m
▸▸ Comput **p. device** unité f périphérique;

Comput **p. equipment** matériel *m* périphérique, périphériques; *Comput* **p. interchange program** logiciel *m* de commutation de périphérique; *Comput* **p. unit** unité périphérique

periphery [pə'rɪfərɪ] N périphérie *f*; **on the p. of one's vision** à la périphérie de son champ de vision; **on the p. of the crowd** en bordure de la foule; **on the p. of society** en marge de la société

periphrasis, *pl* **periphrases** [pə'rɪfrəsɪs, -iːz] N *Liter* périphrase *f*

periphrastic [perɪ'fræstɪk] ADJ *Liter* périphrastique

periscope ['perɪskəʊp] N périscope *m*
▸▸ *TV, Cin* **p. shot** plan *m* en contreplongée

perish ['perɪʃ] VI **1** *(of person)* périr; *Fam* **p. the thought!** loin de moi cette pensée!; **if, p. the thought, you should die …** si, Dieu nous en préserve, vous deviez mourir … **2** *(of rubber, leather)* se détériorer; *(of fresh food)* s'avarier
▸ VT *(rubber, leather)* détériorer; *(fresh food)* avarier

perishability [perɪʃə'bɪlɪtɪ] N *Com* périssabilité *f*

perishable ['perɪʃəb(ə)l] ADJ périssable
▸ NPL **perishables** denrées *fpl* périssables

perished ['perɪʃt] ADJ détérioré, usé; *Fam* **I'm p.** *(very cold)* je meurs de froid

perisher ['perɪʃər] N *Br Sl (pest)* saligaud *m*; **little p.** petit coquin *m*

perishing ['perɪʃɪŋ] ADJ **1** *Fam (very cold)* très froid; **it's p.** il fait un froid de canard; **I'm p.** je meurs de froid **2** *Br Sl (intensifier)* sacré; *(car, machine)* satané; **p. idiot** sacré idiot; **it's a p. nuisance** c'est sacrément ennuyeux

peristalsis [perɪ'stælsɪs] N péristaltisme *m*

peristyle ['perɪstaɪl] N *Archit* péristyle *m*

peritoneum [perɪtə'niːəm] N *Anat* péritoine *m*

peritonitis [perɪtə'naɪtɪs] N *Med* péritonite *f*; **to have p.** avoir une péritonite

periwig ['perɪwɪɡ] N *Hist* perruque *f*

periwinkle¹ ['perɪwɪŋk(ə)l] N *(plant)* (petite) pervenche *f*; *(colour)* bleu pervenche *m inv*
▸▸ **p. blue** bleu pervenche

periwinkle² N *(mollusc)* bigorneau *m*

perjure ['pɜːdʒər] VT *Law* **to p. oneself** faire un faux témoignage

perjurer ['pɜːdʒərər] N *Law* faux témoin *m*

perjury ['pɜːdʒərɪ] N *Law* faux témoignage *m*; **to commit p.** faire un faux témoignage; **the penalty for p.** la peine encourue quand on fait un faux témoignage

perk¹ [pɜːk] N *Br Fam* à-côté *m*, *pl* à-côtés, avantage *m*; **perks include …** les avantages acquis comprennent …; **free tickets are one of the perks of the job** un des avantages de ce travail est que l'on peut obtenir des billets gratuits; **clean air is a p. of working in the country** l'air pur est un des avantages du travail à la campagne

perk² *Fam* VI *(of coffee)* passer
▸ VT *(coffee)* faire
▸ **perk up** VI *(become more cheerful, after illness)* se requinquer; *(of party)* s'animer; **I don't know what to do to make him p. up** je ne sais pas quoi faire pour lui remonter le moral
▸ VT SEP **1** *(revive) (person)* requinquer, ragaillardir; *(cheer up)* remonter le moral à; **the coffee perked her up** le café l'a requinquée *ou* ravigotée **2** *(raise)* **to p. up its ears** *(of dog)* dresser les oreilles

perkily ['pɜːkɪlɪ] ADV d'un air animé; *(to answer, say)* d'un ton dégagé *ou* désinvolte

perky ['pɜːkɪ] ADJ *(lively)* plein d'entrain, animé; *(cheerful)* guilleret; *(tone)* dégagé, désinvolte; *(remark)* désinvolte

perm¹ [pɜːm] N *(in hair)* permanente *f*, **to have a p.** se faire faire une permanente
▸ VT **to p. sb's hair** faire faire une permanente à qn; **to have one's hair permed** se faire faire une permanente

perm² N *Br (in football pools)* permutation *f*

permafrost ['pɜːməfrɒst] N *Geol* permafrost *m*

permanence ['pɜːmənəns] N permanence *f*

permanency ['pɜːmənənsɪ] N permanence *f*

permanent ['pɜːmənənt] ADJ permanent; *(residence, address)* fixe; *(ink, stain)* indélébile; **p. hearing loss** perte *f* définitive de l'ouïe; **she was in a p. state of depression** elle était continuellement déprimée
▸ N *(in hair)* permanente *f*
▸▸ *Fin* **p. credit** accréditif *m* permanent; *Ins* **p. health insurance** assurance *f* longue maladie; *Com* **p. inventory** stock *m* de sécurité, stock stratégique, inventaire *m* permanent; **p. press** *(for clothes)* plissé *m* permanent; *Pol* **p. representation** représentation *f* permanente; *Pol* **p. representative** représentant, -ante permanent(e); **p. site** *(caravan site)* terrain *m* de caravaning permanent; **p. wave** permanente *f*; *Br* **p. way** voie *f* ferrée

permanganate [pə'mæŋɡəneɪt] N *Chem* permanganate *m*

permeability [pɜːmɪə'bɪlɪtɪ] N perméabilité *f*

permeable ['pɜːmɪəb(ə)l] ADJ perméable

permeate ['pɜːmɪeɪt] VT **1** *(penetrate)* filtrer *ou* passer à travers; **the soil was permeated with water** le sol était saturé d'eau; **a smell of flowers permeated the room** une odeur de fleurs embaumaient la pièce; **his clothes were permeated by a smell of napthalene** ses vêtements étaient imprégnés d'une odeur de naphtaline; **the house was permeated by damp** la maison était imprégnée d'humidité **2** *Fig (of feeling, idea etc)* imprégner; **this attitude permeated 18th-century thought** la pensée du 18e siècle a été imprégnée par cette attitude; **the country was permeated with fear** le pays était plongé dans la peur; **doubt had permeated the organization** le doute s'était infiltré dans l'organisation
▸ VI passer; **to p. through sth** filtrer *ou* passer à travers qch; **water permeates everywhere** l'eau s'infiltre partout

Permian ['pɜːmɪən] ADJ *Geol* permien

permissible [pə'mɪsɪb(ə)l] ADJ admissible, acceptable

permission [pə'mɪʃən] N permission *f*, autorisation *f*; **to ask/give/refuse sb p. to do sth** demander/donner/refuser à qn la permission *ou* l'autorisation de faire qch; **with your p.** avec votre permission *ou* autorisation; **you have my p.** je te donne la permission, je t'y autorise; **published by kind p. of …** publié avec l'aimable autorisation de …; *St Exch* **p. to deal** visa *m* (de la COB) VOIR GRAMMAIRE A58–9; B39–40

permissive [pə'mɪsɪv] ADJ *(tolerant)* permissif
▸▸ **p. society** société *f* permissive

permissively [pə'mɪsɪvlɪ] ADV de manière permissive

permissiveness [pə'mɪsɪvnɪs] N permissivité *f*

permit¹ ['pɜːmɪt] N permis *m*; *(allowing entry)* laissez-passer *m inv*; *(at Customs)* acquit-à-caution *m*, *pl* acquits-à-caution, passavant *m*; **export p.** autorisation *f* d'exporter; **work p.** permis de travail; **p. holders only** *(on sign)* réservé aux personnes autorisées

permit² [pə'mɪt] (**-tt-**) VT permettre; **to p. sb to do sth** permettre à qn de faire qch, autoriser qn à faire qch; **larger telescopes p. us to …** des télescopes plus performants nous permettent de …; **if I may be permitted** si vous me le permettez; **p. me to tell you …!** *(angrily)* laissez-moi vous dire que …!; *Br Admin* **permitted hours** *(for selling alcohol)* = heures *fpl* légales de vente des boissons alcoolisées
▸ VI **if time permits** si j'ai/nous avons/*etc* le temps; **weather permitting** si le temps le permet
▸ **permit of** VT INSEP *Fml (admit possibility of)* admettre; **this permits of only one explanation** ceci n'admet qu'une explication

permutation [pɜːmjʊ'teɪʃən] N permutation *f*

permute [pə'mjuːt] VT *Ling, Math* permuter

pernicious [pə'nɪʃəs] ADJ pernicieux
▸▸ *Med* **p. anaemia** anémie *f* pernicieuse

perniciously [pə'nɪʃəslɪ] ADV pernicieusement

pernickety [pə'nɪkɪtɪ] ADJ *Fam (person)* tatillon, pointilleux; *(job)* délicat, minutieux; **to be p. about one's food** être difficile sur la nourriture; **soufflé can be rather a p. thing to make** le soufflé est un plat assez délicat à préparer

perorate ['perəreɪt] VI *Fml* **1** *(conclude speech)* faire la péroraison **2** *(speak at length)* discourir longuement

peroration [perə'reɪʃən] N *Fml* **1** *(conclusion)* péroraison *f* **2** *(long speech)* long discours *m*, discours de longue haleine

peroxide [pə'rɒksaɪd] N *Chem* peroxyde *m*
▸ VT *(hair)* (faire) blondir à l'eau oxygénée
▸▸ *Pej* **p. blonde** *(woman)* blonde *f* décolorée

perp [pɜːp] N *Am Sl (perpetrator)* auteur *m*

perpendicular [pɜːpən'dɪkjʊlər] ADJ perpendiculaire (**to** à); *(wall etc)* vertical, -aux; *(upright, straight)* à plomb; *(cliff)* à pic; **line p. to another** ligne perpendiculaire à une autre
▸ N **1** *(plumb line)* fil *m* à plomb; **out of (the) p.** hors d'aplomb, hors d'équerre **2** *Geom* perpendiculaire *f*
▸▸ *Archit* **p. style** style *m* (gothique) perpendiculaire

perpendicularly [pɜːpən'dɪkjʊlərlɪ] ADV perpendiculairement; *(to rise, fall, drop)* verticalement, à la verticale; *(to be built)* d'aplomb; **the cliff rose p.** la falaise s'élevait tout droit

perpetrate ['pɜːpɪtreɪt] VT *(crime)* commettre, perpétrer; *(fraud, error)* commettre

perpetration [pɜːpɪ'treɪʃən] N *(of crime)* perpétration *f*, *(of fraud, deception)* accomplissement *m*

perpetrator ['pɜːpɪtreɪtər] N *(of crime)* auteur *m*; **the p.** l'auteur du délit

perpetual [pə'petjʊəl] ADJ *(eternal)* perpétuel, éternel; *(incessant)* sans fin, continuel, incessant
▸▸ *Chess* **p. check** échec *m* perpétuel; *Fin* **p. inventory** stock *m* stratégique; *Fin* **p. loan** emprunt *m* perpétuel; **p. motion** mouvement *m* perpétuel; **p. snow** neiges *fpl* éternelles

perpetually [pə'petjʊəlɪ] ADV *(eternally)* perpétuellement, éternellement; *(ceaselessly)* sans cesse; *(continually)* continuellement, perpétuellement

perpetuate [pə'petjʊeɪt] VT perpétuer; **to p. the species** perpétuer l'espèce

perpetuation [pəpetjʊ'eɪʃən] N perpétuation *f*

perpetuity [pɜːpɪ'tjuːɪtɪ] N **1** perpétuité *f*, **in** *or* **for p.** à perpétuité **2** *Law (of property)* jouissance *f* à perpétuité; **(annuity in)** p. rente *f* perpétuelle

perplex [pə'pleks] **VT** laisser *ou* rendre perplexe; **she was perplexed by his lack of enthusiasm** son manque d'enthousiasme la laissait *ou* rendait perplexe

perplexed [pə'plekst] **ADJ** perplexe

perplexing [pə'pleksɪŋ] **ADJ** *(problem etc)* troublant; *(book, play etc)* difficile (à comprendre); *(person)* déconcertant; **it's very p.** on n'y comprend rien; **I find his attitude most p.** son attitude me laisse totalement perplexe

perplexity [pə'pleksɪtɪ] **N** perplexité *f*

perquisite ['pɜːkwɪzɪt] **N** *Br Fml* = **perk**[1]

perry ['perɪ] **N** *(drink)* poiré *m*

persecute ['pɜːsɪkjuːt] **VT** persécuter; **to be persecuted in the press** faire l'objet d'attaques répétées dans la presse

persecution [pɜːsɪ'kjuːʃən] **N** persécution *f*, *Psy* **p. complex** *or* **mania** complexe *m* de persécution

persecutor ['pɜːsɪkjuːtər] **N** persécuteur, -trice

perseverance [pɜːsɪ'vɪərəns] **N** persévérance *f*

persevere [pɜːsɪ'vɪər] **VI** persévérer **(with** *or* **in sth** dans qch; **with sb** avec qn); **to p. in one's belief that ...** persister à croire que ...; **to p. in doing sth** persister à faire qch

persevering [pɜːsɪ'vɪərɪŋ] **ADJ** persévérant; **thanks to our p. staff** grâce à la persévérance de notre personnel

Persia ['pɜːʃə] **N** Perse *f*

Persian ['pɜːʃən] **ADJ** persan; *Antiq* perse; *(cat, horse)* persan; *(carpet)* de Perse **N 1** *(person)* Persan, -ane; *Antiq* Perse *mf* **2** *(cat)* chat *m* persan **3** *Ling* persan

Persian Gulf (the) **N** le Golfe persique

persimmon [pɜːs'sɪmən] **N 1** *(fruit)* plaquemine *f*, *(from Japan)* kaki *m* **2** *(tree)* plaqueminier *m*
▶▶ **p. tree** plaqueminier

persist [pə'sɪst] **VI 1** persister, s'obstiner **(in doing sth** à faire qch); **to p. in one's opinion** persister *ou* s'obstiner dans son opinion; **to p. in one's belief that ...** persister à croire que ... **2** *(of fog, fever etc)* persister, continuer; *(of belief)* persister

persistence [pə'sɪstəns] **N 1** persistance *f*, ténacité *f*, obstination *f* **(in doing sth** à faire qch) **2** *(of fog, fever, belief etc)* persistance *f*

persistent [pə'sɪstənt] **ADJ** *(person)* persistant, opiniâtre, tenace; *(doubts, problems, pain etc)* continuel, incessant; *(rumours)* persistant; *(rain)* continuel, qui s'obstine; **to be in p. pain** souffrir continuellement; **to have a p. belief in sth** persister à croire à qch; *Com* **p. demand for ...** demande suivie *ou* soutenue pour ...
▶▶ **p. offender** récidiviste *mf*, *Med* **p. vegetative state** état *m* végétatif chronique

persistently [pə'sɪstəntlɪ] **ADV** avec persistance; *(to fail, refuse, warn)* à plusieurs reprises; *(to be late, short of funds)* continuellement; **she p. offended** elle récidivait sans cesse

persnickety [pə'snɪkɪtɪ] **ADJ** *Am Fam* = **pernickety**

person ['pɜːs(ə)n] **N 1** personne *f*, *Pej* individu *m*, type *m*; **what's he/she like as a p.?** il/elle est comment sur le plan personnel?; **I like her as a p.** je l'aime bien en tant que personne; **he/she is a kind/strange p.** c'est une personne gentille/étrange, c'est quelqu'un de gentil/d'étrange; **a coffee/football p.** un amateur de café/de foot; **are you a cat p. or a dog p.?** est-ce que tu préfères les chats ou chiens?; **there is no p. of that name here** il n'y a personne de ce nom ici; *Law* **some p. or**

persons unknown un certain quidam; **in p. en propre, en personne; he came in p. il est venu en personne; to deliver sth in p.** remettre qch en main(s) propre(s); **help came, in the p. of Amanda** on a trouvé de l'aide, en la personne d'Amanda; **to carry weapons on one's p.** porter des armes sur soi; **to be one's own p.** vivre à sa façon *ou* à son idée; *Tel* **p. to p. call** appel *m* avec préavis *ou* de personne à personne
2 *Gram* verb in the first **p.** verbe *m* à la première personne; **the second p. plural** la deuxième personne du pluriel; **the story is told in the first p.** l'histoire est racontée à la première personne
3 *Rel* (one) God in three Persons la Trinité

persona [pɜː'səʊnə] **N** *also Psy* personnage *m*; **p. grata/non grata** persona grata/non grata; *Fig* **you'll be p. non grata unless you bring a present** tu ne seras pas bien vu si tu n'apportes pas de cadeau; **to be p. non grata with sb** ne pas être dans les petits papiers de qn

personable ['pɜːsənəb(ə)l] **ADJ** bien (fait) de sa personne; **he's a very p. young man** c'est un jeune homme qui présente très bien

personage ['pɜːsənɪdʒ] **N** personnage *m*

personal ['pɜːsən(ə)l] **ADJ** personnel; **to be careless about one's p. appearance** négliger sa tenue; **to make a p. appearance** venir *ou* paraître en personne; **for p. reasons** pour des raisons personnelles; **don't be p., don't make p. remarks** ne faites pas d'allusions personnelles; **it's nothing p. but ...** ça n'a rien de personnel mais ...; **to do sb a p. favour** rendre un service à qn à titre personnel; **it's a p. matter** c'est une affaire privée *ou* personnelle; **my p. opinion** *or* **view is that ...** à mon avis ...; **this is not my p. opinion** ce n'est pas mon opinion personnelle; **to give a p. touch to sth** donner une touche personnelle à qch; **I want it for my p. use** j'en ai besoin pour mon usage personnel; **articles for p. use** *(at customs)* objets à usage personnel
▶▶ **p. accident insurance** assurance *f* contre les accidents corporels; **have you got any p. accident insurance?** est-ce que vous avez une assurance contre les accidents?; **p. account** *Banking* compte *m* personnel; *St Exch* compte de tiers; *Acct* compte propre; *Law* **p. action** *(relating to property)* action *f* mobilière; *Fam* **p. ad** petite annonce *f* *(pour rencontres)*; *Banking* **p. assets** patrimoine *m*; *Banking* **p. assets profile** profil *m* patrimonial; **p. assistant** *(of executive)* assistant, -ante; *(with secretarial duties)* secrétaire *mf* de direction; *Sport* **p. best** record *m* personnel; **3 mins 22 secs is my p. best** mon record *(personnel)* est 3 min 22; **p. column** petites annonces *(pour rencontres)*; **p. computer** ordinateur *m* individuel *ou* personnel, PC *m*; **p. data** données *fpl* nominatives; **p. effects** effets *mpl* personnels; *Br Fin Formerly* **p. equity plan** ≃ plan *m* d'épargne en actions; **p. estate** biens *mpl* mobiliers personnels; **p. financial statement** état *m* de fortune; **p. friend** ami, -ie personnel(elle); *Comput* **p. home page** page *f* personnelle, page perso; **p. hygiene** hygiène *f* corporelle; *Banking* **p. identification number** code *m* confidentiel *(d'une carte bancaire)*; **p. liberty** liberté *f* individuelle; **p. loan** prêt *m* personnel, prêt personnalisé; *Mktg* **p. observation** observation *f* en situation; **p. organizer** organiseur *m*; *(electronic)* agenda *m* électronique, organiseur; *Gram* **p. pronoun** pronom *m* personnel; **p. property** biens mobiliers personnels; **p. property insurance** assurance sur les objets personnels; *Mktg* **p. selling** ventes *fpl* personnelles; **p. shopper** acheteur, -euse personnel(elle); **p. stereo** Walkman® *m*, baladeur *m*; **p. trainer** entraîneur, -euse per-

sonnel(elle); *Acct* **p. wealth statement** état *m* de fortune

personality [pɜːsə'nælɪtɪ] **N 1** *(character)* personnalité *f*; **he's got no p.** il n'a aucune personnalité **2** *(well-known person)* personnalité *f*; **TV/sports p.** personnalité célèbre de la télévision/du monde du sport **3** *Old-fashioned (personal remark)* **to indulge in personalities** faire des remarques personnelles
▶▶ **p. cult** culte *m* de la personnalité; **p. disorder** trouble *m* de la personnalité; **p. profile** profil *m* de personnalité; *Mktg* **p. promotion** promotion *f* par une personnalité; **p. test** test *m* de personnalité, *Spec* test projectif

personalize ['pɜːsənəlaɪz] **VT** personnaliser; **a personalized shirt** une chemise personnalisée; **personalized letter** lettre *f* personnelle; **I don't want to p. the issue** je ne veux pas donner un tour personnel à ce problème

personally ['pɜːsən(ə)lɪ] **ADV** personnellement; *(to intervene, see sb)* en personne; **to attend to sth p.** s'occuper de qch en personne *ou* personnellement; **p. I think ...** pour ma part je pense ...; **that belongs to me p.** cela m'appartient en propre; **to deliver sth to sb p.** remettre qch à qn en main(s) propre(s); **don't take it p.** *(what was said, done)* n'en faites pas une affaire personnelle, ne le prenez pas personnellement; **I didn't mean it p.** ma remarque n'avait rien de personnel

personalty ['pɜːsənltɪ] **N** *Law* biens *mpl* meubles, biens mobiliers

personification [pɜːsɒnɪfɪ'keɪʃən] **N** personnification *f*; **to be the p. of meanness** être l'avarice même *ou* l'avarice personnifiée *ou* l'avarice en personne; **he is the p. of this new trend in English fiction** il incarne cette nouvelle tendance de la fiction anglaise

personify [pɜː'sɒnɪfaɪ] **VT** personnifier; **he's meanness personified** il est *ou* c'est l'avarice même *ou* l'avarice personnifiée *ou* l'avarice en personne

personnel [pɜːsə'nel] **N** personnel *m*; **I work in p.** *(the department)* je travaille au service du personnel; *(the field)* je suis dans la branche du personnel
▶▶ *Mil* **p. carrier** *(véhicule m de)* transport *m* de troupes; *(aircraft)* avion *m* de transport de personnel; **p. consultant** conseiller, -ère du travail; **p. department** service *m* du personnel; **p. director** directeur, -trice du personnel; **p. file card** fiche *f* signalétique; **p. files** fichiers *mpl* des salariés; **p. management** direction *f* *ou* administration *f* du personnel; **p. manager** directeur du personnel; **p. representative** délégué, -ée du personnel

perspective [pə'spektɪv] **N 1** *Math, Art* perspective *f*; **to draw an object in/out of p.** dessiner un objet en perspective/en faussant la perspective **2** *Fig (relative importance)* **to see a matter in its true p.** voir une affaire sous son vrai jour; **to put sth in(to) p.** remettre qch à sa *(vraie)* place; **let's keep things in p.** n'exagérons rien; **to see events in a historical p.** voir des événements dans une perspective *ou* optique historique **3** *Fml (view)*, *Fig (prospect)* perspective *f*; **a fine p. opened out before his eyes** une belle perspective s'ouvrit devant ses yeux
ADJ *Art (drawing etc)* en perspective, perspectif; **p. lines of a picture** fuyants *mpl* d'un tableau

Perspex® ['pɜːspeks] **N** plexiglas®® *m*

perspicacious [pɜːspɪ'keɪʃəs] **ADJ** *Fml (person)* perspicace; *(comment, analysis etc)* clairvoyant, lucide, fin

perspicaciously [pɜːspɪ'keɪʃəslɪ] **ADV** *Fml* avec perspicacité *ou* clairvoyance *ou* discernement

perspicacity [pɜːspɪˈkæsɪtɪ] N *Fml* perspicacité *f*

perspicuity [pɜːspɪˈkjuːɪtɪ] N *Fml (of person)* perspicacité *f, (of style etc)* clarté *f,* netteté *f,* lucidité *f*

perspicuous [pəˈspɪkjʊəs] ADJ *Fml* clair, net, *f* nette, lucide

perspicuously [pəˈspɪkjʊəslɪ] ADV *Fml* clairement, nettement

perspiration [pɜːspəˈreɪʃən] N **1** *(sweat)* transpiration *f,* sueur *f,* **beads of p.** gouttes *fpl* de sueur; **bathed in** or **dripping with p.** trempé de sueur, en nage **2** *(act)* transpiration *f,* perspiration *f*

perspire [pəˈspaɪər] VI transpirer

persuadable [pəˈsweɪdəb(ə)l] ADJ **easily p.** facile à persuader

persuade [pəˈsweɪd] VT persuader, convaincre (**to do** de faire); **to p. sb not to do sth** dissuader qn de faire qch; **to p. sb that ...** persuader qn que ... + *ind*; **nothing could p. her** aucun argument n'a pu la convaincre; **she persuaded herself that everything would work out** elle s'est persuadée ou convaincue elle-même que tout marcherait bien

VI *Fml* **the argument fails to p.** cet argument n'est pas très convaincant

persuasion [pəˈsweɪʒən] N **1** *(act of persuading, ability to persuade)* persuasion *f,* **powers of p.** force *f ou* pouvoir *m* de persuasion; **the art of p.** l'art *m* de la persuasion **2** *(beliefs)* **(religious) p.** *(religion)* religion *f,* confession *f,* **political p.** opinions *fpl* politiques; **he was of a different political p. altogether** ses opinions politiques étaient complètement différentes; **to be of the Catholic p.** être de religion catholique; *Hum* **a person of the male/female p.** un homme/ une femme; *Old-fashioned* **it's my p. that ...** je suis persuadé ou convaincu que ...

persuasive [pəˈsweɪzɪv, -sɪv] ADJ *(person)* persuasif; *(argument)* convaincant

persuasively [pəˈsweɪzɪvlɪ, -sɪvlɪ] ADV *(to say)* d'un ton persuasif; *(to argue, write)* de façon convaincante

persuasiveness [pəˈsweɪzɪvnɪs, -sɪv-] N *(of person)* force *f* persuasive ou de persuasion; *(of argument)* caractère *m* convaincant; **the p. of her tone** son ton persuasif

pert [pɜːt] ADJ **1** *(cheeky)* effronté **2** *(of clothing)* *(stylishly neat)* pimpant **3** *(nose, breasts)* pointu; *(bottom)* petit et ferme

pertain [pəˈteɪn] VI *Fml* **1** *(belong)* appartenir (**to sth** à qch); **the house and the land pertaining to it** la maison et le terrain qui font partie de la propriété **2** *(have reference)* **to p. to sth** se rapporter à qch, avoir un rapport avec qch, avoir rapport à qch

pertinacious [pɜːtɪˈneɪʃəs] ADJ *Fml* obstiné, opiniâtre

pertinaciously [pɜːtɪˈneɪʃəslɪ] ADV *Fml* obstinément, opiniâtrement

pertinence [ˈpɜːtɪnəns] N *(of question, criticism)* pertinence *f,* à-propos *m inv; (of remark)* pertinence, à-propos, justesse *f*

pertinent [ˈpɜːtɪnənt] ADJ *(question, criticism)* pertinent; *(remark)* pertinent, juste; **to be p. to** *(question)* avoir un rapport avec, avoir rapport à

pertinently [ˈpɜːtɪnəntlɪ] ADV d'une manière pertinente, avec à-propos

pertly [ˈpɜːtlɪ] ADV **1** *(cheekily)* avec effronterie **2** *(in a lively way)* d'un air guilleret

pertness [ˈpɜːtnɪs] N **1** *(cheekiness)* effronterie *f* **2** *(liveliness)* air *m* guilleret **3** **the p. of her breasts** ses petits seins bien fermes

perturb [pəˈtɜːb] VT **1** *(worry)* troubler, inquiéter; **to be perturbed** être troublé ou inquiet; **if you are perturbed by this idea** si

cette idée vous inquiète **2** *Lit (put into confusion) (kingdom etc)* jeter le désordre ou la perturbation dans **3** *Astron (star)* dévier; *Phys (compass needle)* affoler

perturbation [pɜːtəˈbeɪʃən] N **1** *Fml (of mind)* agitation *f,* inquiétude *f,* trouble *m* **2** *Phys (of magnetic needle)* affolement *m*

perturbed [pəˈtɜːbd] ADJ troublé, inquiet

Peru [pəˈruː] N Pérou *m*

perusal [pəˈruːz(ə)l] N *Fml* lecture *f,* **for your p. and approval** pour que vous l'étudiez et l'approuviez; **for your p. when you have time** pour que vous y jetiez un coup d'œil, quand vous en aurez le temps

peruse [pəˈruːz] VT **1** *(read carefully)* lire attentivement, prendre connaissance de **2** *(read quickly) (magazine, newspaper)* feuilleter; *(letter, article)* survoler

Peruvian [pəˈruːvɪən] ADJ péruvien
N Péruvien, -ienne

perv [pɜːv] N *Fam* = **pervert**[1]

pervade [pɜːˈveɪd] VT s'infiltrer dans, se répandre dans; **the scent of pine trees pervaded the air** l'air était embaumé de l'odeur des pins; **the novel is pervaded by a sense of gloom** le roman est imprégné d'une atmosphère lugubre; **minor errors p. the entire dictionary** le dictionnaire est parsemé de petites erreurs; **such attitudes p. British business** ces attitudes sont omniprésentes dans ou se retrouvent à tous les niveaux dans les entreprises britanniques

pervading [pɜːˈveɪdɪŋ] ADJ *(smell)* pénétrant; **(all-)p.** qui se répand partout; *(influence, feeling etc)* dominant; **the p. nostalgia of his work** la nostalgie qui est omniprésente dans son œuvre

pervasive [pɜːˈveɪsɪv] ADJ qui se répand partout; *(gloom, smell)* envahissant

perverse [pəˈvɜːs] ADJ **1** *(wicked)* pervers, perverti; *(stubborn)* entêté; *(contrary)* contrariant; **to take a p. pleasure in doing** prendre un malin plaisir à faire; **then it would be p. to deny that ...** *(illogical)* alors ce serait illogique de nier que ... **2** *(sexually deviant)* pervers

Note that the French word **pervers** never means **stubborn** or **contrary**.

perversely [pəˈvɜːslɪ] ADV *(wickedly)* perversement, avec perversité; *(contrarily)* d'une manière contrariante; **to p. believe that ...** s'entêter à croire que ...

perverseness [pəˈvɜːsnɪs] N *(wickedness)* perversité *f, (contrariness)* esprit *m* contraire ou contrariant; *(cantankerousness)* caractère *m* revêche ou acariâtre

perversion [pəˈvɜːʃən] N **1** *(act of corrupting)* pervertissement *m; (perverted action, form)* perversion *f,* **a p. of the truth** un travestissement de la vérité **2** *(sexual)* perversions perversions *fpl* sexuelles

perversity [pəˈvɜːsɪtɪ] N = **perverseness**

pervert[1] [ˈpɜːvɜːt] N *Psy (sexual)* **p.** pervers, -erse *(sexuel(elle))*; *Fam* **your brother is such a p.!** ton frère est un véritable obsédé!

pervert[2] [pəˈvɜːt] VT *(corrupt morally) (person)* pervertir; *(distort) (facts)* altérer, dénaturer; *Law* **to p. the course of justice** entraver le bon fonctionnement de la justice; **to p. the truth** déformer la vérité

perverted [pəˈvɜːtɪd] ADJ pervers

pervious [ˈpɜːvɪəs] ADJ perméable *(à l'eau etc)*

pervy [ˈpɜːvɪ] ADJ *Br Fam* pervers

peseta [pəˈseɪtə] N *Formerly (Spanish currency)* peseta *f*

pesky [ˈpeskɪ] ADJ *esp Am Fam* embêtant, empoisonnant; **what are those p. kids up**

to now? que font ces maudits ou sacrés gosses maintenant?

peso [ˈpeɪsəʊ] *(pl* **pesos)** N *(Mexican currency)* peso *m*

pessary [ˈpesərɪ] N *Med* ovule *m*

pessimism [ˈpesɪmɪz(ə)m] N pessimisme *m*; **there is growing p. about the prospects for peace** on est de plus en plus pessimiste quant aux chances de paix

pessimist [ˈpesɪmɪst] N pessimiste *mf*; **don't be such a p.!** ne sois pas si pessimiste!

pessimistic [pesɪˈmɪstɪk] ADJ pessimiste

pessimistically [pesɪˈmɪstɪklɪ] ADV avec pessimisme

PEST [pest] N *Mktg (abbr* **political economic sociological technological)** = facteurs *mpl* politiques, économiques, sociaux et technologiques (considérés comme les aspects les plus importants lors de l'analyse de l'environnement d'une entreprise)

pest [pest] N **1** *(animal, insect, plant)* animal *m*/insecte *m*/plante *f* nuisible; **rabbits are a p. here** ici les lapins sont un fléau **2** *Fam (nuisance)* **stop being a p.!** arrête d'embêter le monde!; **he's a perfect p.!** c'est un vrai poison!; **having to take the dog for a walk is a real p.** c'est vraiment embêtant d'avoir à promener le chien

► ► **p. control** *(action) (of rats)* dératisation *f, (of insects)* désinsectisation *f, (department) (for rats)* service *m* de dératisation; *(for insects)* service de désinsectisation

Note that the French word **peste** also means **plague**.

pester [ˈpestər] VT tourmenter, importuner; **to p. sb to do sth** harceler qn pour qu'il fasse qch; **to p. sb with questions** importuner ou assommer ou harceler qn de (ses) questions; **to p. sb for money** harceler qn pour obtenir de l'argent

pesticide [ˈpestɪsaɪd] N pesticide *m*

pestiferous [peˈstɪfərəs] ADJ *Lit (air)* pestilentiel; *(doctrine)* pernicieux

pestilence [ˈpestɪləns] N *Lit* peste *f*

pestilential [pestɪˈlenʃəl] ADJ *Med (disease)* pestilentiel; *(smell)* pestilentiel, infect; *Fam (irritating)* assommant, empoisonnant

pestle [ˈpes(ə)l] N *Culin* pilon *m*

pet[1] [pet] N **1** *(animal)* animal *m* domestique ou familier ou de compagnie; **do you have any pets?** est-ce que tu as un animal?; **a p. monkey/budgerigar** un singe/une perruche apprivoisé(e) **2** *(favourite child)* enfant *mf* gâté(e); **mother's/teacher's p.** le chouchou de sa maman/du professeur; **my p.!** mon chéri!, mon petit chou!; **my p. hate** ma bête noire; **p. subject** sujet *m* de prédilection

VT (-tt-) **1** *(make a pet of) (person)* choyer, chouchouter **2** *(stroke, pat) (person, dog etc)* caresser, câliner

VI *Fam (sexually)* se caresser, *Fam* se peloter
► ► **p. food** aliments *mpl* pour animaux (domestiques); **p. name** surnom *m* affectueux; **p. passport** = sorte de passeport pour animal domestique, visant à éviter la période de quarantaine après un séjour à l'étranger; **p. shop** magasin *m* d'animaux domestiques, animalerie *f*

pet[2] N *Old-fashioned Fam* **to be in a p.** *(to sulk)* faire la tête, être de mauvaise humeur (**about** à cause de); **to go in a p.** faire la tête

petal [ˈpet(ə)l] N **1** *(of flower)* pétale *m* **2** *Fam (term of affection)* **thanks p.** merci mon chou

petard [peˈtɑːd] N **to be hoist with one's own p.** être pris à son propre piège

Pete [piːt] N *Fam* **for P. 's sake!** pour l'amour du ciel!

Peter ['pi:tər] **N** he's a real P. Pan c'est un vrai gosse
▸▸ **P. Pan collar** col *m* Claudine

peter ['pi:tər] **N 1** *Sl (safe)* coffre-fort *m*, *pl* coffres-forts **2** *Am Sl (penis)* quéquette *f*, zizi *m*
▸ **peter out** **VI** *Fam (of conversation, interest, enthusiasm etc)* tarir; *(of scheme, plan)* n'aboutir à rien; *(of path, stream)* disparaître; *(of flame etc)* mourir; **the party gradually petered out** les gens ont quitté la fête peu à peu

peterman ['pi:təmæn] **N** *Sl (safe-breaker)* casseur *m* de coffres-forts

petersham ['pi:təʃəm] **N** *Tex* gros-grain *m*, *pl* gros-grains

petite [pə'ti:t] **ADJ** *(woman)* menu

petition [pɪ'tɪʃən] **N 1** *(request)* requête *f*, supplique *f*; *(document)* pétition *f*; **to grant a p.** faire droit à une pétition; **to hand in/sign a p.** remettre/signer une pétition; **to get up a p.** faire signer une pétition **2** *Law* **p. for mercy** recours *m* en grâce; **p. for a divorce** demande *f* en divorce; **p. in bankruptcy** *(made by creditors)* requête *f* des créanciers; *(made by bankrupt)* requête du négociant insolvable **3** *(to God)* prière *f*
VT *(court, sovereign etc)* adresser *ou* présenter une pétition à
VI *(with document)* pétitionner; **to p. for sth** *(collect signatures)* faire signer une pétition pour qch; *(present petition)* adresser une pétition pour qch; *Fml* **to p. for mercy** se pourvoir *ou* recourir en grâce; *Law* **to p. for divorce** faire une demande de divorce

petitioner [pɪ'tɪʃənər] **N** pétitionnaire *mf*; *Law* requérant, -ante

petrel ['petrəl] **N** *(bird)* pétrel *m*

petrifaction [petrɪ'fækʃən], **petrification** [petrɪfɪ'keɪʃən] **N** pétrification *f*

petrified ['petrɪfaɪd] **ADJ** *(wood etc)* pétrifié; *Fam* **p. with fear** pétrifié *ou* paralysé de terreur; *Fam* **I was p. he would shoot me** j'étais mort de peur à l'idée qu'il me tire dessus

petrify ['petrɪfaɪ] **VT** *(wood etc)* pétrifier; *Fam (with fear)* pétrifier, paralyser
VI se pétrifier

petrifying ['petrɪfaɪɪŋ] **ADJ** *Fam (frightening)* paralysant

petrochemical [petrəʊ'kemɪk(ə)l] **ADJ** *(industry etc)* pétrochimique
NPL **petrochemicals** produits *mpl* pétrochimiques

petrocurrency ['petrəʊkʌrənsɪ] **N** pétromonnaies *fpl*

petrodollar ['petrəʊdɒlər] **N** pétrodollar *m*

petrol ['petrəl] **N** *Br Aut* essence *f*, *Suisse* benzine *f*; **to fill up with p.** faire le plein d'essence; **to run out of p.** tomber en panne d'essence; **high-grade** *or* **four-star p.** = supercarburant *m*, *Fam* super *m*
▸▸ **p. bomb** cocktail *m* Molotov; **p. can** bidon *m* d'essence; **p. cap** bouchon *m* d'essence; **p. company** compagnie *f* pétrolière; **p. filler cap** bouchon d'essence; **p. filler pipe** tuyau *m* de remplissage d'essence; **p. gauge** jauge *f* à essence; **p. pump** *(at service station)* pompe *f* à essence; **p. station** station-service *f*, *pl* stations-services; *Aut* **p. tank** réservoir *m* (d'essence); **p. tanker** *(lorry)* camion-citerne *m*, *pl* camions-citernes; *(ship)* pétrolier *m*, tanker *m*

Note that the French word **pétrole** is a false friend and is never a translation for the English word **petrol**. It means **oil**.

petrol-bomb **VT** jeter des cocktails Molotov sur

petroleum [pə'trəʊlɪəm] **N** pétrole *m*

▸▸ **p. industry** industrie *f* pétrolière; *Br* **p. jelly** vaseline *f*

petrolhead ['petrəlhed] **N** *Br Fam* dingue *mf* de bagnoles

petrology [pe'trɒlədʒɪ] **N** pétrologie *f*

petticoat ['petɪkəʊt] **N** *(skirt length)* jupon *m*; *(full length)* combinaison *f*
▸▸ *Fam* **p. government** gouvernement *m* de femmes

pettifogging ['petɪfɒgɪŋ] **ADJ** *Old-fashioned (detail)* insignifiant; *(objection)* de pure chicane; *(person)* chicanier; **p. lawyer** avocassier, -ière

pettiness ['petɪnɪs] **N** *(insignificance)* insignifiance *f*; *(small-mindedness)* mesquinerie *f*

petting ['petɪŋ] **N** *Fam* pelotage *m*; **heavy p.** attouchements *mpl*

pettish ['petɪʃ] **ADJ** *(person)* de mauvaise humeur, maussade, irritable; *(behaviour, reaction)* maussade, morose

pettishly ['petɪʃlɪ] **ADV** avec mauvaise humeur

petty ['petɪ] **ADJ 1** *(insignificant, minor)* petit, insignifiant; **p. annoyances** tracasseries *fpl*, petits ennuis *mpl* **2** **p. (-minded)** mesquin
▸▸ **p. cash** petite caisse *f*; **p. cash book** livre *m* de petite caisse; **p. cash box** petite caisse; **p. cash voucher** bon *m* de petite caisse; **p. crime** actes *mpl* délictueux; **p. larceny** larcin *m*; **p. offences** contraventions *fpl*; *Br Naut* **p. officer** ≃ second maître *m*

petty-mindedness [petɪ'maɪndɪdnɪs] **N** mesquinerie *f*

petulance ['petjʊləns] **N** irascibilité *f*, mauvaise humeur *f*; **an outburst of p.** un accès de mauvaise humeur

petulant ['petjʊlənt] **ADJ** irritable, susceptible; *(frown)* irrité; **he became quite p.** il s'est montré vraiment susceptible; **you're in a p. mood today!** tu es vraiment susceptible aujourd'hui!

Note that the French word **pétulant** is a false friend and is never a translation for the English word **petulant**. It means **exuberant**.

petulantly ['petjʊləntlɪ] **ADV** *(to look at)* d'un air irrité; *(to say)* d'un ton irrité; *(to react)* avec humeur

petunia [pɪ'tju:nɪə] **N** *(plant)* pétunia *m*

pew [pju:] **N** banc *m* d'église; *Fam* **take** *or* **have a p.!** assieds-toi!

pewter ['pju:tər] **N** étain *m*; **p. (ware)** étains, vaisselle *f* d'étain; **I like p. (ware)** j'aime les étains

PFI [pi:ef'aɪ] **N** *(abbr* **private finance initiative***)* partenariat *m* public-privé

PG [pi:'dʒi:] **ADJ** *Br Cin (abbr* **parental guidance***) (film)* = qui exige une autorisation parentale

PGCE [pi:dʒi:si:'i:] **N** *Br Sch (abbr* **Postgraduate Certificate in Education***)* = diplôme *m* d'enseignement

PgDn *Comput (abbr* **page down***)* PgSv

PGP [pi:dʒi:'pi:] **N** *Comput (abbr* **Pretty Good Privacy***)* (logiciel *m* de chiffrement) PGP *m*

PgUp *Comput (abbr* **page up***)* PgPr

pH [pi:'eɪtʃ] **N** *Chem* pH *m*; **a pH of 9** un pH de 9

phalanx ['fælæŋks] **N 1** *(pl usu* **phalanxes** ['fælæŋksɪz]*) (in ancient armies)*, *Fig* armée *f* **2** *Anat, Bot (pl usu* **phalanges** [fə'lændʒi:z]*)* phalange *f*

phallic ['fælɪk] **ADJ** phallique
▸▸ **p. symbol** symbole *m* phallique

phallocentric [fæləʊ'sentrɪk] **ADJ** phallocentrique

phallus ['fæləs] **N** phallus *m*

phantasm ['fæntæz(ə)m] **N** *Lit (illusion)* illusion *f*; *(ghost)* apparition *f*

phantasmagoria [fæntæzmæ'gɒrɪə] **N** *Lit* fantasmagorie *f*

phantasy ['fæntəsɪ] **N** = **fantasy**

phantom ['fæntəm] **N** fantôme *m*, spectre *m*
▸▸ *Tel* **p. circuit** circuit *m* fantôme; *Med* **p. limb** membre *m* fantôme; *Br* **p. pregnancy** grossesse *f* nerveuse; **p. ship** vaisseau *m* fantôme

Pharaoh ['feərəʊ] **N** *Antiq* pharaon *m*

Pharisee ['færɪsi:] **N** *Antiq, Fig* pharisien, -ienne

pharmaceutical [fɑ:mə'sju:tɪk(ə)l] **ADJ** pharmaceutique; **p. rep(resentative)** visiteur, -euse médical(e)
NPL **pharmaceuticals** *(medicines)* produits *mpl* pharmaceutiques; *(industry)* industrie *f* pharmaceutique; **I'm in pharmaceuticals** je suis dans l'industrie pharmaceutique
▸▸ **pharmaceuticals company** société *f* pharmaceutique

pharmacist ['fɑ:məsɪst] **N** pharmacien, -ienne

pharmacological [fɑ:məkə'lɒdʒɪk(ə)l] **ADJ** pharmacologique

pharmacologist [fɑ:mə'kɒlədʒɪst] **N** pharmacologiste *mf*, pharmacologue *mf*

pharmacology [fɑ:mə'kɒlədʒɪ] **N** pharmacologie *f*

pharmacopoeia [fɑ:məkəʊ'pi:ə] **N** *(book)* pharmacopée *f*, *(collection of drugs)* pharmacopée, pharmacie *f*

pharmacy ['fɑ:məsɪ] **N** pharmacie *f*

pharyngitis [færɪn'dʒaɪtɪs] **N** *Med* pharyngite *f*

pharynx ['færɪŋks] **N** *Anat* pharynx *m*

phase [feɪz] **N** *(of phenomenon, process, moon etc)* phase *f*; **it's still in the development p.** c'est encore en cours de développement; **initial/final p.** phase initiale/finale; *Rugby* **second p.** deuxième temps *m*; **to enter upon a new p.** entrer dans une nouvelle phase; **it's just a p. (he's/she's going through)** ça lui passera; *Phys, Tech* **in p.** en phase (**with sth** avec qch); **out of p.** *Phys, Tech* hors de phase, déphasé; *Fig* déphasé; *Elec* **single/two/three-p. current** courant *m* monophasé/diphasé/triphasé
VT 1 *(changes, new methods)* introduire progressivement; *(project)* développer en phases successives; *(schedule, introduction of technology etc)* échelonner; **the negotiations have to be properly phased** les diverses phases des négociations doivent être correctement planifiées **2** *Elec etc* mettre en phases, caler en phase
▸▸ *TV* **p. distortion** déphasage *m*
▸ **phase in** **VT SEP** *(changes, new methods etc)* introduire progressivement; *(new systems, equipment etc)* mettre en place progressivement
▸ **phase out** **VT SEP 1** *(get rid of gradually) (methods, equipment, jobs etc)* éliminer progressivement; *Hum (boyfriend)* faire sortir de sa vie; **the system is being phased out** ce système est en cours d'abandon **2** *(get rid of)* éliminer; **that's all been phased out now** ça n'existe plus maintenant

phased [feɪzd] **ADJ 1** par phases, progressif; *(evacuation)* progressif **2** *Elec* phasé; *(light)* cohérent

phasing ['feɪzɪŋ] **N 1** *(planning)* planification *f* par phases; *(of manufacturing schedule etc)* échelonnement *m*; *(phasing in) (of measures, new methods)* introduction *f* progressive **2** *Elec etc* mise *f* en phase, calage *m* en phase

▸▸ **p. in** *(of new methods)* adoption *f* ou introduction progressive; *(of new systems, new equipment)* mise en place progressive; **p. out** *(of old methods, systems, equipment etc)* abandon *m* progressif; *(of jobs)* suppression *f* progressive

phat [fæt] **ADJ** *Am Sl* super, génial, -aux

PhD [piːeɪtʃ'diː] **N** *Univ (abbr* **Doctor of Philosophy**) *(diploma)* = doctorat *m*; *(person)* docteur *m*, titulaire *mf* d'un doctorat; **to have a P. in Maths** avoir un doctorat en maths

pheasant ['fez(ə)nt] **N** faisan *m*; **cock p.** (coq *m*) faisan; **hen p.** (poule *f*) faisane *f*; **young p.** faisandeau *m*
▸▸ **p. poult** faisandeau *m*; **p. shoot** faisanderie *f*; **p. shooting** chasse *f* au faisan

phenix ['fiːnɪks] **N** *Am Myth* = **phoenix**

phenobarbitone [fiːnəʊ'bɑːbɪtəʊn] **N** *Pharm* phénobarbital *m*

phenol ['fiːnɒl] **N** *Chem* phénol *m*

phenomenal [fɪ'nɒmɪn(ə)l] **ADJ** *(very great)* phénoménal, -aux, prodigieux; *Phil* phénoménal

phenomenally [fɪ'nɒmɪn(ə)lɪ] **ADV** prodigieusement; **he's p. rich/stupid** il est phénoménalement riche/d'une insondable bêtise

phenomenological [fənɒmənə'lɒdʒɪk(ə)l] **ADJ** phénoménologique

phenomenologist [fənɒmə'nɒlədʒɪst] **N** phénoménologue *mf*

phenomenology [fənɒmə'nɒlədʒɪ] **N** phénoménologie *f*

phenomenon, *pl* **phenomena** [fɪ'nɒmɪnən, -mɪnə] **N** phénomène *m*

pheromone ['ferəməʊn] **N** phérormone *f*, phéromone *f*

phew [fjuː] **INT** *(when hot)* pfff!; *(disgust)* pouah!; *(relief)* ouf!

phial ['faɪəl] **N** fiole *f*, flacon *m*, ampoule *f*

Phil *abbr* **Philadelphia**

Philadelphia [fɪlə'delfɪə] **N** Philadelphie

philander [fɪ'lændər] **VI** *Lit Pej* courir le jupon

philanderer [fɪ'lændərər] **N** *Pej* coureur *m* de jupons

philandering [fɪ'lændərɪŋ] *Pej* **N she had had enough of his p.** elle en avait assez qu'il coure le jupon
ADJ *(ways, habits)* de coureur de jupon; **her p. husband** son coureur de mari

philanthropic [fɪlən'θrɒpɪk] **ADJ** philanthropique; *(person)* philanthrope

philanthropist [fɪ'lænθrəpɪst] **N** philanthrope *mf*

philanthropy [fɪ'lænθrəpɪ] **N** philanthropie *f*

philatelic [fɪlə'telɪk] **ADJ** philatélique

philatelist [fɪ'lætəlɪst] **N** philatéliste *mf*

philately [fɪ'lætəlɪ] **N** philatélie *f*

-phile [faɪl] **SUFF** -phile; **Anglop.** anglophile *mf*, **Francop.** francophile *mf*

philharmonic [fɪlə'mɒnɪk] **ADJ** philharmonique
N philharmonie *f*, société *f* philharmonique

-philia ['fɪlɪə] **SUFF** -philie; **necrop.** nécrophilie *f*, **anglop.** anglophilie *f*

Philippine ['fɪlɪpiːn] **ADJ** philippin
N the Philippines les (îles *fpl*) Philippines *fpl* VOIR GRAMMAIRE A12

philistine ['fɪlɪstaɪn] **N** *Art, Liter* béotien, -ienne, philistin *m*; *Bible* **P.** Philistin *m*
ADJ *Art, Liter* béotien, philistin

philistinism ['fɪlɪstɪnɪz(ə)m] **N** philistinisme *m*

Phillips® ['fɪlɪps] **ADJ**
▸▸ **P. screw** vis *f* à empreinte cruciforme; **P. screwdriver** tournevis *m* à empreinte cruciforme

philodendron [fɪlə'dendrən] **N** *(plant)* philodendron *m*

philological [fɪlə'lɒdʒɪk(ə)l] **ADJ** philologique

philologist [fɪ'lɒlədʒɪst] **N** philologue *mf*

philology [fɪ'lɒlədʒɪ] **N** philologie *f*

philosopher [fɪ'lɒsəfər] **N** philosophe *mf*; **the p.'s stone** la pierre philosophale

philosophic(al) [fɪlə'sɒfɪk, -ɪk(ə)l] **ADJ** *Phil* philosophique; *Fig (person, attitude)* philosophe; **she was p. about her defeat** elle a pris sa défaite en philosophe ou avec philosophie

philosophically [fɪlə'sɒfɪklɪ] **ADV** *Phil* philosophiquement; *Fig (to react etc)* en philosophe, avec philosophie

philosophize [fɪ'lɒsəfaɪz] **VI** philosopher

philosophy [fɪ'lɒsəfɪ] **N** philosophie *f*; **a personal p.** une philosophie personnelle; **one's own p. about sth** sa conception personnelle de qch; **my p. is …** ma philosophie c'est …; **with p.** *(to endure hardship)* avec philosophie, en philosophe

philtre, *Am* **philter** ['fɪltər] **N** philtre *m*

phiz [fɪz], **phizog** ['fɪzɒg] **N** *esp Br Old-fashioned Sl (face)* binette *f*, tronche *f*

phlebitis [flɪ'baɪtɪs] **N** *Med* phlébite *f*; **to have p.** avoir une phlébite

phlegm [flem] **N 1** *(mucus)* flegme *m*, pituite *f* (bronchiale); **to cough up p.** tousser gras **2** *Fml (composure)* flegme *m*, calme *m*

phlegmatic [fleg'mætɪk] **ADJ** flegmatique

phlegmatically [fleg'mætɪklɪ] **ADV** flegmatiquement

phlox [flɒks] **N** *(plant)* phlox *m*

-phobe [fəʊb] **SUFF** -phobe *mf*

phobia ['fəʊbɪə] **N** phobie *f*; **to have a p. about sth** avoir une phobie pour qch

-phobia ['fəʊbɪə] **SUFF** -phobie *f*

phobic ['fəʊbɪk] **ADJ, N** *Med* phobique *mf*; *Fig* **he's really p. about tidiness** c'est un vrai maniaque du rangement

-phobic ['fəʊbɪk] **SUFF** -phobe

Phoenician [fɪ'niːʃən] *Antiq* **ADJ** phénicien **N 1** Phénicien, -ienne **2** *Ling* phénicien *m*

phoenix, *Am* **phenix** ['fiːnɪks] **N** *Myth* phénix *m*; **to rise, p.-like, from …** renaître, tel un phénix, de …

phone[1] [fəʊn] **N** téléphone *m*; **to be on the p.** *(talking)* être au téléphone; *(have a telephone)* avoir le téléphone; *Fam* **to give sb a p.** donner un coup de téléphone ou de fil à qn; **he was on the p. for an hour** il a passé une heure au téléphone; **he's on the p.** *(in office)* il est en ligne; **quiet, Mummy's on the p.** tais-toi, maman a quelqu'un au bout du fil; **I've got Mummy on the p.** j'ai Maman au bout du fil; **to get on the p. to sb** téléphoner à qn; **I couldn't get her on the p.** je n'ai pas réussi à l'avoir au téléphone ou à la joindre; **could you get Maria on the p. for me?** est-ce que tu pourrais m'appeler Maria (au téléphone)?; **get off the p.!** raccroche!; **to speak to sb on** *or* **over the p.** parler à qn au téléphone
VT 1 to p. sb téléphoner à qn, appeler qn au téléphone, donner un coup de téléphone ou *Fam* de fil à qn; **to p. the office/police** téléphoner au bureau/à la police **2 to p. a piece of news** téléphoner une nouvelle
VI téléphoner; **to p. home** téléphoner à la maison
▸▸ **p. bill** facture *f* de téléphone; **p. book** annuaire *m* (téléphonique); **p. booth** cabine *f* téléphonique; *Br* **p. box** cabine téléphonique; **p. call** coup *m* de téléphone, appel *m* (téléphonique); **p. number** numéro *m* de téléphone; **p. tap** écoute *f* téléphonique; **p. tapping** écoutes téléphoniques

▸ **phone in VI** téléphoner; **to p. in sick** téléphoner pour dire qu'on est malade
▸ **phone up VT SEP = phone VT**

phone[2] **N** *Ling* phonème *m*

-phone [fəʊn] **SUFF** -phone; **Anglop./Francop.** anglophone/francophone

phonecard ['fəʊnkɑːd] **N** *Br Tel* télécarte *f*, carte *f* téléphonique

phone-in N p. (programme) émission *f* à ligne ouverte, émission au cours de laquelle les téléspectateurs/auditeurs peuvent intervenir par téléphone

phoneme ['fəʊniːm] **N** *Ling* phonème *m*

phonemic [fə'niːmɪk] **ADJ** phonémique

phonetic [fə'netɪk] **ADJ** phonétique
▸▸ **p. alphabet** alphabet *m* phonétique

phonetically [fə'netɪklɪ] **ADV** phonétiquement

phonetician [fəʊnə'tɪʃən] **N** phonéticien, -ienne

phonetics [fə'netɪks] **N** VOIR GRAMMAIRE A10 **1** *(science)* phonétique *f* **2** *(symbols)* phonétique *f*

phoney, *esp Am* **phony** ['fəʊnɪ] *Fam* **ADJ** *(comp* **phonier;** *superl* **phoniest)** faux, *f* fausse; *(story, excuse etc)* bidon; **he's p. (Am as a two-dollar bill)** il est faux comme un jeton, il est faux jeton
N *(impostor)* imposteur *m*; *(insincere person)* faux jeton *m*; *(fake object)* faux *m*
▸▸ *Hist* **p. war** drôle *f* de guerre

phonic ['fɒnɪk, 'fəʊnɪk] **ADJ** phonique

phonograph ['fəʊnəgræf] **N** *Am* phonographe *m*

phonology [fə'nɒlədʒɪ] **N** phonologie *f*

phony ['fəʊnɪ] **ADJ, N** *esp Am Fam* = **phoney**

phooey ['fuːɪ] **INT** peuh!

phosgene ['fɒzdʒiːn] **N** *Chem* phosgène *m*

phosphate ['fɒsfeɪt] **N** *Chem* phosphate *m*; **p. of lime, calcium p.** phosphate de chaux; **p. mine** *or* **works** phosphaterie *f*

phosphide ['fɒsfaɪd] **N** *Chem* phosphure *m*

phosphite ['fɒsfaɪt] **N** *Chem* phosphite *m*

phosphoresce [fɒsfə'res] **VI** être phosphorescent, luire par phosphorescence

phosphorescence [fɒsfə'resəns] **N** phosphorescence *f*

phosphorescent [fɒsfə'resənt] **ADJ** phosphorescent

phosphoric [fɒs'fɒrɪk] **ADJ** *Chem* phosphorique

phosphorous ['fɒsfərəs] **ADJ** *Chem* phosphoreux

phosphorus ['fɒsfərəs] **N** *Chem* phosphore *m*

photo ['fəʊtəʊ] **N** photo *f*; **to take good photos** prendre de bonnes photos; **to take a good p.** *(be photogenic)* être photogénique
▸▸ **p. album** album *m* de photos; *Cin, TV* **p. call** séance *f* de photos; *Comput* **p. CD** CD-Photo *m inv*, Photo-CD *m inv*; *Comput* **p. editing** retouche *f* d'images; **p. finish** *Sport* arrivée *f* groupée; *Fig* partie *f* serrée; **p. library** photothèque *f*; **p. opportunity** séance de photo; **p. shoot** séance photos

photo- ['fəʊtəʊ] **PREF** photo-

photobooth ['fəʊtəʊbuːð] **N** Photomaton® *m*

photocard ['fəʊtəʊkɑːd] **N** carte *f* portant une photo d'identité du titulaire

photocell ['fəʊtəʊsel] **N** photocellule *f*

photocompose [fəʊtəʊkəm'pəʊz] **VT** photocomposer

photocomposer [fəʊtəʊkəm'pəʊzər] **N** *(person)* photocompositeur, -trice

photocomposition [fəʊtəʊkɒmpə'zɪʃən]

N photocomposition *f*
▸▸ **p. machine** photocomposeuse *f*

photocompositor [fəʊtəʊkəm'pɒzɪtər] **N** *(machine)* photocomposeuse *f*

photocopier ['fəʊtəʊkɒpɪər] **N** photocopieur *m*, photocopieuse *f*

photocopy ['fəʊtəʊkɒpɪ] **N** photocopie *f*; **to take** *or* **make a p. of sth** faire une photocopie de qch, photocopier qch
VT photocopier
VI **these pictures won't p. very well** ces dessins ne donneront pas de bonnes photocopies; **to do some photocopying** faire des photocopies

photoelectric [fəʊtəʊɪ'lektrɪk] **ADJ** photoélectrique
▸▸ **p. cell** cellule *f* photoélectrique

photoelectron [fəʊtəʊɪ'lektrɒn] **N** *Phys* photoélectron *m*

photoengraving [fəʊtəʊɪn'greɪvɪŋ] **N** photogravure *f*

Photofit® ['fəʊtəʊfɪt] **N** *(picture)* portrait-robot *m*, *pl* portraits-robots
▸▸ **P. picture** portrait-robot

photogenic [fəʊtə'dʒenɪk] **ADJ** photogénique

photograph ['fəʊtəʊgrɑːf] **N** photo *f*, photographie *f*, **in the p.** sur la photo; **to have a p. of sth** avoir qch en photo; **to take sb's p.** prendre une photo de qn; **he had his p. taken** il s'est fait photographier; **she takes a good p.** *(is photogenic)* elle est photogénique
VT photographier, prendre en photo
VI **to p. well** *(be photogenic)* être photogénique; **it won't p. well in this light** cela ne fera pas une bonne photo dans cette lumière
▸▸ **p. album** album *m* de photos; **p. library** photothèque *f*

Note that the French word **photographe** is a false friend and is never a translation for the English word **photograph**. It means **photographer**.

photographer [fə'tɒgrəfər] **N** photographe *mf*; **she's a good/bad p.** elle prend de bonnes/mauvaises photos

photographic [fəʊtə'græfɪk] **ADJ** *(process, description etc)* photographique; **to have a p. memory** avoir une mémoire photographique
▸▸ **p. agency** agence *f* photographique; **p. library** photothèque *f*, **p. paper** papier *m* photo

photographically [fəʊtə'græfɪklɪ] **ADV** photographiquement

photography [fə'tɒgrəfɪ] **N** photographie *f*

photogravure [fəʊtəʊgrə'vjʊər] **N** photogravure *f*

photojournalism [fəʊtəʊ'dʒɜːnəlɪz(ə)m] **N** photoreportage *m*

photojournalist [fəʊtəʊ'dʒɜːnəlɪst] **N** reporter *m* photographe, photojournaliste *mf*

photolithograph [fəʊtəʊ'lɪθəʊgrɑːf] **N** photolithographie *f*

photolithography [fəʊtəʊlɪ'θɒgrəfɪ] **N** photolithographie *f*

photoluminescence [fəʊtəʊluːmɪ'nesəns] **N** photoluminescence *f*

photometer [fəʊ'tɒmɪtər] **N** *Phys* photomètre *m*

photometry [fəʊ'tɒmɪtrɪ] **N** *Phys* photométrie *f*

photomontage ['fəʊtəʊmɒn'tɑːʒ] **N** photomontage *m*

photon ['fəʊtɒn] **N** *Phys* photon *m*

photonovel ['fəʊtəʊnɒv(ə)l] **N** roman-photo *m*, *pl* romans-photos

photosensitive [fəʊtəʊ'sensɪtɪv] **ADJ** photosensible

photoset ['fəʊtəʊset] **VT** *Br* photocomposer

photosetter ['fəʊtəʊsetər] **N** *Br* photocomposeuse *f*, photocompositeur *m*

photosetting ['fəʊtəʊsetɪŋ] **N** *Br* photocomposition *f*
▸▸ **p. machine** photocomposeuse *f*

Photostat® ['fəʊtəʊstæt] **N** photostat *m*
VT faire un photostat de
VI faire des photostats

photo-story **N** roman-photo *m*, *pl* romans-photos

photosynthesis [fəʊtəʊ'sɪnθɪsɪs] **N** photosynthèse *f*

photosynthesize [fəʊtəʊ'sɪnθɪsaɪz] **VT** photosynthétiser

phototropism [fəʊtəʊ'trəʊpɪz(ə)m] **N** *Biol* phototropisme *m*

phototypesetter [fəʊtəʊ'taɪpsetər] **N** *Br* photocompositeur *m*

phototypesetting [fəʊtəʊ'taɪpsetɪŋ] **N** *Br* photocomposition *f*

photovoltaic [fəʊtəʊvɒl'teɪɪk] **ADJ** photovoltaïque
▸▸ **p. cell** cellule *f* photovoltaïque, photopile *f*; **p. effect** effet *m* photovoltaïque

phrasal ['freɪzəl] **ADJ**
▸▸ *Gram* **p. verb** verbe *m* à particule, verbe composé **VOIR GRAMMAIRE A61–3; B65**

phrase [freɪz] **N** expression *f*, *Mus* phrase *f*, *Gram* locution *f* (adverbiale *etc*), membre *m* de phrase; **noun p.** syntagme *m* nominal; **could you describe it for us in a p. or two?** est-ce que vous pourriez nous le décrire en quelques phrases?; **in Voltaire's p.** comme dirait Voltaire
VT 1 *(verbally)* exprimer, donner un tour à; *(letter, invitation, question, answer)* tourner; **that is how he phrased it** voilà comment il s'est exprimé, voilà comment il a tourné cela **2** *Mus* phraser
▸▸ **p. book** manuel *m* *ou* guide *m* de conversation

Note that the French noun **phrase** is a false friend. It means **sentence**.

phraseology [freɪzɪ'ɒlədʒɪ] **N** phraséologie *f*

phrasing ['freɪzɪŋ] **N 1** *(of text)* phraséologie *f*, *(of thought)* expression *f*, *(of answer, notice etc)* tournure *f* **2** *Mus* phrasé *m*

phreaker ['friːkər] **N** *Comput, Tel Fam* pirate *m* du téléphone

phreaking ['friːkɪŋ] **N** *Comput, Tel Fam* piratage *m* du téléphone

phrenic nerve ['frenɪk] **N** *Med* nerf *m* phrénique

phrenology [frɪ'nɒlədʒɪ] **N** phrénologie *f*

phthisis ['θaɪsɪs] **N** *Med* phtisie *f*

phut [fʌt] **ADV** *Fam* **to go p.** *(of business, engine etc)* claquer; **the light went p.** la lumière s'est éteinte

phwoar [fwɔːr] **INT** *Fam* wouaouh!; **p.! he's a bit of all right** wouaouh! il n'est pas mal

phylactery [fɪ'læktərɪ] **N** *Jewish Rel* phylactère *m*

phylloxera [fɪlɒk'sɪərə] **N** *(insect)* phylloxéra *m*

phylum, *pl* **phyla** ['faɪləm, -lə] **N** *Biol* phylum *m*

physic ['fɪzɪk] **N** *Arch* remède *m*

physical ['fɪzɪk(ə)l] **ADJ 1** *(relating to the body)* physique; *Med (symptoms)* somatique; **rugby is a very p. sport** le rugby est un sport dans lequel il y a beaucoup de contacts physiques; **the game got very p.** le jeu est devenu très physique; **it left him**

a p. wreck ça lui a détruit la santé **2** *(concrete, material)* physique; *Geog* **p. features** topographie *f*
N *Med Fam* visite *f* médicale; **to have a p.** passer une visite médicale
▸▸ **p. access control** contrôle *m* d'accès physique; *Fin* **p. assets** immobilisations *fpl* non financières; *Fin* **p. capital** capital *m* existant; **p. chemistry** chimie *f* physique; **p. contact** contact *m* physique; *Comput* **p. disk cache** cache *m* disque physique; *Mktg* **p. distribution** distribution *f* physique; *Mktg* **p. distribution management** gestion *f* de la distribution physique; **p. education** éducation *f* physique; *Med* **p. examination** visite médicale; **p. exercises** (exercices *mpl* de) gymnastique *f*, **p. fitness** (bonne) forme *f* physique; **p. geography** géographie *f* physique; **p. handicap** infirmité *f*, **p. impossibility** impossibilité *f* matérielle *ou* physique; *Com* **p. inventory** inventaire *m* effectif; *Old-fashioned Br Fam* **p. jerks** (exercices de) gymnastique; **p. presence** présence *f* physique; **p. property** propriété *f* physique; **p. sciences** sciences *fpl* physiques; **p. strength** force *f* physique; **p. training** (exercices de) gymnastique

physically ['fɪzɪklɪ] **ADV 1** physiquement; **p. attractive** attirant sur le plan physique; **p. fit** en bonne forme physique; **to be p. handicapped** être handicapé physique **2** *(materially)* physiquement, matériellement; **seeing it on TV isn't the same as being p. there** le voir à la télévision ce n'est pas la même chose que d'y assister en personne

physician [fɪ'zɪʃən] **N** médecin *m*

Note that the French word **physicien** is a false friend and is never a translation for the English word **physician**. It means **physicist**.

physicist ['fɪzɪsɪst] **N** physicien, -ienne

physics ['fɪzɪks] **N** physique *f* **VOIR GRAMMAIRE A10**

physio ['fɪzɪəʊ] **N** *Med Fam* **1** *(abbr* **physiotherapist)** kiné *mf* **2** *(abbr* **physiotherapy)** kiné *f*

physiognomy [fɪzɪ'ɒnəmɪ] **N** *Fml (of person)* physionomie *f*, *Geog (of region)* configuration *f*

physiological [fɪzɪə'lɒdʒɪk(ə)l] **ADJ** physiologique

physiologically [fɪzɪə'lɒdʒɪklɪ] **ADV** physiologiquement

physiologist [fɪzɪ'ɒlədʒɪst] **N** physiologiste *mf*, physiologue *mf*

physiology [fɪzɪ'ɒlədʒɪ] **N** physiologie *f*

physiopathology [fɪzɪəʊpə'θɒlədʒɪ] **N** *Med* physiopathologie *f*

physiotherapist [fɪzɪəʊ'θerəpɪst] **N** kinésithérapeute *mf*

physiotherapy [fɪzɪəʊ'θerəpɪ] **N** kinésithérapie *f*, rééducation *f*, **to have p.** faire de la rééducation

physique [fɪ'ziːk] **N** physique *m*; **fine p.** beau physique; **poor p.** physique ingrat; **he hasn't the p. for it** il n'a pas le physique de l'emploi

pi [paɪ] **N** *(in Greek alphabet)*, *Math* pi *m*

PIA [piːaɪ'eɪ] **N** *Fin (abbr* **personal investment authority)** = organisme *m* chargé de surveiller les activités des conseillers financiers indépendants et de protéger les petits investisseurs

pianissimo [pɪə'nɪsɪməʊ] **ADV**, **N** pianissimo *m*

pianist ['pɪənɪst] **N** pianiste *mf*

piano¹ [pɪ'ænəʊ], *Fml* **pianoforte** [pɪænəʊ'fɔːtɪ] **N** piano *m*; **sonata for p. and violin** sonate pour piano et violon

▸▸**p. accordion** accordéon m (à touches); **p. concerto** concerto m pour piano; **p. duet** duo m pour piano; **p. key** touche f; **p. player** pianiste mf; **p. stool** tabouret m de piano; **p. tuner** accordeur m de pianos

piano² [pɪˈɑːnəʊ] ADJ, ADV Mus piano

piastre [pɪˈæstər] N (currency) piastre f

piazza [pɪˈætsə] N (esp in Italy) place f (publique); Br (covered) galerie f

PIBOR [ˈpaɪbɔːr] N (abbr Paris interbank offered rate) TIOP m, PIBOR m

pic [pɪk] N Fam 1 (picture) image f, (photograph) photo f 2 Br Cin film m; **the pics** (the cinema) le ciné, le cinoche

pica [ˈpaɪkə] N Typ pica m

picador [ˈpɪkədɔːr] N picador m

Picardy [ˈpɪkədɪ] N Picardie f

picaresque [pɪkəˈresk] ADJ (novel) picaresque

piccalilli [pɪkəˈlɪlɪ] N Culin pickles mpl à la moutarde

piccaninny [pɪkəˈnɪnɪ] N Old-fashioned Offensive Sl (negro child) négrillon, -onne

piccolo [ˈpɪkələʊ] N Mus piccolo m

piccy [ˈpɪkɪ] N Fam (snapshot) photo f

pick¹ [pɪk] N 1 (tool) pic m, pioche f; (miner's) **p.** pic à main 2 Mus (plectrum) plectre m, médiator m

pick² N **the p.** (best) (of people) l'élite f, la crème; (of apples, new films etc) le meilleur, pl les meilleurs; **the p. of the bunch** le meilleur de tous ou Fam du lot; (several people) le dessus du panier, Fam le gratin; **we had first p.** nous avons été les premiers à choisir; **take your p.** choisissez

PICK³ VT 1 (choose) choisir, sélectionner; **to p. one's words (carefully)** (bien) choisir ses mots; Horseracing etc **to p. a winner** choisir ou désigner un gagnant; Fig **we've certainly picked a winner in Paul Rodger** nous avons vraiment tiré le bon numéro avec Paul Rodger; **he was picked for Scotland** il a été choisi pour représenter l'Écosse; **to p. one's way through a field** traverser un champ en regardant où on met les pieds; **you picked a fine time to tell me** tu as bien choisi ton moment pour me le dire; **to p. a fight** chercher la bagarre (**with sb** à qn) 2 (gather) (flowers, fruit etc) cueillir 3 (lock) crocheter; **to p. rags** détisser ou effilocher des chiffons; **to p. sb's pocket** faire les poches à qn; **she picked a hole in her jumper** elle a fait un trou à son pull en tirant sur la laine; Fig **to p. holes in sth** (in argument, theory, book etc) trouver des failles dans qch; Fam **she's constantly picking holes (in everything)** elle n'arrête pas de chercher la petite bête; **to p. sb's brains** avoir recours aux lumières de qn; **can I p. your brains a minute?** est-ce que je peux faire appel à tes connaissances une minute?; **to p. a bone** décortiquer un os; Fig **to have a bone to p. with sb** avoir un compte à régler avec qn; **to p. one's nose/teeth** se curer le nez/les dents; **to p. a spot/scab** gratter un bouton/une croûte 4 (of birds) (corn etc) picoter, becqueter 5 Mus **to p. a guitar** pincer la guitare

VI (choose) choisir; **you p. first** choisis d'abord; **to p. and choose** faire le/la difficile ▸**pick at** VT INSEP **to p. at one's food** picorer; **to p. at a scab** gratter une croûte ▸**pick off** VT SEP 1 (remove) (flowers, leaves etc) enlever, ôter; **p. those papers off the ground** ramassez ces papiers qui sont par terre; **to p. the meat off a bone** décortiquer un os; **she picked herself off the floor** elle s'est relevée 2 (of gunman, sniper) descendre, abattre; (several people) descendre ou abattre un à un; Fig (opponent etc) éliminer; (several op-

ponents) éliminer les uns après les autres ▸**pick on** VT INSEP 1 (victimize) s'en prendre à; **stop picking on her** arrête de t'en prendre à elle; **why p. on me?** pourquoi s'en prendre à moi?; **p. on sb your own size!** ne t'attaque pas à qn de plus faible que toi! 2 (choose) (person, thing) choisir; **I always get picked on for the worst jobs** c'est toujours à moi que reviennent les tâches les plus ingrates ▸**pick out** VT SEP 1 (remove) (something) extirper, enlever 2 (select) (something) choisir; **he picked out the best peaches** il a choisi les meilleures pêches; **to p. out a criminal** (in identification parade) identifier un criminel 3 (recognize) repérer; **she was easy to p. out in her orange coat** elle était facilement reconnaissable ou facile à repérer avec son manteau orange 4 (highlight) **picked out in gold** rehaussé d'or 5 Mus **to p. out a tune** essayer de retrouver un air ▸**pick over** VT INSEP (fruit etc) trier; Fig (performance, exam, details) débattre de ▸**pick up** VT SEP 1 (lift up) prendre; (sth from the ground) ramasser; (sth that has fallen over) relever; (telephone) décrocher; Knitting (stitch) relever; **to p. up survivors** (of ship, helicopter) recueillir des survivants; **to p. up the odd pound here or there** (earn) gagner un peu d'argent par ci par là; **to p. up a child** (in one's arms) prendre un enfant dans ses bras; (after falling) relever un enfant; **to p. oneself up** (after falling) se relever; **to p. up the pieces** (after breaking sth), Fig ramasser les morceaux; **we were left to p. up the bill** c'est nous qui avons dû casquer; **let me p. up the bill** laisse-moi payer 2 (collect) aller prendre ou chercher; **I'll p. you up at the station** je viendrai vous chercher ou vous prendre à la gare; **the train stops to p. up passengers** le train s'arrête pour prendre des voyageurs 3 (catch) **to p. up a cold** ramasser ou attraper un rhume 4 (acquire) **to p. sth up cheap** acheter qch bon marché; **she's good at picking up bargains** elle a du flair pour les bonnes affaires; **to p. up a parking ticket** attraper un PV 5 Fam (initiate casual sexual relationship with) **to p. up a man/woman** lever ou emballer un homme/une femme; **he tried to p. her up** il l'a draguée; **to p. up a customer** (of prostitute) racoler ou raccrocher un client 6 (arrest) (person) arrêter 7 (message) capter, recevoir; Radio (station) capter; Elec (current) prendre, capter; (of searchlight) (plane etc) repérer; **the police have picked up a trail** la police a trouvé une piste 8 (learn) (trick, language, fact) apprendre; (news, information) recueillir; **to p. up a habit** prendre une habitude; **I don't know where he's picking up these funny ideas from** je ne sais pas où il va chercher ces idées bizarres; **she seems to have picked up the idea that …** elle a l'air de s'être mis dans la tête que … 9 (notice) (error) relever 10 (continue) (discussion) reprendre; **we soon picked up the road again** nous avons vite retrouvé notre chemin 11 (reprimand) **to p. sb up sharply** reprendre qn vertement; **I'd like to p. Chris Jones up on that (point)** j'aimerais reprendre Chris Jones sur ce point; **to p. sb up for a mistake** réprimander qn pour avoir fait une erreur 12 Aut etc **to p. up speed** reprendre de la vitesse; **to p. up strength** (of person) reprendre des forces

13 (make better) (person) remonter; **that will p. you up** voilà qui vous remonte

VI 1 (improve) s'améliorer; (after illness) retrouver la santé ou ses forces, se rétablir; **business is picking up** les affaires reprennent; **the weather looks like picking up** le temps a l'air de se remettre; **the game certainly picked up in the second half** la partie s'est animée dans la deuxième mi-temps 2 (continue) (of conversation, negotiations etc) reprendre; (in relationship) recommencer; **let's p. up where we left off** reprenons là où nous nous étions arrêtés 3 Sport etc **to p. up on sb** rattraper qn; **this engine picks up well** ce moteur a de bonnes reprises

pick-a-back ADV, ADJ, N = **piggyback**

pickaninny [pɪkəˈnɪnɪ] N Old-fashioned Offensive Sl = **piccaninny**

pickaxe, Am **pickax** [ˈpɪkæks] N (tool) pioche f, pic m

VT piocher

picker [ˈpɪkər] N 1 (of fruit etc) cueilleur, -euse 2 (of cotton etc) démêleur, -euse

pickerel [ˈpɪkərəl] N (fish) doré m

picket [ˈpɪkɪt] N 1 Ind etc (of strikers) piquet m de grève; (one person) gréviste mf en faction 2 Mil etc (detachment) piquet m (d'hommes); (one soldier) factionnaire m; **to be on p.** être de piquet 3 (stake) (of fence etc) piquet m, pieu m; (for horses etc) piquet d'attache

VT (-t-) 1 Ind etc **to p. a factory** mettre un piquet de grève aux portes d'une usine 2 (fence) (area) entourer de piquets ou de pieux 3 (fasten) (horses) mettre au(x) piquet(s)

VI Ind etc faire le piquet de grève ▸▸**p. duty** piquet; **p. fence** clôture f de piquets, palissade f; **p. line** piquet de grève

picketing [ˈpɪkɪtɪŋ] N Ind etc blocage m par des piquets de grève

picking [ˈpɪkɪŋ] N 1 (choosing) choix m 2 (of fruit, flowers etc) cueillette f 3 (of lock) crochetage m

▸▸**p. season** cueillette

pickings [ˈpɪkɪŋz] NPL (money etc) bénéfices mpl; **to make rich p. from a scheme** tirer de gros bénéfices d'une affaire

pickle [ˈpɪk(ə)l] N 1 **pickles** pickles mpl, conserves fpl au vinaigre; **mixed pickles** mélange m de pickles 2 (marinade) saumure f 3 Fam (predicament) **to be in a bit of a p.** être dans de beaux draps ou dans le pétrin

VT saumurer, conserver (au vinaigre ou à la saumure)

pickled [ˈpɪk(ə)ld] ADJ 1 saumuré, en saumure 2 Fam (drunk) gris, pompette

▸▸**p. cabbage** chou m rouge au vinaigre; **p. onions** oignons mpl au vinaigre

pickling [ˈpɪk(ə)lɪŋ] N saumurage m, conservation f au vinaigre

▸▸**p. onions** petits oignons mpl

picklock [ˈpɪklɒk] N 1 (person) crocheteur m (de serrures) 2 (key) crochet m, rossignol m

pick-me-up N Fam remontant m

pickpocket [ˈpɪkpɒkɪt] N voleur, -euse à la tire, pickpocket m

pick-up N 1 (collection) ramassage m; Electron, Radio (of signal) captage m 2 (device) (on record player) lecteur m (phonographique), pick-up m inv; Electron etc (of waves, vibrations) capteur m, détecteur m 3 (truck) pick-up m inv, camionnette f à plateau 4 Fam (man, woman) conquête f 5 Fam (improvement) amélioration f; (of business etc) reprise f; (of optimism) regain m

►► **p. arm** (on record player) pick-up; **p. point** (for passengers on coach journey, goods etc) point m de ramassage; **p. truck** pick-up, camionnette à plateau

picky ['pɪkɪ] ADJ Fam difficile; **to be p. about one's food** être difficile sur la nourriture

picnic ['pɪknɪk] N pique-nique m, pl pique-niques; **to go on a p.** aller faire un pique-nique, aller pique-niquer; Fig Fam **it was no p.** cela n'a pas été une partie de plaisir; **we had a p. lunch** nous avons pique-niqué à midi; **we'll take a p. lunch with us** nous emporterons un pique-nique (pour le déjeuner) VI (pt, pp **picnicked**) pique-niquer, faire un pique-nique

►► **p. area** aire f de pique-nique; **p. basket, p. hamper** panier m à pique-nique; (filled) panier garni; **p. site** aire de pique-nique

picnicker ['pɪknɪkər] N pique-niqueur, -euse, pl pique-niqueurs, -euses

Pict [pɪkt] N Hist Picte mf

Pictish ['pɪktɪʃ] ADJ Hist picte, pictique

pictogram ['pɪktəɡræm] N pictogramme m

pictograph ['pɪktəɡrɑːf] N pictographe m

pictorial [pɪk'tɔːrɪəl] ADJ (magazine etc) illustré; (representation) en images N périodique m illustré, journal m illustré ►► **p. dictionary** dictionnaire m en images

pictorially [pɪk'tɔːrɪəlɪ] ADV en images

PICTURE ['pɪktʃər] N 1 (image) (painting) tableau m, peinture f; (drawing) dessin m; (in picture book etc), TV image f; (illustrating text) illustration f; (photograph) photo f; **to paint a p.** faire ou peindre un tableau; **to draw a p.** faire un dessin; **to get one's p. in the paper** avoir sa photo dans le journal

2 Cin Fam (film) film m; **to make a p.** faire un film; **to go to the pictures** aller au cinéma

3 Fig **to get the political/economic p.** la situation politique/économique; Med **we don't know the clinical p.** nous ne savons pas quelle est la situation clinique; **to get a mental p. of sth** se représenter qch; **to paint a bleak p. of the future** présenter une triste image de l'avenir; **this book gives a more accurate p. of the General** ce livre offre un portrait plus fidèle du général; **a clearer p. is emerging of what is taking place in the city** une image plus nette de ce qui se passe dans la ville est en train de se dessiner

4 (phrases) **she's a p.**, **she looks a p.** elle est belle; **he's no p.!** ce n'est pas une beauté!; **she looked an absolute p. in her new dress** elle était à croquer avec sa nouvelle robe; **he's the p. of health** il respire la santé; **she looked a p. of misery** elle faisait pitié; **his face was a p.** il a fait une tête à mourir de rire; **to be in the p.** être au courant ou au fait; **put/keep me in the p.** mets/tiens-moi au courant; **I get the p.** je vois; **to be out of the p.** être dépassé, être en dehors du coup; **it doesn't come into the p.** cela n'entre pas en ligne de compte; **when did he come into the p.?** quand a-t-il commencé à être question de lui?

VT **1** (imagine) **to p. (to oneself)** s'imaginer, se figurer, se représenter; **I can't p. him as a teacher** je ne me l'imagine ou le figure pas professeur; **p. yourself as leader/at 80** imagine-toi dirigeant/à 80 ans

2 (represent, portray) représenter; (in words) dépeindre, décrire; Fig Orwell **pictures a world where …** Orwell décrit ou dépeint un monde où …

►► **p. book** livre m d'images; Cards **p. card** figure f; **p. cheque** image-chèque f, pl images-chèques; Mktg **p. completion** images à compléter; **p. dealer** marchand, -ande de tableaux; Journ **p. desk** bureau m des illustrations; **p. dictionary** dictionnaire m en images; **p. editor** illustrateur, -trice; **p. frame** cadre m (pour tableaux); **p. framer**

encadreur, -euse; **p. gallery** musée m de peinture; **p. hat** capeline f; **p. library** banque f d'images; Comput **p. memory** mémoire f d'images; Tel **p. messaging** envoi m de photos par téléphone portable; Br Old-fashioned **p. palace** cinéma m; Old-fashioned **p. postcard** carte f postale (illustrée); **p. puzzle** rébus m; TV **p. quality** qualité f des images; **p. research** documentation f iconographique; **p. researcher** documentaliste mf iconographique; **p. story** roman-photo m, pl romans-photos; TV **p. tube** tube m image; **p. window** fenêtre f ou baie f panoramique; **p. writing** écriture f idéographique

picturesque [pɪktʃə'resk] ADJ pittoresque; (descriptions etc) imagé; Euph **she told him in p. language to leave** elle lui a ordonné de partir dans un langage assez cru

picturesquely [pɪktʃə'resklɪ] ADV pittoresquement; (to describe, write) de façon imagée

picturesqueness [pɪktʃə'resknɪs] N pittoresque m

piddle ['pɪd(ə)l] Fam VI faire pipi N pipi m; **to have a p.** faire pipi

piddling ['pɪdlɪŋ] ADJ Fam insignifiant, ridicule

pidgin ['pɪdʒɪn] N Ling pidgin m; **p. English** etc ≃ petit nègre m

pie [paɪ] N (with meat) = pâté m en croûte; (apple etc) **p.** = tourte f (aux pommes etc); esp Am (without top) tarte f (aux pommes etc); **chicken p.** = croustade f de volaille; **cottage** or **shepherd's p.** hachis m parmentier; **fish p.** = timbale f de poissons; Fam **p. in the sky** des châteaux en Espagne; **easy as p.** simple comme bonjour

►► **p. chart** graphique m circulaire, camembert m; **p. dish** plat m à tarte; (for meat) terrine f; (oven-proof) plat allant au four

piebald ['paɪbɔːld] ADJ (horse) pie N (cheval m) pie m

PIECE [piːs]

| morceau 1 ▪ bout 1 ▪ parcelle 1 |
| ▪ pièce 1–4 ▪ article 1 ▪ pion 2 |

N **1** (of paper, bread etc) morceau m, bout m; (of string, ribbon) bout m; (of land) parcelle f; (of cloth) morceau, coupon m; (of glass etc) morceau, fragment m, éclat m; (of machine etc) partie f, pièce f; (of music, poetry) morceau; (in book) passage m; Journ article m, papier m; **to do a p. to camera** s'adresser directement à la caméra (pour un reporter de télévision); **a p. of clothing** un vêtement; **a p. of furniture** un meuble; **a p. of luggage** (suitcase) une valise; (bag) un sac; **how many pieces of luggage do you have?** combien de bagages avez-vous?; **one p. of hand-luggage** un bagage à main; **to do a p. of work** faire un travail; **to show sb a p. of one's work** montrer un échantillon de son travail à qn; **he's a nasty p. of work** c'est un sale type; **a p. of advice** un conseil; **p. of bravery/folly** acte m de bravoure/folie; **a p. of cruelty** une cruauté; **p. of (good) luck** coup m de chance; **what a p. of luck!** quelle chance!; **a p. of news** une nouvelle; Fig Fam **it was a p. of cake** c'était de la tarte; Fig **everyone wants a p. of the cake** tout le monde veut sa part du gâteau

2 (in games) (in backgammon) dame f; (in dominoes) domino m; (in draughts) pion m; (of jigsaw puzzle) pièce f; Chess pièce f

3 esp Br (coin) **five/fifty-pence p.** pièce f de cinq/cinquante pence

4 (weapon) (of artillery) pièce f; (firearm) arme f, Fam **to be carrying a p.** porter une arme, être armé

5 Sl (girl) nana f; **she's a nice** or **tasty p.** c'est une belle nana ou nénette

6 Metal **punched/shaped p.** pièce f estampée/profilée; **to cast cylinders in one p.** couler des cylindres d'un seul jet ou en bloc; **cast** or **pressed** or **made in one p.** monobloc inv

7 esp Am (short distance) **he lives down the road a p.** il n'habite pas loin d'ici; **I'll walk with you down the road a p.** je vais faire un petit bout de chemin avec toi

8 Sl (gun) flingue m

9 (in phrases) **they are all of a p.** (of people) ils sont tous du même genre ou acabit; **it's all of a p. to me** pour moi c'est la même chose ou ça revient au même; **to be still in one p.** (of person, car etc after accident) être encore entier; **all in one p.** (made, constructed) tout d'une pièce, d'un seul morceau, d'un seul tenant; **to give sb a p. of one's mind** dire ses quatre vérités à qn; **to say one's p.** dire ce qu'on a à dire; **p. by p.** morceau par morceau; Com **to sell sth by the p.** vendre qch à la pièce; Fam **to go to pieces** (of person) s'effondrer (complètement), Fam craquer; Sport (of team etc) s'effondrer; **to fall to pieces** (of bicycle, furniture, plans etc) tomber en morceaux; (of house etc) se délabrer, crouler; **my coat is falling to pieces** mon manteau part en morceaux; **her life was falling to pieces** toute sa vie s'effondrait; **to take a machine to pieces** démonter une machine; **to break sth in** or **to pieces** briser qch, mettre qch en morceaux

►► Tex **p. goods** marchandises fpl ou tissus mpl à la pièce; **p. rate** paiement m à la pièce

► **piece together** VT SEP (assemble) (model, jigsaw etc) joindre, assembler les morceaux de; (broken vase, chair, torn letter) recoller les morceaux de; (facts etc) coordonner; **to p. together what happened** reconstituer ce qui s'est passé; **detectives are piecing together a picture of the events** les enquêteurs sont en train de se faire une idée des événements

-piece [piːs] SUFF **one-p. overall** combinaison f; **a three-p. suite** un salon trois pièces; **two-/three-p. suit** costume m deux/trois pièces; **a twenty-four-p. dinner service** un service de table vingt-quatre pièces; **three-p. ensemble** trio m; **a four-p. band** un groupe de quatre éléments; **a twenty-p. orchestra** un orchestre de vingt musiciens ou éléments

piecemeal ['piːsmiːl] ADV par morceaux; (gradually) petit à petit, peu à peu; **the collection was sold p.** les pièces de la collection ont été vendues séparément ADJ fragmentaire, parcellaire; (work) fait petit à petit; (funding, transformation) morcelé, fragmenté

piecework ['piːswɜːk] N Ind travail m à la tâche ou à la pièce

pieceworker ['piːswɜːkər] N Ind travailleur, -euse à la tâche ou à la pièce

piecrust ['paɪkrʌst] N croûte f de pâté

pied [paɪd] ADJ bigarré, panaché; **the P. Piper of Hamelin** le Joueur de flûte d'Hamelin

pied-à-terre, pl **pieds-à-terre** [pjeɪdɑː'teər] N pied-à-terre m inv

Piedmont ['piːdmɒnt] N Piémont m

pie-eyed ADJ Sl (drunk) rond, bourré; **to get p.** se saouler

pier [pɪər] N **1** (at seaside resort) jetée f; (of stone) môle m, digue f; (on piles) estacade f **2** Constr (of stonework) pilier m

pierce [pɪəs] VT percer, transpercer; **to p. a hole in sth** faire ou percer un trou dans qch; **to have one's ears pierced** se faire percer les oreilles; **to p. the darkness** (of light) trouer l'obscurité; **to p. the air with one's cries** percer l'air de ses cris

VI to p. through the enemy's lines pénétrer les lignes de l'ennemi

piercing ['pɪəsɪŋ] **ADJ** (tool, cry) aigu, perçant; (look) perçant, pénétrant; (cold, wind) pénétrant

pierhead ['pɪəhed] **N** musoir m

pierrot ['pɪərəʊ] **N** Theat pierrot m

piety ['paɪətɪ] **N** piété f

piffle ['pɪf(ə)l] **N** Fam futilités fpl, bêtises fpl, niaiseries fpl; **to talk p.** dire des futilités ou des bêtises

piffling ['pɪflɪŋ] **ADJ** Fam (objection, mistake) insignifiant; (sum, wage) ridicule, insignifiant; (occupation, activity) futile; (speech etc) creux; **some p. little assistant** un petit assistant insignifiant

pig [pɪg] **N 1** (animal) porc m, cochon m; Am (young pig) cochonnet m, porcelet m; Fam (glutton) goinfre mf, glouton, -onne; **to eat like a p., to make a p. of oneself** s'empiffrer, se goinfrer; Fam **he's a greedy p.** c'est un goinfre; Fig Fam **to buy a p. in a poke** acheter chat en poche; Fig Fam **to make pigs fly** quand les poules auront des dents; Br Fam **to make a p.'s ear of sth** saloper qch; **wild p.** sanglier m; Am (piglet) marcassin m, jeune sanglier **2** Fam (unpleasant person) salaud m, salope f, sale type m; Fam (ugly person) mocheté f; Sl Pej (police officer) flic m; Br Fam (unpleasant thing, task) truc m chiant; Fam **you dirty little p.!** petit cochon!; Fam **what a selfish p.!** quel sale égoïste!; Fam **the filing cabinet was a p. to move** ça a été vachement difficile de déplacer le classeur **3** Metal (of casting) gueuse f, (of lead, tin etc) saumon m

VI (-gg-) (of sow) mettre bas, cochonner **VT** Fam **1 to p. oneself** (eat excessively) s'empiffrer, se goinfrer (**on sth** de qch) **2 to p. it** (be untidy, dirty) vivre comme des cochons

▸▸**p. farm** porcherie f, élevage m de porcs; **p. iron** fonte f brute; **P. Latin** = argot m codé utilisé en milieu scolaire, ≃ javanais m

▸**pig out** **VI** Fam (eat excessively) s'empiffrer, se goinfrer (**on sth** de qch)

pigeon ['pɪdʒɪn] **N 1** (bird) pigeon m **2** Br Fam **that's not my p.** (concern) ce n'est pas mon truc

▸▸**p. fancier** colombophile mf; **p. loft** pigeonnier m; **p. post** transport m de dépêches par pigeons voyageurs

pigeon-breasted [-'brestɪd], **pigeon-chested** [-'tʃestɪd] **ADJ** à la poitrine saillante

pigeonhole ['pɪdʒɪnhəʊl] **N 1** (in desk) case f, casier m; Fig **to put sb in a p.** cataloguer qn, étiqueter qn **2** (in dovecote) boulin m **VT 1** (classify) (papers etc) caser, classer; (complaint etc) classer; (file away in memory) reléguer dans sa mémoire **2** (defer) remettre à plus tard; **the scheme had been pigeonholed until further notice** le projet avait été remis jusqu'à nouvel ordre **3** (person) étiqueter, cataloguer, mettre une étiquette à; **I don't like being pigeonholed** je n'aime pas qu'on me catalogue

pigeon-toed **ADJ** qui marche les pieds tournés en dedans

piggery ['pɪgərɪ] **N** porcherie f, Fam (gluttony) goinfrerie f

piggish ['pɪgɪʃ] **ADJ** Fam (person) (dirty) sale, malpropre; (gluttonous) goinfre

piggy ['pɪgɪ] Fam **N** (in children's language) cochonnet m, petit cochon m; **p. in the middle** (children's game) = jeu m d'enfants dans lequel l'un des participants doit attraper la balle que les autres s'envoient; Fig **I've had enough of being p. in the middle** j'en avais assez d'être pris entre deux feux

ADJ (gluttonous) goinfre; (behaviour) de goinfre; (eyes) porcin; **that was p. of you!** tu t'es goinfré!

▸▸**p. bank** tirelire f

piggyback ['pɪgɪbæk] **ADV 1** (on one's back) sur le dos; **to ride p. on sb** monter sur le dos de qn **2** Comput **to mount sth p. on sth** superposer qch sur qch

N to give sb a p. porter qn sur son dos; **can I have a p.?** est-ce que je peux monter sur ton dos?

▸▸Comput **p. board** carte f fille

piggybacking ['pɪgɪbækɪŋ] **N 1** Com exportation f kangourou **2** Banking portage m

pig-headed **ADJ** obstiné, entêté

pigheadedly [pɪg'hedɪdlɪ] **ADV** obstinément

pigheadedness [pɪg'hedɪdnɪs] **N** obstination f, entêtement m

piglet ['pɪglɪt] **N** cochonnet m, porcelet m

pigment ['pɪgmənt] **N 1** Art etc couleur f, colorant m, pigment m **2** Physiol pigment m

▸▸**p. cell** cellule f pigmentaire

pigmentation [pɪgmən'teɪʃən] **N** pigmentation f

pigmented [pɪg'mentɪd] **ADJ** pigmenté

pigmy ['pɪgmɪ] **N, ADJ** = **pygmy**

pigpen ['pɪgpen] **N** Am = **pigsty**

pigskin ['pɪgskɪn] **N** (leather) peau f de porc; **p. purse** bourse f en peau de porc

pigsty ['pɪgstaɪ] **N 1** porcherie f **2** Fig Fam (house, room) porcherie f; **your room is a p.** ta chambre est une vraie porcherie

pigswill ['pɪgswɪl] **N** pâtée f pour les porcs; Fam (food) pâtée pour chiens

pigtail ['pɪgteɪl] **N** natte f

pig-thick **ADJ** Br Fam con comme un balai

pig-ugly **ADJ** Br Fam moche comme un pou

pike¹ [paɪk] **N 1** (weapon) pique f **2** Br Dial (peak in the Lake District) pic m

▸▸**p. bearer** piquier m

pike² **N** (fish) brochet m

pike³ **N** esp Am = **turnpike**

pikestaff ['paɪksta:f] **N 1** (weapon) bois m ou hampe f de pique **2** (for walking) bâton m à pointe de fer

pikey ['paɪkɪ] **N** Br Sl casseur m

pilaf(f) ['pi:læf] **N** Culin pilaf m, pilau m

pilaster [pɪ'læstər] **N** Archit pilastre m

pilates [pɪ'lɑ:teɪz] **N** Pilates m, méthode f Pilates; **to do p.** pratiquer la méthode Pilates

pilau, pilaw ['pi:laʊ, -ləʊ, -lɔ:] **N** = **pilaf**

pilchard ['pɪltʃəd] **N** (fish) pilchard m

PILE [paɪl]

N	tas **1** ▪ pile **1, 2** ▪ édifice **3** ▪ pieu **4** ▪ poil **5**
VT	entasser ▪ empiler

N 1 (heap) (of wood, stones, rubbish etc) tas m; (of objects, goods etc) tas, amas m, amoncellement m; (of gold) monceau m; (of plates, laundry etc) pile f; **to put in(to) a p.,** **to make a p. of** mettre en tas, empiler; Fam **he made his p. in the fur trade** (fortune) il a fait fortune dans le commerce de fourrure; Fam **she must have made a p. out of that deal** elle a dû gagner une fortune dans ce contrat; Fam **to have piles** or **a p. of ironing/work to do** avoir un tas de repassage/travail à faire; Fig Fam **to be at the top/bottom of the p.** être favorisé/défavorisé **2** Elec (electric) **p.** pile f (électrique); Nucl (atomic) **p.** pile, réacteur m (atomique) **3** (building) édifice m; Fam Hum **the family p.** la cabane familiale **4** Constr pieu m; **to drive piles** enfoncer des pieux; **built on piles** bâti sur pilotis **5** Tex (of carpet etc) poil m

VT (earth etc) entasser, amonceler; (objects) mettre en tas; (wood, books etc) empiler; **they piled food onto my plate** ils ont amoncelé de la nourriture dans mon assiette; **the table was piled high with dishes** des assiettes s'empilaient sur la table

VI Fam **seven of them piled into the car** sept d'entre eux se sont entassés dans la voiture

▸▸**p. dwelling** habitation f lacustre ou sur pilotis; **p. fabrics** tissus mpl à poil

▸**pile in** **VI** Fam (of people) entrer en masse; **p. in everybody!** (into car etc) allez-y, montez tout le monde!

VT SEP Fam (cause to enter in large numbers, quantity) entasser

▸**pile off** **VI** Fam descendre en masse

▸**pile on** **VT SEP** (give in large numbers, quantity) amonceler; **my plate was full, but they piled on more** mon assiette était pleine mais ils m'ont resservi une platée; **to p. on the pressure** faire monter la pression; **to p. on the agony** dramatiser; **to p. on the runs** marquer un grand nombre de points; Fam **to p. it on** exagérer, en rajouter

▸**pile out** **VI** Fam (of people) partir en masse; (from vehicle) sortir en masse; **fifteen people piled out of the compartment** quinze personnes ont quitté le compartiment en masse

▸**pile up** **VI** (form into pile(s)) s'amonceler, s'entasser, s'empiler; (of cars) se caramboler; **dirty dishes were piling up** la vaisselle sale s'empilait ou s'amoncelait; **work was piling up on her desk** le travail s'amoncelait sur son bureau; **the clouds are piling up** les nuages s'amoncellent

VT SEP 1 (form into pile(s)) entasser, empiler; **p. the leaves up here** entasse les feuilles ici; **to p. up money** amasser de l'argent **2** Fam (crash, wreck) **to p. up one's plane/a car** bousiller son appareil/une voiture; **ship piled up on the rocks** navire échoué sur les rochers

---

pile-driver **N** Constr sonnette f, Fam (blow) coup m d'assommoir; Ftbl shoot m vigoureux

piles [paɪlz] **NPL** Med hémorroïdes fpl, **to have p.** avoir des hémorroïdes

pile-up **N** Aut carambolage m, télescopage m en série

pilfer ['pɪlfər] **VT & VI** chaparder (**sth from sb** qch à qn)

pilferage ['pɪlfərɪdʒ] **N** = **pilfering**

pilferer ['pɪlfərər] **N** chapardeur, -euse

pilfering ['pɪlfərɪŋ] **N** petits vols mpl, larcins mpl; **the percentage lost through p.** le pourcentage perdu imputable aux petits vols

pilgrim ['pɪlgrɪm] **N** pèlerin, -ine; **pilgrims to Lourdes/Mecca** les pèlerins de Lourdes/de la Mecque

▸▸**the P. Fathers** les (Pères) Pèlerins mpl; Liter **The P.'s Progress** Le Voyage du pèlerin

pilgrimage ['pɪlgrɪmɪdʒ] **N** Rel, Fig pèlerinage m; **to go on a p., to make a p.** aller en pèlerinage, faire un pèlerinage

pill [pɪl] **N** Pharm pilule f, **the p.** (contraceptive) la pilule; **she's on the p.** elle prend la pilule; (sugar-coated) **p.** dragée f, Fam **to be a p. popper** se bourrer de médicaments

pillage ['pɪlɪdʒ] Lit **N** pillage m

VT (town) piller, saccager, mettre à sac

VI se livrer au pillage, piller

pillager ['pɪlɪdʒər] **N** pilleur, -euse, pillard, -arde

pillar ['pɪlər] **N** Archit pilier m; (of table, pedestal table) pied m central; Fig **a p. of the Church/of society** un pilier de l'Église/de la société; **to be a p. of strength** être d'un grand appui; **I've been rushing around from p. to post** je n'ai pas arrêté de courir d'un endroit à l'autre ou à droite et à gauche; **p. of**

fire/smoke colonne *f* de feu/fumée; **p. of rock** colonne rocheuse; **p. of salt** statue *f* de sel; *Aut* door p. montant *m* de porte
▸▸*Br* **p. box** boîte *f* à lettres

pillared ['pɪləd] **ADJ** *Archit* à piliers

pillbox ['pɪlbɒks] **N 1** *(for pills)* boîte *f* à pilules **2** *(hat)* petit chapeau *m* rond sans bord **3** *Mil* blockhaus *m*
▸▸**p. hat** petit chapeau rond sans bord

pillhead ['pɪlhed] **N** *Sl* accro *mf* aux tranquillisants ou aux speeds

pillion ['pɪljən] **N** *(seat on motorcycle)* siège *m* arrière, selle *f* tandem, tan-sad *m*, *pl* tan-sads; **to ride p.** monter derrière
▸▸**p. passenger, p. rider** passager, -ère (de derrière); **p. seat** siège arrière, selle tandem, tan-sad

pillock ['pɪlək] **N** *Br Sl (fool)* abruti *m*, con *m*

pillory ['pɪlərɪ] **N** pilori *m*
VT *Hist, Fig (person)* mettre au pilori; *Fig (evil, corrupt practice)* dénoncer

pillow ['pɪləʊ] **N** oreiller *m*
VT **to p. one's head on one's arms** poser sa tête sur ses bras; **her head was pillowed on a mound of leaves** sa tête reposait sur un oreiller de feuilles
▸▸**p. fight** bataille *f* de polochons; **p. talk** confidences *fpl* sur l'oreiller

pillowcase, pillowslip ['pɪləʊkeɪs, -slɪp] **N** taie *f* d'oreiller

pilot ['paɪlət] **N 1** *Aviat, Naut* pilote *m* **2** *TV* émission *f* pilote
VT *(ship, plane etc)* piloter; *(person through obstacles)* mener, conduire; **to p. the country through difficult times** aider le pays à traverser une mauvaise passe
▸▸*Met* **p. balloon** ballon-sonde *m*, *pl* ballons-sondes; **p. boat** bateau-pilote *m*, *pl* bateaux-pilotes; **p. burner** veilleuse *f*; **p. cutter** bateau-pilote; **p. factory** usine-pilote *f*, *pl* usines-pilotes; **p. fish** pilote, poisson-pilote *m*, *pl* poissons-pilotes; **p. flame** veilleuse; *Naut* **p. house** poste *m* de pilotage; **p. jet** veilleuse (au gaz); **p. lamp** veilleuse (électrique); **p. light** veilleuse; *Br Aviat* **p. officer** ≃ sous-lieutenant *m*, *pl* sous-lieutenants; **p. plant** usine-pilote; **p. questionnaire** questionnaire *m* pilote; *Aviat, Ind, Com* **p. run** présérie *f*, *Br* **p. scheme** projet-pilote *m*, *pl* projets-pilotes; *Ind, Com* **p. series** présérie; **p. study** étude *f* pilote, avant-projet *m*, *pl* avant-projets, préétude *f*, **p. survey** enquête-pilote *f*, *pl* enquêtes-pilotes; **p. waters** zone *f* de pilotage

PIM [pɪm] **N** *Comput (abbr* **personal information manager)** gestionnaire *m* d'informations personnelles

pimento [pɪ'mentəʊ] **N** *(plant), Culin* piment *m*

pimp [pɪmp] **N** souteneur *m*, proxénète *m*, *Sl* maquereau *m*
VI être proxénète *ou* souteneur; **to p. for sb** maquer qn
VT maquer

pimpernel ['pɪmpənel] **N** *(flower)* mouron *m*; **scarlet p.** mouron rouge

pimple ['pɪmp(ə)l] **N** *(on skin)* bouton *m*; **to come out in pimples** boutonner, bourgeonner

pimply ['pɪmplɪ] **ADJ** boutonneux, couvert de boutons

PIMS [pɪmz] **N** *Mktg (abbr* **profit impact of marketing strategy)** IRSM *m*

PIN [pɪn] **N** *(abbr* **Personal Identification Number)** *(d'une carte bancaire)* code *m* confidentiel
▸▸**P. number** code confidentiel

PIN [pɪn] **N 1** épingle *f*, *(for hair)* épingle (à cheveux); *(brooch)* broche *f*, **(safety) p.** épingle de *ou* à nourrice; **you could have heard a p. drop** on aurait entendu voler une

---

mouche; **as bright** *or* **clean as a new p.** propre comme un sou neuf; **for two pins I'd punch his face** pour un rien je lui casserais la figure; **pins and needles** *(tingling)* fourmillements *mpl*; **I've got pins and needles in my foot** j'ai des fourmis dans le pied
2 *Tech* axe *m*; *(for securing sth)* goupille *f*, clavette *f*; *(of hinge)* gond *m*; *Elec (of plug, on connector)* broche *f*; *(of printhead)* aiguille *f*; *Surg (for fracture)* broche, clou *m*; **(firing) p.** percuteur *m*; **(safety) p.** *(of grenade)* goupille
3 *Golf* drapeau *m* de trou; *(at ninepins)* quille *f*
4 *Fam* **pins** *(legs)* quilles *fpl*, cannes *fpl*; **to feel a bit shaky on one's pins** *(after illness etc)* ne pas se sentir très solide sur ses quilles *ou* cannes
VT **(-nn-) 1** *(fasten with pin)* épingler, attacher avec une/des épingle(s) (**to** à); *(notice to noticeboard, map to wall)* attacher *ou* fixer avec une/des punaise(s), punaiser (**to** à); **to p. papers together** épingler des papiers ensemble
2 *Tech etc* cheviller, goupiller, mettre une goupille à
3 *(hold still)* fixer, clouer; **to p. sb against** *or* **to a wall** clouer *ou* plaquer qn contre un mur; **to p. sb's arms to his sides** coller *ou* plaquer les bras de qn au corps; **to be pinned under a fallen tree** se trouver pris *ou* coincé sous un arbre déraciné; *Fig* **to p. the blame on sb** rejeter la responsabilité sur qn; **you can't p. this on me** tu ne peux pas me mettre ça sur le dos; **to p. one's hopes on sb/sth** mettre tous ses espoirs en qn/dans qch
4 *Constr (wall etc)* étayer, étançonner
▸▸**p. money** argent *m* de poche; *Arch (given to wife)* argent pour le ménage; **p. table** flipper *m*; *Sewing* **p. tuck** nervure *f*, **p. wheel** *(on printer)* roue *f* à picots

▸**pin back VT SEP** *Surg* recoller; *Fig Fam* **to p. back one's ears** tendre l'oreille; *Fig Fam* **pin back your ears** ouvrez bien vos oreilles

▸**pin down VT SEP 1** *(trap)* coincer; **he pinned me down** *(in fight etc)* il m'a coincé; **they were pinned down by the wreckage** ils ont été coincés dans les décombres; *Mil* **to p. down the enemy** coincer l'ennemi; **pinned down by enemy fire** coincé par le feu de l'ennemi
2 *(force to be definite)* obliger à s'engager; **I tried to p. her down to a time** j'ai essayé de l'obliger à donner une heure précise; **to p. sb down to sth** obliger *ou* contraindre qn à faire qch; **without pinning himself down to anything** sans s'engager à rien
3 *(identify)* identifier; **we couldn't p. down the source of the noise** nous ne pouvions pas identifier la source du bruit; **a feeling that's difficult to p. down** un sentiment qu'il est difficile de définir; **it's difficult to p. it down** c'est difficile de mettre le doigt dessus

▸**pin up VT SEP 1** *(fasten to wall etc)* *(photo etc)* fixer au mur etc, punaiser
2 *(fasten)* **to p. up one's hair** relever ses cheveux; **to p. up a hem** rabattre un ourlet avec des épingles

pinafore ['pɪnəfɔːr] **N** *esp Br (apron)* tablier *m*; *(dress)* robe *f* à bretelles, robe-chasuble
▸▸**p. dress** robe à bretelles, robe-chasuble, *pl* robes-chasubles

pinball ['pɪnbɔːl] **N** *(machine, game)* flipper *m*
▸▸**p. machine** flipper

pincer ['pɪnsər] **N** *(of crab, insect etc)* pince *f*
▸▸*Mil* **p. movement** manœuvre *f* *ou* mouvement *m* d'encerclement

pincers ['pɪnsəz] **NPL** *(tool)* **(pair of) p.** pince *f*, tenaille(s) *f (pl)* VOIR GRAMMAIRE A10

pinch [pɪntʃ] **N 1** *(action)* pincement *m*; **to give sb a p.** pincer qn; **the p. of hunger** les tiraillements *mpl* de la faim; *Fam* **to feel the**

---

p. être gêné; **at** *or* **Am in a p.** à la rigueur **2** *(of salt etc)* pincée *f*; *(of snuff)* prise *f*, *Fig* **to take sth with a p. of salt** ne pas prendre qch pour argent comptant
VT 1 *(nip)* *(somebody, somebody's cheek etc)* pincer; **these shoes are pinching my feet** ces chaussures me font mal aux pieds *ou* me blessent; **I had to p. myself** *(I thought I was dreaming)* je me suis pincé **2** *Fam (steal)* piquer, faucher (**from sb** à qn); *(arrest) (thief etc)* épingler, pincer, choper; **I've had my purse pinched** on m'a piqué *ou* fauché mon porte-monnaie; **who's pinched my pen?** qui est-ce qui m'a chipé *ou* piqué mon stylo?; **to get pinched** *(of thief etc)* se faire pincer *ou* épingler *ou* choper
VI 1 *(nip)* blesser; **a shoe that pinches** une chaussure qui blesse *ou* qui serre; *Fig* **that's where the shoe pinches** c'est là que le bât blesse **2** **to p. and scrape** *or* **save** faire des économies de bouts de chandelle
▸**pinch off VT SEP** *(remove)* enlever en pinçant; **to p. off a bud** épincer un bourgeon
▸**pinch out VT SEP** épincer

pinchbeck ['pɪntʃbek] **N** *Lit* toc *m*
ADJ *(sham)* simili, en toc

pinched [pɪntʃt] **ADJ 1** *(face)* tiré, hâve; *(features)* tiré; **to be p. with hunger** être tenaillé par la faim **2** *(restricted)* étroit; **to be (a bit) p. for money/time** être à court d'argent/de temps; **to be (a bit) p. for space** être un peu à l'étroit

pinch-hit **VI** *Am* **to p. for sb** *Baseball* frapper à la place de qn; *Fig* remplacer qn

pinch-hitter **N** *Am Baseball* frappeur *m* d'urgence *ou* suppléant

pinch-runner **N** *Am Baseball* coureur *m* d'urgence *ou* suppléant

pincushion ['pɪnkʊʃən] **N** pelote *f* à épingles

pine¹ [paɪn] **N 1** *(tree)* pin *m* **2** *(wood)* (bois *m* de) pin *m*; **p. furniture** meubles *mpl* en pin
▸▸**p. cone** pomme *f* de pin, *Can* cocotte *f*, **p. forest** forêt *f* de pins, pinède *f*, **p. kernel** pignon *m*, pigne *f*, **p. marten** martre *f*, **p. needle** aiguille *f* de pin; **p. nut** pignon, pigne; **p. tree** pin

pine² **VI** languir; **to p. with grief** languir de tristesse
▸**pine away VI** = **pine²**
▸**pine for VT INSEP** languir pour *ou* après; **to p. for home/the good old days** avoir la nostalgie du foyer/du bon vieux temps; **he's pining for a good plate of sauerkraut** il meurt d'envie de manger une bonne assiette de choucroute

pineapple ['paɪnæp(ə)l] **N** ananas *m*; **p. juice** jus *m* d'ananas

ping [pɪŋ] **N** *(of sth hitting wine glass, small bell etc)* tintement *m*, petit bruit *m* clair; *(of bullet etc)* cinglement *m*
VI *(of sth hitting wine glass, small bell etc)* tinter, faire un petit bruit clair; *(of bullet etc)* cingler

Pinger® ['pɪŋər] **N** *(timer)* minuteur *m*

Ping-Pong® **N** ping-pong *m*
▸▸**P. ball** balle *f* de ping-pong; **P. table** table *f* de ping-pong

pinhead ['pɪnhed] **N 1** tête *f* d'épingle **2** *Fam (stupid person)* idiot, -ote, abruti, -ie

pinhole ['pɪnhəʊl] **N 1** trou *m* d'épingle; *Opt (in screen etc)* ouverture *f* minuscule; *Phot* sténopé *m*; **p. source of light** source *f* de lumière punctiforme *ou* ponctuelle **2** *Tech* trou *m* de cheville *ou* de goujon
▸▸**p. camera** appareil *m* à sténopé

pining ['paɪnɪŋ] **N** langueur *f*, languissement *m*; *(strong desire)* désir *m* ardent (**for** sth de qch); *(for home)* nostalgie *f*

pinion¹ ['pɪnɪən] **N** *Orn (flight feathers)* penne *f*, rémige *f*

VT 1 *(hold)* **to p. sb to the ground/against a wall** clouer qn au sol/contre un mur; **to p. sb's arms** *(tie)* attacher *ou* lier les bras de qn; *(hold)* tenir les bras de qn **2** *(bird)* rogner les ailes à

pinion² N *Tech* pignon *m*
▸▸ **p. wheel** roue *f* à pignon

pink¹ [pɪŋk] N **1** *(colour)* rose *m*; **in the p. of condition** *or* **health** en excellente *ou* parfaite santé; *(of racehorse etc)* entraîné à fond; *(of person)* se porter à merveille **2** *(flower)* œillet *m*; **garden p.** (œillet) mignardise *f*

ADJ 1 *(colour)* rose; **to turn** *or* **go p.** *(with embarrassment etc)* rosir; **to see p. elephants** voir double; **p. eyes** *(of albino)* yeux *mpl* rouges **2** *Fam* = **pinko**
▸▸ **p. champagne** champagne *m* rosé; *Am Fam* **p. collar job** = emploi *m* typiquement féminin; *Am Fam* **p. collar workers** employés *fpl* de bureau; **p. gin** = cocktail *m* à base de gin et d'angustura; **p. lady** = cocktail à base de gin et de grenadine; **the p. pound** = le pouvoir d'achat de la communauté homosexuelle; *Am Fam* **p. slip** lettre *f ou* avis *m* de licenciement; **to get one's p. slip** être licencié

pink² VT *Sewing etc (with pinking shears)* denteler, cranter; *(leather etc)* travailler à jour, évider

pink³ VI *(of engine)* cliqueter

pinkeye ['pɪŋkaɪ] N *Med* conjonctivite *f* aiguë contagieuse

pinkie ['pɪŋkɪ] N *Am, Scot Fam* petit doigt *m*, auriculaire *m*

pinking¹ ['pɪŋkɪŋ] N *Sewing etc* découpage *m*, découpure *f*
▸▸ **p. scissors, p. shears** ciseaux *mpl* à cranter *ou* à denteler

pinking² N *(of engine)* cliquetis *m (produit par les autoallumages)*

pinkish ['pɪŋkɪʃ] ADJ rosé, rosâtre

pinko ['pɪŋkəʊ] N, ADJ *Pol Fam* gauchisant, -ante

pinky¹ ['pɪŋkɪ] N *Am, Scot Fam* = **pinkie**

pinky² ADJ *Fam* rosé, rosâtre; **p. grey** gris *m inv* rosâtre *ou* rosé

pinnace ['pɪnɪs] N *Naut* chaloupe *f*, grand canot *m*

pinnacle ['pɪnək(ə)l] N **1** *(of mountain)* cime *f*; **a p. of rock** un piton rocheux; *Fig* **on the highest p. of fame** à l'apogée *ou* au sommet de la gloire **2** *Archit* pinacle *m*, clocheton *m*; *(of ridge)* couronnement *m*

pinny ['pɪnɪ] N *esp Br Fam* tablier *m*

pinout ['pɪnaʊt] N *Comput* broche *f* de sortie

pinpoint ['pɪnpɔɪnt] N *(tip of a pin)* pointe *f* d'épingle; *(very small point)* point *m* infime *ou* infinitésimal
VT *(point out)* indiquer exactement; *(locate)* *(place, fact, argument, consideration)* localiser *ou* repérer exactement; *(source of rumour, cause of problem)* déterminer, identifier; *Mil (aim at)* viser avec précision; *(fire on, bomb)* effectuer un tir/un bombardement de précision sur; **to p. a problem** isoler un problème, mettre le doigt sur un problème
▸▸ **p. accuracy** haute précision *f*; *Mil* **p. bombing** bombardement *m* de précision

pinprick ['pɪnprɪk] N piqûre *f* d'aiguille; *Fam* **pinpricks** *(annoying things)* tracasseries *fpl*

pinstripe ['pɪnstraɪp] N *Tex* rayures *fpl* fines; **pinstripes** costume *m* rayé
▸▸ **p. suit** costume rayé

pint [paɪnt] N **1** *(measurement)* pinte *f* (= 0,568 litre; *Am* = 0,473 litre) **2** *Br Fam* **a p.** *(beer)* une pinte de bière; **I'm going for a p.** je vais prendre une bière
▸▸ **p. mug, p. pot** chope *f* d'une pinte

pinta ['paɪntə] N *Br Fam* pinte *f* de lait

pintail ['pɪnteɪl] N **1** *(wild duck)* pilet *m* **2** *(grouse)* tétras *m* à longue queue, *Can* gelinotte *f* à queue fine

pinto ['pɪntəʊ] N *Am (horse)* (cheval *m*) pie *m*
▸▸ *Culin* **p. beans** haricots *mpl* pinto; *Am* **p. horse** (cheval) pie

pint-size(d) ADJ *Fam* minuscule

pin-up N *Fam (woman, picture of woman)* pin-up *f inv*

Pinyin ['pɪn'jɪn] N *Ling* pinyin *m*

pioneer [paɪə'nɪər] N pionnier, -ière; **a p. researcher in the field of ...** un chercheur qui est à l'avant-garde des travaux dans le domaine de ...; **her p. work in the study of radioactivity** ses travaux innovateurs dans le domaine de la radioactivité
VT to p. a new method être le premier/l'un des premiers à développer une nouvelle méthode; **to p. research into ...** être à l'avant-garde de la recherche dans ...

pioneering [paɪə'nɪərɪŋ] ADJ *(work)* innovateur, -trice; *(scientist etc)* qui fait œuvre de pionnier; **to do p. work in a science** faire œuvre de pionnier dans une science, ouvrir la voie dans une science; **in p. days** au temps des pionniers; **p. company** entreprise *f* innovatrice

pious ['paɪəs] ADJ pieux; **p. fraud** pieux mensonge *m*; *Fam (person)* hypocrite *mf*; **p. hope** espoir *m* vain; **these p. hopes** ces vains espoirs

piously ['paɪəslɪ] ADV pieusement, avec piété

piousness ['paɪəsnɪs] N piété *f*

PIP [pɪp] N *Comput (abbr peripheral interchange program)* logiciel *m* de commutation de périphérique

pip¹ [pɪp] N *(of fruit)* pépin *m*

pip² N **1** *(on card, die etc)* point *m* **2** *Br Mil Fam* **to get one's third p.** ≃ recevoir sa troisième ficelle **3** *Radio (sound)* top *m*; *(on radar)* top d'écho; **the pips** *Radio* = les bips *mpl* sonores; *Tel* la tonalité de crédit épuisé

pip³ VT (-pp-) *Fam* **to be pipped at the post** se faire coiffer *ou* battre sur le poteau

pip⁴ N *Old-fashioned Br Fam* **to give sb the p.** embêter qn

pipe [paɪp] N **1** *(tube)* tuyau *m*, conduit *m*, conduite *f*, canalisation *f*; **pipes and fittings** tuyauterie *f* et accessoires *mpl* de tuyauterie **2** *Mus* chalumeau *m*; *Naut (of boatswain)* sifflet *m*; *(of bird)* chant *m*; **the pipes** *(bagpipes)* la cornemuse

3 *(for smoking)* pipe *f*; **to smoke a p.** fumer une pipe; *Fam* **put that in your p. and smoke it!** mettez ça dans votre poche et votre mouchoir par-dessus!
VI *Mus* jouer du chalumeau; *(play the bagpipes)* jouer de la cornemuse; *(of bird etc)* siffler; *(speak shrilly)* parler d'une voix flûtée; *Naut* donner un coup de sifflet
VT 1 *(house etc)* installer *ou* poser des canalisations dans; *(water, oil etc)* canaliser; **piped water** eau *f* courante; **to p. oil to a refinery** amener le pétrole à une raffinerie par oléduc *ou* par pipeline; *Fam* **piped music** musique *f* de fond
2 *Mus (tune)* jouer au chalumeau; *(on bagpipes)* jouer à la cornemuse; *(sing)* chanter d'une voix flûtée; *Naut (order)* siffler; *Naut* **to p. sb aboard** rendre les honneurs du sifflet à qn
3 *Sewing etc (cushion etc)* passepoiler
4 *Culin (cake)* décorer avec une (poche à) douille
5 *Comput (commands)* chaîner
▸▸ *Mus* **p. band** orchestre *m* de cornemuses; **p. bomb** = bombe *f* artisanale fabriquée à partir d'un morceau de tuyau contenant

des explosifs; **p. cleaner** cure-pipe *m*, *pl* cure-pipes; **p. dream** chimère *f*; **p. of peace** calumet *m* de la paix; **p. rack** râtelier *m* à pipes; **p. tobacco** tabac *m* à pipe
▸ **pipe down** VI *Fam* **1** *(make less noise)* faire moins de bruit; **p. down!** moins de bruit! **2** *(not talk so much)* rabattre son caquet; **p. down!** boucle-la!; **he piped down when he realized she knew a lot more about it** il a fermé son clapet quand il s'est rendu compte qu'elle en savait bien plus que lui
▸ **pipe in** VT SEP **to p. in the guests** *(in Scotland)* jouer de la cornemuse en tête de la procession (lors de l'entrée solennelle des invités)
▸ **pipe up** VI *(start to speak)* commencer à parler; **a little voice piped up** une petite voix s'est fait entendre

pipeclay ['paɪpkleɪ] N terre *f* de pipe

pipeline ['paɪplaɪn] N **1** *(large pipe)* canalisation *f*, conduite *f*; *(for gas)* conduite de gaz naturel, gazoduc *m*; *(for petrol)* oléoduc *m*, pipeline *m* **2** *Fig (for news, technology etc)* canal *m ou* voie *f* d'acheminement; **it's in the p.** c'est en route; **there's a pay rise in the p.** il y a une augmentation de salaire en perspective

piper ['paɪpər] N *Mus* joueur, -euse de chalumeau; *(of bagpipes)* joueur, -euse de cornemuse, cornemuseur *m*, cornemuseux *m*; *Prov* **he who pays the p. calls the tune** c'est celui qui paye qui décide

pipette [pɪ'pet] N *Chem etc* pipette *f*, compte-gouttes *m inv*

piping ['paɪpɪŋ] ADJ *(sound)* flûté, aigu, *f* aiguë; *(voice)* flûté
ADV p. hot tout chaud, bouillant
N 1 *(system)* canalisations *fpl*, *(pipes collectively)* conduites *fpl*, tuyaux *mpl*, tuyauterie *f*, canalisations
2 *Mus etc (sound of pipe)* son *m* du chalumeau; *(sound of bagpipes)* son de la cornemuse; *(of birds)* gazouillement *m*, gazouillis *m*; *Naut* coups *mpl* de sifflet
3 *Sewing etc (material)* passepoil *m*
4 *Culin (of cake)* décoration *f* faite à la (poche à) douille
5 *Comput (of commands)* chaînage *m*
▸▸ *Culin* **p. bag** poche *f* à douille; *Culin* **p. nozzle** douille *f*

pipistrelle [pɪpɪ'strel] N *(bat)* pipistrelle *f*
▸▸ **p. bat** pipistrelle

pipit ['pɪpɪt] N *(bird)* pipit *m*

pippin ['pɪpɪn] N *(apple)* (pomme *f*) reinette *f*

pipsqueak ['pɪpskwiːk] N *Fam (person)* petit bonhomme *m* de rien du tout, gringalet *m*

piquancy ['piːkənsɪ] N **1** *(of food)* goût *m* piquant **2** *Fig (of tale, affair etc)* sel *m*, piquant *m*

piquant ['piːkənt] ADJ *(flavour, story)* piquant

piquantly ['piːkəntlɪ] ADV d'une manière piquante, avec du piquant

pique [piːk] N dépit *m*, ressentiment *m*; **in a fit of p.** dans un accès de dépit
VT 1 *(offend) (person)* piquer, dépiter; **to feel piqued by sth** être dépité par qch; **to p. sb's pride** piquer *ou* blesser qn dans son orgueil **2** *(arouse) (sb's curiosity, interest)* piquer, exciter

piquet [pɪ'ket] N *Cards* piquet *m*

piracy ['paɪrəsɪ] N **1** *Naut etc* piraterie *f*; **an act of p.** un acte de piraterie; **air p.** piraterie de l'air **2** *(of copyright)* atteinte *f* au droit d'auteur; *(of ideas etc)* pillage *m*, vol *m*; *(of software etc)* piratage *m*; **film p.** piratage de films

piranha [pɪ'rɑːnə] N *(fish)* piranha *m*, piraya *m*

pirate ['paɪrɪt] N **1** *Naut (person)* pirate *m*;

(ship) navire *m* pirate **2** *Radio (person)* pirate *m* **3** *(of literary work etc)* contrefacteur *m*; *(of ideas etc)* voleur, -euse; *(of software, cassette etc)* pirate *m*

VT 1 *Naut (ship)* s'emparer de **2** *(invention, ideas etc)* s'approprier, voler; *(brand)* contrefaire; *(cassette, film, software etc)* pirater; **to p. a book** *(republish without permission)* republier un livre sans autorisation; *(copy)* contrefaire *ou* démarquer un livre

► ► **p. cassette** cassette *f* pirate; **p. edition** édition *f* pirate; **p. program** programme *m* pirate; **p. radio** radio *f* pirate; **p. software** logiciel *m* pirate; **p. station** poste *m ou* émetteur *m* pirate; **p. tape** cassette pirate; **p. video** vidéo *f* pirate

pirated ['paɪrɪtɪd] **ADJ** pirate; **a p. edition** une édition pirate

piratical [paɪ'rætɪk(ə)l] **ADJ 1** *Naut* de pirate **2** *Com (reproduction etc)* de contrefacteur, de contrefaçon

pirating ['paɪrɪtɪŋ] **N** *(of software etc)* piratage *m*

pirouette [pɪrʊ'et] **N** pirouette *f*
VI pirouetter, faire une/des pirouette(s)

Pisa ['pi:zə] **N** Pise *f*

piscatorial [pɪskə'tɔːrɪəl] **ADJ** *Fml* halieutique

Pisces ['paɪsiːz] **N** *Astrol* les Poissons *mpl*; **to be (a) P.** être (des) Poissons

pish [pɪʃ] *Scot* = **piss**

piss [pɪs] *Sl* **N** pisse *f*; **to have a p.** pisser; **to take the p. out of sb** se foutre (de la gueule) de qn; **to take the p. out of sth** se foutre de qch; **you're taking the p.!** tu te fous de moi!, tu déconnes!; **the artist is taking the p.** cet artiste se fout de la gueule du monde; *Br* **to go on the p.** *(go out drinking)* aller se bourrer la gueule, aller prendre une cuite; **it was p. easy** c'était de la tarte; **p. poor** *(very bad)* complètement nul

VI pisser; **it's pissing (with rain or down)** il pleut comme vache qui pisse; *Am* **p. on it!** *(forget it)* laisse béton!; *(I'm fed up)* j'en ai plein le cul!; **to p. all over sb** *(defeat)* battre qn à plates coutures

VT *(blood etc)* pisser; **to p. oneself, to p. one's pants** pisser dans son froc; **to p. the bed** pisser au lit; **I almost pissed myself laughing** j'ai tellement rigolé que j'ai failli en pisser dans mon froc

► ► *Br* **p. artist** *(drunkard)* poivrot, -ote

► **piss about, piss around** **VI** *Sl (behave foolishly)* faire le con, déconner; *(waste time)* glandouiller; **we don't have time to p. about** on n'a pas de temps à perdre en conneries; **don't p. around with my stuff** arrête de tripoter mes affaires *ou* de foutre le bordel dans mes affaires

VT SEP *Sl (waste time of)* **to p. sb about** *or* **around** faire perdre son temps à qn

► **piss down** **VI** *Sl (rain)* **it's pissing down** il pleut comme vache qui pisse

► **piss off** *Sl* **VI** *(go away)* foutre le camp; **p. off!** fous le camp!

VT *(annoy)* faire chier; **that really pisses me off** ça me fait vraiment chier; **to be pissed off** en avoir ras le cul; **to be pissed off with sb/sth** *(have had enough of)* en avoir ras le bol de qn/qch; **to be pissed off at/about sth** être en pétard contre qn/à cause de qch

pissbucket ['pɪsbʌkɪt] **N** *Sl* **1** *(toilet)* chiottes *fpl* **2** *(person)* ordure *f*, raclure *f*

pissed [pɪst] **ADJ 1** *Br Sl (drunk)* soûl, bourré, plein; **to get p.** se soûler la gueule; **as p. as a fart** *or* **a newt, p. out of one's head** comme une queue de pelle **2** *Am Sl (angry)* en rogne, en boule; **to be p. at sb** être en rogne contre qn; **I was pretty p. about it** ça m'a vraiment foutu en rogne

pisser ['pɪsər] **N** *Sl* **1** *(annoying situation)* **what a p.!** quelle merde!; **it was a real p. that the weather wasn't better** c'était vraiment chiant qu'il fasse pas plus beau **2** *Am (remarkable situation)* **what a p.!** c'est génial ou super! **3** *Am (annoying person)* emmerdeur, -euse; *(remarkable person)* **to be a p.** être un mec/une nana génial(e)

pisshead ['pɪshed] **N** *Br Sl (drunkard)* soûlard, -arde

pisshole ['pɪshəʊl] **N** *Sl* **his eyes are like pissholes in the snow** il a des petits yeux

piss-take **N** *Br Sl (joke)* blague *f*, *(parody)* parodie *f*; **this is a p. isn't it?** non mais tu te fous de ma gueule ou quoi?

piss-taker **N** *Br Sl (mocker)* personne *f* qui se fout du monde; **he's a real p.** il se fout vraiment de la gueule du monde

piss-up **N** *Br Sl (drinking spree)* **to go on** *or* **have a p.** (aller) se soûler la gueule; **they couldn't organize a p. in a brewery** ils ne sont pas foutus d'organiser quoi que ce soit correctement

pistachio [pɪ'stɑːʃɪəʊ] **N** *(nut)* pistache *f*, *(tree)* pistachier *m*

► ► **p. nut** pistache; **p. tree** pistachier

piste [piːst] **N** *Ski* piste *f*

pistil ['pɪstɪl] **N** *Bot* pistil *m*

pistol ['pɪst(ə)l] **N 1** *(gun)* pistolet *m*; **to hold a p. to sb's head** tenir un pistolet braqué contre la tempe de qn; *Fig* mettre le couteau sous la gorge à qn; *Fig* **to make a decision with a p. to one's head** prendre une décision avec le couteau sous la gorge **2** *Tech (of pneumatic tool)* pistolet *m*

► ► **p. grip** *(of tool, camera)* crosse *f*, **p. shot** coup *m* de pistolet

pistol-whip **VT** (**-pp-**) frapper avec un pistolet

piston ['pɪstən] **N** *Tech, Mus (of brass instrument)* piston *m*

► ► **p. dwell** temps *m* d'immobilité du piston; **p. engine** moteur *m* à pistons; **p. head** tête *f ou* fond *m* du piston; **p. ring** segment *m* (de piston); **p. walls** parois *fpl* du piston

pit¹ [pɪt] **N 1** *(hole in ground)* fosse *f*, *Min* puits *m*; *(coal mine)* mine *f*, **to dig a p.** creuser une fosse; *Aut etc* inspection **p.** fosse de visite; *Lit* **the (bottomless) p.** *(hell)* l'enfer *m*, les enfers; *Min* **to work in the pits** travailler à la mine; **he went down the pits when he was 16** il est descendu à la mine à 16 ans

2 *Fig Sl* **it's/he's the pits** *(awful)* c'est/il est nul

3 *Theat (seating, spectators)* parterre *m*; *(at Stock Exchange)* corbeille *f*, *(for cock fight)* arène *f*, *(for bears)* fosse *f*, **(orchestra) p.** fosse d'orchestre; *Sport* **the pits** les stands *mpl* de ravitaillement

4 *(mark) (on metal, glass etc)* piqûre *f*, alvéole *m*

5 *Med (from smallpox etc)* cicatrice *f*, marque *f*, *Anat* **the p. of the stomach** le creux de l'estomac; *Fig* **her rejection hit him in the p. of his stomach** son rejet lui a fait l'effet d'un coup de poing dans l'estomac

6 *Br Sl (bed)* pieu *m*; **in one's p.** au pieu

7 *Sl (untidy place)* foutoir *m*

VT (**-tt-**) **1** **to p. sb against sb** mettre qn aux prises avec qn, opposer qn à qn; **to p. oneself against sb** se mesurer à qn; **to p. one's wits against sb** se mesurer avec qn **2** *(of acids etc) (metal etc)* piquer, trouer; *Med (of smallpox etc) (sb's face)* grêler, marquer

► ► **p. pony** cheval *m* de mine; **p. prop** poteau *m ou* étai *m* de mine, étançon *m*

pit² **N** *(stone) (of cherry etc)* noyau *m*
VT (**-tt-**) *(cherries etc)* dénoyauter

pita ['pɪtə] **N** = **pitta**

pit-a-pat **ADV** **to go p.** *(of rain etc)* crépiter; *(of feet)* trottiner; *(of the heart)* faire toc-toc

N *(of rain)* crépitement *m*; *(of feet)* trottinement *m*; *(of heart)* battement *m*

pitch¹ [pɪtʃ] **N 1** *(act of throwing) (of stone, ball etc)* lancement *m*

2 *Br (place) (in market)* place *f*, emplacement *m*; *(of stallholder, beggar etc)* place habituelle

3 *Sport (for football etc)* terrain *m*; *Cr* terrain entre les guichets

4 *Mus (of note)* hauteur *f*, **to have perfect p.** avoir l'oreille absolue; **to give the orchestra the p.** donner le ton à l'orchestre; **to rise in p.** monter de ton

5 *(degree)* **to such a p. that ...** à tel point que ...; **expectation had reached fever p.** l'attente était fébrile

6 *(talk)* **(sales) p.** baratin *m*, boniment *m* publicitaire; *(of advertising agency)* spéculative *f*, *Am Sl* **to make a p. for** *(express support for)* vanter les mérites de

7 *Cin* présentation *f*, soumission *f*, pitch *m*

8 *Constr (slope) (of staircase)* pente *f*, rampant *m*; *(of roof)* pente, inclinaison *f*, *Tech (of plane)* inclinaison, basile *f*

9 *Archit (of ceiling)* hauteur *f*

10 *(of ship, aircraft) (type of movement)* tangage *m*; *(instance)* coup *m* de tangage; **angle of p.** angle *m* de tangage

11 *Tech (spacing) (of rivets, holes)* espacement *m*, écartement *m*; *(of cogwheel, screw, propeller etc)*, *Typ (of characters)* pas *m*

VT 1 *(throw) (ball, stone etc)* jeter, lancer; *(in baseball)* lancer; **to p. the hay onto the cart** jeter le foin sur la charrette

2 *(set up) (tent)* dresser, monter; *(camp)* établir; *Cr* **to p. wickets** planter *ou* dresser les guichets

3 *Mus* jouer dans une clef donnée; **to p. one's voice higher/lower** hausser/baisser le ton de sa voix

4 *(aim)* **to p. an estimate too low** arrêter un devis trop bas; **to p. one's aspirations too high** viser trop haut; **stories pitched at older children** histoires écrites pour des enfants plus âgés

5 *Cin* présenter, soumettre, pitcher

6 *Fam* **to p. a yarn** raconter des histoires

VI 1 *(in baseball)* lancer **2** *(fall)* tomber; **to p. forward** *(be thrown)* être projeté en avant; *(fall)* piquer du nez; **he pitched into the water** il est tombé dans l'eau; **the ball pitched on a stone** le ballon a rebondi sur une pierre **3** *(of ship, aircraft)* tanguer

► ► **p. angle** angle *m* de tangage; *Tech* **p. circle** cercle *m* primitif; *(of wheel)* ligne *f* d'engrènement; *Mus* **p. pipe** diapason *m* (sifflet)

► **pitch in** **VI** *(contribute to a task)* s'y mettre; *(contribute money etc)* payer son écot; **they all pitched in to help** ils ont tous donné un coup de main

► **pitch into** **VT INSEP** *Fam (attack) (physically)* attaquer, se lancer sur; *(verbally)* dire son fait à; **to p. into a task** se mettre à une tâche

► **pitch on** **VT INSEP** *(choose)* choisir

► **pitch out** **VT SEP** *(person) (from house)* expulser; *(from competition)* éliminer; *(rubbish)* balancer, jeter; **to p. sb out of office** démettre qn de ses fonctions

pitch² **N** *(substance)* poix *f*, *(from coal tar)* brai *m*; **black** *or* **dark as p.** *(hair, eyes)* noir comme le jais; *(room, night)* noir comme dans un four

VT *(coat with pitch)* brayer, enduire de poix *ou* de brai

► ► *Bot* **p. pine** pitchpin *m*

pitch-black **ADJ** noir comme le jais; **her p. hair** ses cheveux noirs de jais; **it's p.** *(I can't see)* il fait noir comme dans un four

pitch-dark **ADJ** **it's p.** *(outside)* il fait nuit noire; *(in cellar etc)* il fait noir comme dans un four

pitched [pɪtʃt] **ADJ**

► ► *Mil, Fig* **p. battle** bataille *f* rangée

pitcher¹ ['pɪtʃər] N (jug) cruche f, pichet m; (large) broc m; esp Am (small jug) pot m; Prov **little pitchers have big ears** = pas devant les enfants

pitcher² N Baseball lanceur m

pitchfork ['pɪtʃfɔːk] N Agr fourche f, (two-pronged) bident m
VT (hay) lancer avec une fourche; Fig Fam (force) (person) parachuter (**into a job** à un poste)

pitching ['pɪtʃɪŋ] N Naut, Aviat (of ship, plane) tangage m

piteous ['pɪtɪəs] ADJ pitoyable, piteux; **he was a p. sight** il faisait pitié

piteously ['pɪtɪəslɪ] ADV pitoyablement, piteusement

pitfall ['pɪtfɔːl] N (pit) trappe f, fosse f; Fig (trap) piège m; **the pitfalls of English** les pièges de l'anglais

pith [pɪθ] N 1 (of orange etc) peau f blanche; Bot (medulla) moelle f 2 Fig (of argument, idea etc) essence f, (piquancy) (of story) piquant m
▸▸ **p. helmet** casque m colonial

pithead ['pɪthed] N Min bouche f de puits
▸▸ **p. ballot** vote m des mineurs (de fond); **p. baths** bains mpl/douches fpl de la mine

pithiness ['pɪθɪnɪs] N (of style etc) concision f

pithy ['pɪθɪ] ADJ 1 (orange etc) couvert de peau blanche; (stem etc) moelleux 2 (style etc) concis; **p. phrase** phrase f lapidaire

pitiable ['pɪtɪəb(ə)l] ADJ pitoyable, piteux; (appearance, object) minable, lamentable; **she was in a p. state** elle était dans un état à faire pitié, elle était dans un état pitoyable ou dans un piteux état

pitiful ['pɪtɪfʊl] ADJ 1 (arousing pity) pitoyable; **it's p. to see him like this** ça fait pitié de le voir comme ça 2 Pej (deplorable) lamentable, pitoyable

pitifully ['pɪtɪfʊlɪ] ADV 1 (arousing pity) pitoyablement; **she was p. thin** elle était d'une maigreur pitoyable 2 Pej (deplorably) lamentablement, pitoyablement; **he was p. bad at drawing** il était lamentable en dessin; **she sings p.** elle chante lamentablement mal; **p. small** (salary) de misère; (house etc) si petit que c'en est lamentable

pitiless ['pɪtɪlɪs] ADJ impitoyable; (wind, cold) cruel

pitilessly ['pɪtɪlɪslɪ] ADV impitoyablement, sans pitié; **p. cruel** d'une cruauté impitoyable; **to behave p. towards sb** se montrer impitoyable envers qn

piton ['piːtɒn] N (in mountaineering) piton m

pitta ['pɪtə] N
▸▸ **p. bread** pita m

pittance ['pɪtəns] N (wages) salaire m de misère; (income) maigre revenu m, revenu misérable; **his pension is a p.** sa retraite est dérisoire

Note that the French word **pitance** is a false friend and is never a translation for the English word **pittance**. It means **sustenance**.

pitted ['pɪtɪd] ADJ 1 (metal etc) piqué, alvéolé; (surface of moon) alvéolé; (skin) (by smallpox) grêlé; (by acne) couvert de marques 2 (olives) dénoyauté

pitter-patter ['pɪtə-] N (of rain, hail) crépitement m; (of feet) trottinement m; (of heart) battement m
ADV **to go p.** (feet) trottiner; (heart) palpiter; **the rain fell p. on the leaves** la pluie tombait doucement sur les feuilles

pitting ['pɪtɪŋ] N (on metal surface) piquage m

pituitary [pɪˈtjuːɪt(ə)rɪ] Anat N (gland) hypophyse f, glande f pituitaire
ADJ pituitaire
▸▸ **p. gland** hypophyse, glande pituitaire

pity ['pɪtɪ] N 1 (compassion) pitié f, **to have** or **take p. on sb** avoir pitié de qn, prendre qn en pitié; **to take p. on sb** (be moved to pity) s'apitoyer sur qn; **she deserves no p.** elle ne mérite pas qu'on s'apitoie sur elle; **are you entirely without p.?** es-tu incapable du moindre sentiment de pitié?; **to show no p.** ne manifester aucune pitié; **the thought moved him to p.** cette pensée lui inspira de la pitié; **to do sth out of p. for sb** faire qch par pitié pour qn; **for p.'s sake** par pitié
2 (misfortune) **what a p.!** quel dommage!; **it's a great p. that ...** il est bien malheureux ou dommage que ... + subj, **it's no great p. that ...** ce n'est pas si grave que ... + subj, (quite a good thing) encore heureux que ... + subj, **more's the p.** c'est bien dommage
VT (person) plaindre, avoir pitié de; **he is to be pitied** il est à plaindre

pitying ['pɪtɪɪŋ] ADJ compatissant; (look) compatissant, de pitié

pityingly ['pɪtɪɪŋlɪ] ADV (to look) avec pitié, d'un air compatissant; (to say) d'un ton compatissant

Pius ['paɪəs] N Pie m

pivot ['pɪvət] N 1 Tech etc pivot m, axe m; (of crane) pivot; (of axle etc) tourillon m 2 Fig (person in company etc) pivot m, cheville f ouvrière; Mil (man) pivot, guide m, homme m de base
VI (-t-) pivoter, tourner (**on sth** sur qch); **she pivoted on her left leg** elle pivota sur sa jambe gauche; Fig **their plans pivoted around her** leurs projets reposaient sur elle
VT (turn) (something) faire pivoter; (set on a pivot) (gun) monter sur pivot
▸▸ Mil **p. man** pivot, guide, homme de base

pivotal ['pɪvət(ə)l] ADJ (point) cardinal, -aux; Fig (position etc) clef inv; (importance) capital, -aux; **she is p. in their plans** elle joue un rôle central dans leurs projets

pix [pɪks] NPL Fam = **pics**, see **pic**

pixel ['pɪksəl] N Comput pixel m
▸▸ **p. density** densité f en pixels

pixelated ['pɪksəleɪtəd] ADJ = **pixellated**

pixelation ['pɪksəleɪʃən], **pixelization** ['pɪksəlaɪˈeɪʃən] N TV (to hide identity) mosaïquage m

pixelize ['pɪksəlaɪz] VT TV (to hide identity) mosaïquer

pixellated ['pɪksəleɪtəd] ADJ Comput (image) pixélisé, bitmap, en mode point

pixie ['pɪksɪ] N (elf) lutin m; (fairy) fée f

pixil(l)ated ['pɪksɪleɪtəd] ADJ Am Sl (drunk) bourré, plein

pixy ['pɪksɪ] N = **pixie**

pizza ['piːtsə] N Culin pizza f
▸▸ **p. base** pâte f à pizza; **p. parlour** pizzeria f

pizzazz [pəˈzæz] N Fam = **pzazz**

pizzeria [piːtsəˈriːə] N pizzeria f

PJs ['piːdʒeɪz] NPL Fam (abbr pyjamas) pyjama m

Pk abbr Park

pkg N abbr package

pkt N abbr packet

P & L [piːənˈel] N 1 (abbr profit and loss) pertes fpl et profits mpl 2 (abbr profit and loss account, profit and loss statement) compte m de résultat; **we can see from the P. that developing the product is not a viable option** le compte de résultat montre clairement qu'il ne serait pas rentable de développer ce produit 3 (abbr profit and loss form) compte m d'exploitation

Pl (abbr **Place**) = rue

pl Gram (abbr **plural**) pl

placard ['plækɑːd] N (written notice) écriteau m; (poster) affiche f, (carried by protester) pancarte f
VT (wall) placarder

Note that the French word **placard** is a false friend and is never a translation for the English word **placard**. Its most common meaning is **cupboard**.

placate [pləˈkeɪt] VT apaiser, calmer

PLACE [pleɪs]

| **N** endroit **1** ▪ lieu **1, 3** ▪ place **2, 6–10** ▪ avoir lieu (to take place) **4** ▪ maison **5** |
| **VT** placer **1, 3, 4** ▪ mettre **1** |

N 1 (location) endroit m, lieu m; (in street names) rue f, **an ideal p. for a picnic** un endroit idéal pour pique-niquer; **a good p. to meet people** un bon endroit pour rencontrer des gens; **this is the p.!** (here we are) nous voilà arrivés!; **to move from one p. to another** se déplacer d'un endroit à un autre; **the village/museum was an interesting p.** le village/musée était intéressant; **I'm looking for a p. to stay** je cherche un logement; **can you recommend a p. to eat?** pouvez-vous me recommander un restaurant?; **this is no p. for you** ce n'est pas un endroit pour vous; **I've broken my arm in two places** je me suis cassé le bras en deux endroits; **I can't be in two places at once** je ne peux pas être à deux endroits à la fois; **the book was good in places** le livre était bon par endroits; **all over the p.** (in many different places) partout; Fig (in disorder) dans tous les sens; Fig Fam **the team were all over the p.** l'équipe a joué n'importe comment; Fig Fam **these figures are all over the p.** (are inaccurate) ces chiffres ont été calculés n'importe comment; Fig Fam **at the interview he was all over the p.** (panicking, unclear) il a raconté n'importe quoi à l'entretien; Fig Fam **this paragraph is all over the p.** ce paragraphe a été écrit n'importe comment; Fig Fam **to go places** (succeed) réussir (dans la vie); Br Fam **the other p.** Univ (at Oxford) Cambridge; (at Cambridge) Oxford; Parl (in House of Commons) la Chambre des lords; (in House of Lords) la Chambre des communes; **Belmont P.** rue Belmont

2 (assigned to somebody, something) place f, **everything in its p.** chaque chose à sa place; **in its proper time and p.** en temps et lieu; **to find a p. for sth** trouver une place pour qch; **this town has a special p. in my affections** j'ai une tendresse particulière pour cette ville; **to hold sth in p.** tenir qch en place; **to lose/find one's p.** (in a book) perdre/retrouver sa page; **his anger gave p. to pity** sa colère a fait place à un sentiment de pitié; **to take sb's p.** remplacer qn; (oust) prendre la place de qn; **a woman's p. is in the home** la place d'une femme est à la maison

3 (for specific purpose) **p. of amusement** lieu m de divertissement; **p. of payment** lieu de paiement; **p. of refuge** lieu de refuge

4 **to take p.** (happen) avoir lieu; **the marriage will not take p.** le mariage n'aura pas lieu ou ne se fera pas; **many changes have taken p.** il y a eu beaucoup de changements; **while this was taking p.** tandis que cela se passait

5 (residence) **a little p. in the country** une petite maison à la campagne; Fam **nice p. you've got here** c'est bien chez vous!; Fam **come round to my p.** venez chez moi; Fam **your p. or mine?** on va chez toi ou chez moi?

6 (seat etc) **is this p. taken?** est-ce que cette

place est prise?; **to book a p.** réserver une place; **to change places with sb** changer de place avec qn; **to give up** or **offer one's p. to sb** laisser sa place à qn; **if I get there first I'll keep a p. for you** si j'arrive le premier je te garderai une place; **to keep sb's p. in a queue** garder la place de qn dans une file d'attente; **to set** or **lay an extra p. at table** mettre une assiette de plus à table

7 (vacancy etc) **to get a p. at university** être admis à l'université; **the school still has five places left** cette école a encore cinq places de libres

8 this remark is out of p. (inappropriate) cette observation est déplacée ou hors de propos; **to look out of p.** (of person) ne pas être à sa place ou dans son élément; (of thing) ne pas être à sa place; **he didn't look out of p.** il ne déparait pas; **it's not my p. to do it** ce n'est pas à moi de le faire

9 (situation) **put yourself in my p.** mettez-vous à ma place; **if I were in your p. I'd go** à votre place, j'irais

10 (in society, competition etc) place f, rang m; **to keep sb in his p.** montrer à qn où est sa place; **to know one's p.** savoir où est sa place; Iron **I know my p.** je sais où est ma place; Fig **to put sb in his p.** remettre qn à sa place; **in first/second p.** en premier/second lieu; Sport **to finish in second/last p.** finir à la deuxième/dernière place ou en deuxième/dernière position; Horseracing **to back a horse for a p.** jouer un cheval placé; Math **to three decimal places** à trois décimales

11 (parts of an argument etc) **in the first p. ..., in the second p. ...** en premier lieu ..., en second lieu ...; **I don't know why they gave him the job in the first p.** d'ailleurs je ne sais même pas pourquoi ils l'ont embauché

vt 1 (put) placer, mettre; **to p. a book back on a shelf** remettre un livre (en place) sur un rayon; **to p. a book with a publisher** confier un livre à un éditeur; **to p. a matter in sb's hands** mettre une affaire dans les mains de qn; **I p. myself at your disposal** je me mets à votre disposition; **to p. a child in sb's care** confier un enfant à la garde de qn; **to p. a child in care/with foster parents** placer ou mettre un enfant à la DDASS/dans une famille d'acceuil

2 the house is well placed (situated) la maison est bien située; **how are we placed for time?** combien de temps avons-nous?; **how are you placed for money?** comment ça va côté finances?; **you're better placed than I am to answer that** tu es mieux placé que moi pour répondre à cela; **British industry is well placed to ...** l'industrie britannique est à même de ...; **strategically placed airfields** des terrains d'aviation stratégiquement situés

3 Com, Fin etc (goods, shares) placer, vendre; (loan) placer, négocier; (invest) (funds) placer; (contract) adjuger, concéder; **to p. an order** passer une commande; **to p. an order for sth** passer commande de qch; **to p. an order with sb** passer commande à qn; **to p. a bet** faire un pari; **to p. a bet on sb/sth** parier sur qn/qch

4 (find a job for) placer

5 (class, Sch, Sport etc **to be placed third** se classer troisième; **I would p. him among the outstanding biographers of the century** je le classerais parmi les meilleurs biographes du siècle; Horseracing **was your horse placed?** est-ce que votre cheval s'est classé dans les trois premiers?

6 (identify) (sound) localiser; **I know his face but I can't p. him** je l'ai déjà vu mais je n'arrive pas à le remettre

vi Am esp Horseracing se classer entre les trois premiers

▸▸**p. of birth** lieu de naissance; **p. of business** lieu de travail; **p. card** = carte f marquant la place de chaque convive à table; **p. of death** lieu de décès; Fin **p. of issue** lieu d'émission; Sport **p. kick** coup m de pied placé; **p. mat** set m (de table); **p. name** nom m de lieu; **p. of residence** résidence f, domicile m (réel); Br Law **p. of safety order** = ordonnance f autorisant une personne ou un organisme à garder des enfants maltraités en lieu sûr; **p. setting** couvert m; **p. of work** lieu de travail; **p. of worship** lieu de culte

placebo [plə'si:bəʊ] N Med, Fig placebo m; **the p. effect** l'effet m placebo

placement ['pleɪsmənt] N **1** (putting in place) placement m, mise f en place; (siting) localisation f; (of funds, bet, shares) placement; (of contract) adjudication f; (of order) passage m; (finding job) placement; **the p. of children in care/with foster parents** le placement d'enfants à la DDASS/dans des familles d'accueil **2** (of trainee etc) stage m; **to get a p.** (of trainee) trouver un stage

placenta [plə'sentə] N Anat, Bot placenta m

placid ['plæsɪd] ADJ placide, calme, tranquille

placidity [plə'sɪdɪtɪ], **placidness** ['plæsɪdnɪs] N placidité f, calme m, tranquillité f

placidly ['plæsɪdlɪ] ADV placidement, calmement, tranquillement

placing ['pleɪsɪŋ] N **1** = **placement 1**
2 p. of an order passation f de commande
3 Sport etc (ranking) classement m

placket ['plækɪt] N Sewing patte f

plagiarism ['pleɪdʒərɪz(ə)m] N plagiat m; **student accused of p.** étudiant accusé d'avoir copié

plagiarist ['pleɪdʒərɪst] N plagiaire mf

plagiarize ['pleɪdʒəraɪz] VT (author) plagier; (work) plagier, faire un plagiat de, contrefaire; (student's essay) copier (from dans)
vi se livrer à des plagiats

plague [pleɪg] N Med peste f, Bible, Fig (scourge) fléau m, plaie f; **to avoid sb/sth like the p.** éviter qn/qch comme la peste; Arch **a p. on both your houses!** allez tous au diable!; Arch **a p. on you and your statistics!** allez au diable, toi et tes statistiques!; **p. ridden** or **stricken** infesté par la peste
vt (person) tourmenter, harceler; **she was plagued by illness** la maladie la poursuivait sans relâche; **to p. sb's life** empoisonner l'existence de qn; **to p. sb with questions** harceler qn de questions; **our journey was plagued by minor problems** nous avons été accablés de petits ennuis pendant notre voyage; **the team was plagued by injury** l'équipe a collectionné les blessures

plaice [pleɪs] N (fish) carrelet m, plie f (franche)

plaid [plæd, Scot pleɪd] N **1** (material) tartan m, tissu m écossais **2** (part of Highland costume, travelling rug) plaid m

PLAIN [pleɪn]

ADJ clair **1** ▪ simple **2** ▪ nature **2** ▪ uni **3** ▪ quelconque **4**		
ADV simplement **1** ▪ franchement **2**		
N plaine		

ADJ 1 (clear, unambiguous) clair, évident; **to make sth p. to sb** faire comprendre qch à qn; **to make one's feelings p.** exprimer clairement ses sentiments; **they made their contempt for him p.** ils n'ont pas caché leur mépris pour lui; **it's as p. as (plain) can be** or **as p. as a pikestaff** or **as the nose on your face** c'est on ne peut plus clair, c'est clair comme le jour; **it's p. (to see) that you don't like me** il est évident que vous ne m'aimez

pas; **I'll be quite p. with you** je vais être franc avec toi; **in p. English** clairement; **what is that in p. English?** = qu'est-ce que ça veut dire en bon français?; **p. answer** réponse f carrée; **p. speaking** franc parler m; **the p. truth** la pure ou simple vérité

2 (simple) (style, furniture, dress, sewing) simple, sans recherche; (cigarettes) sans filtre; (unadorned) (rice, yoghurt etc) nature; **that's just p. foolishness/ignorance** c'est de la pure bêtise/ignorance; Knitting **one p. one purl** une maille à l'endroit, une maille à l'envers; **p. country people** de simples campagnards; **in p. clothes** en civil; **p. cooking** cuisine f simple; **p. living** vie f simple

3 (uniformly coloured) (wallpaper, carpet, material etc) uni; (paper) non réglé

4 (unattractive) (woman) pas particulièrement belle, plutôt quelconque; **she's rather a p. Jane** c'est une jeune fille plutôt quelconque

ADV Fam **1** (simply) simplement; **he's just p. ignorant** il est tout simplement ignorant
2 (frankly) franchement; **to speak p.** parler franc ou sans détours; **she told me p. what she thought about him** elle lui a dit franchement ou sans détours ce qu'elle pensait de lui

N Geog plaine f; **alluvial p.** plaine alluviale; **the Great Plains** la Prairie (américaine)

▸▸**p. chocolate** chocolat m noir; **p.-clothes policeman** agent m en civil; **p. flour** farine f (sans levure); **p. knitting** tricot m à l'endroit; **p. paper fax** télécopieur m ou fax m sur papier ordinaire

plainchant ['pleɪntʃɑːnt] N = **plainsong**

plainly ['pleɪnlɪ] ADV **1** (clearly) (to see) clairement, nettement; **to speak p.** (be frank) parler franchement ou sans détours; **I can p. see that I am not welcome here** je vois bien que je ne suis pas le bienvenu ici; **p. visible/audible** qui se voit/s'entend clairement; **p. I was not wanted** il était clair que j'étais de trop; **they were p. exhausted** ils étaient de toute évidence épuisés **2** (simply) (to live) simplement; (to dress) simplement, sans recherche

plainness ['pleɪnnɪs] N **1** (clarity) (of concise language) clarté f, simplicité f; (of frank language) franchise f, rondeur f **2** (simplicity) (of lifestyle etc) simplicité f **3** (lack of beauty) manque m de beauté

plainsong ['pleɪnsɒŋ] N Mus plain-chant m, pl plains-chants

plain-spoken ADJ franc, f franche

plaint [pleɪnt] N Law plainte f

plaintiff ['pleɪntɪf] N Law demandeur, -eresse, plaignant, -ante

plaintive ['pleɪntɪv] ADJ plaintif

plaintively ['pleɪntɪvlɪ] ADV plaintivement

plaintiveness ['pleɪntɪvnɪs] N ton m plaintif

plait [plæt] N (of hair) natte f, tresse f; **she had her hair in plaits** elle avait des nattes
vt (hair etc) natter, tresser

plan [plæn] N **1** (proposal, intention) projet m, plan m; (timetable) planning m; (for the future) projet; **p. of battle** plan de bataille; **p. of campaign** plan d'action; Fin **investment p.** plan d'investissement; Econ **five-year p.** plan quinquennal; Aviat **flight p.** plan de vol; **to change one's plans** changer ses projets; **to have no fixed plan(s)** ne pas avoir de projet bien déterminé; **everything went according to p.** tout a marché comme prévu; **the best p. would be to ...** la meilleure solution serait de ...; **it would be a good p. to ...** ce serait une bonne idée de ...; **what are your plans for the summer?** quels sont vos projets pour cet été?; **I've thought of a p.** j'ai imaginé un plan; **to have other plans** avoir d'autres projets; **they had other plans for us** ils avaient autre chose en vue en ce qui nous concernait

2 *(drawing etc) (of building, town)* plan *m*; *(in surveying) (of area)* plan, levé *m*; *(outline) (of novel etc)* plan; **ground p.** plan géométral **vt** (**-nn-**) **1** *(arrange) (trip)* projeter; *(attack etc)* combiner; *(crime)* comploter, tramer; **everything had been planned down to the last detail** tout avait été planifié dans les moindres détails; **to p. to do sth** projeter de faire qch; **we don't have anything planned tomorrow afternoon** nous n'avons rien de prévu demain après-midi; **things did not go as planned** les choses ne se sont pas passées comme prévu; **this had been planned** cela avait été prévu

2 *(make a plan of)* faire *ou* dessiner le plan de; *Econ (production etc)* planifier; *(new novel etc)* faire *ou* établir *ou* élaborer le plan de; **to p. one's lessons** *(of teacher)* préparer ses cours; **the school was planned for 500 pupils** l'école a été prévue pour 500 élèves **vi** faire des projets; **to p. for the future** faire des projets d'avenir; **they had planned for six** ils avaient prévu pour six personnes

▶ **plan ahead** **vi** faire des projets; *(for lunch, party)* s'y prendre à l'avance

▶ **plan on** **vt insep** *(have intention of) (something)* prévoir; **to p. on doing sth** prévoir *ou* projeter *ou* avoir l'intention de faire qch; **we're planning on going to Brazil** *or* **on a trip to Brazil** nous projetons *ou* nous avons l'intention de partir au Brésil, nous projetons un voyage au Brésil; **don't p. on being able to persuade him** ne compte pas arriver à le persuader; **we hadn't planned on staying long** nous n'avions pas prévu de *ou* ne comptions pas rester longtemps

▶ **plan out** **vt sep** *(make detailed plans for)* prévoir (en détail); **he had planned it all out** il avait tout prévu, il en avait établi tous les détails

plane¹ [pleɪn] **adj** *(angle, geometry etc)* plan **n 1** *Geom* plan *m*; **horizontal/vertical p.** plan horizontal/vertical; *Opt* **focal p.** plan focal; *Geol* **fault p.** plan de faille

2 *Fig* plan *m*, niveau *m*; **on the economic p.** sur le plan économique; **a higher p. of intelligence** un niveau intellectuel supérieur

3 *Aviat* **tail p.** plan *m* fixe horizontal

4 *(aeroplane)* avion *m*; **by p.** en avion; **it's just a short p. ride** c'est un court voyage en avion

vi *(of bird, aircraft)* planer; **to p. down** descendre en vol plané *ou* en planant; **to p. along the water** *(of hydroplane)* glisser à la surface de l'eau

▶▶ *Geom* **p. surface** surface *f* plane; **p. ticket** billet *m* d'avion; *Math* **p. trigonometry** trigonométrie *f* rectiligne

plane² **n** *(tool)* rabot *m*
vt *Carp etc (wood)* raboter, aplanir, planer; *(metal)* aplanir, planer; **to p. a surface smooth** aplanir une surface; *(also wood)* raboter une surface

plane³ **n** *(tree)* platane *m*
▶▶ **p. tree** platane

planet ['plænɪt] **n** *Astron* planète *f*; **the biggest country on the p.** le plus grand pays de la planète

planetarium [plænɪ'teərɪəm] **n** planétarium *m*

planetary ['plænɪt(ə)rɪ] **adj** *Astron (system, time, movement)* planétaire

plangent ['plændʒənt] **adj** *Lit* élégiaque

planing ['pleɪnɪŋ] **n** *Carp etc (of wood)* rabotage *m*, planage *m*, aplanissage *m*; *(of metal)* planage, aplanissage
▶▶ **p. machine** raboteuse *f*

planisphere ['plænɪsfɪər] **n** planisphère *m* céleste

plank [plæŋk] **n 1** *Carp, Constr etc* planche *f* (épaisse), madrier *m*; *Naut* **to walk the p.** passer à la planche **2** *Pol Fig* **this was a main p. in the party platform** c'était un des principaux articles du programme du parti
vt *Constr (floor)* planchéier

▶ **plank down** **vt sep** *(put down heavily)* poser brusquement

planking ['plæŋkɪŋ] **n** *(planks)* planches *fpl*, madriers *mpl*

plankton ['plæŋktən] **n** plancton *m*

planned ['plænd] **adj 1** prévu, projeté; **the p. meeting never took place** la réunion qui avait été prévue n'a jamais eu lieu; **well/badly p.** bien/mal conçu; *(plot, crime)* bien/mal concerté *ou* organisé; **was it a p. pregnancy?** c'était vraiment votre/leur intention d'avoir un enfant? **2** *Econ etc* planifié; **p. takeover of** projet *m* d'OPA sur
▶▶ *Econ* **p. economy** économie *f* planifiée

planner ['plænər] **n 1** *(person)* planificateur, -trice; **(town) p.** urbaniste *mf* **2** *(on wall of office etc)* planning *m*; *(chart)* chronogramme *m*; *(diary)* agenda *m*

planning ['plænɪŋ] **n 1** *(of project, plot etc)* conception *f*, élaboration *f*; *(of menus)* élaboration; **the expedition will require careful p.** il faudra une organisation minutieuse pour mener à bien cette expédition; **it's still at the p. stage** c'est encore à l'état de projet; **the project was halted at the p. stage** le projet n'a pas dépassé le stade de la planification **2** *Econ* planification *f*, *Fam* planning *m*; *Admin* **to get p. permission to build sth** *or* **for sth** obtenir le permis de construire qch; **town p.** urbanisme *m*; **family p.** planning familial

plant [plɑːnt] **n 1** plante *f*; **flowering p.** plante à fleurs; **pot p., house p.** plante d'appartement; **bedding p.** plant *m* à repiquer

2 *Ind (equipment)* équipement *m*, matériel *m* (industriel); *(facility)* installation *f* (industrielle); *(factory)* usine *f*; **cooling p.** appareil *m* de refroidissement; **(electric) power p., generating p.** centrale *f* électrique

3 *Sl (spy)* taupe *f*; *(from police)* mouchard *m*; *(of magician, memory man)* compère *m*; *(something planted in order to incriminate)* coup *m* monté; **the drugs were a p.** la drogue avait été placée là pour me/le/*etc* mettre en cause

vt 1 *(tree etc)* planter; **to p. a field with wheat** mettre un champ en blé

2 *(insert, place) (stake in the ground etc)* planter; *Mil etc (bomb)* poser; *Fam (spy)* planter; **to p. an idea in sb's mind** implanter une idée dans l'esprit de qn; *Fam* **a well planted blow** un coup bien asséné *ou* bien appliqué; *Fam* **he planted a big kiss on her cheek** il lui planta un gros baiser sur la joue; *Fam* **to p. oneself in front of sb** se planter devant qn; **to p. incriminating evidence on sb** fabriquer de fausses preuves contre qn

▶▶ **p. biology** phytobiologie *f*; **p. breeder** phytogénéticien, -ienne; **p. hire** location *f* de matériel industriel; **p. life** flore *f*, **p. physiology** physiologie *f* végétale; **p. stand** jardinière *f*

▶ **plant out** **vt sep** *Agr (seedling)* repiquer

plantain¹ ['plæntɪn] **n** *(plant)* plantain *m*

plantain² **n 1** *(fruit)* banane *f* des Antilles **2** *(tree)* bananier *m* du paradis
▶▶ **p. tree** bananier du paradis

plantar ['plæntər] **adj** *Anat* plantaire

plantation [plæn'teɪʃən] **n** *(of trees, cotton etc)* plantation *f*

planter ['plɑːntər] **n 1** *(plantation owner, worker)* planteur, -euse; **coffee/sugar/cotton p.** planteur, -euse de café/de sucre/de coton **2** *(tool)* planteuse *f* **3** *(pot for house plant)* cache-pot *m inv*; *(for outside)* jardinière *f*

plaque [plæk] **n 1** *(bronze, marble etc)* plaque *f* (commémorative) **2** *(on teeth)* plaque *f* dentaire

plash [plæʃ] **n** *(of waves, stream etc)* clapotement *m*, clapotis *m*; *(of object falling into water)* flac *m*
vi *(of liquids)* clapoter, faire un clapotis; *(of falling object etc)* faire flac *(sur l'eau etc)*

plasm ['plæz(ə)m] **n** *Biol* protoplasme *m*

plasma ['plæzmə] **n** plasma *m*; **(blood) p.** plasma (sanguin)
▶▶ *Comput* **p. display** affichage *m* à plasma; *Comput* **p. screen** écran *m* (à) plasma

plasmapheresis [plæzməfə'resɪs] **n** *Med* plasmaphérèse *f*, échange *m* plasmatique

plaster ['plɑːstər] **n 1** *Constr etc* plâtre *m*; **to put a leg in p.** plâtrer une jambe, mettre une jambe dans le plâtre **2** *Br Med* **(sticking) p.** pansement *m* adhésif, sparadrap *m*; **corn p.** pansement coricide

vt 1 *Constr etc (wall)* plâtrer, enduire de plâtre **2** *Fig* **the wall was plastered with advertisements** le mur était tapissé d'affiches; **plastered with mud** *(person, shoes, car etc)* couvert de boue; **her face was plastered with make-up** elle avait un peu forcé sur le maquillage; **he plastered his hair down** il aplatit ses cheveux; **her name was plastered over the front pages** son nom s'étalait en première page **3** *Med (leg etc)* plâtrer

▶▶ **p. cast** *Med* plâtre; *Art* moule *m* (en plâtre); **p. of Paris** plâtre de Paris *ou* à mouler

plasterboard ['plɑːstəbɔːd] **n** *Constr* Placoplâtre® *m*

plastered ['plɑːstəd] **adj** *Fam* beurré, pinté; **to get p.** se beurrer, se pinter

plasterer ['plɑːstərər] **n** plâtrier *m*

plasterwork ['plɑːstəwɜːk] **n** *Constr* plâtres *mpl*

plastic ['plæstɪk] **n 1** plastique *m*; **laminated p.** (plastique) stratifié *m*, lamifié *m*; **moulded p.** plastique moulé; **wrapped in p.** emballé dans du plastique; **the plastics industry** l'industrie *f* des plastiques **2** *Fam (money)* monnaie *f* électronique; **he paid for it with p.** il l'a payé avec une carte de crédit

adj 1 *(made of plastic) (bag, cup)* en plastique **2** *Art etc* plastique **3** *(artificial)* synthétique, artificiel; **p. smile** sourire *m* artificiel

▶▶ **the p. arts** les arts *mpl* plastiques; **p. bomb** charge *f* de plastique, bombe *f* au plastique; **to blow up a house with a p. bomb** plastiquer une maison; **p. bullet** balle *f* en plastique; **p. explosive** plastic *m*; *Fam* **p. money** monnaie électronique; **p. surgeon** *(cosmetic)* chirurgien, -ienne esthétique; *(therapeutic)* plasticien, -ienne; **p. surgery** *(cosmetic)* chirurgie *f* esthétique; *(therapeutic)* chirurgie plastique *ou* réparatrice

Plasticine® ['plæstɪsiːn] **n** pâte *f* à modeler

plasticity [plæs'tɪsɪtɪ] **n** plasticité *f*, *Art, Cin* effet *m* plastique

plate [pleɪt] **n 1** *(for food)* assiette *f*; **dinner/soup p.** assiette plate/creuse; *Fig Fam* **to have a lot on one's p.** avoir du pain sur la planche; *Fig Fam* **I've already got far too much on my p.** j'ai déjà largement à faire; *Fig Fam* **I've got enough on my p. without him causing problems** j'ai déjà assez à faire sans qu'il ne crée des problèmes; *Fig Fam* **to hand sth to sb on a p.** apporter qch à qn sur un plateau; *Fig Fam* **he got it handed to him on a p.** on le lui a apporté sur un plateau; *Rel etc* **(collection) p.** plateau *m* de quête; *Rel etc* **to pass round the p.** faire la quête

2 *(small piece) (of metal, glass, plastic etc)* petite plaque *f*, lamelle *f*, *Geol, Med* plaque; **(dental) p.** *(for straightening teeth)* appareil *m* (dentaire); *(dentures)* dentier *m*

3 *Metal (large piece)* plaque *f*, *Ind* (grande) feuille *f*; *(of armour)* plaque, plate *f*; *(of door*

hinge) paumelle *f*, **hot p.** *(on cooker)* plaque chauffante; *(single plate)* réchaud *m*; *(plate warmer)* chauffe-assiettes *m inv*; **name p.** *(on door)* plaque de porte; *(of street)* plaque de rue; *(of machine)* plaque d'identification ou de série; *Br Aut etc* **number p.** plaque d'immatriculation

4 *Elec (of battery etc)* plaque *f*, lame *f*, *Electron (of electron tube)* plaque, anode *f*

5 *(in engraving), Typ* plaque *f*, *(in engraving), Phot etc* cliché *m*; *(engraving)* planche *f*, gravure *f*, estampe *f*; *Phot* **(photographic) p.** plaque (photographique); **p. 12 (a)** *(in book)* planche 12 (a)

6 *Constr (wall) p. (of beam)* plaque *f* d'assise **7** *(plated metal) (gold)* orfèvrerie *f*, **silver p.** argenterie *f*, **it's (only) p.** c'est du plaqué **8** *Sport* coupe *f* (d'or, d'argent donnée en prix)

VT 1 *(protect with plates of metal)* blinder, recouvrir *ou* garnir de plaques **2** *(add layer of metal to)* métalliser; *(with gold)* plaquer en or; *(with silver)* plaquer en argent

▸▸ **p. armour** armure *f* (en plaques de fer); *Aut* **p. clutch** embrayage *m* à disque *ou* à plateau; *Typ* **p. cylinder** cylindre *m* porteplaque, *pl* cylindres porte-plaques; **p. glass** verre *m* (à vitres); **p.-glass window** *(of shop)* vitrine *f*, *(of house)* baie *f* vitrée; **p. rack** égouttoir *m*; **p. service** *(in restaurant)* service *m* à l'assiette; *Geol* **p. tectonics** tectonique *f* des plaques; **p. warmer** chauffeassiettes

plateau, *pl* **plateaux, plateaus** ['plætəʊ, -əʊz] **N** *Geog* plateau *m*; *Fig* **to reach a p.** atteindre un palier

plated ['pleɪtɪd] **ADJ 1** *(protected with metal plates)* recouvert *ou* garni de plaques; **armour p.** blindé **2** *(coated with metal)* plaqué; **gold p.** plaqué or; **silver p.** argenté; **chromium p.** chromé

plateful ['pleɪtfʊl] **N** assiettée *f*, (pleine) assiette *f*

platelayer ['pleɪtleɪər] **N** *Br Rail* poseur *m* de rails

plateless printing ['pleɪtlɪs] **N** impression *f* sans presse

platelet ['pleɪtlɪt] **N** *(in blood)* plaquette *f*

plate-making **N** *Typ* préparation *f* des plaques offset

platen ['plæt(ə)n] **N** rouleau *m*; *Typ* platine *f*

plate-room manager **N** *Typ* conducteur *m* de presse

platform ['plætfɔːm] **N 1** *(raised flat surface)* plate-forme *f*, *pl* plates-formes; *Rail (where passengers stand)* quai *m*; *(where train stops)* voie *f*, *(of weighing machine)* tablier *m*; *(of crane)* passerelle *f*, *Petr* **drilling p.** plateforme de forage; **launching/firing p.** plateforme de lancement/de tir (de missiles); *Rail* **the train waiting at p. one** le train au départ voie n° 1; *Rail* **to wait on the p.** *(of person)* attendre sur le quai; *Rail* **what p. is it for London?** quel quai est-ce pour Londres?; *Rail* **arrival/departure p.** quai d'arrivée/de départ

2 *(at public meeting)* estrade *f*, tribune *f*; *Pol Fig (of party)* plate-forme *f*, *pl* plates-formes, programme *m*; **he used his programme on TV as a p. for promoting his political views** son émission télévisée lui servait de tribune pour promouvoir ses opinions politiques

3 *Comput* plate-forme *f*, *pl* plates-formes **4** **platforms** *(shoes)* chaussures *fpl* à semelles compensées

▸▸ *Am Rail* **p. car** (wagon *m*) plate-forme; **p. shoes** chaussures à semelle compensée; **p. soles** semelles *fpl* compensées; *Rail* **p. ticket** ticket *m* de quai

plating ['pleɪtɪŋ] **N 1** *(protective)* blindage *m*; **steel** *or* **armour p.** blindage **2** *(coating with metal)* placage *m*; *(copper)* cuivrage *m*;

(gold) dorage *m*, dorure *f*; *(silver)* argentage *m*, argenture *f*

platinum ['plætɪnəm] **N** platine *m*; **p. blond hair** cheveux blond platiné *ou* blond platine *ou* platinés; **she's a p. blonde** c'est une blonde platinée

ADV to go p. *(of record)* devenir disque de platine

▸▸ **p. disc** disque *m* de platine

platitude ['plætɪtjuːd] **N** *(remark)* platitude *f*, banalité *f*, lieu *m* commun

platitudinous [plætɪ'tjuːdɪnəs] **ADJ** *(style, speech)* plat, banal, -als

Plato ['pleɪtəʊ] **N** Platon

Platonic [plə'tɒnɪk] **ADJ** *(philosophy etc)* platonicien; *(love)* platonique; **he wanted to keep things platonic** il voulait que leur relation reste platonique

platoon [plə'tuːn] **N** *Mil (in infantry)* section *f*, *(in tanks)* peloton *m*; *Fig (of assistants, students)* armée *f*

▸▸ **p. commander** chef *m* de section; *(in tanks)* chef de peloton

platter ['plætər] **N 1** *(plate)* plat *m* **2** *esp Am Fam (record)* disque *m*

platypus ['plætɪpəs] **N** *(animal)* ornithorynque *m*

plaudits ['plɔːdɪts] **NPL** *esp Lit* (salve *f* d')applaudissements *mpl*; **the new menus on trains have won the p. of passengers** les nouveaux menus servis dans les trains ont été accueillis avec enthousiasme par les passagers

plausibility [plɔːzə'bɪlɪtɪ] **N** *(of argument, excuse etc)* plausibilité *f*, **the plot is lacking in p.** l'intrigue n'est guère plausible; **I would question the p. of someone doing …** il ne me semble guère plausible que quelqu'un fasse …; **she argued, with some p., that …** elle a avancé, de façon assez convaincante, que …

plausible ['plɔːzəb(ə)l] **ADJ 1** *(excuse etc)* plausible, vraisemblable; *(pretext etc)* spécieux **2** *(person, argument)* convaincant

plausibly ['plɔːzəblɪ] **ADV** plausiblement; *(to argue etc)* de façon convaincante

PLAY [pleɪ]

N pièce (de théâtre) **1** ▪ jeu **2, 3, 5**	
VI jouer **1–4**	
VT jouer **1–3** ▪ jouer à **1** ▪ jouer de **3** ▪ mettre **3**	

N 1 *Theat* pièce *f* de théâtre; **Shakespeare's plays** les pièces *ou* le théâtre de Shakespeare; **(radio) p.** pièce radiophonique; **(television) p.** dramatique *f*

2 *(movement) (of mechanical part)* course *f*, *(unwanted slack)* jeu *m*; *(of light)* jeu, reflets *mpl*; **a complex p. of forces** un rapport de forces complexe; **there's still too much p. in the brakes** il y a encore trop de jeu dans les freins; **to come into p.** entrer en jeu, intervenir; **to bring** *or* **call** *or* **put sth into p.** mettre qch en jeu *ou* en œuvre; *(one's faculties)* exercer qch; *Fam* **to make a p. for sth** jouer le grand jeu pour obtenir qch; *Fam* **to make a p. for sb** *(try to seduce)* jouer le grand jeu à qn, faire des avances à qn; **to give** *or* **allow full p. to one's imagination** donner libre cours à son imagination; **to make great p. of sth** beaucoup insister sur qch

3 *(of children etc)* jeu *m*; **I didn't want to interrupt the children's p.** je ne voulais pas interrompre les enfants alors qu'ils étaient en train de jouer; **at p.** en train de jouer; **the aristocracy at p.** l'aristocratie en train de se détendre; **to say sth in p.** dire qch en plaisantant *ou* pour rire; **p. on words** calembour *m*, jeu de mots

4 *Sport* **p. began at one o'clock** la partie a

commencé à une heure; **after some very boring p. in the first half …** après une première mi-temps très ennuyeuse …; *Tennis* **there was some incredibly fast p. in the final set** il y a eu des échanges très rapides au dernier set; **what a good piece of p.!** quel beau coup!, bien joué!; *Cr* **rain stopped p.** la partie a été interrompue par la pluie; **in p.** *(of ball)* en jeu; **out of p.** hors jeu

5 *(gambling)* jeu *m* (de hasard); **to lose at p.** perdre au jeu

VI 1 *(have fun)* jouer; *(of animals)* jouer, folâtrer, gambader

2 *(participate in game)* jouer; **to p. against sb/a team** jouer contre qn/une équipe; **to p. in goal** être goal; **who plays first?** à qui de commencer?; *(at bowling)* à qui la boule?; *Golf* **à qui l'honneur?**; **to p. hard to get** se faire désirer; **to p. for money** *(in gambling)* jouer pour de l'argent; **to p. high** *or* **for high stakes** *(in gambling)* jouer gros (jeu); *Cards* **to p. high/low** jouer une forte/basse carte; **do you p.?** est-ce que tu sais jouer?

3 *(move) (of light, colour, fountain)* jouer, chatoyer; **the sun is playing on the water** le soleil joue sur l'eau

4 *Theat etc (act)* jouer; **to p. on the stage** *(of actor)* jouer *ou* se produire sur la scène; **production/film now playing at …** pièce/film qui passe actuellement à …; **to p. to packed houses** jouer *ou* se produire à guichets fermés

5 *Mus (of instrument, musician, band)* jouer; **they always have music playing full blast** ils mettent toujours leur musique plein pot; **I could hear the radio playing in the next room** j'entendais (le son de) la radio dans la pièce à côté

VT 1 *Sport etc (game of tennis etc)* faire, jouer; *(match)* jouer, disputer; *(include on one's team)* inclure dans son équipe; **to p. football/tennis** jouer au football/tennis; **to p. cards/chess** jouer aux cartes/échecs; **to p. sb at chess** faire une partie d'échecs avec qn; **Real Madrid played Dynamo Kiev** le Real de Madrid a affronté *ou* a joué contre le Dynamo de Kiev; *Ftbl etc* **to p. left back** jouer arrière gauche; **the team was playing two substitutes** l'équipe jouait avec deux remplaçant(e)s; *Sport* **to p. a shot/ball** jouer un coup/une balle; *Cards* **to p. a card** jouer une carte; **to p. clubs/spades** jouer trèfle/pique; *Chess etc* **to p. a move** jouer; *Fam* **to p. a hunch** jouer *ou* agir sur une intuition; **I'll p. you for the drinks** le perdant paie les consommations, d'accord?

2 *Theat, Cin (part)* jouer; *(tragedy)* jouer, représenter; **to p. Macbeth** jouer *ou* tenir le rôle de Macbeth; *Fig* **to p. an important part** jouer un rôle important; *Fam* **to p. the fool** faire l'idiot(e) *ou* l'imbécile; *Fam* **don't p. the innocent with me!** ne fais pas l'innocent avec moi!

3 *Mus* **to p. the piano/the flute** jouer du piano/de la flûte; **to p. a piece** jouer un morceau; **to p. a record-player** faire marcher un tourne-disques; **to p. a record/a tape** passer *ou* mettre un disque/une cassette; **can you p. some Pink Floyd?** tu peux mettre quelque chose des Pink Floyd?; **the neighbours were playing loud music** les voisins avaient mis la musique à fond

4 **to p. a joke** *or* **a trick on sb** jouer un tour à qn

5 *esp Lit* **to p. sb false** trahir qn

6 *(direct)* diriger (**upon, over** sur); **to p. the hose on the fire** diriger la lance sur le feu

▸▸ **p. area** aire *f* de jeux

▸ **play about, play around** **VI 1** *(play)* jouer, s'amuser; **stop playing around with that gun!** arrête de jouer avec ce revolver!

2 *(not be serious)* s'amuser; **it's time he stopped playing about and settled down** il est temps qu'il arrête de s'amuser et qu'il se fixe

3 *(consider possibilities)* **to p. around with an idea** retourner une idée dans sa tête; **to p. around with a tune** expérimenter avec un air; **they played around with the words to find a good slogan** ils jonglaient avec les mots pour trouver un bon slogan; **they played around with various names** ils ont envisagé plusieurs noms

4 *(sexually)* avoir des aventures; **to p. around with sb** avoir une aventure avec qn; **you're just playing around (with me)** tu joues avec moi

▸ **play along** VI **1** *(accompany)* **I played the fiddle while he played along on the accordeon** je jouais du violon tandis qu'il m'accompagnait à l'accordéon

2 *(cooperate)* coopérer (**with** avec)

VT SEP *(manipulate)* *(person)* manipuler

▸ **play at** VT INSEP **1 to p. at soldiers** jouer aux soldats; **to p. at keeping shop** jouer au marchand/à la marchande

2 *(dabble in)* **to p. at doing sth** faire qch en amateur; **they played at being revolutionaries** ils jouaient aux petits révolutionnaires; **they're just playing at being married** ils voient le mariage comme un jeu; *Fam* **what do you think you're playing at?** à quoi tu joues?

▸ **play back** VT SEP *(tape)* écouter, passer

▸ **play down** VT SEP *(importance of sth)* minimiser; *(problem)* dédramatiser; **the government is trying to p. down its role** le gouvernement tente de minimiser l'importance de son rôle

▸ **play in** VT SEP **1** *Sport* **to p. oneself in** *(become accustomed)* se faire au jeu

2 *(with music)* accueillir en musique

▸ **play into** VT INSEP **to p. into sb's hands** faire le jeu de qn

▸ **play off** VT SEP *(oppose)* **to p. sb off against sb** opposer qn à qn; **they played their enemies off against each other** ils ont dressé leurs ennemis les uns contre les autres

VI *Sport (attempt to break tie)* faire *ou* jouer la belle

▸ **play on** VI *(continue to play)* continuer à jouer

VT INSEP **1** *(exploit)* **to p. on sb's feelings** jouer sur les sentiments de qn

2 *(pun on)* **to p. on words** jouer sur les mots; **the title plays on a line from Shakespeare** le titre est un jeu de mots sur une phrase de Shakespeare

▸ **play out** VT SEP **1** *(act)* **the events being played out on the world's stage** les événements qui se déroulent dans le monde

2 *Fam (usu passive) (exhaust)* **to be played out** *(of person, horse etc)* être vanné *ou* éreinté; *(of idea etc)* être vieux jeu *ou* démodé; *(of story)* avoir perdu tout intérêt

3 *(with music)* **they were played out to the strains of ...** leur départ a été accompagné par l'air de ...

▸ **play up** VI **1** *Br Fam (of car, child, horse etc)* faire des siennes; **my back/war wound is playing up again** mon dos/ma blessure de guerre recommence à me faire souffrir

2 *Fam (flatter)* **to p. up to sb** flatter qn

VT SEP **1** *Br Fam (cause difficulties to)* énerver, *Fam* taper sur le système de; **my rheumatism is playing me up** mes rhumatismes me font souffrir

2 *(emphasize)* faire ressortir; *(incident, scandal)* exploiter

▸ **play upon** VT INSEP = **play on** VT INSEP

▸ **play with** VT INSEP **1** *(to amuse oneself with)* **to p. with a doll/dolls** jouer *ou* s'amuser avec une poupée/jouer à la poupée; **to p. with one's glasses** jouer (distraitement) avec ses lunettes; **to be playing with fire** jouer avec le feu; **to p. with sb's affections** jouer avec l'affection de qn; **to p. with words** jouer sur les mots

2 *(to have at one's disposal)* **we've got plenty of time to p. with** nous avons beaucoup de temps à nous; **we don't have a lot of money to p. with** nous n'avons pas beaucoup d'argent à notre disposition

3 *Fam* **to p. with oneself** *(masturbate)* se toucher

playable ['pleɪəb(ə)l] ADJ *(football pitch etc)* praticable; *(shot, ball, music)* jouable

play-act VI *(pretend)* jouer la comédie; *(clown around)* faire le clown

play-acting N **it's just p.** *(pretence)* c'est de la comédie; *(clowning around)* c'est pour rire

playback ['pleɪbæk] N réécoute f, *TV etc* présonorisation f, play-back m inv, présono f; **we watched the p. after the programme** nous avons regardé l'enregistrement après l'émission

▸▸ **p. deck** magnétoscope m de lecture; **p. head** tête f de lecture

playbill ['pleɪbɪl] N *Theat (poster)* affiche f (de théâtre); *Am (programme)* programme m

playboy ['pleɪbɔɪ] N playboy m

player ['pleɪər] N **1** *Sport* joueur, -euse; *(team member)* équipier, -ière, joueur, -euse; **card/billiards p.** joueur, -euse de cartes/billard

2 *Mus* musicien, -ienne; *(of instrument)* joueur, -euse; **a good guitar p.** un(e) bon(ne) guitariste; **the band's piano p.** le pianiste du groupe

3 *(machine)* **record p.** tourne-disque m, pl tourne-disques; **cassette p.** lecteur m de cassettes, magnétophone m (à cassettes)

4 *Theat* acteur, -trice; *(of part)* interprète mf

5 *Com, Mktg* acteur m; **who are the key players in this market?** qui sont les acteurs principaux sur ce marché?

▸▸ **p. piano** piano m mécanique

playfellow ['pleɪfeləʊ] N *Old-fashioned* = **playmate**

playful ['pleɪfʊl] ADJ *(person, cat)* espiègle; *(mood)* enjoué, badin; *(remark)* espiègle, enjoué; **she gave him a p. push** elle l'a poussé pour jouer *ou* par espièglerie

playfully ['pleɪfʊlɪ] ADV *(to say, remark)* en badinant, d'un ton enjoué; *(to smile)* d'un air enjoué; *(to push sb etc)* pour jouer, par espièglerie

playfulness ['pleɪfʊlnɪs] N *(of remark)* caractère m badin; *(of person, cat)* espièglerie f

playgoer ['pleɪgəʊər] N habitué, -ée du théâtre

playground ['pleɪgraʊnd] N *Sch* cour f (de récréation); *(outside of school)* parc m de jeu; *Fig* **St Tropez is the p. of the rich** St Tropez est le lieu de villégiature des riches

playgroup ['pleɪgruːp] N ≃ (école f) maternelle f

playhouse ['pleɪhaʊs] N **1** *Theat* théâtre m **2** *(for children)* maison f

playing ['pleɪɪŋ] N **1** *(by children etc)* jeu m; **I'm not in the mood for p.** je ne suis pas d'humeur à jouer **2** *Sport* jeu m; **the team's p.** le jeu de l'équipe; **p. is more important than winning** il est plus important de jouer que de gagner **3** *Mus* jeu m; **his p. is superb** son jeu est magnifique; **her p. of the sonata was superb** elle a joué la sonate de façon magnifique

▸▸ **p. card** carte f à jouer; *Br* **p. field** terrain m de sport

playlist ['pleɪlɪst] N *TV etc* liste f de disques à programmer

playmaker ['pleɪmeɪkər] N *Sport* meneur, -euse de jeu

playmate ['pleɪmeɪt] N camarade mf (de jeu); *(friend)* copain m, copine f

play-off N *Sport* belle f

playout music ['pleɪaʊt] N musique f (de générique) de fin

playpen ['pleɪpen] N parc m (pour bébé)

playroom ['pleɪruːm] N salle f de jeux

playschool ['pleɪskuːl] N ≃ (école f) maternelle f

plaything ['pleɪθɪŋ] N jouet m; *Fam* **she's just his p.** il se sert d'elle comme d'un jouet

playtime ['pleɪtaɪm] N *Sch* récréation f, *Fam* récré f

playwright ['pleɪraɪt] N auteur m dramatique, dramaturge mf

plaza ['plɑːzə] N *Am* **1** *(square)* place f **2** *(shopping centre)* centre m commercial **3** *Aut (service area)* aire f de service

plc, PLC [piːel'siː] N **1** *Br Com (abbr* **public limited company)** ≃ SA f; **Smith p.** Smith SA **2** *Mktg (abbr* **product life-cycle)** cycle m de vie du produit

plea [pliː] N **1** *(appeal)* appel m; **p. for mercy** appel à la clémence; **to make a p. for tolerance** en appeler à *ou* implorer la tolérance **2** *(excuse)* excuse f, prétexte m (**for doing sth** pour faire qch); **on the p. that he had a prior engagement** sous prétexte d'un autre engagement; **they did not accept his p. that he had simply forgotten** il a allégué qu'il avait simplement oublié mais ils n'ont pas accepté cette excuse **3** *Law* défense f; **special p.** exception f péremptoire; **to enter a p. of guilty/not guilty** plaider coupable/non coupable; **to put forward a p. of insanity** *(of counsel)* plaider la folie

▸▸ *Law* **p. bargaining** = possibilité f pour un inculpé de se voir notifier un chef d'inculpation moins grave s'il accepte de plaider coupable

plead [pliːd] *(pt, pp* **pleaded,** *occ Am* **pled** [pled])* VI **1 to p. with sb for sb/sth** intervenir *ou* intercéder *ou* plaider auprès de qn pour qn/qch; **to p. for mercy** implorer la clémence, en appeler à la clémence; **to p. for justice** demander que justice soit faite; **they were pleading with him to stop** ils le suppliaient de s'arrêter **2** *Law* plaider (**for** pour; **against** contre); **to p. guilty/not guilty** plaider coupable/non coupable; **how do you p.?** plaidez-vous coupable ou non coupable?

VT **1** *Law, Fig (case)* plaider; *Fig* **to p. sb's cause with sb** intercéder pour qn auprès de qn, plaider la cause de qn auprès de qn; **to p. insanity** *(of counsel)* plaider la folie **2** *(claim) (ignorance etc)* prétexter; *(excuse)* invoquer, alléguer

pleading ['pliːdɪŋ] ADJ suppliant, implorant

N **1** prières fpl (**for sb** en faveur de qn) **2** *Law (speech)* plaidoyer m; *(action)* plaidoirie f; *(art)* l'art m de plaider

pleadingly ['pliːdɪŋlɪ] ADV *(to say)* d'un ton suppliant *ou* implorant; *(to look)* d'un regard suppliant *ou* implorant

pleasant ['plezənt] ADJ agréable; *(person)* agréable, affable, aimable; **p. breeze** brise f douce *ou* agréable; **it's a p. day** il fait bon aujourd'hui; **to have a p. day** *(relaxing etc)* passer agréablement la journée; **I had a p. day at the office** tout s'est bien passé au bureau; **to make oneself p.** *or* **to be p. (to sb)** se rendre agréable (auprès de qn); **he was very p.** il s'est montré très affable *ou* très gentil; **the account of the trial does not make p. reading** le récit du procès n'est pas une lecture des plus agréables; **p. dreams!** fais de beaux rêves!

pleasantly ['plezəntlɪ] ADV agréablement, d'une manière agréable; **she smiled p. at him** elle lui sourit d'un air affable; **p. situated** agréablement situé, d'une situation agréable; **to be p. surprised** être agréablement surpris

pleasantness ['plezntnɪs] N (of place etc) agrément m, charme m; (of person, manner etc) affabilité f

pleasantry ['plezntrɪ] N **1** (joke) plaisanterie f **2** pleasantries (polite remarks) civilités fpl

please [pliːz] INT s'il vous plaît/s'il te plaît; **come in, p.** entrez, s'il vous plaît, entrez, je vous prie; **p. don't cry** ne pleurez pas, je vous en supplie; **p., daddy, p.** s'il te plaît, papa; **p. tell me …** voudriez-vous bien me dire …; **may I? – p. do!** vous permettez? – je vous en prie!; **p. sit down** or **take a seat** veuillez vous asseoir; **p. don't interrupt!** veuillez bien ne pas m'/nous interrompre; **p. do not walk on the grass** (on sign) prière de ne pas marcher sur le gazon; **would you like some cake/to come with me?** – **yes, p.** est-ce que vous voulez un peu de gâteau/venir avec moi? – oh, oui, avec plaisir; **p. let me win the lottery!** Mon Dieu, j'aimerais tant gagner au loto!; Sch **p., sir!** pardon, monsieur!; **(oh) p.!** (in indignation, disgust etc) c'est vrai!
  VT (give pleasure to) plaire à, faire plaisir à; (make content) contenter, satisfaire; **the news pleased her immensely** cette nouvelle lui a fait immensément plaisir; **to try to p. sb** chercher à faire plaisir à qn; **you can't p. everybody** on ne peut plaire à tout le monde; Prov **you can't p. all of the people all of the time** on ne peut pas faire plaisir à tout le monde; **he's hard to p.** il est difficile (à contenter); **she's easy to p., she's easily pleased** elle n'est pas difficile; **music that pleases the ear** musique qui flatte l'oreille; **p. yourself!** faites comme il vous plaira ou comme vous voudrez; Fml **His Majesty has been graciously pleased to …** il a plu à sa gracieuse Majesté de …
  VI **1** (like) to do as one pleases agir à sa guise ou à son gré; **do as you p.** faites comme vous voudrez; **he will only do as he pleases** il n'en fait jamais qu'à sa tête; **just as you p.** comme vous voudrez; **if you p.** s'il vous/te plaît; **and then, if you p., he blamed me for it!** et le comble c'est qu'il a dit que c'était de ma faute! **2** (give pleasure) faire plaisir; **he tries hard to p.** il fait tout pour me/te/etc faire plaisir
  V IMPERS Arch, Lit **may it p. your Majesty** plaise ou n'en déplaise à votre Majesté; **p. God!** plaise à Dieu!, Dieu le veuille!
  N without so much as a **p.** or **thank you** sans même dire merci

pleased [pliːzd] ADJ (satisfied) satisfait, content; (happy) heureux; (smile) de satisfaction; **to be p. with sth/sb** être content de qch/qn; **to be p. to do sth** faire qch avec plaisir; **he's very p. with himself** il est très content ou fort satisfait de lui-même ou Pej de sa petite personne; **I'm very p. (that) she's coming** cela me fait énormément plaisir qu'elle vienne, je suis ravi ou très content qu'elle vienne; **I'll be p. to come** je viendrai avec plaisir; **p. to meet you** enchanté de faire votre connaissance; **I'm so p. to see you** je suis très content ou cela me fait grand plaisir de vous voir; **she didn't exactly look p. to see me** elle n'avait pas vraiment l'air contente de me voir; **I'm p. to say that …** je suis heureux de pouvoir vous dire que …; Fml **I am p. to inform you that …** j'ai le plaisir de vous aviser que …; **to be p. for sb** être content pour qn; Fam **he's as p. as Punch** il est heureux comme un roi

pleasing ['pliːzɪŋ] ADJ (news, result) qui fait plaisir; (meal, film, conversation etc) agréable; (person, manner) agréable, plaisant

pleasingly ['pliːzɪŋlɪ] ADV agréablement

pleasurable ['pleʒərəb(ə)l] ADJ agréable

pleasurably ['pleʒərəblɪ] ADV agréablement

pleasure ['pleʒər] N **1** (contentment) plaisir m; **to take** or **find p. in doing sth** éprouver du plaisir à faire qch, prendre ou avoir (du) plaisir à faire qch; **it gave me great p.** m'a fait énormément plaisir; **her books gave p. to many people** beaucoup de gens ont pris du plaisir à lire ses livres; Fml **I have p. in informing you that …** j'ai le plaisir ou je suis heureux de vous apprendre que …; **it gives me no p. to inform you that …** j'ai la triste tâche de vous apprendre que …; **it's a real p. to see you looking so cheerful** cela me fait vraiment plaisir de vous voir si gai; **it is a p. to listen to him** on a plaisir à l'écouter; **thank you very much – (it was) a p.** merci beaucoup – de rien; **the p. was all mine** tout le plaisir était pour moi; **I haven't the p. of knowing her** or **of your acquaintance** je n'ai pas le plaisir de la connaître; **with p.** avec plaisir, volontiers; **with the greatest (of) p.** avec le plus grand plaisir; Fml **Mr Stevens requests the p. of the company of Miss Miller at …** (invitation) M. Stevens prie Mlle Miller de lui faire le plaisir d'assister à …
  2 (enjoyment) plaisir(s) m(pl); **life given up to p., life of p.** vie consacrée aux plaisirs; **to take one's p.** s'amuser, se divertir; **to travel for p.** voyager pour son plaisir
  3 Old-fashioned (will) volonté f, bon plaisir m; **at sb's p.** au gré de qn, au bon plaisir de qn; **during the King's p.** pendant le bon plaisir du roi
  VT Arch faire plaisir à
  VI Arch se plaire, prendre plaisir (**in sth** à qch; **in doing sth** à faire qch)
  ▸▸ **p. boat** bateau m de plaisance; **p. cruising** navigation f de plaisance; **the p. principle** le principe de plaisir; **p. seeker** jouisseur, -euse; **p. seeking** recherche f des plaisirs; **p. trip** excursion f

pleat [pliːt] Sewing etc N pli m
  VT (skirt etc) plisser, faire des plis à

pleated ['pliːtɪd] ADJ (skirt etc) plissé

pleating ['pliːtɪŋ] N (no pl) (pleats) plis mpl, plissé(s) m(pl)

pleb [pleb] N Fam prolo mf

plebby ['plebɪ] ADJ Fam prolo

plebeian [plə'biːən] ADJ, N plébéien, -ienne

plebiscite ['plebɪsɪt] N plébiscite m; **to hold a p.** organiser un plébiscite; **to vote for sb/sth by p.** plébisciter qn/qch

plectrum ['plektrəm] N Mus (for guitar etc) médiator m

pled PT, PP see plead

pledge [pledʒ] N **1** (oath) promesse f, vœu m; **a p. of loyalty/support** une promesse ou un serment de loyauté/soutien; **the Opposition has sworn a p. to repeal this law** l'opposition a fait le serment d'abroger cette loi; Old-fashioned **to take** or **sign the p.** (of abstainer) promettre de s'abstenir d'alcool
  2 (object of value) gage m, nantissement m; **to hold in p.** (dé)tenir en gage ou en nantissement; **to redeem a p.** retirer un gage; Fin **p. over property** gage immobilier
  3 (sign) **p. of good faith** garantie f de bonne foi
  VT **1** (promise) (one's word etc) engager; **to p. oneself** or **one's word to do sth** s'engager à faire qch; **to be pledged to do sth** avoir pris l'engagement de faire qch; **to p. one's loyalty/support** accorder sa loyauté/son soutien; **to p. one's honour** donner sa parole d'honneur, s'engager sur l'honneur (**to do sth** à faire qch); **to p. one's allegiance to the king** vouer obéissance au roi; **to p. money** (in radio, television appeal) promettre un don
  2 (give as pledge or security) donner ou mettre en gage, déposer en gage ou en nantissement, engager; **to p. one's property** engager son bien; **to p. securities** déposer des titres en garantie
  ▸▸ Fin **p. holder** détenteur, -trice de gage(s)

pledgee [ple'dʒiː] N Fin gagiste mf

pledgor ['pledʒər] N Fin gageur, -euse

pleiad, pl pleiads, pleiades ['plaɪəd, -ædz, -ədiːz] N **1** Liter pléiade f **2** Myth, Astron **the Pleiads, the Pleiades** les Pléiades fpl

plenary ['pliːnərɪ] ADJ complet, -ète, entier; ▸▸ **p. assembly** assemblée f plénière; **p. power** (of dictator) pouvoir m absolu; (of president) pleins pouvoirs; **p. session** (at conference) séance f plénière

plenipotentiary [plenɪpə'tenʃ(ə)rɪ] ADJ, N plénipotentiaire m

plenitude ['plenɪtjuːd] N plénitude f

plentiful ['plentɪfʊl] ADJ abondant, copieux; **to be p.** abonder

plentifully ['plentɪfʊlɪ] ADV abondamment, copieusement

plenty ['plentɪ] N abondance f; **p. of …** beaucoup de …, Fam plein de …; **you've got p. of time** vous avez largement le temps; **to arrive in p. of time** arriver de bonne heure; **to have p. to live on** avoir largement de quoi vivre; **that's p.** (when being served food, drink) ça suffit; Fam **there's p. more where that came from!** (food etc) quand il y en a plus, il y en a encore; **take as much as you like, there's p. more** prenez-en autant que vous voulez, il en reste beaucoup; **land of p.** pays m de cocagne; **year of p.** année f d'abondance
  ADV Fam **it's p. big enough** c'est bien assez gros
  ADV Arch, Am abondant; **money is p.** l'argent ne manque pas ou abonde

pleonasm ['pliːənæz(ə)m] N pléonasme m

pleonastic [pliːə'næstɪk] ADJ pléonastique, redondant; **to be p.** (of word) être un pléonasme

plethora ['pleθərə] N pléthore f, surabondance f

pleural ['plʊər(ə)l] ADJ Med pleural, -aux
  ▸▸ **p. membrane** plèvre f

pleurisy ['plʊərɪsɪ] N Med pleurésie f; **to have p.** avoir ou faire une pleurésie

plexus ['pleksəs] N **1** Anat plexus m **2** Fig (maze) enchevêtrement m

pliability [plaɪə'bɪlɪtɪ] N (of stem etc) flexibilité f, souplesse f; (of character) docilité f, souplesse

pliable ['plaɪəb(ə)l] ADJ pliable, pliant, flexible; (leather) souple; Fig (character etc) docile, malléable, souple

pliers ['plaɪəz] NPL (tool) pince(s) f(pl), tenaille(s) f(pl); **a pair of p.** des tenailles VOIR GRAMMAIRE A10

plight [plaɪt] N condition f ou état m critique; **to be in a sorry** or **sad p.** (of person, country, economy) être dans une mauvaise passe; **she saw my p. and helped me get up** elle a vu que ça n'allait pas et m'a aidé à me relever; **what a p. you're in!** comme vous voilà fait!

plight [plaɪt] VT **to p. one's troth to sb** Arch donner sa foi à qn; (promise to marry) se fiancer à qn

Plimsoll ['plɪmsəl] N
  ▸▸ Naut **P. line, P. mark** ligne f de Plimsoll

plimsolls ['plɪmsəlz] NPL Br (chaussures fpl de) tennis mpl

plinth [plɪnθ] N Archit plinthe f; (of statue, column) socle m

Pliny ['plɪnɪ] N **P. the Elder/the Younger** Pline m l'Ancien/le Jeune

plip key [plɪp] N Aut plip m

PLO [piː'el'əʊ] N (abbr Palestine Liberation Organization) OLP f; **P. representatives** représentants de l'OLP

plod [plɒd] N **1** (walking) démarche f lourde ou lente; **it's a long p.** il faut marcher longtemps **2** *(heavy work)* travail *m* pénible **3** *Sl (police officer)* flic *m*, poulet *m*; **the p.** *(the police)* les flics, les poulets

vi *(-dd-)* **1** *(walk)* marcher lourdement *ou* péniblement; **to p. on** continuer sa marche pénible; **he plodded home alone** *(dejected)* seul et malheureux, il est rentré chez lui **2** *(work)* = **plod away**

vt to p. one's way avancer *ou* marcher d'un pas lent

▸ **plod along** **vi 1** *(walk slowly)* avancer *ou* marcher d'un pas lent **2** *(work slowly)* travailler laborieusement **(with** à)

▸ **plod away** **vi** *(work slowly)* travailler laborieusement **(at** à), peiner, trimer **(at** sur)

▸ **plod on** **vi** = **plod along**

▸ **plod through** **vt insep** *(work slowly at)* travailler laborieusement à; **I'm plodding through a rather boring book just now** j'avance péniblement dans un livre plutôt barbant en ce moment

plodder ['plɒdər] **n** *Pej* besogneux, -euse

plodding ['plɒdɪŋ] **adj** *(steps)* pesant, lourd

plonk[1] [plɒŋk] **n** *(sound)* bruit *m* sourd
vt = **plonk down**

▸ **plonk away** **vi** *Fam* **to p. away on the piano** pianoter

▸ **plonk down** **vt sep** poser lourdement; **just p. it down there** pose-le par là; **he plonked his glass down** il posa son verre bruyamment; **to p. oneself down in an armchair** se laisser tomber dans un fauteuil

▸ **plonk out** **vt sep** *Fam* **to p. out a tune on a guitar/piano** jouer maladroitement un air à la guitare/au piano

plonk[2] **n** *Br Fam (wine)* pinard *m*; *(poor quality wine)* piquette *f*

plonker ['plɒŋkər] **n** *Br Sl* **1** *(penis)* bite *f*, *Hum* zizi *m* **2** *(fool)* branleur *m*

plook [pluk] **n** *Scot, North Eng Fam (pimple)* bouton *m*

plop [plɒp] **n 1** *(splash)* flac *m*, plouf *m* **2** *(soft sound)* pouf *m*
adv to go p. *(of sth falling into water etc)* faire plouf; *(of sth landing softly)* faire pouf
vi *(-pp-)* **1** *(splash)* faire flac *ou* plouf, tomber en faisant flac *ou* plouf **2** *(land softly)* tomber; **she plopped exhausted onto the bed** épuisée, elle s'est laissée tomber sur le lit

plosive ['pləusɪv] *Ling* **adj** *(consonant)* explosif
n explosive *f*

plot [plɒt] **n 1** *(conspiracy)* complot *m*, conspiration *f*; **a p. on sb's life** un complot pour tuer qn; **to hatch a p.** tramer *ou* ourdir un complot
2 *Liter, Theat, Cin (of play, novel etc)* intrigue *f*, action *f*; *Fig* **the p. thickens** l'affaire se corse
3 *Math etc* tracé *m*; *(graph)* graphe *m*, graphique *m*; *Aviat, Naut (of ship's or plane's route)* tracé, graphe; *(on radar)* pointé *m*
4 *(land)* (parcelle *f* *ou* lot *m* de) terrain *m*; *(small)* lopin *m* de terre; **building p.** terrain à bâtir; **(vegetable) p.** *(in garden)* potager *m*
vt *(-tt-)* **1** *(plan)* *(person's downfall)* machiner, combiner; **to p. sb's murder** comploter de tuer qn, combiner le meurtre de qn
2 *Liter, Cin etc* **a well plotted novel/film** un roman/film qui a une bonne intrigue
3 *Math, Phys (curve, diagram, graph)* tracer; *(in surveying etc)(area of land)* dresser *ou* lever le plan de, faire le levé de; *(geometric figure)* tracer, rapporter; *(point on map)* marquer, tracer, repérer; *(on radar)* marquer, relever; *Comput* tracer; *Fig (progress, development)* suivre; **to p. a course** *(for plane, ship)* relever *ou* tracer une route; *Aviat, Naut* **to p. the position** faire le point
vi *(conspire)* comploter, conspirer **(against sb** contre qn)

plotter ['plɒtər] **n 1** *(conspirator)* conspirateur, -trice, comploteur, -euse **2** *(on radar)* marqueur, -euse, plotteur *m*; *Comput (device)* traceur *m*

plotting ['plɒtɪŋ] **n** *(conspiring)* complot(s) *m(pl)*, conspiration(s) *f(pl)*
▸▸ *Comput* **p. board, p. table** table *f* traçante, traceur *m* de courbes

plough, *Am* **plow** [plau] **n 1** charrue *f*, **under the p.** *(of land)* cultivé; *Fig* **to put one's hand to the p.** mettre la main à la pâte **2** *Astron* **the P.** la Grande Ourse
vt 1 *(field)* labourer; *(furrow)* tracer, creuser; *(of ship)(waves)* fendre, sillonner; **to p. the soil** labourer la terre, retourner la terre (à la charrue); **ploughed land** terres *fpl* labourées **2** *Sch Old-fashioned Br Fam* **to p. an exam** se planter à un examen; **to be** *or* **get ploughed in an exam** être recalé *ou* collé à un examen
vi *Agr* labourer la terre

▸ **plough back,** *Am* **plow back** **vt sep** *Com, Fin* réinvestir **(into** dans); **profits ploughed back into the business** bénéfices réinvestis dans l'affaire

▸ **plough in,** *Am* **plow in** **vt sep** *(manure etc)* enterrer *ou* enfouir dans le sol en labourant; *Com, Fin etc (money etc)* investir

▸ **plough into,** *Am* **plow into** **vt insep 1** *(of vehicle)* rentrer dans, foncer dans **2** *(attack)(physically)* se jeter sur; *(verbally)* s'en prendre à
vt sep *(money etc)* investir dans

▸ **plough on,** *Am* **plow on** **vi** *(continue laboriously)* **to p. on with one's work/a book** poursuivre laborieusement son travail/sa lecture; **let's p. on another fifteen minutes** encore un petit effort d'un quart d'heure; **as negotiations p. on** tandis que les négociations se poursuivent laborieusement

▸ **plough through,** *Am* **plow through** **vt insep** *(move laboriously)* **to p. through the snow** avancer péniblement dans la neige; *Fig* **to p. through a book** lire un livre avec peine; **to p. through some work** faire un travail laborieusement; **they were ploughing through their work** ils avançaient laborieusement dans leur travail; **I've got all this to p. through** j'ai tout ça à me taper
vt sep to p. one's way through the snow avancer péniblement dans la neige; **to p. one's way through a book** lire un livre à grand peine; **I'm ploughing my way through this** *(book)* je suis en train de lire ce pavé; **he was ploughing his way through a huge plate of spaghetti** il s'efforçait de finir une énorme assiette de spaghettis

▸ **plough up,** *Am* **plow up** **vt sep 1** *(turn over)*, *Fig (churn up)(field etc)* labourer **2** *(remove)(weeds etc)* déraciner *ou* arracher à la charrue

ploughback, *Am* **plowback** ['plaubæk] **n** bénéfices *mpl* réinvestis

ploughing, *Am* **plowing** ['plauɪŋ] **n** labourage *m*, labour *m*; **p. back of profits** réinvestissement *m* des bénéfices

ploughland, *Am* **plowland** ['plaulænd] **n** *(cultivated land)* terres *fpl* cultivées; *(ploughed land)* terres labourées; *(arable land)* terre *f* arable *ou* labourable

ploughman, *Am* **plowman,** *pl* **ploughmen, plowmen** ['plaumən] **n** laboureur *m*
▸▸ *Br* **p.'s lunch** = plat *m* à base de pain, de fromage et de pickles

ploughshare, *Am* **plowshare** ['plauʃeər] **n** soc *m* de charrue

plover ['plʌvər] **n** *(bird)* pluvier *m*; **golden p.** pluvier doré; *Culin* **p.'s eggs** œufs *mpl* de vanneau

plow, plowland *etc Am* = **plough, ploughland** *etc*

ploy [plɔɪ] **n** stratagème *m*, *Fam* truc *m*

pluck [plʌk] **n 1** *(courage)* cran *m*, courage *m*; **she's got plenty of p.** elle a du cran *ou* du courage, elle a du cœur au ventre **2** *(pull)(at guitar string etc)* pincement *m*
vt 1 *(pull out)(hair, feathers etc)* arracher; *(flower)* cueillir; *Fig* **they were plucked from danger by a helicopter** un hélicoptère les a arrachés au danger; *Fig* **to p. sb from obscurity** faire sortir qn de l'anonymat; *Fig* **these figures have been plucked from the air** ces chiffres ne reposent sur rien de concret
2 *(pull)* **to p. sb's sleeve** tirer qn par la manche; *Mus* **to p. a guitar** pincer les cordes d'une guitare
3 *(remove feathers from)(poultry)* plumer; **to p. one's eyebrows** s'épiler les sourcils
vi to p. at sb's sleeve tirer qn par la manche

▸ **pluck up** **vt sep to p. up (one's) courage to do sth** rassembler son courage pour faire qch

pluckily ['plʌkɪlɪ] **adv** courageusement, avec cran *ou* courage

pluckiness ['plʌkɪnɪs] **n** cran *m*, courage *m*

plucky ['plʌkɪ] **adj** courageux; **to be p.** être courageux, avoir du courage *ou* du cran

plug [plʌg] **n 1** *(for sink, bath, tank etc)* bonde *f*, *(stopper)* bouchon *m*, tampon *m*; *(dentistry)*, *Surg* tampon *(d'ouate, de coton)*; *Geol* culot *m* volcanique; **to pull the p. out** *(of sink etc)* enlever la bonde
2 *Elec* fiche *f*, prise *f* de courant, prise mâle; *Tech (for nail, screw in wall)* fiche *f*, *(spark)* p. bougie *f*, *Elec* **two-/three-pin p.** fiche à deux/trois broches; **to pull the p. out** *(disconnect electrical appliance)* débrancher; *Fig Fam* **to pull the p. on sb** couper tous ses moyens à qn; **to pull the p. on a project** annuler un projet
3 *Am (fire)* **p.** bouche *f* d'incendie
4 *(of toilet)* chasse *f* d'eau; **to pull the p.** tirer la chasse
5 **p. of tobacco** chique *f* de tabac
6 *Com Fam (publicity)* pub *f*, **the DJ gave the album a p.** l'animateur a fait de la pub pour l'album
vt *(-gg-)* **1** *(block)(opening, pipe)* boucher, obturer; *(wound)* tamponner; *(of dentist)(cavity)* obturer; **to p. a leak** arrêter une fuite
2 *Com Fam (promote)(product)* faire du battage *ou* de la pub pour
3 *esp Am Sl (shoot)(person)* fusiller, flinguer
▸▸ *Comput* **p. compatible** compatible au niveau du matériel; **p. socket** prise de courant, prise femelle; *Aut* **p. spanner** clé *f* à bougies

▸ **plug away** **vi** *Fam (persevere)* persévérer **(at sth** dans qch), s'acharner **(at sth** sur qch)

▸ **plug in** *Elec* **vt sep** *(lamp etc)* brancher; *(printer to computer etc)* connecter
vi *(insert plug)* brancher

▸ **plug into** **vt sep** *Elec (connect)* **to p. sth into sth** brancher qch sur qch
vt insep *Elec (connect)* **the TV plugs into that socket** la télé se branche sur cette prise; *Fig* **to p. into a computer network** avoir accès à un réseau informatique; **to p. into public opinion** se mettre à l'écoute de l'opinion publique

▸ **plug up** **vt sep** = plug **vt 1**

plug-and-play **adj** *Comput* prêt à brancher

plughole ['plʌghəul] **n** *(in sink, bathtub)* bonde *f*, trou *m* d'écoulement; *Fam* **that's £300 down the p.!** voilà 300 livres par la fenêtre!; *Fam* **his company's going down the p.** sa société se casse la figure

plug-in **n** *Comput* module *m* d'extension

plug-in-and-go **adj** *Comput* prêt à brancher

plug-ugly **adj** *Fam (person)* affreux

plum [plʌm] **n 1** *(fruit)* prune *f*, *(tree)* prunier *m*; **p. jam** confiture *f* de prunes **2** *Fam (job)* boulot *m* en or; *(part in play etc)* rôle *m* en or

ADJ (colour) prune inv
▸▸**p. brandy** (eau f de vie de) prune; **p. cake** cake m; **p. pudding** pudding m de Noël; **p. tomato** olivette f; **p. tree** prunier

plumage ['pluːmɪdʒ] N plumage m

plumb [plʌm] N **1** (perpendicular) aplomb m; **out of p.** hors d'aplomb **2** (of plumb line) plomb m
ADJ droit, vertical, -aux, d'aplomb
ADV perpendiculairement (**with sth** à qch), à la verticale, à l'aplomb (**with sth** de qch); Fam **p. in the centre** en plein milieu, au beau milieu; (of target) en plein dans le mille; Am Fam **p. crazy** complètement fou
VT 1 (in surveying) vérifier l'aplomb de; (wall) vérifier l'aplomb de, plomber **2** Naut, Fig sonder; Fig **to p. the depths** toucher le fond
▸▸**p. bob** plomb; **p. line** Constr fil m à plomb; Naut sonde f
▸ **plumb in** VT SEP (install) (washing machine etc) raccorder

plumbago [plʌm'beɪɡəʊ] N **1** Bot plumbago m **2** Miner plombagine f

plumber ['plʌmər] N plombier m; **p.'s mate** aide m plombier

plumbing ['plʌmɪŋ] N **1** (action, job) plomberie f **2** (pipes) plomberie f, tuyauterie f, tuyaux mpl; (toilets, washbasins etc) installations fpl sanitaires; Fam Hum **to inspect the p.** (urinate) aller aux toilettes

plume [pluːm] N **1** Arch, Lit (feather) plume f, **a p. of smoke** une volute de fumée; **a p. of spray** un jet d'eau; Fig Lit **plumes** paré des plumes du paon **2** (ornament) panache m, aigrette f, (on helmet) plumet m, panache
VT 1 (ornament) orner ou garnir de plumes; **black-plumed** aux plumes noires; **plumed helmet** casque m empanaché **2** (preen) **to p. itself** (of bird) se lisser les plumes; **to p. oneself on sth** (of person) se glorifier de qch

plummet ['plʌmɪt] N (weight) (of plumb line, fishing line, sounding line) plomb m
VI plonger, tomber à la verticale; (of morale, popularity, standards) chuter; (of prices etc) s'effondrer; (of blood pressure etc) tomber soudainement; **the aircraft plummeted to the ground** l'avion s'est écrasé au sol

plummy ['plʌmɪ] ADJ Br Fam **1** usu Pej (voice) de la haute, snobinard **2** Old-fashioned (job) agréable, bien payé

plump [plʌmp] ADJ (person) grassouillet, -ette, dodu, boulot, -otte, bien en chair; (baby, chicken, cheeks) dodu; (hands) potelé
VT to p. oneself into an armchair s'affaler dans un fauteuil
▸ **plump down** VT SEP (suitcase etc) laisser tomber lourdement; **she plumped herself down on the sofa** elle s'est affalée sur le sofa
▸ **plump for** VT INSEP Fam (choose) choisir
▸ **plump out** VI = plump up VI
▸ **plump up** VT SEP (shake) (pillow) secouer
VI (become fat) devenir dodu

plumpness ['plʌmpnɪs] N embonpoint m, rondeur f, **to be inclined to p.** avoir tendance à prendre de l'embonpoint; **the p. of the baby's arms** les bras potelés du bébé

plunder ['plʌndər] N (booty) butin m; (act) pillage m
VT (country etc) piller, mettre à sac; Fig (bookshelves, fridge) faire une descente dans
VI piller

plundering ['plʌndərɪŋ] ADJ pillard
N pillage m

plunge [plʌndʒ] N plongeon m; Fig baisse f radicale, chute f (**in** de); **to take a p.** faire un plongeon, plonger (**into** dans); Fig (of profits etc) s'effondrer; Fam **to take the p.** (resolve to do sth) prendre le taureau par

les cornes; (get married) se marier
VT (into water) plonger, immerger; **to p. a dagger into sb's back** plonger un poignard dans le dos de qn; **plunged in darkness** plongé dans l'obscurité; **to p. sb into despair** plonger qn dans le désespoir
VI (of person) (into water) plonger, se jeter (la tête la première); (into forest etc) s'enfoncer; (into affair etc) se jeter à corps perdu; (into conversation) se lancer; (in gambling) jouer sans compter ou gros jeu; (of ship) tanguer, piquer du nez; (of profits) s'effondrer; St Exch (of speculator, investor) risquer de grosses sommes; **the lorry plunged over the cliff** le camion plongea par-dessus la falaise; **the aircraft plunged to the ground** l'avion s'est écrasé au sol; **the aircraft was plunging to the ground** l'avion tombait en chute libre; **she plunged to her death** elle fit une chute mortelle; **sales have plunged by 30%** les ventes ont chuté de 30%; **necklines have plunged this year** cette année les décolletés sont plus profonds; **to p. forward** s'élancer en avant

plunger ['plʌndʒər] N **1** (device) (on pump, in coffee-maker, syringe) piston m; Aut piston plongeur; (in lock) bonhomme m de verrouillage; (of detonator) manette f, (rubber) **p.** (for clearing sink etc) ventouse f **2** Fam (gambler) flambeur, -euse

plunging ['plʌndʒɪŋ] ADJ (prices) en chute libre; **p. neckline** décolleté m plongeant
N (of boat) tangage m

plunk [plʌŋk] VT **1** (banjo etc) pincer les cordes de **2** (drop heavily) laisser tomber lourdement
▸ **plunk down** VT SEP laisser tomber lourdement

pluperfect ['pluːpɜːfɪkt] VOIR GRAMMAIRE A50; B30 Gram ADJ plus-que-parfait
N plus-que-parfait m, pl plus-que-parfaits; **in the p.** au plus-que-parfait
▸▸**p. subjunctive** plus-que-parfait du subjonctif

plural ['plʊər(ə)l] ADJ Gram pluriel
N Gram pluriel m; **in the p.** au pluriel VOIR GRAMMAIRE A9–15; B8
▸▸Pol **p. vote** vote m plural

pluralism ['plʊərəlɪz(ə)m] N **1** Phil etc pluralisme m **2** (holding of several posts) cumul m de(s) fonctions

plurality [plʊə'rælɪtɪ] N **1** pluralité f **2** (of functions) cumul m **3** Am Pol (relative majority) majorité f relative ou simple

plus [plʌs] PREP plus; **seven p. nine** sept plus neuf; **two floors p. an attic** deux étages plus un grenier; **remember this, p. what she told you** rappelle-toi de ça, en plus de ce qu'elle t'a dit
ADJ on the p. side of the account à l'actif du compte; **on the p. side, the bicycle is very light** à sa légèreté est l'un des avantages de cette bicyclette; **fifteen p.** (quantity) plus de quinze; (age) au-dessus de quinze ans
N (pl **plusses** ['plʌsɪz]) Math (symbol) plus m; (positive quantity) quantité f positive; Fig (advantage) avantage m, atout m; **it's a p.** c'est un plus ou avantage ou atout
▸▸**p. fours** pantalon m de golf; Comput **p. key** touche f plus; **p. sign** signe m plus, plus

plush [plʌʃ] N Tex peluche f
ADJ 1 Tex en peluche **2** Fam (apartment etc) somptueux, luxueux; (restaurant, hotel) de luxe

plushy ['plʌʃɪ] ADJ Fam = plush ADJ 2

Plutarch ['pluːtɑːk] N Plutarque

Pluto ['pluːtəʊ] N **1** Myth Pluton **2** Astron Pluton f

plutocracy [pluː'tɒkrəsɪ] N ploutocratie f

plutocrat ['pluːtəkræt] N often Pej ploutocrate mf

plutocratic [pluːtə'krætɪk] ADJ ploutocratique

plutonium [pluː'təʊnɪəm] N Chem plutonium m

pluviometer [pluːvɪ'ɒmɪtər] N pluviomètre m

ply [plaɪ] N **1** (of plywood) placage m, épaisseur f, (of tyre) pli m; **two-p. paper handkerchief** mouchoir m en papier double épaisseur
2 (strand) (of wool, rope) fil m, brin m; **three-p. wool** laine f trois fils; **what p. is it?** c'est de la laine à combien de fils?
3 Fam (plywood) contreplaqué m; **three-p.** contreplaqué à trois plis
VT 1 (use) (tool) manier vigoureusement; (needle) faire courir; (trade) exercer
2 (supply) **to p. sb with questions** presser qn de questions; **to p. sb with drink** ne pas arrêter de verser à boire à qn, verser force rasades à qn; **to p. sb with food** donner abondamment à manger à qn
3 to p. an ocean (of ship) faire la traversée; **to p. a route** (of ship, bus etc) assurer une liaison
VI (of ship, bus etc) faire le service ou la navette (**between ... and ...** entre ... et ...); **to p. for hire** (of taxi etc) prendre des clients

plywood ['plaɪwʊd] N contreplaqué m

PM [piː'em] N Br, Can Pol (abbr **Prime Minister**) Premier ministre m

pm, p.m. ['piːem] ADV (abbr **post meridiem**) **6 pm** 18h; **10 am or pm?** 10 heures du matin ou du soir? VOIR GRAMMAIRE A80; B60

PMS [piːem'es] N Med (abbr **premenstrual syndrome**) syndrome m prémenstruel

PMT [piːem'tiː] N Med (abbr **premenstrual tension**) syndrome m prémenstruel

P/N [piː'en] N Com (abbr **promissory note**) billet m à ordre

pneumatic [njuː'mætɪk] ADJ pneumatique; Fam (bosom) plantureux, généreux
▸▸**p. brakes** freins mpl à air comprimé; **p. drill** marteau-piqueur m, pl marteaux-piqueurs; **p. tyre** pneu m

pneumatically [njuː'mætɪklɪ] ADV **p. operated** (machine) à air comprimé

pneumatics [njuː'mætɪks] N Phys pneumatique f VOIR GRAMMAIRE A10

pneumonia [njuː'məʊnɪə] N Med pneumonie f, **to have p.** avoir une pneumonie

PO [piː'əʊ] N **1** (abbr **Post Office**) PO Box BP **2** (abbr **postal order**) mandat m postal **3** Naut (abbr **petty officer**) second maître m

po [pəʊ] N Old-fashioned Br Fam pot m de chambre, Jules m

POA ['piːəʊ'eɪ] N (abbr **Prison Officers' Association**) = syndicat m des agents pénitentiaires en Grande-Bretagne

poach[1] [pəʊtʃ] VT Culin (eggs etc) pocher; **poached egg** œuf m poché

poach[2] VT (steal) (game etc) braconner; (steal from) (woods etc) braconner dans; Fig (employee) débaucher
VI braconner; Ftbl etc rester près des buts de l'équipe adverse; **to p. on sb's preserves** braconner sur la chasse gardée de qn; Fig empiéter sur le domaine de qn

poacher[1] ['pəʊtʃər] N (egg) **p.** pocheuse f (à œufs)

poacher[2] N (thief) braconnier, -ière

poaching ['pəʊtʃɪŋ] N (thieving) braconnage m

pock [pɒk] N Med pustule f (de la petite vérole)

pocket ['pɒkɪt] N **1** (of jacket etc) poche f, **waistcoat p.** gousset m; **to put one's hands in one's pockets** mettre les mains dans ses poches; **to go through sb's pockets** faire les

poches à qn; *Fam* **to have sb in one's p.** avoir qn dans sa poche; *Fam* **to live in each other's** *or* **one another's pockets** ne pas se lâcher d'une semelle; **prices to suit every p.** des prix à la portée de tout le monde; *Fig Fam* **to line one's pockets** se remplir les poches; *Fig* **he's always got his hand in his p.** il a toujours la main sur le portefeuille, il est toujours à débourser; **to be in p.** y gagner; **to be out of p.** *(over a transaction)* y être de sa poche, ne pas rentrer dans ses fonds; **how much are you out of p.?** combien est-ce que vous avez dépensé?; **to pay for sth out of one's own p.** payer qch de sa poche
2 *(bag)* *(for hops, wool)* sac *m*; *Billiards* blouse *f*
3 *Min (of ore, water, gas)* poche *f*, *(of firedamp)* nid *m*
4 *(small area) (of resistance, rebellion etc)* poche *f*
VT (**-t-**) **1** *(put in pocket)* empocher, mettre dans sa poche; *Pej (steal) Fam* chiper
2 *(insult)* avaler, encaisser
3 *(one's feelings)* faire taire; **to p. one's pride** faire taire son amour-propre
4 *Billiards (ball)* blouser
▸▸ **p. battleship** cuirassé *m* de poche; *Br* **p. billiards** *(pool)* billard *m* américain; *Sl Hum* **to play pocket billiards** jouer avec ses cacahuètes; **p. calculator** calculatrice *f* de poche; **p. comb** peigne *m* de poche; **p. computer** ordinateur *m* de poche; **p. dictionary** dictionnaire *m* de poche; **p. handkerchief** mouchoir *m* de poche; **p. modem** modem *m* de poche; *Br* **p. money** argent *m* de poche; **p. notebook** carnet *m*; **p. size** *(in bookbinding)* format *m* de poche

pocketbook ['pɒkɪtbʊk] **N** *Am* **1** *(handbag)* sac *m* à main **2** *(small book)* livre *m* de poche

pocketful ['pɒkɪtfʊl] **N** pleine poche *f*, **pocketfuls of sweets** de pleines poches *ou* des poches pleines de bonbons

pocketknife ['pɒkɪtnaɪf] **N** couteau *m* de poche, canif *m*

pockmark ['pɒkmɑːk] **N** marque *f* de la petite vérole

pockmarked ['pɒkmɑːkt] **ADJ** *(face)* grêlé; *(surface of the moon etc)* plein de trous

pod [pɒd] **N 1** *(of beans, peas etc)* cosse *f*, gousse *f* **2** *(of silkworm)* cocon *m* **3** *Aviat (of jet engine)* nacelle *f*; **engine p.** nacelle-moteur *f*, *pl* nacelles-moteur
VT (**-dd-**) *(peas)* écosser

podgy ['pɒdʒɪ] **ADJ** *(person)* boulot, -otte; *(finger)* boudiné, rondelet; *(knees)* grassouillet; **to get p.** engraisser

podiatrist [pə'daɪətrɪst] **N** *Am* pédicure *mf*

podium, *pl* **podia** ['pəʊdɪəm, -ɪə] **N** estrade *f*, *(for medallist)* podium *m*

poem ['pəʊɪm] **N** poème *m*, poésie *f*

poet ['pəʊɪt] **N** poète *m*
▸▸ **p. laureate** poète lauréat

poetaster [pəʊɪ'tæstər] **N** *Pej* mauvais poète *m*, rimailleur, -euse

poetess ['pəʊɪtɪs] **N** *Old-fashioned* femme *f* poète, poétesse *f*

poetic [pəʊ'etɪk] **ADJ** poétique
▸▸ **p. justice** justice *f* divine; **p. licence** licence *f* poétique

poetical [pəʊ'etɪk(ə)l] **ADJ** poétique

poetically [pəʊ'etɪklɪ] **ADV** poétiquement; **p. gifted** doué pour la poésie

poetics [pəʊ'etɪks] **N** poétique *f* VOIR GRAMMAIRE A10

poetry ['pəʊɪtrɪ] **N** poésie *f*, **to write p.** écrire des poèmes; **the art of p.** l'art *m* poétique; **it was p. in motion** c'était un vrai plaisir pour les yeux
▸▸ **p. reading, p. recital** lecture *f* de poèmes

po-faced [-feɪst] **ADJ** *Fam Pej* avec une tête d'enterrement; **why are you looking so p.** pourquoi fais-tu une telle tête d'enterrement?; **the p. old cow!** elle fait une de ces tronches!

pogo ['pəʊgəʊ] **VI** *(dance)* danser le pogo
▸▸ **p. stick** bâton *m* sauteur

pogrom ['pɒgrəm] **N** pogrom(e) *m*

poignancy ['pɔɪnjənsɪ] **N** *(of an emotion etc)* caractère *m* poignant; **a moment of great p.** un moment très poignant

poignant ['pɔɪnjənt] **ADJ** *(feeling)* poignant, vif; *(regret etc)* amer, -ère

poignantly ['pɔɪnjəntlɪ] **ADV** d'une façon poignante

poinsettia [pɔɪn'setɪə] **N** *(plant)* poinsettia *m*

POINT [pɔɪnt]

N point **1, 3, 6–8** ▪ moment **2** ▪ but **4**
▪ virgule **6** ▪ pointe **9**
VT pointer **1** ▪ diriger **1** ▪ indiquer **2**
VI montrer du doigt **2**

N 1 *(in space)* point *m*; **p. of arrival/departure** point d'arrivée/de départ; **at that p. on the road** à cet endroit de la route; **the train goes to Taunton and all points west** le train dessert Taunton et toutes les gares dans cette direction; **p. of contact** point de contact
2 *(precise moment)* **at this p. in time** en ce moment même; **at this p. the phone rang** c'est alors que le téléphone a sonné, à ce moment-là le téléphone a sonné; **at one p. I thought we would all be killed** à un certain moment, j'ai cru que nous allions tous être tués; **to be on the p. of doing sth** être sur le point de faire qch; **on** *or* **at the p. of death** sur le point de mourir, à l'article de la mort; **to be on the p. of departure** être sur le point de partir; **the p. of no return** le point de non-retour; **a high/low p. in sb's life** un moment fort/difficile de la vie de qn; **when it came to the p.** quand le moment critique est arrivé; **there comes a p. in everyone's life when ...** dans la vie de chacun il arrive un moment où ...; **up to a (certain) p.** jusqu'à un certain point; **she had reached the p. where she was no longer interested** elle en était arrivée à perdre tout intérêt; **severe to the p. of cruelty** sévère jusqu'à la cruauté
3 *(of argumentation etc)* point *m*; **the chief p. of an argument** le point essentiel d'un raisonnement; **figures that give p. to his argument** chiffres qui ajoutent du poids à sa thèse; **on that p. we disagree** là-dessus nous ne sommes pas d'accord; **I take your p.** je vois ce que vous voulez dire; **p. taken!** *(agreeing)* très juste!; **OK, OK p. taken!** ça va, ça va, j'ai compris!; **she has a p.** elle a raison; **to make a p.** faire une remarque; **to make a p. of doing sth** ne pas manquer de faire qch; **my p.** *or* **the p. I'm making is that ...** là où je veux en venir c'est que ...; **you've made your p.!** ça va, j'ai compris!; **the teacher went through the essay p. by p.** le professeur a repris la dissertation point par point; **in p. of fact** en fait, à vrai dire; **p. of grammar/of law** question *f* de grammaire/de droit; **p. of honour** point d'honneur; **the p. (subject)** le sujet, la question; **the p. at issue** le sujet dont il est question; **the p. is (that) ...** c'est que ...; **get** *or* **come to the p.!** (venons-en) au fait!; **that's the p.** c'est bien de cela qu'il s'agit; **that's not the p.** il ne s'agit pas de cela; **that's beside the p.!** ce n'est pas le problème *ou* la question!; **you're missing the p.** tu n'as pas compris ce que je voulais dire; **on this p.** à cet égard, à ce propos; **this is very much to the p.** c'est bien parlé *ou* bien dit

4 *(purpose)* but *m*; **what would be the p. (of doing that)?** à quoi bon (faire cela)?; **there is no p. in (doing) it** cela ne servirait à rien; **I can't see the p.** *(of doing it)* je ne vois pas l'intérêt
5 *(characteristic)* **a p. of interest** un détail intéressant; **a p. of similarity/difference** une similarité/différence; **to have its good points** avoir ses bons côtés; **tact has never been one of your strong points** la délicatesse n'a jamais été ton fort; **its price is a p. in its favour** son prix est un de ses atouts
6 *Gram* **(full) p.** point *m*; *Math* **(decimal) p.** virgule *f* (décimale); **three p. five (3.5)** trois virgule cinq (3,5)
7 *(in game, exam etc)* point *m*; **to score so many points** marquer *ou* obtenir tant de points; **you get three points for a correct answer** une bonne réponse vaut trois points; *Cards etc* **to play ten pence a p.** jouer à dix pence le point; *Boxing* **to win on points** gagner aux points; *Boxing* **beaten on points** battu aux points; *Boxing* **a points decision** une décision aux points
8 *Typ etc (measure)* point *m*; **6-p. type** caractères *mpl* de 6 points; **the thermometer went up/down two points** le thermomètre a monté/a baissé de deux degrés; *St Exch* **rise/fall of one p.** *(of price)* hausse *f*/baisse *f* d'un point
9 *(sharp end) (of needle, nail, sword, tool etc)* pointe *f*, *(of drill)* mouche *f*, *(of quill pen)* bec *m*; *Geog* pointe, promontoire *m*; **to dance on points** faire des pointes; **on (full) p.** *(of dancer)* sur la pointe; **on demi-p.** *(of dancer)* sur la demi-pointe; **to end in a p.** aller *ou* se terminer en pointe; **to give a p. to a pencil** tailler un crayon; **a p. of a joke** piquant *m ou* sel *m* d'une plaisanterie; **points** *(of horse etc)* extrémités *fpl*; *(in hunting) (of deer)* cors *mpl*; *Fig* **not to put too fine a p. on it ...** pour dire les choses clairement ...
10 *Br Elec (off mains)* prise *f* de courant; **eight-p. distributor** *(in engine)* distributeur *m* (d'allumage) à huit plots
11 *Aut* **points** contacts *mpl* de rupteur
12 *Br Rail* **points** aiguillage *m*
13 **the points of the compass** les aires *fpl* du vent; **to alter course 16 points** venir de 16 quarts
14 *(in backgammon)* flèche *f*, pointe *f*, case *f*

VT 1 *(aim) (gun)* pointer, braquer; *(telescope)* diriger, orienter, braquer (**at** sur); *(finger)* pointer; **to p. one's finger at sb** montrer qn du doigt; *Fig* **to p. the finger at sb** montrer qn du doigt; **to p. a gun at sb** braquer *ou* pointer une arme sur qn; **to p. a camera at sth/sb** braquer un appareil photo sur qch/qn; *Fam* **just p. me in the right direction** dites-moi simplement quelle direction je dois prendre; **she pointed the car/the boat towards home** elle a pris la direction de la maison
2 *(indicate)* **to p. the way** indiquer *ou* montrer le chemin (**to sb** à qn; **to a place** vers un endroit); *Fig* indiquer la direction à suivre (**towards sth** pour parvenir à qch); **the ship/car was pointing the wrong way** le navire/la voiture était tourné(e) du mauvais côté
3 *(in ballet)* **to p. the toe** *or* **the foot** pointer le pied
4 *Constr (wall)* jointoyer
5 *(of hunting dog) (game)* arrêter

VI 1 *(indicate)* **the magnetic needle always points north** l'aiguille aimantée est toujours tournée vers le nord; **the hour hand is pointing to 10** la petite aiguille indique 10 heures; **the arrow points in the direction of the entrance** la flèche indique la direction de l'entrée; **this points to the fact that ...** ceci montre *ou* indique que ...; **everything seems to p. to success** tout semble indiquer que tout ira bien; **everything points to sui-cide** tout semble privilégier l'hypothèse du suicide

2 *(with finger etc)* **to p. at sb/sth** montrer *ou* désigner qn/qch du doigt *etc*; **don't p., it's rude** ne montre pas du doigt; **it's not polite** ne montre pas du doigt, c'est mal poli
3 *(of hunting dog)* tomber en arrêt
▸▸ *Cycling* **points competition** classement *m* par points; *Br* **p. duty** *(of police officer, traffic warden)* service *m* de la circulation; **policeman on p. duty** agent *m* de circulation; **to be on p. duty** être à la circulation; *Br Rail* **p. lever** levier *m* d'aiguille; **p. of order** point de procédure; *Mktg* **p. of purchase** lieu *m* d'achat, lieu de vente; *Mktg* **p. of sale** lieu de vente, point de vente; *Typ, Comput* **p. size** corps *m*; **p. source** source *f* ponctuelle; **p. system** *(at school etc)* barème *m*, système *m* de notation *f*, *(in game etc)* système d'attribution des points; **p. of view** *TV, Cin* angle *m* du regard; *(opinion)* point de vue, opinion *f*; **to consider sth from all points of view** considérer qch sous tous ses aspects; **p. work** *(of ballet dancer)* pointes
▸ **point off** VT SEP *Math (decimals)* séparer par une virgule
▸ **point out** VT SEP **1 to p. sb/sth out to sb** montrer qn/qch à qn; *(with one's finger)* montrer *ou* désigner qn/qch du doigt à qn
2 *(indicate, show)* *(error etc)* signaler, relever; *(fact)* faire remarquer; **to p. out sth to sb** attirer l'attention de qn sur qch, signaler *ou* faire remarquer qch à qn; **to p. out to sb that he is wrong** faire remarquer à qn qu'il a tort; **to p. out to sb the advantages of sth** montrer à qn les avantages de qch; **might I p. out that ...?** permettez-moi de vous faire observer *ou* remarquer que ...; **he has been pointed out to me as a capable man** on me l'a signalé comme un homme capable
▸ **point up** VT SEP *(highlight)* mettre en évidence

point-blank ADJ *Mil etc (firing)* direct, à bout portant; *(refusal, denial)* catégorique; **to fire at p. range** tirer à bout portant; **he was shot at p. range** on lui a tiré dessus à bout portant
ADV **to fire p. at sb** tirer sur qn à bout portant; **he asked me p. whether ...** il m'a demandé de but en blanc si ...; **to deny sth p.** nier qch catégoriquement; **to refuse p.** refuser catégoriquement *ou* (tout) net (**to do sth** de faire qch)

point-by-point ADJ **p. analysis** analyse *f* point par point

pointed ['pɔɪntɪd] ADJ **1** *(having a sharp point)* pointu; *(beard)* (taillé) en pointe **2** *(remark)* sarcastique, mordant; *(allusion, look)* peu équivoque, peu voilé
▸▸ **p.-nose pliers** pince *f* à bec pointu

pointedly ['pɔɪntɪdlɪ] ADV *(to say)* d'un ton sarcastique *ou* mordant; *(to refer)* explicitement, nettement; **not too p.** sans appuyer; **she stared p. at the ceiling during the speech** elle fixa ostensiblement son regard au plafond pendant le discours

pointedness ['pɔɪntɪdnɪs] N *(of remark)* mordant *m*; *(of allusion)* caractère *m* explicite

pointer ['pɔɪntər] N **1** *(of clock)* aiguille *f*, *(of scales)* aiguille, languette *f*, *Sch (at blackboard)* baguette *f*; *Comput* pointeur *m*; **optical** *or* **illuminated p.** *(for slides)* flèche *f* lumineuse
2 *Fam (advice)* tuyau *m*; **to give sb a few pointers on sth** donner à qn quelques indications *ou* tuyaux à propos de qch; **a p. to the future** un signe précurseur
3 *(dog)* pointer *m*
4 *Constr (bricklayer's tool)* pointe *f*

pointillism ['pwæntɪlɪz(ə)m] N *Art* pointillisme *m*

pointing ['pɔɪntɪŋ] N *Constr (of wall)* jointoiement *m*
▸▸ *Comput* **p. device** pointeur *m*

pointless ['pɔɪntlɪs] ADJ *(story etc)* qui ne rime à rien; *(joke)* fade, sans sel; *(remark etc)* qui n'a rien à voir avec la question; *(action, suffering)* inutile; *(violence)* gratuite; *(existence)* sans but; **it would be p.** ce serait inutile, cela ne servirait à rien (**to do** de faire); **it is a p. exercise** ça ne sert à rien

pointlessly ['pɔɪntlɪslɪ] ADV *(to argue, work, die etc)* inutilement, vainement

pointlessness ['pɔɪntlɪsnɪs] N *(of joke etc)* fadeur *f*, *(of remark etc)* manque *m* d'à-propos; *(of action, changes)* inutilité *f*, *(of violence)* gratuité *f*, *(of existence)* futilité *f*

point-of-purchase ADJ *Mktg* sur le point *ou* sur le lieu de vente;
▸▸ **p. advertising** publicité *f* sur le lieu de vente, PLV *f*; **p. competition** concurrence *f* entre points de vente; **p. display** exposition *f* sur le lieu de vente; **p. information** informations *fpl* sur le lieu de vente; **p. material** matériel *m* de publicité sur le lieu de vente, matériel de PLV; **p. promotion** promotion *f* sur le lieu de vente

point-of-sale ADJ *Mktg* sur le point *ou* sur le lieu de vente
▸▸ **p. advertising** publicité *f* sur le lieu de vente, PLV *f*; **p. competition** concurrence *f* entre points de vente; **p. display** exposition *f* sur le lieu de vente; **p. information** informations *fpl* sur le lieu de vente; **p. material** matériel *m* de publicité sur le lieu de vente, matériel de PLV; **points-of-sale network** réseau *m* de points de vente; **p. promotion** communication *f* ou promotion *f* ou publicité sur le lieu de vente, CLV *f*, PLV; **p. terminal** terminal *m* point de vente, TPV *m*

point-of-view shot N *Cin, TV* plan *m* subjectif

pointsman ['pɔɪntsmən] N *Br Rail* aiguilleur *m*

point-to-point ADJ *Br Sport* cross *m* à cheval
▸▸ *Tel* **p. audioconference** audioconférence *f* point à point; *Comput* **p. protocol** protocole *m* point à point; *Br Sport* **p. race** cross à cheval

pointy-headed [pɔɪntɪ-] ADJ *Am Pej* intello

poise [pɔɪz] N **1** *(balance)* équilibre *m*; *(state of composure)* aplomb *m*; **to recover one's p.** retrouver son aplomb; **to have p.** *(of person)* avoir de la prestance; **a man of p.** un homme pondéré **2** *(of head, body)* port *m*
VT *(equilibre)*, *(in hand)* tenir en équilibre; **to be poised** être en équilibre; *(of person)* être équilibré; **her hand was poised over the telephone** sa main était suspendue au-dessus du téléphone; **she poised herself on the edge of the desk** elle s'assit délicatement sur le bord du bureau; **the cat was poised ready to spring** le chat se tenait prêt à bondir; **Rome was poised to conquer the known world** Rome se tenait prête à conquérir le monde connu; **to be poised on the brink of sth** être à deux doigts de qch

poised [pɔɪzd] ADJ posé; **she's very p. for one so young** elle est très posée pour quelqu'un d'aussi jeune

poison ['pɔɪz(ə)n] N poison *m*; **to take p.** s'empoisonner; *Fam* **what's your p.?** *(drink)* qu'est-ce que tu veux boire?
VT *(of person)* *(somebody, something)* empoisonner; *(of substance)* *(somebody)* intoxiquer; *Fig (the mind)* corrompre, pervertir; *(sb's life)* empoisonner; **to p. sb's mind against sb** monter qn contre qn; **poisoned arrow** flèche *f* empoisonnée; *Fig* **poisoned chalice** cadeau *m* empoisonné; **poisoned food** nourriture *f* empoisonnée
▸▸ **p. gas** gaz *m* toxique; *Zool* **p. gland** glande *f* à venin; *Bot* **p. ivy** sumac *m* vénéneux, *Can* herbe *f* à puces *ou* à la puce; **p. pen letter** lettre *f* anonyme *(d'insulte ou de menace)*; *Fin Fam* **p. pill** *(strategy)* pilule *f* empoisonnée

poisoner ['pɔɪzənər] N empoisonneur, -euse

poisoning ['pɔɪzənɪŋ] N *(by person)* *(of person, food)* empoisonnement *m*; *(by substance)* *(of person)* intoxication *f*, *(of mind)* corruption *f*

poisonous ['pɔɪzənəs] ADJ *(substance)* toxique, intoxicant; *(gas)* asphyxiant, toxique; *(animal)* venimeux; *(plant)* vénéneux; *Fig (doctrine)* pernicieux; *(remark, allegation)* pernicieux; *(atmosphere)* malfaisant; *(coffee, liquid)* répugnant

> When translating the English word **poisonous**, note that the French words **vénéneux** and **venimeux** are not interchangeable. **Vénéneux** applies to plants whereas **venimeux** applies to animals.

poke¹ [pəʊk] N **1** *(push)* poussée *f*, *(with elbow)* coup *m* de coude; **to give sth a p. with one's finger/a stick** pousser qch du doigt/du bout d'un bâton; **to give sb a p. in the eye** *(with finger)* mettre le doigt dans l'œil à qn; *(with umbrella)* mettre un coup de parapluie dans l'œil à qn; **to give sb a (friendly) p. in the ribs** donner une bourrade (amicale) à qn
2 *Vulg (act of sexual intercourse)* partie *f* de jambes en l'air; **to give sb a p.** sauter qn, tirer un coup avec qn
VT **1 to p. one's finger in sb's eye** mettre le doigt dans l'œil à qn; **he poked his finger at the map** il a pointé le doigt vers la carte; **to p. one's umbrella in sb's eye** mettre un coup de parapluie dans l'œil à qn; **he poked the ice with a stick** il a tâté la glace du bout d'un bâton; **to p. sb in the ribs** *(friendly gesture)* donner une bourrade (amicale) à qn; **to p. a hole in sth** faire un trou dans qch, crever qch
2 *(insert)* *(finger in cake, thermometer in mouth)* enfoncer, planter; *(finger up nose)* fourrer (**in(to)** dans); **to p. one's head through the window** passer la tête par la fenêtre; *Fam* **to p. one's nose into other people's business** fourrer son nez dans les affaires des autres
3 *(fire)* tisonner, attiser
4 to p. fun at sb/sth se moquer de qn/qch
5 *Vulg (have sexual intercourse with)* sauter, tirer un coup avec
VI **to p. at sth** *(with one's finger/a stick)* tâter qch du bout du doigt/d'un bâton; *Fam* **to p. into other people's business** fourrer son nez dans les affaires des autres
▸ **poke about, poke around** VI **1** *(search)* fouiller, fureter; **a dog was poking about in the bushes** un chien fouinait *ou* furetait dans les buissons; **she was poking about in the wardrobe for something to wear** elle fouillait dans l'armoire pour trouver quelque chose à mettre **2** *(make unwanted enquiries)* fourrer son nez partout, fouiner; **that social worker is always poking about** cette assistante sociale est toujours en train de fourrer son nez partout
VT INSEP *(search in)* *(antique shop etc)* fouiller dans
▸ **poke out** VI *(protrude)* sortir, dépasser (**of, from** de); **her umbrella was poking out (of her bag)** son parapluie sortait *ou* dépassait de son sac; **his stomach was poking out** son ventre dépassait
VT SEP **1** *(push out)* **to p. one's head out (of the window)** passer *ou* sortir la tête par la fenêtre; **to p. one's tongue out** tirer la langue (**at sb** à qn) **2 to p. sb's eye out** éborgner qn

poke ² N *Dial esp Scot (bag)* sac *m*, sachet *m*

poker ['pəʊkər] N **1** *(for fire)* tisonnier *m* **2** *Cards* poker *m*
▸▸ **p. dice** dés *mpl* pour jouer au poker d'as; *(game)* poker d'as; **p. face** visage *m* impassible *ou* impénétrable; **p. game** partie *f* de poker; **p. work** pyrogravure *f*

poker-faced [-feɪst] ADJ *(person)* au visage impassible; *(reply, response)* qui ne trahit aucune émotion

poky ['pəʊkɪ] ADJ *(room)* exigu, -uë; **to live in a p. little place** être logé à l'étroit

pol [pɒl] N *Am Fam (abbr* **politician**) politicien *m*

Polack ['pəʊlæk] N *Offensive Sl* Polack *mf*

Poland ['pəʊlənd] N Pologne *f*

polar ['pəʊlər] ADJ *Geog, Math, Phys* polaire
▸▸ **p. bear** ours *m* polaire *ou* blanc

polarity [pəʊ'lærɪtɪ] N *Phys* polarité *f*

polarization [pəʊlərɪ'zeɪʃən] N *Phys* polarisation *f*; *esp Pol Fig* radicalisation *f*

polarize ['pəʊləraɪz] VT **1** *Phys (light, iron bar etc)* polariser **2** *(make extreme) (opinions)* radicaliser
VI **1** *Phys* se polariser **2** *(of opinions ec)* se radicaliser

polarizing filter ['pəʊləraɪzɪŋ] N *TV, Cin* filtre *m* polarisant

Polaroid® ['pəʊlərɔɪd] N **1** *Phot (camera)* Polaroïd® *m*; *(photograph)* photographie *f* instantanée **2** *Opt* Polaroïd® *m*; **Polaroids**® *(sunglasses)* lunettes *fpl* de soleil (à verre) polaroïd
ADJ *(camera)* Polaroïd®; *(film)* pour Polaroïd®

polder ['pəʊldə(r)] N polder *m*

Pole [pəʊl] N *(person)* Polonais, -aise VOIR GRAMMAIRE A19

pole ¹ [pəʊl] N **1** *(stick, rod)* perche *f*; *(fixed in ground)* poteau *m*; *(for plants)* échalas *m*, rame *f*; *(of scaffolding)* mât *m*; *(for flag)* hampe *f*; *(of stretcher)* bras *m*; *Naut (of mast)* flèche *f*; *(of tent)* piquet *m*; *(of circus tent)* mât; *Br Fam* **to be up the p.** *(mad)* être timbré *ou* toqué; **to be up the p. with worry** être fou *ou* malade d'inquiétude
2 *Arch (measurement)* perche *f*
3 *Vulg (penis)* queue *f*, bite *f*
▸▸ **p. dancing** = style de danse de strip-tease qui s'exécute autour d'une barre verticale

pole ² N *Elec, Geog* pôle *m*; **North P.** pôle Nord, pôle arctique *ou* boréal; **South P.** pôle Sud, pôle antarctique *ou* austral; **magnetic/true p.** pôle magnétique/géographique; *Fig* **to be poles apart** *(of people)* être aux antipodes l'un de l'autre; *(of views etc)* être diamétralement opposés; **opposite poles** *(of magnet)* pôles contraires
▸▸ **P. Star** (étoile *f*) Polaire *f*

poleaxe, *Am* **poleax** ['pəʊlæks] N merlin *m*
VT *(hit) (person)* assommer; *(animal)* abattre avec un merlin; *Fig* **she was poleaxed by the news** la nouvelle l'a abasourdie *ou* assommée

polecat ['pəʊlkæt] N *(animal)* putois *m*

polemic [pə'lemɪk] N polémique *f*
ADJ *Fml* polémique

polemical [pə'lemɪk(ə)l] ADJ polémique

polemicist [pə'lemɪsɪst] N polémiste *mf*

polemics [pə'lemɪks] N polémique *f* VOIR GRAMMAIRE A10

polenta [pə'lentə] N polenta *f*

pole-vault *Sport* VI sauter à la perche
N saut *m* à la perche

pole-vaulter N *Sport* sauteur, -euse à la perche, perchiste *mf*

police [pə'liːs] N INV *(with pl verb)* **the p.** la police; **twenty p. were on duty** vingt agents

---

mpl (de police) étaient de service; **to be a member of the p., to be in the p.** être de *ou* dans la police; **hours of careful p. work** des heures d'un travail poussé de la part de la police VOIR GRAMMAIRE A11
VT **1** *(the country)* maintenir l'ordre dans; **to p. a football match/demonstration** assurer l'ordre à un match de football/une manifestation; **the area is heavily policed** la zone est sous haute surveillance **2** *Fig (institution etc)* surveiller, contrôler; *(measures etc)* veiller au respect de; **should the press p. itself?** la presse doit-elle être autorisée à s'auto-réglementer?
▸▸ *Am* **p. captain** ≃ commissaire *m* de police; **p. car** voiture *f* de police; *Br* **p. constable** ≃ gardien *m* de la paix, ≃ agent *m* (de police); *Am* **the p. department** la Police; **p. dog** chien *m* policier; *Br* **the Police Federation** = syndicat *m* de la police britannique; **p. force** police *f*; **to be a member of the p. force** être de *ou* dans la police; **p. informer** indicateur, -trice; **p. inspector** inspecteur, -trice de police; *Br (in the CID)* commissaire *m* de police; **p. officer** policier, -ière, agent *m* de police; **p. state** État *m ou* régime *m* policier; **p. station** *(urban)* poste *m* de police, commissariat *m* (de police); *(rural)* gendarmerie *f*, **p. van** *(for transporting prisoners)* voiture cellulaire; *(for transporting police)* car *m* de police

policeman, *pl* **policemen** [pə'liːsmən] N agent *m* (de police)

policewoman, *pl* **policewomen** [pə'liːswʊmən, -wɪmɪn] N femme *f* agent (de police)

policing [pə'liːsɪŋ] N **1** *(by police)* maintien *m* de l'ordre; **the p. of the match/demonstration was inadequate** le service d'ordre du match/de la manifestation était inadéquat **2** *Fig* **the p. of these regulations** la responsabilité de veiller au respect de cette réglementation
▸▸ **p. policy** politique *f* de maintien de l'ordre

policy ¹ ['pɒlɪsɪ] N politique *f*; *(measure)* mesure *f*; **foreign p.** politique étrangère *ou* extérieure; **economic/agricultural p.** politique économique/agricole; **we have the right policies** nous avons les mesures adéquates; **the company's success is essentially down to their inspired marketing p.** le succès de l'entreprise est dû en grande partie à l'intelligence de leur politique de commercialisation; **my p. is not to tell him anything** ma politique, c'est de ne rien lui dire; **sales p.** politique de vente; **changes of p.** changements *mpl* de politique
▸▸ **p. adviser** conseiller, -ère politique; **p. changes** changements de politique; **p. meeting** séance *f* de concertation; **p. paper** = document *m* énonçant une position de principe; **p. position** position *f* de principe; **p. statement** déclaration *f* de principe; **p. unit** comité *m* politique; *Am Pej* **p. wonk** conseiller, -ère politique

policy ² N *(in insurance)* police *f* (d'assurance); **(fully) comprehensive** *or* **all-risks p.** police tous risques; **to take out a p.** souscrire à une police d'assurance

policyholder ['pɒlɪsɪhəʊldər] N assuré, -ée

polio ['pəʊlɪəʊ] N *Med* polio *f*; **to have p.** avoir la polio

poliomyelitis [pəʊlɪəʊmaɪə'laɪtɪs] N *Med* poliomyélite *f*

Polish ['pəʊlɪʃ] VOIR GRAMMAIRE A19 ADJ polonais
N *Ling* polonais *m*

polish ['pɒlɪʃ] N **1** *(finish of surface etc)* poli *m*, brillant *m*, lustre *m*; *(of metals)* poli, brunissure *f*; **high p.** poli brillant; **to lose its p.** se dépolir, se ternir; **to take the p. off sth** dépolir qch, ternir qch; **to give the table a p.** cirer la table

---

2 *(substance)* crème *f ou* pâte *f* à polir; **boot** *or* **shoe p.** cirage *m*, crème pour chaussures; **floor p.** encaustique *f ou* cire *f* à parquet; **metal p.** produit *m* pour faire briller les métaux; **nail p.** vernis *m* à ongles
3 *Fig (refinement) (of person)* belles manières *fpl*, savoir-vivre *m inv*; *(of novel, style, performance)* élégance *f*; **to have a certain p.** *(of person)* avoir un certain savoir-vivre; *(of novel, style etc)* avoir une certaine élégance; **to lack p.** *(of person)* manquer d'éducation *ou* de savoir-vivre; *(of novel, style etc)* manquer d'élégance; **to give sth a final p.** mettre la dernière main à qch
VT **1** *(wood, metal etc)* polir; *(gold, silver)* brunir; *(shoes)* cirer; *(brass)* astiquer, faire briller; *(stone etc)* lisser; *(parquet floor, tiles)* cirer, encaustiquer; *(rice)* glacer, polir
2 *Fig (make more refined) (person, manners)* polir, dégrossir; *(style, interpretation)* polir, perfectionner; **to p. one's French** perfectionner son français
▸ **polish off** VT SEP *Fam (course, dish)* finir; *(meal, bottle, job)* expédier; *(put finishing touch to) (job)* mettre la dernière main à; *(get rid of, defeat) (rebels, competitor etc)* liquider, régler son compte à; **to p. off one's drink** vider son verre; **such hard work at his age polished him off** un travail aussi dur à son âge l'a achevé
▸ **polish up** VT SEP **1** faire reluire; *(brass objects)* astiquer, brunir, lustrer **2** *(improve) (language)* perfectionner; *(style)* parfaire

polished ['pɒlɪʃt] ADJ **1** poli; *(wood, floor, shoes)* ciré **2** *(manners etc)* poli, distingué **3** *(style etc)* châtié, raffiné

polisher ['pɒlɪʃər] N **1** *(person) (of metals etc)* polisseur, -euse, brunisseur, -euse; *(of brass)* astiqueur, -euse **2** *(tool)* instrument *m* à polir, polissoir *m*; *(for metal)* brunissoir *m*; **electric floor p.** cireuse *f* électrique à parquet

Politburo ['pɒlɪtbjʊərəʊ] N *Pol* Politburo *m*

polite [pə'laɪt] ADJ *(courteous)* poli (**to sb** envers *ou* avec qn); **I was just being p.** j'ai fait/dit ça par politesse; **p. refusal** refus *m* poli
▸▸ **p. society** la bonne société, le beau monde; **this word is not used in p. society** ce mot ne s'utilise pas chez les gens bien élevés

politely [pə'laɪtlɪ] ADV poliment

politeness [pə'laɪtnɪs] N politesse *f*

politic ['pɒlɪtɪk] ADJ **1** *Fml (person, conduct)* politique, avisé, *Pej* rusé, astucieux; **it would not be p. to …** ce ne serait pas prudent de … **2** **the body p.** le corps politique; *(the state)* l'État *m*

political [pə'lɪtɪk(ə)l] ADJ **1** *Pol (party etc)* politique; **he isn't very p.** il n'a pas une forte conscience politique; **p. beliefs** opinions *fpl* politiques **2** *Fig* **she's a p. animal** c'est quelqu'un de très politisé; **things are getting far too p. in the office** ça devient vraiment intenable au bureau avec toutes ces manigances *ou Fam* magouilles; **it was a p. decision** c'était une décision qui relevait de la politique interne de l'entreprise/du service/*etc*
▸▸ **p. analyst** analyste *mf* politique; **p. asylum** asile *m* politique; **to request/be granted p. asylum** demander/se voir accorder l'asile politique; **p. correctness** le politiquement correct; **p. correspondent** journaliste *mf* politique; **p. economy** économie *f* politique; **p. editor** rédacteur, -trice en chef politique; **p. map** carte *f* politique; **p. prisoner** prisonnier, -ière politique; **p. science** sciences *fpl* politiques; **p. theory** théorie *f* politique

politically [pə'lɪtɪklɪ] ADV **1** politiquement; **p. informed** au courant des choses de la politique; **to be p. aware** avoir une conscience

politique, être politisé; **p. radical** radical sur le plan politique **2** *Fig* **p. that wouldn't be a wise thing to say** du point de vue tactique, ce ne serait pas une chose à dire
▸▸ **p. correct** politiquement correct

politician [pɒlɪ'tɪʃən] **N 1** homme *m*/femme *f* politique; *esp Pej* politicien, -ienne **2** *esp Am Pej (self-interested)* politicard, -arde

politicize [pə'lɪtɪsaɪz] **VT** *(debate, problem, person etc)* politiser

politicking ['pɒlɪtɪkɪŋ] **N** activité *f* électorale menée pour obtenir des suffrages; **the issue has been bogged down by last-minute p.** les tractations de politique politicienne ont fait s'enliser la discussion

politico [pə'lɪtɪkəʊ] **N** *esp Am Pej* politicard, -arde

politico-economic **ADJ** politico-économique

politics ['pɒlɪtɪks] **N** politique *f*; **to be interested in p.** s'intéresser à la politique; **to talk p.** parler politique; **his p. are right of centre** (politiquement parlant) il se situe à droite; **what are her p.?** de quel bord est-elle?, politiquement, où est-ce qu'elle se situe?; **foreign p.** politique étrangère; *Fig* **office p.** intrigues *fpl* de bureau ❙VOIR GRAMMAIRE A10❙

polity ['pɒlɪtɪ] **N** *Pol* **1** *(constitution)* constitution *f* politique; *(form of government)* régime *m*; *(state)* État *m* **2** *(management)* administration *f* politique

polka ['pɒlkə] **N** *Mus* polka *f*
▸▸ *Tex* **p. dots** pois *mpl*

polka-dot **ADJ** à pois; **blue p.-dot tie** cravate *f* bleue à pois (blancs)

poll¹ [pəʊl] **N 1** *(voting)* vote *m* (par bulletins), scrutin *m*; **to go to the polls** aller aux urnes; **to head the p.** arriver en tête de scrutin; **heavy/light p.** forte/faible participation *f* électorale; **a 76% p.** un taux de participation de 76%; **to get a large share of the p.** remporter *ou* réunir une grande proportion des voix *ou* suffrages
2 *(survey)* sondage *m*; **(public) opinion p.** sondage d'opinion; **to carry out a p.** faire un sondage; **the latest poll puts the Socialists in the lead** le dernier sondage donne les socialistes en tête
VT 1 *(of polling clerk) (person)* recueillir le bulletin de vote de; *(of candidate) (votes)* réunir; **the Conservatives polled 41% nationally** les conservateurs ont remporté 41% des voix *ou* suffrages au niveau national; **to p. a vote for sb** donner sa voix à qn, voter pour qn
2 *(in opinion poll)* sonder; **most of those polled were in favour of the plan** la plupart des personnes sondées étaient favorables au projet
3 *(tree)* étêter, écimer; *(bull)* décorner
4 *Comput* interroger
VI **the party polled well** le parti a remporté une bonne proportion des suffrages *ou* des voix
▸▸ **p. tax** *(in UK)* = impôt *m* aboli en 1993, regroupant taxe d'habitation et impôts locaux, payable par chaque occupant adulte d'une même habitation; *(in US)* = impôt, aboli en 1964, donnant droit à être inscrit sur les listes électorales; *Hist* capitation *f*

poll² **N** *(animal)* vache *f* etc sans cornes

pollack ['pɒlək] **N** = **pollock**

pollard ['pɒləd] **N** *(tree)* arbre *m* étêté; *(animal)* animal *m* sans cornes
VT *(tree)* étêter, élaguer

pollen ['pɒlən] **N** *Bot* pollen *m*
▸▸ **p. count** taux *m* de pollen; **p. sac** sac *m* pollinique

pollinate ['pɒlɪneɪt] **VT** *Bot* polliniser

pollination [pɒlɪ'neɪʃən] **N** *Bot* pollinisa-

tion *f*, fécondation *f*; **self-p.** pollinisation directe; **cross-p.** pollinisation croisée

polling ['pəʊlɪŋ] **N 1** scrutin *m*, élections *fpl* **2** *(for opinion poll)* sondage *m* **3** *Comput (querying)* interrogation *f*
▸▸ **p. booth** isoloir *m*; **p. company** institut *m* de sondage; **p. day** jour *m* des élections *ou* du scrutin; **p. station** bureau *m* de vote

polliwog ['pɒlɪwɒg] **N** *Am (tadpole)* têtard *m*

pollock ['pɒlək] **N** colin *m*

pollster ['pəʊlstər] **N** enquêteur, -euse; **according to the pollsters** selon les sondages

pollutant [pə'luːtənt] **N** polluant *m*

pollute [pə'luːt] **VT** *(river, atmosphere etc)* polluer; *(language, mind)* contaminer

polluted [pə'luːtəd] **ADJ** *Am Fam (drunk)* pété, bourré

polluter [pə'luːtər] **N** pollueur, -euse

pollution [pə'luːʃən] **N 1** *(contamination) (of river, atmosphere)* pollution *f*, *(of language, mind)* contamination *f*; **p. policy** politique *f* antipollution; **atmospheric p., p. of the atmosphere** pollution atmosphérique *ou* de l'air **2** *(pollutants)* polluants *mpl*; **the river is full of p.** la rivière est très polluée

pollution-free **ADJ** non pollué

Polly ['pɒlɪ] **N** *Fam (parrot)* **(pretty) P.** Jacquot *m*

Pollyanna [pɒlɪ'ænə] **N** *esp Am* optimiste *mf*

pollywog ['pɒlɪwɒg] **N** *Am (tadpole)* têtard *m*

polo ['pəʊləʊ] **N** *Sport* polo *m*; **to play p.** jouer au polo
▸▸ *Br* **p. neck** *(collar)* col *m* roulé; *(sweater)* (pull m à) col roulé; *Br* **p. neck sweater** pull à col roulé; *Sport* **p. pony** poney *m* de polo; **p. shirt** polo *m* (chemise); *Sport* **p. stick** maillet *m*

polonaise [pɒlə'neɪz] **N** *Mus* polonaise *f*

poltergeist ['pɒltəgaɪst] **N** esprit *m* frappeur

poly ['pɒlɪ] **N** *Br Formerly Fam* = **polytechnic**

poly- ['pɒlɪ] **PREF** poly-

polyandrous [pɒlɪ'ændrəs] **ADJ** polyandre

polyandry ['pɒlɪændrɪ] **N** polyandrie *f*

polyanthus [pɒlɪ'ænθəs] **N** primevère *f* des jardins

poly bag **N** *Fam* sac *m* en plastique

polychromatic [pɒlɪkrəʊ'mætɪk] **ADJ** polychrome

polychrome ['pɒlɪkrəʊm] **ADJ** polychrome
N *(statue)* statue *f* polychrome; *(colouring)* polychromie *f*

polychromy ['pɒlɪkrəʊmɪ] **N** polychromie *f*

polyclinic [pɒlɪ'klɪnɪk] **N** *Med* polyclinique *f*

polyester [pɒlɪ'estər] **N** *Chem* polyester *m*

polyethylene [pɒlɪ'eθɪliːn] **N** *esp Am Chem* polyéthylène *m*, polythène *m*

polygamist [pə'lɪgəmɪst] **N** polygame *mf*

polygamous [pə'lɪgəməs] **ADJ** polygame

polygamy [pə'lɪgəmɪ] **N** polygamie *f*

polyglot ['pɒlɪglɒt] **ADJ, N** polyglotte *mf*

polygon ['pɒlɪgən] **N** *Geom* polygone *m*

polygonal [pə'lɪgən(ə)l] **ADJ** *Geom* polygonal, -aux

polygraph ['pɒlɪgrɑːf] **N** détecteur *m* de mensonges; **to take a p. test** subir un test au détecteur de mensonges

polyhedron [pɒlɪ'hiːdrən] **N** *Geom* polyèdre *m*

polymath ['pɒlɪmæθ] **N** esprit *m* universel

polymer ['pɒlɪmər] **N** *Chem* polymère *m*

polymerization [pɒlɪməraɪ'zeɪʃən] **N** *Chem* polymérisation *f*

polymorphic [pɒlɪ'mɔːfɪk] **ADJ** *Biol, Chem* polymorphe, polymorphique

polymorphism [pɒlɪ'mɔːfɪz(ə)m] **N** *Biol, Chem* polymorphisme *m*, polymorphie *f*

polymorphous [pɒlɪ'mɔːfəs] **ADJ** = **polymorphic**

Polynesia [pɒlɪ'niːzɪə] **N** Polynésie *f*

Polynesian [pɒlɪ'niːzɪən] **ADJ** polynésien **N** Polynésien, -ienne

polyneuritis [pɒlɪnjʊ'raɪtɪs] **N** *Med* polynévrite *f*

polynomial [pɒlɪ'nəʊmɪəl] **N** *Math* polynôme *m*

polyp ['pɒlɪp] **N** *Zool, Med* polype *m*

polyphase ['pɒlɪfeɪz] **ADJ** *Elec* polyphasé

polyphonic [pɒlɪ'fɒnɪk] **ADJ** *Mus, Ling* polyphonique

polyphony [pə'lɪfənɪ] **N** *Mus, Ling* polyphonie *f*

polypropylene [pɒlɪ'prəʊpɪliːn] **N** *Chem* polypropène *m*, polypropylène *m*

polypus ['pɒlɪpəs] **N** *Med* polype *m*

polysaccharide [pɒlɪ'sækəraɪd] **N** *Chem* polysaccharide *m*, polyoside *m*

polystyrene [pɒlɪ'staɪriːn] **N** *Chem* polystyrène *m*; **p. packaging** emballage *m* en polystyrène

polysyllabic [pɒlɪsɪ'læbɪk] **ADJ** polysyllabe, polysyllabique

polysyllable ['pɒlɪsɪləb(ə)l] **N** polysyllabe *m*

polytechnic [pɒlɪ'teknɪk] **ADJ** *Formerly* polytechnique
N *Br Univ Formerly* ≃ Institut *m* universitaire de technologie

> Note that the French noun **Polytechnique** is a false friend and is never a translation for the word **polytechnic**. It is the name of one of France's most prestigious **Grandes écoles**.

polytheism ['pɒlɪθiːɪz(ə)m] **N** polythéisme *m*

polytheistic [pɒlɪθiː'ɪstɪk] **ADJ** polythéiste

polythene ['pɒlɪθiːn] **N** *esp Br* polyéthylène *m*, polythène *m*
▸▸ **p. bag** sac *m* en plastique

polyunsaturated [pɒlɪʌn'sætjʊreɪtɪd] **ADJ** *Chem* polyinsaturé
▸▸ **p. fats** graisses *fpl* polyinsaturées

polyurethane [pɒlɪ'jʊərɪθeɪn] **N** *Chem etc* polyuréthane *m*

polyvalent [pɒlɪ'veɪlənt] **ADJ** *Chem* polyvalent

polyvinyl [pɒlɪ'vaɪnɪl] **N** *Chem* polyvinyle *m*
▸▸ **p. chloride** chlorure *m* de polyvinyle

pom [pɒm] **N** *Austr Fam* Anglais, -aise

pomegranate ['pɒmɪgrænɪt] **N 1** *(fruit)* grenade *f* **2** *(tree)* grenadier *m*
▸▸ **p. tree** grenadier

Pomerania [pɒmə'reɪnɪə] **N** Poméranie *f*

Pomeranian [pɒmə'reɪnɪən] **N** *(dog)* loulou *m* (de Poméranie)
ADJ de Poméranie
▸▸ **P. dog** loulou (de Poméranie)

pommel ['pʌm(ə)l] **N** *(of sword, saddle)* pommeau *m*
VT (-ll-, *Am* -l-) = **pummel** **VT**
▸▸ **p. horse** cheval-d'arçons *m inv*

pommie, pommy ['pɒmɪ] **N** *Austr Fam* Anglais, -aise; **p. bastard** salaud *m* d'Anglais, sale Anglaise *f*

pomp [pɒmp] **N** pompe *f*, éclat *m*, faste *m*; **p. and circumstance** (grand) apparat *m*

Pompeii [pɒm'peɪiː] **N** Pompéi

pompom, pompon ['pɒmpɒm, -pɒn] **N** *(tuft)* pompon *m*

pom-pom N *Mil* canon-mitrailleuse *m, pl* canons-mitrailleuses *(système Maxim)*

pomposity [pɒm'pɒsɪtɪ] N *Pej (of person)* suffisance *f, (of remark, style)* emphase *f*

pompous ['pɒmpəs] ADJ *Pej (person)* plein de suffisance; *(style, remark)* emphatique, pompeux

pompously ['pɒmpəslɪ] ADV *Pej (to behave, talk etc)* avec suffisance; *(to write)* avec emphase

pompousness ['pɒmpəsnɪs] N *Pej (of person)* suffisance *f, (of style, remark)* emphase *f*

ponce [pɒns] *esp Br Sl* N **1** *(effeminate man)* gonzesse *f*, pédé *m* **2** *(pimp)* maquereau *m*
▸ VI *(live off earnings)* vivre aux crochets d'une prostituée
▸ **ponce about, ponce around** VI *Br Sl* **1** *(waste time)* glandouiller **2** *(of effeminate man)* se pavaner
▸ **ponce up** VT SEP *Sl (dress up)* **to get all ponced up** se mettre sur son trente-et-un

poncey ['pɒnsɪ] ADJ *esp Br Sl* = **poncy**

poncho, *pl* **ponchos** ['pɒntʃəʊ, -əʊz] N poncho *m*

poncy ['pɒnsɪ] ADJ *esp Br Sl (effeminate) (manner etc)* efféminé, de gonzesse

pond [pɒnd] N étang *m; (in park)* bassin *m*, pièce *f* d'eau; *(in village)* mare *f, (for fish)* vivier *m*, réservoir *m; (of mill)* réservoir; *Fam* **the P.** *(the Atlantic)* l'Atlantique *m*
▸▸ **p. life** la faune des étangs; *Fam Hum Pej (disreputable people)* minables *mpl*

ponder ['pɒndər] VT *(question)* réfléchir sur; *(opinion, proposal)* considérer, peser; *(situation)* méditer (sur), réfléchir à; *(idea)* considérer; **to p. whether …** se demander si …
▸ VI réfléchir, méditer; **to p. over or on sth** réfléchir à *ou* méditer sur qch

ponderable ['pɒndərəb(ə)l] ADJ pondérable

ponderous ['pɒndərəs] ADJ **1** *(large)* massif, énorme; *(movements, person)* lourd **2** *(task, work)* laborieux **3** *(style)* lourd, pesant; *(joke, remark)* lourd

ponderously ['pɒndərəslɪ] ADV *(to move)* lourdement; *(to make progress)* laborieusement

pondweed ['pɒndwiːd] N *(plant)* épi *m* d'eau

pone [pəʊn] N *Am* **(corn) p.** *(bread)* pain *m* de maïs
▸▸ **p. bread** pain de maïs

pong [pɒŋ] *Br Fam* N *(smell)* puanteur *f*, **what a p.!** ça pue!, ça schlingue!; **there's a terrible p. of fish!** ça pue le poisson à plein nez!
▸ VI *(smell)* puer, schlinguer; **the room still pongs of cigarettes** la pièce pue encore la cigarette

pongy ['pɒŋɪ] ADJ *Br Fam (smelly)* **it's a bit p. in here** ça pue *ou* schlingue là-dedans

pontiff ['pɒntɪf] N *Rel* pontife *m*; **the sovereign p.** le souverain pontife

pontifical [pɒn'tɪfɪk(ə)l] ADJ *Rel* pontifical, -aux
▸ N *Rel (book)* pontifical *m*

pontificate¹ [pɒn'tɪfɪkɪt] N *Rel* pontificat *m*

pontificate² [pɒn'tɪfɪkeɪt] VI *Rel, Fig Pej* pontifier; **to p. about sth** pontifier à propos de *ou* sur qch

Pontius Pilate ['pɒnʃəs'paɪlət] N *Bible* Ponce Pilate

pontoon [pɒn'tuːn] N **1** *(float)* ponton *m; Aviat (on aeroplane)* flotteur *m* **2** *Br Cards* vingt-et-un *m inv*
▸▸ **p. bridge** pont *m* flottant

pony ['pəʊnɪ] N **1** *(animal)* poney *m; Am (small horse)* petit cheval *m; Am* **cow p.** che-

val de ranch **2** *Br Sl (£25)* vingt-cinq livres *fpl* sterling **3** *Am Sch Fam (in exam)* traduction *f* (juxtalinéaire) **4** *(drinking glass)* petit verre *m* (sans pied)
▸▸ **p. trekking** randonnées *fpl* à dos de poney

ponytail ['pəʊnɪteɪl] N *(hairstyle)* queue *f* de cheval; **to wear one's hair in a p.** avoir une queue de cheval

poo [puː] *Fam* N **1** *(excrement)* caca *m*; **to do** *or Br* **have a p.** faire caca **2** *Br (worthless things)* **it's a load of p.** ça vaut pas un clou; **he's talking a load of p.** il raconte n'importe quoi
▸ VI faire caca

pooch [puːtʃ] N *Sl (dog)* cabot *m*, clebs *m*

poodle ['puːd(ə)l] N caniche *mf, Fig (servile follower)* larbin *m*

poof¹ [pʊf] N *Br Offensive Sl* pédé *m*, tante *f*

poof² INT pouf; **and then suddenly, p., it disappeared!** et puis pouf! il a disparu!

poofter ['pʊftər] N *Br Offensive Sl* pédé *m*, tante *f*

poofy ['pʊfɪ] ADJ *Br Offensive Sl* de gonzesse, de pédé; **some p. guy** une espèce de pédé; **it's p. to …** c'est bon pour les gonzesses *ou* les pédés de …; **to look p.** avoir l'air d'un pédé

pooh [puː] INT bah!, peuh!
▸ N *(in children's language) (faeces)* caca *m*

pooh-pooh¹ N = **pooh** N

pooh-pooh² VT *(idea, warning, piece of advice)* se moquer de, faire peu de cas de

pool¹ [puːl] N *(pond)* mare *f, (puddle)* flaque *f* d'eau; *(ornamental)* pièce *f* d'eau; *(left on beach by tide)* bâche *f, (in river)* clame *m;* **(swimming) p.** piscine *f*, **lying in a p. of blood** étendu dans une mare de sang; **a p. of light** une flaque de lumière

pool² N **1** *(group etc)* groupe *m; Com (of companies)* groupement *m*, pool *m; Econ* fonds *m* commun; *(of company cars, computers etc)* parc *m; Fig (of ideas, talent etc)* réservoir *m*; **a p. of experience** une mine d'expériences bigarrées; **a p. of experts/advisers** un groupe *ou* une équipe d'experts/de conseillers; **a p. of funds** un fonds commun; **typing p.** central *m* dactylographique, pool de dactylos **2** *(in games) (kitty)* cagnotte *f, Billiards* poule *f* **3** *(game)* billard *m* américain **4** *Br* **football pools,** *Fam* **pools** = concours *m* de pronostics de matchs de football; **to do the pools** faire des concours de pronostics (sur des matchs de football)
▸ VT *(capital, profits, ideas)* mettre en commun; *(resources)* grouper, mettre en commun; *Com etc (orders)* grouper; **pooled services** services *mpl* en commun
▸▸ **p. cue** queue *f* de billard; **p. hall** salle *f* de billard; **p. table** (table *f* de) billard

pooling of interests ['puːlɪŋ] N *Am Fin* (absorption-)fusion *f, pl* (absorptions-)fusions, unification *f*

poolroom ['puːlrʊm] N salle *f* de billard

poon [puːn], **poontang** ['puːntæŋ] N *Am Vulg* **1** *(female genitals)* chatte *f*, chagatte *f* **2** *(women)* gonzesses *fpl*, meufs *fpl*; **he's gone out looking for p.** il cherche une meuf à se mettre sur le bout

poonani [puː'nænɪ] N *Vulg (female genitals)* chatte *f*, chagatte *f*

poop [puːp] N **1** *Am Fam (excrement)* caca *m*; **to take a p.** faire caca **2** *Naut (deck)* (pont *m* de) dunette *f*, gaillard *m* d'arrière **3** *Naut (raised part)* poupe *f*
▸ VI *Am Fam (defecate)* faire caca
▸▸ *Naut* **p. deck** (pont de) dunette, gaillard d'arrière

pooped [puːpt] ADJ *esp Am Fam (exhausted)* claqué, vanné

pooper-scooper ['puːpəˌskuːpər] N *Fam* ramasse-crottes *m inv*

POOR [pɔːr] ADJ **1** *(having little wealth)* pauvre; **a p. man/woman** un pauvre/une pauvre; **as p. as a church mouse** pauvre comme Job; **I'm poorer by a thousand euros, I'm a thousand euros poorer** j'en suis pour mille euros; **the p. man's champagne** le champagne du pauvre

2 *(inferior)* mauvais, médiocre; *(quality)* inférieur; *(health)* fragile; *(soil)* maigre, peu fertile; *(weather)* mauvais; **I've a p. memory** je n'ai pas une bonne mémoire; **to have p. sight** avoir une mauvaise vue; **her hearing is very p.** elle entend très mal, elle est très dure d'oreille; **to be p. at maths** être faible en math(s); **his French is very p.** son français est très faible; **to cut a p. figure** faire piètre figure; **the patient had a p. night** le malade a passé une mauvaise nuit; **to be a p. sailor** ne pas avoir le pied marin; **he gave a p. account of himself** il ne s'en est pas très bien tiré; **in p. condition** en mauvais état; **p. excuse** piètre excuse; **p. harvest** mauvaise récolte; **p. light** mauvais éclairage; **p. loser** mauvais perdant; **p. performance** *(of company)* contre-performance *f, pl* contre-performances; **p. reception** *(unwelcoming)* mauvais accueil; *Radio etc* mauvaise transmission; *Com* **p. sales (figures)** mauvais chiffre de ventes; **to come a p. second** *(in race)* se classer deuxième, loin derrière le vainqueur; **in terms of exports, Britain comes a p. second to Japan** en matière d'exportations, la Grande-Bretagne est en deuxième position, loin derrière le Japon; **I come a very p. second in his affections** je n'ai qu'une misérable deuxième place dans son cœur; **it's a p. substitute for the real thing** c'est loin de valoir l'original; **in p. taste** de mauvais goût; **there was a p. turnout** peu de gens sont venus

3 *(to be pitied)* pauvre; **p. creature!, p. thing!** pauvre petit!, pauvre petite!; **the p. soul!** le pauvre!, la pauvre!; **p. Philippe!** pauvre Philippe!; **I'm so sorry for the p. man** comme je le plains, le pauvre homme; **when p. Alice was alive** du vivant de la pauvre Alice; **p. you, you p. thing** *(to man)* mon pauvre vieux; *(to woman)* ma pauvre vieille
▸ NPL **the p.** les pauvres *mpl*
▸▸ **p. box** tronc *m* des pauvres; *Hist* **p. law** = loi *f* sociale dictant les conditions dans lesquelles les pauvres étaient pris en charge par les communes; **p. relation** parent *m* pauvre; *Am Pej* **p. White** petit blanc, petite blanche

poorhouse ['pɔːhaʊs] N *Hist* asile *m* des pauvres

poorly ['pɔːlɪ] ADV pauvrement; **p. dressed** pauvrement vêtu; **to be p. off** *(financially)* avoir des problèmes d'argent; **p. lit** mal éclairé; **he did p. in his exams** il a eu de mauvais résultats à ses examens; **p. suited to these conditions** mal adapté à ces conditions; **to perform p. at low temperatures** donner de mauvais résultats à basse température
▸ ADJ PRED *Fam (person)* souffrant, indisposé; **she's looking p.** elle n'a pas l'air bien, elle a mauvaise mine; **I'm feeling p.** je ne suis pas dans mon assiette

poorness ['pɔːnɪs] N **1** *(of person)* pauvreté *f* **2** *(inferiority)* médiocrité *f*

POP ['piːəʊ'piː] N **1** *Comput (abbr* **post office protocol)** protocole *m* POP **2** *Comput (abbr* **point of presence)** point *m* de présence, point d'accès **3** *Mktg (abbr* **point of purchase)** point *m* de vente

pop¹ [pɒp] INT crac!, pan!; **to go p.** éclater,

crever; **p. goes the cork!** paf! le bouchon saute

N**1** *(sound of cork etc)* bruit *m* sec **2** *Fam (fizzy drink)* boisson *f* gazeuse **3** *Fam* **to take a p. at sb/sth** critiquer qn/qch

VI *(-pp-)* **1** éclater, péter; *(of cork)* sauter, péter; *(of balloon, corn)* éclater; *(of ears)* se déboucher tout d'un coup

2 *Fam (go quickly)* **to p. over** *or* **across** *or* **down to the grocers** faire un saut (jusque) chez l'épicier; **they popped by** *or* **round to see us** ils sont passés nous voir; **I'm going to p. into town** je vais faire un saut en ville; **to p. into bed** se mettre vite au lit

VT **1** *(balloon)* crever; *(cork)* faire sauter; **to p. corn** faire du pop-corn

2 *(put quickly)* mettre; **to p. sth into a drawer** mettre *ou* glisser qch dans un tiroir; **to p. one's head out of the window** passer la tête par la fenêtre

3 *Fam* **then he popped the question** alors il lui a/m'a demandé de l'épouser

4 *Fam* **to p. pills** se bourrer de comprimés

5 *Old-fashioned Br Sl (pawn)* mettre en gage *ou* au clou

▸ **pop in** VI *Fam* entrer en passant *ou* un instant (**at sb's** chez qn); **I've just popped in** je ne fais que passer; **he popped in to say hello** il est passé (me/nous/*etc*) dire bonjour

VT SEP porter; **could you p. these trousers in at the dry cleaners?** est-ce que tu peux porter ce pantalon au pressing?

▸ **pop off** VI **1** *Fam (leave abruptly)* filer, partir **2** *Br Sl (die)* claquer

▸ **pop out** VI *Fam (go out)* sortir; **I only popped out for five minutes** je ne suis sorti que cinq minutes; **his eyes were popping out of his head** les yeux lui sortaient de la tête

▸ **pop up** VI *Fam* **1** *(rise suddenly)* surgir; **a head popped up through the trap door** une tête a surgi de la trappe **2** **this question has popped up again** cette question est revenue sur le tapis; **he popped up again some years later in Miami** il est réapparu quelques années après à Miami

pop² ADJ pop

N *Mus* (musique *f*) pop *m ou f*

▸▸ **p. art** pop art *m*; **p. music** musique pop, pop music *f*; **p. psychology** psychologie *f* de pacotille; **p. singer** chanteur, -euse de pop; **p. song** chanson *f* pop

pop³ N *Am Fam (father)* papa *m*

pop⁴ *(abbr* **population)** pop

popcorn ['pɒpkɔ:n] N pop-corn *m inv*

pope [pəʊp] N *(in Catholic Church)* pape *m*; *(in Eastern Orthodox Church)* pope *m*; *Fam Hum* **is the P. Catholic?** à ton avis?

▸▸ *Culin* **p.'s nose** croupion *m*

popemobile ['pəʊpməbi:l] N *Fam* papamobile *f*

popery ['pəʊpərɪ] N *Pej* papisme *m*

popeyed ['pɒpaɪd] ADJ *Fam (having protuberant eyes)* aux yeux exorbités; *(with surprise)* aux yeux écarquillés

popgun ['pɒpgʌn] N *(toy) (rifle)* fusil *m* à bouchon; *(handgun)* pistolet *m* à bouchon

popinjay ['pɒpɪndʒeɪ] N *Old-fashioned* fat *m*, freluquet *m*

popish ['pəʊpɪʃ] ADJ *Pej* papiste

poplar ['pɒplər] N *(tree)* peuplier *m*

poplin ['pɒplɪn] N *Tex* popeline *f*

popover ['pɒpəʊvər] N *Culin* beignet *m*

poppadom, poppadum ['pɒpədəm] N *Culin* poppadum *m*

popper ['pɒpər] N **1** *Br Fam (on clothing, bag etc)* bouton-pression *m*, *pl* boutons-pression **2** *Fam (drug)* poppers *mpl*

poppet ['pɒpɪt] N *Old-fashioned Fam* **she's a p.** elle est charmante; **my p.** *(to boy, man)*

mon chéri; *(to girl, woman)* ma chérie; *(to boy or girl)* mon (petit) chou

▸▸ **p. valve** soupape *f* à champignon

popping ['pɒpɪŋ] N *(of microphone)* saturation *f* acoustique

poppy ['pɒpɪ] N *(plant)* pavot *m*; *(flower)* coquelicot *m*; *(worn on Armistice Day)* = coquelicot en papier porté le jour de l'Armistice, vendu au profit des anciens combattants; **p. (coloured), p. red** rouge coquelicot *inv*

▸▸ *Br* **P. Day** = journée *f* de commémoration (le dimanche suivant *ou* précédant le 11 novembre) pendant laquelle on porte un coquelicot en papier en souvenir des soldats britanniques morts lors des guerres mondiales; **p. seed** graine *f* de pavot

poppycock ['pɒpɪkɒk] N *Fam* bêtises *fpl*, inepties *fpl*

Popsicle® ['pɒpsɪk(ə)l] N *Am Culin* ≃ Esquimau® *m*

popsy ['pɒpsɪ] N *Old-fashioned Br Fam* pépée *f*, nana *f*

populace ['pɒpjʊləs] N *Fml* **the p.** le peuple, *Pej* la populace

popular ['pɒpjʊlər] ADJ **1** *(generally liked) (person, action etc)* populaire; *(in vogue)* à la mode, en vogue; *(music, song)* populaire; **to make oneself p.** se rendre populaire (**with** auprès de); **his views have not made him p. with the authorities** à cause de ses opinions, il est mal vu des autorités; **she is p. with her colleagues** elle est très populaire auprès de ses collègues, elle est très appréciée de ses collègues; **this was not a p. decision** cette décision n'était pas populaire

2 *(of or for the people)* populaire, du peuple; **with p. appeal** qui plaît au grand public; **by p. demand** à la demande générale; **contrary to p. belief** contrairement à ce que les gens croient; **p. misconception** idée *f* fausse et très répandue; **p. prices** prix *mpl* à la portée de tous; **p. support** soutien *m* populaire; **to be chosen by p. vote** rencontrer l'adhésion du public; **p. work** *or* **treatise** ouvrage *m* de vulgarisation

▸▸ **p. culture** culture *f* populaire; *Hist* **P. Front** Front *m* populaire; **the p. press** la presse à grand tirage et à sensation

popularity [pɒpjʊ'lærɪtɪ] N popularité *f*, *Com (of product etc)* succès *m* auprès du (grand) public; **the president's p. has fallen** *or* **diminished** la popularité du président a baissé; **to experience a rise/fall in p.** voir sa popularité augmenter/baisser; **to grow/decline in p.** devenir plus/moins populaire (**among** parmi); **the sport has gained in p.** le sport est de plus en plus populaire

▸▸ **p. rating** taux *m* de popularité

popularization [pɒpjʊləraɪ'zeɪʃən] N popularisation *f*, *(of science etc)* vulgarisation *f*

popularize ['pɒpjʊləraɪz] VT *(game, activity, form of music)* populariser; *(knowledge, idea, science etc)* vulgariser; *(method)* propager; *(fashion)* mettre en vogue

popularizer ['pɒpjʊləraɪzər] N *(of science, ideas)* vulgarisateur, -trice

popularly ['pɒpjʊləlɪ] ADV communément, généralement; **p. known as ...** *(of plant etc)* dont le nom vulgaire est ...; *(of person)* familièrement appelé ...; **it is p. believed that ...** les gens croient que ..., il est communément admis que ...

populate ['pɒpjʊleɪt] VT peupler; **densely** *or* **thickly populated country** pays très peuplé; **sparsely populated** *(region)* peu densément peuplé

population [pɒpjʊ'leɪʃən] N population *f*; **the town has a p. of 85,000** la ville compte 85 000 habitants; **world p. figures are rising** la population mondiale augmente

▸▸ **p. census** recensement *m* démographique *ou* de la population; **p. control** contrôle *m* démographique; **p. explosion** explosion *f* démographique; **p. growth** croissance *f* démographique; **p. statistics** statistiques *fpl* démographiques

populism ['pɒpjʊlɪz(ə)m] N *Pol* populisme *m*

populist ['pɒpjʊlɪst] *Pol* N populiste *mf*

ADJ populiste; **p. support** support *m* populaire

populous ['pɒpjʊləs] ADJ populeux, très peuplé

pop-up ADJ *(toaster)* automatique

▸▸ **p. book** livre *m* en relief; *Comput* **p. menu** menu *m* local; *Aut* **p. sunroof** toit *m* ouvrant dépliant

porcelain ['pɔ:s(ə)lɪn] N porcelaine *f*; **a p. collection** une collection d'objets en porcelaine; **p. plate** assiette *f* en porcelaine

▸▸ **p. manufacturer** porcelainier, -ière; **p. ware** porcelaine

porch [pɔ:tʃ] N **1** *(over door)* porche *m*; **(glass) p.** *(of hotel etc)* marquise *f* **2** *Am (veranda)* véranda *f*

▸▸ **p. roof** auvent *m*

porchscreen ['pɔ:tʃskri:n] N *Am* moustiquaire *f (autour d'une véranda)*

porchswing ['pɔ:tʃswɪŋ] N *Am* balançoire *f* *(sur une véranda, typique de certaines maisons aux États-Unis)*

porcine ['pɔ:saɪn] ADJ porcin, de porc

porcupine ['pɔ:kjʊpaɪn] N porc-épic *m*, *pl* porcs-épics

▸▸ **p. fish** poisson *m* porc-épic

pore [pɔ:r] N *Anat, Bot etc* pore *m*

▸ **pore over** VT INSEP *(examine closely) (book)* être absorbé par; *(map, contract)* étudier soigneusement; *(problem)* méditer longuement

pork [pɔ:k] N *Culin* porc *m*

▸▸ *Am Pol Fam* **the p. barrel** = fonds *mpl* alloués par le gouvernement à une circonscription et destinés à s'attirer les bonnes grâces des électeurs; **p. chop** côtelette *f* de porc; **p. pie** ≃ paté *m* en croûte *(à la viande de porc)*; *Br Sl* **to tell p. pies** *(tell lies)* raconter des bobards; **p. scratchings** grattons *mpl*

porker ['pɔ:kər] N = jeune porc *m* engraissé, destiné à la boucherie

porkpie hat ['pɔ:kpaɪ-] N = chapeau *m* de feutre rond à forme aplatie

porky ['pɔ:kɪ] ADJ *Fam* gras, gros

N *Sl (lie)* bobard *m*

porn [pɔ:n] *Fam* N pornographie *f*; **soft/hard p.** pornographie soft/hard

ADJ porno *inv*

▸▸ **p. dealer** vendeur *m* de matériel pornographique; **p. shop** sex-shop *m*, *pl* sex-shops; *Br* **p. squad** = branche *f* de la police chargée de réprimer la production et la distribution illégales de matériel pornographique

porno ['pɔ:nəʊ] ADJ porno *inv*

pornographer [pɔ:'nɒgrəfər] N pornographe *mf*

pornographic [pɔ:nə'græfɪk] ADJ pornographique; *Fig* indécent

pornography [pɔ:'nɒgrəfɪ] N pornographie *f*

▸▸ **p. dealer** vendeur *m* de matériel pornographique; **p. shop** sex-shop *m*, *pl* sex-shops

porosity [pɔ:'rɒsɪtɪ] N porosité *f*

porous ['pɔ:rəs] ADJ poreux

porousness ['pɔ:rəsnɪs] N porosité *f*

porphyry ['pɔ:fɪrɪ] N *Miner* porphyre *m*

porpoise ['pɔ:pəs] N *(animal)* marsouin *m*

porridge ['pɒrɪdʒ] N **1** *Culin* bouillie *f* d'avoine, porridge *m* **2** *Br Sl* **to do p.** purger sa peine en prison
▸▸ **p. oats** flocons *mpl* d'avoine

porringer ['pɒrɪndʒər] N écuelle *f*

port[1] [pɔːt] N *(harbour, town)* port *m*; **the p. of London** le port de Londres; **in p.** au port; **to put into p.** relâcher; **to call at a p.** faire escale à un port; *Prov* **any p. in a storm** *(any will do)* nécessité fait loi; **p. to p. shipment** expédition *f* port à port
▸▸ **p. of arrival** port d'arrivée; **p. authorities** autorités *fpl* portuaires, administration *f* portuaire; **p. of call** *Naut* escale *f*, *Fig* arrêt *m*; **p. charges** droits *mpl* de port, frais *mpl* portuaires; **p. of departure** port de départ; **p. of discharge** port d'arrivée; **p. dues** droits de port, frais portuaires; **p. of embarkation** port d'embarquement; **p. of entry** port de débarquement; **p. of loading** port d'embarquement; **p. of refuge** port de refuge; **p. of registry** port d'attache

port[2] N **1** *Naut (opening for loading)* sabord *m*; **p.(-lid)** mantelet *m* ou panneau *m* ou volet *m* de sabord, contre-sabord *m*, *pl* contre-sabords; **air** or **ventilation p.** sabord d'aération **2** *Tech (of cylinder etc)* orifice *m*, lumière *f*; **admission** or **inlet p.** orifice ou pipe *f* d'admission **3** *Comput* port *m*; **input/output p.** port entrée/sortie
VT *Comput* transférer, transporter

port[3] N *Naut* **p. (side)** bâbord *m*; **land to p.!** la terre par bâbord!; **on the p. bow** par bâbord devant

port[4] N *(wine)* porto *m*
▸▸ *Old-fashioned* **p. wine stain** *(birthmark)* tache *f* de vin

portability [pɔːtə'bɪlɪtɪ] N portabilité *f*

portable ['pɔːtəb(ə)l] ADJ portatif, portable; *Fin (pension, mortgage)* transférable; *Comput (program)* portable
N *(television)* téléviseur *m* portatif ou portable; *(computer)* (ordinateur *m*) portable *m*

portage ['pɔːtɪdʒ] N *Fml* **1** *(transport) (of goods)* transport *m*, port *m*; *(of canoe etc between waterways)* portage *m* **2** *(costs)* frais *mpl* de port ou de transport

Portakabin® ['pɔːtəkæbɪn] N = baraquement *m* préfabriqué

portal ['pɔːt(ə)l] N **1** *Archit (of cathedral)* portail *m* **2** *Comput* portail *m*
▸▸ *Anat* **p. vein** veine *f* porte

Portaloo® ['pɔːtəluː] N toilettes *fpl* provisoires

portcullis [pɔːt'kʌlɪs] N *(of castle)* herse *f*, sarrasine *f*

portend [pɔː'tend] VT *Fml* présager, faire pressentir

portent ['pɔːtent] N *Fml* **1** *(sign)* présage *m* **2** *(importance)* portée *f*

portentous [pɔː'tentəs] ADJ **1** *(prodigious) (event, happening)* prodigieux; *(ominously so)* de mauvais présage ou augure **2** *(solemn)* solennel; *Pej (over-serious)* pompeux, pontifiant

portentously [pɔː'tentəslɪ] ADV solennellement; *Pej* pompeusement

porter ['pɔːtər] N **1** *Rail* porteur, -euse; *(at hotel)* chasseur *m*, garçon *m*; *Am Rail (of sleeper)* garçon **2** *esp Br (doorkeeper) (of museum etc)* portier, -ière, concierge *mf*; *(of building)* concierge; **p.'s desk** comptoir *m* du concierge; **p.'s lodge** loge *f* de concierge; *(at entrance to large estate)* maisonnette *f* du portier **3** *Br Old-fashioned (beer)* bière *f* brune (anglaise), porter *m*

porterage ['pɔːtərɪdʒ] N **1** *(carrying)* transport *m*, factage *m* **2** *(cost)* prix *m* de transport, factage *m*

porterhouse ['pɔːtəhaʊs] N
▸ *Culin* **p. steak** chateaubriand *m*, châteaubriant *m*

portfolio [pɔːt'fəʊlɪəʊ] N **1** *(for documents etc)* serviette *f*; *(for drawings, prints)* carton *m*; **candidates are asked to bring a p. of their recent work** on a demandé aux candidats d'apporter un dossier contenant leurs travaux récents; **minister's p.** portefeuille *m* de ministre; **minister without p.** ministre sans portefeuille **2** *Fin (of shares)* portefeuille *m*; **securities in p.** valeurs *fpl* en portefeuille
▸▸ **p. analysis** analyse *f* de portefeuille; **p. diversification** diversification *f* de portefeuille; **p. insurance** assurance *f* de portefeuille; **p. management** gestion *f* de portefeuille; **p. manager** gestionnaire *mf* de portefeuille; **p. mix** portefeuille d'activités; **p. securities** valeurs de portefeuille; **p. worker** = personne *f* ayant plusieurs emplois ou travailleur *m* indépendant ayant plusieurs employeurs

porthole ['pɔːthəʊl] N *Naut* hublot *m*

portico ['pɔːtɪkəʊ], *pl* **porticos, porticoes** ['pɔːtɪkəʊ, -əʊz] N *Archit* portique *m*

portion ['pɔːʃən] N **1** *(part)* partie *f*, *(of inheritance)* part *f*, *Culin (of meat etc)* portion *f*; **this p. to be given up** *(on ticket)* côté *m* à détacher; *Law* **p. (of inheritance)** part *f* d'héritage; *(marriage)* **p.** dot *f* **2** *Lit (destiny)* destinée *f*, sort *m*
VT = **portion out**
▸ **portion out** VT SEP *(property, sum)* partager, répartir

portliness ['pɔːtlɪnɪs] N corpulence *f*

portly ['pɔːtlɪ] ADJ corpulent

portmanteau, *pl* **portmanteaus, portmanteaux** [pɔːt'mæntəʊ, -əʊz] N *Old-fashioned* valise *f*
▸▸ **p. word** mot-valise *m*, *pl* mots-valises

portrait ['pɔːtreɪt] N **1** *Art*, *Fig* portrait *m*; **to have one's p. painted, to sit for one's p.** se faire peindre **2** *Typ*, *Comput* **to print sth in p.** imprimer qch en portrait
ADV *(to print)* en mode portrait, à la française
▸▸ **p. bust** (portrait en) buste *m*; *Comput* **p. format** format *m* portrait; **p. gallery** galerie *f* de portraits; **p. lens** objectif *m* pour portraits; *Comput* **p. mode** mode *m* portrait; **p. painter** portraitiste *mf*

portraitist ['pɔːtrətɪst] N portraitiste *mf*

portraiture ['pɔːtrətjər] N *(art)* (art *m* du) portrait *m*

portray [pɔː'treɪ] VT **1** *(depict)* dépeindre, décrire; **in the film the soldiers are portrayed as monsters** dans le film les soldats sont dépeints comme des monstres **2** *Arch, Lit (paint portrait of)* faire le portrait de

portrayal [pɔː'treɪəl] N **1** *(depiction)* description *f*, peinture *f*; *Theat, Cin (by actor, actress)* interprétation *f* **2** *Arch, Lit (portrait)* portrait *m*

Portugal ['pɔːtjʊg(ə)l] N Portugal *m*

Portuguese [pɔːtjʊ'giːz] ADJ portugais
N 1 Portugais, -aise **2** *Ling* portugais *m*
▸▸ *Zool* **P. man-of-war** physalie *f*, **P.-speaking** lusophone

POS [piːəʊ'es] N *Mktg (abbr* **point of sale**) PDV *m*

pose [pəʊz] N **1** *(of body)* pose *f*, attitude *f*, *(of model)* pose; **to strike a p.** *(of model)* prendre une pose **2** *(affectation)* pose *f*, affectation *f*; **it's just a p.** c'est juste un air qu'il/elle/*etc* se donne
VT 1 *Art (model)* faire poser; **to p. sb** faire prendre une pose à qn pour son portrait **2** *(problem)* poser, soulever; *(question, difficulty)* soulever; *(danger)* présenter (**to** pour); **to p. a threat to sth** menacer qch
VI *(for one's portrait, as model)* poser; *(be-*

have affectedly) poser, se donner des airs (affectés); **to p. for sb** *(as a model)* poser pour qn; **young men posing in biker jackets** *(affectedly)* des jeunes gens se donnant des airs avec leurs blousons de moto; **to p. as a Frenchman/a socialist** se faire passer pour un Français/un socialiste

poser ['pəʊzər] N *Fam* **1** *Pej (person)* poseur, -euse **2** *(difficult question)* colle *f*; **to give sb a p.** poser une colle à qn

poseur [pəʊ'zɜːr] N *Pej* = **poser 1**

posh [pɒʃ] *Br Fam* ADJ *(upper-class)* très comme il faut, *Pej* snob; *(hotel, restaurant)* chic, de luxe; **a p. accent** un accent snob; **a p. area** un quartier chic ou bourgeois; **you do look p.!** comme tu es chic!; **it looks p.** ça fait bien
ADV **to talk p.** parler comme un snob
N *Br Sl (cocaine)* coke *f*

posit ['pɒzɪt] VT *Phil etc, Fml (proposition)* avancer, poser en principe (**that ...** que ... + *ind*)

N 1 *(of body) (posture etc)* position *f*, posture *f*; **in a horizontal/vertical** or **upright p.** en position horizontale/verticale; **in the off/on p.** dans la position arrêt/marche
2 *(mental attitude)* position *f*, point *m* de vue; **to take up an uncompromising p.** adopter une attitude intransigeante (**about sth** à l'égard de qch); **I have no p. on the matter** je n'ai pas d'idée bien arrêtée sur le sujet; **what is the American p. on this issue?** quelle est la position des Américains sur ce problème?; **her p. is that ...** ce qu'elle pense c'est que ..., son point de vue est que ...
3 *(place)* position *f*, *(of object)* place *f*, *(of town etc)* situation *f*, *Banking etc (window)* guichet *m*; *Aviat, Naut (of plane, ship)* position *f*; *Mil* emplacement *m*, position *f*; **in p.** en place; **out of p.** déplacé; **to put** or **get sth into p.** mettre qch en place; *Aviat, Naut* **to fix** or **work out one's p.** faire le point; **to change the p. of sth** changer qch de position; *Ftbl* **what p. do you play?** en quelle position jouez-vous?, quelle est votre position sur le terrain?; *Naut* **to take up p. ahead/astern** prendre poste en tête/derrière; *Mil* **to move into p.** se mettre en place ou en position; **to bring guns into p.** mettre des pièces en batterie ou en position; **p. closed** *(in bank etc)* guichet fermé
4 *(situation)* situation *f*, *Old-fashioned (social status)* rang *m* social, condition *f*, état *m*; **to be in an awkward p.** se trouver dans une situation difficile ou délicate; **to be in a strong p.** être bien placé; **put yourself in my p.** mettez-vous à ma place; **try to see this from my/their/our p.** essayez de voir ceci de mon/leur/notre point de vue; **to be in a p. to do sth** être à même ou en mesure de faire qch; **you're in no p. to criticize** tu es vraiment mal placé pour faire des critiques; **what is the financial p. of the firm?** quelle est la situation financière de la maison?; **to keep up one's p.** *(in society)* tenir son rang; **to be in seventh p.** *(in race etc)* être en septième position
5 *esp Fml (job)* poste *m*, emploi *m*, situation *f*; **it's a p. of great responsibility** c'est un poste à haute responsabilité; **there were four candidates for the p. of manager** il y avait quatre candidats au poste de directeur; **to work one's way up to a good p.** se faire une belle situation; **p. of trust** poste de confiance
VT 1 *(place) (objects)* mettre en place, pla-

cer; *(troops)* mettre en position, poster; **to p. oneself** *(of troops, military observer, police etc)* se poster; *(of spectators)* se placer; **the town is positioned on the top of a basalt rock** la ville est située au sommet d'un rocher de basalte; **we are well positioned to take advantage of this opportunity** nous sommes bien placés pour tirer parti de cette opportunité

2 *(locate)* déterminer la position de

3 *Mktg (product)* positionner

▸▸**p. finding** orientation *f*; *Mil* goniométrie *f*; *St Exch* **p. limit** limite *f* de position; *Pol* **p. paper** déclaration *f* de principe; *St Exch* **p. taking** prise *f* de position

positioning [pə'zɪʃənɪŋ] N *Mktg* positionnement *m*

▸▸*Comput* **p. macro** macro-commande *f* de position, *pl* macro-commandes; *Mktg* **p. study** étude *f* de positionnement

positive ['pɒzɪtɪv] ADJ **1** *(affirmative)* positif; *Med* **the test was p.** le test était positif; **p. answer** *(yes)* réponse *f* affirmative; *(indicating willingness to do sth)* réponse positive *ou* favorable; **p. proof, proof p.** preuve *f* formelle; **there was a tremendously p. response to this idea** cette idée a été extrêmement bien accueillie *ou* reçue

2 *Fam (for emphasis)* **a p. miracle** un véritable miracle; **it's a p. shame** c'est une véritable honte

3 *(certain)* certain, sûr **(of** de**); I'm p. on that point** je n'ai aucun doute à ce sujet; **I'm p. (that) I saw him** je suis certain *ou* sûr de l'avoir vu; **are you sure? – p.!** tu es sûr? – absolument!

4 *(constructive)* *(person, philosophy)* positif; *(proposition, help)* constructif; **he described the talks as 'p.'** il a qualifié les discussions de 'positives'; **but on the p. side, ...** mais d'un autre côté, ...

5 *Math, Elec* positif

N **1 to accentuate the p.** mettre l'accent sur le côté positif des choses

2 *Phot* positif *m*, épreuve *f* positive

3 *Gram* degré *m* positif; **in the p.** à la forme affirmative

▸▸**p. action** *(discrimination)* = mesures *fpl* anti-discriminatoires en faveur de l'égalité des races et des sexes, *Can* action *f* positive; *Gram* **p. degree** *(of adjective, adverb)* degré positif; **p. discrimination** = mesures anti-discriminatoires en faveur de l'égalité des races et des sexes, *Can* action positive; *Fin* **p. prescription** prescription *f* acquisitive; *Phot* **p. print** positif, épreuve positive; *Med etc* **p. reaction** réaction *f* positive; **p. thinking** idées *fpl* constructives; **p. vetting** contrôle *m ou* enquête *f* de sécurité *(sur un candidat à un poste touchant à la sécurité nationale)*

positively ['pɒzɪtɪvlɪ] ADV **1** *(affirmatively)* positivement; **try to think p. about the situation** essaie de voir la situation d'une manière constructive; **people have responded quite p. to our suggestions** nos suggestions ont été fort bien accueillies; **he had been p. vetted on three occasions** il avait fait l'objet de trois enquêtes de sécurité qui s'étaient avérées satisfaisantes; **the body has been p. identified** le corps a été identifié de façon certaine

2 *(for emphasis)* assurément, certainement, sûrement; **I'm p. convinced it was him** je suis absolument convaincu que c'était lui; *Fam* **p. not** absolument pas; **smiling? – she was p. beaming!** souriante? – elle était littéralement radieuse!

3 *Elec* **p. charged** à charge positive; *Tech* **p. driven** à commande directe

positivism ['pɒzɪtɪvɪz(ə)m] N *Phil* positivisme *m*

positivist ['pɒzɪtɪvɪst] ADJ, N *Phil* positiviste *mf*

posology [pə'sɒlədʒɪ] N *Med* posologie *f*

poss *abbr* **possible**

posse ['pɒsɪ] N *(of people)* troupe *f*, bande *f*; *Am Hist (under sheriff)* = détachement *m* d'hommes aux ordres du shérif; *Fam (group of friends)* bande; *(entourage)* clique *f*; *(criminal gang)* gang *m*; **he's out with the p.** il est sorti avec ses potes *ou* avec sa bande

possess [pə'zes] VT **1** *(property etc)* posséder; *(quality, faculty)* avoir, posséder; **all I p.** tout ce que je possède; *Lit* **to be possessed of a property** posséder un bien **2** *(of evil spirit)* posséder; **possessed by fear/rage** pris de terreur/de rage; **what possessed you to do that?** qu'est-ce qui vous a pris de faire cela?; **to be possessed with an idea** être obsédé par une idée; **to scream like one possessed** crier comme un possédé **3** *Lit* **to p. oneself in patience** se munir de patience

possession [pə'zeʃən] N **1** *(ownership)* possession *f*, jouissance *f* **(of** de**); to have sth in one's p.** avoir qch en sa possession; **to be in p. of sth** être en possession de qch; **how did the car come into your p.?** comment la voiture est-elle entrée en votre possession?; **to take p. of an estate, to come** *or* **enter into p. of an estate** entrer en possession *ou* en jouissance d'un bien; **to take** *or* **get p. of sth** *(forcefully)* s'emparer de qch; **the information in my p.** les renseignements dont je dispose; **in full p. of one's faculties** en pleine possession de ses facultés; **he's been arrested for p.** *(of drugs)* il a été arrêté pour détention de drogue; **sorry, p. is nine points** *or* **tenths of the law!** la possession vaut titre; *Ftbl* **to lose p. of the ball** perdre le ballon; *Sport* **to have p.** être en possession du ballon

2 *(object possessed)* possession *f*; **possessions** possessions, biens *mpl*; *(colonies)* possessions, colonies *fpl*

3 *(by demon)* possession *f*

possessive [pə'zesɪv] ADJ **1** *(parent etc)* possessif **(about** avec**); she's very p. about her children** c'est une mère très possessive **2** *Gram* **the p. case** le cas possessif VOIR GRAMMAIRE A30; B21–2

N *Gram* adjectif *m*/pronom *m* possessif; **the p.** *(case)* le possessif

▸▸*Gram* **p. adjective** adjectif possessif; **p. pronoun** pronom possessif

possessiveness [pə'zesɪvnɪs] N possessivité *f* **(about** à propos de**)**

possessor [pə'zesər] N possesseur *m*

possibility [pɒsɪ'bɪlɪtɪ] N **1** *(of event)* possibilité *f*, éventualité *f*; **have you considered the p. of his being dead?** avez-vous envisagé la possibilité qu'il soit mort?; **within the range** *or* **the bounds of p.** dans la limite du possible; **there's a p. that it will rain** il est possible qu'il pleuve; **there's a definite** *or* **a strong p. that he'll say yes** il est fort probable qu'il dise oui; **there is little p. that he will win** il n'a guère de chances de gagner, il est peu probable qu'il gagne VOIR GRAMMAIRE A59–60; B40

2 *(possible event, outcome)* éventualité *f*; **that is a distinct p.** c'est bien possible; **to allow for all possibilities** parer à toute éventualité; **the possibilities are endless!** les possibilités sont innombrables!

3 *(potential)* *(usu pl)* **the plan has possibilities** ce projet offre des chances de succès; **the flat has possibilities** l'appartement a un bon potentiel

POSSIBLE ['pɒsɪb(ə)l] ADJ possible; **it's p.** c'est possible; **that's quite p.** c'est très *ou* fort possible; **it's just p. that ...** il y a des chances pour que ... + *subj*; **anything's p.** tout est possible; **it is p. that he will come** il est pos-

sible *ou* il se peut qu'il vienne; **is it p. to see her?** y a-t-il moyen *ou* est-il possible de la voir?; **as cheap/soon as p.** aussi bon marché/tôt que possible; **the best p.** le meilleur possible; **the shortest p. route** l'itinéraire le plus court possible; **to give as many details as p.** donner le plus de détails possible *ou* tous les détails possibles; **what p. interest can you have in it?** mais quel intérêt cela peut-il donc avoir pour vous?; **there's no p. reason why he should have done it** il n'avait absolument aucune raison de le faire; **if p.** *(I will do it)* si possible; **if it's p. to ...** si c'est possible de ...; **whenever/wherever p.** toutes les fois que/partout où c'est possible; **as far as p.** dans la mesure du possible; **the p. nomination of ...** la nomination éventuelle de ...; **to insure against p. accidents** s'assurer contre les accidents éventuels

N **1 it's in the realms of the p.** c'est dans le domaine du possible

2 *Fam (candidate)* candidat, -ate possible *ou* acceptable; **only two of the jobs/flats are possibles** seuls deux des emplois/appartements sont à considérer

possibly ['pɒsɪblɪ] ADV **1 I can't p. do it** je ne peux vraiment pas le faire, il ne m'est vraiment pas possible de le faire; **I'll do all I p. can** je ferai tout mon possible; **you can't p. mean that!** vous ne pouvez pas dire ça sérieusement!; **I can't p. allow you to do that!** je ne peux vraiment pas vous permettre de faire cela!; **they can't p. have left yet!** il est tout à fait impossible qu'ils soient déjà partis!; **it can't p. cost that much!** c'est absolument impossible que ça coûte aussi cher que ça! **2** *(perhaps)* peut-être (bien); **he has p. heard of you** il se peut qu'il ait entendu parler de vous; **p.!** c'est possible, cela se peut; **p. not** peut-être pas

possum ['pɒsəm] N *Fam (animal)* opossum *m*; **to play p.** faire le mort; *(keep low profile)* se tenir coi

post¹ [pəʊst] N **1** *(of fence)* pieu *m*; *(of frame)* montant *m*; *Constr etc* poteau *m*, pilier *m*; *(of door, window)* montant *m*, jambage *m*; *Ftbl* poteau; **(bed) p.** colonne *f* de lit; **(telegraph) p.** poteau télégraphique

2 *(starting)* **p.** *(poteau m de)* départ *m*; **(winning) p.** (poteau d')arrivée *f*; *Sport, Fig* **to be left at the p.** rater le départ; *Sport, Fig* **to be beaten** *or Fam* **pipped at the p.** se faire coiffer *ou* battre sur le poteau

VT **1** *(on wall etc)* *(bills, notice etc)* afficher, placarder, coller; **p. no bills** *(on sign)* défense d'afficher; **to p. prices** afficher des prix

2 *(on list)* *(person)* inscrire *ou* porter sur une liste; *(in marine insurance)* *(ship)* porter disparu; **to be posted for night duty** être sur la liste (du personnel) de service de nuit; **to be posted missing** être porté disparu *ou* manquant; *St Exch* **to p. security** déposer des garanties

POST²

N courrier **1** ▪ poste **1, 3, 4**
VT poster **1, 5** ▪ affecter **4**

N *Br* **1** *(mail)* courrier *m*; *(service)* poste *f*; **by return of p.** par retour du courrier; **when does the next p. go?** à quelle heure est la prochaine levée?; **to miss the p.** manquer la levée; *(in office)* manquer le courrier; **the first p.** la première distribution; **to catch the p.** poster une lettre/un paquet/*etc* à temps *(pour une levée déterminée)*; **there's no p. today** *(no letters for you, no delivery service)* il n'y a pas de courrier aujourd'hui; **to put sth in the p.** mettre qch à la poste; **to send sth by p.** envoyer qch par la poste; **has the p. been yet?** est-ce que le facteur est passé?; **was there any p. for me?** est-ce que j'ai du courrier?

2 *Hist (coach)* (malle-)poste *f, pl* malles-poste(s)

3 *Fml (job)* poste *m*, emploi *m*; **to take up a p.** commencer un travail, débuter dans un poste, *Fml* entrer en fonction

4 *Mil etc* poste *m*; *Am (permanent station)* camp *m*, fort *m*; *(garrison)* garnison *f*; **to be/die at one's p.** être/mourir à son poste; **advanced** *or* **outlying p.** *(place, group of men)* poste avancé; **lookout p.** poste de guet *ou* d'observation; **frontier p.** poste frontière

5 *Br Mil (bugle call)* **first p.** première partie *f* de la sonnerie de la retraite; **last p.** dernière partie (de la sonnerie); *(for the dead)* sonnerie *f* aux morts; **to sound the last p. (over the grave)** jouer la sonnerie aux morts

VT 1 *Br (letter) (put in the post)* mettre à la poste *ou* à la boîte, poster; *(send)* envoyer par la poste, poster; **I'll p. it to you** je vous l'enverrai par la poste, je vous le posterai

2 *Acct (in bookkeeping)* passer écriture de; *(in computerized accounts)* valider; **to p. an amount** passer un montant

3 *Fam* **I'll keep you posted** *(informed)* je vous tiendrai au courant

4 *(assign), Mil etc* désigner *ou* affecter à un commandement; *Com etc* **to be posted to a different branch** être muté dans une autre succursale; *Mil* **to be posted to a unit/a ship** être affecté à une unité/un navire

5 *Mil etc (position)* poster, placer; *(guard)* poster, placer, mettre en faction; *Fig* **she posted herself at the window** elle s'est postée à la fenêtre

▸▸ **p. chaise** chaise *f* de poste; *Hist* **p. coach** (malle-)poste; **p. office** *(place)* (bureau *m* de); *(service)* (service *m* des) postes *fpl*, poste; *Am (game)* = jeu *m* d'enfant dans lequel un des joueurs fait semblant de distribuer des lettres, en échange desquelles il reçoit un baiser; **the P. Office** *(government department)* ≃ la Poste; **p. office account** compte *m* chèque postal; **p. office box** boîte *f* postale; **p. office cheque** chèque *m* postal; **p. office van** ≃ camionnette *f* de la Poste

▸ **post on** VT SEP *(forward)* faire suivre; **I'll p. your mail on to you** je te ferai suivre ton courrier

postage ['pəʊstɪdʒ] N *(for mail)* affranchissement *m*, port *m*; **add 10% (for) p. and packing** ajouter 10% pour les frais d'emballage et d'expédition; **additional p.** *(on insufficiently stamped letter)* surtaxe *f* (postale); **p. included** port compris; **p. paid** port payé

▸▸ **p. rates** tarifs *mpl* postaux; **p. stamp** timbre *m*, timbre-poste *m*, *pl* timbres-poste

postal ['pəʊst(ə)l] ADJ **1** postal, -aux **2** *Am Fam* **to go p.** *(get angry)* péter les plombs

▸▸ *Am* **p. card** carte *f* postale; **p. charges** *(system of charges)* tarifs *mpl* postaux; *(actually charged)* frais *mpl* d'envoi *ou* de port; *Br* **p. order** mandat *m* postal, mandat poste; **p. rates** tarifs postaux; **p. services** services *mpl* postaux; *Mktg* **p. survey** enquête *f* postale

postbag ['pəʊstbæg] N *esp Br* sac *m* postal; *Radio, TV etc* **our p. has been heavy this week** vous avez été nombreux à nous écrire cette semaine

postbox ['pəʊstbɒks] N *esp Br* boîte *f* aux *ou* à lettres

postcard ['pəʊstkɑːd] N carte *f* postale

postcode ['pəʊstkəʊd] N *Br* code *m* postal

post-colonial ADJ post-colonial, -aux

post-colonialism N post-colonialisme *m*

post-colonialist ADJ, N post-colonialiste *mf*

postdate ['pəʊst'deɪt] VT postdater

postedit ['pəʊst'edɪt] VT *(in machine translation)* post-éditer

posted price ['pəʊstɪd] N prix *m* affiché

poster ['pəʊstər] N affiche *f*; *(decorative)* poster *m*; **to be a p. boy/girl for sth** incarner qch

▸▸ *Mktg* **p. advertising** publicité *f* par affichage, publicité par voie d'affiches; *Mktg* **p. campaign** campagne *f* d'affichage; **p. paint** gouache *f*

poste restante ['pəʊstres'tɒnt] N, ADV *Br* poste *f* restante

posterior [pɒ'stɪərɪər] ADJ *Fml* postérieur (**to** à); *Anat (towards back of body)* dorsal, -aux

N *Fam Hum (person's bottom)* postérieur *m*, derrière *m*

posterity [pɒ'sterɪtɪ] N postérité *f*; **to preserve sth for p.** garder qch pour la postérité; **p. will remember her as …** elle entrera dans la postérité comme …

postern ['pəʊstɜːn] N poterne *f*

postgrad [pəʊst'græd] N *Fam* = **postgraduate** N

postgraduate [pəʊst'grædjʊɪt] ADJ *(degree, student, qualifications)* de troisième cycle; *(club)* pour les étudiants de troisième cycle

N *(student)* étudiant, -ante de troisième cycle

▸▸ **p. studies** = (études *fpl* de) troisième cycle *m*

posthaste ['pəʊst'heɪst] ADV en toute hâte

posthumous ['pɒstjʊməs] ADJ *(works)* posthume

posthumously ['pɒstjʊməslɪ] ADV *(to be awarded a medal)* à titre posthume; *(to publish a book, piece of music etc)* après la mort de l'auteur/du compositeur/*etc*

post-ignition N autoallumage *m*

postil(l)ion [pɒ'stɪlɪən] N postillon *m*

postimpressionism [pəʊstɪm'preʃənɪz(ə)m] N *Art* postimpressionnisme *m*

postimpressionist [pəʊstɪm'preʃənɪst] ADJ, N *Art* postimpressionniste *mf*

postindustrial [pəʊstɪn'dʌstrɪəl] ADJ post-industriel

posting ['pəʊstɪŋ] N **1** *(in diplomatic service, army)* affectation *f (à un poste)*; **he had been given a p. as sales manager in Eastern Europe** on l'avait envoyé en Europe de l'Est comme directeur des ventes **2** *Com (in bookkeeping)* passation *f (d'écritures)* **3** *Mil (of guards)* mise *f* en faction **4** *Br (putting in the post)* mise *f* à la boîte *ou* à la poste; *(sending by mail)* envoi *m* par la poste

▸▸ **p. date** date *f* de la poste

Post-it® N Post-it® *m*

postman, *pl* **postmen** ['pəʊstmən] N facteur *m*

▸▸ **p.'s knock** *(game)* ≃ mariage *m* chinois

postmark ['pəʊstmɑːk] N cachet *m* de la poste, (cachet d')oblitération *f*; **date as p.** cachet de la poste faisant foi

VT oblitérer; **the letter was postmarked London** la lettre était timbrée (au départ) de Londres

postmaster ['pəʊstmɑːstər] N receveur *m* (des postes); *Comput* maître *m* de poste

▸▸ **P. General** ≃ ministre *m* des Postes et Télécommunications, *Can* ministre *m* des Postes

post meridiem [mə'rɪdɪəm] ADV *Fml (in the afternoon)* de l'après-midi; *(in the evening)* du soir

post-millennial ADJ d'après le passage au troisième millénaire

postmistress ['pəʊstmɪstrɪs] N receveuse *f* des postes

postmodern ['pəʊst'mɒdən] ADJ *Archit, Art etc* postmoderne

postmodernism [pəʊst'mɒd(ə)nɪz(ə)m] N *Archit, Art etc* postmodernisme *m*

postmodernist [pəʊst'mɒd(ə)nɪst] ADJ, N *Archit, Art etc* postmoderniste *mf*

postmortem [pəʊst'mɔːtəm] N autopsie *f*; *Fig* analyse *f* rétrospective *ou* après coup; *Fig* **please, no postmortems** inutile de revenir sur ce qui est terminé

▸▸ **p. examination** autopsie *f*; **to hold a p. examination (on)** faire une autopsie (sur)

postnatal [pəʊst'neɪt(ə)l] ADJ postnatal, -als *ou* -aux

▸▸ **p. depression** dépression *f* postnatale

post-op ADJ postopératoire

N salle *f* de réveil

postoperative [pəʊst'ɒpərətɪv] ADJ *Med* postopératoire

post-paid ADJ port payé

postpartum [pəʊst'pɑːtəm] N *Med* postpartum *m*

postpone [pəʊst'pəʊn] VT *(departure, project, decision etc)* remettre, reporter, renvoyer à plus tard; *(deadline)* reculer; *Sport (match)* différer, ajourner, remettre; *(payment)* différer; **to p. a matter for a week** remettre *ou* renvoyer une affaire à huitaine; **the meeting is postponed until next week** la réunion a été remise à *ou* ajournée jusqu'à la semaine prochaine

postponement [pəʊst'pəʊnmənt] N *(of meeting, decision etc)* report *m*; *(of match, trial)* ajournement *m*

postposition [pəʊstpə'zɪʃən] N *Gram* postposition *f*

postprandial [pəʊst'prændɪəl] ADJ *usu Hum* après le repas; **to go for a p. stroll** faire une promenade digestive

postproduction [pəʊstprə'dʌkʃən] N *Cin, TV* postproduction *f*; **the film is in p.** le film est en postproduction

▸▸ **p. editing** montage *m* de postproduction; **p. mixer** mélangeur *m* de postproduction; **p. studio** studio *m* de postproduction

post-purchase ADJ *Mktg* post-achat

▸▸ **p. behaviour** comportement *m* post-achat; **p. dissonance** discordance *f* post-achat; **p. evaluation** évaluation *f* post-achat

PostScript® ['pəʊstskrɪpt] N *Comput* PostScript® *m*; **PostScript® font** police *f* de caractères PostScript®; **PostScript® printer** imprimante *f* PostScript®

postscript ['pəʊstskrɪpt] N **1** *(in letter)* post-scriptum *m inv*; **by way of p.** en post-scriptum **2** *(in book)* postface *f*; *Fig (additional events)* suite *f*

post-sync(h)ing ['pəʊstsɪŋkɪŋ] N *TV etc* postsynchro *f*

post-synchronization N *TV etc* postsonorisation *f*, postsynchronisation *f*

post-test *Mktg* N post-test *m*, *pl* post-tests

VT post-tester

post-traumatic stress disorder N *Med* névrose *f* post-traumatique

postulant ['pɒstjʊlənt] N *Rel* postulant, -ante

postulate¹ ['pɒstjʊlɪt] N *(in logic), Math* postulat *m*

postulate² ['pɒstjʊleɪt] VT **1** *(in logic), Math* postuler, poser en postulat **2** *(put forward existence of)* postuler

posture ['pɒstʃər] N **1** posture *f*, pose *f*, attitude *f*; **to have good p.** avoir une bonne posture, bien se tenir **2** *Fig (attitude)* attitude *f*, position *f* (**on** en ce qui concerne)

VI *(physically)* poser; *(in behaviour, attitude) (show off)* se donner des airs; *(adopt position) (in negotiations, making threat etc)* user de roublardise

posturing ['pɒstʃərɪŋ] N *(physical)* poses *fpl*, *(in behaviour, attitude) (showing off)* affectation *f*, airs *mpl*, *(of politician, negotiator etc)* roublardise *f*

postwar ['pəʊst'wɔːr] ADJ d'après-guerre; **the p. period** l'après-guerre m

posy ['pəʊzɪ] N petit bouquet m

pot [pɒt] N **1** (receptacle) pot m; (for cooking) marmite f; (saucepan) casserole f; Sport Sl (trophy) coupe f; **pots and pans** batterie f de cuisine; **a p. of tea** un thé (servi dans une théière); **it's (a case of) the p. calling the kettle black** c'est l'hôpital qui se moque de la charité; Fam **to go to p.** (of country, economy) aller à la ruine; (of hopes, chances) tomber en poussière; **his health has gone to p.** sa santé s'est délabrée; **her marriage has gone to p.** ça ne va plus du tout avec son mari; Sl **he hasn't got a p. to piss in** il est complètement fauché; Fam **to take a p. shot at sb/sth** (fire at) tirer à l'aveuglette sur qn/qch; Fig **I'll take a p. shot at it** je vais tenter ma chance; **he took a p. shot at the answer** il a répondu au petit bonheur (la chance) ou au pif; **to take a p. shot at sb** lancer une critique à qn; **taking a p. shot, I'd say ...** au pif, je dirais ...

2 Fam **pots of...** (a lot of) des tas de ...; **to have pots of money** rouler sur l'or; **we have pots of time** nous avons tout le temps **3** Sl (marijuana) herbe f; (hashish) hasch m **4** (kitty) cagnotte f **5** Fam (potbelly) bedon m **6** (potentiometer) potentiomètre m

VT (-tt-) **1** (butter, salted meat etc) mettre en pot; (plant) mettre en pot, empoter; (baby) mettre sur son pot; Billiards (ball) blouser **2** (shoot) (rabbit, pheasant etc) abattre

VI (shoot) **to p. at** (rabbit, pheasant etc) lâcher un coup de fusil à
► ► Br **p. plant** plante f d'intérieur
► **pot on** VT SEP (plant) rempoter
► **pot up** VT SEP (plant) mettre en pot, empoter

potable ['pəʊtəb(ə)l] ADJ Fml, Hum potable, buvable

potash ['pɒtæʃ] N potasse f

potassium [pə'tæsɪəm] N Chem potassium m
► ► **p. chloride** chlorure m de potassium

potato, pl **potatoes** [pə'teɪtəʊ, -əʊz] N pomme f de terre; **to dig up** or **lift potatoes** arracher des pommes de terre
► ► Am **p. chips**, Br **p. crisps** (pommes) chips fpl, **p. masher** presse-purée m inv; **p. peeler** (tool) éplucheur m, épluche-légumes m inv, (couteau m) économe m; (machine) éplucheuse f; **p. salad** salade f de pommes de terre

potbellied [pɒt'belɪd] ADJ Fam ventru, bedonnant

potbelly ['pɒtbelɪ] N Fam gros ventre m, bedaine f, bedon m

potboiler ['pɒtbɔɪlər] N Fam œuvre f alimentaire

poteen [pɒ'tiːn] N = whisky m irlandais distillé en fraude

potency ['pəʊtənsɪ] N (of argument) force f, puissance f; (of medicine) efficacité f, puissance; (of alcoholic drink) force; **sexual p.** puissance sexuelle

potent ['pəʊtənt] ADJ (drug etc) efficace, puissant; (motive etc) convaincant, décisif; (argument) fort, puissant; (drink) très fort; (poison) violent; (sexually) viril

potentate ['pəʊtənteɪt] N potentat m

potential [pə'tenʃəl] ADJ Math etc potentiel; (danger) possible, latent; (enemy, criminal) en puissance; (client) éventuel

N Phys, Elec potentiel m; Gram **the p.** le potentiel; **human p.** potentiel humain; **to reach** or **fulfil one's p.** atteindre son maximum; **to have p.** avoir du potentiel; **the building has a lot of** or **considerable p.** le bâtiment offre de grandes possibilités d'aménagement; **this**

idea has great p. cette idée ouvre de grandes possibilités; **there is the p. for a major accident** tous les risques d'un grave accident sont réunis
► ► Com, Mktg **p. buyer** acheteur, -euse éventuel(elle); Elec, Phys **p. energy** énergie f potentielle; Econ **p. GDP** PIB m potentiel; **p. market** marché m potentiel; Gram **the p. mood** le potentiel; Mktg **p. user** utilisateur m potentiel

potentiality [pətenʃɪ'ælɪtɪ] N potentialité f

potentially [pə'tenʃəlɪ] ADV potentiellement

potentiometer [pətenʃɪ'ɒmɪtər] N potentiomètre m

pothead ['pɒthed] N Sl gros(se) fumeur, -euse de haschich

pother ['pɒðər] N Dial (confusion) agitation f, confusion f; (din) tapage m, vacarme m

pothole ['pɒthəʊl] N Geol marmite f torrentielle ou de géants; (in road) nid m de poule, fondrière f

potholer ['pɒthəʊlər] N spéléologue mf

potholing ['pɒthəʊlɪŋ] N spéléologie f; **to go p.** faire de la spéléologie

pothook ['pɒthʊk] N Culin crémaillère f

pothunter ['pɒthʌntər] N Sport Fam coureur, -euse de prix

potion ['pəʊʃən] N potion f; **love p.** philtre m d'amour

potluck [pɒt'lʌk] N Fam **to take p.** choisir au hasard; **it was just p.** c'était un pur hasard; **come round for a meal, but you'll have to take p.** venez manger à la maison, mais ça sera à la fortune du pot

potpourri [pəʊ'pʊərɪ, -pə'riː] N (dried flowers) fleurs fpl séchées; Mus, Liter potpourri m, pl pots-pourris

pot-roast N morceau m de viande cuit à l'étouffée
VT cuire à l'étouffée

potsherd ['pɒtʃɜːd] N Archeol fragment m de poterie

pottage ['pɒtɪdʒ] N Arch potage m (épais); (with meat and vegetables) potée f; Bible **mess of p.** = plat m de lentilles

potted ['pɒtɪd] ADJ **1** Culin (conservé) en pot, en terrine; Fam (biography etc) abrégé, condensé **2** Am Fam (drunk) pété, bourré
► ► **p. meat** ≃ terrine f, **p. palm** palmier m en pot; **p. plant** plante f verte; **p. shrimps** crevettes fpl en conserve

potter [1] ['pɒtər] N Art potier, -ière
► ► **p.'s clay** terre f de potier ou à potier; **p.'s wheel** tour m de potier

potter [2] VI Br **1** (do odd jobs) bricoler **2** (walk about slowly) traîner, traînasser; **to p. down to the shops** aller faire un tour dans les magasins
► **potter about**, **potter around** VI Br **1** (do odd jobs) bricoler; **to p. about at odd jobs** bricoler, faire des petits travaux; **to p. about the house** faire des petits travaux ou bricoler dans la maison **2** (move about slowly) traîner, traînasser; **pottering about in country lanes in her car** en se baladant dans les chemins de campagne au volant de sa voiture
► **potter along** VI (move slowly, work slowly) (of person) aller sans se presser; (of car) aller doucement; **he's just pottering along** (in life) il va son petit bonhomme de chemin; **he just potters along** (in job) il avance tranquillement; **I think I'll p. along to the pub** je crois que je vais aller faire un petit tour au pub

pottery ['pɒtərɪ] N (art, place) poterie f; **a piece of p.** une poterie; **some p.** des poteries; **a p. vase** un vase en terre ou en poterie

potting shed ['pɒtɪŋ] N cabane f de jardin

potty [1] ['pɒtɪ] ADJ Br Fam (crazy) toqué, timbré, dingue; **to go p.** devenir timbré ou dingue; **to be p. about sb/sth** être toqué de qn/qch; **you're driving me p.** tu me rends dingue, tu me fais tourner en bourrique

potty [2] N (in children's language) pot m (de chambre) (d'enfant); **to p. train one's child** apprendre à son enfant à être propre ou à aller sur le pot; **is she p. trained?** est-ce qu'elle est propre?
► ► **p. training** apprentissage m de la propreté

pouch [paʊtʃ] N **1** (small bag) (petit) sac m; (for money) bourse f, (of dispatch rider, courier) sacoche f, (for ammunition) étui m; **tobacco p.** blague f à tabac **2** (of marsupial) poche f ventrale

pouf(fe) [puːf] N (furniture) pouf m

poult [pəʊlt] N (young chicken) (jeune) poulet m; (young turkey) dindonneau m; (young pheasant, partridge) pouillard m

poulterer ['pəʊltərər] N marchand, -ande de volaille, volailler, -ère

poultice ['pəʊltɪs] N Med cataplasme m

poultry ['pəʊltrɪ] N (no pl) volaille f
► ► **p. dealer** marchand, -ande de volaille, volailler, -ère; **p. farm** élevage m de volaille ou de volailles; **p. farmer** éleveur, -euse de volaille ou de volailles, aviculteur, -trice; **p. farming** élevage de volaille ou de volailles, aviculture f

pounce [paʊns] N bond m; **to make a p. on** (of bird, animal) fondre ou s'abattre ou bondir sur; Fam (of person) se précipiter ou se jeter sur
VI **1** (of bird, animal) bondir, attaquer; **to p. on the prey** fondre ou s'abattre ou bondir sur la proie **2** Fam (of person) se précipiter, se jeter (on sur); (of police etc) faire une descente (on sur); Fig **he pounced on her mistake** il a sauté sur son erreur; **to p. on an opportunity** saisir une chance à la volée; **when the shares are low, we'll p.** quand les actions auront baissé, nous attaquerons

pound [1] [paʊnd] N <small>VOIR GRAMMAIRE A13</small> **1** (measurement of weight) livre f (= 453,6 grammes); **to sell sth by the p.** vendre qch à la livre; **40 pence a p.** quarante pence la livre; Fig **to demand one's p. of flesh from sb** exiger son dû de qn

2 (currency unit) **p. (sterling)** livre f (sterling)
► ► Culin **p. cake** ≃ quatre-quarts m inv; **p. coin** pièce f d'une livre; Hist **p. note** billet m d'une livre; **p. sign** (£) symbole m de la livre (sterling); Am (on telephone) dièse m

pound [2] N (for stray animals, cars) fourrière f

pound [3] VT Law saisir

pound [4] VT (crush etc) (stones etc) broyer, piler, concasser; (salt, sugar, drug) piler, broyer; (lumps of earth) casser, briser; (earth) pilonner; (person) (with fists) battre, rosser; (in competition) mettre la pâtée à; Mil (position) pilonner, marteler; **to p. sth to pieces** réduire qch en miettes ou en morceaux; **to p. sb into submission** s'acharner sur qn jusqu'à ce qu'il se soumette; **to p. the beat** (of policeman) patrouiller; **you'll be back to pounding the beat** (demoted) on vous remettra à la circulation; **to p. the streets** battre le trottoir
VI frapper ou taper dur; (of heart) battre à grands coups; (of drum, music) résonner; **to p. at** or **on sth** cogner dur sur qch; **to p. on the door** donner de grands coups à la porte; **the waves pounded against the shore** les vagues s'abattaient ou se brisaient sur le rivage; **feet were heard pounding on the stairs** on entendit des pas résonner lourdement dans l'escalier; **she pounded down the road after them** elle s'élança derrière eux sur la route

▶ **pound along** VI they're really pounding along ils vont à fond de train; he was pounding along after them il les poursuivait à toute allure

▶ **pound away** VI (of waves) se briser (at, against sur); we heard the guns pounding away nous entendions le bruit incessant des canons; the guns pounded away at their position les canons pilonnaient sans relâche leur position; he sat pounding away at the piano il martelait le piano, il jouait du piano comme un forcené; he was pounding away at the typewriter il tapait comme un fou sur la machine à écrire

poundage ['paʊndɪdʒ] N 1 (weight) poids m en livres 2 (tax, commission) taxe f/commission f proportionnelle au poids/à la valeur

-pounder ['paʊndər] SUFF two/three-p. (fish) poisson m de deux/de trois livres (de poids); Mil thirty-p. canon m ou pièce f de trente

pounding ['paʊndɪŋ] N (of heart) battement m frénétique; (of drums) battement; the p. of the waves le martellement des vagues; to take a p. (of boat) être fortement secoué; (of troops, city etc) être pilonné; Fig (of team etc) être battu à plate(s) couture(s); Fig the economy has taken quite a p. l'économie a subi des coups de boutoir; Fig the euro took a p. l'euro a été attaqué

POUR [pɔːr] VT verser (into dans); Metal couler; to p. sb a drink verser un verre à qn; p. the water down the sink versez l'eau dans l'évier; Fig the government poured money into the industry le gouvernement a investi des sommes énormes dans l'industrie; Fig she looked as if she'd been poured into her jeans elle portait un jean extrêmement moulant

VI 1 it's pouring (with rain), the rain's pouring down il pleut à verse, la pluie tombe à torrents; there were tears pouring down her cheeks son visage était baigné de larmes; blood was pouring from the cut on her forehead le sang s'écoulait en abondance de l'entaille qu'elle avait au front; the sunlight poured into the room les rayons du soleil inondaient la pièce; water was pouring into the cellar l'eau entrait à flots dans la cave; sweat was pouring off him il ruisselait de sueur; reinforcements poured in to the area des renforts sont arrivés en masse dans la région; tourists were pouring into the palace les touristes entraient en foule dans le palais

2 this jug doesn't p. well ce broc ne verse pas bien; shall I p.? puis-je faire le service?

▶ **pour down** VI (of rain) tomber à verse; it's been pouring down for days il pleut à verse depuis des jours et des jours

▶ **pour in** VI (of water) se déverser, entrer à flots; the crowd came pouring in on entrait à flots ou en foule; invitations came pouring in ça a été une avalanche d'invitations
VT SEP (liquid) verser; Fig the government poured money in le gouvernement a investi des sommes énormes

▶ **pour off** VT SEP vider

▶ **pour out** VI (of water) se déverser, sortir à flots; (of people) sortir en foule; smoke was pouring out of the window des nuages de fumée s'échappaient de la fenêtre; the words just poured out les mots sont sortis en flots; all his feelings came pouring out il a laissé libre cours à ses émotions
VT SEP (tea, coffee etc) verser; (anger, feelings) donner libre cours à; (of chimney) (clouds of smoke) cracher, vomir; Fig he poured out all his frustrations to me il m'a déballé toutes ses frustrations; to p. out a torrent of abuse at sb déverser un torrent d'injures sur qn; she poured out her feelings to me elle m'a ouvert son cœur; Japanese

products are being poured out onto the market les produits japonais inondent le marché

pouring ['pɔːrɪŋ] ADJ (rain) torrentiel

pout [paʊt] N moue f
VI faire la moue; (sulk) bouder; her pouting lips ses lèvres boudeuses

pouter ['paʊtər] N (pigeon) pigeon m boulant
▶ ▶ **p. pigeon** pigeon boulant

POV [piːəʊ'viː] N TV, Cin (abbr point of view) angle m du regard

poverty ['pɒvətɪ] N 1 pauvreté f; extreme or abject p. misère f; to live in p. vivre dans la gêne ou (stronger) la misère 2 (lack) (of food etc) disette f, manque m, pénurie f; (poor quality) (of soil) pauvreté f; p. of ideas pénurie f d'idées
▶ ▶ **p. line** seuil m de pauvreté; to live below the p. line vivre en-dessous du seuil de pauvreté; **p. trap** = situation f inextricable de ceux qui dépendent de prestations sociales qu'ils perdent pour peu qu'ils trouvent une activité, même très peu rémunérée

poverty-stricken ADJ (person) indigent, réduit à la misère; (dwelling, area etc) misérable; a. p. country un pays souffrant de la misère

POW [piːəʊ'dʌb(ə)ljuː] N (abbr prisoner of war) prisonnier m de guerre

powder ['paʊdər] N poudre f; (gunpowder) poudre, explosif m; to reduce sth to p. réduire qch en poudre, pulvériser qch; Fig (destroy) réduire qch en poussière ou en miettes; (face) p. poudre (de riz); Am Sl to take a p. (disappear) ficher le camp
VT 1 (cake etc) saupoudrer (with de); a landscape powdered with snow un paysage saupoudré de neige; to p. one's face se poudrer (le visage); Fam Euph to go and p. one's nose aller se laver les mains 2 (convert to powder) (milk etc) réduire en poudre
▶ ▶ **p. blue** bleu m pastel; **p. compact** poudrier m; **p. keg** (of gunpowder) baril m de poudre; Fig poudrière f; **p. puff** houppette f; Euph **p. room** toilettes fpl (pour dames)

powdered ['paʊdəd] ADJ 1 (milk etc) en poudre; (coal etc) pulvérisé; in p. form sous forme de poudre 2 (face) poudré

powdery ['paʊd(ə)rɪ] ADJ poudreux; (crumbly) friable

POWER ['paʊər]

| N pouvoir 1, 2, 6 • faculté 2 • force 3 |
| • puissance 3, 4, 8, 9 • courant 7 |
| VT faire marcher |

N 1 Pol etc (authority, control) pouvoir m, autorité f; to come (in)to p. arriver au pouvoir; to be in/out of p. être/ne pas être au pouvoir; to lose p. perdre le pouvoir; the party in p. le parti au pouvoir; to be voted into/out of p. être nommé au pouvoir/chassé du pouvoir par un vote; to be in sb's p. être à la merci de qn; also Fig to be the real p. behind the throne tirer les ficelles; also Hum the powers that be les autorités fpl; Rel the powers of darkness les puissances des ténèbres; to have sb in one's p. avoir qn à sa merci; absolute/executive/legislative p. pouvoir absolu/exécutif/législatif; they constitute his p. base ils constituent le groupe d'où il tire son pouvoir

2 (capacity) pouvoir m; to have the p. to do sth avoir le pouvoir ou la faculté de faire qch; I'll do everything in my p. je ferai tout ce qui est en mon pouvoir ou tout mon possible; it is beyond my p. ce n'est pas en mon pouvoir; to be at the height or peak of one's powers être à l'apogée de sa puissance; her powers were failing her les forces lui manquaient; mental or intellectual powers fa-

cultés fpl intellectuelles; a man of great mental or intellectual powers un homme doté de grandes facultés intellectuelles; Phys, Chem **p. of absorption** capacité f d'absorption; **p. of observation** facultés d'observation; the p. of reason (faculty) la raison; (strength, force) la puissance de la raison; the p. of speech (faculty) la parole; (force) le pouvoir de la parole; **powers of concentration** facultés de concentration; **powers of persuasion** dons mpl de persuasion

3 (physical strength) force f, puissance f; Fam more p. to your elbow! allez-y!

4 (nation etc) puissance f, **sea/air/industrial/nuclear/world p.** (country) puissance maritime/aérienne/industrielle/nucléaire/mondiale; the great powers (countries) les grandes puissances

5 Fam that'll do you a p. of good ça vous fera énormément de bien

6 Law procuration f, mandat m, pouvoir m; p. of life and death droit m de vie et de mort; Law delegation of powers délégation f de pouvoirs; Law to furnish sb with full powers donner pleins pouvoirs à qn; to act with full powers agir de pleine autorité; the police have been given greater powers la police a reçu des pouvoirs plus importants

7 (electricity) courant m; **nuclear/wind/hydroelectric p.** énergie f nucléaire/éolienne/hydroélectrique; to shut off/turn on the p. couper/mettre le courant

8 Tech (of machine etc) puissance f, (of magnet) force f, Tech etc full p. puissance maximale

9 Math (of a number) puissance f, three to the p. of ten trois (à la) puissance dix

VT (provide with power) (machine) actionner, faire marcher; (propel) propulser; powered by two engines actionné par deux moteurs

VI Fam (move fast) he powered round the bend il avala la courbe à toute allure; she powered into the lead elle accéléra et prit la tête de la course; the rocket powered up into the sky la fusée s'éleva vers le ciel

▶ ▶ **p. amplifier** amplificateur m de puissance; Law **p. of attorney** procuration f; to give sb p. of attorney donner procuration à qn; Aut **p. box** (for airbag) boîtier m d'alimentation; Aut **p. brakes** freins mpl assistés; **p. broker** décideur, -euse politique; **p. cut** coupure f de courant; Br **p. dressing** = façon f de s'habiller qu'adoptent certaines femmes cadres dans le but de projeter une image d'autorité; she goes in for p. dressing elle s'habille pour donner une image imposante; Tech **p. driven** à propulsion mécanique; **p. failure** panne f de courant; **p. line** ligne f à haute tension; **p. lunch** déjeuner m d'affaires entre personnes importantes; Am **p. outage** rupture f de l'alimentation; Elec **p. pack** bloc m d'alimentation électrique; **p. plant** (factory) centrale f électrique; (generator) groupe m électrogène; (engine) groupe moteur; **p. point** prise f de courant; **p. politics** politique f du coup de force; Comput **p. save mode** mode m repos; **p. station** centrale (électrique); Aut **p. steering** direction f assistée; **p. strike** grève f des employés de l'électricité; Aut **p. stroke** temps m explosion ou détente; **p. structure** (system) hiérarchie f, répartition f des pouvoirs; (people with power) = ensemble m des personnes qui détiennent le pouvoir; **p. struggle** lutte f pour le pouvoir; **p. supply** Elec alimentation f (électrique); Comput transformateur m; **p. switch** bouton m marche-arrêt; **p. tool** outil m électrique; Comput **p. unit** dispositif m d'alimentation; **p. user** gros utilisateur, grosse utilisatrice; Comput = personne f qui sait utiliser au mieux les ressources de son ordinateur

▶ **power down** VT SEP mettre hors tension

VI *(of computer, machine)* se mettre hors tension

▸ **power up** VT SEP mettre sous tension

VI *(of computer, machine)* se mettre sous tension, s'allumer

power-assisted [-əsɪstɪd] ADJ *Aut (steering)* assisté

power-down N *Comput* mise *f* hors tension

-powered ['paʊəd] SUFF nuclear-p. à propulsion atomique *ou* nucléaire

powerful ['paʊəfʊl] ADJ **1** puissant; *(blow)* grand; *(argument, incentive)* puissant, de poids; *(language, prose style)* vigoureux, qui a de l'impact; *(music, passage)* puissant, plein de vigueur; *(speaker, actor)* qui a de la présence, qui en impose; **to become more p.** *(of State, ruler)* devenir plus puissant; *(of hurricane etc)* augmenter en puissance; **p. dose** *(of drug)* forte dose; **a p. new novel / film** un nouveau roman/film très puissant *ou* fort; **a p. image** une image chargée de force, une image-choc; **there's a p. smell of cats in here** ça pue les chats ici

2 *Old-fashioned Fam* **a p. lot of …** un tas de …

ADV *esp Am Fam* **I was p. tired** j'étais rudement fatigué

powerfully ['paʊəfʊlɪ] ADV puissamment; *(influenced, affected)* fortement; *(to argue)* vigoureusement; **p. built** *(man)* à forte carrure; **it smells p. of cabbage** ça sent le chou à plein nez

powerhouse ['paʊəhaʊs] N *Elec* centrale *f* électrique; *Fam (person)* personne *f* vigoureuse et dynamique; **she's the p. of the organization** c'est le moteur de l'organisation; **he's a p. of new ideas** il ne tarit pas d'idées nouvelles

powerless ['paʊəlɪs] ADJ impuissant; **in a p. state** dans un état d'impuissance totale; **p. to act** impuissant à agir; **I am p. to help you** je ne peux *ou Fml* puis rien faire pour vous aider

power-on key N *Br Comput* touche *f* d'alimentation

powertrain ['paʊətreɪn] N *Aut* groupe *m* motopropulseur

power-up N *(of computer, machine)* mise *f* sous tension; **on p.** à la mise sous tension

powwow ['paʊwaʊ] N *(of American Indians)* assemblée *f*, *Fam (talk, discussion)* palabre *f*, discussion *f*

VI *(of American Indians)* tenir une assemblée; *Fam (talk)* palabrer; *Fam* **to p. about sth** discuter de qch

pox [pɒks] N *Med Fam* **the p.** la vérole; *Arch* **a p. on …!** maudit soit …!/maudits soient …!

poxy ['pɒksɪ] ADJ *Br Sl (worthless)* merdique; *(unpleasant)* dégueulasse; **he only gave me a p. five pounds for it** il me l'a acheté cinq malheureuses livres

pp¹ [piː'piː] *(abbr per procurationem)* ADV pp **Jane Smith** p.p. Jane Smith

VT **shall I pp it?** est-ce que je signe à votre/sa place?

pp² *(abbr pages)* pp; **see pp 44–47** voir pp 44 à 47

p & p [piːən'piː] N *Br Com (abbr postage and packing)* port *m* et emballage

PPB [piːpiː'biː] N *Acct (abbr planning-programming-budgeting system)* système *m* de planification-programmation-budgétisation, rationalisation *f* des choix budgétaires

PPD [piːpiː'diː] N *Com (abbr prepaid)* port payé par le destinataire

PPE [piːpiː'iː] N *Univ (abbr philosophy, politics and economics)* études *fpl* de philosophie, sciences politiques et économie

ppi [piːpiː'aɪ] N *Comput (abbr pixels per inch)* ppp *mpl*

ppm [piːpiː'em] N *Comput (abbr pages per minute)* ppm

PPP [piːpiː'piː] N **1** *Comput (abbr point-to-point protocol)* protocole *m* PPP, protocole point à point **2** *(abbr public-private partnership)* partenariat *m* public-privé

pps [piːpiː'es] N *(abbr post postscriptum)* pps

PQ [piː'kjuː] N *Can* **1** *abbr* **Province of Quebec 2** *abbr* **Parti québécois**

PR [piː'ɑːr] N **1** *(abbr public relations)* relations *fpl* publiques, RP *fpl*; **we need better PR** il nous faut améliorer nos relations publiques; **a skilful PR man** un homme qui excelle dans les relations publiques **2** *Pol (abbr proportional representation)* RP *f*

▸▸ **PR agency** agence *f* conseil en communication; **PR company** société *f* conseil en communication; **PR consultancy** agence conseil en communication; **PR consultant** conseil *m* en communication

practicability [præktɪkə'bɪlɪtɪ] N faisabilité *f*, *(of road etc)* praticabilité *f*

practicable ['præktɪkəb(ə)l] ADJ **1** *(feasible)* faisable, réalisable; **as far as is p.** autant que possible **2** *(road, ford)* praticable

practical ['præktɪk(ə)l] ADJ **1** *(mind, solution, clothing, appliance)* pratique; *(proposition)* réalisable; **he's very p.** il a l'esprit pratique; **we must be p.** il faut que nous soyons raisonnables; **the p. thing to do would be to …** il serait raisonnable de …; **I know it's a very boring and p. question** je sais que c'est une question très ennuyeuse et pragmatique; **for all p. purposes** en fin de compte; **of no p. use** *or* **value** inutilisable dans la pratique; **p. application** *(of theory etc)* mise *f* en pratique; *(of invention etc)* réalisation *f* (pratique)

2 *(virtual)* **with p. unanimity** d'un consentement presque unanime; **it's a p. certainty** c'est quasiment certain

N *Sch (lesson)* travaux *mpl* dirigés *ou* pratiques; *(examination)* épreuve *f* pratique

▸▸ **p. joke** farce *f*, **p. joker** farceur, -euse; *Sch* **p. work** travaux dirigés *ou* pratiques

practicality [præktɪ'kælɪtɪ] N **1** *(feasibility)* aspect *m* pratique, caractère *m* pratique **2** *(of person)* sens *m ou* esprit *m* pratique **3** **practicalities** *(details)* détails *mpl ou* aspects *mpl* pratiques

practically ['præktɪklɪ] ADV **1** *(based)* sur la pratique; *(useful)* dans la pratique, en pratique; **to be p. minded** avoir un esprit pratique; **p. speaking** en pratique **2** *(almost)* pour ainsi dire, pratiquement; **there has been p. no snow** il n'y a presque *ou* pratiquement pas eu de neige; **p. the whole of the audience** la quasi-totalité de l'auditoire; **we're p. there** nous y sommes presque, nous sommes pratiquement arrivés

practice ['præktɪs] N **1** *(action)* pratique *f*; **to put one's ideas into p.** mettre ses idées en pratique; **in p.** en *ou* dans la pratique

2 *(of profession etc)* exercice *m*; *(of doctor etc)* *(surgery)* cabinet *m*; *(patients)* clientèle *f*, *(of solicitor)* étude *f*, **to be in p.** *(of doctor etc)* exercer; **to set up in** *or* **go into p.** commencer à exercer

3 *(custom)* coutume *f*, usage *m*; *Ind etc* technique *f*, méthodes *fpl*; **to make a p. of doing sth** se faire une habitude *ou* une règle de faire qch; **it's the usual p.** c'est l'usage; **in hospitals it's standard p. to throw needles away** dans les hôpitaux, la règle est de jeter les seringues usagées; **it's good/bad p. to do this** il est conseillé *ou* recommandé/déconseillé de faire cela

4 *(exercise, training)* exercice(s) *m(pl)*; *Sport etc* entraînement *m*; **it takes years of p.** cela demande des années de pratique *ou*

Sport etc d'entraînement; **I don't get much p.** *(at driving, playing sport, music etc)* je ne m'exerce pas souvent; **I need more p.** j'ai besoin de plus de pratique *ou Sport etc* de m'entraîner davantage; **to do 2 hours' a day** s'entraîner *ou* s'exercer deux heures par jour; **to keep in p.** continuer à s'exercer; *Sport* se maintenir en forme; **I have to get back into p.** il faut que je m'y remette; **to get out of p.** perdre l'habitude *ou* la main, se rouiller; **I'm out of p.** je manque de pratique; *Sport* **Schumacher did 3.25 in p.** Schumacher a fait 3 mn. 25 aux essais; **he refuses to do his piano p.** il refuse de travailler son piano; *Prov* **p. makes perfect** c'est en forgeant qu'on devient forgeron

VT & VI *Am* = **practise**

▸▸ *Sport* **p. match** match *m* d'entraînement

practiced, practicing ADJ *Am* = **practised, practising**

practise, *Am* **practice** ['præktɪs] VT **1** *(carry out)* *(witchcraft, self-denial etc)* pratiquer; *(method)* suivre; *(principle etc)* mettre en pratique *ou* en action; **to p. what one preaches** mettre en pratique ce que l'on prêche; **to p. a custom** suivre une coutume

2 *(work at)* *(profession)* pratiquer, exercer; *(medicine)* exercer; *Law* **to p. law** exercer le métier de notaire/d'avocat; **he studied law/ medicine, but never practised** il a étudié le droit/la médecine, mais n'a jamais exercé

3 *(do exercises etc on)* *(the piano, flute etc)* travailler, s'exercer à; *Tennis, Billiards etc (shot)* s'exercer à; **to p. one's backhand** travailler son revers; *Mus* **to p. one's scales** faire des gammes; **to p. one's French** pratiquer son français (**on sb** avec qn)

VI **1** *(of doctor, lawyer)* exercer **2** *(do exercises etc)* s'exercer; *Sport* s'entraîner

practised, *Am* **practiced** ['præktɪst] ADJ *(teacher, nurse, speaker etc)* expérimenté; *(ear, eye)* exercé; *Pej (charm)* étudié, compassé; **with a p. hand** d'une main exercée *ou* habile; **with p. ease** avec une grande aisance; **p. in the arts of seduction/deception** rompu aux arts de la séduction/ tromperie

practising, *Am* **practicing** ['præktɪsɪŋ] ADJ *(doctor, solicitor etc)* en exercice; *(Christian, Catholic)* pratiquant; **a p. homosexual** un homosexuel actif, une homosexuelle active

practitioner [præk'tɪʃənər] N médecin, *Fml* praticien, -ienne; **a skilled p. of acupuncture / osteopathy** un acupuncteur/ostéopathe exercé

praetorian [priː'tɔːrɪən] ADJ

▸▸ *Hist, Fig* **p. guard** garde *f* prétorienne

pragmatic [præg'mætɪk] ADJ pragmatique

pragmatism ['prægmətɪz(ə)m] N pragmatisme *m*

pragmatist ['prægmətɪst] N pragmatiste *mf*

prairie ['preərɪ] N *(North American)* prairie *f*, **the Prairies** les Prairies

▸▸ *Zool* **p. dog** chien *m* de prairie; **p. oyster** *(drink)* = boisson *f* à base d'œuf cru *(remède contre les excès d'alcool)*; *(offal)* = délices *mpl* de brebis; *Zool* **p. wolf** coyote *m*

praise [preɪz] N *(deserved)* éloge(s) *m(pl)*, louange(s) *f(pl)*; *(adulatory or in worship)* louange(s); **in p. of sb/sth** à la louange de qn/qch; **to be full of p. for sb/sth** ne pas tarir d'éloges sur qn/qch; **to sing the praises of sth/sb** chanter *ou* célébrer les louanges de qch/qn; **to sing one's own praises** chanter ses propres louanges, faire son propre éloge; **I have nothing but p. for him** je n'ai rien pour lui que des éloges *ou* louanges; **she deserves special p.** elle mérite tous les éloges *ou* toutes les louanges; **his conduct is beyond all p.** sa conduite est au-dessus de tout éloge; *Arch* **p. be (to God)!** Dieu soit loué!

VT louer, faire l'éloge de; **to p. sb to the skies** porter qn aux nues; **to p. God** louer *ou* glorifier Dieu

praiseworthiness ['preɪzwɜːðɪnɪs] **N** mérite *m*, valeur *f*

praiseworthy ['preɪzwɜːðɪ] **ADJ** digne d'éloges, louable, méritoire; **that was very p. of you** c'est très louable de votre part

praline ['prɑːliːn] **N** *Culin* **1** *(filling)* pralin *m* **2** *(sweet) (almond)* amande *f* pralinée, praline *f*

pram [præm] **N** *Br* landau *m*, voiture *f* d'enfant

prance [prɑːns] **VI 1** *(of horse)* caracoler; **a prancing horse** un cheval fringant **2** *(of person) (to strut)* se pavaner; *(to skip)* avancer en sautillant; **to p. in/out** entrer/sortir en se pavanant/en sautillant; **she pranced in and calmly announced that …** elle est entrée d'un pas léger et a annoncé calmement que …
▸ **prance about** **VI** *(of horse)* caracoler; *(of person)* se pavaner

prang [præŋ] *Br Fam* **N to have a p.** *(in car)* avoir un accrochage
VT *(aeroplane, car)* amocher

prank [præŋk] **N** *(escapade)* frasque *f*, fredaine *f*, *(practical joke)* tour *m*, farce *f*; **to get up to all sorts of pranks** faire les cent coups; **to play pranks on sb** jouer des tours à qn, faire des farces à qn

prankster ['præŋkstər] **N** farceur, -euse

prat [præt] **N** *Br Sl (idiot)* andouille *f*, imbécile *mf*; **I feel like a right p.** j'ai vraiment l'air d'une andouille *ou* d'un imbécile
▸ **prat about, prat around** **VI** *Br Sl (act foolishly)* faire l'idiot; *(waste time)* glander, glandouiller

prate [preɪt] **VI** *Pej (self-importantly)* débiter des niaiseries *ou* des absurdités; *(chatter)* jaser, bavarder

pratfall ['prætfɔːl] **N** *Am* **to do a p.** tomber sur les fesses; *Fig* se planter

prattish ['prætɪʃ] **ADJ** crétin, idiot

prattle ['præt(ə)l] **N** *(of children)* babil *m*, babillage *m*; *(of busybodies)* bavardage *m*, papotage *m*
VI *(talk nonsense) (of child)* babiller; *(of adult)* jacasser; *(converse)* bavarder, papoter (**to** avec); **they never stop prattling to one another about …** ils n'arrêtent pas de bavarder *ou* de papoter ensemble à propos de …

prawn [prɔːn] **N** crevette *f* (rose); *(bigger)* bouquet *m*; **Dublin Bay p.** langoustine *f*; *Austr Fam* **don't come the raw p. with me!** n'essaie pas de m'embobiner!
▸ ▸ **p. cocktail** cocktail *m* de crevettes; **p. crackers** beignets *mpl* de crevettes

pray [preɪ] **VI 1** prier; **to p. to God** prier Dieu; **to p. for sb** prier pour qn; **to p. for** *(peace, person's safety etc)* prier pour; **they're praying for a child** ils prient pour avoir un enfant; **to p. for rain/good weather** prier pour qu'il pleuve/pour qu'il fasse beau; **to p. for sb's soul** prier pour (le repos de) l'âme de qn; **I've been praying for you to say that** j'espérais de tout mon cœur que tu dises cela; *Fam* **he's past praying for** il est perdu
2 *Arch* **p. be seated** veuillez (bien) vous asseoir; *Lit, Iron* **and what, p., would you have me say?** et que voudrais-tu donc que je dise?; *Lit, Iron* **and what, p., would you suggest I do?** et que suggèrerais-tu donc que je fasse?
VT I prayed that they wouldn't hear me j'ai prié pour qu'ils ne m'entendent pas; **I p. we are on time** je prie pour que nous arrivions à l'heure

prayer [preər] **N** prière *f*; **p. for the dead** prière pour les morts; **to say one's prayers**

faire *ou* dire *ou* réciter ses prières; *Sch* **prayers** la prière du matin en commun; *Church of Eng* **Morning/Evening P.** office *m* du matin/du soir; **his p. was granted** sa prière a été exaucée; **they knelt in p.** ils se sont agenouillés pour prier; **his head was bowed in p.** sa tête était inclinée dans une prière; *Fam* **he doesn't have a p.** il n'a aucune chance
▸ ▸ **p. beads** chapelet *m*; **p. book** livre *m* de prières; **p. mat** tapis *m* à prières; **p. meeting** réunion *f* de prière; **p. wheel** moulin *m* à prières

praying ['preɪɪŋ] **ADJ** en prières
N prière(s) *f(pl)*
▸ ▸ *Entom* **p. mantis** mante *f* religieuse

pre- [priː] **PREF** pré-

preach [priːtʃ] **VI** prêcher; **to p. to sb** prêcher qn; *Fig* **to p. to the converted** prêcher un converti; **to p. against sb** prêcher contre qn; *Fig Fam* **he's always preaching at me** il est toujours à me faire la leçon *ou* à me sermonner; **stop preaching!** arrête ton sermon!
VT *(sermon)* prononcer; **to p. a new doctrine** prêcher une doctrine nouvelle; **she preaches austerity and lives in luxury** elle prêche l'austérité mais elle vit dans le luxe

preacher ['priːtʃər] **N** prédicateur *m*; *Am (clergyman)* pasteur *m*; *Fig Pej* prêcheur, -euse; **he's a poor p.** il prêche mal

preachify ['priːtʃɪfaɪ] **VI** *Fam Pej* faire la morale

preaching ['priːtʃɪŋ] **ADJ** prêcheur, -euse
N prédication *f*, *Fig Pej* sermons *mpl*

preachy ['priːtʃɪ] **ADJ** *Fam Pej* prêcheur, -euse, sermonneur, -euse

preamble [priː'æmb(ə)l] **N 1** *Fml (to legal text)* préambule *m*; *(of book)* introduction *f*, préface *f*, *(of treaty)* préliminaires *mpl*; *(to speech)* préambule, entrée *f* en matière **2** *Law (of bill)* exposé *m*

preamplifier [priː'æmplɪfaɪər] **N** préamplificateur *m*

prearrange [priːə'reɪndʒ] **VT** arranger au préalable *ou* d'avance; **at a prearranged signal** sur un signal convenu

prebend ['prebənd] **N** *Rel (stipend)* prébende *f*, *(person)* prébendier *m*

prebendary ['prebənd(ə)rɪ] **N** *Rel* prébendier *m*

prebill [priː'bɪl] **VT** *Acct* préfacturer

prebilling [priː'bɪlɪŋ] **N** *Acct* préfacturation *f*

pre-board **VT** *(unaccompanied children etc)* pré-embarquer

precancerous ['priː'kænsərəs] **ADJ** précancéreux

precarious [prɪ'keərɪəs] **ADJ** précaire; **to make a p. living** gagner sa vie précairement; **a p. life** une vie précaire

precariously [prɪ'keərɪəslɪ] **ADV** précairement; **p. balanced** dans un équilibre précaire

precariousness [prɪ'keərɪəsnɪs] **N** précarité *f*

precast ['priːkɑːst] **ADJ** *(concrete)* prémoulé

precaution [prɪ'kɔːʃən] **N** *(act)* précaution *f*, *(attitude)* prévoyance *f*; **to take precautions** prendre des précautions (**against sth** contre qch); *(use contraceptive)* se protéger; **despite all our precautions** en dépit de toutes les précautions que nous avions prises; **as a p.** par mesure de précaution

precautionary [prɪ'kɔːʃən(ə)rɪ] **ADJ** *(measure)* préventif (**against** contre)

precede [prɪ'siːd] **VT 1** *(in time)* précéder; **the conference was preceded by a reception** une réception a eu lieu avant la conférence; **she preceded me as secretary** elle m'a pré-

cédé au poste de secrétaire **2** *(in space)* précéder, être devant **3** *(take precedence over)* avoir le pas *ou* la préséance sur

precedence ['presɪdəns] **N** *(in rank)* préséance *f*, *(in priority etc)* priorité *f*; **in order of p.** par ordre de préséance; **to have** *or* **take p. over sb** avoir le pas *ou* la préséance sur qn, prendre le pas sur qn; **a duty that takes p. over all others** un devoir qui prime tout; **this job takes p. over everything else** ce travail est à faire en priorité

precedent ['presɪdənt] **N 1** précédent *m*; **to create** *or* **set a p.** créer un précédent; **to break with p.** rompre avec la tradition; **there's no p. for it** il n'y en a pas d'exemple; **according to p.** conformément à la tradition; **without p.** sans précédent **2** *Law* décision *f* judiciaire faisant jurisprudence; **to set p.** faire jurisprudence

preceding [prɪ'siːdɪŋ] **ADJ** précédent; **the p. day** la veille; **in the p. article/chapter** dans l'article/le chapitre ci-avant

precentor [prɪ'sentər] **N** *Rel* maître *m* de chapelle

precept ['priːsept] **N** précepte *m*

pre-check-in **N** préinscription *f*

precinct ['priːsɪŋkt] **N 1** *(enclosed area)* enceinte *f*, enclos *m*; **precincts** *(of cathedral etc)* enceinte, enclos; **(shopping) p.** centre *m* commercial *(fermé à la circulation automobile)* **2** *(boundary)* **within the precincts of** dans l'enceinte de **3** *Am (electoral district)* circonscription *f* électorale; *(police district)* circonscription administrative

preciosity [preʃɪ'ɒsɪtɪ] **N** *Fml* préciosité *f*

precious ['preʃəs] **ADJ** *(metals, stones)*, *Pej (affected)* précieux; **we wasted a lot of p. time** nous avons perdu un temps précieux; **a few p. drops of water** quelques précieuses gouttes d'eau; **that photo is very p. to me** je tiens beaucoup à cette photo; *Fam Iron* **you and your p. project!** toi et ton sacré projet!
N *(term of endearment)* **my p.!** mon trésor!, mon amour!
ADV *Fam* **there are p. few of them** il y en a très peu; **there's p. little chance of that happening** il y a très peu de chances que cela se produise
▸ ▸ **p. stones** *(in raw state)* pierres *fpl* précieuses; *(cut)* pierreries *fpl*, pierres précieuses

precipice ['presɪpɪs] **N** précipice *m*; **to fall over a p.** tomber dans un précipice

precipitance [prɪ'sɪpɪtəns], **precipitancy** [prɪ'sɪpɪtənsɪ] **N** *Fml (suddenness, abruptness)* précipitation *f*, *(haste)* empressement *m*; *(rashness)* irréflexion *f*

precipitant [prɪ'sɪpɪtənt] **ADJ** = **precipitate**[1] **ADJ**
N *Chem* précipitant *m*

precipitate[1] [prɪ'sɪpɪtɪt] **N** *Chem* précipité *m*; **to form a p.** (se) précipiter
ADJ *Fml (sudden, abrupt, hasty)* précipité; **let's not be p.** ne précipitons pas les choses

> Attention: ne pas confondre avec **precipitous.**

precipitate[2] [prɪ'sɪpɪteɪt] **VT 1** *(hasten) (crisis, person's downfall)*, *Chem (solid substance)* précipiter; **to p. a war/an argument** faire éclater une guerre/une dispute; **to p. matters** précipiter *ou* hâter les choses **2** *(throw)* précipiter
VI *Chem* (se) précipiter; *Met* se condenser

precipitately [prɪ'sɪpɪtətlɪ] **ADV** précipitamment

precipitation [prɪsɪpɪ'teɪʃən] **N 1** *Chem* précipitation *f*, *Met* précipitations; *Met* **annual p.** précipitations annuelles **2** *Fml*

m, prix *m ou* prime du change; *St Exch* **to pay a p.** verser *ou* acquitter un premium; **to issue shares at a p.** émettre des actions au-dessus du pair *ou* de leur valeur nominale; **to sell sth at a p.** vendre qch à prime *ou* à bénéfice; **antiques are at a p.** *(are sought after)* les antiquités sont très recherchées; *(sell at high prices)* les antiquités se vendent à prix d'or; **time is at a p.** le temps presse; **her time is at a p.** son temps est précieux; **good translators are at a p.** les bons traducteurs ne courent pas les rues *ou* sont rares; *Fig* **to put** *or* **place a p. on sth** *(of people, government etc)* accorder beaucoup d'importance à qch; *(of circumstances, nature of work etc)* mettre l'accent sur qch
▸▸*Br* **p. bonds** obligations *fpl* à lots; *Am* **p. fuel**, *Am* **p. gasoline**, *Br* **p. grade petrol** supercarburant *m*, *Fam* super *m*; *Com* **p. price** prix de prestige; *Mktg* **p. product** produit *m* de prestige; *Com* **p. rebate** ristourne *f* de prime; *Mktg* **p. selling** vente *f* avec prime; *Mktg* **p. service** service *m* premier

premium-rate ADJ *Tel (call)* vers un numéro surtaxé; *(number)* surtaxé

premolar [priːˈməʊlər] N *Anat* prémolaire *f*
▸▸**p. tooth** (dent *f*) prémolaire

premonition [premǝˈnɪʃǝn, priː-] N *(of misfortune etc)* prémonition *f*, pressentiment *m*; **to have a p.** avoir un pressentiment; **to have a p. of disaster** pressentir un désastre; **to have a p. that …** avoir le pressentiment que …, pressentir que …

premonitory [prɪˈmɒnɪtǝrɪ] ADJ prémonitoire

prenatal [priːˈneɪt(ǝ)l] ADJ prénatal, -als *ou* -aux

prenup [ˈpriːnʌp] N *Fam* contrat *m* de mariage

prenuptial [priːˈnʌpʃǝl] ADJ prénuptial, -aux
▸▸**p. agreement** contrat *m* de mariage

preoccupation [priːɒkjʊˈpeɪʃǝn] N préoccupation *f* (**with** à l'égard de); **to have a p. with sth** être préoccupé par qch

preoccupied [priːˈɒkjʊpaɪd] ADJ préoccupé (**with, by** par); **to be p. with** *or* **by sth** se préoccuper de qch

preoccupy [priːˈɒkjʊpaɪ] VT *(person, the mind)* préoccuper

preordain [priːɔːˈdeɪn] VT *(destine)* prédéterminer; **it was preordained** c'était prédestiné

prep [prep] N *Br Sch Fam (esp in private school) (period)* étude *f* (du soir); *(homework)* devoirs *mpl* (du soir)
VT (**-pp-**) *Am Fam* préparer; *Med* **to p. sb for an operation** préparer qn pour une opération
▸▸**p. period** (heure *f* de) permanence *f*; **p. room** (salle *f* d') étude; **p. school** *(in UK)* école *f* primaire privée *(pour enfants de sept à treize ans, préparant généralement à entrer dans une "public school")* ; *(in US)* = école privée qui prépare à l'enseignement supérieur

prepack [priːˈpæk] VT *Com* préconditionner, préemballer

prepaid [priːˈpeɪd] ADJ prépayé; *Acct* payé *ou* constaté d'avance
▸▸**p. card** carte *f* prépayée; **p. envelope** enveloppe *f* affranchie; **p. income** produit *m* constaté d'avance

preparation [prepǝˈreɪʃǝn] N **1** *(action) (of food, medication etc)* préparation *f*, *(of plane, car etc)* mise *f* en état; **they broke the news to her without any p.** ils lui ont annoncé la nouvelle sans aucune préparation; **p. of accounting entries** précomptabilisation *f*, préimputation *f*; **in p. for the summer holidays** en prévision des vacances d'été

2 preparations *(measures)* préparatifs *mpl*; **preparations for war** préparatifs de guerre; **to make (one's) preparations for sth** prendre ses mesures *ou* ses dispositions en vue de qch, faire des préparatifs en vue de qch; **to make (one's) preparations for a journey** se préparer à *ou* pour un voyage, faire ses préparatifs de voyage

3 *Br Sch (esp in private school) (period)* étude *f* (du soir); *(homework)* devoirs *mpl* (du soir)

4 *(substance) (pharmaceutical etc)* préparation *f*

> When translating the English word **preparation**, note that the French words **préparatifs** and **préparation** are not interchangeable.

preparatory [prɪˈpærǝtǝrɪ] ADJ préparatoire; *(steps, measures)* préalable; **p. to** *(departure, invasion etc)* en préparation pour; **p. to going abroad/resigning** avant d'aller à l'étranger/de démissionner
▸▸**p. school** *(in UK)* école *f* primaire privée *(pour enfants de sept à treize ans, préparant généralement à entrer dans une "public school"); (in US)* = école privée qui prépare à l'enseignement supérieur

prepare [prɪˈpeǝr] VT *(meal etc)* préparer; *(attack etc)* monter, préparer; *(plane, car etc)* mettre en état; **to p. a surprise for sb** préparer *ou* ménager une surprise à qn; **to p. the way for negotiations** préparer la voie pour des négociations; **to p. sb for an exam** préparer qn à un examen; **to p. sb for bad news** préparer qn à recevoir une mauvaise nouvelle; **to p. oneself for sth** se préparer à qch; **their training had prepared them for most eventualities** leur entraînement les avait préparés à presque toutes les éventualités; **prepared from the finest ingredients** préparé avec les meilleurs ingrédients
VI se préparer, s'apprêter (**for sth** à qch; **to do sth** à faire qch); **to p. for departure** faire ses préparatifs de départ; **to p. for an examination** préparer un examen

prepared [prɪˈpeǝd] ADJ **1** *(willing)* **I am (quite) p. to …** je suis prêt *ou* disposé à …; **he was/was not p. to lie** il était/n'était pas disposé à mentir

2 *(ready)* **to be p. for anything** être prêt à tout; **to be p. for bad news** être préparé à recevoir une mauvaise nouvelle; **be p.** *(Scout's motto)* toujours prêt; **I wasn't p. for this reaction** je ne m'attendais pas à cette réaction

3 *(made)* préparé; **to have a p. excuse/explanation** avoir une excuse/explication toute prête; **a well p. dish** un plat bien préparé; **a p. speech** un discours préparé (à l'avance); **p. timber** bois *m* refait

preparedness [prɪˈpeǝrɪdnɪs] N état *m* de préparation; **I am unsure of their p. to deal with such an eventuality** je doute qu'ils soient prêts à faire face à une telle éventualité; *Mil* **to be in a state of p.** être en état d'alerte (préventive)

prepay [priːˈpeɪ] VT *(pt, pp* **prepaid***)* payer *ou* régler d'avance; *(letter etc)* affranchir; **a prepaid envelope** une enveloppe affranchie
▸▸*Tel* **p. package** *(for mobile phone)* coffret *m* avec carte prépayée

prepayment [priːˈpeɪmǝnt] N paiement *m* à l'avance, paiement préalable; *Acct* charge *f* constatée d'avance
▸▸*Acct* **p. and accrued income** compte *m* de régularisation; *Acct* **p. clause** clause *f* de remboursement par anticipation; *Fin* **p. penalty** indemnité *f* de remboursement par anticipation

preponderance [prɪˈpɒndǝrǝns] N prépon-

dérance *f* (**over** sur); **there was a p. of French books on the shelf** il y avait une majorité de livres français sur l'étagère

preponderant [prɪˈpɒndǝrǝnt] ADJ prépondérant; **boys tend to be p.** il tend à y avoir une majorité de garçons

preponderantly [prɪˈpɒndǝrǝntlɪ] ADV à un degré prépondérant; **the guests were p. French** les invités étaient pour la majeure partie français

preponderate [prɪˈpɒndǝreɪt] VI l'emporter (**over** sur)

preposition [prepǝˈzɪʃǝn] N *Gram* préposition *f*

prepositional [prepǝˈzɪʃǝn(ǝ)l] ADJ prépositif

prepositionally [prepǝˈzɪʃǝn(ǝ)lɪ] ADV *(used)* comme préposition

prepossess [priːpǝˈzes] VT *Fml* **1** *(engross)* préoccuper **2** *(influence)* influencer

prepossessing [priːpǝˈzesɪŋ] ADJ *(face)* agréable, avenant; **p. appearance** aspect *m* engageant; *(of person)* air *m* sympathique *ou* avenant; **he's not the most p. of people** ce n'est pas l'homme le plus avenant du monde

preposterous [prɪˈpɒstǝrǝs] ADJ absurde; **that's a p. lie!** c'est complètement absurde!

preposterously [prɪˈpɒstǝrǝslɪ] ADV d'une façon absurde; **it was p. easy** ça a été un jeu d'enfant

preposterousness [prɪˈpɒstǝrǝsnɪs] N absurdité *f*

preppy [prepɪ] *esp Am Fam* ADJ *(look, clothes etc)* ≃ bon chic bon genre, BCBG
N **to be a p.** être *ou* faire très BCBG

pre-press N prépresse *m*

pre-printed form N pré-imprimé *m*, *pl* pré-imprimés

preproduction [priːprǝˈdʌkʃǝn] N *TV etc* préproduction *f*; **the film is in p.** le film est en préproduction

preprogram [priːˈprǝʊgræm] VT *Comput etc* préprogrammer; **humans are preprogrammed to behave in certain ways** les êtres humains sont conditionnés à se comporter d'une certaine façon

preprogrammed [priːˈprǝʊgræmd] ADJ *Comput etc* préprogrammé

prepubescent [priːpjuːˈbesǝnt] ADJ prépubère; *Fig Pej (immature)* puéril

prepublication [priːpʌblɪˈkeɪʃǝn] N prépublication *f*

prepuce [ˈpriːpjuːs] N *Anat* prépuce *m*

prequel [ˈpriːkwǝl] N = film *m* qui reprend des thèmes et des personnages d'un film réalisé plus tôt, mais dont l'action se déroule antérieurement aux événements exposés dans le premier film

Pre-Raphaelite [priːˈræfǝlaɪt] ADJ, N *Art* préraphaélite *m*

prerecord [priːrɪˈkɔːd] VT préenregistrer; *TV, Radio* **prerecorded broadcast** émission *f* en différé; **prerecorded cassette** cassette *f* préenregistrée; **prerecorded telephone message service** audiphone *m*

prerecording [priːrɪˈkɔːdɪŋ] N préenregistrement *m*; *TV, Radio* (émission *f* en) différé *m*

preregistration [priːredʒɪˈstreɪʃǝn] N *Univ* préinscription *f*, *pl* avant-premières

prerelease [priːrɪˈliːs] *Cin* N *(of film)* avant-première *f*, *pl* avant-premières
▸▸**p. publicity** = publicité *f* qui précède la sortie d'un film, d'un livre, d'un disque etc

prerequisite [priːˈrekwɪzɪt] ADJ préalablement nécessaire, indispensable
N condition *f* préalable

prerogative [prɪˈrɒgǝtɪv] N prérogative *f*,

privilège *m*; **the royal p.** la prérogative royale; **to exercise the royal p.** faire acte de souverain

▸▸*Pol* **p. powers** = pouvoir *m* de décision d'un chef d'État ne nécessitant pas l'approbation du pouvoir législatif

Pres *Pol etc abbr* President

presage¹ ['presɪdʒ] **N** *Lit (sign)* présage *m*; *(foreboding)* pressentiment *m*; **to be a p. of sth** présager qch, être le présage de qch

presage² ['presɪdʒ, prɪ'seɪdʒ] **VT** *Lit (catastrophe etc)* présager, faire pressentir

pre-sales service **N** service *m* pré-vente

Presbyterian [prezbɪ'tɪərɪən] **ADJ, N** *Rel* presbytérien, -ienne

Presbyterianism [prezbɪ'tɪərɪənɪz(ə)m] **N** *Rel* presbytérianisme *m*

presbytery ['prezbɪt(ə)rɪ] **N** *Rel* **1** *(in church)* sanctuaire *m* **2** *Cathol (residence)* presbytère *m* **3** *(in Presbyterian Church) (court)* consistoire *m*

preschool [priː'skuːl] **ADJ** *(age etc)* préscolaire

prescience ['presɪəns] **N** *Fml* prescience *f*

prescient ['presɪənt] **ADJ** *Fml* prescient

prescoring [priː'skɔːrɪŋ] **N** *(of sound)* préenregistrement *m*

prescribe [prɪ'skraɪb] **VT 1** prescrire; **prescribed task** tâche *f* imposée; **in the prescribed time** dans le délai prescrit **2** *Med* **to p. sth for sb** prescrire qch à qn

prescription [prɪ'skrɪpʃən] **N 1** *(order)* prescription *f* **2** *Med* ordonnance *f*; **available only on (a doctor's) p.** délivré seulement sur ordonnance; **repeat p.** = ordonnance renouvelable

▸▸**p. charges** frais *mpl* de médicaments *ou* pharmaceutiques; **p. drugs** médicaments *mpl* délivrés uniquement sur ordonnance

prescriptive [prɪ'skrɪptɪv] **ADJ 1** *(prescribing action)* normatif **2** *(established by custom)* consacré par l'usage *ou* par la coutume

prescriptivism [prɪ'skrɪptɪvɪz(ə)m] **N** *Phil* normativisme *m*

preselect [priːsə'lekt] **VT** *(tracks, channels)* prérégler

pre-selector **N** *Aut* présélecteur *m*

▸▸**p. gearbox** boîte *f* à présélection

presence ['prezəns] **N 1** présence *f*; **in the p. of ...** en présence de ...; **say nothing about it in his p.** n'en parlez pas devant lui; *Fml* **to be admitted to the p.** *(to see monarch etc)* être admis en présence; **your p. is requested at ...** vous êtes prié d'assister à ...; **the police maintained a discreet p.** *(at demonstration etc)* la police a assuré une surveillance discrète; **the American military p.** la présence militaire américaine; **to make one's p. felt** se faire remarquer, faire sentir sa présence

2 p. of mind présence *f* d'esprit; **to keep one's p. of mind** garder son sang-froid; **to have the p. of mind to do sth** avoir la présence d'esprit de faire qch

3 *(bearing)* présence *f*, prestance *f*; **to have stage p.** avoir de la présence sur scène; **he has p.** il a de la présence *ou* de la prestance, il en impose

present¹ ['prezənt] **ADJ 1** *(in attendance)* présent; **to be p. at a ceremony** être présent *ou* assister à une cérémonie; **he cannot be interviewed without a lawyer being p.** on ne peut pas l'interroger sans la présence d'un avocat; **all (those) p. heard it** toute l'assistance l'a entendu; **some of you p. here** quelques-uns d'entre vous, ici présents; **minerals which are p. in the solution** minéraux qui sont présents dans la solution; **p. company excepted** à l'exception des personnes ici présentes, bien sûr

2 *(in time)* actuel; *(under discussion)* en question; **the p. king** le roi actuel; **at the p. time** *or* **moment** *(at this very moment)* en ce moment; *(in this period of time)* actuellement, aujourd'hui; **up to the p. time** jusqu'ici; **in the p. case** dans le cas qui nous occupe; **the p. year** l'année *f* courante

▸ **N 1** *(time)*,*Gram* présent *m*; **the p.** le présent; **up to the p.** jusqu'à présent, jusqu'ici; **at p.** *(at this very moment)* en ce moment; *(now)* à présent; *(in this period of time)* actuellement, aujourd'hui; **that's all I can tell you at p.** c'est tout ce que je peux vous dire pour l'instant *ou* pour le moment; **no more at p.** rien de plus pour le moment *ou* pour l'instant; **as things are at p.** *(at the stage things have reached)* au point où en sont les choses; *(nowadays)* par les temps qui courent; **for the p.** pour le moment, pour l'instant

2 *Law* **by these presents** par la présente

▸▸*Gram* **p. perfect** passé *m* composé **VOIR GRAMMAIRE A50; B30** ; *Gram* **p. subjunctive** présent du subjonctif **VOIR GRAMMAIRE A53-4; B32-3** ; *Gram* **p. tense** présent **VOIR GRAMMAIRE A49; B30** ; *Acct* **p. value** valeur *f* actuelle *ou* actualisée

present² **N** *(gift)* cadeau *m*; **to make sb a p. of sth, to give sth to sb as a p.** faire cadeau de qch à qn, donner qch en cadeau à qn; **it's for a p.** *(when buying)* c'est pour offrir

present³ [prɪ'zent] **VT 1** *(introduce, put forward)* présenter; **to p. sb to sb** présenter qn à qn; *Fml* **allow me to p. Miss Lorna Johnston** permettez-moi de vous présenter Miss Lorna Johnston; **to p. sb at court** présenter qn à la cour; *Theat* **to p. a play** *(of company etc)* présenter *ou* donner une pièce; *TV, Radio* **to p. a programme** *(of presenter)* présenter une émission; **to p. oneself at** *or* **for an examination** se présenter à *ou* pour un examen; **a good opportunity presents itself** une bonne occasion se présente (**for doing sth** de faire qch); **to p. sb/sth in a good/bad light** présenter qn/qch sous un jour favorable/défavorable; **his attempts to mount the horse presented a strange spectacle** ses tentatives pour se mettre en selle offraient un curieux spectacle

2 *(give)* *(gift)* donner; *(award, certificate)* remettre; **to p. sth to sb, to p. sb with sth** donner/remettre qch à qn; **the mayor will be presenting the prizes** le maire distribuera les prix; **to p. one's compliments to sb** présenter ses compliments à qn; **they were presented with an empty goalmouth** ils se trouvèrent devant un but vide; **this presented her with no option but to agree** ceci ne lui a pas laissé d'autre alternative que d'accepter; *Mil, Fig* **to p. sb with an easy target** offrir une bonne cible à qn

3 *Com* **to p. a bill for acceptance** présenter une traite à l'acceptation; *Law* **to p. a plea** introduire une instance; *Com* **to p. invoices** présenter des factures

4 *Parl (bill)* présenter, introduire; **to p. a plan to a meeting** soumettre un plan à une assemblée

5 *Mil* **to p. arms** présenter les armes; **arms!** présentez armes!

▸ **VI** *Obst (of foetus)* se présenter; *Med* **to p. with sth** avoir qch, présenter qch

presentable [prɪ'zentəb(ə)l] **ADJ** *(person, thing)* présentable; *(garment)* portable, mettable; **am I p.?** je suis présentable?

presentation [prezən'teɪʃən] **N 1** *(of person, theory, business plan, sales proposal etc)* présentation *f*; *(of play)* présentation, représentation *f*; *(of thesis, dissertation)* soutenance *f*; **to give a p.** faire un exposé; **p. of accounts for audit** reddition *f* de comptes

2 *(giving)* *(of gift, medal etc to somebody)* remise *f*; *(gift)* cadeau *m* *(offert à qn)*; **to make**

a p. to sb remettre un cadeau/une médaille/*etc* à qn

3 *Com* **payable on p. of the coupon** payable contre remise du coupon; **on p. of the invoice** au vu de *ou* sur présentation de la facture; **p. for acceptance** présentation *f* à l'acceptation; **p. for payment** présentation au paiement

4 *Obst (of foetus)* présentation *f*

▸▸**p. ceremony** cérémonie *f* de remise *(d'un prix)*; **p. copy** *(specimen)* spécimen *m* (gratuit); *(from writer)* exemplaire *m* gratuit; *Fin* **p. date** date *f* de présentation; *Comput* **p. graphics** graphiques *mpl* de présentation; *Mktg* **p. pack** paquet *m* de présentation; **p. slides** diapositives *fpl* de présentation; *Comput* **p. software** logiciel *m* de présentation *ou* de préAO

present-day **ADJ ATTRIB** actuel; **p. London/ Brazil** le Londres/Brésil d'aujourd'hui

presenteeism [prezən'tiːɪzm] **N** = fait, pour un employé, de travailler également en dehors des heures de bureau pour se faire bien voir de ses supérieurs

presenter [prɪ'zentər] **N** *Radio, TV etc* présentateur, -trice

presentiment [prɪ'zentɪmənt] **N** *esp Fml* pressentiment *m*; **to have a p. of danger** avoir le pressentiment qu'il y a du danger

presently ['prezəntlɪ] **ADV 1** *(soon)* bientôt; *(in past)* au bout d'un certain temps **2** *esp Am (now)* actuellement, à présent

Note that the French word **présentement** always means **at present**.

presentment [prɪ'zentmənt] **N** *Com (of bill of exchange etc)* présentation *f*

preservation [prezə'veɪʃən] **N 1** *(maintenance)* conservation *f*, préservation *f*; *(of peace, order)* maintien *m*; *(in laboratory) (of a flower, specimen)* naturalisation *f*; *Com (of goods etc)* traitement *m* avant stockage; **in a good state of p.** en bon état de conservation **2** *(protection)* préservation *f* (**from a danger** d'un danger)

▸▸*Br* **p. order** classement *m* (à titre de monument historique); **p. society** = association *f* pour la protection des sites et monuments

preservative [prɪ'zɜːvətɪv] **N** conservateur *m*; *(in foods)* agent *m* de conservation, conservateur, préservateur *m*; **it acts as a p. for the wood** cela conserve le bois

Note that the French word **préservatif** is a false friend and is never a translation for the English word **preservative**. It means **condom**.

preserve [prɪ'zɜːv] **N 1** *(apricot etc)* preserve(s) *(jam)* confiture *f* (d'abricots *etc*); **preserves** *(bottled fruit)* conserves *fpl* **2** *(area)* **(game) p.** réserve *f*, *Fig* **engineering is no longer a male p.** le métier d'ingénieur n'est plus réservé aux hommes; **the kitchen is his p. entirely** la cuisine c'est son domaine à lui

▸ **VT 1** *(maintain) (custom, sense of humour etc)* conserver, préserver; *(peace etc)* maintenir; *(appearance, illusion)* préserver; *(silence etc)* garder, observer **2** *(leather, wood, building etc)* protéger, préserver; *Culin (fruit etc)* conserver, mettre en conserve; *(in laboratory) (plant, animal)* naturaliser **3** *(protect) (person)* préserver (**from sth** de qch); **saints p. us!** grands dieux!

preserved [prɪ'zɜːvd] **ADJ 1** *(fruit)* en conserve; **p. food** conserves *fpl*; *Old-fashioned* **p. meat** conserve *f* de viande **2** **well/badly p.** *(building etc)* en bon/mauvais état de conservation; **well p.** *(person)* bien conservé

preserver [prɪˈzɜːvər] N *(person) (of traditions etc)* conservateur, -trice

preserving [prɪˈzɜːvɪŋ] N = **preservation**
▸▸ *Old-fashioned* p. pan bassine f à confitures

preset [priːˈset] VT *(pt, pp preset; prp presetting)* Tech, Electron *(machine etc)* prérégler
ADJ préréglé; *Comput* présélectionné

preshrink [priːˈʃrɪŋk] VT *(pt preshrank* [-ˈʃræŋk]; *pp preshrunk* [-ˈʃrʌŋk]) *(fabric)* rendre irrétrécissable

preshrunk [priːˈʃrʌŋk] ADJ *(fabric)* irrétrécissable

preside [prɪˈzaɪd] VI présider; **to p. at** *or* **over a meeting** présider une réunion; **the man who presided over the collapse of the company** l'homme qui était président lors de la chute de l'entreprise; **to p. over events** *(direct)* diriger les événements

presidency [ˈprezɪdənsɪ] N présidence f; **to assume the p.** assumer la présidence

president [ˈprezɪdənt] N président m; *(of American company)* président-directeur m général, *pl* présidents-directeurs généraux, P.-D.G. m; **P. Truman** le président Truman; **Mr P.** Monsieur le Président; *EU* **P. of the Commission** président de la Commission; *Am* **P. of the Senate** président du Sénat

president-elect N *Pol* président m élu

presidential [prezɪˈdenʃəl] ADJ présidentiel; **to nurse p. ambitions** *or* **aspirations** aspirer à *ou* ambitionner la présidence
▸▸ p. appointment = poste m à pourvoir sur nomination présidentielle; **p. elections** (élections fpl) présidentielles fpl; **p. hopeful** présidentiable mf

presidium [prɪˈsɪdɪəm, -ˈzɪd-] N *Pol* présidium m

PRESS [pres]

N	pression 1 ▪ presse 2–4
VT	appuyer sur 1 ▪ presser 1, 3, 4 ▪ repasser 3
VI	appuyer 1 ▪ exercer une pression 1

N 1 *(act of pushing) (of something)* pression f; *(crowd)* foule f; *Lit (of battle)* mêlée f; **at the p. of a button, it …** il suffit d'appuyer sur un bouton pour qu'il …; **give it a slight p.** appuyez légèrement là-dessus; **give your trousers a p.** donne un coup de fer à ton pantalon; **to force one's way through the p.** fendre la foule, se frayer un chemin à travers la foule
2 *(device) (for trousers, tennis racquet, coins etc)* presse f; *(for wine, cider, oil)* pressoir m; **hydraulic p.** presse hydraulique
3 *Typ (printing)* p. presse f (d'imprimerie); **to go to p.** être mis sous presse, aller à l'impression; **we go to p. at 5.00** on est mis sous presse à 5.00; *(copy deadline)* on boucle à 5.00; **at the time of going to p.** au moment d'être mis sous presse; **hot** *or* **straight from the p.** tout frais; **ready for p.** prêt à mettre sous presse; **to pass a proof for p.** donner le bon à tirer; **the Conway P.** *(printing firm)* l'Imprimerie f Conway; *(publishing firm)* les Éditions fpl Conway
4 *Journ* **the p.** *(newspapers)* la presse, les journaux mpl; *(journalists)* la presse; **p. freedom, freedom of the p.** la liberté de la presse; **to write for the p.** écrire pour les journaux; **she's a member of the p.** elle a une carte de presse; **to have** *or* **get a good/bad p.** avoir bonne/mauvaise presse; **the story appeared in the p.** on a parlé de cette affaire dans la presse; **they managed to keep her name out of the p.** ils ont réussi à ce que son nom ne paraisse pas dans la presse
5 *(in weightlifting)* développé m

6 *Scot (cupboard)* **(linen** *or* **clothes) p.** armoire f à linge

VT 1 *(push) (something)* appuyer sur; *(squeeze)* presser, serrer; *(into clay, wet cement etc)* enfoncer; *(grapes)* pressurer; *(with feet)* fouler; **he pressed my hand in his** il a serré ma main dans la sienne; **she pressed the child to her** elle a serré l'enfant contre elle; **she pressed her nose against the window** elle a collé son nez à la vitre; **to p. sth home** enfoncer qch; **to p. sth shut** fermer qch en appuyant dessus; **to p. sth flat** aplatir qch; **to p. sth (back) into shape** rendre sa forme à qch; **to p. a lemon** presser un citron; **to p. flowers** presser des fleurs
2 *Tech* mettre sous presse; *(metal)* matricer, estamper; *(record)* matricer, presser; *(holes)* percer; *(paper)* calandrer
3 *(trousers, skirt)* repasser, donner un coup de fer à; *Sewing* **to p. a seam** rabattre une couture
4 *(put pressure on)* **to p. the enemy hard** *or* **closely** serrer l'ennemi de près, talonner l'ennemi; **to p. sb hard** harceler qn; **pressed by one's creditors** harcelé par ses créanciers; **to be pressed for time/money** être à court de temps/d'argent; **to p. sb for an answer/a decision** presser qn pour qu'il réponde/prenne une décision; **to p. sb to do sth** presser qn de faire qch; **if you p. her she'll tell you** si tu insistes, elle te le dira; **if pressed, he would admit …** quand on insistait *ou* le poussait, il admettait …; **to p. sth into service (as sth)** utiliser qch (comme qch)
5 *(persist with sth)* **to p. an analogy/a comparison too far** pousser une analogie/une comparaison trop loin; **to p. (home) one's advantage** profiter de son avantage; **to p. one's attentions on sb** faire des avances à qn; **to p. a claim** insister sur une demande; **to p. a gift on sb** forcer qn à accepter un cadeau; **can I p. another piece of cake on you?** vous mangerez bien une autre part de gâteau?; **to p. a point** insister sur un point; *Law* **to p. charges** porter plainte

VI 1 *(push)* appuyer, exercer une pression; **don't p. too hard** n'appuyez pas trop fort; **the crowd was pressing forward towards the exit** la foule se pressait pour gagner la sortie; **to p. close against sb** se serrer contre qn; **stop pressing!** *(pushing me)* ne poussez pas!
2 *time is pressing* le temps presse; **nothing presses** rien ne presse; **to p. for an answer** insister pour avoir une réponse immédiate; **to p. for an adjournment/the law to be tightened up** exiger un ajournement/que la loi soit renforcée
▸▸ p. advertising publicité f dans la presse; **p. agency** agence f de presse; **p. agent** attaché, -ée de presse; **p. attaché** attaché, -ée de presse; **p. badge** macaron m de presse; **p. baron** magnat m de la presse; **p. box** tribune f de (la) presse; **p. campaign** campagne f de presse; **p. card** carte f de presse *ou* de journaliste; **p. clipping** coupure f de presse *ou* de journal; *Br* **the P. Complaints Commission** = organisme m britannique de contrôle de la presse; **p. conference** conférence f de presse; **p. copy** *(of book)* exemplaire m de service de presse; **p. corps** journalistes mpl; **p. coverage** couverture f médiatique; *Br* **p. cutting** coupure de presse *ou* de journal; **p. day** jour m de tirage; **p. gallery** tribune de (la) presse; *Hist* **p. gang** enrôleurs mpl, racoleurs mpl; **p. handout** communiqué m de presse; **p. insert** encart m presse; **p. kit** dossier m de presse *(distribué aux journalistes)*; **p. lord** magnat de la presse; **p. office** service m de presse; **p. officer** responsable mf des relations avec la presse; **p. pack** dossier de presse; **p. pass** carte f de presse; **p. photogra-**

pher photographe mf de presse; *Typ* **p. proof** tierce f; **p. relations** relations fpl presse; **p. release** communiqué de presse; **p. report** reportage m; **p. reporter** reporter m de la presse écrite; **p. run** tirage m; *Pol* **p. secretary** ≃ porte-parole m inv du gouvernement; **p. stand** tribune de (la) presse; *Br* **p. stud** bouton-pression m, *pl* boutons-pression, pression
▸ **press down** VT SEP appuyer sur; *(with force)* enfoncer
VI **to p. down on sb** peser sur qn
▸ **press on** VI *(walk faster)* presser *ou* forcer le pas; *(travel faster)* se presser, se dépêcher; *(continue journey)* continuer son chemin; *(persevere with activity)* persévérer, ne pas abandonner; *(continue activity)* continuer; **to p. on** *or* **ahead with one's work** poursuivre son travail; **p. on regardless!** allez-y quand même
▸ **press out** VT SEP 1 *(juice etc)* exprimer
2 *Tech (holes)* percer (**out of** dans); *(shapes, parts)* découper (**out of** dans)

press-button ADJ
▸▸ *Tel* p. dialling numérotation f à touches

pressed [prest] ADJ
▸▸ *Old-fashioned* p. beef = bœuf m salé, bouilli et moulé en forme; **p. flowers** fleurs fpl pressées; **p. steel** acier m embouti

press-gang VT *Hist* **to p. sb into the navy/army** enrôler qn de force dans la marine/l'armée; *Fig Fam* **to p. sb into doing sth** forcer la main à qn pour qu'il fasse qch

pressie [ˈprezɪ] N *Br Fam* cadeau m

pressing [ˈpresɪŋ] ADJ *(danger, invitation)* pressant; *(work, matters)* urgent, pressant; *(debt)* criard; **the matter is p.** il y a urgence; **there is a p. need for action** il faut agir vite
N 1 *(act of pressing) (on something)* pression f; *(of grapes)* pressurage m; *(with feet)* foulage m; *(of record, metal)* estampage m, matriçage m; *(of paper)* calandrage m; *(of clothes)* pressing m 2 *(pressed metal piece)* pièce f matricée

pressman, *pl* **pressmen** [ˈpresmən] N *(journalist)* journaliste m, reporter m

pressmark [ˈpresmɑːk] N *(of book in library)* cote f

press-up N *Gym* traction f, *Fam* pompe f; **to do press-ups** faire des tractions *ou Fam* des pompes

pressure [ˈpreʃər] N 1 *(on something, somebody)* pression f; **I felt the slight p. of his hand on my arm** j'ai senti la légère pression de sa main sur mon bras; *Fig* **to bring p. to bear** *or* **to put p. on sb** faire pression sur qn; **to act under p.** agir sous la pression des circonstances; **I can't take all this p.** je ne supporte pas d'être sous une telle pression; **he's been under a lot of p. lately** il est très stressé *ou* vraiment sous pression ces derniers temps; **financial p.** pressions financières; **the p. of business/work/modern life** la pression des affaires/du travail/de la vie moderne; **he pleaded p. of work to excuse his absence** il a excusé son absence en invoquant un excès de travail; **to work at high p.** être débordé; **there's no p., don't come if you don't want to** rien ne t'oblige, si tu ne veux pas venir, ne viens pas
2 *Phys, Tech etc* pression f; *(of fluid, heavy body)* poussée f; *Elec* pression (électrique), tension f, voltage m; *Met* **high/low-p. area** zone f anticyclonique/cyclonique, zone de hautes/basses pressions
VT *(person)* exercer une pression sur; **stop pressuring me!** arrête de me presser comme ça!; **to p. sb to do** *or* **into doing sth** forcer *ou* obliger qn à faire qch, exercer des pressions sur qn pour qu'il/elle fasse qch
▸▸ *Tech* p. chamber réservoir m d'air comprimé; *Culin* **p. cooker** cocotte-minute®

f, pl cocottes-minute, autocuiseur *m*; **p. gauge** jauge *f* de pression, manomètre *m*; **p. group** groupe *m* de pression; *Physiol* **p. point** *(on artery)* point *m* de compression; **p. pump** pompe *f* à pression; *Med* **p. sore** escarre *f*; **p. suit** scaphandre *m* pressurisé; **p. switch** *(for oil pressure)* manocontact *m*

pressure-charged [-tʃɑːdʒd] ADJ *Aut* suralimenté

pressure-cook VT *Culin* (faire) cuire sous pression *ou* à la cocotte-minute®

pressurization [preʃəraɪˈzeɪʃən] N *Tech* pressurisation *f*, mise *f*/maintien *m* sous pression

pressurize [ˈpreʃəraɪz] VT **1** *Tech* pressuriser; *Aviat, Astronaut* **pressurized cabin/suit** cabine *f*/combinaison *f* pressurisée; *Nucl* **pressurized water reactor** réacteur *m* à eau sous pression **2** *(put moral pressure on)(person)* exercer une pression sur; **to p. sb into doing sth** faire pression sur qn pour qu'il/elle fasse qch; **don't p. me** ne me force pas; **a pressurized environment** un environnement stressant

Prestel® [ˈprestel] N *Br TV* ≃ Minitel® *m*

prestidigitation [prestɪdɪdʒɪˈteɪʃən] N *Fml, Hum* prestidigitation *f*

prestidigitator [prestɪˈdɪdʒɪteɪtər] N *Fml, Hum* prestidigitateur, -trice

prestige [presˈtiːʒ] N prestige *m*; **it would mean a loss of p.** ce serait déchoir *ou* déroger; **p. flats** appartements *mpl* de grand standing; **a p. job** un poste prestigieux; **the p. value of the address** le caractère prestigieux de l'adresse, l'adresse prestigieuse; **it has p. value** c'est prestigieux
▸▸*Mktg* **p. advertising** publicité *f* de prestige; **p. goods** produits *mpl* prestigieux; **p. model** modèle *m* de prestige; *Com* **p. price** prix *m* de prestige; *Mktg* **p. product** produit *m* de prestige; *Mktg* **p. promotion** *f* de prestige

prestigious [presˈtɪdʒəs] ADJ prestigieux

presto [ˈprestəʊ] ADJ, ADV, N *Mus* presto *m*
INT hey p.! et le tour est joué!

prestressed [priːˈstrest] ADJ *(concrete)* précontraint

presumably [prɪˈzjuːməblɪ] ADV vraisemblablement; **p. she will come** il est probable qu'elle vienne, elle viendra vraisemblablement; **p. you told him that …** je suppose que vous lui avez dit que …; **have they left? – p.** ils sont partis? – je pense *ou* vraisemblablement

presume [prɪˈzjuːm] VT présumer; **you're presuming rather a lot** tu es bien présomptueux; **to p. sb innocent** présumer qn innocent *ou* que qn est innocent; **he was presumed dead** *(by family etc)* on le croyait mort; *(by authorities)* on a présumé qu'il était mort, on l'a considéré comme décédé; **I p. (that) you've written to him** je suppose que vous lui avez écrit; **I p. so** je suppose que oui; *Fml* **I wouldn't p. to question her decision** je n'aurais pas la présomption de mettre sa décision en question; *Fml* **I wouldn't p. so far as to …** je n'aurais pas la présomption de …
VI *Fml* se montrer présomptueux; **to p. on one's friendship with sb** abuser de l'amitié de qn

presumption [prɪˈzʌmpʃən] N **1** *(assumption)* présomption *f*; **to make a p. that …** présumer que …; **I agreed on the p. that …** j'ai dit que j'étais d'accord parce que je supposais que …; **the p. is that she is dead** on présume qu'elle est morte; *Law* **p. of law** présomption légale; *Law* **p. of fact** présomption de fait **2** *Fml (arrogance)* présomption *f*

presumptive [prɪˈzʌmptɪv] ADJ **heir p.** hé-

ritier *m* présomptif, héritière *f* présomptive
▸▸*Law etc* **p. evidence** (preuve *f* par) présomption *f*

presumptuous [prɪˈzʌmptjʊəs] ADJ présomptueux

presumptuously [prɪˈzʌmptjʊəslɪ] ADV présomptueusement; **she p. assumed that … elle** a eu la présomption de croire que …

presumptuousness [prɪˈzʌmptjʊəsnɪs] N présomption *f*; **her p. in assuming that …** sa présomption à croire que …

presuppose [priːsəˈpəʊz] VT présupposer

presupposition [priːsʌpəˈzɪʃən] N présupposition *f*

pre-tax ADJ avant impôt
▸▸**p. margin** marge *f* avant impôt; **p. profit** bénéfice *m* avant impôt

pretence, *Am* **pretense** [prɪˈtens] N **1** *(feigning)* faux-semblant *m*, *pl* faux-semblants, simulation *f*; **to make a p. of doing sth** faire semblant de faire qch; **under the p. of friendship** sous prétexte d'amitié; **under the p. that …** sous prétexte que …; **under** *or* **on the p. of consulting me** sous prétexte de me consulter; **she makes no p. to photographic skills** elle ne prétend pas avoir des dons de photographe; **he made no p. of his boredom/his scepticism** il n'a pas caché son ennui/son scepticisme; **she made no p. of being interested/of feeling anything for him** elle n'a aucunement feint d'être intéressée/de ressentir quoi que ce soit envers lui
2 *(pretension)* **devoid of all p.** sans aucune prétention

pretend [prɪˈtend] VT **1** *(feign)* feindre, simuler; **to p. ignorance** simuler l'ignorance, faire l'ignorant(ante); **to p. to be ill** faire semblant d'être malade, faire le/la malade; **to p. to do sth** faire semblant *ou* mine de faire qch; **they pretended that nothing had happened** ils ont fait comme si rien ne s'était passé *ou* comme si de rien n'était; **let's p. that we're astronauts** on dirait qu'on était astronautes; **p. you haven't seen him** fais semblant de ne pas l'avoir vu; **I'll p. I didn't hear that last remark** je vais faire comme si je n'avais pas entendu cette dernière remarque; **it's no use pretending (that) I'm still young** ce n'est pas la peine de prétendre que je suis encore jeune; **he pretended he was a doctor** *(in order to deceive)* il s'est fait passer pour médecin; **pretending that he had a lot of work to do, he left early** sous prétexte d'avoir beaucoup de travail à faire, il est parti de bonne heure
2 *(claim)* **she does not p. to be artistic** elle ne prétend pas être artiste
VI **1** *(put on act)* faire semblant, jouer la comédie; **to play at 'let's p.'** jouer à faire semblant; **I can't go on pretending to her like this** je ne peux pas continuer à lui jouer la comédie comme ça; **don't worry, I was only pretending, I still want to do it!** mais non, c'était pour rire, je suis toujours d'accord!; **he appeared interested, but he was just pretending** il s'est montré intéressé mais il faisait semblant *ou* jouait la comédie
2 *Fml (lay claim)* **to p. to sth** prétendre à qch; **I don't p. to great knowledge on the matter/any special expertise** je ne prétends pas savoir grand-chose sur la question/avoir des connaissances particulières; *Arch* **to p. to the throne** prétendre au trône
ADJ *Fam* **it was only p.!** c'était pour rire!; **a p. slap** une claque pour rire; **it's only p. money/a p. gun** ce n'est pas du vrai argent/un vrai pistolet

> Note that the French verb **prétendre** is a false friend and is rarely a translation for the English verb **to pretend**. It means **to claim**.

pretended [prɪˈtendɪd] ADJ *(emotion, interest)* feint, simulé; *(doctor, wealth, ignorance etc)* soi-disant, prétendu

pretender [prɪˈtendər] N **1** *(person who puts on act)* simulateur, -trice **2** *(claimant)* prétendant, -ante (**to** à); *Hist* **the Old P.** le Prétendant; *Hist* **the Young P.** le Jeune Prétendant

pretense [prɪˈtens] N *Am* = **pretence**

pretension [prɪˈtenʃən] N **1** *(claim, esp a false one)* prétention *f* (**to** à); **man of no pretension(s)** homme sans prétentions; **to have pretensions to literary taste** se piquer de littérature; **to have social pretensions** vouloir arriver; **I make no pretensions to being impartial** je ne prétends pas être impartial **2** = **pretentiousness**

pretentious [prɪˈtenʃəs] ADJ prétentieux

pretentiously [prɪˈtenʃəslɪ] ADV prétentieusement

pretentiousness [prɪˈtenʃəsnɪs] N prétention *f*

preterite [ˈpretərɪt] N *Gram* prétérit *m*, passé *m* simple VOIR GRAMMAIRE A39

preternatural [priːtəˈnætʃərəl] ADJ *Lit* hors du commun, exceptionnel

pre-test N pré-test *m*, *pl* pré-tests
VT pré-tester

pre-testing N pré-tests *mpl*

pretext [ˈpriːtekst] N prétexte *m*; **to give sth as a p.** alléguer qch comme prétexte; **he came under** *or* **on the p. of consulting his sister** il est venu sous prétexte de consulter sa sœur

Pretoria [prɪˈtɔːrɪə] N Prétoria

prettify [ˈprɪtɪfaɪ] VT *esp Pej* enjoliver

prettily [ˈprɪtɪlɪ] ADV *(decorated, dressed)* joliment; **to smile p.** faire un/des sourire(s) charmeur(s); **she sang very p.** elle a chanté avec beaucoup de charme

prettiness [ˈprɪtɪnɪs] N *(of woman)* charmes *mpl*; *Pej (of style etc)* mignardise *f*; **the p. of her smile** son joli sourire

pretty [ˈprɪtɪ] ADJ *(woman, child)* joli, mignon; *(thing)* joli; **p. picture/song** joli tableau/jolie chanson; *(with pejorative nuance)* joli petit tableau/jolie petite chanson; **as p. as a picture** joli *ou* mignon comme tout; *usu Pej* **his p.-boy good looks** ses charmes de joli garçon; *Pej* **to make p. speeches** dire des gentillesses; **(it was) not a p. sight** ce n'était pas beau à voir; *Iron* **a p. state of affairs!, a p. mess!** c'est du joli *ou* du propre!; *(that we're in)* nous voilà dans de beaux draps!; *Fam* **that'll cost me a p. penny!** ça va me coûter cher!; *Fam* **to make a p. penny out of sth** tirer une petite fortune de qch; *Fam* **I'm not just a p. face** qu'est-ce que tu crois?, il y en a là-dedans!
ADV **1** *(fairly)* assez, passablement; **I was p. certain that …** j'étais à peu près sûr que …; **I'm p. well** ça ne va pas trop mal; **p. good** *(not bad)* pas mal *ou* mauvais; *(very good)* vraiment bon; **it's p. difficult** c'est plutôt difficile; **p. nearly** *or* **much** *or* **well the same thing** à peu près la même chose **2** *Fam* **to be sitting p.** ne pas avoir à s'en faire
▸ **pretty up** VT SEP enjoliver; **to p. oneself up** se faire beau/belle

pretty-pretty ADJ *Pej (actor)* insipide, sans caractère; *(paintings, style)* gentillet; *(dress)* cucul la praline; **his p. good looks** son charme presque efféminé

pretzel [ˈpretz(ə)l] N *Culin* bretzel *m*

prevail [prɪˈveɪl] VI **1** *(come out strongest)* prévaloir, avoir l'avantage; **let us hope that justice/reason prevails** espérons que la justice/la raison l'emportera; **to p. over** *or* **against sb** prévaloir sur *ou* contre qn, avoir l'avantage *ou* l'emporter sur qn **2 to p. on sb**

to do sth *(persuade)* amener *ou* décider qn à faire qch; **he was prevailed (up)on by his friends to …** il se laissa persuader par ses amis de … **3** *(predominate)* prédominer, régner; *(of theory etc)* prédominer, avoir cours; **the conditions prevailing in France** les conditions qui règnent en France

prevailing [prɪˈveɪlɪŋ] ADJ **1** *(widespread)* (pré)dominant; **the p. opinion** l'opinion la plus répandue **2** *(current)* actuel; **in the then p. moral climate** dans le climat moral qui régnait alors; **the p. cold** le froid qui règne en ce moment; **p. fashions** la mode actuelle; **p. winds** vents *mpl* dominants

prevalence [ˈprevələns] N *(of opinion etc)* prédominance *f*; *Med* prévalence *f*; **p. of bribery** caractère *m* généralisé de la corruption; **p. of typhus** fréquence *f* des cas de typhus

prevalent [ˈprevələnt] ADJ **1** *(widespread)* (pré)dominant; *(opinion)* le plus répandu; **this opinion is p. among teenagers** cette opinion est très répandue parmi les adolescents; **the disease is p. here** la maladie est très répandue ici **2** *(current, prevailing)* *(conditions)* actuel; *(in the past)* de l'époque

prevaricate [prɪˈværɪkeɪt] VI user d'équivoques, tergiverser

prevarication [prɪværɪˈkeɪʃən] N tergiversation *f*

prevaricator [prɪˈværɪkeɪtər] N personne *f* qui tergiverse *ou* qui use d'équivoques

prevent [prɪˈvent] VT *(wedding etc)* empêcher, faire obstacle à; *(accident, misfortune etc)* empêcher, prévenir, parer à; **to p. sb (from) doing sth, to p. sb's doing sth** empêcher qn de faire qch, empêcher que qn ne fasse qch; **to p. a disease from spreading** empêcher une maladie de s'étendre, éviter qu'une maladie ne s'étende; **there is nothing to p. our doing so** il n'y a rien qui nous en empêche; **to be unavoidably prevented from doing sth** être dans l'impossibilité matérielle de faire qch; **I cannot p. him** je ne peux pas l'en empêcher; **to p. any scandal** pour éviter tout scandale; **the police prevented the murderer from being lynched** la police a empêché que l'assassin ne soit lynché

preventable [prɪˈventəb(ə)l] ADJ évitable; **it would have been easily p.** ç'aurait été facile à éviter; **a p. disease** une maladie que l'on peut prévenir

preventative [prɪˈventətɪv] ADJ, N = **preventive**

prevention [prɪˈvenʃən] N prévention *f*; **p. of accidents** prévention des accidents; **p. of disease** prévention de la maladie; **rust / fire / crime p.** protection *f* contre la rouille / les incendies / le crime; **society for the p. of cruelty to children / to animals** société *f* protectrice des enfants / des animaux; *Prov* **p. is better than cure** mieux vaut prévenir que guérir

preventive [prɪˈventɪv] ADJ **p. measures** mesures *fpl* préventives *ou* de précaution N *(measure)* mesure *f* préventive; *(medication)* médicament *m* préventif
▸ ▸ *Br Law* **p. detention** détention *f* préventive; **p. medicine** médecine *f* préventive, prophylaxie *f*

preventively [prɪˈventɪvlɪ] ADV préventivement; **to act p. against sth** prendre des mesures préventives contre qch

preview [ˈpriːvjuː] N *Cin, Theat* avant-première *f*, *pl* avant-premières; *(of art exhibition)* vernissage *m*; *esp Am Cin (advertising film)* bande-annonce *f*, *pl* bandes-annonces; **we got a p. of the latest computers** on a eu un aperçu des derniers ordinateurs

VT *Cin, Theat (of person)* voir en avant-première; *(of cinema)* donner *ou* présenter en avant-première; *TV etc* pré-visionner; *(film)* passer en avant-première
▸ ▸ *Comput* **p. mode** mode *m* de prévisualisation; *TV etc* **p. monitor** écran *m* de preview

previous [ˈpriːvɪəs] ADJ précédent; *(in time)* antérieur **(to** à); *(coming immediately before)* précédent; **they have returned to their p. intransigence** ils sont retournés à leur intransigeance passée; **my p. belief was that …** mon sentiment était auparavant que …; **on a p. occasion** une autre fois; **on the p. occasion we had met** la dernière fois que nous nous étions rencontrés; **the p. day** le jour précédent, la veille; **the p. evening** la veille au soir; **in the days/weeks p. to his departure** pendant les jours/semaines qui ont précédé son départ; **in the programme p. to this one** dans l'émission antérieure à celle-ci; **her p. job** son travail précédent; **tell me about your p. jobs** parlez-moi de vos emplois antérieurs; **in a p. existence** dans une vie antérieure; **have you had any p. experience?** avez-vous de l'expérience dans ce domaine?; **p. engagement** engagement *m* antérieur; **p. convictions** condamnations *fpl* antérieures; *(for motoring offences)* contraventions *fpl* antérieures; *Sl* **you're being a bit p.!** vous êtes trop pressé!, vous allez trop vite!
ADV **p. to my departure** avant mon départ N *Br Sl (previous convictions)* casier *m* judiciaire; **he's got p. for drink-driving** il a déjà été arrêté pour conduite en état d'ivresse

previously [ˈpriːvɪəslɪ] ADV auparavant; **three days p.** trois jours auparavant; **I was going to introduce them, but they'd met p.** j'allais les présenter l'un à l'autre, mais ils s'étaient déjà rencontrés

prewar [priːˈwɔːr] ADJ *(prices etc)* d'avant-guerre; **the p. period/years** l'avant-guerre *m*/les années *fpl* d'avant-guerre

prey [preɪ] N proie *f*; **birds of p.** oiseaux *mpl* de proie, rapaces *mpl*; **beasts of p.** bêtes *fpl* de proie; **to pursue its p.** *(of beast)* poursuivre sa proie; **to be a p. to** être la proie de; *(fear, doubt etc)* être en proie à, être la proie de; **to fall p. to temptation** céder à la tentation
▸ **prey on, prey upon** VT INSEP *(be predator of)* *(something, somebody)* faire sa proie de; *Fig* **something is preying on his mind** il y a quelque chose qui le tourmente *ou* *Fam* le travaille; **to p. on old people** *(of confidence trickster etc)* abuser des personnes âgées; **to p. on sb's fears/insecurity** exploiter les craintes/l'insécurité de qn

prezzie [ˈprezɪ] N *Br Fam* cadeau *m*

PRICE [praɪs] N prix *m*; *(of shares)* cours *m*, cote *f*; *Horseracing* cote; **to rise** *or* **increase** *or* **go up in p.** *(of goods)* augmenter; **what p. is that article?** quel est le prix de cet article?; **petrol has come down** *or* **gone down in p.** le prix de l'essence a baissé; **car prices have fallen** le prix des voitures a chuté; **he charges reasonable prices** il pratique des prix raisonnables; **to quote** *or* **name a p.** faire le prix; **his pictures fetch huge prices** ses tableaux atteignent des sommes phénoménales *ou* se vendent à prix d'or; **what p. can you put on good health?** la santé n'a pas de prix; **to be beyond** *or* **without p.** être (d'un prix) inestimable *ou* hors de prix, ne pas avoir de prix; **you can buy it at a p.** vous pouvez l'acheter en y mettant le prix; **this must be done at any p.** il faut que cela se fasse à tout prix *ou* coûte que coûte; **not at any p.** à aucun prix; **I got a good p. for it** j'en ai eu un bon prix; *Fig* **to pay the p. (for sth)** faire les frais (de qch); *Fig* **the p. paid for progress/fame** la rançon du progrès/de la gloire; *Fig* **to set a high p. on sth** faire grand

cas de qch; **it's too high a p. (to pay)** c'est trop cher; *Fig* c'est trop cher payé; **to put** *or* **set a p. on sb's head** mettre la tête de qn à prix; **she's got a p. on her head** sa tête a été mise à prix; **everyone has their p.** il n'y a pas d'homme qu'on ne puisse acheter; *Horseracing* **long/short p.** forte/faible cote; *Fam* **what p. my chances of being appointed?** quelles sont mes chances d'être nommé?; **what p. glory!** pour ce qu'elle rapporte, la gloire!; **p. inclusive of tax** prix taxe comprise SEE GRAMMAR B59

VT **1** *(indicate cost of)* mettre un prix à; *(decide cost of)* fixer le prix de; **all goods must be clearly priced** le prix des marchandises doit être clairement indiqué; **the book is priced at £10** le livre est vendu (au prix de) dix livres
2 *(of customer)* s'informer du prix de
3 *Com* **to p. competitors out of the market** éliminer la concurrence en pratiquant des prix déloyaux; **to p. oneself out of the market** perdre sa clientèle en demandant des prix inabordables; **we've been priced out of the Japanese market** nous avons perdu le marché japonais à cause de nos prix; **he priced himself out of the job** il n'a pas été embauché parce qu'il a demandé un salaire trop élevé
▸ ▸ **p. agreement** accord *m* sur les prix; *Fin* **p. bid** offre *f* de prix; **p. break** baisse *f* de prix; **p. ceiling** plafond *m* de prix; **p. comparison** comparaison *f* des prix; **p. competitiveness** compétitivité-prix *f*, *pl* compétitivités-prix; **p. control** contrôle *m* des prix; **p. cut** rabais *m*, réduction *f* (des prix), baisse des prix; **p. cutting** baisse de prix; *Mktg* **p. differential** écart *m* de prix; **p. discount** remise *f* sur les prix; **p. discrimination** tarif *m* discriminatoire; *St Exch* **p./earnings ratio** ratio *m* cours-bénéfice; **p. effect** effet *m* de prix; **p. elasticity** élasticité *f* des prix; **p. escalation** flambée *f* des prix; **p. ex-works** prix départ usine; **p. floor** prix plancher; **p. freeze** blocage *m* des prix, gel *m* des prix; **p. hike** hausse *f* de prix; **prices and incomes policy** politique *f* des prix et des salaires; **p. increase** hausse *f* des prix, augmentation *f* des prix; **p. index** indice *m* de prix; **p. indicator** indicateur *m* de prix; *Fin* **p. inflation** inflation *f* des prix; **p. instability** instabilité *f* des prix; *Mktg* **p. label** étiquette *f* de prix; **p. labelling** étiquetage *m* des prix; *Mktg* **p. leader** prix directeur; *Mktg* **p. leadership** commandement *m* des prix; **p. level** niveau *m* de prix; **p. list** tarif, liste *f* des prix; *St Exch* **p. maker** inflation *f* des prix; **p. markup** majoration *f* de prix; *Fin* **p. of money** prix *ou* loyer *m* de l'argent; *Fin* **p. plan** plan *m* prix; *Mktg* **p. point** prix (de référence); *Mktg* **p. policy** politique de prix; *Mktg* **p. positioning** positionnement *m* de prix; *Mktg* **p. promotion** promotion *f*, *Mktg* **p. proposal** proposition *f* de prix; **p. range** gamme *f* *ou* échelle *f* des prix; **what is your p. range?** combien voulez-vous mettre?; **it's not in my p. range** ce n'est pas dans mes prix; **p. reduction** réduction (des prix); **p. regulation** réglementation *f* des prix; *Fin* **p. ring** monopole *m* des prix; *Mktg* **p. scale** barème *m* des prix, échelle des prix; *Mktg* **p. sensitivity** sensibilité *f* aux prix; *Mktg* **p. setting** détermination *f* des prix, fixation *f* des prix; *St Exch* **p. spreads** écarts de cours; *Mktg* **p. stability** stabilité *f* des prix; *Mktg* **p. step** écart de prix; *Fin* **p. structure** structure *f* des prix; **p. support** soutien *m* des prix; *Mktg* **p. survey** enquête *f* sur les prix; **p. tag** *(label)* étiquette de prix; *(value)* prix, valeur *f*; **p. theory** théorie *f* des prix; *Mktg* **p. undercutting** gâchage *m* des prix; **p. war** guerre *f* des prix
▸ **price down** VT SEP *Com* baisser le prix de
▸ **price up** VT SEP *Com* augmenter le prix de

price-conscious ADJ attentif aux prix

priced [praɪst] ADJ **1** high-p. cher, coûteux; **low-p.** bon marché, à bas prix **2** *(marked with price)* marqué d'un prix; **everything in the window is p.** tous les prix des articles qui se trouvent dans la vitrine sont indiqués

price-elastic ADJ *Mktg* au prix élastique

price-fixing N *(by companies, cartel)* alignement m des prix

price-inelastic ADJ *Mktg* au prix stable

priceless ['praɪslɪs] N **1** *(invaluable)* inestimable, qui n'a pas de prix **2** *Fam (funny) (joke, person etc)* impayable

> Attention: ne pas confondre avec **worthless**, qui signifie **sans aucune valeur**.

price-sensitive ADJ sensible au prix

pricey ['praɪsɪ] ADJ *Fam* cher, coûteux

pricing ['praɪsɪŋ] N *(setting price(s))* fixation f du prix (**of sth** de qch); **anticipatory p.** fixation des prix par anticipation

▸▸ **p. policy** politique f de(s) prix; **p. research** recherche f sur les prix

prick [prɪk] N **1** *(of needle etc)* piqûre f; **pricks of conscience** remords mpl (de conscience), scrupules mpl; **to have a p. of conscience** être titillé par sa conscience **2** *Vulg (penis)* bite f, queue f; *(man)* connard m; **stop making such a p. of yourself!** arrête de faire le con!; **to feel like a spare p. (at a wedding)** tenir la chandelle

VT *(make holes in) (sausages, potatoes)* piquer; *(balloon)* crever, percer; *(blister)* crever; **to p. one's finger** se piquer au *ou* le doigt; **the nurse pricked my arm with a needle** l'infirmière m'a piqué le bras avec une aiguille; **his conscience is pricking him** sa conscience l'aiguillonne *ou* le tourmente; **to p. a hole in sth** faire un trou dans qch

VI **his skin was pricking with the heat** sa peau lui picotait à cause de la chaleur

▸▸ *Vulg* **p. teaser** allumeuse f

▸ **prick out** VT SEP *(seedlings)* repiquer

▸ **prick up** VT SEP **to p. up one's ears** *(of animal)* dresser les oreilles; *(of person)* tendre *ou* dresser l'oreille

VI **his ears pricked up** *(of dog)* ses oreilles se sont dressées; *(of person)* il a dressé l'oreille

pricking ['prɪkɪŋ] ADJ piquant; **a p. sensation** un picotement, un fourmillement

N *(piercing)* piquage m; *(sensation) (of skin etc)* picotement m, fourmillement m; **prickings of conscience** remords mpl (de conscience)

▸▸ **p. out** *(of seedlings)* repiquage m

prickle ['prɪk(ə)l] N **1** *(of animal)* piquant m; *(of plant)* épine f, piquant **2** *(sensation) (of skin etc)* picotement m; *Fig (of anticipation, excitement)* fourmillement m

VT piquer, picoter, aiguillonner

VI *(of skin, parts of body)* fourmiller; *Fig* **to p. with indignation** se hérisser

prickling ['prɪklɪŋ] ADJ *(sensation)* de picotement, de fourmillement

N picotement m

prickly ['prɪklɪ] ADJ **1** *(animal)* hérissé de piquants; *(plant)* épineux, piquant; *Fig (reply etc)* sec; *(person)* difficile; *Fig* **he's very p. today** il est très susceptible *ou* irritable aujourd'hui **2** *(sensation)* de picotement, de fourmillement

▸▸ *Med* **p. heat** fièvre f miliaire, miliaire f, suette f miliaire; **p. pear** *(fruit)* figue f de Barbarie; *(tree)* figuier m de Barbarie

pride [praɪd] N **1** *(satisfaction)* fierté f, orgueil m; *(self-esteem)* amour-propre m, pl amours-propres, orgueil; *Pej (vanity)* orgueil, vanité f; **her children were a source of great p. to her** elle était très fière de ses enfants, ses enfants étaient sa grande fierté; **the sin of p.** le péché d'orgueil; **puffed up** or

blown up or **swollen with p.** bouffi d'orgueil; **I have my p.!** j'ai ma fierté!; **to have too much p. to do sth** être trop fier pour faire qch; **to hurt** or **wound sb's p.** blesser l'amour-propre *ou* l'orgueil de qn; **to take (a) p. in sth** être fier de qch; **to take p. in one's work** mettre tout son amour-propre *ou* toute sa fierté dans son travail; **he takes great p. in his daughter's achievements** il est très fier des succès de sa fille; *Prov* **p. comes before a fall** l'arrogance précède la ruine et l'esprit altier la chute

2 *(person, thing)* fierté f; **he is the p. of the family** il fait la fierté de la famille; **the p. of my collection** le clou de ma collection; **the p. of the fleet** l'orgueil m de la flotte; **she's his p. and joy** elle fait toute sa fierté; **that antique table is her p. and joy** elle est très fière de cette table ancienne

3 to have p. of place avoir *ou* tenir la place d'honneur

4 *(of lions)* troupe f

VT **to p. oneself (up)on sth/doing sth** être fier de qch/de faire qch; *Pej* s'enorgueillir *ou* se piquer *ou* se faire gloire de qch/de faire qch; **to p. oneself on one's knowledge of literature** se piquer de littérature

priest [priːst] N prêtre m; **the priests** *(as a body)* le clergé; *Cathol* **parish p.** ≃ curé m; **assistant p.** vicaire m; **to become a p.** devenir prêtre

priestess ['priːstes] N prêtresse f

priesthood ['priːsthʊd] N **1** *(state)* prêtrise f, sacerdoce m; **to enter the p.** entrer dans les ordres, se faire prêtre **2** *(priests)* **the p.** le clergé

priestly ['priːstlɪ] ADJ sacerdotal, -aux, de prêtre; **p. duties** fonctions fpl sacerdotales

prig [prɪg] N **he's a real little p.** il fait toujours le petit saint; **don't be such a p.!** ne sois pas aussi bégueule!

priggish ['prɪgɪʃ] ADJ *(person)* collet monté inv; *(objection, criticism)* pudibond; **she's very p.** elle est très collet monté *ou* très bégueule

priggishness ['prɪgɪʃnɪs] N bégueulerie f, pudibonderie f

prim [prɪm] ADJ **1** *usu Pej (person)* collet monté inv; *(manner)* guindé, compassé; **she's so p. and proper** *(morally)* elle est tellement prude *ou* collet monté; *(in appearance, tidiness etc)* elle est tellement correcte **2** *(garden)* méticuleusement entretenu

prima ['priːmə] ADJ

▸▸ **p. ballerina** danseuse f étoile; **p. donna** *(opera singer)* prima donna f, pl prime donne *ou* prima donna; *Pej (temperamental person)* diva f, *Fig* **he's a real p. donna** il joue à la star

primacy ['praɪməsɪ] N **1** primauté f, prééminence f **2** *Rel* primatie f

primaeval [praɪ'miːv(ə)l] ADJ = **primeval**

prima facie ['praɪmə'feɪʃɪ] ADV de prime abord

ADJ *Law* **p. case** = affaire f qui, d'après les premiers témoignages, paraît bien fondée; *Fig* **this is a p. case of ...** à première vue c'est une affaire de ...; *Law* **p. evidence** commencement m de preuve

primal ['praɪm(ə)l] ADJ **1** *(first)* primitif, originel **2** *(most important) (duty etc)* principal, -aux, fondamental, -aux

▸▸ *Psy* **p. scream** cri m primal

primarily ['praɪmərɪlɪ, praɪ'merɪlɪ] ADV **1** *(principally)* principalement, essentiellement **2** *(originally)* à l'origine, originairement

primary ['praɪmərɪ] ADJ *(original)* primitif, originel; *(first)* premier; *(fundamental, main)* premier, principal, -aux; *Elec, Phys etc (coil,*

current, electron etc) primaire; **the p. meaning of a word** le sens premier d'un mot

N **1** *Astron* planète f principale, grande planète **2** *Elec* bobine f primaire **3** *(colour)* couleur f fondamentale **4** *Orn (feather)* rémige f **5** *Am Pol (election)* (élection f) primaire f; *(assembly)* assemblée f primaire

▸▸ **p. cause** cause f première; *Elec* **p. cell** pile f primaire; **p. colours** couleurs fondamentales; *Mktg* **p. data** informations fpl primaires, données fpl primaires; *Fin* **p. dealer** spécialiste mf en valeurs du Trésor; *Mktg* **p. demand** demande f primaire; *Am St Exch* **p. earnings per share** bénéfices mpl premiers par action; *Sch* **p. education** enseignement m primaire; *Pol* **p. election** *(in US)* (élection) primaire; *Comput* **p. file** fichier m primaire *ou* principal; *Econ* **p. industries** secteur m primaire; *Med* **p. infection** primo-infection f, pl primo-infections; *Med* **p. lesion** lésion f *ou* accident m primaire; *St Exch* **p. market** marché m primaire, marché du neuf; *Astron* **p. planet** planète principale *ou* primaire; *Com* **p. product** matière f première, produit m brut; *Geol* **p. rocks** roches fpl primaires; **p. school** école f primaire; *Gram* **p. tenses** temps mpl primitifs

> ## Primaries
> Les élections primaires américaines (directes ou indirectes selon les États) aboutissent à la sélection des candidats qui seront en lice pour représenter les deux grands partis nationaux à l'élection présidentielle.

primate ['praɪmeɪt] N **1** *Rel* primat m; **the P. of All England** l'archevêque m de Cantorbéry **2** *Zool* primate m

prime¹ [praɪm] ADJ **1** *(most important)* premier, principal, -aux; **of p. importance** d'importance capitale, de (toute) première importance; **p. motive** principal mobile m (**of** de) **2** *(excellent) (wines etc)* excellent, de qualité supérieure, de première qualité; *(example, condition, building land etc)* excellent; **p. quality meat** viande f de premier choix

N **1** *(best time)* **p. of youth** fleur f de la jeunesse; **in the p. of life, in one's p.** à *ou* dans la fleur de l'âge; **to be past one's/its p.** ne plus être de la première jeunesse **2** *Rel* prime f; **to say/sing the p.** dire/chanter prime **3** *Math* nombre m premier

▸▸ *Fin* **p. bill** papier m commercial de premier ordre; *Fin* **p. bond** obligation f de premier ordre; **p. cost** prix m de revient; **p. meridian of Greenwich** méridien m (d')origine de Greenwich; **p. minister** Premier ministre m; **p. ministerial** de/du premier ministre; **p. ministership** poste m de premier ministre; **p. mover** *Phys* force f motrice; *Phil* cause f première; *Fig (person)* instigateur, -trice; *Math* **p. number** nombre premier; *Fin* **p. rate** taux m d'escompte bancaire préférentiel, prime rate m; *TV* **p. time** heures fpl de grande écoute, prime time m

prime² VT **1** *(warhead, pump, gun etc)* amorcer; **to p. oneself for battle/for a fight** se préparer au combat; *Fig* **to p. the pump** donner son appui (dans un premier temps) **2** *(provide with information) (person)* renseigner; **to p. sb for a speech** préparer qn à faire son discours; **the witnesses had all been primed by the police** les dépositions des témoins leur avaient été suggérées par la police; **to be well primed (with alcohol)** être bien imbibé **3** *(prepare) (surface to be painted)* apprêter

primer¹ ['praɪmər] N **1** *(of explosive)* amorce f **2** *(paint)* apprêt m

▸▸ **p. detonator** amorce-détonateur f, pl amorces-détonateurs

primer² N *Old-fashioned (reading book)* premier livre *m* de lecture; *(for mathematics etc) (junior level)* premier livre; *(more advanced)* introduction *f*

prime-time ADJ *TV* diffusé à une heure de grande écoute *ou* de prime time
▸▸ **p. advertising** publicité *f* aux heures de grande écoute *ou* en prime time

primeval [praɪˈmiːv(ə)l] ADJ primitif

priming [ˈpraɪmɪŋ] N **1** *(of pump)* amorçage *m*; *(explosive powder)* amorce *f* **2** *(in painting) (of wood etc)* apprêtage *m*, apprêt *m*; *(paint)* apprêt
▸▸ **p. charge** charge *f* d'amorçage; **p. powder** *(explosive)* amorce

primitive [ˈprɪmɪtɪv] ADJ primitif; *(manners)* grossier, rude; *(understanding)* rudimentaire; **p. language** langue *f* primitive; **the plumbing is very p.** les installations sanitaires sont plutôt rudimentaires
▸ N *Art (painter, picture)* primitif *m*; *(in anthropology)* primitif, -ive; *Math* primitive *f*

primitively [ˈprɪmɪtɪvlɪ] ADV primitivement; *(constructed, equipped)* de manière rudimentaire

primitiveness [ˈprɪmɪtɪvnɪs] N caractère *m* primitif; *(of plumbing, understanding etc)* caractère rudimentaire; *(of manners)* grossièreté *f*, rudesse *f*

primitivism [ˈprɪmɪtɪvɪz(ə)m] N primitivisme *m*

primly [ˈprɪmlɪ] ADV *(to smile, remark)* d'un air collet monté, d'un air guindé; *(to dress, behave)* avec pruderie *ou* pudibonderie, très correctement

primness [ˈprɪmnɪs] N *(of person's behaviour, manner)* pruderie *f*, pudibonderie *f*; *(of person's appearance)* côté *m* très correct, air *m* guindé *ou* compassé; *(of garden)* ordre *m* méticuleux

primogeniture [praɪməʊˈdʒenɪtʃər] N primogéniture *f*; **(right of) p.** droit *m* d'aînesse

primordial [praɪˈmɔːdɪəl] ADJ primordial, -aux, originel

primordially [praɪˈmɔːdɪəlɪ] ADV primordialement, originellement

primp [prɪmp] *Old-fashioned Fam* VI *(dress up)* se mettre sur son trente-et-un; *Pej* s'attifer
▸ VT **to p.** *oneself up* se mettre sur son trente-et-un; *Pej* s'attifer

primrose [ˈprɪmrəʊz] N *(plant)* primevère *f*; *(yellow)* jaune *m* pâle
▸▸ *Fig Lit* **the p. path** le chemin de la facilité; **p. yellow** jaune pâle

primula [ˈprɪmjʊlə] N *(plant)* primula *f*, primevère *f*

Primus® [ˈpraɪməs] N *(stove)* réchaud *m* portatif
▸▸ **P. stove** réchaud portatif

prince [prɪns] N prince *m*; **to live like a p.** vivre comme un prince; **P. Charles** le Prince Charles; *Hist* **the Black P.** le Prince Noir
▸▸ **p. of the blood** prince du sang; **P. Charming** le Prince Charmant; **p. consort** prince consort; *Fig* **the P. of Darkness** le prince des ténèbres; **P. Edward Island** l'île *f* du Prince-Édouard; **p. regent** prince régent; **the P. of Wales** le Prince de Galles

princeling [ˈprɪnslɪŋ] N principicule *m*

princely [ˈprɪnslɪ] ADJ princier; *(gift)* magnifique; **to get a p. salary** être payé princièrement; **a p. sum** une somme princière

princess [prɪnˈses] N princesse *f*; **P. Anne** la Princesse Anne
▸▸ **p. dress** robe *f* princesse; **the p. royal** la princesse royale *(fille aînée du monarque)*; **the P. of Wales** la Princesse de Galles

principal [ˈprɪnsɪp(ə)l] ADJ principal, -aux; **p. events in one's life** événements *mpl* capitaux de la vie

▸ N **1** *(person) (of college)* principal, -ale; *(of school)* directeur, -trice; *Com, Law (in transaction)* mandant, -ante, commettant *m*; *St Exch* donneur, -euse d'ordre; *Law (of crime)* auteur *m*; *Mus* soliste *mf*; *Theat* acteur, -trice qui tient le rôle principal; *Law* **p. and agent** commettant et préposé; **principals in a duel** adversaires *mpl* dans un duel
2 *Fin (of debt)* capital *m*, principal *m*; **p. and interest** principal et intérêts
▸▸ **p. boy** = jeune héros *m* d'une pantomime dont le rôle est traditionnellement joué par une femme; *Gram* **p. clause** (proposition *f*) principale *f*

principality [prɪnsɪˈpælɪtɪ] N principauté *f*

principally [ˈprɪnsɪplɪ] ADV principalement, surtout

principle [ˈprɪnsɪp(ə)l] N **1** *(idea)* principe *m*; **fundamental p.** principe premier *ou* fondamental; **in p.** en principe; **to reach an agreement in p.** parvenir à un accord de principe; **machines that work on the same p.** machines qui fonctionnent sur *ou* d'après le même principe
2 *(moral rule)* principe *m*; **to have high principles** avoir des principes; **man of no principles** homme sans principes; **on p.** par principe; **to do sth on p.** faire qch par principe; **to stick to one's principles** rester fidèle à ses principes; **it's the p. of the thing** c'est une question de principe
3 *Phil (law)* loi *f*; **p. of causality** loi de causalité

principled [ˈprɪnsɪp(ə)ld] ADJ *(behaviour)* dicté par des principes; *(person)* qui a des principes; **to be p.** *(of person)* avoir des principes; **it was very p. of her to refuse** elle a démontré de hauts principes en refusant; *Fam* **he doesn't have a p. bone in his body!** il est complètement dépourvu de principes!

print [prɪnt] N **1** *(imprint)* empreinte *f*; *(of foot)* marque *f*, trace *f*; **thumb p.** empreinte du pouce
2 *(printed matter)* matière *f* imprimée; **to read several pages of p.** lire plusieurs pages de texte; **to appear in p.** *(of writings)* paraître; *(of author)* se faire imprimer; **to see one's name appear in p.** voir son nom apparaître dans un livre/journal/*etc*; **he refused to believe the story until he saw it in p.** il a refusé de croire à l'histoire tant qu'il ne l'a pas vue publiée; **edition in p.** édition en vente (courante); **his unguarded comments got into p.** ses propos irréfléchis ont été publiés ou imprimés; **the newspapers had already gone to p. when the news broke** les journaux étaient déjà sous presse lorsque la nouvelle est tombée; **out of p.** épuisé
3 *(characters)* caractères *mpl*; **large/small p.** gros/petits caractères; **the p. was so small I could barely read it** il était imprimé en caractères si petits que j'avais du mal à le lire; **always read the small p.** *(of contract, guarantee etc)* il faut toujours lire ce qu'il y a d'écrit en petits caractères
4 *(engraving etc)* estampe *f*
5 *Phot* épreuve *f*; *Cin* copie *f*; **to take a p. from a negative** tirer une épreuve d'un cliché; **contact p.** épreuve par contact
6 *(material)* indienne *f*; **(cotton) p.** imprimé *m*

▸ VT **1** *(book etc)* imprimer; *(copies)* tirer; *(newspaper)* imprimer, tirer; **the novel is being printed** le roman est sous presse *ou* en cours d'impression; **1,000 copies of the book have already been printed** on a déjà tiré le livre à 1000 exemplaires; **printed in France** imprimé en France; **the story was printed in all the national newspapers** la nouvelle a été relatée par tous les grands quotidiens; **the papers refused to p. the story** les journaux ont refusé de publier cette histoire

2 *(imprint)* imprimer (**sth on sth** qch sur qch); **incidents that p. themselves on the memory** incidents qui se gravent dans la mémoire
3 *(write) (address, name etc)* écrire en lettres d'imprimerie
4 *Phot* **to p. a negative** tirer une épreuve d'un cliché
5 *Tex (cotton etc)* imprimer

▸ VI **1** *(of printer)* imprimer; *(of document)* s'imprimer; *Phot* **the negative hasn't printed very well** le cliché n'a pas donné un très bon résultat au tirage; **the book is now printing** le livre est à l'impression *ou* est actuellement sous presse
2 *(when writing)* écrire en lettres d'imprimerie; **please p.** *(on form etc)* veuillez écrire en lettres d'imprimerie
▸▸ *Mktg* **p. ad, p. advertisement** publicité *f* presse; *Mktg* **p. advertising** publicité *f* presse; *Comput* **p. buffer** mémoire *f* tampon d'imprimante; *Comput* **p. code** code *m* d'impression; *Comput* **p. drum** tambour *m* d'impression; *Comput* **p. file** fichier *m* d'impression; *Comput* **p. format** format *m* d'impression; *Comput* **p. head** tête *f* d'impression; *Comput* **p. job** *(file)* fichier à imprimer; *Comput* **p. list** liste *f* de fichiers à imprimer; **the p. media** la presse écrite et l'édition; *Comput* **p. menu** menu *m* d'impression; *Comput* **p. option** option *f* d'impression; *Comput* **p. preview** prévisualisation *f*, aperçu *m* avant impression; *Comput* **p. quality** qualité *f* d'impression; *Comput* **p. queue** liste de fichiers à imprimer; *Comput* **p. queuing** mise *f* en attente à l'impression; **p. ribbon** ruban *m* d'impression; **p. room** cabinet *m* d'estampes; **p. run** tirage *m*; *Comput* **p. screen** copie *f* d'écran; **to do a p. screen** imprimer un écran; *Comput* **p. screen key** touche *f* d'impression d'écran; **p. shop** imprimerie *f*; *Comput* **p. speed** vitesse *f* d'impression; **the p. unions** les syndicats *mpl* des typographes; **p. wheel** roue *f* d'impression

▸ **print off** VT SEP **1** *(book)* imprimer; *(copy)* tirer; *(magazine)* tirer, imprimer **2** *Phot* tirer
▸ **print out** VT SEP *Comput* imprimer

printable [ˈprɪntəb(ə)l] ADJ publiable, imprimable

printed [ˈprɪntɪd] ADJ imprimé; **such is the power of the p. word** tel est le pouvoir de l'écrit
▸▸ *Elec* **p. circuit** circuit *m* imprimé; *Elec* **p. circuit board** carte *f* de *ou* à circuits imprimés; *Tex* **p. cotton** coton *m* imprimé; **p. directory** annuaire *m* papier; **p. form** imprimé *m*, formulaire *m*; **p. matter** imprimés; **p. paper rate** *(at post office)* tarif *m* imprimés

printer [ˈprɪntər] N **1** *Typ etc (person)* imprimeur *m*; *(machine)*, *Comput* imprimante *f*; *Tel* téléscripteur *m*; **it's at the p.'s** c'est chez l'imprimeur *ou* à l'impression **2** *Phot (person)* tireur, -euse d'épreuves; *(machine)* tireuse *f*
▸▸ *Comput* **p. buffer** mémoire *f* tampon d'imprimante; *Comput* **p. cable** câble *m* d'imprimante; **p. carriage** chariot *m* d'imprimante; *Comput* **p. code** code *m* d'impression; **p.'s devil** apprenti *m* imprimeur; *Comput* **p. driver** programme *m* de commande d'impression; **p. drum** tambour *m* d'impression; **p. engine** mécanique *f* d'impression; **p.'s error** faute *f* d'impression, coquille *f*; **p. font** fonte *f* imprimante; **p.'s ink** encre *f* d'imprimerie; *Comput* **p. interface** interface *f* imprimante; **p. language** langage *m* d'impression; **p.'s mark** marque *f* d'imprimeur; **p. output** sortie *f* d'imprimante; **p. paper** papier *m* d'impression; *Comput* **p. port** port *m* d'imprimante; **p.'s proofs** épreuves *fpl* d'imprimerie; **p.'s reader** correcteur,

-trice d'épreuves; **p. sharing** partage *m* d'imprimantes; **p. speed** vitesse *f* d'impression; **p. spooler** spouleur *m* d'imprimante, pilote *m* de mise en attente des fichiers à imprimer; **p. spooling** mise *f* en attente des fichiers à imprimer; **p. stand** table *f* d'imprimante

printing ['prɪntɪŋ] N 1 *(action) (of book)* impression *f*, tirage *m*; *(craft)* imprimerie *f*, typographie *f*; *(writing)* écriture *f* en lettres d'imprimerie; **he works in p.** il travaille dans l'imprimerie; **fourth p.** quatrième impression 2 *Phot* tirage *m* 3 *Tex* **cotton p.** impression *f* sur coton
▸▸ **p. error** erreur *f* typographique; **p. ink** encre *f* d'imprimerie; **p. paper** papier *m* d'impression; **p. press** presse *f* (d'imprimerie)

printout ['prɪntaʊt] N *Comput* impression *f*, sortie *f* (sur) imprimante, copie *f*, *(continuous)* listing *m*, listage *m*

print-through paper N *Comput* papier *m* à effet d'empreinte, liasse *f* carbonnée

prior ['praɪər] ADJ précédent, antérieur; **p. to** avant; **p. to his winning/appointment** avant qu'il ne gagne/ne soit nommé; **to have a p. claim** avoir des prétentions antérieures; **p. engagement** engagement *m* antérieur; **I have a p. engagement** je suis déjà pris; **to have p. knowledge of sth** être déjà au courant de qch
N *Rel* prieur *m*

prioress ['praɪəres] N *Rel* prieure *f*

prioritization [praɪɒrɪtaɪ'zeɪʃən] N **the p. of all these jobs** la définition d'un ordre de priorité pour toutes ces tâches; **they opted for a p. of expansion** ils ont décidé de donner la priorité à l'expansion

prioritize [praɪ'ɒrɪtaɪz] VT 1 *(arrange according to priority) (several tasks etc)* donner un ordre de priorité à; **it depends how you p. them** tout dépend de l'ordre de priorité que tu établis; **it was wrongly prioritized** on a mal jugé de son importance 2 *(give priority to) (one task etc)* donner la priorité à
VI *(evaluate priorities)* établir un ordre de priorités

priority [praɪ'ɒrɪtɪ] N priorité *f*; **to give p. to sb/sth** donner la priorité à qn/qch; **to have p.** *(of job etc)* être prioritaire; *(of person when driving)* avoir la priorité; **to have or take p. over sb** avoir la préséance ou la priorité sur qn; **hygiene has a high p.** l'hygiène est tout à fait prioritaire; **our first p. is to buy the tickets** il faut que nous achetions les billets, c'est une priorité absolue; **p.** *(on message)* urgent; **to have one's priorities right/wrong** savoir/ne pas savoir ce qui est important; **p. of claim** priorité *f*
ADJ ATTRIB **to get p. treatment** *(of task)* être exécuté ou fait en priorité
▸▸ **p. booking** réservation *f* prioritaire; **p. holder** prioritaire *mf*; *Law* **p. rights** droits *mpl* de priorité ou de préférence; *St Exch* **p. share** action *f* privilégiée, action de priorité

priory ['praɪərɪ] N *Rel* prieuré *m* *(de couvent)*

prise [praɪz] VT *Br* = **prize²**

prism ['prɪz(ə)m] N prisme *m*
▸▸ **p. binoculars** jumelle(s) *f(pl)* prismatiques ou à prismes

prismatic [prɪz'mætɪk] ADJ *(shape, colour etc)* prismatique
▸▸ **p. binoculars** jumelle(s) *f(pl)* prismatiques ou à prismes

prison ['prɪz(ə)n] N *also Fig* prison *f*; **to send sb to p., to put sb in p.** mettre qn en prison; **to throw sb into p.** jeter qn en prison; **he's been in p.** il a fait de la prison; *Fig* **to escape from the p. of one's marriage** mettre fin à un mariage qui était devenu une prison VOIR GRAMMAIRE A6

▸▸ **p. camp** camp *m* de prisonniers; **p. officer** gardien, -ienne de prison; **p. visitor** visiteur, -euse de prison; **p. yard** cour *f* de prison

prisoner ['prɪz(ə)nər] N 1 *(captive)* prisonnier, -ière; **to take/hold sb p.** faire/retenir qn prisonnier; **to take prisoners** faire des prisonniers; *Fig* **to take no prisoners** être impitoyable; *Fig* **to be a p. of one's past** être prisonnier de son passé 2 *Law* détenu, -ue; *(after sentence)* détenu, -ue, prisonnier, -ière; **p. at the bar** prévenu, -ue; *(for serious crimes)* accusé, -ée
▸▸ **p. of conscience** prisonnier, -ière d'opinion; **p. of war** prisonnier, -ière de guerre; **p. of war camp** camp *m* de prisonniers de guerre

prissy ['prɪsɪ] ADJ *(person) (fussy)* pointilleux, maniaque; *(prudish)* collet monté *inv*, bégueule; *(language)* pudibond

pristine ['prɪstiːn] ADJ *(spotless)* impeccable, sans tache; **in p. condition** comme neuf

prithee ['prɪðɪ] INT *Arch* je te prie

privacy ['praɪvəsɪ, 'prɪ-] N intimité *f*, **the p. of one's home** l'intimité de son foyer; **a desire for p.** un désir d'échapper aux regards indiscrets; **I like my p.** j'aime avoir un peu d'intimité; **to disturb sb's p.** faire intrusion chez qn; **there is no p. here** on n'est jamais seul ici
▸▸ *Can* **P. Commissioner** Commissaire *m* à la protection de la vie privée

PRIVATE ['praɪvɪt] ADJ 1 *(personal)* privé; **can I talk to you about something p.?** puis-je discuter avec vous de quelque chose de personnel?; **can we go somewhere p.?** est-ce que nous pourrions discuter en privé?; **a p. joke** une plaisanterie entre nous/eux/*etc*; **the p. life of an actor** la vie privée d'un acteur; **in one's p. life** dans la vie privée, dans le privé; **p. motives** motifs *mpl* personnels
2 *(secret)* secret, -ète; **to keep a matter p.** tenir une affaire secrète; **she is a very p. person** c'est quelqu'un de très discret ou réservé; **he is very p. about his affairs** il est très réservé ou secret pour ce qui est de ses affaires; **p. and confidential** secret et confidentiel; **to mark a letter p.** marquer sur une lettre 'confidentiel' ou 'personnel'; **you stay out of this! — it's p. between John and me** reste en dehors de tout ça! — ça ne regarde que John et moi; **to be received in p. audience** être reçu en audience particulière
3 *(for personal use)* **p. bathroom** salle *f* de bain particulière; **this is his own p. room** c'est sa pièce à lui; **for my p. use** pour mon usage personnel
4 *(to which public not admitted)* **the funeral will be p.** les obsèques auront lieu dans la plus stricte intimité; **P.** *(on sign)* entrée interdite au public
5 *(not state-run)* privé
N 1 **in p.** *(in private life)* dans la vie privée; *(with close family)* dans l'intimité; *(with friends etc, not in public)* dans le privé; *(confidentially)* en privé; **married in p.** marié dans l'intimité; **to sit in p.** *(of assembly)* se réunir en séance privée; *Law* **to hear a case in p.** juger une affaire à huis clos; **to speak to sb in p.** parler à qn en privé; **in p. she admitted she was worried** en privé elle a admis qu'elle était inquiète; *(to herself)* dans son for intérieur elle a admis qu'elle était inquiète
2 *Mil* simple soldat *m*; **the privates and the NCOs** la troupe et les gradés; **p. Jones!** soldat Jones!
3 *Fam* **privates** *(genitals)* parties *fpl* (génitales)
▸▸ **p. bank** banque *f* privée; *Tel* **p. branch exchange** autocommutateur *m* privé; **p. bus** bus *m* réservé; **p. car** voiture *f* particulière;

p. citizen simple particulier *m*; **p. company** entreprise *f* ou société *f* privée; **p. dance** bal *m* sur invitation; **p. detective** détective *m* privé; **p. education** enseignement *m* privé; **p. enterprise** entreprise *f* privée; *(principle)* libre entreprise; *Fam* **p. eye** *(private detective)* privé *m*; **p. finance initiative** partenariat *m* public-privé; **p. fishing** pêche *f* gardée; **p. function** réception *f* privée; **p. health insurance** assurance *f* maladie privée; **p. house** maison *f* particulière; **p. income** rentes *fpl*; **p. individual** particulier *m*; **p. industry** privé *m*; **p. investigator** détective *m* privé; *Fin* **p. investment** investissement *m* ou placement *m* privé; *Fin* **p. investor** investisseur, -euse privé(e); **p. lessons** cours *mpl* particuliers; *Fin* **p. limited company** société *f* à responsabilité limitée; *Tel* **p. line** ligne *f* privée; **p. means** rentes, fortune *f* personnelle; *Parl* **p. member** = simple député *m*; *Parl* **p. member's bill** = proposition *f* de loi faite par un simple député; **p. nursing home** clinique *f* privée; **p. office** cabinet *m* particulier; **p. ownership** propriété *f* privée; *Fam Euph* **p. parts** parties génitales; **p. party** *(gathering)* réunion *f* privée ou intime; *(group)* groupe *m* de particuliers; **p. patient** = patient *m* d'un médecin dont les consultations ne sont pas prises en charge par les services de santé; *Fin* **p. pension** retraite *f* complémentaire; **they operate a p. pension scheme** ils ont leur propre caisse de retraite; *Theat* **p. performance** représentation *f* privée; *Med* **p. practice** médecine *f* privée ou non conventionnelle; **p. property** propriété privée; **p. road** voie *f* privée; **p. room** *(in hospital)* chambre *f* particulière; **p. sale** vente *f* à l'amiable; **p. school** école *f* privée; *Cin* **p. screening** projection *f* privée, séance *f* privée; **p. secretary** secrétaire *mf* particulier(ière); *Br Pol* = haut fonctionnaire *m* dont le rôle est d'assister un ministre; **p. sector** *(secteur m)* privé *m*; **p. sector salaries** salaires *mpl* du secteur privé; *Cin* **p. showing** projection privée, séance privée; **p. soldier** simple soldat, (soldat de) deuxième classe *m*; *Law* **p. wrong** atteinte *f* aux droits d'un individu

privateer [praɪvə'tɪər] N *Hist (ship)* (bâtiment *m* armé en) corsaire *m*; *(man)* corsaire

private-label brand N *Mktg* marque *f* de distributeur

privately ['praɪvɪtlɪ] ADV 1 *(as/by a private individual) (to act, speak etc)* en simple particulier; *(to sell)* de gré à gré; **to benefit p. from sth** bénéficier personnellement de qch; *(hotel)* familial, -aux; *(not state-owned)* **p. owned** qui appartient à un particulier; du (secteur) privé
2 *(in private)* en privé; **to speak to sb p.** parler à qn en privé ou en particulier
3 *(inwardly) (to think, suspect etc)* intérieurement
4 *(not through state system)* **I had it done p.** *(of treatment at doctor's, dentist's etc)* je l'ai fait faire à mes frais; **she was p. educated** elle a fait sa scolarité dans le privé; **he had them p. educated** il les a mis dans une école privée

privation [praɪ'veɪʃən] N privation *f* (**of** de); **to live in p.** vivre dans la privation, vivre de privations

privatization [praɪvɪtaɪ'zeɪʃən] N privatisation *f*

privatize ['praɪvɪtaɪz] VT privatiser

privet ['prɪvɪt] N *(plant)* troène *m*
▸▸ **p. hedge** haie *f* de troènes

privilege ['prɪvɪlɪdʒ] N 1 *also Comput* privilège *m*; **to grant sb certain privileges** octroyer certains privilèges ou avantages à qn; **to enjoy the p. of doing sth** jouir du privilège ou avoir le privilège de faire qch; **it is**

my p. to introduce ... j'ai le grand honneur *ou* le privilège de vous présenter ...; **it was a p. to have known her** c'est un privilège de l'avoir connue; **I had the p. of knowing him personally** j'ai eu le privilège de le connaître personnellement **2** *Law (of lawyer)* droit *m* de tenir une information secrète; *Parl* immunité *f* parlementaire
VT *(usu passive) (person)* privilégier; **I am privileged to be able to present to you ...** j'ai l'honneur *ou* le privilège de vous présenter ...

privileged ['prɪvɪlɪdʒd] **ADJ** privilégié; **the p. classes** les classes *fpl* privilégiées; **a p. few** quelques privilégiés; **p. information** informations *fpl* confidentielles
NPL the p. les privilégiés *mpl*
▸▸*Fin* **p. debt** dette *f* privilégiée

privily ['prɪvɪlɪ] **ADV** *Arch* en secret

privy ['prɪvɪ] **ADJ** *Fml* **to be p. to sth** *(have knowledge of)* avoir connaissance de qch
N *Old-fashioned (toilet)* cabinets *mpl* (souvent en dehors de la maison)
▸▸**the P. Council** le Conseil privé *(du souverain)*; **the P. Purse** = la cassette du souverain

prize[1] [praɪz] **N 1** *(award)* prix *m*; *(what is at stake, to be won)* enjeu *m*; *Fam* **no prizes for guessing** ce n'est pas difficile à deviner; **to win the p., to carry off the p.** remporter le prix **2** *(in a lottery)* lot *m*; **to win first p.** gagner le gros lot; **the first p. is a week in London** le premier prix est une semaine à Londres **3** *Naut (ship)* prise *f*, capture *f*
ADJ ATTRIB *(example)* excellent, parfait; *(tulips, sheep etc)* primé; **p. bull** taureau *m* primé; *Fam* **he's a p. idiot** c'est un abruti de première; **it's my p. possession** c'est l'objet que je prise au-dessus de tout
VT *(value)* priser; **to p. sth highly** faire grand cas de qch; **her most prized possession** l'objet qu'elle prise au-dessus de tout
▸▸*Fin* **p. bond** obligation *f* à lots, valeur *f* à lots; **p. draw** tombola *f*, loterie *f*; **p. list** liste *f* des gagnants; **p. money** prix *(en argent)*; **the p. money is £5000** le prix se monte à 5000 livres; **what did you do with the p. money?** qu'est-ce que tu as fait avec l'argent de la récompense?; *Boxing* **p. ring** ring *m (pour la boxe professionnelle)*

prize[2] **VT** *Br (force)* **to p. sth up** soulever qch à l'aide d'un levier *etc*; **I managed to p. the plaque off the wall** j'ai réussi à décrocher *ou* détacher la plaque du mur; **to p. a lid open** forcer un couvercle avec un levier *etc*; **they had to p. his hand open to get the key** ils ont dû ouvrir sa main de force pour avoir la clé; **to p. sth out of sb** *(money)* soutirer qch à qn; *(secret, information)* arracher qch à qn; **to p. sth out of sb's grasp** arracher qch à qn

prizefight ['praɪzfaɪt] **N** match *m* de boxe professionnel

prizefighter ['praɪzfaɪtər] **N** boxeur, -euse professionnel(elle)

prizefighting ['praɪzfaɪtɪŋ] **N** boxe *f* professionnelle

prizegiving ['praɪzgɪvɪŋ] **N** distribution *f* des prix
▸▸*Sch* **p. day** jour *m* de la distribution des prix

prizewinner ['praɪzwɪnər] **N** *(in game, lottery etc)* gagnant, -ante (du prix); *Sch, Art etc* lauréat, -ate

prizewinning ['praɪzwɪnɪŋ] **ADJ** *(novel etc)* primé; *(ticket, number)* gagnant

PRO [piːɑːˈrəʊ] **N 1** *(abbr* **public relations officer)** responsable *mf* des relations publiques **2** *Br (abbr* **Public Record Office)** ≃ Archives *fpl* nationales

pro[1] [prəʊ] **N 1** *Sport etc Fam (professional*

person) pro *mf inv*; **to turn p.** passer pro; **she was a real p.** *(actress, singer etc)* c'était une vraie pro **2** *Sl (prostitute)* professionnelle *f*

pro[2] **ADJ, PREP** pour; **he was very p. (the idea)** il était tout à fait pour (cette idée)
NPL the pros and cons le pour et le contre

pro- [prəʊ] **PREF** pro-; **to be p.-hanging/-abortion** être partisan de la pendaison/de l'interruption volontaire de grossesse; **a p.-hanging demonstration** une manifestation en faveur de la pendaison; **to be p.-Europe/American** être pro-européen/pro-américain; **the p.-Yeltsin forces** les forces de Yeltsin

proactive [prəʊˈæktɪv] **ADJ** dynamique, qui prend les devants, plein d'initiative; **you should be more p.** prends plus souvent des initiatives
▸▸*Mktg* **p. marketing** marketing *m* proactif; *Admin* **p. staffing** dotation *f* par anticipation

pro-am **ADJ** *Golf (abbr* **professional-amateur)**
▸▸**p. tournament** = tournoi *m* opposant des équipes composées chacune d'un professionnel et d'un amateur

prob [prɒb] **N** *Fam (abbr* **problem)** problème *m*, blème *m*; *Br* **no probs!** pas de problèmes!

probability [prɒbəˈbɪlɪtɪ] **N** probabilité *f*; **in all p.** selon toute probabilité *ou* vraisemblance; **the p. is that it will get hotter** il est probable qu'il fasse encore plus chaud; **there is a strong p./not much p. that ...** il est fort probable/il n'est guère probable que ...; **there would be little p. of our succeeding** nous aurions peu de chances de réussir; **there is every p. that events will prove him right** selon toute probabilité les événements lui donneront raison; *Math* **calculation of probabilities, calculus of p.** calcul *m* des probabilités; **what is the p. of 10% proving defective?** quelle probabilité y a-t-il que 10% s'avèrent défectueux? **VOIR GRAMMAIRE A58–60; B39**
▸▸**p. laws** lois *fpl* des probabilités; *Mktg* **p. method** *(of sampling)* méthode *f* probabiliste; *Mktg* **p. sample** échantillon *m* probabiliste; *Mktg* **p. sampling** échantillonnage *m* probabiliste

probable ['prɒbəb(ə)l] **ADJ** probable; *(story, excuse)* vraisemblable; **it's p. that he'll come** il est probable qu'il viendra; **p. cause of death** cause *f* probable de la mort
N *(likely candidate, participant)* candidat, -ate/participant, -ante qui a de bonnes chances; *esp Am (probable thing, event)* probabilité *f*; **certainties and probables** certitudes *fpl* et probabilités
▸▸*Math* **p. error** erreur *f* probable

probably ['prɒbəblɪ] **ADV** probablement; **will they come? – p. not** est-ce qu'ils viendront? – probablement pas

probate ['prəʊb(e)ɪt] **N** *Law* **1 (grant of) p.** *(for will)* validation *f*, homologation *f*; **to grant p. (of a will)** homologuer un testament; *Am* **p. court, court of p.** tribunal *m* des successions et des tutelles **2** *(will)* testament *m* revêtu de la formule exécutoire

probation [prəˈbeɪʃən] **N 1** *(trial period)* **(period of) p.** période *f* d'essai; *Rel (of novice)* probation *f*; **to be on p.** faire une période d'essai; *Rel* être en probation **2** *Law* (mise *f* en) liberté *f* surveillée; **he'll probably get p.** on lui accordera probablement la liberté surveillée; **on p.** en liberté surveillée
▸▸**p. officer** ≃ agent *m* de probation; **p. system** régime *m* de la liberté surveillée

probationary [prəˈbeɪʃən(ə)rɪ] **ADJ**
▸▸**p. period** période *f* d'essai; *Rel* probationaire

probationer [prəˈbeɪʃənər] **N 1** *(person on trial period)* stagiaire *mf*, personne *f* (qui

est) à l'essai; *Rel* novice *mf* **2** *Law* délinquant, -ante en liberté surveillée

probe [prəʊb] **N 1** *(instrument)* sonde *f*; *(act)* coup *m* de sonde; **space p.** sonde spatiale **2** *Fam (enquiry)* enquête *f* (into sur)
VT *Med (wound etc)* sonder, explorer; *Fig (person)* sonder; *(the past)* fouiller (dans); *(mystery etc)* approfondir, fouiller
VI to p. into the past fouiller dans le passé; **to p. deeply into the human heart** *(of novelist)* sonder le cœur humain; **if you'd probed more deeply** *(to journalist etc)* si vous aviez fait des recherches plus approfondies; **to p. into people's private lives** fouiller dans la vie des gens; **to p. into the circumstances surrounding the accident** analyser *ou* explorer les circonstances dans lesquelles l'accident s'était produit

probing ['prəʊbɪŋ] **ADJ** *(investigation, enquiry)* approfondi; *(eyes, look)* scrutateur; **she felt the doctor's p. fingers on her arm** elle sentait les doigts du docteur qui sondaient son bras
N *Med (of wound)* sondage *m*, exploration *f*; *(enquiries, questions)* questions *fpl* (into sur); **to do some p.** poser des questions; **I'll do some p. and try to find out why she's so reluctant** je ferai ma petite enquête pour savoir pourquoi elle est si réticente; **no amount of p. will persuade him to reveal the truth** on aura beau insister, rien ne le persuadera à révéler la vérité

probity ['prəʊbɪtɪ] **N** *Fml* probité *f*, honnêteté *f*

problem ['prɒbləm] **N** *Math, Fig* problème *m*; **that's your p.** ça, c'est ton problème; **their p. is that they don't have enough time** leur problème c'est qu'ils n'ont pas assez de temps; **money isn't a p.** l'argent n'est pas un problème; **and I thought I had problems!** moi qui pensais que j'avais des problèmes!; **I can't pay until next week – that's not a p.** je ne pourrai pas payer avant la semaine prochaine – ce n'est pas un problème *ou* pas de problème; *Fam* **I haven't got a car – no p., I'll take you** je n'ai pas de voiture – pas de problème, je t'emmènerai; **social problems** problèmes sociaux; **the housing p.** la crise du logement; **it's a p. to know what to do** il est bien difficile de savoir quoi faire; **he's a p.** c'est un cas *ou* c'est un problème, celui-là; **I don't want to be a p.** je ne veux pas causer *ou* créer de problème(s); **what seems to be the p.?** qu'est-ce qu'il y a?, où est le problème?; **has anyone got a p. with that?** est-ce que quelqu'un a une objection?, est-ce que ça dérange quelqu'un?; *Fam* **what's your p.?** tu as un problème ou quoi?; **to have a drink/drug p.** (trop) boire/se droguer; **to have a weight p.** avoir tendance à prendre du poids; **the LX31 always was a p. car** la LX31 nous/leur/*etc* a toujours posé des problèmes
▸▸**p. area** *(in town)* quartier *m* à problèmes; *(in project)* source *f* de problèmes; **p. child** *(child)* enfant *mf* à problèmes, enfant difficile; *Mktg (company, product)* dilemme *m*; **p. families** familles *fpl* à problèmes; *Br* **p. page** courrier *m* du cœur; **p. recognition** reconnaissance *f* du problème

problematic(al) [prɒblɪˈmætɪk, -ɪk(ə)l] **ADJ** *(question, opinion, result etc)* problématique

problematically [prɒblɪˈmætɪklɪ] **ADV** problématiquement

problem-orient(at)ed **ADJ**
▸▸*Comput* **p. language** langage *m* orienté problème

problem-solving **N** résolution *f* de problèmes
▸▸**p. skills** capacités *fpl* à résoudre les problèmes

pro bono [-'bəʊnəʊ] ADJ *Am Law (legal work)* à titre gratuit; *(lawyer)* exerçant à titre gratuit

proboscis, *pl* **proboscises** [prəʊ'bɒsɪs, -ɪsɪz] N **1** *(of elephant, insect)* trompe *f* **2** *Hum (nose)* appendice *m*
▸ ▸ *Zool* **p. monkey** nasique *m*

procedural [prə'siːdʒər(ə)l] ADJ de procédure; *Law* procédural, -aux
▸ ▸ *Comput* **p. language** langage *m* de procédures

procedure [prə'siːdʒər] N procédure *f*; *Med (for administering treatment etc)* protocole *m*; **the correct p.** la marche à suivre, la bonne procédure; **what's the p. for renewing a passport?** quelle est la marche à suivre pour faire renouveler un passeport?; **p. in case of fire** marche à suivre en cas d'incendie; **rules** *or* **order of p.** règles *fpl* de procédure; *(of assembly)* règlement *m* intérieur; **code of criminal p.** code *m* de procédure pénale

procedure-orient(at)ed ADJ *Comput* orienté procédure
▸ ▸ **p. language** langage *m* procédural

proceed [prə'siːd] VI **1** *esp Fml (walk)* marcher; *(drive)* rouler; **in which direction were you proceeding?** dans quelle direction vous dirigiez-vous?; **to p. to a place** *(go to a place)* aller *ou* se rendre à un endroit; *(go towards a place)* se diriger vers un endroit; **to p. with caution** *(go)* avancer prudemment **2** *(act)* procéder; **how shall we p.?** comment allons-nous procéder?; **how does one p.?** quelle est la marche à suivre?, comment procède-t-on?; **to p. with caution** procéder *ou* agir avec prudence **3** **to p. to do sth** *(begin)* se mettre à faire qch, commencer à faire qch; **you may p. to remove the outer casing** vous pouvez maintenant enlever le carter; **to p. to business** *(at meeting etc)* passer aux affaires; **I will now p. to another matter** je passe maintenant à une autre question **4** *(continue)* se poursuivre, (se) continuer; **to p. (on one's way)** continuer son chemin, poursuivre sa route; **the play proceeded without further interruption** la pièce se poursuivit sans autre interruption; **the project is proceeding well** le projet se déroule bien; **negotiations are now proceeding** des négociations sont en cours; **to pay as the work proceeds** payer au fur et à mesure que l'ouvrage avance; **he immediately proceeded to say the opposite** et le voilà qui se met à dire le contraire; **to p. with sth** poursuivre qch, continuer qch; **before we p. any further** avant d'aller plus loin; **she is proceeding with her complaint** elle maintient sa plainte; **p.!** continuez! **5** *Law* **to p. against sb** poursuivre qn (en justice) **6** *(originate)* **sounds proceeding from a room** bruits qui sortent *ou* proviennent d'une pièce; **the social problems proceeding from lack of education** les problèmes sociaux qui découlent du manque d'éducation **7** *Comput (in dialog box)* continuer

proceeding [prə'siːdɪŋ] N **1** *Fml (way of acting)* manière *f* de procéder, façon *f* d'agir **2** *(event, operation)* opération *f*; **proceedings** *(of assembly)* débats *mpl*; *(of conference)* actes *fpl*; **proceedings were interrupted by …** le déroulement des événements a été interrompu par …; **to co-ordinate proceedings** coordonner les opérations; *Admin* **the entire proceedings were disgraceful** toute l'affaire a été menée d'une façon indigne; *Admin* **to conduct the proceedings** diriger les débats; *Admin* **the proceedings were orderly** la réunion s'est déroulée dans le calme **3** *Law (legal)* **proceedings** procès *m*, pour-

suites *fpl* judiciaires *ou* en justice; **to take** *or* **institute proceedings against sb** intenter une action contre qn, intenter un procès à qn, poursuivre qn en justice; **to order proceedings to be taken against sb** instrumenter contre qn

proceeds ['prəʊsiːdz] NPL *(from sale etc)* produit *m*, montant *m*; *(of charity)* bénéfices *mpl*; **all the p. of the album will go to charity** tous les bénéfices faits grâce à cet album iront à des œuvres de bienfaisance

process[1] ['prəʊses] N **1** processus *m*; **it's a slow p.** c'est un processus lent; *(persuading sb, adopting new system etc)* ça va prendre longtemps; **by a p. of elimination/of trial and error** en procédant par élimination/par tâtonnements *ou* approximations successives; **to be in the p. of doing sth** être en train de faire qch; **he lost most of his friends in the p.** il a perdu presque tous ses amis en faisant cela; **but you ruined the carpet in the p.** mais tu as abîmé la moquette par la même occasion; **during the p. of dismantling** au cours du démontage; **the work is in p.** le travail est en cours; **the building is in the p. of construction/of being repaired** le bâtiment est en cours de construction/de réparation; **the peace p.** le processus de paix **2** *Tech (industrial)* procédé *m*; *(chemical)* réaction *f*; *Typ, Phot* procédés photoméca-niques; *Comput* procédé, opération *f*, traitement *m*; *Metal* **Bessemer p.** procédé Bessemer **3** *Law* procès *m*, action *f* en justice; *(summons)* sommation *f* de comparaître; **by due p. of law** par voies légales

VT **1** *Ind (raw material, product)* traiter, transformer; *(food)* préparer *ou* confectionner industriellement; *(mail)* acheminer; *Comput (information)* traiter; *Admin (documents, job applications)* traiter; **to p. an order** donner suite à une commande, traiter une commande; **your request is being processed** votre demande est en cours de traitement; **processed cheese** fromage *m* fondu *ou* à tartiner; *(in slices)* fromage en tranches; **processed food** aliment(s) *m(pl)* conditionné(s); *(precooked)* plat(s) *m(pl)* cuisiné(s) industriellement **2** *Law (person)* intenter un procès à, pour-suivre (en justice) **3** *Phot* développer
▸ ▸ *Phot* **p. camera** tireuse *f* optique; *Comput, Typ* **p. colours** impression *f* en quadrichromie; **p. engineering** ingénierie *f* de procédés; **p. printing** impression en couleurs

> Note that the French noun **procès** is a false friend. It only means **trial**.

process[2] [prə'ses] VI *(walk in line)* défiler (en cortège); *Rel* défiler en procession

processing ['prəʊsesɪŋ] N *(of raw material, product)* traitement *m*, transformation *f*; *(of food)* confection *f ou* préparation *f* industrielle; *Comput (of data)* traitement; *Phot (of film)* développement *m*, traitement; *Admin (of application)* traitement; **p. of mail** acheminement *m* du courrier
▸ ▸ **p. industry** industrie *f* de transformation; *Comput* **p. language** langage *m* de traitement; **p. plant** *(for sewage, nuclear waste etc)* usine *f* de traitement; *Comput* **p. power** puissance *f* de traitement; *Comput* **p. speed** vitesse *f* de traitement; *Comput* **p. time** temps *m* de traitement; *Comput* **p. unit** unité *f* de traitement

procession [prə'seʃən] N *(of people)* cortège *m*, défilé *m*; *(of cars)* file *f*; *(religious)* procession *f*; **to go** *or* **walk in p.** aller en cortège *ou* en procession, défiler; *Fig* **a p. of**

people came through his office throughout the day les gens n'ont pas arrêté de défiler dans son bureau de toute la journée

processional [prə'seʃən(ə)l] ADJ processionnel
N *Rel (book)* processionnal *m*; *(hymn)* hymne *m* processionnel

processor ['prəʊsesər] N *Comput* processeur *m*
▸ ▸ **p. speed** vitesse *f* du processeur

process-server N *Law* huissier *m* (qui dresse des exploits)

pro-choice ADJ *(pro-abortion)* en faveur du droit à l'avortement

proclaim [prə'kleɪm] VT **1** *(declare) (one's innocence, guilt, despair etc)* proclamer; *(one's love)* déclarer; **to p. that one is innocent** proclamer que l'on est innocent; **to p. sb king** proclamer qn roi; **to have sth proclaimed through the town** faire annoncer *ou* faire crier qch par la ville; **to p. a state of emergency/one's independence** déclarer l'état d'urgence/son indépendance **2** *Fig (show) (one's guilt, anger, joy)* révéler

proclamation [prɒklə'meɪʃən] N proclamation *f*, déclaration *f* (publique); *(of banns etc)* publication *f*; **to make** *or* **issue a p.** faire une proclamation

proclivity [prə'klɪvɪtɪ] N *esp Fml* penchant *m* (**for sth** pour *ou* à qch)

proconsul [prəʊ'kɒnsəl] N *Hist* proconsul *m*

procrastinate [prəʊ'kræstɪneɪt] VI remettre les choses au lendemain; **stop procrastinating** arrêtez de remettre les choses au lendemain

procrastination [prəʊkræstɪ'neɪʃən] N **I've had enough p.** j'en ai assez qu'on remette toujours tout au lendemain; **there's too much p.** on a trop tendance à remettre les choses au lendemain; *Prov* **p. is the thief of time** il ne faut pas remettre au lendemain ce que l'on peut faire le jour même

procrastinator [prəʊ'kræstɪneɪtər] N **she's a terrible p.** il faut toujours qu'elle remette les choses au lendemain

procreate ['prəʊkrɪeɪt] VI procréer

procreation [prəʊkrɪ'eɪʃən] N procréation *f*

proctor ['prɒktər] N **1** *Univ (at Oxford, Cambridge)* membre *m* exécutif du conseil de discipline; *Am (invigilator)* = personne *f* chargée de surveiller un/des examen(s) **2** *Law* avoué *m* *(devant une cour ecclésiastique)*; **Queen's/King's p.** procureur *m* de la reine/du roi **3** *Rel* procureur *m*
VT & VI *Am Univ (invigilate)* surveiller

procurable [prə'kjʊərəb(ə)l] ADJ que l'on peut se procurer; **they're easily p.** on peut se les procurer facilement; **it is no longer p.** on ne peut plus s'en procurer

procuration [prɒkjʊ'reɪʃən] N *Law* procuration *f*; **letters of p.** procuration, mandat *m*

procurator ['prɒkjʊreɪtər] N *Law* fondé, -ée de pouvoir(s)
▸ ▸ **p. fiscal** = en Écosse, magistrat *m* qui fait office de procureur et qui remplit les fonctions du 'coroner' en Angleterre

procure [prə'kjʊər] VT **1** *(obtain)* obtenir, procurer; **to p. sth for sb** procurer qch à qn; **to p. sth (for oneself)** se procurer qch **2** *(for prostitution) (woman)* offrir les services de
VI faire du proxénétisme

procurement [prə'kjʊərmənt] N *Fml* acquisition *f* (**of** de); *Ind* achat *m*; *(department)* service *m* des achats
▸ ▸ **p. department** service des achats; *Mil* **p. officer** agent *m* des achats

procurer [prə'kjʊərər] N *Fml* **1** *(of prostitutes)* proxénète *mf* **2** *(one who obtains)* personne *f* chargée des acquisitions

procuress [prəˈkjʊərɪs] N *Lit* entremetteuse *f*

procuring [prəˈkʊərɪŋ] N **1** *(for prostitution)* proxénétisme *m* **2** *(of supplies)* acquisition *f*, *Ind* achat *m*

Prod [prɒd] N *esp Ir, Scot Offensive Sl* protestant, -ante

prod [prɒd] N **1** *(act)* coup *m (donné du bout du doigt etc)*; **to give sb a p.** pousser qn (du doigt/avec un baton/*etc*); **she gave him an encouraging p. with her elbow** elle l'a poussé du coude pour l'encourager; *Fig Fam* **give him a p.** aiguillonnez-le un peu; *Fig Fam* **he needs an occasional p.** il a besoin qu'on le pousse de temps en temps; **thanks for the p.** *(reminder)* merci de me l'avoir rappelé **2** *(object)* aiguillon *m*

VT (**-dd-**) **1 to p. sb/sth** pousser qn/qch (**with sth** du bout de qch) **2** *Fig Fam (person)* aiguillonner, pousser (**into doing sth** à faire qch); **they were finally prodded into action by the news** cette nouvelle les a finalement poussés *ou* incités à entrer en action; **he needs a lot of prodding** il faut toujours le pousser

VI **to p. at** = prod VT **1**

prodigal [ˈprɒdɪɡ(ə)l] ADJ prodigue; *Fml* **to be p. with** *or* **of sth** être prodigue de qch N prodigue *mf*
▸▸ *Bible* **the P. Son** l'enfant *m* prodigue

prodigality [prɒdɪˈɡælɪtɪ] N prodigalité *f*

prodigally [ˈprɒdɪɡ(ə)lɪ] ADV *(to spend etc)* avec prodigalité

prodigious [prəˈdɪdʒəs] ADJ prodigieux

prodigiously [prəˈdɪdʒəslɪ] ADV prodigieusement; *(to eat, drink)* énormément

prodigy [ˈprɒdɪdʒɪ] N prodige *m*, merveille *f*, **child** *or* **infant p.** enfant *mf* prodige

produce[1] [ˈprɒdjuːs] N *(no pl) Agr (products)* produits *mpl*, denrées *fpl*; **p. of Spain** *(on packaging)* produit d'origine espagnole; **agricultural/dairy p.** produits agricoles/laitiers

PRODUCE[2] [prəˈdjuːs]

produire **1–5**	▪ fabriquer **1**
▪ rapporter **2**	▪ présenter **3**
▪ fournir **3**	▪ provoquer **4**

VT **1** *(manufacture, make)* produire, fabriquer; *(cheese, sausages)* faire; *(wine)* produire; *(sound)* émettre
2 *(yield) (profit)* rapporter; *(milk, apples, steam etc)* produire; *Phys (energy)* produire, générer; *Elec (spark)* faire jaillir
3 *(present) (one's ticket, passport)* présenter, montrer; *(reasons)* fournir, donner; *(objection)* émettre; *Law (documents, alibi)* produire, fournir; *(witness)* faire comparaître; **she produced a ten-pound note/a gun** elle a sorti un billet de dix livres/un revolver
4 *(create)* créer; *(children)* faire; *(reaction)* produire, provoquer, entraîner; *(denial)* entraîner, provoquer; *(anger, despair, uncertainty)* susciter, provoquer, donner lieu à; *(interest)* susciter; *(effect)* provoquer; **to p. a vacuum** produire *ou* faire le vide; **to p. a sensation** *(of book etc)* faire sensation; **the drug produces a sensation of well-being** cette drogue procure une sensation de bien-être; **this writer has produced about thirty novels** cet auteur a écrit *ou* produit une trentaine de romans; **the publishers produced a special edition** les éditeurs ont publié *ou* sorti une édition spéciale
5 *Theat (play) (of person) (organize generally)* produire; *Br (direct)* mettre en scène; *(of company)* produire, représenter; *Cin, Radio, TV (film, radio or TV programme, record)* produire; *Theat* **a badly produced play** une pièce mal montée

producer [prəˈdjuːsər] N **1** *Agr, Ind* producteur, -trice; *(of manufactured goods)* producteur, -trice, fabricant, -ante (**of** de); **the company/country is an important p. of coffee** *or* **coffee p.** cette entreprise/ce pays est un important producteur de café **2** *Theat* producteur, -trice; *Br (director)* metteur *m* en scène; *Cin, Radio, TV* producteur, -trice
▸▸ **p. goods** biens *mpl* de production; *Econ* **p. price index** indice *m* des prix à la production

-producing [prəˈdjuːsɪŋ] SUFF **coffee**/**oil-p.** producteur, -trice de café/de pétrole; **oil-p. country** pays producteur de pétrole

product [ˈprɒdʌkt] N **1** *(result), Com* produit *m*; **the p. of ten years' work** le produit de dix années de travail; **the disaster was the p. of bad planning** ce désastre était le résultat d'une mauvaise organisation; **she was a p. of her age** c'était un pur produit de son époque **2** *Math* produit *m*
▸▸ **p. advertising** publicité *f* de produit; **p. analysis** analyse *f* de produit; **p. attribute** attribut *m* du produit; **p. augmentation** amélioration *f* du produit; **p. awareness** notoriété *f* du produit, mémorisation *f* du produit; **p. awareness advertising** publicité de sensibilisation au produit; **p. awareness level** degré *m* de mémorisation d'un produit; **p. budget** budget *m* de production; **p. bundling** groupage *m* de produits; **p. bundling pricing** fixation *f* des prix par lot; **p. category** catégorie *f* de produit; **p. champion** champion *m* de produit; **p. depth** profondeur *f* de produit; **p. design** conception *f* du produit; **p. development** élaboration *f* du produit; **p. development cost** coût *m* de l'élaboration du produit; **p. development programme** programme *m* de mise au point du produit; **p. differentiation** différenciation *f* du produit; **p. display** présentation *f* du produit; **p. diversification** diversification *f* des produits; **p. features** caractéristiques *fpl* du produit; **p. form** type *m* de produit; **p. group manager** directeur, -trice de groupe de produits; **p. hierarchy** hiérarchie *f* des produits; **p. image** image *f* de produit; **p. improvement** amélioration du produit; **p. information sheet** fiche *f* technique; **p. innovation** innovation *f* de produit; *EU* **p. liability** responsabilité *f* du produit; **p. liability insurance** assurance *f* de responsabilité du produit; **p. life-cycle** cycle *m* de vie du produit; **p. life-cycle curve** courbe *f* du cycle *m* de vie d'un produit; **p. line** ligne *f* de produits; **p. line manager** directeur, -trice de ligne de produits; **p. management** gestion *f* de produits; **p. manager** chef *m* *ou* directeur, -trice de produit, responsable *mf* produit; **p. mapping** carte *f* perceptuelle de produits; **p. market** marché *m* de produit; **p. marketing** marketing *m* du produit; **p. mix** assortiment *m* *ou* mix *m* de produits; **p. mix depth** profondeur *f* de l'assortiment de produits; **p. mix width** largeur *f* de l'assortiment de produits; **p. orientation** optique *f* produit; **p. overheads** frais *mpl* généraux de production; **p. placement** placement *m* de produit; **p. planning** plan *m* de développement des produits; **p. policy** politique *f* de lancement de produit; **p. portfolio** portefeuille *m* de produits; **p. positioning** positionnement *m* du produit; **p. positioning map** carte de positionnement des produits, carte de l'univers des produits; **p. profile** profil *m* du produit; **p. promotion** communication *f* produit; **p. range** gamme *f* de produits; **p. specialist** spécialiste *mf* produit; **p. test** test *m* de produit, essai *m* de produits; **p. testing** essais *ou* tests de produit

production [prəˈdʌkʃən] N **1** *(of cars, appliances etc)* production *f*, fabrication *f*, *(of milk, apples etc)* production; **to go into p.**

entrer en production; **to go out of p.** cesser d'être produit; **to take sth out of p.** cesser de produire qch; **when do we go into p.?** quand est-ce que nous lançons la production?; **is it in p. yet?** est-ce qu'on en a commencé la production?; **to move** *or* **shift p.** relocaliser son unité de production; **drop in p.** chute *f* *ou* baisse *f* de la production
2 *(presentation) (of documents)* production *f*, présentation *f*; *(of ticket)* présentation
3 *Phys (of energy)* production *f*, génération *f*
4 *Cin, Radio, TV, Theat* production *f*; *Br (directing)* mise *f* en scène; *(finished work)* pièce *f*; **the film goes into p. in the autumn** le tournage du film commence en automne; *Fam* **to make a p. (number) (out) of sth** *(make fuss)* faire tout un fromage de qch; *Cin* **a film with high/low p. values** un film à gros/petit budget
▸▸ **p. assistant** assistant, -ante de production; **p. associate** producteur, -trice associé(e); *Ind* **p. budget** budget *m* de production; **p. buyer** responsable *mf* des achats; **p. capacity** capacité *f* de production; **p. car** voiture *f* de série; **p. company** société *f* de production; **p. control** direction *f* de la production; **p. control room** salle *f* de contrôle de production; **p. cost** coût *m* de production; **p. department** service *m* (de) production; **p. designer** directeur, -trice artistique; **p. director** directeur, -trice de production; *Journ* directeur, -trice de la fabrication; *TV* administrateur, -trice de la production; **p. editor** rédacteur, -trice en chef technique; **p. flowchart** organigramme *m* de production; **p. leadtime** délai *m* de production; **p. line** chaîne *f* de fabrication; **to work on a p. line** travailler à la chaîne; **p. manager** directeur, -trice de la production; **p. meeting** conférence *f* de production; **p. mixer** mélangeur *m* (de production); **p. platform** plate-forme *f* de production, *pl* plates-formes; **p. secretary** secrétaire *mf* de production; **p. switcher** mélangeur (de production); **p. talkback system** réseau *m* d'ordres, intercom *m* de production; **p. team** équipe *f* de production

productive [prəˈdʌktɪv] ADJ **1** productif; *(discussions)* positif; *(land etc)* productif, fertile; *(mine etc)* qui rend; **p. period of an author** années *fpl* productives d'un auteur; **the meeting wasn't very p.** la réunion n'a pas été très productive **2** *Econ (work)* productif **3** *Fml* **to be p. of** *(give rise to)* engendrer, produire
▸▸ *Econ* **p. labour** travail *m* productif; **p. life** *(of machine)* vie *f* physique

productively [prəˈdʌktɪvlɪ] ADV **to use one's time p.** employer son temps de façon efficace

productivity [prɒdʌkˈtɪvɪtɪ] N productivité *f*
▸▸ **p. agreement** accord *m* de productivité; **p. bargaining** négociation *f* syndicale d'un contrat de productivité; **p. bonus** prime *f* de rendement; **p. deal** accord de productivité; **p. drive** campagne *f* de productivité

product/market pair N *Mktg* couple *m* produit/marché

product/price policy N *Mktg* politique *f* de produit/prix

Prof *(abbr* **Professor***) (in title)* Prof

prof [prɒf] N *Fam (at university)* prof *mf*, *(at hospital)* professeur *m*

profanation [prɒfəˈneɪʃən] N *Rel* profanation *f*

profane [prəˈfeɪn] ADJ **1** *(blasphemous) (act)* profane; *(language)* impie, blasphématoire; *(person)* qui blasphème à tout propos **2** *Lit (secular)* profane; **things sacred and p.** le sacré et le profane
VT *(something sacred, one's talent)* profaner

profanity [prə'fænɪtɪ] N **1** *(word, remark)* blasphème *m*, juron *m*; **to utter profanities** blasphémer **2** *(of language)* grossièreté *f*; *(of text)* nature *f* profane; *(of action)* impiété *f*

profess [prə'fes] VT **1** *(declare) (one's faith etc)* professer, faire profession de; *(enthusiasm, hatred, disbelief)* professer; **to p. oneself a socialist** se déclarer socialiste, faire profession de socialisme; **to p. oneself satisfied** se déclarer satisfait; **to p. one's ignorance** avouer son ignorance **2** *(allege, claim)* prétendre; **he professes to be a socialist but …** il se prétend *ou* se déclare socialiste, mais …; **I do not p. to be a scholar** je ne prétends pas être savant; **to p. a lack of understanding of sth** prétendre ne pas comprendre qch

professed [prə'fest] ADJ **1** *(enemy)* déclaré; *(Marxist etc)* déclaré; *(pretended)* prétendu **2** *(monk, nun)* profès, -esse

professedly [prə'fesɪdlɪ] ADV *(on one's own admission)* de son propre aveu; *(according to one's claims)* soi-disant

profession [prə'feʃən] N **1** *(occupation)* profession *f*; **the p.** *(people)* (les membres *mpl* de) la profession; **the teaching p.** le corps enseignant, les enseignants *mpl*; **the (learned) professions** les professions libérales; **writer by p.** écrivain professionnel; **she is a doctor by p.** elle est médecin de (sa) profession; *Hum* **the oldest p. (in the world)** le plus vieux métier du monde VOIR GRAMMAIRE A6; B5 **2** *(declaration)* profession *f*, déclaration *f*; **p. of faith** profession de foi

professional [prə'feʃən(ə)l] ADJ **1** *(paid) (dancer, photographer, footballer etc)* professionnel; *(soldier, diplomat)* de carrière; *Fig* **a p. liar/hypochondriac** un menteur/un hypocondriaque professionnel; *Sport etc* **to turn** *or* **go p.** passer *ou* devenir professionnel; **p. man/woman** homme *m*/femme *f* qui exerce une profession libérale **2** *(relating to job)* professionnel; **to take a p. interest in sth** s'intéresser professionnellement à qch; **to take p. advice on sth** consulter une personne du métier *ou* un professionnel sur qch; *(on legal, medical matter)* consulter un avocat/un médecin à propos de qch; *Euph* **I think she needs p. help** je pense qu'elle a besoin d'aller voir un psychiatre **3** *(competent)* professionnel; **she is very p.** elle est très professionnelle; **they made a very p. job of the repair** la réparation qu'ils ont faite est digne de professionnels; **his manner was very p.** il s'est comporté en professionnel

N professionnel, -elle; **it's best to leave such work to the professionals** il vaut mieux laisser ce genre de travail à des professionnels *ou* à des gens du métier; **a golf/rugby p.** un golfeur/rugbyman professionnel

▶▶ **p. army** armée *f* de métier; **p. association** association *f* professionnelle; **p. body** organisme *m* professionnel; **p. certificate** certificat *m* d'aptitude professionnelle; **p. code of ethics** déontologie *f*; **p. football** football *m* professionnel; *Ftbl* **p. foul** faute *f* délibérée; **p. hospitality** industrie *f* de l'hôtellerie; **p. indemnity insurance** assurance *f* d'indemnisation professionnelle; **p. misconduct** faute professionnelle

professionalism [prə'feʃənəlɪz(ə)m] N professionnalisme *m*; **his air of spurious p.** ses airs de faux professionnel

professionally [prə'feʃənəlɪ] ADV **1** *(as a job)* professionnellement; **to sing/dance/play football** être un chanteur/danseur/footballeur professionnel **2** *(competently)* comme un professionnel, en professionnel; **it was very p. done** c'est du travail de professionnel

professor [prə'fesər] N *Univ Br* professeur *m* (de faculté) titulaire d'une chaire; *Am* enseignant, -ante, professeur (de faculté); **she's a p.** elle est professeur; **he's the p. of German** c'est le professeur titulaire de la chaire d'allemand; **P. Martin** le Professeur Martin; *(as address)* Monsieur/Madame Martin, Professeur; *(as address to medical doctor)* Monsieur/Madame le Professeur Martin

professorial [prɒfɪ'sɔːrɪəl] ADJ professoral, -aux

professorship [prə'fesəʃɪp] N *Univ* chaire *f*; **a p. in Modern History** une chaire d'histoire moderne; **to get a p.** obtenir une chaire

proffer ['prɒfər] VT *(-r-) Fml (advice)* offrir, présenter; *(opinion, observation)* avancer; *(resignation)* présenter; **to p. one's hand** tendre la main (**to sb** à qn)

proficiency [prə'fɪʃənsɪ] N *(in a subject)* compétence *f*, capacités *fpl* (**in** dans); *(in a language)* maîtrise *f* (**in** de)

proficient [prə'fɪʃənt] ADJ compétent; *(swimmer)* excellent; **to be p. at German** avoir une bonne maîtrise de l'allemand; **to be a p. liar** avoir le mensonge facile

proficiently [prə'fɪʃəntlɪ] ADV avec compétence; *(to speak a language)* couramment; **to swim p.** être un excellent nageur; **to lie p.** avoir le mensonge facile

profile ['prəʊfaɪl] N *(of person, face, mountain)* profil *m*; *TV, Journ (of celebrity)* portrait *m*, profil; *(of company)* profil; *Tech (of land, aircraft wing)* profil; *(on graph)* graphique *m*, courbe *f*; **she has the right p. for the job** elle a le profil qui convient pour cet emploi; *Art* **drawn in p.** dessiné de profil; *Fig* **to keep a low p.** *(of person)* garder un profil bas; *Fig* **to have a high p.** *(of person)* être (très) en vue; *(of issue)* être d'actualité; *Fig* **to raise one's p.** se mettre plus en vue; **to raise a party's/sb's p.** promouvoir l'image du parti/de qn

VT *(draw in profile)* dessiner *ou* montrer de profil; *TV, Journ* faire le portrait de; **she was profiled in a TV programme** une émission télévisée a présenté son portrait; **the trees are profiled against the horizon** les arbres se profilent sur l'horizon

▶▶ **p. characteristics** *(of tourists)* caractéristiques *fpl*; *TV, Cin* **p. shot** plan *m* de profil; *TV, Cin* **p. spotlight** spot *m* de profil

profit ['prɒfɪt] N *Com* bénéfice *m*, profit *m*; *Fig (advantage)* avantage *m*; **what p. is there in it for her?** quel avantage cela présente-t-il pour elle?, qu'est-ce que cela peut lui rapporter?; **to make a p.** *(of seller, company)* faire un *ou* des bénéfice(s); *(of goods)* rapporter; **we made a p. on the sale of** *or* **on selling the house** nous avons fait *ou* réalisé un bénéfice sur la vente de la maison; **to turn sth to p.** tirer profit *ou* bénéfice de qch; *Com* **gross/net p.** bénéfice brut/net; **£100 clear p.** 100 livres de bénéfice net; **p. on a transaction** rendement *m* d'une opération; **profits were down/up this year** les bénéfices ont diminué/augmenté cette année; **at a p.** *(to sell sth)* à profit; *(to work a mine)* avec profit; **to derive (a) p. from sth** retirer un bénéfice *ou* un profit de qch; **p. and loss** pertes et profits *mpl*; **p. and loss account, p. and loss statement** compte *m* de résultat; **p. or loss** résultat *m*; **p. or loss for the financial year** résultat de l'exercice

VI *(-t-)* **to p. by** *or* **from sth** bénéficier de qch, tirer profit de qch; **to p. by** *or* **from sb's advice** mettre à profit le conseil de qn; **you could well p. by being more careful** vous avez tout intérêt à faire plus attention

VT *Lit (person)* rapporter *ou* profiter à

▶▶ *Acct* **p. balance** solde *m* bénéficiaire;

Acct **p. centre** centre *m* de profit; *Acct* **p.-centre accounting** = comptabilité *f* par centres de profits; *Fin* **p. equation** équation *f* de bénéfice; *Mktg* **p. impact of marketing strategy** impact *m* sur la rentabilité de la stratégie marketing; *Fin* **p. indicator** indice *m* de profit; *Fin* **p. margin** marge *f* bénéficiaire; *Fin* **p. motive** motivation *f* par le profit; *Fin* **p. opportunity** occasion *f* de profit; *Fin* **p. optimization** optimisation *f* du *ou* des profits; *Fin* **p. outlook** perspectives *fpl* de profit; *Fin* **p. rate** taux *m* de profit *ou* de bénéfice; *Fin* **p. squeeze** compression *f* des bénéfices, étranglement *m* des marges; *Fin* **p. tax** impôt *m* sur les bénéfices; *Fin* **p. warning** = annonce *f* d'une baisse prochaine des bénéfices d'une entreprise

profitability [prɒfɪtə'bɪlɪtɪ] N rentabilité *f*

▶▶ **p. index** indice *m* de rentabilité; **p. ratio** ratio *m* de rentabilité; **p. value** *(of a company)* valeur *f* de rendement

profitable ['prɒfɪtəb(ə)l] ADJ *(deal, agreement)* profitable, avantageux; *(speculation, company)* rentable, lucratif; **it will be more p. for us to sell it** ce sera plus avantageux pour nous de le vendre; **it would be a more p. use of your time** ça serait pour vous une meilleure manière d'utiliser votre temps

profitably ['prɒfɪtəblɪ] ADV *(at a profit)* profitablement, avantageusement; *(to invest)* avec bénéfice; **to sell a house p.** vendre une maison à profit; **to use one's time p.** employer utilement son temps

profit-driven ADJ poussé par les profits

profiteer [prɒfɪ'tɪər] *Pej* N affairiste *mf*; **war profiteers** profiteurs *mpl* de guerre VI faire des bénéfices immoraux

profiteering [prɒfɪ'tɪərɪŋ] N *Pej* mercantilisme *m*, affairisme *m*

profitless ['prɒfɪtlɪs] ADJ sans profit; **we spent a p. week investigating the possibilities** nous avons perdu une semaine à étudier les diverses possibilités

profit-making ADJ *(company)* rentable; *(association)* à but lucratif; **this is supposed to be a p. company** cette entreprise est censée être à but lucratif

profit-sharing N participation *f* aux bénéfices, intéressement *m*

▶▶ **p. scheme** plan *m* de participation aux bénéfices, plan d'intéressement

profit-taking N prise *f* de bénéfices

profit-volume ratio N *Fin* rapport *m* profit sur ventes

profligacy ['prɒflɪgəsɪ] N **1** *(debauchery)* débauche *f* **2** *(extravagance)* prodigalité *f*

profligate ['prɒflɪgət] ADJ **1** *(debauched)* débauché **2** *(extravagant)* prodigue, dissipateur, -trice

N **1** *(debauchee)* débauché, -ée **2** *(extravagant person)* prodigue *mf*

pro forma [-'fɔːmə] ADV pour la forme
N *(invoice)* facture *f* pro forma
▶▶ *Fin* **p. bill** traite *f* pro forma; **p. invoice** facture pro forma

profound [prə'faʊnd] ADJ profond

profoundly [prə'faʊndlɪ] ADV **1** *(grateful, deaf, wise)* profondément **2** *(to write, express sth)* avec profondeur

profundity [prə'fʌndɪtɪ] N profondeur *f*

profuse [prə'fjuːs] ADJ *(copious)* abondant, *Lit* profus; **to offer p. thanks** remercier avec profusion; **to be p. in one's apologies** se confondre en excuses; **to be p. in one's praise** se répandre en compliments; **p. bleeding** hémorragie *f* abondante

profusely [prə'fjuːslɪ] ADV profusément; **to apologize p.** se confondre en excuses; **to bleed p.** saigner en abondance; **to perspire**

p. transpirer abondamment; **to praise sb p.** ne pas tarir d'éloges sur qn; **to thank sb p.** remercier qn avec profusion

profuseness [prəˈfjuːsnɪs] N profusion f

profusion [prəˈfjuːʒən] N (abundance) profusion f, abondance f; **flowers in p.** des fleurs à profusion

prog [prɒg] N TV, Radio Old-fashioned Fam émission f

progenitor [prəʊˈdʒenɪtər] N (ancestor) ancêtre m, aïeul, -eule, pl aïeux; Fig (forerunner) précurseur m; (founder) fondateur m; Fml, Hum (parent) géniteur, -trice

progeny [ˈprɒdʒɪnɪ] N Fml (offspring) progéniture f; (descendants) descendants mpl; Hum **is this another of your p.?** est-ce que c'est un de tes rejetons?

progesterone [prəʊˈdʒestərəʊn] N Biol, Chem progestérone f

prognosis, pl **prognoses** [prɒgˈnəʊsɪs, -əʊsiːz] N **1** Med pronostic m; (art) prognose f **2** (forecast) prévision(s) f(pl), pronostic m; **to make a p.** faire un pronostic ou des prévisions

prognostic [prɒgˈnɒstɪk] ADJ (test etc) de pronostic
N Med signe m pronostique

prognostication [prɒgnɒstɪˈkeɪʃən] N prédiction f, présage m

program¹ [ˈprəʊgræm] N Comput programme m
VT & VI Comput programmer; **to p. a computer to do sth** programmer un ordinateur pour qu'il fasse qch; **to be programmed to do sth** être programmé pour faire qch
▸▸**p. card** carte f programme; **p. disk** disquette f programme; **p. error** erreur f de programmation; **p. file** fichier m programme; **p. language** langage m de programmation; **p. library** bibliothèque f de programmes; **p. line** ligne f de programme

program² N, VT Am = **programme**

programmable [prəʊˈgræməb(ə)l] ADJ (computer, oven etc) programmable
▸▸Comput **p. ROM** mémoire f morte programmable

programme, Am **program** [ˈprəʊgræm] N **1** (for play, concert, of political party etc) programme m; **what's the p. for today?** quel est le programme aujourd'hui?; **training p.** programme d'instruction ou de formation
2 TV, Radio émission f, programme m; **current affairs p.** émission ou programme d'actualités; **in a change to the advertised p.** contrairement à ce qu'annonçait le programme
3 TV (channel) chaîne f, Radio (station) station f
VT programmer; **to p. sth to do sth** programmer qch pour faire qch; **programmed teaching** or **learning** enseignement m programmé
▸▸**p. billing** = position f d'un programme dans la grille de programmation; **p. bus** tableau m de programmation; **p. controller** directeur, -trice des programmes ou d'antenne; **p. grid** grille f de programmes; **p. music** musique f à programme; **p. planner** programmateur, -trice; **p. planning** programmation f, **p. schedule** grille f de programmes; **p. scheduler** programmateur, -trice; **p. seller** vendeur, -euse de programmes; **p. supervisor** chef m d'antenne; **p. trail** annonce f de programme

programme-maker N TV etc réalisateur, -trice

programmer [ˈprəʊgræmər] N **1** (person) Comput programmeur, -euse; TV, Radio, Tech programmateur, -trice **2** (device) programmateur m

programming [ˈprəʊgræmɪŋ] N **1** Comput

programmation f **2** TV, Radio programmation f
▸▸Comput **p. error** erreur f de programmation; Comput **p. language** langage m de programmation

progress¹ [ˈprəʊgres] N (no pl) **1** (improvement) progrès mpl; **age of p.** époque f ou siècle m de progrès; **to make p. in one's studies** faire des progrès dans ses études; **he was making slow/rapid p. with the language** il progressait lentement/rapidement dans son apprentissage de la langue; **to make great p.** avancer à pas de géant; (of industry) prendre un grand essor; **negotiations are making good p.** les négociations sont en bonne voie; **the patient is making good p.** le patient donne de bons signes de récupération; Iron **that's p. for you!** c'est ça le progrès!
2 (movement) (of time, disease etc) marche f, (of events) cours m; (of plan, project) déroulement m; (of work) progrès m, avancement m; Chess **the knight's p.** la marche du cavalier; **the work is now in p.** le travail est en cours; **the negotiations in p.** les négociations en cours; **do not enter while a lecture is in p.** défense d'entrer pendant le déroulement d'un cours
▸▸Ind **p. chart** diagramme m de l'avancement des travaux; Ind **p. payment** paiement m proportionnel (à l'avancement des travaux); **p. report** compte-rendu m, pl comptes-rendus; (on work) rapport m sur l'avancement des travaux; (on patient) bulletin m de santé; (on pupil) bulletin scolaire

progress² [prəˈgres] VI **1** (improve) (of person) faire des progrès, progresser; (of project) progresser, avancer; **her English has progressed a lot** elle a fait de gros progrès en anglais, elle a beaucoup progressé en anglais; **to p. with one's studies** progresser dans ses études; **the patient is progressing satisfactorily** le malade fait des progrès satisfaisants **2** (move forwards) (in space, time etc) avancer; **as the inquiry progresses** à mesure que l'enquête avance; **as the year progresses** au fur et à mesure que l'année progresse; **to p. towards a place** s'approcher d'un endroit (par étapes successives); **to p. onto more difficult tasks** passer à des tâches plus difficiles; **I never progressed beyond the first lesson** je ne suis jamais allé au-delà de la première leçon
VT esp Com (advance) faire progresser

progression [prəˈgreʃən] N (movement), Math, Mus progression f; (of star) marche f; Mil avance f

progressive [prəˈgresɪv] ADJ **1** (movement) progressif, en avant **2** (forward-looking) (ideas, methods) avancé, progressiste; (literature, music) d'avant-garde; **to be p.** (of person) avoir des idées avancées ou progressistes; Pol **the p. party** le parti progressiste **3** Gram **the p. form** la forme progressive
N **1** Pol progressiste mf **2** Gram (temps m) progressif VOIR GRAMMAIRE A49–51
▸▸Med **p. disease** maladie f dégénérative; Mus **p. jazz** jazz m progressif; Fin **p. taxation** imposition f progressive

progressively [prəˈgresɪvlɪ] ADV progressivement

progressiveness [prəˈgresɪvnɪs] N progressivité f

prohibit [prəˈhɪbɪt] VT (forbid) défendre, interdire, prohiber; **it is prohibited by law** c'est interdit ou défendu par la loi; **smoking prohibited** défense de fumer; **to p. sb from doing sth** (of person) défendre ou interdire à qn de faire qch; (of cause, quality etc) empêcher qn de faire qch; **prohibited goods** marchandises fpl prohibées

prohibition [prəʊɪˈbɪʃən] N interdiction f, prohibition f (**from doing sth** de faire qch); Hist **P.** la Prohibition
▸▸Pol **p. party** parti m prohibitionniste

prohibitionist [prəʊɪˈbɪʃənɪst] ADJ, N prohibitionniste mf

prohibitive [prəˈhɪbɪtɪv] ADJ prohibitif; **the price of flowers is p.** les fleurs sont hors de prix
▸▸**p. price** prix m prohibitif ou inabordable

prohibitively [prəˈhɪbɪtɪvlɪ] ADV **p. expensive** à un prix prohibitif

project¹ [ˈprɒdʒekt] N projet m; Sch (of pupil, group of pupils) étude f pratique; (for drainage, irrigation etc) travaux mpl; Am (housing) **p.** lotissement m
▸▸**p. leader** responsable mf de projet; **p. management** gestion f de projets; Comput **p. management package** gestionnaire m de projets; **p. manager** chef m de projet; Constr maître m d'œuvre; **p. milestones** étapes fpl principales du projet

project² [prəˈdʒekt] VT **1** (plan) projeter; **the Minister's projected visit had to be cancelled** la visite que le Ministre avait prévue a dû être annulée
2 (propel) projeter; (missile etc) lancer; **to p. one's voice** projeter sa voix
3 Cin etc (image, film) projeter (**onto a screen** sur un écran); Math (line) projeter; (plane) projeter, tracer la projection de; **he projected himself as France's saviour** il s'est présenté comme le sauveur de la France; **she projects an image of self-confidence** elle donne d'elle-même l'image d'une personne pleine d'assurance; **the country has successfully projected itself as a stable economy** le pays a réussi à donner de lui l'image d'une économie stable
4 (predict) (results) prévoir; **the projected sales figures** le chiffre d'affaires escompté; **he's projecting a 40% slide in May** il prévoit une baisse de 40% au mois de mai
5 (imagine) **to p. oneself into the past/the future** se transporter dans le passé/l'avenir; Psy **to p. one's needs onto other people** projeter ses besoins sur les autres
VI **1** (protrude) déborder, dépasser, faire saillie; **the balcony projects over the pavement** le balcon surplombe le trottoir
2 (with voice) projeter sa voix

projected [prəˈdʒektɪd] ADJ (legislation, undertaking) en projet, prévu
▸▸Geom **p. angle** angle m projeté; TV etc **p. background** fond m projeté, transparence f, Com, Fin **p. growth** croissance f prévue; Art **p. shadow** ombre f portée; Fin **p. turnover** chiffre m d'affaires prévisionnel

projectile [prəˈdʒektaɪl] ADJ (force) impulsif, projectif
N projectile m
▸▸**p. vomiting** vomissements mpl violents; Mil **p. weapons** armes fpl de jet

projecting [prəˈdʒektɪŋ] ADJ Archit saillant, en saillie; **p. part of a roof** avancée f d'un toit

projection [prəˈdʒekʃən] N **1** (of image, one's voice etc) projection f, (of projectile) lancement m **2** (in mapmaking) projection f **3** (prediction) prévision f; **demographic projections** projections fpl démographiques **4** Psy projection f **5** (protruding part) saillie f, (of roof etc) avancée f, (of façade) avant-corps m inv
▸▸Cin **p. booth, p. room** cabine f de projection

projectionist [prəˈdʒekʃənɪst] N Cin projectionniste mf

projective [prəˈdʒektɪv] ADJ Math (plane) de projection; (geometry) projectif
▸▸Psy **p. test** test m projectif

projector [prə'dʒektər] N *Cin* projecteur *m*

prolapse ['prəʊlæps] *Med* N *(of womb etc)* prolapsus *m*
▸ VI *(of organ)* descendre, tomber

prolapsed ['prəʊlæpst] ADJ *Med* prolabé

prole [prəʊl] N *Fam Pej* prolo *mf*

proletarian [prəʊlɪ'teərɪən] ADJ prolétarien, prolétaire
N prolétaire *mf*

proletarianize [prəʊlɪ'teərɪənaɪz] VT prolétariser

proletariat [prəʊlɪ'teərɪət] N prolétariat *m*
VOIR GRAMMAIRE A11

pro-life ADJ
▸▸ **p. movement** mouvement *m* pour le respect de la vie *(adversaire de l'interruption volontaire de grossesse)*

pro-lifer N *Fam* adversaire *mf* de l'interruption volontaire de grossesse

proliferate [prə'lɪfəreɪt] VI proliférer; *(of human beings)* se multiplier

proliferation [prəlɪfə'reɪʃən] N prolifération *f*

prolific [prə'lɪfɪk] ADJ prolifique, fécond, fertile (**in, of** en); *(writer, composer)* prolifique, fécond; **the country has been a p. producer of inventors** le pays a été fécond en inventeurs; **a p. goalscorer** un bon buteur

prolifically [prə'lɪfɪklɪ] ADV *(to write, compose)* abondamment; **she is a p. productive writer** c'est un écrivain prolifique *ou* fécond; **he has been a p. successful goalscorer** il a marqué énormément de buts

prolix ['prəʊlɪks] ADJ *Fml* prolixe, diffus

prolixity [prəʊ'lɪksɪtɪ] N *Fml* prolixité *f*

prologue ['prəʊlɒg] N prologue *m* (**to** de)

prolong [prə'lɒŋ] VT *(life etc)* prolonger; *(line)* continuer, prolonger; **don't p. the agony** ne me/le/*etc* faites pas souffrir plus longtemps

prolongation [prəʊlɒŋ'geɪʃən] N *(of the time sth lasts)* prolongation *f*, *(of line etc)* prolongement *m*

prolonged [prə'lɒŋgd] ADJ prolongé

PROM [prɒm] N *Comput (abbr* **Programmable Read Only Memory)** mémoire *f* morte programmable

prom [prɒm] N *Fam* **1** *Br (at seaside)* front *m* de mer **2** *Br Mus (concert)* concert-promenade *m*, *pl* concerts-promenades; **the Proms** = série *f* de concerts-promenades, qui a lieu au mois de juillet au Albert Hall de Londres **3** *Am Sch (dance)* = bal *m* d'étudiants
▸▸ *Am Sch, Univ* **p. queen** reine *f* du bal

pro-marketeer N *Pol* = partisan *m* de l'appartenance de la Grande-Bretagne au Marché commun

promenade ['prɒmənɑːd] N *(place for walking)* promenade *f*, *Br (at seaside)* front *m* de mer; *Theat Old-fashioned (in pit)* promenoir *m*
VI se promener
VT exhiber
▸▸ **p. concert** concert-promenade *m*, *pl* concerts-promenade; *Naut* **p. deck** pont *m* promenade

promenader ['prɒmənɑːdər] N *Br Mus Fam* auditeur, -trice d'un concert-promenade

Promethean [prə'miːθɪən] ADJ *Myth* prométhéen

Prometheus [prə'miːθɪəs] N *Myth* Prométhée

prominence ['prɒmɪnəns] N **1** *(of issue, person etc)* éminence *f*, **to bring sth into p., to give sth p.** faire ressortir qch, donner une place importante à qch; **to come** *or* **rise to p.** prendre de l'importance; **she came to international p. with that song** c'est grâce à

cette chanson qu'elle a percé au niveau international; **to occupy a position of some p.** *(of politician etc)* occuper une position éminente; *(of house)* être situé sur une éminence **2** *(of land, feature etc)* proéminence *f*, *(part sticking up)* saillie *f*, protubérance *f*

prominent ['prɒmɪnənt] ADJ **1** *(projecting)* saillant, en saillie, proéminent; *(cheekbone)* saillant; *(nose)* proéminent **2** *(obvious)* saillant, frappant; *(well-known)* éminent; **p. feature** trait *m* saillant; **in a p. position** dans une position éminente; *(house)* situé sur une éminence; **to hold a p. position** occuper une position éminente; **p. people** personnages *mpl* éminents *ou* en vue

prominently ['prɒmɪnəntlɪ] ADV *(to place etc)* bien en vue; **to display sth p.** mettre qch bien en évidence *ou* en vue

promiscuity [prɒmɪ'skjuːɪtɪ] N promiscuité *f* sexuelle

> Note that the French word **promiscuité** is a false friend and is never a translation for the English word **promiscuity**. It means lack of privacy.

promiscuous [prə'mɪskjʊəs] ADJ **1** *(behaviour)* dissolu; *(person)* aux mœurs dissolues; **to be p.** *(of person)* coucher avec n'importe qui *ou* tout le monde; *(of society, group)* être permissif **2** *Fml (mixed)* confus, mêlé; *(crowd)* hétérogène

promiscuously [prə'mɪskjʊəslɪ] ADV **1** to behave p. avoir des mœurs dissolues **2** *Fml (in a random or confused way)* confusément

promise ['prɒmɪs] N **1** *(pledge)* promesse *f*, **to make a p.** faire une promesse; **to keep one's p.** tenir sa promesse; **to break one's p.** manquer à sa parole, ne pas tenir sa promesse; **I'm not making any promises but I'll try my best** je ne promets rien, mais je ferai de mon mieux; **a p. is a p.** chose promise, chose due; **promises, promises!** rien que des promesses!; **empty promises** promesses vaines; **to hold out a p. of sth to sb** laisser espérer qch à qn, faire miroiter qch à qn
2 *(potential) (no pl)* **to show p.** être prometteur, promettre; **child who shows p., child full of p.** enfant qui promet; **young man with every p. of a brilliant future** jeune homme promis à un brillant avenir
VT **1** *(make a promise of)* promettre; **to p. sb sth** promettre qch à qn; **to p. (sb) to do sth** promettre (à qn) de faire qch; **he promised me he'd do it** il m'a promis qu'il le ferait *ou* de le faire; **they were promised help** on leur a promis de l'aide; **to p. oneself sth** se promettre qch; *Fam* **you'll be sorry, I p. you** je vous promets que vous le regretterez
2 *(indicate)* promettre; **it promises to be hot** le temps promet d'être *ou* s'annonce chaud
VI promettre; **I'll pay you back, I p.** je te rembourserai, je te le promets *ou* c'est promis; **I'll wait for you – (do you) p.?** je t'attendrai – tu le promets? *ou* promis?; **but you promised!** mais tu avais promis!; **the scheme promises well** le projet s'annonce bien

promised ['prɒmɪst] ADJ promis
▸▸ *Bible, Fig* **the P. Land** la Terre promise

promising ['prɒmɪsɪŋ] ADJ prometteur, -euse, qui promet; **she's made a p. start** elle a fait des débuts prometteurs; **the future looks p.** l'avenir promet, l'avenir s'annonce bien

promisingly ['prɒmɪsɪŋlɪ] ADV d'une façon prometteuse *ou* qui promet

promissory ['prɒmɪsərɪ] ADJ
▸▸ *Com* **p. note** billet *m* à ordre

promo ['prəʊməʊ] N *Fam* **1** *(video)* vidéo *f* promotionnelle; *(for record)* clip *m* **2** *Com (promotion)* promo *f*

promontory ['prɒmənt(ə)rɪ] N promontoire *m*

promote [prə'məʊt] VT **1** *(raise in rank)* promouvoir, donner de l'avancement à; **to be promoted to (the rank of) captain** être promu (au grade de) capitaine, passer capitaine; **to be promoted** être promu, monter en grade; *Ftbl (of team)* passer dans la division supérieure; **to be promoted to the first division** passer *ou* monter en première division **2** *(encourage) (peace, growth, justice, cause)* promouvoir; *(the arts, a project)* encourager; *(success)* favoriser; *(person's interests)* servir; *(result)* amener, contribuer à; *Com (product)* promouvoir, faire la promotion de; *Chem (reaction)* amorcer, provoquer; *Parl* **to p. a bill** prendre l'initiative d'un projet de loi

promoter [prə'məʊtər] N *(of construction project)* promoteur, -trice; *Sport, Theat* organisateur, -trice; *(sponsor)* parrain *m*; **to be a p. of** *(theory, idea, cause)* promouvoir; **the main promoters of this idea** les principaux défenseurs de cette idée; **sales p.** promoteur, -trice de ventes

promotion [prə'məʊʃən] N **1** *(in rank)* promotion *f*, avancement *m*; *Ftbl (of team)* ascension *f*, promotion; **to get p.** être promu, avoir *ou* obtenir de l'avancement; *Ftbl (of team)* passer dans la division supérieure; **to get p. to captain** être promu au grade de capitaine; **to get p. to manager** être promu directeur **2** *Com (of product)* promotion *f*, **to have a Chanel® p.** avoir des produits Chanel® en promotion; **sales p.** promotion des ventes
▸▸ **promotions agency** agence *f* de promotion; **p. budget** budget *m* promotionnel; **p. campaign** campagne *f* de promotion; **p. team** équipe *f* promotionnelle; **p. techniques** techniques *fpl* de promotion des ventes

promotional [prə'məʊʃən(ə)l] ADJ *Com* promotionnel
▸▸ **p. campaign** campagne *f* de promotion; **p. costs** coûts *mpl* de promotion; **p. discount** remise *f* promotionnelle; **p. literature** prospectus *mpl* promotionnels; **p. material** matériel *m* de promotion; **p. offer** offre *f* promotionnelle; **p. policy** politique *f* de communication, politique de promotion; **p. price** prix *m* promotionnel; **p. sample** échantillon *m* promotionnel; **p. target** cible *f* de communication; **p. video** (cassette *f*) vidéo *f* promotionnelle

prompt [prɒmpt] ADJ **1** *(swift)* rapide, prompt; **the article elicited a p. denial** cet article a été promptement démenti; **to take p. action** prendre des mesures immédiates; **her p. action saved his life** la rapidité de sa réaction lui a sauvé la vie; **to be p. to act** être prompt à agir, agir rapidement; **he was always very p. to understand** il comprenait toujours très vite; **p. reply** *(to letter etc)* prompte réponse *f*, réponse rapide; **p. service** service *m* rapide
2 *(on time)* ponctuel
ADV **at three o'clock p.** à trois heures précises
VT **1** *(cause) (reaction, reply)* provoquer; **to p. sb to do sth** pousser *ou* porter qn à faire qch; **what prompted you to come?** qu'est-ce qui vous a donné l'idée de venir?; **these events prompted her to ...** ces événements l'ont poussée à ...; **to be prompted by a feeling of pity** être animé par un sentiment de pitié
2 *(actor, pupil, speaker)* **to p. sb** *Theat* souffler sa réplique à qn; *(provide with correct response, answer)* souffler à qn; **she needed no prompting when asked her opinion on the subject** elle n'avait pas besoin d'encouragement pour donner son opinion sur le sujet; **'where did you go?', the teacher prompted** 'où es-tu allé?' dit le professeur pour

l'encourager à parler; **the teacher prompted him with another question** le professeur lui posa une autre question pour le mettre sur la voie

N 1 *Theat (reminder)* **to give an actor a p.** souffler une réplique à un acteur **2** *Comput* invite *f*, indicatif *m*; *(with wording)* message *m* d'invite; **DOS p.** invite du DOS; **return to the C:\ p.** revenir au message d'attente du DOS

▸▸ *Theat* **p. box** trou *m* (du souffleur); *TV* **p. card** aide-mémoire *m inv*, carton *m* de prompteur; *Theat* **p. copy** exemplaire *m ou* manuscrit *m* du souffleur; *Fin* **p. note** rappel *m* d'échéance; *Com* **p. payment** paiement *m* dans les délais; *Theat* **p. side** *(in UK)* côté *m* cour; *(in US)* côté jardin; **opposite p. side** *(in UK)* côté jardin; *(in US)* côté cour

prompter ['prɒmptər] **N 1** *Theat* souffleur, -euse; **p.'s box** trou *m* du souffleur **2** *TV* téléprompteur *m*

prompting ['prɒmptɪŋ] **N 1** *(persuasion, encouragement)* insistance *f*; **they will not do it without the p. of the international community** ils ne le feront pas si la communauté internationale ne les y pousse pas; **I wonder whose p. lies behind these questions** je me demande qui est à l'origine de ces questions; **to do sth at sb's p.** faire qch sur les instances *ou* à l'instigation de qn; **the promptings of conscience** l'aiguillon *m* de la conscience; **he needed no p.** il n'a pas été nécessaire de le pousser **2** *(of actor, pupil, speaker)* **he needed a lot of p.** *(of actor)* on devait lui souffler tout le temps; **to answer a question without p.** répondre à une question sans que personne ne souffle; *Sch* **no p.!** ne soufflez pas!

promptitude ['prɒmptɪtjuːd] **N** = **promptness**

promptly ['prɒmptlɪ] **ADV 1** *(rapidly)* promptement, rapidement **2** *(punctually)* ponctuellement **3** *(immediately)* sur-le-champ, immédiatement

promptness ['prɒmptnɪs] **N** promptitude *f*

promulgate ['prɒməlgeɪt] **VT** *Fml* **1** *(law, edict)* promulguer **2** *(idea, doctrine etc)* propager, répandre

promulgation [prɒməl'geɪʃən] **N** *Fml* **1** *(of law, edict)* promulgation *f* **2** *(of idea, doctrine)* propagation *f*

prone [prəʊn] **ADJ 1** *(lying) (person, animal etc)* couché sur le ventre, étendu face contre terre; **to be in a p. position** être couché sur le ventre **2** *(inclined)* **p. to sth/do sth** enclin *ou* porté à qch/faire qch; **p. to a disease** prédisposé à une maladie

-prone [prəʊn] **SUFF** **to be accident-/disaster-p.** être enclin aux accidents/désastres; **a strike-p. industry** une industrie sujette aux grèves

proneness ['prəʊnnɪs] **N** propension *f* **(to** à**);** *(to disease)* prédisposition *f*; **he has a certain p. to accidents/to letting himself be influenced** il est assez enclin aux accidents/à se laisser influencer

prong [prɒŋ] **N** *(of fork)* dent *f*; *(on stag's antler)* pointe *f*

pronged [prɒŋd] **ADJ** **two-p. fork** fourchette *f* à deux dents; *Mil* **two/three-p. attack** attaque *f* sur deux/trois fronts; **it's a two-p. argument** c'est un argument qui porte sur deux fronts

pronominal [prəʊ'nɒmɪn(ə)l] **ADJ** *Gram* pronominal, -aux

pronominally [prəʊ'nɒmɪn(ə)lɪ] **ADV** *Gram* pronominalement

pronoun ['prəʊnaʊn] **N** *Gram* pronom *m*
VOIR GRAMMAIRE A27–38; B14–23

pronounce [prə'naʊns] **VT 1** *(word etc)* prononcer; **this letter is not pronounced** cette

lettre ne se prononce pas; **is that how you p. it** *or* **how it's pronounced?** est-ce que c'est comme ça que ça se prononce? **2** *Fml (declare)* déclarer (**that** que); *Law (sentence)* prononcer; *(judgment)* rendre, prononcer; **to p. sb (to be) a genius** déclarer que qn est un génie; **I now p. you man and wife** *(in marriage service)* je vous déclare mari et femme

VI to p. on a subject se prononcer sur un sujet; *(of tribunal)* statuer sur une question; **to p. for** *or* **in favour of sb/against sb** se prononcer *ou* se déclarer pour/contre qn

pronounceable [prə'naʊnsəb(ə)l] **ADJ** prononçable; **a barely p. name** un nom tout juste prononçable; **easily p.** facile à prononcer

pronounced [prə'naʊnst] **ADJ** *(squint, accent, liking)* prononcé, marqué; *(features)* accusé; *(views, opinions)* arrêté; **the change is becoming more p.** le changement s'accentue; **he walks with a p. limp** il boite de façon prononcée

pronouncement [prə'naʊnsmənt] **N** *esp Fml* déclaration *f*

pronouncing [prə'naʊnsɪŋ] **N** *Law (of sentence)* prononcé *m*

▸▸ **p. dictionary** dictionnaire *m* de prononciation

pronto ['prɒntəʊ] **ADV** *Fam* illico

pronuclear [prəʊ'njuːklɪər] **ADJ** *(policy, statement etc)* en faveur du nucléaire; **he is p.** il est pour le nucléaire

pronunciation [prənʌnsɪ'eɪʃən] **N** *(of word, language)* prononciation *f*; **his French p. was good** il avait une bonne prononciation en français

proof [pruːf] **N 1** *(evidence)* preuve *f*; **you have no p.** tu n'as pas de preuve; **positive p., p. positive** preuve patente; **clear p. of guilt** preuve évidente de culpabilité; **to give p. of** *(guilt, innocence)* prouver, démontrer; *(commitment, loyalty)* faire preuve de; *(intelligence)* montrer, indiquer; **this is p. that he is lying** cela prouve qu'il ment; **in p. of** *or* **as a p. of one's good faith** comme preuve *ou* en témoignage de sa bonne foi; **to produce p. to the contrary** fournir la preuve du contraire; *Law* **the onus** *or* **the burden of p. lies with …** la charge de la preuve incombe à …; **p. of one's identity** preuve d'identité **2** *(test)* épreuve *f*; **to put sth/sb to the p.** mettre qch/qn à l'épreuve; *Prov* **the p. of the pudding is in the eating** c'est à l'œuvre que l'on connaît l'artisan **3** *Typ (printer's)* **p.** épreuve *f* (d'imprimerie); **to read proofs** corriger des épreuves; **to pass the proofs** donner le bon à tirer; **at the p. stage** à la correction des épreuves **4** *Phot* épreuve *f* **5** *(of alcoholic drink)* teneur *f* en alcool

ADJ 1 *(resistant)* **p. against sth** résistant à qch, à l'épreuve de qch; **p. against damp** imperméable, étanche; *Tech* hydrofuge; **to be p. against danger/disease** être à l'abri du danger/immunisé contre la maladie; **p. against temptation** *(person)* insensible à la tentation

2 to be 0.9% p. *(of alcohol)* contenir 0,9% d'alcool

VT 1 *Typ (take proof from)* tirer une épreuve de **2** *(check proofs of)* corriger **3** *(fabric etc)* imperméabiliser; *(against acid etc)* rendre résistant *ou* inattaquable

▸▸ *Typ* **p. correction marks** signes *mpl* de correction sur épreuve; *Com* **p. of debt** affirmation *f* de créance; **p. of identity** pièce *f* d'identité; **p. of insurance** attestation *f* d'assurance; *Typ* **p. marks** signes de correction sur épreuve; **p. of payment** justificatif *m* de paiement; **p. of purchase** reçu *m*

-proof [pruːf] **SUFF** **bulletp./heatp.** à l'épreuve des balles/de la chaleur

proofing ['pruːfɪŋ] **N 1** *(action) (of fabric etc)* imperméabilisation *f* **2** *(coating)* enduit *m* imperméable **3** *Typ (production)* tirage *m* des épreuves; *(reading)* correction *f* des épreuves

proofread ['pruːfriːd] *Typ* **VI** corriger des épreuves

VT corriger, relire, corriger les épreuves de; **once it's been p.** une fois les épreuves corrigées

proofreader ['pruːfriːdər] **N** *Typ* correcteur, -trice

proofreading ['pruːfriːdɪŋ] **N** *Typ* correction *f* d'épreuves

▸▸ **p. mark** signe *m* de correction

prop[1] [prɒp] **N 1** *(support)* appui *m*, support *m*; *(of wall)* étançon *m*, étai *m*; *Rugby (player)* pilier *m*; *Min (pit)* **p.** étai *ou* étançon de mine; *Fig* **he was the p. of his father's old age** c'était lui qui soutenait son père âgé; **this fact serves as a p. to her argument** ce fait étaye son argument; **it is one of the props of his existence** c'est une des choses qui l'aident à vivre **2** *Theat etc* accessoire *m*; **props** *(person)* accessoiriste *mf*; *Fig* **the rock star's guitar was just a p.** la guitare du chanteur de rock n'était qu'un accessoire

VT (**-pp-**) *(support)* appuyer, soutenir; **to p. a ladder/a person against a wall** appuyer une échelle/une personne contre un mur; **she propped her chin on her hand** elle posa son menton sur sa main

▸▸ *Theat etc* **props department** service *m* des accessoires; *Rugby* **p. forward** pilier; *Theat etc* **props person** accessoiriste

▸ **prop open VT SEP** maintenir ouvert; **she propped the door open with a chair** elle a calé *ou* bloqué la porte avec une chaise pour qu'elle reste ouverte

▸ **prop up VT SEP** *(support) (tunnel, building)* appuyer, soutenir; *(wall)* étançonner, étayer; *Fig (currency, system etc)* soutenir; **propped up on one's elbows** accoudé; **to p. up a patient on his pillow** redresser un malade sur son oreiller; **to p. a ladder/a person up against a wall** appuyer une échelle/une personne contre un mur; **to p. oneself up against sth** s'appuyer contre qch; **propped up by a pile of books** calé par une pile de livres; *Fig* **the regime is being propped up by the military** le régime est maintenu en place par l'armée; *Hum* **a group of boys propping up a wall** un groupe de jeunes appuyés contre un mur; **are you propping up the wall?** tu as peur que le mur s'écroule?; *Br* **he's always propping up the bar** c'est un vrai pilier de bar; **he'll be out propping up a bar somewhere** il doit être dans un bar quelque part

prop[2] **N** *Aviat Fam* = **propeller**

prop[3] *Com (abbr* **proprietor**) propriétaire *mf*

propaganda [prɒpə'gændə] **N** propagande *f*
▸▸ **p. film** film *m* de propagande

propagandist [prɒpə'gændɪst] **N, ADJ** propagandiste *mf*

propagandize [prɒpə'gændaɪz] *Fml* **VI** faire de la propagande

VT *(one's ideas, theories)* faire de la propagande pour; *(the masses, one's colleagues etc)* faire de la propagande à

propagate ['prɒpəgeɪt] **VT** *Bot, Phys etc* propager; *Fig (ideas etc)* propager, disséminer

VI *(of animal, plant)* se propager

propagation [prɒpə'geɪʃən] **N** *Bot, Phys, Fig* propagation *f*

propagator ['prɒpəgeɪtər] **N** *(for seedlings)* = mini-serre *f*, *pl* mini-serres

propane ['prəʊpeɪn] **N** *Chem* propane *m*

propel [prə'pel] **VT** (**-ll-**) *(something)* propulser; *Fig (urge on)* pousser (**towards** vers);

propelled by ambition poussé *ou* animé par l'ambition

propellant, propellent [prə'pelənt] N *(fuel)* combustible *m*; *(for rocket)* propergol *m*; **liquid/solid (rocket) p.** propergol liquide/solide
ADJ propulseur *(no f)*, propulsif

propeller [prə'pelər] N *Naut, Aviat* hélice *f*
▶▶ **p. blade** pale *f* d'hélice; **p. shaft** *Aviat* arbre *m* porte-hélice; *Naut* arbre d'hélice; *Aut* arbre de transmission

propelling [prə'pelɪŋ] ADJ propulsif
▶▶ **p. pencil** porte-mine *m inv*

propensity [prə'pensɪtɪ] N propension *f* (**to sth** à qch; **to do** *or* **for doing sth** à faire qch)

PROPER ['prɒpər]

ADJ vrai **1** ▪ proprement dit **1**
▪ convenable **2** ▪ bon **2** ▪ correct **2**

ADJ **1** *(true, real)* vrai; **it'll be good to sleep in a p. bed** ça va être agréable de dormir dans un vrai lit; **the p. word** le mot juste; **p. meaning of a word** signification *f* propre d'un mot; **what's its p. name?** comment ça s'appelle au juste?; **to get a p. night's sleep** avoir une bonne nuit de sommeil; **it's more a course in design than in architecture p.** c'est plus un cours de design que d'architecture proprement dite; **we're still not in London p. yet** nous ne sommes pas encore arrivés à Londres même
2 *(most suitable, suited)* convenable; *(behaviour, model etc)* approprié; *(correct in behaviour)* convenable, comme il faut; **is that the p. way to treat your sister?** est-ce que c'est comme ça qu'on traite sa sœur?; **at the p. time** en temps utile, au moment voulu; **to apply to the p. person** s'adresser à qui de droit; **to put sth in the p. place** mettre qch à sa place; **to think it p. to do sth** juger bon *ou* à propos de faire qch; **do as you think p.** faites comme bon vous semblera; *Fam* **to do the p. thing by sb** faire son devoir, faire ce qu'il faut; **the p. way to do it** la bonne façon de le faire; **the p. use of the subjunctive** l'emploi *m* correct du subjonctif; **paid at the p. rate** payé au taux *ou* au prix convenable; **a very p. old lady** une vieille dame très comme il faut; *(very dignified)* une vieille dame très digne; *Fam* **a p. little madam** une vraie petite madame; *Old-fashioned* **it's not the p. thing to do** cela ne se fait pas; **it's not p.** ce n'est pas bien; **that's not the p. way to behave!** en voilà des manières!, tiens-toi convenablement!; **she thanked him, as is only p.** elle l'a remercié, comme il se devait
3 *(characteristic)* **p. use of a drug** emploi *m* rationnel d'un remède; **to put sth to its p. use** utiliser qch correctement *ou* de la bonne façon; *Fml* **p. to sth** propre *ou* particulier à qch
4 *Br Fam (intensifier)* **we're in a p. mess** nous voilà dans de beaux draps!; **he's a p. fool** c'est un parfait imbécile *ou* une vraie andouille; **we gave him a p. kicking** nous lui avons mis une bonne raclée
ADV *Fam* **they got it good and p.** ils ont reçu ce qu'ils méritaient; *Fam* **to talk p.** parler correctement; *Br Dial* **he was p. angry** il était drôlement en colère
▶▶ *Math* **p. fraction** fraction *f* inférieure à l'unité; *Gram* **p. name** nom *m* propre; *Gram* **p. noun** nom propre

Note that the French word **propre** never means **right** or **adequate**. Its most common meaning is **clean**.

properly ['prɒplɪ] ADV **1** *(correctly)* correctement; **p. speaking** proprement dit, à proprement parler; **speak p.!** tu pourrais

t'exprimer convenablement!; **do it p. or not at all** faites-le correctement *ou* comme il faut ou pas du tout; **I haven't been sleeping p.** je dors mal ces temps-ci
2 *(suitably)* convenablement; *(correctly in behaviour)* comme il faut; **he very p. refused** il a refusé, comme il le fallait
3 *Fam (intensive)* **he was p. fed up** il en avait carrément marre
4 *Law (to act)* de bon droit

propertied ['prɒpətɪd] ADJ possédant

property ['prɒpətɪ] N **1** *(possessions)* propriété *f*, biens *mpl*; *(buildings)* immeuble(s) *m(pl)*; *(land)* propriété (foncière), terrain *m*; *(house)* propriété; **that's my p.** cela m'appartient; **they have p. in Scotland** *(land)* ils ont des terres en Écosse; **personal p.** affaires *fpl* personnelles, *Lit* effets *mpl* personnels; **damage to p.** dommages *mpl* matériels; **get off my p.!** sortez de ma propriété!; **p. is theft** la propriété, c'est le vol; **this television is stolen p.** cette télévision a été volée
2 *Law (right)* (droit *m* de) propriété *f*; **literary/intellectual p.** propriété littéraire/intellectuelle
3 *(quality)* *(of thing)* propriété *f*; **(inherent) p.** attribut *m*; **plants with healing properties** plantes qui ont des propriétés *ou* des vertus thérapeutiques
4 *Theat etc* accessoire *m*
5 *Comput* **properties** *(of file, drive)* propriétés *fpl*
▶▶ *Br* **p. assets** patrimoine *m* immobilier; **p. developer** promoteur, -trice (immobilier (ière)); **p. development** promotion *f* immobilière; *Acct* **p. improvement cost** impense *f*; *Br* **p. loan** prêt *m* immobilier; *Theat* **p. man** accessoiriste *m*; **p. market** marché *m* immobilier; *Theat* **p. mistress** accessoiriste *f*; **p. owner** propriétaire *mf*; **p. pages** section *f* immobilier; **p. shares** valeurs *fpl* immobilières; **p. speculation** spéculation *f* immobilière; **p. tax** impôt *m* foncier

Attention: ne pas confondre avec **propriety**, qui signifie **bienséance**.

prophecy ['prɒfɪsɪ] N prophétie *f*

prophesy ['prɒfɪsaɪ] VI prophétiser, faire des prophéties; **exactly as she had prophesied** exactement comme elle l'avait prédit
VT *(event)* prophétiser, prédire

prophet ['prɒfɪt] N prophète *m*; *Bible* **the major/minor prophets** les grands/petits prophètes; **the P.** *(in Islam)* le Prophète (Mahomet); *Prov* **no man is a p. in his own country** nul n'est prophète en son pays; *Fam* **the prophets of doom** les prophètes de malheur

prophetess ['prɒfɪtes] N prophétesse *f*

prophetic [prə'fetɪk] ADJ prophétique; **these deeds were p. of his future greatness** ces actions annonçaient sa grandeur future

prophetically [prə'fetɪklɪ] ADV prophétiquement

prophylactic [prɒfɪ'læktɪk] *Med* ADJ prophylactique
N prophylactique *m*; *(condom)* préservatif *m*

prophylaxis [prɒfɪ'læksɪs] N *Med* prophylaxie *f*

propinquity [prə'pɪŋkwɪtɪ] N *Fml* **1** *(proximity)* proximité *f* (de lieu); **to live in close p. to sb** habiter tout à proximité de qn **2** *(of blood relationship)* (proche) parenté *f* **3** *(similarity)* affinité *f* (**of ideas** entre les idées)

propitiate [prə'pɪʃɪeɪt] VT *Fml (person whom one has offended)* apaiser

propitiation [prəpɪʃɪ'eɪʃən] N *Fml (of the gods)* propitiation *f*, *Fig* apaisement *m*

propitiatory [prə'pɪʃɪət(ə)rɪ] ADJ *Fml* propitiatoire

propitious [prə'pɪʃəs] ADJ *Fml (to person, undertaking)* propice, favorable

propitiously [prə'pɪʃəslɪ] ADV *Fml* d'une manière propice

propman ['prɒpmæn] N *Theat* accessoiriste *m*

proponent [prə'pəʊnənt] N adepte *mf*, partisan *m*

proportion [prə'pɔːʃən] N **1** *(relationship)* rapport *m*, proportion *f*; *Math (arithmetic, geometric)* proportion; **friction in p. to the load** frottement proportionnel à la charge; **the same ingredients in different proportions** les mêmes ingrédients dans des proportions différentes; **in p. to ...** proportionnellement à ...; **out of all p. to ...** sans commune mesure avec ...; **the payment is out of all p. to the work involved** la rétribution n'est pas du tout proportionnelle au travail requis; **it has grown out of all p. to the original design** cela n'a plus aucune commune mesure avec le plan initial; **in perfect p.** en parfaite harmonie (**to** avec); **out of p.** mal proportionné, disproportionné; **he has no sense of p.** il n'a pas le sens de la mesure; **to lose all sense of p.** ne garder aucune mesure; **let's keep a sense of p.** remettons les choses à leur place; **you're getting this all out of p.** tu as une impression complètement déformée de tout cela; **in direct/inverse p. to sth** en rapport direct/inverse à qch SEE GRAMMAR B59
2 *(part)* *(of ingredient in mixture)* part *f*, proportion *f*, *(of work, time, money etc)* part, partie *f*; **a large p. of them are students** une grande part *ou* partie d'entre eux sont étudiants; **what p. of the group is French?** quelle est la proportion de Français dans le groupe?
3 *(dimensions)* **proportions** *(of building, human body, crisis)* proportions *fpl*; *(of machine)* dimensions *fpl*; **a Greek temple of classical proportions** un temple grec de proportions classiques
VT proportionner

proportional [prə'pɔːʃən(ə)l] ADJ proportionnel (**to** à), en proportion (**to** de); **inversely/directly p. to ...** inversement/directement proportionnel à ...
N *Math* proportionnelle *f*
▶▶ *Admin* **p. assessment** coéquation *f*; *Typ* **p. font** police *f* proportionnelle; *Pol* **p. representation** représentation *f* proportionnelle; *Typ* **p. spacing** espacement *m* proportionnel; **p. tax** impôt *m* proportionnel

proportionally [prə'pɔːʃən(ə)lɪ] ADV en proportion, proportionnellement (**to** à); **they spend p. more of their budget on research than does ...** ils accordent à la recherche une proportion de leur budget supérieure à celle que dépense ...

proportionate [prə'pɔːʃənɪt] ADJ proportionné, proportionnel (**to** à); **a p. response** une réponse en conséquence

proportionately [prə'pɔːʃənɪtlɪ] ADV proportionnellement, en proportion (**to** à)

proportioned [prə'pɔːʃənd] ADJ **well/badly p.** bien/mal proportionné

proposal [prə'pəʊz(ə)l] N **1** *(offer)* proposition *f*, offre *f*; **to make a p.** faire *ou* formuler une proposition; **p. (of marriage)** demande *f* en mariage; **p. of peace, peace p.** proposition de paix **2** *(plan)* projet *m*; **the p. to turn the building into a museum** le projet de transformer le bâtiment en musée

propose [prə'pəʊz] VT *(candidate, motion)* proposer; **to p. sb for treasurer** proposer qn pour le poste de trésorier; **he proposed that ...** il a proposé que ... + *subj*; **to p. a toast** porter un toast (**to sb** à la santé de qn); **to p. sb's health** porter un toast à la santé de qn; **to p. to do sth** *or* **doing sth** *(in-*

tend) avoir l'intention de *ou Fml* se proposer de faire qch; **they p. making the street one-way** *(suggest)* ils suggèrent de mettre cette rue en sens unique
▸ **VI 1** *(make offer of marriage)* faire une demande en mariage; **he proposed to her** il lui a demandé de l'épouser; **when did he p.?** quand a-t-il fait sa demande en mariage? **2** *Prov* **man proposes, God disposes** l'homme propose et Dieu dispose

proposed [prə'pəʊzd] **ADJ** proposé

proposer [prə'pəʊzər] **N** auteur *m* d'une offre *ou* d'une proposition; *(at club etc) (of candidate)* parrain *m*, marraine *f*; **p. of a motion** promoteur, -trice d'une motion

proposition [prɒpə'zɪʃən] **N 1** *(offer)* proposition *f*, offre *f*; *(sexual)* avances *fpl*; *Fam (matter)* affaire *f*, **that's quite a p.!, it's a tough p.!** ce n'est pas une mince affaire!; **I've got a p. (to put to you)** j'ai une proposition (à te faire); *Fam* **paying p.** affaire rentable *ou* qui rapporte; *Fam* **that's a very different p.** c'est tout à fait autre chose, c'est une autre histoire; *Fam* **he's a tough p.** il n'est pas commode
2 *(in logic), Gram* proposition *f*
▸ **VT** *(sexually)* faire des avances à

propound [prə'paʊnd] **VT** *(idea)* émettre; *(programme, theory)* exposer

proprietary [prə'praɪɪt(ə)rɪ] **ADJ** *(right etc)* de propriété, de propriétaire; *(air, attitude)* possessif
▸ *Com* **p. article** article *m* de marque (déposée); *Com* **p. brand** marque *f* déposée; **p. medicines** spécialités *fpl* pharmaceutiques; *Com* **p. name** marque déposée

proprietor [prə'praɪətər] **N** propriétaire *mf*

proprietorial [prəpraɪə'tɔːrɪəl] **ADJ** *(attitude, rights)* de propriétaire; **he's very p. about it** il est très possessif avec ça

proprietorship [prə'praɪətəʃɪp] **N** *Fml* **to dispute the p. of sth** disputer la propriété de qch; **under his p.** alors qu'il est/était propriétaire

proprietress [prə'praɪətrɪs] **N** propriétaire *f*

propriety [prə'praɪətɪ] **N 1** *(correctness) (of language, manners, behaviour)* bienséance *f*, correction *f*; *(of action, measure)* opportunité *f* **2** *(standard of behaviour)* **to observe the proprieties** observer les convenances

Note that the French word **propriété** is a false friend and is never a translation for the English word **propriety**. It means **property**.

Attention: ne pas confondre avec **property**, qui signifie **propriété**.

propshaft ['prɒpʃɑːft] **N** *Aut* arbre *m* de transmission

propulsion [prə'pʌlʃən] **N** *Tech* propulsion *f*, **means of p.** moyen(s) *m(pl) ou* mode *m* de propulsion

propulsive [prə'pʌlsɪv] **ADJ** propulsif; *(movement, effort)* de propulsion; *(force)* moteur, -trice

pro rata [-'rɑːtə] **ADJ** proportionnel, au prorata; **p. payment** paiement *m* proportionnel ▸ **ADV** proportionnellement, au prorata

prorogation [prəʊrə'geɪʃən] **N** *Fml* prorogation *f*

prorogue [prə'rəʊg] **VT** *Fml* proroger

prosaic [prəʊ'zeɪɪk] **ADJ** *(style, mind etc)* prosaïque

prosaically [prəʊ'zeɪɪklɪ] **ADV** prosaïquement

proscenium [prə'siːnɪəm] **N** *Theat* avant-scène *f*, *pl* avant-scènes
▸ **p. arch** ≃ manteau *m* d'Arlequin

proscribe [prəʊ'skraɪb] **VT** proscrire

proscription [prəʊ'skrɪpʃən] **N** proscription *f*

prose [prəʊz] **N 1** prose *f*, **poem in p.** poème *m* en prose **2** *Sch, Univ (translation)* thème *m* ▸ **VI** *Pol Old-fashioned Pej* tenir des discours ennuyeux
▸ **p. poem** poème en prose; **p. writer** prosateur *m*

prosecute ['prɒsɪkjuːt] **VT 1** *Law (person)* poursuivre (en justice); **the prosecuting counsel** *or Am* **attorney** ≃ le Ministère public **2** *Fml (pursue) (claim, activities, war etc)* poursuivre
▸ **VI** *Law* **to decide to p.** décider d'engager des poursuites judiciaires; **who's prosecuting?** qui plaide pour le Ministère public?

prosecution [prɒsɪ'kjuːʃən] **N 1** *Law (proceedings)* poursuites *fpl* judiciaires, accusation *f*, **the p.** *(lawyers)* les plaignants *mpl*; *(in Crown case)* ≃ le Ministère public; **who's appearing for the p.?** qui plaide pour le Ministère public?; **witness for the p.** témoin *m* à charge; **to bring a p. against sb** engager des poursuites judiciaires contre qn **2** *Fml (of activity etc)* poursuite *f*

prosecutor ['prɒsɪkjuːtər] **N** *Law* plaignant, -ante; **she was p. in several famous trials** elle a plaidé pour le Ministère public dans plusieurs grands procès

proselyte ['prɒsɪlaɪt] **N** prosélyte *mf*

proselytism ['prɒsɪlɪtɪz(ə)m] **N** prosélytisme *m*

proselytize ['prɒsɪlɪtaɪz] **VT** *(person)* convertir, faire un/une prosélyte de ▸ **VI** faire du prosélytisme *ou* des prosélytes

proselytizing ['prɒsɪlɪtaɪzɪŋ] **N** prosélytisme *m*

prosodic [prə'sɒdɪk] **ADJ** prosodique

prosody ['prɒsədɪ] **N** prosodie *f*

prospect¹ ['prɒspekt] **N 1** *(expectation, thought)* perspective *f*, **to open up a new p. to sb** ouvrir une nouvelle perspective à qn; **there is very little p. of it** on ne peut guère y compter; **there is every p. that we shall succeed/of his becoming Prime Minister** tout semble indiquer que nous réussirons/qu'il deviendra Premier ministre; **no p. of agreement** aucune perspective d'accord; **in p.** en perspective
2 *(chance, likelihood)* **future prospects** perspectives *fpl* d'avenir; **prospects of success** chances *fpl* de succès; **his prospects are brilliant** un brillant avenir l'attend; **to have prospects** *(of person)* avoir de l'avenir *ou* un avenir prometteur; **a job with prospects** un poste qui offre des perspectives d'avenir
3 *Com (prospective customer)* client *m* éventuel, prospect *m*
4 *Fml (view)* vue *f*, perspective *f*
▸ *Mktg* **p. pool** groupe *m* de prospects

prospect² [prə'spekt] **VI** *Min, Mktg* prospecter; **to p. for gold** chercher de l'or ▸ **VT** *(land, mine)* prospecter

prospecting [prə'spektɪŋ] **N** *Min, Mktg* prospection *f*; **oil/gold p.** prospection pétrolière/d'or

prospective [prə'spektɪv] **ADJ** *(likely)* en perspective; **my p. son-in-law** mon futur gendre; **p. buyer** acheteur, -euse éventuel(le) *ou* potentiel(le); **the p. sale of the painting at auction** la possibilité d'une vente aux enchères du tableau; **the p. Conservative candidate** l'éventuel candidat des conservateurs

prospector [prə'spektər] **N** prospecteur, -trice; **oil p.** chercheur, -euse de pétrole, *(géologue mf)* pétrolier(ière); **gold p.** chercheur, -euse d'or

prospectus, *pl* prospectuses [prə'spektəs, -təsɪz] **N** *Com* prospectus *m*, réclame *f*; *Fin* appel *m* à la souscription publique; *Sch, Univ* brochure *f* d'information

prosper ['prɒspər] **VI** prospérer, réussir; **how's he doing, still prospering?** comment va-t-il, ça marche toujours bien pour lui?

prosperity [prɒ'sperɪtɪ] **N** prospérité *f*

prosperous ['prɒspərəs] **ADJ 1** *(wealthy)* prospère **2** *Lit (favourable)* favorable; **p. winds** vents *mpl* favorables

prosperously ['prɒspərəslɪ] **ADV** d'une manière prospère; **he lives quite p.** il vit dans la prospérité

prosperousness ['prɒspərəsnɪs] **N** prospérité *f*

prostaglandin [prɒstə'glændɪn] **N** *Physiol* prostaglandine *f*

prostate ['prɒsteɪt] **N** *Anat* prostate *f*
▸ **p. gland** prostate

prosthesis ['prɒsθɪsɪs, prɒs'θiːsɪs] **N** *Surg, Gram* prothèse *f*

prosthetics [prɒs'θetɪks] **N** prothétique *f*
VOIR GRAMMAIRE A10

prostitute ['prɒstɪtjuːt] **N** prostituée *f*, **male p.** prostitué *m*
▸ **VT** *(one's body, talent etc)* prostituer; **to p. oneself** se prostituer

prostitution [prɒstɪ'tjuːʃən] **N** prostitution *f*

prostrate¹ ['prɒstreɪt] **ADJ 1** *(lying down)* couché; *(submissively)* prosterné; **to lie p.** être couché; *(submissively)* être prosterné **2** *(exhausted)* abattu, accablé; *Med* prostré; **p. with grief** terrassé par le chagrin

prostrate² [prɒ'streɪt] **VT 1** *(lay down) (on ground)* coucher *ou* étendre par terre; **to p. oneself before sb** se prosterner devant qn **2** *(exhaust)* abattre, accabler; *Med* mettre dans un état de prostration; **prostrated by the heat** accablé de chaleur

prostration [prɒ'streɪʃən] **N 1** *(lying down)* prosternation *f* **2** *(exhaustion)* abattement *m*, accablement *m*; *Med* prostration *f*

prosy ['prəʊzɪ] **ADJ** *Fam (style)* fastidieux; *Old-fashioned (person)* verbeux, ennuyeux

protagonist [prəʊ'tægənɪst] **N** protagoniste *mf*; *(of idea, view)* partisan *m*

protean [prəʊ'tiːən, 'prəʊtɪən] **ADJ** *Lit* protéiforme

protease ['prəʊtɪeɪz] **N** protéase *f*
▸ *Pharm* **p. inhibitor** antiprotéase *f*, inhibiteur *m* de protéase

protect [prə'tekt] **VT 1** protéger; *(person's interests etc)* sauvegarder; **to p. sb/sth from** *or* **against** protéger qn/qch de *ou* contre; *(rain etc)* protéger *ou* abriter qn/qch de; **well protected against the cold** bien protégé contre le froid, bien protégé du froid; **to p. sb against sb's anger** soustraire qn à la colère de qn **2** *Econ (industry)* protéger

protected [prə'tektɪd] **ADJ** *(area, species etc)* protégé

protection [prə'tekʃən] **N 1** protection *f* (**against** contre); *(of person's interests etc)* sauvegarde *f*, *Fam (money)* = argent *m* versé à un racket en échange de sa soi-disant protection; **to be under sb's p.** être sous la protection de qn; **under police p.** sous la protection de la police; **to claim the p. of the law** demander la protection de la loi; **p. against attack** protection en cas d'attaque; **society for the p. of birds** société *f* protectrice des oiseaux; **suntan lotion gives** *or* **provides some p. against the sun** le lait solaire protège du *ou* contre le soleil **2** *Econ* protectionnisme *m*; *(of industry)* protection *f*
▸ **p. factor** *(of suntan lotion)* indice *m* de protection; *Fam* **p. money** = argent versé à un racket en échange de sa soi-disant protection; **p. racket** racket *m*

protectionism [prə'tekʃənɪz(ə)m] **N** *Econ* protectionnisme *m*

protectionist [prə'tekʃənɪst] ADJ, N Econ protectionniste mf

protective [prə'tektɪv] ADJ protecteur, -trice; (clothing, mask etc) de protection, protecteur; **he is very p. towards his children** il se montre très protecteur envers ses enfants; **to be p. of one's interests** sauvegarder ses intérêts

▸▸ Aut **p. cage** cage f de sécurité; Biol **p. coloration**, **p. colouring** mimétisme m des couleurs; Econ **p. duties** droits mpl protecteurs; Econ **p. tariff** tarif m protecteur

protectively [prə'tektɪvlɪ] ADV d'une manière protectrice; (with protective gesture) d'un geste protecteur; **he put an arm p. around her shoulder** il entoura son épaule d'un bras protecteur; **to behave p. towards sb** se montrer protecteur envers qn

protector [prə'tektər] N **1** (person) protecteur, -trice **2** (device) (for machine, equipment etc) dispositif m de protection; **ear p.** protège-oreilles m inv

protectorate [prə'tektərɪt] N Pol protectorat m

protectress [prə'tektrɪs] N protectrice f

protégé, protégée ['prɒteʒeɪ] N protégé, -ée

protein ['prəʊtiːn] N protéine f

proteinaceous [prəʊtiː'neɪʃəs] ADJ Med protéique

protest[1] ['prəʊtest] N **1** protestation f; **to make a p.** protester, élever des protestations (**about sth** à propos de qch); **to register a p.** protester (**with** auprès de); **to raise a strong p.** élever des protestations énergiques; **to give rise to protests** (of action) soulever des protestations; **to stage a p.** (demonstration) organiser ou monter une manifestation; **she has strong grounds for p. at the way she was treated** elle a de bons motifs de protester contre la manière dont elle a été traitée; Law **p. in writing** réserve f, **under p.** (to do something) à son corps défendant, en protestant; (to sign etc) sous réserve; Law **to act under p.** protester de violence; **she resigned in p. (at this decision)** elle a démissionné en signe de protestation (contre cette décision)

2 Law, Fin protêt m; **p. for non-acceptance** protêt faute d'acceptation

▸▸ **p. march** marche f de protestation; **p. meeting** réunion f de protestation; **p. singer** chanteur, -euse engagé(e); **p. song** chanson f engagée; **p. strike** grève f de protestation; **p. vote** vote m de protestation

protest[2] [prə'test] VT **1** (one's innocence etc) protester de; **to p. that ...** protester en disant que ...; Fin **to p. a bill** (faire) protester un effet ou une lettre de change **2** Am (protest against) (decision, measure) protester contre

VI protester (**against** contre); **the demonstrators protesting against or about the new tax** les manifestants qui protestent contre le nouvel impôt; **really, I p., that's too much!** non, vraiment, je proteste, c'est trop!

protestable [prə'testəb(ə)l] ADJ Fin protestable

Protestant ['prɒtɪstənt] ADJ, N Rel protestant, -ante

▸▸ **the P. Church** l'Église f protestante ou réformée; **P. work ethic** éthique f protestante du travail

Protestantism ['prɒtɪstəntɪz(ə)m] N Rel protestantisme m

protestation [prɒtes'teɪʃən] N protestation f; **in spite of his protestations of innocence** en dépit de ses protestations d'innocence; **her reaction provoked protestations of love/loyalty from him** sa réaction la poussé à protester de son amour/de sa loyauté

protester [prə'testər] N protestataire mf; **anti-nuclear/peace p.** manifestant, -ante contre le nucléaire/pour la paix

protocol ['prəʊtəkɒl] N (in diplomacy etc), Law, Comput protocole m

proton ['prəʊtɒn] N Nucl proton m

protoplasm ['prəʊtəplæz(ə)m] N Biol protoplasme m, protoplasma m

prototype ['prəʊtətaɪp] N prototype m; **p. aircraft/car** prototype d'avion/de voiture

protozoa [prəʊtə'zəʊə] NPL Biol protozoaires mpl

protozoan [prəʊtə'zəʊən] N, ADJ Biol protozoaire m

protract [prə'trækt] VT prolonger; (matter, business) faire traîner en longueur

protracted [prə'træktɪd] ADJ prolongé

protraction [prə'trækʃən] N **1** (of trial etc) prolongation f, (of procedure etc) longueur f **2** Anat (of muscle) protraction f

protractor [prə'træktər] N **1** Geom rapporteur m **2** Anat (muscle) (muscle m) protracteur m

▸▸ Anat **p. muscle** (muscle) protracteur

protrude [prə'truːd] VI (of brick, beam etc) dépasser; (of shelf, balcony, rock etc) dépasser, avancer; **his teeth p. (too far)** il a les dents qui avancent; **there was a notebook protruding from her pocket** un carnet dépassait de sa poche

VT (faire) sortir, pousser en avant, avancer

protruding [prə'truːdɪŋ] ADJ en saillie, saillant; (jaw, teeth) qui avance; (eyes) exorbité, saillant; (stomach, ribs) protubérant

protrusion [prə'truːʒ(ə)n] N **1** (state) sortie f, saillie f **2** (thing) saillie f, protubérance f; Anat protrusion f

protuberance [prə'tjuːbərəns] N protubérance f

protuberant [prə'tjuːbərənt] ADJ protubérant

proud [praʊd] ADJ **1** (justifiably) fier; **to be p. of sth/of having done sth** être fier ou s'enorgueillir de qch/d'avoir fait qch; **to be p. of oneself** être fier de soi; Iron **I hope you're p. of yourself!** tu peux être fier de toi!; **I'm p. to have known her** je suis fier de l'avoir connue; **it made me feel p. to be Welsh** cela m'a rendu fier d'être gallois; **we're all p. of you** nous sommes tous fiers de toi; **he's the p. owner of ...** il est l'heureux propriétaire de ...; **it was her proudest possession** c'était ce qu'elle avait de plus précieux; **a p. moment** un moment d'intense fierté; **a picture of the p. parents** une photo des parents, débordants de fierté; **as p. as a peacock** or **as Punch** fier comme Artaban

2 Pej (arrogant) orgueilleux, fier; **too p. to apologize** trop fier pour s'excuser; **I'll sit here, I'm not p.** je m'assiérai là, je ne suis pas exigeant

3 (noble) fier, digne; (impressive) (city etc) imposant, magnifique; Old-fashioned, Hum **a p. beauty** une beauté orgueilleuse; Lit **a p. and noble race** or **people** un peuple fier et noble

4 Tech (protruding) **to stand p. of a surface** dépasser ou déborder d'une surface

ADV Fam **to do sb p.** faire honneur à qn; (entertain lavishly) se mettre en frais pour qn; **the caterers did us p.** les traiteurs nous ont fait un festin de rois; **they do you p. at that restaurant** on se régale dans ce restaurant; **to do oneself p.** se dépasser

proudly ['praʊdlɪ] ADV **1** (with justifiable pride) fièrement; **we p. present the Rolling Stones in concert** nous avons le plaisir ou nous sommes heureux de vous présenter les Rolling Stones en concert; **the banners waved p. in the wind** les drapeaux flottaient fièrement dans le vent **2** Pej (haughtily) orgueilleusement

prove [pruːv] (pp **proved**, esp Am, Scot **proven** ['pruːv(ə)n, 'prəʊ-]) VT **1** (demonstrate) (the truth of something) prouver, démontrer; (fact) constater; (one's identity) justifier de; (one's good will) témoigner de; Law (a will) homologuer; **I can't p. it** je ne peux pas le prouver; **to p. that ...** prouver que ...; **the evidence goes to p. that ...** les témoignages concourent à prouver que ...; **she/this assertion was proved wrong** on a prouvé qu'elle avait tort/que cette affirmation était fausse; **subsequent developments proved me right** la suite des événements m'a donné raison; **to p. oneself** faire ses preuves; **what are you trying to p.?** qu'est-ce que tu cherches à prouver?; **to do sth to p. a point** faire qch pour démontrer un point de vue; **that proves my point** ceci confirme ce que je disais; **that doesn't p. anything!** cela ne prouve rien!; Math **to p. a sum** faire la preuve d'un calcul **2** Culin (dough) faire lever

VI (of person) se montrer; **she proved (to be) ideal for the job** elle s'est révélée être la personne idéale pour cet emploi; **if what you say proves (to be) true** si ce que vous dites se confirme; **many of his observations have proved correct** beaucoup de ses observations se sont avérées ou révélées justes; **to p. unequal to one's task** se montrer au-dessous de sa tâche

proven ['pruːv(ə)n, 'prəʊ-] PP esp Am, Scot see **prove**

ADJ (demonstrated) (courage, method, remedy etc) éprouvé; Scot Law **a verdict of p./not p.** un verdict de culpabilité prouvée/non prouvée

provenance ['prɒvənəns] N provenance f, origine f

Provençal [prɒvɒn'sɑːl] ADJ provençal, -aux N **1** Provençal, -ale **2** Ling provençal m

provender ['prɒvɪndər] N Agr fourrage m

proverb ['prɒvɜːb] N proverbe m; Bible **(the Book of) Proverbs** le livre des Proverbes

proverbial [prə'vɜːbɪəl] ADJ proverbial, -aux; **as happy as the p. sandboy** gai comme le pinson du proverbe

proverbially [prə'vɜːbɪəlɪ] ADV proverbialement

provide [prə'vaɪd] VT **1** (supply) fournir; **to p. sb with sth, to p. sth for sb** fournir qch à qn, pourvoir qn de qch; **they were well provided with food** ils étaient bien approvisionnés ou ravitaillés; **this provided her with an excuse** ça lui a fourni une excuse; **please write your name and address in the space provided** veuillez écrire vos nom et adresse dans le blanc prévu à cet effet; **to p. an explanation** donner ou fournir une explication; **to p. an exit** (of passage) offrir une sortie; (of architect) ménager une sortie; **to p. a regular bus service** assurer un service d'autobus régulier; **to p. jobs** fournir des emplois; **this factory will p. 500 new jobs** cette usine créera 500 emplois **2** (stipulate) stipuler (**that** que); **the law provides that ...** la loi stipule ou prévoit que ...

VI **the Lord will p.** Dieu y pourvoira

▸ **provide against** VT INSEP (attack etc) se prémunir contre; (danger) parer à

▸ **provide for** VT INSEP **1** (supply needs of) pourvoir ou subvenir aux besoins de; **to p. for oneself** pourvoir ou subvenir à ses propres besoins; **to be well** or **amply provided for** avoir grandement de quoi vivre; **he provided for everything** il a subvenu à tout; **he left his family well provided for** il laissa sa famille à l'abri du besoin **2** (allow for) **to p. for an eventuality** pourvoir à ou parer à une éventualité; **expenses provided for in the budget** dépenses prévues au budget; **this has been provided for** on y a pourvu; **they had failed to p. for that possibility** ils ne s'étaient pas prémunis contre cette possibilité

provided [prə'vaɪdɪd] **CONJ p. (that)** pourvu que + *sub*, à condition que + *sub*; **p. there is enough** pourvu qu'il y en ait assez, à condition qu'il y en ait assez, seulement s'il y en a assez

providence ['prɒvɪdəns] **N 1** *Rel* providence *f* (divine); **by a special p.** par une intervention providentielle; **P.** smiled on us la chance *ou* la fortune nous a souri **2** *Old-fashioned (foresight)* prévoyance *f*, prudence *f*

provident ['prɒvɪdənt] **ADJ** prévoyant
▸▸ *Br* **p. society** société *f* de prévoyance

providential [prɒvɪ'denʃəl] **ADJ** *(help etc)* providentiel

providentially [prɒvɪ'denʃəlɪ] **ADV** providentiellement

providently ['prɒvɪdəntlɪ] **ADV** avec prévoyance; **he had p. set aside a considerable sum** il avait eu la prévoyance de mettre une somme considérable de côté

provider [prə'vaɪdər] **N** pourvoyeur, -euse; *Com* fournisseur, -euse; **the region was one of the main providers of unskilled labour** cette région était l'une des principales réserves de main-d'œuvre non qualifiée

providing [prə'vaɪdɪŋ] **CONJ** = **provided**

province ['prɒvɪns] **N 1** *(of country)* province *f*; **in the provinces** en province **2** *Law (of court)* juridiction *f*, ressort *m*, compétence *f*; **that is not (within) my p.** ce n'est pas de mon ressort

provincial [prə'vɪnʃəl] **ADJ** provincial, -aux; *(theatre)* de province
N provincial, -ale

provincialism [prə'vɪnʃəlɪz(ə)m] **N** provincialisme *m*

proving ['pruːvɪŋ] **N** *(of truth of sth)* preuve *f*, démonstration *f*; *(of fact)* constatation *f*; *Law (of a will)* homologation *f*; **the p. of a theory/ a hypothesis** la démonstration d'une théorie/d'une hypothèse
▸▸ **p. ground** terrain *m* d'essai

provirus ['prəʊvaɪrəs] **N** *Med* provirus *m*

provision [prə'vɪʒən] **N 1** *(supply)* provision *f*, réserve *f*; **provisions** *(food)* provisions *(de bouche)*; **to lay in a store of provisions** faire provision de vivres; **wholesale p. business** maison *f* d'alimentation en gros
2 *(act of supplying)* **p. of capital/services** prestation *f* de capitaux/de services; **the p. of free education is under threat** l'éducation gratuite est menacée; **the p. of food to the refugees** l'approvisionnement des réfugiés en nourriture; **the p. of housing to the refugees** le logement des réfugiés; **there was little p. for education in the budget** la part du budget consacrée à l'éducation était faible
3 *(allowance)* **p. for/against sth** *(prise f des)* dispositions *fpl* nécessaires pour assurer qch/pour parer à qch; **to make p. for sth** pourvoir à qch; **the law makes no p. for a case of this kind** la loi ne prévoit pas un cas semblable; **to make p. for one's family** assurer l'avenir de sa famille; **to make p. against sth** prendre des mesures contre qch, se prémunir contre qch
4 *(stipulation) (of treaty)* article *m*; *(of contract)* clause *f*, stipulation *f*, **provisions of an act** dispositions *fpl* d'une loi; **to come within the provisions of the law** être prévu par la loi
VT *(army, ship etc)* approvisionner
▸▸ *Acct* **p. for charges** provision pour frais; *Acct* **p. for depreciation** provision pour dépréciation *ou* amortissement; *Acct* **p. for liabilities** provision pour sommes exigibles

provisional [prə'vɪʒən(ə)l] **ADJ** provisoire;

Law provisionnel; *(finding)* par provision
N *Pol* **the Provisionals** les membres *mpl* de l'IRA provisoire
▸▸ *Fin* **p. budget** budget *m* prévisionnel; *Br Aut* **p. driving licence** permis *m* de conduire provisoire; **p. government** gouvernement *m* provisoire; **the P. IRA** l'IRA *f* provisoire

provisionally [prə'vɪʒən(ə)lɪ] **ADV** provisoirement; *Law* provisionnellement; *(to appoint sb)* à titre provisoire

proviso, *pl* **provisos** [prə'vaɪzəʊ, -əʊz] **N 1** *(in document)* clause *f* conditionnelle; *(of contract)* condition *f* **2** *(stipulation)* stipulation *f*, **with the p. that he gives his consent** à condition qu'il soit d'accord

provisory [prə'vaɪzərɪ] **ADJ** conditionnel

Provo ['prəʊvəʊ] **N** *Pol Fam* membre *m* de l'IRA provisoire

provocation [prɒvə'keɪʃən] **N** provocation *f*, **at the slightest p.** à la moindre provocation; **to act under p.** agir en réponse à une provocation; **without p.** sans provocation

provocative [prə'vɒkətɪv] **ADJ** provocateur, -trice, provocant; *(smile, dress etc)* provocant, aguichant; **he's just being p.** il ne fait cela que pour provoquer

provocatively [prə'vɒkətɪvlɪ] **ADV** *(to smile, be dressed)* d'une manière provocante, ...; **he said p.** ..., dit-il d'un air provocant; **a p. low-cut dress** une robe au décolleté provocant

provoke [prə'vəʊk] **VT 1** *(person)* provoquer, pousser, inciter (**to do sth** à faire qch); *(irritate)* irriter, agacer, exaspérer; *(dog)* exciter; **to p. sb to anger** mettre qn en colère; **I was provoked** on m'a provoqué *ou Fam* cherché; **don't p. her** ne la provoque *ou Fam* cherche pas **2** *(arouse) (curiosity)* exciter, faire naître; *(gaiety)* provoquer; *(passion, indignation, interest)* soulever; **to p. a reaction** provoquer une réaction

provoking [prə'vəʊkɪŋ] **ADJ** *(irritating)* irritant, agaçant, exaspérant

provost ['prɒvəst] **N 1** *Sch, Univ* principal *m* **2** *Scot Admin* maire *m*
▸▸ *Mil* **p. duty** ['prɒvəʊ] service *m* prévôtal, prévôté *f*; *Mil* **p. marshal** ['prɒvəʊ] prévôt *m*

prow [praʊ] **N** *(of ship)* proue *f*

prowess ['praʊɪs] **N 1** *(skill)* talent *m*, habileté *f*, **her p. at tennis** *or* **as a t. player** son talent au tennis; **she has shown great p.** elle a fait des prouesses; **his sexual/intellectual p.** ses prouesses sexuelles/intellectuelles **2** *Lit (courage)* vaillance *f*

prowl [praʊl] **N to go on the p.** *(of lion etc)*, *Fig* partir en chasse; **to be on the p. for sth** être en quête *ou* à la recherche de qch; **let's have a p. around** et si on zyeutait?
VI *(of animal, person)* rôder; **to p. about the streets** rôder dans les rues; **to p. about the shops** tourner dans les magasins
VT to p. the streets rôder dans les rues
▸▸ *Am* **p. car** voiture *f* de police en patrouille

prowler ['praʊlər] **N** rôdeur, -euse; **there's a p. in the neighbourhood** il y a quelqu'un qui rôde dans le voisinage

prox [prɒks] **ADV** *Com Old-fashioned (abbr* **proximo)** *(du mois)* prochain

proximity [prɒk'sɪmɪtɪ] **N** *(closeness)* proximité *f*, **its p. to London** sa situation à proximité de Londres; **in p. to** à proximité de, près de; **in close p. to** juste à proximité *ou* tout près de; *Fig* **p. of blood** proche parenté *f*
▸▸ *Mil* **p. fuse** fusée *f* à influence, fusée de proximité; *Pol* **p. talks** négociations *fpl* rapprochées

proximo ['prɒksɪməʊ] **ADV** *Com Old-fashioned (du mois)* prochain

proxy ['prɒksɪ] **N 1** *(power)* procuration *f*,

délégation *f* de pouvoirs, pouvoir *m*, mandat *m* **2** *(person)* mandataire *mf*, fondé, -ée de pouvoir, délégué, -ée; *Com* mandataire; **to make sb one's p.** déléguer ses pouvoirs à qn; **to vote by p.** voter par procuration
▸▸ **p. bomb** = bombe *f* amenée sur les lieux par une personne agissant sous la contrainte; *Comput* **p. server** serveur *m* proxy, serveur mandataire *ou* de procuration; **p. vote** vote *m* par procuration

Prozac® ['prəʊzæk] **N** Prozac® *m*

PRP [piːɑː'piː] **N** *(abbr* **performance-related pay)** salaire *m* au rendement

prude [pruːd] **N** prude *mf*, bégueule *f*, **don't be such a p.!** ne soyez pas si prude *ou* si bégueule!

prudence ['pruːdəns] **N** prudence *f*, *(common sense)* sagesse *f*
▸▸ *Acct* **p. concept** principe *m* de prudence

prudent ['pruːdənt] **ADJ** prudent; *(sensible)* sage

prudential [pruː'denʃəl] **ADJ**
▸▸ *Am* **p. committee** *(of municipality, company)* = comité *m* de surveillance

prudently ['pruːdəntlɪ] **ADV** prudemment

prudery ['pruːdərɪ] **N** pruderie *f*, pudibonderie *f*

prudish ['pruːdɪʃ] **ADJ** prude, pudibond

prudishness ['pruːdɪʃnɪs] **N** = **prudery**

prune [pruːn] **N** pruneau *m*; *Fig Fam* **old p.** *(old woman)* vieille bique *f* ratatinée
VT 1 *(rose bush, fruit tree)* tailler; *(tree roots)* rafraîchir; *(tree)* émonder; *(branch)* élaguer **2** *Fig (article etc)* faire des coupures dans, élaguer; *(list of tasks, demands)* réduire; *(army, bureaucracy)* dégraisser
▸ **prune away, prune off** **VT SEP** *(branch)* élaguer

> Note that the French word **prune** is a false friend and is never a translation for the English word **prune**. It means **plum**.

pruning ['pruːnɪŋ] **N 1** *(of rose bush, fruit tree)* taille *f*; *(of tree)* émondage *m*; *(of branch)* élagage *m* **2** *Fig (of article etc)* élagage *m*
▸▸ **p. hook** ébranchoir *m*; **p. knife** serpette *f*; **p. shears** cisailles *fpl*

prurience ['prʊərɪəns], **pruriency** ['prʊərɪənsɪ] **N** lasciveté *f*, lubricité *f*

prurient ['prʊərɪənt] **ADJ** *(à l'esprit)* lascif; **to take a p. interest in sth** porter un intérêt lascif à qch

Prussia ['prʌʃə] **N** Prusse *f*

Prussian ['prʌʃən] **ADJ** prussien
N Prussien, -ienne
▸▸ **P. blue** bleu *m* de Prusse

prussic ['prʌsɪk] **ADJ** *Chem (acid)* prussique, cyanhydrique

pry[1] [praɪ] **VI** *(pt, pp* **pried)** *(into particular matter)* fouiller, fureter (**into sth** dans qch); *(generally)* fourrer son nez partout; **I don't mean to p., but why did you do it?** je sais que ça ne me regarde pas, mais pourquoi est-ce que tu as fait ça?; **to p. into a secret** chercher à pénétrer un secret

pry[2] **VT** *(pt, pp* **pried)** *Am* = **prize**[2]
▸ **pry loose** **VT SEP** *Am* décoller, détacher
▸ **pry open** **VT SEP** *Am (door, safe etc)* forcer

prying ['praɪɪŋ] **ADJ** curieux, indiscret, -ète; **safe from p. eyes** à l'abri des regards indiscrets

PS [piː'es] **N** *(abbr* **postscript)** PS *m*; **to add a PS to a letter** ajouter un PS à une lettre; **PS see you next week** PS à la semaine prochaine

psalm [sɑːm] **N** psaume *m*; *Bible* **(the Book of) Psalms** (le livre des) Psaumes
▸▸ **p. book** livre *m* de psaumes, psautier *m*

psalmist ['sɑːmɪst] N psalmiste m

psalmody ['sɑːmədɪ] N psalmodie f

psalter ['sɔːltər] N psautier m

PSB [piːes'biː] N Am TV (abbr **public service broadcasting**) émissions fpl de service public

PSBR [piːesbiː'ɑːr] N Br Econ (abbr **public sector borrowing requirement**) = besoins mpl d'emprunt du secteur public non couverts par les rentrées fiscales

psephological [sefəˈlɒdʒɪk(ə)l] ADJ relatif à l'étude scientifique des élections

psephologist [seˈfɒlədʒɪst] N spécialiste mf de l'étude des élections

psephology [seˈfɒlədʒɪ] N étude f scientifique des élections

pseud [sjuːd] N Br Fam Pej crâneur, -euse; **P.'s Corner** = section f de la revue humoristique Private Eye où des articles prétentieux sont publiés pour l'amusement général

pseudo ['sjuːdəʊ] ADJ, PREF Fam faux, f fausse, pseudo-

pseudonym ['sjuːdənɪm] N pseudonyme m; **to write sth under a p.** écrire qch sous un pseudonyme

pseudonymous [sjuːˈdɒnɪməs] ADJ (writer) qui écrit sous un pseudonyme; (column, article) écrit sous un pseudonyme

pseudy ['sjuːdɪ] ADJ Fam Pej prétentieux

pshaw [(p)ʃɔː] INT Old-fashioned (indicating disgust) peuh!

psi [saɪ] N Phys (abbr **pounds per square inch**) livres par pouce carré

psittacosis [sɪtəˈkəʊsɪs] N Med, Vet psittacose f

psoriasis [səˈraɪəsɪs] N Med psoriasis m

psst [pst] INT (to attract attention) psitt!, pst!; (to warn) chut!

▸ **PST** [piːesˈtiː] N Am (abbr **Pacific Standard Time**) PST

▸ **PSV** [piːesˈviː] N Formerly (abbr **public service vehicle**) véhicule m de transport en commun

psych out [saɪk] VT SEP Fam = psyche out

psych up VT SEP Fam = psyche up

psyche ['saɪkɪ] N psychisme m; Phil psyché f

▸ **psyche out** [saɪk] VT SEP Fam (unnerve) déstabiliser; (guess) (sb's intentions, motives etc) deviner, percer à jour

▸ **psyche up** VT SEP Fam (prepare) **to p. one-self up (for sth/to do sth)** se préparer mentalement (à qch/à faire qch); **to p. sb up for sth** préparer qn mentalement pour qch

psychedelic [saɪkəˈdelɪk] ADJ psychédélique

psyched-up [saɪkt-] ADJ Fam gonflé à bloc; **to get oneself p.** se préparer mentalement

psychiatric [saɪkɪˈætrɪk] ADJ psychiatrique
▸ Br **p. social worker** assistant, -ante social(e) en psychiatrie

psychiatrist [saɪˈkaɪətrɪst] N psychiatre mf

psychiatry [saɪˈkaɪətrɪ] N psychiatrie f

psychic(al) [saɪkɪk, ɪk(ə)l] ADJ psychique; (phenomenon etc) métapsychique; **to have p. powers** avoir des dons mpl de voyance, être un peu médium; Fam **I'm not p.!** je ne suis pas devin!
N médium m

psycho ['saɪkəʊ] ADJ, N Fam psychopathe mf

psychoanalyse, Am **psychoanalyze** [saɪkəʊˈænəlaɪz] VT psychanalyser

psychoanalysis [saɪkəʊəˈnælɪsɪs] N psychanalyse f

psychoanalyst [saɪkəʊˈænəlɪst] N psychanalyste mf

psychoanalytic(al) [saɪkəʊænəˈlɪtɪk, -ɪk(ə)l] ADJ psychanalytique

psychoanalyze Am = psychoanalyse

psychobabble ['saɪkəʊbæb(ə)l] N Fam jargon m de psy

psychodrama ['saɪkəʊdrɑːmə] N psychodrame m, jeu m de rôle

psychographic [saɪkəʊˈgræfɪk] N psychographique
▸ Mktg **p. segmentation** segmentation f psychographique

psychographics [saɪkəʊˈgræfɪks] N psychographie f VOIR GRAMMAIRE A10

psychological [saɪkəˈlɒdʒɪk(ə)l] ADJ psychologique
▸ **p. contract** contrat m psychologique; **the p. moment** le moment psychologique; Mktg **p. price** prix m psychologique ou d'acceptabilité; **p. profile** profil m psychologique; **p. warfare** guerre f psychologique

psychologically [saɪkəˈlɒdʒɪklɪ] ADV psychologiquement

psychologist [saɪˈkɒlədʒɪst] N psychologue mf; **child p.** psychologue pour enfants

psychology [saɪˈkɒlədʒɪ] N psychologie f; **the p. of the football hooligan** la psychologie des hooligans du football; Fam **to use p.** faire preuve de psychologie

psychometric [saɪkəˈmetrɪk] ADJ psychométrique

psychomotor [saɪkəʊməʊtər] ADJ psychomoteur, -trice

psychoneurosis [saɪkəʊnjʊˈrəʊsɪs] N psychonévrose f

psychopath ['saɪkəʊpæθ] N psychopathe mf

psychopathic [saɪkəʊˈpæθɪk] ADJ (person) psychopathe; (condition, personality) psychopathique

psychopathology [saɪkəʊpəˈθɒlədʒɪ] N psychopathologie f

psychophysiology [saɪkəʊfɪzɪˈɒlədʒɪ] N psychophysiologie f

psychosis, pl **psychoses** [saɪˈkəʊsɪs, -əʊsiːz] N psychose f

psychosomatic [saɪkəʊsəˈmætɪk] ADJ psychosomatique

psychotherapist [saɪkəʊˈθerəpɪst] N psychothérapeute mf

psychotherapy [saɪkəʊˈθerəpɪ] N psychothérapie f

psychotic [saɪˈkɒtɪk] ADJ, N psychotique mf

psychotropic [saɪkəʊˈtrɒpɪk] ADJ Pharm psychotrope
▸ **p. drug** psychotrope m

PT [piːˈtiː] N Old-fashioned (abbr **physical training**) EPS f

PTA [piːtiːˈeɪ] N Sch (abbr **Parent-Teacher Association**) = association f de parents d'élèves et de professeurs

ptarmigan ['tɑːmɪgən] N (bird) **p.,** Am **rock p.** lagopède m muet, Can lagopède des rochers

Pte Mil (abbr **private**) simple soldat m

pterodactyl [terəʊˈdæktɪl] N ptérodactyle m

PTO [piːtiːˈəʊ] (abbr **please turn over**) TSVP

ptomaine ['təʊmeɪn] N Chem ptomaïne f
▸ **p. poisoning** intoxication f alimentaire

P2P ['piːtuːˈpiː] ADJ (abbr **peer to peer**) P2P

Pty (abbr **proprietary company**) SARL

pub [pʌb] N Br Fam pub m
▸ **p. food,** Fam **p. grub** = nourriture f (relativement simple) servie dans un pub; **p. lunch** déjeuner m simple (servi dans un pub); **to go out for a p. lunch** aller déjeuner dans un pub; **p. quiz** jeu m de culture générale dans un pub

pub-crawl N Br Fam tournée f des bars; **to go on a p.** faire la tournée des bars, aller de bar en bar, Can Fam partir sur une brosse

puberty ['pjuːbətɪ] N Physiol puberté f; **at p.** à la puberté; **to reach p.** atteindre l'âge de la puberté

pubescence [pjuːˈbesəns] N **1** Bot pubescence f **2** Physiol puberté f

pubescent [pjuːˈbesənt] ADJ **1** Bot pubescent **2** Physiol pubère

pubic ['pjuːbɪk] ADJ Anat pubien
▸ **p. bone** symphyse f pubienne; **p. hair** poils mpl pubiens ou du pubis; (single) poil m pubien ou du pubis

pubis ['pjuːbɪs] N Anat pubis m

public ['pʌblɪk] ADJ public, f publique; **to go p. (of firm)** émettre ou placer des actions dans le public; (reveal information) tout dire ou raconter; **to go p. with the story** raconter toute l'histoire; **to make sth p.** rendre qch public; (news etc) publier qch; **to make a p. appearance** paraître en public; **at p. expense** aux frais du contribuable; **to be in the p. eye** être très en vue; **to work for the p. good** travailler pour le bien public; **to be in the p. interest** servir le bien public; **of p. interest** d'intérêt public; **p. interest in the matter was flagging** l'intérêt du public pour cette affaire faiblissait; **it's p. knowledge** tout le monde sait cela; **to be in p. ownership** être nationalisé; **in a p. place** dans un lieu public; **to make a p. protest** protester publiquement
N **the (general) p.** le (grand) public; **book aimed at a wide p.** livre qui s'adresse à un large public; **my p. like the old songs** mon public aime les vieilles chansons; **there isn't much of a p. for that kind of thing** ce genre de choses n'attire pas un grand public; **in p.** en public, publiquement; Fin **to issue shares to the p.** placer des actions dans le public VOIR GRAMMAIRE A11
▸ Am TV **p. access channel** = chaîne f du réseau câblé sur laquelle des particuliers peuvent diffuser leurs propres émissions; **p. accountability** transparence f, Br Pol **P. Accounts Committee** = comité m chargé d'examiner les comptes publics; **p. address system** sonorisation f, Fam sono f, Am **p. assistance** aide f sociale; **p. authorities** pouvoirs mpl publics; Br **p. bar** salle f de bar (dans un pub qui contient deux bars séparés, l'expression désigne le plus populaire des deux); **p. body** corporation f de droit public; Am Radio, TV **p. broadcaster** diffuseur m public; Br **p. call box** cabine f (téléphonique) publique; **p. carrier** transporteur m public; **p. company** ≃ société f anonyme; **p. company law** loi f sur les sociétés anonymes; Br **p. convenience** toilettes fpl publiques; Br, Can **p. corporation** entreprise f publique; **p. data network** réseau m public de données; Fin **p. debt** dette f publique ou de l'État; Am Law **p. defender** avocat m commis d'office; Fin **p. deposits** = dépôts mpl des différents services du gouvernement britannique à la Banque d'Angleterre; **p. domain** domaine m public; **to be p. domain** être dans le domaine public; **in the p. domain** dans le domaine public; Comput **p. domain software** logiciel m (du domaine public), Can publiciel m; **p. enemy number one** ennemi m public numéro un; **p. examination** examen m national de l'enseignement public; **p. excursion fare** tarif m excursion; **p. figure** personnalité f très en vue; **p. foreign debt** dette publique extérieure; **p. funds** fonds mpl publics; **p. health official** représentant, -ante de la santé publique; **p. holiday** jour m férié, fête f légale; **p. house** Br (pub) pub m, bar m; Am (inn) auberge f, Am **p. housing** logements mpl sociaux, ≃ HLM f inv; **p. information broadcast** message m de grande cause nationale; Br **p. lavatory** toilettes publiques; **p. lending right** = droits mpl que touche un auteur ou un éditeur pour le prêt de ses li-

vres en bibliothèque; **p. liability** responsabilité *f* civile; **p. liability insurance** assurance *f* responsabilité civile; **p. life** la vie publique; **p. limited company** ≃ société anonyme; **p. loan** emprunt *m* public; **p. money** deniers *mpl ou* fonds publics; *St Exch* **p. offering** offre *f* publique; **p. opinion** opinion *f* publique; **p. opinion poll** sondage *m* (d'opinion); **p. park** jardin *m* public; *Br* **P. Record Office** ≃ Archives *fpl* nationales; **p. relations** relations *fpl* publiques; **p. relations consultant** conseil *m* en relations publiques, conseil en communication; **p. relations department** service *m* des relations publiques; **p. relations director** directeur, -trice des relations publiques; **p. relations exercise** opération *f* de relations publiques; **p. relations manager** directeur, -trice des relations publiques; **p. relations officer** responsable *mf* des relations publiques; **p. sales office** (of an airline etc) agence *f* commerciale; **p. school** (in UK) public school *f*, école *f* privée (prestigieuse); (in US) école publique; *Br* a **p.-school education** une scolarité *ou* des études *fpl* dans le privé; *Br* **he's very p.-school** il fait très école privée; **p. sector** secteur *m* public; *Br Econ* **p. sector borrowing requirement** = besoins *mpl* d'emprunt du secteur public non couverts par les rentrées fiscales; **p. sector earnings** revenus *mpl* du secteur public; **p. service** (amenity) service public *ou* d'intérêt général; *Br* (civil service) fonction *f* publique; **the p. services** les services publics; **the organization performs a useful p. service** cette organisation offre un service public fort utile; *Am TV* **p. service broadcasting** émissions *fpl* de service public; **p. service vehicle** véhicule *m* de transport en commun; *St Exch* **p. share offer** offre publique de vente; **p. speaking** art *m* oratoire; *Fin* **p. spending** dépenses *fpl* publiques *ou* de l'État; **p. spirit** sens *m* civique, civisme *m*; **p. transport** transports *mpl* en commun; **p. transport advertising** affichage *m* transport; **p. transport vehicle** véhicule *m* des transports en commun; **p. utility** *Am* (company) = société privée assurant un service public et réglementée par une commission d'État; *Br* (amenity) service public; *Br* **p. utility company** société d'utilité publique; **p. works** travaux *mpl* publics

> Note that the French expression **école publique** is never a translation for the British sense of the expression **public school**. It means **state school**.

Public schools

En Angleterre et au pays de Galles, le terme "public school" désigne une école privée de type traditionnel. Certaines de ces écoles (Eton et Harrow, par exemple) sont très prestigieuses et élitistes. Les "public schools" sont censées former l'élite de la nation. Aux États-Unis et parfois en Écosse, le terme désigne une école publique.

publican ['pʌblɪkən] N *Br* patron, -onne d'un/du pub

publication [pʌblɪ'keɪʃən] N **1** (of book, news, the banns etc) publication *f*, (of order, decree) promulgation *f*; **my article has been accepted for p.** mon article va être publié; **this is not for p.** ceci n'est pas destiné à la publication **2** (published work) publication *f* ▶▶ **p. date** (of book) date *f* de parution *ou* de publication; **p. day** jour *m* de parution

publicist ['pʌblɪsɪst] N publicitaire *mf*

publicity [pʌb'lɪsɪtɪ] N (given to a matter) publicité *f*, *Fam* pub *f*, *Com* publicité, réclame *f*; **the football team has received a**

lot of free **p. as a result of this scandal** ce scandale a fait beaucoup de publicité (gratuite) à l'équipe de football; **it's another one of his p.-seeking gimmicks** c'est encore un de ses trucs pour se faire de la publicité; **there's no such thing as bad p.** on ne fait jamais trop parler de soi; **they're very p. conscious** ils sont très conscients de leur image
▶▶ **p. agent** agent *m* publicitaire; **p. brochure** brochure *f* publicitaire; **p. budget** budget *m* publicitaire; **p. campaign** (for new product) campagne *f* publicitaire, campagne de publicité; (by government) campagne d'information; **p. department** service *m* de publicité; **p. expenses** dépenses *fpl* de la publicité; **p. manager** chef *m* de (la) publicité; **p. stunt** coup *m* de pub

publicize ['pʌblɪsaɪz] VT (make known) faire connaître au public; *Com* (advertise) (product) faire de la publicité *ou* de la réclame *ou Fam* de la pub pour; **her resignation was widely publicized** on a fait beaucoup de battage autour de sa démission; **the launch of their new product has been widely publicized** leur nouveau produit a été lancé à grand renfort de publicité; **she doesn't p. the fact** elle ne le crie pas sur tous les toits

publicly ['pʌblɪklɪ] ADV publiquement, en public; *Econ* **p. owned** nationalisé, d'état

public-spirited ADJ (person) qui a le sens civique; (gesture, response) dicté par le sens civique; **that was very p. of them** ils ont fait preuve par là d'un grand civisme *ou* sens civique

publish ['pʌblɪʃ] VT **1** (of publisher, author) (book) éditer, publier; *Comput* (web page) publier; **we're going to p. it next week** on va le publier la semaine prochaine, ça paraîtra chez nous la semaine prochaine; **who publishes Sartre?** qui édite *ou* publie Sartre?; **it's published by Polygon** c'est édité chez Polygon; **the magazine is published quarterly** la revue paraît tous les trois mois; **just published** (of book) vient de paraître; **she's had two novels published** on a publié deux de ses romans; **he's a published author** ses livres sont publiés **2** (edict, the banns) publier; (news) publier, faire paraître
VI **they decided not to p.** ils ont décidé de ne pas faire publier la nouvelle/leur ouvrage/cet article/*etc*; **p. and be damned!** publiez si vous voulez et allez au diable!; **we're going to p. and be damned** on publiera, advienne que pourra

publishable ['pʌblɪʃəb(ə)l] ADJ publiable

publisher ['pʌblɪʃər] N **1** éditeur, -trice; (company) maison *f* d'édition; **p.'s reader** lecteur, -trice de manuscrits (dans une maison d'édition) **2** *Am* (newspaper owner) propriétaire *mf* d'un/du journal

publishing ['pʌblɪʃɪŋ] N **1** (of book, report, accounts etc) publication *f*, (profession, business) édition *f*; **to work** *or* **be in p.** travailler dans l'édition **2** (of the banns etc) publication *f*
▶▶ **p. firm, p. house** maison *f* d'édition; **the p. trade** l'édition

puce [pju:s] ADJ, N puce *m inv*

puck[1] [pʌk] N (elf) lutin *m*, farfadet *m*

puck[2] N *Sport* (in ice hockey) palet *m*

pucker ['pʌkər] N (in face) (wrinkle) ride *f*, (fold) pli *m*; (in material) faux pli, godet *m*
VT (one's face) rider; (material) froncer, faire goder *ou* godailler; (one's brow, forehead etc) froncer; (one's lips) plisser
VI = **pucker up** VI
▶ **pucker up** VI (of garment, material) faire des faux plis, goder, godailler; **his face puckered up** sa figure s'est crispée; **she puckered up for his kiss** elle tendit les lèvres, se préparant à son baiser
VT SEP (one's lips) tendre

puckish ['pʌkɪʃ] ADJ malicieux, espiègle

pud [pʊd] N *Br Fam* pudding *m*; (dessert) dessert *m*; **what's for p.?** qu'est-ce qu'il y a comme dessert?; **there's ice-cream for p.** il y a de la glace en dessert

pudding ['pʊdɪŋ] N **1** (dish) (suet) p. pudding *m*, pouding *m*; *Sl Hum* **to be in the p. club** (be pregnant) avoir un polichinelle dans le tiroir **2** (dessert) dessert *m*; **what's for p.?** qu'est-ce qu'il y a comme *ou* pour le dessert? **3** *Fam* (chubby person) petit gros *m*, petite grosse *f*, (baby) gros bébé *m*
▶▶ **p. basin, p. bowl** moule *m* à puddings *ou* à poudings; **p. basin haircut, p. bowl haircut** coupe *f* au bol

puddingface ['pʊdɪŋfeɪs] N *Fam* visage *m* empâté

puddinghead ['pʊdɪŋhed] N *Fam* idiot, -ote, andouille *f*

puddingstone ['pʊdɪŋstəʊn] N *Geol* poudingue *m*

puddle ['pʌd(ə)l] N (of water, oil) flaque *f*, (small pool) petite mare *f*, *Fam* **the dog's made a p. on the carpet** le chien a fait pipi sur le tapis
VT *Metal* (iron) puddler

pudenda [pju:'dendə] NPL *Fml* parties *fpl* génitales

pudgy ['pʌdʒɪ] ADJ *Fam* (person) rondelet, dodu

puerile ['pjʊəraɪl] ADJ *Pej* puéril; **he's being utterly p. about it** il a une attitude complètement puérile à cet égard

puerility [pjʊə'rɪlɪtɪ] N *Fml* puérilité *f*

puerperal [pju:'ɜ:pərəl] ADJ *Med* puerpéral, -aux

Puerto Rican [pweətəʊ'ri:kən, pwɜ:təʊ-] ADJ portoricain
N Portoricain, -aine

Puerto Rico [pweətəʊ'ri:kəʊ, pwɜ:təʊ-] N Porto Rico *m*

puff [pʌf] N **1** (of breath) souffle *m*; (of air) souffle, bouffée *f*, (of smoke, steam) bouffée; **to take a p. at one's pipe** tirer une bouffée de sa pipe; **give me a p.** (of your cigarette) passe-moi une bouffée *ou Fam* une taffe; *Fam* **out of p.** essoufflé, à bout de souffle; *Fam* **let me get my p. back** laissez-moi reprendre mon souffle; *Fig Fam* **our ideas went up** *or* **disappeared in a p. of smoke** nos idées sont parties en fumée
2 *Sewing* (of dress) bouillon *m*; (of sleeve) bouffant *m*; *Am* (quilt) édredon *m*
3 (in media) reportage *m* flatteur; *Old-fashioned Fam* (advertisement) pub *f*, réclame *f* (tapageuse); **I managed to get in a p. about my new book** j'ai réussi à faire de la pub *ou* de la réclame pour mon nouveau livre
4 *Culin* cream p. chou *m* à la crème
5 *Br Sl* (marijuana) herbe *f*, beu *f*, (cannabis) shit *m*, hasch *m*
VI (of person) souffler; (of steam engine) lancer des bouffées de vapeur; **to p. and blow** *or* **pant** haleter; **to p. (away) at one's pipe** tirer sur sa pipe, tirer des bouffées de sa pipe; **the steam engine puffed into view** la fumée indiqua l'arrivée du train; **to p. into the station** entrer en gare dans un nuage de fumée
VT **1** (smoke, air) émettre, envoyer; (pipe etc) fumer par petites bouffées; (rice) (faire) gonfler; **to p. smoke into sb's face** envoyer de la fumée à la figure de qn
2 *Old-fashioned Fam* (advertise) (one's wares) pousser, vanter
▶▶ *Zool* **p. adder** vipère *f* heurtante; *Culin* **p. pastry** pâte *f* feuilletée; **p. sleeves** manches *fpl* ballon

▶ **puff out** VT SEP **1** (one's cheeks) gonfler; (sleeve etc) faire ballonner *ou* bouffer; **to p. out one's chest** bomber le torse **2** (emit) (smoke) émettre, envoyer **3** *Fam* (exhaust) crever; **that walk has puffed me out** cette marche m'a crevé

▸ **puff up** VT SEP *(one's cheeks)* gonfler; **he was puffed up with pride** il était bouffi d'orgueil

Puffa jacket® ['pʌfə] N blouson *m* de rappeur

puffball ['pʌfbɔːl] N *Bot* vesse-de-loup *f, pl* vesses-de-loup

puffed [pʌft] ADJ **1** p. out *(of skirt etc)* ballonné; **p. up (with pride)** bouffi d'orgueil **2** *Fam* p. (out) *(person)* essoufflé, à bout de souffle; *(tired)* fatigué

▸▸ **p. rice** riz *m* gonflé; **p. sleeves** manches *fpl* ballon

puffer ['pʌfər] N *Fam (train)* train *m* à vapeur; *(boat)* bateau *m* à vapeur

puffin ['pʌfɪn] N *(bird)* macareux *m* moine, puffin *m*

puffiness ['pʌfɪnɪs] N *(of face etc)* aspect *m* bouffi

puffy ['pʌfɪ] ADJ **1** *(swollen) (face, clouds)* bouffi, boursouflé; *(eyes)* gonflé, bouffi; **to be p. under the eyes** avoir les yeux bouffis *ou* gonflés **2** *Fam (person) (short-winded)* à l'haleine courte, poussif; *(out of breath)* hors d'haleine

pug [pʌg] N *(dog)* carlin *m*

▸▸ **p. dog** carlin *m*; **p. nose** nez *m* camus

pugilism ['pjuːdʒɪlɪz(ə)m] N *Fml* boxe *f*

pugilist ['pjuːdʒɪlɪst] N *Fml* pugiliste *m*

pugnacious [pʌg'neɪʃəs] ADJ querelleur, -euse, batailleur, -euse, *Lit* pugnace

pugnaciously [pʌg'neɪʃəslɪ] ADV d'une manière querelleuse *ou* batailleuse *ou Lit* pugnace; *(to defend sth)* avec pugnacité

pugnacity [pʌg'næsɪtɪ], **pugnaciousness** [pʌg'neɪʃənɪs] N caractère *m* querelleur *ou* batailleur, *Lit* pugnacité *f*

pug-nosed [-nəʊzd] ADJ au nez écrasé *ou* camus

puke [pjuːk] *Fam* VT & VI dégobiller, dégueuler; **it makes me p.!** c'est à gerber!; **you make me p.!** tu es dégueulasse!

N *(vomit)* dégueulis *m*; **to have a p.** dégobiller, dégueuler

pukey ['pjuːkɪ] ADJ *Sl (disgusting)* merdique

pukka ['pʌkə] ADJ *Br* **1** *(upper-class, posh)* snob **2** *Old-fashioned, Hum (genuine)* authentique; **a p. Englishman** un vrai Anglais d'Angleterre **3** *Fam (excellent)* génial, -aux, super

pulchritude ['pʌlkrɪtjuːd] N *Lit* beauté *f*

PULL [pʊl]

N	traction **1** ▪ attrait **1** ▪ influence **3**
VT	tirer **1, 2, 6** ▪ se déchirer **1**
	▪ traîner **2** ▪ attirer **3** ▪ arracher **4**

N **1** *(act of pulling)* tirage *m*, traction *f*; *(of magnet)* force *f* d'attraction; *(in rowing)* coup *m* (d'aviron); *Fig (attraction) (of foreign places, high salaries etc)* attrait *m*; **give it a hard** *or* **good p.!** tirez fort!; **to give a p. on the rope** tirer sur la corde; **give it one more p.** tire encore un coup; **a few more pulls and I'll be able to reach it** en tirant encore un peu j'arriverai à l'atteindre; **I felt a p. at my sleeve** j'ai senti qu'on me tirait par la manche; *Br Sl* **to be (out) on the p.** *(looking for sexual partner)* draguer

2 *(gulp) (of beer etc)* gorgée *f*, lampée *f*; **to take a p. at one's pipe** tirer une bouffée de sa pipe

3 *(influence)* influence *f*; **to have plenty of p.** avoir le bras long

4 *(climb, effort etc)* **it's a long p. to the top** la montée est rude jusqu'au sommet; **it was a long p. to the shore** *(in rowing boat)* ça a pris du temps pour regagner la rive

5 *(handle)* poignée *f*; **(bell) p.** cordon *m* de sonnette

6 *Golf, Cr* coup *m* tiré

7 *Typ* première épreuve *f*

8 *(catch) (in jumper etc)* accroc *m*; **my cardigan has a p. in it** j'ai fait un accroc à mon cardigan

VT **1** *(rope, person's hair etc)* tirer; *(muscle etc)* se déchirer; *(oar)* manier; **p.** *(notice on door)* tirez, tirer; **pulled muscle** élongation *f*; **he pulled her closer (to him)** il l'a attirée plus près de lui; **he pulled the knot tight(er)** il a resserré le nœud; **she pulled the box from his hands** elle lui a arraché la boîte des mains; **to p. a door/drawer/window open** ouvrir une porte/un tiroir/une fenêtre; **to p. a door shut** *or* **closed** fermer une porte; **to p. the curtains/blinds** tirer les rideaux/stores; **to p. the trigger** presser sur la détente *ou* la gâchette; **p. your chair up to** *or* **nearer the fire** approchez votre fauteuil du feu; **to p. to pieces** déchirer, mettre en morceaux; *(criticize severely)* démolir; **to p. rank on sb** faire valoir son ancienneté sur qn; *Br Fam* **p. the other one! (it's got bells on!)** laisse-moi rire!; **to p. one's hat (down) over one's eyes** enfoncer *ou* rabattre son chapeau sur les yeux; *TV, Cin* **to p. focus** faire la mise au point

2 *(haul) (cart etc)* traîner, tirer; *(of barge etc) (boat)* haler

3 *(attract) (customers, crowd)* attirer; *Sl (pick up) (sexual partner)* lever, emballer

4 *(extract, remove)* **to p. a cork** déboucher une bouteille; **to p. a plant** arracher une plante; **to p. a tooth** arracher *ou* extraire une dent; **to have a tooth pulled** se faire arracher une dent; **it was like pulling teeth** c'était pénible comme tout; **to p. a pint** tirer une bière; **to p. pints** *(for a living)* travailler comme barman/comme serveuse de bar; **to p. a TV programme** retirer une émission de télé; **to p. sth from the files** *(cancel)* retirer qch des fichiers; *Fam* **to p. a gun on sb** mettre un pistolet sous le nez de qn

5 *(do) Fam* **to p. a bank job** se faire une banque; *Fam* **to p. a fast one on sb** avoir qn, rouler qn; **so you thought you could p. a fast one (on me)?** alors comme ça tu voulais me jouer un tour?; **to p. a trick on sb** jouer un tour à qn; **don't ever p. a stunt like that again** ne me/nous/*etc* refais jamais un tour comme ça; **to p. a face** faire une grimace

6 *Typ (proof)* tirer

7 *Sport* **to p. one's shot** envoyer la balle trop loin sur le côté; *Golf* faire un coup tiré

VI **1** tirer; *(in rowing)* ramer, souquer; **she pulled clear of the pack** elle s'est détachée du peloton; **to p. clear of the traffic and sped on** il est sorti du flot de la circulation et a accéléré; **he pulled sharply to the left** il a viré brutalement sur la gauche; **the lorry pulled slowly up the hill** le camion gravissait lentement la côte; **to p. on** *or* **at a rope** tirer sur un cordage; **to p. at one's pipe** tirer sur sa pipe; **they're pulling in different directions** *(they disagree)* ils ne s'entendent pas, ils ne sont pas d'accord, *Fam* ils tirent à hue et à dia

2 the engine is pulling heavily le moteur fatigue *ou* peine; **the brakes p. to the left/right** les freins tirent à gauche/droite

3 *Sport* envoyer la balle trop loin sur le côté; *Golf* faire un coup tiré

4 *Sl (find sexual partner)* faire une touche

▸▸ *Mktg* **p. strategy** stratégie *f* pull; *Comput* **p. technology** recherche *f* individuelle, technologie *f* pull

▸ **pull about** VT SEP *(handle roughly) (object)* tirer dans tous les sens, tirailler; *(person)* malmener; **stop pulling me about!, she said** ne sois pas aussi brutal!, dit-elle

▸ **pull ahead** VI *(in race, election campaign)* prendre la tête; **to p. ahead of one's rival** distancer son rival

▸ **pull along** VT SEP *(person)* tirer par le bras/par l'épaule/*etc*, *(load etc)* tirer derrière soi

▸ **pull apart** VT SEP **1** *(break up) (object)* mettre en petits morceaux; *(clothing etc)* déchirer; *(dismantle for storage etc)* démonter; *(body, flesh)* déchiqueter; *(separate) (two people fighting)* séparer

2 *(criticize) (person)* éreinter; *(performance, argument etc)* démolir

VI **it pulls apart** c'est démontable, ça se démonte

▸ **pull away** VT SEP *(remove forcefully)* **to p. sth away from sth/sb** arracher qch de qch/des mains de qn; **he pulled his hand away** il retira vivement sa main; **they pulled the distraught father away from the burning car** ils ont arraché le père affolé à la voiture en feu

VI **1** *(of train, car)* partir; **the train pulled away from the station** le train a quitté la gare; **as the train began to p. away** alors que le train s'ébranlait; **to p. away from sb** s'écarter de qn; **she's beginning to p. away** *(in race)* elle commence à prendre de l'avance

2 *(in rowing)* **p. away!** souquez!

▸ **pull back** VI *(hesitate)* hésiter; *(not continue with project etc)* se retirer, refuser de continuer; *Mil* décrocher; **they pulled back from committing themselves fully** ils ont renoncé à s'engager complètement

VT SEP *(curtains)* ouvrir; *(covers)* rejeter en arrière; *Mil* retirer; **his father pulled him back from the fire** son père l'a éloigné du feu; **to p. sb/a company back from the brink** faire refaire surface à qn/une entreprise, tirer qn/une entreprise d'affaire

▸ **pull down** VT SEP **1** *(lower) (blind, skirt etc)* baisser; **to p. one's hat down over one's eyes** enfoncer *ou* rabattre son chapeau sur ses yeux; **he's pulling the whole team down** il fait baisser le niveau de toute l'équipe; **my marks in the oral exam will p. me down** mes notes à l'oral vont baisser *ou* descendre ma moyenne

2 *(demolish) (house etc)* démolir, abattre

3 *(of illness, circumstances) (person)* abattre

4 *Comput (menu)* dérouler

5 *Am Fam (earn) (salary)* toucher; *(money)* gagner; **he doesn't p. down much of a salary** il ne gagne pas *ou* touche pas des masses

▸ **pull in** VT SEP **1** *(fishing net etc)* rentrer; *(money)* gagner, *Fam* se faire; **he pulled me in** *(to swimming pool)* il m'a tiré dedans

2 *(attract) (the public)* attirer; **it's really pulling them in** ça attire les foules

3 *Fam (of police) (suspect)* arrêter; **they pulled him in for questioning** ils l'ont arrêté pour l'interroger; **to be pulled in for speeding** être arrêté pour excès de vitesse

4 *Aut* **to p. one's car in to the kerb** se ranger près du trottoir

5 **to p. oneself** *or* **one's stomach in** rentrer son ventre

6 *Horseriding (hold back) (horse)* retenir, tirer sur les rênes de

VI **1** *(stop at side of road) (of vehicle, driver)* s'arrêter, se garer; **p. in here** arrête-toi là; **to p. in to the kerb** se ranger près du trottoir; **we'll p. in at** *or* **to the next garage** on s'arrêtera à la prochaine station-service

2 *(arrive) (of train, bus, person)* arriver; **the express pulled in two hours late** l'express est arrivé avec deux heures de retard

▸ **pull into** VT INSEP *(arrive at) (of train, bus, person etc)* arriver à; **the train was pulling into the station** le train entrait en gare; **the bus pulled into view** le bus apparut; *Sport* **to p. into the lead** prendre la tête

▸ **pull off** VT SEP **1** *(remove) (clothes, wrapping etc)* enlever; *(detach)* détacher (**from** de); **to p. sth off sth** *(detach from)* détacher qch de qch; **to p. the sheets off the bed** retirer *ou* enlever les draps du lit

2 *Fam (win) (prize)* décrocher, gagner, remporter; **to p. off a deal** réussir une opération, boucler une affaire; **to p. off a bank raid/a project** réussir un hold-up/un projet; **he pulled it off** il a réussi

VI the lid simply pulls off il suffit de tirer pour enlever le couvercle; **the top pulls off to reveal ...** le dessus se retire et on peut voir ...

▸ **pull on** VT SEP *(sweater, one's hat etc)* mettre; **to p. sth on over sth else** enfiler qch par-dessus qch d'autre

▸ **pull out** VT SEP **1** *(extract) (tooth)* arracher, extraire; **to p. a wallet out of one's pocket** tirer *ou* sortir un portefeuille de sa poche; **to p. a nail out of a plank** arracher un clou d'une planche; **to p. a cork out of a bottle** enlever un bouchon d'une bouteille; **to p. a car out of a ditch** sortir une voiture d'un fossé; **to p. the country/economy out of the recession** faire sortir le pays/l'économie de la récession; **p. me out, I'm stuck in the mud!** sors-moi de là, je suis enlisé dans la boue!; **he was pulled out of the burning car** il a été arraché de la voiture en feu; *Fam* **to p. out all the stops** faire le maximum (**to do sth** pour faire qch)

2 *(withdraw) (troops)* retirer

3 *(drawer) (open)* ouvrir; *(remove)* enlever, dégager; *(leaf of table, shelf)* tirer

VI 1 *Aut (move out to overtake)* déboîter; **to p. out from behind a car** déboîter de derrière une voiture

2 *(leave) (of train, bus, person etc)* partir; **when do we p. out?** quand est-ce qu'on part?

3 *(withdraw) (of troops)* se retirer; *(of firm from project, buyer)* se désister; *(of firm from place)* quitter une/la région/ville/*etc*

4 *(be extendible or detachable) (of drawer)* s'ouvrir; *(of handle) (be telescopic)* s'allonger; *(of map)* se déplier; **the table pulls out to seat ten** avec les rallonges c'est une table de dix personnes; **the sofa pulls out so you can sleep on it** on peut déplier le sofa pour dormir dedans

▸ **pull out of** VT INSEP **1** *(leave) (of train, bus, person etc)* partir de; **the train was pulling out of the station** le train sortait de la gare; *Aviat* **to p. out of a dive** arrêter de piquer; **the country is pulling out of the recession** le pays est en train de sortir de la récession

2 *(withdraw from) (agreement, deal, country)* se retirer de

▸ **pull over** VT SEP **1** tirer; *(cause to fall)* faire tomber; **careful you don't p. that wardrobe over on top of you!** attention de ne pas te faire tomber l'armoire sur la tête!

2 **she pulled her sweater over her head** *(putting it on)* elle a enfilé son pull; *(taking it off)* elle a enlevé son pull

VI she's pulling over to let the other runners past elle se met sur le côté pour laisser passer les autres coureurs; *Aut* **to p. over to the kerb** se ranger le long du trottoir

▸ **pull round** VT SEP *(chair, object)* tourner; *(boat) (turn)* faire tourner; *(turn through 180 degrees)* faire demi-tour à; *(person) (help regain consciousness)* ranimer; *(help recover from illness)* remonter, remettre sur pied

VI *(of ship)* tourner; *(through 180 degrees)* faire demi-tour; *(of person) (regain consciousness)* revenir à soi; *(recover from illness)* se remettre

▸ **pull through** VT SEP **1** *(of doctor etc) (person)* remettre sur pied

2 *(help survive difficulty) (person)* tirer d'embarras *ou* d'affaire; **he says his faith pulled him through** il dit que c'est sa foi qui lui a permis de s'en sortir

VI 1 *(recover from illness)* s'en tirer

2 *(survive difficulty)* se tirer d'affaire, s'en tirer, surmonter ses difficultés

▸ **pull to** VT SEP *(door)* tirer, fermer

▸ **pull together** VT SEP *(information)* rassembler, réunir; **he pulled them together into a team** il a réussi à faire d'eux une équipe; **to p. oneself together** *(become calm, more organized)* se ressaisir, se reprendre, reprendre ses esprits; **p. yourself together!** ressaisissez-vous!

VI *(co-operate)* s'entendre; **if we all p. together on this** si nous y mettons tous du nôtre; **p. together!** *(in rowing)* avant partout!

▸ **pull up** VT SEP **1** *(raise) (blind)* hausser, lever; *(one's skirt)* retrousser, relever; *(plant, weeds)* arracher; **p. up a chair!** prends une chaise!; **to p. one's socks up** tirer *ou* remonter ses chaussettes; *Fig Fam* se remuer, s'activer; **his good marks in maths pulled him up again** ses bonnes notes en maths ont remonté sa moyenne

2 *(stop)*, *Horseriding (horse)* arrêter; **to p. oneself up (short)** s'arrêter *(quand on est sur le point de dire ou faire qch d'indiscret)*; **to p. sb up (short)** arrêter qn net

3 *(reprimand) (person)* rembarrer; **he pulled me up for being late** il m'a rembarré parce que j'étais en retard; *Aut* **to be pulled up (by the police)** se faire arrêter (par un agent)

VI 1 *(stop)* s'arrêter; **the horse pulled up lame** le cheval s'est arrêté en boitant

2 *(close gap)* **to p. up (on another competitor)** réduire la distance (qui vous sépare d'un autre concurrent)

pull-back N *(withdrawal) (of troops)* retrait *m*

pull-down ADJ
  ▸▸ *Comput* **p. menu** menu *m* déroulant; *Comput* **p. window** fenêtre *f* déroulante

pullet ['pʊlɪt] N poulette *f*, *(fattened)* poularde *f*

pulley ['pʊlɪ] N poulie *f*
  ▸▸ **p. block** palan *m*, moufle *f*; **p. wheel** réa *m*, rouet *m*

pull-in N *Br (café)* = restoroute® *m*; *(for parking)* parking *m* *(surtout près d'un restaurant)*

Pullman ['pʊlmən] N *Rail (carriage)* voiture *f* Pullman
  ▸▸ **P. car**, **P. carriage** voiture Pullman

pull-off N *Am Aut (rest area)* aire *f* de repos

pull-out ADJ ATTRIB *(section in magazine)* détachable
  N *Journ* supplément *m* détachable
  ▸▸ **p. leaf** *(on desk, table)* rallonge *f*

pullover ['pʊləʊvər] N pull-over *m*, *pl* pull-overs, *Fam* pull *m*

pullulate ['pʌljʊleɪt] VI *Lit* pulluler (**with** life de vie)

pull-up N **1** *(of car etc)* arrêt *m* **2** *(café)* = restoroute® *m* **3** *Gym* traction *f*

pulmonary ['pʌlmənərɪ] ADJ ATTRIB *Anat, Med* pulmonaire

pulp [pʌlp] N *(of fruit)* pulpe *f*, chair *f*; **dental p.** pulpe dentaire; **paper p.** pâte *f ou* pulpe à papier; **to reduce to (a) p.** *(wood etc)* réduire en pulpe *ou* en pâte; *Fam* **to beat sb to a p.** mettre qn en bouillie
  VT *(wood etc)* réduire en pulpe *ou* en pâte; *(fruit)* écraser, réduire en purée; *(books)* mettre au pilon; **pulping machine** *(in papermaking)* pilon *m*
  ▸▸ **p. fiction** romans *mpl* de gare; **p. novels** romans de ou à quatre sous; **p. writer** auteur *m* de romans de gare

pulpit ['pʊlpɪt] N *(of minister)* chaire *f*; **condemned from the p.** condamné par l'église

pulpwood ['pʌlpwʊd] N *(for papermaking)* bois *m* à pâte

pulpy ['pʌlpɪ] ADJ pulpeux, charnu

pulsar ['pʌlsər] N *Astron* pulsar *m*

pulsate [pʌl'seɪt] VI palpiter; *(vibrate)* vibrer; *(of heart etc)* battre; *Fig* **his novels p. with life** ses romans bouillonnent de vie

pulsation [pʌl'seɪʃən] N *Physiol, Elec, Astron* pulsation *f*; *(of heart)* battement *m*, pulsation

pulse [pʌls] N **1** *Physiol* pouls *m*; **quick p.** pouls fréquent *ou* précipité; **strong/weak p.** pouls fort/faible; **to feel** *or* **take sb's p.** prendre le pouls à qn; **his p. quickened** son pouls s'est accéléré; *Fig* **to have one's finger on the p.** être à la page; *Fig* **to keep one's finger on the p. of ...** se tenir étroitement au courant de ... **2** *(of heart)* pulsation *f*, battement *m*; *Phys (of light, sound etc)* vibration *f*; *Electron, Radio* impulsion *f*, *Mus* cadence *f*, rythme *m*
  VI **1** *(of heart)* battre; *(beat hard)* palpiter; **a vein pulsed above his right eye** une veine se gonflait au-dessus de son œil droit; **to p. through the arteries** *(of blood)* circuler dans les artères par pulsations rythmées **2** *Fig* vibrer (**with** energy d'énergie); **her novels p. with life** ses romans bouillonnent de vie; **the pulsing music** le rythme saccadé de la musique
  VT *Elec etc (current)* moduler en impulsions
  ▸▸ **p. rate** fréquence *f* du pouls

pulse [pʌls] N *(plant)* (plante *f*) légumineuse *f*, légume *m* à gousse; *(lentils, beans etc)* légume sec, *Spec* graine *f* de légumes à gousse

pulverization [pʌlvəraɪ'zeɪʃən] N pulvérisation *f*

pulverize ['pʌlvəraɪz] VT pulvériser, réduire en poudre; *Fam* **to p. sb** *(beat up)* démolir qn; *(defeat heavily)* pulvériser qn; *(criticize severely)* éreinter qn

puma ['pjuːmə] N *(animal)* puma *m*, couguar *m*

pumice ['pʌmɪs] N *(pierre f)* ponce *f*
  VT *(surface)* poncer, passer à la pierre ponce
  ▸▸ **p. stone** *(pierre)* ponce

pummel ['pʌm(ə)l] VT *(-ll-, Am -l-) (person)* battre, rosser; *(door, sb's chest)* battre; *(mixture into dough)* pétrir; **to be pummelled by the waves** être battu par les vagues; **to be pummelled by artillery** être pilonné par les tirs d'artillerie
  N = **pommel** N

pummelling, *Am* **pummeling** ['pʌm(ə)lɪŋ] N volée *f* de coups, raclée *f*; **to give sb a good p.** donner une bonne raclée à qn; **to get a p.** *(of boxer)* se faire taper dessus

pump [pʌmp] N **1** *(device)* pompe *f* **2** *(shoe) (for dancing)* escarpin *m*; *(for sports)* (chaussure *f* de) tennis *f*
  VT *(water etc)* pomper; **to p. a well dry** assécher *ou* épuiser un puits; **to p. sb's stomach** faire un lavage d'estomac à qn; **to p. air into sb's lungs** insuffler de l'air dans les poumons de qn; **to p. air into a balloon** gonfler un ballon *(à l'aide d'une pompe)*; **to p. water into a cavity** amener de l'eau à la pompe dans une cavité; *Fam* **to p. sb's hand** serrer vigoureusement la main à qn; *Fam* **to p. sb** *(for information)* tirer les vers du nez à qn; **to p. water into a boiler** refouler de l'eau dans une chaudière; *Fam* **the athletes were pumped full of drugs** les athlètes étaient complètement dopés; *Sl* **to p. sb full of lead** *(shoot)* trouer la peau à qn; *Fam* **to p. iron** faire de la gonflette; **he looks as if he pumps iron** on dirait un haltérophile; *Fig* **the government pumped money into the region** le gouvernement a injecté des capitaux dans cette région
  VI **1** *(of heart, machine etc)* pomper **2** *Br Sl (pass wind)* péter
  ▸▸ **p. attendant** *(at petrol station)* pompiste

mf; **p. room** *(building)* pavillon *m*; *(room)* buvette *f (dans une station thermale)*; **p. water** eau *f* de pompe

▶ **pump in** VT SEP *(water etc)* faire entrer à l'aide d'une pompe; *Fig* **more money will have to be pumped in** il faudra injecter plus d'argent

▶ **pump out** VT SEP *(water etc)* pomper; *Naut* **to p. out the holds** assécher les cales; **to p. out sb's stomach** faire un lavage d'estomac à qn

▶ **pump up** VT SEP *(tyre)* gonfler; *(oil, water)* pomper

pump-action shotgun N fusil *m* à pompe

pumped [pʌmpt] ADJ *Am Fam (excited)* surexcité; *(enthusiastic)* emballé

pumping ['pʌmpɪŋ] N *(of water etc)* pompage *m*
▶▶ **p. station** station *f* de pompage

pumpkin ['pʌmpkɪn] N potiron *m*, citrouille *f*
▶▶ **p. pie** tarte *f* au potiron

pun [pʌn] N calembour *m*, jeu *m* de mots (**on sth** sur qch); **if you'll forgive or pardon the p.** pardonnez-moi ce jeu de mots
VI (-nn-) faire des calembours *ou* des jeux de mots; **…, he punned** …, plaisanta-t-il

Punch [pʌntʃ] N ≃ Polichinelle *m*, Guignol *m*; **P. and Judy show** ≃ (théâtre *m* de) Guignol

---

Punch and Judy

En Grande-Bretagne, le "Punch and Judy show" est un spectacle pour enfants semblable aux Guignols en France. Il est souvent présenté dans un jardin public ou sur une plage. On y retrouve Punch le bossu, sa femme Judy avec laquelle il se querelle constamment, et leur chien Toby.

---

punch¹ [pʌntʃ] N **1** *(blow)* coup *m* de poing; **I got quite a p.** je me suis pris un sacré coup de poing; **to pack quite a p.** *(hit hard)* cogner dur; *Boxing* avoir du punch; *Fig (of drink)* être corsé; **to pull a p.** retenir un coup; **he didn't pull his punches** *(he hit hard)* il n'y est pas allé de main morte; *Fig (he spoke frankly)* il n'a pas mâché ses mots; *Fig* **a documentary that pulls no punches** un documentaire sans complaisance

2 *Fam (energy)* punch *m*; **style that has p.** style qui a du punch, style incisif

3 *Tech etc (tool)* poinçon *m*; *(machine)* poinçonneuse *f*; *(for making holes)* perforatrice *f*; **(ticket) p.** *(of ticket inspector)* poinçon; *(for use by passenger)* composteur *m*

VT **1** *(hit) (person)* donner un/des coup(s) de poing à, cogner sur; *(ball, wall etc)* donner un/des coup(s) de poing à, cogner dans; *(typewriter keys, telephone)* taper sur; *(number)* taper, frapper (**into** sur); **to p. a number into a phone** composer un numéro; **to p. sb on the nose** donner un coup de poing sur le nez de qn; **he punched him on the chin** il lui a donné un coup de poing au menton; **the goalie punched the ball clear** le goal a écarté la balle d'un coup de poing; **to p. the air** lever le bras en signe de victoire; *Am* **to p. cattle** être cowboy

2 *Tech (with tool)* percer, découper à l'emporte-pièce; *(hole)* faire, percer; *(leather etc)* perforer; *(iron sheet)* estamper, étamper; *Comput (card, tape)* perforer; **to p. a ticket** *(of ticket inspector etc)* poinçonner un billet; *(of passenger)* composter un billet; *Comput* **punched card** carte *f* perforée
▶▶ *Comput* **p. card** carte *f* perforée; **p. card reader** machine *f* interprète de cartes perforées; **p. line** chute *f (d'une histoire drôle)*; *Ind* **p. operator** mécanographe *mf*; **p. tape** bande *f* perforée

▶ **punch away** VT SEP *(ball etc)* détourner d'un coup de poing
VI donner des coups de poing

▶ **punch in** VT SEP **1** *(box etc)* cabosser (d'un/de coup(s) de poing); *Fam* **to p. sb's face in** casser la gueule à qn **2** *(enter) (number, details)* taper; **p. your number in** composez votre numéro

▶ **punch out** VT SEP **1** *Tech (pin)* chasser; *(shape, pattern etc)* découper à la matrice **2** **to p. it out with sb** échanger des coups de poing avec qn

punch² N *(drink)* punch *m*

punchbag ['pʌntʃbæg] N *Boxing* punching-bag *m*, *pl* punching-bags; *Fig* souffre-douleur *m inv*

punchball ['pʌntʃbɔːl] N *Boxing* punching-ball *m*, *pl* punching-balls

punchbowl ['pʌntʃbəʊl] N **1** bol *m* à punch **2** *Br Geog (between two hills)* cuvette *f*

punch-drunk ADJ *esp Boxing* sonné, abruti *(par les coups)*; *Fig* sonné

puncher ['pʌntʃər] N **1** *Tech (person)* *(of sheet metal etc)* poinçonneur, -euse, perceur, -euse; *Comput (of cards, tapes)* perforeur, -euse; *(in metalworking)* estampeur, -euse **2** *Tech (device) (for sheet metal)* poinçonneuse *f*, *(for cardboard, leather etc)* emporte-pièce *m inv*, *Comput (for cards, tapes)* perforatrice *f* **3** *Boxing* puncheur *m*; *Am* **cow p.** cowboy *m*

punching ['pʌntʃɪŋ] N *Tech (action)* perçage *m*, poinçonnage *m*; **p. (out)** découpage *m (à l'emporte-pièce)*
▶▶ *Am* **p. bag** *Sport* sac *m* de sable, punching-bag *m*, *pl* punching-bags; *Fig (victim)* souffre-douleur *m inv*; **p. machine** machine *f* poinçonneuse

punchtape reader ['pʌntʃteɪp] N lecteur *m* de ruban perforé

punch-up N *Br Fam* bagarre *f*; **to have a p.** se bagarrer, se battre; **he looked as if he'd been in a p.** on aurait dit qu'il s'était battu *ou* bagarré

punchy ['pʌntʃɪ] ADJ *Fam* **1** *(slogan etc)* incisif, marquant; *(speech, novel)* plein de punch **2** = **punch-drunk**

punctilious [pʌŋk'tɪlɪəs] ADJ pointilleux, méticuleux

punctiliously [pʌŋk'tɪlɪəslɪ] ADV scrupuleusement, dans les moindres détails

punctiliousness [pʌŋk'tɪlɪəsnɪs] N grande attention *f* portée aux détails, méticulosité *f*

punctual ['pʌŋktjʊəl] ADJ *(person)* ponctuel, à l'heure; *(train, bus etc)* à l'heure; **to make a p. start** partir à l'heure

punctuality [pʌŋktjʊ'ælɪtɪ] N *(of person)* ponctualité *f*, exactitude *f*; *(of train, bus etc)* exactitude

punctually ['pʌŋktjʊəlɪ] ADV *(to arrive) (of person)* ponctuellement, à l'heure; *(of train, bus etc)* à l'heure; **we intend to leave p. at 7.30** nous comptons partir à 7h30 précises

punctuate ['pʌŋktjʊeɪt] VT **1** *(sentence etc)* ponctuer **2** *Fig* **speech punctuated with anecdotes** discours ponctué *ou* agrémenté d'anecdotes; **speech punctuated with applause** discours entrecoupé d'applaudissements; **a landscape punctuated with clumps of trees** un paysage avec çà et là un bouquet d'arbres

punctuation [pʌŋktjʊ'eɪʃən] N ponctuation *f*
▶▶ **p. mark** signe *m* de ponctuation

puncture ['pʌŋktʃər] N **1** *(in tyre)* crevaison *f*, *(hole in surface, skin etc)* perforation *f*; **to have a p.** *(action)* crever; *(state)* être crevé **2** *Med (action)* ponction *f*; *(of abscess)* ponction
VT *(tyre)* crever, perforer; *Mil, Sport (defence)* percer; *Med (blister, abscess)* ponc-

tionner; **a punctured lung** un poumon perforé; *Fig* **to p. sb's pride/self-confidence** entamer la fierté/la confiance en soi de qn; **to p. sb's self-esteem** rabattre le caquet à qn
VI *(of tyre)* crever
▶▶ **p. patch** *(for repairing inner tube)* rustine® *f*, **p. repair kit** trousse *f* de réparation pour crevaisons; *Med* **p. wound** blessure *f* pénétrante

pundit ['pʌndɪt] N **1** *(expert) (political etc)* spécialiste *mf*, expert *m*, *Fam* pontife *m*, ponte *m*; **according to the pundits** si l'on en croit les spécialistes *ou Fam* les grands pontes **2** *(in India)* pandit *m*

pungency ['pʌndʒənsɪ] N **1** *(of spice etc) (in taste)* saveur *f* piquante; *(in smell)* odeur *f* forte *ou* piquante **2** *Fig (of words)* âcreté *f*, aigreur *f*, *(of story)* saveur *f*, *(of style etc)* saveur, causticité *f*

pungent ['pʌndʒənt] ADJ **1** *(smell etc)* fort, âcre, piquant; *(taste)* piquant; **p. sauce** sauce *f* relevée *ou* épicée **2** *(style, wit etc)* mordant, caustique

pungently ['pʌndʒəntlɪ] ADV d'une manière piquante

Punic ['pjuːnɪk] ADJ *Hist* punique

puniness ['pjuːnɪnɪs] N faiblesse *f*

punish ['pʌnɪʃ] VT **1** *(child, wrongdoer, mistake)* punir; **to p. sb with imprisonment** punir qn d'une peine d'emprisonnement; **to p. sb for a crime** punir qn pour un crime; **to p. sb for having done sth** *or* **for doing sth** punir qn pour avoir fait qch; *Law* **to p. sb by** *or* **with a fine** frapper qn d'une amende **2** *Sport etc Fam (boxer) (hit hard)* taper dur sur; *(opponent's mistake)* ne pas pardonner; *(horse)* malmener; *Aut (engine)* fatiguer, forcer; **he really punishes himself in training** il se donne à fond à l'entraînement

punishable ['pʌnɪʃəb(ə)l] ADJ punissable; *Law* délictueux; **p. by a fine/by death** passible d'amende/d'une peine de mort

punishing ['pʌnɪʃɪŋ] ADJ dur; *(blow)* violent; *(game)* rude; *(work)* épuisant, éreintant; **a p. race** une course épuisante; **a p. schedule** un emploi du temps extrêmement serré
N punition *f*

punishment ['pʌnɪʃmənt] N **1** punition *f*, châtiment *m*; *Law* peine *f*; **as a p. for sth** en punition de qch; **to inflict a p. on sb** donner *ou* infliger une punition à qn; **to escape p.** échapper à la punition; **to make the p. fit the crime** proportionner la punition au crime; **to take one's p. like a man** recevoir sa punition sans broncher **2** *Fam (blows etc)* **to take a lot of p.** *(of boxer etc)* encaisser; *(of army, warship, tank, car, boat etc)* être malmené; *(of shoes, clothes etc)* être soumis à rude épreuve; **it has to be able to take a lot of p.** *(of footwear, paint etc)* il faut que ça soit résistant; *(of car)* il faut qu'elle soit bien solide; **to inflict severe p. on a team** administrer une cruelle défaite à une équipe

punitive ['pjuːnɪtɪv], **punitory** ['pjuːnɪt(ə)rɪ] ADJ répressif; *(taxation)* très sévère
▶▶ *Law* **p. damages** dommages et intérêts *mpl* dissuasifs; *Mil* **p. expedition** expédition *f* punitive; *Law* **p. justice** justice *f* répressive

Punjab ['pʌndʒɑːb] N Pendjab *m*

Punjabi [pʌn'dʒɑːbɪ] ADJ du Pendjab
N **1** habitant, -ante du Pendjab; *(by birth)* originaire *mf* du Pendjab **2** *Ling* pendjabi *m*

punk [pʌŋk] N **1** *(music fan, rebel etc)* punk *mf*; *(music)* le punk (rock) **2** *Am Fam Pej (worthless person)* vaurien *m*, crapule *f*
ADJ **1** *(music, hairstyle etc)* punk *inv*; **a p. band** un groupe punk **2** *Am Fam (worthless)* nul, qui ne vaut rien
▶▶ *Mus* **p. rock** le punk rock

punnet ['pʌnɪt] N *esp Br (for strawberries etc)* petit carton *m*, barquette *f*

punster ['pʌnstər] N faiseur, -euse de calembours *ou* de jeux de mots

punt[1] [pʌnt] N *(boat)* bateau *m* à fond plat
VT *(boat)* conduire à la perche; *(person)* transporter dans un bateau à fond plat
VI **to go punting** faire un tour dans un bateau à fond plat
▸▸ **p. pole** perche *f (pour la conduite d'un bateau à fond plat)*

punt[2] *Ftbl, Rugby* VT *(ball)* envoyer d'un coup de volée
VI donner un coup de pied de volée
N coup *m* de volée

punt[3] VI **1** *Cards* ponter; **to p. high** ponter gros **2** *Br Horseracing* parier

punt[4] N *Formerly (Irish currency)* livre *f* irlandaise

punter[1] ['pʌntər] N *Br***1** *Horseracing* parieur, -euse **2** *Fam (consumer, customer)* client, -ente; **the punters** *(the public)* le public, les gens; **the average p.** l'homme de la rue **3** *Fam (prostitute's client)* miché *m*, micheton *m* **4** *St Exch Fam (speculator)* boursicoteur, -euse, boursicotier, -ière **5** *Cards* ponte *m*

punter[2] N *(in boat)* canotier *m (qui conduit à la perche)*

puny ['pjuːnɪ] ADJ *(person)* chétif; *(arms, chest)* frêle, maigre; *(hands)* tout petit; *(effort)* malheureux; *(argument, excuse)* piètre; **a p. little fellow** un petit gringalet; **our p. little guns** nos pauvres *ou* malheureux petits canons; **a p. 50p** cinquante malheureux pence

pup [pʌp] N **1** *(of dog)* jeune chien, -ienne, chiot *m*; *(of seal)* jeune phoque *m*; *(of wolf)* louveteau *m*; *(of rat)* raton *m*; **a bitch and her pups** une chienne et ses petits; **to be in p.** *(of bitch)* être grosse; **Fig to be sold a p.** se faire rouler **2** *Fam (young man) (self-important)* freluquet *m*; *(impertinent)* petit impertinent, *m*
VI mettre bas

pupa, *pl* **pupae** ['pjuːpə, -iː] N *(insect)* nymphe *f*

pupate [pjuː'peɪt] VI *(of insect)* se métamorphoser en nymphe

pupil ['pjuːp(ə)l] N **1** *Sch* élève *mf* **2** *Law* pupille *mf* **3** *Anat (of eye)* pupille *f*

pupil(l)age ['pjuːpɪlɪdʒ] N *Law* pupillarité *f*; **child in p.** enfant en pupille *ou* en tutelle

pupilometer [pjuː'pɪl'ɒmɪtər] N pupillomètre *m*

puppet ['pʌpɪt] N marionnette *f*; *Fig (person)* marionnette, fantoche *m*; **glove** *or* **hand p.** marionnette à gaine
▸▸ *Fig* **p. government** gouvernement *m* fantoche; **p. play, p. show** (spectacle *m* de) marionnettes; **p. theatre** théâtre *m* de marionnettes

puppeteer [pʌpɪ'tɪər] N marionnettiste *mf*

puppetry ['pʌpɪtrɪ] N art *m* des marionnettes; *(puppet making)* fabrication *f* de marionnettes

puppy ['pʌpɪ] N **1** *(dog)* jeune chien, -ienne, chiot *m* **2** *Fam (young man)* = **pup** N **2**
▸▸ **p. dog** jeune chien, -ienne, chiot; *Br* **p. fat** rondeurs *fpl* de l'adolescence; **p. love** amourette *f*, amour *m* d'adolescent

purblind ['pɜːblaɪnd] ADJ **1** *(almost blind)* presque aveugle **2** *Fml (obtuse)* obtus; *(policy, refusal)* aveugle

purchase ['pɜːtʃɪs] N **1** *(act of buying, thing bought)* achat *m*; *(of company)* rachat *m*; **to make some purchases** faire des achats **2** *(grip)* prise *f*; **to get** *or* **secure a p. on sth** trouver prise sur qch
VT *(object)* acheter, *Fml* acquérir, faire l'ac-

quisition de; *Acct* **to p. a debt** racheter une créance
VI acheter; **now is the time to p.** c'est maintenant qu'il faut acheter
▸▸ *Acct* **p. account** compte *m* d'achats; *Am Acct* **p. accounting** = méthode *f* de comptabilité utilisée lors de l'acquisition d'une entreprise, dans laquelle les résultats de la filiale n'apparaissent pas dans le bilan de la société mère; *Mktg* **p. behaviour** comportement *m* d'achat; *Acct* **p. budget** budget *m* des approvisionnements; **p. contract** contrat *m* d'achat; **p. cost** coût *m* d'achat; *Acct* **p. of debts** rachat des créances; *Mktg* **p. decision** décision *f* d'achat; *Mktg* **p. diary** relevé *m* d'achat journalier; *Acct* **p. entry** écriture *f* d'achats; *Mktg* **p. environment** environnement *m* d'achat; *Mktg* **p. frequency** fréquence *f* d'achat; *Acct* **p. invoice** facture *f* d'achat; *Acct* **p. invoice ledger** journal *m* factures-fournisseurs; *Acct* **p. ledger** (grand-) livre *m* d'achats, *pl* grands-livres, journal des achats; *Acct* **p. ledger clerk** facturier, -ière *m* d'entrée; *Acct* **p. method** méthode d'achat; *Fin* **p. note** bordereau *m* d'achat; *Mktg* **p. occasion** occasion *f* d'achat; **p. order** *Fin (for goods, service)* bon *m* de commande; *St Exch (for shares)* ordre *m* d'achat; **p. price** prix *m* d'achat; *Fin* **p. value** valeur *f* d'achat; *Mktg* **p. volume** volume *m* d'achat

> Note that the French verb **pourchasser** is a false friend and is never a translation for the English word **to purchase**. It means **to chase**.

purchaser ['pɜːtʃəsər] N acheteur, -euse, *Fml* acquéreur, -euse
▸▸ *Mktg* **p. behaviour** comportement *m* de l'acheteur

purchasing ['pɜːtʃəsɪŋ] N achat *m*; *(of company)* rachat *m*; *(department)* service *m* des achats
▸▸ *Am* **p. agent** acheteur, -euse; *Mktg* **p. behaviour** comportement *m* d'achat; *Mktg* **p. behaviour model** modèle *m* de comportement d'achat; **p. co-operative** groupement *m* d'achat; **p. costs** frais *mpl* de passation de commande; *Mktg* **p. decision** décision *f* d'achat; **p. department** service *m* des achats; **p. manager** chef *m* des achats; *Mktg* **p. motivator** mobile *m* d'achat; *Fin* **p. power** capacité *f* d'achat, pouvoir *m* d'achat; *Mktg* **p. process** processus *m* d'achat; **p. rights** droits *mpl* d'achat

purdah ['pɜːdə] N *Rel* = système *m* qui astreint les femmes à une vie retirée; *Fig* **to go into p.** se retirer, ne voir personne

pure [pjʊər] ADJ *(unadulterated, morally uncorrupted)* pur; **as p. as the driven snow** pur comme l'enfant qui vient de naître; **p.-minded** pur d'esprit; **the p. and simple truth** la vérité pure et simple; *Bible* **the p. in heart** ceux qui ont le cœur pur; **p. Arab (horse)** (cheval *m*) arabe *m* de race pure; **by p. chance** un pur hasard; **p. English** anglais *m* pur; *Phil* **p. reason** la raison pure; **p. thoughts** pensées *fpl* pures; **p. silk/wool** pure soie *f*/laine *f*
▸▸ **p. mathematics** les mathématiques *mpl* pures

pure-blood ADJ *(horse)* pur sang *inv*
N *(horse)* pur-sang *m inv*

pure-blooded ADJ *(of animal, person)* pur sang *inv*

purebred ['pjʊəbred] ADJ *(dog, bull)* de race (pure), pur sang *inv*
N animal *m* de race; *(horse)* pur-sang *m inv*

purée ['pjʊəreɪ] *Culin* N purée *f*; **tomato p.** concentré *m* de tomate
VT *(apples, potatoes etc)* réduire *ou* écraser en purée; **puréed potatoes/spinach** purée *f* de pommes de terre/d'épinards

purely ['pjʊəlɪ] ADV purement; **he is p. concerned with ...** il est uniquement préoccupé de ...; **p. routine questioning** interrogatoire *m* de simple routine; **it was p. by chance that we met** notre rencontre n'était qu'un pur hasard; **it was p. accidental** c'était un pur hasard; **p. and simply** purement et simplement

pureness ['pjʊənɪs] N pureté *f*

purgation [pɜː'geɪʃən] N **1** *Med (of intestine)* purge *f* **2** *Rel (in purgatory)* purgation *f* de l'âme

purgative ['pɜːgətɪv] ADJ, N *Med* purgatif *m*

purgatory ['pɜːgət(ə)rɪ] N *Rel* purgatoire *m*; **the souls in p.** les âmes du purgatoire, les âmes en peine; **to live a life of p.** souffrir les peines du purgatoire de son vivant; *Fig* **it was sheer p.** c'était l'enfer, c'était atroce

purge [pɜːdʒ] N **1** *(drug etc)* purgatif *m*, purge *f* **2** *(action) Med* purge *f*; *Pol etc (of political party etc)* épuration *f*, nettoyage *m*, purge
VT *Med (person)* purger; *(political party etc)* nettoyer, épurer; *Rel* **to p. oneself** *of or* **from sin** se laver de ses péchés; *Law* **to p. oneself of a charge** se disculper, se justifier; *Am Law* **to p. one's contempt** faire amende honorable *(pour outrage aux magistrats)*

purging ['pɜːdʒɪŋ] N *Med etc (of body)* purge *f*, purification *f*; *(of political party etc)* épuration *f*

purification [pjʊərɪfɪ'keɪʃən] N purification *f*; *(of gas, oil, water etc)* épuration *f*; *Rel* **the Feast of the P. (of the Virgin Mary)** (la fête de) la Purification

purifier ['pjʊərɪfaɪər] N *(for gas, oil etc)* épurateur *m*; *(for air)* assainisseur *m*

purify ['pjʊərɪfaɪ] VT *(air etc)* assainir, purifier; *(gas, oil etc)* épurer; *(language)* purifier; *(blood)* dépurer; *(heart, mind etc)* purifier; **to p. sb of** *or* **from his sins** laver qn de ses péchés

purist ['pjʊərɪst] N puriste *mf*; **a linguistic p.** un puriste en matière de linguistique

puritan ['pjʊərɪt(ə)n] ADJ, N **1** puritain, -aine **2** *Hist* P. puritain, -aine

puritanical [pjʊərɪ'tænɪk(ə)l] ADJ puritain

puritanism ['pjʊərɪtənɪz(ə)m] N puritanisme *m*

purity ['pjʊərɪtɪ] N pureté *f*; **degree of p.** *(of water etc)* (degré *m* de) pureté; *(of gold)* titre *m*; **the p. of sb's motives** la pureté des motifs de qn

purl [pɜːl] *Knitting* N maille *f* à l'envers
VT *(row)* tricoter à l'envers; **knit one, p. one** une maille à l'endroit, une maille à l'envers
▸▸ **p. stitch** maille *f* à l'envers

purlieus ['pɜːljuːz] NPL *Lit (surrounding area)* alentours *mpl*, environs *mpl*; **in the p. of** aux alentours *ou* environs de

purloin [pɜː'lɔɪn] VT *Fml* voler, dérober

purple ['pɜːp(ə)l] ADJ violet; **he turned** *or* **went p.** il est devenu rouge
N *(colour)* violet *m*; *(dye)* pourpre *f*; **born to the p.** né dans la pourpre
▸▸ *Mil* P. Heart = médaille *f* décernée aux blessés de guerre de l'armée américaine; *Pharm Fam* **p. heart** pilule *f* d'amphétamine; *Liter* **p. patch** morceau *m* de bravoure; *Liter* **p. prose** prose *f* héroïque

purplish ['pɜːplɪʃ] ADJ violacé, violâtre; *(face)* cramoisi

purport[1] ['pɜːpɔːt] N *Fml (of document) (intention)* esprit *m*; *(of argument)* portée *f*, force *f*

purport[2] [pɜː'pɔːt] VT **to p. to be sth** *(of person)* prétendre être qch; *(of thing)* être présenté comme étant qch

purpose ['pɜːpəs] N **1** *(object, aim)* but *m*, objectif *m*; **fixed p.** dessein *m ou* objectif bien arrêté; **to gain** *or* **achieve one's p.** atteindre son but *ou* objectif, accomplir son dessein; **for** *or* **with the p. of doing sth** dans l'intention *ou* le but de faire qch; **what is the p. of your visit?** quel est le but *ou* l'objet de votre visite?; **it does not suit her p. to have it widely known** ça ne l'arrangerait pas que ça se sache; **to do sth on p.** faire qch exprès; **to have a sense of p.** être motivé; **his life lacked any real sense of p.** sa vie était dépourvue de but précis; **to give sb a sense of p.** motiver qn; **man of p.** homme *m* résolu *ou* décidé **2** *(use) (of object)* but *m*, objet *m*; **the buildings were not built for this p.** ces bâtiments n'ont pas été construits dans ce but *ou* à cette fin; **I've never understood their p.** je n'ai jamais compris à quoi ils servaient; **does it serve any useful p.?** est-ce que ça sert à quelque chose?; **intended p.** *(of building, amount of money)* destination *f*, affectation *f*; **they were never used for their intended p.** ils n'ont jamais servi à l'usage auquel on les destinait; **to serve no p.** ne servir à rien; **once she had served her p. they abandoned her** une fois qu'elle eut tenu son rôle, ils l'abandonnèrent; **this will suit** *or* **serve your p.** cela fera votre affaire; **made for that very p.** fait tout exprès; **for all purposes** à toutes fins, à tous usages; **intended for practical purposes** destiné à des usages pratiques; **to set up a commission for the p. of investigation** former un comité à des fins d'enquête; **for the p. of this article …** *(in lease, contract etc)* au sens du présent article …; **for our purposes we can assume this is true** en ce qui nous concerne, nous pouvons admettre que c'est vrai **3 to speak to the p.** parler à propos; **very much to the p.** fort à propos; **to some p.** utilement, avantageusement, efficacement; **all that will have been to no p.** tout cela n'aura servi à rien; **we're (talking) at cross purposes** il y a malentendu (entre nous), nous ne parlons pas de la même chose/personne; **in order to avoid talking at cross purposes** afin d'éviter tout malentendu

vt *Fml* **to p. to do sth** *or* **doing sth** se proposer de faire qch

purpose-built **ADJ** *(conference centre, sports complex)* construit (tout) spécialement; **it's not exactly p. but …** ce n'est pas exactement fait pour mais …

purposeful [ˈpɜːpəsfʊl] **ADJ** *(determined)* résolu, déterminé

purposefully [ˈpɜːpəsfʊlɪ] **ADV** *(determinedly) (to act)* résolument, avec détermination; *(to walk out etc)* d'un air résolu *ou* déterminé

> Attention: ne pas confondre avec **purposely**, qui signifie **délibérément**.

purposeless [ˈpɜːpəslɪs] **ADJ** *(existence)* sans but; *(lacking determination) (atmosphere)* d'indécision; *(attempts, person)* qui manque de conviction; **the p. air which seems to surround this government** le manque de détermination qui semble caractériser ce gouvernement

purposely [ˈpɜːpəslɪ] **ADV** exprès, à dessein, délibérément; **he p. looked the other way** il a regardé exprès de l'autre côté; **I came to p. see her** je suis venu exprès pour la voir

> Attention: ne pas confondre avec **purposefully**, qui signifie **avec détermination**.

purr [pɜːr] **N** *(of cat)* ronron *m*, ronronnement *m*; *(of machine)* ronflement *m*; *(of car engine etc)* ronronnement *m*; **she's got a very loud p.** *(of cat)* elle ronronne très fort

vi *(of cat, car, person)* ronronner

purring [ˈpɜːrɪŋ] **ADJ** *(cat)* qui ronronne, qui fait ronron

N = **purr** N

purse [pɜːs] **N** porte-monnaie *m inv*; *Am (handbag)* sac *m* à main; **the public p.** le Trésor public; *Old-fashioned* **it is beyond my p.** c'est au-dessus de mes moyens; *Sport* **to put up a p.** offrir un prix; *Sport* **how big is the p.?** à combien se monte le prix?; *Fam* **she holds the p. strings** c'est elle qui tient les cordons de la bourse

vt to p. (up) one's lips *or* **mouth** pincer les lèvres; **she pursed her lips in disapproval** elle pinça les lèvres en signe de désapprobation

▸▸ *Zool* **p. crab** crabe *m* des cocotiers; *Fishing* **p. net, p. seine** senne *f ou* seine *f* à poche

purser [ˈpɜːsər] **N** *Naut (in merchant navy)* commissaire *m*; **p.'s mate** cambusier *m*

pursuance [pəˈsjuːəns] **N** *Fml* exécution *f*; **in p. of one's duty** dans l'exercice de ses fonctions; **in p. of your instructions** conformément à vos instructions

pursuant [pəˈsjuːənt] **ADV** *Fml* **p. to your instructions** conformément à vos instructions

pursue [pəˈsjuː] **vt 1** *(chase) (person, animal)* poursuivre; *(pleasure, happiness)* rechercher; *(aim)* chercher à atteindre; **to be pursued by misfortune** être poursuivi par le malheur **2** *(continue) (one's path, studies)* continuer, poursuivre; *(policy)* poursuivre; *(course of action)* suivre; *(trade, profession)* faire, exercer; *(enquiry, matter)* donner suite à, poursuivre; **the subject was pursued no further** on ne s'attacha pas davantage à débattre ce sujet; **to p. a career in medicine/the law/journalism** faire carrière dans la médecine/le droit/le journalisme

pursuer [pəˈsjuːər] **N 1** poursuivant, -ante **2** *Scot Law* plaignant, -ante

pursuit [pəˈsjuːt] **N 1** *(chase)* poursuite *f*, *Fig (of pleasure, knowledge, happiness etc)* recherche *f*, quête *f*; **to be in p. of sb** être à la poursuite de qn; **the dogs were in hot p.** les chiens avaient engagé la chasse; **with two policemen in hot p.** avec deux agents à ses/mes/*etc* trousses; **in p. of his aim** en poursuivant son but; **in p. of happiness** à la poursuite *ou* en quête du bonheur **2** *(occupation)* occupation *f*, *(leisure)* passe-temps *m inv*; **literary pursuits** travaux *mpl* littéraires

▸▸ *Mil, Aviat* **p. plane** avion *m* de chasse; *Cycling* **p. race** poursuite

purulence [ˈpjʊərʊləns] **N** *Med* **1** purulence *f* **2** *(pus)* pus *m*

purulent [ˈpjʊərʊlənt] **ADJ** *Med* purulent

purvey [pəˈveɪ] **vt** *Com Fml (provisions)* fournir; **we p. a selection of fine wines** nous offrons une sélection de vins fins; **to p. information** diffuser l'information

purveyance [pəˈveɪəns] **N** fourniture *f* de provisions, approvisionnement *m*

purveyor [pəˈveɪər] **N** *Com Fml* fournisseur, -euse *(of provisions)*, approvisionneur, -euse **(of** en; **to** de)

purview [ˈpɜːvjuː] **N 1** *Law (of a law)* corps *m* **2** *Fml (scope) (of inquiry)* limites *fpl*, portée *f*; **it is not within my p. to …** il n'est pas dans mes compétences de …

pus [pʌs] **N** *Med* pus *m*

PUSH [pʊʃ]

N	poussée **1** = effort **2**
VT	pousser **1, 4** = appuyer sur **1** = enfoncer **2** = préconiser **3**
VI	pousser **1** = avancer **2**

N 1 poussée *f*, *Billiards (stroke)* coup *m* queuté; **to give sth/sb a p.** pousser qch/qn; *Fig* **to give sb a p.** pousser qn; **she just needs a little p.** elle a besoin qu'on la pousse un peu; *Fam* **to get the p.** *(from job)* se faire virer, être flanqué à la porte; *(from relationship)* se faire plaquer; *Fam* **to give sb the p.**

(from job) virer qn, flanquer qn à la porte; *(from relationship)* plaquer qn; **to give a car a p. start** faire démarrer une voiture en la poussant;

2 *(effort)* effort *m*, coup *m* de collier; *Mil (attack)* attaque *f* en masse; **to make a p. for change** lutter pour le changement; **the club's p. for promotion** les efforts soutenus du club pour être promu; **the final p. for the summit** le dernier effort pour atteindre le sommet

3 *(drive)* dynamisme *m*

4 *Fam (difficult moment)* **at a p.** à la limite; **when it comes to the p., you can always rely on her** aux moments critiques, on peut toujours compter sur elle; **if it comes to the p., he'll choose Sarah not Henry** s'il fallait qu'il choisisse, il prendrait Sarah et pas Henry; **if p. comes to shove** si la situation l'exige

5 *esp Austr Sl (gang)* bande *f*, clique *f (de voyous, de pickpockets)*

vt 1 *(person, wheelbarrow etc)* pousser; *(button)* appuyer sur; **to p. sb into the room** pousser qn (pour le faire entrer) dans la pièce; **to p. the door shut/open with one's foot** fermer/ouvrir la porte du pied; **don't p. (me)!** ne (me) poussez pas!, ne (me) bousculez pas!; **did he fall or was he pushed?** il est tombé ou on l'a poussé?; **did he leave or was he pushed?** *(from job)* il est parti de lui-même ou on l'y a poussé?; **to p. sb into a corner** acculer qn; **to p. sb out of the way** écarter qn; **to p. one's way through the crowd** se frayer *ou* s'ouvrir un chemin à travers la foule; **to p. one's way in** *(party, conversation etc)* s'immiscer; **to p. an attack home** pousser à fond une attaque; **to p. home one's advantage** tirer le meilleur parti possible de son avantage; *Fig* **to p. oneself** *(make an effort)* forcer; *Fig* **he needs pushing** il faut toujours le pousser

2 *(thrust) (knife, stick, hands etc)* enfoncer *(into* dans*)*

3 *Fig (goods)* faire (de) la réclame pour; *(theory, system)* préconiser; *(drugs)* vendre, fournir; **the government is pushing the idea of people setting up small businesses** le gouvernement favorise la création de petites entreprises; **he's pushing himself as a compromise candidate** il se présente comme le candidat du compromis; **to p. one's demands** revendiquer ses droits; *St Exch* **to p. shares** placer des valeurs douteuses; **to p. the line that …** insister sur le fait que …

4 *(force)* **to p. sb into doing sth** pousser qn à faire qch; **don't p. me!** ne me presse pas!; **her parents didn't p. her into the law** ses parents ne l'ont pas poussée à faire du droit; **to p. sb for payment/an answer** harceler qn pour se faire payer/pour qu'il réponde; **don't p. him too far** ne le poussez pas à bout; **I don't want to p. the comparison too far, but …** je ne veux pas pousser la comparaison trop loin, mais …; *Fam* **to p. one's luck** y aller un peu fort; *Fam* **that's pushing it a bit** tu y vas/il y va/*etc* un peu fort; **I'm terribly pushed (for time)** je suis très pressé; **to be pushed for money** être à court d'argent

5 *Fam* **he's pushing sixty** il frise la soixantaine

vi 1 pousser; *(sign on door)* poussez, pousser; **to p. against sth** pousser qch; *Aut* **we'll have to get out and p.** il va falloir descendre pousser; **stop pushing!** arrêtez de pousser!; *Fig* **you have to p. to get your way** pour réussir il faut savoir se mettre en avant

2 *(move forward)* avancer (avec difficulté); **the crowd pushed towards the exits** la foule se pressait vers la sortie; **to p. through the crowd** se frayer *ou* s'ouvrir un chemin à travers la foule; **he pushed past me** il m'a bousculé et m'a passé devant

▸▸ **p. button** bouton-poussoir *m*, *pl* boutons-poussoirs; *Com* **p. money** prime *f* au vendeur; *Mktg* **p. strategy** stratégie *f* push; *Billiards* **p. stroke** coup queuté; *Comput* **p. technology** technologie *f* du push de données

► **push about, push around** VT SEP *Fam (bully) (person)* marcher sur les pieds de, mener par le bout du nez; **we're sick and tired of being pushed about** *or* **around** nous en avons marre d'être menés par le bout du nez *ou* de nous faire marcher sur les pieds

► **push ahead** VI **1** *(continue)* continuer, persévérer; **to p. ahead with the work** poursuivre les travaux

2 *(advance)* avancer, progresser (**with** dans); **research is pushing ahead** les recherches avancent

► **push along** VT SEP *(move by pushing) (pram etc)* pousser

VI *Fam (leave)* partir, y aller; **I suppose I should be pushing along soon** il va bientôt falloir que j'y aille

► **push around** = **push about**

► **push aside** VT SEP *(shove out of way)* écarter

► **push away** VT SEP *(shove from oneself)* écarter, repousser

► **push back** VT SEP *(shove away) (person)* repousser; *(crowd, enemy etc)* faire reculer, refouler; *(attack)* réprimer; *(curtains)* écarter

► **push down** VT SEP *(lever, switch)* abaisser; *(prices)* faire baisser; **he pushed down the lid but it wouldn't shut** il a appuyé sur le couvercle mais il ne voulait pas fermer

VI **1** *(of lever etc)* s'abaisser; *(of person)* appuyer

2 *(press down) (of weight)* peser (**on** sur)

► **push for** VT INSEP faire campagne pour; **the unions are pushing for 10%** les syndicats font pression pour obtenir 10%; **to p. for a decision** exiger qu'une décision soit prise

VT SEP **to p. sb for an answer** presser qn pour qu'il/elle donne une réponse

► **push forward** VT SEP *(cause to move)* pousser en avant, (faire) avancer; **he was pushed forward by the crowd** la foule l'a poussé en avant; *Fig* **to p. oneself forward** se mettre en avant, chercher à s'imposer

VI *(move forward)* avancer

► **push in** VT SEP *(insert)* enfoncer; **the side of the car was pushed in** le flanc de la voiture était enfoncé; **he was standing by the pool and someone pushed him in** il était au bord de la piscine et quelqu'un l'a poussé dedans; **they opened the door and pushed me in** ils ont ouvert la porte et m'ont poussé à l'intérieur; *Sl* **to p. sb's face in** casser la gueule à qn

VI *(jump queue)* resquiller; **she's always pushing in where she's not wanted** il faut toujours qu'elle s'immisce *ou* s'impose là où on ne veut pas d'elle

► **push off** VT SEP **1** *(cause to fall)* faire tomber; **he pushed me off the wall** il m'a fait tomber du mur, il m'a poussé du haut du mur; **they tried to p. her (car) off the road** ils ont essayé de faire sortir sa voiture de la route; **to p. sb off a committee** exclure *ou* écarter qn d'un comité

2 *(remove by pushing)* pousser; **p. the lid off** soulève le couvercle

VI **1** *Fam (leave)* partir, se casser; *Naut* pousser au large; *Fam* **p. off!** fiche le camp!, tire-toi!

2 the lid pushes off le couvercle glisse

► **push on** VI *(continue with work, journey etc)* continuer; **to p. on to** *or* **as far as a place** pousser jusqu'à un endroit; **it's time to p. on** *(with journey)* il est temps de nous remettre en route; **to p. on with the work** se remettre au travail

VT SEP **1** *(press into place) (lid, cover etc)* appuyer sur

2 *(encourage)* encourager

► **push onto** VT SEP **to p. sth onto sb** *(blame, work etc)* mettre qch sur le dos de qn

► **push out** VT SEP **1** *(cause to leave) (physically)* pousser dehors, faire sortir; **he was pushed out of the group** il a été exclu du groupe; **to p. one's way out** se frayer un chemin vers la sortie

2 *(launch) (boat)* mettre à l'eau; *Fig Fam* **to p. the boat out** ne pas regarder à la dépense

► **push over** VT SEP *(cause to fall)* faire tomber

► **push through** VT SEP **1** *(cause to pass through)* faire passer; **to p. sth through sth** faire passer qch à travers qch; *Pol* **to p. a bill through Parliament** faire accepter un projet de loi au parlement

2 *Pol (get accepted) (bill etc)* faire accepter

3 *(bring to completion) (work)* mener à bien, parvenir à terminer

VI *(shove through)* se frayer un chemin

VT INSEP *(shove through)* se frayer *ou* se faire un chemin à travers; **to p. through a crowd** se frayer un chemin dans la foule

► **push to** VT SEP *(door, shutters)* pousser, fermer

► **push up** VT SEP **1** *(lift by pushing) (lid etc)* relever, soulever

2 *(help climb by pushing) (person)* aider à monter (en le poussant)

3 *(increase) (prices etc)* faire monter

push-bike N *Br Fam* vélo *m*, bécane *f*

push-button ADJ

► ► **p. controls** commandes *fpl* automatiques; **p. operation** fonctionnement *m* automatique; **p. telephone** téléphone *m* à touches; **p. war** guerre *f* presse-bouton

pushcart ['pʊʃkɑːt] N voiture *f* à bras, charrette *f* à bras

pushchair ['pʊʃtʃeər] N *Br (for baby)* poussette *f*

pusher ['pʊʃər] N **1** *Fam (drug)* **p.** dealer *m* **2** *(ambitious person)* ambitieux, -euse, *Pej* arriviste *mf* **3** *Br (baby's)* **p.** *(utensil)* raclette *f* **4** *TV* machiniste *m* chargé du travelling

pushiness ['pʊʃɪnɪs] N *Fam* **they didn't like his p.** ils le trouvaient trop ambitieux; **you need a bit of p.** il faut insister un peu, il faut jouer des coudes

pushing ['pʊʃɪŋ] ADJ = **pushy**

N poussée *f*; **no p.!** ne poussez pas!; **there was a lot of p. and shoving** ça poussait et ça se bousculait dans tous les sens

pushover ['pʊʃəʊvər] N **1** *Fam (thing)* **it's a p.** c'est un jeu d'enfant, c'est de la tarte **2** *Fam (opponent)* adversaire *mf* facile; *(gullible person)* bonne poire *f*; **when it comes to redheads, I'm a p.** quand je rencontre une rousse, je ne peux pas me retenir

pushpin ['pʊʃpɪn] N *Am (for drawing board etc)* punaise *f*

push-pull N *Electron* push-pull *m inv*

► ► **p. amplifier** amplificateur *m* push-pull; **p. circuit** circuit *m* push-pull; *Aut* **p. hand control** *(for disabled driver)* commande *f* manuelle pousser-tirer; **p. train** train *m* réversible

pushrod ['pʊʃrɒd] N *Aut (in engine)* poussoir *m*, tige *f* poussoir *ou* de poussée *ou* de culbuteur

push-start VT *Aut (car etc)* faire démarrer en le poussant

push-up N *Gym* traction *f*, *Fam* pompe *f*; **to do push-ups** faire des tractions *ou Fam* des pompes

pushy ['pʊʃɪ] ADJ *Fam* **1** *(self-assertive)* **you have to be pretty p. in this work** il faut savoir insister dans ce travail **2** *(ambitious)* ambitieux, *Pej* arriviste; **I had very p. parents** mes parents m'ont beaucoup poussé

pusillanimity [pjuːsɪlə'nɪmɪtɪ] N *Fml* pusillanimité *f*

pusillanimous [pjuːsɪ'lænɪməs] ADJ *Fml* pusillanime

puss [pʊs] N **1** *Fam (cat)* minet *m*, minette *f*, minou *m*; **P. in Boots** le Chat botté **2** *Sl (face)* figure *f*

pussy[1] ['pʊsɪ] N **1** *Fam (cat)* minet *m*, minette *f*, minou *m* **2** *Vulg (female genitals)* chatte *f*; **he hadn't had any p. for months** *(sex)* il n'avait pas baisé depuis des mois

► ► *Fam* **p. cat** minet, minette, minou; *Bot* **p. willow** saule *m* blanc

pussy[2] ['pʌsɪ] ADJ *(containing pus)* suintant

pussyfoot ['pʊsɪfʊt] VI *Fam (avoid committing oneself)* ne pas se mouiller; **stop pussyfooting around!** arrête de tergiverser!; **we could do without all this pussyfooting about** on se passerait bien de toutes ces tergiversations

pussy-whipped [-wɪpt] ADJ *Sl* dominé par sa femme

pustule ['pʌstjuːl] N *Med, Vet* pustule *f*

PUT [pʊt] *(pt, pp* **put;** *prp* **putting)**

VT mettre **1, 4–6** ▪ poser **1, 2**
▪ soumettre **2** ▪ dire **3** ▪ estimer **4**

VT **1** *(place)* mettre; **p. it on the table** mettez-le *ou* posez-le sur la table; **to p. one's arms around sb/sth** prendre qn/qch dans ses bras; **she p. her head through the window/round the door** elle a passé la tête par la fenêtre/dans l'encoignure de la porte; **to p. a hem on a skirt** faire un ourlet à une jupe; **to p. the telescope to one's eye** porter le télescope à son œil; **to p. a child in a home** placer un enfant dans une maison d'accueil; **to p. sb on the street** *(leave destitute)* mettre qn à la rue; **to p. an advertisement in the paper** mettre *ou* insérer une annonce dans le journal; **to p. a man on the moon** envoyer un homme sur la lune; **to p. a man into orbit** mettre un homme en orbite; **to p. a bowl/a chair into sb's hands** mettre un bol/une chaise entre les mains de qn; **to p. a coin/a letter/a gun into sb's hand** glisser une pièce/une lettre/un revolver dans la main de qn; **to p. a limit/tax on sth** mettre une limite à/une taxe sur qch; **to p. a ban on sth** interdire qch; **to p. a ban on sb doing sth** interdire à qn de faire qch; *Fam* **p. it there!** *(shake hands)* touchez là!; **to p. oneself into sb's hands** s'en remettre à qn; **to p. a matter into sb's hands** confier une affaire à qn; *Fig* **to p. sb in his/her place** *(reprimand)* remettre qn à sa place; *Fig* **he didn't know where to p. himself** il ne savait plus où se mettre; **p. yourself in my position** *or* **place** mettez-vous à ma place; **p. it out of your mind** *or* **head** sors-le-toi de la tête; **I had long p. this thought out of my mind** ça faisait longtemps que je m'étais sorti cette idée de la tête; **to p. one's signature to sth** apposer sa signature sur *ou* à qch; **to p. one's name to sth** prêter son nom à qch; **to p. honour before riches** préférer l'honneur à l'argent; **to p. a matter right** arranger une affaire, remettre les choses au point; **to p. sb out of suspense** tirer qn du doute; **to p. sb against sb** monter qn contre qn; **to p. an article on the market** mettre un article en vente *ou* sur le marché; **to p. a play on the stage** monter une pièce; **to p. one's thoughts into words** traduire ses pensées par des mots; **to p. money into an undertaking** mettre de l'argent dans une affaire; **to p. money on a horse** miser *ou* parier sur un cheval; **to p. some energy into finishing a job** mettre de l'énergie à achever une tâche; **to p. a lot of work into sth/doing sth** beaucoup travailler à qch/pour faire qch

2 *(present)* **to p. a question to sb** poser une question à qn; **to p. a case before sb** soumettre un cas à qn; **to p. a resolution to the meeting** présenter une résolution à l'assemblée; *Law* **I p. it to you that …** n'est-il pas vrai que …?; **I p. it to him that it would be better to …** je lui ai suggéré qu'il vaudrait mieux …; **to p. the case clearly** exposer clairement la situation; **what did you p. for question three?** qu'est-ce que tu as mis à la troisième question?

3 *(express)* **to p. it bluntly** pour parler franc; **you could have p. that better** tu aurais pu tourner cela un peu mieux; **if one may p. it in that way** si l'on peut s'exprimer ainsi; **I wouldn't p. it quite like that** je ne dirais pas cela; **I don't know how to p. it** je ne sais comment dire; **to p. it another way, …** en d'autres termes, …; **'to encourage the others', as Voltaire puts it** 'pour encourager les autres' comme dirait Voltaire

4 *(estimate)* estimer, évaluer; **to p. the population at 10,000** estimer *ou* évaluer la population à 10 000; **I would p. her on a par with** *or* **in the same class as Henry James** je la mettrais dans la même catégorie que Henry James; **I wouldn't have p. her age at more than 25** je ne lui aurais pas donné plus de 25 ans; **what would you p. it at?** quelle est votre estimation?

5 to p. an end to sth mettre fin à qch; **to p. a stop to sth** mettre un terme à qch

6 *(cause to do, go, be etc)* **to p. sb to do sth** *(to make, have sb do sth)* faire faire qch à qn; *(to designate sb to do sth)* désigner qn pour faire qch; **to p. sb in(to) a good/bad mood** mettre qn de bonne/mauvaise humeur; **to p. a guard on the door** faire surveiller la porte; **to p. a child to bed** mettre un enfant au lit; **to p. sth to (a) good use** faire bon usage de qch, bien employer *ou* utiliser qch; **to p. sb to the test** mettre qn à l'épreuve; **to p. a resolution to the vote** mettre une résolution aux voix; **to p. the enemy to flight** mettre l'ennemi en fuite; **to p. sb to sleep** endormir qn; *Euph* **to have a dog p. to sleep** faire piquer un chien; **I'm putting you to a lot of trouble** je vous cause beaucoup d'ennuis; **to p. sb to work** mettre qn au travail (**on sth** sur qch)

7 *(direct, force)* **to p. a bullet through sb's head** mettre *ou* loger une balle dans la tête de qn; **to p. one's fist through the window** enfoncer la fenêtre d'un coup de poing; *Sport* **to p. the shot** lancer le poids

VI *Naut* **to p. (out) to sea** prendre la mer *ou* le large; **to p. into port** faire escale, relâcher, faire relâche

N1 *Sport (of shot)* lancer *m*, lancement *m*

2 *St Exch (option)* option *f* de vente, put *m*
▸▸*St Exch* **p. band** période *f* de validité d'une option de vente; *St Exch* **p. bond** emprunt *m* à fenêtre; *St Exch* **p. option** option de vente, put; *St Exch* **p. warrant** warrant *m* à la vente

▸ **put about VT SEP 1** *(spread) (rumour)* faire circuler; **to p. it about that …** faire circuler le bruit que …; **it's being p. about by her rivals that …** ses rivaux font circuler le bruit que …; **it is being p. about that …** il paraîtrait que …, le bruit court que …

2 *Naut* **to p. a ship about** virer de bord

3 *Fam (be sexually promiscuous)* **to p. oneself about, to p. it about** coucher avec tout le monde

VI *Naut* virer de bord

▸ **put across VT SEP 1** *(communicate) (feeling)* communiquer; *(message, idea)* faire passer; **to p. sth across to sb** faire comprendre qch à qn; **she knows how to p. her ideas across** elle sait bien faire passer ses idées; **he's good at putting himself across at interviews** il sait se faire valoir dans les entretiens; **he p. himself across badly at the interview** il a donné une mauvaise image de lui-même à l'entretien; **it doesn't p.**

across the sense of size you get from the place cela ne restitue pas le sentiment d'immensité qu'on ressent à cet endroit

2 *Fam* **to p. one across on sb** *(trick)* rouler qn, avoir qn

▸ **put around VT SEP = put about VT SEP 1**

▸ **put aside VT SEP** *(place on one side) (one's book etc)* poser à côté de soi; *(keep)* mettre de côté; *Fig (hope, idea)* renoncer à; *Fig (save) (money etc)* mettre de côté; **if we p. aside the emotional trauma caused** mis à part le choc émotionnel provoqué; **p. aside all gloomy thoughts** oublie toutes ces pensées maussades; **let's try to p. aside our differences** essayons de laisser nos différends de côté

▸ **put away VT SEP 1** *(tidy away)* ranger; *(return to its place)* remettre à sa place; *(car)* garer; **p. your money/wallet away** *(I'm paying)* range ton argent/ton portefeuille

2 *(save)* mettre de côté; **to p. something away for one's old age** mettre quelque chose de côté pour sa retraite

3 *Fam (lock up) (in prison)* mettre en taule; *(in asylum etc)* (faire) enfermer

4 *Fam (consume) (food)* avaler, expédier; *(drink)* siffler; **he can really p. it away** *(drink)* il a une bonne descente; *(food)* il a un appétit d'ogre

▸ **put back VT SEP 1** *(restore to its position)* remettre à sa place; **to p. sth back where one found it** remettre qch là où on l'a trouvé

2 *(postpone) (meeting etc)* reporter; *(turn back hands of) (clock, watch)* retarder; *Fig* **this decision has p. the clock back** cette décision nous a ramenés en arrière; *Sch* **his absence has p. him back** son absence l'a retardé dans ses études

VI *Naut* retourner *ou* revenir *ou* rentrer au port

▸ **put by VT SEP** *(money)* mettre de côté; *(supplies etc)* mettre en réserve; **to have something p. by** *(savings)* avoir des économies

▸ **put down VT SEP 1** *(set down)* poser; **to p. sth down on the ground** poser *ou* déposer qch par terre; *Tel* **to p. down the receiver** *or* **the phone** raccrocher; **p. that gun down!** pose ce revolver!; **to p. down passengers** *(of bus etc)* débarquer *ou* déposer *ou* laisser descendre des voyageurs; **to p. the baby down** *(put to bed)* mettre le bébé au lit, coucher le bébé; **to p. down roots** *(of plant)*, *Fig (of person)* s'enraciner; **I couldn't p. it down** *(book)* je l'ai lu d'un trait

2 *(suppress) (revolt, opposition)* réprimer

3 *(close) (umbrella)* fermer

4 *(write)* noter; **to p. sth down in writing** mettre *ou* *Fml* coucher qch par écrit; **to p. down one's name** *(enrol)* s'inscrire, se faire inscrire (**for** pour); *Fam* **p. me down for a ticket/to play** mets-moi sur la liste pour les tickets/des joueurs; **p. it down to me** *or* **to my account** inscrivez-le *ou* mettez-le sur mon compte; **we'll have to p. it down to experience** au moins on a appris quelque chose; **to p. sb/sth down as sth** classer qn/qch comme qch; **I should p. her down as thirty** je lui donne trente ans

5 *(attribute)* **to p. sth down to sb/sth** attribuer *ou* imputer qch à qn/qch; **I p. his success down to luck** j'attribue son succès à la chance

6 *(pay)* **to p. some money down (as a deposit)** verser *ou* déposer une caution; **how much can you p. down?** combien pouvez-vous verser *ou* déposer en caution?; **I've p. £500 down on my new car** j'ai versé 500 livres d'arrhes pour ma nouvelle voiture

7 *(kill) (animal)* abattre; *Vet* **to have a dog p. down** faire piquer un chien

8 *(say negative things about)* dire du mal de; **you're always putting me down** tu n'arrêtes pas de me critiquer; **you shouldn't p. your-**

self down tu ne devrais pas te sous-estimer

9 *esp Parl* **to p. down a motion of censure** déposer une motion de censure

10 *(wine)* mettre en cave

VI *Aviat* atterrir

▸ **put forward VT SEP 1** *(suggest) (plan, theory etc)* avancer, mettre en avant; *(claim)* émettre; **to p. sb** *or* **sb's name forward (for a post)** suggérer qn *ou* le nom de qn (pour un poste); **to p. oneself forward** *(get oneself noticed)* se mettre en avant; **to p. one's best foot forward** *(walk faster)* presser le pas; *Fig* se mettre en devoir de faire de son mieux

2 *(advance) (clock, time of meeting etc)* avancer

▸ **put in VT SEP 1** *(place in)* mettre; **to p. one's contact lenses in** mettre ses lentilles de contact; **to p. one's head in at the window** passer la tête par la fenêtre; **you only get out what you p. in** on ne récolte que ce qu'on sème; **and it was before twelve, she p. in spitefully** et il n'était pas midi, ajouta-t-elle méchamment; **to p. in a (good) word for sb** dire un mot en faveur de qn

2 *(install)* installer; **we're having a new telephone p. in** on nous installe un nouveau téléphone; **the voters p. the Tories in** les électeurs ont mis les conservateurs au pouvoir

3 *(enter)* présenter; **to p. in a claim/an application** déposer une réclamation/une candidature; **we're putting him in for the 500 metres** nous le présentons pour le 500 mètres; **to p. pupils in for an examination** présenter des élèves à un examen

4 *(spend time doing)* **to p. in an hour's work** faire une heure de travail; **she's p. in a lot of time on this project** elle a passé beaucoup de temps sur ce projet; **they've p. in a tremendous amount of work** ils ont fourni une quantité de travail remarquable

VI *Naut* **to p. in at a port** faire escale *ou* relâcher dans un port

2 *(apply)* **to p. in for an election/for a job** poser sa candidature à une élection/à un poste; **to p. in for two days' leave** demander un congé *ou* *Mil* une permission de 48 heures

▸ **put off VT SEP 1** *(postpone) (meeting, appointment)* remettre *ou* renvoyer à plus tard, ajourner, repousser; *(decision, payment)* remettre à plus tard, différer; *(work)* remettre à plus tard; *(guests)* décommander; **to p. off doing sth** remettre à plus tard de faire qch; **he p. off telling her for as long as possible** il a repoussé le plus possible le moment de lui dire; **don't keep putting things off** ne remettez pas toujours à plus tard; *Prov* **never p. off till tomorrow what you can do today** il ne faut jamais remettre au lendemain ce que l'on peut faire le jour même; **let's p. lunch off to another time** nous déjeunerons ensemble une autre fois

2 *(make excuses to)* **to p. sb off** donner le change à qn, entortiller qn; **to p. sb off with an excuse** se débarrasser de qn *ou* renvoyer qn avec une excuse; **I won't be p. off any longer** j'en ai assez qu'on m'entortille

3 *(allow to get off bus etc)* laisser descendre; *(force to get off)* faire descendre; **could you p. me off at the High Street?** pourriez-vous me laisser descendre *ou* m'arrêter à High Street?

4 *(switch off) (television, radio etc)* éteindre

5 *(cause dislike in) (person)* dégoûter; **there's something about him that puts me off** il y a quelque chose en lui qui me dégoûte; **the mere smell of that cheese puts me off** l'odeur de ce fromage suffit à m'écœurer; **don't be p. off by his gruff manner** ne te laisse pas décourager *ou* rebuter par ses manières rébarbatives

6 *(disturb) (person)* déconcerter, dérouter, troubler; **these interruptions p. me off** ces interruptions me déconcentrent; **the noise was putting her off her tennis** le bruit l'empêchait de bien jouer au tennis; **the worry was putting me off my food** l'inquiétude me coupait l'appétit

vi *Naut* déborder du quai, pousser au large; **to p. off from the shore** quitter la côte, prendre le large

▶ **put on vt sep 1** *(clothes, shoes)* mettre; **to p. on one's make-up** se maquiller

2 *(assume)* **to p. on an air of innocence** prendre *ou* se donner un air innocent; **to p. on an act** jouer la comédie; **to p. on an accent** prendre un accent; *Fam* **you're putting it on!** tout ça c'est du chiqué!

3 *Fam (deceive)* **she's putting you on** elle te fait marcher

4 *(present) Theat (play)* monter; *TV, Radio (programme)* diffuser, passer; *TV, Radio* **why can't they p. something decent on for a change?** ils ne pourraient pas passer quelque chose d'intéressant pour une fois?

5 *(add to weight, price etc)* grossir, prendre du poids; **I've p. on five kilos** j'ai pris cinq kilos, j'ai grossi de cinq kilos; **they've p. 2p on (the price)** on a augmenté le prix de 2 pence

6 *(switch on) (light, gas)* allumer; *(radio, television)* allumer, mettre; **he p. on some Vivaldi/the news** il a mis du Vivaldi/les informations; **to p. the kettle on** mettre la bouilloire à chauffer; **to p. the potatoes on** *(to cook)* mettre les pommes de terre à cuire; *(to heat up)* faire chauffer les pommes de terre; **to p. on a record/a tape** passer un disque/une cassette; **to p. on the brake(s)** freiner

7 *(put into service) (train)* mettre en service; **to p. on speed** prendre de la vitesse

8 *Horseracing etc (bet)* **to p. on £1** miser 1 livre

9 *(advance) (clock)* avancer

10 *(on telephone)* **could you p. him on, please?** pouvez-vous me le passer, s'il vous plaît?

▶ **put on to vt sep 1** *(provide with information about)* **to p. sb on to sth** indiquer qch à qn; **who p. you on to it?** *Fam* qui est-ce qui vous a donné le tuyau?; **who p. the police on to me?** qui m'a dénoncé à la police?

2 *Tel* **would you p. me on to Mr Lawrence?** voulez-vous me passer M. Lawrence?

▶ **put out vt sep 1** *(place outside)* mettre dehors; **to p. the cat out** mettre le chat dehors; **to p. the rubbish out** sortir la/les poubelle(s); *Naut* **to p. out a boat** mettre un canot à l'eau; **to p. one's head out of the window** passer la tête par la fenêtre; **the snail p. out its horns** l'escargot a sorti ses cornes; **to p. out peace feelers** envoyer des sondages de paix; **to p. sb's eyes out** crever les yeux à qn, éborgner qn

2 *(arrange for use)* sortir, préparer; **I've p. your clothes out** je t'ai sorti *ou* préparé tes vêtements

3 *(extend) (one's hand)* avancer, tendre; *(one's arm)* allonger, tendre; **to p. out one's tongue** tirer la langue; **she p. out a foot to trip him up** elle a mis un pied en avant pour le faire trébucher

4 *(issue) (new record, edition, model etc)* sortir; *(appeal, request)* faire; *(statement)* émettre

5 *(extinguish) (candle, fire, light)* éteindre; *(gas)* fermer

6 *(make unconscious) (patient)* endormir

7 *(make angry) (person)* ennuyer, fâcher, contrarier; **to be p. out about sth** être mécontent de qch; **she gets terribly p. out if you don't agree with her** elle s'énerve si on n'est pas d'accord avec elle

8 *(inconvenience) (person)* déranger, incommoder, gêner; **you mustn't p. yourself out for me** il ne faut pas vous déranger pour

moi; **would one more guest p. you out?** est-ce qu'un invité de plus te dérangerait?; **I don't want to p. anyone out** je ne veux déranger personne

9 *(dislocate)* **to p. one's back/shoulder out** se démettre le dos/l'épaule

10 **to p. a cow out to grass** mettre une vache en pâture; **to p. money out (to interest)** placer de l'argent (à intérêt); **to p. work out** *(subcontract)* mettre du travail en sous-traitance; **to p. work out to tender** mettre du travail en adjudication

vi 1 *Naut* **to p. out (to sea)** prendre le large *ou* la mer

2 *Am Sl (of woman)* accepter de coucher (**for** avec); **did she p. out?** est-ce qu'elle a bien voulu coucher?; **she puts out for anyone** *(is promiscuous)* elle coucherait avec le premier venu

▶ **put over vt sep 1** *(communicate)* = **put across 1**

2 *Am (postpone)* remettre à plus tard, différer

3 *Fam* **to p. one over on sb** avoir qn

▶ **put through vt sep 1** *(carry through) (project)* mener à bien, faire aboutir; *(have accepted) (deal)* faire accepter

2 *Tel (connect)* **to p. sb through to sb** mettre qn en ligne avec qn, passer qn à qn; **p. him through, please** mettez-le en ligne *ou* passez-le moi, s'il vous plaît; **I'll p. you through to him** je vous le passe

3 *(cause to suffer)* **you've p. your mother through a lot of worry** tu as causé beaucoup d'inquiétude à ta mère; **I've p. myself through hell for you** j'ai souffert le martyre pour toi; *Fam* **to p. sb through it** *(at interview etc)* mettre qn à l'épreuve; **to p. sb through an ordeal** faire subir une rude épreuve à qn; **have you any idea what you're putting him through?** as-tu la moindre idée de ce que tu lui fais subir?

4 *(subject to)* **to p. sb/sth through sth** soumettre qn/qch à qch, faire subir qch à qn/qch; **to p. oneself through sth** endurer qch

5 **she p. herself through university** elle s'est payé ses études à l'université

▶ **put to vt sep** *(only in passive)* **to be hard p. to it to do sth** avoir beaucoup de mal à faire qch

▶ **put together vt sep 1** *(place side by side) (two objects)* mettre côte à côte; *(facts)* rapprocher, comparer

2 *(assemble) (parts, components)* assembler, mettre ensemble; *(machine etc)* monter, assembler; *(meal)* préparer, confectionner; *(menu)* élaborer; *(report, story, programme)* mettre sur pied; *(team, show)* monter; *(different elements, contrasting things)* réunir, rassembler; **the programme is nicely p. together** ce programme est bien fait; **to p. together a convincing picture of what happened** reconstituer une idée convaincante de ce qui s'est passé; **Fam to p. two and two together** tirer ses conclusions; **I'll just p. a few things together (in my bag)** je vais faire rapidement ma valise; **she's got more brains than the rest of them p. together** elle est plus intelligente qu'eux tous mis ensemble

▶ **put up vt sep 1** *(raise) (one's hair, collar of coat etc)* relever; *(umbrella)* ouvrir; *(rocket, distress flare)* envoyer; **could all those going p. up their hands?** que tous ceux qui y vont lèvent la main; **p. up your hands!, p. your hands up!** haut les mains!; *Fam* **p. them up!** *(in robbery)* haut les mains!; *(before fight)* défends-toi!; **I'm going to p. my feet up for a few minutes** je vais me reposer un peu

2 *(erect) (ladder, tent etc)* dresser; *(house etc)* construire, bâtir; *(monument)* ériger; *(scaffolding)* installer, monter

3 *(attach to wall) (painting)* fixer, accrocher; *(poster) (with paste)* coller; *(notice etc)*

afficher; *(curtain)* poser, accrocher; *(wallpaper)* poser

4 *(increase) (prices)* augmenter

5 *(provide accommodation for)* loger, héberger; **to p. you up** je ne peux pas vous loger *ou* vous héberger

6 *(offer) (candidate)* proposer (**for the elections** aux élections); **to p. sth up for sale** mettre qch en vente; **to p. a picture up for auction** mettre un tableau aux enchères; **to p. up resistance** *or* **a fight** *or* **a struggle** *(physically)* opposer une résistance; *(morally)* s'opposer; **to p. up a good case for sth** présenter de bons arguments en faveur de qch

7 *(provide) (sum of money)* fournir; **to p. up the money for an undertaking** fournir les fonds d'une entreprise

8 *(sword)* baisser

vi 1 *(stay)* **to p. up at a hotel** descendre dans un hôtel; **I've been putting up at a hotel for three weeks** ça fait trois semaines que je suis à l'hôtel; **where are you putting up?** où est-ce que tu loges?; *(in hotel)* où es-tu descendu?

2 *(of candidate)* **to p. up for the council** poser sa candidature comme conseiller; **to p. up for re-election** se présenter pour être réélu

3 *Fam* **p. up or shut up!** montrez la couleur de votre argent d'abord!

▶ **put upon vt insep** **to p. upon sb** *(abuse)* abuser de qn; *(exploit)* exploiter qn; **I won't be p. upon** je refuse qu'on abuse de moi

▶ **put up to vt sep** **to p. sb up to doing sth** *(incite)* inciter qn à faire qch; **who p. you up to it?** *(put the idea into your head)* qui vous a donné l'idée de faire ça?; *(made you do it)* qui vous a fait faire ça?

▶ **put up with vt insep** *(tolerate)* supporter, tolérer; **we'll have to p. up with it** il faut l'accepter *ou* nous y résigner; **I don't know how you p. up with the noise** je ne sais pas comment tu peux supporter tout ce bruit; **I'll have to p. up with him** il faudra bien que je le supporte

putative ['pju:tətɪv] **adj attrib** *Fml* putatif

put-down **n** *Fam* affront *m*

put-in **n** *Rugby* introduction *f*

put-on **adj** *(air, smile)* affecté; *(joy)* affecté, feint

n *esp Am Fam (deception)* **it's just a p.** c'est du chiqué, c'est de la comédie; **the whole thing was a p. to gain sympathy** toute l'histoire n'était qu'un subterfuge pour s'attirer de la sympathie

put-put ['pʌtpʌt] **n** *(sound)* teuf-teuf *m, pl* teufs-teufs

vi *(of small engine etc)* faire teuf-teuf

putrefaction [pju:trɪ'fækʃən] **n** putréfaction *f*

putrefy ['pju:trɪfaɪ] **vt** putréfier, pourrir

vi se putréfier, pourrir, suppurer, s'envenimer; **a putrefying corpse** un cadavre en état de putréfaction

putrescence [pju:'tresəns] **n** *Fml* putrescence *f*

putrescent [pju:'tresənt] **adj** *Fml* putrescent, en putréfaction

putrid ['pju:trɪd] **adj 1** putride **2** *Fam (disgusting, horrible)* dégoûtant, dégueulasse

putsch [pʊtʃ] **n** putsch *m*

putt [pʌt] *Golf* **n** putt *m*; **to hole a long p.** rentrer un long putt

vt & vi putter

putter¹ ['pʌtər] **n** *Golf (club)* putter *m*; **good/bad p.** *(person)* joueur, -euse qui putte bien

putter² **vi** *Am* = **potter²**

putting ['pʌtɪŋ] **n** *(game), Golf* putting *m*; **to practise p.** s'exercer à putter

▶ ▶ **p. green** green *m*; **p. iron** putter *m*

putto, pl **putti** ['pʊtəʊ, -tiː] N Art putto m, pl putti

putty ['pʌtɪ] N mastic m; **to fill a hole with p.** boucher un trou au mastic, mastiquer un trou; **my legs felt like p.** j'avais les jambes en coton; **p.-coloured** grisâtre; **she's like p. in my hands** j'en fais ce que je veux
VT (hole) mastiquer, boucher au mastic
▸▸ **p. knife** couteau m à mastiquer, spatule f de vitrier

put-up ADJ
▸▸ Fam **p. job** affaire f préparée à l'avance; (trap) coup m monté

put-upon ADJ **she was feeling p.** elle avait l'impression qu'on abusait de sa gentillesse; **a p. expression** une tête de martyr

put-you-up N canapé-lit m, pl canapés-lits

putz [pʌts] N Am Fam andouille f, truffe f
▸ **putz around** VI Am Fam (act foolishly) faire l'idiot, faire l'imbecile; (waste time) glander, glandouiller

puzzle ['pʌz(ə)l] N **1** (game) (manual) casse-tête m inv; (mental) devinette f **2** (mystery) énigme f
VT (person) intriguer, laisser perplexe; **puzzled look** air m perplexe; **I was puzzled** j'étais perplexe, je ne savais que penser; **he puzzles me** il m'intrigue, c'est une énigme pour moi; **I am puzzled to know why you have done this** ça m'intrigue de savoir pourquoi tu as fait ça; **to p. one's head over sth** se casser la tête sur qch, chercher à comprendre qch
VI **to p. about sth** chercher à comprendre qch
▸▸ **p. book** livre m de jeux; (of crosswords) livre de mots croisés
▸ **puzzle out** VT SEP (problem) résoudre; (solution, meaning) trouver; **I'm still trying to p. out how he did it** je cherche toujours à comprendre comment il l'a fait

▸ **puzzle over** VT INSEP (wonder about) chercher à comprendre, se casser la tête sur

puzzlement ['pʌz(ə)lmənt] N perplexité f; **to look at sb in p.** regarder qn d'un air perplexe; **an expression of p.** un air perplexe; **much to my p.** à ma grande surprise

puzzler ['pʌzlər] N Fam (mystery) énigme f; **that's a p.!** (problem) voilà une question difficile!

puzzling ['pʌzlɪŋ] ADJ curieux, bizarre

PVC [piːviːˈsiː] N (abbr **polyvinyl chloride**) PVC m; **a P. belt** une ceinture en PVC

PVS [piːviːˈes] N (abbr **persistent vegetative state**) état m végétatif chronique

PW [piːˈdʌb(ə)ljuː] N (abbr **policewoman**) femme f policier

PWR [piːdʌb(ə)ljuːˈɑːr] N Nucl (abbr **pressurized-water reactor**) REP m (réacteur à eau pressurisée)

PX [piːˈeks] N Am Mil (abbr **post exchange**) foyer m

pygmy ['pɪgmɪ] N pygmée m
ADJ pygmée

pyjamas [pəˈdʒɑːməz] N esp Br (pair of) pyjamas pyjama m; **he's in pyjamas** il est en pyjama VOIR GRAMMAIRE A10
▸▸ **p. bottoms** pantalon m de pyjama; **p. jacket** veste f de pyjama; **p. party** = fête f où tous les invités portent un pyjama; **p. top** (jacket) veste de pyjama; (pull-on type) haut m de pyjama; **p. trousers** pantalon de pyjama

pylon ['paɪlən] N **1** (of metal, reinforced concrete) pylône m; (electricity) p. pylône (de transformateur électrique) **2** Archit (gateway) pylône m

pyorrhea [paɪəˈrɪə] N Med pyorrhée f

pyramid ['pɪrəmɪd] N Archit, Math pyramide f

▸▸ Com **p. scheme** plan m commercial en cascade; Com **p. selling** vente f pyramidale

pyramidal [pɪˈræmɪd(ə)l] ADJ Fml pyramidal, -aux

pyre ['paɪər] N (funeral) p. bûcher m (funéraire)

Pyrenean [pɪrəˈniːən] ADJ pyrénéen, des Pyrénées
▸▸ **P. mountain dog** chien m ou berger m des Pyrénées

Pyrenees (the) [ðəpɪrəˈniːz] NPL les Pyrénées fpl

pyrethrum [paɪˈriːθrəm] N (plant) pyrèthre m

pyretic [paɪˈretɪk] ADJ Med pyrétique

Pyrex® ['paɪreks] N Pyrex® m; **P. dish** plat m en Pyrex®

pyrites [paɪˈraɪtiːz] N Miner pyrite f; **iron p.** pyrite de fer, fer m sulfuré

pyritic [paɪˈrɪtɪk] ADJ Miner pyriteux

pyromaniac [paɪrəʊˈmeɪnɪæk] N pyromane mf

pyrotechnic [paɪrəʊˈteknɪk] ADJ USU ATTRIB pyrotechnique; **p. display** feu m d'artifice

pyrotechnics [paɪrəʊˈteknɪks] N pyrotechnie f, (fireworks) feux mpl d'artifice; Fig (of style etc) fioritures fpl VOIR GRAMMAIRE A10

Pyrrhic ['pɪrɪk] ADJ Antiq de Pyrrhus
▸▸ Fig **P. victory** victoire f à la Pyrrhus, victoire désastreuse

Pythagoras [paɪˈθægərəs] N Pythagore m

Pythagorean [paɪθægəˈriːən] ADJ pythagoricien

python ['paɪθən] N python m

pyx [pɪks] N Rel ciboire m

pzazz [pəˈzæz] N Fam (flair) punch m

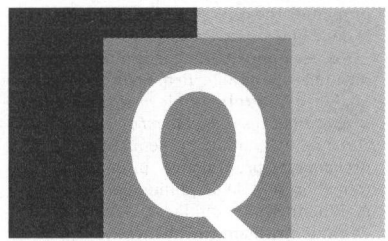

Q, q¹ [kjuː] N *(letter)* Q, q *m*; **two Q's** deux Q

q² *Sch etc (abbr* **question***)* q.

Qatar [kæˈtɑː(r)] N le Qatar

Qatari [kæˈtɑːrɪ] N habitant, -ante du Qatar
ADJ du Qatar

QC [kjuːˈsiː] N *Br Law abbr* **Queen's Counsel**

QE2 [kjuːiːˈtuː] N *Br Naut (abbr* **Queen Elizabeth II**) = le paquebot Queen Elizabeth II

QED [kjuːiːˈdiː] *(abbr quod erat demonstrandum)* CQFD (ce qu'il fallait démontrer)

QIP [kjuːaɪˈpiː] N *(abbr* **quality improvement programme***)* programme *m* d'amélioration de la qualité

QM [kjuːˈem] N *Mil abbr* **Quartermaster**

QMG [kjuːemˈdʒiː] N *Mil (abbr* **Quartermaster General***)* = Directeur *m* de l'Intendance (militaire)

QMV [kjuːemˈviː] N *EU (abbr* **qualified majority voting***)* vote *m* à la majorité qualifiée

qt, *pl* **qts** *abbr* **quart,** *pl* **quarts**

q.t. [kjuːˈtiː] N *Fam (abbr* **quiet***)* **to do sth on the q.t.** faire qch en douce; **to tell sb sth on the q.t.** dire qch à qn discrètement *ou* en confidence; **this is strictly on the q.t.** c'est confidentiel

Q-tip® N *Am* coton-tige® *m, pl* cotons-tiges

qty *Com abbr* **quantity**

qua [kwɑː] PREP *Fml* **alcohol q.** alcool l'alcool en tant que tel

quack¹ [kwæk] INT **q.! q.!** coin-coin!
N **1** *(cry)* coin-coin *m inv* **2** *(in children's language)* **q.-q.** *(duck)* canard *m*
VI **1** *(of duck)* cancaner, *Fam* faire coin-coin **2** *Fam (of person)* jacasser

quack² N *Pej* **1** *(charlatan)* charlatan *m* **2** *Br, Austr Fam (doctor)* toubib *m*
▸▸ **q. doctor** *(unqualified)* charlatan; **q. remedy** remède *m* de charlatan; *Fig* fausse solution *f*

quackery [ˈkwækərɪ] N charlatanisme *m*, charlatanerie *f*

quad¹ [kwɒd] N *Sch Fam* cour *f*

quad² N *Fam (child)* quadruplé, -ée
▸▸ **q. bike** quad *m*; **q. biking** quad; **to go q. biking** faire du quad; *Comput* **q. density** densité *f* quadruple

quadragenarian [kwɒdrədʒəˈneərɪən] ADJ, N quadragénaire *mf*

Quadragesima [kwɒdrəˈdʒesɪmə] N *Rel* Quadragésime *f*
▸▸ **Q. Sunday** le dimanche de la Quadragésime

quadrangle [ˈkwɒdræŋg(ə)l] N **1** *Geom* figure *f* quadrangulaire, quadrilatère *m* **2** *(courtyard) (at school, college etc)* cour *f*, *Archit* cour carrée

quadrangular [kwɒˈdræŋgjʊlər] ADJ quadrangulaire

quadrant [ˈkwɒdrənt] N *Astron, Geom (of*

circle*)* quart *m* de cercle; *(of surface)*, *Naut* quadrant *m*

quadraphonic [kwɒdrəˈfɒnɪk] ADJ quadriphonique, tétraphonique

quadraphonics [kwɒdrəˈfɒnɪks] N SING quadriphonie *f*, tétraphonie *f* VOIR GRAMMAIRE A10

quadrasonic [kwɒdrəˈsɒnɪk] ADJ tétraphonique

quadratic [kwɒˈdrætɪk] ADJ *Math (equation)* quadratique, du second degré

quadrature [ˈkwɒdrətʃər] N *Math, Astron* quadrature *f*; **q. of the circle** quadrature du cercle

quadrennial [kwɒˈdrenɪəl] ADJ quadriennal, -aux

quadri- [ˈkwɒdrɪ] PREF quadri-

quadrilateral [kwɒdrɪˈlætər(ə)l] *Geom etc* ADJ quadrilatéral, -aux
N quadrilatère *m*

quadrille [kwəˈdrɪl] N *Mus* quadrille *m*

quadrillion [kwɒˈdrɪlɪən] N *Br (10^{24})* quadrillion *m*; *Am (10^{15})* mille billions

quadriplegia [kwɒdrɪˈpliːdʒɪə] N *Med* tétraplégie *f*, quadriplégie *f*

quadriplegic [kwɒdrɪˈpliːdʒɪk] ADJ, N *Med* tétraplégique *mf*, quadriplégique *mf*

quadroon [kwɒˈdruːn] ADJ, N quarteron, -onne

quadruped [ˈkwɒdrʊped] ADJ, N quadrupède *m*

quadruple [kwɒˈdruːp(ə)l] ADJ, N quadruple *m* VT & VI quadrupler

quadruplet [kwɒˈdruːplɪt, ˈkwɒdrʊplɪt] N **1** *(child)* quadruplé, -ée **2** *Mus* quartolet *m*

quadruplicate¹ [kwɒˈdruːplɪkət] ADJ quadruple; **in q.** en quatre exemplaires

quadruplicate² [kwɒˈdruːplɪkeɪt] VT **1** *(multiply by four)* quadrupler, multiplier par quatre **2** *(make four copies of) (letter etc)* faire *ou* tirer quatre exemplaires de

quaff [kwɒf] VT *Lit (wine)* boire à longs traits; *(glass)* vider d'un trait

quagmire [ˈkwægmaɪər, ˈkwɒg-] N *(bog)* marécage *m*; *Fig (awkward situation)* bourbier *m*

quail¹ [kweɪl] N INV *(bird)* caille *f* (des blés), *Can* colin *m*; **q.'s eggs** œufs *mpl* de caille

quail² VI *Lit (of person)* fléchir, faiblir (**before** devant); **his heart quailed** son cœur défaillit

quaint [kweɪnt] ADJ *(unusual)* curieux; *(attractively old-fashioned)* suranné, vieillot, -otte; *(picturesque)* pittoresque; mignon, -onne; **he has this q. hope that he'll find a permanent job** il croit naïvement qu'il va trouver un emploi permanent; **a q. little cottage** une petite chaumière pittoresque

quaintly [ˈkweɪntlɪ] ADV *(unusually)* curieusement; *(picturesquely)* de façon pittoresque; **q. old-fashioned** d'un charme vieillot; **rather q. worded** formulé de façon assez mignonne

quaintness [ˈkweɪntnɪs] N *(unusualness)* étrangeté *f*, *(old-fashioned charm)* pittoresque *m* suranné; **the q. of the wording** la façon assez mignonne dont c'était formulé

quake [kweɪk] N **1** *Fam (earthquake)* tremblement *m* de terre **2** *(shaking)* tremblement *m*
VI **1** *(of person)* trembler, frémir (**with fear** de crainte); **to q. in one's shoes** trembler de peur; **he was quaking with laughter** il était secoué de rires **2** *(of thing)* trembler, branler; **quaking grass** brize *f*

Quaker [ˈkweɪkər] N *Rel* quaker *m*, quakeresse *f*

Quakerism [ˈkweɪkərɪz(ə)m] N *Rel* quakerisme *m*

qualification [kwɒlɪfɪˈkeɪʃən] N **1** *(diploma etc)* diplôme *m*, qualification *f*; **to have the necessary qualifications for a job** *(skills etc)* avoir les qualités *ou* les compétences requises pour remplir une fonction; *(diplomas)* avoir les diplômes requis *ou* les qualifications requises pour remplir une fonction; **paper** *or* **formal qualifications** diplômes; **professional q.** qualification professionnelle; **what are your qualifications?** quels diplômes avez-vous?; **a q. in translation** un diplôme de traduction; **one of the qualifications for this job is a sense of humour** une des qualités requises pour ce poste est le sens de l'humour

2 *(successful completion of studies)* obtention *f* d'un diplôme; **on q.** une fois le diplôme obtenu

3 *Sport* qualification *f*, **on q. for the World Cup** après s'être qualifié pour la Coupe du monde

4 *(reservation)* réserve *f*, restriction *f*; *(condition)* condition *f*; **to accept without q.** *(without reservation)* accepter sans réserve; *(without conditions)* accepter sans conditions; **to add a few qualifications** *(to a statement, remarks etc)* apporter quelques modifications

5 *Fml (description)* qualification *f*; **the report's q. of them as 'mercenaries'** le fait que le rapport les qualifiait de mercenaires

qualified [ˈkwɒlɪfaɪd] ADJ **1** *(competent) (for position etc)* qualifié, compétent, qui a les capacités requises; *(having diploma etc)* qualifié, diplômé; *(for position etc)* qui a les diplômes requis *ou* les qualifications requises; *(pilot etc)* breveté; *Law* capable (**to do** de faire); **she's very highly q.** elle est très qualifiée; **to be q. to do sth** *(be competent)* avoir les compétences voulues *ou* les capacités requises pour faire qch; *(have diploma etc)* avoir les diplômes requis *ou* les qualifications requises pour faire qch; **I am q. to speak about it** *(I know about it)* je suis bien placé pour en parler; **to be q. to speak** *(at meeting etc)* avoir voix au chapitre; **q. persons** personnes *fpl* compétentes

2 *(modified)* *(approval, support etc)* modéré; *(praise)* mitigé

▸▸*EU* **q. majority voting** vote *m* à la majorité qualifiée; *Acct* **q. report** rapport *m* réservé; **q. success** demi-succès *m inv*

qualifier ['kwɒlɪfaɪər] N **1** *Sport (person, team that qualifies)* qualifié, -ée; *(qualifying round)* série *f* éliminatoire **2** *Gram* qualificatif *m* **3** *(reservation)* restriction *f*, réserve *f*; *(condition)* condition *f*

qualify ['kwɒlɪfaɪ] VT **1** to q. sb for sth/for doing *or* to do sth *(of course, training etc)* donner à qn les compétences voulues pour qch/pour faire qch, qualifier qn pour qch/pour faire qch; *Law* donner qualité à qn pour qch/pour faire qch; **my knowledge qualifies me to undertake this work** j'ai les connaissances pour entreprendre cet ouvrage; **what do you think qualifies you for this job?** en quoi vous considérez-vous comme qualifié pour cet emploi?

2 *(modify)* *(consent etc)* apporter des réserves à; *(statement)* apporter des précisions à, préciser; *(enjoyment)* modérer, diminuer

3 *Fml (describe)* to q. sb/sth as sth qualifier qn/qch de qch

4 *Gram* qualifier

VI obtenir son diplôme; *Sport* se qualifier (for pour); **to q. for sth** obtenir les diplômes *ou* les qualifications nécessaires pour qch; **to q. as an engineer/a nurse/an accountant** obtenir son diplôme d'ingénieur/d'infirmière/de comptable; **to q. as a doctor** être reçu médecin; **to q. as a pilot** obtenir son brevet de pilote; **you don't q. for a grant** vous ne remplissez pas les conditions requises pour recevoir une bourse; **that doesn't q. as news** *(nobody is interested)* ça n'intéresse personne; *(the information is out of date)* ça n'a rien de nouveau; **it hardly qualifies as a mountain** on ne peut pas vraiment appeler cela une montagne

qualifying ['kwɒlɪfaɪɪŋ] ADJ **1** *(modifying)* modificateur, -trice **2** *Gram (adjective)* qualificatif; *(adverb)* modificatif

▸▸**q. examination** *(at end of course)* examen *m* de fin d'études; *(to get onto course)* examen d'entrée; *Sport* **q. round** *(épreuve f)* éliminatoire *f*; **q. statement** déclaration *f* corrective

qualitative ['kwɒlɪtətɪv] ADJ qualitatif

▸▸**q. analysis** analyse *f* qualitative; *Mktg* **q. forecasting** prévisions *fpl* qualitatives; *Mktg* **q. research** études *fpl* qualitatives; *Mktg* **q. study** étude *f* qualitative

qualitatively ['kwɒlɪtətɪvlɪ] ADV qualitativement

quality ['kwɒlɪtɪ] N **1** *(degree of excellence)* qualité *f*; **of good q.** de bonne qualité; **of high/poor q.** de qualité supérieure/inférieure; **high/poor q. goods** marchandises *fpl* de bonne/mauvaise qualité; **a q. service/magazine** un service/magazine de qualité; **q. matters more than quantity** la qualité importe plus que la quantité; **the q. of life** la qualité de la vie; **q./price ratio** rapport *m* qualité/prix; *esp Am* **to spend q. time together** passer de bons moments ensemble

2 *(characteristic)* *(of person)* qualité *f*, trait *m*; *(of thing)* qualité *f*; *(of sound, voice)* qualité, timbre *m*; **one of the qualities I look for in a friend** une des qualités que je recherche chez un ami; **moral/intellectual qualities** qualités morales/intellectuelles; **he has many (good) qualities** il a beaucoup de qualités

3 *Fml* **to act in the q. of ...** agir en qualité de ...

4 *Arch (high status)* **person of q.** personne *f* de qualité; **the q.** les gens *mpl* de qualité, *Pej* le beau linge

▸▸**q. assurance** garantie *f* de qualité; **q. audit** audit *m* de qualité; *Br* **q. circle** cercle *m* de qualité; **q. control** contrôle *m* de (la) qualité; **q. controller** responsable *mf* du contrôle de (la) qualité, qualiticien, -ienne; *Com* **q. improvement programme** programme *m* d'amélioration de la qualité; *Com* **q. goods** marchandises de qualité; **q. label** label *m* de qualité; **q. management** gestion *f* qualité; *Br* **q. newspaper** = quotidien *m* ou journal *m* du dimanche de qualité (par opposition à la presse populaire); *Mktg* **q. positioning** positionnement *m* par la qualité; **q. press** presse *f* de qualité

quality-assurance manager N directeur, -trice de l'assurance-qualité

qualm [kwɑ:m] N **1** *(pang of conscience)* scrupule *m*; **to have no qualms about doing sth** n'avoir aucun scrupule à faire qch; **I sometimes have qualms about what I did** j'ai parfois des remords pour ce que j'ai fait **2** *(premonition)* pressentiment *m* de malheur; *(anxiety)* inquiétude *f*; **don't you feel any qualms about getting married?** n'éprouves-tu aucune inquiétude à l'idée de te marier?

quandary ['kwɒnd(ə)rɪ] N dilemme *m*; **to be in a q.** *(unable to decide what to do)* ne pas trop savoir que faire; **it put him in a q.** il ne savait que faire, il était face à un dilemme

quango ['kwæŋgəʊ] N *Br (abbr* **quasi-autonomous non-governmental organization)** = organisme *m* créé par le gouvernement et doté de pouvoirs quasi autonomes

---

Quango

En Grande-Bretagne, un "quango" est un organisme semi-public principalement financé par l'État mais disposant d'une certaine autonomie. Certains de ces organismes ont un rôle purement consultatif. D'autres sont habilités à prendre des décisions, notamment au niveau local, et c'est pourquoi au cours de ces dernières années les "quangos" ont fait l'objet de critiques, car leurs membres sont nommés par le gouvernement et non pas élus.

---

quantifiable [kwɒntɪ'faɪəb(ə)l] ADJ quantifiable

quantifier ['kwɒntɪfaɪər] N *(in logic)*, *Math, Ling* quantificateur *m*

quantify ['kwɒntɪfaɪ] VT **1** *(losses, damage)* quantifier, calculer; *(influence, contribution)* quantifier, évaluer; **happiness is hard to q.** le bonheur est difficile à quantifier **2** *(in logic)* quantifier

quantitative ['kwɒntɪtətɪv] ADJ quantitatif

▸▸**q. analysis** analyse *f* quantitative; *Mktg* **q. forecasting** prévisions *fpl* quantitatives; *Mktg* **q. research** études *fpl* quantitatives; *Mktg* **q. study** étude *f* quantitative

quantitatively ['kwɒntɪtətɪvlɪ] ADV quantitativement

quantity ['kwɒntɪtɪ] N **1** quantité *f*; **a small q. of** une petite quantité de; **to buy sth in large quantities** acheter qch en grande quantité; **they would drink quantities of beer** ils buvaient des litres et des litres de bière; **negligible q.** quantité négligeable; **to produce sth in q.** produire qch en quantité; *Constr* **bill of quantities** devis *m* [SEE GRAMMAR B58–60] **2** *(in prosody)* quantité *f*

▸▸**q. discount** remise *f* ou escompte *m* sur la quantité *ou* sur les achats en gros; **q. mark** signe *m* de quantité; **q. surveying** métrage

m; **q. surveyor** métreur, -euse; *Econ* **q. theory** théorie *f* quantitative

quantum, *pl* **quanta** ['kwɒntəm, -ə] N *Maths, Phys* quantum *m*

▸▸**q. leap** saut *m* quantique; *Fig* bond *m* en avant; **q. mechanics** mécanique *f* quantique; **q. number** nombre *m* quantique; **q. physics** physique *f* quantique; **q. theory** théorie *f* des quanta *ou* quantique

quarantine ['kwɒrənti:n] N quarantaine *f*; **to be in q.** *(of person, animal)* être en quarantaine

VT *(person, ship)* mettre en quarantaine; *Comput (infected file)* mettre en quarantaine

quark [kwɑ:k] N **1** *Nucl* quark *m* **2** *(soft cheese)* ≃ fromage *m* blanc

quarrel ['kwɒr(ə)l] N *(dispute)* dispute *f*, querelle *f*; **to pick a q. with sb** faire une scène à qn, se quereller avec qn; **to try to pick a q. with sb** chercher querelle *ou* noise à qn; **they've had a q.** ils se sont disputés *ou Fml* querellés; **what was their q. about?** pourquoi se sont-ils disputés?; **to make up a q.** se réconcilier; **I have no q. with him** je n'ai rien à lui reprocher; **my q. with you is that ...** ce que je te reproche c'est que ...; **she has no q. with that** elle n'a rien à redire là-dessus

VI *(-ll-, Am -l-)* **1** se disputer, *Fml* se quereller **(with sb over** *or* **about sth** avec qn à propos de qch); **they've been quarrelling** ils se sont disputés *ou Fml* querellés; **I don't want to q.** je ne veux pas me disputer *ou Fam* me bagarrer **2** to q. with sb for doing sth *(find fault with)* reprocher à qn de faire qch; **to q. with sth** *(take exception to)* ne pas être d'accord avec qch; **I can't q. with that** je n'ai rien à redire à cela; **while I wouldn't q. with your figures ...** bien que je ne conteste pas vos chiffres ...

quarrelling, *Am* **quarreling** ['kwɒr(ə)lɪŋ] ADJ querelleur, -euse

N disputes *fpl*, querelles *fpl*

quarrelsome ['kwɒr(ə)lsəm] ADJ querelleur, -euse, batailleur, -euse; **in a q. mood** d'humeur batailleuse *ou* querelleuse

quarrier ['kwɒrɪər] N = quarryman

quarry¹ ['kwɒrɪ] N *(animal, bird)*, *Fig (person)* proie *f*

quarry² N *(for stone, slate etc)* carrière *f*; **open q.** carrière à ciel ouvert

VT *(stone, slate etc)* extraire

VI exploiter une carrière; **to q. for granite** extraire du granite

▸▸**q. stone** moellon *m*; **q. tile** carreau *m*

▸ **quarry out** VT SEP *(stone, slate etc)* extraire

quarrying ['kwɒrɪɪŋ] N exploitation *f* de carrières

quarryman, *pl* **quarrymen** ['kwɒrɪmən] N *(ouvrier m)* carrier *m*; **slate q.** perrayeur *m*, perrier *m*

quart [kwɔ:t] N *(liquid measurement) (in UK)* = 1,136 litres; *(in US)* = 0,946 litre; *Prov* **you can't fit a q. into a pint pot** à l'impossible, nul n'est tenu

quarte [kɑ:t] N *Fencing* quarte *f*

quarter ['kwɔ:tər] N **1** *(portion)* *(of apple, circle, century etc)* quart *m*; *(of orange, moon)* quartier *m*; *Culin (of beef, lamb)* quartier; **to divide sth in(to) quarters** diviser qch en quatre; **three quarters** trois quarts; **three and a q.** trois et quart; **a q. (of a pound) of coffee** un quart (de livre) de café, ≃ cent grammes de café; **bottle one q.** *or* **a q. full** bouteille au quart pleine; *Culin* **fore/hind q.** quartier de devant/de derrière; **moon at the first q.** lune au premier quartier; **moon in its last q.** lune dans son dernier quartier *ou* sur son décroît; **I can get it for you for a q. of the price** je peux vous l'avoir pour le quart du prix

2 *(of time) (three-month period)* trimestre *m*; **profits were up during the last q.** les bénéfices ont augmenté au cours du dernier trimestre; **to be paid by the q.** être payé par trimestre; **in the first q. of 2004** pendant le premier trimestre de l'année 2004; **in the first q. of the century** pendant le premier quart du siècle; **a q. to six,** *Am* **a q. of six** six heures moins le quart; **it's a q. to** il est moins le quart; **a q. past six,** *Am* **a q. after six** six heures et quart; **it's a q. past** il est le quart; **there's a train at a q. to and a q. past every hour** il y a un train à moins le quart et au quart; **a q. of an hour** un quart d'heure

3 *Naut (direction)* aire *f* de vent, quart *m*, côté *m*; **the wind is in the right q.** le vent vient du bon côté

4 *(area) (of town)* quartier *m*; **the slum q.** le quartier des taudis; **the residential q.** le quartier résidentiel; **from the four quarters of the globe** des quatre coins du monde; **news from all quarters** des nouvelles de partout; **what is he doing in these quarters?** que fait-il dans ces parages?; **an order from high quarters** un ordre d'en haut; **in some quarters there is talk of rebellion** on parle de rébellion dans certains milieux; **you'll get no help from that q.** vous n'obtiendrez aucune aide de ce côté; **it is rumoured in certain quarters that …** on murmure dans certains milieux que …

5 quarters *(lodgings) Mil* quartier *m*, cantonnement *m*, logement *m*; *(for servants)* appartements *mpl* *(domestiques)*; *Aviat* **crew's quarters** locaux *mpl* affectés au personnel de bord

6 *Naut* **quarters** *(stations)* postes *mpl*; *Naut* **to beat** *or* **pipe to quarters** battre *ou* sonner le branle-bas; *Naut* **general quarters** branle-bas de combat

7 *esp Lit (mercy)* quartier *m*, merci *f*; **to give q.** faire quartier, accorder merci; **to give no q.** ne pas faire de quartier

8 *Am (coin)* pièce *f* de vingt-cinq cents; *(sum)* quart *m* de dollar

VT 1 *(apple etc)* diviser en quatre; *(beef etc)* diviser par quartiers, équarrir; *(time, amount)* réduire des trois quarts; *Hist (condemned man)* écarteler; **to q. the ground** *(of hunting dogs)* quêter **2** *Mil (lodge) (troops)* cantonner, caserner, loger; **to be quartered with sb** loger chez qn

▸▸ **q. binding** *(in bookbinding)* demi-reliure *f*, *pl* demi-reliures; *Br Fin* **q. day** *(jour m* du) terme *m*; *Am Mus* **q. note** noire *f*; *Law* **q. sessions** *(in England and Wales)* ≃ cour *f* d'assises *(remplacée en 1972 par la "Crown Court"); (in US)* = dans certains États, tribunal *m* local à compétence criminelle, pouvant avoir des fonctions administratives; *Mus* **q. tone** quart de ton

quarterback ['kwɔːtəbæk] **N** *Am Ftbl* arrière *m*; *Fam* **to be a Monday morning q.** être sage a posteriori

quarterdeck ['kwɔːtədek] **N** *Naut* **1** plage *f* arrière **2** *(no pl)* **the q.** *(officers)* les officiers *mpl*

quarterfinal [kwɔːtə'faɪnəl] **N** *Sport* quart *m* de finale; **he's in the quarterfinals** il est en quarts de finale, il dispute les quarts de finale

quarterfinalist [kwɔːtə'faɪnəlɪst] **N** quart-de-finaliste *mf*, *pl* quart-de-finalistes

quartering ['kwɔːtərɪŋ] **N 1** *(division)* division *f* en quatre; *(of beef, tree trunk)* équarrissage *m* **2** *Mil (lodging) (of troops)* logement *m*, cantonnement *m*, stationnement *m*

quarterlight ['kwɔːtəlaɪt] **N** *Aut* déflecteur *m* de porte avant

quarterly ['kwɔːtəlɪ] **ADJ** trimestriel; *(subscription)* au trimestre

N publication *f* trimestrielle

ADV trimestriellement, tous les trimestres, tous les trois mois

quartermaster ['kwɔːtəmɑːstər] **N** *Naut* maître *m* de timonerie; *Mil* commissaire *m*; intendant *m*

▸▸ *Mil* **Q. General** Directeur *m* de l'Intendance *(militaire)*; **q.'s store** magasin *m*

quarter-pounder [-'paʊndər] **N** *Culin* = hamburger *m* d'environ 100 grammes

quarterstaff ['kwɔːtəstɑːf] **N** *Hist (weapon)* bâton *m*; **to fence with quarterstaffs** jouer du bâton

quarterwindow ['kwɔːtəwɪndəʊ] **N** *Aut* glace *f* de custode, custode *f*

quartet(te) [kwɔː'tet] **N 1** *(players, music, group of four)* quatuor *m*; *(jazz band)* quartette *m*; **string q.** quatuor à cordes **2** *Liter* tétralogie *f*

quartile ['kwɔːtaɪl] **N** quartile *m*

quarto ['kwɔːtəʊ] **ADJ, N** in-quarto *m inv*

quartz [kwɔːts] **N** *Miner* quartz *m*

▸▸ **q. clock** pendule *f* à quartz; **q. crystal** cristal *m* de quartz; **q. lamp** lampe *f* (à vapeur de mercure) à tube de quartz; **q. watch** montre *f* à quartz

quartz-halogen N halogène *m* à quartz

quartzite ['kwɔːtsaɪt] **N** *Miner* quartzite *m*

quasar ['kweɪzɑːr] **N** *Astron* quasar *m*

quash [kwɒʃ] **VT 1** *(feeling, plan)* étouffer; *(revolt)* écraser; *Fam* **to q. sb** écraser qn **2** *Law (verdict, decision)* casser, infirmer, annuler; **to q. proceedings** *or* **an action** arrêter les poursuites

quasi- ['kweɪsaɪ, 'kwɑːzɪ] **PREF** quasi-; **q.-contract** quasi-contrat *m*, *pl* quasi-contrats; *Fin* **q.-money** quasi-monnaie *f*, *pl* quasi-monnaies; **q.-scientific** quasi-scientifique, presque scientifique

quatercentenary [kwɒtəsen'tiːnərɪ] **N** quatrième centenaire *m*

quaternary [kwə'tɜːnərɪ] **ADJ** *Chem, Geol, Math* quaternaire; *Geol* **the Q. era** l'ère *f* quaternaire

N *Geol* **the Q.** le quaternaire

quatrain ['kwɒtreɪn] **N** *(of poem)* quatrain *m*

quaver ['kweɪvər] **N 1** *Br Mus (note)* croche *f* **2** *(trembling) (in voice)* tremblement *m*, chevrotement *m*; *Mus* tremolo *m*; **to have a q. in one's voice** parler d'une voix tremblante

VI *(of voice)* chevroter, trembloter; *Mus* faire un tremolo; **quavering voice** voix *f* tremblotante *ou* chevrotante, voix mal assurée

VT **to q. (out)** *(song)* chevroter

quay [kiː] **N** quai *m*; **alongside the q.** à quai; *Com* **ex-q.** *(goods)* à prendre *ou* livrable à quai

quayside ['kiːsaɪd] **N** quai *m*; **we walked along the q.** nous nous sommes promenés le long du quai; **on the q.** sur le quai

queasiness ['kwiːzɪnɪs] **N** *Med* nausées *fpl*; *Fig* malaise *m*

queasy ['kwiːzɪ] **ADJ** *(stomach)* délicat; **I feel q.** j'ai la nausée, j'ai mal au cœur; **the drugs make him q.** les médicaments lui donnent des nausées; **the very sight of meat makes her feel q.** la simple vue de la viande lui donne la nausée; **she was looking rather q.** elle avait l'air d'avoir mal au cœur; *Fig* **to feel q. about sth** se sentir mal à l'aise en ce qui concerne qch

Quebec [kwɪ'bek] **N** Québec *m*; **I'm from Q.** je suis Québecois, -oise, je suis du Québec

Quebecer [kɪ'bekər] **N** Québecois, -oise

queen [kwiːn] **N 1** reine *f*; **the kings and queens of England** les souverains *mpl* d'Angleterre; *Br* **the Q.'s Christmas message** = discours *m* télévisé et radiodiffusé de la reine le jour de Noël; **Q. of heaven** reine du ciel; *esp Iron* **she is the q. of my heart** elle règne sur mon cœur; **the rose is the q. of flowers** la rose est la reine des fleurs

2 *Cards* dame *f*, *Chess* reine *f*, dame; **Q. of hearts** reine de cœur

3 *(insect) (of ants etc)* reine *f*

4 *Offensive Sl (male homosexual)* tante *f*, folle *f*

VT 1 *Fam* **to q. it** faire la reine *ou* jouer les personnages importants (**over sb** avec qn) **2** *Chess (pawn)* damer

VI *Chess (of pawn)* aller à dame

▸▸ **Q. Anne** = style *m* d'architecture et de mobilier du XVIIIème siècle caractérisé par des lignes sobres; **a Q. Anne house** une maison de l'époque de la reine Anne; *Entom* **q. bee** reine des abeilles; *Fig* **she's the q. bee around here** c'est elle qui commande ici, c'est elle la patronne ici; *Law* **Queen's Bench** = en Angleterre et au pays de Galles, l'une des trois divisions de la High Court, ≃ tribunal *m* de grande instance; *Law* **Queen's Counsel** ≃ bâtonnier *m* de l'ordre *(en Angleterre)*; **the Q.'s English** l'anglais *m* britannique correct; **she speaks the Q.'s English** elle s'exprime dans un anglais très soigné; **Q. Mother** reine mère; *Br Parl* **Q.'s Speech** = allocution *f* prononcée par la reine *(mais préparée par le gouvernement)* lors de la rentrée parlementaire et dans laquelle elle définit les grands axes de la politique gouvernementale

queencake ['kwiːnkeɪk] **N** *Am* = petit gâteau *m* aux raisins secs

queenly ['kwiːnlɪ] **ADJ** de reine

queen-size bed N grand lit *m* double

queer ['kwɪər] **N 1** *Offensive Sl (male homosexual)* pédé *m*, pédale *f* **2** *Am Sl (counterfeit money)* fausse monnaie *f*

ADJ 1 *(strange)* bizarre, étrange, singulier; **she's a q.-looking person** elle a une drôle de tête; **she has a q.-sounding name** elle a un drôle de nom; **q. ideas** idées *fpl* bizarres *ou Fam* biscornues; *Fam* **q. in the head** toqué, timbré; *Br Fam* **to be in Q. Street** être dans une situation *(financière)* délicate

2 *(suspicious)* suspect, louche

3 *Offensive Sl (homosexual)* pédé, homo

4 *Fam (unwell)* pas bien; **I feel very q.** je me sens tout chose *ou* tout drôle; **to come over** *or* **to be taken q.** avoir un malaise

VT *Fam* **to q. the pitch for sb, to q. sb's pitch** bouleverser *ou* faire échouer les plans de qn

▸▸ *Am Fam* **q. money** *(counterfeit)* fausse monnaie

queer-basher [-bæʃər] **N** *Br Offensive Sl (assaults on homosexuals)* = individu *m* qui se livre à des violences à l'encontre d'homosexuels

queer-bashing N *Br Offensive Sl (assaults on homosexuals)* chasse *f* aux pédés

queerly ['kwɪəlɪ] **ADV** bizarrement, étrangement

queerness ['kwɪənɪs] **N** étrangeté *f*

quell [kwel] **VT** *Lit (revolt, emotion)* réprimer; *(rioters)* mater; *(person, passion)* dompter

quench [kwentʃ] **VT 1 to q. one's thirst** se désaltérer, étancher sa soif **2** *(extinguish) (fire, flame)* éteindre **3** *(cool) (in metalwork) (metal)* tremper; *Fig (person's enthusiasm)* atténuer **4** *(suppress) (desire)* réprimer, étouffer

querulous ['kwerʊləs] **ADJ** *(person)* qui se plaint toujours, grognon; *(tone)* plaintif, dolent

querulously ['kwerʊləslɪ] **ADV** d'un ton plaintif *ou* dolent

query ['kwɪərɪ] **N** *(question)* question *f*; *Comput* interrogation *f*; **I have a q.** j'ai une question; **to raise a q.** soulever une question; **to settle a q.** résoudre une question;

there was a note of q. in her voice il y avait une note d'interrogation dans sa voix; **q.: is this accurate?** *(in margin of document etc)* question: est-ce exact?

VT 1 *(ask)* **to q. if** *or* **whether ...** demander si ...; **how much is that?, he queried** combien est-ce?, demanda-t-il

2 *(put in doubt) (question, statement)* mettre en question *ou* en doute; *(mark with question mark)* marquer d'un point d'interrogation; *Am (question) (person)* poser des questions à; **she queried the bill** elle a dit qu'ils s'étaient trompés dans l'addition; **I would q. it if I were you** à votre place je vérifierais qu'ils ne se sont pas trompés

3 *Comput* **to q. a database** interroger une base de données

▸▸ *Comput* **q. language** langage *m* d'interrogation

quest [kwest] *Lit* **N** quête *f*, recherche *f*; **to go in q. of sb/sth** se mettre *ou* aller *ou* partir à la recherche de qn/qch *ou* en quête de qn/qch; **her q. for justice** sa bataille pour que justice soit faite; **the q. for the Holy Grail** la quête du Graal

VI to q. after *or* **for sth** être à la recherche de qch

QUESTION [ˈkwestʃən]

N question **1, 3** ▪ doute **2**
VT interroger **1** ▪ mettre en doute **2**

N VOIR GRAMMAIRE A46–7; B63–4 **1** *(interrogation)* question *f*, demande *f*; *(in exam)* question; **to ask sb a q., to ask a q. of sb, to put a q. to sb** poser une question à qn; *Parl* adresser une interpellation à qn; **does anyone have any questions?** quelqu'un a-t-il une question?; **I have a q.** j'ai une question; **the q. is, did she know?** la question est de savoir si elle était au courant; *Gram* **direct/indirect q.** interrogation *f* directe/indirecte; *Sch etc* **list** *or* **set of questions** questionnaire *m*; **a q. and answer session** une séance questions-réponses

2 *(doubt)* doute *m*; **without q.** sans aucun doute, sans contredit; **to obey without q.** obéir aveuglément; **her courage/dedication is beyond q.** son courage/dévouement est indiscutable; **that is beyond q.** c'est incontestable; **his honesty has never been in q.** son honnêteté n'a jamais été mise en doute; **to call sb's honesty into q.** mettre en question l'honnêteté de qn; **there is no q. about it** il n'y a pas de doute là-dessus; **it's open to q. whether ...** on peut se demander si ...; **the wisdom of this decision is open to q.** le bien-fondé de la décision est discutable

3 *(matter, issue)* question *f*; **that's the q.** c'est bien là la question; **that's another** *or* **a different q.** c'est une autre histoire; **that is not the q., that is beside the q.** ce n'est pas là la question, il ne s'agit pas de cela; **the q. is whether ...** il s'agit de savoir si ...; **it is out of the q.** c'est hors de question; **it is quite out of the q. for us to ...** il ne saurait être question pour nous de ...; **there's no q. of you(r) going back to work at the moment** il n'est pas question que vous repreniez le travail pour le moment; **there is no q. of going back now** il n'est pas question de revenir en arrière; **it's not a q. of who's right** la question n'est pas de savoir qui a raison; **the Palestinian q.** la question palestinienne; **a q. of life or death** une question de vie ou de mort; **a q. of money/time** une question d'argent/de temps; **it's only a q. of time before it happens** ça arrivera tôt ou tard; **the matter/person in q.** l'affaire/la personne en question; *Law* **the case in q.** le cas en litige; **there was some q. of ...** il a été question de ...

4 *Hist* **to put sb to the q.** *(torture)* mettre qn

à la question, appliquer la question à qn

VT 1 *(person)* questionner, interroger (**about** sur, à propos de); **to be questioned** être interrogé; *(of suspect)* subir un interrogatoire; **the people questioned in the survey** les personnes interrogées dans le cadre du sondage; **she was questioned on her views** *(in interview etc)* on l'a interrogée sur ses opinions

2 *(cast doubt on)* mettre en question *ou* en doute *ou* en cause, contester; **nobody is questioning your ...** personne ne met en doute *ou* en question votre/vos ...; **I q. whether he will come** je doute qu'il vienne; **I q. whether it would not be better to ...** je me demande s'il ne vaudrait pas mieux ...

▸▸ *Gram* **q. form** forme *f* interrogative; **q. mark** *(punctuation mark)* point *m* d'interrogation; *Mktg (product)* point d'interrogation, dilemme *m*; *Fig* **a q. mark hangs over the project** il y a un point d'interrogation quant au projet; **q. master** meneur, -euse de jeu; *Radio, TV* animateur, -trice *(d'un jeu)*; *Ling* **q. tag** question tag *m*, = tournure *f* interrogative en fin de phrase, équivalent du "n'est-ce pas" français VOIR GRAMMAIRE A47; B64 ; *Parl* **q. time** heure *f* consacrée aux questions; **q. word** mot *m* interrogatif

questionable [ˈkwestʃənəb(ə)l] **ADJ 1** *(doubtful)* contestable, discutable, douteux; **of q. authenticity** *(document etc)* d'une authenticité (fort) douteuse; **this is the most democratic country – that's very q.** c'est le pays le plus démocratique – c'est très discutable **2** *Pej (conduct etc)* suspect, équivoque; **in q. taste** d'un goût douteux

questioner [ˈkwestʃənər] **N** interrogateur, -trice; *(who likes asking questions)* questionneur, -euse; *(calling in to TV programme)* téléspectateur, -trice; *(calling in to radio programme)* auditeur, -trice; *(in studio audience)* spectateur, -trice

questioning [ˈkwestʃənɪŋ] **ADJ** *(look etc)* interrogateur, -trice; **to have a q. mind** avoir un esprit curieux

N questions *fpl*, interrogation *f*; *Mil etc (of prisoner)* interrogatoire *m*; **to be held for q.** *(by police)* être détenu pour un interrogatoire

questioningly [ˈkwestʃənɪŋlɪ] **ADV** *(to look at sb)* d'un air interrogateur; *(to say sth)* d'un ton interrogateur

questionnaire [kwestʃəˈneər] **N** questionnaire *m*

▸▸ **q. analysis** dépouillement *m* de questionnaire; **q. construction** construction *f* de questionnaire; **q. survey** enquête *f* par questionnaire

quetzal [ˈketsəl] **N** *(bird)* quetzal *m*, *pl* quetzals

queue [kjuː] **N 1** *esp Br (line) (of people)* queue *f*, file *f*; *(of cars)* file; **is this the q.?** *(for tickets etc)* est-ce que c'est la queue?; **to form a q., to stand in a q.** faire la queue; **there is a q., you know!** il faut faire la queue!; **to join the q.** se mettre à la queue; *Fig* **join the q.!** vous n'êtes pas le seul/la seule; **to jump the q.** passer avant son tour **2** *Comput* file *f* d'attente **3** *Arch (of hair, wig)* queue *f*

VI faire la queue; **I spent ages queuing for a bus** j'ai passé des heures à attendre le bus

VT *Comput (print jobs)* mettre en file d'attente

▸ **queue up VI** faire la queue; **people queued up to shake his hand** les gens faisaient la queue pour lui serrer la main; **people are queuing up for a job like yours** les gens se battent pour décrocher un emploi comme le vôtre

queue-jump VI resquiller

queue-jumper N resquilleur, -euse

quibble [ˈkwɪb(ə)l] **N** argutie *f*, chicane *f* sur les mots

VI *(equivocate)* ergoter, chicaner; *(split hairs)* chipoter, couper les cheveux en quatre; **he didn't q. about the price** il n'a pas chipoté sur le prix

quibbler [ˈkwɪblər] **N** ergoteur, -euse, chicaneur, -euse

quibbling [ˈkwɪb(ə)lɪŋ] **N** arguties *fpl*, chicanerie *f*, ergoterie *f*

ADJ qui porte sur des vétilles

quiche [kiːʃ] **N** *Culin* quiche *f*

quick [kwɪk] **ADJ** *(movement, growth etc)* rapide; *Mus* animé, vif; **that was q.!** ça a été rapide!; **as q. as lightning** *or* **as a flash** aussi vite que l'éclair, en un clin d'œil; **be q. (about it)!** faites vite!, dépêchez-vous!; **he's q.** *(of worker)* il court vite; *(he understands etc quickly)* il est vif; **q. to act/to anger** prompt à agir/à se fâcher; **she's very q. to take offence** elle se vexe très facilement; **don't be so q. to criticize** ne critique donc pas si vite; **she was q. to realize what had happened** elle s'est vite rendu compte de ce qui s'était passé; **to be q. off the mark** *(in race)* démarrer vite; *(to start sth)* démarrer sans perdre de temps; *(to understand)* avoir l'esprit vif; **he wasn't exactly q. off the mark when it came to ordering drinks** il était plutôt lent à la détente quand il s'agissait de commander les boissons; *Fam* **let's have a q. one** *(drink)* si on prenait un petit verre?; **they've gone upstairs for a q. one** *(sex)* ils sont montés (pour) tirer un petit coup; **the quickest way there** le chemin le plus court (pour y arriver); **what's the q. way to find a job?** comment trouve-t-on un emploi rapidement?; **I'll just have a q. bath** je vais juste prendre un bain en vitesse; **can I ask you a q. question?** je peux vous poser une petite question?; **q. mind** esprit *m* prompt *ou* vif; **q. recovery (from an illness)** prompt rétablissement *m* (d'une maladie); **q. temper** tempérament *m* emporté, irascibilité *f*; **she has a q. temper** elle s'emporte facilement

N 1 *(flesh)* vif *m*; **to bite one's nails to the q.** se ronger les ongles jusqu'au vif; *Fig* **to sting** *or* **cut sb to the q.** blesser *ou* piquer qn au vif **2** *Rel* **the q. and the dead** *(pl)* les vivants *mpl* et les morts

ADV 1 *Fam* vite, rapidement; **as q. as possible** aussi vite que possible; **to run quicker** courir plus vite; **he just wants to get rich q.** il ne pense qu'à s'enrichir rapidement; **q.! over here!** vite! par ici!

2 *(in compounds)* **q.-acting, q.-action** *(mechanism)* à action rapide *ou* immédiate; *(drug, medication)* à action rapide; **q.-drying paint** peinture *f* qui sèche rapidement; **q.-firing rifle** fusil *m* à tir rapide; **q.-growing** *(plant etc)* à croissance rapide; *Constr, Culin* **q.-setting** *(cement, jelly)* à prise rapide

▸▸ *Acct* **q. assets** liquidités *fpl*, actif *m* liquide; **q. fix** solution *f* miracle; *Comput* **q. launch bar** barre *f* de lancement rapide; *Acct* **q. ratio** ratio *m* de liquidité immédiate; **q. reference guide** aide-mémoire *m inv*; **q. sale** vente *f* rapide; *Cards* **q. trick** levée *f* assurée

quick-change artiste N *Theat* = acteur *m* qui change de costume souvent au cours d'un spectacle; *Fig* personne *f* versatile

quicken [ˈkwɪk(ə)n] **VT** *(step, pace)* hâter, presser, accélérer; *Med (pulse)* accélérer; *(stimulate) (imagination)* stimuler; *(interest)* exciter; *(appetite)* aiguiser; *(feelings)* provoquer; *Sport* **to q. the pace** accélérer le pas *ou* le rythme

VI *(of pace, pulse etc)* devenir plus rapide, s'accélérer; *Lit (of nature, hope etc)* s'animer, se ranimer; *(of foetus)* bouger

quickening [ˈkwɪkənɪŋ] **ADJ** *(pace)* qui s'accélère; *Lit* **her q. hope** ses espoirs grandissants

N *(of pace, pulse)* accélération *f*; *(of nature etc)* renouveau *m*; *Obst* premiers mouvements *mpl* du fœtus

quickfire ['kwɪkfaɪər] **ADJ ATTRIB** *(questions, repartee)* rapide, au rythme soutenu

quick-freeze **VT** *Culin* surgeler

quickie ['kwɪkɪ] **N** *Fam (quick drink)* consommation *f* prise sur le pouce; *(something done quickly)* chose *f* faite à la hâte; **let's have a q.** *(drink)* si on prenait un petit verre?; *(sex)* on fait l'amour en vitesse?; **OK, but make it a q.** si tu veux, mais en vitesse
► ► **q. divorce** divorce *m* express

quicklime ['kwɪklaɪm] **N** chaux *f* vive

quickly ['kwɪklɪ] **ADV** vite, rapidement; **q.!** vite!

quickness ['kwɪknɪs] **N 1** *(rapidity)* vitesse *f*, rapidité *f*; *(of pulse)* rythme *m* rapide **2** *(sharpness) (of sight)* acuité *f*; *(of hearing)* finesse *f*; *(of mind)* vivacité *f*; **q. of temper** caractère *m* emporté *ou* irascible

quicksand ['kwɪksænd] **N** sables *mpl* mouvants; **to get caught** *or* **stuck in q.** *or* **in the quicksands** être pris dans des sables mouvants

quickset ['kwɪkset] **N** *Br* haie *f* vive
► ► **q. hedge** haie vive

quickshift gear change ['kwɪkʃɪft] **N** changement *m* de vitesse rapide

quicksilver ['kwɪksɪlvər] **N** vif-argent *m*, *pl* vifs-argents; **he's/she's just like q.** c'est du vif-argent

quickstep ['kwɪkstep] **N** *(dance)* fox-trot *m* inv rapide

quick-tempered **ADJ** emporté, colérique, coléreux, irascible; **to be q.** s'emporter facilement

quick-witted **ADJ** vif, éveillé, à l'esprit vif

quid[1] [kwɪd] **N** *Br Fam (inv in pl) (pound)* livre *f*, **it cost me 10 q.** ça m'a coûté 100 balles; **to be quids in** être tranquille *ou* peinard

quid[2] **N** *(of tobacco)* chique *f*

quid pro quo [kwɪdprəʊ'kwəʊ] **N** compensation *f*, contrepartie *f*, **what did she get as a q. for her silence?** qu'est-ce qu'elle a reçu en contrepartie de son silence?

quiescence [kwɪ'esəns] **N** *Fml* tranquillité *f*

quiescent [kwɪ'esənt] **ADJ** *Fml* inactif, passif

QUIET ['kwaɪət]

N tranquillité ▪ calme ▪ silence
ADJ doux **1, 2** ▪ tranquille **1, 4**
▪ calme **1, 4** ▪ silencieux **1** ▪ discret **3** ▪ dans l'intimité **3**

N *(calm)* tranquillité *f*, calme *m*; *(silence)* silence *m*; **to enjoy perfect peace and q.** jouir d'une parfaite tranquillité; **the q. of the night** le calme de la nuit; *Br Fam* **to do sth on the q.** faire qch discrètement, *Pej* faire qch en cachette *ou* à la dérobée

ADJ 1 *(with little sound or motion) (music)* doux, *f* douce; *(voice)* bas, doux; *(neighbour, neighbourhood)* tranquille, calme; *(sea)* calme; *(engine)* silencieux; **can we go somewhere q.?** est-ce que nous pouvons aller dans un endroit tranquille?; **the wind grew q.** le vent s'est apaisé; **to keep q.** *(make no noise)* rester *ou* se tenir tranquille; *(say nothing)* se taire, ne rien dire, garder le silence; **we must keep q. about it** il ne faut pas en parler; **keep it q.** pas un mot; **she was very q. about her background** elle n'a pas dit grand-chose de ses antécédents; **to keep a child q.** faire taire un enfant; **to keep sb q.** tenir qn tranquille; **be q.!** tais-toi! taisez-vous!; **q. please!** silence, s'il vous

plaît!; **to be as q. as a mouse** *(of person)* être très silencieux; **the house was as q. as the grave** il n'y avait pas un bruit dans la maison; **it's as q. as the grave here on a Saturday** c'est complètement mort ici le samedi; **could I have a q. word (with you)?** est-ce que je peux vous prendre à part pour vous dire deux mots?

2 *(calm)* doux, *f* douce; **he's a very q. kind of chap** c'est un type très tranquille; **q. disposition** caractère *m* doux *ou* calme; **q. horse** cheval *m* doux *ou* tranquille *ou* sage

3 *(subdued, discreet) (dress, colours etc)* simple, discret, -ète, sobre; **we had a q. laugh over it** nous en avons ri entre nous; **you're very q., is anything wrong?** tu es drôlement silencieux, il y a quelque chose qui ne va pas?; **it's very pretty countryside, in a q. sort of way** c'est un très joli paysage, dans le genre paisible; **q. irony** ironie *f* voilée; **q. optimism** optimisme *m* modéré; **q. wedding** mariage *m* célébré dans l'intimité

4 *(undisturbed)* calme, tranquille, paisible; **to lead a q. life** mener une vie calme; *Fam* **anything for a q. life!** n'importe quoi du moment qu'on me fiche la paix!; *Com* **business is very q.** les affaires ne marchent pas très fort; **it's very q. in here tonight** *(in the pub, shop etc)* c'est très calme ce soir; **to have a q. drink** boire un coup tranquillement; **to spend a q. evening (in)** passer une soirée tranquille; *Fam* **all q. on the western front** à l'ouest rien de nouveau

VT = **quieten**

► **quiet down** = **quieten down**

quieten ['kwaɪət(ə)n] **VT** *Br (uproar etc)* apaiser, calmer; *(person, one's conscience)* tranquilliser; *(child)* faire taire; *(fears, suspicions)* dissiper; *(of business)* calmer

► **quieten down** *Br* **VI 1** *(become silent)* se taire **2** *(become calm) (of person)* se calmer; *(of business)* ralentir
VT SEP 1 *(make silent)* faire taire **2** *(make calm) (person, animal)* calmer

quietly ['kwaɪətlɪ] **ADV 1** *(with little sound or motion)* silencieusement, sans bruit **2** *(calmly)* tranquillement, doucement; **to be q. determined to do sth** être froidement décidé à faire qch **3** *(discreetly) (dressed etc)* simplement, discrètement; **to get married q.** se marier sans cérémonie *ou* dans l'intimité **4** *(with little excitement)* **we live very q.** nous menons une vie très calme

quietness ['kwaɪətnɪs] **N 1** *(lack of sound)* silence *m* **2** *(calmness) (of person)* calme *m* **3** *(of dress, colour etc)* sobriété *f* **4** *(of life)* tranquillité *f*; *(of business)* manque *m* d'activité

quietude ['kwaɪətjuːd] **N** *Lit* quiétude *f*

quietus [kwaɪ'iːtəs] **N** *Lit (death)* mort *f*

quiff [kwɪf] **N** *Br (hairstyle)* banane *f*

quill [kwɪl] **N 1** *(feather)* penne *f*; *(shaft of feather)* tuyau *m*; *(pen)* plume *f* (d'oie) **2** *(of porcupine etc)* piquant *m*
► ► **q. feather** penne *f*; **q. pen** plume d'oie

quilt [kwɪlt] **N** couverture *f* piquée *ou* matelassée; *(eiderdown)* édredon *m* piqué; **(continental) q.** couette *f*, *Suisse* duvet *m*
VT 1 *(garment etc)* matelasser, ouater, ouatiner et piquer; **quilted jacket** veste *f* matelassée **2** *(two pieces of material)* piquer
VI faire du matelassage
► ► **q. cover** housse *f* de couette

quilting ['kwɪltɪŋ] **N** matelassage *m*

quin [kwɪn] **N** *Br Fam (child)* quintuplé, -ée

quince [kwɪns] **N 1** *(fruit)* coing *m* **2** *(tree)* cognassier *m*
► ► **q. jelly** gelée *f* de coings; **q. tree** cognassier

quincentenary [kwɪnsen'tiːnərɪ] **N** cinquième centenaire *m*

quinine [kwɪ'niːn] **N** *Chem* quinine *f*

quinquagenarian [kwɪŋkwədʒə'neərɪən] **ADJ, N** quinquagénaire *mf*

Quinquagesima [kwɪŋkwə'dʒesɪmə] **N** *Rel* Quinquagésime *f*
► ► **Q. Sunday** le dimanche de la Quinquagésime

quinsy ['kwɪnzɪ] **N** *Med Old-fashioned* angine *f* phlegmoneuse

quintal ['kwɪnt(ə)l] **N** *(measurement)* quintal *m* métrique *(de 100 kg)*

quinte [kænt] **N** *Fencing* quinte *f*

quintessence [kwɪn'tesəns] **N** *Fml* quintessence *f*

quintessential [kwɪntɪ'senʃəl] **ADJ** *Fml* quintessenciel

quintessentially [kwɪntɪ'senʃəlɪ] **ADV** *Fml* fondamentalement

quintet(te) [kwɪn'tet] **N** *Mus* quintette *m*

quintillion [kwɪn'tɪljən] **N** *Br* (10^{30}) quintillion *m*; *Am* (10^{18}) trillion *m*

quintuple [kwɪn'tjʊp(ə)l] **ADJ, N** quintuple *m*
VT & VI quintupler

quintuplet [kwɪn'tjuːplɪt, 'kwɪntjʊplɪt] **N** *(child)* quintuplé, -ée

quip [kwɪp] **N** *(sarcastic remark)* sarcasme *m*, raillerie *f*; *(witty remark)* trait *m ou* mot *m* d'esprit; *(riposte)* repartie *f*
VI (**-pp-**) *(make sarcastic remark)* railler; *(be witty)* faire des mots d'esprit
VT *(say sarcastically)* dire de façon sarcastique; *(say wittily)* dire avec esprit

quire ['kwaɪər] **N 1 q. of paper** *(24 sheets)* ≃ main *f* de papier *(25 feuilles)* **2** *Typ* **in quires** en feuilles

quirk [kwɜːk] **N** *(of character)* particularité *f*, bizarrerie *f* de caractère; **he's got a lot of little quirks** il y a plein de choses bizarres chez lui; **a q. of fate** un caprice du sort; **by a q. they both went to Rome** par un effet du hasard, ils sont tous les deux allés à Rome

quirky ['kwɜːkɪ] **ADJ** *(sense of humour etc)* bizarre

quisling ['kwɪzlɪŋ] **N** *Pej* collaborateur, -trice

quit [kwɪt] **VI** *(pt, pp quitted, Dial, Am quit; prp quitting)* *(resign)* démissionner; *(in fight)* abandonner; *Comput* sortir; **you can't fire me, I q.!** vous ne pouvez pas me mettre à la porte, je démissionne!; **to receive notice to q.** *(of tenant)* recevoir son congé
VT 1 *(leave) (person, place)* quitter **2** *Comput (database, programme)* sortir de, quitter **3 to q. office** se démettre de ses fonctions **4** *Fam* **to q. one's job** quitter son emploi, démissionner; **to q. doing sth** arrêter *ou* cesser de faire qch; **q. annoying me, will you!** tu vas arrêter de m'ennuyer!; **to q. work** arrêter de travailler, cesser le travail
ADJ *Fml* quitte, libéré; **to be q. of sb/sth** être débarrassé de qn/qch

---
QUITE [kwaɪt]

vraiment **1** ▪ tout à fait **1** ▪ assez **2**

ADV VOIR GRAMMAIRE A5 **1** *(entirely)* vraiment; **she's q. happy** elle est tout à fait heureuse; **he's q. happy to let others do the work** ça ne le dérange absolument pas de laisser les autres faire le travail; **q. finished** entièrement *ou* complètement fini; *Iron* **have you q. finished?** c'est pas bientôt fini?; **q. recovered** tout à fait *ou* complètement rétabli; **he was q. obviously drunk** il était manifestement ivre; **q. the best story of its kind** sans aucun doute la meilleure histoire de ce genre; **q. as much** autant; **q. enough** bien assez; **that's q. enough of that!** ça suffit comme ça!; **q. apart from the fact that ...**

en dehors du fait que …; **q. right** *(of sum)* parfaitement juste; *(of clock)* bien à l'heure; **you are q. right** vous avez bien *ou* tout à fait raison; **q. (so)!** parfaitement!, d'accord!; **I'm afraid I'll be a bit late – that's q. all right** je crains d'être un peu en retard – ce n'est pas grave; **not q.** pas tout à fait; **not q. 300** pas tout à fait 300; **it's not q. 2 o'clock** il n'est pas tout à fait 2 heures; **q. the opposite** bien au contraire; **I don't q. know what he will do** je ne sais pas trop ce qu'il fera; **you know q. well what I mean** vous savez très bien ce que je veux dire; **I q. understand** je comprends bien, je me rends parfaitement compte; **I don't q. understand** je ne comprends pas bien; **I can't q. remember when it happened** je ne me souviens pas bien *ou* tout à fait quand ça s'est passé; **in q. another tone** sur un tout autre ton; **that's q. another matter!** c'est tout autre chose! **2** *(fairly, rather)* assez; **q. big/small** assez gros/petit; **q. frequently/recently** assez fréquemment/récemment; **this furniture is q. sought after** ces meubles sont assez recherchés; **I q. like him** je l'aime bien; **she is q. happy** elle est assez heureuse; **q. a lot of people/money** un assez grand nombre de gens/une assez grosse somme d'argent; **q. a few people** pas mal de gens **3** *(really)* **q. a beauty** une vraie beauté; **it was q. a surprise** c'était une véritable surprise; **it's been q. a day** quelle journée!; **she's q. a girl** elle est formidable; **that film was q. something** ce film c'était vraiment quelque chose; **it's q. something when …** c'est vraiment quelque chose quand …; **it was q. something (to do sth)** c'était vraiment quelque chose (de faire qch)

quits [kwɪts] **ADJ now we're q.** maintenant nous sommes quittes; **double or q.** quitte ou double; **I'll be q. with him yet** il me le paiera; **let's call it q.** *(agree to end game, dispute)* restons-en là

quittance ['kwɪt(ə)ns] **N** *Fin* quittance *f*, décharge *f*, acquit *m*

quitter ['kwɪtər] **N** *Fam Pej* personne *f* qui abandonne facilement; **she's not a q.** elle n'est pas du genre à abandonner *ou* à se laisser abattre

quiver¹ ['kwɪvər] **N** *(of person)* tremblement *m*, frisson *m*, frémissement *m*; *(of leaves, lips)* frémissement, tremblement; *(of flesh)* palpitation *f*, frémissement; **with a q. in one's voice** d'une voix frémissante *ou* mal assurée
VI *(of person)* trembler, frémir, frissonner; *(of leaves, lips)* frémir, trembler; *(of voice, light)* trembloter; *(of flesh)* palpiter, frémir; **to q. with fear** trembler de peur; **voice quivering with emotion** voix vibrante d'émotion
VT *(of bird)* **to q. its wings** agiter ses ailes

quiver² **N** *(arrow holder)* carquois *m*; *esp Lit Fig* **to have an arrow** *or* **a shaft left in one's q.** n'être pas à bout de ressources

quivering ['kwɪvərɪŋ] **ADJ** *(person)* tremblant, frissonnant, frémissant; *(leaves, lips)* frémissant, tremblant; *(flesh)* palpitant, frémissant; **the experience had reduced him to a q. mass** *or* **jelly** l'épreuve l'avait réduit à l'état de loque
N *(of person)* tremblement *m*, frémissement *m*, frissonnement *m*; *(of leaves, lips)* frémissement, tremblement; *(of flesh)* palpitation *f*, frémissement; *(of eyelashes)* battement *m*

qui vive [ki:'vi:v] **N on the q.** sur le qui-vive

Quixote, Don Quixote [dɒn'kwɪksəʊt, -ki:'həʊtɪ] **N** *Liter* Don Quichotte *m*

quixotic [kwɪk'sɒtɪk] **ADJ** *(person)* chimérique; *(plan, idea, character etc)* donquichottesque; *(behaviour)* chimérique, donquichottesque

quixotically [kwɪk'sɒtɪklɪ] **ADV** en Don Quichotte, à la manière de Don Quichotte

quiz [kwɪz] **N 1** *(on radio)* jeu *m* radiophonique; *(on TV)* jeu télévisé; *(in magazine etc)* quiz *m*, questionnaire *m* **2** *(questioning)* interrogatoire *m*; *esp Am Sch* examen *m* oral
VT *(-zz-)* questionner; *Am Sch (candidate)* faire passer un/l'oral à; **they quizzed me on my political views** ils m'ont interrogé sur mes opinions politiques
▸▸**q. programme, q. show** *(on radio)* jeu radiophonique; *(on TV)* jeu télévisé

quizmaster ['kwɪzmɑːstər] **N** *Radio, TV etc* animateur, -trice, meneur, -euse de jeu

quizzical ['kwɪzɪk(ə)l] **ADJ** *(look, air)* interrogateur, -trice; *(mocking)* railleur

quizzically ['kwɪzɪk(ə)lɪ] **ADV** d'un air interrogateur; *(mockingly)* d'un air railleur

quod [kwɒd] **N** *Br Sl (prison)* taule *f*; **in q.** en taule

quoin [kɔɪn] **N** *Constr (cornerstone)* pierre *f* d'angle; *(of wall)* coin *m*; *(internal)* encoignure *f*

quoit [kɔɪt] **N** palet *m*; **to play (at) quoits** jouer au palet

quorate ['kwɔːreɪt] **ADJ** *Admin, Fml* **to be q.** être en nombre

Quorn® [kwɔːn] **N =** aliment *m* aux protéines végétales de substitut à la viande

quorum ['kwɔːrəm] **N** quorum *m*; **to have a q.** être en nombre; **to form a q.** constituer un quorum

quota ['kwəʊtə] **N** *(stipulated quantity, number)* quota *m*; *(share)* quote-part *f*, *pl* quotes-parts; *Fin* quotité *f*; **import/export quotas** contingents *mpl ou* quotas d'importation/ d'exportation; **to apportion** *or* **fix quotas for import** déterminer les quotas d'importation; **I've had my q. of bad luck** j'ai eu ma dose *ou* part de malchance; **we've had more than our q. of rain recently** nous avons eu plus que notre quota *ou* dose de pluie dernièrement

▸▸*Mktg* **q. method** *(of sampling)* méthode *f* des quotas; *Mktg* **q. sample** échantillon *m* par quotas; *Mktg* **q. sampling** échantillonnage *m* par quotas

quotable ['kwəʊtəb(ə)l] **ADJ 1** *(worth quoting)* qui vaut la peine d'être cité, digne d'être cité; *(able to be quoted)* que l'on peut *ou* qu'il est permis de citer; **a very q. phrase** une formule qui vaut la peine d'être citée; **the press find him very q.** les journalistes adorent ses petites phrases **2** *St Exch* cotable

quotation [kwəʊ'teɪʃən] **N 1** *(from author etc)* citation *f* **2** *Com* prix *m*; *(for repair work etc)* devis *m*; *St Exch* cotation *f*, cote *f*, cours *m*, prix; **to ask for a q.** *(for proposed work)* demander un devis; **they gave me a q. of £500** ils m'ont fait un devis de 500 livres; **to seek a share q.** faire une demande d'admission *ou* d'inscription à la cote
▸▸**q. marks** guillemets *mpl*; **in q. marks** entre guillemets

quote [kwəʊt] **N 1** citation *f*; **a q. from Shakespeare** une citation de Shakespeare **2** **quotes, q. marks** guillemets *mpl*; **in quotes** entre guillemets **3** *Com Fam* = **quotation 2**
VT 1 *(author, passage etc)* citer; *(authority, proof)* alléguer, citer; **he was quoted as saying that …** il aurait dit que …; **she said q. …** et voici exactement ce qu'elle a dit …; **his q. unquote 'friends'** ses amis entre guillemets; **can I q. you on that?** est-ce que je puis vous citer?; **don't q. me (on this) but …** ce n'est pas encore officiel *ou* définitif mais …; **q. sb as an example** citer qn pour *ou* en exemple; *Admin, Com* **in reply please q. this number** prière de rappeler ce numéro dans toute correspondance ultérieure
2 *Com (price)* établir, faire; **to q. a price** faire *ou* indiquer un prix; **they quoted me £500 for the work** ils m'ont fait un devis de 500 livres pour ce travail
3 *St Exch (share, expiry)* coter; **stock officially quoted** valeurs *fpl* admises à la cote officielle; **quoted on the Stock Exchange** coté en Bourse; *Br* **quoted company** société *f* cotée en Bourse; **quoted investment** valeur *f* cotée en Bourse; **quoted price** cours *m* inscrit à la cote officielle; **quoted securities** valeurs de Bourse; **quoted share** action *f* cotée, action inscrite à la cote officielle
VI 1 *Com* faire un devis, donner un prix **2** **to q. from a book/an author/memory** citer un livre/un auteur/de mémoire

quoth [kwəʊθ] **VT** *Arch, Hum* **no, q. I** non, dis-je

quotidian [kwəʊ'tɪdɪən] **ADJ** *Lit* quotidien

quotient ['kwəʊʃənt] **N** *Math* quotient *m*

qv [kjuː'viː] *(abbr* **quod vide)** cf

qwerty ['kwɜːtɪ] **N**
▸▸**q. keyboard** clavier *m* QWERTY

qwertz [kwɜːts] **N**
▸▸**q. keyboard** clavier *m* QWERTZ

R, r [ɑːr] N *(letter)* R, r *m*; **two r's** deux r; **the three Rs** = la lecture, l'écriture et l'arithmétique *(qui constituent les fondements de l'enseignement primaire)*

ADJ *Am Cin (abbr* **Restricted***)* interdit aux moins de 17 ans

RA [ɑːˈreɪ] N *Br (abbr* **Royal Academy***)* = académie *f* royale des beaux-arts

rabbet [ˈræbɪt] N *Carp* feuillure *f*

rabbi [ˈræbaɪ] N *Rel* rabbin *m*; **chief r.** grand rabbin

rabbinic(al) [rəˈbɪnɪk, -ɪk(ə)l] ADJ rabbinique

rabbit [ˈræbɪt] N **1** *(animal, fur)* lapin *m*; *Fig* **they breed like rabbits** ils se reproduisent comme des lapins; **to produce a r. out of a hat** *(of conjuror)* faire sortir un lapin d'un chapeau; *Fig* trouver une solution miracle; **to run like a scared r.** courir *ou* détaler comme un lapin; **young r.** lapereau *m*; **wild r.** lapin de garenne; **I'm fed up with all this r. food** je vais finir par me transformer en lapin avec toutes ces crudités **2** *Culin* lapin *m*; **stewed r.** ragoût *m* de lapin **3** *Sport Old-fashioned (poor performer)* nullard, -arde
▸▸ **r. burrow** terrier *m* (de lapin); *Am* **r. ears** antenne *f* téléscopique; **r. food** aliments *mpl* pour lapins; *Fam Hum Pej (salad, green vegetables)* verdure *f*; **r.'s foot** *(lucky charm)* patte *f* de lapin; **r. hole** terrier de lapin; **r. hutch** clapier *m*, cage *f ou* cabane *f* à lapins; *Br Fam Fig (accommodation)* cage à lapins; **r.'s paw** *(lucky charm)* patte de lapin; **r. punch** coup *m* du lapin; **r. warren** garenne *f*, *Fig* labyrinthe *m*, dédale *m*
▸ **rabbit on** VI *Br Fam (talk)* jacasser, bavasser (**about** à propos de); **what's she rabbiting on about?** qu'est-ce qu'elle raconte *ou* bave?; **do stop rabbitting on** tais-toi un peu

rabbiting [ˈræbɪtɪŋ] N **to go r.** faire la chasse au lapin, chasser le lapin

rabble [ˈræb(ə)l] N **1** *(disorderly mob)* foule *f* **2** *Pol Old-fashioned Pej (lower classes)* **the r.** la populace, la canaille

rabble-rouser [-raʊzər] N agitateur, -trice

rabble-rousing N incitation *f* à la révolte
ADJ *(speech)* incendiaire; *(leader)* qui incite à la révolte

Rabelaisian [ræbəˈleɪzɪən] ADJ *(humour etc)* rabelaisien

rabid [ˈræbɪd, ˈreɪ-] ADJ *Vet (dog etc)* enragé; *Fig (socialist etc)* enragé, fanatique; *(hatred)* farouche

rabies [ˈreɪbiːz] N *Med, Vet* rage *f*; **the dog is a r. carrier** le chien est porteur de la rage; **r. vaccine** vaccin *m* contre la rage

RAC [ɑːriːˈsiː] N *Br Aut (abbr* **Royal Automobile Club***)* ≃ Touring-Club *m*

raccoon [rəˈkuːn] N *(animal)* raton *m* laveur; **r. skin hat** toque *f* en raton laveur

race¹ [reɪs] N **1** *Sport* course *f*; **a hundred metres r.** une course sur cent mètres, un

cent mètres; **it's anybody's r.** il n'y a pas de favori; *Sport, Fig* **a r. against time** une course contre la montre; *Horseracing* **the races** les courses; **to go to the races** aller aux courses; **he loves the races** c'est un passionné des courses

2 *(channel for water)* canal *m*; **mill r.** bief *m* de moulin

3 *(tide)* raz *m*

VI **1** *(move quickly) (of person, animal)* courir à toute vitesse, galoper; **to r. by** *(of time)* filer; **the weekend just raced by** le weekend a passé très vite; **to r. for a bus/train** courir *ou* galoper pour attraper un bus/train; **to r. down the street** dévaler la rue à toute vitesse; **she raced to answer the door** elle se précipita pour ouvrir la porte; **the ambulance raced to the scene of the accident** l'ambulance fonça sur les lieux de l'accident; **the car was racing along** la voiture allait à toute vitesse; **to r. up the stairs** monter les escaliers quatre à quatre; **he raced through his meal** il a avalé son repas à toute vitesse; **the horse raced towards the winning post** le cheval a foncé vers la ligne d'arrivée; **the work is racing ahead** le travail avance très vite; **the clouds are racing across the sky** les nuages filent dans le ciel

2 *Sport (of cyclist, driver)* participer à une épreuve *ou* à des épreuves de vitesse; *(of jockey)* monter; *(of athlete, horse)* courir; *Horseracing (of owner)* faire courir des chevaux

3 *(of engine)* s'emballer

4 *(of pulse)* être rapide; **my heart is racing** mon cœur bat la chamade

VT **1** *(against person, car etc)* faire la course avec; **I'll r. you home!** le premier arrivé à la maison a gagné!; **come on, r. you!** le premier arrivé là-bas!; **he raced me round the block** il a fait la course avec moi autour du pâté de maisons; **the car raced the bus to the traffic lights** la voiture a fait la course avec le bus pour arriver la première aux feux

2 *(enter for races) (horse)* faire courir; **to r. pigeons** faire des courses de pigeons

3 *(transport quickly)* **he raced me to the airport** il m'a emmené à l'aéroport à toute vitesse

4 *Aut (engine)* emballer
▸▸ *Am* **r. car** voiture *f* de course; *Horseracing* **r. card** programme *m* (des courses); *Am* **r. driver** pilote *m* de course; *Horseracing* **r. meeting** courses *fpl*; **there's a r. meeting at Newmarket tomorrow** on court *ou* il y a des courses demain à Newmarket

race² N *(species)* race *f*; **the human r.** la race humaine
▸▸ **r. relations** relations *fpl* interraciales; **r. riot** émeute *f* raciale

racecourse [ˈreɪskɔːs] N champ *m* de courses, hippodrome *m*, turf *m*

racegoer [ˈreɪsɡəʊər] N turfiste *mf*

racehorse [ˈreɪshɔːs] N cheval *m* de course

raceme [rəˈsiːm] N *Bot* grappe *f*

racer [ˈreɪsər] N *(person)* coureur, -euse; *(horse, bicycle, car, motorcycle)* cheval *m*/vélo *m*/voiture *f*/moto *f* de course; *(yacht)* yacht *m* de course, racer *m*

racetrack [ˈreɪstræk] N *(for cars)* circuit *m*; *(for bikes)* piste *f*; *Horseracing* champ *m* de courses, hippodrome *m*

raceway [ˈreɪsweɪ] N **1** *(channel for water)* canal *m* **2** *esp Am Elec* conduite *f* pour câbles **3** *(car racing)* circuit *m* **4** *esp Am Horseracing* champ *m* de courses, hippodrome *m* **5** *esp Am Tech (for ball bearings)* chemin *m* de roulement à billes

racial [ˈreɪʃəl] ADJ **1** *(concerning a race)* racial, -aux, ethnique **2** *(between races)* racial, -aux
▸▸ **r. discrimination** discrimination *f* raciale; **r. violence** violence *f* raciale

racialism [ˈreɪʃəlɪz(ə)m] N racisme *m*

racialist [ˈreɪʃəlɪst] ADJ, N raciste *mf*

racially [ˈreɪʃəlɪ] ADV **r. biased policy** politique *f* de discrimination raciale; **they were r. discriminated against** ils ont souffert de discrimination raciale; **a r. slanted article** un article à tendance raciste

raciness [ˈreɪsɪnɪs] N **1** *(liveliness) (of writing, style)* verve *f* **2** *(suggestiveness) (of story, joke)* grivoiserie *f*

racing [ˈreɪsɪŋ] N *Sport* course *f*; *Horseracing* courses (de chevaux), hippisme *m*, turf *m*; **motor r.** course automobile
ADJ **1** *Fig* **it's a r. certainty** c'est certain, c'est une certitude; **if anyone is a r. certainty for divorce, it's them!** s'il y a un couple qui est sûr de divorcer, c'est (bien) eux **2** **r. pulse** pouls *m* élevé; **a r. heart may be a warning sign of a heart attack** avoir des palpitations peut être le signal avant-coureur d'une crise cardiaque
▸▸ **r. bicycle** vélo *m* de course; **r. car** voiture *f* de course; *Horseracing.* **r. colours** couleurs *fpl* de l'écurie; **r. driver** coureur, -euse automobile, pilote *mf* (de course); **r. man** turfiste *m*; **r. pigeon** pigeon *m* voyageur *(de compétition)*; **r. stable** écurie *f* de courses; **r. tip** pronostic *m*

racism [ˈreɪsɪz(ə)m] N racisme *m*

racist [ˈreɪsɪst] ADJ, N raciste *mf*

rack¹ [ræk] N **to be going to r. and ruin** *(of country, company)* courir à la ruine; *(of house etc)* se délabrer, tomber en ruines; *(of health, economy, business)* aller de mal en pis; **this country/the economy/this house has gone to r. and ruin** ce pays/l'économie/la maison est dans un état lamentable

rack² N **1** *(for hay etc)* râtelier *m*; *(sectioned)* casier *m*; *(set of shelves)* étagère *f*, *(bicycle)* support *m ou* râtelier *m* à vélos; **(bottle) r.** casier à bouteilles; **(display) r.** présentoir *m*; **(luggage) r.** porte-bagages *m inv* **2** *Hist (for torture)* chevalet *m* (de torture); *Fig* **to be on**

the r. être au supplice; **to keep sb on the r., to have sb on the r.** mettre qn au supplice **3** *Comput* châssis *m*; *Tech* crémaillère *f* **4** *Culin* **r. of lamb** carré *m* d'agneau **5** *Am Fam* **to hit the r.** *(go to bed)* se pieuter, se bâcher

▪ **VT** *(person) (of disease, pain, guilt etc)* tourmenter, torturer, faire souffrir le martyre à; **to be racked with pain** être perclus de douleur; **to be racked by doubts** être en proie au doute; **to be racked by guilt** être tourmenté par un sentiment de culpabilité; **her body was racked with sobs** son corps était secoué de sanglots; **to r. one's brains** se creuser la tête *ou Fam* les méninges

▸▸**r. and pinion** crémaillère; **r. and pinion railway** chemin *m* de fer à crémaillère; **r. railway** chemin *m* de fer à crémaillère; **r. rate** *(in hotel)* plein tarif *m*; **r. slip** fiche *f* de réservation

▸ **rack back** **VT SEP** *Am Fam* **to r. sb back** passer un savon à qn, remonter les bretelles à qn

▸ **rack up** **VT SEP** *Sport etc (points)* accumuler

racket[1] N *(bat)* raquette *f*, **rackets** *(game)* jeu *m* de paume

▸▸*Sport* **r. cover** housse *f* de raquette; *Sport* **r. press** presse-raquette *m inv*; presse *f*

racket[2] N *Fam* **1** *(noise)* vacarme *m*, tintamarre *m*, *Fam* boucan *m*; **to make a r.** faire du tapage *ou* du vacarme *ou Fam* du boucan; **will you turn that r. off!** arrêtez ce vacarme! **2** *(criminal activity)* escroquerie *f*, racket *m*; **it's a r.** c'est du racket *ou* de l'escroquerie *ou* du vol; **this lottery is such a r.** cette loterie, c'est de l'arnaque; **he's involved in some money-laundering r.** il trempe dans des affaires de blanchiment d'argent **3** *Hum (occupation)* métier *m*; **how did you get into this r.?** comment est-ce que tu es arrivé dans cette branche?; **the teaching r.** le métier d'enseignant

racketeer [rækɪ'tɪər] N racketter *m*, racketteur, -euse

racketeering [rækɪ'tɪərɪŋ] N racket *m*

racking ['rækɪŋ] ADJ *(pain etc)* atroce; *(doubts, guilt)* affreux

rack-rent N loyer *m* excessif *ou* exorbitant

racoon [rə'ku:n] N = **raccoon**

racquet ['rækɪt] N = **racket**[1]

racy ['reɪsɪ] ADJ **1** *(lively) (description, writing)* piquant **2** *(person)* plein de vie, très vivant; *(style)* plein de verve **3** *(suggestive) (story, joke)* osé

rad 1 *(abbr **radiation**) (unit)* rd *f* **2** *esp Am (abbr **radiator**)* radiateur *m*

RADA ['rɑːdə] N *Br (abbr **Royal Academy of Dramatic Art**)* = Conservatoire *m* national d'art dramatique

radar ['reɪdɑːr] N radar *m*; **ground r.** radar au sol

▸▸**r. detection** détection *f* radar; **r. gun** radar gun *m*; **r. operator** radariste *mf*, opérateur, -trice radar; **r. screen** écran *m* (de) radar; **r. speed trap** contrôle *m* radar; **r. station** station *f* radar; **r. trap** contrôle radar

raddled ['ræd(ə)ld] ADJ *(face) (worn-out)* ravagé; *(over made-up)* peinturluré

radial ['reɪdɪəl] ADJ **1** *Tech, Math* radial, -aux **2** *Anat (artery etc)* radial, -aux

▪ N **1** *(tyre)* pneu *m* radial *ou* à carcasse radiale **2** *(line)* rayon *m*

▸▸**r. engine** moteur *m* en étoile; **r. road** radiale *f*, **r. tyre** pneu radial

radially ['reɪdɪəlɪ] ADV radialement

radiance ['reɪdɪəns] N *(of light, sun)* rayonnement *m*, éclat *m*; *(of beauty, smile)* éclat *m*

radiant ['reɪdɪənt] ADJ **1** *(light, sun)* éclatant **2** *(beauty, smile)* radieux, rayonnant; **a woman of r. beauty** une femme d'une beauté éblouissante; **the bride was r.** la mariée était radieuse *ou* rayonnante; **to be r. with joy** rayonner de joie

▪ N **1** *Phys* point *m* radiant **2** *(of heater)* foyer *m* de rayonnement **3** *Astron* radiant *m*

▸▸*Phys* **r. energy** énergie *f* de rayonnement; *Phys* **r. heat** chaleur *f* rayonnante; **r. heating** chauffage *m* par rayonnement; **r. point** point radiant

radiantly ['reɪdɪəntlɪ] ADV radieusement; **to be r. beautiful** être rayonnant de beauté; **she smiled r.** elle eut un sourire radieux; **r. happy** rayonnant de bonheur

radiate ['reɪdɪeɪt] VI *(of heat, light), Med (of pain)* rayonner, irradier

▪ **VT** *(heat, light)* émettre; **to r. happiness** rayonner de bonheur

radiation [reɪdɪ'eɪʃən] N **1** *(radioactivity)* radiation *f*; **to be exposed to r.** être exposé à des radiations **2** *(heat)* rayonnement *m* **3** *(light)* irradiation *f*; **ultraviolet r.** rayons *mpl* ultraviolets

▸▸**r. sickness** mal *m* des rayons; **r. therapy** radiothérapie *f*

radiator ['reɪdɪeɪtər] N **1** *(for heating)* radiateur *m* **2** *Aut* radiateur *m*

▸▸*Aut* **r. cap** bouchon *m* du radiateur; *Aut* **r. core** faisceau *m* de radiateur; *Aut* **r. grille** calandre *f*; *Aut* **r. matrix** faisceau de radiateur

radical ['rædɪk(ə)l] ADJ **1** *(opinion, policy etc)* radical, -aux; **to make a r. alteration in sth** changer qch radicalement **2** *Ling, Math, Bot* radical, -aux

▪ N **1** *Pol* radical, -ale **2** *Chem, Ling, Math* radical *m*

▸▸**r. chic** ≃ socialisme *m* de salon

radicalism ['rædɪkəlɪz(ə)m] N *Pol* radicalisme *m*

radicalize ['rædɪkəlaɪz] VT radicaliser

radically ['rædɪklɪ] ADV radicalement

radicle ['rædɪk(ə)l] N **1** *Bot (embryo)* radicule *f*, *(root)* radicelle *f* **2** *Chem* radical *m*

radio ['reɪdɪəʊ] N **1** *(set)* poste *m* (de radio), radio *f*; **to put** *or* **switch** *or* **turn the r. on/off** allumer/éteindre la radio; **she was on the r. last night** elle est passée à la radio hier soir; **R. Moscow** Radio Moscou **2** *(service, system)* **French r.** radiodiffusion *f* française **3** *Tel* radio(télégraphie) *f*; *(in taxi, ship etc)* radio *f*; **to communicate by r.** communiquer par radio; **to send a message by r.** envoyer un message radio

▪ **VT** *(information etc)* envoyer par radio; **to r. a person/ship** contacter une personne/un bateau par radio; **to r. one's position** signaler sa position par radio

▪ **VI** **to r. for assistance** *or* **help** demander de l'aide par radio

▸▸*Mktg* **r. advertising** publicité *f* à la radio; **r. alarm** radio-réveil *m*, *pl* radio-réveils; **r. announcer** présentateur, -trice de radio; **r. astronomy** radioastronomie *f*, **r. beacon** radiobalise *f*; **r. broadcast** émission *f* de radio; **r. broadcasting** radiodiffusion; **r. bulletin** bulletin *m* radiophonique; **r. button** bouton *m* radio, bouton d'option; **r. car** voiture *f* radio; **r. cassette** radiocassette *f*, **r. communication** contact *m* radio, liaison *f* radio, radiocommunications *fpl*; **r. data system** *(for motorists)* système *m* radio de transmission de données; **r. drama** pièce *f* radiophonique; **r. engineer** ingénieur *m* radio; **r. frequency** fréquence *f* radioélectrique, radiofréquence *f*; **r. ham** radioamateur *m*; **r. journalism** journalisme *m* de radio; **r. journalist** journaliste *mf* de radio; *Tel* **r. link** liaison radio; **r. listener** auditeur, -trice; **r. mast** antenne *f* radio; **r. message** message *m* radio; **r. microphone** microphone *m* sans fil; **r. navigation** radionavigation *f*, **r. officer** radionavigant *m*; **r. operator** *(on plane)* radio; *(on ship)* radionavigant; **r. play** pièce radiophonique; **r. producer** producteur, -trice d'émissions de radio; **r. programme** programme *m* radiodiffusé *ou* radiophonique,

émission de radio; **r. receiver** radiorécepteur *m*; **r. reporter** reporter *m* radio; *Naut* **r. room** poste radio de bord; **r. satellite** satellite *m* radio; **r. set** poste (de radio), radio *f*; **r. signal** signal *m* radiophonique; **r. spectrum** spectre *m* radio *ou* radioélectrique *ou* des fréquences radioélectriques; **r. station** station *f* de radio; **r. taxi** radio-taxi *m*, *pl* radio-taxis; **r. telescope** radiotélescope *m*; **r. transmitter** (poste) émetteur *m* radio; **r. vehicle** véhicule *m* radio; **r. waves** ondes *fpl* hertziennes, ondes radio

Radio

Les principales stations de radio de la BBC sont: Radio 1 (bulletins d'information, musique pop et rock); Radio 2 (variétés); Radio 3 (musique classique); Radio 4 (actualités, reportages, théâtre, programmes éducatifs); Radio 5 Live (sports, programmes éducatifs, musique pop et rock). La BBC comprend également trente-neuf stations locales. Il existe d'autre part plus de cent stations indépendantes.

radioactive [reɪdɪəʊ'æktɪv] ADJ *(substance, material)* radioactif

▸▸**r. dust** poussières *fpl* radioactives; **r. fallout** retombées *fpl* radioactives; **r. waste** déchets *mpl* radioactifs *ou* nucléaires

radioactivity [reɪdɪəʊæk'tɪvɪtɪ] N radioactivité *f*

radiocarbon [reɪdɪəʊ'kɑːbən] N radiocarbone *m*, carbone *m* 14

▸▸**r. dating** datation *f* au carbone 14

radio-controlled ADJ télécommandé

radiogram ['reɪdɪəʊgræm] N **1** *Br Old-fashioned (radio and record player)* = meuble *m* qui incorpore un poste de radio et un pick-up **2** *Radio (message)* radiogramme *m*, radiotélégramme *m* **3** *Med* = **radiograph**

radiograph ['reɪdɪəʊgrɑːf] N *Med* radiographie *f*

radiographer [reɪdɪ'ɒgrəfər] N *Med* radiologue *mf*

radiographic [reɪdɪəʊ'græfɪk] ADJ *Med* radiographique

radiography [reɪdɪ'ɒgrəfɪ] N *Med etc* radiographie *f*

radioisotope [reɪdɪəʊ'aɪsətəʊp] N radioisotope *m*, *pl* radio-isotopes

radiological [reɪdɪəʊ'lɒdʒɪk(ə)l] ADJ radiologique

radiologist [reɪdɪ'ɒlədʒɪst] N radiologue *mf*

radiology [reɪdɪ'ɒlədʒɪ] N radiologie *f*

radio-pager N récepteur *m* d'appel *ou* de poche

radioscopic [reɪdɪəʊ'skɒpɪk] ADJ *Med* radioscopique

radioscopy [reɪdɪ'ɒskəpɪ] N *Med* radioscopie *f*

radiotelegram [reɪdɪəʊ'telɪgræm] N radiotélégramme *m*, radiogramme *m*, *Fam* radio *m*

radiotelephone [reɪdɪəʊ'telɪfəʊn] N radiotéléphone *m*

radiotelephony [reɪdɪəʊtɪ'lefənɪ] N radiotéléphonie *f*, *Old-fashioned* téléphonie sans fil, TSF *f*

radiotherapist [reɪdɪəʊ'θerəpɪst] N radiothérapeute *mf*

radiotherapy [reɪdɪəʊ'θerəpɪ] N radiothérapie *f*

radish ['rædɪʃ] N radis *m*

radium ['reɪdɪəm] N *Chem* radium *m*

▸▸**r. treatment** curiethérapie *f*

radius, *pl* **radii** ['reɪdɪəs, -ɪaɪ] N **1** *(of circle)* rayon *m*; *Aviat* rayon (d'action), autonomie *f*; **within a r. of ten miles** dans un rayon de seize kilomètres **2** *(of crane)* portée *f* **3** *Anat (bone)* radius *m*

radix, *pl* **radices** ['reɪdɪks, -ɪsiːz] **N 1** *Math (in logarithms etc)* base *f* **2** *Ling* radical *m*

radon ['reɪdɒn] **N** *Chem* radon *m*

RAF [ɑːreɪ'ef] **N** *Br Mil (abbr* **Royal Air Force)** Armée *f* de l'air britannique

raffia ['ræfɪə] **N** *Bot* raphia *m*
▸▸ **r. mat** tapis *m* en raphia

raffish ['ræfɪʃ] **ADJ** dissolu; *(look)* canaille

raffle ['ræf(ə)l] **N** tombola *f*; **I won it in a r.** je l'ai gagné dans une tombola
VT to r. (off) mettre en tombola
▸▸ **r. ticket** billet *m* de tombola

raft [rɑːft] **N 1** radeau *m*; **(inflatable) life r.** canot *m* (pneumatique) de sauvetage **2** *(in logging)* timber r., *Am* lumber r. train *m* de bois ou de flottage **3** *Fam (large quantity)* **I have a r. of papers on my desk** j'ai une montagne de papiers sur mon bureau; **a r. of new measures** un paquet de nouvelles mesures
VT *(wood)* flotter en trains; **they rafted the logs to the paper mill** ils ont flotté les troncs jusqu'à la papeterie
VI to r. across the river traverser le fleuve sur un radeau

rafter ['rɑːftər] **N** *Constr* chevron *m*; **main r.** arbalétrier *m*; **the rafters** le chevronnage

rafting ['rɑːftɪŋ] **N** *Sport* rafting *m*

rag¹ [ræg] **N 1** *(piece of cloth)* chiffon *m*; *Fig* **to feel like a wet r.** être lessivé *ou* ramollo *ou* vidé; *Fig Fam* **to lose the** *or* **one's r.** sortir de ses gonds; *Sl* **to be on the r.** *(menstruating)* avoir ses ragnagnas **2** *(old garment)* guenille *f*, **rags** haillons *mpl*, guenilles, loques *fpl*; **to be in rags** être en guenilles *ou* en haillons; **to go from rags to riches** passer de la pauvreté à la richesse; **a rags to riches story** l'histoire d'une réussite sociale fulgurante **3** *Fam Pej (newspaper)* feuille *f* de chou, torchon *m*; **you don't read that r., do you?** tu ne lis pas ce torchon quand même?; **the local r.** le journal du coin
▸▸ **r. book** livre *m* en tissu; **r. content** *(of paper)* pourcentage *m* de peille; **r. doll** poupée *f* de chiffon; **r. paper** papier *m* à base de peille; **r. picker** chiffonnier, -ière; **r. rug** catalogne *f*, *Fam* **r. trade** confection *f*; **he's in the r. trade** il est *ou* travaille dans les fringues

rag² **VT** (**-gg-**) *Br (tease)* taquiner (**about** sur); *Sch (teacher etc)* chahuter, asticoter, *Fam* mettre en boîte; **to r. sb mercilessly** asticoter qn sans arrêt
N *Br Old-fashioned (joking etc)* blague *f*, farce *f*, **I did it for** *or* **as a r.** je l'ai fait pour blaguer, c'était une blague
▸▸ **r. week** = semaine *f* annuelle du calendrier universitaire où les étudiants organisent des kermesses dont les bénéfices vont à des œuvres de charité

raga ['rɑːgə] **N** *Mus* raga *m*

ragamuffin ['rægəmʌfɪn] **N** *(child)* gamin *m* des rues; **you little r.!** petit polisson!

rag-and-bone **ADJ**
▸▸ *Br* **r. man** chiffonnier *m*

ragbag ['rægbæg] **N** *(jumble) (of things, ideas etc)* fatras *m*, ensemble *m* hétéroclite; **they were a r. team** ils formaient une équipe hétéroclite; **this file's just a r.** ce fichier, c'est un fourre-tout

rage [reɪdʒ] **N 1** *(of person)* colère *f*, fureur *f*, rage *f*; **to be in a r.** être furieux *ou* fou de rage; **to get** *or* **fly into a r.** se mettre en colère, piquer une colère; **to have a fit of r.** avoir un accès de fureur; **to weep with r.** pleurer de rage **2** *Fam* **to be all the r.** *(of dance, music etc)* faire fureur, être la grande mode

VI 1 *(of person)* être furieux, rager; **to r. against** *or* **at sb/sth** être furieux *ou* tempêter contre qn/qch **2** *(of river, ocean)* être déchaîné *ou* démonté; *(of epidemic, war)* régner, sévir; *(of battle, fire, storm)* faire rage; *(of wind)* souffler en tempête

ragga ['rægə] **N** *Mus* ragga *m*

ragged ['rægɪd] **ADJ** *(garment etc)* en lambeaux, en loques; *(person)* en haillons, en guenilles, déguenillé; **a shirt with r. cuffs** une chemise aux poignets élimés; **she was beginning to look rather r.** elle commençait à avoir l'air dépenaillé; *Mus* **the execution is r.** l'exécution manque d'ensemble; *Fam* **to run oneself r.** s'éreinter; **she's run r. with those kids** les gosses l'épuisent; *Typ* **r. right/left** non-justifié à droite/à gauche; *Typ* **to print sth r.** imprimer qch sans justification
▸▸ *Bot* **r. robin** fleur *f* de coucou *(lychnis)*

ragging ['rægɪŋ] **N** *(teasing)* taquineries *fpl*; **to give sb a r.** mettre qn en boîte, taquiner qn; **he took a lot of r.** on l'a beaucoup taquiné

raggle-taggle ['ræg(ə)l'tæg(ə)l] **ADJ** *(army etc)* hétéroclite

raghead ['ræghed] **N** *Am Fam (Arab)* raton *m*, bicot *m*; *(gypsy)* romanichel, -elle

raging ['reɪdʒɪŋ] **ADJ** *(person)* furieux, en colère; *(fever)* très fort; *(thirst)* terrible; *(sea)* déchaîné, démonté; *(storm, wind)* déchaîné; **I had a r. headache** j'avais affreusement mal à la tête; **to be in a r. temper** être furieux; **r. toothache** rage *f* de dents
N *(of person)* colère *f*, fureur *f*, rage *f*; *(of sea, wind)* fureur *f*

raglan ['ræglən] **N** *(coat)* raglan *m*
ADJ raglan *inv*
▸▸ **r. coat** (manteau *m*) raglan; **r. sleeves** manches *fpl* raglan; **r. sweater** pull *m* raglan

ragman, *pl* **ragmen** ['rægmən] **N** chiffonnier *m*

ragout ['ræguː] **N** *Culin* ragoût *m*

rag-roll **VT** *(wall etc)* = appliquer de la peinture (sur un mur etc) à l'aide d'un chiffon

ragtag ['rægtæg] **N** **the r. and bobtail** la racaille
ADJ hétéroclite

ragtime ['rægtaɪm] **N** *Mus* ragtime *m*

ragtop ['rægtɒp] **N** *Am Fam* décapotable *f*

ragweed ['rægwiːd] **N** *Bot* herbe *f* à poux

ragwort ['rægwɜːt] **N** *Bot* séneçon *m*, *Fam* herbe *f* de saint-Jacques

rah-rah ['rɑːrɑː] **ADJ** *Am* enthousiaste; *Fig* **he's very r. about the President** c'est un fervent admirateur du Président

raid [reɪd] **N** *(on bank etc)* hold-up *m* *inv*, *Fam* braquage *m*; *(by police)* descente *f*, *St Exch* raid *m*; *Mil, Aviat* raid (**on** sur, contre); *Mil, Aviat* **daylight/night r.** attaque *f* (aérienne) de jour/de nuit
VT *(attack) (bank, post office)* attaquer, *Fam* braquer; *(bar, club etc) (of police)* faire une descente dans; *Mil* faire un raid *ou* des raids dans; *Aviat* faire un raid *ou* des raids sur; **the terrorists raided the presidential palace** les terroristes ont fait un raid sur le palais présidentiel; *Fig* **the children raided the fridge** les enfants ont fait une razzia dans le frigo

raider ['reɪdər] **N** *St Exch* raider *m*; *(of banks)* voleur, -euse, *Fam* braqueur, -euse de banques; *Mil (boat)* raider *m*; *(plane)* bombardier *m*; *(soldier)* membre *m* d'un commando

rail¹ [reɪl] **N 1** *(for protection, support) (of escalator, stairway)* main *f* courante; *(of balcony)* balustrade *f*, *(banister)* rampe *f*, *Naut* lisse *f*
2 *(for hanging things)* **curtain r.** tringle *f* à rideaux; **picture r.** cimaise *f*, **towel r.** porte-serviettes *m* *inv*

3 *Rail (track)* rail *m*; **to travel by r.** voyager en train; **to send goods by r.** envoyer des marchandises par chemin de fer
4 rails *Horseracing* corde *f*, *Naut* bastingage *m*, garde-corps *m* *inv*, rambarde *f*; **he was pushed to the rails by the other jockeys** il a été forcé de tenir la corde par les autres jockeys; *Rail* **to jump** *or* **leave the rails** dérailler, sortir des rails; *Fig* **to go off the rails** dérailler; *(morally)* s'écarter du droit chemin; **to get the economy back on the rails** remettre l'économie sur les rails; **I did my best to get him back on the rails after his breakdown** j'ai fait de mon mieux pour le remettre sur pieds après sa dépression nerveuse
▸▸ **r. network** réseau *m* ferroviaire *ou* de chemin de fer; **r. pass** carte *f* de train; **r. strike** grève *f* des chemins de fer; **r. transport** transport *m* par chemin de fer *ou* par train; **r. worker** employé, -ée des chemins de fer; *(for track, rolling stock)* cheminot *m*
▸ **rail against, rail at** **VT INSEP** *Fml (person)* s'en prendre à; **to r. against fate** s'en prendre au destin
▸ **rail in** **VT SEP** clôturer, entourer d'une clôture
▸ **rail off** **VT SEP** fermer avec une clôture *ou* une barrière; **the path down to the beach was railed off after the accident** le chemin qui mène à la plage a été fermé après l'accident

rail² **N** *(bird)* râle *m*; **water r.** râle d'eau

railcar ['reɪlkɑːr] **N** *Am Rail* autorail *m*

railcard ['reɪlkɑːd] **N** *Br* carte *f* de chemin de fer

railfreight ['reɪlfreɪt] **N** **to send r.** envoyer par chemin de fer

railhead ['reɪlhed] **N** *Rail etc* tête *f* de ligne

railing¹ ['reɪlɪŋ] **N** *(also* **railings) 1** *(barrier) (of metal)* grille *f*, *(of wood)* palissade *f*, **iron railings** grille **2** *(in dangerous place)* garde-fou *m*, *pl* garde-fous, garde-corps *m* *inv* **3** *(for support) (on staircase)* rampe *f*, *(on balcony)* balustrade *f*

railing² **N** *(complaints)* invectives *fpl* (**at, against** contre)

raillery ['reɪlərɪ] **N** *(teasing)* raillerie *f*

railman, *pl* **railmen** ['reɪlmən] **N** = **railwayman**

railroad ['reɪlrəʊd] **N** *Am (system)* chemin *m* de fer; *(track)* voie *f* ferrée; **to travel by r.** voyager en chemin de fer
VT 1 *Fam (force acceptance of)* **to r. a bill through Parliament** imposer un projet de loi au Parlement **2** *Fam (force into action)* **to r. sb into doing sth** faire pression sur qn pour qu'il fasse qch; **to be railroaded into doing sth** être forcé à faire qch; **I don't want to r. you, but …** je ne voudrais pas te forcer mais …; **she was railroaded into this job** on a fait pression sur elle pour qu'elle prenne ce poste **3** *esp Am Law Fam (convict by false charges)* condamner à l'aide de fausses inculpations; *(hastily)* juger sommairement **4** *Am (transport)* transporter par chemin de fer
▸▸ *Am* **r. apartment** = appartement *m* dont les pièces sont en enfilade; **r. car** wagon *m*

railway ['reɪlweɪ] **N** *Br, Can (system)* chemin *m* de fer; *(track)* voie *f* ferrée; **to travel by r.** voyager en chemin de fer; **to work on the railway(s)** être employé des chemins de fer; **Canadian National Railways** Chemins de fer nationaux du Canada
▸▸ **r. bridge** pont *m* ferroviaire; **r. carriage** wagon *m*, voiture *f*, **r. company** société *f* des chemins de fer; **r. crossing** passage *m* à niveau; **r. cutting** traversée *f* en déblai; **r. embankment** remblai *m*; **r. engine** locomotive *f*, **r. engineer** ingénieur *m* des chemins de fer; **r. guide** indicateur *m* des chemins de fer; **r. line** *(route)* ligne *f* de chemin de fer; *(track)* voie ferrée; *(rail)* rail *m*; **r. network**

réseau *m* ferroviaire *ou* de chemin de fer; **r. signal** signal *m* ferroviaire; **r. station** gare *f* (de chemin de fer); *(in France)* gare SNCF; **r. strike** grève *f* des chemins de fer; **r. system** réseau ferroviaire *ou* de chemin de fer; **r. ticket** billet *m* de train; **r. timetable** horaires *mpl* des chemins de fer; *(printed)* fiche *f* horaire; **r. track** voie ferrée; **r. worker** employé, -ée des chemins de fer; *(for track, rolling stock)* cheminot *m*; **r. yard** dépôt *m*

railwayman, *pl* **railwaymen** ['reɪlweɪmən] N *Br, Can (administrative employee)* employé, -ée des chemins de fer; *(technical employee)* cheminot *m*; *Br Formerly* **National Union of Railwaymen** = syndicat *m* des employés de chemins de fer de Grande-Bretagne

raiment ['reɪmənt] N *Arch, Lit* vêtements *mpl*, habits *mpl*

rain [reɪn] N **1** pluie *f*; **in the r.** sous la pluie; **it looks like r.** on dirait qu'il va pleuvoir, le temps est à la pluie; **it's pouring with r.** il pleut à verse, il pleut des cordes; **they had some r. during their holiday** ils ont eu de la pluie pendant leurs vacances; **a river swollen with r.,** **a r.-swollen river** une rivière gonflée par les pluies; **the rains** la saison des pluies; **(come) r. or shine** *(whatever the weather)* qu'il pleuve ou qu'il vente; *(whatever the circumstances)* quoiqu'il arrive; *Br Fam* **two days in bed and you'll be as right as r.** deux jours au lit et tu seras remis; *Fig* **he doesn't have the sense to come in out of the r.** il n'a pas inventé le fil à couper le beurre; **driving/fine r.** pluie battante/fine; **freezing r.** pluie verglaçante; **heavy r.** forte *ou* grosse pluie; **light r.** pluie fine

2 *Fig (large quantity) (of abuse, blows etc)* pluie *f*, avalanche *f*

V IMPERS pleuvoir; **it rains/is raining** il pleut; **it is raining hard** il pleut à verse; *Br Fam* **it's raining cats and dogs** il tombe des cordes, il pleut comme vache qui pisse; *Prov* **it never rains but it pours** un malheur ne vient jamais seul

VI *(of abuse, blows etc)* pleuvoir (**on** sur)

VT **to r. gifts/flowers on sb** couvrir qn de cadeaux/fleurs; **to r. blows on sb** rouer qn de coups

▸▸ *Geog* **r. belt** zone *f* des pluies; **r. cape** pèlerine *f*; *Am* **r. check** = bon *m* pour un autre match (ou spectacle) donné par suite d'une annulation à cause de la pluie; *Fam Fig* **I'll take a r. check on that** ça sera pour une autre fois; **r. cloud** nuage *m* de pluie; **r. dance** danse *f* de la pluie; **r. gauge** pluviomètre *m*; **r. hat** capuche *f*, **r. hood** capuche *f*; *(attached to anorak, jacket etc)* capuchon *m*, capuche; **r. shower** averse *f*

▸ **rain down** VI = **rain** VI
VT SEP = **rain** VT

▸ **rain off** VT SEP *Br Sport etc* **to be rained off** *(of match etc)* être annulé à cause du mauvais temps

▸ **rain out** VT SEP *Am* = **rain off**

rainbow ['reɪnbəʊ] N arc-en-ciel *m*, *pl* arcs-en-ciel; **all the colours of the r.** toutes les couleurs de l'arc-en-ciel; **a dress in all the colours of the r.** une robe arc-en-ciel; *Fig* **to chase rainbows** se nourrir d'illusions; **r.-coloured** aux couleurs de l'arc-en-ciel

▸▸ *Pol* **r. coalition** = coalition *f* représentant un large éventail de tendances; **r. trout** truite *f* arc-en-ciel

raincoat ['reɪnkəʊt] N imperméable *m*, *Fam* imper *m*

raindrop ['reɪndrɒp] N goutte *f* de pluie

rainfall ['reɪnfɔːl] N *(amount)* précipitations *fpl*; **average r.** précipitations moyennes, taux *m* de pluviosité; **low/high r.** précipitations faibles/importantes

rainforest ['reɪnfɒrɪst] N **(tropical) r.** forêt *f* tropicale humide

rainless ['reɪnlɪs] ADJ *(day etc)* sans pluie

rainmaker ['reɪnmeɪkər] N *(magician)* faiseur, -euse de pluie

rainmaking ['reɪnmeɪkɪŋ] ADJ *(ritual etc)* pour faire pleuvoir

rainout ['reɪnaʊt] N *Am Sl* match *m* annulé à cause du mauvais temps

rainproof ['reɪnpruːf] ADJ *(coat, fabric etc)* imperméable
VT *(fabric)* imperméabiliser

rainslicker ['reɪnslɪkə(r)] N *Am* ciré *m*

rainstorm ['reɪnstɔːm] N pluies *fpl* torrentielles

rainwater ['reɪnwɔːtər] N eau *f* de pluie

rainwear ['reɪnweər] N *(clothing)* vêtements *mpl* de pluie

rainy ['reɪnɪ] ADJ *(climate, weather)* pluvieux; **a r. day** un jour de pluie; **it has been very r. recently** il a beaucoup plu récemment; *Fig* **to put something by** *or* **keep something for a r. day** garder une poire pour la soif; *Fig* **she puts by ten pounds a week for a r. day** elle met dix livres de côté par semaine au cas où elle en aurait besoin

▸▸ **r. season** saison *f* des pluies

RAISE [reɪz]

VT	lever 1, 6, 13 ▪ soulever 1, 5, 12
▪ remonter 1 ▪ augmenter 2 ▪ faire monter 2 ▪ élever 8 ▪ cultiver 8
N	augmentation 1

VT **1** *(lift, cause to rise) (one's hand, eyes, anchor)* lever; *(veil)* relever; *(weight)* lever, soulever; *(blind)* remonter; *(flag)* hisser; *(sunken ship)* renflouer; **to r. a cloud of dust** soulever un nuage de poussière; *Theat* **to r. the curtain** lever le rideau; **to r. an eyebrow** *or* **one's eyebrows** *(in disapproval)* froncer les sourcils, sourciller; *(in surprise)* ouvrir des yeux ronds; **he raised an eyebrow at the news** il eut l'air étonné d'entendre cette nouvelle; **that will r. a few eyebrows** *or* **an eyebrow or two** *(cause surprise)* cela va en surprendre plus d'un; *(cause disapproval)* cela va en faire tiquer plus d'un; **eyebrows were raised yesterday when …** *(in surprise)* cela en a surpris plus d'un hier quand; *(in disapproval)* la désapprobation s'est lue sur les visages hier quand …; **to r. one's fist to sb** menacer qn du poing; **to r. one's glass** lever son verre (**to sb** à la santé de qn); **to r. one's glass to one's lips** porter son verre à ses lèvres; **to r. sb's hackles** hérisser qn; **to r. one's hand to sb** lever la main sur qn; **to r. one's hat to sb** soulever son chapeau pour saluer qn; *Fig* **tirer son chapeau à qn**; **to r. one's head** *(from lowered position)* lever la tête; *(hold erect)* dresser la tête; **to r. a patient to a sitting position** soulever un malade pour l'asseoir; **to r. sb's hopes** donner de l'espoir à qn; **don't r. your hopes too much** n'espère pas trop; *Mil, Fig* **to r. one's sights** viser plus haut; **to r. standards** *(of education, morality)* élever le niveau; *(of cleanliness, safety)* améliorer les conditions; **to r. the standard of living** améliorer le niveau de vie; **to r. sb's spirits** remonter le moral à qn; **to r. the tone** *or* **level of the conversation** élever le niveau de la conversation; **to r. the tone** *or* **level of the neighbourhood** rehausser le prestige du quartier; **to r. the rafters** *(make noise)* faire un foin d'enfer *ou* un boucan de tous les diables; **to r. the roof** *(make noise)* faire un foin d'enfer *ou* un boucan de tous les diables; *(complain)* faire une scène terrible *ou* de tous les diables

2 *(increase in amount) (wages, price)* augmenter; *(temperature)* faire monter; **to r. a credit limit** déplafonner un crédit; **to r. production to a maximum** porter la production

au maximum; **to r. the school-leaving age** prolonger la scolarité; **they've raised the age limit to …** l'âge limite est passé à …; **to r. the stakes** faire monter les enjeux; **to r. the pass mark** élever le niveau requis; *Fig* **she raised the temperature (of the room) by her condemnation of party policy** les esprits se sont échauffés lorsqu'elle a condamné la politique du parti; *Am* **to r. a cheque** falsifier le montant d'un chèque; *Cards* **I'll r. you ten** *(at poker)* plus dix; *Math* **to r. a number to the ninth power** élever un nombre à la puissance neuf

3 *(increase in height)* **to r. (the level of) a wall** rehausser *ou* surélever un mur; **to r. the level of the ground** rehausser le niveau du sol; **to r. the ceiling on wage increases** augmenter le plafond des salaires; **she raised herself to her full height and replied …** elle se redressa et, de toute sa hauteur, répondit …

4 *(increase in intensity)* **to r. sb's consciousness (of sth)** *(inform)* sensibiliser qn (à qch); *(emphasize)* faire prendre conscience à qn (de qch); **to r. one's voice** *(speak more loudly)* élever la voix; *(speak in anger)* hausser le ton; **no one raised their voice (to answer** *or* **speak)** personne ne souffla mot

5 *(create, produce) (problem, matter for discussion)* soulever (**with** auprès de); *(fears, doubts, distrust)* susciter; *Br* **to r. a cheque** faire un chèque; **to r. an objection** élever *ou* soulever une objection; **to r. a question** *(make query)* poser une question; **his attitude raises certain questions** son attitude pose *ou* soulève *ou* suscite certaines questions; **his attitude raises questions about his loyalty** son attitude remet en question sa loyauté; *Fam* **to r. hell** *(complain)* faire une scène terrible *ou* de tous les diables (**about sth** à propos de qch); **to r. a blush/laugh** faire rougir/rire; **to r. a cheer** *(of people)* crier hourra; *(of announcement, speech etc)* soulever des hourras; **to r. a shout** *(of people)* pousser un cri; **to r. a smile** *(in oneself)* esquisser un sourire; *(in others)* provoquer *ou* faire naître un sourire; **to r. a storm of laughter/protest** déclencher *ou* soulever une tempête de rires/protestations; **to r. the alarm** donner *ou* sonner l'alarme; **to r. a loan** *(of government)* émettre *ou* lancer un emprunt; *(of individual)* faire un emprunt (**on** sur); **to r. steam** *(in boiler)* chauffer la chaudière

6 *(collect together) (money)* rassembler; **to r. money for charity** mobiliser des fonds pour une œuvre de bienfaisance; **to r. an army** réunir une armée, mettre une armée sur pied; **to r. funds** *(for charity) (of volunteers)* collecter des fonds (**for** pour, au profit de); *(for business, government programme)* se procurer des fonds; **to r. signatures** *(for petition)* rassembler des signatures; **how much (money) did you r. on the car when you sold it?** combien est-ce que tu t'es fait sur la vente de la voiture?; **he wanted a new motorbike but couldn't r. the money** il voulait une moto neuve mais il n'a pas pu trouver l'argent nécessaire; **to r. taxes** lever des impôts

7 *(erect) (building, barn etc)* construire; *(statue)* ériger (**to** à l'effigie de)

8 *(rear, grow) (children)* élever; *(cattle, poultry etc)* élever, faire l'élevage de; *(wheat, vegetables)* cultiver, faire pousser

9 *(promote) Mil, Fig* **to r. sb from the ranks** promouvoir qn; *Mil* **to r. sb to the rank of lieutenant** promouvoir qn lieutenant; **to r. sb from the gutter** sortir qn du caniveau; **to r. sb to the peerage** *(give hereditary title to)* anoblir qn; *(give life title to)* conférer à qn un titre de pair

10 *(contact) (by telephone) (person)* joindre, contacter; *(by radio) (ship)* entrer en contact (radio) avec; *Naut* **to r. land** apercevoir la terre

11 *(awaken, rouse)* **to r. Cain** *(make noise)* faire un foin d'enfer *ou* un boucan de tous les diables; *(complain)* faire une scène terrible *ou* de tous les diables; **to r. the devil** *(complain)* faire une scène terrible *ou* de tous les diables; **to r. sb from his/her bed** faire lever qn, sortir qn du lit; **to r. sb from the dead** ressusciter qn; **to r. a ghost** faire apparaître un fantôme; **to r. a spirit** évoquer un esprit

12 *(stir up) (nation)* soulever; *(rebellion)* provoquer

13 *(end) (blockade, embargo, siege)* lever

N 1 *Am (pay increase)* augmentation *f* (de salaire); **to get a r.** être augmenté, avoir une augmentation

2 *Cards (poker)* relance *f, (bridge)* enchère *f*

▸ **raise up VT SEP** lever, soulever; **she raised herself up out of her chair** elle se leva de son fauteuil

Attention: ne pas confondre avec le verbe **to rise**, qui n'est jamais suivi d'un complément d'objet.

raised [reɪzd] **ADJ 1** *(lifted) (arm etc)* levé; **we could hear r. voices from the next room** on entendait les gens qui se disputaient dans la pièce d'à côté; **to say sth in a r. voice** dire qch en haussant le ton **2** *(elevated) (deck, flowerbed)* surélevé; *(embossed) (design, letter, motif)* en relief **3** *Am Culin* au levain

raiser ['reɪzər] **N** *(breeder) (of cattle etc)* éleveur, -euse

raisin ['reɪz(ə)n] **N** raisin *m* sec
▸▸ **r. bread** pain *m* aux raisins *(miche)*

Note that the French word **raisin** is a false friend and is never a translation for the English word **raisin**. It means **grapes**.

raising ['reɪzɪŋ] **N 1** *(lifting) (of curtain)* lever *m; (of sunken ship)* renflouage *m; (of standards)* élévation *f* **2** *(of prices, rents, salaries)* augmentation *f,* **r. of the school-leaving age** prolongation *f* de la scolarité **3** *(of army)* levée *f, (collecting) (of funds for charity)* collecte *f, (of taxes)* levée; **r. of money** mobilisation *f* de fonds **4** *(of barn, building)* construction *f, (of monument, statue)* érection *f* **5** *(of animals)* élevage *m; (of children)* éducation *f; (of crops)* culture *f* **6** *(of blockade, embargo, siege)* levée **7 r. of the dead** résurrection *f* des morts
▸▸ *Culin* **r. agent** levure *f*

Raj [rɑːdʒ] **N** *Hist* **the R.** l'empire *m* britannique en Inde

rajah ['rɑːdʒə] **N** ra(d)ja(h) *m*

rake¹ [reɪk] **N 1** *(for gardener, croupier)* râteau *m* **2** *(for grate)* râble *m,* ringard *m;* **as thin as a r.** maigre comme un clou

VT 1 *(collect or level with rake) (leaves, ground, path)* ratisser **2** *Mil (fire on with machine gun) (enemy forces, trenches)* mitrailler **3** *(search) (with eyes) (group, crowd)* détailler minutieusement; *(with searchlights) (sky, sea)* balayer; **to r. one's memory** fouiller dans ses souvenirs

▸ **rake about, rake around VI** *(search)* fouiller (**among, in** dans)

▸ **rake in VT SEP 1** *Fam (money) (acquire)* amasser; **you must be raking it in!** tu dois t'en mettre plein les poches!; **that shop is raking in a fortune** ce magasin ramasse une fortune **2** *(in garden) (compost)* enfouir au râteau; *(in casino) (stakes)* ratisser

▸ **rake off VT SEP 1** *(remove) (pebbles, leaves)* enlever au râteau **2** *Fam (take)* empocher; **he raked off £50** il a empoché 50 livres, il s'est mis 50 livres dans la poche

▸ **rake out VT SEP 1** *(remove ashes from)* reti-

rer *ou* enlever les cendres de **2** *Fam (find) (scarf, gloves etc)* dégoter, dénicher (**from** dans)

▸ **rake over VT SEP** *(ground)* ratisser; *Fig* **to r. over the ashes** *or* **the past** *(revive)* remuer le passé

▸ **rake through VT INSEP** *(search) (pockets, drawer)* fouiller dans; **the down-and-out was raking through the dustbins** le clochard fouillait dans *ou* faisait les poubelles

▸ **rake up VT SEP 1** *(collect with rake) (leaves)* ratisser **2** *(revive) (fire)* attiser; *Fig* **to r. up an old quarrel** raviver une ancienne querelle; **to r. up the past** remuer le passé; **to r. up sb's past** fouiller dans le passé de qn **3** *Fam (find with difficulty) (money, story etc)* dégoter, dénicher

rake² **N** *(slope) (of aircraft wings, funnel, mast etc) (angle* m d')inclinaison *f, (of stage)* pente *f,* inclinaison; **stage with a steep r.** scène fortement inclinée

VI *(of aircraft wings, funnel, mast etc)* être incliné; *(of stage)* être en pente *ou* incliné

VT *(funnel, mast etc)* incliner; *(stage)* construire en pente; **a steeply raked stage** une scène fortement inclinée

rake³ **N** *Lit (dissolute man)* coureur *m,* débauché *m,* libertin *m, Old-fashioned* roué *m*

rake-off **N 1** *Fam (share of profits) (legal)* commission *f, (illegal)* ristourne *f,* **what's her r.?** *(legal)* quelle est sa part?; *(illegal)* combien est-ce qu'elle se met dans la poche? **2** *Am (deduction)* rabais *m,* réduction *f* (**on** sur)

raki [rɑːˈkiː, ˈrækɪ] **N** *(drink)* raki *m*

rakish ['reɪkɪʃ] **ADJ 1** *Old-fashioned (dissolute) (behaviour, life)* débauché **2** *(jaunty) (air)* cavalier, désinvolte; **to wear one's hat at a r. angle** porter son chapeau avec l'air canaille; *Naut* **a ship built on r. lines** un navire à la forme élancée *ou* effilée

rakishly ['reɪkɪʃlɪ] **ADV** d'un air désinvolte

rally ['rælɪ] **N 1** *(meeting)* grand rassemblement *m; (protest gathering)* manifestation *f* **2** *(improvement) (in health)* amélioration *f* passagère, mieux *m* momentané; *St Exch* redressement *m,* rally *m* **3** *Sport (in tennis etc)* long échange *m* **4** *(car race)* rallye *m*

VT 1 *(unite, win over) (troops, supporters)* rallier; **to r. support for a cause** s'assurer un soutien pour une cause **2** *(recover) (one's strength)* reprendre; **to r. one's spirits** reprendre courage; **to r. sb's spirits** redonner courage à qn

VI 1 *(unite, support)* se rallier (**to, round** à); **to r. for the attack** se regrouper pour attaquer; **to r. round sb** *(help)* venir en aide à qn; **all the neighbours rallied round to help** tous les voisins sont venus apporter leur soutien; **to r. to sb's defence** accourir au secours de qn **2** *(recover) (of shares)* se redresser; *(of patient)* se remettre momentanément; *(of athlete)* se reprendre, se ressaisir; **the pound rallied in the afternoon** la livre est remontée dans l'après-midi; **the market rallied** les cours ont repris **3** *Sport (enter car rallies)* courir *ou* participer à des rallyes; *Tennis* **they've been rallying for five minutes** l'échange dure depuis cinq minutes
▸▸ **r. driver** pilote *m* de rallye

rallycross ['rælɪkrɒs] **N** *Aut* rallycross *m*

rallyer ['rælɪər] **N** *Sport* concurrent, -ente d'un rallye

rallying ['rælɪɪŋ] **N 1** *(of troops, supporters)* ralliement *m* **2** *Sport, Aut* rallyes *mpl;* **to go r.** faire un rallye
▸▸ **r. cry** cri *m* de ralliement; **r. point** point *m* de ralliement

ralph [rælf] **VI** *Fam (vomit)* gerber, dégueuler

RAM **N 1** [ræm] *Comput (abbr* **random access**

memory) mémoire *f* vive; **R.-resident** résident en mémoire vive **2** [ɑːreɪˈem] *Br (abbr* **Royal Academy of Music**) = Conservatoire *m* national de musique
▸▸ *Comput* **R. chip** puce *f* de mémoire vive; *Comput* **R. disk** mémoire à disque

ram [ræm] **N 1** *(animal)* bélier *m; (astrological sign)* Bélier **2** *Tech (part of pile driver)* marteau *m; (part of hydraulic press)* (piston *m*) plongeur *m;* **(hydraulic) r.** bélier *m* hydraulique **3** *Hum Sl (sexually active man)* viril *m,* macho *m*

VT (-mm-) **1** *(crash into) (of ship) (another ship, submarine)* entrer en collision avec, aborder; *Hist (galleon)* éperonner; *(of car) (tree, lorry)* heurter, percuter; **he rammed the gates with a lorry** *(knocked down)* il a défoncé le portail avec un camion; **he rammed the trolley into my ankles** il m'a heurté les chevilles avec son caddie® **2** *(force into place)* enfoncer (**into** dans)
▸▸ *Aut* **r. air** air *m* forcé; *Aut* **r. air induction** introduction *f* d'air par forçage; **r. cylinder** vérin *m*

▸ **ram down VT SEP** *(compact) (earth)* tasser; *Fig* **to r. one's hat down on one's head** enfoncer son chapeau (sur la tête); **she's always ramming religion down my throat** elle me rebat toujours les oreilles avec sa religion

▸ **ram home VT SEP** *(emphasize) (the importance of sth)* insister sur; **he kept ramming it home that we should ...** il n'arrêtait pas de répéter que nous devions ...; *Mil* **to r. home a charge** bourrer un canon *ou* un fusil

▸ **ram into VT SEP** *(force)* **to r. clothes into a suitcase** bourrer une valise de vêtements; **to r. a charge into a gun** bourrer un fusil; *Fig* **the teacher rammed the dates into them** le professeur leur enfonçait *ou* leur faisait entrer les dates dans la tête; **to r. food into one's mouth** se gaver

VT INSEP *(collide with)* emboutir, percuter; **a Jag rammed into the back of me** une Jag a embouti l'arrière de ma voiture; **they rammed into each other** ils se sont percutés

▸ **ram through VT SEP** *(force acceptance of) (appointment)* imposer

Ramadan [ræməˈdɑːn] **N** *Rel* ramadan *m;* **during R.** pendant le ramadan

ramble ['ræmb(ə)l] **N** *(walk) (spontaneous)* balade *f,* grande promenade *f, (planned)* randonnée *f,* **to go on** *or* **for a r.** *(spontaneously)* faire une balade *ou* une grande promenade; *(planned)* partir en randonnée

VI 1 *(walk) (spontaneously)* se balader, faire une grande promenade (**over, through** dans); *(planned)* faire une randonnée (**over, through** dans) **2** *(talk in disconnected fashion)* parler sans suite, dire n'importe quoi (**about** de) **3** *(be delirious)* divaguer, *Fam* battre la campagne **4** *(meander) (of stream)* serpenter (**through** dans); **there was ivy rambling all over the ruins** le lierre rampait sur les ruines; **the path that rambles through the fields** le chemin sinueux qui traverse les champs

▸ **ramble on VI** tenir des discours sans fin, discourir; **to r. on about nothing in particular** parler pour ne rien dire; **what are you rambling on about now?** qu'est-ce que tu racontes maintenant?

rambler ['ræmblər] **N 1** *(hiker)* randonneur, -euse **2** *(rose)* rosier *m* grimpant **3** *Am (house)* ranch *m*

rambling ['ræmblɪŋ] **ADJ 1** *(conversation, letter, speech etc)* décousu **2** *(path, stream etc)* sinueux; **a r. house** une maison pleine de coins et de recoins; **a r. town** une ville construite au hasard

N 1 *(hiking)* randonnées *fpl;* **to go r.** partir en randonnée **2 ramblings** *(delirium)* divagations *fpl;* **the ramblings of old age**

les radotages *mpl* de la vieillesse
▸▸ **r. rose** rosier *m* sarmenteux

rambunctious [ræm'bʌŋkʃəs] **ADJ** *Am Fam*
1 *(boisterous) (behaviour, child)* turbulent,
chahuteur, -euse, tapageur **2** *(noisy) (meet-ing)* bruyant, mouvementé; *(party)* bruyant

RAMC [ɑːreɪem'siː] **N** *Br Mil (abbr* **Royal Ar-my Medical Corps)** ≃ service *m* de santé de
l'armée

ramee ['ræmɪ] **N** *Tex* = **ramie**

ramekin, ramequin ['ræmɪkɪn] **N** *Culin* ramequin *m*

ramie ['ræmɪ] **N** *Tex* ramie *f*

ramification [ræmɪfɪ'keɪʃən] **N** ramification *f*

ramify ['ræmɪfaɪ] **VT** ramifier
VI se ramifier

ramjet ['ræmdʒet] **N** *Aviat (engine)* statoréacteur *m*, tuyère *f* thermopropulsive; *(aircraft)*
avion *m* à statoréacteur
▸▸ **r. engine** statoréacteur, tuyère thermopropulsive

rammer ['ræmər] **N** *(for road-making)* dame
f, *(for metal-working)* fouloir *m*, batte *f*, *(for
civil engineering)* engin *m* de compactage
du sol

ramp [ræmp] **N 1** *(slope)* rampe *f* **2** *Aut (in
garage)* pont *m* élévateur; *(connecting road)*
bretelle *f* (d'accès); *(bump on road)* dos *m*
d'âne; *(difference in level)* dénivellation *f*, dénivellement *m*; *(to slow traffic down)* ralentisseur *m*; *Aviat* **boarding r.** passerelle *f*
▸▸ *Comput* **r. access** accès *m* aléatoire;
Comput **r. access file** fichier *m* à accès aléatoire; *Comput* **r. access memory** mémoire *f*
vive; *Mktg* **r. check** contrôle *m* par sonda-
ge(s); *Comput* **r. error** erreur *f* aléatoire; **r. kil-
lings** tuerie *f* aveugle *ou* au hasard; *Mktg* **r.
sample** échantillon *m* aléatoire; *Mktg* **r.
sampling** échantillonnage *m* aléatoire; *Mktg*
r. selection sélection *f* au hasard; *Math* **r. variable** variable *f* aléatoire; **r. violence** violence *f* aveugle

rampage¹ ['ræmpeɪdʒ] **N** *Fam* **to be** *or* **go on
the r.** *(lose control)* se déchaîner; *(cause damage)* tout saccager; *Hum* **the boss is on the
r.** le patron est complètement déchaîné; **the
hooligans went on a r.** les hooligans ont tout
saccagé sur leur passage

rampage² [ræm'peɪdʒ] **VI to r. (about** *or*
around) se déchaîner; **they were rampaging through the streets** ils saccageaient
tout dans les rues

rampaging [ræm'peɪdʒɪŋ] **ADJ** *(bulls, protestors etc)* déchaîné

rampancy ['ræmpənsɪ] **N** *(of corruption,
vice)* prolifération *f*, *(of plant)* exubérance *f*

rampant ['ræmpənt] **ADJ 1** *(corruption, poverty, vice)* qui sévit, endémique; *(plant)* exubérant, luxuriant; **to be r.** *(of corruption etc)*
régner, sévir; *Fam* **he's a bit r. tonight** *(sexually)* il est émoustillé ce soir; **r. inflation** inflation *f* galopante **2** *Her* rampant; **the Lion
R.** le Lion rampant

rampart ['ræmpɑːt] **N** *(fortification)*, *Fig* rempart *m*

ram-raid **VT to r. a shop** = dévaliser un magasin après en avoir brisé la vitrine à l'aide
d'un véhicule

ramrod ['ræmrɒd] **N** *(for cleaning rifle)* écouvillon *m*; *(for loading cannon)* refouloir *m*; **to
be as stiff as a r.** être raide comme un piquet; **to sit as straight as a r.** *or* **r.-straight**
être raide comme un piquet sur sa chaise

ramshackle ['ræmʃæk(ə)l] **ADJ** *(building,
farm)* délabré, qui tombe en ruines; *(economy, government)* qui s'effrite *ou* s'effondre,
délabré; **r. old car** vieille guimbarde *f*

ran [ræn] **PP** *see* **run VT, VI**

ranch [rɑːntʃ] **N** ranch *m*, ferme *f* d'élevage;
cattle/mink r. ferme d'élevage de bétail/du
vison
VI avoir *ou* exploiter *ou* tenir un ranch
VT *(cattle, mink)* élever, faire l'élevage de
▸▸ *Culin* **r. dressing** = mayonnaise *f* cré-
meuse à l'ail; **r. hand** ouvrier, -ière agricole;
r. house *(bungalow)* maison *f* sans étage; *(on
ranch)* maison; *Am* **r. mink** vison *m* d'élevage

rancher ['rɑːntʃər] **N** propriétaire *mf* de
ranch; **cattle/mink r.** éleveur, -euse de bé-
tail/visons

ranching ['rɑːntʃɪŋ] **N** *(of cattle, mink)* élevage *m*

rancid ['rænsɪd] **ADJ** rance; **to go r.** rancir; **to
smell r.** sentir le rance

rancidity [ræn'sɪdɪtɪ], **rancidness** ['rænsɪd-
nɪs] **N** *(of butter, fat etc)* rancidité *f*

rancorous ['rænkərəs] **ADJ** *(attitude)* rancunier, plein de rancœur; *(remark)* amer, plein
de rancœur

rancour, *Am* **rancor** ['rænkər] **N** rancune *f*,
rancœur *f*; **full of r.** *(remark etc)* amer; **the r.
of her remarks/criticisms** l'amertume de ses
remarques/critiques; **he is full of r.** *(permanent condition)* il est aigri; **to be full of r.
against sb** avoir beaucoup de rancœur
contre qn

rand [rænd] **N 1** *(South African currency)* rand
m **2** *Geog* **the R.** le Rand

random ['rændəm] **ADJ** *(choice)* fait au hasard; *(sample)* prélevé au hasard; *(pattern)*
irrégulier; *Math (error, number)* aléatoire; **I
just made a r. guess** j'ai deviné tout à fait
par hasard; **a r. selection of people were
asked if ...** on a demandé à des gens choisis
au hasard si ...; **a r. shot** une balle perdue;
to be killed by a r. shot *or* **bullet** être tué
par une balle perdue
N at r. au hasard; **to fire at r.** tirer au hasard
ou à l'aveuglette
▸▸ *Comput* **r. access** accès *m* aléatoire;
Comput **r. access file** fichier *m* à accès aléatoire; *Comput* **r. access memory** mémoire *f*
vive; *Mktg* **r. check** contrôle *m* par sonda-
ge(s); *Comput* **r. error** erreur *f* aléatoire; **r. kil-
lings** tuerie *f* aveugle *ou* au hasard; *Mktg* **r.
sample** échantillon *m* aléatoire; *Mktg* **r.
sampling** échantillonnage *m* aléatoire; *Mktg*
r. selection sélection *f* au hasard; *Math* **r. variable** variable *f* aléatoire; **r. violence** violence *f* aveugle

randomize ['rændəmaɪz] **VT** randomiser

randy ['rændɪ] **ADJ** *Br Fam* émoustillé, allumé; **to get** *or* **become r.** commencer à s'exciter; **to make sb r.** allumer qn; **to be feeling
r.** être excité; **he's a r. devil** c'est un chaud
lapin

ranee ['rɑːnɪ] **N** rani *f*

RANGE [reɪndʒ]		
N portée **1**	▪ échelle **3**	▪ étendue **4**
▪ gamme **5**		
VT ranger **1**	▪ parcourir **2**	
VI aller de ... à **1**	▪ parcourir **2**	

N 1 *(of missile, telescope, weapon)* portée *f*;
(of car, plane) autonomie *f*, *Mil* **out of r.** hors
de portée (de tir); *Mil* **within r.** à portée de tir;
at point blank r. à bout portant; **at a r. of
1,000 metres** à une distance de 1000 mètres;
to fire at short/long r. tirer à petite/grande
distance *ou* à courte/longue portée; **short/
medium/long-r. aircraft** court/moyen/long-
courrier *m*; *Met* **short/long-r. forecast** prévisions *fpl* météorologiques à court/long
terme; **to be within hearing r.** être à portée
de voix; **r. of vision** champ *m* visuel

2 *(target practice area)* **rifle** *or* **shooting r.**
Mil champ *m* de tir; *(at funfair)* stand *m* de
tir; **rocket/torpedo r.** zone *f* d'essai de fu-
sées/torpilles

3 *(scale) (of prices, salaries)* échelle *f*, éventail *m*; *(of instrument, voice)* étendue *f*, registre *m*, tessiture *f*; **beyond one's r.** *(of price)*
au-dessus de ses moyens; *(of note)* hors de
son registre; **within one's r.** *(of price)* dans
ses prix; *(of note)* dans son registre; **what is
your price r.?** quel prix voulez-vous mettre?;
a house at the lower end of the r. une maison bas de gamme; **an actor with a wide r.
of expressions** un acteur qui a une gamme
d'expressions très variée

4 *(scope) (of knowledge, research)* étendue

f, *(of inquiry, investigation)* domaine *m*; **she
has a wide r. of interests** elle s'intéresse à
beaucoup de choses

5 *(collection, series) (of colours, feelings,
products)* gamme *f*, *(of patterns, sizes)* choix
m; **the shop carries a wide/limited r. of ...** le
magasin offre un grand choix/choix limité
de ...; **the coat comes in a wide r. of co-
lours/sizes** le manteau existe dans une
gamme variée de couleurs/un grand choix
de tailles; **a top of the r. sports car** une voiture de sport haut de gamme; **to experience
the full r. of emotions** passer par toute la
gamme des émotions

6 *(of hills, mountains)* chaîne *f*

7 *(territory) (of animal, plant)* habitat *m*; *Am
(grazing area)* prairie *f*, pâturages *mpl*

8 *(in surveying)* alignement *m*, direction *f*

9 *(cooker)* **kitchen r.** fourneau *m* de cuisine

VT 1 *(arrange in row) (troops, pupils)* faire
aligner; *(tanks along border)* déployer;
(plates, books) ranger (**along** le long de);
Fig **to r. oneself with sb** se ranger du côté
de qn; *(in political, scientific etc matters)* s'aligner sur la position de qn; *Fig* **to r. oneself
against sb** s'opposer à qn; **the forces which
were ranged against them** les forces alliées
contre eux

2 *(travel) (forest, sea)* parcourir, sillonner
(**in search of, looking for** à la recherche de)

3 *(aim) (weapon, telescope)* braquer (**on**
sur)

4 *Am* **to r. cattle** élever du bétail dans la
prairie

VI 1 *(extend) (of ages, colours, marks)* aller
(**from ... to** de ... à); *(of prices, temperatures)* varier (**from ... to** entre ... et); **incomes ranging from £12,000 to £15,000** *or*
between £12,000 and £15,000 revenus *mpl*
de l'ordre de 12 000 à 15 000 livres; **their discussions will r. over a great many topics**
leurs discussions couvriront un grand nombre de sujets

2 *(travel) (of animals, people)* parcourir; *(of
projectiles)* porter (**over a given distance** à
une distance donnée); **these guns r. over
six miles** ces canons ont une portée de six
mil(l)es; **they ranged over a large area**
(were found) leur habitat était très étendu;
(roamed across) ils parcouraient de larges
étendues; *Fig* **his eyes ranged over the audience** il parcourut l'auditoire des yeux

3 *Mil (adjust aim)* régler le tir
▸▸ *Mktg* **r. addition** ajout *m* à la gamme; *Am*
r. cattle bétail *m* élevé dans la prairie; **r. finder** télémètre *m*; **r. finding** télémétrie *f*, **r.
pole** *(surveying instrument)* jalon *m*; **r. rod**
(surveying instrument) jalon; *Mktg* **r. stretching** extension *f* de la gamme

rangefinder ['reɪndʒfaɪndər] **N** télémètre
m

rangeland ['reɪndʒlænd] **N** *Am* prairie *f*

ranger ['reɪndʒər] **N 1** *(in forest, park)* garde
m forestier **2** *Am (State police officer)* ≃ gendarme *m* **3** *Am Mil* ranger *m* **4 R.** *(senior Girl
Guide)* (guide *f*) aînée
▸▸ *Br* **R. Guide** (guide) aînée

ranging ['reɪndʒɪŋ] **ADJ**
▸▸ *Mil* **r. fire** tir *m* de réglage; **r. pole** *(surveying instrument)* jalon *m*; **r. rod** *(surveying
instrument)* jalon

rangy ['reɪndʒɪ] **ADJ** *(thin)* élancé

rani ['rɑːnɪ] **N** rani *f*

rank¹ [ræŋk] **N 1** *(position) (in army, navy)*
grade *m*; *(in society)* rang *m* (social); *Fin (of
debt, mortgage)* rang; *Br* **badge of r.** insigne
m de grade; **officer of high r.** officier *m* supérieur; **to hold the r. of colonel** avoir le grade
de colonel; **to reduce in r.** rétrograder; *Mil*
the ranks les hommes *mpl* (du rang); *Mil*,
Fig **to have risen from the ranks** être sorti
du rang; **to reduce an NCO to the ranks** cas-

ser un sous-officier; **to have served in the ranks** avoir servi comme simple soldat; *Mil* **all ranks** les militaires *mpl* de tous grades; *Br Mil* **officers and other ranks** gradés et simples soldats; **the higher ranks of the civil service** les hauts fonctionnaires; **person of (high) r.** personne de haut rang; **actor/dancer of the first r.** comédien/danseur de premier ordre; *Br* **a Minister of Cabinet r.** un ministre du cabinet; *Fig* **to pull r. (on sb)** faire jouer son grade (avec qn); *Fig* **the ranks of the homeless/unemployed** les rangs des sans-abri/chômeurs

2 *(row) (of trees, on chessboard etc)* rangée *f*, *(of people)* rang *m*; **r. upon r.** *(of objects)* rangée après rangée; *(of people)* rang après rang; **to arrange in ranks** *(objects)* mettre en rangées; *(people)* (faire) mettre en rangs; *Mil* **close ranks!** serrez!; *Mil* **to break/close ranks** rompre/serrer les rangs; *Fig* **to break ranks** se désolidariser (**with** de, d'avec); *Fig* **to close ranks** se montrer solidaire; *Mil* **front r.** premier rang; *Br* **(taxi) r.** station *f* de taxis

vt 1 *(classify) (athlete, book etc)* classer (**among** parmi, au nombre de)

2 *Am (outrank) (in army)* occuper un rang supérieur à; *(in office, organization etc)* être le supérieur de

3 *(arrange in rows) (pieces of game)* mettre en rangées; *(troops)* (faire) mettre en rangs

vi 1 *(occupy position)* compter (**among** parmi); **to r. above sb** être le supérieur de *ou* occuper un rang supérieur à qn; **to r. below sb** occuper un rang inférieur à qn; **to r. equally** être au même niveau (**with** que); **to r. with sb** être du même niveau que qn; **in chess, a castle ranks above a bishop** aux échecs, la tour est plus forte que le fou; **this must** *or* **has to r. as the best/biggest/worst ...** ceci doit être le meilleur/plus grand/pire ...; **a car does not r. high in my order of priorities** une voiture ne vient pas en tête de mes priorités

2 *Fin* **to r. before/after sb** *(of creditor, claimant)* prendre rang *ou* passer avant/après qn; **to r. equally (with sb)** prendre *ou* avoir le même rang (que qn); **to r. after sth** *(of share)* être primé par qch; **to r. before sth** *(of share)* avoir la priorité sur qch

3 *Am Mil (be most senior)* être le plus haut en grade; *Fig* **he doesn't r.** ce n'est pas quelqu'un d'important

rank² **ADJ 1** *Fml (excessive) (vegetation, weeds)* envahissant, luxuriant; **to grow r.** pousser (très) rapidement **2** *(foul-smelling)* fétide, qui sent fort; **to be r. with sweat** sentir fort la sueur; **to smell r.** sentir fort **3** *(absolute)* complet, -ète, absolu; *(ignorance, stupidity, incompetence)* crasse; **he's a r. outsider** *(in competition)* c'est un outsider; **r. beginner** parfait(e) novice *mf*; **r. imposter** fieffé imposteur *m*; **r. injustice** injustice *f* flagrante **4** *Br Fam (worthless)* merdique; **his last film was totally r.!** son dernier film était complètement merdique!

▸ **rank on vt insep** *Am* **to r. on sb** agonir qn d'injures, traiter qn de tous les noms

rank-and-file n 1 *Mil (soldiers)* simples soldats *mpl*; **ten officers and two hundred r.** dix officiers et deux cents hommes **2** *(ordinary members) (in political party, union)* base *f*; **r. feelings/opinions** sentiments/opinions des membres *ou* de la base

rank-and-filer n *(in army)* simple soldat *m*; *(in political party, union)* membre *m* de la base

ranker ['ræŋkər] **n** *Mil (soldier)* simple soldat *m*; *(officer)* officier *m* sorti du rang

ranking ['ræŋkɪŋ] **n** *(classification)* classement *m*; **his r. is number four** il est classé quatrième

adj 1 *Am (authority, economist)* éminent **2** **high/low r.** *(officer)* de haut grade/grade in-

férieur; *(diplomat, official)* de haut rang/ rang inférieur; **a low r. civil servant** un petit fonctionnaire

▸▸ *Am Mil* **r. officer** officier *m* responsable

rankle ['ræŋk(ə)l] **vi** rester sur le cœur; **it rankled with me** je ne l'ai pas digéré; **what they did still rankles with her** elle n'a toujours pas digéré ce qu'ils ont fait

rankness ['ræŋknɪs] **n 1** *Fml (of vegetation)* exubérance *f*, luxuriance *f* **2** *(foul smell)* odeur *f* forte *ou* fétide

ransack ['rænsæk] **vt 1** *(search) (room, drawer)* mettre sens dessus dessous **2** *(pillage) (store, town)* piller, mettre à sac; *(house) (of burglar)* dévaliser

ransom ['rænsəm] **n** *(money)* rançon *f*; **to hold sb to r.** demander une rançon pour la libération de qn; *Fig* **the strikers were holding the country to r.** les grévistes exerçaient un chantage sur le pays

vt *(captive)* racheter

rant [rænt] **vi** déclamer avec véhémence, *Fam* déblatérer (**about, at** contre); **to r. and rave** fulminer, tempêter (**about, at** contre)

▸ **rant on vi** = **rant**

ranting ['ræntɪŋ] **adj** *(style)* déclamatoire; *(speech)* tonitruant

n ranting(s) déclamation *f*; **to listen to sb's r. about sth** écouter qn s'échauffer à propos de qch; **sectarian rantings** propos *mpl* d'un sectarisme hystérique; **r. and raving, rantings and ravings** discours *m* délirant

ranunculus, *pl* **ranunculuses, ranunculi** [ræ'nʌŋkjʊləs, -əsɪz, -aɪ] **n** *Bot* renoncule *f*

rap [ræp] **n 1** *(slight blow)* petit coup *m* sec; **I heard a r. at the door** j'ai entendu frapper à la porte; **to give sb a r. on** *or* **over the knuckles** *(hit)*, *Fig* taper sur les doigts à qn; *Fig* **the saleswoman was given a r. over the knuckles for being rude to a customer** la vendeuse s'est fait taper sur les doigts pour avoir été impolie avec un client

2 *esp Am Sl (accusation, charge)* **he's up on a murder/drugs r.** il est accusé de meurtre/ dans une affaire de drogue; **to beat the r.** échapper à la condamnation; **to take the r. for sth** trinquer pour qch; **you let me take the r. for you** tu m'as laissé trinquer à ta place

3 *Am Fam (conversation, speech)* **don't give me that r.!** raconte pas n'importe quoi!; **r. session** bavardage *m*; **we had a good r. session** on a discuté pendant un bon bout de temps; **he was laying down some r. about the new model** il était en train de faire un baratin sur le nouveau modèle

4 *Fig Fam (small amount)* **he doesn't care** *or* **give a r.** il s'en moque *ou* s'en fiche éperdument **5** *Mus* rap *m*

vt *(-pp-) (strike) (window, door)* frapper à; **to r. sb's knuckles** *or* **sb on** *or* **over the knuckles** *(hit)*, *Fig* taper sur les doigts à qn; *Am* **to r. sb** *(criticize)* éreinter qn

vi 1 **to r. at/on sth** frapper sur *ou* contre qch **2** *Am Fam (talk)* papoter, bavarder

▸▸ *Mus* **r. artist** chanteur, -euse de rap; *Mus* **r. music** rap *m*; *Am Fam* **r. sheet** casier *m* judiciaire

▸ **rap out vt sep 1** *(order, instruction)* lancer **2** **to r. out a message** *(by tapping)* communiquer au moyen de coups

rapacious [rə'peɪʃəs] **adj** rapace

rapaciously [rə'peɪʃəslɪ] **adv** avec rapacité

rapacity [rə'pæsɪtɪ] **n** rapacité *f*

rape¹ [reɪp] **n 1** viol *m*; **to commit r.** violer; *Fig* **the r. of the tropical forests** la destruction des forêts tropicales **2** *Arch (abduction)* enlèvement *m*; **the R. of the Sabine Women** l'enlèvement des Sabines

vt *(person)* violer; *Fig (forest, environment, region)* détruire

▸▸ **r. crisis centre** centre *m* d'accueil pour femmes violées; **r. suite** pièce *f* réservée aux victimes de viols *(dans un commissariat)*; **r. victim** personne *f* violée, victime *f* d'un viol

rape² **n 1** *Bot (crop)* colza *m* **2** *(remains of grapes)* marc *m* (de raisin)

▸▸ **r. oil** huile *f* de colza

rapeseed ['reɪpsiːd] **n** graine *f* de colza

▸▸ **r. oil** huile *f* de colza

raphia ['ræfɪə] **n** *Bot* raphia *m*

adj en raphia

rapid ['ræpɪd] **adj** *(developments, improvement, progress)* rapide; **a r. pulse** un pouls rapide; **r. strides** longues enjambées *fpl*, *Fig* **we are making r. strides towards a cure for cancer** la recherche contre le cancer fait des progrès rapides; **they have had six children in r. succession** ils ont eu six enfants très rapprochés

▸▸ *Mil* **r. deployment force** force *f* d'intervention rapide; **r. eye movement** mouvements *mpl* oculaires rapides; *Mil* **r. reaction force** forces *fpl* d'action rapide

rapid-fire **adj** *Mil* à tir rapide; *Fig (questions, jokes)* qui se succèdent à toute allure

rapidity [rə'pɪdɪtɪ] **n** rapidité *f*

rapidly ['ræpɪdlɪ] **adv** rapidement

rapids ['ræpɪdz] **npl** *Geog* rapides *mpl*; **to shoot the r.** descendre les rapides

rapier ['reɪpɪər] **n** rapière *f*

▸▸ **r. thrust** coup *m* de rapière; **r. wit** esprit *m* acerbe

rapist ['reɪpɪst] **n** violeur *m*, auteur *m* d'un viol/de viols

▸ **rappel down** **vi** *(in mountaineering)* descendre en rappel

rapper ['ræpər] **n** *Mus* chanteur, -euse de rap

rapport [ræ'pɔːr] **n** bons rapports *mpl*, affinités *fpl*; **there was an instant r. between them** ils ressentirent une sympathie immédiate l'un pour l'autre; **he had a r. with his music teacher** il avait des affinités avec son professeur de musique

rapprochement [ræ'prɒʃmɒn] **n** rapprochement *m*; **to effect a r.** se rapprocher (**with sb** de qn)

rapscallion [ræp'skælɪən] **n** *Arch, Hum* garnement *m*

rapt [ræpt] **adj** *(attention, interest)* profond; *(look, smile)* ravi, d'extase; **a r. face** un visage attentif; **there was a r. look on her face as she listened** elle écoutait, l'air très absorbé; **to be r. in contemplation** être plongé dans ses pensées, *Litt* s'abîmer dans la contemplation

raptor ['ræptər] **n** *Orn* rapace *m*

rapture ['ræptʃər] **n** ravissement *m*, extase *f*; **to be in raptures** être ravi *ou* enchanté (**with, over** de); **in raptures of delight** transporté de joie; **he was filled with r. at the thought/the idea** il était en extase à cette pensée/cette idée; **to go into raptures** s'extasier (**over** devant); **he goes into raptures over his new grandchild** il s'extasie *ou* il est en extase devant son dernier petit-enfant; **she went into raptures at the prospect of meeting him** elle est tombée en extase à l'idée de le rencontrer

rapturous ['ræptʃərəs] **adj** *(cries)* d'extase, de ravissement; *(applause)* frénétique; *(reception, welcome)* enthousiaste; **his face was r. with joy** il rayonnait de joie; **they were r. about their daughter's success** le succès de leur fille les rendait fous de joie

rare [reər] **adj 1** *(uncommon)* rare; **very** *or* **extremely r.** très *ou* extrêmement rare, rarissime; **it is r. for him to do that** c'est rare qu'il fasse ça; *Fig* **he's a r. bird** *(strange)* il est bizarre; *Fam* **you're a r. bird in these parts since you got that promotion** vous vous faites rare depuis que vous avez été promu **2** *Culin (meat)* saignant; **medium r.** à point; **very rare** bleu **3** *(lacking oxygen) (air, atmosphere)* raréfié **4** *(exceptional)* rare, exceptionnel; **he has a rare gift** il a un don exceptionnel **5** *(excellent)* super, génial, -aux; **we had a r. night out last night** on a passé une super soirée hier **6** *Fam (extreme)* énorme; **you gave me a r. fright!** tu m'as fait une peur bleue ou une de ces peurs!

▸▸*Chem* **r. earth** terre *f* rare; *Chem* **r. gas** gaz *m* rare

rarebit ['ræbɪt, 'reəbɪt] N *Culin* **Welsh r.** = tranche *f* de pain grillée recouverte de fromage fondu souvent mélangé à de la moutarde et de la bière

rarefied ['reərɪfaɪd] ADJ *(thin) (air, gas)* raréfié; *Fig* **to live in a r. atmosphere** vivre dans un monde à part

rarefy ['reərɪfaɪ] VT *(air, gas)* raréfier

VI *(of air, gas)* se raréfier

rarely ['reəlɪ] ADV rarement; **r. have I** or **I have r. encountered anyone like him** j'ai rarement rencontré quelqu'un comme lui; **she is r. ill** elle est rarement malade, il est rare qu'elle soit malade

rareness ['reənɪs] N *(uncommonness)* rareté *f*

raring ['reərɪŋ] ADJ *(eager)* **r. to start** impatient de commencer; **to be r. to go** *(of person, animal)* trépigner *ou* piaffer d'impatience

rarity ['reərɪtɪ] N *(uncommonness)* rareté *f*; **a fine day is a r. here** une belle journée est un événement rare ici; **wild flowers are becoming (something of) a r.** les fleurs sauvages se font de plus en plus rares

rascal ['rɑːsk(ə)l] N **1** *(child)* coquin, -ine, fripon, -onne; **you little r.!** petit coquin!, petite canaille! **2** *Old-fashioned (scoundrel)* coquin *m*, vaurien *m*

rascally ['rɑːskəlɪ] ADJ *Old-fashioned (behaviour)* de coquin; *(person)* coquin

rase [reɪz] VT = **raze**

rash[1] [ræʃ] N **1** *Med* rougeur *f*, éruption *f* (cutanée); *(caused by allergy)* urticaire *f*, *(caused by chickenpox, measles, scarlet fever)* exanthème *m*, *Fam* boutons *mpl*; **to come out** or **break out in a r.** attraper des boutons; *(because of allergy)* avoir une crise d'urticaire; **strawberries bring me out in a r.** les fraises me donnent de l'urticaire; *Fig* **the very thought of him brings me out in a r.!** rien que de penser à lui ça me donne des boutons! **2** *Fig (of anonymous letters, resignations etc)* vague *f*, épidémie *f*

rash[2] ADJ *(person)* imprudent, téméraire; *(action, words)* imprudent, inconsidéré, irréfléchi; **don't make any r. promises!** ne faites pas de promesses en l'air!; **we decided in a r. moment to …** nous avons décidé dans un moment de folie de …; **that was a bit r. of you** c'était un peu risqué de ta part; *Hum* **don't do anything r., will you?** surtout, ne fais pas de folies!

rasher ['ræʃər] N *Br* tranche *f* de bacon

rashly ['ræʃlɪ] ADV *(to behave, act, speak)* sans réfléchir, imprudemment; *(to agree, decide)* dans un moment de folie

rashness ['ræʃnɪs] N *(of person, action)* imprudence *f*, inconséquence *f*; **I paid for my r.** j'ai payé cher mes imprudences; **the r. of the chairman's statement** la déclaration inconsidérée du président

rasp [rɑːsp] N **1** *(file)* râpe *f* **2** *(sound)* grincement *m*; **the r. in his voice** le ton rauque de sa voix **3** *Scot Fam (abbr* **raspberry***)* framboise *f*

VT**1** *(use file on)* râper; *Fig* **the cat rasped its tongue over my face** le chat m'a léché la figure de sa langue râpeuse; **he rasped his hand over his unshaven chin** il frotta sa main sur son menton râpeux **2** *(say hoarsely)* **to r. (out)** dire d'une voix rauque; **to r. out an answer/a plea** répondre/supplier d'une voix rauque

VI**1** *(make hoarse sound)* **her breath rasped in her lungs** elle avait une respiration sifflante **2** *(be irritating)* **to r. on the ears** écorcher les oreilles; **the constant creaking of the door was rasping on their nerves** le grincement constant de la porte leur portait sur les nerfs

raspberry ['rɑːzb(ə)rɪ] N **1** *(fruit, flavour)* framboise *f* **2** *Fam* **to blow** or **give sb a r.** *(jeer)* siffler qn; **to get a r.** se faire siffler

▸▸**r. bush** framboisier *m*; **r. cane** framboisier; **r. jam** confiture *f* de framboise; **r. tart** tarte *f* à la framboise; **r. vinegar** vinaigre *m* de framboise

rasping ['rɑːspɪŋ] N **1** *(noise)* grincement *m*, crissement *m* **2** *(shaved-off piece of metal)* copeau *m*

ADJ *(noise)* grinçant, crissant; *(voice)* rauque, grinçant

raspings ['rɑːspɪŋz] NPL *Culin (breadcrumbs)* chapelure *f*

Rasta ['rɑːstə] N, ADJ *(abbr* **Rastafarian***)* rasta *mf inv*

Rastafarian [ræstə'feərɪən] N, ADJ rastafari *mf inv*

Rastafarianism [ræstə'feərɪənɪz(ə)m] N rastafarianisme *m*

raster ['ræstər] N trame *f*

▸▸*Comput, Typ* **r. image** image *f* tramée; *Comput, Typ* **r. scan** balayage *m* de trame

rasterize ['ræstəraɪz] VT *Comput, Typ* convertir en mode point à point

rat [ræt] N **1** *(animal)* rat *m*; **to be caught like a r. in a trap** être fait comme un rat; **with her hair all in rats' tails** avec ses mèches collées; *Fig* **I smell a r.** il y a quelque chose de louche; *Am Sl* **I don't give a r.'s ass** je m'en fous pas mal, je m'en balance **2** *Fam Pej (unreliable person)* lâcheur, -euse; **you r.!** salaud!, ordure! **3** *Am Fam Pej (informer)* mouchard, -arde, indic *m* **4** *Fam Pej (strikebreaker)* jaune *mf*, briseur, -euse de grève **5** *Old-fashioned Br Fam* **rats!** *(exclamation of irritation)* zut!

VI **(-tt-)** *Fam Pej (reveal information)* moucharder, cafarder

▸▸*Am Fam* **r. cheese** fromage *m* ordinaire; **r. pack** *(paparazzi)* paparazzi(s) *mpl*; **r. poison** mort-aux-rats *f inv*; **r. race** foire *f* d'empoigne; **r. run** = rue *f* résidentielle empruntée par les automobilistes qui veulent éviter les bouchons aux heures de pointe

▸**rat on** VT INSEP *Fam Pej (person) (to friends, parents etc)* dénoncer; *(to police)* balancer; **to r. on a promise** revenir sur une promesse; **they ratted on our deal** ils nous ont laissé tomber dans cette affaire

▸**rat out** VT SEP *Am Fam* **to r. sb out** balancer qn, moucharder qn

ratable ['reɪtəb(ə)l] ADJ = **rateable**

ratafia [rætə'fɪə] N *(liqueur)* ratafia *m*; *(biscuit)* macaron *m*

▸▸**r. biscuit** macaron *m*

ratan [ræ'tæn] N = **rattan**

rat-arsed [-ɑːst] ADJ *Br Sl (drunk)* rond comme une queue de pelle

rat-a-tat(-tat) [rætə'tæt(-tæt)] N *(on door)* toc toc *m*; *(on drum)* rantanplan *m*; *(of machine gun)* pétarade *f*, *(of typewriter)* tac-tac-tac *m*

VI **(-tt-)** *(on door)* frapper; *(of machine gun)* pétarader

ratatouille [rætə'tuːɪ] N *Culin* ratatouille *f*

ratbag ['rætbæg] N *Sl (obnoxious person)*

con *m*, conne *f*; *Hum* **you r.!** petit saligaud, petite garce!

rat-catcher N chasseur, -euse de rats

ratchet ['rætʃɪt] N *Tech* rochet *m*; *Fig* **this had a r. effect on prices** cela a entraîné une augmentation irréversible des prix

▸▸**r. mechanism** *(dispositif m d')*encliquetage *m*; **r. screwdriver** tournevis *m* à cliquet; **r. wheel** roue *f* à rochet, **r. wrench** clé *f* à rochet

rate [reɪt] N **1** *(of inflation, tax etc)* taux *m*; *Fin* **birth/crime/death r.** taux de natalité/criminalité/mortalité; **pass** or **success/failure r.** *(in exam etc)* pourcentage *m* de réussites/d'échecs; **at the r. of** *(amount)* à raison de; **to be paid at the r. of five pounds an hour** être payé (à raison de) cinq livres de l'heure; **to strike for higher rates of pay** faire la grève pour obtenir une augmentation de salaire; **the r. is 60p in the pound** le taux est de soixante pence par livre

2 *(speed)* vitesse *f*, *Comput, Tel* débit *m*; **the fearful r. of technological advance** le rythme effrayant du progrès technologique; **at the r. of …** au rythme de …; *Fam* **at a r. of knots** à toute allure; **at this r.** à ce rythme-là; *(slow speed)* à ce train-là; **at the r. things are going** du train où vont les choses; *Fig* **at any r.** en tout cas

3 *(price, charge)* tarif *m*; **what are your rates?** *(for hotel room, service)* quels sont vos tarifs *ou* prix?; **to pay the full r.** payer plein tarif

4 *Br Formerly (tax) (usu pl)* **rates** impôts *mpl* locaux; **rates and taxes** impôts et contributions; **rates office** recette *f* municipale

VT **1** *(consider)* considérer *(as* comme); *(classify) (athlete, pianist etc)* classer *(among* parmi); *(evaluate) (pupil, concert, film etc)* évaluer; **I r. him among my closest friends** je le compte au nombre de *ou* le considère comme un de mes amis les plus proches; **to r. sb/sth highly** apprécier beaucoup qn/qch; **to be highly rated** être très apprécié; **how do you r. their chances of winning the contract?** à votre avis, quelles sont leurs chances de décrocher le contrat?; **I r. this restaurant very highly** je trouve ce restaurant excellent; *Br Fam* **I don't r. him** je ne l'apprécie pas beaucoup

2 *(deserve)* mériter; **that performance should r. him third place** cette prestation devrait lui assurer la troisième place; **a battle that didn't r. a mention in the history books** une bataille qui n'a pas mérité d'apparaître dans les livres d'histoire

3 *Br (set amount of taxes on) (property)* établir *ou* calculer le montant des impôts locaux sur; **their house has been rated higher this year** leur maison a été classée dans la tranche supérieure cette année

VI *(be classified)* se classer, être classé *(as* comme); **in terms of efficiency, she rates higher than anyone else** en ce qui concerne l'efficacité, elle bat tout le monde; **to r. with** *(impress)* plaire à, impressionner

▸▸*Mktg* **r. of adoption** *(of product)* taux d'adoption; *Aviat* **r. of climb** vitesse ascensionnelle; *Mktg* **r. of awareness** taux de notoriété; *Fin* **r. band** plage *f ou* fourchette *f* de taux; *Mktg* **r. of churn** taux de clients passés à la concurrence; *Br Formerly* **r. collector** receveur, -euse municipal(e); *Fin* **r. of depreciation** taux d'amortissement; **r. of exchange** cours *m ou* taux de change; **r. of flow** *(of rivers, turbines)* débit *m*; *Fin* **r. of growth** taux d'accroissement *ou* de croissance; *Fin* **r. of increase** taux d'accroissement; *Fin, Econ* **r. of inflation** taux d'inflation; *Mktg* **r. of penetration** taux de pénétration; **r. of production** taux de production; *Br Formerly* **r. rebate** dégrèvement *m* d'impôts locaux; *Mktg* **r. of renewal** taux de renouvellement; *Fin* **r. of return** *(on investment)* taux de rendement; *Fin* **r. of return pricing** fixation *f* de prix au taux de rendement établi; **r. of uptake** taux de succès

-rate [reɪt] SUFF **first/second -r.** de premier/second ordre

rateable ['reɪtəb(ə)l] ADJ *Br Admin (house, property)* imposable
▸▸ **r. value** ≃ valeur *f* locative imposable

rate-cap VT *Br Admin (local authority)* fixer un taux plafond pour les impôts locaux de

rate-capping [-kæpɪŋ] N *Br Admin* plafonnement *m* des impôts locaux

rated ['reɪtɪd] ADJ *Tech (load, speed, voltage)* nominal, -aux

rate-of-return analysis N analyse *f* du rendement

ratepayer ['reɪtpeɪər] N *Br Formerly (local taxpayer)* contribuable *mf* (assujetti(e) aux impôts locaux)

ratfink ['rætfɪŋk] N *Am Pej Sl (obnoxious person)* salaud *m*, ordure *f*

rather ['rɑːðər] ADV **1** *(preferably)* plutôt (**than** que); **I'd r. stay** j'aimerais mieux *ou* je préférerais rester (**than** que); **I would r. that you came** je préférerais que vous veniez; **I'd r. not** je n'y tiens pas; **I'd r. you didn't do it** je préférerais que tu ne le fasses pas; **r. than leave/stay** plutôt que de partir/rester; **anything r. than that** tout sauf ça; **r. you than me!** plutôt toi que moi!; **accept? I'd r. die!** accepter? plutôt mourir!
2 *(more precisely)* **or r.** ou plutôt, ou pour être plus précis
3 *(fairly)* plutôt, assez; *(to a degree)* un peu; **she's a r. *or* r. a beautiful woman** elle est plutôt belle femme; **she is r. plain** elle n'est pas très jolie; **r. a lot of people** pas mal de monde; **I r. think you know him** je crois bien *ou* il me semble que vous le connaissez; **it tastes r. like a pear** *(but I know it's not)* ça rappelle le goût de la poire; *(I'm guessing)* on dirait de la poire; **I am r. inclined to agree with you** je suis plutôt de votre avis; **I r. liked it** ça m'a assez *ou Fam* pas mal plu; **it's r. nice** c'est bien, *Fam* c'est pas mal!; **r. more tired** un peu plus fatigué (**than** que) VOIR GRAMMAIRE A5
4 ['rɑːðɜː] *Old-fashioned (certainly) (when accepting offer)* oui alors, et comment; *(when answering question)* et comment

ratification [rætɪfɪ'keɪʃən] N *(by government)* ratification *f*, *(by sports authorities)* homologation *f*

ratify ['rætɪfaɪ] VT *(treaty)* ratifier; *(record)* homologuer; **to r. a contract** approuver un contrat

ratine [ræ'tiːn] N *Tex* ratine *f*

rating ['reɪtɪŋ] N **1** *(classification)* classement *m* **2** *(evaluation) (of employee, student etc)* appréciation *f*, *(of candidates, politicians)* cote *f* de popularité; *(for credit)* notation *f* **3** *TV* **the ratings** l'indice *m* d'écoute, le taux *m* d'audience, le taux d'écoute; **to boost the ratings** améliorer l'indice d'écoute; **to stand high in the ratings** avoir un indice d'écoute élevé; **ratings success** succès *m* d'audience; **ratings war** guerre *f* de l'audimat®, course *f* à l'audimat® **4** *Br Admin (of property) (setting of tax)* calcul *m* du montant des impôts locaux; *(tax)* montant *m* des impôts locaux **5** *Br (sailor)* matelot *m*; **the ratings** les matelots et gradés
▸▸ **r. agency** agence *f* de notation *ou* de rating; *Am Mil* **r. badge** insigne *m* de grade; *Mktg* **r. scale** *(in market research)* échelle *f* de classement; *Cin* **r. system** = système *m* de classement des films en fonction de l'âge du public autorisé

ratio, *pl* **ratios** ['reɪʃɪəʊ, -əʊz] N *(proportion,*

relationship) proportion *f*, rapport *m*; **in a r. of 25 to 1** dans une proportion *ou* un rapport de 25 pour 1; **in direct r.** directement proportionnel, en rapport direct (**to** avec), en raison directe (**to** de); **the school has a teacher-pupil r. of 1 to 10** l'école a un rapport professeur-élève de 1 pour 10

ratiocination [rætɪɒsɪ'neɪʃən] N *Fml* raisonnement *m*

ration ['ræʃən, *Am* 'reɪʃən] N *(of bread, sugar etc)* ration *f*; **you've had your r. of TV for this evening** tu as eu ta dose de télévision pour ce soir; **rations** *(food supplies)* provisions *fpl*; **to be on short rations** avoir des rations réduites; **to put sb on short rations** réduire les rations de qn; **full rations** rations complètes; *Mil* **to draw rations** toucher sa ration; *Am Mil* **C rations** vivres *mpl*; *Br Mil* **iron rations** vivres de réserve
VT *(bread, sugar etc)* rationner; **I was rationed to …** ma ration était de …; **she rations herself to one film a week** elle se limite à un film par semaine; **I'll r. you to an hour's television a day** je ne t'autoriserai à regarder la télévision qu'une heure par jour
▸▸ **r. book** carte *f* de rationnement; **r. card** carte de rationnement

rational ['ræʃənəl] ADJ **1** *(sensible) (behaviour, person)* raisonnable, sensé; **it seemed like the r. thing to do** il me semblait que c'était ce qu'il y avait de plus logique à faire **2** *(sane)* rationnel; *(lucid)* lucide; **to be quite r.** avoir toute sa tête **3** *(based on or using reason) (decision)* sensé; *(thought)* rationnel; *(animal, creature)* doué de raison; **she is not quite r. when the subject of divorce comes up** elle ne pense pas très clairement lorsqu'on parle de divorce **4** *Math (number)* rationnel

rationale [ræʃə'nɑːl] N *(reasoning)* raisonnement *m* (**for** de); *(written or spoken)* exposé *m* raisonné; **what's the r. for the decision?** comment peut-on expliquer cette décision?

rationalism ['ræʃənəlɪz(ə)m] N rationalisme *m*

rationalist ['ræʃənəlɪst] ADJ, N rationaliste *mf*

rationalistic [ræʃənə'lɪstɪk] ADJ rationaliste

rationality [ræʃə'nælɪtɪ] N *(of decision, thought)* rationalité *f*

rationalization [ræʃənəlaɪ'zeɪʃən] N **1** *(of action, behaviour etc)* justification *f*, rationalisation *f* (**of** de) **2** *Br Ind (of company etc)* rationalisation *f*

rationalize ['ræʃənəlaɪz] VT **1** *(action, behaviour, dislike, fear etc)* justifier, rationaliser, trouver une explication logique *ou* rationnelle à **2** *Br Ind (company etc)* rationaliser
VI *(do)* **stop rationalizing!** arrête de chercher des excuses!

rationally ['ræʃənəlɪ] ADV **1** *(sensibly)* raisonnablement **2** *(sanely)* rationnellement **3** *(using reason) (to decide, think)* rationnellement

rationing ['ræʃənɪŋ, *Am* 'reɪʃənɪŋ] N *(of bread, sugar etc)* rationnement *m* (**of** de); **(food) r.** rationnement alimentaire

ratlin(e) ['rætlɪn] N *Naut* enfléchure *f*

ratrack ['rætræk] N *Ski* ratrack *m*

rat-tail N *(file)* lime *f*) queue-de-rat *f*, *pl* (limes) queues-de-rat

rattan [ræ'tæn] N *Bot* rotang *m*; *(substance)* rotin *m*; **r. furniture** meubles *mpl* en rotin

rat-tat N, VI = **rat-a-tat(-tat)**

ratted ['rætɪd] ADJ *Br Sl (drunk)* bourré comme un coing, pété à mort; **to get r.** se péter, se torcher

ratteen [ræ'tiːn] N *Tex* = **ratine**

ratter ['rætər] N *(dog)* ratier *m*

rattiness ['rætɪnɪs] N *Br Fam (irritability)* irritabilité *f*

rattling ['rætɪŋ] N **to go r.** faire la chasse aux rats

rattle ['ræt(ə)l] N **1** *(for baby)* hochet *m*; *(on pram)* boulier *m*; *(for sports fan)* crécelle *f*; *(of snake)* sonnette *f* **2** *(noise) (of bottles, chains, coins, keys)* cliquetis *m*; *(in engine)* bruit *m* (de ferraille); *(of gunfire, hailstones)* crépitement *m*; *(of door, window)* vibration *f*; **(death) r.** râle *m*
VI *(make noise)* faire du bruit; *(of bottles)* cliqueter, s'entrechoquer; *(of chains, coins, keys)* cliqueter; *(of door, window)* vibrer; *(of engine)* faire un bruit de ferraille; *(of gunfire, hailstones)* crépiter; **the door rattled in the wind** le vent faisait vibrer la porte
VT **1** *(make noise with) (box)* secouer; *(bottles)* entrechoquer; *(chains, coins, keys)* faire du bruit avec; *(door, window)* ébranler, faire vibrer **2** *Fam (make nervous) (person)* démonter, ébranler, faire perdre son sang froid à; **to get rattled** perdre son sang froid; **don't get rattled!** pas de panique!; **we got them rattled** on a semé la panique parmi eux; **she was badly rattled by the news** la nouvelle l'a beaucoup secouée *ou* l'a complètement démontée; **to be easily rattled** être facilement démonté
▸ **rattle along** VI **1** *(move noisily) (of car, train)* rouler dans un bruit de ferraille **2** *(move quickly) (in car, train)* rouler à toute allure
▸ **rattle around** VI **he's been rattling around in that enormous house since his wife died** il est perdu dans cette grande maison depuis la mort de sa femme
▸ **rattle away** VI *(talk rapidly)* jacasser
▸ **rattle down** VI *(of stones etc)* tomber avec fracas
▸ **rattle off** VT SEP *(lines, recitation etc)* débiter
▸ **rattle on** VI *(speak at length)* ne pas arrêter de parler (**about** de)
▸ **rattle through** VT INSEP *(homework, task etc)* expédier

rattlebrain ['ræt(ə)lbreɪn] N *Old-fashioned Fam (foolish person)* cervelle *f* d'oiseau, tête *f* de linotte

rattlesnake ['ræt(ə)lsneɪk], *Am* **rattler** ['rætlər] N serpent *m* à sonnette, crotale *m*

rattletrap ['ræt(ə)ltræp] N *Old-fashioned Fam (car)* vieille guimbarde *f ou* bagnole *f*

rattling ['ræt(ə)lɪŋ] N = **rattle** N 2
ADJ **1** *(noisy)* bruyant; **r. noise** cliquetis *m* **2** *(fast)* rapide; **to set a r. pace** imposer un rythme très rapide; *(in race)* mener à une cadence rapide
ADV *Old-fashioned (extremely)* **we had a r. good time** on s'est drôlement amusés; **this book is a r. good read** ce livre est vraiment formidable

rat-trap N **1** *(for animals)* piège *m* à rats, ratière *f* **2** *Am (rundown building)* taudis *m*

ratty ['rætɪ] ADJ **1** *Br Fam (irritable)* irritable, grincheux; *(annoyed)* irrité, grincheux; **to get r.** *(of adult)* prendre la mouche; *(of child)* devenir grognon **2** *Am Fam (shabby) (building, clothes)* miteux

raucous ['rɔːkəs] ADJ **1** *(hoarse)* rauque; **r. voice** voix *f* rauque *ou* éraillée **2** *(loud, rowdy)* **r. laughter** rires *mpl* gras; **a r. party** une soirée tapageuse *ou* bruyante; **things got a bit r. as the evening wore on** la soirée est devenue de plus en plus bruyante

raucously ['rɔːkəslɪ] ADV **1** *(to shout etc)* d'une voix rauque **2** *(to celebrate)* bruyamment, de façon tapageuse

raucousness ['rɔːkəsnɪs] N **1** *(hoarseness)* raucité *f* **2** *(rowdiness)* **the r. of the party**

was not to his liking il n'aimait pas le côté tapageur *ou* bruyant de la soirée

raunch(iness) [rɔːntʃ, ˈrɔːntʃɪnɪs] N *Fam* **1** *(of joke, song)* grivoiserie f **2** *(of dance, voice)* sensualité f

raunchy [ˈrɔːntʃɪ] ADJ *Fam* **1** *(joke, song)* *(dirty)* cochon; *(in more light-hearted way)* grivois; **that's much too r. for our viewers** c'est beaucoup trop grivois pour nos téléspectateurs **2** *(sexy)* *(dance, voice)* sexy *inv*; **there is something a little r. about her** elle a un petit quelque chose de sexy

ravage [ˈrævɪdʒ] N *(damage)* *(caused by alcohol, disease, grief, time etc)* *(usu pl)* **ravages** ravages *mpl*
▶ VT *(destroy)* *(crops, region)* ravager, dévaster; *(person)* ravager; **the invading army ravaged the land** l'armée ennemie a mis le pays à feu et à sang; **ravaged face** visage *m* ravagé

rave [reɪv] N **1** *Fam (praise)* éloge *m* enthousiaste; *Br Fam* **to have a r. about sb/sth** parler avec beaucoup d'enthousiasme de qn/ qch; **r. notice** *or* **review** critique f *ou* revue f dithyrambique **2** *(party)* rave f
▶ VI **1** *(be delirious)* délirer **2** *(talk nonsense)* divaguer, délirer (**about** à propos de); **to r. (on)** *(rage)* tempêter (**about, at** contre); **to r. at** *or* **against sb** s'emporter contre qn, être *ou* se mettre en colère contre qn **3** *Fam* **to r. about sb/sth** *(praise)* ne pas tarir d'éloges sur qn/qch, faire l'éloge de qn/qch

raven [ˈreɪv(ə)n] N *(bird)* corbeau *m*
▶ ADJ *(colour)* (noir comme du) jais, de jais; **a r.-haired beauty** une beauté aux cheveux noir corbeau *ou* de jais

ravening [ˈræv(ə)nɪŋ] ADJ *(hungry)* vorace; *Hum* **the r. hordes** les morfales *mpl*

ravenous [ˈræv(ə)nəs] ADJ *(animal)* vorace; *(person)* affamé; *(appetite)* vorace, féroce; *Fig* **to be r.** avoir une faim dévorante *ou* de loup; *Fig* **to be r. for** *(fame, power)* être assoiffé *ou* avide de

ravenously [ˈræv(ə)nəslɪ] ADV *(to eat)* voracement; **to be r. hungry** avoir une faim dévorante *ou* de loup

raver [ˈreɪvər] N *Br* **1** *Fam (socially active person)* fêtard, -arde, noceur, -euse; **he's a bit of a r.** il est noceur; *(trendy)* il est dans le coup, il est branché **2** *(who goes to raves)* raver *m*

rave-up N *Br Fam (party)* fiesta f, nouba f; **to have a r.** faire la fiesta *ou* nouba; **the neighbours had a right old r. last night** les voisins ont fait une de ces fiestas *ou* noubas hier soir

ravine [rəˈviːn] N ravin *m*

raving [ˈreɪvɪŋ] ADJ ATTRIB **1** *(delirious)* délirant **2** *(angry)* furieux; **a r. lunatic** un fou furieux, une folle furieuse; **I'd have to be a r. lunatic to …** il faudrait que je sois complètement fou pour …; **to be r. mad** *(crazy)* être complètement fou; *Fam (angry)* être furax (**about** au sujet de; **with** contre); *Br Fam* **you are stark r. mad** *or* **bonkers** tu es complètement givré *ou* fêlé; *Fig* **she is a r. beauty** elle est d'une grande beauté; **she is no r. beauty** ce n'est pas une beauté; **to be a r. success** avoir un succès fou
▶ N **1** *(delirium)* délire *m* **2** *(wild talk)* divagation f; **the ravings of a madman** les divagations d'un fou

ravioli [rævɪˈəʊlɪ] N *(pasta)* ravioli *mpl* VOIR GRAMMAIRE A14

ravish [ˈrævɪʃ] VT *Fml* **1** *Lit (delight)* *(person)* enchanter, ravir **2** *(rape)* violenter, violer; *Arch (woman)* *(abduct)* enlever, ravir

ravishing [ˈrævɪʃɪŋ] ADJ *(sight, view)* magnifique, ravissant; **a r. woman, a woman of r. beauty** une femme ravissante *ou* d'une grande beauté

ravishingly [ˈrævɪʃɪŋlɪ] ADV *(to play, sing)* à ravir; **r. beautiful** d'une beauté ravissante

raw [rɔː] ADJ **1** *(uncooked)* *(meat, shellfish, vegetables)* cru
2 *(untreated)* *(sugar, latex, leather)* brut; *(spirits)* pur; *(cotton, linen)* écru; *(silk)* grège, écru; *(sewage)* non traité
3 *(unprocessed)* *(data, statistics)* brut
4 *(inexperienced)* inexpérimenté; **a r. recruit** un bleu
5 *(sore)* *(wound)* à vif; *(skin)* écorché; **her hands were r. with the cold** ses mains étaient bleues à cause du froid; *Fig* **the memory was still r.** le souvenir était encore cuisant *ou* douloureux; *Fig* **my nerves are r.** j'ai les nerfs à vif *ou* à fleur de peau; *Fig* **a r. deal** *(unfair treatment)* traitement *m* injuste; **to give sb a r. deal** être dur avec qn; **he's had a r. deal out of life** il n'a pas été gâté par la vie; **working mothers get a r. deal from the government** les mères qui travaillent sont très défavorisées par le gouvernement; *Fig* **to touch a r. nerve** toucher un point sensible
6 *(unpleasant)* *(climate, weather)* âpre, glacial, -als *ou* -aux; **a r. wind** un vent âpre *ou* pénétrant; **it's a r. day** il fait glacial
7 *Am (frank)* cru, brutal, -aux, réaliste; **the film paints a r. picture of penitentiary life** le film peint la vie carcérale de façon crue *ou* brutale *ou* réaliste
▶ N **life in the r.** la vie telle qu'elle est; **to get** *or* **touch sb on the r.** piquer *ou* toucher qn au vif; *Fam* **in the r.** *(naked)* nu, tout nu, *Fam* à poil
▶▶ **r. edge** *(of material)* bord *m* coupé; **r. material** matière f première; *Fig* **he uses his former colleagues as r. material for his plays** il s'inspire de ses anciens collègues pour ses pièces

rawboned [ˈrɔːbəʊnd] ADJ *(thin and strong-looking)* mince et vigoureux

rawhide [ˈrɔːhaɪd] N **1** *(untreated leather)* cuir *m* brut *ou* vert; **r. bag/belt** sac *m*/ceinture f en cuir vert **2** *(whip)* fouet *m* à lanières

Rawlplug® [ˈrɔːlplʌg] N cheville f, tampon *m*

rawness [ˈrɔːnɪs] N **1** *(inexperience)* *(of recruit etc)* inexpérience f **2** *(soreness)* *(of skin)* écorchure f, éraflure f **3** *(unpleasantness)* *(of climate, weather)* âpreté f, rudesse f, *(of wind)* âpreté f **4** *Am (frankness)* réalisme *m*, brutalité f

ray [reɪ] N **1** *(of light, sun etc)*, *Phys* rayon *m*; *Fig* **that child has brought a r. of sunshine into my life** cet enfant, c'est mon rayon de soleil; *Iron* **you're a real little r. of sunshine, aren't you!** tu as vraiment le mot pour rire, toi! **2** *Fig (of hope, intelligence)* lueur f **3** *(fish)* raie f; **electric r.** torpille f
▶▶ **r. gun** pistolet *m* à rayons

rayon [ˈreɪɒn] N *Tex* rayonne f, **r. dress/shirt** robe f/chemise f en rayonne

raze [reɪz] VT **to r. (to the ground)** *(building)* raser

razor [ˈreɪzər] N rasoir *m*; **electric r.** rasoir électrique; **lady's r.** rasoir pour femme; **r. edge** fil *m* tranchant; *(mountain ridge)* arête f effilée *ou* aiguë; *Fig* **to be (balanced) on a r.'s edge** *(election, match, fate)* être très incertain; **on a r.'s edge** *(in difficulty)* au bord du précipice *ou* du gouffre; **her life was on a r.'s edge for days** sa vie n'a tenu qu'à un fil pendant plusieurs jours; **she gave him a r. slash across the face** elle lui a donné un coup de rasoir au visage
▶▶ **r. blade** lame f de rasoir; *Am Zool* **r. clam** couteau *m* à rasoir; **r. cut** *(hairstyle)* coupe f au rasoir; *Am* **r. ribbon** barbelés *mpl* tranchants; **r. wire** barbelés tranchants

razorback [ˈreɪzəbæk] N **1** *(whale)* rorqual *m* **2** *Am (wild pig)* cochon *m* sauvage

razorbill [ˈreɪzəbɪl] N *(bird)* petit pingouin *m*

razor-cut VT *(hair)* couper au rasoir

razor-sharp ADJ *(knife)* coupant comme un rasoir; *Fig (intelligence, mind)* vif; *(wit, reply)* acerbe

razor-shell N *Br (shellfish)* couteau *m*, solen *m*

razz [ræz] VT *Am Fam (tease)* taquiner, railler, tourner en ridicule

razzamatazz [ˈræzəmətæz] N = **razzmatazz**

razzle [ˈræz(ə)l] N *Br Fam* **to be** *or* **go on the r.** faire la bringue *ou* la fête *ou* la nouba

razzle-dazzle N *Fam (flashy display)* tape-à-l'œil *m inv*; clinquant *m*; *Br* **to be** *or* **go on the r.** faire la bringue *ou* la fête *ou* la nouba

razzmatazz [ˈræzmətæz] N *Fam (flashy display)* tape-à-l'œil *m inv*; clinquant *m*

R & B [ɑːrənˈbiː] N *Mus (abbr* **rhythm and blues***)* rhythm and blues *m*

RC [ɑːˈsiː] N, ADJ *Rel (abbr* **Roman Catholic***)* catholique *mf*

RCMP [ɑːsiːemˈpiː] N *Can (abbr* **Royal Canadian Mounted Police***)* GRC f

R & D [ɑːrənˈdiː] N *(abbr* **research and development***)* recherche f et développement; **R. department** bureau *m* d'études; **R. director** directeur, -trice de recherche et développement; **R. expenditure** dépenses *fpl* pour la recherche et le développement

Rd *abbr* **Road**

RDA [ɑːdiːˈeɪ] N *(abbr* **recommended daily allowance***)* recommandation f quotidienne officielle *(en vitamines, sels, minéraux etc)*

RDBMS [ɑːdiːbiːemˈes] N *Comput (abbr* **relational database management system***)* SGBDR *m*

RDS [ɑːdiːˈes] N *(abbr* **radio data system***)* RDS *m*

re¹ [reɪ] N *Mus* ré *m*

re² [riː] PREP *(with reference to)* *(at top of letter)* objet *m*; *(in body of letter etc)* en référence à, suite à
▶ N *Law* **(in) re Martin v Thomas** dans l'affaire Martin contre Thomas

re- [riː-] PREF **1** *(before consonant)* re-, ré-; **rebaptize** rebaptiser; **to reheat** réchauffer **2** *(before vowel)* r-, ré-; **to reassure** rassurer; **to readjust** rajuster, réajuster

REACH [riːtʃ]

N	portée **1, 5** ▪ extension **2**
VT	arriver à **1, 3** ▪ atteindre **1, 2**
	▪ parvenir à **1** ▪ joindre **2**
VI	s'étendre

N **1** *(accessibility)* atteinte f, portée f; **beyond the r. of the authorities** à l'abri des *ou* hors de la portée des autorités; **he was beyond the r. of human help** on ne pouvait plus rien faire pour lui; **a subject beyond my r.** une matière qui dépasse mon entendement; **out of r.** *(object)* hors de portée; **I'll be out of r. for a week** on ne pourra pas me contacter pendant une semaine; **keep out of the r. of children** *(instruction on medicine bottles, plastic bags etc)* ne pas laisser à la portée des enfants; **within r. of** à portée de; *(near)* à proximité de, proche de; **within arm's r.** à portée de la main; **within easy r.** *(object)* à portée de la main; *(banks, shops etc)* facilement accessible; **within everyone's r.** *(affordable)* à la portée de tous *ou* de toutes les bourses; **fifty pounds for a meal is not within my r.** je ne peux pas me permettre de mettre cinquante livres dans un repas
2 *(length of arm)* extension f, *Boxing* allonge f; **he has a longer r. than any of the other contenders** il a la meilleure allonge de tous ses concurrents
3 *(action)* **she made a r. for the gun** elle étendit la main pour prendre le revolver

4 (*area, region*) (*of river*) partie *f*; **the upper reaches of a river** le cours supérieur d'une rivière; **in the further reaches of the empire** au fin fond de l'empire

5 *TV etc* (*audience size*) portée *f*

VT 1 (*arrive at*) (*conclusion, destination*) arriver à; (*goal, height*) atteindre; (*of letter, news, parcel*) parvenir à; **to r. (an) agreement** aboutir à un accord (**on** sur); **to r. a decision** prendre une décision; **to r. a ceiling** (*of imports, wages*) plafonner; **to r. the end of one's journey** arriver au bout de son voyage; **which page have you reached?** à quelle page en es-tu?; **it has reached my ears that ...** j'ai entendu dire *ou* appris que ...; **production has reached rock bottom** *or* **an all time low** la production est descendue à son niveau le plus bas; **unemployment is reaching the two million mark** le nombre de chômeurs atteint le seuil des deux millions

2 (*gain access to*) (*beach, house*) atteindre; (*contact*) joindre, contacter; **to r. sb by telephone** joindre qn par/*ou* au téléphone; **easy/difficult to r.** (*house etc*) facile/difficile d'accès; **the town could only be reached by sea** on ne pouvait accéder à *ou* atteindre la ville que par la mer; *Fig* **nobody can r. him** (*get through to him*) on ne peut pas communiquer avec lui; **the adverts are intended to r. the over-40s** les publicités sont destinées aux *ou* sont à l'intention des plus de 40 ans; **to r. a younger/wider audience** toucher un public plus jeune/large

3 (*stretch as far as*) (*one's shoulder, waist*) arriver (jusqu')à; **can you r. the ceiling?** est-ce que vous pouvez toucher le plafond?; **are the curtains long enough to r. the floor?** est-ce que les rideaux sont suffisamment longs pour descendre jusqu'au sol?

4 (*hand*) **to r. sb sth** passer qch à qn

5 *Am Fam* (*corrupt*) (*witness*) corrompre, suborner

VI (*extend*) (*of forest, property etc*) s'étendre (**to** jusqu'à); (*of noise, voice*) porter (**to** jusqu'à); **as far as the eye can r.** à perte de vue; **can you r.?** est-ce que tu peux y arriver?; **to r. for sth** *or* **to get sth** allonger *ou* étendre le bras pour prendre qch; **the policeman reached for his gun** l'agent de police mit la main sur son revolver; *Fig* **to r. for the sky** *or* **the stars** être très ambitieux, viser très haut; *Am* **r. (for the sky)!** haut les mains!; **to r. into** (*drawer, pocket*) mettre la main dans (**for** pour prendre)

▸ **reach across** **VI** allonger *ou* (é)tendre le bras

▸ **reach back** **VI** *Fig* (*of records, files etc*) remonter (**to** à)

▸ **reach down** **VI** (*of coat, curtains, hair etc*) descendre (**to** jusqu'à); (*of person*) allonger *ou* (é)tendre le bras (**for** pour prendre) **VT SEP** (*object*) (*from cupboard, shelf*) descendre; **can you r. me down that saucepan?** est-ce que tu peux me passer la casserole là-haut?; **he reached it down to her** il le lui a passé

▸ **reach out** **VI** allonger *ou* (é)tendre le bras (**for** pour prendre) **VT SEP** **he reached out his hand for the glass** il tendit la main vers le verre

▸ **reach over** **VI** = **reach across** **VT SEP** **to r. sb over sth** passer qch à qn; **could you r. me over the salt?** est-ce que tu peux me passer le sel?

▸ **reach up** **VI** (*of person*) lever le bras (**for** pour prendre); (*of snow, water*) monter (**to** jusqu'à); **her boots reached halfway up her legs** ses bottes lui montaient à mi-jambe **VT SEP** **to r. sb up sth** passer qch à qn

---

reachable ['ri:tʃəb(ə)l] **ADJ** (*place, object*) accessible; (*goal, objective*) que l'on peut atteindre; **put it where it won't be r. by the kids** mets-le hors de portée des enfants

reach-me-down **N** *Br Old-fashioned* vieux vêtement *m*

react [rɪˈækt] **VI** réagir (**against** contre; **on** sur; **to** à); **to be slow to r.** (*of chemical*) avoir une réaction lente; (*of person*) être lent à réagir; **he reacted well to the treatment** il a bien réagi au traitement; **an acid can r. with a base to form a salt** un acide et une base peuvent réagir ensemble et former un sel **VT** *Chem* faire réagir (**sth with sth** qch avec qch)

reactance [rɪˈæktəns] **N** *Elec* réactance *f*

reactant [rɪˈæktənt] **N** *Chem* réactif *m*

reaction [rɪˈækʃən] **N 1** (*response*) (*of chemical, person*) réaction *f*; **to show no r.** rester sans réaction; **what was her r.?** quelle a été sa réaction?, comment a-t-elle réagi?; **in r. to** en *ou* par réaction contre; *Med* **if there is any adverse r.** en cas d'effets indésirables; **the patient's adverse r.** le fait que le malade ait mal réagi **2** *Pol Pej* **the forces of r.** les réactionnaires *mpl*, *Fam* les réacs *mpl*

▸ *Aviat* **r. engine** moteur *m* à réaction, réacteur *m*; *Aviat* **r. motor** moteur *m* à réaction, réacteur; *Cin, TV* **r. shot** plan *m* de coupe; **r. time** temps *m* de réaction; *Tech* **r. turbine** turbine *f* à réaction

reactionary [rɪˈækʃən(ə)rɪ] **ADJ, N** *Pol* réactionnaire *mf*; **the reactionaries** les réactionnaires *mpl*, *Fam* les réacs *mpl*

reactivate [rɪˈæktɪveɪt] **VT 1** (*start again*) (*group, club*) reconstituer, reformer **2** *esp Am Mil* (*return to active status*) (*ship*) remettre en service

reactive [rɪˈæktɪv] **ADJ** *Chem, Phys* réactif; *Elec* (*load, power*) réactif, déwatté

▸ *Elec* **r. current** courant *m* réactif; *Mktg* **r. marketing** marketing *m* réactif

reactivity [rɪækˈtɪvɪtɪ] **N** *Chem, Phys* réactivité *f*

reactor [rɪˈæktər] **N** *Chem* réacteur *m*; *Nucl* réacteur atomique

read[1] [ri:d] **N** **to have a r.** faire un peu de lecture; *Fam* **just have a r. of this!** (*expression of astonishment, disgust*) lis-moi ça!; *Br Fam* **can I have a r. of your magazine?** est-ce que je peux jeter un coup d'œil à votre magazine?; *Fam* **this book's a good r.** ce livre est agréable à lire; **I've always enjoyed a good r.** j'ai toujours aimé avoir un bon livre à lire; **he was having a quiet r.** il lisait tranquillement; *Theat* **we'll have a r. through this afternoon** nous lirons la pièce cet après-midi

▸ *Comput* **r. error** erreur *f* de lecture; *Comput* **r. head** tête *f* de lecture

---

READ[2] (*pt, pp* **read** [red])

VT	lire **1–4** ■ interpréter **2** ■ étudier
	5 ■ indiquer **6**
VI	lire **1, 2**

VT 1 (*newspaper, book, Braille etc*), *Comput* lire; (*writing, score*) lire, déchiffrer; **have you got anything to r.?** avez-vous de quoi lire *ou* quelque chose à lire?; **have you got enough to r.?** avez-vous assez de lecture?; **to r. sth over** *and* **over (again)** lire et relire qch; **I r. Italian** je lis *ou* je peux lire l'italien; **to r. Proust in the original** lire Proust dans le texte; **her novels have been r.** [red] **and enjoyed by millions** ses romans ont été lus et appréciés par des millions de personnes; **to be widely r.** [red] (*of magazine, author etc*) être très lu (**by** parmi); (*of scholar etc*) avoir beaucoup lu; **she is widely r.** [red] **in history** elle a lu beaucoup de livres d'histoire; **for 'least', r. 'lease'** il faut lire 'lease' au lieu de 'least'; **do you r. me?** *Radio* est-ce que vous me recevez?; *Fig* est-ce que tu me comprends?; **I r. you loud and clear** *Radio* je vous reçois cinq sur cinq; *Fig* oui, oui j'ai compris; **he was reading my lips** il lisait sur mes lèvres; *Fig* **r. my lips!** (*believe me*) je te jure!; *Admin* **r.** [red] **and approved** (*stamp on document*) lu et approuvé; *Fig* **to take sth as r.** [red] (*evident*) considérer qch comme allant de soi; (*agreed upon*) considérer qch comme entendu; *Admin* **to take the minutes as r.** [red] passer sur la lecture du procès-verbal

2 (*interpret*) (*situation, sb's actions etc*) interpréter; **to r. sb's mind** *or* **thoughts** lire dans les pensées de qn; **to r. the future** lire *ou* prédire l'avenir; **she can r. him like a book** elle sait toujours ce qu'il pense; *Sport* **to r. the game well** anticiper sur les mouvements de l'adversaire; **he r.** [red] **that well** (*of sportsman*) il a bien anticipé; **I r.** [red] **it as 24, but it was actually 224** j'ai vu 24 mais en fait c'était 224; **to r. the temperature/a thermometer** lire la température/un thermomètre; **to r. an electricity meter** relever un compteur d'électricité; **to r. sb's palm** *or* **hand** lire les lignes de la main de qn

3 (*say aloud*) (*letter, poem*) lire (à haute voix); **to r. sb sth, to r. sth to sb** lire qch à qn; **r. me that last bit again** relis-moi le dernier passage; **to r. a child a bedtime story** lire une histoire à un enfant pour qu'il s'endorme; *Rel* **to r. the lesson** lire un passage de l'Évangile; *Fig* **to r. sb a lesson** *or* **a lecture** faire la leçon à qn; **to r. a paper at a conference** présenter un exposé à une conférence; **to r. the news** *Radio* lire les informations; *TV* présenter le journal; *Law* **to r. a will** exécuter la lecture d'un testament

4 **to r. oneself to sleep** lire jusqu'à ce qu'on s'endorme; **he r.** [red] **me to sleep** il m'a fait la lecture jusqu'à ce que je m'endorme

5 *Br Univ* (*study*) (*French, history etc*) étudier; **to r. law/medicine** faire son droit/sa médecine

6 (*show*) (*of measuring instrument*) indiquer; **the inscription on the monument reads ...** on peut lire sur le monument ...; **the sign on the door r.** [red] **No Entry** sur l'écriteau on pouvait lire 'Défense d'entrer'

VI 1 lire; **she taught her daughter (how) to r.** elle a appris à lire à sa fille; **to r. to sb** faire la lecture à qn; **I'm very fond of reading** j'aime beaucoup lire *ou* la lecture *ou Fam* bouquiner; **to r. aloud** lire à haute voix; **r. quietly to yourselves** lisez en silence; **to r. about sb/ sth** lire quelque chose sur qch/qn; **what are you reading about?** qu'est-ce que tu lis?; **we r.** [red] **of his death in the newspaper** nous avons appris sa mort dans le journal

2 (*interpret*) **to r. between the lines** lire entre les lignes; **she r.** [red] **in the cards that I would be famous** elle a lu dans les cartes que je serais célèbre

3 *Br Univ* **to r. for a degree** préparer un diplôme; **to r. for the Bar** faire des études de droit

4 (*be worded*) **to r. well/badly** (*of text*) être bien/mal écrit; **his text reads like a translation** son texte sent la traduction; **the telegram reads as follows** le télégramme est libellé comme suit; **Arabic reads from right to left** l'arabe se lit de droite à gauche; **her life story reads like a fairytale** sa vie ressemble à un conte de fées

▸ **read in** **VT SEP** *Comput* (*data*) emmagasiner, lire et stocker en mémoire

▸ **read into** **VT SEP** **to r. sth into sth** voir qch dans qch; **don't r. too much into what she says** ne donne pas à ce qu'elle dit plus de signification que ça n'en a; **you're reading far too much into it** tu interprètes beaucoup trop

▸ **read off** **VT SEP** (*names etc*) énumérer (**from** sur)

▸ **read on** **VI** (*continue to read*) now **r. on** lisez la suite; **to r. on from ...** lire à partir de ...

▸ **read out** VT SEP *(names, list, passage etc)* lire (à haute voix); *Comput (data)* sortir, extraire de la mémoire

▸ **read over** VT SEP *(quickly)* parcourir; *(with special care)* examiner; *esp Am (read again)* relire

▸ **read through** VT SEP *(skim)* parcourir; *(examine closely)* lire en détail, examiner; *Theat* **to r. through a play** faire la lecture d'une pièce

▸ **read up** VT SEP *(subject)* étudier

▸ **read up on** VT INSEP = **read up**

---

readability [riːdəˈbɪlɪtɪ] N *(of book, handwriting)* lisibilité *f*

readable [ˈriːdəb(ə)l] ADJ **1** *(book, style etc)* lisible; **highly** *or* **very r.** d'une lecture très agréable **2** *(legible) (handwriting, disk)* lisible; **not r.** illisible

readdress [riːəˈdres] VT *(forward) (letter)* faire suivre

reader [ˈriːdər] N **1** *(of books, newspapers etc)* lecteur, -trice; *Am (company librarian)* documentaliste *mf*; **she is a great** *or* **an avid r.** c'est une grande liseuse, elle lit beaucoup; **he's not much of a r.** il n'aime pas beaucoup la lecture, il ne lit pas beaucoup; *(proof)* **r.** correcteur, -trice d'épreuves; **publisher's r.** lecteur, -trice dans une maison d'édition **2** *Univ Br* ≃ maître *m* de recherches; *Am* ≃ assistant, -ante, *Can* ≃ chargé, -e de cours **3** *(book) (for teaching reading)* livre *m* de lecture; *(textbook)* livre, manuel *m*; *(anthology)* recueil *m*; **French/geography r.** livre de français/géographie; **a Melville r.** un recueil d'extraits de Melville **4** *(machine)* lecteur *m*

readership [ˈriːdəʃɪp] N **1** *(of magazine, author etc)* lecteurs *mpl*; *(esp of paper)* lectorat *m*; **what is the paper's r.?** combien de personnes lisent le journal? **2** *Br Univ* **she holds a r. in mathematics** elle est maître de recherches en mathématiques

▸▸ **r. survey** étude *f* du lectorat

readies [ˈrediz] NPL *Br Fam (cash)* fric *m*; **£500 in r.** 500 livres en liquide; **I want the r. first** je veux le fric d'abord

readily [ˈredɪlɪ] ADV *(willingly)* de bonne grâce, volontiers; *(easily)* facilement

readiness [ˈredɪnɪs] N **1** *(willingness)* empressement *m* (**to do** à faire) **2** *(agility) (of speech, tongue)* facilité *f* d'expression; *(of mind, wit)* vivacité *f* d'esprit **3** *(preparedness)* **to be in r.** être prêt (**for** pour); **to have everything in r.** avoir tout prêt

reading [ˈriːdɪŋ] N **1** *(action, pastime)* lecture *f*; **r. is not his favourite activity** la lecture n'est pas son passe-temps favori; **I have a lot of r. to catch up on** j'ai beaucoup de retard à rattraper dans mes lectures; **I like a bit of light r.** j'aime bien un livre facile à lire de temps en temps; **his thesis makes (for) boring r.** sa thèse est ennuyeuse à lire; **a young woman of wide r.** une jeune femme très cultivée *ou* érudite *ou* lettrée; *Comput* **r. to disk** lecture *f* sur disque

2 *(saying aloud) (of play, poetry, will)* lecture *f*; *Parl* **first/second/third r.** *(of bill)* première/seconde/troisième lecture

3 *(measurement) (of meter)* relevé *m*; *(by instrument)* indication *f*; **the fuel gauge is giving the wrong r.** la jauge d'essence n'est pas fiable; **to take a barometric/temperature r.** lire le baromètre/le thermomètre

4 *(interpretation) (of facts, situation, character)* interprétation *f*; **this is one of two possible readings of the poem/novel** c'est l'une des deux lectures possibles du poème/roman

ADJ **to have a r. age of ten** lire comme un enfant de dix ans; **she has a r. age well in advance of her years** elle est très en avance

---

sur son âge pour ce qui est de la lecture; **children of r. age** des enfants en âge de lire; **I have a r. knowledge of Arabic** je peux lire l'arabe; **take some r. material** *or* **matter** prends de la lecture *ou* de quoi lire; **the r. public** les lecteurs *mpl*

▸▸ **r. book** livre *m* de lecture; **r. glasses** *(spectacles)* lunettes *fpl* pour lire; *Comput* **r. head** tête *f* de lecture; **r. lamp** lampe *f* de bureau; *(by bed)* lampe de chevet; **r. light** liseuse *f*, **r. list** *(syllabus)* liste *f* des ouvrages au programme; *(for further reading)* liste des ouvrages recommandés; **r. room** salle *f* de lecture **r. speed** *(of child, computer)* vitesse *f* de lecture

readjust [riːəˈdʒʌst] VT *(correct) (prices, wages)* rajuster, réajuster; *(microscope, telescope)* remettre au point; **to r. one's clothing** se rajuster

VI *(of person)* se réadapter (**to** à)

readjustment [riːəˈdʒʌstmənt] N **1** *(of prices, wages)* rajustement *m*, réajustement *m*; **some r. of the telescope is necessary** il faut régler à *ou* de nouveau le télescope **2** *(of person)* réadaptation *f*

read-me ADJ

▸▸ *Comput* **r. document** fichier *m* lisez-moi, ouvrez-moi *m inv*; *Comput* **r. file** fichier lisez-moi, ouvrez-moi *m*

readmission [riːədˈmɪʃən] N *(to club, political party)* réintégration *f* (**to** dans); **to gain r. to a party** réintégrer un parti; **his r. to hospital was seen as a bad sign** le fait qu'il soit réadmis à l'hôpital a été interprété comme un mauvais signe

readmit [riːədˈmɪt] VT *(take in again) (person)* réintégrer (**to** dans); **he was readmitted (to hospital) last night** il a été réadmis à l'hôpital la nuit dernière

read-only ADJ *Comput* (à) lecture seule; **that file is r.** ce fichier est protégé en écriture; **to make a file r.** mettre un fichier en lecture seule

▸▸ **r. disk** *(hard)* disque *m* en lecture seule; *(floppy)* disquette *f* en lecture seule; **r. file** fichier *m* en lecture seule; **r. memory** mémoire *f* morte; **r. mode** mode *m* lecture seule

read-out N *Comput* lecture *f*; *(on screen)* affichage *m*; *(on paper)* sortie *f* papier ou sur imprimante, listing *m*

▸▸ **r. device** unité *f* d'affichage

read-through N *(of script)* lecture *f* du scénario; **to give sth a quick r.** parcourir qch rapidement

readvertise [riːˈædvətaɪz] VT *(job)* repasser une annonce pour

VI **they're readvertising** ils ont repassé l'annonce

readvertisement [riːədˈvɜːtɪsmənt] N deuxième annonce *f*; **this is a r.** *(notice on jobs page)* deuxième annonce d'offre d'emploi

read-write ADJ *Comput*

▸▸ **r. head** tête *f* de lecture-écriture; **r. memory** mémoire *f* lecture-écriture; **r. protection notch** encoche *f* de protection lecture-écriture

ready [ˈredɪ] ADJ **1** *(prepared)* prêt (**to do** à faire; **for sth** pour qch); **to get r.** se préparer, s'apprêter (**to do** à faire; **for sth** à qch); *Old-fashioned* **to make r.** faire des préparations, se préparer (**for** pour); **to get sth r.** préparer qch; **dinner is r.** le dîner est servi, *Fam* à table; **I'm r. if you are, r. when you are** quand tu veux; *Sport* **r.! steady! go!** à vos marques! prêts! partez!; **to get r. for school** se préparer pour aller à l'école; **to get r. for bed** se préparer à aller se coucher; **to get a patient r. for an operation** préparer un malade pour une opération; **to get some food r.** préparer à manger; **to get a room r. for a guest** préparer une chambre pour un invité;

---

r. for delivery livrable; *Com* **r. for shipping** sous palan; **r. for use** prêt à l'usage; **she's r. for anything** elle est prête à tout; **r. to go to press** bon à tirer, BAT; **are you r. to order?** *(in restaurant)* avez-vous choisi *ou* fait votre choix?; **r. to serve** *(food)* prêt à servir, tout prêt; **I'm r. to drop** *(exhausted)* je tombe de fatigue; **r. to hand** sous la main, à portée de (la) main

2 *(willing)* prêt, disposé (**to do** à faire); **she's always r. to help** elle est toujours prête à rendre service

3 *(quick)* prompt, facile; **to have a r. wit** avoir l'esprit prompt *ou* d'à-propos *ou* de repartie; **to be always r. with an answer** avoir la réplique prompte; **you're always a bit too r. with advice** tu donnes toujours trop de conseils; **he's very r. with his fists** il est prompt à se battre; **don't be too r. to condemn him** ne le condamnez pas trop rapidement, ne soyez pas trop prompt à lui jeter la pierre; **a r. source of income** une source de revenu facile; **the story found r. acceptance** l'histoire a été acceptée sans difficulté

N **1** *Fam* **the r.** *(money)* argent *m* liquide; **have you enough of the r. on you?** est-ce que tu as assez de liquide?

2 **the reporter had her notebook at the r.** la journaliste avait son carnet tout prêt; **with camera at the r., she ...** son appareil photo tout prêt, elle ...; **with their guns at the r.** prêts à tirer

VT *(the house)* préparer; **to r. oneself for action** se préparer à l'action

▸▸ **r. meal** plat *m* cuisiné; **r. money** argent liquide; **to pay in r. money** payer en espèces ou en argent liquide; *Br* **r. reckoner** barème *m*

ready- [redɪ-] PREF **r.-cut** précoupé

ready-made ADJ *(clothes)* de prêt-à-porter; *(food)* précuit; *(curtains, excuse, argument, solution)* tout fait; **a r. cake** un gâteau tout fait; *Fig* **to have a r. family** avoir une famille déjà constituée

N *(garment)* vêtement *m* de prêt-à-porter

ready-mix ADJ *(buns, cake etc)* fait à partir d'une préparation; *(concrete)* prémalaxé

ready-to-wear ADJ

▸▸ **r. clothing** prêt-à-porter *m*, *pl* prêts-à-porter

reaffirm [riːəˈfɜːm] VT *(one's loyalty, a belief, one's intentions)* réaffirmer

reafforest [riːəˈfɒrɪst] VT = **reforest**

reafforestation [riːəfɒrɪˈsteɪʃən] N = **reforestation**

Reaganite [ˈreɪɡənaɪt] N partisan *m* de Reagan; **R. budget/programme** budget *m*/programme *m* reaganien

Reaganomics [reɪɡəˈnɒmɪks] NPL *(usu with sing verb)* reaganisme *m*

reagent [rɪˈeɪdʒənt] N *Chem* réactif *m*

REAL [rɪəl] ADJ **1** *(authentic) (diamond, pearl, mother)* vrai; *(gold, leather)* véritable; *(silk, flowers)* naturel; **a r. friend/idiot** un véritable ami/idiot; **a r. disaster/shock** un véritable *ou* vrai désastre/choc; **he's made a r. effort** il a fait un véritable effort, il a fait un effort réel; **that's what I call a r. man!** ça, c'est ce que j'appelle un (vrai) homme; **the r. reason** la vraie raison (**for** pour); **she has no r. feeling for poetry** elle n'a pas le sens de la poésie; **what is his r. name?** quel est son vrai nom?; **he's a r. gentleman** c'est un vrai gentleman; *Fam* **it's the r. McCoy** *or* **thing** c'est du vrai de vrai; **this orange drink is not bad but it's poor stuff compared to the r. thing** cette boisson à l'orange n'est pas mauvaise, mais ça ne vaut pas le vrai jus d'orange; *Fam* **she swears it's the r. thing this time** *(true love)* elle jure que cette fois-ci c'est le grand

amour; *Fam* **this is not a drill, it's the r. thing or for r.** ce n'est pas un exercice, c'est pour de vrai; *Fam* **is that man for r.?** il est pas vrai, ce type!; *Fam* **is that for r.?** c'est vrai?; *Fam* **get r.!** tu délires!
 2 *(actual) (cost, salary, world etc), Math, Phys* réel; **in r. life** dans la réalité *ou* la vie
 ADV *Am Fam (very)* vraiment, très; **a r. fine day** une très belle journée; **that's r. nice of you** c'est vraiment *ou* très gentil de votre part; **I'll see you r. soon** à très bientôt
 N *Phil* **the r.** le réel
 ▸▸*Fin* **r. accounts** comptes *mpl* de valeur; *Br* **r. ale** bière *f* artisanale; *Fin* **r. assets** biens *mpl* immobiliers; **r. estate** *Br Law* biens fonciers; *Am* biens immobiliers; **she works in r. estate** elle travaille dans l'immobilier; *Econ* **r. GDP** PIB *m* réel; *Econ* **r. growth** croissance *f* réelle; *Econ* **r. income** revenu *m* réel; *Rel* **r. presence** présence *f* réelle; *Econ* **r. purchasing power** pouvoir *m* d'achat réel; *Mktg* **r. repositioning** repositionnement *m* réel; **r. salary** salaire *m* réel; **r. tennis** jeu *m* de paume; **to play r. tennis** jouer à la paume; *Fin* **r. terms** termes *mpl* réels; **what does that mean in r. terms?** qu'est-ce que ça signifie au bout du compte?; *Comput* **r. time** temps *m* réel; *Fin* **r. value** valeur *f* effective

real-estate ADJ
 ▸▸**r. agency** agence *f* immobilière; **r. agent** agent *m* immobilier; **r. developer** promoteur *m* immobilier

realign [riːə'laɪn] VT aligner (de nouveau); *Fin (currencies)* réaligner; *Pol* regrouper
 VI s'aligner (de nouveau); *Pol* se regrouper

realignment [riːə'laɪnmənt] N (nouvel) alignement *m*; *Fin* réalignement *m*; *Pol* regroupement *m*
 ▸▸*Fin* **r. of currencies** réalignement monétaire

realism ['rɪəlɪz(ə)m] N *Art, Phil etc* réalisme *m*

realist ['rɪəlɪst] ADJ, N *Art, Phil etc* réaliste *mf*

realistic [rɪə'lɪstɪk] ADJ *(person, proposal)* réaliste; *(style)* plein de réalisme

realistically [rɪə'lɪstɪklɪ] ADV *(to act, behave)* avec réalisme

reality [rɪ'ælɪtɪ] N réalité *f*; **in r.** en réalité; **to bring sb back to r.** ramener qn à la réalité; **they refuse to face the r. of their situation** ils refusent de voir la situation telle qu'elle est; **to become a r.** *(of dream, hope etc)* se réaliser, devenir réalité; **to make a dream/project (a) r.** réaliser un rêve/projet; **the realities of everyday life** les réalités de la vie quotidienne; **it was a r. check for him** ça l'a ramené à la réalité
 ▸▸*Am TV* **r. show** reality show *m*; **r. television** télé-vérité *f*

realizable ['rɪəlaɪzəb(ə)l] ADJ *(plan, project etc), Fin* réalisable
 ▸▸**r. assets** actif *m* réalisable; **r. securities** valeurs *fpl* réalisables

realization [rɪəlaɪ'zeɪʃən] N **1** *(of plan, project etc), Fin* réalisation *f* **2** *(awareness)* prise *f* de conscience; **there is a growing r. that ...** on commence à se rendre compte que ...; **the sudden r. that ... made her weep** elle s'est mise à pleurer quand tout d'un coup elle s'est rendu compte que ...

realize ['rɪəlaɪz] VT **1** *Fin (asset, profit)* réaliser; **to r. a high price** *(of goods)* atteindre un prix élevé; *(of seller)* obtenir un prix élevé; **how much did they r. on the sale?** combien est-ce qu'ils ont gagné sur la vente?; **these shares cannot be realized** il n'y a pas de marché pour ces titres **2** *(make real)* **our worst fears have been realized** nos pires craintes se sont réalisées; **our hopes were realized** nos espoirs se sont réalisés *ou* concrétisés; **he hasn't yet realized his full potential** il n'a

pas encore atteint son maximum **3** *(know, be aware of)* se rendre compte de, réaliser; **I r. that, but ...** je sais bien, mais ... **4** *(become aware of)* se rendre compte de/que, prendre conscience de/que; **we realized that he was blind** nous nous sommes aperçus *ou* rendu compte qu'il était aveugle; **I realized it at the first glance** je m'en suis aperçu *ou* rendu compte au premier coup d'œil
 VI **I'm sorry, I didn't r.** je suis désolé, je ne m'en étais pas rendu compte *ou Fam* je n'avais pas réalisé

really ['rɪəlɪ] ADV **1** *(actually)* vraiment; **things that r. exist** choses qui existent réellement; **that is r. a matter for the manager** c'est là proprement l'affaire du gérant; **is it r. true?** est-ce bien vrai? **2** *(intensifier)* **he r. likes you** il t'aime beaucoup; **you r. must go to** il faut absolument que vous y alliez; **I r. have** *or* **ought to be going** il faut vraiment que j'y aille **3** *(very)* vraiment; **she's r. nice** elle est vraiment sympa
 INT **r.?** vraiment?; **r.!** *(indignation)* vraiment!

realm [relm] N **1** *Fml (kingdom)* royaume *m* **2** *Fig (of dreams, fancy etc)* monde *m*; *(of politics, science etc)* domaine *m*; **within the realms of possibility** dans le domaine du possible; **health is no longer exclusively the r. of doctors** la santé n'est plus l'apanage du médecin

real-time ADJ *(processing, system, control)* en temps réel
 ▸▸**r. clock** horloge *f* (en) temps réel; **r. graphics** graphiques *mpl* en temps réel; **r. management** gestion *f* en temps réel; **r. operating system** système *m* d'exploitation en temps réel; *St Exch* **r. trading** cotation *f* en temps réel

Realtor® ['rɪəltər] N *Am* agent *m* immobilier

realty ['rɪəltɪ] N *Law* biens *mpl* immobiliers, (biens) immeubles *mpl*

ream¹ [riːm] N *(of paper)* rame *f*; *Fam* **to write reams** écrire des pages et des pages; *Fam* **reams of statistics/information** des quantités *fpl* de statistiques/d'informations

ream² VT **1** *Tech (bore) (part)* aléser **2** *Am (squeeze) (lemon)* presser
 ▸ **ream out** VT SEP *Am Sl* **to r. sb out** *(scold)* passer un savon à qn, remonter les bretelles à qn

reamer ['riːmər] N **1** *Tech* alésoir *m* **2** *Am (for lemon)* presse-citron *m inv*

reanimate [riː'ænɪmeɪt] VT *Med* r(é)animer

reap [riːp] VT *(corn, field)* moissonner; *Prov* **he who sows the wind shall r. the whirlwind** qui sème le vent récolte la tempête; *Fig* **to r. the rewards of one's labours** recueillir le fruit de ses travaux; *Fig* **I r. no benefit from it** je n'en retire aucun avantage
 VI moissonner, faire la moisson

reaper ['riːpər] N *(machine)* moissonneuse *f*; *(person)* moissonneur, -euse; *Fig* **the (Grim) R.** la Faucheuse
 ▸▸**r. binder** moissonneuse-lieuse *f*, *pl* moissoneuses-lieuses

reaping ['riːpɪŋ] N *(of corn etc)* moisson *f*
 ▸▸**r. hook** faucille *f*; **r. machine** moissonneuse *f*

reappear [riːə'pɪər] VI réapparaître

reappearance [riːə'pɪərəns] N réapparition *f*

reapply [riːə'plaɪ] VT *(cream, lotion etc)* réappliquer
 VI *(for grant, job, loan etc)* renouveler sa demande (**for** de)

reappoint [riːə'pɔɪnt] VT *(person)* renommer

reappointment [riːə'pɔɪntmənt] N **nobody opposed his r.** personne ne s'opposa à ce qu'il soit reconduit dans ses fonctions

reappraisal [riːə'preɪz(ə)l] N **1** *Fin (of property)* réévaluation *f* **2** *(of policy)* réexamen *m*

reappraise [riːə'preɪz] VT **1** *Fin (property)* réévaluer **2** *(policy)* réexaminer

rear¹ [rɪər] N **1** *(back part) (of building, car, train)* arrière *m*; **in the r.** en arrière, à l'arrière; **in the r. of the train** en queue du train; **at** *or Am* **in the r. of** *(behind)* derrière; **from the r.** par derrière; *(to recognize)* de derrière; **to bring up the r.** *(of procession)* venir en queue; *(be in last place)* être à la queue, *Pej* être la lanterne rouge; **r. legs** *(of dog, cat etc)* pattes *fpl* de derrière; *(of horse)* jambes *fpl* de derrière; *Aut* **r.-view** *or Am* **r.-vision mirror** rétroviseur *m*, rétro *m* **2** *(military column)* queue *f*; **to bring up the r.** *(come at end)* *(of military column)* fermer la marche; **to protect one's r.** *Mil* protéger ses arrières; *Fig* assurer ses arrières **3** *Fam (buttocks)* **r. (end)** derrière *m*, fesses *fpl*; **he needs a kick in the r.** il lui faut un coup de pied au derrière *ou* dans les fesses
 ADJ *(door, wheel)* arrière *inv*, de derrière; *(engine)* arrière; *(carriages)* de queue; **is there a rear entrance?** est-ce qu'il y a une entrée par derrière?
 ▸▸*Naut* **r. admiral** contre-amiral *m*, *pl* contre-amiraux; *Aut* **r. drive axle** pont *m* arrière; *Br Aut* **r. lamps** feux *mpl* arrière; *Br Aut* **r. lights** feux arrière; *Cin, TV* **r. projection** projection *f* en transparence; *Aut* **r. spoiler** aileron *m ou* spoiler *m* arrière; *Aut* **r. window** lunette *f* arrière

rear² VT **1** *(nurture) (child, sheep)* élever; *(plants)* cultiver **2** *(lift) (one's head)* relever; *Fig* **to r. its ugly head** *(of racism, violence etc)* faire son apparition
 VI **to r. (up) (on its hind legs)** *(of horse)* se cabrer; **cliffs r. (up) above the shore** des falaises se dressent au-dessus du rivage

rear-drive ADJ à traction arrière

rear-end VT *esp Am Aut* **to r. sb** *(collide with)* emboutir l'arrière de la voiture de qn

rear-engined [rɪər'endʒɪnd] ADJ *(car etc)* avec le moteur à l'arrière, à moteur arrière

rearguard ['rɪəgɑːd] N *Mil* arrière-garde *f*, *pl* arrière-gardes
 ▸▸**r. action** combat *m* d'arrière-garde; *also Fig* **to fight** *or* **mount a r. action** mener un combat d'arrière-garde

rearing ['rɪərɪŋ] N **1** *(of children)* éducation *f*; *(of animals)* élevage *m*; *(of plants)* culture *f* **2** **r. (up)** *(of horse)* cabrage *m*

rearm [riː'ɑːm] VT & VI réarmer

rearmament [riː'ɑːməmənt] N *(of country, soldiers etc)* réarmement *m*

rearmost ['rɪəməʊst] ADJ dernier; *(carriage, compartment on train)* dernier, de queue

rear-mounted ADJ *(engine, gun)* monté à l'arrière

rearrange [riːə'reɪndʒ] VT *(books, furniture, flowers)* changer la disposition de; *(room, office)* aménager de façon différente; *(one's clothing)* réajuster; *(schedule)* modifier; *(appointment)* changer, reporter; **they've rearranged everything in here** tout a changé de place ici; **could we r. things?** est-ce qu'on peut s'organiser autrement?; *Fam* **to r. sb's face** casser la gueule à qn

rearrangement [riːə'reɪndʒmənt] N *(of books, flowers, room etc)* réarrangement *m*; *(of schedule)* modification *f*; *(of appointment)* changement *m*

rearward ['rɪəwəd] ADJ **1** *(at back) (compartment etc)* (situé à l')arrière **2** *(backward) (glance, movement)* vers l'arrière
 ADV *esp Am* = **rearwards**

rearwards ['rɪəwədz] ADV *esp Br (be situated)* à l'arrière; *(to glance, move)* vers l'arrière

rear-wheel drive N *Aut* propulsion *f* arrière; **car with r.** voiture *f* à traction arrière

rear-wheel steering N *Aut* roues *fpl* arrière directrices

REASON ['riːz(ə)n] **N 1** *(cause)* raison *f* (**for** de); **there is a r. for his doing so** il y a une raison pour qu'il fasse ça; **to state one's reasons for a decision** motiver une décision; **for reasons of health** pour raisons de santé; **reasons of state** la raison d'État; *usu Iron* **for reasons best known to themselves** pour des raisons qu'eux seuls connaissent *ou* qu'ils sont les seuls à connaître; **for some** *or* **one r. or other** pour une raison ou pour une autre; **for no other r. than that I forgot** pour la simple raison que j'ai oublié; **for no particular r.** sans raison particulière; **for no r. at all** sans aucune raison; **that's no r. for refusing to help me!** ce n'est pas une raison pour refuser de m'aider!; **for that very r.** pour cette raison même; **for the very r. that he had been asked not to do it** précisément parce qu'on l'avait prié de ne pas le faire; **the r. why** la raison; **I don't know the r. why** je ne sais pas pourquoi; **the r. (why) he left** la raison pour laquelle il est parti; **the r. (why** *or* **for which) he came, his r. for coming** la raison pour laquelle il est venu; **what's the r. for it?** à quoi cela tient-il?, quelle en est la raison?; **what r. did you give for your absence?** comment as-tu expliqué ton absence?; **what r. could they give for such inhuman acts?** comment peuvent-ils justifier des actes d'une telle cruauté?; **to have every r. to believe …** avoir tout lieu de croire …; **I have (good) r. to believe that he's lying** j'ai de bonnes raisons de croire qu'il ment; **to have r. enough (to do sth)** avoir de bonnes raisons (de faire qch); **she complains and with (good) r.** elle se plaint et pour cause; **it's not without (good) r. that I detest him** ce n'est pas pour rien que je le déteste; **to give sb good r. for doing sth** donner de bonnes raisons à qn de faire qch; **give me one good r. why I should!** donne-moi une raison valable pour que je le fasse!; **all the more r. for going there** *or* **why I should go there** raison de plus pour y aller *ou* pour que j'y aille; *Fml* **by r. of his infirmity** en raison de son infirmité; **to be found not guilty by r. of insanity** être déclaré non-coupable pour cause de démence

2 *(sanity, common sense)* raison *f*; **he lost his r.** il a perdu la raison; **to listen to** *or* **hear** *or* **see r.** entendre raison; **it stands to r.** il va de soi *ou* sans dire (**that …** que … + *ind*); **that stands to r.** ça va de soi *ou* sans dire, c'est logique; **within r.** dans des limites raisonnables

VI raisonner (**about** sur); **to r. with sb** raisonner (avec) qn; **there's no reasoning with him** il n'y a pas moyen de lui faire entendre raison, on ne peut pas raisonner avec lui; *Hum* **ours is not to r. why** il ne faut pas chercher à comprendre; **to r. from past experience** raisonner en fonction de ses expériences passées

VT to r. that … estimer que … + *ind*; **to r. sb into/out of doing sth** convaincre qn de faire/de ne pas faire qch

▸ **reason out** VT SEP *(maths problem)* résoudre; *(one's differences)* résoudre en discutant; **to r. out that …** déduire que …

reasonable ['riːz(ə)nəb(ə)l] ADJ *(person, price, demand)* raisonnable; *(offer)* acceptable, raisonnable; *(effort)* acceptable; **(do) be r.** soyez *ou* tâchez d'être raisonnable; **as is only r.** ce qui est parfaitement normal; **to believe sth beyond all r. doubt** croire qch en son âme et conscience; **r. suspicions** soupçons *mpl* fondés; **r. excuse** excuse *f* valable (**for** de); **with a r. amount of luck** avec un peu de chance; **the weather/meal/film**

was r. le temps/le repas/le film était passable

reasonableness ['riːz(ə)nəb(ə)lnɪs] N *(of person, offer etc)* caractère *m* raisonnable; *(of effort)* caractère acceptable; *(of suspicion)* bien-fondé *m, pl* bien-fondés

reasonably ['riːz(ə)nəblɪ] ADV **1** *(to behave, act)* raisonnablement, de façon raisonnable; **r. priced** d'un prix raisonnable **2** *(fairly, rather)* assez; **r. fit** en assez bonne forme; **if we are r. lucky** avec un peu de chance

reasoned ['riːzənd] ADJ *(analysis, decision etc)* raisonné

reasoning ['riːzənɪŋ] N raisonnement *m*; **power of r.** *(ability)* capacité *f* de raisonnement; **the r. behind the decision** les raisons de cette décision; **such r. is dangerous** un tel raisonnement est dangereux

ADJ *(creature etc)* doué de raison; *(ability, process etc)* de raisonnement

reassemble [riːə'semb(ə)l] VT **1** *(gather)* *(troops)* rassembler **2** *(put together)* *(machine)* remonter; *(frame)* rassembler

VI *(of troops)* s'assembler de nouveau; **Parliament will r. on …** le Parlement rouvrira le …

reassembly [riːə'semblɪ] N *(gathering together)* rassemblement *m*; *Pol* rentrée *f*; *(of machine, gun)* remontage *m*

reassert [riːə'sɜːt] VT *(conviction, belief)* réaffirmer; **her self-confidence reasserted itself** sa confiance est revenue

reassess [riːə'ses] VT **1** *(policy, situation)* reconsidérer, réexaminer **2** *Fin (damages)* réévaluer; **you have been reassessed** votre situation fiscale a été réexaminée

reassessment [riːə'sesmənt] N **1** *(of policy, situation)* réexamen *m* **2** *Fin (of damages)* réévaluation *f*

reassign [riːə'saɪn] VT *(transfer) (employee, police officer etc)* muter (**to** à); *(funds)* réaffecter; *(work, project etc)* confier (**to** à); **the work has been reassigned** le travail a été confié à quelqu'un d'autre

reassignment [riːə'saɪnmənt] N **1** *(transfer) (of employee, police officer etc)* mutation *f*; *(of funds)* réaffectation *f* **2** *(duties)* nouveau poste *m*, nouvelles fonctions *fpl*

reassume [riːə'sjuːm] VT *(one's duties)* reprendre

reassurance [riːə'ʃʊərəns] N **1** *(comfort)* réconfort *m*; *(guarantee)* assurance *f*; **the boss gave (them) reassurances about their jobs** le patron les a rassurés quant à leur emploi **2** *Br Fin* réassurance *f*

reassure [riːə'ʃʊər] VT **1** *(person)* rassurer (**about** à propos de); **to r. sb of one's esteem** assurer qn de son estime; **to feel reassured** se sentir rassuré (**about** sur) **2** *Br Fin* réassurer

reassuring [riːə'ʃʊərɪŋ] ADJ *(person, news etc)* rassurant

reassuringly [riːə'ʃʊərɪŋlɪ] ADV *(to behave, act)* d'une manière rassurante

reawaken [riːə'weɪk(ə)n] VT *(sleeper)* réveiller; *(interest, feeling)* ranimer, faire renaître; *(hope)* faire renaître

VI *(of person)* se réveiller de nouveau; *(of affection, feelings, interest)* se ranimer

reawakening [riːə'weɪk(ə)nɪŋ] N *(of person, feeling etc)* réveil *m*; *(of interest)* regain *m*; *(of idea)* renaissance *f*

rebate ['riːbeɪt] N *Com etc* **1** *(refund)* remboursement *m* (partiel); *(of tax)* dégrèvement *m* **2** *(discount on purchase)* rabais *m*, ristourne *f*

rebel [¹ 'reb(ə)l] N *(opponent) (of government)* rebelle *mf*; *(armed)* rebelle, insurgé, -ée; *(in society)* rebelle, révolté, -ée; *Hist* **the**

Rebels *(Confederates)* les confédérés

ADJ *(soldier)* rebelle; *(camp, territory)* des rebelles; *(attack)* de rebelles

▸▸ **r. forces** forces *fpl* rebelles; **r. leader** chef *m* des rebelles; **r. MP** parlementaire *mf* rebelle

rebel [² rɪ'bel] VI *(-ll-)* *(against government)* se rebeller, se soulever (**against** contre); *(against society)* se rebeller, se révolter (**against** contre); **to r. against one's fate** se révolter *ou* s'insurger contre son destin; **her stomach rebelled at the thought of more food** elle avait l'estomac qui se soulevait rien que de penser à de la nourriture

rebellion [rɪ'beljən] N *(against government)* rébellion *f*, soulèvement *m* (**against** contre); *(against society)* rébellion, révolte *f* (**against** contre); **to be in r. against** être en rébellion contre; **to rise up in r.** se soulever (**against** contre)

rebellious [rɪ'beljəs] ADJ *(soldier, troops etc)* insubordonné; *(student, inhabitants)* révolté, en révolte; *(behaviour, child, hair)* rebelle; **r. act** acte *m* de rébellion

rebelliously [rɪ'beljəslɪ] ADV *(to behave, act)* d'une façon rebelle

rebelliousness [rɪ'beljəsnɪs] N *(of troops)* insubordination *f*; *(of students etc)* esprit *m* de rébellion

rebirth [riː'bɜːθ] N *(of country etc)* renaissance *f*

reboot [riː'buːt] *Comput* VT réamorcer

VI se réamorcer

rebore ['riːbɔːr] *Aut* N réalésage *m*; **my car needs a r.** le cylindre de ma voiture a besoin d'être réalésé *ou* d'un réalésage

VT réaléser

reborn [riː'bɔːn] ADJ USU PRED né à nouveau; **to be r.** renaître; **hope was r.** l'espoir est revenu; **to feel r.** *(physically)* se sentir revigoré; *(spiritually)* se sentir renaître

rebound [¹ 'riːbaʊnd] N *(of ball)* rebond *m*; **to hit a ball on the r.** frapper une balle au rebond; **he headed in the r.** il a marqué un but de la tête en prenant la balle au rebond; *Fig* **she married him on the r.** elle l'a épousé à cause d'une déception amoureuse; *Fig* **he caught her on the r.** il a commencé à la fréquenter au moment où elle sortait d'une déception amoureuse

rebound [² rɪ'baʊnd] VI **1** *(of ball etc)* rebondir; *(of stone)* ricocher; *(of cry, noise)* faire écho (**from** contre); *Fig (of joke, lie etc)* se retourner (**on** contre); **the trick he played rebounded on him** son mauvais tour s'est retourné contre lui **2** *(recover) (of person)* se ressaisir (**from** après); *(of share prices, business)* reprendre, se redresser (**from** après)

rebrand [riː'brænd] VT *Mktg (product)* changer la marque de

rebranding [riː'brændɪŋ] N *Mktg (of product)* changement *m* de marque

rebuff [rɪ'bʌf] N *(of person)* rebuffade *f*; *(of suggestion etc)* refus *m*; **to meet with** *or* **suffer a r.** *(of person)* essuyer une rebuffade; *(of suggestion etc)* être repoussé

VT *(reject) (advances)* repousser; *(person)* repousser, rejeter; *(offer, suggestion)* rejeter; *(allegation)* démentir; **to feel rebuffed** se sentir repoussé *ou* rejeté

rebuild [riː'bɪld] VT *(pt, pp* **rebuilt** [riː'bɪlt]*)* *(house, company)* reconstruire; *(one's life)* reconstruire, refaire; *(machine, engine)* remettre à neuf, refaire

rebuilding [riː'bɪldɪŋ] N *(of house, company)* reconstruction *f*; *(of machine, engine)* réfection *f*, remise *f* à neuf

rebuke [rɪ'bjuːk] N réprimande *f*; **to administer** *or* **deliver a r. to sb** réprimander qn, faire une réprimande à qn

vt *(person)* réprimander (**for doing sth** pour avoir fait qch)

rebus ['riːbəs] **n** rébus *m*

rebut [rɪ'bʌt] **vt** (**-tt-**) *Fml (accusation, hypothesis etc)* réfuter

rebuttal [rɪ'bʌt(ə)l] **n** *Fml* réfutation *f*

rebuy ['riːbaɪ] **n** *Mktg* réachat *m*
➤➤ **r. rate** taux *m* de réachat

rec [rek] **n** *Fam* **1** *Br (ground)* terrain *m* de jeux **2** *Am Sch (break)* récré *f*
➤➤ *Br* **r. ground** terrain de jeux; *Am* **r. room** *(in home)* salle *f* de jeux

recalcitrance [rɪ'kælsɪtrəns] **n** *Fml* récalcitrance *f*

recalcitrant [rɪ'kælsɪtrənt] **adj** *Fml (horse, person)* récalcitrant; *(disease)* rebelle

recall¹ ['riːkɔːl] **n 1** *(remembering)* **she has remarkable powers of r.** elle a une mémoire remarquable; **to have instant r.** avoir une excellente mémoire; **to have total r.** (être capable de) se souvenir de tous les détails de quelque chose **2** *(calling back) (of troops, library book, defective goods etc)* rappel *m*; *(of Parliament)* reconvocation *f*, *Mil* **to sound the r.** battre le rappel; **lost beyond r.** perdu irrévocablement
➤➤ *Mktg* **r. rate** taux *m* de mémorisation; *Mktg* **r. score** score *m* de mémorisation; **r. slip** *(for library book)* fiche *f* de rappel; *Mktg* **r. test** test *m* de rappel *ou* de mémorisation

recall² [rɪ'kɔːl] **vt 1** *(remember)* se souvenir de, se rappeler; **to r. doing sth** se rappeler avoir fait qch; **to r. sth to sb** rappeler qch à qn; **legends that r. the past** légendes évocatrices du passé *ou* qui évoquent le passé; **how vividly I r. the scene!** avec quelle netteté je revois ce spectacle! **2** *(call back) (troops, defective goods etc)* rappeler; *(library book)* demander le retour de; **the sound of the telephone recalled her to the present** la sonnerie du téléphone la ramena à la réalité

vi as I r. si je me rappelle bien; **as you may r.** comme vous vous en souvenez *ou* le rappelez peut-être; **as you will r.** comme vous vous en souvenez sans doute

recant [rɪ'kænt] **vt** *(opinion)* rétracter, revenir sur; *(doctrinal error)* abjurer; *(doctrine)* désavouer
vi se rétracter

recantation [riːkæn'teɪʃən] **n** *(of faith, statement)* abjuration *f* (**of** de)

recap ['riːkæp] **n 1** *Fam (summary)* récapitulation *f*, **let's do a r.** faisons le point **2** *Am Aut* pneu *m* rechapé
vt (**-pp-**) *Fam* **= recapitulate vt 1**
2 *Am Aut (tyre)* rechaper
vi *Fam* récapituler

recapitalization [riːkæpɪtəlaɪ'zeɪʃən] **n** recapitalisation *f*

recapitalize [riː'kæpɪtəlaɪz] **vt** changer la structure financière de

recapitulate [riːkə'pɪtjʊleɪt] **vt 1** *(summarize) (discussion etc)* récapituler; **let us r. the facts** faisons le point **2** *Mus (theme)* reprendre
vi récapituler

recapitulation [riːkəpɪtjʊ'leɪʃən] **n 1** *(of discussion etc)* récapitulation *f* **2** *Mus* reprise *f*

recapture [riː'kæptʃər] **n** *(of town)* reprise *f*, *(of prisoner)* capture *f*
vt 1 *(take again) (prisoner, town)* reprendre **2** *(recreate) (era, age, atmosphere)* faire revivre, recréer; *(one's youth)* retrouver

recarpet [riː'kɑːpɪt] **vt** changer la moquette de, remoquetter

recast [riː'kɑːst] **vt** *(pt, pp* **recast***)* **1** *(reshape) (sentence, piece of writing)* remanier **2** *Theat (find new cast for) (play)* changer la distribu-

tion de; *(find new part for) (actor)* donner un nouveau rôle à; **the part has been r.** le rôle a été donné à quelqu'un d'autre

recce ['rekɪ] **n** *Fam (exploration)* reconnaissance *f*, **to make a quick r.** faire une reconnaissance rapide (**of** de)

recede [rɪ'siːd] **vi 1** *(of tide, sea)* se retirer, descendre; *(of coastline, person, thing)* s'éloigner, reculer; **as memories of the past r.** à mesure que les souvenirs du passé s'effacent **2** *(slope backwards)* **to have a receding chin/forehead** avoir le menton/front fuyant *ou* qui fuit; **his hair(line)** *or* **he is receding** son front se dégarnit **3** *(lose value)* perdre de la valeur; **the company's shares have receded five points** les actions de la société ont reculé de *ou* perdu cinq points

receipt [rɪ'siːt] **n 1** *(receiving) (of letter, parcel etc)* réception *f*, **on r. of this letter** dès réception de cette lettre; **on r. of the news** à la nouvelle *(about de)*; **within one week of r.** dans un délai d'une semaine après réception; **to pay on r.** payer à (la) réception; **to acknowledge r.** accuser réception (**of** de); **we are in r. of ...** nous avons reçu ...; *Com* **r. at domicile** prise *f* à domicile; *Fin* **r. of a dividend** perception *f* de dividende **2** *(for payment)* reçu *m* (**for** de); *(in supermarket, bar)* ticket *m* de caisse; *(for letter, parcel)* récépissé *m*, accusé *m* de réception; **to give a r.** *(for meal, taxi fare etc)* donner un reçu; *(for rent)* donner une quittance **3 receipts** *(takings)* recettes *fpl*, rentrées *fpl*; **receipts and expenditure** recettes et dépenses *fpl*
vt *Com* acquitter, quittancer; **to r. a bill** *(in writing)* acquitter une facture; *(with stamp)* apposer le tampon 'pour acquit' sur une facture
➤➤ *Fin* **r. book** carnet *m* de quittances; *Com* **r. stamp** timbre-quittance *m*, *pl* timbres-quittances

receivable [rɪ'siːvəb(ə)l] *Com* **adj** *(account, bill etc)* à recevoir
n compte *m* *ou* effet *m* à recevoir

receive [rɪ'siːv] **vt 1** *(take delivery of) (gift, news, letter)* recevoir; *(money etc)* recevoir, toucher; *(salary etc)* toucher; **I have received your letter** j'ai reçu votre lettre, votre lettre m'est parvenue; **received with thanks** *(on bill)* pour acquit; *Radio, TV* **to r. a broadcast** recevoir une émission; *St Exch* **to r. a premium** encaisser un premium; **to r. a station** capter un poste; **are you receiving me?** *(on radio)* est-ce que vous me recevez?; **to r. (the) service** *(of tennis or badminton player)* recevoir le service; *Law* **to r. stolen goods** receler des objets volés

2 *(be given) (greeting, blow, communion etc)* recevoir; *(refusal)* essuyer; *(criticism)* faire l'objet de; *(commission, unemployment benefit, interest)* percevoir; *Law* **to r. thirty days** être condamné à un mois de prison; **I received the distinct impression that ...** j'ai eu la nette impression que ...; *Prov* **it is better** *or* **more blessed to give than to r.** il y a plus de joie à donner qu'à recevoir; **we don't want them to r. a bad impression of us** nous ne voulons pas leur faire mauvaise impression; *St Exch* **to r. a premium** encaisser un premium

3 *(welcome) (guests)* recevoir; **to be cordially received** *(of visitor etc)* trouver un accueil chaleureux, être bien reçu; **the proposal was badly received** la proposition reçut un accueil favorable/défavorable *ou* a été bien/mal reçue; **the film was well received by the critics** le film a été bien accueilli par la critique; **to r. sb into the Church** admettre qn dans l'Église; **to r. sb into one's family** admettre *ou* recevoir qn dans sa famille
vi *(of tennis or badminton player)* recevoir le service

received [rɪ'siːvd] **adj** *(idea)* reçu; *(opinion)* admis; **the r. view is that ...** il est communément admis *ou* accepté que ..., on admet communément que ...
➤➤ *Br* **R. Pronunciation** prononciation *f* standard (de l'anglais); *Com* **r. stamp** cachet *m* d'arrivée; **r. wisdom** sagesse *f* populaire

receiver [rɪ'siːvər] **n 1** *(of stolen goods)* receleur, -euse **2** *Tel* récepteur *m*; **to lift** *or* **pick up the r.** décrocher; **to replace the r.** raccrocher **3** *Radio, TV* récepteur *m* **4** *Law, Fin* **r. in bankruptcy, official r.** administrateur, -trice judiciaire, syndic *m* de faillite; **to be in the hands of the r.** être en règlement judiciaire
➤➤ *Radio, TV* **r. aerial** antenne *f* de réception; *Am* **r. general** receveur *m* des impôts; **r. rest** *(for telephone)* berceau *m* (du combiné)

receivership [rɪ'siːvəʃɪp] **n** *Law, Fin* liquidation *f* judiciaire; **to go into r.** être placé sous administration judiciaire

receiving [rɪ'siːvɪŋ] **n** *(of stolen goods)* recel *m*
adj *Fam* **to be at** *or* **on the r. end** écoper; **to be on the r. end of sb's temper** faire les frais du mauvais caractère de qn; *Fam* **I've been on the r. end of customers' complaints all day** c'est moi qui me suis occupé des réclamations des clients toute la journée; *Fam* **it's different when you're on the r. end** c'est tout autre chose quand c'est à toi que ça arrive
➤➤ *Radio, TV* **r. aerial** antenne *f* de réception; *Am* **r. blanket** petite couverture *f* légère pour bébé; *Com* **r. depot** dépôt *m* de réception; *Radio, TV* **r. set** poste *m* récepteur; *Radio, TV* **r. station** station *f* réceptrice

recent ['riːsənt] **adj** *(development, event, past)* récent; *(acquaintance)* nouveau, *f* nouvelle; **event of r. date** événement *m* récent; **all that is quite r.** tout cela est très récent; **in r. months** au cours des derniers mois; **r. news** nouvelles *fpl* récentes *ou* fraîches; **in r. times** récemment; **the most r. edition** *(of book etc)* la dernière édition; **her most r. novel** son dernier roman

recently ['riːsəntlɪ] **adv** récemment; **as r. as yesterday** pas plus tard qu'hier; **until quite r.** jusqu'à récemment *ou* ces derniers temps; **I saw her r.** je l'ai vue tout dernièrement

receptacle [rɪ'septək(ə)l] **n 1** *(for litter, paper, water etc)* récipient *m* **2** *Am Elec* prise *f* de courant (femelle)

reception [rɪ'sepʃən] **n 1** *(welcome)* accueil *m*; **to give sb a chilly/warm r.** réserver à qn un accueil glacial/chaleureux; **what kind of r. did you get?** quel accueil est-ce qu'ils t'ont réservé?, comment est-ce qu'ils t'ont reçu?; **the play has had a favourable r.** la pièce a été accueillie favorablement *ou* bien reçue **2** *(party)* réception *f*, *(in the evening)* réception, soirée *f*, **wedding r.** réception de mariage **3** *(in hotel)* réception *f*, *(in office, hospital)* accueil *m*; **at** *or* **to r.** à la réception/à l'accueil **4** *Radio, TV* réception *f*
➤➤ *Br* **r. centre** centre *m* d'accueil; *Br Sch* **r. class** première année *f* de maternelle; *Am* **r. clerk** réceptionniste *mf*, *also Fig Hum* **r. committee** comité *m* d'accueil; **r. desk** *(in hotel)* réception; *(in office, hospital)* accueil; **r. room** *(in hotel)* salle *f* de réception; *Br (in house)* salon *m*

receptionist [rɪ'sepʃənɪst] **n** réceptionniste *mf*, *(at trade fair)* hôtesse *f* d'accueil

receptive [rɪ'septɪv] **adj** *(audience, listener)* réceptif (**to an idea** à une idée); **r. to sb** compréhensif envers qn

receptiveness [rɪ'septɪvnɪs], **receptivity** [riːsep'tɪvɪtɪ] **n** *(of audience, listener)* réceptivité *f* (**to** à)

receptor [rɪ'septər] **n 1** *(for antibody, drug)*

récepteur *m* **2** *(for radio signals)* récepteur *m*

▸▸*Physiol* r. **site** (site *m*) récepteur

recess [rɪˈses, *Am* ˈriːses] **N 1** *Br (holidays) (of law courts, Parliament)* vacances *fpl*; **while Parliament is in r.** pendant les vacances parlementaires **2** *Am Sch (break)* récréation *f* **3** *Am Law (break)* suspension *f* d'audience; **the court is now in r.** l'audience est maintenant suspendue; **we will take a ten minute r.** nous allons suspendre l'audience pendant dix minutes **4** *(nook)* recoin *m*; *(for bed etc)* renfoncement *m*; *(for statue)* niche *f*; **dining r.** coin *m* repas, coin salle à manger; **in the innermost recesses of the soul** dans les replis *ou* recoins les plus secrets de l'âme

VT *(place in a recess) (lighting, switch etc)* encastrer

VI 1 *Br* **Parliament will r. next week** les vacances parlementaires commenceront la semaine prochaine **2** *Am (of assembly)* suspendre la séance; *(of court)* suspendre l'audience

recession [rɪˈseʃən] **N** *Econ* récession *f*; **in (a) r.** en récession

recessionary [rɪˈseʃənərɪ] **ADJ** *Econ (conditions, policy etc)* de récession; **to have a r. effect** entraîner une récession

▸▸r. **gap** écart *m* déflationniste

recessive [rɪˈsesɪv] **ADJ** *Biol (gene)* récessif

recharge [riːˈtʃɑːdʒ] **VT** *(battery)* recharger; *Fig* **to r. one's batteries** recharger ses batteries, reprendre du poil de la bête

VI *(of battery)* se recharger

rechargeable [riːˈtʃɑːdʒəb(ə)l] **ADJ** *(battery)* rechargeable

recharger [riːˈtʃɑːdʒər] **N** *(for battery)* chargeur *m*

recherché [rəˈʃeəʃeɪ] **ADJ** *(film, topic)* recherché

recidivism [rɪˈsɪdɪvɪz(ə)m] **N** *Law* récidivisme *m*

recidivist [rɪˈsɪdɪvɪst] **ADJ, N** *Law* récidiviste *mf*

recidivistic [rɪsɪdɪˈvɪstɪk] **ADJ** *Law (tendency etc)* à récidiver

recipe [ˈresɪpɪ] **N** *Culin, Fig* recette *f*; *Pharm* formule *f*, recette; **r. for a happy life** recette pour vivre heureux; **a r. for failure** le meilleur moyen pour échouer; **those two working together would be a r. for disaster** si ces deux-là travaillaient ensemble ce serait l'échec *ou* la catastrophe assuré(e)

▸▸r. **book** livre *m* de recettes; r. **card** fiche-recette *f*, *pl* fiches-recettes, fiche-cuisine *f*, *pl* fiches-cuisines

recipient [rɪˈsɪpɪənt] **N** *(of gift, letter etc)* destinataire *mf*; *(of cheque, money)* bénéficiaire *mf*; *(of award, honour)* récipiendaire *mf*; *Med (of organ transplant)* receveur, -euse

> Note that the French word **récipient** is a false friend and is never a translation for the English word **recipient**. It means **container**.

reciprocal [rɪˈsɪprək(ə)l] **ADJ 1** *(mutual)* mutuel, réciproque; *(bilateral)* réciproque, bilatéral, -aux; **he dislikes me and it's r.** il ne m'aime pas et c'est réciproque *ou* je le lui rends bien **2** *Gram* réciproque **3** *Math* réciproque, inverse

N *Math* réciproque *f*, inverse *f*

▸▸r. **agreement** accord *m* réciproque; r. **marketing** marketing *m* bilatéral; *Mktg* r. **relationships model** modèle *m* de relations réciproques; r. **trading** commerce *m* réciproque

reciprocally [rɪˈsɪprəklɪ] **ADV** *(to trade)* réciproquement

reciprocate [rɪˈsɪprəkeɪt] **VT** *(return) (compliment)* retourner; **to r. sb's kindness** payer la gentillesse de qn de retour; **he had great admiration for her but his feelings were never reciprocated** il avait beaucoup d'admiration pour elle mais ce n'était pas réciproque

VI 1 *(do the same)* en faire autant; *(counterattack)* riposter **2** *Tech (of piston etc)* avoir un mouvement alternatif *ou* de va-et-vient

reciprocating [rɪˈsɪprəkeɪtɪŋ] **ADJ** *Tech (movement)* alternatif; *(machine)* à mouvement alternatif *ou* de va-et-vient

▸▸r. **engine** moteur *m* alternatif

reciprocation [rɪsɪprəˈkeɪʃən] **N 1** *(of feeling)* réciprocité *f*; **I think some r. of her compliment is called for** je pense qu'il faudrait lui retourner le compliment; **these feelings met with no r.** ces sentiments n'ont pas été payés de retour; **in r. for ...** en retour de ... **2** *Tech* mouvement *m* alternatif, va-et-vient *m inv*

reciprocity [resɪˈprɒsɪtɪ] **N** réciprocité *f*

recirculated air [riːˈsɜːkjʊleɪtɪd] **N** *Aut* air *m* recyclé

recital [rɪˈsaɪt(ə)l] **N 1** *(of poetry)* récitation *f* **2** *Mus* récital *m*; **to give a r.** donner un récital; **Bach r.** récital Bach **3** *(of events etc)* récit *m*, narration *f*; *(of complaints, details etc)* énumération *f*

recitation [resɪˈteɪʃən] **N** *(of poem etc)* récitation *f*; **to give a r.** réciter; **to give a r. from Burns** réciter du Burns

recitative [resɪtəˈtiːv] **N** *Mus* récitatif *m*

recite [rɪˈsaɪt] **VT 1** *(poem etc)* réciter **2** *(complaints, details etc)* énumérer

VI réciter; **will you r. to us?** voulez-vous nous réciter quelque chose?

reckless [ˈreklɪs] **ADJ** *(foolhardy) (person)* inconscient, téméraire; *(attempt, action, decision etc)* téméraire; *(driving, gambler)* imprudent; **to be a r. spender** dépenser sans compter; **to be r. with one's money** dépenser son argent inconsidérément

▸▸*Admin, Law* r. **driver** conducteur, -trice imprudent(e), *Fam* chauffard *m*; r. **driving** conduite *f* imprudente

recklessly [ˈreklɪslɪ] **ADV** *(to attempt)* témérairement; *(to drive, gamble)* imprudemment; *(to spend)* sans compter

recklessness [ˈreklɪsnɪs] **N** *(of attempt, person)* témérité *f*; *(of driving, gambling)* imprudence *f*

reckon [ˈrekən] **VT 1** *(consider) (person)* considérer (**as** comme); **to r. sb among the greatest writers** mettre qn au rang *ou* au nombre des plus grands écrivains; **he is reckoned to be one of the richest men in England** il paraît *ou* ce serait l'un des hommes les plus riches d'Angleterre **2** *(calculate, count) (amount etc)* calculer, compter; **the cost has been reckoned at £100** le coût a été estimé à 100 livres **3** *Fam (think)* penser; **I r. he's forty** je lui donne quarante ans; **I r. he'll consent** à mon avis, il consentira; **maybe we should go, what do you r.?** nous devrions peut-être y aller, qu'est-ce que tu en penses?; **the Government obviously reckons it has a good chance of winning an early election** le gouvernement a bon espoir de gagner une élection anticipée **4** *Fam (regard favourably)* **I don't r. her chances** je ne donne pas cher de sa réussite

VI 1 *(calculate)* compter, calculer; **reckoning from today** à partir *ou* à compter d'aujourd'hui **2** *(expect, plan)* compter (**to go** partir); **you should r. to be there by 6 o'clock at the latest** il faut que tu prévoies d'arriver à six heures au plus tard

▸ **reckon in VT SEP** compter

▸ **reckon on VT INSEP** **to r. on sth** compter sur

qch; **they had not reckoned on finding me here** ils ne comptaient pas me trouver ici

▸ **reckon up VT SEP** *(column of figures)* additionner; *(change, coins)* compter; **to r. up the cost of sth** calculer le coût de qch; **to r. up a bill** faire une facture

VI *(prepare bill)* faire la note

▸ **reckon with VT INSEP** compter avec; **to have sb to r. with** avoir affaire à qn; **she's a force to be reckoned with** c'est une femme avec laquelle il faut compter; **he hadn't reckoned with this response** il ne s'attendait pas à cette réaction

▸ **reckon without VT INSEP** compter sans; **he had reckoned without his rivals** il n'avait pas tenu compte de ses rivaux

reckoner [ˈrek(ə)nər] **N** **ready r.** barème *m*

reckoning [ˈrekənɪŋ] **N** *(of bill, interest etc)* calcul *m*; **by my r.** d'après mes calculs; **to be out in one's r.** s'être trompé dans ses calculs; **you're a long way out in your r.** vous êtes loin du compte; **to the best of my r.** autant je puisse en juger; **day of r.** *Rel* jour *m* du Jugement dernier; *Fig* instant *m* de vérité

reclaim[1] [rɪˈkleɪm] **VT 1** *(land)* mettre en valeur; *(from undergrowth)* défricher; *(marsh)* assécher; **to r. land from the sea/the desert** conquérir du terrain sur la mer/le désert **2** *(lost property, suitcase etc)* récupérer; *(tax, expenses)* se faire rembourser; **to r. VAT** récupérer la TVA **3** *Ind (rubber etc)* régénérer; *(by-product)* récupérer

> Note that the French verb **réclamer** is a false friend and is never a translation for the English verb **to reclaim**. It means **to claim, to demand**.

reclaim[2] [ˈriːkleɪm] **N** **luggage** *or* **baggage r.** *(in airport)* retrait *m* des bagages

reclamation [rekləˈmeɪʃən] **N 1** *(of land)* mise *f* en valeur; *(from undergrowth)* défrichement *m*; *(of marsh)* assèchement *m* **2** *(of tax, expenses)* remboursement *m* **3** *Ind (of rubber etc)* régénération *f*; *(of by-product)* récupération *f*

reclassify [riːˈklæsɪfaɪ] **VT** *(plant etc)* reclasser; *(document etc)* reclassifier

recline [rɪˈklaɪn] **VT** *(one's head)* appuyer (**against** contre; **on** sur); *(seat)* incliner le dossier de

VI *(of person) (be lying)* être allongé *ou* étendu (**on** sur); *(lie down)* s'allonger, s'étendre; *(of head)* être appuyé (**on** sur); *(of seat)* avoir un dossier inclinable *ou* réglable

recliner [rɪˈklaɪnər] **N** *(for sunbathing)* chaise *f* longue; *(armchair)* fauteuil *m* à dossier inclinable, fauteuil relax

reclining [rɪˈklaɪnɪŋ] **ADJ** *(seat)* inclinable, à dossier inclinable; **to be in a r. position** *(of person)* être en position allongée *ou* couchée; *(of seat)* être incliné

▸▸r. **chair** chaise *f* longue

recluse [rɪˈkluːs] **N** reclus, -use; **to live** *or* **lead the life of a r.** vivre en reclus *ou* ermite; **she has become a bit of a r.** elle est devenue assez solitaire

recognition [rekəgˈnɪʃən] **N 1** *(identification) (of person, style etc)* reconnaissance *f*; **she gave no sign of r.** elle n'a pas eu l'air de me/le/*etc* reconnaître; **to change beyond** *or* **out of all r.** devenir méconnaissable; *Mktg* **brand r.** identification *f* de la marque **2** *(acknowledgement) (of fact, government, speaker etc)* reconnaissance *f*; **to win r.** *(of artist etc)* s'imposer (**from** aux yeux de); **her work has won her international r.** son œuvre lui a permis de s'imposer sur le plan international; **to withhold r. from** *(government)* refuser de reconnaître; **in r. of his courage** en reconnaissance de son courage; **she re-**

ceived **no r.** on ne lui accordait aucune considération
▶▶ *Mktg* **r. score** score *m* de reconnaissance; *Mktg* **r. test** test *m* de reconnaissance
recognizable [rekəg'naɪzəb(ə)l] ADJ *(person, style etc)* reconnaissable; **he's so changed as to be no longer r.** il est devenu méconnaissable
recognizably [rekəg'naɪzəblɪ] ADV **she is r. your daughter** on voit bien que c'est votre fille
recognizance [rɪ'kɒgnɪzəns] N *Law (promise)* engagement *m*; *(money paid)* caution *f* personnelle; **to enter into recognizances** donner caution; **to enter into recognizances for sb** se porter garant *ou* caution pour qn, cautionner qn; **to be released on one's own recognizances** être remis en liberté sur engagement personnel
recognize ['rekəgnaɪz] VT **1** *(know again)* *(person, town etc)* reconnaître; **to r. the truth when one sees it** être capable de savoir si quelque chose est vrai ou non, savoir discerner le vrai du faux; **he can certainly r. a good business opportunity** il sait repérer les bonnes affaires **2** *(acknowledge)* *(government, fact etc)* reconnaître; *Sport (record)* homologuer; **to r. sb as king** reconnaître qn comme *ou* en tant que roi; **to r. defeat** accepter *ou* admettre sa défaite; **to be the first to r. a fact** être le premier à reconnaître un fait **3** *Am* **to r. a member** *(of chairman of a meeting etc)* donner la parole à un membre; *Am* **to be recognized** *(of speaker)* avoir la parole
recognized ['rekəgnaɪzd] ADJ *(government etc)* reconnu; *(truth)* admis, accepté; *(method etc)* classique; **it is a r. fact that …** c'est un fait avéré *ou* reconnu que …; **the r. term** le terme consacré **(for** pour); **to be a r. authority** être une autorité reconnue (par tous) **(on** en)
▶▶ *Com* **r. agent** agent *m* accrédité **(for** pour); *Fin* **r. investment exchange** marché *m* d'investissement agréé
recoil[1] ['riːkɔɪl] N *(of gun, rifle)* recul *m*; *(of spring)* détente *f*; *(of person)* mouvement *m* de recul
recoil[2] [rɪ'kɔɪl] VI *(of gun, rifle)* reculer; *(of spring)* se détendre; *(of person)* reculer **(from doing sth** à l'idée de faire qch); *Fig (of joke etc)* se retourner **(on** contre); **to r. (in horror/disgust)** avoir un mouvement de recul
recoilless [rɪ'kɔɪllɪs] ADJ *(rifle etc)* sans recul
recollect [rekə'lekt] VT se rappeler, se souvenir de; **she was unable to r. what had happened** elle était incapable de se souvenir de ce qui s'était passé
VI **as far as I r.** autant que je m'en souvienne
recollection [rekə'lekʃən] N souvenir *m*; **my earliest recollections** mes premiers souvenirs; **her r. differs from mine** nos souvenirs ne concordent pas, ses souvenirs et les miens ne concordent pas; **I have some r. of it** j'en ai un vague souvenir; **I have no r. of it** je n'en ai *ou* je n'en garde aucun souvenir; **I have no r. of doing it** je ne me souviens pas de *ou* je ne me rappelle pas l'avoir fait; **to the best of my r.** pour autant que je me souvienne
recombinant [riː'kɒmbɪnənt] ADJ *Biol*
▶▶ **r. DNA** ADN *m* recombinant; **r. technology** recombinaison *f* génétique
recommend [rekə'mend] VT **1** *(praise)* *(book, restaurant, doctor)* recommander **(to** à; **for** pour); **the hotel is to be recommended for its cooking** on recommande cet hôtel pour sa cuisine; **the film has little to r. it** on

ne peut pas dire grand-chose en faveur de ce film (**apart from, except** en dehors de); **the place has little to r. it apart from the weather** cet endroit n'a pas grand intérêt à part qu'il y fait beau; **the proposal has a lot to r. it** la proposition a beaucoup d'avantages *ou* d'attrait; **the hotel comes recommended** on dit beaucoup de bien de cet hôtel **2** *(advise) (caution)* conseiller; **to r. sb to do sth** recommander *ou* conseiller à qn de faire qch; **I r. going** *or* **that you go via Leeds** je vous recommande *ou* conseille de passer par Leeds; **this is not to be recommended** ce n'est pas recommandé; **recommended (retail) price** prix *m* (public) conseillé **3** *Old-fashioned (entrust)* **to r. sth to the care of sb** *or* **to sb's care** recommander qch aux soins de qn; **to r. one's soul to God** recommander son âme à Dieu
recommendable [rekə'mendəb(ə)l] ADJ *(book, person etc)* recommandable; **highly r.** très recommandable
recommendation [rekəmen'deɪʃən] N **1** *(advice)* recommandation *f*; **I have come on the r. of one of your customers** je viens sur la recommandation d'un de vos clients; **through personal r.** par recommandation personnelle; **one can only join the club through personal r.** on ne peut devenir membre du club qu'en étant recommandé personnellement; **my r. is that …** ce que je recommande *ou* conseille c'est que …; **to follow/ignore sb's recommendations** suivre/ne pas suivre les recommandations de qn; **the report's recommendations** les recommandations contenues dans le rapport **2** *(commendation)* recommandation *f*; **the hotel's sole r. is its location** l'emplacement de l'hôtel est son seul intérêt
recompense ['rekəmpens] N **1** *(reward)* récompense *f* (**for** de); **in r. for …** en récompense de … **2** *Law (for damage, loss)* dédommagement *m* (**for** de, pour); **as r.** en dédommagement
VT **1** *(reward)* récompenser (**for** de) **2** *Law (compensate)* dédommager (**for sth** de qch)
reconcilable [rekən'saɪləb(ə)l] ADJ *(ideas, opinions)* compatible, conciliable (**with** avec); **not r.** irréconciliable
reconcile ['rekənsaɪl] VT **1** *(person)* réconcilier (**with** avec); **to be reconciled with sb** se réconcilier avec qn; **to r. sb to sth** faire accepter qch à *ou* par qn; **to r. oneself** *or* **become reconciled to sth** se résigner à quelque chose **2** *(settle) (quarrel)* régler, mettre fin à; **let us r. our differences** essayons de nous entendre **3** *(make agree)* *(opinions, facts)* concilier; *Fin (figures, bank statement)* rapprocher; *Acct (accounts, entries)* faire cadrer, faire accorder; **evidence which cannot be reconciled with the known facts** témoignage qui ne cadre pas avec les faits connus

> When translating the English verb **to reconcile**, note that the French verbs **concilier** and **réconcilier** are not interchangeable.

reconciliation [rekənsɪlɪ'eɪʃən] N **1** *(of people)* réconciliation *f* (**between** entre; **with** avec) **2** *(of differences, of opinions)* conciliation *f* **3** *Fin (of figures, bank statements)* rapprochement *m*; *Acct (of accounts, entries)* ajustement *m*
▶▶ *Fin* **r. account** compte *m* collectif; *Acct* **r. statement** état *m* de rapprochement
recondite [rɪ'kɒndaɪt, 'rekəndaɪt] ADJ *Fml (subject, knowledge)* abscons
recondition [riːkən'dɪʃən] VT *(engine etc)* refaire, remettre à neuf
reconditioned [riːkən'dɪʃənd] ADJ *(engine etc)* remis en état, refait

reconditioning [riːkən'dɪʃənɪŋ] N *(of engine etc)* remise *f* à neuf
reconfiguration [riːkənfɪgə'reɪʃən] N *Comput (of keyboard, system etc)* reconfiguration *f*
reconfigure [riːkən'fɪgər] VT *Comput (keyboard, system)* reconfigurer
reconnaissance [rɪ'kɒnɪsəns] N *Mil, Fig* reconnaissance *f*; **to make a r.** faire une reconnaissance; **to be on r.** être en reconnaissance; **r. flight/mission/satellite** vol *m*/mission *f*/satellite *m* de reconnaissance
reconnect [riːkə'nekt] VT *(telephone, cable etc)* rebrancher; *(pipe)* raccorder; **to r. the water supply** rétablir l'alimentation en eau; *Tel* **to r. sb** *(of operator)* rétablir la communication; *(of telephone company)* rebrancher le téléphone
VI se reconnecter
reconnection [riːkə'nekʃən] N *(of cable, telephone etc)* rebranchement *m*; *(of pipe)* raccordement *m*; *(of water supply, telephone call)* rétablissement *m*
▶▶ *Tel* **r. charge** frais *mpl* de rebranchement
reconnoitre, *Am* **reconnoiter** [rekə'nɔɪtər] VT *Mil, Fig* reconnaître
VI faire une reconnaissance
reconquer [riː'kɒŋkər] VT *(country etc)* reconquérir
reconquest [riː'kɒŋkwest] N *(of country etc)* reconquête *f*
reconsider [riːkən'sɪdər] VT *(question)* reconsidérer, repenser; *(decision)* reconsidérer, réexaminer
VI reconsidérer la question; **I advise you to r.** je vous conseille de revoir votre position
reconsideration [riːkənsɪdə'reɪʃən] N *(of question)* reconsidération *f*; *(of decision)* reconsidération, réexamen *m*
reconstitute [riː'kɒnstɪtjuːt] VT reconstituer
reconstitution [riːkɒnstɪ'tjuːʃən] N reconstitution *f*
reconstruct [riːkən'strʌkt] VT *(house etc)* reconstruire, rebâtir; *(company, corrupt computer file etc), Fig (facts, crime)* reconstituer; *(one's life, a country)* reconstruire
reconstruction [riːkən'strʌkʃən] N *(of house, country, life etc)* reconstruction *f*, *(of file, company etc), Fig (of crime)* reconstitution *f*; **economic and financial r.** restauration *f* économique et financière
reconstructive [riːkən'strʌktɪv] ADJ
▶▶ **r. surgery** chirurgie *f* réparatrice
reconvene [riːkən'viːn] VT convoquer de nouveau
VI se réunir à nouveau

RECORD[1] ['rekɔːd]

> N registre **1, 2** ▪ procès-verbal **1**
> ▪ dossier **2** ▪ antécédents **4** ▪ disque **5** ▪ record **6**
> ADJ ATTRIB record

N **1** *(of attendance)* registre *m*; *(of proceedings)* procès-verbal *m*, pl procès-verbaux; *(of verdict, fact)* enregistrement *m*; **to keep a r. of sth** garder une trace de qch; **I can find no r. of it** je n'en trouve aucune mention; **to be on r.** *(of verdict, fact)* être enregistré; *Law* **to strike sth from the r.** rayer qch du procès-verbal; **to be on r. as saying sth** avoir déclaré qch publiquement; **to go on r. as a pacifist** se déclarer pacifiste; **to put sth on r.** noter qch, consigner qch; **it is on r. that …** *or* **it is a matter of r.** c'est un fait établi (**that** que); **this is the coldest winter on r.** c'est l'hiver le plus froid que l'on ait jamais enregistré; **to say sth off the r.** dire qch en confidence; **this is strictly off the r.** ceci est strictement confidentiel, ceci doit rester entre nous; **(just) for the r.,**

to keep the r. straight pour que les choses soient claires; **is this for the r.?** est-ce que cela est officiel?; **to put** or **set the r. straight** mettre les choses au clair, dissiper tout malentendu; **to leave few records** (of ancient civilization) laisser peu de témoignages écrits; **the Etruscans left little r. of their religious beliefs** les Étruscans n'ont laissé que peu de traces de leurs croyances

2 (file) dossier m; Hist, Law archive f, Admin registre m; **our records do not go back that far** nos registres ou nos archives ne remontent pas aussi loin; Admin **records management** gestion fdes dossiers

3 Comput (in database) article m, enregistrement m

4 (personal history) antécédents mpl; (of criminal) casier m judiciaire; (achievements) résultats mpl; **to have a good/bad safety r.** (of company etc) avoir une bonne/mauvaise réputation en ce qui concerne la sécurité; Mil, Fig **he has a good r.** ses états de service sont bons; **his past r.** (behaviour) ses antécédents; (achievements) ses résultats antérieurs; **given your r. as a late payer** vu vos antécédents de mauvais payeur; Law **to have a clean r.** avoir un casier judiciaire vierge; Law **he has a r.** il a déjà été condamné, il a des condamnations antérieures; Med **case r.** fiche fde patient ou d'observation

5 Mus (recording) disque m; **to make a r.** faire ou enregistrer un disque; **to play** or **put on a r.** mettre ou passer un disque; **to change a r.** changer un disque; Fig Hum **change the r., will you?** change de disque!

6 (best performance) record m; **to set a r.** établir un record; **to hold the r.** détenir le record (**for** de); **to break** or **beat the r.** battre le record (**for, by** de); **to break all records** battre tous les records

ADJ ATTRIB record inv; **in r. time** en un temps record; **unemployment is at a r. high/low** le chômage a atteint son chiffre le plus haut/bas

▸▸**r. buff** discophile mf, collectionneur, -euse de disques; **r. card** fiche; **r. company** maison f de disques; **r. deck** platine f (tourne-disque); **r. form** (for keeping records) bordereau m de saisie; **r. label** label m; **r. library** discothèque f (de prêt); **r. office** bureau m des archives; Law greffe m; **r. player** tourne-disque m, pl tourne-disques, platine (disques); **r. producer** producteur m de disques; **r. shop** magasin m de disques; **r. token** chèque-disque m, pl chèques-disques

RECORD² [rɪˈkɔːd]

VT noter **1** ▪ enregistrer **1–3**
▪ rapporter **1**
VI enregistrer

VT 1 (write down) (fact) noter (par écrit), consigner, enregistrer; (give account of) (events) rapporter, relater; (thoughts, ideas etc) noter (par écrit), consigner, mettre sur papier; (temperature, rainfall, hours of sunshine etc) relever; (of policeman) consigner; Law (judgment) minuter; Parl **to r. a vote** voter; **throughout recorded history** aussi loin que les archives remontent; Br **to send a letter (by) recorded delivery** envoyer une lettre en recommandé; **to r. one's opposition** indiquer par écrit son opposition; (in speech) faire part de son opposition

2 (tape) (song, programme) enregistrer; **recorded** (not live) (programme) différé; **this is a recorded message** (on telephone) ceci est un message enregistré; **recorded highlights** extraits mpl pré-enregistrés

3 (register) (earthquake, drop in sales, increase in accidents etc) enregistrer; **the ther-**

mometer records ten degrees le thermomètre marque dix degrés

4 (be evidence of) (battle etc) rappeler, commémorer

VI (of machine, performer) enregistrer; (of sound) s'enregistrer; **his voice doesn't r. well** sa voix ne se prête pas bien à l'enregistrement; **r./replay head** tête f de lecture/enregistrement

record-breaker N (person) personne qui a battu un/des record(s); (sporting etc performance) **it was a splendid run but I don't think it's a r.** c'était une belle prestation mais je ne pense pas que le record soit battu

record-breaking ADJ (jump, success etc) qui bat tous les records

recorder [rɪˈkɔːdər] N **1** (machine) (appareil m) enregistreur m; (tape) r. magnétophone m; radio-cassette r. radiocassette m **2** Mus flûte f à bec **3** Eng Law = avocat m nommé pour remplir certaines fonctions de juge

record-holder N détenteur, -trice du/d'un record

recording [rɪˈkɔːdɪŋ] N **1** (on tape etc) enregistrement m; **to play a r.** passer un enregistrement **2** (writing down) relation fpar écrit; (giving account) consignation f

▸▸**r. artist** musicien, -ienne (qui enregistre des disques); **r. contract** contrat m avec une maison de disques; **r. deck** magnétoscope m d'enregistrement; **r. engineer** ingénieur m du son; **r. head** tête f d'enregistrement; **r. instrument** appareil m enregistreur; **r. session** séance f d'enregistrement; **r. studio** studio m d'enregistrement; **r. tape** ruban m ou bande f d'enregistrement

recount [rɪˈkaʊnt] VT (relate) raconter (**to** à)

re-count¹ [ˈriːkaʊnt] N (of people, money, votes etc) recomptage m, nouveau comptage m; **to do a r.** (of money, people, votes etc) recompter; **to call for** or **demand a r.** exiger un nouveau compte des voix

re-count² [riːˈkaʊnt] VT (money etc) recompter; (votes) compter de nouveau

recoup [rɪˈkuːp] VT (money, loss) récupérer; Law défalquer, faire le décompte de; **to r. one's investment** rentrer dans ses fonds

recourse [rɪˈkɔːs] N **1** recours m; **to have r. to sth/sb** avoir recours ou recourir à qch/qn; **my only r. is …** mon seul recours est … (**to do** de faire); **she cannot remember without r. to her notes** elle ne peut pas se souvenir sans avoir recours à ses notes; **right of r.** droit m de recours **2** Fin recours m; **endorsement without r.** endossement m à forfait

recover [rɪˈkʌvər] VT **1** (get back, find again) retrouver, Lit recouvrer; (one's appetite, voice) retrouver; Comput (file, data) récupérer; **to r. one's breath/courage** reprendre haleine/courage; **to r. consciousness** reprendre connaissance, revenir à soi; **I am recovering my strength** mes forces me reviennent; **to r. one's money** (lent to sb) récupérer son argent; (invested in project etc) rentrer dans ses fonds; **to r. sth from sb** reprendre qch à qn; **to r. one's health** guérir, se rétablir, recouvrer la santé; **to r. oneself** or **one's composure** se ressaisir; **to r. one's balance** retrouver son équilibre **2** (obtain, collect) (bodies, Ind (by-product) récupérer; (from sea) (body, space ship) repêcher

VI (of person) (from shock etc) se remettre (**from** de); (from illness) guérir, se remettre, se rétablir (**from** de); (in competition, race etc) se ressaisir; (of market, business) reprendre; (of stock market, economy, country) se redresser; (of currency) remonter; **to be quite recovered** (of patient) être tout à fait remis ou guéri ou rétabli

re-cover VT (chair etc) recouvrir

recoverable [rɪˈkʌvərəb(ə)l] ADJ (something lost) récupérable; (money) recouvrable; (by-product, computer file etc) récupérable

▸▸Com **r. packaging** emballage m récupérable; Petr **r. resources** ressources fpl exploitables

recovery [rɪˈkʌvərɪ] N **1** (of something lost) récupération f; (of money, deposit) recouvrement m; Comput (of file, data) récupération; **beyond** or **past r.** irrécupérable; Law **action for r. of property** (action fen) revendication f, **r. of damages** obtention f de dommages-intérêts

2 (from illness) guérison f; **to be on the way** or **road to r.** être en voie de guérison; **the patient is making a good r.** le malade fait des progrès rapides; **she made a quick r.** elle s'est vite rétablie; **he is past** or **beyond r.** (patient) on ne peut plus rien faire pour lui, il est dans un état désespéré; **I wish you a speedy r.** je vous souhaite un prompt rétablissement

3 (of economy) redressement m; (of export market, business) reprise f; (of currency) remontée f; **the textile industry has declined beyond r.** l'industrie textile connaît un déclin irrémédiable; **to make a r.** (in competition, race etc) se ressaisir

▸▸Med **r. position** position f latérale de sécurité; Med **r. room** salle f de réanimation; Br Aut **r. service** service m de dépannage; **r. ship** navire m de récupération; Br **r. vehicle** dépanneuse f, **r. vessel** navire de récupération

re-create VT (in film, play etc) (age, era etc) reconstituer, recréer

recreation [rekrɪˈeɪʃən] N loisirs mpl; Sch (break) récréation f, Sch **during (the) r.** pendant la récréation; **I only write poetry for r.** j'écris des poèmes uniquement pour le plaisir

▸▸**r. centre** centre m de loisirs; Br **r. ground** terrain m de jeux; **r. room** (in school, hospital) salle f de récréation; (in hotel) salle de jeux; Am (at home) salle de jeux

re-creation N Cin, Theat etc (of era etc) reconstitution f, recréation f

recreational [rekrɪˈeɪʃən(ə)l] ADJ (activities, facilities) de loisirs

▸▸**r. area** aire f de jeux; **r. centre** centre m de loisirs; **r. drug** drogue f à usage récréatif; **r. therapy** thérapie f par le jeu; Am **r. vehicle** camping-car m, pl camping-cars

recriminate [rɪˈkrɪmɪneɪt] VI récriminer

recrimination [rɪkrɪmɪˈneɪʃən] N récrimination f (**against** contre)

recriminatory [rɪˈkrɪmɪnət(ə)rɪ] ADJ (remark etc) de récrimination

recrudescence [riːkruːˈdesəns] N Fml recrudescence f

recrudescent [riːkruːˈdesənt] ADJ Fml recrudescent

recruit [rɪˈkruːt] N Mil (in organization, company etc) recrue f

VT (army) recruter; (employee) embaucher (as pour le poste de); **to r. sb to do sth** embaucher ou recruter qn pour faire qch

VI Mil recruter; (of company) recruter, embaucher (**for** pour)

recruiting [rɪˈkruːtɪŋ] N (of soldier) recrutement m; (of employee) recrutement, embauche f

▸▸**r. agent** agent m de recrutement; **r. office** bureau m de recrutement; **r. officer** Mil recruteur, -euse; Hist racoleur m; Mil **r. sergeant** sergent m recruteur

recruitment [rɪˈkruːtmənt] N (of soldier, employee etc) recrutement m

▸▸**r. agency** cabinet m de recrutement; **r. campaign** campagne f de recrutement; **r. consultant** conseil m en recrutement; **r. of-**

ficer recruteur, -euse; **r. scheme** programme *m* de recrutement

rectal ['rekt(ə)l] ADJ *Med, Anat* rectal, -aux
▸▸**r. cancer** cancer *m* du rectum; **r. examination** examen *m* rectal *ou* du rectum

rectangle ['rektæŋg(ə)l] N rectangle *m*

rectangular [rek'tæŋgjʊlər] ADJ rectangulaire; **to be r. in shape** être rectangulaire

rectification [rektɪfɪ'keɪʃən] N *(of calculation, situation etc)* rectification *f*; *(of oversight)* réparation *f*; *Elec* redressement *m*; *Acct (of entry)* modification *f*, rectification

rectifier ['rektɪfaɪər] N *Chem* rectificateur *m*; *Elec* redresseur *m*

rectify ['rektɪfaɪ] VT *(calculation)* rectifier, corriger; *(mistake, situation), Chem, Math* rectifier; *(oversight)* réparer; *Elec* redresser; *Acct (entry)* modifier, rectifier

rectilineal [rektɪ'lɪnɪəl], **rectilinear** [rektɪ'lɪnɪər] ADJ rectiligne
▸▸*TV* **r. scanning** analyse *f* par lignes

rectitude ['rektɪtjuːd] N rectitude *f*

recto ['rektəʊ] N *Typ* recto *m*

rector ['rektər] N **1** *(in Church of England)* pasteur *m* anglican; *(in Catholic church) (of seminary)* supérieur *m* **2** *Univ* président *m*; *Scot Sch* proviseur *m*; *Scot Univ* = personne *f* élue par les étudiants pour les représenter

rectorial [rek'tɔːrɪəl] ADJ *(decision, duties)* rectoral, -aux; *Scot Univ* **r. election** = élection *f* d'une personnalité dont le rôle est de représenter les étudiants

rectory ['rektərɪ] N *Rel (residence)* presbytère *m*

rectoscope ['rektəskəʊp] N *Med* rectoscope *m*

rectum, *pl* **rectums, recta** ['rektəm, -əmz, -ə] N *Anat* rectum *m*

recumbent [rɪ'kʌmbənt] ADJ *Lit* couché, étendu; **to be r.** être couché (**on** sur)
▸▸*Art* **r. figure** figure *f* couchée, gisant *m*

recuperate [rɪ'kuːpəreɪt, -'kjuː-] VT *(one's strength, money, heat)* récupérer
VI *(of person)* se remettre, se rétablir, récupérer (**from** de); **he had gone to the South of France to r.** il était allé en convalescence dans le Midi; **she is still recuperating** elle est encore en convalescence

recuperation [rɪkuːpə'reɪʃən, -'kjuː-] N **1** *(of strength, money, heat)* récupération *f* **2** *(from illness)* rétablissement *m*; **powers of r.** capacités *fpl* de rétablissement

recuperative [rɪ'kuːpərətɪv, -'kjuː-] ADJ *(powers)* de rétablissement

recur [rɪ'kɜːr] VI **(-rr-)** *(of theme)* revenir, être répété; *(of event), Math (of figures)* se reproduire; *(of illness)* réapparaître; **to r. to the mind** revenir à la mémoire; **a festival that recurs every ten years** une fête qui a lieu tous les dix ans

recurrence [rɪ'kʌrəns] N *(of illness)* réapparition *f*; *(of infectious disease)* récurrence *f*, récidive *f*; *(of theme)* répétition *f*, réapparition; *(of event)* répétition; **has there been any r. of the symptoms?** les symptômes se sont-ils manifestés à nouveau?

recurrent [rɪ'kʌrənt] ADJ **1** *(event)* périodique, qui revient *ou* se répète périodiquement; *(fever, symptom, theme)* récurrent; *(dream, nightmare)* qui revient souvent **2** *Med, Anat* récurrent
▸▸**r. expenses** dépenses *fpl* courantes; *Com* frais *mpl* généraux; *Math* **r. series** série *f* récurrente

recurring [rɪ'kɜːrɪŋ] ADJ *(event)* périodique; *(theme)* qui se répète, qui réapparaît; *(dream, nightmare)* qui revient souvent; **33. 33 r.** 33, 33 à l'infini
▸▸**r. decimal** fraction *f* périodique

recusant ['rekjʊzənt] ADJ *Rel* réfractaire

recyclable [riː'saɪkləbəl] ADJ *(container etc)* recyclable

recycle [riː'saɪk(ə)l] VT *(waste, water, paper etc)* recycler; **recycled paper/glass/plastic** papier *m*/verre *m*/plastique *m* recyclé; *Fin* **to r. funds** remettre des fonds en circulation
▸▸*Comput* **r. bin** corbeille *f*

recycling [riː'saɪklɪŋ] N *(of paper etc)* recyclage *m*; *(of funds)* remise *f* en circulation
▸▸**r. facility** installation *f* de recyclage; **r. plant** usine *f* de recyclage

red [red] ADJ *(comp* **redder**, *superl* **reddest)* **1** *(dress, wine, lips etc)* rouge; *(beard, hair)* roux, *f* rousse; **r.(-rimmed) eyes** yeux *mpl* rouges; **to turn** *or* **go r.** *(of person, litmus paper)* rougir, devenir rouge; *(of leaves etc)* roussir; *(of sky)* rougeoyer; **wait till the lights turn r.** attend que le feu passe au rouge; **to be r. in the face** *or* **have a r. face** *(permanent state)* être rougeaud; **to be r. (in the face) with anger/embarrassment** être rouge de colère/gêne; **was my face r.!** ce que j'étais gêné!; **there will be some r. faces on the Opposition benches** cela va causer de l'embarras dans les rangs de l'Opposition; **to be as r. as a beetroot** *(with embarrassment)* être rouge comme une tomate; **to be as r. as a lobster** *(with sunburn)* être rouge comme une écrevisse; *Am Fam* **it isn't worth a r. cent** ça ne vaut pas un centime; **the mere mention of his name was like a r. rag to a bull (to him)** le simple fait d'entendre son nom le mettait dans une colère noire; **Little R. Riding Hood** Le Petit Chaperon rouge
2 *Fam (communist)* rouge
N **1** *(colour)* rouge *m*; **r. is my favourite colour** le rouge est ma couleur préférée; **dressed in r.** habillé de *ou* en rouge; *Fam* **to see r.** *(be angry)* voir rouge
2 *Fin Fam* **to be in the r.** *(of company, person)* avoir un découvert, être dans le rouge; *(of account)* avoir un solde déficitaire; **to go into the r.** passer dans le rouge; **at last I'm out of the r.** enfin je ne suis plus à découvert
3 *Pol Fam* rouge *mf*; **to see reds under the bed** avoir la phobie des communistes; **the reds-under-the-bed syndrome** la phobie anti-communiste
4 *(in billiards)* bille *f* rouge; *(on roulette table)* rouge *m*
5 *(red wine)* rouge *m*
▸▸*Mil, Fig* **r. alert** alerte *f* rouge; **to be on r. alert** être en état d'alerte maximale; **R. Army** Armée *f* rouge; **r. card** *(in football, rugby)* carton *m* rouge, *Belg* carte *f* rouge; **r. carpet** tapis *m* rouge; *Fig* **to put** *or* **roll out the r. carpet for sb** recevoir quelqu'un en grande pompe, dérouler le tapis rouge pour recevoir quelqu'un; **I got the r.-carpet treatment wherever I went** on m'a reçu en grande pompe partout où je suis allé; **r. channel** *(at airport etc)* = file *f* pour les passagers qui ont des objets à déclarer à la douane; *Fam* **R. China** la Chine communiste *ou* populaire; **the R. Crescent** le Croissant-Rouge; **R. Cross** Croix-Rouge *f*, *Astron* **r. dwarf** naine *f* rouge; *Br Naut* **R. Ensign** = pavillon *m* de la marine marchande britannique; **the R. Flag** = hymne *f* du parti travailliste britannique; **r. flag** drapeau *m* rouge; *Astron* **r. giant** géante *f* rouge; **R. Guard** *(in China)* garde *m* rouge; **r. herring** *(fish)* hareng *m* saur; *Fig* diversion *f*, **it's just a red herring** ce n'est qu'un truc pour nous dépister ou pour brouiller les pistes; **R. Indian** Peau-Rouge *mf*, *pl* Peaux-Rouges; *Am Fin Fam* **r. ink** déficit *m*; **to go into r. ink** *(of person)* se mettre à découvert; *(of company)* être en déficit; *Aut* **r. light** feu *m* rouge; **to go through a r. light** brûler le feu rouge; *Fig* **to get** *or* **be given the r. light** être rejeté; **r.-light district** quartier *m* des prostituées,

quartier chaud; **r. meat** viande *f* rouge; **r. pepper** *(spice)* (poivre *m* de) cayenne *m*; *(vegetable)* poivron *m* rouge; **the R. Sea** la mer Rouge; **r. setter** setter *m* irlandais; *Hist* **R. Shirts** Chemises *fpl* rouges; **r. snapper** vivanneau *m*; **R. Square** la place Rouge; *Zool* **r. squirrel** écureuil *m* roux; **r. tape** *(bureaucracy)* paperasserie *f*

red-blooded ADJ *(person)* vigoureux, robuste; *(policy, response etc)* musclé; **the average r. male** n'importe quel homme digne de ce nom

redbreast ['redbrest] N *(bird)* **(robin)** r. rouge-gorge *m*, *pl* rouges-gorges

redbrick ['redbrɪk] ADJ *(house, building)* en brique rouge
▸▸*Br Fig* **r. university** = université *f* de province (par opposition à Oxford et Cambridge) construites à la fin du XIXᵉ siècle

redcap ['redkæp] N **1** *Br Mil Fam* soldat *m* de la police militaire **2** *Am Rail* porteur *m*

redcoat ['redkəʊt] N **1** *Br* **1** *Hist* soldat *m* anglais (du dix-huitième siècle) **2** *(at holiday camp)* animateur, -trice

redcurrant ['redkʌrənt] N groseille *f* (rouge)
▸▸**r. bush** groseillier *m* rouge; **r. jelly** gelée *f* de groseille

redden ['red(ə)n] VT rougir, rendre rouge
VI *(of sky)* rougeoyer; *(of leaves)* roussir; *(of person)* rougir

reddish ['redɪʃ] ADJ *(light, colour)* rougeâtre; *(hair)* rougeâtre, qui tire sur le roux

redecorate [riː'dekəreɪt] VT *(flat etc)* refaire
VI refaire la peinture et les papiers

redecoration [riːdekə'reɪʃən] N *(of house etc)* remise *f* à neuf de la peinture et des papiers

redeem [rɪ'diːm] VT **1** *(recover) (pawned item)* dégager; **to r. one's good name** sauver son honneur **2** *Fin (pay off) (mortgaged property)* racheter, dégager; *(debt)* amortir, se libérer de; *(bill)* honorer; *(loan)* rembourser, amortir; *Fig Fml (obligations)* s'acquitter de; **to r. a mortgage** *(of mortgagor)* éteindre une hypothèque; *(of mortgagee)* purger une hypothèque; *Fml* **to r. one's promise** tenir sa promesse (**to do sth** de faire qch) **3** *(convert) (bond)* obtenir le remboursement de; *(gift token)* échanger; *(coupon)* rembourser; **to r. a bond** racheter une obligation **4** *(compensate for) (fault)* racheter, rattraper; **to r. oneself** se racheter; **it's his sole redeeming feature** c'est sa seule qualité **5** *Fml (free) (slave, prisoner)* libérer, racheter; *Rel (of Christ) (mankind)* racheter

redeemable [rɪ'diːməb(ə)l] ADJ **1** *Fin (loan, mortgage)* remboursable; *(voucher)* encaissable; *(share)* réalisable, rachetable; *(debt)* remboursable, amortissable; *Fig (manuscript)* qui peut être sauvé; **coupons are r. for cash** les coupons sont remboursables en espèces **2** *(mistake)* réparable; *(sin, crime)* expiable; *(sinner)* rachetable

redeemer [rɪ'diːmər] N *Rel* **the R.** le Rédempteur

redefine [riːdɪ'faɪn] VT redéfinir

redefinition [riːdef'nɪʃən] N redéfinition *f*

redemption [rɪ'dem(p)ʃən] N **1** *(of item pawned)* dégagement *m* **2** *(of property)* rachat *m*; *Fin (of mortgage) (by mortgagor)* extinction *f*, *(by mortgagee)* purge *f*, *(of loan)* amortissement *m* **3** *(of gift token)* échange *m*; *Fin (of coupon)* remboursement *m* **4** *(of fault)* rachat *m*; **to be beyond** *or* **past r.** être irrécupérable; *(of smashed car, broken toy etc)* être irréparable **5** *(of slave, prisoner)* rachat *m*; *Rel* rédemption *f*, *Fig* **this setback proved his r.** ce revers de fortune fut son salut
▸▸*Fin* **r. date** date *f* d'échéance; *Fin* **r. fee** prime *f* de remboursement; *Fin* **r. premium**

prime de remboursement; *Fin* **r. price** prix *m* de rachat; *Fin* **r. value** valeur *f* de remboursement *ou* de rachat; *Fin* **r. yield** rendement *m* à l'échéance

redemptive [rɪ'demtɪv] ADJ *esp Rel* rédempteur, -trice

redeploy [ri:dɪ'plɔɪ] VT *Mil (troops etc)* redéployer; *Admin (employees)* réaffecter

redeployment [ri:dɪ'plɔɪmənt] N *(of troops etc)* redéploiement *m*; *(of staff)* réaffectation *f*

redesign [ri:dɪ'zaɪn] VT reconcevoir

redevelop [ri:dɪ'veləp] VT *(poor district)* réaménager, revaloriser; **the docks are being redeveloped** les docks sont en cours de réaménagement

redevelopment [ri:dɪ'veləpmənt] N *(of town, street etc)* réaménagement *m*, remise *f* en valeur; **scheduled for r.** dont le réaménagement est prévu
▸▸ **r. area** zone *f* de réaménagement

red-eye N **1** *Am Fam* whisky *m* bon marché **2** *Aviat Fam (night flight)* vol *m* de nuit **3** *Phot* = phénomène *m* provoquant l'apparition de taches rouges dans les yeux des personnes photographiées au flash; **to avoid the r. effect** ... pour éviter que le sujet n'apparaisse avec les yeux rouges ...
▸▸ *Aviat Fam* **r. flight** vol de nuit

red-eyed ADJ aux yeux rouges; **to be r.** avoir les yeux rouges (**with, from** de); **she's r. from crying/staying up all night** elle a les yeux rouges d'avoir pleuré/d'avoir passé une nuit blanche

red-faced ['red'feɪst] ADJ *(naturally)* rougeaud, rubicond; *(with anger, embarrassment)* rouge, rougissant (**with** de); **a r. admission** un aveu confus

red-haired ADJ aux cheveux roux; **a r. man** un roux; **a r. girl** une rousse

red-handed [-'hændɪd] ADJ **to be caught r.** être pris en flagrant délit *ou Fam* la main dans le sac

redhead ['redhed] N **1** *(person)* roux *m*, rousse *f* **2** *TV, Cin (lighting)* mandarine *f*

red-headed ADJ **1** *(person)* = **red-haired 2** *(bird, animal)* à tête rouge

red-hot ADJ *(very hot)* brûlant; *(metal)* chauffé au rouge; *Fig (supporter, revolutionary etc)* ardent; *(enthusiasm)* débordant; *Fam (news, information)* de dernière minute; *Fam (very good)* excellent, sensass *inv*; **to make sth r.** *(by heating)* porter qch au rouge; **Rangers are the r. favourites to win the cup** Rangers sont les grandissimes favoris de la coupe
▸▸ *Bot* **r. poker** tritoma *m*

redial[1] [ri:'daɪəl] (**-ll-**, *Am* **-l-**) *Tel* VT **to r. a number** refaire un numéro
VI refaire le numéro

redial[2] ['ri:daɪəl] N *Tel* rappel *m* du dernier numéro; **the latest model has automatic r.** le dernier modèle est muni du système de rappel du dernier numéro
▸▸ **r. feature** rappel du dernier numéro

redirect [ri:dɪ'rekt, -daɪ-] VT **1** *(letter etc)* faire suivre; *(telephone call etc)* réacheminer **2** *(plane etc)* dérouter **3** *Fig* **to r. one's energies (into sth)** réorienter son énergie (dans qch)

redirection [ri:dɪ'rekʃən, -daɪ-] N **1** *(of letter etc)* réacheminement *m*, réexpédition *f* **2** *(of plane)* déroutement *m* **3** *Fig* **the situation demands the r. of some of our attention to ...** la situation exige que l'on réoriente nos efforts vers ...

rediscount [ri:'dɪskaʊnt] N réescompte *m*
VT *Am Com* réescompter

rediscover [ri:dɪ'skʌvər] VT redécouvrir

redistribute [ri:dɪ'strɪbju:t] VT *(wealth,*

tasks) redistribuer; *Pol* **to r. seats** redécouper les circonscriptions électorales

redistribution [ri:dɪstrɪ'bju:ʃən] N *(of wealth, labour)* redistribution *f*; *Pol* **r. of seats** nouveau découpage *m* des circonscriptions

red-letter ADJ
▸▸ **r. day** jour *m* à marquer d'une pierre blanche; **this has been a r. day for everyone** ceci a été un jour mémorable pour tout le monde

redneck ['rednek] N *Am Fam Pej* plouc *mf*, bouseux, -euse *(du Sud des États-Unis)*; **a r. politician** un homme politique tout ce qu'il y a de plus réactionnaire; **a r. attitude** une attitude réactionnaire

redness ['rednɪs] N *(of face, sky etc)* rouge *m*; *(of hair)* rousseur *f*

redo [ri:'du:] VT *(pt* **redid** [ri:'dɪd]; *pp* **redone** [ri:'dʌn])* (task, flat)* refaire; *Comput* rétablir, refaire

redolent ['redələnt] ADJ *Lit (sweet-smelling)* odoriférant, parfumé; *(strong-smelling)* qui a une odeur forte (**of** de); *Fig (reminiscent)* évocateur, -trice, suggestif; **r. of spring** qui exhale une odeur de printemps; **a house r. of the past** une maison qui évoque le passé

redouble [ri:'dʌb(ə)l] VT *(one's cries, entreaties)* redoubler; **to r. one's efforts** redoubler d'efforts *ou* de zèle; *Cards* **to r. spades** surcontrer pique
VI *(of noise, efforts, criticism etc)* redoubler; *Cards* surcontrer

redoubt [rɪ'daʊt] N *Mil* redoute *f*; *Fig* bastion *m*

redoubtable [rɪ'daʊtəb(ə)l] ADJ *(fearsome)* formidable; *(opponent)* redoutable

redound [rɪ'daʊnd] VI *Fml (of deeds)* se retourner (**upon, on** contre); **to r. to sb's credit** être à l'honneur de qn; **to r. to sb's advantage** tourner à l'avantage de qn

red-pencil VT (**-ll-**, *Am* **-l-**) *(text)* corriger, réviser

redraft[1] ['ri:drɑ:ft] N **1** *(action) (of proposal, submission)* refonte *f* **2** *(resulting text)* texte *m* revu; **this is the third r.** c'est la troisième version

redraft[2] [ri:'drɑ:ft] VT *(proposal, submission)* rédiger à nouveau

redress [rɪ'dres] N *(of grievance)* réparation *f*, **to seek r.** demander réparation (**for** de); **there is no r.** il n'y a pas de recours
VT *(rectify) (a wrong)* réparer; **to r. the balance** rétablir l'équilibre

re-dress VT **to r. a wound** refaire le pansement d'une blessure

redshank ['redʃæŋk] N *(bird)* chevalier *m* gambette

redskin ['redskɪn] N *Pol Old-fashioned Pej* Peau-Rouge *mf*, *pl* Peaux-Rouges

redstart ['redstɑ:t] N *(bird)* rouge-queue *m* à front blanc, *pl* rouges-queues à front blanc

redtop ['redtɒp] N *Br Journ Fam* tabloïde *m*, journal *m* à sensation *(dont le titre est imprimé en rouge)*

reduce [rɪ'dju:s] VT **1** *(lessen) (price)* baisser, diminuer, réduire; *(drawing, photograph)* réduire; *(tax)* baisser, alléger; *(spending)* diminuer, réduire; *(temperature)* faire baisser; *Culin (sauce)* faire réduire; **oranges have been reduced** les oranges ont baissé *ou* diminué; *Com* **reduced to £10 from £15** soldé de 15 à 10 livres; **are these shoes reduced?** est-ce que ces chaussures sont soldées *ou* en solde?; **to buy sth at a reduced price** acheter qch à prix réduit; *Ind* **to r. output** ralentir la production; **to r. the risk** réduire le risque (**of sth** de qch); **to r. speed** diminuer *ou* réduire la vitesse, ralentir; **to r. stocks** dé-

stocker des marchandises; **to r. a prison sentence** accorder *ou* consentir une remise de peine; **his prison sentence was reduced to two years** sa peine de prison a été ramenée à deux ans
 2 *(bring to a certain state)* **to r. sth to ashes/dust** réduire qch en cendres/poussière; **to r. sb to despair/silence** réduire qn au désespoir/silence; **his words reduced her to tears** ses paroles l'ont fait fondre en larmes; **to r. sb to helpless laughter** faire mourir qn de rire; **to r. sb to the ranks/the rank of ...** rétrograder *ou* casser qn/descendre qn au rang de ...; **to be reduced to doing sth** en être réduit à faire qch; **is this what I've been reduced to?** j'en suis donc réduit à cela?
 3 *(simplify) (problem, question)* ramener (**to** à); *(fraction, equation)* réduire; **to r. sth to a percentage** exprimer qch en pourcentage; **to r. a fraction to its lowest terms** simplifier une fraction, ramener une fraction à sa plus simple expression; **to r. two fractions to the same denominator** réduire deux fractions au même dénominateur
VI *(slim)* maigrir; *Culin (of sauce)* se réduire

reduced [rɪ'dju:st] ADJ *(smaller)* réduit; **on a r. scale** à une échelle réduite; **at r. prices** au rabais, en solde; **at greatly r. prices** à prix très réduits; **at (a) r. rate** *(bus or theatre ticket etc)* à tarif réduit; **r. rate loan** prêt *m* à taux réduit; **everything r. by ten per cent** remise de dix pour cent sur tous nos articles; **r. to clear** *(sign)* (soldes) coup de balai; **to be/live in r. circumstances** être/vivre dans la gêne

reducer [rɪ'dju:sər] N *Elec* réducteur *m*; *Phot* affaiblisseur *m*

reducible [rɪ'dju:sɪb(ə)l] ADJ réductible (**to** à)

reduction [rɪ'dʌkʃən] N **1** *(of prices)* baisse *f*, diminution *f*, réduction *f*; *(of taxes)* allègement *m*; *(of costs, speed, spending)* diminution, réduction; *(of drawing, photograph, scale)* réduction; *(of temperature, voltage)* baisse; **I'll give you a r.** *(on purchase)* je vous fais un prix; **big reductions** *(sale notice)* rabais, soldes; *Law* **r. of sentence** remise *f* de peine; *Fin* **r. in borrowings** désendettement *m*; **r. in staff** compression *f* de personnel; **r. in stocks** déstockage *m*; **r. of capital** réduction de capital **2** *(of equation)* réduction *f* **3** *Med (of fracture)* réduction *f*
▸▸ *Tech* **r. gear** (engrenage *m*) démultiplicateur *m*

reductionism [rɪ'dʌkʃənɪz(ə)m] N *Phil* réductionnisme *m*

reductionist [rɪ'dʌkʃənɪst] N, ADJ *Phil* réductionniste *mf*

redundancy [rɪ'dʌndənsɪ] N **1** *Br Ind (dismissal)* licenciement *m*; **redundancies have been heavy** il y a eu beaucoup de licenciements; **the strike caused over three hundred redundancies** la grève a causé le licenciement de plus de trois cents personnes; **voluntary r.** départ *m* volontaire **2** *(of details, factory etc)* inutilité *f*, *Comput, Ling etc* redondance *f*
▸▸ *Br* **r. notice** préavis *m* de licenciement; *Br* **r. payment** indemnité *f* de licenciement

redundant [rɪ'dʌndənt] ADJ **1** *Br (worker)* licencié; **to make sb r.** *(of employer)* licencier qn, mettre qn au chômage; *(of technology etc)* entraîner le licenciement de qn; **to be made r.** être licencié, être mis au chômage **2** *(details, factory etc)* superflu; *(information, knowledge)* inutile; *Comput, Ling (file, information)* redondant; **I just feel r. round here now** j'ai l'impression de ne plus servir à rien ici

redwood ['redwʊd] N *(tree)* séquoia *m*

re-echo VT *(repeat) (sound)* répercuter, renvoyer; *Fig* répéter
VI *(of noise, voice etc)* retentir, résonner; **the**

hall echoed and re-echoed to the sound of applause la salle retentissait d'acclamations

reed [ri:d] **N 1** (plant) roseau m; Fig **broken r.** personne f sur laquelle on ne peut (pas) compter **2** Mus (of instrument) anche f
▶▶**r. bed** roselière f; Orn **r. bunting** bruant m des roseaux; **r. pipe** pipeau m, chalumeau m; **r. stop** jeu m d'anches; Orn **r. warbler** fauvette f des roseaux, rousserolle f effarvatte

re-edit **VT** (text) rédiger à nouveau; Comput rééditer

re-educate **VT** (criminal etc), Med (limb) rééduquer

re-education **N** (of criminal etc), Med (of limb) rééducation f

reedy ['ri:dɪ] **ADJ 1** (covered in reeds) plein ou couvert de roseaux **2** (shrill) (instrument) aigu, f aiguë; (voice) flûté, grêle

reef¹ [ri:f] **N** (rocks) écueil m, récif m; Fig écueil m; **to hit a r.** (of ship) faire naufrage sur un récif; Fig **his plans had hit a r.** ses projets s'étaient heurté à un écueil

reef² Naut **N** (of sail) ris m
VT (sail) prendre un ou des ris à; **to r. the sails** prendre les ris
▶▶**r. knot** nœud m plat

reefer ['ri:fər] **N 1** (jacket) caban m, vareuse f **2** Old-fashioned Fam (marijuana cigarette) joint m **3** Am (for transporting goods) camion m/navire m/wagon m frigorifique; (refrigerator) chambre f frigorifique
ADJ (truck etc) réfrigéré

reek [ri:k] **N** (bad smell) puanteur f
VI puer; also Fig **to r. of sth** puer qch; **this room reeks** ça pue ici; Fig **the whole affair reeks of corruption** toute cette affaire sent la corruption à plein nez

reel [ri:l] **N 1** Br (for film, paper, thread) bobine f, (film itself) pellicule f, (for fishing line) moulinet m; (for cable, hose etc) dévidoir m; **r. to r. tape** bande f en bobine; **r. to r. (tape recorder)** magnétophone m à bobines; Am Fam **(right) off the r.** (continuously) d'une seule traite, d'affilée; (immediately) sans hésiter, sur-le-champ **2** (dance, music) reel m, quadrille m écossais
VI (sway) chanceler; (not walk straight) tituber; **to go reeling down the street** descendre la rue en titubant; Fig **to make sb's senses r.** donner le vertige à qn; Fig **my head is reeling** la tête me tourne; Fig **I'm still reeling** (after news) je n'en suis toujours pas revenu; Fig **she was still reeling from shock at what had happened** elle était encore toute retournée par ce qui venait de se passer; **to send sb reeling** (of punch) envoyer valser qn; Fig (of news, scene etc) abasourdir qn; Fig **his mind** or **brain reeled at the thought** cette pensée lui donnait le vertige; Fig **the whole room was reeling** toute la salle tournoyait autour de moi/lui/etc
▶**reel in** **VT SEP** **to r. a fish in** remonter un poisson (avec le moulinet)
▶**reel off** **VT SEP** (speech etc) débiter

re-elect **VT** (MP etc) réélire; **she is sure to be re-elected** sa réélection est assurée; **he was re-elected (as) president** on l'a réélu président

re-election **N** réélection f; **to stand** or Am **run for r.** se représenter

reeling ['ri:lɪŋ] **ADJ** (gait) titubant

re-embark **VT** (passengers) rembarquer
VI rembarquer; Fig **to r. on sth** recommencer qch

re-embarkation **N** rembarquement m

re-emerge **VI** (of person) ressortir; (of sun) reparaître; **when the country re-emerges into prosperity** quand le pays connaîtra à nouveau la prospérité

re-employ **VT** (former employee) réembaucher

re-employment **N** (of former employee) réembauchage m

re-enact **VT 1** (enforce) (law) remettre en vigueur **2** (depict) (accident, crime, battle) reconstituer; (scene, mistakes) reproduire

re-enactment **N 1** (of law) remise f en vigueur **2** (of accident, crime, battle) reconstitution f; (of scene, mistakes) reproduction f

re-engage **VT 1** (former employee) réembaucher **2** Tech (cogwheel) rengrener; Aut **to r. the clutch** rembrayer

re-engagement **N 1** (of former employee) réembauchage m **2** Tech (of cogwheel) rengrènement m; Aut (of clutch) rembrayage m

re-enlist **VI** Mil se rengager

re-enter **VI** (of person, spacecraft) rentrer; (of musical instrument) faire une ou sa rentrée; **to r. for an examination** se présenter de nouveau à un examen; Theat **r. Macbeth** Macbeth rentre
VT 1 (a room etc) rentrer dans; **he never re-entered that house** il n'a jamais remis les pieds dans cette maison; **to r. the job market** se remettre à chercher du travail; **the spacecraft re-entered the atmosphere** le vaisseau spatial est rentré dans l'atmosphère **2** (date, name) réinscrire, inscrire de nouveau

re-entrant **ADJ** (angle etc) rentrant
N angle m rentrant

re-entry **N** (of person, spacecraft) rentrée f, **to make its r.** (of spacecraft) rentrer dans l'atmosphère

re-establish **VT** (communications, diplomatic relations etc) rétablir

re-establishment **N** (of communications, relations etc) rétablissement m

reeve [ri:v] **VT** (pt **rove** [rəʊv], **reeved**; pp **reeved, rove**) Naut (rope) passer (**through a block** dans une poulie)

re-examination **N 1** (of file, question etc) réexamen m **2** Law (of witness) nouvel interrogatoire m

re-examine **VT 1** (review) (file, question etc) réexaminer **2** Law (witness) interroger de nouveau

re-export¹ [ri:'ekspɔ:t] **N** (of goods) réexportation f

re-export² ['ri:ekspɔ:t] **VT** (goods) réexporter

re-exportation **N** réexportation f

ref **N** [ref] **1** Br Sport Fam (abbr **referee**) arbitre m **2** Com (abbr **reference**) (at head of letter) réf; **your r.** v/réf; **our r.** n/réf

re-face **VT** (building) ravaler les façades de; (wall) refaire

refashion [ri:'fæʃən] **VT** remodeler

refectory [rɪ'fekt(ə)rɪ] **N** réfectoire m
▶▶**r. table** = table f longue et étroite (souvent en chêne massif)

REFER [rɪ'fɜːr] **VT** (**-rr-**) (direct) (matter, proposal etc) soumettre (**to** à); **to r. a cheque to drawer** (of bank) retourner un chèque au tireur; **r. to drawer** (notice on cheque) voir le tireur; **he referred me to an article on the subject** il m'a renvoyé à un article sur la question; **to r. a matter to sb** soumettre une question à qn; **to r. a question to sb for (a) decision** soumettre une question à la décision de qn; **to r. a matter to a tribunal** soumettre une affaire à un tribunal; **the reader is referred to ...** (in book) se reporter à ...; **to r. a patient to a specialist** envoyer un malade chez un spécialiste; Med **she's going to r. me** elle va m'envoyer chez un spécialiste; **to r. a customer to another department** renvoyer un client à un autre service; **he just referred me back to you** il m'a renvoyé à vous; Med **referred pain** douleur f irradiée
▶**refer to** **VT INSEP 1** (consult) se référer ou se

reporter à; **to r. (back) to an expert** consulter un expert
2 (allude to) faire allusion à; (speak of) parler de; **who are you referring to?** de qui parlez-vous?; **it's you I'm referring to** c'est de toi que je parle; **referred to as ...** désigné sous le nom de ...; **he never refers to it** il n'en parle jamais; **we won't r. to it again** nous n'en reparlons plus; Com **referring to ...** nous référant à ...; **referring to your letter** suite à votre lettre
3 (apply to) s'appliquer à; **these measures r. to large enterprises only** ces mesures ne concernent que les grandes entreprises; **this remark refers to you** (is aimed at) cette remarque s'adresse à vous; (is about) cette remarque vous concerne

referee [refə'riː] **N 1** Sport, Fig arbitre m **2** (for job etc) please give at least two referees veuillez fournir aux moins deux références; **will you act as my r.?** voulez-vous me fournir des références? **3** Fin **r. in case of need** (on bill of exchange) adresse f au besoin
VT & VI (pt, pp **refereed**) Sport, Fig arbitrer

reference ['ref(ə)rəns] **N 1** (to higher authority) renvoi m; **without r. to the Board** sans consulter le conseil d'administration; **I'll have to make r. to my superior** il faudra que j'en réfère à mon supérieur; **terms of r.** (of person, investigating body) compétence f, (of law) étendue f, **outside the committee's terms of r.** hors de la compétence du comité **2** (consultation) consultation f, (source) référence f, **for r. only** (on library book) consultation sur place; (on document etc in circulation) pour information seulement; **to keep sth for future r.** garder qch à titre d'information; **for future r., please note ...** pour votre information à l'avenir, veuillez noter ...
3 (allusion) allusion f (**to** à); (mention) mention f (**to** de); (connection) rapport m (**to** avec); (in book) (allusion) référence f, (cross-reference) renvoi m; (on map) coordonnées fpl, **to make r. to a fact** faire mention d'un fait; **if any r. is made to me** si on parle de moi; **with r. to what was said ...** en référence à ce qui a été dit ...; **a talk on the environment with particular r. to ...** un exposé sur l'environnement abordant tout particulièrement ...; **with r. to my letter of the 20th March** me référant ou suite à ma lettre du 20 mars; **in r.** or **with r. to your letter** en ce qui concerne votre lettre; **with r. to what was said at the meeting** à propos de ou en ce qui concerne ce qui a été dit au cours de la réunion; **r. AB** (at head of letter) référence AB; **our/your r.** (on letter) notre/votre référence
4 (testimonial) (from bank etc) référence f, (from employer) référence, lettre f de recommandation, certificat m de travail; **to give sb a r.** donner son avis sur qn; **to have good references** avoir de bonnes références; **he got a very bad r. from his previous employer** son ancien employeur ne l'a pas du tout recommandé; **to take up references** prendre contact avec ou contacter les personnes dont un candidat se recommande; **to give sb as a r.** se recommander de qn; **you may use my name as (a) r.** vous pouvez donner mon nom comme référence, vous pouvez vous recommander de moi
VT 1 (refer to) faire référence à **2** (thesis) établir la liste des citations dans; (quotation) donner la référence de **3** Comput référencer
▶▶**r. book** ouvrage m de référence; Mktg **r. customer** client, -ente de référence; Mktg **r. group** groupe m de référence; **r. library** bibliothèque f d'ouvrages de référence; **r. number** numéro m de référence; Banking **r. period** période f de référence; **r. point** point m de repère; Mktg **r. price** prix m de réfé-

rence; *Fin* **r. rate** taux *m* de référence; **r. room** *(in public library)* salle *f* de lecture; *(in university)* salle de consultation; *Mktg* **r. sale** vente *f* de référence; **r. work** ouvrage *m* de référence

referendum [refə'rendəm] N *Pol* référendum *m*, referendum *m*; **to hold a r.** organiser un référendum; **decided in a** *or* **by r.** décidé par référendum

referral [rɪ'fɜːrəl] N **1** *(forwarding)* renvoi *m* **2** *(consultation)* consultation *f* **3** *Univ (of the-sis)* renvoi *m* pour révision **4** *(person)* patient *m* *(envoyé par son médecin chez un spécialiste)*

refill[1] ['riːfɪl] N *(for lighter, pen)* recharge *f*, cartouche *f*, *(for propelling pencil)* mine *f* de rechange; *(for notebook)* feuilles *fpl* de rechange; *(of drink)* autre verre *m*; **I'll have a r.** tu me remets la même chose?; **would you like a r.?** je vous ressers?; **she handed me her glass for a r.** elle m'a tendu son verre pour que je la reserve

refill[2] [riː'fɪl] VT *(glass etc)* remplir (à nouveau) **(with** de); *(lighter, pen etc)* recharger; *(shelves)* regarnir (**with** de)

refillable [riː'fɪləb(ə)l] ADJ *(lighter, pen)* rechargeable

refinance [riː'faɪnæns] *Fin* VT *(loan)* refinancer
VI *(of company)* se refinancer (**on the money market** auprès du marché monétaire)

refinancing [riː'faɪnænsɪŋ] N *Fin* refinancement *m*; **to get r. from a bank** se refinancer auprès d'une banque

refine [rɪ'faɪn] VT **1** *(process, purify)* *(sugar, petroleum)* raffiner; *(metal)* affiner **2** *(develop)* *(technique, machine)* perfectionner
▸ **refine on, refine upon** VT INSEP *(improve)* parfaire

refined [rɪ'faɪnd] ADJ *(petroleum, sugar)* raffiné; *(metal)* affiné; *Fig (person, taste)* raffiné, *Pej* maniéré

refinement [rɪ'faɪnmənt] N **1** *(of manners, taste, person)* raffinement *m*; **of great r.** *(person)* très raffiné; **lack of r.** vulgarité *f* **2** *(of technique)* perfectionnement *m*; **machine with all the latest refinements** machine dotée des derniers perfectionnements; **to make refinements to** *(machine)* perfectionner; *(plan, tactics etc)* parfaire **3** *(of metal etc)* = **refining**

refiner [rɪ'faɪnər] N *(of petroleum, sugar)* raffineur *m*; *(of metal)* affineur *m*

refinery [rɪ'faɪnərɪ] N *(for petroleum, sugar)* raffinerie *f*, *(for metal)* affinerie *f*

refining [rɪ'faɪnɪŋ] N *(of petroleum, sugar)* raffinage *m*; *(of metal)* affinage *m*

refit[1] ['riːfɪt] N *(of ship)* réparation *f*, remise *f* en état; *(of factory)* réaménagement *m*; **the yacht is under r.** le yacht est en cours de réparation

refit[2] [riː'fɪt] (**-tt-**) VT *(ship)* remettre en état; *(factory)* réaménager
VI *(of ship)* être en cours de réparation; *(of factory)* être en cours de réaménagement; **while we're refitting** *(the ship)* pendant les réparations; *(the factory)* pendant le réaménagement

reflate [riː'fleɪt] VT **to r. the economy** relancer l'économie
VI relancer l'économie

reflation [riː'fleɪʃən] N relance *f*

reflationary [riː'fleɪʃənərɪ] ADJ *Econ* de relance; **r. pressure** pression *f* de relance

reflect [rɪ'flekt] VT **1** *(image)* réfléchir, refléter, renvoyer; *(light)* réfléchir, renvoyer; *(heat)* renvoyer; **to be reflected** se réfléchir (**in** sur); *TV etc* **reflected light** lumière *f* réfléchie; *Fig* **to bask** *or* **bathe in reflected glory** se parer des plumes du paon; **they basked**

or **bathed in the reflected glory of their famous daughter** ils se glorifiaient de la célébrité de leur fille; *Fig* **her personal problems are reflected in her poor performance at school** elle a des problèmes personnels et ses résultats scolaires s'en ressentent **2** *(think)* **to r. that …** penser *ou* se dire que … + *ind*
VI *(think)* réfléchir (**on** à, sur)
▸ **reflect on** VT INSEP **to r. well on sb** *(of action etc)* faire honneur à qn; **to r. badly on sb** *(of action etc)* faire du tort à qn, nuire à (la réputation de) qn; **how is that going to r. on the company?** quelles en seront les conséquences *ou* répercussions pour la société?

reflecting [rɪ'flektɪŋ] ADJ *(surface etc)* réfléchissant

reflection [rɪ'flekʃən] N **1** *(image)* *(in mirror)* reflet *m*, image *f* (réfléchie); *Fig* reflet (**of** de); **to see one's r. in a mirror** voir son image dans un miroir; *Fig* **the final score was a fair r. of the Italians' superiority** le score final reflétait bien la supériorité des Italiens; **this report is not an accurate r. of the situation** ce rapport ne donne pas un aperçu exact de la situation
2 *(action)* *(of light, sound, image)* réflexion *f* **3** *Fig (on honesty, character etc)* *(negative)* blâme *m*, critique *f* (**on** de); **their conduct is a (bad) r. on all of us** leur conduite nous fait du tort à tous; **it's a good r. on the school** c'est bon pour la réputation de l'école; **it's a r. on your popularity** ça veut dire beaucoup quant à ta popularité; **it's no r. on your performance** il ne s'agit pas d'une remise en cause de votre performance, cela ne remet pas votre performance en cause
4 *(thought)* réflexion *f* (**on** sur); **on r.** à la réflexion, en y réfléchissant, tout bien réfléchi; **to do sth without due r.** faire qch sans avoir suffisamment réfléchi; **reflections** réflexions, pensées *fpl*; **reflections on the history of …** considérations *fpl* sur l'histoire de …

reflective [rɪ'flektɪv] ADJ **1** *(thoughtful)* *(person)* réfléchi **2** *(surface)* réfléchissant, réflecteur; *(power, angle)* réflecteur; *(light)* réfléchi

reflectively [rɪ'flektɪvlɪ] ADV *(to look at)* d'un air pensif; *(to say)* d'un ton pensif

reflector [rɪ'flektər] N *(on bicycle, vehicle)* réflecteur *m*, cataphote® *m*, catadioptre *m*; *(on sign, of heat)* réflecteur
▸▸ **r. board** panneau *m* réflecteur

reflex ['riːfleks] N *(reaction)* réflexe *m*; **to have good reflexes** avoir de bons réflexes; **to test sb's reflexes** tester les réflexes de qn; **your reflexes aren't what they should be** vos réflexes sont défaillants
ADJ **1** réflexe **2** *Math (angle)* rentrant
▸▸ *Physiol* **r. action** réflexe *m*; *Phot* **r. camera** (appareil *m*) reflex *m*

reflexion [rɪ'flekʃən] N = **reflection**

reflexive [rɪ'fleksɪv] VOIR GRAMMAIRE A29–30; B28–9 *Gram* ADJ *(pronoun, verb)* réfléchi
N *(verb)* verbe *m* réfléchi; *(pronoun)* pronom *m* (personnel) réfléchi

reflexively [rɪ'fleksɪvlɪ] ADV *Gram* au sens réfléchi

reflexology [riːflek'sɒlədʒɪ] N réflexologie *f*

refloat [riː'fləʊt] VT **1** *(ship)* renflouer, (re-)mettre à flot **2** *Fin (loan)* émettre de nouveau; *(company)* renflouer, remettre à flot; *Fig (proposals)* présenter à nouveau

reflux ['riːflʌks] N reflux *m*

refocus [riː'fəʊkəs] (**-s-**) VT *Cin, TV (camera)* refaire la mise au point de

reforest [riː'fɒrɪst] VT *(region, land)* reboiser

reforestation [riːfɒrɪ'steɪʃən] N reboisement *m*

reform [rɪ'fɔːm] N *(of law, institution etc)* réforme *f*, *(of person)* retour *m* à la vertu *ou* à une conduite meilleure; *(of alcoholics, criminals, delinquents)* réinsertion *f*; **to introduce reforms** introduire *ou* apporter des réformes; **to make reforms** faire des réformes; **to be beyond r.** être irrécupérable
VT *(improve)* *(institution, law etc)* réformer; *(system)* réformer, améliorer; *(person)* corriger, ramener à la vertu; **he's a reformed character** il s'est assagi, il a changé en bien; **a reformed alcoholic** un ancien alcoolique
VI *(of person)* se corriger, s'amender
▸▸ **Reformed Church** Église *f* réformée; *Am* **r. school** ≃ centre *m* d'éducation surveillée

re-form VT *(battalion, group etc)* reformer
VI *(of group, troops etc)* se reformer

reformat [riː'fɔːmæt] (**-tt-**) *Comput, Typ* VT *(text, disk, page etc)* reformater
VI reformater

reformation [refə'meɪʃən] N **1** *(of calendar, society etc)* réforme *f*; *Rel, Hist* **the R.** la Réforme **2** *(of person)* retour *m* à la vertu *ou* à une conduite meilleure

reformatory [rɪ'fɔːmət(ə)rɪ] ADJ *(measures etc)* réformateur, -trice
N *Am* ≃ centre *m* d'éducation surveillée; *Br Formerly* maison *f* de correction *ou* de redressement

reformatting [riː'fɔːmætɪŋ] N *Comput, Typ* *(of text, disk, page etc)* reformatage *m*

reformer [rɪ'fɔːmər] N *(of religion, society)* réformateur, -trice

reformism [rɪ'fɔːmɪz(ə)m] N réformisme *m*

reformist [rɪ'fɔːmɪst] ADJ, N réformiste *mf*

refract [rɪ'frækt] VT *(light)* réfracter; **to be refracted** être réfracté

refracting [rɪ'fræktɪŋ] ADJ *(material, prism)* réfringent; *(angle)* de réfraction
▸▸ **r. telescope** réfracteur *m*, lunette *f* astronomique

refraction [rɪ'frækʃən] N *Phys, Opt* réfraction *f*; **double r.** biréfringence *f*

refractive [rɪ'fræktɪv] ADJ *Phys* réfringent
▸▸ **r. index** indice *m* de réfraction

refractivity [riːfræk'tɪvɪtɪ] N *Phys* réfringence *f*

refractor [rɪ'fræktər] N **1** *Phys (material)* milieu *m* réfringent; *(object)* dispositif *m* réfringent **2** *(telescope)* réfracteur *m*, lunette *f* astronomique

refractory [rɪ'frækt(ə)rɪ] ADJ *Fml (person)* réfractaire, récalcitrant; *(animal)* récalcitrant; *(illness)* rebelle
N réfractaire *m*

refrain[1] [rɪ'freɪn] N *Mus, Fig* refrain *m*

refrain[2] VI se retenir, s'abstenir (**from doing** de faire); **to r. from comment** s'abstenir de tout commentaire; **he couldn't r. from smiling** il n'a pu s'empêcher de sourire; **kindly r. from smoking/talking** *(on notice)* prière de ne pas fumer/parler

refrangible [rɪ'frændʒɪb(ə)l] ADJ *Phys, Opt* réfrangible

re-freeze VT *(food)* recongeler

refresh[1] [rɪ'freʃ] N *Comput* actualisation *f*, rafraîchissement *m*
▸▸ **r. rate** taux *m* d'actualisation *ou* de rafraîchissement

refresh[2] VT *(person)* *(of bath, drink)* rafraîchir, *Fam* requinquer; *(of rest, amusement)* reposer, délasser; *Comput* rafraîchir, actualiser; **to r. oneself** *(with food)* se restaurer; *(with drink)* se rafraîchir; *(by taking bath)* se délasser; **to awake refreshed** s'éveiller frais et dispos *ou* bien reposé; *Hum* **to r. the inner man** se désaltérer; **to r. one's memory** se rafraîchir la mémoire; *Fam* **let me r. your memory!** je vais vous rafraîchir la mémoire!;

can I r. your drink for you? voulez-vous que je vous resserve?

refresher [rɪ'freʃər] N
▸▸ **r. course** stage m ou cours m de recyclage

refreshing [rɪ'freʃɪŋ] ADJ (breeze, drink) rafraîchissant; (sleep) réparateur, -trice, reposant; (bath, shower, cup of tea) revigorant, ravigotant; **it is r. or a r. change to encounter such honesty** cela change agréablement de ou il est réconfortant de rencontrer une telle honnêteté; **his honesty is r.** son honnêteté est comme une bouffée d'air frais ou est réconfortante

refreshingly [rɪ'freʃɪŋlɪ] ADV d'une manière qui repose ou fait du bien; **r. honest** d'une honnêteté réconfortante; **a r. original style** un style dont l'originalité est comme une bouffée d'air frais

refreshments [rɪ'freʃmənts] NPL (drinks) rafraîchissements mpl, (snacks) collation f, **to order some r.** commander à manger/à boire; **r. will be served** une collation sera servie

refrigerant [rɪ'frɪdʒərənt] N (mélange m) réfrigérant m

refrigerate [rɪ'frɪdʒəreɪt] VT (food etc) réfrigérer; **r. after opening** (notice on packet) conserver au réfrigérateur après ouverture; **keep refrigerated** (notice on packet) conserver au réfrigérateur; **refrigerated lorry** camion m frigorifique; **refrigerated meat** viande f frigorifiée; **refrigerated ship** navire m frigorifique

refrigeration [rɪfrɪdʒə'reɪʃən] N (of food etc) réfrigération f
▸▸ **r. plant** installation f frigorifique

refrigerator [rɪ'frɪdʒəreɪtər] N (domestic) réfrigérateur m, frigidaire® m; (industrial) réfrigérateur, chambre f ou appareil m frigorifique

refuel [riː'fjuːəl] (-ll-, Am -l-) VT (ship, aircraft, racing car) ravitailler en carburant; Fig **to r. speculation** alimenter les conjectures
VI (of ship, aircraft, racing car) se ravitailler en carburant; **to r. in flight** se ravitailler en vol

refuelling, Am **refueling** [riː'fjuːəlɪŋ] N (of ship, aircraft, racing car) ravitaillement m en carburant
▸▸ **r. stop** (of aircraft, ship) escale f pour se ravitailler en carburant; (of racing car) arrêt m pour se ravitailler en carburant

refuge ['refjuːdʒ] N (from danger) refuge m, asile m; (from weather) abri m (from contre); (for battered women) foyer m; Br (island in road) refuge; **place of r.** lieu m de refuge ou d'asile; **to seek r.** chercher refuge ou asile; **to take r.** (from danger) se réfugier (with chez); **to take r. from the storm** s'abriter de l'orage; Fig **to take r. in lying/drugs/ religion** se réfugier dans le mensonge/la drogue/la religion; Fig **to seek r. in lying/ drugs/religion** chercher refuge dans le mensonge/la drogue/la religion; **he has been accused of taking r. in evasive language** on l'a accusé de pratiquer la langue de bois; Lit **God is my r.** Dieu est mon refuge

refugee [refjʊ'dʒiː] N réfugié, -ée; **economic r.** migrant, -ante économique
▸▸ **r. camp** camp m de réfugiés; **r. status** statut m de réfugié

refund[1] ['riːfʌnd] N (for ticket, tax etc) remboursement m; **to obtain a r. for sth** se faire rembourser qch; **I'm due a r.** je dois être remboursé

refund[2] [riː'fʌnd, rɪ-] VT (money, payment etc) rembourser; **to r. sb** rembourser qn (**sth** de qch)

refundable [riː'fʌndəbl] ADJ **to charge a r. deposit on sth** consigner qch

refunding [riː'fʌndɪŋ] N remboursement m
▸▸ Fin **r. clause** clause f de remboursement; Fin **r. loan** prêt m de remboursement

refurbish [riː'fɜːbɪʃ] VT (flat, restaurant etc) remettre à neuf

refurbishment [riː'fɜːbɪʃmənt] N remise f à neuf

refusal [rɪ'fjuːz(ə)l] N (of offer, invitation etc) refus m (**to do** de faire); (of cheque) rejet m; **to give a flat r.** refuser (tout) net; **to meet with a r.** (of person) se heurter à ou essuyer un refus; (of offer, invitation etc) se heurter à un refus; **she shook her head in r.** elle a fait non de la tête; **that's his third r.** (of show-jumper) c'est la troisième fois qu'il refuse l'obstacle; **to have first r.** avoir la priorité (**on sth** sur qch); **to give sb first r.** donner la priorité à qn; **you promised me first r. on the car** tu m'as promis que je serais le premier à qui tu proposerais (d'acheter) la voiture
▸▸ Mktg **r. rate** taux m de refus

refuse[1] ['refjuːs] N (rubbish) ordures fpl, détritus m; **household r.** ordures ménagères
▸▸ **r. bag** sac m à ordures; Br **r. bin** poubelle f, Br **r. chute** vide-ordures m inv; Br **r. collection** ramassage m d'ordures; Br **r. collector** éboueur m; Br **r. disposal** traitement m des ordures; Br **r. disposal unit** broyeur m d'ordures; Br **r. dump** (public) décharge f (publique), dépotoir m; **r. material** détritus

> Note that the French word **refus** is a false friend and is never a translation for the English word **refuse**. It means **refusal**.

refuse[2] [rɪ'fjuːz] VT (invitation, offer), Horseriding (fence etc) refuser; (request) rejeter, repousser; **to r. to do sth** refuser de ou Fml se refuser à faire qch; **I r. to believe that** je ne peux pas le croire; **to r. to comment** se refuser à tout commentaire; **to r. to fight** refuser le combat; **the car refuses to start** la voiture ne veut pas démarrer; **to r. sb sth** refuser qch à qn; **to r. sb admittance** refuser (de laisser entrer) qn; **they were refused admittance** on ne les a pas laissés entrer; **to be refused** essuyer un refus; **I don't see how we can r. them** je ne vois pas comment on peut le leur refuser; **she made me an offer I couldn't r.** elle m'a fait une proposition que je ne pouvais pas refuser; **she refused him** (would not marry him) elle l'a rejeté
VI (of person) refuser; (of horse) refuser l'obstacle

refus(e)nik [rɪ'fjuːznɪk] N Pol refuznik mf

refutation [refjʊ'teɪʃən] N (disproving) réfutation f

refute [rɪ'fjuːt] VT **1** (disprove) (argument, theory etc) réfuter; **to r. a statement** démontrer la fausseté d'une déclaration **2** (deny) **to r. an allegation** nier une allégation

regain [rɪ'geɪn] VT **1** (get back) (person's confidence) regagner; (strength, money) récupérer; (strength, health, sight, balance, freedom) retrouver, recouvrer; **to r. possession of sth** rentrer en ou reprendre possession de qch; **to r. consciousness** reprendre connaissance, revenir à soi; **to r. (lost) ground** regagner du terrain **2** (reach) (a place, one's seat) regagner

regal ['riːg(ə)l] ADJ (offer, salary, splendour etc) royal, -aux; (air, person) majestueux, royal

regale [rɪ'geɪl] VT (person) régaler (**with** de)

regalia [rɪ'geɪlɪə] NPL (of monarch) insignes mpl royaux; (of Freemason etc) insignes; **the mayor came first in all his r.** le maire venu en premier avec tous les insignes de ses fonctions; Hum **here comes Mrs Smith in full r.** voilà Mme Smith dans ses plus beaux atours

regally ['riːg(ə)lɪ] ADV (to entertain) royalement; (to behave, act) majestueusement

regard [rɪ'gɑːd] N **1** (admiration, respect) (for person) respect m, estime f, (for skill, talent etc) respect; **to have great r. for sb** avoir beaucoup d'estime pour qn; **I have great r. for him but I don't particularly like him** j'ai beaucoup de respect pour lui mais je ne l'apprécie pas particulièrement; **to hold sb in great or high r.** tenir qn en grande ou haute estime; **out of r. for sb** par respect pour qn
2 (consideration) égard m, considération f (**for** pour); **out of r. for** par égard pour; **without or with no r. to** sans égard pour; **without r. to race or colour** sans distinction de race ni de couleur; **to pay r. to** avoir égard à, faire attention à; **to pay no r. to** ne faire aucune attention à; **to have no r. for human life** faire peu de cas de la vie humaine
3 (connection) **in this or that r.** à cet égard; **in all regards** à tous (les) égards; **with r. to** en ce qui concerne, quant à; **with r. to your letter of …** relativement à votre lettre du …; **having r. to** si l'on tient compte de, eu égard à
4 (in message etc) **to give or send one's regards** transmettre son bon souvenir, Fml faire ses hommages; **(please give) my kindest or best regards to the family** (présentez) mon meilleur souvenir ou mes sincères amitiés à toute la famille; **kind or best regards** (at end of letter) cordialement
VT **1** (admire, respect) avoir de l'estime pour; **to r. sb highly** avoir beaucoup d'estime pour qn; **to be highly regarded** être tenu en haute estime
2 (consider) considérer (**as** comme), tenir (**as** pour)
3 (concern) regarder, concerner; **as regards …** en ce qui concerne …, pour ce qui est de …, quant à …; **she is very strict as regards discipline** elle est très sévère pour ce qui est de ou sur le chapitre de la discipline

> Note that the French word **regard** is a false friend and is never a translation for the English word **regard**. It means **look, gaze**.
>
> Note that the French verb **regarder** is a false friend and is never a translation for the English verb **to regard**. It means **to look at, to watch**.

regardful [rɪ'gɑːdfʊl] ADJ **to be r. of** se soucier de

regarding [rɪ'gɑːdɪŋ] PREP (about) en ce qui concerne, pour ce qui est de; Fam **what's it r.?** de quoi s'agit-il?

regardless [rɪ'gɑːdlɪs] ADV **1 r. of** (consequences, danger, noise etc) sans se soucier de; **to be r. of the danger of infection** ne pas se soucier du risque d'infection; **r. of expense** sans regarder à la dépense **2** (despite everything) quand même; **press on r.!** allez-y quand même!, continuez!

regatta [rɪ'gætə] N régate f

regency ['riːdʒənsɪ] N régence f, Hist **the R.** la Régence; **R. armchair/furniture** fauteuil m/meubles mpl Régence

regenerate [rɪ'dʒenəreɪt] VT régénérer; **to r. an industry/a political party** régénérer une industrie/un parti politique; **to r. interest in sth** raviver l'intérêt pour qch; Fig **to feel regenerated** se sentir régénéré
VI (of industry, party etc) se régénérer; (of tail, organ etc) repousser

regenerating [rɪ'dʒenəreɪtɪŋ] ADJ régénérateur, -trice

regeneration [rɪdʒenə'reɪʃən] N régénération f

regenerative [rɪ'dʒenərətɪv] ADJ régénérateur, -trice; *Med* régénératif
▸▸ *Aut* **r. braking** freinage *m* à régénération

regent ['riːdʒənt] ADJ *Hist* régent
N **1** *Hist* régent, -ente; **prince r.** prince *m* régent **2** *Am* = membre *m* du conseil d'administration d'une université

reggae ['regeɪ] N *Mus* reggae *m*

regicide ['redʒɪsaɪd] N *(crime)* régicide *m*; *(person)* régicide *mf*

regime, régime [reɪ'ʒiːm] N *Pol* régime *m*; **the old r.** l'ancien régime

regimen ['redʒɪmen] N *Med* régime *m*

regiment ['redʒɪmənt] N *Mil, Fig* régiment *m*; **there's enough to feed a r.** il y a de quoi nourrir un régiment
VT *(people)* enrégimenter, embrigader; *(education system, organization)* réglementer

regimental [redʒɪ'ment(ə)l] *Mil* ADJ *(badge, flag etc)* régimentaire, du régiment
NPL **regimentals** *(uniform)* uniforme *m* (militaire), tenue *f* militaire; **in full regimentals** en grande tenue d'apparat
▸▸ **r. band** fanfare *f* du régiment; **r. sergeant major** ≃ adjudant-chef *m*, *pl* adjudants-chefs

regimentation [redʒɪmen'teɪʃən] N *Pej* discipline *f* excessive

regimented ['redʒɪmentɪd] ADJ strict; **it's a very r. organization** c'est une organisation très rigide

region ['riːdʒ(ə)n] N *(of country, body etc)* région *f*, *Fig* **in the r. of** environ; **somewhere in the r. of £500** dans les 500 livres

regional ['riːdʒən(ə)l] ADJ régional, -aux
▸▸ *Br* **r. development** *(building, land development)* aménagement *m* du territoire; *(for jobs)* action *f* régionale; *Br* **r. development corporation** = organisme *m* pour l'aménagement du territoire

regionalism ['riːdʒənəlɪz(ə)m] N *Ling* *(word, expression)* régionalisme *m*

regionalization [riːdʒən(ə)laɪ'zeɪʃən] N régionalisation *f*

━━━━━━━━━━━━━━━━━━
REGISTER ['redʒɪstər]
┌─────────────────────────────────┐
│ **N** registre **1-4, 6** ▪ liste **1** ▪ caisse **5** │
│ **VT** inscrire **1** ▪ immatriculer **1** │
│ ▪ déclarer **1** ▪ indiquer **2** ▪ manifester **2** │
│ **VI** s'inscrire **1** │
└─────────────────────────────────┘

N **1** *(book)* registre *m*; *(list)* liste *f*, *Sch* cahier *m* d'appel; **to enter sth in a r.** inscrire qch sur *ou* dans un registre; **to keep a r.** tenir un registre; *Sch* **to take the r.** faire l'appel; **r. of births, marriages and deaths** registre de l'état civil; **electoral r., r. of voters** liste électorale; **r. of shareholders** livre *m* des actionnaires
2 *(range)* *(of instrument)* registre *m*; *(of voice)* registre, tessiture *f*
3 *(style)* *(of speaking, writing)* registre *m*
4 *Comput* registre *m*
5 (cash) r. caisse *f* enregistreuse
6 *Typ* registre *m*; **to be in/out of r.** être/ne pas être en registre
VT **1** *(enter in records)* *(member, student)* inscrire; *(vehicle, ship, goods)* immatriculer; *(company)* faire enregistrer; *(birth, marriage, death)* déclarer; *(trademark)* déposer; **to r. a complaint** se plaindre (**with sb** auprès de qn); **to r. a protest** protester; **to r. a letter** recommander une lettre; **I want to send it registered** je voudrais l'envoyer en recommandé; **is the car registered in your name?** est-ce que la voiture est à votre nom?; **she is not registered at this hotel** elle n'est pas descendue à cet hôtel
2 *(indicate, make known)* *(of thermometer*

etc) (temperature etc) indiquer; *(of person) (astonishment, displeasure)* manifester, exprimer; **his face registered disappointment/disapproval** son visage exprimait *ou* reflétait la déception/la désapprobation; **the earthquake registered seven on the Richter scale** le séisme a atteint sept sur l'échelle de Richter; **winds registering a hundred miles an hour** des vents atteignant 160 kilomètres/heure
3 *(realize)* se rendre compte de, prendre la mesure de; **she hadn't registered the danger she was in** elle ne s'était pas rendue compte du danger qu'elle courait
4 *(achieve) (progress, victory)* réaliser
VI **1** *(for course etc)* s'inscrire (**for** à); *(at hotel)* signer le registre; *(of voter)* se faire inscrire sur la liste électorale; **to r. with the police** se faire inscrire à la police
2 *(of gauge, machine)* marcher, fonctionner; *(of amount, measurement)* être indiqué, apparaître; **the quake was so small it barely even registered** la secousse a été à peine perceptible
3 *Fam (of fact, joke etc)* être compris; **he explained it to me yesterday but it didn't r.** il me l'a expliqué hier, mais je n'ai pas fait attention; **I don't think the bad news has registered (with him/her) yet** on lui a annoncé la mauvaise nouvelle mais je ne crois pas qu'il/elle ait bien réalisé; **I've been so busy his absence has barely registered** je suis tellement occupé que je me suis à peine aperçu de son absence; **I did give them the address but I don't think it registered** je leur ai bien donné l'adresse mais je ne crois pas qu'ils l'aient retenue
▸▸ *Admin* **r. office** bureau *m* de l'état civil

registered ['redʒɪstəd] ADJ *(member, voter)* inscrit; *(vehicle)* immatriculé; **to send sth by r. mail** envoyer qch en recommandé; **the r. unemployed** les personnes inscrites au chômage; *Br* **to be r. disabled** avoir une carte d'invalidité
▸▸ *Com* **r. agent** agent *m* agréé; *Fin* **r. bond** obligation *f* nominative; *Fin* **r. capital** capital *m* déclaré; **r. charity** organisme *m* de bienfaisance reconnu par l'État; **r. childminder** nourrice *f* agréée; **r. company** société *f* inscrite au registre du commerce; *Fin* **r. debenture** obligation nominative; *Mktg* **r. design** modèle *m* déposé; **r. letter** lettre *f* recommandée; **r. name** nom *m* déposé; *Br* **r. nurse** infirmière *f* diplômée (d'État); *Br* **r. office** siège *m* social; *Can Fin* **r. retirement savings plan** régime *m* enregistré d'épargne-retraite; *Fin* **r. securities** titres *mpl* nominatifs, valeurs *fpl* nominatives; *St Exch* **r. share** action *f* nominative; *Fin* **r. share certificate** certificat *m* nominatif d'action(s); *St Exch* **r. stock** titres nominatifs, valeurs nominatives; **r. trademark** marque *f* déposée; *Comput* **r. user** = utilisateur, -trice disposant d'une licence

registrar ['redʒɪstrɑːr] N **1** *Br (in registry office)* officier *m* de l'état civil **2** *Am Univ* chef *m* du service *ou* du bureau des inscriptions; *Br Univ* secrétaire *m* général **3** *Com* **r. of companies** directeur *m* du registre des sociétés **4** *Br Med* chef *m* de clinique
▸▸ **the R. General** le Conservateur des actes de l'état civil

registration [redʒɪs'treɪʃən] N *(of student for course etc)* inscription *f*; *(of voter)* inscription sur la liste électorale; *(of vehicle)* immatriculation *f*; *(of birth, death, marriage)* déclaration *f*; *(of trademark)* dépôt *m*; **when does r. start?** *(for university, evening classes)* quand les inscriptions commencent-elles?
▸▸ *St Exch* **r. body** chambre *f* d'enregistrement; **r. card** *(for enrolling on course etc)* fiche *f* d'inscription; *(for foreign guests)* fiche

voyageur; *(for non-EU guests)* fiche de police; *Comput* licence *f*, **r. certificate** matricule *f*, *Br Aut* **r. document** ≃ carte *f* grise; **r. fees** droits *mpl* d'inscription; **r. form** bulletin *m* d'inscription; **r. number** *(of car)* numéro *m* minéralogique *ou* d'immatriculation; *(of student)* (numéro) matricule *m*; **r. and transfer fees** droits d'inscription et de transfert

registry ['redʒɪstrɪ] N **1** *(office)* bureau *m* d'enregistrement **2** *Naut* **a ship of Canadian r.** un navire immatriculé au Canada; **port of r.** port *m* d'attache
▸▸ *Br Admin* **r. office** bureau *m* de l'état civil; **to be married at a** *or* **the r. office** se marier civilement, ≃ se marier à la mairie

regrade [riː'greɪd] VT **1** *(nurse, employee, officer etc)* reclasser **2** *Am Sch (homework)* renoter

regrading [riː'greɪdɪŋ] N *(of nurse, employee, officer etc)* reclassement *m*

regress [rɪ'gres] VI régresser

regression [rɪ'greʃən] N régression *f*

regressive [rɪ'gresɪv] ADJ *Biol, Fin* régressif
▸▸ *Econ* **r. taxation** imposition *f* régressive

regret [rɪ'gret] N regret *m* (**for** de); **to feel r.** éprouver du regret (**at, about** à; **about doing** d'avoir fait); **to express one's r.** exprimer ses regrets; **to have** *or* **feel a pang of r.** éprouver une pointe de regret; **to have no regrets** n'avoir aucun regret, ne rien regretter (**about** au sujet de, quant à); **my only r. is that I didn't resign earlier** je n'ai qu'un regret, c'est de ne pas avoir donné ma démission plus tôt; **(much) to my r.** à mon grand regret; **it is with deep r. that we inform you that …** c'est à grand regret que nous vous informons que …; **she sends (you/us) her regrets** *(is unable to come)* elle vous/nous prie de l'excuser
VT (**-tt-**) *(be sorry for)* regretter; **to r. doing** *or* **having done sth** regretter d'avoir fait qch; **we r. any inconvenience to passengers** nous prions les voyageurs de bien vouloir nous excuser pour ce désagrément; **you'll r. this!** tu le regretteras!; **I r. (have) to inform you that …** j'ai le regret *ou* je regrette de (devoir) vous annoncer que …; **then, I r. to say, she …** puis, malheureusement, elle …; **he bitterly regretted having spoken** il a amèrement regretté d'avoir parlé; **I r. to hear that …** je suis désolé d'apprendre que …; **it is to be regretted that …** il est regrettable *ou* à regretter que … + *sub*

regretful [rɪ'gretfʊl] ADJ *(glance, expression)* plein de regrets; *(feeling)* de regret; **to be r.** *(of person)* avoir des regrets (**about** au sujet de, quant à)

regretfully [rɪ'gretfəlɪ] ADV *(to say)* avec regret; **r., I cannot** je regrette, je ne peux pas

regrettable [rɪ'gretəb(ə)l] ADJ *(sad)* regrettable; *(inconvenient)* fâcheux; **it is r. that …** il est regrettable *ou* à regretter *ou* fâcheux que … + *sub*

regrettably [rɪ'gretəblɪ] ADV malheureusement; **r. few people were present** il est regrettable que si peu de personnes soient venues; **a joke in r. poor taste** une plaisanterie dont le mauvais goût est à déplorer; **that's r. short-sighted of him** c'est, de sa part, un manque de perspicacité regrettable

regroup [riː'gruːp] VT regrouper
VI se regrouper, se rassembler

regrouping [riː'gruːpɪŋ] N regroupement *m*

━━━━━━━━━━━━━━━━━━
REGULAR ['regjʊlər]
┌─────────────────────────────────┐
│ **ADJ** régulier **1-3** ▪ uni **1** ▪ habituel **2** ▪ fidèle **2** ▪ permanent **2** ▪ normal **2, 5** │
│ **N** habitué **1** │
└─────────────────────────────────┘

ADJ 1 *(steady, even) (features, pulse, service etc)* régulier; *(surface)* régulier, uni; **on a r. basis** régulièrement; **to have r. bowel movements** aller régulièrement à la selle; **bran will keep you r.** le son vous fera aller régulièrement à la selle; **to be as r. as clockwork** être réglé comme du papier à musique; **to do sth as r. as clockwork** faire qch avec une régularité infaillible; **he's there every Tuesday, (as) r. as clockwork** il est là tous les mardis, il est réglé comme du papier à musique; **to keep r. hours** *(have strict timetable)* avoir un emploi du temps précis, avoir des horaires réguliers; *(go to bed and rise at reasonable time)* se lever et se coucher à heures régulières; **you should keep more r. hours** *(go to bed earlier)* vous devriez vous coucher plus tôt; **he was a man of r. habits** il avait ses habitudes

2 *(usual) (doctor etc)* habituel; *(verb)* régulier; *(price, size)* normal, -aux, *Can* régulier; *(reader, listener)* fidèle; *(staff)* permanent; *Am Aut (gas)* ordinaire; **my r. bedtime** l'heure à laquelle je me couche habituellement; **you can stay up past your r. bedtime** tu peux te coucher plus tard que d'habitude; **a r. visitor to the house** un/une des habitué(e)s de la maison; *Ind* **r. model** modèle *m* courant; **r. supplier** fournisseur *m* habituel

3 *(professional) (army, soldier)* régulier **4** *Fam (real, thorough) (fool, slave etc)* vrai, véritable; **a r. hero** un vrai héros; *esp Am* **a r. guy** un type réglo *ou* sympa **5** *(normal) (procedure, behaviour etc)* normal, -aux

N 1 *(in bar, restaurant etc)* habitué, -ée **2** *Am Aut (gas)* ordinaire *m* **3** *Mil (professional)* régulier *m*
▸▸ *Journ* **r. column** chronique *f*; **r. customer** client, -ente habitué(e); **r. price** prix *m* de règle

regularity [regjʊˈlærɪtɪ] **N** *(of features, pulse etc)* régularité *f*; **to do sth with unfailing r.** faire qch avec une régularité infaillible
regularize [ˈregjʊləraɪz] **VT** *(situation)* régulariser
regularly [ˈregjʊləlɪ] **ADV** *(to attend, visit etc)* régulièrement; *Am* **the coat is r. priced at …** le manteau coûte normalement …
regulate [ˈregjʊleɪt] **VT 1** *(adjust) (working of a machine, watch, flow of water etc)* régler; *(of valve)* contrôler **2** *(control) (people)* contrôler; **he leads a well-regulated life** il mène une vie très réglée; **rules regulating the use of additives** les réglementations qui régissent l'emploi des additifs
regulating [ˈregjʊleɪtɪŋ] **ADJ** *(knob, switch, valve)* de réglage; *(hormone, mechanism)* régulateur, -trice; **self-r.** à réglage automatique
▸▸ **r. body** autorité *f* de régulation
regulation [regjʊˈleɪʃən] **N 1** *(action) (of machine, watch etc)* réglage *m*; *(of voltage)* régulation *f*; *(of food additives etc)* réglementation *f*; *(of information)* contrôle *m* **2** *(rule)* règlement *m*; **r. dress/speed/uniform** tenue *f*/vitesse *f*/uniforme *m* réglementaire; **black shoes are r. wear** le port de chaussures noires est réglementaire; **regulations** règlement(s); **contrary to** *or* **against (the) regulations** contraire au règlement; **in accordance with the regulations** selon le règlement; **it's not in accordance with the regulations** ce n'est pas réglementaire; **under the regulations** en vertu du règlement; **EU regulations** règlements de l'UE; **safety regulations** règles *fpl* de sécurité
regulator [ˈregjʊleɪtər] **N 1** *(person)* régulateur, -trice **2** *(apparatus)* régulateur *m*
▸▸ **r. valve** régulateur
regulatory [ˈregjʊlətərɪ, regjʊˈleɪtərɪ] **ADJ**

(framework) réglementaire; *(authority)* de contrôle
▸▸ **r. body** instance *f* de contrôle
Regulo® [ˈregjʊləʊ] **N** *Br Culin* thermostat *m*
regurgitate [rɪˈgɜːdʒɪteɪt] **VT** *(food)* régurgiter; *Fig Pej* **to r. one's lecture notes** régurgiter ses cours
regurgitation [rɪgɜːdʒɪˈteɪʃən] **N** *(of food)*, *Fig Pej (of lecture notes)* régurgitation *f*
rehab [ˈriːhæb] **N** *Fam* désintoxication *f*; **to be in r.** être en cure de désintoxication
▸▸ **r. unit** centre *m* de désintoxication
rehabilitate [riːəˈbɪlɪteɪt, riːh-] **VT 1** *(criminal, drug addict, alcoholic)* réinsérer; *Med (stroke victim etc)* rééduquer **2** *(restore reputation of) (politician)* réhabiliter **3** *(restore) (building, area)* réhabiliter, remettre en état, rénover
rehabilitation [riːəbɪlɪˈteɪʃən, riːh-] **N 1** *(of criminal, drug addict, alcoholic)* réinsertion *f*, *Med (of stroke victim etc)* rééducation *f* **2** *(restoring of reputation) (of politician)* réhabilitation *f* **3** *(restoring) (of building, area)* réhabilitation *f*, remise *f* en état, rénovation *f*
▸▸ **r. centre** *(for work training)* centre *m* de réadaptation; *(for drug addicts)* centre *m* de désintoxication
rehash¹ [ˈriːhæʃ] **N** *Fam (of book, script etc)* resucée *f*; **it was a r. of her first novel** c'était une resucée de son premier roman; **it's just a r.** c'est du réchauffé
rehash² [riːˈhæʃ] **VT** *Fam (rework) (old story etc)* remanier; *(old arguments etc)* ressasser, rabâcher
rehearsal [rɪˈhɜːs(ə)l] **N** *(of play, speech etc)* répétition *f*; **to have** *or* **hold a r.** faire une répétition; **to put a play into r.** commencer les répétitions d'une pièce; **we go into r. next week** nous commençons les répétitions la semaine prochaine; *Fig* **the naval exercises were just a r. for the real thing** les exercices navals n'étaient qu'un entraînement; *Theat* **dress r.** *(répétition)* générale *f*
▸▸ **r. room** salle *f* de répétition; **r. script** scénario *m* de répétition
rehearse [rɪˈhɜːs] **VT 1** *(play, part, piece of music, ballet)* répéter; *(actor, orchestra)* faire répéter; **I rehearsed what I was going to say** j'ai préparé ce que j'allais dire; **her indignation struck me as rather rehearsed** son indignation me sembla forcée; **the cast were well rehearsed** les acteurs connaissaient bien leur rôle; **she had been carefully rehearsed by her advisers** ses conseillers lui avaient soigneusement fait répéter ce qu'elle devait dire **2** *(list) (complaints, arguments etc)* répéter, rabâcher
VI *(of actor, musician etc)* répéter
reheat [riːˈhiːt] **VT & VI** réchauffer
rehouse [riːˈhaʊz] **VT** reloger
rehousing [riːˈhaʊzɪŋ] **N** relogement *m*
rehydration [riːhaɪˈdreɪʃən] **N** *Med* réhydratation *f*
reign [reɪn] **N** *(of monarch, champion etc)* règne *m*; **in** *or* **during the r. of …** sous le règne de …; **r. of terror** règne de la terreur; **their r. of terror/violence is at an end** la terreur/violence qu'ils faisaient régner a pris fin
VI *(of monarch, champion, silence etc)* régner; **to r. supreme** *(of monarch)* régner en maître absolu; *(of champion)* être inégalé *ou* sans rival; **to r. for ten years** régner (pendant) dix ans; **silence reigned** le silence régnait; **it's the usual situation in the office: chaos reigns** c'est comme d'habitude au bureau: il y règne le plus grand chaos
▸ **reign over** **VT INSEP** *(of monarch, silence etc)* régner sur
reigning [ˈreɪnɪŋ] **ADJ** *(monarch)* régnant; *(champion)* en titre

reimburse [riːɪmˈbɜːs] **VT** *(money)* rembourser; **to r. sb (for) sth** rembourser qn de qch
reimbursement [riːɪmˈbɜːsmənt] **N** *(of money, person)* remboursement *m*
reimport [riːɪmˈpɔːt] **VT** réimporter
reimportation [riːɪmpɔːˈteɪʃən] **N** réimportation *f*
reimpose [riːɪmˈpəʊz] **VT** réimposer
rein [reɪn] **N** *(for rider, on child)* rêne *f*; *(for coachman)* guide *f*; **to pull at** *or* **on the reins** *(of horse, rider)* tirer sur les rênes; **the reins of power** les rênes du pouvoir; *Fig* **to assume** *or* **take over/hold the reins of government** prendre/tenir les rênes du gouvernement; *Fig* **to hand over the reins** *(of politician, businessman etc)* passer les rênes du pouvoir *(* **to** à*)*; **to give a horse the reins** *or* **free r.** lâcher les rênes *ou* la bride à un cheval; *Fig* **to give sb a free r.** donner carte blanche à qn *(* **to do sth** pour faire qch*)*; *Fig* **to give free r. to one's imagination** donner libre cours à son imagination; *Fig* **to keep a tight r. on** *or* **over sb** tenir la bride haute à qn; *Fig* **to keep a tight r. on one's spending** surveiller étroitement ses dépenses; *Fig* **to keep a tight r. on one's emotions** ne pas se laisser aller à ses émotions, maîtriser ses émotions; *Fig* **to keep a tight r. on one's imagination** ne pas se laisser emporter par son imagination
▸ **rein back** **VT SEP** *(horse)* faire arrêter
VI *(of rider)* faire arrêter son cheval
▸ **rein in** **VT SEP** *(horse)* serrer la bride *ou* les rênes à; *Fig (enthusiasm, emotions, feelings)* modérer; *Fig* **to r. sb in** *(of person in authority)* serrer la bride *ou* la vis à qn; *(of colleague, friend)* faire se modérer; **to r. in one's spending** mettre un frein à *ou* modérer ses dépenses
VI *(of rider)* ramener son cheval au pas
reincarnate¹ [riːɪnˈkɑːnɪt, -eɪt] **ADJ** réincarné
reincarnate² [riːɪnkɑːˈneɪt] **VT** **to be reincarnated** se réincarner *(* **as** sous les traits de, sous la forme de*)*
reincarnation [riːɪnkɑːˈneɪʃən] **N** réincarnation *f*
reindeer [ˈreɪndɪər] **N** renne *m*; **r. moss** *or* **lichen** cladonie *f*
reinforce [riːɪnˈfɔːs] **VT** *(army, wall, fabric)* renforcer; *(foundations)* consolider; *(concrete, glass)* armer; *Fig (argument)* étayer *(* **with** avec*)*; *(prejudices)* renforcer; *(request)* appuyer *(* **with** avec*)*; **that just reinforces what I've been saying** ça ne fait que renforcer ce que j'ai dit
reinforcement [riːɪnˈfɔːsmənt] **N 1** *(action) (of army, wall, fabric)* renforcement *m*; *(of foundations)* consolidation *f*; *(of concrete, glass)* armature *f* **2** *(troops etc)* reinforcements renforts *mpl*; **to await reinforcements** attendre un renfort *ou* des renforts; **to call up reinforcements** demander des renforts
reinitialize [riːɪˈnɪʃəlaɪz] **VT** *Comput* réinitialiser
reinsert [riːɪnˈsɜːt] **VT** *(advert, coin, clause)* réinsérer
reinstall [riːɪnˈstɔːl] **VT** *Comput* réinstaller
reinstallation [riːɪnstəˈleɪʃən] **N** *Comput* réinstallation *f*
reinstate [riːɪnˈsteɪt] **VT** *(person)* réintégrer, rétablir (dans ses fonctions); *(clause etc)* réintroduire
reinstatement [riːɪnˈsteɪtmənt] **N** *(of person)* réintégration *f*, rétablissement *m* *(* **as** en tant que, au poste de*)*; *(of clause etc)* réintroduction *f*
reinstitute [riːˈɪnstɪtjuːt] **VT** réintroduire

reinstitution [ri:ɪnstɪ'tjuːʃən] N réintroduction f

reinsurance [ri:ɪn'ʃʊərəns, -'ʃɔːr-] N réassurance f

reinsure [ri:ɪn'ʃʊər, -'ʃɔːr] VT réassurer

reinsurer [ri:ɪn'ʃʊərər, -'ʃɔːr-] N réassureur m

reintegrate [ri:'ɪntɪgreɪt] VT *(into society etc)* réinsérer

reintegration [ri:ɪntɪ'greɪʃən] N réinsertion f

reinterpret [ri:ɪn'tɜːprɪt] VT réinterpréter

reinterpretation [ri:ɪntɜːprɪ'teɪʃən] N ré-interprétation f

reintroduce [ri:ɪntrə'djuːs] VT réintroduire

reintroduction [ri:ɪntrə'dʌkʃən] N réintroduction f

reinvent [ri:ɪn'vent] VT *Fig* **to r. the wheel** refaire ce qui a déjà été fait

reinvest [ri:ɪn'vest] VT réinvestir

reinvestment [ri:ɪn'vestmənt] N *Fin* nouveau placement m, réinvestissement m

reinvigorate [ri:ɪn'vɪɡəreɪt] VT *(usu passive)* revigorer

reissue [ri:'ɪʃuː] N *(of book, recording)* ré-édition f, *(of banknotes, shares, stamps)* nouvelle émission f
VT *(book, recording)* rééditer; *(banknotes, shares, stamps)* émettre de nouveau

reiterate [ri:'ɪtəreɪt] VT *(request, promise etc)* réitérer

reiteration [ri:ɪtə'reɪʃən] N réitération f

reiterative [ri:'ɪtərətɪv] ADJ réitératif

reject[1] ['riːdʒekt] N *Com (in factory)* article m de rebut, rebut m; *(in shop)* (article de) second choix m; *Fig (person)* personne f marginalisée; *Fig (for job)* candidat m refusé ou qui a échoué; *Fam* **he's a bit of a (social) r.!** il n'est pas sortable!; *Fig* **I'm not going out with one of your rejects!** *(former boyfriend or girlfriend)* ne crois pas que je vais sortir avec un/une de tes ex!; *Fig* **export rejects** marchandises fpl impropres à l'exportation
▸▸ **r. shop** magasin m d'articles de second choix

reject[2] [rɪ'dʒekt] VT *(refuse) (advice, offer, proposal)* rejeter, repousser; *(doctrine)* réprouver; *(goods, manuscript, applicant)* refuser; *(suitor)* éconduire; *(of animal, parent) (young, child)* rejeter; **to feel rejected** se sentir rejeté; **to r. one's food** *(not want)* refuser la nourriture; *Med (vomit)* rendre la nourriture; *Ind* **to r. a part** mettre une pièce au rebut; *Med* **to r. a transplant** rejeter un greffon; **the machine keeps rejecting this coin** pas moyen que la machine accepte cette ou ma pièce

rejection [rɪ'dʒekʃən] N **1** *(of advances, demands)* rejet m; *(of offer, manuscript)* refus m; **to meet with r.** *(of applicant etc)* essuyer un refus; *(of offer, suggestion)* être rejeté; **letter of r.** lettre f de refus **2** *Med (of transplant)* rejet m; *(of food)* régurgitation f
▸▸ **r. letter** lettre de refus; **r. slip** lettre de refus

rejig [ri:'dʒɪɡ] VT **(-gg-) 1** *Fam (rearrange) (text etc)* remanier **2** *(re-equip) (factory)* réaménager

rejoice [rɪ'dʒɔɪs] VI se réjouir (**at, over** de; **in doing** de faire); **to r. in one's freedom/independence** jouir de sa liberté/son indépendance; **we r. to hear that you are safe** nous sommes ravis d'apprendre que vous êtes sain et sauf; *Hum Iron* **he rejoiced in the name of Winterbottom** il répondait au nom délicieux de Winterbottom

rejoicing [rɪ'dʒɔɪsɪŋ] N **1** *(joy)* réjouissance f, allégresse f (**at, over** à); **there was much r. at the announcement** la nouvelle a suscité une très grande joie; **it was an occasion for general r.** ce fut la grande liesse ou la liesse générale **2 rejoicings** *(festivities)* réjouissances fpl, festivités fpl; **there were great rejoicings on the day of the Coronation** il y a eu de grandes réjouissances le jour du couronnement

rejoin[1] [rɪ'dʒɔɪn] VT & VI *(retort)* répliquer

rejoin[2] [ri:'dʒɔɪn] VT **1** *(attach)* rejoindre, réunir (**to** à) **2** *(return to) (person)* rejoindre, retrouver; *Mil (unit, regiment)* rallier, rejoindre; **to r. one's ship** rallier le bord; **to r. a political party** se réinscrire à un parti politique
VI *(of roads, lines etc)* se rejoindre

rejoinder [rɪ'dʒɔɪndər] N *(retort)* réplique f, sharp f, riposte f

rejuvenate [rɪ'dʒuːvɪneɪt] VT *(person)* rajeunir; **I feel rejuvenated after a week off** je me sens rajeuni ou revigoré ou *Fam* requinqué après une semaine de vacances; *Fig* **to r. the economy** donner un coup de fouet à l'économie

rejuvenating [rɪ'dʒuːvɪneɪtɪŋ] ADJ rajeunissant

rejuvenation [rɪdʒuːvɪ'neɪʃən] N rajeunissement m

rekey [riː'kiː] VT *Comput* refrapper

rekeying [riː'kiːɪŋ] N *Comput* refrappe f

rekindle [riː'kɪnd(ə)l] VT *(fire)* rallumer; *Fig (enthusiasm, hope)* ranimer, raviver; *(hatred)* ranimer, raviver, rallumer; *Fig* **a romantic dinner to r. the flame** or **spark** un dîner en amoureux pour ranimer la flamme
VI se rallumer

relapse [rɪ'læps] *Med* N rechute f; **to have** or **suffer a r.** avoir ou faire une rechute, rechuter; **his r. into alcoholism came as no surprise** le fait qu'il soit retombé dans l'alcoolisme n'a surpris personne
VI avoir ou faire une rechute, rechuter; **to r. into unconsciousness** reperdre connaissance; *Fig* **to r. into alcoholism** retomber dans l'alcoolisme

relate [rɪ'leɪt] VT **1** *(narrate) (story etc)* raconter, *Fml* conter; *(one's adventures)* faire le récit de; **strange to r. ...** chose étonnante à dire ... **2** *(connect) (two facts)* établir un rapport entre; **to r. sth to sth** *(link)* rattacher qch à qch
VI **1** *(of question etc)* se rapporter, avoir rapport, avoir trait (**to** à); **agreement relating to ...** convention ayant trait à ... **2** *(of person)* **he finds it difficult to r., he can't r.** *(to others)* il lui est difficile de communiquer avec les autres; **I can't r. to modern music** je n'arrive pas à apprécier la musique moderne; **I don't r. to my home town any more** je ne me sens plus d'attaches avec ma ville natale

related [rɪ'leɪtɪd] ADJ **1** *(languages, styles)* apparenté; **the cost of the project is directly r. to ...** le coût du projet est directement lié à ...; **questions r. to a subject** questions relatives à un sujet; **the two events are r.** les deux événements sont liés; **closely r. species** espèces fpl voisines; **r. activity** activité f annexe; **r. ideas** idées fpl connexes **2** *(people)* apparenté (**to** à); *(by blood)* parent (**to** de); *(by marriage)* parent par alliance (**to** à); **are you two r.?** êtes-vous apparentés ou parents ou de la même famille?; **we are not really r., I just call her 'aunt'** nous ne sommes pas parents ou de la même famille, je l'appelle juste Tatie comme ça; **we're r. by marriage** nous sommes parents par alliance; **he is closely/distantly r. to me** nous sommes proches parents/parents éloignés

-related [rɪ'leɪtɪd] SUFF space-/industry-r. lié à l'espace/l'industrie

relating [rɪ'leɪtɪŋ] ADJ **r. to** *(about)* relatif à, qui se rapporte à; *Admin, Law* afférent à

relation [rɪ'leɪʃən] N **1** *(relative)* parent,

-ente; **r. by marriage** parent, -ente par alliance; **what r. is he to you?** quel est son lien de parenté avec vous?; **are you any r. to ...?** avez-vous un lien de parenté avec ...?; **he's no r. to me** or **of mine** il n'est pas de ma famille; **she is my closest living r.** c'est la plus proche parente qui me reste; **I have relations in Montreal** j'ai de la famille à Montréal; **we've invited all the relations** nous avons invité toute la famille
2 *(connection, relationship)* relation f, rapport m *(between* entre; **in** or **with** r. to relativement à, par rapport à; **to bear no r. to** n'avoir aucun rapport avec; **to bear little r. to** avoir peu de rapport avec; **relations between us are rather strained** nos relations sont plutôt tendues; **to have** or **enjoy friendly relations** entretenir des relations amicales ou des rapports amicaux (**with** avec); **how are relations between you?** comment est-ce que vous vous entendez?; **to enter into relations with sb** entrer ou se mettre en rapport ou en relations avec qn; **to break off all relations with sb** rompre toute relation ou cesser tout rapport avec qn; *Fml* **to have (sexual) relations** avoir des rapports sexuels (**with** avec)
3 *(telling) (of adventures, story etc)* relation f, récit m

relational [rɪ'leɪʃ(ə)l] ADJ relationnel
▸▸ *Comput* **r. database** base f de données relationnelle; *Comput* **r. operator** opérateur m relationnel

relationship [rɪ'leɪʃənʃɪp] N **1** *(relations)* rapports mpl, *(sexual)* liaison f; **to have a love-hate r. with sb/sth** avoir avec qn/qch des relations ou des rapports dans laquel(elle)s se mêlent l'amour et la haine; **she has a good r. with her mother-in-law** elle s'entend bien avec sa belle-mère; **she's been trying to get out of the r. for months** elle essaye de rompre depuis des mois; **our r. is going nowhere** notre relation ne nous mène nulle part; **patient-doctor r.** rapports patient-médecin ou entre le patient et le médecin; **to have a r.** *(affair)* avoir une liaison (**with** avec); **I'm already in a r.** j'ai déjà quelqu'un, je suis déjà avec quelqu'un; **he finds it difficult to have relationships with people** ça lui est difficile d'avoir des relations ou des rapports avec les autres; **our r. is purely professional** nos rapports ou relations sont purement professionnel(elle)s; **what exactly is your r. with her?** quelle est la nature de ou quels sont vos rapports ou relations avec elle?
2 *(kinship) (between people of same family)* lien(s) m(pl) de parenté; *(by marriage)* parenté f par alliance; *(between languages, styles etc)* parenté f; **family r.** lien de parenté; **blood r.** parenté, *(degré* m de) consanguinité f, **what was your r. to the deceased?** quel était votre lien de parenté avec le défunt?
3 *(connection) (between things)* rapport m, relation f (**between ... and** entre ... et); **in r. to** relativement à
▸▸ **r. marketing** marketing m relationnel

relative ['relətɪv] ADJ relatif; **r. to** *(compared to)* relativement à, comparé à; *(in terms of)* en fonction de, par rapport à
N **1** *(person)* parent, -ente; **r. by marriage** parent, -ente par alliance; **he's no r. of mine** il n'est pas de ma famille; **she is my closest living r.** c'est la plus proche parente qui me reste; **I have relatives in Montreal** j'ai de la famille à Montréal; **we've invited all the relatives** nous avons invité toute la famille **2** *Phil* **the r.** le relatif
▸▸ *Gram* **r. clause** (proposition f) relative f, *Mktg* **r. market share** part f de marché relative; *Gram* **r. pronoun** pronom m relatif VOIR GRAMMAIRE A32–3; B22–3

Note that the French word **relatif** is never used to refer to members of one's family.

relatively ['relətɪvlɪ] ADV (fairly) relativement, assez; **r. few people were there** il y avait assez ou relativement peu de gens; **r. speaking** relativement parlant

relativism ['relətɪvɪz(ə)m] N Phil relativisme m

relativistic [relətɪ'vɪstɪk] ADJ relativiste

relativity [relə'tɪvɪtɪ] N relativité f; **r. theory, theory of r.** théorie f de la relativité

relaunch[1] ['riː'lɔːntʃ] N Mktg relancement m

relaunch[2] [riː'lɔːntʃ] VT Mktg relancer

relax [rɪ'læks] VT 1 (person) (of bath, meditation etc) (physically) détendre, délasser, relaxer; (mentally) détendre, relaxer 2 (loosen) (muscles) relâcher, décontracter, relaxer; (discipline) relâcher; (policy, law) assouplir; **to r. one's hold** or **grip** desserrer son étreinte; Fig **to r. one's grip on** relâcher son emprise sur; **to r. one's efforts** relâcher ses efforts

VI 1 (of person) (physically) se détendre, se délasser, se relaxer; (mentally) se détendre, se relaxer; **r.!** (calm down) du calme!; **r.!, I'm not going to hurt you** détends-toi, je ne vais pas te faire mal 2 (of muscles) se relâcher, se détendre

relaxant [rɪ'læks(ə)nt] N (drug, drink etc) relaxant m; Med **muscle r.** myorelaxant m, décontracturant m

relaxation [riːlæks'eɪʃən] N 1 (of person) (physical) détente f, délassement m, relaxation f; (mental) détente, relaxation; **fishing is his only r.** la pêche est sa seule détente; **she finds r. in reading** elle se détend en lisant; **reading is one of my favourite forms of r.** lire est une de mes façons préférées de me détendre 2 (of muscles) décontraction f, relaxation f; (of discipline) relâchement m; (of policy, law) assouplissement m
▸ ▸ **r. therapy** relaxation

relaxed [rɪ'lækst] ADJ (atmosphere, person) décontracté, détendu, Fam **relax** inv; **she takes a very r. approach** or **is very r. in her approach to bringing up her children** elle élève ses enfants de façon très décontractée

relaxing [rɪ'læksɪŋ] ADJ (climate, medication) relaxant; **a very r. day** une vraie journée de détente; **a r. place for a holiday** un endroit tranquille pour passer des vacances

relay[1] ['riːleɪ] N 1 (of people, horses) relais m; (of workers) relève f; **to work in relays** travailler par relais, se relayer; **they worked in r. all night to put out the fire** ils se sont relayés toute la nuit pour éteindre l'incendie; **they were organized into relays** ils étaient répartis en équipes et ils se relayaient 2 Sport (race) (course f de) relais m; **the 4 x 100 m relay** le relais 4 x 100 m 3 Elec, Electron, Tel relais m; Radio, TV (transmitter) relais, réémetteur m; (broadcast) émission f relayée
▸ ▸ Sport **r. race** (course de) relais; Radio, TV **r. station** relais; Radio, TV **r. transmitter** réémetteur

relay[2] [rɪ'leɪ, riː-] VT (pt, pp **relayed**) Elec, Tel, Radio etc (telephone message, broadcast etc) relayer; **to r. information to sb** transmettre des informations à qn

re-lay VT (carpet, tiles etc) reposer

RELEASE [rɪ'liːs] N 1 (of hostage, prisoner) libération f; (from care, worry) délivrance f, libération (**from** de); (from obligation, responsibility) libération (**from** de); **it was a merciful r.** (when he or she died) ça a été une véritable délivrance; Law **order of r.** (ordre m de) levée f d'écrou; Law **r. on bail** mise f en liberté sous caution; Br **day r.**

= jour m de liberté accordé aux employés d'une entreprise pour faire un stage de formation

2 (of bomb) largage m; (of balloons, pigeons) lâcher m; (of gas etc) dégagement m; (of steam) échappement m; (of pressure) relâchement m; Phys (of energy) libération f; (of spring) détente f; (of mechanism) déclenchement m; (of clutch) débrayage m; (on typewriter) levier m de dégagement du chariot; Phot (**shutter**) **r.** (action) déclenchement m; (mechanism) déclencheur m

3 (of book, record etc) sortie f, mise f en vente; (of film) sortie; (of document) diffusion f; (of computer software) version f, (**press**) **r.** communiqué m de presse; **is the film on general r.?** est-ce que le film passe dans les salles?; **it's a new r.** ça vient de sortir; **latest r.** (record) dernier disque m; (film) dernier film m

4 Fin (of credits, funds) déblocage m, dégagement m

VT 1 (liberate) (hostage, prisoner) libérer; (patient) (from hospital) laisser sortir (**from** de); (from work) libérer; **to r. a debtor** libérer un débiteur; **to r. sb from his** or **her promise** délier qn de sa promesse; **to r. sb from a duty** dispenser qn d'une corvée; Law **released on bail** remis en liberté sous caution **2** (let go) (balloon, carrier pigeon) lâcher; (bomb) lâcher, larguer; **to r. sb's hand** lâcher la main de qn; **to r. one's hold** desserrer son étreinte, Law **prise**; **playing squash is a good way of releasing tension** le squash est un bon moyen de se détendre **3** (emit) (gas) dégager, laisser échapper; (fumes etc) émettre; **to be released** (of energy etc) se libérer **4** (unblock) (jammed part etc) dégager; (spring) détendre; (brake) desserrer; Phot (shutter) déclencher; **to r. the safety catch** (on gun) libérer le cran de sûreté; Aut **to r. the clutch** débrayer **5** (make available) (book, record etc) sortir, mettre en vente; (film) sortir; (news) rendre public; (document) diffuser **6** Fin (funds) débloquer, dégager
▸ ▸ Tech **r. lever** (on clutch) levier de débrayage; (on typewriter) levier de dégagement du chariot; Cin **r. print** copie f d'exploitation

relegate ['religeɪt] VT (downgrade) reléguer (**to** à); Ftbl **to r. a team** (to the next division) reléguer une équipe en division inférieure; Fig **we relegated the old bed to the spare room** on a relégué le vieux lit dans la chambre d'amis

relegation [reli'geɪʃən] N (of person etc) relégation f (**to** à); (of soccer club) relégation en division inférieure; **the r. struggle** la lutte pour rester dans la division supérieure

relent [rɪ'lent] VI (of person) s'adoucir, se radoucir; (as result of argument, persuasion) fléchir, se laisser amadouer; (of storm, wind, rain) diminuer de violence, se calmer

relentless [rɪ'lentlɪs] ADJ (person) implacable, inflexible, intransigeant; (hatred) implacable; (persecution, pain etc) sans rémission; (criticism) incessant, constant; **to be r. in doing sth** mettre de l'acharnement à faire qch

relentlessly [rɪ'lentlɪslɪ] ADV (to beat etc) implacablement; (to continue, persecute etc) sans rémission, avec acharnement; (to argue) continuellement, sans arrêt; (to blow, rain) sans interruption, continuellement

relet [riː'let] VT (house etc) relouer

relevance ['reləvəns], **relevancy** ['reləvənsɪ] N 1 (aptness) (of facts, remarks etc) pertinence f; **to have** or **bear some r.** avoir un rapport (**to** avec); **I don't see what r. his re-**

marks have to the situation je ne vois pas le rapport entre ses remarques et la situation; **what r. does that have to anything?** quel rapport est-ce que ça a? 2 (significance) intérêt m; **Latin no longer has any r. in the school curriculum** le latin ne sert plus à rien dans les programmes scolaires; **Shakespeare's plays are still full of r.** les pièces de Shakespeare sont toujours d'actualité; **whether I happen to agree or not is of no r.** (makes no difference) mon avis n'a aucune importance

relevant ['reləvənt] ADJ 1 (apt) (fact, detail etc) pertinent; **r. to** qui a un rapport avec; **to be r.** avoir un rapport (**to sth** avec qch); **that's not r.** ça n'a rien à voir (**to** avec); **opinions are not r.** ce n'est pas une question d'opinions; **that's hardly r.** ça n'a pas grand intérêt; **that's hardly r. to the discussion** ça n'a pas grand-chose à voir avec la discussion

2 (appropriate, proper) approprié; **you should report the matter to the r. department** vous devriez en référer au service compétent; **the r. documents** les documents qui se rapportent à l'affaire; Law les pièces justificatives; **to refer sb to the r. chapter of a book** renvoyer qn au chapitre correspondant; **she did not have the r. experience for the job** elle n'avait pas l'expérience requise pour le poste

3 (significant) important; (useful) utile; **is a knowledge of Latin r. to employers?** est-ce que la connaissance du latin a encore un intérêt quelconque pour les chefs d'entreprise?; **all r. information** tous renseignements utiles; **to be highly r.** (of experience, qualifications) être très utile (**for** pour); **to be/remain r.** (of book, play, idea, ideology etc) être/rester d'actualité
▸ ▸ Acct **r. costs** coûts mpl attribuables; **r. range** fourchette f pertinente d'activité

reliability [rɪlaɪə'bɪlɪtɪ] N (of person, firm etc) sérieux m; (of information) sérieux, sûreté f; (of source, testimony) sûreté; (of device, machine, car) fiabilité f; **I'm not altogether sure about the r. of our witnesses** je ne suis pas vraiment sûr qu'on puisse faire confiance à nos témoins

reliable [rɪ'laɪəb(ə)l] ADJ (firm) sérieux; (information) sérieux, sûr; (person) fiable, sur qui on peut compter; (source, testimony) sûr; (car, machine etc) fiable; **to have sth from a r. source** or **on r. evidence** tenir qch de source sûre; **my memory isn't r.** je n'ai pas bonne mémoire; **the weather is not very r.** on ne peut pas se fier au temps

reliably [rɪ'laɪəblɪ] ADV (to operate, perform etc) de façon fiable; **to be r. informed that ...** savoir de source sûre que ... + ind

reliance [rɪ'laɪəns] N 1 (dependence) dépendance f (**on** vis à vis de); **r. on alcohol** dépendance à l'alcool; **because of the country's r. on the arms industry** parce que l'économie du pays dépend de l'industrie de l'armement **2** (trust) confiance f; **to place r. in** or **on sb/ sth** se fier à qn/qch

reliant [rɪ'laɪənt] ADJ **to be r. on** (dependent on) dépendre de (**for** pour)

relic ['relɪk] N 1 (reminder of past, remnant) vestige m; **the last surviving r. of** les derniers vestiges de; **relics of the past** vestiges du passé; Hum **their old r. of a car** leur vieille bagnole toute pourrie; Lit **relics** (corpse) dépouille f mortelle **2** Rel relique f

relief [rɪ'liːf] N 1 (from pain, anxiety, poverty etc) soulagement m (**from** de); **to bring r. to sb** apporter du soulagement à qn; **that's** or **what a r.!** quel soulagement!; **for the r. of pain** (of pills etc) pour soulager la douleur; **to my great r., much to my r.** à mon grand soulagement; **to feel r.** se sentir soulagé, ressentir du soulagement (**at** à; **about, over** à propos de); **his feelings of r. were short-lived** son soulagement a été de courte durée; **you can imagine my r.** or **the r. that I felt** tu peux imaginer mon soulagement; **to provide light** or **comic r.** détendre l'atmosphère, introduire une note comique; **by way of light r.** pour se détendre un peu

2 (help) secours m, assistance f, aide f; Am **to be on r.** recevoir une aide sociale; **disaster/famine r.** secours ou assistance ou aide aux victimes d'un désastre/d'une famine; **tax r.** dégrèvement m fiscal

3 (replacement) personne f qui assure la relève, remplaçant, -ante; **my r. didn't show up** mon remplaçant/ma remplaçante ne s'est pas présenté(e)

4 (liberation) (of city etc) libération f

5 Art relief m, modelé m; **printed in r.** imprimé en relief; **to stand out in r.** ressortir, se détacher (**against** sur); **to stand out in bold** or **sharp r.** ressortir ou se détacher nettement; **to bring** or **throw sth into r.** faire ressortir qch; Art **high/low r.** haut/bas-relief

6 Geog relief m (terrestre); **an area of low r.** une zone au relief peu élevé

▸▸ **r. agency** organisme m d'aide humanitaire; **r. driver** chauffeur m qui assure la relève; **r. fund** caisse f de secours; **r. map** carte f en relief; **r. official** responsable mf d'un organisme d'aide humanitaire; **r. road** itinéraire m bis, route f de délestage; **r. staff** (cover staff) personnel m extra; **r. train** train m supplémentaire; **r. troops** la relève; **r. valve** soupape f de sûreté, clapet m de décharge; **r. work** coopération f; **r. worker** = membre m d'une organisation humanitaire qui travaille sur le terrain

> Note that the French word **relief** never means **assistance**.

relieve [rɪˈliːv] VT **1** (alleviate) (pain, anxiety, poverty) soulager; (boredom) tromper; (the situation) remédier à; (pressure) réduire; **to do sth to r. the boredom** faire qch pour tromper l'ennui; **to r. oneself** (urinate) se soulager; **black dress relieved by** or **with white lace** robe noire agrémentée de dentelle blanche; **to r. the monotony we went for a walk** pour nous changer les idées nous sommes allés nous promener; Aut, Med **to r. congestion in sth** décongestionner qch **2** (replace) (person) remplacer, relayer; Mil, Naut (the guard, watch) relever **3** (liberate) Mil (city) libérer; (person) (from obligation) dégager, affranchir (**from** de); **to r. sb of a burden** soulager qn d'un fardeau; **to r. sb of their coat** débarrasser qn de son manteau; **to r. sb of their duties** relever qn de ses fonctions; Fam Hum **to r. sb of sth** (steal) soulager qn de qch

relieved [rɪˈliːvd] ADJ soulagé; **I'm very r. to hear it** je suis très soulagé de l'apprendre, c'est un grand soulagement pour moi de l'apprendre; **to feel r.** se sentir soulagé; **to be r. at the news** être soulagé en apprenant la nouvelle

religion [rɪˈlɪdʒən] N religion f; (Catholic, Protestant) religion, culte m; (heading on form) confession f; Fam Pej **to get r.** attraper le virus de la religion; **it's against my r. to work on Sundays** c'est contraire à ma religion de travailler le dimanche; Hum **it's against his r. to do the washing-up!** c'est contraire à sa religion de faire la vaisselle!; Fig **to make a r. of (doing) sth** se faire une obligation de (faire) qch; Fig **football is a r. with some people** le football est une religion pour certains

religiosity [rɪlɪdʒɪˈɒsɪtɪ] N Pej religiosité f

religious [rɪˈlɪdʒəs] ADJ (person) pieux, croyant; (fanatic, order, service, leader, life)

religieux; (war, book) de religion; Fig (care) méticuleux; Fig **his r. attendance at every football match** sa fréquentation scrupuleuse de tous les matches de football; Fig **to be r. about doing sth** faire qch avec un soin méticuleux

N INV Rel religieux, -ieuse

▸▸ **r. beliefs** croyances fpl religieuses; **r. education** instruction f religieuse; **r. instruction** instruction religieuse; **r. persuasion** confession f; **r. programme** programme m à caractère religieux

religiously [rɪˈlɪdʒəslɪ] ADV (to behave, act) religieusement, pieusement; Fig (to attend, obey) religieusement, scrupuleusement

religiousness [rɪˈlɪdʒəsnɪs] N (of person) piété f, dévotion f; (of music, art) caractère m religieux; Fig (of attendance, obedience) caractère scrupuleux; (in carrying out task) extrême méticulosité f

reline [riːˈlaɪn] VT (coat) remettre une doublure à; Aut **to r. the brakes** changer les garnitures de freins

relinquish [rɪˈlɪŋkwɪʃ] VT (give up) (habit, hope) abandonner; (plan, right, inheritance) renoncer à; **to r. all thoughts of doing sth** abandonner toute pensée de faire qch; **to r. (one's hold on) sth** (let go) lâcher qch, renoncer à qch; **to r. one's hold on one's children** laisser partir ses enfants; **her mind was beginning to r. its hold on reality** elle commençait à perdre le sens de la réalité

relinquishment [rɪˈlɪŋkwɪʃmənt] N Fml (of hope etc) abandon m (**of** de); (of right etc) renonciation f (**of** à)

reliquary [ˈrelɪkwərɪ] N Rel reliquaire m

relish [ˈrelɪʃ] N **1** (liking, taste) goût m (**for** pour); **to eat sth with r.** manger qch de bon appétit, savourer qch **2** (pleasure) plaisir m; **danger gives r. to an adventure** le danger donne du piquant à une aventure; **he used to tell the story with great r.** il se délectait à raconter cette histoire; **..., she said with great r.** ... dit-elle avec délectation **3** Culin (pickle) condiment m, Can achar m

VT (enjoy) apprécier; (dish) goûter, savourer; Fig (victory, moment) savourer; **to r. doing sth** trouver du plaisir à ou aimer faire qch; **I didn't r. the prospect** cette perspective ne me disait rien; **I didn't r. the prospect/thought/idea of telling her** j'appréhendais de le lui dire; **we didn't r. the idea** l'idée ne nous souriait pas

relive [riːˈlɪv] VT (one's life, the past) revivre

rellies [ˈrelɪz] NPL Br Fam (relatives) famille f; **are you seeing your r. at Christmas?** tu vas voir ta famille à Noël?

reload [riːˈləʊd] VT (ship, camera, rifle, software etc) recharger

VI (of ship, photographer etc) recharger; (of gun, software) se recharger

relocate [riːləʊˈkeɪt] VT (move) (factory, company) réimplanter, déménager

VI (of person, shop) déménager; (of company) se réimplanter, déménager; **the firm is relocating out of Glasgow** la société se réimplante hors de Glasgow

relocation [riːləʊˈkeɪʃən] N (of person, shop) déménagement m; (of company) réimplantation f

▸▸ **r. allowance** (for employee) indemnité f de déménagement; **r. assistance** (from employer) contribution f aux frais de déménagement; **r. expenses** (for employee) frais mpl de déménagement

reluctance [rɪˈlʌktəns] N (unwillingness) réticence f, (strong) répugnance f; **to do sth with a show of r.** faire qch avec une réticence feinte; **to show (some) r. to do sth** se montrer peu disposé ou empressé à faire

qch; **to do sth with r.** faire qch à regret ou à contrecœur

reluctant [rɪˈlʌktənt] ADJ (consent, greeting, promise etc) accordé à contrecœur; **to be r. to do sth** hésiter ou être peu disposé ou peu empressé à faire qch; **to feel r.** hésiter, éprouver de la répugnance (**to do** à faire); **a r. teacher** un professeur malgré lui; **I was a r. witness of their quarrel** j'étais le témoin involontaire de leur querelle

reluctantly [rɪˈlʌktəntlɪ] ADV (to consent, greet, promise etc) avec répugnance, à contrecœur; **I say it r.** il m'en coûte de le dire

▸ **rely on, rely upon** [rɪˈlaɪ] VT INSEP **1** (count on) (person's help, discretion) compter sur; (have confidence in) (person, judgment etc) avoir confiance en; **I'm relying on it** j'y compte (bien); **it's a car you can r. on** c'est une voiture fiable; **he's a lawyer you can r. on** c'est un avocat sur lequel on peut compter; **we can't r. on the weather** on ne peut jamais savoir quel temps il va faire; Iron **you can always rely on him to be late** tu peux compter sur lui pour arriver en retard à chaque fois **2** (be dependent on) (person) dépendre de (**for sth** pour qch)

REM [ɑːriːˈem] (abbr rapid eye movement) sommeil m paradoxal, phase f de mouvements oculaires

remailer [riːˈmeɪlər] N Comput service m de courrier électronique anonyme

remain [rɪˈmeɪn] VI **1** (stay behind) rester **2** (continue to be) (of doubts) rester, subsister; **to r. silent** garder le silence; **to r. faithful to sb/sth** rester fidèle à qn/qch; **please r. in your seats** veuillez rester assis; **let it r. as it is** laissez-le comme cela; **one thing remains certain** une chose demeure certaine; **to r. a problem** demeurer un problème; **to r. the same** demeurer inchangé; **the crime remains unsolved** le crime n'a toujours pas été élucidé; **the fact remains that ...** il n'en est pas moins vrai que ..., toujours est-il que ...; Br Old-fashioned **I r., Sir, yours truly** (at end of letter) veuillez agréer, Monsieur, l'expression de mes sentiments distingués **3** (be left) rester, subsister; **all that remains of ...** tout ce qui reste ou subsiste de ...; **much yet remains to be done** il reste encore beaucoup à faire; **it (only) remains for me to ...** il ne me reste qu'à ..., je n'ai plus qu'à ...; **it remains to be seen whether ...** reste à savoir si ...; **that remains to be seen** c'est ce que nous verrons, Fam ça reste à voir

remainder [rɪˈmeɪndər] N **1** (of time, wine etc) reste m; (of salary, specific quantity) restant m, reste; (of amount due) reliquat m; **the r. of his life** le reste ou le restant de sa vie; **the r. (remaining people)** les autres mfpl **2** Math reste m; **division with no r.** division f sans reste; **the r. is one** il reste un **3** (book) invendu m soldé

VT (book) solder

remaindered [rɪˈmeɪndɜːd] ADJ (book) soldé

remaining [rɪˈmeɪnɪŋ] ADJ (food, money, wine etc) qui reste, restant; **the r. travellers** le reste des voyageurs, les autres voyageurs; **our only r. hope** le seul espoir qui nous reste

remains [rɪˈmeɪnz] NPL (of fortune, meal) restes mpl; (of old building) ruines fpl, vestiges mpl; Fig **the last r. of his self-respect** les derniers vestiges de son amour-propre; **(human) r.** restes humains; Old-fashioned (literary) **r.** œuvres fpl posthumes

remake[1] [ˈriːmeɪk] N (of film, TV series) remake m, nouvelle version f; **to do a r. of** faire un remake de

remake[2] [riːˈmeɪk] VT (pt, pp **remade** [riː-

'meɪd]) (film) refaire, faire un remake de; (bed) refaire

remand [rɪ'mɑːnd] Law N to be on r. (in custody) être en détention préventive; (on bail) être en liberté provisoire (sous caution)
▪ VT to r. (in custody) placer en détention préventive; to r. on bail mettre en liberté provisoire sous caution
► ► r. centre, r. home maison f de détention préventive

remark [rɪ'mɑːk] N 1 (comment) remarque f, commentaire m; to make or pass a r. faire une remarque ou une observation ou un commentaire (about sur); to let sth pass without r. laisser passer qch sans commentaire; to venture or hazard a r. se permettre ou risquer une remarque ou une observation ou un commentaire; no remarks, please! pas de commentaires, s'il vous plaît! 2 Fml (notice) attention f, worthy of r. digne d'attention; it could not escape r. that … on ne pouvait pas ne pas remarquer que …, le fait que … ne pouvait pas passer inaperçu; her reaction could not escape r. sa réaction n'a pu passer inaperçue
▪ VT 1 (comment) faire remarquer (that … que … + ind) 2 Fml (note) (somebody) remarquer; (something) remarquer, noter; it may be remarked that … constatons que …
▪ VI to r. on sth (on weather, food etc) parler de qch; I remarked on it to my mother j'en ai fait la remarque à ma mère; I remarked to her father on how well she was looking j'ai fait remarquer à son père qu'elle avait l'air très en forme

> Note that the French verb **remarquer** is a false friend and is never a translation for the English verb **to remark**. Its most common meaning is **to notice**.

remarkable [rɪ'mɑːkəb(ə)l] ADJ (change, coincidence, progress etc) remarquable (for par)

remarkably [rɪ'mɑːkəblɪ] ADV (to change, progress etc) remarquablement, notablement; (good, intelligent) remarquablement; (bad, stupid) incroyablement

remarket [riː'mɑːkɪt] VT recommercialiser

remarketing [riː'mɑːkɪtɪŋ] N marketing m de relance

remarriage [riː'mærɪdʒ] N remariage m

remarry [riː'mærɪ] VT 1 (first spouse) se remarier avec, épouser de nouveau 2 (of registrar etc) (divorced couple) remarier
▪ VI se remarier

remaster [riː'mɑːstər] VT (album) remasteriser

rematch ['riːmætʃ] N Sport match m retour

remediable [rɪ'miːdɪəb(ə)l] ADJ Fml (situation) remédiable; (illness) curable; an easily r. fault un défaut auquel on peut facilement remédier

remedial [rɪ'miːdɪəl] ADJ 1 (measures, action) de redressement; to take r. action prendre des mesures de redressement; the public is demanding for r. action to halt the destruction of the environment le public demande que des mesures soient prises pour stopper la destruction de l'environnement 2 Br Sch (classes) de rattrapage, de soutien; (education) spécialisé; (pupil, student) qui n'a pas le niveau; she teaches r. maths elle donne des cours de rattrapage ou de soutien en maths 3 (treatment) curatif, correctif
► ► Br Sch r. class classe f de rattrapage; Br Sch r. education éducation f spécialisée; Med r. exercises gymnastique f corrective; Br Sch r. teacher enseignant, -ante chargé(e) d'une classe de rattrapage; Br Sch r. teaching rattrapage m scolaire

remedy ['remɪdɪ] N (for illness), Fig remède m (for pour, contre); it's past or beyond r. c'est irrémédiable ou sans remède
▪ VT (situation) remédier à; the situation hasn't been remedied yet on n'a pas encore remédié à la situation

remember [rɪ'membər] VT 1 (recall) (somebody) se souvenir de; (something) se souvenir de, se rappeler; I r. him as being very generous je me souviens de lui comme de quelqu'un de très généreux; they r. me as a child ils se souviennent de moi lorsque j'étais enfant; she will long be remembered for her achievements on se souviendra longtemps d'elle pour ses exploits; he will be remembered as the man who … on se souviendra de lui comme de l'homme qui …; do you r. turning off the lights? est-ce que tu te souviens (d') avoir éteint les lumières?; do you r. me turning off the lights? tu te souviens si j'ai éteint la lumière?; to r. that … se souvenir ou se rappeler que … + ind; the chairman, you will r., cannot vote le président, ne l'oubliez pas, ne peut pas voter; I can't r. his name for the moment son nom m'échappe pour l'instant; I'll r. his name in a minute son nom me reviendra dans une minute; it will be something to r. you by ce sera un souvenir de vous; I'll give him something to r. (me by)! il se souviendra de moi! VOIR GRAMMAIRE A43-4
   2 (not forget) (lesson) retenir, ne pas oublier; it was a night/a holiday to r. c'était une nuit/des vacances mémorable(s); I'll r. to do it je n'oublierai pas de le faire; that's worth remembering c'est à noter; r. or you must r. (that) he's only ten years old n'oubliez pas qu'il n'a que dix ans; did you r. to turn off the lights? est-ce que tu as pensé à éteindre les lumières?; r. that we're going to the theatre next week n'oublie pas que nous allons au théâtre la semaine prochaine; r. where we are! reprends-toi!; I remembered myself just in time je me suis ressaisi juste à temps VOIR GRAMMAIRE A43-4
   3 (give gift to) ne pas oublier; she always remembers the children at Christmas elle n'oublie jamais les enfants à Noël; he remembered me in his will il ne m'a pas oublié dans son testament
   4 (speak of) let us r. them in our prayers prions pour eux; r. me (kindly) to them rappelez-moi à leur bon souvenir, dites-leur bien des choses de ma part; esp Fml he asked to be remembered to you il me prie de le rappeler à votre bon souvenir
   5 (of service, monument etc) (the dead) rendre hommage à
▪ VI se souvenir, se rappeler; as I r. d'après mes souvenirs; as far as I (can) r. pour autant que je me souvienne; if I r. rightly si je m'en souviens bien, si j'ai bonne mémoire; for as long as I can r. aussi loin que remontent mes souvenirs

remembrance [rɪ'membrəns] N 1 (memory) souvenir m; in r. of sb/sth en souvenir de qn/qch; garden of r. jardin m commémoratif 2 Old-fashioned (keepsake) souvenir m 3 Old-fashioned (greeting) give my kind remembrances to him rappelez-moi à son bon souvenir
► ► R. Day, Br R. Sunday (commémoration f de l')Armistice m (le dimanche avant ou après le 11 novembre)

REMIC [ɑːriːmaɪ'siː] N Am Fin (abbr real estate mortgage investment conduit) obligation f garantie par hypothèque

remind [rɪ'maɪnd] VT (person) rappeler à (that … que … + ind); to r. sb of sth rappeler qch à qn; he reminds me of my brother il me fait penser à ou me rappelle mon frère; that reminds me of my childhood cela me rappelle mon enfance; to r. sb to do sth faire

penser à qn à faire qch; he reminded them of their duty to … il leur rappela qu'il était de leur devoir de …; r. me about it tomorrow rappelle-le-moi demain; that or which reminds me! à propos!; I would r. you that … permettez-moi de vous rappeler que …

reminder [rɪ'maɪndər] N (letter, of event) rappel m; (to jog memory) pense-bête m, pl pense-bêtes; to send/give sb a r. about sth envoyer un rappel à qn à propos de qch; the exhibition is a stark r. of the horrors of war l'exposition rappelle la guerre dans toute son horreur; such events are a r. that … de tels événements nous rappellent que …; it's a r. to myself to … c'est pour me rappeler de …; Fin r. of account due rappel m d'échéance
► ► Acct r. entry poste m de mémoire

reminisce [remɪ'nɪs] VI évoquer ou raconter ses souvenirs (about de); (in thoughts) évoquer le passé, repenser au passé; to r. about the good old days évoquer le bon vieux temps; to r. about sb parler de qn (en se souvenant)

reminiscence [remɪ'nɪsəns] N (of past) souvenir m (about, of de); to write one's reminiscences écrire ses souvenirs

reminiscent [remɪ'nɪsənt] ADJ 1 (nostalgic) nostalgique; to be in a r. mood être enclin à ou d'humeur à évoquer des souvenirs 2 (suggestive) r. of qui fait penser à ou rappelle ou évoque; in a voice reminiscent of that of her mother or of her mother's d'une voix qui fait penser à ou qui rappelle celle de sa mère

reminiscently [remɪ'nɪsəntlɪ] ADV to smile r. sourire en pensant à qch; to talk r. of sth évoquer des souvenirs de qch

remiss [rɪ'mɪs] ADJ (negligent) négligent (in doing de faire); that was very r. of her c'était de la négligence de sa part

remission [rɪ'mɪʃən] N 1 Law remise f de peine 2 Med rémission f, to go into r. (of disease, patient) entrer en phase de rémission 3 Rel rémission f; to pray for the r. of sins prier pour la rémission des péchés 4 (of debt) remise f, (of duty, fee, payment) dispense f, (of tax) dispense, exemption f

remit¹ [rɪ'mɪt] (-tt-) VT 1 (send back) renvoyer; Law (case) renvoyer à un autre tribunal; Fin to r. a sum to sb remettre une somme à qn 2 (lessen), Law (sentence) remettre; Fig Fml (efforts) relâcher 3 (forgive) (sin) pardonner, absoudre 4 (cancel) (debt) remettre, faire remise de; to r. sb's fees dispenser qn de ses frais; to r. sb's income tax dispenser ou exempter qn de l'impôt sur le revenu 5 Fml (postpone) (matter) remettre, différer
▪ VI 1 (of debtor) régler, payer; please r. by cheque veuillez régler ou payer par chèque 2 Fml (abate) (of efforts, zeal etc) diminuer; (of pain, storm) se calmer

remit² [riː'mɪt] N (area of authority) attributions fpl; to exceed one's r. aller au-delà de ses attributions; it is outside or not part of our r. ceci ne relève pas de nos attributions

remittance [rɪ'mɪtəns] N Com (payment) versement m; (settlement) paiement m, règlement m; return the form with your r. renvoyez le formulaire avec votre règlement ou paiement
► ► Fin r. advice avis m de remise; Fin r. date date f de remise; Fin r. of funds remise f de fonds

remix¹ ['riːmɪks] N Mus (record) remix m

remix² [riː'mɪks] VT Mus remixer, refaire le mixage de

remnant ['remnənt] N 1 (of food) reste m; Fig (of imperialism, former glory) vestige m; Fig the remnants of one's dignity/an army ce qui subsiste ou reste de sa dignité/d'une armée **2** (of fabric) coupon m; (of carpet) chute f; **remnants** (of fabric) coupons, fins fpl de série; **r. sale** (of fabric) soldes mpl de fins de série

remodel [riːˈmɒd(ə)l] VT (**-ll-**, Am **-l-**) (bill, draft) remanier; (structure) Fig (legislation) modifier; **to have one's nose/chin remodelled** se faire refaire le nez/le menton

remonstrate [ˈremənstreɪt] VI **to r. with sb** faire des remontrances à qn (**about** au sujet de); **there's no point in trying to r. with her about it** ça ne sert à rien d'en discuter avec elle; **to r. against sth** protester contre qch; VT **to r. that ...** protester en disant que ...

remorse [riˈmɔːs] N remords m (**for, about** de); **without r.** (not sorry) sans remords; (to do sth) sans scrupules; **to feel r.** éprouver ou avoir du ou des remords (**for having done** d'avoir fait); **a feeling/twinge of r.** un sentiment/une pointe de remords; **in a fit of r.** dans un accès de remords; **to show r.** manifester des remords

remorseful [riˈmɔːsfʊl] ADJ plein de remords

remorsefully [riˈmɔːsfəlɪ] ADV (to say) d'un ton plein de remords

remorseless [riˈmɔːslɪs] ADJ (person, wind) impitoyable; (cruelty, persecution) incessant; Fig (ambition, logic, self-interest) implacable; **he was r. in the demands that he made on his employees** il ne laissait aucun répit à ses employés; **she was r. with herself** elle était très dure avec elle-même; **he was r. in his pursuit of the criminal** il n'avait de cesse qu'il n'arrête le criminel

remorselessly [riˈmɔːslɪslɪ] ADV (to hit, pursue etc) impitoyablement; (ambitious, logical etc) implacablement

remorselessness [riˈmɔːslɪsnɪs] N (of person, criticisms, attack) acharnement m

remortgage [riːˈmɔːgɪdʒ] VT (house, property) hypothéquer de nouveau, prendre une nouvelle hypothèque sur

remote [riˈməʊt] ADJ **1** (far-off) (house, village etc) reculé; (ancestor) lointain; (cousin) éloigné, lointain; **r. from** loin ou éloigné de; **in the remotest part of Asia** au fin fond de l'Asie; **in the r. future/past** dans un avenir/un passé lointain

2 (removed, not connected) éloigné (**from** de); **his plays are r. from everyday life** ses pièces sont éloignées de la vie quotidienne

3 Comput (terminal) distant; (user) à distance

4 (aloof) distant, réservé; (with mind elsewhere) absent; **she had a rather r. look on her face** (looked aloof) elle avait une expression plutôt distante; (was thinking of other things) elle avait un air absent

5 (slight) (chance, connection, possibility, resemblance) vague; (prospect) peu probable; **I haven't the remotest idea of what he meant** je n'ai pas la moindre idée de ce qu'il voulait dire; **there is a r. possibility that ...** il y a une vague possibilité que ... + subj; **in the r. event of a water shortage** dans l'hypothèse improbable d'une pénurie d'eau; **he hasn't the remotest chance of winning** il n'a pas la moindre chance de gagner

N Fam (remote control) télécommande f

▸▸ Comput **r. access** accès m à distance; **r. antiquity** la haute antiquité; **r. control** télécommande, commande à distance; Comput **r. data entry** entrée f de données à distance; Comput **r. data processing** télétraitement m; Comput **r. help** téléassistance f; Comput **r. interrogation** interrogation f à distance; Comput **r. job entry** télésoumission f de travaux; Comput **r. loading** téléchargement m; Comput **r. management** télégestion f; Comput **r. processing** télétraitement; Comput **r. reading** lecture f à distance; Comput **r.**

sensing télédétection f; Comput **r. satellite** satellite m de télédétection; TV etc **r. station** télestation f; Comput **r. terminal** terminal m distant; Comput **r. troubleshooting** télédépannage m; TV etc **r. van** voiture f de reportage

remote-controlled ADJ (model aircraft, door, television etc) télécommandé; (bomb) commandé à distance

remotely [riˈməʊtlɪ] ADV **1** (distantly) (situated) loin, au loin; (related) de loin **2** (absent-mindedly) (to answer etc) d'un ton absent **3** (slightly) (possible) vaguement; **it's only r. connected with the subject** cela n'a qu'un faible rapport avec le sujet; **it isn't even r. connected with the subject** cela n'a même pas le moindre rapport avec le sujet; **I'm not r. interested in science fiction** la science-fiction ne m'intéresse pas le moins du monde; **not r. aware** nullement conscient; **it isn't even r. possible** c'est rigoureusement impossible

remoteness [riˈməʊtnɪs] N **1** (distance) (of house, past etc) éloignement m; (isolation) isolement m **2** (aloofness) distance f, her air of r. (aloofness) son air distant; (absent-mindedness) son air absent; **the r. of her manner** son côté distant **3** (of resemblance) faible degré m; **the r. of her chances of success** l'improbabilité f de sa réussite

remould[1] [ˈriːməʊld] N Br Aut pneu m rechapé

remould[2] [riːˈməʊld] VT Br **1** Aut (tyre) rechaper **2** (clay figure), Fig (image, character etc) remodeler

remount [riːˈmaʊnt] VT **1** (get on again) **to r. one's horse/bicycle** remonter à cheval/bicyclette, remonter sur son cheval/sa bicyclette **2** (go up again) (stairs) remonter **3** (place on new support) (picture) rentoiler; (jewel) remonter

VI remonter à cheval/à bicyclette

removable [riˈmuːvəb(ə)l] ADJ **1** (component, lid, lining etc) amovible **2** (mark, spot, stain etc) qui peut partir; **the stain's not r.** la tache est indélébile

▸▸ Comput **r. disk** disque m amovible ou extractible

removal [riˈmuːv(ə)l] N **1** (taking away) (of rubbish, plate) enlèvement m; (of stain etc) nettoyage m; (of appendix, kidney, tumour etc) ablation f; (of doubt, fear) dissipation f; (of burden, worry, obstacle, threat, word) suppression f; **r. of customs barriers** suppression des barrières douanières; **the r. of stains from a jacket** le détachage d'une veste; **for stain r., for the r. of stains** pour enlever les taches, pour détacher **2** (taking off) (of coat, glove etc) enlèvement m; (of tyre) démontage m; (of seal) levée f; **after r. of the bandages** une fois les bandages enlevés; **after the r. of her make-up** une fois démaquillée **3** (dismissal) révocation f, renvoi m; (of civil servant, judge etc) destitution f **4** (moving house) déménagement m

▸▸ **r. company** entreprise f de déménagement; **r. expenses** frais mpl de déménagement; Br **r. man** déménageur m; **r. van** camion m de déménagement

remove [riˈmuːv] VT **1** (take away) (rubbish, plate) enlever; (stain) enlever, faire partir (**from** de); (source of infection) éliminer; (appendix, kidney, tumour) procéder à l'ablation de, enlever; (person) emmener (**to** à); Fig (doubt, fear) dissiper; (worry, obstacle, threat, word) supprimer, éliminer; **to have a mole/wart removed** se faire enlever un grain de beauté/une verrue; **to r. sb's name from a list** rayer qn d'une liste; **she's having the plaster removed tomorrow** on lui enlève son plâtre demain; **to r. a burden from sb** soulager qn d'un fardeau; **to r. a child from**

school retirer un enfant de l'école; **police removed the demonstrators** la police a fait partir les manifestants; **the judge ordered her to be removed from the court room** le juge a ordonné qu'on la fasse sortir de la salle d'audience; **he has been removed to hospital** il a été transporté à l'hôpital; **death has removed him from our midst** la mort nous l'a enlevé

2 (take off) (coat, gloves, hat) enlever, retirer (**from sb** à qn); (tyre) démonter; (seal) lever; **to r. one's make-up** se démaquiller; **to r. the hair from one's legs** s'épiler les jambes

3 (dismiss) (executive, director) révoquer, renvoyer; (civil servant, magistrate) destituer; **to r. sb from his or her position** démettre qn de ses fonctions (**as** de)

4 (of furniture movers) (furniture etc) déménager

5 Euph (kill) (person) supprimer

VI Old-fashioned (of people, company) déménager (**to** à)

N (degree of difference) distance f, **at a certain r.** à une certaine distance; **at one r.** de façon interposée; **it is but or only one r. from ...** cela est tout près de ...; **her account is several removes from the truth** son récit est assez loin de la vérité

removed [riˈmuːvd] ADJ (distant) **his feeling was not far r. from love** son sentiment n'était pas très éloigné de l'amour; **her explanation is far r. from the truth** son explication est très éloignée de la vérité; **first cousin once r.** cousin, -ine issu(e) de germain

remover [riˈmuːvər] N **1** (company, person) déménageur m; **a company of furniture removers** une entreprise de déménagement **2** (substance) **paint r.** décapant m; **stain r.** détachant m; **hair r.** (d)épilatoire m; **nail varnish r.** dissolvant m; **make-up r.** démaquillant m

removing [riˈmuːvɪŋ] ADJ

▸▸ **r. cream** (for hair) crème f (d)épilatoire; (for make-up) crème démaquillante; (for wrinkles) crème antirides

remunerate [riˈmjuːnəreɪt] VT Fml (person) rémunérer (**for** de); (service) rémunérer

remuneration [rɪmjuːnəˈreɪʃən] N Fml (for service etc) rémunération f (**for** de)

▸▸ **r. package** = salaire m et avantages mpl complémentaires

remunerative [riˈmjuːnərətɪv] ADJ Fml rémunérateur, -trice

Renaissance [riˈneɪsəns] N renaissance f, Art, Hist **the R.** la Renaissance; **R. art/literature** art m/littérature f de la Renaissance

▸▸ **R. man** esprit m universel

renaissance [riˈneɪsəns] N (of industry etc) renaissance f

renal [ˈriːn(ə)l] ADJ Anat (artery etc) rénal, -aux

▸▸ **r. failure** insuffisance f rénale

rename [riːˈneɪm] VT (person, street) rebaptiser; Comput (file) changer le nom de, renommer

renascence [riˈnæsəns, -ˈneɪ-] N Lit (of nationalism) renaissance f, (of interest) regain m

renascent [riˈnæsənt, -ˈneɪ-] ADJ Lit (interest, nationalism etc) renaissant

renationalization [riːnæʃənəlaɪˈzeɪʃən] N renationalisation f

renationalize [riːˈnæʃənəlaɪz] VT renationaliser

rend [rend] VT (pt, pp **rent** [rent]) **1** (pierce) (the silence) déchirer; **the air was rent with her screams** l'air était déchiré par ses hurlements **2** Lit (tear) déchirer; **to r. sth asunder or apart** (in two parts) déchirer ou fendre qch en deux; (in several parts) (car, ship etc) déchiqueter qch; **he was rent from my arms** il fut arraché à mes bras; **a country rent by civil war** un pays déchiré par la guerre civile

render ['rendər] **VT 1** *Fml (give) (homage, service)* rendre; *(description)* faire; *(explanation)* donner; **to r. thanks to God** rendre grâce à Dieu; *Bible* **r. unto Caesar the things which are Caesar's** rendez à César ce qui appartient à César; **to r. an account of sth** *(describe)* faire le récit de qch; *Fin* **to r. an account to sb** remettre un compte à qn; *Fin* **as per account rendered** suivant compte remis; **to r. assistance to sb** prêter secours à qn; **to r. (up) a fortress** rendre une forteresse; *Lit* **to r. one's soul** *(die)* rendre l'âme **2** *(make, cause to be)* rendre; **the blow rendered her unconscious** le coup lui a fait perdre connaissance; **the news rendered her speechless** la nouvelle l'a laissée sans voix **3** *(depict)* *(light)* rendre; *(perform)* *(piece of music)* interpréter **4** *(translate)* rendre, traduire (**in, into** en) **5** *(plaster)* *(wall etc)* plâtrer, enduire de plâtre **6** *Culin* **to r. (down) fat** faire fondre de la graisse

rendering ['rendərɪŋ] **N 1** *Fin (of account)* reddition *f* **2** *(of expression, features in painting)* rendu *m*; *(of music)* interprétation *f*; **his r. of what happened** sa version des faits **3** *(translating) (of phrase)* traduction *f* **4** *(of wall)* enduit *m* **5** *(of fat)* fonte *f*
▸▸ **r. plant** usine *f* d'équarrissage

rendezvous ['rɒndɪvuː, *pl* -vuːz] **N** *(meeting, meeting-place)* rendez-vous *m inv* (**for** de); **to make a r. with sb** prendre rendez-vous avec qn; **to keep a r.** se rendre à un rendez-vous
VI *(pt, pp* **rendezvoused** [-vuːd]; *prp* **rendezvousing** [-vuːɪŋ]) se réunir, se retrouver; **to r. with sb** retrouver qn

rendition [ren'dɪʃən] **N** *(of role etc)* interprétation *f*, *to give a r. of (role etc)* interpréter; **they finished with a r. of the Marseillaise** ils ont terminé en chantant/jouant la Marseillaise

renegade ['renɪɡeɪd] **N 1** *(traitor)* renégat, -ate **2** *(outlaw)* hors-la-loi *m inv*
▸▸ **r. priest** prêtre *m* parjure

renege, renegue [rɪ'neɪɡ] **VI 1** manquer à *ou* revenir sur sa promesse (**on doing sth** de faire qch); **she has reneged (on her promise)** elle a manqué à sa promesse; **she has reneged (on our deal)** elle est revenue sur notre marché **2** *Cards* faire une fausse renonce

renegotiate [riːnɪ'ɡəʊʃɪeɪt] **VT** renégocier
renegotiation [riːnɪɡəʊʃɪ'eɪʃən] **N** renégociation *f*

renew [rɪ'njuː] **VT 1** *(resume) (conversation)* reprendre; **to r. one's acquaintance with sb** renouer connaissance avec qn; **to r. pressure on sb** recommencer à faire pression sur qn (**to do** pour qu'il fasse); *Mil* **to r. an attack** attaquer de nouveau; *Fig* **to r. one's attack** revenir à la charge *ou* à l'attaque (**on** concernant) **2** *(restate) (request, promise)* renouveler **3** *(extend) (lease, passport, bill of exchange)* renouveler; **to r. a lease** reconduire un bail; **to r. one's subscription** se réabonner, renouveler son abonnement (**to** à); **to r. a library book** faire renouveler *ou* prolonger le prêt d'un livre de bibliothèque; **to r. one's wardrobe** renouveler sa garde-robe **4** *(revive) (hope, enthusiasm etc)* raviver

renewable [rɪ'njuːəb(ə)l] **ADJ** *(passport etc)* renouvelable; *(lease, contract)* reconductible, renouvelable; **your subscription is r. at the end of the year** *(must be renewed)* votre abonnement doit être renouvelé à la fin de l'année; *(may be renewed)* votre abonnement peut être renouvelé à la fin de l'année
▸▸ **r. energy** énergie *f* renouvelable; **r. resources** ressources *fpl* renouvelables

renewal [rɪ'njuːəl] **N 1** *(of acquaintance)* renouement *m*; *(of hostilities, violence, bombing)* reprise *f*; *(of enthusiasm, hopes)* regain *m*; **r. of activity** reprise *ou* regain d'activité **2** *(of promise, request)* renouvellement *m* **3** *(of lease, passport etc)* renouvellement *m*; *(of library book)* renouvellement de prêt; **r. of subscription** réabonnement *m*, renouvellement d'abonnement (**to** à)
▸▸ **r. clause** clause *f* de reconduction; **r. notice** avis *m* de renouvellement; **r. premium** prime *f* de renouvellement

renewed [rɪ'njuːd] **ADJ** *(effort, enthusiasm, vigour)* renouvelé; *(attempt, hope)* nouveau; *(activity, efforts)* redoublé; **r. bombing/outbreaks of violence** reprise *f* des bombardements/de la violence; **doctors are expressing r. concern about her condition** son état inspire de nouvelles inquiétudes aux médecins; **there is r. interest in …** il y a un regain d'intérêt pour …; **there has been r. military activity in the region** il y a eu un regain d'activité militaire dans la région

rennet ['renɪt] **N** présure *f*

re-nose **VT** *Journ (story)* réorienter

renounce [rɪ'naʊns] **VT 1** *(abandon, give up) (right, title, alcohol, violence etc)* renoncer à; *Law (nationality, inheritance)* répudier; **to r. all thought of doing sth** renoncer à toute idée de faire qch; *Lit* **to r. the world** renoncer au monde **2** *(disown) (treaty)* répudier, dénoncer; *(friend)* renier, désavouer; *(one's principles)* renier; **to r. one's faith** renoncer à sa foi, apostasier; **to r. Satan and all his works** renoncer à Satan, à ses pompes et à ses œuvres

renouncement [rɪ'naʊnsmənt] **N** = **renunciation**

renovate ['renəveɪt] **VT** *(house etc)* rénover

renovation [renə'veɪʃən] **N** *(of house etc)* rénovation *f*, **closed for r.** *(notice in shop window)* fermé pour cause de travaux de rénovation; **to be under r.** être en cours de rénovation; **to undergo renovations** subir des rénovations, être en rénovation; **r. project/work** projet *m*/travaux *mpl* de rénovation

renovator ['renəveɪtər] **N** rénovateur, -trice

renown [rɪ'naʊn] **N** renommée *f*, renom *m*; **woman of great** *or* **high r.** femme *f* de grand renom; **to win r.** acquérir une renommée, se faire une renommée (**as** en tant que; **for** pour)

renowned [rɪ'naʊnd] **ADJ** *(town, person)* renommé, célèbre (**for** pour; **as** comme); *(wine)* fameux; *(artist, writer)* célèbre, illustre; **Dr Hector Smith, the r. psychiatrist** le Dr Hector Smith, le célèbre psychiatre; **he is r. for being late** il est réputé pour être toujours en retard

rent¹ [rent] **N** *(on flat, house etc)* loyer *m*; **for r.** à louer; **how much do you pay in r.?, how much r. do you pay?** combien est-ce que tu paies de loyer?; **to live somewhere free of r.** habiter quelque part sans payer de loyer; **to be behind with the r.** être en retard pour (payer) le loyer; **Friday is r. day, it's r. day on Friday** on doit payer le loyer vendredi
VT *(flat, video, car)* louer (**from, to** à); **to r. (out) rooms** louer des chambres (**from, to** à); **she lives in a rented house** elle habite dans une maison qu'elle loue; **rented accommodation** logement *m* en location, location *f*, **to r.** à louer
VI **it rents at** *or* **for …** cela se loue à …
▸▸ **r. book** carnet *m* de quittances de loyer; *Fam* **r. boy** jeune prostitué *m* homosexuel; **r. collector** receveur, -euse des loyers; **r. strike** grève *f* des loyers
▸ **rent out** **VT INSEP** = **rent¹ VT**

rent² **N** *(in clothing)* déchirure *f*, accroc *m*; *(in clouds)* déchirure, trouée *f*; *(in relations)* rupture *f*

rent³ **PT, PP** *see* **rend**

rental ['rent(ə)l] **N 1** *(hire) (of car, flat, house etc)* location *f* **2** *(money paid) (for flat, house)* loyer *m*; *(for car, equipment, television, holiday flat)* (prix *m* de) location *f*, *(for telephone)* abonnement *m*; *Tel* **fixed r.** redevance *f* d'abonnement
▸▸ **r. car** voiture *f* de location; **r. company** société *f* de location; **r. charge** *(for telephone)* abonnement *m*; *(for TV, car)* prix *m* de location; **r. expenses** charges *fpl* locatives; **r. income** revenus *mpl* locatifs; **r. office** *(for car)* bureau *m* de location; **r. property** propriété *f* à louer

rent-a-mob **N** *Fam* agitateurs *mpl*

rent-free **ADJ** *(accommodation, flat etc)* exempt de loyer; **to live somewhere r.** habiter quelque part sans payer de loyer; **a house is available r.** il y a une maison où l'on peut habiter gratuitement *ou* sans payer de loyer

rents [rents] **NPL** *Am Fam (parents)* vieux *mpl*, renps *mpl*

renunciation [rɪnʌnsɪ'eɪʃən] **N 1** *(of right, title, alcohol, violence etc)* renonciation *f* (**of** à); *Law (of nationality, inheritance)* répudiation *f* **2** *(of treaty)* répudiation *f*, dénonciation *f*, *(of beliefs)* reniement *m*; *(of friend)* reniement, désaveu *m*; *(of world)* renoncement *m* (**of** à)

reoccupy [riː'ɒkjʊpaɪ] **VT** *(territory)* réoccuper; *(house)* habiter à nouveau; **the house is reoccupied** la maison est réhabitée

reopen [riː'əʊp(ə)n] **VT 1** *(book, frontier, investigation etc)* rouvrir; *Fig* **to r. an old wound** rouvrir une plaie **2** *(resume) (hostilities)* recommencer, reprendre; *(talks)* reprendre
VI *(of wound)* se rouvrir; *(of shop, theatre etc)* rouvrir; *(law court)* rentrer; *(of schools, talks)* reprendre; **the border has reopened** la frontière a été rouverte

reopening [riː'əʊp(ə)nɪŋ] **N** *(of shop, theatre, border, investigation etc)* réouverture *f*, *(of hostilities, talks)* reprise *f*, *Fig* **this will merely lead to the r. of old wounds** ça ne fera que rouvrir d'anciennes blessures

reorder [riː'ɔːdər] **N** *(to obtain more supplies)* nouvelle commande *f*, *(reminder to supplier)* commande renouvelée; **to send** *or* **put a r. in** envoyer *ou* passer une nouvelle commande (**for** de); **r. form/procedure** formulaire *m*/procédure *f* de renouvellement de commande
VT *(order more)* faire une nouvelle commande de; *(order again)* renouveler la commande de
▸▸ *Com* **r. level** seuil *m* de réapprovisionnement

reorganization [riːɔːɡənaɪ'zeɪʃən] **N** *(of company, system, files etc)* réorganisation *f*

reorganize [riː'ɔːɡənaɪz] **VT** *(company, system, files etc)* réorganiser
VI *(of company etc)* se réorganiser

Rep [rep] *Am Pol* **1** *abbr* **Representative 2** *abbr* **Republican**

rep¹ [rep] *Fam* **N** *(abbr* **representative)** *(door to door)* représentant, -ante; *(for large company)* représentant, -ante, VRP *m* (**for** chez); **sales r.** représentant, -ante de commerce, VRP
VI travailler comme représentant, -ante (**for** chez)

rep² **N** *Br Theat Fam (abbr* **repertory)** *(theatre)* théâtre *m*; **what's on at the local r.?** qu'est-ce qu'on joue au théâtre municipal?; **to work in r.** faire du théâtre

repackage [riː'pækɪdʒ] **VT** *Mktg* reconditionner, repenser l'emballage de

repaginate [riː'pædʒɪneɪt] **VT** remettre en pages; *(renumber)* repaginer

repaint [riːˈpeɪnt] **VT** repeindre

repair [rɪˈpeər] **N 1** (of shoes, watch etc) réparation f; (of building, road) réparation, réfection f; (of machine) réparation, remise f en état; (of clothing) réparation, raccommodage m; **to be in need of r.** avoir besoin d'être réparé; **to be in for r.** (of car etc) être en réparation; **to be (damaged) beyond r.** être irréparable; **road under r.** (road sign) travaux; **(shoe) repairs while you wait** (notice in shop) cordonnerie minute; **to make repairs to sth** (machine, car, bike) faire des réparations sur qch; (shoes, garment) réparer; **to carry out repairs** effectuer des réparations; **he does all his own repairs** il fait toutes ses réparations lui-même; **to undergo repairs** or **be under r.** être en réparation **2** (condition) **to be in good/bad r.** être en bon/mauvais état, être bien/mal entretenu; **to keep a road/car/property in (good) r.** entretenir une route/voiture/propriété
▸ **VT** (mend) (shoes, watch, building, road) réparer; (machine) réparer, remettre en état
▸▸ **r. kit** trousse f à outils; **r. shop** atelier m de réparations

repairer [rɪˈpeərər] **N** (of shoes) cordonnier, -ière; (of watch, machine etc) réparateur, -trice

repairman, pl **repairmen** [rɪˈpeəmæn, -men] **N** (of televisions, washing machines etc) réparateur m; **a computer/TV/washing machine r.** un réparateur d'ordinateurs/de télévisions/de machines à laver

repaper [riːˈpeɪpər] **VT** (room) retapisser

reparation [repəˈreɪʃən] **N** Fml (of wrong, omission) réparation f; **in r. of …** en réparation de …; **to make r. for sth** réparer qch; **(war) reparations, r. payments** réparations

repartee [repɑːˈtiː] **N** repartie f, **to be good** or **quick at r.** avoir la repartie facile, avoir de la repartie; **to engage in r.** faire de l'esprit

repast [rɪˈpɑːst] **N** Lit repas m

repatriate[1] [riːˈpætrieɪt] **VT** (prisoner of war, capital etc) rapatrier (**to** vers)

repatriate[2] [riːˈpætriət] **N** rapatrié, -ée

repatriation [riːpætriˈeɪʃən] **N** (of prisoner of war, capital etc) rapatriement m

repay [riːˈpeɪ, rɪ-] **VT** (pt, pp **repaid** [riːˈpeɪd, rɪ-]) **1** (pay back) (money) rendre, rembourser; (loan, person) rembourser **2** (reward) (person) récompenser (**for** de); (give same in return for) (favour) rendre; **is this how you r. me?** c'est comme ça que tu me récompenses ou remercies?; **to r. sb with ingratitude** payer qn d'ingratitude; **to r. a kindness** payer une gentillesse de retour; **I can never r. you for all you've done** je ne pourrai jamais vous remercier assez pour tout ce que vous avez fait; **how can I ever r. you?** pourrais-je jamais vous remercier?

repayable [riːˈpeɪəb(ə)l, rɪ-] **ADJ** (loan) remboursable

repayment [riːˈpeɪmənt, rɪ-] **N 1** (of loan, mortgage etc) remboursement m; **the repayments are spread over five years** les remboursements sont échelonnés sur cinq ans **2** (of kindness) récompense f; **in r. of your helpfulness/support** pour te remercier de ton aide/soutien
▸▸ Br **r. mortgage** prêt-logement m, pl prêts-logement (aux remboursements échelonnés); **r. plan** calendrier m des paiements

repeal [rɪˈpiːl] **N** (of law) abrogation f, (of decree) révocation f
▸ **VT** (law) abroger; (decree) révoquer

repeat [rɪˈpiːt] **VT 1** (do again) (action, motif) répéter; (one's efforts, prescription, attempt) renouveler; (as encore) (song, piece of music) bisser; Radio, TV (programme) rediffuser; Sch **to r. a year** redoubler; **history repeats itself** l'histoire se répète **2** (say again)

(question) répéter; (threat, order, promise) réitérer; **it can't be repeated too often** on ne saurait trop le répéter; Mus **r.** (after a line of a song etc) bis; **to r. oneself** se répéter; **am I repeating myself?** est-ce que je me répète?, Fam est-ce que je radote?; **I don't want to have to r. myself** je ne veux pas avoir à le répéter; **r. after me …** répétez après moi … **3** (say to others) (secret) répéter; **don't r. this, but …** ne le répète pas, mais …
▸ **VI 1** (of decimal figure) se répéter **2** (of food) donner des renvois; **it's repeating on me** ça me donne des renvois
▸ **N** (of event, motif, attempt) répétition f, Mus (passage) reprise f, Mus (mark) barre f de reprise, renvoi m; Radio, TV rediffusion f; **there's nothing on (television) but repeats** il n'y a que des rediffusions; **a r. of the attempt to assassinate him** une nouvelle tentative d'assassinat sur sa personne; **we get a lot of r. business** beaucoup de nos clients reviennent; **it will be a r. of last year's final** ça sera comme la finale de l'année dernière
▸▸ Tel **r. dial** recomposition f, renumérotation f; Comput **r. function** fonction f de répétition; Law **r. offender** récidiviste mf; Com **r. order** commande f renouvelée; Theat **r. performance** deuxième représentation f, Fig **we don't want a r. performance of last year's chaos** nous ne voulons pas que le désordre de l'année dernière se reproduise; **r. prescription** ordonnance f (de renouvellement d'un médicament); Mktg **r. purchase** achats mpl répétés; **r. run** (of adverts etc) passage m répété; Mktg **r. sale** ventes fpl répétées

repeat-action key **N** Comput touche f de répétition

repeated [rɪˈpiːtɪd] **ADJ** (action etc) répété; (question etc) réitéré; (effort) renouvelé; **after r. failures/warnings** après des échecs/des avertissements répétés

repeatedly [rɪˈpiːtɪdlɪ] **ADV** à maintes reprises

repeater [rɪˈpiːtər] **N** (rifle) fusil m à répétition

repeating [rɪˈpiːtɪŋ] **ADJ 1** (rifle) à répétition **2** (decimal) périodique
▸ **N** (of word, action) répétition f

repel [rɪˈpel] **VT** (-ll-) **1** (repulse) (assailant) repousser; **to r. moisture** empêcher l'infiltration de l'humidité; **like poles r. (each other)** les pôles semblables se repoussent; **a spray that repels greenfly** un aérosol qui éloigne les pucerons **2** (disgust) répugner à, dégoûter; **she was repelled by the sight** elle a été dégoûtée par ce qu'elle a vu

repellent [rɪˈpelənt] **ADJ** (person, sight etc) repoussant, répugnant; **he finds her/the idea quite r.** elle/l'idée lui répugne; **r. (to water)** imperméable
▸ **N** (for insects) insecticide m

-repellent [rɪˈpelənt] **SUFF** moth/rust-**r.** antimites/antirouille

repent [rɪˈpent] **VI** se repentir (**of** de)
▸ **VT** se repentir de

repentance [rɪˈpentəns] **N** repentir m (**for** pour); **to show r.** manifester du repentir; Rel venir à résipiscence, se repentir; **to show no sign of r.** ne manifester aucun signe de repentir

repentant [rɪˈpentənt] **ADJ** (sinner etc) repentant (**of** de)

repentantly [rɪˈpentəntlɪ] **ADV** (to say, look at) d'un ton/d'un air repentant

repercussion [riːpəˈkʌʃən] **N 1** (indirect effect) répercussion f, (of scandal) retentissement m; (consequence) contrecoup m; **to have repercussions** avoir des répercussions (**for, on** sur); **the repercussions are still be-**

-ing felt on en ressent encore les répercussions **2** (from impact, of sound) répercussion f

repertoire [ˈrepətwɑːr] **N** (of jokes, songs etc), Theat répertoire m; **to have a wide/limited r.** avoir un vaste répertoire/un répertoire restreint; Theat **the two plays will be performed in r.** les deux pièces seront jouées en alternance

repertory [ˈrepət(ə)rɪ] **N 1** Theat **to work in r.** faire du théâtre de répertoire; (theatre) théâtre m de répertoire; **what's on at the local r.?** qu'est-ce qu'on joue au théâtre municipal? **2** (repertoire) répertoire m
▸▸ Theat **r. company** compagnie f ou troupe f de répertoire; Theat **r. theatre** théâtre de répertoire

répétiteur [repetiˈtɜːr] **N** Theat (of opera singer etc) maître m de musique

repetition [repɪˈtɪʃən] **N** (of word, action etc) répétition f; (of effort) renouvellement m; Mus reprise f, Sport **it was an exact r. of last year's final** c'était exactement comme la finale de l'année dernière; **I don't want any r. of your behaviour!** que cela ne se produise pas!

repetitious [repɪˈtɪʃəs] **ADJ** (book, speech etc) plein de répétitions

repetitive [rɪˈpetɪtɪv] **ADJ** (person) rabâcheur; (job) répétitif
▸▸ Med **r. strain injury, r. stress injury** = douleur f due à la répétition d'un même mouvement lors d'une activité telle que taper à la machine, jouer du violon etc

rephrase [riːˈfreɪz] **VT** (question) formuler à nouveau, reformuler; **perhaps I should r. that …** peut-être devrais-je m'exprimer autrement …

repine [rɪˈpaɪn] **VI** Lit être mécontent (**at** de)

replace [rɪˈpleɪs] **VT 1** (put back) (object) replacer, remettre (en place); **I replaced the book on the shelf** j'ai replacé ou remis le livre sur l'étagère; **r. the book when you've finished with it** remets le livre à sa place quand tu n'en auras plus besoin; Tel **to r. the receiver** raccrocher (le combiné) **2** (substitute for) (person, object) remplacer (**as** en tant que; **with** par); **to be replaced by** or **with** être remplacé par; **it can be replaced** (of broken cup etc) on peut retrouver le/la même; Comput **r. all** tout remplacer

> When translating the English verb **to replace**, note that the French verbs **replacer** and **remplacer** are not interchangeable. **Replacer** means **to put back** and **remplacer** means **to take the place of**.

replaceable [rɪˈpleɪsɪb(ə)l] **ADJ** (broken cup etc) remplaçable

replacement [rɪˈpleɪsmənt] **N 1** (putting back) (of object) remise f en place **2** (substitution) (of person, object) remplacement m (**of … by** de … par) **3** (substitute) (for person) remplaçant, -ante; (for component) pièce f de rechange; **we are looking for a r. for our secretary** nous cherchons quelqu'un pour remplacer notre secrétaire
▸▸ **r. cost** coût m de remplacement; Med **r. hip joint** prothèse f de (la) hanche; Med **r. knee joint** prothèse de (la) rotule; Mktg **r. sale** vente f de remplacement; **r. teacher** professeur m suppléant, suppléant, -ante, remplaçant, -ante; **r. value** valeur f de remplacement

replant [riːˈplɑːnt] **VT** (shrub, garden) replanter

replay[1] [ˈriːpleɪ] **N** Sport second match m, nouvelle rencontre f, TV instant or Br action **r.** répétition f immédiate d'une séquence; TV **(slow-motion) r.** répétition au ralenti; TV **to give** or **show a r.** repasser une séquence; *(in slow motion)* repasser une séquence au ralenti; **the r. clearly shows the foul** on voit bien la faute au ralenti

replay [2] [riː'pleɪ] **VT 1** *Sport (match)* rejouer; *Tennis* **to r. a point** rejouer un point **2** *(recording)* repasser

replenish [rɪ'plenɪʃ] **VT** *(cup etc)* remplir de nouveau (**with** de); **to r. one's supplies** se réapprovisionner (**with** de); *Banking* **to r. an account** approvisionner un compte; **she kept his glass replenished** elle veillait à ce que son verre fût toujours plein; **do you need replenishing?** est-ce que je remplis ton verre?

replenishment [rɪ'plenɪʃmənt] **N** *(of cup etc)* remplissage *m*; **r. of supplies** réapprovisionnement *m*

replete [rɪ'pliːt] **ADJ** *Fml* **1** *(full up)* rassasié; **r. with** gorgé de **2** *(well-supplied)* rempli, plein (**with** de)

repletion [rɪ'pliːʃən] **N** *Fml* satiété *f*; **to eat to r.** manger à satiété *ou* jusqu'à être rassasié

replica ['replɪkə] **N** *(of statue, painting, building)* réplique *f*; *(of document)* copie *f*; *Fig (of person)* portrait *m*; *(of match, dispute etc)* répétition *f*; **she is a r. of her grandmother** c'est (tout) le portrait de sa grand-mère

replicate ['replɪkeɪt] **VT** *(document)* copier; *(experiment, cell, gene)* reproduire; *Comput (in spreadsheet)* recopier à l'identique; **the gene can r. itself** le gène peut se reproduire

reply [rɪ'plaɪ] **N** *(to letter, query etc)* réponse *f*; **I made no r.** je n'ai rien répondu; **his r. to that was ...** *(in speech)* il a répondu à cela que ...; **his r. to that was to march out of the room** il a réagi à cela en sortant d'un air furieux de la pièce; **what did you say in r.?** qu'est-ce que tu as répondu?; **what did you do in r.?** comment est-ce que tu as réagi?; **there was no r.** *(to telephone call)* on n'a pas répondu, ça ne répondait pas; *(to knock on door)* on n'a pas ouvert; **in r. to your letter** en réponse à votre lettre; **r. paid** réponse payée ▪ **VT & VI** répondre (**to** à); *(retort)* répliquer (**to** à); **yes, madam, he replied** oui, madame, a-t-il répondu
▸ ▸ *Mktg* **r. card** carte-réponse *f*, *pl* cartes-réponses; *Mktg* **r. coupon** coupon-réponse *m*, *pl* coupons-réponses; **r. slip** talon *m* à retourner

reply-paid **N** *Br* avec réponse payée
▸ ▸ *Mktg* **r. card** carte *f*T; **r. envelope** enveloppe *f*T, enveloppe-retour *f*, *pl* enveloppes-retour; **r. letter** lettre *f* avec réponse payée

repo ['riːpəʊ] **N 1** *Am Fam (abbr repossession)* saisie *f* **2** *(abbr repurchase)* rachat *m*; *St Exch, Banking* réméré *m*
▸ ▸ *St Exch, Banking* **r. agreement** opération *f* de réméré *ou* de prise en pension, opération repo; *Am Fam* **r. man** ≃ huissier *m* *(chargé par une société de saisir des meubles etc non payés)*; *St Exch, Banking* **r. operation** opération de réméré *ou* de prise en pension, opération repo; *St Exch, Banking* **r. rate** taux *m* de réméré *ou* de prise en pension

REPORT [rɪ'pɔːt]

N rapport **1** ▪ compte rendu **1**
▪ procès-verbal **1** ▪ reportage **1**
▪ bulletin **1**
VT rendre compte de **1** ▪ faire un
reportage sur **1** ▪ signaler **2, 3**
▪ annoncer **2**
VI se présenter **1** ▪ faire un rapport **2**

N 1 *(account)*, *Com* rapport *m* (**on** sur); *(of meetings)* compte rendu *m*; *(in writing)* procès-verbal *m*, *pl* procès-verbaux; *(in newspaper)* *(short)* compte rendu; *(long)* reportage *m*; *(on radio, television)* repor-

tage; *(by eyewitness)* témoignage *m*; *Comput* état *m*; **there was a short r. of the incident in the newspaper** l'incident a fait l'objet d'un petit article *ou* d'un entrefilet dans le journal; **according to reports in the newspapers** selon les journaux/les services de renseignements; **to draw up** *or* **make a r. on sth** faire *ou* rédiger un rapport sur qch; *(of police officer)* dresser procès-verbal de qch; **r. of the board of directors** *(in annual account)* rapport de gestion; *Sch* **book r.** compte rendu de lecture; *Sch* **end-of-term r.** bulletin *m* (trimestriel); **progress r.** rapport périodique *ou* d'avancement (des travaux); *Sch* **school r.** bulletin scolaire; *Mil* **sick r.** rôle *m* des malades

2 *(rumour)* bruit *m* (qui court), rumeur *f*

3 *(sound)* *(of shot)* détonation *f*, coup *m* de fusil/de canon; *(of explosion)* bruit *m* d'explosion, détonation

4 *Old-fashioned (reputation)* renom *m*; **man of good r.** homme *m* de bonne réputation

VT 1 *(give account of)* rendre compte de; *(fact, incident)* rapporter; *(speech etc)* faire le compte rendu de; *Journ* faire un reportage sur; **to r. one's findings** rendre compte des résultats de ses recherches (**to sb** à qn); **the newspapers r. heavy casualties** les journaux font état de nombreuses victimes; **little progress has been reported so far** jusqu'à présent on n'a obtenu que peu de résultats; **the president was reported by the newspapers to have ...** les journaux ont rapporté *ou* raconté que le président avait ...; **her resignation is reported in several papers** sa démission est annoncée dans plusieurs journaux; **she is reported to be dead** elle serait morte, on dit qu'elle est morte, on la dit morte; **it is reported that ...** on dit que ... + *ind*; **the version reported in the press** la version parue dans la presse; **they are reported to be in France** ils seraient en France

2 *(make known)* *(accident, theft)* signaler (**to** à); *(announce)* *(change, developments, profits, loss etc)* annoncer; *Mil* **to r. sb sick/missing** porter qn malade/absent; **to r. sb missing** *(to police)* signaler la disparition de qn; **she has been reported missing** on a signalé sa disparition; **she was reported missing five years ago** elle a été portée disparue il y a cinq ans; **nothing to r.** rien à signaler; *(on form)* néant, RAS

3 *(denounce)* **I'm going to r. you** *(to authorities)* je vais te signaler; **to r. sb to the police** dénoncer qn à la police; **to r. a pupil to the headmaster** *(of teacher)* signaler la mauvaise conduite d'un élève au directeur; **to r. a pupil for smoking** signaler le nom d'un élève surpris en train de fumer; **I'm going to r. you for smoking** je dirai au directeur que je t'ai surpris en train de fumer

VI 1 *(present oneself)* se présenter (**to sb** à *ou* devant qn; **to a place** à un endroit); **please r. to reception** veuillez vous présenter à la réception; **you've to r. to the headmaster** tu dois aller chez le directeur; *Mil* **to r. sick** se faire porter malade; *Mil* **to r. fit** reprendre son service (après une maladie); *Mil* **to r. to one's unit** rallier son unité; **to r. for duty** prendre son service; **you will r. for duty on Monday** vous vous présenterez à votre poste lundi; **to r. back from leave** reprendre son service après un congé

2 *(give account)* faire un rapport (**on** sur); *(of journalist)* faire un reportage (**on** sur); **to r. (for a newspaper)** faire des reportages (pour un journal); *Parl* **to r. on a bill** rapporter un projet de loi; *TV, Radio* **reporting from Geneva is our foreign affairs correspondent ...** de Genève, notre correspondant pour les affaires étrangères ...; **this is Mary Smith reporting for ITN news** Mary Smith pour le journal d'ITN

▸ ▸ *Sch* **r. card** bulletin *ou* carnet *m* scolaire; *Comput* **r. form** rapport (d'édition), fiche *f* d'état; *Comput* **r. form generator** générateur *m* d'états; *Br Parl* **r. stage** = examen *m* d'un projet de loi avant la troisième lecture; **the bill has reached the r. stage** le projet de loi a été présenté au Parlement

▸ **report back VI 1** *(announce return)* se présenter **2** *(announce findings)* rendre compte (**on sth** de qch); **to r. back to a committee** faire son rapport à un comité; **they r. back to head office once a week** ils font un rapport pour le siège une fois par semaine

▸ **report to VT INSEP 1** *(be accountable to)* *(person)* rendre compte à; **who do you r. to?** qui est votre supérieur?; **you'll be reporting to Mr Jones** vous travaillerez sous la direction de M. Jones; **I r. directly to the board** je n'ai pas de supérieur hiérarchique à part le conseil d'administration **2** *(inform of developments)* **to r. to sb** faire son rapport à qn (**on** sur), rendre compte à qn (**on** de)

> Note that the French word **report** is a false friend and is never a translation for the English word **report**. Its most common meaning is **postponement**.
>
> Note that the French verb **reporter** is a false friend and is never a translation for the English verb **to report**. Its most common meaning is **to postpone**.

reportage [repɔ'tɑːʒ] **N** *Journ etc* reportage *m*

reported [rɪ'pɔːtɪd] **ADJ ATTRIB** **their last r. position was south of the river** *(given by themselves)* la dernière fois qu'ils ont donné leur position, ils étaient au sud de la rivière; *(given by third party)* ils ont été vus pour la dernière fois au sud de la rivière; **her r. lack of interest in her children** son soi-disant manque d'intérêt pour ses enfants
▸ ▸ *Gram* **r. speech** style *m* *ou* discours *m* indirect

reportedly [rɪ'pɔːtɪdlɪ] **ADV** à ce qu'on dit; **the President r. said that ...** le Président aurait dit que ...; **she is r. unharmed** elle serait indemne; **he is r. resident in Paris** il résiderait à Paris

reporter [rɪ'pɔːtər] **N** reporter *mf*, journaliste *mf*; *(correspondent)* envoyé, -ée, reporter; *Radio, TV* reporter

reporting [rɪ'pɔːtɪŋ] **N** *(of news)* reportage *m*; **his r. of the facts is always accurate** il rapporte toujours fidèlement les faits; **she is noted for her objective r.** elle est connue pour l'objectivité de ses reportages
▸ ▸ *St Exch* **r. limit** seuil *m* d'annonce obligatoire; **r. restrictions** restrictions *fpl* journalistiques; *esp Jur* **r. restrictions have been imposed** on a imposé des restrictions quant aux reportages; **r. structure** *(within company)* structure *f* hiérarchique

repose [rɪ'pəʊz] **VT** *Fml* **1** **to r. trust in sb** placer *ou* mettre sa confiance en qn **2** *(rest)* *(one's head)* reposer
VI 1 *(of argument, plan)* reposer (**on** sur) **2** *Fml (rest)* reposer
N *Fml, Lit (rest)* repos *m*; *(sleep)* sommeil *m*; **her face is beautiful in r.** son visage est très beau lorsqu'elle est détendue; **to pray for the r. of sb's soul** prier pour le repos de l'âme de qn

reposition [riːpə'zɪʃən] **VT 1** *(move)* **she repositioned herself nearer the door** elle a changé de place pour aller se placer près de la porte **2** *Com (product, party)* repositionner

repositioning [riːpə'zɪʃənɪŋ] **N** *Com (of product, party)* repositionnement *m*

repository [rɪ'pɒzɪt(ə)rɪ] **N** *(for books, fur-*

niture etc) dépôt m, entrepôt m; Fig Lit (of knowledge etc) mine f

repossess [riːpəˈzes] **VT** (for non-payment) (furniture, car etc) saisir

repossession [riːpəˈzeʃən] **N** (of furniture etc) saisie f

repot [riːˈpɒt] **VT** (plant) rempoter

reprehend [repriˈhend] **VT** Fml réprimander

reprehensible [repriˈhensɪb(ə)l] **ADJ** (behaviour, act) répréhensible; **that was most r. of you** c'était très répréhensible de votre part

reprehensibly [repriˈhensɪblɪ] **ADV** (to behave, act) de façon répréhensible

represent [repriˈzent] **VT 1** (depict, portray) (person, object) représenter **2** (act as agent for) (person, company etc), Law, Pol représenter; **the Queen will be represented by …** la Reine sera représentée par … **3** (constitute) représenter, constituer; **this represents a great improvement** cela constitue un grand progrès **4** (symbolize, embody) (nation, love etc) symboliser **5** (typify) représenter; **the government's policy does not r. my opinions** la politique du gouvernement n'est pas représentative de mes opinions **6** (describe) (person, object) présenter (**to be, as** comme); **he represents himself as a model of virtue** il se présente comme ou il se donne pour un modèle de vertu **7** Fml (state, express) faire remarquer, signaler (**to** à); **I will r. your grievances to management** je ferai part de vos griefs à la direction

re-present VT (bill etc) présenter à ou de nouveau; **to r. a cheque** représenter un chèque à l'acceptation

representation [reprizenˈteɪʃən] **N 1** Pol représentation f, **they have increased their r. to six** le nombre de leurs délégués est passé à six; **they still lacked r. in Parliament** ils n'étaient toujours pas représentés au Parlement **2** (in painting) représentation f **3** (of facts) exposé m des faits; **this is a fair r. of their point of view** cela représente bien leur point de vue **4** (complaints) protestations fpl; Fml **to make representations** faire des démarches (**about** concernant; **to** auprès de)

representational [reprizenˈteɪʃən(ə)l] **ADJ** (art) figuratif

representative [repriˈzentətɪv] **N 1** (of group, company, organization etc) représentant, -ante; (for mail-order firm) délégué, -ée; (sales) **r.** représentante, -ante, VRP m; **to send a r. to a conference** envoyer un(e) représentant, -ante ou se faire représenter à une conférence; **sole representatives of a firm** représentants ou agents exclusifs d'une maison **2** Am Pol député m
  ADJ 1 (typical) représentatif, typique; **a r. cross-section of the population** un échantillon représentatif de la population **2** Pol (government) représentatif
  ▸▸ **r. sample** échantillon m type

repress [riˈpres] **VT 1** (desire, passions, uprising) réprimer; (tears) retenir **2** Psy (unconsciously) refouler; (consciously) réprimer

repressed [riˈprest] **ADJ** (person, feelings) refoulé; (laughter) étouffé; **he is very r.** il est très refoulé ou Fam coincé; **she had a very r. adolescence** elle a été refoulée à l'adolescence

repression [riˈpreʃən] **N 1** (of desire, uprising etc) répression f **2** Psy (unconscious) refoulement m; (conscious) répression f

repressive [riˈpresɪv] **ADJ** (government, law) répressif; (measures) répressif, de répression

reprieve [riˈpriːv] Law **N** (for condemned prisoner) (definitive) commutation f de la peine capitale; (temporary), Fig sursis m; Law **to grant a r.** accorder une commuta-

tion de peine/un sursis; Fig **this is a r. for the government** cela constitue un sursis pour le gouvernement; **we've got a r.** (for project etc) on nous a donné un peu plus de temps
  VT (prisoner) accorder une commutation de la peine capitale à; (temporary) accorder un sursis à; Fig **the shipyard has been reprieved** le chantier naval bénéficie d'un sursis

reprimand [ˈreprimɑːnd] **N** (of child) réprimande f, (of employee, accused person) blâme m; **to be given a r.** (of child) recevoir une réprimande; (of employee etc) recevoir un blâme; **she was let off with a r.** elle s'en est tirée avec une réprimande/un blâme
  VT (child) réprimander (**for** pour); (employee, accused person) blâmer (**for** pour)

reprint¹ [ˈriːprɪnt] **N** (of book) réimpression f, (of article) nouvelle parution f, nouvelle publication f, **the book is going into its fourth r.** le livre va être réimprimé pour la quatrième fois; **separate r.** (of article from journal) tirage m à part

reprint² [riːˈprɪnt] **VT** (book) réimprimer; (article) faire paraître ou publier à nouveau; **article reprinted from The Times** article reproduit du Times
  VI (of book) être en réimpression

reprisal [riˈpraɪz(ə)l] **N** représailles fpl; **to carry out or take reprisals** exercer des représailles, user de représailles (**against** contre); **to threaten reprisals** menacer de représailles; **there have been threats of r.** il y a eu des menaces de représailles; **as a or in r. for …** en ou par représailles pour …; **r. attack/raid** attaque f/raid m de représailles

reprise [riˈpriːz] Mus reprise f

repro [ˈriːprəʊ] **N** Fam (abbr **reproduction**, **reprography**) repro f
  ▸▸ **r. head** tête f de lecture

reproach [riˈprəʊtʃ] **N 1** (blame) reproche m; **she heaped reproaches on him** elle l'a accablé de reproches; **a look of r.** un regard plein de reproche; **there was a note of r. in his voice** il y avait une pointe ou une nuance de reproche dans sa voix; **a letter of r.** une lettre de reproches; **beyond or above r.** irréprochable **2** (shame) honte f, **to be a r. to …** être la honte de…; **it is a r. to the government that …** c'est une honte pour le gouvernement que …; **things that have brought r. upon him** choses qui ont jeté le discrédit sur lui
  VT reprocher (**sb for** or **with sth** qch à qn); **to r. oneself** s'en vouloir; **I have nothing to r. myself with** or **for** je n'ai rien à me reprocher; **she reproached him for not keeping his promise** elle lui a reproché de n'avoir pas tenu sa promesse

reproachful [riˈprəʊtʃfʊl] **ADJ** (tone) de reproche; (look) plein de reproche

reproachfully [riˈprəʊtʃfəlɪ] **ADV** (to say, look at) d'un ton/d'un air de reproche ou plein de reproche

reprobate [ˈreprəbeɪt] **N** Fml réprouvé, -ée, Old-fashioned Hum vaurien, -ienne

reprocess [riːˈprəʊses] **VT** Ind etc (waste etc) retraiter

reprocessing [riːˈprəʊsesɪŋ] **N** (of waste) retraitement m; **nuclear r.** retraitement des déchets nucléaires
  ▸▸ **r. plant** usine f de retraitement

reproduce [riːprəˈdjuːs] **VT** (copy) (painting) reproduire; (document) copier
  VI Biol, Bot se reproduire; (of photocopier) reproduire; **this print will r. well** cette estampe se prêtera bien à la reproduction

reproduction [riːprəˈdʌkʃən] **N** (of document, picture etc), Biol, Bot reproduction f, **thousands of reproductions have been made of this picture** ce tableau a été reproduit à des milliers d'exemplaires

▸▸ **r. furniture** reproduction ou copie f de meubles d'époque; **r. rights** droits mpl de reproduction

reproductive [riːprəˈdʌktɪv] **ADJ** Biol reproducteur, -trice
  ▸▸ **r. organs** organes mpl reproducteurs; **r. system** appareil m reproducteur

reprogram [riːˈprəʊɡræm] **VT** Comput reprogrammer; **to r. a computer to do sth** reprogrammer un ordinateur pour qu'il fasse qch

reprogrammable [ˈriːprəʊˈɡræməbəl] **ADJ** Comput (key) reprogrammable

reprographic [reprəˈɡræfɪk] **ADJ** reprographique

reprography [reˈprɒɡrəfɪ] **N** reprographie f

reproof¹ [riˈpruːf] **N** esp Fml réprobation f, (in speech, writing) blâme m; **he looked at her with r.** il l'a regardée avec réprobation; **word/look of r.** mot m/regard m de réprobation

reproof² [riːˈpruːf] **VT** (raincoat) réimperméabiliser

reprove [riˈpruːv] **VT** esp Fml (child) réprimander, reprendre; (person) réprimander (**for** pour); (action) condamner

reproving [riˈpruːvɪŋ] **ADJ** esp Fml (look, tone) réprobateur, -trice

reprovingly [riˈpruːvɪŋlɪ] **ADV** (to say, look at) d'un ton/d'un air réprobateur

reptile [ˈreptaɪl] **N** reptile m
  ▸▸ **r. house** vivarium m

reptilian [repˈtɪlɪən] **ADJ** (animal) reptilien, Pej (features) de reptile
  N reptile m

republic [riˈpʌblɪk] **N** république f

Republican [riˈpʌblɪkən] **ADJ, N** Pol républicain, -aine

Republican

Aux États-Unis, un "Republican" est un partisan du Parti républicain. En Irlande, le terme "Republican" désigne une personne qui souhaite le rattachement de l'Irlande du Nord à la république d'Irlande. Au Royaume-Uni et en Australie, le terme désigne les personnes favorables à l'abolition de la monarchie et à l'établissement d'une république.

---

republican [riˈpʌblɪkən] **ADJ, N** républicain, -aine

republicanism [riˈpʌblɪkənɪz(ə)m] **N** républicanisme m

republication [riːpʌblɪˈkeɪʃən] **N** réédition f

republish [riːˈpʌblɪʃ] **VT** rééditer

repudiate [riˈpjuːdɪeɪt] **VT** Fml (spouse, idea, treaty etc) répudier; (friend, opinion) désavouer; (offer) repousser; (debt, accusation) nier; **to r. the authorship of a book** désavouer la paternité d'un livre

repudiation [ripjuːdɪˈeɪʃən] **N** (of spouse, idea etc) répudiation f, (of friend, opinion) désaveu m; (of offer) refus m; (of debt, accusation) reniement m

repugnance [riˈpʌɡnəns] **N** (abhorrence) répugnance f (**for** pour); **to have a r. for sth/for doing sth** avoir de la répugnance pour qch/à faire qch

repugnant [riˈpʌɡnənt] **ADJ** (deed, person etc) répugnant (**to** à); **to be r. to sb** répugner à qn

repulse [riˈpʌls] **N** (of assistance, offer etc) refus m; Mil échec m; **to meet with a r.** (of person, offer) essuyer un refus
  VT (person, request), Mil (assault) repousser; Mil (enemy) repousser, refouler; **to be repulsed by sth** (disgusted) être révolté par qch

to be at r. *(be dead)* reposer en paix; *Euph* **to be laid to r.** *(buried)* être enterré; *Euph* **to be or lie at r.** *(dead)* reposer en paix; *Euph* **to lay sb to r.** porter qn en terre, enterrer qn; *Fig* **to lay** *or* **put a plan to r.** *(not carry any further)* renoncer à *ou* abandonner un projet; **to lay** *or* **put allegations/doubts/suspicions to r.** dissiper des allégations/des doutes/des suspicions; **perhaps we could lay the matter to r.** *(not discuss any further)* peut-être qu'on pourrait arrêter de parler de cette affaire une bonne fois pour toutes; **the matter should be laid to r. as quickly as possible** *(resolved)* cette affaire doit être résolue au plus vite
2 *(support)* support *m*; *(for billiard cue)* chevalet *m*; *Tel (for receiver)* étrier *m*
3 *Mus (silence)* silence *m*
VI 1 *(relax)* se reposer, prendre du repos; **you need to r. (up)** il vous faut le repos complet; **to r. from one's work** se reposer de son travail; **to r. easy** se détendre; **to be resting** *(of actor)* = se trouver sans engagement; **she is resting comfortably** *(after operation etc)* son état est satisfaisant; **I won't r. until ...** je n'aurai de cesse que ... + *subj*; **to r. on** *(of roof etc)* reposer sur; **he was resting on his shovel** il s'appuyait sur sa pelle; **his head was resting on her shoulder** il avait la tête appuyée contre son épaule; *Fig* **to r. on one's oars** se reposer, *Fam* souffler; *Fig* **to r. on one's laurels** se reposer *ou* s'endormir sur ses lauriers
2 *(be buried)* être enterré, reposer; **may they r. in peace!** qu'ils reposent en paix!; **r. in peace** *(inscription on gravestone)* qu'il(s)/qu'elle(s) repose(nt) en paix
3 *(remain)* **there the matter rests** l'affaire en reste *ou* en est là; **I won't let it r. at that** cela ne se passera pas ainsi; **let it r.!** *(stop talking about it)* n'en parlons plus!; *(stop pursuing the matter)* ça suffit; **can't we let it r.?** *(stop talking about it)* restons-en là, je vous en prie; **r. assured** soyez certain *ou* assuré; **(that** que) **a heavy responsibility rests (up)on them** une lourde responsabilité pèse sur eux; **to r. with** *(of decision, responsibility etc)* incomber à; **it rests with you to ...** il vous incombe de ...; **it doesn't r. with me to decide** ce n'est pas à moi qu'il incombe de décider
4 *(be based)* **to r. on** *(of argument, fame)* reposer sur
5 *Law* **the defence/prosecution rests** = plaise au tribunal d'adopter mes conclusions
VT 1 *(repose)* **to r. oneself** se reposer; **to r. one's men/horses** laisser ses hommes/chevaux se reposer; **the coach wanted to r. his players** l'entraîneur voulait que son équipe se repose; **to r. one's eyes/legs** se reposer les yeux/les jambes; *Agr* **to r. a field** mettre un champ en jachère; **(God) r. his soul!** que Dieu ait son âme!, qu'il repose en paix!
2 *(lean)* *(one's elbows)* appuyer (**on** sur); *(one's head)* reposer (**on** sur); *(one's hopes, confidence etc)* fonder (**on** sur)
3 *(base)* *(argument, theory)* fonder (**on** sur)
4 *esp Am Law* **to r. one's case** conclure son plaidoyer; *Fig* **I r. my case** j'ai dit ce que j'avais à dire
▸▸*Aut* **r. area** aire *f* de repos; *Am* **r. room** toilettes *fpl*; *Am Aut* **r. stop** aire de stationnement *ou* de repos

rest² N **the r.** *(remainder)* le reste (**of** de); *(others)* les autres *mfpl*; **where's the r. (of it)?** *(of money, food etc)* où est le reste?; **the r. of the men/cups** les autres hommes/tasses; **I'm keeping the r. of it for tomorrow** je garde le reste *ou* le restant pour demain; **do you want to watch the r. of the news?** est-ce que tu veux regarder le reste des actualités?; **(as) for the r.** quant au reste, pour le

reste; **and (all) the r. of it** et tout le reste; **the r. of us** nous autres, le reste (d'entre nous); **it's just another day like all the r.** c'est un jour comme un autre

restart [riː'stɑːt] **VT** *(work etc)* recommencer, reprendre; *(machine)* (re)mettre en marche; *(engine)* remettre en marche, relancer; *(computer)* réamorcer
VI *(of job etc)* recommencer, reprendre; *(of machine, engine)* se remettre en marche; *(of computer)* se réamorcer

restate [riː'steɪt] **VT 1** *(repeat)* *(theory, viewpoint)* exposer de nouveau; *Mus (theme)* reprendre; **she restated her concern about the child's safety** elle a réitéré ses inquiétudes à propos de la sécurité de l'enfant **2** *(rephrase)* *(question)* reformuler, formuler de nouveau

restatement [riː'steɪtmənt] **N 1** *(repetition)* *(of theory, viewpoint)* nouvel exposé *m*; **it's a point that bears r.** c'est une chose qui mérite d'être répétée **2** *(rephrasing)* *(of question)* nouvelle formulation *f*

restaurant ['restrɒnt] **N** restaurant *m*
▸▸*Br* **r. car** wagon-restaurant *m*, *pl* wagons-restaurants, voiture-restaurant *f*, *pl* voitures-restaurants; **r. chain** chaîne *f* de restaurants; **r. manager** gérant, -ante de restaurant

restaurateur [restərə'tɜːr] **N** restaurateur, -trice

rest-cure N cure *f* de repos; *Fig* **this job is no r.** ce travail n'est pas une sinécure

rest-day N *(of cricketer, tennis player etc)* jour *m* de repos; *(of shift worker)* jour de congé

rested ['restɪd] **ADJ** reposé; **to feel r.** se sentir *(bien)* reposé *ou* frais et dispos

restful ['restfʊl] **ADJ** *(holiday, weekend, place etc)* reposant; **r. to the eyes** *(colour, lighting)* qui repose les yeux, reposant pour la vue

restfully ['restfəlɪ] **ADV** *(to spend time)* paisiblement, tranquillement

rest-home N **1** *(for convalescents)* maison *f* de repos **2** *(for elderly)* maison *f* de retraite; **to go into/to put sb in a r.** aller en/mettre qn en maison de retraite

resting ['restɪŋ] **N**
▸▸ **r. place** lieu *m* de repos; *Fig Literary (grave)* dernière demeure *f*, **last r. place** dernière demeure

restitution [restɪ'tjuːʃən] **N** *Fml (of stolen property)* restitution *f*; *(compensation)* réparation *f*; **to make r. of sth** *(give back)* restituer qch; **to make r. for sth** *(make up for)* réparer qch; *(by providing monetary compensation)* verser des dommages-intérêts pour qch; **he should make full r.** il devrait verser une compensation intégrale

restive ['restɪv] **ADJ** *(nervous)* *(person, crowd)* agité; *(apt to rebel)* *(person, child)* récalcitrant, indocile, rétif; *(horse)* rétif

restively ['restɪvlɪ] **ADV** nerveusement

restiveness ['restɪvnɪs] **N** *(of population, because of individual's nervousness)* agitation *f*, *(because of boredom)* *(of audience)* impatience *f*, *(of child)* nature *f* turbulente; *(of horse)* nature rétive

restless ['restlɪs] **ADJ** *(person)* nerveux, agité; *(child)* agité, remuant; *(sea)* agité; *(wind)* incessant; **to be r. in one's sleep** *or* **a r. sleeper** avoir un *ou* le sommeil agité; **I've had** *or* **spent a r. night** j'ai passé une nuit agitée; **r. mind** esprit *m* agité; **she's feeling a bit r.** *(in present job, situation etc)* elle a envie de voir *ou* de faire autre chose; **the audience was getting r.** l'auditoire s'impatientait

restlessly ['restlɪslɪ] **ADV** *(to move)* (of

person) avec agitation; *Lit (of wind)* sans cesse

restlessness ['restlɪsnɪs] **N** *(of person, sea)* agitation *f*, *(of mind)* nervosité *f*, état *m* fiévreux; *(of audience)* impatience *f*

restock [riː'stɒk] **VT** *(shelves, shop)* réapprovisionner (**with** en); *(freezer)* refaire le plein de; **to r. a river (with fish)** rempoissonner une rivière
VI *(of shop)* se réapprovisionner

restocking [riː'stɒkɪŋ] **N** réapprovisionnement *m*

restoration [restə'reɪʃən] **N 1** *(of monument, building, furniture etc)* restauration *f* **2** *(of communications, law and order)* rétablissement *m* **3** *(of lost property, fortune)* restitution *f*, *(of dynasty)* restauration *f*, rétablissement *m* sur le trône; *Hist* **the R.** la Restauration
▸▸*Br* **R. comedy** *(genre)* théâtre *m* de la Restauration anglaise *(caractérisé par la satire des mœurs du temps)*; *(play)* comédie *f* de l'époque de la Restauration anglaise *(caractérisée par la satire des mœurs du temps)*; *Fin* **r. fund** caisse *f* de restauration; **r. project** projet *m* de restauration; **r. work** travail *m* de restauration

restorative [rɪ'stɔːrətɪv, -'stɒr-] **N** *(medicine)* cordial *m*
ADJ **the r. powers of sleep** les pouvoirs reconstituants du sommeil

restore [rɪ'stɔːr] **VT 1** *(monument, building, furniture etc)* restaurer; **to r. sth to its former glory** redonner son éclat d'antan à qch; **to be restored to its former glory** retrouver son éclat d'antan **2** *Comput (files)* restaurer **3** *(bring back)* *(law and order, calm)* rétablir; *(peace)* rétablir, restaurer; *(confidence)* faire renaître; *(discipline, dynasty)* restaurer; **order is being restored** l'ordre est en train d'être rétabli; **to r. sb to health** rétablir la santé de qn; **to r. sb to power** remettre quelqu'un au pouvoir; **to r. a company to profitability** permettre à une entreprise de redevenir bénéficiaire; **I feel quite restored** je me sens revigoré; **to r. sb to life** ramener qn à la vie; **to r. sb's strength** redonner des forces à qn; **to r. sb's sight/hearing** rendre la vue/l'ouïe à qn; **to r. the circulation** réactiver la circulation **4** *(give back)* restituer, rendre (**to sb** à qn); **to r. sth to its place/former condition** remettre qch à sa place *ou* en place/en état
N *Comput* **to do a r.** faire une restauration

restorer [rɪ'stɔːrər] **N 1** *(of building, picture etc)* restaurateur, -trice **2** *(for hair)* régénérateur *m* capillaire

restrain [rɪ'streɪn] **VT** *(person, dog, one's curiosity)* retenir; *(passions)* refréner; *(crowd, tears)* retenir, contenir; *(anger)* contenir, refouler; **to r. oneself** se maîtriser, se contenir; **I had to r. an impulse to laugh out loud/to hit him** il a fallu que je me retienne pour ne pas rire tout haut/pour ne pas le frapper; **to r. sb from doing sth** empêcher qn de faire qch; **he had to be forcibly restrained** il a fallu le retenir de force; **to r. sb's activities** mettre un frein aux activités de qn

restrained [rɪ'streɪnd] **ADJ** *(feelings)* contenu; *(tone, terms)* mesuré; *(style)* sobre; *(silence)* prudent; *(response)* mitigé; **her manner was very r.** son attitude était très réservée

restraining [rɪ'streɪnɪŋ] **ADJ** *(influence)* modérateur; *Law* qui retient, restrictif
▸▸*Law* **r. order** injonction *f*

restraint [rɪ'streɪnt] **N 1** *(moderation)* *(of person)* modération *f*, mesure *f*, *(of style)* sobriété *f*, **to throw aside all r.** abandonner toute mesure; **to show** *or* **exercise great r.** faire preuve de beaucoup de modération;

to urge r. demander instamment qu'on fasse preuve de modération (**in doing** en faisant) **2** *(restriction)* restriction *f*; *(of powers, wages)* limitation *f*; **to put a r. on sb** contraindre qn; **to break free of all r.** se déchaîner; **to be under no r.** avoir ses coudées franches; **without r.** *(to laugh, cry, speak etc)* sans se retenir; **to impose restraints** imposer des restrictions (**on** sur); **r. of trade** restrictions commerciales; **to put sb under r.** *(mental patient)* mettre la camisole de force à qn; *(prisoner)* mettre les menottes à qn

restrict [rɪ'strɪkt] **VT** *(speed etc)* limiter, restreindre (**to** à); **to r. oneself to ...** se limiter à ..., se restreindre à ...; **he is restricted to one glass of wine a day** il n'a droit qu'à un verre de vin par jour; **fog is restricting visibility** le brouillard limite la visibilité; **membership is restricted to the over-20s** la qualité de membre est réservée aux personnes âgées de plus de 20 ans; *Banking* **to r. the supply of a currency** raréfier une monnaie

restricted [rɪ'strɪktɪd] **ADJ** *(sense, space, use)* restreint, limité; *(sale)* contrôlé; *(speed)* limité; **to be on a r. diet** suivre un régime sévère *ou* strict; **she feels less r. wearing trousers** elle se sent plus libre (de ses mouvements) lorsqu'elle porte un pantalon; **r. access** *(sign)* accès réservé; *Comput* **r.-access system** système *m* à accès restreint; **r. area** *(out of bounds)* zone *f* interdite; *Br Aut* *(with parking restrictions)* zone à stationnement réglementé; *(with speed limit)* zone à vitesse limitée; **r. document** document *m* secret; *Theat* **seats with a r. view (of the stage)** des places depuis lesquelles on ne voit pas toute la scène
▸▸ *Comput* **r. users group** = nombre *m* restreint d'utilisateurs ayant accès à des informations confidentielles

restriction [rɪ'strɪkʃən] **N** restriction *f*; *(of speed etc)* limitation *f*; **to place** *or* **set** *or* **impose restrictions on sth** apporter des restrictions à qch

restrictive [rɪ'strɪktɪv] **ADJ 1** *(clause, measure)* restrictif **2** *Ling* *(clause)* déterminatif
▸▸ **r. clause** clause *f* restrictive; **r. practice** *(by union)* pratique *f* restrictive; *(by traders)* atteinte *f* à la libre concurrence

restring [riː'strɪŋ] **VT** *(pt, pp* **restrung** [riː-'strʌŋ]*)* *(pearls)* enfiler de nouveau; *(violin)* remonter; *(guitar)* remplacer les cordes de; *(racket)* recorder

restructure [riː'strʌktʃər] **VT** *(company, industry, economy)* restructurer

restructuring [riː'strʌktʃərɪŋ] **N** restructuration *f*

restyle [riː'staɪl] **VT** *(car)* changer le style de; *(hair)* changer la coupe de

result [rɪ'zʌlt] **N 1** *(of action, behaviour etc)*, *Math, Sport etc* résultat *m* (**of** de); **the r. is that ...** il en résulte que ...; **as a r. of ...** à la suite de ...; **without r.** sans résultat; **results** *(of exam etc)* résultats; **I tried making some jam with disastrous results** j'ai essayé de faire des confitures mais ça a été un désastre; **if they get a good r. in this match** s'ils font un bon match; *Br Fam* **to get a r.** *(in sport)* gagner, l'emporter; **this paint gives excellent results** cette peinture donne d'excellents résultats; **to be a** *or* **the r. of sth** résulter *ou* être le résultat de qch; **as a r.** en conséquence; **to have little or no r.** avoir peu ou pas de résultats; *Comput* **results page** page *f* de résultats
2 *(good outcome)* **to yield** *or* **show results** donner des résultats; **she knows how to get results** elle sait comment s'y prendre pour arriver à quelque chose *ou* pour avoir des résultats; *Br Fam* **we need a r.** il faut qu'on fasse un résultat; *Br Fam* **a 20% pay**

rise? what a r.! 20% d'augmentation? tu as fait fort!
VI résulter (**from** de); **it results from this that ...** il s'ensuit que ...; **consequences resulting from ...** conséquences de ...; **to r. in** *(unpleasantness, increase, decrease)* entraîner, engendrer; *(loss of life)* entraîner, provoquer; **the summit talks resulted in a treaty** le sommet a abouti à la signature d'un traité

resultant [rɪ'zʌltənt] **ADJ ATTRIB** qui en résulte, résultant
▸ *Math* **résultante** *f*

resume [rɪ'zjuːm] **VT** *(relations)* reprendre, renouer; *(after short break)* *(speech, negotiations, discussions, trip)* continuer, poursuivre; **to r. one's seat** reprendre sa place, se rasseoir; **to r. doing sth** se remettre à faire qch; **to r. work** se remettre au travail; **to r. one's duties** reprendre son service *ou* ses fonctions; **she resumed her maiden name** elle a repris son nom de jeune fille
VI *(of music, speaker etc)* continuer, reprendre; **we/the meeting will r. after lunch** nous reprendrons/la réunion reprendra après le déjeuner; *Cr* **play resumed at four** le match a repris à quatre heures

> Note that the French verb **résumer** is a false friend and is never a translation for the English verb **to resume**. It means **to summarize**.

résumé ['reɪzjʊmeɪ, -uːmeɪ] **N 1** *(summary)* résumé *m*, abrégé *m*; **to give a r. of sth** faire un résumé de qch **2** *Am (curriculum vitae)* curriculum vitae *m inv*

resumption [rɪ'zʌmpʃən] **N** *(of relationship, negotiations etc)* reprise *f*

resurface [riː'sɜːfɪs] **VT** *(road)* refaire le revêtement de
VI *(of submarine)* faire surface, revenir à la surface; *esp Hum* **when did he eventually r.?** *(return)* quand est-ce qu'il a fini par refaire surface?

resurgence [rɪ'sɜːdʒəns] **N** *(of nationalism, trend, idea, ideology)* résurgence *f*, réapparition *f*; *(of disease)* réapparition; *(of company etc)* reprise *f*

resurgent [rɪ'sɜːdʒənt] **ADJ USU ATTRIB** *(idea, nationalism etc)* renaissant; *(company etc)* qui connaît une reprise

resurrect [rezə'rekt] **VT** *(the dead)*, *Fig (fashion)* ressusciter; *(era)* faire revivre; *(quarrel, argument)* réveiller; *(hopes, fears)* ranimer

resurrection [rezə'rekʃən] **N** *(of the dead)*, *Fig* résurrection *f*; **the R.** la résurrection du Christ; **this resulted in the r. of their old argument** cela a relancé leur querelle

resuscitate [rɪ'sʌsɪteɪt] **VT** *Med (person)* ranimer; *Fig (plan)* ressortir; *(ailing company)* faire repartir

> Note that the French verb **ressusciter** is a false friend and is never a translation for the English verb **to resuscitate**. It means **to resurrect** or **to revive**.

resuscitation [rɪsʌsɪ'teɪʃən] **N** *Med* réanimation *f*, ranimation *f*; **all attempts at r. failed** toutes les tentatives de réanimation *ou* de ranimation ont échoué; *Fig* **there was a r. of interest** il y a eu un regain d'intérêt

resuscitator [rɪ'sʌsɪteɪtər] **N** *(machine)* appareil *m* de réanimation

retail ['riːteɪl] **N** *Com* (vente *f* au) détail *m*; **to buy/sell goods r.** *or Am* **at r.** acheter/vendre des marchandises au détail; **wholesale and r. business** commerce *m* de gros et de détail
VT 1 *(goods)* vendre au détail **2** *(spread)* *(gossip)* colporter
VI *(of goods)* se vendre au détail (**at, for** à)
▸▸ **r. audit** audit *m* des détaillants; **r. audi-**

tor audit *m* des détaillants, auditeur, -trice des détaillants; **r. bank** banque *f* de détail; **r. banking** banque de détail; **r. chain** chaîne *f* de vente au détail, chaîne de détail; **r. customer** client, -ente qui achète au détail; **r. dealer** détaillant, -ante; **r. goods** marchandises *fpl* vendues au détail, marchandises au détail; **r. outlet** magasin *m* de (vente au) détail, point *m* de (vente au) détail; **r. panel** panel *m* de détaillants; *Br* **r. park** zone *f* commerciale; **r. price** prix *m* de *ou* au détail; *Br Fin* **R. Price Index** indice *m* des prix de détail; **r. price maintenance** prix imposé; **r. sales** ventes au détail; **r. selling** vente au détail; **r. shipment** expédition *f* de détail; **r. shop** magasin de (vente au) détail; *Fam* **r. therapy** = le shopping envisagé comme remède à la dépression; **r. trade** commerce (de détail); **r. wholesale** demi-gros *m inv*

retailer ['riːteɪlər] **N** détaillant, -ante; **retailers' group** groupement *m* de détaillants
▸▸ **r. brand** marque *f* de revendeur *ou* de détaillant *ou* de distributeur; **r. margin** marge *f* du détaillant

retailing ['riːteɪlɪŋ] **N** vente *f* au détail
▸▸ *Com, Mktg* **r. mix** marchéage *m* de distribution

retain [rɪ'teɪn] **VT 1** *(keep) (property, control etc)* conserver, garder; *(custom, heat etc)* conserver; **to r. the right to do sth** se réserver le droit de faire qch **2 to r. sb's services** s'assurer les services de qn; *Br Law* **to r. a barrister** *or* **counsel** retenir un avocat (à l'avance); *Law* **retaining fee** avance *f*, provision *f* **3** *(hold in place) (object)* retenir, maintenir; *Constr* **retaining wall** mur *m* de soutènement *ou* de retenue **4** *(remember)* garder en mémoire, mémoriser

retained [rɪ'teɪnd] **ADJ** *Acct*
▸▸ **r. earnings** revenu *m* non distribué; **r. profit** bénéfices *mpl* non distribués

retainer [rɪ'teɪnər] **N 1** *(fee)* avance *f*, provision *f*; **to pay sb a r.** verser une avance *ou* provision à qn **2** *Old-fashioned (servant)* serviteur *m*

retake[1] ['riːteɪk] **N 1** *Cin, TV* nouvelle prise *f*, **it took several retakes** il a fallu plusieurs prises **2** *esp Univ (exam)* examen *m* à repasser; *(candidate)* candidat, -ate qui repasse un examen; **how many retakes did you have to do?** combien d'examens est-ce que tu as dû repasser?; **the r. of the history exam** *or* **the history r. will be held on ...** l'examen d'histoire de la session de rattrapage aura lieu le ...

retake[2] [riː'teɪk] **VT** *(pt* **retook** [riː'tʊk]; *pp* **retaken** [riː'teɪk(ə)n]*)* **1** *Cin, TV (shot)* refaire, filmer à nouveau; *(scene)* refaire une prise (de vues) de **2** *esp Univ (exam)* repasser **3** *(stronghold etc)* reprendre

retaliate [rɪ'tælɪeɪt] **VI** riposter, rendre la pareille; *(in speech)* riposter; *esp Mil* user de représailles (**with** par); **to r. for an attack** riposter à une attaque (**by doing** en faisant)

retaliation [rɪtælɪ'eɪʃən] **N** riposte *f*, représailles *fpl* (**against** contre); **r. for the attack** représailles contre l'attaque; **in r.** par mesure de représailles; **in r. for** en représailles de

retaliatory [rɪ'tælɪət(ə)rɪ] **ADJ ATTRIB** de représailles, de rétorsion; **to take r. measures** exercer des représailles, riposter
▸▸ **r. attack** riposte *f*; **r. bombing** des représailles *fpl* sous forme de bombardements

retard[1] ['riːtɑːd] **N** *Fam Pej (retarded person)* demeuré, -ée

retard[2] [rɪ'tɑːd] **VT** *(delay growth or development of)* retarder, retarder la croissance *ou* le développement de; **to be severely (mentally) retarded** être très attardé *ou* arriéré; **mentally retarded person** (personne *f)* attardé(e) *ou* arriéré(e); **the retarded** *(used as pl)* les attardés *mpl*, les arriérés *mpl*

-retardant [rɪ'tɑːdənt] **SUFF** **heat/flame-r.** qui ralentit la propagation de la chaleur/ des flammes

retardation [riːtɑːˈdeɪʃən] **N** *(of growth)* retard *m*; *(of mechanism)* retardement *m*; **(mental)** **r.** arriération *f* mentale

retch [retʃ] **VI** avoir des haut-le-cœur; *Fig* **to make sb r.** soulever le cœur à qn

retching ['retʃɪŋ] **N** haut-le-cœur *mpl*; **r. noises were coming from the bathroom** on entendait quelqu'un vomir dans la salle de bain

retd *(abbr* **retired)** retraité, à la retraite

retell [riːˈtel] **VT** *(pt, pp* **retold** [riːˈtəʊld]*)* *(story)* raconter de nouveau

retelling [riːˈtelɪŋ] **N** **the number of his assailants grew with each r.** chaque fois qu'il racontait l'histoire le nombre de ses attaquants augmentait

retention [rɪˈtenʃən] **N** *(of custom)* conservation *f*; *(of authority, provisions, restrictions)* maintien *m*; *(of fact, impression etc)* mémoire *f*; *Med (of urine etc)* rétention *f*; **to have limited powers of r.** *(memory)* avoir peu de mémoire; **to have great powers of r.** *(memory)* avoir une excellente mémoire; *Com* **r. of title** réserve *f* de propriété

retentive [rɪˈtentɪv] **ADJ** *(memory)* fidèle; *(person)* qui a une bonne mémoire

retentiveness [rɪˈtentɪvnɪs] **N** *(of memory)* fidélité *f*

rethink[1] ['riːθɪŋk] **N** **to have a r. (about sth)** réfléchir à nouveau (à qch); **we need a complete r. of our strategy** il nous faut revoir entièrement notre stratégie; **the plan needs a complete r.** le projet doit être complètement repensé

rethink[2] [riːˈθɪŋk] **VT** *(pt, pp* **rethought** [riːˈθɔːt]*)* *(matter, plan)* repenser, reconsidérer

reticence ['retɪsəns] **N** *(on one occasion)* réticence *f*; *(character trait)* réserve *f*; **the r. of his manner** sa réticence/réserve; **without any r.** sans réticence(s); **this r. isn't like her** elle n'est pas aussi réservée d'habitude

reticent ['retɪsənt] **ADJ** peu communicatif, réservé; **to be r. about sth** ne pas vouloir parler de qch, faire mystère de qch

Note that the French word **réticent** is a false friend and is never a translation for the English word **reticent**. It means **hesitant**.

reticently ['retɪsəntlɪ] **ADV** avec réticence *ou* réserve

reticular [rɪˈtɪkjʊlər], **reticulate, reticulated** [rɪˈtɪkjʊlət, -leɪtɪd] **ADJ** *esp Biol* réticulé

reticulation [rɪtɪkjʊˈleɪʃən] **N** *esp Biol* réticulation *f*

reticule ['retɪkjuːl] **N 1** *Opt* réticule *m* **2** *Hist (bag)* réticule *m*

retina, *pl* **retinas, retinae** ['retɪnə, -əz, -iː] **N** *(of eye)* rétine *f*

retinal ['retɪnəl] **ADJ** rétinien
▸▸ *Med* **r. detachment** décollement *m* de la rétine

retinitis [retɪˈnaɪtɪs] **N** rétinite *f*

retinue ['retɪnjuː] **N** *(of prince etc)*, *Hum* suite *f*

retire [rɪˈtaɪər] **VI 1** *(of employee)* prendre sa retraite; **to r. from a company** prendre sa retraite d'une société; **to r. from teaching** prendre sa retraite de l'enseignement; **when I r.** quand je prendrai ma retraite; **to r. early** prendre une retraite anticipée; **to have retired** être à la retraite **2** *(withdraw)* se retirer (**to** dans, à; **from** de); *(of troops)*

reculer, se replier (**to** vers); *(from match, competition etc)* se retirer, abandonner; **to r. from boxing/the race** abandonner la boxe/la course; **to r. into oneself** se replier sur soi-même; *Fml* **to r. from the room** quitter la pièce; *Fml* **to r. (to bed/for the night)** (aller) se coucher
▸ **VT 1** *(person) (from work)* mettre à la retraite **2** *(withdraw), Mil (troops)* retirer **3** *Fin (coins, bill, bonds, shares)* retirer

retired [rɪˈtaɪəd] **ADJ 1** *(police officer, doctor etc)* retraité, à la retraite; **to be r.** être à la retraite; *Mil* **to put** *or* **place sb on the r. list** mettre qn à la retraite; **Admiral John Smith, r.** Amiral John Smith, retraité **2** *(secluded) (life)* retiré; *(place etc)* retiré, isolé **3** *Fin (coins, bill, bonds, shares)* retiré

retiree [retaɪəˈriː] **N** *Am* retraité, -ée

retirement [rɪˈtaɪəmənt] **N 1** *(from work, army etc)* retraite *f*; **on my r.** *(when I retire)* quand je serai à la retraite; *(when I retired)* quand j'ai pris ma retraite; **to take early r.** prendre une retraite anticipée; **she's been offered early r.** on lui a proposé de prendre *ou* de faire valoir ses droits à une retraite anticipée; **to come out of r.** reprendre sa carrière; **to live in r.** *(no longer employed)* être à la retraite; *(in seclusion)* vivre retiré du monde; **compulsory r.** retraite d'office **2** *(withdrawal) (of troops)* repli *m*; *(from match, competition etc)* abandon *m* **3** *Fin (of coins, bill, bonds, shares)* retrait *m*
▸▸ **r. age** âge *m* de la retraite; *Br* **r. flat** appartement *m* pour retraités; **r. pension** (pension *f* de) retraite *f*; *Am* **r. plan** régime *m* de retraite; **r. present** cadeau *m* de départ en *ou* à la retraite; *Fin* **r. savings plan** plan *m* d'épargne retraite

retiring [rɪˈtaɪərɪŋ] **ADJ 1** *(reserved)* réservé; **to have** *or* **be of a r. nature** avoir un *ou* être d'un naturel réservé **2** *(employee)* qui prend sa retraite; *(elected official)* sortant; **to reach r. age** atteindre l'âge de la retraite

retool [riːˈtuːl] **VT** *Ind (factory)* rééquiper; *Am Fam (company)* réorganiser
▸ **VI** *Ind (of factory)* se rééquiper; *Am Fam (of company)* se réorganiser

retort[1] [rɪˈtɔːt] **N** *(answer)* réplique *f* (**to** à), riposte *f*; **to make a r.** lancer une réplique
▸ **VT & VI** répliquer, rétorquer

retort[2] **N** *Chem, Ind* cornue *f*

retouch[1] ['riːtʌtʃ] **N** *(of photograph)* retouche *f*

retouch[2] [riːˈtʌtʃ] **VT** *(photograph)* retoucher

retouching [riːˈtʌtʃɪŋ] **N** *(of photograph etc)* retouche *f*

retrace [rɪˈtreɪs] **VT** *(events)* reconstituer; **to r. one's steps** revenir sur ses pas, rebrousser chemin; **to r. sb's movements** *(of police etc)* reconstituer les faits et gestes de qn

retract [rɪˈtrækt] **VT 1** *(what one said)* rétracter; *(statement, offer etc)* revenir sur; *(opinion etc)* désavouer, rétracter **2** *(of animal) (claws)* rentrer; *Aviat* **to r. the undercarriage** escamoter *ou* rentrer le train d'atterrissage
▸ **VI 1** *(of person)* se rétracter **2** *(of cat's claws)* rentrer; *Aviat (of undercarriage)* s'escamoter, rentrer; *(of blade)* s'escamoter

retractable [rɪˈtræktəb(ə)l] **ADJ** *Aviat (undercarriage)* rentrant, escamotable; *(handle etc)* escamotable; *(ballpoint pen)* à pointe rétractable

retraction [rɪˈtrækʃən] **N 1** *(of statement)* rétractation *f*; *(of opinion)* désaveu *m*, reniement *m*; **to publish a r.** *(of newspaper)* publier un désaveu **2** *(of claws etc)* rétraction *f*

retrain [riːˈtreɪn] **VT** *(employee)* recycler; *Med (muscle)* rééduquer
▸ **VI** *(of employee)* se recycler

retraining [riːˈtreɪnɪŋ] **N** *(of person)* recyclage *m*; *Med (of muscle)* rééducation *f*

retread[1] ['riːtred] **N** *Aut* (pneu *m*) rechapé *m*

retread[2] [riːˈtred] **VT** *Aut (tyre)* rechaper

retreat [rɪˈtriːt] **N 1** *Mil, Fig* retraite *f*; *Mil* **to sound/beat the r.** sonner/battre la retraite; *Fig* **to beat a (hasty) r.** battre en retraite **2** *(of flood waters)* retrait *m*, recul *m* **3** *Rel (seclusion)* retraite *f*; **to go into** *or* **on r.** faire une retraite **4** *(place)* abri *m*, retraite *f*, refuge *m*; **a holiday/weekend r.** une maison paisible pour les vacances/le week-end; **a country r.** une maison paisible à la campagne
▸ **VI 1** *Mil* battre en retraite, reculer; *(of crowd, spectators etc)* battre en retraite, reculer (**from** de); **to r. a few hundred yards** reculer de quelques centaines de mètres; **to r. into a world of one's own** s'isoler dans son petit monde (à soi); **to r. from the public eye** se retirer du monde **2** *(of flood waters, glacier)* reculer

retrench [rɪˈtrentʃ] **VT** *Fin (expenditure)* restreindre; *Liter (literary work)* faire des coupures dans
▸ **VI** *Fin* restreindre ses dépenses, faire des économies

retrenchment [rɪˈtrentʃmənt] **N** *Fin (of expenditure)* réduction *f*; **policy of r.** politique *f* d'économies

retrial [riːˈtraɪ(ə)l] **N** *Law* nouveau procès *m*

retribution [retrɪˈbjuːʃən] **N** châtiment *m*; **in r. for sth** comme châtiment pour qch; **to exact r.** se venger; **the Day of R.** le Jugement dernier; **just r. of** *or* **for a crime** juste châtiment pour un crime

Note that the French word **rétribution** is a false friend and is never a translation for the English word **retribution**. It means **remuneration** or **reward**.

retributive [rɪˈtrɪbjʊtɪv] **ADJ** *(measure etc)* punitif

retrievable [rɪˈtriːvəb(ə)l] **ADJ** *(loss, error)* réparable; *Comput* accessible; *Fin (amount)* recouvrable

retrieval [rɪˈtriːv(ə)l] **N** *(recovery) (of lost object)* récupération *f*, *(of error, loss)* réparation *f*, *(of fortune)* rétablissement *m*, *Fin* recouvrement *m*; *Comput (of data)* recherche *f*, *(of lost data)* récupération; **information r. system** système *m* de recherche documentaire; *(computer system)* système de recherche d'information; **beyond** *or* **past r.** irréparable
▸▸ *Comput* **r. system** système de recherche

retrieve [rɪˈtriːv] **VT** *(property)* récupérer; *(freedom)* retrouver; *(loss, error etc)* réparer; *(honour, fortune)* rétablir; *(of dog) (ball, game bird etc)* rapporter; *Fin (assets)* recouvrer; *Comput (file)* retrouver, extraire; **to r. one's losses** se refaire; **to r. the situation** sauver la situation
▸ **VI** *(in hunting) (of dog)* rapporter

retriever [rɪˈtriːvər] **N** *(dog)* retriever *m*

retro ['retrəʊ] **ADJ** *(fashion etc)* rétro *inv*

retro- ['retrəʊ-] **PREF** rétro-

retroactive [retrəʊˈæktɪv] **ADJ** *(increase, measure etc)* rétroactif; **the increase is r. to last January** l'augmentation a un effet rétroactif à compter de janvier dernier

retroactively [retrəʊˈæktɪvlɪ] **ADV** *(to increase, come into effect etc)* rétroactivement

retrofit ['retrəʊfɪt] **VT** *Aviat (aircraft, machine)* moderniser (**with** en y intégrant)

retroflex ['retrəʊfleks] **ADJ** *Ling* rétroflexe

retroflexion [retrəʊˈflekʃən] **N** *Med* rétroflexion *f*

retrograde ['retrəgreɪd] **ADJ** *(movement, step etc)* rétrograde

retrogress [retrəˈgres] **VI** rétrograder

retrogression [retrə'greʃən] N rétrograda-tion f, rétrogression f; Biol régression f

retrogressive [retrə'gresɪv] ADJ rétrograde; Biol régressif

retrorocket ['retrəʊrɒkɪt] N Astronaut ré-trofusée f

retrospect ['retrəspekt] N **in r.** rétrospecti-vement, après coup; **when I consider these events in r.** quand je pense à ces événe-ments rétrospectivement ou après coup

retrospective [retrə'spektɪv] ADJ (review) rétrospectif; (measure) à effet rétroactif
▪ N (of film director's, artist's etc work) rétro-spective f

retrospectively [retrə'spektɪvlɪ] ADV (to consider etc) rétrospectivement, après coup; (to take effect) rétroactivement

retroussé [rə'truːseɪ] ADJ (nose) retroussé

retrovirus ['retrəʊvaɪrəs] N Biol rétrovirus m

retry [riː'traɪ] VT Law juger à ou de nouveau
▪ VI esp Comput réessayer

retsina [ret'siːnə] N retsina m

retune[1] ['riːtjuːn] N Aut (of engine) réglage m; **the engine needs a r.** il faut faire régler le moteur

retune[2] [riː'tjuːn] VT Aut (engine) régler; Mus (instrument) accorder; Radio régler
▪ VI Radio **to r. to medium wave** régler son poste sur ondes moyennes

RETURN [rɪ'tɜːn]

N retour **1**	▪ aller et retour **2**
▪ renvoi **3**	▪ rapport **4**
VI revenir	▪ retourner ▪ rentrer
VT rendre **1**	▪ renvoyer **1**
▪ remettre **1**	▪ rapporter **1, 2**

N **1** (of person, peace, spring etc) retour m; **on my r.** dès ou à mon retour; **on his r. to France** à son retour en France; **by r. (of post)** par retour (du courrier); **the r. to school** la ren-trée (des classes); **many happy returns (of the day)!** bon anniversaire!

2 Br (ticket) aller (et) retour; Br **day r. =** aller (et) retour valable pour la journée seule-ment; Br **cheap day r.** billet m d'aller (et) re-tour à tarif réduit valable pour la journée seulement; **I've lost the r. half of my ticket** j'ai perdu mon billet ou coupon de retour; **how much is the r. fare?** combien coûte l'al-ler (et) retour?; Br **r. air fare** tarif m aérien aller-retour; **point of no r.** point m de non-retour

3 (of goods to supplier) renvoi m; (of stolen property) restitution f; (of overpayment) remboursement m; Tennis (of service) renvoi (de la balle); (library book) livre m (de bi-bliothèque) que l'on rapporte; (election) (of politician) élection f; Comput (on keyboard) touche f (de) retour; (carriage) **r.** (on type-writer, keyboard) retour m (de chariot); Ten-nis **to make a good r. (of service)** bien renvoyer le service; **r. to office** (of politi-cian) reprise f de fonctions; **on his r. to office** quand il a été réélu; Com **on sale or r.** (goods) vendu avec possibilité de retour; **no deposit, no r.** (on bottle) ni retour, ni consigne; Theat **returns may be available on the day of the performance** des places peuvent se libérer le jour de la représenta-tion; **are there any returns?** est-ce que des places se sont libérées?; Com **returns** ren-dus mpl; (of books, newspapers) invendus mpl, bouillons mpl; Pol Fam **to announce the returns of the election** annoncer les ré-sultats du scrutin; **early returns indicate a win for the incumbent** les premiers résul-tats laissent prévoir une victoire du candi-dat sortant

4 Fin (yield) rapport m (on de); **how much r. do you get on your investment?** combien

est-ce que ton investissement te rapporte?; **returns** (profit) bénéfices mpl; Acct **returns ledger** journal m des rendus; **quick returns** bénéfices réalisés rapidement; **small pro-fits and quick returns** faibles bénéfices et ventes rapides; **to bring (in) a fair r.** rappor-ter un bénéfice raisonnable; **r. on capital** re-tour m sur capital; Acct **r. on capital employed** rendement m sur capital immobi-lisé; **r. on investment** retour sur investisse-ment; **r. on sales** retour sur ventes

5 (form) rapport m officiel; (for tax) déclara-tion f

6 to give sth in r. donner qch en échange; (for favour, service) donner qch en guise de récompense ou de remerciement; **in r. for which ...** moyennant quoi ...; **if you will do sth in r.** si vous voulez bien faire qch en re-tour; **in r. for this service ...** en récompense de ce service ...; **you must expect the same treatment in r.** il faut vous attendre à la pa-reille; **it's a small r. for all your kindness** c'est une modeste récompense pour votre bonté
▪ VI (come back) revenir; (go back) retourner; (of anxiety, fear) revenir, reprendre; **to r. home** rentrer (chez soi); **I was returning from a journey** je rentrais de voyage; **he/ spring has returned** il/le printemps est reve-nu ou est de retour; **to r. from the dead** res-susciter d'entre les morts; **her colour returned** elle a repris des couleurs; **to r. to office** (be re-elected) être réélu; Naut **to r. to port** rentrer au port; **to r. to a task** reprendre une tâche; **to r. to a subject** revenir à un su-jet; **to r. to one's old habits** reprendre ses vieilles habitudes; **to r. to work** reprendre le travail; **r. to sender** (on undelivered letter) retour à l'envoyeur
▪ VT **1** (give or send back) (book, compliment, verdict etc) rendre; (something stolen etc) restituer; (gift, ball etc) renvoyer; (loan) rem-bourser; (elect) (MP) élire; **a returned letter** une lettre renvoyée à l'expéditeur; **returned cheque** chèque m retourné; **to r. a book to its place** remettre un livre à sa place; **to r. a purchase to a shop** rendre ou rapporter un article à un magasin; Tennis **to r. (the) ser-vice** renvoyer le service; Law **the jury retur-ned a verdict of guilty/not guilty** le jury a déclaré l'accusé coupable/non coupable; **to r. an animal to the wild** remettre un ani-mal en liberté; Mil **to r. fire** riposter (au feu adverse); **to r. the favour** rendre la pareille; **to r. sb's greeting** rendre un salut à qn; **to r. good for evil** rendre le bien pour le mal; **to r. sb's love** aimer qn en retour; Tel **to r. a call** rappeler; Pol **to r. the result of the poll** an-noncer les résultats du scrutin

2 Com, Fin (produce) (profit) rapporter, dé-gager

3 Old-fashioned (answer) répondre, répliquer
▸▸ **r. address** adresse f de l'expéditeur; **r. flight** vol m de retour; **r. journey** (voyage m du) retour; Comput **r. key** touche (de) retour; Sport **r. match** match m retour, revanche f; **I'll give you a r. match next week** on dispu-tera le match retour ou la revanche la se-maine prochaine; Br **r. ticket** (billet d')aller m (et) retour

returnable [rɪ'tɜːnəb(ə)l] ADJ Com (pur-chase, ticket etc) qui peut être rendu; (bottle) consigné; **sale items are not r.** (notice in shop) les articles en solde ne sont ni échan-gés ni repris; **empties are not r.** on ne re-prend pas les bouteilles, les bouteilles ne sont pas consignées
▸▸ Com **r. packaging** emballage m consi-gné

returning [rɪ'tɜːnɪŋ] N
▸▸ Pol **r. officer** président, -ente du bureau de vote

reunification [riːjuːnɪfɪ'keɪʃən] N (of coun-try) réunification f

reunify [riː'juːnɪfaɪ] VT (country) réunifier

reunion [riː'juːnɪən] N retrouvailles fpl, réu-nion f; Am **class r.** réunion d'anciens élèves de la même classe ou promotion; **to have or hold a r.** organiser une réunion ou des re-trouvailles; **r. celebration** célébration f de retrouvailles; **r. dinner** dîner m de retrou-vailles

reunite [riːju'naɪt] VT (after quarrel) (family etc) réconcilier; **the freed hostage was re-united with his wife** l'otage libéré a retrou-vé sa femme; **the dog was reunited with its owner** le chien a retrouvé son maître; **he reunited the band for one last gig** il a re-formé le groupe pour un ultime concert
▪ VI (of band) se reformer

reupholster [riːʌp'həʊlstər] VT (chair etc) rembourrer et recouvrir

reusable [reː'juːzəb(ə)l] ADJ (paper, bottle etc) réutilisable; (battery) rechargeable

reuse[1] [riː'juːs] N (of paper, bottle etc) réutili-sation f

reuse[2] [riː'juːz] VT (paper, bottle etc) réutili-ser

Rev N Rel (abbr **Reverend**) révérend

rev [rev] Aut Fam N (abbr **revolution**) tour m (à la minute ou minute); **to do three thou-sand revs** faire trois mille tours (à la) minute
▪ VT (-vv-) (engine) emballer; **he revs the en-gine too hard** il fait tourner le moteur trop vite
▪ VI (of engine) s'emballer; (of driver) emballer le moteur
▸▸ **r. counter** compte-tours m inv; **r. limiter** limiteur m de régime
▸ **rev up** VT SEP, VI = rev VT, VI

revalidate [rɪ'vælɪdeɪt] VT revalider
▸▸ **r. sticker** autocollant m de revalidation

revaluation [riːvæljʊ'eɪʃən] N Econ, Fin (of currency, property etc) réévaluation f

revalue [riː'væljuː] VT Econ, Fin (currency, property) réévaluer

revamp[1] ['riːvæmp] N Fam (of method, play etc) remaniement m; (of policy) modifica-tion f, remaniement; (of company) réorgani-sation f, restructuration f; (of house etc) retapage m, remise f en état

revamp[2] [riː'væmp] VT Fam (method, play etc) remanier; (policy) modifier, remanier; (company) réorganiser, restructurer; (house etc) retaper, remettre en état

revanchisme [rɪ'vɑ̃ntʃɪz(ə)m] N revan-chisme m

revanchiste [rɪ'vɑ̃ntʃɪst] N, ADJ revan-chiste mf, revanchard, -arde

Revd Rel (abbr **Reverend**) révérend

reveal [rɪ'viːl] VT (something hidden, secret, one's sources, name) révéler; (fact) révéler, faire connaître; (quality etc) laisser voir; **to r. one's identity** révéler son identité, dire ou donner son nom, se faire connaître; **the po-lice do not want to r. the identity of the vic-tim** la police ne veut pas révéler l'identité de la victime; **a medical examination revealed two cracked ribs** un examen médical a per-mis de découvrir deux côtes fêlées; **it was revealed that ...** on a révélé que ...

revealing [rɪ'viːlɪŋ] ADJ (sign, comment etc) révélateur, -trice; (dress) (low-cut) décolleté; (skirt, dress) (short) très court, qui ne cache pas grand-chose; (blouse) (transparent) transparent; **that was very r. about his in-tentions** cela en disait long sur ses intentions

revealingly [rɪ'viːlɪŋlɪ] ADV (to say) d'un ton révélateur; **a r. low dress** une robe très décolletée

reveille [rɪ'vælɪ] N Mil réveil m; **to sound (the) r.** sonner ou battre le réveil

revel ['rev(ə)l] VI (-ll-, Am -l-) se réjouir, se dile ridicule; **from the sublime to the r.** du sublime au ridicule

ridiculously [rɪ'dɪkjʊləslɪ] ADV *(to act, dress etc)* d'une façon ridicule, ridiculement; *(easy, expensive, low etc)* ridiculement

ridiculousness [rɪ'dɪkjʊləsnɪs] N *(of appearance, behaviour, situation etc)* ridicule *m*

riding ['raɪdɪŋ] N **1** *(of horse)* équitation *f*; *(skill)* monte *f*; **r. is her favourite hobby** l'équitation est son passe-temps favori **2** *Aut* **smooth r.** suspension *f* douce **3** *(in Canada, New Zealand)* circonscription *f* électorale; *(in Yorkshire)* division *f* administrative
►►**r. boots** bottes *fpl* de cheval; **r. breeches** culotte *f* de cheval; **r. cap** bombe *f*; **r. crop** cravache *f*; **r. habit** tenue *f* d'amazone; **r. instructor** professeur *m* d'équitation; **r. kit** tenue de cheval; **r. lesson** leçon *f* d'équitation; **r. school** école *f* d'équitation; **r. whip** cravache

RIE [ɑːraɪ'iː] N *Fin (abbr* **recognized investment exchange)** marché *m* d'investissement agréé

rife [raɪf] ADJ *(widespread)* répandu; **to be r.** *(of corruption, crime, disease etc)* régner, sévir; *(of rumours)* aller bon train; **the city was r. with disease** la ville était en proie à la maladie, la maladie régnait dans la ville; **the city was r. with rumour** les rumeurs allaient bon train dans la ville; **the police force is r. with corruption** la corruption règne dans la police

riff [rɪf] N *Mus* riff *m*

riffle ['rɪf(ə)l] N *Am (ripple)* rides *fpl* sur l'eau, ondulations *fpl* de l'eau; *(shoal)* banc *m*
VT *(cards)* battre; *(pages)* feuilleter
► **riffle through** VT INSEP feuilleter

riffraff ['rɪfræf] N *Pej* racaille *f*; **he's just r.** c'est un vaurien

rifle[1] ['raɪf(ə)l] VT *(flat, office etc)* mettre sens dessus dessous; *(person's pockets, filing cabinet, drawer)* fouiller; *(tomb)* violer

rifle[2] N fusil *m*; *(for hunting)* fusil (de chasse); **within r. shot** à portée de fusil
►► **r. club** société *f* de tir; *Mil* **R. Corps** corps *m* des fusiliers *ou* des chasseurs à pied; *TV, Radio* **r. mike** micro *m* canon; **r. practice** (exercice *m* de) tir *m* au fusil; **r. shot** coup *m* de fusil

rifleman, *pl* **riflemen** ['raɪf(ə)lmən] N *Mil* fusilier *m*, fantassin *m*

rifling ['raɪflɪŋ] N *(on gun barrel)* *(grooves)* rayures *fpl*

rift [rɪft] N *(in earth, rock etc)* fissure *f*, crevasse *f*, *(in clouds etc)* éclaircie *f*, *Fig (in relationship)* rupture *f*, *Pol (in party)* scission *f*, *Fig* **to heal the r. between two people** réconcilier deux personnes; **to heal the r. in a party** réconcilier les adversaires au sein d'un parti
►► **r. valley** fossé *m* d'effondrement

rig [rɪg] N **1** *(of ship)* gréement *m* **2** *(oil)* **r.** derrick *m*; *(at sea)* plate-forme *f* pétrolière, *pl* plates-formes pétrolières **3** *Am (truck)* semi-remorque *m*, *pl* semi-remorques **4** *Fam (outfit)* = **rigout 5** *St Exch Fam (rise)* hausse *f* factice; *(fall)* baisse *f* factice
VT (**-gg-**) **1** *Naut (ship)* gréer **2** *Fam (manipulate dishonestly) (election etc)* truquer; **to r. the market** *Com* manipuler le marché; *St Exch* manipuler la Bourse; **to r. prices** fixer illégalement les prix; **to r. a game** truquer un jeu
► **rig out** VT SEP *(dress) (person)* attifer, accoutrer (**as** en); **to r. oneself out** s'accoutrer (**in** dans, avec)
► **rig up** VT SEP *(aerial, shelter)* monter, installer; *Fam* **to r. something up** faire une installation de fortune

rigamarole ['rɪgəmərəʊl] N *Fam* = **rigmarole**

rigger ['rɪgər] N **1** *(of ship)* gréeur *m*; **square r.** *(ship)* navire *m* gréé en carré **2** *(of plane)* monteur-régleur *m*, *pl* monteurs-régleurs

rigging ['rɪgɪŋ] N **1** *(on ship)* gréement *m*; *(of ship)* gréage *m* **2** *Fam (election)* truquage *m*; *St Exch (of market)* hausse *f ou* baisse *f* factice; *(of prices)* fixation *f* illégale

RIGHT [raɪt]

ADJ	bon **1, 3** ▪ juste **1, 2** ▪ bien **2, 4** ▪ vrai **5** ▪ droit **6**
N	droit **1, 2, 5** ▪ bien **1** ▪ droite **4, 6**
ADV	droit **1** ▪ juste **3, 4** ▪ bien **4, 5** ▪ à droite **6**
VT	redresser **1**

ADJ **1** *(correct, accurate) (answer etc)* bon, *f* bonne, exact, juste; *(word)* exact, juste; **that can't be r.** ça ne peut pas être ça, ça ne peut pas être juste; **have you got the r. amount?** avez-vous le compte exact?; **is this the r. house?** est-ce la bonne maison?; **what's the r. time?** quelle heure est-il (exactement)?, quelle est l'heure juste *ou* exacte?; **my watch is r.** ma montre est à l'heure; **to be r.** *(of person)* avoir raison (**to do** de faire); **you're quite r.!** vous avez bien raison!; **to be r. about sth** avoir raison à propos de qch; **you were r. about him being a crook** vous aviez raison de dire que c'est une canaille; **you were quite r. to call the police** vous avez bien fait d'appeler la police; **it doesn't look r.** *(of answer, dress etc)* ça ne va pas; **the r. side of the material** l'endroit *m* du tissu; **r. side** *ou* **way up** à l'endroit; **we're on the r. road** nous sommes sur le bon chemin *ou* la bonne route; *Fig* **to be on the r. lines** être dans la bonne direction; **that's r.!** parfaitement!, c'est ça!; **r. (you are)!** entendu!, d'accord!; *Fam* **r.?** d'accord?; **r. on!**, *Br, Austr* **too r.!** exactement!, bien parlé!; **he's on the r. side of forty** il n'a pas encore quarante ans; **to get on the r. side of sb** s'insinuer dans les bonnes grâces de qn; **to keep on the r. side of the law** respecter la loi
2 *(morally good)* bien; *(fair)* juste; **it's not r. to steal** ce n'est pas bien de voler; **it's not r. that ...** ce n'est pas juste que ... + *sub*; **I can't accept the money – it wouldn't look r.** je ne peux pas accepter l'argent, ça ferait mauvais effet; **it's only r.** ce n'est que justice; **I thought it r. to attend** j'ai jugé bon *ou* à propos d'y aller; **to do the r. thing** se conduire honnêtement *ou* honorablement; *Br Old-fashioned* **I hope he's going to do the r. thing by you** *(marry you)* j'espère qu'il va agir honorablement à ton égard (et demander ta main)
3 *(most appropriate)* **the r. thing to do** la meilleure chose à faire; **in the r. place** à la bonne place; **to be in the r. place at the r. time** être là où il faut quand il le faut; **the r. man/woman in the r. place** l'homme/la femme qu'il faut pour la tâche; **you came at the r. time** vous êtes venu au bon moment; **now is not the r. time to mention it** ce n'est pas le moment d'en parler; **to wait for the r. moment** attendre le bon moment *ou* le moment opportun; **to know the r. people** avoir des relations, connaître les gens qu'il faut
4 *(mentally, physically well)* bien; **to be in one's r. mind** avoir toute sa raison, être en possession de toutes ses facultés; **no one in their r. mind would do such a thing** aucune personne sensée ne ferait une chose pareille; *Fam* **he's not quite r. in the head** il n'a pas toute sa tête; **I'm not feeling quite r.** je ne me sens pas très bien, *Fam* je ne me sens pas dans mon assiette; *Fam* **as r. as** *Br* **rain** *or Am* **a trivet** en parfaite santé
5 *Br Fam (as intensifier)* vrai; **I felt a r. fool** je

me suis senti vraiment stupide; **he's all r.** c'est un brave type; *Sl* **she's a bit of all r.!** voilà une jolie pépée!

6 *(righthand)* droit; **on the r. side** *ou* sur la droite; **r. hand** main *f* droite; **on my r. hand** sur *ou* à ma droite; **he's my r. hand** c'est mon bras droit; **r. justified** justifié à droite
N **1** *(morality)* droit *m*, bien *m*; **r. and wrong** le bien et le mal; **to know r. from wrong** faire la différence entre le bien et le mal; **to teach sb r. from wrong** apprendre à qn la différence entre le bien et le mal; **to be in the r.** avoir raison; **by rights** en toute justice
2 *(entitlement)* droit *m* (**to** à; **to do** de faire); **by what r.?** de quel droit?, à quel titre?; **what r. have you to do that?** de quel droit faites-vous cela?; **to exercise a r.** exercer un droit; **r. to know** droit de savoir; **r. to vote** droit de vote; *Law* **r. of abode** *(of refugee etc)* droit de séjour; **r. of reply** droit de réponse *ou* de rectification; **to hold the film/translation rights to a book** détenir les droits d'adaptation cinématographique/de traduction d'un livre; **all rights reserved** tous droits réservés; **it belongs to him by r.** cela lui appartient de droit; **to possess sth in one's own r.** avoir qch en propre; **she is famous in her own r.** c'est elle-même une célébrité; **the rights of man** les droits de l'homme; **human/animal rights** les droits de l'homme/l'animal; **women's rights** les droits de la femme; **to be within one's rights** être dans son droit (**in doing** en faisant); **to know one's rights** connaître ses droits; *St Exch* **rights issue** émission *f* de nouvelles actions à taux préférentiel, émission de droits
3 *(order)* **to put** *or* **set sth to rights** arranger qch, mettre qch en ordre; **I'll soon have this kitchen set to rights** j'aurai vite fait de remettre de l'ordre dans la cuisine; **to put** *or* **set the world to rights** refaire le monde; **to put** *or* **set things to rights** remettre de l'ordre
4 *(right-hand side)* droite *f*, côté *m* droit; **on the r.** à droite; **on your r.** sur *ou* à votre droite; **to drive on the r.** rouler *ou* conduire à droite; **to keep to the r.** tenir sa droite
5 *Boxing etc (blow)* droit *m*; **with a r. to the jaw** d'un droit à la mâchoire
6 *Pol* **the r.** la droite; **a government of the r.** un gouvernement de droite; **to be to** *or* **on the r.** être à droite; **to be to the r. of sb** *(more right-wing than)* être plus à droite que qn
ADV **1** *(straight)* (tout) droit; **he went r. at him** il est allé droit vers lui; **to put a mistake r.** corriger *ou* rectifier une erreur; **to put things r.** arranger les choses; **to put one's watch r.** mettre sa montre à l'heure; **to put sb r.** *(give directions)* aider qn; *(open eyes)* détromper qn, désabuser qn (**about** au sujet de); **drink this, it'll soon put you r.** bois ça, ça te remettra d'aplomb; **to do sth r. away** *or* **off** *(immediately)* faire qch sur-le-champ *ou* immédiatement; *(at the first attempt)* faire qch du premier coup; **I'll be r. back** je reviens tout de suite; *(at the moment)* en ce moment; **r. now** *(immediately)* tout de suite; **he was here r. now** il était là il y a une minute
2 *(completely)* **r. to the end of the peninsula** jusqu'au bout de la presqu'île; **a wall r. round the house** un mur tout autour de la maison; **he turned r. round** il a fait un tour complet; **r. at the top** tout en haut; *Fig* **you have to go r. to the top if you want to get anything done** il faut aller tout en haut de la hiérarchie pour arriver à quelque chose; **r. at the back** tout au fond; **to go r. through sth** traverser qch de part en part; **somebody had cut r. through the cable** quelqu'un avait sectionné le câble; **she walked r. up to me** elle se dirigea tout droit vers moi; **the water came r. up to her shoulders** l'eau lui arrivait jusqu'aux épaules; **r. up until the last mo-**

ment jusqu'à la dernière minute; **the dress came r. down to her ankles** la robe lui arrivait jusqu'aux chevilles

3 *(exactly)* exactement; **r. in the middle** au beau *ou* en plein milieu; **r. behind** juste derrière; **r. in the middle of the harvest** en pleine moisson; **the wind was r. behind us** nous avions le vent en plein dans le dos; **to be r. behind sb** *(in support)* soutenir qn à fond; **he parked r. in front of the gate** il s'est garé en plein devant le portail; **I'll be waiting r. here** j'attends ici, je ne bouge pas; **it was r. here on the table** il était là sur la table

4 *(correctly) (to answer)* correctement; *(to guess)* juste; **if I remember r.** si je me souviens bien; **did I hear r.?** est-ce que j'ai bien entendu?; **you did r. to wait** vous avez bien fait d'attendre; **to act r.** bien agir

5 *(well)* bien; **nothing goes r. with me** rien ne me réussit; **I'm sure it'll all come r. for you** je suis sûr que tout s'arrangera pour vous; **I got your letter all r.** j'ai bien reçu votre lettre; **to see sb r.** *(financially)* veiller à ce que qn ne soit pas à court d'argent; **r. enough, she could have been more tactful** *(I agree with you)* c'est vrai elle aurait pu être plus délicate; **it was a mistake r. enough** c'était bien une erreur; **he's to blame r. enough** c'est bien de sa faute (à lui)

6 *(to the right-hand side) (to look, turn)* à droite; *Fam* **r., left and centre** *(everywhere)* de tous les côtés; *Fam* **he owes money r., left and centre** il doit de l'argent à droite et à gauche; *Fam* **he cheated us r., left and centre** il nous a eus sur tous les tableaux

7 *Br Dial Fam (very)* très; **I was r. glad to hear it** j'étais très heureux de l'apprendre

vt 1 *(put upright) (boat, car etc)* redresser; **to r. itself** *(of boat)* se redresser

2 *(correct) (a wrong)* réparer; *(mistake)* corriger, rectifier; **to r. itself** *(of situation)* s'arranger; *(of problem)* se résoudre

▸▸ **r. angle** angle *m* droit; *Comput* **r. arrow** flèche *f* vers la droite; *Comput* **r. arrow key** touche *f* de déplacement vers la droite; **r. bank** *(of river)* rive *f* droite; *Typ* **r. justification** justification *f* à droite; *Br* **R. Honourable** titre *m* utilisé pour s'adresser à certains hauts fonctionnaires ou à quelqu'un ayant un titre de noblesse; *TV, Cin* **r. pan** panoramique *m* horizontal GD; **r. of recourse** droit de recours; *Br* **r. to roam** = droit d'emprunter des sentiers sur des terres appartenant à de grands propriétaires terriens; *Am Geom* **r. triangle** triangle *m* rectangle; **r. of way** *Aut* priorité *f*; *(right to cross land)* droit de passage; *(path, road)* chemin *m*; *Am (for power line, railroad etc)* voie *f*; **there is no r. of way across this land** il n'y a pas de droit de passage sur cette terre; **to have r. of way** *(on road)* avoir (la) priorité; *Zool* **r. whale** baleine *f* franche; **r. wing** *Pol* droite; *Sport (position)* aile *f* droite; *(player)* ailier *m* droit

right-angled ADJ à angle droit; *(triangle etc)* rectangle

right-click *Comput* VT cliquer avec le bouton droit de la souris sur

vi cliquer avec le bouton droit de la souris (on sur); **r. on the icon to start the program** cliquez sur l'icône avec le bouton droit de la souris pour faire démarrer le programme

righteous ['raɪtʃəs] ADJ **1** *(person)* droit, vertueux; *Bible* juste; *(anger, indignation)* juste, justifié; *Pej* **in a r. tone of voice** d'un ton satisfait **2** *Am Fam (genuine)* authentique; *(excellent)* génial, -aux, super

NPL **the r.** les bons *mpl*, les justes *mpl*

righteously ['raɪtʃəslɪ] ADV *(to live, behave)* vertueusement; *(to deny, protest)* de manière offensée; *Pej (to say)* d'un ton satisfait; **he became r. indignant** il s'indigna

righteousness ['raɪtʃəsnɪs] N *(of person)*

droiture *f*, vertu *f*; *Bible* **those who hunger and thirst after r.** ceux qui ont soif de justice

rightful ['raɪtfʊl] ADJ *(heir, king, claim, owner)* légitime; *(inheritance)* auquel on a droit; **to have one's r. share** avoir sa juste part; **she insisted on being given her r. share** elle insista pour qu'on lui donne la part à laquelle elle avait droit

rightfully ['raɪtfəlɪ] ADV légitimement; *(inherited)* à juste titre; **it is r. mine** cela m'appartient légitimement

right-hand ADJ *(glove etc)* de la main droite; *(bend, drawer etc)* de droite; **on the r. side** sur le côté droit

▸▸ *Aut* **r. drive** conduite *f* à droite; **to have r. drive** avoir la conduite à droite, avoir le volant à droite; **r. man** bras *m* droit

right-handed [-'hændɪd] ADJ *(person)* droitier; *(punch)* du droit; *(tool, scissors etc)* pour droitiers; **r. screw** vis *f* dont le pas est à droite

ADV *(to play, hit etc)* de la main droite

right-hander [-'hændər] N **1** *(person)* droitier, -ière **2** *(blow)* coup *m* du droit, droit *m*

righting ['raɪtɪŋ] N *(of boat, wrong)* redressement *m*

rightism ['raɪtɪz(ə)m] N *Pol* idées *fpl* de droite; *(extreme right)* extrême droite *f*

rightist ['raɪtɪst] N *(person)* homme *m*/ femme *f* de droite

ADJ *(ideas, politics etc)* de droite; *(extremely right-wing)* d'extrême droite

rightly ['raɪtlɪ] ADV *(correctly) (to act, judge, guess)* bien; *(to choose)* avec raison; *(justifiably) (to believe, be annoyed, concerned)* à juste titre, avec raison; **r. or wrongly** à tort ou à raison; **I can't r. say** je ne saurais dire au juste; **I don't r. know** je ne sais pas exactement *ou* au juste; **and r. so** et à juste titre, et avec raison

right-minded ADJ sensé

rightness ['raɪtnɪs] N *(of decision, cause)* légitimité *f*; *(of answer)* justesse *f*, exactitude *f*

righto [raɪ'təʊ] INT *Br Fam* OK!, d'accord!

right-of-centre ADJ *Pol* de centre-droite; **her political beliefs are r.** politiquement, elle se situe au centre-droit

right-on ADJ *Fam* politiquement correct

rightsize ['raɪtsaɪz] VT dégraisser

rightsizing ['raɪtsaɪzɪŋ] N dégraissage *m*

right-thinking ADJ sensé

right-to-lifer N *Am* personne *f* qui est contre l'avortement

right-wing ADJ *Pol (attitude, government, policy etc)* de droite; **he is very r.** il est très à droite

right-winger N *Pol* personne *f* de droite

righty-ho [raɪtɪ'həʊ] INT *Br Fam* OK!, d'accord!

rigid ['rɪdʒɪd] ADJ *(metal, plastic etc)* rigide; *Fig (discipline, principles, rules etc)* rigide, strict, inflexible; *(etiquette)* rigide; **she's very r. in her ideas** elle a des idées très rigides *ou* inflexibles; **r. with fear** pétrifié; *Br Fam* **to be bored r.** s'ennuyer ferme; *Br Fam* **it shook me r.** *(shocked me)* ça m'a fichu un sacré coup

rigidity [rɪ'dʒɪdɪtɪ] N *(of metal, plastic)* rigidité *f*, raideur *f*; *Fig (of discipline, principles, rules etc)* rigidité, inflexibilité *f*; *(of etiquette)* rigidité

rigidly ['rɪdʒɪdlɪ] ADV rigidement; *(censored, controlled)* sévèrement, strictement; **r. opposed to ...** rigoureusement opposé à ...

rigmarole ['rɪgmərəʊl] N *Fam* **1** *(process)* procédure *f* compliquée; **to go through a whole r.** faire tout un tas de démarches **2** *(speech)* galimatias *m*

rigor ['rɪgər] N *Am* = rigour

▸▸ **r. mortis** ['mɔːtɪs] rigidité *f* cadavérique

rigorous ['rɪgərəs] ADJ *(discipline, training, climate, analysis etc)* rigoureux

rigorously ['rɪgərəslɪ] ADV rigoureusement

rigorousness ['rɪgərəsnɪs] N rigueur *f*

rigour, *Am* **rigor** ['rɪgər] N rigueur *f*; **the r. of the law** la sévérité de la loi; **the rigours of prison life/the Scottish climate** les rigueurs de la vie en prison/du climat écossais

rigout ['rɪgaʊt] N *Fam (outfit)* tenue *f*, *Pej* accoutrement *m*; **to be in full r.** être en grande tenue

rile [raɪl] VT *Fam (person)* agacer, exaspérer; **to r. sb (up) about sth** faire (en)rager qn à propos de qch; **don't get riled!** ne t'énerve pas!

Riley ['raɪlɪ] N *Fam* **to lead** *or* **live the life of R.** mener la grande vie

rill [rɪl] N *Lit* ruisselet *m*, petit ruisseau *m*

rim [rɪm] N *(of cup, glass, crater etc)* bord *m*; *(of wheel)* jante *f*, *(of dirt, soap etc)* dépôt *m*, trace *f*; **spectacle rims** monture *f* de lunettes; **countries on the Pacific R.** pays *mpl* de la ceinture pacifique; **Pacific R. economy** économie *f* des pays de la ceinture pacifique

VT *(-mm-) (wheel)* janter; *(of hills etc) (valley)* border; **nails rimmed with dirt** des ongles ourlés de crasse

▸▸ *TV, Cin* **r. light** éclairage *m* rasant

rime¹ [raɪm] N *Lit (frost)* givre *m*, gelée *f* blanche

rime² N, VT & VI *Arch* = **rhyme**

rimless ['rɪmlɪs] ADJ *(spectacles)* sans monture

-rimmed ['rɪmd] SUFF **horn/steel-r.** *(spectacles)* avec une monture en écaille/en acier

rimming ['rɪmɪŋ] N *TV, Cin* éclairage *m* frisant

rind [raɪnd] N *(of fruit)* écorce *f*, *(of cheese)* croûte *f*, *(of bacon)* couenne *f*, **a piece of orange/lemon r.** un zeste *ou* un morceau d'écorce de citron/d'orange

---

RING¹ [rɪŋ]

N	anneau **1** ▪ bague **1** ▪ cercle **2, 4** ▪ arène **3**
VT	entourer **2**

N 1 *(band) (for finger)* anneau *m*; *(with stone, for marking birds)* bague *f*; *(for keys)* porte-clés *m inv*; *(for napkin)* rond *m* de serviette; *Gym* **the rings** les anneaux *mpl*; *Tech* **retaining r.** plaquette *f* de fixation

2 *(circle) (of people, chairs etc)* cercle *m*; *(in water, of smoke)* rond *m*; *(burner on stove)* feu *m*, brûleur *m*; *(around planet)* anneau *m*; *(around sun, moon)* halo *m*; *(of tree)* anneau *ou* cercle annuel; *(stain)* marque *f*, trace *f*; **the cup will leave a r.** la tasse va faire une marque; **sitting in a r.** assis en cercle *ou* en rond; *Geol* **R. of Fire** ceinture *f* de feu; **to have rings round one's eyes** avoir des cernes sous les yeux *ou* les yeux cernés; **they formed a r. round her** ils ont formé un cercle autour d'elle; **to draw** *or* **put a r. round sth** entourer qch d'un cercle; *Fig* **to make** *or* **run rings round sb** *(at chess, tennis etc)* complètement dominer qn; *(in quiz game, general knowledge test etc)* être bien meilleur que qn; **(swimming)** r. bouée *f*

3 *(enclosure) (at circus)* arène *f*, piste *f*, *(for boxing, wrestling)* ring *m*; *(for bullfight)* arène; *(for showjumping)* enceinte *f*, **the r.** *(boxing as sport)* la boxe *f*, *Boxing* **to retire from the r.** abandonner la boxe; *St Exch* **the R.** le Parquet; *Fig* **to throw** *or* **toss one's hat into the r.** faire connaître son intention de participer

4 *(organization) (of people)* groupe *m*, cercle *m*; *(gang)* bande *f*; *Com* cartel *m*; *(of spies, drug traffickers)* réseau *m*

VT 1 *(bird)* baguer

2 *(of police, troops etc) (building etc)* encercler; *(item on list etc)* entourer d'un trait de crayon; **to r. sb/sth round** *or* **about** *or* **in** *(surround)* encercler *ou* entourer qn/qch (**with** de)

▸▸ **r. binder** classeur *m* (à anneaux); *Mus* **The R. Cycle** La Tétralogie; **r. finger** annulaire *m*; *Comput* **r. network** réseau en anneau; *Br* **r. road** périphérique *m*; *Br* **r. spanner** clé *f* polygonale; *Comput* **r. structure** structure *f* en anneau

RING²

| **N** sonnerie **1** ▪ tintement **1** ▪ coup de fil **2** |
| **VI** sonner **1** ▪ tinter **1** ▪ téléphoner **2** ▪ résonner **3** |
| **VT** sonner **1** ▪ téléphoner à **2** |

N 1 *(sound) (of bells, telephone)* sonnerie *f*; *(of small bell, coins)* tintement *m*; *(of voice)* timbre *m*; **there was a r. at the door** on a sonné; **a r. of bells** *(set of bells)* un carillon; *Tel* **I hung up on the sixth r.** j'ai raccroché à la sixième sonnerie; *Fig* **the name has a familiar r. to it** ce nom me dit quelque chose; **the r. of truth** l'accent *m* de la vérité; *Fig* **it has a hollow r.** cela sonne creux

2 *Br Tel Fam (communication)* coup *m* de fil; **to give sb a r.** passer un coup de fil à qn

VI *(pt* **rang** *[ræŋ]; pp* **rung** *[rʌŋ])* **1** *(of bell, telephone, person)* sonner; *(of small bell)* tinter; *(of alarm)* retentir; **this will cause the alarm to r.** cela déclenchera l'alarme; **to r. at the door** sonner à la porte; **the bell is ringing for dinner** on sonne pour le dîner; **to r. for sb** sonner qn; **to r. for some coffee** *(by pushing bell)* sonner pour demander du café; *(by telephoning)* téléphoner pour demander du café; **to r. for room service** sonner pour appeler le service en chambre

2 *esp Br Tel* téléphoner; **to r. round** passer une série de coups de fil

3 *(resonate) (of street etc)* résonner, retentir (**with** de); *(of ears)* bourdonner; **her words still r. in my ears** ses paroles résonnent encore à mes oreilles

4 *Fig* **to r. true** être convaincant; **to r. false** sonner faux; *Fig* **his answer did not r. true** sa réponse sonnait faux

VT 1 *(bell)* (faire) sonner; *(alarm)* déclencher; **to r. the doorbell** sonner à la porte; *Fig* **does that r. a bell?** est-ce que cela vous rappelle *ou* vous dit quelque chose?; *Fig* **the name rings a bell** ce nom me dit quelque chose; *Fig* **to r. the changes** introduire des changements

2 *esp Br Tel* téléphoner à, appeler, passer un coup de fil à

▸ **ring back** *esp Br Tel* **VI** rappeler
  VT SEP *(person)* rappeler

▸ **ring down VT SEP** *Theat* **to r. down the curtain** sonner pour faire baisser le rideau; *Fig* **to r. down the curtain on sth** marquer la fin de qch

▸ **ring in VI** *esp Br Tel* **to r. in sick** appeler pour dire qu'on est malade; **the boss wants her to r. in every hour** le patron veut qu'elle appelle toutes les heures
  VT SEP **to r. in the New Year** marquer la nouvelle année par une volée de cloches

▸ **ring off VI** *esp Br Tel* raccrocher

▸ **ring out VI** *(of bell, telephone)* sonner; *(of voice, shot)* retentir
  VT SEP **to r. out the Old Year** marquer la fin de l'année en sonnant les cloches

▸ **ring up** *esp Br* **VI** *Tel* téléphoner
  VT SEP 1 *Tel (person)* téléphoner à, appeler, passer un coup de fil à
  2 *Theat* **to r. up the curtain** sonner pour

faire lever le rideau; *Fig* **to r. up the curtain on sth** marquer le début de qch
  3 **to r. an amount up** *(on cash register)* enregistrer une somme; **to r. up a profit** réaliser un bénéfice

ring-bound ADJ *(notebook, file)* à anneaux

ringed [rɪŋd] **ADJ 1** *(wearing ring) (bird)* bagué **2** *(with marking) (plover etc)* à collier

ringer ['rɪŋər] **N 1** *(of bell)* sonneur, -euse, carillonneur, -euse **2** *Am Horseracing* cheval *m* substitué à un autre **3** *Fam* **to be a dead r. for sb** être le sosie de qn **4** *Sl (stolen car with altered plates)* voiture *f* maquillée

ringing ['rɪŋɪŋ] **ADJ** *(bell)* qui tinte *ou* sonne; *(voice, laughter etc)* sonore, retentissant; **I still have a r. sound in my ears** j'ai encore les oreilles qui sifflent; **in r. tones** d'une voix vibrante

  N *(of large bell, telephone)* sonnerie *f*; *(of small bell)* tintement *m*; *(in ears)* bourdonnement *m*

  ▸▸ *Br Tel* **r. tone** sonnerie, signal *m* d'appel

ringleader ['rɪŋliːdər] **N** *Pej (of gang)* chef *m* de bande; *(of rebellion, in mischief etc)* meneur, -euse

ringlet ['rɪŋlɪt] **N** *(curl)* anglaise *f*, boucle *f* (de cheveux); **to wear one's hair in ringlets** porter les cheveux en boucles, porter des anglaises

ringmaster ['rɪŋmɑːstər] **N** *(of circus)* ≃ Monsieur Loyal

ring-necked [-nekt] **ADJ** *(bird, snake)* à collier
  ▸▸ **r. dove** pigeon *m* ramier, palombe *f*

ring-pull N anneau *m*, bague *f* *(sur une boîte de conserve, de boisson etc)*
  ▸▸ **r. can** cannette *f*, boîte *f* *(qu'on ouvre en tirant sur une bague)*

ringside ['rɪŋsaɪd] **N** premier rang *m*; **at the r.** au premier rang; **to have a r. seat** *(at circus, boxing match)* avoir une place au premier rang; *Fig* être aux premières loges; **to have a r. view of sth** être bien placé pour voir qch

ring-tailed ADJ à queue zébrée
  ▸▸ **r. lemur** maki *m*

ringtone ['rɪŋtəʊn] **N** *Tel* tonalité *f* de sonnerie

ringworm ['rɪŋwɜːm] **N** *Med* teigne *f*

rink [rɪŋk] **N** *(for ice-skating)* patinoire *f*; *(for roller-skating)* piste *f*

rinkydink [ˈrɪŋkɪˈdɪŋk] **ADJ** *Am Fam (poor quality)* à la gomme

rinse [rɪns] **N 1** *(of bottle, hands etc)* rinçage *m*; **to give sth a r.** rincer qch **2** *(hair colouring)* rinçage *m* (colorant); **to have a r.** se faire faire un rinçage (colorant)

  VT 1 *(washing, cup etc)* rincer; **to r. soap out of a sponge/clothes** rincer une éponge/des vêtements pour enlever le savon; **to r. one's hands** se passer les mains à l'eau; *(remove soap)* se rincer les mains; **to r. one's mouth** se rincer la bouche **2** *(with hair colouring)* **to r. one's hair** se faire un rinçage (colorant); **to r. sb's hair** faire un rinçage (colorant) à qn
  ▸▸ **r. cycle** *(in washing machine)* cycle *m* de rinçage, rinçage

▸ **rinse down VT SEP** *(meal, pill)* **can I have some water to r. the pill down with?** puis-je avoir de l'eau pour avaler mon cachet?; **a little glass of something to r. it down?** un petit verre de quelque chose pour le faire passer?

▸ **rinse out VT SEP** *(cup, bucket etc)* rincer; **to r. out the dirt/soap** rincer pour enlever la saleté/le savon; *Fig* **go and r. your mouth out!** va te laver la bouche!
  VI *(of stain, dye)* partir à l'eau

riot ['raɪət] **N** *(uprising)* émeute *f*; *Fig* **there will be a r.** *(when people find out)* ça va faire

scandale; *Fig* **a r. of colour** une explosion de couleurs; **to run r.** *(of person)* se déchaîner; *(of plants, inflation)* devenir incontrôlable; **my imagination was running r.** j'ai commencé à imaginer toutes sortes de choses; *Fam* **he's/it's a r.** *(amusing)* il est/c'est tordant

  VI *(-t-)* faire une émeute; *(of football supporters, demonstrators) (to fight)* se battre; *(to destroy things)* se livrer à de violentes manifestations; *(of prisoners)* se mutiner

  ▸▸ *Hist* **R. Act** loi *f* antiémeutes, loi contre les rassemblements séditieux; *Fig* **to read sb the r. act** souffler dans les bronches à qn, passer un savon à qn; **r. gear** matériel *m* antiémeutes; **r. police** police *f* *ou* forces *fpl* antiémeutes

rioter ['raɪətər] **N** émeutier, -ière; *(football fans, demonstrators)* vandale *mf*, casseur, -euse; *(prisoners)* mutin *m*

rioting ['raɪətɪŋ] **N r. football hooligans** des hooligans qui cassent tout sur leur passage; **r. mob** bande *f* d'émeutiers; *(of football fans)* bande des vandales *ou* des casseurs
  N émeutes *fpl*; *(fighting)* bagarres *fpl*; **r. broke out when ...** des *ou* les bagarres ont éclaté quand ...

riotous ['raɪətəs] **ADJ 1** *(crowd etc)* violent; *Law* **to charge sb with r. behaviour** accuser qn d'avoir eu un comportement séditieux; **r. living** vie *f* déréglée **2** *Fam (amusing) (party, occasion)* très gai et très bruyant; *(laughter)* exubérant; **we had a r. time** on a bien rigolé; **a r. success** un franc succès, un succès retentissant

riotously ['raɪətəslɪ] **ADV** violemment; *Fam* **to be r. funny** être à se tordre de rire; **a r. funny film** un film extrêmement drôle

RIP [ɑːraɪˈpiː] *(abbr* **Rest In Peace)** Repose en paix

rip [rɪp] **N** *(in fabric)* déchirure *f*; **there's a r. in your jacket** il y a une déchirure à ta veste
  VT *(-pp-)* *(fabric etc)* déchirer; **to r. to pieces** *or* **shreds** *(garment)* déchirer en lambeaux; *(letter)* déchirer en mille morceaux; *Fig (play, film, director etc)* éreinter; *(argument)* mettre en pièces; **it's ripped to pieces** *or* **shreds** *(garment, carpet)* il est en lambeaux
  VI 1 *(of fabric etc)* se déchirer

  2 *Fam* **to r. along** aller *ou* avancer à toute vitesse *ou* à fond de train; **the explosion ripped through the building** le choc de l'explosion s'est propagé dans tout le bâtiment; **let her** *or* **it r.!** *(of car, motorboat etc)* mets les gaz!, fonce!

  3 *Fam (be angry)* **to let r.** laisser éclater sa colère (**about** au sujet de); **to let r. (with) a stream of abuse** lancer une bordée d'injures; **to let r. at sb** s'en prendre à qn (**about** au sujet de); **to let r. against the government** s'en prendre *ou* s'attaquer au gouvernement (**for** au sujet de); **she really let r.** *(spoke her mind, let hair down etc)* elle s'est déchaînée

▸ **rip apart VT SEP** déchirer; *Fig* éreinter, mettre en pièces
  VI se déchirer

▸ **rip away VT SEP** arracher

▸ **rip into VT INSEP** *Fam (person)* attaquer violemment

▸ **rip off VT SEP 1** *(by tearing, remove quickly)* arracher; *(one's jacket)* enlever en toute hâte; **they ripped off their clothes** ils se sont déshabillés en toute hâte **2** *Fam (steal)* piquer; *Fam* **to r. sb off** *(cheat)* arnaquer qn; *Fam* **you were ripped off** tu t'es fait arnaquer

▸ **rip open VT SEP** *(person)* éventrer; *(cheek)* déchirer; *(garment) (open quickly)* ouvrir d'un mouvement; **the bayonet ripped open his stomach** la baïonnette l'a éventré; **to r. open a letter** décacheter une lettre en la déchirant; **to r. open a package** ouvrir un paquet en le déchirant; **jeans ripped open at the knee** un jean déchiré au genou ▪ **vi** se déchirer

▸ **rip out vt sep** (remove) (fireplace, light fittings etc) enlever; (page from book) arracher

▸ **rip up vt sep 1** (tear) (letter) déchirer **2** (remove) (floorboards) arracher; (pavement) creuser

riparian [raɪ'peərɪən] **adj, n** Fml riverain, -aine; (wildlife) des rivières

ripcord ['rɪpkɔːd] **n** (on parachute) corde f d'ouverture, cordelette f de déclenchement; (on hot-air balloon) corde de déchirure

ripe [raɪp] **adj** (fruit, grain) mûr; (cheese) bien fait, bien à point; (vulgar) grossier; **to live to a r. old age** vivre vieux, vivre jusqu'à un âge avancé; Hum **the r. old age of sixteen** l'âge avancé de seize ans; **the time is r. for speaking the truth** le temps est venu de dire la vérité; **the time is not yet r.** le temps n'est pas encore venu; **r. for change/revolution** mûr ou prêt pour le changement/la révolution; **the company is r. for takeover** la société est prête pour être rachetée; **a site r. for development** un site bon à exploiter; **to smell r.** (of fruit) avoir un parfum de fruit mûr; Pej (of person) sentir mauvais

ripen ['raɪp(ə)n] **vt** (fruit, grain) (faire) mûrir; (cheese) affiner
▪ **vi** (of fruit, grain) mûrir; Fig (of plan etc) mûrir; (of cheese) se faire; Fig **to r. into manhood** atteindre l'âge d'homme

ripeness ['raɪpnɪs] **n** (of fruit, grain etc) maturité f, Fig (of comments, language) grossièreté f

ripening ['raɪp(ə)nɪŋ] **adj 1** Lit (sun) qui fait mûrir **2** (fruit, grain) mûrissant, qui mûrit; (cheese) qui se fait
▪ **n** (of fruit, grain) maturation f, mûrissage m, mûrissement m; (of cheese) affinage m

rip-off n Fam **1** (swindle) escroquerie f, arnaque f; **that restaurant's a r.** ce restaurant est une arnaque; **what a r.!** quelle arnaque!; **r. prices** des prix astronomiques; **r. merchant** arnaqueur, -euse **2** (theft) vol m, fauche f; **it's a r. from an Osborne play** ils ont pompé l'idée dans une pièce d'Osborne

riposte [rɪ'pɒst] **n** Fencing riposte f, **to make a r.** riposter
▪ **vi** (in argument etc), Fencing riposter

ripped [rɪpt] **adj** Fam (drunk) bourré, pété; (on drugs) raide, défoncé; Br Sl **r. to the tits** (drunk) bourré comme un coing, plein comme une barrique; (on drugs) complètement raide ou défoncé

ripper¹ ['rɪpər] **n** (killer) éventreur m

ripper² Austr Fam **n** (excellent person, thing) he's a r. c'est quelqu'un de super; **it's a r.** c'est super ou génial; **you little r.!** super!, génial!
▪ **adj** (excellent) super, génial, -aux

ripping ['rɪpɪŋ] **adj** Old-fashioned Br Fam épatant, formidable; **a r. yarn** une histoire épatante

ripple ['rɪp(ə)l] **n 1** (wave) (on water) ride f, (in corn, hair) ondoiement m, ondulation f, Fig **a r. of excitement ran through the crowd** un frémissement d'excitation a parcouru la foule **2** (noise) (of stream) murmure m, gazouillement m; (of conversation, voices) murmure(s); (of laughter, applause) vague f **3** (ice-cream) raspberry/strawberry r. = glace f vanille panachée à la framboise/fraise
▪ **vi 1** (form ripples) (of water) se rider; (of corn, hair) onduler, ondoyer; (of muscles) saillir **2** (make sound) (of stream) murmurer, gazouiller; **laughter/applause rippled through the audience** des vagues de rires/d'applaudissements ont traversé le public
▪ **vt** (of wind) (water, sand) rider; **he rippled his muscles** il a fait saillir ses muscles

▸▸ TV, Cin **r. dissolve** fondu m par ondulation; **r. effect** répercussions fpl

rip-roaring adj Fam (party) tumultueux; **a r. success** un succès retentissant

ripsaw ['rɪpsɔː] **n** scie f à refendre

riptide ['rɪptaɪd] **n** courant m de retour

RISC [rɪsk] **n** Comput (abbr reduced instruction set chip/computer) RISC

RISE [raɪz]

n lever **1, 2** ▪ ascension **2**	
▪ éminence **2** ▪ montée **3** ▪ hausse **3**	
vi se lever **1–4** ▪ se relever **1** ▪ monter **3, 4** ▪ s'élever **3, 4** ▪ augmenter **4**	

n 1 (appearance) (of sun, moon) lever m; Fig **to give r. to sth** donner lieu à qch

2 (ascent) (of theatre curtain) lever m; (of leader, party) ascension f, (to power) accession f, (in rank) avancement m, promotion f, (of industry, technology) essor m; (in ground) éminence f, **her r. to fame came overnight** elle est devenue célèbre du jour au lendemain; Fam **to take** or **get a r. out of sb** (tease) faire enrager qn

3 (increase) (in pressure etc) hausse f (in de); (in level of river) crue f, (of temperature) augmentation f, élévation f, (of tide) montée f, (of price) hausse, augmentation; Br (pay) augmentation (de salaire); Br **to get a r.** (in salary) être augmenté; **the r. and fall** (of empire, politician etc) la grandeur et la décadence; **the book charts his r. and fall** le livre retrace son ascension et sa chute; **the r. and fall of the tide** le flux et le reflux; **food prices are on the r.** le prix des denrées est en hausse; **a big r. in house prices is on the way** une hausse ou augmentation importante des prix de l'immobilier se prépare
▪ **vi** (pt rose [rəʊz]; pp risen ['rɪz(ə)n]) **1** (get up) Fml (from bed, chair) se lever; (from knees, after fall) se relever; (from the dead) ressusciter; (of Parliament, court) (at end of day) lever ou clore la séance; (at end of session) entrer en vacances; (on entry of judge) se lever; **all r.!** (in courtroom) levez-vous s'il vous plaît!; **to r. from the table** se lever de table; **to r. on its hind legs** (of horse) se cabrer; **to r. early/late** (from bed) se lever tôt/tard; Fam **r. and shine!** debout!; **Christ is risen** le Christ est ressuscité

2 (appear, emerge) (of sun, star, moon) se lever; **a picture rose in my mind** une image s'est présentée à mon esprit; **a feeling of panic rose in me** un sentiment de panique s'est emparé de moi; **to r. from the ashes of sth** renaître des cendres de qch; **new buildings are rising all the time** on n'arrête pas de construire

3 (ascend) (of theatre curtain) se lever; (of road, ground, sap etc) monter; (of smoke, balloon) monter, s'élever (from de); Fig (in society) s'élever; Theat **the curtain rose at 7.30** le lever de rideau a eu lieu à 19h30; **to r. off the ground** (of plane) quitter le sol, décoller; **to r. in the saddle** faire du trot enlevé; **to r. to the surface** (of fish), Fig (of anger) faire surface; (of doubts, conflict) se faire jour; **to r. to the bait** mordre à l'hameçon; **a murmur rose from the crowd** une rumeur s'est élevée parmi la foule; **the boat rose and fell on the water** le bateau se balançait sur l'eau; **trees rising a hundred feet above the plain** arbres qui s'élèvent à trente mètres au-dessus de la plaine; **his voice rose above the noise of the crowd** sa voix s'élevait au-dessus du bruit de la foule; **this book never rises above the level of potboiler** ce livre n'est que de la littérature alimentaire; Fig **to r. above events/one's difficulties** ne pas se laisser abattre par les événements/ses problèmes; **she seems to r. above that kind of petty jealousy** elle semble être au-dessus

de ce genre de jalousie mesquine; **try to r. above it** tâche de rester au-dessus de la mêlée; **to r. to the occasion/challenge/task** se montrer à la hauteur de la situation/du défi/de la tâche; **to r. to fame** devenir célèbre; **to r. to power** accéder au pouvoir; **to r. in the world** faire son chemin; **he rose from nothing** il est parti de rien; **to r. to the rank of colonel** monter jusqu'au grade de colonel; **to r. through the ranks** monter les échelons un à un; **to r. in sb's esteem** monter dans l'estime de qn

4 (increase in amount, intensity) (of temperature) monter, augmenter; (of wind) se lever; (of voice) s'élever; (of hope) grandir; (of tide, pressure, river, water level) monter; (of dough) lever; (of prices) monter, augmenter; **prices are rising** les prix montent ou sont à la ou en hausse; **everything has risen in price** tout a augmenté, tous les prix ont augmenté; **the river has risen by two metres** la rivière est montée de deux mètres; **the wind has risen to gale force** le vent se mit à souffler en tempête; **my spirits rose at the sight of the mountains** j'ai repris courage à la vue des montagnes; **her colour rose** ses joues s'empourprèrent

5 (become erect) (of hair) se hérisser; **the dog's hackles rose** le chien s'est hérissé de colère; **the hair on the back of her neck rose** ses poils se sont hérissés

6 (revolt) se soulever, se révolter (against contre); **to r. in arms** prendre les armes; **to r. in protest against sth** se soulever ou se révolter contre qch

7 (originate) (of river) prendre sa source (at à; in dans); (of difficulty, quarrel) provenir, naître (from de)
▸▸ Comput **r. time** temps m de montée
▸ **rise up vi** (revolt) = **rise vi 6**

> Attention: ne pas confondre avec le verbe **to raise**, qui est toujours accompagné d'un complément d'objet.

riser ['raɪzər] **n 1** early r. lève-tôt mf inv; late r. lève-tard mf inv **2** (on staircase) contremarche f **3** (pipe) tuyau m de montée

risibility [rɪzɪ'bɪlɪtɪ] **n** Lit (of situation etc) caractère m risible ou ridicule; (of offer) caractère dérisoire

risible ['rɪzɪb(ə)l] **adj** Lit (idea, plan etc) risible, ridicule; (offer) dérisoire

rising ['raɪzɪŋ] **adj 1** (sun) levant **2** (road, artist, politician etc) qui monte; **the r. generation** la nouvelle ou la jeune génération; **r. ground** élévation f du terrain, éminence f **3** (pressure, temperature) en hausse; (tide) montant; (stock market) orienté à la hausse; **r. prices** la hausse des prix
▪ **n 1** (of Parliament) levée f, clôture f, **I don't like early r.** je n'aime pas me lever tôt **2** (of sun, moon) lever m; (of star) lever, ascension f **3** (of theatre curtain) lever m; (of sap) montée f **4** (of river) montée f **5** (revolt) insurrection f, révolte f, soulèvement m
▪ **prep** he's r. sixty il va sur (ses) soixante ans
▸▸ **r. damp** humidité f ascensionnelle ou par capillarité; **r. star** Astron étoile f montante; Mktg (product) produit m d'avenir; Horseriding **r. trot** trot m enlevé ou à l'anglaise

risk [rɪsk] **n** (danger) risque m (of doing faire); (in insurance) risque m; (to life, person, child) en danger; Med (person, population) à risque; (job) menacé; **to place** or **put sth at r.** risquer qch; **to place** or **put sb at r.** faire courir un danger à qn; **is there any r. of that happening?** est-ce qu'il y a un risque que cela se produise?; **there's no r. of that happening** pas de danger que ça se passe, ça ne risque pas d'arriver; **to be full of risks** comporter beaucoup de risques; **to run**

longues heures en selle; *(on horse)* écorchure *f ou* excoriation *f* sous la selle
▶ **saddle up** VI *(of rider)* seller
VT SEP *(horse)* seller

saddleback ['sæd(ə)bæk] N **1** *Archit* toit *m* en bâtière **2** *(of hill)* ensellement *m* **3** *(pig)* cochon *m* noir avec une ceinture blanche

saddlebag ['sæd(ə)bæg] N *Horseriding, Cycling etc* sacoche *f* de selle

saddlecloth ['sæd(ə)lklɒθ] N couverture *f ou* tapis *m* de selle

saddler ['sædlər] N sellier *m*

saddlery ['sædlərɪ] N *(trade, articles)* sellerie *f*, bourrellerie *f*

saddle-sore ADJ **to be s.** *Horseriding* avoir mal aux fesses (d'avoir été en selle); *Cycling* avoir mal aux fesses (d'avoir fait du vélo)

saddling ['sædlɪŋ] N *(of horse)* sellage *m*

saddo ['sædəʊ] N *Br Fam* nul *m*, nulle *f*

Sadducee ['sædjʊsi:] N Saducéen, -enne

sadism ['seɪdɪz(ə)m] N sadisme *m*

sadist ['seɪdɪst] N sadique *mf*

sadistic [sə'dɪstɪk] ADJ sadique

sadistically [sə'dɪstɪklɪ] ADV sadiquement, avec sadisme

sadly ['sædlɪ] ADV **1** *(in an unhappy way) (to reply, smile)* tristement, d'un air triste **2** *(deplorably)* malheureusement; **s.,** this is so c'est, hélas *ou* malheureusement, le cas **3** *(greatly)* vraiment; **you're s. mistaken** tu te trompes lourdement; **he is s. missed** il nous/leur manque beaucoup; **compassion is s. lacking in our society** la compassion fait tristement défaut dans notre société

sadness ['sædnɪs] N tristesse *f*, mélancolie *f*

sadomasochism [seɪdəʊ'mæsəkɪz(ə)m] N sadomasochisme *m*

sadomasochist [seɪdəʊ'mæsəkɪst] N sadomasochiste *mf*

sadomasochistic [seɪdəʊmæsəˈkɪstɪk] ADJ sadomasochiste

s.a.e. [eseɪ'i:] N *Com etc (abbr* **stamped addressed envelope)** enveloppe *f* timbrée avec son adresse

safari [sə'fɑːrɪ] N safari *m*; **on s.** en safari; **to go on s.** faire un safari, aller en safari
▶▶ **s. holiday** safari *m*; **s. jacket** saharienne *f*; **s. park** réserve *f* d'animaux sauvages; **s. suit** ensemble *m* avec saharienne

SAFE [seɪf]

ADJ	en sécurité **1** ▪ sûr **2–4**
	▪ sans danger **2** ▪ solide **2**
N	coffre-fort

ADJ **1** *(not in danger)* en sécurité; **s. from sth** à l'abri de qch; **to be s. from recognition** ne pas risquer d'être reconnu; **at last we are s.** enfin nous voilà en sécurité *ou* saufs *ou* hors de danger; **I'm glad to hear you're s.** je suis content d'apprendre qu'il ne t'est rien arrivé; **your daughter's not s. with him** votre fille court un risque en le fréquentant; **to come home s.** rentrer sain et sauf; **s. and sound** sain et sauf

2 *(not dangerous) (street, town)* sûr; *(chemical, water etc)* sans danger; *(building, bridge etc)* solide; **she assured me the water was perfectly s. for drinking** elle m'a assuré qu'on pouvait boire l'eau sans danger; **not s. dangereux; is it s. to leave him alone?** est-ce qu'il n'y a pas de danger à le laisser seul?; **is the meat/water s. (to eat/drink)?** est-ce qu'on peut manger la viande/boire l'eau sans risque?; **to make a bomb s.** désamorcer une bombe; **it's as s. as houses** *(not dangerous)* cela ne présente pas le moindre risque; **a s. beach for children** une plage où les enfants peuvent se baigner en (toute) sécurité; **at a s. distance** à distance

respectueuse; *Med* **s. dose** dose *f* inoffensive; **s. driver** conducteur, -trice prudent(ente)

3 *(not entailing risk) (conversation, novel etc)* sûr; **it's a s. guess that ...** on ne prend pas beaucoup de risques en disant que ...; **it is s. to say that ...** on peut dire à coup sûr que ...; **(in order) to be on the s. side** pour plus de sûreté, pour être plus sûr; **s. investment** placement sûr *ou* de tout repos; **it's as s. as houses** *or Br* **as the Bank of England** *(of investment)* c'est de l'or en barres; *Prov* **better s. than sorry** deux précautions valent mieux qu'une; **it's a pretty s. assumption** *or* **bet that ...** il y a fort à parier que ...; **to wish sb a s. journey** souhaiter bon voyage à qn; **to have a s. journey** faire bon voyage

4 *(secure) (place etc)* sûr; **in s. keeping** en lieu sûr, en sûreté; **to give sth to sb for s. keeping** confier qch à qn; **it's in his s. keeping** c'est sous sa garde; **in s. hands** entre (de) bonnes mains; **he's a s. pair of hands** *(of goalkeeper)* il a les mains très sûres; *(of manager, minister etc)* il est très fiable; **to put sb/sth in a s. place** mettre qn/qch en lieu sûr; **a s. retreat** un asile assuré *ou* sûr

5 *Br Sl (good)* chouette, cool; **are we still on for tonight?** – **yeah, s.** ça marche toujours pour ce soir? – ouais, pas de problème

ADV **to play (it) s.** ne rien risquer

N **1** *(strongbox)* coffre-fort *m*, *pl* coffres-forts; *Banking* **night** *or* **deposit s.** coffre *m* de nuit

2 *(meat)* **s.** garde-manger *m inv*
▶▶ **s. area** zone *f* de sécurité; *Fin* **s. custody** garde *f* en dépôt de titres; **s. deposit** dépôt *m* en coffre-fort; **s. haven** refuge *m*; *Mil* zone *f* de sécurité; **s. house** refuge *m*; **s. load** *(for lorry)* charge *f* admissible; *(for lift)* charge maximum; *Elec* charge de sécurité; *Br Pol* **s. seat** = siège *m* de député qui traditionnellement va toujours au même parti; **s. sex** rapports *mpl* sexuels protégés; **to practise s. sex** se protéger *(contre les maladies sexuellement transmissibles)*; **a s. sex campaign** une campagne visant à promouvoir l'utilisation du préservatif

safe-blower N perceur, -euse de coffres-forts à l'explosif

safe-breaker N perceur, -euse de coffres-forts

safe-conduct N sauf-conduit *m*, *pl* sauf-conduits

safe-cracker N = **safe-breaker**

safeguard ['seɪfɡɑːd] N garantie *f* (**against** contre)
VT *(sb's interests, rights)* sauvegarder, protéger
VI **to s. against sth** se protéger contre qch
▶▶ **s. clause** clause *f* de sauvegarde

safekeeping [seɪf'ki:pɪŋ] N **in s.** en lieu sûr, en sûreté; **to give sth to sb for s.** confier qch à qn; **it's in his s.** c'est sous sa garde

safelight ['seɪflaɪt] N *Phot* lampe *f* inactinique

safely ['seɪflɪ] ADV **1** *(to work, play, use a tool etc)* en toute sécurité; *(to drive, ride)* sans danger; **to arrive s.** *(of person)* bien arriver; *(after dangerous journey)* arriver sain et sauf; *(of parcel etc)* arriver sans dommage; *(of ship etc)* arriver à bon port; **to land s.** atterrir sans problème; **to put sth s. away** mettre qch en lieu sûr *ou* en sûreté; **the bomb has been s. defused** la bombe a été désamorcée et ne présente plus aucun danger; **the kids are s. tucked up in bed** les enfants sont bien sagement au lit **2** *(with certainty)* avec certitude; **I can s. say that ...** je puis dire avec certitude *ou* à coup sûr que ...; **you can s. expect her to remember** vous pouvez être sûr qu'elle s'en souviendra

safeness ['seɪfnɪs] N **1 a feeling of s.** un

sentiment de sécurité *ou* de sûreté **2** *(of bridge)* solidité *f*, *(of nuclear power, electrical appliances)* sûreté *f* **3** *(certainty) (of deal, investment, choice etc)* sûreté *f*, *(cautiousness) (of style, writing)* assurance *f*

safety ['seɪftɪ] N *(of person)* sécurité *f*; *(of thing)* sûreté *f*; **to seek s. in flight** chercher son salut dans la fuite; **to guarantee sb's s.** *(of police etc)* assurer la protection de qn; *Prov* **there's s. in numbers** plus on est nombreux, moins on court de risques; **for s.'s sake** pour plus de sûreté; **in a place of s.** en lieu sûr; **road s.** sécurité routière; **she's very s. conscious** elle se préoccupe beaucoup de la sécurité; **s. first!** ne prenez pas de risques!
▶▶ **s. belt** ceinture *f* de sécurité; *Aut* **s. cage** habitacle *m* de sécurité; **s. catch** *(on gun)* cran *m* de sécurité; *(on window, door)* cran de sûreté; *(on bonnet)* crochet *m* de sécurité; *Aut* **s. cell** cellule *f* de sécurité; **s. chain** *(on door)* chaîne *f* de sûreté; *(on bracelet)* chaînette *f* de sûreté; **s. deposit box** coffre(-fort) *m*, *pl* coffres(-forts); **s. device** dispositif *m* de sécurité; **s. drill** exercice *m* d'évacuation; **s. feature** *(device)* dispositif de sécurité; *(characteristic)* caractéristique *f* pour assurer la sécurité; **s. features** *(on car)* aménagements *mpl ou* dispositifs de sécurité; **s. glass** verre *m* de sécurité; **s. lamp** lampe *f* de mineur; **s. lock** verrouillage *m* de sécurité; **s. margin** marge *f* de sécurité; **s. matches** allumettes *fpl* de sûreté; **s. measures** consignes *fpl* de sécurité; **s. mechanism** mécanisme *m* de sécurité; **s. net** filet *m*; *Fig* filet (de sécurité); **s. pin** *(fastener)* épingle *f* de nourrice *ou* de sûreté; *(of grenade, bomb)* goupille *f* de sûreté; **s. regulations** consignes de sécurité; **s. standards** normes *fpl* de sécurité; *Com* **s. stock** stock *m* de sécurité; **s. valve** *Tech* soupape *f* de sûreté; *Fig* soupape

safety-first ADJ *(campaign, measures)* de sécurité

saffron ['sæfrən] N **1** *Bot, Culin, Pharm* safran *m*; **wild** *or* **meadow s.** safran des prés **2** *(colour)* safran *m inv*
ADJ safran *inv*
▶▶ **s. crocus** safran; **s. yellow** jaune *m* safran

sag [sæg] N **1** *(of roof etc)* affaissement *m*, fléchissement *m*; *(in line, rope etc)* flèche *f*, ventre *m* **2** *(drop) (in prices, support etc)* baisse *f*
VI (-gg-) *(of platform, roof etc)* s'affaisser, fléchir; *(of cheek, breast etc)* pendre; *(of cable, rope) (state)* être détendu, pendre; *(action)* se détendre; *(of curtain)* pendre au milieu; *(of prices, support etc)* baisser, fléchir; **the gate was sagging on its hinges** le portail était branlant; **he's beginning to s. a little** il faiblit un peu

saga ['sɑːɡə] N *Liter* saga *f*; *Fam* **the continuing s. of our washing machine** le feuilleton de notre machine à laver

sagacious [sə'ɡeɪʃəs] ADJ *Fml (person, mind, remark etc)* sagace, avisé; *(action)* plein de sagesse

sagaciously [sə'ɡeɪʃəslɪ] ADV *Fml* avec sagacité

sagacity [sə'ɡæsɪtɪ] N *Fml (of person, remark)* sagacité *f*, perspicacité *f*

sage¹ [seɪdʒ] *Lit* ADJ *(person, conduct etc)* sage, prudent
N *(wise man)* philosophe *m*, sage *m*

sage² N **1** *Bot, Culin* sauge *f* **2** *(colour)* vert *m* cendré
▶▶ **s. green** vert cendré *inv*; **s. tea** tisane *f* de sauge

sagely ['seɪdʒlɪ] ADV *Lit* sagement, prudemment

sagging ['sæɡɪŋ] ADJ *(roof etc)* affaissé;

(gate etc) penché d'un côté; *(breast, cheek etc)* pendant; *(line etc)* courbe; *(rope)* lâche; *(prices, market, support etc)* en baisse; *(enthusiasm, demand)* fléchissant, faiblissant

Sagittarius [sædʒɪ'teərɪəs] N *Astron* Sagittaire *m*; **to be (a) S.** être (du) Sagittaire

sago ['seɪɡəʊ] N *Culin* sagou *m*
▸▸ *Bot* **s. palm** sagoutier *m*; *Culin* **s. pudding** sagou au lait

Sahara [sə'hɑːrə] N **the S. (Desert)** le Sahara

sahib ['sɑːɪb] N sahib *m*

said PT, PP *see* say VT, VI

sail [seɪl] N **1** *(on boat)* voile *f*; **square s.** voile carrée; **to hoist/lower a s.** hisser/amener une voile; **to make s.** *(set sail)* prendre la mer; *(spread sails)* hisser les voiles; **under s.** *(of ship)* sous voile(s), à la voile; **under full s.** toutes voiles dehors; **to set s.** prendre la mer; **to set s. for ...** partir pour ...; **s. ho!** voilier en vue!; **a fleet of twenty s.** une flotte de vingt voiles *ou* de vingt voiliers
2 *(journey)* traversée *f*; **it will be a three hours' s.** la traversée durera trois heures; **to go for a s.** faire de la voile
3 *(of windmill)* aile *f*, volant *m*, toile *f*
VI **1** *(of sailing ship)* faire voile; *(of any ship)* naviguer, faire route; *Sport* **do you s.?** est-ce que vous faites de la voile?; *Fig* **to s. (a bit) close to the wind** prendre des risques
2 *(start voyage)* prendre la mer; **we s. at noon** nous partons à midi
3 *(travel by sea)* voyager par mer; **to s. over the seas** parcourir les mers; **they sailed around the Mediterranean** ils ont fait le tour de la Méditerranée; **to s. round a cape** contourner un promontoire
4 *(of glider)* planer; **there were clouds sailing by** des nuages voguaient dans le ciel; **the ball/stone sailed through the air** le ballon/caillou vola; **his toupee went sailing out of the open window** son postiche s'est envolé par la fenêtre ouverte
5 to s. into a room entrer majestueusement dans une pièce; *Fam* **to s. through an examination** réussir un examen sans problèmes *ou Fam* les doigts dans le nez
VT *(sailing boat)* manœuvrer; *(ship)* piloter, commander; **to s. a toy boat on a pond** faire naviguer un petit bateau sur un bassin; **to s. the seas** parcourir les mers

sailboard ['seɪlbɔːd] *Sport* N planche *f* à voile
VI faire de la planche à voile *ou* du véliplanche

sailboarder ['seɪlbɔːdər] N *Sport* (véli)-planchiste *mf*

sailboarding ['seɪlbɔːdɪŋ] N *Sport* planche *f* à voile, véliplanchisme *m*

sailboat ['seɪlbəʊt] N *Am* voilier *m*, bateau *m* à voile

sailcloth ['seɪlklɒθ] N *Tex (for sails)* toile *f* à voile(s); *(for clothes)* toile

sailing ['seɪlɪŋ] N **1** *(activity) (in sailing ship, sailing boat)* navigation *f* à voile; *(in any ship)* navigation; *Sport* voile *f*; **to go s.** faire de la voile; *Fig* **it's (all) plain s.** cela va tout seul **2** *(departure)* départ *m*, appareillage *m*; **the 12 o'clock s.** le bateau de midi
▸▸ **s. boat** voilier *m*, bateau *m* (à voiles); **s. card** liste *f* des navires en partance; **s. orders** ordre *m* d'appareiller, instructions *fpl* pour l'appareillage; **s. schedule** horaires *mpl* de départ; **s. ship** (grand) voilier, navire *m* à voile *ou* à voiles

sailmaker ['seɪlmeɪkər] N voilier *m*

sailor ['seɪlər] N marin *m*; **to be a good s.** avoir le pied marin; **to be a bad s.** être sujet au mal de mer
▸▸ **s. hat** *(for boys)* béret *m* de marin; *(for women)* canotier *m*; **s. suit** costume *m* marin

sainfoin ['sænfɔɪn] N *(plant)* sainfoin *m*

saint [seɪnt] N **1** saint *m*, sainte *f*; **s.'s day** fête *f* de saint, fête patronale; **All Saints' (Day)** la Toussaint; *Fig* **I'm no s.** je ne suis pas un saint; *Fam* **to try the patience of a s.** lasser la patience d'un saint **2 the Communion of Saints** la Communion des Saints
▸▸ **S. Andrew's Day** La Saint-André *(fête nationale de l'Écosse, le 30 novembre)*; **S. Bernard** *(dog)* saint-bernard *m inv*; **S. David's Day** la Saint-David *(fête nationale du pays de Galles, le 1 mars)*; **S. George's Day** la Saint-Georges *(fête nationale de l'Angleterre, le 23 avril)*; **S. Helena** *(island)* Sainte-Hélène; **S. John the Baptist** saint Jean-Baptiste; **the S. Lawrence (River)** le (fleuve) Saint-Laurent; **S. Patrick's Day** la Saint-Patrick *(fête nationale d'Irlande, le 17 mars)*; **S. Pierre and Miquelon** Saint-Pierre-et-Miquelon; **S. Sylvester** Saint Sylvestre

---

Saint Patrick's Day

Patrick, le saint patron de l'Irlande, est célébré le 17 mars, qui est le jour de sa mort, en l'an 461. Saint Patrick convertit les Irlandais au christianisme et établit monastères, églises et écoles dans tout le pays. Selon la légende, il aurait également réussi à chasser tous les serpents d'Irlande. Chômée en Irlande, la St Patrick est également fêtée dans certaines villes américaines comptant une forte proportion de personnes d'origine irlandaise.

---

sainted ['seɪntɪd] ADJ *Old-fashioned Fam* **my s. aunt!** mes aïeux!

sainthood ['seɪnthʊd] N sainteté *f*

saintliness ['seɪntlɪnɪs] N sainteté *f*

saintly ['seɪntlɪ] ADJ *(life, action etc)* de saint; *Iron* **to put on a s. air** prendre un air de petit saint

sake¹ [seɪk] N **1 to do sth for the s. of sb** *or* **for sb's s.** faire qch pour qn *ou* par égard pour qn; **I forgive you for her s.** je vous pardonne par égard pour elle; **do it for the s. of your family** faites-le pour (l'amour de) votre famille; **they stayed together for the s. of the children** *or* **for the children's s.** ils sont restés ensemble à cause des enfants; **for all our sakes, tell no one** ne le dis à personne dans notre intérêt à tous; **do it for my s.** *(do it to please me)* faites-le pour me faire plaisir; **for God's s., for goodness' s., for heaven's s., for Pete's s., for pity's s.** pour l'amour de Dieu *ou* du ciel; **all for the s. of a few pence!** tout ça pour quelques malheureux pence!; **for the s. of peace** dans l'intérêt de la paix; **for old times' s.** en souvenir du passé; **for economy's s.** par économie; **art for art's s.** l'art pour l'art; **this is talking for talking's s.** *or* **for the s. of talking** c'est parler pour parler; **let's say, for the s. of argument** *or* **for argument's s. ...** admettons que ...; **you're just saying that for the s. of an argument** *or* **of arguing!** tu dis cela uniquement par provocation!
2 *Am Fam* **sakes alive!, sakes!** grand Dieu!, par exemple!

sake² ['sɑːkɪ] N *(drink)* saké *m*

sal [sæl] N
▸▸ **s. ammoniac** sel *m* ammoniac; **s. volatile** sel volatile, sels (anglais)

salaam [sə'lɑːm] *Fam* N salutation *f* (chez les musulmans)
VT & VI saluer

salacious [sə'leɪʃəs] ADJ *(story, person)* salace

salaciousness [sə'leɪʃəsnɪs] N *(of story, person)* salacité *f*

salad ['sæləd] N salade *f*; **cheese/ham s.** salade au fromage/jambon; **green s.** salade

(verte); **fruit s.** macédoine *f ou* salade de fruits
▸▸ **s. bar** *(restaurant)* = restaurant *m* où l'on mange des salades; *(area)* salad bar *m*; **s. bowl** saladier *m*; *Br* **s. cream** = sorte *f* de mayonnaise (vendue en bouteille); **s. days** années *fpl* de jeunesse; **s. dressing** sauce *f* *(pour salade)*; *(French dressing)* vinaigrette *f*; **s. oil** huile *f* pour assaisonnement; **s. spinner** essoreuse *f* à salade

salamander ['sæləmændər] N salamandre *f*

salami [sə'lɑːmɪ] N salami *m*

salaried ['sælərɪd] ADJ *Ind, Com* **1** *(personnel)* salarié **2** *(employment)* rémunéré
▸▸ **s. employee** salarié, -ée; **s. staff** salariés *mpl*

salary ['sælərɪ] N salaire *m*; *(of civil servant)* traitement *m*; **s. plus commission** salaire fixe plus commission
▸▸ **s. earner** salarié, -ée; **s. level** niveau *m* de rémunération *ou* de salaires; **s. scale** échelle *f* de salaires

salaryman, *pl* **salarymen** ['sælərɪmæn, -men] N employé *m* de bureau japonais

sale [seɪl] N **1** *(act, event)* vente *f*; **sales** *(turnover)* chiffre *m* d'affaires; **house for s.** maison à vendre; **business for s.** fonds à céder; **to put sth up for s.** mettre qch en vente; **on s.** *Br (available to buy)* en vente; *Am (at reduced price)* en solde; *Com* **s. at arrival/departure** vente à l'arrivée/au départ; **s. by private agreement** vente à l'amiable; **s. of stock** écoulement *m* de stocks; **s. or return basis** vente avec faculté de retour; **bill of s.** acte *m* de vente; **s. by auction, auction s.** vente aux enchères; *Law* **compulsory s.** adjudication *f* forcée
2 *Com (clearance)* **s.** *or* **sales** soldes *mpl*; **in the s.,** *Am* **on s.** *(article)* en solde; **I got it in a s.** je l'ai acheté en solde; **I got it in the sale(s)** je l'ai acheté pendant les soldes
▸▸ **sales acumen** sens *m* du commerce; **sales agent** agent *m* commercial; **s. agreement** compromis *m* de vente; **sales analysis** analyse *f* des ventes; **sales area** *(in store)* surface *f* de vente; *(district)* région *f* desservie; *Br* **sales assistant** vendeur, -euse; **sales audit** audit *m* de vente; **sales campaign** campagne *f* de vente; **sales commission** commission *f* de vente; **sales consultant** conseiller, -ère commercial(ale); **sales contract** contrat *m* de vente; **sales counter** comptoir *m* de vente; **sales department** service *m* commercial, service des ventes; **sales director** directeur, -trice des ventes; **sales drive** campagne de vente; **sales engineer** ingénieur *m* technico-commercial, ingénieur commercial, ingénieur des ventes; **sales figures** chiffre de vente; **sales floor** surface de vente; **sales force** force *f ou* équipe *f* de vente; **sales forecast** prévision *f* des ventes; **sales goal** objectif *m* de vente; **sales invoice** facture *f* de vente; *Acct* **sales ledger** grand livre *m* des ventes, journal *m* des ventes; **sales letter** lettre *f* de vente; **sales licence** licence *f* de vente; **sales literature** prospectus *mpl*; **sales manager** directeur, -trice commercial(ale), responsable *mf* des ventes; **sales and marketing** vente-marketing *f*; **sales and marketing department** service vente-marketing; **sales and marketing director** directeur, -trice des ventes et du marketing; **sales meeting** réunion *f* de représentants; **sales monopoly** monopole *m* de vente; **sales network** réseau *m* de vente; **sales objective** objectif de vente; **sales outlet** point *m* de vente; **sales pitch** arguments *mpl* de vente; *(verbal)* boniment *m*, argumentation *f*; **s. price** *(selling price)* prix *m* de vente; *(reduced price)* prix soldé; **sales promoter** promoteur, -trice de ventes; **sales promotion** promotion *f* des ventes, animation *f* des ventes; **sales quota** quota *m* de ventes; **sales rally** rallye *m* de sti-

mulation; **sales representative,** *Fam* **sales rep** représentant, -ante commercial(ale); *Am* **sales slip** ticket *m* de caisse; **sales target** objectif de vente; **sales tax** taxe *f* sur le chiffre d'affaires, TCA *f*; **sales team** équipe *f* de vente; **sales technician** agent technico-commercial; **sales technique** technique *f* de vente; **sales tool** instrument *m* de vente; **sales volume** volume *m* des ventes; *Mktg* **sales wave** vague *f* de vente; **s. of work** vente de charité

saleability [seɪlə'bɪlɪtɪ] N *Com* facilité *f* d'écoulement

saleable ['seɪləb(ə)l] ADJ *(goods etc)* vendable

saleroom ['seɪlru:m] N salle *f* de(s) vente(s)

salesclerk ['seɪlzklɑ:k] N *Am* vendeur, -euse

salesgirl ['seɪlzgɜ:l] N vendeuse *f*

salesman, *pl* **salesmen** ['seɪlzmən] N vendeur *m*; *(sales representative)* représentant *m* (de commerce)

salesmanship ['seɪlzmənʃɪp] N technique *f* de vente

salesperson, *pl* **salespeople** ['seɪlzpɜ:sən, -pi:p(ə)l] N **1** *(for company)* représentant, -ante (de commerce) **2** *(in shop)* vendeur, -euse

saleswoman, *pl* **saleswomen** ['seɪlzwʊmən, -wɪmɪn] N **1** *(for company)* représentante *f* (de commerce) **2** *(in shop)* vendeuse *f*

Salic law ['seɪlɪk] N *Hist* loi *f* salique

salient ['seɪlɪənt] ADJ **1** *(angle etc)* saillant **2** *(characteristic)* saillant, frappant; **the s. points of an argument** les points forts d'une argumentation
N *(in trench warfare etc)* saillant *m*

saline ['seɪlaɪn] ADJ *(spring, water)* salin, salé
N *Med (salt solution)* sérum *m* physiologique
▸▸ *Med* **s. drip** perfusion *f* saline; **s. solution** solution *f* saline

salinity [sə'lɪnɪtɪ] N salinité *f*

saliva [sə'laɪvə] N salive *f*

salivary [sə'laɪvərɪ] ADJ *(glands etc)* salivaire

salivate ['sælɪveɪt] VI *also Fig* saliver

salivation [sælɪ'veɪʃən] N salivation *f*

sallow[1] ['sæləʊ] N *(willow)* saule *m*

sallow[2] ADJ *(complexion)* jaunâtre

sallowness ['sæləʊnɪs] N *(of complexion)* ton *m* jaunâtre

Sally ['sælɪ] N *Br Fam* **the S. Army** l'Armée *f* du salut

sally ['sælɪ] N **1** *Mil* sortie *f*, *(excursion)* excursion *f*, sortie *f*; **his first s. into travel writing** sa première tentative de récit de voyage **2** *Old-fashioned* **s. (of wit)** boutade *f*, trait *m* d'esprit
▸ **sally forth, sally out** VI **1** *(go out)* sortir; *Hum (go for walk)* partir en promenade **2** *Mil* faire une sortie **3** *Lit (go out)* sortir; **young students who are now about to s. forth into the world** de jeunes étudiants sur le point de se lancer dans le monde

salmon ['sæmən] N *(usu inv in pl)* *(fish)* saumon *m*; **young s.** tacon *m*, saumoneau *m*
ADJ *(colour)* (rose *m*) saumon *m inv*
▸▸ **s. ladder, s. leap, s. pass** échelle *f* à saumon(s); **s. pink** (rose) saumon; **s. steak** darne *f* de saumon; **s. trout** truite *f* saumonée

salmonella [sælmə'nelə] N salmonelle *f*; **to have s. (poisoning)** avoir une salmonellose

salon ['sælɒn] N **1** *(of fashion designer, hairdresser etc)* salon *m*; *Art* **the S.** le Salon; **(beauty) s.** institut *m ou* salon de beauté; **hairdressing s.** salon de coiffure **2** *Liter* salon *m* **3** *(drawing room)* salon *m*

saloon [sə'lu:n] N **1** *Am (bar)* saloon *m*, bar *m*; **billiard s.** salle *f* de billard **2** *Naut (of steamship)* salon *m*; *(on yacht)* cabine *f* **3** *Br Aut (car)* berline *f*, **two-door s.** coach *m*; **four-door s.** berline
▸▸ *Br* **s. bar** salle de pub *(plus confortable que le bar principal)*; *Br Aut* **s. car** berline; *Am* **s. keeper** patron, -onne de saloon *ou* de bar

salopettes [sælə'pets] NPL *Ski (garment)* combinaison *f*

salsa ['sælsə] N **1** *(sauce)* salsa *f* méxicaine **2** *(music, dance)* salsa *f*

salsify ['sælsɪfɪ] N *(plant)* salsifis *m*

SALT [sɔ:lt] N *Mil (abbr* **Strategic Arms Limitation Talks)** SALT *m*
▸▸ **S. talks** négociations *fpl* SALT

salt [sɔ:lt] N **1** *(on roads)*, *Culin, Chem* sel *m*; **kitchen s.** gros sel; **rock s.** sel gemme; **sea s.** sel marin, sel de mer; **table s.** sel de table; **(bath) salts** sels de bain; *Old-fashioned* **(liver) salts** sels; **to take a story with a pinch** *or* **grain of s.** ne pas prendre une histoire au pied de la lettre; **he's not worth his s.** il ne vaut rien; **any athlete worth his/her s.** n'importe quel(elle) athlète digne de ce nom, n'importe quel athlète qui se respecte; *Old-fashioned* **to sit (at table) above/below the s.** être assis au haut bout/au bas bout de la table; *Fig* **to rub s. in the wound** remuer le couteau dans la plaie; *Fig* **the s. of the earth** le sel de la terre
2 *(interest)* **to add s. to sth** mettre un peu de sel à qch, mettre du piment à qch
3 *Naut Fam* **old s.** vieux loup *m* de mer
ADJ **1** *(food)* salé; **too s.** trop salé **2** *(rocks, ground)* salifère
VT **1** *(food)* saler **2** = **salt down**
▸▸ **s. beef** bœuf *m* salé; **s. cod** morue *f* salée; **s. flats** marais *m* salant; **s. lake** lac *m* salé; **s. lick** *(stone)* pierre *f* salée; **s. marsh** marais salant; **s. mine** mine *f* de sel; **s. pan** marais salant, salin *m*; **s. spoon** cuiller *f* à sel; *Hist* **s. tax** gabelle *f*; **s. water** eau *f* salée
▸ **salt away** VT SEP *(save) (money etc)* économiser, mettre en lieu sûr
▸ **salt down** VT SEP *(preserve with salt) (meat, fish etc)* saler

saltbox ['sɔ:ltbɒks] N boîte *f* à sel; *Am (house)* = maison *f* à toit penchant *(avec deux étages à l'avant et un étage à l'arrière)*

saltcellar ['sɔ:ltselər] N *(for salt)* salière *f*

salted ['sɔ:ltɪd] ADJ *(butter, herring etc)* salé

salt-free ADJ *(diet etc)* sans sel

saltine [sɔ:l'ti:n] N *Am Culin* biscuit *m* salé

saltiness ['sɔ:ltɪnɪs] N *(of water etc)* salinité *f*, *(of food etc)* salure *f*

salting ['sɔ:ltɪŋ] N *(of meat etc) (for preserving)* salaison *f*, *(for flavouring)* salage *m*

saltmill ['sɔ:ltmɪl] N moulin *m* à sel

saltpetre, *Am* **saltpeter** [sɔ:lt'pi:tər] N salpêtre *m*

saltwater ['sɔ:ltwɔ:tər] ADJ ATTRIB **s. fish** poisson *m* de mer

saltworks ['sɔ:ltwɜ:ks] N *(for sea salt)* salin *m*; *(for rock salt)* saline *f*, *(salt refinery)* raffinerie *f* de sel

saltwort ['sɔ:ltwɜ:t] N *Bot* **1** soude *f*, **prickly s.** kali *m* **2** *(salicornia)* salicorne *f*

salty ['sɔ:ltɪ] ADJ **1** *(taste, sauce, water etc)* salé **2** *Fam (anecdote, book)* piquant; *(licentious)* salé, corsé

salubrious [sə'lu:brɪəs] N *Fml* salubre, sain; *Fig* **one of his less than s. friends** un de ses amis pas très fréquentables

salubriousness [sə'lu:brɪəsnɪs] N *Fml* salubrité *f*

saluki [sə'lu:kɪ] N *(dog)* sloughi *m*

salutary ['sæljʊt(ə)rɪ] ADJ salutaire; **to have a s. effect on sb** faire du bien à qn

salutation [sæljʊ'teɪʃən] N *Fml* salutation *f*, *(in letter)* titre *m* de civilité; **in s.** en guise de salut

salute [sə'lu:t] N *Mil, Naut etc (gesture)* salut *m*; **to return sb's s.** rendre son salut à qn; **to take the s.** *(at march past)* passer les troupes en revue; **to fire a s.** tirer une salve; **to fire a ten-gun s.** saluer de dix coups
VT *(person)* saluer; *Lit* **to s. sb's achievements** saluer les exploits de qn; **I s. you** je te tire mon chapeau
VI *Mil, Naut* saluer, faire le salut militaire

salvage ['sælvɪdʒ] N **1** *(salvaging) (of ship etc)* sauvetage *m*; *(of waste material)* récupération *f* **2** *(objects salvaged)* objets *mpl* sauvés *(après une catastrophe)* **3** *(money)* indemnité *f ou* prime *f* de sauvetage; *(paid to salvage tug)* indemnité de remorquage
VT *(ship etc)* sauver; *(items from fire etc)* sauver, récupérer; *(car etc)* récupérer; *Fam (dish, essay etc)* rattraper; **to s. something from the ruins of one's career** sauver quelque chose de la faillite qu'a été sa carrière; **salvaged goods** matériel *m* récupéré
▸▸ **s. company** = compagnie *f* spécialisée dans le remorquage et le renflouage de navires; **s. tug** remorqueur *m* *(pour les sauvetages)*; **s. vessel** navire *m* de relevage

salvation [sæl'veɪʃən] N salut *m*; **to work out one's own s.** travailler à son (propre) salut; **you've been my s.** vous m'avez sauvé; **beyond s.** irrécupérable
▸▸ **the S. Army** l'Armée *f* du salut

salvationist [sæl'veɪʃənɪst] N salutiste *mf*

salve [sælv, sɑ:v] N *Pharm* baume *m*, onguent *m*; *Fig* baume
VT *Fml* adoucir, apaiser; *(conscience)* soulager

salver ['sælvər] N *(tray)* plateau *m* *(en argent etc)*

salvia ['sælvɪə] N *(plant)* sauge *f* (ornementale)

salvo ['sælvəʊ] N *Mil, Naut, Fig* salve *f*; **to fire a s.** tirer une salve; **s. of applause** salve d'applaudissements

SAM [sæm] N *Mil (abbr* **surface-to-air missile)** missile *m* sol-air

Samaritan [sə'mærɪt(ə)n] ADJ samaritain
N Samaritain, -aine; *Bible* **the Good S.** le bon Samaritain; **to be a good S.** se conduire en bon Samaritain; **the Samaritans** *(telephone service)* ≃ SOS *m* Amitié

samba ['sæmbə] N *(dance)* samba *f*
VI danser la samba

sambo ['sæmbəʊ] N *Offensive, Sl* bougnoul *m*

SAME [seɪm] ADJ même; **at the s. time that ...** au moment même où ...; **he's the s. age as me** il est du même âge que moi; **in the s. way** de la même façon; **we are going the s. way** nous allons dans la même direction; **do you still feel the s. way?** est-ce que vos sentiments sont toujours les mêmes?; **she's still the s. (old)** Sarah c'est toujours notre bonne vieille Sarah; **one and the s. thing** une seule et même chose; **the very s. thing** tout à fait *ou* exactement la même chose; **the** *or* **that very s. day** le jour même; **the very s. situation** la même situation exactement; **it is always/it is no longer the s. thing** c'est toujours/ce n'est plus la même chose; **it all amounts** *or* **comes to the s. thing** tout cela revient au même; *Fam* **it's the s. difference** c'est bonnet blanc et blanc bonnet; **at the s. time** en même temps; *(at once)* à la fois, du même coup; **that s. man is now a millionaire** ce même homme est maintenant millionnaire
PRON **the s.** le même, la même, *pl* les mêmes; *Fml (that one)* celui-là même, celle-là même, *pl* ceux-là mêmes, celles-là mêmes;

it's the s. everywhere c'est la même chose *ou* c'est pareil *ou Fml* il en est de même partout; it's all the s., it's just the s. c'est exactement la même chose, *Fam* c'est tout comme; if it's all the s. to you si cela ne vous fait rien, si ça vous est égal; it's much the s. c'est à peu près la même chose; low-alcohol lager just isn't the s. la bière à faible teneur en alcool, ça n'est tout simplement pareil *ou* pas la même chose; the house isn't the s. without her la maison n'est pas pareille sans elle; he had an accident and he's never been the s. since il a eu un accident et il n'est plus le même depuis; *Fam* (the) s. again? *(whisky etc)* encore un?; *Fam* s. again! remettez ça!; *Fam* s. here! et moi aussi!, et moi de même!; a Happy New Year to you! – (the) s. to you! je vous souhaite une bonne année! – vous de même!; *Fam* (the) s. to you, you bastard! toi pareil, espèce de salaud!; I would have done the s. j'aurais fait la même chose *ou* de même, j'aurais agi de la même façon

ADV the s. de la même façon; to think/feel/act the s. penser/sentir/agir de même; they taste all the s. ils ont tous le même goût; all these houses look the s. to me je trouve que ces maisons se ressemblent toutes; all her songs sound the s. toutes ses chansons se ressemblent; all the s. *(nevertheless)* quand même, tout de même; when I am away, things go on just the s. quand je suis absent, tout continue à marcher comme d'habitude

same-day delivery N *Com* livraison *f* le jour même

same-day value N *Banking* valeur *f* jour

sameness ['seɪmnɪs] N **1** *(being identical)* identité *f*, similitude *f* **2** *(monotony)* monotonie *f*

samey ['seɪmɪ] ADJ *Fam* monotone

Samoa [sə'məʊə] N Samoa *m*

Samoan [sə'məʊən] N **1** *(person)* Samoan, -ane **2** *(language)* samoan *m*
▪ ADJ samoan

samosa [sə'məʊsə] N samosa *m*

samovar ['sæməvɑ:r] N samovar *m*

sampan ['sæmpæn] N *(boat)* sampan(g) *m*

sample ['sɑ:mp(ə)l] N **1** *Com etc (of cloth etc)* échantillon *m*; *(of ore, blood, urine)* prélèvement *m*; a s. of one's work un échantillon de son travail; *Com* up to s. pareil *ou* conforme à l'échantillon; *Com* not up to s. non conforme à l'échantillon; to take a s. faire un prélèvement; to take a blood s. faire une prise de sang **2** *Mus* sample *m*
▪ VT **1** *(wine, dish)* goûter à, déguster; *(experience)* essayer **2** *Mktg (public opinion)* sonder **3** *Mus* échantillonner, sampler
▪ VI *Mus* échantillonner, sampler
▪▪s. book catalogue *m* d'échantillons; s. card carte *f* d'échantillons; *Mktg* s. survey enquête *f* par sondage

sampler ['sɑ:mplər] N **1** *Sewing* = modèle *m* de broderie **2** *Mus (equipment)* échantillonneur *m*

sampling ['sɑ:mplɪŋ] N **1** prélèvement *m ou* prise *f* d'échantillons, échantillonnage *m*; *(of food, wine etc)* dégustation *f*, *Com, Ind* random s. prélèvement d'échantillons au hasard **2** *Mus* sampling *m*
▪▪s. error erreur *f* d'échantillonnage

samurai ['sæmʊraɪ] N INV samouraï *m*

San Andreas Fault [sænæn'dreɪəs-] N the S. la faille de San Andreas *(faille géologique à l'origine de nombreux tremblements de terre en Californie)*

sanatorium, *pl* **sanatoriums, sanatoria** [sænə'tɔ:rɪəm, -ɪəmz, -ɪə] N sanatorium *m*

sanctification [sæŋ(k)tɪfɪ'keɪʃən] N sanctification *f*

sanctified ['sæŋ(k)tɪfaɪd] ADJ *(person)* sanctifié; *(thing)* consacré

sanctify ['sæŋ(k)tɪfaɪ] VT **1** *(person, thing)* sanctifier; *(day, land etc)* consacrer **2** sanctified by time consacré par le temps

sanctimonious [sæŋ(k)tɪ'məʊnɪəs] ADJ d'une piété suffisante; *(air)* de petit saint; don't be so s. ne sois pas si moralisateur

sanctimoniously [sæŋ(k)tɪ'məʊnɪəslɪ] ADV d'un air de petit saint

sanction ['sæŋ(k)ʃən] N **1** *Law (punitive)* s. sanction *f* (pénale); *Pol* to impose (economic) sanctions on a country prendre des sanctions économiques contre un pays; accused of sanctions busting accusé de ne pas respecter des sanctions *(contre un pays, une organisation etc)* **2** *Fml (consent)* sanction *f*, autorisation *f*; without their s. sans leur consentement
▪ VT **1** *Law (ratify) (law etc)* ratifier **2** *(authorize)* sanctionner, autoriser; sanctioned by usage consacré par l'usage

sanctity ['sæŋ(k)tɪtɪ] N **1** *Rel (of person, life etc)* sainteté *f* **2** *(of land, oath etc)* caractère *m* sacré; *(of private life etc)* inviolabilité *f*

sanctuary ['sæŋ(k)tjʊərɪ] N **1** *Rel (place)* sanctuaire *m* **2** *(refuge)* sanctuaire *m*, refuge *m*; to take s. trouver asile **3** *(for birds)* refuge *m*; wildlife s. réserve *f* zoologique

sanctum ['sæŋ(k)təm] N *Rel, Fig (room etc)* sanctuaire *m*

Sanctus ['sæŋ(k)təs] N *Rel, Mus* sanctus *m*

sand [sænd] N sable *m*; the coast offers mile after mile of shining sands la côte vous offre des kilomètres de sable doré; *Constr, Fig* to build on s. bâtir sur le sable; on the sand(s) *(on the beach)* sur la plage; *(on sandbank)* sur un banc de sable; *Prov* the sands of time are running out for us nous n'aurons bientôt plus le temps, le temps qui nous est imparti sera bientôt écoulé
▪ VT **1** *(with sandpaper) (make smoother)* poncer; *(remove paint, varnish from)* décaper au papier de verre **2** *(cover with sand) (pathway etc)* sabler; *(floor)* répandre du sable sur
▪▪s. bar ensablement *m*; s. castle château *m* de sable; s. dune dune *f*, *Zool* s. eel lançon *m*, équille *f*, *Zool* s. flea *(sandhopper)* puce *f* de mer, talitre *m*; *(chigoe)* chique *f*, s. hopper *(crustacean)* puce de mer; *Br Orn* s. martin hirondelle *f* de rivage; *Am Golf* s. trap bunker *m* (de sable)

▸ **sand down** VT SEP = **sand** VT **1**

sandal ['sænd(ə)l] N sandale *f*

sandalwood ['sænd(ə)lwʊd] N (bois *m* de) santal *m*

sandbag ['sændbæg] N *Mil etc* sac *m* de sable
▪ VT (-gg-) **1** *Mil (building)* protéger avec des sacs de sable **2** *(hit)* assommer *(d'un coup de gourdin sur la nuque)*

sandbank ['sændbæŋk] N banc *m* de sable

sandblast ['sændblɑ:st] VT décaper au jet de sable, sabler

sandblasting ['sændblɑ:stɪŋ] N *(of surface)* décapage *m ou* décapement *m* au (jet de) sable

sandboy ['sændbɔɪ] N as happy as a s. gai comme un pinson, heureux comme un poisson dans l'eau

sander ['sændər] N *(tool)* ponceuse *f*

sandglass ['sændglɑ:s] N sablier *m*

Sandhurst ['sændhɜːst] N *Br Mil* ≃ Saint-Cyr

sanding ['sændɪŋ] N **1** *(with sandpaper) (smoothing)* ponçage *m*; *(removal of paint, varnish)* décapage *m* au papier de verre **2** *(spreading of sand)* sablage *m*
▪▪s. disc disque *m* en papier de verre; s. down *(smoothing)* ponçage; *(removal of paint, varnish)* décapage *m* au papier de verre

sandman ['sændmæn] N *Fig* marchand *m* de sable

sandpail ['sændpeɪl] N *Am* seau *m* *(pour faire des châteaux de sable)*

sandpaper ['sændpeɪpər] N papier *m* de verre
▪ VT frotter *ou* poncer au papier de verre

sandpiper ['sændpaɪpər] N *(bird)* bécasseau *m*

sandpit ['sændpɪt] N sablière *f*, sablonnière *f*, carrière *f* de sable; *(for children)* bac *m* à sable

sandshoes ['sændʃu:z] NPL *Br* rythmiques *fpl*

sandstone ['sændstəʊn] N grès *m*; s. buildings bâtiments *mpl* en grès

sandstorm ['sændstɔ:m] N tempête *f* de sable

sandwich ['sændwɪtʃ] N sandwich *m*, *pl* sandwichs, sandwiches; *Culin (cake)* génoise *f* fourrée; ham/cheese s. sandwich au jambon/fromage; open s. canapé *m*; *Am* hero *or* submarine s. gros sandwich coupé dans une baguette; *Br Fam Hum* to be one s. short of a picnic ne pas être net
▪ VT intercaler (between entre), *Fam* coincer (between entre); to be sandwiched between two people être coincé entre *ou Fam* pris en sandwich entre deux personnes
▪▪*Br* s. bar ≃ snack *m (où on vend des sandwichs)*; s. board panneau *m* publicitaire *(porté par un homme-sandwich)*; *Culin* s. cake génoise fourrée; *Br* s. course = stage *m* de formation professionnelle en alternance; s. filling garniture *f*, S. Islands îles *fpl* Sandwich; s. loaf ≃ pain *m* de mie; s. man homme-sandwich *m*, *pl* hommes-sandwichs; s. toaster appareil *m* à croque-monsieur

sandy ['sændɪ] ADJ **1** *(earth etc)* sableux, sablonneux; *(path)* sablonneux, de sable; *(beach)* de sable; are the beaches s.? est-ce que ce sont des plages de sable?; s. bottom *(of river, sea)* fond de sable; my hair is all s. *(full of sand)* mes cheveux sont pleins de sable **2** *(in colour) (hair etc)* roux pâle *inv*, blond roux *inv*

sane [seɪn] ADJ *(person)* sain d'esprit; *(views, speech etc)* raisonnable, sensé; to be s. *(of person)* avoir toute sa raison

sanely ['seɪnlɪ] ADV raisonnablement; he spoke quite s. il a dit des choses très sensées

sang PT *see* sing

sang-froid [sɒŋ'frwɑ:] N sang-froid *m inv*

sanguinary ['sæŋgwɪnərɪ] ADJ *Lit (battle)* sanglant; *(tyrant)* sanguinaire

sanguine ['sæŋgwɪn] ADJ *Lit* **1** *(complexion etc)* d'un rouge sanguin, rubicond **2** *(person, disposition etc)* confiant, optimiste (about quant à); to be of a s. disposition être porté à l'optimisme

> Note that the French adjective **sanguin** is a false friend and is never a translation for the English adjective **sanguine**.

sanguinely ['sæŋgwɪnlɪ] ADV avec confiance, avec optimisme

sanitarium [sænɪ'teərɪəm] N *Am* = **sanatorium**

sanitary ['sænɪt(ə)rɪ] ADJ hygiénique, sanitaire
▪▪s. disposal bag sachet *m* pour garniture périodique; s. engineer technicien, -ienne du service sanitaire; s. inspector inspecteur, -trice de la santé publique; *Am* s. napkin, s. pad, *Br* s. towel serviette *f* hygiénique; s. ware appareils *mpl* sanitaires

sanitation [sænɪ'teɪʃən] N *(system)* système *m* sanitaire; the s. here is appalling les conditions sanitaires ici sont affreuses; there's no s. in the camps il n'y a pas d'installations sanitaires dans les camps

sanitize ['sænɪtaɪz] VT *esp Am (clean)* aseptiser; *(sterilize)* stériliser; *Fig (document, novel etc)* expurger

sanity ['sænɪtɪ] N **1** *(of person)* santé *f* mentale; **there are doubts about his s.** on se demande s'il est sain d'esprit **2** *(of plan, policy etc)* bon sens *m*

sanserif [sæn'serɪf] *Typ* N caractères *mpl* sans empattement
   ADJ sans empattement

Sanskrit ['sænskrɪt] ADJ, N *Ling* sanscrit *m*, sanskrit *m*

Santa, Santa Claus ['sæntə(klɔːz)] N le père Noël

sap¹ [sæp] N **1** *(of plant)* sève *f*; **the s. is rising** la sève monte; *Fig* **to feel the s. rising** être tout ragaillardi **2** *Fam (gullible person)* poire *f*, *(idiot)* andouille *f*

sap² N *Mil etc (trench)* sape *f*
   VT (-pp-) *Mil, Fig* saper, miner; **the fever has sapped (him of) his strength** la fièvre l'a miné

sap³ N *Am (cosh)* gourdin *m*

saphead ['sæphed] N *Am Fam* andouille *f*

sapless ['sæplɪs] ADJ *(plant, wood)* sans sève, desséché

sapling ['sæplɪŋ] N *(young tree)* jeune arbre *m*

sapper ['sæpər] N *Mil* sapeur *m*; *(in charge of laying mines)* mineur *m*; *Fam* **the sappers** le génie

sapphic ['sæfɪk] ADJ *(in prosody)* saphique; *Lit (lesbian)* saphique
   ▸▸ *Old-fashioned* **s. vice** saphisme *m*

sapphire ['sæfaɪər] N **1** *(precious stone)* saphir *m* **2** *(colour)* (couleur *f* de) saphir *m*
   ADJ *(in colour)* (couleur de) saphir *inv*

sappiness ['sæpɪnɪs] N *(of tree etc)* abondance *f* de sève, teneur *f* en sève

sappy ['sæpɪ] ADJ **1** *(tree etc)* plein de sève; *(timber)* vert **2** *Old-fashioned Fam (stupid)* bête, stupide

saraband ['særəbænd] N *(dance, music)* sarabande *f*

Saracen ['særəs(ə)n] *Hist* ADJ sarrasin
   N Sarrasin, -ine

sarcasm ['saːkæz(ə)m] N *(characteristic, remark)* sarcasme *m*; **his constant s.** ses sarcasmes continuels

sarcastic [saː'kæstɪk] ADJ sarcastique; **a s. remark** un sarcasme, une remarque sarcastique

sarcastically [saː'kæstɪklɪ] ADV d'une manière sarcastique

sarcoma [saː'kəʊmə] N *Med* sarcome *m*

sarcophagus, *pl* **sarcophagi** [saː'kɒfəgəs, -fədʒaɪ] N sarcophage *m*

sardine [saː'diːn] N *(fish)* sardine *f*; **the passengers were packed in like sardines** les passagers étaient serrés comme des sardines
   ▸▸ **s. boat** sardinier *m*

Sardinia [saː'dɪnɪə] N Sardaigne *f*

Sardinian [saː'dɪnɪən] ADJ sarde
   N **1** Sarde *mf* **2** *Ling* sarde *m*

sardonic [saː'dɒnɪk] ADJ *(expression, laugh)* sardonique

sardonically [saː'dɒnɪklɪ] ADV d'une manière sardonique, sardoniquement

sarge [saːdʒ] N *Mil Fam* sergent *m*

sari ['saːrɪ] N *(garment)* sari *m*

Sark [saːk] N *(île f* de) Sercq

sarky ['saːkɪ] ADJ *Fam* sarcastique

sarnie ['saːnɪ] N *Br Fam* casse-croûte *m inv*, casse-dalle *m inv*

sarong [sə'rɒŋ] N *(garment)* sarong *m*

SARS [saːz] N *Med* SRAS *m*

sarsaparilla [saːsəpə'rɪlə] N *(plant)* salsepareille *f*, *(drink)* boisson *f* à la salsepareille

sartorial [saː'tɔːrɪəl] ADJ *Fml (matters, taste)* vestimentaire; *(trade)* de tailleur; **s. elegance** élégance *f* vestimentaire; *Fam* **he is a s. disaster area** il n'a aucun sens de l'élégance vestimentaire

SAS [eseɪ'es] N *Br Mil (abbr* **special air service**) ≃ GIGN *m*

SASE [eseɪes'iː] N *Am (abbr* **self-addressed stamped envelope**) enveloppe *f* timbrée libellée à ses nom et adresse

sash¹ [sæʃ] N *(on dress)* large ceinture *f* à nœud bouffant; *(worn by officer)* écharpe *f*

sash² N *Constr (of window)* châssis *m* à guillotine
   ▸▸ **s. window** fenêtre *f* à guillotine

sashay ['sæʃeɪ] VI *Am Fam* **he sashayed across to the bar** *(walked affectedly)* il s'est approché du bar avec une nonchalance affectée; **I'll just s. down to Joe's place** *(go)* je vais juste faire un tour chez Joe

sashcord ['sæʃkɔːd] N corde *f* de fenêtre

sashimi ['sæʃɪmɪ] N sashimi *m*

Sask *abbr* **Saskatchewan**

sasquatch ['sæskwætʃ] N = géant *m* des légendes du Nord-Ouest des États-Unis et du Sud-Ouest du Canada

sass [sæs] VT *Am Fam (be insolent to)* répondre à

Sassenach ['sæsənæk] *Scot Hum or Pej* N Anglais, -aise
   ADJ anglais

sassy ['sæsɪ] ADJ *Am Fam* effronté, insolent

Sat *abbr* **Saturday**

sat PT, PP *see* **sit**

Satan ['seɪt(ə)n] N Satan *m*

satanic [sə'tænɪk] ADJ satanique, diabolique

satanically [sə'tænɪklɪ] ADV sataniquement, diaboliquement

satanism ['seɪtənɪz(ə)m] N satanisme *m*

satanist ['seɪtənɪst] N sataniste *mf*

satay ['sæteɪ] N *Culin* satay *m*
   ▸▸ **s. sauce** sauce *f* satay

satchel ['sætʃəl] N sacoche *f*, *Sch* cartable *m*

sate [seɪt] VT **1** *Fml (hunger)* rassasier, assouvir; *(desire etc)* assouvir; *(person)* rassasier **2** = **satiate**

sateen [sə'tiːn] N *Tex* satinette *f*, satin *m* de coton

satellite ['sætəlaɪt] N **1** *(natural, man-made)* satellite *m*; **artificial s.** satellite artificiel; **manned/unmanned s.** satellite habité/non habité; **(tele)communications s.** satellite de télécommunications; **meteorological** *or* **weather s.** satellite météorologique; **to watch sth on s.** regarder qch sur satellite **2** *(town)* ville *f* satellite; *(state)* (État *m*) satellite *m*
   ▸▸ **s. antenna** antenne *f* satellite; **s. broadcast** émission *f* retransmise par satellite; **s. broadcasting** retransmission *f* par satellite; **s. channel** chaîne *f* par satellite; **s. communication system** système *m* de communication par satellite; **s. dish** antenne parabolique; **s. link** liaison *f* par satellite; **s. network** réseau *m* satellite; **s. photo** photo *f* satellite; **s. picture** photo satellite; *Met* animation *f* satellite; **s. speaker** enceinte *f* satellite; **s. state** (État) satellite; **s. station** station *f* satellite; **s. television** télévision *f* par satellite; **s. town** ville satellite; **s. transmission** transmission *f* par satellite; **s. transponder** transpondeur *m* satellite; **s. uplink** liaison *f* par satellite

satiate ['seɪʃɪeɪt] VT *Fml* rassasier (**with** de)

satiated ['seɪʃɪeɪtɪd] ADJ *Fml (with food)* rassasié; *(with pleasure)* comblé

satiation [seɪʃɪ'eɪʃən] N *Fml* **1** *(process)* assouvissement *m* **2** *(state)* satiété *f*; **to reach (a point of) s.** *(when eating, drinking)* être rassasié; **to eat until one has reached (a point of) s.** manger à satiété

satiety [sə'taɪɪtɪ] N = **satiation 2**

satin ['sætɪn] N *Tex* satin *m*; **s. paper** papier *m* satiné
   ▸▸ **s. finish** *(of paper etc)* apprêt *m* satiné; **s. flower** stellaire *f*

satinette [sætɪ'net] N *Tex* satinette *f*

satire ['sætaɪər] N satire *f*; **a s. on sth** une satire de qch

satirical [sə'tɪrɪk(ə)l] ADJ satirique

satirically [sə'tɪrɪklɪ] ADV satiriquement

satirist ['sætɪrɪst] N *(writer)* satiriste *mf*; *(comedian)* chansonnier, -ière, comédien, -ienne satirique

satirize ['sætɪraɪz] VT faire la satire de; *(in literature)* satiriser

satisfaction [sætɪs'fækʃən] N **1** *(pleasure)* satisfaction *f*, contentement *m* (**at, with** de); **to have the s. of doing sth** avoir la satisfaction de faire qch; **it gives me great s. to know that …** je suis très satisfait d'apprendre que …; **to one's complete s.** à la satisfaction totale; *Com* **s. or your money back** remboursement garanti; *Com* **s. guaranteed** satisfaction garantie **2** *(act) (of creditor)* désintéressement *m*; *(of condition)* accomplissement *m*; *(of hunger, desire)* assouvissement *m*; **to demand s.** *(in duel)* demander réparation

satisfactorily [sætɪs'fækt(ə)rɪlɪ] ADV de manière *ou* de façon satisfaisante

satisfactory [sætɪs'fækt(ə)rɪ] ADJ satisfaisant; *(pupil)* qui donne satisfaction; **the result is not very s.** le résultat n'est pas très satisfaisant *ou* laisse à désirer; **to bring negotiations to a s. conclusion** mener à bien des négociations; *Med* **the patient is s.** *or* **in a s. condition** l'état du malade est satisfaisant

> Attention: ne pas confondre avec **satisfying**.

satisfied ['sætɪsfaɪd] ADJ *(customer etc)* content, satisfait (**with** de); *Iron* **not s. with that, she then broke the other chair** comme ça ne lui suffisait pas, elle a cassé l'autre chaise

satisfy ['sætɪsfaɪ] VT **1** *(make happy)* satisfaire, contenter; *Sch* **to s. the examiners** *(of examinee)* être reçu à l'examen; **(in order) to s. your curiosity** pour satisfaire votre curiosité **2** *(convince)* convaincre, assurer; **I am satisfied that he was telling the truth** je suis convaincu *ou* persuadé *ou* sûr qu'il disait la vérité **3** *(creditors)* désintéresser; *(condition)* remplir; *Math (equation)* satisfaire à; *(sb's honour)* faire réparation à, satisfaire à; **to s. demand** satisfaire à la demande

satisfying ['sætɪsfaɪɪŋ] ADJ *(job, outcome, evening)* satisfaisant; *(meal)* substantiel

> Attention: ne pas confondre avec **satisfactory**.

satsuma [sæt'suːmə] N satsuma *f*

saturate ['sætʃəreɪt] VT **1** *(soak)* imprégner, saturer (**with** de) **2** *Chem, Phys (solution)* saturer; *Com* **to s. the market** saturer le marché

saturated ['sætʃəreɪtɪd] ADJ **1** *(ground, clothing etc)* détrempé, saturé d'eau; **to become s. with sth** s'imprégner de qch; *Fig* être saturé de qch; *Com* **the market is s.** le marché est saturé **2** *Chem, Phys (solution, compound etc)* saturé, intense **3** *(colour)* saturé, intense
   ▸▸ **s. fat** graisse *f* saturée

saturation [ˌsætʃəˈreɪʃən] N imprégnation f, saturation f; Chem, Phys saturation; **the media's s. coverage of the affair** la couverture médiatique outrancière de l'affaire

▸▸ **s. bombing** bombardement m intensif; **s. point** point m de saturation; **the market has reached s. point** le marché est saturé, le marché est arrivé à saturation

Saturday [ˈsætədɪ] N samedi m; **S. 14 June** samedi 14 juin; **S. morning/evening** samedi matin/soir; **it's S. today** nous sommes samedi aujourd'hui; **he comes on Saturdays** il vient le samedi; **he's coming on S.** il vient samedi; **every S.** tous les samedis VOIR GRAMMAIRE A81–2; B61–2

Saturn [ˈsætɜːn] N Astron Saturne f; Myth Saturne m

saturnalia [ˌsætəˈneɪlɪə] N saturnales fpl

saturnine [ˈsætənaɪn] ADJ Lit (gloomy) taciturne, sombre

saturnism [ˈsætənɪz(ə)m] N Med saturnisme m

satyr [ˈsætər] N Myth etc satyre m

sauce [sɔːs] N **1** Culin sauce f, **tomato s.** sauce tomate; **white s.** sauce blanche ou béchamel; **caper s.** sauce aux câpres; Prov **what's s. for the goose is s. for the gander** ce qui est bon pour l'un l'est aussi pour l'autre **2** Old-fashioned Fam (impudence) culot m, toupet m **3** Fam (alcohol) alcool m, bibine f; **to hit the s.** se mettre à picoler; **to be on the s.** s'être remis à picoler; **to be off the s.** être au régime sec

▸▸ **s. boat** saucière f

sauced [sɔːst] ADJ Fam (drunk) bourré, pété

saucepan [ˈsɔːspən] N casserole f, **double s.** bain-marie m, pl bains-marie

▸▸ **s. lid** couvercle m de casserole

saucer [ˈsɔːsər] N soucoupe f, **flying s.** soucoupe volante; Fam **eyes like saucers** yeux comme des soucoupes

saucily [ˈsɔːsɪlɪ] ADV Fam (in risqué manner) d'un air coquin

sauciness [ˈsɔːsɪnɪs] N Fam **1** (impertinence) impertinence f **2** (risqué quality) (of joke, nightdress etc) côté m coquin

saucy [ˈsɔːsɪ] ADJ Fam **1** (impertinent) impertinent, effronté **2** (risqué) (person, joke, nightdress etc) coquin; Old-fashioned **s. little hat** petit chapeau coquet

Saudi [ˈsaʊdɪ] ADJ saoudien
N Fam **1** (person) Saoudien, -ienne **2** (country) Arabie f séoudite ou saoudite

Saudi Arabia N Arabie f saoudite

Saudi Arabian N Saoudien, -ienne
ADJ saoudien

sauerkraut [ˈsaʊəkraʊt] N choucroute f

sauna [ˈsɔːnə] N sauna m

saunter [ˈsɔːntər] N balade f, **to go for a s. in the park** aller se balader dans le parc; **at a s.** (to arrive) tranquillement
VI to s. (along) se balader; **to s. along** or **down the street** descendre la rue en flânant; **to s. up to sb** s'approcher de qn tranquillement; **she sauntered in, half an hour late** elle est arrivée tranquillement, une demi-heure en retard; **she sauntered past as if nothing had happened** elle est passée d'un pas tranquille comme si elle ne s'était rien passé

saurian [ˈsɔːrɪən] ADJ, N (reptile) saurien m

sausage [ˈsɒsɪdʒ] N Culin (fresh) saucisse f; (preserved, hard, dry) saucisson m; Br Fig Fam **not a s.** que dalle; **I was left without a s.** il ne me restait que dalle; Fam Hum **you silly s.!** que tu es bête ou nigaud!

▸▸ Br Fam **s. dog** saucisse f à pattes, teckel m; **s. roll** = sorte f de friand à la saucisse; **s. skin** boyau m

sausagemeat [ˈsɒsɪdʒmiːt] N chair f à saucisse

sauté [ˈsəʊteɪ] ADJ sauté
N sauté m
VT (faire) sauter
▸▸ **s. potatoes** pommes fpl de terre sautées

sautéed [ˈsəʊteɪd] ADJ sauté

savage [ˈsævɪdʒ] ADJ **1** (fierce) (animal, criticism) féroce; (blow) brutal, -aux, féroce; (person) enragé; **to make a s. attack on sb** attaquer sauvagement qn **2** (primitive) (people, custom etc) sauvage, barbare
N sauvage mf
VT **1** (attack physically) (of animal) attaquer sauvagement **2** (criticize) (person, play) éreinter; (proposal, plan) critiquer violemment

savagely [ˈsævɪdʒlɪ] ADV (to beat, attack) sauvagement, férocement; (to criticize) violemment

savageness [ˈsævɪdʒnɪs], **savagery** [ˈsævɪdʒ(ə)rɪ] N (fierceness) (of animal, blow, attack, criticism) férocité f

savanna(h) [səˈvænə] N savane f

SAVE [seɪv]

VT	sauver **1** ▪ garder **2** ▪ mettre de côté **2** ▪ économiser **2, 3** ▪ sauvegarder **5**
VI	économiser, épargner
N	arrêt
PREP	sauf, à l'exception de

VT **1** (rescue) (person, animal) sauver; **to s. sb's life** sauver la vie à ou de qn; Fig **she can't run to s. her life** elle est incapable de courir; Fig **to s. one's (own) neck** or **skin** sauver sa peau; **the doctors could not s. him** les médecins n'ont pas pu le sauver; **to s. sb from falling** empêcher qn de tomber; **this saved us from financial disaster** ça nous a sauvé d'une catastrophe financière; Ftbl etc **to s. a goal** arrêter le ballon; Sport **to s. the game** sauver le match; **to s. the situation** sauver la situation; Rel **to s. one's soul** sauver son âme; **to s. sth from a fire** récupérer qch des décombres d'un incendie; **God s. the King/the Queen!** vive le Roi/la Reine!

2 (keep for future) (old jars, old wrapping paper etc) garder, mettre de côté; (money) économiser, épargner, mettre de côté; (collect) (stamps, cigarette coupons, petrol vouchers etc) collectionner; **I s. £100 a month in a special account** j'économise 100 livres par mois sur un compte spécial; **how much money have you got saved?** combien d'argent avez-vous mis de côté?; **I'm saving this one for later** je garde celui-ci pour plus tard; **to s. oneself for sth** se réserver pour qch; **s. a dance for me** réservez-moi une danse

3 (not waste) (money, work etc) économiser; (expenditure, effort) éviter; (space) gagner; **to s. time** gagner du temps, économiser du temps; **I am saving my strength** je me ménage, je ménage mes forces; **I might as well have saved my breath** j'aurais mieux fait d'économiser ma salive; **I saved £10 by buying it there** j'ai économisé dix livres en l'achetant là; **s. pounds on washing machines** faites des économies sur l'achat d'une machine à laver

4 (spare) **to s. sb sth** éviter ou épargner qch à qn; **this has saved him a great deal of expense/trouble** cela lui a évité ou épargné beaucoup de dépense/peine; **this will s. us having to do it again** ça nous évitera de devoir le refaire; **to s. sb the trouble of doing sth** éviter ou épargner à qn la peine de faire qch; **to s. sb from sth** épargner qch à qn; **to s. sb from doing sth** épargner à qn la peine de faire qch

5 Comput sauvegarder; **to s. sth to disk** sauvegarder qch sur disquette

VI (save money) économiser, épargner; **I've never been able to s.** je n'ai jamais pu éco-

nomiser ou épargner; **they are saving for their holiday/a new car** ils économisent pour leurs vacances/pour acheter une voiture neuve; **s. on heating costs by insulating your house** économisez sur vos frais de chauffage en isolant votre maison
N Ftbl arrêt m; **to make a s.** arrêter la balle
PREP Arch, Lit sauf, excepté, à l'exception de
CONJ Arch, Lit **s. that ...** sauf que ..., excepté que ...
▸▸ Comput **s. command** commande f de sauvegarde

▸ **save up** VI (save money) économiser, faire des économies (**for** pour); **we're saving up to go to Canada/buy a fridge** nous économisons pour aller au Canada/pour acheter un réfrigérateur
VT SEP (keep for future) (money etc) économiser, mettre de côté; (collect) (stamps, petrol vouchers etc) collectionner

save-as-you-earn ADJ
▸▸ Br Fin **s. scheme** = plan m d'épargne à contributions mensuelles produisant des intérêts exonérés d'impôts

saveloy [ˈsævəlɔɪ] N Culin cervelas m

saver [ˈseɪvər] N (person who saves money) épargnant, -ante

saving [ˈseɪvɪŋ] ADJ (redeeming) **her/its s. grace** ce qui la/le rachète
N **1** (rescue) (of lives etc) sauvetage m; (of person, souls) salut m; **this was the s. of him** cela a été son salut **2** (act of saving money) économie f, épargne f, **we made a s. of £500 on the usual price** nous avons fait une économie de 500 livres sur le prix habituel; **savings** économies; Econ dépôts mpl d'épargne; **to live on one's savings** vivre de ses économies; **to make savings** faire des économies **3** Comput sauvegarde f
CONJ Arch, Lit = **save** CONJ
PREP Arch, Lit sauf; **s. your presence** sauf votre respect
▸▸ **savings account** compte m d'épargne; **Savings Bank** ≃ Caisse f (nationale) d'épargne; **savings certificate** ≃ bon m d'épargne; **savings club** club m d'épargne; Am **savings and loan association** caisse d'épargne-logement; **savings plan** plan m d'épargne; Econ **savings ratio** taux m d'épargne; Fin **savings scheme** plan d'épargne

saviour, Am **savior** [ˈseɪvjər] N sauveur m; Rel **Our S.** Notre Sauveur

savory [ˈseɪvərɪ] N Bot, Culin sarriette f

savour, Am **savor** [ˈseɪvər] N saveur f, goût m
VT (success, moment etc) savourer
VI (of thing) **to s. of sth** sentir qch; **the whole affair savours of corruption** tout cela sent la corruption

savoury, Am **savory** [ˈseɪvərɪ] ADJ **1** (appetizing) (taste, dish) savoureux, appétissant; **he looked even less s. than the other tramps** il avait l'air encore plus repoussant que les autres clochards; **he doesn't have a very s. reputation** il a une sale réputation **2** Culin (not sweet) salé
N Culin (hors d'œuvre) hors-d'œuvre m inv (chaud ou froid); (course) entremets m salé

Savoy [səˈvɔɪ] N **1** Geog Savoie f **2** (cabbage) chou m frisé de Milan
▸▸ **s. cabbage** chou frisé de Milan

savvy [ˈsævɪ] Sl N (common sense) jugeote f
VT piger; **s.?** tu piges?

saw¹ [sɔː] N (tool) scie f, **metal s.** scie à métaux; **circular s.** scie circulaire
VT (pt **sawed** [sɔːd]; pp **sawn** [sɔːn], **sawed**) scier
▸▸ **s. blade** lame f de scie; **s. tooth** dent f de scie
▸ **saw off** VT SEP couper ou enlever à la scie
▸ **saw up** VT SEP (wood) débiter

saw² N Lit (saying) adage m, dicton m

saw³ PT see see¹

sawbones ['sɔːbəʊnz] N Old-fashioned Fam chirurgien m

sawbuck ['sɔːbʌk] N Am 1 = sawhorse 2 Fam (ten-dollar bill) billet m de dix dollars

sawdust ['sɔːdʌst] N sciure f (de bois)

sawfish ['sɔːfɪʃ] N poisson-scie m, pl poissons-scies

sawhorse ['sɔːhɔːs] N Carp chevalet m de sciage, chèvre f

sawing ['sɔːɪŋ] N (of wood) sciage m
▸▸ s. up (of wood) débitage m

sawmill ['sɔːmɪl] N scierie f

sawn-off shotgun N carabine f à canon scié

sawyer ['sɔːjər] N scieur m (de long)

sax [sæks] N Mus Fam saxo m
▸▸ s. player saxophoniste mf

saxifrage ['sæksɪfreɪdʒ] N (plant) saxifrage f

Saxon ['sæks(ə)n] ADJ saxon
N 1 Saxon, -onne 2 Ling saxon m

Saxony ['sæksənɪ] N Saxe f

saxophone ['sæksəfəʊn] N Mus saxophone m

saxophonist [sæk'sɒfənɪst] N Mus saxophoniste mf

SAY [seɪ]

| VT | dire 1, 2 ▪ indiquer 1 ▪ penser 1 |
| VI | dire |

VT (pt, pp said [sed]; 3rd sing pr says [sez]) 1 (utter) dire; to s. sth to sb dire qch à qn; to s. sth again répéter qch, redire qch; to s. hello/goodbye (to sb) dire bonjour/au revoir (à qn); s. hello to her from me dis-lui bonjour de ma part; to s. goodbye to one's chances of winning dire adieu à ses chances de gagner; to s. yes/no to an offer accepter/refuser une offre; Fam I wouldn't s. no to a glass of beer je boirais bien ou volontiers un verre de bière; to s. a word dire un mot; you have only to s. the word vous n'avez qu'un mot à dire; I didn't s. a word je n'ai pas dit un mot; it's for him/not for him to s. c'est/ce n'est pas à lui de décider; Tel who shall I s. is calling? c'est de la part de qui?; why he did it I can't or couldn't s. (I have no idea) je ne sais pas pourquoi il l'a fait; I can't s. (I'm not allowed to tell you) je ne peux pas le dire; there's no saying what might happen if ... on ne sait pas ce qui pourrait se passer si ...; it goes without saying that ... il va de soi ou cela va sans dire que ...; what did you s.? (repeat what you said) pardon?, qu'avez-vous dit?; whatever he may s. quoi qu'il en dise; what do you s. to a drink? ça te dit de prendre un verre?; 'good morning', she said 'bonjour', dit-elle; he said that you were here il a dit que vous étiez ici; as I said in my letter comme je l'ai dit dans ma lettre; the Bible says or it says in the Bible that ... comme il est écrit dans la Bible ...; it says in the newspaper that ... on dit dans le journal que ...; the church clock says ten le cadran de l'église marque dix heures; what does your watch s.? quelle heure est-il à ta montre?; the sign said ten more kilometres la pancarte indiquait qu'il restait dix kilomètres; let it be said soit dit en passant; you don't mean to s. he's 86 vous n'allez pas me dire qu'il a 86 ans; one might as well s. ... autant dire ...; I must s. that ... j'avoue que ...; je dois dire que ...; it has to or must be said il faut le dire; that's to s. c'est-à-dire; have you said anything about it to him? est-ce que vous lui en avez parlé?; the less said the better moins nous parlerons, mieux cela vaudra; to s. nothing of ... et je

ne parle pas de ...; getting there will be difficult enough, to s. nothing of getting home again se rendre là-bas va déjà être assez difficile, alors je ne parle pas de revenir ici; he has very little to s. for himself il est peu communicatif; what have you got to s. for yourself? eh bien, expliquez-vous!; there's a lot to be said for it c'est une bonne idée; there is little/much to be said for beginning now on n'a pas/on a intérêt à commencer dès maintenant; you're honest, I'll s. that for you je dirais en votre faveur que vous êtes honnête; the way you dress says something about you as a person la manière dont les gens s'habillent est révélatrice de leur personnalité; his response says a lot about ... sa réponse en dit long sur ...; don't s. you've forgotten already! ne (me) dis pas que tu as déjà oublié!; Fam you don't s. (so)! pas possible!, ça alors!; you can s. that again!, you said it! vous l'avez dit!, comme vous dites!; need I s. more? est-il besoin d'en dire davantage?; they s. that ..., it is said that ... on dit que ..., on prétend que ...; I've heard it said that ... j'ai entendu dire que ...; he is said to be rich, they s. he is rich on le dit riche, on dit qu'il est riche; what do you s., Amanda, should we go? qu'en penses-tu Amanda, on y va?; what do you s. to that? qu'en dites-vous ou pensez-vous?; is he stupid? – I wouldn't s. that est-ce qu'il est bête? – je n'irais pas jusque-là; on the whole, I should s. not je crois que non ou je crois bien que non; it is difficult to s. (when/where/which) il est difficile de dire (quand/où/quel); didn't I s. so! je vous l'avais bien dit!; I should s. so! et comment donc!; what did I s.? (I was right) qu'est-ce que j'avais dit?; let us or shall we or shall I s. disons; if I had, s., £100,000 to spend si j'avais, mettons ou disons, £100,000 livres à dépenser; other countries such as Germany, s., or France d'autres pays comme, par exemple, l'Allemagne ou la France; she didn't accept their offer – I should s. not! elle n'a pas accepté leur offre – il ne manquerait plus que ça! VOIR GRAMMAIRE A78

2 (recite) (prayer etc) dire; to s. one's prayers dire ou faire ses prières; to s. Mass dire la messe

VI I'm not saying je ne dis rien; Fam says you! que tu dis!; I mean to s.! tout de même!, quand même!; as they s., as people s. comme on dit; as one might s. comme qui dirait; Fam s., I've got an idea dites donc, j'ai une idée; Br Old-fashioned I s.! Am s.! (exclamatory) dites donc!; Br Old-fashioned I s.! (expressing surprise) pas possible!, fichtre!; I'll s.! et comment donc!

N to have one's s. dire ce qu'on a à dire; to have a s. in a discussion avoir son mot à dire dans un débat; let me have my s. laissez-moi parler; I have no s. in the matter je n'ai pas voix au chapitre

SAYE [eseɪwaɪ'iː] N Br Fin (abbr save as you earn) = plan m d'épargne à contributions mensuelles produisant des intérêts exonérés d'impôts

saying ['seɪɪŋ] N proverbe m, dicton m; as the s. goes (according to the proverb) comme dit le proverbe

say-so N Fam (permission) permission f; I can't do it without her s. je ne peux pas le faire sans sa permission; on sb's s. avec la permission de qn

S-bend N Br double virage m, virage en S

SBU [esbiː'juː] N (abbr strategic business unit) DAS m

SC [es'siː] N (abbr South Carolina) Caroline f du Sud

scab [skæb] N 1 (on wound) croûte f 2 Vet (disease) gale f 3 Ind Sl (person) jaune mf, bri-

seur, -euse de grève; s. miner mineur m qui ne fait pas grève
VI (-bb-) 1 (of wound) former une croûte 2 Ind Sl (replace strikers) remplacer les grévistes; (betray workmates) trahir ses camarades
▸▸ s. labour des briseurs de grève
▸ scab over VI = scab VI 1

scabbard ['skæbəd] N (for sword) fourreau m; (for dagger) gaine f

scabby ['skæbɪ] ADJ 1 Vet (sheep etc) galeux 2 (sore etc) croûteux, scabieux 3 Fam (contemptible) (behaviour etc) dégoûtant 4 Fam (grotty) (coat, room etc) pouilleux 5 Br Fam (worthless) merdique; you can keep your s. car! tu peux la garder, ta caisse de merde!

scabies ['skeɪbiːz] N Med gale f

scabious ['skeɪbɪəs] N (plant) scabieuse f

scabrous ['skeɪbrəs] ADJ 1 (surface etc) rugueux, raboteux 2 (topic, tale etc) scabreux, risqué

scads [skædz] NPL Am Fam des tas (of de)

scaffold ['skæf(ə)ld] N 1 (for execution) échafaud m; to go to the s. monter à ou sur l'échafaud 2 Constr échafaudage m

scaffolding ['skæfəldɪŋ] N échafaudage m

scag [skæg] N Sl 1 (heroin) héro f, blanche f 2 Am (ugly woman) boudin m, cageot m

scalable font ['skeɪləb(ə)l] N Typ police f de taille variable

scalawag ['skæləwæg] N esp Am Fam = scallywag

scald [skɔːld] VT 1 (burn) (hand etc) ébouillanter; to s. oneself s'ébouillanter 2 Culin (fruit, vegetables) échauder, ébouillanter; (milk etc) faire chauffer sans bouillir; (pot, container) échauder, ébouillanter
N (on hand etc) brûlure f

scalding ['skɔːldɪŋ] ADJ a s. hot day une journée torride; Lit s. tears larmes brûlantes; s. (hot) (liquid) brûlant
N (burning) brûlure f; the boiling water caused s. on her arms and face elle s'est ébouillanté les bras et le visage

scale¹ [skeɪl] N 1 (on fish, reptile etc) écaille f; Med (on skin) squame f 2 Metal scale(s) écailles fpl de fer 3 (incrustation) (in pipes, kettle etc) tartre m, incrustation f; (on teeth) tartre; boiler s. tartre
VT (fish) écailler; (teeth) détartrer; (boiler, pipe) désincruster, détartrer
VI (of skin) (se) desquamer; (of paint etc) s'écailler
▸▸ s. remover (for teeth) détartrant m

scale² N (for weighing) balance f; (for letters) pèse-lettres m inv; (in bathroom etc) pèse-personne m, pl pèse-personnes; (for baby) pèse-bébé m, pl pèse-bébés; (pan) plateau m (de balance); (deep) bassin m; pair of scales balance à plateaux; to tip the scales at 100 kilos peser 100 kilos; Fig to tip the scales faire pencher la balance; platform scales bascule f, letter scales pèse-lettres; bathroom scales pèse-personne; baby scales pèse-bébé
▸▸ s. pan plateau (de balance); (deep) bassin

scale³ N 1 (grading system) échelle f; (of thermometer) échelle (graduée), graduations fpl; sliding s. (of salaries, prices) échelle mobile; sliding s. tariff tarif m dégressif; at the top of the (social) s. en haut ou au sommet de l'échelle (sociale); to judge sth on a s. of one to ten noter qch sur dix 2 (size) (of map, drawing etc) échelle f; small-/large-scale map échelle f; petite/à grande échelle; to draw sth to s. dessiner qch à l'échelle; to be in/out of s. être/ne pas être à l'échelle; on a national s. à l'échelle nationale; the s. of a problem/crisis/disaster/project l'ampleur ou l'importance d'un problème/d'une crise/d'un sinistre/d'un projet

3 *Mus* gamme *f*; **major/minor s.** gamme majeure/mineure; **to practise one's scales** faire des gammes

VT 1 *(climb) (wall etc)* escalader; *(mountain, cliff)* escalader, faire l'ascension de **2** *Typ (font)* ajuster la taille de

▸▸ **s. drawing** dessin *m* à l'échelle; **s. model** *(of car, plane)* modèle *m* réduit; *(of building, town centre)* maquette *f*

▸ **scale down VT SEP 1** *(draw to smaller scale)* réduire l'échelle de; *Typ (font)* réduire (la taille de) **2** *(prices, demands etc)* réduire; *(expectations)* calmer; **to s. down production** ralentir la production

▸ **scale up VT SEP** *(prices, demands etc)* augmenter; *Typ (font)* agrandir

scales [skeɪlz] **NPL** *see* **scale²**

scaling¹ [ˈskeɪlɪŋ] **N 1** *(action) (of teeth)* détartrage *m*; *(of boiler, pipes)* détartrage, désincrustation *f* **2** *(deposit inside pipe, boiler, kettle etc)* tartre *m*, calcaire *m*; *(process of incrustation)* formation *f* du tartre, entartrage *m*

scaling² **N 1** *(climbing)* escalade *f* **2** *(grading) (of prices, salaries etc)* graduation *f*; *Typ (of font)* ajustement *m* de la taille

▸▸ **s. down** réduction *f*, diminution *f*; *(proportionately)* réduction proportionnelle; **s. up** augmentation *f*

scallion [ˈskæljən] **N** *Bot* échalote *f*

scallop [ˈskɒləp, ˈskæl-] **N 1** *(mollusc)*, *Culin* coquille *f* Saint-Jacques; *Culin (of veal etc)* escalope *f* **2** *Sewing etc* feston *m*

VT 1 *Culin (fish etc)* faire cuire en coquille(s) **2** *Sewing* festonner; **a scalloped handkerchief** un mouchoir festonné

scally [ˈskælɪ] **N** *Br Fam* arnaqueur, -euse

scallywag [ˈskælɪwæg] **N 1** *Fam* chenapan *m*; **little s.** *(child)* petit(e) coquin, -ine **2** *Hist* = partisan *m* des républicains après la guerre de Sécession

scalp [skælp] **N** *Anat* cuir *m* chevelu; *(war trophy)* scalp *m*

VT 1 *(in war)* scalper; *Hum (of hairdresser)* ratiboiser **2** *esp Am Fam (tickets)* revendre au noir

scalpel [ˈskælp(ə)l] **N** *Surg* scalpel *m*

scalper [ˈskælpər] **N 1** *St Exch Sl* spéculateur, -trice sur variation minimale **2** *esp Am Fam (ticket tout)* = revendeur, -euse de billets au marché noir

scaly [ˈskeɪlɪ] **ADJ** *(fish)* écailleux; *(skin)* squameux

scam [skæm] **N** *Fam* arnaque *f*

VT arnaquer

scammer [ˈskæmər] **N** *Fam* arnaqueur, -euse

scamp [skæmp] **N** fripouille *f*; *Fam* **little s.** *(child)* petit(e) coquin, -ine

scamper [ˈskæmpər] **VI** *(run playfully)* gambader; **it scampered up the tree** il a grimpé à l'arbre en un clin d'œil; **they all scampered across the bridge** ils ont traversé le pont à toute vitesse; *Fig* **the programme scampered through the 18th century in ten minutes** l'émission a survolé le XVIIIᵉ siècle en dix minutes

N *(playful run)* course *f* folâtre *ou* allègre; *(quick run)* course rapide

▸ **scamper away, scamper off VI** *(of mice)* filer; *(of animals)* détaler; *(of person)* décamper

scampi [ˈskæmpɪ] **N** *Culin* scampi *mpl*

scan [skæn] **N 1** *(look)* regard *m* appuyé; **after a quick s. around the room, they left** ils examinèrent rapidement la pièce et s'en allèrent **2** *Electron, Radio etc* balayage *m*; *Comput* lecture *f* au scanne(u)r **3** *Med* examen *m* au scanne(u)r; *(in pregnancy)* écho-

graphie *f*; **to have a s.** se faire faire un examen au scanne(u)r; *(in pregnancy)* se faire faire une échographie

VT (-nn-) 1 *(in prosody) (verse)* scander **2** *(examine closely)* scruter, examiner minutieusement; *(the horizon)* scruter **3** *(glance at, over)* jeter un coup d'œil sur; *(book etc)* feuilleter, parcourir **4** *Electron, Radio etc (image, soundtrack)* balayer; *Med* examiner au scanne(u)r; *(in pregnancy)* faire une échographie à; *Comput (text, graphics)* passer *ou* lire au scanne(u)r, scanner; **scanned input** entrée *f* (à partir du) scanne(u)r

VI *(in prosody)* **this line doesn't s.** ce vers est faux

▸ **scan in VT SEP** *Comput (graphics)* insérer par scanne(u)r, capturer au scanne(u)r

scandal [ˈskænd(ə)l] **N 1** *(outrage)* scandale *m*; **it's a s.** c'est un scandale; **to create** *or* **cause a s.** causer un scandale **2** *(gossip)* médisance *f*

▸▸ *Fam* **s. sheet** journal *m* à scandale

scandalize [ˈskændəlaɪz] **VT** scandaliser, choquer

scandalmonger [ˈskænd(ə)lmʌŋgər] **N** colporteur, -euse d'histoires scandaleuses

scandalmongering [ˈskænd(ə)lmʌŋgərɪŋ] **N** it's just s. c'est fait exprès pour faire du scandale; **to put a stop to this s.** mettre un terme à tous ces racontars

ADV *(journalist etc)* qui cherche le scandale

scandalous [ˈskændələs] **ADJ** *(conduct, event, prices etc)* scandaleux

scandalously [ˈskændələslɪ] **ADV** scandaleusement

Scandinavia [skændɪˈneɪvɪə] **N** Scandinavie *f*

Scandinavian [skændɪˈneɪvɪən] **ADJ** scandinave

N Scandinave *mf*

scanner [ˈskænər] **N** *Med, Comput* scanne(u)r *m*; **radar s.** explorateur *m ou* balayeur *m* radar; *(radar aerial)* antenne *f* (de) radar

scanning [ˈskænɪŋ] **N 1** *(in prosody) (of verse)* scansion *f* **2** *(close examination)* examen *m* minutieux; *Electron, Radio etc (of image, soundtrack)* balayage *m*; *Comput* passage *m* au scanne(u)r, scannérisation *f*; **radar s.** exploration *f ou* balayage radar

scansion [ˈskænʃən] **N** *(in prosody)* scansion *f*

scant [skænt] **ADJ ATTRIB** insuffisant, peu abondant; **they paid s. regard to what he said** ils ont à peine fait attention à ce qu'il disait

scantily [ˈskæntɪlɪ] **ADV** peu abondamment; *(insufficiently)* insuffisamment; **s. dressed** *or* **clad** très peu vêtu; **she came to the party rather s. clad** elle est venue à la soirée dans une tenue des plus légères

scantiness [ˈskæntɪnɪs] **N** *(of supplies etc)* insuffisance *f*; *(of vegetation)* rareté *f*, pauvreté *f*

scants [skænts] **NPL** *Br Fam (men's)* calcif *m*; *(women's)* petite culotte *f*

scanty [ˈskæntɪ] **ADJ** *(supply etc)* peu abondant; *(insufficient)* insuffisant, à peine suffisant; **a s. meal** un maigre repas; **a s. little dress** une robe qui ne cache pas grand-chose

scapegoat [ˈskeɪpgəʊt] **N** *(who takes the blame)* bouc *m* émissaire; *(on whom frustrations are taken out)* souffre-douleur *m inv*

scapegrace [ˈskeɪpgreɪs] **N** *Old-fashioned (good-for-nothing)* vaurien, -ienne, bon *m*/bonne *f* à rien

scapula, *pl* **scapulae** [ˈskæpjʊlə, -iː] **N** *Anat* omoplate *f*

scapular [ˈskæpjʊlər] **ADJ** *Anat* scapulaire

scar¹ [skɑːr] **N** *(mark of wound)* cicatrice *f*; *(on face, caused by knife etc)* balafre *f*; **the scars that the old mine workings have left on the hills** les cicatrices laissées sur les collines par les anciennes mines; **he carried the (mental) scars for the rest of his life** il est resté marqué à vie

VT (-rr-) *(leg, face etc)* marquer d'une cicatrice; *(face) (with knife etc)* balafrer; **to be scarred** porter *ou* avoir des cicatrices; *Fig* **to be scarred for life** *(by experience etc)* être marqué à vie; **war-scarred** *(of country etc)* dévasté par la guerre

VI *(of wound)* faire une cicatrice

▸▸ **s. tissue** tissu *m* cicatriciel

▸ **scar over VI** cicatriser

scar² **N** *(in mountain range etc)* rocher *m* escarpé

scarab [ˈskærəb] **N** *(precious stone)*, *Entom* scarabée *m*

scarce [skeəs] **ADJ** *(animal, water, edition, substance, news etc)* rare; *(commodities)* rare, peu abondant; *Fam* **to make oneself s.** s'éclipser, s'esquiver

ADV *Arch, Lit* = **scarcely**

scarcely [ˈskeəslɪ] **ADV** à peine, *Fml* guère; **I have s. any left** il ne m'en reste presque plus, *Fml* il ne m'en reste guère; **she could s. speak** c'est à peine si elle pouvait parler, elle pouvait à peine parler; **s. ever** presque jamais; **he had s. come in** *or* **s. had he come in when the telephone rang** à peine était-il rentré que le téléphone sonna; **she was s. 21 years old** elle avait à peine 21 ans; **it is s. likely that …** il est peu vraisemblable que …; **they would s. destroy their own home, would they?** ils n'iraient pas jusqu'à détruire leur propre maison! VOIR GRAMMAIRE A78

scarcity [ˈskeəsɪtɪ], **scarceness** [ˈskeəsnɪs] **N** *(rarity)* rareté *f*; *(lack)* manque *m*, disette *f*; **to have s. value** être précieux parce que rare; **because of their s. value** parce qu'ils sont rares

scare [skeər] **N** panique *f*; *Fam* **you gave me an awful s.** vous m'avez fait une drôle de peur; **a bomb s.** une alerte à la bombe; **a s. over poisoned food** une panique à propos de nourriture empoisonnée

VT *(alarm)* effrayer, alarmer; *(frighten)* faire peur à, effrayer; **they scared him into leaving** *(intentionally)* ils lui ont fait peur jusqu'à ce qu'il parte; *(unintentionally)* ils lui ont fait peur au point qu'il est parti; **the high costs scared them off the idea** les coûts élevés leur en ont fait abandonner l'idée; *Fam* **to s. the pants off sb** faire une peur bleue à qn

VI s'effrayer, s'alarmer; **I don't s. easily** je ne m'effraie pas facilement *ou* pour rien

▸ **scare away, scare off VT SEP** *(frighten) (person)* faire fuir; *(birds, deer etc)* effaroucher; *(discourage, put off)* faire fuir, effrayer

scarecrow [ˈskeəkrəʊ] **N** *Agr, Fig* épouvantail *m*; **to be dressed like a s.** être habillé à faire peur

scared [skeəd] **ADJ** *(look)* apeuré, effrayé; **to be s. of sb/sth** avoir peur de qn/qch; **I'm not s. of you** tu ne me fais pas peur, je n'ai pas peur de toi; **he's s. of his own shadow** il a peur de son ombre; **to be s. to death** *or* **out of one's wits**, *Fam* **to be s. stiff** avoir une peur bleue (**of** de)

scaredy-cat [ˈskeədɪ-] **N** *Fam (in children's language)* froussard, -arde

scaremonger [ˈskeəmʌŋgər] **N** alarmiste *mf*

scaremongering [ˈskeəmʌŋgərɪŋ] **N** alarmisme *m*

scarf, *pl* **scarfs, scarves** [skɑːf(s), skɑːvz] **N** écharpe *f*; *(of silk)* foulard *m*; **football s.** écharpe aux couleurs d'une équipe de football

VT 1 *Constr (join)* joindre par enture; *(cut)* entailler **2** *Am Fam (eat)* bouffer, boulotter

scarface ['skɑːfeɪs] N balafré, -ée

scarification [skærɪfɪ'keɪʃən] N *Agr, Med* scarification *f*

scarify ['skærɪfaɪ] VT **1** *(skin, ground)* scarifier **2** *Fam* = **scare** VT

scarily ['skeərɪlɪ] ADV à faire peur; **we came s. close to being killed** on est passé à deux doigts de la mort

scarlatina [skɑːlə'tiːnə] N *Med* scarlatine *f*

scarlet ['skɑːlɪt] ADJ écarlate; **to blush** *or* **go** *or* **turn s.** devenir cramoisi *ou* écarlate ▪ N écarlate *m*
▸ ▸ *Med* **s. fever** scarlatine *f*; *Cathol* **s. hat** chapeau *m* de cardinal; *Bot* **s. pimpernel** mouron *m* rouge; *Br Bot* **s. runner** haricot *m* (à rames); *Br Hum* **s. woman** femme *f* de mauvaise vie

scarp [skɑːp] N **1** *Geog (of hill)* escarpement *m* **2** *Mil (in fortifications)* escarpe *f*

scarper ['skɑːpər] VI *Br Fam* se tirer, déguerpir

SCART [skɑːt] N *(abbr* **Syndicat des Constructeurs d'Appareils Radiorécepteurs et Téléviseurs)**
▸ ▸ **S. cable** câble *m* péritel®; **S. plug** prise *f* péritel®

scary ['skeərɪ] ADJ *Fam (frightening)* effrayant, qui fait peur; **it's s. here** ça fiche la frousse ici

scat [skæt] INT *Fam* filez!, fichez le camp!

scathing ['skeɪðɪŋ] ADJ *(remark, sarcasm etc)* acerbe, mordant, cinglant; **she was s. about security arrangements** elle a fait des remarques acerbes au sujet des mesures de sécurité

scathingly ['skeɪðɪŋlɪ] ADV d'une manière acerbe; *(to remark)* d'un ton cinglant *ou* acerbe

scatological [skætə'lɒdʒɪk(ə)l] ADJ *(joke etc)* scatologique

scatology [skə'tɒlədʒɪ] N scatologie *f*

scatter ['skætər] VT *(army etc)* disperser; *(clouds etc)* dissiper; *(birds etc)* faire envoler; *(leaves, papers etc)* éparpiller; *(sow) (corn, seed)* semer à la volée; *Phys (of surface) (light)* diffuser
▪ VI *(of crowd etc)* se disperser; *(of birds etc)* s'égailler; *(of army)* se débander; *(of clouds etc)* se dissiper; *(of shot)* s'éparpiller
▪ N *(of shot etc)* éparpillement *m*, dispersion *f*, écartement *m*
▸ ▸ **s. cushion** petit coussin *m*; **s. rug** petit tapis *m*, carpette *f*; *(by bed)* descente *f* de lit

scatterbrain ['skætəbreɪn] N *Fam* étourdi, -ie, tête *f* de linotte

scatterbrained ['skætəbreɪnd] ADJ *Fam* étourdi, écervelé

scattered ['skætəd] ADJ dispersé, éparpillé, épars; *(light)* diffus; **s. over the floor** éparpillé sur le sol; **houses s. here and there on the plain** des maisons çà et là dans la plaine
▸ ▸ *Met* **s. showers** averses *fpl* éparses

scattering ['skætərɪŋ] N *(small number)* petit nombre *m*; *(small quantity)* petite quantité *f*; **there was a s. of snow on the mountains** il y avait de la neige çà et là sur les montagnes; **he only has a s. of followers** il n'a qu'un petit nombre de disciples

scattiness ['skætɪnɪs] N *Br Fam (absentmindedness)* étourderie *f*, *(craziness)* loufoquerie *f*

scatty ['skætɪ] ADJ *Br Fam (absent-minded)* étourdi, écervelé; *(crazy)* barjo, barge

scavenge ['skævɪndʒ] VI *(hunt)* fouiller; **to s. in the dustbins** fouiller *ou* faire les poubelles; **to s. for information/news** être à l'affût des informations/nouvelles

---

▪ VT récupérer; *(in engine) (burnt gas)* balayer, refouler

scavenger ['skævɪndʒər] N **1** *(person, animal)* fouilleur, -euse d'ordures; *(animal living off dead prey)* animal *m* nécrophage; **he's a real s.** *(gets things from other people's rubbish)* c'est le roi de la récupération **2** *Arch (street cleaner)* éboueur *m*

scenario [sɪ'nɑːrɪəʊ] N *Cin, Theat, Fig* scénario *m*

scene [siːn] N **1** *Theat, Cin (place of action)* scène *f*, *Fig (of event)* théâtre *m*, lieu *m*; *Theat* **change of s.** changement de décor *ou* de scène; *Fig* **a change of s. would do him good** un changement d'air *ou* de décor lui ferait du bien; *Theat* **the s. is set in London** l'action se passe à Londres; **to set the s.** planter le décor; *Fig* **her success set the s. for more women to enter music** son succès a permis à un plus grand nombre de femmes d'avoir une carrière musicale; **the political/sporting s.** la scène politique/sportive; **the modern poetry s. in Paris** la poésie moderne à Paris; **this athlete is a newcomer to the international s.** cet athlète est nouveau sur la scène sportive internationale; **to arrive or come on the s.** faire son apparition; *(of police)* arriver sur les lieux (du crime/de l'accident/*etc*); **to be first on the s.** être le premier sur les lieux; **the s. of the crime/accident** les lieux du crime/de l'accident; *Fam* **it's not my s.** ce n'est pas mon genre
2 *Theat (subdivision of play)* scène *f*, **s. two** scène deux
3 *Theat (scenery)* décor *m*; **scenes painted by ...** décors par ...; *also Fig* **behind the scenes** dans la *ou* les coulisse(s)
4 *Fig (episode)* scène *f*, spectacle *m*; **it was a touching s.** c'était une scène émouvante *ou* un spectacle émouvant; **I can just picture the s.** je vois d'ici la scène
5 *(sight)* vue *f*, **the s. from the window** la vue de la fenêtre; **a s. of devastation** un spectacle de désolation
6 *Fam (fuss)* **now don't make a s.!** ne fais pas une scène!
▸ ▸ *Theat* **s. change** changement de décor *ou* de scène; *Theat* **s. dock** case *f* à décor *ou* décors; *Theat* **s. painter** décorateur, -trice de théâtre

scene-of-crime officer N = agent *m* responsable de l'enquête sur le lieu du crime

scenery ['siːnərɪ] N **1** *Theat* décor(s) *m(pl)*; *Fig Fam* **you need a change of s.** vous avez besoin de changer d'air *ou* de décor **2** *(countryside)* paysage *m*; *(view)* vue *f*

scene-set N *TV etc* mise *f* en place

sceneshifter ['siːnʃɪftər] N *Theat* machiniste *mf*

scenic ['siːnɪk] ADJ **1** *(countryside)* pittoresque; *(route etc)* panoramique; **an area of great s. beauty** une région qui offre de très beaux panoramas **2** *Theat* scénique
▸ ▸ *Theat* **s. cloth** rideau *m* de fond scénique; *Theat* **s. designer** décorateur, -trice de théâtre, scénographe *mf*, **s. railway** *(for tourists)* petit train *m* (touristique); *(in fairground)* montagnes *fpl* russes; **s. route** *(for tourists)* route *f* touristique, itinéraire *m* panoramique; *TV etc* **s. treatment** scénographie *f*, *Theat* **s. workshop** atelier *m* de décors

scent [sent] N **1** *(smell)* parfum *m*; *(of flowers)* odeur *f*, *Lit* senteur *f*
2 *(liquid)* parfum *m*
3 *(in hunting)* fumet *m*, vent *m*; **s. gland** *or* **organ** glande *f* à sécrétion odoriférante; **to pick up the s.** *(of hounds)* trouver la piste; **to be on the s.** être sur la piste *(* **of** de); **to lose** *or* **be thrown off the s.** perdre la trace *ou* la piste; **to throw the police off the s.** mettre la police en déroute, semer la police
4 *(sense of smell) (of dog)* odorat *m*, flair *m*

▪ VT **1** *(of hounds etc)* **to s. game** flairer *ou* sentir le gibier; *Fig* **to s. dishonesty/etc** flairer la malhonnêteté/etc, **a keen-scented dog** un chien au nez *ou* à l'odorat fin **2** *(of flower etc) (the air)* parfumer, embaumer; **to s. sth with sth** *(with perfume etc)* parfumer *ou* imprégner qch de qch

scented ['sentɪd] ADJ *(soap etc)* parfumé

scentless ['sentlɪs] ADJ *(flower)* inodore, sans odeur

sceptic, *Am* **skeptic** ['skeptɪk] N sceptique *mf*

sceptical, *Am* **skeptical** ['skeptɪk(ə)l] ADJ sceptique

sceptically, *Am* **skeptically** ['skeptɪklɪ] ADV sceptiquement, avec incrédulité

scepticism, *Am* **skepticism** ['skeptɪsɪz(ə)m] N scepticisme *m*

sceptre, *Am* **scepter** ['septər] N sceptre *m*

schedule ['ʃedjuːl, *Am* 'skedjuːl] N **1** *(plan)* programme *m*; *(for work)* plan *m* (de travail), planning *m*; *Rail etc (timetable)* horaire *m*; **to be behind/ahead of s.** être en retard/en avance sur les prévisions; **we're on s. (for March)** nous sommes dans les délais (pour mars); **everything went off according to s.** tout a marché comme prévu; **I work to a very tight s.** mon emploi du temps est très chargé; **on s.** *(train, bus etc)* à l'heure
2 *Com (list) (of items)* nomenclature *f*, *(of machines)* inventaire *m*; *(of prices)* barème *m*; *Admin (of taxes)* cédule *f*
3 *Law (to law, articles of association etc)* annexe *f*
▪ VT **1** *(make plan for)* programmer, inscrire au programme, faire le programme de; *(put in timetable) (train etc)* inscrire à l'horaire; **the mayor is scheduled to make a speech** le maire doit prononcer un discours; **it's scheduled for three o'clock** c'est prévu pour quinze heures
2 *Br (class)* **to s. as an ancient monument** classer (comme) monument historique
3 *Com (list) (item)* inscrire sur une liste
4 *Law (add as appendix)* ajouter en annexe

scheduled ['ʃedjuːld, *Am* 'skedjuːld] ADJ *(flight, services etc)* régulier; **to arrive at the s. time** arriver à l'heure prévue *ou* annoncée *ou* indiquée; *TV* **a change to our s. programme** un changement dans notre grille des programmes
▸ ▸ *Fin* **s. territories** zone *f* sterling

scheduler ['ʃedjuːlər, *Am* 'skedjuːlər] N *Comput (package)* logiciel *m* de planification (de projets)

scheduling ['ʃedjuːlɪŋ, *Am* 'skedjuːlɪŋ] N ordonnancement *m*; *TV, Radio* programmation *f*
▸ ▸ *TV, Radio* **s. director** directeur, -trice des programmes

schema, *pl* **schemata** ['skiːmə, -ətə] N *Fml* schéma *m*

schematic [skɪ'mætɪk] ADJ schématique

scheme [skiːm] N **1** *(arrangement)* arrangement *m*, combinaison *f*, *(system)* système *m*; **colour s.** combinaison de(s) couleurs; **I like the colour s. on this carpet** j'aime le mélange de couleurs de ce tapis; **where does mankind fit into the s. of things?** quelle est la place de l'humanité dans l'univers?; **where does it come in your s. of things?** quelle place cela a-t-il dans votre conception des choses?
2 *(plan)* plan *m*, projet *m*
3 *Pej (intrigue)* intrigue *f*, *Fam* magouille *f*; **the best laid schemes** les combinaisons *fpl* *ou Fam* les combines *fpl* les mieux étudiées
4 *esp Br* **pension s.** caisse *f* de retraite; **(housing) s.** cité *f*
▪ VI intriguer, *Fam* magouiller
▪ VT *(plot)* machiner, combiner; **to s. sb's downfall** comploter pour renverser qn

schemer ['skiːmər] N *Pej* intrigant, -ante
scheming ['skiːmɪŋ] ADJ intrigant
▪ N intrigues *fpl*, machinations *fpl*
scherzo ['skeətsəʊ] N *Mus* scherzo *m*
schilling ['ʃɪlɪŋ] N *Formerly (Austrian currency)* schilling *m*
schism ['s(k)ɪz(ə)m] N schisme *m*
schismatic [s(k)ɪz'mætɪk] ADJ, N schismatique *mf*
schist [ʃɪst] N *Miner* schiste *m*; **mica s.** micaschiste *m*
schizo ['skɪtsəʊ] ADJ, N *Fam* schizo(phrène) *mf*
schizoid ['skɪtsɔɪd] ADJ, N *Psy* schizoïde *mf*
schizophrenia [skɪtsəʊ'friːnɪə] N *Psy* schizophrénie *f*
schizophrenic [skɪtsəʊ'frenɪk] ADJ, N schizophrène *mf*, schizophrénique *mf*
schlemiel [ʃlə'miːl] N *Am Fam* minable *mf*
schlep(p) [ʃlep] *esp Am Fam* N **1** *(person)* lourdaud, -aude **2** *(journey)* trotte *f*; **it's a bit of a s. to the supermarket** ça fait une trotte jusqu'au supermarché
▪ VT *(carry, drag)* trimballer, transbahuter; **I've got to s. all this stuff over to the office** il faut que je trimballe *ou* transbahute tous ces trucs au bureau
▪ VI faire un tour, traîner; **to s. home** rentrer chez soi à pinces; **I had to s. to the grocery store** il a fallu que je crapahute jusqu'à l'épicerie
schlock [ʃlɒk] N *Am Fam* **1** *(junk)* camelote *f*, saloperies *fpl* **2** *(lazy person)* flemmard, -arde
▪ ADJ *(worthless)* qui ne vaut pas un clou, nul; **s. jewelry** bijoux *mpl* en toc
schlong [ʃlɒŋ] N *Am Sl (penis)* zob *m*
schlub [ʃlʌb] N *Am Fam* crétin, -ine, andouille *f*
schmal(t)z [ʃmɔːlts] N *Fam* guimauve *f*
schmaltzy ['ʃmɔːltsɪ] ADJ *Fam (film, novel, music etc)* à l'eau de rose, à la guimauve
schmo [ʃməʊ] N *Am Fam (unlucky person)* guignard, -arde; *(stupid person)* nul *m*, *f* nulle
schmooze [ʃmuːz] VI *Fam (at party, function etc)* faire des mondanités
schmuck [ʃmʌk] N *Am Sl (fool)* andouille *f*
schnapps [ʃnæps] N schnaps *m*
schnitzel ['ʃnɪts(ə)l] N côtelette *f* de veau
schnook [ʃnʊk] N *Am Fam* poire *f*, pigeon *m*
schnozzle ['ʃnɒz(ə)l] N *Sl (nose)* naze *m*
scholar ['skɒlər] N **1** *(learned person)* savant, -ante, érudit, -ite; **I'm not much of a s.** je ne suis pas très savant; **Latin s.** latiniste *mf* **2** *Sch, Univ (winner of scholarship)* boursier, -ière **3** *Arch (pupil)* élève *mf*, écolier, -ière
scholarly ['skɒləlɪ] ADJ savant, érudit
scholarship ['skɒləʃɪp] N **1** *(learning)* savoir *m*, érudition *f* **2** *Sch, Univ (sum of money)* bourse *f* (d'études)
scholastic [skə'læstɪk] ADJ *(philosophy, theology)* scolastique; *Sch Fml (work, success etc)* scolaire
▪ N *Phil, Rel* scolastique *m*
school[1] [skuːl] N **1** *(for children)* école *f*; *Admin* établissement *m* scolaire; *(from 11 to 15)* collège *m*; *(from 15 to 18)* lycée *m*; **to go to s.** aller en classe *ou* à l'école/au collège/au lycée; **which s. do you go to?** à quelle école/à quel collège/à quel lycée est-ce que tu vas?; **I went to** *or* **was at s. with her** je suis allé à l'école/au collège/au lycée avec elle; **I'm still at s.** je vais encore à l'école; **at s.** à l'école *ou* en classe/au collège/au lycée; **there is no s. tomorrow** il n'y a pas d'école *ou* il n'y a pas classe demain; **when does s.**

start? *(primary)* à quelle heure est-ce que la classe commence?; *(secondary)* à quelle heure est-ce que les cours commencent?; **nursery s.** *(école)* maternelle *f*; *Br* **primary** *or Am* **elementary s.** école primaire; *Admin* établissement d'enseignement primaire; *Br* **comprehensive s.** établissement d'enseignement secondaire polyvalent; **grammar s.** *Br* ≃ lycée, *Am* ≃ école primaire; **high s.** *(from 11 to 15)* collège; *(from 15 to 18)* lycée; **independent** *or* **private s.** école *ou* collège libre; **public s.** *Br* école privée, *Am* école publique; **state s.** école publique *ou* d'Etat, établissement public; *Br Formerly* **approved s.** centre *m* d'éducation surveillée; **Sunday s.** catéchisme *m*; **the whole s. knew it** toute l'école le savait; **the upper/lower s.** *(the pupils)* les grandes/petites classes; **of s. age** d'âge scolaire VOIR GRAMMAIRE A6–7
  2 *(part of university)* département *m*, institut *m*; *Am (college, university)* faculté *f*, université *f*; *Am* **to be at s.** être à l'université; **s. of art, art s.** école *f* des beaux-arts; **s. of dancing** académie *f ou* école de danse; **fencing s.** académie *ou* salle *f* d'escrime; *Br* **driving s., s. of motoring** auto-école *f*, *pl* auto-écoles; **summer s.** cours *m* de vacances, université d'été VOIR GRAMMAIRE A6–7
  3 *Art, Phil etc (group)* école *f*; *(following a master)* disciples *mpl*; **the Flemish s.** l'école flamande; **the Platonic s.** l'école de Platon; *Fam* **to be brought up in the s. of hard knocks** être élevé à la dure; **she is one of the old s.** elle est de la vieille école
▪ VT **1** *(educate) (person)* instruire, faire l'éducation de **2** *(train) (child, sb's mind)* former; *(horse)* dresser; **to s. oneself** se discipliner
  ▸▸ **s. attendance** *(going to school)* scolarisation *f*; *(not being absent)* présence *f* à l'école; **s. board** conseil *m* d'établissement; **s. book** livre *m* de classe, livre scolaire; **schools broadcasting** émissions *fpl* scolaires; **s. building** bâtiment *m* scolaire; **s. day** journée *f* scolaire *ou* d'école; **s. friend** camarade *mf* de classe *ou* d'école; **s. hours** heures *fpl* de classe *ou* d'école; **s. leaver** jeune *mf* qui a terminé ses études secondaires; **s. magazine** journal *m* de l'école; **schools programmes** programmes *mpl* éducatifs; **schools radio** radio *f* scolaire; **s. report** bulletin *m* scolaire; **Br s. run** conduites *fpl* (scolaires); **s. of thought** école *f* de pensée; **s. trip** voyage *m* scolaire; *Fig* théorie *f*; **s. uniform** uniforme *m* scolaire; **s. year** année *f* scolaire
school[2] N *(of fish)* banc *m*; *(of porpoises)* bande *f*
schoolboy ['skuːlbɔɪ] N écolier *m*; *(11 to 15)* collégien *m*; *(15 to 18)* lycéen *m*
  ▸▸ **s. slang** argot *m* scolaire
schoolchild, *pl* **schoolchildren** ['skuːltʃaɪld, -tʃɪldrən] N écolier, -ière
schooldays ['skuːldeɪz] N *(period of life)* vie *f* scolaire; **in my s.** quand j'étais à l'école
schoolfellow ['skuːlfeləʊ] N *Old-fashioned* camarade *mf* de classe *ou* d'école
schoolgirl ['skuːlɡɜːl] N écolière *f*; *(11 to 15)* collégienne *f*; *(15 to 18)* lycéenne *f*
schoolhouse ['skuːlhaʊs] N **1** *(school building)* école *f* **2** *(head's residence)* maison *f* du directeur/de la directrice *(faisant corps avec l'école)*
schooling ['skuːlɪŋ] N **1** *(education)* instruction *f*, éducation *f*; *(sending up to school)* scolarisation *f*; **he paid for his nephew's s.** il a subvenu aux frais d'études de son neveu; **compulsory s.** scolarisation obligatoire **2** *(of horse)* dressage *m*
schoolkid ['skuːlkɪd] N *Fam* écolier, -ière
school-leaving age N âge *m* de fin de scolarité
schoolma'am, **schoolmarm** ['skuːlmɑːm]

N *Old-fashioned Fam* institutrice *f*; *still current in Fig* **she's a real s.** elle est tellement pédante
schoolmaster ['skuːlmɑːstər] N *Old-fashioned (in primary school)* instituteur *m*, maître *m* (d'école); *(in secondary school)* professeur *m*
schoolmate ['skuːlmeɪt] N camarade *mf* de classe
schoolmistress ['skuːlmɪstrɪs] N *Old-fashioned (in primary school)* institutrice *f*, maîtresse *f* (d'école); *(in secondary school)* professeur *m*
schoolroom ['skuːlruːm] N salle *f* de classe
schoolteacher ['skuːltiːtʃər] N *(in primary school)* instituteur, -trice, maître *m*/maîtresse *f* (d'école); *(in secondary school)* professeur *m*
schoolteaching ['skuːltiːtʃɪŋ] N enseignement *m*
schooner[1] ['skuːnər] N *Naut* schooner *m*, goélette *f*
schooner[2] N *(sherry glass)* grand verre *m* à xérès; *Am (beer glass)* grand verre à bière
schtuk [ʃtʊk] N *Br Fam* **to be in s.** être dans le pétrin, être dans la panade
sciatic [saɪ'ætɪk] ADJ *Anat (nerve)* sciatique
sciatica [saɪ'ætɪkə] N *Med* sciatique *f*
science ['saɪəns] N science *f*; **pure/applied s.** science pure/sciences appliquées; **natural s.** sciences naturelles; **social s.** sciences sociales; **s. teacher** professeur *m* de science
  ▸▸ **s. fiction** science-fiction *f*, *pl* sciences-fictions; **s. park** parc *m* scientifique
scientific [saɪən'tɪfɪk] ADJ scientifique; **let's be s. about this** faisons preuve d'esprit scientifique; **s. research** recherche *f* scientifique
scientifically [saɪən'tɪfɪklɪ] ADV scientifiquement
scientist ['saɪəntɪst] N scientifique *mf*, savant, -ante
scientistic [saɪən'tɪstɪk] ADJ *Pej* prétendument scientifique
sci-fi ['saɪfaɪ] *Fam* N SF *f*
  ▪ ADJ de SF
Scilly ['sɪlɪ] N **the S. Isles, the Scillies** les Sorlingues *fpl*
scimitar ['sɪmɪtər] N cimeterre *m*
scintillate ['sɪntɪleɪt] VI scintiller; **scintillating with wit** pétillant d'esprit
scintillating ['sɪntɪleɪtɪŋ] ADJ *(wit, conversation etc)* étincelant, pétillant; *(book, match etc)* brillant; *Iron* **it wasn't exactly s.** ce n'était pas particulièrement brillant
scintillation [sɪntɪ'leɪʃən] N *(of wit etc)* éclat *m*
scion ['saɪən] N **1** *(of plant)* scion *m*, greffon *m* **2** *Lit (of noble family etc) (descendant)* descendant *m*, rejeton *m*
scissor ['sɪzər] VT (dé)couper avec des ciseaux
  ▸▸ *Orn* **s. bill** bec-en-ciseaux *m*, *pl* becs-en-ciseaux
scissors ['sɪzəz] N **(pair of) s.** ciseaux *mpl*; **s.** *(in wrestling), Gym etc* ciseaux; *(in high jump)* saut *m* en ciseaux; *Fig* **it's a s.-and-paste job** *(of book etc)* c'est du réchauffé VOIR GRAMMAIRE A11
  ▸▸ *Sport* **s. kick** ciseau *m*
sclerosis, *pl* **scleroses** [sklɪə'rəʊsɪs, -əʊsiːz] N *Med* sclérose *f*
scoff[1] [skɒf] VI *(mock)* se moquer; **to s. at** *(somebody)* railler, se moquer de; *(something)* se moquer de; **don't s.!** ne te moque pas!; **to s. at danger** faire fi du danger
  ▪ N *(mocking)* **we had a good s. at his expense** nous nous sommes bien moqués de lui

scoff² *esp Br Fam* **VT** *(eat)* bouffer; **he scoffed the whole packet** il s'est enfilé tout le paquet
N *(food)* boustifaille *f*, bouffe *f*

scoffing ['skɒfɪŋ] **ADJ** *(mocking)* moqueur, -euse, railleur, -euse
N moquerie(s) *f(pl)*, raillerie(s) *f(pl)*

scold [skəʊld] **VI** gronder, criailler
VT gronder, réprimander; **to s. sb for doing sth** gronder qn d'avoir fait qch; **she scolded him for being late** elle l'a grondé à cause de son retard
N *Old-fashioned (woman)* mégère *f*

scolding ['skəʊldɪŋ] **ADJ** *(tone)* de réprimande
N *(reprimand)* gronderie(s) *f(pl)*, réprimande *f*, semonce *f*; **to give sb a good s.** sermonner qn, *Fam* remonter les bretelles à qn; **constant s.** des réprimandes continuelles

scoliosis [skɒlɪ'əʊsɪs] **N** *Med* scoliose *f*

scollop ['skɒləp] **N, VT** = **scallop**

sconce [skɒns] **N 1** *(with handle)* bougeoir *m* **2** *(on wall)* applique *f*

scone [skɒn, skəʊn] **N** *Culin* = sorte *f* de petit pain sucré que l'on consomme avec ou sans beurre

scooby ['sku:bɪ] **N** *Br Fam* **he hasn't got a s.** *(is incompetent)* il est vraiment nul; *(doesn't suspect)* il se doute de rien; *(doesn't know)* il en a pas la moindre idée

scoop [sku:p] **N 1** *(device)* *(for flour, rice etc)* pelle *f*, *(for ice-cream)* cuiller *f* à glace, portionneuse *f*, *(for mashed potato)* cuiller à faire des boules de purée; *Naut (bailer)* épuisette *f*, écope *f*; *(of dredger)* godet *m* **2** *(portion)* cuillerée *f*; **a s. of ice-cream/mashed potato**/*etc* une boule de glace/purée/*etc* **3** *Journ Fam* scoop *m*, exclusivité *f*; **to make a s.** faire un scoop
VT 1 *(shovel)* *(water from a boat)* écoper; *(earth)* enlever; **to s. sth into sth** évider qch dans qch; **to s. ice-cream into a cone** mettre de la glace dans un cornet **2** *Journ* **to s. a story** avoir un scoop; **to s. the other papers** publier avant les autres journaux
▸▸ **s. neck** décolleté *m* rond; *Fishing* **s. net** drague *f*
▸ **scoop out VT SEP** *(wood, tomato etc)* évider; **to s. the water out of a boat** écoper un bateau
▸ **scoop up VT SEP** *(sand, coal, flour etc)* *(with hands)* prendre à pleines mains; *(with scoop)* *(sand, mud etc)* ramasser; *(water)* puiser; *(ice-cream, mashed potato)* faire des boules de; **she scooped up the last of her soup** elle finit son assiette d'un coup de cuillère; **he scooped up the book from the floor** il ramassa le livre qui était par terre; **the helicopter scooped him up** l'hélicoptère le repêcha; **she scooped the baby up (in her arms)** elle a saisi le bébé (dans ses bras)

scoot [sku:t] **VI** *Fam* **to s. (off** or **away)** filer, déguerpir; **he came scooting up to me** il se précipita sur moi; **it's time to s.!** allez, on se casse!

scooter ['sku:tər] **N** *(for child)* trottinette *f*, patinette *f*, **(motor) s.** scooter *m*

scope [skəʊp] **N** *(of action, law etc)* portée *f*, étendue *f*; *(of science etc)* domaine *m*; *(of undertaking)* envergure *f*; *(for sb's movements etc)* espace *m*, place *f*; **s. of cover** *(in insurance)* objet *m* de garantie; **the guidelines leave a lot of s. for interpretation** les instructions laissent une grande place à l'interprétation; **it's beyond** or **outside my s.** cela n'est pas de mon ressort, cela n'est pas ou ne rentre pas dans ma compétence; **it is beyond the s. of my comprehension how ...** je ne comprends absolument pas comment ...; **to have no/a lot of s. for manoeuvre** n'avoir aucune/avoir une grande marge de

manœuvre; **it's outside the s. of this enquiry** cela n'entre pas dans les limites de cette enquête; **to give full** or **free s. to sb** laisser le champ libre à qn; **to give full** or **free s. to one's imagination** laisser libre cours à son imagination; **there's little s. for people with your qualifications** il y a peu de possibilités pour des gens avec des qualifications telles que les vôtres
VT *Am Fam (look at)* mater, reluquer; *(see)* voir; **he's at the beach scoping the babes** il est à la plage en train de mater les nanas; **did you s. that ring he was wearing?** t'as vu un peu la bague qu'il avait au doigt?

scorch [skɔ:tʃ] **VT** *(of fire etc)* *(clothes etc)* (légèrement) brûler; *(of sun)* *(grass etc)* brûler, dessécher; *Culin (meat etc)* laisser brûler
VI 1 *(of material etc)* brûler **2** *Br Fam (move quickly)* **he scorched after her** il courut après elle; **to s. down the road** *(of person, car)* descendre la rue à toute vitesse; **she scorched past the other competitors** elle a dépassé les autres concurrents à toute vitesse; **she went scorching past us in her new car** elle passa devant nous comme une fusée dans sa nouvelle voiture
N trace *f* de brûlure
▸▸ *Mil* **scorched earth policy** tactique *f ou* politique *f* de la terre brûlée; **s. mark** trace de brûlure
▸ **scorch along VI** *Br Fam (of car, runner)* passer à toute allure

scorcher ['skɔ:tʃər] **N** *Fam (hot day)* journée *f* torride; **today's been a s.** il en a fait un plat aujourd'hui

scorching ['skɔ:tʃɪŋ] **ADJ** *(sun)* brûlant, ardent; *(wind)* brûlant; *(heat, day)* torride
ADV *(day)* torride; **s. hot** *(water, drink, saucepan etc)* brûlant; *Fam* **it's s. hot here** il fait une chaleur à crever ici

SCORE [skɔ:r]

N score 1	▪ marque 1	▪ rayure 2
▪ rainure 2	▪ entaille 2	▪ strie 2
▪ critère 4	▪ partition 5	▪ vingt 6
VT marquer 1	▪ rayer 2	▪ composer la
	musique de 3	▪ acheter 4
VI marquer 1	▪ compter les points 2	
▪ découper 4	▪ faire une touche 5	

N 1 *Sport etc* score *m*, marque *f*; *(in quiz)* score; **after 20 minutes, there was still no s.** après 20 minutes, le score était toujours zéro à zéro; **what's the s.?** quel est le score ou la marque?; *Fig Fam* on en est où?, qu'est-ce qui se passe?; **to keep the s.** marquer ou compter les points; *Cards* tenir la marque; **what was your s.?** combien tu as fait ou marqué?; *Fig Fam* **to know the s.** savoir ce qu'il en est
2 *(line made by cutting)* rayure *f*, rainure *f*, *(deeper)* entaille *f*, *(on rock etc)* strie *f*
3 **old s.** or **scores** *(dispute)* vieille(s) rancœur(s) *f(pl)*; **to have an old s. to settle with sb** avoir un vieux compte à régler avec qn; **to pay off** or **settle old scores** régler de vieux comptes
4 *(reason, grounds)* critère *m*; **on what s. was her application rejected?** sur quels critères sa candidature a-t-elle été rejetée?; **don't worry on that s.** n'ayez aucune crainte sur ce point ou à ce sujet
5 *Mus* partition *f*; **full s.** partition d'orchestre
6 *(pl* score) *(twenty)* **a s.** vingt, une vingtaine; *Arch* **three or four s. people** entre soixante et quatre-vingts personnes; *Fam* **you can find them by the s.** on les trouve à la pelle; *Fam* **scores** *(a large number)* un grand nombre; *Fam* **scores of people** une foule de gens **VOIR GRAMMAIRE A12–13; B59**
VT 1 *Sport (goal, try, points)* marquer; **to s. a hit** *(with song)* faire un tube; *Fig (of idea etc)* faire un tabac; *(of person)* faire des ravages;

Fig **to s. a success** remporter un succès; *Fig Fam* **to s. points off sb** river son clou à qn; *Fig Fam* **to s. an own goal** se faire du tort à soi-même
2 *(cut line in)* *(cylinder, ground, paper, wood etc)* rayer; *(leather etc)* inciser; *(rock etc)* strier; **she scored her name on the bench** elle grava son nom sur le banc; **s. the meat/fish with a sharp knife** faites des petites entailles dans la viande/le poisson avec un couteau bien aiguisé; **a mountainside scored by torrents** un flanc de montagne creusé ou raviné par les torrents; **water had scored grooves into the rock** l'eau avait creusé des rainures dans le rocher
3 *Mus (film, play etc)* composer la musique de; **scored for piano, violin and flute** pour piano, violon et flûte
4 *Sl (drugs)* acheter
VI 1 *Sport (of football player, team)* marquer; *(in rugby)* marquer un essai; *(in basketball)* marquer un panier
2 *(keep the score)* compter ou marquer les points
3 *Fig* **that's where he scores** *(that's where he has the advantage)* c'est là qu'il est le plus fort; **this is where the new Renault really scores** c'est là que la nouvelle Renault est vraiment super; **he scores on looks but not much else** il est mignon mais ça s'arrête là
4 *(with knife, scissors)* découper; **s. along the dotted line** découper le long des pointillés
5 *Sl (find sexual partner)* faire une touche
6 *Sl (buy drugs)* acheter de la dope
▸ **score off VT INSEP** *Fam (win point in argument etc)* **to s. off sb** river son clou à qn
VT SEP *(delete)* rayer; **s. his name off the list** rayez son nom de la liste
▸ **score out VT SEP** *(delete)* rayer

scoreboard ['skɔ:bɔ:d] **N** tableau *m* d'affichage

scorecard ['skɔ:kɑ:d] **N** *Sport* carte *f ou* fiche *f* de score; *Golf* carte du parcours; *(at shooting range)* carton *m*

scorer ['skɔ:rər] **N** *Sport* **1** *(person who keeps score)* personne *f* qui marque les points **2** *Ftbl etc (person who scores goal, point etc)* buteur, -euse; **the team's top (goal) s.** le meilleur buteur de l'équipe

scoring ['skɔ:rɪŋ] **N 1** *Sport* **to open the s.** ouvrir la marque; **there was no s. until ...** aucun point ou *Ftbl etc* but n'avait été marqué jusqu'à ce que ... **2** *(grooves etc)* *(on surface)* rayure *f*; *(on rock)* stries *fpl*, striation *f*, *(on cylinder etc)* rayures **3** *Mus (of piece of music)* orchestration *f*, arrangement *m*

scorn [skɔ:n] **VT 1** dédaigner, mépriser; **she scorned their help** elle a dédaigné leur aide **2** **to s. to do sth** dédaigner de faire qch
N dédain *m*, mépris *m*; **to pour s. on sth** rejeter qch avec mépris

scornful ['skɔ:nfʊl] **ADJ** *(person, smile etc)* dédaigneux, méprisant; **to be s. of sb/sth** dédaigner ou mépriser qn/qch, traiter qn/qch avec mépris ou dédain

scornfully ['skɔ:nfʊlɪ] **ADV** dédaigneusement, avec mépris

Scorpio ['skɔ:pɪəʊ] **N** *Astrol* Scorpion *m*; **to be (a) S.** être (du) Scorpion

scorpion ['skɔ:pɪən] **N** *(animal)* scorpion *m*

Scot [skɒt] **N** Écossais, -aise **VOIR GRAMMAIRE A19**

Scotch [skɒtʃ] **VOIR GRAMMAIRE A19** **ADJ** *(not used in Scotland)* écossais
N 1 *(whisky)* scotch *m* **2** *(not used in Scotland)* **the S.** les Écossais *mpl*
▸▸ *Culin* **S. broth** = soupe *f* écossaise à base de légumes et d'orge perlée; *Culin* **S. egg** = œuf *m* dur entouré de chair à saucisse et en-

robé de chapelure; **S. fir** pin *m* d'Écosse; **S. mist** bruine *f*, *Fam* **what do think that is, then, S. mist?** si tu allais à la mer, tu n'y trouverais pas d'eau; **S. pine** pin d'Écosse; *Am* **S. tape**® Scotch® *m*; **S. terrier** scottish-terrier *m*, *pl* scottish-terriers, Scotch-terrier *m*, *pl* Scotch-terriers; **S. whisky** scotch, whisky *m* écossais

scotch [skɒtʃ] **vt** *(project etc)* mettre fin à, faire échouer; *(rumour)* mettre fin à, mettre un terme à

scot-free ['skɒt-] **ADJ** *Fam* **to get off s.** *(unpunished)* s'en tirer à bon compte

Scotland ['skɒtlənd] **N** Écosse *f*
▸▸ **S. Office** = ministère *m* des affaires écossaises; **S. Secretary** =ministre des affaires écossaises à Westminster; **S. Yard** = ancien nom *m* du siège de la police à Londres (aujourd'hui "New Scotland Yard"), ≃ Quai *m* des Orfèvres

Scots [skɒts] VOIR GRAMMAIRE A19 **ADJ** écossais
N *Ling* écossais *m*
▸▸ **S. fir** pin *m* d'Écosse; **the S. Guards** la Garde écossaise; **S. pine** pin d'Écosse

Scotsman, *pl* **Scotsmen** ['skɒtsmən] **N** Écossais *m* VOIR GRAMMAIRE A19

Scotswoman, *pl* **Scotswomen** ['skɒtswʊmən, -wɪmɪn] **N** Écossaise *f* VOIR GRAMMAIRE A19

Scott [skɒt] **INT** *Old-fashioned* **Great S.!** Grand Dieu!

Scotticism ['skɒtɪsɪz(ə)m] **N** expression *f* écossaise

Scottie (dog) ['skɒtɪ] **N** *Fam* scottish-terrier *m*, *pl* scottish-terriers

Scottish ['skɒtɪʃ] **ADJ** écossais VOIR GRAMMAIRE A19
▸▸ **S. Executive** = gouvernement *m* semi-autonome de l'Écosse; **S. Office** = ministère *m* des affaires écossaises; **S. Parliament** parlement *m* écossais; **S. terrier** scottish-terrier *m*, *pl* scottish-terriers, Scotch-terrier *m*, *pl* Scotch-terriers

---

Scottish Parliament
Le Parlement écossais fut établi dans le cadre du projet de décentralisation ("devolution") du gouvernement travailliste et fut inauguré à Édimbourg en mai 1999. Les 129 membres du Parlement écossais (MSP) siègent sous la houlette du "First Minister". Le Parlement est pourvu d'une grande autonomie en matière de fiscalité mais ses pouvoirs législatifs sont néanmoins limités.

---

scoundrel ['skaʊndr(ə)l] **N** scélérat *m*, vaurien *m*; *Fam (child, puppy etc)* chenapan *m*

scour[1] ['skaʊər] **vt** *(saucepan etc)* récurer; *(floor etc)* frotter; *(in metalwork) (metal surface)* décaper; **the stream had scoured a channel in the hillside** le cours d'eau avait creusé un passage dans la colline
N **to give a saucepan/the bath a good s.** bien récurer une casserole/la baignoire

scour[2] **vi** = **scour about**
vt *(search) (countryside)* parcourir, battre; *(woods, house)* fouiller; **to s. the country for sb** battre la campagne à la recherche de qn
▸ **scour about** **vi** *(search widely)* battre la campagne

scourer ['skaʊərər] **N (pan** or **pot) s.** *(metal)* tampon *m* à récurer; *(sponge)* éponge *f* à récurer

scourge [skɜːdʒ] **N 1** *(affliction)* fléau *m* **2** *Arch, Lit (whip)* fouet *m*; *Rel (for self-flagellation)* discipline *f*; *Fig* **he was the s. of ...** il était la terreur de ...

---

vt 1 *Arch, Lit (whip)* fouetter, flageller; *Rel* **to s. oneself** se donner la discipline **2** *Lit (afflict) (of war, famine, drought)* dévaster; *(of corruption)* accabler

scouring ['skaʊərɪŋ] **N, ADJ** *(scrubbing)* récurage *m*, frottage *m*; *(in metalwork)* décapage *m*
▸▸ **s. pad** *(metal)* tampon *m* à récurer; *(sponge)* éponge *f* à récurer; **s. powder** poudre *f* à récurer

Scouse [skaʊs] *Br Fam* **ADJ** de Liverpool
N *Ling* dialecte *m* de Liverpool

Scouser ['skaʊsər] **N** *Fam* personne *f* originaire de Liverpool

scout [skaʊt] **N 1** *(person)*, *Mil* éclaireur *m*; *Br Aut Old-fashioned* dépanneur *m* *(employé par les organismes d'assistance automobile)*; **(boy) s.** *(Catholic)* scout *m*; *(non-Catholic)* éclaireur *m*; *Am* **(Girl) S.** guide *f*, éclaireuse *f*, *Cin, Sport etc* **(talent) s.** dénicheur, -euse de talents; *Am Fam* **a good s.** *(fellow)* un bon gars
2 *(aircraft)* avion *m* de reconnaissance
3 *Fam (search)* tour *m* de reconnaissance; **to have a s. around for sth** chercher qch; **I had a good s. around** j'ai bien cherché
4 *Univ (servant)* garçon *m* de service *(spécialement à Oxford)*
vi *Mil etc* aller en reconnaissance; *Cin, Sport etc* **to s. for talent** être à la recherche de futurs talents
▸▸ **s. camp** camp *m* scout
▸ **scout about, scout around** **vi** *(search)* chercher **(for sth** qch)

scouting ['skaʊtɪŋ] **N** scoutisme *m*
▸▸ **the S. Movement** le mouvement scout

scoutmaster ['skaʊtmɑːstər] **N** chef *m* de troupe

scow [skaʊ] **N** *Naut* chaland *m*

scowl [skaʊl] **N** air *m* renfrogné; **to look at sb with a s.** regarder qn d'un air renfrogné
vi se renfrogner; **to s. at sb** menacer qn du regard, regarder qn d'un air menaçant

scowling ['skaʊlɪŋ] **ADJ** renfrogné

Scrabble® ['skræb(ə)l] **N** Scrabble® *m*

scrabble ['skræb(ə)l] **vi** **to s. (about** or **around)** *(scrape)* gratter; *(grope)* tâtonner; **I was scrabbling about in the dark, trying to find my key** je tâtonnais dans le noir pour trouver ma clef; **beggars were scrabbling about in the dirt for coins** des mendiants grattaient dans la saleté pour trouver des pièces; **to s. about for work** chercher du travail désespérément

scrag [skræg] **N the s. of the neck** la nuque; *Culin* **s. (end) of mutton** collet *m* de mouton
vt **(-gg-)** *Old-fashioned Fam (tease, rag)* tourmenter

scraggy ['skrægɪ] **ADJ** *(person etc)* maigre, maigrichon, maigrelet; *(piece of meat)* maigrichon, maigrelet

scram [skræm] **vi** **(-mm-)** *Fam* filer, ficher le camp; **s.!** file!, fiche le camp!

scramble ['skræmb(ə)l] **N 1** *(rush, struggle)* bousculade *f*, *Hist* **the s. for Africa** la lutte des puissances coloniales pour se répartir l'Afrique; **a s. for jobs** une bataille pour l'emploi; **a s. for profits** une course effrénée aux profits; **there was a s. for the door** il y a eu une ruée vers la porte
2 *(climb)* ascension *f* difficile
3 *Aviat Fam (takeoff)* décollage *m* d'urgence
4 *Br Sport* **(motorcycle) s.** motocross *m inv*
vi 1 to s. for sth *(struggle)* se battre *ou* se bousculer pour avoir qch
2 *(move, often with difficulty)* **to s. up/down/in/out** monter/descendre/entrer/sortir péniblement; **we scrambled over the rocks** nous avons grimpé par-dessus les rochers; **to s. up a hill** grimper une colline à quatre pattes

---

3 *(move with speed)* **to s. up a ladder/tree** monter à une échelle/un arbre à toute vitesse; **he scrambled into his trousers** il a enfilé son pantalon à toute vitesse
4 *Aviat Fam (take off)* décoller d'urgence
5 *Sport* faire du motocross
vt 1 *Culin (eggs)* brouiller; **scrambled eggs** œufs *mpl* brouillés **2** *Tel, Electron etc (message)* brouiller; **scrambled** *(encoded)* brouillé, codé, crypté **3** *Aviat Fam (aircraft)* faire décoller d'urgence

scrambler ['skræmblər] **N 1** *Tel etc (device)* brouilleur *m* **2** *Br Sport (on motorbike)* motard *m* de motocross

scrambling ['skræmblɪŋ] **N 1** *Tel, Electron etc (of message)* brouillage *m* **2** *Br Sport* **(motorcycle) s.** motocross *m*

scramjet ['skræmdʒet] **N** statoréacteur *m* à combustion supersonique

scran [skræn] **N** *Br Fam (food)* bouffe *f*, graille *f*

scrap[1] [skræp] **N 1** *(piece) (of paper)* morceau *m*, bout *m*; *(of land etc)* parcelle *f*, *(of ribbon, information, evidence)* bout; *(of bread etc)* petit morceau; *(for scrapbook)* image *f*, *(cutting from newspaper)* coupure *f*, **to fight over the scraps** se disputer les restes; **to tear sth into scraps** déchirer qch en morceaux; **scraps** *(of food)* restes *mpl*, *(of cloth)* bouts; **not a s. of evidence** pas la moindre preuve; **there isn't a s. of truth in what she says** il n'y a pas une parcelle de vérité dans ce qu'elle dit; **to catch scraps of a conversation** saisir des bouts *ou* des bribes de conversation **2 to sell sth for s.** vendre qch à la casse
vt (-pp-) 1 *(discard) (part etc)* mettre au rebut; *(machine)* mettre hors service; *(nuclear missiles etc)* abandonner la construction de; *(project)* laisser tomber, abandonner **2** *(send for scrap) (car, lorry etc)* mettre à la ferraille *ou* à la casse
▸▸ **s. dealer** ferrailleur *m*; **s. iron** ferraille *f*, *Br* **s. merchant** ferrailleur *m*; **s. metal** ferraille; **s. paper** *(papier m)* brouillon *m*

scrap[2] **N** *Fam (fight)* bagarre *f*, *(quarrel)* dispute *f*, **to have a s.** *(fight)* se bagarrer; *(quarrel)* se disputer; **to get into a s.** *(fight)* se bagarrer; *(quarrel)* se disputer **(with sb** avec qn)
vi (-pp-) *Fam (fight)* se bagarrer; *(quarrel)* se disputer

scrapbook ['skræpbʊk] **N** album *m* *(de découpages)*

scrape [skreɪp] **vt 1** *(scratch) (skin, polished surface etc)* érafler; **to s. one's shins** s'érafler les tibias; **to s. the bottom** *(of ship)* sillonner *ou* talonner le fond
2 *(clean) (dirt, burnt part)* racler **(off** de); *(paint, wallpaper, surface)* gratter **(off** de); *(wall)* ravaler; *Culin (carrots etc)* gratter; *(in tanning) (skin)* racler, dépiler; **to s. one's shoes** racler *ou* décrotter ses chaussures; **to s. one's plate clean** racler son assiette; *Naut* **to s. a ship's bottom** nettoyer la carène d'un navire; *Fig* **to s. the (bottom of the) barrel** *(with money)* racler les fonds de tiroir; *(be reduced to extremes)* être tombé bien bas
3 with her hair scraped back les cheveux tirés
4 *(achieve laboriously)* **to s. a living** gagner tout juste sa vie *ou Fam* sa croûte; **to s. a win** arracher une victoire; **to s. a pass** *(in exam)* réussir de justesse
vi 1 *(scratch)* gratter; *(make sound) (of wheel, pen, violin etc)* grincer; **branches that s. against the shutters** branches qui frottent contre les volets
2 to s. or **s. away (on the fiddle)** gratter du violon
3 *Fam (succeed with difficulty)* **to s. home** *(win game, race)* gagner de justesse; **to s. in-**

to college réussir de justesse à rentrer à l'université

N 1 *(action with scraper)* coup *m* de grattoir *ou* de racloir; *(wound on skin)* éraflure *f*, *(thin layer)* *(of butter etc)* mince couche *f*, *(sound)* *(of violin etc)* grincement *m*; **to give sth a s. with one's nail** gratter qch avec son ongle; **she had given the car a nasty s. on the side** elle avait fait une belle éraflure sur le côté de la voiture

2 *Fam (difficulty)* embarras *m*; **to get into a s.** se mettre dans l'embarras *ou Fam* le pétrin; **to get out of a s.** se tirer d'affaire *ou* d'embarras

▸ **scrape along** VI *(just manage financially etc)* vivoter, s'en tirer péniblement

▸ **scrape by** VI **1** = **scrape along**

2 *(just succeed) (in an exam)* réussir de justesse

▸ **scrape in** VI *(just succeed) (in entering university etc)* entrer de justesse; *(in winning election)* gagner de justesse; *Sport (in qualifying)* se qualifier de justesse

▸ **scrape off** VT SEP *(remove) (paint etc)* racler, gratter

▸ **scrape out** VT SEP *(saucepan)* récurer; *(pipes)* nettoyer

▸ **scrape through** VI = **scrape by 2**

VT INSEP **s. through an examination** être reçu de justesse à un examen; **the bill only just scraped through its first reading** le projet de loi a été adopté de justesse en première lecture

▸ **scrape together** VT SEP *(save with difficulty) (sum of money)* rassembler

▸ **scrape up** VT SEP **1** = **scrape together**

2 *Hum* he scraped himself up off the floor il a fini par se relever; **we had to s. him up off the ground** il a fallu le ramasser à la petite cuillère

scraper ['skreɪpər] N racloir *m*, grattoir *m*; *Aut etc* **(ice) s.** raclette *f*, grattoir *(pour parebrise)*; **door** *or* **shoe s.** décrottoir *m*, grattoir

scrapheap ['skræphiːp] N tas *m* de ferraille; **to throw sth on the s.** mettre qch à la ferraille *ou* au rebut; *Fig* **to throw sb on the s.** laisser tomber qn comme une vieille savate; **he ended up on the s.** *(through redundancy etc)* on l'a mis au rebut; **to consign ideas/projects to the s.** mettre des idées/projets au rebut; **lots of companies are on the s.** beaucoup d'entreprises sont hors de combat

scrapie ['skreɪpɪ] N *Vet* tremblante *f*

scraping ['skreɪpɪŋ] N **1** *(sound) (of pen, saw, violin etc)* grattement *m*; *Fig* **bowing and s.** salamalecs *mpl* **2** *(thin layer) (of butter etc)* mince couche *f*

scrapman, *pl* **scrapmen** ['skræpmən] N ferrailleur *m*, casseur *m*

scrapple ['skræp(ə)l] N *Am Culin* = (genre de) friand *m* fait de farine de maïs et de morceaux de porc que l'on fait frire à la poêle

scrappy ['skræpɪ] ADJ *(collection etc)* hétérogène, hétéroclite; *(speech, film, novel)* décousu; *(work, performance)* inégal, -aux; *Sport* **a s. second half** une seconde mi-temps inégale; **s. knowledge** connaissances *fpl* fragmentaires

scratch [skrætʃ] N **1** *(mark, cut)* égratignure *f*, éraflure *f*; *(made by claw)* griffure *f*; *(on polished surface, record etc)* rayure *f*; **it's nothing, just a s.** ce n'est rien, juste une égratignure; **he came out of it without a s.** il s'en est sorti indemne, il s'en est sorti sans la moindre égratignure

2 *(blow) (with fingernail)* coup *m* d'ongle; *(with claw)* coup de griffe

3 *(repeated action) (of pen)* grincement *m*; **could you give my back a s.?** tu peux me gratter le dos?; **to give one's head a s.** se gratter la tête

4 *Fig Fam* **to start from s.** partir de rien; *(restart)* repartir à zéro; **to build a house from s.** construire une maison de bout en bout; **to write a dictionary from s.** écrire un dictionnaire totalement nouveau; **she built the business up from s.** elle a monté l'affaire à partir de rien; **to come up to s.** être à la hauteur, faire le poids; **to bring sb up to s.** mettre qn à niveau; *(prepare for exam)* préparer qn; **to bring sth up to s.** mettre qch à niveau; **he's not up to s.** il ne fait pas le poids, il n'est pas à la hauteur; **the work was not up to s.** le travail n'était pas à la hauteur

5 *Am Fam (money)* fric *m*, pognon *m*

ADJ *(meal etc)* improvisé, sommaire

VT **1** *(of cat, person etc)* griffer; *(of thorn etc) (skin)* égratigner, érafler; *(glass, record etc)* rayer; **he was badly scratched** il était tout écorché; **to s. oneself** s'égratigner, s'érafler; *(with nails)* se griffer; **to s. one's name on a bench** graver son nom sur un banc; *Fig* **she quickly scratched a few notes on her pad** elle griffonna rapidement quelques notes sur son calepin; **to s. a hole** creuser un trou avec les griffes; *Fig* **to s. the surface (of the problem)** ne faire qu'effleurer le problème; *Fig* **s. a cynic and you'll often find an idealist** si l'on gratte un peu, on trouve souvent un idéaliste derrière un cynique

2 *(rub) (metal, itchy skin)* gratter; **to s. one's head** se gratter la tête; *Fig* **you s. my back and I'll s. yours** rends-moi service et je te renverrai l'ascenseur

3 *(of bird, animal) (ground)* gratter

4 *(delete)* **to s. sb off** *or* **from a list** rayer *ou* biffer qn d'une liste; **to s. sb from a team** exclure qn d'une équipe; *Horseracing* **to s. a horse** déclarer forfait pour un cheval; *(of stewards)* scratcher un cheval

VI **1** *(of person, animal) (to relieve itch)* se gratter; *(of bird, animal) (in the ground)* gratter; *(of thorns, branches etc)* piquer; *(of wool, new clothes)* gratter; **don't s.!** *(yourself)* arrête de te gratter!; *(stop scratching me)* arrête de me griffer!; **a cat that scratches** un chat qui griffe; **to s. at the door** gratter à la porte

2 *(of pen etc)* grincer, gratter

3 *Sport (of entrant)* déclarer forfait

▸▸ **s. card** carte *f* à gratter; *Golf* **s. golfer** *(in tournament)* joueur, -euse classé(e) zéro; *Am* **s. paper** *(papier m)* brouillon *m*; *Sport* **s. team** équipe *f* improvisée

▸ **scratch about, scratch around** VI **to s. about** *or* **around for sth** essayer de dénicher qch

▸ **scratch out** VT SEP **1** *(remove by scratching)* **to s. sb's eyes out** arracher les yeux à qn

2 *(delete) (word)* rayer, biffer, raturer; *(with penknife)* gratter, effacer

▸ **scratch together** VT SEP = **scrape together**

scratching ['skrætʃɪŋ] N **1** *(with fingernail)* coups *mpl* d'ongle; *(damaging) (action)* rayage *m*; *(on surface)* rayures *fpl* **2** *(to relieve itch)* grattement *m* **3** *(sound)* grattement *m*; *(of pen nib)* grincement *m*; *(of record)* craquement(s) *m(pl)*

scratchpad ['skrætʃpæd] N *Am Comput* bloc-notes *m*, *pl* blocs-notes

▸▸ **s. memory** mémoire *f* bloc-notes

scratchy ['skrætʃɪ] ADJ **1** *(drawing)* peu assuré; **s. writing** pattes *fpl* de mouche **2** *(pen etc) (messy)* qui gratte; *(noisy)* qui grince *(sur le papier)*; *(material etc) (coarse)* rugueux, grossier; *(that irritates skin)* qui gratte (la peau); *(record)* qui craque

scrawl [skrɔːl] *Pej* N *(writing)* griffonnage *m*, gribouillage *m*; **this s. is supposed to be your answer?** ces gribouillages-là?

VT *(letter etc)* griffonner, gribouiller

VI écrire comme un chat

scrawny ['skrɔːnɪ] ADJ *(neck)* maigre, décharné; *(piece of meat)* maigrichon

scream [skriːm] N **1** *(cry)* cri *m* perçant *ou* aigu, hurlement *m*; **a s. of pain** un cri *ou* un hurlement de douleur; **screams of laughter** de grands éclats *mpl* de rire **2** *Fam (amusing thing, person)* **it was a s.** c'était à se tordre (de rire); **he's a s.** il est tordant

VI *(once)* pousser un cri perçant *ou* aigu, hurler; *(repeatedly)* pousser des cris aigus, hurler; *(of rabbit, hare)* couiner; *(of jet, missile)* faire un bruit perçant; **jets screamed overhead** des jets sont passés au-dessus de nos têtes dans un bruit assourdissant; **to s. with pain** crier *ou* hurler de douleur; **to s. with laughter** rire à gorge déployée *ou* aux éclats; **everyone's screaming about high prices** tout le monde pousse les hauts cris à propos des prix élevés; **the poster screams at you** l'affiche vous saute à la figure

VT **to s. abuse** hurler des injures; **to s. oneself hoarse** crier à en avoir la voix rauque; **the headlines screamed 'guilty'** le mot 'coupable' s'étalait en grosses lettres sur les premières pages des journaux

screaming ['skriːmɪŋ] ADJ *(person)* criard; *(headlines)* tape-à-l'œil *inv*, *(missile, jet)* qui fait un bruit perçant

N *(of terror etc)* cris *mpl*, hurlements *mpl*, *(of birds etc)* cris perçants

screamingly ['skriːmɪŋlɪ] ADV *Fam* **s. funny** tordant, à se tordre (de rire)

scree [skriː] N *Geol* éboulis *m*

screech [skriːtʃ] N *(cry)* cri *m* perçant *ou* aigu; *(of tyres, brakes etc)* crissement *m*; **a s. of laughter** un éclat de rire perçant

VI *(of person, parrot etc)* pousser des cris perçants *ou* aigus; *(of tyres)* crisser; **the car screeched to a halt** la voiture s'est arrêtée dans un crissement de pneus; **she does tend to s. on the high notes** elle a tendance à hurler les notes aiguës

VT *(orders, insults)* hurler

▸▸ Orn **s. owl** chat-huant *m*, *pl* chats-huants, hulotte *f*

screeching ['skriːtʃɪŋ] ADJ *(laugh)* perçant, aigu; *(tyres)* qui crissent

N *(cries)* cris *mpl* perçants *ou* aigus; *(of tyres)* crissement *m*

screed [skriːd] N *usu Pej (long book)* pavé *m*; *(long article)* article *m* à rallonge; **to write screeds** en écrire des tartines; **she wrote me a s.** *(long letter)* elle m'a écrit une lettre qui fait des kilomètres

screen [skriːn] N **1** *(in front of fire)* écran *m*; *(against draught)* paravent *m*; *(partition)* cloison *f*; *(wrought iron etc)* grille *f*; **choir s.** *(in church)* grille de chœur; **rood s.** jubé *m*; **s. of trees** rideau *m* d'arbres; **to act as a s. for a criminal** couvrir un criminel; **the shop was just a s. for her criminal activities** le magasin n'était qu'une couverture pour ses activités criminelles; **protective/safety s.** écran de protection/de sécurité; **fire s.** écran ignifuge

2 *Cin, TV etc* écran *m*; **the s.** *(cinema)* l'écran; **television s.** écran de télévision; **the big s.** *(cinema)* le grand écran; **the small s.** *(television)* le petit écran; **the multiplex has twelve screens** le multiplexe a douze salles; **stars of stage and s.** des vedettes de théâtre et de cinéma; **a picture/a face appeared on the s.** une image/un visage est apparu(e) sur l'écran

3 *Comput* écran *m*; **on s.** sur (l')écran; **to bring up the next s.** amener l'écran suivant; **this takes you back/forwards a s.** *or* **s. by s.** ceci vous fait reculer/avancer écran par écran; **s.-oriented** orienté écran

4 *Elec, Electron* écran *m*; **fluorescent s.** écran fluorescent

5 *Constr, Min (sieve)* crible *m*, tamis *m*, sas *m*; *Am (ventilation grill in door)* grille *f* de ventilation

VT 1 *(conceal) (something)* masquer, dissimuler, cacher; *(behind a screen)* cacher derrière un écran *ou* un paravent; *(protect)* abriter, protéger; *(from harmful influences etc)* mettre à l'abri *(from* de); **to s. sth from view** cacher *ou* masquer *ou* dérober qch aux regards *ou* à la vue

2 *Cin (film)* projeter, passer; *(show on television)* passer à l'écran

3 *(personnel)* trier, sélectionner; *(job applicants)* examiner; *(immigrants etc)* filtrer; *(news etc)* filtrer, passer au crible; *Med (person)* faire passer un test de dépistage à; **to s. sb for security** contrôler qn pour des raisons de sécurité

4 *(sieve etc) (gravel, coal, ore, grain etc)* cribler, passer au crible

▸▸ *Cin* **s. actor** acteur *m* de cinéma; *Cin* **s. actress** actrice *f* de cinéma; *Cin, TV* **s. adaptation** adaptation *f* à l'écran; *Comput* **s. capture** capture *f* d'écran; *Comput* **s. controller** contrôleur *m* d'écran; *Comput* **s. display** affichage *m*; *Am* **s. door** porte *f* avec moustiquaire; *Comput* **s. down command** commande *f* écran vers le bas, commande écran suivant; *Comput* **s. dump** capture d'écran; *Comput* **s. font** fonte *f* écran; *Comput* **s. generation** génération *f* d'écrans; *Cin, TV* **s. image** image *f* à l'écran; *Psy* **s. memory** souvenir-écran *m, pl* souvenirs-écrans; *Comput* **s. painting** modification *f* du papier peint; *Comput* **s. refresh** actualisation *f ou* régénération *f* de l'écran; *Cin* **s. rights** droits *mpl* d'adaptation à l'écran; *Comput* **s. saver** économiseur *m* d'écran; *Comput* **s. shot** capture d'écran; *Cin* **s. test** bout *m* d'essai; *Comput* **s. up command** commande écran vers le haut, commande écran précédent; *Aut* **s. wash** lave-glace *m, pl* lave-glaces; *Cin, TV* **s. writing** écriture *f* de scénarios

▸ **screen off** VT SEP *(part of room)* séparer par un paravent/une cloison/un rideau/*etc*; **their house is screened off (from ours) by a row of trees** nous ne pouvons voir leur maison de la nôtre à cause de la rangée d'arbres qui les sépare; **the nurses screened off the dying man** les infirmières ont tiré les rideaux/ont mis des paravents autour du lit du mourant

▸ **screen out** VT SEP éliminer, écarter

screening ['skri:nɪŋ] **N 1** *Cin (of film)* projection *f*, passage *m* à l'écran; *(on television)* passage à l'écran; **when the film had its first s.** quand le film est passé pour la première fois à l'écran **2** *(of personnel)* triage *m*, sélection *f*; *(of immigrants, news etc)* filtrage *m*; *(of job applicants)* examen *m* sélectif; *Med (of contagious patients)* dépistage *m*; **s. for a disease** dépistage d'une maladie; *Med* **to have a s.** se faire faire un test de dépistage **3** *(sieving) (of gravel, coal etc)* criblage *m*; *(of grain)* sassement *m*

▸▸ *Cin* **s. room** salle *f* de projection

screenplay ['skri:npleɪ] **N** *Cin* scénario *m*

screenporch ['skri:npɔ:tʃ] **N** *Am* véranda *f (entourée d'une moustiquaire)*

screenwriter ['skri:nraɪtər] **N** *Cin* scénariste *mf*

screw [skru:] **N 1** *(for fixing)* vis *f*; *Tech* **Archimedes' *or* Archimedean s.** vis d'Archimède; *Fam* **to have a s. loose** avoir une case de vide *ou* une araignée au plafond; *Fam* **to put the screws on sb, to tighten the s. on sb** mettre la pression sur qn

2 *Aviat, Naut* hélice *f*; **twin-s.** hélice double

3 *(turn of screw)* tour *m* de vis; *(turn of screwdriver)* coup *m* de tournevis; **give it another s.** serrez-le encore un peu

4 *Old-fashioned (twist) (of tobacco)* papillote *f*; *(of paper)* tortillon *m*

5 *Billiards* effet *m*; **to put (a *or* some) s. on the ball** donner de l'effet à la balle

6 *Br Sl (prison officer)* maton, -onne

7 *Vulg (sexual intercourse)* baise *f*; **what she needs is a good s.** c'est une mal-baisée; **to have a good s.** baiser un bon coup; **she's a good s.** c'est un bon coup

8 *Br Old-fashioned Fam (salary)* salaire *m*, paye *f*; **to be on a good s.** avoir un bon salaire

VT 1 *(fix)* visser; **to s. sth (on) to sth** visser qch à *ou* sur qch; **screwed together** vissés l'un(s) à l'autre; **to s. one's head round to see sth** se tordre le cou pour voir qch; **to s. one's face into a smile *or* grin** se forcer à sourire, faire une grimace plutôt qu'un sourire

2 *Fam (cheat) (person)* avoir, rouler; **we've been screwed!** on s'est fait avoir!; **to s. money from *or* out of sb** extorquer de l'argent à qn; **they're out to s. you for every penny you've got** ils essayent de vous extorquer tout l'argent que vous avez

3 *Billiards (ball)* donner de l'effet à

4 *Vulg (have sexual intercourse with)* s'envoyer, sauter, baiser; *Fig* **s. you!** va te faire foutre!; **s. him!** qu'il aille se faire foutre!; **s. the expense!** et merde, je peux bien m'offrir ça!

5 *Am Fam* **to s. the pooch** *(blunder)* faire une gaffe *ou* une boulette

VI 1 *(of tap etc)* tourner; **the knobs s. into the drawer** les boutons se vissent sur le tiroir **2** *Billiards (of ball)* rebondir de travers, dévier **3** *Vulg (have sexual intercourse)* baiser, s'envoyer en l'air

▸▸ **s. cap** *(of bottle)* bouchon *m* à vis; *(of jar)* couvercle *m* à vis; *Aviat, Naut* **s. propeller** hélice; **s. thread** pas *m ou* filet *m* de vis; **s. top** *(of bottle)* bouchon à vis; *(of jar)* couvercle à vis

▸ **screw around** VT SEP *Fam* **to s. sb around** *(treat badly)* se foutre de la gueule de qn; *(waste time of)* faire perdre son temps à qn

VI 1 *Fam (mess around)* glander **2** *Vulg (be promiscuous)* baiser *ou* coucher avec tout le monde

▸ **screw back** VI *Billiards (of player)* faire de l'effet rétrograde, faire un rétro; *(of ball)* revenir en arrière

▸ **screw down** VT SEP *(secure)* fixer *ou* tenir avec une/des vis

▸ **screw off** VT SEP *(lid)* dévisser

VI se dévisser

▸ **screw on** VT SEP *(attach)* visser; *Fam* **he's got his head screwed on, his head's screwed on the right way** il a la tête solide *ou* la tête sur les épaules

VI se visser

▸ **screw up** VT SEP **1** *(tighten by screwing)* visser; *(nut)* serrer; **to s. sth up tight** visser qch à bloc; **to s. up a piece of paper** froisser une feuille de papier; **to s. up one's eyes** plisser les yeux; **to s. up one's face** grimacer; **to s. up one's courage** prendre son courage à deux mains **2** *Sl (spoil) (job)* bousiller, foutre en l'air; **this has screwed up my plans** ça m'a foutu mes plans en l'air; **he screwed up the interview** il a complètement merdé à l'entretien **3** *Sl (make neurotic)* **to s. sb up** foutre qn en l'air; **her parents' divorce has really screwed her up** le divorce de ses parents l'a vraiment foutue en l'air

VI 1 *(of lid, nut etc)* se visser **2** **her face screwed up in distaste *or* disgust** elle fit une grimace de dégoût **3** *Sl (make a mess of sth)* merder

screwball ['skru:bɔ:l] **ADJ, N** *esp Am Fam* dingue *mf*

screwdriver ['skru:draɪvər] **N 1** *(tool)* tournevis *m*; **crossheaded s.** tournevis cruciforme **2** *(cocktail)* vodka-orange *f, pl* vodkas-orange

▸▸ **s. blade** lame *f* de tournevis; **s. handle** poignée *f* de tournevis

screwed [skru:d] **ADJ** *Fam* **1** *(in trouble)* **to be s.** être foutu **2** *Br (drunk)* bourré, rond

screw-loose ADJ *Am Fam* loufoque, loufedingue

screw-on ADJ *(earrings)* à vis; *Phot (lens)* détachable, mobile

screwy ['skru:ɪ] ADJ *Fam* dingue, loufoque

scribble ['skrɪb(ə)l] **VT** *(a few words, notes)* griffonner, gribouiller

VI gribouiller; *(write quickly, in notebook etc)* griffonner; **don't s. on the walls** ne gribouille pas sur les murs; **I used to s. a bit** j'écrivais un peu, quoi, autrefois

N 1 *(act of scribbling)* griffonnage *m*, gribouillage *m* **2** *(bad handwriting)* écriture *f* illisible, pattes *fpl* de mouche; **that's not drawing, it's just (a) s.** ce n'est pas du dessin, c'est du gribouillage

▸ **scribble down** VT SEP *(write)* = **scribble** VT

scribbler ['skrɪblər] **N 1** *(person who scribbles)* griffonneur, -euse, gribouilleur, -euse **2** *Fam (inferior writer)* écrivailleur, -euse

scribbling ['skrɪblɪŋ] **N** *(bad handwriting)* griffonnage *m*, gribouillage *m*; *Fam* **scribblings** *(inferior writings)* écrits *mpl* de deuxième zone

▸▸ **s. pad** bloc-notes *m, pl* blocs-notes; **s. paper** *(papier m)* brouillon *m*

scribe [skraɪb] **N** *Hist (person)* scribe *m*

scrim [skrɪm] **N** *Cin* diffuseur *m*

scrimmage ['skrɪmɪdʒ] **N 1** *(struggle)* mêlée *f*, bagarre *f*, bousculade *f* **2** *Am Ftbl* mêlée *f*

VI se bousculer

VT *Am Ftbl (ball)* mettre en mêlée

scrimp [skrɪmp] **VI** **to s. (and save)** faire des économies de bouts de chandelle

scrip [skrɪp] **N** *Fin (share)* titre *m* provisoire

▸▸ **s. certificate** certificat *m* d'actions provisoire; **s. issue** émission *f* d'actions gratuites

script [skrɪpt] **N 1** *(manuscript)* manuscrit *m*; *Sch (in exam)* copie *f*; *Theat* texte *m*; *Cin* scénario *m*, script *m*; **to read from a s.** *(of newsreader, politician etc)* lire ses notes; *also Fig* **that's not in the s.** ce n'est pas prévu au programme **2** *(as opposed to print)* écriture *f*; script; **Gothic s.** écriture gothique

▸▸ *Cin, TV* **s. department** équipe *f* des scénaristes; *Cin, TV* **s. development** développement *m* du scénario; *Cin, TV* **s. editor** scénariste *mf* (de réécriture); *Cin, TV* **s. girl** scripte *f*, script girl *f*; *Typ* **s. type** cursive *f*

scripted ['skrɪptɪd] ADJ *(remark etc)* préparé à l'avance

scriptural ['skrɪptʃər(ə)l] ADJ *Rel* scripturaire

scripture ['skrɪptʃər] **N 1** **(Holy) S., the Scriptures** l'Écriture *f* sainte, les (saintes) Écritures **2** *Sch* instruction *f* religieuse

▸▸ *Sch* **s. lesson** cours *m* d'histoire sainte

scriptwriter ['skrɪptraɪtər] **N** *Cin etc* scénariste *mf*

scriptwriting ['skrɪptraɪtɪŋ] **N** écriture *f* de scénarios

scrofula ['skrɒfjʊlə] **N** *Med* scrofule *f*

scrofulous ['skrɒfjʊləs] ADJ **1** *Med* scrofuleux **2** *(corrupt)* dépravé

scroll [skrəʊl] **N 1** *(roll of paper, parchment)* rouleau *m*; **the Dead Sea Scrolls** les manuscrits *mpl* de la mer Morte **2** *(decoration), Archit etc* spirale *f*; *(of Ionic capital)* volute *f*; *(in writing)* enjolivement *m*, arabesque *f*; *(in engraving etc)* cartouche *m* (encadrant un titre); *(of violin)* crosse *f* **3** *Comput* défilement *m*

VI *Comput* défiler

VT *Comput* faire défiler

▸▸ *Comput* **s. arrow** flèche *f* de défilement; *Comput* **s. bar** barre *f* de défilement; *Comput* **s. box** ascenseur *m*; *Comput* **s. button** bouton *m* de défilement; *Comput* **s. lock (key)** touche *f* d'arrêt de défilement; *Comput* **s. wheel** *(on mouse)* roue *f* de défilement

▶ **scroll down** Comput **VI** (of operator) faire défiler de haut en bas; (of text) défiler de haut en bas

VT INSEP to s. down a page passer à la page suivante

▶ **scroll through VT INSEP** Comput (text) parcourir

▶ **scroll up** Comput **VI** (of operator) faire défiler de bas en haut; (of text) défiler de bas en haut

VT INSEP to s. up a page passer à la page précédente

scrolling ['skrəʊlɪŋ] **N** Comput défilement m

Scrooge [skru:dʒ] **N** Fam grippe-sou m, pl grippe-sous

scrotal ['skrəʊtəl] **ADJ** Anat scrotal, -aux

scrotum ['skrəʊtəm] **N** Anat scrotum m

scrounge [skraʊndʒ] Fam **VT** (meal, cigarette) se faire offrir; **to s. money** taper les gens; **to s. sth from** or **off sb** se faire offrir qch par qn; **to s. money from sb** taper qn; **can I s. a cigarette off you?** tu m'offres une cigarette?; **could I s. a lift from someone?** est-ce que quelqu'un peut m'emmener?; **she managed to s. together the money** elle a réussi à trouver l'argent en tapant les gens **VI to s. round for sth** essayer de se faire offrir ou payer qch; **to s. off sb** vivre aux crochets de qn, profiter de qn

N he's on the s. il cherche quelqu'un à taper; **he's always on the s.** c'est un tapeur

scrounger ['skraʊndʒər] **N** Fam tapeur, -euse; (living off state etc) profiteur, -euse; (getting invitations to meals) pique-assiette mf inv

scrub¹ [skrʌb] **N** (bushes) broussailles fpl; (land) brousse f, (in Mediterranean country) garrigue f

scrub² **VT** (-bb-) **1** (clean) (pot) récurer; (floor) frotter (avec une brosse ou à la brosse); Naut (deck etc) briquer; **to s. one's hands** bien se laver ou se frotter les mains **2** Fam (cancel) annuler; (tape) effacer; **she's been scrubbed from the team** on l'a virée de l'équipe

N give your hands a good s. frottez-vous bien les mains; **to give the table a good s.** frotter la table (à la brosse)

▶▶ Am **s. brush** brosse f à récurer; Am **s. team** équipe f de deuxième ordre

▶ **scrub down VT SEP** (walls etc) lessiver; **go and s. yourself down** va te décrasser

▶ **scrub off VT SEP** enlever, frotter (pour faire partir)

VI s'enlever

▶ **scrub out VT SEP** (stain, mud, dirt etc) faire partir; (pots) récurer

▶ **scrub up VI** Med (wash) (of surgeon) se brosser les mains (avant d'opérer)

scrubber ['skrʌbər] **N 1** (implement) (pan) s. tampon m à récurer **2** Br Fam (promiscuous woman) pute f, putain f, marie-couche-toi-là f inv

scrubbing ['skrʌbɪŋ] **N 1** (cleaning) (of pot) récurage m; (with brush) nettoyage m avec une brosse dure **2 = scrub²** N

▶▶ Br **s. brush** brosse f à récurer

scrubland ['skrʌblænd] **N** brousse f

scruff [skrʌf] **N 1** (part of neck) nuque f; (skin) peau f du cou; **to take sb by the s. of the neck** saisir qn par la peau du cou **2** Fam (scruffy person) **he's a real s.!** il est vraiment peu soigné!, il fait vraiment négligé!; **a s. like you** quelqu'un d'aussi peu soigné que toi

scruffily ['skrʌfɪlɪ] **ADV** Fam dépenaillé; **s. dressed** débraillé

scruffiness ['skrʌfɪnɪs] **N** (in dress, appearance) négligence f, (of district) état m de délabrement

scruffy ['skrʌfɪ] **ADJ** (person) (badly dressed) peu soigné, débraillé, Fam dépenaillé; (clothes etc) sale, en piteux état; (hotel) minable; (district) délabré; **this jacket's getting a bit s.** cette veste commence à s'user; **a s. old van** un vieux camion tout pourri ou déglingué

scrum [skrʌm] **N** Rugby mêlée f, Fam (pushing, shoving) mêlée, bousculade f

▶▶ **s. cap** protège-oreilles m inv; **s. half** demi m de mêlée

scrummage ['skrʌmɪdʒ] **N = scrum**

scrummy ['skrʌmɪ] **ADJ** Br Fam (delicious) délicieux, super bon

scrump [skrʌmp] **VI** Br Fam chiper des fruits (dans un verger etc)

scrumptious ['skrʌm(p)ʃəs] **ADJ** Fam épatant, fameux

scrumpy ['skrʌmpɪ] **N** Br cidre m fermier

scrunch [skrʌntʃ] **VT** (with teeth) croquer avec les dents; **to s. a cigarette into the ground** écrabouiller une cigarette sur le sol; **to s. a piece of paper into a ball** faire une boule avec une feuille de papier

VI (make scrunching sound) craquer; (of snow) crisser

N (of boots on snow etc) crissement m

▶ **scrunch up VT SEP** (paper) écraser; **to s. one's face up in disgust** faire une grimace de dégoût

scrunchy¹ ['skrʌntʃɪ] **ADJ** (cereal etc) qui craque sous la dent

scrunchy² **N** (for hair) chouchou m

scruple ['skru:p(ə)l] **N** scrupule m; **to have scruples about sth** avoir des scrupules à propos de qch; **to have scruples about doing sth** avoir des scrupules à faire qch; **he has no scruples about lying to them** il n'a aucun scrupule à leur mentir

VI Fml **not to s. to do sth** ne pas avoir de scrupules à faire qch

scrupulous ['skru:pjʊləs] **ADJ 1** (person, conscience etc) scrupuleux; **the newspaper was s. about checking its sources** le journal vérifiait très soigneusement ses sources **2** (care, work) scrupuleux, minutieux

scrupulously ['skru:pjʊləslɪ] **ADV 1** (with moral correctness) scrupuleusement **2** (carefully) scrupuleusement, minutieusement; **s. clean** d'une propreté rigoureuse

scrupulousness ['skru:pjʊləsnɪs] **N** (quality) esprit m scrupuleux; **his s. in noting down all his expenses** les scrupules qu'il avait à relever toutes les dépenses

scrutineer [skru:tɪ'nɪər] **N** (of votes) scrutateur, -trice

scrutinize ['skru:tɪnaɪz] **VT** scruter, sonder; (examine in depth) examiner soigneusement; (votes) vérifier

scrutiny ['skru:tɪnɪ] **N** (examination) examen m minutieux ou attentif; **to come under s.** faire l'objet d'un examen

SCSI ['skʌzɪ] **N** Comput (abbr small computer systems interface) SCSI f

▶▶ **S. address** adresse f SCSI; **S. card** carte f SCSI; **S. chain** chaîne f SCSI

scuba ['sku:bə] **N** scaphandre m autonome

▶▶ **s. diver** plongeur, -euse sous-marin(e); **s. diving** plongée f sous-marine

scud [skʌd] **VI** (-dd-) filer comme le vent; **the clouds were scudding across the sky** les nuages filaient à travers le ciel

scuff [skʌf] **VT** frotter, racler (avec les pieds); (leather, shoes etc) érafler

VI marcher en traînant les pieds; **to s. through the autumn leaves** marcher dans les feuilles mortes

N (mark) éraflure f, (on floor) rayure f

▶▶ **s. mark** éraflure; (on floor) rayure

▶ **scuff up VT SEP** (raise into the air) (snow, dust) soulever (en traînant les pieds)

scuffed [skʌft] **ADJ** (shoe) éraflé; (floor) rayé

scuffing ['skʌfɪŋ] **N** (on piston) rayures fpl (d'usure)

scuffle ['skʌf(ə)l] **N** échauffourée f, bagarre f

VI se battre, se bagarrer

scull [skʌl] **N** (oar) (one of a pair) aviron m de couple; (used at stern) godille f, (boat) scull m

VI (row in pair) ramer ou nager en couple; (at stern) godiller

VT (row in pair) faire avancer en couple; (at stern) faire avancer à la godille

scullery ['skʌlərɪ] **N** Br arrière-cuisine f, pl arrière-cuisines

▶▶ Br **s. maid** fille f de cuisine

sculling ['skʌlɪŋ] **N** (rowing) (in pair) nage f à couple; (at stern) nage f à la godille

sculpt [skʌlpt] Art **VT** (statue) sculpter **VI** faire de la sculpture

sculptor ['skʌlptər] **N** Art sculpteur m

sculptress ['skʌlptrɪs] **N** Art femme f sculpteur, sculptrice f

sculptural ['skʌlptʃər(ə)l] **ADJ** (art) sculptural, -aux

sculpture ['skʌlptʃər] **N** (art or object) sculpture f

VT (carve) (statue, stone etc) sculpter; **she has finely sculptured features** elle a le visage très fin

VI faire de la sculpture

scum [skʌm] **N 1** (film of dirt) pellicule f de crasse; (froth) écume f, mousse f, **to take the s. off sth** (off boiled food) écumer qch, enlever l'écume de qch; (off bath etc) enlever la crasse de qch **2** Pej (people) **the s. of society** le rebut de la société; **the s. of the earth** la lie de la société; **he's/they're s.** c'est une ordure/ce sont des ordures; **she treats him like s.** elle le traite comme de la merde

scumbag ['skʌmbæg] **N** Fam (person) salaud m, ordure f

scunner ['skʌnər] **N** Scot dégoût m; **to take a s. to sb/sth** prendre qn/qch en dégoût

scunnered ['skʌnəd] **ADJ** Scot **to be s. (with)** en avoir marre (de)

scupper ['skʌpər] **N** Naut dalot m

VT Fam (ship, project etc) couler, saborder; **we're scuppered!** on est fichus!

scurf [skɜ:f] **N** (on head) pellicules fpl; (on skin) désquamation f

scurfy ['skɜ:fɪ] **ADJ** (head etc) pelliculeux; (skin) squameux

scurrility [skə'rɪlɪtɪ] **N** (of language, person) grossièreté f, (of attack) ignominie f

scurrilous ['skʌrɪləs] **ADJ** (language etc) grossier, injurieux; (person) grossier; (attack) ignoble

scurrilously ['skʌrɪləslɪ] **ADV** (coarsely) grossièrement; (insultingly) injurieusement

scurrilousness ['skʌrɪləsnɪs] **N = scurrility**

scurry ['skʌrɪ] **N** (dash) course f précipitée, débandade f

VI (dash) aller à pas précipités, Fam filer

▶ **scurry away, scurry off VI** (of mice) filer; (of people) décamper; (of animals) détaler

S-curve N Am double virage m, virage en S

scurvy ['skɜ:vɪ] **N** Med scorbut m; **to get s.** attraper le scorbut

scutcheon ['skʌtʃən] **N** Her écu m, écusson m

scuttle¹ ['skʌt(ə)l] **N** (container) **(coal) s.** seau m à charbon

scuttle² **N** Naut (hatch) écoutille f, Am (in ceiling) trappe f

VT Naut (ship) saborder

scuttle³ **VI** (run) courir

▶ **scuttle away, scuttle off VI** (of crab, insect etc) déguerpir; (of person) décamper

scuttling ['skʌtlɪŋ] N (of ship) sabordage m

scuzzy ['skʌzɪ] ADJ Fam crade, cradingue

Scylla ['sɪlə] N Lit **to be between S. and Charybdis** être tiraillé entre deux maux

scythe [saɪð] N Agr faux f
VT (corn etc) faucher
▸ **scythe through** VT INSEP (with a weapon) faucher; **her stick scythed through the air** son bâton fendit l'air

SDI [esdi:'aɪ] N Mil (abbr **strategic defence initiative**) initiative f de défense stratégique

SDLP [esdi:el'pi:] N (abbr **Social Democratic and Labour Party**) = parti m politique d'Irlande du Nord

SDP [esdi:'pi:] N (abbr **Social Democratic Party**) Parti m social démocrate

SDRAM [esdi:'ræm] N Comput (abbr **synchronous dynamic random access memory**) SDRAM f

SE (abbr **south east**) SE

SEA [esi:'eɪ] N (abbr **Single European Act**) AUE m

sea [si:] N **1** mer f; **at the bottom of the s.** au fond de la mer; **by the s.** au bord de la mer; **by s.** par (voie de) mer; **beyond** or **over the sea(s)** au delà des mers; **to go to s.** (become sailor) devenir marin; (set sail) (of person, ship) prendre la mer; **to put (out) to s.** (of ship) prendre la mer ou le large; **the open s., the high seas** le large, la haute mer; **on the high seas, out at s.** en haute mer, en pleine mer, au grand large; Fig **to be all at s.** (perplexed) être complètement perdu; **heavy** or **strong s.** grosse mer, mer grosse ou houleuse; **there's a heavy s.** il y a de la mer; Naut **to run before the s.** avoir la mer de l'arrière; Fam **old s. dog** vieux loup m de mer; **to find** or **get one's s. legs** s'habituer à la mer; **he hasn't found his s. legs** il n'a pas encore le pied marin; **a room with a s. view** une chambre avec vue sur la mer
2 Fig (of faces) mer f; (of blood) bain m; Lit (of troubles) multitude f
▸▸ **s. air** air m marin ou de la mer; Zool **s. anemone** anémone f de mer; **s. bass** bar m, loup m; **s. bathing** bains mpl de mer; **s. battle** bataille f navale; **s. breeze** (wind) brise f marine; (cocktail) sea breeze m; Zool **s. calf** veau m marin, phoque m; **s. captain** capitaine m de la marine marchande; **s. change** changement m radical, profond changement; **s. chest** coffre m de marin ou de bord; **s. coast** côte f; Zool **s. cow** vache f marine, sirénien m; **s. crossing** traversée f; **s. cucumber** concombre m de mer, holothurie f; Orn **s. eagle** aigle m des mers; Zool **s. elephant** éléphant m de mer; **s. fight** combat m naval; **s. fish** poisson m de mer; **s. fishery** pêche f maritime; **s. fishing** pêche maritime; **s. floor** fond m de la mer; **s. fog** brouillard m (en mer); **s. freight** fret m maritime; **s. freight services** messageries fpl maritimes; **s. god** dieu m marin ou de la mer; **s. kayak** kayak m de mer; **s. kayaking** kayak de mer; **to go s. kayaking** faire du kayak de mer; **s. lane** couloir m de navigation; **s. level** niveau m de la mer; Zool **s. lion** otarie f; Scot **s. loch** bras m de mer; Br Mil **S. Lord** lord m de l'Amirauté; **s. mile** mille m marin; **s. mist** brume f de mer; **s. monster** monstre m marin; Zool **s. otter** loutre f de mer; **s. power** puissance f navale; **s. salt** sel m marin ou de mer; **s. scout** scout m marin; Zool **s. serpent** serpent m de mer; **s. shanty** chanson f de marins; Zool **s. snake** serpent m de mer; **s. travel** voyages mpl en mer; **s. trout** truite f de mer; Zool **s. urchin** oursin m; **s. voyage** voyage m en mer; **s. wall** digue f

seabed ['si:bed] N fond m de la mer

seabird ['si:bɜ:d] N oiseau m de mer

seaboard ['si:bɔ:d] N (coastline) littoral m;

(coastal region) bord m de la mer, région f côtière

seaboots ['si:bu:ts] NPL bottes fpl de marin ou de mer

seaborne ['si:bɔ:n] ADJ (trade) maritime; (goods) transporté par mer

seafarer ['si:feərər] N (sailor) marin m

seafaring ['si:feərɪŋ] ADJ **a s. people** un peuple de navigateurs

seafood ['si:fu:d] N (no pl) fruits mpl de mer; **s. restaurant** restaurant m de fruits de mer

seafront ['si:frʌnt] N (area facing sea) bord m de (la) mer; (promenade) esplanade f, front m de mer; **house on the s.** maison sur le front de mer

seagoing ['si:gəʊɪŋ] ADJ (ship) de mer; (nation) de navigateurs

sea-green N, ADJ bleu-vert m inv

seagull ['si:gʌl] N (bird) mouette f, goéland m

seahorse ['si:hɔ:s] N hippocampe m

seal[1] [si:l] N **1** (animal) phoque m; **elephant s.** éléphant m de mer; **grey s.** phoque gris; **fur s.** otarie f à fourrure; **s. cull** abattage m de phoques **2** (skin) (peau f de) phoque m
VI (hunt seals) chasser le phoque; **to go sealing** aller à la chasse au phoque

seal[2] N **1** (on deed etc) sceau m; (on letter, bottle of wine etc) cachet m; (on door etc) scellés mpl; Com (on goods for export) plomb m; Law **given under my hand and s.** signé et scellé par moi; **under the s. of silence/secrecy** sous le sceau du silence/du secret; **to give one's s. of approval to sth** donner son approbation à qch; **to set one's s. to sth** (to mark with one's seal) mettre son sceau sur qch; (to authorize) autoriser qch, confirmer qch; (to give approval to) donner son approbation à qch; **to set the s. on sth** (on alliance, friendship) sceller qch; (on fate, defeat) décider de qch; **this event set the s. on their fate** cet événement allait décider de leur sort; **under s.** sous scellés; Rel **under the s. of confession** dans le secret de la confession; Law **official s.** (affixed to property etc) scellé m
2 (instrument) sceau m; Admin **the Great S.** le grand sceau (employé pour les actes publics)
3 Tech (device for making airtight) joint m d'étanchéité; (airtight join) joint étanche; **in order to get a good s.** pour obtenir une bonne étanchéité
VT **1** (put seal on) (deed etc) sceller; (letter, bottle) cacheter; (at customs) (goods) (faire) plomber; Law (door etc) apposer les scellés sur; **to s. sb's fate** (of event etc) décider du sort de qn; **his fate is sealed** son sort est décidé
2 (close) (letter etc) cacheter; (block) (mineshaft, pipe) obturer, boucher; (jar) fermer hermétiquement; (box) sceller; (make airtight) rendre étanche, étancher; (of joint etc) assurer l'étanchéité de; Culin (meat) saisir; **sealed with a kiss** (of letter) fermé avec un baiser; **the frontier has been sealed** la frontière est fermée; **my lips are sealed** (I am not allowed to say) il m'est défendu de parler; (I shall not say) je ne dirai pas un mot
▸ **seal in** VT SEP (contain) enfermer; **fry the meat at a high temperature to s. in the flavour** faites revenir la viande à feu vif afin de lui conserver toute sa saveur
▸ **seal off** VT SEP (isolate) isoler; **the area was sealed off by the police** le quartier a été bouclé par la police
▸ **seal up** VT SEP = seal[2] VT 2

sealant ['si:lənt] N produit m d'étanchéité

sealed [si:ld] ADJ (envelope) cacheté; (train) plombé; (box, door) scellé; **in a s. jar** dans un bocal fermé hermétiquement

---

▸▸ Com **s. bid** soumission f cachetée; Com **s.-bid pricing** fixation f d'un prix de soumission; Aut **s. cooling system** circuit m de refroidissement pressurisé; **s. envelope** pli m cacheté; Mil, Naut **s. orders** ordres mpl cachetés

sealer ['si:lər] N **1** (ship) bateau m pour la chasse aux phoques **2** (seal hunter) chasseur m de phoques

sealing[1] ['si:lɪŋ] N (seal hunting) chasse f au phoque

sealing[2] N **1** (putting on seal) (on deed etc) scellage m; (of letter etc) cachetage m; (at customs) (of goods) plombage m **2** (closing) (of letter) cachetage m; (of pipe etc) obturation f
▸▸ **s. compound** lut m, mastic m; Aut (for radiator) anti-fuite m inv; **s. wax** cire f à cacheter

sealskin ['si:lskɪn] N (peau f de) phoque m; **s. coat** manteau m en (peau de) phoque

seam [si:m] N **1** Sewing couture f; (in metal pipe, between boards etc) joint m; (weld) soudure f; **flat s.** couture rabattue ou plate; **French s.** couture double ou anglaise; **a ship's seams** les coutures d'un navire; Fig **bursting at the seams** (of room, building etc) plein à craquer; **to be coming apart at the seams** (of garment) craquer de partout; Fig (of economy, system etc) aller à vau-l'eau **2** (wrinkle) (on face etc) ride f **3** Min etc (of coal etc) veine f
VT **1** Sewing (garment) faire une couture à **2** **a face seamed with scars** un visage couvert de cicatrices
▸▸ **s. bowler** (in cricket) = lanceur m qui utilise les coutures de la balle pour la faire dévier

seaman, pl **seamen** ['si:mən] N marin m; (ordinary sailor) matelot m, marin; Br **ordinary s.** matelot de troisième classe ou de pont; Br **able(-bodied) s.** matelot de deuxième classe; Br **leading s.** matelot (breveté) de première classe, quartier-maître m, pl quartiers-maîtres

seamanship ['si:mənʃɪp] N qualités fpl de navigateur; **thanks to his s.** grâce à ses qualités de navigateur

seamless ['si:mlɪs] ADJ **1** (stocking) sans couture; (in metalworking) (tube etc) sans soudure **2** Fig (changeover, whole) continu; **a s. transition** un passage très progressif

seamlessly ['si:mlɪslɪ] ADV Fig très progressivement

seamstress ['semstrɪs] N couturière f

seamy ['si:mɪ] ADJ sordide; **one of the city's seamier districts** l'un des quartiers les plus sordides de la ville; **the s. side of life/politics** le côté sordide de l'existence/la politique

seance[1] ['seɪɒns] N (of spiritualists) séance f de spiritisme

seaplane ['si:pleɪn] N Aviat hydravion m

seaport ['si:pɔ:t] N port m maritime ou de mer

SEAQ [esi:eɪ'kju:] N (abbr **Stock Exchange Automated Quotations System**) système m de cotation automatisé

sear [sɪər] VT **1** (to burn) brûler; (a wound) cautériser; Fig **the image would forever be seared on his memory** l'image resterait à tout jamais gravée dans sa mémoire **2** Culin (meat etc) saisir **3** Fig Lit (harden) (conscience etc) endurcir; (heart) durcir, dessécher
ADJ Lit (withered) flétri, desséché

search [sɜ:tʃ] N recherche(s) f(pl); (in a drawer etc) fouille f; Law perquisition f; (at customs) visite f; **to have a s. for sth** chercher qch; **her s. for her son/the truth** la recherche de son fils/la vérité; **in s. of sth** à la recherche de qch; **to be in s. of sth** être en quête de qch, être à la recherche de qch;

Comput **to do a s.** faire une recherche; *Comput* **to do a s. for sth** rechercher qch; *Comput* **s. and replace** recherche *f* et remplacement *m*; *Comput* **s. and replace command** commande *f* de recherche et remplacement; *Comput* **s. and replace function** fonction *f* recherche et remplacement; **to make a s.** faire des recherches; **right of s.** droit *m* de visite; *(at sea)* droit de recherche

VT *(place, house, drawer, box, suspect, sb's pockets, one's memory)* fouiller; *(face)* scruter; *(at customs) (ship, sb's bags)* visiter; *Comput (file, directory)* rechercher dans; *Comput* **to s. and replace sth** rechercher et remplacer qch; *Law* **to s. a house** faire une perquisition *ou* une visite domiciliaire; *Law* **to s. the scene of a crime** fouiller le lieu d'un crime; *Fam* **s. me!** je n'ai pas la moindre idée!

VI faire des recherches; *Comput* effectuer une recherche; **to s. after the truth** rechercher la vérité; **to s. for sb/sth** (re)chercher qn/qch

▸▸ *Comput* **s. command** commande de recherche; *Comput* **s. direction** direction *f* de la recherche; *Comput* **s. engine** moteur *m* de recherche; **s. party** équipe *f* de secours; *Comput* **s. time** temps *m* de recherche; **s. warrant** mandat *m* de perquisition

▸ **search out** VT SEP chercher
▸ **search through** VT INSEP fouiller

searchable ['sɜːtʃəb(ə)l] ADJ *Comput* **s. by name/price/date** sur lequel/laquelle on peut effectuer une recherche par nom/prix/date

searcher ['sɜːtʃər] N *(member of search party)* sauveteur *m*; **he was a s. after truth** c'était un homme qui recherchait la vérité

searching ['sɜːtʃɪŋ] ADJ *(examination)* minutieux; *(look)* scrutateur, -trice; **s. questions** questions *fpl* de fond
N *(of suspect, house, ship etc)* fouille *f*, *(at customs)* visite *f*, *Law* perquisition *f*

searchlight ['sɜːtʃlaɪt] N projecteur *m*; *(beam)* faisceau *m* d'un/du projecteur; **to turn a s. on sth** braquer un projecteur sur qch

searing ['sɪərɪŋ] ADJ *(pain)* fulgurant; *(criticism, indictment etc)* virulent

seascape ['siːskeɪp] N **1** *(view)* vue *f* sur la mer **2** *(picture)* marine *f*

seashell ['siːʃel] N coquille *f* de mer, coquillage *m*

seashore ['siːʃɔːr] N bord *m* de (la) mer; *(beach)* plage *f*

seasick ['siːsɪk] ADJ **to be s.** avoir le mal de mer; **to be a little/very s.** avoir un léger/fort mal de mer

seasickness ['siːsɪknɪs] N mal *m* de mer, *Spec* naupathie *f*

seaside ['siːsaɪd] N bord *m* de (la) mer; **at the s.** au bord de la mer; **a s. village/boarding house** un village/une pension au bord de la mer
▸▸ **s. resort** station *f* balnéaire

season ['siːz(ə)n] N [VOIR GRAMMAIRE A7; A81–2; B4; B61-2] **1** *(period of year)* saison *f*; **the four seasons** les quatre saisons; **the rainy s.** la saison des pluies; **hunting s.** saison de la chasse; **close/open s.** *(in hunting)* chasse fermée/ouverte; *Fishing* pêche *f* fermée/ouverte; **the tourist s.** la saison touristique; **S.'s Greetings** meilleurs vœux de fin d'année
2 *(for fruit, vegetables etc)* saison *f*, **oysters are in/out of s.** c'est/ce n'est pas la saison des huîtres; **strawberries are in s.** c'est la saison des fraises; **in s.** *(of animal)* en rut; *(of female animal)* en chaleur; *Com* **the high s.** la haute saison; *Com* **the slack s., the off s.** la morte-saison, *pl* mortes-saisons
3 *Fam (season ticket)* abonnement *m*
4 *Theat* saison *f*, *TV, Cin* cycle *m*; **a s. of**

French films un cycle de films français
5 *Sport* saison *f*, **the football/cricket/etc s.** la saison de football/cricket/*etc*
VT *(dish)* assaisonner; *(wood)* dessécher; *(barrel)* aviner; *(wine)* mûrir
VI *(of wood)* se sécher; *(of wine etc)* mûrir, faire
▸▸ **s. ticket** (carte *f* d')abonnement; **s. ticket holder** abonné, -ée

seasonable ['siːzənəb(ə)l] ADJ **1 s. weather** un temps de saison **2** *Lit (help, advice)* opportun, à propos

seasonal ['siːzən(ə)l] ADJ *(changes etc)* des saisons; *(trade, occupation)* saisonnier, -ière
▸▸ *Econ* **s. adjustment** ajustement *m* saisonnier; *Med* **s. affective disorder** dépression *f* saisonnière; **s. employment** emploi *m* saisonnier; **s. fluctuation** fluctuation *f* saisonnière; **s. worker** saisonnier, -ière

seasonally ['siːzən(ə)lɪ] ADV selon la saison; **s. adjusted unemployment figures** chiffres *mpl* du chômage en données corrigées des variations saisonnières

seasoned ['siːzənd] ADJ **1** *Culin (dish)* assaisonné; **highly s. dish** plat *m* relevé *ou* épicé **2** *(wood, cigar etc)* sec, *f* sèche; *(wine)* mûr, fait **3** *Fig (soldier)* aguerri; **a s. political campaigner** un militant politique chevronné; **s. traveller** voyageur, -euse expérimenté(e)

seasoning ['siːzənɪŋ] N **1** *(act)* *Culin (of dish)* assaisonnement *m*; *(of wood)* séchage *m*; *(of wine)* maturation *f*, *(of troops)* aguerrissement *m* **2** *Culin (condiment)* assaisonnement *m*, condiment *m*

seat [siːt] N **1** *(chair)* (in Parliament, on bus, train etc) siège *m*; *(in theatre)* place *f*, *(of toilet)* lunette *f*, siège; *(bench) (in park etc)* banc *m*; *Aut* **car s.** siège de voiture; *Aviat* **ejection or ejector s.** siège éjectable; *Aut, Theat etc* **flap or folding s.** strapontin *m*; *Fam* **to be in the hot s.** être sur la sellette; **to book a s.** *(on train, in theatre)* réserver une place
2 *(somewhere to sit)* place *f*, **there were no seats left** il n'y avait plus de places; **to take a s.** s'asseoir; **to keep one's s.** rester assis; **keep a s. for me** gardez-moi une place; *Pol* **to have a s. in the House** avoir un siège à l'Assemblée; **to have a s. on the Council** être conseiller (municipal); **to have a s. on the board** avoir un siège au conseil d'administration
3 *(part) (of chair)* siège *m*, fond *m*; *Fam (of person)* derrière *m*, fesses *fpl*; *(of trousers)* fond
4 *(centre) (of government)* siège *m*; *(of disease)* foyer *m*; *Med (of pain etc)* siège; **s. of learning** haut lieu *m* du savoir; **the s. of the emotions** le siège des émotions; **country s.** château *m*
5 *Horseriding (way of sitting)* assiette *f*, **to have a good s.** avoir une bonne assiette
6 *Tech (of valve)* siège *m*
VT **1** *(cause to sit)* (child etc) (faire) asseoir; *(guests) (show where to place)* placer; *(show to seat)* faire asseoir; **you will be seated in five minutes, madam** votre table sera prête dans cinq minutes, madame; **to remain seated** rester assis; *Fml* **please be seated** veuillez vous asseoir, je vous prie de vous asseoir
2 *(accommodate)* **bus which seats thirty** autobus à trente places (assises); **this table seats twelve** on tient à douze à cette table; **the hall seats two hundred** deux cents personnes peuvent tenir dans la salle
3 *Tech (valve)* assurer *ou* ajuster l'assise de
▸▸ **s. number** numéro *m* de place (assise); *Aviat* **s. pitch** espacement *m* des sièges

seatback ['siːtbæk] N dossier *m*

seatbelt ['siːtbelt] N *Aut, Aviat* ceinture *f* de sécurité

-seater ['siːtər] SUFF a **two/single/etc -s.** *Aut* une voiture à deux places/une place/*etc*;

Aviat un avion biplace *ou* à deux places/à une place/*etc*

seating ['siːtɪŋ] N *(allocation of seats)* allocation *f* des sièges *ou* des places; *(positioning)* placement *m*; *(seats) (in hall etc)* sièges *mpl*, *Tech (of valve)* siège *m*; **there is more s. upstairs** il y a encore des places en haut
▸▸ **s. arrangements** le placement *ou* la disposition des gens; **s. capacity** nombre *m* de places assises; *(of car park etc)* capacité *f* d'accueil; **s. plan** *(in theatre)* plan *m* de la disposition des places; *(at table)* plan de table

SEATO ['siːtəʊ] N *Mil (abbr* **Southeast Asia Treaty Organization)** OTASE *f*

seat-of-the-pants [siːtəvðə'pænts] ADJ *Fam* **the project has been a bit of a s. operation** le projet a été mené au pif

seaward ['siːwəd] ADV *(also* **seawards)** vers la mer, du côté du large
ADJ de (la) mer
N **to s.** du côté du large, vers le large
▸▸ **s. breeze** brise *f* de mer

seawater ['siːwɔːtər] N eau *f* de mer
▸▸ **s. therapy** thalassothérapie *f*

seaway ['siːweɪ] N *Naut* route *f*, **the St Lawrence S.** la voie maritime du Saint-Laurent

seaweed ['siːwiːd] N algue *f*

seaworthiness ['siːwɜːðɪnɪs] N (état *m* de) navigabilité *f*

seaworthy ['siːwɜːðɪ] ADJ *(of ship)* en (bon) état de navigabilité

sebaceous [sɪ'beɪʃəs] ADJ *(gland, cyst)* sébacé

sebum ['siːbəm] N *Physiol* sébum *m*

SEC [esiː'siː] N *(abbr* **Securities and Exchange Commission)** = commission *f* américaine des opérations de Bourse, ≃ COB *f*

sec [sek] N *Fam* = **second** N **1**; **half a s.!, just a s.!** une seconde!, deux secondes!

secant ['siːkənt] *Math* ADJ sécant
N sécante *f*

secateurs [sekə'tɜːz] NPL *Br* sécateur *m*

secede [sɪ'siːd] VI faire sécession; *(from party)* se séparer, faire scission (**from** de)

secession [sɪ'seʃən] N sécession *f*, *(from party)* scission *f*, *Hist* **the War of S.** la guerre de Sécession

secessionist [sɪ'seʃənɪst] ADJ, N scissionniste *mf*, *Hist* sécessionniste *mf*

seclude [sɪ'kluːd] VT tenir retiré *ou* éloigné *ou* écarté (**from** de)

secluded [sɪ'kluːdɪd] ADJ *(place)* écarté, retiré; **s. life** vie *f* retirée *ou* de reclus; **to live a s. life** vivre une vie retirée *ou* de reclus

seclusion [sɪ'kluːʒən] N solitude *f*, *(of village, farm)* isolement *m*; **in s.** retiré du monde; **to live in s.** vivre dans la solitude, vivre en reclus

---

SECOND[1] ['sekənd]

N seconde **1–3**	▪ second **3**
▪ deuxième **3**	▪ témoin **6**
ADJ second **1**	▪ deuxième **1**
▪ deuxièmement **1**	
VT seconder **1**	▪ appuyer **1**

N **1** *(of time)* seconde *f*, **in a split s.** en une fraction de seconde; **for a s.** pendant une seconde; **wait a s.!** attendez une seconde *ou* un instant!; **I won't be a s.** je reviens tout de suite, j'en ai pour deux secondes
2 *Math, Astron* seconde *f*
3 *(in order)* second *m*, seconde *f*, deuxième *mf*; *Sport etc* **to come in a good s.** arriver second en très bonne position derrière le vainqueur; *Mil etc* **s. in command** commandant *m* en second; *Br Univ* **to get a s.** être reçu à la licence avec mention assez bien; *Br Univ* **upper/lower s.** *(degree)* mention *f*

bien/assez bien; *Aut* **to start in s.** démarrer en seconde; *Fam* **anyone for seconds?** *(at meal)* qui veut se resservir?, *Fam* qui veut du rab ou du rabiot?
4 *Mus* **major/minor s.** seconde *f* majeure/mineure
5 *Com* **seconds** articles *mpl* de deuxième choix, produits *mpl* de second choix
6 *(in duel)* témoin *m*; *Boxing* soigneur *m*
▶ **ADJ 1** second, deuxième; **the s. of March** le deux mars; **twenty-/thirty-s.** vingt-/trente-deuxième; **Charles the S.** Charles Deux *ou* II; **our roads are s. to none** nos routes sont les meilleures du monde; **to be s. in line for the throne** être deuxième prétendant au trône; **I'm s. in line for promotion** je suis deuxième sur la liste des gens à promouvoir; **to be s. in command** commander en second; **to marry a s. time** *or* **for the s. time** se marier pour la deuxième *ou* seconde fois; **Spain's s. city** la deuxième ville d'Espagne; **the s. largest city in the world/in Portugal** la deuxième ville du monde/du Portugal; **to take a s. helping** *(at meal)* se resservir; **he's the s. oldest player in the team** après le doyen de l'équipe, c'est lui le plus vieux; **she knew she would never be more than s. best** *(in person's affection)* elle savait qu'elle ne serait jamais plus qu'un second choix; *(of athlete)* elle savait qu'elle serait toujours deuxième; **we're not happy with s. best** nous ne nous contenterons pas d'un pis-aller; **in a fight with him, you'll come off s. best** si tu t'affrontes à lui, tu n'en sortiras pas vainqueur; **to take a s. holiday** reprendre des vacances; **it has become s. nature to her** elle le fait presque par instinct; **in s. place** deuxièmement, en second lieu; **to take s. place** passer second; **on s.** *Br* **thoughts** *or Am* **thought** tout bien réfléchi; **to have s. thoughts** avoir des hésitations (**about sth** au sujet de qch); **are you having s. thoughts?** est-ce que vous hésitez?; **I've had s. thoughts** j'ai bien réfléchi, j'ai changé d'avis; **to get one's s. wind** *(in race etc)* trouver un second souffle; *Fig (after feeling tired)* trouver un second souffle, se remettre
2 *(another)* **a s. Camus/Churchill** un nouveau Camus/Churchill
▶ **VT** *(support)* *(person)* seconder; *(in debate etc)* *(motion)* appuyer
▶▶ **s. ballot** deuxième tour *m*; *Pol* **s. chamber** deuxième chambre *f*, *(in UK)* Chambre *f* des lords; *(in US)* Sénat *m*; **s. chance** deuxième chance *f*, **s. childhood** gâtisme *m*, seconde enfance *f*, *Rail* **s. class** seconde (classe *f*); *Rel* **the S. Coming** le second avènement; **s. cousin** cousin, -ine issu(e) de germains; *Cin* **s. feature** deuxième film *m* *(d'un programme où figurent deux longs métrages)*; **s. floor** *(in UK)* deuxième étage *m*; *(in US)* premier étage; *Sch* **s. form** ≃ (classe de) cinquième *f*, *Aut* **s. gear** seconde *f*, **s. hand** *(of watch, clock)* aiguille *f* des secondes, trotteuse *f*, **s. home** résidence *f* secondaire; **my s. home** *(country)* mon deuxième pays; *(family)* ma deuxième famille; **s. language** deuxième langue *f*, *Journ* **s. lead** gros titre *m* de deuxième ordre; **s. name** nom *m* de famille; **s. nature** seconde nature *f*, **s. opinion** deuxième avis *m*; *Gram* **s. person** deuxième personne *f*, *Parl* **s. reading** deuxième lecture *f*, **s. sight** seconde *ou* double vue *f*, *Mus* **s. violin** deuxième violon *m*

second² [sɪ'kɒnd] **VT** *Br (detach) Mil (officer)* mettre en disponibilité *ou* hors cadre *(pour fonctions spéciales etc)*; *(employee)* détacher, envoyer en détachement; **she's been seconded to head office** elle a été détachée au siège social

secondary ['sekənd(ə)rɪ] **ADJ** secondaire; *(evidence)* indirect; *(rôle etc)* peu important, accessoire; **the s. meaning of a word** le sens

dérivé d'un mot; **of s. importance** d'importance secondaire
▶▶ *Med* **s. cancer** métastase *f*, **s. education** enseignement *m* secondaire *ou* du second degré; *Med* **s. infection** surinfection *f*; **s. legislation** législation *f* secondaire; *Br Formerly* **s. modern** = collège *m* offrant un enseignement semi-professionnel; **s. road** route *f* secondaire *ou* départementale; **s. school** = établissement *m* secondaire, *Can, Suisse* école *f* secondaire; *Econ* **s. sector** secteur *m* secondaire

second-class **ADJ** *(ticket, carriage)* de seconde (classe)
▶▶ **s. citizen** citoyen, -enne de seconde zone; *Br Univ* **s. degree** = licence *f* avec mention assez bien; **s. mail** courrier *m* (à tarif) non urgent

second-degree burns **NPL** *Med* brûlures *fpl* au deuxième degré

seconder ['sekəndər] **N** personne *f* qui soutient une proposition; **I need a s.** il me faut quelqu'un qui soutienne ma proposition

second-generation **ADJ** *(immigrant etc)* de la deuxième génération; *(computer, mobile phone etc)* de deuxième génération

second-guess **VT to s. sb** anticiper ce que qn va dire/faire

second-hand **ADV** *(to buy)* d'occasion; **to hear news s.** recevoir des nouvelles de seconde main *ou* d'un tiers
▶ **ADJ** *(car, book, furniture etc)* d'occasion; *(news etc)* de seconde main; **s. bookshop** librairie *f* d'occasion; **s. clothes shop** boutique *f* de vêtements d'occasion; **the s. market** le marché de l'occasion
▶▶ **s. dealer** marchand, -ande d'articles d'occasion; *(in clothes)* fripier, -ière; *(in books)* bouquiniste *mf*, **s. shop** magasin *m* d'articles d'occasion

secondly ['sekəndlɪ] **ADV** deuxièmement, en second lieu

secondment [sɪ'kɒndmənt] **N** *Br Mil etc* détachement *m* (**to** à; **from** de); **to be on s. to another department** être détaché auprès d'un autre service

second-rate **ADJ** *(goods, equipment)* de qualité inférieure; *(movie, book)* médiocre; *(politician, player)* médiocre, de second ordre

second-row forward **N** *Rugby* avant *m* de deuxième ligne

secrecy ['siːkrɪsɪ] **N** secret *m*; **in s.** en secret; **why all the s.?** pourquoi tous ces secrets?; **there's no s. about it** ça n'a rien de secret; **business conducted in complete s.** affaires menées dans le plus grand secret; **to swear sb to s.** faire jurer le silence à qn

secret ['siːkrɪt] **ADJ** secret, -ète; *(place)* secret, caché; **to keep sth s.** tenir *ou* garder qch secret, cacher qch, taire qch; **he'd kept it s. from me for years** il me l'avait caché pendant des années; **a desk with a s. compartment** un bureau à secret
▶ **N** secret *m*; **in s.** en secret; **can you keep a s.?** est-ce que tu peux garder un secret?; **it can be our little s.** ça sera notre petit secret à nous; **I make no s. of it** je n'en fais pas mystère, je ne le cache pas; **to let sb into the s.** mettre qn dans le secret; **the s. is not to press too hard** l'astuce consiste à ne pas appuyer trop fort; **it's no s.** ce n'est un secret; **an open s.** un secret de Polichinelle
▶▶ **s. admirer** admirateur, -trice secret(ète); **s. agent** agent *m* secret; **s. ballot** vote *m* à bulletin secret; **s. door** porte *f* cachée *ou* dérobée; **s. meeting** réunion *f* secrète; **s. police** police *f* secrète; **the S. Service** = service *m* de protection des hauts fonctionnaires américains et de leurs familles; *Mil, Fig* **s. weapon** arme *f* secrète

secretarial [sekrə'teərɪəl] **ADJ** *(work)* de secrétariat
▶▶ **s. college** école *f* de secrétariat; **s. course** cours *m* de secrétariat; **s. post** poste *m* de secrétaire; **s. service** service *m* de secrétariat; **s. skills** notions *fpl* de secrétariat; **the s. staff** le secrétariat

secretariat [sekrə'teərɪət] **N** secrétariat *m*

secretary ['sekrət(ə)rɪ] **N 1** secrétaire *mf*; **private s.** secrétaire particulier(-ière); *Br* **company s.** secrétaire *mf* général(e); **(1st/2nd/3rd) s. (to ambassador)** ≃ secrétaire d'ambassade **2** *(bird)* serpentaire *m*, secrétaire *m*
▶▶ **s. bird** serpentaire, secrétaire; **S. of State** *Br* ≃ ministre *m*, *Am* ≃ ministre des Affaires étrangères

secretary-general **N** secrétaire *mf* général(e)

secrete [sɪ'kriːt] **VT 1** *(of gland etc)* sécréter **2** *(hide)* cacher

secretion [sɪ'kriːʃən] **N** *Physiol* sécrétion *f*

secretive ['siːkrɪtɪv] **ADJ** *(person)* secret, -ète; *(in negative sense)* cachottier; *(behaviour)* fermé; **why are you being so s. about it?** pourquoi fais-tu tant de cachotteries là-dessus?

secretively ['siːkrɪtɪvlɪ] **ADV** avec dissimulation

secretiveness ['siːkrɪtɪvnɪs] **N** caractère *m* secret; *(on particular occasion)* cachotterie *f*

secretly ['siːkrɪtlɪ] **ADV** en secret; *(to think etc)* secrètement

sect [sekt] **N** secte *f*

sectarian [sek'teərɪən] **ADJ** *(attitude, cult)* sectaire
▶ **N** sectaire *mf*
▶▶ **s. killing** = meurtre *m* motivé par le sectarisme religieux

> Note that, unlike the word **sectarian** in British English, the French word **sectaire** does not specifically refer to tensions between Catholics and Protestants.

sectarianism [sek'teərɪənɪz(ə)m] **N** sectarisme *m* religieux; *(attitude)* esprit *m* sectaire

> Note that, unlike the word **sectarianism** in British English, the French word **sectarisme** does not specifically refer to tensions between Catholics and Protestants.

section ['sekʃən] **N 1** *(part)* section *f*, portion *f*, *(of structure, company)* division *f*, partie *f*, *(of tube, railway etc)* tronçon *m*; *Com (of store)* rayon *m*; *(in shop)* secteur *m*; *Am Rail (of sleeping car)* compartiment *m*; *(component, prefabricated part)* élément *m*; *(of document, text etc)* partie *f*; *(of law etc)* article *m*; *Mus (in orchestra)* section *f*; *Mil (fighting unit)* groupe *m* de combat; *(of fusiliers, grenadiers)* équipe *f*, *Am (area)* lotissement *m*; *Aviat* **nose s.** partie avant, nez *m*; **tail s.** partie arrière, queue *f*; **the bookcase comes in sections** la bibliothèque est démontable; *Journ* **sports/travel/financial/TV s.** rubrique *f* sport/voyage/finances/télé; **all sections of the population** toutes les couches de la population, toutes les catégories sociales **2** *(cut) Geom* section *f*, *Archit, Constr etc* coupe *f*, profil *m*, section; *(in metalwork)* *Constr* profilé *m*; *(thin slice)* tranche *f*, lamelle *f*, **microscopic s.** mince lame *f*, plaque *f* *(pour examen au microscope)*; **conic/plane s.** section conique/plane; **horizontal s.** coupe *ou* section horizontale
▶ **VT 1** *(cut)* sectionner **2** *(send to psychiatric hospital)* faire interner
▶▶ **s. manager** chef *m* de section

sectional ['sekʃən(ə)l] **ADJ 1** *(interests)* particulier; *(rivalries)* interne **2** *(drawing etc)* en coupe, en profil; *(area)* de section **3** *(furniture)* modulaire

sectionalism [ˈsekʃənəlɪz(ə)m] N *Am* régionalisme *m*, esprit *m* de clocher

sector [ˈsektər] N **1** *Geom, Astron, Mil, Comput* secteur *m*; *Admin* **public/private s.** secteur public/privé; **public s. spending** dépenses *fpl* publiques **2** *Geom (instrument)* compas *m* de proportion

secular [ˈsekjʊlər] ADJ *Rel (history, art etc)* laïque, séculier; *(music)* profane; **s. priest** (prêtre *m*) séculier *m*

secularism [ˈsekjʊlərɪz(ə)m] N **1** laïcisme *m* **2** *Phil* laïcité *f*

secularization [sekjʊlərɑɪˈzeɪʃən] N *(of church property etc)* sécularisation *f*; *(of school)* laïcisation *f*

secularize [ˈsekjʊlərɑɪz] VT *(property, priest)* séculariser; *(school)* laïciser

secure [sɪˈkjʊər] ADJ **1** *(free from anxiety) (person)* tranquille, en paix; *Psy* sûr de soi; *(future, nomination)* assuré; **you make me feel s.** tu me donnes confiance; **to feel s. of victory** être assuré *ou* certain de la victoire; *Fml* **s. in the knowledge that …** sachant avec certitude que …
2 *(safe) (valuables)* en sûreté; *(investment, place, job)* sûr; **s. communications** communications *fpl* inviolables; **s. from attack** à l'abri d'une attaque; **the prisoner is s.** le prisonnier est en lieu sûr
3 *(door, plank, foundations, lock etc)* solide; *(foothold, grasp)* ferme, sûr; **that rope doesn't look very s.** cette corde n'a pas l'air très solide; **to make the boat s.** bien amarrer le bateau
VT **1** *(keep out of danger)* mettre en sûreté; *(prisoner)* mettre en lieu sûr; **to s. a pass** *(in mountains)* garder un défilé
2 *(immobilize) (sth which is loose)* bien fixer; *(flapping shutter etc)* attacher, fixer; *(cargo)* arrimer; **doors and windows should be properly secured** les portes et les fenêtres doivent être bien fermées
3 *Law, Com (borrower)* garantir; **to s. a debt by mortgage** hypothéquer une créance; *Fin* **to s. a loan** garantir un emprunt, nantir un prêt; *Fin* **to s. by warrant** warranter
4 *(obtain)* obtenir; *(objective)* atteindre; **to s. sth for sb** *(future, victory, holiday etc)* assurer qch pour qn; **he secured his future with the company by …** il a assuré son avenir dans l'entreprise en …
▸▸*Comput* **s. electronic transaction** protocole *m* SET; *Comput* **s. HTTP** protocole HTTP sécurisé; *Comput* **s. server** serveur *m* sécurisé; *Comput* **s. sockets layer** protocole SSL; **s. unit** *(in psychiatric hospital)* quartier *m* de haute sécurité; *(in children's home)* section *f* surveillée; *Comput* **s. Web site** site *m* sécurisé

secured [sɪˈkjʊəd] ADJ *Fin (loan)* garanti; *(bond)* cautionné

securely [sɪˈkjʊəlɪ] ADV **1** *(safely)* en sécurité; **to be s. protected** être parfaitement protégé; **he is s. behind bars** il est hors d'état de nuire **2** *(firmly)* solidement; **s. tightened** bien serré; **make sure your seat belt is s. fastened** assurez-vous que vous avez bien attaché votre ceinture de sécurité

securitization [sɪkjʊərɑɪtɑɪˈzeɪʃən] N *St Exch* titrisation *f*

securitize [sɪˈkjʊərɑɪtɑɪz] VT *St Exch* titriser

security [sɪˈkjʊərɪtɪ] N **1** *(of lock, person etc)* sécurité *f*, sûreté *f*; **to live in s.** vivre en sécurité; **s. of tenure** *(in job)* sécurité de l'emploi; *(as tenant)* jouissance *f* d'une location; **(job)** s. sécurité de l'emploi
2 *(at military base, during state visit etc)* sécurité *f*; **a s. cordon has been thrown around**

the airport un déploiement de forces de l'ordre a été organisé autour de l'aéroport; **the (United Nations) S. Council** le Conseil de sécurité (des Nations unies); **he's/it's a s. risk** il/cela constitue un danger *ou* un risque pour la sécurité; **(maximum) s. wing** quartier *m* de haute sécurité
3 *(safeguard)* sécurité *f*; **there's a further s. against theft** il y a un dispositif de sécurité antivol supplémentaire
4 *Com, Law (financial guarantee)* garantie *f*; *(for payment of debt)* caution *f*, cautionnement *m*; *(collateral)* nantissement *m*; *(person)* garant, -ante; **s. for a debt** *(money etc)* garantie d'une créance; **to stand s. for sb** se porter garant *ou* caution pour qn; **to give sth as (a) s.** donner qch en cautionnement; **to lend money on s./without s.** prêter de l'argent sur nantissement/sur gage à découvert
5 *St Exch* **securities** titres *mpl*, papiers *mpl* valeurs, valeurs *fpl*; **government securities** fonds *mpl* d'État; **securities lodged as collateral** titres déposés en nantissement; **securities issued** valeurs émises
6 **(social) s.** sécurité *f* sociale; **to live on s.** vivre des allocations
▸▸**s. alert** alerte *f* au danger; **s. blanket** doudou *m*; *Psy* objet *m* transitionnel; *Comput* **s. certificate** certificat *m* de sécurité; *Admin, Mil* **s. clearance** habilitation *f*; *(document)* laissez-passer *m inv*; **s. code** code *m* confidentiel; *Fin* **s. deposit** dépôt *m* de garantie; **s. device** sécurité *f*; *Am St Exch* **Securities and Exchange Commission** = commission *f* américaine des opérations de Bourse, ≃ COB *f*; **s. firm** société *f* de gardiennage; **s. forces** forces *fpl* de sécurité; **s. guard** garde *m* (chargé de la sécurité); *(for armoured van)* convoyeur, -euse de fonds; *St Exch* **securities house** société *f* de Bourse; *Comput* **s. level** niveau *m* de sécurité; *St Exch* **securities market** marché *m* des valeurs, marché des titres; **s. measures** mesures *fpl* de sécurité; **s. officer** *(on ship)* officier *m* chargé de la sécurité; *(in firm)* employé, -ée chargé(e) de la sécurité; *(inspector)* inspecteur, -trice de la sécurité; *Comput* **s. password** mot *m* de passe sécuritaire; **s. patrol** patrouille *f* de sûreté *ou* de protection; **s. personnel** personnel *m* de sécurité

security-coded ADJ *(radio)* codé, à code de sécurité
▸▸*Aut* **s. immobilizer** antidémarrage *m* codé

sedan [sɪˈdæn] N *Am Aut* voiture *f* de tourisme; **four-door s.** berline *f*
▸▸*Hist* **s. chair** chaise *f* à porteurs

sedate [sɪˈdeɪt] ADJ *(person)* posé, pondéré, réfléchi; *(lifestyle)* calme; *(deportment)* composé, calme
VT *Med* donner un sédatif à

sedately [sɪˈdeɪtlɪ] ADV posément

sedation [sɪˈdeɪʃən] N *Med* sédation *f*; **to be under s.** être sous sédatifs *ou* sous calmants

sedative [ˈsedətɪv] ADJ, N *Med* sédatif *m*, calmant *m*

sedentary [ˈsedəntrɪ] ADJ *(posture)* assis; *(job, life)* sédentaire

sedge [sedʒ] N *(plant)* joncs *mpl*, roseaux *mpl*
▸▸*Orn* **s. warbler** phragmite *m* des joncs

sediment [ˈsedɪmənt] N sédiment *m*; *(in bottle)* dépôt *m*; *(in wine)* lie *f*; *Chem* résidu *m*

sedimentary [sedɪˈment(ə)rɪ] ADJ *Geol (layer, rock)* sédimentaire

sedimentation [sedɪmenˈteɪʃən] N sédimentation *f*

sedition [sɪˈdɪʃən] N sédition *f*

seditious [sɪˈdɪʃəs] ADJ séditieux

seduce [sɪˈdjuːs] VT séduire; **they seduced**

him away from the company with … ils ont réussi à le convaincre de quitter l'entreprise en lui faisant miroiter …; **to s. sb into doing sth** convaincre qn de faire qch

> Note that the most common meaning of the French verb **séduire** is **to charm** or **to appeal to**, depending on the context.

seducer [sɪˈdjuːsər] N séducteur, -trice

seduction [sɪˈdʌkʃən] N **1** *(sexual)* séduction *f* **2** *(attractiveness) (usu pl)* attrait *m*, charme *m*; **the seductions of such a lifestyle** les attraits *ou* charmes d'un tel style de vie

seductive [sɪˈdʌktɪv] ADJ *(look, charm)* séducteur, -trice; *(music, argument, speech)* charmeur, -euse; *(smile)* aguichant; *(offer)* séduisant, attrayant, alléchant

seductively [sɪˈdʌktɪvlɪ] ADV avec séduction; **s. attractive** très attirant

seductiveness [sɪˈdʌktɪvnɪs] N *(of offer etc)* caractère *m* séduisant *ou* attrayant *ou* alléchant; *(of woman)* séduction *f*, charme *m*; *(of style)* charme

sedulous [ˈsedjʊləs] ADJ *Fml* assidu, scrupuleux

sedulously [ˈsedjʊləslɪ] ADV *Fml* scrupuleusement

SEE¹ [siː] VOIR GRAMMAIRE A41; B35 (*pt* **saw** [sɔː]; *pp* **seen** [siːn])

> **VT** voir **1, 4, 5, 9, 10** ▪ comprendre **2** ▪ reconnaître **2** ▪ percevoir **4** ▪ s'assurer que **8** ▪ recevoir **9** ▪ consulter **9** ▪ reconduire **11** ▪ accompagner **11**
> **VI** voir **1–6**

VT **1** *(with eyes)* voir; **I saw it with my own eyes** je l'ai vu de mes propres yeux, je l'ai de mes yeux vu; **the cathedral can be seen from a long way off** on voit la cathédrale de très loin; **to s. the sights of the town** visiter les monuments de la ville; **there's nothing to s.** il n'y a rien à voir; **I can't s. anything** je ne vois rien; **the moment I saw him** dès que je l'ai aperçu *ou* vu; **did you s. that programme last night?** tu as vu cette émission hier soir?; **now s. what you've done!** regarde ce que tu as fait!; **s. page 50** voir page 50; **s. above** se reporter plus haut; **s. (on) the back** voir au verso; **I'm not fit to be seen** je ne suis pas présentable; **to s. things** *(hallucinate)* avoir des hallucinations *ou* des visions; **it has to be seen to be believed** il faut le voir pour le croire; **the squalor in which they live has to be seen to be believed** ils vivent dans une misère, il faut le voir pour le croire; **to s. sb do** *or* **doing sth** voir qn faire qch; **I saw him fall** je l'ai vu tomber; **to s. sb coming** voir venir qn; *Fig* **they saw you coming a mile off** ils t'ont vu arriver de loin; **to s. one's way** voir où l'on va; **I can't s. a way out of this problem** je ne vois pas d'issue à ce problème; **could you s. your way to lending me your car?** est-ce que, par hasard, tu pourrais me prêter ta voiture?; **to s. the back of sb** se débarrasser de qn; **to s. sense** *or* **reason** entendre raison; **I'll s. him in hell first!** qu'il aille au diable!, qu'il aille se faire pendre!; **he has seen a great deal of the world** *(he has travelled a great deal)* il a beaucoup voyagé; *(he has a great deal of experience)* il a une vaste expérience; **the city hasn't seen such crowds in decades** la ville n'a pas connu une foule pareille depuis des dizaines d'années; **the country saw many changes** le pays a connu de grands changements; *Mil* **the first time he saw action** quand il a reçu le baptême du feu; *Mil* **he saw action in the desert** il a combattu dans le désert
2 *(understand)* comprendre, saisir; *(the er-*

ror of one's ways etc) reconnaître; **I don't s. how/why/where …** je ne vois pas comment/pourquoi/où …; **I don't s. the need** *or* **necessity for …** je ne vois pas l'intérêt de …; **they cannot s. the truth** la vérité leur échappe; **I can't s. the difference** je ne vois pas la différence; **I don't s. the point** je ne vois pas l'intérêt; **he can't s. a joke** il ne comprend pas la plaisanterie; **I s. what you mean** je vois ce que vous voulez dire; **I don't s. that at all!** *(I don't agree)* je ne suis pas du tout d'accord!

3 *(observe)* **to s. oneself in one's children** se reconnaître dans ses enfants; **I don't know what you s. in her** je ne vois pas ce que tu lui trouves; **it remains to be seen whether …** (il) reste à savoir si …; **whether this is true remains to be seen** (il) reste à savoir si ceci est vrai; **I can't s. any sense** *or* **the sense in continuing this discussion** je ne vois pas l'intérêt de continuer cette discussion; **I s.** *or* **saw in the paper that …** j'ai vu dans le journal que …; **he never lived to s. the project finished** il est mort avant que le projet ne soit achevé; **I s. (that) you're a sports fan** je vois que vous êtes un fan de sport

4 *(perceive sth in a certain way)* voir, percevoir; **I s. things differently now** aujourd'hui, je vois les choses autrement; **this is how I s. it** voici comme je perçois la chose

5 *(envisage)* voir; **what do you s. happening next?** d'après vous, qu'est-ce qui va se passer ensuite?; **how do you s. the situation in a year's time?** comment pensez-vous que la situation aura évolué dans un an?; **I don't s. myself still doing this in a year's time** je ne me vois *ou* m'imagine pas faire encore cela dans un an; **how do you s. things developing?** comment est-ce que vous envisagez l'avenir?; **I can't s. them accepting this** je ne peux pas croire qu'ils vont accepter cela; **they say this will be more efficient, but I don't s. it** ils disent que cela sera plus efficace, mais je n'y crois pas; **I don't s. any chance of that** à mon avis, c'est peu probable; **I can't s. you as a boxer** je ne te vois pas en boxeur; **I can't s. myself doing this** je ne me vois *ou* m'imagine pas en train de faire cela

6 *(examine)* examiner; **let me s. that letter again** repassez-moi cette lettre (pour que je la relise)

7 *(investigate, enquire, discover)* **I'll s. what I can do** je vais voir ce que je peux faire; **let's s. what happens if …** voyons ce qu'il se passe si …

8 *(make sure)* **to s. (to it) that everything is in order** s'assurer que tout est en ordre; **I shall s. (to it) that he comes** je me charge de le faire venir; **s. (to it) that you don't miss the train!** faites attention de ne pas manquer le train!; *Fam* **he'll s. you (all) right** il s'occupera de toi

9 *(meet)* *(person)* voir; *(visitor)* recevoir; *(doctor, solicitor etc)* consulter, voir; **he sees a great deal of the Longs** il fréquente *ou* voit beaucoup les Long; **we don't s. much of each other** nous ne nous voyons pas souvent; **when shall I s. you again?** quand est-ce que je vais vous revoir?; **are you seeing another woman?** est-ce que tu as *ou* vois une autre femme?; **s. you soon!, (I'll) be seeing you!** à bientôt!; **(I'll) s. you Thursday!** à jeudi!; *Fam* **s. you!** salut!, à plus! [aplys]; **to go to** *or* **and s. sb** aller voir qn; **I can't s. him today** *(visitor)* je ne peux pas le recevoir aujourd'hui

10 *(speak to)* **I want to s. the manager** je veux voir le directeur; **can I s. you for a minute in my office?** je peux vous voir un instant dans mon bureau?; **I'd like to s. you on business** je voudrais vous parler affaires

11 *(escort, accompany)* **to s. sb home** reconduire qn *ou* accompagner qn jusque chez

lui/elle; **I saw him to the station** je l'ai accompagné jusqu'à la gare; **I'll s. you to the door** je vous accompagne jusqu'à la porte
12 *(at cards)* **I'll s. you** je te demande à voir; **I'll s. your hundred** je vous suis à cent

VI 1 voir; **she can't s. very well** *(her sight is poor)* elle ne voit pas très bien, sa vue n'est pas très bonne; *(on specific occasions)* elle ne voit pas très bien; **cats can s. in the dark** les chats voient clair la nuit; **as far as the eye can s.** à perte de vue; **to s. into the future** voir l'avenir; **to s. into sb's heart** lire dans le cœur de qn; *Old-fashioned Fam* **s. here!** *(annoyance)* dites donc!, voyons!

2 *(understand)* voir; **as far as I can s.** autant que je puisse en juger; **I s.** je vois, je comprends; **ah, I s.!** ah, je vois!; **do you see?,** *Fam* **s.?** tu vois?; **you s., I never liked them** voyez-vous, je ne les ai jamais aimés

3 *(observe)* voir; **s. for yourself** voyez par vous-même; **seeing is believing** on ne peut nier ce qu'on voit de ses propres yeux; **we shall s.** nous verrons (bien); **we'll soon s.** on le saura vite; **we'll soon s. if …** on saura vite si …; **I'll be a good musician one day, you'll s.** je serai un bon musicien un jour, vous verrez; **s.! I told you he wouldn't let us down** tu vois! je t'avais dit qu'il ne nous laisserait pas tomber

4 *(examine)* voir; **can I s.?** je peux voir?; **let me s.!, let's s.!** fais voir!; **have you got a free room?** – **let me s.** est-ce que vous avez une chambre libre? – voyons (voir); **it was, let me s., in 1998** c'était, voyons (voir), en 1998
5 *(consider)* voir; **can we go to the beach, Mummy?** – **we'll** *or* **I'll s.** est-ce qu'on peut aller à la plage, maman? – on verra
6 *(find out)* (aller) voir

▶ **see about** VT INSEP **1** *(attend to)* s'occuper de; **I'll have to s. about that old door** il faudra que je m'occupe de cette vieille porte
2 *(consider)* voir; **I'll s. about it** je verrai ça; *Iron* **we'll (soon) s. about that!** c'est ce qu'on va voir!

▶ **see across** VT SEP *(escort to other side of)* **to s. sb across the road** aider qn à traverser la rue

▶ **see in** VI *(look in)* voir à l'intérieur; **the curtains were drawn, so we couldn't s. in** les rideaux étaient tirés, nous ne pouvions rien voir à l'intérieur

VT SEP *(escort in)* *(person)* faire entrer; **to s. the new year in** faire le réveillon du nouvel an

▶ **see into** VT INSEP **to s. into sth** *(investigate)* se renseigner sur qch, examiner qch

▶ **see off**
VT SEP **1 to s. sb off at the station** accompagner qn (jusqu')à la gare; **we'll come to s. you off** nous viendrons vous dire au revoir
2 to s. sb off (the premises) *(escort)* accompagner qn jusqu'à la sortie; *(make sure they go)* s'assurer du départ de qn
3 *(in fight etc)* **she saw off two bigger girls** elle a battu deux filles plus grandes qu'elle; **the dogs saw them off** les chiens les ont fait fuir

▶ **see out** VT SEP **1** *(escort to door)* accompagner jusqu'à la porte; **I'll s. myself out** je connais le chemin, ce n'est pas la peine de me raccompagner
2 *(stay until end of)* voir la fin de; *(undertaking)* mener à bonne fin; **I's. another year out here, then go home** je vais passer une autre année ici, puis je rentrerai; **I don't think these boots will s. the winter out** je ne crois pas que ces bottes feront l'hiver; **he isn't expected to s. out the week** il y a peu de chances qu'il survive jusqu'à la fin de la semaine; **he'll s. us all out!** *(will survive us)* il nous enterrera tous!

▶ **see over, see round** VT INSEP *(tour)* *(house etc)* visiter, voir

▶ **see through** VT INSEP *(not be deceived by)*

(person) deviner les intentions de; **I saw through him** j'ai deviné ses intentions, je l'ai percé à jour; **I saw through their little game** j'ai vite compris leur petit jeu

VT SEP **1** *(stay until end of)* **to s. a show/film through** assister à un spectacle/regarder un film jusqu'au bout; **to s. a matter through** mener une affaire à bonne fin *ou* jusqu'au bout; **I'll s. it through** je tiendrai jusqu'au bout

2 *(help to cope)* aider; **£20 should s. me through (to Monday)** 20 livres devraient me suffire (jusqu'à lundi); **friends and relatives are seeing her through this bad time** ses amis et sa famille l'aident à traverser cette période difficile; **200 gallons should s. us through the winter** 200 gallons devraient nous suffire pour l'hiver

▶ **see to** VT INSEP *(deal with)* s'occuper de; **I'll have to get it seen to** il faut que je m'en occupe; **I'll s. to it** je vais m'en occuper, je m'en charge; **I'll s. to it that you're not disturbed** je ferai en sorte que vous ne soyez pas dérangé

▶ **see up** VT SEP *(accompany)* **to s. sb up** faire monter qn

see² N *Rel (of bishop)* siège *m* épiscopal, évêché *m*; *(of archbishop)* archevêché *m*; **the Holy S.** le Saint-Siège

seed [si:d] N **1** graine *f*, *(of apple, pear, grapes etc)* pépin *m*; **mustard s.** graine de moutarde; **seed(s)** *(in gardening, agriculture)* semence(s) *f(pl)*, graine(s); **to go** *or* **run to s.** *(of plant)* monter en graine; *(of land)* tomber en friche; *(of person)* se laisser aller; *Fig* **the seeds of discord** les germes *mpl* de la discorde; **to sow (the) seeds of discord/doubt** semer la discorde/le doute

2 *Arch, Lit* = semen

3 *Bible Lit (descendants)* descendance *f*, lignée *f*; **the s. of Abraham** la descendance d'Abraham

4 *Tennis* tête *f* de série

VI *(of plant)* monter en graine; *(of cereals)* venir à graine

VT **1** *(sow with seeds)* *(field etc)* semer; *Met* **to s. clouds** provoquer la pluie **2** *(remove seeds from)* *(melons, grapes etc)* épépiner **3** *Tennis* **to s. the players** classer les joueurs; **seeded players** têtes *fpl* de série; **she was seeded tenth** elle était classée dixième

▶ ▶ **s. bed** *(couche f* de) semis *m*, germoir *m*; **s. box** boîte *f* à semis; *Fin* **s. capital** capital *m* initial *ou* de départ, mise *f* de fonds initiale; **s. corn** grain *m* de semence; *Br* **s. merchant** grainetier, -ière; *Fin* **s. money** capital initial *ou* de départ, mise de fonds initiale; **s. pearls** semence de perles; **s. potatoes** pommes *fpl* de terre de semence; **s. tray** terrine *f* à semis; *Bot* **s. vessel** péricarpe *m*

seedcake ['si:dkeɪk] N *Culin* gâteau *m* parfumé au carvi

seediness ['si:dɪnɪs] N **1** *(of clothes)* état *m* miteux; *(of building)* état minable; **the s. of the area surprised him** il fut surpris de voir à quel point l'endroit était minable **2** *Fam (feeling of being unwell)* indisposition *f*

seedless ['si:dlɪs] ADJ *(grapes etc)* sans pépins

seedling ['si:dlɪŋ] N *(plant grown from seed)* (jeune) plant *m*; **seedlings** semis *m*

seedsman, *pl* **seedsmen** ['si:dzmən] N grainetier *m*

seedy ['si:dɪ] ADJ **1** *(shabby)* *(person)* miteux; *(hotel etc)* minable, miteux **2** *Fam (unwell)* mal fichu, patraque; **to feel s.** se sentir patraque, être mal fichu, ne pas être dans son assiette **3** *(full of seeds)* plein de pépins

seeing ['si:ɪŋ] CONJ **s. (that** *or* *Fam* **as how)** … vu que … + *ind*, étant donné que … + *ind*; **s. as how it's all so simple, why don't you do**

it yourself? pourquoi ne le fais-tu pas toi-même puisque c'est si simple?

▸ **N s. is believing** voir c'est croire

▸▸ *Am* **s. eye dog** chien *m* d'aveugle

seeing-to N *Br Sl* **to give sb a good s.** *(beat up)* tabasser qn; *(have sex with)* faire passer qn à la casserole

seek [siːk] *(pt, pp* **sought** [sɔːt]*)* VT **1** *(look for) (sth lost, job etc)* chercher; *(sb's friendship, promotion etc)* rechercher; *(somebody)* chercher; **to be actively seeking employment** être en recherche effective d'emploi; **to s. one's fortune** chercher fortune; **to s. shelter** chercher un abri; **they sought shelter under a tree** ils se sont réfugiés sous un arbre

2 *(request)* **to s. sth from** *or of* **sb** demander qch à qn; **to s. sb's help** rechercher *ou* demander l'aide de qn; **to s. advice** demander conseil

3 to s. to do sth essayer *ou* tenter de faire qch; **she sought in vain to convince them of her innocence** elle tenta en vain de les convaincre de son innocence

▸ VI **s.!** *(to dog)* cherche!; *Prov* **s. and you** *or Arch* **ye shall find** quand on cherche, on trouve

▸▸ *Comput* **s. time** temps *m* d'accès

▸ **seek after** VT INSEP *(look for) (truth)* chercher; **to be much sought after** être très recherché *ou* demandé

▸ **seek out** VT SEP *(find) (person)* trouver

seeker ['siːkər] N chercheur, -euse; **a s. after truth** un chercheur/une chercheuse de vérité; **pleasure seekers** gens *mpl* en quête de plaisirs

SEEM [siːm] VI sembler, paraître, avoir l'air; **to s. tired** paraître *ou* sembler *ou* avoir l'air fatigué; **how did she s. to you?** comment l'as-tu trouvée?; **do whatever seems best (to you)** fais au mieux; **how does it s. to you?** qu'en pensez-vous?; **it seems like a dream** on croit rêver; **it all seems a long time ago now** ça me paraît loin maintenant; **it doesn't s. right, them getting away with it** ça ne semble pas juste qu'ils s'en tirent à bon compte; **she seems to be** *or* **she seems (like) a nice person** elle a l'air bien; **I s. to have heard his name somewhere** il me semble avoir entendu son nom quelque part; **I seemed to be floating on a cloud** j'avais l'impression de flotter sur un nuage; **I s. to have dropped your vase** je crois (bien) que j'ai laissé tomber votre vase; **I can't s. to get it right** je n'y arrive pas; **she seemed to be trying to say something** elle semblait essayer de dire quelque chose

▸ V IMPERS **it seems (that) …, it would s. that** … il paraît que … + *ind*, il semble que … + *ind ou subj*; **it seemed best to …** il semblait préférable de …; **it seems like only yesterday** c'est comme si c'était hier; **it seems likely that this will happen soon** cela risque d'arriver bientôt; **it seems to me that …** il me semble que …; **it seemed to me (that) I was dreaming** il me semblait *ou* j'avais l'impression que je rêvais; **it seemed as though** *or* **as if …** il semblait que … + *sub*, on aurait dit que … + *ind*; **it seems so, it would s. so** à ce qu'il paraît; **it seems not, it wouldn't s. so** il paraît que non; **it seems to be raining** on dirait qu'il pleut; **there doesn't s. to be any butter left** j'ai l'impression qu'il n'y a plus de beurre

seeming ['siːmɪŋ] ADJ apparent

seemingly ['siːmɪŋlɪ] ADV apparemment

seemliness ['siːmlɪnɪs] N *Fml* bienséance *f*

seemly ['siːmlɪ] ADJ *Fml* convenable, bienséant

seen [siːn] PP *see* see[1]

▸ ADJ ATTRIB *Sch* **a s. translation** une traduction préparée

seep [siːp] VI suinter; *(into sth)* s'infiltrer; **the water was seeping into the earth** l'eau s'infiltrait dans la terre; **information was seeping out** des renseignements filtraient

seepage ['siːpɪdʒ] N **1** *(act)* suintement *m*; *Fig (of workers)* fuite *f* **2** *(lost liquid)* fuite *f*, déperdition *f*

seer [sɪər] N *Lit* prophète *m*, prophétesse *f*

seersucker ['sɪəsʌkər] N *Tex* coton *m* gaufré

seesaw ['siːsɔː] N bascule *f*, tapecul *m*

▸ ADJ *(movement)* de bascule, de va-et-vient

▸ VI **1** *(play on a seesaw)* jouer à la bascule, faire du tapecul **2** *(of machine part etc)* basculer; *Fig (oscillate)* osciller

▸▸ *Fin* **s. effect** effet *m* balançoire

seethe [siːð] VI *(of liquid)* bouillonner; *(of crowd etc)* s'agiter; **the street is seething with people** la rue grouille de monde; **to be seething (with anger)** bouillir de colère; **he's absolutely seething** il est fou de rage; **the country was seething with discontent** le mécontentement agitait tout le pays

seething ['siːðɪŋ] ADJ *(liquid)* bouillonnant; **a s. mass of worms** une masse grouillante de vers

see-through ADJ transparent

segment[1] ['segmənt] N **1** *(of sphere, circle, worm)* segment *m*; *(of orange)* quartier *m*; *(of population, public opinion)* partie *f*, **s. of a line** segment linéaire **2** *Mktg (of market, population)* segment *m*

segment[2] [seg'ment] VT **1** *(divide)* couper en segments, segmenter **2** *Mktg (market, population)* segmenter

▸ VI *(of worm)* se segmenter

segmentation [segmən'teɪʃən] N *Biol, Mktg* segmentation *f*

segregate ['segrɪgeɪt] VT *(something)* isoler, mettre à part; *(somebody)* séparer (**from** de); *(races)* soumettre à la ségrégation

segregation [segrɪ'geɪʃən] N séparation *f*, isolement *m*; *Pol* ségrégation *f*, **policy of s.** ségrégationnisme *m*

segregationist [segrɪ'geɪʃənɪst] ADJ, N *Pol* ségrégationniste *mf*

segue ['segweɪ] N *TV etc* transition *f* musicale

▸ VI enchaîner; **to s. into** enchaîner sur

sei whale [seɪ] N *Zool* rorqual *m* boréal

seismic ['saɪzmɪk] ADJ sismique; *Fig (shock waves, changes)* gigantesque

seismograph ['saɪzməgrɑːf] N sismographe *m*

seismologist [saɪz'mɒlədʒɪst] N sismologue *mf*

seismology [saɪz'mɒlədʒɪ] N sismologie *f*

seize [siːz] VT **1** *(grab)* saisir; **to s. hold of sb/sth** saisir *ou* empoigner qn/qch; **to s. hold of an idea** se jeter sur une idée; **to s. sb by the throat** saisir qn à la gorge; **to s. the opportunity of doing sth** saisir *ou* saisir l'occasion de faire qch; **to be seized with fright/panic/doubt** être saisi de peur/panique/doute

2 *(take for oneself)* s'emparer de; *(fortress)* prendre; *(enemy ship)* capturer; *Law (drugs, stolen goods etc)* saisir; *(person)* arrêter

3 *(understand) (meaning, implication etc)* saisir; **to s. the meaning of sth** prendre *ou* saisir le sens de qch

▸ **seize on** VT INSEP *(grasp) (idea)* saisir; **to s. on a pretext for leaving** saisir *ou* sauter sur un prétexte pour partir

▸ **seize up** VI *Tech etc (become stuck) (of part, machine etc)* (se) gripper, coincer; *(of engine)* caler; **my knee's seized up** *(completely)* mon genou est coincé; *(partially)* mon genou est ankylosé

▸ **seize upon** VT INSEP = seize on

seizing ['siːzɪŋ] N *Mil (of fortress)* prise *f*, *(of enemy ship)* capture *f*, *Law (of property, goods)* saisie *f*

seizure ['siːʒər] N **1** *(of fortress)* prise *f*, *(of enemy ship)* capture *f*, *Law (of property, goods)* saisie *f* **2** *Med* crise *f*, attaque *f*, **(apoplectic) s.** attaque d'apoplexie; *Fam* **he just about had a s. when he found out!** il a failli faire une crise quand il a su!

seldom ['seldəm] ADV rarement; **he is s. seen** on le voit rarement; **such things are s. seen now** de telles choses se font rares de nos jours; **s. have I heard such nonsense** j'ai rarement entendu des bêtises pareilles VOIR GRAMMAIRE A78

select [sɪ'lekt] VT choisir, sélectionner; *Comput, Sport* sélectionner; **to s. from …** choisir parmi …; *Comput* **s. 'enter'** tapez 'entrée'; *Comput* **to s. an option** activer une option

▸ ADJ *(exclusive)* de (premier) choix, d'élite; *(club)* très fermé, sélect; *(audience)* choisi

▸▸ *Pol* **s. committee** commission *f* d'enquête parlementaire

selectable [sɪ'lektəb(ə)l] ADJ *Comput* qui peut être sélectionné

selected [sɪ'lektɪd] ADJ choisi; *Com* de choix; *Liter* **s. passages** morceaux *mpl* choisis

selection [sɪ'lekʃən] N **1** *(act of choosing)* choix *m*, sélection *f*, *(for team)* sélection; **to make a s.** faire un choix; *Biol* **natural s.** sélection naturelle **2** *(range)* choix *m*; **a wide s.** un grand choix; **a narrow s.** un choix limité; **a good s. of wines** un bon choix de vins; **they don't have a very good s.** ils n'ont pas beaucoup de choix **3** *(thing(s) chosen)* **selections from Byron** morceaux *mpl* choisis de Byron; *Horseracing* **our selections** nos pronostics

▸▸ **s. box** *(of chocolate bars)* assortiment *m* de barres chocolatées; *Mktg* **s. method** méthode *f* de sélection; **s. procedure** procédure *f* de sélection; *(for staff)* démarche *f* de sélection

selective [sɪ'lektɪv] ADJ sélectif; **to be s.** *(of person)* savoir choisir, choisir avec discernement; **he's very s. about what he eats** il est très difficile sur la nourriture; **you should be more s. about your friends** tu devrais mieux choisir tes amis; **to be s. in the application of a law** appliquer la loi en fonction de ses intérêts

▸▸ **s. breeding** élevage *m* sélectif; *Sch* **s. entry** sélection *f*

selectively [sɪ'lektɪvlɪ] ADV de manière sélective

selectivity [sɪlek'tɪvɪtɪ] N sélectivité *f*

selectman, *pl* **selectmen** [sɪ'lektmən] N *Am (in New England)* = conseiller *m* municipal

selector [sɪ'lektər] N **1** *Sport* sélectionneur, -euse **2** *Tel, Aut* sélecteur *m*

▸▸ *Aut* **s. lever** *(in automatic gearbox)* levier *m* de sélection

selenium [sɪ'liːnɪəm] N sélénium *m*

self, *pl* **selves** [self, selvz] N **1** **that wasn't his real s.** il n'était pas lui-même; **he's quite his old** *or* **former s. again** *(he has recovered)* il est complètement rétabli; *(his character has returned to normal)* il est tout à fait comme auparavant; **she is a shadow of her former s.** elle n'est plus que l'ombre d'elle-même; **she was her usual cheerful/tactless s.** comme à son habitude, elle était gaie/blessante; **preoccupation with s.** préoccupation *f* de sa propre personne; *Old-fashioned* **your good selves** vous-mêmes, vous

2 *Psy* **the s.** *(personality)* la personnalité; *(ego)* le moi; **two selves in one body** deux personnalités dans une seule personne; **the notion of the s.** la notion du moi

3 *(flower)* fleur *f* de couleur uniforme

PRON *(on cheque)* **pay s.** payez à moi-même

self- [self] PREF **1** *(of and by oneself)* auto-; **s.-analysis** autoanalyse *f* **2** *(in oneself)* de soi-même; **s.-belief** confiance *f* en soi **3** *(automatic)* automatique; **s.-closing** à fermeture automatique

self-abasement N rabaissement *m* de soi-même

self-abnegation N = self-denial

self-absorbed [-əb'zɔːbd] ADJ égocentrique

self-abuse N *Old-fashioned* masturbation *f*

self-acting ADJ automatique

self-addressed [ə'drest] ADJ
▸▸ **s. envelope** enveloppe *f* à son propre nom

self-adhesive ADJ autocollant
▸▸ **s. label** étiquette *f* autocollante

self-adjusting ADJ à autoréglage, à réglage automatique
▸▸ **s. tappet** poussoir *m* autorégleur

self-advertisement N publicité *f* qu'on se fait à soi-même; **to indulge in s.** aimer se faire de la publicité

self-advocacy N *esp Am Admin (of mentally handicapped person)* affirmation *f* de soi

self-aggrandizement N autoglorification *f*

self-analysis N autoanalyse *f*

self-apparent ADJ évident

self-appointed ADJ **a s. critic of the régime** une personne qui s'érige en critique du régime; **a s. spokesperson** un porte-parole qui s'est lui-même désigné; **s. moral guardians** des moralisateurs qui s'érigent en censeurs

self-appraisal N auto-évaluation *f*, *pl* auto-évaluations
▸▸ **s. scheme** système *m* d'auto-évaluation

self-assembly ADJ *(furniture etc)* à monter soi-même
N **flat-packed for s.** en pièces détachées à monter soi-même

self-assertive ADJ décidé; **be more s.** vous devriez vous affirmer davantage

self-assertiveness N affirmation *f* de soi

self-assessment N **1** auto-évaluation *f*, *pl* auto-évaluations **2** *Br (for tax purposes)* = système *m* de déclaration des revenus pour le paiement des impôts, par opposition au prélèvement à la source

self-assurance N assurance *f*

self-assured ADJ sûr de soi, plein d'assurance

self-aware ADJ conscient de soi-même

self-awareness N conscience *f* de soi

self-belief N confiance *f* en soi; **to have s.** croire en soi-même

self-betterment N *(material)* amélioration *f* de sa condition; *(spiritual)* progrès *mpl* spirituels

self-catering ADJ *(holiday)* en appartement meublé; *(flat)* meublé avec cuisine équipée
ADV **to go s.** louer un meublé pour ses vacances
▸▸ **s. accommodation** meublé *m* de tourisme; **s. apartment** meublé, location *f* de vacances, appartement *m* en location; **s. holiday** vacances *fpl* en location; **to be on a s. holiday** être en location

self-censorship N autocensure *f*; **to practise s.** s'autocensurer

self-centred, *Am* **self-centered** [-'sentəd] ADJ égocentrique

self-centredness, *Am* **self-centeredness** [-'sentədnɪs] N égocentrisme *m*

self-certification N = système *m* dans lequel les employés n'ont pas besoin de certificat médical pour justifier d'une absence

self-check routine N *Comput* routine *f* d'autotest

self-cleaning ADJ *(oven)* autonettoyant

self-coloured, *Am* **self-colored** ADJ uni

self-composed ADJ posé, calme

self-composure N calme *m*

self-concept N *(self-image)* image *f* de soi

self-confessed [-kən'fest] ADJ **as a s. pervert, I ...** tout perverti que je suis, je ...; **he is a s. workaholic** de son propre aveu, c'est un bourreau de travail

self-confidence N confiance *f* en soi, assurance *f*

self-confident ADJ sûr de soi, plein d'assurance

self-congratulation N autosatisfaction *f*

self-congratulatory ADJ *(person)* qui fait de l'autosatisfaction; *(remarks, tone)* d'autosatisfaction, dénotant l'autosatisfaction

self-conscious ADJ **1** *(person)* embarrassé, gêné, contraint; **he's very s. about his large nose** il est très complexé par son gros nez **2** *(affected) (writing style etc)* affecté **3** *Phil* conscient, qui a conscience de soi

self-consciously ADV avec gêne *ou* embarras

self-consciousness N **1** *(embarrassment)* contrainte *f*, embarras *m*, gêne *f* **2** *(affectedness) (of writing style etc)* affectation *f* **3** *Phil* conscience *f* de soi

self-contained [-kən'teɪnd] ADJ **1** *(person)* réservé; *(uncommunicative)* peu communicatif; *(independent)* indépendant **2** *(apartment)* indépendant, avec entrée particulière

self-contempt N mépris *m* de soi-même; **to be full of s.** se mépriser

self-contradictory ADJ contradictoire

self-control N maîtrise *f* de soi; **to exercise s.** faire un effort sur soi-même; **to have no s.** ne pas savoir se maîtriser; **to lose one's s.** perdre tout empire sur soi-même, ne plus se maîtriser *ou* se contrôler; **to regain one's s.** se ressaisir

self-controlled ADJ **to be s.** *(of person)* avoir du sang-froid

self-correcting [-kə'rektɪŋ] ADJ à correction automatique, autocorrecteur, -trice

self-critical ADJ **to be s.** être critique à l'égard de soi-même; **you're too s.** tu es trop sévère avec toi-même

self-criticism N autocritique *f*

self-deception N aveuglement *m*; **it's pure s. on his part** il se fait des illusions

self-defeating [-dɪ'fiːtɪŋ] ADJ **that would be s.** cela irait à l'encontre du but recherché

self-defence, *Am* **self-defense** N *Law* légitime défense *f*; **to kill sb in s.** tuer qn en (état de) légitime défense; **a course in s.** un cours d'autodéfense *ou* de self-défense

self-delusion N illusion *f*; **it is nothing but s. on her part** elle se fait des illusions

self-denial N abnégation *f*

self-denying [-dɪ'naɪɪŋ] ADJ qui fait preuve d'abnégation; **a s. life** une vie de sacrifice

self-deprecation [-deprɪ'keɪʃən] N dénigrement *m* de soi-même

self-deprecatory ADJ *(person)* qui se dénigre; *(remarks)* critique envers soi-même

self-destruct VI s'autodétruire

self-destruction N autodestruction *f*

self-destructive ADJ *(behaviour, character)* suicidaire

self-determination N *Pol* autodétermination *f*

self-discipline N autodiscipline *f*

self-doubt N manque *m* de confiance en soi

self-drive ADJ *(car)* sans chauffeur

self-educated ADJ autodidacte

self-effacing [-ɪ'feɪsɪŋ] ADJ effacé

self-employed ADJ qui travaille à son (propre) compte, indépendant
NPL **the s.** les travailleurs *mpl* indépendants

self-employment N travail *m* à son propre compte, travail en indépendant

self-esteem N estime *f ou* respect *m* de soi, amour-propre *m*; **to suffer from low s.** avoir peu d'estime de soi

self-evident ADJ évident en soi, qui saute aux yeux

self-evidently ADV à l'évidence

self-examination N *(of conscience)* examen *m* de conscience; *(of breast)* autopalpation *f*

self-explanatory ADJ qui s'explique de soi-même

self-expression N libre expression *f*

self-fertilization N *Biol* autofécondation *f*

self-fertilizing [-'fɜːtɪlaɪzɪŋ] ADJ *Biol* autofécondant

self-financing ADJ *(entreprise)* qui s'autofinance
N autofinancement *m*

self-fulfilling ADJ
▸▸ **s. prophecy** = prophétie *f* défaitiste qui se réalise

self-fulfilment N accomplissement *m* de soi, épanouissement *m*

self-funding ADJ qui s'autofinance

self-governing ADJ autonome

self-government N autonomie *f*

self-hatred N haine *f* de soi

self-help N efforts *mpl* personnels
▸▸ **s. book** = manuel *m* prodiguant des conseils au lecteur pour améliorer un aspect particulier de sa vie; **s. group** groupe *m* d'entraide

self-hypnosis N autohypnose *f*

self-ignition N *Aut* auto-allumage *m*

self-image N image *f* qu'on a de soi-même, image de soi

self-importance N suffisance *f*, présomption *f*

self-important ADJ suffisant, présomptueux

self-imposed [-ɪm'pəʊzd] ADJ *(task etc)* dont on a pris de soi-même la responsabilité; *(exile)* volontaire

self-improvement N amélioration *f* personnelle; *(material)* amélioration de sa condition

self-induction N *Elec* self-induction *f*, auto-induction *f*
▸▸ **s. coil** bobine *f* de self-induction, *Fam* self *f*

self-indulgence N sybaritisme *m*, habitude *f* de ne rien se refuser; **a typical example of the author's stylistic s.** un exemple typique de la complaisance stylistique de l'auteur envers lui-même

self-indulgent ADJ sybarite, qui ne se refuse rien; *(writer, artist etc)* complaisant envers soi-même; *(novel, film etc)* complaisant

self-inflicted [-ɪn'flɪktɪd] ADJ *(damage etc)* que l'on s'inflige à soi-même; **s. wound** mutilation *f* volontaire

self-interest N intérêt *m* (personnel); **to act from** *or* **out of s.** agir dans un but intéressé

self-interested ADJ intéressé

selfish ['selfɪʃ] ADJ égoïste

selfishly ['selfɪʃlɪ] ADV égoïstement; **to act s.** agir en égoïste

selfishness ['selfɪʃnɪs] N égoïsme *m*

self-justification N justification *f* (de ses propres actes); **his attempts at s.** ses tentatives pour se justifier

self-knowledge N connaissance *f* de soi

selfless ['selflɪs] ADJ désintéressé, altruiste

selflessness ['selflɪsnɪs] N désintéressement *m*, altruisme *m*

self-loading ADJ *(gun)* automatique

self-loathing N dégoût *m* de soi-même

self-locking ADJ *(door etc)* à verrouillage *ou* fermeture automatique; *Tech* à blocage automatique, auto-bloqueur, -euse; *(nut)* indesserrable

self-love N narcissisme *m*

self-made ADJ
▸▸ **s. man** self-made-man *m*, *pl* self-made-men

self-mockery N moquerie *f* à l'égard de soi-même

self-mocking ADJ *(tone, remarks)* empreint d'ironie à l'égard de soi-même

self-motivated ADJ capable de prendre des initiatives

self-motivation N motivation *f*

self-obsessed [əb'sest] ADJ obsédé par soi-même

self-opinionated ADJ entêté; **he's very s.** il veut toujours avoir raison

self-op studio N *(in broadcasting)* studio *m* de reportage

self-parking ADJ *Aut (wipers)* à retour automatique

self-perpetuating [-pə'petjʊeɪtɪŋ] ADJ qui se reproduit indéfiniment

self-pity N attendrissement *m* sur soi-même; **full of s.** attendri sur soi-même; **to wallow in s.** s'apitoyer sur son sort

self-pitying ADJ qui s'apitoie sur son sort

self-pollination N *Bot* autopollinisation *f*

self-portrait N autoportrait *m*

self-possessed [-pə'zest] ADJ maître de soi, qui a beaucoup de sang-froid

self-possession N sang-froid *m*, maîtrise *f* de soi

self-praise N éloge *m* de soi-même; **I'm not saying that in s.** ce n'est pas laudatif à mon égard

self-preservation N **(instinct for) s.** instinct *m* de conservation

self-proclaimed [-prə'kleɪmd] ADJ autoproclamé

self-propelled, self-propelling [-prə'peld] ADJ *(vehicle)* automoteur, -trice, auto-propulsé

self-publicist N **he is an accomplished s.** il sait soigner sa publicité

self-raising, *Am* **self-rising** ADJ *(flour)* contenant de la levure chimique

self-regard N = **self-esteem**

self-regulating ADJ *Tech* autorégulateur, -trice, à autoréglage; *(economy)* qui se régule d'elle-même

self-regulation N autorégulation *f*

self-reliance N indépendance *f*

self-reliant ADJ indépendant

self-repairing bumper [-rɪ'peərɪŋ] N *Aut* pare-chocs *m inv* auto-réparable

self-replicate VI s'autoreproduire

self-replicating [-'replɪkeɪtɪŋ] ADJ autoreproducteur, -trice

self-replication [-replɪ'keɪʃən] N autoreproduction *f*

self-respect N respect *m* de soi, amour-propre *m*; **have you no s.?** tu n'as pas d'amour-propre?; **to lose all s.** perdre toute dignité

self-respecting ADJ qui se respecte; **no s. journalist/doctor** aucun journaliste/médecin qui se respecte

self-restraint N retenue *f*; **to exercise s.** se contenir, se retenir

self-righteous ADJ pharisaïque, content de soi; **stop being so s.!** cesse d'être aussi content de toi!

self-righteousness N pharisaïsme *m*, satisfaction *f* de soi

self-righting ADJ *(lifeboat etc)* à redressement automatique

self-rule N *Pol* autonomie *f*

self-sacrifice N abnégation *f*

selfsame ['selfseɪm] ADJ même; **the s. thing** exactement la même chose

self-satisfaction N contentement *m* de soi, fatuité *f*, suffisance *f*

self-satisfied ADJ *(person)* content de soi, suffisant; *(look)* suffisant; **to look s.** avoir l'air content de soi-même

self-sealing ADJ *(envelope)* autocollant

self-seeking [-'siːkɪŋ] ADJ *(person)* égoïste

self-service N *Com* libre-service *m*, *pl* libres-services; **s. petrol station** station *f* libre-service
▸▸ **s. restaurant** self-service *m*, *pl* self-services

self-serving ADJ égoïste, intéressé

self-starter N **1** *Aut Old-fashioned* démarreur *m* (automatique) **2** *(person)* personne *f* très motivée et capable d'initiatives

self-styled [-staɪld] ADJ soi-disant *inv*, prétendu

self-sufficiency N indépendance *f*, *Econ* national **s.** autarcie *f*

self-sufficient ADJ *(independent)* indépendant, autosuffisant; **the country is s. in foodstuffs** le pays pourvoit à ses propres besoins en denrées alimentaires

self-supporting ADJ indépendant; *(person)* qui pourvoit à ses besoins; *(business)* qui couvre ses frais; *Archit (vault)* autoportant

self-tapping ADJ
▸▸ **s. screw** vis *f* autotaraudeuse

self-taught ADJ **1** *(person)* autodidacte **2** *(skills)* que l'on a acquis tout seul

self-test *Comput* N autotest *m*; **the printer does a s.** l'imprimante procède à une vérification de ses fonctions
VI s'autotester
▸▸ **s. button** bouton *m* d'autotest; **s. program** programme *m* d'autotest

self-timer N *Phot* retardateur *m*

self-willed [-wɪld] ADJ obstiné, volontaire

self-winding [-waɪndɪŋ] ADJ *(watch)* à remontage automatique

SELL [sel]

VT	vendre **1** ▪ faire vendre **2, 4**
VI	se vendre **1** ▪ faire vendre **2**

VT *(pt, pp* **sold** [səʊld]) **1** vendre; *(goods)* vendre, placer; **to s. sb sth, to s. sth to sb** vendre qch à qn; **he sold it to me for £10** il me l'a vendu (pour) 10 livres; **to s. sth for cash** vendre qch au comptant; **to s. sth on credit** vendre qch à crédit; **to s. sth privately** vendre qch de gré à gré; **a shop that sells clothes/furniture** un magasin de vêtements/meubles; **the album/book sold nearly a million copies** l'album/le livre s'est vendu à près d'un million d'exemplaires; **the Guardian** sells roughly 400,000 copies a day le Guardian tourne à environ 400 000 exemplaires par jour; **to s. sb into slavery/prostitution** vendre qn comme esclave/prostituée; **to s. sth at a loss** vendre qch à perte; **to s. sth at a profit** faire un bénéfice en vendant qch; *Lit* **to s. one's life dearly** vendre chèrement sa vie; **to s. one's soul** vendre son âme

2 *(cause to be sold)* faire vendre; **scandal sells newspapers** ce sont les scandales qui font vendre les journaux; **you need at least one major star to s. the film** il faut au moins une star pour que le film fasse recette

3 **to s. oneself** *(in interview etc)* se faire valoir, *Fam* se vendre; **to s. oneself short** ne pas se montrer à sa juste valeur; **you have to s. yourself more to the electorate** il faudrait vous vendre mieux auprès des électeurs; **to s. an idea to the electorate** faire passer une idée auprès des électeurs; **to s. a party to the electorate** vendre les idées d'un parti auprès des électeurs; **they had difficulty selling the changes to the workforce** ils ont eu des difficultés à faire accepter les changements aux ouvriers; **I couldn't s. my father the idea** je n'ai pas pu faire accepter l'idée à mon père; *Fam* **to be sold on an idea** être emballé par une idée

4 *(betray) (secret, one's country etc)* vendre; **to s. oneself** se vendre; **to s. sb down the river** *(betray)* trahir qn

VI **1** *(of product etc)* se vendre; **to s. well/badly** se vendre bien/mal; **to s. like hot cakes** se vendre comme des petits pains; **shares in the company are selling at 109 pence** les actions de cette compagnie s'échangent à 109 pence

2 *(helps sales)* faire vendre; **sex sells** le sexe fait vendre

3 *(work in sales)* être dans la vente; **to be good at selling** être (un) bon vendeur; **I'm not selling** *(my car etc)* je ne ne suis pas vendeur

N **1** **hard s.** vente *f* par des méthodes agressives; **soft s.** vente par des méthodes de suggestion *ou* de persuasion

2 *Old-fashioned Fam (trick)* attrape-nigaud *m*, *pl* attrape-nigauds
▸▸ *St Exch* **s. order** injonction *f* à la vente

▸ **sell forward** VT SEP, VI *Fin* vendre à terme

▸ **sell off** VT SEP *(dispose of at low price) (of shop)* solder; *(stock)* liquider; *(of person)* vendre; **to s. off goods** écouler *ou* liquider des marchandises

▸ **sell out** VT SEP **1** **the concert is sold out** il n'y a plus de billets pour le concert; **the tickets are sold out** tous les billets ont été vendus; **the edition is sold out** l'édition est épuisée; **I'm sold out** j'ai tout vendu; **the supermarket was sold out of butter** le supermarché était à court de beurre

2 *St Exch (portfolio of shares)* réaliser

3 *(betray) (person, principles etc)* vendre, trahir

VI **1** *(sell all stocks)* **to s. out (of sth)** se trouver à court (de qch); **have you got any bread? – no, I'm afraid we've sold out** est-ce que vous avez du pain? – non, nous n'en avons plus

2 *(sell business)* liquider; *(sell shares)* retirer sa participation d'une/de la société; **to s. out to sb** vendre sa participation à qn

3 *(betray cause)* trahir sa cause

▸ **sell up** VT SEP **to s. up a business/property** vendre (complètement) une affaire/propriété

VI *(sell property)* vendre ses effets; *(sell business)* vendre son fonds; **he sold up and went to Canada** il a tout vendu et est parti au Canada

sell-by date N *Com* date *f* limite de vente; *Fig Fam* **to be past one's s.** avoir fait son temps

seller ['selər] N **1** *(person)* vendeur, -euse; *(stockist)* marchand, -ande (**of** de); *Fin (of stocks)* réalisateur *m*; **s.'s market** marché *m* à la hausse **2** *(item)* **good/bad s.** article *m* qui se vend bien/mal; **it's one of our biggest sellers** c'est un de nos articles qui se vend le mieux

selling ['selɪŋ] N *(of goods etc)* vente *f*, écoulement *m*; **buying and s.** la vente et l'achat; **the job doesn't involve much s.** le travail ne fait pas intervenir beaucoup de vente
▸▸ **s. off** *(of stock)* liquidation *f*; **s. point** point *m* fort; **s. price** prix *m* de vente; **s. rate** *(of currency)* taux *m* de vente

sell-off N *(of state-owned company)* vente *f*

Sellotape® ['seləteɪp] N ruban *m* adhésif, Scotch® *m*

sellotape VT **to s. sth to sth** scotcher qch à qch

sellout ['selaʊt] N **1 this play's a s.** on joue à guichets fermés; **this line has been a s.** cet article s'est vendu à merveille (et il ne nous en reste plus) **2** *(act of betrayal)* trahison *f*

selvage, selvedge ['selvɪdʒ] N *(of fabric)* lisière *f*

semantic [sɪ'mæntɪk] ADJ *Ling* sémantique; **a purely s. distinction** une distinction purement sémantique

semantically [sɪ'mæntɪklɪ] ADV sémantiquement, du point de vue sémantique

semantics [sɪ'mæntɪks] NPL *(usu with sing verb)* sémantique *f*, *Fig* **that's just s.** ce ne sont que des discours VOIR GRAMMAIRE A10

semaphore ['seməfɔ:r] N sémaphore *m* VT *(message)* transmettre par sémaphore
▸▸ *Rail etc* **s. signal** signal *m* à bras

semblance ['sembləns] N *(appearance)* apparence *f*, semblant *m*; **to re-establish a** or **some s. of order** rétablir un semblant d'ordre; **a (mere) s. of friendship** un semblant d'amitié

semen ['si:men] N *Physiol* sperme *m*

semester [sɪ'mestər] N *Am* semestre *m*

semi ['semɪ] N *Br Fam (house)* maison *f* jumelée

semi- ['semɪ] PREF semi-, demi-

semiautomatic ['semɪɔ:tə'mætɪk] ADJ semi-automatique, *pl* semi-automatiques N arme *f* semi-automatique

semibreve ['semɪbri:v] N *Br Mus* ronde *f*

semicircle ['semɪsɜ:k(ə)l] N demi-cercle *m*, *pl* demi-cercles

semicircular ['semɪ'sɜ:kjʊlər] ADJ demi-circulaire, *pl* demi-circulaires, semi-circulaire, *pl* semi-circulaires

semicolon ['semɪ'kəʊlən] N point-virgule *m*, *pl* points-virgules

semiconductor ['semɪkən'dʌktər] N *Elec* semi-conducteur *m*, *pl* semi-conducteurs

semiconscious ['semɪ'kɒnʃəs] ADJ à demi conscient

semiconsciousness ['semɪ'kɒnʃəsnɪs] N demi-inconscience *f*

semidarkness ['semɪ'dɑ:knɪs] N demi-jour *m*, pénombre *f*

semidetached ['semɪdɪ'tætʃt] ADJ *(house)* jumelé, jumeau, *f* jumelle; *Fig* **a s. member of the Government** = un membre du gouvernement en qui le Premier ministre ne peut pas totalement avoir confiance
N maison *f* jumelée

semi-documentary N film *m* semi-documentaire

semifinal ['semɪ'faɪn(ə)l] N *Sport* demi-finale *f*, *pl* demi-finales; **to reach the semifinals** atteindre les demi-finales

semifinalist ['semɪ'faɪnəlɪst] N *Sport* demi-finaliste *mf*, *pl* demi-finalistes

semi-finished goods NPL produits *mpl* semi-finis

semi-graphics N *Comput* semi-graphisme *m* VOIR GRAMMAIRE A10

semi-invalid N **he's a s.** il ne peut presque plus se déplacer

semiliterate ['semɪ'lɪtərɪt] ADJ quasi illettré

semi-manufactured product [mænjʊ'fæktʃəd] N demi-produit *m*, *pl* demi-produits

semimonthly ['semɪ'mʌnθlɪ] ADJ *Am (publication)* bimensuel

seminal ['semɪnəl] ADJ **1** *Anat, Bot* séminal, -aux **2** *(event, work)* fructueux
▸▸ *Anat, Bot* **s. fluid** liquide *m* séminal

seminar ['semɪnɑ:r] N *Univ* séminaire *m*

seminarist ['semɪnərɪst] N *Cathol* séminariste *m*

seminary ['semɪnərɪ] N *Cathol* séminaire *m*

semi-obscurity N *(darkness)* pénombre *f*, *Fig* quasi-obscurité *f*

semi-official ADJ semi-officiel, *pl* semi-officiels

semiological [semɪə'lɒdʒɪk(ə)l] ADJ sémiologique

semiology [semɪ'ɒlədʒɪ] N sém(é)iologie *f*

semiotic [semɪ'ɒtɪk] ADJ sémiotique

semiotician [semɪə'tɪʃən] N sémioticien, -ienne

semiotics [semɪ'ɒtɪks] NPL *(usu with sing verb)* sémiotique *f* VOIR GRAMMAIRE A10

semi-precious ADJ semi-précieux, fin

semiquaver ['semɪkweɪvər] N *Br Mus* double croche *f*

semi-retired ADJ **he is s.** il est en retraite partielle

semi-retirement N retraite *f* partielle

semi-skilled ADJ *(worker)* spécialisé

semi-skimmed ['skɪmd] ADJ
▸▸ **s. milk** lait *m* demi-écrémé

Semite ['semaɪt] N Sémite *mf*

Semitic [sɪ'mɪtɪk] ADJ sémitique

semitone ['semɪtəʊn] N *Br Mus* demi-ton *m*, *pl* demi-tons

semitropical ['semɪ'trɒpɪkəl] ADJ = subtropical

semivowel ['semɪ'vaʊəl] N semi-voyelle *f*, *pl* semi-voyelles

semolina [semə'li:nə] N semoule *f*

SEN [esɪ'en] N *Br Med (abbr* **State Enrolled Nurse)** infirmier, -ière diplômé(e) d'État

Sen 1 *(abbr* **senator)** sénateur *m* **2** *(abbr* **senior)** aîné, père

senate ['senɪt] N **1** *Pol* Sénat *m* **2** *Univ* conseil *m* d'université
▸▸ **s. house** Sénat

Senate
Le Sénat constitue, avec la Chambre des représentants, l'organe législatif américain; composé de 100 membres (deux par État), il détient l'exclusivité du droit d'impeachment.

senator ['senətər] N *Pol* sénateur *m*

senatorial [senə'tɔ:rɪəl] ADJ sénatorial, -aux

SEND [send] VT *(pt, pp* **sent** [sent]) **1** *(dispatch) (something)* envoyer; *(in business letters, administration etc)* faire parvenir; *(by post) (letter etc)* envoyer, expédier; *(money)* remettre; *(person)* envoyer; **to s. word to sb** avertir qn; **to s. one's love to sb** envoyer ou faire ses amitiés à qn; **to s. clothes to the laundry** donner du linge à blanchir; **to s. a child to school** envoyer un enfant à l'école; **to s. sb to prison** envoyer qn en prison; **to s. sb on an errand** envoyer qn faire une cour-

se; **to s. sb for sth** envoyer qn chercher qch; *Comput* **s. to the printer** envoyer à ou vers ou sur l'imprimante
2 *(cause to move, change etc)* **force that sends sth in a certain direction** force qui fait marcher ou qui pousse qch dans une certaine direction; **it sends a current down the wire** cela fait passer un courant dans le fil; **it sent a shiver down my spine** cela m'a fait un frisson dans le dos; **the blow sent him sprawling** le coup l'a renversé; **that sent him into fits of laughter** cela l'a fait éclater de rire; **you'll s. me mad** vous allez me rendre fou; **the rain sent us scurrying for shelter** nous avons couru nous abriter dès que la pluie a commencé; **to s. sb into a panic/a fit of depression/a rage** paniquer/déprimer/faire enrager qn; **to s. sb's profits tumbling** faire chuter les bénéfices de qn; *Fam* **to s. sb packing, to s. sb about his/her business** envoyer promener qn
3 *Lit (grant) (something)* accorder, envoyer; **s. him/her victorious** que Dieu lui donne ou lui accorde la victoire; **what fortune sends us** ce que la fortune nous envoie
4 *Old-fashioned Fam (thrill)* **it sends me** ça me transporte
▸ **send along** VT SEP envoyer; **s. him along** *(send him to see me)* envoyez-le-moi; *(tell him to see me)* dites-lui de venir me voir
▸ **send away** VT SEP **1** *(send to another place)* envoyer; **to be sent away to school** être envoyé à l'école
2 *(dismiss)* renvoyer, congédier
VI *(write to obtain something)* écrire
▸ **send away for** VT INSEP *(write to obtain)* demander par courrier; **s. away for your free copy now** demandez dès maintenant votre exemplaire gratuit
▸ **send back** VT SEP *(return) (somebody, something)* renvoyer; *(food in restaurant)* renvoyer à la cuisine
▸ **send down** VT SEP **1** *(send to lower place)* faire descendre
2 *(cause to fall) (prices, temperature etc)* faire descendre
3 *Br Univ (expel)* renvoyer, expulser
4 *Br Fam (send to prison)* envoyer en prison, coffrer
▸ **send for** VT INSEP **1** *(summon) (somebody, something)* envoyer chercher; **we sent for a couple of pizzas** nous nous sommes fait livrer deux pizzas; **we sent for the doctor** nous avons appelé le médecin, nous avons envoyé chercher le médecin
2 = **send away for**
▸ **send in** VT SEP *(send to a place) (invoice, bill)* soumettre; *(request etc)* remettre; *(dinner)* (faire) servir; **he has sent in his bill (to us/them)** il nous/leur a envoyé sa note; **many viewers sent in comments on the programme** de nombreux spectateurs ont envoyé leurs commentaires sur l'émission; **s. Mrs Jones in** faites entrer Mme Jones; **to s. the army in** envoyer l'armée
VI *(write to obtain sth)* faire une demande écrite (**for sth** de qch)
▸ **send off** VT SEP *(by post)* envoyer, expédier; *Ftbl etc (player)* renvoyer ou expulser du terrain
VI = **send away 2**
▸ **send on** VT SEP *(forward) (letter)* faire suivre; *(order)* transmettre; *(luggage)* expédier à l'avance; *Ftbl etc (player)* envoyer sur le terrain
▸ **send on ahead** VT SEP *(luggage etc)* envoyer à l'avance; *(person)* envoyer en reconnaissance
▸ **send out** VT SEP **1** *(person)* envoyer dehors; *(pupil)* mettre à la porte; **to s. sb out for more food/wine** envoyer qn chercher de la nourriture/du vin
2 *(leaflets)* lancer, expédier; *(invitations)* envoyer

3 *(signals, heat etc)* émettre; **the chimney/engine sent out billows of smoke** la cheminée/le moteur crachait des tourbillons de fumée
VI *(for food, wine)* envoyer chercher
▶ **send up VT SEP 1** *(send to higher place)* *(person, object)* faire monter; *(rocket)* lancer
2 *(prices, temperature etc)* faire monter *ou Fam* grimper
3 *Br Fam (parody)* se moquer de, parodier; *(play, part)* faire une parodie de; **he sent her up as an eccentric duchess** il l'avait caricaturée sous les traits d'une duchesse excentrique
4 *Am Fam (send to prison)* envoyer en taule, coffrer

sender ['sendər] **N** *(of letter, fax, goods)* expéditeur, -trice; *(of radio message)* transmetteur *m*

sending ['sendɪŋ] **N** envoi *m*; **s. by rail** expédition *f* par chemin de fer
▶▶ **s. depot** dépôt *m* d'expédition

send-off N *Fam* **we went to the station to give her a good s.** nous sommes allés à la gare pour marquer son départ; **to give sb a good s.** *(funeral)* faire à qn de belles funérailles; **to give sb a big s.** venir nombreux pour dire au revoir à qn

send-up N *Br Fam* satire *f*, parodie *f*; **is this a s.?** est-ce qu'on se moque de moi?

Senegal [senɪ'gɔːl] **N** Sénégal *m*

Senegalese [senɪgə'liːz] **ADJ** sénégalais **N** Sénégalais, -aise

senescence [sɪ'nesəns] **N** *Med* sénescence *f*

senile ['siːnaɪl] **ADJ** sénile
▶▶ **s. dementia** démence *f* sénile

senility [sɪ'nɪlɪtɪ] **N** sénilité *f*

senior ['siːnjər] **ADJ** *(in age)* aîné; *(in rank, position etc)* plus haut placé; *(longer-serving)* plus ancien; *Mil etc (officer)* supérieur; **Bernard Long s.** Bernard Long père; **he's two years s. to me** il est mon aîné de deux ans; **s. in rank** de grade supérieur; **the s. boys/girls of a school** les garçons/filles des grandes classes
N 1 *(in age)* aîné, -ée; **she is his s. by three years, she is three years his s.** elle est son aînée de trois ans; **to be sb's s.** *(in age)* être l'aîné de qn; *(in rank)* être d'un rang plus élevé que qn; **the seniors** *(pupils)* les grand(e)s **2** *Am Sch* étudiant, -ante de quatrième (et dernière) année
▶▶ **s. citizen** personne *f* âgée ou du troisième âge; **s. executive** cadre *m* supérieur; **s. management** la direction; **s. officer** l'officier *m* commandant; **I'll report you to your s. officer** je vais vous signaler à votre supérieur; **s. official** haut fonctionnaire *m*; **s. partner** associé, -ée principal(e); **s. reporter** grand reporter *m*; *Br* **the S. Service** la marine

seniority [siːnɪ'ɒrɪtɪ] **N 1** *(in age)* priorité *f* d'âge, supériorité *f* d'âge; **he was chairman by virtue of s.** il était président en raison de son âge **2** *(in rank)* ancienneté *f* (de grade); **to be promoted by s.** avancer (de grade) *ou* être promu à l'ancienneté; **to have s. over sb** avoir plus d'ancienneté que qn

senna ['senə] **N** *Bot* séné *m*
▶▶ *Pharm* **s. pods** follicules *mpl* de séné

sensation [sen'seɪʃən] **N 1** *(power of feeling)* sensibilité *f*, *(feeling)* *(of wellbeing, discomfort, heat, cold etc)* sensation *f*, **I had the s. of falling** j'avais la sensation de tomber **2** *(excitement)* **to create** *ou* **make** *ou* **cause a s.** *(of event etc)* faire sensation; **the film was the s. of the year** le film a été l'événement de l'année; **s.-hungry readers** des lecteurs avides de sensationnel

sensational [sen'seɪʃən(ə)l] **ADJ 1** *(film, novel, press etc)* à sensation **2** *Fam (excellent)* sensationnel, fantastique

sensationalism [sen'seɪʃənəlɪz(ə)m] **N 1** recherche *f* du sensationnel **2** *Phil* sensualisme *m*, sensationnisme *m*

sensationalist [sen'seɪʃənəlɪst] **N** *(with news)* colporteur *m* de nouvelles à sensation; *(who overdramatizes)* personne *f* ayant tendance à dramatiser; *(writer)* auteur *m* à sensation; *(journalist)* journaliste *mf* qui fait du sensationnel
ADJ *(article, style, journalism)* à sensation; **to be s.** *(of tabloids, reporting)* faire du sensationnel

sensationalize [sen'seɪʃənəlaɪz] **VT** *(event etc)* faire du sensationnel sur; **it's been so sensationalized that ...** on a fait tant de battage là-dessus que ...

sensationally [sen'seɪʃ(ə)nəlɪ] **ADV 1** **the murder was treated s. in the tabloids** les tabloïdes ont fait du meurtre une histoire à sensations **2** *Fam (successful, good)* d'une manière sensationnelle *ou* fantastique; **they did s. well in the first round** ils ont été fantastiques dans les premières épreuves

SENSE [sens]

N sens **1, 3, 5** ▪ sensation **3**	
▪ sentiment **3** ▪ conscience **3** ▪ bon	
sens **4** ▪ signification **5**	
VT sentir **1** ▪ avoir l'impression que **1**	

N 1 *(faculty)* sens *m*; **the five senses** les cinq sens; **to have a keen s. of smell/hearing** avoir l'odorat fin/l'ouïe fine; **she seemed to have a sixth s.** elle semblait posséder un sixième sens; **to be in possession of all one's senses** jouir de toutes ses facultés; **pleasures of the senses** plaisirs sensuels *ou* des sens
2 have you taken leave of your senses? avez-vous perdu l'esprit *ou* la raison?; **to come to one's senses** *(be sensible again)* revenir à la raison; *(regain consciousness)* revenir à soi; **to bring sb to his senses** ramener qn à la raison
3 *(feeling)* sensation *f*, sens *m*; *(awareness)* sentiment *m*, conscience *f*; **she has a s. for what is likely to sell** elle a du flair pour deviner ce qui se vendra; **a s. of achievement** un sentiment d'accomplissement; **to have a s. of belonging** avoir le sentiment d'être intégré; **s. of colour/beauty** sens des couleurs/de la beauté; **s. of injustice** sentiment d'injustice; **a s. of pleasure/warmth** une sensation de plaisir/chaleur; **to lose all s. of reality/time** perdre la notion de la réalité/du temps
4 *(rationality)* bon sens *m*; **common s.** sens *m* commun; **good s.** bon sens; **to talk s.** parler raison; **there's no s. in that, that doesn't make s.** cela n'a pas de sens, cela ne rime à rien; **it would make more s. if ...** cela serait plus intelligent si ...; **there's a lot of s. in what she says** ce qu'elle dit est très sensé; **it doesn't make s. to do that** cela n'a pas de sens de faire une chose pareille; **it makes good political/business s. to ...** il est bon sur le plan politique/commercial de ...; **it makes more s. to do this first** c'est plus logique de commencer par cela; **that makes good s.** c'est logique, c'est une bonne idée; **where's the s. in that?** à quoi ça sert?; **there's no s. in doing that** ça ne sert à rien; **to have the (good) s. to do sth** avoir l'intelligence *ou* le bon sens de faire qch; **to have more s. than to do sth** avoir assez de bon sens pour ne pas faire qch
5 *(meaning)* *(of word etc)* sens *m*, signification *f*; **these words don't make s.** ces mots n'ont pas de sens *ou* sont incompréhensibles; **now the sentence makes more s.** maintenant la phrase a plus de sens; **does this sentence make s.?** cette phrase veut-elle dire quelque chose?; **you're not making s.**

vous êtes illogique; **make s.!** sois logique!; **I can't make s. of it** je n'arrive pas à le comprendre; **in the literal/figurative s.** au sens propre/figuré; **in every s. of the word, in more senses than one** dans tous les sens du terme; **in a s.** d'une certaine façon, dans un (certain) sens; **in the s. that ...** en ce sens que ..., au sens où ...; **in the normal s. (of the word)** à proprement parler; **in no s., not in any s.** en aucun cas; **this is not in any real s. a change of policy** ça ne représente pas du tout un changement de politique; **in a very real s.** véritablement
VT 1 *(know intuitively)* sentir; *(have premonition)* pressentir; **I sensed no difference in his mood from last time** je n'ai décelé chez lui aucun changement d'humeur par rapport à la dernière fois; **I sensed that she was hiding something** j'avais l'impression qu'elle cachait quelque chose
2 *Phil* percevoir par le sens
3 *Electron etc* détecter
▶▶ **s. impression** sensation *f*; **s. organ** organe *m* des sens *ou* sensoriel

senseless ['senslɪs] **ADJ 1** *(unconscious)* sans connaissance, inanimé; **to fall s.** tomber sans connaissance; **to knock/beat sb s.** assommer qn **2** *(pointless)* *(action)* insensé, stupide, absurde; **a s. killing** un meurtre gratuit; **a s. remark** une remarque stupide; **what a s. waste (of human life)** *(one person)* voilà une vie humaine absurdement gâchée; *(more than one person)* que de vies humaines gâchées

senselessly ['senslɪslɪ] **ADV** absurdement

senselessness ['senslɪsnɪs] **N** *(stupidity)* absurdité *f*

sensibility [sensɪ'bɪlɪtɪ] **N 1** *(of person)* sensibilité *f*, émotivité *f*; **I do not want to offend anyone's sensibilities** je ne veux pas heurter la susceptibilité de qui que ce soit **2** *(of organ etc)* sensibilité *f*

sensible ['sensɪb(ə)l] **ADJ 1** *(rational)* *(person, decision)* sensé, raisonnable; *(choice)* judicieux; **it would be more s. to ...** il serait plus raisonnable de ...; **be s.** soyez raisonnable **2 s. clothes** vêtements commodes *ou* pratiques; **s. shoes** chaussures confortables et pratiques **3** *Arch, Lit (aware)* conscient (**of** de); **to be s. of the fact that ...** être sensible au *ou* apprécier le fait que ... **4** *Fml (perceptible)* *(quantity, difference etc)* sensible, appréciable

Note that the French word **sensible** is a false friend and is almost never a translation for the English word **sensible**. It means **sensitive**.

sensibly ['sensɪblɪ] **ADV 1** *(rationally)* *(to behave, discuss)* raisonnablement; *(to decide, divide)* judicieusement; **to be s. dressed** porter des vêtements pratiques **2** *(perceptibly)* sensiblement, perceptiblement

sensitive ['sensɪtɪv] **ADJ 1** *(person, skin)* sensible; *(portrayal, interpretation)* plein de sensibilité; **he's very s. about his accent** il est très susceptible sur son accent; **to be s. to noise** être sensible au bruit; **to be s. to the cold** *(of person)* être frileux **2** *Fin (market)* sensible; *Phot (plate)* impressionnable, sensible à la lumière; *(paper)* sensible, sensibilisé; **s. to sth** sensible à qch **3** *(question, issue etc)* délicat, sensible; *(document, information)* confidentiel
▶▶ *Phot etc* **s. layer** couche *f* sensible

sensitively ['sensɪtɪvlɪ] **ADV** sensiblement, d'une manière sensible; *(to write etc)* avec sensibilité

sensitiveness ['sensɪtɪvnɪs], **sensitivity** [sensɪ'tɪvɪtɪ] **N** *(of person, skin, machine, instrument etc)* sensibilité *f*, *Phot* impressionnabilité f, rapidité f; (of question etc) caractère m délicat; (of document, information etc) caractère confidentiel

sensitization [sensɪtaɪ'zeɪʃən] N Med, Phot sensibilisation f

sensitize ['sensɪtaɪz] VT sensibiliser; Phot **sensitized paper** papier m sensible ou sensibilisé

sensitizer ['sensɪtaɪzər] N Phot sensibilisateur m

sensor ['sensər] N Electron détecteur m, capteur m

sensory ['sensərɪ] ADJ (nerve etc) sensoriel ▸▸ **s. organs** organes mpl des sens

sensual ['sensjʊəl] ADJ 1 sensuel; (instinct) animal, -aux; **s. pleasures** plaisirs mpl des sens 2 (person, art) sensuel, voluptueux

> Attention: ne pas confondre avec **sensuous**.

sensualism ['sensjʊəlɪz(ə)m] N 1 sensualité f 2 Phil sensualisme m

sensualist ['sensjʊəlɪst] N 1 sensualiste mf, voluptueux, -euse 2 Phil sensualiste mf

sensuality [sensjʊ'ælɪtɪ] N sensualité f

sensuous ['sensjʊəs] ADJ (pleasure, life, charm etc) sensuel, voluptueux

> Attention: ne pas confondre avec **sensual**.

sensuously ['sensjʊəslɪ] ADV voluptueusement, avec volupté

sensuousness ['sensjʊəsnɪs] N volupté f

sent PT, PP see **send**

sentence ['sentəns] N 1 Gram phrase f VOIR GRAMMAIRE A78–9; B62–4 2 Law (conviction) condamnation f, sentence f; (period in prison) peine f; **life s.** condamnation à perpétuité; **s. of death, death s.** condamnation à mort, arrêt m de mort; **under s. of death** condamné à mort; **to pass (a) s.** prononcer une condamnation ou une sentence; **while he was serving his s.** pendant qu'il purgeait sa peine ▸ VT Law condamner; **to s. sb to a month's imprisonment/to death** condamner qn à un mois de prison/à mort ▸▸ Mktg **s. completion** (in market research) phrases fpl à compléter

sententious [sen'tenʃəs] ADJ Fml (person, speech etc) sentencieux

sententiousness [sen'tenʃəsnɪs] N Fml (of person) caractère m sentencieux; (of writing etc) ton m sentencieux

sentient ['sentɪənt] ADJ Fml sensible

sentiment ['sentɪmənt] N 1 (opinion) sentiment m, opinion f, avis m; **these are my sentiments** voilà mon sentiment ou mon opinion; **my sentiments exactly** je partage entièrement votre avis; **noble sentiments** sentiments nobles 2 (sentimentality) sentimentalité f; (mawkish) sensiblerie f 3 Arch, Lit (emotion) sentimentalité f

sentimental [sentɪ'ment(ə)l] ADJ sentimental, -aux; **don't be so s.!** ne sois pas si sentimental! ▸▸ **s. value** valeur f sentimentale

sentimentalism [sentɪ'mentəlɪz(ə)m] N sentimentalisme m; (mawkishness) sensiblerie f

sentimentalist [sentɪ'mentəlɪst] N personne f sentimentale; **he's/she's a s.** c'est un sentimental/une sentimentale

sentimentality [sentɪmen'tælɪtɪ] N sentimentalité f; (mawkishness) sensiblerie f

sentimentalize [sentɪ'mentəlaɪz] VI faire du sentiment ▸ VT (novel, work, situation etc) romancer

sentimentally [sentɪ'ment(ə)lɪ] ADV sentimentalement; (mawkishly) avec sensiblerie

sentinel ['sentɪn(ə)l] N Mil factionnaire m, sentinelle f; Fig **the s. of democracy** le garant ou gardien de la démocratie; **to stand s. over sth** être de garde à qch; Fig protéger qch

sentry ['sentrɪ] N Mil factionnaire m, sentinelle f; **to be on or to do s. duty, to stand s.** être en sentinelle ou de faction; **to relieve a s.** relever une sentinelle ▸▸ **s. box** guérite f

Seoul [səʊl] N Séoul

sepal ['sep(ə)l] N Bot sépale m

separable ['sep(ə)rəb(ə)l] ADJ séparable

separate¹ ['sep(ə)rət] ADJ (parts, box, booklet etc) séparé, détaché (**from** de); (distinct) distinct; (independent) indépendant; (times, days) différent; **the two issues are quite s.** les deux problèmes sont distincts; **to keep sth s. (from sth else)** séparer qch (de qch d'autre); **to sleep in s. rooms/beds** (of married couple) faire chambre/lit à part; **use a s. piece of paper** utilisez une feuille séparée; **it's now become a s. company** c'est maintenant une société indépendante; **they went their/we went our s. ways** ils sont partis chacun de leur côté/nous sommes partis chacun de notre côté ▸ N 1 (print) tiré m à part 2 Com (items of dress) **separates** coordonnés mpl

separate² ['sepəreɪt] VT séparer (**from** de); (milk) écrémer; (members of a family etc) désunir; (sb from his family etc) détacher (**from** de); **to s. eggs** séparer les blancs des jaunes; **two eggs** prenez deux œufs, séparez les blancs des jaunes; **murder cases can be separated under four headings** on distingue quatre types de meurtres; **to s. two boxers** séparer deux boxeurs; **he is separated (from his wife)** il est séparé (de sa femme); **the Channel separates England from France** la Manche sépare la France et l'Angleterre; **the gulf that separates him from his colleagues** l'abîme entre lui et ses collègues, l'abîme qui le sépare de ses collègues; **what separates their language from other African languages is ...** ce qui distingue leur langue des autres langues africaines, c'est ...; **to s. the men from the boys** faire un tri ▸ VI (of group of people, man and wife) se séparer; **when we separated for the night** quand nous nous sommes quittés pour la nuit; **to s. from sb** se séparer de qn, rompre avec qn
▸ **separate off** VT SEP séparer
▸ **separate out** VI se séparer ▸ VT SEP séparer (**from** de)

separately ['sep(ə)rətlɪ] ADV séparément; **are you paying s.?** (in shop, restaurant etc) est-ce que vous payez séparément?; **not to be sold s.** (on multiple pack, promotional item etc) ne peut être vendu séparément; **wash s.** (on garment label etc) laver séparément; **keep this s.** gardez ceci à part

separation [sepə'reɪʃən] N séparation f (**from sb** d'avec qn); (judicial) **s.** séparation (judiciaire) ▸▸ **s. allowance** Mil allocation f mensuelle (versée par l'armée à la femme d'un soldat); (alimony) pension f alimentaire; Psy **s. anxiety** peur f de l'abandon; Pol **s. of powers** séparation f des pouvoirs

separatism ['sepərətɪz(ə)m] N séparatisme m

separatist ['sepərətɪst] ADJ, N séparatiste mf

separator ['sepəreɪtər] N Tech, Comput séparateur m

sepia ['si:pɪə] N Art sépia f ▸▸ **s. drawing** dessin m à la sépia

sepoy ['si:pɔɪ] N Mil cipaye m

sepsis ['sepsɪs] N Med septicité f

Sept abbr September

September [sep'tembər] N septembre m; **in**

S. au mois de septembre, en septembre; (on) the first/the seventh of S. le premier/le sept septembre VOIR GRAMMAIRE A81–2; B60–2

septet [sep'tet] N Mus septuor m

septic ['septɪk] ADJ Med septique; (wound) infecté; **to become or go s.** s'infecter; **I have a s. finger** j'ai un doigt infecté ▸▸ **s. poisoning** septicémie f; **s. tank** fosse f septique

septicaemia, Am septicemia [septɪ-'si:mɪə] N Med septicémie f

septuagenarian [septjʊədʒɪ'neərɪən] N, ADJ septuagénaire mf

Septuagesima [septjʊə'dʒesɪmə] N Rel septuagésime f ▸▸ **S. Sunday** le dimanche de la Septuagésime

Septuagint ['septjʊədʒɪnt] N version f (de la Bible) des Septante, Septante f

septum, pl septa [septəm, -ə] N Anat septum m; Bot cloison f

sepulchral [sɪ'pʌlkrəl] ADJ Lit sépulcral, -aux

sepulchre, Am sepulcher ['sepəlkər] N sépulcre m; **the Holy S.** le Saint Sépulcre

sequel ['si:kwəl] N (to novel etc) suite f; **as a s. to these events** comme suite à ces événements; **action that had an unfortunate s.** acte qui a entraîné des suites malheureuses

sequelize ['si:kwəlaɪz] VT esp Am (movie) donner une suite à

sequence ['si:kwəns] N 1 (order) ordre m; (in time) ordre, succession f; **what's the s. of events going to be?** quelle est le programme?; **in some sort of s.** dans un ordre quelconque; **in s.** 1 un après l'autre; **out of s.** (one item) mal rangé; (set of pictures, items) dans le désordre; **the films were deliberately shown out of s.** les films ont été présentés dans le désordre exprès; **logical s.** enchaînement m logique 2 (series) (of events, disasters etc) suite f, série f 3 Cards, Mus, Cin, Comput séquence f; Mus **a chord s.** une suite d'accords ▸▸ Comput **s. check** contrôle m de séquence; Comput **s. checking** contrôle de séquence; Gram **s. of tenses** concordance f des temps

sequencer ['si:kwənsər] N Comput coordonnateur m, séquenceur m

sequencing ['si:kwənsɪŋ] N Comput mise f en séquence

sequential [sɪ'kwenʃəl] ADJ 1 Comput séquentiel 2 Fml (following) séquentiel ▸▸ Comput **s. file** fichier m séquentiel; Comput **s. processing** traitement m séquentiel; Cin, TV **s. shooting** tourné-monté m, pl tournés-montés

sequentially [sɪ'kwenʃəlɪ] ADV séquentiellement

sequester [sɪ'kwestər] VT 1 Fml (confiscate) confisquer; Law (property of debtor) séquestrer, mettre sous séquestre 2 Lit **to s. oneself (from the world)** se retirer (du monde); **to lead a sequestered life** vivre une vie de reclus; **a sequestered corner of the property** un coin isolé de la propriété

sequestrate [sɪ'kwestreɪt] VT confisquer; Law (property of debtor) séquestrer, mettre sous séquestre

sequestration [si:kwe'streɪʃən] N confiscation f, Law séquestration f, mise f sous séquestre

sequin ['si:kwɪn] N (on dress etc) paillette f

sequined ['si:kwɪnd] ADJ à paillettes

sequoia [sɪ'kwɔɪə] N (tree) séquoia m

seraglio [se'rɑ:lɪəʊ] N sérail m, pl -ails

seraph, pl seraphs, seraphim ['serəf, -əfs, -əfɪm] N séraphin m

seraphic [sɪˈræfɪk] ADJ séraphique

Serb [sɜːb] ADJ serbe
N Serbe *mf*

Serbia [ˈsɜːbɪə] N Serbie *f*

Serbian [ˈsɜːbɪən] ADJ serbe
N 1 Serbe *mf* 2 *Ling* serbe *m*

Serbo-Croat [sɜːbəʊˈkrəʊæt], **Serbo-Croatian** [-krəʊˈeɪʃən] ADJ serbo-croate, *pl* serbo-croates
N 1 Serbo-croate *mf*, *pl* Serbo-croates 2 *Ling* serbo-croate *m*

sere [sɪər] ADJ *Lit (vegetation)* desséché; *(lake)* asséché

serenade [serəˈneɪd] N sérénade *f*
VT donner une sérénade à

serendipitous [serənˈdɪpɪtəs] ADJ *Lit* génial et fortuit

serendipity [serənˈdɪpɪtɪ] N *Lit* don *m* de faire des trouvailles

serene [sɪˈriːn] ADJ 1 *(sky, sea, person)* serein, calme, tranquille; *(sky)* clair; **her face wore a s. look** son visage exprimait le calme *ou* la sérénité 2 *(in title)* sérénissime; **His S. Highness** son Altesse sérénissime

serenely [sɪˈriːnlɪ] ADV calmement, avec sérénité

serenity [sɪˈrenɪtɪ] N sérénité *f*, calme *m*

serf [sɜːf] N serf *m*, serve *f*

serfdom [ˈsɜːfdəm] N servage *m*

serge [sɜːdʒ] N *Tex* serge *f*; **cotton s.** sergé *m*
▸▸ **s. suit** costume *m* en sergé

sergeant [ˈsɑːdʒənt] N *(in infantry, air force)* sergent *m*; *(in artillery, armoured corps, cavalry)* maréchal *m* des logis; **(police) s.** brigadier *m*; **quartermaster s., staff s.** *(in infantry, air force)* sergent fourrier *ou* comptable; *(in artillery, armoured corps, cavalry)* maréchal des logis fourrier *ou* comptable; *Law* **s. at arms** huissier *m*

sergeant-major N *Mil* adjudant *m*; **regimental s.** adjudant-chef *m*, *pl* adjudants-chefs

serial [ˈsɪərɪəl] ADJ 1 *Mus (belonging to series)* sériel 2 *(arranged in series)* en série; *(from series)* d'une série; *(forming series)* formant série 3 *Comput (processing, transmission, data)* série *inv*; **s. to parallel convertor** convertisseur *m* série-parallèle
N *(story published in parts)* *(in magazine)* feuilleton *m*, roman-feuilleton *m*, *pl* romans-feuilletons; *Radio* feuilleton *(radiophonique)*; *TV* feuilleton *(télévisé)*; **it was first published in s. form** cela a d'abord été publié sous forme de feuilleton
▸▸ *Comput* **s. access** accès *m* séquentiel; *Comput* **s. cable** câble *m* série; **s. data** données *fpl* série; **s. device** périphérique *m* série; **s. drama** feuilleton *m*; **s. input** entrée *f* série; *Comput* **s. interface** interface *f* série; **s. killer** tueur, -euse en série; **s. monogamist** = personne *f* qui a une succession de relations monogamiques; **s. monogamy** = succession *f* de relations monogamiques; **s. number** *(of product, publication)* numéro *m* de série; *(of cheque, voucher)* numéro; *(of soldier)* (numéro) matricule *m*; **s. output** sortie *f* série; *Comput* **s. port** port *m* série; *Comput* **s. printer** imprimante *f* série; *Comput* **s. printer port** port *m* d'imprimante série; **s. rights** droits *mpl* de reproduction en feuilleton; **s. writer** feuilletoniste *mf*

serialization [sɪərɪəlaɪˈzeɪʃən] N mise *f* en feuilleton, publication *f* en feuilleton; *TV, Radio* adaptation *f* en feuilleton
▸▸ **s. rights** droits *mpl* de reproduction en feuilleton

serialize [ˈsɪərɪəlaɪz] VT *(novel etc)* publier en feuilleton, adapter en feuilleton; *TV, Radio* diffuser en feuilleton; **serialized in six parts** *(novel etc)* publié en six épisodes; *TV,*

Radio diffusé en six parties; **it's being serialized in the Observer** ça sort en feuilleton dans l'Observer

serially [ˈsɪərɪəlɪ] ADV 1 en *ou* par série 2 *Journ* en feuilleton

seriatim [sɪərɪˈeɪtɪm] ADV *Fml* point par point

sericulture [ˈserɪkʌltʃər] N sériciculture *f*

series [ˈsɪəriːz] N 1 série *f*; *(of colours)* échelle *f*, gamme *f*; *(of books)*, *TV, Radio* série; *(in magazine, newspaper)* série d'articles; **a s. of terrorist attacks** une série d'attaques terroristes; **in s.** en série, en succession 2 *Elec* série *f*; **connection in s.** montage *m* en série
▸▸ *Elec* **s. connection** montage en série; *TV* **s. producer** producteur *m* de série télévisée; *Elec* **s. winding** enroulement *m* en série

series-connected ADJ *Comput* connecté en série

series-wound ADJ *Elec* à enroulements série
▸▸ **s. motor** moteur *m* à enroulements série

serif [ˈserɪf] N *Typ* empattement *m*

seriocomic [sɪərɪəʊˈkɒmɪk] ADJ moitié sérieux moitié comique

serious [ˈsɪərɪəs] ADJ 1 *(grave, critical)* sérieux, grave; **things are becoming s.** cela devient sérieux; **s. injury** blessure grave; **s. mistake** grosse faute
2 *(in earnest, thoughtful)* *(person, decision, newspaper etc)* sérieux; **she's not really a s. novelist** *(not considered a real novelist)* ce n'est pas un écrivain majeur; **to be s. about sth** parler sérieusement à propos de qch; **is he s. about emigrating?** est-ce qu'il envisage sérieusement d'émigrer?; **I have never seen him so s. about a girl** je ne l'ai jamais vu aussi sérieux avec une fille; **I'm s.** je ne plaisante pas; **are you s.?** tu parles sérieusement?; **surely you're not s.?** vous n'êtes pas sérieux?, vous plaisantez?; **I was being s. when I said ...** je ne plaisantais pas quand j'ai dit ...; **I have never given the subject s. thought** je n'ai jamais pensé sérieusement; *Fam* **an evening of s. drinking** une soirée bien arrosée; *Fam* **they go in for some really s. drinking at the weekends** le week-end, qu'est-ce qu'ils descendent!; *Fam* **that is one s. computer!** c'est que c'est une gnognotte, cet ordinateur!; *Fam* **s. money** beaucoup de fric; **the s. press** la presse sérieuse
▸▸ *Br* **s. crime squad** brigade *f* criminelle; *Br* **S. Fraud Office** ≃ Service *m* de la répression des fraudes

seriously [ˈsɪərɪəslɪ] ADV 1 *(gravely, critically)* sérieusement, gravement; **s. ill** gravement malade; **s. wounded** grièvement blessé; *Mil* **the s. wounded** les grands blessés; **the project is s. late** le projet est vraiment en retard; **he got it s. wrong** il s'est complètement trompé; *Fam* **her boyfriend is s. gorgeous** son petit ami est super beau
2 *(in earnest)* *(to talk)* sérieusement; **to take sth s.** prendre qch au sérieux; **to take oneself s.** se prendre au sérieux; **she takes everything far too s.** elle prend tout bien trop au sérieux; **if we are to be taken s. as a world-class football team** pour qu'on nous prenne au sérieux en tant qu'équipe de football de niveau international; **you can't s. expect them to believe that** vous ne pouvez pas penser sérieusement qu'ils vont croire ça; **but s., what will you do?** plaisanterie à part, qu'allez-vous faire?

serious-minded ADJ *(person)* réfléchi, sérieux

seriousness [ˈsɪərɪəsnɪs] N 1 *(gravity)* *(of situation, illness etc)* gravité *f* 2 *(of tone, personality etc)* sérieux *m*; **in all s.** sérieusement

serjeant [ˈsɑːdʒənt] N **S. at Arms** *Parl*

commandant *m* militaire du Parlement; *Hist (attendant)* huissier *m* d'armes

sermon [ˈsɜːmən] N 1 *Rel* sermon *m*; *(in Protestant church)* prêche *m*; **to deliver a s.** faire un sermon; **collection of sermons** sermonnaire *m*; *Bible* **the S. on the Mount** le Sermon sur la Montagne 2 *Fig* sermon *m*; **to give sb a s.** sermonner qn; **the editor does tend to go in for sermons** le rédacteur en chef a tendance à faire des sermons

sermonize [ˈsɜːmənaɪz] VI *Pej* sermonner, prêcher

sermonizing [ˈsɜːmənaɪzɪŋ] N *Pej* prêchi-prêcha *m inv*

seroconversion [sɪərəʊkənˈvɜːʃən] N *Med* séroconversion *f*

seronegative [sɪərəʊˈnegətɪv] ADJ séronégatif

seronegativity [sɪərəʊnegəˈtɪvɪtɪ] N séronégativité *f*

seropositive [sɪərəʊˈpɒzɪtɪv] ADJ séropositif

seropositivity [sɪərəʊpɒzɪˈtɪvɪtɪ] N séropositivité *f*

serotonin [serəˈtəʊnɪn] N sérotonine *f*

serous [ˈsɪərəs] ADJ *Anat etc (fluid etc)* séreux
▸▸ **s. membrane** séreuse *f*

serpent [ˈsɜːpənt] N serpent *m*

serpentine [ˈsɜːpəntaɪn] ADJ *Lit* serpentin; *(path)* sinueux, tortueux

SERPS [sɜːps] N *Br (abbr* **state earnings-related pension scheme)** = pension *f* de retraite versée par l'État et calculée en fonction des salaires

serrated [seˈreɪtɪd] ADJ *(edge)* en dents de scie, dentelé; *(knife, scissors, instrument)* cranté, en dents de scie

serration [seˈreɪʃən] N denture *f*

serried [ˈserɪd] ADJ *Lit* serré; **in s. ranks** en rangs serrés

serum [ˈsɪərəm] *pl* **serums, sera** [ˈsɪərəm, -əms, -ə] N *Physiol* sérum *m*; **blood s.** sérum sanguin

servant [ˈsɜːvənt] N 1 *(of God, the community etc)* serviteur *m*, servante *f*; **public servants** employés *mpl* d'un service public, employés de la fonction publique; *Arch Fml* **your most humble and obedient s.** votre très humble serviteur
2 *(in household)* domestique *mf*; *(female)* bonne *f*; *(in 19th century and before)* *(male)* serviteur *m*; *(female)* servante *f*; **the servants** les domestiques; *(19th century and before)* les serviteurs; **a large staff of servants** une nombreuse domesticité; **servants' quarters** logement des domestiques

serve [sɜːv] VT 1 *(master, cause etc)* servir; **to s. God/one's country** servir Dieu/sa patrie; **to have served one's country well** avoir bien servi sa patrie, *Lit* bien mériter de la patrie; **he has served the company faithfully** il a rendu de grands services à la société; **to s. one's own interests** servir ses propres intérêts; *Old-fashioned* **he served me very badly** *(treated)* il a très mal agi envers moi
2 *(of thing)* être utile à; **to s. the purpose** faire l'affaire; **that old computer does not really s. my purpose** ce vieil ordinateur ne convient pas à mes besoins; **tool that serves several purposes** outil qui sert à plusieurs usages; **this dictionary should s. the purposes of most users** ce dictionnaire devrait rendre service à la majorité des utilisateurs; **it has served its purpose and has been discarded** il a bien servi et on s'en est débarrassé; **I think this one's served its purpose** *(is useless)* je crois qu'il a fait son temps, celui-ci; **if my memory serves me right** si j'ai bonne mémoire
3 *(complete)* *(prison sentence)* purger; *(apprenticeship)* faire; **to s. one's sentence** *or*

one's time purger sa peine; **he served a sentence of five years' imprisonment** il a fait cinq ans de prison; **to have served ten years** *(in army)* avoir dix ans de service; *(in prison)* avoir fait dix ans de prison; *Pol* **to s. a term of office** exercer un mandat (présidentiel/ de député *etc)*

4 *(of bus, rail service, TV station etc) (region, population etc)* desservir

5 *(in shop)* **to s. a customer** servir un client; **are you being served?** est-ce qu'on s'occupe de vous?; **I'm being served, thank you** on s'occupe de moi, merci; **we don't s. (alcohol to) people under eighteen** *(in bar)* nous ne servons pas d'alcool aux moins de dix-huit ans

6 *(at table etc)* **to s. sb with soup/vegetables** servir du potage/des légumes à qn; **to s. a dish** servir un plat; **dinner is served, madam** Madame est servie; **s. chilled** servir très frais; *Rel* **to s. Mass** servir la messe; **serves four** *(on packet, in recipe)* pour quatre personnes; **beef served in a mushroom sauce** bœuf servi avec une sauce aux champignons

7 *Tennis* **to s. the ball** servir; **he served the ball into ...** il a envoyé la balle de service dans ...; **to s. an ace** faire un ace

8 *Law* **to s. a writ/a summons on sb, to s. sb with a writ/a summons** délivrer *ou* signifier *ou* notifier une assignation/une citation à qn

9 it serves you right! c'est bien fait pour toi!, tu n'as que ce que tu mérites!; **it serves him right for not listening to me** il ne m'a pas écouté, c'est bien fait pour lui; **it would have served you right** tu l'aurais bien mérité

10 *(of male animal) (female)* couvrir

VI 1 *(carry out duty etc)* **to s. in the army** servir dans l'armée; **to s. in the war with sb** faire la guerre avec qn; **she served under three presidents** elle a servi sous trois présidents; **to s. in a government** servir dans un gouvernement

2 *(meet requirements) (of tool, plan etc)* **the boxes s. as tables** les boîtes tiennent lieu de tables; **to s. as a pretext/as an example** servir de prétexte/d'exemple; **it serves to remind us how vulnerable we all are** il est bon de nous rappeler à quel point nous sommes vulnérables; **events in Bosnia s. to demonstrate just how fragile peace is** les événements de Bosnie démontrent à quel point la paix est fragile

3 *(in shop)* être vendeur, -euse

4 to s. (at table) servir à table

5 *Rel* **to s. (at Mass)** servir la messe

6 *Tennis* servir

N *Tennis* service *m*; **(it's) your s.!** à vous de servir!

▸ **serve out VT SEP 1** *(food)* servir **2** *(prison sentence)* purger; *(term of office)* finir, aller jusqu'au bout de; **before she had served out her term of office** avant la fin de son mandat; **to s. out one's time** *(in post etc)* aller jusqu'au bout de son mandat; *Mil* finir son temps de service; *Pej* **the Chairman was just serving out his time** le Président se contentait d'attendre la retraite

▸ **serve up VT SEP** *(dinner etc)* servir; *Fig (programme, excuse etc)* sortir, pondre; *(performance)* servir

VI servir

server ['sɜːvər] **N 1** *(at table)* serveur, -euse **2** *Tennis* serveur, -euse **3** *Rel (at Mass)* servant *m* d'autel **4** *(tray)* plateau *m* (de service) **5** *(utensil)* couvert *m* de service; **(set of) salad/fish servers** service *m* à salade/à poisson **6** *Comput* **(file)** serveur *m*

▸ ▸ *Comput* **s. administrator** administrateur *m* de serveur; *Comput* **s. engine** processeur-serveur *m*, *pl* processeurs-serveurs

SERVICE ['sɜːvɪs] **N 1** service *m*; **in the s. of God/of one's country** au service de Dieu/de son pays; **to die in the King's/Queen's s.** mourir au service du roi/de la reine; **I am**

(entirely) **at your s.** je suis à votre (entière) disposition; **to do sb a s.** rendre (un) service à qn; **to be of some s.** se rendre utile; **to be of s. to sb** être utile à qn; **can I be of any s. to you?** puis-je vous être utile *ou* vous aider en aucune manière?; **to bring** *or* put **into s.** *(piece of machinery, vehicle etc)* mettre en service; **this pen has given me good s.** ce stylo m'a bien servi; **to offer one's services** offrir ses services; **his services to education** les services qu'il a rendus à l'enseignement; **services rendered** services rendus; *Econ* **goods and services** biens *mpl* et services

2 *Old-fashioned* **to be in/go into s.** *(of servant)* être/devenir domestique; **to go into s. with sb** entrer au service de qn

3 *(with army, firm etc)* service *m*; *Com* **promotion according to length of s.** avancement à l'ancienneté; *Com* **to give many years of loyal s. to a company** faire de nombreuses années de bons et loyaux services dans une société; *Mil* **fit/unfit for s.** apte/ inapte au service; *Mil* **to see s.** faire la guerre; *Naut* **afloat/ashore** service à bord/à terre; **military** *or Br Formerly* **national s.** service militaire; **when I was doing my military s.** quand j'étais au régiment; **active s.** service actif; **the civil s.** l'administration *f*, la fonction publique; **to be in the civil s.** être fonctionnaire; **the Foreign** *or* **Diplomatic S.** le service diplomatique, la diplomatie, *Fam* la carrière; **the Secret S.** = le Deuxième Bureau

4 *(in shop, restaurant etc)* service *m*; **the s. there is good/slow** *(in restaurant)* le service y est de qualité/lent; **s. is included** le service est compris; **s. not included** service non-compris; **24-hour s.** *(open 24 hours)* ouvert 24 heures sur 24; *(service carried out within 24 hours)* travail effectué dans les 24 heures

5 *(system) (rail, air, postal etc)* service *m*; *(for water, gas, electricity)* distribution *f*, **bus s.** service d'autobus/de cars; **we have a good bus/train s.** notre ville est bien desservie par les autobus/par le chemin de fer; **goods** *or* **freight s.** service de marchandises; **passenger s.** service de voyageurs; **public services** services publics; **postal/telephone services** services postaux/téléphoniques; **social/medical services** services sociaux/ médicaux; **it provides a s. to the community** cela offre un service aux gens

6 *Mil* **the s.** *(army)* l'armée *f*, *(navy)* la marine; *(air force)* l'armée de l'air; **Joint Services Staff College** ≃ École *f* d'État-major interarmes

7 *(maintenance)* entretien *m*; *Aut* révision *f*; *Mil (of gun)* service *m*; **my car needs a complete s.** ma voiture a besoin d'une révision complète; **after-sales s.** service après-vente; **s. manual** *or* **handbook** manuel *m* d'entretien

8 *Rel* office *m*, culte *m*; **to attend s.** assister à l'office *ou* au culte; **the marriage s.** la cérémonie du mariage

9 *Law (of deed, writ)* délivrance *f*, signification *f*

10 *(crockery)* service *m*; **tea/dinner s.** service à thé/de table

11 *Tennis* service *m*

VT 1 *(do maintenance work on)* entretenir; *(car)* faire la révision de; *(domestic appliance)* assurer l'entretien de

2 *(in breeding) (of bull, stallion) (female)* couvrir

3 *(provide services to)* pourvoir aux besoins de; *Fin (loan, debt)* rembourser

▸ ▸ **s. accommodation** hébergement *m* avec restauration; **s. agreement** contrat *m* de service; **s. area** *Aut (on motorway)* aire *f* de service; *TV, Radio* zone *f* desservie *ou* de réception; *Aut* **s. bay** *(in garage)* zone de travail; **s. bell** *(in hotel)* sonnette *f (pour appeler un employé de l'hôtel)*; *Comput* **s. bureau** so-

ciété *f* de traitement à façon; *Austr, NZ* **s. bus** autocar *m*; *Austr, NZ* **s. car** autocar; *Aviat* **s. ceiling** plafond *m* de fonctionnement normal; *Am Aut* **s. center** aire de services *(au bord d'une autoroute)*; **s. charge** service *m*; *Journ* **s. column** rubrique *f* services; **s. company** entreprise *f* prestataire de services; **s. contract** contrat d'entretien; **s. court** *(in tennis)* rectangle *m* de service; **s. engineer** technicien, -enne de maintenance; **s. fault** *(in tennis)* faute *f* de service; *Br* **s. flat** = appartement *m* avec services ménagers et de restauration; **s. hatch** passe-plat *m*, *pl* passe-plats; *Aut* **s. history** historique *m* d'entretien; **s. industry** industrie *f* de services; **s. life** durée *f* de vie; *Br* **s. lift** monte-charge *m*, *pl* monte-charge(s); **s. line** *(in tennis)* ligne *f* de service; *Mil* **s. personnel** personnel *m* militaire; **s. provider** *(person, company)* prestataire *m* de service(s); *Comput (for Internet)* fournisseur *m* d'accès; *Mil* **s. rifle** fusil *m* réglementaire *ou* de l'armée; **s. road** *(behind shops, factory)* voie *f* d'accès réservée aux livreurs; *(on motorway)* voie d'accès réservée à l'entretien et aux services d'urgence; *Com, Econ* **s. sector** secteur *m* tertiaire, tertiaire *m*; **s. station** station-service *f*, *pl* stations-service; **s. supplier** prestataire *m* de service(s); *Bot* **s. tree** alisier *m*, sorbier *m*; *Mil* **s. vehicle** véhicule *m* militaire *ou* de l'armée

serviceable ['sɜːvɪsəb(ə)l] **ADJ** *(in functioning state)* en état de fonctionner; *(usable)* utilisable; *(useful)* pratique

serviced ['sɜːvɪst] **ADJ** *(apartment etc)* avec service d'entretien

▸ ▸ **s. accommodation** résidence *f* hôtelière; **s. apartment** appartement *m* dans une résidence hôtelière

serviceman, pl servicemen ['sɜːvɪsmən] **N** militaire *m*; *Hist* **national s.** appelé *m*

services ['sɜːvɪsɪz] **NPL 1** *(on motorway)* services *mpl*; *(place)* aire *f* de services; **s. 10 km** *(on sign)* aire de services, 10 km **2 the (armed) s.** les forces *fpl* armées

servicewoman, pl servicewomen ['sɜːvɪswʊmən, -wɪmɪn] **N** femme *f* soldat, *Fam* soldate *f*

servicing ['sɜːvɪsɪŋ] **N** entretien *m*

▸ ▸ **s. manual** manuel *m* d'entretien

serviette [sɜːvɪ'et] **N** *Br* serviette *f* de table

servile ['sɜːvaɪl] **ADJ** *(person, behaviour)* servile

servility [sɜː'vɪlɪtɪ] **N** servilité *f*

serving ['sɜːvɪŋ] **ADJ** *(member, chairman)* actuel, en exercice; **the longest-s. official** la personnalité officielle ayant le plus d'ancienneté

N 1 *(of drinks, meal)* service *m* **2** *(helping)* portion *f*, part *f*

▸ ▸ **s. dish** plat *m*, assiette *f* de service; **s. hatch** passe-plat *m*, *pl* passe-plats

servitude ['sɜːvɪtjuːd] **N** *(slavery)* servitude *f*, esclavage *m*; **to be sold into s.** être vendu comme esclave; *Law* **penal s. for life** *(imprisonment)* travaux forcés à perpétuité

servo ['sɜːvəʊ] **N** *Fam* = **servomechanism** **ADJ**

▸ ▸ *Aut* **s. brake** servofrein *m*

servo-assistance **N** *Tech* servo-assistance *f*

servocontrol [sɜːvəʊkən'trəʊl] **N** *Tech* servocommande *f*

servomechanism [sɜːvəʊ'mekənɪz(ə)m] **N** *Tech* servomécanisme *m*

servomotor [sɜːvəʊ'məʊtər] **N** *Tech* servomoteur *m*

servo-unit **N** *Tech* servocommande *m*

sesame ['sesəmɪ] **N 1** *(plant)* sésame *m* **2 open s.!** *(magic formula)* sésame, ouvre-toi!

▸▸*Culin* s. oil huile *f* de sésame; *Culin* s. seeds graines *fpl* de sésame

sesh [seʃ] N *Br Fam (session)* **to have a drinking s.** se pinter; **we had a bit of a s. last night** on s'en est donné hier soir

session ['seʃən] N **1** *(period of activity)* séance *f*; **morning/evening s.** *(at swimming pool etc)* séance du matin/soir; **skiing tuition at £75 per 3-hour s.** cours de ski à 75 livres par séance de 3 heures; **training s.** séance d'entraînement; **we had a long s. on the phone** nous sommes restés très longtemps au téléphone; **I've just had a long s. with the lawyers** je viens d'avoir un long entretien avec les avocats; *Fam* **she has a complaining s. every morning** tous les matins, il faut qu'elle se plaigne **2** *(meeting)* session *f*, *Parl* **the autumn s.** la session d'automne; **the House is now in s.** la Chambre siège actuellement **3** *Am, Scot Univ (term)* trimestre *m* (universitaire); *(year)* année *f* (universitaire); *Am* **school is in s.** on est en période scolaire

▸▸*Mus* s. artist artiste *mf* de studio; s. musician musicien, -enne de studio

SET® N *Comput (abbr* secure electronic transaction) SET *f*

SET [set]

N jeu **1** ▪ série **1** ▪ service **1**		
▪ collection **1** ▪ groupe **2** ▪ poste **6**		
▪ décor **8** ▪ plateau **8** ▪ manche **11**		
▪ set **11**		
ADJ fixe **1** ▪ prêt **2** ▪ résolu **3**		
▪ prédéterminé **4**		
VT poser **1** ▪ situer **2** ▪ régler **3**		
▪ monter **4** ▪ tendre **5** ▪ fixer **6**		
▪ établir **6** ▪ composer **10**		
VI se coucher **1** ▪ prendre **2**		

N **1** *(group) (of keys, boxes, chesspieces etc)* jeu *m*; *(of problems, rules, symptoms, pans etc)* série *f*; *(of glasses, china)* service *m*; *(of tyres, wheels)* train *m*; *(of turbines)* batterie *f*; *(of stamps, butterflies etc) (collection)* collection *f*; *(series)* série *f*; *(of sb's works)* œuvres *fpl* complètes; *(of lingerie)* parure *f*; *Comput (of characters, instructions)* jeu, ensemble *m*; *Math* ensemble; **s. of bills of exchange** jeu de lettres de change; **s. of data** ensemble de données; **s. of teeth** denture *f*, dentition *f*; *(artificial)* dentier *m*; **s. of golf clubs** jeu de crosses; **s. of bells** sonnerie *f* *(d'église etc)*; *Old-fashioned* **toilet s., dressing-table s.** garniture *f* de toilette; **construction s.** jeu de construction; **a s. of cooking utensils** une batterie de cuisine; **a s. of sheets** une parure de lit; **a s. of screwdrivers** une série de tournevis; **a s. of tests** une batterie de tests; **to collect the (whole) s.** rassembler toute la collection, faire la collection; **chairs, the s. of six, £200** chaises, 200 livres les six

2 *(of people)* groupe *m*; *Pej* **literary/political s.** coterie *f* littéraire/politique; **he got in with the literary/political s.** il s'est mêlé au groupe de ceux qui s'intéressaient à la littérature/politique; **the smart s.** les élégants; **I'm not one of their s.** je ne suis pas de leur monde

3 *Br Sch* **top/bottom s.** classe *f* des forts/des plus faibles

4 *(position) (of public opinion)* tendances *fpl*; **his anxiety was betrayed in the s. of his shoulders** la position de ses épaules trahissait son anxiété; **I could tell she was angry by the s. of her jaw** je voyais sa colère à ses mâchoires serrées

5 *(in hairdressing)* mise *f* en plis

6 *(apparatus)* **(radio) s.** poste *m* de radio; **(television) s.** téléviseur *m*, poste de télévision

7 *Constr* **(paving) s.** pavé *m* d'échantillon

8 *Theat (scenery)* décor *m*; *TV, Cin* plateau *m* (de tournage); **on s.** *Theat* sur scène; *TV, Cin* sur le plateau; **rehearsal on the s.** *Theat* répétition *f* sur scène; *Cin* répétition sur le plateau

9 *Mus etc (performance)* set *m*; **the band played two sets** le groupe a joué deux sets

10 *(tool)* **nail s.** chasse-clou *m*, *pl* chasse-clous; **saw s.** tourne-à-gauche *m inv*

11 *Tennis* manche *f*, set *m*

12 *(of badger)* terrier *m*

ADJ **1** *(face)* immobile, aux traits rigides; *(look)* fixe; *(smile)* figé; **(hard) s.** ferme, figé; *(cement)* bien pris

2 *(prepared)* **to be (all) s. to do sth** être prêt à faire qch; **to be all s.** *(ready to begin)* être prêt à commencer; *Sport* **(get) s.!** en position, attention!; *Journ* **sterling s. to fall** la livre sterling sur le point de chuter

3 *(determined)* **to be (dead) s. on sth** être résolu *ou* déterminé à qch; **to be (dead) s. on doing sth** être résolu *ou* déterminé à faire qch; **to be dead s. against sb/sth** être résolument contre qn/qch

4 *(fixed) (ideas, opinions etc)* arrêté; *(time, price)* fixé; *(way)* prédéterminé; **he has a s. way of doing it** il a sa méthode pour le faire; **to be s. in one's ways** avoir ses habitudes, être coincé dans ses habitudes; **at s. hours** à heures fixes; **with no s. purpose** sans but précis; **s. forms of behaviour** comportements fixés par l'usage; **s. form of prayer** prière liturgique

VT *(pt, pp* set; *prp* setting) **1** *(place) (sth on or against sth, sth before sb)* mettre, poser; **to s. one's glass on the table** poser son verre sur la table; **to s. sth before sb** présenter qch à qn; **to s. a dish in front of sb** servir un plat à qn; **to s. a stake in the ground** enfoncer *ou* planter un pieu dans la terre; **to s. one's hand/seal to a document** apposer sa signature/son sceau à un acte; **to s. sb on his feet again** remettre qn sur pied; **her eyes are s. too close together** elle a les yeux trop rapprochés; **the house is s. in the heart of the woods** la maison est située au milieu des bois; **to s. a match to sth** mettre le feu à qch; **to s. a value on sth** décider de la valeur de qch; **to s. a proposal before the board** présenter un projet au conseil d'administration; **to s. one's heart on sth** avoir qch à cœur, vouloir absolument qch; **to s. the table** mettre le couvert *ou* la table; **to s. the table for two** mettre deux couverts; **to s. a trap (for sb)** tendre un piège (à qn)

2 *(story, film)* situer; **where is the story/film s.?** où est-ce que l'histoire/le film se passe?; *Theat* **to s. a scene** monter un décor; **the second act is s. in a street** le second acte se passe dans une rue

3 *(adjust) (mechanism, watch etc)* régler; **to s. one's watch by the town clock** régler sa montre sur l'horloge de la ville; **to s. the alarm clock for** *or* **at five o'clock** mettre le réveil à cinq heures; **to s. the milometer to zero** remettre le compteur à zéro; **to s. one's hat straight** remettre son chapeau droit; **to have one's hair s.** se faire faire une mise en plis

4 *(mount) (stone)* monter, sertir; **s. with diamonds** orné *ou* incrusté de diamants; **(with) all sails s.** toutes voiles dehors

5 *(prepare) (trap)*, *also Fig* dresser, tendre

6 *(fix) (date, day)* fixer, arrêter; **to s. a date for a meeting** fixer une date de réunion; **to s. a price** fixer *ou* établir un prix; **to s. the rate of sth** tarifer qch; **to s. limits to sth** fixer des limites à qch; **to s. prices high/low** fixer les prix hauts/bas; **to s. an age limit at …** fixer une limite d'âge à …; **to s. oneself a target** se fixer un but; **to s. a fashion/trend** lancer une mode/tendance; **to s. a record** établir un record; **to s. oneself a task** s'imposer une tâche; **to s. sb a problem** poser un

problème à qn; *Sch* **to s. an essay** donner un sujet de dissertation; *Sch* **to s. a book** mettre un livre au programme; **to s. an exam(ination) paper** choisir les questions d'une épreuve écrite; **to s. the page margins** marger la page

7 *(cause to start)* **to s. sb to do sth** faire faire qch à qn; **to s. a man to work** mettre un homme au travail; **that s. me thinking** cela m'a fait réfléchir *ou* m'a donné à réfléchir; **to s. the dog barking** faire aboyer le chien; **to s. people talking** *(provoke comment)* faire parler les gens; **to s. sth going** mettre qch en train; **to s. a mechanism going** mettre un mécanisme en marche; **to s. sb free** libérer qn, rendre sa liberté à qn

8 *Mus* **to s. a melody half a tone higher/lower** transcrire un air un demi-ton plus haut/bas; **to s. words to music** mettre des paroles en musique

9 *Surg (bone, limb)* remettre; *(fracture)* réduire

10 *Typ* composer; **to s. type** composer; **to s. a page** composer une page

11 *(of plant) (fruit)* donner, porter

VI **1** *(of sun, moon)* se coucher; **we saw the sun setting** nous avons vu le coucher du soleil

2 *(become firm) (of jelly)* prendre; *(of broken bone)* se recoller; *(of cement)* prendre, durcir; **her features had s. in an expression of determination** ses traits s'étaient durcis en une expression de très forte détermination; *Fig* **public opinion was beginning to s. against the proposal** l'opinion publique commençait à se durcir contre la proposition

3 *(in hunting) (of dog)* tomber en arrêt

▸▸*Sch* s. books ouvrages *mpl* au programme; **one of our s. books is 'Oliver Twist'** un des ouvrages au programme est 'Oliver Twist'; *Theat, Cin, TV* s. designer décorateur, -trice; s. dressing agencement *m* des éléments du décor; *Gram* s. expression expression *f* figée; s. menu menu *m* fixe; *Gram* s. phrase expression figée; *Sport* s. piece combinaison *f* préparée; *Tennis* s. point balle *f* de set; s. price prix *m* fixe; s. task tâche *f* assignée; **to give sb a s. task to do** assigner à qn une tâche bien précise; *Math* s. theory théorie *f* des ensembles

▸ **set about** VT INSEP **1** *(start)* **to s. about a piece of work** se mettre à *ou* entreprendre un travail; **to s. about doing sth** se mettre à faire qch; **I don't know how to s. about it** je ne sais pas comment m'y prendre

2 *(attack)* **to s. about sb** attaquer qn

▸ **set against** VT SEP **1** *(cause to oppose)* **to s. sb against sb** dresser qn contre qn, *Fam* monter (la tête à) qn contre qn; **it had s. members of the family one against the other** cela avait dressé les membres de la famille les uns contre les autres; **something's s. him against the idea** quelque chose lui en a fait détester l'idée; **to s. oneself** *or* **one's face against sth** s'opposer résolument à qch

2 *(weigh against)* **to s. sth against sth** contrebalancer qch par qch; **to s. the benefits against the costs** évaluer les bénéfices par rapport aux coûts

3 *Fin (offset)* **to s. expenses against taxes** déduire les dépenses des impôts

4 *(compare)* **to s. sth against sth** comparer qch à qch; **we must s. the government's promises against its achievements** nous devons examiner les promesses du gouvernement à la lumière de ses actions

▸ **set apart** VT SEP **1** *(distinguish)* distinguer (**from** de); **what sets them apart from other companies is …** ce qui les distingue des autres sociétés, c'est …

2 *(isolate) (person)* isoler; **they s. themselves apart** ils faisaient bande à part

▸ **set aside** VT SEP **1** *(abandon temporarily)*

(job, task) mettre de côté; **could you s. aside what you're working on for a while?** pouvez-vous laisser ce que vous êtes en train de faire un moment?

2 *(not consider)* ne pas prendre en ligne de compte, laisser de côté; **setting that aspect aside** sans prendre cet aspect en ligne de compte, si on laisse de côté cet aspect; **to s. aside one's personal feelings** mettre de côté tout sentiment personnel

3 *(save)* *(money)* mettre de côté *ou* en réserve; *(hours, weekend etc)* réserver; **to s. aside some money every week** mettre de l'argent de côté chaque semaine

4 *Law (judgement, verdict etc)* casser, infirmer; *(claim)* rejeter; *(will)* annuler

▸ **set back** VT SEP **1** *Constr etc* **house s. back (from the road)** maison en retrait (de la route)

2 *(delay)* retarder le progrès de; **the news may s. him** *or* **his recovery back** la nouvelle risque de retarder sa guérison; **this decision will s. the economy back ten years** cette décision va faire revenir l'économie dix ans en arrière

3 *Fam (cost)* **it s. me back £5,000** ça m'a coûté 5 000 livres; **that new car must have s. her back a bit** cette nouvelle voiture a dû lui coûter un fric fou

▸ **set by** VT SEP **1** = **set aside 3**

▸ **set down** VT SEP **1** *(put down)* poser, déposer; **the train stops to s. down passengers only** ce train ne prend pas de voyageurs

2 to s. sth down in writing coucher qch par écrit; **condition s. down in the contract** condition énoncée dans le contrat; **permissible levels of pollution are s. down in the regulations** les taux de pollution tolérés sont fixés dans les réglementations

▸ **set forth** VI *Arch, Lit (leave)* se mettre en route, partir

VT SEP *(present) (case etc)* présenter, mettre en avant; **the document sets forth a detailed description of …** le document présente une description détaillée de …

▸ **set in** VI *(take hold) (of gangrene, fog, winter, cynicism)* s'installer; **night was setting in** la nuit tombait; **the rain had s. in** la pluie ne s'arrêtait plus

VT SEP *Sewing (sleeve)* monter

▸ **set off** VT SEP **1** *(ignite) (rocket)* faire partir; *(bomb)* faire exploser

2 *(cause) (explosion, alarm, argument, chain of events)* déclencher

3 *(cause to do sth)* **this answer s. them off (laughing)** cette réponse a déclenché les rires; **one look at his face s. me off again** en le voyant, mon fou rire a repris de plus belle; **if you say anything, it'll only s. him off (crying) again** si tu dis quoi que ce soit, il va se remettre à pleurer; **the smallest amount of pollen will s. her off** la moindre dose de pollen lui déclenche une réaction allergique; **don't mention Maradona or you'll s. him off again** surtout ne prononce pas le nom de Maradona, sinon il va recommencer; **someone mentioned the war and, of course, that s. Uncle Arthur off** quelqu'un mentionna le mot guerre et, évidemment, oncle Arthur embraya aussitôt sur le sujet

4 *(enhance)* mettre en relief *ou* en valeur; *(colour, person's best points)* faire ressortir, faire valoir, rehausser; **those curtains really s. the room off** ces rideaux mettent vraiment la pièce en valeur

5 *Fin (debt)* compenser; **to s. off a gain against a loss** compenser une perte par un gain; **can I s. these expenses off against my tax liability?** est-ce que je peux déduire ces frais de mes impôts?

6 *Comput (num lock, insert etc)* désactiver

VI *(depart)* se mettre en route, partir; **to s. off on a journey** partir; **to s. off again** se remettre en route; **to s. off running** partir en courant

▸ **set on** VT INSEP *(attack)* attaquer

VT SEP **1** *Comput (num lock, insert etc)* activer

2 *(cause to follow)* **to s. the police on the tracks of a thief** mettre la police aux trousses d'un voleur; **to s. sb (off) on the wrong track** mettre qn sur une fausse piste; **to s. sb on his way** mettre qn sur les rails

3 *(cause to attack)* **to s. a dog on sb** lâcher un chien sur qn

▸ **set out** VT SEP *(arrange)* disposer; *(goods)* étaler; *(one's ideas)* exposer; **his work is well s. out** son travail est bien présenté

VI **1** *(depart on journey)* se mettre en route, partir; **just as he was setting out** au moment de son départ; **to s. out for school** partir pour l'école; **to s. out again** repartir; **to s. out in pursuit/in search of sb** se mettre à la poursuite/à la recherche de qn

2 *(start job etc)* **I didn't realize when I s. out how difficult it would be** je n'avais pas réalisé combien ce serait difficile lorsque j'ai commencé; **I didn't s. out with any preconceptions** au départ, je n'avais aucune idée préconçue

3 *(intend)* **I didn't s. out to attack the government** je n'avais aucune intention d'attaquer le gouvernement; **they deliberately s. out to cause trouble** ils avaient l'intention de créer des problèmes; **his theory sets out to prove that …** sa théorie a pour objet de prouver que …

▸ **set to** VI **1** *(start working)* se mettre au travail *ou* à l'œuvre

2 *Fam (of two people) (start arguing)* avoir une prise de bec; *(start fighting)* en venir aux mains

VT INSEP *(start doing)* **to s. to work** se mettre au travail *ou* à l'œuvre

▸ **set up** VT SEP **1** *(erect) (mast)* dresser; *(statue)* ériger; *(computer system, stereo system, model train set)* installer; *(machine, tent, tripod etc)* monter; *(barrier)* élever; **to s. sth up again** *(because it has fallen)* relever qch; *Fig* **to s. up a barrier between people** mettre une barrière entre les gens

2 *(arrange) (dinner, meeting, appointment)* organiser; *(system, link)* établir; **I've s. things up (so that …)** j'ai organisé les choses (de telle manière que …); **will you s. things up for the meeting?** veux-tu t'occuper d'organiser la réunion?

3 *(establish) (committee, tribunal)* instituer, constituer; *(business)* créer, fonder; *(programme)* monter; *(distinction, connection)* établir; **to s. up an account** ouvrir un compte; **to s. up house** *or* **home** s'installer dans une maison; **to s. sb up in business** aider qn à monter une affaire; **to s. oneself up as a lawyer** monter un cabinet d'avocat

4 *Med etc (cause) (infection, irritation)* provoquer, causer

5 *Fam (fabricate evidence against sb) (usu passive)* **I've been s. up** on m'a monté un coup, on m'a bien eu

6 *(invigorate) (person)* revivifier; **a fortnight in the country will s. you up** une quinzaine à la campagne va vous remettre d'aplomb

7 *Typ (text)* composer

VI **1** *(establish oneself)* **to s. up in business** se mettre à son compte; **to s. up as a chemist** s'établir pharmacien(ne); **he has s. up for himself** il s'est établi à son compte; **to s. up overseas** s'implanter à l'étranger

2 *(claim to be)* **to s. up as a critic** se poser en critique

▸ **set upon** VT INSEP attaquer; **to be s. upon by sb** être attaqué par qn

set-aside N *EU* gel *m* des terres

setback ['setbæk] N **1** *(reversal, stroke of bad luck)* mésaventure *f*, *Fin, St Exch* tassement *m*, repli *m*; *Med* rechute *f*; **they encountered a number of setbacks** ils ont eu de nom-

breux déboires; **to suffer a s.** *(of patient)* rechuter; **the dollar suffered a s. today** le dollar a connu un repli aujourd'hui; **to suffer a s. in one's plans** voir ses plans compromis; **this will prove a s. in his career** cela va compromettre sa carrière **2** *Archit* décrochement *m*

set-in ADJ

▸▸ *Sewing* **s. sleeve** manche *f* rapportée

setmeter ['setmi:tər] N *TV etc* audimètre *m*

set-square N équerre *f* (à dessin)

sett [set] N **1** *Constr* **(paving) s.** pavé *m* d'échantillon **2** *(of badger)* terrier *m*

settee [se'ti:] N canapé *m*; **bed s.** canapé-lit *m*, *pl* canapés-lits

setter ['setər] N **1** *(person) (of diamonds etc)* sertisseur *m*; *Typ* **(type) s.** compositeur, -trice **2** *(dog)* setter *m*; **Irish s.** setter irlandais

setting ['setɪŋ] ADJ **1** *(sun, star)* couchant **2** **slow-/quick-s. cement** ciment *m* à prise lente/rapide

N **1** *(act of adjusting)* réglage *m* **2** *(act of mounting) (of specimen, jewel)* montage *m*; *(result)* monture *f* **3** *Typ* composition *f* **4** *(act of fixing, arranging) (of date etc)* désignation *f*, **s. up of an account** ouverture *f* d'un compte; **s. up of a business** création *f ou* fondation *f* d'une entreprise **5** *(of sun etc)* coucher *m* **6** *Surg (of broken bone)* recollement *m*; *(of fracture)* réduction *f* **7** *(hardening) (of cement)* affermissement *m*, prise *f* **8** *(location) (of story, festival etc)* cadre *m*; *Theat* mise *f* en scène; **a novel in an 18th century s.** un roman dans un décor XVIIIᵉ siècle **9** *(arrangement)* **s. for violin** arrangement *m* pour violon; **(place) s.** *(at table)* couvert *m*; **the s. to music of …** la mise en musique de … **10** *(on washing machine, iron etc)* réglage *m*; **try a higher s.** *(of oven, iron, microwave etc)* augmentez la température; **what s. was it on?** sur quoi était-elle réglée? **11** *Comput (of tabs etc) (action)* pose *f*, *(position)* positionnement *m*; **printer settings** paramètres *mpl* de l'imprimante

▸▸ **s. lotion** lotion *f* pour mise en plis; *Typ* **s. width** largeur *f* de composition

SETTLE ['set(ə)l]

VT	régler **1, 4**	▪ mettre en place **1**
	▪ coloniser **1**	▪ calmer **2** ▪ fixer **3**
	▪ résoudre **4**	▪ payer **4**
VI	s'établir **1**	▪ se poser **1** ▪ se déposer
	2 ▪ reposer **2**	▪ se calmer **4**

VT **1** *(make stable) (put carefully in place)* mettre bien en place; *(of person, population etc) (country)* coloniser, peupler; *(one's affairs)* régler, mettre de l'ordre dans; **to s. one's feet in the stirrups** bien installer ses pieds dans les étriers; **she had settled herself in an armchair** elle s'était installée dans un fauteuil; **to s. an invalid for the night** installer un malade pour la nuit; **to s. the children for the night** mettre les enfants au lit

2 *(calm) (person, nerves etc)* apaiser, calmer; **give me something to s. my stomach** donnez-moi quelque chose pour l'estomac; **to s. sb's doubts** dissiper les doutes de qn

3 *(fix) (day, venue etc)* fixer, déterminer; **it's as good as settled** c'est comme si c'était fait; **everything is settled, it's settled** l'affaire est conclue; **that's settled, then** c'est entendu *ou* convenu

4 *(resolve) (question)* résoudre, décider; *(quarrel, dispute, account)* régler; *(debt)* payer; **to s. a matter** régler une question; **to s. accounts** *or* **old scores** *or* **an old score with sb** régler des comptes avec qn; **to s. one's differences (with sb)** se mettre d'accord (avec qn); **questions not yet settled** questions en suspens; **that settles it!** voilà qui est réglé!; **s. it among yourselves** arrangez cela entre vous; **to s. a matter out of court** régler une question à l'amiable; **to s. one's bills** payer ses factures; *Fam* **that settled him** *or* **his hash** *(that put a stop to him)* ça lui a réglé son compte; *(that put a stop to his boasting)* ça lui a rabattu le caquet

5 *(bestow)* **to s. an annuity on sb** constituer une rente à qn; **to s. all one's property on one's wife** mettre tous ses biens au nom de sa femme

VI 1 *(of person, people)* s'établir, se fixer (**in a place** dans un lieu); *(of bird, insect etc)* se poser; **to s. in an armchair** s'installer dans un fauteuil; **she had settled in a corner** elle s'était installée dans un coin; **they settled along the Ohio** ils se sont installés au bord de l'Ohio; **she lived here a few years, but didn't s.** elle a vécu ici quelques années, mais ne s'est pas installée définitivement; *(never felt at home)* elle a vécu ici quelques années, mais ne s'est jamais habituée; **the snow is settling** la neige tient; **to s. to work/to do sth** se mettre sérieusement au travail/à faire qch; **he can't s. to anything** il n'arrive pas à se concentrer sur quoi que ce soit; **I couldn't s.** *(in bed)* je n'arrivais pas à m'endormir; *Fig* **a look of despair/contentment had settled on his face** le désespoir/la satisfaction se lisait sur son visage

2 *(of liquid, beer)* reposer; *(of sediment)* se déposer; *(of dust)* retomber; **to let s.** *(dregs etc)* laisser déposer; *(wine)* laisser se rasseoir; *(solution)* laisser reposer; **allow the mixture to s.** laissez reposer le mélange

3 *(of ground, pillar etc)* prendre son assiette, s'asseoir; *(of foundation etc)* s'affaisser; **let your food s. before you go swimming** attendez d'avoir digéré avant d'aller nager

4 *(of excitement)* s'apaiser, se calmer; **the weather is settling** le temps se calme

5 *Law* **to s. (out of court)** régler l'affaire (à l'amiable)

N *(seat)* = banquette *f* en bois avec un dossier

▸ **settle down VI 1** *(make oneself comfortable)* s'installer; **they settled down by the fire/to watch TV** ils s'installèrent près de la cheminée/pour regarder la télévision; **to s. down to sleep** s'apprêter à dormir; **it took the children some time to s. down to sleep** les enfants ont mis du temps à se décider à dormir; **to s. down with a book** s'installer avec un livre

2 *(give serious attention to sth)* **to s. down to work** se mettre sérieusement au travail; **to s. down to a job** s'attaquer *ou* se mettre à une tâche

3 *(adopt regular life)* se ranger, s'assagir; *(of situation)* s'arranger, redevenir normal; *(of excitement)* se calmer; **it's time you settled down and got married** il est temps que tu te ranges et que tu te maries; **he's not someone you could imagine settling down with** ce n'est pas le genre de personne avec qui on peut imaginer se marier; **s. down, children!** calmez-vous, les enfants!, du calme, les enfants!; **he's beginning to s. down at school** il commence à s'habituer à l'école; **things are settling down** *(becoming more definite)* les choses commencent à prendre tournure; *(calming down)* les choses sont en train de se calmer; **as soon as the market settles down** aussitôt que le marché se sera stabilisé

VT SEP 1 *(make comfortable)* **to s. the baby down for the night** installer le bébé pour la nuit

2 *(make calm)* **to s. a class down** calmer une classe

▸ **settle for VT INSEP** *(accept)* accepter; **I settled for £100** j'ai accepté 100 livres; **I insist on the best quality, I never s. for (anything) less** j'exige ce qu'il y a de mieux, je n'accepte

jamais rien en dessous; **we haven't got any brandy, will you s. for Scotch?** nous n'avons pas de cognac, est-ce qu'un whisky fera l'affaire?

▸ **settle in VI** *(become established)* s'installer, s'établir; **to s. in a new school** s'habituer à une nouvelle école; **to s. in at a job** s'habituer à un emploi; **to s. in at a company** s'intégrer à une société

VT SEP *(help become established)* *(new employee, person in new home)* aider à s'installer

▸ **settle on VT INSEP** *(decide on)* décider de; **have you settled on a name for the baby/a date for the wedding?** avez-vous décidé d'un prénom pour le bébé/d'une date pour le mariage?; **they couldn't s. on a price** ils n'ont pas réussi à se mettre d'accord sur un prix

▸ **settle up VI 1** *(pay bill)* payer

2 *(pay debt)* s'acquitter; **I'll s. up with you tomorrow** je vous réglerai demain

▸ **settle with VT INSEP to s. with sb** *(pay debt)* régler ses comptes avec qn

settled ['set(ə)ld] **ADJ 1** *(stable, calm)* *(life)* stable; *(idea, habit)* fixe, enraciné; *(intention)* bien arrêté; *(person, character)* posé, réfléchi; *(bearing etc)* tranquille, calme; **I am a man of s. habits** je suis un homme d'habitudes; **she is s. in her job** elle est habituée à son emploi **2** *(established in home)* *(person)* installé, établi; **to get s.** s'installer **3** *(colonized)* colonisé **4** *Met (calm)* beau, *f* belle; **the weather will remain s.** le temps demeurera au beau fixe

settlement ['set(ə)lmənt] **N 1** *(action)* *(of people in a country)* établissement *m*, installation *f*; *(of country)* colonisation *f* **2** *(of ground)* tassement *m*, affaissement *m* **3** *(of matter)* règlement *m*; *(of question)* résolution *f*, décision *f*; *(of difference)* arrangement *m*; *(of question)* résolution *f*, décision *f*; *(of treaty etc)* conclusion *f*, *Com (of account)* règlement, paiement *m*; *St Exch* liquidation *f*, *Com* **in (full) s.** pour solde de tout compte **4** *(agreement)* accord *m*; **they have reached a s.** ils sont arrivés à un accord; *Law* **s. of an annuity** constitution *f* de rente (**on** en faveur de); **marriage s.** contrat *m* de mariage **5** *(colony)* colonie *f*, **penal s.** colonie pénitentiaire **6** *Am (small community)* village *m*

▸▸ *St Exch* **s. day** jour *m* de (la) liquidation; *Com* **s. discount** remise *f* pour règlement rapide; *Com* **s. period** délai *m* de règlement; *St Exch* **s. price** cours *m* de résiliation; *St Exch* **s. value** valeur *f* liquidative

settler ['setlər] **N** *(colonist)* colon *m*

settling ['setlɪŋ] **N 1** = **settlement 1 2** *(of liquid)* clarification *f* **3** *(of ground)* affaissement *m* **4** = **settlement 3**

set-to **N** *Fam (fight)* bagarre *f*, *(argument)* prise *f* de bec

set-top box **N** boîtier *m* décodeur, décodeur *m*

setup ['setʌp] **N 1** *Fam (organization)* fonctionnement *m*; **it's an odd s.** *(company)* c'est une drôle de boîte; *(marriage, relationship)* c'est un drôle de ménage; *(collection of people)* c'est une drôle d'équipe; **you've got a nice s. here** vous êtes bien installé ici **2** *esp Am Fam (something rigged)* machination *f*, coup *m* monté **3** *Cin, TV* = installation *f* du matériel technique pour le tournage d'une scène

seven ['sev(ə)n] **N** sept *m*; **two sevens are fourteen** deux fois sept font quatorze; **it's s. o'clock** il est sept heures; *Cards* **the s. of hearts** le sept de cœur; **to be s.** *(in age)* avoir sept ans

PRON sept; **s. is not enough** sept, ce n'est pas assez

NUM ADJ sept; **the s. deadly sins** les sept péchés capitaux; **s.-league boots** bottes *fpl* de

sept lieues; *Fam* **the s.-year itch** le cap difficile des sept ans de mariage; *Fam* **to have the s.-year itch** arriver au cap difficile des sept ans de mariage

▸▸ **s. seas** toutes les mers *fpl* (du monde); *Lit* **to sail the s. seas** parcourir les océans

seven-bit character **N** *Comput* caractère *m* à sept bits

seven-bit data **N** *Comput* données *fpl* à sept bits

sevenfold ['sev(ə)nfəʊld] **ADJ** septuple

ADV sept fois autant; **to increase s.** septupler

seventeen [sev(ə)n'ti:n] **NUM ADJ, N** dix-sept *m*; **she's s.** elle a dix-sept ans

seventeenth [sev(ə)n'ti:nθ] **ADJ** dix-septième

N 1 *(of month)* dix-sept *m*; **(on) the s. of May** le dix-sept mai **2** *(person, thing)* dix-septième *mf* **3** *(fraction)* dix-septième *m*

seventh ['sev(ə)nθ] **ADJ** septième; **to be in s. heaven** être aux anges *ou* au septième ciel; **Edward the S.** Édouard Sept; *Rel* **S.-day Adventist** adventiste *mf* du septième jour

N 1 *(of month)* sept *m*; **(on) the s. (of May)** le sept (mai) **2** *(person, thing)* septième *mf*; **you're the s. this morning to ask me that** tu es la septième personne qui me demande *ou* à me demander ça ce matin **3** *(fraction)* septième *m* **4** *Mus (interval)* septième *f*

seventieth ['sev(ə)ntɪɪθ] **ADJ** soixante-dixième, *Belg, Suisse* septantième

N 1 *(person, thing)* soixante-dixième *mf* **2** *(fraction)* soixante-dixième *m*

seventy ['sev(ə)ntɪ] **NUM ADJ, N** soixante-dix *m*, *Belg, Suisse* septante *m*; **s.-one** soixante et onze; **s.-five** soixante-quinze; **s.-nine** soixante-dix-neuf; **to be in one's seventies** être septuagénaire

sever ['sevər] **VT** *(cut off)* *(arm, finger, leg)* sectionner (**at** au niveau de); *(friendship, link, relationship)* rompre; *(communications)* interrompre; **to s. one's connections with sb** couper les liens avec qn; **to s. sth from sth** séparer qch de qch; **a severed head** une tête coupée

VI *(of rope etc)* (se) rompre

several ['sev(ə)rəl] **ADJ 1** *(a number of)* plusieurs; **I've been there s. times** j'y suis allé plusieurs fois; **he and s. others** lui et plusieurs autres SEE GRAMMAR B15 **2** *Lit (respective)* respectif; **they have their s. reasons for wanting …** ils avaient chacun leurs raisons de vouloir …; **they went their s. ways** ils s'en allèrent, chacun de son côté; **we've decided to go our s. ways** nous avons décidé de suivre chacun notre chemin

PRON plusieurs *mfpl*; **s. of us/of them** *etc* plusieurs d'entre nous/d'entre eux *etc*; **s. of our party heard it** plusieurs membres de notre groupe l'ont entendu

severally ['sev(ə)rəlɪ] **ADV** *Fml* séparément, individuellement

severance ['sev(ə)rəns] **N** séparation *f* (**from** de); *(of relations etc)* rupture *f*, cessation *f*; *(of communications, contact)* interruption *f*, rupture

▸▸ **s. pay** indemnité *f* *ou* indemnités *fpl* de licenciement

severe [sɪ'vɪər] **ADJ 1** *(person, measures)* sévère, strict (**with** envers); **a s. reprimand** une verte réprimande **2** *(winter, weather)* rigoureux, rude; *(illness, wound)* grave; **a s. blow** un coup dur; **to suffer s. hardship** connaître de grosses difficultés; **s. loss** grosse *ou* forte perte *f*; **s. pain** douleur *f* violente *ou* vive; **she was in s. pain** elle a énormément souffert **3** *(style etc)* sévère, austère

severely [sɪ'vɪəlɪ] **ADV 1** *(punished, dealt with etc)* sévèrement, avec sévérité **2** *(wounded)* grièvement; *(ill)* gravement; **her**

patience was **s.** tried by his behaviour sa patience a été durement éprouvée par son comportement **3** *(to frown, dress etc)* sévèrement, de façon austère

severity [sɪ'verɪtɪ] N **1** *(of person, punishment, criticism)* sévérité f; *(of conditions)* dureté f **2** *(of weather, climate etc)* rigueur f, rudesse f; *(of illness, loss, injury)* gravité f; *(of pain)* violence f **3** *(of style)* sévérité f, austérité f

Seville [sə'vɪl] N Séville f
▸▸ **S. orange** orange f amère, bigarade f

sew [səʊ] *(pt* sewed [səʊd]; *pp* sewn [səʊn], *occ* sewed*)* VI coudre
VT coudre; *Typ* brocher; **hand/machine sewn** cousu (à la) main/à la machine
▸ **sew on** VT SEP *(button) (put on)* coudre; *(put back on)* recoudre
▸ **sew up** VT SEP **1** *(close by sewing), Surg (wound, cut etc)* recoudre **2** *Fam* it's all sewn up tout est arrangé; **we've got it all sewn up** l'affaire est dans le sac; **to have the elections/the match sewn up** avoir gagné les élections/le match d'avance

sewage ['su:ɪdʒ] N eau(x) f(pl) d'égout(s)
▸▸ **s. disposal** évacuation f des eaux usées; **s. farm** champs *mpl* d'épandage; **s. system** égouts *mpl*; **s. works** champs d'épandage

sewer[1] ['səʊər] N *(person who sews)* couseur, -euse; **to be a good/bad s.** être bon/mauvais couturier

sewer[2] ['su:ər] N *(pipe)* égout *m*; **main s.** égout collecteur; **s. of vice** cloaque *m* de vice; **he's got a mind like a s.** il a l'esprit mal placé; *(he interprets everything sordidly)* c'est un véritable obsédé sexuel
▸▸ **s. rat** rat *m* d'égout

sewerage ['su:ərɪdʒ] N **1** *(system of sewers)* système *m* d'égouts **2** = sewage

sewermouth ['su:əmaʊθ] N *Am Fam* **to be a s.** jurer comme un charretier

sewing ['səʊɪŋ] N **1** *(activity)* couture f **2** *(work)* ouvrage *m* (à l'aiguille); **the s. on this shirt is terrible** cette chemise est très mal cousue
▸▸ **s. basket** boîte f à couture; **s. cotton** fil *m* à coudre; **s. kit** nécessaire *m* de couture; **s. machine** machine f à coudre; **s. needle** aiguille f à coudre; **s. thread** fil à coudre

sewn PP *see* **sew**

sex [seks] N sexe *m*; **to have s. with sb** *(on ongoing basis)* avoir des rapports sexuels avec qn; *(on one occasion)* coucher avec qn; **how many times have you had s. with him?** combien de fois est-ce que vous avez eu des rapports avec lui?; **he's got s. on the brain** il a l'esprit dans la culotte; **a novel full of s.** un roman plein de passages érotiques; **the fair(er) or weaker s.** le beau sexe; **the s. act** l'acte *m* sexuel; **to have a low/high s. drive** avoir un appétit sexuel faible/élevé; *Fam* **s. mad** qui ne pense qu'au sexe; **to be s. mad** ne penser qu'au sexe; **sex-starved** en manque (de sexe); *Psy* **the s. urge** le désir sexuel
VT *(person, animal)* déterminer le sexe de
▸▸ **s. addict** dépendant, -ante sexuel(elle); **s. addiction** dépendance f sexuelle; **s. aid** gadget *m* érotique; **s. appeal** sex-appeal *m*; **s. change** opération f de changement de sexe; **to have a s. change** *(operation)* changer de sexe; **s. change operation** opération de changement de sexe; **s. crime** crime *m* sexuel; *Biol* **s. determination** détermination f du sexe; **s. discrimination** discrimination f sexuelle; **s. education** éducation f sexuelle; **s. fiend** maniaque *mf* sexuel(elle); **the s. industry** l'industrie f du sexe; *Fam* **s. kitten** bombe f sexuelle; **s. life** vie f sexuelle; *Hum* **how's your s. life?** et ta vie amoureuse, comment ça va?; **s. maniac** obsédé, -e sexuel(elle); **s. object** objet *m* sexuel; **s. offen-**

der auteur *m* d'un délit sexuel; **s. organs** organes *mpl* sexuels; *Fam* **s. pest** obsédé *m* *(qui harcèle les femmes)*; **s. scandal** affaire f de mœurs, scandale *m* sexuel; **s. shop** sex-shop *m, pl* sex-shops; **s. symbol** sex-symbol *m, pl* sex-symbols; **s. therapist** sexologue *mf*; **s. tourism** tourisme *m* sexuel; **s. toy** gadget érotique

sexagenarian [seksədʒɪ'neərɪən] ADJ, N sexagénaire *mf*

sexed [sekst] ADJ **1** *Biol* sexué **2** *Psy* **highly s.** qui a une forte libido

sexiness ['seksɪnɪs] N caractère *m* sexy; **the s. of her appearance** son air sexy; **they are all agreed on his s.** elles sont toutes d'accord pour dire qu'il est sexy; **the s. of the way she walks** sa démarche sexy

sexism ['seksɪz(ə)m] N sexisme *m*

sexist ['seksɪst] ADJ sexiste
N sexiste *mf*

sexless ['sekslɪs] ADJ **1** *Biol (neuter)* asexué **2** *(person)* asexué; *(marriage etc)* où il n'y a pas/plus de relations sexuelles

sexologist [sek'sɒlədʒɪst] N sexologue *mf*

sexology [sek'sɒlədʒɪ] N sexologie f

sexploitation [seksplɔɪ'teɪʃən] N *Fam* exploitation f commerciale de la sexualité; **a s. movie** un film dont le propos se résume au sexe

sexploits ['seksplɔɪts] NPL *Fam Hum* aventures *fpl* sexuelles

sexpot ['sekspɒt] N *Fam* femme f/homme *m* très sexy

sextant ['sekstənt] N *Geom, Naut* sextant *m*

sextet [seks'tet] N *Mus* sextuor *m*; *(jazz band)* sextet *m*

sexton ['sekst(ə)n] N *Rel* sacristain *m (qui fait également office de sonneur de cloches et de fossoyeur)*

sextuple ['sekstjʊp(ə)l] ADJ, N sextuple *m*

sextuplet ['sekstjʊplɪt] N **1** *(child)* sextuplé, -ée **2** *Mus* sextolet *m*

sexual ['seksjʊəl] ADJ sexuel; **the s. organs** les organes *mpl* sexuels
▸▸ **s. assault** agression f sexuelle; **s. attraction** attirance f sexuelle; **s. discrimination** discrimination f sexuelle, sexisme *m*; **s. harassment** harcèlement *m* sexuel; **s. intercourse** rapports *mpl* sexuels; **s. reproduction** reproduction f sexuelle

sexuality [seksjʊ'ælɪtɪ] N sexualité f

sexually ['seksjʊəlɪ] ADV sexuellement; **to be s. active** avoir des rapports sexuels; **to be s. attracted to sb** éprouver une attirance sexuelle pour qn
▸▸ *Med* **s. transmitted disease** maladie f sexuellement transmissible, *Can* maladie transmise sexuellement

sex-worker N *(prostitute)* prostitué, -ée

sexy ['seksɪ] ADJ *Fam (person, clothes)* sexy; *(book, film)* érotique; *Mktg (product)* branché; *Fig* **skiing has become very s.** le ski est devenu très chic; **hi there, s.!** *(man)* salut, beau gosse!; *(woman)* salut, ma beauté!

Seychelles [seɪ'ʃelz] NPL **the S.** les Seychelles *fpl*

sez [sez] INT *Sl* **s. you!** *(that's what you think)* tu parles!; *(you're not telling the truth)* et ta sœur!

SF [es'ef] N *(abbr* Science Fiction*)* S.F. f, anticipation f

SFA [ese'feɪ] N *Sport (abbr* Scottish Football Association*)* Fédération f écossaise de football

SFO [esef'əʊ] N *Br (abbr* Serious Fraud Office*)* ≃ Service *m* de la répression des fraudes

sfx [ese'feks] NPL *Cin, TV (abbr* special effects*)* effets *mpl* spéciaux

SGML [esdʒiː'mel] N *Comput (abbr* Standard Generated Markup Language*)* SGML *m*

Sgt *Mil (abbr* Sergeant*)* Sgt

sh [ʃ] INT chut!

shabbily ['ʃæbɪlɪ] ADV **1** *(furnished, dressed etc)* pauvrement **2** *(to treat, behave)* mesquinement

shabbiness ['ʃæbɪnɪs] N **1** *(of clothing etc)* aspect *m* râpé *ou* usé; *(of furniture etc)* piètre état *m*; *(of person)* apparence f pauvre *ou* miteuse **2** *(of conduct etc)* mesquinerie f, petitesse f

shabby ['ʃæbɪ] ADJ **1** *(clothing etc)* râpé, usé; *(furniture, room, house etc)* pauvre, minable; **to become s.** *(of material)* s'élimer; **to look s.** *(of person)* avoir l'air minable *ou* miteux; **s. genteel** pauvre mais digne **2** *(conduct)* mesquin, petit; **a s. excuse** un prétexte mesquin; **s. trick** mesquinerie f

shack [ʃæk] N *(hut)* cabane f, hutte f, *Pej (house)* baraquement *m*; *Fam Hum* **nice little s. you have here** c'est une belle petite baraque que vous avez
▸ **shack up** VI *Sl (cohabit)* **to s. up (together)** se mettre à la colle; **to s. up with sb** *(start to live with)* se mettre à la colle avec qn; **are they still shacking up together?** est-ce qu'ils vivent toujours ensemble?

shackle ['ʃæk(ə)l] VT *(prisoner)* enchaîner, mettre les fers à; *Fig* **shackled by convention** entravé par les conventions

shackles ['ʃæk(ə)lz] NPL *(on prisoner etc)* fers *mpl*; *Fig* **the s. of convention** le carcan des conventions sociales; **to throw off the s. of convention** rejeter le carcan des conventions sociales

shacktown ['ʃæktaʊn] N *Am Fam* bidonville *m*

shade [ʃeɪd] N **1** *(darkness), Art* ombre f; **in the s. of a tree** à l'ombre d'un arbre; **a tree provided some s.** un arbre donnait de l'ombre; **temperature in the s.** température à l'ombre; *Fig* **to put sb in the s.** éclipser qn; *Myth Lit* **the Shades** *(the underworld)* les Enfers *mpl*
2 *(nuance) (of colour, opinion)* nuance f; **different shades of blue** différentes nuances de bleu; *Comput* **shades of grey** niveaux *mpl ou* tons *mpl* de gris; **a s. longer** un tantinet plus long; **a s. too big** un tantinet trop grand; **he is a s. better** il va un tout petit peu mieux; **a s. (too) sweet** un peu (trop) sucré; **a s. of irony** une nuance d'ironie; **just a s.** un petit peu
3 *Lit (ghost)* ombre f, fantôme *m*; *Fig* **shades of 1995** ça rappelle 1995
4 *(device)* **(eye) s.** visière f, **(lamp) s.** abat-jour *m inv*; *Am* **(window) s.** store *m* (de fenêtre); *Fam* **shades** *(sunglasses)* lunettes *fpl* de soleil
VT **1** *(put in darkness)* ombrager, donner de l'ombre à; *(of hat) (face)* obscurcir; **to s. sth from the sun** protéger qch du soleil; **to s. one's eyes with one's hand** s'abriter les yeux de la main; **to s. a light** voiler *ou* masquer une lumière
2 *Art (drawing)* ombrer, mettre des ombres à
VI **blue that shades into green** bleu qui se fond en vert; **these categories s. into one another** ces catégories se confondent
▸ **shade away, shade off** VT SEP *(change by degrees) (colours)* dégrader
VI **red shading off into pink** du rouge qui se fond en rose

shadeband ['ʃeɪdbænd] N *Aut* bande f pare-soleil

shaded ['ʃeɪdɪd] ADJ **1** *(path etc)* ombragé; *(lamp etc)* à abat-jour **2** *Art (drawing)* ombré; *(area on diagram, map)* hachuré

shadeless ['ʃeɪdlɪs] ADJ sans ombre

shadiness ['ʃeɪdɪnɪs] N **1** *(of path etc)* ombre f, ombrage *m* **2** *Fam (suspiciousness) (of* *affair etc)* aspect *m* louche; *(of person)* réputation *f* suspecte

shading ['ʃeɪdɪŋ] **N 1** *Art (on drawing)* ombres *fpl*; *(on map etc)* hachures *fpl* **2 subtle shadings of meaning** *(nuances)* nuances *fpl* de sens subtiles

shadow ['ʃædəʊ] **N 1** ombre *f*; *(dark area)* obscurité *f*; *(on picture, photograph)* noir *m*; **in the s.** *(in the shade)* à *ou* dans l'ombre; *(in dark place)* dans l'obscurité; **to cast a s.** jeter une ombre; *Fig* **this cast a s. over the festivities** cela a jeté une ombre sur la fête; *Fig* **coming events cast their shadows** les événements à venir se font pressentir; *Fig* **to catch at shadows, to run after a s.** se bercer d'illusions; **town nestling in the s. of a mountain** ville nichée à l'ombre d'une montagne; **a figure (standing) in the shadows** une silhouette (se tenant) dans l'ombre; *Fig* **to be afraid of one's own s.** avoir peur de son ombre; **not the s. of a doubt** pas l'ombre d'un doute; **to be a (mere) s. of one's/its former self** *(of person, country)* n'être que l'ombre de soi-même; **the s. of death/war** l'ombre de la mort/guerre; **under the s. of a terrible accusation** sous le coup d'une accusation terrible; *Med* **a s. on the right lung** un voile au poumon droit; **to have (dark) shadows round** *or* **under one's eyes** avoir les yeux cernés; **eye s.** *(make-up)* ombre à paupières

2 *(person) (constant companion)* compagnon *m*/compagne *f* inséparable; *(person following someone)* personne *f* qui prend qn en filature; **the dog was her s.** le chien la suivait comme son ombre; **to put a s. on sb** faire suivre qn

ADJ *Br Pol* fantôme; **the S. Home Secretary** le Ministre de l'Intérieur du cabinet fantôme **VT 1** *(cast shadows over)* ombrager **2** *(follow) (person)* filer, pister, prendre en filature

▸▸ **s. boxing** *Sport* shadow-boxing *m*, boxe *f* dans le vide; *Fig* attaque *f* rituelle *ou* de pure forme; *Br Pol* **s. cabinet** cabinet *m* fantôme; **s. economy** économie *f* parallèle; *Comput* **s. printing** impression *f* ombrée; **s. puppet** = silhouette *f* découpée utilisée dans les spectacles d'ombres chinoises

---

Shadow cabinet

En Grande-Bretagne, le "shadow cabinet" est composé de parlementaires de l'opposition qui deviendraient ministres si l'opposition accédait au pouvoir. Chaque ministre du gouvernement dispose de son homologue "fantôme" dans l'opposition (on parle de "shadow minister"), qui étudie les mêmes dossiers et se spécialise ainsi dans un domaine donné. Les ministres fantômes occupent les "frontbenches" de l'opposition à la Chambre des communes.

---

shadowing ['ʃædəʊɪŋ] **N** *(of suspect etc)* filature *f*

shadowy ['ʃædəʊɪ] **ADJ 1** *(path etc)* ombragé, ombreux **2** *(vague) (project)* indécis, vague; **a s. form** une silhouette vague

shady ['ʃeɪdɪ] **ADJ 1** *(tree etc)* qui donne de l'ombre; *(place, lane etc)* ombragé **2** *Fam (suspicious) (person, transaction, business etc)* louche; *(financier, affair)* véreux; **the s. side of politics** les dessous *mpl* de la politique

shaft [ʃɑːft] **N 1** *(of spear etc)* hampe *f*, bois *m*; *(of golf club, tool)* manche *m* **2** *esp Lit (arrow)* flèche *f*, trait *m*; *Fig* **shafts of wit** des traits d'esprit **3** *(beam) (of light)* rayon *m*; *(of lightning)* éclair *m* **4** *(of column)* fût *m*; *(of feather)* tige *f* **5** *Min* puits *m*; **air** *or* **ventilation s.** puits d'aérage, conduit *m* d'air; **to sink a s.**

creuser *ou Tech* foncer un puits **6** *Br* **lift** *or Am* **elevator s.** cage *f* (d'ascenseur) **7** *Tech* arbre *m*; *(stationary)* axe *m*; **driving s.** arbre moteur; **transmission s.** arbre de transmission; **propeller s.** arbre porte-hélice, arbre d'hélice **8** *(on horse-drawn vehicle)* brancard *m* **9** *Vulg (penis)* chibre *m*, queue *f*

VT 1 *Sl (have sexual intercourse with)* tringler **2** *Sl Fig (cheat)* entuber; **to get shafted** se faire entuber

▸▸ *Aut* **s. pin** fusée *f*

shafted ['ʃɑːftɪd] **ADJ** *Br Sl (drunk)* beurré, bourré

shag [ʃæg] **N 1** *(of carpet)* long poil *m*; **s. pile (carpet)** moquette *f* très moelleuse **2** *(tobacco)* tabac *m* fort *(coupé fin)* **3** *(bird)* cormoran *m* huppé **4** *Br Vulg (sex act)* baise *f*, **to have a s.** tirer un coup; **to be a good s.** *(of person)* être un bon coup **5** *Br Vulg (boring task)* plaie *f*, **it's a real s. having to get up so early every morning** c'est vraiment chiant de devoir se lever si tôt tous les matins

VT & VI *Br Vulg (have sexual intercourse (with))* baiser

▸ **shag out VT SEP** *Br Sl (exhaust)* crever; **I'm shagged out** je suis crevé

shagged [ʃægd] **ADJ** *Br Sl (exhausted)* crevé, claqué

shagger ['ʃægər] **N** *Br Vulg* baiseur *m*

shaggy ['ʃægɪ] **ADJ** *(hairy)* poilu; *(pony etc)* à longs poils; *(hair)* hirsute, ébouriffé; *(beard)* hirsute, touffu; *(eyebrows)* en broussailles; *(carpet)* poilu, à long poil; **s. dog story** = histoire *f* farfelue

shah [ʃɑː] **N** shah *m ou* chah *m* (d'Iran)

SHAKE [ʃeɪk] **VT** *(pt* **shook** [ʃʊk]; *pp* **shaken** ['ʃeɪk(ə)n])* **1** secouer; *(liquid, bottle etc)* agiter; *(building etc)* ébranler, secouer; *Fig (opinion, sb's faith)* ébranler; **s. well (before use)** *(on carton etc)* bien agiter avant l'emploi; **to s. one's head** *(in disbelief etc)* secouer *ou* hocher la tête; *(to indicate 'no')* faire non de la tête; **to s. one's fist at sb** menacer qn du poing; **to s. hands with sb** serrer la main à *ou* de qn; **to s. sb's hand, to s. sb by the hand** donner une poignée de main à qn; **the French s. hands more often** les Français se serrent la main plus souvent; **they shook hands on it** ils ont topé; **to s. oneself free (from sth)** se dégager *(de qch)* d'une secousse; *Fig* se dégager *(de qch)*; **to s. sb out of his/her complacency/apathy** faire sortir qn de sa suffisance/son apathie; **to s. the snow from one's head** secouer sa tête pour se débarrasser de la neige; **that has shaken my faith in him** cela a ébranlé la confiance que j'avais en lui; **event that shook the country** événement qui a bouleversé le pays; **she was badly shaken by the accident** elle a été terriblement bouleversée par l'accident; **to feel shaken after a fall** se ressentir d'une chute; *Fam* **that'll s. him!** ça va le choquer!; *Br Fam* **he's won more awards than you can s. a stick at** on lui a décerné une floppé de prix

2 *Austr Sl (rob)* voler

VI 1 trembler; *(of voice)* trembloter, chevroter; **her hand was shaking** sa main tremblait; **the whole building shook** *(after explosion etc)* tout le bâtiment a tremblé; **the door shakes whenever a bus passes** à chaque fois qu'un bus passe, ça fait trembler la porte; **the ground shook** le sol a tremblé; **to s. with fright/rage** trembler *ou* frémir de crainte/colère; **in a voice shaking with emotion** d'une voix émue *ou* tremblotante; *Fam* **to s. in one's shoes** trembler *ou* grelotter de peur, *Fam* trembler dans ses baskets

2 *Fam* **to s. on it** *(shake hands)* toper

N 1 *(act of shaking)* secousse *f*; *(trembling) (of hand, voice etc)* tremblement *m*; *Am (earthquake)* tremblement de terre; **to give**

sth a good s. bien secouer *ou* agiter qch; **to give oneself a s.** se secouer; **a s. of the head** un hochement de tête; *Fam* **to be all of a s.** trembler de tous ses membres; *Fam* **to have the shakes** *(to be trembling) (with fear)* avoir les chocottes; *(with illness, from alcohol)* avoir la tremblote; **with a s. in his voice** d'une voix tremblotante; *Fig* **in two shakes (of a lamb's tail)** en un rien de temps, *Fam* en moins de deux

2 *Culin* **milk s.** milk-shake *m*, *pl* milk-shakes

3 *Fam* **to be no great shakes** ne pas casser des briques, ne pas casser trois pattes à un canard; *Fam* **he is no great shakes as a writer/at German** comme écrivain/en allemand, il ne casse pas des briques

▸ **shake down VT SEP 1** *(cause to fall)* **to s. down apples** *etc* faire tomber des pommes *etc* en secouant l'arbre

2 *Am Fam (extort money from)* **to s. sb down for ten dollars** faire cracher dix dollars à qn

3 *Am Fam (search) (person, apartment etc)* fouiller

VI 1 *(fall) (of fruits etc)* tomber

2 *(settle down) (get used to routine, job)* s'habituer; *Fam* **to s. down (for the night)** se mettre au pieu, se pieuter

▸ **shake off VT SEP 1** *(remove by shaking)* **to s. the dust off sth** secouer la poussière de qch

2 *(get rid of) (illness, cold, depression etc)* se débarrasser de

3 *Fam (escape from) (person)* se débarrasser de; *(other runner)* semer; **I can't s. him off** il ne me lâche pas d'une semelle; **she's always phoning me up, I can't s. her off** elle me téléphone sans cesse, je n'arrive pas à m'en débarrasser

▸ **shake out VT SEP 1** *(remove dust from) (rug, tablecloth etc)* secouer; *(empty) (bag)* vider en le secouant

2 *(remove by shaking) (dirt, sand etc)* faire sortir en secouant; **he picked up his shoes and shook the sand out** il a ramassé ses chaussures et en a secoué le sable

3 *(unfurl) (sail, flag)* déferler

▸ **shake up VT SEP 1** *(mix by shaking) (liquid, container etc)* secouer; **don't s. the lemonade up** ne secoue pas la limonade

2 *(plump up) (pillow etc)* secouer

3 *(upset) (person)* secouer; **she looks pretty shaken up** elle a l'air assez secouée; **he was badly shaken up after the accident** l'accident lui a fait un coup

4 *(arouse from indifference etc)* secouer; **he needs shaking up** il a besoin qu'on le secoue

shakedown ['ʃeɪkdaʊn] **N 1** *Am Fam (extortion)* chantage *m*, extorsion *f* **2** *Am Fam (search)* fouille *f* **3** *Fam (improvised bed)* lit *m* de fortune

Shaker ['ʃeɪkər] **N** *Rel* = membre *m* d'une secte protestante du XVIIIᵉ siècle, aujourd'hui presque disparue, qui prêchait le célibat

shaker ['ʃeɪkər] **N** **sugar s.** saupoudreuse *f* *(pour le sucre)*; **salad s.** panier *m* à salade; **cocktail s.** shaker *m*

Shakespearian, Shakespearean [ʃeɪks-'pɪərɪən] **ADJ** shakespearien

shake-up **N** *Fam (of staff)* remaniement *m*

shakily ['ʃeɪkɪlɪ] **ADV** *(to walk)* à pas chancelants; *(to write)* d'une main tremblante; *(to speak)* d'une voix chevrotante

shakiness ['ʃeɪkɪnɪs] **N** *(of building, chair etc)* manque *m* de stabilité *ou* de solidité; *(of person, health, knowledge)* faiblesse *f*; *(of hand)* tremblement *m*; *(of voice)* chevrotement *m*; *(of position)* précarité *f*

shaking ['ʃeɪkɪŋ] **N** *Med* tremblement *m*

shako ['ʃækəʊ] **N** *Mil (headgear)* s(c)hako *m*

shaky ['ʃeɪkɪ] **ADJ** *(furniture etc)* branlant, peu solide; *(health)* faible, chancelant; *(position)* précaire; *(hand)* tremblant, vacillant;

(writing) tremblé; *(voice)* mal assuré; *(knowledge)* pas très sûr; **to be s. on one's legs** or *Fam* **one's pins** ne pas tenir sur ses jambes *ou Fam* quilles; **I feel very s.** *(I am trembling)* je suis tout tremblant; *(I feel unsteady on my feet)* je ne me sens pas bien solide sur mes jambes; *(I feel rather unwell)* je suis patraque *ou* tout chose; **his English is s.** il est faible en anglais

shale [ʃeɪl] N *Geol* schiste *m* argileux *ou* ardoiseux, argile *f* schisteuse
▸▸ **s. oil** huile *f* de schiste

shall VOIR GRAMMAIRE A58; B39 *(stressed* [ʃæl], *unstressed* [ʃəl]) MODAL AUX V *(pr* **shall**; *pt, cond* **should** *stressed* [ʃʊd], *unstressed* [ʃəd], *Arch* **shouldst** [ʃʊdst]; *no other parts;* **shall not** *and* **should not** *are often contracted to* **shan't** [ʃɑ:nt], **shouldn't** [ʃʊd(ə)nt]) **1** *(with full meaning, denotes duty or command) Fml* **he s. do it if I order it** il sera obligé de le faire si je le lui ordonne; **he s. not do it** je lui interdis de le faire; **he says he won't do it – he s.!** il dit qu'il ne le fera pas – je l'ordonne!; **you** shall **do it!** vous le ferez, je le veux!; *Law* **ships s. carry three lights** les navires sont tenus de porter trois feux
2 *(making suggestion, asking permission)* **s. I open the window?** voulez-vous que j'ouvre la fenêtre?; **I'll make some coffee, s. I?** je vais faire du café, d'accord?; **let's go in, s. we?** rentrons, voulez-vous?
3 *(future)* **you shan't have any!** tu n'en auras pas!; **you s. pay for this!** vous me le payerez!; **tomorrow I s. go and he will arrive** demain, moi je partirai et lui il arrivera; **will you be there? – I s.** y serez-vous? – oui(, j'y serai); **will you be there? – no, I s. not** or **I shan't** y serez-vous? – non(, je n'y serai pas); **I s. explain the situation to you and you will listen** je vais vous expliquer la situation et vous allez m'écouter; **as we s. see** comme nous le verrons, comme nous allons le voir VOIR GRAMMAIRE A50–1; A78

shallot [ʃəˈlɒt] N échalote *f*

shallow [ˈʃæləʊ] ADJ **1** *(water, dish etc)* peu profond; *(soil)* superficiel; **s.-rooted** *(tree)* à enracinement superficiel; **s. breathing** respiration *f* faible; **the s. end** *(of swimming pool)* le petit bain **2** *Fig (superficial) (person, mind etc)* superficiel; *(friendship)* de surface
▸▸ *Cin, TV* **s. focus** faible profondeur *f* de champ

shallowness [ˈʃæləʊnɪs] N **1** *(of water, dish etc)* peu *m* de profondeur **2** *Fig (of person, mind)* caractère *m* superficiel, superficialité *f*

shallows [ˈʃæləʊz] NPL *(in sea etc)* bas-fond *m, pl* bas-fonds, haut-fond *m, pl* hauts-fonds

shalt [ʃælt] 2ND PERS SING MODAL AUX V *Bible, Arch* **thou s. not kill** tu ne tueras point

shaly [ˈʃeɪlɪ] ADJ schisteux

sham [ʃæm] ADJ faux, *f* fausse, truqué; *(illness etc)* simulé, feint; *(piety)* apparent; **s. peace** paix *f* de pacotille
N feinte *f*, trompe-l'œil *m inv; Fam* chiqué *m*; **it was nothing but a s.** c'était du chiqué; **that's all s.** *Fam* tout ça, c'est de la frime; **he's a s.** c'est un imposteur; **you big s., you're not sad at all!** espèce de comédien, tu n'es pas triste du tout!; **the elections were a s.** les élections n'étaient qu'une imposture
VT (-mm-) feindre, simuler; **to s. sickness** faire semblant d'être malade
VI **he's only shamming** c'est une comédie qu'il nous joue, il fait semblant

shaman [ˈʃæmən] N chaman *m*

shamanism [ˈʃæmənɪz(ə)m] N chamanisme *m*

shamanistic [ʃæməˈnɪstɪk] ADJ relatif au chamanisme

shamateur [ˈʃæmətɜ:r] N *Sport Fam* = athlète *etc* prétendument amateur mais qui, en réalité, perçoit de l'argent

shamble [ˈʃæmb(ə)l] VI **to s. (along)** aller à pas traînants; **to s. up to sb** approcher qn d'un pas traînant

shambles [ˈʃæmb(ə)lz] NPL *(usu with sing verb) (disorder)* désordre *m*, fouillis *m*; *(department, company, accounts)* foutoir *m*; *(reception)* désastre *m*; **what a s.!** quelle pagaille!; **it's a bloody s.!** quel foutoir!; **the match was a s.** le match était totalement nul; **the cupboard was in a s.** le placard était rangé n'importe comment

shambolic [ʃæmˈbɒlɪk] ADJ *Fam* bordélique

shame [ʃeɪm] N **1** *(disgrace, guilt etc)* honte *f*, **hooligans are the s. of our country** les hooligans sont la honte de notre pays; **to bring s. on one's family/country** faire honte à sa famille/son pays; *also Fig* **to put sb to s.** faire honte à qn; **to my s.** à ma grande honte; **s. (up)on you!** quelle honte!; **for s.!** vous n'avez pas honte!; **he hid his face in s.** il s'est caché la face de honte; **to blush for** or **with s.** rougir de honte; **without s.** effronté, éhonté; **she is utterly without s.** elle n'a aucune pudeur; **to be past all s., to be lost to all s.** avoir perdu toute honte; **to have no s.** *(no scruples)* n'avoir aucune honte; **have you no s.?** tu n'as pas honte?; **six cakes! have you no s.?** six gâteaux! tu n'as pas honte?
2 *(pity)* dommage *m*; **it would be a s. to ... il** serait dommage de ...; **it's a s. you can't come** c'est dommage que vous ne puissiez pas venir; **what a s.!** quel dommage!; *Parl* **s.!** = cri *m* des députés anglais à la Chambre des communes pour manifester leur désapprobation ou leur indignation
VT *(cause to feel ashamed)* faire honte à; *(bring shame on)* couvrir de honte; **to be shamed into doing sth** faire qch par amour-propre; **they tried to s. her into donating more** ils ont essayé de lui faire honte pour qu'elle donne davantage

shamefaced [ˈʃeɪmfeɪst] ADJ *(ashamed)* (à l'air) honteux; *(embarrassed)* embarrassé, décontenancé

shamefacedly [ʃeɪmˈfeɪsɪdlɪ] ADV d'un air honteux; *(with embarrassment)* d'un air embarrassé

shameful [ˈʃeɪmfʊl] ADJ honteux, scandaleux

shamefully [ˈʃeɪmfəlɪ] ADV honteusement, scandaleusement; **they've been s. neglected** ils ont été honteusement négligés; **he was s. ignorant about the issue** son ignorance sur la question était honteuse

shamefulness [ˈʃeɪmfʊlnɪs] N honte *f*, infamie *f*

shameless [ˈʃeɪmlɪs] ADJ **1** *(without shame) (person, conduct)* éhonté, effronté; **he was quite s. about it all** il ne montrait aucun scrupule; *usu Hum* **a s. (little) hussy** une diablesse **2** *(immodest) (person)* sans pudeur, dévergondé; *(conduct)* impudique

shamelessly [ˈʃeɪmlɪslɪ] ADV **1** *(without shame)* effrontément **2** *(immodestly) (to carry on, have affair etc)* avec impudeur

shamelessness [ˈʃeɪmlɪsnɪs] N **1** *(lack of shame)* effronterie *f* **2** *(sexual immodesty)* impudeur *f*, *(of conduct)* impudicité *f*

shaming [ˈʃeɪmɪŋ] ADJ humiliant

shammy [ˈʃæmɪ] N *(leather)* peau *f* de chamois
▸▸ **s. leather** peau de chamois

shampoo [ʃæmˈpu:] N shampo(o)ing *m*; li**quid/dry s.** shampo(o)ing liquide/sec; **carpet s.** shampo(o)ing pour moquette; **to give sb a s.** faire un shampo(o)ing à qn; **s. and set** shampo(o)ing et mise en plis
VT **to s. one's hair** se faire un shampo(o)ing; **to s. sb** or **sb's hair** faire un shampo(o)ing à

qn; **to s. a carpet** shampouiner une moquette

shamrock [ˈʃæmrɒk] N *(plant)* trèfle *m*; **the land of the s.** = l'Irlande *f*

shamus [ˈʃeɪməs] N *Am Fam* (détective *m*) privé *m*

shandy [ˈʃændɪ], *Am* **shandygaff** [ˈʃændɪgæf] N panaché *m*; **a lager s.** un panaché à la bière blonde

Shanghai [ʃæŋˈhaɪ] N Shanghai *m*, Changhai *m*

shanghai [ʃæŋˈhaɪ] VT *Naut Fam* **to s. sb** embarquer qn de force sur un navire à court d'équipage; *Fig* **to s. sb into doing sth** *(force)* forcer qn à faire qch

Shangri-La [ʃæŋgrɪˈlɑː] N paradis *m* terrestre

shank [ʃæŋk] N **1** *Culin (of beef)* jarret *m*; *(of horse's leg)* canon *m* **2** *(of key, rivet)* tige *f*, *Typ (of letter)* corps *m*, tige; *Naut (of anchor)* verge *f* **3** *Am Fam (knife)* surin *m*, lame *f*

Shanks [ʃæŋks] N *Fam* **to go** or **ride on S.'s pony** y aller à pinces

shan't CONTR = shall not, *see* shall

shantung [ʃænˈtʌŋ] N *Tex* shant(o)ung *m*

shanty¹ [ˈʃæntɪ] N *(hut)* bicoque *f*, cabane *f*
▸▸ **s. town** bidonville *m*

shanty² N *Naut (sea)* **s.** chanson *f* de marin

SHAPE [ʃeɪp] N *Mil (abbr* **Supreme Headquarters Allied Powers, Europe)** quartier *m* général des forces alliées de l'OTAN en Europe

SHAPE [ʃeɪp] N **1** *(form)* forme *f*, **what s. is it?** de quelle forme est-ce?; **they were the same s.** ils étaient de la même forme, ils avaient la même forme; **a cake in the s. of a ...** un gâteau en forme de ...; **oblong/triangular in s.** de forme oblongue/triangulaire; **spherical in s., of spherical s.** de forme sphérique; **trees of all shapes** des arbres de toutes les formes; **my hat was knocked out of s.** mon chapeau a été déformé; **to get out of s., to lose (its) s.** se déformer; **to mould sth into s.** donner forme à qch; *Journ et Fam* **to knock an article into s.** mettre un article au point; *Fam* **to knock** or **lick a team into s.** faire quelque chose d'une équipe; **to give s. to a plan** donner corps à un projet; **to take s.** prendre forme *ou* tournure; **this is the s. of things to come** c'est ça l'avenir, *esp Pej* voilà ce qui nous attend; **progress, in the s. of motorways/supermarkets** le progrès que représentent les autoroutes/les supermarchés; **wealth in the s. of a large house** la richesse symbolisée par la possession d'une grande maison; **no communication in any s. or form** aucune communication de quelque forme que ce soit; **something in the s. of ...** une espèce *ou* une sorte de ...; **help arrived in the s. of ...** l'aide est arrivée sous la forme de ...
2 *(condition)* **to keep in/get back into s.** *(physically)* garder/retrouver la forme; **to be in good/poor s.** *(of person etc)* être en bonne/petite forme; *Fam* **she was in pretty bad s.** *(very ill, badly injured)* elle était mal en point *ou* dans un sale état; **what sort of s. is he in?** *(after accident, ordeal)* dans quel état est-il?; **he's in no s. to be doing this kind of work!** il n'est pas en état de faire ce genre de travail!
3 *(figure, human figure)* forme *f*, **two shapes loomed up in the darkness** deux formes surgirent dans l'obscurité
VT *(clay etc)* façonner, modeler; *(block of stone etc)* tailler; *Fig (plan)* former; **to s. sth out of sth** façonner qch avec qch; **to s. the clay into an urn** donner à l'argile la forme d'une urne; **to s. sb's character** façonner le caractère de qn; **to s. the destiny of man** diriger *ou* régler la destinée de l'homme; **to**

s. the course of public opinion manipuler l'opinion publique; **the war shaped her perception of the army** la guerre a influencé sa perception de l'armée
VI = shape up 1
▸ **shape up VI 1** *(turn out)* **to s. up well** promettre; *(of affair)* prendre bonne tournure; **let's see how he shapes up in his new job** voyons comment il va s'en tirer dans son nouvel emploi; **the new player is shaping up well** le nouveau joueur promet beaucoup; *esp Am Fam* **s. up or ship out!** secouez-vous, sinon c'est la porte!
2 *(prepare to tackle)* **to s. up to a problem/situation** s'attaquer à un problème/faire face à une situation

shaped [ʃeɪpt] **ADJ 1** façonné, taillé; *(in metalwork) (piece)* profilé, embouti **2 well-/badly s.** bien/mal formé; **an awkwardly s. room** une pièce de forme bizarre; **s. like an egg** en forme d'œuf

-shaped [ʃeɪpt] **SUFF egg/heart/etc -s.** en forme d'œuf/de cœur/etc

shapeless [ˈʃeɪplɪs] **ADJ** informe

shapelessness [ˈʃeɪplɪsnɪs] **N** manque *m* de forme

shapeliness [ˈʃeɪplɪnɪs] **N** *(of woman)* beauté *f* de forme, belles proportions *fpl*; *(of legs)* galbe *m*

shapely [ˈʃeɪplɪ] **ADJ** bien fait; **a s. leg** une jambe bien galbée; **to be s.** *(of woman)* être bien faite *ou Fam* bien roulée

shaper [ˈʃeɪpər] **N** *(who creates projects etc)* personne *f* qui lance des projets

shaping [ˈʃeɪpɪŋ] **N** *(of block of stone etc)* façonnement *m*, façonnage *m*; **the s. of his character** le développement *ou* la formation de son caractère; **the s. of a policy** la conception d'une politique

shard [ʃɑːd] **N** *(of pottery)* tesson *m*

SHARE [ʃeər] **N 1** *(part)* part *f*; **in equal shares** en parts égales; **to have a s. in sth** participer à qch; **to have a s. in the profits** participer aux bénéfices; **you had a s. in this** *(you are partly responsible)* vous y êtes pour quelque chose; *(you contributed)* votre participation a été importante; **I had no s. in this decision** je n'ai aucune responsabilité dans cette décision; **to come in for a s. of the blame** être reconnu responsable; **to take a s. of the profits** prendre sa part des bénéfices; **to take a s. of the blame** reconnaître sa part de responsabilité; **the lion's s.** la part du lion; **s. in profits** *(participation)* participation *f* aux bénéfices; *(amount)* tantième *m*; **to give sb a s. of the profits** donner à qn une part des bénéfices; *Fam* **to go shares** partager (with avec); *Fam* **I went half shares with him** *(in buying sth)* on l'a acheté à deux; **(fair) s.** part équitable; **I'm entitled to a fair s. of the profits** j'ai droit à ma part des bénéfices; **I've had my s. of worries** j'ai eu mon lot de soucis; **she's had more than her (fair) s. of problems** elle a eu largement son lot de problèmes; *Fam* **we've had more than our fair s. of rain and then some** question pluie, nous avons été servis; *Law* **legal s.** *(of inheritance)* réserve *f* légale; **to pay one's s.** payer sa (quote-)part; **to do one's s., to take** *or* **bear one's s. of the burden** participer; **he doesn't do his s.** il ne fait pas sa part; **to have a s. in an undertaking** avoir un intérêt *ou* être intéressé dans une entreprise
2 *Fin* action *f*, titre *m*; **to hold** *or* **have shares** détenir des actions, être actionnaire; **to have shares in a company** détenir des actions dans une société; **to own 51% of the shares** détenir 51% du capital
3 *Agr (of plough)* soc *m* (de charrue)
VT partager; **to s. sth with sb** partager qch

avec qn; **to s. a bathroom** *(of tenants)* partager une salle de bain; **a shared bathroom** une salle de bain commune; **to s. sb's opinion** partager l'avis de qn; **to s. one's ideas/impressions with sb** partager des idées/impressions avec qn; *Iron* **thank you very much for sharing that with me!** c'est vachement intéressant ce que tu dis!; **he shares all his secrets with me** il me fait part de tous ses secrets; **they s. an interest in music** ils s'intéressent tous les deux à la musique
VI partager; **to s. and s. alike** partager équitablement; **to s. in sth** *(in blame, praise etc)* partager qch; **to s. in the profits** participer aux *ou* avoir part aux bénéfices; **to s. in sb's grief/happiness** partager la douleur/le bonheur de qn
▸▸ *Fin* **s. account** compte-titres *m, pl* comptes-titres; *Fin* **s. capital** capital-actions *m, pl* capitaux-actions; *Fin* **s. certificate** certificat *m ou* titre d'actions; *St Exch* **s. dealing** opérations *fpl* de Bourse, négoce *m* de titres; *St Exch* **s. index** indice *m* boursier; **s. issue** émission *f* d'actions; **s. market** marché *m* des valeurs mobilières; **s. option** possibilité *f* d'acheter des actions; *Fin* **s. option scheme** plan *m* de participation par achat d'actions; **s. owner** détenteur, -trice d'actions; **s. ownership** actionnariat *m*; **s. point** point *m* de part de marché; *St Exch* **s. price index** indice des cours d'actions
▸ **share out VT SEP** *(loot etc)* partager, distribuer, répartir; *(work)* répartir, distribuer

sharecropper [ˈʃeəkrɒpər] **N** *Agr* métayer, -ère

sharecropping [ˈʃeəkrɒpɪŋ] **N** *Agr* métayage *m*

shareholder [ˈʃeəhəʊldər] **N** *Fin* actionnaire *mf*; **the shareholders** l'actionnariat *m*, les actionnaires; **minority/majority s.** actionnaire minoritaire/majoritaire; **small s.** petit porteur *m*; **shareholders' funds** capitaux *mpl* propres, haut *m* de bilan; **shareholders' meeting** réunion *f ou* assemblée *f* des actionnaires

shareholding [ˈʃeəhəʊldɪŋ] **N** *Fin (shares)* participation *f*, *(share ownership)* actionnariat *m*

share-out N partage *m*, répartition *f*

shareware [ˈʃeəweər] **N** *Comput* shareware *m*, logiciel *m* en libre essai, logiciel contributif
▸▸ **s. programs** sharewares *mpl*

sharing [ˈʃeərɪŋ] **N 1** *(of loot, property etc)* distribution *f*, partage *m* **2** *(participation)* participation *f*, partage *m*; **profit s.** participation aux bénéfices

shark [ʃɑːk] **N 1** *(fish)* requin *m* **2** *Fam (ruthless person)* requin *m* **3** *Am Fam (talented person)* as *m*; **to be a s. at math** être calé en maths, être une bête en maths

sharkskin [ˈʃɑːkskɪn] **N** peau *f* de requin

sharp [ʃɑːp] **ADJ 1** *(knife, edge)* tranchant, affilé; *(spear, tooth, point)* aigu, f aiguë, pointu
2 *(features etc)* anguleux, tiré; *(peak etc)* pointu; *(angle)* saillant, aigu, f aiguë; *(curve)* prononcé, *(ascent, descent)* raide; *(roof)* pointu, en pointe; *(turning)* brusque; *(outline, focus), Phot (image)* net, f nette; *Fig* **to be at the s. end** être en première ligne; **s. rise/drop in prices** forte *ou* nette hausse/baisse des prix; **s. contrast** contraste marqué *ou* net; **this accident brings into s. relief the need for extra precautions** cet accident démontre à quel point il est nécessaire de prendre des précautions supplémentaires
3 *(sight)* perçant; *(hearing)* fin; *(cunning, shrewd)* rusé, malin; *(unscrupulous)* peu scrupuleux; **to have a s. mind** avoir l'esprit

vif; **he's as s. as a needle** *(quick to understand)* il a l'esprit vif; *(cunning)* il est malin comme un singe; **s. practice(s)** procédés indélicats *ou* peu honnêtes
4 *(wind)* vif, f vive, perçant; *(cold)* pénétrant, piquant; **it's a bit s. this morning** il fait frisquet ce matin; **a s. frost** une forte gelée; **s. pain** douleur aiguë
5 *(fast)* rapide; *(trot)* vif, f vive
6 *(harsh) (voice, words)* cinglant; *(person)* brusque; **to make a s. retort** *(to reply in a sharp tone)* répondre d'une voix cassante; *(to make a cutting reply)* répondre de façon cinglante; **a s. reproof** une verte réprimande; **in a s. tone** d'un ton brusque; **a s. tongue** une langue acérée *ou* caustique
7 *(taste)* âpre, piquant; *(sauce)* piquant; *(apple etc)* acide; *(wine)* vert
8 *(sound)* perçant, aigu, f aiguë
9 *Mus (note)* dièse; **you're s.** *(to singer)* vous chantez trop aigu; *(to violinist)* vous jouez trop aigu; **a semitone s.** un demi-ton trop haut
10 *Fam (in dress)* classe *inv*; **to be a s. dresser** s'habiller classe
N *Mus* dièse *m*; **double s.** double dièse *m*
ADV 1 s. pointed pencil crayon taillé fin; **s. edged** *(knife etc)* tranchant, affilé **2** *(to turn)* brusquement, court; **turn s. right** prenez à angle droit; **the road turns s. right** la route fait un virage serré à droite **3** *(punctually)* **at four o'clock s.** à quatre heures sonnantes *ou* précises *ou Fam* tapantes **4** *Fam* **look s.!** dépêchez-vous!, remuez-vous! **5** *Mus (to sing, play)* trop aigu

sharpen [ˈʃɑːp(ə)n] **VT 1** *(knife, tool etc)* affiler, aiguiser; *(stick etc)* tailler en pointe, aiguiser; *(pencil)* tailler; *(angle)* rendre plus saillant; *(feature, contrast)* accentuer; **to s. its claws** *(of cat etc)* faire ses griffes **2 to s. sb's wits** éveiller l'esprit de qn, *Fam* dégourdir qn **3** *(pain, animosity)* aviver; *(passion, desire)* exciter; *(of walk etc) (appetite)* aiguiser, ouvrir **4 to s. one's voice** prendre un ton plus acerbe *ou* âpre **5** *Culin (sauce)* donner du piquant à **6** *Mus (note)* diéser
VI 1 *(of faculties etc)* s'aiguiser **2** *(of tone)* devenir plus acerbe *ou* âpre **3** *(of sound)* devenir plus perçant *ou* aigu, f aiguë

sharpener [ˈʃɑːp(ə)nər] **N** *(device)* aiguisoir *m*; **(knife) s.** aiguisoir *m* (pour couteaux); **(pencil) s.** taille-crayon *m, pl* taille-crayon(s)

sharpening [ˈʃɑːp(ə)nɪŋ] **N** *(of tool etc)* affilage *m*, aiguisage *m*

sharper [ˈʃɑːpər] **N** escroc *m*; *Cards* tricheur, -euse

sharp-eyed ADJ *(good at finding things)* à qui rien n'échappe; *(keen-sighted)* à la vue perçante

sharply [ˈʃɑːplɪ] **ADV 1 s. pointed** très pointu **2 this contrasts s. with ...** ceci contraste nettement avec ...; **in s. focus** net; **to bring sth s. home, to bring sth s. into focus** faire apparaître qch de façon évidente **3** *(to drop, descend, brake)* brusquement; *(to turn)* brusquement, court; **he looked up s. when I mentioned her name** il a brusquement levé les yeux lorsque j'ai mentionné son nom **4** *(to reprimand)* sévèrement; *(to reply)* d'un ton brusque; **he looked s. at her** *(angrily, warning etc)* il l'a regardée sévèrement; *(trying to understand)* il l'a regardée d'un œil pénétrant

sharpness [ˈʃɑːpnɪs] **N 1** *(of knife edge etc)* tranchant *m*; *(of contours, photograph)* netteté *f*; *(of contrast)* caractère *m* marqué; **s. of focus** *(of photo)* netteté *f*; *(of analysis etc)* précision *f*; *Aut etc* **s. of the turn** raideur *f* du virage **2** *(of mind, hearing)* finesse *f*, *(of child)* intelligence *f*; **s. of sight** acuité *f* visuelle **3** *(of pain)* violence *f*; **there's a s. in**

the air il fait frisquet **4** *(of tone, reprimand)* sévérité *f*, âpreté *f*; *(of tone)* brusquerie *f*; *(of character, voice)* aspérité *f* **5** *(taste) (of sauce)* piquant *m*; *(of apple etc)* acidité *f* **6** *(of sound)* acuité *f*, qualité *f* perçante

sharpshooter ['ʃɑːpʃuːtər] N *Mil* tireur, -euse d'élite

sharp-sighted ADJ *(keen-sighted)* à la vue perçante; *(observant)* observateur, -trice

sharp-tongued ['ʃɑːpˈtʌŋd] ADJ caustique

sharp-witted ADJ vif, *f* vive

shatter ['ʃætər] VT **1** *(smash)* fracasser, briser en éclats; *(bone)* briser en plusieurs morceaux **2** *(hopes)* briser, renverser; *(silence)* rompre **3** *(health, nerves)* détraquer; *Fam* **I was absolutely shattered!** *(stunned)* j'ai été scié!; *(exhausted)* j'étais complètement crevé!
▶ VI se briser (en éclats), se fracasser; **the windscreen shattered** le pare-brise a volé en éclats

shattering ['ʃætərɪŋ] ADJ *(blow)* écrasant; **s. news** des nouvelles renversantes

shatterproof ['ʃætəpruːf] ADJ *(glass, windscreen)* feuilleté

shave [ʃeɪv] VT **1** *(face, legs etc)* raser; *(remove hair from face of) (person)* faire la barbe à; **to s. sb's head** raser la tête à qn; **to s. one's legs** s'épiler les jambes **2** *(wood)* planer; *(corner)* rogner; **to s. prices** rogner les prix **3** *(brush against)* effleurer
▶ VI se raser; **to start shaving** *(of boy)* commencer à se raser
▶ N **1** *(of face, legs etc)* rasage *m*; **to have a s.** se raser; *(be shaved)* se faire raser; **this razor gives you a really close s.** avec ce rasoir, vous pouvez vraiment vous raser de près; *Fam* **that was a close s.!** vous l'avez/il a etc échappé belle!, il était moins une! **2** *(tool)* plane *f*, racloir *m*
▶ **shave off** VT SEP **to s. off one's moustache** se raser la moustache; **to s. off a piece of cheese/sausage** couper une mince tranche de fromage/saucisson; **you'll need to s. a bit more off the drawer** il faut raboter un peu plus le tiroir; **this has shaved a few points off the government's lead in the polls** cela a légèrement rogné l'avance du gouvernement dans les sondages

shaven ['ʃeɪv(ə)n] ADJ *(monk)* tonsuré; *(head, chin)* rasé; **clean s.** *(man)* sans barbe ni moustache; *(face)* glabre

shaver ['ʃeɪvər] N **1** **(electric) s.** rasoir *m* électrique **2** *Old-fashioned Fam* **(young) s.** *(lad)* gosse *m*, gamin *m*
▶▶ **s. socket** prise *f* pour rasoir électrique

Shavian ['ʃeɪvɪən] N admirateur, -trice de George Bernard Shaw
▶ ADJ *(of Shaw)* de George Bernard Shaw; *(like Shaw)* à la George Bernard Shaw

shaving ['ʃeɪvɪŋ] N **1** *(act)* rasage *f* **2** *(small piece shaved off) (of wood, metal)* copeau *m*
▶▶ **s. brush** blaireau *m*; **s. cream** crème *f* à raser; **s. foam** mousse *f* à raser; **s. mirror** miroir *m* à raser; **s. soap** savon *m* à barbe; **s. stick** *(bâton m de)* savon à barbe

shawl [ʃɔːl] N châle *m*

she [ʃiː] PERS PRON VOIR GRAMMAIRE A27–8 **1** elle; *(of ship)* il; **s. was running** elle courait; **what's s. doing?** qu'est-ce qu'elle fait?; **here s. comes!** la voici (qui vient)!; **s. sails at ten o'clock** *(of ship)* il part à dix heures; **s.'s had it, this old car** elle est bonne pour la casse, cette vieille voiture **2** *(stressed)* elle; **s. and I** elle et moi; **she knows nothing about it** elle n'en sait rien, elle; *esp Lit* **s. of whom you speak** celle dont vous parlez
▶ N *Fam* femelle; **it's a s.** *(of newborn child)* c'est une petite fille; *(of animal)* c'est une femelle

she- [ʃiː] PREF **s.-ass** ânesse *f*; **s.-bear** ours *m*

femelle, ourse *f*; **s.-cat** chatte *f*; **s.-devil** diablesse *f*

sheaf [ʃiːf] *pl* **sheaves** [ʃiːf, ʃiːvz] N *(of corn etc)* gerbe *f*; *(of papers)* liasse *f*; **I had a whole s. of letters this morning** j'ai reçu toute une pile de lettres ce matin

shear [ʃɪər] *(pt* **sheared**; *pp* **shorn** [ʃɔːn], **sheared)** VT **1** *(sheep etc)* tondre; *Fig* **to be shorn of sth** être dépouillé *ou* privé de qch **2** *(cut) (branch etc)* couper; **to s. through sth** trancher qch **3** *Phys etc* cisailler
▶ VI *(of material)* se fendre
▶ **shear off** VI se détacher

shearer ['ʃɪərər] N **1** *(person) (of sheep)* tondeur, -euse **2** *(machine) (for sheep)* tondeuse *f*

shearing ['ʃɪərɪŋ] N **1** *(of sheep)* tonte *f* **2** **shearings** *(of wool)* tontes *fpl*

shears [ʃɪəz] N *(pair of)* **s.** *(large scissors)* cisaille(s) *f(pl)*; *(for sheep, at hairdresser)* tondeuse *f*, **(garden) s.** sécateur *m*; *Sewing etc* **pinking s.** ciseaux *mpl* à denteler VOIR GRAMMAIRE A10

sheath [ʃiːθ] N *(pl* [ʃiːðz, ʃiːθs]) *(protective sleeve)* manchon *m* protecteur; *(for sword, umbrella etc)* fourreau *m*; *(for scissors)* étui *m*; *(for knife, electric cable)* gaine *f*, *Anat (of organ)* enveloppe *f*, *(of muscle)* gaine; *Bot* gaine; *(contraceptive)* **s.** préservatif *m*
▶▶ **s. dress** *(robe f)* fourreau *m*; **s. knife** couteau *m* à gaine

sheathe [ʃiːð] VT **1** *(sword etc)* (re)mettre au fourreau, rengainer; *(knife etc)* engainer; **sheathed in** gainé de **2** *Elec (cable)* gainer

sheathing ['ʃiːðɪŋ] N *Elec (sheath) (of cable)* gaine *f*

sheave [ʃiːv] VT *(corn etc)* mettre en gerbes

Sheba ['ʃiːbə] N **the Queen of S.** la reine de Saba

shebang [ʃɪ'bæŋ] N *Sl* **the whole s.** tout le bazar

shebeen [ʃɪ'biːn] N *Dial Irish* débit *m* de boissons clandestin

shed¹ [ʃed] N *(larger)* hangar *m*; *(smaller)* remise *f*, **lean-to s.** appentis *m*; **(garden) s.** cabane *f* de jardin; *Rail* **(engine) s.** remise de locomotives; **tool s.** cabane à outils; **bicycle s.** *(small)* remise à vélo; *(big)* hangar à vélo; **cattle s.** étable *f*

shed² *(pt, pp* **shed**; *prp* **shedding)** VT **1** *(drop, get rid of) (leaves, teeth, skin, horns etc)* perdre; *(of lorry etc) (load)* renverser; **snakes s. their skin** les serpents muent; **its feathers s. water** l'eau lui glisse sur les plumes; **to s. its leaves** *(of plant)* s'effeuiller; **to s. jobs** supprimer des emplois; **to s. labour** licencier de la main-d'œuvre; *Elec* **to s. the load** délester; **he s. 20 pounds in a month** il a perdu neuf kilos en un mois; **to s. one's clothes** se dépouiller de ses vêtements **2** *(spill) (tears, blood)* répandre, verser; *(light)* diffuser; **before more blood is s.** avant que davantage de sang ne soit versé; *Fig* **to s. light on sth** faire *ou* jeter la lumière sur qch
▶ VI *(of cat)* perdre ses poils

she'd [ʃiːd] CONTR **1** = she had, *see* have² **2** = she would, *see* will³

shedding ['ʃedɪŋ] N **1** *(of leaves, teeth etc)* perte *f*, chute *f*, *Elec* **load s.** délestage *m* **2** *(of blood)* effusion *f*

shedload ['ʃedləʊd] N *Br Fam* **a s. of, shedloads of** une tapée de; **she earns a s.** *or* shedloads of dosh elle se fait un fric fou

sheen [ʃiːn] N reflet *m*; **hair with a golden s.** cheveux aux reflets d'or; *Fig* **to take the s. off sb's reputation/image** ternir la réputation/l'image de qn

sheep [ʃiːp] N *(inv in pl)* mouton *m*; *Fig* **the black s. (of the family** *etc*)** la brebis galeuse; *Fig* **lost** *or* **stray s.** brebis perdue *ou* égarée;

they follow one another like s. ce sont des moutons de Panurge; *Fig* **to separate the s. from the goats** *or* **the s. and the goats** séparer les brebis d'avec les boucs; **to make s.'s eyes at sb** faire les yeux doux à qn
▶▶ **s. farmer** éleveur, -euse de moutons; **s. farming** élevage *m* de moutons; **s. pen** parc *m* à moutons; **s. shearer** *(person)* tondeur, -euse; *(machine)* tondeuse *f* mécanique; **s. shearing** tonte *f*

sheep-dip N **1** *(place)* enclos *m* *(avec bain désinfectant)* **2** *(disinfectant)* bain *m* désinfectant *(pour les moutons)*

sheepdog ['ʃiːpdɒg] N *(chien m de)* berger *m*; **Old English s.** berger *m* anglais sans queue
▶▶ **s. trials** concours *m* de chiens de berger

sheepfold ['ʃiːpfəʊld] N parc *m* à moutons

sheepish ['ʃiːpɪʃ] ADJ *(embarrassed)* penaud; **to look s.** rester penaud

sheepishly ['ʃiːpɪʃlɪ] ADV d'un air penaud

sheepishness ['ʃiːpɪʃnɪs] N *(embarrassment)* air *m* penaud

sheepskin ['ʃiːpskɪn] N **1** *(skin)* peau *f* de mouton; *(jacket)* canadienne *f*, veste *f* en peau lainée **2** *esp Am (diploma)* diplôme *m*
▶▶ **s. jacket** canadienne, veste en peau lainée

sheer ADJ **1** *(pure)* pur, véritable; **this accident was caused by s. carelessness** c'est la négligence et elle seule qui est à l'origine de l'accident; **that's s. carelessness!** c'est la négligence pure et simple!; **it's s. madness** *or* **lunacy** *or* **folly** c'est de la folie pure (et simple), c'est de la pure folie; **with a look of s. disbelief** avec un air d'incrédulité absolue; **a s. waste of time** une pure perte de temps; **out of s. malice** par pure méchanceté; **it was s. stupidity** c'était franchement stupide; **in s. desperation, she wrote to him** en désespoir de cause, elle lui écrivit; **by s. chance** tout à fait par hasard; **by s. necessity** par pure nécessité
2 *(perpendicular) (cliff, path etc)* perpendiculaire, à pic, abrupt, escarpé
3 *Tex* fin, transparent; **s. silk stockings** bas *mpl* de soie extra-fins
▶ ADV **1** *(completely) (crazy)* complètement; **this goes s. against everything I've ever been taught** ceci va complètement à l'encontre de tout ce qu'on m'a toujours appris; **the tree was torn s. out by the roots** l'arbre a été littéralement déraciné
2 *(to drop etc)* perpendiculairement, à pic, à plomb
▶ VI *Naut* embarder, faire une embardée
▶ **sheer away** VI *(move away) (of vehicle, boat)* faire une embardée; *Fam* **to s. away from a subject** éviter un sujet

sheesh [ʃiːʃ] INT *Fam (in surprise)* tiens!; *(in exasperation)* allez!

sheet [ʃiːt] N **1** *(on bed)* drap *m*; **fitted s.** drap-housse *m*, *pl* draps-housses; *Fam* **to get between the sheets** se mettre au lit, *Fam* se pieuter; *Fam* **what's he like between the sheets?** comment est-il au lit? **2** *(of paper)* feuille *f*, feuillet *m*; **a s. of newspaper** une feuille de journal; **loose s., fly s.** feuille volante; *Com* **order s.** bulletin *m* de commande; *Ind* **time** *or* **work** *or* **job s.** feuille de présence; *Typ* **the book is still in sheets** le livre n'a pas encore été relié **3** *(of glass)* feuille *f*; *(of metal)* feuille, tôle *f*, plaque *f*; *Culin* **baking s.** plaque à pâtisserie **4** *(of water, foam)* nappe *f*; *(of flame)* rideau *m*; *(of ice)* couche *f*, **the rain was coming down in sheets** la pluie tombait à verse **5** *Br Sl* **sheets** livres *fpl* sterling; **his DVD player cost him 500 sheets** son lecteur de DVD lui a coûté 500 livres **6** *Naut (rope)* écoute *f*, *Old-fashioned Fam* **to be three sheets to the wind** *(drunk)* avoir du vent dans les voiles

▸▸*Naut* **s. bend** nœud *m* d'écoute; *Comput* **s. feeder** bac *m* d'alimentation papier; **s. glass** verre *m* à vitres; **s. lightning** éclair *m* en nappe *ou* en nappes; **s. metal** tôle; **s. mill** laminoir *m* à tôles, tôlerie *f*; **s. music** partitions *fpl*

▸ **sheet down** VI *(of rain)* tomber à verse; **it was sheeting down** il pleuvait à verse

sheet-fed ADJ *Comput* à alimentation feuille par feuille
▸▸ **s. printer** imprimante *f* feuille à feuille

sheetfeed ['ʃiːtfiːd] N *Comput* alimentation *f* feuille par feuille, feuille à feuille *m*; *(device)* dispositif *m* d'alimentation papier

sheeting ['ʃiːtɪŋ] N *(fabric)* toile *f* pour draps; **(plastic) s.** bâche(s) *f(pl)* (en plastique)

sheik(h) [ʃeɪk, ʃiːk] N cheik(h) *m*, scheik *m*

sheik(h)dom ['ʃeɪkdəm, 'ʃiː-] N territoire *m* d'un/du cheik(h)

sheila ['ʃiːlə] N *Austr Sl (girl)* nana *f*

shekel ['ʃek(ə)l] N **1** *Hist (coin, weight)* sicle *m* **2** *Fam* **shekels** *(money)* fric *m*, flouse *m*

shelf, *pl* **shelves** [ʃelf, ʃelvz] N **1** *(in shelving unit)* tablette *f*; *(in cupboard)* planche *f*, rayon *m*; *(in bookcase)* rayon; *(of sideboard)* étagère *f*, *(in oven)* plateau *m*; **(set of) shelves** étagère; **these machines can be bought off the s.** ces machines sont disponibles en stock; **to stay on the shelves** *(of goods) (not get sold)* ne pas se vendre; *(not sell well)* être difficile à vendre; *Fam* **to be on the s.** *(abandoned)* être laissé pour compte; *(of unmarried woman)* être en passe de devenir vieille fille; *Aut* **(window) s.** plage *f* arrière; *(at front)* vide-poche *m*, *pl* vide-poches

2 *(of cliff, rock face)* rebord *m*, saillie *f*; *(in oceanography), Geog* terrasse *f*, plate-forme *f*, *pl* plates-formes; *(of rock, sand)* banc *m*; **continental s.** plate-forme continentale
▸▸ *Mktg* **s. facing** facing *m*, frontale *f*; **s. filler** *(person in supermarket)* réassortisseur, -euse; *Com* **s. life** durée *f* de conservation avant vente; **the s. life is six months** la durée de conservation avant vente est de six mois; *Fig* **to have a short s. life** *(of ideas, pop groups etc)* avoir une durée de vie courte; *Com* **s. space** linéaire *m*, rayonnage *m*; **s. stacker** *(person in supermarket)* réassortisseur, -euse

shell [ʃel] N **1** *(of mollusc, oyster, mussel, snail, egg, nut)* coquille *f*; *(of lobster, turtle)* carapace *f*; *(of pea etc)* cosse *f*; *(of chrysalis)* enveloppe *f*; **shells** *(on beach etc)* coquillages *mpl*; **to come out of/withdraw into one's s.** sortir de/rentrer dans sa coquille; **I'm just an empty s.** je me sens tout vide **2** *Naut (of ship etc)* carcasse *f*, squelette *m*, coque *f*, *Constr (of building)* charpente *f*; *(damaged)* carcasse; **the burnt-out s. of a car/house** la carcasse brûlée d'une voiture/maison **3** *(bomb)* obus *m*

VT **1** *(nuts etc)* écaler, décortiquer; *(peas)* écosser; *(oysters, mussels)* écailler; *(prawns)* éplucher **2** *Mil* bombarder

VI **nuts that s. easily** noix faciles à décortiquer; **peas that s. easily** pois faciles à écosser
▸▸ **s. pink** *(colour)* rose *m* pâle; *Comput* **s. program** logiciel *m* shell; **s. shock** syndrome *m* commotionnel; **s. suit** survêtement *m* (en polyamide froissé et doublé)

When translating the English word **shell**, note that the French words **coquillage** and **coquille** are not interchangeable. **Coquillage** applies mostly to seashells, whereas **coquille** refers to the more general sense of a shell as the outer layer of something.

▸ **shell out** *Fam* VT SEP cracher, casquer; **I was**

shelling out £100 a week on petrol je casquais 100 livres d'essence par semaine
VI casquer, banquer

she'll [ʃiːl] CONTR = **she will**, *see* **will**[3]

shellac [ʃə'læk] N gomme-laque *f*, *pl* gommes-laques; *Chem* shellac *m*
VT (**shellacked**) **1** traiter à la gomme-laque **2** *Am Sport Sl (defeat)* battre à plate(s) couture(s)

shellacking [ʃə'lækɪŋ] N *Am Sport Sl* **to get a s.** se faire battre à plate(s) couture(s)

shelled [ʃeld] ADJ *(nuts etc)* écalé; *(peas)* écossé

shellfire ['ʃelfaɪər] N tir *m* d'obus; **to be under s.** subir des tirs d'obus; **we came under heavy s.** nous avons subi un pilonnage intensif

shellfish ['ʃelfɪʃ] N **1** *(mollusc)* mollusque *m* (comestible), coquillage *m*; *(crustacean)* crustacé *m* **2** *(collectively)* mollusques *mpl* et crustacés *mpl*; *Culin* fruits *mpl* de mer

shelling ['ʃelɪŋ] N *Mil* bombardement *m*

shell-shaped ADJ en forme de coquillage, conchoïde

shellshocked ['ʃelʃɒkt] ADJ *Med, Mil* commotionné; *Fig* **to feel s.** être en état de choc

shelter ['ʃeltər] N **1** *(place)* refuge *m*; *(from rain, bombs, at bus stop etc)* abri *m*; *(bus stop)* Abribus® *m*; *(for the homeless etc)* asile *m*, refuge; *(for guards)* abrivent *m*; *Mil* **air raid s.** abri contre les attaques aériennes, abri de défense passive **2** *(protection)* **under s.** à l'abri, à couvert; **to take s. under/from sth** s'abriter *ou* se mettre à l'abri de qch; **to seek s. under a tree** chercher à s'abriter sous un arbre; **to find s.** trouver un abri; *(of refugee etc)* trouver asile *ou* refuge; **to give s. to sb** abriter qn; *(give asylum etc)* offrir un asile *ou* un refuge à qn

VT abriter; *(lost person etc)* donner asile à, recueillir; **to s. sb/sth from the rain** abriter qn/qch de la pluie

VI s'abriter; **to s. under a tree** s'abriter sous un arbre; **to s. from the wind** s'abriter du vent; **to s. from the rain** s'abriter de la pluie

sheltered ['ʃeltəd] ADJ abrité, protégé (**against**, **from** de); **to have had** *or* **led a s. life** avoir eu une vie protégée, à l'écart des réalités de l'existence; **you've led a s. life!** tu n'as rien vu!
▸▸ **s. housing** foyers *mpl* *(pour personnes handicapées, personnes âgées, femmes battues etc)*; *Am* **s. workshop** = atelier *f* pour personnes handicapées

shelve [ʃelv] VT **1** *(fit with shelves) (cupboard etc)* munir *ou* garnir de rayons **2** *(put on shelves) (books etc)* mettre sur les rayons **3** *(postpone) (question etc)* ajourner; *(project)* mettre en veilleuse; **the project has been shelved for 6 months** le projet a été mis de côté pendant 6 mois

VI *(slope downwards)* **the land shelves down to the sea** le terrain descend en pente douce jusqu'à la mer

shelving ['ʃelvɪŋ] N **1** *(no pl) (shelves)* rayons *mpl*, rayonnage *m*; **adjustable s.** rayons amovibles **2** *(postponing) (of question etc)* ajournement *m*

shemozzle [ʃɪ'mɒz(ə)l] N *Am Fam (fight)* bagarre *f*

shenanigans [ʃɪ'nænɪgənz] NPL *Fam* manigances *fpl*; **he's having s. with my wife** il a une aventure avec ma femme

shepherd ['ʃepəd] N berger *m*, *Lit* pâtre *m*; *Rel* **the Good S.** le bon Pasteur; *Bible* **the Lord is my S.** l'Éternel est mon berger; *German* **s. (dog)** berger allemand

VT *(sheep)* garder; *Fig (of priest) (his flock)* guider; *(tourists etc)* conduire, piloter; **we**

were shepherded into the next room nous avons été conduits dans la pièce suivante
▸▸ **s. dog** (chien *m* de) berger; **s.'s pie** ≃ hachis *m* Parmentier; *Bot* **s.'s purse** capselle *f*, bourse-à-pasteur *f*, *pl* bourses-à-pasteur

shepherdess [ʃepə'des] N bergère *f*

sherbet ['ʃɜːbət] N **1** *(powder) (sweet)* poudre *f* acidulée; *(for drink)* = poudre servant à préparer une boisson gazeuse **2** *Am (water ice)* sorbet *m* **3** *Br Fam (alcoholic drink)* verre *m*; **fancy going for a couple of sherbets?** ça te dirait de sortir prendre un verre?
▸▸ **s. powder** poudre acidulée

sheriff ['ʃerɪf] N **1** *Br Admin* shérif *m (représentant de la Couronne dans un comté)* **2** *Scot Law* juge *m* de première instance **3** *Am* chef *m* de la police *(d'un comté)*, shérif *m*; **deputy s.** = citoyen *m* assermenté faisant fonction d'agent de police

sherry ['ʃerɪ] N vin *m* de Xérès, xérès *m*
▸▸ **s. glass** verre *m* à madère

she's [ʃiːz] CONTR **1** = **she is**, *see* **be 2** = **she has**, *see* **have**[2]

Shetland ['ʃetlənd] N **1** **the Shetlands** les îles *fpl* Shetland **2** *Tex* shetland *m*
▸▸ **the S. Islands** les îles Shetland; **S. pony** poney *m* des Shetland; **S. wool** laine *f* d'Écosse *ou* de Shetland

shew [ʃəʊ] *(pt* **shewed** [ʃəʊd]; *pp* **shewn** [ʃəʊn]) *Arch, Lit* = **show**[2]

Shia ['ʃiːə] N **1** *(religion)* chiisme *m* **2** *(person)* chiite *mf*

shiatsu, **shiatzu** [ʃɪ'ætsuː] N shiatsu *m*

shibboleth ['ʃɪbəleθ] N *Bible* schibboleth *m*; *Fig (of party etc)* mot *m* d'ordre; **outworn shibboleths** *(doctrines)* doctrines vieux jeu *ou* désuètes

shield [ʃiːld] N **1** *(worn on arm)* bouclier *m*; *Her* écu *m*, écusson *m*; **he used his body as a s. to protect the president** il a fait un bouclier de son corps pour protéger le président; *Fig* **a s. against sth** une protection contre qch **2** *(around nuclear reactor)* bouclier *m*; *(on cable)* blindage *m*; *Astron* **heat s.** bouclier thermique; *Aut* **sun s.** pare-soleil *m inv* **3** *(in spray painting)* masque *m*, cache *m* **4** *(police badge)* plaque *f* de policier **5** *Sport (trophy)* plaque *f*

VT **1** protéger (**from**, **against** contre); **to s. sb from criticism** protéger qn des critiques; **to s. sb from punishment** soustraire qn à une punition; **to s. sb from danger** protéger qn contre le danger; **to s. sb with one's (own) body** faire un bouclier de son corps à qn; **to s. one's eyes** se protéger les yeux **2** *(in spray painting) (surfaces)* masquer **3** *Elec, Radio* blinder; **shielded cable** câble *m* blindé
▸▸ **s. bearer** écuyer *m*

SHIFT [ʃɪft]

N	changement **1** ▪ poste **2** ▪ équipe **2**	
VT	déplacer **1** ▪ vendre **2**	
VI	bouger **1** ▪ se magner **2** ▪ se débrouiller **3** ▪ se vendre **4**	

N 1 *(of position etc)* changement *m*; *(of tide, current)* renverse *f*; *(of wind)* saute *f*; **s. in meaning** glissement *m* de sens; **there has been a s. in public opinion** il y a eu un glissement de l'opinion publique; **a s. to the right/left** un glissement à droite/gauche; *Aut* **(gear) s.** levier *m* de vitesses; *Ling* **consonant/vowel s.** mutation *f* consonantique/vocalique; *Astron* **red s.** décalage *m* vers le rouge

2 *Ind etc (work period)* poste *m*; *(group of workers)* équipe *f*, brigade *f* *(d'ouvriers)*; **day/night s.** *(period)* poste de jour/nuit; *(workers)* équipe de jour/nuit; **to work in shifts** travailler par équipes, se relayer; **she**

works long shifts elle fait de longues journées; **to work eight-hour shifts** travailler par poste(s) de huit heures, faire les trois-huit; **we each did three-hour shifts** nous nous sommes relayés toutes les trois heures **3** (*dress*) robe *f* fourreau; *Arch* (*undergarment*) chemise *f* (*de femme*) **4** *Comput* (*on typewriter, computer*) touche *f* majuscule; **press s.** appuyer sur la touche majuscule; **an asterisk is s. 8** pour un astérisque, il faut appuyer simultanément sur la touche majuscule et la touche 8 **5** *Old-fashioned* **to make s.** s'arranger

vt 1 (*move*) changer de place; (*with difficulty*) bouger, déplacer; **could you s. your car?** pouvez-vous déplacer votre voiture?; **the drawer's stuck, I can't s. it** le tiroir est coincé, je ne peux le faire bouger; **they've shifted offices** ils ont déménagé de nouveau; **he keeps getting shifted to a different job** on n'arrête pas de le muter; **he's shifted his position** (*in negotiations*) il a changé de position; **once she's decided on something, it's impossible to s. her** une fois qu'elle a pris une décision, il est impossible de lui faire changer d'avis; **to s. a stain** (*of washing powder etc*) enlever une tache; **to s. the blame onto sb** rejeter la responsabilité sur qn; *Theat* **to s. the scenery** changer le décor; *Aut* **to s. the gears** changer de vitesse

2 *Fam* (*sell*) vendre; **we've been shifting these at 50 a day** (*selling them*) on en vend 50 par jour

vi 1 (*move*) (*of person, object*) bouger, se déplacer; (*change places*) changer de place; *Naut* (*of cargo*) se désarrimer, se déplacer; **it won't s.!** (*of object etc*) ça ne veut pas bouger!; **this stain won't s.** cette tache ne veut pas partir; *Theat* **the scene shifts** la scène change; **the wind has shifted (round)** le vent a tourné *ou* viré; **could you s.?** (*out of the way*) pouvez-vous dégager?; **could you possibly s. a little?** pourriez-vous vous déplacer un peu?; **the building is shifting** l'immeuble bouge; **he wouldn't s.** (*in negotiations etc*) il est resté ferme sur ses positions; **he shifted nervously from foot to foot** il oscillait d'un pied sur l'autre avec nervosité

2 *Fam* (*move quickly*) se magner (le train); **I didn't know she could s. so fast** je ne savais pas qu'elle pouvait aller aussi vite; **this car can really s.!** cette voiture est un vrai bolide!; **that's really shifting** ça, c'est de la vitesse

3 *Fam* **to s. for oneself** (*manage*) se débrouiller; **she can or knows how to s. for herself** elle est débrouillarde

4 *Fam* (*sell*) se vendre; **those TVs just aren't shifting at all** ces télés ne se vendent pas du tout

▸▸ *Comput* **s. key** touche majuscule; *Comput* **s. lock** touche de blocage des majuscules; *Am Aut* **s. stick** levier de (changement de) vitesse; **s. work** travail *m* en équipe; **she does s. work** elle fait les trois-huit; **s. worker** = personne *f* qui fait les trois-huit

▸ **shift about, shift around vt sep** (*object*) changer de place; **we've shifted the office around** nous avons changé la disposition du bureau; **he's always being shifted around** (*in job*) il est tout le temps muté; (*in location in office etc*) on le change tout le temps de place; (*from town to town etc*) on le fait tout le temps déménager

vi 1 (*fidget*) bouger

2 (*move around*) changer de place; (*change jobs*) changer d'emploi

▸ **shift along vi** (*move on seat etc*) se décaler; **s. along a bit** pousse-toi

▸ **shift over vi s. over!** pousse-toi!

▸ **shift up vi 1** = **shift along**

2 *Am Aut* passer à la vitesse supérieure

shift-click *Comput* **n** majuscule-clic *m*, *pl* majuscules-clics

vi faire un majuscule-clic

shift-drag n *Comput* majuscule-glisser *m*

shiftily ['ʃɪftɪlɪ] **adv** sournoisement

shiftiness ['ʃɪftɪnɪs] **n** sournoiserie *f*, fausseté *f*

shifting ['ʃɪftɪŋ] **adj** qui se déplace; (*relationship, scene etc*) changeant; (*wind etc*) inégal, -aux; *Fig* **the s. sands of public opinion** l'opinion publique toujours versatile

n (*moving*) (*of an object by somebody*) déplacement *m*; (*movement*) (*of something*) mouvement *m*, déplacement *m*; (*of cargo*) désarrimage *m*; (*change*) (*of position, direction etc*) changement *m*; *Theat* **scene s.** changement de décors; *Aut* **(gear) s.** changement de vitesse

shiftless ['ʃɪftlɪs] **adj 1** (*lazy*) paresseux **2** (*lacking resourcefulness*) peu débrouillard, qui manque d'initiative *ou* de ressource

shiftlessness ['ʃɪftlɪsnɪs] **n 1** (*laziness*) paresse *f* **2** (*lack of resourcefulness*) manque *m* de ressource *ou* d'initiative

shiftwork ['ʃɪftwɜːk] **n** *Ind* travail *m* par équipes *ou* par roulement

shiftworker ['ʃɪftwɜːkər] **n** *Ind* ouvrier, -ière qui fait les trois-huit

shifty ['ʃɪftɪ] **adj** (*person*) louche; (*look*) sournois; (*behaviour*) ambigu, -uë; **s. eyes** regard *m* fuyant; **there is something s. about him** il y a quelque chose de louche chez lui

Shiism ['ʃiːɪz(ə)m] **n** chiisme *m*

Shiite ['ʃiːaɪt] **n** chiite *mf*

adj chiite

shill [ʃɪl] *Am Fam* **n** baron *m*

vt 1 (*lure into swindle*) arnaquer; **they shilled him into handing over his life savings** ils ont réussi à lui soutirer toutes ses économies **2** (*hype*) faire de la pub pour; **they've got a quarterback shilling their new frozen yoghurt** il y a un joueur de football américain qui fait de la pub pour leur nouveau yaourt glacé

shillelagh [ʃɪˈleɪlə] **n** gourdin *m* irlandais

shilling ['ʃɪlɪŋ] **n** shilling *m*; *Fig* **to cut sb off without a s.** déshériter qn; *Hist* **to take the king's/queen's s.** = s'engager dans l'armée

shillyshally ['ʃɪlɪʃælɪ] **vi** *Fam* hésiter, tergiverser

shillyshallying ['ʃɪlɪʃælɪɪŋ] **n** *Fam* hésitation *f*, tergiversation *f*

shimmer ['ʃɪmər] **n** lueur *f*; (*of sea, silk etc*) miroitement *m*; (*in heat*) reflets *mpl*; (*of TV picture*) scintillement *m*; **a s. of light** une lueur; **the s. of the moon on the lake** les reflets de la lune sur le lac

vi (*of sea*) miroiter; (*of silk*) chatoyer

shimmering ['ʃɪmərɪŋ] **adj** (*sea*) miroitant; (*silk*) chatoyant

shimmy ['ʃɪmɪ] **n 1** *Am Aut* (*movement of front wheels*) flottement *m* des roues avant **2** (*dance*) shimmy *m*

vi 1 *Aut* (*of wheels*) osciller **2** (*dance*) danser le shimmy

shin [ʃɪn] **n** tibia *m*; *Culin* jarret *m* (*de bœuf*), gîte *m* de devant; **to kick sb in the shins** donner un coup de pied dans les tibias à qn; *Sport* **s. guard** *or* **pad** jambière *f*

▸ **shin up** (-nn-) **vt insep** (*climb*) **to s. up a tree** grimper à un arbre

vi (*climb*) grimper

shinbone ['ʃɪnbəʊn] **n** *Anat* tibia *m*

shindig ['ʃɪndɪg] **n** *Fam* **1** (*party*) fête *f* **2** = **shindy 1**

shindy ['ʃɪndɪ] **n** *Fam* **1** (*din*) raffut *m*, ramdam *m*; **to kick up a s.** (*make a din*) faire du raffut *ou* du ramdam; **to kick up a s. about** sth (*protest loudly*) faire du raffut pour protester contre qch **2** *Am* = **shindig 1**

shine [ʃaɪn] **vi** (*pt, pp* shone [ʃɒn]) (*of sun etc*) briller; (*of polished article*) (re)luire; *Fig* (*excel*) briller; **the moon/the sun is shining** il y a un clair de lune/il fait soleil; **the sun was shining straight into my eyes** j'avais le soleil dans les yeux; **the light from the torch shone on a piece of paper** la lumière de la lampe de poche éclaira un morceau de papier; **her face was shining with joy** son visage rayonnait de joie; **her eyes shone with enthusiasm** ses yeux brillaient d'enthousiasme; *Fig* **to s. at maths/Latin** être brillant en maths/latin; *Fig* **he doesn't s. in company** il ne brille pas en société; *Sl* **stick it where the sun don't s.!** tu peux te le mettre où je pense!

vt 1 **to s. a light on sth** (*illuminate*) éclairer qch (*avec une lampe etc*); (*direct at*) braquer une lampe sur qch **2** (*pt, pp* shined [ʃaɪnd]) (*polish*) (*shoes etc*) polir, cirer; (*brass*) astiquer

n 1 (*brightness*) éclat *m*; (*on shoes etc*) brillant *m*; (*on textiles etc*) luisant *m*; **to take the s. off sth** délustrer qch, ternir qch; *Fig* ternir qch, entacher qch **2** (*action*) **to give one's shoes a s.** cirer ses chaussures; **to give the brass a s.** astiquer les cuivres **3** *Fam* **to take a s. to sb** s'enticher de qn **4** *Offensive Sl* (*black man*) nègre *m*, bamboula *m*; (*black woman*) négresse *f*

shiner ['ʃaɪnər] **n** *Fam* (*black eye*) œil *m* poché, *Fam* œil au beurre noir

shingle¹ ['ʃɪŋg(ə)l] **n 1** *Constr* (*wooden tile*) bardeau *m*, aisseau *m* **2** *Am* (*sign*) (*of doctor, lawyer etc*) plaque *f* (*de cuivre*); **to put one's s. up** (*to open business*) s'installer **3** (*hairstyle*) coupe *f* à la garçonne

vt 1 *Constr* (*roof*) couvrir de bardeaux **2** **to s. sb** *or* **sb's hair** couper les cheveux de qn à la garçonne

▸▸ **s. roof** toit *m* en bardeaux

shingle² **n** (*no pl*) (*on beach*) galets *mpl*

▸▸ **s. beach** plage *f* de galets

shingles ['ʃɪŋg(ə)lz] **n** *Med* zona *m* VOIR GRAMMAIRE A10

shingly ['ʃɪŋglɪ] **adj** (*covered in pebbles*) couvert de galets; (*beach*) de galets

shininess ['ʃaɪnɪnɪs] **n** éclat *m*, brillance *f*; (*due to wear*) lustrage *m*

shining ['ʃaɪnɪŋ] **adj** brillant, (re)luisant; (*face*) rayonnant; **a s. example** un parfait exemple (**of sth** de qch)

▸ **shinny up** ['ʃɪnɪ] **vt insep**, **vi** *Am Fam* = **shin up**

Shintoism ['ʃɪntəʊɪz(ə)m] **n** shintoïsme *m*, shinto *m*

shiny ['ʃaɪnɪ] **adj** brillant, luisant; **clothes made s. by long wear** vêtements lustrés par l'usage

ship [ʃɪp] **n 1** navire *m*; (*smaller*) bateau *m*; (*esp warship*) bâtiment *m*; **to go by s.** aller en bateau; **to send sth by s.** envoyer qch par bateau; **is there a doctor/swimming pool on the s.?** y a-t-il un docteur/une piscine à bord?; **sailing s.** voilier *m*, navire à voiles; **passenger s.** paquebot *m*; **merchant s.** navire marchand, cargo *m*; **container s.** navire porte-conteneurs; **depot** *or* **supply s.** ravitailleur *m*; **training s.** navire-école *m*, *pl* navires-écoles; *Fig* **the s. of State** le char de l'État; **the s. of the desert** (*camel*) le vaisseau du désert; *Fig* **when my s. comes home** *or* **in** dès que j'aurai fait fortune; *Fig* **to be like ships that pass in the night** (*of lovers*) être des amants de passage; **s.'s biscuit** biscuit *m* de mer; **s.'s boat** embarcation *f* de bord; **s.'s boy** mousse *m*; **s.'s carpenter** charpentier *m* de bord; **s.'s chandler** shipchandler *m*, fournisseur *m* de navires; **the s.'s company**

l'équipage *m*; **s.'s manifest** manifeste *m* **2** *(spaceship)* vaisseau *m*; *Fam (aeroplane)* avion *m*

vt (**-pp-**) **1** *Com (to send by sea, rail etc)* envoyer, expédier **2** *(to take on board) (cargo etc)* embarquer; **to s. water** *(of ship)* embarquer de l'eau; **to s. oars** rentrer *ou* border les avirons

vi 1 *(of passenger)* s'embarquer; *(of sailor)* armer sur un navire **2** *(be delivered)* sortir des usines

► **ship off vt sep** *Fam (send) (thing, person)* expédier; **his mother shipped him off to boarding school** sa mère l'a expédié dans un pensionnat

► **ship out vt sep** *(send) (goods)* expédier; *(troops etc)* envoyer

vi *esp Am Fam (leave)* mettre les voiles; *see* **shape up**

shipboard ['ʃɪpbɔːd] **adj attrib** à bord d'un/du navire

ship-broker **n** courtier *m* maritime

shipbuilder ['ʃɪpbɪldər] **n** constructeur *m* de navires

shipbuilding ['ʃɪpbɪldɪŋ] **n** construction *f* navale; **a s. firm** une entreprise de construction navale; **the s. industry** l'industrie *f* de la construction navale

shipload ['ʃɪpləʊd] **n** chargement *m*, cargaison *f*, *Fig* **by the s., in shiploads** en masse

shipmate ['ʃɪpmeɪt] **n** compagnon *m ou* camarade *m* de bord

shipment ['ʃɪpmənt] **n** *(sending)* expédition *f*, envoi *m*; *(goods sent)* envoi *m*; **the containers awaiting s.** les conteneurs prêts pour l'expédition; **three shipments of ...** trois cargaisons *ou* chargements de ...

shipowner ['ʃɪpəʊnər] **n** armateur *m*, propriétaire *m* de navires, fréteur *m*

shipped bill [ʃɪpt] **n** *Com* connaissement *m* embarqué

shipped weight **n** *Com* poids *m* embarqué

shipper ['ʃɪpər] **n** expéditeur, -trice

shipping ['ʃɪpɪŋ] **n** *(ships)* navires *mpl (d'un pays, d'un port etc)*; *(sending)* expédition *f*, envoi *m*; **dangerous to** *or* **for s.** dangereux pour la navigation

► ► **s. address** adresse *f* de livraison; **s. agent** agent *m* maritime; **s. bill** connaissement *m*; **s. company** entreprise *f* de transport routier; **s. costs** frais *mpl* d'expédition; *(by ship)* frais d'embarquement; **s. department** service *m* expédition, expéditions; **s. documents** documents *mpl* d'expédition, documents maritimes; **s. exchange** bourse *f* de fret; **s. instructions** instructions *fpl* pour l'expédition; **s. intelligence** nouvelles *fpl* maritimes; **s. lanes** routes *fpl* de navigation; **s. line** ligne *f ou* compagnie maritime; **s. marks** marques *fpl* d'expédition; **s. note** permis *m* d'embarquement; **s. office** bureau *m* d'expédition; **s. routes** routes de navigation

shipshape ['ʃɪpʃeɪp] **adj** *(très)* bien rangé; *(documents etc)* en bon ordre; **everything's s.** tout est à sa place; **to get a room s.** ranger une pièce, mettre de l'ordre dans une pièce; *Old-fashioned* **s. and Bristol fashion!** impeccable!

shipwreck ['ʃɪprek] **n** naufrage *m*; **to suffer s.** *(of ship)* faire naufrage; *Fig* **the s. of one's hopes** le naufrage de ses espoirs

vt *(usu in passive)* **to be shipwrecked** faire naufrage

shipwrecked ['ʃɪprekt] **adj** naufragé

shipwright ['ʃɪpraɪt] **n** constructeur *m* de navires; *(on board ship)* charpentier *m* du bord

shipyard ['ʃɪpjɑːd] **n** chantier *m* naval, chantier de constructions navales; **hundreds of s. workers were sacked** des centaines d'ouvriers des chantiers navals ont été licenciés

shire [ʃaɪər] **n** *Br* **1** comté *m* **2** *(horse)* shire *m*

► ► **s. horse** shire

Shires [ʃaɪəz] **npl** = comtés *mpl* ruraux du centre de l'Angleterre

shirk [ʃɜːk] **vt** *(obligation etc)* manquer à, se soustraire à; *(task)* renâcler à; *(a duty)* esquiver; *(one's duty)* négliger; **to s. doing sth** se défiler (pour ne pas faire qch); **to s. the question** esquiver *ou* éluder la question

vi *(avoid work)* tirer au flanc; **stop shirking!** arrête de tirer au flanc *ou* de te défiler devant le travail!

shirker ['ʃɜːkər] **n** *Fam* tire-au-flanc *m inv*; **she's no s.** elle n'a rien d'un tire-au-flanc

shirr [ʃɜːr] **vt** *Sewing* bouillonner

shirring ['ʃɜːrɪŋ] **n** *Sewing* bouillonné *m*

shirt [ʃɜːt] **n** chemise *f*; *(with short sleeves)* chemisette *f*; *Sport* maillot *m*; **sports** *or* **casual s.** chemise sport; *Fam* **he's a stuffed s.** il est guindé; **to change one's s., to put on a clean s.** changer de chemise; *Fam* **to put one's s. on a horse** parier sa chemise sur un cheval; *Fam* **to take the s. off sb's back** faire cracher jusqu'à son dernier centime à qn; *Fam* **he'd have the s. off your back** il te mangerait la laine sur le dos; *Fam* **he'd give you the s. off his back** il donnerait sa chemise; *Fam* **to lose one's s.** *(lose everything)* y laisser sa chemise; *Am (lose one's temper)* s'emporter, prendre la mouche; *Fam* **keep your s. on!** ne vous emballez pas!, calmez-vous!; *Hist* **Red/Black/Brown Shirts** Chemises rouges/noires/brunes

► ► **s. collar** col *m* de chemise; **s. cuff** poignet *m* de chemise; **s. front** plastron *m ou* devant *m* de chemise

shirting ['ʃɜːtɪŋ] **n** shirting *m*

shirtlifter ['ʃɜːtlɪftər] **n** *Offensive Sl* tantouze *f*, tapette *f*

shirtmaker ['ʃɜːtmeɪkər] **n** chemisier, -ière

shirtsleeve ['ʃɜːtsliːv] **n** manche *f* de chemise; **to be in one's shirtsleeves** être en bras *ou* en manches de chemise

shirt-tail **n** pan *m* de chemise

shirtwaister, *Am* **shirtwaist** ['ʃɜːtweɪst(ər)] **n** *(dress)* robe *f* chemisier

shirty ['ʃɜːtɪ] **adj** *Br Fam* irritable; **to get s.** se fâcher

shit [ʃɪt] **n 1** *Vulg (excrement)*, *Fig (rubbish)* merde *f*; *(nonsense)* conneries *fpl*; **to have a s.** chier; **to have the shits** *(to have diarrhoea)* avoir la chiasse; *(to be frightened)* faire dans son froc; **bird/dog s.** merde d'oiseau/de chien; *Fig* **the s. will really hit the fan** ça va chier; **tough s.!** pas de bol!; **this is a s. book** c'est un livre de merde; **he doesn't give a s.** il s'en fout, *Vulg* il n'en a rien à branler; **to beat the s. out of sb** démolir qn; **to scare the s. out of sb** foutre une trouille bleue à qn; **to bore the s. out of sb** faire crever qn d'ennui; **I'm not taking any more of his s.** je ne le laisserai plus m'emmerder; **to be in the s.** être dans la merde; **to be up s. creek (without a paddle)** être dans la merde jusqu'au cou; *Am* **no s.!** arrête tes conneries!

2 *Vulg (person)* salaud *m*, salope *f*

3 *Sl (heroin)* came *f*, *(marijuana)* shit *m*

int merde!

vi *(pt, pp* **shat** [ʃæt]*, shitted* ['ʃɪtɪd]) *Vulg* chier; **they'll s. on us from a great height** ils vont bien se foutre de nous

vt *Vulg* chier; **I was shitting myself** je chiais dans mon froc; **he'll s. a brick** il va chier dans son froc

► ► **s. stirrer** fouille-merde *mf inv*

shitake mushroom [ʃɪˈtækɪ] **n** champignon *m* shitake

shite [ʃaɪt] **n, vt & vi** *Vulg* = **shit etc**

shit(e)house ['ʃɪthaʊs, 'ʃaɪt-] **n** *Vulg (toilet)* chiottes *fpl*, gogues *mpl*

shitface ['ʃɪtfeɪs] **n** *Vulg* gueule *f* de con

shit-faced **adj** *Sl (drunk)* bourré, pété, beurré; *(on drugs)* défoncé, raide

shithead ['ʃɪthed] **n** *Sl* enfoiré, -ée

shithole ['ʃɪthəʊl] **n** *Sl (dirty place)* porcherie *f*, taudis *m*; **this town's a complete s.** *(boring, ugly)* cette ville est un vrai trou

shit-hot **adj** *Sl* vachement bien

shitless ['ʃɪtlɪs] **adj** *Sl* **to be scared s.** chier dans son froc; **to be bored s.** s'emmerder profondément

shitload ['ʃɪtləʊd] **n** *Sl* **a (whole) s. (of)** une chiée (de)

shit-scared **adj** **to be/look s.** avoir/avoir l'air d'avoir une trouille bleue

shitstorm ['ʃɪtstɔːm] **n** *Am Sl* foin *m*; **the announcement caused a helluva s.** la déclaration a fait un sacré foin

shitty ['ʃɪtɪ] **adj** *Sl (nappies, trousers)* plein de merde; *(weather, job)* merdique, de merde; **I feel s.** je me sens vasouillard; *(feel guilty etc)* je me trouve dégueulasse; **that was a s. thing to say/do to someone** c'était dégueulasse de dire/faire ça à quelqu'un; **he was really s. to her** il a été vraiment dégueulasse avec elle

shitweasel ['ʃɪtwiːzəl] **n** *Am Sl* ordure *f*, raclure *f*

shiv [ʃɪv] *Sl* **n** *(knife)* surin *m*, lame *f*

vt *(stab)* planter

shiver¹ ['ʃɪvər] **vi 1** frissonner, trembler (**with cold/fear** de froid/peur); **to s. like a leaf** *or* **a jelly** trembler comme une feuille **2** *(of sail)* faseyer, ralinguer

n *(from cold, fear)* frisson *m*; **it sent cold shivers down my back** cela m'a fait froid dans le dos; **to feel a s.** avoir un frisson; *Fam* **to have the shivers** avoir la tremblote; *Fam* **it gives me the shivers to think of it** ça me donne des frissons quand j'y pense

shiver² **vt** *(break)* casser en morceaux; *Arch, Hum* **s. me timbers!** tonnerre de Dieu!

vi *(break)* se casser en morceaux

n *(fragment)* éclat *m*, fragment *m*; **to break sth into shivers** casser qch en mille morceaux

shivering ['ʃɪvərɪŋ] **adj** frissonnant; *(with cold)* grelottant

n frissonnement *m*; **to have a s. fit** être pris de frissons

shivery ['ʃɪvərɪ] **adj** = **shivering 1**; **to feel s.** avoir des frissons; *(feverish)* se sentir fiévreux; **it gives you a s. feeling** cela donne le frisson

shoal¹ [ʃəʊl] **n** *(shallow)* haut-fond *m*, *pl* hauts-fonds; *(sandbank)* banc *m* de sable

shoal² **n** *(of fish)* banc *m*; *Fam (of people)* foule *f*, multitude *f*; *(of letters, applications etc)* grande quantité *f*, tas *m*

shock [ʃɒk] **n 1** *(impact)* choc *m*; *(of collision etc)* impact *m*; *(jolt), Geol* secousse *f*; **to stand the s.** résister au choc; **slight (earthquake) shocks were felt** on a senti de petites secousses; *Fig* **the news sent s. waves through the financial world** la nouvelle a provoqué des ondes de choc dans le monde de la finance

2 *(emotional blow)* coup *m*; *(caused by bad news etc), Med* choc *m*; **it was a s. to find out I'd got no money left/I'd won** ça m'a fait un choc de découvrir que je n'avais plus d'argent/que j'avais gagné; **the news of his death came as a terrible s. to all of us** la nouvelle de sa mort nous a tous énormément choqués; **the s. killed him, he died of the s.** le choc l'a tué; **be prepared for a s.** prépare-toi à un choc; *Med* **post-operative s.** choc post-opératoire; **to be in s.** être en état de choc; **to go into s.** entrer en état de choc; **in a state of s.** en état de choc; *Fam Hum* **s. horror story** histoire *f* abominable; *Fam Hum* **s. horror!** l'horreur!

3 *(electric)* **s.** décharge *f*; **to get a(n electric) s.** recevoir une décharge; **electric s. treatment** traitement *m* par électrochocs

4 *(mass)* **s. of hair** tignasse *f*

VT *(person) (scandalize)* choquer; **to s. the eye/ear** choquer la vue/l'oreille; **a book that shocked the public** un livre qui a fait scandale; **easily shocked** qui se choque facilement; **to be shocked at** *or* **by sth** *(scandalized)* être choqué de *ou* scandalisé par qch; **she wanted to s. them into action** elle voulait les choquer pour les faire réagir; **to s. sb out of doing sth** dissuader qn de faire qch en lui faisant peur; **I was shocked to hear that …** j'ai été choqué d'apprendre que …; **millions were shocked by pictures of the famine** des millions de personnes ont été choquées *ou* bouleversées par les images de la famine

▸▸ **s. absorber** amortisseur *m*; *Am Fam* **s. jock** = animateur ou animatrice de radio au ton irrévérencieux et provocateur; **s. tactics** tactique *f ou* action *f* de choc; **s. therapy** *(traitement par)* électrochoc *m*; *Fig* traitement de choc; *Mil* **s. troops** troupes *fpl* de choc; **s. wave** onde *f* de choc

shockable ['ʃɒkəb(ə)l] ADJ **he's easily/not easily s.** il se choque facilement/ne se choque pas facilement

shocked [ʃɒkt] ADJ *(person, voice etc) (scandalized)* choqué; *(stunned)* atterré; **there was a s. silence when …** il y eut un silence atterré lorsque …

shocker ['ʃɒkər] N *Fam* **1** *(shocking news)* **that was a real s.** ça a été un rude coup **2** *(bad mistake)* faute *f* énorme; *(in behaviour)* grosse bourde *f* **3** *(novel)* roman *m* à sensations; *(film)* film *m* à sensations **4** *(person)* **he really is a s.!** il est vraiment impossible!

shocking ['ʃɒkɪŋ] ADJ *(sight etc) (scandalizing)* choquant; *(revolting)* abominable, affreux; *(news)* atterrant, bouleversant; *(weather)* abominable, exécrable; *(pain)* atroce; **to be in a s. state** être dans un état lamentable; **s. behaviour** *(scandalizing)* comportement scandaleux; *(unworthy)* conduite indigne; **how s.!** quelle horreur!; **the s. truth about conditions in our prisons** la terrible vérité sur les conditions de vie dans nos prisons; **their s. ignorance** leur scandaleuse ignorance

ADV *Fam* **he carried on something s.!** il nous a fait une scène abominable!

▸▸ **s. pink** rose *m* bonbon

shockingly ['ʃɒkɪŋlɪ] ADV *(to behave)* scandaleusement; *(to treat)* abominablement; *Fam (extremely) (expensive etc)* affreusement; **they did s. in the exam** leurs résultats à l'examen ont été lamentables; **s. deprived** dans une misère atroce; **s. immoral** d'une immoralité scandaleuse; **a s. low-cut dress** une robe outrageusement décolletée; **in s. bad taste** du dernier mauvais goût

shockproof ['ʃɒkpruːf] ADJ **1** *(scientific instrument etc)* antichoc **2** *Fam (person)* qui ne se choque pas facilement

shod PT, PP *see* **shoe** VT

shoddily ['ʃɒdɪlɪ] ADV **s. made** mal fait; **to treat sb s.** traiter qn peu honorablement; **to behave s. (towards sb)** se conduire mesquinement (envers qn)

shoddiness ['ʃɒdɪnɪs] N *(of material, workmanship)* mauvaise qualité *f*; **the s. of their treatment of him** leur mesquinerie envers lui

shoddy ['ʃɒdɪ] ADJ *(goods etc)* de camelote, de pacotille; *(conduct)* mesquin; *(workmanship)* médiocre; **s. goods** camelote *f*

N *Tex (cloth)* drap *m* de laine d'effilochage, laine *f ou* tissu *m* de récupération

shoe [ʃuː] N **1** *(for foot)* chaussure *f*, soulier *m*; **a pair of shoes** une paire de chaussures; **lace-up shoes** richelieus *m*; **high-heeled shoes** chaussures à talons hauts; **to put on/take off one's shoes** se chausser/se déchausser, mettre/enlever ses chaussures; **to shake** *or* **quake in one's shoes** être dans ses petits souliers; *Fig* **to step into sb's shoes** prendre la place de qn, succéder à qn; *Fig* **I wouldn't like to be in his shoes** je ne voudrais pas être à sa place; **put yourself in my shoes** mets-toi à ma place; *Fig* **to be waiting for dead men's shoes** attendre la mort de qn *(pour le remplacer)*

2 *(horseshoe)* fer *m* à cheval; **to cast** *or* **throw a s.** *(of horse)* perdre un fer, se déferrer

3 *Aut (of brake)* mâchoire *f*

4 *(of sledge etc)* patin *m*

VT *(pt, pp* **shod** [ʃɒd]; *prp* **shoeing)** **1** *(provide with shoes)* chausser; **to be well shod** être bien chaussé **2** *(pt, pp also* **shoed)** *(horse)* ferrer

▸▸ **s. box** boîte *f* à chaussures; **s. cream** cirage *m* en crème; *Aut* **s. expander** écarteur *m* de mâchoire; **s. leather** cuir *m* pour chaussures; **I've worn out a lot of s. leather** j'ai marché des kilomètres; *Fig* **you might as well save your s. leather** c'est inutile que vous y alliez; **s. polish** cirage; **s. rack** porte-chaussures *m inv*; **s. repairs** cordonnerie *f*; **s. scraper** gratte-pieds *m inv*; **s. shop** magasin *m* de chaussures; **s. size** pointure *f*; **s. tree** embauchoir *m*

shoeblack ['ʃuːblæk] N cireur *m*

shoebrush ['ʃuːbrʌʃ] N brosse *f* à chaussures

shoehorn ['ʃuːhɔːn] N chausse-pied *m*, *pl* chausse-pieds

VT *Fig* **we can s. a few more in** on peut en faire tenir encore quelques-uns

shoeing ['ʃuːɪŋ] N *(of horse)* ferrage *m*, ferrure *f*

shoelace ['ʃuːleɪs] N lacet *m* (de chaussure); *Fig* **he's not fit to tie your shoelaces** il n'est pas digne de cirer vos chaussures

shoemaker ['ʃuːmeɪkər] N *(who makes shoes)* fabricant *m* de chaussures; *(who makes and sells shoes)* chausseur *m*; *(shoe repairer)* cordonnier *m*; *Prov* **let the s. stick to his last** cordonnier, mêlez-vous de votre pantoufle!

shoemender ['ʃuːmendər] N cordonnier *m*

shoe-polishing machine N machine *f* à cirer les chaussures

shoeshine ['ʃuːʃaɪn] N *Am* **1** *(action)* cirage *m* de chaussures **2** *(person)* cireur *m* de chaussures

▸▸ **s. boy** (petit) cireur (de chaussures)

shoeshop ['ʃuːʃɒp] N magasin *m* de chaussures

shoestring ['ʃuːstrɪŋ] N lacet *m* de chaussure; *Fig Fam* **on a s.** à peu de frais; *Fam* **they're doing it on a s.** ils tirent sur la corde; *Fam* **a film made on a s. (budget)** un film réalisé à peu de frais

shone PT, PP *see* **shine** VI, VT

shoo [ʃuː] INT *(to animal, children)* allez!, ouste!

▸ **shoo away, shoo off** VT SEP *(scare away) (chickens etc)* chasser

shoo-in N *Fam* **it's a s.** c'est couru d'avance; **they're a s. to win the next election** ils vont gagner les prochaines élections, c'est couru d'avance

shook PT *see* **shake** VT, VI

SHOOT [ʃuːt]

┌───┐
│ **N** pousse **1** ▪ tournage **2** ▪ séance │
│ photo **2** ▪ concours de tir **4** │
│ **VI** se précipiter **1** ▪ tirer **4** ▪ chasser │
│ **4** ▪ tourner **5** ▪ shooter **6** │
│ **VT** franchir **1** ▪ lancer **3** ▪ tirer **3** │
│ ▪ tuer par balle(s) **4** ▪ tirer sur **4** │
│ ▪ tourner **5** ▪ filmer **5** ▪ photographier │
│ **5** │
└───┘

N **1** *Bot (plant)* pousse *f*; *(on a plant)* rejet *m*, scion *m*; *(of vine)* sarment *m*, pampre *m*; **young** *or* **tender s.** tendrille *f*, tendron *m*

2 *Cin, TV* tournage *m*; *Phot* séance *f* photo, prise *f* de vues; **he has a s. all afternoon** il a une prise de vue tout l'après-midi

3 = **chute**

4 *(shooting contest)* concours *m* de tir; *esp Br (hunting party)* partie *f* de chasse; *(land)* chasse *f* gardée

5 *Fam* **the whole (bang) s.** *(everything)* tout le bazar

6 *Fam Euph* **oh s.!** miel!

VI *(pt, pp* **shot** [ʃɒt]) **1** *(move rapidly)* se précipiter; *(of star)* filer; **he shot into the room** il est entré dans la pièce en éclair *ou* en trombe; **to s. forward** foncer *ou* s'élancer à toute allure; **to s. ahead** prendre la tête; **he's always shooting across to New York** il va sans arrêt à New York; **the cat shot out of his arms** le chat bondit de ses bras

2 *(of pain)* élancer; **I've got pains shooting through my shoulder** j'ai des élancements dans l'épaule

3 *(of tree, bud etc)* pousser, bourgeonner; *(of plant)* germer

4 *(fire gun)* tirer; *(hunt)* chasser; **don't s.!** ne tirez pas!; **to s. straight** bien viser; **to s. at sb/sth** tirer *ou* faire feu sur qn/qch; **to be shot at** se faire tirer dessus; *Fig* **to s. from the hip** parler sans réfléchir

5 *Cin* tourner; *Phot (take photo)* prendre la/une photo; *Cin* **s.!** moteur!, on tourne!

6 *Ftbl, Hockey* shooter

7 *esp Am Fam* **s.!** *(say what you want to)* allez-y!

VT **1** *(pass rapidly) (rapids)* franchir; *Aut* **to s. the (traffic) lights** griller *ou* brûler le feu rouge

2 *(move rapidly) (bolt)* pousser; *Fishing (net)* jeter; *Fig* **he had shot his bolt** il avait brûlé ses dernières cartouches; **we were shot out of the car** nous avons été éjectés de la voiture; *Am Fam* **to s. the breeze** *(chat)* bavarder; *(exaggerate)* en rajouter; *Fam* **to s. a line** *(boast)* faire du baratin; **he's just shooting a line** ce qu'il raconte, c'est du baratin

3 *(unleash) (arrow)* décocher; *(projectile)* lancer; *(bullet)* tirer; *Ftbl* **he shot the ball into the net** il a envoyé le ballon dans le filet, il a marqué un but; **to s. a glance at sb** lancer *ou* décocher un regard à qn; **the chimney shot a shower of sparks into the air** la cheminée envoya un jet d'étincelles dans l'air; *Fam* **to s. heroin** se shooter à l'héroïne; *Sl* **to s. one's load** *or* **wad** *(ejaculate)* décharger

4 *(person) (hit with bullet)* atteindre d'un coup de feu; *(kill)* tuer d'un coup de feu; *(wound)* blesser d'un coup de feu; *(spy)* abattre; *(partridge, woodsnipe etc)* tirer; *(hunt) (game)* chasser; **I've been shot** j'ai reçu une balle; **a man was shot (and killed) yesterday** un homme a été tué par balle hier; **everybody remembers the day Kennedy was shot** tout le monde se souvient du jour où Kennedy a été assassiné; **to be shot in the arm** être atteint au bras; **the robbers tried to s. their way out** les voleurs tentèrent de se sauver en tirant des coups de feu; **to s. sb dead** tuer qn par balle; **to s. sb through the head** tirer une balle dans la tête de qn; **she was shot through the heart** elle a été tuée d'une balle en plein cœur; **to s. oneself in the foot** se tirer dans le pied; *Fig (spoil one's chances)* se faire du tort à soi-même; **to s. holes in sb's argument/case** démonter les arguments/la théorie de qn; **to s. sb/sth to pieces** mettre qn/qch en pièces; *Mil* **to be (court-martialled and) shot** être passé par les armes, être fusillé; *Fig Fam* **I'll be shot** je suis foutu; *Fig Fam* **you'll get me shot** tu vas me faire avoir des ennuis

5 *Cin (film)* tourner; *(scene, actor)* filmer; *Phot* photographier; **the photos were all shot on location in Paris** les photos ont toutes été prises à Paris; *TV, Cin* **to s. sound** effectuer une prise de son

6 to s. dice lancer les dés; **to s. pool** faire une partie de billard; **to s. a goal** marquer un but; **to s. a basket** marquer un panier; *Golf* **to s. a 64** faire le parcours en 64 coups

▶ **shoot back** vi **1** *(fire back)* riposter

2 *(into its shell, into office)* disparaître

vt sep *(return quickly)* envoyer; **the candidate shot back his answers** le candidat répondait du tac au tac

▶ **shoot down** vt sep **1** *(cause to fall by gunfire etc) (person)* abattre (par balle); *(plane)* abattre, descendre

2 *(show to be wrong or unacceptable) (person, argument, proposal etc)* descendre; **she was shot down in flames when …** elle a été descendue en flammes lorsque …

▶ **shoot off** vi **1** *(leave quickly)* partir comme une flèche; **I've got to s. off now** il faut que je me sauve

2 *Sl (ejaculate)* décharger

vt sep **1** *(remove by bullet or shell)* emporter par une balle/par un obus; **he had a foot shot off** il a eu un pied fauché par un obus

2 *(fire)* **she shot off a few rounds into the darkness** elle a tiré plusieurs fois dans le noir; **he shot off an entire magazine** il a vidé son chargeur; *Fig* **to s. off a letter/memo to sb** envoyer une lettre/un mémo à qn; *Sl* **to s. one's mouth off** *(be indiscreet)* ouvrir sa grande gueule (**about sth** à propos de qch)

▶ **shoot out** vi *(emerge quickly) (of water, flames)* jaillir; **to s. out of a side street** déboucher brusquement d'une rue latérale

vt sep **1** *(extend quickly) (sparks etc)* lancer; **the snake shot out its tongue** le serpent a dardé sa langue

2 *(extinguish, destroy etc with gunshots) (light, window)* tirer dans; **his right eye had been shot out** il avait perdu l'œil droit dans une fusillade

3 *Fam* **to s. it out** régler ses comptes à coups de feu

▶ **shoot through** vi *Br (leave suddenly)* se tirer, mettre les bouts

▶ **shoot up** vt sep **they shot the bar up** ils ont mitraillé le bar; **he was badly shot up in the war** il a été sérieusement blessé à la guerre; **he's been shot up** il a reçu des balles (dans la peau)

vi **1** *(of plants, children)* pousser; *(of rocket)* s'élever; *(of prices)* monter en flèche; *(of fountain etc)* jaillir; **he's really shot up!** *(he's grown)* qu'est-ce qu'il a poussé!; **new tower blocks are shooting up all over the city** de nouvelles tours poussent dans toute la ville

2 *Sl (with drugs)* se shooter

shoot-'em-up [ˈʃuːtəmʌp] N *Fam* = film *m* ou jeu *m* vidéo ultra-violent

shooter [ˈʃuːtər] N **1** *Sl (gun)* flingue *m*, feu *m* **2** *(drink)* cocktail *m* servi dans un petit verre

shooting [ˈʃuːtɪŋ] ADJ *(pain)* lancinant

N **1** *(gunfire)* coups *mpl* de feu; *(killing)* fusillade *f*, *(of spies, revolutionaries etc)* mise *f* à mort; *(hunting)* chasse *f*; **there was no s.** *(in robbery etc)* aucun coup de feu n'a été tiré; **there was a s.** il y a eu une fusillade; **anyone who witnessed the s. is asked to contact the police** tout témoin de la fusillade est prié de

prendre contact avec la police; **pigeon s.** tir *m* aux pigeons; **the s. season** la saison de la chasse **2** *Cin (of film)* tournage *m*; **s. starts next week on her new film** le tournage de son nouveau film commence la semaine prochaine

▶▶ **s. angle** angle *m* de prise de vue; *Br Aut* **s. brake** break *m*; **s. gallery** *(at fairground)* (stand *m* de) tir; *Sl (for buying drugs)* = lieu *m* où l'on achète, vend et consomme de la drogue; **s. match** concours *m* de tir; *Hunt* **s. party** partie *f* de chasse; **s. plan** plan *m* de travail; **s. range** champ *m* de tir; **s. schedule** plan *m* de tournage; *Cin* **s. script** découpage *m*; **s. star** étoile *f* filante; **s. stick** canne-siège *f*, *pl* cannes-sièges

shoot-out N *Fam* échange *m* de coups de feu, fusillade *f*; **they settled it with a s.** ils ont réglé leurs comptes à coups de feu

shop [ʃɒp] N **1** *Com (building)* magasin *m*; *(small)* boutique *f*; **I'm just going down to the shops** je sors faire des courses; **the ones you buy in shops** ceux que l'on achète en magasin; **you can't get these in the shops** on ne les trouve pas en magasin; **the new book should reach the shops in July** le nouveau livre devrait être en vente en juillet; **grocer's s.** épicerie *f*, **baker's s.** boulangerie *f*, **shoe s.** magasin de chaussures; **duty-free s.** boutique hors taxes; **mobile s.** boutique ambulante; *Old-fashioned* **s.!** il y a quelqu'un?; **to set up s.** *(to open a shop)* ouvrir un magasin; *(to set up as shopkeeper)* s'établir comme commerçant, -ante; **to set up s. as a hairdresser** ouvrir un salon de coiffure; **to set up s. on one's own** se mettre à son compte; **to keep (a) s.** tenir un magasin; **to mind the s.** garder le magasin; *Fig* assurer la permanence; *also Fig* **to shut up s.** fermer boutique; *(at the end of the day)* fermer le magasin; *Fig Fam* **you've come to the wrong s.** vous vous trompez de porte; *Fam* **he was staggering about all over the s.** il titubait fortement; **they're all over the s. on defence policy** leur politique de défense n'est absolument pas cohérente; **my notes are all over the s.** c'est la pagaille dans mes notes; **the defence was all over the s.** c'était la pagaille dans la défense; *Mktg* **s.'s own brand** marque *f* de magasin *ou* de détail(lant)

2 *Fam (act of shopping)* courses *fpl*, shopping *m*; **I do my big s. on a Friday** je fais mes grosses courses le vendredi

3 *Ind etc (workshop)* atelier *m*; **assembly s.** atelier de montage; **pattern s.** atelier de modelage; **repair s.** atelier de réparations; **carpenter's s.** atelier de menuiserie; **closed s.** = entreprise *f* qui n'admet que du personnel appartenant à un certain syndicat

4 *Fam* **to talk s.** parler boutique

vi (-pp-) **to s., to go shopping** (aller) faire ses courses; *(for food)* aller aux provisions; *(at market)* aller faire son marché; **to go shopping for clothes** aller acheter des vêtements, *Can* magasiner

vt *Br Sl (betray) (person)* dénoncer

▶▶ *Br* **s. assistant** vendeur, -euse (de magasin), employé, -ée de magasin; **s. floor** atelier *m*; **the s. floor** *(workforce)* les ouvriers *mpl*; **s. foreman** chef *m* d'atelier; *Br* **s. front** devanture *f*, **s. steward** porte-parole *mf inv* des ouvriers, délégué, -e syndical(e); **s. window** vitrine *f* (de magasin); *(display)* étalage *m*; **in the s. window** dans la *ou* en vitrine; *Fig* **a s. window for British exports** une vitrine pour les exportations britanniques

▶ **shop around** vi comparer les prix; **I shopped around before opening a bank account** j'ai comparé plusieurs banques avant d'ouvrir un compte; **our company is shopping around for new premises** notre société est à la recherche de nouveaux locaux

shopaholic [ˌʃɒpəˈhɒlɪk] N **he's a real s.** il adore faire les boutiques

shopfitter [ˈʃɒpfɪtər] N installateur *m ou* agenceur *m* de magasins

shopgirl [ˈʃɒpgɜːl] N *Old-fashioned* vendeuse *f*, employée *f* de magasin

shop-in-shop N *Com* boutiquage *m*, magasin *m* à l'intérieur d'une grande surface

shopkeeper [ˈʃɒpkiːpər] N commerçant, -ante

shoplifter [ˈʃɒplɪftər] N voleur, -euse à l'étalage

shoplifting [ˈʃɒplɪftɪŋ] N vol *m* à l'étalage

shopman, *pl* **shopmen** [ˈʃɒpmən] N *Am* mécanicien *m (dans un atelier de réparations)*

shopper [ˈʃɒpər] N **1** *(person)* streets crowded with shoppers des rues pleines de gens qui font leurs courses; **for the convenience of shoppers** *(sign in shop)* pour mieux servir nos clients **2** *Fam (bag)* sac *m* à provisions

shopping [ˈʃɒpɪŋ] N courses *fpl*, **to do one's/the s.** faire ses/les courses; *(for food)* aller aux provisions; *(at market)* faire son marché; **I hate s.** *(for food etc)* je déteste faire les courses; *(for clothes, wandering round shops)* je déteste faire du shopping; **to do one's Christmas s.** faire ses achats de Noël; **I had a lot of heavy s.** j'étais lourdement chargé d'achats; **I haven't got much s. to do** je n'ai pas beaucoup de courses à faire; **Saturday is my main s. day** le samedi est le jour où je fais mes grosses courses; **only three s. days to Christmas** il ne reste plus que trois jours pour faire les courses avant Noël; **my weekly s. trip** mes courses hebdomadaires; **for my next s. trip** la prochaine fois que j'irai faire les courses

▶▶ **s. arcade** galerie *f* marchande; **s. bag** sac *m ou* filet *m* à provisions, cabas *m*; **s. basket** panier *m* (à provisions); *Econ* panier de la ménagère; *Comput (for Internet shopping)* caddie *m*; *Am* **s. cart** chariot *m*, Caddie® *m*; *Comput (for Internet shopping)* caddie *m*; **s. centre** centre *m* commercial; *TV* **s. channel** chaîne *f* de télé-achat; **s. list** liste *f* des courses; *Am* **s. mall** galerie marchande; **s. plaza**, *Br* **s. precinct** centre commercial; **s. street** rue *f* commerçante; *Br* **s. trolley** chariot, Caddie®

shopsoiled [ˈʃɒpsɔɪld] ADJ *Br (article)* défraîchi; *(display goods)* qui a fait l'étalage

shoptalk [ˈʃɒptɔːk] N *Fam* **no s., OK?** on ne parle pas métier *ou* affaires *ou Fam* boutique, d'accord?

shopwalker [ˈʃɒpwɔːkər] N *Br* chef *m* de rayon

shopworn [ˈʃɒpwɔːn] ADJ *Am* = **shopsoiled**

shore¹ [ʃɔːr] N *(coast)* côte *f*, *(shoreline)* rivage *m*; *(of sea, lake, river)* bord *m*; **on the s.** sur le rivage; *(on beach)* sur la plage; *(by sea)* au bord de la mer; *Naut* **on s.** à terre; **to go on s.** se rendre à terre; *(disembark)* débarquer; *Lit* **distant shores** de lointains rivages; **she rarely visits our shores** elle visite rarement nos contrées; **to keep rabies from our shores** empêcher la rage d'atteindre nos côtes

▶▶ **s. excursion** excursion *f (lors d'une escale)*; **s. leave** permission *f* à terre

shore² N *Constr etc* étai *m*, étançon *m*

vt = **shore up**

▶ **shore up** vt sep *(support) (house, wall)* étayer, étançonner; *Fig (government)* étayer, consolider

shoreline [ˈʃɔːlaɪn] N rivage *m*; *(by sea)* côte *f*

shoreward(s) [ˈʃɔːwəd(z)] ADV vers la terre

shorn [ʃɔːn] ADJ **1** *(head)* rasé **2** *(sheep)* tondu

PP *see* **shear**

SHORT [ʃɔːt]

> **ADJ** court **1, 2** ▪ petit **1** ▪ bref **2**
> ▪ brusque **3** ▪ insuffisant **4**
> **N** court-métrage **1** ▪ court-circuit **3**

ADJ 1 *(physically)* court; *(person)* petit, de petite taille; **to be s. in the arm/leg** avoir les bras courts/les jambes courtes; *(of garment)* être court au niveau des bras/des jambes; **(at) a s. distance from the station** à peu de distance de la gare; **to have s. hair** avoir les cheveux courts; **to go by the shortest road, to go the shortest way** aller par le chemin le plus court; **a s. history of France** un précis d'histoire de France; **s. back and sides** *(haircut)* coupe *f* dégagée autour des oreilles; **at s. range** à courte portée

2 *(in time)* court, bref, *f* brève; **to take quick s. breaths** respirer à petits coups rapides; **the days are getting shorter** les jours raccourcissent; **s. and sweet** court mais bon; **that was s. and sweet!** c'était court mais c'était bien!; **in s.** *(to sum up)* bref, en résumé, en somme; **Bill is s. for William** Bill est le diminutif de William; **the s. answer is 'no'** en deux mots, la réponse est non; **a s. drink** un petit verre; **we've just got time for a s. game** nous avons juste le temps de faire une petite partie; **at s. intervals** à intervalles rapprochés; **to have a s. memory** avoir la mémoire courte; **to have a s. temper** s'emporter facilement; **for a s. time** pour un petit moment; **a s. time ago** il y a peu de temps; *Ind* **to be on s. time** être en chômage partiel; **to make s. work of sth** *(problem, difficulty)* résoudre qch en un clin d'œil; **he made s. work of his meal** il a avalé son repas en une minute; **you sure made s. work of that!** tu n'y es pas allé par quatre chemins!; **he made s. work of his opponent** il s'est débarrassé de son adversaire en un rien de temps

3 *(abrupt)* **to be s. with sb** être cassant avec qn; **he was very s. with me** il a été très brusque avec moi

4 *(insufficient, lacking)* *(weight, measure etc)* insuffisant; **to give sb s. measure** donner à qn moins que la quantité que l'on lui fait payer; **money is very s.** *or* **is in very s. supply** on est à court d'argent; **water is in s. supply** l'eau se fait rare; **it is two euros s.** il manque deux euros; **I am twenty euros s.** il me manque vingt euros; **50 s. of the thousand** mille moins 50; **to be s. of sth** *(of person)* être à court de qch, manquer de qch; **I'm a bit s. of cash** je suis un peu à court d'argent; **the country is s. of engineers** le pays manque d'ingénieurs; *Fam Hum* **he's one sandwich s. of a picnic** il a une case vide; **he's a bit s. on common sense** il manque un peu de bon sens

5 *(less than)* **little** *or* **not far s. of it** peu s'en faut; **he is not far s. of thirty** il frise la trentaine; **it is little s. of folly** c'est de la folie (pure); **it was nothing s. of a masterpiece** ce n'était rien moins qu'un chef-d'œuvre; **nothing s. of violence would compel him** il n'y a que la violence qui l'y obligerait

6 *St Exch* court, en position courte; *Fin* **bills at s. date** billets *mpl* *ou* traites *fpl* à courte échéance

N 1 *Cin (short film)* court métrage *m*, court *m*
2 *(drink)* alcool *m* fort
3 *Elec Fam (short circuit)* court-circuit *m*, *pl* courts-circuits
4 *(in prosody) (syllable)* brève *f*, *Ling (vowel)* voyelle *f* brève

ADV 1 hair cut s. cheveux coupés court
2 to stop s. s'arrêter (tout) net, *Fam* s'arrêter pile; **to stop s. of doing sth** se retenir de faire qch; **it just stops s. of being criminal** c'est à la limite de la criminalité; **she stopped s. of actually calling him a liar** pour un peu, elle le traitait de menteur; **to cut sb s.** couper la pa-

role à qn; *Fam* **to be caught s.** *(need to relieve oneself)* être pris d'un besoin pressant; *(not have enough money)* être à court d'argent

3 to go s. se priver; **to go s. of sth** se priver de qch; **we're running s. of …** *(supplies etc)* on est presqu'à court de …; **we are running s. of provisions, our provisions are running s.** nos vivres vont bientôt s'épuiser; **to fall s.** *(of arrow, bomb etc)* ne pas arriver jusqu'à la cible; **to fall s. of sb's expectations** décevoir qn; **to fall s. of one's duty** manquer à son devoir; **it falls far s. of what we need** c'est loin de suffire à nos besoins; **s. of a miracle, we are ruined** à moins d'un miracle, nous sommes perdus; **there's not much we can do, s. of selling the house** il n'y a pas grand-chose à faire, à part vendre la maison

4 *Fig* **to sell sb s.** *(betray)* trahir qn; *(trick)* rouler qn; **to sell oneself s.** ne pas se montrer à sa juste valeur

5 *St Exch* **to buy s.** acheter à court terme; **to sell s.** vendre à découvert

VT & VI *Elec Fam* = **short-circuit**

▸▸ *Fin* **s. bills** billets *ou* traites à courte échéance; **s. break** *(holiday)* mini-séjour *m*, *pl* mini-séjours; *Elec* **s. circuit** court-circuit; *pl* courts-circuits; *Horseracing etc* **s. odds** *or* **price** faible cote *f*, **s. order cook** = cuisinier *m* qui prépare les plats au fur et à mesure des commandes; *Culin* **s. pastry** pâte *f* brisée; *Fin* **s. payment** moins-perçu *m*, *pl* moins-perçus; *Fin, St Exch* **s. position** position *f* vendeur, position à découvert; *Horseracing etc* **s. price** faible cote; **s. sale** vente *f* à découvert; *Liter* **s. story** nouvelle *f*, *Ling* **s. syllable** syllabe *f* brève; *Ling* **s. vowel** voyelle brève; *Radio* **s. wave** onde *f* courte

shortage [ˈʃɔːtɪdʒ] **N** *(of money, food etc)* manque *m*, pénurie *f*; **the paper s.** la crise du papier; **we have constant staff shortages** nous manquons constamment de personnel; **there is no s. of applicants** on ne manque pas de candidats

short-arse **N** *Br Sl* nabot, -ote; **he/she is a little s.** il/elle est un peu court(e) sur pattes, *Pej* il/elle a le cul un peu bas

shortbread, shortcake [ˈʃɔːtbred, -keɪk] **N** *Culin* = sablé *m*

short-change **VT** *(intentionally)* voler (en rendant la monnaie); *(accidentally)* ne pas rendre assez de monnaie à; *Fig (cheat)* posséder

short-circuit **N** *Elec* court-circuit *m*, *pl* courts-circuits
VT *Elec, Fig* court-circuiter
VI *Elec* se mettre en court-circuit

shortcode [ˈʃɔːtkəʊd] **N** *Tel* code *m* abrégé
▸▸ **s. dialling** numérotation *f* abrégée

shortcoming [ˈʃɔːtkʌmɪŋ] **N** *(flaw) (usu pl)* **shortcomings** défauts *mpl*, imperfections *fpl*

shortcrust [ˈʃɔːtkrʌst] **ADJ**
▸▸ *Culin* **s. pastry** pâte *f* brisée

shortcut [ˈʃɔːtˈkʌt] **N** raccourci *m*; *Fig* **don't try to take shortcuts** n'essayez pas d'aller trop vite; **there are no shortcuts** on ne peut pas aller plus vite que la musique; **useful shortcuts** des trucs
▸▸ *Comput* **s. key** touche *f* de raccourci

short-dated **ADJ** *Fin (bill)* à courte échéance; *(paper)* court

shorten [ˈʃɔːt(ə)n] **VT** *(skirt etc)* raccourcir; *(text, task)* abréger; *(stay)* écourter; **Albert is often shortened to Bert** on utilise souvent le diminutif Bert à la place d'Albert; *Culin* **to s. pastry** travailler la pâte avec une matière grasse
VI *(of days etc)* raccourcir

shortening [ˈʃɔːtnɪŋ] **N 1** *(of days)* raccour-

cissement *m* **2** *(of text)* raccourcissement *m*, abrègement *m* **3** *Culin* matière *f* grasse

shortfall [ˈʃɔːtfɔːl] **N** manque *m*; *(financial)* déficit *m*; **there's a s. of $100** il manque 100 dollars

short-focus lens **N** *Phot* objectif *m* à courte focale

shorthaired [ˈʃɔːtheəd] **ADJ** *(person)* aux cheveux courts; *(animal)* à poil ras

shorthand [ˈʃɔːthænd] **N** *(writing system)* sténo(graphie) *f*, **to take a speech down in s.** sténographier un discours, prendre un discours en sténo; *Fig* **this is s. for …** c'est l'abréviation de …, en bref, ça signifie …
▸▸ **s. reporter** sténographe *mf*; **s. typing** sténodactylographie *f*, **s. typist** sténodactylo *mf*; **s. writer** sténographe; **s. writing** écriture *f* sténographique

shorthanded [ʃɔːtˈhændɪd] **ADJ** **to be s.** manquer de personnel

short-haul **ADJ** *(flight, route)* court-courrier, *pl* court-courriers
▸▸ **s. aircraft** court-courrier *m*, *pl* court-courriers

shorthorn [ˈʃɔːthɔːn] **N** shorthorn *m*

shortish [ˈʃɔːtɪʃ] **ADJ** assez *ou* plutôt court; *(person)* courtaud

short-legged **ADJ** aux jambes courtes

shortlist [ˈʃɔːtlɪst] **VT** *Br* sélectionner, retenir la candidature de; **to s. a candidate** retenir une candidature *(en vue d'une sélection ultérieure)*; **you've been shortlisted** on a retenu votre candidature
N liste *f* des candidats retenus

short-lived **ADJ** *(joy, triumph etc)* bref, *f* brève, éphémère, de courte durée

shortly [ˈʃɔːtlɪ] **ADV 1** *(soon)* bientôt, prochainement; *(in a couple of minutes)* sous peu; **s. after(wards)** *(soon afterwards)* peu (de temps) après; **President Smith, who was s. to be** *or* **would s. be re-elected** le président Smith, qui allait bientôt être réélu **2** *(abruptly) (to answer etc)* brusquement, sèchement

Attention: ne pas confondre avec **briefly**.

shortness [ˈʃɔːtnɪs] **N 1** *(physical) (of arm, skirt)* peu *m* de longueur; *(of person)* petite taille *f* **2** *(in time) (of life)* brièveté *f*, courte durée *f*; **s. of memory** manque *m* de mémoire **3** *(abruptness)* brusquerie *f* **4** *(lack) (of supplies etc)* manque *m*, insuffisance *f*

short-range **ADJ** *Mil* à courte portée; *(forecast)* à court terme

shorts [ʃɔːts] **NPL** *(short trousers)* short *m*; *Am (underwear)* caleçon *m*; **a pair of s.** un short VOIR GRAMMAIRE A10

shortsheet [ˈʃɔːtʃiːt] **VT** *Am (bed)* mettre en portefeuille

shortsighted [ʃɔːtˈsaɪtɪd] **ADJ 1** *Opt* myope **2** *Fig (approach etc)* imprévoyant; **that was very s. of you/him** *etc* ça n'était pas faire preuve de beaucoup de prévoyance

shortsightedness [ʃɔːtˈsaɪtɪdnɪs] **N 1** *Opt* myopie *f* **2** *Fig (of approach etc)* imprévoyance *f*

short-staffed [-stɑːft] **ADJ** à court de personnel; **to be s.** manquer de personnel

short-stay car park **N** parking *m* courte durée

short-tempered **ADJ** vif, *f* vive, d'un caractère emporté

short-term **ADJ** *(prisoner)* qui purge une peine de prison de courte durée; *(contract)* de courte durée; *(solution, memory), Fin* à court terme
▸▸ **s. borrowings** emprunts *mpl* à court terme; **s. loan** prêt *m* à court terme

short-termism [-'tɜːmɪz(ə)m] N politique f du court terme

short-time N to be on s. être en chômage partiel
ADJ to be on s. working être en chômage partiel
▸▸s. worker chômeur, -euse partiel(elle); s. working chômage m partiel

short-wave ADJ (radio) à ondes courtes

short-winded ADJ au souffle court; to be s. manquer de souffle

shorty ['ʃɔːtɪ] N Fam petit m, petite f; come on, s.! allez, le petit!

shot [ʃɒt] N1 (act of firing, sound) coup m (de feu); **pistol s.** coup de pistolet; **warning s.** coup d'avertissement; Naut coup de semonce; **to fire a s.** tirer un coup de feu; **without firing a s.** sans tirer un (seul) coup de feu; **parting s.** (remark) remarque f ou réplique f qu'on lance en partant, dernière remarque; **he's a good s.** c'est un bon tireur; Fam **a big s.** un type important, un grand manitou, Sl une grosse légume; **a s. across the bows** un tir d'avertissement; Fig un avertissement; **to fire a s. across the bows** tirer un coup en guise d'avertissement; Fig donner un avertissement
2 (inv in pl) (projectiles) (from shotgun) plomb m; **bird s.** cendrée f, Fig like a s. (speedily) comme une flèche; (with no hesitation) d'emblée, sans hésitation; Am Fam the whole s. tout le tremblement; Metal lead s. grenaille f de plomb
3 Sport (of shot putter) poids m; **to put the s.** lancer le poids
4 Sport (in tennis, golf etc) coup m; (in football, hockey) shoot m; **good s.!** bien joué!; Tennis etc drop s. amortie f, passing s. passing-shot m, pl passing-shots; to make a long s. (aim from a distance) viser de loin; Fig (guess wildly) deviner au hasard; (take a risk) prendre un (gros) risque; **not by a long s.** il s'en faut de beaucoup; Fig to take a s. in the dark (make a wild guess) donner une réponse complètement au hasard, Fam y aller au pifomètre; **I'm going to take a s. in the dark and say 1,000** je vais donner un chiffre au hasard, disons 1 000; Fig to call the shots prendre les décisions; Fig they call the shots c'est eux qui décident
5 Phot photo f, Cin, TV plan m, prise f de vue; **you can get a good s. of the castle from here** d'ici vous prendrez bien le château; **the opening shots of the movie** les premières images du film; **in s.** dans le champ; **out of s.** hors champ; **to go out of s.** sortir du champ; **high angle s.** plongée f
6 Fam (injection) piqûre f, Fam (drink) (of brandy etc) petit verre m; **a s. in the arm** (injection) une piqûre au bras; Fig (stimulation) un coup de fouet; **to give sb a s.** faire une piqûre à qn
7 Fig (attempt) **I'll have a s. at it/at doing it** je vais essayer ou tenter le coup; **I had a s. at learning Swahili** j'ai essayé d'apprendre le swahili; **it's worth having a s. at** ça vaut le coup; **her second s. at the presidency** sa deuxième tentative pour obtenir la présidence; **she made** or **had a good s. at it** elle a fait tout ce qu'elle pouvait; esp Am Fam **give it your best s.** fais de ton mieux
8 Fam (turn) tour m; **it's your s.** (in game) à vous de jouer; **to have a s. of sth** essayer qch; **it's my s. next** c'est mon tour; **you've had two shots already** tu as déjà essayé deux fois
ADJ **1 to get s. of sb/sth** se débarrasser de qn/qch; **to be s. of sb/sth** être débarrassé de qn/qch; **I can't wait to be s. of this house** j'ai hâte de me débarrasser de cette maison
2 esp Am Fam (exhausted) épuisé, crevé; (broken, spoilt) fichu, bousillé; **my nerves are s.** je suis à bout de nerfs; **that's another**

day s.! une autre journée de foutue (en l'air)!
▸▸s. glass petit verre; Cin, TV s. list liste f des prises (de vue); Sport s. put lancer m du poids; Sport s. putter lanceur, -euse de poids; Sport s. putting (lancer du) poids; Tex s. silk soie f changeante

shotgun ['ʃɒtgʌn] N fusil m de chasse
▸▸TV, Cin s. mike micro m canon; s. wedding mariage m forcé (lorsque la future mariée est enceinte)

SHOULD [ʃʊd] MODAL AUX V VOIR GRAMMAIRE
A58 **1** (duty or command) **you s. do it at once** vous devriez le faire tout de suite; **you s. have come earlier** vous auriez dû arriver plus tôt; **you/he etc s. not have gone** il ne fallait pas y aller; **a present? oh you shouldn't have!** un cadeau? vous n'auriez pas dû!; **it was an accident that s. have been foreseen** c'était un accident à prévoir; **you s. have seen her!** il fallait la voir!, si vous l'aviez vue!; **you shouldn't laugh at him** vous avez tort de vous moquer de lui; **I shouldn't do that if I were you** je ne ferais pas ça si j'étais toi; **I don't remember – well, you s.** je ne m'en souviens pas – eh bien, tu devrais
2 (expression of opinion) **she s. have arrived by this time** elle devrait être arrivée à l'heure qu'il est; **that s. suit you!** voilà qui fera sans doute votre affaire!; **this weather s. be ideal for anglers** ce temps devrait être idéal pour les pêcheurs; **what s. I have said?** qu'est-ce que j'aurais dû dire?; Iron **I s. worry!** (I don't worry about it) ce n'est pas mon affaire!; Iron **you s. worry about getting fat!** tu ne risques pas de grossir!; Iron **you s. complain!** tu n'as aucune raison de te plaindre!
3 (exclamatory, in rhetorical questions) **why s. you suspect me?** pourquoi me soupçonner?; **how s. I not be happy?** comment ne serais-je pas heureux?; **who s. I meet but Martin!** (et) voilà que je rencontre Martin!
4 (in subordinate clauses) **he ordered that they s. be released** il ordonna qu'on les relâchât; **she insisted that he s. wear his hair short** elle a exigé qu'il porte les cheveux courts; **I didn't want to, but he told me I s.** je ne voulais pas, mais il m'a dit que je devais le faire VOIR GRAMMAIRE A53–4
5 (in conditional clauses) if **he s. come** or Fml **s. he come, let me know** s'il vient, faites-le-moi savoir; **s. the occasion arise, s. it (so) happen** le cas échéant; **in case she s. not be there** au cas où elle ne serait pas là VOIR GRAMMAIRE A52
6 **my holiday was over, the next day I s. be far away** mes vacances étaient finies, le lendemain je serais bien loin
7 (in the main clause of conditional sentences) **we s. come if we were invited** nous viendrions si on nous invitait; **had you written to me I s. have answered you** si vous m'aviez écrit, je vous aurais répondu VOIR GRAMMAIRE A52–3
8 (in softened affirmation) **I s. like a drink** je prendrais bien quelque chose; **I s. have thought that you would have known better** j'aurais pensé que vous auriez été plus avisé; **I shouldn't be surprised (if…)** cela ne me surprendrait pas (que … + pr sub)

shoulder ['ʃəʊldər] N (of person), Culin épaule f, (of hill etc) épaulement m; (of mountain) contrefort m; **round shoulders** dos m rond ou voûté; **he's got broad shoulders** il est large d'épaules; Fig il a bon dos; **too tight across the shoulders** (of coat etc) trop étroit de carrure; **off-the-s. dress** robe f dégageant les épaules; **slung across** or **over the s.** (bag, rifle etc) en bandoulière; **to look over one's s.** vérifier si on est suivi; **to tell sb sth straight from the s.** dire qch carrément ou brutalement à qn; **to have a good head on one's shoulders** avoir la tête sur les épau-

les; **to rub shoulders with millionaires/film stars** côtoyer des millionnaires/stars du cinéma; **to lay the blame on sb's shoulders** rejeter la faute sur qn, Fam mettre la faute sur le dos de qn; Fig **to put one's s. to the wheel** se mettre à l'œuvre avec énergie; **to stand head and shoulders above the rest** (be far taller) dépasser les autres d'une tête; Fig (be far better) surpasser tous les autres; **s. high** à la hauteur des épaules; **to carry sb s. high** porter qn en triomphe; **s. to s.** (side by side) côte à côte, épaule contre épaule; **hard s.** (on road) bas-côté m, pl bas-côtés; **soft s.** (on road) accotement m non stabilisé
VT **1** (push) pousser avec l'épaule; **to s. one's way through the crowd** se frayer un passage à travers la foule à coups d'épaule; **to s. sb out of the way** or **aside** écarter ou repousser qn d'un coup d'épaule; **she shouldered the door open** elle ouvrit la porte d'un coup d'épaule **2** (put on shoulder) (object) mettre sur l'épaule; **to s. one's gun** mettre son fusil sur l'épaule; Fig **to s. the responsibility** endosser la responsabilité; Mil **to s. arms** se mettre au port d'armes; **s. arms!** portez armes!
▸▸s. bag sac m à bandoulière; s. belt ceinture f épaulière; s. blade omoplate f, (of horse etc) paleron m; Mil s. braid fourragère f, s. harness Aviat bretelles fpl; TV, Cin harnais m caméra; s. knot aiguillette f, Am Mil s. loop patte f d'épaule, épaulette f, s. pad (in garment) épaulette (coussinet de rembourrage); Sport protège-épaule m, pl protège-épaules; TV, Cin s. pod crosse f d'épaule; s. rate (in tourism) tarif m moyenne saison; s. season (in tourism) moyenne saison f, s. strap (on dress, bra, accordion) bretelle f, (on bag) bandoulière f, Mil patte d'épaule, épaulette

shout [ʃaʊt] N (of joy, pain etc) cri m; **shouts of laughter** éclats mpl de rire; **there was a s. of 'no more taxes!'** on cria 'plus d'impôts!'; Br, Austr Fam **it's my s.** (my round) c'est ma tournée
VI crier, pousser un cri/des cris; **there's no need to s.** inutile de crier; **to s. at sb** crier contre qn, Fam crier après qn; **don't s. at me!** baisse le ton!, Fam ne me crie pas après!; **to s. for sb** appeler qn de toutes ses forces; **to s. for help** crier ou appeler au secours; **to s. to sb to do sth** crier à qn de faire qch; Fig **it's nothing to s. about** (to boast about) il n'y a pas de quoi se vanter; Fig **to have something to s. about** avoir quelque raison de se réjouir
VT crier; (insults etc) vociférer; **to s. oneself hoarse** s'enrouer à force de crier; **'look out!', he shouted** 'attention!', cria-t-il
▸ **shout down** VT SEP (person) huer, conspuer; (proposal) conspuer; **the speaker was shouted down** l'orateur n'a pas réussi à se faire entendre
▸ **shout out** VI **I shouted out in pain** je hurlais de douleur
VT SEP crier

shouting ['ʃaʊtɪŋ] N cris mpl, (uproar) clameur f, **there was a lot of s.** on criait beaucoup; Fig **it's all over bar the s.** c'est dans le sac, c'est du tout cuit

shove [ʃʌv] N poussée f, (with shoulder etc) coup m; **to give sb/sth a s.** pousser qn/qch, donner une poussée à qn/à qch; Fig **he's lazy, he just needs a little s.** il est paresseux, il a juste besoin qu'on le pousse un peu
VT (person, object) pousser; **to s. sb/sth along** or **forward** pousser qn/qch en avant, faire avancer qn/qch; **to s. sth into a drawer** fourrer qch dans un tiroir
VI pousser; **stop shoving!** arrêtez de pousser!; **she shoved past me** elle m'a bousculé en passant
▸ **shove around** VT SEP **1** (push) bousculer **2**

Fam (bully) malmener; **I don't like being shoved around** je n'aime pas passer pour quantité négligeable

▶**shove aside, shove away** VT SEP *(push away) (person, object)* écarter d'une poussée

▶**shove off** VI *Fam (leave)* décamper; **s. off!** fiche le camp!

VT SEP *(launch) (boat)* pousser au large

▶**shove over** VI *Fam (move over)* se pousser

shove-halfpenny, shove-ha'penny ['ʃʌvheɪpnɪ] N *Br* = (jeu *m* du) galet *m*

shovel ['ʃʌv(ə)l] N pelle *f*, *Constr etc* **power/ steam s.** pelle mécanique/à vapeur

VT (-ll-) *(coal etc)* pelleter, prendre *ou* jeter à la pelle; *Fam* **to s. food into one's mouth** s'empiffrer

▶**shovel away** VT SEP *(snow etc)* déblayer

▶**shovel up** VT SEP *(grain etc)* ramasser *ou* entasser à la pelle

shoveler ['ʃʌvələr] N *(duck)* souchet *m*

shovelful ['ʃʌvəlful] N *(of sand etc)* pelletée *f*

SHOW [ʃəʊ]

N exposition **1** ▪ foire **1** ▪ spectacle **2** ▪ émission **2** ▪ apparence **3** ▪ ostentation **3** ▪ démonstration **3**		
VT montrer **1** ▪ présenter **1** ▪ témoigner **1** ▪ manifester **1** ▪ indiquer **2** ▪ prouver **3** ▪ démontrer **3** ▪ passer **4** ▪ diffuser **4**		
VI se voir **1** ▪ venir **2**		

N **1** *(exhibition)* exposition *f*, *(agricultural etc)* concours *m*, comice *m*; *(of animals)* foire *f*, **to be on s.** être exposé; **motor/air s.** salon *m* de l'automobile/de l'aviation; **fashion s.** présentation *f* de collections; **dog s.** exposition canine

2 *(play etc)* spectacle *m*; *(on television, radio)* émission *f*; **to go to a s.** aller au spectacle; *Theat* **to stop the s.** *(be a success)* faire un tabac; **the s. must go on** *Theat* le spectacle continue; *Fig* il faut continuer *(malgré le décès de qn etc)*; *Theat* **let's get this s. on the road!** allez, c'est parti, on y va!; *Fig* **to run the s.** être à la tête de *ou* diriger l'affaire; *Fig* **to make a s. of oneself** se donner en spectacle; **film s.** séance *f* de cinéma; *Radio, TV* **talk** *or* **chat s.** talk-show *m*, *pl* talk-shows; **one-man s.** solo *m*; **travelling s.** *(at a fair)* spectacle forain

3 *(act of showing) (appearance)* apparence *f*, *(pretence)* semblant *m*, simulacre *m*; *(ostentation)* parade *f*, ostentation *f*; **to vote by s. of hands** voter à mains levées; **it's all a s.** *(not genuine)* ce n'est qu'une façade; **to do sth for s.** *(to impress)* faire qch pour la forme; *(show off skills etc)* faire qch pour épater la galerie; **to be fond of s.** aimer l'éclat *ou* la parade; **s. of generosity** affectation *f* de générosité; **s. of strength** démonstration *f* de force; **to make a s. of resistance** faire semblant *ou* mine de résister; **to make a s. of being angry** faire semblant *ou* faire mine d'être fâché; **to make a great s. of friendship** faire de grandes démonstrations d'amitié; **to make a s. of learning** étaler sa culture

4 to put up a good s. *(of athlete, competitor etc)* bien se défendre; **the party put up a good s.** le parti s'est bien débrouillé; *Old-fashioned Fam* **good s.!** très bien!, bravo!; *Fam* **it was a poor** *or* **bad s.** c'était plutôt manqué; **it's a pretty poor s.** c'est vraiment lamentable

VT (*pt* **showed** [ʃəʊd]; *pp* **shown** [ʃəʊn]) **1** *(display) (thing, quality etc)* montrer; *(allow to be seen)* faire voir, laisser voir; *(passport)* présenter; *(gratitude etc)* témoigner; *(one's feelings)* manifester, laisser voir, laisser pa-

raître; *(courage, enthusiasm)* montrer, faire montre de; **to s. sth to sb, to s. sb sth** montrer *ou* faire voir qch à qn; **to s. sb how to do sth** montrer à qn comment faire qch; **to s. one's wares** étaler ses marchandises; **to s. one's cards** *or* **one's hand** *Cards* découvrir son jeu; *Fig (make one's intentions known)* jouer cartes sur table; **the picture shows three figures** le tableau représente trois personnes; **to have sth to s. for one's money** en avoir pour son argent; **to s. one's legs** montrer ses jambes; *Fam* **that dress shows everything she's got** cette robe ne cache pas grand-chose; **he won't s. his face here again** il ne se montrera plus ici; **a colour that doesn't s. the dirt** une couleur qui n'est pas salissante; **to s. oneself** se montrer, se faire voir; *(at a reception etc)* faire acte de présence; **to s. itself** se montrer; *(of emotion, tendency)* se manifester; **to s. a profit** faire ressortir un bénéfice, dégager des profits; **to s. a loss** accuser *ou* faire ressortir une perte; **to s. great improvement** faire apparaître une grande amélioration; **to s. a taste for sth** témoigner d'un goût pour qch; **his face showed his delight** la joie se voyait sur son visage; **she showed no sign of having heard anything** *(didn't reveal she had)* elle n'a pas montré qu'elle avait entendu; *(didn't seem to have)* elle n'a pas montré si elle avait entendu; **to s. one's age** faire son âge; **to s. oneself (to be) a coward** se montrer lâche; **she showed herself to be a hard worker** s'est révélée *ou* avérée dure à la tâche; **he showed me no mercy** il n'a fait preuve d'aucune pitié envers moi; **to s. willing** faire preuve de bonne volonté

2 *(indicate)* indiquer; **a diagram shows how the system works** un diagramme indique le fonctionnement du système; **place shown on a map** lieu indiqué sur une carte; **to s. the time/the temperature** *(of watch, thermometer etc)* indiquer l'heure/la température

3 *(prove, demonstrate)* prouver, démontrer; **these remarks s. how worried the government is** ces remarques témoignent de l'inquiétude du gouvernement; **a mere glance will s. that …** il suffit d'un coup d'œil pour se rendre compte que …; **which only** *or* **all goes to s. that …** ce qui prouve que …; **it just shows how lucky we are** ça vous montre la chance que nous avons; *Fam* **I'll s. you!** je vais vous apprendre!; *Law* **to s. cause** *or* **reason** *(set out one's reasons)* exposer ses raisons; *(offer valid reasons)* offrir des raisons valables

4 *(film)* passer, projeter; *(TV programme)* diffuser; *TV* **this programme will be shown tomorrow** cette émission passera (à l'écran) demain

5 *(escort, lead)* **to s. sb the way** indiquer *ou* montrer le chemin à qn; **to s. sb to his/her room** conduire qn à sa chambre; **to s. sb round the town** faire visiter *ou* faire voir la ville à qn; **we were shown over the house** on nous a fait visiter la maison; **to s. sb into a room** introduire *ou* faire entrer qn dans une pièce

VI **1** *(be or become visible)* se montrer, paraître, se voir; *(of buds)* sortir; **your slip's showing** votre jupon dépasse; **she lets her feelings s. too much** elle laisse trop voir ses sentiments; **it shows in your face** cela se voit *ou* se lit sur votre visage; **has she started to s. yet?** *(of pregnant woman)* est-ce que ça se voit qu'elle est enceinte?; **she's used to getting what she wants – it shows!** elle a l'habitude d'obtenir ce qu'elle veut – ça se voit!; **it doesn't s.** ça ne se voit pas, on ne dirait pas; **ah well, it just** *or* **all goes to s.!** eh oui, c'est la vie!

2 *Fam (arrive)* se pointer; **he didn't s.** il n'est pas venu

▶▶**s. animal** animal *m* de concours; **s. apartment** appartement *m* témoin; *TV etc* **s. copy** copie *f* antenne *ou* exploitation; **s. format** format *m* de présentation; **s. girl** girl *f*; **s. house** maison *f* témoin; **s. jumper** *(rider)* cavalier, -ère *(participant à des concours de saut d'obstacle)*; *(horse)* sauteur *m*; **s. jumping** jumping *m*, concours *m* de saut d'obstacles; *TV* **s. print** copie antenne *ou* exploitation; *Cin* **s. reel** film *m ou* cassette *f* de démonstration; *Theat Fam* **s. stopper** numéro *m* qui fait un tabac; *Law* **s. trial** procès *m* à grand spectacle; **s. window** vitrine *f (of magasin); (display)* étalage *m*

▶**show in** VT SEP *(escort inside)* faire entrer

▶**show off** VT SEP *(flaunt)* faire montre *ou* étalage de; *(show to advantage)* faire valoir, mettre en valeur; **they like to s. off their culture** ils aiment bien faire étalage de leur culture; **he likes to s. off his muscles/knowledge** il aime bien exhiber ses muscles/ connaissances; **she was showing off her new car** elle exhibait sa nouvelle voiture; **she came in to s. off her new baby** elle est venue faire admirer son nouveau-né; **coat that shows off the figure well** manteau qui marque *ou* dessine bien la taille; **wearing white shows off a tan** porter du blanc met le bronzage en valeur

VI *(try to impress)* se donner des airs, *Fam* faire de l'épate; *(with clothes, possessions etc)* parader, se pavaner; **to s. off in front of sb** chercher à épater qn; **stop showing off!** arrête de faire l'important *ou* de te donner des airs!; **you don't have to drive that fast, you're just showing off** ce n'est pas la peine de conduire aussi vite, tu cherches juste à nous épater

▶**show out** VT SEP *(escort out)* reconduire, accompagner jusqu'à la porte; **it's okay, I'll s. myself out** inutile de vous déranger, je saurai retrouver le chemin (tout seul)

▶**show through** VI se voir au travers; **her knickers showed through under her dress** on voyait sa culotte au travers de sa robe

▶**show up** VT SEP **1** *(reveal) (impostor etc)* démasquer, dénoncer; *(flaw etc)* révéler; **he's been shown up** il est grillé

2 *(shame)* faire honte à, embarrasser; *(deliberately humiliate)* humilier, vexer; **you're always showing me up in front of other people!** *(embarrassing me)* tu me mets toujours dans l'embarras devant les gens!

3 *(escort upstairs)* accompagner en haut

VI **1** *(be evident) (against a background)* se dessiner, se détacher, ressortir; **the dirt really shows up on a white carpet** la saleté ressort vraiment sur une moquette blanche

2 *Fam (arrive)* venir; **to fail to s. up** ne pas se présenter; **they'll s. up at twelve** ils s'amèneront à midi; **you're the boss, you really ought to s. up** tu es le patron, tu devrais vraiment y aller *ou* te montrer

showbiz ['ʃəʊbɪz] N *Fam* industrie *f ou* monde *m* du spectacle, showbiz *m*

▶▶**s. personality** personnalité *f* du showbiz *ou* du monde du spectacle

showboat ['ʃəʊbəʊt] N *Am* bateau-théâtre *m*, *pl* bateaux-théâtres

showbusiness ['ʃəʊbɪznɪs] N industrie *f ou* monde *m* du spectacle; **that's s.!** c'est ça, la vie d'artiste!

▶▶**s. personality** personnalité *f* du monde du spectacle

showcase ['ʃəʊkeɪs] N *Com* vitrine *f*, *Fig* **the exhibition will be a s. for Italy's best furniture designers** l'exposition sera la vitrine de tous les meilleurs créateurs de mobilier d'Italie

showdown ['ʃəʊdaʊn] N *Fam (confrontation)* confrontation *f*

shower ['ʃaʊər] N **1** *(of rain)* averse *f*, *(of*

blows, stones) volée *f*; *(of sparks)* gerbe *f*; *(of insults)* avalanche *f*; **heavy s.** *(of rain)* ondée *f*, grosse averse **2** *(for washing)* *(act, device)* douche *f*; **to have** *or* **take a s.** prendre une douche, se doucher; **he was in the s. for half an hour** il est resté une demi-heure sous la douche **3** *Astron* **meteor s.** essaim *m* de météores **4** *Am Fam (party)* réception *f* où chacun apporte un cadeau **5** *Br Fam Pej (group)* **what a s.!** quelle bande *ou* quel tas de crétins!; **you lazy s!** bande de flemmards!

vt verser; *(water)* faire gicler (**onto** sur); **to s. blows on sb** faire pleuvoir des coups sur qn; **to s. gifts/honours on sb** combler qn de cadeaux/d'honneurs; **I've been showered with invitations** je suis submergé d'invitations; **to s. compliments on sb** inonder qn de compliments

vi *(take a shower)* prendre une douche, se doucher

► *Old-fashioned* **s. bath** bain-douche *m, pl* bains-douches; **s. cabinet** cabine *f* de douche; **s. cap** bonnet *m* de douche; **s. curtain** rideau *m* de douche; **s. gel** gel *m* de douche; **s. head** pomme *f* de douche; **s. room** salle *f* de douches *ou* d'eau; **s. unit** bloc-douche *m, pl* blocs-douches

► **shower down vi** *(of rocks)* tomber; *Fig (of compliments, insults)* pleuvoir; **rocks showered down on us** des pierres s'abattirent sur nous

showerproof ['ʃaʊəpruːf] **ADJ** *Tex* imperméable

showery ['ʃaʊərɪ] **ADJ** *(weather)* pluvieux; **it's s.** *(weather)* le temps est à l'averse

showground ['ʃəʊɡraʊnd] **N** *(fairground)* champ *m* de foire; *(for equestrian event etc)* terrain *m* de concours hippique*etc*

showily ['ʃaʊɪlɪ] **ADV** de façon voyante *ou* ostentatoire; **s. dressed** habillé de façon voyante

showiness ['ʃaʊɪnɪs] **N** faste *m*, ostentation *f*; *(of jewellery)* clinquant *m*; *(of dress, decoration)* luxe *m* criard *ou* tapageur

showing ['ʃəʊɪŋ] **N 1** *(exhibition)* exposition *f* **2** *(of film)* projection *f*; *TV, Cin* présentation *f*; **the first s. will be at ...** la première projection aura lieu à ... **3** *(performance)* performance *f*; **a poor s. by our team** une déplorable performance de la part de notre équipe; **on this s. we don't stand a chance in the championship** vu cette performance, on n'a pas une chance de gagner le championnat **4** *esp Fml* **on your own s.** *(admission)* comme vous le dites vous-même

► ► **s. off** vantardise *f*

showman, *pl* **showmen** ['ʃəʊmən] **N** *(at fair)* forain *m*; *Fig* **he's a real s.** il a le sens du spectacle

showmanship ['ʃəʊmənʃɪp] **N** *(of person)* sens *m* du spectacle; **the s. of his act** son numéro spectaculaire; *Fig Pej* **it's just s.** c'est du cinéma

shown PP *see* **show VT, VI**

show-off N *Fam (person)* m'as-tu-vu *mf inv*; *Fam* frimeur, -euse; **John's a terrible s.** John est un sacré prétentieux; **don't be a s.** *(with clothes, possessions, skills)* arrête de faire de l'épate *ou Fam* de frimer

showpiece ['ʃəʊpiːs] **N** *(in exhibition etc)* œuvre *f*; *Fig* **the locals regarded the new theatre as something of a s.** les gens du quartier considéraient le nouveau théâtre comme leur joyau

showplace ['ʃəʊpleɪs] **N** *(scenic place)* endroit *m* pittoresque

showring ['ʃəʊrɪŋ] **N** *(at auction) (for horses, cattle etc)* arène *f* de vente; *(at equestrian event)* arène *f* de concours hippique

showroom ['ʃəʊruːm] **N** *(for purchasing)* magasin *m*; *(display only)* salle *f ou* salon *m*

d'exposition; *(for cars etc)* salle d'exposition, showroom *m*; **electricity s.** magasin d'électroménager *(où l'on peut aussi payer ses factures d'électricité)*; **in s. condition** à l'état neuf

show-stopping ADJ sensationnel

showy ['ʃəʊɪ] **ADJ** *(appearance, dress)* voyant, *Pej* tapageur, -euse, tape-à-l'œil *inv*; *(jewellery)* clinquant; *(decoration, wallpaper)* criard, tape-à-l'œil; **he's a bit s. in the way he dresses** la façon dont il s'habille est un peu voyante; **he's a bit s. in the way he acts** il se fait un peu trop remarquer

shrapnel ['ʃræpn(ə)l] **N 1** *Mil (fragments)* éclats *mpl* d'obus; *(shell)* shrapnel *m*; **a piece of s.** un éclat d'obus **2** *Fam (loose change)* mitraille *f*

► ► **s. wound** blessure *f* provoquée par des éclats d'obus

shred [ʃred] **N** *(of fabric, paper etc)* lambeau *m*; *(of meat etc)* morceau *m*; **to tear sth (in)to shreds** *(into small pieces)* déchiqueter qch; *(into strips)* mettre qch en lambeaux; **to tear sb's reputation to shreds** démolir la réputation de qn; **to tear sb to shreds** démolir qn; **to tear sb's argument/a play to shreds** démolir l'argument de qn/une pièce; **his reputation was in shreds** sa réputation était ruinée; **his argument was in shreds** son argument était réduit à néant; **her dress was all in shreds** sa robe était tout en lambeaux; **there isn't a s. of evidence** il n'y a pas la moindre preuve; **anyone with a s. of decency would have refused** n'importe qui ayant un minimum de décence aurait refusé; **not a s. of truth** pas un grain de vérité; **without a s. of clothing** on nu comme un ver

vt (**-dd-**) *(something)* déchirer en lambeaux; *(confidential documents)* déchiqueter, broyer, détruire; *Culin (grate)* couper en lamelles

shredded ['ʃredɪd] **ADJ** *Am Fam (drunk)* bourré, pété

shredder ['ʃredər] **N** *(device) (for confidential documents)* destructeur *m* de documents

shreddies ['ʃredɪz] **NPL** *Fam (underwear)* calbute *m*, calcif *m*

shredding ['ʃredɪŋ] **N** *(of fabric, paper)* déchiquetage *m*, broyage *m*; *(confidential documents)* destruction *f*

► ► **s. machine** déchiqueteuse *f*, broyeuse *f*

shrew [ʃruː] **N 1** *Zool (animal)* musaraigne *f* **2** *Pej (woman)* mégère *f*

shrewd [ʃruːd] **ADJ** *(person etc)* sagace; *(businessman)* astucieux; **he's a s. man** c'est une fine mouche; **s. answer** réponse *f* adroite; **that was a s. move** c'était bien joué; **I've got a s. idea that ...** je suis porté à croire que ...; **to make a s. guess** deviner juste; **I could make a pretty s. guess** ce n'est pas difficile à deviner

shrewdly ['ʃruːdlɪ] **ADV** astucieusement

shrewdness ['ʃruːdnɪs] **N** sagacité *f*, finesse *f*

shrewish ['ʃruːɪʃ] **ADJ** *Pej (woman)* acariâtre

shriek [ʃriːk] **N** *(of person, animal)* cri *m* aigu *ou* perçant; **shrieks of joy** cris joyeux; **shrieks of laughter** grands éclats *mpl* de rire; **to give a s.** pousser un cri perçant

vi *(of person)* pousser un cri aigu *ou* perçant; *(of wind)* hurler; **to s. with laughter/pain** hurler de rire/douleur

vt to s. (out) a warning pousser un cri d'avertissement

shrieking ['ʃriːkɪŋ] **N** cris *mpl* aigus *ou* perçants

shrift [ʃrɪft] **N** *Fam* **to give sb short s.** expédier qn, envoyer promener qn; **I got short s. from him** il m'a envoyé promener, *Iron* il m'a bien reçu

shrike [ʃraɪk] **N** *(bird)* pie-grièche *f*, *pl* pies-grièches

shrill [ʃrɪl] **ADJ** *(voice, sound etc)* aigu, *f* aiguë, perçant; *(complaint etc)* véhément; **in a s. voice** d'une voix perçante; **a s. whistle** *(sound)* un coup de sifflet strident

vi *Lit* pousser un son aigu *ou* strident; **a whistle shrilled** un coup de sifflet déchira l'air

shrillness ['ʃrɪlnɪs] **N** *(of sound)* acuité *f*, stridence *f*

shrilly ['ʃrɪlɪ] **ADV** *(to say)* d'un ton aigu; *(to protest)* de façon virulente

shrimp [ʃrɪmp] **N** *(crustacean)* crevette *f* (grise); *Fam Pej (short person)* nabot, -ote

vi to go shrimping, to s. pêcher la crevette, aller à la pêche à la crevette

► ► **s. boat** crevettier *m*; **s. net** haveneau *m*

shrimping net ['ʃrɪmpɪŋ] **N** crevettier *m* *(filet)*

shrine [ʃraɪn] **N 1** *(saint's tomb)* tombeau *m* de saint(e) **2** *(reliquary)* châsse *f*, reliquaire *m* **3** *(place of pilgrimage)* lieu *m* de pèlerinage

shrink [ʃrɪŋk] **vi** *(pt* **shrank** [ʃræŋk]; *pp* **shrunk** [ʃrʌŋk], *as adj* **shrunken** ['ʃrʌŋk(ə)n]) **1** *(become smaller)* (se) rétrécir, rapetisser; *(of income, budget)* diminuer; *(of material etc)* rétrécir; *(of person)* (out of shyness etc) se faire tout petit; **tropical rainforests are shrinking in size** la surface des forêts tropicales humides est en train de diminuer; **he is beginning to s. (with age)** il commence à se tasser; **to s. in the wash** rétrécir au lavage; *Fig* **to s. into oneself** rentrer en soi-même **2** *(move away)* reculer; **to s. from sth** reculer devant *ou* se dérober à qch; **to s. in horror** reculer d'horreur; **to s. from doing sth** reculer *ou* répugner à faire qch

vt *(fabric) (deliberately)* faire rétrécir; **I've shrunk my pullover** *(accidentally)* mon pull a rétréci; **fully shrunk material** tissu irrétrécissable

N *Fam (psychiatrist)* psy *mf*

► **shrink back vi** *(move away)* avoir un mouvement de recul; **to s. back in horror** reculer d'horreur

shrinkage ['ʃrɪŋkɪdʒ] **N 1** *(of wood)* retrait *m*; *Tex etc* rétrécissement *m* **2** *Com (through pilferage)* coulage *m*; *(through damage)* casse *f*

shrinking ['ʃrɪŋkɪŋ] **N 1** *(act of becoming smaller)* = **shrinkage 1 2** *(act of moving back)* **s. from sth** recul *m* devant qch; **she's no s. violet** elle n'est pas timide; **stop acting like a s. violet** arrête de faire ton/ta timide

shrink-wrap vt emballer sous film plastique

shrink-wrapped ADJ sous film plastique

shrink-wrapping N 1 *(process)* emballage *m* sous film plastique **2** *(material)* film *m* plastique

shrive [ʃraɪv] **vt** *(pt* **shrove** [ʃrəʊv]; *pp* **shriven** ['ʃrɪv(ə)n]) *Arch (a penitent)* confesser, absoudre

shrivel ['ʃrɪv(ə)l] (**-ll-**, *Am* **-l-**) **vt** *(skin)* rider; *(apple)* rider, ratatiner; *(of sun) (plants)* dessécher

vi *(of plant, apple)* se rider, se ratatiner

► **shrivel up vi** *(of plant, skin)* se rider, se ratatiner; *Fig* **I shrivelled up with embarrassment** je serais rentré dans un trou de souris, tellement j'étais gêné

vt sep *(apple, skin)* ratatiner; *(plants, leaves)* complètement dessécher

shrivelled ['ʃrɪv(ə)ld] **ADJ** ratatiné

shroud [ʃraʊd] **N 1** *(for dead body)* linceul *m*, suaire *m*; *Fig* **in a s. of mystery** enveloppé de mystère; *Lit* **under a s. of darkness** sous les voiles de la nuit **2** *(rope, cord) (for aerial, mast)* hauban *m*; *(of parachute)* suspente *f*

VT *(body)* ensevelir; *Fig (something)* envelopper, voiler (**in** de); **shrouded in mist/mystery** enveloppé de brume/mystère; **shrouded in gloom** *(meeting, person)* plongé dans la tristesse
▸ ▸ **s. line** *(of parachute)* suspente

Shrove [ʃrəʊv] **ADJ**
▸ ▸ **S. Tuesday** Mardi *m* gras

Shrovetide ['ʃrəʊvtaɪd] **N** *Rel* les jours *mpl* gras

shrub [ʃrʌb] **N** *(plant)* arbrisseau *m*, arbuste *m*

shrubbery ['ʃrʌbərɪ] **N** massif *m* d'arbustes; **the ball disappeared into the s.** la balle disparut dans les massifs (d'arbustes)

shrug [ʃrʌg] **N s. (of the shoulders)** haussement *m* d'épaules; **with a s. (of his shoulders)** en haussant les épaules; **he gave a s. of contempt** il haussa les épaules en signe de mépris
VT (**-gg-**) **to s. one's shoulders** hausser les épaules
VI hausser les épaules
▸ **shrug off VT SEP** *(treat as unimportant)* *(problem, other people's feelings etc)* ignorer; *(danger)* mépriser

shrunken ['ʃrʌŋk(ə)n] **ADJ** *(garment, fabric)* rétréci; *(person, body)* ratatiné; *(head)* réduit; **s. with age** *(person)* tassé par l'âge

shtick [ʃtɪk] **N** *Am Fam* numéro *m*

shuck [ʃʌk] *Am* **N 1** *(of peas, beans)* cosse *f*, gousse *f*; *(of sweetcorn)* spathe *f*; *(of nut)* écale *f*; *(of oyster, clam)* coquille *f* **2** *Fam (trick)* arnaque *f*
INT *Fam* **shucks!** mince (alors)!, flûte (alors)!
VT 1 *(peas, beans)* écosser; *(sweetcorn)* éplucher; *(nuts)* écaler; *(oysters, clams)* écailler **2** *Fam (garment)* ôter; **to s. one's clothes** se déshabiller **3** *Fam (tease)* faire marcher, mener en bateau; *(trick)* arnaquer **4** = **shuck off**
▸ **shuck off VT SEP** *Am (discard)* se débarrasser de; *(rid oneself of) (bad habit)* se défaire de

shudder ['ʃʌdər] **N** *(of person)* frisson *m*, frémissement *m*; *(of engine)* vibration *f*; *Fam* **it gives me the shudders** j'en ai des frissons
VI frissonner (**with** de); *(of machine, vehicle, ship etc)* vibrer; **I s. to think of it** *or* **at the thought of it** j'ai des frissons rien que d'y penser; **I s. to think what went into this soup** je frémis à l'idée de ce qu'il peut y avoir dans cette soupe; **I s. to think** je n'ose y penser; **the bus shuddered to a halt** le bus s'immobilisa en vibrant

shuffle ['ʃʌf(ə)l] **N 1** *(in walking)* traînement *m* de pieds, pas *m* traînant; *(in dancing)* frottement *m* de pieds; **soft shoe s.** = danse *f* de music-hall *(exécutée en chaussons)* **2** *Cards* mélange *m*; **to give the cards a s.** battre *ou* mélanger les cartes
VT *(mix)* *(papers etc)* brasser; *Cards* battre, mélanger; **to s. one's feet** *(in walking)* traîner les pieds; **he stood there shuffling his feet** il était là debout dansant d'un pied sur l'autre
VI 1 *(drag one's feet)* traîner les pieds; **she shuffled into the room** elle entra dans la pièce en traînant les pieds; **the children were shuffling in their seats** les enfants s'agitaient sur leur chaise **2** *Cards* mélanger
▸ **shuffle along VI** *(walk dragging one's feet)* avancer en traînant les pieds
▸ **shuffle off VI** *(walk away dragging one's feet)* s'en aller en traînant les pieds; **the badger shuffled off into the bushes** le blaireau disparut dans les buissons en trottinant
VT SEP *(set aside) (responsibility)* rejeter (**onto sb** sur qn); **to s. a job off onto sb** refiler un boulot à qn; *Hum* **to s. off this mortal coil** mourir

shuffleboard ['ʃʌf(ə)lbɔːd] **N** (jeu *m* de) palet *m*

shuffling ['ʃʌflɪŋ] **ADJ** *(gait)* traînant

shufti, shufty ['ʃʊftɪ] **N** *Br Fam* coup *m* d'œil; **have a s. at this** jettes-y un coup d'œil; **can I have a s.?** je peux jeter un coup d'œil?

shun¹ [ʃʌn] **INT** *Mil etc Fam (attention!)* garde-à-vous!

shun² **VT** (**-nn-**) *(somebody, something)* fuir, éviter; *(publicity)* fuir; **to s. society** fuir le monde; **to s. everybody** éviter tout le monde

shunt [ʃʌnt] **VT 1** *Rail (train, carriages)* manœuvrer; **to s. a train onto a siding** aiguiller un train sur une voie de garage; *Fam* **we were shunted into another room** on nous a parqués dans une autre pièce; *Fam* **the responsibility was shunted back and forth between departments** la responsabilité a été renvoyée de service en service **2** *Elec (circuit etc)* shunter, dériver; *(condenser)* monter en dérivation **3** *Fam (to push)* pousser; **he just shunted me out of his way** il m'a poussé hors de son chemin; **s. that box of files over here, will you?** passe-moi ce carton de dossiers, tu veux!
VI *Fam* **I spent the day shunting back and forth between the two offices** j'ai passé ma journée à faire la navette entre les deux bureaux
N *Elec* shunt *m*, dérivation *f*

shunter ['ʃʌntər] **N** *Rail (train)* locomotive *f* de manœuvre

shunting ['ʃʌntɪŋ] **N 1** *Rail* manœuvre *f* **2** *Elec* dérivation *f*, shuntage *m*
▸ ▸ *Rail* **s. engine** locomotive *f ou* machine *f* de manœuvre; *Rail* **s. operations** manœuvres *fpl* de triage; *Rail* **s. yard** gare *f* de triage

shush [ʃʊʃ] **INT** chut!
VT *(person)* faire taire

shut [ʃʌt] **VT** *(pt, pp* **shut;** *prp* **shutting)** *(door, shop, box, book etc)* fermer; **to s. the door on sb** *or* **in sb's face** fermer la porte au nez de qn; **to s. one's eyes** fermer les yeux; **to s. one's ears to sth** refuser d'entendre qch; **to s. one's mind to the possibility that …** se refuser à l'éventualité que …; **s. your mind to it!** ne pense pas à ça!; **to s. one's finger in the door** se pincer le doigt dans la porte; *Fam* **to s. sb's mouth (for him)** faire taire qn; *Sl* **s. your mouth** *or* **face!** la ferme!, ta gueule!
VI *(of door, lid etc)* (se) fermer; *(of shop, museum etc)* fermer; **the door won't s.** la porte ne ferme pas; **the door s. to** la porte s'est fermée (toute seule)
ADJ fermé; **to find the door s.** trouver la porte fermée, trouver porte close; *Fam* **to keep one's mouth s.** avoir la bouche cousue; **keep your mouth s.!** ferme-la!; **they always keep the door s.** ils gardent toujours la porte fermée; **keep the door s.!** ferme la porte!
▸ **shut away VT SEP to s. oneself away** s'enfermer; **to s. oneself away from the world** s'isoler du monde; **these objects have been s. away for centuries** ces objets sont restés enfermés pendant des siècles
▸ **shut down VT SEP** *(factory, airport etc)* fermer; *(production)* arrêter; *Tech (steam, power)* couper; *Aviat (engine)* couper, arrêter; *Comput (system)* arrêter; *(computer)* éteindre
VI *(of factory etc) (through lack of work)* fermer temporairement; *(for holiday)* fermer; *(permanently)* fermer ses portes; *(of TV station etc for the night)* arrêter ses programmes; *Comput (of system)* s'arrêter
▸ **shut in VT SEP** *(confine) (person, object)* enfermer; **to s. oneself in** s'enfermer; **to feel s. in** avoir un sentiment d'étouffement; **we're s. in by hills** nous sommes entourés de collines

▸ **shut off VT SEP 1** *(stop) (electricity, water)* couper; *Aut (engine)* couper, arrêter; **to s. off funds** couper des crédits **2** *(block) (road)* couper; *(pipe, exit)* boucher **3** *(isolate)* isoler (**from** de); **she s. herself off from other people** elle s'isolait du reste des gens; **to be s. off from society** être exclu du monde; **you shouldn't s. yourself off so** tu ne devrais pas t'isoler comme ça
▸ **shut out VT SEP 1** *(exclude) (person)* exclure; *(air, light, competition)* bloquer; *(memory etc)* chasser; **the trees s. out the view** les arbres bouchent la vue; **to s. sb from** *or* **of sth** exclure qn de qch; **I've s. her out of my life** je l'ai rayée de ma vie **2** *(keep outside)* **to s. sb out (of doors)** fermer la porte à qn; **I've s. myself out (of my house)** je me suis enfermé dehors; **he's taken the keys and has s. me out** il a pris les clefs et du coup je suis enfermé dehors **3** *Am Sl (prevent from scoring)* empêcher de marquer
▸ **shut up VT SEP 1** *(confine) (person, object)* enfermer; **to s. oneself up** s'enfermer chez soi; **to s. sb up (in prison)** emprisonner qn **2** *(close) (room)* fermer; **to s. up shop** *(close shop at end of day)* fermer le magasin; *(close shop permanently)* fermer boutique; *(of theatre etc)* fermer ses portes **3** *(close completely) (west wing etc)* condamner; *(opening etc)* obstruer, boucher; **to s. up a house** *(when going away)* boucler une maison **4** *Fam (make quiet) (person)* faire taire; *(using threats or violence)* réduire au silence; **s. those kids up!** faites taire ces gamins!; **that ought to s. him up** *(stop him boasting)* ça devrait lui rabattre son caquet; *(stop him complaining)* ça devrait le calmer
VI *Fam* se taire; **s. up!** tais-toi!; *(aggressive) Sl* la ferme!, ta gueule!; **he never knows when to s. up** il ne sait pas se taire *ou* la fermer quand il faut; **to s. up about sth** la fermer à propos de qch

shutdown ['ʃʌtdaʊn] **N** *(of factory) (temporary)* fermeture *f* temporaire; *(permanent)* fermeture; *(of machine, computer)* fermeture, arrêt *m* de fin de session

shut-eye **N** *Fam* roupillon *m*; **to have** *or* **catch a bit of s.** roupiller, coincer la bulle

shut-in **ADJ** **to have a s. feeling** *(in room etc)* se sentir enfermé; *(in relationship)* se sentir prisonnier, -ière
N *Am* invalide *mf* confiné chez lui/elle

shut-off **N 1** *(device)* **the automatic s. didn't work** le dispositif d'arrêt automatique n'a pas fonctionné **2** *(action)* arrêt *m*

shut-out **N 1** *Ind* lock-out *m inv* **2** *Am Sl (win)* éclatante victoire *f*
▸ ▸ *Cards* **s. bid** ouverture *f* préventive

shutter ['ʃʌtər] **N 1** *(on window)* volet *m*; *(slatted)* **shutters** persiennes *fpl*; **(folding) shutters** volets pliants; **to open/close the shutters** ouvrir/fermer les volets; **to put up the shutters** *(of shop)* fermer la/les devanture(s), mettre les volets; *Fig (close shop permanently)* fermer boutique **2** *Phot* obturateur *m*; **to release the s.** actionner l'obturateur
▸ ▸ **s. release** déclencheur *m* d'obturateur; **s. speed** vitesse *f* d'obturation

shuttered ['ʃʌtəd] **ADJ** *(window) (with shutters)* à volets; *(with shutters closed)* à volets fermés; **the house has s. windows** la maison a des volets

shuttering ['ʃʌtərɪŋ] **N** *(for concrete)* coffrage *m*

shutting ['ʃʌtɪŋ] **N** fermeture *f*
▸ ▸ **s. down** *(of factory)* fermeture; *(of machine, computer)* fermeture, arrêt *m* de fin de session

shuttle ['ʃʌt(ə)l] **N 1** *Tex, Sewing etc* navette *f* **2** *(vehicle, service)* navette *f*; *Astronaut* **space s.** navette spatiale **3** = **shuttlecock**

VI faire la navette (**between** entre)

VT **to s. sb back and forth** or **to and fro** (of shuttle bus etc) transporter qn d'un endroit à un autre; Pej (from office to office etc) envoyer qn à droite et à gauche, Fam balader qn; **to s. back and forth** (tape) faire avancer et reculer rapidement pour repérer un point précis; **to s. a document to and fro** transbahuter un document d'un endroit à un autre

▶▶ **s. diplomacy** navette diplomatique; **s. service** service m de navettes, navette

shuttlecock ['ʃʌt(ə)lbɒk] N Sport volant m

shy¹ [ʃaɪ] N **1** (throw) (of stone etc) jet m, lancement m; **to take a s. at sth with a stone** tirer sur qch avec un caillou; **5p a s.** (at fairs) 5 pence le coup **2** Old-fashioned Fam (attempt) (to achieve sth) essai m, tentative f; **to have a s. at doing sth** s'essayer à faire qch ▪ VT (pt, pp **shied**; prp **shying**) (throw) (stone etc) lancer, jeter (**at sb** à qn)

shy² ADJ (comp **shyer**, superl **shyest**) **1** (person, child) timide; (bird) sauvage, farouche; **to make sb s.** intimider qn; **to be s. of people** être gêné ou mal à l'aise en société; **to be s. of doing sth** hésiter à faire qch; **he fought s. of admitting his interest** il a fait tout ce qu'il a pu pour ne pas avoir à admettre qu'il était intéressé **2** esp Am **to be s. of** (lack) (something) manquer de; **we're still 500 dollars s.** il nous manque encore 500 dollars

shy³ VI (pt, pp **shied**; prp **shying**) (of horse) s'effaroucher; **to s. at sth** (of horse) s'effaroucher devant qch; Fig (of person) renâcler devant qch

▶ **shy away** VI (retreat in fear, nervousness) **to s. away from sth/doing sth** éviter qch/de faire qch; **to s. away from an idea** se méfier d'une idée; **he has shied away from driving since the accident** il évite de conduire depuis l'accident

Shylock ['ʃaɪlɒk] N Fam Pej usurier, -ière

shyly ['ʃaɪlɪ] ADV (to smile, suggest, look on etc) timidement; (to blush) de timidité

shyness ['ʃaɪnɪs] N (of person, child) timidité f; (of animal) caractère m farouche; **to lose one's s.** s'enhardir

shyster ['ʃaɪstər] N esp Am Pej Fam (lawyer) avocat m marron; (businessman) escroc m

SI [e'saɪ] N Tech (abbr **Système International**) SI m; **SI units** unités fpl de SI

si [si:] N Mus si m

Siam [saɪ'æm] N Hist Siam m

Siamese [saɪə'miːz] ADJ Hist siamois ▪ N **1** Hist (person) Siamois, -oise **2** Ling, Hist siamois m **3** (cat) siamois m

▶▶ **S. cat** chat m siamois; **S. twins** (male) frères mpl siamois; (female) sœurs fpl siamoises; Fam **they're like S. twins, those two!** c'est des vrais siamois, ces deux-là!

siamesed [saɪə'miːzd] ADJ Aut (joined together) siamois

Siberia [saɪ'bɪərɪə] N Sibérie f

Siberian [saɪ'bɪərɪən] ADJ sibérien ▪ N Sibérien, -ienne

sibilance ['sɪbɪləns] N TV, Radio sifflante f

sibilant ['sɪbɪlənt] ADJ sifflant ▪ N Ling sifflante f

sibling ['sɪblɪŋ] N (brother) frère m; (sister) sœur f

▶▶ **s. rivalry** rivalité f entre frères et sœurs

sibyl ['sɪbɪl] N sibylle f

sibylline ['sɪbɪlaɪn] ADJ (book etc) sibyllin

sic [sɪk] ADV sic, ainsi

siccative ['sɪkətɪv] ADJ, N siccatif m

Sicilian [sɪ'sɪlɪən] ADJ sicilien ▪ N Sicilien, -ienne

Sicily ['sɪsɪlɪ] N Sicile f

sick [sɪk] ADJ **1** (ill) malade; (humour) noir; (joke) macabre; **to be s.** (ill) être malade; **to**

report s. se faire porter malade; **to be s. in the head** (mad) être malade de la tête; Fig **you have to be pretty s. to desecrate somebody's grave** il faut être vraiment malade pour profaner la tombe de quelqu'un; Fig **he has a s. mind** c'est quelqu'un de malsain **2 to be s.** (vomit) rendre; **to feel s.** avoir mal au cœur; **to make oneself s.** (on purpose) se faire vomir; (by eating too much chocolate etc) se rendre malade; **he was as s. as a dog** il a été malade comme un chien; Fig il en a fait une maladie; **to be s. to one's stomach** avoir mal au cœur; Fig en être malade, en faire une maladie; Fig **it makes me s.** cela m'écœure; Fig **you make me s.!** tu m'écœures!; Fig **he was very s. at** or **about failing his exam** son échec à l'examen l'a complètement bouleversé; **I'm s. about having to cancel my holiday** je suis malade de devoir annuler mes vacances; Fig **she looked pretty s. when she didn't get the prize** elle avait l'air plutôt écœurée quand elle n'a pas reçu le prix; Fig **to be s. with jealousy** être malade de jalousie; Lit **to be s. at heart** être navré; **s. feeling** malaise m

3 to be s. of sth être las de qch; **to grow s. of sth** se dégoûter de qch; **I'm s. of spaghetti every night/your constant complaining** j'en ai assez de manger des spaghetti tous les soirs/que vous vous plaigniez sans cesse; **I'm s. and tired of it** or **I'm s. to death of it** j'en ai assez, j'en ai marre

▪ N **1** the **s.** (pl) les malades mpl **2** Br Fam (vomit) vomi m

▶▶ **s. bag** = sachet m mis à la disposition des passagers souffrant du mal des transports; **s. bay** infirmerie f, Naut poste m des malades; **s. bed** lit m de malade; **s. benefit** prestations fpl de l'assurance maladie; **s. building syndrome** syndrome m des bâtiments malsains, = syndrome comprenant des maux de tête, qu'on retrouve chez des personnes résidant ou travaillant dans des bâtiments équipés de la climatisation; Br **s. headache** migraine f; **s. leave** congé m (de) maladie; **s. list** liste f des malades; **to be on the s. list** se faire porter malade; Br **s. note** mot m d'absence (pour cause de maladie); Br Mil **s. parade** (soldiers) = ensemble m des soldats se rendant à la consultation; (time) = heure f à laquelle les soldats se rendent à la consultation; **to go on s. parade** se faire porter malade; **s. pay** indemnité f de maladie (versée par l'employeur)

▶ **sick up** VT SEP Br Fam (vomit) vomir, rendre

sicken ['sɪk(ə)n] VI (become ill) tomber malade; (of plants) languir, dépérir; **to be sickening for an illness/for something** couver une maladie/quelque chose; Fig Lit **to s. of sth** se lasser ou se dégoûter de qch ▪ VT (make nauseous) donner mal au cœur à, donner envie de vomir à; Fig (disgust) dégoûter, donner la nausée à; Fig **his business methods s.** mes procédés en affaires me révoltent ou me rendent malade

sickening ['sɪkənɪŋ] ADJ (disgusting) écœurant, dégoûtant; (smell) nauséabond; (sight) révoltant; Fam **how perfectly s.!** (annoying) c'est vraiment écœurant!; Fam **she's so good at maths — I know, it's s.** elle est tellement bonne en maths — je sais, c'est écœurant; **there was a s. crunch as the boats collided** il y a eu un craquement sinistre lorsque les bateaux sont entrés en collision

sickeningly ['sɪkənɪŋlɪ] ADV (de façon) à vous soulever le cœur ou à vous écœurer

sickie ['sɪkɪ] N Br, Austr Fam **to take a s.** se faire porter pâle (lorsqu'on est bien portant)

sickle ['sɪk(ə)l] N faucille f; Med **s. cell anaemia** drépanocytose f

sickliness ['sɪklɪnɪs] N **1** (of person) état m maladif; (of complexion) pâleur f **2** (of cake) goût m écœurant

sickly ['sɪklɪ] ADJ **1** (person) maladif, souffreteux; (plant) étiolé, rabougri; (colour, light) faible, pâle; (complexion) pâle; (pallor) maladif; (sun) blafard; (smile) pâle **2** Old-fashioned (climate) malsain, insalubre **3** (taste) écœurant; Fig (sentiment) qui écœure, qui dégoûte; (story, tune) plein de sensiblerie, à la guimauve; **s. sweet** douceâtre

sickness ['sɪknɪs] N (illness) maladie f, (nausea) mal m de cœur; **you agreed to stay with him in s. and in health** vous aviez accepté de rester avec lui qu'il soit malade ou en bonne santé; (bouts of) **s.** (nausea) nausée(s) f(pl); **sleeping s.** maladie du sommeil; **altitude** or **mountain s.** mal des montagnes; **morning s.** nausées matinales

▶▶ Br **s. benefit** prestations fpl de l'assurance maladie

sicko ['sɪkəʊ] Fam ADJ dérangé, malade ▪ N malade mf, tordu, -ue

sickroom ['sɪkruːm] N chambre f de malade; (in school etc) infirmerie f

SIDE [saɪd]

N	côté **1–6** ▪ flanc **1, 2** ▪ versant **2**
	▪ paroi **2** ▪ face **3** ▪ aspect **4**
	▪ équipe **5**
VI	prendre le parti de (to side with)

N **1** (of person, animal) côté m, flanc m; **to be lying on one's s.** être couché sur le côté; **right/left s.** côté droit/gauche; **by sb's s.** à côté de qn; **by** or **at my s.** à côté de moi, à mes côtés; **they were standing s. by s.** ils se tenaient l'un à côté de l'autre; Fig **they worked s. by s. with their former enemies** ils ont travaillé en étroite collaboration avec leurs anciens ennemis; Fam **to split** or **burst one's sides** (laughing) se tenir les côtes (de rire), se tordre (de rire); **s. of bacon** flèche f de lard; **s. of beef** demi-carcasse f de bœuf **2** (part) (of house, box, triangle etc) côté m; (of mountain) flanc m, versant m; (of ditch, vase) paroi f; (of ship) bord m, côté; Math (of equation) membre m; **to put two boxes s. by s.** mettre deux boîtes l'une à côté de l'autre **3** (surface) côté m; (of record) face f; **the right/wrong s. of a fabric** l'endroit m/l'envers m d'un tissu; **the under/upper s. of sth** le dessous/le dessus de qch; **printed on one s. only** imprimé d'un seul côté; **on the other s. of the paper** (when looking at the front) au verso; (when looking at the back) au recto; **buttered s. up** (of slice of bread) le côté beurré vers le haut; Fig **the other s. of the picture** le revers de la médaille; **the right/wrong s. (of sth)** le bon/mauvais côté (de qch); Com **this s. up** haut!; **on this s. (of)** de ce côté(-ci) (de); **on that s. (of)** de ce côté-là (de); **on the other s. (of sth)** de l'autre côté (de qch); **with a dog on either s.** flanqué de deux chiens; **on both sides** des deux côtés, de part et d'autre; **on all sides, on every s.** de tous les côtés; (everywhere) partout; **on the left-/right-hand s.** à (main) gauche/droite; **on the south s.** du côté sud; **the tower leans on** or **to one s.** la tour penche d'un côté; **to put sth on** or **to one s.** mettre qch de côté; **to take sb on** or **to one s.** prendre qn à part ou en particulier; **to stand on** or **to one s.** se tenir à l'écart ou à part; **from all sides, from every s.** de tous (les) côtés, de toutes parts; **from s. to s.** d'un côté à l'autre; Fig **to get on the right s. of sb** gagner les faveurs de qn; **to be on the right s. of sb** être dans les petits papiers de qn; Fig **to get on the wrong s. of sb** prendre qn à rebrousse-poil; **to be on the right s. of the law** avoir la loi pour soi; **to be on the wrong s. of the law** aller contre la loi; **to be on the right s. of forty** avoir moins de quarante ans; **to be on the wrong s. of forty** avoir quarante ans bien sonnés; **it costs the**

wrong s. of £1,000 ça coûte plus de 1 000 livres; **it's a bit on the expensive/long/hot s.** c'est plutôt cher/long/chaud

4 (aspect) (of situation, argument etc) aspect m, côté m; (of personality) côté; **I could see the funny s. of the situation** je voyais le côté drôle de la situation; **I can't see the funny s. of that** je ne vois pas ce qu'il y a de drôle là-dedans; **his good s.** ses bons côtés; **to have a jealous/thoughtful s.** avoir un côté jaloux/méditatif; **there are many sides to her character** elle a bien des facettes à son caractère; **I had never seen that s. of him before** je n'avais jamais vu cet aspect de sa personnalité; **the good/bad s. of the business** le bon/mauvais côté de l'affaire; **to look on the bright s. (of things)** voir les choses du bon côté, prendre les choses du bon côté; **he always looks on the gloomy s. of things** il voit tout en noir; **to hear/look at both sides of the question** (consider both aspects) considérer les deux aspects de la question; (consider arguments for and against) envisager le pour et le contre; **you haven't heard my s. of the story!** vous n'avez pas entendu ma version de l'histoire!

5 (in dispute) côté m; Sport équipe f, camp m; **the two sides to the dispute will meet on Monday** les deux partis se rencontreront lundi; **to be on the right/wrong s.** être du bon/mauvais côté; **to take sides** choisir son camp, prendre parti; **to refuse to take sides** refuser de prendre parti; **to take sides with sb, to take the s. of sb** se ranger avec ou du côté de qn; **he's on our s.** il est avec nous ou de notre côté; **whose s. are you on?** de quel côté êtes-vous?; **to change sides** changer de camp, virer de bord; Pol etc faire volte-face; **they fought on our s.** ils se sont battus à nos côtés; **they were on the other s.** (in war etc) ils étaient de l'autre côté; **time is on our s.** le temps travaille pour nous; Ftbl **a club/national s.** une équipe locale/nationale; **to pick sides** faire les équipes; **to let the s. down** trahir ou décevoir ses amis etc

6 (lineage) côté m; **on his mother's s.** du côté maternel ou de sa mère

7 Old-fashioned Br Fam (affectation) **to put on s.** se donner des airs; **there's no s. to her at all** c'est quelqu'un de très simple

8 Fig **he does a bit of gardening on the s.** il a un petit boulot: il fait du jardinage; Fam **to make something** or **a bit on the s.** se faire des extras; Fam **profits on the s.** de la gratte; Fam **to have a bit on the s.** (have lover) (of man) avoir une petite amie ou une maîtresse; (of woman) avoir un petit ami ou un amant; **he has his bit on the s. every Tuesday** il a son cinq à sept tous les mardis

9 Billiards **to put s. on a ball** donner de l'effet à une balle

▸ VI **to s. with sb** (support) prendre le parti de qn; **to s. against sb** prendre parti contre qn

▸▸ **s. aisle** (in church) bas-côté m, pl bas-côtés; Theat allée f latérale(s); **s. chair** chaise f (de salle à manger etc); **s. chapel** chapelle f latérale; **s. dish** plat m d'accompagnement; (vegetables) garniture f, **it is served with a s. dish of potatoes** nous le servons avec des pommes de terre en accompagnement; **s. door** porte f latérale; Fig **to enter a profession by the s. door** entrer dans une profession par la petite porte; **s. drum** tambour m; **s. effect** effet m secondaire; **s. entrance** entrée f sur le côté; **s. face** profil m; **s. glance** regard m oblique ou de côté; Fig (allusion) allusion f; **s. issue** question f secondaire; **the s. issues of a question** les à-côtés mpl d'une question; **s. panel** (of vehicle) ridelle f, **s. pocket** poche f extérieure; **s. rail** (on bridge) garde-fou m, pl garde-fous; Naut rambarde f, **s. road** (minor road in country) route f secondaire; (in town) petite rue f; (road at right angles) rue f transversale; **s. sa-**

lad salade f (pour accompagner un plat); **s. street** (minor street) petite rue f; (at right angles) rue transversale; **s. table** petite table f, (for dishes) desserte f; **s. view** vue f de côté; **s. wall** (of tyre) flanc m; **s. whiskers** favoris mpl; **s. window** (of car) vitre f latérale

sideboard ['saɪdbɔːd] N **1** (piece of furniture) buffet m **2** Br **sideboards** (whiskers) favoris mpl

sideburns ['saɪdbɜːnz] NPL (whiskers) favoris mpl

sidecar ['saɪdkɑːr] N **1** (of motorbike) sidecar m, pl side-cars **2** esp Am (cocktail) = cocktail m composé de Cointreau®, de cognac et de jus de citron

-sided [-'saɪdɪd] SUFF **a four-s. figure** une figure à quatre côtés; **a many-s. debate** (with many facets) un débat qui touche à bien des problèmes; (with many participants) un débat auquel on confronte des opinions très diverses; **three-s. contract** contrat à trois parties ou tripartite

side-impact bar N Aut renfort m anti-impact latéral

sidekick ['saɪdkɪk] N Fam acolyte mf; Hum **can I bring along a couple of sidekicks?** est-ce que je peux emmener quelques copains?

sidelight ['saɪdlaɪt] N **1** Phot etc lumière f de côté; Fig **to throw a s. on a subject** donner un aperçu sur un sujet **2** Constr (window) fenêtre f latérale **3 sidelights** Br Aut feux mpl de position; Naut feux de côté

sideline ['saɪdlaɪn] N **1** Ftbl etc ligne f de touche; Fig **to be on the sidelines** (excluded) rester sur la touche; **I prefer to stay on the sidelines** je préfère ne pas m'en mêler; **all his life, he has stayed on the sidelines** toute sa vie, il est resté à l'écart; **to watch from the sidelines** Sport regarder de la ligne de touche; Fig être là en spectateur **2** (secondary job) petit boulot m; **it's just a s.** (which earns money) c'est un petit à-côté; **we sell guide books as a s.** en plus de nos activités principales, nous vendons des guides

▸ VT (usu passive) **to be sidelined** être mis sur ou rester sur la touche; Fig **to be feeling sidelined** avoir l'impression d'avoir été laissé sur la touche

sidelong ['saɪdlɒŋ] ADV (to fall) à l'oblique, obliquement, de côté; (to look at sb) de côté, du coin de l'œil

▸ ADJ (glance) oblique, de côté; **to give sb a s. glance** regarder qn de côté ou du coin de l'œil

sidereal [saɪ'dɪərɪəl] ADJ Astron sidéral, -aux

side-saddle N selle f de dame ou de femme

▸ ADV **to ride s.** monter en amazone

sideshow ['saɪdʃəʊ] N (at fair) (stall) stand m de foire; (show) spectacle m de foire; Fig (secondary matter) affaire f d'importance secondaire

sideslip ['saɪdslɪp] N **1** Aut, Cycling, Ski dérapage m **2** Aviat glissade f (sur l'aile), glissement m latéral

▸ VI **1** Aut, Cycling, Ski déraper **2** Aviat glisser sur l'aile

sidesman, pl **sidesmen** ['saɪdzmən] N Br Rel = marguillier m adjoint

sidesplitting ['saɪdsplɪtɪŋ] ADJ Fam (joke) tordant

sidesplittingly ['saɪdsplɪtɪŋlɪ] ADV Fam **s. funny** drôle à se tordre de rire

sidestep ['saɪdstep] VI faire un pas de côté; Boxing etc esquiver

▸ VT (tackle) éviter; (player) passer; Fig (question) éviter

sidestroke ['saɪdstrəʊk] N Swimming nage f indienne

sideswipe ['saɪdswaɪp] N (blow) coup m sur le côté; **to take a s. at sb** frapper qn sur le côté; Fig faire une remarque désagréable sur qn en passant; Fig **that was a s. at the Prime Minister** c'était une allusion malveillante à propos du Premier ministre

▸ VT Am (car etc) donner un coup dans ou cogner le côté de

sidetrack ['saɪdtræk] N Am Rail voie f secondaire

▸ VT Fig (divert from aim) distraire; (divert from subject) faire dévier (**from** de); **they tried to s. him onto something else** ils ont essayé de le faire dévier sur un autre sujet; **he's easily sidetracked** il se laisse facilement distraire; **to be** or **get sidetracked** (be diverted from one's aim) se détourner de son but; (digress) s'écarter de son sujet

sidewalk ['saɪdwɔːk] N Am trottoir m

▸▸ Am **s. café** café m avec terrasse

sideways ['saɪdweɪz] ADV latéralement; (to look) en biais; (to turn sth) en travers, de biais; **to lean/fall s.** se pencher/tomber sur le côté; **to slide s.** (of door etc) coulisser latéralement; **to walk s.** marcher en crabe; **to put sth s. on to sth** mettre qch à angle droit avec qch

▸ ADJ de côté; **s. motion** mouvement m latéral

sidewinder ['saɪdwaɪndər] N **1** (snake) serpent m à sonnettes cornu **2** Am (blow) coup m sur le côté

siding ['saɪdɪŋ] N Rail voie f de garage; Br (secondary line) embranchement m; (of factory) voie de raccordement; **goods s.** voie de chargement

sidle ['saɪd(ə)l] VI **to s. up to sb** se glisser auprès de qn; **to s. out of the room** se glisser hors de la salle; **to s. along** s'avancer de côté ou Fam de guingois

SIDS [sɪdz] N Med (abbr **sudden infant death syndrome**) mort f subite du nourrisson

siege [siːdʒ] N Mil, Fig siège m; **to lay s. to a town** assiéger une ville; **to raise the s.** lever le siège; **to declare a state of s.** déclarer l'état de siège; **to be under s.** être assiégé; **they have a s. mentality** ils se sentent persécutés

▸▸ **s. gun** (in military history) pièce f de siège

Siena [sɪ'enə] N Sienne

sienna [sɪ'enə] N **1** (earth) terre f de Sienne; **raw/burnt s.** terre de Sienne naturelle/brûlée **2** (colour) ocre m brun

▸ ADJ ocre brun inv

sierra [sɪ'erə] N Geog sierra f

▸▸ **S. Leone** Sierra Leone f

siesta [sɪ'estə] N sieste f, **to take a s.** faire la sieste

sieve [sɪv] N (with coarse mesh) crible m; (with fine mesh) tamis m; (for powders and liquids) sas m; (for liquids) passoire f, **to pass sth through a s.** passer qch au tamis/au crible; Fam **he's got a memory like a s.** il a la tête comme une passoire; **this bucket leaks like a s.** ce seau est une vraie passoire

▸ VT = **sift 1 1**

sift [sɪft] VT **1** (flour) tamiser, passer au tamis; (sand etc) cribler, passer au crible; **to s. sugar over a cake** saupoudrer un gâteau de sucre **2** Fig (examine) (evidence) examiner minutieusement, passer au crible; **to s. the facts** passer les faits au crible

▸ VI (of dust etc) filtrer (**through** à travers); **the sand sifted through his fingers** le sable lui coulait entre les doigts

▸ **sift out** VT SEP (remove by sifting) (impurities) ôter en tamisant; Fig (unsuitable candidates etc) éliminer

▸ **sift through** VT INSEP (facts, evidence) parcourir

sifter ['sɪftər] N **1** (sieve) tamis m, crible m **2** (for sugar) saupoudroir m

sifting ['sɪftɪŋ] N tamisage m, criblage m; Fig (examination) (of evidence etc) examen m minutieux

sigh [saɪ] N soupir m; **heavy/deep/long(-drawn) s.** gros/profond/long soupir; **he breathed** or **heaved a s. of relief** il a poussé un soupir de soulagement; **with a s.** en soupirant, avec un soupir
▪ VI soupirer, pousser un soupir; Lit (of wind) gémir; **to s. with relief** pousser un soupir de soulagement; Old-fashioned **to s. for sb/sth** soupirer pour ou après qn/qch

sighing ['saɪɪŋ] N soupirs mpl; Lit (of wind) plainte f

SIGHT [saɪt]

| N vue 1–3 ▪ viseur 4 ▪ spectacle 5 ▪ site pittoresque 5 |
| VT apercevoir 1 ▪ observer 1 ▪ viser 2 |

N **1** (faculty) vue f; **to have good/bad s.** avoir une bonne/mauvaise vue; **to have long s.** avoir la vue longue, être presbyte; **short s.** myopie f; **to lose one's s.** perdre la vue
2 (act of seeing) **to catch s.** or **get a s. of sb/sth** apercevoir ou entrevoir qn/qch; **to lose s. of sb/sth** perdre qn/qch de vue; **to lose s. of the fact that ...** perdre de vue (le fait) que ...; **I can't bear the s. of him, I hate the very s. of him** je ne peux pas le sentir ou le voir; **I can't stand the s. of blood** je ne supporte pas la vue du sang; **to shoot sb at** or **on s.** faire feu ou tirer sur qn à vue; Mus **to play at s.** déchiffrer; Com, Fin **bill payable at s.** effet payable à vue; Com **we need to have s. of it first** il faut le voir d'abord; **to buy goods s. unseen** acheter des marchandises sans les avoir vues; **at first s.** à première vue, au premier abord; **at first s., everything seemed normal** à première vue, tout semblait normal; **to fall in love at first s.** avoir le coup de foudre (with pour); **it was (a case of) love at first s.** ce fut le coup de foudre; **to know sb by s.** connaître qn de vue; **to find favour in sb's s.** trouver grâce aux yeux de qn; Med **to have a s. test** faire vérifier sa vue
3 (range of vision) **to come into s.** (ap)paraître; **to be within s.** être à portée de vue, être en vue; **to be (with)in s. of land** avoir la terre en vue; **it sank within s. of land** il a coulé près des côtes; **land in s.!** terre!; **keep him in s.** ne le perdez pas de vue; **out of s.** caché aux regards; Old-fashioned Sl (excellent) sensas inv; **to vanish out of s.** disparaître; **to put sth out of s.** faire disparaître qch, cacher qch; **keep it out of s. of the kids** fais attention à ce que les gamins ne le voient pas; **to keep out of s.** se cacher, se dérober; **out of my s.!** hors de ma vue!, hors d'ici!; Prov **out of s. out of mind** loin des yeux, loin du cœur
4 (aiming device) (of firearm) viseur m; **front s.** guidon m; **back s.** cran m de mire; (circular) œilleton m; (of sextant) lumière f; **angle of s.** angle m de visée ou de site, site m; **line of s.** (of optical instrument) ligne f de visée; (of firearm) ligne de mire ou de tir; **to take a s. on sth** viser qch, mirer qch; Mil **telescopic s.** hausse f télescopique, hausse à lunette; **to adjust sights** prendre ou régler la hausse; **to have sb/sth in one's sights** avoir qn/qch en ligne de mire; Fig avoir qn/qch en vue; Fig **to have** or **set one's sights on sb/sth** avoir des vues sur qn/qch; **to set one's sights on becoming rich** avoir la ferme intention de devenir riche; Fig **to lower one's sights** viser moins haut
5 (spectacle) spectacle m; **sad s.** spectacle navrant; **it's a s. to see** cela vaut la peine d'être vu; **it was a s. for sore eyes** cela faisait plaisir à voir; **you're a s. for sore eyes!** c'est un plaisir de te voir!; **what a s. you are!, you**

look a s.! (wet, dirty) te voilà dans un drôle d'état!; (ridiculous) de quoi tu as l'air comme ça!; **the sights** (scenic places) les sites mpl pittoresques; (of a city etc) les monuments mpl, les curiosités fpl; **we're going to see the sights** nous allons visiter la ville/la région/etc
6 Fig Fam **not by a long s.** loin de là; Fam **a damn s. longer/harder/more expensive** vachement plus long/difficile/cher
7 (for inspection purposes) regard m
▪ VT **1** (see) (person, object, land) apercevoir; (star, planet etc) observer; **a golden eagle has been sighted here twice** on a aperçu un aigle royal ici à deux reprises
2 **to s. a gun** (aim) viser; (adjust sights of) régler la lunette d'un fusil
▸▸ Fin **s. bill** effet m à vue; Tech **s. check** contrôle m à vue, contrôle visuel; Fin **s. deposit** dépôt m à vue; Fin **s. draft** traite f à vue; Aut **s. glass** hublot m de contrôle; **s. hole** (for inspection purposes) regard m; Fin **s. letter of credit** crédit m utilisable à vue

sighted ['saɪtɪd] ADJ qui voit
NPL **the s.** les voyants mpl

sighting ['saɪtɪŋ] N **several sightings of teal have been reported** on a vu des sarcelles à plusieurs reprises; **this is the first s. this year** c'est la première fois qu'on le/la/les voit cette année

sightless ['saɪtlɪs] ADJ aveugle; Fig (eyes) éteint

sightlessness ['saɪtlɪsnɪs] N cécité f

sightly ['saɪtlɪ] ADJ **not very s.** pas très beau à voir

sight-read VT & VI Mus déchiffrer

sight-reading N Mus déchiffrage m

sightsee ['saɪtsiː] VI visiter des monuments

sightseeing ['saɪtsiːɪŋ] N **I don't really enjoy s.** je n'aime pas tellement faire le touriste; **we spent the day s.** nous avons passé la journée à visiter le pays/les monuments; **to go s.** visiter la ville/la région/etc; **a s. tour of Paris** un tour de Paris
▸▸ **s. tour** visite f guidée

sightseer ['saɪtsiːər] N touriste mf

SIGN [saɪn]

| N signe 1 ▪ indice 2 ▪ indication 2 ▪ enseigne 3 ▪ panneau 3 ▪ symbole 4 |
| VT signer 1 ▪ embaucher 4 |
| VI signer 1 |

N **1** (gesture) signe m; **to make a s./signs to sb** faire (un) signe/des signes à qn; **s. of the cross** signe de la croix; **to make the s. of the cross** se signer; **s. of recognition** signe de reconnaissance; Tel **call s.** indicatif m d'appel
2 (indication) indice m, indication f; **a sure s.** un signe qui ne trompe pas; **it's a sure s. that ...** à n'en pas douter, c'est le signe que ...; **it's a good/bad s.** c'est bon/mauvais signe; **s. of the times** signe des temps; **as a s. of ...** en signe de ...; **no s. of ...** (no trace of) nulle ou aucune trace de ...; **there is no s. of an end to the recession** il n'y a aucun élément qui indiquerait la fin de la récession; **he gave no s. of having heard anything** il n'a manifesté en aucune façon avoir entendu quoi que ce soit; **to show no s. of life** ne donner aucun signe de vie, ne pas donner signe de vie; **there was no s. of her** elle n'y était pas; **is there any s. of him yet?** il ne serait pas arrivé, par hasard?; **is there any s. of the missing child?** est-ce qu'il y a une trace de l'enfant disparu?; **there is little s. of progress in the negotiations** les négociations ne semblent pas avancer; **if there's the slightest s. of unrest** s'il y a le moindre signe

d'agitation; **all the signs are that ...** tout porte à croire que ...; **the room showed signs of having been recently occupied** il était clair que la pièce avait récemment été occupée
3 (of pub, inn etc) enseigne f; (notice) panneau m; (shop) s. enseigne, écriteau m; **a 'for sale' s.** un écriteau 'à vendre'; **neon s.** enseigne ou réclame f au néon; (road) s. panneau de signalisation (routière); **road signs** (collectively) signalisation f routière; **follow the signs for Manchester** suivre les panneaux indiquant Manchester; **traffic s.** panneau de signalisation (routière)
4 (symbol) symbole m; **plus/minus s.** signe m plus/moins; **s. of the zodiac** signe du zodiaque; **lucky s.** signe de chance
▪ VT **1** (one's name, a document, cheque etc) signer; (bill of exchange) accepter; (contract) signer, passer; Fin **to s. a bill** viser un effet; **to s. a deal** passer un marché; **the letter was signed by the president** la lettre portait la signature du président ou était signée de la main du président; Law **signed, sealed and delivered in the presence of ...** fait et signé en présence de ...
2 (say in sign language) **to s. sth** dire qch dans le langage des sourds-muets
3 Old-fashioned (indicate by gesture) **to s. assent** faire signe que oui; **to s. sb to do sth** faire signe à qn de faire qch
4 Ftbl etc (player) embaucher, engager; **he was signed to United for £1,000,000** il a été embauché par United pour 1 000 000 livres, il a signé un contrat de 1 000 000 livres avec United
▪ VI **1** (write signature) signer; **to s. by proxy, to s. per pro** signer par procuration; **s. here** signez là; Ftbl etc **he signed for United** il a signé avec United
2 (know sign language) connaître le langage des sourds-muets; (use sign language) communiquer dans le langage des sourds-muets
3 (indicate by gesture) **to s. to sb to do sth** faire signe à qn de faire qch
▸▸ **s. language** langue f des signes; **s. painter** (of lettering) peintre m en lettres; (of pub signs etc) peintre d'enseignes; **s. writer** (of lettering) peintre en lettres; (of pub signs etc) peintre d'enseignes

▸**sign away** VT SEP (concede by signing) (right etc) renoncer à (par écrit); **to s. sth away to sb** céder qch par écrit à qn; **you're signing your life away** c'est comme si tu signais ton arrêt de mort; **to s. one's freedom away** renoncer à sa liberté (en signant un contrat etc)
▸**sign for** VT INSEP (acknowledge receipt of) (delivery, registered letter etc) signer pour accuser réception de, émarger
▸**sign in** VI (sign when entering) (of employee) pointer; (of hotel guest) signer à l'entrée; **all visitors must s. in** tous les visiteurs doivent signer en entrant
▪ VT SEP (gain entrance for) signer pour faire entrer; **I'm a member, so I can s. you in** je suis membre, donc je peux vous faire entrer
▸**sign off** VI **1** Radio, TV terminer l'émission (en jouant l'indicatif); **it's time to s. off for today** il est l'heure de nous quitter pour aujourd'hui
2 (close letter) finir une lettre; **I'll s. off now and go to bed** je vais finir cette lettre maintenant et aller au lit
▸**sign on** VT SEP Mil (person) engager; (hire) (worker) embaucher
▪ VI **1** (of worker) être engagé, se faire embaucher; (of soldier) s'engager
2 Br Fam (register for unemployment benefit) s'inscrire au chômage; **Tuesday is my day for signing on** je pointe le mardi
3 Comput ouvrir une session
▸**sign out** VI (sign when leaving) (of employee) pointer; (of hotel guest) signer à la sortie;

visitors must s. out les visiteurs doivent signer en sortant

VT SEP *(indicate departure of)* **could you s. me out?** est-ce que vous pouvez noter que je suis parti?

▸**sign over VT SEP** to s. sth over to sb céder qch à qn (par écrit)

▸**sign up VI 1** *(register)* s'inscrire (**for a course** *etc* à un cours*etc*)

2 *(enlist)* *(of soldier)* s'engager

VT SEP *Sport, Theat etc (player, actor etc) (hire)* donner un contrat à, engager; **can I s. you up as a driver?** est-ce que je peux vous inscrire comme chauffeur?

---

signal ['sɪɡn(ə)l] **N 1** signal *m*, -aux; *Fig* signe *m*; **warning s.** signal avertisseur *ou* d'avertissement; **alarm s.** signal d'alarme *ou* d'alerte; **all clear s.** signal de fin d'alerte; **time s.** signal horaire; *Sport etc* **starting s.** signal de *ou* du départ; *Tel* **call** *or Am* **line s.** indicatif *m* d'appel; *Am* **busy s.** tonalité *f* de ligne occupée; **to give/send/receive a s.** faire/envoyer/recevoir un signal; **when I give the s.** quand je donne/donnerai le signal; *Fig* **he's putting out a lot of confusing signals** son attitude n'est pas claire; *Fig* **we don't want to send the wrong signals** nous ne voulons pas induire les gens en erreur (par notre comportement); **you're sending all the wrong signals if you want her to realize you're attracted to her** si tu veux qu'elle comprenne que tu es attiré par elle, il faut que ton attitude le montre; **his statement sent all the right signals** sa déclaration a clairement laissé voir ses intentions; **the demonstration is a clear s. to the government to change its policy** la manifestation signifie clairement que le gouvernement doit changer de politique; **traffic signals** feux *mpl* de circulation; **light s.** signal lumineux; *Mil* **arm** *or* **hand s.** signal à bras; **semaphore s.** signal sémaphorique; *Naut* signal à bras; **flag s.** *Mil* signal par fanion(s); *Naut* signal à pavillon; *Rail* signal par drapeau; **Morse signals** signaux Morse; **stop s.** signal d'arrêt immédiat; *Br Mil* **Signals** transmissions; *Br Mil* **Signals officer** officier *m* des transmissions

2 *Electron, Radio etc* signal *m*, -aux; **input/output s.** signal *m* d'entrée/de sortie; **I can't get a s.** *(on mobile phone)* je n'ai pas de réception

ADJ ATTRIB *Lit (success)* éclatant, remarquable; *(failure)* notoire; *(service)* insigne; *(importance)* capital, -aux; **a s. lack of sth** un manque flagrant de qch

VI (-**ll**-, *Am* -**l**-) faire un signal/des signaux (**to** à); **I signalled to him (to stop)** je lui ai fait signe (de s'arrêter); **she signalled for the bill** elle a fait signe qu'on lui apporte l'addition; *Aut etc* **to s. before stopping** *(with hand)* prévenir *ou* avertir avant de s'arrêter; *Aut* **he didn't s. before he turned** *(with light)* il n'a pas mis son clignotant avant de tourner; *(with hand)* il n'a pas fait signe avant de tourner

VT *(order)* transmettre; *(train, ship)* faire signe à; *Aut* **to s. that one is turning** *(with hand)* signaler un changement de direction; *(with light)* mettre son clignotant avant de tourner; **the train was signalled to stop** le train a reçu le signal de s'arrêter; **this signals the start of the rainy season** cela indique le début ou c'est le signe du début de la saison des pluies; **her resignation signalled the beginning of the end** sa démission a marqué le début de la fin; **he signalled the car on** il a fait signe à la voiture d'avancer

▸▸*Naut* **s. book** code *m* international des signaux; *Rail* **s. box** poste *m* de signalisation; **s. communications** télécommunications *fpl*, transmissions *fpl*; **s. flag** *Mil* fanion *m* de signalisation; *Naut* pavillon *m* pour signaux; **s. flare** *(rocket)* fusée *f* éclai-

rante; *(stationary)* feu *m* de Bengale; **s. frequency** fréquence *f* du signal; **s. lamp** *(for making signals)* lampe *f* ou projecteur *m* de signalisation; *(serving as a signal)* (lampe) témoin *m*; **s. light** *Naut* fanal *m*, -aux; *Mil* voyant *m* (lumineux); *Am* **s. red** vermillon *m* chinois; **s. rocket** fusée de signalisation; **s. strength** intensité *f* du signal

signalize ['sɪɡnəlaɪz] **VT** *(victory, success)* marquer

signaller ['sɪɡnələr] **N** signaleur *m*

signalling, *Am* **signaling** ['sɪɡnəlɪŋ] **N 1** *(act)* signalisation *f*; *(sending signals)* transmission *f* de signaux; *Naut* pavillon *m* pour signaux; *Rail* drapeau *m* **2** *(signals)* signaux *mpl*

▸▸**s. flag** *Naut* pavillon de signalisation; *Mil* drapeau de signalisation

signally ['sɪɡnəlɪ] **ADV** *Lit* remarquablement, d'une façon éclatante; **... which he had s. failed to do** ... ce qu'il avait totalement manqué de faire; **the performance was s. lacking in enthusiasm** l'interprétation manquait singulièrement d'enthousiasme

signalman, *pl* **signalmen** ['sɪɡnəlmən] **N** signaleur *m*; *(using semaphore)* sémaphoriste *m*; *Rail* bloqueur *m*

signatory ['sɪɡnət(ə)rɪ] **N** signataire *mf* (**to a treaty** d'un traité)

ADJ *(nation)* signataire

signature ['sɪɡnətʃər] **N 1** signature *f*; *Admin* visa *m*; **to put one's s. to a letter** apposer sa signature au bas d'une lettre; **his s. was on the letter** la lettre portait sa signature; *Com etc* **for s.** pour signature; **s. by proxy** signature par procuration **2** *Typ (mark)* signature *f*; *(pages)* cahier *m* d'imprimerie **3** *Mus* **(key) s. armature** *f*

▸▸**s. book** parapheur *m*; **s. file** fichier *m* signature, signature; **s. line** fichier signature, signature; **s. stamp** griffe *f*; *Br Radio, TV* **s. tune** indicatif *m* (musical)

signboard ['saɪnbɔːd] **N** *(of pub, shop etc)* enseigne *f*

signet ['sɪɡnɪt] **N** sceau *m*, cachet *m*

▸▸**s. ring** chevalière *f*; *Hist (for sealing)* anneau *m* sigillaire

significance [sɪɡ'nɪfɪkəns] **N 1** *(importance)* importance *f*, portée *f*; **event of no/ of great s.** événement sans importance/de la plus haute importance **2** *(meaning)* of *(word, gesture etc)* signification *f*; **what is the s. of this ceremony?** que signifie cette cérémonie?; **she gave him a look of deep s.** elle lui glissa un regard très significatif **3** *(in statistics)* signification *f*

significant [sɪɡ'nɪfɪkənt] **ADJ 1** *(event, difference, improvement etc)* important, significatif; *(amount of money)* important; **do you think this is s.?** pensez-vous que cela a de l'importance?; **what's s. about it is that ...** ce qu'il y a d'important là-dedans, c'est que ... **2** *(word, gesture)* significatif; *(look)* lourd de sens **3** *(in statistics)* significatif

▸▸**s. figures** chiffres *mpl* significatifs; **s. other** partenaire *mf* *(dans une relation affective)*; *Psy* = personne *f* dont on se sent très proche

significantly [sɪɡ'nɪfɪkəntlɪ] **ADV 1** *(appreciably)* *(to differ)* sensiblement; **s. cheaper** sensiblement moins cher; **it's not s. different** ça ne fait pas une grosse différence; **there have been s. fewer problems** on a eu nettement moins de problèmes **2** *(in a meaningful way)* *(to look at etc)* d'une manière significative; **she paused s. at this point** à ce moment-là, elle s'est interrompue et son silence était lourd de sens; **s., no one mentioned it** personne n'a mentionné ce point, ce qui, en soi, était très significatif

signification [sɪɡnɪfɪ'keɪʃən] **N** *Fml (of word, event)* signification *f*, sens *m*

significative [sɪɡ'nɪfɪkətɪv] **ADJ** révélateur, -trice (**of** de)

signify ['sɪɡnɪfaɪ] **VT 1** *(indicate)* signifier, indiquer; **a broad forehead signifies intelligence** un front large est (un) signe d'intelligence **2** *(mean)* signifier, vouloir dire; *(make known)* *(one's intentions etc)* signifier, faire connaître

VI importer; **it doesn't s.** cela n'a aucune importance, peu importe

signing ['saɪnɪŋ] **N 1** *(of document etc)* signature *f*; *(of deed)* passation *f*, *Com (of bill)* acceptation *f*; **s. for the post** émargement *m* du courrier; **a manager with s. authority** un fondé de pouvoir **2** *(sign language)* langage *m* des sourds-muets; **her s. is excellent** elle connaît très bien le langage des sourds-muets **3** *Ftbl etc* transfert *m*

signing-in **N** *(of employees)* pointage *m*

sign-off **N** *TV* annonce *f* de la fin des émissions

signpost ['saɪnpəʊst] **N** poteau *m* indicateur; *Fig* jalon *m*, point *m* de repère

VT *(road etc)* signaliser, marquer de poteaux indicateurs; *Fig (thesis, meaning, differences etc)* signaler; **well-/badly signposted road** route qui est bien/mal signalisée; **signposted footpath** sentier *m* balisé

signposting ['saɪnpəʊstɪŋ] **N** signalisation *f* routière; *Fig* **despite obvious s. from the author, some readers failed to spot that ...** bien que l'auteur ait placé des indices très clairs ici et là, certains lecteurs n'ont pas vu que ...

Sikh [siːk] **ADJ, N** *Rel* sikh

silage ['saɪlɪdʒ] **N** *Agr* ensilage *m*

silence ['saɪləns] **N** silence *m*; **s.!** silence!; *(notice in library etc)* défense de parler; **there was a sudden s.** soudain, il y a eu un silence; **to break the s.** rompre le silence; **a shot broke the s.** un coup de feu déchira le silence; **to reduce sb to s.** réduire qn au silence, faire taire qn; **there's been complete s. from head office** le siège est resté totalement silencieux; **a deafening s.** un silence éloquent; **to suffer in s.** souffrir en silence; **to buy sb's s.** acheter le silence de qn; **to write to sb after five years' s.** écrire à qn après un silence de cinq ans; **to pass over sth in s.** passer qch sous silence; **the s. of the night** le silence de la nuit; *Prov* **s. is golden** le silence est d'or

VT *(person)* réduire au silence, faire taire; *(the opposition)* réduire au silence; *(pupils etc)* imposer le silence à; *(one's conscience, criticism)* faire taire; *(complaints)* étouffer; *Mil (enemy fire)* faire cesser, faire taire; *(muffle)* *(noise)* amortir, étouffer; **that really silenced him!** *(made speechless)* ça l'a laissé sans voix!

silencer ['saɪlənsər] **N 1** *Br Aut (on exhaust)* silencieux *m* **2** *(on gun)* silencieux *m*

silent ['saɪlənt] **ADJ 1** *(person, place etc)* silencieux; *(taciturn)* silencieux, taciturne, peu loquace; **to fall s.** devenir silencieux; **he's trying to come across as the strong, s. type** il veut qu'on le prenne pour un mec viril; *Hum* **he's the strong, s. type** c'est un viril; **to keep s.** observer le silence; *(not reveal information)* garder le silence, se taire (**about** sur); **to remain s.** rester muet, -ette; **be s.!** taisez-vous!; **they stood a minute in s. memory of ...** ils ont observé une minute de silence à la mémoire de ...; **to give sb the s. treatment** ne pas adresser la parole à qn; **s. as the grave** muet comme une tombe; **the document is s. on this point** le document ne dit rien sur ce point; **stars of the s. screen** vedettes du cinéma muet

2 *Ling (letter)* muet, -ette; **the k is s.** le k ne se prononce pas, le k est muet

N *Cin* film *m* muet; **the silents** le (cinéma) muet

▸▸ **s. actor** acteur de film(s) muet(s); **s. actress** actrice de film(s) muet(s); **s. camera** caméra *f* muette; **s. film** film muet; **s. majority** majorité *f* silencieuse; **s. movie** film muet; *Rel* **s. order** ordre *m* silencieux; *Am Com* **s. partner** (associé *m*) commanditaire *m*, bailleur *m* de fonds; **s. protest** manifestation *f* silencieuse

silently ['saɪləntlɪ] ADV *(to walk, move, do sth)* sans faire de bruit, silencieusement; *(to nod, sit)* en silence; *(to change sth)* discrètement

silex ['saɪleks] N *Miner* silex *m*

silhouette [sɪluː'et] N silhouette *f*; **in s.** en silhouette
▸ VT silhouetter, projeter en silhouette; **to be silhouetted against a light background** se détacher (en silhouette) sur un fond clair; **a tree silhouetted against the sky** un arbre qui se détachait *ou* qui se découpait sur le ciel
▸▸ *TV, Cin* **s. lighting** éclairage *m* en contre-jour

silica ['sɪlɪkə] N *Chem* silice *f*; **s. gel desiccant crystals** cristaux *mpl* dessiccatifs de Silica gel®

silicate ['sɪlɪkət] N *Chem* silicate *m*

siliceous [sɪ'lɪʃəs] ADJ *Chem* siliceux

silicon ['sɪlɪkən] N *Chem* silicium *m*
▸▸ **s. chip** puce *f*; **S. Glen** = appellation *f*, formée sur le modèle de Silicon Valley ("glen" signifie "vallée" en écossais), d'une région du centre de l'Écosse où sont concentrées un grand nombre de sociétés informatiques; **s. technology** technologie *f* du silicium; **S. Valley** Silicon Valley *f (centre de l'industrie électronique américaine, situé en Californie)*; **s. wafer** tranche *f* de silicium

silicone ['sɪlɪkəʊn] N *Chem* silicone *f*
▸▸ **s. implant** implant *m* mammaire en silicone; **s. rubber** caoutchouc *m* silicone

silicosis [sɪlɪ'kəʊsɪs] N *Med* silicose *f*

silk [sɪlk] N **1** *(fabric, fibre)* soie *f*; *(thread)* fil *m* de soie; **raw s.** soie grège *ou* écrue; **artificial s.** rayonne *f*; **a black s. dress** une robe de soie noire; **fine ladies in their silks and satins** de belles dames dans leurs plus beaux atours **2** *Horseracing* **silks** *(of jockey)* casaque *f* **3** *Br Law Fam* *(King's, Queen's Counsel)* conseiller *m* du roi/de la reine; *(collectively)* conseillers du roi/de la reine; **to take s.** être nommé conseiller du roi/de la reine
▸▸ **s. screen printing** sérigraphie *f*; **s. finish** similisage *m*; **the S. Road** la route de la soie; **s. stockings** bas *mpl* de soie

silken ['sɪlk(ə)n] ADJ *Lit* **1** *Tex* de soie; *Fig (curls)* soyeux, de soie **2** *(voice, words)* doux, *f* douce, *Pej* doucereux, mielleux

silkiness ['sɪlkɪnɪs] N **1** *(of fabric)* nature *f* soyeuse **2** *(of voice, words)* moelleux *m*, *Pej* mielleux *m*

silkworm ['sɪlkwɜːm] N ver *m* à soie
▸▸ **s. breeder** sériciculteur, -trice; **s. breeding** sériciculture *f*; **s. farm** magnanerie *f*; **s. moth** bombyx *m* du mûrier; **s. nursery** magnanerie *f*

silky ['sɪlkɪ] ADJ **1** *(like silk)* *(fabric, hair, cheek)* soyeux **2** *(suave)* *(tone, manner)* doux, *f* douce **3** *(made of silk)* de *ou* en soie

sill [sɪl] N *Constr etc (of door)* seuil *m*; *(of window)* rebord *m*, appui *m*; *(of frame)* sole *f*, semelle *f*; *Aut* bas *m* de marche

sillabub ['sɪləbʌb] N *Culin* = entremets *m* sucré semblable au sabayon

silliness ['sɪlɪnɪs] N sottise *f*, bêtise *f*; **that's enough s. for one morning** assez de bêtises pour ce matin

silly ['sɪlɪ] ADJ *(person)* sot, *f* sotte, stupide; *(question, answer)* stupide; **don't be so s.!** ne

sois pas si bête!; **I'll pay – don't be s.!** je vais payer – il n'en est pas question!; **(you) s. fool** *or* **ass!** imbécile!, espèce d'idiot!; **it would make me look s.** j'aurais l'air bête *ou* ridicule; **that was a s. thing to do!** ça *ou* ce n'était pas très intelligent!; **to say something s.** dire une bêtise; **but that's s.**, **she was here half an hour ago** mais c'est ridicule, elle était ici il y a une demi-heure; **there was a new manager every week, it was** *or* **things were getting s.** il y avait un nouveau gérant chaque semaine, ça en devenait ridicule; **it was s. of me to ask** c'était idiot de ma part de demander; **he's forgotten his umbrella, (the) s. man** il a oublié son parapluie, cet idiot; *Journ Fam* **the s. season** = la période creuse des mois d'été; **to laugh oneself s.** mourir de rire; **to worry sb s.** rendre qn malade d'inquiétude; **she's been worrying herself s.** elle est morte d'inquiétude; **she'll worry herself s.** elle se rendra malade d'inquiétude (**about** à cause de); **to knock sb s.** étourdir *ou* assommer qn
▸ N *Fam* idiot, -ote; **don't be such a s.!** que tu es bête!

sillybilly ['sɪlɪbɪlɪ] N *Fam (to child)* gros bêta *m*, grosse bêtasse *f*; **don't be such a s.!** ne sois pas si bête!; **oh, I am a s.!** oh, que je suis bête!

silo ['saɪləʊ] N *Agr, Mil* silo *m*

silt [sɪlt] N boue *f*; *(in waterway)* dépôt *m*, vase *f*, limon *m*
▸ VT = **silt up**
▸ **silt up** VI *(of harbour etc)* s'envaser
▸ VT SEP *(fill with silt)* *(port, canal)* envaser

silting up N *(of port, canal etc)* envasement *m*

silty ['sɪltɪ] ADJ limoneux

silver ['sɪlvər] N **1** *(metal)* argent *m* **2** *Br (coins)* pièces *fpl* en argent; **a pound in s.** une livre en argent, une livre en pièces *ou* en monnaie d'argent **3** *(silverware)* argenterie *f* **4** *Sport (medal)* médaille *f* d'argent; **to get a s. in the shot put** remporter une médaille d'argent au lancer du poids **5** *(colour)* (couleur *f*) argent *m*
▸ ADJ **1** *(made of silver)* en argent, d'argent; **is that spoon s.?** est-ce que cette cuiller est en argent?; *Prov* **he was born with a s. spoon in his mouth** il est né coiffé **2** *(in colour)* argenté, argent *inv*; **s. hair** des cheveux argentés; *Prov* **every cloud has a s. lining** à quelque chose malheur est bon; **to look for the s. lining** regarder le bon côté des choses **3** *(sound)* argentin; **she has a s. tongue** elle sait parler
▸ VT *(mirror)* étamer; *(cutlery etc)* argenter; *Lit (waves etc)* argenter
▸▸ **s. birch** bouleau *m* blanc; **s. bromide** bromure *m* d'argent; **s. fox** renard *m* argenté; **s. gilt** vermeil *m*, argent recouvert d'or; **s. grey** gris *m* argenté; *Sport etc* **s. medal** médaille d'argent; **s. paper** papier *m* d'argent; **s. plate** *(layer of silver)* plaqué *m* argent; *(tableware)* argenterie *f*; **s. plating** argentage *m*; *(layer)* argenture *f*; **s. service** *(in restaurant)* service *m* de grande classe; **s. service waiter** serveur *m* pour service au guéridon; **s. service waitress** serveuse *f* pour service au guéridon; **the s. screen** le grand écran; *Comput Fam* **s. surfer** internaute *mf* âgé(e); **s. wedding** noces *fpl* d'argent

silverfish ['sɪlvəfɪʃ] N **1** *(fish)* argentine *f* **2** *(insect)* lépisme *m*, petit poisson *m* d'argent

silver-haired ADJ aux cheveux argentés

silver-plate VT argenter

silver-plated ADJ argenté

silverside ['sɪlvəsaɪd] N *Br Culin* gîte *m* à la noix

silversmith ['sɪlvəsmɪθ] N orfèvre *m*

silverware ['sɪlvəweər] N argenterie *f*

silverwork ['sɪlvəwɜːk] N orfèvrerie *f*

silvery ['sɪlvərɪ] ADJ *Lit (cloud, water)* argenté; *(scales etc)* d'argent; *(laugh)* argentin

SIM [sɪm] N *Tel (abbr* **subscriber identity module***)*
▸▸ **S. card** *(in mobile phone)* carte *f* SIM

simian ['sɪmɪən] ADJ *Zool* simien; *Fig (gait, appearance etc)* simiesque
▸ N *Zool* simien *m*

similar ['sɪmɪlər] ADJ semblable (**to** à), pareil (**to** à), similaire; *Math (triangles)* semblable; **your case is s. to mine** votre cas est semblable au mien; **they are s. in appearance** d'apparence, ils sont semblables; **the two women are s.** les deux femmes se ressemblent; **there was a s. mistake on page 1** il y avait une erreur semblable à la page 1; **something s. happened to me** il m'est arrivé quelque chose de semblable

similarity [sɪmɪ'lærɪtɪ] N ressemblance *f*; *Math (of triangles)* similitude *f*; **there the s. ends** c'est là que s'arrête la comparaison

similarly ['sɪmɪləlɪ] ADV pareillement; **they were s. dressed** ils/elles étaient habillé(e)s de la même façon; **s., ...** de même ...

simile ['sɪmɪlɪ] N comparaison *f*

similitude [sɪ'mɪlɪtjuːd] N *Fml (resemblance)* ressemblance *f*, similitude *f*; *(comparison)* comparaison *f*

SIMM [sɪm] N *Comput (abbr* **single in-line memory module***)* SIMM *m*

simmer ['sɪmər] N *Culin* **to keep sth at a s.** *or* **on the s.** (faire) mijoter qch, faire cuire qch à petit feu *ou* à feu doux
▸ VI **1** *Culin etc (of liquid)* frémir; *(of food in pot)* mijoter, cuire à petit feu *ou* à feu doux **2** *Fig (of revolt, discontent etc)* fermenter; **he was simmering with rage** il bouillonnait de rage
▸ VT *Culin (stew etc)* mijoter, mitonner
▸ **simmer down** VI *(of person)* se calmer

simnel ['sɪmn(ə)l] N
▸▸ *Br* **s. cake** gâteau *m* de Pâques *ou* de la mi-carême

simoleon [sɪ'məʊlɪən] N *Am Fam (dollar)* dollar *m*

Simon ['saɪmən] N Simon *m*
▸▸ **S. says** *(game)* Jacques a dit *m*

simon crane ['saɪmən] N *TV, Cin* grue *f* hydraulique

simony ['saɪmənɪ] N *Rel* simonie *f*

simp [sɪmp] N *Am Fam* andouille *f*, crétin, -ine

simper ['sɪmpər] N minauderies *fpl*, ..., **he said with a s.** ..., dit-il en minaudant; **the s. she puts on when ...** la façon dont elle minaude quand ...
▸ VI minauder, mignarder; *(smile affectedly)* sourire avec affectation; **I could hear him simpering down the phone to her** je l'entendais lui dire des minauderies au téléphone

simpering ['sɪmpərɪŋ] ADJ mignard, affecté
▸ N minauderie *f*; **I've had enough of her s.** j'en ai assez de ses minauderies

simple ['sɪmp(ə)l] ADJ *(method etc)* simple, élémentaire; *(character)* simple, naturel; *(naïve)* simple, naïf, -ïve, crédule; **he's a bit s.** il est un peu simplet; **for the s. reason that ...** pour la simple raison que ...; **I'm not so s. as to believe that** je n'ai pas la naïveté de croire cela; **to become simpler** se simplifier; **the simplest thing to do is to ...** le plus simple est de ...; **a meal that is s. to prepare** un repas qui est simple à préparer; **he won't understand, keep it s.** il ne va rien comprendre, reste simple; **let's keep it s.** restons simples; **it's as s. as that** c'est aussi simple que ça; **in s. terms** avec des mots simples; **reduced to its simplest terms** réduit à sa plus simple expression; **to have s. tastes** avoir des goûts simples; **that's the s. truth** c'est la vérité pure et simple

▸▸ *Med* **s. fracture** fracture *f* simple; *Fin* **s. interest** intérêts *mpl* simples; *St Exch* **s. position** position *f* élémentaire; *Gram* **s. sentence** proposition *f* indépendante

simple-hearted [ˈhɑːtɪd] ADJ simple, ingénu, candide

simple-minded ADJ simple (d'esprit), simplet, -ète; *(naive)* naïf, -ïve, candide

simple-mindedness [-ˈmaɪndnɪs] N simplicité *f*, *(naiveness)* naïveté *f*, candeur *f*

simpleness [ˈsɪmp(ə)lnɪs] N = **simplicity**

simple-rank order N *Mktg* classement *m* simple

simpleton [ˈsɪmp(ə)ltən] N nigaud, -aude, niais, -aise

simplex [ˈsɪmpleks] N *Ling (of word)* forme *f* de base

simplicity [sɪmˈplɪsɪtɪ] N **1** *(candour) (of child etc)* candeur *f*, simplicité *f*, *(foolishness)* bêtise *f*, sottise *f* **2** *(of problem, dress etc)* simplicité *f*; **it's s. itself** c'est simple comme bonjour

simplification [sɪmplɪfɪˈkeɪʃən] N simplification *f*

simplify [ˈsɪmplɪfaɪ] VT simplifier

simplistic [sɪmˈplɪstɪk] ADJ simpliste; **am I being too s.?** est-ce que je simplifie trop?

simply [ˈsɪmplɪ] ADV **1** *(in simple manner) (to speak, act)* simplement; *(dressed)* avec simplicité **2** *(absolutely)* absolument; **it's s. impossible** c'est tout bonnement impossible; **I s. won't do it** je refuse absolument de le faire; **I was s. amazed by it** j'en étais tout à fait abasourdi **3** *(just)* tout simplement; **purely and s.** purement et simplement; **it's s. a matter** *or* **question of time** c'est une simple question de temps, c'est tout simplement une question de temps

simulacrum, *pl* **simulacra** [sɪmjʊˈleɪkrəm, -ə] N *Fml* simulacre *m*

simulate [ˈsɪmjʊleɪt] VT **1** *(imitate) (illness etc)* simuler, feindre; *(enthusiasm etc)* affecter; **simulated leather** similicuir *m*; **simulated fur** fausse fourrure *f*, **simulated marble** marbre *m* artificiel; *(painted)* faux marbre **2** *Tech* simuler; **simulated test marketing** marché-test *m* simulé

simulation [sɪmjʊˈleɪʃən] N simulation *f*

simulator [ˈsɪmjʊleɪtər] N *Tech (device)* simulateur *m*; **flight s.** simulateur de vol

simulcast [ˈsaɪməlkɑːst] ADJ radiotélévisé N émission *f* radiotélévisée VT diffuser simultanément sur différents médias

simultaneity [sɪməltəˈneɪɪtɪ] N simultanéité *f*

simultaneous [sɪməlˈteɪnɪəs] ADJ simultané; **s. with ...** qui a lieu en même temps que ...

▸▸ **s. broadcast** émission *f* diffusée simultanément, retransmission *f* simultanée; *Math* **s. equations** système *m* d'équations simultanées; **s. interpreting** interprétation *f* simultanée

simultaneously [sɪməlˈteɪnɪəslɪ] ADV simultanément, en même temps

sin [sɪn] N péché *m*; *Fam (against taste etc)* offense *f*; **sins of omission/commission** péchés par omission/action; **original s.** péché originel; **the seven deadly sins** les sept péchés capitaux; **the forgiveness of sins** le pardon des offenses; *Old-fashioned Hum* **to live in s.** vivre dans le péché; *Fam Hum* **for my sins, I was appointed ...** pour mes péchés, j'ai été nommé ...; *Fam* **if it's not a s. to ask ...** s'il est permis de poser la question ...; *Fam* **it would be a s. to stay indoors on a** day like this c'est un crime de rester à l'intérieur par une si belle journée

VI *(-nn-)* pécher, commettre un péché/des péchés; **to s. against** *(the proprieties)* pécher contre, blesser; *(a rule etc)* manquer à; **more sinned against than sinning** plus à plaindre qu'à blâmer

▸▸ *Sport* **s. bin** banc *m* des pénalités; prison *f*; *Hum* **s. tax** = appellation *f* humoristique de la taxe sur l'alcool et le tabac

Sinai [ˈsaɪnaɪ] N Sinaï *m*; **Mount S.** le mont Sinaï

▸▸ **the S. Peninsula** la presqu'île de Sinaï

since [sɪns] ADV **1** depuis; **I've not seen him s.** je ne l'ai pas revu depuis; **he's been in perfect health ever s.** depuis (lors), il est en parfaite santé **2** *(ago)* **she had long s. given up hope of promotion** elle avait, depuis longtemps, abandonné tout espoir de promotion; **long s.** *(for a long time)* depuis longtemps; *(a long time ago)* il y a longtemps; **not long s.** il n'y a pas très longtemps; **Old-fashioned many years s.** il y a bien des années

PREP depuis; **s. his death** depuis sa mort; **s. early June** dès les premiers jours de juin; **I've been here (ever) s. lunch** je suis là depuis le déjeuner; **she has lived here s. 1998** elle vit ici depuis 1998; **she had lived there s. 1996** elle vivait là depuis 1996; **I haven't seen her s. Christmas** je ne l'ai pas vue depuis Noël; **s. then, s. that time** depuis ce temps-là, depuis lors; *Fam* **s. when do you come into a room without knocking?** depuis quand est-ce qu'on entre sans frapper?; **s. seeing you** depuis que je vous ai vu SEE GRAMMAR B31

CONJ **1** *(in time)* depuis que; **I've been here** depuis que je suis ici; **it's a long time s. I saw her** il y a longtemps que je ne l'ai vue, ça fait longtemps que je ne l'ai pas vue; **(ever) s. I have lived in London** depuis que j'habite (à) Londres; **s. he had been there** depuis qu'il était là SEE GRAMMAR B31 **2** *(because)* puisque; **I'll do it s. it's you that's asking** je le ferai puisque c'est vous qui me le demandez

sincere [sɪnˈsɪər] ADJ sincère; **he is completely s.** il est de bonne foi

sincerely [sɪnˈsɪəlɪ] ADV sincèrement; **it is my s. held conviction that ...** je suis sincèrement convaincu que ...; *Br* **Yours s.,** *Am* **S. yours** *(letter ending)* veuillez agréer, Monsieur *etc*, l'expression de mes sentiments distingués *ou* les meilleurs

sincerity [sɪnˈserɪtɪ] N *(of person)* sincérité *f*, bonne foi *f*, *(of emotion)* sincérité *f*; **in all s.** de la meilleure foi du monde, en toute sincérité

sine [saɪn] N *Math (of angle)* sinus *m*
▸▸ *Law* **s. die** sine die; *Law* **s. qua non** condition *f* sine qua non

sinecure [ˈsaɪnɪkjʊər] N sinécure *f*

sinew [ˈsɪnjuː] N *Anat* tendon *m*

sinewy [ˈsɪnjuːɪ] ADJ **1** *(meat)* tendineux **2** *(arm etc)* musclé, nerveux

sinful [ˈsɪnfʊl] ADJ *(deed, urge, thought)* coupable, honteux; *(world)* plein de péchés, souillé par le péché; **his s. ways** sa vie de pécheur; **s. man** pécheur *m*; **s. woman** pécheresse *f*; **how could such pleasure be s.?** comment un tel plaisir pourrait-il être coupable?; **she thought alcohol was s.** pour elle, boire de l'alcool était un péché; **it's downright s.!** c'est un vrai scandale!

sinfully [ˈsɪnfʊlɪ] ADV *(to act)* d'une façon coupable; **it is s. wasteful to ...** c'est un gaspillage honteux de ...

sinfulness [ˈsɪnfʊlnɪs] N *(of behaviour, act)* caractère *m* scandaleux; **his/her s.** son état de pécheur/pécheresse; **a life of s.** une vie de péché

sing [sɪŋ] *(pt* **sang** [sæŋ]; *pp* **sung** [sʌŋ]) VI **1** *(of person, bird)* chanter; **I can't s.** je ne sais pas chanter **2** *(of the wind etc)* siffler; *(of the ears)* tinter, bourdonner; **the kettle is singing** la bouilloire chante *ou* siffle **3** *Sl (inform)* moucharder, balancer

VT *(song)* chanter; **s. me a song** chante-moi une chanson; **Sinatra sings the Beatles** Sinatra chante les Beatles; *Fig* **to s. another** *or* **a different tune** changer de ton; **to s. sb to sleep** chanter quelque chose pour endormir qn; **to s. sb's praises** chanter les louanges de qn

▸ **sing along** VI **s. along if you like** chantez avec moi/nous *etc* si vous voulez

▸ **sing of** VT INSEP *Lit* chanter

▸ **sing out** VI *(sing loudly)* chanter (plus) fort; *Fam* **s. out if you need me** *(call)* appelle-moi si vous avez/tu as besoin de moi

VT SEP *(note)* chanter clairement

▸ **sing up** VI *(sing louder)* chanter plus fort

singable [ˈsɪŋəb(ə)l] ADJ chantable

Singapore [sɪŋəˈpɔːr] N Singapour *m*

Singaporean [sɪŋəˈpɔːrɪən] ADJ singapourien

N Singapourien, -ienne

singe [sɪndʒ] VT *(accidentally)* brûler légèrement; *(clothes, hair)* roussir; *(deliberately) (poultry, hair)* flamber

N *(burn)* brûlure *f* (légère); *(mark)* marque *f* de brûlure

singer [ˈsɪŋər] N **1** *(artiste)* chanteur, -euse; **s. songwriter** auteur-compositeur-interprète *mf* **2** *Br Sl (informer)* indic *mf*

Singhalese [sɪŋəˈliːz] ADJ, N = **Sinhalese**

singing [ˈsɪŋɪŋ] ADJ *(bird)* qui chante; **to have a fine s. voice** chanter admirablement N *(of person, bird)* chant *m*; **his s. is awful** il chante atrocement

▸▸ **s. lesson** leçon *f* de chant; **s. telegram** = vœux *mpl* présentés sous forme chantée, généralement à l'occasion d'un anniversaire

SINGLE [ˈsɪŋɡ(ə)l]

N 45 tours **1** ▪ single **1** ▪ aller simple **1** ▪ célibataire **2**		
ADJ seul **1** ▪ unique **1** ▪ pour une personne **2** ▪ célibataire **3**		

N **1** *(record)* 45 tours *m*; *(CD or cassette)* single *m*; *(ticket)* aller *m* simple; *(banknote) (one pound)* billet *m* d'une livre; *(one dollar)* billet *m* d'un dollar

2 *(unmarried person)* célibataire *mf*; **a package holiday for singles** des vacances organisées pour célibataires

3 *Tennis etc* **singles** simple *m*; **men's/women's singles** simple messieurs/dames

ADJ **1** *(just one)* seul; **one s. case of ...** un cas unique de ...; **every s. day** tous les jours; **to do sth in a s. movement** faire qch d'un seul geste; **not a s. one** pas un seul, pas un; **I haven't seen a s. soul** je n'ai pas vu âme qui vive; **in a s. sum** en une fois; **don't say a s. word** ne dites pas un (seul) mot

2 *(for one person, not double etc) (bed)* à une place, pour une personne; *(room)* à un lit, pour une personne; *Naut (cabin)* individuel; **in s. rank** sur un rang

3 *(not married)* célibataire, non-marié; **a s. man/woman** un/une célibataire; **he remained s.** il est resté célibataire

▸▸ *Phot* **s. camera** monocaméra *f*, **s. combat** combat *m* singulier; **s. currency** monnaie *f* unique; **S. European Market** Marché *m* unique européen; *Bot* **s. flower** fleur *f* simple; **s. market** marché unique; **s. occupancy** *(of hotel room)* occupation *f* par une seule personne; **s. parent** père *m*/mère *f* célibataire; *Admin* parent *m* isolé; **s. price** prix *m* unique; **s. quotes** guillemets *mpl*; **s. (room) supplement** supplément *m* chambre individuelle; **s. seater** *(vehicle)* monoplace *f*, *Comput* **s. sheet feed** alimentation *f* feuille à feuille; *Typ* **s. spacing** interlignage *m* simple; *Comput* **s. user licence** licence *f* individuelle d'utilisation; **s. yellow line** = ligne *f* jaune indiquant que le stationnement est autorisé à certaines heures

▸ **single out** VT SEP *(choose from many)* isoler, choisir; **she was singled out for praise** elle a fait l'objet de félicitations particulières; **why s. him out (for blame)?** pourquoi le blâmer en particulier?

single-breasted [-'brestɪd] ADJ *(jacket, coat)* droit

single-chamber ADJ *Pol* monocaméral, -aux

single-column ADJ *Typ* à une colonne

single-cylinder ADJ monocylindrique
▸▸*Aut* **s. engine** moteur *m* monocylindrique

single-decker [dekər] N *Br* autobus *m* sans impériale

single-density ADJ *Comput (disk)* à simple densité

single-drive ADJ *(computer)* à un seul lecteur de disquettes

single-engined [-'endʒɪnd] ADJ monomoteur
▸▸ **s. aircraft** *(avion m)* monomoteur *m*

single-handed [-'hændɪd] ADV **I did it s.** je l'ai fait tout seul; **to sail s.** naviguer seul
ADJ **thanks to his s. efforts** grâce aux efforts qu'il a fournis seul

single-handedly [-'hændɪdlɪ] ADV seul, tout seul

single-income ADJ *(family, couple)* à salaire unique

single-lane ADJ *(traffic)* à voie unique

single-lens ADJ
▸▸*Phot* **s. camera** appareil *m* photo monoculaire; *Phot* **s. reflex** reflex *m* (monoobjectif)

single-line ADJ *Aut* **s. traffic only** circulation *f* à une (seule) voie

single-minded ADJ *(in pursuit of a goal) (person)* constant; *(determination, pursuit of power)* farouche; *(convictions)* absolu; *(determined) (attitude, deeds)* résolu; **he was s. in his pursuit of power** sa soif de pouvoir était sans bornes

single-mindedly [-'maɪndɪdlɪ] ADV résolument

single-mindedness [-'maɪndɪdnɪs] N *(constancy)* constance *f*, *(determination)* résolution *f*

single-mode ADJ *Tel* single-mode

singleness ['sɪŋg(ə)lnɪs] N **with s. of purpose** avec un seul but en vue; **his s. of purpose** sa détermination

single-parent family N famille *f* monoparentale

single-phase ADJ *Elec (current)* monophasé
▸▸ **s. current** courant *m* monophasé

singles bar N bar *m* pour célibataires

single-sex ADJ non mixte
▸▸ **s. school** école *f* non-mixte

single-sided ADJ *Comput (disk)* à une seule face

single-spaced [-'speɪst] ADJ *Typ* à interligne simple

single-spoke ADJ *(steering wheel)* monobranche

singlet ['sɪŋglɪt] N *Br* maillot *m* de corps; *(of cotton, flannel)* gilet *m*; *Sport* maillot

single-tasking [-'tæskɪŋ] *Comput* N monotâche *m*
ADJ monotâche

singleton ['sɪŋg(ə)ltən] N *Cards, Math* singleton *m*

single-track ADJ
▸▸ **s. railway** chemin *m* de fer à voie unique; **s. road** route *f* à une seule voie

singly ['sɪŋglɪ] ADV *(one by one)* séparément, un à un; *Com* **articles sold s.** articles qui se vendent séparément *ou* à la pièce; **people entered s. or in pairs** les gens sont entrés seuls ou par deux

singsong ['sɪŋsɒŋ] ADJ *(tone)* chantant; **in a s. voice** d'un ton chantant
N *Fam (singing session)* concert *m* improvisé; **to have a s.** pousser la chansonnette

singular ['sɪŋgjʊlər] ADJ **1** *Gram (number)* singulier, -ière **2** *(remarkable)* rare, remarquable; *(strange)* singulier, -ière, bizarre
N *Gram* singulier *m*; **in the s.** au singulier
VOIR GRAMMAIRE A14–15

singularity [sɪŋgjʊ'lærɪtɪ] N *(remarkableness)* particularité *f*, *(strangeness)* bizarrerie *f*

singularize ['sɪŋgjʊləraɪz] VT singulariser

singularly ['sɪŋgjʊləlɪ] ADV *(remarkably)* singulièrement, remarquablement; **I was s. unimpressed** cela ne m'a vraiment pas impressionné

Sinhalese [sɪn(h)ə'liːz] ADJ cing(h)alais
N **1** *(person)* Cing(h)alais, -aise **2** *Ling* cing(h)alais *m*

sinister ['sɪnɪstər] ADJ **1** *(event, smile, atmosphere, appearance)* sinistre; *(air)* menaçant **2** *Her* senestre, sénestre

sink [sɪŋk] N **1** *(basin) (in kitchen)* évier *m*; **to pour sth down the s.** jeter qch dans l'évier; *Fig Lit* **s. of iniquity** lieu *m* de perdition *ou* de tous les vices
2 *Geol etc* bétoire *f*
VI *(pt* **sank** [sæŋk]; *pp* **sunk** [sʌŋk]; *Arch & as adj* **sunken** ['sʌŋkən])* **1** *(in water)* disparaître dans l'eau; *(of ship)* sombrer, couler; **to s. like a stone** *(of person)* couler à pic; *Fig* **here goes! s. or swim!** allons-y! il faut risquer le tout pour le tout!; **to s. into the mud/the snow** s'enfoncer dans la boue/la neige; **to s. into quicksand** s'enliser dans les sables mouvants
2 **to s. into one's memory** *(of facts etc)* se graver dans la mémoire; **to s. into oblivion** tomber dans l'oubli; **to s. into poverty/a life of crime/depression** s'enfoncer dans la pauvreté/le crime/la dépression; **to s. into a deep sleep** s'endormir profondément; **to s. into a coma** sombrer dans le coma; **sunk in thought** plongé dans ses pensées
3 *(subside)* **to s. (down)** *(of ground)* s'affaisser; *(of wall, building etc)* s'affaisser, se tasser; **to s. (down) into an armchair** *(of person)* se laisser tomber *ou* s'effondrer dans un fauteuil; **to s. to the ground** (se laisser) tomber à terre; **her heart sank at the news** à cette nouvelle, son cœur s'est serré; **his spirits sank** il perdit tout courage; **the sun is sinking** le soleil baisse
4 *(decrease) (of prices etc)* baisser; **the pound has sunk** la livre a chuté *ou* baissé; **they've sunk to the bottom of the league table** ils sont tombés tout en bas du classement; **the patient is sinking fast** le malade baisse *ou* décline rapidement; **her voice sank to a whisper** sa voix s'est réduite à un murmure; **he has sunk in my estimation** il a baissé *ou* diminué dans mon estime; **how could anyone s. so low?** comment peut-on tomber aussi bas?
VT **1** *(ship)* couler, faire sombrer, envoyer au fond; *Fam* **we're sunk** nous sommes fichus
2 *(well)* creuser, forer; *(stake etc)* enfoncer; **stone sunk into the wall** pierre encastrée dans le mur; **to s. one's teeth into sth** enfoncer ses dents dans qch; **they sank their differences** ils ont fait abstraction de leurs différences

3 *Fam (to drink)* s'envoyer; **to s. a pint** s'envoyer une pinte de bière
4 *Fin (debt)* amortir
5 **to s. money in a project** *(invest)* investir des capitaux dans un projet
6 **to s. the ball** *Billiards* mettre la bille dans la blouse; *Golf* envoyer la balle dans le trou
▸▸ **s. unit** bloc-évier *m*, *pl* blocs-éviers

▸ **sink in** VI **1** *(be absorbed) (of liquid)* pénétrer **2** *(be understood)* **her remark didn't s. in until later** ce n'est que plus tard que j'ai/il a etc compris le sens de sa remarque; **the lesson hasn't sunk in** la leçon n'a pas été retenue; **it was beginning to s. in that things had changed** je commençais/il commençait etc à comprendre que les choses avaient changé

sinker ['sɪŋkər] N *(of fishing rod)* plomb *m*

sinkhole ['sɪŋkhəʊl] N *Geol* entonnoir *m*

sinking ['sɪŋkɪŋ] ADJ *(ground)* qui s'enfonce, qui s'affaisse; *(wall etc)* qui se tasse; *(ship)* qui fait naufrage; **with a s. heart** avec un serrement de cœur; **I'm getting that s. feeling that something has happened** j'ai le pressentiment qu'il s'est passé quelque chose; **I get that s. feeling every time I think about what happened** à chaque fois que je pense à ce qui s'est passé, j'ai l'estomac qui se serre
N **1** *(of ship)* engloutissement *m*; *(intentional, in war etc)* torpillage *m* **2** *(subsiding) (of ground etc)* affaissement *m*; *(of building etc)* tassement *m* **3** *(of well)* creusage *m*, forage *m* **4** *Fin (of debt)* amortissement *m*
▸▸ *Fin* **s. fund** caisse *f ou* fonds *mpl* d'amortissement

sinless ['sɪnlɪs] ADJ sans péché; *(pure)* innocent, pur

sinner ['sɪnər] N pécheur *m*, pécheresse *f*

sinning ['sɪnɪŋ] N péché *m*

Sinologist [saɪ'nɒlədʒɪst, sɪ-] N sinologue *mf*

Sinology [saɪ'nɒlədʒɪ, sɪ-] N sinologie *f*

sinuosity [sɪnjʊ'ɒsɪtɪ] N sinuosité *f*

sinuous ['sɪnjʊəs] ADJ **1** *(movement, river etc)* sinueux, tortueux **2** *(supple) (person)* souple, agile

sinus ['saɪnəs] N *Anat* sinus *m*; **I've got a bit of s. trouble** j'ai un problème de sinus

sinusitis [saɪnə'saɪtɪs] N *Med* sinusite *f*

Sioux [suː] ADJ sioux *inv*
N **1** Sioux *mf inv* **2** *Ling* sioux *m*

sip [sɪp] N petite gorgée *f*; **to drink sth in sips** siroter qch, boire qch à petits coups; **have a s. and see if you like it** goûte pour voir si tu aimes
VT *(-pp-) (tea, wine etc)* boire à petites gorgées *ou* à petits coups, siroter
VI **to s. at sth** boire qch à petites gorgées

siphon ['saɪf(ə)n] N siphon *m*
VT *(liquid)* siphonner

▸ **siphon off** VT SEP **1** *(liquid)* siphonner **2** *Fin (money, supplies etc)* détourner; *(staff)* prendre; **they siphoned off all the profits** ils ont détourné *ou Fam* pompé tous les bénéfices

sir [sɜːr, sər] N **1** *(as form of address to a superior, esp to an equal in US)* monsieur *m*; **yes, s.** oui, monsieur; *Mil etc (to superior officer)* oui, mon capitaine/mon colonel etc; *Naut* oui, commandant/amiral etc; **dinner is served, s.** monsieur est servi; **Dear S.** *(in letter)* Monsieur; *(less formal)* Cher Monsieur; **Dear Sirs** Messieurs; *Sch Fam* **s. told me** le maître me l'a dit **2** *(title)* sir (= titre d'un 'baronet' et d'un 'knight'; ne s'emploie jamais sans le prénom, ainsi Sir Walter Scott, Sir Walter)

sire ['saɪər] N **1** *(in breeding)* père *m*; *(stallion)* étalon *m* **2** *Arch, Lit (father)* père *m*; *Arch (address to sovereign)* sire *m*
VT *(of stallion, man)* engendrer

siren ['saɪərən] N **1** *Myth*, sirène *f*; *Fig (temptress)* sirène, femme *f* fatale **2** *(device)* sirène *f*; **ambulance/police s.** sirène d'ambulance/de voiture de police
▸▸ **s. song** chant de sirène

sirloin ['sɜːlɔɪn] N *Culin* aloyau *m (de bœuf)*; **a s. steak** un steak d'aloyau

sirocco [sɪ'rɒkəʊ] N *Met* siroc(c)o *m*

sirup ['sɪrəp] N *Am* = **syrup**

sis [sɪs] N *Fam (sister)* sœurette *f*, *Fam* frangine *f*

sisal ['saɪs(ə)l] N *(plant, fibre)* sisal *m*

sissy ['sɪsɪ] *Pej* N *(cowardly child etc)* poule *f* mouillée; *(effeminate man, boy)* garçon *m* efféminé; **that's a game for sissies!** c'est un jeu de filles!
ADJ *(cowardly)* lâche, peureux; *(effeminate)* efféminé; **he thinks it's s. to ...** il pense que ça fait efféminé de ...

sister ['sɪstər] N **1** *(in family)* sœur *f*; **sisters unite!** *(to female workers, feminists)* sœurs, unissez-vous! **2** *Am Fam (black woman)* = nom *m* donné par les Noirs américains à une femme noire; **you don't treat your sisters like that!** c'est des façons de traiter d'autre Noires! **3** *Rel* religieuse *f*, *(bonne)* sœur *f*; **S. of Mercy** sœur de la Charité; **come in, S.** entrez, ma sœur **4** *(nurse)* infirmière *f* chef; **thank you, s.** merci madame/mademoiselle
ADJ *(publication, hotel)* qui appartient au même groupe; **s. state/party** pays *m*/parti *m* frère; **s. company** société *f* sœur
▸▸ **s. cities** villes *fpl* jumelées; **to be a s. city with** être jumelé avec; **s. ship** *(belonging to same company)* navire *m* de la même ligne; *(identical)* navire-jumeau *m*, *pl* navires-jumeaux, sister-ship *m*, *pl* sister-ships

sisterhood ['sɪstəhʊd] N **1** *Rel* communauté *f* religieuse *(de sœurs)* **2** *(solidarity)* solidarité *f* féminine; **the s.** *(women)* la communauté des femmes

sister-in-law, *pl* **sisters-in-law** N belle-sœur *f*, *pl* belles-sœurs

sisterly ['sɪstəlɪ] ADJ de sœur; **in a s. fashion** en sœur

Sistine ['sɪstiːn, -taɪn] ADJ **the S. chapel** la chapelle Sixtine

Sisyphus ['sɪsɪfəs] N Sisyphe *m*

SIT *(pt, pp* **sat** [sæt]; *prp* **sitting***)*

| VI s'asseoir **1** ▪ être assis **1** ▪ siéger **3** ▪ se trouver, être posé **4** ▪ être perché **5** ▪ couver **5** |
| VT asseoir **1** ▪ passer **2** |

VI 1 *(of person)* s'asseoir; **to be sitting** *(in armchair, on ground etc)* être assis; **s.!** *(to dog)* assis!; **we usually s. in the living room** nous sommes d'ordinaire dans le salon; **where would you like me to s.?, where shall I s.?** où est-ce que je me mets?; **she was sitting reading** elle était assise à lire *ou* en train de lire; **I'm fed up with sitting at home** j'en ai assez de rester enfermé à la maison; **don't just s. there, say something!** mais enfin, dis quelque chose!; **don't just s. there, do something!** eh bien, allez, remue-toi!; **to s. at (the) table** *(take one's seat)* s'asseoir *ou* se mettre à (la) table, s'attabler; **they were sitting at (the) table** ils étaient à table, ils étaient attablés; **we were sitting at lunch/dinner** nous étions en train de déjeuner/dîner; **he sits for hours over his books** il passe des heures penché sur ses livres; *Fam* **to s. tight** *(not move)* ne pas bouger de sa place; *(not give in)* ne pas céder
2 to s. in Parliament = être député
3 *(of assemblies)* siéger, être en séance; **the court is sitting** la séance est ouverte
4 *Fam (of object)* **the diskette was sitting on**

the radiator la disquette était *ou* se trouvait sur le radiateur; **I found it sitting on the fridge** je l'ai trouvé sur le frigo; **the car was sitting in the drive** la voiture était stationnée dans l'allée
5 *(of bird)* être perché; **to s. (on eggs)** *(of hen)* couver
6 *(of responsibility)* **to s. heavy on sb** peser sur qn
7 to s. well/badly *(of jacket etc)* tomber bien/mal; **the jacket sits well/badly on him** la veste lui va bien/ne lui va pas
VT 1 to s. a child on the table asseoir un enfant sur la table
2 *Br Sch etc (exam)* passer
▸ **sit about, sit around** VI *(hang around)* traîner; *(do nothing)* ne rien faire
▸ **sit back** VI **1** *(lean back)* **to s. back in one's chair** s'appuyer contre le dossier de sa chaise/son fauteuil
2 *Fam (relax)* se relaxer; **to s. back and let the others do the work** *(not intervene)* regarder les autres travailler; **the authorities just sat back and did nothing** les autorités n'ont pas daigné faire quoi que ce soit; **we can't just s. back and do nothing** nous ne pouvons pas rester comme ça sans rien faire
▸ **sit down** VI s'asseoir; **to be sitting down** être assis; **please s. down** asseyez-vous, *Fml* veuillez vous asseoir; **to s. down again** se rasseoir; *(at table)* se remettre à (la) table; **to s. down at (the) table** se mettre à table, s'attabler; **to s. down to a meal** se mettre à table pour un repas; **to s. down to a game of bridge** s'installer pour faire une partie de bridge; **I think we should s. down and talk about it** je crois qu'il faut qu'on en discute *ou* parle
VT SEP *(child etc)* asseoir; *Fam* **s. yourself down!** asseyez-vous donc!
▸ **sit for** VT INSEP **1** *Br (be candidate in)* *(exam)* passer
2 *(pose for)* **to s. for one's portrait** se faire faire son portrait
▸ **sit in** VI **1** *(at meeting etc)* assister sans participer; **do you mind if I s. in for a while?** cela vous ennuie-t-il si je reste à écouter un moment?
2 to s. in for sb *(replace)* remplacer qn
3 *(occupy building, office etc)* faire grève avec occupation des locaux
▸ **sit in on** VT INSEP *(attend as observer)* **to s. in on a rehearsal/a meeting** assister à une répétition/une réunion (sans y participer)
▸ **sit on** VT INSEP *Fam* **1** *(not deal with)* *(proposal, suggestion etc)* ne pas s'occuper de; *(deliberately)* faire traîner; **they sat on it for two months** ils ne s'en sont pas occupés pendant deux mois
2 *(repress)* rembarrer
▸ **sit out** VI *(sit down outside)* s'asseoir dehors; *(be seated outside)* être assis dehors
VT SEP 1 *(not participate in)* *(game etc)* ne pas prendre part à; **I'll s. this one out** *(dance)* je ne veux pas danser celle-ci; **I'll s. out this round** *(of card game etc)* je passe mon tour
2 *(wait until end of)* *(conference etc)* rester (patiemment) jusqu'à la fin de; **he sat out the war in Switzerland** il est resté en Suisse en attendant la fin de la guerre
▸ **sit through** VT INSEP *(wait until end of)* rester pendant toute la durée de; **he sat through the whole play** il est resté jusqu'à la fin de la pièce; **to s. through dinner** rester à table jusqu'à la fin du repas; **we had to s. through two hours of Wagner** nous avons dû nous payer deux heures de Wagner
▸ **sit up** VI *(straighten one's back)* se tenir droit *(sur sa chaise, son lit etc)*, se redresser; *(from lying position)* se dresser *ou* se mettre sur son séant; **s. up straight!** tiens-toi droit!; *Fig* **to make sb s. up** étonner qn, épater qn; *Fig* **her competitors are beginning to s. up**

and take notice ses concurrents commencent à prendre conscience de son existence; **to s. up (and beg)** *(of dog)* faire le beau; **to s. up (late)** veiller; **to s. up for sb** *(wait up for)* *(rester debout à)* attendre qn, veiller en attendant le retour de qn; **to s. up with a sick man** garder *ou* veiller un malade; **to s. up to (the) table** *(sit closer)* approcher sa chaise de la table; *(come to table)* venir à table
VT SEP to s. sb up soulever qn pour l'asseoir; **to s. sb up against a wall** adosser qn contre un mur

sitar ['sɪtɑːr, sɪ'tɑːr] N sitar *m*

sitcom ['sɪtkɒm] N *TV, Radio* sitcom *m ou f*

sit-down N *(act)* **come and have a s.** venez vous asseoir
ADJ there are too many guests for a s. meal il y a trop d'invités pour que tout le monde puisse s'asseoir à table
▸▸ **s. meal** dîner *m* pris à table; *Br* **s. strike** grève *f* sur le tas

site [saɪt] N **1** *(position)* *(of building etc)* emplacement *m*, situation *f*; *(archaeological etc)* site *m*; *Med (of pain etc)* siège *m*; **the s. of a battle/a historic meeting** le site d'une bataille/d'une réunion historique; **(camp) s.** *(terrain m de)* camping *m* **2** *(building)* **s.** chantier *m* *(de construction)*; **on s.** sur place; **to be on s.** être à pied d'œuvre **3** *Comput* site *m*
VT *(building, stadium)* placer; *(factory)* implanter; **to be sited** être situé
▸▸ **s. manager** chef *m* de chantier; *Comput* **s. map** plan *m* de navigation; **S. of Special Scientific Interest** = site protégé présentant un intérêt particulier du point de vue de la faune, de la flore ou de la géologie

sit-in N sit-in *m inv*; *(strike)* occupation *f* des locaux

siting ['saɪtɪŋ] N emplacement *m*

sitter ['sɪtər] N **1** *Art* modèle *m* **2** *Fam (childminder)* gardien, -ienne d'enfants **3** *(hen)* couveuse *f* **4** *Sport Fam* **to miss a s.** rater un but/une balle *etc* facile; **you gave him a s.** tu lui as fait une excellente passe

sitting ['sɪtɪŋ] ADJ *(seated)* assis; *(hare)* au gîte; *Art* **a s. figure** une figure assise; **a s. hen** une poule en train de couver; *Parl* **our s. member** le député qui nous représente actuellement
N *(for meal)* service *m*; *(for portrait etc)* pose *f*; *(of committee, court etc)* séance *f*; **s. and standing room** places assises et places debout; **to paint a portrait in three sittings** faire un portrait en trois séances; **first/second s.** *(for meals)* premier/deuxième service; **to serve 500 people in** *ou* **at one s.** servir 500 personnes à la fois; **to write two chapters at one s.** écrire deux chapitres d'un trait *ou* d'un (seul) jet
▸▸ **s. duck** *Fam (target)* cible *m* facile; *(victim)* proie *f* facile, pigeon *m*; **old people are s. ducks for all sorts of confidence tricksters** les personnes âgées sont des proies faciles pour les escrocs en tous genres; *Br* **s. room** salon *m*, salle *f* de séjour; *Br* **s. tenant** locataire *mf* en place

situate ['sɪtjʊeɪt] VT *(house etc)* situer; **from where we were situated ...** d'où nous nous trouvions ...; **pleasantly situated house** maison bien située; **awkwardly situated** *(person)* dans une situation *ou* une position embarrassante; **he's well situated to know what's going on** il est bien placé pour savoir ce qui se passe

situation [sɪtjʊ'eɪʃən] N **1** *(of building, town)* situation *f*, emplacement *m*
2 *(state of affairs)* situation *f*; **to explain the s.** exposer la situation; **to find oneself in an unfortunate s.** se trouver dans une situation

déplorable; *Fam* **what's** *or* **how's the coffee s.?** combien nous reste-t-il de café?; *Fam* **we're in a staff shortage s.** nous n'avons pas assez de personnel; **what to do in an emergency s.** que faire en cas d'urgence

3 *Old-fashioned (employment)* emploi *m*, position *f*; **to look for/find a s.** chercher/trouver un emploi; **situations vacant/wanted** *(in advertisements)* offres *fpl*/demandes *fpl* d'emploi

▸▸ *TV, Radio* **s. comedy** sitcom *m*

sit-up N **to do sit-ups** faire des abdominaux

sit-upon N *Old-fashioned Fam* derrière *m*, postérieur *m*

six [sɪks] N **1** six *m*; **number s.** (le) numéro six; **twenty-s.** vingt-six; **s. fours** *or* **four sixes are twenty-four** six fois quatre *ou* quatre fois six font vingt-quatre; **it's s. o'clock** il est six heures; **at s. thirty** à six heures et demie; **to be s.** *(in age)* avoir six ans; **double s.** *(at dominoes etc)* double-six *m*, *pl* doubles-six; *Cards* **the s. of hearts** le six de cœur; *Fam* **it's s. of one and half a dozen of the other** c'est blanc bonnet et bonnet blanc, c'est kif-kif; **we're all** *or* **everything's at sixes and sevens** tout est sens dessus dessous

2 *Cr* six points *mpl* (marqués par le batteur); **he scored five sixes** il a marqué cinq fois six points; *Fam* **to knock for s.** *(person) (knock down)* étendre; *(flabbergast)* abasourdir; *(enemy etc)* battre à plate(s) couture(s); *(project etc)* ficher en l'air; **that's knocked everything for s.** ça a tout fichu en l'air

PRON six; **I need s. (of them)** il m'en faut six, j'en ai besoin de six

NUM ADJ six; *Fam* **to be s. feet under** être six pieds sous terre; **a s.-cylinder car** une six cylindres; **s.-seater (car)** voiture à six places

▸▸ **the S. Counties** = l'Irlande *f* du Nord; *Hist* **the S. Day War** la guerre des six jours; *Sport* **the S. Nations (tournament)** le tournoi des six nations

sixfold ['sɪksfəʊld] ADJ sextuple
ADV au sextuple; **to increase s.** sextupler

six-foot ADJ *(beam)* de six pieds; **a s. bodyguard** un garde du corps très baraqué

six-footer N homme *m*/femme *f* mesurant six pieds, *Fam* armoire *f* à glace; **he's obviously going to be a s.** on voit bien qu'il sera grand

six-pack N **1** *(of bottles, cans)* pack *m* de six **2** *Hum (stomach muscles)* abdos *mpl*; **he's got a great s.** il a des super abdos

sixpence ['sɪkspəns] N **1** *(sum)* six pence *mpl* **2** *Formerly (coin)* pièce *f* de six pence

sixpenny ['sɪkspənɪ] ADJ *Old-fashioned (costing six pence)* qui coûte six pence; *(stamp)* de six pence

▸▸ **s. piece** pièce *f* de six pence

sixpennyworth [ˌsɪks'penɪwəθ] N *Old-fashioned* **to buy s. of chocolate** acheter pour six pence de chocolat

six-shooter N six-coups *m inv*

six-sided ADJ qui a six côtés, hexagonal, -aux

sixteen [sɪks'tiːn] NUM ADJ, N seize *m*; **she is s.** elle a seize ans

sixteenth [sɪks'tiːnθ] ADJ seizième; **Louis the S.** Louis XVI
N **1** *(in series)* seizième *mf* **2** *(fraction)* seizième *m* **3** *(of month)* seize *m inv*
▸▸ *Am Mus* **s. note** double croche *f*

sixth [sɪksθ] ADJ sixième; **Henry the S.** Henri VI
N **1** *(person, thing)* sixième *mf* **2** *(fraction)* sixième *m* **3** *Mus* sixte *f* **4** *(of month)* six *m inv*
▸▸ *Br Sch* **s. form** ≃ = classe *f* terminale de l'enseignement secondaire en Angleterre et au Pays de Galles, préparant aux A-levels,

≃ classes de première et de terminale; *Br Sch* **s. form college** = établissement *m* préparant aux "A-levels"; *Br Sch* **s. former** = élève *mf* de première ou de terminale; *Am Sch* **s. grade** = classe du primaire pour les 10-11 ans; **s. sense** sixième sens *m*; **some s. sense told me she wouldn't come** j'avais l'intuition qu'elle ne viendrait pas

sixthly ['sɪksθlɪ] ADV sixièmement

sixtieth ['sɪkstɪɪθ] ADJ, N soixantième *mf*

sixty ['sɪkstɪ] NUM ADJ, N soixante *m*; **s.-third** soixante-troisième; **about** *or* **some s. books** une soixantaine de livres; **she's in her sixties** elle a la soixantaine, elle a plus de soixante ans; **in the sixties** dans les années soixante

sixty-four NUM ADJ, N soixante-quatre *m*; *Fam* **the s. (thousand) dollar question** la question cruciale

sixty-nine N *(sexual position)* soixante-neuf *m*

sizable ['saɪzəb(ə)l] ADJ = sizeable

size¹ [saɪz] N **1** *(of building, room)* grandeur *f*, *(of town, country, island)* superficie *f*, *(of carpet, machine, car)* dimensions *fpl*, taille *f*, *(of apple, cake, print)* grosseur *f*, taille; *(of problem, undertaking)* importance *f*, ampleur *f*, *Comput (of file etc)* taille; **of equal** *or* **the same s., of a s.** de (la) même grandeur/taille *etc*; **I was surprised by the s. of the bill** j'ai été étonné par le montant de la note; **bicycles/people come in all shapes and sizes** il y a des bicyclettes/des gens de toutes les formes et de toutes les tailles; **books arranged according to s.** livres disposés par ordre de taille; **it's the s. of an egg** c'est gros comme un œuf; **to grow/decrease in s.** augmenter/diminuer de taille; **actual** *or* **full s.** grandeur nature; **a town of that s.** une ville de cette importance; *Fam* **that's about the s. of it** c'est un peu ça; **to cut a piece to s.** tailler une pièce à la dimension *ou* à la cote; *Fam* **to cut sb down to s.** rabattre le caquet à qn, remettre qn à sa place

2 *(of person)* taille *f*, *Com (of clothes)* taille; *(of shirt)* encolure *f*, *(of shoes, gloves, hat)* pointure *f*, *(of book, paper)* format *m*; **a boy half/twice his s.** un garçon deux fois moins/plus grand que lui; **a s. larger/smaller** *(shoes)* une pointure au-dessus/en-dessous; *(dresses etc)* une taille au-dessus/en-dessous; **what s. do you take?, what's your s.?, what s. are you?** *(in shoes)* quelle pointure chaussez-vous?; *(in dresses, shirts etc)* quelle est votre taille?; **s. ten shoes** ≃ chaussures *fpl* de pointure 44; **I've nothing in your s.** je n'ai rien à votre taille/à votre pointure; **to try sth for s.** essayer qch *(pour voir si la taille va)*; *Fam* **try this one for s.** prends ça

VT *(classify according to size) (objects)* classer par grosseur *ou* par dimension; *(adjust size of)* adapter les dimensions de; *Comput* dimensionner

▸▸ *Comput* **s. box** case *f* de dimensionnement

▸ **size up** VT SEP **to s. sb up** évaluer qn, jauger qn; **they soon sized him up** ils ont eu vite fait de le jauger

size² *Tech* N apprêt *m*; *(glue)* colle *f*, encollage *m*
VT *(wallpaper)* apprêter, encoller

sizeable ['saɪzəb(ə)l] ADJ assez grand, plutôt grand; *(difference)* assez important; *(fine, sum)* assez élevé

sized [saɪzd] ADJ **fair s.** *(quite large)* assez grand; **medium s.** de grandeur *ou* de taille moyenne; **large/small s.** de grande/petite taille; *(book, paper etc)* de grand/petit format

sizing ['saɪzɪŋ] N *Tech* **1** *(process)* apprêtage *m*; *(of wallpaper)* collage *m*, encollage *m* **2** *(substance)* colle *f*, *(in painting)* apprêt *m*

sizzle ['sɪz(ə)l] N *(of something frying)* grésillement *m*
VI *(of frying pan, sausages etc)* grésiller

sizzler ['sɪzlər] N *Fam* journée *f* de canicule; **it was a real s. (of a day)** on se serait cru dans un four, on crevait de chaleur

sizzling ['sɪzlɪŋ] ADJ *(heat, temperature)* torride; *(food)* grésillant
ADV *Fam* **(day)** torride
N grésillement *m*

skank [skæŋk] N *Am Fam (ugly woman)* cageot *m*, boudin *m*

skanky ['skæŋkɪ] ADJ *Am Fam (ugly)* hyper moche

skate¹ [skeɪt] N *(fish)* raie *f*

skate² N **(ice/roller) s.** patin *m* (à glace/à roulettes); *Fig Fam* **to get one's skates on** se dépêcher
VI *(on ice)* patiner, faire du patin; *(on roller skates)* faire du patin à roulettes; **he skated across the lake** il a traversé le lac en patins à glace; *Fig Fam* **to s. round sth** tourner autour du pot

▸ **skate over** VT INSEP **1** *(skate across surface of)* parcourir en patin **2** *(discuss superficially) (subject)* ne faire qu'effleurer; *(difficulties)* passer rapidement sur

skateboard ['skeɪtbɔːd] N *Sport* planche *f* à roulettes, *Fam* skate-board *m*, *pl* skate-boards, skate *m*, *Can* rouli-roulant® *m*, *pl* rouli-roulants
VI *Sport* faire de la planche à roulettes *ou Fam* du skate *ou Can* du rouli-roulant®

skateboarder ['skeɪtbɔːdər] N *Sport* personne *f* pratiquant le skate (-board); **a champion s.** un champion du skate-board

skateboarding ['skeɪtbɔːdɪŋ] N skate(-board) *m*; **to go s.** aller faire du skate-board

skater ['skeɪtər] N patineur, -euse

skating ['skeɪtɪŋ] N *(on ice)* patinage *m*; *(on roller skates)* patin *m* à roulettes
▸▸ **s. rink** *(for ice-skating)* patinoire *f*, *(for roller-skating)* piste *f* pour patin à roulettes

skean-dhu [ˌskiːən'duː] N *Scot* = dague *f* décorative que l'on porte dans la chaussette

skedaddle [skɪ'dæd(ə)l] VI *Fam (run off)* déguerpir, prendre ses jambes à son cou

skeet [skiːt] N *Sport* skeet *m*
▸▸ **s. shooting** *(tir m)* skeet *m*

skeezer ['skiːzər] N *Am Sl Pej (ugly woman)* cageot *m*, boudin *m*; *(promiscuous woman)* pouffiasse *f*, traînée *f*

skein [skeɪn] N **1** *(of silk, wool)* écheveau *m* **2** *(of wild geese)* vol *m*

skeletal ['skelɪt(ə)l] ADJ squelettique; *Fig (presentation etc)* sommaire

skeleton ['skelɪt(ə)n] N **1** *(of human being, animal etc)* squelette *m*; *Fig* **s. in the cupboard** *or Am* **in the closet** secret *m* honteux (de la famille); **to have a s. in the cupboard** *or Am* **in the closet** avoir un squelette dans le placard; **s. at the feast** rabat-joie *m inv*, trouble-fête *m inv*; **he's a living s.** c'est un vrai squelette **2** *Fig (of building etc)* charpente *f*, squelette *m*; *(of novel, essay)* canevas *m*, esquisse *f*
▸▸ **s. crew** personnel *m* réduit; **s. key** passe-partout *m inv*, passe *m*; **s. staff** équipage *m* réduit

skeptic, skeptical *etc Am* = **sceptic, sceptical** *etc*

sketch [sketʃ] N **1** *Art, Liter* croquis *m*, esquisse *f*; **the map is only a s.** la carte n'est qu'un croquis; **character s.** portrait *m* littéraire; **to make a s. of sth** faire le croquis de qch; **preliminary s.** premier jet *m*; **(parliamentary) s. writer** = journaliste *mf* spécialiste de l'actualité parlementaire qu'il/qu'elle présente de façon humoristique **2** *Fig (of project)* exposé *m*, ébauche *f*; **she**

drew a brief **s. of the situation** elle a fait un bref résumé de la situation **3** *Theat, TV* sketch *m*, saynète *f*

VT 1 *Art (landscape, building etc)* esquisser, croquer; *(person, thing)* faire un *ou* le croquis de **2** = **sketch out**

▸▸**s. pad** bloc *m* à croquis

▸**sketch in** VT SEP *(draw roughly)* dessiner sommairement, esquisser; *Fig (details)* esquisser

▸**sketch out** VT SEP *(draw up outline of) (novel)* faire le canevas *ou* l'ébauche de; *(provide outline of) (project etc)* esquisser, ébaucher

sketchbook ['sketʃbʊk] N cahier *m* de croquis

sketchily ['sketʃɪlɪ] ADV sans les détails, *Pej* d'une manière incomplète *ou* vague; *(to remember)* vaguement

sketching ['sketʃɪŋ] N **to do some s.** faire des croquis; **to go s.** aller faire des croquis; **s. block** *or* **pad** bloc *m* à croquis

sketchy ['sketʃɪ] ADJ *(work)* qui manque de fini; *(drawing)* qui manque de détails; *(knowledge)* superficiel, sommaire; *(ideas)* plutôt vague; **I'm a bit s. on this** mes connaissances sont un peu sommaires

skew [skjuː] VI *(of truck etc)* biaiser, obliquer

VT *(distort) (results)* biaiser

ADJ en biais, oblique

ADV de *ou* en biais

N on the s. de *ou* en biais, en oblique

skewbald ['skjuːbɔːld] ADJ *(horse)* pie *inv*

skewer ['skjuːər] *Culin* N *(for pieces of meat, vegetables etc)* brochette *f*, *(larger, for whole pig etc)* broche *f*

VT *(pieces of meat, vegetables etc)* mettre sur une brochette; *(whole pig etc)* embrocher; **his hand had been skewered to the table** il s'est fait clouer la main à la table

skew-whiff ADJ *Br Fam* de travers, *Fam* de traviole

ski, *pl* **skis** [skiː, skiːz] N ski *m*

VI *(pt, pp* **skied***)* skier, faire du ski; *(move)* aller à *ou* en skis; **he skis well** il skie bien; **to learn to s.** apprendre à skier *ou* à faire du ski; **to s. down the slope** descendre la piste à *ou* en skis; **we skied back** nous sommes rentrés à *ou* en skis

▸▸**s. binding** fixation *f*; **s. boots** chaussures *fpl* de ski; *Aut* **s. box** coffre *m* porte-skis; *Aut* **s. carrier** porte-skis *m inv*; **s. centre** station *f* de ski; **s. club** club *m* de ski; *Aut* **s. flap** trappe *f* à skis; **s. instructor** moniteur, -trice de ski; **s. jump** *(ramp)* tremplin *m* de ski; **s. jumper** sauteur *m*; **s. jumping** saut *m* à skis; **s. lift** remontée *f* mécanique; *(chair lift)* télésiège *m*; **s. pants** fuseau *m*, pantalon *m* de ski; **s. pass** forfait *m* de remonte-pente; **s. pole** bâton *m* de ski; *Aut* **s. rack** porte-skis; **s. resort** station *f* de ski; **s. run** piste *f* de ski; **s. slope** piste de ski; **s. stick** bâton de ski; **s. suit** combinaison *f* de ski; **s. tow** téléski *m*; **s. wax** fart *m* (pour skis)

skid [skɪd] N **1** *Aut (action)* dérapage *m*; **to go into a s.** déraper, faire un dérapage; **to correct a s.** redresser **2** *(device)* Com palette *f* sur patins; *Aviat (for landing etc)* patin *m*; *Fig Fam* **to put the skids under sb** *(hurry)* faire se magner qn; *(bring about ruin of)* glisser des peaux de bananes à qn; *Fig Fam* **to be on the skids** *(of economy, company, marriage etc)* battre de l'aile; **he's on the skids** il va mal finir

VI *(-dd-) (of car, tyre etc)* déraper; *(of wheel)* patiner; **his glasses went skidding across the table** ses lunettes ont glissé jusqu'à l'autre bout de la table

VT *(car)* faire faire un dérapage à

▸▸*Am Fam* **s. row** bas-fonds *mpl*, quartier *m* mal famé

skidlid ['skɪdlɪd] N *Aut Sl* casque *m* de moto

skidmark ['skɪdmɑːk] N *(on road)* trace *f* de dérapage; *Fig Fam Hum (on underpants, nappy etc)* trace

skidpan ['skɪdpæn] N *Aut* terrain *m* de dérapages

skier ['skiːər] N skieur, -euse

skiff [skɪf] N esquif *m*, yole *f*, *(in rowing)* skiff *m*

skiffle ['skɪf(ə)l] N *Mus* skiffle *m*

▸▸**s. group** skiffle-group *m inv*

ski-flying N *Ski* vol *m* à ski

skiing ['skiːɪŋ] N ski *m*; **to go s.** faire du ski; **we went on a s. holiday** nous sommes allés aux sports d'hiver

▸▸**s. instructor** moniteur, -trice de ski

skilful, *Am* **skillful** ['skɪlfʊl] ADJ adroit, habile; **to be s. at** *or* **in (doing) sth** être habile à (faire) qch; **to be s. with one's hands** être habile *ou* adroit de ses mains

skilfully, *Am* **skillfully** ['skɪlfʊlɪ] ADV habilement, adroitement

skilfulness, *Am* **skillfulness** ['skɪlfʊlnɪs] N habileté *f*, adresse *f*

skill [skɪl] N **1** *(ability)* habileté *f*, adresse *f*, *(manual)* dextérité *f*, *(as translator, negotiator, footballer, driver)* talent *m*; *(on basis of learning)* connaissances *fpl*; **technical s.** connaissance *f* technique; **s. in doing sth** talent *ou* habileté pour faire qch; **a game involving no s.** un sport/un jeu n'exigeant aucune aptitude particulière; **repairing pianos requires great s.** réparer les pianos demande une grande compétence; **language skills** connaissances en langues; **I don't have the necessary skills** je n'ai pas les connaissances nécessaires; **an archaeologist requires many skills** un archéologue doit posséder de nombreuses aptitudes; **they have very different skills** ils ont des aptitudes très différentes; *Iron* **it's one of my special skills** je suis expert en la matière **2** *(trade)* métier *m*; *(learned technique)* technique *f*; **learn new skills** apprenez un nouveau métier

skilled [skɪld] ADJ habile; *(work)* de spécialiste; **to be s. in doing sth** être habile à faire qch; **highly s. staff** personnel très qualifié; **s. labour** main-d'œuvre *f* qualifiée; **s. manual worker** ouvrier *m* spécialisé, OS *m*; **s. worker** ouvrier qualifié

skillet ['skɪlɪt] N *Am* poêle *f* (à frire)

skillful, skillfully etc *Am* = **skilful, skilfully** etc

skim [skɪm] N **just give it a quick s.** *(read through quickly)* jetez-y un coup d'œil rapide

VT *(-mm-)* **1** *(stock, gravy etc)* écumer; *(milk)* écrémer; *Mktg* écrémer; **skim(med) milk** lait *m* écrémé **2** *(pass lightly over) (surface)* effleurer, raser; **to s. stones on water** faire des ricochets; *Fig* **the book just skims the surface (of the problem)** le livre se contente de survoler le problème

VI **to s. along** *or* **over the ground** *(fly just above)* voler au ras du sol; *(move on surface)* raser le sol; **to s. over the water** *(fly just above)* voler à fleur d'eau; *(move on surface)* raser l'eau; *Fig* **the author skims over the real problems** l'auteur survole les vrais problèmes

▸**skim off** VT SEP *(remove by skimming) (cream, fat etc)* enlever, prélever; *Fig* **to s. the cream off sth** prendre la meilleure partie de qch; **the accounts department skims off the best recruits** la comptabilité récupère les meilleures recrues

▸**skim through** VT INSEP *(read superficially) (novel, document etc)* lire en diagonale

skimmer ['skɪmər] N *(for milk)* écrémeuse *f*

skimp [skɪmp] VT *(food, fabric of dress)* lésiner sur; *Fam (one's work)* bâcler

VI lésiner sur tout; *(live parsimoniously)* vi-

vre chichement; **they skimped on the cost of the new road** ils lésinaient sur le coût de la nouvelle route

skimpily ['skɪmpɪlɪ] ADV *(furnished etc)* parcimonieusement; **s. dressed** légèrement vêtu; **s. made** *(garment)* étriqué

skimpiness ['skɪmpɪnɪs] N insuffisance *f*, *(of garment)* aspect *m* étriqué

skimpy ['skɪmpɪ] ADJ insuffisant; **s. meal** maigre repas; **s. skirt** jupe étriquée; **to be s. with sth** *(be mean)* lésiner sur qch

skin [skɪn] N **1** peau *f*, *Fig* **to have a thin/thick s.** être/ne pas être susceptible; **to cast** *or* **throw its s.** *(of snake etc)* muer; **I always wear cotton next to my s.** je porte toujours du coton sur la peau; **to strip to the s.** se mettre tout nu; **she was soaked to the s.** elle était trempée jusqu'aux os; *Fam* **she's nothing but** *or* **she's all s. and bone** elle n'a que la peau et les os; **I nearly jumped out of my s.** cela m'a fait sursauter; **to escape by the s. of one's teeth** l'échapper belle; **to save one's (own) s.** sauver sa peau; *(escape criticism, scandal etc)* se tirer d'affaire; *Fam* **to get under sb's s.** *(annoy)* ennuyer qn; *(get on sb's nerves)* taper sur les nerfs de qn; *Fam* **I've got her under my s.** je l'ai dans la peau; *Fam* **it's no s. off my nose** ça n'a aucune conséquence pour moi; **s. deep** *(emotions)* à fleur de peau; *(wound)* superficiel; **beauty is only s. deep** la beauté n'est pas tout

2 *(of dead animal)* peau *f*

3 *(of fruit, sausage)* peau *f*, *(of onion)* pelure *f*, *Culin* **potatoes (cooked) in their skins** pommes *fpl* de terre en robe de chambre *ou* en robe des champs

4 *Naut (of canoe)* bordé *m* extérieur; *(of ship)* bordé extérieur, enveloppe *f*, coque *f*, *Aviat (of fuselage)* revêtement *m*

5 *(on milk, sauce, custard etc)* peau *f*, pellicule *f*

6 *Sl (skinhead)* skin *mf*

7 *Sl (cigarette paper)* papier *m* à cigarette

VT *(-nn-)* *(rabbit, cat etc)* écorcher, dépouiller; *(tomato etc)* peler, éplucher; **to s. one's knees** s'écorcher les genoux; *Prov* **there's more than one way to s. a cat** il y a plus d'une façon d'arriver à ses fins; *Fam* **to s. sb alive** écorcher qn, estamper qn; *Am Fam* **s. me!** tape-moi dans la main!

▸▸**s. cancer** cancer *m* de la peau; **s. care** soins *mpl* de la peau; **s. complaint** maladie *f* de peau; **s. cream** crème *f* pour la peau; **s. disease** maladie de peau; **s. diver** plongeur, -euse; **s. diving** plongée *f* sous-marine; *Fam* **s. flick** film *m* porno; *Fam* **s. game** arnaque *f*, **s. graft** greffe *f* de la peau; *Fam* **s. mag(azine)** magazine *m* porno; **s. patch** timbre *m* transdermique; *Med* **s. test** cuti-réaction *f*, *pl* cuti-réactions

▸**skin up** VI *Br Sl* rouler un joint

skinflint ['skɪnflɪnt] N *Fam* pingre *mf*, grippe-sou *m*, *pl* grippe-sous

skinful ['skɪnfʊl] N *Fam* **he's had a s.** *(of alcohol)* il a pris une (bonne) cuite

skinhead ['skɪnhed] N skinhead *mf*

skinless ['skɪnlɪs] ADJ *(sausage etc)* sans peau

skinned [skɪnd] ADJ *(rabbit)* à qui on a enlevé la peau; **to keep one's eyes s.** ouvrir l'œil; **keep your eyes s.** ouvre l'œil (et le bon); **keep one's eyes s. for sb/sth** guetter qn/qch; **I'll keep my eyes s. for one** j'ouvrirai l'œil pour voir si j'en trouve un

-skinned [-skɪnd] SUFF **dark/fair-s.** à la peau mate/claire

skinniness ['skɪnɪnɪs] N maigreur *f*, *(no negative overtones)* minceur *f*

skinny ['skɪnɪ] ADJ maigre; *(without negative overtones)* mince; *(sweater, pullover etc)* collant

N *Am Fam (inside information)* renseignements *mpl*; **what's the s. on the situation?** est-ce qu'il y a du nouveau?

skinny-dip *Fam* N baignade *f* tout nu *ou* à poil
VI nager *ou* se baigner tout nu *ou* à poil

skinny-malinky [-mə'lɪŋkɪ] N *Scot Fam* asperge *f*, grande perche *f*

skin-pop *Sl* VT *(drugs)* se piquer *ou* se shooter à
VI *(inject drugs)* se piquer, se shooter

skint [skɪnt] ADJ *Br Fam* **to be s.** être sans le sou, être fauché

skintight ['skɪntaɪt] ADJ *(garment)* collant, moulant

skip[1] [skɪp] VI (**-pp-**) **1** *(of lambs, children)* sautiller, gambader; *(with rope)* sauter à la corde; **they came skipping out of school** ils sont sortis de l'école en gambadant; **to s. from one subject to another** sauter d'un sujet à un autre; **to read without skipping** lire sans rien sauter
2 *Fam* **I skipped across to Paris** j'ai fait un saut à Paris; **he's just skipped out to the shops** il vient d'aller faire des courses; **if you s. through the work too fast …** si vous travaillez à la va-vite …
3 *Fam (leave without paying)* filer à l'anglaise
VT **1** *(meal, year at school, stage in process)* sauter; *(in planning trip etc) (not go to)* ne pas aller à; *(word, line etc) (intentionally)* omettre; *(accidentally)* sauter (par-dessus), passer; *Comput (command)* sauter; *Sch* **to s. a class** *(play truant)* sécher un cours; *(move up)* sauter une classe; **my heart skipped a beat** mon cœur a fait un bond; *Fam* **to s. bail** se dérober à la justice *(alors qu'on jouit de la liberté provisoire)*; *Fam* **they've skipped the country** ils ont quitté le pays; *Fam* **s. it!** *(that's enough)* ça suffit!; *(forget it)* passons!, laisse courir!
2 *Am* **to s. rope** sauter à la corde
N *(jump)* (petit) saut *m*, gambade *f*
▸▸ *Am* **s. rope** corde *f* à sauter
▸ **skip off** VI *Br Fam (leave)* filer, décamper
▸ **skip over** VT INSEP *(omit) (word, line etc) (intentionally)* omettre; *(accidentally)* sauter (par-dessus), passer

skip[2] N *Constr, Min etc* benne *f*

skip[3] N *Fam (skipper)* cap'taine *m*

skipper ['skɪpər] N **1** *Naut* capitaine *m*, patron *m*; *Aviat* commandant *m* de bord; *Sport Fam* capitaine, chef *m* **2** *Fam (who leaves without paying bill)* client *m* qui part sans payer *ou* qui file à l'anglaise
VT *Fam (ship)* être le commandant de; *(plane)* être le commandant à bord de; *(sports team)* être le chef de

skipping ['skɪpɪŋ] N *(with rope)* saut *m* à la corde
▸▸ **s. rope** corde *f* à sauter

skirl [skɜːl, *Scot* skɪrl] N *Scot (of bagpipes)* son *m* aigu

skirmish ['skɜːmɪʃ] N *Mil* escarmouche *f*, échauffourée *f*; *Fig* altercation *f*
VI *Mil* se livrer à une guerre d'escarmouches; **they are still skirmishing in the hills** il y a encore des escarmouches dans les collines; *Fig* **they've been skirmishing for months** il y a des accrochages depuis des mois entre eux

skirmisher ['skɜːmɪʃər] N *Mil* tirailleur *m*

skirt [skɜːt] N **1** *(garment)* jupe *f*; *(of overcoat, uniform etc)* pan *m*, basque *f* **2** *Br Offensive Sl (women)* nanas *fpl*, gonzesses *fpl*; **they've gone out looking for s.** ils sont allés draguer; **a bit of s.** une nana, une gonzesse **3** *Culin* **s. of beef** = flanchet *m* de bœuf **4** (**saddle**) **s.** petit quartier *m* (de la selle) **5** *(of hovercraft)* jupe *f* **6** *(in engine) (of piston)* jupe *f*

VT *(village, hill, problem)* contourner; *(of person) (wall)* longer, serrer; **the path skirts the wood** le sentier côtoie *ou* contourne le bois
▸▸ **s. clearance** jeu *m* à la jupe
▸ **skirt around** VT INSEP = **skirt**

skirting ['skɜːtɪŋ] N *Br Constr* plinthe *f*
▸▸ **s. board** plinthe *f*

skit [skɪt] N *Liter, Mus, Theat* pièce *f* satirique, satire *f*; **a s. on the current crisis** une satire sur la crise actuelle

skitter ['skɪtər] VI *(move quickly)* **to s. away** *or* **off** *(of spider etc)* s'enfuir; **the pencil skittered across the floor** le crayon glissa sur le sol

skittish ['skɪtɪʃ] ADJ **1** *(horse)* ombrageux **2** *(person) (playful)* espiègle; *(frivolous)* frivole

skittishly ['skɪtɪʃlɪ] ADV *(playfully)* avec espièglerie; *(frivolously)* frivolement

skittishness ['skɪtɪʃnɪs] N **1** *(of horse)* caractère *m* ombrageux **2** *(of person) (playfulness)* espièglerie *f*; *(frivolousness)* frivolité *f*

skittle ['skɪt(ə)l] N quille *f*; (**game of**) **skittles** *(jeu m de)* quilles *fpl*; **to play skittles** jouer aux quilles
▸▸ **s. alley** piste *f* de jeu de quilles; **s. pin** quille *f*

skive [skaɪv] *Br Fam* N *(easy job)* planque *f*; **she's taking PE because it's such a s.** elle a choisi éducation physique parce que c'est pépère
VI tirer au flanc
▸ **skive off** VI *Br Fam (leave work etc)* s'esquiver

skiver ['skaɪvər] N *Br Fam* tire-au-flanc *m inv*

skiving ['skaɪvɪŋ] N *Br Fam* manque *m* de travail; **there's too much s. round here** on tire trop au flanc ici

skivvy ['skɪvɪ] N **1** *Br Pej* bonniche *f*, bonne *f* à tout faire; *Fig* **I'm not your s.!** je ne suis pas ta bonne!
VI *Br* faire la bonne (à tout faire); *Fig* **I'm not skivvying for you** je ne suis pas ta bonne

skua ['skjuːə] N *(bird)* stercoraire *m*

skulduggery [skʌl'dʌgərɪ] N *Fam* magouille *f*; **political/financial s.** magouille politique/financière

skulk [skʌlk] VI **1** *(hide)* se cacher **2** *(move furtively)* rôder; **to s. in/out** entrer/sortir furtivement

skull [skʌl] N crâne *m*; **he's got a thick s.** il a la tête dure; *Fam* **can't you get that into your thick s.?** est-ce que tu ne peux pas te rentrer ça dans le crâne?; *Fam* **I was bored out of my s.** je crevais d'ennui; *Sl* **to be out of one's s.** *(drunk)* être bourré; **to get out of one's s.** se bourrer la gueule
▸▸ **s. and crossbones** *(motif)* tête *f* de mort; *(flag)* pavillon *m* à tête de mort

skullcap ['skʌlkæp] N *(of priest etc)* calotte *f*

skunk [skʌŋk] N *(animal)* mouffette *f*; *(fur)* scons(e) *m*, skons *m*, skun(k)s *m*; *Fam Pej (person)* mufle *m*, salaud *m*

sky [skaɪ] N ciel *m*, *pl* cieux, *(in art)* ciels; **under the open s.** *(to picnic, wander)* au grand air; **to sleep under the open s.** dormir à la belle étoile; *Fig* **the s.'s the limit** il n'y a pas de limite; **to praise sb to the skies** porter qn aux nues; *Prov* **red s. at night, shepherd's delight** rouge le soir, l'espoir; *Prov* **red s. in the morning, shepherd's warning** ≃ araignée du matin, chagrin; **the bridge was blown s. high** le pont a volé en éclats; **his project was blown s. high** son projet a été anéanti; **prices are s. high** les prix sont astronomiques
VT *(pt, pp* **skied***) Cr, Tennis etc (ball)* envoyer en chandelle

▸▸ **s. blue** bleu ciel *m*; *TV* **s. cloth** rideau *m* de fond; **s. marshal** = garde *m* armé embarqué sur un avion de ligne en cas d'attentat

sky-blue ADJ bleu ciel *inv*, bleu azur *inv*

skydiver ['skaɪdaɪvər] N *Aviat, Sport* parachutiste *mf* qui pratique la chute libre

skydiving ['skaɪdaɪvɪŋ] N *Aviat, Sport* parachutisme *m* en chute libre

Skye [skaɪ] N (l'île *f* de) Skye *f*
▸▸ **S. terrier** skye-terrier *m*, *pl* skye-terriers

skyjack ['skaɪdʒæk] VT *Fam (plane)* détourner

skyjacker ['skaɪdʒækər] N *Fam* pirate *m* de l'air

skyjacking ['skaɪdʒækɪŋ] N *Fam* piraterie *f* aérienne

skylark ['skaɪlɑːk] N *(bird)* alouette *f* des champs
VI *Fam (play about)* rigoler, batifoler

skylarking ['skaɪlɑːkɪŋ] N *Fam* rigolade *f*

skylight ['skaɪlaɪt] N *(in roof, ceiling)* jour *m*; *(in attic)* (lucarne *f*) faîtière *f*, *(hinged)* (châssis *m ou* fenêtre *f ou* lucarne à) tabatière *f*

skyline ['skaɪlaɪn] N *(horizon)* (ligne f d') horizon *m*; *(of city)* silhouette *f*; **it radically alters the s.** ça change radicalement le profil de la ville

skypilot ['skaɪpaɪlət] N *Mil Old-fashioned Sl (padre)* aumônier *m* militaire

skyrocket ['skaɪrɒkɪt] N fusée *f*
VI *Fam (of prices etc)* monter en flèche

skyscape ['skaɪskeɪp] N *Art* paysage *m* céleste

skyscraper ['skaɪskreɪpər] N gratte-ciel *m inv*

skyward(s) ['skaɪwəd(z)] ADV *(to fly)* dans le ciel; *(to look)* vers le ciel

skyway ['skaɪweɪ] N *Am* **1** *Aviat* couloir *m* aérien **2** *(flyover)* saut-de-mouton *m*, *pl* sauts-de-mouton; *(raised road)* route *f* surélevée

sky(-)writing N publicité *f* aérienne

S & L [esə'nel] N *Am (abbr* **savings and loan association**) société *f* immobilière

slab [slæb] N **1** *(of stone, marble etc)* plaque *f*, dalle *f*, *(of timber)* plaque; *(in mortuary)* table *f*; (**paving**) **s.** dalle; **butcher's s.** étal *m* de boucher **2** *(of cake)* (grosse) tranche *f*, *(of chocolate)* plaque *f*, tablette *f*, *(of meat)* pavé *m*

slack[1] [slæk] N **1** *(in cable, belt)* mou *m*; *Tech* jeu *m* (nuisible); **to take up the s. in a cable** mettre un câble au raide; *Fig* **to take up the s.** relancer le marché **2** *Naut (sea)* mer *f* étale **3** *(trousers)* **slacks** pantalon *m*
ADJ **1** *(rope etc)* mou, *f* molle, lâche; *(screw)* desserré; *(handshake, grip)* mou; **to be** *or* **hang s.** *(of rope)* avoir du mou; *Fig* **to have a s. rein on sth** diriger qch sans fermeté *ou* mollement **2** *(careless) (person, attitude, work)* négligent; *(lazy)* paresseux, *Fam* flemmard; *(analysis)* flou; **things are getting far too s. around here** il y a beaucoup trop de relâchement ici; **to get** *or* **become s.** *(of person)* se laisser aller, se relâcher; **to be s. in** *or* **about doing sth** être négligent en faisant qch; **security at the base is very s.** les mesures de sécurité à la base militaire ne sont pas du tout strictes **3** *(not busy) (market, economy)* peu actif, *-ive*; *(business)* stagnant; **business is s.** les affaires ne marchent pas fort; **we're s. this afternoon** *(in business etc)* nous ne sommes pas très occupés cet après-midi; **when things are a bit slacker** quand les choses se calmeront; **s. periods** moments de creux, périodes calmes; **the s. season** la morte-saison, la saison creuse; **s. time** période d'accalmie
VI *Fam (of person) (become negligent)* se

laisser aller; *(in one's work, efforts)* se relâcher; **dear me, I must be slacking!** mon Dieu, je vieillis!
▸ **slack off** VI *(diminish) (of pressure, demand, rain etc)* se calmer
VT SEP *Tech (diminish) (pressure)* relâcher

slack² N *(coal)* menu charbon *m*, poussier *m*

slacken ['slæk(ə)n] VT *(pace, efforts)* ralentir; *(rope)* détendre, relâcher, donner du mou à; *(sail)* donner du mou à; **to s. speed** diminuer la vitesse, ralentir (la marche); **to s. the reins** lâcher la bride *ou* les rênes
VI *(of person)* se relâcher, devenir négligent; *(of rope)* prendre du mou; *(of speed)* ralentir; *(of storm)* se calmer; *(of energy, enthusiasm)* retomber; **business is slackening** les affaires stagnent
▸ **slacken off** VI, VT SEP = slack off

slackening ['slæk(ə)nɪŋ] N *(of zeal)* ralentissement *m*, diminution *f*; *(of strength, speed)* diminution; *(of rope, efforts)* relâchement *m*; **s. of speed** ralentissement

slacker ['slækər] N *Fam* paresseux, -euse, *Fam* flemmard, -arde

slackly ['slæklɪ] ADV **1** *(to hang)* mollement **2** *(carelessly)* négligemment

slackness ['slæknɪs] N **1** *(negligence)* négligence *f*, *(laziness)* paresse *f*, *Fam* flemme *f*, *(laxity)* mollesse *f*; *(of discipline)* laxisme *m* **2** *(of muscles etc)* relâchement *m*; *(of rope)* mou *m* **3** *Com (of business)* stagnation *f*

slag [slæg] N **1** *Metal (of metal)* scorie(s) *f(pl)*, *(of blast furnace)* crasse *f*, laitier(s) *m(pl)*, *Min* déchets *mpl* miniers; *Geol* **volcanic s.** scories volcaniques; **s. heap** *Metal* crassier *m*; *Min* terril *m* **2** *Pej Sl (woman)* salope *f*
VT *Br Sl* **1** *(criticize)* débiner, éreinter, descendre en flammes **2** *(make fun of)* se foutre de
▸ **slag off** VT SEP *Br Sl* **1** *(criticize)* débiner, éreinter, descendre en flammes **2** *(make fun of)* se foutre de

slagging ['slægɪŋ] N *Br Sl* **to give sb a s.** débiner qn

slaggy ['slægɪ] ADJ *Br Sl* qui fait pute; **she looks really s. in all that make-up** elle fait vraiment pute avec tout son maquillage

slain [sleɪn] ADJ *Lit* mort
NPL *Lit* **the s.** les morts *mpl*
PP *see* slay

slake [sleɪk] VT **1** *Lit* **to s. one's thirst** étancher *ou* apaiser sa soif, se désaltérer **2** *Chem (lime)* éteindre; **slaked lime** chaux *f* éteinte

slalom ['slɑːləm] N *Ski* slalom *m*

slam² [slæm] VT (-mm-) **1** *(door)* (faire) claquer; **to s. the door in sb's face** claquer la porte au nez de qn; **she slammed the book (down) on the table** elle a flanqué le livre sur la table; **he slammed the phone down** raccrocha d'un geste furieux; *Ftbl* **he slammed the ball into the back of the net** il a logé le ballon au fond des filets; **she slammed her fist into his face** elle lui a flanqué son poing dans la figure; **he slammed the money down on the counter** il jeta rageusement l'argent sur le comptoir **2** *Fam (criticize severely)* critiquer; *(person)* éreinter; **he was slammed in the press** il a été éreinté par la presse **3** *Fam (drink quickly)* descendre, écluser; **let's go s. some beers** allons écluser quelques bières
VI *(of door etc)* claquer; **to s. out of the house** sortir de la maison en claquant la porte
N *(of door etc)* claquement *m*; **he shut the door after him with a s.** il claqua la porte derrière lui

slam² N *Cards (at bridge)* chelem *m*, schelem *m*; *Cards, Sport* **grand s.** grand chelem; **to make a s.** faire (le) chelem
▸ **slam on** VT SEP *Fam* **to s. on the brakes** freiner à fond

slammer ['slæmər] N *Sl (prison)* taule *f*

slander ['slɑːndər] N calomnie *f*, *Law* diffamation *f* verbale
VT calomnier; *Law* diffamer

slanderer ['slɑːndərər] N détracteur, -trice; *Law* diffamateur, -trice

slanderous ['slɑːndərəs] ADJ *(words, article)* calomnieux; *Law* diffamatoire

slanderously ['slɑːndərəslɪ] ADV calomnieusement; *Law* de façon diffamatoire

slang [slæŋ] N *(in general, of specific group)* argot *m*; **prisoners'/schoolboy s.** argot des prisonniers/écoliers; **s. phrase** *or* **expression** expression *f* argotique
VT *Fam (person) (abuse)* injurier; *(reprimand)* engueuler

slangily ['slæŋɪlɪ] ADV *(to express oneself)* en argot

slanging match ['slæŋɪŋ] N *Fam* prise *f* de bec, engueulade *f*; **they were having a s.** ils se sont engueulés

slangy ['slæŋɪ] ADJ *(style, language, term)* argotique

slant [slɑːnt] N **1** *(oblique angle)* biais *m*, biseau *m*; **on the** *or* **at a s.** de biais, oblique ment **2** *(emphasis)* perspective *f*; **to put a different s. on things** apporter une perspective différente sur les choses; **to put a left-/ right-wing s. on events** interpréter les événements dans une perspective de gauche/ de droite; **these historians put a different s. on events** ces historiens ont envisagé les événements sous un angle différent; **report with a s.** reportage tendancieux **3** *Offensive Sl (Oriental)* bridé, -ée
VI *(slope)* être en pente, être incliné; *(of handwriting)* pencher (**to** à)
VT **1** *(angle)* incliner **2** *Fig (bias)* fausser; **the article was slanted** l'article était orienté; **slanted news** informations tendancieuses *ou* faussées

slant-eyed ADJ aux yeux bridés; **to be s.** avoir les yeux bridés

slanting ['slɑːntɪŋ] ADJ *(roof)* en pente, incliné; *(writing)* couché, penché

slantwise, slantways ['slɑːntwaɪz, -weɪz] ADV en *ou* de biais

slap [slæp] N **1** *(with hand)* claque *f*, tape *f*, *(of waves)* clapotis *m*; **s. in the face** gifle *f*, *Fig (rebuff)* gifle, affront *m*, soufflet *m*; **s. on the back** tape dans le dos; *Fig* félicitations *fpl*; **to get a s. on the back for one's efforts** être félicité pour les efforts que l'on a fournis; *Br Hum Fam* **they were having a bit of s. and tickle on the sofa** ils se faisaient un câlin sur le divan **2** *Br Fam (make-up)* maquillage *m*
ADV *Fam* **s. (bang) in the middle** en plein milieu; **the car went s. bang into the wall** la voiture est rentrée dans le mur de plein fouet; **they ran s. bang into each other** ils se sont rentrés en plein dedans
VT (-pp- [slæpt]) **1** *(person) (with open hand)* donner une claque *ou* une tape à; **to s. sb's face, to s. sb in the face** gifler qn; **to s. sb on the back** donner une tape sur le dos à qn; *Fig (congratulate)* féliciter qn **2** *(put brusquely)* **she slapped the money on the table** elle a jeté *ou* flanqué l'argent sur la table
▸ **slap around** VT SEP battre, *Fam* cogner
▸ **slap down** VT SEP **1** *(put down brusquely)* jeter; *Fam* flanquer, balancer **2** *Fam (repress) (person)* rembarrer; *(put in his place)* remettre à sa place; *(suggestion)* rejeter
▸ **slap on** VT SEP **he slapped on some aftershave** il s'est aspergé de lotion après-rasage; *Fam* **they slapped on another £50** ils ont augmenté le prix de 50 livres; **the paint had been just slapped on** la peinture avait été appliquée n'importe comment

slapdash ['slæpdæʃ] ADJ sans soin(s); *(work)*

à la six-quatre-deux; *(person)* expéditif; **to do sth in a s. manner** faire qch à la va-vite *ou* à la six-quatre-deux
ADV sans soin(s), à la va-vite, à la six-quatre-deux

slap-happy ADJ *Fam (careless)* insouciant; **this work's a bit s.** ce travail a été fait à la va-vite

slaphead ['slæp(h)ed] N *Sl (bald person)* crâne *m* d'œuf

slapper ['slæpər] N *Br Sl* **1** *(promiscuous woman)* pouffiasse *f*, traînée *f*, salope *f* **2** *Pej (any woman)* gonzesse *f*, grognasse *f*

slapping ['slæpɪŋ] N *(blows)* claques *fpl*, gifles *fpl*

slapstick ['slæpstɪk] N grosse farce *f*, bouffonerie *f*
ADJ *(humour)* bouffon
▸▸ **s. comedy** comédie *f* bouffonne, farce *f*

slap-up ADJ *Br Fam* **a s. meal** un repas de derrière les fagots; **he invited me out for a s. lunch** il m'a invité à déjeuner dans un restaurant chic

slash [slæʃ] N **1** *(cut)* entaille *f*, *(on the face)* estafilade *f*, balafre *f* **2** *Sewing (in sleeve)* crevé *m* **3** *Typ* barre *f* oblique **4** *Br Sl* **to have a s.** *(urinate)* pisser un coup
VT *(cut) (flesh)* taillader; *(face)* balafrer; *(rope etc)* couper *ou* trancher net; *Fig (shorten) (text etc)* couper radicalement; *(criticize) (novel etc)* éreinter, *Fam* casser; *(reduce) (prices, interest rates)* casser; *(unemployment, spending)* réduire de façon radicale; **he slashed the sack open** il a fendu le sac d'un coup de couteau; **prices slashed** prix sacrifiés; *Sewing* **slashed sleeve** manche *f* à crevés
VI **to s. at sb with a knife** donner des coups de couteau à qn; **to s. about with a knife** donner des coups de couteau dans tous le sens; **they slashed through the undergrowth** ils se sont taillés un chemin dans les sous-bois

slasher film ['slæʃər] N *Fam* = film *m* d'horreur particulièrement sanglant

slashing ['slæʃɪŋ] ADJ *(criticism)* mordant, cinglant

slat [slæt] N *(of shutter etc)* lame *f*, lamelle *f*, planchette *f*; *(of bed)* traverse *f*

slate¹ [sleɪt] N **1** *Geol* ardoise *f*, *Constr* (feuille *f* d')ardoise; *Br Fam* **to have a s. loose** avoir une case de vide, avoir une araignée au plafond **2** *(writing)* s. ardoise *f*, *Br Fam* **put it on my s.** *(as debt)* mettez-le-moi sur mon ardoise; *Fig* **to wipe the s. clean** faire table rase (du passé); **I have a clean s.** *(have no debts)* je n'ai pas de dettes; *(have committed no offence)* mon casier judiciaire est vierge; **to start again with a clean s.** repartir sur de nouvelles bases **3** *TV etc* clap *m*
VT *Constr (roof)* couvrir d'ardoises *ou* en ardoise; **slated roof** toit d'ardoises **2** *Am Pol (candidate)* inscrire sur la liste; **to be slated to do sth** être susceptible de faire qch; **he was slated for promotion but ...** il aurait dû être promu mais ...
▸▸ **s. blue** bleu ardoise *m inv*; **s. pencil** crayon *m* d'ardoise; **s. quarry** ardoisière *f*, **s. roof** toit *m* d'ardoises

slate² VT *Br Fam (criticize severely) (person, book, decision, government)* critiquer, éreinter, *Fam* casser

slate-blue ADJ bleu ardoise *inv*

slate-coloured ADJ ardoise *inv*

slate-grey ADJ gris ardoise *inv*

slater ['sleɪtər] N **1** *(person)* couvreur *m* (en ardoises) **2** *Dial (woodlouse)* cloporte *m*

slating ['sleɪtɪŋ] N *Br Fam* **1** *(reprimand)* savon *m*; **he got a s. from the PM** il s'est fait passer un savon par le Premier ministre **2** *(severe criticism)* critique *f* acerbe; **the play**

got a s. in the press la pièce a été éreintée *ou Fam* cassée par la presse

slatted ['slætɪd] ADJ *(shutters etc)* à lames, à planchettes

slattern ['slætən] N femme *f* mal soignée, souillon *f*

slatternly ['slætənlɪ] ADJ *(woman)* mal soigné; *(habit, dress)* négligé

slaty ['sleɪtɪ] ADJ *Geol* ardoisier; *(colour)* ardoisé

slaughter ['slɔːtər] N 1 *(of cattle, sheep etc)* abattage *m* 2 *(of people)* tuerie *f*, carnage *m*, massacre *m*; **the senseless s. of innocent civilians** le massacre insensé de civils innocents
   VT 1 *(cattle, sheep)* abattre 2 *(kill) (people)* tuer, massacrer; *Fam (defeat heavily) (opponent)* battre à plate(s) couture(s), massacrer

slaughtered ['slɔːtəd] ADJ *Br Fam (drunk)* bourré, beurré, pété

slaughterer ['slɔːtərər] N 1 *(of cattle, sheep)* abatteur *m*, tueur *m* 2 *(of people)* tueur, -euse

slaughterhouse ['slɔːtəhaʊs] N abattoir *m*

slaughtering ['slɔːtərɪŋ] N 1 *(of cattle, sheep)* abattage *m* 2 *(of people)* tuerie *f*, carnage *m*, massacre *m*

Slav [slɑːv] ADJ slave
   N Slave *mf*

slave [sleɪv] N esclave *mf*; **to be sb's s.** être l'esclave de qn; **to be the s. of** *or* **a s. to one's passion** être esclave de sa passion; **to be a s. to duty** ne connaître que son devoir; **to be a s. to convention** être esclave des conventions; **to be a s. to one's work** être esclave de son travail; *Fam Hum* **what did your last s. die of?** je ne suis pas ta bonne!
   ▸ ▸ **s. camera** caméra *f* asservie *ou* esclave; **s. cylinder** cylindre *m* récepteur; **s. driver** meneur *m* d'esclaves; *Fig* négrier *m*; **s. labour** *(work)* travail *m* fait par des esclaves; *Fig* travail de forçat; *(workers)* = personnes *fpl* que l'on utilise comme esclaves; **s. trade** commerce *m* des esclaves; *(of Africans)* traite *f* des Noirs; **s. trader** marchand *m* d'esclaves, négrier

slave VI travailler comme un nègre (**over** à); **to s. over a hot stove** trimer à ses fourneaux
   ▸ **slave away** VI *(work hard)* trimer (**over, at** sur)

slaver[1] ['sleɪvər] N 1 *(ship)* (bâtiment *m*) négrier *m* 2 *(person)* marchand *m* d'esclaves; *(of Blacks)* négrier *m*; **White s.** personne *f* pratiquant la traite des Blanches

slaver[2] ['slævər] N *(saliva)* bave *f*, salive *f*
   VI *(dribble)* baver (**over** sur)

slavery ['sleɪvərɪ] N esclavage *m*; **to sell sb into s.** vendre qn comme esclave; **to reduce to s.** *(person)* réduire en esclavage; *(a people)* asservir; **White s.** traite *f* des Blanches; **this work is sheer s.** ce travail est un véritable esclavage

Slavic ['slɑːvɪk] ADJ, N slave *m*

slavish ['sleɪvɪʃ] ADJ *(submission)* d'esclave; *(imitation)* servile

slavishly ['sleɪvɪʃlɪ] ADV *(to imitate)* servilement

slavishness ['sleɪvɪʃnɪs] N servilité *f*

Slavonic [slə'vɒnɪk] ADJ slave; **student of S. languages** slavisant, -ante
   N *Ling* slave *m*; **Church S., Old S.** slavon *m*

slaw [slɔː] N *esp Am Culin* salade *f* de chou cru

slay [sleɪ] VT *(pt* slew [sluː]; *pp* slain [sleɪn]) *Lit* tuer; *Am Journ* assassiner; **the slain** *(npl)* les morts *mpl*; *Fam* **this one will really s. you** *(of joke etc)* celle-là va vous faire mourir de rire

slayer ['sleɪər] N *Lit (killer)* tueur, -euse; *esp Am Journ (murderer)* assassin *m* (**of** de)

slaying ['sleɪɪŋ] N *Lit (killing)* *(of dragon)* destruction *f*, *(of person)* meurtre *m*; *esp Am Journ (murder)* assassinat *m*, meurtre *m*

sleaze [sliːz] N *Fam* corruption *f*, *(gossip in newspapers, on TV)* ragots *mpl* sordides; *(dirt, immorality)* perversité *f*; **the s. factor will affect his chances in the election** tous les ragots sordides qui ont circulé à son sujet risquent de compromettre son succès aux élections; **the s. factor in politics** la corruption de la vie politique

sleazebag ['sliːzbæg], *Am* **sleazeball** ['sliːzbɔːl] N *Sl* ordure *f*, raclure *f*

sleaziness ['sliːzɪnɪs] N *Fam (of place etc)* sordide *m*

sleazo ['sliːzəʊ] N *Fam* personne *f* louche; **he's a s.** c'est un type louche

sleazy ['sliːzɪ] ADJ *Fam* sordide, glauque

sled [sled] N, VI *Am* = **sledge**[1,2]

sledge[1] [sledʒ] N *(means of transport)* traîneau *m*; *(toy)* luge *f*
   VI *(travel)* aller en traîneau; *(play)* faire de la luge; **to go sledging** se promener en traîneau, faire une promenade en traîneau; *(of children)* aller faire de la luge

sledge[2] N = **sledgehammer**

sledgehammer ['sledʒhæmər] N *(tool)* masse *f*; **to have (all) the subtlety of a s.** manquer totalement de subtilité; **a s. blow** *(punch)* un coup de massue; *Fig (to industry etc)* un coup fatal; **to use a s. to crack a walnut** employer les grands moyens (pour régler un problème mineur)
   ▸ ▸ *Fam* **s. arguments** arguments massue(s)

sleek [sliːk] ADJ 1 *(smooth) (hair, fur etc)* lisse et brillant; *(person) (well-groomed)* trop pomponné; **a s. black limousine** une limousine d'un noir brillant; **the car's s. lines** la ligne aérodynamique de la voiture 2 *(unctuous) (manner)* mielleux, onctueux
   VT *(hair, horse's coat)* lisser

▸ **sleek down** VT SEP **to s. down one's hair** se lisser les cheveux; *(with oil)* se brillantiner les cheveux

sleekly ['sliːklɪ] ADV 1 **to glisten s.** luire 2 *(unctuously) (to talk, act)* mielleusement, onctueusement

sleekness ['sliːknɪs] N 1 *(of skin, satin)* luisant *m* 2 *(of manners)* onctuosité *f*

SLEEP [sliːp] N sommeil *m*; *Fam (substance in eye)* chassie *f*, **short s.** somme *m*; **deep** *or* **sound s.** sommeil profond; **beauty s.** sommeil avant minuit *(considéré comme le plus réparateur)*; **to go to** *or* **drop off to s.** s'endormir, s'assoupir; **to go to** *or* **drop off to s. again** se rendormir; **to send sb to s.** endormir qn; *Med* **to put sb to s.** endormir qn; *Vet* **to put an animal to s.** piquer un animal; **to read oneself to s.** lire pour s'endormir; **to rouse sb from his/her s.** réveiller qn, arracher qn au sommeil; **to have a good (night's) s.** bien dormir; **I need my s.** j'ai besoin de beaucoup de sommeil; **to get two hours' s.** dormir deux heures; **I didn't get a wink of s. all night** je n'ai pas fermé l'œil de la nuit; *(stayed up working etc)* j'ai passé une nuit blanche; **a night without s.** une nuit blanche; **to rub the s. out of one's eyes** se frotter les yeux pour se réveiller; **I won't lose any s. over it** cela ne m'empêchera pas de dormir; **in my s.** *(to cry, talk, call out)* en dormant; **to walk in one's s.** être somnambule; **my foot's gone to s.** j'ai des fourmis dans le pied, j'ai le pied engourdi
   VI *(pt, pp* slept [slept]) 1 *(not be awake)* dormir; **to s. like a log** dormir à poings fermés, dormir comme une souche *ou* comme un loir; **to s. soundly** dormir profondément; **to s. the night through** dormir toute la nuit; **to s. through a noise** ne pas être réveillé par un bruit; **I slept right through the alarm** je n'ai

pas entendu le réveil; **I haven't slept a wink all night** je n'ai pas fermé l'œil de (toute) la nuit; **to s. (for) six hours** dormir six heures; **to try to s.** chercher le sommeil; **he can't s. for thinking about it** il n'en dort pas; **to s. late** faire la grasse matinée; **I'll s. on it** je déciderai demain, la nuit porte conseil; **s. on it** la nuit porte conseil
   2 *(spend a night)* coucher; **to s. rough** coucher à la dure; **to s. on the floor/in a bed** coucher par terre/dans un lit; **the bed had not been slept in** le lit n'avait pas été défait
   VT 1 **a house that sleeps ten people** une maison où l'on peut coucher à dix; **this room sleeps four** on peut coucher à quatre dans cette chambre
   2 *Lit* **to s. the sleep of the just** dormir du sommeil du juste
   ▸ ▸ *Comput* **s. mode** veille *f*

▸ **sleep around** VI *Fam (be promiscuous)* coucher avec n'importe qui

▸ **sleep away** VT SEP **to s. the day/the hours away** passer la journée/les heures à dormir

▸ **sleep in** VI 1 *(have a lie-in)* faire la grasse matinée; *(wake up too late)* ne pas se réveiller à l'heure
   2 *(of servant)* coucher à la maison

▸ **sleep off** VT SEP *Fam (remove by sleeping)* *(headache)* faire passer en dormant; **to s. off one's hangover, to s. it off** cuver son vin/sa bière *etc*

▸ **sleep out** VI *(not sleep at home)* découcher; *(in open air)* coucher à la belle (étoile); *(of servant)* coucher à domicile, venir en journée

▸ **sleep together** VI coucher ensemble

▸ **sleep with** VT INSEP **to s. with sb** coucher avec qn

sleeper ['sliːpər] N 1 *(person)* dormeur, -euse; **a late s.** un couche-tard; **to be a light/heavy s.** avoir le sommeil léger/profond; **to be a good s.** *(of baby)* bien dormir 2 *Br Rail (on track)* traverse *f* 3 *Rail (carriage)* wagon-lit *m*, *pl* wagons-lits; *(train)* train-couchettes *m inv* 4 *Am (pajamas)* sleeper(s) pyjama *m* d'enfant 5 *(spy)* espion *m* en sommeil 6 *(earring)* dormeuse *f* 7 *Fam (unexpected success)* = film *m*, livre *m*, chanson *f etc* qui rencontre un succès inattendu et tardif
   ▸ ▸ **s. cell** cellule *f* terroriste dormante *ou* en sommeil

sleepily ['sliːpɪlɪ] ADV d'un air endormi; **a village nestled s. in the hills** un village blotti tranquillement contre les collines

sleepiness ['sliːpɪnɪs] N 1 *(desire to sleep)* envie *f* de dormir, somnolence *f* 2 *(of town)* calme *m*, *Pej* apathie *f*

sleeping ['sliːpɪŋ] ADJ dormant, endormi; *Prov* **let s. dogs lie** ne réveillez pas le chat qui dort
   N sommeil *m*; **the house has s. accommodation for ten** c'est une maison où dix personnes peuvent dormir; **there's no s. accommodation here** il n'y a rien pour dormir; **this is the s. accommodation here** c'est ici qu'on dort; **what are the s. arrangements?** et pour dormir, comment on fait?; **she was a bit vague about the s. arrangements** elle est restée vague concernant les lits
   ▸ ▸ **s. bag** sac *m* de couchage; *Rail* **s. car** wagon-lit *m*, *pl* wagons-lits; *Br* **s. draught** soporifique *m*; *Br Com* **s. partner** (associé *m*) commanditaire *m*, bailleur *m* de fonds; **s. pill** somnifère *m*; *Br* **s. policeman** casse-vitesse *m inu*, ralentisseur *m*; **s. quarters** chambres *fpl* à coucher; *Mil* chambrées *fpl*; *Sch* dortoir *m*; **s. sickness** maladie *f* du sommeil; *Am* **s. suit** grenouillère *f*, **s. tablet** somnifère

sleepless ['sliːplɪs] ADJ sans sommeil; *(night)* d'insomnie; **to have a s. night** ne pas fermer l'œil de la nuit, passer une nuit blanche; *Lit* **s. vigilance** vigilance sans faille

sleeplessly ['sli:plɪslɪ] ADV sans dormir

sleeplessness ['sli:plɪsnɪs] N insomnie f

sleepsuit ['sli:psju:t] = **sleeping suit**

sleepwalk ['sli:pwɔ:k] VI (be a sleepwalker) être somnambule; **he's sleepwalking** il marche en dormant; **I was sleepwalking last night** j'ai eu une crise de somnambulisme la nuit dernière; Fig **we are sleepwalking into disaster** nous allons tout droit à la catastrophe sans nous en rendre compte

sleepwalker ['sli:pwɔ:kər] N somnambule mf

sleepwalking ['sli:pwɔ:kɪŋ] N somnambulisme m

sleepy ['sli:pɪ] ADJ **1** somnolent; **to be** or **feel s.** avoir envie de dormir, avoir sommeil; **to make sb (feel) s.** endormir qn; **s. look** air endormi **2 little town** petite ville endormie

sleepyhead ['sli:pɪhed] N Fam endormi, -ie; **wake up, s.!** debout, paresseux/paresseuse!

sleet [sli:t] N **1** (icy rain) pluie f mêlée de neige **2** Am (ice) verglas m
▸ V IMPERS **it's sleeting** il tombe de la neige fondue

sleeve [sli:v] N **1** (of garment) manche f; **short s.** manche courte; Fig Fam **he's got something up his s.** il a une idée derrière la tête; **he's got a surprise up his s.** il nous/leur etc réserve une surprise; **to have more than one trick up one's s.** avoir plus d'un tour dans son sac **2** Tech chemise f, fourreau m, gaine f (souple); (tubular casing) douille f **3** (of record) pochette f
▸▸ **s. board** jeannette f; **s. hole** (in clothing) emmanchure f, Br **s. notes** = texte m figurant au dos des pochettes de disques

sleeved [sli:vd] ADJ (garment) à manches

-sleeved [-sli:vd] SUFF **long/short-s.** à manches longues/courtes

sleeveless ['sli:vlɪs] ADJ (dress, pullover etc) sans manches

sleigh [sleɪ] N traîneau m
▸▸ **s. bell** grelot m (de traîneau); **s. ride** promenade f en traîneau

sleight [slaɪt] N (conjuring trick) tour m de passe-passe; **it's done by s. of hand** c'est de la prestidigitation; **by s. of hand** par un tour de passe-passe

slender ['slendər] ADJ **1** mince; (figure) svelte, fluet, -ette; **s. waist** taille fine **2** (hope) ténu; (income) modique, maigre, modeste; **the slenderest of margins** une marge des plus étroites; **there is a very s. chance that ...** il y a une chance très faible que ...; **s. means** de maigres ressources; **of s. means** qui a de petits moyens

slenderize ['slendəraɪz] VT Am amincir

slenderly ['slendəlɪ] ADV **s. built** mince, svelte

slenderness ['slendənɪs] N **1** minceur f, (of person, waist) sveltesse f **2** (of fortune) modicité f, (of resources) maigreur f

slept PT, PP see **sleep** VI, VT

sleuth ['slu:θ] N Fam usu Hum limier m, détective m; **a good bit of s. work** un travail de fin limier
▸ VI Fam faire le détective

sleuthhound ['slu:θhaʊnd] N (dog) limier m, Fam (detective) limier, détective m

slew¹ [slu:] N (turn) virage m; Aut (180-degree turn) tête-à-queue m inv
▸ VT faire pivoter
▸ VI pivoter; (of car) (turn right round) faire un tête-à-queue; **the car slewed off the track** la voiture a dérapé hors de la piste
▸ **slew around, slew round** VT SEP (rotate) faire pivoter; **she slewed the car round** elle a fait pivoter la voiture; (180-degree turn) elle a fait un tête-à-queue

slew² N Fam (large number) tas m

slew³ PT see **slay**

slice [slaɪs] N **1** (of bread, cake, meat etc) tranche f, (of pizza) part f, (of apple) quartier m; (round) **s.** (of lemon, sausage etc) rondelle f, **s. of bread and butter** tartine f beurrée; **apple s.** tartelette f aux pommes; **to take a large s. of the credit for sth** s'attribuer une large part du mérite de qch; **a. s. of the profits** une part des bénéfices; **a s. of life** une tranche de vie **2** (utensil) **fish s.** pelle f (à poisson); **cake s.** pelle f à tarte **3** Sport coup m qui fait dévier la balle; Tennis balle coupée
▸ VT **1** couper ou découper en tranches; **to s. thinly** (meat) couper en tranches fines; (onions etc) émincer; **to s. sth in two** or **in half** couper qch en deux; Am **no matter how thin you s. it, it's still baloney** par quelque bout que tu le prennes, c'est un bobard **2** (ball) Tennis couper; Golf, Rugby faire dévier
▸ VI **this meat slices easily** cette viande est facile à couper
▸ **slice into** VT INSEP (cut easily) couper facilement; **the knife sliced into the flesh** le couteau a pénétré dans la chair
▸ **slice off** VT SEP (remove by slicing) (piece) trancher, couper, détacher; **to s. off the tip of one's finger** se trancher le bout du doigt
▸ **slice through** VT INSEP (cut easily) couper sans effort; **the knife sliced through the rope** le couteau a tranché la corde; Fig **the river slices through the city** la rivière coupe la ville en deux; **to s. through the enemy lines** transpercer les lignes adverses; **he sliced through the red tape** il a éliminé toute la paperasserie d'un seul coup
▸ **slice up** VT SEP (cut into slices) couper ou découper en tranches

slice-and-dice movie N Fam = film m d'horreur particulièrement sanglant

sliced [slaɪst] ADJ (bread, ham etc) en tranches; Fam **he thinks it's the best thing since s. bread** il pense que c'est ce qu'on a fait de mieux depuis l'invention du fil à couper le beurre

slicer ['slaɪsər] N Culin (device) couteau m à découper; (electric) couteau électrique; (bacon) **s.** coupe-jambon m inv

slick [slɪk] ADJ Fam (skilful, deft) habile, adroit; (catch, changeover) adroit; (movie) bien fait, Pej malin, -igne; **s. talker** beau parleur m
▸ N (oil) **s.** nappe f de pétrole; (on beach and sea) marée f noire
▸ **slick back** VT SEP (comb back with oil etc) **to s. back one's hair** se lisser les cheveux en arrière
▸ **slick down** VT SEP (comb down with oil etc) **to s. one's hair down** se lisser les cheveux
▸ **slick up** VI Fam (make oneself attractive) se faire beau

slicker ['slɪkər] N Am **1** (raincoat) imperméable m; (oilskin) ciré m **2** (person) (city) **s.** homme m de finance habile, Pej requin m

slickly ['slɪklɪ] ADV usu Pej (skilfully) habilement; (cunningly) habilement, adroitement

slickness ['slɪknɪs] N usu Pej (skill, deftness) habileté f, adresse f, (cunning) ruse f

slide [slaɪd] N **1** (action) glissade f, glissement m; (of land) glissement de terrain; **to have a s.** (of person) faire une glissade; **the alarming s. of the economy** le dérapage alarmant de l'économie; **a s. in prices/popularity** une chute des prix/de la popularité; **a mud s.** une coulée de boue; **a rock s.** un éboulement **2** (place) (on snow or ice) glissoire f, (in playground) toboggan m; Aviat (escape) **s.** toboggan d'évacuation **3** Mus (or-

nament) coulé m; (in violin playing etc) glissade f, (part of trombone etc) coulisse f **4** Tech (sliding part) pièce f qui glisse ou qui coulisse; (of slide rule) coulisseau m, réglette f, (in rowing) glissière f **5** (of microscope) (object) **s.** (plaque f ou lame f) porte-objet m, pl porte-objet(s); (what is on the slide) préparation f **6** Phot (colour) **s.** diapositive f (en couleur), Fam diapo f (en couleur); **lecture illustrated with slides** conférence f avec projections **7** Br (hair) **s.** barrette f
▸ VI (pt, pp slid [slɪd]) **1** (slip) (of mechanism between runners etc) coulisser; (of person) glisser; **to s. (on ice)** (of person) glisser (sur la glace), faire une glissade/des glissades; **she slid on the floor** elle a glissé sur le parquet; **the dish slid off the table/onto the floor** le plat a glissé de la table/sur le sol; Fig **to let things** or **everything s.** laisser tout aller à la dérive; (lose interest in everything) se désintéresser de tout; **the country was sliding into anarchy** le pays glissait vers l'anarchie; **prices/profits had begun to s.** les prix/profits avaient commencé à chuter **2** (move quietly) (into room, behind curtain etc) se glisser; **the snake slid through the grass** le serpent s'est glissé entre les herbes; **the pilot slid into the cockpit** le pilote s'est glissé dans le cockpit; **to s. over a delicate subject** glisser sur un sujet délicat
▸ VT (faire) glisser; **to s. sth into one's pocket** glisser qch dans sa poche
▸▸ Am **s. fastener** fermeture f à glissière, fermeture Éclair®; **s. guitar** slide guitar f, TV etc **s. matter** cache m latéral; **s. projector** projecteur m de diapositives; **s. show** diaporama m; Comput diaporama, projection f de diapositives
▸ **slide down** VI (go down by sliding) descendre en glissant; (of prices) chuter
▸ VT INSEP (go down by sliding) descendre en glissant; **to s. down a rope** se laisser couler ou glisser le long d'une corde; **to s. down the banisters** glisser le long de la rampe; **it's sliding down the charts** il perd des places au hit-parade
▸ **slide off** VI **1** (be removed by sliding) the lid **slides off** pour enlever le couvercle, il faut le faire glisser ou coulisser; **it keeps sliding off** ça n'arrête pas de glisser **2** Fam (sneak away) filer en douce
▸ VT SEP (lid etc) faire glisser
▸ **slide out** VI **1** (come out by sliding) sortir en glissant **2** Fam (sneak outside) se glisser dehors
▸ VT SEP (drawers, battery) enlever en faisant glisser
▸ **slide out of** VT INSEP (evade) se sortir de; **to s. out of doing the housework** échapper aux tâches ménagères; **I'd like to see him s. out of that one** j'aimerais bien voir comment il va se tirer d'affaire

sliding ['slaɪdɪŋ] ADJ (part) qui glisse; (movement) glissant; (panel) mobile; (door) coulissant
▸▸ **s. roof** toit m ouvrant; **s. scale** (for salaries) échelle f mobile; (for prices) barème m des prix; (for tax) barème des impôts; **s. seat** (in rowing boat) banc m à coulisses ou à glissières; (in car) siège m réglable ou mobile; **s. sunroof** toit ouvrant coulissant

slight [slaɪt] ADJ **1** (small) (pain, mistake etc) léger, -ère, petit; (intelligence, difference etc) faible; (damage) peu important; (wound) sans gravité; **a s. accident** un petit incident; **a s. improvement** un léger mieux; **not the slightest danger/interest** etc pas le moindre danger/intérêt etc; **to take offence at the slightest thing** se vexer pour un rien; **I haven't the slightest (idea)** je n'en ai pas la moindre idée; **not in the slightest** pas du tout, pas le moins du monde; **they weren't**

(in) the slightest bit interested, they weren't interested in the slightest ils n'étaient pas le moins du monde intéressés; **there's a s. chance of some sunshine tomorrow** il y a une petite chance qu'il fasse beau demain **2** *(thin)* ténu; *(person)* menu; *(figure)* frêle

N *(affront)* affront *m*

VT *(person)* *(affront)* faire un affront à; *(treat without consideration)* traiter sans considération, manquer d'égards pour *ou* à; **to feel slighted** se sentir vexé *ou* froissé

slighting ['slaɪtɪŋ] **ADJ** *(tone)* de mépris, de dédain; *(remark)* plein de mépris

slightingly ['slaɪtɪŋlɪ] **ADV** avec dédain, dédaigneusement

slightly ['slaɪtlɪ] **ADV 1** *(to a small degree)* légèrement, un peu; **s. better** un (petit) peu mieux; **I know him s.** je le connais un peu **2** *(thinly)* **s. built** menu

slightness ['slaɪtnɪs] **N 1** *(small extent)* *(of mistake etc)* légèreté *f*, *(of difference)* petitesse *f*, *(of damage)* insignifiance *f* **2** *(thinness)* **the s. of her arms** ses bras menus; **her s.** son corps menu

slim [slɪm] **ADJ** *(comp* **slimmer**, *superl* **slimmest)** *(person)* svelte; *(fingers etc)* fuselé, menu; *(book etc)* mince; *(chance, hope etc)* petit; **tall and s.** élancé; **his first s. volume** son premier petit opuscule

VT (-mm-) amincir

VI maigrir; **to be slimming** être au régime, suivre un régime amaigrissant; **dress that is slimming** robe qui mincit

▸ **slim down VT SEP** *(reduce)* *(labour force)* réduire; **the company is slimming down its electronics operation** la société réduit ses activités dans le domaine de l'électronique

VI 1 *(lose weight)* maigrir **2** *(become smaller in size)* *(of company, army etc)* diminuer de taille

slime [slaɪm] **N 1** *(mud)* vase *f* **2** *(on fish etc)* humeur *f* visqueuse; *(of slug)* bave *f*; **what's this horrible s.?** qu'est-ce que c'est ce truc dégueulasse? **3** *Fam (person)* ordure *f*

slimebag ['slaɪmbæg], **slimeball** ['slaɪmbɔːl] **N** *Fam (despicable person)* ordure *f*, raclure *f*, *(repulsive man)* gros dégueulasse *m*

sliminess ['slaɪmɪnɪs] **N 1** *(of fish etc)* viscosité *f* **2** *Fam (servility)* servilité *f*, obséquiosité *f*

slimly ['slɪmlɪ] **ADV s. built** svelte

slimmer ['slɪmər] **N** personne *f* qui suit un régime amaigrissant; **ideal for slimmers** l'idéal pour maigrir

slimming ['slɪmɪŋ] **N** amincissement *m*; **s. can be bad for you** les régimes peuvent parfois nuire à la santé

▸▸ **s. club** centre *m* d'amaigrissement; **s. course** cure *f* d'amaigrissement; **s. diet** régime *m* amaigrissant; **s. pill** pilule *f* amaigrissante

slimness ['slɪmnɪs] **N** *(of person)* minceur *f*, sveltesse *f*, *(of book etc)* minceur *f*

slimy ['slaɪmɪ] **ADJ 1** *(consistency)* vaseux; *(mud)* gras, *f* grasse; *(paste etc)* visqueux, gluant; **the frog felt all s.** la grenouille était toute visqueuse **2** *(tracks of slug)* visqueux; *(covered in slime)* couvert de vase; *(fish)* couvert d'une sécrétion visqueuse; *(slug etc)* couvert de bave; **it was a horrible s. mess** c'était parfaitement dégueulasse **3** *Fam (person)* servile, obséquieux; **he's a real s. creep** c'est un vrai lèche-bottes

sling [slɪŋ] **N 1** *Med* écharpe *f*, *(of rifle etc)* bretelle *f*, *(for hoisting)*, *Naut etc* élingue *f*, *(for hoisting people)* agui *m*; **to have one's arm in a s.** avoir le bras en écharpe **2** *(weapon)* fronde *f*

VT *(pt, pp* **slung** [slʌŋ]*)* **1** *(hang)* suspendre; **to s. sth over one's shoulder** jeter qch sur l'épaule; **to s. sth across one's chest** mettre

qch en bandoulière; *Fam* **to s. one's hook** mettre les bouts **2** *(throw)* lancer, jeter; **s. that paper over, will you?** lance-moi le journal, s'il te plaît; **they were slinging insults at each other** ils se lançaient des insultes

▸ **sling off VT SEP** *Fam* **to s. sb off a course** virer qn d'un cours

▸ **sling out VT SEP** *Fam* **1** *(dismiss)* *(person)* flanquer dehors; **he was slung out of the army** il s'est fait jeter de l'armée **2** *(throw away)* jeter, balancer

▸ **sling up VT SEP** *(hoist)* hisser *(avec une grue)*

slingback ['slɪŋbæk] **N** chaussure *f* à talon ouvert, sandale *f*

ADJ *(shoe)* à talon ouvert

slingshot ['slɪŋʃɒt] **N** *esp Am* fronde *f*

slink [slɪŋk] **VI** *(pt, pp* **slunk** [slʌŋk]*)* **to s. off** *or* **away** partir en catimini, s'éclipser; **to s. in/out** entrer/sortir furtivement; **she was slinking about in a velvet dress** elle ondulait dans sa robe en velours

slinkily ['slɪŋkɪlɪ] **ADV** *Fam (to move)* avec des ondulations; **s. cut dress** robe qui épouse bien les courbes du corps; **she sidled s. up to him** elle s'est dirigée vers lui en roulant des hanches

slinking ['slɪŋkɪŋ] **ADJ** furtif

slinky ['slɪŋkɪ] **ADJ** *Fam (figure)* svelte, mince; *(clothing)* collant, ajusté; *(walk)* ondulant

SLIP [slɪp] **N** *Comput (abbr* **serial line Internet protocol)** protocole *m* SLIP

SLIP¹ [slɪp]

N chute **1, 5**	▪ faute d'inattention **2**
▪ lapsus **2**	▪ glissement **4, 5**
▪ éboulement **4**	▪ baisse **5**
▪ combinaison **6**	
VI glisser **1**	▪ chuter **1** ▪ baisser **1**
▪ patiner **1**	▪ se glisser **2**
VT échapper à **1**	▪ glisser **2**

N 1 *(fall)* **he had a s. on the ice** il a fait une chute sur la glace; **he had a nasty s.** il est mal tombé, il a fait une mauvaise chute

2 *(error)* faute *f* d'inattention *ou* d'étourderie; *(in speaking)* lapsus *m*; **to make a s.** faire une erreur; *(in speaking)* faire un lapsus; **s. of the pen** petite erreur *f* d'orthographe; **she made a s. of the tongue** sa langue a fourché; **it was a s., I meant to say …** ma langue a fourché, je voulais dire …; *Prov* **there's many a s. 'twixt cup and lip** il y a loin de la coupe aux lèvres

3 to give sb the s. fausser compagnie à qn

4 *Geol (of land)* glissement *m*; *(of rocks)* éboulement *m*

5 *(by thing)* glissement *m*; *(in share values etc)* chute *f*, *(in standards)* baisse *f*, *Aut (of clutch)* patinage *m*

6 *(garment)* combinaison *f* *(de femme)*; **half** *or* **waist s.** jupon *m*; **your s.'s showing** votre jupon dépasse; **(pillow) s.** taie *f* d'oreiller

7 *(of ferry)* cale *f* de chargement; **the ship is still on the slips** le navire est toujours sur cale(s) *ou* en construction

8 *Theat* **the slips** les coulisses *fpl*

9 *Cr (player)* chasseur *m* posté à droite du garde-guichet; **the slips** *(position)* la station à droite du garde-guichet

10 *(in pottery)* *(for decoration)* engobe *m*

VI (-pp-) 1 *(slide)* glisser; *(of knot)* couler, courir; *(of earth etc)* s'ébouler; *(of prices)* chuter; *Tech etc (of clutch, belt etc)* patiner, glisser; *TV* **the picture keeps slipping** l'image descend; **his foot slipped** son pied a glissé; **I slipped on a banana skin** j'ai glissé sur une peau de banane; **to s. from sb's hands** *or* **grasp** *(of vase, book etc)* glisser des mains *ou* des doigts de qn; **to s. through sb's fingers** filer entre les doigts de qn; **to s.**

into bad habits prendre de mauvaises habitudes; **an error that has slipped into the text** une faute qui s'est glissée dans le texte; **the patient slipped into a coma** le malade est tombé dans le coma; **money just slips through his fingers** l'argent lui file entre les doigts; **they let the terrorists s. through their fingers** ils ont laissé filer les terroristes; **he let his guard s.** il a baissé sa garde; **don't let your concentration s.** ne relâche pas ta concentration; **the record has slipped to number 22** le disque est descendu en 22ème position; **the quality is slipping** la qualité baisse

2 *(move quickly, smoothly etc)* **to s. into bed** se glisser *ou* se couler dans son lit; **to s. into one's dressing gown** passer *ou* *Fam* enfiler sa robe de chambre; **she slipped into the next room** elle s'est glissée dans la pièce voisine; **just s. round** *or* **over to the post office** fais un saut jusqu'au bureau de poste

3 *(make mistake)* faire une (faute d')étourderie; **you're slipping!** *(performing below one's usual standard)* tu baisses!; **he slipped and said 'twenty' by mistake** sa langue a fourché et il a dit 'vingt' par erreur

4 to let s. *(opportunity, word, secret)* laisser échapper; **she let s. a few swearwords** elle a laissé échapper quelques jurons; **to let (it) s. that …** laisser échapper que …

VT 1 *Aut* **to s. the clutch** laisser patiner l'embrayage; **to s. its chain** *or* **leash** *or* **lead** *(of animal)* se détacher; **the dog has slipped its collar** le chien s'est dégagé de son collier; **his name has slipped my mind** son nom m'échappe; **to s. sb's attention** échapper à qn **2** *(put)* *(sth into sb's hand, a letter into the postbox)* glisser; **he slipped it into his pocket** il l'a glissé dans sa poche; **to s. sth into the conversation** glisser qch dans la conversation; **to s. the bolt (home)** pousser le verrou à fond; **I slipped my arm round her waist** j'ai glissé mon bras autour de sa taille; *Fam* **to s. something** *or* **one over on sb** rouler qn

3 *Naut* **to s. a cable** larguer *ou* filer une amarre par le bout; **to s. one's moorings** filer le corps-mort

4 *Knitting (stitch)* glisser

5 *Med* **to s. a disc** se faire une hernie discale

▸▸ *Br* **s. road** bretelle *f* d'accès; *Sewing* **s. stitch** point *m* perdu

▸ **slip away VI** *(of person)* *(get away)* filer; *(leave work early)* s'éclipser; *(of lead in elections etc)* s'effriter; **the patient was slipping away** le malade s'éteignait doucement; **control of the party was slipping away from her** elle perdait peu à peu son emprise sur le parti; **my life seemed to be slipping away from me** ma vie m'échappait; **you're slipping away from me** *(in relationship)* tu t'éloignes de moi

▸ **slip back VI 1** *(return)* revenir (**into** dans)

2 *(get worse)* *(of work)* se dégrader

VT SEP *(put back)* remettre

▸ **slip by VI 1** *(of time, years etc)* passer; *(fast)* fuir

2 *(pass unnoticed)* *(of person)* passer sans se faire remarquer

VT INSEP **to s. by sb** *(of errors, escapee)* échapper à qn

▸ **slip down VI** *(slide down)* descendre en glissant; *(of socks)* descendre; **this whisky slips down very nicely** ce whisky descend tout seul

VT INSEP **to s. down a pole** glisser le long d'un poteau; **they've slipped down the league** ils sont descendus au classement

▸ **slip in VI** *(enter quickly, inconspicuously)* entrer sans se faire remarquer; **a few mistakes slipped in** *(in text)* quelques erreurs se sont glissées dans le texte

VT *(insert inconspicuously)* glisser; **she slipped in several references to …** elle a placé plusieurs allusions à …

▸ **slip off** VT SEP (jacket, shoes) enlever
VI (of person) s'éclipser

▸ **slip on** VT SEP (put on quickly) (garment)
passer, Fam enfiler

▸ **slip out** VI **1** (escape) s'échapper; **the soap
slipped out of my hands** le savon m'a glissé
des mains; **to let sth s. out** laisser échapper
qch; **the secret has slipped out** le secret a
transpiré; **it slipped out that …** le bruit s'est
répandu selon lequel …
2 (leave quickly, inconspicuously) (to avoid
somebody or something) filer (à l'anglaise);
I'm just slipping out for a few minutes je
m'éclipse quelques minutes, je reviens dans
une minute; **could you s. out and buy me
some chocolate?** tu pourrais faire un saut à
l'épicerie etc pour m'acheter du chocolat?

▸ **slip past** VI passer
VT INSEP **to s. past sb/sth** se glisser devant
qn/qch
VT SEP Fam **to s. one past sb** rouler qn

▸ **slip through** VI (of errors etc) échapper à
l'attention; **too many mistakes are slipping
through** il y a trop d'erreurs qui nous/leur etc
échappent

▸ **slip up** VI (make mistake) se tromper; (socially etc) faire une gaffe, gaffer

> Note that the French word **slip** is a false
> friend and is never a translation for the
> English word **slip**. It means **underpants**
> or **briefs**.

slip² N **1** (piece) (of paper) bout m; (coupon)
bon m; (docket) fiche f; (of land etc) bande f
étroite; **pay s.** bulletin m de paie; **sales s.** récépissé m
2 Old-fashioned Fam **s. of a girl** jeune fille
fluette; (young) fillette f
3 (in horticulture) bouture f; (for grafting)
scion m
▸▸ Journ **s. page** page f volante; Typ **s. sheet**
feuille f intercalaire

slipcase ['slɪpkeɪs] N (for books) étui m

slipcover ['slɪpkʌvər] N esp Am **1** (for furniture) housse f **2** (book cover) jaquette f

slipknot ['slɪpnɒt] N nœud m coulant

slip-on N Fam **1** slip-ons (shoes) mocassins
mpl **2** Am (sweater) pull-over m, pl pull-
overs, pull m
ADJ (shoe) sans lacets
▸▸ **s. shoes** mocassins

slipover ['slɪpəʊvər] N débardeur m

slippage ['slɪpɪdʒ] N (in production) retard
m; **there's too much s.** (loss of time) on perd
de plus en plus de temps; **s. in prices** dérapage m des prix

slipped disc [slɪpt] N Med hernie f discale

slipper ['slɪpər] N **1** (footwear) (backless)
mule f; (with back) chausson m, pantoufle f
2 Tech (of brake) patin m
▸▸ Old-fashioned **s. baths** bains mpl publics

slipperiness ['slɪpərɪnɪs] N **1** (of surface)
nature f glissante **2** (of person) caractère m
rusé

slippery ['slɪpərɪ] ADJ **1** (pavement, fish etc)
glissant; (difficult) (subject, concept) délicat;
it's s. (underfoot) ça glisse; Fig **to be on s.
ground** être sur un terrain glissant; Fig **it's a
s. slope** nous sommes/il est etc sur une
pente glissante; **this was the start of the s.
slope that led to (his) alcoholism** ce fut le
début de la déchéance qui l'a mené à l'alcoolisme **2** (devious) (person) retors; **he's as
s. as an eel** il glisse comme une ou est aussi
insaisissable qu'une anguille

slippy ['slɪpɪ] ADJ Fam **1** (slippery) glissant **2**
Old-fashioned Br Fam (quick) **you'll have to
be pretty s. about it** il va falloir que tu fasses
ficelle; **look s.!** grouille-toi!

slipshod ['slɪpʃɒd] ADJ (negligent) (person,
attitude) négligent; (work) négligé, bâclé;

book written in a s. manner livre écrit sans
soin

slipstream ['slɪpstriːm] N (of car, boat etc)
sillage m, remous mpl; Aviat souffle m ou
vent m de l'hélice; Fig **to be dragged along
in sb's s.** se laisser entraîner par qn
VT (car) se mettre dans le sillage de

slip-up N Fam gaffe f; **there's been a s.** il y a
eu une gaffe de faite; **to make a s.** faire une
gaffe

slipway ['slɪpweɪ] N Naut (for building, repairing) cale f ou chantier m de construction; (for launching) slip m

slit [slɪt] N fente f; (between curtains etc) entrebâillement m; (for shooting through)
meurtrière f
ADJ (skirt) fendu; (eyes) bridé
VT (pt, pp slit; prp slitting) (make slit in) fendre; (envelope) ouvrir; Surg (flesh) inciser;
the knife had s. his leg open le couteau lui
avait ouvert la cuisse; **the blow s. his cheek**
le coup lui a déchiré la joue; **to s. sb's throat**
couper la gorge à qn; **to s. open a sack** éventrer un sac
▸▸ **s. pocket** poche f fendue; Mil **s. trench**
tranchée f étroite

slither ['slɪðər] N glissement m
VI glisser; (of snake, worm) ramper; **the dog
was slithering about on the ice** le chien dé-
rapait sur la glace; **to s. down a hill** déraper
dans une pente

sliver ['slɪvər] N (thin slice) petite tranche f;
(of wood) éclat m

Sloane, Sloane Ranger [sləʊn('reɪndʒər)] N
Br Fam jeune fille f BCBG

Sloaney ['sləʊnɪ] ADJ Br Fam BCBG

slob [slɒb] N Fam (untidy, rude) rustaud,
-aude; (lazy) flemmard, -arde; **big fat s.** gros
lard m

slobber ['slɒbər] N (saliva) bave f, salive f
VI (salivate) baver; **stop slobbering on me**
arrête de me baver dessus

▸ **slobber over** VT INSEP (of dog, baby) (person, shoulder) baver; (kiss etc) (person) faire
des bises baveuses à; **he doesn't like them
slobbering all over him** il n'aime pas qu'ils
lui bavent dessus

sloe [sləʊ] N **1** (fruit) prunelle f **2** (tree) prunellier m
▸▸ **s. gin** gin m à la prunelle

slog [slɒg] Fam N **1** (blow) coup m (violent);
to give the ball a real s. frapper dans la balle
un bon coup **2** (hard work) boulot m pénible; **it was a bit of a s.** on en a bavé; **a hard
s.** (great effort, reading book) un gros effort;
(walk, ride) un trajet pénible; **it's a long s. to
the top** (of hill, in organization) on en bave
pour arriver en haut
VT (-gg-) (hit) (person, object) cogner, battre;
Cr (ball) frapper fort sur; **he slogged his way
through the text** il a déchiffré le texte avec
grande difficulté
VI (work hard) turbiner, trimer; **they
slogged for miles** (walking) ils marchèrent
à grand-peine pendant des kilomètres

▸ **slog along** VI Fam (keep walking) marcher
d'un pas lourd ou péniblement

▸ **slog away** VI Fam (keep working, trying)
trimer

▸ **slog away at** VT INSEP Fam **1** (work hard at)
travailler avec acharnement à **2** (keep hitting) continuer à frapper

▸ **slog on** VI Fam **1** = slog along **2** (keep
working) continuer à trimer; **I think I'll s. on
a little longer** je pense que je vais continuer
à bosser encore un peu

slogan ['sləʊgən] N Pol, Com slogan m; **elec-
tion/advertising s.** slogan électoral/
publicitaire

slogger ['slɒgər] N Fam **1** Boxing, Cr cogneur m **2** (hard worker) bûcheur, -euse

slo-mo ['sləʊməʊ] N, ADJ Fam abbr slow-
motion

sloop [sluːp] N Naut sloop m

slop [slɒp] VT (-pp-) (spill) (liquid) renverser
(**over the table** sur la table)
VI (of liquids) déborder
N **1** slops (pig food) soupe f à cochons; Pej
(food) brouet m; (spilt drinks) (on table etc)
boissons fpl renversées **2** Fam (sentimentality) bêtises fpl à l'eau de rose
▸▸ Br **s. basin** vide-tasses m inv; **s. bucket**
seau m (à ordures); (in prison) seau hygiénique; (for pigs) seau à pâtée

▸ **slop about, slop around** VI **1** Fam (walk
in water, mud etc) patauger, barboter **2** (of liquid) clapoter **3** Fig Fam **he just slops around
the house all day** il passe toute la journée à
traîner ou Fam à glandouiller chez lui

▸ **slop out** VI (in prison) vider les seaux hygiéniques

▸ **slop over** VI = slop

slope [sləʊp] N **1** (incline) pente f, inclinaison f; (in road, railway) rampe f; **steep/
gentle s.** pente raide/douce; Mil **with rifle
at the s.** l'arme sur l'épaule **2** (hill) pente f;
(of mountain) versant m; Ski piste f; **on the
slopes of the Himalayas** sur les pentes de
l'Himalaya; **on the northern s.** sur le versant
nord; **halfway down/up the s.** à mi-pente
VI (of ground etc) être en pente; (not be
straight) (of picture etc) pencher; **to s. forward** or **to the right/backward** or **to the left**
(of writing) pencher à droite/à gauche; **the
garden slopes down to the river** le jardin
descend (en pente) vers la rivière; **the
ground slopes up to the house** le terrain
monte en pente vers la maison
VT incliner; Mil **to s. arms** mettre l'arme sur
l'épaule; **s. arms!** arme sur l'épaule!

▸ **slope away, slope off** VI Fam (leave furtively) décamper, filer

sloping ['sləʊpɪŋ] ADJ (table, roof) en pente;
(writing) penché; (shoulders) tombant

sloppily ['slɒpɪlɪ] ADV **1** (carelessly) sans
soin **2** Fam (sentimentally) avec sensiblerie

sloppiness ['slɒpɪnɪs] N **1** (carelessness) (in
work) manque m de soin, négligence f; (of
style) négligence **2** Fam (sentimentality) sentimentalité f excessive

slopping out ['slɒpɪŋ] N (in prison) vidange f des seaux hygiéniques

sloppy ['slɒpɪ] ADJ (careless) (work, person) négligé; (worker) négligent; (organization, approach) nul, f nulle; (language,
spelling) relâché **2** Fam (sentimental) (novel)
guimauve; (person) fleur bleue
▸▸ Br Fam **s. joe** (sweater) pull-over m très
ample, pl pull-overs très amples; Am (hamburger) steak m haché servi en sandwich

slosh [slɒʃ] VI (of liquid) (move around) clapoter
VT **1** (spill) (water etc) renverser **2** Fam (apply liberally) (paint on wall etc) flanquer **3**
Br Sl (hit) (person) flanquer un coup à, tabasser

▸ **slosh about, slosh around** VI **1** Fam (walk
in water, mud etc) patauger, barboter **2** (of liquid) clapoter

sloshed [slɒʃt] ADJ Br Sl (drunk) bourré, rond

slot [slɒt] N **1** (groove) (in vending machine,
head of screw etc) fente f; Comput emplacement m; **to put a coin in the s.** (of vending
machine etc) introduire une pièce de monnaie dans la fente; Comput **expansion s.** emplacement pour carte d'extension **2** (in
broadcasting schedule, waiting list etc) créneau m horaire; (for aircraft in flight control)
créneau m; **we could put the new series in the
7:30 s.** on pourrait caser ou placer le nouveau feuilleton dans le créneau de 19 heures
30; **we've missed our s.** nous avons raté notre créneau; **there's a s. for somebody with**

editorial skills il y a un créneau pour quelqu'un ayant une formation de rédacteur; **to fill a s.** boucher un trou; *Radio, TV* **prime time s.** heure *f* de grande écoute
VT (-tt-) to s. sth into sth insérer *ou* mettre qch dans qch; **to s. sb into a job** caser qn dans un travail; **where can we s. him in?** comment est-ce qu'on peut l'intégrer?
VI s'introduire, se glisser (**into sth** dans qch); **it slots well into our programme** cela s'insère bien dans notre programme; **she slotted into the department well** elle s'est bien intégrée au service
▸▸ **s. machine** *(for vending)* distributeur *m* (automatique); *(for gambling)* machine *f* à sous; *Br* **s. meter** compteur *m* à pièces
▸ **slot in VT SEP** *(fit in) (patient, customer etc)* prendre; **to s. a book in a space on a shelf** glisser un livre dans un espace sur une étagère
VI *(fit in)* **the book will s. in here** le livre rentrera là-dedans
▸ **slot together VT SEP** *(pieces)* encastrer l'un dans l'autre/les uns dans les autres
VI s'encastrer l'un dans l'autre/les uns dans les autres

sloth [sləʊθ] **N 1** *(laziness)* paresse *f* **2** *(animal)* paresseux *m*
▸▸ **s. bear** ours *m* lippu; **s. monkey** loris *m* lent

slothful [ˈsləʊθfʊl] **ADJ** paresseux, -euse
slothfully [ˈsləʊθfəlɪ] **ADV** paresseusement
slothfulness [ˈsləʊθfʊlnɪs] **N** paresse *f*
slot-in card N *Comput* carte *f* enfichable
slouch [slaʊtʃ] **N 1** *(way of walking)* démarche *f* molasse; *(deportment)* allure *f* avachie *ou* molle; **s. of the shoulders** épaules tombantes **2** *Fam* **he's no s.** il n'est pas empoté
VI *(hold oneself badly)* être avachi; *(walk badly)* avoir une démarche molasse; **don't s.!** tenez-vous droit!
▸▸ **s. hat** chapeau *m* à larges bords
▸ **slouch about, slouch around VI** *(in town)* traîner; *(at home, in front of television)* traînasser

slough[1] [slaʊ] **N** *(bog)* bourbier *m*, fondrière *f*, *Lit* **to be in a s. of despair/gloom** sombrer dans le désespoir/la tristesse
slough[2] [slʌf] **N** *(of reptile, insect)* mue *f*; **to cast its s.** muer
VI *(of reptile etc)* muer
VT to s. its skin *(of reptile, insect)* muer; *Lit* **to s. a bad habit** se débarrasser d'une mauvaise habitude
▸ **slough away VI** = **slough off**
▸ **slough off VT SEP** = **slough**[2]
VI *(become detached) (of scab etc)* se détacher, tomber

Slovak [ˈsləʊvæk] **ADJ** slovaque
N 1 *(person)* Slovaque *mf* **2** *Ling* slovaque *m*
Slovakia [sləʊˈvækɪə] **N** Slovaquie *f*
Slovakian [sləʊˈvækɪən] **ADJ, N** = **Slovak**
sloven [ˈslʌvən] **N 1** *(untidy person)* mal soigné, -ée; *(woman)* souillon *f* **2** *Old-fashioned (careless worker)* saboteur, -euse
Slovene [ˈsləʊviːn] **ADJ, N** = **Slovenian**
Slovenia [sləʊˈviːnɪə] **N** Slovénie *f*
Slovenian [sləʊˈviːnɪən] **ADJ** slovène
N 1 *(person)* Slovène *mf* **2** *Ling* slovène *m*
slovenliness [ˈslʌv(ə)nlɪnɪs] **N** *(of work, appearance)* négligence *f*
slovenly [ˈslʌv(ə)nlɪ] **ADJ 1** *(untidy) (person)* mal soigné; *(dress)* débraillé **2** *(negligent) (person)* négligent; *(work)* négligé, bousillé; *(style)* débraillé; **done in a s. way** fait sans soin

SLOW [sləʊ] **ADJ 1** *(not fast)* lent; *(boring) (film, show etc)* ennuyeux; *(stupid) (person)* simple; **I'm being a bit s. this morning** je suis un peu lent ce matin; **to be s. over doing sth**

mettre longtemps à faire qch; **business is s.** les affaires languissent *ou* ne vont pas fort; **to be s. to do sth** *(of person)* être lent à faire qch; **s. to act** *or* **to take action** lent à agir; **progress has been s.** les progrès ont été lents; **this method is s. but sure** cette méthode est lente mais sûre; **he wasn't s. to respond** *or* **in responding** il n'a pas été long à réagir; **he's been s. to get it done** il a mis du temps à le faire; **sorry I was s. getting back to you** désolé d'avoir mis du temps à vous rappeler; **you're very s. today** tu es très lent aujourd'hui; *Fam* **to be as s. as treacle** *or Am* **molasses (in winter)** être lent comme un escargot *ou* une tortue; **to be s. off the mark** *(in race)* démarrer en douceur; *(to start sth)* prendre son temps pour faire qch; *(to understand)* être lent à la détente; **a s. child** un enfant attardé; **to cook sth in a s. oven** faire cuire qch à four doux; *Am Sl* **to do a s. burn** avoir la moutarde qui vous monte au nez; **it's s. work** ça ne va pas vite; **she's a s. worker** elle travaille lentement
2 *(clock, watch)* en retard; **my watch is five minutes s.** ma montre retarde de cinq minutes
ADV lentement; **to go s.** aller lentement; *(as industrial action)* faire la grève perlée; **to run s.** *(of engine)* tourner au ralenti; *(of clock)* retarder; **s.!** *(on road sign)* ralentir!; *Naut* **s. ahead/astern!** en avant/en arrière doucement!; **s. spoken** qui parle lentement; **s. moving** *(traffic)* au ralenti; *(queue, crowd, river, film, etc)* lent; **s. burning** à combustion lente; *(in explosives) (powder)* lent
VT & VI = **slow down, slow up**
▸▸ *Culin* **s. burner** feu *m* doux; **s. cooker** mijoteuse *f*; **the s. lane** *(when driving on left)* la file de gauche; *(when driving on right)* la file de droite; *Cin, TV* **s. motion** ralenti *m*; **in s. motion** au ralenti; *Tech* **s. running** ralenti; **s. train** omnibus *m*
▸ **slow down, slow up VI** *(go more slowly)* ralentir; *Aut (of engine)* prendre le ralenti; **to s. down** *or* **up (to a stop)** s'arrêter; *Fig* **s. down a bit!** doucement!; **as he got older, he slowed down** à mesure qu'il prenait de l'âge, il a ralenti son rythme
VT SEP ralentir; **I'll only s. you down** je vais vous retarder

slowcoach [ˈsləʊkəʊtʃ] **N** *Br Fam* lambin, -ine, traînard, -arde
slow-cook VT mijoter, faire cuire à feu doux
slowdown [ˈsləʊdaʊn] **N** *(slowing) (in business etc)* ralentissement *m*; *Am (industrial action)* travail *m* au ralenti
slowing [ˈsləʊɪŋ] **N s. (down** *or* **up)** ralentissement *m*
slowly [ˈsləʊlɪ] **ADV** lentement; **the time/ morning has gone very s.** le temps/la matinée a passé très lentement; **to run s.** *(engine)* tourner au ralenti; **he's s. realizing that ...** il se rend compte peu à peu que ...; **s. but surely** lentement mais sûrement; **to cook sth s.** faire cuire qch à feu doux
slow-motion replay N ralenti *m*
slowness [ˈsləʊnɪs] **N** *(lack of speed)* lenteur *f*, *(of mind)* lourdeur *f*, lenteur *f*; *(of film, show etc)* lenteur; *(of clock etc)* retard *m*
slowpoke [ˈsləʊpəʊk] **N** *Am Fam* lambin, -ine, traînard, -arde
slow-release ADJ *Med (medicine)* retard *inv*
slow-running jet N *Aut* gicleur *m* de ralenti
slow-witted ADJ à l'esprit lent
slow-worm N orvet *m*, serpent *m* de verre
SLR [eselˈɑːr] **N** *Phot (abbr* **single-lens reflex)** reflex *m* monoculaire
sludge [slʌdʒ] **N** *(mud)* vase *f*, fange *f*, *Ind*

boue *f*; *(in engine)* cambouis *m*; **sewage s.** vidanges *fpl*
sludgy [ˈslʌdʒɪ] **ADJ** *(muddy)* vaseux; *Ind* boueux
slug[1] [slʌg] **N** *Zool* limace *f*
▸▸ **s. pellet** pastille *f* anti-limace
slug[2] **N 1** *(bullet)* balle *f*, plomb *m* **2** *Fam (of brandy etc)* goutte *f*, coup *m*
slug[3] *esp Am Fam* **N** *(blow)* coup *m* violent
VT *(hit) (person, ball)* frapper; **he slugged me with a piece of wood** il m'a frappé avec un bâton
▸ **slug out VT SEP** *Fam, also Fig* **to s. it out** *(of two people)* se rentrer dedans; **he slugged it out with him** il s'est battu avec lui
slugfest [ˈslʌgfest] **N** *Am Fam* **1** *Boxing* combat *m* **2** *(fight)* baston *m ou f*, castagne *f*
sluggard [ˈslʌgəd] **ADJ, N** *Lit* paresseux, -euse, fainéant, -ante
sluggish [ˈslʌgɪʃ] **ADJ** *(person, day) (lazy)* paresseux, *Fam* flemmard; *(not energetic)* léthargique; *(mind)* lent, engourdi; *(response, attempt, engine)* mou, *f* molle; *(river, pulse etc)* lent, paresseux; *(market)* stagnant; *(sales)* médiocre; *(organization, bureaucracy)* lourd; **the economy is s.** l'économie tourne au ralenti; **at a s. pace** au ralenti
sluggishly [ˈslʌgɪʃlɪ] **ADV 1** *(lazily)* paresseusement **2** *(slowly)* lentement
sluggishness [ˈslʌgɪʃnɪs] **N 1** *(of person)* paresse *f*, *Fam* flemme *f*, *(of mind)* lenteur *f* **2** *(of river etc)* lenteur *f*, *Aut (of engine)* mollesse *f*, *(of organization, bureaucracy)* lourdeur *f*
sluice [sluːs] **N 1** *(structure)* écluse *f* **2** = **sluicegate 3** *(action) Fam* **to give sth a s. down** laver qch à grande eau
VT *(wash)* laver à grande eau
▸ **sluice down VT SEP** *(wash down)* laver à grande eau; **to s. oneself down with cold water** s'asperger d'eau fraîche
▸ **sluice out VT SEP 1** *Tech (release) (water from reservoir)* laisser échapper (par les vannes) **2** *(rinse) (cup, pot etc)* rincer
VI *(of water etc) (flow out in great quantity)* couler à flots
sluicegate [ˈsluːsgeɪt] **N** porte *f* d'écluse, vanne *f*
sluiceway [ˈsluːsweɪ] **N** canal *m*, -aux à vannes
slum [slʌm] **N** *(district)* bas quartiers *mpl*, quartier *m* pauvre; *also Fig (house)* taudis *m*
VT (-mm-) *Fam* **to s. it** s'encanailler; *Fig Hum* **I'm slumming it tonight** j'ai décidé d'aller m'encanailler ce soir
▸▸ *Br* **s. clearance** rénovation *f ou* aménagement *m* des quartiers insalubres; **s. landlord** marchand *m* de sommeil
slumber [ˈslʌmbər] **N** *Lit* sommeil *m*; **her s. was** *or* **her slumbers were interrupted by ...** son sommeil a été interrompu par ...; *Fig* **the country had finally awoken from its slumbers** le pays était enfin sorti de sa torpeur; *Fig Lit* **he awoke from his intellectual slumbers** il est sorti de ses hibernations intellectuelles
VI sommeiller, dormir (paisiblement)
▸▸ *Am* **s. party** soirée *f* entre copines *(au cours de laquelle on regarde des films, on discute et on dort dans la même pièce)*; **s. wear** vêtements *mpl* de nuit
slumlord [ˈslʌmlɔːd] **N** *esp Am Fam* marchand *m* de sommeil
slummy [ˈslʌmɪ] **ADJ** sordide; **the s. area of town** les bas quartiers
slump [slʌmp] **N** *Econ (of prices etc)* effondrement *m*; **s. in prices** dégringolade *f* des prix; **the s. in oil prices** l'effondrement des prix du pétrole; **there's been a s. in the**

pound la livre a chuté; *Econ* **the s.** la crise *ou* dépression économique

VI 1 *(of person)* s'effondrer, s'affaisser (**into a chair** dans un fauteuil); **the editor was slumped unconscious over his desk** le rédacteur était effondré sans connaissance sur son bureau **2** *Econ (of prices, pound) (fall suddenly)* s'effondrer, *Fam* dégringoler; *(of economy, demand)* chuter

slumpflation [slʌmpˈfleɪʃən] **N** *Econ* forte récession *f* accompagnée d'une inflation des prix et des salaires

slung PT, PP *see* **sling** VT

slunk PT, PP *see* **slink**

slur [slɜːr] **N 1** *(insult)* insulte *f*; *(on reputation)* tache *f*; **a racial s.** une réflexion raciste; **to cast a s. on sb's reputation** porter atteinte à *ou* ternir la réputation de qn **2** *Mus (sign)* liaison *f*; *(passage)* coulé *m* **3** *(in speech)* mauvaise articulation *f*; **in a drunken s.** de la voix traînante d'un ivrogne; **to speak with a s.** mal articuler; *(as result of stroke etc)* parler d'une voix traînante

VT (**-rr-**) **1** *(words)* mal articuler; **his speech was slurred** il articulait mal; *(because of stroke etc)* il parlait d'une voix traînante **2** *Mus (two notes)* lier; *(passage)* couler; **slurred notes** notes liées coulant

VI *(speak indistinctly)* mal articuler ses mots, manger la moitié de ses mots

▸ **slur over** VT INSEP *(not deal with fully)* **to s. over a fact** passer *ou* glisser sur un fait

slurp [slɜːp] **VT** *(soup etc)* faire du bruit en mangeant; *(tea)* faire du bruit en buvant

VI *(eating)* faire du bruit en mangeant; *(drinking)* faire du bruit en buvant

▸ **slurp up** VT SEP *(soup)* avaler en faisant du bruit

slush [slʌʃ] **N 1** *(snow)* neige *f* fondue **2** *Fam (sentimentality)* sensiblerie *f*

▸▸ **s. fund** caisse *f* noire *(servant généralement au paiement des pots-de-vin)*; *Fam* **money** dessous-de-table *mpl*

slushy [ˈslʌʃɪ] **ADJ 1** *(from snow)* détrempé par la neige **2** *Fam (novel, film etc)* guimauve; *(person)* fleur bleue *inv*

slut [slʌt] **N 1** *(dirty woman)* souillon *f* **2** *(promiscuous woman)* salope *f*

sluttish [ˈslʌtɪʃ] **ADJ 1** *(dirty)* sale; **to lead a s. existence** vivre salement **2** *(morals)* dépravé; *(behaviour)* débauché, dépravé; **a s. woman** une salope

sluttishness [ˈslʌtɪʃnɪs] **N 1** *(dirtiness)* saleté *f* **2** *(promiscuity)* conduite *f* immorale

slutty [ˈslʌtɪ] **ADJ** *Fam (promiscuous)* coucheuse; *(clothes, behaviour, make-up)* qui fait pute

sly [slaɪ] **ADJ** *(comp* **slyer,** *superl* **slyest) 1** *(cunning)* rusé; **he's a s. dog** c'est un fin matois **2** *(dishonest)* sournois **3** *(mischievous)* malin, *f*-igne, espiègle; **s. grin** sourire espiègle

N on the s. à la dérobée, en cachette

slyboots [ˈslaɪbuːts] **N** *Fam* petit malin *m*, petite maligne *f*

slyly [ˈslaɪlɪ] **ADV 1** *(cunningly)* avec ruse **2** *(dishonestly)* sournoisement **3** *(mischievously)* d'une manière espiègle, avec espièglerie

slyness [ˈslaɪnɪs] **N 1** *(cunning)* ruse *f* **2** *(dishonesty)* sournoiserie *f* **3** *(mischievousness)* espièglerie *f*

smack¹ [smæk] **N 1** *(blow)* claque *f*, **s. in the face** gifle *f*, *Fig Fam* **s. (in the eye)** affront *m*, rebuffade *f*, **to give a child a s. on the bottom** donner une fessée à un enfant **2** *(sound)* claquement *m*; **with a s. of his lips** avec un claquement de langue; **the s. of the waves** le fouettement des vagues **3** *Fam (loud kiss)* gros baiser *m* retentissant, grosse bise *f*

ADV to go s. *(make sound)* faire clac; *Fam* **bump s. into a tree** rentrer en plein dans un arbre; **to bump s. into a lamppost** se prendre un lampadaire; **s. in the middle** en plein milieu, au beau milieu; **he caught him s. on the chin** il l'a frappé en plein sur le menton

VT *(hit)* frapper, taper *(avec le plat de la main)*; *(person)* donner une claque à; **to s. sb's face** donner une gifle à qn, gifler qn; **to s. a child's bottom** donner une fessée à un enfant

smack² **N** *Naut* **(fishing) s.** bateau *m* de pêche

smack³ **N** *Sl (heroin)* héro *f*

smack⁴ **N** *(slight taste) (of garlic etc)* léger goût *m*

▸ **smack of** VT INSEP *(have slight taste of)* avoir un léger goût de; *Fig* **to s. of heresy** sentir l'hérésie *ou* le brûlé *ou* le fagot

smacker [ˈsmækər] **N 1** *Fam (big kiss)* grosse bise *f*, gros baiser *m* **2** *Sl (pound)* livre *f*, *(dollar)* dollar *m*; **fifty smackers** cinquante livres/dollars

smacking [ˈsmækɪŋ] **N** *(spanking)* fessée *f*, **to give sb a s.** donner une fessée à qn

small [smɔːl] **ADJ 1** *(not large)* petit; *(dose etc)* petit, faible; **to make sth smaller** rapetisser qch; **to make oneself s.** se faire tout petit; **s. child** *(young)* enfant en bas âge, petit enfant; *(small in size)* enfant de petite taille; **a s. coffee** une petite tasse (de café); **a s. white coffee please!** un petit crème, s'il vous plaît!; **s. details** de menus détails; **the smallest details** les moindres détails; **of s. dimensions** de petites dimensions; **he's a s. eater** il a un petit appétit; **a s. hotel** un hôtel modeste; **s. income** revenu modique *ou* modeste; **in s. numbers** en petit nombre; **the smallest number of people possible** le moins de gens possible; **s. voice** voix fluette, petite voix

2 *(not important)* peu important; *Br Fam* **to be s. beer** être insignifiant; **this was s. beer** c'était de la petite bière; **of no s. consequence** très important, qui porte à conséquence; **she took no s. pride in ...** elle n'était pas peu fière de ...; **it makes not the smallest difference** ça ne fait pas la moindre différence; **it was no s. surprise to me** cela m'a beaucoup surpris; **it's s. wonder that ...** ce n'est guère étonnant que ... + *subj*, **a s. matter** une bagatelle; **I do some acting, in a s. way** je fais un peu de théâtre; **he's a farmer in a s. way** il tient une petite exploitation agricole; **in her own s. way, she had ...** dans la limite de ses moyens, elle avait ...

3 *(petty)* mesquin; **I felt very s.** *(ashamed)* je n'étais pas fier; *(humiliated)* je me suis senti très humilié; **to make sb look** *or* **feel s.** humilier qn, rabaisser qn; **s. mind** esprit mesquin

N 1 s. of the back creux *m ou* chute *f* des reins **2** *Fam* **smalls** lingerie *f*, sous-vêtements *mpl*; **to wash one's smalls** faire sa petite lessive **3** *(small size) (in T-shirt etc)* petite taille *f*, **this T-shirt is a s.** ce T-shirt est une petite taille

ADV 1 *(to chop etc)* menu, fin **2** *(to write)* petit; **to think s.** voir petit

▸▸ **s. ad** petite annonce *f*, **s. arms** armes *fpl* portatives; **s. business** *(firm)* petite entreprise *f*, PME *f*, *(shop)* petit commerce *m*; **s. businessman** petit entrepreneur *m ou* patron *m*; *Typ Fam* **s. caps** petites capitales *fpl*; **s. capitals** capitales *fpl*; **s. change** petite monnaie *f*, *Aut* **s. end** *(of connecting rod)* pied *m*; **s. fry** menu fretin *m*; **s. hours** petit matin *m*; **in the s. hours** au petit matin; *Anat* **s. intestine** intestin *m* grêle; *Fin* **s. investor** petit porteur *m*; *Typ* **s. letters** minuscules *fpl*, **s. print** petits caractères *mpl*; **s. scale** petite échelle *f*, **s. screen** petit écran *m*; **s. shopkeeper** petit commerçant *m*; **s. talk** banalités *fpl*, *Typ* **s. type** petits corps *mpl*

smallholder [ˈsmɔːlhəʊldər] **N** *Agr* petit cultivateur *m*

smallholding [ˈsmɔːlhəʊldɪŋ] **N** *Agr* petite ferme *f*

smallish [ˈsmɔːlɪʃ] **ADJ** assez *ou* plutôt petit

small-minded **ADJ** à l'esprit mesquin *ou* étroit

smallness [ˈsmɔːlnɪs] **N 1** *(of income)* petitesse *f*, modicité *f*, *(of sum)* faible montant *m* **2** *(pettiness)* **the s. of his mind** sa mesquinerie

smallpox [ˈsmɔːlpɒks] **N** *Med* petite vérole *f*, variole *f*, **a s. case** un cas de variole

small-scale **ADJ 1** *(model)* réduit; *(map)* à petite échelle **2** *(business)* peu important, de peu d'importance

▸▸ *Comput* **s. integration** intégration *f* à petite échelle

small-time **ADJ** *Fam* insignifiant, médiocre; **s. crook** petit escroc *m*

small-town **ADJ** *Fam* provincial, -aux, de province; **a s. attitude** une mentalité provinciale

▸ **smarm down** [smɑːm] VT SEP **to s. down one's hair** se brillantiner les cheveux

▸ **smarm up to** VT INSEP *Fam Pej* lécher les bottes à

smarminess [ˈsmɑːmɪnɪs] **N** *Fam Pej* caractère *m* doucereux; **his s. gets on my nerves** ses flagorneries me tapent sur les nerfs

smarmy [ˈsmɑːmɪ] **ADJ** *Fam Pej* doucereux, flagorneur; **a s. git** un lèche-bottes *inv*

smart [smɑːt] **ADJ 1** *(clever)* habile, intelligent; *(shrewd)* malin, *f*-igne, rusé; *(quick-thinking)* à l'esprit vif; *(resourceful)* qui a des idées, *Fam* dégourdi, débrouillard; *Comput* intelligent; **it isn't s. to break the law** ce n'est pas malin d'enfreindre la loi; **to be too s. for sb** être trop intelligent pour qn; **trying to be s., eh?** tu essaies de faire le malin, hein?; **don't try to be s. with me** n'essaie pas de faire le malin avec moi; **that wasn't very s., was it?** ce n'était pas très malin, tu ne trouves pas?; **s. lad wanted** on recherche un jeune garçon intelligent; **s. businesswoman** femme d'affaires habile; **s. answer** réponse habile; **the s. money is on JJ for chairman** les gens au parfum prédisent JJ comme PDG; *Fam* **s. a. one** c'est un malin

2 *(dress, person, building etc) (elegant)* élégant, chic *inv*; *(attractive)* coquet, pimpant; **to make oneself s.** se faire beau/belle; *(for interview etc)* bien s'habiller; **you do look s.!** comme tu es beau/belle!; **the s. set** la haute; **to be a s. dresser** bien s'habiller

3 *(quick)* vif, *f* vive, rapide; *(prompt)* prompt; **s. pace** allure vive; **that's s. work** vous avez vite fait; **a s. box on the ear** une bonne gifle; **s. reprimand** réprimande assez sèche

ADV look s. (about it)! dépêchez-vous!, remuez-vous!

N *(pain)* douleur *f* cuisante

VI 1 *(of wound, graze etc)* brûler; **my eyes are smarting** les yeux me brûlent **2** *(of person)* souffrir; **to s. under an insult** souffrir sous le coup d'une insulte

▸▸ *Fam* **s. Alec, s. Aleck** petit malin *m*; **s. bomb** bombe *f* intelligente; **s. card** carte *f* à puce; **s. card reader** lecteur *m* de cartes à puce *ou* de cartes à mémoire; **s. drug** psychotrope *m*; **s. missile** engin *m* intelligent

smartarse, *Am* **smartass** [ˈsmɑːtɑːs, -æs] *Fam* **N** petit malin *m*, petite maligne *f*, **don't be such a s.!** arrête de faire le malin!

ADJ *(answer)* malin, *f*-igne

smarten [ˈsmɑːt(ə)n] **VT to s. (the appearance of) sth** arranger qch; **to s. one's pace** accélérer, activer

▸ **smarten up** VT SEP **1** *(make more elegant)*

(something) donner du chic à; *(make more presentable)* arranger; **to s. oneself up** se faire beau **2** *Fam (improve)* **you'd better s. up your ideas** *or* **your act!** tu ferais bien de te reprendre!; *(to lazy person)* tu ferais bien de te secouer!

VI 1 *(make oneself elegant)* se faire beau **2** *Fam (improve performance)* se reprendre

smarting ['smɑːtɪŋ] **ADJ** *(pain, eyes)* brûlant **N** douleur *f* cuisante

smartish ['smɑːtɪʃ] **ADV** *Br Fam* vite fait, en vitesse; **you'd better get ready pretty s.** tu ferais mieux de te préparer vite fait

smartness ['smɑːtnɪs] **N 1** *(cleverness)* habileté *f*, intelligence *f*; *(shrewdness)* ruse *f*; *(quickness of thought)* vivacité *f* (d'esprit); *(resourcefulness)* débrouillardise *f* **2** *(elegance)* élégance *f*, chic *m* **3** *(speed)* rapidité *f*

smarts [smɑːts] **NPL** *Am Fam (intelligence)* intelligence *f*; **to have s.** en avoir dans le ciboulot; **he's pretty low on s.** c'est pas une lumière

smarty-pants ['smɑːtɪ] **N** *Fam* petit malin *m*, petite maligne *f*

smash [smæʃ] **N 1** *(heavy blow)* coup *m* violent; *(loud noise)* fracas *m*; *Tennis* smash *m* **2** *(collision)* collision *f*; *(accident)* accident *m*; *(pile-up)* télescopage *m* **3** *(failure) (in business)* débâcle *f*; *(bankruptcy)* faillite *f* **4** *Fam (success)* succès *m* bœuf; **it was a s.** ça a fait un tabac

ADV to go s. *(of firm, bank)* faire faillite

VT 1 to s. sth on *or* **against sth** heurter *ou* lancer qch contre qch avec violence; **to s. sth open** ouvrir qch d'un coup violent; **she smashed him over the head with a chair** elle lui a cassé une chaise sur la tête; **she smashed her fist into his face** elle lui a fichu son poing dans la figure; **he smashed the ball into the back of the net** d'un tir terrible, il a envoyé le ballon au fond des filets; *Tennis* **to s. the ball** faire un smash, smasher **2 to s. sth** *(to pieces)* briser qch (en mille morceaux); *(shatter)* fracasser qch; **to s. the door open** enfoncer la porte **3** *(destroy) (object, person)* anéantir; *(army etc)* écraser; *Sport (record)* pulvériser; **to s. a drugs ring** démanteler un réseau de trafiquants de drogue

VI 1 *(strike)* se heurter violemment (**into sth** contre qch); **the car smashed into the wall** la voiture est allée s'écraser contre le mur **2 to s. (in pieces)** éclater (en mille morceaux) **3** *(of firm etc)* faire faillite

▸▸ **s. hit** *(song, record)* gros succès *m*

▸ **smash down VT SEP** *(door etc)* défoncer
▸ **smash in VT SEP 1** *(break open) (door etc)* enfoncer, défoncer; *(safe)* forcer **2** *Fam* **to s. sb's face in** casser la figure *ou Fam* la gueule à qn; **I'll s. your face in** je vais te casser la gueule
▸ **smash open VT SEP 1** = **smash in 1 2** *(box etc)* ouvrir en cassant d'un coup de marteau *etc*; **he smashed his head open on a rock** il s'est ouvert la tête en heurtant un rocher
▸ **smash up VT SEP** *(something)* briser en morceaux; *(car etc)* démolir; **they smashed the place up in revenge** ils ont tout démoli pour se venger

smash-and-grab ADJ pillage *m* de vitrine
▸▸ **s. raid** pillage de vitrine

smashed [smæʃt] **ADJ** *Sl (drunk)* bourré, rond; *(on drugs)* camé; **to get s.** *(drunk)* se bourrer; *(on drugs)* se camer

smasher ['smæʃər] **N** *Br Fam* **what a s.!** *(attractive person)* il/elle est vachement bien!; **that's a s.!** *(car etc)* il/elle est génial(e)!

smashing ['smæʃɪŋ] **ADJ 1** *(blow)* violent **2** *Br Fam (excellent)* super, génial, -aux; **we had a s. time** c'était vachement bien

smash-up N *Aut, Rail etc Fam (collision)* télescopage *m*

smattering ['smæt(ə)rɪŋ] **N** *(of French, maths etc)* connaissances *fpl* sommaires; **to have a s. of English** savoir un peu d'anglais; **to have a s. of chemistry** avoir quelques notions de chimie

SME [esem'iː] **N** *(abbr small and medium-sized enterprise)* PME *f*

smear [smɪər] **N 1** *(stain)* tache *f*, souillure *f*; *(defamation)* diffamation *f*, *(spoken)* calomnie *f*; **they resorted to s. tactics** ils eurent recours à la diffamation/la calomnie **2** *Med* frottis *m*

VT 1 *(stain)* barbouiller, salir (**with** avec); *(non-pejorative sense, cover)* enduire (**with** de); **their faces were smeared with coaldust** ils avaient le visage tout barbouillé de charbon; **to s. sth with grease, to s. grease on sth** étaler de la graisse sur qch; **the walls were smeared with blood** les murs étaient tout maculés de sang; **to s. oneself with grease, to s. grease on oneself** s'enduire de graisse **2** *(page of writing etc)* maculer, barbouiller; **don't s. the paint!** ne salis pas la peinture!; **the colours had been smeared into one another** les couleurs s'étaient mélangées; **to get smeared** *(of outline)* s'estomper; **the rain has smeared the address** la pluie a en partie effacé l'adresse **3** *(defame)* diffamer; *(verbally)* calomnier; *(person's reputation)* salir

VI *(of paint etc)* couler; *(of ink)* baver

▸▸ **s. campaign** campagne *f* de diffamation *ou* dénigrement; *Med* **s. test** frottis (vaginal), *Can* test *m* de Papanicolaou

smeary ['smɪərɪ] **ADJ** *(stained)* taché, barbouillé; *(with blurred outlines)* aux contours estompés; *(windows etc)* sale

smell [smel] **N 1** *(sense of)* **s.** odorat *m*; *(of animals)* flair *m*; **to have a keen sense of s.** avoir l'odorat très développé; *(of dog etc)* avoir beaucoup de flair **2** *(odour) (of flowers)* odeur *f*, parfum *m*, senteur *f*; **(bad) s.** mauvaise odeur; **there's a bad s.** ça sent mauvais; **what's that s.?** quelle est cette odeur?; **stale s.** *(of beer etc)* relent *m*; **it has no s.** ça n'a pas d'odeur; **(pleasant) s. of cooking** bonne odeur de cuisine; **the s. was unbearable** l'odeur était intolérable; **to take a s. at sth** sentir qch, renifler qch; *Fig* **a s. of death** une odeur de mort; *Fig* **I don't like the s. of this at all** ça ne me plaît pas du tout, c'est louche

VT *(pt, pp smelt* [smelt], *occ* **smelled)** *(inhale smell of) (something)* sentir; *(flowers)* respirer l'odeur de; *(of dog) (something)* flairer, renifler; *(perceive smell of) (something)* sentir l'odeur de; *(odour)* sentir; *Fig (danger etc)* sentir, flairer; **I can s. something burning** je sens quelque chose qui brûle; **I can s. gas** ça sent le gaz; **I can s. cooking/chocolate** je sens une odeur de cuisine/chocolat; *Fig* **I s. a rat** il y a quelque chose de louche

VI 1 *(of flower etc)* sentir; **to s. good/bad/strong(ly)** sentir bon/mauvais/fort; **to s. of violets** sentir la violette; **it smells like lemon** ça sent le citron, on dirait du citron; **to s. of gas** sentir le gaz; **these flowers don't s.** ces fleurs n'ont pas d'odeur, ces fleurs ne sentent rien **2** *(have bad smell)* sentir (mauvais); **it smells (awful)!** ça pue!; **his breath smells** il a mauvaise haleine **3** *(have sense of smell)* **he can't s.** il n'a pas d'odorat

▸ **smell out VT SEP 1** *(discover by smelling) (of dog)* flairer; *Fig (of person) (secret)* découvrir **2 his cigarettes are smelling the office out** ses cigarettes empestent *ou* empuantissent le bureau

smelliness ['smelɪnɪs] **N** mauvaise odeur *f*, puanteur *f*

smelling ['smelɪŋ] **ADJ**
▸▸ **s. salts** sels *mpl*

smelly ['smelɪ] **ADJ 1** malodorant, puant; **it's**

s. in here ça sent mauvais ici; **to be s.** sentir mauvais; **he's got s. feet** il pue des pieds; **am I still s.?** je sens encore (mauvais)? **2** *Fam (objectionable, unpleasant)* dégueulasse

smelt¹ [smelt] **N** *(fish)* éperlan *m*

smelt² **VT** *(ore)* fondre; *(metal)* extraire par fusion

smelter ['smeltər] **N** haut-fourneau *m*, *pl* hauts-fourneaux

smelting ['smeltɪŋ] **N** *(of ore)* fonte *f*, fusion *f*, *(of metal)* extraction *f* par fusion
▸▸ **s. works** fonderie *f*

smidgen ['smɪdʒən] **N** *Fam* **a s. of sth** un tout petit peu de qch

smile [smaɪl] **N** sourire *m*; **with a s.** en souriant, avec un sourire; **with a s. on his lips** le sourire aux lèvres; **to give sb a s.** adresser un sourire à qn, sourire à qn; **she was all smiles** elle était toute souriante *ou* tout sourire; *(pretence)* elle était tout sucre tout miel; **that'll take** *or* **wipe the s. off his face!** cela va lui faire passer l'envie de sourire!

VI sourire; **to s. at sb** sourire à qn, adresser un sourire à qn; **fortune smiles on him** la fortune lui sourit; **to keep smiling,** *Lit* **to s. in the face of adversity** garder le sourire; **he always comes up smiling** il garde toujours le sourire; *Phot* **s.!** souriez!; **she smiled back (at him)** elle lui rendit son sourire

VT to s. a bitter s. sourire amèrement, avoir un sourire amer; **to s. a welcome to sb** accueillir qn avec *ou* par un sourire; **to s. one's gratitude** exprimer sa gratitude par un sourire

smiley ['smaɪlɪ] **N** *Comput* souriant *m*, émoticon *m*

smiling ['smaɪlɪŋ] **ADJ** souriant

smilingly ['smaɪlɪŋlɪ] **ADV** en souriant, avec un sourire

smirch [smɜːtʃ] **N** tache *f*, salissure *f*, souillure *f*
VT salir, souiller

smirk [smɜːk] **N** *(affected smile)* sourire *m* affecté; *(mocking)* petit sourire supérieur; *(gloating)* petit sourire narquois
VI *(affectedly)* sourire d'un air affecté; *(mockingly)* sourire d'un air supérieur; *(gloatingly)* sourire d'un air narquois

smite [smaɪt] **VT** *(pt* **smote** [sməʊt]; *pp* **smitten** ['smɪt(ə)n])** **1** *Arch, Lit (strike) (the enemy)* frapper, battre **2 to be smitten with blindness** être frappé de cécité; **to be smitten with remorse** être pris de remords; **to be smitten with a desire to do sth** être pris d'un *ou* du désir de faire qch; *Fam* **to be smitten with a girl** être amoureux fou d'une jeune fille; **he's totally smitten** il est sous le charme

▸ **smite down VT SEP** *Arch, Lit* abattre

smith [smɪθ] **N** forgeron *m*; *(who shoes horses)* maréchal-ferrant *m*, *pl* maréchaux-ferrants

smithereens [smɪðə'riːnz] **NPL** **the ship was blown to s.** l'explosion a réduit le navire en miettes; **he was blown to s. in the explosion** il a été déchiqueté dans l'explosion; **to smash sth to s.** briser qch en mille morceaux

Smithsonian Institution [smɪθ'səʊnɪən] **N** = complexe *m* culturel à Washington

smithy ['smɪðɪ] **N** forge *f*; *(for shoeing horses)* (atelier *m* de) maréchalerie *f*

smitten PP *see* **smite**

smock [smɒk] **N** *(garment)* blouse *f*, sarrau *m*
VT *Sewing (dress etc)* orner de smocks

smocking ['smɒkɪŋ] **N** smocks *mpl*

smog [smɒg] **N** smog *m*

smoke [sməʊk] **N 1** *(substance)* fumée *f*; **tobacco s.** fumée de tabac; *Fig Fam* **to go up in s.** *(of building, papers etc)* partir en fumée;

Fam **he had s. coming out of his ears** *(was angry)* ses yeux lançaient des éclairs; *Prov* **(there's) no s. without fire** il n'y a pas de fumée sans feu

2 *(act of smoking)* **let's have a s.** si on fumait (une cigarette/une pipe/un cigare)?; **I always have a s. at about 10** je me fume toujours ma petite cigarette aux alentours de dix heures

3 *Fam (cigarette)* cigarette *f*; *(cigar)* cigare *m*
4 *(cannabis cigarette)* joint *m*; *(cannabis)* chichon *m*, shit *m*
5 *Br Sl* **the (Big) S.** Londres *m*

VI 1 *(smoke tobacco)* fumer; **do you s.?** (est-ce que) vous fumez?; **do you mind if I s.?** est-ce que ça vous dérange si je fume?; *Fam* **to s. like a chimney** *(of person)* fumer comme un pompier *ou* un sapeur
2 *(emit smoke, vapour)* fumer; *(of lamp)* fumer; **the horses' flanks were smoking** les chevaux étaient tout fumants

VT 1 *(tobacco)* fumer; **to s. a pipe/cigarettes** fumer la pipe/des cigarettes; **to s. twenty a day** fumer vingt cigarettes par jour
2 *Culin (ham, meat, fish)* fumer
▸▸ **s. alarm** détecteur *m* de fumée; **s. bomb** bombe *f* fumigène; **s. detector** détecteur de fumée; **s. screen** *Mil* rideau *m ou* écran *m* de fumée; *Fig (comments, action etc)* tentative *f* de dissimulation; **s. signal** signal *m* de fumée
▸ **smoke out** VT SEP **1** *(flush out with smoke) (insects)* enfumer pour les chasser; *Fig* faire sortir; *(bandits, snipers)* débusquer **2** *(fill with smoke)* enfumer **3 my pipe is smoked out** j'ai fini ma pipe

smoked [sməʊkt] ADJ *Culin* fumé
▸▸ **s. glass** verre *m* fumé; **s. salmon** saumon *m* fumé

smoke-filled [-fɪld] ADJ plein de fumée, enfumé

smokeless ['sməʊklɪs] ADJ *(fuel)* sans fumée
▸▸ **s. zone** = zone *f* où il est interdit de brûler du charbon afin de limiter la pollution atmosphérique

smoker ['sməʊkər] N **1** *(of tobacco)* fumeur, -euse; **cigarette/pipe s.** fumeur de cigarettes/pipe; **heavy s.** gros fumeur; **s.'s cough** toux *f* de fumeur **2** *Rail etc Fam (compartment)* compartiment *m* fumeurs

smokestack ['sməʊkstæk] N cheminée *f*
▸▸ *esp Am* **s. industry** industrie *f* lourde

smoking ['sməʊkɪŋ] ADJ fumant, qui fume
N **1** *(of tobacco) (habit)* tabagisme *m*; **the effects of s. on the foetus** les effets du tabagisme sur le fœtus; **s. can damage your health** fumer nuit à votre santé; **no s. (allowed)** défense de fumer **2** *Culin (of ham etc)* fumage *m*
▸▸ **s. area** zone *f* fumeurs; **s. carriage** voiture *f* fumeurs; **s. compartment** compartiment *m* fumeurs; *Fig* **s. gun** *(clue)* indice *m* flagrant; **s. jacket** veste *f* d'intérieur; **s. room** fumoir *m (pour fumeurs)*

smoky ['sməʊkɪ] ADJ **1** *(atmosphere, room, town)* enfumé **2** *(ceiling etc)* noirci par la fumée **3** *(fire, lamp)* qui fume **4** *(taste)* qui a un goût de fumée
▸▸ **s. blue** gris bleu *m inv*; **s. grey** gris fumée *m inv*; *Geol* **s. quartz** quartz *m* fumé

smolder, smoldering *Am* = **smoulder, smouldering**

smooch [smuːtʃ] *Fam* VI **1** *(kiss)* se bécoter; *(cuddle)* se peloter **2** *(dance)* danser un slow
N **to have a s.** *(kiss)* se bécoter; *(cuddle)* se peloter; *(dance)* danser un slow

smoochy ['smuːtʃɪ] ADJ *Fam (music)* doux, *f* douce, et romantique

smooth [smuːð] ADJ **1** *(surface, paper)* lisse; *(skin)* doux, *f* douce; *(road etc)* uni, égal, -aux; *(forehead)* sans rides; *(mixture, sauce*

etc) onctueux; **to make s.** *(jagged edges)* lisser; *(hair)* défriser; *(road, surface)* aplanir; **the steps were worn s.** les marches étaient devenues lisses; *Br Fam* **as s. as a baby's bottom** *(skin, face etc)* doux comme une peau de bébé; **as s. as a millpond** *(sea)* d'un calme plat; **s. chin** *(without a beard)* menton glabre; *(close-shaven)* menton rasé de près; **a s. shave** un rasage parfait

2 *(gentle)* doux, *f* douce; *(trip, flight etc) (comfortable)* confortable; *(without problems)* sans anicroches; *(wine)* moelleux; *(style)* coulant; *(person)* doucereux, mielleux; **the conference got off to a s. start** la conférence a commencé très bien; **to ensure a s. passage for a bill** s'assurer qu'un projet de loi sera adopté sans difficulté; **to make things s. for sb** faciliter les choses pour qn; **he's a s. operator** il sait s'y prendre; *TV etc* **s. cut** montage *m* régulier; **s. ride** conduite aisée; *Fig* **the bill had a s. ride** le projet de loi est passé sans problème; **s. running** *(of machine)* fonctionnement doux *ou* régulier; *(of project)* déroulement sans anicroches; **the s. running of the department** le bon fonctionnement du service; **s. talker** beau parleur *m*; **to have a s. tongue** être doucereux; *Fam* **s. character** personne mielleuse
N **to give one's hair a s. (down)** lisser ses cheveux, se lisser les cheveux; **to give sth a s. down with sandpaper** égaliser qch avec du papier de verre; **you have to take the rough with the s.** il faut prendre le bon avec le moins bon
VT *(feathers, hair etc)* lisser; *(plank)* aplanir; *(ground)* égaliser; *(garment)* défroisser; **to s. one's brow** dérider son front; **to s. the way for sb/sth** faciliter les choses pour qn/qch
▸ **smooth away** VT SEP *(problems, fears etc)* faire oublier
▸ **smooth back** VT SEP **to s. back one's hair** mettre ses cheveux en arrière
▸ **smooth down** VT SEP *(make smooth) (feathers, hair etc)* lisser; *(wood)* égaliser
▸ **smooth off** VT SEP *(make smooth) (angle)* adoucir
▸ **smooth out** VT SEP **1** *(map, sheets)* défroisser; *(remove by smoothing) (crease)* faire disparaître **2** = **smooth over**
▸ **smooth over** VT SEP *(make easier)* **to s. over difficulties** aplanir les difficultés; **to s. things over** arrondir les angles

smoothbore ['smuːðbɔːr] ADJ à canon lisse

smoothie ['smuːðɪ] N **1** *Fam (smooth talker)* baratineur, -euse **2** *(drink)* smoothie *m*, = jus *m* de fruit épais avec sa pulpe

smoothly ['smuːðlɪ] ADV *(to work, function)* sans heurts, sans problèmes; *(of car, engine etc)* en douceur; **to run s.** *(of car)* rouler en douceur; *(of meeting, project)* se dérouler sans heurts; **everything's going s.** tout va bien, *Fam* tout marche comme sur des roulettes, tout baigne; **the journey went s.** le voyage s'est déroulé sans problèmes; **the interview went quite s. until I …** l'entretien s'est bien passé jusqu'à ce que je …

smoothness ['smuːðnɪs] N **1** *(of surface)* égalité *f*; *(of skin, fur)* douceur *f*, satiné *m*; *(of sea)* calme *m* **2** *(of operation of machine)* douceur *f*, régularité *f*; *(of machine, administration etc)* bon fonctionnement *m*; *(of style)* fluidité *f* **3** *(suavity) (of person)* air *m* doucereux

smooth-running ADJ *(machine etc)* qui marche bien; *(project)* qui se déroule sans anicroches

smooth-spoken ADJ doucereux, mielleux

smooth-talk VT **to s. sb** prendre qn par les sentiments, *Fam* embobiner qn; **to s. sb into doing sth** embobiner qn pour qu'il fasse

qch; **let's see if he can s. his way out of this one** voyons si cette fois-ci il réussit à s'en sortir à force de baratin

smooth-talking ADJ doucereux, mielleux
smooth-tongued [-'tʌŋd] ADJ doucereux, mielleux

smoothy ['smuːðɪ] N *Fam* = **smoothie**

smote PT *see* **smite**

smother ['smʌðər] VT **1** *(stifle) (person)* étouffer, suffoquer; *(fire)* étouffer; *(sound)* éteindre, étouffer; *(cry)* étouffer, retenir; *(oath, groan, yawn)* réprimer; *Fig (person, criticism, call for inquiry, scandal)* étouffer; *(one's feelings)* cacher; **to s. sb with kisses** étouffer qn de baisers **2** *(cover)* couvrir; **strawberries smothered in** *or* **with cream** fraises recouvertes de crème; **to be smothered in furs** être emmitouflé dans des fourrures
VI suffoquer, étouffer

smothered ['smʌðəd] ADJ *(cry)* sourd, étouffé; *(sound)* étouffé

smother-love N *Fam* amour *m* étouffant d'une mère

smoulder, *Am* **smolder** ['sməʊldər] VI *(of coal etc)* brûler lentement *ou* sans flamme; *(of fire, rebellion etc)* couver (sous la cendre); **to s. with anger/passion** se consumer de colère/passion

smouldering, *Am* **smoldering** ['sməʊldərɪŋ] ADJ *(coal etc)* qui brûle sans flamme; *(fire, dissent, passion, jealousy etc)* qui couve (sous la cendre)

SMS [eseˈmes] N *Tel (abbr* **short message service)** *(service)* texte *m*; *(message)* message *m* texte

SMTP [esemtiˈpiː] N *Comput (abbr* **Simple Mail Transfer Protocol)** protocole *m* SMTP

smudge [smʌdʒ] N tache *f*, salissure *f*; *(slip with pen)* bavure *f* de stylo; **you've got a s. on your nose** tu as une tache sur le nez; **the house was just a white s. in the distance** la maison n'était qu'une tache blanche dans le lointain
VT *(ink)* étaler; *(drawing, paint)* salir; *(eye make-up)* faire couler; **don't kiss me or you'll s. my lipstick** ne m'embrasse pas, sinon mon rouge à lèvres va s'en aller
VI *(of ink, writing)* s'étaler; *(of paint)* couler

smudgy ['smʌdʒɪ] ADJ *(face etc)* sali; *(text)* taché; *(handwriting, drawing)* sale; **the heat had made her make-up s.** la chaleur avait fait couler son maquillage

smug [smʌg] ADJ *(tone, look)* suffisant, satisfait de soi-même; **he has a s. look** il a un air suffisant, il a l'air content de lui; **stop looking so s.** arrête de te croire supérieur; **he was s. about his success** sa réussite le rendait plein de suffisance

smuggle ['smʌg(ə)l] VT *(arms, drugs etc)* faire de la contrebande de; *(when coming through customs)* faire passer en fraude; **to s. sth into/out of the country** (faire) entrer/sortir qch en contrebande; **to s. sb into/out of a country** faire entrer qn clandestinement dans un pays/sortir qn clandestinement d'un pays; **they are being smuggled into France by boat** on les fait entrer clandestinement en France par bateau; **to s. sth into a room** apporter qch subrepticement dans une pièce
VI *(of arms or drugs smuggler)* faire de la contrebande; *(when coming through customs)* frauder
▸ **smuggle in** VT SEP *(into country) (arms, drugs etc)* introduire en contrebande; *(when coming through customs)* faire passer en fraude; *(into prison etc)* introduire illégalement
▸ **smuggle out** VT SEP *(from country) (arms,*

drugs etc) faire sortir en contrebande; *(when coming through customs)* faire sortir en fraude; *(from prison etc)* faire sortir illégalement

smuggler ['smʌglər] **N** *(of drugs, arms etc)* contrebandier, -ière; *(when coming through customs)* fraudeur, -euse

smuggling ['smʌglɪŋ] **N** *(of drugs, arms etc)* trafic *m*, contrebande *f*; *(when coming through customs)* fraude *f*; **drug s.** trafic *m* de stupéfiant; **s. operation** opération *f* de contrebande

smugly ['smʌglɪ] **ADV** *(to look at)* d'un air suffisant; *(to say)* d'un ton suffisant; **he's so s. self-righteous** il est tellement suffisant

smugness ['smʌgnɪs] **N** suffisance *f*

smut [smʌt] **N 1** *(soot)* parcelle *f* de suie; *(soot mark)* tache *f* de suie (**on the face** au *ou* sur le visage) **2** *(obscenity)* cochonneries *fpl*, grivoiseries *fpl*; **to talk s.** dire des cochonneries *fpl*; **that book's/film's just s.** il n'y a que des cochonneries dans ce livre/film **3** *Agr (on grain crops)* charbon *m*

smuttiness ['smʌtɪnɪs] **N** *(lewdness) (of remark etc)* grivoiserie *f*, grossièreté *f*

smutty ['smʌtɪ] **ADJ 1** *(remark, conversation etc)* grossier, grivois **2** *(dirty)* noirci, noir, sali *(de suie)*

snack [snæk] **N** casse-croûte *m inv*; collation *f*; **if you eat too many snacks between meals …** si vous grignotez (trop) entre les repas …; **to have a s.** casser la croûte, manger un morceau sur le pouce

VI manger entre les repas; **I've been snacking on chocolates all day** aujourd'hui je me suis nourri de chocolat

▸▸ **s. bar** snack *m*, snack-bar *m*, *pl* snack-bars; **s. food** amuse-gueules *mpl*

snaffle ['snæf(ə)l] **N** *Horseriding* mors *m* brisé, bridon *m*

VT *Br Fam (take, steal)* piquer; **who's snaffled my pen?** qui est-ce qui m'a piqué mon stylo?

▸▸ *Horseriding* **s. bit** mors brisé, bridon

▸ **snaffle up VT SEP** *Br Fam (bargains, cakes etc)* rafler

snafu [snæ'fuː] *Sl* **ADJ** en (grand) désordre, chaotique

N grosse gaffe *f*

snag [snæg] **N 1** *(protrusion) (of tree)* aspérité *f* **2** *Fig (problem)* accroc *m*; *Fig* **to strike a** *or* **hit a** *or* **come across a s.** se heurter à un obstacle *ou* à une anicroche; **that's the s.!** voilà le hic!; **the s. is that it's too expensive** le hic, c'est que c'est trop cher **3** *(tear) (in garment)* accroc *m* **4** *Austr Fam (sausage)* saucisse *f*

VT *(-gg-) (dress etc)* faire un accroc à; *(stocking etc)* accrocher

VI *(of clothes)* s'accrocher

snail [sneɪl] **N** escargot *m*; **at a s.'s pace** à pas d'escargot

▸▸ *Aut* **s. cam** came *f* en colimaçon; *Fam* **s. mail** courrier *m* escargot, = courrier postal

snake [sneɪk] **N 1** *(reptile)* serpent *m*; *Fig (person)* faux jeton *m*; **common s., grass s.** couleuvre *f* à collier; *Fig* **a s. in the grass** un faux jeton; **snakes and ladders** *(game)* ≃ le jeu de l'oie; *Am Fam* **snakes alive!** grand Dieu! **2** *Fin* serpent *m* monétaire

VI *(of road etc)* serpenter

▸▸ **s. charmer** charmeur, -euse de serpent; **s. oil** remède *m* de charlatan; *Am Fig* **s. pit** fosse *f* aux serpents, nid *m* de vipères

snakebite ['sneɪkbaɪt] **N 1** *(wound)* morsure *f* de serpent **2** *Fam (drink)* = boisson *f* comprenant une mesure de bière et une mesure de cidre

snakeskin ['sneɪkskɪn] **N** peau *f* de serpent

SNAP [snæp]

| **N** coup de dents **1** ▪ claquement **2** ▪ crac **2** ▪ photo **5** |
| **ADJ** instantané |
| **VI** essayer de mordre **1** ▪ faire un bruit sec **2** ▪ se casser net **3** ▪ parler sèchement **4** ▪ prendre des photos **5** |
| **VT** faire claquer **1** ▪ casser **2** ▪ prendre (en photo) **3** ▪ dire sur un ton sec **4** |

N 1 *(action) (of teeth)* coup *m* de dents; **to have a s. at sth** *(of dog etc)* essayer de happer qch; **with a s. of the fingers** claquant ses doigts

2 *(sound) (of teeth, whip etc)* coup *m* sec, claquement *m*; *(of sth breaking)* crac *m*; **I heard a s.** j'ai entendu un crac

3 *(cold weather)* **cold s.** courte période *f* de temps froid, coup *m* de froid

4 *Culin* **ginger s.** biscuit *m* sec au gingembre

5 *Phot Fam* instantané *m*; **holiday snaps** photos *fpl* de vacances

6 *Cards* ≃ (jeu *m* de) bataille *f*

ADJ instantané, imprévu; **s. decision** décision *f* immédiate; **to call a s. election** procéder à une élection surprise

ADV **to go s.** *(make sound)* faire clac; *(break cleanly)* (se) casser net; **s. went my stick!** et crac! ma canne s'est cassée!

INT 1 *Cards* **s.!** ≃ bataille!

2 *Fam (in identical situation)* **I'm going to Paris – s.!** je vais à Paris – ça par exemple! moi aussi!; **do you like my new tie? – yes, but look, s.!** tu aimes ma nouvelle cravate? – oui, mais regarde, j'ai la même!

VI *(-pp-)* **1** *(of dog etc)* **to s. at sb/sth** essayer de mordre qn/qch

2 *(of teeth, whip etc)* claquer, faire un bruit sec; **to s. (shut)** *(of fastener, door etc)* se fermer avec un bruit sec; **he snapped to attention** il se mit au garde-à-vous en un quart de seconde

3 *(of stick, rope etc)* **to s. (in two)** *(break cleanly)* (se) casser net; *(break with sound)* se rompre avec un bruit sec

4 *(speak abruptly)* parler sèchement; **to s. at sb** s'adresser à qn d'un ton sec *ou* cassant; **there's no need to s.** ce n'est pas la peine de me parler sur ce ton

5 *Phot* **tourists snapping away with their cameras** des touristes qui n'arrêtent pas de prendre des photos

VT 1 *(whip etc)* faire claquer; **to s. one's fingers** (faire) claquer ses doigts; **to s. one's fingers at sb** narguer qn, faire la nique à qn

2 *(break) (stick etc)* casser, rompre; **to s. sth in two** casser qch en deux

3 *Phot Fam (take photo of)* prendre; *(facial expression etc)* saisir; **she snapped him eating a cake** elle l'a pris en photo en train de manger un gâteau

4 *(say sharply)* **to s. an order at sb** lancer un ordre à qn d'un ton sec; **'mind your own business!', he snapped (at me)** 'occupe-toi de ce qui te regarde', dit-il d'un ton cassant

▸▸ **s. fastener** *(press stud)* bouton-pression *m*, *pl* boutons-pression, pression *f*; *(clasp on handbag, necklace)* fermoir *m* (à pression); **s. lock** serrure *f* à ressort

▸ **snap back VI** *(of trigger etc)* revenir brusquement

▸ **snap off VT SEP** *(break off) (with hands etc)* arracher; *(with teeth)* enlever d'un coup de dents; *(accidentally) (end of stick etc)* casser; *Fig Fam* **to s. sb's head off** rembarrer qn vivement

VI *(break off)* se casser

▸ **snap out VT SEP** *(say sharply) (order)* donner d'un ton sec

VI *Fam (return to normal mood)* **s. out of it!** fais pas la tête *ou* la gueule!; **I'm sure she'll s.**

---

out of it soon je suis sûr qu'elle va finir par se dérider

▸ **snap to VI** *(close with snap) (of lid, door etc)* se (re)fermer avec un bruit sec

VT SEP (re)fermer (avec un bruit sec)

▸ **snap up VT SEP 1** *(seize in jaws)* saisir, happer

2 *(buy, take quickly etc)* rafler; **to s. up a bargain** sauter sur *ou* saisir une occasion; **the tickets are being snapped up like hot cakes** les billets s'arrachent comme des petits pains

snapdragon ['snæpdræg(ə)n] **N** *(flower)* muflier *m*, gueule-de-loup *f*, *pl* gueules-de-loup

snapper ['snæpər] **N 1** *(fish)* vivaneau *m* **2** *Ir Fam* môme *mf*, gosse *mf*

snappily ['snæpɪlɪ] **ADV** *(to reply)* d'un ton hargneux

snappish ['snæpɪʃ] **ADJ** *(person, dog)* hargneux

snappishly ['snæpɪʃlɪ] **ADV** *(to reply)* d'un ton hargneux

snappishness ['snæpɪʃnɪs] **N** hargne *f*

snappy ['snæpɪ] **ADJ 1** *(person, tone, reply, dog)* hargneux **2** *(style, prose etc)* vif, *f* vive, plein d'allant; *(organization)* dynamique; *(slogan, campaign)* plein de punch; *Fam* **make it s.!** grouille-toi!, magne-toi!; **he's a s. dresser** il s'habille chic *ou Fam* classe

snapshot ['snæpʃɒt] **N** *Phot, Fig Fam* instantané *m*; *Comput (of screen)* instantané *m*, impression *f* immédiate

snare [sneər] **N** *(in hunting)* lacet *m*, collet *m*; *Fig* piège *m*; **to lay** *or* **set a s.** *(for animal)* poser un collet; *(for opponent)* tendre un piège; **to be caught in a s.** *(of animal)* être pris au lacet; *Fig (of person)* être pris au piège

VT *(bird)* prendre au filet; *(rabbit)* prendre au collet *ou* au lacet; *Fig (person)* prendre au piège

▸▸ *Mus* **s. drum** caisse *f* claire

snarl¹ [snɑːl] **N** *(sound) (of dog, person)* grondement *m*, grognement *m*; *(of tiger)* feulement *m*

VI *(show teeth)* montrer les dents; *(make sound) (of person, dog)* grogner, gronder; *(of tiger)* feuler; **to s. at sb** *(of person, dog)* grogner *ou* gronder contre qn; **'go away!', he snarled** 'va-t'en', gronda-t-il

snarl² **N** *(entanglement) (of ropes, wires etc)* enchevêtrement *m*; *(of traffic)* embouteillage *m*

VI *(become entangled)* s'emmêler, s'enchevêtrer

VT *(entangle)* emmêler, enchevêtrer

▸ **snarl up VT SEP** **to s. up the traffic** provoquer des embouteillages; **to s. up a system** paralyser un système; **the traffic gets snarled up at the traffic lights** la circulation bouchonne aux feux; **I got snarled up on the ringroad** je suis resté coincé dans un bouchon sur le périphérique

VI *(of traffic)* bouchonner; *(of system, country etc)* être paralysé

snarling ['snɑːlɪŋ] **ADJ** grondant, grognant

N *(sound)* grondement *m*, grognement *m*

snarl-up **N** *(of traffic)* embouteillage *m*, bouchon *m*; *(in system etc)* paralysie *f*; **there's a s. in the switchboard** le standard est saturé

snatch [snætʃ] **N 1** *(grab)* mouvement *m* vif *(pour saisir qch)*; *Fam (kidnapping)* kidnapping *m*, enlèvement *m*; *Fam (robbery)* vol *m*; *Sport (in weightlifting)* arraché *m*; **to make a s. at** *or* **for sth** chercher à saisir qch; **to carry out a wages/jewellery s.** *(theft)* voler la paye/des bijoux

2 *(short period)* courte période *f*; *(small piece)* fragment *m*; **s. of sleep** petit somme *m*; **in** *or* **by snatches** *(to sleep)* par intervalles; *(to work)* de façon intermittente, à bâtons rompus; **to overhear snatches of conversation** surprendre des bouts *ou* des bribes de conversation; **I could hear a s. of music** quelques notes de musique me parvenaient

3 *Sl (female genitals)* chatte *f*

VT *(object)* saisir, empoigner; *(kidnap)* *(baby)* kidnapper; *(steal)* voler; *Sport (in weightlifting) (weight)* arracher; **to s. sth from sb** arracher qch à qn; **to s. sth out of sb's hands** arracher qch des mains de qn; **to s. an opportunity** saisir une occasion; **to s. something to eat** manger sur le pouce; **to s. a bit of sleep** faire un petit somme; **I snatched three hours' sleep** j'ai fait un petit somme de trois heures

VI saisir brusquement *ou* arracher les objets; **don't s.!** on n'arrache pas les choses des mains des gens!

▸▸ *Br* **s. squad** = groupe *m* de policiers chargé d'arrêter les meneurs (lors d'une manifestation)

▸ **snatch at** **VT INSEP** *(try to grab)* tâcher de saisir; **to s. at an opportunity** saisir une occasion (au vol)

▸ **snatch away** **VT SEP** *(grab)* arracher, enlever (**from** de); **he snatched away the book I was reading** il m'a arraché des mains le livre que je lisais; **he snatched it away from me/George** il me l'a arraché des mains/il l'a arraché des mains de George

▸ **snatch up** **VT SEP** *(pick up quickly)* ramasser vivement; **she snatched up the baby** elle s'est emparée vivement du bébé

snazzy ['snæzɪ] **ADJ** *Fam (shirt, tie, car)* classe *inv*; **he's a s. dresser** il s'habille classe

sneak [sniːk] **N 1** *esp Br Fam (telltale)* cafard, -arde, mouchard, -arde **2** *Fam (devious person)* faux jeton *m*

VI 1 *esp Br Fam (tell tales)* moucharder, cafarder **2** *(move furtively)* **to s. past the guard** passer devant la garde sans se faire voir; **to s. into the cinema without paying** entrer au cinéma sans payer

VT *(remove surreptitiously) (from desk, room etc)* subtiliser; *(deliver surreptitiously) (cigarettes, whisky etc)* donner en cachette; *(letter)* glisser; **to s. a glance at sb** glisser un œil vers qn; **they sneaked him past the guards** ils le firent passer sans que les gardes le voient; **someone must have sneaked it into my suitcase** quelqu'un a dû le glisser dans ma valise; **she sneaked her boyfriend into her bedroom** elle fit subrepticement entrer son petit ami dans sa chambre

▸▸ **s. preview** avant-première *f* privée, *pl* avant-premières privées; **to have a s. preview of sth** *(of exhibition, film etc)* voir qch en avant-première; *(of book, product etc)* avoir la primeur de qch; *Br* **s. thief** chapardeur, -euse

▸ **sneak about, sneak around** **VI** *(move furtively)* rôder

▸ **sneak away** **VI** = sneak off

▸ **sneak in** **VI** *(enter furtively)* entrer sans se faire repérer; **to s. in without paying** entrer sans payer

VT SEP *(bring in furtively) (object)* introduire furtivement *ou* subrepticement; **I'll s. you in after dark** je te ferai entrer discrètement à la nuit tombée

▸ **sneak off** **VI** *(leave furtively)* filer; **he sneaked off and joined another team** il a filé en douce et a rejoint une autre équipe

▸ **sneak on** **VT INSEP** *esp Br Fam (tell tales on)* moucharder

▸ **sneak out** **VI** *(leave furtively)* filer; **to s. out of a room** sortir d'une pièce sans se faire voir

VT SEP *(take out furtively) (object)* emporter subrepticement; *(person)* faire sortir subrepticement

sneakers ['sniːkəz] **NPL** *esp Am* tennis *fpl*

sneaking ['sniːkɪŋ] **ADJ I have a s. respect**

for him j'avoue que j'ai un certain respect pour lui; **to have a s. feeling** *or* **suspicion that ...** avoir comme une vague impression que ...

sneaky ['sniːkɪ] **ADJ** sournois

sneer [snɪər] **N** *(smile)* sourire *m* de mépris; *(laugh)* ricanement *m*; *(remark)* sarcasme *m*

VI *(smile)* sourire d'un air moqueur; *(laugh)* ricaner; **to s. at sb** se moquer de qn; *(address scornful remarks to)* lancer des sarcasmes à qn

VT 'you couldn't do that', he sneered 'tu n'en serais pas capable', a-t-il lancé en ricanant

sneerer ['snɪərər] **N** moqueur, -euse, ricaneur, -euse

sneering ['snɪərɪŋ] **ADJ** *(face, look)* ricaneur; *(remark, laughter)* sarcastique

N *(laughing)* ricanement *m*; *(remarks)* sarcasmes *mpl*

sneeringly ['snɪərɪŋlɪ] **ADV** *(contemptuously)* avec mépris; *(sarcastically)* d'un air sarcastique; *(laughing scornfully)* en ricanant

sneeze [sniːz] **N** éternuement *m*

VI éternuer; **she sneezed all over her plate** elle a éternué sur son assiette

▸ **sneeze at VT INSEP** *Fam* **that's not to be sneezed at** il ne faut pas cracher dessus

sneezing ['sniːzɪŋ] **N** éternuement *m*; **his s. irritates me** ses éternuements m'agacent

▸▸ **s. fit** crise *f* d'éternuements; **s. powder** poudre *f* à éternuer

snick [snɪk] **N** *(notch)* entaille *f*, encoche *f*

VT 1 *(wood etc)* entailler, faire une entaille dans; *(fabric)* faire une fente dans **2** *Cr (ball)* couper légèrement

snicker ['snɪkər] **N, VI = snigger etc**

snide [snaɪd] **ADJ** *Fam (scornful)* méprisant; *(sarcastic)* sarcastique; **she was very s. about it** elle s'est montrée très méprisante/très sarcastique à ce sujet

sniff [snɪf] **N** reniflement *m*; **to take a s. at sth** renifler qch; **with a s. of disgust** avec un reniflement de dégoût; **I caught a s. of his aftershave** j'ai senti son after-shave; **there's still a s. of gas** ça sent toujours le gaz; **to have a little s.** *(smell)* renifler un petit coup; *Fam (have a slight cold)* avoir un léger rhume

VI renifler; **he sniffed with disdain** il a reniflé avec dédain

VT 1 *(investigate by smelling)* flairer, renifler; *(detect) (good meal, danger etc)* flairer; **the dog sniffed my hand** le chien m'a flairé la main **2** *(inhale) (snuff etc)* humer, renifler; *(cocaine, glue)* sniffer

▸ **sniff at VT INSEP 1** *Fam (disdain)* **the offer is not to be sniffed at** il ne faut pas cracher sur une proposition comme celle-ci **2** *(smell)* flairer, renifler; **the dog sniffed at my hand** le chien m'a flairé la main

▸ **sniff out VT SEP** *(discover by smelling) (of dog) (person, object)* détecter, flairer; *Fig (scandal etc)* déterrer

sniffer dog ['snɪfər] **N** chien *m* renifleur

sniffle ['snɪf(ə)l] **N** *(slight cold)* petit rhume *m* (de cerveau); **to have a s.** *or* **the sniffles** avoir un petit rhume

VI 1 *(sniff repeatedly)* renifler **2** *(cry)* pleurnicher

sniffy ['snɪfɪ] **ADJ** *Fam* **1** *(disdainful)* dédaigneux; **to be s. about sth** *(take exception to sth)* voir qch d'un mauvais œil; *(regard with contempt)* considérer qch avec mépris **2** *(bad-smelling)* **it's a bit s. in here** ça pue un peu ici **3** *(with cold)* **I'm still a bit s.** je renifle encore

snifter ['snɪftər] **N 1** *Old-fashioned Fam (drink)* goutte *f*, petit verre *m* **2** *Am (glass)* verre *m* à cognac

snigger ['snɪgər] **N** *(stifled laughter)* ricane-

ment *m*; *(at dirty story etc)* petit rire *m* grivois

VI *(stifle laughter)* ricaner (**at** à propos de)

sniggering ['snɪgərɪŋ] **N** *(stifled laughter)* ricanement *m*; **her s. irritates me** ses ricanements m'agacent

snip [snɪp] **N 1** *(cut)* petite entaille *f*, *(act of cutting with scissors)* coup *m* de ciseaux **2** *(piece cut off) (of paper, fabric)* morceau *m* coupé, bout *m* **3** *Br Fam (bargain)* affaire *f* (avantageuse), occasion *f*; **to get a s.** faire une affaire; **at £25 it's a s.** à 25 livres c'est une affaire

VT (**-pp-**) couper *(en donnant de petits coups de ciseaux)*

▸ **snip off VT SEP** couper

snipe [snaɪp] **N INV** *(bird)* bécassine *f*

VI *Mil* tirer; *Fig (criticize)* critiquer; **to s. at sb** *Mil* tirer sur qn *(d'une position embusquée)*; *Fig* critiquer qn sournoisement; **to s. at the enemy** canarder l'ennemi; **to be sniped at** se faire canarder

sniper ['snaɪpər] **N** *Mil* tireur *m* embusqué; **to be killed by a s.'s bullet** être tué par un tireur embusqué

▸▸ **s. fire** tir *m* d'embuscade

sniping ['snaɪpɪŋ] **N** *Mil* tir *m* d'embuscade; *Fig* critique *f* sournoise (**at sb** de qn)

ADJ *(criticism, remarks etc)* sournois

snippet ['snɪpɪt] **N** *(small piece)* bout *m*, morceau *m* (coupé); *(of book etc)* court extrait *m*; *(of conversation)* bribes *fpl*

snit [snɪt] **N** *Am* **to be in a s.** faire la gueule

snitch [snɪtʃ] *Sl* **N 1** *(informer)* balance *f* **2** *(nose)* pif *m*

VI *(inform)* moucharder; **to s. on sb** balancer qn

VT *(steal)* chaparder

snivel ['snɪv(ə)l] **N** *(whine)* pleurnichement *m*; **to say sth with a s.** dire qch en pleurnichant

VI (**-ll-**, *Am* **-l-**) *(whine)* pleurnicher

sniveller, *Am* **sniveler** ['snɪv(ə)lər] **N** pleurnicheur, -euse

snivelling, *Am* **sniveling** ['snɪv(ə)lɪŋ] **ADJ** *(person) (whining)* pleurnicheur, -euse; **you s. little idiot!** espèce de pleurnicheur!

N *(whining)* pleurnicherie *f*

snob [snɒb] **N** snob *mf*; **she's a bit of a s.** c'est une snobinarde; **a music s.** un snob en matière de musique

snobbery ['snɒbərɪ] **N** snobisme *m*; **inverted s.** snobisme à rebours; **intellectual s.** snobisme intellectuel

snobbish ['snɒbɪʃ] **ADJ** snob *inv*

snobbishness ['snɒbɪʃnɪs] **N** snobisme *m*

snockered ['snɒkəd] **ADJ** *Am Fam (drunk)* bourré, pété

snog [snɒg] *Br Fam* **VI** se bécoter

VT bécoter

N **to have a s.** se bécoter

snogging ['snɒgɪŋ] **N** *Br Fam* bécotage *m*

snood [snuːd] **N** *(hairnet)* résille *f*

snook [snuːk] **N** *Fam* **to cock a s. at sb** *(make gesture at)* faire un pied de nez à qn; *Fig (defy)* faire la nique à qn

snooker ['snuːkər] **N** *(game)* billard *m* snooker; *(shot)* snooker *m*

VT **to s. sb** *(in game)* empêcher qn de frapper la boule directement; *Fig Fam* mettre qn dans une impasse; *Fig Fam* **now I've snookered myself** je suis coincé maintenant; **to be snookered** *(in game)* se trouver dans l'impossibilité de frapper la boule directement; *Fig* être coincé, être dans une impasse

snoop [snuːp] *Fam* **N 1** = snooper **2 I'll have a s. around** je vais jeter un petit coup d'œil

VI fourrer son nez partout, fouiner; **he was snooping behind the lab** il fouinait derrière le labo

▸ **snoop around VI** *Fam* fourrer son nez partout; **to s. around in sb's papers/desk** fouiller dans les papiers/le bureau de qn

▸ **snooper** ['snu:pər] N *Fam* **1** *(official investigator)* fouine *f* **2 he's a terrible s.** il fourre son nez partout

snoot [snu:t] N *Fam (nose)* blaire *m*, tarin *m*

snooty ['snu:tɪ] ADJ *Fam* arrogant, hautain

snooze [snu:z] *Fam* N **1** petit somme *m*; **to have a s.** faire un petit somme **2** *(on alarm clock)* (position *f*) sommeil *m*
VI sommeiller, faire un petit somme; *(be not quite asleep)* somnoler
▸▸ **s. button** bouton *m* de veille; **s. position** *(on alarm clock)* (position) sommeil

snore [snɔ:r] N ronflement *m*
VI ronfler

snorer ['snɔ:rər] N ronfleur, -euse

snoring ['snɔ:rɪŋ] N ronflement *m*; **the sound of his s.** le bruit de ses ronflements; **his s. could be heard halfway down the corridor** on l'entendait ronfler du milieu du couloir

snorkel ['snɔ:k(ə)l] N *Swimming* tuba *m*; *(of submarine)* schnorchel *m*, schnorkel *m*
VI **to s., to go snorkelling** faire de la plongée avec un tuba

snort [snɔ:t] N **1** *(exhalation)* reniflement *m*; *(of horse etc)* ébrouement *m* **2** *(expressing impatience, disgust)* grognement *m* d'impatience/de dégoût; *(of anger)* grommellement *m*; **s. of laughter** court éclat *m* de rire; **she gave a s. of disbelief** elle a reniflé *ou* pouffé en signe d'incrédulité **3** *Sl (of drink)* petit coup *m*; *(of cocaine)* prise *f*; **he had a quick s. of whisky** il s'est jeté un petit whisky derrière la cravate
VI *(exhale)* renifler bruyamment; *(of horse)* s'ébrouer; **to s. with laughter** pouffer de rire; **to s. in disbelief** pouffer en signe d'incrédulité; **to s. with anger** s'étrangler de colère; *Fig Fam* **to s. at sth** dédaigner qch
VT **1** *(answer)* grogner; **'that's preposterous!', she snorted** 'c'est absurde!', a-t-elle jeté **2** *Sl (cocaine)* sniffer

snorter ['snɔ:tər] N *Sl* **1** *Br (strong letter)* lettre *f* carabinée; **that's a real s. (of a problem)** ça va nous/vous/*etc* donner du fil à retordre **2** *(short drink)* *(of alcohol)* goutte *f*, petit verre *m*

snot [snɒt] N *Fam (from nose)* morve *f*; **a bit of s.** de la morve
▸▸ **s. rag** tire-jus *m inv*, tire-moelle *m inv*

snotty ['snɒtɪ] ADJ *Fam* **1** *(handkerchief)* sale, dégoûtant; *(nose)* couvert de morve; **s.(-nosed)** cradingue, crade; **some s.(-nosed) little brat** un petit morveux **2** *(arrogant)* arrogant; **one of those incredibly officials** un de ces officiels qui pètent plus haut que leur cul

snout [snaʊt] N **1** *(of animal)* museau *m*; *(of pig, hedgehog)* groin *m*; *(of boar)* boutoir *m*; *(of gun)* bout *m* (du canon); *Fam (nose)* naze *m*, tarin *m*, pif *m* **2** *Br Sl (tobacco)* tabac *m* **3** *Br Sl (police informer)* indic *m*

snow [snəʊ] N **1** neige *f*; **the roads are covered with s.** les routes sont enneigées; **to be s. blind** souffrir de cécité des neiges **2** *TV, Radio* neige *f* **3** *Sl (cocaine)* neige *f*, *(heroin crystals)* cristaux *mpl* d'héroïne
V IMPERS neiger; **it's snowing** il neige
▸▸ **s. blindness** cécité *f* des neiges; **s. chains** chaînes *fpl* (à neige); **s. fence** pare-neige *m inv*; **s. goggles** lunettes *fpl* de ski; *Orn* **s. goose** oie *f* des neiges; **s. hole** *(in mountaineering)* trou *m* de neige; *Am Fam* **s. job** baratin *m*; **to give sb a s. job** baratiner qn, rouler qn dans la farine; **s. leopard** léopard *m* des neiges, once *f*, **s. tyre** pneu *m* neige

▸ **snow in** VT SEP *(usu passive)* **to be snowed in** être bloqué par la neige
▸ **snow off** VT SEP *(usu passive)* **the match was snowed off** le match a été annulé à cause de la neige
▸ **snow under** VT SEP *(usu passive)* **snowed under with work** débordé de travail
▸ **snow up** VT SEP *(usu passive)* **to be snowed up** être bloqué par la neige

snowball ['snəʊbɔ:l] N **1** boule *f* de neige; *Can* balle *f* de neige; *Fam* **he hasn't a s.'s chance (in hell)** il n'a pas l'ombre d'une chance **2** *(drink)* snowball *m*
VI *(of story, debts etc)* faire boule de neige **2** *(fight with snowballs)* se battre à coups de boules de neige
▸▸ **s. effect** effet *m* boule de neige; **s. fight** bataille *f* de boules de neige

snowbank ['snəʊbæŋk] N congère *f*

snowbike ['snəʊbaɪk] N motoski *m*

snowboarding ['snəʊbɔ:dɪŋ] N snowboard *m*; **to go s.** faire du snowboard

snowboot ['snəʊbu:t] N après-ski *m*, *pl* après-skis

snowbound ['snəʊbaʊnd] ADJ *(person, airport)* bloqué par la neige

snowcapped ['snəʊkæpt] ADJ couronné de neige

snowdrift ['snəʊdrɪft] N congère *f*

snowdrop ['snəʊdrɒp] N *(flower)* perce-neige *m ou f inv*

snowfall ['snəʊfɔ:l] N chute *f* de neige

snowfield ['snəʊfi:ld] N champ *m* de neige

snowflake ['snəʊfleɪk] N flocon *m* de neige

snowline ['snəʊlaɪn] N limite *f* des neiges éternelles

snowman [, *pl* snowmen ['snəʊmæn, -men] N bonhomme *m* de neige; **they built *or* made a s.** ils ont fait un bonhomme de neige; **the abominable s.** l'abominable homme des neiges

snowmobile ['snəʊməʊbi:l] N *Am (open)* motoneige *f*, *(enclosed)* autoneige *f*

snowplough, *Am* **snowplow** ['snəʊplaʊ] N *Rail, Ski etc* chasse-neige *m inv*

snowshoe ['snəʊʃu:] N raquette *f (pour la neige)*

snowstorm ['snəʊstɔ:m] N tempête *f* de neige

snowsuit ['snəʊsu:t] N combinaison *f* de ski

snow-white ADJ **1** *(in colour)* blanc comme neige **2** *Fig* pur, innocent

snowy ['snəʊɪ] ADJ neigeux; *(day etc)* de neige; *(field etc)* enneigé; *(season)* des neiges; **s. (white) hair** cheveux blancs (comme la neige)

SNP [esen'pi:] N *Pol (abbr* **Scottish National Party)** parti *m* nationaliste écossais

snub [snʌb] N *(refusal)* rebuffade *f*, *(insult)* affront *m*; **to meet with a s.** être rejeté d'une rebuffade
VT *(-bb-)* *(person)* faire un affront à; **I said hello but he just snubbed me** je lui ai dit bonjour mais il m'a ignoré *ou* m'a snobé
ADJ *(nose)* (plat et) retroussé

snub-nosed ['snʌbnəʊzd] ADJ au nez retroussé
▸▸ **s. revolver** revolver *m* au canon court

snuff [snʌf] N tabac *m* à priser; **to take s.** priser; **a pinch of s.** une prise
VT **1** *(extinguish)* *(candle)* moucher; *(hope, enthusiasm etc)* éteindre **2** *Br Sl* **to s. it** *(die)* clamecer, clamser, passer l'arme à gauche **3** *(sniff)* *(air)* humer
▸▸ *Fam* **s. movie** = film *m* pornographique au cours duquel un participant est réellement assassiné
▸ **snuff out** VT SEP *(life)* mettre un terme à; *(opposition)* étouffer; *Fam (person)* éliminer

snuffbox ['snʌfbɒks] N tabatière *f*

snuffer ['snʌfər] N *(for candle)* mouchette *f*

snuffle ['snʌf(ə)l] N **1** *(sniff)* reniflement *m*; *Fam* **snuffles** *(cold)* rhume *m* **2** *(nasal tone)* voix *f* nasillarde
VI **1** *(sniff)* renifler; *(have a cold)* avoir un rhume **2** *(speak in nasal tone)* nasiller, parler en nasillant

snug [snʌg] ADJ *(house etc)* confortable, où l'on est bien; *(person)* *(sheltered)* bien à l'abri; *(warm)* bien au chaud; *(bed)* douillet, -ette; *(jacket)* bien chaud; **to make oneself s.** se mettre à son aise; **to lie s. in bed** être bien au chaud dans son lit; *Fam* **as s. as a bug in a rug** tranquille comme Baptiste; **it's a s. fit** *(of machine part etc)* ça s'emboîte parfaitement; *(of clothing)* c'est bien ajusté; **it's a bit of a s. fit, it's a bit too s.** *(of clothing)* c'est un peu trop serré
N *Br* petite arrière-salle *f (dans un pub)*, *pl* petites arrière-salles

snuggery ['snʌgərɪ] N petite pièce *f* intime (et confortable); *Br (in pub)* petite arrière-salle *f*, *pl* petites arrière-salles

snuggle ['snʌg(ə)l] VI **to s. under the covers** se pelotonner sous les couvertures; **village snuggling in the valley** village niché dans la vallée
VT **to s. a child close to one** serrer un enfant dans ses bras
▸ **snuggle down** VI *(make oneself comfortable)* **to s. down in bed** se blottir (bien au chaud) dans son lit
▸ **snuggle up** VI *(come close)* se pelotonner, se blottir (**to sb** contre qn); **to s. up with a good book** s'installer bien confortablement avec un bon livre

snugly ['snʌglɪ] ADV confortablement; *(warmly)* bien au chaud; **s. wrapped** *(in blanket etc)* douillettement enveloppé; **garment that fits s.** vêtement bien ajusté; **this piece should fit s. into ...** cette pièce devrait s'emboîter parfaitement *ou* exactement dans ...

So. **1** *(abbr* **South)** S. **2** *(abbr* **Southern)** S.

SO [səʊ]

ADV si **1** ▪ tellement **1** ▪ ainsi **2** ▪ environ *(or so)* **2** ▪ pour que *(so that)* **3** ▪ de sorte que *(so that)* **4** ▪ comme si comme ça *(so so)* **5**		
CONJ donc **1, 2**		

ADV 1 *(to such an extent)* si, tellement; **it's so easy** c'est si *ou* tellement facile; **I was so disappointed** j'étais tellement déçu; **we're so pleased you could come** nous sommes tellement *ou* si contents que vous ayez pu venir; **she isn't so very old** elle n'est pas tellement *ou* si vieille; **the young and the not so young** les jeunes et les moins jeunes; **I'm not so sure of that** je n'en suis pas si sûr; **so serious a wound** une blessure aussi grave; **what is so important about this case?** qu'est-ce que cette affaire a de si important?; **he's not so clever as she is** il n'est pas aussi intelligent qu'elle; **she wouldn't be so stupid as to do that** elle ne serait pas bête au point de faire cela, elle ne serait pas assez bête pour faire cela; **would you be so kind as to ...?** voudriez-vous avoir la gentillesse de ...?; **I was so hungry I could have eaten it all** j'avais si faim que j'aurais pu tout manger; **he's so rich that he doesn't know what he's worth** il est riche au point d'ignorer le montant de sa fortune; **I loved her so (much)** je l'aimais tant; **we enjoyed ourselves so much** nous nous sommes tellement amusés; **it's not so much that I dislike them, more that I don't like them** ce n'est pas tant qu'ils me déplaisent, ça serait plutôt qu'ils ne me plaisent pas; **you do exaggerate so!** tu

exagères tellement! VOIR GRAMMAIRE A5

2 *(in this way)* ainsi, de cette façon, de cette manière; **stand just so** tenez-vous ainsi *ou* comme ça; **while he was so occupied ...** pendant qu'il était ainsi occupé ...; **as X is to Y, so Y is to Z** X est à Y ce que Y est à Z; **she so arranged things that ...** elle a fait en sorte que ... + *subj*; **I have been so informed** c'est ce que l'on m'a dit; **so I believe** c'est ce que je crois; **it so happened that I was there** le hasard a voulu que je fusse là, il s'est trouvé que j'étais là; **and so on, and so forth** et ainsi de suite; **so to speak** *or* **say** pour ainsi dire; **has the train gone? – I think so** le train est parti? – je crois *ou* je pense que oui; **he's clever – do you think so?** il est intelligent – vous trouvez?; **I suppose so, I expect so** je (le) suppose; **I hope so** je l'espère bien, j'espère bien; **I'm afraid so** j'en ai bien peur, je le crains; **I didn't say so** moi, je n'ai pas dit cela; **is she really ill? – so it seems** elle est donc vraiment malade? – à ce qu'il paraît; **so I told him** c'est ce que je lui ai dit; **there is a train at six, so I was told** il y a un train à six heures, ou du moins c'est ce qu'on m'a dit; **I'm not very organized – so I see!** je ne suis pas très organisé – c'est ce que je vois!; **I told you so!** je vous l'avais bien dit!; **so much so that ...** à tel point que ..., tellement que ...; **(much) more so** (bien) plus encore; **that's so** c'est bien vrai; **is that so?** vraiment?; **that being so** *(as this is the case)* puisqu'il en est ainsi; *(should this prove the case)* dans ces conditions; **so be it!** soit!, qu'il en soit ainsi!; **if so** s'il en est ainsi; **why so?** pourquoi cela?; **how so?** comment cela?; **perhaps so** cela se peut; **quite so** parfaitement, absolument; **a hundred pounds or so** une centaine de livres; **a week or so** une huitaine de jours; **a little girl so high** une petite fille grande comme ça; **she's right and so are you** elle a raison et vous aussi; **and so am I/are we** et moi/et nous aussi; **he thinks he can do it – so he can** il pense qu'il peut le faire – en effet il le peut; **you're late! – so I am!** vous êtes en retard! – c'est vrai!; **it was Mr Smith – so it was!** c'était Monsieur Smith – en effet!; *Fam* **they aren't French – they are so!** ils ne sont pas français – si! VOIR GRAMMAIRE A29

3 *(purpose)* **so that, so as to** afin que + *subj*, pour que + *subj*, afin de + *inf*, pour + *inf*; **she stood up so as to** *or* **so that she could see better** elle s'est levée afin de *ou* pour mieux voir; **she sat down so that I could see better** elle s'est assise afin que *ou* pour que je puisse mieux voir; **we hurried so as not to be late, we hurried so that we shouldn't be late** nous nous sommes dépêchés pour ne pas être *ou* afin de ne pas être en retard VOIR GRAMMAIRE A75; B58

4 *(consequence)* **so that** de sorte que; **the flight was cancelled so that we had to stay at home** le vol a été annulé de sorte que *ou* si bien que nous avons dû rester à la maison; **the crates had fallen over so that we couldn't get past** comme les caisses étaient tombées, nous n'avons pas pu passer VOIR GRAMMAIRE A75; B58

5 *Fam* **so so** *(not too bad)* comme ci comme ça; **the cooking is only so so** la cuisine n'est pas terrible

CONJ 1 *(therefore)* donc, c'est pourquoi; **she has a bad temper, so be careful** elle a un mauvais caractère, donc faites attention; **he wasn't there, so I came back again** il n'était pas là, donc je suis revenu; **so what?** et alors?; **it's very expensive – so? what am I supposed to do about it?** c'est très cher – et alors? que voulez-vous que j'y fasse?; **so, we're a bit late, what difference does that make?** et alors, nous sommes un peu en retard, quelle différence cela fait-il?

2 so there you are! vous voilà donc!; **so**

that's **what it is!** ah! c'est comme ça!; **so you're not coming?** vous ne venez donc pas?; **so, what do we do?** eh bien, qu'est-ce qu'on fait?

soak [səʊk] **VT 1** *(of liquid, person)* tremper (**in sth** dans qch); *(beans etc)* faire tremper; **the rain soaked me to the skin** la pluie m'a trempé jusqu'aux os; **soaked with blood/sweat** plein de sang/trempé de transpiration; **I got soaked** je me suis tout trempé; *(by rain)* je me suis fait tremper **2** *Fam (customer)* écorcher; **to s. the rich** faire payer les riches

VI baigner, tremper (**in sth** dans qch); *(of liquid)* s'infiltrer, s'imbiber (**into sth** dans qch); **to leave a saucepan to s.** laisser une casserole tremper

N 1 give them a good s. mets-les bien à tremper; **to have a good s. (in the bath)** prendre un bon bain **2** *Fam (drunkard)* poivrot, -ote

▸ **soak in VI** *(of liquid)* pénétrer, être absorbé; *Fig* **has it soaked in yet?** est-ce qu'il a/est-ce que tu as/*etc* pigé?

VT SEP *(absorb)* **to s. in water** s'imprégner d'eau, absorber l'eau; **she went to the main square to s. in the atmosphere** elle est allée sur la place principale pour s'imprégner de son atmosphère

▸ **soak through VI 1** *(seep through to other side)* s'infiltrer à travers **2** *(be absorbed)* pénétrer, s'infiltrer

▸ **soak up VT SEP** *(liquid)* absorber, boire; **to s. up water** s'imprégner d'eau, absorber l'eau; *Fig* **to s. up the sun** se rôtir au soleil; **to s. up the atmosphere** s'imprégner de l'atmosphère

soaked [səʊkt] **ADJ** trempé; *(ground)* détrempé; **s. to the skin, s. through** trempé jusqu'aux os

soaking [ˈsəʊkɪŋ] **N** trempage *m*; **give the beans a good s.** faites tremper les haricots pendant plusieurs heures; **give the clothes a good s.** mettez le linge à tremper pendant un bon moment; **to get a s.** se faire tremper

ADJ *(wet)* trempé; **you're absolutely s.!** vous êtes tout trempé!

ADV s. wet trempé; **to get s. wet** se tremper; *(in rain)* se faire tremper

so-and-so N *Fam* **1** *(unspecified person)* Untel *m*, Unetelle *f*; **Mr S.** Monsieur Untel; **Mrs S.** Madame Unetelle **2** *Pej (unpleasant person)* type *m*; **a crafty s.** une fine mouche, un malin; **you old s.!** *(reproving)* espèce de vilain!; **the old s.!** *(angry)* le salaud!; *(admiring, surprised)* le bougre!; **you greedy old s.** espèce de gourmand!; **don't cry, you silly old s.!** faut pas pleurer, espèce d'idiot!

soap [səʊp] **N** savon *m*; **a bar** *or* **cake of s.** un savon; *(small)* une savonnette; **shaving s.** savon à barbe; **to wash sth with s.** savonner qch **2** *Fam (flattery)* flagornerie *f*, flatterie *f* **3** *Radio, TV Fam* feuilleton *m* (populaire), soap opera *m* **4** *Am Sl* **no s.!** des clous!, des nèfles!

VT *(clothes etc)* savonner

▸ ▸ **s. bubble** bulle *f* de savon; *Radio, TV* **s. opera** feuilleton (populaire), soap opera; **s. powder** lessive *f* (en poudre), poudre *f* à laver; *Radio, TV* **s. star** vedette *f* de feuilleton

▸ **soap down VT SEP** savonner

Soap opera

Le soap opera est un genre radiophonique et télévisé très populaire dans les pays anglophones. Il s'agit de feuilletons diffusés à raison de trois ou quatre épisodes par semaine sur une très longue période. Les soap operas sont ainsi nommés car les premiers d'entre eux étaient financés par des marques de détergents, aux États-Unis. Il n'est pas rare que les soap operas alimen-

tent les conversations de tous les jours, ou soient le sujet d'articles de journaux. Les soap operas britanniques ('Eastenders' et 'Coronation Street' par exemple) ont souvent pour cadre le milieu ouvrier et diffèrent en cela de leurs équivalents américains et australiens dont le ton est beaucoup moins réaliste et dont l'action se déroule le plus souvent dans des milieux privilégiés.

soapbox [ˈsəʊpbɒks] **N 1** *(container)* caisse *f* à savon; *Fig (for speaker)* tribune *f* improvisée *ou* de fortune; **to get up on a s.** faire un discours improvisé, haranguer les foules; **get off your s.!** ne monte pas sur tes grands chevaux! **2** *(go-kart)* chariot *m*, ≃ kart *m* *(sans moteur)*

▸ ▸ **s. orator** personne *f* qui harangue les foules

soapdish [ˈsəʊpdɪʃ] **N** porte-savon *m*, *pl* porte-savons

soap-dodger N *Br Fam Hum (man)* mec *m* cradingue; *(woman)* bonne femme *f* cradingue

soapflakes [ˈsəʊpfleɪks] **NPL** savon *m* en paillettes

soapiness [ˈsəʊpɪnɪs] **N** *(of something)* caractère *m* savonneux

soapstone [ˈsəʊpstəʊn] **N** stéatite *f*

soapsuds [ˈsəʊpsʌdz] **NPL** *(lather)* mousse *f* de savon; *(water)* eau *f* savonneuse

soapy [ˈsəʊpɪ] **ADJ 1** *(water)* savonneux; *(body)* couvert de savon; *(taste)* de savon; **this beer tastes s.** cette bière a un goût de savon **2** *Fam (flattering) (person, voice)* doucereux, onctueux

soar [sɔːr] **VI** *esp Lit (fly up)* prendre son essor, s'élever; *(glide)* planer; *(of spirits)* remonter en flèche; **rents have soared** les loyers ont augmenté de façon vertigineuse

soaring [ˈsɔːrɪŋ] **ADJ** *(bird, arrow)* qui monte *ou* s'élève dans les airs; *(steeple)* élancé; *(price, popularity etc)* qui monte en flèche; **the s. flight of the eagle** le vol majestueux de l'aigle

N *(rising)* *(of bird)* essor *m*; *(of prices)* hausse *f*

sob [sɒb] **N** sanglot *m*; **with a s. in her voice** la voix étouffée par un sanglot

VI (-bb-) sangloter

VT *(say)* dire en sanglotant; **she sobbed herself to sleep** elle s'est endormie en sanglotant

▸ ▸ *Am Fam* **s. sister** journaliste *f* qui fait le courrier du cœur; *Fam Pej* **s. story** histoire *f* larmoyante, histoire à vous fendre le cœur; *Fam* **to tell sb a s. story** raconter une histoire pour apitoyer qn; *Fam Pej* **s. stuff** sensiblerie *f*, mélo *m*

▸ **sob out VT SEP 1** *(say)* dire en sanglotant **2 to s. one's heart out** pleurer à chaudes larmes

s.o.b. [esəʊˈbiː] **N** *esp Am Sl (abbr* **son of a bitch)** fils *m* de pute, salaud *m*

sobbing [ˈsɒbɪŋ] **ADJ in a s. voice** d'une voix brisée par les sanglots

N sanglots *mpl*

sober [ˈsəʊbər] **ADJ 1** *(not drunk)* sobre; **as s. as a judge** *(temperate)* sobre comme un chameau; *(serious)* sérieux comme un pape; **when he's s. (again)** quand il sera dessoûlé **2** *(moderate)* sobre, modéré; *(calm)* calme, posé; *(face)* grave; *(colours, dress)* sobre; **s. opinion** opinion *f* réfléchie; **the s. truth** la simple vérité

VT dessoûler; **this news sobered him** cette nouvelle l'a dégrisé

▸ **sober down VI** *(become calmer)* s'assagir

VT SEP dégriser

▸**sober up** VI *(become less drunk)* se dégriser; **s. up!** reprends-toi!
VT SEP dessoûler; *(of news etc)* dégriser

sobering ['səʊbərɪŋ] ADJ qui dégrise; **it's had a s. effect on him** ça l'a dégrisé; **it's a s. thought** ça vous fait réfléchir

sober-minded ADJ *(serious)* sérieux, réfléchi

soberness ['səʊbənɪs] N **1** *(not drinking)* sobriété f **2** *(of style, dress, character)* sobriété f, *(seriousness)* sérieux m

sobersides ['səʊbəsaɪdz] N *Old-fashioned Fam (solemn person)* bonnet m de nuit

sobriety [səʊ'braɪətɪ] N *also Fig* sobriété f

Soc 1 *abbr* **society 2** *abbr* **Socialist**

so-called [-'kɔːld] ADJ **1** *(so named)* appelé ainsi, ainsi nommé; **the s. temperate zone** la zone dite tempérée **2** *(supposed)* **a s. doctor** un soi-disant *ou* un prétendu docteur; **s. progress** de prétendus progrès

soccer ['sɒkər] N football m, foot m
▸▸**s. match** match m de football *ou* de foot; *Am* **s. mom** = femme f de milieu bourgeois qui accompagne et encourage ses enfants lors de leurs séances d'entraînement de foot; **s. pitch** terrain m de football; **s. player** footballeur, -euse

sociability [səʊʃə'bɪlɪtɪ] N sociabilité f

sociable ['səʊʃəb(ə)l] ADJ sociable; **I had a drink with them to be s.** j'ai pris un verre avec eux pour me montrer sociable; **to become more s.** *(of person) (become less shy)* s'apprivoiser; *(become more friendly)* devenir plus sociable; **I'm not feeling very s. at the moment** je n'ai pas envie de voir du monde en ce moment; **I'm not in a s. mood** je ne suis pas d'humeur à voir du monde

sociably ['səʊʃəblɪ] ADV sociablement; **she's not very s. inclined** elle n'est pas très mondaine

social ['səʊʃəl] ADJ **1** social, -aux; **to have a busy s. life** *(see a lot of people)* voir beaucoup de monde; *(go out a lot)* sortir beaucoup; **work is getting in the way of my s. life** j'ai trop de travail pour pouvoir sortir; **since he's been married, he's had to give up his s. life** depuis son mariage, il ne voit presque plus personne; **to be sb's s. equal** être l'égal de qn sur le plan social; **the s. ladder** l'échelle f sociale; **to take sth into s. ownership** nationaliser qch
2 *Zool* social, -aux; **man is a s. animal** l'homme est un animal grégaire
N *(party)* soirée f
▸▸**s. benefits** prestations fpl sociales; *EU* **the S. Chapter** le volet social *(du traité de Maastricht)*; **s. class** classe f sociale; **s. climber** arriviste mf; **s. climbing** arrivisme m; **s. democrat** social-démocrate m, pl sociaux-démocrates, sociale-démocrate f, pl sociales-démocrates; **s. disease** = maladie f provoquée par des facteurs socio-économiques; *Euph (venereal)* maladie vénérienne; **s. drinker** = personne f qui ne boit d'alcool qu'en société; **s. drinking** = consommation f d'alcool lors de réunions entre amis; **s. engineering** manipulation f des structures sociales; **s. evening** *(party)* soirée f; *(gathering)* réunion f, **s. fund** = caisse f d'aide sociale; **s. group** catégorie f socio-professionnelle, CSP f, **s. marketing** marketing m social; **s. movement** mouvement m social; **s. order** ordre m social; **s. outcast** paria m; **s. position** rang m dans la société; **s. reformer** réformateur, -trice de la société; **s. sciences** sciences fpl humaines; **to be on** *or* **get s. security** toucher une aide sociale; *Am* **s. security number** numéro m de Sécurité sociale; **s. services** services mpl sociaux; **s. work** assistance f sociale, travail m

social; **s. worker** assistant, -ante social(e), travailleur, -euse social(e)

socialism ['səʊʃəlɪz(ə)m] N socialisme m

socialist ['səʊʃəlɪst] ADJ, N socialiste mf

socialite ['səʊʃəlaɪt] N membre m de la haute société, homme m/femme f du monde

socialize ['səʊʃəlaɪz] VI **to s. with sb** fréquenter qn; *(chat)* bavarder avec qn; **he won't s.** il n'accepte jamais une invitation; **they do a lot of socializing** ils voient beaucoup de gens
VT *Econ (property)* nationaliser
▸▸*Am* **socialized medicine** médecine f d'État

socially ['səʊʃəlɪ] ADV socialement; **to be s. active** *(go out a lot)* sortir beaucoup; *(see a lot of people)* voir beaucoup de monde; **we don't do much s.** nous sortons peu, nous fréquentons peu de gens; **I saw her s. for a while, but nothing beyond that** je l'ai vaguement fréquentée pendant un temps, mais rien de plus; **I don't know him s. at all, just at work** en dehors du travail, je ne le connais pas du tout; **s. mobile** mobile sur le plan social; **s. disadvantaged** défavorisé

society [sə'saɪətɪ] N **1** *(social community, company)* société f; **he's a danger** *or* **menace to s.** c'est un danger pour la société; **to avoid the s. of one's colleagues** éviter la compagnie de ses collègues; **this word isn't used in polite s.** on n'utilise pas ce mot chez les gens bien élevés; **consumer s.** société de consommation
2 *(nation, group)* société f, **primitive/industrial societies** des sociétés primitives/industrielles
3 *(fashionable circles)* **(high) s.** la haute société, le *(beau ou grand)* monde; **s. people** gens mpl du monde; **a s. wedding** un mariage dans le grand monde
4 *(body)* société f, *(association)* association f, charitable f œuvre f de bienfaisance *ou* de charité; *Br* **National S. for the Prevention of Cruelty to Children** organisation f de protection de l'enfance
▸▸*Journ* **s. column** chronique f mondaine; *Rel* **the S. of Friends** la Société des Amis, les Quakers mpl; **the S. of Jesus** la Compagnie de Jésus; **S. for the Protection of the Unborn Child** = ligue f contre l'avortement

> Note that the French word **société** is also used as a translation for the English words **company** and **firm**.

sociocultural [səʊsɪəʊ'kʌltʃər(ə)l] ADJ socioculturel

socioeconomic [səʊsɪəʊiːkə'nɒmɪk] ADJ socio-économique
▸▸**s. grouping** classification f socio-économique

sociolinguistic [səʊsɪəʊlɪŋ'gwɪstɪk] ADJ sociolinguistique

sociolinguistics [səʊsɪəʊlɪŋ'gwɪstɪks] N sociolinguistique f VOIR GRAMMAIRE A10

sociological [səʊsɪə'lɒdʒɪk(ə)l] ADJ sociologique

sociologist [səʊsɪ'ɒlədʒɪst] N sociologue mf

sociology [səʊsɪ'ɒlədʒɪ] N sociologie f

sociometry [səʊsɪ'ɒmɪtrɪ] N sociométrie f

sociopath ['səʊsɪəpæθ] N inadapté, -ée

socioprofessional [səʊsɪəʊprə'feʃən(ə)l] ADJ socioprofessionnel
▸▸**s. group** catégorie f socioprofessionnelle, CSP f

sock¹ [sɒk] N *(Am pl also* **sox)** *(garment)* chaussette f, **(ankle) socks** socquettes fpl; *Br Fig Fam* **to pull one's socks up** se secouer; *Br Fam* **put a s. in it, will you!** ferme-la!

sock² *Fam* N *(blow)* gnon m, beigne f, *(in the*

eye*)* cocard m; **to give sb a s. on the jaw** flanquer une beigne à qn
VT *(hit) (person)* flanquer une beigne à; **s. it to me!** *(show me what you can do)* montre-moi ce que tu sais faire!

socket ['sɒkɪt] N *Anat (of eye)* orbite f, *(of tooth)* alvéole f, *(of bone)* cavité f articulaire, glène f, *(of pipe) (in plumbing)* emboîtement m, manchon m; *esp Br (for electric plug)* prise f (de courant); *(of lightbulb)* douille f, *Comput (slot)* prise (femelle); *(on Internet)* socket f, port m; *(tool)* douille f, embout m; **ball and s. joint** *Anat* énarthrose f, *Tech* articulation f, **microphone s.** prise microphone
▸▸**s. set** coffret m de douilles

Socrates ['sɒkrətiːz] N Socrate

Socratic [sɒ'krætɪk] ADJ socratique

sod¹ [sɒd] N *(piece of turf)* motte f de gazon; **to cut** *or* **turn the first s.** donner le premier coup de bêche; **under the s.** *(buried)* enterré

sod² *esp Br Sl* N *(obnoxious person or thing)* **he's a real s.** c'est un vrai salaud; **you silly s.!** espèce d'imbécile!; **you stupid s.!** andouille!; **poor s.!** pauvre bougre!; **he's a rude s.!** quel ours!; **the kid's being an absolute little s.!** ce gosse est une vraie peste!; **this problem/screw is a real s.!** ce putain de problème/cette putain de vis!; **odds and sods** petits bouts mpl, bribes fpl et morceaux mpl
VT *(to damn)* **s. you!** va te faire foutre!; **s. them!** ils peuvent toujours aller se faire voir!; **s. the party, I'm tired** la soirée, je m'en fous, je suis fatigué; **s. it!** merde, alors!
▸**sod off** VI *esp Br Sl (go away)* foutre le camp; **s. off!** fous-moi le camp!; **I told him to s. off** je lui ai dit d'aller se faire voir

soda ['səʊdə] N **1** *Chem etc* soude f, **caustic s.** soude caustique; **washing s.** carbonate m de soude; **bicarbonate of s., baking s.** bicarbonate m de soude **2** *(fizzy water)* eau f de Seltz **3** *Am (soft drink)* soda m
▸▸**s. bread** pain m à la levure chimique; *Am* **s. cracker** = biscuit m sec à la levure chimique; *Am* **s. fountain** *(café)* ≃ café m; *(device)* siphon m (d'eau de Seltz); **s. water** eau de Seltz

sod-all *esp Br Sl* N *(nothing)* que dalle; **that's got s. to do with it!** ça n'a foutrement rien à voir avec ça!; **they do s. all day** ils n'en fichent pas une rame de la journée
ADJ ATTRIB **I have s. money** je n'ai pas un putain de rond; **they've got s. hope of winning** ils n'ont pas une putain de chance de gagner

sodden ['sɒd(ə)n] ADJ *(field)* (dé)trempé; *(clothes etc)* trempé; **s. with drink** imbibé d'alcool

sodding ['sɒdɪŋ] *esp Br Sl* ADJ *(as intensifier)* **this s. weather/government/car** ce putain de temps/de gouvernement/cette putain de voiture; **he's a s. nuisance!** c'est un sacré emmerdeur!
ADV vachement; **you can s. well do it yourself!** démerde-toi tout seul pour le faire!; **don't be so s. lazy!** ce que tu peux être flemmard!

sodium ['səʊdɪəm] N *Chem* sodium m
▸▸**s. chloride** chlorure m de sodium

Sodom ['sɒdəm] N Sodome f

sodomite ['sɒdəmaɪt] N sodomite m

sodomize ['sɒdəmaɪz] VT sodomiser

sodomy ['sɒdəmɪ] N sodomie f

Sod's law [sɒdz] N loi f de l'emmerdement maximum

sofa ['səʊfə] N canapé m
▸▸**s. bed** canapé-lit m, pl canapés-lits

SOFT [sɒft]

| ADJ mou **1** • doux **1, 2** • tendre **1, 2** • souple **1** • indulgent **3** • tranquille **3** • stupide **4** |

ADJ 1 *(substance, ground, cheese etc)* mou, *f* molle; *(pillow, carpet, fabric, toilet paper etc)* doux, *f* douce, moelleux; *(rock, pencil etc)* tendre; *(hat)* mou; *(leather)* souple; **a nice s. bed** un lit moelleux; **this bed is too s.** ce lit est trop mou; **as s. as silk** doux comme de la soie; **s. to the touch** doux au toucher; **s. skin** peau douce *ou* veloutée; **to become** *ou* **get s.** s'amollir

2 *(gentle) (voice, music, rain, wind etc)* doux, *f* douce; *(shade, blue etc)* tendre; **s. step** pas feutré *ou* de loup; **s. words** mots doux *ou* tendres

3 *(person) (not strict)* indulgent, coulant; *(easy) (job, life etc)* tranquille; **Fam to be s. on sb** *(fond of)* être amoureux *ou* entiché de qn; *(lenient towards)* être coulant avec qn; **you mustn't be so s. with** *or* **on them** il faut les traiter plus sévèrement; **to have a s. spot for sb** avoir un faible pour qn; *Fam* **to be a s. touch** *(of person) (easy to get money from)* être facile à taper; *(easy to take advantage of)* être bonne poire; **to have a s. heart** avoir le cœur tendre

4 *Fam (stupid)* stupide, bête; **don't be s.!** ne sois pas bête!; **he's gone s. in the head!** il a perdu la boule!

ADV *Fam* **don't talk s.!** ne dis pas de bêtises!
► ► *Ling* **s. consonant** consonne *f* douce; *Comput* **s. copy** visualisation *f* sur écran; *Fin* **s. currency** devise *f* faible; **s. drinks** boissons *fpl* non alcoolisées; **s. drugs** drogues *fpl* douces; *Phot* **s. focus** flou *m* artistique, point *m* diffus; **s. fruit** ≃ fruits *mpl* rouges; *Br* **s. furnishings** tissus *mpl* d'ameublement; *Comput* **s. hyphen** césure *f* automatique, tiret *m* conditionnel; *Comput* **s. key** touche *f* programmable; *Aviat, Astronaut, Econ* **s. landing** atterrissage *m* en douceur; **s. lighting** éclairage *m* diffus; *Econ, Fin* **s. loan** prêt *m* avantageux *ou* à des conditions avantageuses; **s. option** solution *f* de facilité; **s. outline** contour *m* flou; **s. page break** changement *m* conditionnel de page; **s. porn** pornographie *f* peu explicite, *Fam* soft *m*; *Comput* **s. reset** simple réinitialisation *f*, *Comput* **s. return** saut *m* de ligne automatique; *Comput* **s. sectoring** formatage *m* logiciel; *Com* **s. sell** = méthodes *fpl* de vente non agressives; **s. shoulder** *(on road)* accotement *m* non stabilisé; **s. space** espace *m* ressort; *Anat* **s. tissue** parties *fpl* charnues; **s. verge** *(on road)* accotement *m* non stabilisé; **s. water** eau *f* douce *ou* non calcaire

softback ['sɒftbæk] **N** (livre *m* de) poche *m*
► ► **s. version** version *f* poche

softball ['sɒftbɔːl] **N** *Am Sl* = variante *f* du baseball qui se joue avec une balle plus grande et plus molle

soft-boiled ADJ *(egg)* mollet

soft-centre, *Am* **soft-center N** *(chocolate)* chocolat *m* fourré

soft-centred, *Am* **soft-centered ADJ** *(chocolate, sweet)* fourré

soft-core ADJ *(pornography)* soft *inv*

soft-cover N *esp Am* (livre *m* de) poche *m*

soften ['sɒf(ə)n] **VT** *(wax etc)* ramollir; *(skin)* adoucir; *(leather)* assouplir; *(person) (physically)* ramollir; *(emotionally)* attendrir; *(colour)* adoucir, atténuer; *(voice, personality, water etc)* adoucir; *(light, contrast etc)* atténuer; *(one's tone)* radoucir; *(person's anger)* calmer, atténuer; **troops softened by idleness** troupes amollies par l'oisiveté; **the government has softened its stance in its talks with the unions** le gouvernement a adouci sa position lors des négociations avec les syndicats; *Fig* **to s. the blow** amortir le choc
VI *(of wax etc)* se ramollir; *(of skin etc)* s'adoucir; *(of meat)* s'attendrir; *(of person)* se radoucir; *(of anger)* se calmer; **the union's stance has softened** le syndicat a adouci sa position

► **soften up VT SEP 1** *(make softer)* adoucir **2** *Mil etc (prisoner, suspect etc)* réduire la résistance de **3** *(hard-hearted person)* amadouer
VI = soften VI

softener ['sɒf(ə)nər] **N water s.** adoucisseur *m* d'eau; **fabric s.** adoucissant *m*

softening ['sɒf(ə)nɪŋ] **N** *(of wax etc)* ramollissement *m*; *(of leather)* assouplissement *m*; *(of character, attitudes, water)* adoucissement *f*; *(of light, contrast, outlines)* atténuation *f*; *Hum* **he has suffered from a s. of the brain** son cerveau s'est ramolli; **there has been a s. of attitudes** il y a eu un adoucissement *ou* un fléchissement des attitudes

soft-faced hammer [-feɪst] **N** maillet *m*

soft-focus ADJ
► ► **s. lens** objectif *m* pour créer des effets de flou

softheaded [sɒft'hedɪd] **ADJ** *Fam* bête, niais

softhearted [sɒft'hɑːtɪd] **ADJ** au cœur tendre, sensible; **he's too s.** il a trop de cœur

softie ['sɒftɪ] **N** *Fam* = **softy**

softly ['sɒftlɪ] **ADV** *(to talk, whisper, tap etc)* doucement; *(to walk)* sans bruit; *(tenderly)* tendrement; *(to land)* en douceur; **the room is s. lit** l'éclairage de la pièce est doux; **the prisoners are treated too s.** les prisonniers ne sont pas traités assez sévèrement

softly-softly ADJ *(approach etc)* doux, *f* douce

softness ['sɒftnɪs] **N 1** *(of skin, fabric, climate etc)* douceur *f* **2** *(of character)* mollesse *f*; *(of outlines)* flou *m* **3** *Fam (foolishness)* niaiserie *f*

soft-pedal VI 1 *Mus* mettre la pédale douce **2** *Fam (not emphasize strongly)* y aller doucement, ne pas trop insister
VT *Fig* atténuer, amoindrir

soft-sectored [-sektəd] **ADJ** *Comput (disk)* formaté par programme, à secteurs logiciels

soft-soap VT *Fam* flatter, passer la pommade à

soft-spoken ADJ to be very s. avoir la voix très douce

soft-top N *Aut* décapotable *f*

software ['sɒftweər] **N** *Comput* logiciel *m*, software *m*; **all the s. written for ...** tous les logiciels réalisés pour ...; **a piece of s.** un logiciel
► ► **s. company** éditeur *m* de logiciels; **s. developer** développeur, -euse; **s. engineer** ingénieur *m* logiciels; **s. error** erreur *f* de logiciel; **s. house** éditeur *m* de logiciel; **s. package** logiciel *m*; **s. piracy** piratage *m* de logiciels; **s. platform** plate-forme *f* logicielle, *pl* plates-formes logicielles; **s. problem** problème *m* de logiciel; **s. tool** outil *m* logiciel; **s. writer** concepteur *m* de logiciel

software-compatible ADJ compatible du point de vue logiciel

softwood ['sɒftwʊd] **N** *Carp etc* bois *m* tendre

softy ['sɒftɪ] **N** *Fam (gentle person)* cœur *m* sensible; *(coward)* couard, -arde; **to be a terrible s.** *(sentimental)* être sentimental à l'excès; **you know I'm a big s.** *(can't say no)* tu sais que je suis trop gentil

SOGAT ['səʊɡæt] **N** *Br abbr* **Society of Graphical and Allied Trades**

soggy ['sɒɡɪ] **ADJ** *(ground)* détrempé, imbibé; *(clothes, carpet, shoes, bread)* trempé; *(cake)* imbibé

soh [səʊ] **N** *Mus* sol *m inv*

soil [sɔɪl] **N 1** *(earth)* terre *f*; **to cultivate the s.** cultiver la terre; **alluvial s.** terrain *m* d'alluvion(s); *Lit* **one's native s.** sa terre natale **2** *Old-fashioned* **night s.** *(excrement)* excréments *mpl* humains

VT *(clothes, sheet, underwear)* souiller, salir; **they had soiled the carpet with mud** ils avaient maculé la moquette de boue; *Fig* **to s. one's hands** se salir les mains; *Fig* **to s. sb's reputation** salir la réputation de qn
VI fabric that soils easily tissu salissant *ou* qui se salit facilement

soiled [sɔɪld] **ADJ** *(dressings)* usagé; *(bedlinen)* souillé; *(goods)* défraîchi; *Fig (reputation)* entaché; **if it's s., the shop won't exchange it** si c'est sale, la boutique ne fera pas l'échange; **some slightly s. items at reduced prices** des articles légèrement salis à prix réduits

soirée ['swɑːreɪ] **N** soirée *f*

soixante-neuf [swæsɑːnt'nɜːf] **N** soixante-neuf *m*

sojourn ['sɒdʒɜːn] *Lit* **N** séjour *m*
VI séjourner

sol [sɒl] **N** *Mus* sol *m inv*

solace ['sɒləs] *Lit* **N** consolation *f*, soulagement *m*; **to find s. in sth** trouver une consolation dans qch
VT *(person)* consoler; **I solaced myself with this thought** cette pensée m'a consolé

sola of exchange ['səʊlə] **N** *Fin* seule *f* de change

solar ['səʊlər] **ADJ** *(system, energy etc)* solaire
► ► **s. battery** batterie *f* solaire; **s. cell** pile *f* solaire, photopile *f*; **s. eclipse** éclipse *f* solaire; **s. panel** panneau *m* solaire; *Anat* **s. plexus** plexus *m* solaire; **s. power** énergie *f* solaire

solarium, *pl* **solaria** [səʊ'leərɪəm, -ɪə] **N** solarium *m*

solar-powered ADJ à énergie solaire

sold PT, PP *see* **sell**

solder ['sɒldər, 'səʊldər] **N** soudure *f*
VT souder

soldering ['sɒldərɪŋ, 'səʊldərɪŋ] **N** soudure *f*
► ► **s. iron** fer *m* à souder

soldier ['səʊldʒər] **N** soldat *m*, militaire *m*; **private s.** simple soldat, (soldat de) deuxième classe *m*; **to become a s.** se faire soldat, entrer dans l'armée; **an old s.** un ancien soldat, un vétéran; **tin s.** soldat de plomb
VI *(be a soldier)* faire le métier de soldat
► ► **s. ant** (fourmi *f*) soldat; **s. of fortune** soldat de fortune

► **soldier on VI** *Br (persevere)* persévérer; **we soldiered on through the blizzard** nous avons progressé à grand-peine dans le blizzard; **I'll s. on with this for another half hour** je vais encore m'escrimer là-dessus pendant une demi-heure

soldiering ['səʊldʒərɪŋ] **N** la carrière militaire *ou* des armes; **he was tired of s.** il avait assez du métier de soldat; **to go s.** se faire soldat

soldierlike, soldierly ['səʊldʒəlaɪk, -lɪ] **ADJ** de soldat

soldiery ['səʊldʒərɪ] **N** *(no pl) Old-fashioned (soldiers)* soldats *mpl*, militaires *mpl*

sole¹ [səʊl] **N** *(of foot)* plante *f*; *(of shoe)* semelle *f*
VT *(shoe) (fit with sole)* mettre une semelle à; *(resole)* ressemeler

sole² **N** *(fish)* sole *f*; **Dover s.** (vraie) sole

sole³ **ADJ 1** *(only)* seul, unique; **his s. reason** son unique raison **2** *(exclusive)* exclusif; **to have s. responsibility for sth** être entièrement responsable de qch
► ► **s. agency** représentation *f* exclusive; **s. agency contract** contrat *m* de représentation exclusive; **s. agent** agent *m* exclusif; **s. contract** contrat exclusif; **s. right** droit *m* exclusif; *Br Com* **s. trader** entreprise *f* individuelle *ou* unipersonnelle

solecism ['sɒlɪsɪz(ə)m] **N** *Ling* solécisme *m*; *Fml (social error)* bévue *f*

solely [ˈsəʊllɪ] ADV seulement, uniquement; **I went there s. to see it** j'y suis allé dans le seul but de le voir

solemn [ˈsɒləm] ADJ **1** (oath etc) solennel; (duty) sacré; (question) grave; Law **s. agreement** contrat m solennel; **s. warning** avertissement m formel **2** (person) grave, sérieux; (tone, atmosphere) solennel; **to look s.** avoir l'air solennel

solemness [ˈsɒləmnɪs] N = **solemnity 1**

solemnity [səˈlemnɪtɪ] N **1** (of occasion, ceremony) solennité f; (of expression, attitude) gravité f, sérieux m; **with all s.** en toute solennité **2** Lit **the solemnities** (religious festival) les fêtes fpl solennelles, les solennités fpl

solemnization [sɒləmnaɪˈzeɪʃən] N (of marriage) célébration f

solemnize [ˈsɒləmnaɪz] VT (religious festival) solenniser, célébrer; (marriage) célébrer

solemnly [ˈsɒləmlɪ] ADV **1** (to promise etc) solennellement **2** (seriously) gravement; (to speak) avec solennité

solenoid [ˈsɒlənɔɪd] N Elec solénoïde m ►► **s. switch** contacteur m à solénoïde

solfa [ˈsɒlfɑː] N Mus **tonic s.** solfège m

solicit [səˈlɪsɪt] VT **1** solliciter (**from sb** de qn); (votes) solliciter, briguer **2** (of prostitute) (customers) racoler ▸ VI (of prostitute) racoler

solicitation [səlɪsɪˈteɪʃən] N sollicitation f

soliciting [səˈlɪsɪtɪŋ] N Law (of prostitute) racolage m

solicitor [səˈlɪsɪtər] N **1** Br Law (for drawing up documents, conveyancing) ≃ notaire m; (for court work, divorce cases) avocate, -ate **2** (seeking trade etc) solliciteur, -euse ►► Br **S. General** conseiller m juridique de la Couronne

solicitous [səˈlɪsɪtəs] ADJ Lit (eager) soucieux, désireux (**of sth** de qch); (concerned) préoccupé; (caring) plein de sollicitude; **s. attention to detail** soin méticuleux des détails

solicitously [səˈlɪsɪtəslɪ] ADV avec sollicitude

solicitousness [səˈlɪsɪtəsnɪs], **solicitude** [səˈlɪsɪtjuːd] N sollicitude f, préoccupation f

solid [ˈsɒlɪd] ADJ **1** (brick, stone, business), Fig (business) solide; (mass, line) compact; (gold, silver) massif; (tyre) plein; (wall) plein, sans ouvertures; (in a single piece) en une seule pièce, d'un seul tenant; Fig **a s. wall of demonstrators** un mur compact de manifestants; **frozen s.** (water, pond) gelé jusqu'au fond; Fig **there is s. support for the proposal** il y a une majorité de gens en faveur de la proposition; Pol etc **the union was s. behind him** le syndicat était tout entier derrière lui; **the town was s. for Labour** la ville a massivement voté Travailliste; **the workers were s. behind the strike** les employés étaient tous pour la grève; **to become s.** (of fluid) se solidifier; **s. as a rock** (ice, mud) dur comme de la pierre; Fig solide comme le roc; **to build on s. foundations** bâtir sur des fondations solides; Fig construire sur des bases solides; **on s. ground** sur un terrain ferme; **man of s. build** homme bien charpenté; **s. common sense** solide bon sens; **to have s. reasons for believing sth** avoir de bonnes raisons de croire qch; **a good s. meal** un repas consistant; **some good s. research** des recherches bien concrètes; **to sleep/work for nine s. hours** dormir/travailler neuf heures d'affilée; **three days' s. rain** trois jours de pluie continue; **s. vote** vote m massif

2 Am Fam (excellent) génial, -aux, super ▸ N solide m; **solids** (food) aliments mpl solides; **is the baby on solids yet?** le bébé mange-t-il déjà des aliments solides?
▸ ADV **1 to sleep/work for nine hours s.** dormir/travailler neuf heures d'affilée **2** Am Fam (absolutely) absolument; **I s. gotta do it!** il faut absolument que je le fasse!
►► Math **s. angle** angle m solide; **s. food** nourriture f solide; **s. fuel** combustible m solide

solidarity [sɒlɪˈdærɪtɪ] N solidarité f; **to show s. with sb** faire preuve de solidarité envers qn

solidification [səlɪdɪfɪˈkeɪʃən] N solidification f; (of oil) congélation f

solidify [səˈlɪdɪfaɪ] VT **1** solidifier; (oil) congeler **2** Fig (union, fact) consolider ▸ VI **1** se solidifier; (of oil) se congeler **2** Fig (of opinions etc) se consolider

solidity [səˈlɪdɪtɪ] N solidité f

solidly [ˈsɒlɪdlɪ] ADV **1** solidement; (without interruption) sans interruption, sans s'arrêter; **s. held** tenu fermement ou solidement; **s. built man** homme bien charpenté **2** (to vote) massivement; **we're s. behind you** nous vous soutenons à fond

solid-state ADJ (physics) des solides; (electronics, circuit, device) à semi-conducteurs ►► **s. electronics** semi-conducteurs mpl

solidus [ˈsɒlɪdəs], pl **solidi** [-daɪ] N Typ barre f oblique

soliloquize [səˈlɪləkwaɪz] VI faire un monologue, soliloquer

soliloquy [səˈlɪləkwɪ] N soliloque m, monologue m

solitaire [sɒlɪˈteər] N **1** (game with pegs etc) solitaire m; Am Cards (jeu m de) patience f, réussite f **2** (gem) solitaire m

solitary [ˈsɒlɪt(ə)rɪ] ADJ solitaire; (on one's, its own) seul, solitaire; (isolated) isolé; **not a s. one** pas un seul ▸ N Fam régime m (d'isolement) cellulaire; **he got three months' s.** il a pris trois mois de cachot ►► **s. confinement** isolement m cellulaire; **to be kept in s. confinement** être détenu en régime (d'isolement) cellulaire

solitude [ˈsɒlɪtjuːd] N solitude f; **to live in s.** vivre dans la solitude

solo [ˈsəʊləʊ] N **1** Mus solo m; **violin s.** solo de violon **2** (flight) vol m solo **3** Cards solo m (variante du whist) ▸ ADV **1** Mus en solo; **to play/to sing s.** jouer/chanter en solo **2** (unaided) seul, en solitaire, en solo; **to fly s.** voler en solo; **to go s.** Cards jouer solo; (of business partner, member of rock group etc) faire une carrière en solo ▸ ADJ **1** Mus solo; **she plays s. violin** elle est soliste de violon, elle est violon solo **2** (unaided) en solitaire; **a s. act** un one-man-show ►► **s. album** album m solo; **s. flight** vol solo; **her first s. flight** son premier vol en solo; Cards **s. whist** solo (variante du whist)

soloist [ˈsəʊləʊɪst] N Mus soliste mf

Solomon Islands [ˈsɒləmən] NPL îles fpl Salomon

solstice [ˈsɒlstɪs] N solstice m; **the winter/summer s.** le solstice d'hiver/d'été

solubility [sɒljʊˈbɪlɪtɪ] N (of a salt etc) solubilité f

soluble [ˈsɒljʊb(ə)l] ADJ **1** soluble (**in water** dans l'eau) **2** (problem) soluble

solution [səˈluːʃən] N **1** (act of solving) (of difficulty, equation) résolution f, solution f **2** (answer) (to problem) solution f; **there is no real s. to this** il n'y a aucune solution dans ce cas **3** (fluid) solution f; **salt in s.** sel m en solution

solvable [ˈsɒlvəb(ə)l] ADJ (problem) soluble

Note that the French adjective **solvable** is a false friend and is never a translation for the English adjective **solvable**. It means **financially solvent**.

solve [sɒlv] VT (problem, equation, riddle) résoudre; (mystery) éclaircir

solvency [ˈsɒlvənsɪ] N Com, Law solvabilité f

solvent [ˈsɒlvənt] ADJ **1** Com, Law solvable **2** (liquid) dissolvant, solvant ▸ N dissolvant m, solvant m ►► **s. abuse** usage m de solvants hallucinogènes; **s. abuser** toxicomane mf utilisant des solvants hallucinogènes

Som abbr Somerset

Somali [səˈmɑːlɪ] ADJ somali, somalien ▸ N **1** Somali, -ie; **the S.** (pl) les Somalis mpl **2** Ling somali m

Somalia [səˈmɑːlɪə] N Somalie f

Somaliland [səˈmɑːlɪlænd] N Hist Somalie f

somatic [səˈmætɪk] ADJ Biol somatique

sombre, Am **somber** [ˈsɒmbər] ADJ (colour etc) sombre; (person, look) sombre; (mood) maussade; **to be in a s. mood** être d'humeur maussade

sombrely, Am **somberly** [ˈsɒmbəlɪ] ADV (to look at sb etc) d'un air sombre; **s. dressed** habillé de couleurs sombres

sombrero [sɒmˈbreərəʊ] N sombrero m

SOME [sʌm] VOIR GRAMMAIRE A34–5; B14–15

ADJ	quelconque **1** ▪ certains **1** ▪ de, du, de la, des **2** ▪ intensive **3**
PRON	certains **1** ▪ quelques-uns **1, 2** ▪ un peu **2**
ADV	environ

ADJ **1** (not specified) **s. (sort of)** excuse une excuse quelconque; **he'll come s. day** il arrivera un de ces jours; **s. days she is better** certains jours elle va mieux; **s. books are difficult to read** certains livres sont difficiles à lire, il y a des livres qui sont difficiles à lire; **s. people say ...** certaines personnes disent ..., il y en a qui disent ...; **s. fool left the door open** un imbécile a laissé la porte ouverte; **s. bureaucrat decided the road would be here** un bureaucrate quelconque a décidé que la route passerait ici; **s. book or other** un livre quelconque

2 (certain quantity, number) de; **to drink s. water** boire de l'eau; **I ate s. fruit** j'ai mangé des fruits; **s. strange people appeared** d'étranges personnes ou des personnes étranges ont fait leur apparition; **s. people** des personnes; (a few) quelques personnes; **s. people think ...** il y a des gens qui pensent ...; **I felt s. uneasiness** je ressentais quelque inquiétude; **that would be s. help** cela faciliterait un peu les choses; **in s. measure, to s. degree** jusqu'à un certain point, dans une certaine mesure; **s. distance away** à quelque distance, à une certaine distance; **s. days ago** il y a quelques jours; **for s. time** pendant quelque temps ou un certain temps; **he has been waiting for s. time** il attend depuis quelque temps ou depuis un certain temps; **it will be s. time** or **s. little while before it's finished** ça va prendre un certain temps ou un moment avant que ça soit fini; **at s. length** assez longuement SEE GRAMMAR B5

3 Fam (intensive) **(that was) s. storm!** quelle tempête!; **she's s. girl!** c'est une fille formidable!; **that was s. meal!** ce que nous avons bien mangé!, Fam ce qu'on s'est mis!; **s. people!** il y a des gens, vraiment! Iron **s. father you are!** quel père tu fais!; **s. hope!** tu peux toujours rêver!

PRON **1** (people) certain(e)s, quelques-uns,

quelques-unes; **s. or all of them** tous ou seulement certains d'entre eux; **s. believe that …** certains croient que …, il y en a qui croient que …; **they went off, s. one way, s. another** ils se sont dispersés, les uns d'un côté, les autres de l'autre *ou Lit* qui d'un côté, qui de l'autre; **s. of my friends** certains de mes amis

2 *(things, quantity) (referring to countable nouns)* quelques-uns, quelques-unes; *(referring to uncountable nouns)* un peu; **s. of the guests had already left** quelques invités étaient déjà partis; **s. of the money has been recovered** on a retrouvé une partie de l'argent; **I have s.** j'en ai; **give me s.** donnez-m'en; **I've s. more** *(I have some left)* j'en ai encore; *(I have some others)* j'en ai d'autres; **s. of the time** une partie du temps; **Norway has s. of the most beautiful scenery in the world** les paysages de la Norvège sont parmi les plus beaux du monde; **at least there's** <u>some</u> **left** *(not nothing)* il en reste quand même un peu

ADV **1** *(approximately)* environ, quelque *inv*; **s. thirty pounds** une trentaine de livres, quelque trente livres; **s. fifteen minutes** un bon quart d'heure; **s. few minutes ago** il y a quelques minutes

2 *Am Fam (intensive)* **to go it s.** y aller en plein; **it annoyed him s.** ça l'a plutôt énervé

somebody ['sʌmbədɪ] PRON *(some person)* quelqu'un; **s. told me so** quelqu'un *ou* on me l'a dit; **s. I know told me** quelqu'un que je connais me l'a dit; **he's not s. you can trust** ce n'est pas quelqu'un en qui on peut avoir confiance; **s. is knocking** on frappe; **s. is missing** il manque quelqu'un; **s. (or other) has told him** quelqu'un lui a dit; **is this s.'s wallet?** est-ce que ce portefeuille est à quelqu'un?; **s. important** quelqu'un d'important; **we need s. a bit taller/who speaks Russian** il nous faut quelqu'un d'un peu plus grand/qui parle russe; *Fam* **Mr S. (or other)** quelqu'un; **there was a Mr S. (or other) to see you** il y a a M. Machin (Truc) qui voulait te voir; **s. else** quelqu'un d'autre; **he went and s. else came along** il est parti et un autre est venu VOIR GRAMMAIRE A34; B16

PRON, N *(pl* **somebodies** ['sʌmbədɪz]*) (important person)* **he's (a) s.** c'est un personnage, ce n'est pas le premier venu; **she thinks she's s.** elle se croit quelqu'un, elle ne se prend pas pour n'importe qui; **I want to be s.** je veux être quelqu'un

someday ['sʌmdeɪ] ADV un jour

somehow ['sʌmhaʊ] ADV **1** *(in some way or other)* d'une façon ou d'une autre, d'une manière ou d'une autre; **we'll manage it s. (or other)** nous y parviendrons tant bien que mal; **s. we got there on time** nous nous sommes débrouillés pour arriver à l'heure **2** *(for some reason or other)* **I never liked her s.** pour une raison ou pour une autre, elle ne m'a jamais été sympathique; **s. (or other) it's different** il y a pourtant une différence; **s. it doesn't seem right** je ne sais pas pourquoi mais j'ai l'impression que c'est faux

someone ['sʌmwʌn] PRON = **somebody**

someplace ['sʌmpleɪs] ADV *Am* = **somewhere**

somersault ['sʌməsɔːlt] N *(on ground or accidental)* culbute *f*; *(in air)* saut *m* périlleux; **to turn** *or* **do a s.** *(on ground or accidentally)* faire la culbute; *(in air)* faire un saut périlleux; *(of car)* faire un tonneau

VI *(of person) (on ground or accidentally)* faire la/des culbute(s); *(in air)* faire un/des saut(s) périlleux; *(of car)* faire un/des tonneau(x); **the car somersaulted twice** la voiture a fait deux tonneaux; **he's good at somersaulting** il est doué pour les culbutes/les sauts périlleux

['sʌmθɪŋ] VOIR GRAMMAIRE A34; B16

N, PRON **1** quelque chose *m*; **I've brought you a little s.** je vous ai apporté un petit quelque chose *ou* une bricole; **say s.** dites quelque chose; **s. or other was bothering her** quelque chose l'ennuyait; **Anne s. (or other)** Anne je ne sais plus quoi; **there's s. about him I don't like** il y a en lui quelque chose qui me déplaît; **s. tells me she'll come** quelque chose me dit qu'elle viendra; **s. has happened** il est arrivé quelque chose; **was it s. I said?** est-ce que j'ai dit quelque chose (qu'il ne fallait pas)?; **s. to drink/eat/read** quelque chose à boire/manger/lire; **to ask for s. to drink** demander (quelque chose) à boire; **can I get you s.?** est-ce que je peux vous offrir quelque chose (à manger/à boire)?; **let's have s. to eat** mangeons quelque chose; **it must have been s. he ate that made him ill** ça doit être quelque chose qu'il a mangé qui l'a rendu malade; **s. to live for** une raison de vivre; **to have s. to cry/be annoyed about** avoir une bonne raison de pleurer/se fâcher; **to have s. to hang on to** avoir quelque chose à quoi se raccrocher; **s. new** quelque chose de nouveau *ou* de neuf; **I've s. else to do** j'ai autre chose à faire; **he's in a bank** il travaille dans une banque; **in the year eleven hundred and s.** en l'an onze cent et quelque chose; **she's eighty s.** elle a quatre-vingts ans et quelques, *Fam* elle a quatre-vingts ans et des poussières; **a certain (indefinable) s.** un je-ne-sais-quoi; **he has seen s. of the world** *(is mature, experienced)* il connaît la vie; *(has travelled)* il a pas mal voyagé; **her plan has s. in it, there's s. in her plan** son projet mérite considération; **there's s. in what you say** il y a de la vérité dans ce que vous dites; **she has s. to do with it** elle y est pour quelque chose; **it's s. to do with the way he speaks** ça a un rapport avec la façon dont il parle; **well, that's s.!** c'est déjà quelque chose!; **that was quite s.!** c'était vraiment quelque chose!; *Fam* **that meal was s. else!** c'était quelque chose, ce repas; *Fam* **he really is s. else!** il est pas possible!; **she's an accountant or s.** elle est comptable ou quelque chose comme ça; **is it broken or s.?** c'est cassé ou quoi?; **she's off work with a cold or s.** elle n'est pas venue travailler à cause du rhume, je crois; **he bought it from a man in a bar or s.** je crois qu'il l'a acheté à un type dans un bar

2 there's s. of an improvement il y a une certaine amélioration; **she's s. of a miser** elle est un peu *ou* quelque peu avare

ADV **1 it looks s. like a guinea pig** ça ressemble à un cochon d'Inde; **s. like 500** 500 environ, quelque chose comme 500; **is this s. like him?** est-ce que ça lui ressemble un peu?; **s. like that** quelque chose comme ça

2 *Fam (intensifying)* **he treated me s. awful** il m'a traité d'une façon abominable; **he fancies her s. rotten** il en est amoureux comme pas possible

sometime ['sʌmtaɪm] ADV *(often written as two words)* **s. (or other)** un jour ou l'autre; **you'll have to make your mind up s.** tôt ou tard, il faudra que tu prennes une décision; **the last time I saw him was s. in August** la dernière fois que je l'ai vu, c'était en août; **we'll talk about it s. before/after Christmas** on en reparlera à un moment ou à un autre avant/après Noël; **I'll do it s.** je vais le faire; **I hope to go there s.** j'espère y aller un jour; **s. before 7 o'clock** avant 7 heures; **s. last year** au cours de l'année dernière; **s. in August** pendant le mois d'août; **s. before last Tuesday** avant mardi dernier; **s. between 1997 and 2001** entre 1997 et 2001; **s. soon** bientôt; *Fam* **see you s.!** à bientôt!

ADJ ATTRIB *Lit* **Mr Martin, my s. tutor** M. Martin, autrefois mon professeur

> Attention: ne pas confondre avec **sometimes**.

sometimes ['sʌmtaɪmz] ADV quelquefois, parfois; **s. one, s. the other** tantôt l'un, tantôt l'autre

> Attention: ne pas confondre avec **sometime**.

somewhat ['sʌmwɒt] ADV un peu, quelque peu; **it's s. difficult** c'est assez difficile

N **he was s. of a coward** il était assez poltron; **this was s. of a relief** ce fut, en quelque sorte, un soulagement

somewhere ['sʌmweər] ADV **1** *(in or to some place)* quelque part; **it's s. in the Bible** cela se trouve quelque part dans la Bible; **s. near us** pas bien loin de nous; **s. along the way** sur le chemin, quelque part en chemin; **now we're getting s.!** voilà un premier résultat!, enfin nous avançons!; **I need s. quiet to work** j'ai besoin d'un endroit calme pour travailler; **s. in the world** quelque part (dans le monde); **s. in France** quelque part en France; **s. else** ailleurs, autre part; **s. or other** je ne sais où; **he lives s. near Oxford** il habite dans les environs d'Oxford

2 *(approximately)* **he is s. around fifty** il a à peu près cinquante ans; **it costs s. in the region of £500** cela coûte environ 500 livres; **there were s. around 50 kilobytes left** il restait environ 50 kilo-octets

sommelier ['sɒməljeɪ] N sommelier *m*

somnambulism [sɒm'næmbjʊlɪz(ə)m] N somnambulisme *m*

somnambulist [sɒm'næmbjʊlɪst] N somnambule *mf*

somniferous [sɒm'nɪfərəs] ADJ somnifère, soporifique; *Fig* soporifique

somnolence ['sɒmnələns] N *Fml* somnolence *f*

somnolent ['sɒmnələnt] ADJ *Fml* somnolent

son [sʌn] N **1** *(family member)* fils *m*; **she's got two sons** elle a deux garçons; *Fig* **a s. of the people** un fils du peuple; *Am Sl* **s. of a bitch** *(obnoxious person)* fils *m* de pute, salaud *m*; *Am Fam* **s. of a gun** coquin *m*; *Rel* **the S. of God** le fils de Dieu; *Rel* **the S. of Man** le fils de l'homme

2 *Fam (term of address)* fiston *m*; **OK, s.?** *(lad)* OK, mon petit gars?

sonar ['səʊnɑ:r] N *Naut* sonar *m*

sonata [sə'nɑ:tə] N *Mus* sonate *f*

sonatina [sɒnə'ti:nə] N *Mus* sonatine *f*

sonde [sɒnd] N *Met etc* sonde *f*

son et lumière ['sɒneɪ'lu:mjeə(r)] ADJ spectacle *m* son et lumière, son et lumière *m*

song [sɒŋ] N **1** chanson *f*, *Lit* chant *m*; *Rel* cantique *m*; **marching s.** chanson de route; **give us a s.** chantez-nous quelque chose; *Fam* **to buy sth for a s.** acheter qch pour rien *ou* pour une bouchée de pain; *Fam* **it went for a s.** cela s'est vendu pour une bouchée de pain; *Fam* **he made a great s. and dance about it** il en a fait tout un plat; *Lit* **s. of victory** chant de victoire; **s. of praise** *Lit* louanges *fpl*; *Rel* cantique *m*; *Lit* **with a s. in one's heart** la joie au cœur, le cœur léger; *Bible* **the S. of Songs, the S. of Solomon** le Cantique des Cantiques; **a festival of French s.** un festival de la chanson française; *Fam* **to be on s.** *(of engine)* tourner rond; *(of team)* être en bonne forme

2 *(singing)* chant *m*; **to burst** *or* **break into s.** se mettre à chanter; **the s. of the birds** le chant *ou* le ramage des oiseaux

▸▸ **s. book** recueil *m* de chansons, chansonnier *m*

songbird ['sɒŋbɜːd] N oiseau *m* chanteur

songster ['sɒŋstər] N **1** *(singer)* chanteur *m* **2** *(poet)* poète *m*, chantre *m* **3** = **songbird**

songstress ['sɒŋstrɪs] N *(singer)* chanteuse *f*

songwriter ['sɒŋraɪtər] N *Mus (writes the music)* compositeur, -trice (de chansons); *(writes the words)* parolier, -ière; *(writes both)* auteur-compositeur *m*, *pl* auteurs-compositeurs

sonic ['sɒnɪk] ADJ *Phys* acoustique, audible; *Aviat (speed)* sonique
  ▸ ▸ **s. boom** bang *m*

son-in-law, *pl* **sons-in-law** N gendre *m*, beau-fils *m*, *pl* beaux-fils

sonnet ['sɒnɪt] N *(in poetry)* sonnet *m*

sonny ['sʌnɪ] N *Fam* mon petit gars *m*, fiston *m*; **look here, s. Jim** *or* **boy** attention, mon petit gars

sonority [sə'nɒrɪtɪ] N sonorité *f*

sonorous ['sɒnərəs] ADJ **1** *(resonant)* sonore **2** *(grandiloquent)* grandiloquent

> Note that the French adjective **sonore** only applies to sounds.

sonorously ['sɒnərəslɪ] ADV *(to speak)* d'une voix sonore; **the organ boomed s.** l'orgue résonnait

sonorousness ['sɒnərəsnɪs] N sonorité *f*

soon [suːn] ADV VOIR GRAMMAIRE A21 **1** *(within a short time)* bientôt; **how s. can you get here?** combien de temps vous faut-il pour y aller?; **s. after** peu après; **s. after four** (un) peu après quatre heures; **it will s. be three years since ...** voici bientôt trois ans que ..., cela fera bientôt trois ans que ...; **he'll be here very s.** il sera ici sous peu, il sera ici très bientôt; **must you leave so s.?** vous faut-il partir si tôt?; **too s.** trop tôt, avant l'heure; **an hour too s.** *(to arrive etc)* avec une heure d'avance; **they were s. making friends** ils se sont bien vite fait des amis; **it ended all too s.** cela a fini bien trop tôt; **none too s.** juste à temps

2 as s. as aussitôt que, dès que; **I'll see him as s. as he comes** je le verrai aussitôt *ou* dès qu'il arrivera; **as s. as I arrived in London** dès mon arrivée à Londres; **as s. as he saw them** dès qu'il les a vus; **as s. as possible** le plus tôt possible, aussitôt que possible, dès que possible SEE GRAMMAR B31–2

3 sooner *(earlier)* plus tôt; **we would have got there sooner if ...** nous serions arrivés plus tôt si ...; **the sooner you begin, the sooner you will have finished** plus tôt vous commencerez, plus vite vous aurez fini; **the problem should be dealt with sooner rather than later** il faut faire face au problème le plus tôt possible; **the sooner the better** le plus tôt sera le mieux; **sooner or later** tôt ou tard; **no sooner said than done** (aus)sitôt dit, (aus)sitôt fait; **no sooner had he finished than he was arrested** à peine eut-il fini qu'il fut arrêté

4 *(preference)* **I would just as s. stay** j'aime autant rester; **I would die sooner than give in** je mourrais plutôt que de céder; **I would sooner die** j'aimerais mieux mourir; **someone will have to do it – sooner you than me!** quelqu'un devra le faire – il vaudrait mieux que ce soit vous, plutôt que moi!

5 soonest *(to do sth)* aussitôt que possible; **it will be next week at the soonest** ce sera la semaine prochaine au plus tôt; *Prov* **least said soonest mended** moins on en dit, mieux ça vaut

soot [sʊt] N suie *f*

sooth [suːθ] N *Arch* **in s.** en vérité

soothe [suːð] VT *(pain, burn etc)* calmer, apaiser; *(the mind)* tranquilliser; *(person)* apaiser; **to s. sb's anger** apaiser la colère de qn

▸ **soothe down** VT SEP *(make less angry, worried) (person)* calmer

soothing ['suːðɪŋ] ADJ calmant, apaisant; *Med* lénitif; **in a s. voice** d'une voix apaisante

soothingly ['suːðɪŋlɪ] ADV *(to say)* d'un ton apaisant

soothsayer ['suːθseɪər] N *Arch* devin *m*, devineresse *f*

soothsaying ['suːθseɪɪŋ] N *Arch* divination *f*

sooty ['sʊtɪ] ADJ **1** *(covered in soot)* couvert de suie; *(black)* noir de suie **2** *(deposit)* de suie; *(resembling soot)* fuligineux

sop [sɒp] N **1** *(bread)* morceau *m* de pain trempé **2** *Lit (concession)* concession *f*; **as a s. to his conscience** pour soulager sa conscience; **he just said that as a s. to her feelings** il a dit ça seulement pour lui plaire *ou (if she is angry etc)* pour l'amadouer; **a concession that was not much more than a s. to the unions** une concession qui n'avait pour but que d'amadouer les syndicats
  VT (**-pp-**) *(bread)* (faire) tremper

▸ **sop up** VT SEP *(mop up) (liquid)* éponger; **the paper towel sopped up the water** l'essuie-tout a absorbé toute l'eau

soph [sɒf] N *Am Fam (sophomore)* étudiant, -ante de deuxième année

sophism ['sɒfɪz(ə)m] N sophisme *m*

sophist ['sɒfɪst] N sophiste *mf*

sophistical [sə'fɪstɪk(ə)l] ADJ sophistique, captieux

sophisticate [sə'fɪstɪkɪt] N personne *f* sophistiquée

sophisticated [sə'fɪstɪkeɪtɪd] ADJ *(person)* sophistiqué; *(in matters of food, wine, conversation, tastes etc)* raffiné; *(style)* recherché, sophistiqué; *(plan)* subtil; *(machinery)* (très) perfectionné; *(technology)* sophistiqué; **for the s. look this winter ...** si vous voulez être élégante cet hiver ...; **our more s. readers** nos lecteurs les plus cultivés; **teenagers think it's very s. to ...** les adolescents pensent que ça fait très bien de ...

sophistication [səfɪstɪ'keɪʃən] N *(of person) (appearance)* raffinement *m*, sophistication *f*; *(tastes)* goûts *mpl* raffinés; *(of style, dress)* recherche *f*; *(of machinery)* (degré *m* de) perfectionnement *m*

sophistry ['sɒfɪstrɪ] N **1** *(reasoning)* sophistique *f*, **to indulge in s.** se laisser aller à la sophistique **2** *(example)* sophisme *m*

Sophocles ['sɒfəkliːz] N Sophocle *m*

sophomore ['sɒfəmɔːr] N *Am Univ* étudiant, -ante de seconde année; **I'm a s.** je suis en deuxième année (de fac)

soporific [sɒpə'rɪfɪk] ADJ somnifère, soporifique
  N somnifère *m*

soppiness ['sɒpɪnɪs] N *Br Fam (sentimentality)* sentimentalisme *m*, sensiblerie *f*

sopping ['sɒpɪŋ] ADJ **s. (wet)** *(person)* trempé jusqu'aux os; *(shirt, cloth)* détrempé

soppy ['sɒpɪ] ADJ *Br Fam* **1** *(sentimental) (person)* gnangnan *inv*; *(sentiment)* fadasse; *(story, film etc)* à l'eau de rose **2** *(silly)* stupide, bête; **don't be s.!** ne sois pas si bête!

soprano, *pl* **sopranos, soprani** [sə'prɑːnəʊ, -əʊz, -iː] N *Mus (singer)* soprano *mf*, *(voice, part, instrument)* soprano *m*; **to sing s.** avoir une voix de soprano
  ADJ *(voice, part)* de soprano; *(music)* pour soprano
  ▸ ▸ **s. saxophone** saxophone *m* soprano; **s. voice** voix *f* de soprano

sorb [sɔːb] N **1** *(fruit)* sorbe *f* **2** *(tree)* sorbier *m*

sorbet ['sɔːbeɪ] N *Culin (water ice)* sorbet *m*

sorbitol ['sɔːbɪtɒl] N sorbitol *m*

sorcerer ['sɔːs(ə)rər] N sorcier *m*

sorceress ['sɔːs(ə)rɪs] N sorcière *f*

sorcery ['sɔːs(ə)rɪ] N sorcellerie *f*

sordid ['sɔːdɪd] ADJ sordide; *(place etc)* sale, crasseux; *(business, motives)* bas, *f* basse, vil

sordidly ['sɔːdɪdlɪ] ADV sordidement

sordidness ['sɔːdɪdnɪs] N sordidité *f*, *(of place etc)* saleté *f*, *(of business, motives)* bassesse *f*

sore [sɔːr] ADJ **1** *(painful)* douloureux, endolori; *(eyes, throat, gums)* irrité; **s. to the touch** douloureux au toucher; **s. throat** mal *m* de gorge; **I've (got) a s. throat** j'ai mal à la gorge, j'ai la gorge irritée; **to have a s. finger** avoir mal au doigt; **it's still s.** ça fait toujours mal; *Fig* **it's a s. point** *or* **subject with him** il est très sensible sur ce point

2 *esp Am Fam (annoyed)* embêté (**about** au sujet de); *(upset)* chagriné (**about** par); **Mom's s. because I forgot her birthday** Maman a de la peine parce que j'ai oublié son anniversaire

3 *Am Fam (angry)* en rogne; **to be** *or* **get s.** se ficher en rogne

4 *Lit* **to be in s. need of sth** avoir grandement besoin de qch
  N *Med* plaie *f*, *Fig* **to (re)open an old s.** raviver une plaie ancienne; **(running) s.** ulcère *m*

sorehead ['sɔːhed] N *esp Am Fam* ronchon, -onne

sorely ['sɔːlɪ] ADV **1** *Lit (painfully)* **s. wounded** gravement *ou* grièvement blessé **2** *(greatly)* gravement, grandement; **s. distressed** dans une grande *ou* profonde détresse; **s. needed** dont on a grandement besoin; **s. tempted** fortement tenté; **s. tried** cruellement éprouvé

soreness ['sɔːnɪs] N *Med* douleur *f*

sorghum ['sɔːgəm] N *(plant)* sorgho *m*

sorrel[1] ['sɒrəl] N *(plant)* oseille *f*

sorrel[2] ADJ *(horse)* alezan
  N *(colour, horse)* alezan *m*

sorrow ['sɒrəʊ] N douleur *f*, chagrin *m*; **to my s.** à mon (grand) regret; **more in s. than in anger** avec plus de tristesse que de colère; *Bible* **the Man of Sorrows** l'Homme *m* de douleur
  VI *esp Lit* s'affliger, être affligé (**over** *or* **at** *or* **about sth** de qch); **to s. for** *or* **after sb/sth** pleurer qn/qch

sorrowful ['sɒrəfʊl] ADJ *(person)* triste, affligé, chagriné; *(look, smile)* affligé; *(news, situation)* triste, attristant

sorrowfully ['sɒrəfʊlɪ] ADV tristement

sorrowing ['sɒrəʊɪŋ] ADJ affligé

SORRY ['sɒrɪ]

> désolé **1** ▪ pardon **1** ▪ regretter *(to be sorry)* **1** ▪ piteux **2**

ADJ **1** *(regretful)* fâché, chagriné, désolé (**about sth** de qch); **she's s. she did it** *or* **for having done it** elle regrette de l'avoir fait; **to be s. not to have done sth** regretter *ou* avoir du regret de ne pas avoir fait qch; **I'm only s. we couldn't have stayed longer** je regrette que nous n'ayons pas pu rester plus longtemps; *Fam* **you'll be s.!** il vous en cuira!, vous vous en repentirez!; **you'll be s. you ever came here!** vous allez regretter d'être venu ici!; **I'll make him s.** je le lui ferai regretter; **I'll make him s. (that) he ever came here** je lui ferai regretter d'être venu ici; **I'm s. I ever let him in the house** je regrette de l'avoir laissé entrer dans la maison; **I'm (very) s. to hear that ...** je regrette (infiniment) que ..., je suis désolé d'apprendre que ...; **you won't be s. you bought a ...** vous ne regretterez pas d'avoir acheté un ...; **I'm s. to say that ...** je regrette d'avoir à vous dire que ...; **I'm so s. to keep you waiting** excusez-moi de vous faire attendre; **(I'm) s.!** pardon!, excusez-moi!; **s.?** *(what?)* pardon?; **s., did you really mean what you said earlier?** à propos, parliez-vous sérieusement tout à l'heure?; **I'm s., but that's crap!** je suis désolé, mais c'est de la merde!; **so s.!** vraiment désolé!; **s., I can't help** désolé, je ne peux rien pour vous; **to feel s. for sb** *(take pity on)* avoir pitié de qn; *(feel sympathy for)* plaindre qn; **I'm s. for him** *(I feel pity for him)* il me fait pitié; *(I sympathize with him)* je le plains; **to look s. for oneself** faire grise mine; **he's just feeling s. for himself** il s'apitoie sur son sort; **once you've stopped feeling s. for yourself** une fois que tu auras fini de te plaindre; **I'm just feeling a bit s. for myself** je suis un peu déprimé; **I don't usually feel this s. for myself** d'habitude, je ne me laisse pas aller comme ça; **to say one is s. (for sth)** demander pardon (pour qch); **say s. to the lady** *(to child)* demande pardon à la dame

2 *(pitiful)* misérable, piteux; **to be in a s. plight** être dans une mauvaise passe; **to be in a s. state** être dans un piteux état; **to cut a s. figure** faire piètre figure; **it was/they were a s. sight** c'était/ils offraient un spectacle navrant; **the whole s. tale** toute cette malheureuse affaire

---

sorry-ass, sorry-assed ADJ *Am Sl (inferior, contemptible)* à la con; **that s. son-of-a-bitch stole my woman!** cet enfoiré m'a piqué ma gonzesse!

SORT [sɔːt]

N sorte **1** ▪ genre **1** ▪ espèce **1** ▪ un peu *(sort of)* **2** ▪ tri **4**	
VT trier, classer	
VI trier	

N 1 *(kind)* sorte *f*, genre *m*, espèce *f*; **all sorts of people** des gens de toutes sortes; **it takes all sorts (to make a world)** il faut de tout (pour faire un monde); **what s. of tree is it?** quelle sorte d'arbre est-ce?; **what s. of day did you have?** comment s'est passée ta journée?; **what s. of a man is he?** quelle sorte d'homme est-ce?; **she's not the s. to give in easily** elle n'est pas du genre à abandonner facilement; **I know your s.!** je connais les gens comme toi!; *Fam* **she's a good s.** c'est une fille sympa; **we don't want your s. here** nous ne voulons pas de gens comme vous ici; **these s. of people** ces gens-là; **you get all sorts at these parties** on rencontre toutes sortes de gens dans ces soirées; **I've heard all sorts of things about him** j'en ai entendu de toutes les couleurs sur son compte; **I can't stand that s. of thing** je ne peux pas souffrir ce genre de chose; **something of the s.** *or* **of that s.** quelque chose de pareil *ou* de semblable *ou* dans ce genre-là; **nothing of the s.!** *(not in the least)* pas du tout!; **he's a liar – he's nothing of the s.!** c'est un menteur – pas du tout!; **I've a s. of feeling that …** j'ai comme l'impression que …; **the trees formed a s. of arch** les arbres formaient comme une arche; **that's my s. of holiday** voilà des vacances comme je les aime; *Pej* **coffee of a s.** du soi-disant café; **a peace of sorts** une paix, si l'on peut dire; **he is some s. of writer** il est écrivain mais je ne sais pas quel genre de livres il écrit; *Pej* **a writer of sorts** un écrivaillon; **to make some s. of (a) reply** répondre d'une façon quelconque *ou* tant bien que mal; **to be out of sorts** *(a little unwell)* être mal fichu, ne pas être dans son assiette; *(in a bad mood)* être de mauvaise humeur VOIR GRAMMAIRE A13

2 *Fam (used adverbially)* **s. of** *(a bit)* plutôt, un peu; *(in a way)* d'une certaine façon; **it's s. of heavy** c'est un peu lourd, c'est plutôt lourd; **I s. of feel that …** j'ai dans l'idée que

…, j'ai comme l'impression que …; **I s. of expected it** je m'en doutais un peu; **it's getting s. of late** il se fait tard, quoi; **did he say sorry? – s. of** il s'est excusé? – en quelque sorte; **he s. of apologized** d'une certaine façon, il s'est excusé

3 *Old-fashioned (manner)* **in this s.** de cette manière *ou* façon; **in some s.** en quelque sorte, d'une certaine manière

4 *(order)*, *Comput* tri *m*; **to have a quick s. through the mail** faire un tri rapide du courrier, trier rapidement le courrier; **to do a s.** trier

VT *(make selection from)* *(something)* trier, faire le tri de; *(put together)* assortir; *(papers etc)* classer; *Comput* trier; **to s. sth in ascending/descending order** trier qch par ordre croissant/décroissant; **to s. the letters** *(in post office)* trier les lettres; **to s. things into categories** classer des choses par catégories; **s. these documents into piles** triez ces documents et faites-en des piles; **it's the kind of drink that sorts the men from the boys** c'est une boisson d'hommes; **situations like this s. the men from the boys** des situations comme celle-ci vous permettent de savoir qui est un homme

VI *Comput (arrange in list)* trier; *(of file, data)* se trier; **s. on this field to a new file** trier à partir de ce champ et sauvegarder les données réordonnées dans un nouveau fichier

▸▸ *Banking* **s. code** code *m* guichet; *Comput* **s. routine** routine *f* de tri

▸ **sort out** VT SEP **1** *(eliminate by sorting)* trier, sélectionner; **to s. out the foreign stamps from the British ones** séparer les timbres étrangers des timbres britanniques

2 *(organize)* *(papers, desk etc)* mettre de l'ordre dans; **it's time she sorted herself out** il est temps qu'elle se reprenne; **give me a few minutes to get (myself) sorted out** *or* **to s. myself out** *(on arrival in office, at home etc)* donnez-moi quelques minutes pour souffler; *(arrange papers for meeting etc)* donnez-moi quelques minutes pour m'organiser; **to s. out who's sleeping where** décider qui dort où; **to s. out a room/some clothes for sb** *(allocate)* préparer une chambre/des vêtements pour qn; **I'll go and s. the tickets out** *(make arrangements for, obtain)* je vais m'occuper des billets; **I've sorted out the tickets** j'ai tout arrangé en ce qui concerne les billets

3 *(establish, clarify)* **we never sorted out what really happened** nous n'avons jamais compris ce qui s'était vraiment passé; **let's s. out how much we owe you** voyons combien nous vous devons; **to s. out the details** mettre au clair les détails; **you've got to s. out your priorities** il faut que tu définisses ce qui prime pour toi

4 *Fam (deal with)* *(problem)* régler; *(difficult person)* régler son compte à; **everything's sorted out now** tout est arrangé *ou* réglé maintenant; **two aspirins ought to s. out that headache** deux aspirines devraient avoir raison de ce mal de tête

▸ **sort through** VT INSEP *(search among)* *(old clothes, papers etc)* faire un *ou* le tri dans; **to s. through the mail** dépouiller le courrier

sorta [ˈsɔːtə] CONTR *Fam* = **sort of**

sorted [ˈsɔːtɪd] *Br Fam* ADJ **to be s.** *(psychologically)* être bien dans ses baskets; *(have everything one needs)* être paré; **to be s. for sth** disposer de qch; **are you s. for whizz?** t'as ce qu'il te faut comme speed?; **if I get that pay rise, I'll be s.** si j'obtiens cette augmentation j'aurai plus à m'en faire INT super!, génial!

sorter [ˈsɔːtər] N **1** *(person)* trieur, -euse; *(who classifies)* classeur, -euse **2** *(device)* machine *f* trieuse; **(letter) s.** trieur *m* de lettres

sortie [ˈsɔːtɪ] N *Mil, Aviat etc* sortie *f*; **I make the occasional s. to the shops** de temps en temps, je vais faire un tour dans les magasins

sorting [ˈsɔːtɪŋ] N triage *m*, tri *m*; *(classifying)* classement *m*; *Comput* tri

▸▸ *Comput* **s. algorithm** algorithme *m* de tri; **s. office** centre *m* de tri

SOS [esəʊˈes] N SOS *m*; **to send (out) an S.** envoyer un SOS; *Fig* **relief organizations are sending out an S. for food and clothing** les organisations d'aide demandent d'urgence de la nourriture et des vêtements

▸▸ **S. call** appel *m* de détresse

sot [sɒt] N ivrogne *m*

> Note that the French word **sot** is a false friend and is never a translation for the English word **sot**. It means **fool**.

sottish [ˈsɒtɪʃ] ADJ *(person)* abruti par l'alcool; *(behaviour)* d'ivrogne

sotto voce [sɒtəʊˈvəʊtʃɪ] ADV *(to speak)* tout bas

soufflé [ˈsuːfleɪ] N *Culin* soufflé *m*; **cheese/spinach s.** soufflé au fromage/aux épinards

▸▸ **s. dish** moule *m* à soufflé

sough [saʊ] *Lit* N *(of wind)* murmure *m* VI *(of wind)* murmurer

sought PT, PP *see* **seek**

sought-after ADJ *(job, car etc)* recherché; **much s.** très recherché

soul [səʊl] N **1** *(spirit)* âme *f*; **to throw oneself body and s. into sth** se donner corps et âme à qch; *Old-fashioned* **upon my s.!** sur mon âme!; **he's the s. of discretion** il est la discrétion même; **departed souls** les âmes des trépassés *ou* des disparus; **to pray for sb's s.** prier pour l'âme de qn; **to sell one's s.** vendre son âme; *Fig* **this music's/drama's got no s.** cette musique/ce théâtre n'a pas d'âme; **God rest her s.!** que Dieu ait son âme!; **All Souls' Day** la Fête des Morts

2 *(person)* âme *f*; **population of two thousand souls** population de deux mille âmes; **without meeting a (living) s.** sans rencontrer âme qui vive; **there wasn't a s. in the street** il n'y avait pas un chat dans la rue; **I promise I won't tell a s.** je promets que je ne le dirai à personne; **he's a good s.** c'est une bonne âme; **she's a happy s.** elle a un tempérament heureux *ou* optimiste; **poor s.!** le/la pauvre!; **poor little s.!** pauvre petit(e)!

3 *(music)* soul *f*, soul music *f*

▸▸ **s. brother** = nom *m* que les Noirs américains donnent aux hommes noirs; *Fam* **s. food** cuisine *f* afroaméricaine; **s. music** soul, soul music; **s. singer** chanteur, -euse de soul; **s. sister** = nom que les Noirs américains donnent aux femmes noires

soul-destroying [-dɪstrɔɪɪŋ] ADJ *(job etc)* abrutissant, d'une monotonie mortelle

soulful [ˈsəʊlfʊl] ADJ *(with deep feeling)* tendre; *(music)* qui touche l'âme

soulfully [ˈsəʊlfəlɪ] ADV *(to sing)* tendrement; *Pej (sentimentally)* avec sensiblerie

soulless [ˈsəʊllɪs] ADJ **1** *(person)* sans âme **2** *(job)* abrutissant

soullessly [ˈsəʊllɪslɪ] ADV sans émotion; **the house had been s. renovated** on a rénové la maison sans aucune sensibilité

soullessness [ˈsəʊllɪsnɪs] N *(of person)* manque *m* de sensibilité; *(of building)* côté *m* inhumain; **the s. of my surroundings** le décor inhumain qui est le mien

soulmate [ˈsəʊlmeɪt] N âme *f* sœur

soul-searching N examen *m* de conscience; **after a lot of s.** après un profond examen de conscience

soul-stirring ADJ émouvant

SOUND¹ [saʊnd]

> **N** son ▪ bruit ▪ sonorité
> **VI** résonner **1** ▪ retentir **1** ▪ sembler
> **2** ▪ avoir l'air **2** ▪ sonner **2**
> **VT** sonner **1** ▪ prononcer **2**
> ▪ ausculter **3**

N Phys, Mus etc son m; (of door, car engine, wind etc) bruit m; **the device recognizes the s. of your voice** l'appareil reconnaît le son de votre voix; **the s. of one's own voice** le son de sa (propre) voix; **he likes (listening to) the s. of his own voice** il aime s'écouter parler; **there was not a s. to be heard** on n'entendait pas le moindre bruit; **no s. escaped his lips** pas un son ne sortait de ses lèvres; **not a s. could be heard** le silence était total; **the s. of a dog barking/a door closing** le bruit d'un chien qui aboie/d'une porte qui se ferme; **every violin has its own s.** chaque violon a sa propre sonorité; **within (the) s. of ...** à portée du son de ...; *TV etc* **to turn up/turn down the s.** augmenter/diminuer le volume; **I don't like the s. of it** cela ne me dit rien qui vaille; **he's angry by the s. of it** on dirait bien qu'il est fâché; *Fam* **today's sounds** (music) les sons d'aujourd'hui; **it has a sixties s. to it** ça ressemble à la musique des années soixante

VI 1 (make sound) sonner, résonner; (resound) retentir; **the trumpet sounded** la trompette retentit *ou* sonna

2 (seem) paraître, sembler, avoir l'air; **name that sounds French** nom qui sonne français; **she sounds French** elle a l'air d'être française; **the translation still sounds a bit French** la traduction sonne toujours un peu français; **that sounds like trouble!** voilà les ennuis!; **he sounds like my kind of guy** c'est le genre de type avec qui je m'entendrais; **you s. like the kind of person we're looking for** je crois que vous êtes la personne qu'il nous faut; **it still sounds a bit wrong** (of words, music) ça sonne encore un peu faux; **that sounds odd!** cela paraît bizarre!; **what about an omelette? – that sounds good!** que dirais-tu d'une omelette? – bonne idée!; **'attractive four-bedroomed house', how does that s.?** 'belle maison avec quatre chambres à coucher', qu'est-ce que tu en penses?; **their suggestion sounds interesting** leur suggestion semble intéressante; **how does that s. to you?** (referring to suggestion) qu'est-ce que tu en dis?; **she sounded interested/happy** elle semblait intéressée/heureuse; **the noise sounded a long way off** le bruit semblait venir de loin; **it sounds like Mozart** on dirait du Mozart; **he doesn't s. like a man to ...** d'après ce que vous dites, il ne serait pas homme à ...

VT 1 (trumpet, retreat) sonner; (the alert, the alarm) donner; *Aut* **to s. one's horn** klaxonner; *Lit* **to s. sb's praises** chanter les louanges de qn

2 (pronounce) (letter) prononcer; **the h is not sounded** l'h ne se prononce pas *ou* est muet

3 *Med* (person, person's chest) ausculter; **he sounded my chest** il m'a ausculté

▸▸**s. archives** phonothèque f; **s. barrier** mur m du son; **s. board** (of piano) table f d'harmonie; (of organ) tamis m; *Mus* **s. box** caisse f de résonance; *Comput* **s. card** carte f son; **s. check** soundcheck m; **s. effects** bruitage m; **s. engineer** ingénieur m du son; **s. camera** caméra f sonore; *Cin, TV, Radio* **s. crew** équipe f du son; **s. designer** concepteur m sonore; **s. detector** (of missile) détecteur m par le son; **s. editing** montage m sonore; **s. editor** monteur m son; **s. film** film m sonore; **s. generator** générateur m de son; **s. hole** (of violin, viola etc) ouïe f, esse f; (of guitar, lute etc) rosace f, rose f; **s. level** niveau m sonore;

s. logo logo m sonore; **s. man** preneur m de son, opérateur m du son; **s. mixer** table f *ou* console f de mixage; **s. mixing** mixage m sonore; **s. plot** = liste f des sons et bruitages nécessaires pour la production d'une pièce de théâtre ou radiophonique; **s. quality** qualité f du son, qualité sonore; **s. recording** enregistrement m du son, enregistrement sonore; **s. recordist** preneur de son; **s. reel** bande f son; **s. stage** studio m insonorisé; **s. studio** auditorium m *ou* studio d'enregistrement; **s. system** (hi-fi) chaîne f hifi; (PA system) sonorisation f; **s. wave** onde f sonore

▸**sound off** **VI** *Fam* (express opinions forcefully, complain) **to s. off** faire de grands laïus sur qch; **to s. off at sb** engueuler qn; **she's always sounding off about rude shop assistants** elle est toujours en train de se plaindre des vendeuses peu aimables

sound² **N** *Med* (probe) sonde f
VT 1 *Naut, Med* sonder **2 to s. public opinion** sonder l'opinion publique
VI (of whale) plonger au fond
▸**sound out** **VT SEP** (ascertain opinion, allegiance of) (person) sonder

sound³ **N** (channel) détroit m, bras m de mer

sound⁴ **ADJ 1** (lungs, foundations) sain; (wood) sans tare; (bridge, engine) (in good condition) en bon état; (not damaged) non endommagé; **s. in body and mind** sain de corps et d'esprit; **of s. mind** sain d'esprit; *Fam* **to be s. in wind and limb** (of person) avoir un bon pied bon œil; **I'm as s. as a bell** je suis en parfaite santé

2 (argument, knowledge, basis) solide; (reason, reasoning) valable; (policy etc) sage; (investment) sûr, solide, fiable; (goalkeeper, manager, musician, lawyer etc) bon, f bonne, fiable; **ecologically s. legislation** législation juste du point de vue écologique; **s. doctrine** doctrine saine; *Rel* (orthodox) doctrine orthodoxe; **a s. piece of advice** un bon conseil; **s. financial position** situation financière saine; **s. business** entreprise saine *ou* solide; **he's pretty s. on his grammar** il a de bonnes bases en grammaire; **it makes good s. sense** c'est tout à fait raisonnable

3 a s. sleep un sommeil profond; **I'm a s. sleeper** je dors bien; **to give sb a s. thrashing** administrer une bonne correction à qn
ADV **to be s. asleep** être profondément endormi, dormir à poings fermés

soundbite ['saʊndbaɪt] **N** petite phrase f

sounder ['saʊndər] **N** *Naut* sondeur m

sounding¹ ['saʊndɪŋ] **N** *Mil* **the s. of the retreat** le signal de la retraite

sounding² **N 1** *Naut* (act) sondage m; **echo s.** sondage par ultra-sons **2** *Naut* **soundings** (measurements) sondages mpl; (bottom) fonds mpl; **to take soundings** sonder, prendre le fond; *Fig* sonder
▸▸**s. board** (of pulpit etc) abat-voix m inv; (of piano) table f d'harmonie; (of organ) tamis m; *Fig* **to use sb as a s. board** tester ses idées sur qn; **s. lead** (plomb m de) sonde f; **s. line** sonde

soundless ['saʊndlɪs] **ADJ** muet, -ette, silencieux

soundlessly ['saʊndlɪslɪ] **ADV** silencieusement, sans bruit

soundly ['saʊndlɪ] **ADV 1** (solidly) solidement **2** (to reason) sainement; (wisely) judicieusement; **to invest s.** investir dans des valeurs sûres; **he argued s.** son argumentation était solide **3** (to sleep) profondément; **to thrash sb s.** (with stick etc) administrer une bonne correction à qn; *Sport* **we were s. beaten** nous avons été battus à plate(s) couture(s)

soundness ['saʊndnɪs] **N 1** (of merchandise, mind etc) bon état m; (of company) solidité f;

(solvency) solvabilité f **2** (of argument, reasoning, decision etc) validité f; (of judgment) justesse f; (of advice, policy) sagesse f; (of doctrine) orthodoxie f

soundproof ['saʊndpruːf] **ADJ** (room etc) insonorisé; (material) insonore
VT (room etc) insonoriser
▸▸**s. hood** capot m antibruit

soundproofing ['saʊndpruːfɪŋ] **N** (material) matériau m isolant *ou* insonore; (act) insonorisation f

soundtrack ['saʊndtræk] **N** *Cin* bande f sonore; **s. (album)** bande originale

soup [suːp] **N** soupe f, (thin) potage m; **onion/fish s.** soupe à l'oignon/de poisson; *Fig Fam* **to be in the s.** être dans le pétrin; *Fig Fam* **to land sb in the s.** mettre qn dans le pétrin
▸▸**s. kitchen** soupe populaire; **s. ladle** louche f, **s. plate** assiette f creuse *ou* à soupe; **s. spoon** cuillère f *ou* cuiller f à soupe; *Am Fam Hum* **s. strainer** (large moustache) grosses bacchantes fpl; **s. tureen** soupière f
▸**soup up** **VT SEP** *Fam* (car, engine) gonfler

soupçon ['suːpsɒn] **N** (of garlic, sarcasm) soupçon m, pointe f

souped-up ['suːpt-] **ADJ** *Fam* gonflé; **a s. job** (car, motorcycle) une bagnole/une moto au moteur gonflé

sour ['saʊər] **ADJ 1** (fruit etc) aigre, acide; (milk, cream, bread etc) aigre; (wine) suret, -ette, verjuté; (soil) acide; **to turn s.** (of food) (s')aigrir, surir; *Fig* (of situation, relationship) tourner à l'aigre, *Fam* tourner au vinaigre; **to turn sth s.** (faire) aigrir qch; **to smell s.** sentir l'aigre; *Fig* **the plan went s. on him** (went wrong) le projet a mal tourné pour lui
2 (person) revêche, aigre; **he's s. about being left out** il est amer parce qu'on l'a laissé à l'écart
VI surir, (s')aigrir; **her temper has soured** son caractère s'est aigri
VT (milk, character etc) aigrir; *Culin* **soured cream** crème f aigre; **soured by disappointment** (person) aigri par une déception; **these events have soured their relationship** ces événements ont aigri leur relation
▸▸**s. cream** crème aigre; **s. grapes** dépit m; **it was just s. grapes that made her say that** elle a simplement dit ça par rancœur

source [sɔːs] **N** (of river, misfortune, light etc) source f, (of heat, infection etc) foyer m; **the Rhone has its s. in the Alps** le Rhône prend sa source dans les Alpes; **a good s. of vitamin C** une bonne source de vitamine C; **this book is a good s. of information about ...** ce livre est une bonne source d'informations sur ...; **I have it from a good s.** je le sais *ou* tiens de source sûre; **a historian's/reporter's sources** les sources d'un historien/reporter
▸▸*Comput* **s. disk** disque m source; (floppy) disquette f source; *Comput* **s. document** document m de base, document source; *Comput* **s. drive** unité f source *ou* d'origine; *Comput* **s. file** fichier m source; **s. language** (in translation, interpreting) langue f de départ; *Comput* langage m source; **s. materials** (of book) sources fpl; *Comput* **s. program** programme m source; *Comput* **s. text** texte m de départ

sourdough ['saʊədəʊ] **N**
▸▸**s. bread** pain m au levain

surface ['saʊəfeɪs] **N** *Fam* = **sourpuss**

surfaced ['saʊəfeɪst] **ADJ** (person) au visage rébarbatif; (look) revêche; (reply) aigre

sourly ['saʊəlɪ] **ADV** (to answer) aigrement; (to look at sb) d'un air revêche

sourness ['saʊənɪs] **N 1** (of fruit etc) aigreur f, acidité f, (of milk) aigreur f **2** (of person) aigreur f

sourpuss ['saʊəpʊs] N *Fam* grincheux, -euse; *(kill-joy)* rabat-joie *m inv*

sousaphone ['suːzəfəʊn] N *Mus* sousaphone *m*

sous chef ['suːʃef] N second *m*, assistant *m* du chef de cuisine

souse [saʊs] N *Culin* saumure *f*, marinade *f*
▪ VT plonger, immerger (**in** dans); *Culin (herring)* faire mariner; **to s. sth with water** arroser qch d'eau

soused [saʊst] ADJ **1** *Culin* mariné **2** *Sl (drunk)* bourré, pété; **to get s.** se soûler
▸▸ *Culin* **s. herrings** harengs *mpl* marinés

south [saʊθ] N sud *m*, midi *m*; **the house faces the s.** la maison est exposée au sud *ou* au midi; **to the s.** au sud (**of** de); **the s.** *(region of a country)* le sud, le midi; **the S. of France** le sud *ou* le Midi (de la France); *Hist* **the S.** *(of United States)* le Sud, les États *mpl* du sud
▪ ADV au sud; **to travel s.** voyager vers le sud; **it's s. of here** c'est au sud d'ici; **I'm going down s.** *(to southern part of country)* je vais dans le sud; **s. by east** sud-quart-sud-est; **s. by west** sud-quart-sud-ouest
▪ ADJ sud *inv*; *(wind)* du sud; *(wall, window)* exposé au sud; **s. side** côté *m* sud; **on the s. side** du côté sud; **the s. coast** la côte sud
▸▸ **S. Africa** l'Afrique *f* du Sud; **S. African** sud-africain, -aine; **S. America** l'Amérique *f* du Sud; **S. American** sud-américain, -aine; **S. Korea** la Corée du Sud; **S. Pacific** Pacifique *m* sud; **S. Pole** le pôle Sud; **S. Sea Islands** l'Océanie *f*, **S. Seas** mers *fpl* du Sud; **S. Vietnam** le Viêt Nam du Sud; **S. Yemen** le Yémen du Sud

southbound ['saʊθbaʊnd] ADJ *(traffic)* en direction du sud; *(lane, carriageway)* du sud; *(road)* vers le sud; **s. traffic is subject to delays** la circulation est ralentie dans le sens sud; **there's a jam on the s. carriageway** il y a un bouchon en direction du sud

southeast [saʊθ'iːst] N sud-est *m*; *Naut* suet *m*
▪ ADJ **1** *Geog* sud-est *inv*, du sud-est; **in s. England** dans le sud-est de l'Angleterre **2** *(wind)* de sud-est, du sud-est
▪ ADV au sud-est; *(to travel)* vers le sud-est; **it's 50 miles s. of Liverpool** c'est à 80 kilomètres au sud-est de Liverpool
▸▸ **S. Asia** Asie *f* du Sud-Est; **the S. Asian Treaty Organization** l'Organisation *f* du traité de l'Asie du Sud-Est

southeaster ['saʊθ'iːstə(r)] N *(wind)* vent *m* de *ou* du sud-est; *Naut* suet *m*

southeasterly [saʊθ'iːstəlɪ] ADJ **1** *Geog* sud-est *inv*, du sud-est; **to travel in a s. direction** aller vers le sud-est; *Naut* **to steer a s. course** faire route vers le sud-est; *(when setting out)* mettre le cap au sud-est **2** *(wind)* de sud-est, du sud-est
▪ ADV vers le sud-est
▪ N vent *m* de *ou* du sud-est; *Naut* suet *m*

southeastern [saʊθ'iːstən] ADJ sud-est *inv*, du sud-est, *(wind)* de sud-est, du sud-est; **the s. suburbs** la banlieue sud-est

southerly ['sʌðəlɪ] ADJ **1** *Geog* sud *inv*, du sud; **to travel in a s. direction** voyager vers le sud; **s. point** point situé au sud *ou* vers le sud; **the most s. point of the United States** le point situé le plus au sud des États-Unis; **a room with a s. aspect** une pièce exposée au sud *ou* au midi; *Naut* **to steer a s. course** faire route vers le sud; *(change course)* mettre le cap au sud **2** *(wind)* de sud, du sud
▪ ADV vers le sud

southern ['sʌðən] ADJ **1** *Geog* sud *inv*, du sud, méridional, -aux; **he has a s. accent** il a un accent du sud; *(in France)* il a l'accent méridional; **the s. wing of the castle** l'aile sud

du château; **in s. India** dans le sud de l'Inde; **the s. hemisphere** l'hémisphère *m* sud *ou* austral **2** *(wind)* de sud, du sud **3** *Hist (in American Civil War)* sudiste
▸▸ **s. Africa** l'Afrique *f* australe; *Astron* **the S. Cross** la Croix du Sud; **s. Europe** l'Europe *f* méridionale; **S. Ireland** l'Irlande *f* du Sud; **s. lights** aurore *f* australe

southerner ['sʌðənər] N **1** habitant, -ante du sud; *(in continental Europe)* méridional, -ale; **she's a s.** elle vient du sud **2** *Hist (of United States)* sudiste *mf*

south-facing ADJ *(house, wall)* (exposé) au sud *ou* au midi

southpaw ['saʊθpɔː] N *Boxing etc* gaucher, -ère

south-south-east, *Naut* sou'sou'east [saʊ(θ)saʊ(θ)'iːst] N sud-sud-est *m inv*
▪ ADJ **1** *Geog* sud-sud-est *inv*, du sud-sud-est **2** *(wind)* de *ou* du sud-sud-est
▪ ADV au sud-sud-est; *(to travel)* vers le sud-sud-est

south-south-west, *Naut* sou'sou'west [saʊ(θ)saʊ(θ)'west] N sud-sud-ouest *m*; *Naut* susuroît *m*
▪ ADJ **1** *Geog* sud-sud-ouest *inv*, du sud-sud-ouest **2** *(wind)* de *ou* du sud-sud-est
▪ ADV au sud-sud-ouest; *(to travel)* vers le sud-sud-ouest

southward ['saʊθwəd] ADJ vers le sud, en direction du sud
▪ ADV vers le sud, en direction du sud
▪ N sud *m*

southwards ['saʊθwədz] ADV vers le sud

southwest, *Naut* sou'west [saʊ(θ)'west] N sud-ouest *m*; *Naut* suroît *m*
▪ ADV au sud-ouest; *(to travel)* vers le sud-ouest; **s. by west** sud-ouest-quart-ouest; **s. by south** sud-ouest-quart-sud
▪ ADJ **1** *Geog* sud-ouest *inv*, du sud-ouest; **in s. Scotland** dans le sud-ouest de l'Écosse **2** *(wind)* de *ou* du sud-ouest

southwester, *Naut* sou'wester ['saʊ(θ)-'westər] N *(wind)* vent *m* de *ou* du sud-ouest; *Naut* suroît *m*

southwesterly, *Naut* sou'westerly [saʊ(θ)-'westəlɪ] ADJ **1** *Geog* sud-ouest *inv*, du sud-ouest; **in a s. direction** vers le sud-ouest; *Naut* **to steer a s. course** faire route vers le sud-ouest; *(when setting out)* mettre le cap au sud-ouest **2** *(wind)* de *ou* du sud-ouest
▪ ADV vers le sud-ouest
▪ N = **southwester**

southwestern [saʊθ'westən] ADJ sud-ouest *inv*, du sud-ouest; **to travel in a s. direction** voyager vers le sud-ouest

souvenir [suːvə'nɪər] N souvenir *m*
▸▸ **s. shop** boutique *f* de souvenirs

> Note that the French word **souvenir** also means **memory**.

sovereign ['sɒvrɪn] ADJ souverain, suprême; **the s. good** le bien souverain; **s. rights** droits *mpl* de souveraineté
▪ N **1** *(monarch)* souverain, -aine, monarque *m* **2** *Hist (coin)* souverain *m (pièce d'or de la valeur d'une livre)*

sovereignty ['sɒvrəntɪ] N souveraineté *f*

Soviet ['səʊvɪət] N **1** *(council)* soviet *m*; **Supreme S.** Soviet suprême **2 the Soviets** *(people)* les Soviétiques *mpl*
▪ ADJ soviétique; *Formerly* **the Union of S. Socialist Republics** l'Union *f* des Républiques socialistes soviétiques
▸▸ *Formerly* **S. Union** Union *f* soviétique

sovietization [səʊvɪətaɪ'zeɪʃən] N soviétisation *f*

sow[1] [səʊ] *(pt* **sowed** [səʊd]; *pp* **sown** [səʊn], **sowed)** VT *(seeds, field)* semer; **to s. a field with wheat** ensemencer un champ de blé;

Fig **to s. (the seeds of) discord/doubt** semer la discorde/le doute
▪ VI semer

sow[2] [saʊ] N *(female pig)* truie *f*, *(wild)* laie *f*

sower ['səʊər] N *(person)* semeur, -euse; *(device)* semoir *m*

sowing ['səʊɪŋ] N *(task)* ensemencement *m*; **s. time** *or* **season** *(saison f des)* semailles *fpl*

sown PP *see* **sow**[1]

sox [sɒks] NPL *Am* = **socks**, *see* **sock**[1]

soya ['sɔɪə] N soja *m*
▸▸ *Br* **s. bean** graine *f* de soja; **s. flour** farine *f* de soja; **s. milk** lait *m* de soja; **s. sauce** sauce *f* de *ou* au soja

soybean ['sɔɪbiːn] N *Am* graine *f* de soja

soy sauce [sɔɪ] N sauce *f* de *ou* au soja

sozzled ['sɒz(ə)ld] ADJ *Br Sl (drunk)* pété, bourré; **to get s.** se soûler

SP [es'piː] N *Horseracing (abbr* **starting price**) dernière cote *f* avant le départ; *Br Fam* **to give sb the SP** mettre qn au parfum (**on** à propos de *ou* concernant)

spa [spɑː] N **1** *(spring)* source *f* thermale; *(in sports centre, health farm etc)* Jacuzzi® *m*
▸▸ **s. bath** bain *m* bouillonnant; **s. hotel** hôtel *m* médicalisé; **s. resort** station *f* hydrominérale; **s. town** ville *f* d'eau, station thermale

space [speɪs] N **1** espace *m*; *(room)* place *f*; **he sat staring into s.** il était assis le regard perdu dans le vide; **open spaces** *(green)* espaces verts; *(not built on)* étendues *fpl* non bâties; **wide open spaces** grands espaces; **living s.** espace vital; **in a confined s.** dans un espace restreint; *Com* **to sell s.** *(in a newspaper)* vendre de l'espace (dans un journal); **to take up a lot of s.** prendre *ou* occuper beaucoup de place; **there's no s. left** il n'y a plus de place; **this cupboard is a great s. saver** avec ce placard, on gagne beaucoup de place
2 *Astron* espace *m*; **the conquest of s.** la conquête de l'espace; **outer s.** espace extra-atmosphérique
3 *(free area, place)* espace *m* libre; *(interval)* espacement *m*, intervalle *m*; *(on form etc)* blanc *m*, espace; **a s. in the timetable** un créneau dans l'emploi du temps; **a (parking) s.** une place de parking
4 *(between lines of writing etc)* interligne *m*; *Typ* espace *m* blanc; **blank s.** *(between letters)* intervalle *m* entre les lettres
5 *(period)* espace *m*, intervalle *m*; **in the s. of a year** dans *ou* en l'espace d'un an; **after a short s. of time** après un court intervalle
▪ VT *(trees, words, visits)* espacer; *(troops, payments)* échelonner; **evenly spaced** régulièrement espacés; **the posts are spaced ten feet apart** les poteaux sont plantés à dix pieds d'intervalle
▸▸ **s. age** ère *f* de l'exploration spatiale; **s. bar** *(on keyboard)* barre *f* d'espacement; **s. blanket** couverture *f* de survie; *Fam* **s. cadet** allumé, -ée; *Fam* **s. cake** gâteau *m* au cannabis, space cake *m*; **s. flight** vol *m ou* voyage *m* spatial; **s. heater** radiateur *m*; **S. Invaders®** Space Invaders® *m*; **s. mission** mission *f* spatiale; **s. probe** sonde *f* spatiale; **s. rocket** fusée *f* spatiale *ou* interplanétaire; *Typ* **s. rule** filet *m* maigre; **s. shot** lancement *m* spatial; **s. shuttle** navette *f* spatiale; **s. station** station *f* spatiale *ou* orbitale; **s. suit** scaphandre *m ou* combinaison *f* de cosmonaute; **s. travel** voyages *mpl* dans l'espace, *Spec* astronautique *f*
▸ **space out** VT SEP **1** *(arrange at intervals)* = **space** VT **2** *Sl* **to be** *or* **feel spaced out** *(dazed)* être dans le coaltar; *(after taking drugs)* être raide, planer

spaceage ['speɪseɪdʒ] ADJ *(technology etc)* futuriste

spacebar ['speɪsbɑːr] N *Typ* barre f d'espacement

spacecraft ['speɪskrɑːft] N véhicule m ou vaisseau m spatial, astronef m

spacelab ['speɪslæb] N laboratoire m spatial

spaceman, pl **spacemen** ['speɪsmæn, -men] N astronaute m

spacer ['speɪsər] N *Tech* pièce f d'écartement

space-saving ADJ qui permet de gagner de la place; *(furniture etc)* compact; **if you're looking for some s. ideas** si vous cherchez des idées pour gagner de la place

spaceship ['speɪsʃɪp] N véhicule m ou vaisseau m spatial, astronef m

space-time N *Phys* espace-temps m inv

spacewalk ['speɪswɔːk] N *Astronaut* marche f dans l'espace

spacewoman, pl **spacewomen** ['speɪswʊmən, -wɪmɪn] N astronaute f

spacing ['speɪsɪŋ] N *(of trees etc)* espacement m, écartement m; *Typ (of letters, lines)* espacement m; **in single/double s.** *(with typewriter)* à simple/double interligne

spacious ['speɪʃəs] ADJ *(kitchen, house, car boot)* spacieux, vaste; *(clothes)* ample

spaciousness ['speɪʃəsnɪs] N *(of kitchen, house, car boot)* dimensions fpl spacieuses

spade¹ [speɪd] N *(tool)* bêche f; *(child's)* pelle f; **to call a s. a s.** appeler les choses par leur nom, appeler un chat un chat
  VT *(earth etc)* bêcher

spade² N 1 *Cards* pique m; **ace of spades** as m de pique; **to play a s., to play spades** jouer pique 2 *Offensive Sl (black person)* nègre m, négresse f

spadeful ['speɪdfʊl] N pelletée f

spadework ['speɪdwɜːk] N *(with spade)* travaux mpl à la bêche; *Fig* travaux préliminaires

spag bol [spæg'bɒl] N *Br Fam (spaghetti bolognese)* spaghettis mpl (à la) bolognaise

spaghetti [spə'getɪ] N *Culin* spaghetti mpl; *Elec Fam (cables, wires)* souplisseau m VOIR GRAMMAIRE A14
  ▸▸ **S. Junction** = surnom d'un échangeur sur l'autoroute M6 au nord de Birmingham; *Fig* **it's like S. Junction around here!** tous ces échangeurs, c'est compliqué!; **s. western** western-spaghetti m, pl westerns-spaghetti

Spain [speɪn] N Espagne f

spam [spæm] *Comput* N messages mpl publicitaires, pourriels mpl; **a s. e-mail** un message publicitaire, un pourriel
  VT envoyer des messages publicitaires ou des pourriels à
  VI spammer

spammer ['spæmə] N *Comput* = personne f qui envoie des messages publicitaires en masse

spamming ['spæmɪŋ] N *Comput* spamming m

span¹ [spæn] N 1 *(of hand)* empan m; **wing s.** *(of bird, aircraft)* envergure f
  2 *(between two points of support)* portée f; *(of arch)* largeur f; *(of bridge)* travée f; **single s. bridge** pont m à travée unique
  3 *(duration, period of time)* durée f; **the party's twenty-year s. in power is coming to an end** les vingt années de pouvoir du parti arrivent à leur fin
  4 *(extent) (of knowledge, interests, activity etc)* étendue f
  VT (-nn-) 1 *(of bridge etc) (river etc)* enjamber; **once the river had been spanned** une fois qu'on a eu construit un pont pour traverser la rivière
  2 *(include)* couvrir; **her knowledge spans a wide range of subjects** ses connaissances couvrent une grande variété de sujets; **his**

life spans nearly the whole century sa vie embrasse presque tout le siècle; *Mus* **to s. an octave** couvrir une octave

span² N *(pair) (of horses, oxen)* paire f, couple m

spangle ['spæŋ(ə)l] N *Tex etc* paillette f; *(large)* paillon m
  VT pailleter (**with** de); **spangled with silver** pailleté d'argent

Spaniard ['spænjəd] N Espagnol, -ole VOIR GRAMMAIRE A19

spaniel ['spænjəl] N épagneul m; **cocker/springer s.** épagneul cocker/springer

Spanish ['spænɪʃ] VOIR GRAMMAIRE A19 ADJ espagnol
  N 1 *Ling* espagnol m 2 **the S.** *(pl)* les Espagnols mpl
  ▸▸ **S. America** Amérique f hispanophone; **S. fly** mouche f d'Espagne, cantharide f; **S. guitar** guitare f classique; **the S. Inquisition** l'Inquisition f espagnole; **S. moss** tillandsia m; **S. omelette** omelette f à l'espagnole; **S. onion** oignon m d'Espagne

Spanish-American ADJ hispano-américain
  ▸▸ *Hist* **the S. war** la guerre hispano-américaine

Spanish-speaking ADJ hispanophone

spank [spæŋk] N fessée f
  VT *(child)* fesser, donner une fessée à
  ▸ **spank along** VI *(go fast)* aller bon train

spanking ['spæŋkɪŋ] N fessée f; **to give a child a s.** donner une fessée à un enfant
  ADJ *Old-fashioned Fam* 1 *(excellent)* épatant
  2 **to go at a s. pace** aller bon train
  ADV *Fam* **s. new** flambant neuf; **a s. good time was had** on s'est diablement bien amusé

spanner ['spænər] N *Br* clef f; **adjustable s.** clef à molette; **box s.** clef à douille ou à tire-fonds; *Fig* **to throw a s. in the works** causer des problèmes; **that's really thrown a s. in the works!** cela nous/leur/etc a vraiment mis des bâtons dans les roues!; **so that's the s. in the works** alors, c'est ça le hic

spar¹ [spɑːr] N *Naut* espar m; *Aviat* **wing s.** longeron m d'aile

spar² N *Miner* spath m

spar³ VI (-rr-) **to s. with sb** *Boxing* s'entraîner avec qn; *Fig (argue)* jouter avec qn

SPARE ['speər]

ADJ en plus **1** ▪ disponible **1** ▪ libre **1** ▪ frugal **2** ▪ dépouillé **2** ▪ sec **3**	
N pièce de rechange ▪ roue de secours	
VT se passer de **2** ▪ ménager **3** ▪ faire grâce à **3**	

ADJ 1 *(surplus) (copy, trousers)* en plus; *(free)* disponible; **have you got a s. plastic bag?** est-ce que tu as un sac en plastique qui ne te sert pas?; **with the s. cash, they bought a table** avec l'argent qui leur restait, ils ont acheté une table; **that left a few hours s.** ça a laissé quelques heures libres; **is this bed s.?** est-ce que ce lit est libre?; **we have a s. bed** *(can put you/him up for the night)* nous avons un lit qui ne sert pas; *Fam* **is this cake going s.?** si vous ne savez pas quoi faire de ce gâteau, je le prends; *Fam* **if you have any tickets going s.** si vous avez des tickets en trop; *Fam* **if you hear of any flats going s.** si vous entendez parler d'appartements qui se libèrent
  2 *(frugal) (meal etc)* frugal, -aux; *(style, room)* dépouillé
  3 *(thin) (person)* sec, f sèche; **he was tall and s.** il était grand et mince
  4 *Br Fam (mad)* **to drive sb s.** rendre qn dingue; **he'll go s. if he finds out** il va être fou s'il apprend ça

N *(spare part)* pièce f de rechange, pièce détachée; *(tyre)* roue f de secours; **I've lost my pencil, have you got a s.?** j'ai perdu mon crayon, en as-tu un à me prêter?
  VT 1 *(in negative constructions) (be grudging of)* **to s. no expense** ne pas regarder à la dépense; **to s. no pains** se donner beaucoup de mal; **to s. no effort** ne pas ménager ses efforts
  2 *(go without)* se passer de; **can you s. that much money?** pouvez-vous vous en passer?; **can you s. the time?** avez-vous le temps?; **we can't s. him** il nous est indispensable, nous ne pouvons pas nous passer de lui; **to have nothing to s.** n'avoir que le strict nécessaire, ne rien avoir de superflu; **to have enough and to s. (of sth)** avoir plus qu'il n'en faut (de qch); **there is room to s.** la place ne manque pas; **I cannot s. the time to finish it** je n'ai pas le temps de le finir; **to have no time to s.** ne pas avoir le temps; **to have no time to s. for sb/sth** ne pas avoir de temps à consacrer à qn/qch; **when I have time to s.** quand j'ai des loisirs, quand j'ai du temps libre; **whenever I have a minute to s.** dès que j'ai une minute; **I have a minute to s., so send her in** j'ai une minute à lui consacrer, faites-la donc entrer; **to catch a train with five minutes to s.** prendre un train avec cinq minutes de battement; **we caught the plane with absolutely no time to s.** nous avons attrapé l'avion vraiment de justesse; **we'll have at least half an hour to s.** nous aurons au minimum une demi-heure de battement; **to s. sb some sugar/ten pounds** donner à qn du sucre/dix livres; **are you sure you can s. it?** tu es sûr que ça ne te dérange pas?; *Iron* **tu es sûr que ça ne vas pas te manquer?; can you s. a couple of people this afternoon?** est-ce que vous pourriez vous passer de quelques personnes cet après-midi?; **can you s. me a few moments?** pouvez-vous m'accorder quelques minutes?; **to s. a thought for sb** penser à qn
  3 *(show mercy towards) (person, horse)* ménager; *(person condemned to die)* faire grâce à; **to s. sb's life** épargner la vie de qn; **s. me!** *(do not kill me)* de grâce!, épargnez-moi!; *Fig (don't expose me to that etc)* par pitié, pas ça!; **if she is spared** *(lives)* si elle vit; **death spares no one** la mort n'épargne personne; **the flood spared nothing** l'inondation n'a rien épargné; **to s. sb's feelings** ménager qn, épargner qn; **tell me, don't s. my feelings** dis-moi, n'essaye pas de me ménager; **the report spared no one** le rapport ne ménageait personne; **s. my blushes!** ne me faites pas rougir!; **he doesn't s. himself** il ne se ménage pas; **to s. sb the trouble of doing sth** éviter à qn la peine de faire qch; **you could have spared yourself/us the trouble** vous auriez pu vous/nous éviter cette peine; **s. me the details!** *(don't tell me)* épargne-moi les détails!; **I'll s. you the rest** je vous fais grâce du reste
  ▸▸ **s. parts** fpl de rechange, pièces détachées; **s. room** chambre f d'amis; **s. time** temps m libre; **in my s. time** à mes heures perdues; **I don't get much s. time** je n'ai pas beaucoup de temps libre; *Am* **s. tire,** *Br* **s. tyre** pneu m de rechange; *Fam (around waist)* bourrelet m de graisse, pneu; *Br* **s. wheel** roue f de secours

sparing ['speərɪŋ] ADJ *(economical)* économe; **to be s. with the butter** ménager le beurre; **she is very s. with her money** elle fait très attention à son argent; **he is s. with his praise** il est avare de louanges

sparingly ['speərɪŋlɪ] ADV *(to eat)* sobrement; *(moderately)* modérément, avec modération; **to use sth s.** utiliser qch avec modération; **apply the cream s. to the affected area** appliquer la crème en couche fine sur la région touchée

spark [spɑːk] N **1** *(glowing particle)* étincelle *f*; *(from fire)* flammèche *f*; **the s. of life** l'étincelle de la vie; *Fig* **sparks flew** ça a fait des étincelles; **he hasn't a s. of imagination** il manque totalement d'imagination; **he hasn't a s. of generosity in him** il n'est pas généreux pour deux sous; **a bright s.** *(intelligent person)* une tête; *Fam Iron* **you're a bright s.!** tu es un rapide, toi!; **who's the bright s. who …?** qui est le petit malin qui …?

2 *Elec etc* étincelle *f*; *(in engine)* éclateur *m*, pont *m* d'allumage

3 *Fam* **sparks** *(radio operator)* radio *m*; *(electrician)* électricien *m*

VI jeter des étincelles; *(of dynamo etc)* cracher; **to s. across the terminals** *(of current)* jaillir entre les bornes

▸▸ *Aut* **s. advance** correcteur *m* d'avance; *Aut* **s. gap** écartement *m* des électrodes; *Aut* **s. plug** bougie *f*; *Aut* **s. plug spanner** clé *f* à bougie

▸ **spark off** VT SEP *(initiate)* *(revolution, reaction etc)* déclencher, provoquer; *(idea etc)* donner naissance à; **this remark sparked off a discussion about …** cette remarque a déclenché *ou* donné lieu à une discussion au sujet de …

sparkle [spɑːk(ə)l] N **1** *(spot of light)* étincelle *f*; *(lasting only short time)* brève lueur *f* **2** *(act, state of sparkling)* scintillement *m*; *(of eyes)* éclat *m*, pétillement *m*; *(of diamond)* feux *mpl*; **wine that has lost its s.** vin qui ne pétille plus; *Fig* **if the s. has gone out of your marriage …** si la magie a disparu de votre mariage …; **he's got no s. about him** il est plutôt terne; **he's lost his s.** il a perdu sa joie de vivre

VI *(of jewel, tinsel, metal, snow etc)* étinceler, scintiller; *(of surface of lake)* miroiter; *(of wine)* pétiller, mousser; **her eyes sparkled (with joy)** ses yeux pétillaient (de joie); **sparkling with wit** *(book)* plein d'esprit

sparkler [spɑːklər] N **1** *(firework)* cierge *m* magique **2** *Fam (diamond)* diam *m*

sparkling [spɑːklɪŋ] ADJ étincelant, brillant; *(conversation)* brillant; *(wine)* mousseux, pétillant; *(lemonade)* gazeux; **he was a s. conversationalist** sa conversation était des plus brillantes

ADV **s. clean** étincelant de propreté, d'une propreté étincelante

sparring [spɑːrɪŋ] N *Boxing* entraînement *m*; *(arguing)* échanges *mpl* verbaux; **it was just a little good-natured s.** *(verbal)* ce n'était qu'une petite bagarre amicale

▸▸ **s. match** *(in boxing)* match *m* d'entraînement; *Fig (argument)* discussion *f* animée; **I could hear them having a s. match in the corridor** je les entendais se disputer dans le couloir; **s. partner** *(in boxing)* partenaire *m* d'entraînement, sparring-partner *m*, *pl* sparring-partners; *Fig* adversaire *m*

sparrow [spærəʊ] N *(bird)* moineau *m*; **hedge s.** fauvette *f* d'hiver

sparrowhawk [spærəʊhɔːk] N *(bird)* épervier *m*

sparse [spɑːs] ADJ *(trees, population)* clairsemé, épars; **s. hair** cheveux rares *ou* clairsemés

sparsely [spɑːslɪ] ADV peu abondamment; **s. covered with trees** aux arbres clairsemés; **s. furnished** à peine meublé; **s. populated** peu peuplé

sparseness [spɑːsnɪs] N *(of population)* faible densité *f*; *(of vegetation)* manque *m*

Sparta [spɑːtə] N Sparte

Spartan [spɑːtən] ADJ *Hist*, *Fig* spartiate; *Fig* **to lead a s. life** vivre en spartiate, mener une vie de spartiate

N *Hist* Spartiate *mf*

spasm [spæz(ə)m] N *Med* spasme *m*; *Fig (of coughing, jealousy)* accès *m*; *Med* **to go into spasms** avoir des spasmes; **to work in spasms** travailler par à-coups; **after a sudden s. of feverish activity** après un accès soudain d'activité fébrile

spasmodic [spæzˈmɒdɪk] ADJ *Med* spasmodique; *Fig (irregular)* irrégulier, -ère; *(intermittent)* intermittent; **s. work** travail fait par à-coups

spasmodically [spæzˈmɒdɪklɪ] ADV *Med* spasmodiquement; *Fig (irregularly)* irrégulièrement; *(intermittently)* de façon intermittente; *(to work)* par à-coups

spastic [spæstɪk] ADJ *Med* spastique; *(paralysis etc)* spasmodique; *Offensive Sl (performance, attempt etc)* minable, nul, *f* nulle

N *Med* handicapé, -ée moteur; *Offensive Sl (clumsy person)* gol *mf*, gogol *mf*

spat¹ [spæt] N *(of oysters etc)* naissain *m*

spat² N *(item of clothing)* demi-guêtre *f*, *pl* demi-guêtres

spat³ *Fam* N *(quarrel)* querelle *f*

VI *(-tt-)* *(quarrel)* se quereller

spat⁴ PT, PP *see* spit² VI, VT

spate [speɪt] N *(of river)* crue *f*; *Fig (of letters etc)* avalanche *f*; *(of abuse)* torrent *m*; **river in (full) s.** rivière en crue; *Fig* **to be in full s.** être en plein dans son sujet; **a s. of burglaries** une série de cambriolages; **there's been a sudden s. of orders** il y a eu une soudaine avalanche *ou* un soudain déluge de commandes

spatial [speɪʃəl] ADJ *Math*, *Phys etc* spatial, -aux

▸▸ **s. awareness** perception *f* de l'espace

spatiotemporal [speɪʃɪəʊˈtempərəl] ADJ spatio-temporel, *pl* spatio-temporels

spatter [spætər] N *(of liquid)* éclaboussure *f*; *Ind (of solder)* projection *f*

VT éclabousser (**with** de); **the wall was spattered with grease** le mur était couvert d'éclaboussures *ou* tout éclaboussé de graisse

VI *(of liquid)* jaillir, gicler; **the rain spattering down on the pavement** la pluie qui rebondit sur le trottoir

-spattered [-spætəd] SUFF blood-/mud-/oil-spattered couvert d'éclaboussures de sang/de boue/d'huile

spatula [spætjʊlə] N *Pharm*, *Surg*, *Culin etc* spatule *f*

spavin [spævɪn] N *Vet* éparvin *m*

spawn [spɔːn] N **1** *(of frog, fish etc)* frai *m*, œufs *mpl*; *Lit*, *Pej (offspring)* progéniture *f* **2** *(mushroom)* **s.** blancs *mpl* de champignon, mycélium *m*

VI *(of fish etc)* frayer; *Fam (of people)* se multiplier

VT *(of fish, frog etc)* *(eggs)* déposer; *Fig* engendrer, donner naissance à; **the organization/movement spawned various offshoots** l'organisation/le mouvement a donné naissance à plusieurs ramifications

spawning [spɔːnɪŋ] N *Zool* frai *m*

▸▸ **s. ground** frayère *f*; **s. season** frai

spay [speɪ] VT *Vet* châtrer

spaz [spæz] N *Fam* gol *mf*, gogol *mf*

▸ **spaz out** VT SEP *Fam* faire le con

SPEAK [spiːk] *(pt* **spoke** [spəʊk]; *pp* **spoken** [spəʊk(ə)n])

VI	parler **1** ▪ se parler **1** ▪ faire un discours **2**
VT	dire **1** ▪ parler **2** ▪ indiquer **3**

VI **1** *(talk)* *(of person)* parler; **can he s.?** est-ce qu'il parle?, est-ce qu'il sait parler?; **without speaking** sans parler, sans rien dire; **to s. to sb** parler à qn *(about sth* de qch); **he spoke slowly/hesitatingly/too quickly** il s'est ex-

primé *ou* il a parlé lentement/avec hésitation/trop rapidement; **she hasn't spoken to me since** elle ne m'a pas adressé la parole depuis; **I can't give you a rise, you'll have to s. to the boss** je ne peux pas vous donner une augmentation, il va falloir que vous vous adressiez au patron; **they're not speaking (to each other)** ils ne s'adressent pas *ou* plus la parole; **I hate it when Mum and Dad aren't speaking** j'ai horreur des fois où Papa et Maman refusent de se parler; **isn't it about time you two started speaking again?** est-ce que vous ne devriez pas faire la paix?; **I'll s. to him about it** je lui en toucherai un mot, je lui en parlerai; **I know her/him to s. to** on se dit bonjour; **roughly speaking** approximativement; **legally/morally speaking** légalement/moralement parlant; **so to s.** pour ainsi dire; *Tel* **who's speaking?** qui est à l'appareil?; *(before transferring call)* c'est de la part de qui?; **Mr Thomas? – yes, speaking** M. Thomas? – lui-même

2 *(give a speech)* faire un discours; **he spoke on the subject of …** il a parlé *ou* traité de …; **to have the right to s.** avoir le droit de se faire entendre, avoir droit à la parole

VT **1** *(a word, the truth)* dire; **she has never spoken a word to me** elle ne m'a jamais adressé la parole, elle ne m'a jamais dit un mot; **he didn't s. a word about it** il n'en a pas soufflé mot; **to s. one's mind** dire ce qu'on pense; **to s. one's lines** *(in play)* dire son rôle

2 *(language)* parler; **do you s. French?** parlez-vous français?; **English is spoken everywhere** l'anglais est parlé partout; **English spoken** *(on sign)* on parle anglais; *also Fig* **to s. the same language** parler le même langage

3 *Lit (show)* *(feeling, emotion)* indiquer, témoigner de; **eyes that s. affection** yeux qui témoignent de l'amitié

▸ **speak against** VT INSEP *(motion, bill, proposal)* se prononcer contre; **she spoke passionately against the practice** elle a condamné cette pratique avec virulence

▸ **speak for** VT INSEP **1** *(person)* *(speak on behalf of)* parler pour; *(speak in support of)* plaider pour; **I'm sure I s. for everyone when I say …** je suis sûr que j'exprime la pensée générale lorsque je dis …; **speaking for myself** pour ma part, en ce qui me concerne; **I'll tell him when to leave, I can s. for myself!** c'est moi qui lui dirai de partir, je suis parfaitement capable de le faire moi-même!; **he is old enough to s. for himself** *(ask for something)* il est assez grand pour le demander tout seul; *(say something)* il est assez grand pour le dire lui-même; *Fam usu Hum* **s. for yourself!** parle pour toi!; **the facts s. for themselves** ces faits se passent de commentaires *ou* parlent d'eux-mêmes; **it doesn't s. very well for her chances of winning** ça ne laisse présager rien de bon quant à ses chances de victoire

2 to be spoken for *(to be reserved)* être réservé; *(of man, woman)* *(at dance etc)* être accompagné; *(have girlfriend, boyfriend)* avoir un(e) petit(e) ami(e); *(have wife, husband)* être marié(e)

▸ **speak of** VT INSEP **1** *(talk about)* parler de; **speaking of …** à propos de …, en parlant de …; **it's nothing to s. of** ce n'est rien, n'en parlons plus; **there's nothing on television/in the town, or nothing to s. of anyway** il n'y a rien de spécial à la télévision/en ville; **to s. well/highly of sb/sth** dire du bien/beaucoup de bien de qn/qch; **he is well spoken of** il a une bonne réputation, on dit du bien de lui; **to s. ill of sb** dire du mal de qn, médire de qn

2 *(indicate)* être significatif de; **this speaks of large-scale corruption** c'est le signe d'une corruption à grande échelle

▶**speak out** VI **1** *(speak with courage)* oser parler, oser prendre la parole; **to s. out against injustice** oser dénoncer l'injustice
2 *(speak loudly)* parler (plus) fort
▶**speak up** VI **1** *(speak louder)* parler plus fort *ou* plus haut
2 *(take active part in discussion etc)* prendre la parole, participer à la discussion; **she speaks up in class/meetings** elle prend la parole en classe/lors de réunions
3 = **speak out 1**
▶**speak up for** VT INSEP *(person)* parler en faveur de; **why don't you s. up for yourself?** pourquoi est-ce que tu ne te défends pas?; **you've got to learn to s. up for yourself** il faut que tu apprennes à défendre tes intérêts

speakeasy ['spiːkiːzɪ] N *Am* débit *m ou* bar *m* clandestin

speaker ['spiːkər] N **1** *(in dialogue)* interlocuteur, -trice; **as a s. of Italian** *or* **an Italian s. myself** ... moi qui parle italien ...; **there are very few surviving speakers of the language** il reste très peu de personnes qui parlent cette langue; **there were three speakers on the tape** il y avait trois personnes (qui parlaient) sur la bande; **I'm a plain s.** j'appelle les choses par leur nom, je dis ce que je pense, je dis les choses comme elles sont
2 *(at meeting, in discussion programme)* intervenant, -ante; *(at conference)* conférencier, -ière; *(political, orator)* orateur, -trice; *Am TV (announcer)* speaker *m*, speakerine *f*; **we have three speakers this evening** nous avons trois intervenants ce soir; **the next s. will be** ... la parole est maintenant à ...; **to be a good s.** s'exprimer très bien
3 *Parl* **the S.** *Br, Can* = le Président (des Communes); *Am* = le Président du Congrès; **Mr/Madam S.** Monsieur/Madame le Président
4 *(loudspeaker)* haut-parleur *m*, *pl* haut-parleurs, enceinte *f*

speaking ['spiːkɪŋ] ADJ **1** *(involving speech)* **do you have a s. part in the play** est-ce que vous avez du texte?; **she has a good s. voice** elle a une belle voix **2** *(which speaks) (doll, robot etc)* parlant
N **plain s.** franchise *f*, franc-parler *m*; **public s. art** *m* oratoire; **unaccustomed as I am to public s.** bien que je n'aie pas l'habitude de parler en public; **s. a foreign language is easier than writing it** parler une langue étrangère, c'est plus facile que de l'écrire; **he finds s. very difficult** il a du mal à parler; **we're no longer on s. terms** on ne s'adresse plus la parole
▶▶*Br* **s. clock** horloge *f* parlante; **s. tube** tuyau *m* acoustique

-speaking [-'spiːkɪŋ] SUFF **Chinese-/Russian-s.** *(as mother tongue)* de langue maternelle chinoise/russe; *(as learnt language)* qui parle chinois/russe; **slow-s.** qui s'exprime lentement; **plain-s.** qui appelle les choses par leur nom

spear [spɪər] N **1** *Mil* lance *f*, *(in hunting)* épieu *m*; *(for throwing)* javelot *m*; **to be a s.-carrier** *Theat* être figurant; *Fig* avoir un rôle mineur **2** *Fishing* harpon *m* **3** *(of grass)* brin *m*; **spears of asparagus, asparagus spears** pointes *fpl* d'asperges
VT **1** *(pierce) (person)* transpercer *ou (kill)* tuer d'un coup de lance; *(olive, piece of food etc)* piquer *(avec une fourchette etc)* **2** *Fishing (fish)* harponner
▶▶**s. fishing** pêche *f ou* chasse *f* (sous-marine) au harpon; *Bot* **s. grass** pâturin *m*

spearhead ['spɪəhed] N *(of spear)* fer *m* de lance; *Mil (of attack)* pointe *f*, *Fig (of organization etc)* fer de lance
VT *Mil* **they spearheaded the crossing of the river** ils ont forcé les premiers le passage du

fleuve; *Fig* **to s. a movement** être le fer de lance d'un mouvement

spearmint ['spɪəmɪnt] N *(plant, flavour)* menthe *f* verte; *(sweet)* bonbon *m* à la menthe

spec [spek] N *Fam* **we've got it on s. for a week** on l'a à l'essai pour une semaine; **to buy sth on s.** acheter qch à tout hasard

speccy ['spekɪ] *Br Fam* N binoclard, -arde
ADJ binoclard

special ['speʃəl] ADJ spécial, -aux, particulier, -ère **(to** à); *(friend)* intime; **nothing s.** rien de particulier; **the food was OK but nothing s.** la nourriture était assez bonne mais elle n'avait rien d'exceptionnel; **are you doing anything s. for your birthday?** tu fais quelque chose de spécial pour ton anniversaire?; **what's so s. about the 19th of November?** qu'est-ce que le 19 novembre a de si spécial?; **to pay s. attention** faire particulièrement attention **(to** sth à qch); **for someone s.** *(on card)* pour quelqu'un qui m'est cher; **for s. occasions** pour les jours de fête, pour les occasions spéciales; **to get s. treatment** bénéficier d'un traitement de faveur; **s. case** cas *m* particulier; **s. characteristic** particularité *f*, **s. feature** particularité *f*
N *(train)* train *m* spécial; *(newspaper)* édition *f* spéciale; *(programme)* émission *f* spéciale; **today's s.** *(in restaurant)* plat *m* du jour
▶▶**s. agent** *(spy etc)* agent *m* secret; **S. Air Service** = commando *m* d'intervention spéciale de l'armée britannique; *EU* **S. Area of Conservation** zone *f* spéciale de conservation; **S. Branch** = service *m* de police britannique chargé des crimes contre la sûreté de l'État, ≈ Renseignements *mpl* généraux; *Typ* **s. character** caractère *m* spécial; **s. clause** clause *f* particulière; *Br* **s. constable** auxiliaire *mf* de police; *Journ* **s. correspondent** envoyé, -ée spécial(e); **s. delivery** = service postal britannique garantissant la distribution du courrier sous 24 heures; **to mail sth s. delivery** envoyer qch en exprès; *Fin* **s. drawing rights** droits *mpl* de tirage spéciaux; **s. edition** édition spéciale, hors m série; *Cin, TV* **s. effects** effets *mpl* spéciaux; **s. indications** *(on ticket)* indications *fpl* spéciales; *Comput* **s. interest group** groupe *m* d'intérêt; **s. interest holidays** vacances *fpl* à thème; *Journ* **s. issue** numéro *m* spécial; *Br* **s. licence** dispense *f* de bans; *Br* **they were married by s. licence** ils se sont mariés avec dispense de bans; **s. offer** promotion *f*; **s. pleading** argument *m* spécieux; *Law* plaidoyer *m* partial; *Pol* **s. powers** pouvoirs *mpl* extraordinaires; *Com* **s. price** prix *m* spécial; **s. rate** tarif *m* préférentiel *ou* spécial; *Br* **s. school** établissement *m* d'enseignement spécialisé *(pour enfants handicapés ou inadaptés)*

Note that the French adjective **spécial** also means **peculiar, odd**.

specialist ['speʃəlɪst] N spécialiste *mf*; **to become a s. in electronics** *or* **an electronics s.** se spécialiser dans l'électronique; *Med* **heart/lung/cancer s.** cardiologue *mf*/pneumologue *mf*/cancérologue *mf*
ADJ *(skills, vocabulary, knowledge)* spécialisé, de spécialiste; *(writing, publication)* pour spécialistes; *(bookshop, TV channel, dictionary)* spécialisé; **what are your s. subjects?** dans quels sujets vous spécialisez-vous?; **it requires s. skills** ça demande les compétences d'un spécialiste; **if you don't have the s. knowledge** si vous n'avez pas les connaissances d'un spécialiste
▶▶*Com* **s. retailer** détaillant, -ante spécialisé(e); **s. teacher** professeur *m* spécialisé

speciality [speʃɪ'ælɪtɪ], *Am* **specialty** ['speʃəltɪ] N **1** *(of store, restaurant, region etc)*

spécialité *f*, *(area of study) (of student)* matière *f* principale; *(of researcher)* sujet *m* de recherches; **his s. is Vietnamese art** il se spécialise dans l'art du Vietnam; *also Iron* **that's my s.** c'est ma spécialité, je suis spécialiste; **skiing holidays are s.** *(in advertisement)* les sports d'hiver sont notre spécialité; **s. goods** produits *mpl* de spécialité, produits spécialisés; **s. restaurant** restaurant *m* de spécialités; **s. shop** magasin *m* spécialisé **2** *Law* = **specialty 1**

specialization [speʃəlaɪ'zeɪʃən] N spécialisation *f* **(in** dans)

specialize ['speʃəlaɪz] VI *(of shop, researcher etc)* se spécialiser **(in** dans); *Iron* **she specializes in that sort of blunder** elle est spécialiste de ce genre de gaffes

specialized ['speʃəlaɪzd] ADJ *(work, subject)* spécialisé

specially ['speʃəlɪ] ADV *(in particular)* spécialement, particulièrement; **I'm s. interested in antique furniture** je m'intéresse plus particulièrement *ou* surtout aux antiquités; **I went there s. to see them** j'y suis allé dans le seul but de les voir, j'y suis allé exprès pour les voir; **I waited up s.** je suis resté debout exprès; **s. designed to ...** spécialement conçu pour ...; **I s. asked you not to ...** je t'avais bien demandé de ne pas ...; **it's not s. good** ce n'est pas particulièrement bon; **s. at night** surtout le soir; **they had a cake s. made** ils ont fait faire un gâteau spécialement

Attention: ne pas confondre avec **especially**.

specialty ['speʃəltɪ] N **1** *Law* contrat *m* par acte scellé **2** *Am* = **speciality 1**

specie ['spiːʃiː] N *(no pl) Fin* espèces *fpl* (monnayées)

species ['spiːʃiːz] N INV **1** *Biol* espèce *f*, **the human s.** l'espèce humaine; **the origin of s.** l'origine *f* des espèces **2** *(type)* espèce *f*, sorte *f*

specific [spɪ'sɪfɪk] ADJ *(particular)* spécifique; *(clear) (statement, example, rule, aim)* précis; *(command)* explicite; **or, to be s., ...** ou, pour être précis ...; **in this s. case** dans ce cas précis *ou* particulier; **to be s.** *(of person)* être explicite; **she was pretty s. about her intentions** elle a été très précise quant à ses intentions; **could you be a bit more s.?** pourriez-vous être plus précis?, pourriez-vous préciser?
N *Med* spécifique *m* **(for** contre); *Am Ind* **specifics** *(precise description)* description *f* précise; *(characteristics)* caractéristiques *fpl*, *Fam* **to get down to specifics** en venir aux faits précis
▶▶*Phys* **s. gravity** densité *f*

specifically [spɪ'sɪfɪk(ə)lɪ] ADV spécifiquement; *(precisely)* précisément; **your name was mentioned s.** votre nom a été bien précisément mentionné; **you must state quite s. what the requirements are** vous devez bien spécifier les conditions requises; **I s. told you not to ...** je t'ai dit très précisément de ne pas ...; **I s. asked for a small portion** j'ai bien demandé une petite portion; **we were s. forbidden to ...** il nous était expressément défendu de ...; **it is s. designed for use in ...** c'est (tout) spécialement conçu pour une utilisation dans ...; **a book which is s. written for people who ...** un livre écrit tout particulièrement pour les gens qui ...

specification [spesɪfɪ'keɪʃən] N **1** *(act) (of details etc)* spécification *f* **2** *(description) (of car)* caractéristiques *fpl*, *(of work to be done)* prescriptions *fpl*; *Constr, Ind* **specifications** *(of contract)* cahier *m* des charges **3** *(condition, stipulation)* spécification *f*, **there's no**

s. about the number of times you can enter on ne précise pas combien de fois on peut participer; **their only s. was that the press should not be told** la seule condition qu'ils avaient posée était que la presse ne devait pas être informée

▸▸ *Com* **s. buying** achats *mpl* spécifiés

specificity [spesɪˈfɪsɪtɪ] **N** spécificité *f*

specify [ˈspesɪfaɪ] **VT** *(conditions etc)* spécifier, préciser; **I specified blue** j'ai spécifié la couleur bleue; **specified load** charge prévue *ou* prescrite; **unless otherwise specified** sauf indication contraire

specimen [ˈspesɪmɪn] **N** spécimen *m*; *(sample)* spécimen, échantillon *m*; **the finest specimens in his collection** les plus belles pièces de sa collection; **that's a magnificent s.** *(butterfly etc)* c'est un très beau spécimen; **a s. of sb's handwriting** un échantillon *ou* exemple de l'écriture de qn; *Med* **to take a s. of sb's blood, to take a blood s. from sb** faire une prise de sang à qn; *Fam* **a s. (of urine)** un prélèvement d'urine; *Fam* **an odd s.** *(person)* un drôle de type; *Fam* **you're a pretty pathetic s., aren't you!** tu es vraiment lamentable!

▸▸ **s. bottle** flacon-échantillon *m*, *pl* flacons-échantillons; **s. copy** spécimen *m* *(livre, magazine)*; **s. page** page *f* spécimen, page type; **s. signature** spécimen de signature

specious [ˈspiːʃəs] **ADJ** *(appearance)* spécieux, trompeur; *(argument, promises)* captieux, spécieux

speciousness [ˈspiːʃəsnɪs] **N** *(of argument, promises)* caractère *m* spécieux

speck [spek] **N** **1** *(mark)* petite tache *f*, *(of colour, ink)* point *m*; *(on fruit)* tavelure *f*; *Med* **specks (in front of the eyes)** mouches *fpl*, taches *fpl* *(devant les yeux)* **2** *(small piece)* *(of dust)* grain *m*, atome *m*; **the ship was only a s. on the horizon** le navire n'était qu'un point à l'horizon

speckle [ˈspek(ə)l] **N** petite tache *f*, *(of colour)* point *m*; *(on animal, egg)* moucheture *f*, tacheture *f*

VT tacheter, moucheter

speckled [ˈspek(ə)ld] **ADJ** tacheté, moucheté; *(plumage)* grivelé; *(hen)* tacheté; **bird s. with white** oiseau tacheté de blanc

specs [speks] **NPL** *Fam* **1** *(spectacles)* carreaux *mpl* **2** *Ind* *(specifications)* spécifications *fpl*

spectacle [ˈspektək(ə)l] **N** **1** *(show, sight)* spectacle *m*; **to make a s. of oneself** se donner en spectacle **2** **(pair of) spectacles** (paire *f* de) lunettes *fpl*; **to put on one's spectacles** mettre *ou* chausser ses lunettes VOIR GRAMMAIRE A10

spectacled [ˈspektək(ə)ld] **ADJ** à lunettes

spectacular [spekˈtækjʊlər] **ADJ** spectaculaire **N** *Theat, Cin* superproduction *f*; **an ice-skating s.** une revue de patinage artistique

spectacularly [spekˈtækjʊləlɪ] **ADV** *(to improve, collapse etc)* de façon spectaculaire

spectate [spekˈteɪt] **VI** *esp Sp* **to s. at** *(match etc)* assister à; **I prefer to s.** je préfère être spectateur/spectatrice

spectator [spekˈteɪtər] **N** spectateur, -trice; **the spectators** les spectateurs; **we don't want any spectators** nous ne voulons pas qu'on nous regarde

▸▸ **s. sport** sport *m* grand public; **swimming is not a very good s. sport** la natation n'est pas un sport très intéressant à regarder; *Fig* **television has turned war into a s. sport** la télévision a transformé la guerre en spectacle

specter [ˈspektər] **N** *Am* = spectre

spectral [ˈspektr(ə)l] **ADJ** **1** *Phys (analysis, band, density)* spectral, -aux **2** *(ghostly)* spectral, -aux

▸▸ *Phys* **s. colours** couleurs *fpl* spectrales; *Phys* **s. range** domaine *m* spectral

spectre [ˈspektər] **N** spectre *m*, fantôme *m*; *Fig* **the s. of war/famine** *(threat)* le spectre de la guerre/famine

spectrogram [ˈspektrəʊgræm] **N** spectrogramme *m*

spectrograph [ˈspektrəʊgræf] **N** spectrographe *m*

spectrometer [spekˈtrɒmɪtər] **N** spectromètre *m*

spectroscope [ˈspektrəskəʊp] **N** spectroscope *m*

spectroscopy [spekˈtrɒskəpɪ] **N** spectroscopie *f*

spectrum, *pl* **spectra** [ˈspektrəm, -trə] **N** **1** *Phys etc* spectre *m*; **the colours of the s.** les couleurs spectrales *ou* du spectre **2** *(of opinions)* éventail *m*; **a wide s. of opinions** un large éventail d'opinions; **the whole s. of political opinion** tout l'éventail des opinions politiques; **across the political s.** dans l'ensemble des tendances politiques

▸▸ **s. analysis** analyse *f* spectrale

speculate [ˈspekjʊleɪt] **VI** **1 to s. on** *or* **about sth** *(wonder)* spéculer *ou* méditer sur qch; *(conjecture)* faire des conjectures sur qch **2** *Fin* spéculer; **to s. on the Stock Exchange** spéculer en Bourse

speculating [ˈspekjʊleɪtɪŋ] **N** *Fin* spéculation *f*

speculation [spekjʊˈleɪʃən] **N** **1** *(wondering)* spéculation *f*, méditation *f*, *(conjecture)* conjecture *f* (**on, about** sur); **it was pure s. on his part** c'était (une) pure conjecture de sa part **2** *Fin* spéculation *f*; **to buy sth on s.** acheter qch à titre de spéculation

speculative [ˈspekjʊlətɪv] **ADJ** spéculatif; **these are merely s. assumptions** ce sont là de pures hypothèses *ou* de pures conjectures

▸▸ *St Exch* **s. securities, s. shares** valeurs *fpl* spéculatives

speculatively [ˈspekjʊlətɪvlɪ] **ADV** *(to suggest, argue)* à titre d'hypothèse; *(to invest)* spéculativement

speculator [ˈspekjʊleɪtər] **N** spéculateur, -trice; *St Exch* joueur, -euse en Bourse, spéculateur, -trice

speculum, *pl* **speculums, specula** [ˈspekjʊləm, -əmz, -ə] **N** *Med* spéculum *m*

sped **PT, PP** *see* **speed VI, VT**

speech [spiːtʃ] **N** **1** *(faculty)* la parole; **to lose the power of s.** perdre la parole; **her s. was slow and deliberate** elle parlait lentement en pesant ses mots; **to be slow of s.** parler lentement; **to be abrupt in one's s.** parler d'une manière brusque

2 *(language)* *(of a people)* langue *f*, *(of a region etc)* parler *m*; **things which people say in everyday s.** des choses que les gens disent dans la langue de tous les jours

3 *(address)* discours *m*, allocution *f*; **to give** *or* **make a s.** faire *ou* prononcer un discours *ou* une allocution; **s.! s.!** un discours! un discours!

4 *Gram* **part of s.** partie *f* du discours; **direct/indirect s.** discours *m ou* style *m* direct/indirect; **figure of s.** figure *f* de rhétorique VOIR GRAMMAIRE A63; A78

▸▸ *Comput* **s. chip** puce *f* de traitement de la parole; *Ling* **s. community** communauté *f* linguistique; *Br Sch* **s. day** distribution *f* des prix; **s. defect** défaut *m* de prononciation, *Spec* trouble *f* du langage; **s. impediment** défaut d'élocution *ou* de prononciation; *Comput* **s. recognition** reconnaissance *f* de la parole; *Radio* **s. station** station *f* de radio à vocation culturelle; **s. synthesizer** synthétiseur *m* de parole; **s. therapist** orthophoniste *mf*, *Belg, Suisse* logopède *mf*; **s. therapy** orthophonie *f*

Speech day

À la fin de l'année scolaire en Grande-Bretagne, certaines écoles invitent une personnalité à prononcer un discours et à distribuer des prix.

speechify [ˈspiːtʃɪfaɪ] **VI** *Pej* discourir, pérorer

speechifying [ˈspiːtʃɪfaɪɪŋ] **N** *Pej* beaux discours *mpl*, laïus *m*

speechless [ˈspiːtʃlɪs] **ADJ 1** *(struck dumb)* interdit, interloqué, muet, -ette; **to be s. with anger/fear/rage** être muet de colère/peur/rage; **emotion left him s.** l'émotion l'a laissé muet; **I was s.** *(with anger, surprise etc)* j'étais sans voix; **I'm s.!** je ne sais pas quoi dire! **2** *(for physiological reasons)* incapable de parler

speechlessly [ˈspiːtʃlɪslɪ] **ADV** sans voix

speechwriter [ˈspiːtʃraɪtər] **N** rédacteur, -trice de discours

speed [spiːd] **N** **1** vitesse *f*, rapidité *f*; *(of engine, machine)* vitesse, régime *m*; *Phot (of film, shutter)* vitesse; *(of lens)* rapidité; **the s. of light/sound** la vitesse de la lumière/du son; *Lit* **to make all s.** faire diligence, se hâter; **with all possible s.** aussi rapidement *ou* aussi vite que possible; **the s. with which she learnt/the building was completed** la vitesse à laquelle elle a appris/le bâtiment a été terminé; *Aut etc* **at s. (to travel)** à grande vitesse; **at top** *or* **full s.** à toute vitesse; *(of runners)* à toutes jambes; **to drive at top s.** rouler à toute vitesse *ou* à toute allure; *Naut* **full s. ahead/astern!** en avant/en arrière toute!; **car with a maximum s. of 150 km an hour** voiture qui plafonne à 150 km à l'heure; **cruising s.** vitesse *ou* régime de croisière; *Aviat* **take-off s.** vitesse de décollage; **to gather/lose s.** prendre/perdre de la vitesse; **to reduce s.** ralentir; **to pick up s.** *(of train, car)* prendre de la vitesse; *Fam* **to be up to s. on sth** être au courant de qch; *Fam* **to bring sb up to s. on sth** mettre qn au courant de qch

2 *(gear)* vitesse *f*; **five-s. gearbox** boîte *f* à cinq vitesses

3 *Comput* vitesse *f*; **32 s. CD-ROM** lecteur *m* de CD-ROM 32 x

4 *Arch* **to wish sb good s.** souhaiter bonne chance à qn

5 *Fam (amphetamines)* amphets *fpl*, amphés *fpl*, speed *m*

VI 1 *(pt, pp* **sped** *or* **speeded***) (hasten)* se hâter, se presser; *(go fast)* aller vite; *Aut etc (go fast)* faire de la vitesse; **the car was speeding towards us** la voiture arrivait sur nous à toute vitesse; **we are speeding towards a crisis** nous allons à grands pas vers une crise

2 *(pt, pp* **speeded***) Aut (exceed speed limit)* faire un excès de vitesse; **I was caught speeding** j'ai eu une contravention pour excès de vitesse

3 *Fam* **to be speeding** *(be under effect of amphetamines)* être sous amphés, speeder

VT *(pt, pp* **sped** *or* **speeded***) Arch, Lit* **to s. sb on his/her way** *(wish a good journey)* souhaiter bon voyage à qn; *esp Hum (encourage to leave)* encourager *ou* presser qn à partir plus vite; *Arch* **God s. (you)!** bon voyage!

▸▸ **s. bump** casse-vitesse *m inv*, ralentisseur *m*; **s. camera** radar *m*; *Am Fam* **s. cop** motard *m* (de la police); **s. dating** speed dating *m*, = soirées *fpl* de rencontre dont chaque participant dispose d'un temps limité pour s'entretenir avec tous les autres; *Tel* **s. dial** numérotation *f* abrégée; **s. limit** limitation *f* de vitesse; *Br, Austr Fam* **s. merchant** mordu, -ue de vitesse; *Aut* **s. sensor** capteur *m* de vitesse; **s. trap** contrôle *m* de vitesse

▸ **speed along** VI *(in car, on bike)* rouler vite, *Fam* foncer; *(on foot)* marcher *ou* courir vite; **the work is speeding along** le travail avance à bonne allure

VT SEP *(work)* faire avancer *ou* progresser en vitesse

▸ **speed back** VI *(of person, driver)* rentrer à toute vitesse; **she sped back to Edinburgh** elle est retournée à Édimbourg à toute vitesse

VT SEP *(person)* ramener à toute vitesse

▸ **speed off** VI *(on foot, in car)* partir à toute allure

VT SEP **they sped him off to hospital** ils l'ont transporté à l'hôpital à toute vitesse

▸ **speed up** VI *(of driver, runner etc)* accélérer; *(of work, pace)* s'accélérer; *(work faster)* travailler plus rapidement

VT SEP *(staff, project)* activer; *(job)* activer, accélérer; **to s. things up** accélérer *ou* activer les choses

speedball ['spi:dbɔ:l] N *Sl* speedball *m (mélange d'héroïne et de cocaïne)*

speedboat ['spi:dbəʊt] N vedette *f*; *(with outboard motor)* hors-bord *m inv*

speedfreak ['spi:dfri:k] N *Sl* **to be a s.** consommer beaucoup d'amphets

speedily ['spi:dɪlɪ] ADV rapidement

speediness ['spi:dɪnɪs] N rapidité *f*

speeding ['spi:dɪŋ] N *Aut (exceeding speed limit)* excès *m* de vitesse

▸▸ **s. fine** contravention *f* pour excès de vitesse; **s. ticket** P-V *m inv* pour excès de vitesse; **s. up** accélération *f*

speedo ['spi:dəʊ] N *Fam* = **speedometer**

speedometer [spi:'dɒmɪtər] N *Aut etc* compteur *m* (de vitesse)

speedster ['spi:dstər] N *(car)* bolide *m*; *(driver)* fou *m* du volant, *Pej* chauffard *m*

speed-up N accélération *f*

speedway ['spi:dweɪ] N **1** *Sport (motorcycle racing)* speedway *m*; *(track)* circuit *m* de speedway; *Am (for cars)* circuit automobile **2** *Am (fast road)* autoroute *f*

▸▸ **s. rider** pilote *m* de speedway

speedwell ['spi:dwel] N *(plant)* véronique *f*

Speedwriting® ['spi:draɪtɪŋ] N écriture *f* abrégée

speedy ['spi:dɪ] ADJ *(person, work, response etc)* rapide, prompt; *(car)* rapide

speleologist [spi:lɪ'ɒlədʒɪst] N spéléologue *mf*

speleology [spi:lɪ'ɒlədʒɪ] N spéléologie *f*

spell¹ [spel] N *(magic words)* formule *f* magique, charme *m*; *(enchanted state)* sort *m*, maléfice *m*, charme; **to cast a (magic) s. over sb, to put a (magic) s. on sb** jeter un sort à qn, ensorceler qn; **to break the s.** rompre le charme; **under a s.** sous un charme, ensorcelé

spell² *(pt, pp* **spelt, spelled** [spelt, speld]*)* VT **1** *(out loud)* épeler; *(in writing)* orthographier; **how is it spelt?, how do you s. it?** comment ça s'épelle *ou* s'écrit?; **how do you s. 'Mississippi'?** comment écrit-on 'Mississippi'?; **can you s. that for me?** *(on telephone etc)* pouvez-vous me l'épeler?; **it's spelt** *or* **you s. it with an 'o'** ça s'écrit avec un 'o' **2** **what do these letters s.?** quel mot forment ces lettres? **3** *(signify)* signifier; **to s. disaster** être un désastre; **this spells disaster** on est perdu; **it would s. disaster** cela serait un désastre

VI orthographier *ou* écrire correctement; **he can't s.** il est nul en orthographe; **she can't s. very well** elle n'est pas très bonne en orthographe

▸ **spell out** VT SEP *(address, name etc) (pro-*nounce individual letters of)* épeler; *(have difficulty in reading)* déchiffrer péniblement; *Fig (explain explicitly)* expliquer bien clairement; **... even though I spelled my name out for him ...** bien que je lui aie épelé mon nom; *Fig* **do I have to s. it out for you?** faut-il que je te fasse un dessin?; *Fig* **I'll s. it out for you** je vais te le dire clairement

spell³ N **1** *(period)* période *f*, *Austr (rest period)* repos *m*; **to rest for a (short) s.** se reposer pendant quelque temps; **a long s. of cold weather** une longue période de froid; **during the cold s.** pendant le coup de froid; **we're in for a s. of wet weather** le temps se met à la pluie; **to suffer from dizzy spells** être sujet à des vertiges; **it's his second s. in prison** c'est son deuxième séjour en prison; **the end of the party's long s. in power is in sight** le parti est en train de vivre ses derniers moments au pouvoir

2 *(turn) (of duty)* tour *m*; **to do a s. of duty** faire un tour de service; **to take spells at the pumps** se relayer aux pompes; **do you want to take a s. at the wheel?** tu veux en relayer au volant?

VT **1** *Am Fam (relieve) (person)* relayer, relever *(dans son travail)* **2** *Austr (allow to rest) (horse)* laisser reposer

spellbinder ['spelbaɪndər] N *(speaker)* orateur, -trice captivant(e)

spellbinding ['spelbaɪndɪŋ] ADJ envoûtant

spellbound ['spelbaʊnd] ADJ *(fascinated)* envoûté, fasciné; **to hold sb s.** envoûter qn, fasciner qn

spellcheck ['speltʃek] *Comput* N correction *f* orthographique; **to do** *or* **run a s. on a document** effectuer une correction orthographique sur un document

VT faire la vérification orthographique de

spellchecker ['speltʃekər] N *Comput* correcteur *m* orthographique *ou* d'orthographe

spellchecking ['speltʃekɪŋ] N *Comput* correction *f* orthographique *ou* d'orthographe

speller ['spelər] N **1** *(person)* **to be a good/a bad s.** être fort/faible en orthographe **2** *(book)* alphabet *m*

spelling ['spelɪŋ] N orthographe *f*; **his s. is atrocious** son orthographe est déplorable
VOIR GRAMMAIRE A79–80

▸▸ **s. mistake** faute *f* d'orthographe; **s. test** test *m* d'orthographe

spelt PT, PP *see* **spell**²

spend [spend] VT *(pt, pp* **spent** [spent]*)* **1** *(money)* dépenser; **to s. one's money on cigarettes** dépenser son argent en cigarettes; **her father has spent a great deal on her education** son père a dépensé beaucoup pour ses études; **to s. money on sb** dépenser son argent pour qn; **she spends money like water** l'argent lui fond *ou* glisse entre les mains; *Br Fam* **to s. a penny** *(urinate)* faire pipi

2 *(pass) (time)* passer; **to s. the night** passer la nuit; **to s. Sunday in the country** passer le dimanche à la campagne; **haven't you got any better ways of spending your time?** c'est tout ce que tu trouves à faire pour t'occuper?; **could you please s. a little time talking to her about it?** pourrais-tu prendre un peu de temps pour lui en parler?; **how do you s. your weekends?** qu'est-ce que tu fais le week-end?

3 *(expend) (time, energy)* consacrer; **to s. time on (doing) sth** consacrer *ou* employer du temps à (faire) qch; **to s. a lot of effort on a job** se donner beaucoup de mal pour un travail; **if you spent a bit more care on ...** si tu apportais *ou* mettais un peu plus de soin à ...

4 *(usu passive) (use up) (one's strength, ammunition)* épuiser; **her strength/energy was**

all but spent elle n'avait presque plus de forces/d'énergie

VI dépenser

N *esp Com* dépenses *fpl*

spendable ['spendəb(ə)l] ADJ

▸▸ **s. income** revenu *m* dépensable

spender ['spendər] N **to be a big s.** être très dépensier; **they are the biggest arms s.** ce sont eux qui dépensent le plus en armement

spending ['spendɪŋ] N dépense *f*, **public s.** dépenses *fpl* publiques

▸▸ **s. cuts** réductions *fpl* des dépenses; **s. money** argent *m* de poche; **s. power** pouvoir *m* d'achat; **s. spree** vague *f* de dépenses; **to go on a s. spree** faire des folies

spendthrift ['spendθrɪft] N dépensier, -ière; **s. habits** habitudes *fpl* dépensières

spent [spent] ADJ **1** *(tired)* épuisé **2** *(used up)* épuisé; **s. bullet** balle *f* morte; **s. match** allumette *f* usagée

PT, PP *see* **spend**

sperm [spɜ:m] N **1** *Physiol* sperme *m* **2** *(cell)* spermatozoïde *m*

▸▸ **s. bank** banque *f* de sperme; **s. cell** spermatozoïde; **s. donor** donneur *m* de sperme; **s. oil** blanc *m* de baleine, spermaceti *m*; *Zool* **s. whale** cachalot *m*

spermaceti [spɜ:mə'setɪ] N spermaceti *m*, blanc *m* de baleine

spermatozoon, *pl* **spermatozooa** [spɜ:mətəʊ'zəʊɒn, -əʊə] N spermatozoïde *m*

spermicidal [spɜ:mɪ'saɪd(ə)l] ADJ spermicide

spermicide ['spɜ:mɪsaɪd] N spermicide *m*

spew [spju:] *Br Fam* VT & VI *(vomit)* dégueuler; **it makes you want to s.!** ça fait gerber!

N *(vomit)* dégueulis *m*

▸ **spew forth, spew out** VI *(of lava, flames etc)* jaillir, fuser *(from, of* de*)*; *Fig (of propaganda, lies, etc)* fuser

VT SEP *(lava, propaganda)*, *Fig (propaganda)* déverser

▸ **spew up** VI, VT SEP *Br Fam (vomit)* dégueuler

spewing ['spju:ɪŋ] ADJ *Br Fam (angry)* furmasse, furax

sphagnum, *pl* **sphagna** ['sfægnəm, -ə] N *Bot* sphaigne *f*

▸▸ **s. moss** sphaigne

sphere [sfɪər] N **1** *Astron, Geom* sphère *f*; **the celestial s.** la sphère céleste **2** *(field)* domaine *m*, sphère *f*; *(social circle)* milieu *m*, sphère; **to extend one's s. of activity** étendre sa sphère d'activité; **that is not within my s.** cela n'est pas de mon domaine *ou* mon ressort; **in the political s.** sur le plan politique; **in political/academic spheres** dans les milieux politiques/universitaires; **s. of influence** sphère *ou* zone *f* d'influence

spherical ['sferɪk(ə)l] ADJ sphérique

spheroid ['sfɪərɔɪd] N sphéroïde *m*

sphincter ['sfɪŋktər] N sphincter *m*

sphinx, *pl* **sphinxes** [sfɪŋks, 'sfɪŋksɪz] N *Myth* sphinx *m*

sphinx-like ADJ de sphinx; *(smile)* énigmatique

spic [spɪk] N *Am Offensive Sl* métèque *mf* *(d'origine latino-américaine)*

spice [spaɪs] N **1** *Culin* épice *f*, **mixed spice(s)** épices mélangées **2** *Fig* sel *m*, piquant *m*; **to give s. to a story** pimenter un récit; **the s. of life** le sel *ou* le piquant de la vie; **the s. of adventure** le piment de l'aventure

VT **1** *(cake, drink etc)* épicer **2** *Fig (story etc)* pimenter, relever

▸▸ **s. rack** étagère *f ou* présentoir *m* à épices

spiciness ['spaɪsɪnɪs] N **1** *(of food)* caractère *m* épicé **2** *Fig (of story)* piquant *m*, sel *m*

spick [spɪk] ADJ **s. and span** reluisant de propreté, propre comme un sou neuf; *(person)* tiré à quatre épingles

N *Am Offensive Sl (Spanish-American)* latino *mf*

spicy ['spaɪsɪ] ADJ **1** *Culin (spiced)* épicé; *(taste)* relevé **2** *Fig (story, conversation etc)* piquant, croustillant; *(risqué)* salé, épicé, poivré; **to tell s. stories** en dire de vertes

spider ['spaɪdər] N **1** araignée *f* **2** *Br (for luggage)* araignée (à bagages)**3** *Am Culin* poêle *f* (à trépied) **4** *Comput* araignée
▸▸**s. crab** araignée (de mer); **s. monkey** singe *m* araignée; **s. plant** chlorophytum *m*; *Br* **s.'s web, s. web** toile d'araignée

spiderman, *pl* **spidermen** ['spaɪdəmæn, -men] N *Br* = ouvrier *m* qui travaille au sommet des édifices

spidery ['spaɪdərɪ] ADJ *(resembling a spider)* qui ressemble à une araignée; **s. handwriting** pattes *fpl* de mouches

spiel [ʃpiːl, spiːl] N *Fam* baratin *m*, speech *m*; *(of salesman)* boniment *m*; **he gave me some s. about having been held up at the airport** il m'a servi tout un baratin comme quoi il avait été bloqué à l'aéroport
▸**spiel off** VT SEP *Am Fam (recite)* débiter

spiffing ['spɪfɪŋ] ADJ *Old-fashioned Br Fam* épatant

spigot ['spɪgət] N **1** *(stopper) (of barrel)* fausset *m* **2** *Am (faucet for water etc)* robinet *m* **3** *(handle of tap)* clef *f* (de robinet)

spike [spaɪk] N **1** *(of railing, helmet)* pointe *f*, *(of barbed wire etc)* piquant *m*; **impaled on the spikes of the railings** empalé sur la grille; *Sport* **spikes** *(running shoes)* chaussures *fpl* à pointes
2 *Bot* épi *m*
3 *Elec* pointe *f ou* crête *f* de tension
4 *Journ* page *f*, **on the s.** rejeté
5 *Sl (hypodermic needle)* shooteuse *f*, pompe *f*
6 *(nail)* gros clou *m*
VT **1** *(fit with spikes)* armer de pointes; **spiked gate** grille *f* à pointes *ou* garnie de pointes; *Sport* **spiked shoes** chaussures *fpl* à pointes
2 *(thwart) (affair)* faire avorter; *(plan)* contrecarrer, entraver; *Fig* **to s. sb's guns** priver qn de ses moyens d'action, mettre qn hors d'action
3 *(add alcohol to) (drink)* corser
4 *Journ (story, article)* rejeter, *Fam* balancer
▸▸**s. heel** *(on woman's shoes)* talon *m* aiguille; **s. lavender** lavande *f* aspic *m*, spic *m*; **s. nail** gros clou

spiked [spaɪkt] ADJ *Journ* rejeté

spikenard ['spaɪknɑːd] N *Lit (ointment)* nard *m* (indien)

spiky ['spaɪkɪ] ADJ **1** *(with sharp points)* piquant; **s. hair** *(short)* cheveux *mpl* en brosse; *(of punk etc)* cheveux hérissés **2** *Fam (touchy, irritable)* susceptible, chatouilleux

spill¹ [spɪl] VT *(pt, pp* **spilt, spilled** [spɪlt, spɪld]) *(liquid, salt)* renverser; *(blood)* verser; **without spilling a drop** sans laisser tomber une goutte; *Fig Fam* **to s. the beans** révéler un secret; *(under interrogation)* cracher *ou* lâcher le morceau
VI **1** *(of liquid)* se répandre, couler; **some wine had spilled on the carpet** du vin s'était répandu sur le tapis **2** *Fig Fam (reveal information)* vendre la mèche; *(under interrogation)* cracher *ou* lâcher le morceau; **come on, s.!** allez, accouche!
N *(fall)* **to have** *or* **take a s.** culbuter; *(from bicycle, horse)* tomber, faire une chute, *Fam* ramasser *ou* se prendre une pelle
▸**spill out** VI *(of liquid etc)* déborder; *Fig (of words)* sortir; **the crowd started spilling out of the stadium** la foule commença à se déverser hors du stade

VT SEP *(liquid)* renverser; *Fig (story)* répandre
▸**spill over** VI *(of liquid)* déborder, se déverser; *Fig (of scandal, conflict)* se répandre (**into** dans); **the population has spilled over into the surrounding areas** la population s'est déversée sur les zones avoisinantes; **the conflict could s. over into neighbouring countries** le conflit risquerait de s'étendre aux pays voisins

spill² N *(for lighting fire etc)* allume-feu *m, pl* allume-feux
▸▸*TV* **s. light** lumière *f* parasite, mouche *f*

spillage ['spɪlɪdʒ] N *(action)* déversement *m* accidentel; *(liquid)* liquide *m* déversé; **there's been a diesel s. on the M25** un chargement de gasoil s'est renversé sur la M25

spillover ['spɪləʊvər] N *(excess population)* surpopulation *f*

spillway ['spɪlweɪ] N *Tech* déversoir *m*

spilt PT, PP *see* **spill¹** VT, VI

SPIN [spɪn]

| N tournoiement **1** ▪ essorage **1** |
| ▪ promenade **2** ▪ manipulation **3** |
| VT filer ▪ faire tourner |
| VI tourner **1** ▪ tournoyer **1** ▪ patiner **2** ▪ manipuler l'information **3** |

N **1** *(turning movement)* tournoiement *m*; *(of ball etc)* mouvement *m* de) rotation *f*, *(of washing machine)* essorage *m*; *Aviat* vrille *f*, **to give sth a s.** *(in spin-dryer)* essorer qch; **give the washing a quick s.** donne un petit coup d'essorage au linge; *Sport* **to put s. on a ball** donner de l'effet à une balle; **there was a lot of s. on that ball** il y avait beaucoup d'effet dans cette balle; **to go into a s.** *Aut* faire un tête-à-queue; *Fig* perdre la tête; *Fig* **the news sent him into a s.** la nouvelle l'a complètement paniqué; *Fam* **to have the spins** avoir le tournis *(généralement après avoir trop bu)*; *Aviat* **flat s.** vrille à plat, tonneau *m*; *Fig Fam* **to be in a flat s.** ne pas savoir où donner de la tête; *Br Fam* **on the s.** *(in a row)* de suite; *Br Fam* **they've won seven games on the s.** ils ont gagné sept matchs de suite
2 *Fam (short journey) (in car etc)* tour *m*, promenade *f*, **to go for a s.** aller faire un tour
3 *Fam (on information)* **to put the right s. on a story** présenter une affaire sous un angle favorable; **the government put its own s. on the situation** le gouvernement a présenté la situation sous un angle qui lui convenait; **the government has been criticized for indulging in too much s.** on a reproché au gouvernement de trop manipuler les informations fournies au public
4 *Austr Fam (luck)* coup *m* de chance; *(bad luck)* malchance *f*
VT *(pt, pp* **spun** [spʌn]; *prp* **spinning) 1** *(wool, cotton etc)* filer; **to s. its web** *(of spider)* tisser sa toile; **to s. a top** lancer *ou* faire tourner une toupie; **to s. a coin** jouer à pile ou face
2 = spin-dry
VI **1** *(of top etc)* tourner; *(of suspended object)* tournoyer; *(of compass)* être affolé, s'affoler; **my head's spinning** la tête me tourne; **the room's spinning** *(because I'm dizzy, drunk etc)* la pièce tourne (autour de moi); **the blow sent him spinning** le coup l'a envoyé rouler
2 *(of wheel)* patiner *(sur place)*; *Fishing* pêcher à la cuillère; **to s. for fish** pêcher, lancer
3 *Fam (of spin doctor)* manipuler l'information, présenter les choses sous un angle favorable
▸▸*Sport* **s. bowler** = lanceur *m* qui donne de l'effet à la balle; *Pol Fam Pej* **s. doctor** = chargé *m* des relations publiques d'un parti politique
▸**spin out** VT SEP *(prolong) (speech)* délayer;

(discussion) faire durer, prolonger; *(affair, story)* faire traîner en longueur; **to s. out one's money** économiser; **to s. out one's drink** faire durer sa boisson
▸**spin round** VI *(turn) (of car)* faire un tête-à-queue; *(of person)* pivoter, virevolter; *(turn around sharply)* se retourner vivement, faire volte-face; **she spun round in her chair** elle pivota sur sa chaise; **to s. round and round** tournoyer, tourbillonner
VT SEP *(turn fast) (wheel, person etc)* faire tourner; *(several times) (person)* faire tournoyer

spina bifida [spaɪnə'bɪfɪdə] N *Med* spina-bifida *m*

spinach ['spɪnɪtʃ] N *(plant)* épinard *m*; *Culin* épinards *mpl*

spinal ['spaɪn(ə)l] ADJ spinal, -aux, vertébral, -aux
▸▸**s. column** colonne *f* vertébrale; *Spec* rachis *m*; **s. cord** moelle épinière; **s. curvature** déviation *f* de la colonne vertébrale; **s. injury** lésion *f* de la colonne vertébrale

spindle ['spɪnd(ə)l] N **1** *Tex* fuseau *m*; **s.-shaped** fusiforme, fuselé **2** *Tech etc* arbre *m*, axe *m*, mandrin *m*; *(of potter's wheel etc)* pivot *m*; *(of axle, shaft)* fusée *f*

spindleshanks ['spɪnd(ə)lʃæŋks] N *Old-fashioned Fam (person)* grand échalas *m*

spindly ['spɪndlɪ] ADJ *(person)* maigrelet; *(legs)* grêle; *(furniture etc)* peu solide, peu robuste

spindrift ['spɪndrɪft] N embrun(s) *m(pl)*, poudrin *m*

spin-dry VT *(clothes)* (faire) essorer

spin-dryer N essoreuse *f* (centrifuge)

spin-drying N essorage *m*

spine [spaɪn] N **1** *Anat* épine *f* dorsale, colonne *f* vertébrale, *Spec* rachis *m* **2** *Geog* arête *f* **3** *(of book)* dos *m* **4** *(of plant, fish, hedgehog etc)* piquant *m*, épine *f*

spine-chiller N *(story)* histoire *f* à vous glacer le sang; *(novel, film)* roman *m*/film *m* d'épouvante

spine-chilling ADJ à vous glacer le sang

spineless ['spaɪnlɪs] ADJ **1** *(person) (lacking character)* mou, *f* molle, sans caractère; *(lacking courage)* poltron, lâche **2** *(without spines) (plant, fish etc)* sans épines, sans piquants

spinelessness ['spaɪnlɪsnɪs] N lâcheté *f*

spinet [spɪ'net] N *Mus* épinette *f*

spinnaker ['spɪnəkər] N *Naut* spinnaker *m*, spi *m*

spinner ['spɪnər] N **1** *Tex* fileur, -euse; *Fig* **s. of tales** *or* **yarns** conteur, -euse **2** *Fishing* cuillère *f* **3** *Cr (bowler)* lanceur *m* qui donne de l'effet à la balle; *(ball)* balle *f* avec de l'effet

spinneret ['spɪnəret] N *(of spider etc)* filière *f*

spinney ['spɪnɪ] N *Br* petit bois *m*, bosquet *m*

spinning ['spɪnɪŋ] ADJ tournant, tournoyant; **my s. head** ma tête qui tourne/tournait
N **1** *Tex (of wool, cotton etc)* filage *m*, *Ind* filature *f* **2** *(in fishng)* pêche *f* à la cuiller *ou* cuillère
▸▸**s. factory** filature; **s. jenny** jenny *f*, **s. mill** filature; **s. top** toupie *f*, **s. wheel** rouet *m*

spin-off N *(advantage)* retombée *f*, avantage *m ou* bénéfice *m* supplémentaire; *(byproduct)* sous-produit *m*, *Ind* sous-produits, *(produit m)* dérivé *m*; **the film is a s. from a TV series** le film est tiré d'une série télévisée; **a s. of the Olympics was meant to be the creation of permanent jobs** on estimait qu'une des retombées des Jeux olympiques serait la création d'emplois permanents

spinster ['spɪnstər] N célibataire *f*, femme *f*/ fille *f* non mariée, *Pej* vieille fille

spinsterhood ['spɪnstəhʊd] N état m de vieille fille

spiny ['spaɪnɪ] ADJ Biol, Zool épineux; (covered in spines) épineux, couvert d'épines ou de piquants
▸▸Zool **s. anteater** échidné m; Zool **s. lobster** langouste f

spiracle ['spaɪərək(ə)l] N (of whale etc) évent m; (of insect) stigmate m

spiral ['spaɪər(ə)l] N spirale f; (single curve) spire f, tour m; **in a s.** en spirale; **wage-price** or **inflationary s.** course f ou spirale des prix et des salaires
ADJ (motif, shell, curve) en (forme de) spirale; (descent, spring) en spirale; **the plane went into a s. descent** l'avion amorça une descente en vrille
VI (-ll-, Am -l-) (form a spiral) former une spirale; (turn) tourner en spirale; (rise) (of steam, smoke) s'élever en spirale; **spiralling prices** dérapage m des prix
▸▸**s. binding** reliure f à spirale; **s. staircase** escalier m en colimaçon
▸ **spiral down** VI (of plane) descendre en spirale ou en vrille; (of steps) descendre en spirale ou en colimaçon
▸ **spiral up** VI (of rocket etc) s'élever ou monter en spirale; (of smoke) s'élever en spirale; (of steps) monter en spirale ou en colimaçon; (of prices) monter en vrille

spirally ['spaɪərəlɪ] ADV en spirale

spire ['spaɪər] N Archit (of church) aiguille f, flèche f

SPIRIT ['spɪrɪt] N **1** (soul) esprit m, âme f; **I'll be with you in s.** je serai avec vous en pensée; Bible **the poor in s.** les pauvres d'esprit; Rel, Prov **the s. is willing but the flesh is weak** l'esprit est prompt, mais la chair est faible
2 (incorporeal being) esprit m; **the (Holy) S.** le Saint-Esprit, l'Esprit saint; **evil s.** esprit malin, mauvais génie m; **to raise a s.** évoquer un esprit; **to believe in spirits** croire aux esprits ou aux revenants
3 (person) esprit m; **the leading s.** (in undertaking) l'âme f, le chef; (of revolt) le meneur, la meneuse
4 (mood, attitude) esprit m, disposition f; **the s. of the age** l'esprit du siècle; **the s. of liberty** l'esprit de liberté; **that was not the s. of the agreement** ce n'était pas l'esprit de cet accord; **to have the party s.** avoir envie de s'amuser; **to enter into the s. of sth** entrer dans l'esprit de qch; **to enter into the s. of the thing** entrer de bon cœur dans la partie; **to take sth in the right/wrong s.** prendre qch bien/mal; **he took it in the s. in which it was intended** il l'a pris comme il fallait; Fam **that's the s.!** à la bonne heure!
5 (courage) caractère m, courage m; (ardour) ardeur f, entrain m; **man of unbending s.** homme au caractère inflexible; **woman of s.** (having strong character) femme de caractère; (brave) femme courageuse; **to show s.** montrer du caractère ou du courage; **to have s.** avoir de l'allant; **the pianist played with more s. than skill** le pianiste jouait avec plus d'ardeur que de talent; **his s. was broken** quelque chose s'était brisé en lui; **to be in good spirits** (cheerful) être gai; (in a good mood) être de bonne humeur; **to be in high spirits** être en train ou en verve; **to be in low spirits** (depressed) être abattu; (feel sad) se sentir tout triste; **to keep up one's spirits** ne pas perdre courage; **to raise** or **revive sb's spirits** remonter le moral à qn; **their spirits rose** ils reprirent courage; **with s.** (to say sth, react) énergiquement; **... she replied with s.** ... répondit-elle avec beaucoup de verve
6 spirits (drinks) spiritueux mpl; **wines and spirits** vins mpl et spiritueux; **methylated**

spirits alcool m dénaturé ou à brûler; **surgical s.** alcool à 90°
VT **they spirited him out of the back door** ils l'ont fait sortir discrètement par la porte de derrière; **to s. weapons into a building** introduire des armes dans un bâtiment; **the film spirits us back to 18th century France** le film nous transporte dans la France du XVIIIᵉ siècle
▸▸**s. gum** colle f gomme; **s. lamp** lampe f à alcool; **s. level** niveau m à bulle; **s. stove** réchaud m à alcool; **s. writing** = écrits mpl dictés au médium par les esprits
▸ **spirit away, spirit off** VT SEP (remove secretly, quickly) (person) faire disparaître ou enlever comme par enchantement; (object) subtiliser, escamoter

spirited ['spɪrɪtɪd] ADJ **1** (person) (lively) vif, f vive, animé; (passionate) plein de fougue ou de verve; (intrepid) intrépide; (horse) fougueux **2** (style, reply etc) plein de verve; **s. attack** attaque pleine de fougue; **s. discussion** discussion vive ou animée; Mus **to give a s. performance** jouer avec brio ou avec verve

spiritless ['spɪrɪtlɪs] ADJ **1** (style) sans vie; (conversation etc) qui manque d'entrain **2** (person) (lacking courage, character) sans courage, sans caractère; (cowardly) lâche; (lacking vigour, passion) sans vigueur, sans ardeur; (weak) mou, f molle

spiritual ['spɪrɪtjʊəl] ADJ Rel spirituel; (not material, physical) spirituel, immatériel; **s. father** père m spirituel; **France is my s. home** la France est ma terre spirituelle; **Cambridge is his s. home** Cambridge, c'est la ville où il se sent chez lui; **his s. home is probably 18th century Holland** c'est probablement dans la Hollande du XVIIIᵉ siècle qu'il se sentirait le plus à l'aise
N Mus (negro) **s.** negro spiritual m, pl negro spirituals
▸▸**s. life** vie f spirituelle

spiritualism ['spɪrɪtjʊəlɪz(ə)m] N **1** (belief in spirits) spiritisme m **2** Phil spiritualisme m

spiritualist ['spɪrɪtjʊəlɪst] N, ADJ **1** (believing in spirits) spirite mf **2** Phil spiritualiste mf

spirituality [spɪrɪtjʊ'ælɪtɪ] N (of soul, person) spiritualité f

spiritually ['spɪrɪtjʊəlɪ] ADV spirituellement

spirituous ['spɪrɪtjʊəs] ADJ Fml spiritueux, alcoolique
▸▸**s. liquor** alcool m fort, spiritueux m

spirt [spɜːt] N, VT & VI = spurt

spit¹ [spɪt] N **1** Culin broche f **2** Geog **s.** (of land) pointe f (de terre), langue f (de terre)
VT (-tt-) Culin (put on a spit) (meat etc) embrocher, mettre à la broche

spit² N **1** (saliva) salive f; (act of spitting) crachement m; **he wiped the s. from his face** il essuya le crachat de son visage; **a gob of s.** un crachat; Fam **he's the s. of his father** c'est son père tout craché; Fam **s. and polish** astiquage m, fourbissage m; **a s. and sawdust bar** un bar tout simple **2** (of rain) crachin m
VI (pt, pp **spat** [spæt]; prp **spitting**) (of person, cat, pen) cracher; (of fire) crépiter; (of hot fat) grésiller; **to s. in sb's face, to s. at sb** cracher au visage à qn; **I wouldn't trust him further than I could s.** je n'ai pas la moindre confiance en lui; **it's spitting (with rain)** il crachine, il fait du crachin
VT (saliva, blood, insults) cracher
▸ **spit back** VI (of engine) avoir des retours de flamme (au carburateur)
▸ **spit out** VT SEP (expel from mouth) cracher; (something bad) recracher; **'you're fired!', he spat out** 'vous êtes viré!', lança-t-il; Fam **s. it out!** (say what you want to) accouche!, vide ton sac!
▸ **spit up** VT SEP (blood) cracher

spit³ N (depth of spade) profondeur f de fer de bêche; **to dig the ground two spits deep** labourer la terre à deux fers de bêche

spite [spaɪt] N **1** (malice) rancune f, (ill will) malveillance f; (pique) dépit m; **from** or **out of s.** (out of maliciousness) par pure malice ou méchanceté; **he broke her toy out of pure** or **sheer s.** il a cassé son jouet par pure méchanceté envers elle; **she went to a different university out of s.** (to annoy sb) elle est allée dans une autre université pour ennuyer son monde
2 in s. of ... en dépit de ..., malgré ...; **in s. of everything** malgré tout; **in s. of the fact that I had warned her, in s. of my having warned her** en dépit du fait que je l'avais prévenue, bien que je l'aie prévenue
VT (person) vexer, contrarier; **he does it to s. me** il le fait pour me tracasser ou m'ennuyer

spiteful ['spaɪtfʊl] ADJ méchant, malveillant; (because of a grudge) rancunier, vindicatif; **s. remark** observation f méchante; **s. tongue** langue f de vipère

spitefully ['spaɪtfəlɪ] ADV par malveillance, méchamment, par dépit ou rancune; **'that's a stupid idea', he said s.** 'c'est une idée stupide', dit-il méchamment

spitefulness ['spaɪtfʊlnɪs] N méchanceté f, malveillance f; (because of grudge) rancœur f

spitfire ['spɪtfaɪər] N (person) furie f

spitroast ['spɪtrəʊst] VT Culin cuire à la broche; **s. lamb** agneau à la broche

spitting ['spɪtɪŋ] N crachement m; **no s.** (on sign) défense de cracher; Fam **within s. distance of the front door** à deux pas de la porte d'entrée; Fam **he's the s. image of his father** c'est son père tout craché

spittle ['spɪt(ə)l] N (saliva) salive f; (of animal) bave f; **she was covered in s.** elle était couverte de crachats

spittoon [spɪ'tuːn] N crachoir m

spitz [spɪts] N (dog) loulou m

spiv [spɪv] N Br Fam filou m; (on black market) profiteur m ou trafiquant m du marché noir

spivvy ['spɪvɪ] ADJ Br Fam (appearance, clothes) tape-à-l'œil inv, tapageur; **do I look a bit s. in this?** n'ai-je pas l'air un peu filou avec ça?

splash [splæʃ] N **1** (action) (of water, molten metal) éclaboussement m; (of waves) clapotement m, clapotis m; **to fall into the water with a s.** tomber dans l'eau en faisant floc ou flac; Fig Fam **to make a (big) s.** faire sensation **2** (mark, amount) (of mud, ink etc) éclaboussure f, (of colour, light) tache f, Fam **a whisky and s.** un whisky soda; **just a s., please** (of water etc) très peu ou juste un soupçon, s'il vous plaît
INT floc!, flac!, ploc!
VT éclabousser (**with water** d'eau); Journ étaler; **to s. water at one another** se jeter de l'eau; Journ **a photo was splashed across the front page** une photo s'étalait en première page; **to s. one's way across a river** traverser une rivière en pataugeant; **to s. oneself** (with water etc) s'éclabousser; (with paint etc) se tacher; **to s. oneself/one's face with water** s'asperger/s'asperger la figure d'eau; **he really splashes the aftershave on** il s'asperge de lotion après-rasage
VI (of liquid) faire des éclaboussures; (of waves) clapoter; (of tap) cracher; (of person, animal) barboter, patauger
▸▸**s. back** (for sink etc) panneau m protecteur; **s. headline** manchette f, Comput **s. page** page f de garde; Comput **s. screen** splash screen m; Journ **s. story** sujet m à sensation
▸ **splash about, splash around** VT SEP

(spread by splashing) (water) faire jaillir, faire gicler; *Fam* **to s. one's money about** claquer son argent

vi *(of person, animal)* barboter, patauger

▸ **splash down vi** *Astronaut (land in sea)* amerrir

▸ **splash out** *Br Fam* **vi** *(spend more money than usual)* claquer des ronds; **I've splashed out on a new car** je me suis offert une nouvelle voiture; **you** have **been splashing out, haven't you!** tu as fait des frais *ou* des folies, dis-moi!

vt sep **we splashed out £500 on a new camera** nous avons dépensé *ou Fam* claqué 500 livres dans un nouvel appareil-photo

▸ **splash up vi** *(be thrown up) (of liquid, mud etc)* gicler

vt sep *(liquid, mud etc)* faire gicler

splashdown ['splæʃdaʊn] **n** *(of spacecraft)* amerrissage *m*

splat [splæt] **int** floc!; **the fruit landed s. on the ground** le fruit tomba sur le sol en faisant floc

splatter ['splætər] **n** éclaboussure *f*

vt **to s. sb with mud, to s. mud over sb** éclabousser qn de boue; **blood was splattered everywhere** tout était éclaboussé de sang **vi** *(of liquid)* jaillir, gicler; **the tomato splattered against the wall** la tomate a giclé sur le mur

▸ ▸ *Fam* **s. movie** = film *m* violent et sanglant

splay [spleɪ] **vt** *(one's fingers)* écarter; *Archit etc* **to s. the sides of a window** ébraser *ou* évaser une fenêtre; **to walk with splayed feet** marcher en canard; **splayed opening** ouverture ébrasée *ou* évasée

adj *(knees etc)* tourné en dehors

▸ **splay out vt sep** *(spread) (one's fingers)* écarter

vi *Archit etc* s'évaser

splayfooted [spleɪ'fʊtɪd] **adj** *(person)* **to be s.** marcher en canard

spleen [spliːn] **n 1** *Anat* rate *f* **2** *Fml (anger)* bile *f*, **in a fit of s. ...** dans un accès de mauvaise humeur ...; **to vent one's s. on sb** décharger sa mauvaise humeur sur qn **3** *Arch, Lit (melancholy)* spleen *m*

splendid ['splendɪd] **adj** *(gown, occasion, view)* splendide, superbe, magnifique; *(meal)* magnifique; *(opportunity)* splendide; **we had a s. time** c'était formidable; **a policy of s. isolation** une politique isolationniste; *Fig* **he sat in s. isolation** il était assis, superbe dans sa solitude; **that's s., thanks very much!** c'est formidable, merci beaucoup!

splendidly ['splendɪdlɪ] **adv** splendidement, magnifiquement; **s. dressed** superbement vêtu; **they got along s.** ils s'entendirent magnifiquement bien

splendiferous [splen'dɪfərəs] **adj** *Fam usu Hum* magnifique, rutilant

splendour, *Am* **splendor** ['splendər] **n** splendeur *f*, magnificence *f*; **the mountains in all their s.** les montagnes dans toute leur splendeur

splice [splaɪs] **n** *(in rope, cable etc)* épissure *f*, *Carp* enture *f*, *Cin (in film)* (point *m* de) collage *m*; *(in magnetic tape)* raccord *m*

vt *Naut etc (rope, cable)* épisser; *Carp (two pieces of wood)* enter; *Cin (film)* coller; *(tape)* raccorder, faire un raccord à; *Old-fashioned Fam* **to s. the mainbrace** boire un coup; *Fam* **to get spliced** *(marry)* se caser

splicer ['splaɪsər] **n** *(for tape, film)* colleuse *f*

splicing ['splaɪsɪŋ] **n** *Naut (of rope, cable)* épissage *m*; *Carp (of two pieces of wood)* enture *f*, *Cin (of film)* collage *m*; *(of tape)* raccordement *m*

▸ ▸ **s. table** table *f* de montage (de films); **s. unit** presse *f* à coller

spliff [splɪf] **n** *Sl* joint *m*

splint [splɪnt] *Med* **n** attelle *f*, éclisse *f*; **to put a limb in splints** éclisser un membre

vt *(broken limb)* éclisser

splinter ['splɪntər] **n** *(of wood, glass, shrapnel)* éclat *m*; *(in finger etc)* écharde *f*, *Surg (of fractured bone)* esquille *f*; **I've got a s. in my finger** je me suis enfoncé une écharde dans le doigt

vt *(something)* briser en mille morceaux; *(violently)* faire voler en éclats; *(oar, mast)* craquer

vi *(shatter)* éclater; *(violently)* voler en éclats; *(of oar, mast etc)* craquer, éclater; *(of bone)* se briser; *Fig (of political party)* éclater

▸ ▸ **s. group** groupe *m* dissident *ou* scissionniste

splinterproof ['splɪntəpruːf] **adj** *(glass)* se brisant sans éclats

SPLIT [splɪt] **n 1** *(in floorboard etc)* fente *f*, *(small)* fissure *f*, *(in rock etc)* crevasse *f*, *(in dress, robe etc)* déchirure *f*, *(in skin)* gerçure *f*

2 *(division) (in group)* division *f*, scission *f*, *(in personality)* dédoublement *m*; *(of screen)* éclatement *m*; **a three-/four-way s. (in the voting)** division en trois/quatre (de l'électorat); **there was a s. in the party over ...** il y avait une division *ou* une scission dans le parti à propos de ...; **to heal the s.** effacer les divisions

3 *(share in profits, loot etc)* part *f*, **they suggested a fifty-fifty s. of the profits** ils ont proposé de partager les bénéfices fifty-fifty

4 banana **s.** banana split *m inv*

5 *Gym* **to do the splits** faire le grand écart

6 *(in meaning of word etc)* distinction *f*

adj *(lip, skirt)* fendu; **in a s. second** en une fraction de seconde; **it only took a s. second** cela n'a demandé qu'une fraction de seconde; **to work a s. shift** avoir une journée de travail discontinue

vt *(pt, pp* split; *prp* splitting) **1** *(wood etc)* fendre; *(slate)* (re)fendre; *(rock etc)* cliver; *(tear)* déchirer; *Comput (file, image)* découper; **to s. one's head** s'ouvrir la tête (**on sth** sur qch); *Fam* **to s. one's sides laughing** *or* **with laughter** se tenir les côtes; *Fig* **to s. hairs** ergoter, couper les cheveux en quatre

2 *(divide) (amount of money, people into groups etc)* diviser (**into equal shares** en parts égales); **to s. sth in two** *or* **in half** *or* **down the middle** couper qch en deux; *Nucl* **to s. the atom** fissionner l'atome; **to s. a company** scinder une société; *Pol* **to s. the party** provoquer une scission dans le parti; **this s. the party three ways** ceci a divisé *ou* scindé le parti en trois; **to s. the vote** disperser les voix; **the Labour Party paid the price of a s. vote** le parti travailliste a fait les frais de la division; **to s. one's vote,** *esp Am* **to s. the ticket** partager ses votes entre plusieurs candidats; **to s. shares** fractionner des actions; **to s. a bottle** *(share)* partager une bouteille; **to s. the difference** partager la différence; *Fam* **can you s. a fiver for me?** pouvez-vous me faire la monnaie de cinq livres?

vi 1 *(of wood etc)* se fendre; *(of rock)* se cliver; *(of skin etc)* se gercer; *(of dress etc)* se déchirer; *(of seam in dress etc)* craquer; *Fig (of political party etc)* se scinder; *Fam* **my head's splitting** j'ai un mal de tête fou

2 *Sl (leave)* mettre les bouts

▸ ▸ **s. end** fourches *f*, **I tend to get s. ends** j'ai des cheveux qui ont tendance à fourcher; *Gram* **s. infinitive** = infinitif *m* où un adverbe ou une expression adverbiale est intercalé entre "to" et le verbe; **s. peas** pois *mpl* cassés; *Psy* **s. personality** double personalité *f*, dédoublement *m* de personalité; **he has a s. personality** il souffre d'un dédoublement de personalité; *Br* **s. pin** goupille *f* fendue; *Cin, Comput* **s. screen** écran *m* divisé; **s. second** fraction *f* de seconde

▸ **split away vi** = **split off vi**

▸ **split off vi** *(become detached)* se séparer, se détacher *(par clivage)*; *Fig (leave group)* se séparer

vt sep *(break off)* détacher *(par clivage)*

▸ **split on vt insep** *Br Sl (inform on) (person)* dénoncer; *(accomplice, friend)* donner

▸ **split open vi** *(burst open)* se fendre, s'ouvrir

vt sep *(break open)* ouvrir; **to s. one's head open** s'ouvrir la tête

▸ **split up vt sep 1** *(divide) (money, work, loot)* répartir, partager; *(couple, people fighting)* séparer; *(organization, party)* diviser, scinder; *(break up into several parts) (party etc)* fragmenter; **we s. the work up amongst ourselves** nous nous sommes réparti le travail; **I don't want to s. you and Joyce up** je ne veux pas te séparer de Joyce; **the police tried to s. the crowd up** la police a essayé de disperser la foule

2 *(break down, analyse) (meaning of a word)* analyser, décomposer; **it should be s. up into paragraphs** il faudrait le décomposer *ou* diviser en paragraphes; *Chem* **to s. up a compound into its elements** dédoubler un composé en ses éléments

vi *(divide)* **the compound had s. up into its elements** le composé s'était divisé en ses éléments; **the party s. up (into three groups)** le parti s'est divisé (en trois groupes); **Paul and Anne have s. up** Paul et Anne se sont séparés *ou* ont rompu; **the rock group s. up in 1992** le groupe de rock s'est séparé en 1992

split-level adj *Archit (building, room etc)* à deux niveaux

▸ ▸ **s. cooker** cuisinière *f* à éléments de cuisson séparés

split-second adj **with s. timing** avec un minutage réglé au dixième de seconde; **trapeze work requires s. timing** le trapèze requiert une synchronisation réglée au dixième de seconde

splitter, splitter box ['splɪtər] **n** *Aut* doubleur *m* de gamme

splitting ['splɪtɪŋ] **adj** *Fam* **to have a s. headache** avoir un mal de tête fou

n 1 *Nucl* **s. of the atom** fission *f* de l'atome **2** = **splitting up**

▸ ▸ **s. up** *(of wood)* fendage *m*; *(division)* division *f*, *(of two people)* séparation *f*, *(of political party)* scission *f*

split-up n *(in political party)* division *f*, scission *f*, *(of couple)* séparation *f*, rupture *f*, *(of friends)* séparation

split-view mirror n *Aut* rétroviseur *m* à double miroir

splodge [splɒdʒ] *Fam* **n** *(stain) (of colour, ink)* pâté *m*; *(piece) (of ice cream, ketchup etc)* plâtrée *f*

vt *(stain)* tacher, barbouiller (**with** de); **he splodged a great lump of cream on top** il balança une grosse cuillerée de chantilly par-dessus

splotch [splɒtʃ] *Fam* **n** *(of colour, ink)* pâté *m*

vt tacher, barbouiller (**with** de)

splurge [splɜːdʒ] *Fam* **n 1** *(ostentation)* esbroufe *f*, épate *f* **2** *(extravagant spending)* folles dépenses *fpl*; **I have a bit of a s. from time to time** je m'autorise quelques folies de temps en temps; **let's have a s. and give the biggest party ever** et si on claquait du fric et qu'on organisait la plus grande fête qu'on ait jamais vue

vi = **splurge out**

▸ **splurge out vi** *Fam (spend extravagantly)* faire des dépenses extravagantes; **to s. out on sth** faire des folies pour qch

splutter ['splʌtər] **n 1** *(speech)* bredouillement *m* **2** *(of engine)* bafouillage *m*; **the engine gave a s. and died** le moteur a toussé, puis est mort

vt *(excuse, threat)* bredouiller

VI *(of person) (because of surprise, emotion)* bafouiller; *(because of anger)* s'étrangler; *(of engine)* bafouiller; **the engine finally spluttered into life** finalement, le moteur a toussé, puis a démarré

▸ **splutter out VT SEP** = **splutter VT**

VI *(of fire, firework etc)* s'éteindre avec un crépitement

spoil [spɔɪl] **VT** *(pt, pp* **spoiled, spoilt** [spɔɪld, spɔɪlt]*)* **1** *(ruin) (evening, holiday, view)* gâcher; *(goods, decorations etc)* abîmer; **her hat was spoilt by the rain** son chapeau a été abîmé par la pluie; **the picnic was spoilt by the rain** le pique-nique a été gâché par la pluie; **to get spoilt** *or* **spoiled** *(of object)* s'abîmer; **to s. sb's fun** gâter *ou* gâcher le plaisir de qn; **it spoils (the beauty of) the view** ça gâche la vue; **to s. sb's appetite** couper l'appétit *ou* la faim à qn; **to s. the market** gâter le marché; **to s. the surprise** tout gâcher *(en dévoilant une surprise)*; **don't s. the surprise for me** ne me gâche pas tout; **to s. the ending of a film/book (for sb)** gâcher un film/livre (à qn) en lui révélant la fin; **spoiled goods** marchandises *fpl* avariées; *Pol* **spoilt paper** bulletin *m* nul **2** *(indulge) (person)* gâter; **a spoilt child** un enfant gâté; **we're spoilt here, not many cities have 20 theatres** nous sommes gâtés ici, peu de villes comptent 20 théâtres; **to be spoilt for choice** avoir l'embarras du choix

VI 1 *(of fruit, fish etc)* s'abîmer **2 to be spoiling for a fight** avoir envie de se battre, *Fam* chercher la bagarre

N *(usu pl)* butin *m*; *Fig* **to claim one's share of the spoil(s)** demander sa part du gâteau; **one of the spoils of war** une prise de guerre

spoilage [ˈspɔɪlɪdʒ] **N** *Typ* déchets *mpl* de tirage

spoiler [ˈspɔɪlər] **N 1** *Aviat* déporteur *m*; *Aut* béquet *m*, becquet *m*, spoiler *m* **2** *Pol etc (candidate)* = candidat *m* qui se présente dans le seul but de compromettre les chances d'un autre candidat **3** *Journ* = tactique *f* utilisée pour s'approprier le scoop d'un journal rival

spoilsport [ˈspɔɪlspɔːt] **N** *Fam* trouble-fête *mf inv*; rabat-joie *mf inv*; **don't be a s.!** ne joue pas les trouble-fête *ou* les rabat-joie!

spoke[1] [spəʊk] **N 1** *(of wheel)* rayon *m* **2** *(airport)* aéroport *m* d'apport **3** *Br Fig* **to put a s. in sb's wheel** mettre des bâtons dans les roues à qn

▸ ▸ **s. wheel** roue *f* à rayons

spoke[2] *PT see* **speak**

spoken [ˈspəʊk(ə)n] *PP see* **speak**
ADJ *(dialogue)* parlé, oral, *-aux*; **the s. word** la parole; **s. language** langue *f* parlée; **my s. French is quite good** en français, je suis assez bon à l'oral

spoken-voice ADJ *(record)* parlé

spokeshave [ˈspəʊkʃeɪv] **N** *Carp (tool)* vastringue *f*

spokesman, *pl* **spokesmen** [ˈspəʊksmən] **N** *(of party etc)* porte-parole *m inv*; **to act as s. for sb** être le porte-parole de qn; *(on one occasion)* prendre la parole au nom de qn

spokesperson [ˈspəʊkspɜːsən] **N** porte-parole *mf inv*

spokeswoman, *pl* **spokeswomen** [ˈspəʊkswʊmən, -wɪmɪn] **N** *(femme f)* porte-parole *f inv*

spoliation [spəʊlɪˈeɪʃən] **N** *Fml (despoiling)* spoliation *f*

spondaic [spɒnˈdeɪɪk] **ADJ** *(in prosody)* spondaïque

spondee [ˈspɒndiː] **N** *(in prosody)* spondée *m*

spondulicks, spondulix [spɒnˈdjuːlɪks] **NPL** *Fam* fric *m*

sponge [spʌndʒ] **N 1** *(for washing etc), Zool* éponge *f*; **to throw in the s.** *Boxing* jeter l'éponge; *Fig* s'avouer vaincu, abandonner la partie **2** *(action)* coup *m* d'éponge; **to give sth a s.** passer l'éponge sur un coup d'éponge à qch **3** *(cake)* gâteau *m* de Savoie

VT 1 éponger, passer l'éponge sur **2** *Fam (cadge) (meal etc)* écornifler, grappiller; **to s. sth off** *or* **from sb** chiper *ou* taper qch à qn
VI *Fam (be parasite)* faire le parasite

▸ ▸ *Br* **s. bag** trousse *f ou* sac *m* de toilette; **s. bath** toilette *f* à l'éponge; **s. biscuit** ≃ madeleine *f*; **s. cake** gâteau de Savoie, génoise *f*; *Tex* **s. cloth** tissu *m* éponge; **s. fisher** pêcheur, -euse d'éponges

▸ **sponge down VT SEP** *(wash) (person)* doucher avec une éponge; *(horse)* éponger; *(car)* nettoyer à l'éponge

▸ **sponge off VT SEP** *(stain)* enlever à l'éponge

VT INSEP *Fam (parents, friends etc)* vivre aux crochets *ou* aux dépens de; **they're just sponging off the state!** ce ne sont que des parasites de l'État!

▸ **sponge on VT INSEP** *Fam* = **sponge off VT INSEP**

▸ **sponge out VT SEP** *(blood etc)* enlever à l'éponge; *(wound)* nettoyer à l'éponge

▸ **sponge up VT SEP** *(liquid)* éponger

sponger [ˈspʌndʒər] **N** *Fam* parasite *m*

sponginess [ˈspʌndʒɪnɪs] **N** spongiosité *f*; *(of cake, pastry)* moelleux *m*; *(of road surface)* caractère *m* mou; *(of soles)* souplesse *f*

spongy [ˈspʌndʒɪ] **ADJ** spongieux; *(cake, pastry)* moelleux; *(road surface)* mou, *f* molle; *(soles)* souple

sponsor [ˈspɒnsər] **N** *(for athlete, team, festival, programme, giving money)* sponsor *m*; *(introducing new member to club, for student)* parrain *m*; *(at baptism)* parrain, marraine *f*, *Law* garant *m*, répondant *m*, caution *f* **(for sb** de qn*)*; **to stand s. to a child** *(at baptism)* tenir un enfant sur les fonts (baptismaux)

VT 1 *(athlete, team, charity walker, festival etc)* sponsoriser; *(student, candidate)* parrainer; *Radio, TV (programme)* sponsoriser, parrainer; **sponsored walk** marche *f* sponsorisée (pour aider une œuvre de charité) **2** *Law (act as guarantor for)* être le garant de, répondre de, se porter caution pour **3** *Rel (act as godparent to)* parrainer

---

Sponsored event

La Grande-Bretagne compte de très nombreuses organisations caritatives ("charities"). L'un des moyens employés pour rassembler des fonds est de s'engager auprès d'autres gens (généralement des amis, voisins et collègues de travail) à accomplir une épreuve en échange d'une somme d'argent déterminée. Il peut s'agir d'épreuves physiques ("sponsored walk", "sponsored swim") ou de défis saugrenus, tels que se rendre au bureau en pyjama ou bien encore garder le silence pendant toute une journée ("sponsored silence"). Des "sponsored events" sont également organisés par des écoles et des clubs sportifs afin d'obtenir de l'argent pour acheter du matériel.

---

sponsoring [ˈspɒnsərɪŋ] **N** *Mktg* parrainage *m*, mécénat *m*

sponsorship [ˈspɒnsəʃɪp] **N 1** *(of athlete, team, festival etc), Radio, TV (of programme)* parrainage *m*, sponsorat *m*; *(of student, candidate)* parrainage; *Mktg* **under the s. of** sous le patronage de **2** *Law* garantie *f*, caution *f* **3** *Rel (by godparent)* parrainage *m*

▸ ▸ **s. agreement, s. deal** contrat *m* de sponsoring

spontaneity [spɒntəˈniːɪtɪ, -ˈneɪ-] **N** spontanéité *f*

spontaneous [spɒnˈteɪnɪəs] **ADJ** *(person, gesture)* spontané; *(act, confession)* volontaire

▸ ▸ **s. combustion** combustion *f* spontanée

spontaneously [spɒnˈteɪnɪəslɪ] **ADV** spontanément; **she s. offered to help** elle a spontanément proposé son aide

spoof [spuːf] *Fam* **N 1** *(play, film etc)* satire *f* **(on** de*)*; **s. thriller** satire de film à sensations **2** *(trick)* blague *f*; **they erected some s. factories to fool the enemy** ils ont installé des usines factices pour tromper l'ennemi; **he sent round a s. memo about redundancies** il a fait passer une fausse circulaire *ou Fam* une circulaire bidon parlant de licenciements

VT *(parody, satirize)* parodier, caricaturer

spook [spuːk] *Fam* **N 1** *(ghost)* fantôme *m* **2** *esp Am Fam (spy)* espion, -ionne **3** *Am Offensive Sl (black man)* nègre *m*, bamboula *m*; *(black woman)* négresse *f*

VT *(startle)* foutre la trouille à; *(frighten, disturb)* donner la chair de poule à

spooky [ˈspuːkɪ] **ADJ** *Fam (story etc)* qui fait peur; *(place)* sinistre; *(strange)* dingue; **it's s. here at night** c'est sinistre ici le soir; **he's a s. sort of person** il est du genre sinistre

spool [spuːl] **N 1** *Tex* bobine *f*, can(n)ette *f*; *(of sewing machine)* can(n)ette; **s. of thread** bobine de coton (à coudre) **2** *Fishing* tambour *m* (de moulinet) **3** *Elec (corps m de)* bobine *f*, *Phot, Cin* bobine (de film); **take-up s.** bobine enrouleuse; **(ribbon) s.** *(for typewriter)* bobine du ruban

VT *Tex* bobiner; *Comput* spouler, mettre en (file d')attente

spooler [ˈspuːlər] **N** *Comput (for printing)* spouleur *m*, pilote *m* de mise en file d'attente

spoon [spuːn] **N 1** *(utensil)* cuillère *f*, cuiller *f*; **serving s.** cuillère de service *ou* à service **2** *Golf* bois *m* numéro 3, spoon *m*; *Fishing* **s. (bait), trolling s.** cuillère *f*

VT 1 *(liquid)* prendre *ou* verser à l'aide d'une cuillère; **to s. syrup/gravy onto sth** verser un sirop/une sauce sur qch à l'aide d'une cuillère; **he spooned soup into his mouth** il enfournait de grandes cuillerées de soupe **2** *Fishing* pêcher à la cuillère

VI *Old-fashioned Fam (of couple)* se faire des mamours

▸ **spoon out VT SEP** *(serve) (sauce etc)* servir (avec une cuillère)

▸ **spoon up VT SEP** *(eat)* manger à la cuillère

spoonbill [ˈspuːnbɪl] **N** *(bird)* spatule *f* (blanche)

spoonerism [ˈspuːnərɪz(ə)m] **N** contrepèterie *f*

spoon-feed VT *(pt, pp* **spoon-fed** [-fed]*)* nourrir à la cuillère; *Fig (student etc)* mâcher le travail à

spoonful [ˈspuːnfʊl] **N** cuillerée *f*

spoor [spʊər] **N** *(in hunting)* foulées *fpl*, piste *f*

sporadic [spəˈrædɪk] **ADJ** sporadique; *(showers)* épars, isolé; *(work), Mil (firing)* intermittent

sporadically [spəˈrædɪk(ə)lɪ] **ADV** sporadiquement; *(to fire, work)* par intervalles, à intermittence

spore [spɔːr] **N** *Biol* spore *f*

sporran [ˈspɒrən] **N** *Scot* = aumônière *f* en cuir parfois agrémentée de fourrure, portée sur le devant du kilt

sport [spɔːt] **N 1** sport *m*; **aquatic/winter sports** sports nautiques/d'hiver
2 *Fam* **he's a (good** *or* **real) s.** *(good loser)*

c'est un beau joueur; *(generous, fair, lively person)* c'est une personne sympa; **you're a real s.** tu es vraiment sympa; **a bad s.** *(bad loser)* un mauvais perdant, une mauvaise perdante; **come on, be a s.!** allez, sois sympa!; *esp Austr* **hello, (old) s.!** salut, mon vieux!

3 *Old-fashioned (amusement)* jeu *m*, divertissement *m*, amusement *m*; **in s.** pour rire, par plaisanterie; **to make s. of sth** s'amuser *ou* se moquer de qch; **to have good s.** *(in hunting)* faire bonne chasse; *(in fishing)* faire bonne pêche *ou* bonne prise

4 *Bot, Biol* variété *f* anormale, type *m* anormal

VT *(wear)* *(red waistcoat, carnation etc)* arborer

VI 1 *Old-fashioned (amuse oneself)* se divertir, s'amuser **2** *Biol, Bot (of plants, animals)* produire une variété anormale

▸▸ **sports car** voiture *f* de sport; **sports coat,** *Am* **s. coat** veste *f* sport; **sports commentator** commentateur *m* sportif; **sports correspondent** journaliste *m* sportif, journaliste *f* sportive; **sports centre** complexe *m* *ou* centre *m* sportif; **sports club** club *m* de sport; **sports day** = réunion *f* sportive annuelle où les parents sont invités; **sports editor** rédacteur *m* en chef sportif; **sports facilities** installations *fpl* sportives; **sports ground** terrain *m* de sport *ou* de jeux; **sports jacket,** *Am* **s. jacket** veste *f* sport; **sports journalist** journaliste *m* sportif, journaliste *f* sportive; *Journ* **sports page** rubrique *f* sportive, page *f* des sports; **sports paper** journal *m* sportif; **sports press** presse *f* sportive; **sports programme** émission *f* sportive; **sports reporter** reporter *m* sportif; *TV etc* **sports results** résultats *mpl* sportifs; *Aut* **sports saloon** berline *f* sport; **sports shoes** trainings *mpl*; **sports shop** magasin *m* de sport

sporting ['spɔːtɪŋ] **ADJ 1** *(to do with sport)* sportif **2** *(fair, reasonable)* **it's very s. of him** c'est très chic de sa part; **you've got a s. chance** tu as tes chances; **to give sb a s. chance** donner sa chance à qn; **I'll make you a s. offer** je vais vous faire une offre honnête; **in a s. spirit** avec un esprit sportif, sportivement **3** *Old-fashioned (fond of hunting or fishing)* amateur de chasse/de pêche

▸▸ **s. event** manifestation *f* sportive; **s. man, s. woman** *(horseracing enthusiast)* turfiste *mf*

sportingly ['spɔːtɪŋlɪ] **ADV** sportivement

sportive ['spɔːtɪv] **ADJ** *Old-fashioned (joking)* badin; *(playful)* folâtre

sportscast ['spɔːtskɑːst] **N** *Am Radio, TV* émission *f* sportive

sportscaster ['spɔːtskɑːstər] **N** *Am Radio, TV* journaliste *m* sportif, journaliste *f* sportive

sportsman, *pl* **sportsmen** ['spɔːtsmən] **N 1** *(player)* sportif *m*; *(hunter)* chasseur *m*; *(angler)* pêcheur *m* **2 he's a real s.** *(fair-minded person)* il a l'esprit sportif; *(good loser)* il est beau joueur

sportsmanlike ['spɔːtsmənlaɪk] **ADJ** sportif; **in a s. way** sportivement

sportsmanship ['spɔːtsmənʃɪp] **N 1** *(skill)* habileté *f ou* qualités *fpl* de sportif **2** *(fair-mindedness)* esprit *m* sportif, sportivité *f*

sportsperson ['spɔːtspɜːsən] **N** *(player)* sportif, -ive

sportswear ['spɔːtsweər] **N** vêtements *mpl* de sport

sportswoman, *pl* **sportswomen** ['spɔːtswʊmən, -wɪmɪn] **N** *(player)* sportive *f*

sporty ['spɔːtɪ] **ADJ** *Fam* **1** *(fond of sport)* sportif **2** *(jacket etc)* gai; *(car)* sportif; **it's a bit too s.** c'est un peu trop sport

---

SPOT [spɒt]

N endroit **1**	lieu **1**	tache **2**
bouton **3**	pois **4**	point **4**
goutte **5**	projecteur **6**	numéro **7**
créneau **7**		
VT tacher **1**	repérer **2**	
VI pleuvioter		

N 1 *(place)* endroit *m*, lieu *m*; **a remote s.** un endroit écarté *ou* isolé; **beauty s.** site *m* touristique; *Aut* **a black s.** *(on road)* un point noir; **an unemployment black s.** une zone particulièrement touchée par le chômage; **X marks the s.** *(of crime etc)* la croix indique le lieu; **the police are on the s.** la police est sur les lieux; **to have sb on the s.** *(reporter, representative, agent etc)* avoir qn sur place; **our reporter on the s., Mary Smith** notre correspondante sur place, Mary Smith; *Fam* **to put sb on the s.** *(put in difficult position)* mettre qn dans une situation difficile; *(force to answer difficult question)* embarrasser qn par des questions; **to be fined on the s.** recevoir une amende sur-le-champ; **to do sth on the s.** *(straightaway)* faire qch sur place *ou* sur-le-champ; **to be killed on the s.** être tué sur le coup, être tué net; *Fam* **her performance failed to hit the high spots** sa représentation n'a pas été brillante; *Fam* **to be in a (tight) s.** *(in predicament)* être dans le pétrin; *Fam* **to get into a bit of a s.** se ficher dans le pétrin; **night s.** boîte *f* de nuit; **weak s.** point faible; **to find sb's weak s.** trouver le défaut dans la cuirasse de qn, trouver le point faible de qn; **blind s.** *Anat* point aveugle; *Aut* angle *m* mort; *(in road)* endroit *m* sans visibilité; *Fam* **that's your blind s.** c'est là où vous refusez de voir clair; **I have a blind s. about maths** je ne comprends rien aux mathématiques

2 *(stain)* tache *f*, macule *f*; *(on fruit etc)* tavelure *f*

3 *(pimple)* bouton *m*; **to come out in spots** se couvrir de boutons; **it makes me come out in spots** ça me donne des boutons

4 *(dot) (of colour) (on shirt, tie etc)* pois *m*; *(on playing card, domino)* point *m*; *Billiards* mouche *f*; **blue tie with red spots** cravate bleue à pois rouges; **a leopard's spots** la tacheture *ou* la moucheture d'un léopard; *Fam* **to knock spots off sb** *(beat)* battre qn à plate(s) couture(s); **she knocks spots off him** *(is much better than)* il ne lui arrive pas à la cheville; **the new Peugeot knocks spots off the ...** face à la nouvelle Peugeot, le ... ne fait pas le poids; *Med* **a s. on the lung** un voile au poumon

5 *Br Fam (small amount) (of rain, wine)* goutte *f*; **a s. of whisky** une larme de whisky; **what about a s. of lunch?** si nous déjeunions?; **to do a s. of work** faire un peu de travail; **a s. of bother** *or* **trouble** un petit ennui; **to get into a s. of bother** s'attirer des ennuis

6 *(spotlight), Theat* projecteur *m*; *(in home, on exhibition stand)* spot *m*

7 *TV, Radio (for artist, interviewee)* numéro *m*; *(time reserved for adverts, specific commentator)* créneau *m*; **he got a s. on the Margie Warner show** *(as singer, comedian)* il a fait un numéro dans le show de Margie Warner; *(interview)* il s'est fait interviewer ou il est passé dans le show de Margie Warner

VT (-tt-) 1 *(mark with spots)* tacher, moucheter; *(stain, mark)* tacher, souiller; *Billiards (ball)* mettre sur la mouche

2 *(notice) (person, object)* repérer, apercevoir; *Horseracing etc (winner)* prédire, repérer; *Mil (enemy positions etc)* repérer, observer; *(trains etc)* repérer; *(talent)* dénicher; **to s. sb doing sth** apercevoir qn en train de faire qch; **I spotted her in the crowd** je l'ai repérée au milieu de la foule; **to s. a**

mistake détecter une erreur; **to s. an opportunity** repérer une occasion; **well spotted!** *(when noticing mistake)* bien vu!; *(when finding sb in crowd)* quel œil!; **I'd never have spotted it** je ne l'aurais jamais remarqué; **she was last spotted in the pub** la dernière fois qu'on l'a vue, elle était au pub; **I spotted him as a potential troublemaker** j'ai très vite repéré qu'il était un agitateur

VI it's spotting (with rain) il pleuviote

▸▸ *Fin* **s. buying** achat *m* au comptant; *Br* **s. cash** argent *m* liquide; **s. check** *(investigation)* contrôle *m* surprise; *(for quality)* contrôle par sondage; *(by customs)* fouille *f* au hasard; *Fin* **s. deal** opération *f ou* transaction *f* au comptant; *Geog* **s. height** altitude *f*; *Fin* **s. market** marché *m* au comptant; **s. news** brève *f*; *Fin* **s. price** cours *m* spot; *Fin* **s. rate** cours à vue, cours spot; *Fin* **s. trading** négociations *fpl* au comptant; *Fin* **s. transaction** opération *ou* transaction au comptant

spot-check VT *(randomly)* contrôler par sondage(s); *(at random intervals)* contrôler à intervalles irréguliers; *(without notice)* faire des contrôles surprises de; **athletes are regularly spot-checked for anabolic steroids** on effectue souvent des contrôles surprises sur les athlètes pour détecter les anabolisants

spotless ['spɒtlɪs] **ADJ** *(shirt, reputation)* sans tache, immaculé; *(house, kitchen)* impeccable

spotlessly ['spɒtlɪslɪ] **ADV** **s. clean** impeccable; **s. white** d'une blancheur immaculée *ou* parfaite

spotlessness ['spɒtlɪsnɪs] **N** propreté *f*

spotlight ['spɒtlaɪt] **N** *Theat, Cin (beam)* lumière *f* de projecteur; *(device)* spot *m*, projecteur *m* (à faisceau concentré); *(in home, on exhibition stand etc)* Aut projecteur auxiliaire orientable; **to hold the s.** *Theat* occuper le centre de la scène *(dans la lumière du projecteur)*; *Fig* avoir *ou* tenir la vedette; *Fig* **she has always been in** or **has never been out of the s.** elle n'a pas cessé de tenir la vedette *ou* d'être sur la sellette

VT *(person, object), Theat* diriger les projecteurs sur; *Fig* mettre en vedette

spotlighting ['spɒtlaɪtɪŋ] **N** *(in home), Theat, Cin* éclairage *m* à effet

spot-on *Fam* **ADJ** exact, au point; **that's s.** c'est exact; **his answer was s.** sa réponse était parfaitement exacte *ou* correcte; **the missiles were s.** les missiles ont atterri en plein dans la mille

ADV *(guess)* en plein dans le mille; **he timed it s.** il a calculé son coup à la seconde près

INT *(excellent)* super!, génial!

spotter ['spɒtər] **N** *Mil, Aviat* observateur *m*; **train s.** = personne *f* qui regarde passer des trains *(pour repérer les différents modèles)*; **talent s.** dénicheur, -euse de talent

▸▸ **s. plane** avion *m* d'observation

spotting ['spɒtɪŋ] **N** **train/plane s.** repérage *m* de trains/d'avions

spotty ['spɒtɪ] **ADJ 1** *(marked with spots)* moucheté, tacheté; *(covered with stains)* plein de taches **2** *(pimply) (face, person)* couvert de boutons, boutonneux; **a s. adolescent** un adolescent boutonneux

N *Fam* **hi there, s.!** salut, le boutonneux/la boutonneuse!

spot-weld VT souder par points

N soudure *f* par points

spot-welding N soudure *f* par points

spouse [spaʊz, spaʊs] **N** *Admin, Law* conjoint, -ointe; *Arch, Lit* époux *m*, épouse *f*

spout [spaʊt] **N 1** *(of teapot, kettle etc)* bec *m*; *(of watering can)* canon *m*, goulot *m*; *(of whale)* évent *m*; *Constr* **rainwater s.** *(of gutter)* tuyau *m* de décharge, gargouille *f*, chantepleure *f*, *Sl* **to be up the s.** *(ruined)* être fichu *ou* foutu; *(pregnant)* être en cloque; **our plans are up the s.** nos projets sont tombés à l'eau; **now we're really up the s.** maintenant nous sommes vraiment dans de beaux draps *ou* dans le pétrin **2** *(jet of liquid)* jet *m*; **a s. of water shot up** un jet d'eau partit

VI 1 *(of liquid)* jaillir, rejaillir; *(more forcefully)* gicler; *(of whale)* lancer un jet d'eau/d'air, souffler **2** *Fig Fam (of person)* parler à jet continu, dégoiser; **what's he spouting on about now?** qu'est-ce qu'il est en train de débiter maintenant?

VT 1 *(of person) (water etc)* faire jaillir, lancer; **the pipe spouted water everywhere** de l'eau jaillissait du tuyau **2** *Fig Fam (speech, nonsense)* dégoiser *ou* débiter à jet continu

▸ ▸ **s. hole** *(of whale)* évent

▸ **spout out** **VI** *(of water, lava etc)* jaillir, sortir en giclant; **the liquid was spouting out of the barrel** le liquide sortait du tonneau en giclant, le liquide jaillissait du tonneau

VT SEP 1 *(lava)* cracher; **the pipe spouted out water** de l'eau jaillissait du tuyau et éclaboussait partout **2** *Fig Fam (utter) (statistics etc)* débiter

sprain [spreɪn] **N** *Med* entorse *f*, *(less serious)* foulure *f*

VT *(ankle, wrist)* se fouler; *(more seriously)* se faire une entorse à; **sprained ankle** foulure *f* à la cheville; *(more serious)* entorse *f* à la cheville

sprang PT *see* **spring** **VI, VT**

sprat [spræt] **N** *(fish)* sprat *m*, harenguet *m*

sprawl [sprɔːl] **N 1** *(position)* position *f* affalée **2** *(of houses etc)* étendue *f*; **an urban s.** une agglomération

VI 1 *(of person)* s'affaler, s'étaler; **he was lying sprawled (out) on the sofa** il était affalé sur le divan; **to send sb sprawling** faire tomber qn de tout son long; **to go sprawling** s'étaler par terre **2** *(of town etc)* s'étendre de tous les côtés; *(of plant)* s'étendre, se déployer

sprawling [ˈsprɔːlɪŋ] ADJ **1** *(person)* affalé **2** *(suburbs, plants)* tentaculaire; **s. handwriting** écriture *f* irrégulière et étalée

spray[1] [spreɪ] **N** *(of plant)* brin *m*, ramille *f*; **s. of flowers** branche *f* de fleurs, rameau *m* fleuri; *Archit, Sewing etc* chute *f* de fleurs; **s. of diamonds** aigrette *f* de diamants

spray[2] **N 1** *(liquid) (of seawater)* embrun *m*, poudrin *m*; *(water in particles)* poussière *f* d'eau, eau *f* vaporisée; *(of perfume, fuel etc)* jet *m* atomisé *ou* pulvérisé; *(for hair)* spray *m* coiffant, laque *f*

2 *(act of spraying)* coup *m* de vaporisateur; *(of perfume, paint etc)* jet *m*; **to give sth a s.** *(fields, roses etc)* pulvériser qch; *(walls etc)* peindre qch au pistolet; *(hair)* mettre du spray *ou* de la laque sur qch

3 *(device) (for hair spray, paint etc)* bombe *f*, *(non-gas operated)* atomiseur *m*, vaporisateur *m*; **deodorant s.** désodorisant *m* atomiseur; **perfume s.** atomiseur à parfum; **fly s.** atomiseur *ou* bombe insecticide

VT 1 *(perfume, hair conditioner, deodorant)* atomiser, vaporiser; *(paint, chemicals)* pulvériser; **he sprayed water all over me** il m'a aspergé d'eau; **to s. a solution up one's nostrils** se vaporiser un liquide dans le nez; *Ind* **to s. dry** sécher par atomisation; **slogan sprayed on a wall** slogan écrit à la bombe sur un mur; **this liquid is sprayed on the oil slick** ce liquide est pulvérisé sur le pétrole; **three layers of paint are sprayed onto the metal** on passe trois couches de peinture au pistolet sur le métal

2 *(cover with spray)* asperger, arroser; *(plants etc)* bassiner; *(tree)* passer au vaporisateur; *(with paint-sprayer)* peindre au pistolet; **she sprays her hair in position** elle se

coiffe en se mettant du spray; **to s. the crops/the fields** pulvériser les récoltes/champs; **to s. sth with machine-gun fire** mitrailler qch

VI water sprayed up in our faces de l'eau éclaboussait nos visages

▸ ▸ **s. can** *(for aerosol)* bombe, aérosol *m*; *(refillable)* vaporisateur; *Ind* **s. drying** *(of milk etc)* séchage *m* par atomisation; **s. gun** *(for paint)* pistolet *m* (à peinture); **s. nozzle** gicleur *m*; **s. paint** peinture *f* en bombe; **a can of s. paint** une bombe de peinture

sprayer [ˈspreɪər] **N 1** vaporisateur *m*, pulvérisateur *m*; *(for paint)* pistolet *m* **2** *(vehicle, plane)* arroseuse *f*

SPREAD [spred]

N	étendue **1**	▪ diffusion **2**
	▪ propagation **2**	▪ pâte à tartiner **5**
VT	étendre **1, 3**	▪ tendre **1**	▪ déployer
1	▪ répandre **2**	▪ propager **2**	▪ étaler
3	▪ enduire **4**		
VI	s'étendre **1, 2**	▪ se répandre **2**	▪ se
propager **2**	▪ s'étaler **3**		

N 1 *(of land etc)* étendue *f*, *(of wings, sails etc)* envergure *f*, *Com (between two rates)* différence *f*, *(in interest rates)* différentiel *m* de taux d'intérêt; *St Exch* écart *m*; *Am (ranch)* ranch *m*, *St Exch* **s. of investments** diversification *f* des placements; **we have a good s. of products** *(range)* nous avons un bel éventail *ou* une belle gamme de produits

2 *(expansion) (of education)* diffusion *f*, *(of doctrine, disease)* propagation *f*, *(of ideas)* expansion *f*, dissémination *f*

3 *Fam (big meal)* festin *m*, repas *m* somptueux; **cold s.** repas froid

4 *Journ etc* double page *f*, *(advertisement)* double page publicitaire

5 *Culin* pâte *f* à tartiner; **cheese s.** fromage *m* à tartiner; **chocolate s.** chocolat *m* à tartiner

VT *(pt, pp spread)* **1** *(one's arms etc)* étendre; *(net)* tendre; *(sails)* déployer; *(one's fingers)* écarter; **a bird with its wings s.** un oiseau aux ailes déployées; **to s. one's wings** *(of bird)*, *Fig* déployer ses ailes

2 *(distribute) (sand, straw)* répandre; *(manure, fertilizer)* épandre; *(terror)* semer; *(news)* répandre, rapporter; *(lies etc)* colporter; *(disease)* propager; **to s. sb's fame (abroad)** faire connaître la réputation de qn; *Fig* **he's in danger of spreading himself too thin** il risque de faire trop de choses à la fois; **the payments are s. over several months** les paiements sont échelonnés *ou* étalés *ou* répartis sur plusieurs mois; **if we can s. the work over three months** si nous pouvons répartir le travail sur trois mois; **could you s. the word?** voulez-vous passer le mot?

3 *(apply)* **to s. butter on a slice of bread** étendre *ou* étaler du beurre sur une tranche de pain, tartiner une tranche de pain de beurre; **to s. ointment on a burn** appliquer *ou* mettre de la pommade sur une brûlure; **to s. the paint evenly** étendre *ou* étaler la peinture en couches égales

4 **to s. a surface with sth** recouvrir *ou* enduire une surface de qch; *Am Old-fashioned* **to s. the table** dresser *ou* mettre la table, mettre le couvert

VI 1 *(stretch) (of forest, city, suburbs)* s'étendre, s'étaler; *(of desert)* s'étendre

2 *(of rumour, news, ideas etc)* se répandre, se propager; *(of disease, fire, theory, epidemic etc)* se propager, s'étendre (**to** à, jusqu'à); *(of smell, smoke, sound)* se répandre (**throughout** dans); *(of fame)* s'étendre (**throughout** dans); *(of cancer)* se généraliser; *(of evil)* s'étendre, se généraliser; *(of group of people)* se disperser; **the fire is**

spreading l'incendie gagne; **her ideas are spreading** ses idées font tache d'huile

3 *(of butter, paste, cheese etc)* s'étaler; **it spreads easily** c'est facile à tartiner

▸ ▸ **s. betting** = système *m* de paris portant sur le résultat d'un événement sportif ou autre, où les gains sont proportionnels à la justesse des prédictions, selon une fourchette de résultats préétablie; **s. eagle** *Her* aigle *f* éployée; *(in skating)* grand aigle *m*

▸ **spread about, spread around** VT SEP **1** *(rumour, disease etc)* répandre; **have you been spreading it around that I'm pregnant?** est-ce que tu as été raconter partout que je suis enceinte?

2 *Euph* **he spreads himself about a bit** *(is promiscuous)* il couche à droite et à gauche

▸ **spread out** VT SEP **1** *(open out) (map etc)* déployer, étaler; **the plain lay s. out in front of us** la plaine s'étalait *ou* se déployait devant nous; **a bird with its wings s. out** un oiseau aux ailes déployées; **to s. oneself out** *(on sofa etc)* s'étendre, s'allonger; **he s. his papers out on the desk** il étala ses papiers sur le bureau

2 *(space out in time) (deliveries, payments)* échelonner; **to s. out over several financial years** étaler sur plusieurs exercices

VI *(of person) (on sofa etc)* s'étendre, s'allonger; *(of troops, rescue party etc)* se disperser; **give yourself room to s. out** *(doing craft work etc)* accordez-vous de l'espace pour vous étaler

spread-eagled [-ˈiːg(ə)ld] ADJ étalé de tout son long

spreader [ˈspredər] **N 1** *(person) (of idea)* propagateur, -trice; *(of news)* rapporteur, -euse; *(of rumour)* colporteur, -euse, propagateur, -trice **2** *Agr, Constr* épandeur *m*, épandeuse *f*, *(for putty, plaster etc)* spatule *f*

spreading [ˈspredɪŋ] ADJ **under a s. chestnut tree** sous un châtaignier bien déployé

N *(act of spreading) (of lies)* colportage *m*; *(of disease, doctrine, rumours)* propagation *f*, *(of ideas)* dissémination *f*, *(of paint etc)* étendage *m*

spreadsheet [ˈspredʃiːt] **N** *Comput* feuille *f* de calcul; *(software)* tableur *m*

spree [spriː] **N** nouba *f*, **to have a s., to go (out) on a s.** faire la nouba; **to go on a shopping** *or* **spending s.** aller claquer son argent dans les magasins; **a s. of looting** des saccages

sprig [sprɪg] **N** brin *m*

sprightliness [ˈspraɪtlɪnɪs] **N** vivacité *f*

sprightly [ˈspraɪtlɪ] ADJ *(person, tune)* vif, *f* vive; *(old person)* alerte, fringant; **her s. commentary on current events** ses commentaires pétillants sur l'actualité; **he's very s. for 80** il est très fringant pour ses 80 ans

spring [sprɪŋ] **N 1** *(of water)* source *f*, *Fig Lit (of custom etc)* source, origine *f*, **hot** *or* **thermal s.** source thermale; **hot** *or* **thermal springs** eaux thermales; **mineral s.** source d'eau minérale

2 *(season)* printemps *m*; **in (the) s.** au printemps; **a lovely s. evening** une belle soirée de printemps; **to have s. fever** être amoureux, *Can* avoir la fièvre du printemps; **s. flowers** fleurs printanières VOIR GRAMMAIRE A7

3 *(leap)* saut *m*, bond *m*

4 *(elasticity)* élasticité *f*, **the s. of a bow** la force *ou* la souplesse d'un arc; **with a s. in his step** d'un pas léger; **the s. had gone out of her step** sa démarche avait perdu de sa souplesse; *Carp* **there's too much s. in this type of wood** ce type de bois est trop souple

5 *(device)* ressort *m*; **(watch) s.** ressort (de montre); **springs, s. suspension** *(of car etc)* suspension *f* à ressort(s)

VI (*pt* **sprang** [spræŋ]; *pp* **sprung** [sprʌŋ]) **1** (*jump*) bondir, sauter; **to s. to one's feet** se lever vivement *ou* d'un bond; **to s. into action** (*of person*) passer à l'action; **he sprang into life when I mentioned the subject** il a semblé revivre quand j'ai mentionné le sujet; **the engine sprang to life** le moteur partit d'un coup; **to s. to sb's defence** (*in words*) prendre vivement la défense de qn; (*in case of assault etc*) se précipiter pour porter secours à qn; **the lid sprang open** le couvercle a sauté; **the door sprang open** la porte s'est ouverte d'un coup; **the lever springs out** le levier sort tout d'un coup; **to s. into public view** être propulsé sur la scène publique; **he sprang to fame overnight** il est devenu célèbre du jour au lendemain; **they sprang to attention** d'un bond, ils se mirent au garde-à-vous; **one thing that immediately springs to mind is …** une chose qui vient immédiatement à l'esprit est …; *Lit* **a tear sprang to her eye** une larme surgit dans ses yeux; *Lit* **an oath sprang to his lips** un juron lui est monté aux lèvres

2 (*to originate, come into being*) **to s. from** venir de, provenir de; **hope springs eternal** l'espérance reste toujours vivace; **to s. into existence** surgir, apparaître soudain; *Fam* **where did you s. from?** d'où sortez-vous?

3 (*warp*) (*of wood*) gauchir, se déformer, se déjeter

VT 1 to s. a leak faire une voie d'eau **2** (*partridge etc*) (faire) lever **3** (*trap*) faire jouer; (*mine*) faire sauter **4** (*car*) munir de ressorts; **sprung carriage** voiture suspendue **5** *Fam* (*help to escape from prison*) faire échapper de prison

▸▸ *Br* **s. balance** peson *m* à ressort; *Culin* **s. chicken** poussin *m*; *Fam Fig* **she's no s. chicken** elle n'est plus toute jeune; **s. lock** serrure *f* à fermeture automatique; **s. mattress** matelas *m* à ressorts; *Br* **s. onion** petit oignon *m*; **s. roll** rouleau *m* de printemps; **s. tide** grande marée *f*, (*at equinox*) marée d'équinoxe (de printemps); **s. vegetables** primeurs *fpl*; **s. water** eau *f* de source

▸ **spring back VI** (*move back suddenly*) (*of object*) se redresser, repartir en arrière; **the branch sprang back** la branche s'est redressée; **she sprang back in horror** elle recula d'un bond, horrifiée

▸ **spring forward VI** (*rush forward*) s'élancer *ou* se précipiter en avant

▸ **spring on VT SEP** (*confront with*) **to s. a question on sb** (*unexpectedly*) poser à qn une question inattendue; (*point-blank*) poser une question à brûle-pourpoint à qn; **to s. a surprise on sb** faire une surprise à qn; **I wish you wouldn't s. things on me like that** (*without warning*) j'aimerais bien que tu arrêtes de me prendre par surprise; **sorry to have to s. this on you** désolé de vous demander ça à la dernière minute

▸ **spring up VI 1** (*jump to one's feet*) se lever vivement *ou* d'un bond **2** (*appear suddenly*) **a breeze sprang up** une brise s'est levée; **an intimacy sprang up between them** l'intimité naquit entre eux; **a doubt sprang up in his mind** un doute a germé dans son esprit; **the company sprang up almost overnight** la société s'est montée quasiment du jour au lendemain; **to (begin to) s. up** (*of plant etc*) (commencer à) pousser; **McDonalds are springing up all over the place** les McDonald poussent partout comme des champignons

springboard ['sprɪŋbɔːd] **N** *Gym, Swimming, Fig* tremplin *m*

springbok ['sprɪŋbɒk] **N** (*antelope*) springbok *m*

spring-clean N nettoyage *m* de printemps; **to give a house a s.** faire le nettoyage de printemps dans une maison

VT (*house*) nettoyer à fond

VI faire le nettoyage de printemps, *Can* faire le grand ménage

spring-cleaning N grand nettoyage *m* de printemps

springe [sprɪndʒ] **N** (*snare*) lacet *m*, collet *m*

springer ['sprɪŋər] **N** (*dog*) springer *m*

▸▸ **s. spaniel** springer

springiness ['sprɪŋɪnɪs] **N** effet *m* de ressort; (*of hair*) gonflant *m*; (*of mattress*) élasticité *f*; (*of turf, ground*) souplesse *f*

springing ['sprɪŋɪŋ] **N** (*of car, bed*) suspension *f*

springless ['sprɪŋlɪs] **ADJ** *Tech* sans ressort(s)

springlike ['sprɪŋlaɪk] **ADJ** (*weather etc*) de printemps; (*dress*) printanier, -ère

spring-loaded ADJ à ressort

springtide ['sprɪŋtaɪd] **N** *Lit* = **springtime N**

springtime ['sprɪŋtaɪm] **N** printemps *m*; **in s.** au printemps

ADJ ATTRIB (*weather, feeling*) printanier, -ère

springy ['sprɪŋɪ] **ADJ** élastique, qui fait ressort; (*brake pedal*) flexible; (*carpet*) moelleux; (*wood*) élastique; (*hair*) qui ont du volume; **with a s. step** (*to walk*) d'un pas léger

sprinkle ['sprɪŋk(ə)l] **VT** (*cake, pie etc*) (*with sugar, salt etc*) saupoudrer (**with sth** de qch); (*with liquid*) arroser légèrement (**with sth** de qch); **to s. the floor with sand** répandre du sable par terre; **he should s. a few well-known names in the text** il devrait introduire quelques noms fameux par-ci par-là dans le texte; **a house or two was sprinkled here and there on the hillside** quelques maisons étaient éparpillées sur la colline

N (*of salt, sugar, nutmeg etc*) pincée *f*, **a s. of rain** quelques gouttes *fpl* d'une pluie

sprinkler ['sprɪŋklər] **N 1** (*for lawns etc*) arroseur *m*; (**rotary**) **s.** arroseur (rotatif); (**fire**) **s.** (*extinguisher*) extincteur *m* (automatique) d'incendie **2** *Rel* goupillon *m*, aspersoir *m* **3** (*for sugar*) saupoudreuse *f*

▸▸ **s. head** (*of shower*) pommeau *m*; (*of watering can*) pomme *f*, (*buried in ground*) arroseur; **s. system** installation *f* d'extinction automatique d'incendie, installation sprinkler

sprinkling ['sprɪŋklɪŋ] **N 1** (*action*) (*with sugar etc*) saupoudrage *m*; (*with water*) arrosage *m* léger; *Rel* **s.** of holy water aspergès *m*, aspersion *f* **2** (*quantity*) (*of nutmeg, sugar etc*) pincée *f*, **a s. of gravel** une légère couche de gravier; **a s. of knowledge** quelques connaissances; **with a liberal s. of literary references** avec moult références littéraires données ici et là; **with a larger than usual s. of mistakes** avec çà et là encore plus de fautes que d'habitude; **a s. of new faces in the congregation** quelques nouvelles têtes ici et là dans la congrégation; **there was now a s. of grey among the auburn hair** il y avait maintenant quelques fils d'argent dans la chevelure auburn

▸▸ *Am* **s. can** arrosoir *m*

sprint [sprɪnt] **N** *Sport* sprint *m*; (*acceleration, spurt*) pointe *f* de vitesse; *Sport, Fig Fam* **to put on a s.** (*run*) piquer un sprint; **you'll need to put on a bit of a s. if you're going to finish that translation in time** il va falloir que tu passes la seconde si tu veux finir cette traduction à temps; **there was a s. finish** il y a eu un sprint à l'arrivée; **he has a good s. finish** il est très rapide dans les sprints de fins de courses

VI *Sport* sprinter; **I was good at sprinting** j'étais bon dans les courses de vitesse; **to s. past sb** sprinter pour dépasser qn; **the little boy sprinted off** le petit garçon s'élança à

toutes jambes; **he sprinted upstairs** il est monté en courant; **he sprinted after her** il a couru derrière elle à toute vitesse; **I had to s. for the bus** j'ai dû courir *ou* *Fam* piquer un sprint pour attraper le bus

sprinter ['sprɪntər] **N** *Sport* sprinter *m*

sprite [spraɪt] **N** lutin *m*, esprit *m* (follet), farfadet *m*

sprocket ['sprɒkɪt] **N** *Tech* **1** (*cog*) dent *f* (de pignon) **2** (*wheel*) pignon *m*

▸▸ **s. hole** (*for film*) perforation *f*, **s. wheel** pignon

sprog [sprɒg] **N** *Sl* (*child*) môme *mf*, gosse *mf*

sprout [spraʊt] **N** *Bot* **1** (*shoot*) pousse *f* **2** (**Brussels**) **sprouts** choux *mpl* de Bruxelles

VI 1 (*of plant*) pousser; (*of branch, shrub*) bourgeonner; (*of seed*) germer **2** = **sprout up**

VT 1 to s. horns (*of animal*) pousser des cornes; *Fam* **to s. a moustache** se laisser pousser la moustache **2** (*seeds*) faire germer

▸ **sprout up VI** (*of plants*), *Fam* (*of child*) pousser; *Fig* (*of new buildings, towns etc*) pousser comme un champignon/des champignons, (*of new community, sect*) surgir, naître

spruce[1] [spruːs] **ADJ** (*person*) (très) soigné, tiré à quatre épingles; (*house, room*) (très) soigné, bien entretenu

▸ **spruce up VT SEP** (*make neat*) (*house, room*) donner de l'éclat à; **to s. oneself up** se faire beau/belle; **all spruced up** sur son trente et un

spruce[2] **N** (*tree*) épicéa *m*; **Norway s.** sapin *m* de Norvège

▸▸ **s. fir** (*sapin*) épicéa

spruceness ['spruːsnɪs] **N** (*of person*) mise *f* soignée; (*of house, room etc*) propreté *f*

sprung [sprʌŋ] **ADJ** (*mattress etc*) à ressorts

PP see spring VI, VT

spry [spraɪ] **ADJ** (*comp* **spryer**, *superl* **spryest**) vif, *f* vive, actif, plein d'allant

spud [spʌd] **N 1** *Fam* (*potato*) patate *f* **2** (*weeding hoe*) sarcloir *m*

▸▸ *Mil Sl* **s. bashing** corvée *f* de patates, (corvée) *ou* pluches *fpl*

spume [spjuːm] **N** *Arch, Lit* (*of sea*) écume *f*

spun [spʌn] **ADJ** filé

PT, PP see spin[2] **VT, VI**

▸▸ **s. silk** schappe *f*, *Culin* **s. sugar** sucre *m* filé

spunk [spʌŋk] **N 1** *Old-fashioned Fam* (*courage*) cran *m*; **to have plenty of s.** avoir du cran **2** *Br Vulg* (*semen*) foutre *m*

spunky ['spʌŋkɪ] **ADJ** *Fam* **1** *Old-fashioned* (*brave*) courageux, qui a du cran **2** *Br, Austr* (*attractive*) canon

spur [spɜːr] **N 1** (*for riding*) éperon *m*; *Fig* **to win one's spurs** faire ses preuves **2** *Fig* (*stimulus*) stimulant *m*; **this hope was the s. that drove her on** cet espoir fut l'aiguillon qui la fit aller de l'avant; **to do sth on the s. of the moment** faire qch sous l'impulsion du moment *ou* sur un coup de tête; **it was a s.-of-the-moment decision** j'ai pris/il a pris/*etc* cette décision sur un coup de tête **3** (*of cock*) ergot *m*; (*of fighting cock*) éperon *m* **4** *Geog* éperon *m*, contrefort *m*; (*of railway line*) épi *m*; (*to motorway*) bretelle *f* d'accès, voie *f* d'accélération **5** *Bot* éperon *m*

VT (**-rr-**) (*horse*) éperonner, talonner; *Fig* **to s. sb into action** pousser qn à agir; **booted and spurred** botté et éperonné

▸ **spur on VT SEP 1** (*horse*) éperonner, talonner **2** *Fig* (*motivate*) aiguillonner, stimuler; **spurred on by a desire to …** stimulé *ou* aiguillonné par un désir de …; **this spurred us on to redouble our efforts** ceci nous a stimulés et fait redoubler d'efforts

spurge [spɜːdʒ] **N** (*plant*) euphorbe *f*, épurge *f*

spurious ['spjʊərɪəs] ADJ *(false)* faux, *f* fausse; *(argument, objection)* non valable; *(distinction, reasoning)* douteux; *(writings)* apocryphe; *(edition)* de contrefaçon

spuriously ['spjʊərɪəslɪ] ADV faussement

spuriousness ['spjʊərɪəsnɪs] N fausseté *f* (**of** de); *(of distinction)* non-validité *f*; *(of text)* caractère *m* apocryphe

spurn [spɜːn] VT *(offer)* rejeter avec mépris; *(person, person's advances)* repousser avec mépris; **she's feeling spurned** *(by lover, boyfriend)* elle se sent rejetée

spurt [spɜːt] N **1** *(of liquid)* jaillissement *m*, jet *m*, giclée *f* **2** *(sudden effort)* effort *m* soudain; *(burst of energy)* poussée *f* d'énergie; *Sport (of speed)* effort de vitesse; *Cycling Fam* emballage *m*; **a s. of anger/jealousy** un bref moment de colère/jalousie; **a s. of energy** une poussée d'énergie; **to put on a s.** *(when running)* démarrer; *Cycling Fam* emballer; *(in work etc)* donner un coup de collier; **there's been a sudden s. of activity** il y a eu un regain d'activité; **she tends to work in spurts** elle a tendance à travailler par à-coups; *Sport* **final s.** pointe *f* finale, rush *m*
  VI **1** *(of liquid)* jaillir, gicler **2** *Sport* produire son effort; **she spurted past the other competitors** elle a produit son effort et a dépassé les autres concurrents; **he spurted into the lead** *Sport* il a produit son effort et s'est placé en tête de la course; *Fig* il est soudain venu se placer en tête
  VT *(of person) (liquid)* faire jaillir, faire gicler; *(of fountain pen)* gicler; **the pipe spurted water everywhere** de l'eau jaillissait du tuyau et éclaboussait partout; **the pen spurted ink onto the carpet** l'encre jaillit du stylo et tacha la moquette
  ► **spurt out** VI = **spurt** VI **1**
  VT SEP = **spurt** VT

sputnik ['spʊtnɪk] N *Astronaut* spoutnik *m*

sputter ['spʌtər] VT *(say while spitting saliva)* dire en lançant des postillons
  VI *(mumble)* bredouiller; *(talk while spitting saliva)* lancer des postillons en parlant; *Aut (of engine)* tousser; *(of pen)* fuir irrégulièrement; *(of kindling wood)* pétiller; *(of meat on grill, candle)* grésiller; *(of flame)* grésiller, crépiter; **the engine sputtered into life** le moteur toussa avant de démarrer
  ► **sputter out** VI *(stop burning)* **the candle sputtered out** la bougie s'est éteinte en grésillant

sputum, *pl* **sputa** ['spjuːtəm, -ə] N *Med* crachat *m*

spy, *pl* **spies** [spaɪ, spaɪz] N *Pol, Ind* espion, -ionne; *(for police, prison warden etc)* *Fam* mouchard, -arde; **another s. scandal would ruin us** la découverte d'un autre espion et le scandale qui en résulterait équivaudrait à notre perte
  VI espionner; **to s. on sb** épier *ou* espionner qn; **I had the feeling I was being spied on all the time** j'avais l'impression qu'on m'épiait tout le temps
  VT *(notice)* apercevoir, voir
  ► ► **s. network** réseau *m* d'espionnage; **s. plane** avion-espion *m*, *pl* avions-espions; **s. ring** réseau d'espionnage; **s. satellite** satellite *m* espion, *pl* satellites-espions
  ► **spy out** VT SEP **to s. out the land** explorer le terrain

spyglass ['spaɪglɑːs] N *Old-fashioned* lunette *f* d'approche, longue-vue *f*, *pl* longues-vues

spyhole ['spaɪhəʊl] N *(in wall, floor)* trou *m*; *(in door)* judas *m*

spying ['spaɪɪŋ] N espionnage *m*

spyware ['spaɪweər] N *Comput* logiciel *m* espion

Sq *(abbr* **Square)** place, square

sq *(abbr* **square)** carré

sq. ft. *(abbr* **square foot/feet)** pied(s) carré(s)

SQL [eskjuːˈel] N *Comput abbr* **structured query language**

SQL engine N *Comput* processeur *m* SQL

Sqn. Ldr. *Br Mil, Aviat abbr* **Squadron Leader**

squab [skwɒb] N **1** *(young pigeon)* pigeonneau *m* sans plumes **2** *Br Aut* coussin *m*

squabble ['skwɒb(ə)l] N querelle *f*, chamaillerie *f*
  VI se quereller, se chamailler (**with** avec)

squabbler ['skwɒblər] N querelleur, -euse, chamailleur, -euse

squabbling ['skwɒblɪŋ] N querelles *fpl*, chamailleries *fpl*

squad [skwɒd] N **1** *(of workmen etc)* brigade *f*, équipe *f*; *Sport* équipe *f*; **rescue s.** équipe de secours **2** *Mil* escouade *f*; **firing s.** peloton *m* d'exécution
  ► ► **s. car** voiture *f* de patrouille de police

squaddie ['skwɒdɪ] N *Br Fam (private soldier)* bidasse *m*

squadron ['skwɒdrən] N **1** *Mil, Aviat* escadron *m*; **fighter/bomber s.** escadron de chasse/bombardiers **2** *Naut* escadre *f*
  ► ► *Br* **s. leader** *(in air force)* ≃ commandant *m*, *Belg, Can* ≃ major *m*

squalid ['skwɒlɪd] ADJ *(dirty)* sale; *(sordid)* sordide

squalidly ['skwɒlɪdlɪ] ADV de façon sordide

squalidness ['skwɒlɪdnɪs] N = **squalor**

squall [skwɔːl] N **1** *(cry)* cri *m* rauque *ou* discordant **2** *(gust)* bourrasque *f*, rafale *f*, *Naut* grain *m*
  VI *(cry)* crier, *Fam* brailler

squalling ['skwɔːlɪŋ] ADJ criard, *Fam* braillard
  N criaillerie *f*

squally ['skwɔːlɪ] ADJ *(weather)* à rafales; *Naut* à grains; **it's s. today** il y des bourrasques *ou Naut* des grains aujourd'hui

squalor ['skwɒlər] N *(dirtiness)* saleté *f*; *(poverty)* misère *f*; **to die in s.** mourir dans la misère

squander ['skwɒndər] VT *(money, time), Fig (talents)* gaspiller; *(fortune)* dissiper, dilapider, *Fam* claquer; *Fig (natural resources)* dilapider

squandering ['skwɒndərɪŋ] N *(of money, time)* gaspillage *m*; *(of fortune)* dissipation *f*

SQUARE [skweər]

N carré **1, 2** ▪ case **1** ▪ place **1** ▪ square **3** ▪ équerre **4**	
ADJ carré **1** ▪ catégorique **2** ▪ quitte **2** ▪ honnête **2** ▪ ringard **3**	
ADV à angle droit **1** ▪ honnêtement **2**	
VT régler **2** ▪ élever au carré **5** ▪ quadriller **6**	
VI s'accorder	

N **1** *(shape) (of chocolate etc), Geom* carré *m*; *(on chessboard etc)* case *f*, *(on map)* carreau-module *m, pl* carreaux-modules; **to divide a map into squares** quadriller une carte; **to fold sth into a s.** plier qch en carré; *Fig* **to be back at s. one** être revenu à son point de départ; *Fig* **let's start again from s. one** repartons du point de départ; *(in relationship)* repartons à zéro; **(silk) s.** carré *ou* foulard *m* (de soie)
  2 *Math (of number)* carré *m*; **magic s.** carré magique
  3 *(of town, village)* place *f*; *(with garden)* square *m*; *Mil* terrain *m* de manœuvre(s)
  4 *(for drawing, measuring angles)* équerre *f*; **set s.** équerre à dessin; **to cut sth on the s.** couper qch à angles droits; **out of s.** qui n'est pas d'équerre
  5 *Fam* ringard, -arde

ADJ **1** *(figure, shoulders, neckline), Naut (sail), Math (metre, centimetre etc)* carré; **nine metres s.** de neuf mètres sur neuf, de neuf mètres au carré; **nine s. metres** neuf mètres carrés; **a s. mile** = 2,5 kilomètres carrés; *Fig* **to be a s. peg in a round hole** ne pas être à sa place VOIR GRAMMAIRE B59
  2 *Fig (refusal, denial)* net, *f* nette, catégorique; *(meal)* copieux; **what he needs is a good s. meal** tout ce dont il a besoin, c'est d'un vrai repas; **to get things s.** *(arrange)* arranger les choses; *(put in order)* mettre tout en ordre; **to make an account s.** régler un compte; **to be s. with sb** être quitte envers qn; **they are (all) s.** *(in competition)* ils sont à égalité; *(debts to each other have been paid)* ils sont quittes; **to get s. with sb** *(get even)* régler son compte à qn; *(settle bills etc)* être quitte envers qn; **to get things s. with sb** *(arrange matters)* arranger les choses avec qn; **a s. deal** une affaire honnête; **he always gives you a s. deal** il est toujours loyal en affaires
  3 *Fam* ringard; **you're so s.** qu'est-ce que tu peux être ringard
  ADV **1** *(at right angles)* à angle droit; *Tech* d'équerre (**to, with** avec); **set s. upon its base** d'aplomb sur sa base; **he hit him (fair and) s. on the jaw** il l'a frappé en plein sur le menton
  2 *(to act)* honnêtement; **fair and s.** loyalement, carrément
  VT **1** *(block of marble, wood)* carrer, équarrir
  2 *(account)* régler; **to s. accounts with sb** *(pay money owed)* régler (ses comptes avec) qn; *(get revenge)* régler son compte à qn; **to s. matters** arranger les choses; **to s. one's practice with one's principles** accorder ses actions avec ses principes; **how do you s. it with your conscience?** comment arrangez-vous cela avec votre conscience?; **it's OK, I'll s. it with him** ça va, j'arrangerai ça avec lui
  3 *Fam (bribe)* acheter, soudoyer, *Fam* graisser la patte à
  4 *Geom, Fig* **to s. the circle** faire la quadrature du cercle; **it's like squaring the circle** c'est la quadrature du cercle
  5 *Math (number, expression)* élever *ou* mettre au carré; **four squared** quatre au carré
  6 *(divide into squares) (sheet of paper)* quadriller; **squared paper** papier quadrillé *ou* à carreaux
  7 *Sport* **to s. the match** *(of team, player)* égaliser; **that goal squares the match** avec ce but, ils ont égalisé
  VI **1** **the end and the side should s. with each other** le bout et le côté doivent se raccorder
  2 *(coincide)* s'accorder (**with** avec); **the theory does not s. with the facts** la théorie ne correspond pas aux faits
  ► ► *Typ* **s. brackets** *(right-angled)* crochets *mpl*; **s. corner** coin *m* à angle droit; **s. dance** quadrille *m*, *Can* danse *f* carrée; *Fam* **s. eyes** *(person)* téléphage *m*; **s. measure** mesure *f* de surface *ou* de superficie; **the S. Mile** = City de Londres *(dont la superficie fait environ un mile carré)*; **s. number** carré *m*; *Naut* **s. rigger** navire *m* gréé en carré; **s. root** racine *f* carrée; **s. ruler** carrelet *m*, règle *f* quadrangulaire; *Am Fam* **s. shooter** personne *f* franche; *Electron* **s. wave** onde *f* carrée *ou* rectangulaire
  ► **square away** VT SEP *Am (tidy) (books)* ranger; *(room)* arranger
  ► **square off** VT SEP **1** *(divide into squares) (sheet of paper)* quadriller
  2 *Carp etc (make square) (end of a plank)* mettre d'équerre, équarrir
  VI *esp Am (assume fighting position)* se mettre en position de combat
  ► **square up** VI **1** *(settle debts)* régler ses dettes *ou* comptes; **can we s. up later?** pouvons-nous nous arranger *ou* faire nos

comptes plus tard?; **to s. up with sb** *(pay money owed)* régler (ses comptes avec) qn; *Fig (get even with)* se venger de qn, régler son compte à qn **2** *(face up)* **to s. up to the difficulties/to sb** faire face aux difficultés/à qn **3** *(assume fighting position)* se mettre en position de combat **4** *Am Fam (of criminal)* raccrocher, se ranger des voitures; *(of drug addict)* décrocher **VT SEP** *Carp etc (make square) (end of plank)* mettre d'équerre, équarrir

square-bashing N *Br Mil Sl* ≃ exercice *m*
square-built ADJ *(person)* aux épaules carrées; *(short and sturdy)* trapu; *(building)* carré
square-headed ADJ à tête carrée
squarely ['skweəlɪ] ADV **1** *(directly)* carrément; **look me s. in the eyes** regarde-moi bien dans les yeux; **stand it s. on its base** placez-le bien en équilibre sur son socle **2** *(honestly)* carrément, honnêtement; *(to act)* loyalement
squareness ['skweənɪs] N **1** *(shape)* forme *f* carrée **2** *Fam (of person, views)* conservatisme *m*
square-shouldered [-'ʃəʊldəd] ADJ aux épaules carrées
square-toed ADJ *(shoes)* à bout carré
squaring ['skweərɪŋ] N **1** *(of account)* règlement *m* **2 the s. of the circle** la quadrature du cercle
squash¹ [skwɒʃ] N **1** *(crush)* **there was a dreadful s. at the doors** la foule s'écrasait aux portes; **it was a s., but everyone got in the car** nous étions serrés comme des sardines mais tout le monde a tenu dans la voiture **2** *(crowd)* cohue *f* **3** *Br* **orange/lemon s.** *(concentrate, drink)* sirop *m* d'orange/de citron **4** *Sport* squash *m* **VT** écraser, aplatir; *Fig (revolt etc)* écraser, étouffer; *Fig (person)* remettre à sa place, rembarrer; *Fig* **she looked rather squashed** *(humiliated)* elle avait l'air plutôt dépité **VI** *(become squashed)* s'écraser, s'aplatir; **to s. into a room/car** se serrer dans une pièce/voiture
   ▸▸ *Sport* **s. court** court *m* de squash; *Old-fashioned* **s. hat** chapeau *m* mou; *Br Sport* **s. rackets** squash
▸ **squash up** VI *(sit, stand together closely)* se serrer **VT SEP** écraser
squash² N *(vegetable)* courge *f*
squashy ['skwɒʃɪ] ADJ *(fruit)* trop mûr; *(easily squashed)* qui s'écrase facilement; *(ground)* bourbeux, détrempé
squat [skwɒt] VI (-tt-) **1** *(crouch down)* s'accroupir; *(of animal)* se tapir; **she was squatting by the fire** elle était accroupie au coin du feu **2** *(occupy house illegally)* squatter; **to s. on a piece of land** occuper un terrain illégalement **VT** *(occupy illegally) (house)* squatter **N 1** *(posture)* posture *f* accroupie **2** *(place)* squat *m* **ADJ** *(person)* ramassé, trapu; *(object, building etc)* écrasé; *(arc)* surbaissé
squatter ['skwɒtər] N squatter *m*
squaw [skwɔ:] N squaw *f*
squawk [skwɔ:k] N *(of bird)*, *Fam (of person)* cri *m* rauque; **a s. of protest** un tollé; **to give a s. of outrage** pousser un cri d'indignation **2** *Am Fam (complaint)* rouspétance *f*; **what's your s.?** c'est quoi ton problème? **VI 1** *(of bird)* pousser des cris rauques; *Fam (of person, baby)* brailler; **to s. with rage/in protest** pousser des cris de rage/en signe de protestation **2** *Fam (complain)* rouspéter **3** *Sl (inform)* moucharder
   ▸▸ *Am Fam* **s. box** *(loudspeaker)* haut-

parleur *m*, *pl* haut-parleurs; *(intercom)* interphone *m*; *(telephone)* bigophone *m*
squeak [skwi:k] N **1** *(noise) (of animal, person)* couinement *m*, cri *m* aigu; *(of unoiled door, wheel etc)* grincement *m*; **to let out a s.** pousser un couinement; *Fam* **I don't want to hear another s. out of you** je ne veux pas entendre le moindre murmure **2** *Fam* **that was a near or narrow s.!** nous l'avons/il l'a/ *etc* échappé belle! **VI** *(of animal)* couiner; *(of person)* pousser des cris aigus, couiner; *(of machine part etc)* grincer; *(of shoes)* crisser **VT** crier d'une petite voix aiguë
squeaking ['skwi:kɪŋ] N *(of animal)* couinements *mpl*; *(of door etc)* grincement *m*
squeaky ['skwi:kɪ] ADJ *(floorboard, bed, hinge)* grinçant; *(voice)* aigu, -uë; *Fam* **s. clean** *(hands, hair)* extrêmement propre; *(image, reputation)* sans tache
squeal [skwi:l] N cri *m* aigu; *(of animal)* cri perçant; *(of brakes)* grincement *m*; *(of tyres)* crissement *m* **VI 1** *(scream)* pousser des cris aigus, couiner; *(of tyres)* crisser; *(of brakes)* grincer; **to s. like a stuck pig** crier comme un porc qu'on égorge **2** *Fam (complain)* protester, jeter les hauts cris **3** *Sl (inform)* moucharder; **to s. on sb** dénoncer qn **VT** crier d'une voix aiguë *ou* perçante
squealer ['skwi:lər] N *Sl (informer)* mouchard, -arde
squealing ['skwi:lɪŋ] N cris *mpl* aigus; *(of tyres)* crissement *m*; *(of brakes)* grincement *m*
squeamish ['skwi:mɪʃ] ADJ sensible, *Fam* chochotte; **to feel s.** avoir des nausées, avoir mal au cœur; **it makes me feel s.** ça me donne mal au cœur; **I'm s. about seeing blood** je ne supporte pas la vue du sang; **don't be so s.!** ne fais pas le dégoûté!, *Fam* ne fais pas ta chochotte!
   NPL the s. les petites natures *fpl*; **this programme/film is not for the s.** cette émission/ce film est réservé à ceux qui ont l'estomac bien accroché
squeamishness ['skwi:mɪʃnɪs] N sensibilité *f*
squeegee ['skwi:dʒi:] N **1** *(mop)* balai *m* en caoutchouc; *(for window cleaning)* racloir *m (avec bordure de caoutchouc)* **2** *Phot etc* raclette *f*; **roller s.** rouleau *m* en caoutchouc
SQUEEZE [skwi:z] N **1** *(pressure)* compression *f*, *(of hand)* serrement *m*; *(hug)* étreinte *f*; **a s. of lemon** quelques gouttes *fpl* de citron; **to give sth a s.** *(toothpaste)* serrer qch; *(cloth)* essorer qch; *(lemon)* presser qch; **to give sb's hand a s.** serrer la main à qn; **to give sb a s.** serrer qn dans ses bras; **credit s.** restriction *f* de crédit; *Fam* **to put the s. on sb** mettre la pression sur qn; **to put the s. on prices/wages** bloquer les prix/salaires; **it'll be a s. but I think we should all fit in** on sera serrés mais je crois que tout le monde tiendra; **it was a tight s.** *(but we fitted in)* on tenait tout juste; **it's something of a s. getting into these jeans** quelle gymnastique pour enfiler ce jean!; *Fam* **(main) s.** *(boyfriend)* mec *m*, Jules *m*; *(girlfriend)* nana *f*, gonzesse *f*
   2 *(in bridge)* squeeze *m*
   VT 1 *(sponge, lemon)* presser; *(hug) (person)* embrasser, étreindre; *(wring) (cloth)* essorer; **to s. sb's hand** serrer la main à qn; **to s. the life out of sb** *(of bear, person)* étouffer qn; **to s. liquid out of sth** faire sortir un liquide de qch; **to s. the water out of a sponge** essorer une éponge; **to s. the juice out of a lemon** extraire le jus d'un citron; **to s. sth into a box** faire entrer qch de force dans une boîte; **he squeezed his way under the fence** il s'est glissé *ou* faufilé sous le

prices/wages bloquer les prix/salaires; **I think we can just s. you in** *(find time for in schedule etc)* je crois qu'on pourra vous trouver un petit moment; *(in class, car etc)* je crois qu'on pourra vous trouver une petite place; **to s. money out of sb** extorquer de l'argent à qn
   2 *Fig (put pressure on)* pressurer; **we'll have to s. him a bit harder** il va falloir qu'on augmente encore la pression sur lui; **to s. the working class/rich** pressurer les classes ouvrières/les riches; **the British car industry has been squeezed by foreign competition** l'industrie automobile britannique subit la pression de la concurrence étrangère
   VI to s. into a crowded train entrer de force dans un train bondé; **to find a little parking space to s. into** trouver une petite place de parking où se faufiler; **any room for one more to s. in?** y a-t-il encore une toute petite place?; **we squeezed under the fence** nous nous sommes glissés *ou* faufilés sous le grillage
▸ **squeeze out** VT SEP *(juice etc)* extraire; **to s. out a tear** y aller de sa (petite) larme; *Fam* **they're trying to s. me out** *(off company board etc)* ils essaient de se débarrasser de moi
▸ **squeeze through** VI se faufiler, se glisser **VT INSEP to s. through a narrow window** se glisser par une fenêtre étroite
▸ **squeeze up** VI *(sit, stand together closely)* **to s. up (together)** se serrer (les uns contre les autres); **s. up a bit so Jane can sit down** serrez-vous un peu pour que Jane puisse s'asseoir

squeezebox ['skwi:zbɒks] N *Fam* accordéon *m*, concertina *m*
squeezer ['skwi:zər] N presse *f*, **lemon s.** presse-citron *m inv*
squelch [skweltʃ] N *(of mud)* bruit *m* de succion; *(of wet shoes etc)* gargouillement *m*, gargouillis *m* **VI to s. through the mud** patauger dans la boue; **they squelched across the muddy farmyard** ils ont traversé la cour de la ferme en pataugeant; **the water squelched in his shoes** l'eau gargouillait dans ses chaussures
squib [skwɪb] N **1** *(firework)* pétard *m*, serpenteau *m*; *Fig* **to be a damp s.** faire l'effet d'un pétard mouillé **2** *(satire)* satire *f*, brocard *m*
squid [skwɪd] N calmar *m*, calamar *m*
squiffy ['skwɪfɪ] ADJ *Old-fashioned Br Fam* un peu ivre, gris, éméché
squiggle ['skwɪg(ə)l] N *(mark, line)* trait *m ou* ligne *f* en paraphe; *(writing)* gribouillis *m*
squiggly ['skwɪglɪ] ADJ tortueux, -euse, sinueux, -euse
squillion ['skwɪljən] N *Br Fam Hum* **squillions (of)** une foultitude (de), une ribambelle (de)
squint [skwɪnt] N **1** *(eye defect)* strabisme *m*; **he has a slight s.** il louche légèrement **2** *(sideways glance)* regard *m* de côté *ou* de travers; **I had a s. at his paper** j'ai jeté un coup d'œil oblique sur son journal; *Fam* **let's have a s. at it!** faites voir! **ADJ 1** *(eyes)* louche **2** *Fam (crooked)* de travers, *Fam* de traviole **VI 1** *(have eye defect)* loucher **2** *(look through half-closed eyes)* plisser les yeux; **they're all squinting because of the sun** ils font tous la grimace à cause du soleil **3** *(look sideways)* **to s. at sb/sth** regarder qn/ qch de côté *ou* de travers *ou* furtivement
squint-eyed ADJ au regard louche
squinting ['skwɪntɪŋ] N strabisme *m*
squire ['skwaɪər] N **1** *Br (local landowner)* châtelain *m* **2** *Hist (attendant to knight)* écuyer *m* **3** *Br Fam* **evening, s.** 'soir, patron **VT** *(lady)* servir de cavalier à, escorter

squirearchy ['skwaɪəɾɑːkɪ] N classe f des châtelains

squirm [skwɜːm] VI (of worm etc) se tordre, se tortiller; (with embarrassment) être très mal à l'aise; **he was squirming with embarrassment** il se tordait d'embarras; **to s. with delight** se tortiller de joie; **to s. out of a situation** se sortir d'une situation; **to s. out of one's commitments** se défiler de ses obligations; **his over-politeness makes me s.** sa politesse excessive me met extrêmement mal à l'aise; **the sight of all that blood made me s.** tout ce sang m'a donné la nausée
▸ VT **to s. one's way out of a situation** se sortir d'une situation; **to s. one's way out of one's commitments** se défiler de ses obligations
▸ N (of pain etc) tortillement m

squirrel ['skwɪɾ(ə)l] N **1** (animal) écureuil m **2** Fig (hoarder) **she's a real s.** c'est une vraie fourmi
▸ **squirrel away** VT SEP mettre de côté

squirrelly ['skwɪɾ(ə)lɪ] ADJ Am Fam (eccentric) loufedingue

squirt [skwɜːt] N **1** (of liquid) jet m, giclée f; **to add a s. of soda** ajouter une giclée d'eau de Seltz; **to give sb a s. with a water pistol** arroser qn avec un pistolet à eau **2** Fam (insignificant person) morveux, -euse, péteux, -euse
▸ VT (liquid etc) faire gicler; **to s. soda water into a glass** mettre une giclée d'eau de Seltz dans un verre; **he squirted a little deodorant under each arm** il se vaporisa du déodorant sur chaque aisselle
▸ VI (of liquid etc) gicler, jaillir; **water was squirting out everywhere** l'eau giclait de partout

squish [skwɪʃ] Fam N (sound) bruit m d'écrabouillement; **the s. of mud underfoot** le gargouillement de la boue sous les pieds
▸ VT (squash) écraser
▸ VI **the mud squished beneath his feet** la boue gargouillait sous ses pieds

squishy ['skwɪʃɪ] ADJ Fam (ground) détrempé; (fruit etc) mou, f molle; **the ground's s. underfoot** le sol gargouille sous les pas

squits [skwɪts] NPL Br Fam **the s.** la courante

Sr (abbr **Senior**) Sr

SRAM ['esræm] N Comput (abbr **static random access memory**) mémoire f vive statique

Sri Lanka [sriː'læŋkə] N Sri Lanka m

Sri Lankan [sriː'læŋkən] ADJ srilankais
▸ N Sri Lankais, -aise

SRN [esɑːr'en] N Br Med abbr **State Registered Nurse**

SS [es'es] N Naut (abbr **steamship**) = initiales précédant le nom des navires de la marine marchande; **the SS Normandie** le Normandie

S-shaped ADJ en S; **S. hook** crochet m en S

SSL [eses'el] N Comput (abbr **secure sockets layer**) protocole m SSL

SSN N abbr **social security number**

SSSI ['eses'es'aɪ, 'trɪpəles'aɪ] N (abbr **Site of Special Scientific Interest**) = en Grande-Bretagne, site m déclaré d'intérêt scientifique

St 1 (abbr **Street**) rue **2** (abbr **Saint**) S(t), f Ste

st (abbr **stone**) = 6,35 kg

stab [stæb] N **1** (with dagger) coup m de poignard; (with knife) coup m de couteau; Fig **s. in the back** coup de Jarnac, attaque f déloyale; **s. of pain** élancement m; **a s. of remorse/envy** une pointe de remords/de jalousie; (with knife) coup(s) de couteau; **he had severe s. wounds in the chest** il était dans un état grave, ayant reçu des coups de couteau dans la poitrine
2 Fam (attempt) **to have a s. at sth** essayer

de faire qch; **I'll have a s.** je vais essayer
▸ VT (**-bb-**) (person) (with dagger) poignarder; (with knife) donner un coup/des coups de couteau à; **to s. sb with a fork/pair of scissors** donner un coup/des coups de fourchette/ciseaux à qn; **to s. sb to death** tuer qn à coups de couteau, poignarder qn; **to s. sb in the back** poignarder qn dans le dos; Fig tirer dans le dos de qn; **he's been stabbed** il a été poignardé; **he stabbed his knife into the tabletop** il planta son couteau dans la table; **she stabbed a piece of sausage with her fork** elle piqua un morceau de saucisse avec sa fourchette
▸ VI **to s. at sb** (with knife) porter un coup de couteau à qn; (with dagger) porter un coup de poignard à qn; **he stabbed at the map with his finger** il a indiqué un point sur la carte avec son doigt; **to s. at sb with one's finger** menacer qn du doigt

stabbing ['stæbɪŋ] ADJ (pain) lancinant
▸ N (act) (with dagger) coups mpl de poignard; (with knife) coups de couteau; (murder) meurtre m à coups de couteau; (attack) coup(s) de couteau; **there was a s. in the pub last night** quelqu'un s'est fait poignarder au pub hier soir; **to die in a s.** mourir poignardé; **the number of stabbings has increased** le nombre d'attaques à l'arme blanche est en hausse

stability [stə'bɪlɪtɪ] N (of building) stabilité f, solidité f; (economic, of aircraft, chemical compound etc) stabilité; **mental s.** équilibre m mental

stabilization [steɪbɪlaɪ'zeɪʃən] N (of economy, aircraft), Phys, Elec stabilisation
▸ ▸ Econ **s. fund** fonds m de stabilisation

stabilize ['steɪbɪlaɪz] VT (economy, ship, exchange rate) stabiliser
▸ VI se stabiliser

stabilizer ['steɪbɪlaɪzər] N **1** Naut stabilisateur m; Aviat stabilisateur, empennage m **2** (on bicycle) stabilisateur m **3** (in foodstuffs, explosives etc) stabilisant m
▸ ▸ Aut **s. bar** barre f stabilisatrice

stabilizing ['steɪbɪlaɪzɪŋ] ADJ stabilisateur, -trice; **to have or exert a s. effect on prices** exercer une action stabilisatrice sur les prix; **her new job had a s. effect on her** son nouvel emploi a eu un effet stabilisateur ou équilibrant sur elle
▸ ▸ **s. agent** (in foodstuffs) agent m stabilisant

stable 1 ['steɪb(ə)l] N **1** (building) écurie f; Fig **to lock the s. door after the horse has bolted** fermer la cage quand les oiseaux se sont envolés **2** (horses) chevaux mpl (d'une certaine écurie); Horseracing, Aut etc écurie f, Fig (of boxers, film stars) équipe f, (of publications, newspapers) empire m; **racing s.** écurie de courses; **s. companion** or **mate** (horse) cheval m de la même écurie; Fig (person) (in sport, film) membre m de la même équipe; **they are political s. mates** ils partagent les mêmes idées politiques
▸ VT (horse) loger dans une écurie; **we can s. three horses** nous avons de la place pour trois chevaux

Note that the French word **étable** is a false friend and is never a translation for the English word **stable**. It means **cowshed**.

stable 2 ADJ **1** (steady) (marriage, job, surface, economy, political situation), Chem, Phys stable; (ground, stairs, stepladders) solide; **s. currency** monnaie stable; **the government is becoming more s.** le gouvernement se stabilise; **to be in a s. condition** (of patient) être dans un état stationnaire; **s. state** état stable, état de stabilité **2** (well-balanced) (person) équilibré; **he's perfectly s.** il est parfaitement équilibré; **he's not s.** il n'est pas équilibré, il est instable

stableboy ['steɪblbɔɪ] N garçon m d'écurie

stablelad ['steɪblblæd] N lad m

stabling ['steɪblɪŋ] N **1** (of horses) logement m dans une écurie **2** (space in stables) **we have plenty of s.** nous ne manquons pas de place aux écuries

staccato [stə'kɑːtəʊ] Mus ADJ (note) staccato; Fig (style, dialogue of play) haché; (voice) saccadé
▸ ADV staccato
▸ N staccato m; **she replied in a rapid s.** elle répondit d'un ton rapide et saccadé

stache [stæʃ] N Am Fam (moustache) bacchantes fpl, moustagache f

stack [stæk] N **1** (of hay etc) meule f; (of wood, coal, plates etc) pile f, tas m; (of weapons) faisceau m; **stacks** (in library) rayonnages mpl
2 Fam **stacks of ...** (a lot of) des tas de ..., beaucoup de ...; **I've stacks of work to do** j'ai plein de boulot; **I've got stacks of things to read** j'ai une tonne de choses à lire; **we've got stacks of time** on a largement le temps; **to make stacks of money** ramasser l'argent à la pelle; **stacks** or **a s. of letters/complaints** des tonnes de courrier/plaintes
3 (of chimney) souche f, corps m; (of locomotive etc) cheminée f
4 Geog (rock formation) haut rocher m (au large d'une côte)
5 Aviat (aircraft waiting to land) = avions mpl dans le ciel en attente d'un créneau d'atterrissage
6 Comput pile f
▸ VT 1 (put in stacks) (hay) mettre en meule(s); (wood, coal, plates etc) empiler, entasser; (weapons) mettre en faisceaux; **the odds were stacked against them** tout était contre eux; SI **a woman stacked the way she is** une femme roulée comme elle
2 Am **to s. the cards** tricher aux cartes; **the jury was stacked against him** le jury avait un parti pris contre lui
3 Aviat (aircraft waiting to land) mettre en attente d'atterrissage
4 (fill) (shelf, room) bourrer
▸ ▸ **s. room** (in library) réserve f
▸ **stack up** VT SEP (objects, books etc) empiler

stacker ['stækər] N (on printer) dispositif m d'alimentation feuille à feuille; (for output) récepteur m (de sortie d'imprimante)

stacking chairs ['stækɪŋ] NPL chaises fpl superposables

stadium, pl **stadiums**, **stadia** ['steɪdɪəm, -ɪəmz, -ɪə] N Sport etc stade m

staff [stɑːf] N **1** (stick) bâton m; (of banner, lance) hampe f; (of bishop) crosse f; Naut (of flag) mât m; (in surveying) mire f; Am **at half s.** (of flag) en berne; Lit **the s. of life** (bread) le pain
2 (personnel, employees) personnel m; **when he joined the s.** quand il est entré dans le personnel; **how many people are there on the s.?** combien de personnes y a-t-il en tout?; **s. cutbacks** réduction f de personnel; **domestic s.** domestiques mfpl; Journ **editorial s.** rédaction f; **teaching s.** personnel enseignant; **nursing s.** infirmiers mpl, infirmières fpl; **office s.** personnel de bureau; **sales-support s.** personnel de soutien commercial; **senior** or **managerial s.** cadres mpl supérieurs; **s.-student ratio** rapport m entre le nombre de professeurs et le nombre d'étudiants VOIR GRAMMAIRE A11
3 Mil (officers) état-major m, pl états-majors; **general s.** état-major général; **chief of s.** chef d'état-major; **joint chiefs of s.** état-major interarmées
4 Mus (pl **staves** [steɪvz]) portée f
▸ VT (office etc) pourvoir en personnel; **the office is almost entirely staffed by women** le personnel du bureau est presque entière-

ment composé de femmes; **the office is only staffed between the hours of 2 and 4** il y a quelqu'un au bureau de 14 h à 16 h seulement

▸▸ **s. association** ≃ comité *m* d'entreprise; *Mil* **s. college** école *f* supérieure de guerre; *Journ* **s. correspondent** envoyé *m* de la rédaction, correspondant *m* permanent; *Br* **s. nurse** infirmier, -ière diplômé(e); *Mil* **s. officer** officier *m* d'état-major; *Sch* **s. room** salle *f* des professeurs; **s. turnover** roulement *m* du personnel

staffer ['stɑːfər] N *Fam* membre *m* du personnel; *Journ* journaliste *mf* permanent(e)

staffing ['stɑːfɪŋ] N *(finding staff)* recrutement *m* de personnel; **the delay is due to s.difficulties** le retard est dû à des problèmes de recrutement

▸▸ **s. arrangements** organisation *f* du personnel; **s. levels** effectifs *mpl*; **s. policy** politique *f* de recrutement du personnel

Staffs *abbr* **Staffordshire**

stag [stæg] N **1** *(animal)* cerf *m* **2** *Br St Exch Fam (premium hunter)* loup *m*

▸▸ *Entom* **s. beetle** cerf-volant *m, pl* cerfs-volants, *Spec* lucane *m*; **s. night** *(before wedding)* enterrement *m* de la vie de garçon

---

STAGE [steɪdʒ]

| **N** scène **1** ▪ plateau **1** ▪ estrade **2** |
| ▪ échafaudage **2** ▪ stade **3** ▪ étape **3,** |
| **4** ▪ diligence **5** |
| **VT** mettre en scène **1** ▪ organiser **1** |
| ▪ monter **1** |

N 1 *Theat (place)* scène *f*; *TV, Cin* plateau *m*; **the s.** *(theatre)* le théâtre; **to go on the s.** *(take up acting)* devenir acteur/actrice; **front of the s.** avant-scène *f*; **to come on (the) s.** entrer en scène; **to set the s.** monter les décors; *Fig* préparer le terrain; *Fig* **now the s. was set for …** maintenant tout était prêt pour …; **s. left/right** côté cour/jardin **2** *(platform)* estrade *f*, *(for workmen)* échafaudage *m*; *(of microscope)* platine *f* **3** *(phase)* stade *m*, étape *f*; **to be at a particular s.** *(in one's development etc)* en être à un certain stade; **to go through a particular s.** *(in one's development etc)* traverser un certain stade; **at this s.** à ce point, à ce moment; **in the larval s.** à l'état de larve, au stade larvaire; **to do sth in (successive) stages** faire qch par étapes (successives); **at what s. in its development?** à quel moment *ou* stade de son développement?; **at this s. in the project** à ce stade du projet; **at a later s. in his life** à un stade plus avancé de sa vie; **to pay in easy stages** payer en petits versements; **to do sth one s. at a time** faire qch étape par étape; **s. of production** phase *f* de production **4** *(part of journey)* étape *f*, *Hist (for stagecoach etc)* relais *m*; **s. by s.** d'étape en étape; **we did the journey in easy stages** nous avons fait le voyage en petites étapes; *Br* **fare s.** (changement *m* de) section *f* *(de l'itinéraire d'un autobus)* **5** *(stagecoach)* diligence *f* **6** *Astronaut (of rocket)* étage *m*

VT 1 *Theat etc* mettre en scène; *(play)* monter, porter à la scène; *(demonstration etc)* organiser, faire; *(coup)* monter; **to s. a comeback** faire un come-back; **the whole incident had been staged** l'incident avait été monté de toutes pièces **2** *(phase)* **staged payments** paiements *mpl* échelonnés; **carefully staged reduction of nuclear weapons** réduction soigneusement planifiée des armes nucléaires

▸▸ **s. direction** indication *f* scénique; **s. diving** = fait de se jeter dans la foule depuis la scène; **s. door** entrée *f* des artistes; **s. effects** effets *mpl* scéniques; **s. fright** trac *m*;

s. lighting éclairage *m* de plateau; **s. manager** régisseur *m*; **s. name** nom *m* de scène; **s. school** école *f* d'art dramatique; **s. whisper** aparté *m*; **'it's midnight', he announced in a loud s. whisper** 'il est minuit', chuchota-t-il, suffisamment fort pour que tout le monde l'entende

---

Note that the French word **stage** is a false friend and is never a translation for the English word **stage**. It means **training course**.

---

stagecoach ['steɪdʒkəʊtʃ] N diligence *f*

stagecraft ['steɪdʒkrɑːft] N *Theat* technique *f* de la scène

stagehand ['steɪdʒhænd] N *Theat* machiniste *mf*; *TV* machiniste de plateau

stage-manage VT *Theat* mettre en scène; *Fig Pej (demonstration etc)* organiser depuis les coulisses

stager ['steɪdʒər] N **old s.** vieux routier *m*

stage-struck ADJ épris *ou* féru de théâtre

stagey ['steɪdʒɪ] ADJ *Pej* = **stagy**

stagflation [stæg'fleɪʃən] N *Econ* stagflation *f*

stagger ['stægər] VI chanceler, tituber; **she staggered beneath the weight** elle chancela sous le poids; **s. along** marcher en chancelant *ou* en titubant; **to s. to one's feet** se relever en chancelant

VT 1 *(overwhelm) (person)* stupéfier; **to be staggered** tomber à la renverse; **I'm staggered!** je n'arrive pas à le croire! **2** *(hours of work, holidays etc)* échelonner

N 1 pas *m* chancelant **2** *Vet* **staggers** vertigo *m*

staggered ['stægəd] ADJ *Fam (amazed)* estomaqué

▸▸ **s. junction** carrefour *m* décalé; **s. payments** paiements *mpl* échelonnés

staggering ['stægərɪŋ] ADJ *(news)* renversant, atterrant; *(price)* incroyable; **s. blow** coup *m* de massue; **s. increase in prices** hausse vertigineuse des prix; **it cost a s. £4,000** ça a coûté la somme incroyable de 4000 livres

N *(of hours of work, holidays)* échelonnement *m*

staghorn ['stæghɔːn] N bois *mpl* de cerf

staghunt(ing) ['stæghʌnt(ɪŋ)] N chasse *f* au cerf

staging ['steɪdʒɪŋ] N **1** *Theat (of play)* mise *f* à la scène **2** *(scaffolding)* échafaudage *m*; *(shelving)* rayonnage *f* **3** *Astron* largage *m* *(d'un étage de fusée)*

▸▸ *Mil* **s. area, s. point** lieu *m* de rassemblement; *Br* **s. post** lieu *ou* point *m* de ravitaillement; *Aviat* escale *f* aérienne; *Hist (for coaches)* relais *m* (de diligences)

stagnant ['stægnənt] ADJ *(water)* stagnant; *(trade, business)* en stagnation, dans le marasme

stagnate [stæg'neɪt] VI *(of water, trade, business), Fig (of person)* stagner

stagnation [stæg'neɪʃən] N *(of water)* stagnation *f*, *(of trade)* stagnation, marasme *m*

stagy ['steɪdʒɪ] ADJ *Pej* théâtral, -aux

staid [steɪd] ADJ sérieux

staidness ['steɪdnɪs] N sérieux *m*

stain [steɪn] N **1** *(mark)* tache *f*; **to remove a s.** enlever une tache *(from* de*)*; *Fig* **without a s. on his character** sans atteinte à sa réputation; **to leave a s. on sb's reputation** entacher la réputation de qn; **a grease/blood s.** une tache de graisse/sang **2** *(dye)* colorant *m*; **(wood) s.** teinture *f* (pour bois)

VT 1 *(mark)* tacher *(with* de*)*; *Fig (person's reputation)* entacher, souiller, ternir; **hands stained with blood** mains tachées *ou* souillées de sang; *Fig* **hands stained with the**

blood of innocent people mains tachées du sang d'innocents **2** *(dye) (wood)* teindre, teinter; *(glass)* peindre

VI **material that stains easily** tissu qui se tache facilement

▸▸ **s. remover** détachant *m*

stained glass [steɪnd] N *(material)* verre *m* coloré; *(windows)* vitraux *mpl*

stained-glass window N vitrail *m, pl* -aux

staining ['steɪnɪŋ] N *(of wood)* teinture *f*

stainless ['steɪnlɪs] ADJ **1** *(rust-resistant)* inoxydable **2** *Fig (reputation)* sans tache

▸▸ **s. steel** acier *m* inoxydable

stair ['steər] N **1** stair(s) *(flight of stairs)* escalier *m*; **she took the stairs** elle prit l'escalier; **I met him on the stairs** je l'ai rencontré dans l'escalier; **back stairs** escalier de service **2** *(step)* marche *f*, degré *m*

▸▸ **s. carpet** tapis *m* d'escalier

staircase ['steəkeɪs] N *(stairs)* escalier *m*; *(structure)* cage *f* d'escalier; **secret s.** escalier dérobé

stairway ['steəweɪ] N = **staircase**

stairwell ['steəwel] N cage *f* d'escalier

stake [steɪk] N **1** *(piece of wood, metal)* pieu *m*; *(for marking land)* jalon *m*, fiche *f*, *(for tethering animal)* piquet *m*, *(in horticulture)* tuteur *m*, *(for vine)* échalas *m*, *(in surveying)* jalon; *Fam* **to pull up stakes** *(leave)* partir; *(leave one's home)* déménager **2** *(for execution)* **to die** *ou* **be burned at the s.** mourir sur le bûcher; **she went to the s. for her beliefs** on l'a brûlée pour ses croyances; *Fig* **but I'm not going to go to the s. for it** mais je n'ai aucune intention de mourir pour ça **3** *(in gambling), Fig* mise *f*, enjeu *m*; **the stakes are down** les jeux sont faits; **to play for high stakes** jouer gros jeu; **our honour is at s.** il y va de notre honneur, notre honneur est en jeu; **there's a lot at s.** de lourds intérêts sont en jeu; **to have large sums at s. in an enterprise** avoir de fortes sommes engagées dans une entreprise; **to have a s. in sth** avoir des intérêts dans qch; *Horseracing* **stakes** *(prize)* prix *m*

VT 1 *(mark out) (piece of land etc)* jalonner, piqueter; *(in surveying) (line, road etc)* jalonner; **to s. a claim** *Min* jalonner une concession; *Fig* faire valoir ses droits **2** *(support with stakes) (object)* soutenir avec des pieux; *(vine etc)* échalasser; *(tomatoes)* tuteurer **3** *(in gambling) (amount of money)* mettre en jeu, jouer; *Fig (reputation, job etc)* risquer; **to s. twenty euros** miser *ou* jouer vingt euros; **to s. everything** *or* **one's all** jouer son va-tout, mettre tout en jeu; **I'd s. my life on it** j'en mettrais ma tête à couper **4** *Am Fam (person) (provide with money)* financer; *(provide needs of)* subvenir aux besoins de

▸▸ **s. boat** bateau *m* de ligne de départ

▸ **stake off** VT SEP = **stake** VT **1**

▸ **stake out** VT SEP **1** = **stake** VT **1**

2 *(keep under observation) (building etc)* surveiller

stakeholder ['steɪkhəʊldər] N personne *f* participant à une affaire, partie *f* prenante

▸▸ **s. pension** = système *m* de retraite accessible aux salariés (notamment ceux qui ont de faibles revenus) ne bénéficiant pas d'une retraite complémentaire; **s. society** = terme popularisé par Tony Blair, qui désigne un type de société où chaque citoyen a un rôle à jouer car il y va de son propre intérêt

stakeout ['steɪkaʊt] N surveillance *f*; **to be on s.** faire le guet; **he was caught in a s.** la police faisait le guet et on l'a arrêté

staking ['steɪkɪŋ] N **1** *(marking off) (of piece of land etc)* jalonnement *m*, piquetage *m* **2** *(support) (of vine)* échalassage *m*; *(of tomatoes)* tuteurage *m*

stalactite ['stælæktaɪt, *Am also* stə'læktaɪt] N *Geol* stalactite *f*

stalagmite ['stæləgmaɪt, *Am also* stə'lægmaɪt] N *Geol* stalagmite *f*

stale [steɪl] ADJ **1** *(not fresh)* qui n'est pas frais, *f* fraîche; *(bread, cake)* rassis; *(air)* vicié; **s. breath** mauvaise haleine *f*, **s. smell** odeur *f* de renfermé; *(of beer, perfume etc)* relent *m*
2 *Fig (old) (excuse, cliché, argument etc)* vieux, *f* vieille; **s. joke** plaisanterie éculée; **s. news** nouvelle plus très fraîche; **it soon becomes s. and boring** on s'en lasse rapidement et ça devient ennuyeux
3 *(person)* qui a perdu sa fraîcheur; **to go s.** *(of athlete etc)* se surentraîner; *(of actor, musician etc)* perdre son inspiration; **I'm s.** *(of athlete, executive)* je suis vidé; *(of actor, writer, musician)* je n'ai plus d'inspiration; **I'm feeling a bit s.** j'ai un peu perdu de ma fraîcheur; *Fam* **it's gone s. on me** ça ne m'intéresse plus, j'ai perdu mon enthousiasme; **her marriage had gone s.** son mariage avait perdu de sa passion
4 *Fin (market)* lourd, plat
VI *(of news etc)* perdre de son intérêt; **pleasure that never stales** plaisir toujours nouveau
▸▸ *Fin* **s. cheque** chèque *m* prescrit

stalemate ['steɪlmeɪt] N *Chess* pat *m*; *Fig* **negotiations have reached a s.** les négociations sont dans l'impasse; *Fig* **it's s. between them** ils sont dans une impasse; *Fig* **it's s.** c'est l'impasse
VT *Chess* **Black is stalemated** les Noirs sont pat; *Fig* **this has stalemated the talks** cela a mis les négociations dans l'impasse; **stalemated industry** industrie *f* dans l'impasse

staleness ['steɪlnɪs] N **1** *(of bread)* état *m* rassis; *(of beer etc)* évent *m*; *(stale smell)* odeur *f* de renfermé; *(of beer, perfume etc)* relent *m* **2** *(of news)* manque *m* de fraîcheur

Stalinism ['stɑːlɪnɪz(ə)m] N stalinisme *m*

Stalinist ['stɑːlɪnɪst] ADJ, N stalinien, -ienne

stalk¹ [stɔːk] VI *(walk haughtily)* marcher *ou* s'avancer l'air hautain; **to s. out of a room** sortir d'une pièce l'air hautain
VT **1** *(of animal) (prey)* être sur les traces de; *(of hunter) (game)* traquer; *(deer)* chasser à l'approche; *Fig (person)* suivre furtivement; *(of private detective)* filer; *(of murderer)* traquer **2** *(prowl about in) (corridor, street)* rôder dans
N *(way of walking) (imposing)* démarche *f* majestueuse; *(disdainful)* démarche hautaine

stalk² N **1** *(of plant)* tige *f*, *(of fruit)* queue *f*, *(of wheat, corn)* chaume *m*; *(of bunch of grapes)* rafle *f*, râpe *f*, *(of cabbage)* trognon *m*; *Zool* pédoncule *m*, pédicule *m*; **s.-eyed** aux yeux pédonculés; **her eyes came out/ were (out) on stalks** les yeux lui sont sortis/sortaient de la tête **2** *(of wineglass)* pied *m* **3** *Aut (for controls)* tige *f*, manette *f*

stalker ['stɔːkər] N *(hunter)* chasseur *m* à l'approche; *(criminal)* = criminel *m* suivant sa victime à la trace; *(obsessive fan)* = admirateur *m* obsessionnel qui harcèle une célébrité ou une de ses connaissances

stalking ['stɔːkɪŋ] N **1** *(in hunting)* chasse *f* à l'approche **2** *(form of harassment)* = forme de harcèlement qui consiste à suivre quelqu'un en permanence
▸▸ **s. horse** *(in hunting)* cheval *m* d'abri; *Fig (pretext)* prétexte *m*; *Pol* **we'll use him as a s. horse** on va se servir comme d'un candidat bidon

stall [stɔːl] N **1** *(in stable)* stalle *f*, *(in byre)* case *f* **2** *(for selling etc)* étalage *m* (en plein vent), éventaire *m*; *(at exhibition etc)* stand *m*; **(market) s.** place *f ou* emplacement *m* (au marché); **newspaper s.** kiosque *m* à journaux; **I bought it at a fruit s.** je l'ai acheté chez le petit marchand de fruits; *also Fig* **to set out one's s.** déballer sa marchandise
3 *choir* **s.** stalle *f*, *Theat* **(orchestra) stalls** fauteuils *mpl* d'orchestre; **a seat in the stalls** un fauteuil d'orchestre
4 *Med (for finger)* doigtier *m*
5 *(act of stalling) Aut (of engine)* calage *m*; **I thought his story was just a s. to gain time** j'ai pensé qu'il ne cherchait qu'à gagner du temps avec son histoire
6 *Horseracing* **(starting) stalls** stalle *f* (de départ)
VT **1** *Aut (engine)* caler **2** *(put in stalls) (cattle)* mettre à l'étable **3** *(hold off) (cattle)* **s. them for half an hour** essaie de les retenir une demi-heure; **I think he's deliberately stalling us** je crois qu'il nous fait attendre délibérément; **they tried to s. us with some nonsense** ils ont tenté de nous retarder avec des bêtises
VI **1** *(of engine)* caler; *Aviat, Fig (of campaign)* être en perte de vitesse **2** **to s. (for time)** chercher à gagner du temps; **stop stalling!** arrête de tergiverser!; **we'll have to s. on this for another week or so** il faudra que nous gagnions environ une semaine de plus pour ça

stall-feed VT *(pt, pp* **stall-fed** [-fed]*) (cattle)* engraisser à l'étable

stallholder ['stɔːlhəʊldər] N étalagiste *mf*, marchand, -ande en plein vent; **I've agreed to be a s. at the fête** j'ai accepté de tenir un stand à la fête

stalling ['stɔːlɪŋ] N *Aut* **to prevent s.** pour empêcher que le moteur ne cale

stallion ['stæljən] N étalon *m*

stalwart ['stɔːlwət] ADJ *(strong)* robuste, vigoureux; *(brave)* vaillant; *Fig (defender)* résolu; *(supporter)* fidèle; *(refusal)* inébranlable; **they put up a s. defence** ils se sont défendus d'arrache-pied
N *Pol* **a party s.** un pilier du parti

stamen ['steɪmən] N *Bot* étamine *f*

stamina ['stæmɪnə] N résistance *f*

stammer ['stæmər] N *(permanent)* bégaiement *m*; *(out of nervousness etc)* bégaiement, balbutiement *m*; **man with a s.** homme qui bégaie, bègue *m*
VI *(normally)* bégayer; *(out of nervousness etc)* bégayer, balbutier
VT = **stammer out**
▸ **stammer out** VT SEP *(excuse etc)* bégayer, balbutier

stammerer ['stæmərər] N bègue *mf*

stammering ['stæmərɪŋ] N bégaiement *m*; *(through nervousness etc)* bégaiement, balbutiement *m*

STAMP [stæmp] N **1** **(postage) s.** timbre(-poste) *m*, *pl* timbres(-poste); *Br* **(National Insurance) s.** = mois *m* de cotisation à l'assurance chômage
2 *(device for marking)* tampon *m*; *(esp for metal)* estampe *f*, étampe *f*, *(esp for gold etc)* poinçon *m*; **signature s.** griffe *f*, **date s.** (timbre *m*) dateur *m*; **rubber s.** tampon *ou* timbre de caoutchouc
3 *(mark)* marque *f* (apposée); *Ind* estampille *f ou* marque de contrôle; *Fig* **it needs his s. of approval** il faut son approbation; **to bear the s. of genius** porter l'empreinte du génie; **to leave one's s. on sth** marquer qch de son empreinte; **there are few politicians of her s.** *(calibre)* il y a peu de politiciens de sa trempe, *Pej* il y a peu de politiciens de son espèce

4 *(in metalwork)* étampeuse *f*, estampeuse *f*
5 *(of foot)* battement *m* de pied *(d'impatience, de colère)*; **with a s. of the foot** en frappant du pied; **the ceaseless s. of feet past my window** le bruit continuel des pas devant ma fenêtre
VT **1** **to s. one's foot** taper du pied; **he stamped the toy to pieces** il a écrabouillé le jouet à coups de talon; **he stamped the snow/mud off his boots** il tapait du pied pour faire tomber la neige/boue; **he stamped the earth down** il a tassé la terre avec le pied
2 *(imprint mark on) (object)* imprimer sur; *(gold, silver)* poinçonner; *(coins etc)* frapper, estamper; *(leather)* frapper, estamper, gaufrer; **each article is stamped with the manufacturer's mark** chaque article porte la marque du fabricant; **a design is stamped on the butter** un dessin est imprimé dans le beurre; *Fig* **he was determined to s. his mark on the party** il était déterminé à marquer le parti de son empreinte
3 *(mark with ink) (document)* timbrer, estampiller; *(passport)* viser; *(letter)* affranchir; *(goods)* estampiller; *Fin* **to s. a bill** viser un effet; **they s. the details on your cheque** ils tamponnent les détails sur votre chèque; **a machine that stamps the date on …** une machine qui marque *ou* tamponne la date sur …
4 *(put postage stamp on) (letter, parcel)* timbrer, affranchir
5 *(in metalwork) (metal objects)* étamper, estamper
6 *Fig* **to s. sb/sth (as)** … donner à qn/qch le caractère de …; **this stamped him (as) a rebel** à partir de là, on lui a collé l'étiquette de rebelle
VI **to s. upstairs/outside** monter l'escalier/ sortir d'un pas bruyant
▸▸ **s. album** album *m* de timbres-poste; **s. collecting** philatélie *f*, **s. collector** collectionneur, -euse de timbres *ou* de timbres-poste, philatéliste *mf*; *Law* **s. duty** droit *m* de timbre, timbre fiscal; **s. hinge** charnière *f*, **s. machine** distributeur *m* automatique de timbres-poste; **s. pad** tampon (encreur)
▸ **stamp about, stamp around** VI *(stamp feet)* trépigner, piétiner; *(for warmth)* battre la semelle
▸ **stamp on** VT INSEP **1** *(step on) (cockroach, worm)* écraser (avec le talon)
2 *Fig (repress) (person)* écraser, bafouer; *(suggestions)* fouler aux pieds
VT SEP *(date etc)* tamponner, marquer
▸ **stamp out** VT SEP **1** *(eradicate) (rebellion)* écraser; *(abuse, resistance, independence etc)* éradiquer; *(epidemic, inflation)* enrayer
2 *(extinguish by stamping) (fire)* éteindre en piétinant
3 *(in metalwork) (sheet metal)* découper à la presse *ou* à l'emporte-pièce

stamped [stæmpt] ADJ *(with seal)* estampillé
▸▸ **s. addressed envelope** enveloppe *f* timbrée

stampede [stæm'piːd] N *(rush, flight) (of troops, horses etc)* fuite *f* précipitée, débandade *f*, **several people were injured in the s.** plusieurs personnes ont été blessées dans la panique; **there was a s. for the door** tout le monde s'est précipité vers la porte
VI *(rush)* se ruer, se précipiter (**for, towards** vers, sur); *(flee)* fuir en désordre *ou* à la débandade; *(of cattle etc)* partir à la débandade
VT *(cattle, people)* semer la panique parmi; **to s. a nation into war** précipiter un peuple dans la guerre; **to s. sb into doing sth** presser qn à faire qch, bousculer qn pour qu'il fasse qch; **I don't want to s. you into (making) a decision** je ne veux pas te presser *ou* te bousculer dans ta décision

stamping ['stæmpɪŋ] N **1** (with feet) piétinement m, trépignement m **2** (in metalwork) estampage m, étampage m; (item) pièce festampée **3** (of letters, parcels) affranchissement m, timbrage m

▸▸ Fam s. ground lieu m favori; this was one of my old s. grounds j'y allais tout le temps; s. out (of disease, crime, corruption, abuse) éradication f; (of strike, movement, rebellion) répression f; (of dissent, protest) étouffement m; s. press estampeuse f

stance [stæns] N (posture) position f; Fig position, attitude f; Golf, Cr etc (of player) posture f; she took up her usual s. at the window elle s'est mise à la fenêtre comme à son habitude; the government's s. on this la position ou l'attitude du gouvernement là-dessus

stanch [stɑːntʃ] VT = staunch²

stanchion ['stɑːnʃən] N étançon m, étai m

STAND [stænd]

N	position **1** ▪ représentation **2** ▪ station **3** ▪ support **4** ▪ béquille **4** ▪ étalage **5** ▪ stand **5** ▪ tribune **6** ▪ barre des témoins **8**
VI	être debout **1** ▪ se lever **1** ▪ se trouver **2**, **5** ▪ être **2**, **5** ▪ être valable **4** ▪ tenir **4** ▪ reposer **6**
VT	mettre **1** ▪ placer **1** ▪ supporter **3** ▪ subir **3** ▪ offrir **4**

N **1** (position) position f (on concernant); to take up a s. near the door se poster ou prendre position près de la porte; to take a s. prendre position et s'y tenir; to take a firm s. ne pas transiger; you should take a firmer s. with them tu devrais adopter une attitude plus ferme envers eux; to make a s. against an abuse s'opposer résolument à un abus; to make a s. (against the enemy) (of troops) faire face (à l'ennemi)

2 Theat représentation f; (by band) concert m

3 (for taxis) station f

4 (support) (of lamp etc) support m, pied m; (for motorbike etc) béquille f; (revolving) s. (for books, postcards etc) tourniquet m

5 (stall) (in open air) étalage m, étal m; (at exhibition etc) stand m

6 (at sports ground, for watching procession) tribune f; the stands les tribunes

7 Agr (crop) récolte f sur pied; (of trees) peuplement m

8 Law (witness box) barre f des témoins; to take the s. venir à la barre

VI (pt, pp stood [stʊd]) **1** (have upright position) être debout, se tenir debout; (maintain upright position) rester debout; (assume upright position) se lever; she stood with her back to me elle se tenait debout en me tournant le dos; to be/keep standing être/rester debout; I was too weak to s. j'étais trop faible pour me tenir debout; I could hardly s. je pouvais à peine me tenir debout; Fig to s. on one's own two feet se débrouiller tout seul; Fam he hasn't/you haven't/etc a leg to s. on ça ne tient pas; I've lost everything but what I s. up in j'ai tout perdu sauf ce que j'ai sur le dos; to s. six feet high (of object) avoir six pieds de haut, mesurer six pieds; (of person) mesurer six pieds; the house is still standing la maison tient toujours debout; not a stone (of the building) was left standing le bâtiment avait été complètement détruit; Sch s.! levez-vous!; Mil to s. to attention se mettre au garde-à-vous

2 (be situated, be) se trouver, être; a chapel stands at the top of the hill une chapelle se dresse au sommet de la colline; a car was standing at the door il y avait une voiture à la porte; the monument stands as a memorial to his life's work le monument a été

érigé pour célébrer l'œuvre de sa vie; I found the door standing open j'ai trouvé la porte ouverte; nothing stands between you and success rien ne s'oppose à votre succès; a man stood in the doorway un homme se tenait à la porte; I'll s. at or by the window je me mettrai à la fenêtre; I didn't know where to s. je ne savais où me mettre; I stood and looked at him, I stood looking at him je suis resté à le regarder; I was standing a few feet away from him je me tenais à quelques pas de lui; to s. talking/watching rester à parler/regarder; don't just s. there! do something! ne reste pas là avec les bras ballants! fais quelque chose!; don't s. in the passage! ne reste pas là, tu gênes le passage!; if you insist on leaving school at 16, I won't s. in your way si tu veux vraiment arrêter tes études à 16 ans, je ne m'y opposerai pas; to leave sb standing (there) laisser qn planté (là); Sport etc to be left standing être laissé sur place; to leave the competition standing Sport griller la concurrence; Fig laisser les autres très loin derrière; s. and deliver! la bourse ou la vie!; we're standing right behind you nous sommes avec vous; with the union standing behind him/her/etc avec le soutien du syndicat

3 (maintain position) to s. fast or firm (not retreat) tenir, tenir bon; to s. still se tenir immobile; time seemed to s. still le temps semblait s'être arrêté; we s. or fall together nous sommes solidaires (les uns des autres); I shall s. or fall by the issue mon sort dépend du résultat; to s. alone faire face ou tenir tête seul; to s. on ceremony faire des manières; she's standing on her dignity elle exige le respect qui lui est dû; she doesn't s. on her dignity at these occasions elle ne fait pas la fière dans de telles circonstances

4 (remain valid) tenir, se maintenir; the passage must s. le passage doit rester comme il est ou sans modification; the bet stands le pari tient; the objection stands cette objection est toujours valable; what you said last week, does that still s.? et ce que tu as dit la semaine dernière, ça tient toujours?

5 (be in certain state) être, se trouver; to s. convicted of ... avoir été déclaré coupable de ..., être convaincu de ...; to s. in need of ... avoir besoin de ...; you s. in danger of getting killed vous risquez de vous faire tuer; to s. to lose £5,000 risquer de perdre 5 000 livres; to s. to win a lot of money avoir des chances de gagner beaucoup d'argent; no one stands to gain from a quarrel like this personne n'a rien à gagner d'une telle querelle; to s. as security for a debt assurer une créance; to s. guarantor or surety for sb se porter garant envers qn, cautionner qn; the thermometer stood at 30° le thermomètre marquait 30°; the debt now stands at $3.5 billion la dette s'élève à présent à $3,5 milliards; the balance stands at £50 le reliquat de compte est de cinquante livres; the amount standing to your credit votre solde créditeur; how do we s.? (in work etc) où en sommes-nous?; (financially) où en sont nos comptes?; as matters s., as it stands au point où en sont les choses, dans l'état actuel des choses; to know how things s. être au fait de la situation; I don't know where I s. j'ignore quelle est ma situation ou ma position; how do you s. with him? quelle est votre position vis-à-vis de lui?; you never know how or where you s. with her on ne sait jamais sur quel pied danser avec elle; I s. corrected je reconnais mon erreur

6 (remain motionless) to allow a liquid to s. laisser reposer ou laisser déposer un liquide

VT **1** (place upright) mettre, poser, placer; to s. sth on the table mettre ou poser qch sur la

table; to s. sth against the wall dresser qch contre le mur; to s. sth upright mettre qch debout

2 to s. one's ground tenir bon ou ferme; s. your ground! (don't retreat) ne reculez pas d'une semelle!; (don't give up opposition) tenez ferme!, ne lâchez pas prise!

3 (endure) supporter, soutenir, subir; to s. the cold supporter le froid; to s. a shock résister à ou supporter un choc; his argument does not s. investigation son argument ne tient pas; to s. comparison with sb/sth soutenir la comparaison avec qn/qch; he can't s. her il ne peut pas la souffrir ou la sentir; I won't s. such behaviour je ne supporterai pas une pareille conduite; I can't s. it any longer (heat, cold, discomfort etc) je ne tiens plus; (emotional tension, cruelty etc) je n'en peux plus

4 Fam (pay for) payer, offrir; to s. sb a drink payer à boire à qn; to s. sb a dinner payer un dîner à qn; I'll s. you c'est moi qui paie

5 to s. a chance (of doing sth) avoir de bonnes chances (de faire qch); if this initiative is to s. a chance ... si vous voulez que cette initiative ait la moindre chance de succès ...

▸▸ TV etc s. lamp lumière f sur pied; TV etc s. microphone microphone m sur pied

▸ **stand about, stand around** VI (be standing, doing nothing) se tenir là; there were a lot of people standing around talking il y avait beaucoup de monde qui se tenait là à parler; I can't afford to pay people to s. around all day doing nothing je n'ai pas les moyens de payer les gens à ne rien faire

▸ **stand aside** VI **1** (be standing apart) se tenir à l'écart

2 (move aside) s'écarter; to s. aside to let sb pass s'effacer pour laisser passer qn; Fig to s. aside in favour of sb se désister en faveur de qn

▸ **stand away** VI (move away) s'éloigner (from de)

▸ **stand back** VI **1** (of person) (move away) (se) reculer; (keep in background) se tenir en arrière; s. well back, please! reculez(-vous) bien, s'il vous plaît

2 (of building etc) être situé en retrait; a house standing back from the road une maison située en retrait de la route

▸ **stand by** VI **1** (be ready) se tenir prêt; Naut se tenir paré; Mil the troops are standing by les troupes sont en état d'alerte; Naut s. by! paré!, attention!; Radio s. by to receive prenez l'écoute

2 (wait) attendre, patienter; viewers were told to s. by for further developments on demanda aux téléspectateurs de patienter et d'attendre la suite des événements

3 (not get involved) se tenir là (sans intervenir); people just stood by and watched him being beaten up les gens restèrent là à le regarder se faire cogner

VT INSEP **1** (stand next, near to) (of person) se tenir près de ou à côté de

2 (person) (support, defend) soutenir, défendre; (take side of) se ranger du côté de; she stood by her friend throughout the trial elle a soutenu son amie tout au long du procès

3 (keep, honour) (promise) rester fidèle à; I s. by what I said je m'en tiens à ce que j'ai dit

▸ **stand down** VI (retire) (from team, position etc) se retirer; (of candidate) retirer sa candidature (in favour of en faveur de); Mil quitter son service; Law (of witness) quitter la barre

▸ **stand for** VT INSEP **1** esp Br (present oneself as candidate for) se présenter à; to s. for parliament se présenter aux élections parlementaires; to s. for the chairmanship se présenter à la présidence; to s. for election se présenter aux élections; half the committee are standing for re-election la moitié des membres du comité se représente

2 *(mean, represent) (something)* signifier, vouloir dire; **'tsp' stands for 'teaspoonful'** 'tsp' signifie 'teaspoonful'; **the letters AA s. for 'Alcoholics Anonymous'** les lettres AA veulent dire 'Alcooliques anonymes'; **our party stands for freedom and democracy** notre parti est celui de la liberté et de la démocratie

3 *(tolerate) (something)* supporter, tolérer; **I won't s. for it** je ne supporterai pas cela

▸ **stand in** VI *(act as replacement)* assurer le remplacement

▸ **stand in for** VT INSEP *(act as replacement for) (person)* remplacer; *Cin (actor)* doubler; **sparkling wine will have to s. in for champagne** le vin mousseux tiendra lieu de champagne

▸ **stand off** VI *(remain at a distance)* se tenir éloigné *ou* à l'écart

VT INSEP *Naut* **to s. off the coast** être au large

▸ **stand out** VI **1** *(be noticeable) (of objects)* ressortir; *Pej* détonner; *(protrude)* faire saillie; **to s. out in sharp relief** ressortir, se détacher; *Fig* se distinguer; **to s. out against sth** faire contraste avec qch; **mountains that s. out against the horizon** montagnes qui se dessinent *ou* sur l'horizon; **the qualities that s. out in his work** les qualités marquantes de son œuvre; **she stands out in a crowd** on la remarque dans la foule; *Fig* **characteristics that make him s. out in the crowd** traits qui le caractérisent; *Fam* **that stands out a mile!** *(is very obvious)* ça se voit comme le nez au milieu de la figure!; **it really stands out that he's not a local** ça se voit *ou* se remarque vraiment qu'il n'est pas d'ici

2 *(adopt firm position)* résister (**against** à), tenir bon *ou* ferme (**against** contre)

▸ **stand out for** VT INSEP *(something)* insister sur

▸ **stand over** VI *(be postponed)* rester en suspens; **to let a question s. over, to allow a question to s. over** remettre une question à plus tard, laisser une question en suspens

VT INSEP **to s. over sb** *(lean over)* se pencher sur qn; *(watch)* surveiller qn de près; **if I don't s. over him, he does nothing** si je ne suis pas toujours sur son dos, il ne fait rien

▸ **stand to** VI *Mil etc* être prêt, être en état d'alerte; **s. to!** aux armes!

VT SEP *Mil etc* mettre en état d'alerte

▸ **stand together** VI **1** *(form a group)* être en groupe; **they were standing together in a line** ils formaient une colonne

2 *Fig (show solidarity)* être *ou* rester solidaire

▸ **stand up** VI **1** *(rise to one's feet)* se lever, se mettre debout; *(to be standing up)* se tenir debout; **this lamp won't s. up straight** cette lampe ne tient pas droite; **s. up!** levez-vous!, debout!; **we must s. up and be counted!** il ne faut pas nous laisser faire!

2 *(be valid)* se tenir, être valide; **there isn't enough evidence for the charge to s. up in court** il n'y a pas suffisamment de preuves pour que l'accusation tienne au tribunal

VT SEP **1** *Fam (fail to meet)* poser un lapin à

2 *(put in upright position) (object)* mettre debout; **to s. a child up (again)** (re)mettre un enfant sur ses pieds

▸ **stand up for** VT INSEP *(defend) (person)* soutenir, défendre; **only Chris stood up for her** seul Chris l'a soutenue *ou* s'est mis de son côté; **s. up for what you believe in** défendez ce en quoi vous croyez

▸ **stand up to** VT INSEP *(resist, oppose) (person)* tenir tête à; *(endure) (of object)* résister à; **it won't s. up to that sort of treatment** ça ne résistera pas à ce genre de traitement; **it doesn't s. up to close analysis** ça ne résiste pas à une analyse poussée

stand-alone *Comput* N poste *m* autonome, monoposte *m*

ADJ *(system)* autonome

▸▸ **s. computer** ordinateur *m* autonome; **s. workstation** station *f* de travail autonome

STANDARD ['stændəd] N **1** *(flag etc)* bannière *f*, *Mil* étendard *m*; *Naut* pavillon *m*

2 *(accepted length, quantity etc)* étalon *m*, référence *f*; **to use sth as a s.** prendre qch comme référence; *Fin* **gold/silver s.** étalon (d')or/d'argent; **s. model** *(of car)* voiture *f* de série; *(of machine)* modèle *m* standard *ou* de série

3 *(set requirement)* norme *f*; **to meet government standards** être conforme aux normes établies par le gouvernement; **to make a product comply with standards** adapter un produit aux normes; **standards and practices** normes et usages; **standards catalogue** catalogue *m* de normes

4 *(level, quality)* niveau *m*; **to have high/low standards** *(of person)* être exigeant/ne pas être exigeant; *(of school)* exiger un bon niveau/ne pas exiger un bon niveau; **they have no standards** ils ne sont pas exigeants du tout; **s. of living** niveau de vie; **everyone has his own standards** chacun voit midi à sa porte; **to raise the standards of behaviour** améliorer la discipline; **a high s. of playing/academic achievement** un niveau de jeu/de réussite académique élevé; **he sets very high standards for his students** il exige de ses étudiants un niveau très élevé; **not to come up to s.** ne pas atteindre le niveau exigé; **my cooking isn't up to your s.** ma cuisine n'est pas à la hauteur de la vôtre

5 *(in horticulture)* **s. rose (tree)** rosier *m* sur tige

ADJ **1** *(length, width etc)* standard *inv*, normalisé; **s. thickness** *(of iron etc)* épaisseur *f* type *ou* courante; **s. weight** poids *m* normal; **British S. Time** heure *f* légale anglaise

2 *(usual) (criticism, problem, behaviour, approach)* classique; *(price)* normal, -aux; **headrests are s.** *or* **are fitted as s.** les appuis-têtes sont montés en série; **s. spelling/pronunciation** orthographe *f*/prononciation *f* correcte; **a s. French dictionary** un dictionnaire général de la langue française; **one of his s. jokes** une de ses plaisanteries habituelles; **to come in s. sizes** *(of clothes)* exister dans les tailles standards; **the cooking is fairly s.** c'est normal; **s. closure** *(for letter)* formule *f* de politesse pour terminer une lettre; **s. cost** coût *m* standard *ou* préétabli; **s. opening** *(for letter)* formule de politesse pour commencer une lettre; **s. service** service *m* standard

▸▸ **s. bearer** *(of cause)* porte-drapeau *m*, *pl* porte-drapeau(x); *(of political party)* chef *m* de file; *(of flag)* porte-étendard *m*, *pl* porte-étendard(s); **s. class** deuxième classe *f*; **standards committee** organisme *m* de normalisation; **standards conversion** *(in broadcasting)* transcodage *m*; **standards converter** *(in broadcasting)* transcodeur *m*; **s. deviation** *(in statistics)* écart-type *m*, *pl* écarts-types; **s. document** document *m* type; **s. edition** *(of an author)* édition *f* courante; **s. English** l'anglais *m* standard; *Rail* **s. gauge** voie *f* normale, écartement *m* normal; *Br* **s. lamp** lampadaire *m* (de salon); **s. measure** mesure *f* étalon; *Comput* **s. memory** mémoire *f* standard; **s. practice** pratique *f* courante; **s. rate** *(of tax)* taux *m* standard

standardization [stændədaɪ'zeɪʃən] N standardisation *f*, *(of weights etc)* étalonnage *m*, étalonnement *m*; *(of methods etc)* uniformisation *f*

standardize ['stændədaɪz] VT normaliser, standardiser; *(weights etc)* étalonner; *(methods, conditions)* uniformiser

VI **to s. on sth** adopter qch comme standard

stand-by N **1** *(substitute person)* **to act as a s.** remplacer qn

2 *(sth held in reserve)* réserve *f*; **to have a sum in reserve as a s.** avoir une somme en réserve en cas de besoin; **a fruitcake can be a useful s. for unexpected guests** il est toujours bon d'avoir un cake en réserve pour les invités surprises

3 *Mil etc (state of readiness)* (état *m* d')alerte *f*; **to be on s.** *(of troops, firemen etc)* être en état d'alerte

4 *Aviat (passenger)* passager, -ère (en) stand-by; *(ticket)* stand-by *m inv*; **to be on s.** être en stand-by

ADV **to fly s.** voler en stand-by

▸▸ **s. mode** *(of printer etc)* veille *f*, **in s. mode** en veille; *Aviat* **s. passenger** passager, -ère (en) stand-by; *Aviat* **s. ticket** stand-by; **s. time** *(of mobile phone)* autonomie *f* en veille

standee [stæn'diː] N *esp Am (in bus)* voyageur, -euse debout; *Theat* spectateur, -trice debout

stand-in N *(person)* remplaçant, -ante; *(actor)* doublure *f* ; *(stunt person)* cascadeur, -euse

ADJ remplaçant; **a s. teacher/speaker/***etc* un remplaçant

standing ['stændɪŋ] ADJ **1** *(in upright position)* debout **2** *(permanent) (price)* fixe; *(on bill)* frais *mpl* d'abonnement; **I have a s. invitation** je peux aller chez lui/elle/eux quand je veux; **you have a s. invitation** tu peux venir chez moi/nous quand tu veux

N **1** *(upright position)* station *f* debout; **no s.!** *(in bus etc)* défense de voyager debout **2** *of long s. (friends)* de longue date; **friend of twenty years'** ami de vingt ans **3** *(position) (of country, firm)* rang *m*, position *f*, *(of party, person)* popularité *f*, **financial s.** situation *f* financière; **social s.** position sociale

▸▸ **Mil s. army** armée *f* de métier; **s. charges** *(on bill)* frais *mpl* d'abonnement; **s. committee** comité *m* permanent; **s. crop** récolte *f* sur pied; *Com* **s. expenses** frais *mpl* généraux; **s. joke** grosse plaisanterie *f*, **he's become a s. joke** il est devenu un objet de risée; *Sport* **s. jump** saut *m* à pieds joints; *Br Banking* **s. order** virement *m* automatique; *Br Pol* **s. orders** règlement *m* intérieur *(d'une assemblée délibérative)*; **s. ovation** ovation *f*; **s. places, s. room** places *fpl* debout; **it was s. room only on the train** il n'y avait plus de places assises dans le train; **s. rule** règle *f* fixe; **s. start** *Sport* départ *m* debout; *Aut* départ arrêté; **s. stone** pierre *f* levée; **s. water** eau *f* stagnante *ou* dormante

stand-off N *(between opponents)* impasse *f*

stand-off, stand-off half N *Rugby* demi *m* d'ouverture

stand-offish [-'ɒfɪʃ] ADJ *(person)* peu accessible, distant, réservé; **to be s.** se mettre *ou* se tenir sur son quant-à-soi

stand-offishness [-'ɒfɪʃnɪs] N raideur *f*, réserve *f*

standout ['stændaʊt] N *Am* **his article was a real s.** son article sortait vraiment du lot

standpipe ['stændpaɪp] N *(in street)* colonne *f* d'alimentation

standpoint ['stændpɔɪnt] N point *m* de vue; **from the s. of ...** du point de vue de ...; **from a late 20th century s.** dans une perspective de fin de XXᵉ siècle

standstill ['stændstɪl] N arrêt *m*, immobilisation *f*, **traffic has come to a s.** la circulation est immobilisée; **to bring to a s.** arrêter; *(railways, production etc)* paralyser; **many factories are at a s.** beaucoup d'usines chôment; **the railways are at a s.** les chemins de fer sont paralysés

stand-up ADJ **1** *(collar)* droit, montant **2** *(meal)* pris debout **3** **a s. fight** *(physical)* une bagarre en règle; *(verbal)* une discussion violente

ɴ *(comedy)* spectacle *m* comique; **to do s.** faire des spectacles comiques

▸▸ **s. comedian** comique *mf* (de scène); **s. comedy** spectacles *mpl* comiques; **s. comic** comique (de scène); *Boxing* **s. fight** combat *m* en règle

stank PP *see* **stink**

Stanley knife® ['stænlɪ] ɴ cutter *m*

stannic ['stænɪk] ADJ *Chem* stannique

stanza, *pl* **stanzas** ['stænzə, -əz] ɴ *(in poetry)* strophe *f*

staphylococcus, *pl* **staphylococci** [stæfɪləʊ'kɒkəs, -'kɒksaɪ] ɴ staphylocoque *m*

staple[1] ['steɪp(ə)l] ɴ *(for papers)* agrafe *f*, *(for cable etc)* crampon *m*; **wire s.** (clou *m*) cavalier *m*

▪ VT *(piece of paper, cheque etc)* agrafer (**to** à); *Constr etc* fixer avec un crampon, agrafer; **to s. two pieces of paper together** agrafer deux morceaux de papier

▸▸ **s. gun** agrafeuse *f* (professionnelle); **s. remover** arrache-agrafes *m inv*

staple[2] ɴ *(basic foodstuff)* aliment *m* de base; *Com, Econ (item)* article *m* de base; *(raw material)* matière *f* première; **staples** *(goods)* biens *mpl* de première nécessité; **sex scandals are a s. of the tabloid press** la presse à sensation se nourrit des scandales sexuels; **such accusations are a s. of the annual conference** ces accusations reviennent régulièrement à chaque conférence annuelle; **s. convenience goods** produits *mpl* de première nécessité; *Fig* pain *m* quotidien; **I grew up on a s. diet of television and violence** j'ai grandi nourri de télévision et de violence

▸▸ **s. crop** culture *f* de base; **s. diet** alimentation *f* de base

stapler ['steɪplər] ɴ *(device)* agrafeuse *f*

stapling ['steɪplɪŋ] ɴ *(of papers)* fixation *f* à l'aide d'agrafes, agrafage *m*; *(of cables etc)* fixation à l'aide de crochets *ou* crampons

star [stɑːr] ɴ **1** *Astron* étoile *f*; **shooting s.** étoile filante; **the morning s.** l'étoile du matin; **the pole s.** l'étoile polaire, la polaire; **he was born under a lucky s.** il est né sous une bonne étoile; *Fig* **to reach for the stars** essayer d'atteindre les sommets; *Fig Fam* **to see stars** voir les étoiles en plein midi, voir trente-six chandelles; **the Stars and Stripes** *(American flag)* la bannière étoilée

2 *(insignia) (of order)* plaque *f*, *Mil (on shoulder of uniform)* étoile *f*; **S. of David** étoile de David; **three s. brandy** cognac *m* trois étoiles; **three s. hotel** hôtel *m* trois étoiles

3 *(shape) (on horse's forehead)* étoile *f*; *Typ* astérisque *m*; *Comput* **in a s. configuration** connecté en étoile

4 *Cin etc (person)* étoile *f*, vedette *f*, star *f*, *Mktg* vedette, star; **film** *or* **movie s.** étoile *ou* star *ou* vedette du cinéma; **rock s.** star du rock; **s. presenter** animateur, -trice vedette; **the s. attraction of tonight's show** la principale attraction du spectacle de ce soir; **to get s. billing** tenir le haut de l'affiche; *Fam (of performance, conference, evening)* clou *m*

▪ VT (-rr-) **1** *(mark with asterisk) (word etc)* marquer d'un astérisque

2 *Cin, Theat, TV etc (of film, play etc) (actor)* mettre en scène dans le rôle principal, avoir pour vedette; **the film/play stars Katharine Hepburn (as** *or* **in the role of)** le film/la pièce met en scène Katharine Hepburn dans le rôle principal (de); **'The Last Metro', starring Catherine Deneuve and Gérard Depardieu** 'le Dernier Métro', avec Catherine Deneuve et Gérard Depardieu dans les rôles principaux

▪ VI *Cin, Theat, TV etc (of actor, actress)* être en vedette; **who starred with Redford in 'The Sting'?** qui jouait avec Redford dans 'l'Arnaque'?; **'Othello', with Laurence Olivier starring in the title role** 'Othello', avec Laurence Olivier dans le rôle principal; **he's starring in a new TV serial** il est la vedette d'un nouveau feuilleton télévisé; **he starred as a gangster** il avait un rôle de gangster; **to have a starring role** avoir un des premiers rôles

▸▸ **s. part** rôle *m* de vedette; *Sport* **s. player** joueur, -euse vedette; **s. rating** *(of hotel)* classement *m* par étoiles *Comput* **s. structure** structure *f* en étoile; *Cin, Theat* **s. system** star-system *m*, *pl* star-systems; **s. turn** numéro *m* de premier ordre; *Fam (of performance, conference, evening)* clou *m*

starboard ['stɑːbəd] ɴ *Naut* tribord *m*; **on the s. side, to s.** à tribord; **on the s. bow** par tribord devant; **hard a-s.!** tribord toute!

starch [stɑːtʃ] ɴ *(for collar, tablecloth etc)* amidon *m*, empois *m*; *Culin (from potatoes)* fécule *f*; *(from rice, corn, wheat etc)* amidon *m*

▪ VT *(collar, tablecloth etc)* empeser, amidonner

starched [stɑːtʃt] ADJ *Literary* maudit par le sort empesé, amidonné

starchy ['stɑːtʃɪ] ADJ **1** *(diet)* riche en féculents; *(taste)* farineux; **s. foods** féculents *mpl* **2** *Fam (person, manner)* guindé

star-crossed ADJ

▸▸ **s. lovers** amants *mpl* maudits

stardom ['stɑːdəm] ɴ *Cin, Theat etc (state)* célébrité *f*, vedettariat *m*; **to rise to s.** devenir une vedette, atteindre la célébrité; **dreams of s.** rêves *mpl* de célébrité

stardust ['stɑːdʌst] ɴ **1** *Astron* amas *m* stellaire **2** *(magic dust)* poudre *f* magique; **to have s. in one's eyes** être plein d'illusions

stare [steər] ɴ regard *m* fixe; **glassy/stony s.** regard terne/dur; **vacant s.** regard vague; **to have a long s. at sb/sth** fixer longuement qn/qch

▪ VI regarder fixement; *(with astonishment)* ouvrir de grands yeux; **to s. into the distance** regarder au loin; **don't s.!** ne regarde pas comme ça!; **it's rude to s.** ce n'est pas poli de dévisager les gens; **to s. at sb/sth** *(look at hard)* regarder qn/qch fixement, fixer qn/qch; *(begin to look at)* porter son regard sur qn/qch; *(be stupefied by)* regarder qn/qch d'un air hébété; **to s. at sb** *(look at insolently)* regarder qn effrontément, dévisager qn; **what are you staring at?** que regardez-vous comme ça?

▪ VT **to s. sb in the face** dévisager qn; **it's staring you in the face** *(it's obvious)* ça vous saute aux yeux; **the answer was staring me in the face all the time** la réponse était sous mon nez depuis le début

▸ **stare out** VT SEP **to s. sb out** fixer qn jusqu'à ce qu'il/elle détourne les yeux

starfish ['stɑːfɪʃ] ɴ étoile *f* de mer, astérie *f*

stargaze ['stɑːgeɪz] VI **1** *Fam (look at stars)* regarder les étoiles **2** *(daydream)* rêvasser, bayer aux corneilles

stargazer ['stɑːgeɪzər] ɴ **1** *(astrologist)* astrologue *mf*; *Fam (astronomer)* passionné, -ée d'astronomie **2** *(daydreamer)* rêveur, -euse, rêvasseur, -euse

stargazing ['stɑːgeɪzɪŋ] ɴ **1** *(astrology)* astrologie *f*, *Fam (looking at stars)* étude *f* des étoiles **2** *(daydreaming)* rêvasserie(s) *f(pl)*

staring ['steərɪŋ] ADJ *(bystanders)* curieux; **with s. eyes** *(fixedly)* aux yeux fixes; *(wide-open)* aux yeux écarquillés; *(blank)* aux yeux vides

stark [stɑːk] ADJ *(contrast)* absolu, fort; *(light)* cru; *(furnishing, black and white)* austère, sobre; *(truth, facts)* brut; *(landscape)*

nu; **this stands in s. contrast to ...** ceci se démarque nettement de ...; **s. realism** *(of novel, painting)* réalisme *m* brut; **a very s. flat** un appartement très nu *ou* sobre; **the s. simplicity of ...** la sobre *ou* l'austère simplicité de ...; **the s. desolation of the region** l'absolue désolation de la région; **s. madness** folie *f* pure; **the s. towns of the North** les mornes villes du Nord

▪ ADV **s. staring mad** complètement fou; **s. naked** tout nu

starkers ['stɑːkəz] ADJ, ADV *Br Fam* à poil

starkness ['stɑːknɪs] ɴ *(of furnishing etc)* austérité *f*, sobriété *f*; *(of landscape)* nudité *f*; **the s. of the contrast between ...** le contraste violent entre ...

starless ['stɑːlɪs] ADJ sans étoiles

starlet ['stɑːlɪt] ɴ *Cin etc* starlette *f*, starlet *f*

starlight ['stɑːlaɪt] ɴ lumière *f* des étoiles; **in the** *or* **by s.** à la lumière des étoiles

starling ['stɑːlɪŋ] ɴ *(bird)* étourneau *m*

starlit ['stɑːlɪt] ADJ *(sky)* étoilé; **a s. night** une nuit étoilée

star-of-Bethlehem ɴ *(plant)* ornithogale *m* (à ombelle), *Fam* dame *f* d'onze heures

starred [stɑːd] ADJ *Typ (asterisked)* marqué d'un astérisque

starry ['stɑːrɪ] ADJ *(sky)* étoilé, *(par)*semé d'étoiles

▸▸ **s. night** nuit *f* étoilée

starry-eyed ADJ *(person)* naïf, *f* naïve; **the children stood s. in front of the Christmas tree** les enfants étaient debout devant le sapin de Noël, émerveillés; **a s. scheme** un projet utopique; **she was all s. about him until ...** elle était tout émerveillée par lui jusqu'à ce que ...

starshell ['stɑːʃel] ɴ *Mil* obus *m* éclairant *ou* à étoiles

star-spangled [-spæŋg(ə)ld] ADJ étoilé

▸▸ **the S. Banner** *(flag)* la bannière étoilée; *(national anthem)* l'hymne *m* national des États-Unis

START [stɑːt]

ɴ	commencement 1 ▪ début 1
	▪ départ 1, 2 ▪ démarrage 1 ▪ sursaut 3
VI	commencer 1 ▪ débuter 1
	▪ sursaut 2 ▪ se mettre en route 3
	▪ partir 3, 4 ▪ démarrer 4
VT	commencer 1 ▪ entamer 1
	▪ lancer 1, 3, 4 ▪ fonder 3 ▪ mettre en marche 4 ▪ démarrer 4

ɴ **1** *(beginning)* commencement *m*, début *m*; *(of journey, race)* départ *m*; *Aut* démarrage *m*; *Aviat* envol *m*; **for a s.** pour commencer; **at the s.** au début; **at the very s.** au tout début; **from the s.** dès le début; **there were problems from the s.** il y a eu des problèmes dès le début; **I never liked him, right from the s.** il m'a toujours déplu, dès le début; **from s. to finish** du début (jusqu')à la fin; **£5 isn't much, but it's a s.** 5 livres ce n'est pas grand-chose, mais c'est un début; **I've cleaned the kitchen – well, it's a s.** j'ai nettoyé la cuisine – eh bien, c'est déjà ça; **she had a good s. in life** elle a bien débuté dans la vie; **to make a s.** *(begin work)* commencer; *(begin journey)* se mettre en route; **to make a s. on sth** commencer qch; **to make a fresh s. in one's life** refaire sa vie; **to make a good s.** bien commencer; **to make a fresh s.** recommencer; *Sport* **false s.** faux départ; **to give sb a s.** *(in business etc)* lancer qn; *Sport* laisser qn partir le premier, donner un peu d'avance à qn; **to give sb a 60 metre(s) s.** donner à qn 60 mètres d'avance; **to have a s. on sb** être en avance sur qn

2 *(starting place)* départ *m*; **the runners**

lined up at the s. les coureurs se rangèrent sur la ligne de départ

3 *(sudden movement) (with fear, surprise)* tressaillement *m*, sursaut *m*, soubresaut *m*; **to wake with a s.** se réveiller en sursaut; **he gave a s.** il a tressailli, il a sursauté; **to give sb a s.** faire sursauter qn; **you gave me such a s.!** tu m'as fait peur!

VI 1 *(begin)* commencer; *(in career)* débuter; **to s. again** recommencer; **the story starts with a murder** l'histoire commence par un meurtre; **well, to s. at the beginning …** bon, commençons par le commencement …; **you'd better s. by telling me your name** vous devriez commencer par me dire votre nom; **let's s. with the cost** commençons par le coût; **to s. the way one means to go on** donner la mesure dès le début; **starting Monday** à partir de lundi; **she had started as a doctor** elle avait débuté *ou* commencé en tant que médecin; **to s. in business** se mettre *ou* se lancer dans les affaires; **to s. with** *(in the first place)* au début; **there were only six members to s. with** il n'y avait que six membres au début; **to s. on a job** commencer *ou* entamer un travail; **she started on $500 a week** elle a débuté à 500 dollars par semaine; *Fam* **now don't you s.!** tu ne vas pas t'y mettre aussi!

2 *(move suddenly) (with surprise, fear etc)* sursauter, tressaillir, tressauter; **he started at the sound of my voice** il a tressailli au son de ma voix; **she started with surprise** surprise, elle sursauta; **to s. out of one's sleep** se réveiller en sursaut

3 *(begin journey)* partir, se mettre en route; **to s. again** repartir, se remettre en route; **to s. on a journey** commencer un voyage; **we s. tomorrow** nous partons demain

4 *(begin to move) (of car)* démarrer; *(of train)* partir, s'ébranler; *(of engine)* partir, démarrer; **the engine won't s.** le moteur refuse de partir *ou* de démarrer

VT 1 *(work, campaign etc)* commencer; *(conversation, talks etc)* entamer; *(a fashion, rumour etc)* lancer; **to s. a job** démarrer un travail; **to s. a meeting** débuter une séance; **to s. legal proceedings** engager une action en justice; **to s. a fire** provoquer un incendie; **you started it** c'est toi qui as commencé; **to s. doing sth, to s. to do sth** commencer *ou* se mettre à faire qch; **to s. crying again** se remettre à pleurer; **it's just started raining** il se met à pleuvoir; **now you've started something!** en voilà une affaire!; **if you s. him on this subject, he will never stop** si vous le lancez sur ce sujet, il ne tarira pas; **we started him in the sales department** nous l'avons fait débuter au service des ventes; **to get started** *(of person) (on task)* commencer, s'y mettre; *(on journey)* partir, se mettre en route; *(in career etc)* débuter, démarrer; **to help sb get started in life** aider qn à démarrer dans la vie; **when does he s. school?** quand est-ce qu'il commence l'école?

2 *Sport (runners etc)* donner le signal du départ à; *(in hunting) (stag, hare)* lever; *Horseriding* **to s. a horse at a gallop** faire partir un cheval au galop

3 *(set up) (company, newspaper)* lancer; *(business)* fonder; **to s. sb in business** lancer qn dans les affaires

4 *(cause to function) (machine)* mettre en marche, lancer; *(car)* démarrer; *(engine)* mettre en marche; *(computer, pump)* amorcer

▸▸ *Comput* **s. bit** bit *m* de départ; *Comput* **s. button** *(in Windows)* bouton *m* Démarrer; *Comput* **s. code** code *m* de départ; *Comput* **s. menu** *(in Windows)* menu *m* Démarrer

▸ **start in on** VT INSEP *esp Am (attack)* s'attaquer à

▸ **start off** VI **1** *(begin journey)* = **start** VI **4**

2 *(begin)* commencer; **you s. off** *(in discussion etc)* commencez; **she started off by talking about …** elle commença en parlant de …

VT SEP **1** *(begin)* commencer; **s. your talk off with a reference to …** commencez votre discours en mentionnant …; **he lent us a couple of thousand pounds to s. us off** *(in business etc)* il nous a prêté quelques milliers de livres pour nous aider à démarrer; **here are three specimens to s. you off** *(with your collection)* voici trois spécimens pour commencer; **the pianist played a few bars to s. them off** *(in singing etc)* le pianiste a joué quelques mesures d'introduction; **what started the whole thing off?** comment tout a-t-il commencé?

2 to s. sb off *(on a subject)* lancer qn sur un sujet; **don't s. him off on that!** *(get him talking about it)* ne le lance pas sur ce sujet!; **the baby's crying again, what started him off this time?** le bébé s'est remis à pleurer, qu'est-ce qu'il a cette fois?; **dad's finally calmed down, don't you s. him off again** papa s'est enfin calmé, ne va pas l'énerver

▸ **start on** VT INSEP *(begin quarrelling with, shouting at etc)* s'en prendre à

▸ **start out** VI *(begin)* commencer, débuter; *(begin journey)* se mettre en route (**for** pour); **she started out as a postwoman/ driving a van** elle a commencé *ou* débuté comme factrice/conductrice de camion; **he started out to write a novel** au départ, il voulait écrire un roman

▸ **start over** VI *Am (start again)* recommencer

▸ **start up** VI **1** *(start functioning) (of engine)* démarrer, se mettre en marche; *(of machine)* démarrer, se mettre en marche; *(of computer, program)* se mettre en route

2 *(in business)* s'installer; **to s. up in business** monter sa propre affaire; **he decided to s. up by himself** il a décidé de se mettre à son compte

VT SEP **1** *(cause to function) (engine, car)* mettre en marche, démarrer; *(machine)* mettre en marche; *(computer, program)* mettre en route

2 *(company, newspaper)* lancer; *(business)* fonder; *(restaurant, school)* ouvrir

starter ['stɑːtər] N **1** *Sport (runner, horse)* partant *m*; **to be an early s.** *(start work early)* commencer son travail de bonne heure; **to be a slow s.** être lent à démarrer **2** *Sport etc (official)* starter *m*; **to be under s.'s orders** attendre le signal du starter **3** *(device), Aut* démarreur *m*; *Tech* dispositif *m* de mise en marche; *Elec* (rhéostat *m*) démarreur, rhéostat de démarrage **4** *esp Br Culin* entrée *f*, hors-d'œuvre *m inv*; **would you like as?** désirez-vous une entrée?; *Fig Fam* **for starters** *(for a start)* pour commencer, (tout) d'abord

▸▸ *Br* **s. flat** = appartement *m* convenant à ceux qui achètent pour la première fois; **s. motor** démarreur *m*; *Tech* **s. solenoid** électrovalve *f* de starter

> Note that the most common meaning of the French word **starter** is **choke** (in an engine).

starting ['stɑːtɪŋ] N **1** *(beginning)* commencement *m*, début *m*; *(causing to start) (of war, fight etc)* instigation *f* **2** *(of business etc)* mise *f* en route *ou* en train **3** *(of engine etc)* mise *f* en marche, démarrage *m*; *(of machine)* lancement *m*

▸▸ **s. block** *(in athletics)* starting-block *m, pl* starting-blocks; *(for swimmers)* plot *m* de départ; *Br Aut* **s. handle** manivelle *f*, *Sport* **s. line** ligne *f* de départ; *Tech* **s. motor** moteur *m* de démarrage; **s. pistol** pistolet *m* du starter; **s. place, s. point** point *m* de départ; *Sport*

s. post ligne de départ; **s. price** prix *m* initial; *Horseracing* cote *f* au départ; *(at auction)* mise *f* à prix, prix d'appel; **s. salary** salaire *m* d'embauche; **s. signal** signal *m* de *ou* du départ; **s. up** *(of business etc)* mise en route *ou* en train; *(of engine)* mise en marche, démarrage *m*; *(of machine)* lancement *m*

startle ['stɑːt(ə)l] VT *(alarm)* effrayer, alarmer; *(cause to jump)* faire sursauter; **she was startled to see him so pale** sa pâleur l'alarma

startled ['stɑːt(ə)ld] ADJ effrayé; **to give a s. cry** crier d'effroi

startling ['stɑːtlɪŋ] ADJ étonnant, surprenant; *(contrast, resemblance)* saisissant; **s. green eyes** des yeux d'un vert saisissant

start-up N **1** *(of machine)* démarrage *m* **2** *(of new business)* ouverture *f*, lancement *m*; **there have been 500 start-ups this year** il y a eu 500 créations d'entreprises cette année

▸▸ *Fin* **s. capital** capital *m* initial, capital de départ; *Fin* **s. costs** frais *mpl* d'établissement; *Comput* **s. disk** disquette *f* de démarrage; *Comput* **s. screen** écran *m* d'accueil

starvation [stɑːˈveɪʃən] N privation *f ou* manque *m* de nourriture, inanition *f*; **millions are threatened with s. if …** des millions de gens vont peut-être mourir de faim si …; **to die of s.** mourir de faim; **prisoners were kept on a s. diet** les prisonniers étaient presque entièrement privés de nourriture; **a s. diet of rice and a few vegetables** une alimentation très pauvre à base de riz et de quelques légumes; **I'm on a s. diet** *(to slim)* je suis un régime draconien

▸▸ **s. wages** salaire *m* de famine *ou* de misère

starve [stɑːv] VI *(lack food)* manquer de nourriture; *(endure hunger)* souffrir de la faim; **to s. (to death)** mourir de faim; *Fam* **I'm starving** *(hungry)* je meurs *ou* je crève de faim

VT *(deprive of food) (person)* priver de nourriture; **to s. sb (to death)** faire mourir qn de faim; **they were prepared to s. themselves to death rather than give in** ils étaient prêts à se laisser mourir de faim plutôt que de capituler; **to s. a city into surrender** affamer une ville pour l'amener à se rendre; *Fig* **to s. sb/sth of sth** priver qn/qch de qch

▸ **starve out** VT SEP *Mil etc (town, garrison)* affamer *(pour le/la/etc faire sortir)*

starved [stɑːvd] ADJ affamé; **she looks half s.** elle a l'air famélique; **s. of affection** privé d'affection; **I'm feeling s. of affection** je suis en manque d'affection; *Fam* **I'm s.** *(hungry)* je crève de faim

starving ['stɑːvɪŋ] ADJ affamé; **the s. millions** tous ceux qui souffrent de la faim

Star Wars NPL *Mil* guerre *f* des étoiles

stash [stæʃ] *Fam* N **1** *(of arms)* cache *f*, *(of biscuits etc)* réserve *f* (secrète); **a s. of drugs was discovered** de la drogue a été découverte; **I hid my s.** *(of drugs)* j'ai caché ma part de drogue **2** *(place)* planque *f*

VT *(object) (hide)* cacher, planquer; *(put)* ficher

▸ **stash away** VT SEP = **stash** VT

stasis ['steɪsɪs] N stase *f*

STATE [steɪt]		

N état **1**	▪ condition **1**	▪ situation **1**
▪ rang **2**	▪ État **3, 4**	
VT déclarer **1**	▪ formuler **1**	

N 1 *(condition)* état *m*, condition *f*, *(situation)* situation *f*, **to be in a good s. of repair** être en bon état; *Iron* **here's a nice s. of affairs!** nous voilà bien!, c'est du joli *ou* du propre!; **a body in a s. of rest/motion** un corps au repos/en mouvement; **to declare a s. of war/ emergency** déclarer l'état de guerre d'urgence; **s. of consciousness** état de conscience; **s. of health** état de santé; **what's the current s. of play?** où en sont-ils?; **what's the current s. of play on our project?** où en est notre projet?; **I am not in a fit s. to travel** je ne suis pas en état de voyager; **he was in a s. of panic** il a été pris de panique; **she was in a s. of terror** elle était terrifiée; **the married s.** le mariage; **the single s.** le célibat; **in a solid/liquid s.** à l'état solide/liquide; **nitrogen is more easily transportable in its liquid s.** l'azote est plus facilement transportable à l'état liquide; **to be in a terrible s.** *(emotionally)* être dans tous ses états; *(of room, papers etc)* être dans un état désastreux; **this represents the s. of the art in …** c'est la pointe de la technologie en matière de …

2 *(rank)* rang *m*; *(ceremony)* pompe *f*, apparat *m*; **she lived in a style befitting her s.** elle avait un train de vie digne de son rang; **to live in s.** mener grand train; **to travel in s.** voyager en grand apparat; **to dine in s.** dîner en grande pompe; **to lie in s.** *(of body)* être exposé; **lying in s.** *(of body)* exposition *f*; **he was in his robes of s.** il était en costume d'apparat

3 *Pol (country, nation)* État *m*; **the S.** l'État; **Church and S.** l'Église et l'État; **Secretary of S.** *Br* secrétaire *m* d'État, *Am* ≃ ministre *m* des Affaires étrangères; **affairs of S.** affaires *fpl* d'État; **s.-run** public

4 *(administrative region in some countries)* État *m*; **the United States of America,** *Fam* **the States** les États-Unis (d'Amérique)

vt 1 *(declare)* déclarer; *(conditions, demands, reasons, objections)* énoncer; *(claim etc)* exposer, formuler; *Math, Fig (problem)* poser, énoncer; **this condition was expressly stated** cette condition était clairement énoncée; **the receipt should s. the source of payment** le reçu doit stipuler l'origine du paiement; **please s. below …** veuillez noter en bas …; **I have stated my opinion** j'ai donné mon opinion; **they stated their opposition to that measure** ils ont clairement fait savoir leur opposition à cette mesure; **I can s. with certainty that …** je peux affirmer avec certitude que …; *Law* **to s. the case** faire l'exposé des faits; **please s. your name and address (and qualifications)** veuillez décliner vos nom et adresse (et qualités)

2 *(fix) (time, date)* **at the stated times** aux heures indiquées; **on the stated dates** aux jours indiqués; **at stated intervals** à intervalles fixes

▸ ▸ **s.-aided industry** industrie *f* subventionnée par l'État; **s. apartments** appartements *mpl* de parade; **s. ball** grand bal *m* officiel; **s. capitalism** capitalisme *m* d'État; **s. carriage** voiture *f* d'apparat; **s. church** église *f* d'État; **s. coach** voiture d'apparat; **s. control** contrôle *m* étatique; *(doctrine)* étatisme *m*; **to bring an industry under s. control** étatiser une industrie; *Am* **S. Department** ≃ ministère *m* des Affaires étrangères; **s. documents** documents *mpl* officiels; **the s. education system** l'enseignement *m* public; *Br* **S. Enrolled Nurse** aide-soignant, -ante diplômé(e), *pl* aides-soignant(e)s diplômé(e)s; **s. funeral** funérailles *fpl* nationales; *Hist* **the States General** les États généraux; **s. government** gouvernement *m* d'État; **s. intervention** intervention *f* de l'État; **s. of mind** état d'esprit; **the S. Opening of Parliament** = l'ouverture *f* officielle du Parlement britannique en présence du souverain; **s.-owned company** entreprise *f* publique; **s.-owned industry** industrie du secteur public; **s. paper** imprimé *m* officiel; **s. pension** pension *f* de l'État; **s. planning** planification *f* nationale; **s. police** police *f* de l'État; *Br Formerly* **S. Registered Nurse** infirmier, -ière diplômé(e)

(remplacé en 1992 par 'Registered Nurse'); *Br* **s. school** école *f* publique; **s. secret** secret *m* d'État; *Br* **s. sector** secteur *m* public; **s. subsidy** subvention *f* d'État; *Law* **S. Supreme Court** = instance *f* judiciaire suprême dans chaque État américain; **the s. system** *(education)* le public, l'enseignement public; *Am* **s. trooper** ≃ gendarme *m*; **S. of the Union address** discours *m* sur l'état de l'Union; *Am* **S. university** = université *f* subventionnée et contrôlée par un État; *Pol* **s. visit** visite *f* officielle

---

State of the Union
Ce discours radiotélévisé, dans lequel le président des États-Unis dresse le bilan de son programme et en définit les orientations, est prononcé devant le Congrès. L'allocution présidentielle a lieu tous les ans en janvier.

---

statecraft ['steɪtkrɑːft] N savoir *m* d'un homme d'État

Statehouse ['steɪthaʊs] N *Am* = bâtiment *m* où siège le corps législatif d'un État

stateless ['steɪtlɪs] ADJ apatride
▸ ▸ **s. person** apatride *mf*; **s. society** société *f* sans État

statelessness ['steɪtlɪsnɪs] N apatridie *f*

stateliness ['steɪtlɪnɪs] N **1** *(grandeur)* majesté *f*, grandeur *f* **2** *(dignity)* dignité *f*

stately ['steɪtlɪ] ADJ **1** *(imposing)* majestueux, imposant **2** *(dignified)* plein de dignité; *(noble)* noble, élevé; **s. bearing** allure pleine de majesté
▸ ▸ **s. home** = château *m* ou manoir *m* à la campagne, généralement ouvert au public

statement ['steɪtmənt] N **1** déclaration *f*, *(of facts)* exposé *m*, énoncé *m*; *(official, to Press, House of Commons)* communiqué *m*; *Law (made by witness etc)* déposition *f*; **she made the following s.: …** elle a déclaré que …; **I have no further statement(s) to make** je n'ai plus rien à ajouter; *Fig* **the film is making a s.** il y a un message dans ce film; *Fig* **someone who wears jeans to a wedding reception is making a s.** quelqu'un qui va à un mariage en jeans veut faire comprendre quelque chose; **a s. appeared in the press to the effect that …** il fut affirmé dans la presse que …; **a bare s. of the facts** un simple énoncé des faits; *Law* **to take sb's s.** prendre la déposition de qn; **to volunteer a s.** faire une déposition de son propre gré; **to call him a thief is nothing more than a s. of fact** le traiter de voleur, c'est une constatation

2 *(received from bank, credit card company) (of account)* relevé *m* de compte; **monthly s.** fin *f* de mois
▸ ▸ **s. of account** relevé de compte; **s. of affairs** *(in bankruptcy)* bilan *m* de liquidation

state-of-play report N état *m* de situation

state-of-the-art ADJ *(technology, design etc)* de pointe, très avancé; **it's very s.** c'est le nec plus ultra, c'est très moderne

stateroom ['steɪtruːm] N **1** *Naut* cabine *f*, *Am Rail Old-fashioned* (compartiment *m* de) wagon-lit *m*, *pl* wagons-lits **2** *esp Br (in palace etc)* chambre *f* d'apparat, grand appartement *m*

stateside ['steɪtsaɪd] ADV aux États-Unis
ADJ des États-Unis, américain

statesman, *pl* **statesmen** ['steɪtsmən] N homme *m* d'État

statesmanlike ['steɪtsmənlaɪk] ADJ *(attitude etc)* d'homme d'État; *Fig* stratégique

statesmanship ['steɪtsmənʃɪp] N art *m* de gouverner; **a decision which shows considerable s.** une décision qui prouve des qualités d'homme d'État

statewide ['steɪtwaɪd] ADJ, ADV partout dans un/l'État

static ['stætɪk] N **1** électricité *f* statique; *(on telephone line, radio)* parasites *mpl* **2** *Am Fam (insolence)* insolence *f*, *(hassle, interference)* embêtements *mpl*; **I'm not taking that s. from you!** arrête de faire l'insolent! **you can expect plenty of s. from mom** tu vas avoir Maman sur le dos
ADJ **1** *(electricity)* statique **2** *(not moving)* statique; *(unchangeable)* immuable; *Pej (relationship etc)* qui stagne; **the situation remains s.** la situation reste inchangée
▸ ▸ *Aut* **s. lap belt** ceinture *f* ventrale statique; *Comput* **s. RAM, s. random access memory** mémoire *f* vive statique; *TV, Cin* **s. shot** plan *m* fixe

statics ['stætɪks] NPL *Phys (usu with sing verb)* statique *f* VOIR GRAMMAIRE A10

station ['steɪʃən] N **1** *(railway)* **s.** gare *f*, **underground** *or Am* **subway s.** station *f* de métro; **bus** *or Br* **coach s.** gare routière; *Rail* **passenger/goods s.** gare de voyageurs/de marchandises

2 *(place)* position *f*, place *f*, *(post)* poste *m*; **to take up one's s.** *(take one's place)* prendre sa place; *(go to one's post)* se rendre à son poste; *Rel* **the stations of the Cross** le chemin de la Croix; *Mil etc* **action stations** postes de combat; *Mil, Fig* **action stations!** à vos postes!; **naval s.** station *f* navale; *(port)* port *m* de guerre; **military s.** poste militaire; *(garrison)* garnison *f*; *Naut* **lifeboat s.** station de sauvetage; *Met* **weather s.** station météo(rologique); **(police) s.** commissariat *m* (de police), poste (de police); **fire s.** poste *ou* caserne *f* de pompiers; **power s.** centrale *f* électrique; **atomic power s.** centrale atomique; *Aut* **filling s., petrol s.,** *Am* **gas s.** poste d'essence, station-service *f*, *pl* stations-service

3 *(radio)* **s.** station *f* (de radio); **(television) s.** chaîne *f* (de télévision)

4 *Austr (farm)* = ferme *f* (et ses dépendances); **sheep s.** élevage *m* de moutons

5 *(social condition)* position *f*, condition *f*, *(rank)* rang *m*; **s. in life** situation *f* sociale; *Old-fashioned* **to marry below** *or* **beneath one's s.** faire une mésalliance, se mésallier
vt *(person in a place)* placer, mettre; *(soldier)* désigner son poste à; *(troops)* poster; **to be stationed at …** *Mil* être stationné *ou* être en garnison à …; *Naut* être en station à …; **he stationed himself behind a door** il s'est posté derrière une porte
▸ ▸ *TV, Radio* **s. ident, s. identification** indicatif *m* de chaîne; *Rail* **s. manager** chef *m* de gare; *Rail* **s. master** chef de gare; **s. presetting** *Radio* programmation *f* des stations; *TV* programmation des chaînes; *Am Aut* **s. wagon** break *m*; **s. waiter** chef de rang

stationary ['steɪʃən(ə)rɪ] ADJ **1** *(not moving)* immobile; *(car) (parked)* en stationnement; *(not moving)* à l'arrêt; **to remain s.** rester immobile **2** *(fixed)* fixe; *(permanent)* à demeure
▸ ▸ *Mil* **s. target** cible *f* fixe

Attention: ne pas confondre avec **stationery.**

---

stationer ['steɪʃənər] N papetier *m*; **s.'s (shop)** papeterie *f*

stationery ['steɪʃən(ə)rɪ] N papeterie *f*, *(writing paper)* papier *m* à lettres; **office/school s.** fournitures *fpl* de bureau/scolaires; **hotel s.** = papier à lettres à en-tête d'un hôtel; **headed s.** papier à en-tête
▸ ▸ *Br Admin* **the S. Office** = maison *f* d'édition britannique publiant les documents approuvés par le Parlement, les ministères et autres organismes officiels, ≃ l'Imprimerie *f* nationale

Attention: ne pas confondre avec **stationary**.

statism ['steɪtɪz(ə)m] N étatisme m

statist ['steɪtɪst] ADJ étatiste

statistic [stə'tɪstɪk] N *(statistical item)* élément m d'un/du tableau statistique; **statistics** statistiques *fpl*; **a worrying s.** un chiffre inquiétant; **to become just another s.** *(unimportant person)* n'être plus qu'un numéro; **he became just another s.** *(was killed)* il est juste venu s'ajouter aux statistiques (des morts); **vital statistics** statistiques démographiques; *Fam (of woman)* mensurations *fpl*

statistical [stə'tɪstɪk(ə)l] ADJ statistique
▸▸ **s. data** données *fpl* statistiques; **s. tables** statistiques *fpl*

statistically [stə'tɪstɪk(ə)lɪ] ADV statistiquement

statistician [stætɪs'tɪʃən] N statisticien, -ienne

statistics [stə'tɪstɪks] NPL *(usu with sing verb) (science)* statistique f VOIR GRAMMAIRE A10

stator ['steɪtər] N *Tech, Elec (of turbine)* stator m

statuary ['stætjʊərɪ] ADJ *(art, marble etc)* statuaire
N 1 *(art)* statuaire f, art m statuaire 2 *(statues)* statues *fpl*

statue ['stætjuː] N statue f; **don't stand there like a s.!** ne reste pas là comme une souche!

statuesque [stætjʊ'esk] ADJ sculptural, -aux

statuette [stætjʊ'et] N statuette f

stature ['stætjər] N stature f, taille f; **to be short of s.** être de petite taille; **it will increase her s.** *(of author etc)* sa réputation y gagnera; **he grew in s. as he …** *(in reputation)* il acquit une certaine réputation à mesure qu'il …; **a writer of some international s.** un écrivain ayant une certaine renommée internationale; **a politician of his s.** un homme politique de son envergure

status ['steɪtəs] N *(position)* statut m; *(marital)* situation f de famille; *(prestige, standing)* prestige m, standing m; **(personal) s.** statut (personnel); *Admin* **civil s.** état m civil; **social s.** rang m social; **with no official s.** sans titre officiel; **he's only interested in the job because of the s. that's attached to it** cet emploi ne l'intéresse qu'en raison du prestige qui y est attaché
▸▸ *Comput* **s. bar** barre f d'état; *Comput* **s. box** zone f d'état; **s. enquiry** *(about creditworthiness)* prise f de renseignements sur la solvabilité; **s. enquiry department** service m des renseignements commerciaux; *Comput* **s. line** ligne f d'état; **s. meeting** réunion f de bilan; *Comput* **s. printout** *(of printer)* impression f des paramètres de l'imprimante; **s. quo** statu quo m; **to maintain the s. quo** maintenir le statu quo; *Comput* **s. report** état m du projet; **s. symbol** marque f de prestige

status-conscious ADJ attaché à son standing

statute ['stætjuːt] N *Law* loi f, ordonnance f; *Br Pol (act)* acte m du Parlement; **statutes** *(of company)* statuts *mpl*, règlements *mpl*
▸▸ *Br* **s. book** code m (des lois), recueil m de lois; **to put sth in the s. book** faire passer qch en loi; *(of trade union etc)* faire passer qch dans le règlement; **s. law** droit m écrit; **s. of limitations** loi de prescription, prescription f légale; **the s. of limitations in this country is ten years** dans ce pays, il y a une prescription de dix ans

statutory ['stætjʊt(ə)rɪ] ADJ **1** *(established by law)* établi par la loi; *(by regulations)* réglementaire; *(offence)* prévu par la loi; **there**

is no s. obligation to … il n'y a aucune obligation légale de … **2** *(according to law)* statutaire, conforme aux statuts
▸▸ **s. duty** devoir m défini par la loi; **s. holiday** jour m férié, fête f légale; *Am* **s. rape** détournement m de mineur; **s. regulations** règlements *mpl* statutaires; **s. reserve** réserve f statutaire; **s. rights** droits *mpl* statutaires; **s. sick pay** = indemnité f de maladie versée par l'employeur

staunch¹ [stɔːntʃ] ADJ *(person)* sûr, dévoué; *(supporter)* dévoué, loyal; **a s. Catholic** un(e) catholique à tout crin; **a s. socialist** un(e) socialiste convaincu(e)

staunch² VT *(blood)* étancher; **to s. a wound** étancher le sang d'une blessure

staunchly ['stɔːntʃlɪ] ADV avec fermeté; *(with resolve)* avec résolution; **s. Catholic/republican area** région résolument catholique/républicaine

staunchness ['stɔːntʃnɪs] N *(of person)* fermeté f; *(loyalty)* dévouement m

stave [steɪv] N **1** *(wooden stick)* bâton m; **staves** *(of barrel)* douves *fpl* **2** *(in prosody) (of poem)* stance f, strophe f **3** *Mus* portée f
▸ **stave in** VT SEP *(pt, pp staved, stove* [stəʊv]) *(break) (barrel, ship's sides)* défoncer, enfoncer
▸ **stave off** VT SEP *(keep away) (problem etc)* détourner, écarter; *(danger)* prévenir, parer à; *(disaster)* conjurer; **to s. off a cold** éviter un rhume; **to s. off hunger** tromper la faim

STAY¹ [steɪ]

VI	rester **1** ▪ séjourner **2** ▪ loger **2** ▪ s'arrêter **4** ▪ habiter **5**
VT	arrêter **1** ▪ enrayer **1** ▪ ajourner **2** ▪ tenir **3**
N	séjour ▪ visite

VI **1** *(not move, remain)* rester; **s. there!** tenez-vous là!; **s. where you are!** restez où vous êtes!; *Fam* **to s. put** ne pas bouger; *(refuse to move)* refuser de bouger; *Fam* **I'll s. put, I'm staying put** j'y suis, j'y reste; **to s. still** rester tranquille; **to s. at home** rester à la maison ou chez soi; **to s. in bed** rester au lit; *(when ill)* garder le lit; **to s. to or for dinner** rester à ou pour) dîner; **computers are here to s.** les ordinateurs sont entrés dans les mœurs; **this word is here to s.** ce mot est entré dans la langue; **these changes are here to s.** ces changements sont passés dans les mœurs; **the weather stayed fine/wet all week** le temps est resté au beau/à la pluie toute la semaine; **it stays dark until after eight in winter** il fait nuit jusqu'à plus de huit heures en hiver; **if the weather stays like this** si le temps se maintient; **s.! (to dog)** pas bouger!; **it won't s. in position** impossible de le/la faire tenir en place
2 *(reside) (for short time)* séjourner; **I stayed five years in the States** j'ai passé ou habité cinq ans aux États-Unis; **where are you staying?** où loges-tu?; **he has come to s.** *(for a visit)* il est venu passer quelques jours chez nous; *(for good)* il est venu habiter chez nous; **to s. at a hotel** être à l'hôtel; **I'm staying at a hotel** je suis descendu à l'hôtel; **to s. with sb** loger chez qn; *(for holiday)* passer quelque temps chez qn; **we're staying with relations** nous sommes chez des parents
3 *Sport (endure)* **a horse that can s.** un cheval qui a du fond; **to s. with sth** s'atteler à qch; **it won't be finished unless you s. with it** ce ne sera jamais fini à moins que tu ne t'y tiennes
4 *Arch (stop)* s'arrêter
5 *Scot (live)* habiter, demeurer
VT **1** *esp Lit (stop) (person's progress)* arrêter; *(epidemic)* enrayer; **to s. sb's arm** *or* **hand** retenir le bras de qn; **to s. one's hand** se retenir

2 *Law etc* remettre; *(decision etc)* ajourner; **to s. judgement** surseoir à un/au jugement
3 *(endure)* **she can s. five kilometres** elle peut tenir cinq kilomètres; **to s. the course** tenir le rythme; *Sport* **will he s. the distance?** tiendra-t-il la distance?
N *(in a town etc)* séjour m; *(at friend's house)* visite f; **fortnight's s.** séjour de quinze jours
▸▸ **s. of execution** *Law* ordonnance f à surseoir (à un jugement), sursis m; *Fig* sursis; *Law* **s. of proceedings** suspension f d'instances

▸ **stay away** VI *(not approach)* ne pas s'approcher (**from** de); *(not attend)* ne pas assister (**from** à); **to s. away from school** ne pas aller à l'école; **to s. away from danger** se tenir à l'écart du danger; **you can play outside, but s. away from the road** tu peux jouer dehors, mais ne va pas sur la route
▸ **stay behind** VI rester en arrière; *(after school, work)* rester plus tard
▸ **stay down** VI **1** *Sch (repeat year)* redoubler
2 *(of hair, lid etc)* tenir en place; **I've tried to eat but nothing will s. down** j'ai essayé de manger mais je ne garde rien
3 *(under water)* **the turtle/diver can s. down for …** la tortue/le plongeur peut rester sous l'eau pendant …
▸ **stay in** VI **1** *(not go out)* ne pas sortir; *(stay in house)* rester à la maison
2 *(of screw, fitting etc)* rester en place
▸ **stay off** VI **1** *(not go to work, school)* rester à la maison
2 *(hold off) (of bad weather)* ne pas arriver; **we're hoping the rain will s. off a little longer** nous espérons que la pluie attendra encore un peu
VT INSEP **1** *(keep away from) (main roads, private property etc)* éviter, ne pas passer par; *(alcohol, drugs, sweets etc)* ne pas prendre, éviter; **s. off the whisky!** pas de whisky!
2 *(not attend) (school, work etc)* ne pas aller à
▸ **stay on** VI **1** *(remain longer)* rester plus longtemps
2 *(remain in place) (of hat, wig etc)* tenir ou rester en place; *(of sticker etc)* tenir
▸ **stay out** VI *(stay outside)* rester dehors; *(not come home)* ne pas rentrer; **to s. out all night** découcher; **to s. out late** rentrer tard; **to s. out until all hours of the night** rester dehors jusque très tard dans la nuit
2 *Ind (continue strike)* poursuivre ou continuer la grève
3 *(not interfere)* **to s. out of sth** ne pas se mêler de qch; **s. out of this!** ne t'en mêle pas!
▸ **stay over** VI prolonger son séjour, rester plus longtemps; **you can s. over if you like** *(spend the night)* tu peux dormir ici si tu veux
▸ **stay up** VI **1** *(not go to bed)* ne pas se coucher, veiller; **to s. up late** se coucher ou veiller tard; **we stayed up all night talking** nous sommes restés à parler toute la nuit; **my parents always s. up until I get home** mes parents attendent toujours jusqu'à ce que je sois rentré pour aller se coucher; **don't s. up for me** ne m'attends pas pour aller dormir
2 *(remain in place) (of picture, shelf, tent, trousers)* tenir; **the decorations stayed up until February** les décorations sont restées en place jusqu'en février
3 *Br (at university)* **he used to s. up over the vacations** il restait (travailler) à l'université pendant les vacances

stay² N **1** *(support)* soutien m; *Constr, Tech etc* étai m, étançon m; *Naut (for mast)* étai m; *Aut (for bonnet)* béquille f
2 **stays** *(corset)* corset m

stay-at-home ADJ, N casanier, -ière

stayer ['steɪər] N **1** *Sport (runner)* coureur m de fond; *(cyclist)* stayer m; *(horse)* stayer, cheval m qui a du fond **2** *(person who perseveres)* personne f persévérante; **she's a real**

s. elle va jusqu'au bout de ce qu'elle entreprend; **gifted but not a s.** doué mais manque de suivi *ou* de persévérance

staying ['steɪɪŋ] **N**
▸▸ **s. power** résistance *f*, endurance *f*; **to have good s. power** *(of horse)* avoir du fond

stay-over **N** *(reused hotel room)* chambre *f* en recouche, recouche *f*

stays list **N** *(at hotel)* liste *f* des clients en recouche

STD [estiː'diː] **N 1** *Br Tel* (*abbr* **subscriber trunk dialling**) automatique *m* (interurbain) **2** *Med* (*abbr* **sexually transmitted disease**) MST *f*
▸▸ *Br Tel* **S. code** indicatif *m* de zone

stead [sted] **N 1 to stand sb in good s.** être fort utile à qn **2** *esp Lit* **in sb's s.** à la place *ou* au lieu de qn

steadfast ['stedfɑːst] **ADJ** ferme, stable; **s. in love/in adversity** constant en amour/dans l'adversité; **they were s. in their refusal to compromise** ils se sont montrés très déterminés dans leur refus du compromis
ADV *(to hold, stand)* sans fléchir

steadfastly ['stedfɑːstlɪ] **ADV** *(to refuse)* fermement; *(to love, serve etc)* avec constance; **she has s. refused to identify her sources** elle a toujours refusé de désigner ses sources

steadfastness ['stedfɑːstnɪs] **N** *(determination)* fermeté *f*, *(constancy)* constance *f*

Steadicam® ['stedɪkæm] **N** *TV, Cin* Steadicam® *f*
▸▸ **S. operator** opérateur *m* Steadicam®

steadily ['stedɪlɪ] **ADV 1** *(solidly)* fermement **2** *(at regular rate)* régulièrement; *(without stopping)* sans arrêt; *(without jolting)* sans à-coups; *(constantly)* continuellement; *(to work)* assidûment; **to walk s.** *(not stagger)* bien tenir sur ses jambes; **s. increasing output** rendement augmentant de façon régulière; **his health grows s. worse** sa santé empire régulièrement; **to work s. at sth** travailler assidûment à qch; **they were s. gaining on us** inexorablement, ils nous rattrapaient **3** *(calmly)* d'une manière posée; **she looked at him s.** elle l'a fixé du regard, elle l'a regardé fixement

steadiness ['stedɪnɪs] **N 1** *(of table, hand etc)* fermeté *f*; **s. of hand** sûreté *f* des gestes; **s. of hand is vital for surgeons** il est vital que les chirurgiens aient la main sûre **2** *(regularity)* *(of movement, action)* régularité *f*, *(perseverance)* assiduité *f*, persévérance *f*, *(stability)* stabilité *f*, **s. of purpose** constance *f* (avec laquelle l'on poursuit ses objectifs); *St Exch* **s. of prices** bonne tenue *f* des prix **3** *(calm)* *(of person)* calme *m*; *(non-volatility)* régularité *f*

steady ['stedɪ] **ADJ 1** *(stable, solid)* *(table, ladder etc)* stable; **to make a bookshelf s.** rendre une étagère stable; **to hold sth s.** bien tenir qch; **to keep s.** ne pas bouger; **to be s. on one's feet** *or* **legs** être d'aplomb sur ses jambes; **to have a s. hand** avoir la main sûre; **with a s. hand** d'une main sûre *ou* ferme
 2 *(regular)* *(rate, increase, growth)* continu, soutenu; *(income)* fixe, régulier; *(pulse)* égal; *Com (market)* soutenu; *(person)* *(in work, lifestyle etc)* régulier; **s. breeze** brise *f* étale; *Com* **s. demand** demande suivie (**for** pour); *Sport* **to play a s. game** avoir un jeu régulier; **beneath her s. gaze** sous son regard soutenu; **s. increase** augmentation frégulière; **s. pace** allure frégulière; **to drive at a s. 90** rouler constamment à 90; **s. prices** prix *mpl* stables; **s. progress** progrès *mpl* constants; **s. rain** pluie *f* persistante; **s. worker** travailleur *m* régulier *(concernant la productivité)*; **to be s. in one's affections** être constant dans ses affections; **he hasn't been**

in s. work for years il n'a pas (eu) de travail stable depuis des années
 3 *(calm)* posé; **s. horse** cheval *m* calme; **in a s. voice** d'une voix posée
 4 **he has a s. girlfriend** il a la même copine depuis longtemps; **I don't have a s. boyfriend** je n'ai pas vraiment de petit ami
ADV *Fam* **they are going s. now** ça devient sérieux entre eux deux; **they've been going s. for two years now** ça fait deux ans qu'ils sortent ensemble
INT s.! *(don't move)* ne bougez pas!; *(watch out you don't fall)* attention (de ne pas tomber)!; *Fam* **s. (on)!** *(gently)* doucement!
N *Fam* **my s.** *(boyfriend)* mon petit ami; *(girlfriend)* ma petite amie
VT raffermir, affermir; **to s. one's hand** s'assurer que sa main ne tremble pas; **to s. oneself** retrouver son équilibre; **to s. oneself against sth** s'appuyer contre qch; **to s. one's nerves** calmer ses nerfs; **marriage has steadied him** le mariage lui a donné un certain équilibre
VI *(of boat etc)* retrouver son équilibre; **prices are steadying** les prix se raffermissent
▸ **steady down** **VI** *(become a calmer person)* se calmer

steak [steɪk] **N** *Culin (beef)* bifteck *m*, steak *m*; *(cut from the ribs)* entrecôte *f*, *(of meat, fish)* tranche *f*, *(of salmon)* darne *f*, **fillet s.** *(beef)* tournedos *m*; **s. and chips** steak frites
▸▸ **s. and kidney pie** tourte *f* à la viande et aux rognons de bœuf; **s. and kidney pudding** pudding *m* à la viande et aux rognons de bœuf; **s. knife** couteau *m* à steak *ou* à viande; **s. tartare** steak *m* tartare

steakhouse ['steɪkhaʊs] **N** grill *m*

steal [stiːl] **VT** *(pt* **stole** [stəʊl]; *pp* **stolen** ['stəʊl(ə)n]) *(property, person's idea, husband)* voler (**from sb** à qn); **I've had my purse stolen** on m'a volé mon porte-monnaie; **to s. money from the till** *(of employee)* prendre de l'argent *ou* se servir dans la caisse; **to s. sb's heart** prendre le cœur de qn; **to s. a kiss** voler un baiser; **to s. a few hours from one's studies** laisser ses études de côté pendant quelques heures; **to s. a glance at sb** jeter un coup d'œil furtif à qn; **to s. a march on sb** devancer qn; *Theat* **to s. the show** ravir la vedette; **to s. sb's thunder** couper l'herbe sous le pied de qn
VI 1 voler (**from sb** qn); *Bible* **thou shalt not s.** tu ne voleras point; **to be caught stealing** être pris en train de voler **2** *(move quietly)* **to s. away/in/out** s'en aller/entrer/sortir sans bruit; **she stole into the room** elle s'est faufilée *ou* glissée dans la pièce; **to s. up on sb** se glisser vers qn; *Fig (of old age etc)* prendre qn par surprise
N *Fam (bargain)* affaire *f*; **at $35, it's a s.!** à 35 dollars, c'est une affaire!

stealing ['stiːlɪŋ] **N** vol *m*; **s. is wrong** c'est mal de voler

stealth [stelθ] **N** ruse *f*, **by s.** par la ruse; *(furtively)* à la dérobée, furtivement; **to do good by s.** faire le bien en restant dans l'ombre
▸▸ *Mil* **s. bomber** avion *m* furtif; **s. tax** = mesure *f* visant à augmenter les recettes du gouvernement par un moyen détourné, afin d'éviter une hausse directe et visible des impôts qui mécontenterait les citoyens

stealthily ['stelθɪlɪ] **ADV** furtivement, à la dérobée

stealthiness ['stelθɪnɪs] **N** *(of action etc)* caractère *m* furtif; *(of person)* manières *fpl* furtives; **his s. in defaming his rivals** la ruse avec laquelle il parvenait à diffamer ses rivaux

stealthy ['stelθɪ] **ADJ** furtif; *(look)* dérobé, à la dérobée; **with a s. step** à pas furtifs *ou* feutrés *ou* de loup

steam [stiːm] **N** vapeur *f* (d'eau); *(condensa-*

tion) buée *f*; *Tech etc* **to get up** *or* **to raise s.** mettre la chaudière sous pression; **to get up s.** *(of person)* rassembler toutes ses forces *ou* toute son énergie; **at full s.** à toute vapeur; *Naut* **full s. ahead!** en avant toute!; **to run out of s.** *(of engine etc)* ne plus être sous pression; *Fam (of project, campaign etc)* s'essouffler; *Fam (of person)* manquer de souffle; *Fam* **I'm running out of s.** je commence à peiner; *Fig* **to let off s.** se défouler; **to proceed under its own s.** *(of damaged ship etc)* parvenir à naviguer sans être remorqué; *Fig* **I'll get there under my own s.** j'irai par mes propres moyens
VT passer à la vapeur, étuver; *Culin (vegetables etc)* cuire à la vapeur *ou* à l'étuvée; **to s. open an envelope** décacheter une lettre à la vapeur
VI 1 *(give off steam)* fumer; **horses steaming with sweat** chevaux fumants (de sueur) **2** *(cook in steam)* *(of vegetables etc)* cuire à la vapeur **3** **to s. ahead** *(of ship, locomotive)* avancer (à la vapeur); *Fig (make rapid progress)* avancer à toute vapeur; **the train steamed out of the station** le train quitta la gare dans un nuage de fumée; **the ferry steamed into port** le ferry entra dans le port; *Fig Fam* **he came steaming into the room** *(fast)* il est entré dans la pièce à toute pompe; *(angry)* il est entré dans la pièce en fulminant
▸▸ **s. bath** bain *m* de vapeur; **s. cooking** cuisson *f* à la vapeur; **s. engine** *Tech* moteur *m* à vapeur; *Rail* locomotive *f* à vapeur; **s. iron** fer *m* (à repasser) à vapeur; **s. power** vapeur; *Old-fashioned Br Fam* **s. radio** *(broadcasting)* ≃ la bonne vieille radio *(par opposition à la télévision)*; *(set)* poste *m* de radio antédiluvien; **in the days of s. radio** aux débuts de la radio; **s. room** hammam *m*; *Am* **s. shovel** bulldozer *m*
▸ **steam off** **VT SEP** *(stamp)* décoller à la vapeur
 VI *(of ship)* s'éloigner (en fumant)
▸ **steam up** **VI** *(become covered in condensation)* *(of window, windscreen, glasses etc)* s'embuer
 VT SEP *(usu passive)* **to get all steamed up** *(of windows, glasses etc)* se couvrir de buée, s'embuer; *Fig Fam (lose one's composure)* s'énerver

steamboat ['stiːmbəʊt] **N** (bateau *m* à) vapeur *m*

steamboats ['stiːmbəʊts] **ADJ** *Br Fam (drunk)* rond comme une queue de pelle, pété à mort

steamed [stiːmd] **ADJ** *(vegetables etc)* à la vapeur

steamer ['stiːmər] **N 1** *(ship)* (bateau *m* à) vapeur *m* **2** *Culin (saucepan)* cuiseur *m* à vapeur; *(insert for saucepan)* panier *m* de cuisson à la vapeur

steaming ['stiːmɪŋ] **ADJ 1** *(emitting steam)* fumant **2** *Fig Fam (angry)* fumant de colère; *Br (drunk)* bourré, pété
 ADV **s. hot** bien chaud; *Br Fam* **s. drunk** bourré, pété
 N 1 *Culin* cuisson *f* à la vapeur *ou* à l'étuvée **2** *Sl (street robbery by gangs)* = vol *m* de sacs à main pratiqué en bande

steamroller ['stiːmrəʊlər] **N** *Constr* rouleau *m* compresseur; *Fig* force *f* écrasante
 VT *Constr (road)* passer au rouleau compresseur; *Fig (the opposition etc)* écraser; **to s. a bill through Parliament** imposer un projet de loi au Parlement; **he steamrollered his plans through the committee** il a imposé ses projets au comité

steamship ['stiːmʃɪp] **N** bateau *m* à vapeur

steamy ['stiːmɪ] **ADJ** *(full of steam)* plein de vapeur; *(covered in steam)* couvert de buée; *Fig Fam (novel, movie, scene)* torride

steed [stiːd] **N** *Lit* coursier *m*, destrier *m*

steel [stiːl] **N 1** *(metal)* acier *m*; **rolled s.** acier laminé; **a grip/a will of s.** une poigne/une volonté de fer; **nerves of s.** nerfs *mpl* d'acier; **s. knife/ladder** couteau *m*/échelle *f* en acier; **s. plate** plaque *f* d'acier **2** *Arch, Lit (sword)* fer *m*, épée *f*; *(blade)* lame *f* **3** *(for sharpening knives)* affiloir *m*, fusil *m*
VT to s. oneself *or* **one's heart to do sth** s'armer de courage pour faire qch; **to s. oneself against sth** se blinder contre qch
▸▸*Mus* **s. band** steel band *m*; **the s. industry** la sidérurgie; **s. mill** aciérie *f*; **s. wool** paille *f* de fer

steelclad ['stiːlklæd] **ADJ** couvert *ou* revêtu d'acier; *(knight)* bardé de fer

steel-plated **ADJ** cuirassé

steelwork ['stiːlwɜːk] **N 1** *Tech* tôleries *fpl*; **constructional s.** profilés *mpl* pour constructions **2** *(usu with sing verb)* **steelworks** *(factory)* aciérie *f*

steelworker ['stiːlwɜːkər] **N** ouvrier *m* de l'industrie sidérurgique

steely ['stiːlɪ] **ADJ 1** *(of steel)* d'acier; **s. blue** bleu *m* acier **2** *(hard)* dur; *(gaze etc)* d'acier; *(determination)* inflexible

steelyard ['stiːljɑːd, 'stɪljəd] **N** (balance *f*) romaine *f*

steep¹ [stiːp] **ADJ 1** *(path, hill, street)* escarpé, raide; *(slope)* raide; *(cliff)* à pic; **s. climb** *(hill)* pente *f* raide; **the plane went into a s. climb/dive** l'avion monta à la verticale/descendit en piqué; **s. gradient** forte pente, pente raide *ou* rapide; **s. rise in prices** hausse *f* considérable des prix **2** *Fam (excessive) (price etc)* excessif; **that's pretty s.!** *(of price)* c'est un peu raide!; **that's a bit s.!** *(unreasonable)* c'est un peu fort!

steep² **VT** *(clothes, food)* faire tremper; *(hides)* tremper; **terrace steeped in sunshine** terrasse baignée de soleil; **steeped in prejudice** imbibé de préjugés; **steeped in history** imprégné d'histoire; **to s. oneself in the atmosphere of the Middle Ages** se tremper *ou* se plonger dans l'atmosphère du Moyen Âge
VI tremper; *Culin* macérer, mariner

steepen ['stiːpən] **VI** *(of slope etc)* devenir plus raide; *(of prices)* augmenter

steeple ['stiːpəl] **N** *(bell tower)* clocher *m*; *(spire)* flèche *f* (de clocher)

steeplechase ['stiːpəltʃeɪs] **N** *Sport, Horseracing* steeple-chase *m, pl* steeplechases, steeple *m*

steeplechaser ['stiːpəltʃeɪsər] **N** *Sport, Horseracing (rider)* cavalier *m* qui monte en steeple-chases; *(horse, athlete)* steeplechaser *m, pl* steeple-chasers

steeplechasing ['stiːpəltʃeɪsɪŋ] **N** *Sport, Horseracing* steeple-chases *mpl*

steeplejack ['stiːpəldʒæk] **N** réparateur *m* de clochers et de cheminées d'usines

steeply ['stiːplɪ] **ADV** *(to drop)* en pente raide, à pic; *(to climb)* à pic; **road that climbs s.** route à forte pente; **to rise s.** *(of path)* monter à pic; *Fig (of prices)* monter en flèche

steepness ['stiːpnɪs] **N** *(of slope)* escarpement *m*

steer [stɪər] **VT** *(car)* conduire, diriger; *(ship)* gouverner; *(yacht)* barrer; *(person)* diriger (**towards** vers); **to s. sb out of trouble** sortir qn du pétrin; **to s. a northerly course, to s. north** faire route vers le nord; *(turn north)* mettre le cap sur le nord; *Fig* **to s. a middle course** trouver un compromis; **he tried to s. the conversation away from the subject** il a essayé de détourner la conversation; **to s. the conversation round to another subject** aiguiller la conversation sur un autre sujet; **to s. a country out of a crisis** faire sortir un pays de la crise
VI *(of person)* conduire; *(of ship)* gouverner;

to s. for sth se diriger vers qch; **to s. clear of sb/sth** éviter qn/qch
▸ **N** *(bull)* bœuf *m*

steerage ['stɪərɪdʒ] **N** *Naut Old-fashioned (third-class accommodation)* entrepont *m*; **to travel s.** voyager dans l'entrepont

steerageway ['stɪərɪdʒweɪ] **N** *Naut* vitesse *f* nécessaire pour gouverner

steering ['stɪərɪŋ] **N** *(act) (of car)* direction *f*; *(mechanism) (of car)* timonerie *f*, *(boîte f de)* direction; *(of ship)* appareil *m* à gouverner; *(of plane)* direction
▸▸*Aut* **s. arm** bras *m* de direction; *Aut* **s. box** boîtier *m* de direction; **s. column** colonne *f* de direction; **s. column lock** antivol *m* de direction; *Br* **s. committee** comité *m* directeur; *Aut* **s. geometry** géométrie *f* du train avant; *Aut* **s. lock** *(turning circle)* rayon *m* de braquage; *(antitheft device)* antivol *m* de direction; **s. play** jeu *m* à la direction; **s. rod** bielle *f* de direction; **s. wheel** *Aut* volant *m*; *Naut* roue *f* du gouvernail, barre *f*

steersman, *pl* **steersmen** ['stɪəzmən] **N** *Naut* homme *m* de barre, timonier *m*

stellar ['stelər] **ADJ** stellaire

stem¹ [stem] **N 1** *Bot (of plant)* tige *f*, *Spec* pédoncule *m*; *(of leaf)* queue *f*, *Spec* pétiole *m*; *Am Fam* **stems** *(legs)* quilles *fpl*, gambettes *fpl* **2** *(of glass)* pied *m*; *(of tobacco pipe)* tuyau *m*; *(of valve)* tige *f*, *Mus (of note)* queue *f*, *Typ (of letter)* hampe *f* **3** *Ling (of word)* radical *m* **4** *(of ship)* étrave *f*; **from s. to stern** de l'avant à l'arrière; *Fig* **the party is split from s. to stern on this issue** le parti est totalement divisé sur cette question
VI (**-mm-**) **to s. from sth** *(of problems, errors, theories etc)* provenir de qch; *(of models, versions, designs etc)* être issu de qch; **much harm stemmed from this** il en est résulté beaucoup de mal
▸▸*Biol* **s. cell** cellule *f* souche; **s. glass** verre *m* à pied

stem² **VT** *(hold back) (flow of liquid etc)* arrêter, contenir; *Fig* **to s. an epidemic** enrayer une épidémie; *Fig* **to s. the tide of …** arrêter le flot de …; *Fig* **to s. the rise in unemployment/crime** enrayer la montée du chômage/de la criminalité; *Fig* **to s. the advance of fascism/an army** bloquer l'avancée du fascisme/d'une armée
VI *Ski* faire un stem
▸ **N** *Ski (virage m en)* stem *m*
▸▸*Ski* **s. Christie** stem christie; **s. parallel** stem parallèle

stemmed [stemd] **ADJ** *(glass)* à pied

stemware ['stemweər] **N** *Am (glasses)* verres *mpl*

stench [stentʃ] **N** odeur *f* nauséabonde, puanteur *f*; *Fig* **the s. of corruption** l'odeur nauséabonde de la corruption

stencil ['stensəl] **N 1** *(device)* pochoir *m*; **coloured by s.** colorié au pochoir **2** *(work)* peinture *f* au pochoir **3** *(typewritten copy etc)* stencil *m*
VT (**-ll-,** *Am* **-l-**) *(leaf, flower etc)* peindre au pochoir; *Ind, Com (packing case)* marquer; *(letter etc)* polycopier, tirer au stencil
VI peindre au pochoir
▸▸**s. paper** papier *m* stencil; **s. plate** pochoir

sten gun [sten] **N** mitraillette *f*

stenographer, *Am* **stenographist** [stə'nɒɡrəfər, -fɪst] **N** sténographe *mf*, *Fam* sténo *mf*

stenography [stə'nɒɡrəfɪ] **N** sténographie *f*

stenotyper ['stenətaɪpər] **N** sténotype *m*

stenotypist ['stenətaɪpɪst] **N** sténotypiste *mf*

stenotypy ['stenətaɪpɪ] **N** sténotypie *f*

stentorian [sten'tɔːrɪən] **ADJ** *(voice)* de stentor

STEP [step]

N pas **1, 2** ▪ démarche **3** ▪ mesure **3** ▪ marche **4** ▪ échelon **4** ▪ étape **5**	
VI faire un pas ▪ marcher	

N 1 *(movement, sound)* pas *m*; **with quick steps** d'un pas rapide; **to take a s.** faire un pas (**back** en arrière; **forward** en avant); **one s. forward, two steps back** un pas en avant et deux pas en arrière; *esp Lit* **to turn one's steps towards a place** diriger ses pas *ou* se diriger vers un lieu; **a child's first steps** les premiers pas d'un enfant; **at every s.** à chaque pas; **s. by s.** pas à pas; *(little by little)* petit à petit, graduellement, progressivement; **within a few steps of the house** à quelques pas de la maison; **it's quite a s.** *(quite a long way)* ce n'est pas tout près; *(quite a big change)* c'est une décision importante; **that's a great s. forward** c'est déjà un grand pas de fait, c'est déjà un grand progrès; **a s. in the right direction** un pas dans la bonne voie; **you'll have to watch your s.** il va falloir que tu fasses attention où tu mets les pieds; *Fig* fais attention à ce que tu fais; *Fig* **they fought us every s. of the way** ils nous ont combattu sans répit *ou* sur chaque point; *Fig* **we're behind you every s. of the way** nous sommes avec vous sur toute la ligne **2** *(in walking, dancing)* pas *m*; **marching s.** pas ordinaire; **to be in s.** marcher au pas, être au pas; **to fall into s.** se mettre au pas; **to keep (in) s.** rester au pas; **to break s.** rompre le pas; *Fig* **to be out of s. with sb** être à contre-courant de qn; *Fig* **supply has got out of s. with demand** l'offre ne correspond plus à la demande **3** *(action, measure)* démarche *f*, mesure *f*; **to take the necessary steps** faire *ou* entreprendre les démarches nécessaires; **to take steps to do sth** prendre des mesures pour faire qch; **the first s. will be to …** la première chose à faire, ce sera de … **4** *(of staircase)* marche *f*, degré *m*; *(of ladder)* échelon *m*; *(of stepladders)* marche; **flight of steps** escalier *m*, volée *f* de marches; *(outside building)* perron *m*; **mind the s.** attention à la marche; **to go up a s.** *(be promoted)* monter en grade; **it's a s. up from the old house** c'est un peu mieux que la vieille maison; **this new job is a s. up for me** ce nouveau travail va me permettre de progresser dans ma carrière; **to cut steps** *(in mountaineering)* tailler **5** *(stage)* étape *f*; **it is a simple two-s. procedure** c'est une procédure simple en deux étapes; **the next s. is to …** l'étape suivante consiste à … **6** *(ladder)* **(pair of) steps** escabeau *m*, échelle *f* double; *Aviat* **steps** passerelle *f* **7** *(type of exercise)* step *m*; **I go to s. twice a week** je vais à un cours de step deux fois par semaine
VI (**stepped** [stept]) *(take a step, steps)* faire un pas/des pas; *(walk)* marcher, aller; **to s. on sb's foot** marcher sur le pied de qn; **s. this way** venez par ici; **s. inside for a moment** entrez pour un moment; **he stepped carefully over the cat** il enjamba soigneusement le chat; **to s. off a ladder** descendre d'une échelle; *Fam Hum* **he stepped under a bus** il est passé sous un bus
▸ **step aside** **VI** s'écarter; **to s. aside to let sb pass** s'écarter pour laisser passer qn; **it's time the chairman stepped aside** il est temps que le président se retire et laisse la place à quelqu'un d'autre
▸ **step back** **VI** faire un pas en arrière; *Fig* **if we could s. back into the last century** si nous pouvions revenir au siècle passé; **sometimes it helps to s. back and look at things** il est parfois bon de prendre du recul

▸**step down** VT SEP *(decrease) Elec (current)* dévolter; *Tech* **to s. down the gear** démultiplier la transmission

VI **1** *(resign)* démissionner; **he stepped down in favour of the other candidate** *(withdrew)* il s'est retiré en faveur de l'autre candidat

2 *(descend)* descendre (**from** de)

▸**step forward** VI faire un pas en avant; *Fig (of volunteer etc)* se désigner, se porter volontaire

▸**step in** VI entrer (**to** dans); *(intervene)* intervenir, s'interposer

▸**step on** VT INSEP *(tread on)* marcher sur; *Fam* **to s. on the gas, to s. on it** *Aut* appuyer sur l'accélérateur *ou Fam* sur le champignon; *(hurry)* se dépêcher, *Fam* se grouiller; **to s. on the brakes** donner un coup de frein brusque

▸**step out** VI **1** *(go outside house etc)* sortir

2 *(walk faster)* allonger *ou* forcer le pas; **to s. out briskly** marcher rapidement

3 *Old-fashioned* **to be stepping out with sb** *(courting)* sortir avec qn

▸**step up** VI **to s. up to sb/sth** s'approcher de qn/qch; **s. up! s. up! come and see ...** approchez! approchez! venez voir ...; **he stepped up onto the platform** il est monté sur le podium

VT SEP *(increase, intensify)* accroître, augmenter

stepbrother ['stepbrʌðər] N demi-frère m, pl demi-frères *(fils du beau-père ou de la belle-mère)*

stepchild, pl **stepchildren** ['steptʃaɪld, -tʃɪldrən] N beau-fils m, belle-fille f, pl beaux-fils, belles-filles

stepdaughter ['stepdɔːtər] N belle-fille f, pl belles-filles

stepfather ['stepfɑːðər] N beau-père m, pl beaux-pères

stepladder ['steplædər] N escabeau m

stepless transmission ['steplɪs] N *Aut* transmission f à variation continue

stepmother ['stepmʌðər] N belle-mère f, pl belles-mères

steppe [step] N *Geog* steppe f

stepper ['stepər] N

▸▸*Elec* **s. motor** moteur m pas-à-pas

stepping stone ['stepɪŋ] N pierre f (pour passer une rivière/etc à gué); *Fig* tremplin m

stepping up N *(of production etc)* augmentation f, *(of campaign etc)* intensification f

stepsister ['stepsɪstər] N demi-sœur f, pl demi-sœurs *(fille du beau-père ou de la belle-mère)*

stepson ['stepsʌn] N beau-fils m, pl beaux-fils

stereo, pl **stereos** ['sterɪəʊ, -əʊz, 'stɪə-] N **1** *(equipment)* chaîne f stéréo **2** *(sound)* stéréo f; **to listen to sth in s.** écouter qch en stéréo **3** *Typ* = **stereotype** N **2**

ADJ *(equipment, record, cassette)* stéréo *inv*; *(recording, broadcast)* en stéréo

▸▸**s. signal** signal m stéréo; **s. system** chaîne f stéréo; **s. transmitter** émetteur m stéréo

stereophonic [sterɪə'fɒnɪk, stɪə-] ADJ stéréophonique

stereoscope ['sterɪəskəʊp, 'stɪər-] N *Opt* stéréoscope m

stereoscopic [sterɪəʊ'skɒpɪk, stɪə-] ADJ stéréoscopique

stereotype ['sterɪətaɪp, 'stɪə-] N **1** *Fig* stéréotype m **2** *Typ* cliché m

VT **1** *Fig* stéréotyper **2** *Typ* stéréotyper, clicher

stereotyped ['sterɪətaɪpt, 'stɪə-] ADJ *Typ, Fig* stéréotypé; **the s. idea of a farmer** le stéréotype de l'agriculteur

stereotypical [sterɪə'tɪpɪkəl, stɪə-] ADJ stéréotypé; **the s. image of an American tourist** le stéréotype du touriste américain

stereotyping ['sterɪətaɪpɪŋ, 'stɪə-] N **1** *Fig* fabrication f de stéréotypes; **the s. of women** les stéréotypes que l'on colle aux femmes **2** *Typ* clichage m

sterile ['steraɪl] ADJ stérile

sterility [ste'rɪlɪtɪ] N stérilité f

sterilization [sterɪlaɪ'zeɪʃən] N stérilisation f

sterilize ['sterɪlaɪz] VT stériliser; **sterilized milk** lait m stérilisé

sterilizer ['sterɪlaɪzər] N *(device)* stérilisateur m

sterilizing ['sterɪlaɪzɪŋ] N stérilisation f

sterling ['stɜːlɪŋ] ADJ *(silver)* de bon aloi, fin; *Fig* vrai, solide; **a s. fighter** un combattant inlassable; **s. qualities** qualités fpl solides; **pound s.** livre f sterling

N *(currency)* (livre f) sterling m; **to pay in s.** payer en livres sterling

▸▸**s. area** zone f sterling

stern[1] [stɜːn] ADJ sévère; **we are made of sterner stuff** nous, nous sommes d'une autre trempe

stern[2] N *Naut* arrière m

sternly ['stɜːnlɪ] ADV sévèrement

sternness ['stɜːnnɪs] N sévérité f

sternum, pl **sterna, sternums** ['stɜːnəm, -ə, -əmz] N *Anat* sternum m

steroid ['stɪərɔɪd, 'ste-] N *Biol, Chem* stéroïde m

stertorous ['stɜːtərəs] ADJ *Med, Lit* stertoreux, ronflant

stet [stet] *Typ* N bon m

VT (-**tt**-) *(text)* maintenir

stethoscope ['steθəskəʊp] N *Med* stéthoscope m

Stetson® ['stets(ə)n] N chapeau m mou à larges bords

stevedore ['stiːvɪdɔːr] N docker m, arrimeur m

stew [stjuː] N **1** *Culin* ragoût m; **Irish s.** ragoût de mouton à l'irlandaise; *Fam* **to be in a s.** *(of person)* être dans tous ses états **2** *Arch (brothel)* bordel m

VT *Culin (meat etc)* faire cuire en ragoût; **to s. apples** faire une compote de pommes

VI **1** *Culin (of meat)* mijoter; *Fam* **to let sb s. in his/her own juice** laisser qn cuire dans son jus, laisser mariner qn **2** *Br Fam (of person)* **to be stewing** crever de chaleur; **it's stewing in here** il fait une chaleur à crever ici

steward ['stjʊəd] N **1** *(of estate)* régisseur m, intendant m; *Naut (manager of provisions)* distributeur m, commis m *ou* agent m aux vivres; *Naut, Aviat (attendant)* steward m; *Naut* **s.'s mate** cambusier m **2** *(at sporting event)* commissaire m; *(at demonstration etc)* membre m du service d'ordre; *(at dance)* organisateur, -trice; *Ind* **shop s.** délégué m d'atelier *ou* d'usine *ou* du personnel

▸▸*Horseracing* **s.'s inquiry** enquête f des commissaires

stewardess [stjʊə'des] N *Naut* hôtesse f, *Aviat* **air s.** hôtesse de l'air

stewardship ['stjʊədʃɪp] N économat m, intendance f, *Fig* **under his s., the situation improved markedly** quand il était responsable, les choses s'étaient nettement améliorées

stewed [stjuːd] ADJ **1 this tea is s.** ce thé a trop infusé **2** *Fam (drunk)* **s. (to the gills)** rond comme une queue de pelle

▸▸**s. beef** ragoût m de bœuf, bœuf m (à la) mode; **s. fruit** compote f de fruits

stewing ['stjuːɪŋ] N

▸▸**s. beef** bœuf m à braiser; **s. pan** (grande) casserole f, **s. pears** poires fpl à cuire

stewpan ['stjuːpæn] N (grande) casserole f

stewpot ['stjuːpɒt] N cocotte f, fait-tout m inv

St. Ex. *Fin (abbr* **Stock Exchange**) Bourse f

STICK [stɪk]

N bâton **1, 3** ▪ morceau de bois **1** ▪ canne **1** ▪ bâtonnet **1** ▪ branche **4** ▪ critiques **6**
VT piquer **1** ▪ planter **1** ▪ mettre **2** ▪ coller **3** ▪ supporter **4**
VI coller **2** ▪ tenir **2** ▪ rester **2** ▪ (se) coincer **3**

N **1** *(piece of wood)* bâton m; *(small piece of wood)* morceau m de bois; *Fig* **the big s.** la manière forte, (la politique de) la force; *Fig* **you're giving him a s. to beat you with** vous lui donnez des verges pour vous faire fouetter *ou* le bâton pour vous faire battre; **(walking) s.** canne f; **to gather sticks** ramasser du bois sec *ou* du petit bois; **cocktail s.** curedents m inv *(utilisé à l'apéritif)*; **(swizzle) s.** *(for cocktails etc)* agitateur m; **not a s. was left standing** tout était rasé; **my few sticks of furniture** mes quelques meubles; *Prov* **sticks and stones may break my bones (but words will never hurt me)** = les chiens aboient, la caravane passe; *Fam* **he lives out in the sticks** il habite un trou perdu, il vit dans la brousse; *Sl* **to be up the s.** *(pregnant)* être en cloque

2 *Old-fashioned Fam (person)* **he's/she's a funny old s.** c'est un drôle de personnage; **he's/she's a good old s.** c'est un type/une fille bien; **a dry old s.** un pince-sans-rire; **Jeremy, old s.!** Jeremy, vieille branche!

3 *(of barley sugar, chewing gum, glue etc)* bâton m; *(of deodorant)* applicateur m; *(of dynamite)* bâtonnet m

4 *Culin* **s. of celery** branche f de céleri; **s. of rhubarb** tige f de rhubarbe

5 *Mil, Aviat* **s. of bombs** chapelet m de bombes

6 *Fam (criticism)* critiques; **to take a lot of s.** *(to be criticized)* se faire taper sur les doigts; *(to be mocked)* se faire mettre en boîte; *Fam* **to give sb s.** *(criticize)* taper sur les doigts de qn (**for sth** à cause de qch); *(laugh at)* se payer la tête de qn (**for sth** à cause de qch); *Fam* **to give it some s.** *(exert oneself)* s'y mettre

VT (*pt, pp* **stuck** [stʌk]) **1** *(insert)* piquer, enfoncer (**sth into sth** qch dans qch), planter, fixer (**sth on a spike** qch sur une pointe); **to s. a pin into sth** enfoncer une épingle dans qch; **she stuck the spade into the ground** elle a planté la bêche dans le sol; **to s. pigs** chasser le sanglier à l'épieu

2 *Fam (put)* mettre; **to s. one's hat on one's head** mettre *ou* planter son chapeau sur sa tête; **s. it in your pocket** fourrez-le dans votre poche; **s. it in the corner** collez ça dans le coin; **s. it on the table** mettez ça sur la table

3 *(attach with glue, sticky tape)* coller; **to s. sth on(to) sth** coller qch à *ou* sur qch; **their trunk was stuck all over with labels** leur malle était couverte d'étiquettes

4 *Br Fam (endure)* supporter, endurer; **to s. it** tenir le coup, tenir bon; **I can't s. it any longer** je n'en peux plus; **I can't s. him** je ne peux pas le sentir

5 *(in horticulture) (peas etc)* ramer; *(plants)* mettre des tuteurs à

6 to be stuck *(unable to move)* être coincé; *(in mud etc)* être embourbé; *(mentally, in a problem etc)* être bloqué *ou* en panne; **to get stuck in a bog** s'embourber dans un marécage; **he got his head stuck** sa tête est restée coincée; **I got stuck on the last question** j'ai séché sur la dernière question; **there's something stuck in the pipe** il y a quelque chose de coincé dans le tuyau; **here I am**

stuck in hospital for six weeks me voilà cloué à l'hôpital pour six semaines; **I was stuck at Heathrow for six hours** j'ai été bloqué six heures à Heathrow; **to be stuck in a job** être coincé dans un emploi; **the book's finished but I'm stuck for a title** le livre est fini mais je ne trouve pas de titre; **stuck for money** à court d'argent; *Fam* **I'm stuck with it/him** *(can't get rid of)* je ne peux pas m'en débarrasser; *Fam* **we're stuck with it** *(decision etc)* il faut s'y résigner

7 *Fam* **you can s. your job** ton boulot tu peux te le mettre où je pense; **he can s. his money!** son fric, il peut se le mettre où je pense!; **s. it!** va te faire voir!

VI 1 the point was sticking through the lining la pointe avait percé la doublure; **don't leave the spade sticking in the ground** ne laisse pas la pelle plantée dans le sol

2 *(adhere)* (se) coller, s'attacher, tenir (**to** à); *Culin (of rice etc)* attacher; **the stamp won't s.** le timbre ne colle pas; **the name stuck** ce nom leur/lui/*etc* est resté

3 *(of key, drawer, mechanism)* (se) coincer; *(in sand, bog etc)* s'enfoncer; *Aut (of valve, cut-out)* rester collé; *Fig* **the words stuck in his throat** les mots lui restèrent dans la gorge; **it sticks in my throat** *(of situation, sb's arrogance etc)* c'est dur à digérer; **to s. fast** *(of boat)* s'enliser; **the lift has stuck** l'ascenseur est coincé

➤➤ **s. deodorant** déodorant *m* en stick; **s. figure** personnage *m* stylisé; **s. insect** phasme *m*; *TV* **s. mike** micro *m* tenu à la main

➤ **stick around** VI *Fam (wait)* attendre; *(stay)* rester

➤ **stick at** VT INSEP **1** *(persevere with)* s'acharner à (faire); **s. at it!** persévérez!

2 *(stop in face of)* **to s. at nothing** ne reculer devant rien

➤ **stick by** VT INSEP **1** *(remain loyal to)* **to s. by a friend** ne pas abandonner un ami

2 *(continue to affirm)* maintenir; **I s. by what I said** je maintiens ce que j'ai dit

➤ **stick down** VT SEP **1** *Fam (put down)* **s. it down anywhere** mettez-le *ou* collez-le n'importe où; **to s. sth down in a notebook** inscrire qch sur un carnet

2 *(with glue) (envelope)* coller

➤ **stick in** VT SEP **1** *(with glue)* coller

2 *Fam (put in)* mettre, *Fam* coller; *(knife etc)* enfoncer

3 *Fam* **to get stuck in** *(start working)* s'y mettre; *(start eating)* se mettre à manger; **to get stuck into sth** *(work etc)* se mettre à qch; *(food)* se mettre à manger qch; **let's get stuck in!** allons, on s'y met!

VI 1 *(of knife etc)* s'enfoncer; **she threw the knife at the wall and it stuck in** elle a lancé le couteau contre le mur et il s'y est planté

2 *Fam (persevere)* **just s. in there!** tenez bon!

➤ **stick on** VT SEP *(stamp etc)* coller, fixer; *Sl* **to s. one on sb** *(hit)* coller *ou* ficher un marron à qn; *Fam* **to be stuck on sb** être fou de qn; *Fam* **he is stuck on the idea** il s'enthousiasme pour cette idée

VI *(adhere)* adhérer; *(to stay stuck on)* rester collé

➤ **stick out** VT SEP **1** *(cause to protrude)* faire dépasser, sortir; **to s. out one's tongue** tirer la langue; **to s. out one's hand** tendre la main; **to s. out one's chest** bomber la poitrine; **he stuck his head out (of the window)** il sortit la tête (par la fenêtre); *Fam* **to s. one's neck out** prendre des risques (**for sb** pour qn)

2 *Fam* **to s. it out** *(persevere)* persévérer

VI 1 *(protrude)* faire saillie, ressortir; **to s. out** dépasser (**beyond sth** de qch); **his ears s. out** il a les oreilles décollées; **her teeth s. out** elle a les dents qui avancent

2 *Fam (be noticeable)* se voir, se remarquer; **the way she dresses makes her s. out** la manière dont elle s'habille fait qu'elle ne passe

pas inaperçue; **it sticks out a mile** c'est clair comme le jour; **it sticks out like a sore thumb** ça détonne, ça jure

➤ **stick out for** VT INSEP *Fam (insist on)* **to s. out for sth** s'obstiner à demander qch

➤ **stick to** VT INSEP **1** *(adhere to)* coller à; **the rice had stuck to the pan** le riz avait collé *ou* attaché à la casserole; **her shirt stuck to her back** elle avait la chemise collée au dos; **the name stuck to him** ce nom lui est resté; **to s. to sb like a limpet** *or* **like a leech** *or* **like glue** se cramponner *ou* s'accrocher à qn, *Fam* coller qn

2 *(remain true to)* **to s. to one's promise** tenir sa promesse; **s. to it!** *(don't give in)* persévérez!; *Fam* **to s. to one's guns** ne pas en démordre; **to s. to an opinion** maintenir une opinion, ne pas démordre d'une opinion

3 *(restrict oneself to)* **to s. to the facts** s'en tenir aux faits; **to s. to the point** ne pas s'écarter de la question; **to s. to the text** serrer le texte de près

4 *(continue to affirm)* **I s. to what I said** je maintiens ce que j'ai dit; **she's sticking to her version of what happened** elle maintient sa version des faits; **that's my story and I'm sticking to it** c'est ma version et je m'y tiens

5 *(keep)* **s. to what you've got!** contente-toi de ce que tu as!

6 *(not leave)* **to s. to one's post** rester à son poste; **he sticks to his room** il ne sort pas de sa chambre

➤ **stick together** VI **1** *(with glue etc)* être collé

2 *(of friends etc)* **it's amazing they've stuck together** c'est incroyable qu'ils soient restés ensemble; **they always s. together** ils sont inséparables; *(show solidarity)* ils sont toujours solidaires

VT SEP coller (ensemble)

➤ **stick up** VT SEP **1** *Fam (erect) (fence)* ériger; *(signpost)* mettre, planter

2 *Sl (raise)* **s. 'em up!** haut les mains!

3 *Fam (attach to wall etc) (notice, poster etc)* afficher

4 *Fam* **to s. up a bank** attaquer une banque à main armée

VI *(point upwards)* se dresser; **his hair's sticking up** il est ébouriffé; **an overturned table with its legs sticking up in the air** une table à l'envers avec les pieds en l'air

➤ **stick up for** VT INSEP *(defend)* prendre la défense de, soutenir; **to s. up for one's rights** défendre ses droits; **she can s. up for herself** elle peut se défendre toute seule

➤ **stick with** VT INSEP **1** *(remain loyal to)* rester fidèle à

2 *(stay near)* rester avec; **the other runners couldn't s. with him** les autres coureurs ne pouvaient pas le suivre

3 *(persevere with) (English, tennis etc)* continuer; **to s. with doing sth** continuer à faire qch; **I'm sticking with my old car for now** je garde ma vieille voiture pour le moment

sticker ['stɪkər] N **1** *(label)* étiquette *f* gommée; *Am Fam (poster)* affiche *f*; *Am Fam (election poster)* affiche électorale **2** *Fam (determined person)* personne *f* persévérante; **she's a s.** elle ne manque pas de persévérance

stickiness ['stɪkɪnɪs] N *(of substance, hands etc)* moiteur *f*; *(of product)* nature *f* gluante *ou* collante

sticking ['stɪkɪŋ] ADJ

➤➤ *Br* **s. plaster** pansement *m* adhésif, sparadrap *m*; *Fig* **s. point** point *m* de désaccord, point de friction

stick-in-the-mud *Fam* N **he's an old s.** *(killjoy)* c'est un rabat-joie; *(fogey)* c'est un vieux réac

ADJ *(attitude, person etc) (killjoy)* rabat-joie *inv*; *(fogey)* réac

stickleback ['stɪklbæk] N *(fish)* épinoche *f*

stickler ['stɪklər] N **to be a s. for discipline** être à cheval sur la discipline

stick-on ADJ *(label)* adhésif

➤➤ **s. soles** semelles *fpl* autocollantes

stick-up N *Fam* attaque *f* à main armée, braquage *m*; **this is a s.!** ceci est un hold-up!

stickweed ['stɪkwiːd] N *Bot* jacobée *f*

sticky ['stɪkɪ] ADJ **1** *(substance, hands)* poisseux, gluant; *(paper etc)* collant, adhésif; *(climate)* moite; **to have s. fingers** avoir les doigts poisseux; *Fam (be a thief)* être voleur; **s. weather** temps *m* lourd; *Br Fig Fam* **to be on a s. wicket** être dans une situation difficile **2** *Fam (awkward) (problem, situation)* difficile; **is he being s. about it?** est-ce qu'il fait des histoires (à ce sujet)?; **he'll come to a s. end** il finira mal

➤➤ *Fam* **s. bun** petit pain *m* sucré; *Comput* **s. key** touche *f* à auto-maintien; **s. label** étiquette *f* autocollante, étiquette gommée; **s. tape** ruban *m* adhésif; **s. toffee pudding** = pudding *m* au caramel cuit à la vapeur

stickybeak ['stɪkɪbiːk] *Austr Fam* N fouineur, -euse, fouinard, -arde
VI fouiner

stiff [stɪf] ADJ **1** *(rigid, hard)* raide, rigide, dur; *(brush)* dur; *(person, manner)* raide, guindé; *(stubborn)* inflexible, obstiné; *(style)* guindé, empesé; *Fin (market, commodity)* ferme; **s. joint** articulation *f* ankylosée; **to grow s.** *(of joint)* s'ankyloser; **to be quite s.** *(with sitting still)* être engourdi; *(after exercise)* être tout courbaturé; *(through lack of exercise)* être raide, manquer de souplesse; **he is very s.** *(formal)* il est d'un abord difficile; *Fam* **exams scare me s.** j'ai une peur bleue des examens; **I was bored s.** je m'ennuyais à mourir; **I was frozen s.** j'étais frigorifié; **a s. smile** un sourire forcé; **book bound in s. covers** livre relié en carton; **s. neck** torticolis *m*; **to offer s. resistance** *(of person)* résister opiniâtrement, tenir bon; *(of thing)* tenir bon

2 *(door-handle, hinge etc)* qui fonctionne mal; *(paste, batter)* ferme; *(soil, clay)* dur; **the handle is s.** la poignée est dure; *Naut* **s. breeze** forte brise *f*

3 *(exam)* difficile; **I sent them a s. letter** je leur ai envoyé une lettre bien sentie; **s. price** prix *m* élevé; **s. sentence** peine *f* sévère; **you need a s. drink** tu as besoin d'un remontant; **a s. whisky** un whisky bien tassé; **that's a bit s.!** *(going too far)* c'est un peu fort!

4 *Br Fam (full)* plein (à craquer); **the place was s. with men in suits** l'endroit était plein de messieurs en costume

5 *Am Fam (drunk)* bourré, rond

N **1** *Sl (corpse)* macchabée *m* **2** *Am Fam (tramp)* clodo *mf*; *(stupid person)* nul *m*, nulle *f*; *(ordinary working man)* prolo *m*
VT *Sl (kill)* buter

stiffen ['stɪf(ə)n] VT **1** *(wall, beam, plate etc)* renforcer; *(with starch) (collar etc)* empeser; **age has stiffened his joints** l'âge lui a raidi les articulations; **this action stiffened their resolve** cette action a raffermi leur résolution **2** *(paste)* rendre ferme, donner de la consistance à; *(drink)* corser **3** *(exam, test)* rendre plus difficile

VI **1** *(become rigid)* (se) raidir, devenir raide; *(of person)* se raidir; **opposition is stiffening** l'opposition se durcit **2** *(of paste etc)* devenir ferme, prendre de la consistance; *Naut (of wind)* fraîchir

stiffener ['stɪf(ə)nər] N **1** *(in shoe)* contrefort *m*; *(in collar)* baleine *f* (de col) **2** *Fam (drink)* remontant *m*

stiffening ['stɪf(ə)nɪŋ] N **1** *(action)* raidissement *m*, renforcement *m*; *(of resistance)* durcissement *m*; **s. of the joints** ankylose *f* **2** *(for cloth)* amidon *m*

stiffly ['stɪflɪ] ADV (to bow) avec raideur; (to answer, greet etc) avec froideur; (to resist) obstinément

stiff-necked [-nekt] ADJ (stubborn) obstiné, entêté

stiffness ['stɪfnɪs] N 1 (of limbs, beam etc) raideur f, rigidité f; (of spring etc) dureté f; Fin (of market) fermeté f; s. of the legs (after exercise) courbatures fpl dans les jambes; (through lack of exercise) raideur, manque m de souplesse; (after sitting) engourdissement m des jambes; s. of manner raideur, air m guindé 2 (of paste) fermeté f, consistance f, (of soil) dureté f, fermeté 3 (of price) montant m élevé; (of exam) difficulté f

stiffy ['stɪfɪ] N Sl to have a s. (erection) triquer, avoir la trique

stifle ['staɪf(ə)l] VT (person) étouffer, suffoquer; (shouts, cries, yawn, laugh) étouffer; (rebellion) réprimer; (cry) retenir
VI suffoquer, étouffer

stifled ['staɪf(ə)ld] ADJ (cry etc) étouffé; with a s. voice d'une voix éteinte

stifling ['staɪflɪŋ] ADJ étouffant, suffocant; (sensation) d'étouffement; it's s. here! on étouffe ici!

stigma, pl **stigmas, stigmata** ['stɪgmə, -əz, 'stɪgmətə, stɪg'mɑːtə] N 1 (pl usu **stigmas**) (social disgrace) honte f; there is no longer any s. in being a single mother il n'y a plus de honte à être mère célibataire 2 stigmata (of saint) stigmates mpl 3 (pl **stigmata**) Biol (of insect etc) stigmate m 4 (pl **stigmas**) Bot (of pistil) stigmate m

stigmatic [stɪg'mætɪk] N Rel stigmatisé, -ée

stigmatize ['stɪgmətaɪz] VT stigmatiser; stigmatized as a coward marqué comme lâche; stigmatized as illegitimate entaché de bâtardise

stile[1] [staɪl] N 1 (in fence, hedge etc) échalier m 2 (turnstile) tourniquet m

stile[2] N Constr (of door etc) montant m

stiletto, pl **stilettos, stilettoes** [stɪ'letəʊ, -əʊz] N 1 (dagger) stylet m 2 s. heels, stilettos talons mpl aiguille 3 Sewing etc poinçon m

still[1] [stɪl] ADJ (motionless) immobile; (calm) calme; (silent) silencieux; (wine) non mousseux; (orange juice, mineral water) non gazeux; s. water eau f dormante; Prov s. waters run deep il faut se méfier de l'eau qui dort
ADV to keep s. ne pas bouger, se tenir ou rester tranquille; sit s.! restez ou tenez-vous tranquille!; to stand s. (not move) ne pas bouger, se tenir immobile; (of science etc) ne pas faire de progrès; her heart stood s. son cœur cessa de battre
N 1 in the s. of the night dans le calme de la nuit 2 Cin photo f (tirée du film)
VT (person) tranquilliser, calmer, apaiser; to s. sb's fears calmer les craintes de qn
▸▸ TV, Cin s. frame image f fixe; s. life nature f morte

still[2] ADV 1 (up to now) encore; he is s. here il est encore ou toujours ici; he's s. not here il n'est toujours pas là; it's stuck – s.? c'est coincé – encore?; I s. have 500 euros il me reste 500 euros, j'ai encore 500 euros; I have s. to thank you il me reste à vous remercier; it s. remains to be seen ça reste à voir; I s. can't see what was wrong with my suggestion je ne vois toujours pas en quoi ma suggestion était mauvaise; in spite of his faults, I love him s. malgré ses défauts, je l'aime toujours
2 (even) encore; s. more/less encore plus/ moins; s. more worrying ... plus inquiétant encore ...; if you can reduce the price s. further si vous pouvez réduire encore le prix
3 (nonetheless, all the same) pourtant; he's s. the boss c'est pourtant lui le patron; but

that s. doesn't justify ... mais cela ne justifie pourtant pas ...; OK, but I s. think we ought to do it d'accord, mais je pense qu'on devrait quand même le faire; it s. won't make me change my mind je ne vais pas changer d'avis pour autant; but s., if she **did** accept, wouldn't it be marvellous! peut-être, mais si elle acceptait, ce serait formidable!
CONJ cependant, pourtant, néanmoins, toutefois; the fact remains that ... toujours est-il que ..., il n'en reste pas moins vrai que ...; s., what else could I have done? qu'aurais-je pu faire d'autre, enfin?

still[3] N (for distilling) alambic m

stillbirth ['stɪlbɜːθ] N enfant m mort-né; the number of stillbirths la mortinatalité

stillborn ['stɪlbɔːn] ADJ mort-né, -ée, pl mort-nés, -ées; Fig (project etc) avorté, mort-né

stillness ['stɪlnɪs] N tranquillité f, (of person) calme m, repos m; (of place, atmosphere) tranquillité, paix f

stilt [stɪlt] N 1 (for walking) échasse f; to walk on stilts marcher sur des échasses 2 Constr pilotis m

stilted ['stɪltɪd] ADJ (style, manner etc) guindé, raide

Stilton® ['stɪlt(ə)n] N fromage m de Stilton, stilton m

stimulant ['stɪmjʊlənt] N (tea, coffee etc) excitant m; Med stimulant m; (for heart) tonicardiaque m
ADJ ATTRIB it has a s. effect ça a un effet stimulant

stimulate ['stɪmjʊleɪt] VT 1 (person, enthusiasm) stimuler; (mind, appetite etc) aiguiser; Ind (production) encourager, activer 2 Med (liver etc) stimuler

stimulating ['stɪmjʊleɪtɪŋ] ADJ (competition, work) stimulant; (music) entraînant; (book) stimulant, qui donne à penser; it's s. to work with talented people c'est stimulant de travailler avec des gens qui ont du talent

stimulation [stɪmjʊ'leɪʃən] N stimulation f, to need s. avoir besoin d'être stimulé
▸▸ s. marketing marketing m de stimulation

stimulative ['stɪmjʊlətɪv] ADJ stimulant
N stimulant m

stimulus, pl **stimuli** ['stɪmjʊləs, -aɪ] N 1 (incentive) encouragement m; to give a s. to trade donner un coup de fouet au commerce 2 Physiol stimulus m; to apply a s. to a muscle exciter un muscle
▸▸ Physiol s. response réponse f stimulée

sting [stɪŋ] N 1 (of bee) dard m, aiguillon m; (of scorpion) aiguillon; (of nettle) poil m piquant
2 (injury) (from bee etc) piqûre f, Fig (of joke) pointe f, (of wound) douleur f cuisante; (of attack) vigueur f, mordant m; with the s. of the wind in our faces le visage fouetté par le vent; joke with a s. in it plaisanterie qui comporte une pointe; to have a s. in the tail (of story etc) avoir une fin inattendue; Lit the s. of remorse l'aiguillon du remords; Fig to take the s. out of sth affaiblir qch
3 esp Am Sl (con trick) arnaque f, (by police) coup m monté
VT (pt, pp stung [stʌŋ]) 1 (of bees, nettles etc) piquer; a bee stung her finger ou stung her on the finger une abeille lui a piqué le doigt; that reply stung her (to the quick) cette réponse l'a piquée (au vif); smoke that stings the eyes fumée qui picote les yeux; this stung him into action cela l'a incité à agir
2 Fam (cheat) to s. sb for £50 rouler qn en lui faisant payer 50 livres, dépouiller qn de 50 livres; to get stung essuyer le coup de fusil; could I s. you for a tenner? (borrow) est-

ce que je peux te taper dix livres?
VI (of parts of the body) cuire; (of cut, graze) picoter, brûler; (of bees, nettles etc) piquer; my eyes were stinging les yeux me brûlaient; this is going to s. a bit ça va faire un peu mal; Fig that stung! (of remark etc) c'est blessant!

stingily ['stɪndʒɪlɪ] ADV mesquinement, chichement

stinginess ['stɪndʒɪnɪs] N (of person) pingrerie f, (of portion etc) insuffisance f

stinging ['stɪŋɪŋ] ADJ (pain etc) cuisant; (blow, answer) cinglant; s. remark remarque f blessante
▸▸ s. nettle ortie f

stingray ['stɪŋreɪ] N (fish) pastenague f

stingy ['stɪndʒɪ] ADJ (person) chiche, pingre; a s. portion une portion peu généreuse; to be s. with one's money être avare (avec son argent); to be s. with the cream lésiner sur la crème

stink [stɪŋk] N 1 (smell) puanteur f 2 Fam (trouble) grabuge m; to raise ou kick up a s. faire un esclandre ou du grabuge; there'll be a s.! il va y avoir du grabuge!
VI (pt stank [stæŋk], stunk [stʌŋk]; pp stunk) (of place, person etc) puer, empester; it stinks in here ça pue ici; to s. of garlic puer ou empester l'ail; Fam s. of money puer le fric; Fam this film/book stinks! ce film/livre est nul!; the whole business stinks of corruption tout ça sent la corruption à plein nez
▸ stink out VT SEP (fill with bad smell) (room etc) empester

stinkbomb ['stɪŋkbɒm] N boule f puante

stinker ['stɪŋkər] N Fam 1 to be a s. (unpleasant, difficult thing) être vachement dur, être coton; (worthless thing) être nul, être merdique; the algebra paper was a s. on a eu une composition d'algèbre carabinée; I had a s. of a cold j'avais un rhume carabiné 2 (person) individu m méprisable, salaud m

stinkhorn ['stɪŋkhɔːn] N Bot phallus m impudique

stinking ['stɪŋkɪŋ] ADJ 1 (smelly) puant 2 Fam (disgusting) dégueulasse; (worthless) nul, merdique; a s. cold un rhume carabiné
ADV Fam to be s. rich puer le fric

stinko ['stɪŋkəʊ] ADJ Am Fam (drunk) pété, bourré

stinkpot ['stɪŋkpɒt] N Old-fashioned Fam (unpleasant person) salaud m; what a s.! (smelly) qu'est-ce qu'il pue!

stint [stɪnt] N 1 (period) temps m, période f, (amount of work) besogne f assignée; to do one's daily s. accomplir sa tâche quotidienne; if you do a regular s. (with the weights/your clarinet) si tu travailles régulièrement (tes haltères/ta clarinette); do you want a s. at the wheel? est-ce que tu veux prendre un peu le volant?; I did the last s. c'est moi qui ai pris le dernier tour; after a long s. at the keyboard après être resté longtemps au clavier; she had a two-year s. in the army elle a fait deux ans dans l'armée 2 (restriction) restriction f, without s. sans limite; (to spend money) sans compter
VT (money, effort) épargner; don't s. the cream/whisky ne lésine pas sur la crème/le whisky; to s. oneself se sacrifier; to s. sb of sth priver qn de qch, refuser qch à qn; to give without stinting donner sans compter; he doesn't s. his praise il n'est pas avare de compliments
▸ stint on VT INSEP lésiner sur

stipend ['staɪpend] N traitement m, appointements mpl (d'un ecclésiastique, d'un magistrat)

stipendiary [staɪ'pendjərɪ] ADJ qui reçoit des appointements fixes

N *Br* juge *m* d'un tribunal d'instance *(à Londres et dans les grandes villes)*
▸▸*Br* **s. magistrate** juge *m* d'un tribunal d'instance *(à Londres et dans les grandes villes)*

stipple ['stɪp(ə)l] *Art* VT *(drawing)* faire en pointillé
VI pointiller

stipulate ['stɪpjʊleɪt] VT *(date, condition etc)* stipuler; **to s. (in writing) that ...** stipuler *(par écrit)* que ...; **within the period stipulated** dans le délai prescrit; **to s. the terms of a contract** fixer les conditions d'un contrat

stipulation [stɪpjʊ'leɪʃən] N condition *f*; *Law* stipulation *f*; **the only s. I make is that ...** la seule condition que je pose, c'est que ...; **on the s. that ...** à condition que ...

stir¹ [stɜːr] N **1** *(act of stirring liquid etc)* **to give sth a s.** remuer *ou* tourner qch **2** *(agitation)* agitation *f*, émoi *m*; **there was a great s.** il y eut un grand remue-ménage; **to make or cause a s.** faire du bruit, faire sensation; **the news caused a s. in the town** la nouvelle a mis la ville en émoi
VT **(-rr-)** *(set in motion) (leaves, water)* remuer, faire bouger; *(tea etc)* remuer, tourner; *(move emotionally) (person)* émouvoir, remuer; *(emotions)* agiter; *(curiosity, interest)* éveiller; *Culin (sauce, cream etc)* tourner; *(mixture)* agiter; *(fire)* activer, attiser; **not a breath stirs the leaves** pas un souffle ne remue *ou* ne fait trembler les feuilles; **to s. sb to pity** provoquer la compassion de qn; **events that s. the soul** événements qui remuent l'âme; **these words stirred her to action** ces mots l'ont fait agir; *Fam* **s. yourself or your stumps!** remue-toi!; *Br Fam* **to s. it** *(make trouble)* fomenter la discorde
VI **1** *(move)* bouger, remuer; **don't s. from here** ne bougez pas d'ici; **he didn't s. out of the house** il n'est pas sorti de la maison; **he hasn't stirred yet** *(is still in bed)* il n'est pas encore levé; **to s. in one's sleep** remuer dans son sommeil; **the audience were stirring in their seats** les spectateurs s'agitaient dans leur fauteuil
2 *Br Fam (set people against each other)* semer la zizanie
▸ **stir up** VT SEP **1** *(of wind)* remuer, faire bouger; *(fire)* ranimer, activer **2** *(rebellion, dissent)* fomenter **3** *(workers, crowd etc)* inciter à la révolte; **to s. up hatred** attiser les haines; **to s. up trouble** fomenter la discorde; **to s. things up** semer la zizanie

stir² N *Sl (prison)* taule *f*; **in s.** en taule

stir-crazy ADJ *esp Am Sl* fou, *f* folle, détraqué *(à cause d'une longue période de détention)*

stir-fry *Culin* N sauté *m*
VT faire sauter *ou* frire rapidement; **stir-fried vegetables** légumes *mpl* sautés

stirrer ['stɜːrər] N **1** *Br Fam (person who provokes trouble)* personne *f* qui sème la zizanie **2** *Chem, Phot (device)* agitateur *m*

stirring ['stɜːrɪŋ] ADJ *(moving)* émouvant; **s. times** une époque passionnante; **it's s. stuff** c'est passionnant
N **1** *Br Fam (troublemaking)* **s. is her speciality** semer la zizanie, c'est sa spécialité **2** *stirrings (beginnings)* frémissement *m*; **the first stirrings of passion** les premiers frémissements de la passion; **the first stirrings of revolt/resistance** les premiers signes de la révolte/de la résistance

stirrup ['stɪrəp] N **1** *Horseriding* étrier *m*; **to put one's feet in the stirrups** chausser les étriers **2** *Med* **stirrups** étriers *mpl*
▸▸**s. cup** coup *m* de l'étrier; **s. leather** étrivière *f*, **s. pump** seau-pompe *m*, *pl* seaux-pompes; **s. strap** étrivière *f*

stitch [stɪtʃ] N **1** *Sewing* point *m*; *(in knitting, crochet)* maille *f*, *Surg* (point de) suture *f*,

(machine) s. piqûre *f* (à la machine); **to put a few stitches in a garment** faire un point à un vêtement; *Fam* **he hasn't got a dry s. on him** il est trempé jusqu'aux os; *Fam* **without a s. on** nu comme un ver; **to drop a s.** *(in knitting, crochet)* sauter une maille; **dropped s.** *(in knitting, crochet)* maille coulée; **to make a s.** *(in knitting, crochet)* faire une maille; **to put stitches in a wound** faire une suture à *ou* suturer une plaie, recoudre une plaie; **she had to have ten stitches** ils ont dû lui faire dix points de suture; **when are you having the stitches out?** quand allez-vous vous faire retirer vos points de suture?; *Prov* **a s. in time saves nine** un point à temps en épargne cent, un point fait à temps en vaut mille
2 *(pain)* point *m* de côté; **I've got a s.** j'ai un point de côté
3 *Fam* **we were in stitches** *(laughing)* on se tordait de rire; **his story/the film had us in stitches** son histoire était tordante/le film était tordant *ou* à se tordre de rire; **he had us in stitches** il nous a fait (nous) tordre de rire
4 *Am Fam (amusing person, thing)* **to be a s.** être tordant *ou* crevant
VT **1** *(clothing)* coudre; *(leather)* piquer; **to (machine) s.** piquer (à la machine); **to s. sth onto sth** coudre qch sur qch **2** *Surg (wound)* suturer **3** *(in bookbinding) (book)* brocher
▸ **stitch down** VT SEP coudre; *(repair)* recoudre
▸ **stitch up** VT SEP **1** *(repair by sewing) (bag etc)* recoudre **2** *(of surgeon) (person, wound)* recoudre; **we'll soon have you stitched up** on va vous faire quelques points de suture et ce sera fini **3** *Sl (falsely incriminate)* faire porter le chapeau à; **I've been stitched up** on m'a fait porter le chapeau

stitching ['stɪtʃɪŋ] N **1** *(act) Sewing* couture *f*, *(in leather)* piqûre *f*, *(ornamental)* broderie *f*, *Surg* suture *f*, *(in bookbinding)* brochage *m*, brochure *f* **2** *Sewing (stitches)* points *mpl*, piqûres *fpl*; **the s.'s coming undone** les piqûres se sont défaites

St John's wort [wɜːt] N millepertuis *m*

stoat [stəʊt] N hermine *f*

stoater ['stəʊtər] N *Scot Fam* **1** *(excellent thing)* **what a s. of a goal!** quel but d'enfer!; **we had a s. of an idea** on a eu une idée géniale **2** *(beautiful person)* canon *m*; **his new girlfriend's a s.!** sa nouvelle copine est canon!

stochastic [stɒ'kæstɪk] ADJ stochastique

stock [stɒk] N **1** *(supply)* provision *f*, approvisionnement *m*, stock *m*; *(in forestry)* peuplement *m*; *Com* marchandises *fpl* (en magasin), stock; *Ind* stock; **to lay in a s. of food** faire provision de vivres, s'approvisionner en vivres; **old s.** fonds *mpl* de boutique; **surplus s.** surplus *mpl*; **stocks are low** il y a peu de marchandises en stock; **while stocks last** jusqu'à épuisement des stocks; **to take s.** faire *ou* dresser l'inventaire; *Fig* faire le bilan; *Fig* **to take s. of sb** évaluer qn; *(by looking at)* toiser qn; **to take s. of the situation** faire le bilan de la situation, faire le point de la situation; **in s.** en magasin, en stock; **to be out of s.** *(of goods)* manquer en magasin; *(of book)* être épuisé; **we're out of s.** nous sommes en rupture de stock; *Rail* **locomotive s.** effectif *m ou* dotation *f* en locomotives; *Cin (film)* **s.** film *m* vierge, films *ou* bandes *fpl* vierges
2 *(livestock)* bétail *m*; **grazing s.** bétail, animaux *mpl* sur pied; **fat s.** bétail de boucherie
3 *Fin* fonds *mpl*, valeurs *fpl*, actions *fpl*; **government s.** fonds d'État, fonds *ou* effets *mpl* publics, rentes *fpl* (sur l'État); **stocks and shares** valeurs mobilières, valeurs de Bourse, titres *mpl*; *Fig* **her s. is going up/down** sa cote est en hausse/en baisse

4 *(of tree) (trunk)* tronc *m*; *(stump)* bloc *m*; *(in horticulture)* sujet *m*, ente *f*, porte-greffe *m*, *pl* porte-greffe(s); *Fig (lineage)* souche *f*; **he's of German s.** il est d'origine allemande
5 *(of rifle)* fût *m*, bois *m*, monture *f*, *(of whip)* manche *m*; *(of plough)* macheron *m*; *Naut (of anchor)* jas *m*
6 *Naut* **stocks** cales *fpl*; **to be on the stocks** être sur cales, être en construction; *Fig (of new novel etc)* être en chantier
7 **stocks** *(for punishment)* pilori *m*
8 *Ind (raw materials)* matières *fpl* premières
9 *Culin* bouillon *m*; **beef/chicken/vegetable s.** bouillon *m* de bœuf/poulet/légumes
10 *(plant)* matthiole *f*, giroflée *fdes* jardins
11 *(neckwear)* col-cravate *m* (d'équitation), *pl* cols-cravates; *(of English clergy)* plastron *m* en soie noire
ADJ *(conventional)* habituel; **he has three s. speeches** il a, en tout et pour tout, trois discours qu'il ressort périodiquement; **s. answer** réponse *f* classique; **s. phrase** expression *f* toute faite, expression consacrée
VT **1** *(supply) (shop)* approvisionner (**with** de, en); *(farm)* monter en bétail; *(house)* approvisionner (**with** de); *(pond)* empoissonner; *(forest)* peupler (**with** de); **this shop is well stocked** ce magasin est bien approvisionné; **to have a well-stocked cellar** avoir une cave bien remplie
2 *(have, keep in stock) (goods)* avoir *ou* tenir *ou* garder en magasin *ou* en dépôt, stocker; **I don't s. this article** je ne vends pas cet article; **we s. all leading makes of furniture** nous faisons toutes les grandes marques de meubles
▸▸**s. availability** disponibilité *f* en stock; **s. book** livre *m* des inventaires; **s. breeder** éleveur *m*; **s. breeding** élevage *m*; *Fin* **s. check** contrôle *m* des stocks; *Theat* **s. company** troupe *f* à demeure *(dans une ville)*; **s. control** contrôle *m* des stocks; **s. control system** système *m* de contrôle de stocks; *Culin* **s. cube** bouillon *m* Kub®; **S. Exchange** Bourse *(de Londres)*; **s. exchange** Bourse; **s. farm** élevage (de bétail); **s. farmer** éleveur; **s. farming** élevage (de bétail) *(activité)*; *Cin, TV* **s. footage** séquences *fpl* d'archives; **s. index** indice *m* de la Bourse; **s. in hand** marchandises en stock, marchandises en magasin; *Com* **s. in trade** marchandises (en magasin), stock; *Fig* **the double entendre was her s. in trade** l'ambiguïté, c'était sa spécialité; *Com* **s. issued docket** bon *m* de sortie; *Com* **s. keeper** magasinier *m*; *Com* **s. keeping** tenue *f* des stocks; **s. level** niveau *m* de stock; **s. list** *St Exch* cours *mpl* de la Bourse; *Com* inventaire *m*, inventaire des stocks; **s. market** Bourse (des valeurs), marché *m* financier; **s. market gamble** spéculation *f* boursière; **s. market crash** krach *m* boursier; **s. market value** valeur *f* en Bourse; **s. outage** rupture *f* de stock; *Theat* **s. piece, s. play** pièce *f* de *ou* du répertoire; *Com* **s. received docket** bon d'entrée; **s. replacement** renouvellement *m* des stocks; *Austr* **s. rider** cow-boy *m*, *pl* cow-boys; **s. sheet** fiche *f* de stock; *TV* **s. shot** image *f ou* document *m* d'archives; **s. shrinkage** coulage *m* de stock; *Com* **s. take** inventaire *m* des stocks; **s. turnaround, s. turnover** rotation *f* des stocks
▸ **stock up** VI *(build up a stock)* faire des provisions *ou* des réserves; **to s. up with sth** bien s'approvisionner en *ou* de qch
VT SEP *(larder, cellar)* approvisionner

stockade [stɒ'keɪd] N **1** *(fort)* palissade *f*, palanque *f* **2** *Am Mil (prison)* bloc *m*; **to be in the s.** être au bloc
VT palissader, palanquer

stockboy ['stɒkbɔɪ] N magasinier *m*

stockbroker ['stɒkbrəʊkər] N agent *m* de change
▸▸*Br Fam* **the s. belt** la banlieue aisée

stockbroking ['stɒkbrəʊkɪŋ] N commerce m des valeurs en Bourse

stock-car N Sport stock-car m
▸▸ s. racing course f de stock-cars

stockfish ['stɒkfɪʃ] N stockfisch m, merluche f

stockgirl ['stɒkgɜːl] N magasinière f

stockholder ['stɒkhəʊldər] N Fin actionnaire mf, porteur m ou détenteur m de titres

stockily ['stɒkɪlɪ] ADV s. built trapu

stockiness ['stɒkɪnɪs] N stature f trapue

stockinet(te) [stɒkɪ'net] N Tex wool/cotton s. jersey m de laine/coton

stocking ['stɒkɪŋ] N (garment) bas m; Old-fashioned (knee-length sock) chaussette f; Med elastic ou support s. bas à varices; body s. combinaison f (une pièce)
▸▸ s. filler = petit cadeau m destiné à remplir le 'Christmas stocking' à Noël; s. mask bas (utilisé par un bandit masqué); Knitting s. stitch point m de jersey

stockist ['stɒkɪst] N Com revendeur m; (agent) stockiste m

stockjobber ['stɒkdʒɒbər] N Br St Exch Formerly = avant 1986, intermédiaire mf en Bourse qui traitait directement avec les agents de change et non avec le public

stockman, pl **stockmen** ['stɒkmən] N 1 (man who works with livestock) gardien m de bestiaux; (owner) bouvier m 2 Am (warehouseman) magasinier m

stockpile ['stɒkpaɪl] N (of sugar, ammunition etc) stocks mpl de réserve ou de sécurité; nuclear s. réserve(s) f(pl) d'armements nucléaires
VT (goods) stocker; (arms) entasser, accumuler

stockpiling ['stɒkpaɪlɪŋ] N stockage m, constitution f de réserves; (of nuclear weapons) accumulation f

stockpot ['stɒkpɒt] N Culin marmite f

stockroom ['stɒkruːm] N Com magasin m, réserve f, resserre f

stock-still ADV to stand s. rester (complètement) immobile; he suddenly stood s. soudain, il s'immobilisa

stocktaking ['stɒkteɪkɪŋ] N Com, Ind (établissement m ou levée f d')inventaire m, inventaire des stocks; s. is in February on fait l'inventaire en février

stocky ['stɒkɪ] ADJ trapu; (horse) ragot

stockyard ['stɒkjɑːd] N parc m à bétail ou à bestiaux

stodge [stɒdʒ] N Fam (food) aliment m bourratif, étouffe-chrétien m inv; the s. we get in the canteen les trucs bourratifs qu'on nous sert à la cantine

stodgy ['stɒdʒɪ] ADJ 1 (meal, food) bourratif 2 (book) indigeste; (style) lourd; (person) ennuyeux à force de sérieux, assommant

stogie ['stəʊgɪ] N Am cigare m bon marché

stoic ['stəʊɪk] ADJ, N stoïque mf, Antiq S. stoïcien, -ienne

stoical ['stəʊɪk(ə)l] ADJ stoïque

stoically ['stəʊɪklɪ] ADV stoïquement

stoicism ['stəʊɪsɪz(ə)m] N stoïcisme m

stoke [stəʊk] VT (fire) entretenir; (furnace) alimenter, entretenir le feu de; (steam engine) chauffer le foyer de; Fig Fam the way he stokes his food in la façon dont il engouffre sa nourriture
▸ stoke up VT SEP = stoke
VI 1 Naut pousser les feux; Rail alimenter le feu 2 Fam (eat heavily) bouffer (comme quatre), bâfrer
▸ stoke up on VT INSEP Fam (eat a lot of) se bourrer de

stoker ['stəʊkər] N Rail chauffeur m; Naut mécanicien m; (of blast furnace) chargeur m

STOL [stɒl] N Mil, Aviat (abbr short takeoff and landing) 1 (system) décollage m et atterrissage m courts 2 (aircraft) ADAC m

stole[1] [stəʊl] N 1 Rel étole f 2 (garment) étole f (de vison etc)

stole[2] PT see steal VT, VI

stolen ['stəʊlən] ADJ (car, property etc) volé
PP see steal VT, VI
▸▸ s. goods objets mpl volés; he was charged with receiving s. goods on l'a inculpé de recel (de marchandises volées)

stolid ['stɒlɪd] ADJ flegmatique, impassible; his s. exterior concealed … sous des dehors impassibles, il cachait …

stolidity [stɒ'lɪdɪtɪ] N flegme m

stolidly ['stɒlɪdlɪ] ADV flegmatiquement

stolidness ['stɒlɪdnɪs] N flegme m

stoma, pl **stomata** ['stəʊmə, -ətə] N stomate m

stomach ['stʌmək] N (organ) estomac m; (front of abdomen) ventre m; pain in the s. mal m d'estomac; upset s. troubles mpl de la digestion; Pharm to be taken on an empty s. à prendre à jeun; to drink on an empty s. boire lorsqu'on a l'estomac vide, boire à jeun; to turn sb's s. soulever le cœur à qn, écœurer qn; to have a cast iron s. avoir un estomac à toute épreuve ou d'autruche; an army marches on its s. une armée ne se bat pas le ventre vide; first s. (of ruminants) panse f; to have a large s. (be fat) avoir un gros ventre; Fig to have no s. for sth (not feel like) ne pas se sentir d'humeur à qch; Fig he had no s. for a fight il n'avait pas le cœur à se battre
VT (support) (something) supporter, endurer; (person) supporter; I can't s. it any longer j'en ai plein le dos, j'en ai ras le bol; I can't s. oysters je ne peux pas avaler les huîtres; I can't s.the way he looks at me il a une façon de me regarder qui me débecte
▸▸ s. ache douleurs fpl d'estomac, Fam mal m de ventre; to have s. ache avoir mal au ventre; s. pump pompe f stomacale; s. upset troubles mpl de la digestion

stomp [stɒmp] VI frapper du pied; to s. out of the room quitter la pièce en martelant des pieds; I wish you wouldn't s. around like that j'aimerais que tu arrêtes de marteler des pieds comme ça; he was stomping up and down the room il arpentait la pièce d'un pas lourd; she stomped off elle est partie en tapant des pieds
VT Am Fam (defeat) flanquer une peignée ou une déculottée à

stomping ground ['stɒmpɪŋ] = **stamping ground**

stone [stəʊn] N 1 (piece of rock) pierre f; (pebble) caillou m, -oux; Constr mœllon m, pierre de taille; (gravestone) pierre tombale; not to leave a s. standing tout raser ou démolir; to throw stones at sb lancer des pierres sur ou à qn; Fig who's going to cast the first s. (at him)? qui lui jettera la (première) pierre?; Fig to leave no s. unturned mettre tout en œuvre, remuer ciel et terre (to do sth pour accomplir qch); a s.'s throw from here à deux pas d'ici
2 (precious stone) pierre f, precious stones (in raw state) pierres précieuses; (cut) pierreries fpl, pierres précieuses
3 (material) pierre f (à bâtir); s. coloured beige; s. floor sol m dallé; s. jug cruche f de grès
4 Med calcul m
5 (of fruit) noyau m
6 Br (unit of weight) = 6,348 kg
ADJ Am Fam (absolute, real) véritable, total; she is a s. babe! c'est une supernana! this is turning into a s. drag! ça devient vraiment galère!

VT 1 (fruit) dénoyauter
2 (person) attaquer ou assaillir à coups de pierres, lapider; (as punishment) lapider; (car etc) lancer des pierres contre; to s. sb to death lapider qn (jusqu'à ce que mort s'ensuive); Br Sl s. the crows!, s. me! ça alors!
▸▸ the S. Age l'âge m de (la) pierre; s. axe hache f de pierre; s. cutter (person who cuts blocks) tailleur m ou équarrisseur m de pierres; Zool s. marten fouine f; (jusqu'à la s. saw scie f à pierre ou de carrier; Journ s. sub correcteur m de mise en page

stone-blind ADJ complètement aveugle

stonechat ['stəʊntʃæt] N (bird) traquet m pâtre

stone-cold ADJ froid comme le marbre; the tea is s. ce thé est complètement froid ou glacé
ADV s. sober complètement sobre

stonecrop ['stəʊnkrɒp] N (plant) orpin m

stoned [stəʊnd] ADJ 1 Sl to be s. (on drugs) être pété ou défoncé; Old-fashioned (drunk) être bourré 2 (fruit) dénoyauté

stone-dead ADJ raide mort
ADV raide mort; the blow killed him s. le coup l'a tué instantanément; Fig to kill a proposal s. sonner le glas d'une proposition; the teacher killed French s. for her le professeur l'a complètement dégoûtée du français

stone-deaf ADJ complètement sourd, sourd comme un pot

stoneground ['stəʊngraʊnd] ADJ (flour) à l'ancienne

stonemason ['stəʊnmeɪs(ə)n] N maçon m

stoner ['stəʊnər] N Sl adepte mf de la fumette

stonewall [stəʊn'wɔːl] VI 1 Sport = pratiquer un jeu défensif pour tenir jusqu'à la fin 2 Parl, Fig faire de l'obstruction

stonewalling [stəʊn'wɔːlɪŋ] N 1 Sport jeu m défensif 2 Parl, Fig obstructionnisme m

stoneware ['stəʊnweər] N poterie f de grès

stonewashed ['stəʊnwɒʃt] ADJ (jeans etc) délavé

stonework ['stəʊnwɜːk] N maçonnerie f

stonily ['stəʊnɪlɪ] ADV froidement; (to look at sb) d'un air glacial; (to reply) d'un ton glacial

stoniness ['stəʊnɪnɪs] N 1 (of soil) nature f pierreuse 2 (of heart) dureté f; (of look) froideur f

stoning ['stəʊnɪŋ] N (of person) lapidation f

stonker ['stɒŋkər] N Br Fam 1 (impressive thing) what a s. of a goal! quel but d'enfer!; their latest album's a complete s.! leur dernier album est absolument génial! 2 (large thing) mastodonte m; that new skyscraper is a s.! ce nouveau gratte-ciel est un vrai mastodonte

stonking ['stɒŋkɪŋ] ADJ Br Fam super, génial, -aux; he scored a s. goal il a marqué un but d'enfer

stony ['stəʊnɪ] ADJ 1 (full of, covered in stones) pierreux, rocailleux 2 (hard like stone) dur comme la pierre 3 (lacking in emotion) dur; (reception) froid; (look, stare, silence) glacial, -als ou -aux; s. heart cœur m de glace ou de marbre 4 Br Fam s. broke sans le sou, dans la dèche; I'm s. broke je n'ai pas un sou, je suis fauché (comme les blés)

stony-hearted [-'hɑːtɪd] ADJ au cœur de pierre; to be or remain s. être ou rester de glace ou marbre; he's s. il a un cœur de pierre

stood PT, PP see stand[2] VI, VT

stooge [stuːdʒ] N 1 Theat faire-valoir m inv (d'un comique) 2 Fig, Fam (lackey) larbin m; (dupe) pigeon m, poire f; (idiot) andouille f, crétin, -ine
VI Theat to s. for a comedian servir de faire-valoir à un comique

stook [stuːk] *Agr* N tas *m* de gerbes, moyette *f*

VT mettre en moyettes

stool [stuːl] N 1 *(seat)* tabouret *m*; *(with steps)* escabeau *m*; **folding s.** pliant *m*; **piano s.** tabouret de piano; *Fig* **to fall between two stools** être assis entre deux chaises; **prayer s.** prie-Dieu *m inv* 2 *Med* selles *f* 3 *(in horticulture)*, *Agr* pied *m* mère, plante *f* mère

▸ ▸ *Fam* **s. pigeon** indic *mf*, mouchard, -arde

stoop [stuːp] VI *(bend down)* se pencher, se baisser; *(have bent back)* avoir le dos rond, être voûté; *Fig (abase oneself)* s'abaisser, s'avilir (**to do sth** à *ou* jusqu'à faire qch); *(deign)* daigner (**to do sth** faire qch); *Lit* **to s. to conquer** s'abaisser pour triompher; **she stooped to pick up the pin** elle s'est baissée pour ramasser l'épingle; **he was beginning to s.** il commençait à se voûter; *Fig* **he would s. to anything** c'est un homme prêt à toutes les bassesses; *Fig* **I never thought they'd s. so low as to …** je ne pensais pas qu'ils s'abaisseraient jusqu'à …

VT *(head)* pencher, incliner; *(back)* courber, arrondir

N 1 *(posture)* dos *m* rond, épaules *fpl* voûtées; **to have a s.** avoir le dos rond *ou* les épaules voûtées; **to walk with a s.** marcher les épaules voûtées, marcher voûté 2 *Am (porch)* porche *m (avec perron)*; *(platform)* terrasse *f* surélevée *(devant une maison)*

stooping [stuːpɪŋ] ADJ penché (en avant); *(permanently)* voûté

STOP [stɒp]

| N arrêt 1 ▪ halte 1 ▪ pause 1 |
| ▪ escale 1 ▪ arrêt d'autobus 1 ▪ point 2 |
| VT arrêter 1, 2 ▪ interrompre 1 |
| ▪ cesser 2 ▪ boucher 3 ▪ obstruer 3 |
| VI s'arrêter 1, 2 ▪ stopper 1 ▪ cesser 2 ▪ rester 3 |

N 1 *(halt)* arrêt *m*; *(pause)* arrêt, halte *f*, pause *f*, *Aviat (in flight)* escale *f*; **to put a s. to sth** arrêter *ou* faire cesser qch, mettre fin à qch; **ten minutes' s.** dix minutes d'arrêt; **to come to a s.** s'arrêter; *(of car)* stopper; **to make a s.** faire (une) halte; *(for short period)* faire une pause; **we made four stops along the way** nous nous sommes arrêtés *ou* nous avons fait halte quatre fois en chemin; **the bus/train makes a s. at …** le bus/le train s'arrête à …; **let's have a s. for lunch** faisons une pause pour le déjeuner; **we travelled without a s.** nous avons voyagé sans escale; **we had a s. at the castle on the way back** nous nous sommes arrêtés au château sur le chemin du retour; **(bus) s.** arrêt (d'autobus); **request s.** arrêt facultatif

2 *(full stop)* point *m*; *(in telegram)* stop *m* 3 *Mus (on organ)* jeu *m*, registre *m*; **to pull out a s.** tirer un registre; *Fig Fam* **to pull out all the stops** faire un effort surhumain (**to do sth** pour faire qch)

4 *Carp*, *Tech etc* dispositif *m* de blocage, arrêt *m*, taquet *m*, butée *f*, *(for door)* heurtoir *m*; *Tech (for end of travel)* butoir *m* 5 *Opt*, *Phot (of lens)* diaphragme *m* 6 *Ling* occlusive *f*

VT (-pp-) 1 *(halt)* arrêter; *(traffic)* arrêter, interrompre; *(clock)* arrêter; *(machine)* arrêter, stopper; *Boxing (blow)* parer; *(fight)* interrompre; *(abuse, evil practice, rumours)* mettre fin à, faire cesser; *(strike)* briser, enrayer; **s. thief!** au voleur!; **to s. an opponent** *Ftbl* arrêter un adversaire; *Boxing* mettre un adversaire K.O.; **this bullet will s. a man at 200 metres** cette balle arrêtera un homme à 200 mètres; *Mil Sl* **to s. a bullet** prendre une balle; **the curtains s. the light** les rideaux cachent la lumière; **to s. sb's**

doing sth *or* **sb (from) doing sth** empêcher qn de faire qch; **I couldn't s. myself** je n'ai pas pu m'en empêcher; **to s. sth being done** empêcher que qch (ne) se fasse; **nothing will s. her** rien ne l'arrêtera; **what's stopping you?** qu'est-ce qui vous retient?, qu'est-ce qui vous en empêche?; **to s. the bleeding** arrêter l'hémorragie; **dumping nuclear waste should be stopped** il faut qu'on arrête de jeter n'importe où les déchets nucléaires; **it ought to be stopped** *(put an end to)* il faut que cela cesse

2 *(cease) (efforts, visits, work)* cesser; *Com* **to s. payment** cesser les paiements; **to s. doing sth** arrêter *ou* cesser de faire qch; **to s. smoking/drinking** s'arrêter *ou* cesser de fumer/boire; **he never stops talking** il n'arrête pas de parler, il parle sans cesse; **s. that noise!** arrête ce bruit!; **s. it!** *(to naughty child)* ça suffit!, assez!; *(you're hurting me)* arrête!; **it has stopped raining** il a cessé de pleuvoir, la pluie a cessé

3 *(block) (hole)* boucher, fermer; *(pipe)* obstruer, obturer; *Br (tooth)* plomber; **to s. one's ears** se boucher les oreilles; **to s. a gap** *(around door etc)* boucher un espace; *Fig* combler une lacune; *Com* **to s. (payment of) a cheque** faire opposition à un chèque; **to s. sb's wages** retenir le salaire de qn; **to s. £100 out of sb's wages** faire une retenue de 100 livres sur le salaire de qn; **to s. sb's pension** supprimer la pension de qn; *Mil* **all leave is stopped** toutes les troupes sont consignées, toutes les permissions sont suspendues

4 *(in horticulture) (plant)* pincer

5 *Mus* **to s. a string** presser une corde; **to s. a flute** boucher les trous d'une flûte

VI 1 *(halt)* s'arrêter; *(of ship, car)* s'arrêter, stopper; **to s. short** *or* **dead** s'arrêter net *ou* *Fam* pile; **to s. and talk to sb** s'arrêter pour parler à qn; **to do a hundred kilometres without stopping** faire cent kilomètres sans s'arrêter *ou* sans arrêt *ou* (tout) d'une traite; **we stopped in Caen** nous nous sommes arrêtés à Caen; **to go through a station without stopping** passer dans une gare sans s'y arrêter; *Naut* **to s. at a port** faire escale à *ou* dans un port

2 *(cease) (of rain, pain, headache, person doing sth)* s'arrêter, cesser; **my watch has stopped** ma montre s'est arrêtée; **to work fifteen hours without stopping** travailler pendant quinze heures d'affilée *ou* de suite; **to s. for lunch** faire une pause pour déjeuner; **he never stops** *(working, talking etc)* il ne s'arrête jamais; **she stopped in the middle of a sentence** elle s'arrêta au milieu d'une phrase; **he never stops to think** il ne prend jamais le temps de réfléchir; **she doesn't know when to s.** elle ne sait pas s'arrêter; **she didn't s. at that** elle ne s'en tint pas là; **he'll s. at nothing** rien ne l'arrêtera; **s. a moment!** arrêtez un instant!; **the matter will not s. there** l'affaire n'en demeurera pas là; **the rain has stopped** la pluie a cessé

3 *Br Fam (stay)* rester; **to s. at home** rester à la maison; **she's stopping with us for a few days** elle est venue passer quelques jours chez nous; **we decided to s. at a hotel** nous avons décidé de descendre à l'hôtel; **we stopped at a hotel for two weeks** nous avons passé deux semaines à l'hôtel

▸ ▸ *Phot* **s. bath** bain *m* d'arrêt; *Comput* **s. bit** bit *m* d'arrêt; *Comput* **s. button** bouton *m* arrêt; *Comput* **s. code** code *m* d'arrêt; *Cin* **s. frame** arrêt *m* sur image; *Br* **s. sign** *(signal m de)* stop; *Am* **s. street** = rue *f* non prioritaire

▸ **stop away** VI *Br Fam (not come)* ne pas venir; *(not go)* ne pas y aller

▸ **stop by** VI *(visit briefly)* faire une petite visite; **s. by any time** tu peux passer quand tu veux; **I'll s. by at the post office on my way home** je passerai à la poste en rentrant à la

maison; **we'll s. by and see you next week** nous passerons te voir la semaine prochaine

▸ **stop down** *Phot* VT SEP diaphragmer

VI réduire l'ouverture

▸ **stop in** VI *Fam* 1 *(visit)* **to s. in to see sb** passer voir qn

2 *Br (stay at home)* rester chez soi

▸ **stop off** VI *(stay briefly)* faire (une) halte; **they're stopping off at Bali for a couple of days on their way home** ils font étape à Bali pour quelques jours en rentrant

▸ **stop out** VI *Br Fam (not come home)* **to s. out all night** découcher, ne pas rentrer de toute la nuit; **to s. out (till) late** rentrer tard

▸ **stop over** VI *(stay briefly)* faire escale, faire halte; **we stopped over at Manchester on the flight to Toronto** nous avons fait escale à Manchester en route pour Toronto

▸ **stop up** VT SEP *(block) (hole)* boucher; *(pipe)* obstruer, obturer

VI 1 *Br Fam (not go to bed)* **to s. up late** veiller tard; **to s. up all night** veiller toute la nuit

2 *Phot* augmenter l'ouverture

stop-go, stop-and-go ADJ

▸ ▸ *Br Econ* **s. policy** politique f économique en dents de scie *(alternant arrêt de la croissance et mesures de relance)*, politique du stop-and-go

stopcock [stɒpkɒk] N robinet *m* d'arrêt

stopgap [stɒpgæp] N bouche-trou *m*, *pl* bouche-trous; **s. measure** pis-aller *m inv*

stoplight [stɒplaɪt] N 1 *(in street)* feu *m* rouge 2 *(on car)* stop *m*

stop-limit order N *St Exch* ordre *m* stop à cours limité

stop-list N *Banking (for lost cheques)* liste *f* de chèques volés ou perdus

stop-motion photography N prise *f* de vues image par image

stop-off N escale *f*

stopover [stɒpəʊvər] N *(break in journey)* escale *f*, *Rail (option of breaking journey)* faculté *f* d'arrêt

▸ ▸ **s. ticket** billet *m* avec (faculté d')arrêt

stoppage [stɒpɪdʒ] N 1 *(of traffic)* arrêt *m*, interruption *f*; *Mil etc (of pay, leave)* suspension *f*, *(of work)* arrêt, interruption; *(by discontented employees)* débrayage *m*; *(longer)* grève *f* 2 *(obstruction) (of pipe)* obstruction *f*, engorgement *m*; *Med* occlusion *f* 3 *(of salary)* retenue *f*

stopper [stɒpər] N *(of bottle etc)* bouchon *m*; *(of pipe)* obturateur *m*

VT *(carafe, flask etc)* boucher

stopping [stɒpɪŋ] N 1 *(act of ending)* cessation *f*, *(of service)* suppression *f*, **s. of payment** suspension *f* de paiement 2 *Br (in tooth)* plombage *m*

▸ ▸ **s. place** *(point m d')* arrêt *m*, halte *f*, *Br* **s. train** omnibus *m*

stop-press N *Br Journ (news)* informations *fpl* de dernière heure

▸ ▸ **s. news** informations de dernière heure

stopwatch [stɒpwɒtʃ] N chronomètre *m*; **they used a s. to time them** ils les ont chronométrés

storage [stɔːrɪdʒ] N 1 *(act of storing)*, *Com*, *Elec* emmagasinage *m*, emmagasinement *m*; *(of heat)* accumulation *f*, *Comput* stockage *m*; **to put sth into s.** mettre qch en dépôt 2 *(available space)* *(in store, for storing)* espace *m* disponible; *(of business)* entrepôts *mpl*, magasins *mpl*; **the kitchen has plenty of s. space** la cuisine a beaucoup d'espace de rangement; **there is additional s. for luggage in the rack above your head** vous pouvez également déposer vos bagages dans les casiers au-dessus de vos têtes 3 *(cost)* frais *mpl* d'entrepôt, magasinage *m*

▸ ▸ *Comput* **s. capacity** capacité *f* de stockage; *Elec* **s. cell** accumulateur *m*, batterie *f* secondaire; *Com* **s. costs** frais *mpl* d'entreposage; *Comput* **s. device** dispositif *m* de stockage; **s. heater** radiateur *m* à accumulation; *Comput* **s. medium** support *m* de stockage; **s. room** *(small)* cagibi *m*; *(larger)* débarras *m*; **s. tank** *(for fuel)* réservoir *m* (de stockage); *(for rainwater)* citerne *f*; **s. tray** *(in car)* vide-poche *m inv*; **s. unit** meuble *m* de rangement

store [stɔːr] **N 1** *(supply)* provision *f*, approvisionnement *m*; **to have a good s. of wine** avoir une bonne cave; **a s. of jokes** un stock d'histoires drôles; **his vast s. of knowledge** ses vastes connaissances, sa culture impressionnante; **to lay in a s. of sth** faire une provision de qch, s'approvisionner en qch; **to lay in stores** s'approvisionner; **to hold** *or* **keep sth in s.** tenir *ou* garder qch en réserve; **what the future holds in s. for us** ce que l'avenir nous réserve; **I have a surprise in s. for her** je lui ménage *ou* réserve une surprise; **to set great/little s. by sth** faire grand/peu de cas de qch

2 stores *(supplies)* provisions *fpl*, approvisionnement *m*; *(food and drink)* provisions, vivres *mpl*

3 *Com, Ind (warehouse etc)* entrepôt *m*, magasin *m*; *(for furniture)* garde-meuble *m*, *pl* garde-meubles; *Mil, Naut (in barracks)* magasin

4 *(large shop)* grand magasin *m*; *Am (shop)* magasin; **general s.** épicerie *f*; **the village s.** l'épicerie du village; **toy/book s.** magasin de jouets/librairie *f*; **(department) s.** grand magasin

5 *Comput* mémoire *f*

VT 1 *(put in a store)* *(hay, corn)* emmagasiner; *(beetroot etc)* mettre en silo; *(take into store)* *(furniture)* prendre en dépôt; *(put in store)* *(furniture)* mettre en dépôt; **squirrels s. food for the winter** les écureuils font des provisions pour l'hiver

2 *(accumulate)* amasser, accumuler; *(put in reserve)* mettre en réserve; *(electricity, heat)* emmagasiner; **s. in a cool place** conserver au frais

3 *Comput* stocker

4 *(supply)* approvisionner (**with** en); **he stored the larder with enough tinned goods to last the winter** il a rempli le placard avec assez de boîtes de conserve pour passer l'hiver

VI goods that don't s. well marchandises qui ne se conservent *ou* ne se gardent pas bien

▸▸ **s. audit** contrôle *m* des points de vente; **s. brand** marque *f* de magasin; **s. card** carte *f* de crédit *(d'un grand magasin)*; **s. detective** vigile *m* *(dans un magasin)*; **s. manager** chef *m* de magasin

▸ **store away VT SEP** *(put away for future)* emmagasiner; *Fig* **he's storing it all away** il enregistre tout

▸ **store up VT SEP** = **store VT 2**; **to s. up problems for oneself** se garantir des problèmes pour l'avenir; **feelings of resentment that have been stored up over the years** des sentiments d'amertume qui se sont accumulés au fil des ans

store-bought ADJ de commerce; *(clothes)* de confection; **a s. cake** un gâteau de pâtisserie

storefront ['stɔːfrʌnt] **N** *Am* devanture *f* de magasin

storehouse ['stɔːhaʊs] **N** magasin *m*, entrepôt *m*, dépôt *m*; *Fig* **a s. of information** une mine de renseignements

storekeeper ['stɔːkiːpər] **N** magasinier *m*; *(in hospital)* dépensier, -ière; *Am (shop-keeper)* commerçant, -ante

storeroom ['stɔːruːm] **N** *(for food)* office *m*; *(for old furniture etc)* débarras *m*; *(in school, offices etc)* réserve *f*; *Ind* halle *f* de dépôt;

Naut soute *f* aux vivres *ou* à provisions, magasin *m*, cambuse *f*

store(s)man, *pl* **store(s)men** ['stɔː(z)mən] **N** manutentionnaire *m*, magasinier *m*

storey, *Am* **story** ['stɔːrɪ] **N** *(of building)* étage *m*; *Br* **on the third s.**, *Am* **on the fourth s.** au troisième étage; **single** *or* **one s. house** maison sans étage *ou* de plain-pied

Attention: ne pas confondre avec **story**.

-storeyed, *Am* **-storied** ['stɔːrɪd] **SUFF two-s. house** maison à un étage; **one-s.** *or* **single-s. house** maison sans étage *ou* de plain-pied

storing ['stɔːrɪŋ] **N** *Com* magasinage *m*

stork [stɔːk] **N** *(bird)* cigogne *f*

storm [stɔːm] **N 1** *Met* orage *m*; *(wind)* tempête *f*; **rain s.** tempête de pluie; **there's a s. coming** le temps est à l'orage; *Fig* **a s. in a tea-cup** une tempête dans un verre d'eau; *Fig* **political s.** ouragan *m* *ou* tourmente *f* politique; *Fig* **to bring a s. about one's ears** déclencher un tollé général; *Fig* **to cause a s.** faire l'effet d'une bombe; **to go down a s.** *(be very successful)* faire un tabac, faire un malheur

2 *(of insults)* bordée *f*; *(of applause, protest)* tempête *f*; **to raise a s. of laughter** déchaîner l'hilarité générale

3 *Mil* assaut *m*; **to take a stronghold by s.** prendre d'assaut une place forte; *Fig* **to take the audience by s.** soulever l'auditoire; **the play took Broadway by s.** la pièce a connu un succès foudroyant à Broadway; *Fig* **to take sb by s.** *(emotionally)* bouleverser qn

VI *(of person)* tempêter, pester; **to s. at sb** s'emporter contre qn; **to s. into/out of the room** entrer dans/quitter la pièce comme un ouragan; **she was storming about the place like a madwoman** elle se démenait dans la pièce comme une folle; **she went storming into the lead** elle est venue prendre la tête comme un ouragan

VT 1 *Mil (attack)* donner l'assaut à; *(capture)* prendre d'assaut, emporter d'assaut, enlever **2** *(say angrily)* fulminer

▸▸ **s. cloud** *Met* nuage *m* d'orage; *Fig* nuage menaçant; **s. cone** cône *m* de tempête; **s. damage** dommages *mpl ou* dégâts *mpl* causés par l'orage *ou* la tempête; *Am* **s. door** porte *f* extérieure *(qui double la porte de la maison pour éviter les courants d'air)*; **s. drain** égout *m* pluvial; **s. lantern** lampe *f* tempête; **s. sewer** égout pluvial; **s. troops** troupes *fpl* d'assaut; **s. warning** avis *m* de tempête

stormbound ['stɔːmbaʊnd] **ADJ** bloqué par une tempête

storming ['stɔːmɪŋ] **N** *Mil* prise *f* d'assaut *(of* de); **the s. of the Bastille** la prise de la Bastille

stormy ['stɔːmɪ] **ADJ** *(weather, sky)* orageux; *(sea)* démonté; **the weather is s.** le temps est orageux *ou* à l'orage; *Fig* **s. discussion** discussion *f* orageuse; **s. life** vie *f* tumultueuse; **s. marriage** mariage *m* orageux; **s. meeting** réunion *f* houleuse

▸▸ *Orn* **s. petrel** pétrel-tempête *m*, *pl* pétrels-tempête

story¹ ['stɔːrɪ] **N 1** *(tale, account)* histoire *f*; **to tell a s.** raconter *ou* conter une histoire; **there is a s. that ...** on raconte que ...; **as the s. goes** à ce que l'on raconte; *Fig* **that is quite another s.** ça, c'est une autre histoire; *Fam* **it's the (same) old s.** *or* **the old, old s.** c'est toujours la même histoire; *Fam* **it's the s. of my life** c'est le genre de chose qui m'arrive tout le temps; **it's a long s.** c'est toute une histoire; **it's a long story** ; **these bruises tell their own s.** ces meurtrissures en disent long; **each photo tells its** *or* **a s.** toutes les photos racontent une histoire; **she can tell a good s.** elle en connaît de bonnes; **so, to cut a long s. short ...** bref, pour résumer ...

2 short s. nouvelle *f*, conte *m*; **short s. writer** nouvelliste *mf*

3 *(plot) (of novel, play etc)* intrigue *f*

4 *Journ Fam* affaire *f*, information *f*; **who have we got on the s.?** qui est sur l'affaire?; **they decided to publish the s.** ils ont décidé de publier l'information; **all the papers ran** *or* **carried the s.** tous les journaux en ont parlé; **the s. broke just after the morning papers had gone to press** on a appris la nouvelle juste après la mise sous presse des journaux du matin

5 *Fam (lie)* histoire *f*, conte *m*; **to tell stories** raconter des histoires

▸▸ *Mktg* **s. completion** histoire *f ou* scénario *m* à compléter

Attention: ne pas confondre avec **storey**.

story² **N** *Am (of building)* = **storey**

storyboard ['stɔːrɪbɔːd] **N** story-board *m*, *pl* story-boards, scénarimage *m*

storybook ['stɔːrɪbʊk] **N** livre *m* de contes, livre d'histoires; **it looks like a s. castle** cela ressemble à un château de conte de fées; **it had a s. ending** ça s'est terminé comme un conte de fées

storyline ['stɔːrɪlaɪn] **N** intrigue *f*; **it was quite hard to follow the s.** j'ai/il a/*etc* eu du mal à suivre le fil de l'histoire

storyteller ['stɔːrɪtelər] **N 1** conteur, -euse; **to be a good/bad s.** être bon/mauvais conteur **2** *Fam (liar)* menteur, -euse; **you big s.!** gros menteur!, grosse menteuse!

storytelling ['stɔːrɪtelɪŋ] **N 1** art *m* de conter; **to be good at s.** avoir l'art de raconter des histoires **2** *Fam (telling lies)* mensonges *mpl*

stoup [stuːp] **N** *Rel* bénitier *m*

stout [staʊt] **ADJ 1** *(fat)* corpulent, fort; **to grow s.** prendre de l'embonpoint **2** *(solid)* *(door, shoes, beam)* solide; *(cloth)* renforcé **3** *(strong)* *(shoulders, legs, arms etc)* fort, vigoureux; *(brave)* brave, vaillant; *(resolute)* ferme, résolu; *Old-fashioned* **s. fellow** *(brave)* homme vaillant *ou* courageux; *(sturdy)* costaud *m*; **s. heart** cœur *m* vaillant; **to put up a s. resistance** se défendre vaillamment

N *(beer)* stout *m*, bière *f* brune forte

stouthearted [staʊt'hɑːtɪd] **ADJ** *Lit* courageux, intrépide

stoutly ['staʊtlɪ] **ADV 1** *(vigorously)* fortement, vigoureusement; *(to deny sth)* catégoriquement; **she s. maintained that ...** elle affirmait énergiquement que ... **2** *(sturdily)* *(built)* solidement

stoutness ['staʊtnɪs] **N 1** *(fatness)* embonpoint *m* **2** *(solidity)* solidité *f* **3** *(vigorousness)* *(of resistance etc)* fermeté *f*, vigueur *f*

stove [staʊv] **N 1** *(cooker)* cuisinière *f*, *(oven)* fourneau *m*; *(small, portable)* réchaud *m*; **electric/gas s.** cuisinière électrique/à gaz; **oil s.** poêle *m* à pétrole; *(heater)* calorifère *m* à mazout **2** *Chem, Ind* étuve *f*, four *m*

stovepipe ['staʊvpaɪp] **N** tuyau *m* de poêle

▸▸ **s. hat** chapeau *m* tuyau de poêle

stow [staʊ] **VT 1** *(put away)* ranger, mettre; *Sl* **s. it!** *(shut up)* la ferme!; *(that's enough)* ça suffit! **2** *Naut (cargo)* arrimer; *(anchor, ship's boats)* saisir **3 to s. sth full of sth** remplir qch de qch

▸ **stow away VT SEP** = **stow**; *Fam* **to s. away a huge meal** s'envoyer un repas énorme; *Fam* **he can certainly s. it away** il a un bon coup de fourchette

VI *(hide)* s'embarquer clandestinement

stowage ['staʊɪdʒ] **N** *Naut (of goods)* arrimage *m*; *(space)* espace *m* utile; *(cost)* frais *mpl* d'arrimage

▸▸ *Aut* **s. bin** vide-poches *m inv*; bac *m* de rangement

stowaway ['stəʊəweɪ] N *Naut, Aviat* passager *m ou* voyageur *m* clandestin

strabismus [stræˈbɪzməs] N *Med* strabisme *m*

straddle ['stræd(ə)l] VT **1** *(be on both sides of) (horse)* enfourcher; *(chair)* se mettre à califourchon sur; *(wall)* se mettre à califourchon *ou* à cheval sur; **their empire straddled the Mediterranean** leur empire couvrait la Méditerranée; **to s. a river** *(of bridge)* enjamber une rivière; **the village straddles the border** le village est à cheval sur la frontière; **her life straddled two centuries** sa vie est à cheval sur deux siècles; **a company that straddles two continents** une entreprise qui a des intérêts dans deux continents **2** *Am Pol etc (question)* refuser de se compromettre sur; **to s. the fence** ne pas prendre parti, ne pas s'engager

N **1** *Sport (in high jump)* rouleau *m* ventral **2** *St Exch* stellage *m*

strafe [streɪf] VT *Mil* mitrailler en rasemottes

straggle ['stræg(ə)l] VI **1** *(walk in disorderly fashion)* marcher sans ordre; *(not keep up)* rester en arrière, traîner; **other climbers straggled behind and got lost** d'autres grimpeurs sont restés à la traîne et se sont perdus; **his hair straggled over his jacket collar** les mèches de sa nuque pendouillaient sur le col de son veston **2** *(of plants)* pousser en désordre; **the roses are straggling everywhere** les roses poussent dans tous les sens

straggler ['stræglər] N *(person)* traînard, -arde; *Naut (ship, sailor)* retardataire *m*, lanterne *f* rouge

straggling ['stræglɪŋ] ADJ **a few s. houses** quelques maisons *fpl* éparpillées; **s. hairs** mèches *fpl* rebelles

straggly ['stræglɪ] ADJ *(branches, hair)* épars; *(beard)* rare; **a s. line of refugees** une file étirée de réfugiés

---

STRAIGHT [streɪt]

ADJ droit **1, 7**	▪ rectiligne **1**	▪ raide **1**
▪ honnête **2**	▪ franc **2**	▪ hétéro **4**
▪ pur **5**		
N ligne droite **1**	▪ hétéro **3**	
▪ personne sérieuse **4**		
ADV droit **1**	▪ directement **2, 3**	
▪ honnêtement **4**	▪ clair **5**	

ADJ **1** *(not curved) (back, leg, line etc)* droit; *(trajectory)* rectiligne; *(movement)* en ligne droite; *Tennis* **to win in three s. sets** gagner en trois sets; *Am* **she got s. As in the exam** *(all As)* elle n'a obtenu que des mentions très bien à l'examen; **a s. A student** un étudiant brillant; *Fig* **to play with** *or* **keep a s. bat** se conduire honorablement; **to have a s. back** avoir le dos bien droit, se tenir bien droit; **s. hair** cheveux *mpl* raides; *Am* **he's a s. arrow** *(person of integrity)* il est un peu coincé; **2** *(honest)* honnête, loyal; *(frank)* franc, *f* franche; *(answer)* sans équivoque, franc; **s. as a die** d'une droiture absolue; **to be s. with sb** agir loyalement avec qn *ou* envers qn; **be s. with me, is he ...?** sois franc avec moi, est-il ...?; **I want a s. answer!** je veux une réponse franche!; **to play a s. game** jouer franc jeu; **it's time for some s. talking** il est temps que nous ayons une conversation très franche

3 *(serious, conventional)* **to keep a s. face** garder son sérieux; **I couldn't keep a s. face** je n'ai pas pu m'empêcher de rire

4 *Fam (heterosexual)* hétéro(sexuel)

5 *(neat)* pur; **s. whisky** whisky *m* sec; **to drink one's whisky s.** boire son whisky sec

6 *Fam (not on drugs)* **to be s.** ne pas avoir pris de drogue; *Am* **to get s.** = prendre une dose d'héroïne (ou d'une drogue comparable) de façon à éviter l'effet de manque

7 *(aligned)* droit; **your tie isn't s.** votre cravate n'est pas droite *ou* est de travers; **your skirt isn't s.** ta jupe est de travers; **to put a picture s.** redresser un tableau; **to put the room s.** remettre de l'ordre dans la pièce; *Fig* **to put things** *or* **matters s.** arranger les choses; *(sort problem out)* débrouiller l'affaire; **to put sb s.** révéler son erreur à qn; **you ought to put her s. about what he's (really) like** tu devrais lui dire la personne qu'il est vraiment; **let's try to get things s.** essayons d'y voir clair; **let's get this s., he left at two o'clock?** mettons les choses au clair, il est parti à deux heures?; *Fam* **get this s.!** comprends-moi bien!; *Fam* **I need five hundred pounds to get me s.** il me faut cinq cents livres pour me remettre d'aplomb *ou* me refaire

N **1** **to be out of (the) s.** n'être pas d'aplomb, être de travers; **to cut a material on the s.** couper une étoffe de droit fil; **the s. and narrow** le droit chemin; **to keep on** *or* **stick to the s. and narrow** rester dans le droit chemin

2 *Sport* **the s.** *(on race track)* la ligne droite; **the back s.** la ligne opposée *ou* d'en face; **the home s.** la (dernière) ligne droite; *Fig* **we're on the home s. now** nous sommes dans la dernière ligne droite

3 *Sl (heterosexual)* hétéro *mf*

4 *Sl (conventional person)* personne *f* conventionnelle *ou* sérieuse; **don't be such a s.!** sois pas si sérieux!

ADV **1** *(in straight line)* droit; **to fly s. as an arrow** voler droit comme une flèche; **to shoot s.** tirer juste; **to go s.** aller droit; *Fam (of criminal)* se ranger des voitures; **keep** *or* **go s. on** continuez tout droit; **to read a book s. through** *(from beginning to end)* lire un livre d'un bout à l'autre; *(without stopping)* lire un livre d'une traite

2 *(without delay)* directement; **it comes s. from Paris** ça vient directement *ou* tout droit de Paris; **I'll be s. back** je reviens directement; **to come/go** *or* **get s. to the point** venir/aller droit au fait; **to get s. on with one's work** se mettre directement au travail; **to walk s. in** entrer sans frapper; **s. away** immédiatement, aussitôt, tout de suite; *Fam* **s. off** sur-le-champ, tout de suite; *Fam* **I can't tell you s. off** je ne peux pas vous le dire tout de suite

3 *(directly)* directement; **to drink s. from the bottle** boire à (même) la bouteille; **it is s. across the road** c'est juste en face; **s. above sth** juste au-dessus de qch; **to look sb s. in the face** regarder qn bien en face; **he looked s. through me** il m'a regardé sans me voir; **we drove s. through Nantes** nous avons traversé Nantes sans nous arrêter; *Fam* **to let sb have it s.** dire son fait à qn; **I told him s. (out) what I thought of it** je lui ai dit carrément *ou* tout net ce que j'en pensais; **to come s. out with sth** dire qch tout net; **to tell** *or* **give sb sth s. from the shoulder** dire qch carrément à qn; *Theat* **to play a part s.** jouer un rôle de façon classique

4 *(honestly)* honnêtement; **to deal s. with people** être loyal en affaires; **to play s.** jouer franc jeu; *Br Sl* **s. up!** sans blague!

5 *(clearly)* **I can't see s.** je ne vois pas clair; **I can't think s.** mon cerveau refuse de fonctionner

▸▸ *Theat* **s. actor** acteur, -trice sérieux(euse); **s. edge** *(tool)* règle *f* (à araser); *Pol* **s. fight** campagne *f* électorale à deux candidats; *Cards* **s. flush** quinte *f* flush; *Boxing* **s. left** direct *m* du gauche; **s. line** (ligne *f*) droite *f*; *Theat* **s. man** *(of comedian)* faire-valoir *m inv*; *Theat* **s. part** rôle *m* sérieux;

Am **s. razor** rasoir *m* à main; *Boxing* **s. right** direct du droit; *Am Pol* **s. ticket** liste *f* non panachée; *Horseracing, Fin* **s. tip** tuyau *m* sûr *ou* de source sûre

straightaway ['streɪtəweɪ] ADV immédiatement, tout de suite
ADJ *Am* en ligne droite

straight-edged ADJ *(knife, blade)* à tranchant droit

straighten ['streɪt(ə)n] VT *(make straight)* rendre droit; *(nail, rod etc)* redresser; *(bar)* défausser; *(put in order)* ranger, mettre en ordre; **to s. one's back** se redresser; **to s. one's hair** se recoiffer; *(take curls out)* se défriser les cheveux; **to s. one's tie** arranger sa cravate; **to s. one's affairs** mettre de l'ordre dans ses affaires
VI *(of person)* se redresser; *(of thing, road etc)* devenir droit
▸ **straighten out** VT SEP **1** *(make straight)* redresser; *(bar)* défausser; **he straightened out the crumpled bedclothes** il a remis les draps en place **2** *(put right) (one's affairs)* arranger, mettre en ordre; **I will try to s. things out** je vais essayer d'arranger les choses
VI *(become straight) (of river, road etc)* redevenir droit
▸ **straighten up** VT SEP **1** *(put straight) (picture etc)* redresser **2** *(put in order) (room etc)* mettre de l'ordre dans
VI *(straighten one's back)* se redresser

straight-faced [-'feɪst] ADJ impassible

straightforward [streɪt'fɔːwəd] ADJ **1** *(person, conduct)* franc, *f* franche; **to give a s. answer to a question** répondre sans détours à une question; **to be quite s. about it** y aller franc jeu **2** *(simple)* simple; **it's a very s. cooker to use** c'est une cuisinière très simple à utiliser **3** *(clear)* manifeste; **a case of s. racism** un exemple de racisme manifeste

straightforwardly [streɪt'fɔːwədlɪ] ADV **1** *(to act)* avec droiture, loyalement; *(to speak)* franchement, d'une manière franche, sans détours **2** *(simply)* facilement; **it can be assembled s. enough** le montage est assez facile; **you then quite s. remove the lid** puis vous ôtez le couvercle tout simplement *ou* très facilement **3** *(clearly)* manifestement; **to be s. wrong** *(of person)* avoir manifestement tort

straightforwardness [streɪt'fɔːwədnɪs] N *(of person)* franchise *f*, *(of matter, question)* simplicité *f*

straightline depreciation ['streɪtlaɪn] N *Acct* amortissement *m* linéaire

straightness ['streɪtnɪs] N **1** *(of line)* rectitude *f* **2** *(of conduct)* droiture *f*, rectitude *f*

straight-to-video ADJ *(movie)* sorti directement sur cassette vidéo

STRAIN[1] [streɪn] N **1** *(tension)* tension *f*, *Phys (ratio)* rapport *m* de la déformation, allongement *m* unitaire; **the s. on the rope was too great** la corde était soumise à une trop grande tension; **to relieve the s. on** *or* **take the s. off a beam** soulager une poutre; *Tech* **breaking s.** force *f ou* contrainte *f* à la rupture, effort *m* de rupture; **to take the s.** *(of beam) (be subjected to)* être soumis à une tension; *(to support)* supporter la tension; *(of person)* supporter la tension nerveuse; **it would be** *or* **put too great a s. on my finances** ce serait trop lourd pour ma bourse; **the long hours put a s. on her marriage** ses horaires impossibles ont occasionné des tensions dans son mariage; **the s. of modern life** la tension de la vie moderne; **the s. of business life** la fatigue propre au monde des affaires; **all this driving's getting a bit of a s.** tous ces déplacements en voiture commencent à me fatiguer; **I find it a s.** je trouve cela fatigant; **the s. was beginning to tell**

(on them/etc) la tension devenait visible; **mental s.** surmenage *m* (intellectuel); **eye s.** fatigue *f* des yeux

2 *Med* entorse *f*, *(less serious)* foulure *f*; **s. in the back** tour *m* de reins

vt 1 *(cable)* tendre, surtendre; **to s. one's ears** tendre l'oreille; **to s. one's eyes** *(overuse)* se fatiguer *ou* s'abîmer les yeux *ou* la vue (**doing sth** à faire qch); *(make effort)* s'efforcer (**to see sth** pour voir qch); **to s. one's voice** *(overuse)* se fatiguer la voix; *(make effort)* forcer sa voix; **to s. every nerve to do sth** mettre toute sa force à faire qch; **to s. relations** tendre les rapports (**between** entre); **to s. one's resources** grever ses ressources jusqu'à la limite

2 *Tech (part)* déformer; **I've strained my wrist/ankle** je me suis foulé le poignet/la cheville; *(more seriously)* je me suis fait une entorse au poignet/à la cheville; **to s. one's back** se faire mal au dos; **to s. one's heart** se fatiguer le cœur; **to s. a muscle** se froisser un muscle; **to s. oneself** *(overexert oneself)* se surmener, s'éreinter (**doing sth** à faire qch); *Iron* **he doesn't (exactly) s. himself** on ne peut pas dire qu'il se foule (la rate); *Iron* **don't s. yourself, will you!** surtout ne te foule pas!

3 *(liquid)* filtrer, passer; *(stock)* tamiser, passer; *(vegetables)* faire égoutter

vi 1 *(make great effort)* peiner; **to s. at a door** essayer d'ouvrir une porte; **to s. at a rope/at the oars** tirer sur une corde/sur les rames; **to s. at the leash** *(of dog)* tirer sur la laisse; *Fig (be restless)* ne pas tenir en place; *(be rebellious)* se rebeller

2 *(of beam)* fatiguer, travailler; *(of rope)* être trop tendu

3 *Tech (of piece of metal)* gauchir, se fausser

4 *Lit* **to s. at sth** *(be unwilling)* se faire un scrupule de qch; **to s. at doing sth** avoir des scrupules à faire qch

5 *(of liquid)* filtrer (**through** à travers)

---

strain² **n 1** *Biol (of virus)* souche *f*, *(of grain, plant)* variété *f*, *(of animal)* race *f*, lignée *f*

2 a s. of weakness un fond de faiblesse; **he said much more in the same s.** il s'est étendu longuement dans ce sens; **other stories/films in the same s.** d'autres histoires/films dans la même veine

3 *esp Lit* **strains** *(sounds, music)* accents *mpl*; **sweet strains** doux accords *mpl*

strained [streɪnd] **adj 1** *(rope, conversation, atmosphere etc)* tendu; **s. nerves** nerfs *mpl* tendus; **s. relations** rapports *mpl* tendus **2** *Med* **s. ankle** cheville *f* foulée **3** *(forced)* *(laughter)* forcé, contraint; *(language, interpretation)* forcé, exagéré **4** *(liquid)* filtré; *(stock)* tamisé; *(vegetables)* égoutté

strainer ['streɪnər] **n** *Culin* passoire *f*; **tea s.** passe-thé *m inv*, passette *f* à thé; **milk s.** passoire

strait [streɪt] **n 1** détroit *m* **2 to be in dire** *or* **desperate straits** être dans une situation désespérée; *(financially)* avoir de gros problèmes financiers

▶▶ **the Straits of Dover** le Pas de Calais; **the Straits of Gibraltar** le détroit de Gibraltar

straitened ['streɪtənd] **adj in s. circumstances** dans une situation (financière) difficile

straitjacket ['streɪtdʒækɪt] **n** camisole *f* de force; *Fig* carcan *m*; *Fig* **a financial s.** un carcan financier

vt *Fig* gêner, entraver; **to be straitjacketed by a lack of investment/by censorship** être bloqué par le manque d'investissement/par la censure

straitlaced ['streɪt'leɪst] **adj** collet monté *inv*

strand¹ [strænd] **n** *Lit (shore)* rive *f*, grève *f*
vt *(ship)* échouer; **tourists stranded by the**

air controllers' strike touristes bloqués à cause de la grève des aiguilleurs du ciel

strand² **n 1** *(piece) (of rope)* brin *m*, toron *m*; *Sewing (of cotton)* brin; *(of cloth)* fil *m*; *(of hair)* mèche *f* **2** *Fig (of plot)* fil *m*; **to unravel the strands of a complicated affair** démêler les fils d'une affaire compliquée

stranded ['strændɪd] **adj 1** *(ship)* échoué; **s. whale** baleine échouée (sur la plage) **2** *(person)* **to leave sb s.** laisser qn en rade; **to be s.** rester en rade; **s. tourists** touristes bloqués

strange [streɪndʒ] **adj 1** *(unusual)* étrange, bizarre; **they didn't write – (that's) s.** ils n'ont pas écrit – (c'est) bizarre; **s. beasts** bêtes *fpl* fantastiques; **she wears the strangest clothes** elle porte les vêtements les plus bizarres; **she's a s. girl** c'est une fille bizarre; **it's a s. thing** c'est (une chose) étrange; **s. to say, I've never met him** bien que cela paraisse bizarre, je ne l'ai jamais rencontré; **it's s. that you haven't heard of it** c'est bizarre que tu n'en aies pas entendu parler; **it was s. to see her in a dress** ça faisait bizarre *ou* drôle de la voir en robe; **s. how some faces stick in your mind** c'est bizarre *ou* drôle comme certains visages restent gravés dans la mémoire; **they've got a s. way of saying thank you** ils ont une drôle de façon de dire merci; **it felt s. to be back in Scotland again** cela m'a fait bizarre de revenir en Écosse

2 *(unfamiliar)* **s. faces** des visages *mpl* nouveaux *ou* inconnus; **a s. place/house** un endroit/une maison qu'on ne connaît pas; **I can't work with s. tools** je ne peux pas travailler avec des outils qui ne sont pas les miens; **don't talk to s. men** ne parle pas aux étrangers

3 *Arch (foreign)* étranger; **in a s. land** dans un pays étranger

strangely ['streɪndʒlɪ] **adv** bizarrement; **it all seemed s. familiar** tout avait un étrange goût de déja-vu; **he's behaving very s.** il se conduit de manière très étrange; **s. enough, he felt nothing** ce qui est bizarre c'est qu'il n'a rien senti

strangeness ['streɪndʒnɪs] **n 1** *(unusual quality)* bizarrerie *f* **2** *(unfamiliarity) (of surroundings etc)* étrangeté *f*

stranger ['streɪndʒər] **n** *(from somewhere else)* étranger, -ère; *(someone not known)* inconnu, -ue; **don't talk to strangers** ne parle pas aux inconnus; **I'm a s. here** je ne suis pas d'ici; **they're strangers (to us)** nous ne les connaissons pas; **you're quite a s. these days!** vous vous faites rare!; *Fam* **hello, s.!** salut toi! on ne te voit plus!; *(to unknown person)* bonjour, l'étranger!; **to become a s. to sb** devenir étranger à qn; **they had become complete strangers to one another** ils étaient devenus des étrangers l'un pour l'autre; **to become a s. to sth** perdre l'habitude de qch; **he's a s./no s. to fear** il ne connaît pas/il connaît bien la peur; **she's no s. to controversy/success** elle a l'habitude de la polémique/du succès

> Attention: ne pas confondre avec **foreigner**.

strangle ['stræŋ(g)l] **vt** *(person)*, *Fig* étrangler; *(laugh)* étouffer

strangled ['stræŋ(g)ld] **adj** *(person)* étranglé; *(voice, laughter)* étouffé

stranglehold ['stræŋ(g)lhəʊld] **n 1** *(in wrestling)* étranglement *m* **2** *Fig* **to have a s. on sb** tenir qn à la gorge; **to have a s. on sth** avoir la mainmise sur qch; **economic s.** mainmise économique; **to break the s. on a country's economy** mettre fin à la mainmise sur l'économie d'un pays

strangler ['stræŋglər] **n** *(person)* étrangleur, -euse

strangling ['stræŋglɪŋ] **n** étranglement *m*

strangulate ['stræŋgjʊleɪt] **vt 1** *Med (intestine)* étrangler; **strangulated hernia** hernie *f* étranglée **2** = **strangle**

strangulation [stræŋgjʊ'leɪʃən] **n** strangulation *f*; *Fig* **economic s.** asphyxie *f* économique

strap [stræp] **n** *(of leather, canvas)* sangle *f*, lanière *f*, courroie *f*; *(on bra etc)* bretelle *f*; *(on shoe)* lanière, patte *f*, *(for watch)* bracelet *m*; *(on underground train, bus)* poignée *f*; **watch s.** bracelet de montre; **(trouser) s.** *(under foot)* sous-pied *m*, *pl* sous-pieds; **to give sb the s.** *(punishment)* fouetter qn (avec une sangle)

vt (**-pp-** [stræpt]) **1** *(attach) (object)* attacher avec une sangle, sangler; *(trunk)* boucler; **to s. sth to sth** attacher **2** *(punish)* **to s. a child** frapper un enfant avec une sangle **3** *Med (broken limb etc)* bander

▶ **strap down vt sep** *(containers etc)* arrimer; *(prisoner, patient)* attacher

▶ **strap in vt sep** *(passenger)* attacher; **to s. oneself in** s'attacher, attacher sa ceinture

▶ **strap up vt sep 1** *(suitcase)* sangler **2** *Med* = **strap vt 3**

straphang ['stræphæŋ] **vi** voyager debout *(en se tenant à la courroie ou à la poignée)*

straphanger ['stræphæŋər] **n** *(in underground etc)* voyageur, -euse debout; **after 15 years of being a s.** *(commuting)* après être allé au travail pendant 15 ans en métro

strapless ['stræplɪs] **adj** *(dress, bra etc)* sans bretelles; **s. top** bustier *m*

strapline ['stræplaɪn] **n** *Journ* surtitre *m*

strapped [stræpt] **adj** *Fam* **1 to be s. (for cash)** être à court d'argent, être fauché **2** *Am (armed)* armé, chargé

strapping ['stræpɪŋ] **adj** solide, robuste; **s. fellow** grand gaillard; **tall s. girl** fille grande et costaude

strata ['strɑːtə] **npl** *see* **stratum**

stratagem ['strætədʒəm] **n** stratagème *m*

strategic [strə'tiːdʒɪk] **adj** stratégique

▶▶ **s. business area** domaine *m* d'activité stratégique; **s. business plan** plan *m* stratégique d'entreprise; **s. business unit** domaine d'activité stratégique; **s. management** gestion *f* stratégique; **s. marketing** marketing *m* stratégique; **s. planning** planification *f* stratégique; *Br* **S. Rail Authority** = organisme *m* chargé de résoudre les problèmes posés par le système de transport ferroviaire

strategically [strə'tiːdʒɪk(ə)lɪ] **adv** stratégiquement; **s. placed** placé à un endroit/aux endroits stratégique(s)

strategist ['strætədʒɪst] **n** stratège *m*

strategy ['strætɪdʒɪ] **n** stratégie *f*

stratification [strætɪfɪ'keɪʃən] **n** stratification *f*

stratified ['strætɪfaɪd] **adj** *(formation, society)* stratifié

stratify ['strætɪfaɪ] **vt** stratifier
vi se stratifier

stratosphere ['strætəsfɪər] **n** stratosphère *f*

stratum, *pl* **strata** ['strɑːtəm, -ə] **n** *Geol* strate *f*, couche *f*; *Fig* couche; **the various strata of society** les différentes couches sociales VOIR GRAMMAIRE A13

straw [strɔː] **n 1** paille *f*; **it's not worth a s.** cela ne vaut pas un clou *ou* un pet de lapin; *Fig* **to clutch** *or* **grasp at straws** se raccrocher à de faux espoirs; *Prov* **a drowning man will clutch at a s.** = quand on se noie, on est prêt à se raccrocher à n'importe quoi; *Fig* **straws in the wind** un signe, un indice; *Prov* **it's the last s. that breaks the camel's back** c'est la goutte d'eau qui fait déborder le vase; **it's the last s.!** ça c'est le comble *ou* le bouquet!; *Fig* **man of s.** homme *m* de paille **2** *(for drinking)* paille *f*; **to drink lemonade through a s.** boire de la limonade avec une paille **3** *(colour)* jaune *m* paille

▸▸ **s. hat** chapeau *m* de paille; *Am Fig* **s. man** homme de paille; **s. mat** paillasson *m*; **s. mattress** paillasse *f*; **s. poll** sondage *m* d'opinion

strawberry ['strɔːb(ə)rɪ] N *(fruit, flavour)* fraise *f*; **s. (plant)** fraisier *m*; **wild s.**, *Am* **field s.** fraise des bois; **s. ice cream** glace *f* à la fraise; **s. jam** confiture *f* de fraises

▸▸ **s. bed** planche *f ou* plant *m* de fraisiers; **s. blonde** blonde *f* qui tire sur le roux; **s. field** fraiseraie *f*; **s. mark** tache *f* de vin, envie *f*

Strawberries and cream

En Grande-Bretagne, les fraises à la crème sont traditionnellement consommées lors de certaines manifestations en plein air, notamment au tournoi de tennis de Wimbledon.

strawberry-blonde ADJ blond vénitien *inv*

straw-coloured ADJ jaune paille *inv*

stray [streɪ] N **1** *(animal)* animal *m* égaré; *(dog)* chien *m* errant; *Law* animal sans maître **2 waifs and strays** *(children)* enfants *mpl* abandonnés **3** *Radio* **strays** parasites *mpl*, friture *f*

ADJ **1** *(animal)* égaré, perdu; *Law* sans maître **2** *Fig (example, specimen)* isolé; **s. bullet** balle *f* perdue; **here are a few s. thoughts on the project** voilà quelques idées en vrac concernant le projet; **any s. thoughts you might have …** si vous avez des idées …

VI *(of person, animal)* s'égarer, errer; *(of sheep)* s'écarter du troupeau; **the plane had strayed off course** l'avion s'était écarté de sa route; **the sheep will s. onto the road** les moutons vont se sauver sur la route; *Fig* **to s. from the right path** s'écarter du droit chemin; **to let one's thoughts s.** laisser vagabonder *ou* vaguer ses pensées; **to s. from the point** s'écarter du sujet

streak [striːk] N **1** *(stripe)* raie *f*, rayure *f*; *(of mist, vapour, dirt)* traînée *f*; *(of light)* rai *m*, trait *m*; **a s. of sunlight** un rayon de soleil; **the first streaks of dawn** les premières lueurs de l'aube; **like a s. of lightning** comme un éclair; **streaks of grey hair** mèches *fpl* de cheveux gris; **I've had a s. of luck** je tiens le filon; **winning/losing s.** *(in sport)* suite *f* de victoires/défaites; **to be on a winning s.**, **to hit a winning s.** être en veine; **there's a s. of Irish blood in her** elle a un peu de sang irlandais; *Br Sl* **he's a long s. of piss** *(tall and thin)* c'est une grande perche; *(insipid in character)* c'est une lavette **2** *Fig (tendency)* tendance *f*; **to have a jealous/mean/cruel s.** être d'une nature jalouse/avare/cruelle; **there was a s. of cowardice in him** il avait un côté lâche **3** *Fam (act of running naked)* **to do a s.** courir nu (en public)

VT rayer, strier **(with** de); **fur streaked with black** pelage rayé de noir; **streaked with tears** strié de larmes; **her face was streaked with dirt/blood** elle avait des traces de saleté/sang sur le visage; **wall streaked with damp** mur plein de traces d'humidité; **white marble streaked with red** marbre blanc veiné de rouge; **his hair was streaked with silver** ses cheveux étaient parsemés de fils d'argent; **to have one's hair streaked** se faire faire des mèches

VI **1** *(run, move etc fast)* **to s. along/past** aller/passer comme un éclair; **to s. off** partir à toute allure; **the Ferrari streaked past him** la Ferrari le dépassa en trombe; **the rocket streaked up into the sky** la fusée partit comme un éclair dans le ciel **2** *Fam (run naked)* courir nu (en public)

streaker ['striːkər] N *Fam* = personne *f* qui court nu(e) (en public)

streaking ['striːkɪŋ] N *(streaks)* raies *fpl*, rayures *fpl*, bandes *fpl*; *(in hairdressing)* effet *m* de mèches

streaky ['striːkɪ] ADJ *(paint)* irrégulier; *(pattern)* strié; *(mirror, plates etc)* couvert de traces; *(cloud)* effiloché; **her make-up had gone s.** son maquillage avait dégouliné

▸▸ *Br Culin* **s. bacon** bacon *m* entrelardé

stream [striːm] N **1** *(brook)* ruisseau *m*; **mountain s.** torrent *m*

2 *(flow)* *(of light, blood, water)* flot(s) *m(pl)*, jet *m*; *(of lava)* coulée *f*; *(of tears, words, congratulations, insults)* flot, torrent *m*; *(of people, cars)* flot; **in one continuous s.** à jet continu

3 *(current)* courant *m*; **with the s.** dans le sens du courant, au fil de l'eau; **against the s.** contre le courant, à contre-courant; *Fig* **to go with the s.** suivre le mouvement; *Fig* **to go against the s.** aller à contre-courant; **the main s. of public opinion** le courant de l'opinion publique

4 to come on s. *(of oil)* commencer à couler; *(of new power station etc)* entrer en production; **to go off s.** *(of oil)* cesser de couler; *(of power station etc)* cesser de produire

5 *Br Sch* groupe *m* de niveau

VI **1** *(of liquid)* couler à flots, ruisseler; **people were streaming over the bridge** un flot continu de gens traversait le pont; **people streamed out of the stadium** des flots de gens sortaient du stade; **the sunlight streams in(to the room)** le soleil entre à flots (dans la chambre)

2 *(of surface)* ruisseler **(with** de); **his eyes were streaming** *(he was crying)* il était ruisselant de larmes; *(his eyes were watering)* il avait les yeux qui pleuraient

3 *(of hair, garment, banner)* flotter (au vent)

VT **1 to s. blood** ruisseler de sang **2** *Br Sch* **s. pupils** répartir les élèves selon leur niveau d'aptitude **3** *(audio, video)* transmettre en continu *(sur l'Internet)*

▸▸ **s. feed** *(on photocopier)* alimentation *f* automatique; *Liter* **s. of consciousness** monologue *m* intérieur

streamer ['striːmər] N **1** *(flag)* banderole *f*; **(paper) streamers** serpentins *mpl* (de carnaval) **2** *Journ (headline)* titre *m* flamboyant, bandeau *m*, cinq colonnes *fpl* à la une **3** *Comput* streamer *m*, dévideur *m*

streaming ['striːmɪŋ] ADJ *(liquid)* qui coule; *Fam* **to have a s. cold** avoir un gros rhume

N **1** *Br Sch* répartition *f* par niveaux **2** *(of audio, video)* streaming *m*, transmission *f* en continu *(sur l'Internet)*

streamline ['striːmlaɪn] VT **1** *(car etc)* caréner **2** *Fig (method, economy)* rationaliser; *(department, company, army etc)* dégraisser

streamlined ['striːmlaɪnd] ADJ **1** *Aut, Aviat* caréné; *(fuselage)* aérodynamique; *(ship)* hydrodynamique **2** *Fig (system, economy)* rationalisé; *(department, organization, army etc)* dégraissé

streamlining ['striːmlaɪnɪŋ] N **1** *(of bodywork)* carénage *m*, profilage *m* **2** *Fig (of system, economy)* rationalisation *f*; *(of department, organization, army etc)* dégraissage *m*

street [striːt] N rue *f*; **back s.** petite rue écartée; *Pej* rue pauvre; *(dangerous)* rue mal fréquentée; **the High S.** la Grand-rue; **to turn** *or* **throw sb (out) into the s.** jeter qn à la rue; **to walk the streets** courir les rues, battre le pavé; *(of prostitute)* faire le trottoir; **on the s.** dans la rue; **to be on the street(s)** *(of prostitute)* faire le trottoir; *(of homeless person)* être à la rue; **the whole s. heard the row** toute la rue a entendu la dispute; **the man in the s.** Monsieur Tout-le-Monde, l'homme

de la rue; *Fam* **she's streets ahead of the rest of the class** elle est largement en tête de la classe; *Fig* **that's right up my s.** c'est tout à fait mon rayon

▸▸ *Br Old-fashioned* **s. Arab** gamin, -ine *ou* gosse *mf* des rues; **s. art** peintures *fpl* murales *(dans la rue)*; **s. cred** image *f* de marque; **to have a lot of s. cred** être très branché; **it gives him a lot of s. cred** ça lui donne une bonne image de marque; **they're gaining s. cred** leur image de marque s'améliore; **this won't do much for my s. cred** ça va craindre pour mon image de marque; **s. furniture** mobilier *m* urbain; **s. guide** plan *m* de la ville; *Am Sport* **s. hockey** hockey *m* sur roulettes; **s. interview** micro-trottoir *m*, *pl* micros-trottoirs; **s. lamp** réverbère *m*; **s. level** rez-de-chaussée *m inv*; **below s. level** au sous-sol; **s. life** *(activity)* animation *f* (des rues); **s. light** réverbère; **s. lighting** éclairage *m* public; **s. map** plan de la ville; **s. market** marché *m* en plein air *ou* à ciel ouvert; *St Exch* marché hors Bourse; **s. musician** musicien, -ienne des rues; **s. party** = fête *f* de rue organisée pour célébrer un événement; **s. person** SDF *mf*; **s. photographer** photostoppeur, -euse; **s. plan** plan de la ville; **s. sweeper** *(person)* balayeur, -euse; *(machine)* balayeuse *f*; **s. theatre** théâtre *m* de rue *ou* de foire; **s. trader** marchand, -ande ambulant(e); *Old-fashioned* **s. urchin** gamin, -ine *ou* gosse des rues; **s. value** *(of drugs)* valeur *f* marchande

streetcar ['striːtkɑːr] N *Am* tramway *m*

streetwalker ['striːtwɔːkər] N racoleuse *f*

streetwise ['striːtwaɪz] ADJ averti, malin

strength [streŋθ] N **1** *(of person, acid, player, team)* force *f*; *Chem (of solution)* titre *m*; *Elec (of current)* intensité *f*; *(of beam, rope)* solidité *f*; *(of emotion)* force, intensité; *(of market)* fermeté *f*; **solution at full s.**, **full-s. solution** solution *f* concentrée; **s. of character** force de caractère; **s. of purpose** détermination *f*; **s. of will** résolution *f*, volonté *f*; **by sheer (physical) s.** uniquement grâce à la force physique; **to recover** *or* **regain one's s.** reprendre des forces; **you must keep up your s.** il faut garder vos forces; **she doesn't know her own s.** elle ne connaît pas sa force; **to build up one's s. again** reprendre des forces; **to lose s.** s'affaiblir; *Fig* **to do sth on the s. of what one has been told** faire qch en se fiant à *ou* en s'appuyant sur ce qu'on vous a dit; **convicted on the s. of eyewitness evidence** condamné sur la foi des déclarations de témoins oculaires; **he got a good job on the s. of his qualifications** il a obtenu un bon emploi grâce à ses diplômes; **s. of a friendship** solidité d'une amitié; **s. of materials** résistance *f* des matériaux; **to go from s. to s.** *(of person's health)* aller de mieux en mieux; *(of project etc)* avancer à pas de géant; *(of company, new writer etc)* connaître une réussite de plus en plus remarquable; **we went from s. to s.** *(in business or political relationship)* nous avons progressé à pas de géant; *(in personal relationship)* nous nous entendions de mieux en mieux; *Mktg* **strengths and weaknesses** forces et faiblesses *fpl*; *Fam* **give me s.!** pitié!

2 *(numbers)* **to be present in great s.** être présents en grand nombre; **they were there in full s.** ils y étaient au grand complet

3 *Mil (of army)*, *Fig* effectif(s) *m(pl)*; **wartime/peacetime s.** effectif de guerre/de paix; **to be under s.** avoir un effectif insuffisant; **to bring a battalion/department up to s.** compléter l'effectif d'un bataillon/service; **there are 30 of us when we're at full s.** nous sommes 30 quand nous sommes au complet

strengthen ['streŋθ(ə)n] VT *(wall, house, position, friendship)* consolider; *(beam, ma-*

terial, law, pound sterling) renforcer; (person, body) fortifier; (sb's authority) (r)affermir; Chem (solution) augmenter la concentration de; Typ (colour) charger; **it would s. my hand** or **position** cela renforcerait ma position; **this merely strengthened their resolve** ça n'a fait que renforcer leur détermination

VI (of resolve, position etc) se renforcer, s'affermir; (of sterling etc) se raffermir; (of patient, industry, country etc) prendre ou reprendre des forces

strengthening ['streŋθ(ə)nɪŋ] **ADJ** (tonic) fortifiant

N (of material) renforcement m; (of wall, building) consolidation f; (of sb's authority) (r)affermissement m; **there was a s. of opposition** l'opposition s'est renforcée; **there was a slight s. of the pound on foreign markets** il y a eu un léger renforcement de la livre sur les marchés étrangers

strenuous ['strenjʊəs] **ADJ** (work, match, day at the office) fatigant; (campaigner) zélé; (effort, opposition) acharné; (denial) formel, énergique; **to make s. efforts to get sth done** faire des efforts acharnés pour accomplir qch; **a s. advocate of sth** un défenseur passionné de qch; **a s. opponent of sth** un adversaire acharné de qch; **s. life** vie f harassante

strenuously ['strenjʊəslɪ] **ADV** vigoureusement; (to work, oppose) avec acharnement; (to deny) formellement, énergiquement

strenuousness ['strenjʊəsnɪs] **N** (of work) dureté f (de l'effort physique exigé); (of opposition) acharnement m

strep throat [strep] **N** Am **to have a s.** avoir mal à la gorge

streptococcal [streptəʊ'kɒk(ə)l] **ADJ** Med streptococcique

streptococcus, pl **streptococci** [streptəʊ-'kɒkəs, -'kɒk(s)aɪ] **N** Med streptocoque m

streptomycin [streptəʊ'maɪsɪn] **N** Med streptomycine f

stress [stres] **N 1** (mental) stress m, tension f; **to be under a lot of s.** être en proie au stress, être très tendu; **how does he react under s.?** comment réagit-il sous le stress ou sous la pression?; **I work better under s.** je travaille mieux sous la pression; **this puts our relationship under s.** ça crée des tensions dans nos relations; **how to cope with s.** comment vivre avec le stress; **some people thrive on s.** certaines personnes travaillent mieux sous la pression; **a major s. factor** un important facteur de stress ou de tension; **the stresses and strains of modern life** les tensions et les pressions de la vie moderne

2 Tech etc (tension) tension f, travail m; Tech (in components) sollicitation f; **to be in s.** (of beam) travailler

3 (emphasis) insistance f, Ling accent m tonique; (in prosody) accentuation f; **to put s. on sth** insister sur qch; **to lay s. on** (fact) insister sur, faire ressortir; (word) insister sur; **the s. falls on the last syllable** l'accent tonique tombe sur la dernière syllabe; **there was too much s. on memorization of facts** on demandait d'apprendre trop de faits par cœur

VT 1 (emphasize) insister sur; (fact) faire ressortir; (word) souligner, insister sur; **she stressed that no decision had been taken** elle a insisté sur ou souligné le fait qu'aucune décision n'avait été prise

2 Ling (syllable) accentuer, appuyer sur; **stressed syllable** syllabe f accentuée

3 Tech (beam) charger, fatiguer, faire travailler; **to be stressed** (of beam) travailler

▸▸ Med **s. fracture** fracture f de surmenage; Tech etc **s. limit** limite f de travail ou de fatigue; Ling **s. mark** marque f d'accent

stressed [strest] **ADJ** Tech sollicité; (beam etc) sous tension; (person) stressé, sous tension, tendu; (syllable) accentué; **to let oneself get s.** se laisser gagner par le stress

stressed-out **ADJ** (complètement) stressé

stressful ['stresfʊl] **ADJ** (situation, job) stressant

stress-related **ADJ** dû au stress
▸▸ **s. illness** maladie f due au stress

STRETCH [stretʃ] **N 1** (act of stretching) étirement m; **with a yawn and a s.** en bâillant et en s'étirant; **to have a s.** s'étirer; **at full s.** au maximum de ses capacités; **by no s. of the imagination could it be called a democracy** même avec beaucoup d'imagination ou même en faisant un gros effort d'imagination, on ne pourrait pas dire qu'il s'agit d'une démocratie; **it's not ready yet, not by a long s.** ce n'est pas encore prêt, et il s'en faut de beaucoup; Mus **s. of the fingers** (at the piano) écart m des doigts

2 (elasticity) élasticité f; **with two-way s.** (of elastic fabric) extensible dans les deux sens

3 (of country, water) étendue f; (of land) bande f; (of road) section f; (of time, silence etc) période f; **for a long s. of time** (pendant) longtemps, pendant une longue période de temps; **at a s., at one s.** (tout) d'un trait, d'affilée; **she's been working for hours at a s.** voilà des heures qu'elle travaille sans désemparer; Fam **to do a five-year s.** (in prison) faire cinq ans de taule

VT 1 (extend) (elastic, belt, cable, spring) tendre; (shoes, gloves) détendre, élargir; (sb's patience) éprouver, exercer; (meaning of a word) forcer; (arm) allonger; (hand) tendre, avancer; (leg) étirer; **to s. oneself** s'étirer; **to s. one's neck to see sth** tendre le cou pour voir qch; **to s. one's legs** (take short walk etc) se dégourdir les jambes; **to s. its wings** (of bird) déployer ses ailes; Fig **to s. one's wings** voler de ses propres ailes; **he stretched his arm through the broken window** il allongea le bras à travers le carreau cassé; **to s. the truth** exagérer; **to s. a point** faire une exception (**for sb** en faveur de qn); Fam **that's stretching it a bit!** vous y allez/il y va/etc un peu fort!; Art **to s. the canvas on the frame** tendre la toile sur le châssis; **to s. a rope across a room** tendre une corde à travers une pièce; **to s. an awning over the deck** établir une tente sur le pont

2 (put demands on) demander un effort maximum à; (resources) grever jusqu'à la limite; **to be fully stretched** (of person) être à son rendement maximum; (of resources, services) être sollicité à fond; **she needs a job that will s. her** elle a besoin d'un travail qui la pousse à donner le maximum

3 (make last) (income, supplies etc) tirer au maximum sur; **we should be able to s. the food until the weekend** nous devrions pouvoir faire durer les provisions jusqu'au week-end; **our money could be stretched to last until Christmas** nous pourrions faire durer notre argent jusqu'à Noël

VI 1 (become longer) s'allonger; (of person, rope) s'étirer; (of elastic) se détendre; (of gloves etc) se détendre, s'élargir; **the rope stretched across the ravine** la corde allait d'un côté à l'autre du ravin; **it's rude to s.!** (with arm) il est impoli d'allonger le bras comme ça!; **she stretched across the table** elle allongea le bras ou tout le corps en travers de la table; **he stretched down under the table to pick up …** il allongea le bras ou le corps sous la table pour ramasser …; **I have to s. up to reach the top shelf** il faut que je m'étire pour atteindre l'étagère du haut

2 (of terrain, road etc) s'étendre; **the road stretches away into the distance** la route s'étire dans le lointain

3 **my resources won't s. to that** mes moyens (pécuniaires) ne vont pas jusque-là; **the dish will s. to six helpings** on pourra faire six portions; **there is enough material here to s. to two books** il y a assez de matière pour en faire deux livres
▸▸ **s. fabric** Stretch ® m; **s. mark** vergeture f
▸ **stretch out** **VI 1** (extend limbs) s'étirer; (of horse when racing) aller ventre à terre

2 (extend) (of road, valley etc) s'étendre; **a barren future stretched out ahead of her** un avenir sombre se profilait devant elle

VT SEP (extend) (arm) allonger; (hand) tendre, avancer; **to lie stretched out on the ground** être étendu par terre; **we could s. the meat out till Sunday** nous pourrions faire durer la viande jusqu'à dimanche

stretcher ['stretʃər] **N 1** (for casualty) brancard m, civière f; **he was carried** or **taken off on a s.** on l'a emmené sur une civière ou un brancard; **he's a s. case** Med il faut l'emporter sur une civière; Fig Fam (having been beaten up etc) il est bon pour l'hôpital **2** Art (canvas) **s.** châssis m
▸▸ **s. bearer** brancardier m; **s. party** détachement m de brancardiers
▸ **stretcher off** **VT SEP** (remove on stretcher) emmener sur une civière

stretching ['stretʃɪŋ] **N 1** Sport (warm-up) étirement m (musculaire) **2 s. of the rules** entorse f au règlement

stretchy ['stretʃɪ] **ADJ** élastique, extensible

strew [struː] **VT** (pp **strewed** [struːd] or **strewn** [struːn]) **to s. sth over the floor** (on purpose) jeter ou répandre qch sur le plancher, (re)couvrir le plancher de qch; (accidentally) répandre qch sur le plancher; **the ground was strewn with rushes** une jonchée de roseaux recouvrait le sol, le sol était jonché de roseaux; **the bomb exploded, strewing the crowd with pieces of broken glass** la bombe explosa, couvrant la foule de débris de verre; **his clothes were strewn everywhere in the house** ses vêtements étaient éparpillés partout dans la maison; **toys were strewn over** or **around** or **on the floor** des jouets jonchaient le plancher; **references to classical literature are strewn throughout his work** son œuvre est émaillée de références à la littérature classique

strewth [struːθ] **INT** Br Sl ça alors!

striated [straɪ'eɪtɪd] **ADJ** strié

stricken ['strɪk(ə)n] **ADJ** esp Lit (person, voice, look) affligé; **he looked s.** il avait l'air affligé; **s. with grief** accablé de douleur; **s. with guilt** accablé par les remords; **s. by** or **with polio** atteint de polio; **s. by** or **with blindness** frappé de cécité; **the s. city** la ville sinistrée; **the s. vessel** le vaisseau en détresse ou naufragé; **the s. animal hid in the bushes** l'animal blessé se cacha dans les fourrés

PP see **strike VT, VI**

strict [strɪkt] **ADJ 1** (teacher, boss, parent etc) strict, sévère; **to be s. with sb** être sévère ou strict avec ou envers qn **2** (ruling, etiquette) strict, péremptoire; (discipline, regime) sévère, strict; (fast) strict, austère; **s. deadline** délai m de rigueur; **s. morals** morale f rigide, mœurs fpl sévères; **s. Muslim** musulman de stricte obédience; **she gave s. orders not to be woken** elle a donné l'ordre formel ou strict qu'on ne la réveille pas **3** (exact) exact, strict; **the s. minimum** le strict minimum; **in the s. sense of the word** au sens strict du mot; **to observe s. neutrality** observer une neutralité la plus stricte; **in strictest confidence** à titre tout à fait ou strictement confidentiel

strictly ['strɪktlɪ] **ADV 1** (sternly) strictement, sévèrement; (treated, brought up) avec rigueur **2** (totally) strictement; **s. confi-**

dential strictement confidentiel; **smoking (is) s. prohibited** il est strictement *ou* formellement interdit de fumer; **it is s. forbidden** c'est strictement défendu, c'est formellement interdit **3** *(exactly)* exactement, rigoureusement; **s. (speaking)** à proprement parler; **this rule was s. observed** cette règle a été rigoureusement *ou* strictement observée

strictness ['strɪktnɪs] N **1** *(of discipline)* sévérité f **2** *(of rules)* rigueur f; **their s. in applying the rules** la rigueur avec laquelle ils appliquaient le règlement **3** *(of interpretation)* exactitude f

stricture ['strɪktʃər] N *Fml* **1** *(usu pl)* **strictures** *(criticism)* critiques fpl; **to pass strictures (up)on sb/sth** diriger ses critiques contre qn/qch **2** *(restriction)* restriction f, limitation f **3** *Med (of ureter)* rétrécissement m; *(of intestine)* étranglement m

stride [straɪd] N **1** (grand) pas m, enjambée f; *(when running)* foulée f; **to shorten/lengthen one's s.** ralentir/allonger le pas; *Fig* **to make great strides** faire de grands progrès *ou* des progrès rapides; *Fig* **to take sth in one's s.** *or Am* **in s.** *(do easily)* faire qch sans le moindre effort; *(not be disconcerted by)* ne pas se laisser troubler par qch; **she left him after 6 months, but he took it all in his s.** après 6 mois, elle l'a quitté brusquement, mais il ne s'est pas laissé troubler pour autant; **these things happen, you just have to learn to take them in your s.** ce sont des choses qui arrivent, il faut savoir les accepter; **eventually you come to take it all in your s.** on finit par s'y faire; **to get into** *or Fam* **to hit one's s.** *(in walking)* prendre son allure normale; *Sport (of runner)* trouver son rythme; *(in working)* prendre la cadence; *Fig* **to put sb off his/her s.** faire perdre la cadence à qn **2** *esp Austr Fam* **strides** *(trousers)* fute m, futal m

▸ VI *(pt* **strode** [strəʊd]; *pp* **stridden** ['strɪd(ə)n])* marcher à grands pas *ou* à grandes enjambées; **she strode into the room** elle est entrée dans la pièce à grandes enjambées; **to s. along/away** avancer/s'éloigner à grands pas; **science is striding further ahead each year** chaque année, la science avance *ou* progresse à pas de géant; **she just strode straight up to him and said …** elle se dirigea droit vers lui et dit …; **Bonaparte strode impatiently up and down the room** Bonaparte arpentait impatiemment la pièce; **to s. over sth** enjamber qch

▸ VT *Lit* **he strode the deck/the streets** il arpentait le pont/les rues

stridency ['straɪdənsɪ] N stridence f; *(of protests)* véhémence f

strident ['straɪdənt] ADJ strident; *(colour)* criard; *(protest)* véhément

stridently ['straɪdəntlɪ] ADV *(to talk)* d'une voix stridente; *(to laugh, shout)* de façon stridente; *(to protest)* avec véhémence

strife [straɪf] N contestation f; **domestic s.** querelles fpl de ménage; **political/sectarian s.** des luttes fpl politiques/sectaires; **after years of industrial s.** après des années de conflits sociaux

---

STRIKE [straɪk]

N grève **1** ▪ rencontre **2** ▪ coup **3** ▪ sonnerie **3**	
VT frapper **1, 3, 12** ▪ heurter **2** ▪ frotter **4** ▪ impressionner **5** ▪ découvrir **6** ▪ démonter **7** ▪ supprimer **9**	
VI attaquer **1** ▪ frapper **1** ▪ survenir **1** ▪ sonner **2** ▪ se mettre en grève **3**	

N **1** *Ind* grève f; **teachers'/miners' s.** grève des professeurs/mineurs; **postal s.** grève des

---

postiers; **power s.** = grève dans le secteur de l'électricité; **an unofficial s.** = grève qui n'est pas soutenue par les syndicats; **lightning s.** grève surprise; **sit-down s.** grève sur le tas; **sympathy s.** grève de solidarité; **to be on s.** être en grève, faire grève; **to go on** *or* **come out on s.** se mettre en grève; **to bring people out on s.** amener des gens à faire grève; **to go on hunger s.** *(of prisoner)* faire la grève de la faim; **there have been calls for s. action** on a appelé à la grève; **the dispute could easily lead to s. action** le conflit pouvait très facilement amener une grève

2 *Min (of ore, oil)* rencontre f; *(of bed)* découverte f; **there has been a major oil s.** il y a eu une découverte d'un important gisement de pétrole; *Fig Fam* **lucky s.** coup m de veine

3 *(blow)* coup m; *(of clock)* sonnerie f; *Mil* raid m (**on** sur); *Fishing (by angler)* ferrage m; *(by fish)* mordage m; *(in baseball)* balle f manquée *(par le batteur)*; *(in tenpin bowling)* honneur m double; *Mil* **first s. weapon** arme f de première frappe; *Mil, Aviat* **air s.** raid, intervention f aérienne

▸ VT *(pt* **struck** [strʌk]; *pp* **struck,** *Arch, Lit* **stricken** ['strɪk(ə)n])* **1** *(hit) (person, piano key)* frapper; **to s. sb in the face** frapper qn à la figure; **to be struck by a stone** être frappé par une pierre; **to s. sb a blow** porter *ou* assener un coup à qn; **they got what they wanted without striking a blow** ils ont obtenu ce qu'ils voulaient sans coup férir; **to be struck by a huge wave** essuyer un coup de mer; **ready to s. a blow for freedom of speech** prêt à se battre pour défendre la liberté de parole; **who struck the first blow?** qui a frappé le premier?; *Fig* **in his speech, he struck a blow for freedom/those who …** par son discours, il a fait avancer la cause de liberté/de ceux qui …; *Fig* **to s. a blow at sth** taper sur qch; *Mus* **to s. a chord (with me)** je me retrouve là-dedans; *Fig* **that strikes a familiar note** cela fait l'effet du déjà vu/du déjà entendu, ça me rappelle des choses; **to s. the right/wrong note** sonner juste/faux; **the clock strikes the hour and half hour** l'horloge sonne l'heure et la demi-heure; **the clock struck the hour** l'horloge sonna l'heure juste; **as the clock struck ten** lorsque l'horloge sonna dix heures

2 *(collide with)* frapper contre, heurter; **his head struck the pavement** sa tête a heurté le trottoir; **to s. (the) bottom** *(of ship)* toucher (le fond), talonner; **struck by lightning** *(house)* frappé par la foudre; *(tree, person)* foudroyé; **lightning had struck the house** la foudre était tombée sur la maison; **to s. a mine** *(of ship)* heurter une mine; **to s. a pedestrian** *(of car)* heurter un piéton; **a sound struck my ear** un bruit attira mon attention

3 to s. terror into sb frapper qn de terreur; **it struck fear into their hearts** ils furent glacés d'effroi; **to s. sb with surprise** frapper qn d'étonnement; **struck with panic/terror** pris de panique/terrorisé; **to be struck dumb/blind** être frappé de mutisme/cécité; **he was struck dead by a heart attack** il a été emporté par une crise cardiaque; **the bullet hit her in the head, striking her dead** la balle l'a frappée en pleine tête, la tuant sur le coup; *Lit* **he struck his opponent dead** il a tué son adversaire d'un coup

4 *(match)* allumer, frotter; *(sparks)* faire jaillir; *Old-fashioned Br Sl* **s. a light!** nom de Dieu!

5 *(impress)* impressionner; *(the eye, imagination)* frapper; **how does she s. you?** quelle impression vous fait-elle?; **he strikes me as (being) sincere** il me paraît sincère; **the place struck her as familiar** l'endroit lui a paru familier; **that is how it struck me** voilà l'effet que cela m'a fait; **did it never s. you that you weren't wanted there?** ne vous est-il ja-

---

mais venu à l'esprit que vous étiez de trop?; **what struck me was his brazen impudence** ce qui m'a frappé, c'est son impudence sans nom; **the thought struck me that …** l'idée m'est venue *ou* il m'est venu à l'idée que …; **it strikes me that we'd do better to say no** j'ai la nette impression que nous ferions mieux de dire non

6 *(discover) (path)* tomber sur, découvrir; *(gold)* découvrir; **to s. oil** atteindre une nappe de pétrole, rencontrer *ou* toucher le pétrole; *Fig* trouver un filon; *Fam* **she has struck it rich** elle a fait fortune

7 *(lower) (tent)* démonter; *Naut (sail)* amener, caler; *Theat* **to s. the set** démonter le décor; **to s. camp** lever le camp; **to s. one's flag** *or* **one's colours** *Naut* amener *ou* rentrer son pavillon, mettre pavillon bas; *Fig (surrender)* se rendre

8 to s. an attitude poser

9 to s. a bargain faire *ou* conclure un marché; **to s. a balance between X and Y** trouver un équilibre entre X et Y; **to s. an agreement/deal** conclure un accord/un marché (**with sb** avec qn)

10 *(delete)* enlever, supprimer; **that remark must be struck** *or Am* **stricken from the record** cette remarque doit être retirée du procès-verbal

11 *(of plant)* **to s. root** prendre racine

12 *(coin, medal)* frapper

▸ VI **1** *(attack) (of enemy)* attaquer; *(of assassin, burglar etc)* frapper; *(of disaster, earthquake etc)* survenir; *(with dagger, club etc)* frapper; *(of serpent)* foncer; *Fig* **to s. at sth** menacer qch; **these reforms s. deep at the heart of our traditional way of life** ces réformes mettent en péril notre mode de vie traditionnel; **to s. home** faire mouche; *Prov* **s. while the iron is hot** il faut battre le fer tant qu'il est chaud; **the terrorists struck twice** les terroristes ont frappé deux fois; **where the missile struck** là où le missile a frappé

2 *(of clock)* sonner

3 *Ind* se mettre en grève; **to s. for better conditions** se mettre en grève pour de meilleures conditions de travail; **striking workers** ouvriers en grève

4 *(travel, head)* prendre *(une certaine direction)*; **to s. across country** prendre à travers champs; **they then struck west** ils sont ensuite partis vers l'ouest

5 *(of cutting)* prendre (racine)

▸▸ **s. aircraft** avion(s) *m(pl)* d'assaut; **s. ballot** = vote m avant que les syndicats ne décident d'une grève; **s. force** *(nuclear capacity)* force f de frappe; *(of police, soldiers, squad)* détachement m *ou* brigade f d'intervention; *(larger force)* force d'intervention; **s. fund** = caisse f de prévoyance permettant d'aider les grévistes; **s. notice** préavis m de grève; **s. pay** salaire m de gréviste *(versé par le syndicat ou par un fonds de solidarité)*; *Fin* **s. price** *(for share)* prix m d'exercice

▸ **strike back** VT SEP *(hit with return blow)* **to s. sb back** rendre son coup à qn; **if anyone strikes me, I s. him back** si quelqu'un me frappe, je rends le coup

▸ VI *(hit return blow)* rendre le coup; *Fig (retaliate)* effectuer des représailles; **to s. back at the enemy** répliquer à l'ennemi, contre-attaquer; **the government struck back at its critics** le gouvernement a répondu à ceux qui le critiquaient

▸ **strike down** VT SEP *(knock down)* renverser; *(kill)* abattre; *Fig* **struck down by disease** terrassé par la maladie

▸ **strike off** VT SEP **1** *(remove by hitting)* enlever d'un coup; *(sb's head)* trancher

2 *(delete)* **to s. off a name from a list, to s. a name off a list** biffer *ou* rayer un nom d'une liste; **to be struck off** *(of doctor, solicitor)* être radié

3 *Com (deduct)* **to s. off £5** faire une réduction de *ou* déduire 5 livres
4 *Typ (number of copies)* tirer
vi *(travel, head)* **to s. off to the left** *(of person)* prendre à gauche; *(of road)* tourner à gauche; **we left the path and struck off into the depths of the forest** nous avons quitté le sentier et nous nous sommes enfoncés dans la forêt
▸ **strike on vt insep** *(discover)* tomber sur
▸ **strike out vt sep** *(delete)* *(word)* rayer, biffer, barrer; **s. out whichever does not apply** rayer la mention inutile
vi 1 *(hit out)* **to s. out at sb** allonger *ou* porter un coup à qn; *Fig (criticize, attack)* attaquer qn; **to s. out right and left** frapper à droite et à gauche
2 *(travel, head)* **I struck out for the shore** *(swimming)* j'ai commencé à nager dans la direction du rivage; *(rowing)* j'ai commencé à ramer dans la direction du rivage; *Fig* **to s. out in a new direction** *(in life, thinking etc)* prendre une direction nouvelle
3 *(become independent)* **to s. out for oneself, to s. out on one's own** voler de ses propres ailes
4 *(in baseball)* sortir (du jeu)
▸ **strike up vt sep** *(song)* entonner; *(piece of music)* commencer de *ou* à jouer; **to s. up a friendship with sb** se lier d'amitié avec qn, se prendre d'amitié pour qn; **to s. up an acquaintance with sb** lier connaissance avec qn; **to s. up a conversation with sb** entrer en conversation avec qn; **they immediately struck up a conversation** ils sont immédiatement entrés en conversation
vi on his arrival the band struck up à son arrivée, la fanfare attaqua un morceau

strikebound ['straɪkbaʊnd] **adj** paralysé par une/la grève; *(commuters)* coincé par une/la grève

strikebreaker ['straɪkbreɪkər] **n** *Ind* briseur, -euse de grève

strike-out mode n *Comput* mode *m* barré

striker ['straɪkər] **n 1** *Ind* gréviste *mf* **2** *Ftbl* buteur *m*; *Cr* = batteur *m* qui reçoit; *(in baseball)* batteur *m* **3** *(device)* frappeur *m*; *(of clock)* marteau *m*; *(of firearm)* percuteur *m*
▸ ▸ *Aut* **s. plate** gâche *f* de porte

strike-thru mode n *Comput* mode *m* barré

striking ['straɪkɪŋ] **adj 1** *(sight, similarity, difference, appearance)* frappant, saisissant; *(feature)* saillant; *(situation)* dramatique; **he was a s. figure** c'était un personnage impressionnant; **of s. beauty** d'une beauté frappante **2** *(workers)* en grève
n 1 *(of coins)* frappe *f* **2 within s. distance** à quelques kilomètres; **we were within s. distance of the summit** nous étions tout près du sommet; **we haven't finished, but we're within s. distance** nous n'avons pas encore fini, mais on en est tout près **3** *(of clock)* sonnerie *f*
▸ ▸ **s. clock** pendule *f* à sonnerie; **s. mechanism** sonnerie *f* (des heures); **s. off** *(of name)* suppression *f*; *(of lawyer, doctor)* radiation *f*; **s. surface** *(for match)* frottoir *m*

strikingly ['straɪkɪŋlɪ] **adv** d'une manière frappante *ou* saisissante; **s. beautiful** d'une beauté frappante

Strine [straɪn] **n** *Fam Hum* anglais *m* australien

string [strɪŋ] **n 1** *(cord)* ficelle *f*; *(piece of string)* bout *m* de ficelle; *(of puppet)* fil *m*; **ball of s.** pelote *f* de ficelle; *Fig* **to have sb on a s.** mener qn par le bout du nez; *Fig* **to keep sb on a s.** *(in uncertainty)* laisser qn dans l'incertitude; *(keep control over)* tenir qn en laisse; *Fig* **(with) no strings (attached)** sans conditions, sans condition aucune; **with strings attached** avec des conditions;

Fig **to pull the strings** tirer les ficelles; *Fig* **to pull strings** faire jouer ses relations *ou Fam* le piston; *Fig* **somebody pulled strings to get him the job** il a eu le poste par piston
2 *(of violin, piano, bow)* corde *f*; *Tennis* **strings** *(of racket)* cordes, cordage *m*; **the strings of a violin** la monture d'un violon; **guitar/violin s.** corde de guitare/de violon; **the strings** *(in orchestra)* *(instruments, players)* les cordes; **a s. of horses** un groupe de chevaux; **our first s.** *(athlete, horse etc)* le meilleur; **our second s.** *(athletes, horse)* nos athlètes/notre cheval numéro deux; *Fig* **to have more than one s. to one's bow** avoir plus d'une corde à son arc
3 *(of onions, islands)* chapelet *m*; *(of medals)* brochette *f*; *(of vehicles)* file *f*; *(of barges)* train *m*; *(of words, shops, defeats)* série *f*; **s. of beads** collier *m*; *Rel* chapelet *m*; **s. of pearls** collier de perles; **a whole s. of children/names** toute une kyrielle d'enfants/de noms
4 *Comput* suite *f*, chaîne *f*; **s. of characters** suite de caractères
vt *(pp, pt strung* [strʌŋ]*)* **1** *(fit with strings)* *(tennis racket)* corder; *(violin)* mettre les cordes à, monter; *(bow)* bander; **to be highly strung** *(of person, horse etc)* être nerveux; *(likely to suffer for emotional reasons)* être émotif
2 *(pearls)* enfiler; **to s. fairy lights across a garden** accrocher des guirlandes de lampions dans un jardin; *Fig* **to s. sentences together** enfiler des phrases; **he can't s. two sentences together** il est incapable d'aligner trois mots
3 *Culin* **to s. beans** ôter les fils des haricots
▸ ▸ **s. bag** filet *m* à provisions; **s. band** orchestre *m* à cordes; **s. bass** contrebasse *f*; **s. bean** haricot *m* vert; **s. orchestra** orchestre *m* à cordes; **s. quartet** quatuor *m* à cordes; *Comput* **s. variable** variable *f* alphanumérique; **s. vest** tricot *m* de corps à grosses mailles
▸ **string along vt sep** *Fam (deceitfully encourage)* duper, tromper; **they're just stringing you along** ils se moquent de toi; **let's s. them along a bit longer** et si on les faisait marcher encore un peu
▸ **string along with vt insep** *Fam (accompany)* accompagner, faire route avec
▸ **string out vt** *(form long line)* s'espacer; *Sport* **the field strung out behind** le peloton des coureurs s'effilochait
vt sep 1 *(in time)* **to s. sth out** faire durer qch; **the TV series was strung out over six weeks** le feuilleton (de) télé a traîné pendant six semaines **2** *(in space)* **the troops were strung out over 200 kilometres** les troupes s'échelonnaient sur 200 kilomètres; **you're all too strung out, get closer together** vous êtes trop clairsemés, rapprochez-vous les uns des autres
▸ **string up vt sep** *Fam (hang)* pendre haut et court

stringboard ['strɪŋbɔːd] **n** *Constr* limon *m* (d'escalier)

stringed [strɪŋd] **adj** *Mus (instrument)* à cordes

stringency ['strɪndʒənsɪ] **n** *(of rules)* rigueur *f*, sévérité *f*; *Fin (of market)* resserrement *m*

stringent ['strɪndʒənt] **adj** *(rules)* rigoureux, -euse, strict; *Fin (market)* tendu, serré

stringently ['strɪndʒəntlɪ] **adv** rigoureusement, strictement

stringer ['strɪŋər] **n** *(journalist)* reporter *m* local, stringer *m*, stringman *m*

stringing ['strɪŋɪŋ] **n** *(act)* *(of violin)* montage *m*; *(of racket)* cordage *m*; *(of bow)* bandage *m*

stringpiece ['strɪŋpiːs] **n** *Constr* longrine *f*

string-puller [-pʊlər] **n** *Fam* **he could be a**

useful s. il peut nous/leur/etc être utile s'il fait jouer ses relations

stringy ['strɪŋɪ] **adj 1** *(vegetables)* fibreux, -euse, filandreux, -euse; **s. meat** viande *f* filandreuse **2** *(person)* élancé

STRIP [strɪp] **n 1** *(of cloth, paper)* bande *f*; *(of metal)* lame *f*, lamelle *f*; *(of ground)* bande, langue *f*, **narrow s.** bandelette *f*; *Fig* **to tear sb off a s.** donner *ou* passer un savon à qn, laver la tête à qn; *Med* **dressing s.** bande à pansement; *Aviat* **(landing) s.** piste *f* (d'atterrissage); **comic s.** bande dessinée, BD *f*
2 *Sport (clothes)* *(of football team)* tenue *f*
3 **to do a s.** *(undress)* se déshabiller, se dévêtir; *(for show)* faire un strip-tease
vt (-pp-) 1 *(undress)* déshabiller, dévêtir; **to s. sb to the skin, to s. sb naked** mettre qn à poil; **stripped to the waist** nu jusqu'à la ceinture, torse nu
2 *(deprive)* **to s. sb of sth** dépouiller *ou* déposséder qn de qch; **to s. sb of his/her clothes** dépouiller qn de ses vêtements; **trees stripped of their leaves** arbres dépouillés de leurs feuilles; **stripped of all his worldly goods** dépouillé de tous ses biens; **to be stripped of one's title/rank/office** être dépouillé de son titre/rang/poste
3 *(bed)* défaire; *Elec (cable)* dénuder; *Phot (plate)* pelliculer; **to s. a tree** *(of leaves)* effeuiller un arbre; *(of bark)* écorcer un arbre; *(of branches)* ébrancher un arbre; *(of fruit)* *(of person)* cueillir les fruits sur un arbre; *(of bird)* manger tous les fruits d'un arbre; **to s. a wall** *(remove wallpaper)* arracher le papier d'un mur; *(remove paint)* enlever *ou* gratter la peinture d'un mur; **thieves have stripped the house** les cambrioleurs ont complètement vidé la maison; *Mil Fam* **to s. an NCO** dégrader un sous-officier; **to s. an engine/a gun** démonter un moteur/un fusil; *Aut* **stripped chassis** châssis *m* nu
4 *(remove)* **to s. sth from sth** enlever *ou* ôter qch de qch
vi *(undress)* se déshabiller, se dévêtir; **to s. to the waist** se mettre nu jusqu'à la ceinture
▸ ▸ **s. cartoon** bande dessinée, BD; **s. club** boîte *f* de strip-tease; *Br* **s. light** néon *m*, tube *m* (au) néon; *Br* **s. lighting** éclairage *m* fluorescent *ou* au néon; *esp Am* **s. mining** exploitation *f* à ciel ouvert; **s. poker** strip-poker *m*; **s. show** *(spectacle m de)* strip-tease *m*, *pl* strip-teases
▸ **strip down vt sep** *(dismantle)* *(engine, gun)* démonter; *(remove non-essential parts from)* *(bike etc)* enlever les parties non essentielles de; *Fig* **to s. a theory down to (its) essentials** simplifier une théorie pour n'en garder que l'essentiel
vi *(undress)* se déshabiller; **to s. down to one's underwear** se mettre en sous-vêtements
▸ **strip off vi 1** *(undress)* se déshabiller, *Fam* se dépoiler
2 *(of wallpaper etc)* se décoller, s'enlever
vt sep *(remove)* *(paint)* gratter; *(wallpaper)* décoller; **to s. the paint off a wall** enlever *ou* gratter la peinture d'un mur

stripe [straɪp] **n 1** *(on cloth)* rayure *f*, raie *f*; *(on animal's coat)* rayure, zébrure *f*; *Mil* galon *m*; *(magnetic)* piste *f*; **black with a red s.** noir à raie rouge; **to mark sth with stripes** rayer *ou* zébrer qch; *Mil* **long service s.** chevron *m*; *Mil* **to get/lose a s.** être promu/dégradé **2** *Am* **a man of that s.** un homme de ce genre

striped [straɪpt] **adj** *(socks, material etc)* à raies, à rayures; *(animal's coat)* rayé, zébré; **red and blue s. jacket** veston rayé rouge et bleu

stripling ['strɪplɪŋ] **n** tout jeune homme *m*

strippagram ['strɪpəgræm] **n** = message *m* d'adieu ou d'anniversaire etc délivré par une jeune fille ou un jeune homme qui fait un strip-tease

stripped-down [strɪpt-] ADJ s. version version *f* simplifiée

stripper ['strɪpər] N **1** *(striptease artist)* strip-teaseuse *f, pl* strip-teaseuses; **(male)** s. strip-teaseur *m, pl* strip-teaseurs **2 (paint)** s. décapant *m*; **wallpaper s.** produit *m* pour décoller le papier peint

strip-search N fouille *f* d'une personne dévêtue; **to undergo a s.** devoir se déshabiller afin d'être fouillé
▸ VT **to s. sb** faire déshabiller qn pour le/la fouiller

striptease ['strɪptiːz] N (spectacle *m* de) strip-tease *m, pl* strip-teases; **to do a s.** faire un strip-tease
▸▸**s. artist** strip-teaseur *m, pl* strip-teaseurs, strip-teaseuse *f, pl* strip-teaseuses

stripy ['straɪpɪ] ADJ = **striped**

strive [straɪv] VI *(pt* **strove** [strəʊv]; *pp* **striven** ['strɪv(ə)n]*)* **to s. to do sth** s'efforcer de faire qch, faire des efforts pour faire qch; **to s. for** *or* **after sth** essayer d'obtenir qch; **to s. after effect** chercher à faire de l'effet; **s. as we might** malgré tous nos efforts; **to s. against sb** lutter contre qn

strobe [strəʊb] N *Phys etc* stroboscope *m*
▸▸**s. lighting** lumière *f* stroboscopique

stroboscope ['strəʊbəskəʊp] N stroboscope *m*

strode PT *see* **stride** VI, VT

stroke[1] [strəʊk] N **1** *(blow)* coup *m*; **to receive twenty strokes** *(with whip, cane etc)* recevoir vingt coups; *Fig* **at a s.** d'un coup; **to abolish a practice at a s.** abolir un usage d'un seul coup; **s. of lightning** coup de foudre
2 *(movement) (of wing, oar)* coup *m*; *Tech (of piston etc)* mouvement *m*, course *f*; *Cr, Tennis etc* coup; *Swimming (style)* nage *f*; *(arm movement)* mouvement des bras; *(in breast stroke)* brasse *f*; **she was only a few strokes from the bank** elle était à quelques mètres seulement de la rive; **to lengthen the s.** *(in rowing)* allonger la nage; **to keep s.** *(in rowing)* nager ensemble, garder la cadence; *Fig* **to be off one's s.** n'être pas au mieux de sa forme; *Fig* **to put sb off his/her s.** déconcerter qn; **not to do a s. of work** ne rien faire; **s. of (good) luck** coup de chance, aubaine *f*; **s. of wit/of genius** trait *m* d'esprit/de génie; **bold s.** coup hardi
3 *(of clock)* coup *m*; **on the s. of nine** sur le coup de neuf heures, à neuf heures sonnantes *ou* tapantes; **to arrive on the s.** arriver à l'heure juste
4 *Med* attaque *f*; **to have a s.** avoir une attaque
5 *(mark)* trait *m*; *Typ* barre *f* oblique; *(of pencil, brush)* coup *m* de crayon/de pinceau; *(of pen)* trait de plume; **at the s. of a pen** d'un coup de crayon; **with a few bold strokes of the brush** de trois coups de pinceau; *Fig* **to put the finishing strokes to one's work** apporter les dernières touches *ou* mettre la dernière main à son travail
6 *(oarsman)* chef *m* de nage; **to row s.** donner la nage, être chef de nage
▸ VT *(in rowing)* être chef de nage de
▸ VI *(in rowing)* être chef de nage, donner la nage
▸▸**s. oar** *(oar)* aviron *m* du chef de nage; *(person)* chef de nage; *Golf* **s. play** partie *f* par coups

stroke[2] N **1** *(caress)* caresse *f*; **to give sb/sth a s.** caresser qn/qch **2** *esp Am (remark) (positive)* **s.** encouragement *m*; **to give sb a s.** encourager qn
▸ VT *(caress) (fur, sb's hair)* caresser; **to s. one's chin** se caresser le menton; **to s. one's hair down** *or* **into place** lisser ses cheveux; **s.**

the ointment evenly over the ... passer la pommade en couche régulière sur le ...; **he just stroked the ball into the net** il fit glisser le ballon dans les buts
▸▸*Am Sl* **s. magazine** magazine *m* de cul

-stroke [-strəʊk] SUFF **two/four-s. engine** moteur *m* à deux/à quatre temps

stroll [strəʊl] N tour *m, Fam* balade *f*; **to take** *or* **go for a s.** aller faire un tour
▸ VI flâner, *Fam* se balader; **to s. around town** flâner en ville; **she strolled in an hour late and didn't even say sorry** elle est arrivée tranquillement avec une heure de retard et ne s'est même pas excusée; **he strolled across to me** il s'avança tranquillement vers moi

stroller ['strəʊlər] N **1** *(person)* flâneur, -euse, promeneur, -euse **2** *Am (pushchair)* poussette *f* (d'enfant)

strolling ['strəʊlɪŋ] ADJ
▸▸*Theat* **s. player** comédien, -ienne ambulant(e); **s. players** troupe *f* ambulante

STRONG [strɒŋ]

ADJ	fort **1, 2** ▪ robuste **1** ▪ solide **2**
	▪ puissant **2** ▪ ferme **2** ▪ vigoureux **2**
	▪ énergique **2** ▪ résistant **3**

ADJ *(comp* **stronger** ['strɒŋgər]; *superl* **strongest** ['strɒŋgɪst]*)* **1** *(physically powerful) (person, horse etc)* fort; **he's not very s.** *(not muscular)* il n'est pas très fort; *(not healthy)* il n'est pas très robuste; **to be s. in the arm** avoir beaucoup de force dans le bras; **she's as s. as a horse** *or* **an ox** elle est forte comme un cheval *ou* un bœuf; **to be getting stronger** *(after illness)* reprendre ses forces; **his eyesight is not as s. as it was** sa vue a baissé, sa vue n'est pas aussi bonne qu'elle était
2 *(belief, will, currency, feelings, food, tastes, drink)* fort; *(wind, voice, light)* fort, puissant; *(character)* fort, ferme; *(nerves, constitution)* solide; *(country)* puissant; *(colour)* vif; *(protest, plea)* puissant, énergique; *Com (market)* ferme; *Elec (current)* fort, intense; *(supporter)* ardent, vigoureux; **there's s. evidence that he committed suicide/the economy is recovering** tout porte à croire qu'il s'est suicidé/qu'il va y avoir une reprise de l'économie; **she's a s. character** elle a une forte personnalité; **he's a s. candidate for the post** il a le profil idéal pour le poste; **this is a s. possibility** il y a de fortes chances; **to have s. reasons for doing sth** avoir de bonnes raisons de faire qch; **if you have s. feelings about it** si cela vous tient très à cœur; **he comes from a s. Catholic family** il vient d'une famille très catholique; **the religion which is strongest in Scandinavia** la religion qui prédomine en Scandinavie; **the pound is getting stronger** la livre sterling se raffermit; **to be in a s. position** *(politically, financially, militarily)* être dans une position de force; **s. conviction** ferme conviction *f*; **you've got to be s. and say 'no'** il faut être ferme et dire 'non'; **be s.** *(be brave)* sois courageux *ou* fort; **company two hundred s.** société forte de deux cents personnes; **the wind is growing stronger** le vent forcit; **to give s. support to sb/a measure** appuyer fortement qn/une mesure; **to be s. on sth** *(good at)* être fort en qch; *Mus* **s. beat** temps *m* fort; **a s. chance** une forte chance; **a s. accent** un fort accent; **s. verb** verbe *m* fort; **s. syllable** syllabe *f* accentuée; **s. likeness** grande *ou* forte ressemblance *f*; **s. measures** mesures *fpl* draconiennes; *Fig* **I found the book rather s.** j'ai trouvé ce livre plutôt salé; **s. point** point fort; **politeness is not her s. point** la politesse n'est pas son fort; **to have a s. smell** sentir fort; *Chem* **s. solution** solution forte *ou* concentrée; *Cards* **s. suit** *(couleur f)* longue *f*; *Fig* **languages are not**

my s. suit les langues ne sont pas mon fort; **s. wind** grand vent
3 *(resistant) (rope, cloth, shoes)* solide, résistant
4 s. language *(forceful)* langage *m* énergique *ou* vigoureux; *(swearwords)* grossièretés *fpl*; **to write in s. terms to sb** écrire une lettre énergique à qn; **to put sth in the strongest possible terms** exprimer qch dans des termes les plus énergiques possible
NPL **the s.** les forts *mpl*, les puissants *mpl*
ADV *Fam* **to be still going s.** *(be in good condition etc) (of athlete)* avoir encore un bon rythme; *(of old person, party, company etc)* se porter toujours bien; **how's grandfather? – still going s.** comment va le grand-père? – toujours solide; **you're pitching it a bit s.** vous y allez un peu fort

strong-arm ADJ **to use s. methods** *or* **tactics** utiliser la manière forte; **by s. methods** à la méthode forte
▸ VT **1** *Am Fam (beat)* rouer de coups **2** *(use forceful methods on)* **Labour strong-armed the union leaders into calling off the strike** le parti travailliste a forcé la main aux dirigeants syndicaux pour qu'ils mettent fin à la grève

strong-box N coffre-fort *m, pl* coffres-forts

stronghold ['strɒŋhəʊld] N *(fortress)* forteresse *f, Fig* bastion *m*; **s. of trade unionism** bastion du syndicalisme

strongly ['strɒŋlɪ] ADV **1** *(solidly)* solidement **2** *(forcefully) (to believe)* fortement; *(to support, oppose, endorse)* vigoureusement, énergiquement; **the sun shone s.** le soleil brillait fort; **he argued s. in favour of/against** ... il s'est montré très partisan de/opposé à ...; **to be s. in favour of sth** être fortement en faveur *ou* chaud partisan de qch; **s. worded letter** lettre dans laquelle on ne mâche pas ses mots; **I don't feel s. about it** je n'y attache pas une grande importance; **I feel very s. that they should be punished** je suis convaincu qu'ils devraient être punis

strongman ['strɒŋmæn] N **1** *(powerful man)* homme *m* à poigne **2** *(in circus)* Monsieur Muscle *m*; **could you do your s. act with this coffee jar?** viens nous faire admirer ta force, on a besoin d'ouvrir un pot de café

strong-minded ADJ **to be s.** *(of person)* avoir de la volonté; **s. person** forte tête *f*

strong-mindedness [-'maɪndɪdnɪs] N force *f* de caractère

strongroom ['strɒŋruːm] N chambre *f* forte

strong-willed [-'wɪld] ADJ = **strong-minded**

strontium ['strɒntɪəm] N *Chem* strontium *m*

strop [strɒp] N **1 (razor) s.** cuir *m* (à repasser *ou* à rasoir), affiloir *m* **2** *Br Fam* **to be in a s.** être mal luné, être de mauvais poil
▸ VT *(-pp-) (razor)* affiler *ou* repasser sur le cuir

strophe ['strəʊfɪ] N *(in poetry)* strophe *f*

stroppiness ['strɒpɪnɪs] N *Br Fam (insolence)* insolence *f, (awkwardness)* mauvais caractère *m; (aggressiveness)* agressivité *f*

stroppy ['strɒpɪ] ADJ *Br Fam (insolent)* insolent; *(not cooperative)* contrariant; *(aggressive)* agressif, hargneux; **she got a bit s. when I asked her if ...** elle est montée sur ses grands chevaux quand je lui ai demandé si ...; **don't get s. with me!** ce n'est pas la peine de monter sur tes grands chevaux!

strove PT *see* **strive**

struck PT, PP *see* **strike** VT, VI

structural ['strʌktʃər(ə)l] ADJ **1** *Phil, Geol etc* structural, -aux; *(relating to structure)* structurel **2** *Constr* de construction
▸▸*Econ* **s. adjustment** ajustement *m* struc-

turel; **s. damage** dégâts *mpl* de structure; **s. engineer** ingénieur *m* civil; **s. fault** défaut *m* de construction; **s. iron** fer *m* de construction; **s. linguistics** linguistique *f* structurale; **s. steel** acier *m* de construction

structuralism ['strʌktʃər(ə)lɪz(ə)m] N *Psy, Ling* structuralisme *m*

structurally ['strʌktʃər(ə)lɪ] ADV **1** *(to think, analyse)* structurellement; **s., the novel is …** du point de vue de la structure, le roman est … **2 the building is sound s.** la structure du bâtiment est saine

structure ['strʌktʃər] N **1** *(composition, framework) (of building, society, language etc)* structure *f*, *Mil etc* **command s.** structure *f* de commandement; *Econ* **price s.** structure des prix **2** *(building, monument)* construction *f*, édifice *m*, bâtiment *m*; *Fig* **the social s.** l'édifice social
▪ VT *(organization)* structurer; *(novel etc)* structurer, architecturer

structured ['strʌktʃəd] ADJ structuré; **highly s.** très structuré
▸▸ **s. interview** entretien *m* structuré *ou* centré; *Comput* **s. query language** langage *m* d'interrogation structuré; **s. questionnaire** questionnaire *m* structuré

struggle ['strʌg(ə)l] N lutte *f* (**for** pour; **against** contre); **fierce/desperate s.** lutte acharnée/désespérée; **he gave in without a s.** il n'a opposé aucune résistance; **the class s.** la lutte des classes; **s. for freedom** lutte pour la liberté; **life is a s.** la vie est un combat; **the s. for life/for existence** la lutte pour la vie/pour l'existence; **it's a s. getting the kids to wash properly** il faut se battre pour que les enfants se lavent correctement; **it'll be a s. but I think we'll make it** ce sera difficile *ou* dur, mais je crois que nous y arriverons; **I finished the book but it was a real s.** j'ai terminé le livre mais ça a été très dur; **I had a s. getting him to change his mind** j'ai eu du mal à le faire changer d'avis; **he's not worried about the s. that many people have just to make ends meet** il se fiche que des tas de gens doivent se battre pour arriver à joindre les deux bouts
▪ VI lutter (**with** avec; **against** contre; **for** pour; *(move violently)* se débattre, se démener; **to s. to do sth** avoir du mal à faire qch; **she struggled to control her temper** elle a eu du mal à ne pas s'emporter; **the child struggled and kicked** l'enfant se débattait des pieds et des mains; **she was struggling with her umbrella** elle se débattait avec son parapluie; **he struggled to his feet** il s'est levé avec difficulté; **to s. along** *(walking etc)* marcher *ou* avancer péniblement; **we're struggling along** *(in life, with work etc)* nous nous débrouillons tant bien que mal; **he struggled through the hole in the wall** avec difficulté, il réussit à passer par le trou du mur; **the more he struggled, the deeper he sank in the mud** plus il se débattait, plus il s'enfonçait dans la boue; **let's s. on for another month/couple of kilometres or so** essayons de tenir encore un mois/kilomètre ou deux; **the climbers struggled back to camp** les grimpeurs sont rentrés au camp tant bien que mal; **we had to struggle through the crowd to get to the bar** il a fallu que l'on se fraie un chemin à travers la foule pour accéder au bar; *Fig* **we struggled through** nous avons surmonté tous les obstacles; **to be struggling (badly)** *(in one's job, university course etc)* avoir du mal; **the team is struggling** *(in match, to retain position in league etc)* l'équipe a des difficultés; **to s. against circumstances** lutter contre les événements; **to s. with death** lutter contre la mort; **to s. with one's conscience/homework** être aux prises avec sa conscience/ ses devoirs; **we have to s. to make ends**

meet nous avons du mal à joindre les deux bouts; **many companies are struggling** *(financially)* beaucoup d'entreprises ont du mal *ou* sont en difficulté; **I had to s. to make myself understood** j'ai eu de la peine *ou* du mal à me faire comprendre; **he was obviously struggling for** *or* **to find the right word** il avait visiblement de la peine à trouver le mot juste

struggling ['strʌglɪŋ] ADJ *(artist etc)* qui vit péniblement; *(masses)* laborieux; **when I was a s. young actor** quand je débutais comme acteur

strum [strʌm] N **the s. of a guitar** le son d'une guitare
▪ VT *(-mm-)* *(guitar)* pincer les cordes de; **to s. (out) a tune** *(on guitar)* jouer un air
▪ VI *(on a guitar)* pincer les cordes

strumming ['strʌmɪŋ] N **a gentle s. from the guitar** les doux accords de la guitare; *Pej* **his s. gets on my nerves** les raclements de sa guitare me tapent sur les nerfs

strumpet ['strʌmpɪt] N *Arch, Lit* prostituée *f*

strung PT, PP *see* **string** VT

strung-out ADJ *Sl (on heroin)* en manque

strung-up ADJ *(person)* tendu

strut[1] [strʌt] N *Constr (support)* étai *m*; *(crosspiece)* traverse *f*; *(in roofing)* jambe *f* de force; *(of roof truss)* contrefiche *f*, *Aviat* pilier *m*, mât *m*

strut[2] N *(walk)* démarche *f* affectée
▪ VI *(-tt-)* se pavaner; *(after victory, compliment etc)* se rengorger; **to s. in/out** entrer/ sortir en pavanant
▪ VT *esp Am Fam* **to s. one's stuff** frimer
▸ **strut about, strut around** VI *(parade oneself)* se pavaner; *(walk around self-importantly)* parader

struth [stru:θ] INT *Br Sl* = **strewth**

strychnine ['strɪkni:n] N strychnine *f*

stub [stʌb] N **1** *(of pencil)* bout *m*; *(of cigarette, cigar)* mégot *m*; *(of dog's tail)* bout de queue **2** *(of cheque)* talon *m*, souche *f*
▪ VT *(-bb-)* **to s. one's toe** *(on* or *against sth)* se heurter *ou* se cogner le pied *(contre* qch*)*
▸▸ **s. axle** essieu *m* à chapes fermées
▸ **stub out** VT SEP *(cigarette)* écraser

stubble ['stʌb(ə)l] N **1** *Agr* chaume *m*, éteule *f*, **to clear a field of s.** chaumer un champ; **to burn the s.** brûler les chaumes **2** *(on face)* barbe *f* piquante *(de plusieurs jours)*
▸▸ *Agr* **s. field** chaume

stubbly ['stʌblɪ] ADJ **1** *Agr (field)* couvert de chaume *ou* d'éteule **2 s. beard** barbe *f* piquante *(de plusieurs jours)*; **s. chin** menton *m* qui pique

stubborn ['stʌbən] ADJ **1** *(person)* entêté, têtu, obstiné; *(determination, resistance)* farouche; **their s. refusal to surrender** leur refus obstiné de se rendre; **as s. as a mule** têtu comme un mulet *ou* une mule **2** *(stain, infection)* rebelle

stubbornly ['stʌbənlɪ] ADV obstinément, avec entêtement; **she s. refused to give up hope** elle a refusé obstinément d'abandonner espoir

stubbornness ['stʌbənnɪs] N *(of person)* entêtement *m*, obstination *f*, opiniâtreté *f*, *(of determination, resistance)* inflexibilité *f*

stubby ['stʌbɪ] ADJ *(person)* trapu; *(finger)* boudiné
▪ N *Br, Austr Fam (bottle of beer)* canette *f*

stucco ['stʌkəʊ] N stuc *m*
▪ VT *(pt, pp* **stuccoed**; *prp* **stuccoing)** stuquer; **stuccoed decorations** des décorations en stuc
▸▸ **s. work** *(act, process)* stucage *m*; *(result)* stuc *m*

stuck PT, PP *see* **stick**[2] VT, VI

stuck-up ADJ *Fam Pej* snob; *(conceited)* prétentieux

stud[1] [stʌd] N **1** *(nail)* clou *m* à grosse tête; *(as ornament)* clou doré; *(of pedestrian crossing)* clou; **studs** *(on football boots)* crampons *mpl* **2** *(of dress shirt)* bouton *m* (double); **(collar) s.** bouton de col **3** *Tech (short pin)* goujon *m*, tourillon *m*; *(bolt)* goujon **4** *Constr* poteau *m*, montant *m* **5** *(earring)* clou *m* (d'oreille)
▪ VT *(-dd-)* **1** *(fit with studs)* garnir de clous, clouter; **studded door** porte garnie de clous *ou* cloutée; **studded tyre** pneu *m* clouté; *Fig* **studded with stars** *(sky)* parsemé d'étoiles; **her dress was studded with jewels** sa robe était constellée de pierreries **2** *Constr (partition)* établir la charpente de
▸▸ **s. bolt** goujon; **s. earring** clou *m* (d'oreille); **s. fastener** pression *f* (bouton); *Constr* **s. wall** mur *m* de séparation

stud[2] N **1 to be at s.** *(of horse)* être à la monte; *(of dog)* faire des saillies; **to put a horse to s.** utiliser un cheval comme étalon **2** *(stallion)*, *Fig Sl (man)* étalon *m*; **he's a real s.** *(promiscuous)* c'est un vrai tombeur **3** *Cards* poker *m*
▸▸ **s. farm** haras *m*; **s. mare** (jument *f*) poulinière *f*, *Am Fam* **s. muffin** super beau mec *m*; *Cards* **s. poker** poker

studbook ['stʌdbʊk] N stud-book *m*, *pl* studbooks

student ['stju:dənt] N **1** *Univ* étudiant, -ante; *Sch* élève *mf*; **law/medical/arts s.** étudiant en droit/en médecine/en lettres **2** *(observer etc) (of human nature etc)* observateur, -trice *(of* de); **students of Middle East politics will know that …** ceux qui étudient la politique du Moyen-Orient savent que …
▸▸ **the s. body** les étudiants *mpl*; *Am* **s. driver** apprenti, -ie conducteur(trice); **s. flat** appartement *m* d'étudiants; **s. grant** bourse *f* (d'études); **s. house** maison *f* d'étudiants; **s. life** vie *f* d'étudiant; **s. loan** prêt *m* bancaire pour étudiants; **s. nurse** élève *mf* infirmier(ière); **s. radio** radio *f* universitaire; **s. rate** *(for travel etc)* tarif *m* étudiant; **s. riots** émeutes *fpl* étudiantes; **s. teacher** *(in primary school)* instituteur, -trice stagiaire; *(in secondary school)* professeur *m* stagiaire; **students' union** syndicat *m* étudiant; *(premises)* ≃ foyer *m* des étudiants

---

Students' union

Dans les universités britanniques et américaines, on appelle "students' union" à la fois le syndicat et les locaux où il se trouve. Le syndicat est chargé de défendre les intérêts des étudiants, sert de centre d'information et de conseil en matière de logement, de santé et de financement, et organise des événements culturels et des activités.

---

studhorse ['stʌdhɔ:s] N étalon *m*

studied ['stʌdɪd] ADJ *(style, attitude, posture)* étudié, recherché; *(move, act)* prémédité, calculé; *(negligence)* voulu; **s. elegance** élégance *f* recherchée

studio ['stju:dɪəʊ] N *(of artist, photographer)* atelier *m*, studio *m*; **(film/television) s.** studio de cinéma/de télévision; **recording s.** studio d'enregistrement; *Radio* auditorium *m*
▸▸ *Am* **s. apartment** studio; **s. audience** public *m* (présent lors de la diffusion ou de l'enregistrement d'une émission); **s. bed** canapé-lit *m*, *pl* canapés-lits; **s. broadcast camera, s. camera** caméra *f* en studio; **s. couch** canapé-lit, canapé *m* convertible; *Br* **s. flat** studio; **s. manager** directeur *m* de studio; **s. monitor** écran *m* de contrôle studio; **s. rehearsal** répétition *f* en studio; **s. supervisor** chef *m* de studio; *Cin* **the s. system** l'hégémonie *f* des

grands studios (hollywoodiens); **s. talkback** interphone *m* de studio

studious ['stju:dɪəs] **ADJ 1** *(person, atmosphere)* studieux; **person of s. habits** personne studieuse **2** *(careful)* **with s. attention** avec une attention soutenue; **because of his s. avoidance of the topic** parce qu'il évitait soigneusement le sujet

studiously ['stju:dɪəslɪ] **ADV 1** *(listen to teacher)* studieusement **2** *(carefully)* attentivement; **she s. avoided me** elle s'ingéniait à m'éviter; **he was s. polite** il était d'une politesse étudiée

studiousness ['stju:dɪəsnɪs] **N 1** *(eagerness to study)* amour *m* de l'étude **2** *(carefulness)* empressement *m*, zèle *m* (**in doing sth** à faire qch)

study ['stʌdɪ] **N 1** *(investigation)* étude *f* (**of** de); *(report)* étude, rapport *m*; **to make a s. of sth** étudier qch; **I've made a special s. of** … je me suis spécialisé dans …; *Sch, Univ* **studies** études; **Department of Classical Studies** Section des lettres classiques **2** *(room)* cabinet *m* de travail, bureau *m*; *Sch* salle *f* d'étude **3** *Old-fashioned* **brown s.** *(reverie)* rêverie *f*, **to be (lost) in a brown s.** être plongé *ou* absorbé dans ses réflexions *ou* dans de vagues rêveries **4** *Art, Mus* étude *f*, *Fam* **her face was a s.!** il fallait voir sa tête!

VT *(language, music, part)* étudier; *(terrain, stars)* observer; *Scol, Univ (French, law)* faire des études de; *(plans)* examiner, étudier; *(question)* mettre à l'étude; **she studied history at Yale** elle a étudié l'histoire à Yale; **he studied her face for signs of emotion** il examina son visage pour y détecter des signes d'émotion

VI étudier; **you ought to s. harder** tu devrais étudier davantage; **he's studying** il étudie; *(he's at college etc)* il fait ses études; **she's studying to be a doctor** elle fait des études de médecine; **to s. for an examination** se préparer pour un examen, préparer un examen; **he studied under Professor Green** il a étudié avec le Professeur Green, il a été l'élève du Professeur Green

▸▸ **s. group** groupe *m* de travail *ou* d'étude; *Am* **s. hall** *(place)* salle d'étude; *(period)* heure *f* d'étude; **s. period** heure de permanence *ou* d'étude; **s. tour** voyage *m* d'étude; **s. trip** voyage d'études

---

STUFF [stʌf]

| **N** matière **1** ▪ substance **1** ▪ truc **1, 2** ▪ affaires **2** ▪ étoffe **4** |
| **VT** bourrer **1** ▪ rembourrer **1** ▪ farcir **1** ▪ empailler **1** |

N 1 *(substance)* matière(s) *f(pl)*, substance *f*, *Fam* truc *m*; **here's some s. to put on that burn** voilà de quoi soigner cette brûlure; **there's some sticky s. in the sink** il y a quelque chose qui colle dans l'évier; **he is of the s. that heroes are made of** il est du bois dont on fait les héros; *Fam* **she writes good s.** elle écrit de bons trucs; *Fam* **there was some s. about unions on the news** ils ont dit un truc sur les syndicats aux informations; **dangerous s., acid** c'est dangereux, l'acide; *Fam* **this wine is good s.** ce vin, c'est du bon; **I don't like that s. you gave me** je n'aime pas ce que vous m'avez donné là **2** *(objects)* truc *m*; *(possessions)* affaires *fpl* **3** *(more vaguely)* **come on, do your s.!** allons, montre-nous ce que tu sais faire!; **he knows his s.** il s'y connaît; **that's the s.!** voilà ce qu'il faut!; **good s.!** *(well done etc)* bien!; **old s.** vieilleries *fpl*, **silly s.** sottises *fpl*, balivernes *fpl*, *Old-fashioned* **s. and nonsense!** ça, c'est de la bêtise!; *Sl* **she's a nice bit of s., she's hot s.** elle est vraiment bien balan-

cée, elle est canon; *Sl* **he was there with his bit of s.** il était là avec sa petite copine **4** *Tex* (woollen) **s.** étoffe *f* de laine **5** *Sl (drug)* came *f*

VT 1 *(fill)* bourrer (**with** de); *(chair, cushion)* rembourrer (**with** de); *Culin (chicken etc)* farcir; *(zoological specimen)* empailler, naturaliser; *Vulg (have sex with)* se faire; **her pockets are stuffed with sweets** elle a des bonbons plein les poches; *Fam* **to s. oneself, to s. one's face** s'empiffrer; **his head was stuffed with romantic ideas** il avait la tête bourrée *ou* farcie d'idées romanesques; *Br Vulg* **get stuffed!** va te faire foutre!; *Br Vulg* **he can get stuffed** il peut aller se faire foutre; *Pol* **to s. the ballot box** *(fill with false ballot papers)* remplir les urnes de faux bulletins de vote; *(rig election)* truquer les élections; **the only way he'll win is if they s. the ballot box** sa seule chance de gagner, c'est la fraude électorale

2 *(shove)* **to s. sth into sth** fourrer qch dans qch; **to s. one's fingers in one's ears** se boucher les oreilles (avec les doigts); *Br Vulg* **you can s. it (up your arse)!** tu peux te le mettre où je pense!; *Br Vulg* **s. your job!** ton boulot, tu peux te le mettre où je pense!; *Br Vulg* **s. this, I'm going home!** et puis merde, je rentre!

▸ **stuff up VT SEP** *(hole etc)* boucher; **I'm all stuffed up with a cold** j'ai le nez complètement bouché avec ce rhume; **I'm or my nose is stuffed up** j'ai le nez bouché

stuffed [stʌft] **ADJ 1** *(olives, peppers etc)* farci; *(owl, fox, rabbit etc)* empaillé **2** *Br, Austr Fam (in trouble)* cuit, fichu; **if that cheque doesn't arrive soon, we're s.** si ce chèque n'arrive pas bientôt, on est cuits

▸▸ **s. shirt** prétentieux, -ieuse

stuffing ['stʌfɪŋ] **N** *(filling for meat, poultry etc)* farce *f*, *(for upholstery)* bourre *f*, rembourrage *m*; **horsehair s.** matelassure *f* de crin; *Fam* **to knock the s. out of sb** *(defeat heavily)* mettre la pâtée à qn; *(of blow, attacker, illness)* mettre qn K.O.

stuffy ['stʌfɪ] **ADJ 1** *(room etc)* mal ventilé, mal aéré; **to smell s.** sentir le renfermé; **it's a bit s. in here** on manque d'air ici **2** *(standoffish)* collet monté; *(over-conventional)* vieux jeu *inv*; **don't be so s.** *(don't be offended)* il n'y a pas de quoi te scandaliser **3** **to feel s.** *(have blocked nose)* avoir le nez bouché

stultify ['stʌltɪfaɪ] **VT** *(make stupid) (of work)* abrutir, assommer

stultifying ['stʌltɪfaɪɪŋ] **ADJ** *(work)* abrutissant

stumble ['stʌmb(ə)l] **VI 1** *(when walking)* trébucher; *(of horse)* faire un faux pas, broncher; **to s. off** partir en trébuchant; **she stumbled over my briefcase** elle a trébuché sur ma serviette **2 to s. when one speaks** *(hesitate)* hésiter en parlant; *(confuse words etc)* s'embrouiller en parlant; **she stumbled through her speech** elle s'est embrouillée tout au long de son discours

N *(when walking)* trébuchement *m*; *(of horse)* faux pas *m*

▸ **stumble across VT INSEP** *(find)* tomber sur par hasard

▸ **stumble along VI** avancer en trébuchant

▸ **stumble on, stumble upon VT INSEP** = **stumble across**

stumblebum ['stʌmbəlbʌm] **N** *Am Fam (drunken vagrant)* clodo *mf* alcolo; *(clumsy, incompetent person)* manche *m*

stumbling ['stʌmblɪŋ] **ADJ** *(speech)* hésitant; **she took her first s. steps** elle a fait ses premiers pas

▸▸ **s. block** pierre *f* d'achoppement

stump [stʌmp] **N 1** *(of tree)* souche *f*, chicot *m*; *(of tooth)* reste *m* d'une dent cassée, *Fam*

chicot; *(of arm, leg)* moignon *m*; *(of pencil)* bout *m*; *(of cigar)* bout, *Fam* mégot *m*; *(of tail, column, mast)* tronçon *m*; *(of cabbage)* trognon *m*

2 *Fam* **stumps** *(legs)* pattes *fpl*, quilles *fpl*, **stir your stumps!** remuez-vous!, grouillez-vous!

3 *Pol Fam* **to be on the s.** faire campagne **4** *Cr* piquet *m*; **to draw stumps** enlever les piquets, cesser le match

VT 1 *(baffle)* coller; **to be stumped for an answer** ne savoir que répondre, sécher; **it stumped me** ça m'a désarçonné; **this one has got me stumped** alors là, je sèche

2 *Cr* mettre hors jeu *(un batteur qui est sorti de son camp)*

3 *esp Am Pol Fam* **she stumped the country from one end to the other** elle a parcouru le pays d'un bout à l'autre pour sa campagne électorale

VI *esp Am Pol Fam* faire campagne

▸▸ *esp Am Pol Fam* **s. orator, s. speaker** orateur *m*

▸ **stump along VI** *(walk heavily)* marcher *ou* avancer d'un pas lourd; *(limping)* marcher *ou* avancer en clopinant

▸ **stump off VI** *(annoyed)* partir d'un pas lourd

▸ **stump up** *Br Fam* **VT SEP** *(pay)* cracher **VI** casquer

stumpy ['stʌmpɪ] **ADJ** *(person, thing)* trapu; *(figure)* ramassé; **s. pencil** petit bout *m* de crayon

stun [stʌn] **VT** (-nn-) **1** *(make unconscious)* étourdir, assommer **2** *Fig (shock)* abasourdir; **the news stunned us** cette nouvelle nous a fait l'effet d'un coup de massue *ou* nous ont abasourdis; **we were stunned to hear of your accident** nous avons été consternés d'apprendre que vous aviez eu un accident; **to be stunned** être stupéfait; **stunned with surprise** stupéfié, frappé de stupeur

▸▸ **s. grenade** grenade *f* incapacitante; **s. gun** fusil *m* hypodermique

stung **PT, PP** *see* **sting VT, VI**

stunner ['stʌnər] **N** *Fam* **1 he's/she's a s.** il/elle est vachement beau/belle, il/elle est canon **2** *(excellent thing)* chose *f* extraordinaire, *Fam* truc *m* super

stunning ['stʌnɪŋ] **ADJ 1** *(blow)* étourdissant, abrutissant; *(misfortune)* accablant, bouleversant **2** *(shocking)* renversant; *(amazing, excellent)* formidable, épatant; **she's really s.** *(beautiful)* elle est éblouissante; **his/her s. good looks** sa beauté éblouissante

stunningly ['stʌnɪŋlɪ] **ADV s. beautiful** d'une beauté éblouissante; **s. dressed** magnifiquement vêtu

stunt[1] [stʌnt] **VT** *(person, thing)* arrêter dans sa croissance; *(growth)* ralentir très fortement; **the economy had been stunted by the lack of investment** l'économie avait été freinée dans son développement par la faiblesse de l'investissement

stunt[2] **N 1** *(skilful act)* tour *m* de force; *Cin* cascade *f*, **to do one's own stunts** *(of actor, actress)* ne pas se faire doubler dans les scènes dangereuses; *Aviat* **to perform stunts** faire des acrobaties **2** *(sth done to gain attention, for publicity)* coup *m* de pub; *usu Pej* **to pull a s.** faire un coup de pub

▸▸ **s. double** doublure *f* pour les cascades; **s. driver** conducteur, -trice cascadeur(euse); *Aviat* **s. flying** vol *m* acrobatique; **s. man** cascadeur *m*; **s. pilot** pilote *m* de voltige aérienne, voltigeur *m*; **s. woman** cascadeuse *f*

stunted ['stʌntɪd] **ADJ** *(tree, person)* rabougri; *(intellect, development)* atrophié; **to become s.** *(of tree, person)* se rabougrir

stupe [stjuːp] N *Am Fam* andouille f, crétin, -ine

stupefaction [stjuːpɪˈfækʃən] N stupeur f, stupéfaction f

stupefy [ˈstjuːpɪfaɪ] VT 1 *(astound)* abasourdir, stupéfier; **I'm absolutely stupefied (by what has happened)** je n'en reviens pas, j'en suis stupéfait 2 *(make insensitive)* abrutir; *Med* stupéfier, engourdir

stupefying [ˈstjuːpɪfaɪɪŋ] ADJ stupéfiant

stupendous [stjuːˈpendəs] ADJ prodigieux, *Fam* formidable

stupendously [stjuːˈpendəslɪ] ADV prodigieusement

stupid [ˈstjuːpɪd] ADJ bête, idiot; **I did a s. thing** j'ai fait une bêtise; **don't be s.!** ne faites pas l'idiot!; **how s. of me!** que je suis bête!; **I'm not s., you know!** je ne suis pas idiot quand même!; **what a s. place to put it!** c'est idiot de l'avoir mis là!; **a s. film** un film idiot; **I don't want your s. book!** je ne veux pas de ton livre idiot!; *Fam* **to drink oneself s.** s'abrutir d'alcool

N *Fam (term of address)* **of course not, s.!** bien sûr que non, gros bêta/grosse bêtasse!

stupidity [stjuːˈpɪdɪtɪ] N stupidité f, bêtise f

stupidly [ˈstjuːpɪdlɪ] ADV stupidement, bêtement; **rather s., I agreed** bêtement, j'ai accepté

stupor [ˈstjuːpər] N stupeur f, **in a drunken s.** abruti par la boisson

sturdily [ˈstɜːdɪlɪ] ADV 1 *(constructed)* fortement; **s. built** solide 2 *(to refuse, defend etc)* résolument

sturdiness [ˈstɜːdɪnɪs] N 1 *(of person, plant etc)* vigueur f, robustesse f, *(of table, piece of equipment)* solidité f 2 *(of resolve, opposition)* résolution f, fermeté f

sturdy [ˈstɜːdɪ] ADJ 1 *(person)* vigoureux, robuste; *(table, furniture)* solide; **a s. fellow** un gaillard robuste 2 *(opposition, resistance)* résolu, ferme

sturgeon [ˈstɜːdʒ(ə)n] N *(fish)* esturgeon m

stutter [ˈstʌtər] N bégaiement m; **he has a s.** il est bègue, il bégaie

VI bégayer; **the engine stuttered into life** le moteur toussa avant de démarrer

VT bégayer

stutterer [ˈstʌtərər] N bègue mf

stuttering [ˈstʌtərɪŋ] ADJ bègue; **s. machine-gun fire** le crépitement des mitrailleuses

N bégaiement m

sty[1], *pl* **sties** [staɪ, staɪz] N *Agr, Fig* porcherie f

sty[2], **stye**, *pl* **sties, styes** N *Med* orgelet m

Stygian [ˈstɪdʒɪən] ADJ *Lit* d'une noirceur impénétrable

▸▸ **S. gloom** ténèbres fpl impénétrables *ou* insondables

style [staɪl] N 1 *(manner)* style m, manière f, *(of car etc)* type m, modèle f, *(of clothes)* mode f, *(of hair)* coiffure f, **s. of living** style *ou* train m de vie; **Gothic/Byzantine s.** style gothique/byzantin; **building in the classical s.** bâtiment m de style classique; **that's not my s.** ce n'est pas mon genre *ou* style; **that's the s.!** c'est cela!, bravo!; **you've got to admire his s.** on ne peut qu'admirer la façon dont il s'y prend!; **something in that s.** quelque chose de ce genre *ou* style; **in the latest s.** à la (dernière) mode, *Fam* dernier cri

2 *(in writing, speaking)* style m; *(way of writing)* manière f d'écrire; **written in a humorous s.** écrit dans un style humoristique; **written in the s. of a 1940s thriller** écrit dans le style du roman policier des années 1940; **this writer lacks s.** *(good style)* cet écrivain manque de style

3 *(distinction, sophistication)* chic m, classe f, **she has s.** elle a de l'allure *ou* de la classe;

to live in (grand or **great) s.** mener grand train, vivre sur un grand pied; **they arrived in s.** ils ont fait leur entrée en grande pompe; **let's do things in s.** faisons bien les choses; **let's travel in s.** voyageons en grand style

4 *(of calendar)* **old/new s.** vieux/nouveau style m

5 *(tool in engraving)* burin m

6 *Bot* style m

VT 1 *(design)* créer; **dress styled by X** robe créée par X; **hair styled by X** coiffé(e) par X 2 *(designate) (person)* dénommer; *(thing)* appeler; **to s. oneself doctor** se faire appeler docteur

▸▸ *Comput* **s. bar** barre f de style; **s. book** manuel m *ou* protocole m de style; *Comput* **s. sheet** feuille f de style

stylechecker [ˈstaɪltʃekər] N *Comput* correcteur m de style

styling [ˈstaɪlɪŋ] N façon f, *(of car)* ligne f, **hair s.** coiffure f

▸▸ **s. gel** gel m coiffant; **s. mousse** mousse f coiffante

stylish [ˈstaɪlɪʃ] ADJ qui a de la classe; *(clothes)* élégant, chic inv, *(camerawork, design)* artistique; **a s. writer** un écrivain qui a du style

stylishly [ˈstaɪlɪʃlɪ] ADV élégamment, avec chic, avec classe

stylishness [ˈstaɪlɪʃnɪs] N élégance f, chic m, classe f, *(of prose)* élégance

stylist [ˈstaɪlɪst] N styliste mf, **hair s.** coiffeur, -euse (d'art)

stylistic [staɪˈlɪstɪk] ADJ stylistique, du *ou* de style

stylistically [staɪˈlɪstɪk(ə)lɪ] ADV du point de vue de la stylistique

stylistics [staɪˈlɪstɪks] NPL *(usu with sing verb)* stylistique f VOIR GRAMMAIRE A10

stylization [staɪlaɪˈzeɪʃən] N stylisation f

stylize [ˈstaɪlaɪz] VT *Art* styliser; **stylized flowers** fleurs stylisées

stylus, *pl* **styli, styluses** [ˈstaɪləs, -aɪ, -əsɪz] N *(in engraving etc)* style m; *(on record player)* pointe f de lecture; *(made of sapphire)* saphir m; *(made of diamond)* diamant m

stymie [ˈstaɪmɪ] VT *Fam* **this question stymied me** cette question m'a coincé; **to be stymied** être dans une impasse

styptic [ˈstɪptɪk] *Med* ADJ styptique, astringent

N styptique m, astringent m

▸▸ **s. pencil** crayon m hémostatique

suasion [ˈsweɪʒ(ə)n] N *Arch, Lit* persuasion f, **to subject sb to moral s.** agir sur la conscience de qn

suave [swaːv] ADJ affable, courtois, *Lit* urbain, *Pej* doucereux, mielleux

Note that the French word **suave** is a false friend and is almost never a translation for the English word **suave**. It is used to describe something that appeals to the senses in a pleasant way.

suavely [ˈswaːvlɪ] ADV avec affabilité, affablement, *Pej* de façon doucereuse, doucereusement

suaveness [ˈswaːvnɪs], **suavity** [ˈswaːvɪtɪ] N affabilité f, courtoisie f, *Lit* urbanité f, *Pej* manières fpl doucereuses, airs mpl mielleux

sub [sʌb] *Fam* N 1 *(subscription)* (to club, union etc) cotisation f, **to pay one's subs** payer sa cotisation 2 *Sport (substitute)* remplaçant m 3 *Naut (submarine)* sous-marin m, pl sous-marins 4 *Journ (subeditor)* secrétaire mf de rédaction 5 *Br (small loan)* prêt m; **to give sb a s.** dépanner qn; **to get a s.** se faire dépanner

VI (**-bb-**) 1 *(substitute)* **to s. for sb** remplacer

qn 2 *Journ (subedit)* mettre un article au point, travailler comme secrétaire de rédaction

VT 1 *Br (lend)* **to s. sb sth** dépanner qn de qch; **can you s. me a fiver?** tu peux me dépanner de cinq livres? 2 *Journ (article)* mettre au point, corriger

sub-account N *Acct* sous-compte m, pl sous-comptes

subagent [sʌbˈeɪdʒənt] N sous-agent m, pl sous-agents

subalpine [sʌbˈælpaɪn] ADJ subalpin

subaltern [ˈsʌbəltən] N *Mil* (officier m) subalterne m

subaqua [sʌbˈækwə] ADJ sous-marin, subaquatique

▸▸ **s. club** club m de plongée sous-marine; **s. diving** plongée f sous-marine

subatomic [sʌbəˈtɒmɪk] ADJ subatomique

subbed [sʌbd] ADJ *Journ* corrigé

subclass [ˈsʌbklaːs] N sous-classe f, pl sous-classes

subclause [ˈsʌbklɔːz] N *esp Jur (of contract)* paragraphe m

subcommittee [ˈsʌbkəmɪtɪ] N sous-comité m, pl sous-comités; *(in larger organizations)* sous-commission f, pl sous-commissions

subconscious [sʌbˈkɒnʃəs] ADJ, N *Psy* subconscient m

subconsciously [sʌbˈkɒnʃəslɪ] ADV subconsciemment

subcontinent [sʌbˈkɒntɪnənt] N sous-continent m, pl sous-continents; **the Indian s.** le sous-continent indien

subcontract[1] [sʌbˈkɒntrækt] N *(contrat m de)* sous-traitance f, pl sous-traitances

subcontract[2] [sʌbkənˈtrækt] VT *(work, order)* sous-traiter; **to s. a job (out) to sb** sous-traiter un travail avec qn

subcontracting [ˈsʌbkəntræktɪŋ] N sous-traitance f

ADJ sous-traitant, pl sous-traitants; **the s. firm** le sous-traitant

subcontractor [ˈsʌbkəntræktər] N sous-traitant m, pl sous-traitants

subculture [ˈsʌbkʌltʃər] N 1 *(in sociology)* groupe m *ou* phénomène m culturel secondaire; **youth s.** phénomène m culturel propre à la jeunesse 2 *(in bacteriology)* repiquage m, culture f secondaire

subcutaneous [sʌbkjʊˈteɪnɪəs] ADJ sous-cutané, pl sous-cutanés

subdeacon [sʌbˈdiːkən] N *Rel* sous-diacre m, pl sous-diacres

subdirectory [ˈsʌbdɪrektərɪ] N *Comput* sous-répertoire m, pl sous-répertoires

subdivide [sʌbdɪˈvaɪd] VT subdiviser, sous-diviser

VI se subdiviser

subdivision [sʌbdɪˈvɪʒən] N subdivision f

subdominant [sʌbˈdɒmɪnənt] N *Mus* sous-dominante f, pl sous-dominantes

subdue [səbˈdjuː] VT 1 *(tribe, enemy etc)* subjuguer, soumettre, assujettir; *(fire)* maîtriser; *(angry impulse)* dompter, réprimer; *(emotions)* maîtriser, dominer 2 *(light, heat, voice)* adoucir; *(light, pain)* atténuer

subdued [səbˈdjuːd] ADJ *(person) (quieter than usual)* inhabituellement calme; *(sad)* triste; *(heat, sound)* adouci; **s. colours** couleurs fpl douces; **s. conversation** conversation f à voix basse; **s. light** demi-jour m, lumière f tamisée; **in a s. tone** or **voice** à voix basse, à mi-voix

subedit [sʌbˈedɪt] *Journ* VI mettre un article au point, travailler comme secrétaire de rédaction

VT *(article)* mettre au point, corriger

subediting [sʌbˈedɪtɪŋ] N mise f au point, correction f

subeditor [sʌbˈedɪtər] N *Journ* secrétaire mf de rédaction; *(in publishing)* rédacteur, -trice; *Journ* **assistant s.** secrétaire mf adjoint(e)

subfamily [ˈsʌbfæmɪlɪ] N *Biol* sous-famille f, pl sous-familles

subfolder [ˈsʌbfəʊldər] N *Comput* sous-dossier m, pl sous-dossiers

sub-frame N *Aut* faux-châssis m inv, sous-châssis m inv

subfusc [sʌbˈfʌsk] ADJ *(clothing)* sombre

subgenre [ˈsʌbʒɑ̃nrə] N sous-genre m

subgenus, pl **subgenera** [ˈsʌbʒiːnəs, -dʒenərə] N *Biol* sous-genre m, pl sous-genres

subgroup [ˈsʌbgruːp] N sous-groupe m, pl sous-groupes

subhead, subheading [ˈsʌbhed(ɪŋ)] N sous-titre m, pl sous-titres

subhuman [sʌbˈhjuːmən] ADJ sous-humain, pl sous-humains; *(intelligence, behaviour)* inférieur à celui/celle des humains

N sous-homme m, pl sous-hommes

subject[1] [ˈsʌbdʒɪkt] N **1** *(of conversation, book, fugue)* sujet m; *(of legal case)* objet m; *Sch, Univ* matière f; **this will be the s. of my next lecture** ma prochaine conférence portera sur ce sujet; **to wander from the s.** s'écarter du sujet, faire une digression; **while we are on the s.** à ce propos, pendant que nous sommes sur ce sujet; **on the s. of** à propos de; **to change the s.** parler d'autre chose, changer de sujet; **to change the s., has anyone seen Andy?** pour changer de sujet, est-ce que quelqu'un a vu Andy?; **don't try to change the s.!** n'essaie pas de changer de sujet ou de détourner la conversation!; *Sch, Univ* **science subjects** matières fpl scientifiques

2 *Biol, Med etc* sujet m; **to be the s. of an experiment** servir de sujet d'expérience

3 *Gram (of verb)* sujet m VOIR GRAMMAIRE A78; B18

4 *Art, Phot* sujet m

5 *(of monarch)* sujet, -ette; **British s.** sujet britannique

ADJ **1** *(state, country)* assujetti, soumis; **s. to military laws** justiciable des tribunaux militaires

2 *(liable)* **s. to** *(rheumatism, hayfever etc)* sujet à; **to be s. to violent mood swings/fits of jealousy** avoir tendance à avoir des sautes d'humeur/des crises de jalousie; **prices s. to 5% discount** prix bénéficiant d'une remise de 5%; **s. to stamp duty** soumis au timbre; **all trains will be s. to delay** des retards sont à prévoir sur toutes les lignes; **we're all s. to taxation** nous sommes tous assujettis à l'impôt; **an area that is s. to avalanches** une zone d'avalanches; **I'm very s. to colds** j'attrape des rhumes facilement; **s. to variation** variable

3 *(conditional)* **s. to ...** sous réserve de ...; **s. to payment** moyennant paiement; **s. to your consent** sous réserve de votre consentement; **it's all s. to her approval** tout dépend de ou est subordonné à son approbation

▸▸ **s. matter** *(topic)* sujet, thème m; *(substance)* substance f, contenu m

subject[2] [səbˈdʒekt] VT **1** *(subjugate)* *(people, nation)* soumettre, assujettir, subjuguer **2** *(force to undergo)* soumettre, exposer (**sb/sth to sth** qn/qch à qch); **to s. sb to torture** mettre qn à la torture, torturer qn; **to s. sb/sth to an examination** faire subir un examen à qn/qch, soumettre qn/qch à un examen; **to be subjected to much criticism** être en butte à de nombreuses critiques; **metal subjected to great heat** métal exposé à une forte chaleur; **to s. oneself to sth** se soumettre à qch; **to s. sth to tax** soumettre qch à l'impôt

subjection [səbˈdʒekʃən] N soumission f, assujettissement m (**to** à); **in a state of s.** dans la sujétion

subjective [səbˈdʒektɪv] ADJ subjectif

subjectively [səbˈdʒektɪvlɪ] ADV subjectivement

subjectivism [səbˈdʒektɪvɪz(ə)m] N subjectivisme m

subjectivity [sʌbdʒekˈtɪvɪtɪ] N subjectivité f

subjoin [sʌbˈdʒɔɪn] VT *(list)* ajouter, adjoindre

sub judice [ˈsʌbˈdʒuːdɪsɪ] ADJ *Law* **the case is s.** l'affaire n'est pas encore jugée

subjugate [ˈsʌbdʒʊgeɪt] VT *(people, nation)* assujettir, subjuguer

subjugation [sʌbdʒʊˈgeɪʃən] N assujettissement m, subjugation f

subjunctive [səbˈdʒʌŋktɪv] VOIR GRAMMAIRE A53–4; B32–3 *Gram* ADJ subjonctif

N subjonctif m; **in the s. (mood)** au (mode) subjonctif

sublease[1] [ˈsʌbliːs] N **1** *(document, type of contract)* sous-bail m, pl sous-baux; *(of farm)* sous-ferme f, pl sous-fermes **2** *(act)* sous-location f, pl sous-locations

sublease[2] [sʌbˈliːs] VT *(apartment)* sous-louer; *(land)* sous-affermer

sub-lessee N sous-locataire mf, pl sous-locataires

sub-lessor N sous-bailleur, -eresse, pl sous-bailleurs, -eresses

sublet [sʌbˈlet] VT *(pt, pp* sublet; prp subletting)* *(apartment)* sous-louer; *(land)* sous-affermer

sub-letting N sous-location f

sub-lieutenant N *Naut* enseigne m (de vaisseau) de première classe

sublimate [ˈsʌblɪmeɪt] N *Chem* sublimé m
VT **1** *(feeling, instinct)* sublimer **2** *Chem (solid)* sublimer

sublimation [sʌblɪˈmeɪʃən] N sublimation f

sublime [səˈblaɪm] ADJ *(noble, inspiring),* *Fam (very good)* sublime; **s. indifference** suprême indifférence

N **the s.** le sublime; **to go from the s. to the ridiculous** passer du sublime au ridicule
VT *Chem (solid)* sublimer
VI *Chem (of solid)* se sublimer

sublimely [səˈblaɪmlɪ] ADV **1** **s. beautiful** d'une beauté sublime **2** *(indifferent)* suprêmement; **he remained s. unaware of what was going on** il n'a jamais rien su de ce qui se passait

subliminal [sʌbˈlɪmɪn(ə)l] ADJ *Psy* subliminal, -aux, subliminaire
▸▸ **s. advertising** publicité f subliminale ou invisible; **s. message** message m subliminal

sublimity [sʌbˈlɪmɪtɪ] N sublimité f

sub-machine-gun N mitraillette f

submarine [sʌbməˈriːn] ADJ *(cable, volcano)* sous-marin, pl sous-marins

N **1** *Naut* sous-marin m, pl sous-marins; **midget or pocket s.** sous-marin de poche **2** *Am (sandwich)* gros sandwich m

submariner [sʌbˈmærɪnər] N sous-marinier m, pl sous-mariniers

sub-market N sous-marché m, pl sous-marchés

submediant [sʌbˈmiːdɪənt] N *Mus* sous-dominante f, pl sous-dominantes

submenu [ˈsʌbmenjuː] N *Comput* sous-menu m, pl sous-menus

submerge [səbˈmɜːdʒ] VT **1** *(put in liquid)* immerger (**in** dans) **2** *(cover) (field etc)* submerger, inonder; **submerged in details** perdu dans les détails

VI plonger; *(of submarine)* effectuer sa plongée

submerged [səbˈmɜːdʒd] ADJ *(field etc)* submergé, inondé; *(submarine)* en plongée; *(reef)* sous-marin; *Fig* **s. in work** submergé de travail, qui croule sous le travail

submergence [səbˈmɜːdʒəns] N submersion f

submersible [səbˈmɜːsɪb(ə)l] *Naut* ADJ submersible

N (bateau m) submersible m, sous-marin m, pl sous-marins

submersion [səbˈmɜːʃən] N submersion f

submission [səbˈmɪʃən] N **1** *(to person's will, authority)* soumission f; *(to defeat)* résignation f; *(in wrestling)* abandon m; **to starve/beat sb into s.** réduire qn par la famine/violence **2** *(of matter to arbitration)* soumission f; *(of proof of identity)* présentation f **3** *Law* plaidoirie f; **in my s. ...** selon ma thèse ...; **it's my s. that ...** j'ai la conviction que ...

submissive [səbˈmɪsɪv] ADJ *(tone, look)* soumis; *(person)* docile; **to be sexually s.** être soumis sur le plan sexuel

submissively [səbˈmɪsɪvlɪ] ADV avec soumission, docilement

submissiveness [səbˈmɪsɪvnɪs] N soumission f, docilité f

submit [səbˈmɪt] (-tt-) VI *(to sb, sb's will, superior power)* se soumettre; *(to necessity)* se plier; *(to discipline)* s'astreindre; *(to misfortune)* se résigner; *(in wrestling)* abandonner; **to s. to authority** se soumettre à l'autorité

VT se soumettre; **to s. sth for sb's approval/for sb's inspection** soumettre ou présenter qch à l'approbation/à l'inspection de qn; **to s. proof of identity** présenter des pièces d'identité; **to s. that ...** représenter ou alléguer que ...; *Law* **I s. that there is no case against my client** je plaide le non-lieu; **I s. that you are not in fact ...** j'affirme que vous n'êtes pas en fait ...; **the author submits that ...** l'auteur affirme que ...

subnormal [sʌbˈnɔːməl] ADJ *(person, behaviour)* arriéré; *(temperature)* au-dessous de la normale; **educationally s.** arriéré

suborder [ˈsʌbɔːdər] N *Biol* sous-ordre m, pl sous-ordres

subordinate[1] [səˈbɔːdɪnət] ADJ *(rank)* inférieur, subalterne; *(role)* accessoire; **s. to** subordonné à

N subordonné, -ée
▸▸ *Gram* **s. clause** (proposition f) subordonnée f

subordinate[2] [səˈbɔːdɪneɪt] VT subordonner (**to** à); **everything is subordinated to religion** tout est subordonné à la religion

subordination [səbɔːdɪˈneɪʃən] N subordination f (**to** à)

suborn [səˈbɔːn] VT *Law (witness)* suborner

suborning [səˈbɔːnɪŋ] N *Law* subornation f

subplot [ˈsʌbplɒt] N *(of film, play etc)* intrigue f secondaire

subpoena [səˈpiːnə] *Law* N *(of witness)* citation f, assignation f

VT *(pt, pp* subpoenaed) **to s. sb (to appear)** assigner qn à comparaître, citer qn; **to s. sb as witness** citer qn à comparaître; **to s. a witness** assigner un témoin à comparaître; **he has been subpoenaed** il a été cité à comparaître

sub-postmaster N *Br* receveur m d'un bureau de poste *(dans un village)*

sub-postmistress N *Br* receveuse f d'un bureau de poste *(dans un village)*

sub-post office N *Br* petit bureau *m* de poste

sub-prefect N *Admin* sous-préfet *m*, *pl* sous-préfets

subprogram ['sʌbprəʊɡræm] N *Comput* sous-programme *m*, *pl* sous-programmes

subroutine ['sʌbruːtiːn] N *Comput* sous-programme *m*, *pl* sous-programmes

subscribe [səb'skraɪb] VI **1** *(contribute, give money)* souscrire (**to** à); **to s. to a newspaper** *(become a subscriber)* s'abonner à un journal; *(be a subscriber)* être abonné à un journal; *Com* **to s. to a service** s'abonner à un service; **to s. to the Internet** s'abonner à l'Internet; *Fin* **to s. to a loan** souscrire un prêt; *St Exch* **to s. to a share issue** souscrire à une émission d'actions

2 to s. to an opinion souscrire à une opinion; **I don't s. to that theory** je ne souscris pas à cette théorie; **I cannot s. to that** je ne suis pas d'accord avec cela

VT **1** *(money)* verser; **to s. ten pounds** verser dix livres; *St Exch* **to s. to s. shares** souscrire des actions; **subscribed capital** capital *m* souscrit, souscription *f* **2** *Fml (one's name)* souscrire; **to s. one's name to a document** apposer sa signature à un document

subscriber [səb'skraɪbər] N **1** *(to newspaper, Internet)* abonné, -ée; **telephone s.** abonné du *ou* au téléphone **2** *(to charity)* souscripteur *m* **3** *Fml (of document)* signataire *mf*, souscripteur *m*; **the s.** le/la soussigné, -ée
▸▸ *Br* **s. trunk dialling** automatique *m*

subscript ['sʌbskrɪpt] N *Typ* indice *m*; **s. 3** 3 en indice

subscription [səb'skrɪpʃən] N **1** *(to newspaper, Internet)* abonnement *m*; **to take out a s. to a paper** s'abonner à un journal, prendre un abonnement à un journal; **s. to a club** cotisation *f* à un club **2** **s. to a charity** souscription *f* à une œuvre de bienfaisance; **to get up a s.** se cotiser; **monument erected by public s.** monument élevé par souscription publique; *Fin* **s. to a loan** souscription à un emprunt **3** *(to an opinion)* adhésion *f* (**to** à); *(to an act, a decision etc)* approbation *f* (**to** de)
▸▸ *TV* **s. channel** chaîne *f* payante, chaîne à péage; **s. charges** tarifs *mpl* d'abonnement; **s. fee** frais *mpl* d'inscription; *(for share purchase)* droit *m* de souscription; **s. list** liste *f* de souscription *ou* des souscripteurs; **s. renewal** réabonnement *m*; **s. television, s. TV** télévision *f* par abonnement

subsection ['sʌbsekʃən] N subdivision *f*, *(in text)* paragraphe *m*

subsequent ['sʌbsɪkwənt] ADJ suivant, ultérieur, *Law Fml* subséquent; **at a s. meeting** au cours d'une séance ultérieure; **any s. corrections** toutes corrections ultérieures; **the investigation and all the s. recriminations** l'enquête et toutes les plaintes qui s'en sont suivies; **s. events proved us right** la suite des événements a prouvé *ou* les événements ultérieurs ont prouvé que nous avions raison; **s. to this** à la suite de ceci, par la suite

subsequently ['sʌbsɪkwəntlɪ] ADV plus tard, par la suite; **s. to sth** postérieurement à qch

subservience [səb'sɜːvɪəns] N soumission *f*, servilité *f*; *(to fashion)* assujettissement *m*

subservient [səb'sɜːvɪənt] ADJ **1** *(servile)* obséquieux, servile; **s. to sb** soumis à qn **2** *(subordinate)* subordonné; **to make sth s. to sth** subordonner qch à qch

subset ['sʌbset] N *Math* sous-ensemble *m*, *pl* sous-ensembles

subside [səb'saɪd] VI **1** *(of ground, building)* s'affaisser, se tasser; *Fam* **to s. into an armchair** s'affaler dans un fauteuil **2** *(of water)* baisser, diminuer; *(of blister, bump)* dégonfler; **the flood is subsiding** la crue diminue **3** *(of storm, excitement, fever)* s'apaiser, se calmer

subsidence ['sʌbsɪdəns, səb'saɪdəns] N **1** *(of building, road)* affaissement *m*; *(of land, foundations)* tassement *m* **2** *(of river)* décrue *f*, baisse *f*; *Med (of tumour)* délitescence *f*, *(of fever)* apaisement *m* **3** *Geol* subsidence *f*

subsidiarity [səbsɪdɪˈærɪtɪ] N subsidiarité *f*

subsidiary [səb'sɪdɪərɪ] ADJ subsidiaire, auxiliaire
N *Fin (company)* filiale *f*
▸▸ **s. account** sous-compte *m*, *pl* sous-comptes; **s. company** filiale

subsidize ['sʌbsɪdaɪz] VT *(project, industry, person)* subventionner; **to be subsidized by the State** *or* **the government** recevoir une subvention de *ou* être subventionné par l'État; **why should I carry on subsidizing you?** je ne vois pas pourquoi je continuerais à te donner de l'argent!; **subsidized industry** industrie *f* subventionnée

subsidy ['sʌbsɪdɪ] N subvention *f*; **export/building s.** prime *f ou* subvention à l'exportation/à la construction

subsist [səb'sɪst] VI *(stay alive)* tirer sa subsistance, vivre (**on** de); *(remain in existence)* subsister; **custom that still subsists** coutume qui existe *ou* subsiste encore (de nos jours)

subsistence [səb'sɪstəns] N subsistance *f*, *(allowance)* frais *mpl* de subsistance; **means of s.** moyens *m* de subsistance; **to live at s. level** avoir tout juste de quoi vivre; **a bare s. wage** un salaire à peine suffisant pour vivre
▸▸ **s. allowance** frais de subsistance; **s. economy** économie *f* de subsistance; **s. farming** agriculture *f* de subsistance

subsoil ['sʌbsɔɪl] N sous-sol *m*

subsonic [sʌb'sɒnɪk] ADJ *Aviat* subsonique

subspecies ['sʌbspiːʃiːz] N *Biol* sous-espèce *f*, *pl* sous-espèces

substance ['sʌbstəns] N **1** *(matter)* substance *f*, matière *f*; *Rel (spiritual, bodily)* substance **2** *(essential element)* *(of article, argument)* fond *m*, substance *f*, essentiel *m*; **I agree in s.** je suis d'accord sur le fond **3** *(strength, solidity)* solidité *f*; **the candidate was long on image but short on s.** le candidat faisait bonne impression mais manquait d'épaisseur; **book of s.** livre solide; **his argument has little s.** son argument n'a rien de solide; **he's a man of s.** *(financially)* il a du bien; *(intellectually etc)* c'est un homme d'envergure
▸▸ **s. abuse** abus *m* de stupéfiants

substandard [sʌb'stændəd] ADJ de qualité inférieure; **it's s. English/French** ce n'est pas du bon anglais/français

substantial [səb'stænʃəl] ADJ **1** *(significant)* *(point, progress, reduction)* important; *(progress, difference)* grand; *(reason, evidence)* valable; **s. proof** preuve *f* concluante *ou* valable; **a s. number of ...** un nombre important de ... **2** *(meal)* substantiel, copieux; *(structure, book)* solide; *(cloth)* résistant **3** *(company)* solide, bien assis; *(sum of money)* gros; *(profit, loss)* important

┌─────────────────────────────────────┐
│ Attention: ne pas confondre avec   │
│ **substantive**.   │
└─────────────────────────────────────┘

substantially [səb'stænʃəlɪ] ADV **1** *(considerably)* considérablement; **it's now s. improved** cela s'est maintenant considérablement amélioré; **this contributed s. to our success** cela a largement contribué à notre succès **2** *(for the most part)* **they are s. the same** dans l'ensemble *ou* pour l'essentiel, ils sont pareils; **the text is s. unaltered** le texte est dans l'ensemble *ou* pour l'essentiel resté inchangé **3** *(solidly)* *(built)* solidement

substantiate [səb'stænʃɪeɪt] VT *(statement)* prouver, justifier; *(corroborate)* corroborer; *(claim, accusation etc)* prouver *ou* établir le bien-fondé de

substantiation [səbstænʃɪ'eɪʃən] N *(of statement)* justification *f*; *(corroboration)* confirmation *f*; *(of accusation, charge)* preuves *fpl*

substantival [sʌbstən'taɪv(ə)l] ADJ *Gram* substantival

substantive ['sʌbstəntɪv] ADJ **1** *(measures, issue)* important **2** *Gram* substantif
N *Gram* substantif *m*
▸▸ *Law* **s. law** droit *m* positif

┌─────────────────────────────────────┐
│ Attention: ne pas confondre avec   │
│ **substantial**.   │
└─────────────────────────────────────┘

substantively ['sʌbstəntɪvlɪ] ADV **1** *Gram* substantivement **2** *(considerably)* considérablement

substation ['sʌbsteɪʃən] N *Elec etc* sous-station *f*, *pl* sous-stations

substitute ['sʌbstɪtjuːt] N **1** *(foodstuff, drug)* succédané *m*; **as a s. for ...** comme succédané de ...; **coffee s.** ersatz *m* de café; **there's no s. for parental love** rien ne remplace l'amour parental; **low-alcohol lager is a poor s. for the real thing** la bière à faible teneur en alcool n'a rien de comparable avec la vraie bière
2 *(person)* remplaçant, -ante, suppléant, -ante; *Sport* remplaçant; *Law Rel* substitut *m*; **as a s. for ...** en remplacement de ..., pour remplacer ...; **to act as a s. for sb/sth** remplacer qn/qch, se substituer à qn/à qch
VT substituer; *Sport* remplacer; **to s. margarine for butter** remplacer le beurre par la margarine
VI **to s. for sb** remplacer *ou* suppléer qn
▸▸ *Mktg* **s. product** produit *m* de substitution

substitution [sʌbstɪ'tjuːʃən] N substitution *f*, remplacement *m*; *Sport* remplacement; *Sport* **to make a s.** faire un remplacement
▸▸ *Mktg* **s. market** marché *m* de substitution, marché environnant

substitutional market [sʌbstɪtjuːʃən(ə)l] N *Mktg* marché *m* de substitution, marché environnant

substratum, *pl* **substrata, substratums** [sʌb'strɑːtəm, -ə, -əmz] N couche *f* inférieure; *Geol, Phil* substrat *m*

substring ['sʌbstrɪŋ] N *Comput* sous-chaîne *f*, *pl* sous-chaînes

substructure ['sʌbstrʌktʃər] N *(of building)* fondement *m*; *(of road)* infrastructure *f*

subsume [sʌb'sjuːm] VT subsumer; **to s. X under Y** incorporer X à Y

subsystem ['sʌbsɪstəm] N sous-système *m*, *pl* sous-systèmes

subtenancy ['sʌbtenənsɪ] N sous-location *f*, *pl* sous-locations

subtenant ['sʌbtenənt] N sous-locataire *mf*, *pl* sous-locataires

subtend [səb'tend] VT sous-tendre

subterfuge ['sʌbtəfjuːdʒ] N subterfuge *m*; **to resort to s.** user de subterfuge; **this was a s. to ...** c'était un subterfuge pour ...

subterranean [sʌbtə'reɪnɪən] ADJ souterrain

subtext ['sʌbtekst] N message *m* sous-jacent

subtitle ['sʌbtaɪt(ə)l] N *Cin, TV, Typ* N sous-titre *m*, *pl* sous-titres; **film with English subtitles** film sous-titré en anglais
VT sous-titrer

subtitled [ˈsʌbtaɪt(ə)ld] ADJ *Cin, TV* sous-titré, *pl* sous-titrés

subtitler [ˈsʌbtaɪtlər] N *Cin, TV* sous-titreur, -euse

subtitling [ˈsʌbtaɪtlɪŋ] N *Cin, TV* sous-titrage *m*

subtle [ˈsʌt(ə)l] ADJ *(person, mind, reasoning, perfume, charm)* subtil; *(cunning)* rusé, astucieux; **s. distinction** distinction *f* ténue *ou* subtile; **you are being too s.** vous finassez; **s. irony** fine ironie *f*; **s. remark** observation *f* subtile

subtlety [ˈsʌt(ə)ltɪ] N **1** *(of distinction, mind, reasoning)* subtilité *f*; *(of policy)* subtilité, raffinement *m*, finesse *f* **2** *(subtle thing)* subtilité *f*

subtly [ˈsʌt(ə)lɪ] ADV subtilement, avec finesse; *(to argue etc)* avec subtilité; **s. different** légèrement différent

subtonic [sʌbˈtɒnɪk] N *Mus* note *f* sensible, sensible *f*

subtotal [ˈsʌbtəʊt(ə)l] N sous-total *m*, *pl* sous-totaux, total *m* partiel

subtract [səbˈtrækt] VT soustraire, retrancher (**from** de)

subtraction [səbˈtrækʃən] N soustraction *f* (**from** de) VOIR GRAMMAIRE A77; B59

subtropical [sʌbˈtrɒpɪk(ə)l] ADJ subtropical, -aux

subtype [ˈsʌbtaɪp] N sous-type *m*, *pl* sous-types

suburb [ˈsʌbɜːb] N banlieue *f*, *(nearer city)* faubourg *m*; **the suburbs** la banlieue; **in the suburbs** en banlieue; **in the suburbs of Paris** dans la banlieue de Paris; **garden s.** cité-jardin *f*, *pl* cités-jardins

suburban [səˈbɜːbən] ADJ suburbain; *(house, station, train)* de banlieue; *Pej (narrow-minded) (person)* à l'esprit étroit; *(life)* étriqué; **even the city centre's s.** même le centre-ville sent la banlieue

suburbanite [səˈbɜːbənaɪt] N banlieusard, -arde

suburbia [səˈbɜːbɪə] N la banlieue

subvention [səbˈvenʃən] N subvention *f*

subversion [səbˈvɜːʃən] N *Pol etc* subversion *f*

subversive [səbˈvɜːsɪv] ADJ subversif (**of** de) N individu *m* subversif; **a group of subversives** un groupe subversif

subvert [səbˈvɜːt] VT renverser, subvertir

subway [ˈsʌbweɪ] N **1** *Br (walkway under road etc)* passage *m* souterrain, souterrain *m* **2** *esp Am Rail* métro *m*

subwoofer [ˈsʌbˌwuːfər] N caisson *m* de graves, subwoofer *m*

sub-zero ADJ au-dessous de zéro
▸▸**s. temperatures** températures *fpl* en-dessous de zéro

succeed [səkˈsiːd] VI **1** *(be successful)* réussir; **hard workers always s.** les grands travailleurs arrivent *ou* réussissent toujours; **how to s. in business** comment réussir dans les affaires; **young man who will s.** jeune homme qui ira loin; **to s. in doing sth** réussir *ou* arriver à faire qch; **she always succeeds** tout lui réussit; **I/the plan only succeeded in making things worse** je n'ai/le projet n'a réussi qu'à aggraver la situation; **to s. in one's attempt to …** réussir à …; *Prov* **if at first you don't s., try, try again** pour réussir il faut persévérer; *Prov* **nothing succeeds like success** la réussite appelle la réussite **2 to s. to the throne** *or* **the Crown** succéder à la couronne; **to s. to an office/estate** hériter d'une fonction/d'une propriété; *Law* **right to s.** droits *mpl* de succession
VT *(person, thing)* succéder à; **George III was succeeded by George IV** George IV succéda *ou* fut le successeur de George III

succeeding [səkˈsiːdɪŋ] ADJ **1** *(following)* suivant; *(in future)* futur, à venir **2** *(successive)* successif; **with each s. year** d'année en année

success [səkˈses] N succès *m*, réussite *f*; **we wish you s.** bonne chance!; **to meet with** *or* **to achieve s.** avoir *ou* remporter du succès; **the film was a great s. in Italy** le film a eu énormément de succès en Italie; **without s.** sans succès, en vain; **to score a s.** remporter un succès; **to be a s.** *(go well, work out well etc)* réussir, être réussi, être un succès; *(be popular) (of film, book etc)* être un succès; *(of party, cake)* être une réussite, être réussi; **the cake was a big s.** *(everyone liked it)* le gâteau a eu beaucoup de succès; **to be a s. with sb** *(be popular etc)* avoir un *ou* du succès auprès de qn; **it was a huge** *or* **great s.** cela a eu un succès fou; **the company has been one of the few successes of recent years** l'entreprise fait partie des quelques exemples de réussite de ces dernières années; **the film has been his biggest s. to date** ce film a été son plus grand succès à ce jour; **to make a s. of sth** réussir qch; **he made a big s. of it** il a très bien réussi; **a second attempt met with no better s.** une seconde tentative n'a pas eu plus de succès
▸▸**s. fee** prime *f* de rendement; **s. rate** *(of operation, treatment etc)* taux *m* de succès; **s. story** réussite *f*

successful [səkˈsesfʊl] ADJ *(project)* couronné de succès; *(outcome)* heureux; *(play)* qui a du succès; **to be s. in doing sth** réussir à faire qch; *(after an effort)* arriver *ou* parvenir à faire qch; **were you s.?** avez-vous réussi?, *Fam* est-ce que ça a marché?; **he is s. in everything** tout lui réussit, il réussit dans tout ce qu'il entreprend; **a s. businesswoman** une femme d'affaires qui a réussi; **to be s. at the polls** sortir victorieux du scrutin; **s. candidates** *Pol* candidats *mpl* élus; *Sch* candidats reçus; **to bring an operation to a s. conclusion** mener à bien une opération; **a s. evocation of a bygone age** une évocation fort réussie d'une époque révolue; *Com* **s. tenderer** adjudicataire *mf*

successfully [səkˈsesfəlɪ] ADV avec succès; **when we've s. completed this stage of the operation** quand nous aurons mené à bien cette partie de l'opération

succession [səkˈseʃən] N **1** *(series)* *(of victories, visitors etc)* succession *f*, série *f*, suite *f*; **an endless s. of …** une suite ininterrompue de …; **in s.** successivement; **for two years in s.** pendant deux années consécutives *ou* de suite; **in close s.** se succédant de près; **in rapid s.** coup sur coup; **a rapid s. of governments** une succession rapide de gouvernements; **a long s. of kings** une longue suite de rois **2** *(to throne), Law* succession *f*; *(descendants)* lignée *f*; **he was third in s. to the throne** c'était le troisième dans l'ordre de succession au trône; **to settle the s.** régler la succession; **at the time of his s. to the throne** au moment de son avènement; **law of s.** droit *m* des successions; **right of s.** droits de succession

successive [səkˈsesɪv] ADJ successif; **on five s. Sundays** cinq dimanches consécutifs *ou* de suite; **s. generations** les générations *fpl* successives

successively [səkˈsesɪvlɪ] ADV successivement

successor [səkˈsesər] N successeur *m* (**to** à); **the s. to the throne** l'héritier *m* du trône; **my first car and its successors** ma première voiture et celles qui lui ont succédé *ou* qui sont venues ensuite

succinct [səkˈsɪŋ(k)t] ADJ *(account, writer)* succinct

succinctly [səkˈsɪŋ(k)tlɪ] ADV succinctement

succinctness [səkˈsɪŋ(k)tnɪs] N concision *f*

succour, *Am* **succor** [ˈsʌkər] *Lit* N secours *m*, aide *f*; **to give s.** porter secours *ou* assistance
VT venir en aide à, venir à l'aide de; *(the poor)* secourir

succulence [ˈsʌkjʊləns] N succulence *f*

succulent [ˈsʌkjʊlənt] ADJ **1** *(food)* succulent **2** *Bot* **s. leaf** feuille *f* charnue
N *Bot* plante *f* grasse

succumb [səˈkʌm] VI succomber (**to** à), céder (**to** à); **to s. to one's injuries** succomber *ou* mourir de ses blessures; **we have all succumbed to her charm** son charme nous a tous conquis, nous avons tous succombé à son charme; **I eventually succumbed** j'ai fini par céder

SUCH [sʌtʃ] ADJ **1** *(of that kind)* tel, pareil; **animals s. as the lion or the tiger** des animaux tels que le lion ou le tigre; **s. a man** un tel homme; **on s. an occasion** en semblable occasion, en une telle occasion, en une occasion pareille; **why do you ask s. a question?** pourquoi demander une chose pareille?, pourquoi poser une question pareille?; **did you ever see s. a thing!** a-t-on jamais vu pareille chose!; **you wouldn't have s. a thing as a corkscrew, would you?** vous n'auriez pas un tire-bouchon, par hasard?; **s. is not my intention** ce n'est pas là mon intention; **if s. were the case** s'il en était ainsi, si tel était le cas; **the village boasts a bus, s. as it is** le village a un autobus, si l'on peut dire; **s. books as these are always useful** les livres de ce genre sont toujours utiles; **in s. cases** en pareils cas; **in s. weather** par un temps pareil; **how can you tell s. lies?** comment pouvez-vous mentir de la sorte?, comment pouvez-vous dire des mensonges pareils?; **she has s. ideas!** elle a de ces idées!; **s. courage** tant de courage, un tel courage; **some s. plan was in my mind** j'avais dans l'esprit un projet de ce genre; **there is no s. thing** cela n'existe pas; **if there were no s. thing as money** si l'argent n'existait pas; **I said no s. thing** je n'ai rien dit de semblable *ou* de pareil; **no s. thing!** pas du tout!; *Law* **persons guilty of s. offences** personnes coupables des délits susmentionnés

2 on s. (and such) a day in s. (and such) a place tel jour en tel endroit; **your letter of s. and s. a date** votre lettre du tant; **s. a one** un tel, une telle

3 she arranges things in s. a way that she is free on Saturdays elle s'arrange de manière à être libre le samedi; **his kindness was s. as to make us feel ashamed** sa bonté était telle que nous en étions confus; *Fml* **to take s. steps as shall be considered necessary** prendre toutes les mesures qui paraîtront nécessaires; *Fml* **until s. time as is convenient to me** jusqu'à ce que cela me convienne

ADV **s. large houses** de si grandes maisons; **I had never heard s. good music** je n'avais jamais entendu d'aussi bonne musique; **he's not s. a good player as you** ce n'est pas un aussi bon joueur que vous; **s. a clever woman** une femme si intelligente; **it was s. a long time ago** il y a si longtemps de cela; **he is s. a liar** il est tellement menteur, c'est un tel menteur; **s. an enjoyable day** une journée si *ou* tellement agréable; **we had s. a good time** on s'est tellement *ou* si bien amusé(s), on s'est tant amusé(s); **don't be in s. a hurry** ne soyez pas si pressé; **you gave me s. a fright!** vous m'avez fait une (telle) peur! VOIR GRAMMAIRE A5

PRON **1 he enjoys cakes, ice creams and s.** il mange avec plaisir des gâteaux, des glaces et autres choses de ce genre

2 that's not for s. as you cela n'est pas pour quelqu'un comme toi; **s. as have the money can afford it** ceux qui ont de l'argent peuvent se l'offrir; **I haven't many, but I will send you s. as I have** je n'en ai pas beaucoup, mais je vous enverrai ce que j'ai; **s. is life!** c'est la vie!

3 she was a very brave woman and well known as s. c'était une femme très courageuse, et elle était bien connue en tant que telle; **history as s. is too often neglected** l'histoire en tant que telle est trop souvent négligée; **the text as s. is fine but ...** le texte en soi est bien mais ...; **I wasn't scared as s.** je n'avais pas vraiment peur

suchlike ['sʌtʃlaɪk] *Fam* ADJ semblable, pareil
PRON beggars, tramps and s. mendiants, vagabonds et autres gens de la sorte; **concerts, theatres and s.** concerts, théâtres, et autres choses de ce genre

suck [sʌk] VT sucer; *(mother's milk)* téter; *(drink, sweets)* sucer, suçoter; *(handkerchief)* mordiller; *(pipe)* tirer sur; *(not smoking)* sucer; *Tech (liquid, air)* aspirer; **to s. sth through a straw** aspirer qch avec une paille; **to s. one's fingers** se sucer les doigts; **to s. one's thumb** sucer son pouce; **to s. poison out of a wound** extraire le poison d'une blessure en la suçant; *Fig* **to s. sb dry** sucer qn jusqu'à la moelle; **the dust is sucked into the bag** la poussière est aspirée dans le sac; *Fig* **to get sucked into a conspiracy** être entraîné dans une conspiration; *Am Fam* **to s. face** *(kiss)* se rouler des pelles *ou* des patins
  VI **1** *(with mouth)* sucer; *(of baby, animal)* téter (le lait); *(of pump)* aspirer; **to s. at a sweet** sucer *ou* suçoter un bonbon; **to s. on one's pipe** tirer sur sa pipe; *(not smoking)* sucer sa pipe; **to s. on a straw** tirer sur *ou* aspirer avec une paille **2** *Sl (be very bad, unpleasant etc)* être merdique; **this city sucks** cette ville est merdique; **I've got to work all weekend – that sucks!** il faut que je travaille tout le week-end – ça craint!
  N **1 to give sth a s.** sucer qch; **to have or take a s. at a sweet** sucer un bonbon **2 to give a child a s.** donner à téter *ou* la tétée à un enfant
▸ **suck down** VT SEP *(of whirlpool etc)* engloutir, entraîner vers le fond
▸ **suck in** VT SEP *(with mouth)* sucer; *(draw in by vacuum)* aspirer; *(of air pump)* aspirer; *(in vortex)* engloutir; *(cheeks)* creuser; *(knowledge)* absorber; **to get sucked in** *(to conspiracy, plot etc)* se laisser entraîner (**to** dans)
▸ **suck off** VT SEP *Vulg (fellate)* sucer, faire une pipe à
▸ **suck out** VT SEP *(with mouth)* sucer; **to s. out the poison from a wound** aspirer *ou* sucer le poison d'une blessure
▸ **suck up** VT SEP *Tech (liquid, air)* sucer, aspirer, pomper; **these gases get sucked up into the upper atmosphere** ces gaz sont aspirés dans les couches supérieures de l'atmosphère
▸ **suck up to** VT INSEP *Fam Pej (ingratiate oneself with)* faire de la lèche à, lécher les bottes à

sucker ['sʌkər] N **1** *Fam (gullible person)* niais, -aise, nigaud, -aude; **to be a s. for a pretty/handsome face** ne pas savoir résister à un joli visage **2** *(of octopus etc)* suçoir *m*; *(of bloodsucker, on machine)* ventouse *f* **3** *(of plant)* rejeton *m*, rejet *m*; *(of tree)* drageon *m*, surgeon *m*; **to throw out suckers** *(of tree)* drageonner, surgeonner **4** *Am Fam (object)* truc *m*, machin *m*; **what's this s. for?** à quoi ça sert, ce truc?
  VT *esp Am Fam (dupe)* pigeonner; **he suckered them out of a million dollars** il les a eus d'un million de dollars
  VI *(of tree)* drageonner

sucking ['sʌkɪŋ] N *(of baby)* succion *f*, *(of pump)* aspiration *f*
  ▸▸ **s. pig** cochon *m* de lait

suckle ['sʌk(ə)l] VT *(child, young)* allaiter; *(baby)* donner le sein *ou* donner à téter à
  VI *(of baby, animal)* téter

suckling ['sʌklɪŋ] N **1** *(act)* allaitement *m* **2** *Arch (child)* nourrisson, -onne, enfant *mf* au sein; *(animal)* jeune animal *m* qui tète encore
  ▸▸ **s. pig** cochon *m* de lait

sucrose ['su:krəʊs] N *Chem* saccharose *m*

suction ['sʌkʃən] N succion *f*, *(of water in pump)* aspiration *f*, *(of air)* aspiration, appel *m*; **to adhere by s.** faire ventouse
  ▸▸ **s. cup, s. pad** ventouse *f*; **s. pump** pompe *f* aspirante; **s. stroke** temps *m* de l'aspiration

Sudan [ðəsu:'dæn] N (the) **S.** le Soudan

Sudanese [su:də'ni:z] ADJ soudanais, soudanien
  N Soudanais, -aise, Soudanien, -ienne

sudden ['sʌd(ə)n] ADJ **1** soudain, subit; *(movement, bend)* brusque; **this is rather s.** c'est plutôt inattendu; **it was a very s. decision** j'ai/il a /etc pris cette décision très vite; **it's all so s.** tout est arrivé si vite; **their marriage was rather s.** leur mariage s'est fait assez soudainement *ou* brusquement; **s. rise** hausse *f* subite; **s. shower** averse *f* subite **2 all of a s.** soudain, tout à coup, tout d'un coup
  ▸▸ **s. death** mort *f* subite; *(in games), Sport* = jeu *m* pour partager les ex aequo (où le premier point perdu, le premier but concédé etc, entraîne l'élimination immédiate); *Ftbl* **s. death play-off** épreuve *f* des penalties; **s. infant death syndrome** mort *f* subite du nourrisson

suddenly ['sʌd(ə)nlɪ] ADV soudain, tout à coup, tout d'un coup; *(to move)* brusquement; **she died s.** elle est morte subitement; **it happened so s.** c'est arrivé si vite; **then s. he was gone** et puis soudain, il avait disparu; **she very s. changed her mind** elle a changé d'avis très soudainement

suddenness ['sʌd(ə)nnɪs] N soudaineté *f*, *(of movement)* brusquerie *f*

suds [sʌdz] NPL *(soap)* s. *(foam)* mousse *f* de savon; *(soapy water)* eau *f* savonneuse

sue [su:] VT *Law* **to s. sb (at law)** intenter un procès à qn, poursuivre qn en justice; **to s. sb for damages** poursuivre qn en dommages-intérêts; **to s. sb for libel** poursuivre qn pour diffamation
  VI **1** *Law* **to s. for a separation** plaider en séparation; **to s. for libel** attaquer en diffamation; **to s. for a divorce** entamer une procédure de divorce; **if you print that story, I'll s.** si vous publiez cette histoire, je vous fais un procès **2 to s. for peace** demander la paix

suede [sweɪd] N daim *m*, *Spec* suède *m*; **s. gloves/shoes** gants/chaussures en daim
  ▸▸ *Sl* **s. head** crâne *m* rasé

suet ['su:ɪt] N *Culin* graisse *f* de rognon
  ▸▸ **s. dumpling** boulette *f* de graisse de bœuf; **s. pudding** = sorte de pudding sucré *ou* salé à base de farine et de graisse de bœuf

Suez ['su:ɪz, 'sʊɪz] N Suez
  ▸▸ **the S. Canal** le canal de Suez; **the S. crisis** la crise de Suez

suffer ['sʌfər] VT *(undergo)* *(loss, indignity, consequence)* subir; *(pain)* endurer; *(sorrow)* subir, éprouver; *(tolerate, endure)* supporter, tolérer; **to s. defeat** essuyer *ou* subir une défaite; **to s. hunger** souffrir de la faim; **she doesn't s. fools gladly** elle ne peut pas supporter *ou* souffrir les imbéciles
  VI *(of person, business, marriage, relations, health etc)* souffrir; *(of economy)* être perturbé; *(of profits)* subir une perte; **to s. from rheumatism** souffrir de rhumatismes; **to s. for one's misdeeds** supporter les consé-

quences de ses méfaits; **you'll s. for it** il vous en cuira, vous allez le payer; **I'll make (sure) you s. for this!** tu me le paieras!; **to be made to s. for what others have done** payer pour les actions d'autrui; **to s. from neglect** pâtir d'un manque de soins; **the country suffers from labour troubles** le pays est en proie à l'agitation ouvrière; **his good name has suffered** sa réputation a souffert; **she started drinking and her work suffered** elle a commencé à boire et son travail en a pâti; **the vines have suffered from the frost** les vignes ont souffert de la gelée

sufferance ['sʌf(ə)rəns] N tolérance *f* (**of** de); **children are admitted on s.** l'entrée des enfants est tolérée; **I get the feeling I'm just here on s.** j'ai l'impression de n'être ici que parce qu'on m'y tolère

sufferer ['sʌf(ə)rər] N **to be a s. from ill health** avoir une mauvaise santé; **sufferers from asthma/arthritis**, asthma/arthritis sufferers personnes sujettes à l'asthme/ l'arthrite

suffering ['sʌf(ə)rɪŋ] ADJ souffrant, qui souffre
  N souffrance *f*; **the depression caused great s.** la dépression a causé de grandes souffrances; **cheerful in spite of his s.** gai malgré ses souffrances

suffice [sə'faɪs] *Fml* VI suffire; **that will s. (for me)** cela (me) suffira
  VT *(person)* suffire à, être suffisant pour; **s. (it) to say that I got nothing out of it** il suffit de dire que je n'en ai rien obtenu

sufficiency [sə'fɪʃənsɪ] N *Fml* quantité *f* suffisante, *Arch* suffisance *f*; **to have a s. of sth** avoir assez de qch; **to have no more than a bare s.** avoir tout juste assez; *(of food, money)* avoir tout juste de quoi manger/ vivre

sufficient [sə'fɪʃənt] ADJ *(reason, explanation)* suffisant; **s. care/attention** suffisamment de *ou* assez de soins/d'attention; **lack of s. food/funds** insuffisance *f* de nourriture/de moyens; **this is s. to feed them** cela suffit pour les nourrir; **a hundred euros will be s. (for me)** cent euros (me) suffiront; **one light will be s.** une lampe suffira; **this work is not s.** ce travail n'est pas suffisant; **an apology is no longer s.** une excuse ne suffit plus; **it was s. to give her the address and she would find her way there** il suffisait de lui donner l'adresse et elle trouverait son chemin; **this news was s. to make him worry** cette nouvelle suffit à l'inquiéter; **they didn't have s. warning** on ne les a pas prévenus suffisamment à l'avance; **is that s. time for you?** cela vous donne-t-il suffisamment de temps?; **let me know in s. time so that I can ...** prévenez-moi suffisamment à l'avance pour que je puisse ...; **with s. supplies** avec des réserves suffisantes, avec suffisamment de réserves; **there was nowhere near s. heating in the building** l'immeuble était loin d'être suffisamment chauffé
  N assez; **have you had s. (to eat)?** avez-vous assez mangé?; **they don't have s. to live on** ils n'ont pas assez pour vivre

sufficiently [sə'fɪʃəntlɪ] ADV suffisamment, assez; **to be s. tactful to ...** avoir suffisamment de tact pour ...

suffix[1] ['sʌfɪks] N *Gram, Comput* suffixe *m*

suffix[2] ['sʌfɪks, sʌ'fɪks] VT *Gram, Comput* suffixer

suffocate ['sʌfəkeɪt] VT *(kill)* étouffer; *(of smell)* suffoquer; *Fig* **all initiative was suffocated** la moindre initiative était étouffée; *Fig* **the secret police suffocated any dissent** la police secrète étouffa toutes les dissensions
  VI étouffer, suffoquer (**with rage** de colère); **they were suffocating for lack of oxygen** ils étouffaient à cause du manque d'oxygène;

the stowaways suffocated (to death) les passagers clandestins périrent étouffés

suffocating ['sʌfəkeɪtɪŋ] ADJ suffocant, étouffant; **it's s. (in) here** on étouffe ici

suffocation [sʌfə'keɪʃən] N suffocation f, étouffement m; **to die of s.** mourir étouffé ou par asphyxie

suffragan ['sʌfrəgən] ADJ, N Rel bishop s., s. (bishop) (évêque m) suffragant m

suffrage ['sʌfrɪdʒ] N Pol (right to vote) droit m de vote; **universal s.** suffrage m universel; **women's s.** droit de vote pour les femmes

suffragette [sʌfrə'dʒet] N Pol, Hist suffragette f

suffuse [sə'fjuːz] VT esp Lit se répandre sur; **a blush suffused her cheeks** ses joues s'empourprèrent; **eyes suffused with tears** yeux baignés de larmes; **suffused with light** inondé de lumière

sugar ['ʃʊgər] N 1 sucre m; **granulated s.** sucre cristallisé; **lump s.** sucre en morceaux; **lump or cube of s.** morceau m ou carré m de sucre; Br **caster s.** sucre en poudre; **icing s.** sucre glace; **brown s.** sucre roux; **help yourself to s.** prenez donc du sucre; **milk, no s., please** avec du lait, sans sucre, s'il vous plaît; **he takes two spoonfuls of s.** ou **two sugars** il prend deux sucres

2 milk s. sucre m de lait, lactose f; Physiol **blood s.** glucose m sanguin; **blood s. level** taux m de sucre dans le sang

3 Fam (term of address) (mon) trésor m

4 Fam **she's found herself a s. daddy** elle s'est trouvé un vieux friqué qui l'entretient; **I've no intention of being your s. daddy** je n'ai pas l'intention de t'entretenir

5 Euph **oh s.!** oh mercredi!

VT (coffee etc) sucrer; (pill) dragéifier, recouvrir de sucre; **sugared almond** dragée f, Fig **to s. the pill** dorer la pilule

▸▸ **s. almond** dragée f; **s. basin** sucrier m; **s. beet** betterave f sucrière ou à sucre; **s. bowl** sucrier m; **s. cane** canne f à sucre; **s. maple** érable m à sucre; **s. mouse** souris f en sucre; **s. pea** mange-tout m inv; **s. refinery** raffinerie f (de sucre), sucrerie f; **s. shaker** saupoudreuse f (à sucre); **s. tongs** pince f à sucre

sugar-coat VT recouvrir de sucre; Fig (unpleasant measure) faire passer

sugar-coated ADJ recouvert de sucre; (almond) lissé

▸▸ **s. pill** comprimé m dragéifié

sugar-free ADJ sans sucre

sugaring ['ʃʊgərɪŋ] N épilation f au sucre

sugarloaf ['ʃʊgələʊf] N pain m de sucre

▸▸ **s. mountain** montagne f en pain de sucre

sugarplum ['ʃʊgəplʌm] N bonbon m; **yes, my s.** oui, mon petit chou

sugary ['ʃʊgərɪ] ADJ 1 (containing sugar) sucré; (sprinkled with sugar) saupoudré de sucre; **to go s.** (of jam) se cristalliser; **s. taste** goût m sucré 2 (smile, tone) mielleux, sucré; (tone) doucereux

suggest [sə'dʒest] VT 1 (propose) (something) suggérer, proposer (**to sb** à qn); Law **I s. that ...** n'est-il pas vrai que ...?; **she suggested going for a walk** elle a suggéré ou proposé de faire une promenade; **what do you s. I do?** que suggérez-vous que je fasse?; **I shall do as you s.** je ferai comme vous le suggérez; **a solution suggested itself to me** une solution m'est venue à l'esprit; **or was it a conspiracy, as some have suggested?** ou s'agissait-il d'une conspiration, comme on l'avait suggéré auparavant?; Com **suggested retail price** prix m conseillé

2 (inspire, recommend) (idea) inspirer, faire naître; **common sense would s. we give up** le bon sens nous dirait ou conseillerait d'abandonner

3 (insinuate, imply) insinuer; **are you suggesting that I am lying?** est-ce que vous insinuez que je mens?; **which suggests that it was an accident** ce qui semblerait indiquer qu'il s'agissait d'un accident; **are eggs as scarce as the price would s.?** les œufs sont-ils aussi rares que le prix le laisse supposer?; **the marks in the sand s. a person of about ...** les traces sur le sable indiquent la présence d'une personne d'environ ...

4 (evoke) évoquer; **what do these abstract forms s. to you?** que vous suggèrent ou évoquent ces formes abstraites?

suggestible [sə'dʒestɪb(ə)l] ADJ 1 Psy suggestible 2 (easily influenced) influençable

suggestion [sə'dʒestʃən] N 1 (proposal) suggestion f, proposition f; **to be open to suggestions** être prêt à accueillir des suggestions; **at her s., I stayed at home** suivant son conseil, je suis resté chez moi; **to make a s.** faire une suggestion ou proposition; **practical s.** conseil m pratique; **suggestions for improvement** propositions en vue d'une amélioration; **to be full of suggestions** être fécond en idées ou en conseils; **it was only a s.** ce n'était qu'une suggestion VOIR GRAMMAIRE A59-60

2 Law **my s. is that you were not there at the time** n'est-il pas vrai que vous étiez absent à ce moment-là?

3 Psy etc suggestion f, **hypnotic s.** suggestion hypnotique; **adverts work by s.** les publicités fonctionnent à la suggestion

4 (insinuation) indication f, **there is no s. that he might be guilty** rien/personne ne suggère ou dit qu'il est coupable

5 (hint) **to speak with just a s. of a foreign accent** parler avec une pointe d'accent étranger; **s. of regret** nuance f ou pointe f de regret

▸▸ **suggestions box** boîte f à idées

suggestive [sə'dʒestɪv] ADJ 1 (reminiscent, thought-provoking) suggestif; **s. of sth** évocateur de qch 2 (indecent, erotic) (lyrics, dance etc) suggestif; **s. joke** plaisanterie f grivoise

suggestively [sə'dʒestɪvlɪ] ADV d'une façon suggestive

suggestiveness [sə'dʒestɪvnɪs] N (of picture etc) caractère m suggestif

suicidal [suːɪ'saɪd(ə)l] ADJ suicidaire; **it would be s. (to do it)** ce serait du suicide ou ce serait suicidaire (d'agir de la sorte); Fig **as far as your career is concerned, it would be s.** sur le plan professionnel, ça serait du suicide; **s. tendencies** tendances fpl au suicide ou suicidaires; **to be feeling s.** se sentir suicidaire, avoir des idées de suicide; **an absolutely s. bit of driving** une conduite complètement suicidaire

suicide ['suːɪsaɪd] N 1 (act) suicide m; **to commit s.** se suicider; **attempted s.** tentative f de suicide; Fig **to commit political/economic/financial s.** se suicider politiquement/économiquement/financièrement; Fig **it would be s. to go there** ce serait du suicide d'y aller; **mass s.** suicide collectif 2 (person) suicidé, -ée; **there was an attempted s. in the next bed** il y avait quelqu'un qui avait tenté de se suicider dans le lit d'à côté

▸▸ **s. attempt** tentative f de suicide; Mil **s. mission** mission f suicide; **s. note** lettre f (que l'on laisse quand on se suicide); **s. pact** = accord m de suicide collectif entre deux ou plusieurs personnes; **s. squad** équipe f (en mission) suicide

suit [s(j)uːt] N 1 (clothing) ensemble m; (man's) costume m, complet m; (woman's) tailleur m; **two-piece/three-piece s.** costume deux/trois pièces; **s. of armour** armure f complète; Aviat **flying or flight s.** combinaison f de vol; **pressure s.** combinai-

son pressurisée; **space s.** combinaison spatiale

2 Cards couleur f, Fig **politeness is not his strong or long s.** la politesse n'est pas son fort; **to follow s.** fournir à la couleur (demandée); Fig en faire autant, faire de même

3 Law **s. (at law)** (lawsuit) procès m (civil); (act of suing) poursuites fpl judiciaires; **to bring a s. against sb** intenter un procès à qn, poursuivre qn en justice; **criminal s.** action f ou procès criminel(le); **to be a party in a s.** être en cause

4 Old-fashioned, Lit (request) prière f, demande f; **to press one's s. with a girl** (when courting) faire une cour assidue à une jeune fille

5 Fam Pej (person) employé, -ée de bureau (en costume ou tailleur)

VT 1 (of clothes, colours etc) aller à; (of arrangement, time, job etc) convenir à; **to be suited to or for sth** être fait pour qch; **blue suits you** le bleu te va bien; **this climate/this food does not s. me** ce climat/cette nourriture ne me convient pas; **this hat suits you** ce chapeau vous va (bien); **clothes not suited to the climate** vêtements ne convenant pas au climat; **the premises are not suited for display purposes** les locaux ne se prêtent pas à la présentation des marchandises; **he is not suited to be a doctor** il n'est pas fait pour être médecin; **they are suited to or s. each other** ils sont faits l'un pour l'autre; **a small job in the country would s. me very well** un petit emploi en province m'irait ou me conviendrait très bien; **she found a house that suited her** elle a trouvé une maison à son gré; **marriage suits you** le mariage vous réussit; **that suits me best** c'est ce qui m'arrange le mieux; **that suits me (just) fine** or Fam **down to the ground** ça me va à merveille, ça me convient parfaitement; **I shall do it when it suits me** je le ferai quand cela me conviendra; **you can't just come and go when(ever) it suits you** tu ne peux pas aller et venir à ta guise; **(would) two o'clock s. you?** est-ce que deux heures vous conviendrait?; **s. yourself** faites comme vous voudrez; **we have something to s. every taste/pocket** nous en avons pour tous les goûts/toutes les bourses

2 Am (dress in suit) vêtir d'un costume; **his followers were suited in black** ses disciples étaient vêtus d'un costume noir

3 (adapt) adapter (**sth to sth** qch à qch); esp Fml **to s. the action to the word** joindre les gestes à la parole

VI **that date does not s.** cette date ne convient pas; **would tomorrow s.?** demain conviendrait-il?

suitability [s(j)uːtə'bɪlɪtɪ] N (of date, arrangement, character) convenance f, (of comment, translation) à-propos m; (of decision, action etc) bien-fondé m; (of a person for a job) capacité f, **they doubted his s. as a husband for her** ils n'étaient pas sûrs qu'il était le mari qu'il lui fallait; **we've got doubts about the s.** of this film/book for young children nous ne sommes pas sûrs que ce film/livre convienne aux jeunes enfants; **s. of a candidate for a post** aptitude f d'un candidat pour un poste

suitable ['s(j)uːtəb(ə)l] ADJ (subject, work) convenable, qui convient; (candidate) valable; (date, title, clothes, example) adéquat; **we have found nothing s.** nous n'avons rien trouvé qui convienne; **wherever you think s.** où bon vous semblera; **the most s. date** la date qui conviendra le mieux; **is tomorrow s.?** demain te convient-il?; **s. expression** expression f pertinente ou appropriée; **s. marriage** union f bien assortie; **I've nothing s. to wear** je n'ai rien de convenable à me mettre; **with a s. note of sarcasm** avec une touche de sarcasme appropriée; **s. to** or **for sth** bon ou propre ou approprié à qch; **he's not s. for our Christine** ce n'est pas l'homme qu'il faut à notre Christine; **is it a book s. for children?** est-ce un livre pour les enfants?, est-ce que ce livre convient aux enfants?; **s. for children of seven years and under** pour les enfants de sept ans ou moins; **to make sth s. for sth** adapter qch à qch

suitably ['s(j)uːtəblɪ] ADV convenablement; (to say) à propos; **s. impressed/embarrassed** très impressionné/gêné; **s. matched** bien assortis; Iron **I hope you're s. impressed!** j'espère que tu es content maintenant!

suitcase ['s(j)uːtkeɪs] N valise f; **I'm still living out of a s.** je ne suis pas encore installé; **I've been travelling around, living out of a s.** j'ai voyagé un peu partout sans jamais vraiment m'installer

suite [swiːt] N **1 s. (of rooms)** suite f, appartement m **2** (furniture) **(three piece)** canapé m avec deux fauteuils assortis, salon m trois pièces; **bathroom s.** (meubles mpl de) salle f de bains; **bedroom s.** (meubles de) chambre f à coucher **3** Mus suite f; **orchestral s.** suite d'orchestre **4** Comput (of software) suite f logicielle, ensemble m logiciel **5** (of prince) suite f

suiting ['s(j)uːtɪŋ] N Com (cloth) tissu m de confection; **men's suitings** tissus pour complets

suitor ['s(j)uːtər] N **1** Arch, Hum soupirant m **2** Law plaideur, -euse

sulfa, sulfate etc Am = **sulpha, sulphate** etc

sulk [sʌlk] N bouderie f; **to be in a s.** bouder; **to have (a fit of) the sulks** bouder, faire la tête
▸ VI bouder, faire la tête

sulkily ['sʌlkɪlɪ] ADV (to reply) d'un ton bouder; (to look at sb) d'un air bouder; **he retreated s. to his room** il partit dans sa chambre en boudant

sulkiness ['sʌlkɪnɪs] N bouderie f

sulking ['sʌlkɪŋ] N bouderie f

sulky ['sʌlkɪ] ADJ bouder; **to be s.** bouder; **to look s.** avoir un air bouder, faire la tête; (of model) prendre un air bouder

sullen ['sʌlən] ADJ (person) maussade, renfrogné, morose; (silence) obstiné, buté; Lit (sky, clouds) maussade

sullenly ['sʌlənlɪ] ADV d'un air maussade ou renfrogné; (to obey) de mauvaise grâce

sullenness ['sʌlənnɪs] N maussaderie f, air m renfrogné

sullied ['sʌlɪd] ADJ souillé, terni

sully ['sʌlɪ] VT **1** Lit (make dirty) souiller, ternir **2** Fig (reputation) entacher, salir; **to s. one's hands** se salir les mains

sulpha, Am **sulfa** ['sʌlfə] N
▸▸ **s. drug** sulfamide m

sulphate, Am **sulfate** ['sʌlfeɪt] N sulfate m; **copper s.** sulfate de cuivre

sulphide, Am **sulfide** ['sʌlfaɪd] N sulfure m; **hydrogen s.** sulfure d'hydrogène, hydrogène m sulfuré

sulphonamide, Am **sulfonamide** [sʌl'fɒnəmaɪd] N sulfamide m

sulphur, Am **sulfur** ['sʌlfər] N soufre m
▸▸ **s. dioxide** dioxyde m de soufre, anhydride m sulfureux; **s. mine** soufrière f; Geol **s. spring** source f sulfureuse

sulphureous, Am **sulfureous** [sʌl'fjʊərɪəs] ADJ sulfureux; (coloured) couleur de soufre inv, soufré

sulphuric, Am **sulfuric** [sʌl'fjʊərɪk] ADJ (acid) sulfurique

sulphurous, Am **sulfurous** ['sʌlfərəs, -fjʊər-] ADJ **1** = **sulphureous 2** Chem (acid) sulfureux

sultan ['sʌltən] N sultan m

sultana [sʌl'tɑːnə] N **1** Culin (fruit) raisin m de Smyrne **2** (female sultan) sultane f

sultanate ['sʌltəneɪt] N sultanat m

sultriness ['sʌltrɪnɪs] N **1** (of climate etc) chaleur f étouffante; (of atmosphere) lourdeur f; **s. of the weather** le temps lourd **2** Fig (sensuality) sensualité f, volupté f

sultry ['sʌltrɪ] ADJ **1** (heat) étouffant, suffocant; (weather) lourd, orageux; **it's s.** il fait très lourd **2** (voice, look) sensuel, voluptueux

sum [sʌm] N **1** (amount) (of money etc) somme f; (total) somme, total m; (of account) montant m; **in s.** en somme, somme toute; **a nice little s.** une jolie petite somme, une somme rondelette; **the s. of sb's efforts** la somme des efforts de qn; **the whole is greater than the s. of its parts** l'ensemble est encore meilleur que la somme des éléments qui le compose **2** Math (problem) problème m, exercice m (d'arithmétique); Sch **sums** (arithmetic) calcul m; **to do a s. in one's head** faire un calcul de tête; **to do sums** faire du calcul ou de l'arithmétique
▸ VT (-mm-) (numbers) additionner; Math (series) sommer
▸▸ Fin **s. payable** charge f à payer; **s. total** totalité f, somme totale; Fig (of sb's efforts etc) totalité; **is that the s. total of what you've done today?** c'est tout ce que vous avez fait aujourd'hui?
▸ **sum up** VT SEP **1** (summarize) résumer, faire un résumé de; **to s. up what one has said before** se résumer, résumer les faits; Law **to s. up the case** or **the evidence** (of judge) résumer les débats; **to s. up a situation in a word** résumer une situation en un mot **2** (assess quickly) **to s. up the situation at a glance** évaluer la situation d'un coup d'œil; **to s. sb up** juger ou évaluer qn **3** (add) (numbers) faire la somme de, totaliser
▸ VI (summarize) résumer; **to s. up, I will say that ...** en résumé, je dirai que ...; **in summing up, the judge said ...** dans son résumé, le juge a dit ...

sumac(h) ['s(j)uːmæk, 'ʃuː-] N sumac m

summarily ['sʌmərɪlɪ] ADV sommairement

summarize ['sʌməraɪz] VT (book etc) résumer sommairement; (debate etc) récapituler

summary ['sʌmərɪ] ADJ (brief) sommaire; **he was dealt rather s. justice** on lui a rendu une justice plutôt sommaire
▸ N sommaire m, résumé m, aperçu m; (of book) argument m; (of commercial operations) récapitulation f, relevé m; TV, Radio **s. of the news, news s.** rappel m des titres
▸▸ **s. account** (providing summary) résumé; Law référé m; Acct **s. balance sheet** bilan m condensé; **s. dismissal** renvoi m sommaire; Law **s. offences** = délits mpl qui peuvent être jugés en procédure sommaire; **s. proceedings** affaire f sommaire; **s. report** rapport m récapitulatif

summation [sʌ'meɪʃən] N **1** (addition) sommation f, addition f **2** (total) somme f, total m **3** (summary) résumé m; **the exhibition was a s. of his life's work** l'exposition résumait parfaitement son œuvre **4** Am Law résumé m des débats (par le juge)

summer ['sʌmər] N été m; **in s.** en été; **in the s.** pendant l'été; **in the s. of 1995** pendant l'été 1995; **a summer('s) day** un jour d'été; **winter and s. alike, I live in the country** été comme hiver, j'habite la campagne; **next s.** l'été prochain; **Indian s.** été de la Saint-Martin, été indien; Lit **many summers ago** il y a bien longtemps; Lit **a girl of 12 summers** une fille de 12 printemps
▸ VI (by the sea etc) passer l'été; (of cattle) estiver
▸ VT (cattle) estiver
▸▸ **s. break** petites vacances fpl d'été; **s. clothes** habits mpl ou vêtements mpl d'été; **the s. holidays** les vacances ou congés mpl d'été; Scol les grandes vacances; **s. resort** station festivale; **s. school** université f d'été; **s. season** saison f d'été, période f estivale; Admin **s. time** (by clock) heure f d'été; **s. visitor** estivant, -ante

summerhouse ['sʌməhaʊs] N (in garden) pavillon m

summertime ['sʌmətaɪm] N (season) (saison f d')été m

summery ['sʌmərɪ] ADJ d'été, estival, -aux; **you look very s. in that** ça te donne un petit air estival

summing-up ['sʌmɪŋ-] N Law résumé m des débats (par le juge); **in her s. up, the judge said ...** dans son résumé (des débats), le juge a dit ...

summit ['sʌmɪt] N **1** (of mountain) sommet m, cime f, Fig **s. of greatness** le faîte ou sommet des grandeurs; **to be at the s. of one's power/fame** être au sommet ou à l'apogée du pouvoir/de sa gloire **2** Pol sommet m; **talks will be held at s. level** des négociations auront lieu au sommet
▸▸ **s. conference** (conférence f au) sommet

summiteer [sʌmɪ'tɪər] N Pol participant, -ante à un sommet

summon ['sʌmən] VT **1** (call) (servant, help, police, doctor) appeler, faire venir; (assembly, person to meeting, employee) convoquer; Law citer à comparaître; **business summoned him back to London** les affaires l'ont rappelé à Londres; **to s. a defendant/a witness to appear** citer ou assigner un défendeur/un témoin; **s. the next witness!** faites entrer le témoin suivant! **2** = **summon up**
▸ **summon up** VT SEP **1** (courage, help, support etc) faire appel à; **to s. up all one's strength** rassembler toutes ses forces; **summoning up all her courage ...** prenant son courage à deux mains ...; (more serious) rassemblant tout son courage ... **2** (memory) faire resurgir; (spirits) invoquer

summons, pl **summonses** ['sʌmənz, -zɪz] N **1** (order to attend etc) convocation f **2** Law citation f (à comparaître), assignation f (à comparaître); **to issue a s.** lancer une assignation; **to serve a s. on sb** citer qn à comparaître; **to take out a s. against sb** faire assigner qn
▸ VT Law citer à comparaître, assigner, appeler en justice

sump [sʌmp] N **1** (oil) **s.** carter m à huile; **to drain the s.** faire la vidange **2** Min etc puisard m **3** (cesspool) fosse f d'aisance
▸▸ **s. guard** protection f de carter; **s. pan** carter d'huile

sumptuous ['sʌm(p)tjʊəs] ADJ somptueux

sumptuously ['sʌm(p)tjʊəslɪ] ADV somptueusement

sumptuousness ['sʌm(p)tjʊəsnɪs] N somptuosité f

Sun abbr **Sunday**

sun [sʌn] N soleil m; **the s. is shining** il fait (du) soleil, le soleil brille; **the s. rises/sets** le soleil se lève/se couche; **rising/setting s.** soleil levant/couchant; **against the s.** face au soleil; **to have the s. in one's eyes** avoir le soleil dans les yeux; **let's get out of the s.** mettons-nous à l'abri du soleil; **too much s. can be harmful** de trop longues expositions au soleil peuvent être dangereuses; **to take the s.** prendre le soleil; **to catch the s.** (of person) (get suntanned) bronzer; (get sunburnt) prendre des coups de soleil; (of garden etc) voir le soleil; **to get a touch of**

the s. prendre *ou* attraper un coup de soleil; **every species/subject under the s.** toutes les espèces existantes/tous les sujets possibles; **there's nothing new under the s.** (il n'y a) rien de nouveau sous le soleil; **to try everything under the s.** essayer tout ce qu'il est possible d'imaginer; **to call sb every name** *or* **everything under the s.** traiter qn de tous les noms; **nothing under the s. was going to stop her now** rien ni personne n'allait l'arrêter maintenant; *Fig* **to have a place in the s.** avoir une place au soleil; *Br Sl* **she thinks the s. shines out of his arse** elle n'a rien vu d'aussi beau que lui

VT (**-nn-**) exposer au soleil; **to s. oneself** prendre le soleil, *Fam* faire le lézard

▸▸ **s. awning** store *m*; **s. deck** *(of house)* véranda *f*, terrasse *f*; *Naut* pont *m* supérieur, pont-promenade *m*, *pl* ponts-promenades; *Aut* **s. gear** planétaire *m*; **s. helmet** casque *m* (colonial); *Hist* **the S. King** le Roi Soleil; **s. lamp** lampe *f* à bronzer; **s. lotion** lotion *f* solaire; *Br* **s. lounge** solarium *f*; **s. oil** huile *f* solaire; *Am* **s. parlor** solarium, **s. porch** solarium; *Aut* **s. shield** pare-soleil *m inv*; **s. terrace** terrasse *f*, **s. visor** *(on cap, for eyes)* visière *f*, *Aut* pare-soleil; *Aut* **s. wheel** roue *f* solaire

sunbaked ['sʌnbeɪkt] **ADJ** *(earth)* brûlé par le soleil

sunbathe ['sʌnbeɪð] **VI** prendre un bain de soleil, se faire bronzer

sunbather ['sʌnbeɪðər] **N** personne *f* qui prend un bain/des bains de soleil; **suddenly the park was full of sunbathers** soudain le parc s'est rempli de gens venus prendre un bain de soleil

sunbathing ['sʌnbeɪðɪŋ] **N** bains *mpl* de soleil

sunbeam ['sʌnbiːm] **N** rayon *m* de soleil

sunbed ['sʌnbed] **N** *(for tanning)* lit *m* à ultraviolets; *(in garden etc)* (fauteuil *m*) relax *m*

sunblind ['sʌnblaɪnd] **N** store *m*

sunblock ['sʌnblɒk] **N** écran *m* total

sunburn ['sʌnbɜːn] **N** coup *m* de soleil; **suffering from s.** souffrant de coups de soleil

sunburnt, sunburned ['sʌnbɜːnt, -bɜːnd] **ADJ** brûlé par le soleil; **to get s.** attraper *ou* prendre un coup de soleil

sunburst ['sʌnbɜːst] **N** *Met* éclaircie *f*, *(brooch)* broche *f* (en forme de) soleil

sundae ['sʌndeɪ] **N** *Culin* = glace *f* aux fruits recouverte d'un coulis, de noix, de crème Chantilly etc

Sunday ['sʌndɪ] **N** dimanche *m*; **S. 26 July** dimanche 26 juillet; **S. morning/evening** dimanche matin/soir; **it's S. today** nous sommes dimanche aujourd'hui; **he comes on Sundays** il vient le dimanche; **they're coming on S.** ils viennent dimanche; **every S.** tous les dimanches; **to put on one's S. best** s'habiller en dimanche, s'endimancher; **in one's S. best** dans ses habits du dimanche; *Fam* **the Sundays** *(newspapers)* les journaux du dimanche VOIR GRAMMAIRE A81–2; B61–2

▸▸ *Br* **S. lunch** déjeuner *m* du dimanche; **S. newspaper** journal *m* du dimanche; **S. opening** = ouverture *f* des magasins le dimanche; **S. paper** journal *m* du dimanche; **S. school** catéchisme *m*; **S. school teacher** catéchiste *mf*, personne *f* qui fait le catéchisme; **S. supplement** = supplément *m* joint à un journal du dimanche; **S. trading** = ouverture des magasins le dimanche; **S. trading laws** = lois *fpl* réglementant l'ouverture des magasins le dimanche

sunder ['sʌndər] *Lit* **VT** détruire

VI *(of ship's hull)* se rompre; *(of bridge, empire)* s'écrouler

sundial ['sʌndaɪəl] **N** cadran *m* solaire, gnomon *m*

sundown ['sʌndaʊn] **N** coucher *m* du soleil; **at s.** au coucher du soleil

sundowner ['sʌndaʊnər] **N** *Fam* **1** *Br (drink)* = boisson *f* alcoolisée prise le soir **2** *Austr (tramp)* clochard *m*

sun-drenched [-dren(t)ʃt] **ADJ** *(beach etc)* baigné *ou* arrosé de soleil

sun-dried **ADJ** séché au soleil

sundry ['sʌndrɪ] **ADJ** divers; **on s. occasions** à diverses reprises

N 1 all and s. tout le monde; **this is not for all and s. to hear** je ne veux pas que tout le monde entende ça **2 sundries** *(items)* articles *mpl* divers; *(costs)* frais *mpl* divers

▸▸ *Acct* **s. expenses** frais divers

sunfish ['sʌnfɪʃ] **N** môle *f*, poisson-lune *m*, *pl* poissons-lunes

sunflower ['sʌnflaʊər] **N** *(plant)* tournesol *m*, soleil *m*, hélianthe *m*

▸▸ **s. oil** huile *f* de tournesol; **s. seeds** graines *fpl* de tournesol

sung **PP** *see* **sing**

sunglasses ['sʌnglɑːsɪz] **NPL** lunettes *fpl* de soleil

sun-god **N** dieu *m* soleil

sungun ['sʌngʌn] **N** *TV, Cin* sun-gun *m*, *pl* sun-guns, éclairage *m* sur batterie

sunhat ['sʌnhæt] **N** chapeau *m* de soleil

sunk **PT** *see* **sink**

sunken ['sʌŋk(ə)n] **ADJ** *(rock)* immergé; *(wreck)* englouti; *(cheeks)* creux; *(garden etc)* encaissé, en contrebas; **s. eyes** yeux *mpl* creux *ou* enfoncés; **s. chest** poitrine *f* creuse

PP *see* **sink**

sunless ['sʌnlɪs] **ADJ** sans soleil

sunlight ['sʌnlaɪt] **N** *(lumière f du)* soleil *m*; **in the s.** au soleil, en plein soleil; **to keep out of the s.** éviter la lumière du soleil; **keep it out of the s.** protégez-le du soleil, évitez-lui le soleil

sunlit ['sʌnlɪt] **ADJ** éclairé par le soleil; *(full of sunlight)* ensoleillé

sunniness ['sʌnɪnɪs] **N** *(of place)* ensoleillement *m*; *Fig* **the s. of her disposition** ses bonnes dispositions

sunny ['sʌnɪ] **ADJ 1** *(day, place)* ensoleillé; *(building)* éclairé par le soleil; *(side)* exposé au soleil; **it's s.** il fait (du) soleil; *esp Am* **s. side up** *(fried egg)* sur le plat **2** *Fig (face)* radieux, rayonnant; *(person)* joyeux; **to have a s. disposition** être d'une nature joyeuse; *Fig* **to look on the s. side of things** voir le bon côté des choses; *Fam* **to be on the s.**

side of forty ne pas avoir encore atteint la quarantaine

sunray ['sʌnreɪ] **N** rayon *m* de soleil, rayon solaire

▸▸ *Br* **s. lamp** *Med* lampe *f* à rayons ultraviolets; *(for tanning)* lampe à bronzer; *Med* **s. treatment** héliothérapie *f*

sunrise ['sʌnraɪz] **N** lever *m* du soleil; **at s.** au soleil levant, au lever du soleil

▸▸ **s. industry** industrie *f* de pointe

sunroof ['sʌnruːf] **N** *Aut* toit *m* ouvrant; *(of hotel etc)* toiture-terrasse *f*, *pl* toitures-terrasses, solarium *m*

sunset ['sʌnset] **N** coucher *m* du soleil; **at s.** au soleil couchant, au coucher du soleil

▸▸ **s. industry** industrie *f* déclinante

sunshade ['sʌnʃeɪd] **N** *(parasol)* ombrelle *f*; *(for table etc)* parasol *m*; *(in car)* pare-soleil *m inv*

sunshine ['sʌnʃaɪn] **N 1** *(light)* *(clarté f ou lumière f du)* soleil *m*; **in the s.** au soleil; **in the bright** *or* **brilliant s.** en plein soleil; **they need more s.** il leur faut davantage de soleil; **period of s.** période d'ensoleillement **2** *Fam* **hello s.!** *(to girl, woman)* bonjour ma jolie!; *(to boy, man)* salut mon vieux!; *Fam Iron* **where d'you think you're going, s.?** eh, tu vas où comme ça, mon coco?

▸▸ **s. roof** toit *m* ouvrant; **the S. State** = la Floride

sun-soaked **ADJ** *(beach etc)* baigné de soleil

sunspot ['sʌnspɒt] **N 1** *(on the sun)* tache *f* solaire, tache du soleil **2** *(holiday resort etc)* *(for summer holiday)* station *f* estivale; **it's our favourite winter s.** c'est là que nous préférons aller prendre du soleil pendant nos vacances d'hiver

sunstroke ['sʌnstrəʊk] **N** *Med* insolation *f*; **to get s.** attraper une insolation

suntan ['sʌntæn] **N** bronzage *m*, hâle *m*; **to get a s.** (se faire) bronzer; **she's got a tremendous s.** elle a un bronzage magnifique

▸▸ **s. lotion** lotion *f* solaire; **s. oil** huile *f* solaire

suntanned ['sʌntænd] **ADJ** bronzé, hâlé

suntrap ['sʌntræp] **N** coin *m* très ensoleillé

sun-up **N** *Am* lever *m* du soleil; **at s.** au lever du soleil

sun-worship **N** *Rel* culte *m* du soleil

sun-worshipper **N** *Rel* adorateur, -trice du soleil; *Fig (on beach etc)* amateur, -trice de soleil

sup [sʌp] **N** *esp North Eng* petite gorgée *f*; **to take a s. of soup** prendre une goutte de bouillon

VT (**-pp-** [sʌpt]) *esp North Eng* boire à petites gorgées

VI *Old-fashioned (have supper)* souper (**off**, **on** de)

▸ **sup up** *esp North Eng* **VT SEP** *(drink up)* finir **VI** finir son verre

super ['suːpər] **ADJ** *Fam (excellent)* super *inv*, formidable, génial, -aux

N 1 *Am Fam (in apartment block)* concierge *mf*, gardien *m* (d'immeuble) **2** *Fam* = **supervisor 3** *Aut (petrol)* super *m*

▸▸ **S. League** *(in rugby league)* = ligue *f* de rugby composée des meilleures équipes britanniques

superable ['suːpərəb(ə)l] **ADJ** surmontable

superabundance [suːpərə'bʌndəns] **N** surabondance *f* (**of** de)

superabundant [suːpərə'bʌndənt] **ADJ** surabondant

superabundantly [suːpərə'bʌndəntlɪ] **ADV** surabondamment

superannuate [suːpər'ænjʊeɪt] **VT** *(person)* mettre à la retraite; *Fig (thing)* mettre au rancart, remiser

superannuated [suːpərˈænjʊeɪtɪd] ADJ *(person)* (mis) en *ou* à la retraite, retraité; *(ideas)* suranné; *(system, equipment)* démodé

superannuation [suːpərænjʊˈeɪʃən] N retraite *f*
▸▸ s. fund caisse *f* de retraite

superb [suːˈpɜːb] ADJ superbe

superbly [suːˈpɜːblɪ] ADV superbement

supercargo [ˈsuːpəkɑːgəʊ] N *Naut* subrécargue *m*

supercharge [ˈsuːpətʃɑːdʒ] VT *Aut, Aviat etc (engine)* suralimenter, surcomprimer; **supercharged engine** moteur *m* suralimenté *ou* surcomprimé *ou* à compresseur

supercharger [ˈsuːpətʃɑːdʒər] N *Aut, Aviat etc* compresseur *m*, surpresseur *m*

supercilious [suːpəˈsɪlɪəs] ADJ hautain, dédaigneux

superciliously [suːpəˈsɪlɪəslɪ] ADV avec hauteur, dédaigneusement

superciliousness [suːpəˈsɪlɪəsnɪs] N hauteur *f*

superconductor [suːpəkənˈdʌktər] N *Phys, Elec* supraconducteur *m*

supercooling [ˈsuːpəˈkuːlɪŋ] N sous-refroidissement *m*

supercritical [suːpəˈkrɪtɪk(ə)l] ADJ *Nucl* supercritique, surcritique

super-duper [-ˈduːpər] ADJ *Fam* super, superchouette

superego [ˈsuːpərɪgəʊ] N *Psy* surmoi *m*

superelevation [suːpərelɪˈveɪʃən] N *(of road)* dévers *m*

supererogation [suːpərerəˈgeɪʃən] N *Fml* surérogation *f*

superficial [suːpəˈfɪʃəl] ADJ 1 superficiel; **he has a s. charm** il a un charme superficiel; **to have a s. knowledge of sth** avoir des connaissances superficielles de qch; **s. learning** vernis *m* de connaissances 2 *Med* **s. wound** blessure *f* superficielle

superficiality [suːpəfɪʃɪˈælɪtɪ] N superficialité *f*

superficially [suːpəˈfɪʃəlɪ] ADV superficiellement

superfine [ˈsuːpəfaɪn] ADJ 1 *Com etc* surfin, superfin 2 *(mind etc)* raffiné

superfluity [suːpəˈfluːɪtɪ] N superfluité *f*, **s. of good things** surabondance *f* de biens; **s. of words** surabondance de paroles

superfluous [suːˈpɜːfluəs] ADJ superflu, *Lit* superfétatoire; **it would be s. to mention …** il serait superflu de mentionner …; *Fam* **I'm starting to feel a bit s.** je commence à me sentir un peu de trop ici; **s. weight** excédent *m* de poids

superfluously [suːˈpɜːfluəslɪ] ADV d'une manière superflue

superfluousness [suːˈpɜːfluəsnɪs] N superfluité *f*

Superglue® [ˈsuːpəgluː] N super-glu® *f*

superglue [ˈsuːpəgluː] VT coller à la super-glu®

supergrass [ˈsuːpəgrɑːs] N *Br Sl* indic *m* de choc

superhighway [ˈsuːpəhaɪweɪ] N *Comput* autoroute *f*

superhuman [suːpəˈhjuːmən] ADJ surhumain

superimpose [suːpərɪmˈpəʊz] VT superposer, surimposer; *Phot, Cin* faire une surimpression de, surimprimer; **superimposed photos** des photos en surimpression; *Fig* **a Western culture superimposed on an indigenous one** une culture occidentale venue se superposer à une culture indigène

superimposition [suːpərɪmpəˈzɪʃən] N superposition *f*, *Phot, Cin* surimpression *f*

superintend [suːpərɪnˈtend] VT diriger, surveiller; **to s. the election** présider au scrutin

superintendence [suːpərɪnˈtendəns] N direction *f*, surveillance *f*

superintendent [suːpərɪnˈtendənt] N 1 *(director)* directeur, -trice; *(of works etc)* surveillant, -ante, chef *m*; *Am Fam* **sidewalk s.** passant, -ante qui regarde les travaux de construction 2 *(police officer)* commissaire *m* (de police) 3 *Am (of apartment block)* concierge *mf*, gardien *m* (d'immeuble)

superior [suːˈpɪərɪər] ADJ 1 *(position, officer, quality)* supérieur (**to** à); *Geog* **Lake S.** le lac Supérieur; **to be s. in numbers to the enemy** être supérieur en nombre à l'ennemi, avoir la supériorité du nombre sur l'ennemi; **they were overcome by s. numbers** ils ont succombé sous le nombre, ils ont été vaincus par le nombre; **she felt s. to her colleagues** elle se sentait supérieure à ses collègues 2 *(arrogant) (person)* orgueilleux; *(air)* de supériorité; **with a s. smile** avec un sourire condescendant
N supérieur, -ieure; **he is your s.** il est votre supérieur; **to be sb's s. in courage** être plus courageux que qn; **Father S.** père *m* supérieur; **Mother S.** mère *f* supérieure
▸▸ *Typ* **s. letter** lettre *f* supérieure; *Typ* **s. number** chiffre *m* supérieur

superiority [suːpɪərɪˈɒrɪtɪ] N supériorité *f*, **s. in men and materials** supériorité en hommes et en matériel; *Mil, Aviat* **air s.** supériorité aérienne
▸▸ *Psy* **s. complex** complexe *m* de supériorité

superlative [suːˈpɜːlətɪv] ADJ 1 *(excellent)* excellent 2 *Gram* superlatif
N *Gram* superlatif *m*; **in the s.** au superlatif; *Fig* **to speak in superlatives** s'exprimer par superlatifs VOIR GRAMMAIRE A24–6; B11; B13–14

superlatively [suːˈpɜːlətɪvlɪ] ADV extrêmement, au plus haut degré; **s. fit** dans une forme excellente

superman, *pl* **supermen** [ˈsuːpəmæn, -men] N *Phil* surhomme *m*; *Fam* superman *m*

supermarket [ˈsuːpəmɑːkɪt] N supermarché *m*
▸▸ s. **prices** prix *mpl* dans les supermarchés

supermarketing [ˈsuːpəmɑːkɪtɪŋ] N supermarketing *m*

supermini [ˈsuːpəmɪnɪ] N *Aut* citadine *f*

supermodel [ˈsuːpəmɒd(ə)l] N supermodel *m*

supernatural [suːpəˈnætʃərəl] ADJ surnaturel
N surnaturel *m*

supernaturally [suːpəˈnætʃərəlɪ] ADV de manière surnaturelle

supernova [suːpəˈnəʊvə] N *Astron* supernova *f*, *pl* supernovæ

supernumerary [suːpəˈnjuːm(ə)rərɪ] ADJ surnuméraire; *(staff)* en surnombre
N surnuméraire *m*; *Theat, Cin* figurant, -ante *f*

superphosphate [suːpəˈfɒsfeɪt] N superphosphate *m*

superpose [suːpəˈpəʊz] VT superposer (**upon, on** à); *(planks etc)* étager

superpower [ˈsuːpəpaʊər] N *Pol* superpuissance *f*
▸▸ s. **talks** négociations *fpl* entre les superpuissances

superscript [ˈsuːpəskrɪpt] *Typ* ADJ *(number)* en exposant; **s. 3** 3 en exposant
N *(number)* exposant *m*

superscription [suːpəˈskrɪpʃən] N *(on coin)* inscription *f*

supersede [suːpəˈsiːd] VT *(person) (get rid of)* supplanter; *(replace)* remplacer; *(object)* remplacer; **this catalogue supersedes pre-**

vious issues ce catalogue annule les précédents; **method now superseded** méthode périmée; **the RWQ20 has long been superseded by smaller models** la RWQ20 a depuis longtemps été supplantée par des modèles plus petits

supersensitive [suːpəˈsensɪtɪv] ADJ hypersensible

supersonic [suːpəˈsɒnɪk] ADJ *(plane, speed)* supersonique
▸▸ s. **bang, s. boom** bang *m*

superstar [ˈsuːpəstɑːr] N *Cin, Sport* superstar *f*

superstition [suːpəˈstɪʃən] N superstition *f*

superstitious [suːpəˈstɪʃəs] ADJ superstitieux

superstitiously [suːpəˈstɪʃəslɪ] ADV superstitieusement

superstore [ˈsuːpəstɔːr] N hypermarché *m*

superstructure [ˈsuːpəstrʌktʃər] N superstructure *f*

supertanker [ˈsuːpətæŋkər] N *Naut* superpétrolier *m*, supertanker *m*

supertax [ˈsuːpətæks] N surimposition *f*, surtaxe *f*

supertonic [suːpəˈtɒnɪk] N *Mus* sus-tonique *f*, *pl* sus-toniques

superuser [ˈsuːpəjuːzər] N *Comput* gros utilisateur *m*

supervene [suːpəˈviːn] VI *esp Fml* survenir; **if no complications s.** s'il ne survient pas de complications

supervention [suːpəˈvenʃən] N *Fml* survenue *f*

super-VGA [-viːdʒiːˈeɪ] N *Comput* Super-VGA *m*

supervise [ˈsuːpəvaɪz] VT 1 *(keep watch on) (children, prisoners)* surveiller 2 *(department, thesis)* diriger

supervision [suːpəˈvɪʒən] N 1 *(keeping watch on)* surveillance *f*, **children are under the s. of trained instructors at all times** les enfants se trouvent toujours sous la surveillance de moniteurs diplômés 2 *(control) (of department, thesis)* direction *f*

supervisor [ˈsuːpəvaɪzər] N 1 *(in factory etc)* surveillant, -ante 2 *(manager)* directeur, -trice 3 *Univ (of thesis)* directeur, -trice de thèse(s)

supervisory [suːpəˈvaɪz(ə)rɪ] ADJ *(committee etc)* de surveillance; **a s. function** une fonction de surveillance; **a s. role** un rôle de surveillant
▸▸ s. **board** conseil *m* de surveillance

superwoman, *pl* **superwomen** [ˈsuːpəwʊmən, -wɪmɪn] N *Fam* superwoman *f*

supine [ˈsuːpaɪn] N *Gram* supin *m*
ADJ 1 *(lying on back)* couché *ou* étendu sur le dos 2 *(inactive)* mou, *f* molle, indolent

supper [ˈsʌpər] N VOIR GRAMMAIRE A7 *(early evening meal)* dîner *m*; *(snack before going to bed)* souper *m*; **to have s.** dîner; *(before bed)* souper; *Fig* **you'll have to sing for your s.** c'est un prêté pour un rendu, c'est donnant, donnant; **the Last S.** la Cène, le dernier repas (du Seigneur); *Rel* **the Lord's S.** la communion, la cène, l'eucharistie *f*

suppertime [ˈsʌpətaɪm] N l'heure *f* du dîner; *(before bed)* l'heure du souper; **(it's) s.!** à table!

supplant [səˈplɑːnt] VT *(person)* supplanter, prendre la place de, évincer

supple [ˈsʌp(ə)l] ADJ *(limb, object, material)* souple, flexible; *(person)* souple; **to become s.** s'assouplir; **s.-limbed** aux membres souples

supplement¹ [ˈsʌplɪmənt] N *(of newspaper, for travel, of angle)* supplément *m*

supplement² [ˈsʌplɪment] VT *(book)* ajouter un supplément à; **to s. one's income by writing articles** augmenter ses revenus en écrivant des articles

supplementary [sʌplɪ'ment(ə)rɪ] ADJ supplémentaire (**to** de)

▸▸ *Math* **s. angle** angle *m* supplémentaire; *Br Formerly* **s. benefit** = allocation *f* versée par l'État à ceux qui ont les plus faibles revenus; **s. cover** garanties *fpl* complémentaires; **s. income** revenus *mpl* annexes

suppleness ['sʌp(ə)lnɪs] N souplesse *f*

suppliant ['sʌplɪənt] ADJ *(attitude, gesture)* suppliant, de supplication
N suppliant, -ante

supplicant ['sʌplɪkənt] N suppliant, -ante

supplicate ['sʌplɪkeɪt] *Fml, Lit* VT *(person)* supplier (**to do sth** de faire qch); *(sb's protection)* solliciter humblement
VI supplier

supplicating ['sʌplɪkeɪtɪŋ] ADJ suppliant, de supplication

supplication [sʌplɪ'keɪʃən] N **1** *(act)* supplication *f* **2** *(request)* supplique *f*

supplier [sə'plaɪər] N *Com* fournisseur, -euse
▸▸ **s. code** code *m* fournisseur; *Acct* **s. credit** crédit-fournisseur *m*

supply [sə'plaɪ] N **1** *(act of supplying)* approvisionnement *m*, fourniture *f*; **electricity s.** alimentation *f* en électricité; *Econ* **s. and demand** l'offre *f* et la demande

2 *(stock)* provision *f*; **to get (in) a fresh s. of sth** se réapprovisionner en qch; **money/information is in short s.** on manque d'argent/d'informations; **supplies** *(for office, photography)* fournitures *fpl*; **supplies of money** fonds *mpl*, ressources *fpl*; **food supplies** vivres *mpl*; **to cut off** *or* **stop the enemy's supplies** couper l'ennemi de ses approvisionnements; **supplies and services** fournitures et services *mpl*

3 to do s. teaching faire des remplacements
VT **1** fournir, approvisionner (**sb with sth** qn en qch); *(market)* alimenter; *(goods)* fournir, procurer; *(information)* fournir, *(services)* assurer; *(water, gas etc)* amener; **to s. oneself with sth** s'approvisionner en qch; **the tradesmen who s. us** nos fournisseurs; *Elec* **to s. a factory with current** alimenter une usine en courant; **the arteries that s. the brain** les artères qui amènent le sang au cerveau; **to s. proof** fournir des preuves

2 *(omission)* réparer; *(need)* répondre à; **to s. sb's needs** pourvoir *ou* subvenir aux besoins de qn
VI **to s. for sb** *(of teacher etc)* assurer l'intérim *ou* la suppléance de qn
▸▸ *Mil* **s. lines** lignes *fpl* de ravitaillement; **s. pipe** *(for fuel)* conduite *f* d'arrivée du combustible; **s. price** prix *m* d'offre; **s. ship** ravitailleur *m*; **s.-side economics** théorie *f* économique de l'offre; *Br* **s. teacher** remplaçant, -ante

---

Note that the French verb **supplier** is a false friend and is never a translation for the English verb **to supply**. It means **to implore, to beg**.

SUPPORT [sə'pɔːt]

N appui **1, 2** ▪ soutien **2** ▪ support **2**
VT supporter **1** ▪ soutenir **1, 2**
▪ appuyer **2** ▪ sponsoriser **2**
▪ entretenir **3** ▪ pourvoir aux besoins de **3** ▪ permettre l'utilisation de **4**

N **1** *(act of supporting)* appui *m*, soutien *m*; *(of arch, vault)* soutènement *m*; **moral s.** appui *ou* soutien moral; **to give s. to a proposal** appuyer une proposition; **this discovery lends s. to those who have argued ...** cette découverte va dans le sens de ceux qui soutiennent que ...; **the rebels have little s.** les

---

rebelles bénéficient d'un soutien limité; **there is widespread s. for the government** le gouvernement bénéficie d'un très large soutien; **can I expect your s.?** est-ce que je peux compter sur votre soutien?; **to produce documents in s. of an allegation** produire des pièces à l'appui d'une allégation *ou* pour appuyer une allégation; *Law* fournir les pièces au soutien; **to argue in s. of a measure** défendre une mesure; **in s. of this theory** à l'appui de cette théorie; *Mil* **air s.** appui *ou* soutien aérien; **with (financial) s. from the council** avec l'appui (financier) du conseil; **insufficient air for the s. of life** air en quantité insuffisante pour permettre la vie; **their son was their only means of s.** leur fils était leur seul soutien; **to be without means of s.** être sans ressources

2 *(person, thing supporting)* soutien *m*; *(of arch, vault)* appui *m*, support *m*, soutien; *(in horticulture)* tuteur *m*; *Cin (supporting actor)* second rôle *m*; **she is the s. of the family** c'est elle qui fait vivre la famille; *Sport* **(athletic) s.** suspensoir *m*; *Am* **price supports** subventions *fpl*

3 *Mus* groupe *m* en première partie
VT **1** *(hold up)* *(vault, arch)* supporter, soutenir; *Tech (load)* supporter, résister à; *(prices)* soutenir; **I supported him with my arm** je lui ai donné le bras; **he supported himself on a stick/my arm** il s'appuyait sur un bâton/mon bras

2 *(encourage, aid)* *(person, claims)* appuyer; *(theory)* soutenir; *(government, project)* supporter son soutien à; *(charitable event)* sponsoriser; *(charitable organization)* faire une donation à; *Sport (team)* supporter; *Mil (troops)* soutenir; *(of new discoveries etc)* *(theory)* renforcer; **proof that supports a case** preuves à l'appui d'une cause; **his theory is supported by facts** sa théorie est corroborée par les faits; *Parl* **to s. the motion** soutenir la motion; **to be supported by sb** *(in a proposal)* être soutenu par qn; **environmentalists s. the bill** les écologistes soutiennent le projet de loi; **the mayor, supported by the clergy** le maire, avec le soutien du clergé; **supported by a superb cast** avec une distribution superbe; **his parents supported him in his attempt to become an actor** ses parents l'ont soutenu lorsqu'il a essayé de devenir acteur

3 *(help to exist)* *(life)* entretenir; *(person)* soutenir financièrement, pourvoir aux besoins de; **to have a wife and three children to s.** avoir une femme et trois enfants à charge; **it was impossible to s. his family on his meagre salary** il lui était impossible de subvenir aux besoins de sa famille avec son maigre salaire; **hospital supported by voluntary contributions** hôpital financé par les souscriptions volontaires; **to s. oneself** se suffire (à soi-même), gagner sa vie

4 *Comput* permettre l'utilisation de, supporter; **this package, which is supported by all ABC workstations ...** ce progiciel, qui peut être utilisé sur tous les postes de travail ABC ...; **56K supported** gère l'accès en 56 kbit/s
▸▸ **s. band** groupe *m* en première partie; **who was the s. band?** qui est-ce qu'il y avait en première partie?; *Comput* **s. line** assistance *f* technique téléphonique; **s. market** marché *m* support *ou* d'appui; **s. price** prix *m* de soutien; *Admin* **s. services** services *mpl* d'assistance technique; **s. staff** personnel *m* de soutien *ou* des services généraux; **s. stockings** bas *mpl* à varices; *Mil* **s. unit** unité *f* de soutien

---

Note that the English verb **to support** only translates **supporter** when it means **to hold up**. The most common meaning of the French verb **supporter** is **to bear, to withstand**.

---

supportable [sə'pɔːtəb(ə)l] ADJ **1** *(bearable)* supportable, tolérable **2** *(theory etc)* soutenable

supporter [sə'pɔːtər] N **1** *(person)* *(of opinion)* défenseur *m*, tenant *m*; *(of party)* partisan *m*, sympathisant, -ante; *(of politician)* partisan *m*; *Sport (of team)* supporter *m*; **supporters' club** club *m* des supporters **2** *(device)* soutien *m*, support *m*

supporting [sə'pɔːtɪŋ] ADJ *Cin (film, programme)* supplémentaire; *(actor)* qui a un rôle secondaire *ou* de second plan; *Theat* **the s. cast** les seconds *ou* deuxièmes rôles *mpl*; **there is an excellent s. cast** les seconds rôles sont excellents
▸▸ *Theat, Mus* **s. act** première partie *f*; **in the days when the Beatles were one of the s. acts** quand les Beatles se produisaient en première partie; *Theat, Cin* **s. part, s. role** second rôle *m*; **s. wall** mur *m* d'appui *ou* de soutènement

supportive [sə'pɔːtɪv] ADJ *(parent, friend, ally etc)* qui soutient; **to be s.** prêter son appui; **she's been very s.** elle l'a/nous a/*etc* bien soutenu(s); **she's usually so s.** d'habitude, elle fait tout ce qu'elle peut pour les/nous/*etc* aider; **I was trying to be as s. as I could** je faisais de mon mieux pour les/*etc* aider; **you could be more s.!** vous pourriez me/nous/*etc* soutenir un peu plus!; **to be s. of sb's efforts** soutenir qn dans ses efforts

supportiveness [sə'pɔːtɪvnɪs] N soutien *m*, appui *m*

suppose [sə'pəʊz] VT **1** *(assume)* supposer; *(imagine)* imaginer; *(think)* croire, penser; **you mustn't s. that ...** il ne faut pas vous imaginer que ...; **what makes you s. that I trust you?** qu'est-ce qui vous fait croire que j'ai confiance en vous?; **I don't s. he'll do it** je ne crois pas qu'il le fera; **will you go? – I s. so** irez-vous? – probablement; **please can I stay up late? – oh, I s. so** s'il te plaît, est-ce que je peux veiller tard? – oui, si tu veux; **I don't think he'll come – no, I s. not** *or* **I don't s. so** je ne crois pas qu'il viendra – non, sans doute *ou* probablement pas; **I don't s. you remember me** vous ne vous souvenez sans doute pas de moi; **I s. you can't remember *that* either!** tu ne te souviens probablement pas de ça non plus!; **supposing** *or* **(let us) s. (that) you're right** supposons *ou* en supposant *ou* mettons que vous ayez raison; **s.** *or* **supposing you were ill** supposez que vous soyez malade; **s. we do stay another year, what then?** suppose qu'en effet, nous restions une année de plus, et après?; **supposing** *or* **s. he came back** si, par supposition, il revenait, supposons qu'il revienne; **s. I was talking to him, what of it?** et si j'étais en train de lui parler, qu'est-ce que ça peut faire?; **yes, but s. I were to die** oui, mais si je venais à mourir; *Fam* **s. we change the subject** et si nous changions de sujet; **just supposing it did happen** supposons que ça se produise; **the plan supposes we can keep inflation under 1.5%** le projet part du principe que nous arriverons à maintenir l'inflation au-dessous de 1,5%; **that supposes rather more enthusiasm than I think will be forthcoming** cela suppose un enthousiasme qui ne viendra pas, à mon avis VOIR GRAMMAIRE A47–8

2 to be supposed to do sth être censé faire qch; **she's supposed to be in London** *(they say she is, she should be)* elle est censée être à Londres; **the film's supposed to be very good** à ce qu'il paraît, c'est un très bon film; **it's supposed to have been discovered by ...** on dit que cela a été découvert par ...; **there's supposed to be a well in the garden** on dit qu'il y a un puits dans le jardin; **I'm not supposed to do it** je ne suis pas censé le faire; **you're not supposed to know that** *(so* *keep quiet about it)* vous n'êtes pas censé le savoir; *(so I won't tell you)* je n'ai pas à vous le dire; **you're not supposed to park here** vous n'avez pas le droit de vous garer ici; **don't ask me! – you're supposed to be in charge!** ne me demande pas ça! – je croyais pourtant bien que c'était toi le responsable!; **you're supposed to be my friend!** je te croyais mon ami!; **could you lend me the key? – well, I'm not supposed to, but …** pourriez-vous me prêter la clef? – eh bien, je ne devrais pas, mais …; **the computer's not supposed to make a noise like that** l'ordinateur ne devrait pas faire un tel bruit; **how am I supposed to work in conditions like these?** comment veut-on que je travaille dans de telles conditions?; **how is anybody supposed to make sense of that?** comment est-on censé s'y retrouver?

supposed [sə'pəʊzɪd] **ADJ ATTRIB** *(presumed, alleged)* présumé

supposedly [sə'pəʊzɪdlɪ] **ADV** soi-disant

supposition [sʌpə'zɪʃən] **N** supposition *f*, hypothèse *f*; **unfounded s.** supposition gratuite; **on the s. that …** à supposer que … + *sub*, dans l'hypothèse où … + *cond*; **on the s. that she had caught the train** dans l'hypothèse où elle aurait pris le train VOIR GRAM-MAIRE A57

supposititous [sʌpə'zɪʃəs] **ADJ** *Fml* supposé

supposititious [səpɒzɪ'tɪʃəs] **ADJ** *Fml (false)* faux, *f* fausse

suppository [sə'pɒzɪtrɪ] **N** *Pharm* suppositoire *m*

suppress [sə'pres] **VT 1** *(uprising)* réprimer, étouffer; *(newspaper, association)* interdire; *(malpractice)* faire disparaître **2** *(scandal)* étouffer; *(sob)* étouffer, ravaler; *(feelings, emotions)* réprimer, refouler; *(emotion)* dominer; **to s. one's feelings** se contenir, faire taire ses sentiments; **to s. a cough** réprimer son envie de tousser **3** *(hide)* cacher, dissimuler; *(keep silent about)* passer sous silence; *(fact)* ne pas révéler; *Law* faire disparaître; *(name)* taire, ne pas donner **4** *Radio, Elec* déparasiter

> Note that the French verb **supprimer** is a false friend and is almost never a translation for the English verb **to suppress**. Its most common meaning is **to cancel, to abolish**.

suppressed [sə'prest] **ADJ** *(feeling etc)* étouffé, réprimé; **s. anger** colère *f* refoulée; **s. excitement** agitation *f* contenue

suppression [sə'preʃən] **N 1** *(of uprising, malpractice)* répression *f*; *(of book, newspaper)* interdiction *f* **2** *(of emotions)* refoulement *m*; *Med (of sweat, urine)* suppression *f* **3** *(of truth, fact, evidence)* dissimulation *f*; **she could not tolerate this s. of the truth** elle ne pouvait tolérer que l'on dissimule la vérité de cette manière; **the minister demanded the s. of the story** le ministre a exigé que l'on étouffe l'affaire **4** *Radio* antiparasitage *m*

suppressor [sə'presər] **N 1** *(person)* **the s. of the uprising** celui qui dirige/dirigeait/*etc* la répression **2** *Radio (device)* (dispositif *m* ou appareil *m*) antiparasite *m*
> ▸ *Radio* **s. grid** grille *f* d'arrêt

suppurate ['sʌpjʊreɪt] **VI** *(of wound, sore)* suppurer

suppurating ['sʌpjʊreɪtɪŋ] **ADJ** *(of wound, sore)* purulent, suppurant

suppuration [sʌpjʊ'reɪʃən] **N** *(of wound, sore)* suppuration *f*

supranational [suːprə'næʃen(ə)l] **ADJ** supranational, -aux

suprarenal gland [suːprə'riːn(ə)l] **N** *Anat* glande *f* surrénale

supremacist [sʊ'preməsɪst] **N** = personne *f* croyant en la supériorité d'un groupe, racial ou autre

supremacy [sʊ'preməsɪ] **N** suprématie *f*; **white s.** la suprématie de la race blanche

supreme [sʊ'priːm] **ADJ** suprême; **to reign s.** *(of monarch)* régner en souverain absolu; *Fig (of champion etc)* régner; **to make the s. sacrifice** *(die)* se sacrifier
> ▸ *Rel* **the S. Being** l'Être *m* suprême; **S. Commander** commandant *m* en chef; *Am Law* **the S. Court** la Cour suprême *(des États-Unis)*

supremely [sʊ'priːmlɪ] **ADV** suprêmement; **we are s. happy** nous jouissons d'un bonheur suprême, nous sommes suprêmement heureux

supremo, *pl* **supremos** [sʊ'priːməʊ, -məʊz] **N** *Br* grand chef *m*, *Fam* big boss *m*

Supt *abbr* **superintendent**

surcharge ['sɜːtʃɑːdʒ] **N** *(additional charge)* supplément *m*; *(as penalty)* majoration *f* d'impôt; **s. on a letter** surtaxe *f* d'une lettre; **there's a s. for late bookings** il y a un supplément à payer pour les réservations de dernière minute
   VT *(letter etc)* surtaxer; **if motorists were surcharged for …** si on surtaxait les automobilistes pour …

surd [sɜːd] **N 1** *Math* quantité *f* irrationnelle **2** *Ling (consonant)* sourde *f*

SURE [ʃʊər] **ADJ** *(convinced, definite)* sûr, certain; *(judgement, shot)* sûr; *(remedy, cure)* infaillible; *(profit, success)* sûr, assuré; **to be s. of** *or* **about sth** être sûr *ou* certain de qch; **I'm s. of it** j'en suis sûr *ou* certain; **I'm not so s. of** *or* **about that** je n'en suis pas bien sûr *ou* certain; *(implying permission won't be given)* ça, ça m'étonnerait; **I can't be s., but I think it was two o'clock** je n'en suis pas tout à fait sûr, mais je pense qu'il était deux heures; **I'm s. you're mistaken** je suis sûr que vous vous trompez; **are you quite s. he hasn't left yet?** êtes-vous bien sûr qu'il n'est pas encore parti?; **I'm s. you must be** *or* **you're very tired** je suis sûr que vous êtes très fatigué; **to be s. of oneself** être sûr de soi; **I don't know, I'm s.** ma foi, je ne sais pas; **we're all very grateful, I'm s., but …** nous vous/leur/*etc* en sommes certainement très reconnaissants, mais …; **to make s. of sth** s'assurer de qch; **make s. (that) the door is shut** assurez-vous que la porte est fermée, vérifiez que la porte est fermée; **I'll just go and make s.** je vais vérifier; **to make s. of a seat** s'assurer une place; **don't be too** *or* **so s.!** vous êtes bien sûr de vous!; **what makes you so s.?** comment pouvez-vous en être si sûr?; **with a s. hand** d'une main assurée; **there is only one s. way of doing it** il n'y a qu'un moyen sûr de le faire; *Iron* **that's a s. way of failing the interview** c'est un moyen sûr d'échouer à l'entretien; **it's a s. thing** c'est une certitude *ou* une chose certaine; *esp Am Fam* **s. thing!** bien sûr!, pour sûr!; **I don't know for s.** je n'en suis pas bien sûr; **to-morrow for s.** demain sans faute; **she won't come, that's for s.** elle ne viendra pas, c'est certain; **it's s. to be fine** il fera sûrement beau; **he's s. to come** il viendra sûrement *ou* à coup sûr; **be s. to come early** ne manquez pas d'arriver de bonne heure; **be s. not to lose it, be s. that you don't lose it** prenez garde de ne pas le perdre
   ADV 1 *esp Am Fam (really)* vraiment; **it s. is cold** il fait vraiment froid; **it s. was difficult** c'était vraiment ou bien difficile; **you s. do know your history!** vous vous y connaissez vraiment *ou Fam* drôlement bien en histoire! **2 as s. as fate, as s. as eggs are** *or Fam* **is**

eggs aussi vrai qu'il fait jour, aussi sûr que deux et deux font quatre; **s. enough, he was there** il était bien là; **she'll come, s. enough** elle viendra, tu peux compter là-dessus; **no, it's whisky s. enough** non, c'est bien du whisky; *Fam* **for s.!**, *esp Am* **s.!** mais oui!, bien sûr!

surefooted [ʃʊə'fʊtɪd] **ADJ** au pied sûr; **to be s.** avoir le pied sûr; *Fig* **the Prime Minister gave a s. performance in the debate** le Premier ministre a très bien intervenu lors du débat

surely ['ʃʊəlɪ] **ADV 1** *(in a sure manner)* sûrement; **slowly but s.** lentement mais sûrement **2** *(certainly)* assurément, sans doute; **s. he will come** il viendra sûrement; **s. you don't believe that!** vous ne croyez quand même pas cela!; **s. you're not going to leave us?** vous n'allez quand même pas nous quitter?; *esp Am* **will you help me? – s.!** voulez-vous m'aider? – bien sûr!; **it's all gone – s. not!** il n'y en a plus – c'est pas vrai!

sureness ['ʃʊənɪs] **N** *(of hand, judgement etc)* sûreté *f*; *(of remedy)* efficacité *f*; *(certainty)* certitude *f*; **the s. of his aim** la précision de son tir

surety ['ʃʊərətɪ] **N** *Law (person)* caution *f*, garant, -ante; *Com* donneur *m* d'aval; **to stand s. for sb** se porter caution pour qn, se rendre *ou* se porter garant de qn; **s. for a debt** garant d'une dette; **s. for a loan** sûreté *f* en garantie d'un crédit; **in his own s. of £5,000** sous (sa propre) caution de 5000 livres

surf [sɜːf] **N** ressac *m*, vagues *fpl* déferlantes
   VI *(on surfboard)* faire du surf
   VT **to s. the Internet** naviguer *ou* surfer sur l'Internet

surface ['sɜːfɪs] **N 1** *(exterior, face)* surface *f*; **the earth's s.** la surface de la terre; **to rise to the s. of the water** remonter *ou* revenir à la surface de l'eau; **to rise** *or* **come to the s.** *(of submarine)* revenir en surface *ou* à la surface; **to break s.** faire surface; **smooth/even s.** surface lisse/unie; **his politeness is only on the s.** sa politesse est toute de surface; **on the s. she is very calm** en surface, elle est très calme; **meaning that lies below the s.** signification *f* cachée; **we're still very much on the s. of the problem** nous n'avons pas encore attaqué le fond du problème; **to send a letter by s. mail** envoyer une lettre par voie de terre/de mer
   2 *(area)* aire *f*, étendue *f*, superficie *f*; *Geom* **s. of revolution** surface *f* de révolution *ou* de rotation; **working s.** plan *m* de travail; *(in office)* surface utile; *Aviat* **lifting s.** surface portante *ou* de sustentation
   3 *(of road)* revêtement *m*; **temporary s.** chaussée *f* provisoire
   VT *(treat surface of)* apprêter la surface de; *(in papermaking)* calandrer; *Constr (road)* revêtir (**with** de); **they surfaced the back yard with concrete** ils ont recouvert la surface de la cour d'une couche de béton
   VI 1 *(of submarine, whale etc)* faire surface; *(return to surface)* revenir en surface, remonter à la surface
   2 *Fam (of person) (reappear, regain consciousness)* refaire surface
> ▸ *Ling* **s. grammar** grammaire *f* de surface; **s. noise** bruit *m* de surface; **s. speed** *(of submarine)* vitesse *f* en surface; **s. structure** structure *f* superficielle *ou* de surface; **s. tension** tension *f* superficielle; **s. transport** transport *m* terrestre et/ou maritime; **by s. transport** par voie de terre et/ou de mer; **s. water** eau *f* superficielle, eaux de surface; *Min* **s. work** travail *m* au jour; *Min* **s. worker** ouvrier *m* du jour

surface-mounted **ADJ** *Comput (chips)* monté en surface

surface-to-air ADJ
▸▸ *Mil* **s. missile** missile *m* sol-air

surface-to-surface ADJ
▸▸ *Mil* **s. missile** missile *m* sol-sol

surfacing ['sɜːfɪsɪŋ] N *Constr (of/on road etc)* revêtement *m*

surfboard ['sɜːfbɔːd] N planche *f* de surf, surf *m*

surfboarder, surfboarding ['sɜːfbɔːdər, -ɪŋ] = **surfer, surfing**

surfeit ['sɜːfɪt] N *(excess)* surabondance *f*; **to have a s. of oysters/of music** être rassasié d'huîtres/de musique

VT gorger, rassasier (**with** de); **to s. oneself with sth** se gorger de qch jusqu'à s'en dégoûter; **surfeited with pleasure** blasé *ou* écœuré par les plaisirs

surfer ['sɜːfər] N surfeur, -euse; **(Internet) s.** internaute *mf*, navigateur, -trice *ou* surfeur, -euse de l'Internet

surfie ['sɜːfɪ] N *Austr Fam* surfeur, -euse

surfing ['sɜːfɪŋ] N surf *m*

surfrider, surfriding ['sɜːfraɪdər, -ɪŋ] = **surfer, surfing**

surge [sɜːdʒ] N *(of sea)* houle *f*; *Elec (of electricity)* surtension *f*; *Fig (of activity)* poussée *f*; *(of enthusiasm)* accès *m*; *Fig* **the s. of the crowd** les remous *mpl* de la foule; **a s. of anger** un flot *ou* une vague de colère; **there has been a s. of public interest in …** il y a eu un mouvement *ou* une poussée de l'intérêt public pour …; **she felt a s. of fury** elle sentit la fureur monter en elle; **these seasonal surges in production/sales** ces poussées saisonnières de la production/des ventes

VI *(of sea)* être houleux; *(of waters)* se soulever; *Elec (of power)* être en surtension; *Fig* **the crowd surged along the street/onto the pitch** la foule s'est répandue en flots dans la rue/sur le terrain; **the crowd surged back** la foule a reflué

▸ **surge up** VI *(well up)* monter d'un seul coup; **anger surged up within her** un flot de colère est monté en elle; **a figure surged up out of the darkness** une silhouette surgit de l'ombre

surgeon ['sɜːdʒ(ə)n] N chirurgien *m*
▸▸ **s. general** *Mil* médecin-général *m*, *pl* médecins-généraux; *Am Admin* chef *m* des services de santé

surgery ['sɜːdʒərɪ] N **1** *(technique etc)* chirurgie *f*; *(operation)* intervention *f* chirurgicale; **major/minor s.** grande/petite chirurgie; **he'll need s.** il faudra l'opérer; **heart s.** chirurgie du cœur; **he's had heart s.** il a eu une opération du cœur; **the s. was successful** l'opération a réussi; **a clever piece of s.** une opération habile **2** *Br (place) (of doctor)* cabinet *m* (de consultation); *(of dentist)* cabinet; **s. (hours)** heures *fpl* de consultation **3** *Br Pol (of MP etc)* permanence *f* publique; **our MP holds a weekly s.** notre député tient une permanence hebdomadaire

Note that the French word **chirurgie** only has a medical sense.

surgical ['sɜːdʒɪk(ə)l] ADJ chirurgical, -aux; *Fig* **with s. precision** avec une précision mathématique
▸▸ **s. boot** chaussure *f* orthopédique; **s. collar** minerve *f*; **s. instruments** instruments *mpl* de chirurgie; *Br* **s. spirit** alcool *m* à 90°; *Mil* **s. strike** frappe *f* chirurgicale

surging ['sɜːdʒɪŋ] ADJ **a s. sea** une mer houleuse; **a s. mass of people** un flot pressé de gens

surliness ['sɜːlɪnɪs] N *(mood)* humeur *f* maussade; *(of expression)* air *m* bourru; *(of remark)* ton *m* bourru

surly ['sɜːlɪ] ADJ *(person)* revêche; *(tone, look, remark)* bourru

surmise[1] ['sɜːmaɪz] N conjecture *f*

surmise[2] [sɜːˈmaɪz] VT conjecturer; **as you may well have surmised** comme vous l'avez peut-être deviné, comme vous le soupçonnez peut-être

surmount [sɜːˈmaʊnt] VT **1** *(be on top of)* surmonter; **column surmounted by a cross** colonne surmontée d'une croix **2** *(overcome) (obstacle, difficulty)* surmonter; *(emotion)* maîtriser

surmountable [sɜːˈmaʊntəb(ə)l] ADJ surmontable

surname ['sɜːneɪm] N nom *m* de famille; **s. and Christian** *or* **first names** nom et prénoms *mpl* VOIR GRAMMAIRE 88

Note that the French word **surnom** is a false friend and is never a translation for the English word **surname**. It means **nickname**.

surpass [sɜːˈpɑːs] VT **1** *(be superior to) (person)* surpasser; *(rivals)* devancer; **to s. sb in kindness** renchérir sur la bonté de qn; **he has surpassed himself** il s'est surpassé; *Iron* **you've surpassed yourself this time** vous vous êtes surpassé cette fois **2** *(exceed)* dépasser, excéder; **the result surpassed my hopes** le résultat a dépassé mes espérances; **this surpasses all previous records** ceci surpasse tous les records précédents

surpassing [sɜːˈpɑːsɪŋ] ADJ sans égal, sans pareil; **of s. beauty** d'une beauté incomparable *ou* sans pareille

surplice ['sɜːplɪs] N *Rel* surplis *m*

surplus ['sɜːpləs] N surplus *m*, excédent *m*; **to have a s. of sth** avoir qch en excès; **EU grain surpluses** excédents de céréales de l'UE; **government s.** surplus *mpl* du gouvernement

ADJ *(items)* en trop, en surplus, excédentaire; **s. food/wine/oil** excédent *m* alimentaire/de vin/d'huile; **s. to requirements** en trop; **s. population/products** population *f*/produits *mpl* excédentaire(s)

▸▸ *Com* **s. stock** stocks *mpl* excédentaires, surplus

surprise [səˈpraɪz] N surprise *f*; **to take sb by s.** surprendre qn, prendre qn au dépourvu; **to give sb a s.** faire une surprise à qn; **it was a s. to see her there** ce fut une surprise de la voir là; **what a s. to see you here!** je ne m'attendais pas à vous rencontrer ici!; **what a pleasant s.!** quelle bonne surprise!; **the party was meant to be a s.** la fête était censée être une surprise; **to spoil the s.** gâcher la surprise; **it was no s. to learn that he had a criminal record** il n'y avait rien d'étonnant à ce qu'il ait un casier judiciaire; **he's in for a bit of a s.!** s'il savait ce qu'on lui prépare!; **s., s.! it's us!** surprise! c'est nous!; **to my great s., much to my s.** à ma grande surprise, à mon grand étonnement; **imagine my s. when …** imaginez comme j'ai été surpris quand …, imaginez quelle a été ma surprise *ou* quel a été mon étonnement quand …

ADJ surprise; **the President's s. announcement** l'annonce surprise du président

VT **1** *(astonish)* surprendre, étonner; **nothing surprises him** rien ne l'étonne; **you could s. yourself** tu pourrais t'étonner toi-même; **to be surprised at sth** être surpris *ou* étonné de qch; **I am surprised to see you** *or* **at seeing you** je m'étonne de vous voir, je suis surpris de vous voir; **I should be surprised if he came back** cela m'étonnerait qu'il revienne; **there can't be many people who don't have a phone – you'd be surprised** il ne doit pas y avoir beaucoup de gens qui n'ont pas le téléphone – ne crois pas ça; **I wouldn't** *or*

shouldn't be surprised if they knew already cela ne me surprendrait pas qu'ils le sachent déjà; **it doesn't s. me in the least** ça ne m'étonne pas du tout; **I was agreeably surprised** j'ai été agréablement surpris; **I'm surprised at you!** tu m'étonnes! **2** *(catch unawares)* surprendre; **to s. sb in the act** surprendre qn en flagrant délit, prendre qn sur le fait

▸▸ **s. party** = fête *f* organisée pour quelqu'un sans qu'il ou elle le sache; **s. visit** visite *f* surprise; **to pay sb a s. visit** aller chez qn sans le prévenir

surprised [səˈpraɪzd] ADJ *(look)* étonné, surpris; *(expression)* de surprise; **don't look so s.** ne prends pas un air aussi étonné

surprising [səˈpraɪzɪŋ] ADJ surprenant, étonnant; **well, it's not s., is it?** ça n'a vraiment rien de surprenant; **it wouldn't be s. if he was in the plot** ça n'aurait rien de surprenant s'il était du complot; **that's s. coming from him** (venant) de sa part, c'est surprenant

surprisingly [səˈpraɪzɪŋlɪ] ADV étonnamment; **I found him s. young** je lui ai trouvé l'air étonnamment jeune; **s. enough, he agreed** cela peut paraître surprenant, mais il a accepté; **not s., she changed her mind** comme on pouvait s'y attendre *ou* évidemment, elle a changé d'avis

surreal [səˈrɪəl] ADJ surréaliste
N surréalisme *m*

surrealism [səˈrɪəlɪz(ə)m] N surréalisme *m*

surrealist [səˈrɪəlɪst] ADJ, N surréaliste *mf*

surrealistic [sərɪəˈlɪstɪk] ADJ surréaliste

surrealistically [sərɪəˈlɪstɪk(ə)lɪ] ADV d'une manière *ou* dans un style surréaliste

surrender [səˈrendər] N **1** *(act of surrendering) (of army, fortress)* reddition *f*; **no s.!** nous ne nous rendrons pas! **2** *Law (of possessions, rights)* abandon *m*, cession *f*; *(of right to property)* restitution *f*; *(of rights, authority)* abdication *f*; **to make a s. of principle** transiger avec ses principes **3** *(in insurance) (of policy)* rachat *m*

VI se rendre; *Mil* faire (sa) soumission, rendre les armes; **to s. to the police** se constituer prisonnier, se livrer à la police; *Fig* **all right! I s.!** ça va! je me rends!; **to s. to temptation** céder à la tentation

VT **1** *(fortress)* rendre, livrer **2** *(right, possessions)* abandonner, céder; *(right)* abdiquer; **she was instructed to s. her children to the care of the social services** on l'a obligé à laisser la garde de ses enfants à l'autorité des services sociaux; **to s. all hope of sth** abandonner *ou* renoncer à tout espoir de qch; **to s. an advantage** laisser un avantage; **to s. control of sth** abandonner la direction de qch **3** *(in insurance) (policy)* racheter
▸▸ **s. value** *(in insurance)* valeur *f* de rachat

surreptitious [sʌrəpˈtɪʃəs] ADJ subreptice, clandestin

surreptitiously [sʌrəpˈtɪʃəslɪ] ADV subrepticement, clandestinement

surreptitiousness [sʌrəpˈtɪʃnɪs] N caractère *m* subreptice

surrogacy ['sʌrəgəsɪ] N maternité *f* de substitution

surrogate ['sʌrəgɪt] N *(person)* suppléant, -ante, substitut *m*; *Rel, Law* subrogé, -ée; *(thing)* succédané *m* (**for** *or* of sth de qch)
▸▸ **s. mother** *Psy* substitut *m* maternel; *Med* mère *f* porteuse; **s. motherhood** maternité *f* de substitution

surround [səˈraʊnd] N encadrement *m*, bordure *f*

VT entourer; *Mil (enemy)* entourer, cerner; *(town)* investir; **the crowd surrounded the car** la foule a assiégé la voiture; **surrounded by** *or* **with dangers** cerné de dangers; **he li-**

kes to be surrounded by ... il aime être entouré de ...; **give up! you're surrounded!** rendez-vous! vous êtes cernés!; **the decision has been surrounded by controversy** la décision n'a pas cessé d'être controversée ▸▸ *TV, Comput* **s. sound** son *m* 3D

surrounding [səˈraʊndɪŋ] ADJ entourant, environnant; **the s. country** le pays alentour *ou* environnant

surroundings [səˈraʊndɪŋz] NPL **1** *(environment)* environnement *m*, milieu *m*; **in its natural s.** dans son milieu naturel; **to be in familiar s.** être en pays de connaissance **2** *(surrounding area) (of city etc)* environs *mpl*, alentours *mpl*

surtax [ˈsɜːtæks] N surtaxe *f*; *(on income)* = surtaxe progressive sur le revenu
VT surtaxer

surtitle [ˈsɜːtaɪtəl] N surtitre *m*

surveillance [sɜːˈveɪləns] N surveillance *f*, contrôle *m*; **to keep sb under s.** surveiller qn; **to be under s.** être sous surveillance

survey[1] [ˈsɜːveɪ] N **1** *(study) (of subject, situation)* étude *f*; *(of opinions, voting intentions)* sondage *m*; *(for market research)* enquête *f* **2** *(inspection)* inspection *f*, visite *f*; *Br (of house, flat)* expertise *f* **3** *(in surveying) (action)* levé *m*; **aerial s.** levé aérophotogrammétrique; **to make a s. of an estate** relever un domaine; **quantity s.** métrage *m*, métré *m*, toisé *m*
▸▸ *Mktg* **s. research** recherche *f* par sondage

survey[2] [sɜːˈveɪ] VT **1** *(look at) (countryside etc)* regarder, scruter; *(question)* étudier, mettre à l'étude **2** *(in market research) (population)* enquêter; **to s. the scale of the damage** contempler l'ampleur du désastre; **to s. the situation** examiner la situation **3** *(inspect) (ship, building)* inspecter, faire l'expertise de l'état de; *Br* **to have a house surveyed** faire expertiser une maison **4** *(in surveying) (city, property)* relever, lever le(s) plan(s) de; *(coast)* hydrographier, faire l'hydrographie de

Note that the French verb **surveiller** is a false friend and is never a translation for the English verb **to survey**. Its most common meaning is **to supervise, to keep an eye on**.

surveying [sɜːˈveɪɪŋ] N **1** *Constr* expertise *f*; *(for mapmaking)* topographie *f*; **quantity s.** métrage *m*, métré *m*, toisé *m* **2** *(inspection)* inspection *f*, visite *f*
▸▸ **s. instruments** instruments *mpl* topographiques

surveyor [səˈveɪər] N *(of land)* géomètre *mf* expert; **naval s.** (ingénieur *m*) hydrographe *m*; **s.'s table** planchette *f*; *Admin* **land s. and valuer, district s.** cadastreur *m*; **(quantity) s.** métreur *m* vérificateur; *Naut* **marine s.** visiteur *m ou* inspecteur *m* de navires; *Br* **(property) s.** (architecte *mf*) expert *m*

Note that the French word **surveillant** is a false friend and is never a translation for the English word **surveyor**. Its most common meaning is **supervisor**.

survivable [səˈvaɪvəb(ə)l] ADJ **a s. attack** une attaque à laquelle on peut survivre; **the conditions were not s.** il était impossible de survivre dans de telles conditions

survival [səˈvaɪv(ə)l] N **1** *(continued existence) (of tradition)* survivance *f*; *(of injured person etc)* survie *f*; **her s. as party leader** sa survie en tant que tête du parti; **it's a question of s.** c'est une question de survie; *Biol, Fig* **the s. of the fittest** la survie du plus apte **2** *(remaining part) (of ancient custom)* vestige *m*; **a s. of times past** un vestige du passé

▸▸ **s. bag** sac *m* de couchage de survie; **s. kit** équipement *m* de survie

survivalism [səˈvaɪvəlɪz(ə)m] N = préparation *f* à une catastrophe nucléaire ou autre

survivalist [səˈvaɪv(ə)lɪst] N = personne *f* qui se prépare à une catastrophe nucléaire ou autre

survive [səˈvaɪv] VI survivre; *(of custom)* survivre, subsister; **enough to s. on** de quoi survivre; **those who survived** les survivants *mpl*; **those toys wouldn't s. two minutes with our kids** ces jouets ne survivraient pas plus de deux minutes avec nos gamins; *Fam* **it's not serious, you'll s.** ce n'est pas grave, tu t'en remettras; *Fam* **it'll be awful, I don't know how I'll s.!** ça va être horrible, je ne sais pas comment je vais m'en sortir!; *Fam* **how's things? – I'm surviving** comment ça va? – pas trop mal
VT *(of person)* survivre à; *(of house, clothes)* supporter; **he will s. us all** il nous enterrera tous; **he is survived by a family of four** il laisse derrière lui une famille de quatre personnes; **to s. an injury** survivre à une blessure; **to s. an illness** réchapper d'une maladie; **I couldn't s. another meeting with him** je ne supporterais pas une autre réunion avec lui; **to s. a recession** *(of company)* survivre à une récession

surviving [səˈvaɪvɪŋ] ADJ *(person)* survivant; *(remains, copy)* qui reste; **the only s. member of ...** le seul survivant de ...; **there is one s. sister** une des sœurs est encore en vie, il y a une sœur encore en vie

survivor [səˈvaɪvər] N survivant, -ante; **he is the sole s. of his family** il est le seul qui reste de sa famille; **the survivors of the disaster** les rescapés *mpl*; **earthquake/flood s.** rescapé, -ée d'un tremblement de terre/d'une inondation; **she's a s.** *(in politics, business etc)* c'est une battante; *Pej* c'est une miraculée

susceptibility [səseptɪˈbɪlɪtɪ] N **1** *(liability to be affected)* susceptibilité *f*; **s. to a disease** prédisposition *f* à une maladie; **s. to pain** sensibilité *f* à la douleur **2** *Fml (sensitivity)* sensibilité *f*, susceptibilité *f*; **to avoid wounding any susceptibilities** éviter de blesser la susceptibilité de qui que ce soit

susceptible [səˈseptɪb(ə)l] ADJ *(liable to be affected)* sensible (**to** à); *(touchy)* susceptible, qui se froisse facilement; **s. to media influences** sensible à l'influence des médias; **s. to a disease** prédisposé à une maladie; **this will make you less s. to colds** ceci vous rendra plus résistant au rhume; **s. to cold** frileux; *Fml* **s. of proof** qui peut être prouvé, démontrable

suspect[1] [ˈsʌspekt] ADJ suspect
N **1** suspect, -ecte **2** *Mktg* client *m* potentiel, suspect *m*
▸▸ *Mktg* **s. pool** clients *mpl* potentiels

suspect[2] [səˈspekt] VT **1** *(person) (of crime etc)* soupçonner; **to s. sb of sth/of having done sth** soupçonner qn de qch/d'avoir fait qch **2** *(have intuition of) (reason, truth)* soupçonner; *(danger)* flairer, subodorer; **he suspects nothing** il ne se doute de rien; **does your husband s. anything?** est-ce que ton mari se doute de quelque chose?; **I never suspected it for a moment** je n'avais pas le moindre soupçon, je ne m'en suis jamais douté **3** *(doubt) (authenticity of a work etc)* avoir des doutes sur; **to s. sb's motives** mettre en doute les raisons de qn **4** *(consider likely)* croire, penser; **I suspected as much** je m'en doutais; **I s. that what she really means is ...** je pense que ce qu'elle veut vraiment dire, c'est ...; **I s. you're right** je crois bien que tu as raison

suspected [səˈspektɪd] ADJ présumé; **a s. terrorist** un terroriste présumé; *Med* **a s.**

case of typhoid un cas présumé de typhoïde; **he has a s. fracture** on craint qu'il (n')ait une fracture

suspend [səˈspend] VT **1** *(hang)* suspendre, pendre; **to s. sth from the ceiling** suspendre *ou* pendre qch au plafond **2** *(stop) (bus service, work)* suspendre; *Law* **to s. judgment** surseoir au jugement; *Law* **to s. proceedings** suspendre les poursuites; *Com* **to s. payment** suspendre ses paiements **3** *(exclude temporarily) (officer, footballer etc)* suspendre; *(jockey)* mettre à pied; *(newspaper)* suspendre; **to s. sb from his/her office** suspendre qn de ses fonctions; **to s. a pupil (from school)** renvoyer un élève (provisoirement); **suspended on full pay** *Admin* suspendu sans suppression de traitement; *Mil* suspendu sans suppression de solde

suspended [səˈspendɪd] ADJ suspendu; *(particles)* en suspension; *Law* en suspens, suspendu; **she was given a s. prison sentence of six months** elle a été condamnée à six mois de prison avec sursis; **to be in a state of s. animation** *(of person, animal)*, *Fig* être en hibernation; **the scheme is in a state of s. animation** le projet est en suspens

suspender [səˈspendər] N **1** *Br (for stocking)* jarretelle *f*; *(for sock)* fixe-chaussette *m*, *pl* fixe-chaussettes **2** *Am (pair of)* suspenders *(braces)* (paire *f* de) bretelles *fpl*
▸▸ *Br* **s. belt** porte-jarretelles *m inv*

suspense [səˈspens] N **1** *(uncertainty)* suspense *m*, incertitude *f*; *Liter, Cin etc* suspense; **to keep** *or* **hold sb in s.** tenir *ou* garder qn en haleine; **the s. is killing me!** ce suspense me rend fou!; *Iron* quel suspense! **2** *Law* **the question remains in s.** la question reste posée *ou* en suspens
▸▸ *Fin* **s. account** compte *m* d'ordre

suspension [səˈspenʃən] N **1** *(of car etc)* suspension *f* **2** *(of hostilities, supplies etc)* suspension *f*; *Law (of judgement)* surséance *f*; *Com* **s. of payments** suspension de paiements **3** *(of official, officer etc)* suspension *f*; *(of jockey)* mise *f* à pied **4** *Chem* **(substance in) s.** (substance *f* en) suspension *f*
▸▸ **s. bridge** pont *m* suspendu; *Aut* **s. bush** bague *f* de suspension; **s. cable** câble *m* porteur; *Tech* **s. chain** chaîne *f* de suspension; **s. file** hamac *m*, dossier *m* suspendu; *Aut* **s. geometry** géométrie *f* de la suspension; *Typ, Gram* **s. points** points *mpl* de suspension

suspensory [səˈspensərɪ] ADJ *Anat (ligament)* suspenseur
▸▸ *Med* **s. bandage** suspensoir *m*

suspicion [səˈspɪʃən] N **1** *(belief of guilt)* soupçon *m*; *Law* suspicion *f*; **not the shadow** *or* **ghost of a s.** pas l'ombre d'un soupçon; **to be under s.** être soupçonné; **to have (one's) suspicions about sb** avoir des doutes sur qn, soupçonner qn; **to arouse s.** éveiller *ou* faire naître les soupçons; **to arouse** *or* **awaken sb's suspicions** éveiller les soupçons de qn; **above s.** au-dessus de tout soupçon; **praise free from any s. of flattery** louanges aucunement suspectes de flatterie; **to be right in one's suspicions** soupçonner juste; *Law* **to arrest/detain sb on s.** arrêter/détenir qn préventivement; **on s. of arson** sous la présomption d'incendie volontaire; **detention on s.** détention *f* préventive; **I had my suspicions about it** je m'en doutais, j'avais mes soupçons là-dessus; **I had no s. of it** je n'avais pas le moindre soupçon **2** *(characteristic, quality)* défiance *f*, suspicion *f*; **to look at sb with s.** regarder qn avec défiance; **the s. in her eyes/voice** la défiance dans ses yeux/sa voix **3** *(hint)* petite dose *f*, soupçon *m* (**of** de); *(of irony, malice)* pointe *f*

suspicious [sə'spɪʃəs] ADJ **1** (arousing suspicions) suspect, louche; **it looks s.** cela me paraît louche ou suspect; **a s. character** un individu louche ou suspect; **he died in s. circumstances** il est mort dans des circonstances suspectes **2** (having suspicions) méfiant, soupçonneux; **she has a very s. mind** elle est très soupçonneuse ou méfiante; **to be** or **feel s. about** or of **sb/sth** avoir des soupçons à l'endroit ou à l'égard de qn/sur qch; **her behaviour made me s.** sa conduite a éveillé mes soupçons

suspiciously [sə'spɪʃəslɪ] ADV **1** (to act) d'une manière suspecte ou louche; **he was s. eager to leave** l'empressement qu'il avait de partir était suspect; **it sounded s. as though she had lost it** on aurait dit qu'elle l'avait perdu; **it looks s. like the one I lost** il ressemble étrangement à celui que j'ai perdu; **two texts that are s. similar** deux textes qui sont étrangement similaires; **it looks s. like measles (to me)** cela m'a tout l'air d'une rougeole **2** (to watch, ask) d'un air méfiant, avec méfiance; (to think) avec méfiance

suspiciousness [sə'spɪʃəsnɪs] N **1** (causing suspicion) (of behaviour, parcel etc) caractère m suspect ou louche **2** (feeling suspicion) (of person, in voice etc) caractère m soupçonneux, méfiance f

suss [sʌs] VT Br Fam = **suss out**
▸ **suss out** VT SEP Br Fam (work out) (person) classer; (system, technique) piger; **I finally sussed out what she was doing** j'ai fini par piger ce qu'elle faisait; **to have sth sussed out** avoir pigé qch; **I've got him sussed out** j'ai pigé quel genre de type c'est

sussed [sʌst] ADJ Sl **to be s.** (well-informed) être au jus

sustain [sə'steɪn] VT **1** (support) (person, weight, growth, pace, level) soutenir, supporter; **enough oxygen to s. life** suffisamment d'oxygène pour que la vie soit possible; **to s. the body** sustenter le corps; **evidence to s. an assertion** témoignages pour appuyer une affirmation; Mus **to s. a note** tenir ou prolonger une note **2** (suffer, receive) (loss) éprouver, essuyer, subir; (attack) soutenir; **to s. an injury** recevoir une blessure, être blessé **3** Law **to s. an objection** (of court) admettre une objection; **objection sustained** objection admise

sustainable [sə'steɪnəb(ə)l] ADJ **1** (rate, lifestyle) que l'on peut maintenir **2** Ecol (forest) viable; (energy, resources) renouvelable; **s. growth** croissance f durable

sustained [sə'steɪnd] ADJ soutenu; **s. applause** applaudissements mpl prolongés
▸▸ Mil **s. fire** feu m soutenu ou nourri; Mus **s. note** tenue f

sustaining [sə'steɪnɪŋ] ADJ (food, meal) nourrissant; **the s. power of faith** le soutien que constitue la foi

sustenance ['sʌstənəns] N **1** (act) subsistance f, **necessary for the s. of our bodies** nécessaire à notre subsistance; **means of s.** moyens mpl de subsistance **2** (food) aliments mpl, nourriture f

suttee [sʌ'tiː] N Rel (practice) satī m; (widow) satī f

suture ['suːtʃər] N **1** Anat, Bot suture f **2** Surg (action) suture f; (stitch) point m de suture; (thread) fil m pour sutures
VT Surg (wound) suturer

SUV [esjuː'viː] N (abbr **sport utility vehicle**) SUV m

suzerain ['suːzəreɪn] N suzerain, -aine

suzerainty ['suːzərəntɪ] N suzeraineté f

svelte [svelt] ADJ svelte

Svengali [sven'gælɪ] N manipulateur, -trice

SVGA [esviːdʒiːˈeɪ] N Comput (abbr **super video graphics array**) SVGA m
▸▸ **S. monitor** moniteur m SVGA

SW [es'dʌb(ə)ljuː] N Radio (abbr **short wave**) OC

swab [swɒb] N **1** (floorcloth) serpillière f, Naut vadrouille f, Mil écouvillon m **2** Med (material) tampon m; (specimen) prélèvement m; (smear) frottis m; **s. of cotton wool** tampon d'ouate; **to take a s. of sb's throat** faire un prélèvement dans la gorge de qn
VT (-bb-) **1** (clean with floorcloth) nettoyer, essuyer; **to s. the decks** laver le pont **2** = swab down **3** = swab out
▸ **swab down** VT SEP (clean) (courtyard) laver à grande eau; Naut (deck) laver
▸ **swab out** VT SEP (clean out) Mil (firearm) écouvillonner; Med (wound) nettoyer avec un tampon

swacked [swækt] ADJ Am Fam (drunk) bourré

swaddle ['swɒd(ə)l] VT emmailloter (with, in de)

swaddling ['swɒdlɪŋ] N
▸▸ Arch **s. clothes** maillots mpl, langes mpl

swag [swæg] N Fam (of thief) butin m; Austr (of tramp) baluchon m

swagger ['swægər] N (in walk) démarche f balancée et crâneuse; (carefree manner) air m cavalier ou désinvolte; **to walk with a s.** se pavaner
VI **1** (strut) when he walks, he swaggers il marche en se pavanant; **to s.** (about) se pavaner; **to s. in/out** entrer/sortir en se pavanant **2** (boast) fanfaronner, faire le faraud; **to s. about sth** se vanter de qch
▸▸ Mil **s. cane, s. stick** badine f

swaggering ['swægərɪŋ] ADJ (air) crâneur
N **1** = swagger **2** (boasting) fanfaronnades fpl, rodomontades fpl

swagman, pl **swagmen** ['swægmæn, -mən] N Austr Fam chemineau m (qui porte son baluchon)

Swahili [swɑː'hiːlɪ] ADJ souahéli, swahéli, swahili
N **1** (pl **Swahili(s)**) Souahéli, -ie, Swahéli, -ie, Swahéli, -ie, pl -i(es) **2** Ling souahéli m, swahéli m, swahili m

swain [sweɪn] N **1** Lit, Arch (rustic) jeune berger m **2** Old-fashioned, Hum (suitor) soupirant m

SWALK [swɔːlk] (abbr **sealed with a loving kiss**) (written on envelope) = scellée d'un tendre baiser

swallow¹ ['swɒləʊ] VT **1** (food, drink) avaler; **to s. sth whole** avaler qch tout rond; **to s. one's words** (speak indistinctly) avaler ses mots **2** (believe) (story) gober, avaler; **to s. the bait** (of person) se laisser prendre à l'appât; **I told her a lie and she swallowed it** je lui ai raconté un mensonge et elle l'a gobé ou avalé; **her story is hard to s.** son histoire est difficile à avaler **3** (accept without protest) (insult) avaler; (one's anger, pride) ravaler
VI avaler; **to s. hard** (when nervous, afraid) avaler sa salive
N (act of swallowing) déglutition f, (mouthful) (of water) gorgée f, **at one s.** d'un seul coup ou trait
▸ **swallow down** VT SEP (drink, pill) avaler
▸ **swallow up** VT SEP (engulf) engloutir, engouffrer; Fig **they were soon swallowed up by** or **in the mist** ils ont vite été engloutis par le brouillard; **the small country/company was swallowed up** le petit pays/la petite société a été englouti(e)

swallow² N (bird) hirondelle f, Prov **one s. doesn't make a summer** une hirondelle ne fait pas le printemps
▸▸ Br Swimming **s. dive** saut m de l'ange

swallow-dive VI Br Swimming faire le saut de l'ange

swallowtail ['swɒləʊteɪl] N **1** (forked tail) queue f fourchue **2** Old-fashioned Fam (coat) queue-de-morue f, pl queues-de-morue **3** (butterfly) machaon m, grand porte-queue m, pl grands porte-queue(s)
▸▸ **s. butterfly** machaon, grand porte-queue

swallow-tailed ADJ (bird) à queue fourchue
▸▸ **s. coat** = swallowtail 2

swam PT see swim VI, VT

swamp [swɒmp] N marais m, marécage m
VT (flood) inonder; (field) submerger; (boat) remplir d'eau; Fam **to be swamped with sth** (work, orders, requests) être submergé ou débordé de qch; (letters, offers of help) être submergé de qch
▸▸ Am **s. fever** (malaria) paludisme m, malaria f

swampy ['swɒmpɪ] ADJ (terrain) marécageux

swan [swɒn] N cygne m; **mute s.** cygne commun ou muet; **black s.** cygne noir
VI (-nn-) Fam **to s. around** se balader, musarder; **he just sort of swans around the office all day** il ne fait que musarder dans le bureau toute la journée; **she came swanning in at a quarter to ten** elle est arrivée les mains dans les poches à dix heures moins le quart; **where's he swanning off to now?** où est-ce qu'il va encore traîner?; **don't think you can come swanning back just when you feel like it** ne crois pas que tu pourras revenir les mains dans les poches quand tu en auras envie
▸▸ Am Swimming **s. dive** saut m de l'ange; Fig **s. song** chant m du cygne

swank [swæŋk] Fam N **1** (ostentation) épate f, **I've had enough of all this s.** j'en ai assez de toute cette esbroufe **2** (ostentatious person) frimeur, -euse; (boastful person) crâneur, -euse
ADJ esp Am = swanky
VI se donner des airs, faire de l'épate

swanky ['swæŋkɪ] ADJ Fam (person) prétentieux, poseur; (restaurant, dinner, hotel) hyperchic; (car) tapageur

swan-necked [-nekt] ADJ (person) au cou de cygne

swannery ['swɒnərɪ] N réserve f de cygnes

swansdown ['swɒnzdaʊn] N Tex (cotton fabric) molleton m

swap [swɒp] N (exchange) troc m, échange m; (object, article) objet m ou article m à échanger/qu'on a échangé; St Exch swap m, échange financier; **to do a s.** faire un troc ou un échange; **it wasn't a very good s.** ce n'était pas un échange très équitable; **it's a good s.** c'est un échange avantageux; **she took my old car as a s. for this one** elle a pris ma vieille voiture en échange de celle-ci; **swaps** (in stamp collecting etc) doubles mpl
VT (-pp-) **1** to s. sth for sth échanger ou troquer qch contre ou pour qch; **I'll s. you mine for yours** je t'échange le mien contre le tien; Fam **(I'll) s. you!** je te l'échange!; **to s. places with sb** changer de place avec qn; **to s. insults/ideas** échanger des insultes/idées; **to s. stories** échanger ses impressions **2** St Exch swaper
VI faire du troc; **shall we s.?** si nous faisions un échange?

SWAPO ['swɑːpəʊ] N Pol (abbr **South-West Africa People's Organization**) SWAPO f

sward [swɔːd] N Lit gazon m, pelouse f

swarm [swɔːm] N (of bees, people, children) essaim m; (of locusts) vol m; (of gnats, people) nuée f, (of small boats) fourmillement m; **there were swarms of tourists** il y avait des nuées de touristes

vi 1 *(of bees)* essaimer; *(of people)* accourir en masse, se presser (**round** autour de; **in** dans); **the crowd swarmed over the pitch** la foule a fait irruption sur *ou* a envahi le terrain **2** *(of place)* fourmiller, grouiller (**with** de)

vt = **swarm up**

▸ **swarm up vt insep** *(climb)* *(tree, mast)* grimper à; **they all swarmed up the side of the ship** ils grimpèrent comme un seul homme sur les flancs du navire

swarming ['swɔːmɪŋ] **N** *(in beekeeping)* essaimage *m*

swarthiness ['swɔːðɪnɪs] **N** teint *m* basané *ou* bistré

swarthy ['swɔːðɪ] **ADJ** *(complexion)* basané, bistré, *Pej* noiraud

swash [swɒʃ] **N** *(of waves, water)* clapotis *m*
vi *(of waves, water)* clapoter

swashbuckler ['swɒʃbʌklər] **N** bravache *m*

swashbuckling ['swɒʃbʌklɪŋ] **ADJ** fanfaron; **s. film** *(with musketeers)* film *m* de cape et d'épée; *(with pirates)* film de corsaires; **s. tale** fanfaronnade *f*; **s. hero** héros *m* superbe
N fanfaronnades *fpl*, rodomontades *fpl*

swashplate ['swɒʃpleɪt] **N** *Aut* plateau *m* oscillant

swastika ['swɒstɪkə] **N** *Antiq* svastika *m*; *(Nazi)* croix *f* gammée

swat [swɒt] **N** *(blow)* tape *f*; **to take a s. at** *(person, dog etc)* donner une tape à; *(insect)* donner un coup de tapette à; **fly s.** *(swatter)* tapette *f* tue-mouches
vt (**-tt-**) taper; *(insect)* écraser

swath [swɔːθ] **N** *Agr* = **swathe¹**

swathe¹ [sweɪð] **N** *Agr* andain *m*; *Fig* **the cannons had cut great swathes through the troops** les canons avaient décimé les troupes

swathe² **vt** emmailloter, envelopper; **head swathed in bandages** tête enveloppée de bandages; **swathed in mist** baigné de brume

sway [sweɪ] **N 1** *(movement)* balancement *m*, oscillation *f*, mouvement *m* de va-et-vient; *Rail (of trucks)* mouvement de lacet
2 *(control, power)* empire *m*, domination *f*; **under her s.** sous son empire, sous son influence; **to have** *or* **hold s. over a people/country** avoir *ou* tenir un peuple/pays sous sa domination; **emotions that no longer hold any s. over me** des émotions qui n'ont plus aucun empire *ou* aucune emprise sur moi
vi se balancer, osciller; *(of drunkard)* vaciller; *(remain undecided)* rester indécis, hésiter; **to s. in the wind** *(of trees)* se balancer dans le vent; **he swayed back up to the bar** il revint au bar en vacillant; **public opinion is prone to s. this way and that** l'opinion publique oscille souvent d'un côté et de l'autre
vt 1 *(trees)* faire osciller, faire balancer; **she sways her hips when she walks** elle balance *ou* roule les hanches en marchant
2 *(influence)* **considerations that s. our opinions** considérations qui influencent nos opinions; **to s. sb from his/her course** détourner qn de ses projets; **to refuse to be swayed** refuser de se laisser influencer; **what can we say or do to s. you?** *(convince)* que pouvons-nous dire ou faire pour vous convaincre?; *(make you change your mind)* que pouvons-nous dire ou faire pour vous faire changer d'avis?; **what finally swayed them was …** ce qui les a finalement décidés a été …; **it was close but one thing swayed it** *(in vote etc)* la lutte était serrée mais une chose a fait pencher la balance

swaying ['sweɪɪŋ] **ADJ** qui se balance de-ci de-là, qui oscille; **s. motion** balancement *m*, mouvement *m* de va-et-vient

N balancement *m*, oscillation *f*, mouvement *m* de va-et-vient; *(of boat, car)* roulis *m*

Swazi ['swaːzɪ] **ADJ** souazi
N 1 Souazi, -ie **2** *Ling* le dialecte souazi

Swaziland ['swaːzɪlænd] **N** Souaziland *m*

swear [sweər] *(pt* **swore** [swɔːr]; *pp* **sworn** [swɔːn])* **vt 1** jurer; *(on oath)* déclarer sous la foi du serment; **to s. an oath** faire un serment, jurer; **to s. sth on the Bible** jurer qch sur la Bible; **to s. to do sth** jurer de faire qch; **I could have sworn I heard a shout** j'aurais juré avoir entendu un cri; **it wasn't me, I s. (it)!** ce n'était pas moi, je le jure!; **to s. allegiance to sb/sth** prêter serment d'allégeance à qn/qch; **to s. revenge** jurer *ou* faire serment de se venger; **to s. sb to secrecy** faire jurer le secret à qn
2 *(utter swearwords)* **'bloody idiot!', she swore** 'espèce d'abruti!', proféra-t-elle
vi 1 *(use swearwords)* jurer, proférer *ou* lâcher un juron/des jurons; **to s. at sb** injurier qn; **to s. like a trooper** jurer comme un charretier
2 *(give one's word)* jurer
▸ **swear by vt insep** *(invoke)* jurer par; **to s. by one's honour** jurer sur l'honneur; **to s. by all that one holds sacred** jurer sur tout ce qu'on a de plus sacré **2** *(have confidence in)* se fier à; **she swears by him/those vitamin pills** elle ne jure que par lui/par ces vitamines; **it's marvellous stuff, we all s. by it!** c'est merveilleux, nous ne jurons plus que par ça!
▸ **swear in vt sep** *(jury, witness)* faire prêter serment à
▸ **swear off vt insep** *(alcohol etc)* jurer de renoncer à
▸ **swear to vt insep** *(on oath)* attester *ou* certifier sous serment; **I s. to it** je l'atteste; **I would s. to it** je le jurerais, *Fam* j'en mettrais ma main au feu, *Fam* j'en mettrais ma tête à couper; **I couldn't** *or* **wouldn't s. to it** je n'en mettrais pas ma main au feu, je n'en mettrais pas ma tête à couper

swearing ['sweərɪŋ] **N 1** *(use of swearwords)* jurons *mpl*, gros mots *mpl*; **there's too much s. on television** il y a trop de grossièretés à la télévision **2** *Law* **after the s. in of the jury** après que le jury eut prêté serment

swearword ['sweəwɜːd] **N** gros mot *m*, juron *m*

sweat [swet] **N 1** sueur *f*, transpiration *f*; **covered in s.** *(of people, clothes)* couvert *ou* trempé de sueur; **by the s. of one's brow** à la sueur de son front; **the s. was pouring off him** il dégoulinait de sueur; **to be in a s., to be all of a s.** suer, être en nage; *Fig (to be excited)* être tout excité; *Fig* **to be in a s. about sth** avoir des sueurs froides à cause de qch; *Fig* **to work oneself (up) into a s.** se faire du mauvais sang (**about** au sujet de qch); **to break into a s.** se mettre à transpirer; **to be in a cold s.** avoir des sueurs froides; *Fam* **it was a real s. getting this piano up the stairs** monter le piano par l'escalier, c'était vraiment tuant; *Fam* **no s.** pas de problème; *Mil Old-fashioned* **old s.** vieux troupier *m* **2** *(on wall etc)* suintement *m*
vi suer, transpirer; *(of walls)* suinter; *(of cheese)* suer; *Fig Fam (work hard)* peiner; *Fam (worry)* se faire de la bile, se faire un sang d'encre; **to s. profusely** suer à grosses gouttes; **Johnny was sweating over his homework** Johnny potassait ses devoirs; **I've been sweating over this piece of work for the last three hours** ça fait trois heures que je m'escrime à faire ce travail
vt *(person, horse)* faire suer; *(workers)* exploiter; *Culin (onions)* faire revenir *ou* blondir; *Am Fig Fam (suspect)* cuisiner; *Fam* **to s. blood** suer sang et eau; *Fam* **to s. buckets** être en nage
▸▸ *Anat* **s. duct** conduit *m* sudorifère; **s. gland** glande *f* sudoripare

▸ **sweat off vt sep** *(lose by exercise)* *(weight)* perdre en faisant de l'exercice; *(in sauna)* perdre en transpirant
▸ **sweat out vt sep 1** *(cure)* *(cold)* chasser *ou* guérir en transpirant **2** *Fam* **to s. it out** *(endure)* prendre son mal en patience, tenir jusqu'au bout **3** *Sl* **to s. one's guts out** s'échiner

sweatband ['swetbænd] **N** *(of hat)* cuir *m* intérieur; *Sport* bandeau *m* en éponge

sweated ['swetɪd] **ADJ**
▸▸ **s. goods** articles *mpl* produits par des ouvriers exploités; **s. labour** *(staff)* main-d'œuvre *f* exploitée; *(work)* exploitation *f*

sweater ['swetər] **N** *(garment)* pullover *m*, pull *m*

sweatiness ['swetɪnɪs] **N** *(of body etc)* moiteur *f*

sweating ['swetɪŋ] **ADJ** *(person)* en sueur; *(hand, body)* moite; *(wall)* suintant
N transpiration *f*, *Med* sudation *f*; *(of wall)* suintement *m*
▸▸ **s. room** *(in Turkish bath)* étuve *f*, salle *f* de sudation

sweatpants ['swetpænts] **NPL** pantalon *m* de survêtement

sweatshirt ['swetʃɜːt] **N** *Sport* sweat-shirt *m*, *pl* sweat-shirts, sweat *m*

sweatshop ['swetʃɒp] **N** atelier *m* clandestin; *Fig Hum* **it's a real s. here** c'est le bagne ici

sweaty ['swetɪ] **ADJ** *(person)* en sueur; *(hands, palms)* moite; *(work)* qui fait transpirer; *(shirt etc)* imprégné de sueur *ou* de transpiration; *(smell)* de sueur, de transpiration; **to get s.** *(of person)* suer, transpirer; **s. afternoon** après-midi d'une chaleur humide; **s. socks** chaussettes puantes (de sueur)

Swede [swiːd] **N** *(person)* Suédois, -oise **VOIR GRAMMAIRE A19**

swede [swiːd] **N** *(plant)* rutabaga *m*

Sweden ['swiːd(ə)n] **N** Suède *f*

Swedish ['swiːdɪʃ] **VOIR GRAMMAIRE A19** **ADJ** suédois
N *Ling* suédois *m*

SWEEP [swiːp] **N 1** *(single stroke of broom, paintbrush, scythe)* coup *m* de balai/de pinceau/de faux; *(cleaning)* balayage *m*; **at one s.** d'un seul coup; **to give a room a good s. (out)** balayer une chambre à fond; **this room could do with a s.** cette chambre a bien besoin d'un coup de balai; *Fig* **to make a clean s.** *(replace staff etc)* faire table rase; *(in gambling)* rafler le tout; **the thieves made a clean s.** les voleurs ont tout enlevé *ou* raflé
2 *(movement)* *(with arm)* mouvement *m* circulaire; *Mil, Aviat* balayage *m*; **with a wide s. of the arm** d'un geste large; **s. of the eye** regard *m* circulaire
3 *(area covered)* *Mil (of gun)* portée *f*; *(of lighthouse)* balayage *m*, portée; *(of wings)* envergure *f*; *(of knowledge)* étendue *f*
4 *Radio, Electron* **scan(ning) s.** balayage *m*
5 *(rapid flow)* *(of river)* course *f ou* flot *m* rapide
6 *(curve)* courbe *f*, courbure *f*; *(of river)* boucle *f*; *Archit (of arch)* courbe; **to make a wide s. to take a bend** prendre du champ pour effectuer un virage; **s. of a car's lines** galbe *f* d'une voiture; **a fine s. of grass/of country** une belle étendue de gazon/de pays
7 *(chimney)* **s.** *(person)* ramoneur *m*
8 *Fam (sweepstake)* sweepstake *m*
vt *(pt, pp* **swept** [swept])* *(room, streets, dust etc)* balayer; *(chimney)* ramoner; *Naut (channel)* *(for mines)* draguer; **her dress sweeps the ground** sa robe balaie le sol; **a storm swept the town** un orage ravagea la ville; **the deck was swept by a huge wave** une grosse vague balaya le pont; **to s. the**

horizon with a telescope parcourir *ou* balayer l'horizon avec un télescope; **to s. the seas** parcourir les mers; **to s. the board** (*in gambling*) rafler le tout; *Fig* avoir un succès fou; **the latest craze to s. the country** la dernière tocade à envahir le pays; **the most outlandish rumours swept the besieged city** les rumeurs les plus folles parcouraient la ville assiégée; *Fig* **to s. sth under the carpet** enterrer qch; **a wave swept him overboard** une lame l'a entraîné par-dessus bord; **she was swept to power on a wave of nationalism** elle a été propulsée au pouvoir par une vague de nationalisme; **the victorious army swept all before it** l'armée victorieuse a tout balayé sur son passage

VI 1 (*with broom*) balayer

2 (*move rapidly*) avancer avec un mouvement rapide et uni; **she swept into/out of the room** elle est entrée dans/sortie de la salle d'un air majestueux; **to s. round the corner** (*of car*) tourner le coin de la rue en décrivant un large virage; **the plague swept across Europe** la peste a ravagé toute l'Europe; **the beam swept across the sea** le faisceau lumineux balaya la mer; **the rolling prairies s. away into the distance** les prairies ondoyantes se perdent dans le lointain; **the road sweeps round the lake** la route décrit une courbe autour du lac

3 *Naut* **to s. for mines** draguer des mines

▸▸ **s. hand** trotteuse *f*

▸ **sweep along** VI (*move rapidly*) avancer rapidement

VT SEP (*carry forward*) (*of current etc*) entraîner, emporter; **we were swept along by a tide of nationalism** nous avons été balayés par une vague nationaliste

▸ **sweep aside** VT SEP (*move aside*) écarter d'un geste large; **to s. aside opposition** écarter l'opposition; **they were swept aside by the crowd** ils ont été repoussés par la foule

▸ **sweep away** VT SEP (*snow, clouds*) balayer; (*malpractice, abuse*) supprimer; **the bridge was swept away by the torrent** le pont a été emporté par le torrent

▸ **sweep by** VI (*move past rapidly*) (*of car*) passer à toute vitesse; (*of person*) (*majestically*) passer majestueusement; (*disdainfully*) passer dédaigneusement

▸ **sweep down** VT SEP **the current sweeps the logs down with it** le courant emporte *ou* entraîne le bois

VI **1** (*attack*) **the enemy swept down upon us** l'ennemi s'abattit *ou* fonça sur nous

2 (*curve downwards*) **hills sweeping down to the sea** des collines qui descendent vers la mer

▸ **sweep in** VI (*approach, enter rapidly*) **the wind sweeps in** le vent s'engouffre; **she swept in** elle a fait son entrée d'un air majestueux

▸ **sweep off** VT SEP (*remove forcefully*) enlever *ou* emporter avec violence; **he swept her off to Paris for the weekend** il l'a emmenée en week-end à Paris; **to be swept off one's feet by sb** être emballé par qn; **to s. sb off his/her feet** enthousiasmer qn; (*in love affair*) faire perdre la tête à qn

▸ **sweep on** VI (*advance rapidly*) (*of flood*) avancer régulièrement; (*continue*) continuer d'avancer (irrésistiblement)

▸ **sweep out** VT SEP (*clean*) (*room*) balayer (à fond)

VI (*leave majestically*) **she swept out** elle est sortie d'un air majestueux

▸ **sweep past** VI = sweep by

▸ **sweep up** VT SEP (*collect by sweeping*) (*dust, leaves etc*) balayer, ramasser; (*sweep into a pile*) ramasser en tas; **with her hair swept up into a chignon** avec ses cheveux relevés en chignon; **she swept up her two babies and left** en toute hâte, elle prit ses

deux bébés dans ses bras et partit

VI **1** (*clean up*) balayer

2 (*arrive*) **the car swept up to the door** la voiture a roulé majestueusement jusqu'à la porte

sweepback ['swiːpbæk] N *Aviat* (angle *m* de) flèche *f*

sweeper ['swiːpər] N **1** (*person*) balayeur, -euse; *Ftbl* arrière *m* volant **2** (*machine*) (*for industrial use*) balayeuse *f*, (*for domestic use*) balai *m* (mécanique)

sweeping ['swiːpɪŋ] ADJ (*gesture*) large; (*movement*) circulaire; **s. changes** changements *mpl* radicaux; **s. generalization** *or* **statement** généralisation *f* hâtive; *Art* **s. line** ligne *f* allongée *ou* élancée; **low s. lines** (*of car*) lignes basses et allongées; **s. plain** vaste plaine *f*, **s. reform** réforme *f* radicale

N **sweepings** (*refuse*) balayures *fpl*, ordures *fpl*; *Fig* (*of a country, society*) rebut *m*

▸▸ **s. up** balayage *m*, ramassage *m*

sweepingly ['swiːpɪŋlɪ] ADV (*too generally*) (*to describe things, criticize etc*) de façon trop générale *ou* hâtive

sweepstake ['swiːpsteɪk] N *Horseracing* sweepstake *m*

sweet [swiːt] ADJ **1** (*in taste*) sucré; **as s. as honey** doux comme le miel; **to taste s.** avoir une saveur douce; **to have a s. tooth** aimer les sucreries

2 (*fragrant*) **to smell s.** avoir une odeur agréable, sentir bon; (*of rose*) embaumer; *Fig* **the s. smell of success** la douceur du succès; *Fig* **it hardly smells very s.** ça ne sent pas très bon

3 s. breath haleine *f* fraîche

4 (*sound*) doux, *f* douce, mélodieux; (*flattery*) doux à l'oreille

5 (*pleasant*) agréable; (*smile*) doux, *f* douce; **revenge is s.** douce est la vengeance; *Fam* **to keep sb s.** s'assurer les bonnes grâces de qn; **a s. old lady** une vieille dame charmante; **that's very s. of you** c'est bien gentil à vous; **a s. little dress** une gentille petite robe, une petite robe exquise; **a s. girl** une gentille petite fille; **what a s. kitten!** quel petit chat adorable!; **to say** *or* **whisper s. nothings to sb** *or* **in sb's ear** conter fleurette à qn, dire des mots doux à l'oreille de qn; **s. temper** caractère *m* doux *ou* aimable

6 *Old-fashioned Fam* **to be s. on sb** avoir un béguin pour qn

7 (*intensifier*) **she'll do it in her own s. time** elle le fera quand elle le jugera bon; **it's only going to be of benefit to his own s. self** c'est à sa petite pomme qu'ira tout le bénéfice; **he'll go his own s. way** il fera ce qui lui plaira; *Fam* **you bet your s. life I am!** je pense bien!

8 (*engine*) doux, *f* douce; **s. running** (*of machine*) fonctionnement régulier

N *esp Br* (*piece of confectionery*) bonbon *m*; (*dessert*) dessert *m*; **sweets** (*confectionery*) sucreries *fpl*, confiseries *fpl*, friandises *fpl*; **my s.!** mon chéri!, ma chérie!; **be a s.!** sois un amour!

INT *Br Fam* **s. (as a nut)!** cool!, génial!

▸▸ *Bot* **s. cherry** merisier *m*; *Bot* **s. pea** pois *m* de senteur; **s. potato** patate *f* douce; *Br* **s. shop** confiserie *f*, *Culin* **s. and sour sauce** sauce *f* aigre-douce; *Fam* **s. talk** flatteries *fpl*, paroles *fpl* mielleuses; *Bot* **s. violet** violette *f* odorante; *Bot* **s. william** œillet *m* de poète

sweetbread ['swiːtbred] N *Culin* veal/lamb **s.** ris *m* de veau/d'agneau

sweetcorn ['swiːtkɔːn] N *Culin* maïs *m* doux

sweeten ['swiːt(ə)n] VT (*food, drink*) sucrer; (*air*) désodoriser; (*breath*) purifier; (*task*) adoucir, rendre plus agréable; **to s. the pill** dorer la pilule; **to s. sb's temper** adoucir qn; **to s. sb** (*bribe etc*) graisser la patte à qn

sweetener ['swiːt(ə)nər] N **1** *Culin* édulcorant *m*; **artificial s.** édulcorant de synthèse **2** *Fam* (*bribe*) pot-de-vin *m*, *pl* pots-de-vin; **to give sb a s.** graisser la patte à qn, verser un pot-de-vin à qn

sweetening ['swiːt(ə)nɪŋ] N (*substance*) édulcorant *m*; **what s. did you use?** avec quoi l'avez-vous sucré?

sweetheart ['swiːthɑːt] N amoureux, -euse; **(my) s.!** mon amour!, mon cœur!; **they've been sweethearts since childhood** ils s'aiment depuis leur enfance; **a childhood s.** un amour d'enfance

▸▸ *Ind* **s. agreement** = accord *m* entre un employeur et des dirigeants syndicaux dont les termes sont favorables aux deux parties mais pas aux travailleurs concernés

sweetie ['swiːtɪ] N *Fam* **1** *Br* (*confectionery*) bonbon *m* **2 s. (pie)** (*term of endearment*) mon (ma) mignon, -onne; **he's such a s.** il est croquignolet; **be a s. and …** sois mignon tu veux et …

sweetish ['swiːtɪʃ] ADJ sucré; (*unpleasantly*) douceâtre

sweetly ['swiːtlɪ] ADV **1** (*to sing*) mélodieusement; **the engine's running s.** le moteur tourne bien; **he kicked the ball s. into the corner of the net** il a mis la balle dans le coin du filet comme à l'entraînement **2** (*pleasantly*) agréablement, gentiment; **to smile s.** sourire gentiment

sweetmeat ['swiːtmiːt] N *Old-fashioned, Lit* (*sweet*) bonbon *m*; **sweetmeats** sucreries *fpl*, douceurs *fpl*

sweetness ['swiːtnɪs] N **1** (*of honey, victory, revenge etc*) douceur *f*, **I prefer the s. of this beer** je préfère cette bière parce qu'elle est plus douce **2** (*of person, gesture etc*) gentillesse *f*, charme *m*; **she's s. itself when you are there** c'est la douceur personnifiée quand tu es là; **now that he's got what he wanted he's all s. and light** maintenant qu'il a eu ce qu'il voulait il est tout miel

sweet-scented, sweet-smelling ADJ (*flower, plant*) odorant, odoriférant; (*room*) parfumé

sweet-talk VT *Fam* baratiner; **to s. sb into doing sth** baratiner qn pour lui faire faire qch; **you can't s. your way around me this time** cette fois, tu ne m'auras pas par la flatterie *ou* ce n'est pas la peine de me baratiner

sweet-tempered ADJ doux, *f* douce, agréable

swell [swel] N **1** *Naut* houle *f* **2** (*of sound*) augmentation *f*, *Lit* **the majestic s. of the organ** les accents *mpl* majestueux de l'orgue **3** *Mus* (*of organ*) (*device*) soufflet *m* **4** *Old-fashioned Fam* (*well-dressed man*) élégant *m*

ADJ *Am Fam* (*excellent*) épatant; *Iron* **that's just s.!** ça, c'est la meilleure!; **a s. guy** un chic type

VT (*pt swelled; pp swollen* ['swəʊl(ə)n], *occ swelled*) (r)enfler, gonfler; *Mus* (*note*) enfler; **the river was swollen by the rain** la pluie avait grossi la rivière; **eyes swollen with tears** yeux gonflés de larmes; **all this has helped to s. the ranks of the unemployed** tout cela est venu grossir le nombre de chômeurs; **to s. the number(s)** grossir les effectifs

VI enfler; (*of part of the body*) se tuméfier; (*of wood*) gonfler; (*of number, crowd*) augmenter, grossir; (*of sea*) se soulever; (*of music*) enfler; **her arm is swelling** son bras enfle; **his heart swelled with pride** son cœur se gonflait d'orgueil; **the problem had swollen to massive proportions** le problème avait pris des proportions énormes

▸▸ *Mus* **s. box** boîte *f* expressive

▸ **swell out** VI (*be swollen*) être bombé; (*expand*) bomber; **the sails s. out** les voiles se gonflent

▸ **swell up** VI *(of injured part of body etc)* enfler; *esp Lit* **all swollen up with pride** tout bouffi d'orgueil

swellheaded [swel'hedɪd] ADJ *Fam* vaniteux, suffisant

swelling ['swelɪŋ] ADJ qui s'enfle *ou* se gonfle; *(sail)* gonflé; *(numbers)* croissant
  N **1** *(of number)* augmentation f, *(of column)* renflement m **2** *Med (of face)* tuméfaction f, gonflement m, enflure f, *(on forehead)* bosse f, enflure; *(growth)* tumescence f, tumeur f

swelter ['sweltər] VI étouffer *ou* être accablé de chaleur

sweltering ['sweltərɪŋ] ADJ *(heat)* étouffant, accablant; **s. (hot) day** journée f étouffante *ou* d'une chaleur accablante; **it's s. in here** on étouffe ici

swept PT, PP *see* sweep VT, VI

sweptwing ['sweptwɪŋ] ADJ *Aviat (aircraft)* à ailes en flèche

swerve [swɜ:v] VI *(of pedestrian, cyclist, footballer)* faire un écart; *(of horse)* se dérober; *(of car)* faire un écart *ou* une embardée; *(of ball)* décrire une courbe; *Fig (from truth etc)* s'écarter; **the cyclist was swerving in and out of the traffic** le cycliste zigzaguait entre les voitures; **to s. to avoid sb/sth** *(of car, driver)* faire une embardée pour éviter qn/qch; *Fig* **she never swerves from her duty** elle ne s'écarte jamais de son devoir
  VT *(ball)* dévier; **to s. the car** faire un écart avec la voiture
  N écart m, déviation f, *Aut* embardée f, *Sport* **to put a** *or* **some s. on the ball** faire dévier une balle

swift [swɪft] ADJ **1** *(fast)* rapide; *(reaction etc)* prompt; **as s. as an arrow** *ou* rapide comme l'éclair; *Lit* **s. of foot** rapide à la course; *Lit* **s. to anger** toujours prêt à s'emporter, irascible **2** *Am Fam (clever)* malin, -igne; **that was a real s. move** c'était bien joué; **she's not real s.** c'est pas une lumière, elle est pas très maligne
  N *(bird)* martinet m

swift-flowing ADJ *(river)* au cours rapide

swift-footed [-'fʊtɪd] ADJ rapide à la course

swiftly ['swɪftlɪ] ADV *(to run etc)* vite, rapidement; *(to react etc)* promptement

swiftness ['swɪftnɪs] N *(speed)* rapidité f, vitesse f, *(of reply etc)* promptitude f

SWIFT transfer [swɪft] N *Fin* virement m SWIFT

swig [swɪg] *Fam* N lampée f, **to take a s. at the bottle** boire un coup à la bouteille; **he took a s. of whisky** il a bu une lampée *ou* gorgée de whisky; **fancy a s.?** *(passing bottle etc)* un petit coup?
  VT (**-gg-**) *(beer, lemonade etc)* boire à grands traits *ou* à grands coups
▸ **swig down** VT SEP *Fam (beer, lemonade etc)* boire *ou* descendre d'un seul trait

swill [swɪl] N **1** *(for pigs)* pâtée f, *Fig Pej* **this horrible s.** *(food, drink)* cette saloperie **2** *esp Br (act of rinsing)* lavage m à grande eau; **to give sth a s. (out)** laver *ou* rincer qch à grande eau
  VT **1** *Fam (drink)* boire avidement **2** *esp Br =* **swill out**
▸ **swill out** VT SEP *esp Br (rinse)* laver à grande eau; **to s. out a basin** rincer une cuvette à grande eau

swim [swɪm] N **1** *(for leisure)* baignade f, *(for exercise)* nage f, **to have** *or* **take a s.** se baigner; **to go for a s.** *(for leisure)* aller se baigner; *(for exercise)* aller nager; **coming for a s.?** tu viens te baigner?; **did you enjoy your s.?** *(for leisure)* tu t'es bien baigné?; *(for exercise)* tu as bien nagé?; **it was a long s. to the shore** il a fallu nager longtemps pour atteindre le rivage; **I have a big breakfast after my**

morning **s.** le matin je prends un gros petit-déjeuner après avoir nagé; **that's a long s.!** à la nage cela fait loin! **2** *Fig Fam* **to be in the s.** *(of things)* être dans le coup
  VI *(pt* **swam** [swæm]; *pp* **swum** [swʌm]; *prp* **swimming**) *(of person, animal)* nager; *(of fat, scum) (float)* surnager, flotter; *Fig (of eyes, vision)* se brouiller; *Sport* **to s. for one's country** faire partie de l'équipe nationale de natation; **to s. like a fish** nager comme un poisson; **to s. to the shore** gagner le rivage à la nage; **to s. over** *or* **across a river** traverser une rivière à la nage; **they swam under the net** ils sont passés sous le filet (en nageant); **let's s. back** rentrons (à la nage); *Fig* **to s. with the tide** suivre le courant; **to go swimming** *(for leisure)* aller se baigner; *(for exercise)* aller nager; **the meat was swimming in gravy** la viande nageait dans la sauce; **eyes swimming with tears** yeux noyés *ou* baignés de larmes; **to make sb's head s.** faire tourner la tête à qn; **my head is swimming** la tête me tourne, j'ai la tête qui tourne; **everything swam before my eyes** tout semblait tourner autour de moi
  VT *(river)* traverser *ou* passer à la nage; **to s. the Channel** traverser la Manche à la nage; **to s. four lengths** nager *ou* faire quatre longueurs; **to s. the breast stroke** nager la brasse; **she swam one stroke and ...** elle fit une brasse et ...; **to s. a race** faire une course de natation (**with sb** contre qn)
▸▸ **s. bladder** vessie f natatoire

swimmer ['swɪmər] N *(person)* nageur, -euse

swimming ['swɪmɪŋ] N nage f, *esp Sp* natation f
▸▸ *Br* **s. costume** maillot m de bain; **s. instructor** maître-nageur m, *pl* maîtres-nageurs; **s. lesson** leçon f de natation; **s. match** concours m de natation; **s. pool** piscine f, **s. trunks** maillot *ou* slip m de bain

swimmingly ['swɪmɪŋlɪ] ADV *Fam* au mieux, à merveille; **everything is going s.** tout va comme sur des roulettes

swimsuit ['swɪms(j)u:t] N maillot m de bain

swimwear ['swɪmweər] N maillots mpl de bain

swindle ['swɪnd(ə)l] N escroquerie f, filouterie f, **it's a s.** c'est une escroquerie
  VT escroquer, filouter, *Fam* rouler; **to s. sb out of sth** escroquer qch à qn; **I'm afraid you've been swindled** j'ai bien peur que tu ne te sois fait rouler

swindler ['swɪndlər] N escroc m, filou m

swine [swaɪn] N *(inv in pl)* **1** *Sl (man)* salaud m; *(woman)* garce f, **(dirty** *or* **filthy) s.!** sale cochon!; **he's a lazy s.!** c'est une grosse feignasse! **2** *Arch, Dial (pig)* cochon m, porc m, *Arch, Lit* pourceau m
▸▸ **s. fever** peste f porcine

swineherd ['swaɪnhɜ:d] N *Old-fashioned, Lit* porcher m, gardeur m de cochons

SWING [swɪŋ] N **1** *(movement) (of pendulum)* oscillation f, balancement m, va-et-vient m inv; *(of crank)* tour m; *Boxing, Golf* swing m; *Fig* **the s. of the pendulum** le mouvement de balancier; **to give a child a s.** *(on swing)* pousser un enfant (sur une balançoire); *Fam* **to take a s. at sb** balancer un coup de poing à qn; *Golf* **he took a huge s. at the ball** il prit un grand élan pour frapper la balle; **s. of a door** ouverture f d'une porte; **to be in full s.** *(of party etc)* battre son plein; *(of organization)* être en pleine activité; **when the season is in full s.** quand la saison bat son plein; **he has dramatic mood swings** il a des sautes d'humeur incroyables; *Fig* **sudden s. of** *or* **in public opinion** revirement m inattendu de l'opinion publique; *Pol* **s. to the left** glissement m à gauche *ou* vers la gauche; *Econ* **seasonal swings** variations fpl saisonnières

2 *(rhythmic movement)* mouvement m rythmé; *Mus (style of music)* swing m; **to walk with a s.** marcher d'un pas rythmé *ou* d'un pas cadencé; **song that goes with a s.** chanson très rythmée; *Fam* **everything went with a s.** *(of party)* tout a baigné; *Fam* **to get into the s. of things** se mettre au courant *ou* dans le bain

3 *(in playground, hanging from tree etc)* balançoire f, *Fig Fam* **what you gain on the swings, you lose on the roundabouts, it's swings and roundabouts** ce qu'on gagne d'un côté, on le perd de l'autre; *Fam* **it's a swings and roundabouts situation** c'est une situation où l'on n'a rien à perdre ni à gagner
  VI *(pt, pp* **swung** [swʌŋ]) *(on child's swing)* se balancer; *(change direction)* changer de direction; *Mus* swinguer; *Old-fashioned Fam (be up to date)* être dans le vent; *(be going well) (of party)* battre son plein; **to s. (to and fro)** se balancer; *(of bell)* se balancer; *(of pendulum)* osciller; **shop sign that swings (to and fro) in the wind** enseigne de magasin qui ballotte au vent; *Fam* **to s. for a crime** être pendu pour un crime; **to s. (on** *or* **round an axis)** tourner *ou* pivoter sur un axe; **the door swings on its hinges** la porte tourne sur ses gonds; **to s. open** *(of door)* s'ouvrir; **to s. to** *(of door)* se refermer; **to s. (at anchor)** *(of ship)* éviter (sur l'ancre); *Mil* **the whole line swung to the left** toute la ligne fit une conversion vers la gauche; **to s. along** *(walk)* marcher d'un pas balancé; *Fam* **to s. for sb** *(hit out at)* essayer d'en coller une à qn; **to s. into the saddle** sauter à cheval *ou* en selle; **to s. from branch to branch** se balancer d'une branche à une autre; **to s. into action** passer à l'action; *Sl* **to s. both ways** *(be bisexual)* marcher à voile et à vapeur
  VT *(to and fro)* (faire) balancer; *(pendulum)* faire osciller; *(turn)* faire tourner; *Aviat (propeller)* lancer; *(hammock)* suspendre, pendre, accrocher; *Mus (tune etc)* interpréter en swing; **to s. one's arms** balancer les bras; **to s. one's hips** *(in walking)* balancer les hanches; *Boxing* **to s. a blow** balancer un coup; **to s. oneself into the saddle** sauter à cheval *ou* en selle; **to s. a child** faire balancer un enfant; *Cr* **to s. the ball** faire dévier la balle en l'air; **to s. the voting in favour of sb** faire pencher la balance en faveur de qn; *Fam* **to s. a deal** *(bring it off)* mener une affaire à bien; *Fam* **if we get their support I think we can s. it** si on arrive à obtenir leur soutien, je crois qu'on est bon; *Fam* **to s. it so that ...** *(arrange things)* arranger les choses de manière (à ce) que ...
▸▸ **s. boat** balançoire f (en forme de bateau); **s. bridge** pont m tournant; **s. door** porte f battante; **s. glass, s. mirror** miroir m à bascule; *(full length)* psyché f, *Mus* **s. music** swing; *Am Fam* **s. shift** *(work period) =* poste m de 16 heures à minuit; *(team) =* équipe f qui travaille de 16 heures à minuit

▸ **swing at** VT INSEP *(aim blow at)* **to s. at sb** balancer un coup de poing à qn; **he swung wildly at the ball** il a fait un grand mouvement du bras pour atteindre la balle
▸ **swing back** VI *(of door)* se rabattre; *(of pendulum, branch)* revenir; **public opinion swung back** il y eut un revirement d'opinion
▸ **swing out** VI *(of car, driver)* faire un écart; *(from side road)* déboucher
▸ **swing round** VI *(turn around) (of person)* se retourner vivement; *(of public opinion, person etc)* faire volte-face; *(of car)* virer (brusquement), faire un brusque virage; **the car swung right round** la voiture a fait un tête-à-queue; **this part swings round on this pivot** cette pièce tourne autour de ce pivot; *Fig* **to s. round behind the party leadership** se rallier à la direction du parti
  VT SEP *(turn round suddenly) (car)* faire faire un brusque virage à; *(dancer)* faire tourner;

Fig **to s. sb round** convaincre qn; **to s. a car right round** faire faire un tête-à-queue à une auto

swingeing ['swɪndʒɪŋ] ADJ *(increase, reduction etc)* énorme; *(attack, criticism)* violent; **s. blow** coup *m* bien envoyé; **s. cuts** compressions *fpl* budgétaires démesurées; **s. damages** forts dommages-intérêts *mpl*; **s. majority** majorité *f* écrasante

swinger ['swɪŋər] N **1** *Old-fashioned Fam* **to be a s.** *(fashionable)* être dans le vent; *(sociable)* être un(e) fêtard, -arde **2** *(promiscuous person)* débauché, -ée; *(who swaps sexual partners)* échangiste *mf*

swinging ['swɪŋɪŋ] ADJ *(to and fro)* balançant; *(mirror)* à bascule; *Old-fashioned Fam (person)* dans le vent; **with s. arms** les bras ballants; **s. blow** coup *m* balancé; **s. door** porte *f* battante; *Old-fashioned* **s. party** réception *f* endiablée; **s. stride** allure *f* rythmée *ou* cadencée *ou* dégagée; **s. tune** air *m* qui swingue

N *(to and fro)* balancement *m*; *(of pendulum)* oscillation *f*; **s. motion** balancement *m*

▸▸ **s. London** = le Londres branché des années soixante; **the s. sixties** les folles années *fpl* soixante

swingometer [swɪŋ'ɒmɪtər] N tableau *m* des estimations *(des résultats des élections)*

swing-wing ADJ *(aircraft)* à géométrie variable

swinish ['swaɪnɪʃ] ADJ *Fam (behaviour)* dégueulasse; **that s. brother of yours** ton dégueulasse de frère

swipe [swaɪp] N *(with fist or stick)* coup *m* de poing/de bâton; *Cr, Golf* coup à toute volée; **I gave myself a s. round the head with it** je me suis donné un coup sur la tête avec; **to take a s. at sb** *(aim blow at)* balancer un coup *(de poing)* à qn; *Fig (in satire etc)* taper sur qn

VI **to s. at the ball** *(hit it)* frapper la balle de toutes ses forces; **he swiped at the ball but missed** il a voulu frapper la balle de toutes ses forces mais il a frappé dans le vide

VT *Fam* **1** *(hit) (person) (with fist or stick)* donner un coup de poing/de bâton à; *Cr, Golf (ball)* frapper de toutes ses forces; **I managed to s. myself in the eye** j'ai réussi à me donner un coup dans l'œil **2** *(steal)* chiper **3** *(pass through credit card reader)* passer au pressographe

▸▸ **s. card** badge *m*

swirl [swɜ:l] N *(of water)* remous *m*; *(of gases)* tourbillonnement *m*; *(of cream etc)* spirale *f*; **a s. of dust** un tourbillon de poussière; **a s. of skirts** un tournoiement de jupes

VI tournoyer, tourbillonner

VT faire tournoyer

swirling ['swɜ:lɪŋ] ADJ tourbillonnant, tournoyant

swish[1] [swɪʃ] N **1** *(sound) (of water)* bruissement *m*; *(of dress)* froufrou *m*; *(of curtains being drawn)* frôlement *m*; *(of whip)* sifflement *m*; *(of scythe, tyres)* crissement *m* **2** *(blow with whip)* coup *m* de fouet; **the cow flicked away the flies with a s. of its tail** la vache chassait les mouches avec sa queue

VI *(of water)* bruire; *(of silk)* froufrouter; *(of whip)* siffler

VT *(stick, cane)* faire siffler; **to s. its tail** *(of animal)* battre l'air de sa queue

swish[2] ADJ *esp Br Fam (elegant) (person)* élégant, chic; *(flat, car)* super

N *Am Offensive Sl (effeminate homosexual)* folle *f*

swishy ['swɪʃɪ] ADJ *Am Offensive Sl (effeminate)* chochotte

Swiss [swɪs] ADJ suisse; **the S. government** le gouvernement helvétique; **S. French** suisse romand; **S. German** suisse alémanique

N *(inv in pl)* Suisse *m*, Suissesse *f*

▸▸ **S. army knife** couteau *m* suisse; **S. cheese** emmental *m*; **S. cheese plant** monstera *m*; **S. roll** *(gâteau m)* roulé *m*

SWITCH [swɪtʃ]

| N interrupteur **1** ▪ commutateur **1** ▪ revirement **2** ▪ changement **2** ▪ baguette **4** ▪ canne **4** |
| VT changer de **2** ▪ donner un coup de baguette à **4** |
| VI changer |

N **1** interrupteur *m*, *Fam* bouton *m*; *(more than two positions)* commutateur *m*; **two-way s.** va-et-vient *m inv*

2 *(change) (in policy, opinion)* revirement *m*; *(of resources, emphasis)* changement *m*; **to make a s.** effectuer un changement; **to make the s. from gas to electricity** passer du gaz à l'électricité

3 *Am Rail (point)* aiguille *f*; *(siding)* voie *f* de raccordement *ou* de garage

4 *(stick)* baguette *f*, badine *f*; *(for caning pupil)* canne *f*, **(riding) s.** petite cravache *f*

5 *Comput (in DOS)* paramètre *m*

VT **1** *Elec (current)* commuter

2 *(change) (places etc)* changer de; *(lever)* changer la position de; *(exchange)* échanger; **to s. the conversation (to something else)** détourner la conversation; **to s. the conversation to money** faire passer la conversation sur le sujet de l'argent; **why do you always have to s. the conversation to …?** pourquoi faut-il toujours que tu en reviennes à des questions de …?; **can I s. it for another one?** puis-je l'échanger contre un autre?; **he's been switched to another department** il a été muté dans un autre service

3 *Am Rail (train)* aiguiller; **to s. a train onto a branch line** aiguiller un train sur un embranchement

4 *(hit with stick)* donner un coup de baguette à; **to s. its tail** *(of cow)* battre l'air de sa queue

VI *(change)* **to s. (from gas) to electricity** passer (du gaz) à l'électricité; **I see no reason to s. to another brand** je ne vois vraiment pas pourquoi je changerais de marque; **they switched to another topic when I arrived** ils ont changé de conversation quand je suis arrivé; **she later switched to teaching** par la suite, elle s'est réorientée vers l'enseignement

▸▸ **S. card**® = carte *f* de paiement utilisée en Grande-Bretagne, ≃ Carte *f* bleue; **s. gear** appareillage *m* de commutation *ou* de distribution

▸ **switch back** VI *(revert to)* **to s. back (from electricity) to gas** repasser (de l'électricité) au gaz; **we switched back to gas** nous sommes revenus au gaz; **to s. back to BBC2** remettre sur BBC2

▸ **switch off** VT SEP *(radio, light, heating etc)* couper, éteindre; *(printer etc)* éteindre; **it switches itself off** ça s'éteint automatiquement; **they switched off the power** ils ont coupé le courant; **s. the light off when you go out!** éteignez la lampe *ou* n'oubliez pas d'éteindre quand vous sortirez!; *Aut* **to s. off the ignition** *or* **the engine** couper le moteur

VI *(of person) (turn off lights etc)* éteindre; *(of appliance etc)* s'éteindre; **where does it s. off?** où est l'interrupteur?, où est-ce que cela s'éteint?; *Fam* **to s. off (completely)** *(stop listening)* décrocher

▸ **switch on** VT SEP *(radio, TV, heating etc)* mettre (en marche); *(light, current)* mettre; *(electricity, printer)* allumer; *Aut* **to s. on the ignition** *or* **the engine** mettre le contact; **to s. on the charm** faire du charme; **to be swit-**

ched on *Fam (be up to date)* être bien au courant de ce qui se passe; *Sl (be under influence of drugs)* être défoncé; *Fam* **they switched me on to new ideas** ils m'ont initié aux idées nouvelles

VI *(of heating, light, computer, TV)* s'allumer

▸ **switch over** VI **1** *Radio, TV* **to s. over (to another station/channel)** changer de station/chaîne; **let's s. over to Channel 4** et si on mettait la 4?

2 **to s. over to modern languages** *(of student)* réorienter ses études vers les langues vivantes; **we switched over to gas** nous sommes passés au gaz

▸ **switch round** VT SEP *(exchange one for the other)* échanger; **someone's switched these photos round** quelqu'un a échangé ces photos; **why don't we s. the desks round?** et si on changeait les bureaux de place?

VI *(change places)* changer de place; *(in job) (alternate)* tourner

switchback ['swɪtʃbæk] N *(road)* route *f* en lacets; *(railway)* voie *f* ferrée en lacets; *(bend)* virage *m* en lacet; *Br (at fair)* montagnes *fpl* russes

switchblade ['swɪtʃbleɪd] N *Am* couteau *m* à cran d'arrêt

switchboard ['swɪtʃbɔ:d] N **1** *Tel* central *m* (téléphonique); *(in office)* standard *m* **2** *Elec* tableau *m* (commutateur *ou* de distribution)

▸▸ **s. line** ligne *f* principale; **s. operator** standardiste *mf*

switched [swɪtʃt] ADJ

▸▸ **s. line** *(in datacomms)* ligne *f* commutée; *Comput* **s. network** réseau *m* commuté

switcher ['swɪtʃər] N *TV* console *f* vidéo, pupitre *m* de mélange vidéo

switchman, *pl* **switchmen** ['swɪtʃmən] N *Am Rail* aiguilleur *m*

Switzerland ['swɪtsələnd] N Suisse *f*, **German(-speaking) S.** la Suisse alémanique; **French(-speaking) S.** la Suisse romande; **Italian(-speaking) S.** la Suisse italienne

swivel ['swɪv(ə)l] N *(device)* pivot *m*

VI *(-ll-, Am -l-)* pivoter, tourner

VT faire pivoter

▸▸ **s. arm** bras *m* pivotant; **s. base** socle *m* pivotant; **s. chair** siège *m* tournant, chaise *f* pivotante; **s. joint** (joint *m* à) rotule *f*; *Aut* **s. pin** pivot central; **s. seat** siège tournant, chaise pivotante

▸ **swivel round** VI *(turn)* pivoter, tourner; **to s. round on one's heels** pivoter sur ses talons

VT SEP faire pivoter

swivelling, *Am* **swiveling** ADJ *(screen, arm etc)* pivotant, mobile

swiz(z) [swɪz] N *Br Sl* arnaque *f*; **it's a s.!, what a s.!** c'est du vol!

swizzle ['swɪz(ə)l] N **1** *Am Fam (cocktail)* cocktail *m* **2** *Br Sl* = swiz(z)

▸▸ **s. stick** diablotin *m*

swollen ['swəʊl(ə)n] ADJ enflé, gonflé; *(face)* bouffi; *(stomach)* ballonné; **his arm was very s.** il avait le bras très enflé; **s. glands** ganglions *mpl*; **the river is s.** la rivière est en crue; *Fig Fam* **to suffer from** *or* **to have a s. head** avoir la grosse tête

swollen-headed ADJ *Fam* vaniteux, qui a la grosse tête

swoon [swu:n] N *Old-fashioned* N évanouissement *m*, défaillance *f*; **to fall** *or* **go into a s.** s'évanouir, se pâmer

VI **1** *(faint)* s'évanouir **2** *(in rapture)* se pâmer

swoop [swu:p] N *(of plane)* descente *f* en piqué (**upon** sur); *(of falcon on its prey)* descente; **police s.** *(on nightclub etc)* descente de police; **cocaine found in drugs s.** de la cocaïne découverte à la suite d'une descente de police; *Fam* **at one (fell) s.** d'un seul coup

VI **the hawk swooped down on its prey** *(dived)* le faucon a plongé sur sa proie;

(caught it) le faucon a fondu sur sa proie; **the gunship swooped down over the village** l'hélicoptère de combat est descendu en piqué sur le village; **the swallows were swooping and whirling** les hirondelles tourbillonnaient; **the police swooped on the nightclub** la police a fait une descente dans la boîte de nuit

swoosh [swuːʃ] **N** *(of water)* bruissement *m*; *(of wind)* sifflement *m*

VI the water swooshes round the toilet then ... l'eau tourbillonne dans la cuvette des toilettes puis ...; **the waves swooshed over the deck** les vagues déferlaient sur le pont; **you could hear the liquid swooshing around in the tank** on entendait le liquide clapoter dans le réservoir; **the rocket/whip swooshes through the air** la fusée/le fouet siffle dans l'air

VT he swooshed it down the loo il l'a fait disparaître dans les toilettes; **she then swooshed it out with clean water** *(rinsed)* elle l'a ensuite rincé à grande eau; **s. the detergent all over the stain** répandre le détergent généreusement sur la tache

swop [swɒp] **N, VT & VI = swap**

sword [sɔːd] **N** épée *f*, *Arch, Lit* glaive *m*; *Mil, Naut* sabre *m*; **to draw one's s.** tirer son épée, dégainer; **to cross swords with sb** croiser l'épée *ou* le fer avec qn; *Fig (argue)* se disputer avec qn; *(in debate)* se mesurer avec qn; **to put the inhabitants to the s.** passer les habitants au fil de l'épée; *Prov* **those that live by the s. shall die by the s.** ceux qui ont vécu par le fer *ou* par l'épée périront par le fer *ou* par l'épée

▸▸ **s. arm** bras *m* droit; **s. cut** *(blow)* coup *m* de sabre; *(wound)* blessure *f* faite au sabre; *(on face)* balafre *f*; **the S. of Damocles** l'épée de Damoclès; **s. dance** danse *f* du sabre; *Lit* **the S. of Justice** le glaive de la Justice; *Cin Fam* **s. and sandals film, s. and sandals movie** péplum *m*

swordbearer [ˈsɔːdbeərər] **N** *(esp municipal)* officier *m* qui porte le glaive

swordbelt [ˈsɔːdbelt] **N** ceinturon *m*

swordfight [ˈsɔːdfaɪt] **N** combat *m* à l'épée

swordfish [ˈsɔːdfɪʃ] **N** espadon *m*

swordplay [ˈsɔːdpleɪ] **N** *(technique)* escrime *f* à l'épée; **the very realistic s. in the fight scenes** le réalisme des scènes de combat à l'épée; **verbal s.** joute *f* oratoire

swordsman, *pl* **swordsmen** [ˈsɔːdzmən] **N** épéiste *m*, tireur *m* d'épée; **good** *or* **fine s.** fine lame *f*, bonne épée *f*

swordsmanship [ˈsɔːdzmənʃɪp] **N** habileté *f* à l'épée, talents *mpl* d'escrimeur

swordstick [ˈsɔːdstɪk] **N** canne *f* à épée, canne-épée *f*, *pl* cannes-épées

sword-swallower [-swɒləʊər] **N** avaleur *m* de sabres

swore **PT** *see* **swear**

sworn [swɔːn] **ADJ ATTRIB** *(declaration)* sous serment; *(witness)* qui a prêté serment; **s. enemies** ennemis *mpl* jurés
PP *see* **swear**

SWOT [swɒt] **N** *Mktg (abbr* **strengths, weaknesses, opportunities, threats)** forces, faiblesses, opportunités et menaces *fpl*
▸▸ **S. analysis** analyse *f* des forces, faiblesses, opportunités et menaces

swot [swɒt] *Br Sch Fam* **N** *(person)* bûcheur, -euse, bosseur, -euse, *Pej* bachoteur, -euse **VI** *(-tt-)* bûcher, bosser, *Pej* bachoter
▸ **swot up** *Br Sch Fam* **VT SEP** *(maths etc)* potasser, bûcher
VI = swot VI
▸ **swot up on** **VT INSEP** *Br Sch Fam (maths etc)* potasser, bûcher

swotting [ˈswɒtɪŋ] **N** *Br Sch Fam Pej* bacho-

tage *m*; **I'd better do some s.** je ferais mieux de bûcher

swum **PP** *see* **swim** **VI, VT**

swung **PT, PP** *see* **swing** **VI, VT**
▸▸ *Typ* **s. dash** tilde *m*

sybarite [ˈsɪbəraɪt] **ADJ, N** sybarite *mf*

sybaritic [sɪbəˈrɪtɪk] **ADJ** sybaritique, sybarite

sycamore [ˈsɪkəmɔːr] **N** *(maple)* sycomore *m*, faux platane *m*; *Am (plane tree)* platane *m*

sycophancy [ˈsɪkəfənsɪ] **N** *Fml* flagornerie *f*

sycophant [ˈsɪkəfənt] **N** *Fml* flagorneur, -euse

sycophantic [sɪkəˈfæntɪk] **ADJ** *Fml* flagorneur

syllabic [sɪˈlæbɪk] **ADJ** syllabique

syllabification [sɪlæbɪfɪˈkeɪʃən] **N** syllabation *f*

syllabify [sɪˈlæbɪfaɪ] **VT** *(word)* découper en syllabes

syllable [ˈsɪləb(ə)l] **N** syllabe *f*; **short s.** *(in prosody)* brève *f*; **long s.** *(in prosody)* longue *f*; *Fig* **to explain sth in words of one s.** expliquer qch en termes très simples

syllabub [ˈsɪləbʌb] **N** *Culin* sabayon *m*

syllabus, *pl* **syllabi, syllabuses** [ˈsɪləbəs, -aɪ, -əsɪz] **N** *Sch, Univ (of course)* programme *m*; **on the s.** au programme; **to take a subject off the s.** enlever une matière du programme
▸▸ **s. design** conception *f* de programme

syllogism [ˈsɪlədʒɪz(ə)m] **N** *(in logic)* syllogisme *m*

syllogistic [sɪləˈdʒɪstɪk] **ADJ** *(in logic)* syllogistique

sylph [sɪlf] **N 1** *Myth* sylphe *m*, sylphide *f* **2** *Lit (slim woman)* sylphide *f*; *Fam* **she's no s.** elle n'a rien d'une sylphide

sylph-like **ADJ** *(waist etc)* de sylphide; *(woman)* à la taille de sylphide

sylvan [ˈsɪlvən] **ADJ** *Lit* sylvestre

symbiosis, *pl* **symbioses** [sɪmb(a)ɪˈəʊsɪs, -siːz] **N** *Biol, Fig* symbiose *f*

symbiotic [sɪmb(a)ɪˈɒtɪk] **ADJ** *Biol, Fig* symbiotique

symbol [ˈsɪmb(ə)l] **N** symbole *m* (**of, for** de); *Am* **road symbols** pictogrammes routiers **VT** *Am* **= symbolize**

symbolic [sɪmˈbɒlɪk] **ADJ** symbolique
▸▸ **s. logic** logique *f* symbolique

symbolically [sɪmˈbɒlɪklɪ] **ADV** symboliquement

symbolism [ˈsɪmbəlɪz(ə)m] **N** symbolisme *m*

symbolist [ˈsɪmbəlɪst] **ADJ, N** symboliste *mf*

symbolization [sɪmbəlaɪˈzeɪʃən] **N** symbolisation *f*

symbolize [ˈsɪmbəlaɪz] **VT** symboliser

symmetrical [sɪˈmetrɪk(ə)l] **ADJ** symétrique

symmetrically [sɪˈmetrɪklɪ] **ADV** symétriquement

symmetry [ˈsɪmɪtrɪ] **N** symétrie *f*

sympathetic [sɪmpəˈθetɪk] **ADJ 1** *(kind, understanding) (person)* compréhensif, -ive; *(stronger)* compatissant; *(letter)* de sympathie, qui marque la sympathie; *(look, smile)* de sympathie; **he's always very s.** il est toujours prêt à vous écouter; **I didn't find him very s. (about it)** je ne l'ai pas trouvé très compréhensif; **you could try to be more s. (towards her)** tu pourrais essayer de te montrer plus compréhensif (envers elle); **to be s. to a proposal** être bien disposé à l'égard d'une proposition; **s. audience** auditoire *m* bien disposé; **her novel got a very s. reception** son roman a été très bien accueil-

li **2** *(pain)* sympathique; *Phys (vibration)* due à la résonance
▸▸ *Mus* **s. string** corde *f* qui vibre par résonance

Note that the French word **sympathique** is a false friend and is never a translation for the English word **sympathetic**. It means **kind, friendly**.

sympathetically [sɪmpəˈθetɪklɪ] **ADV 1** *(showing understanding)* avec bienveillance; *(showing pity)* avec compassion; **the new play was s. received** la nouvelle pièce a été bien accueillie **2** *Med* par sympathie; *Phys (to vibrate)* par résonance

sympathize [ˈsɪmpəθaɪz] **VI 1** *(show sympathy)* compatir; *(have understanding)* comprendre; **I s. because I used to have similar problems** je compatis car j'ai connu des problèmes du même genre; **I s. with your point of view but ...** je comprends votre point de vue mais ...; **I do s.** *(feel pity etc)* je compatis; *(feel understanding)* je (vous) comprends très bien **2** *(agree)* **those who s. with Professor Smith in his view that ...** ceux qui s'associent au Professeur Smith pour dire que ...; **to s. with a cause** avoir des sympathies pour une cause

Note that the French verb **sympathiser avec** is a false friend and is almost never a translation for the English verb **to sympathize with**. It means **to be friendly with**.

sympathizer [ˈsɪmpəθaɪzər] **N 1** *(person in agreement)* sympathisant, -ante (**with a cause** d'une cause); **a rebel/an IRA s.** un sympathisant des rebelles/de l'IRA **2** *(person who shows sympathy, understanding)* **to be a s. in sb's grief** compatir au chagrin de qn; **we have received many letters from sympathizers** nous avons reçu de nombreuses lettres de personnes qui voulaient nous témoigner leur sympathie

sympathy [ˈsɪmpəθɪ] **N 1** *(compassion)* compassion *f*; **to have s. for sb** éprouver de la compassion pour qn; **to show s. to sb** faire preuve de compassion envers qn; **you have my deepest s.** *Fml (on bereavement etc)* je vous présente toutes mes condoléances; *Hum (on your new girlfriend etc)* je te souhaite bien du plaisir; **a letter of s.** une lettre de condoléances; **we'd all like to express our s. on this tragic loss** nous aimerions tous vous exprimer nos condoléances à la suite de cette perte tragique; **our sympathies are with the families of the dead** nous compatissons avec les familles des victimes; **I don't need s., I need help** ce n'est pas de compassion dont j'ai besoin, c'est d'une aide; **if you do catch a cold, don't expect any s. from me!** si tu attrapes un rhume, ne compte pas sur moi pour te plaindre!

2 *(understanding, support etc)* sympathie *f* (**for** pour); **popular sympathies are on his side** il a l'opinion pour lui; **to view a proposal with s.** regarder une proposition d'un bon œil; **to be in s. with sb's ideas** partager les idées de qn; **my s. is** *or* **my sympathies are with the opposition** ma sympathie va à l'opposition; **she was accused of having communist/federalist sympathies** on l'accusait d'avoir des sympathies pour les communistes/les fédéralistes; **to strike** *or* **come out (on strike) in s.** se mettre en grève de solidarité (**with** avec); **prices went up in s.** les prix sont montés par contrecoup; *Phys* **string that vibrates in s.** corde qui vibre par résonance; *Physiol* **the temperature of the other hand falls in s.** la température de l'autre main tombe par réaction
▸▸ **s. strike** grève *f* de solidarité

Note that the French word **sympathie** is a false friend and is rarely a translation for the English noun **sympathy**. It is usually used to convey the idea of liking somebody.

---

symphonic [sɪm'fɒnɪk] **ADJ** *Mus* symphonique

symphony ['sɪmfənɪ] **N** *Mus* **1** *(composition)*, *Fig* symphonie *f* **2** *Am (orchestra)* orchestre *m* symphonique
▸▸**s. concert** concert *m* symphonique; **s. orchestra** orchestre *m* symphonique

symposium, *pl* **symposia, symposiums** [sɪm'pəʊzɪəm, -ɪə, -ɪəmz] **N** symposium *m*; *(collection)* recueil *m* d'articles *(de spécialistes)*

symptom ['sɪm(p)təm] **N** *Med, Fig* symptôme *m*; **to show all the symptoms of ...** présenter tous les symptômes de ...

symptomatic [sɪm(p)tə'mætɪk] **ADJ** symptomatique **(of** de**)**

synagogue ['sɪnəgɒg] **N** synagogue *f*

synapse ['sɪnæps] **N** synapse *f*

sync [sɪŋk] **N** *(abbr* **synchronization)** **in s.** *(of film etc)* synchronisé; **out of s.** *(of film etc)* mal synchronisé; **the engine is a bit out of s.** le moteur ne tourne pas très rond; **to be in s. with the times** être en harmonie avec son temps; **to be out of s. with the times** être déphasé; **he's somehow out of s. with the others** *(not in tune, not thinking the same way etc)* il est un peu décalé *ou* déphasé par rapport aux autres; **her ideas are out of s. with ...** ses idées sont en décalage par rapport à ...; **the translation is out of s.** il y a un décalage dans cette traduction

synchromarketing [sɪŋkrəʊ'mɑːkɪtɪŋ] **N** synchromarketing *m*

synchromesh ['sɪŋkrəʊmeʃ] **N** *Aut* synchronisation *f*, synchronisateur *m*, synchro *m*; **s. on all gears** boîte de vitesses avec rapports synchronisés
▸▸**s. gearbox** boîte *f* de vitesses à synchroniseur

synchronic [sɪŋ'krɒnɪk] **ADJ** *(synchronous)* synchrone; *Ling (descriptive)* synchronique

synchronism ['sɪŋkrənɪz(ə)m] **N** synchronisme *m*

synchronization [sɪŋkrənaɪ'zeɪʃən] **N** synchronisation *f*

synchronize ['sɪŋkrənaɪz] **VT** *(watches, actions, movements, events)* synchroniser **(sth with sth** qch avec qch**)**; *Elec (generators)* coupler en phase
VI *(of events)* arriver *ou* avoir lieu simultanément; **we'll try to s. with you** nous essaierons de nous synchroniser avec vous

synchronized ['sɪŋkrənaɪzd] **ADJ** synchronisé
▸▸**s. generators** générateurs *mpl* synchronisés *ou* en phase; **s. sound** son *m* synchrone; **s. swimming** natation *f* synchronisée

synchronizer ['sɪŋkrənaɪzər] **N** *Elec, Comput* synchronisateur *m*

synchronizing generator ['sɪŋkrənaɪzɪŋ] **N** *TV etc* générateur *m* de synchro

synchronous ['sɪŋkrənəs] **ADJ** synchrone **(with** de**)**

syncline ['sɪŋklaɪn] **N** *Geol* synclinal *m*

syncopate ['sɪŋkəpeɪt] **VT** syncoper; **syncopated music** musique *f* syncopée; **syncopated rhythm** rythme *m* syncopé

syncopation [sɪŋkə'peɪʃən] **N** *Mus* syncope *f*

syncope ['sɪŋkəpɪ] **N** *Med, Gram* syncope *f*

syncretic [sɪŋ'kretɪk] **ADJ** syncrétique

syncretism ['sɪŋkrətɪz(ə)m] **N** syncrétisme *m*

syndic ['sɪndɪk] **N** syndic *m*

syndicalism ['sɪndɪkəlɪz(ə)m] **N** syndicalisme *m*

syndicalist ['sɪndɪkəlɪst] **N, ADJ** syndicaliste *mf*

syndicate¹ ['sɪndɪkət] **N 1** *Com, Fin* syndicat *m*; *Am (criminal organization)* association *f* de malfaiteurs; *Am (news agency)* agence *f* de presse; *Am (chain of newspapers)* chaîne *f* de journaux; **member of a s., s. member** syndicaliste *mf* **2** *(board of syndics)* conseil *m* de syndics

syndicate² ['sɪndɪkeɪt] **VT** *Journ (article)* publier simultanément dans plusieurs journaux; *Radio* vendre à plusieurs stations; *TV* vendre à plusieurs chaînes; **the photograph was syndicated in all the local newspapers** la photographie a été publiée dans toute la presse régionale; *Fin* **syndicated loan** prêt *m* en participation

syndication [sɪndɪ'keɪʃən] **N** *Journ (of article)* publication *f* simultanée dans plusieurs journaux; *Radio* diffusion *f* simultanée sur plusieurs stations; *TV* diffusion *f* simultanée sur plusieurs chaînes
▸▸**s. agency** agence *f* de presse

syndrome ['sɪndrəʊm] **N** *Med, Fig* syndrome *m*

synectics [sɪ'nektɪks] **N** synectique *f* **VOIR GRAMMAIRE A10**

synergism ['sɪnədʒɪz(ə)m] **N** synergisme *m*

synergy ['sɪnədʒɪ] **N** synergie *f*

synod ['sɪnəd] **N 1** *Rel* synode *m*; **the General S.** = le conseil d'administration de l'Église anglicane **2** *(council)* assemblée *f*, convention *f*

synonym ['sɪnənɪm] **N** synonyme *m*

synonymous [sɪ'nɒnɪməs] **ADJ** synonyme **(with** de**)**; **their name is s. with quality** leur nom est synonyme de qualité

synonymously [sɪ'nɒnɪməslɪ] **ADV** *(to use a word)* comme synonyme **(with** de**)**; **these two words can be used s.** ces deux mots peuvent être employés comme synonymes

synonymy [sɪ'nɒnɪmɪ] **N** synonymie *f*

synopsis, *pl* **synopses** [sɪ'nɒpsɪs, -psiːz] **N** résumé *m*; *(of science, film)* synopsis *m*

synoptic [sɪ'nɒptɪk] **ADJ** synoptique

synovia [sɪ'nəʊvɪə, saɪ-] **N** *Physiol, Anat* synovie *f*

synovial [sɪ'nəʊvɪəl] **ADJ**
▸▸*Med* **s. fluid** liquide *m* synovial; **s. membrane** membrane *f* synoviale

syntactic(al) [sɪn'tæktɪk, -ɪk(ə)l] **ADJ** *Gram, Comput* syntaxique, syntactique

syntax ['sɪntæks] **N** *Gram, Comput* syntaxe *f*
▸▸*Comput* **s. error** erreur *f* de syntaxe

synthesis, *pl* **syntheses** ['sɪnθɪsɪs, -iːz] **N** synthèse *f*

synthesize ['sɪnθəsaɪz] **VT** *(elements)* synthétiser; *(product)* faire la synthèse de

synthesizer ['sɪnθəsaɪzər] **N** synthétiseur *m*

synthetic [sɪn'θetɪk] **ADJ** *(product, fibre etc)* synthétique; *Fam* **s. smile** sourire artificiel *ou* factice
N synthetics matières *fpl* synthétiques **VOIR GRAMMAIRE A10**

synthetically [sɪn'θetɪklɪ] **ADV** synthétiquement

syph [sɪf] **N** *Fam* = **syphilis**

syphilis ['sɪfɪlɪs] **N** *Med* syphilis *f*

syphilitic [sɪfɪ'lɪtɪk] **ADJ, N** *Med* syphilitique *mf*

syphon ['saɪf(ə)n] **N, VT** = **siphon**

Syria ['sɪrɪə] **N** Syrie *f*

Syrian ['sɪrɪən] **ADJ** syrien
N Syrien, -ienne

syringe ['sɪrɪndʒ, sɪ'rɪndʒ] **N** seringue *f*
VT *(wound etc)* seringuer; **to s. (out) the ears** laver les oreilles avec une seringue

syrup ['sɪrəp] **N 1** *(sweet liquid)* sirop *m*; **rosehip/maple s.** sirop d'hibiscus/d'érable; *Pharm* **cough s.** sirop pectoral, sirop pour *ou* contre la toux **2** *(Br golden)* **s.** mélasse *f* raffinée **3** *(sentimentality)* douceur *f* affectée **4** *Br Fam (wig)* moumoute *f*

syrupy ['sɪrəpɪ] **ADJ** sirupeux; *Fig (tone)* mielleux, doucereux; **s. music/prose** musique/prose à l'eau de rose

SYSADMIN [sɪs'ædmɪn] **N** *Comput (abbr* **Systems Administrator)** administrateur *m* du système

SYSOP ['sɪsɒp] **N** *Comput (abbr* **Systems Operator)** sysop *m*, opérateur *m* système

system ['sɪstəm] **N 1** *(structure, organization)* système *m*; **the feudal s.** le régime féodal; **the s.** *(established order)* l'ordre *m* établi, le système; **you can't beat the s.** on ne peut rien contre le système; *Astron* **the solar s.** le système solaire; *Anat* **nervous/muscular s.** système nerveux/musculaire; **the digestive s.** l'appareil *m* digestif; **bad for the s.** mauvais pour l'organisme; **it's a bit of a shock to the s.** ça fait un choc; *Fam* **to get sth out of one's s.** se libérer de qch; *Fam* **to get sb out of one's s.** *(after romance)* se sortir qn de la tête
2 *(network) (railway, telephone etc)* réseau *m*; **road/river s.** réseau routier/fluvial; **s. of pulleys** système *m* de poulies; **central heating s.** installation *f* de chauffage central
3 *Comput* **the XYZ is an excellent s.** le XYZ est un excellent ordinateur; **operating s.** système *m* d'exploitation; **to return to s.** retourner *ou* revenir au système
4 *Comput* **systems** analyse *f* fonctionnelle
5 *(method)* système *m*; *(methodicalness)* méthode *f*; **to lack s.** manquer de méthode *ou* d'organisation
▸▸*Comput* **systems analysis** analyse des systèmes; **systems analyst** analyste-programmeur *m, pl* analystes-programmeurs, analyste-programmeuse *f, pl* analystes-programmeuses; **systems board** carte *f* système; **s. bus** bus *m* système; **s. crash** panne *f* du système; **s. disk** disque *f* système; **systems engineer** ingénieur *m* système; **s. error** erreur *f* système; **s. failure** panne du système; **s. file** fichier *m* système; **s. folder** dossier *m* système; **systems management** direction *f* systématisée; **s. manufacturer** fabricant *m* d'ordinateurs; **s. privilege** privilège *m* d'accès au système; **s. program** programme *m* système; **s. prompt** invite *f* du système, message *m* d'attente du système; **s. software** logiciel *m* d'exploitation, logiciel système; **s. unit** unité *f* système

systematic [sɪstə'mætɪk] **ADJ** systématique, méthodique; **the s. destruction of the forest** la destruction systématique de la forêt; **she's very s.** elle a de l'ordre *ou* de la méthode

systematically [sɪstə'mætɪklɪ] **ADV** systématiquement, avec méthode; *(to destroy etc)* systématiquement

systematization [sɪstəmətaɪ'zeɪʃən] **N** systématisation *f*

systematize ['sɪstəmətaɪz] **VT** systématiser

systemic [sɪs'tiːmɪk] **ADJ** *(insecticide)*, *Ling* systémique

systemization [sɪstəmaɪ'zeɪʃən] **N** = **systematization**

systemize ['sɪstəmaɪz] **VT** = **systematize**

systole ['sɪstəlɪ] **N** *Med* systole *f*

T, t [tiː] N *(letter)* T, t *m*; **to cross one's t's** barrer ses t; **to a T** à la perfection; **she has the accent off to a T** *(of actress etc)* elle maîtrise l'accent à perfection, elle maîtrise parfaitement l'accent; **that's you to a T** c'est tout à fait toi; **my job suits me to a T** mon travail me convient à merveille

TA [tiːˈeɪ] N **1** *Br Mil* *(abbr* **Territorial Army)** = force *f* armée constituée de réservistes volontaires **2** *Am Univ* *(abbr* **teaching assistant)** = étudiant, -ante de deuxième cycle qui assure quelques heures de cours en échange d'une bourse d'étude

ta [tɑː] N, INT *Br Fam* merci *m*

TAB [tæb] N *Med* *(abbr* **typhoid-paratyphoid A and B)** *(vaccin m)* TAB *m*; **he has had a T. injection** on lui a fait le TAB

tab [tæb] N **1** *(on garment) (maker's name tab)* griffe *f*, *(owner's name tab)* étiquette *f*, *(on boot)* tirant *m*; *(on file)* onglet *m*; *(for file, removable)* cavalier *m*; *(on can)* languette *f*, *(on lace)* ferret *m*; *Fig* **to keep tabs on sb/sth** avoir qn/qch à l'œil, ne pas perdre qn/qch de vue; **to keep tabs on expenses** contrôler les dépenses; **to keep tabs on sb's movements** surveiller les moindres mouvements de qn

2 *(loop) (for hanging)* attache *f*, patte *f*

3 *esp Am (bill) (in restaurant)* addition *f*, *(in hotel)* note *f*, *Fam* **to pick up the t.** *(for meal, accommodation)* régler l'addition *ou* la note; *(for government programme, research etc)* payer; *(for damage done by others)* casquer

4 *(on typewriter, word processor etc) (position)* colonne *f*, *(in text, figures)*, *Comput* tabulation *f*; *(key)* tabulateur *m*, touche *f* de tabulation; **to set tabs** régler *ou* positionner les tabulateurs **(at** à)

5 *Sl (of LSD)* buvard *m*

6 *Br Sl (cigarette)* clope *f*

VT *(text)* mettre en colonnes (avec des tabulations); *(figures)* disposer en colonne(s)

▸▸ **t. key** tabulateur, touche de tabulation; **t. points** points *mpl* de tabulation; **t. setting** *(act)* pose *f* de tabulations; *(result)* tabulations; **t. stop** taquet *m* de tabulation

tabard [ˈtæbəd] N *(garment)* tabar(d) *m*

Tabasco® [təˈbæskəʊ] N Tabasco® *m*

tabbing [ˈtæbɪŋ] N *Comput (act)* pose *f* de tabulations; *(result)* tabulations *fpl*

tabbouleh [tæˈbuːleɪ] N taboulé *m*

tabby [ˈtæbɪ] N chat *m* tigré *ou* moucheté

▸▸ **t. cat** chat tigré *ou* moucheté

tab-delimited ADJ *Comput* délimité par des tabulations

tabernacle [ˈtæbənæk(ə)l] N *Rel* **1** *(receptacle)* tabernacle *m* **2** *(place of worship)* temple *m*

table [ˈteɪb(ə)l] N **1** *(piece of furniture)* table *f*, *(small and round)* guéridon *m*; **card** *ou* **gaming t.** table de jeu; **changing/ironing t.** table à langer/repasser; **nest of tables** table

gigogne; **to set** *or Br* **lay the t.** mettre *ou* dresser la table *ou* le couvert; **to sit down to (the) t.** se mettre à table; **to be at (the) t.** être attablé *ou* à table; **to be (sitting) at the breakfast/dinner t.** être à table pour le petit déjeuner/(le) dîner; **to leave the t.** se lever *ou* sortir de table, quitter la table; **he has awful t. manners** il se tient très mal à table; **mind your t. manners!** tiens-toi bien à table!; *Fam* **to drink sb under the t.** mieux tenir l'alcool que qn; **he drank us under the t.** il était encore debout alors que nous roulions sous la table; **I could drink you under the t. any day!** je te parie que je peux boire plus que toi!; **two drinks and I'm under the t.** deux verres et je suis complètement paf!; *Parl* **to lay a bill on the t.** *Br, Can (submit)* déposer un projet de loi; *Am (suspend)* ajourner la discussion d'un projet de loi; *Fig* **to give sb money under the t.** donner un dessous de table *ou* un pot-de-vin à qn; *Fig* **to get back to the negotiating t.** reprendre les pourparlers; *Fig* **management has nothing new to put on the t.** la direction n'a rien de nouveau à proposer; *Fig* **the offer is still on the t.** la proposition tient toujours; *Fig* **to turn the tables on sb** retourner la situation, renverser les rôles; *Fig* **the tables have been turned** les rôles sont renversés; **high** *or Fam* **top t.** *(at banquet etc)* table d'honneur; *Rel* **the Lord's T., the communion t.** la sainte table

2 *(group of diners)* table *f*, tablée *f*, **she kept the entire t. amused** elle a distrait tout le monde à table; *Am* **to wait (on) t.** travailler comme serveur/serveuse; *Am* **I'm not going to wait t. all my life** je ne vais pas être serveur/serveuse toute ma vie

3 *(food)* table *f*, **she keeps a good t.** on mange bien chez elle; **the restaurant has a hot and cold t.** le restaurant propose des plats chauds et des plats froids

4 *(list) (of facts, figures etc)* table *f*, tableau *m*; *(of fares)* liste *f*; *Math* **twelve times t.** table de (multiplication par) douze; *Sport* **(league) t.** classement *m*; **where is the team in the (league) t.?** quel est le classement de l'équipe?; *Chem* **periodic t.** *(of the elements)* tableau de la classification périodique; *Naut* **tide t.** annuaire *m ou* indicateur *m* des marées

5 *Geog (plateau)* plateau *m*

6 *(slab) (of stone)* plaque *f*, tablette *f*, *Rel* **the Tables of the Law** les Tables *fpl* de la Loi

7 *Mus (sounding board)* table *f* d'harmonie

VT **1** *Br, Can Parl (submit) (proposal, resolution)* présenter; *(bill)* déposer; *(amendment)* proposer; **to t. a motion of confidence** poser la question de confiance **2** *Am (suspend) (proposal, resolution, bill)* ajourner la discussion de; *(enquiry)* ajourner

▸▸ *Geog* **T. Bay** la baie de la Table; **t. centre** décor *m* de table; **t. of contents** table des matières; **t. dancing** table dancing *m*, danse *f* aux tables; **t. d'hôte** [ˈtɑːblˈdəʊt] menu *m*; **t. d'hôte dinner** dîner *m* à prix fixe; **t. knife**

couteau *m* de table; **t. lamp** petite lampe *f*, **t. leg** pied *m* de table; **t. linen** linge *m* de table; *Comput* **t. look-up** consultation *f* de table; **t. mat** set *m* de table; *Geog* **T. Mountain** la montagne de la Table; **t. napkin** serviette *f* de table; **t. runner** chemin *m* de table; **t. salt** sel *m* de table, sel fin; **t. service** service *m* à table; **t. talk** menus propos *mpl*, propos légers; **t. tennis** tennis *m* de table, ping-pong *m*; **t.-tennis ball** balle *f* de ping-pong; **t.-tennis bat** raquette *f* de ping-pong; **t.-tennis player** joueur, -euse de ping-pong, pongiste *mf*; **t. top** dessus *m* de table; **t. wine** vin *m* de table

tableau, *pl* **tableaux, tableaus** [ˈtæbləʊ, -əʊz] N *Theat* tableau *m*

▸▸ **t. vivant** tableau vivant

tablecloth [ˈteɪb(ə)lklɒθ] N nappe *f*

table-hop VI = aller de table en table dans un restaurant ou une réception, pour montrer qu'on a des relations

tableland [ˈteɪb(ə)llænd] N *Geog* plateau *m*

table-rapping [-ræpɪŋ] N *(in spiritualism)* coups *mpl* frappés sur un guéridon

tablespoon [ˈteɪb(ə)lspuːn] N **1** *(utensil)* cuiller *f ou* cuillère *f* à soupe **2** *(quantity)* cuillerée *f* à soupe **(of** de)

tablespoonful [ˈteɪb(ə)lspuːnfʊl] N cuillerée *f* à soupe **(of** de)

tablet [ˈtæblɪt] N **1** *(pill) (for swallowing)* comprimé *m*, cachet *m*; *(for sucking)* pastille *f* **2** *(slab) (of clay, slate etc)* tablette *f*, *(inscribed stone)* plaque *f* commémorative **3** *(bar) (of soap)* pain *m* **4** *Scot (sweet)* fondant *m* au caramel

tableware [ˈteɪb(ə)lweər] N vaisselle *f*

tabloid [ˈtæblɔɪd] N *(format)* tabloïd *m*; **the tabloids** les tabloïds; *Pej (popular press)* la presse populaire à scandales *ou* à sensation

ADJ **t., in t. form** *(news etc)* en condensé *ou* raccourci

▸▸ **t. format** format *m* tabloïd; **the t. press** la presse petit format; *Pej (popular press)* la presse populaire à scandales *ou* à sensation; **t. television, t. TV** émissions *fpl* à sensation

---

Tabloids

Dans les pays anglo-saxons, le format tabloïde est caractéristique des journaux populaires. En Grande-Bretagne, les plus connus sont le 'Sun', le 'Daily Mirror', le 'Daily Mail' et le 'Daily Express'. Ces journaux sont très influents en Grande-Bretagne – le 'Sun' affiche ainsi les plus grands tirages de la presse britannique. Les "tabloids" privilégient tout particulièrement les histoires à scandale et à sensation, ce qui a suscité un débat sur le code de conduite de la presse et sur la législation à mettre en place pour protéger la vie privée.

tabloidese [tæbloɪˈdiːz] N style *m* de la presse tabloïde

taboo, tabu [təˈbuː] *Rel, Fig* N tabou *m*, *pl* -ous; **there is a t. on the subject/place** le sujet/l'endroit est tabou
ADJ *(subject, place etc)* tabou *(often inv in pl)*; **to declare sth t.** déclarer qch tabou; **these subjects are t.** ces sujets sont tabou(s)
VT *(something)* interdire, déclarer tabou; *(somebody)* déclarer tabou

tabular [ˈtæbjʊlər] ADJ *(information, statistics)* tabulaire, disposé en table(s) *ou* tableau(x); **in t. form** *(information, statistics etc)* sous forme de table(s) *ou* tableau(x)
▸▸**t. ledger** grand livre *m* (à colonnes)

tabulate [ˈtæbjʊleɪt] VT *(arrange in table)* *(figures, data)* présenter sous forme de table(s) *ou* de tableau(x); *(on word processor etc)* *(figures etc)* mettre en colonnes; **to t. data** classer des données

tabulation [tæbjʊˈleɪʃən] N *(of figures etc)* présentation *f* sous forme de table(s) *ou* tableau(x); *(on typewriter)* mise *f* en colonnes

tabulator [ˈtæbjʊleɪtər] N **1** *(on typewriter, word processor etc)* tabulateur *m* **2** *(machine)* tabulatrice *f*
▸▸**t. key** touche *f* de tabulation

tacheometer [tækɪˈɒmɪtər] N tachéomètre *m*

tachistoscope [təˈkɪstəskəʊp] N tachistoscope *m*

tachograph [ˈtækəʊɡræf] N *Aut* tachygraphe *m*

tachometer [tæˈkɒmɪtər] N *Aut* tachymètre *m*, compte-tours *m inv*

tachycardia [tækɪˈkɑːdɪə] N *Med* tachycardie *f*

tachycardiac [tækɪˈkɑːdɪæk] ADJ *Med* tachycardique

tachymeter [tæˈkɪmɪtər] N tachéomètre *m*

tacit [ˈtæsɪt] ADJ *(admission, consent)* tacite

tacitly [ˈtæsɪtlɪ] ADV *(to admit, consent)* tacitement

taciturn [ˈtæsɪtɜːn] ADJ taciturne

taciturnity [tæsɪˈtɜːnɪtɪ] N taciturnité *f*

Tacitus [ˈtæsɪtəs] N *Hist* Tacite *m*

tack¹ [tæk] N **1** *(fastener)* *(for carpet)* clou *m*; *(for upholstery)* broquette *f*, semence *f*; *(for poster, notice etc)* punaise *f*, *Fam* **to get down to brass tacks** en venir aux faits
2 *Sewing (stitch)* point *m* de bâti; **to take out the tacks** retirer le bâti
3 *(course)*, *Naut* bord *m*, bordée *f*, *Fig* voie *f*, *Naut* **to make a t.** faire *ou* courir *ou* tirer un bord *ou* une bordée; **to be/run/sail on the starboard/port t.** être/courir/faire route tribord amures/bâbord amures; *Fig* **to be on the right t.** être sur la bonne voie; *Fig* **to be on the wrong t.** être sur la mauvaise voie, faire fausse route; *Fig* **let's try another t.** essayons une autre tactique, changeons de tactique; *Fig* **to go off on a fresh t.** *(in career)* changer de voie; *(in conversation)* passer à un autre sujet
VT **1** *(fasten)* **to t. (down)** clouer; *(poster)* punaiser (**to** à); *Fig* **to t. sth on** *(add)* rajouter qch (**to** à) **2** *Sewing* **to t. (down/in/on/together)** bâtir, faufiler; **to t. up a hem** faire le bâti d'un ourlet, faufiler un ourlet
VI *(of ship)* louvoyer, faire *ou* courir *ou* tirer un bord *ou* une bordée; **to t. to port** virer (de bord) sur bâbord

tack² N *Horseriding (harness)* sellerie *f*
▸▸**t. room** sellerie

tack³ N *Naut (ship's biscuits)* biscuits *mpl* de marin

tackiness [ˈtækɪnɪs] N **1** *(stickiness)* *(of paint, varnish)* adhésivité *f*; *(of glue)* viscosité *f* **2** *Fam (shabbiness)* *(of shop, neighbourhood etc)* apparence *f* minable; *(vulgarity)*

(of remark, joke etc) goût *m* douteux; *(of clothes, jewellery)* aspect *m* bon marché; *(of person)* vulgarité *f*

tacking [ˈtækɪŋ] N **1** *(of carpet)* clouage *m* **2** *Sewing* bâti *m*, faufilage *m*; **to take out the t.** retirer le bâti (**from** de) **3** *(of ship)* louvoiement *m*
▸▸**t. about** *(of ship)* louvoiement; **t. stitch** point *m* de bâti; **t. thread** fil *m* à bâtir, faufil *m*

tackle [ˈtæk(ə)l] N **1** *(equipment)* *(for hobby, sport)* attirail *m*, matériel *m*, équipement *m*; *Naut etc (for lifting)* appareil *m* de levage; **under ship's t.** sous palan; **fishing t.** articles *mpl* de pêche **2** *Ftbl, Hockey* tacle *m*; *Rugby* plaquage *m*, placage *m* **3** *Br Fam Hum* **(wedding) t.** *(man's genitals)* service *m* trois-pièces, bijoux *mpl* de famille
VT **1** *(deal with)* *(problem, task)* s'attaquer à; *(pudding etc)* attaquer; *(subject)* aborder; *Sch (homework)* se mettre à; **to t. a thief** attraper un voleur; **I don't know how to t. it** je ne sais pas comment m'y prendre **2** *(speak to)* **to t. sb (about sth)** parler à qn (de qch), dire deux mots à qn (au sujet de qch) **3** *(in hockey)*, *Ftbl* tacler; *Rugby* plaquer

tackler [ˈtæklər] N *Ftbl, Hockey* tacleur *m*; *Rugby* plaqueur *m*

tackling [ˈtæklɪŋ] N *Ftbl, Hockey* tacle *m*; *Rugby* plaquage *m*, placage *m*; **you need to work on your t.** il faut que vous amélioriez vos tacles/vos plaquages

tacky [ˈtækɪ] ADJ **1** *(sticky)* *(paint, varnish)* collant, qui n'est pas sec, *f* sèche; *(glue)* qui commence à prendre; *(surface)* collant, poisseux **2** *Fam (shop, neighbourhood etc)* minable, moche; *(vulgar)* *(remark, joke etc)* d'un goût douteux; *(clothes, jewellery)* minable, à deux sous; *(person)* vulgaire; **a t. colour-scheme** une association de couleurs hideuse; **what a t. way to treat someone** quelle façon minable de traiter quelqu'un

taco [ˈtɑːkəʊ] N *Culin* crêpe *f* de maïs

tact [tækt] N *(of person)* tact *m*; *(in difficult situation)* délicatesse *f*; **a matter requiring t.** un problème qu'il faut aborder avec tact; **to show a lack of/great t.** faire preuve de peu/beaucoup de tact

tactful [ˈtæktfʊl] ADJ *(person)* plein de tact, diplomate; *(in difficult situation)* délicat; *(answer, remark)* plein de tact, diplomatique; *(question, reference)* délicat; **to be t.** *(of person)* avoir du tact; **that wasn't very t. of him** il a manqué de tact, ce n'était pas très délicat de sa part; **she was her usual t. self** elle a fait preuve de son tact habituel; **the t. thing would have been to say nothing** il aurait mieux valu ne rien dire; **that wasn't very t.** quel manque de tact, ce n'était pas très délicat

tactfully [ˈtæktfəlɪ] ADV *(to behave, act)* avec tact *ou* délicatesse *ou* diplomatie; **I t. refrained from asking him** par tact *ou* délicatesse, je me suis retenu de lui poser la question

tactfulness [ˈtæktfʊlnɪs] N = **tact**

tactic [ˈtæktɪk] N *Mil, Fig* tactique *f*, manœuvre *f*, **tactics** la tactique; **to use delaying tactics** utiliser une tactique pour gagner du temps

tactical [ˈtæktɪk(ə)l] ADJ *Mil, Fig* **1** *(move, weapon etc)* tactique; **t. mistake** erreur *f* tactique; **t. withdrawal** retrait *m* stratégique **2** *(person, conduct)* adroit
▸▸**t. voter** = personne *f* qui fait un vote utile; **t. voting** vote *m* utile

tactically [ˈtæktɪklɪ] ADV *(to behave, act)* adroitement; **t. (speaking)** *Mil* du point de vue de la tactique; *Fig* du point de vue tactique

tactician [tækˈtɪʃən] N *Mil, Fig* tacticien, -ienne

tactile [ˈtæktaɪl] ADJ *(organ, reflex etc)* tactile

tactless [ˈtæktlɪs] ADJ *(person)* qui manque de tact; *(answer, remark)* dépourvu de tact, qui manque de tact; *(question, reference)* indélicat; **that was a bit t. of you** tu as fait preuve d'un certain manque de tact, ce n'était pas très délicat de ta part

tactlessly [ˈtæktlɪslɪ] ADV *(to behave, act)* sans tact *ou* délicatesse; **she asked him, rather t., about his first wife** avec un manque de tact évident, elle lui a posé des questions sur sa première femme

tad [tæd] N *Fam* **1 a t.** *(of milk, sugar etc)* un peu; *(somewhat)* quelque peu, un tantinet; **it's a t. long** c'est un peu longuet; **it's a t. worrying** c'est un tantinet inquiétant; **I think you're exaggerating a t.** je crois que t'exagères un tantinet *ou* quelque peu **2** *(child)* gosse *mf*

tadger [ˈtædʒər] N *Br Sl (penis)* chipolata *f*

Tadjik [ˈtɑːdʒɪk, tɑːˈdʒiːk] N = **Tadzhik**

tadpole [ˈtædpəʊl] N têtard *m*

Tadzhik [ˈtɑːdʒɪk, tɑːˈdʒiːk] N Tadjik *mf*; **T. Soviet Socialist Republic** République *f* socialiste soviétique du Tadjikistan

Tadzhiki [tɑːˈdʒiːkiː, -ˈdʒiːkiː] N *Ling* tadjik *m*
ADJ tadjik

Tadzhikistan [tɑːdʒɪkɪˈstɑːn] N Tadjikistan *m*

taffeta [ˈtæfɪtə] N *(fabric)* taffetas *m*; **t. dress/skirt** robe/jupe en *ou* de taffetas

taffrail [ˈtæfreɪl] N *Naut (structure)* couronnement *m*; *(rail)* lisse *f* de couronnement

Taffy [ˈtæfɪ] N *Fam esp Pej (Welshman)* Gallois *m*; **hey, T.!** hé, toi le Gallois!

taffy [ˈtæfɪ] N **1** *Am (sweet)* caramel *m* (dur), *Can* tire *f* **2** *Am Sl (flattery)* flagornerie *f*

tag [tæɡ] N **1** *(for identification)* *(on garment)* marque *f*, *(label)* étiquette *f*, *(on animal)* agrafe *f*, *(on file)* onglet *m*
2 *(end piece)* *(on cord, shoelace)* ferret *m*; *(of material etc)* bout *m*; *Gram (question)* question-tag *f*, *pl* question-tags VOIR GRAMMAIRE A47; B64
3 *(epithet, nickname)* surnom *m*
4 *(quotation)* citation *f*, *(trite saying)* lieu *m* commun, cliché *m*
5 *Am (paper etc flag)* insigne *m*, cocarde *f*
6 *(game)* jeu *m* de chat; *(with sanctuary)* jeu de chat perché; **to play** *or* **have a game of t.** jouer à chat; *(with sanctuary)* jouer à chat perché
7 *Comput (code)* balise *f*
VT (-gg-) **1** *(clothing)* marquer; *(merchandise, software)* étiqueter; *(cattle)* mettre une agrafe à; *(file)* mettre un onglet à; *Comput (code)* baliser
2 *(term)* *(person)* qualifier, traiter (**as** de); *(nickname)* surnommer
3 *Am (for traffic offence)* *(vehicle)* coller une contravention *ou Fam* un papillon sur; *(person)* mettre une contravention à
4 *(in game of tag)* toucher; *Baseball* **to t. sb (out)** mettre un coureur hors jeu
5 *esp Am Fam (follow)* *(person)* suivre; *(of police etc)* filer
VI **to t. after sb** suivre qn
▸▸*Am* **t. day** = journée *f* de vente d'insignes pour une œuvre de bienfaisance; *Am* **t. end** *(oddment of cloth, thread)* bout *m*; *(of goods)* restes *mpl*; *(end of performance, day)* fin *f*; **t. line** *(in play)* mot *m* de la fin; *(in poem)* dernier vers *m*; *(of entertainer)* slogan *m*; *Journ* chute *f*; *Gram* **t. question** question-tag, *pl* question-tags
▸**tag along** VI *(follow)* suivre; **mind if I t. along?** est-ce que je peux venir avec vous?; **to t. along behind** *(lagging)* traîner derrière

▸ **tag on** VI to t. on to sb coller (aux talons de) qn

VT SEP to t. sth on (add) rajouter (to à)

Tagalog [təˈgɑːlɒg] N **1** (person) Tagal m, Tagalog m **2** Ling tagal m, tagalog m

tagboard [ˈtægbɔːd] N Am carton m

tagliatelle [tælʒəˈtelɪ] N Culin tagliatelles fpl

Tahiti [təˈhiːtɪ] N Tahiti m; in T. àTahiti

Tahitian [təˈhiːʃən] ADJ tahitien
N Tahitien, -ienne

tai chi [ˈtaɪtʃiː] N tai-chi m, tai-chi-chuan m

taiga [ˈtaɪgɑː] N Geog taïga f

tail [teɪl] N **1** (of animal, bird, fish, reptile) queue f; **to spread its t.** (of peacock) faire la roue; **with his t. between his legs** (of dog), Fig la queue entre les jambes; Fig **to turn t.** prendre ses jambes à son cou, montrer les talons; Fig **to keep one's t. up** ne pas se laisser abattre; Fig **the t.'s wagging the dog** c'est le monde à l'envers; **the t. of the hostages is wagging the dog of foreign policy** le problème des otages décide de la politique étrangère

2 (of shirt) pan m; (of coat) basque f, pan; **tails** (tail coat) habit m, queue-de-pie f, pl queues-de-pie; **to see sb out of the t. of one's eye** voir qn du coin de l'œil

3 (of comet, kite, plane) queue f; (of car, ski) arrière m; (of coin) pile f, revers m; **story with a sting in the t.** histoire qui se termine sur une pointe de méchanceté; Aut Fam **to sit on sb's t.** coller qn; **tails!** pile!

4 Fam (someone following) personne f en filature; **to put a t. on sb** filer qn; **we've got a t.** quelqu'un nous file, nous sommes suivis; **to be on sb's t.** suivre qn de près; (of detective) filer qn

5 Fam (buttocks) derrière m

6 Am Sl (woman in sexual terms) **she's a great piece of t.** elle est très baisable; **he's looking for some t.** il est en chasse

VT **1** Fam (follow) filer, prendre en filature **2** (lamb etc) couper la queue à

VI to t. after sb suivre qn de près; (of several persons one behind another) suivre qn à la queue leu leu

▸▸ Aviat t. **assembly** dérive f; t. **coat** habit, queue-de-pie; t. **end** (of storm, season, meeting, story) fin f; (of cloth) bout m; (of procession) queue f, fin; t. **feather** penne f; TV t. **slate** clap m de fin; Aviat t. **unit** empennage m

▸ **tail away** VI (of attendance, clientele etc) diminuer, décroître; (of voice) s'affaiblir; (of book etc) se terminer en queue de poisson; (of competitors in race etc) s'espacer, s'égrener; (of column on the march) s'allonger; (of interest, enthusiasm, support) diminuer

▸ **tail back** VI (of traffic) bouchonner; **the traffic tailed back all the way to ...** les voitures étaient pare-chocs contre pare-chocs jusqu'à ...

▸ **tail off** VI = tail away

tailback [ˈteɪlbæk] N Aut (queue) bouchon m, embouteillage m, point m noir

tailboard [ˈteɪlbɔːd] N (on lorry) porte f à rabattement arrière; (on car) hayon m (arrière)

-tailed [teɪld] SUFF short/long-t. à queue courte/longue

tailender [teɪlˈendər] N (in race) dernier, -ière

tailgate [ˈteɪlgeɪt] Aut N (on lorry) porte f à rabattement arrière; (on car) hayon m (arrière)

VT Fam to t. sb coller qn

VI Fam don't t.! ne roulez pas trop près!

tailhopping [ˈteɪlhɒpɪŋ] N Ski ruade f

tailings [ˈteɪlɪŋz] NPL (from mining) déchets mpl

taillamp [ˈteɪllæmp] N Am Aut feu m arrière

taillight [ˈteɪllaɪt] N Am Aut feu m arrière

tailor [ˈteɪlər] N (for men) tailleur m; (for women) couturière f

VT (suit) faire, façonner; Fig (speech) adapter (to, to suit à); (woman's) **tailored suit** tailleur m; **the tailored look is back** la mode des tailleurs ajustés est de retour; **a tailored shirt** une chemise cintrée; **a tailored skirt** une jupe de tailleur

▸▸ t.'s **chalk** craie f de tailleur; t.'s **dummy** mannequin m; Fig Pej **he looks like a t.'s dummy** il est tout endimanché

tailoring [ˈteɪlərɪŋ] N **1** (profession) métier m de tailleur **2** (work) ouvrage m de tailleur

tailor-made ADJ (suit etc) fait sur mesure; t. **for** (specially designed) conçu pour; (suited) fait pour; **it's t. for me** c'est du sur mesure, c'est juste ce qu'il me faut; **the part's t. for her** ce rôle lui va à merveille

tailpiece [ˈteɪlpiːs] N (to document, speech etc) appendice m; (to letter) post-scriptum m inv; Mus (on stringed instrument) cordier m; Typ cul-de-lampe m, pl culs-de-lampe

tailpipe [ˈteɪlpaɪp] N Aut tuyau m d'échappement

tailplane [ˈteɪlpleɪn] N Aviat stabilisateur m

tailrace [ˈteɪlreɪs] N (for mill) bief m d'aval

tailshaft [ˈteɪlʃɑːft] N Aut arbre m de sortie

tailskid [ˈteɪlskɪd] N Aviat béquille f de queue

tailspin [ˈteɪlspɪn] N Aviat (descente f en) vrille f, **to go into a t.** vriller; Fig (panic) s'affoler, paniquer (about de); (of economy, interest rates) s'effondrer; **the news sent her into a t.** la nouvelle l'a affolée ou paniquée

tailwind [ˈteɪlwɪnd] N Aviat vent m arrière

taint [teɪnt] N (of food) corruption f, décomposition f, (of air, water) contamination f, pollution f; (of reputation, corruption) souillure f, Fig (of madness) tare f, **the t. of sin** la tache ou souillure du péché; **book with no t. of bias** livre sans trace de préjugés

VT (contaminate) (food) gâter; (air, water) contaminer, polluer; (minds, morals) infecter, vicier, corrompre; (reputation) souiller, entacher

tainted [ˈteɪntɪd] ADJ (air, water) contaminé, pollué; (food) gâté; (meat) avarié; Fig (reputation) souillé, entaché; (money) sale

Taiwan [taɪˈwɑːn] N Taïwan

Taiwanese [taɪwəˈniːz] ADJ taïwanais
N Taïwanais, -aise

Tajik [ˈtɑːdʒɪk, tɑːˈdʒiːk] N = Tadzhik

Tajikistan [tɑːdʒɪkɪˈstɑːn] N = Tadzhikistan

TAKE [teɪk]

N	prise de vue **1** ▪ enregistrement **1**
▪ prise de son **1** ▪ prise **2** ▪ recette **3**
VT prendre **1, 2, 7–19, 23** ▪ contenir **3**
▪ supporter **4** ▪ emmener **5** ▪ amener **5** ▪ conduire **5** ▪ apporter **6** ▪ consommer **8** ▪ louer **10** ▪ faire **12** ▪ s'emparer de **14** ▪ gagner **14** ▪ passer **21** ▪ se présenter à **21** ▪ emprunter **22** ▪ tirer **22**
VI prendre

N **1** (recording) (of film, scene) prise f de vue(s); (of record) enregistrement m; Radio enregistrement, prise de son; **we'll do that t. again** on va refaire cette prise/cet enregistrement; **they did the scene in one t.** ils ont tourné la scène en une prise

2 (catch) (of fish, game) prise f

3 (money) (of restaurant, shop) recette f; **our t. is up** this week nos recettes sont en hausse cette semaine; Fam **to be on the t.** toucher des pots-de-vin

VT (pt took [tʊk], pp taken [ˈteɪk(ə)n]) **1** (grasp) (knife, somebody's hand) prendre; **to**

t. sth **again** reprendre qch; **to t. sth in one's hand** prendre qch dans la main; **you're taking your life in your hands doing that** c'est ta vie que tu risques en faisant cela; **to t. sb's arm** (lean on etc) prendre le bras de qn; **to t. sb by the arm, to t. sb's arm** (to prevent escape) attraper qn par le bras; **to t. sb in one's arms** prendre qn dans ses bras; **to t. (hold of) sb** saisir ou empoigner qn; **to t. (hold of) sth** se saisir ou s'emparer de qch; **to t. sb by the throat/collar** prendre qn à la gorge/au collet; **to t. the opportunity to do** or **of doing sth** profiter de l'occasion pour faire qch; t. **your partners** (at dance) invitez vos partenaires

2 (remove) (book, pen etc) prendre; **to t. sth (away) from sb** enlever ou prendre qch à qn; (steal) prendre ou voler qch à qn; **to t. one number from another** soustraire ou ôter un chiffre d'un autre; **to t. sth from the table/out of a drawer** prendre qch sur la table/dans un tiroir; **to t. sth from one's pocket** prendre qch dans sa poche; **to t. a saucepan off the heat** ôter ou retirer une casserole du feu; **to t. sth out of sb's hands** prendre qch des mains de qn; Fig **to t. the food out of sb's mouth** retirer le pain de la bouche de qn; **to t. sth off the market** retirer qch du marché

3 (hold) (of container, building etc) contenir, avoir une capacité de; **this bus takes fifty passengers** c'est un car de cinquante places

4 (tolerate) (heat, criticism, insolence, pressure) supporter; **she can't t. a joke** elle ne comprend pas la plaisanterie; **I can't t. any more** je n'en peux plus!; **I can't t. any more of him** je ne peux plus le supporter; **I can't t. much more of this** je commence à en avoir assez, je ne vais pas supporter cela bien longtemps; **he can't t. his drink** il ne supporte pas l'alcool; esp Am **I'm not taking any!** je ne marche pas!; **he can t. it** il sait encaisser

5 (lead) (person) amener (to à); (away) emmener; (in car) conduire (to à); (of road) (person) mener (to à); **to t. the dog for a walk** aller promener le chien; **to t. oneself to bed** aller se coucher; Hum **I can't t. you anywhere** tu n'es pas sortable; **to t. sb home** (on foot, by car etc) raccompagner ou ramener qn; (to meet parents) amener qn chez ses parents ou à la maison; **he's taking me (out) to dinner/the theatre** il m'emmène au restaurant/au théâtre; **to t. sb (along) with one** emmener qn avec soi; **to t. sb round a museum** faire visiter un musée à qn; **she took me round the exhibition** elle m'a fait faire le tour de l'exposition; **to t. sb round a house** faire visiter une maison à qn; **to t. sb across the road** faire traverser la rue à qn; **her job takes her all over the world** son travail l'amène à voyager dans le monde entier; **the scandal has taken her to the top of the best-seller list** le scandale l'a propulsée en haut de la liste des best-sellers; **whatever took him there?** qu'allait-il faire là-bas?; **to t. sb to court** intenter un procès contre qn

6 (carry) (flowers, sweets etc) apporter (to à); (one's coat) prendre; **will this train t. me to Cambridge?** est-ce que ce train va à ou passe par Cambridge?; **to t. sb to hospital** transporter qn à l'hôpital; **to t. sth along** or **over** or **round** apporter qch (to sb à qn); **to t. sth with one** emporter qch; t. **some food with you** emportez des provisions; **to t. sth down(stairs)** descendre qch; Fam **you can't t. it with you** (money when you die) tu ne l'emporteras pas avec toi dans la tombe; **to t. a problem/matter to sb** soumettre un problème/une affaire à qn

7 (go by) (bus, shortcut, road) prendre; t. **the turning on the left** prenez à gauche

8 (require) (of journey, work etc) (time) prendre; (of engine, machine) (diesel, paraffin etc) consommer; **it takes an army/courage** il faut une armée/du courage (**to do** pour faire); **it takes one to know one** il faut en être un/une pour savoir ce que c'est; **it took four of us to carry him** il a fallu s'y mettre *ou* nous avons dû nous y mettre à quatre pour le porter; **that will t. some explaining** voilà qui va demander des explications; **the work took some doing** le travail a été difficile; **it will t. him two hours** il en aura pour deux heures; **it took us longer than I expected** cela nous a pris plus de temps que je ne pensais; **how long does it t. to get there?** combien de temps faut-il pour y aller?; **how long does it t.?** *(for journey, job to be done etc)* combien de temps est-ce que cela prend?; **I took an hour to do it** *or* **over it** j'ai mis une heure à *ou* cela m'a pris une heure pour le faire; **it takes a clever man to do that** bien malin *ou* habile qui peut le faire; **she's got what it takes to be a leader** elle a l'étoffe d'un chef; **she's got what it takes** *(for job etc)* elle a les qualités requises; **he doesn't have what it takes to be a politician** il n'a pas l'étoffe d'un politicien; *Gram* **verb that takes a preposition** verbe qui réclame *ou* nécessite une préposition; **noun that takes an 's' in the plural** nom qui prend un 's' au pluriel

9 *(adopt) (precautions, measures)* prendre; **to t. legal advice** consulter un avocat; **to t. legal proceedings** entamer *ou* engager des poursuites judiciaires; **to t. the veil** prendre le voile; **to t. holy orders** entrer dans les ordres; **to t. a dislike to sb** prendre qn en aversion *ou* en grippe; **to t. a decision about sth** prendre une décision concernant qch; **to t. the view that ...** penser *ou* estimer *ou* considérer que ...

10 *(occupy) (flat, house)* louer; *(seat)* prendre; **all the seats are taken** toutes les places sont prises; **please t. a seat** asseyez-vous, *Fml* veuillez vous asseoir, **t. your seats!** prenez vos places!

11 *(consume) (tablet, sugar etc)* prendre; **to t. something to drink** prendre quelque chose à boire; **how do you t. your coffee?** qu'est-ce que tu prends dans ton café?; **to t. drugs** *(of addicts etc)* se droguer; *(in hospital etc)* prendre des médicaments; **to be taken twice a day** à prendre deux fois par jour; **not to be taken internally** à usage externe; **are you taking anything for that cold?** est-ce que tu soignes ce rhume?, est-ce que tu prends quelque chose pour ce rhume?

12 *(do, perform) (walk, trip)* faire; *(holiday)* prendre; **t. a look at this!** regarde-moi ça!; **t. your pick** faites votre choix; **to t. a bath** *(wash)* prendre un bain; *Am Fam (lose money)* perdre gros; *Ftbl* **to t. a penalty** tirer un penalty; **to t. a print from a negative** tirer une épreuve d'un négatif; **to t. a photograph of sb/sth** prendre qn/qch en photo; **to have one's photograph taken** se faire photographier *ou* prendre en photo; **to t. a good photo(graph)** *(be photogenic)* être photogénique; *Rel* **to t. a service** célébrer un office; *Sch* **he takes them for English** il leur enseigne l'anglais; **to t. the part of Hamlet** jouer (le rôle d')Hamlet

13 *(record) (temperature, letter, notes, name and address)* prendre

14 *(capture) (power, town)* s'emparer de; *(prize)* gagner, remporter; **to t. a woman** *(sexually)* prendre une femme; **t. him alive!** attrapez-le vivant!; **to t. sb prisoner** prendre qn prisonnier; **to t. sb by surprise** prendre qn par surprise, surprendre qn; *Chess etc* **to t. a piece** prendre une pièce; *Cards* **to t. a trick** faire une levée

15 *(experience, feel)* **to t. fright** prendre peur; **to be taken ill** tomber malade

16 *(assume)* **to t. sb/sth for sb/sth** prendre qn/qch pour qn/qch; **I took you for an Englishman** je vous ai pris pour un Anglais; **what do you t. me for?** pour qui tu me

prends?; **to t. the news as** *or* **to be true** tenir la nouvelle pour vraie; **how old do you t. her to be?** quel âge est-ce que tu lui donnes?; **I t. it that you agree** je présume que vous êtes d'accord; **she took your silence to mean refusal** elle a interprété votre silence comme *ou* a pris votre silence pour un refus

17 *(pass successfully) (bend)* prendre; *(obstacle)* sauter

18 *(consider) (case)* prendre; **t. (for example) the pensioners** prenez (par exemple) les *ou* le cas des retraités; **taking one thing with another** l'un dans l'autre

19 *(accept, receive) (client, guest)* prendre; *(cheque)* accepter; *Fam* **t. it or leave it!** c'est à prendre ou à laisser; *Fam* **t. five!** cinq minutes de pause!, reposez-vous cinq minutes!; **to t. sth well/badly** bien/mal prendre qch; **he took the news better than I thought he would** il a pris la nouvelle mieux que je ne l'aurais cru; **to t. sb/sth the wrong way** *(misunderstand)* mal comprendre qn/qch; **don't t. this the wrong way, but ...** *(be offended)* ne le prends pas mal, mais ...; **I wonder how she'll t. it** je me demande quelle tête elle fera *ou* comment elle va le prendre; **I'll t. it here** *(phone call)* je le prends ici; **I took a phone call for her yesterday** j'ai pris un coup de fil pour elle hier; *Old-fashioned* **to t. a wife** prendre femme; **do you t. this man to be your lawful wedded husband?** *(in wedding ceremony)* consentez-vous à prendre M. Lapoire pour époux?; **to t. a chance** *or* **risk** *or* **gamble** risquer le coup; *Com etc* **to t. so much a week** faire (une recette de) tant par semaine; **what** *or* **how much will you t. for it?** combien en voulez-vous?; **does this machine t. pound coins?** cette machine accepte-t-elle les pièces d'une livre?; **to t. the hook** *or* **bait** *(of fish)* mordre à l'hameçon; *Fig* tomber dans le panneau; **to t. a beating** *(be punched)* recevoir une rossée; *(be defeated)* essuyer une défaite; **to t. a bet** tenir un pari; **to t. all responsibility** assumer toute la responsabilité; **we must t. things as we find them** *or* **as they come** il faut prendre les choses comme elles sont *ou* comme elles viennent; **t. it from me!** croyez-moi!; **to t. sb seriously** prendre qn au sérieux; **nylon does not t. dyes well** le nylon ne prend pas bien la teinture; **to t. heavy loads** *(of crane, engine etc)* supporter de lourdes charges; **it won't t. your weight** ça ne supportera pas ton poids

20 *(newspaper, magazine etc)* **what paper do you t.?** *(buy at shop)* quel journal achetez-vous?; *(subscribe to)* à quel journal êtes-vous abonné?

21 *Scol (sit) (exam)* passer, se présenter à; *(study) (subject) (course)* faire; *(course)* suivre; **I didn't t. Latin at school** je n'ai pas fait de latin au lycée; **she took her degree last year** elle a obtenu son diplôme l'an dernier

22 *(copy, quote) (passage from author)* emprunter (**from** à); *(quotation, figures) (from book, report etc)* tirer (**from** de); **the title is taken from the Bible** le titre vient de la Bible; **the word is taken from (the) Latin** ce mot vient du latin

23 *(use) (eggs, flour etc)* prendre; **t. the scissors to it** vas-y avec les ciseaux; **t. a hammer to it** prends un marteau; **I'll have to t. bleach to this stain** il faudra que je nettoie cette tache à l'eau de javel; **his father took a stick to him** son père lui a donné des coups de bâton

VI *(be successful) (of fire, graft, plant cutting, vaccine, dye etc)* prendre

▸▸ *TV, Cin* **t. sheet** liste *f* des prises

▸ **take aback VT SEP** *(surprise)* décontenancer, interloquer (**with** par)

▸ **take after VT INSEP** *(be like) (one's father etc) (in looks)* ressembler à; *(in personality)* tenir de

▸ **take apart VT SEP** *(dismantle) (machine etc)* démonter; *Fig (criticize) (project etc)* démolir; *Fig* **to t. sb apart** *(in fight)* démolir qn; *(scold)* passer un savon à qn

▸ **take away VT SEP 1** *(remove) (from person) (licence)* retirer (**from sb** à qn); *(furniture)* confisquer; *(from place) (person, thing)* enlever (**from** de); *Math (number)* soustraire, ôter (**from** de); **they took his books and files away from him** ils lui ont confisqué ses livres et ses dossiers; **to t. a child away from school** retirer un enfant de l'école; **it takes away the fun** ça gâche tout

2 *(lead) (person)* emmener; *(carry) (thing)* emporter; *(wounded person)* transporter; **what takes you away so soon?** qu'est-ce qui vous fait partir de si bonne heure?; **his work took him away from his family for long periods** son travail le tenait éloigné de sa famille pendant de longues périodes; *Br* **sandwiches to t. away** sandwich(e)s *mpl* à emporter; **not to be taken away** *(on book in library)* à consulter sur place

VI to t. away from the pleasure/value of sth diminuer le plaisir/la valeur de qch; **I don't want to t. away from his achievements in the past, but ...** je ne veux pas minimiser ses performances passées mais ...

▸ **take back VT SEP 1** *(lead) (person)* reconduire, ramener, raccompagner; **they took him back to hospital/his family** ils l'ont reconduit à l'hôpital/dans sa famille

2 *(return) (book etc)* rapporter (**to** à); **that takes me back to my childhood** cela me rappelle mon enfance; **it takes you back a bit, doesn't it?** ça ne nous rajeunit pas tout ça, hein?

3 *(accept) (former employee, unsold goods)* reprendre; **she's a fool to t. him back** *(husband etc)* elle est idiote d'accepter qu'il revienne

4 *(withdraw) (what one said)* retirer; *(one's word)* retirer, reprendre; *(gift)* reprendre; **I t. it (all) back** je retire tout ce que j'ai dit

5 *Typ* transférer à la ligne précédente

▸ **take down VT SEP 1** *(remove) (poster etc)* enlever; *(plate etc) (from cupboard, shelf etc)* descendre; *(coat, picture etc) (from hook)* décrocher

2 *(lower) (one's trousers, one's pants)* baisser

3 *(destroy) (wall etc)* démolir; *Fam* **to t. sb down a peg or two** remettre qn à sa place, rabattre son caquet à qn

4 *(dismantle) (scaffolding, circus tent)* démonter

5 *(record) (name, address, instructions etc)* noter; *(notes)* prendre; **they took down everything she said** ils ont noté tout ce qu'elle disait; **to t. down a letter in shorthand** prendre une lettre en sténo

▸ **take in VT SEP 1** *(lead) (person)* faire entrer; *(carry) (washing, harvest etc)* rentrer

2 *(admit, receive) (orphan)* recueillir; *(lodge) (person)* héberger, loger, recevoir; *(lodgers)* prendre; **to t. in sewing/washing** faire la couture/la lessive à domicile

3 *(reduce) (skirt, sleeve)* reprendre; *Naut* **to t. in sail** prendre un ris; **to t. in the slack** *(on rope)* reprendre du mou

4 *(cover) (several countries etc)* comprendre, englober; *(questions, possibilities)* embrasser; **the tour takes in all the important towns** l'excursion passe par toutes les villes importantes

5 *(understand) (intellectually)* comprendre, se rendre compte de; *(emotionally) (bad news)* réaliser, bien comprendre; **it took me a while to t. in the full implications of this news** il m'a fallu un certain temps pour mesurer entièrement la portée de cette nouvelle; **he took in the situation at a glance** en un clin d'œil il a compris ce qui se passait; **to t. it all** *or* **everything in** *(listen)* être tout oreilles

6 (*deceive*) tromper, rouler (**with** avec); **to be taken in** se faire avoir; **I've been taken in** on m'a eu, je me suis fait rouler; **to allow oneself to be taken in** se laisser avoir *ou* duper *ou* tromper; **to be taken in by appearances** se laisser tromper par les apparences
7 *Am* (*see, visit*) (*museum*) visiter; **to t. in the sights** visiter la ville; **to t. in a movie/show** aller au cinéma/théâtre
▸ **take off** VT SEP **1** (*remove*) (*glasses, hat, make-up, lid*) enlever; (*clothing*) enlever, retirer, ôter; (*leg*) amputer; **t. your feet off the table!** retire *ou* enlève tes pieds de la table!; **to t. sb's attention off sth** détourner l'attention de qn; **he never took his eyes off us** il ne nous quittait pas des yeux; **to t. a couple of pounds off** (*off price*) baisser le prix *ou* faire un rabais de quelques livres; (*by dieting etc*) perdre quelques kilos; **to t. sb off a list** rayer qn d'une liste; **to t. sth off sb's hands** débarrasser qn de qch; **I'll t. the baby off your hands for a few hours** je vais garder le bébé pendant quelques heures, ça te libérera; **to t. sth off the market** retirer qch du marché; **t. your hands off me!** bas les pattes!; **to t. a load off sb's mind** ôter un poids à qn *ou* de la poitrine de qn; **to t. years off sb** (*of clothes, diet etc*) rajeunir qn; **to t. the passengers off** (*from ship*) (*by boat*) débarquer les passagers; **the injured man was taken off the ship by helicopter** le blessé a été évacué du bateau par hélicoptère
2 (*lead*) (*person*) emmener (**to** à, chez, en); **to t. oneself off** s'en aller, *Fam* décamper
3 (*cancel*) (*train, bus etc*) supprimer; (*show, programme*) annuler
4 (*mimic*) imiter
5 **to t. some time off** prendre un congé; **to t. three days off** prendre trois jours de congé; **I'm going to t. the day off tomorrow** demain je prends ma journée
VI **1** (*leave*) (*of plane*) décoller (**for** pour); (*of athlete*) prendre son appel (**from** de); (*of person*) partir (**for** pour); (*hurriedly*) s'en aller, *Fam* décamper, filer; **she's taken off for two weeks in the Caribbean** elle est partie passer deux semaines aux Caraïbes
2 *Fam* (*succeed*) (*of company etc*) prendre un grand essor, être en plein essor; (*of film, book etc*) faire un tabac; **the craze never took off in France** cette mode n'a jamais pris en France
▸ **take on** VT SEP **1** (*accept*) (*task*) entreprendre; (*responsibility*) assumer; **to t. sb on** (*accept challenge of*) se battre contre qn; **to t. sb on at tennis** défier qn au tennis; **to t. it on oneself to do sth** prendre sur soi de faire qch; **to t. on passengers** (*of train etc*) prendre *ou* embarquer des voyageurs
2 (*hire*) (*worker*) engager, embaucher
3 (*acquire*) (*colour, appearance*) prendre (**of** de); **the word takes on another meaning** le mot prend une autre signification
4 (*escort*) (*person*) **in the end, he took me on to the station** en fin de compte, il m'a emmené jusqu'à la gare
VI *Old-fashioned Br Fam* (*be upset*) s'en faire; **she does t. on so** elle s'en fait pour rien
▸ **take out** VT SEP **1** (*remove*) sortir (**of** de); (*tooth*) arracher; (*stain*) ôter, enlever; *Fig Fam* **it really takes it out of you!** (*is tiring*) c'est vraiment épuisant!; *Fig Fam* **to t. it out on sb/sth** passer sa colère sur qn/qch; *Fig* **to t. sb out of himself/herself** changer les idées à qn
2 (*carry*) (*chairs, washing etc*) sortir; *Am* **sandwiches to t. out** sandwich(e)s *mpl* à emporter
3 (*dog*) promener, sortir; **to t. sb out to the theatre/a restaurant** emmener qn au théâtre/restaurant; **why don't you t. me out more often?** pourquoi est-ce qu'on ne sort pas plus souvent tous les deux?; **he's taking**

me out to dinner tonight il m'invite au restaurant ce soir; **he's been taking her out for a couple of months** il sort avec elle depuis quelques mois
4 (*obtain*) (*permit, licence*) prendre, obtenir; (*insurance policy, subscription*) souscrire à; **to t. out insurance** contracter une assurance
5 *esp Am* (*destroy*) détruire; (*kill*) éliminer
▸ **take over** VT SEP **1** (*become responsible for*) (*restaurant, company etc*) prendre la direction de; **to t. over sb's job** remplacer qn; **he took over the family business** il a repris l'entreprise familiale
2 (*buy out*) (*company*) racheter
3 (*overrun*) (*country*) envahir; **she takes over** (*of bossy person etc*) elle est envahissante
4 to t. over the lead (*in race, polls*) prendre la tête
5 *Typ* transférer à la ligne suivante
VI **1** *Mil, Pol* (*assume power*) prendre le pouvoir; (*succeed*) prendre la succession (**from** de); (*of new manager etc*) prendre la direction
2 (*relieve*) prendre la relève (**from** de)
▸ **take to** VT INSEP **1** (*go to*) **to t. to the road** prendre la route; **to t. to one's heels** *or* **to flight** prendre ses jambes à son cou; **to t. to one's bed** prendre le lit, s'aliter; **to t. to the hills** se réfugier dans les collines; **to t. to the boats** monter dans les canots de sauvetage
2 (*adopt*) (*bad habits*) prendre; **he's taken to going for early-morning runs** il a pris l'habitude d'aller courir tous les matins tôt; **to t. to drink** *or* **drinking** se mettre à boire
3 (*like*) (*person*) éprouver de la sympathie pour; **they took to each other instantly** ils se sont tout de suite plu; **I didn't t. to him/it** il/ça ne m'a pas plu; **to t. to a game** prendre goût à un jeu
▸ **take up** VT SEP **1** (*lead*) (*person*) faire monter; **there's a lift to t. you up** vous pouvez monter en ascenseur; **the lift took us up to the 25th floor** l'ascenseur nous a amenés au 25ᵉ étage
2 (*carry*) (*suitcase, shopping etc*) monter
3 (*lift*) (*carpet*) enlever, déclouer; (*paving stones, railway tracks*) enlever; (*street*) dépaver, défoncer; *Rail* (*passengers*) prendre; **to t. up a book from the table** prendre un livre sur la table
4 (*shorten*) (*skirt*) raccourcir; **to t. up the slack** (*in cable*) retendre le câble
5 (*accept*) (*challenge*) relever; (*offer*) accepter; (*suggestion*) retenir; *St Exch* (*shares*) souscrire à; **to t. up a bet** tenir un pari; **to t. sb up on an offer** accepter l'offre de qn; **can I t. you up on your offer?** est-ce que ton offre tient toujours?; **I'll t. you up on that one day** je te prendrai au mot un de ces jours
6 (*discuss*) (*subject, problem etc*) parler de, discuter (**on** de); **I'd like to t. you up on what you said about ...** si vous le permettez, j'aimerais revenir sur ce que vous avez dit à propos de ...; **I'll have to t. you up on that** je ne suis pas du tout d'accord là-dessus
7 (*absorb*) (*water*) absorber
8 (*adopt*) (*idea etc*) adopter; **to t. up an attitude on sth** prendre *ou* adopter une attitude à l'égard de qch
9 (*begin*) (*career*) embrasser; (*hobby, studies*) se mettre à; (*continue*) (*task, book etc*) reprendre, se remettre à; **to t. up one's duties** entrer en fonctions; **to t. up (the thread of) the conversation** reprendre le fil de la conversation
10 (*occupy*) (*space, time*) occuper, prendre; (*attention*) absorber, occuper; **he is entirely taken up with his business** il est complètement absorbé par ses affaires
VI **to t. up with sb** se lier avec qn

takeaway ['teɪkəweɪ] *Br* ADJ (*meal, sandwich etc*) à emporter
N **1** (*café, restaurant*) café *m*/restaurant *m* qui fait des plats à emporter **2** (*sandwich*) sandwich *m* à emporter; (*dish, meal*) plat *m* à emporter; **a Chinese t.** un plat chinois à emporter

take-home ADJ
▸▸ **t. pay** salaire *m* net

taken ['teɪkən] ADJ **1** (*seat, table*) occupé, pris **2** (*impressed*) impressionné (**with** par); **he was very much t. with the idea** l'idée l'enchantait; **I was not t. with her** elle ne m'a pas fait bonne impression

takeoff ['teɪkɒf] N **1** (*mimicry*) imitation *f*; **to do a t. of sb** imiter qn **2** (*departure*) (*of plane*) décollage *m*; (*of high-jumper, long-jumper etc*) appel *m* **3** (*success*) (*of country, industry etc*) essor *m*
▸▸ **t. slot** (*for plane*) créneau *m* horaire de décollage

takeout ['teɪkaʊt] ADJ, N *Am* = **takeaway**

takeover ['teɪkəʊvər] N **1** (*of company*) prise *f* de contrôle, rachat *m* **2** *Pol* prise *f* de pouvoir
▸▸ *Fin* **t. bid** offre *f* publique d'achat, OPA *f*, **to make** *or* **launch a t. bid (for)** faire *ou* lancer une OPA (sur); **to be the subject of a t. bid** être l'objet d'une OPA; **t. fever** opeamania *f*

taker ['teɪkər] N (*of lease*) preneur *m*; (*at auction etc*) acheteur *m*, preneur; **any takers?** (*to go to cinema etc*) est-ce qu'il y a des amateurs?; **I put it up for sale but there were no takers** je l'ai mis en vente mais il n'y a pas eu d'amateurs

take-up N (*of benefits*) réclamation *f*; **the level of t. has been low** peu de gens ont profité de l'offre; **there has been a 10% t. of the grants** 10% des subventions ont été attribuées
▸▸ **t. point** (*of clutch*) point *m* de prise; *Tech* **t. reel** bobine *f* enrouleuse; *Tech* **t. spool** bobine réceptrice

taking ['teɪkɪŋ] ADJ *Old-fashioned* (*person*) attirant, séduisant; (*smile, manners*) engageant
N **1** (*of city etc*) prise *f*; **the money/job is his for the t.** il n'a qu'à accepter l'argent/le poste **2** *Com* **takings** recette *f* **3** *Old-fashioned* **to be in a t.** être agité

talc [tælk] N (*toiletry, mineral*) talc *m*

talcum ['tælkəm] N (*toiletry, mineral*) talc *m*
▸▸ **t. powder** talc

tale [teɪl] N **1** (*story*) conte *m*; (*legend*) légende *f*, **thereby hangs a t.** il y a toute une histoire là-dessous; **his drawn face told the t. of his sufferings** ses traits tirés en disaient long sur ses souffrances; **she lived to tell the t.** elle a survécu **2** (*lie*) histoire *f*; **to tell tales** raconter des histoires **3** (*account, report*) récit *m*; **to tell tales** (*sneak*) rapporter, cafarder; *Fig* **to tell tales out of school** (*be indiscreet*) être indiscret, trop parler

talebearer ['teɪlbeərər] N (*sneak*) rapporteur, -euse, cafard *m*

talent ['tælənt] N **1** (*ability*) talent *m*, don *m*; **to have a t. for sth** être doué en *ou* pour qch, avoir du talent pour qch; **to have a t. for annoying everyone/getting into trouble** avoir le don d'agacer tout le monde/de s'attirer des ennuis; **he has no t. for business** il n'a pas le don des affaires; **a woman of** *or* **with t.** une femme talentueuse *ou* de talent **2** (*person with ability*) talent *m*; *TV Sl* (*actors, presenters etc*) artistes *mpl* **3** *Br Fam* (*people of the opposite sex*) (*women*) belles nanas *fpl*, belles minettes *fpl*; (*men*) beaux mecs *mpl*; **what's the local t. like?** comment sont les nénettes/les mecs par ici?; **where does the t. hang out?** où est-ce qu'on trouve de

belles nanas/de beaux mecs? **4** *Hist (coin)*
talent *m*
▸▸ **t. scout, t. spotter** *(for films)* dénicheur,
-euse de vedettes; *(for sport)* dénicheur,
-euse de futurs grands joueurs

talented ['tæləntɪd] ADJ talentueux, de talent; *(performance)* plein de talent

taletelling ['teɪltelɪŋ] N rapportage *m*, cafardage *m*

talisman, *pl* **talismans** ['tælɪzmən] N talisman *m*

TALK [tɔːk]

| N entretien **1** ▪ conversation **1** |
| ▪ pourparlers *(talks)* **2** ▪ racontars **3** |
| ▪ exposé **6** |
| VI parler **1, 2, 4, 5** ▪ bavarder **1** |
| ▪ jaser **3** ▪ faire un discours **5** |
| VT parler |

N 1 *(conversation)* entretien *m*, conversation
f; **to have a t. with sb** *(chat)* parler *ou* s'entretenir avec qn; **we had an interesting t.** nous
avons eu une conversation intéressante; **it's
time you and I had a little t.** il est temps que
nous ayons une petite conversation; **it's
time we had a t. about your behaviour** il
est temps que nous discutions *ou* parlions
de votre conduite; **that was just sales t.** tout
ça ce n'était que des boniments
2 *(discussion)* **there is some t. of his returning** il est question qu'il revienne; **there has
been t. of it** on en a parlé, il en a été question; *Pol etc* **talks** dialogue *m*, pourparlers
mpl; **to start talks** engager le dialogue, entrer en pourparlers; **peace talks** pourparlers
de paix
3 *(rumour)* **there is some t. of his returning**
le bruit court qu'il va revenir; **it's the t. of
the town** on ne parle que de cela; **she's the
t. of the town** elle défraie la chronique;
their behaviour is causing a lot of t. leur
conduite fait jaser; **it's just t.** ce ne sont que
des racontars
4 *(words, speech)* langue *f*, langage *m*; **baby
t.** babil *m* enfantin; **double t.** *(unclear)* propos *mpl* ambigus; *(false)* propos insincères;
small t. banalités *fpl*, conversation *f* banale,
propos sans importance; **to make** *or* **indulge** *or* **engage in small t.** parler de choses
et d'autres, parler à bâtons rompus; **I'm no
good at small t.** je ne suis pas doué pour
faire la conversation
5 *(bravado)* **to be all t.** *(of person)* être fort
en gueule; **he's all t. and no action** il parle
beaucoup, mais il ne fait pas grand-chose
6 *(lecture)* exposé *m* (**on** sur); **to give a t. on**
or **about sth** faire un exposé sur qch

VI 1 *(converse)* parler; *(chat)* bavarder (**of,
about** de; **with** avec); **to t. to** *or* **with sb** parler à *ou* avec qn, s'entretenir avec qn; **to t. to
oneself** parler tout seul; **she didn't t. to me
the whole evening** elle ne m'a pas dit un mot
de la soirée; **who do you think you are talking to!** à qui croyez-vous donc parler?; **to t.
of** *or* **about doing sth** parler de faire qch; **to
t. and t.** parler sans arrêt; **don't all t. at once**
ne parlez pas tous en même temps; *Iron,
Hum* surtout, ne parlez pas tous en même
temps; **you're the only one I can t. to** tu es
le seul auquel je puisse parler *ou* me
confier; **that's no way to t.!** il ne faut pas
dire des choses pareilles!; *(referring to bad
language)* en voilà un langage!; **he likes to
hear himself t.** il s'écoute parler; **to t.
through one's hat** dire *ou* débiter des sottises; *Fam* **now you're/we're talking!** voilà
qui est mieux!; **can you** *or* **can't t.!** tu
peux (bien) parler, toi!; **to make a prisoner
t.** faire parler un prisonnier; **his accomplices
are afraid he'll t.** ses complices ont peur
qu'il ne parle; *Fam* **he talks big** il fanfaronne;
money talks avec de l'argent on peut tout

faire; **what are you talking about?** *(asking
question)* de quoi parlez-vous?; *(expressing
disbelief)* qu'est-ce que vous racontez?; **I
don't know what you're talking about** *(in
answer to accusation)* je ne sais pas ce que
vous voulez dire; **she knows what she is
talking about** elle sait de quoi elle parle, elle
s'y connaît; **t. about luck/laugh** tu parles
d'une chance/d'un fou rire
2 *(about problem, in reprimanding way)* **to
t. to sb** dire un mot *ou* deux mots à qn, parler à qn; **I'll t. to him!** je vais lui dire deux
mots!, je vais lui en toucher deux mots!
3 *(gossip)* cancaner, jaser; **people will t.** on
va jaser; **you know how people t.** tu sais
comme les gens sont cancaniers *ou* comme
les langues vont bon train; **we don't want
people to t.** il ne faut pas faire jaser; **this will
give them something to t. about** voilà
quelque chose qui va les faire jaser; **the
whole town was talking about it** toute la
ville en parlait; **to get oneself talked about**
faire parler de soi
4 *(speak)* parler; **to learn to t.** apprendre à
parler; **can he t.?** *(of bird)* est-ce qu'il parle?; **is
the baby talking yet?** est-ce que le bébé parle?
5 *(lecture)* **to t. on the radio** faire un discours *ou* parler à la radio
6 how much are we talking about? il faut
compter combien?, ça va chercher dans les
combien?; **we're talking about at least
£10,000** il faut compter au moins 10 000 livres, ça va chercher au moins dans les 10
000 livres

VT *(speak)* *(French etc)* parler; **to t. nonsense** dire des bêtises; **to t. politics** parler
politique; **to t. (common) sense** tenir des
propos raisonnables; **do t. sense!** sois sérieux!; **to t. (some) sense into sb** faire entendre raison à qn; **to t. oneself hoarse**
s'enrouer à force de parler; **to t. oneself into
a job** *(by trying to impress)* obtenir un emploi grâce à son baratin; **you've just talked
yourself into a job** *(by saying that)* ce que
vous avez dit là m'a convaincu et vous avez
le poste; **to t. oneself out of trouble** se tirer
d'affaire grâce à son baratin; **t. yourself out
of that one!** vas-y, essaie de t'en sortir cette
fois-ci!; **she can t. her way out of anything**
avec son bagou elle arrive toujours à se tirer
d'affaire; **to t. sb into/out of doing sth** per-
suader/dissuader qn de faire qch; **to t. sb into a better frame of mind** remonter le moral
à qn en lui parlant; **to t. sb out of a bad
mood** rendre à qn sa bonne humeur en lui
parlant
▸▸ **t. show** causerie *f* (radiodiffusée/télévi-
sée), talk-show *m*, *pl* talk-shows

▸ **talk away VT SEP** **to t. the night away** passer la nuit à parler; **to t. a child's fears away**
rassurer un enfant en lui parlant
VI ne pas s'arrêter de parler

▸ **talk back VI** *(answer cheekily)* répondre
avec insolence (**to** à), répliquer; **don't t.
back to me!** je te défends de me répondre

▸ **talk down VI** **to t. down to sb** parler avec
condescendance *ou* comme à un inférieur à
qn
VT SEP 1 *(silence)* réduire au silence en parlant
2 *(plane, pilot)* donner des instructions d'atterrissage à; **the priest talked the man
down from the parapet** le prêtre a persuadé
l'homme de descendre du parapet

▸ **talk out VT SEP** **to t. things out** discuter la
chose à fond; *Parl* **to t. a bill out** prolonger
les débats de façon qu'un projet de loi ne
puisse être voté avant la clôture

▸ **talk over VT SEP** *(question)* discuter (de),
débattre; **let's t. it over** discutons-en

▸ **talk round VT SEP** *(somebody)* persuader,
faire changer d'avis à; **I talked them round
to my way of thinking** je les ai amenés à
partager mon avis

VT INSEP **to t. round the problem** *or* **issue**
tourner autour du pot
▸ **talk up VT SEP** *(film, book etc)* vanter; **to t.
up sb's chances** surestimer les chances de
qn; **the Chancellor is trying to t. up the economy** le Chancelier s'est montré optimiste
pour tenter de redynamiser l'économie
VI *Am (speak openly, without hesitation)* parler franchement

talkathon ['tɔːkəθɒn] N *Am (in Congress, on
television etc)* débat-marathon *m*, *pl* débats-
marathon

talkative ['tɔːkətɪv] ADJ *(person)* *(chatty)*
causant, loquace; *(chatterbox)* bavard; **he's
very t.** il est très bavard, *Fam* il a la langue
bien pendue, il n'a pas la langue dans sa
poche

talkativeness ['tɔːkətɪvnɪs] N *(of person)*
loquacité *f*

talkback ['tɔːkbæk] N interphone *m*

talker ['tɔːkər] N *(conversationalist)* **to be a
good t.** avoir de la conversation; **to be a brilliant t.** briller dans la conversation; **my father was never much of a t.** mon père n'a
jamais été très bavard

talkie ['tɔːkɪ] N *Cin Old-fashioned Fam* film
m parlant

talking ['tɔːkɪŋ] ADJ parlant
N 1 *(discussion, conversation)* **that's enough
t.** assez parlé; **to do all the t.** *(in conversation)* faire la conversation à soi tout seul;
let me do the t. laisse-moi parler **2** *(chatter)*
bavardage *m*; **no t., please!** pas de bavardage!
▸▸ **t. book** livre *m* enregistré; **t. doll** poupée
f qui parle; *Cin* **t. film** film *m* parlant; *TV* **t.
head** *(presenter)* présentateur, -trice de télévision *(dont on ne voit que la tête et les
épaules)*; *Hum, Pej (interviewee)* = expert *m*
qui s'exprime à la télévision; **t. point** sujet
m de conversation *ou* de discussion; *Br* **t.
shop** lieu *m* de palabres; **the United Nations
is accused of being a t. shop** on accuse les
Nations Unies de ne faire que de la parlotte

talking-to N *Fam (scolding)* réprimande *f*,
semonce *f*; **to give sb a t.** passer un savon à
qn (**about** sur; **for** pour); **he needs a good t.**
il a besoin d'un bon savon

talktime ['tɔːktaɪm] N *Tel* autonomie *f*

talky ['tɔːkɪ] ADJ *Am (book, film etc)* saturé
de dialogues

tall [tɔːl] ADJ *(person)* grand; *(building etc)*
grand, haut, élevé; **how t. are you?** combien
mesurez-vous?; **she's taller than I am** elle
est plus grande que moi; **he was taller by a
head** *or* **stood a (whole) head taller than me**
il me dépassait d'une tête; **she's growing
taller** elle grandit; **he has grown t.** (qu'est-
ce qu')il a grandi; **how t. is that mast?**
quelle est la hauteur de ce mât?; **tree five
metres t.** arbre de cinq mètres de hauteur;
I'd love a t. glass of something cold je boirais
volontiers un grand verre de quelque chose
de bien frais; *Fig* **a t.** *Br* **story** *or Am* **tale** une
histoire invraisemblable *ou* à dormir de-
bout; *Fig* **that's a t. order** voilà qui va être
difficile *ou* compliqué
ADV *Fig* **to walk** *or* **stand t.** marcher la tête
haute

tallboy ['tɔːlbɔɪ] N *Br* grande commode *f*

Tallin(n) ['tælɪn] N Tallinn

tallness ['tɔːlnɪs] N *(of person)* taille *f*, *(of
building etc)* hauteur *f*

tallow ['tæləʊ] N *(fat)* suif *m*
▸▸ **t. candle** chandelle *f*

tally ['tælɪ] N **1** *(record)* *(of merchandise)*
pointage *m*; **to keep a t. of goods/names**
pointer des marchandises/des noms **2** *(calculation)* compte *m*; **to keep (a) t. of one's
score** noter son score; **to keep (a) t. of one's**

spending tenir le compte de ses dépenses; **who's keeping t.?** qui fait les comptes *ou Sport* compte les points?

VT *(goods)* pointer

VI *(of figure, report etc)* correspondre (**with** à), concorder (**with** avec); **these accounts do not t.** ces comptes ne correspondent *ou* ne concordent pas

tally-ho **INT, N** *(in hunting)* taïaut *m*, tayaut *m*

Talmud ['tælmʊd] **N** *Rel* Talmud *m*

Talmudic [tæl'mʊdɪk] **ADJ** *(scholar etc)* talmudique

Talmudist ['tælmʊdɪst] **N** Talmudiste *m*

talon ['tælən] **N** *(of bird)* serre *f*, griffe *f*, *Fig (of person)* griffe

tamable ['teɪməb(ə)l] **ADJ** = **tameable**

tamarind ['tæmərɪnd] **N** *(fruit)* tamarin *m*; *(tree)* tamarinier *m*
▸▸ **t. tree** tamarinier *m*

tamarisk ['tæmərɪsk] **N** *(plant)* tamaris *m*

tambour ['tæmbʊər] **N 1** *Sewing (frame)* tambour *m* à broder **2** *Archit, Mus* tambour *m*
▸▸ *Sewing* **t. frame** tambour à broder; **t. lace** dentelle *f* (brodée) sur tulle

tambourine [tæmbə'riːn] **N** *Mus* tambourin *m*

tame [teɪm] **ADJ 1** *(animal) (unafraid)* familier; *(domesticated)* apprivoisé; *Am (plant, land)* cultivé; **the squirrels are very t.** les écureuils sont très familiers *ou* ne sont pas farouches; **to grow** *or* **become t.** *(of animal)* s'apprivoiser **2** *(person)* soumis, docile; *(story, speech, film, show etc)* fade, banal, -als; **the story's ending was rather t.** l'histoire se terminait sur une note plutôt banale; *Hum* **we have a t. builder who does that sort of thing** on a un ouvrier très serviable qui fait ce genre de choses

VT *(animal)* apprivoiser; *(lion)* dompter; *Am (plant, wilderness)* cultiver; *(person, passion)* dominer; **to t. the elements** dominer les éléments

tameable ['teɪməb(ə)l] **ADJ** *(animal)* qu'on peut apprivoiser; *(lion etc)* domptable

tamely ['teɪmlɪ] **ADV** *(to submit)* sans résistance, docilement; **the story ends very t.** l'histoire se termine de façon très banale; **a t. worded letter of complaint** une lettre de réclamation timide

tamer ['teɪmər] **N** *(of lions etc)* dompteur, -euse

Tamil ['tæmɪl] **ADJ** tamoul, tamil *(no f)*
N 1 *(person)* Tamoul, -oule, Tamil *m* **2** *Ling* tamoul *m*, tamil *m*

taming ['teɪmɪŋ] **N** *(of animal)* apprivoisement *m*; *(of lion)*, *Fig (of person)* domptage *m*; **the T. of the Shrew** la Mégère Apprivoisée

tammy ['tæmɪ] **N** *Fam (cap)* béret *m* écossais

tam-o'-shanter [tæmə'ʃæntər] **N** béret *m* écossais

tamp [tæmp] **VT** *Constr (earth)* damer; *(pipe, tobacco)* bourrer
▸ **tamp down** **VT SEP** = **tamp**

tampax® ['tæmpæks] **N** tampon *m*, tampax® *m*

tamper ['tæmpər] **N 1** *(person)* bourreur *m* **2** *(tool)* dame *f* à fouler **3** *Phys* réflecteur *m* de neutrons
▸ **tamper with** **VT INSEP** *(interfere with) (mechanism etc)* toucher à, *Fam* trifouiller; *(lock)* essayer d'ouvrir; *(rules)* truquer; *(register)* falsifier; *(accounts, document)* truquer, tripatouiller; **to t. with sb's mail** ouvrir le courrier de qn; *Horseracing* **to t. with a horse** doper un cheval; **to t. with a witness** suborner un témoin

tampon ['tæmpɒn] **N** *Surg (of cotton wool,*

gauze) tampon *m*; *(to absorb menstrual flow)* tampon (périodique)

tan [tæn] **N 1** *(on skin)* bronzage *m*, hâle *m*; **to get a (good) t.** bronzer; **to have a t.** être bronzé *ou* hâlé; **to lose one's t.** perdre son bronzage **2** *(colour)* marron *m* clair
ADJ *(colour, shoes)* marron clair *inv*; **t. gloves** des gants *mpl* en cuir marron clair
VT (**-nn-**) *(leather)* tanner; *(of sun) (skin)* hâler, donner un hâle à; *Fam* **to t. sb** *or* **sb's hide** tanner le cuir à qn
VI *(of complexion)* se hâler, bronzer; **I t. easily** je bronze facilement
▸▸ **t. line** marque *f* de bronzage

tanager ['tænədʒər] **N** tangara *m*

tandem ['tændəm] **N** *(bicycle)* tandem *m*; **to do sth in t.** faire qch ensemble; **the party and the unions must work in t.** le parti et les syndicats doivent travailler ensemble; **in t.** *(of horses, turbines etc)* en tandem

tang [tæŋ] **N 1** *(flavour)* saveur *f* piquante, piquant *m*; **a t. of irony** une pointe d'ironie; **the t. of the morning air** l'air *m* vif du matin **2** *(of knife)* soie *f*, *(of file)* queue *f*

tangent ['tændʒənt] **N** *Geom* tangente *f*; **at a t. to a curve** tangentiellement à une courbe; *Fig* **to go off at a t.** changer de sujet

tangential [tæn'dʒenʃəl] **ADJ** *Geom etc* tangentiel; *Fig* secondaire; **that is t. to the main issue** étant donné le sujet, ceci est secondaire

tangerine [tændʒə'riːn, 'tænd-] **N** mandarine *f*
ADJ *(colour)* mandarine *inv*

tangibility [tændʒɪ'bɪlɪtɪ] **N** tangibilité *f*

tangible ['tændʒɪb(ə)l] **ADJ 1** *(palpable)* tangible, palpable **2** *(real)* réel; **t. difference** différence *f* sensible
▸▸ *Fin* **t. assets** actif *m* corporel, valeurs *fpl* matérielles; *Fin* **t. fixed assets** immobilisations *fpl* corporelles

tangibles ['tændʒɪb(ə)lz] **NPL** *Acct* actif *m* corporel, valeurs *fpl* matérielles

tangibly ['tændʒɪblɪ] **ADV 1** *(palpably)* tangiblement **2** *(really)* sensiblement

Tangier(s) [tæn'dʒɪər, -'dʒɪəz] **N** Tanger *m*

tanginess ['tæŋɪnɪs] **N** saveur *f* piquante, piquant *m*

tangle ['tæŋg(ə)l] **N** *(bundle, confusion) (of undergrowth)* fouillis *m*; *(of branches, hair, threads, barbed wire, roads)* enchevêtrement *m*; **to be (all) in a t.** *(of string etc)* être (tout) embrouillé; *(of wool, hair)* être (tout) emmêlé; *Fig (of person)* ne savoir plus où on en est; **his finances are in such a t.** ses comptes sont tellement embrouillés; **her private life is in a terrible t.** sa vie privée est un véritable sac de nœuds; **to get into a t.** *(of string, business)* s'embrouiller; *(of wool, hair)* s'enchevêtrer; *(making speech, explaining sth)* s'embrouiller, s'emmêler; **to get into an emotional t.** se mettre dans une situation compliquée sur le plan affectif
VT = **tangle up**
VI *(of string etc)* s'embrouiller, s'emmêler, s'enchevêtrer
▸ **tangle up** **VT SEP 1** *(make confused) (threads, hair)* emmêler; *(question)* embrouiller; **to get tangled up** *(of threads, wires etc)* s'emmêler; **to get tangled up in sth** *(in rope, net)* *(of animal, person)* être enchevêtré dans qch; **she had got tangled up in some barbed wire** elle était prise dans des barbelés **2** *(involve)* **he got himself tangled up in the Smith case** il s'est retrouvé impliqué dans l'affaire Smith; **they got tangled up in something dishonest** ils ont été mêlés à une affaire malhonnête
▸ **tangle with** **VT INSEP** *Fam (quarrel, fight with)* s'en prendre à; **I wouldn't t. with him if I was you** à ta place je ne me frotterais

pas à lui; **to t. with the law** avoir des démêlés avec la justice

tangled ['tæŋg(ə)ld] **ADJ** *(hair, threads)* emmêlé; *(love life, story)* embrouillé

tango ['tæŋgəʊ] **N** *(dance)* tango *m*
VI danser le tango; *Fig* **it takes two to t.** *(sexual)* il faut être deux pour ces choses-là; *(share responsibility)* tu as ta/il a sa/*etc* part de responsabilité

tangy ['tæŋɪ] **ADJ** *(flavour)* qui a un goût piquant; **the t. sea air** l'air *m* vif de la mer

tank [tæŋk] **N 1** *(container) (for water, petrol etc)* réservoir *m*; **water t.** réservoir à eau *ou* d'eau; *Naut* caisse *f* à eau; *Rail* caisse à eau, soute *f* (à eau); *(alongside track)* château *m* d'eau; **storage t.** réservoir de stockage; **a full t. (of fuel)** un plein *(de carburant)*; *Aut, Aviat* **fuel** *or Br* **petrol** *or Am* **gas(oline) t.** réservoir de carburant **2** *Ind etc (for processing etc)* cuve *f*, bac *m*; *Pol* **think t.** comité *m ou* groupe *m* d'experts; **(air/buoyancy) t.** caisson *m* (à air/de flottabilité) **3** *Mil* char *m*; *Fam* **to be built like a t.** être une armoire à glace; **the tanks** les blindés *mpl*
▸▸ *Am Rail* **t. car** wagon-citerne *m*, *pl* wagons-citernes; **t. commander** commandant *m* de char; **t. regiment** régiment *m* de chars (d'assaut); **t. top** débardeur *m*, pull *m* sans manches; **t. trap** piège *m* à chars; **t. truck** camion-citerne *m*, *pl* camions-citernes; *Rail* **t. wagon** wagon-citerne; **t. warfare** guerre *f* combattue à l'aide de chars
▸ **tank along** **VI** *Fam (go fast) (of driver, car etc)* foncer
▸ **tank up** *Br* **VI** *Aut (fill fuel tank)* faire le plein d'essence
VT SEP *(usu passive) Br Sl* **to get tanked up** *(drunk)* se prendre une biture; **to be tanked up** être bourré *ou* bituré

tankard ['tæŋkəd] **N** chope *f*, *Arch* **a t. of ale** un pot de bière

tanker ['tæŋkər] **N** *Naut* navire-citerne *m*, *pl* navires-citernes; *Rail* wagon-citerne *m*, *pl* wagons-citernes; *Aviat* avion-citerne *m*, *pl* avions-citernes; *(for refuelling)* avion *m* de ravitaillement; *Naut* **oil t.** (navire *m*) pétrolier *m*
▸▸ **t. aircraft** avion-citerne; *(for refuelling)* avion de ravitaillement; **t. lorry**, *Am* **t. truck** camion-citerne *m*, *pl* camions-citernes

tanned [tænd] **ADJ** *(leather)* tanné; *(face, complexion)* hâlé, bronzé; *(deeply, naturally)* basané

tanner[1] ['tænər] **N** *(person)* tanneur *m*

tanner[2] **N** *Hist Sl (coin)* (pièce *f* de) six pence *mpl*

tannery ['tænərɪ] **N** tannerie *f*

tannic ['tænɪk] **ADJ** *(acid)* tannique

tannin ['tænɪn] **N** tan(n)in *m*

tanning ['tænɪŋ] **N 1** *(act of tanning hides)* tannage *m*; **t. (trade)** tannerie *f* **2** *Fam (beating)* raclée *f*; **to give sb a good t.** flanquer une bonne raclée à qn
▸▸ **t. booth** cabine *f* de bronzage; **t. cream** *(self-tanning)* crème *f* autobronzante; *(for natural tan)* crème solaire

Tannoy® ['tænɔɪ] **N** système *m* de haut-parleurs; **an announcement came over the T.** il y a eu une annonce au haut-parleur

tansy ['tænzɪ] **N** *(plant)* tanaisie *f*

tantalize ['tæntəlaɪz] **VT** tourmenter, mettre au supplice

tantalizing ['tæntəlaɪzɪŋ] **ADJ** terriblement alléchant; **it's t.** c'est un vrai supplice de Tantale

tantalizingly ['tæntəlaɪzɪŋlɪ] **ADV** **the cool water was t. near** cette eau fraîche à proximité était un véritable supplice; **we came t. close to solving it** c'était exaspérant *ou* rageant de voir à quel point nous étions près de la solution

tantamount ['tæntəmaʊnt] ADJ équivalent (to à); **to be t. to sth** équivaloir à qch; **that's t. to saying I'm a liar** cela revient à dire que je mens

tantrum ['tæntrəm] N (of child) caprice m; (of adult) colère f; **to throw a t.** (of child) faire un caprice; (of adult) piquer une colère

Tanzania [tænzə'nɪə] N Tanzanie f

Tanzanian [tænzə'nɪən] ADJ tanzanien N Tanzanien, -ienne

Taoism ['taʊɪz(ə)m] N taoïsme m

Taoist ['taʊɪst] N taoïste mf

tap¹ [tæp] N 1 Br (for water) robinet m; (plug) bonde f; **to turn on/turn off the t.** ouvrir/fermer le robinet; Fig **to turn on the t.** (cry) pleurer; Fig **to turn off the t.** fermer le robinet; **on t.** (of beer etc) à la pression; Fig **to be on t.** (of person, thing) être (toujours) disponible; **they've got cheap labour on t.** ils ont de la main-d'œuvre pas chère à volonté **2** esp Am Elec prise f (intermédiaire) **3** (action) (into pipe) branchement m; Tel (of telephone communication) écoute f; Tel **who authorized the t.?** qui a autorisé la mise sur écoute? **4** Fin valeur f du Trésor aux enchères; **long/medium/short t.** valeurs fpl émises à un prix déterminé par l'État à long/moyen/court terme

VT (-pp-) **1** (barrel) percer, mettre en perce; (tree) inciser, entailler; (pine tree) gemmer; (wine) tirer; (natural resources etc) exploiter; (water course) capter; (gas or water pipe) faire un branchement sur; **we must t. all the resources we have** nous devons puiser dans toutes nos ressources; **to t. a telephone conversation** écouter une communication téléphonique à l'aide d'une table d'écoutes; **the phones are tapped** les téléphones sont sur écoute; Fam **to t. sb for fifty euros** taper qn de cinquante euros **2** Tech (nut, screw) tarauder, fileter

▸▸**t. water** eau f du robinet

tap² N **1** (light blow, sound) petit coup m; (with hand) tape f; **t. at the door** coup léger ou discret à la porte; **there was a t. on the window** on frappa à la fenêtre; **a t. on the shoulder** une tape sur l'épaule **2** Mil **to play taps** sonner l'extinction des feux

VT (-pp-) (strike lightly) (surface) taper légèrement, tapoter; (hit gently) (person) donner un petit coup à; **she tapped me on the shoulder** (to attract attention) elle m'a tapé sur l'épaule

VI **1 to t. at** or **on the door** frapper doucement à la porte **2 to t. (dance)** faire des claquettes

▸▸**t. dance** claquettes fpl (danse); **t. dancer** danseur, -euse de claquettes; **t. dancing** claquettes (danse); **to do t. dancing** faire des claquettes

▸**tap out** VT SEP **1 to t. out the rhythm** marquer le rythme; **to t. out the rhythm on the table** taper le rythme sur la table; **to t. out a message** (in morse code) émettre un message; **to t. out a message on the central heating pipes** transmettre un message en tapant sur les tuyaux du chauffage central **2 to t. out one's pipe** débourrer sa pipe

tape [teɪp] N **1** (ribbon) (of cotton) ruban m; (of cloth, paper) bande f; Sport bande d'arrivée; (for measuring) mètre m (ruban); (dressmaker's for measuring) centimètre m; **masking t.** ruban-cache m; ((self-) adhesive or Fam **sticky**) **t.** ruban adhésif, scotch® m; Pharm **adhesive t.** sparadrap m; Elec **insulating t.** ruban isolant, chatterton m; Sport **to breast the t.** franchir la ligne d'arrivée ou arriver le premier; Horseracing **the tapes** (at start) les rubans **2** (in recording) (length of tape) bande f; (cassette) cassette f (audio); (recording) enregistrement m; **magnetic** or **recording t.** bande magnétique; **(video) t.** cassette vidéo; **pre-recorded t.** bande enregistrée; **a classical t.** une cassette de musique classique; **to get** or **put sth on t.** enregistrer qch; **I've got it on t.** je l'ai en cassette

VT **1** (parcel) scotcher; (electric wire) guiper; **to t. sth to sth** scotcher qch à qch **2** Fig **I've got him taped** je sais comment il est ou ce qu'il vaut **3** (record) enregistrer; **she was taped talking to them** elle a été enregistrée en train de leur parler; **taped music** musique f enregistrée

▸▸Comput **t. backup** sauvegarde f sur bande; Comput **t. backup system** système m de sauvegarde sur bande; Comput **t. backup unit** unité f de sauvegarde sur bande; **t. deck** platine f de magnétophone; **t. drive** dérouleur m de bande (magnétique), lecteur m de bande (magnétique); **t. head** tête f de lecture; **t. library** collection f de cassettes; **t. measure** mètre (ruban); (dressmaker's) centimètre m; Comput **t. reader** lecteur de bande; **t. recorder** magnétophone m, lecteur de cassettes; **t. recording** enregistrement (sur bande magnétique); Comput **t. streamer** streamer m; **t. transport** mécanisme m d'entraînement (d'une bande magnétique); Comput **t. unit** unité f de bande

▸**tape up** VT SEP (parcel, broken object) scotcher

taper¹ ['teɪpər] N **1** (candle) bougie f filée; Rel cierge m **2** (to light candle, fire etc) allume-feu m inv

taper² VT tailler en pointe ou en cône; (hair) effiler; Archit (column) fuseler, diminuer

VI s'effiler; **column that tapers upwards** colonne f taillée en pointe; **her hair tapers in to the neck** ses cheveux sont effilés sur son cou; **it tapers to a point** c'est taillé en pointe N Archit, Constr etc (shape) conicité f, cône m

▸**taper off** VI (of line, long thin object) s'amincir, se rétrécir; (get smaller gradually) (of production, numbers etc) diminuer, se réduire

VT SEP (long thin object) effiler; (production etc) réduire, diminuer

tape-record VT enregistrer

tapered ['teɪpəd] ADJ (hair) effilé; (column, candle) en fuseau; **t. trousers** fuseau m

tapering ['teɪpərɪŋ] ADJ en pointe; (finger) effilé, fuselé; Archit (column) en fuseau; Fin **t. rate** tarif m dégressif N (in hairdressing) effilage m

tapestry ['tæpɪstrɪ] N tapisserie f

▸▸**t. maker, t. weaver** tapissier, -ière

tapeworm ['teɪpwɜːm] N ténia m, ver m solitaire

taping ['teɪpɪŋ] N (recording) enregistrement m

tapioca [tæpɪ'əʊkə] N tapioca m

tapir ['teɪpər] N (often inv in pl) (animal) tapir m

tapped out ['tæpt-] ADJ Am Fam crevé, lessivé

tappet ['tæpɪt] N Tech poussoir m

▸▸**t. clearance** jeu m aux culbuteurs

tapping¹ ['tæpɪŋ] N Tel (telephone) **t.** écoutes fpl (de communications téléphoniques)

tapping² N (knocking) petits coups mpl; (with hand) tapotement m

taproom ['tæpruːm] N bar m

taproot ['tæpruːt] N Bot racine f pivotante, pivot m

tar [taːr] N **1** (for roads, in cigarettes) goudron m; Fig Fam **to spoil the ship for a ha'porth of t.** tout gâcher pour des économies de bouts de chandelle **2** Naut Old-fashioned Fam **(Jack) t.** (sailor) loup m de mer

VT (-rr-) (road, wood) goudronner; (pavement) bitumer; Naut (boat) goudronner, brayer; **to t. and feather sb** rouler qn dans le goudron et les plumes; Fig **we're all tarred with the same brush** on nous a tous mis dans le même panier ou sac

▸▸**t. paper** papier m goudronné

ta-ra [tə'raː] INT Br Fam salut!, ciao!

taradiddle ['tærədɪd(ə)l] N Fam (lie) bobard m

tarantella [tærən'telə] N (dance), Mus tarentelle f

tarantula [tə'ræntjʊlə] N (spider) tarentule f

tardily ['taːdɪlɪ] ADV Fml **1** (late) tardivement; (too late) en retard **2** (slowly) lentement

tardiness ['taːdɪnɪs] N Fml **1** (lateness) retard m **2** (slowness) lenteur f (**in doing sth** à faire qch)

tardy ['taːdɪ] ADJ Fml **1** (late) (payment, reaction) tardif **2** (slow) lent; (unhurried) peu empressé

tare¹ [teər] N Bible **tares** (weeds) ivraie f

tare² Com N tare f; (of lorry) poids m net; (of vehicle) poids m à vide

VT (goods) tarer; (vehicle) peser à vide

target ['taːgɪt] N Mil, Fig cible f, objectif m; (person) cible; **moving t.** objectif mobile ou mouvant; **to land on t.** (of bomb etc) atteindre son objectif; **sitting t.** cible facile; Fig **to be an easy t.** être une cible facile; Fig **we're on t.** (to meet the deadline) nous sommes dans les temps (pour ce qui est du respect des échéances); **to set oneself a t.** se fixer un but ou un objectif

VT **1** Mil, Fig (aim at) (place, building etc) viser, prendre pour cible; Com (market) cibler; **they targeted the magazine at 18-to-25-year-olds** le magazine a été conçu pour les 18-25 ans; **services should be better targeted** il faudrait qu'on cible mieux les services **2** (direct) (missiles, advertising campaign) diriger

▸▸Mil **t. area** zone f cible; Mktg **t. audience** audience f cible; Mktg **t. buyer** acheteur, -euse cible; **t. company** société f opéable; Mktg **t. consumer** consommateur, -trice cible; Mktg **t. cost** coût m ciblé; **t. date** (for delivery etc) date f ciblée ou visée; Comput **t. disk** (hard) disque m cible; (floppy) disquette f cible; Comput **t. drive** unité f de destination; **t. figure** objectif m; Comput **t. file** fichier m de destination; Mktg **t. group** groupe m cible; Mktg **T. Group Index** indice m des groupes cibles; **t. language** langue f cible, langue d'arrivée; Mktg **t. market** marché m cible; Mktg **t. marketing** marketing m ciblé; Mktg **t. population** population f cible; Mil **t. practice** exercices mpl de tir; Mktg **t. price** prix m d'équilibre; Mktg **t. pricing** fixation f du prix en fonction de l'objectif; **t. readership** lectorat m cible; Com **t.-return pricing** fixation du prix en fonction du taux de rentabilité souhaité; **t. sales figure** chiffre m de ventes ciblé; **t. setting** arrêt m des objectifs

targeted ['taːgɪtɪd] ADJ visé, ciblé

targetting ['taːgɪtɪŋ] N **1** (setting targets) détermination f d'objectifs; **because of unrealistic t.** en raison d'objectifs non réalistes **2** Mktg ciblage m **3** (of funds, resources etc) **we need better t. of resources** il nous faut mieux cibler les ressources

tariff ['tærɪf] N **1** (at customs) tarif m; **reduced t.** tarif réduit; **full t.** plein tarif **2** (price list) tarif m, tableau m des prix ADJ tarifaire

▸▸**t. barrier, t. wall** barrière f douanière ou tarifaire

Tarmac® ['taːmæk] N **1** Constr macadam m, goudron m **2** Aviat (runway) piste f

VT (*pt, pp* **tarmacked**) *(road etc)* goudronner, macadamiser

tarmacadam [tɑːməˈkædəm] N = **Tarmac 1**

tarn [tɑːn] N *(in mountains)* petit lac *m* de montagne

tarnish [ˈtɑːnɪʃ] N ternissure *f*
   VT *(surface of metal, person's reputation)* ternir
   VI *(of metal etc)* se ternir

tarnishing [ˈtɑːnɪʃɪŋ] N *(of metal)* ternissure *f*

tarot [ˈtærəʊ] N *Cards* tarot *m*
   ▸▸ **t. cards** tarots

tarp [tɑːp] N *Am Fam* = **tarpaulin**

tarpaulin [tɑːˈpɔːlɪn] N *(fabric)* toile *f* goudronnée; *(sheet)* bâche *f*, prélart *m*

tarragon [ˈtærəgən] N *(plant), Culin* estragon *m*
   ▸▸ **t. vinegar** vinaigre *m* à l'estragon

tarry[1] [ˈtɑːrɪ] ADJ **1** *(made of tar)* goudronneux, bitumineux **2** *(covered, stained with tar)* couvert de goudron

tarry[2] [ˈtærɪ] VI *Lit* **1** *(stay)* rester, demeurer (**at** *or* **in a place** dans un endroit) **2** *(delay)* s'attarder (**over sth** sur qch)

tarsus, *pl* **tarsi** [ˈtɑːsəs, -aɪ] N *Anat* tarse *m*

tart[1] [tɑːt] N **1** *esp Br Culin* tarte *f*, *(small)* tartelette *f* **2** *Fam (prostitute)* putain *f*, poule *f*, *Pej (promiscuous woman)* pute *f*, *(woman)* pépée *f*, *Pej* grognasse *f*, *Pej* **the silly t.** cette andouille

tart[2] ADJ *(in taste)* au goût âpre, aigrelet; *(tone)* acerbe, aigre
   ▸ **tart up** VT SEP *Fam usu Pej (room, car etc)* retaper; **to t. oneself up** se faire beau; **this car's just a tarted up version of the …** cette voiture n'est qu'une version améliorée du …

tartan [ˈtɑːt(ə)n] N *Tex (cloth or pattern)* tartan *m*, écossais *m*; **t. shirt** chemise *f* écossaise
   ▸▸ **T. Army** = surnom *m* donné aux supporters de l'équipe de football d'Écosse

Tartar [ˈtɑːtər] ADJ tatar
   N **1** Tatar, *f* Tatare **2** *Fig Pej (man)* homme *m* intraitable; *(woman)* mégère *f*

tartar [ˈtɑːtər] N *(on teeth), Chem* tartre *m*

tartar(e) sauce [ˈtɑːtə] N sauce *f* tartare

tartaric [tɑːˈtærɪk] ADJ *Chem (acid etc)* tartrique

tartly [ˈtɑːtlɪ] ADV *(to say)* d'un ton acerbe

tartness [ˈtɑːtnɪs] N *(of fruit, wine, tone)* aigreur *f*

tarty [ˈtɑːtɪ] ADJ *Sl Pej (clothes etc)* vulgaire; **to look t.** avoir l'air d'une pute

tash [tæʃ] N *Br Fam (abbr* **moustache**) moustache *f*, bacchantes *fpl*

task [tɑːsk] N **1** travail *m*, -aux, tâche *f*; **these are your tasks** voici votre travail; **their t. is to …** leur travail *ou* tâche consiste à …; **the unpleasant t. of informing the parents** la tâche désagréable d'informer les parents; **it's an endless t.** c'est un travail sans fin; **to set sb a t.** imposer une tâche à qn **2 to take sb to t. for (doing) sth** prendre qn à partie *ou* réprimander qn pour (avoir fait) qch
   VT **to t. sb with sth/doing sth** charger qn de qch/faire qch

taskbar [ˈtɑːskbɑːr] N *Comput* barre *f* des tâches

taskforce [ˈtɑːskfɔːs] N *Mil* corps *m* expéditionnaire; *Fig (to investigate)* commission *f*, *(to do special job)* groupe *m* de travail

taskmaster, taskmistress [ˈtɑːskmɑːstər, -mɪstrɪs] N **he is a hard t.** il est terriblement exigeant; *(stronger)* c'est un véritable tyran

Tasmania [tæzˈmeɪnɪə] N Tasmanie *f*

Tasmanian [tæzˈmeɪnɪən] ADJ tasmanien
   N Tasmanien, -ienne

TASS [tæs] N *Formerly (abbr* **telegraphic news agency of the Soviet Union**) TASS *f*

tassel [ˈtæs(ə)l] N **1** *(on furniture, clothing etc)* gland *m* **2** *Bot (on corn)* barbe *f*

tasselled [ˈtæs(ə)ld] ADJ à glands, orné de glands

TASTE [teɪst]

N goût **1, 2, 4, 5** ▪ saveur **1**
VT sentir **1** ▪ percevoir la saveur de **1**
▪ goûter **2** ▪ déguster **2** ▪ goûter à **3**
VI avoir le goût de *(to taste of)*

N 1 *(flavour)* goût *m*, saveur *f*; **it has a burnt t.** cela a un goût de brûlé; **this drink has no t.** cette boisson n'a pas de goût *ou* est insipide; *Fig* **the whole business left a nasty t. in my mouth** toute cette histoire m'a franchement dégoûté *ou* m'a laissé un méchant arrière-goût

   2 *(sense of)* **t.** goût *m*

   3 *(small amount)* **t. of cheese** *etc* un petit peu de fromage *etc*; **a t. of wine** *etc* une petite gorgée de vin *etc*; **have a t. of this claret** goûtez-moi ce bordeaux; *Fig* **to give sb a t. of the whip** faire tâter du fouet à qn; **this was my first t. of freedom** c'était la première fois que je goûtais à la liberté; **she's already had a t. of prison** elle a déjà tâté de la prison; **is this a t. of things to come?** est-ce là un avant-goût de ce qui nous attend?; **to give sb a t. of their own medicine** rendre à qn la monnaie de sa pièce

   4 *(liking)* goût *m* (**for** pour); **to have a t. for** *(music etc)* aimer, avoir le goût de; **to have expensive tastes** avoir des goûts de luxe; **to acquire** *or* **develop a t. for sth** prendre goût à qch; **to find sth to one's t.** trouver qch à son goût; *Culin* **add sugar to t.** on ajoute du sucre à volonté; **it's a matter of t.** c'est une question de goût; *Prov* **everyone to his t.** des goûts et des couleurs on ne discute pas, chacun ses goûts

   5 *(judgement)* goût *m*; **she has excellent t. in dress** elle s'habille avec (beaucoup de) goût; **to be in perfect t.** être d'un goût parfait; **in bad t.** de mauvais goût; **it would be bad t. to wear that to a funeral** il serait de mauvais goût de porter cela à un enterrement

   VT **1** *(distinguish taste of)* sentir, percevoir la saveur de; **I can't t. anything when I have a cold** les aliments n'ont plus aucun goût quand je suis enrhumé; **can't you t. the cinnamon?** tu ne sens pas la cannelle?; **I can t. something like cloves in it** ça sent un peu le clou de girofle

   2 *(sample quality of) (dish)* goûter; *(wines, teas etc)* déguster

   3 *(get a little taste of)* goûter de *ou* à; *(liquid)* boire une petite gorgée de; *Fig (whip, prison etc)* tâter de; **I haven't even tasted it** je n'y ai pas même goûté; **he had not tasted food for three days** il n'avait pas mangé depuis trois jours; **to t. happiness/success** goûter au bonheur/à la réussite

   VI **the cake tasted of lemon** le gâteau avait un goût de citron; **it tastes like spinach** ça a un goût d'épinard; **to t. good/bad** être bon/mauvais, avoir un bon/mauvais goût; **it tastes fine to me** moi je trouve ça bon; **it tastes salty** c'est salé; **it tastes funny** ça a un drôle de goût; **it doesn't t. of anything to me** moi, je trouve que ça ne sent rien; *esp Lit* **to t. of despair/defeat** connaître le désespoir/la défaite
   ▸▸ **t. bud** papille *f* gustative

tasteful [ˈteɪstfʊl] ADJ *(remark, action)* de bon goût; *(decoration)* fait avec goût

tastefully [ˈteɪstfəlɪ] ADV avec goût

tastefulness [ˈteɪstfʊlnɪs] N bon goût *m*

tasteless [ˈteɪstlɪs] ADJ **1** *(food etc)* sans

goût, fade, insipide; **the poison is t. and odourless** le poison est inodore et sans saveur **2** *(clothes, remarks etc)* de mauvais goût

tastelessly [ˈteɪstlɪslɪ] ADV *(to dress, furnish etc)* sans goût

tastelessness [ˈteɪstlɪsnɪs] N **1** *(of food)* insipidité *f*, fadeur *f* **2** *(of person, clothes, remark etc)* manque *m* de goût

taster [ˈteɪstər] N **1** *(person) (of wines, teas etc)* dégustateur, -trice **2** *(foretaste)* **this is just a t. (of what's to come)** ceci n'est qu'un avant-goût (de ce qui va suivre)

tastiness [ˈteɪstɪnɪs] N saveur *f ou* goût *m* agréable

tasting [ˈteɪstɪŋ] N *(of wines)* dégustation *f*

tasty [ˈteɪstɪ] ADJ **1** *(dish, meal)* savoureux; **it's not very t.** ça n'a pas beaucoup de goût; **a t. morsel** un mets succulent **2** *Br Fam (good-looking)* bien foutu; **she's a t. piece** c'est un beau morceau

TAT [tiːeɪˈtiː] N *Mktg (abbr* **thematic apperception test**) TAT *m*

tat[1] [tæt] N *see* **tit**[2]

tat[2] N *Fam (junk)* camelote *f*

ta-ta [tæˈtɑː] INT *Br Fam* au revoir!

Tatar [ˈtɑːtər] ADJ tatar
   N Tatar *m*, Tatare *f*
   ▸▸ **the T. Republic** la République de Tatarie

Tatary [ˈtɑːtərɪ] N Tatarie *f*

tater [ˈteɪtər] N *Br Sl (potato)* patate *f*

tatter [ˈtætər] N lambeau *m*, loque *f*; **in tatters** en lambeaux, en loques; *Fig (reputation, confidence)* anéanti; **to tear sb's reputation to tatters** ruiner la réputation de qn

tattered [ˈtætəd] ADJ *(clothes)* en loques, en lambeaux; *(person)* déguenillé, loqueteux

tattie [ˈtætɪ] N *esp Scot Fam (potato)* patate *f*

tattle [ˈtæt(ə)l] N *(gossip, rumour)* commérages *mpl*, potins *mpl*
   VI *(gossip)* commérer, cancaner

tattler [ˈtætlər] N *(gossip, rumour-monger)* commère *f*, cancanier, -ière

tattle-tale N = **telltale**

tattoo[1] [təˈtuː] N *Mil* **1** *(drum signal)* retraite *f* (du soir); **to beat** *or* **sound the t.** battre *ou* sonner la retraite **2** *(parade)* parade *f* militaire

tattoo[2] N *(design)* tatouage *m*; **a t. of an anchor, an anchor t.** un tatouage représentant une ancre
   VT tatouer
   ▸▸ **t. artist** tatoueur *m*

tattooing [təˈtuːɪŋ] N tatouage *m*

tattooist [təˈtuːɪst] N tatoueur *m*

tatty [ˈtætɪ] ADJ *Fam (in poor condition)* miteux; *(of poor quality)* minable

taught PT, PP *see* **teach**

taunt [tɔːnt] N *(words)* sarcasme *m*, raillerie *f*
   VT accabler de sarcasmes; **to t. sb into action** pousser qn à agir en usant de sarcasmes; **to t. sb with sth** railler qn à propos de qch

taunting [ˈtɔːntɪŋ] ADJ sarcastique, railleur

tauntingly [ˈtɔːntɪŋlɪ] ADV d'un ton sarcastique *ou* railleur

Taurus [ˈtɔːrəs] N *Astrol* Taureau *m*; **to be (a) T.** être (du) Taureau

taut [tɔːt] ADJ *(rope)* tendu; *(muscle)* tendu, contracté; *(prose, style, sentence)* dépouillé; **she looked t.** elle avait l'air tendu; **t. situation** situation *f* tendue

tauten [ˈtɔːt(ə)n] VT *(cable etc)* tendre
   VI se tendre

tautness [ˈtɔːtnɪs] N *(of cable etc)* raideur *f*, *(of muscles)* tension *f*, *(of piece of prose)* caractère *m* dépouillé

tautological [tɔːtəˈlɒdʒɪk(ə)l] ADJ tautologique

tautology [tɔːˈtɒlədʒɪ] N tautologie f

tavern [ˈtæv(ə)n] N (in proper names), Lit taverne f, cabaret m

tawdriness [ˈtɔːdrɪnɪs] N (of piece of jewellery) clinquant m, faux éclat m; (of decor) clinquant; **there was a t. about everything in the hotel** tout dans l'hôtel était clinquant

tawdry [ˈtɔːdrɪ] ADJ **1** (clothing, ornament) tape-à-l'œil, tapageur; (decor) clinquant; **t. jewellery** clinquant m, toc m; **a t. hotel** un hôtel à la décoration tape-à-l'œil **2** (conduct, motive etc) lâche

tawny [ˈtɔːnɪ] ADJ fauve
▸▸ Orn **t. eagle** aigle m ravisseur; Orn **t. owl** chouette f hulotte; **t. port** = porto m qui a jauni dans le fût

tax [tæks] N **1** Admin impôt m, taxe f; **you pay out a small fortune in t.** on paye une petite fortune en impôts; **after t.** net, après impôt; **before t.** hors taxe, HT; (income) avant impôt; **direct/indirect t.** impôt direct/indirect; **income t.** impôt sur le revenu; **capital gains t.** impôt sur les plus-values; **Am value added t., Am processing t.** taxe à la valeur ajoutée; **to levy a t. on sth** frapper qch d'un droit; **t. exempt** exempt d'impôts; **t. paid** net d'impôt **2** (strain) charge f
VT **1** Admin (person) imposer, frapper d'un impôt; (luxury items etc) taxer; **to t. income** imposer le revenu; **to be heavily taxed** être lourdement imposé; **small businesses are being taxed out of existence** accablées d'impôts, les petites entreprises disparaissent; **we're being taxed out of existence** on nous accable d'impôts; Br Aut **taxed** avec vignette
2 (put under strain) mettre à l'épreuve; **to t. sb's intellect/imagination** éprouver l'intelligence/l'imagination de qn; **to t. sb's patience to the limit** abuser sérieusement de la patience de qn
3 esp Lit (accuse) **to t. sb with sth** taxer qn de qch; **to t. sb with doing sth** accuser qn d'avoir fait qch
4 Br Fam (steal) taxer, piquer, chouraver
▸▸ **t. allowance** abattement m fiscal, déduction f fiscale; **t. assessment** avis m d'imposition, fixation f de l'impôt; **t. audit** vérification f fiscale; **t. authorities** administration f fiscale; **t. avoidance** optimisation f ou évasion f fiscale, Can évitement m fiscal; **t. band** tranche f d'imposition; **t. base** assiette f fiscale; **t. benefit** avantage m fiscal; **t. bite** proportion f du revenu pris par l'impôt; **t. bracket** tranche f d'imposition, fourchette f d'imposition; **t. break** réduction f d'impôt, allègement m fiscal; **t. burden** pression f fiscale, poids m de la fiscalité; **t. ceiling** plafond m fiscal, plafond de l'impôt; **t. centre** centre m des impôts, CDI m; **t. clearance** quitus m fiscal; **t. code** barème m fiscal; **t. collection** recouvrement m d'impôts, perception f d'impôts; **t. collector** percepteur m d'impôt, receveur m des contributions; **t. consultant** conseiller, -ère fiscal(e), conseil m fiscal; **t. credit** aide f fiscale, avoir m fiscal; **t. cut** baisse f ou réduction f des impôts; **t. deduction** prélèvement m fiscal, déduction f fiscale; **t. deduction at source** perception f à la source; Br **t. disc** vignette f (automobile); Am **t. dollars** argent m du contribuable; **t. domicile** foyer m ou domicile m fiscal; **t. evasion** fraude f fiscale, évasion f fiscale; **t. exemption** exonération f d'impôt, exemption d'impôt; **t. exile** = personne f qui réside à l'étranger pour minimiser la responsabilité fiscale; **t. expenditure** dépenses fpl fiscales; **t. expert** fiscaliste mf, **t. form** feuille f ou déclaration f d'impôts; **t. fraud** fraude f fiscale; **t. harmonization** harmonisation f fiscale; **t. haven** paradis m fiscal; **t. holiday** période f de grâce (accordée pour le paiement des impôts); **t. impact**

incidence f fiscale; **t. incentive** incitation f fiscale, avantage m fiscal; **t. inspection** contrôle m fiscal; **t. inspector** inspecteur, -trice des contributions directes ou des impôts; **t. law** droit m fiscal; **t. liability** (of person) assujettissement m à l'impôt; (of goods, product) exigibilité f de l'impôt; **t. loophole** échappatoire f fiscale; **t. loss** déficit m fiscal reportable; Br Fam **the t. man** le fisc; **t. office** centre m des impôts; **t. official** agent m du fisc; **t. point** date f de facturation; **t. provision** disposition f fiscale; **t. rate** taux m d'imposition; **t. rebate** dégrèvement m fiscal; **t. reduction** abattement m fiscal; **t. refund** (of income tax) restitution f d'impôts; (on goods) détaxe f; **t. relief** dégrèvement m fiscal; **t. return** déclaration f de revenu, feuille f d'impôts; **to make one's t. return** faire sa déclaration d'impôts; **t. revenue** recettes fpl ou rentrées fpl fiscales; **t. roll** rôle m d'impôt ou des contributions; **t. shelter** échappatoire f fiscale; **t. shield** protection f fiscale; **t. specialist** fiscaliste mf; **t. and spend** = financement m des grandes dépenses budgétaires par des taux d'imposition élevés; **t. stamp** timbre m fiscal; **t. system** régime m fiscal ou d'imposition; **t. threshold** minimum m imposable, seuil m d'imposition; **t. tolerance** tolérance f fiscale; **t. write-off** (expense) dépense f déductible des impôts; (loss) perte f déductible des impôts; **t. year** année f fiscale, année d'imposition (qui commence en avril en Grande-Bretagne)

taxable [ˈtæksəbl] ADJ **1** (revenue, land etc) imposable, taxable; **to make sth t.** imposer qch **2** Law **costs t. to sb** frais mpl à la charge de qn
▸▸ **t. base** base f d'imposition; **t. income** revenu m imposable, assiette f fiscale ou de l'impôt; **t. profit** bénéfice m fiscal ou imposable; **t. transaction** opération f imposable

taxation [tækˈseɪʃən] N (imposing taxes) imposition f, (taxes) charges fpl fiscales; (tax revenue) impôts mpl, taxes fpl; **t. at source** prélèvement m de l'impôt à la source, imposition f à la source

tax-deductible ADJ déductible des impôts

tax-free ADJ (income) exempt d'impôts, (goods) exonéré de taxes
▸▸ **t. shop** boutique f hors taxes; **t. shopping** achats mpl hors taxes

taxi [ˈtæksɪ] N taxi m; **to go by t.** aller en taxi
VI (pt, pp **taxied**; prp **taxiing**) (of aircraft) rouler; **the plane taxied back to the terminal** l'avion regagna le terminal
▸▸ **t. driver** chauffeur m de taxi; **t. fare** (in general) tarif m du taxi; (cost of journey) coût m du taxi, prix m de la course (en taxi); **t. rank**, esp Am **t. stand** station f de taxis

taxicab [ˈtæksɪkæb] N taxi m

taxidermist [ˈtæksɪdɜːmɪst] N taxidermiste mf

taxidermy [ˈtæksɪdɜːmɪ] N taxidermie f

taximeter [ˈtæksɪmiːtər] N taximètre m, compteur m (de taxi)

taxing [ˈtæksɪŋ] ADJ (job, course) ardu; **these long hours are very t.** ces longues journées sont complètement éreintantes

taxiplane [ˈtæksɪpleɪn] N avion-taxi m, pl avions-taxis

taxonomic [tæksəˈnɒmɪk] ADJ taxonomique

taxonomy [tækˈsɒnəmɪ] N taxonomie f

taxpayer [ˈtækspeɪər] N contribuable mf

TB [tiːˈbiː] N Med (abbr **tuberculosis**) tuberculose f

T-bar N Ski téléski m, tire-fesses m inv

T-bone N
▸▸ Culin **T. steak** steak m d'aloyau

tbs, tbsp Culin (abbr **tablespoonful**) cuillerée f à soupe

T-card N fiche f en T

TCP® [tiːsiːˈpiː] N (antiseptic) ≃ Merchryl® m

TCP/IP [tiːsiːpiːaɪˈpiː] N Comput (abbr **transmission control protocol/Internet protocol**) TCP-IP m

TD [tiːˈdiː] N Pol abbr = membre m de la chambre basse du Parlement irlandais

tea [tiː] N **1** (leaves, drink) thé m; (herbal infusion) tisane f, infusion f; **camomile** etc **t.** infusion de camomille etc; **to drink t.** boire ou prendre du thé; **a cup of t.** une tasse de thé; **t. and coffee making facilities** nécessaire m pour préparer le thé et le café; **China t.** thé de Chine; **black/green t.** thé noir/vert
2 esp Br (meal) (afternoon) **t.** thé m, = goûter m; **high t.** repas m du soir; Scot, North Eng **t.** (dinner) dîner m; **to ask sb to t.** inviter qn à (venir) prendre le thé; **to give a t. party** inviter des gens pour le thé; (for children) organiser un goûter
3 (plant) thé m
▸▸ **t. bag** sachet m de thé; **t. blend** mélange m de thés; Br **t. boy** = jeune employé m chargé de préparer le thé pour ses collègues; Br **t. break** pause f pour prendre le thé, pause-thé f, pl pauses-thé; **t. caddy** boîte f à thé; **t. chest** caisse f (à thé); Br **t. cloth** torchon m (à vaisselle); **t. cosy** couvre-théière m, pl couvre-théières; Br **t. lady** = dame f qui prépare ou sert le thé pour les employés d'une entreprise; **t. leaf** feuille f de thé; Br Sl (thief) voleur, -euse; **(used) t. leaves** marc m de thé; **to read the t. leaves** ≃ lire dans le marc de café; **t. plant** arbre m à thé, théier m; **t. plantation** plantation f de thé; **t. planter** planteur m de thé; **t. rose** rose f thé; **t. service, t. set** service m à thé; **t. strainer** passoire f à thé, passe-thé m inv; **t. table** table f (mise) pour le thé, table à thé; Br **t. towel** torchon m (à vaisselle); **t. urn** fontaine f à thé

teacake [ˈtiːkeɪk] N Br Culin = sorte de petit pain

teach [tiːtʃ] VT (pt, pp **taught** [tɔːt]) (subject) enseigner; **to t. sb sth, to t. sth to sb** enseigner ou apprendre qch à qn; **to t. sb (how) to do sth** apprendre à qn à faire qch; **to t. oneself sth** apprendre qch tout seul; **your Japanese is very good, who taught you?** tu parles très bien japonais, qui t'a appris?; **I taught myself** j'ai appris tout seul; **who taught you to drive!** où as-tu appris à conduire!; **can you t. me the butterfly stroke?** est-ce que tu peux m'apprendre la nage papillon?; **he teaches the young pupils** il fait la classe ou l'école aux petits; **she teaches the piano** elle est professeur de piano; **he teaches French** il enseigne le français, il est professeur de français; Am **to t. school** enseigner; (as profession) être dans l'enseignement; **the way history is taught** la manière dont on enseigne l'histoire; Prov **you can't t. your grandmother to suck eggs** ce n'est pas au vieux singe qu'on apprend à faire la grimace; Fam **to t. sb a lesson** donner une leçon à qn; Fam **that'll t. him!** ça lui apprendra!; Fam **to t. sb a thing or two** dégourdir qn; Fam **I'll t. you to speak to me like that!** je vous apprendrai à me parler comme ça!
VI enseigner; (as profession) être dans l'enseignement; **she has taught abroad** elle a enseigné à l'étranger; **when you've been teaching for 25 years …** quand tu as passé 25 ans dans l'enseignement …
N Fam (teacher) prof mf

teachable [ˈtiːtʃəb(ə)l] ADJ **1** (person) qui apprend facilement **2** (subject) enseignable; **it's not t.** c'est impossible à enseigner; **it's not easily t.** cela n'est pas facile à enseigner

teacher ['ti:tʃər] N (at primary school) instituteur, -trice, maître, -esse d'école; (at secondary school) professeur m, enseignant, -ante; **history/French/maths t.** professeur d'histoire/de français/de maths; **to become a t.** devenir professeur
▸▸**t.'s pet** chouchou mf du professeur; **t.-pupil ratio** taux m d'encadrement des élèves; Br **t. training** formation f pédagogique des enseignants; **to do one's t. training** suivre une formation pédagogique; **to get one's t. training certificate** obtenir son certificat d'aptitude pédagogique; Br **t. training college** centre m de formation pédagogique, ≃ école f normale

teach-in N séminaire m

teaching ['ti:tʃɪŋ] N **1** (profession, action) enseignement m; **a low/high standard of maths/language t.** un niveau bas/élevé dans l'enseignement des maths/des langues; **to go into t.** entrer dans l'enseignement **2** (classes) cours mpl; **most of the t. is done in the morning** la plupart des cours ont lieu le matin **3** (doctrine) doctrine f; **teachings** préceptes mpl
▸▸**t. aids** matériel m ou équipement m pédagogique; **t. hospital** centre m hospitalo-universitaire, CHU m; **t. method** méthode f d'enseignement; Br **t. practice** stage m pédagogique (pour futurs enseignants); **the t. profession** (teachers) le corps enseignant; **the t. staff** (of primary school) les instituteurs mpl; (of secondary school) les professeurs mpl

teacup ['ti:kʌp] N tasse f à thé

teacupful ['ti:kʌpfʊl] N (measure) tasse f (of de)

teak [ti:k] N (wood, tree) teck m, tek m

teal [ti:l] N (pl usu **teal**) (duck) sarcelle f

team [ti:m] N (of players, workers etc) équipe f; (of horses, oxen) attelage m; **football t.** équipe de football; **he's one of the t.** il fait partie de l'équipe; **a t. effort** un travail d'équipe; **he's not much of a t. player** (at football), Fig il n'a pas l'esprit d'équipe VOIR **GRAMMAIRE A11**
VT & VI = team up
▸▸**t. games** jeux mpl d'équipe; **t. member** membre m d'une équipe; Sport équipier m; **t. spirit** esprit m d'équipe; **t. sports** sports mpl d'équipe
▸**team up** VI s'associer (**with sb** avec qn); **the two companies have teamed up to work on this project** les deux entreprises se sont associées pour travailler sur ce projet
VT SEP associer, mettre en collaboration (**with** avec)

team-mate N Sport coéquipier m

teamster ['ti:mstər] N **1** (of mules etc) conducteur m (d'attelage), charretier m **2** Am (trucker) camionneur m, routier m; **the Teamsters** (union) = syndicat m américain des camionneurs

teamwork ['ti:mwɜ:k] N (combined effort) travail m d'équipe; (ability to work together) collaboration f, Sport jeu m d'équipe; **success due to t.** réussite due à un travail d'équipe

teapot ['ti:pɒt] N théière f

tear[1] [tɪər] N (from eye) larme f; **in tears** en larmes; **on the verge of tears** au bord des larmes; **to burst into tears** fondre en larmes, éclater en sanglots; **to bring tears to sb's eyes** faire venir des larmes aux yeux de qn; **to shed bitter tears/tears of joy** verser des larmes amères/de joie; **crocodile tears** larmes de crocodile
▸▸**t. duct** canal m lacrymal; **t. gas** gaz m lacrymogène; **t. gas bomb** bombe f lacrymogène

tear[2] [teər] N (rip) déchirure f, (in garment) accroc m

VT (pt **tore** [tɔːr]; pp **torn** [tɔːn]) (dress, letter etc) déchirer; **to t. a muscle** (of person) se déchirer un muscle; **torn tendon** tendon m déchiré; **to t. a hole in sth** faire un trou ou un accroc à qch; **to t. sth in two** ou **in half** déchirer qch en deux; **to t. sth open** ouvrir qch en le déchirant; **to t. sth to pieces** (document, bank note etc) déchirer qch en mille morceaux; Fig (film, argument etc) mettre qch en pièces; **the fox was torn to pieces by the hounds** le renard a été déchiqueté ou mis en pièces par la meute; Fig **to t. sb to pieces** mettre qn en pièces, écharper qn; Fig **they'll t. you to pieces** ils vont vous mettre en pièces, vous allez vous faire écharper; Fig **to t. sb's character to shreds** or **pieces** démolir qn; **country torn by civil war** pays déchiré par la guerre civile; **torn between two feelings** tiraillé entre deux émotions; Fig **that's torn it** il ne manquait plus que ça; Fig **to t. one's hair** s'arracher les cheveux
VI **1** (of material, muscle etc) se déchirer **2 to t. at sth** déchirer qch
▸**tear about, tear around** VI (rush around) courir partout; **I've been tearing around on my bike all day** j'ai pédalé comme un fou toute la journée; **he's always tearing around** il est toujours à se démener; **he tears about from auction to auction** il est toujours à courir d'une vente aux enchères à une autre
VT INSEP **he spends most of his time tearing around the country** il passe la plus grande partie de son temps à sillonner le pays; **to t. around the shops** faire des courses en vitesse; **to t. around a museum** parcourir un musée à toute vitesse
▸**tear along** VI (go fast) aller à toute vitesse, Fam foncer; **to t. along at top speed** aller à toute vitesse; **to t. along at 100 mph** foncer à 100 à l'heure
VT INSEP (go fast on) **he was tearing along the road** (in vehicle, on bike) il dévalait la rue; (on foot) il descendait la rue à toute vitesse
▸**tear away** VT SEP **1** (remove by tearing) arracher (**from** de) **2 to t. oneself away from** (leave reluctantly) (television, book etc) s'arracher de; **I couldn't t. myself away from the place** je n'arrivais pas à me décider à partir
VI (leave at high speed) partir à toute vitesse; (of car) démarrer en trombe
▸**tear down** VT SEP (take down forcefully) (poster etc) arracher (**from** de); (wall, building etc) démolir; (statue) renverser
▸**tear into** VT INSEP **1** (attack physically) attaquer, assaillir; **the lion's teeth tore into the antelope's flesh** le lion lacéra la chair de l'antilope de ou avec ses crocs **2** (attack verbally) incendier, passer un savon à
▸**tear off** VT SEP (detach by tearing) arracher (**from** de); **he had had one of his arms torn off by a machine** il avait eu le bras arraché par une machine; Fam **to t. sb off a strip, to t. a strip off sb** donner ou passer un savon à qn
VI = tear away VI
▸**tear out** VT SEP (remove by tearing) arracher (**from** de); **to t. a page out of a book** arracher une page d'un livre; Fig **he was tearing his hair out** il s'arrachait les cheveux
VI (leave at high speed) partir en trombe; **she tore out of the house after them** elle sortit en trombe de la maison derrière eux
▸**tear up** VT SEP **1** (tear into small pieces) (letter etc) déchirer; (ground, fields etc) (of tanks, car wheels etc) labourer; (deliberately) (of JCB) défoncer; (contract) déchirer; Fig oublier **2** (pull up) (plant, tree) déraciner; (railings, telegraph pole) arracher
VT INSEP (go up fast) **to t. up the stairs** monter l'escalier quatre à quatre

tearaway ['teərəweɪ] N Br casse-cou m inv

teardrop ['tɪədrɒp] N larme f

tearful ['tɪəfʊl] ADJ (person) en pleurs; (farewell) déchirant; **in a t. voice** avec des larmes dans la voix; **she gets all t.** les larmes lui montent aux yeux

tearfully ['tɪəfəlɪ] ADV (crying) en pleurant; (on verge of tears) les larmes aux yeux

tearing ['teərɪŋ] N (of fabric etc) déchirement m; **a t. sound** un bruit de déchirure; Fam **to be in a t. hurry** être terriblement pressé

tearjerker ['tɪədʒɜːkər] N Fam (film, book) mélo m

tearless ['tɪəlɪs] ADJ **t. grief** chagrin m sans larmes

tear-off ADJ (label etc) perforé; (reply slip etc) détachable
▸▸**t. calendar** calendrier m éphéméride; Comput **t. menu** menu m flottant

tearoom ['tɪəruːm] N salon m de thé

tearstained ['tɪəsteɪnd] ADJ (face) (dirty) barbouillé de larmes; (in tears) baigné de larmes

tease [tiːz] N **1** (person) taquin, -ine; **he's a t.** il est taquin **2** (sexual) (woman) allumeuse f; **don't be a t.** arrête de m'allumer
VT **1** (person) taquiner; (dog etc) embêter; (maliciously) tourmenter; **to t. sb about sth** taquiner qn à propos de qch **2** (sexually) allumer **3** Tex (comb out) (fabric etc) effiler, effilocher; (wool) démêler **4 he teased the wire through the slot** avec beaucoup de minutie, il a réussi à mettre le fil dans la fente; **he teased the engine into life** il a réussi à démarrer la voiture à force de la bichonner
VI **don't worry, he's just teasing** ne t'inquiète pas, il fait ça pour rire
▸**tease out** VT SEP **1** Fig **she carefully teases out the important facts** elle prend soin de dégager les faits importants; **to t. information out of sb** faire donner des informations à qn **2** Tex = tease VT **3**

teasel ['tiːz(ə)l] N **1** (plant) cardère f **2** Tex carde f

teaser ['tiːzər] N **1** = tease **2** Fam (problem) question f difficile, colle f; (advert) aguiche f
▸▸Mktg **t. ad** aguiche f, Mktg **t. campaign** campagne f teasing

teashop ['tiːʃɒp] N salon m de thé

teasing ['tiːzɪŋ] ADJ (tone etc) taquin N (provoking) taquinerie f

teasingly ['tiːzɪŋlɪ] ADV (in a teasing tone) sur le ton de la taquinerie; (in order to tease) pour taquiner

teaspoon ['tiːspuːn] N cuillère f ou cuiller f à café

teaspoonful ['tiːspuːnfʊl] N cuillerée f à café

teat [tiːt] N (of woman) mamelon m, bout m de sein, téton m; (of cow etc) trayon m; (of feeding bottle) tétine f

teatime ['tiːtaɪm] N l'heure f du thé

teazel, teazle ['tiːz(ə)l] N = teasel

tech [tek] N Br Fam (abbr **technical college**) ≃ IUT m

techie ['tekɪ] N Comput Fam = terme péjoratif ou humoristique désignant les informaticiens

technical ['teknɪk(ə)l] ADJ (term, dictionary, problem etc) technique; (difficulty) d'ordre technique; **don't get t.** n'emploie pas de termes trop techniques
▸▸Comput **t. assistance** assistance f technique; **t. college** ≃ IUT m; St Exch **t. correction** correction f d'un cours en Bourse; **t. director** directeur m technique; **t. drawing** dessin m industriel; Br **t. hitch** incident m technique; Boxing **t. knockout** knock-out m

inv technique; **t. manager** directeur *m* technique; *Law* **t. offence** quasi-délit *m*, *pl* quasi-délits; *Cin*, *TV* **t. operator** preneur *m* de son, opérateur *m* du son; **t. specifications** spécifications *fpl* techniques; **t. standard** norme *f* technique; *Comput* **t. support** support *m* technique

technicality [tekni'kælɪtɪ] **N 1** (*of term*) technicité *f* **2** (*detail*) détail *m* technique; (*technical term*) terme *m* technique; *Law* **she was acquitted on a t.** elle a été acquittée sur un point de droit

technically ['teknɪklɪ] **ADV 1** techniquement; (*to express oneself*) en termes techniques; **t., it shouldn't be able to fly** d'un point de vue technique, il ne devrait pas pouvoir voler **2** (*strictly, in reality*) en réalité; **t. (speaking), you're not allowed to do that** théoriquement tu n'as pas le droit de faire ça

technician [tek'nɪʃən] **N** technicien, -ienne

Technicolor® ['teknɪkʌlər] **ADJ**, **N** *Cin* Technicolor® *m*

technique [tek'niːk] **N** technique *f*; **his t. is poor** il manque de technique

techno ['teknəʊ] **N** *Mus* techno *f*

technobabble ['teknəʊbæb(ə)l] **N** jargon *m* technique

technocracy [tek'nɒkrəsɪ] **N** technocratie *f*

technocrat ['teknəkræt] **N** technocrate *mf*

technological [teknə'lɒdʒɪk(ə)l] **ADJ** technologique

technologist [tek'nɒlədʒɪst] **N** technologue *mf*, technologiste *mf*

technology [tek'nɒlədʒɪ] **N** technologie *f*; **the lastest t.** la technologie de pointe *ou* la plus avancée
▸▸ **t. transfer** transfert *m* de technologie

technophobia [teknəʊ'fəʊbɪə] **N** technophobie *f*

techy ['tetʃɪ] **ADJ** = tetchy

tectonic [tek'tɒnɪk] **ADJ** tectonique

tectonics [tek'tɒnɪks] **NPL** tectonique *f* VOIR GRAMMAIRE A10

Ted [ted] **N** *Br Fam* (*teddy boy*) ≃ blouson *m* noir

tedder ['tedər] **N** *Agr* (*machine*) faneuse *f*

teddy ['tedɪ] **N** (*toy*) ours *m* en peluche
▸▸ **t. bear** ours en peluche; *Br* **t. boy** ≃ blouson *m* noir (*personne*)

tedious ['tiːdɪəs] **ADJ** (*job, speech etc*) ennuyeux, fastidieux; (*person, film*) ennuyeux; **how t. for you!** comme c'est ennuyeux!; **as he explained in t. detail** comme il l'a expliqué avec force détails fastidieux

tediously ['tiːdɪəslɪ] **ADV** d'une manière ennuyeuse *ou* fastidieuse

tediousness, tedium ['tiːdɪəsnɪs, -dɪəm] **N** (*of job, existence, film*) manque *m* d'intérêt

tee [tiː] *Golf* **N** (*support for ball*) tee *m*; (*piece of ground*) tertre *m ou* point *m* de départ
VT (*ball*) mettre sur un tee
▸ **tee off** **VI** *Golf* jouer le départ
▸ **tee up** **VI** *Golf* placer la balle sur le tee
VT SEP *Golf* **to t. up the ball** placer la balle sur le tee; *Fig* **to t. up a deal** préparer le terrain pour obtenir un contrat; **to t. up a job for sb** apporter un travail à qn sur un plateau

teem [tiːm] **VI 1** grouiller, fourmiller (**with** de); (*with ideas*) regorger (**with** en) **2** **the rain was teeming down** la pluie tombait à verse; **it's teeming with rain** il tombe des cordes

teeming ['tiːmɪŋ] **ADJ 1** grouillant **2 in the t. rain** sous la pluie battante

teen [tiːn] *Fam* **ADJ** = teenage
▸▸ **t. idol** idole *f* des jeunes

teenage ['tiːneɪdʒ] **ADJ** (*boy, girl etc*) adoles-

cent, jeune; (*problems*) de l'adolescence; (*party, novels*) d'adolescents; **in her t. years** quand elle était adolescente; **t. magazine** magazine *m* pour adolescents

teenager ['tiːneɪdʒər] **N** adolescent, -ente

teenpic ['tiːnpɪk] **N** *Cin Fam* film *m* d'ados

teens [tiːnz] **NPL** **one's t.** l'adolescence *f*; **to be in one's t.** être adolescent(e); **to be hardly out of one's t.** avoir juste vingt ans

teeny-bopper ['tiːnɪbɒpər] **N** *Fam* petite minette *f*

teeny(-weeny) ['tiːnɪ('wiːnɪ)], **teensy (weensy)** ['tiːnzɪ('wiːnzɪ)] **ADJ** *Fam* minuscule, tout petit; **just a t. drop, please** juste une toute petite goutte, s'il vous plaît

teeshirt ['tiːʃɜːt] **N** tee-shirt *m*, T-shirt *m*

teeter ['tiːtər] **VI** (*be unsteady*) chanceler; *Fig* **to t. on the brink of ruin/war** être à deux doigts de la ruine/d'un conflit armé
N *esp Am* (*seesaw*) jeu *m* de bascule, tapecul *m*

teethe [tiːð] **VI** (*usu in progressive tenses*) faire ses (premières) dents, percer ses dents

teething ['tiːðɪŋ] **N** dentition *f*, poussée *f* dentaire
▸▸ **t. ring** anneau *m* de dentition; **t. troubles** douleurs *fpl* provoquées par la poussée des dents; *Fig* difficultés *fpl* initiales *ou* de départ

teetotal [tiː'təʊt(ə)l] **ADJ** qui ne boit jamais d'alcool

teetotalism [tiː'təʊtəlɪz(ə)m] **N** abstention *f* de toute boisson alcoolisée; **after two weeks of enforced t.** après une quinzaine de jours au régime sec

teetotaller, *Am* **teetotaler** [tiː'təʊt(ə)lər] **N** personne *f* qui ne boit jamais d'alcool

TEFL ['tef(ə)l] **N** (*abbr* **Teaching of English as a Foreign Language**) enseignement *m* de l'anglais langue étrangère
▸▸ **T. course** formation *f* en anglais langue étrangère

tegument ['tegjʊmənt] **N** tégument *m*

Teh(e)ran [teə'rɑːn] **N** Téhéran

tel (*abbr* **telephone**) tél.

telebanking ['telɪbæŋkɪŋ] **N** monétique *f*, (*home banking*) banque *f* à domicile

telecast ['telɪkɑːst] **N** *TV* émission *f* de télévision
VT (*pt, pp* telecast) téléviser

telecaster ['telɪkɑːstər] **N** (*broadcaster*) téléaste *mf*; (*broadcasting company*) société *f* de télédiffusion

telecine ['telɪsɪnɪ] **N** télécinéma *m*

telecomms ['telɪkɒmz] **NPL** télécommunications *fpl*

telecommunications [telɪkəmjuːnɪ'keɪʃənz] **N** télécommunications *fpl*
▸▸ **t. engineer** technicien *m* des télécommunications; **t. industry** industrie *f* des télécommunications; **t. link** liaison *f* de télécommunications; **t. media** médias *mpl* de télécommunication; **t. network** réseau *m* de télécommunications; **t. satellite** satellite *m* de télécommunications

telecommute ['teləkəmjuːt] **VI** faire du télétravail, télétravailler

telecommuter ['teləkəmjuːtər] **N** télétravailleur, -euse

telecommuting ['teləkəmjuːtɪŋ] **N** télétravail *m*

teleconference ['telɪkɒnf(ə)rəns] **N** téléconférence *f*

teleconferencing ['telɪkɒnf(ə)rənsɪŋ] **N** téléconférences *fpl*

telefilm ['telɪfɪlm] **N** téléfilm *m*, film *m* télévisé

telegenic [telɪ'dʒenɪk] **ADJ** télégénique

telegram ['telɪgræm] **N** télégramme *m*; **greetings t.** télégramme de félicitations
▸▸ **t. form** formule *f* de télégramme

telegraph ['telɪgrɑːf] **N** télégraphe *m*; *Fam* **bush t.** téléphone *m* arabe
VT (*news*) télégraphier; (*person*) télégraphier à; *Sport* **to t. a punch/pass/***etc* télégraphier un coup/une passe/*etc*
VI télégraphier
▸▸ **t. pole** poteau *m* télégraphique; **t. wire** fil *m* télégraphique

telegrapher [tɪ'legrəfər] **N** *Am* télégraphiste *mf*

telegraphese [telɪgrə'fiːz] **N** langage *m ou* style *m* télégraphique

telegraphic [telɪ'græfɪk] **ADJ** télégraphique
▸▸ **t. money order** mandat *m* télégraphique; **t. payment** paiement *m* télégraphique; **t. transfer** transfert *m* télégraphique

telegraphist [tɪ'legrəfɪst] **N** télégraphiste *mf*

telegraphy [tɪ'legrəfɪ] **N** télégraphie *f*

telejector ['telɪdʒektər] **N** *TV* projecteur *m* de télévision

telekinesis [telɪkɪ'niːsɪs] **N** télékinésie *f*

telemarket ['telɪmɑːkɪt] **N** télémarché *m*

telemarketing ['telɪmɑːkɪtɪŋ] **N** télémarketing *m*

telematics [telɪ'mætɪks] **N** télématique *f* VOIR GRAMMAIRE A10

Telemessage® ['telɪmesɪdʒ] **N** *Br* télégramme *m*

telemeter ['telɪmiːtər] **N** (*in surveying*) appareil *m* de télémesure; *Mil etc* télémètre *m*

teleological [telɪə'lɒdʒɪk(ə)l] **ADJ** *Phil* téléologique

teleology [telɪ'ɒlədʒɪ] **N** *Phil* téléologie *f*

telepathic [telɪ'pæθɪk] **ADJ** télépathique; (*person*) télépathe; **you must be t.!** tu dois avoir des dons de télépathie!; **tell me, I'm not t.!** dis-le moi, je ne suis pas médium!

telepathically [telɪ'pæθɪklɪ] **ADV** (*to communicate*) par télépathie

telepathy [tɪ'lepəθɪ] **N** télépathie *f*

telepayment ['telɪpeɪmənt] **N** télépaiement *m*

telephone ['telɪfəʊn] **N** téléphone *m*; **to be on the t.** (*be subscriber*) avoir le téléphone, être abonné au téléphone; (*be speaking on it*) être au téléphone; **to speak to sb on the t.** avoir qn au téléphone; **come on, get off the t.!** allez, raccroche!; **you're wanted on the t.** on vous demande au téléphone; **to have a good t. manner** savoir bien parler au téléphone; *Mil* **field t.** téléphone de campagne; **public t.** téléphone public VOIR GRAMMAIRE A77
VI téléphoner (**to** à); **to t. for a taxi** appeler un taxi (par téléphone)
VT (*message*) téléphoner; (*person*) téléphoner à; **to t. a warning** envoyer un avertissement par téléphone; **to t. a bomb-warning to the police** prévenir la police par téléphone d'une alerte à la bombe
▸▸ **t. banking** opérations *fpl* bancaires par téléphone, banque *f* à domicile; **t. book** annuaire *m* (téléphonique); **t. booking** réservation *f* par téléphone; *Am* **t. booth** cabine *f* téléphonique; **t. box** cabine *f* téléphonique; **t. call** appel *m* téléphonique, coup *m* de téléphone; *Mktg* **t. canvassing** prospection *f* téléphonique, démarchage *m* à distance, télédémarchage *m*; **t. code area** circonscription *f* téléphonique; **t. conversation** conversation *f* téléphonique; **t. directory** annuaire *m* (téléphonique); **t. exchange** central *m* téléphonique; *Mktg* **t. follow-up** relance *f* téléphonique; **t. help desk** assis-

tance *f* téléphonique; **t. interview** entretien *m* téléphonique, entretien par téléphone; **t. interviewing** enquête *f* téléphonique, sondage *m* par téléphone; **t. jack** fiche *f* téléphonique; *Br* **t. kiosk** cabine *f* téléphonique; **t. line** ligne *f* téléphonique; **t. link** liaison *f* téléphonique; **t. marketing** marketing *m* téléphonique, télémarketing *m*; **t. memo** fiche *f* téléphonique; **t. message** message *m* téléphoné *ou* téléphonique; **t. message pad** bloc *m* télé-mémo; **t. network** réseau *m* téléphonique; **t. number** numéro *m* de téléphone; **t. operator** téléphoniste *mf*, standardiste *mf*; **t. order** commande *f* téléphonique *ou* par téléphone; *Mktg* **t. prospecting** télédémarchage *m*, démarchage *m* à distance; **t. reservation** réservation *f* par téléphone *ou* téléphonique; **t. sales** ventes *fpl* par téléphone, téléventes *fpl*; **t. salesman** télévendeur *m*, téléacteur *m*; **t. saleswoman** télévendeuse *f*, téléactrice *f*; **t. selling** vente *f* par téléphone, télévente *f*; **t. services** services *mpl* téléphoniques; **t. subscriber** abonné, -ée du téléphone; **t. survey** enquête *f* téléphonique, enquête par téléphone; **t. switchboard** standard *m* téléphonique

telephonic [telɪˈfɒnɪk] ADJ téléphonique

telephonist [tɪˈlefənɪst] N *Br* téléphoniste *mf*

telephony [tɪˈlefənɪ] N téléphonie *f*

telephotography [telɪfəˈtɒɡrəfɪ] N téléphotographie *f*

telephoto lens [telɪˈfəʊtəʊ] N téléobjectif *m*

teleplay [ˈtelɪpleɪ] N pièce *f* écrite pour la télévision

teleprinter [ˈtelɪprɪntər] N téléimprimeur *m*

teleprocessing [telɪˈprəʊsesɪŋ] N *Comput* télégestion *f*

Teleprompter® [ˈtelɪprɒm(p)tər] N *TV* téléprompteur *m*, télésouffleur *m*

telesales [ˈtelɪseɪlz] N télévente(s) *f(pl)*, phoning *m*
  ▸▸ **t. person** télévendeur, -euse, téléacteur, -trice

telescope [ˈtelɪskəʊp] N **(reflecting) t.** télescope *m* (à réflexion *ou* à miroir); **(refracting) t.** lunette *f* (d'approche), longue-vue *f*, *pl* longues-vues; *Astron* réfracteur *m*; **radio t.** radiotélescope *m*
  VT *(train etc)* télescoper; *Fig (condense)* condenser (**into** en)
  VI *(of train etc)* se télescoper; **parts made to t.** pièces qui s'emboîtent

telescopic [telɪˈskɒpɪk] ADJ **1** télescopique; *(visible with telescope)* visible au télescope **2** *(expanding)* télescopique; *(gangway etc)* coulissant; **t. tripod** trépied *m* télescopique; **t. umbrella** parapluie *m* télescopique; ▸▸ **t. damper** amortisseur *m* télescopique; **t. lens** téléobjectif *m*; **t. sight** lunette *f*

teleselling [ˈtelɪselɪŋ] N télévente *f*

teleshopping [ˈtelɪʃɒpɪŋ] N télé-achat *m*

teletex [ˈtelɪteks] N *Comput* télétex *m*

teletext [ˈtelɪtekst] N *TV* télétexte *m*

telethon [ˈtelɪθɒn] N *TV* téléthon *m*

Teletype® [ˈtelɪtaɪp] N télétype *m*

teletyper [ˈtelɪtaɪpər] N télétype *m*

teletypewriter [telɪˈtaɪpraɪtər] N *Am* = teleprinter

televangelism [telɪˈvændʒəlɪz(ə)m] N = prêche *m* évangéliste à la télévision

televangelist [telɪˈvændʒəlɪst] N = évangéliste *mf* qui prêche à la télévision

televiewer [ˈtelɪvjuːər] N téléspectateur, -trice

televise [ˈtelɪvaɪz] VT téléviser

television [telɪˈvɪʒən] N télévision *f*, *(set)* téléviseur *m*, (poste *m* de) télévision; **closed-circuit t.** télévision *f* à *ou* en circuit fermé; **colour t.** télévision (en) couleur; **colour t. (set)** téléviseur couleur; **pay t.** télévision payante; **what's on t.?** qu'est-ce qu'il y a à la télévision?; **I saw it on t.** je l'ai vu à la télévision; **have you been on t.?** êtes-vous passé à la télévision?; **to watch t.** regarder la télévision; **from a t. point of view** d'un point de vue télévisuel; **it makes/doesn't make good t.** ça n'a/n'a pas un bon impact télévisuel; **a film made for t.** un téléfilm
  ▸▸ **t. advertisement** publicité *f* télévisée; **t. advertising** publicité *f* télévisée; **t. archives** archives *fpl* télévisuelles; **t. audience** *(reached by advertising)* audience *f* télévisuelle; **t. broadcaster** télédiffuseur *m*; **t. broadcasting network** réseau *m* de télédistribution; **t. camera** caméra *f* de télévision; **it's my first time in front of the t. cameras** c'est la première fois que je suis devant les caméras; **t. campaign** campagne *f* télévisuelle; **t. channel** chaîne *f* de télévision; **t. commentary** téléreportage *m*; **t. commercial** spot *m*; **t. crew** équipe *f* de télévision; **t. on demand** télévision *f* à la demande; **t. drama** dramatique *f*; **t. engineer** réparateur *m* de télévisions; **t. guide** journal *m* de télévision; **t. interview** interview *f* télévisée *ou* à la télévision; **t. journalism** journalisme *m* de télévision; **t. journalist** journaliste *mf* de télévision; *Br* **t. licence (fee)** redevance *f*, *(document)* quittance *f* de télévision; **t. movie** téléfilm *m*, film *m* pour la télévision; **t. network** réseau *m* télévisuel; **t. news** journal *m* télévisé, JT *m*; **t. personality** vedette *f* de la télévision; **t. play** pièce *f* de théâtre pour la télévision; **t. programme** émission *f* de télévision; **t. receiver** récepteur *m* de télévision; **t. rights** droits *mpl* de télédiffusion; **t. room** salle *f* de télévision; **t. screen** écran *m* de télévision; **t. series** série *f* télévisée; **t. set** téléviseur *m*, (poste *m* de) télévision *f*; **t. show** spectacle *m* télévisé; **t. sponsoring** parrainage-télévision *m*; **t. station** studios *mpl* de télévision; **t. studio** studio *m* de télévision; **t. tie-in** *(arrangement)* partenariat *m* avec la télévision; **t. tube** tube *m* cathodique; **t. viewer** téléspectateur, -trice; *Mktg* **t. viewing panel** panel *m* de téléspectateurs

televisual [telɪˈvɪʒʊəl] ADJ télévisuel

teleworking [ˈtelɪwɜːkɪŋ] N télétravail *m*

telewriting [ˈtelɪraɪtɪŋ] N téléécriture *f*

telex [ˈteleks] N télex *m*; **to send sth by t.** télexer qch
  VT *(message)* télexer; **I'll t. you** je vous enverrai un télex
  ▸▸ **t. operator** télexiste *mf*; **t. transfer** virement *m* par télex

TELL [tel] *(pt, pp told* [təʊld]*)*

VT	dire **1** ▪ raconter **1** ▪ différencier **2** ▪ reconnaître **2** ▪ compter **4**
VI	se faire sentir **3**

VT **1** *(say)* dire; *(story etc)* raconter; **to t. the truth** dire la vérité; **to t. a lie** dire un mensonge; **to t. sb sth** dire qch à qn; **I know – Dennis told me** je sais – Dennis me l'a dit; **she doesn't t. me anything** elle ne me dit *ou* raconte rien; **to t. sb a joke** raconter une blague à qn; **to t. sb a lie** dire *ou* raconter un mensonge à qn; **can you t. me the way to the station?** pouvez-vous m'indiquer le chemin de la gare?; **I can't t. you how pleased I am** je ne saurais vous dire combien je suis content; **we are told that ...** on nous informe *ou* dit que ...; **I told you no!** je t'ai dit non!; **it's just as I told you** c'est exactement ce que je t'avais dit; **I told you so!, didn't I t. you!, what did I t. you!** je te l'avais bien dit!;

you're telling me! à qui le dis-tu?, tu l'as dit!; **are you telling me (that) you spent £50 on that?** tu ne vas pas me dire que tu as payé 50 livres pour ça?; **t. me another!** à d'autres!; *esp Am Fam* **t. him goodbye (for me)!** dis-lui au revoir de ma part!; **I'll t. you what happened** je vais vous raconter ce qui est arrivé; *Fam* **(I) t. you what!** *(solving problem, making suggestion)* bon!; **t. me something about yourself** parlez-moi un peu de vous(-même); **to hear t. of ...** entendre parler de ...; **to hear t. that ...** entendre dire que ...; **that would be telling!** ça c'est mon secret!; *Fam* **to t. teacher** rapporter, cafarder; **to t. the time** *(of clock)* donner l'heure; **to t. sb the time** *(of person)* dire l'heure qu'il est *ou* donner l'heure à qn; **to t. sb about sb** parler de qn à qn; **she wrote to t. me of her father's death** elle m'a écrit pour m'annoncer la mort de son père; **t. me what you know about it** dites-moi ce que vous en savez; **let me t. you ...** permets-moi de te dire ...; **it's not so easy, let me t. you!** ce n'est pas si facile, je t'assure *ou* je te le dis!; **what does this t. us about his character?** qu'est-ce que cela nous apprend sur son caractère?; **this example tells us nothing about the meaning of the word** cet exemple ne nous renseigne absolument pas sur le sens du mot

2 *(discern)* **it's difficult to t. the difference between them** c'est difficile de les différencier; **to t. good from bad** *or* **right from wrong** discerner le bien du mal; **you can hardly t. him from his brother** c'est à peine si on peut le distinguer de son frère; **in the dark it was hard to t. friend from foe** dans l'obscurité il était difficile de distinguer ses amis de ses ennemis; **one can t. him by his voice** on le reconnaît à sa voix; **she can't t. the time** elle ne sait pas lire l'heure; **one** *or* **you can t. (that) she's lived abroad** on voit qu'elle a vécu à l'étranger; **I can t. it from the look in your eyes** ça se lit dans tes yeux; **I could t. they were lying** je voyais bien qu'ils mentaient; **we couldn't t. if he was angry** *or* **not** nous n'arrivions pas à savoir s'il était en colère ou non; **nobody can t. what the future has in store for us** on ne peut pas savoir ce que l'avenir nous réserve; **there's no telling what he might do!** je ne sais pas comment il va réagir!

3 *(order etc)* **to t. sb to do sth** dire à qn de faire qch; **you can't t. me what to do!** tu n'as pas à me dire ce que je dois faire!; **t. him to come** dis-lui de venir; **do as you are told!** fais ce qu'on te dit; **she'll do as she's told!** elle fera ce qu'on lui dira (de faire)!

4 *(count)* *(votes)* compter; *Rel* **to t. one's beads** égrener son chapelet; **all told** au total; **I made £100 out of it all told** en tout j'ai gagné 100 livres; **I had quite a good holiday all told** en fin de compte *ou* tout compte fait j'ai passé de bonnes vacances

VI **1** *(say)* **please don't t.** ne dis rien, s'il te plaît; **time will t.** qui vivra verra; **more than words can t.** plus qu'on ne saurait dire

2 *(discern)* **it's difficult** *or* **hard to t.** c'est difficile à dire; **it's too early to t.** il est trop tôt pour se prononcer; **who can t.?, there's no telling!** qui sait?; **you never can t.** on ne sait jamais; **it's a male – how can you t.?** c'est un mâle – comment le sais-tu?

3 *(have effect)* *(of drug etc)* produire son effet; *(of sleepless nights etc)* se faire sentir; **breeding will t.** bon sang ne saurait mentir; **it will t. against you** cela vous nuira

▸ **tell apart** VT SEP *(distinguish)* **I can't t. them apart** je n'arrive pas à les distinguer l'un de l'autre *ou* à les différencier

▸ **tell of** VT INSEP **1** *(of story, poem etc)* raconter l'histoire de

2 *(indicate, reveal)* **faces which t. of ...** des visages dans lesquels se lit ...; **rings under her eyes told of sleepless nights** on voyait à ses yeux cernés qu'elle avait passé des nuits blanches

▶ **tell off** VT SEP **1** *Fam (scold)* gronder (**about sth** à propos de qch); **he told them off in no uncertain terms** il leur a dit leurs quatre vérités **2** *Mil etc (assign) (sb for duty)* désigner

▶ **tell on** VT INSEP **1** *(affect badly)* **the heat is telling on him** il commence à souffrir de la chaleur; **his age is beginning to t. on him** il commence à accuser son âge; **the effects of the embargo were beginning to t. on the country's economy** les effets de l'embargo commençaient à se faire sentir sur l'économie du pays **2** *Fam (inform on)* dénoncer; **I'll t. on you!** je le dirai!

teller ['telər] N **1** *(of story etc)* conteur, -euse **2** *(in bank etc)* guichetier, -ière; *Parl (of votes)* scrutateur m

telling ['telɪŋ] ADJ **1** **t. blow** coup m bien asséné *ou* qui porte; **what he said had a t. effect** ce qu'il a dit a porté; **a t. criticism/ remark** une critique/remarque bien sentie; **a t. speech** un discours percutant **2** *(revealing)* révélateur, -trice; **her remarks were very t.** ses remarques étaient très révélatrices ◼ N **the t. of tales plays an important part in their culture** les contes oraux jouent un rôle important dans leur culture; **it loses nothing in the t.** ça ne perd rien à être raconté
▶▶ **t. off** réprimande f; **to give sb a t. off** gronder qn

telltale ['telteɪl] N *(person)* rapporteur, -euse, cafard, cafte ◼ ADJ **a t. sign** un signe révélateur; **a t. odour** une odeur qui ne trompe pas

tellurium [te'lʊərɪəm] N *Chem* tellure m

telly ['telɪ] N *esp Br Fam* télé f; **on the t.** à la télé
▶▶ **t. addict** accro mf de la télé

Telnet ['telnet] N *Comput* Telnet m

temerity [tɪ'merɪtɪ] N témérité f, audace f; **she had the t. to accuse me!** elle a eu l'audace de m'accuser!

temp[1] [temp] *Fam* N intérimaire mf, *(temporary secretary)* secrétaire mf intérimaire; **to do t. work** faire de l'intérim; *(as secretary)* être secrétaire intérimaire ◼ VI faire de l'intérim; *(as secretary)* être secrétaire intérimaire

temp[2] *(abbr* **temperature)** température

temper ['tempər] N **1** *(anger)* colère f, *(bad mood)* mauvaise humeur f; **in an outburst of t.** dans un mouvement de colère; **to be in a t.** être en colère; **to be in a good/bad t.** être de bonne/mauvaise humeur; **to send sb into a t.** mettre qn en colère; *Fam* **t.(, t.)!** du calme!, on se calme!; **to keep one's t.** rester calme, garder son calme; **to lose one's t.** se mettre en colère, s'emporter; **to fly into a t.** piquer une colère **2** *(character)* caractère m, tempérament m; **fiery/even t.** caractère fougueux/égal; **she's got (quite) a t.** elle a un sacré caractère; **to have a quick t.** s'emporter facilement **3** *Metal (of steel)* coefficient m de dureté, trempe f ◼ VT **1** *Tech (steel, blade)* donner la trempe à; *(metal)* recuire, adoucir **2** *(moderate) (action etc)* modérer, adoucir; *(one's grief etc)* maîtriser; *(one's enthusiasm etc)* tempérer, modérer; **to t. justice with mercy** faire preuve de clémence **3** *(piano)* accorder par tempérament

tempera ['tempərə] N *Art* **to paint in t.** peindre à tempera
▶▶ **t. painting** détrempe f

temperament ['temp(ə)rəmənt] N *(character)* caractère m, tempérament m; **an outburst** *or* **show of t.** un coup de colère

temperamental [temp(ə)rə'ment(ə)l] ADJ **1**

(difference etc) du tempérament; **he has a t. aversion to conflict/hard work** fondamentalement il déteste les conflits/le travail **2** *(person)* capricieux, fantasque; *(machine)* capricieux; **his knee has been a bit t. since his accident** son genou lui joue des tours depuis son accident

temperamentally [temp(ə)rə'ment(ə)lɪ] ADV *(by nature)* de nature; **t. different** d'un tempérament différent; **they were t. unsuited** *(of couple)* leurs caractères étaient incompatibles; **she's t. unsuited to this sort of work** elle n'est pas de nature à *ou* elle n'a pas le caractère pour faire ce genre de travail

temperance ['temp(ə)rəns] N **1** *(moderation) (in taking pleasure, eating, drinking etc)* tempérance f, modération f, retenue f **2** *(abstinence from alcohol)* tempérance f, sobriété f
▶▶ **t. hotel** = hôtel m où l'on ne sert pas de boissons alcoolisées; **t. movement** mouvement m antialcoolique; **t. society** ligue f antialcoolique

temperate ['temp(ə)rət] ADJ **1** *(climate, zone etc)* tempéré **2** *(language etc)* modéré, mesuré

temperature ['temp(ə)rətʃər] N température f; **fall in t., t. drop** chute f de température; **room t.** température ambiante; **at room t.** *(of wine)* chambré; **the t. was in the thirties** il faisait plus de trente degrés; *Med* **to take sb's t.** prendre la température de qn; **to have a raised t., to have** *or* **to run a t.** avoir de la température *ou* de la fièvre; **he's got a t. of forty** il a quarante de fièvre; *Fig* **to judge the t. of a meeting** prendre la température d'une réunion; **to raise/lower the t.** faire monter/faire baisser la température
▶▶ **t. chart** feuille f de température; **t. gauge** indicateur m de température; **t. sensor** capteur m de température

tempered ['tempəd] ADJ *(steel)* trempé, recuit; **t. safety glass** verre m de sécurité trempé

-tempered [-'tempəd] SUFF **to be good-/bad-t.** *(habitually)* avoir un bon/mauvais caractère; *(on one occasion)* être de bonne/ mauvaise humeur; **to be quick-t.** s'emporter facilement

tempest ['tempɪst] N *Lit* tempête f, tourmente f

tempestuous [tem'pestjʊəs] ADJ **1** *(weather, wind etc)* de tempête **2** *(meeting etc)* orageux, tempétueux; *(person, mood, relationship etc)* turbulent, agité

tempestuously [tem'pestjʊəslɪ] ADV **1** *Lit* **the winds blew t. outside** un vent de tempête soufflait au dehors **2** *(violently) (to argue etc)* violemment

tempestuousness [tem'pestjʊəsnɪs] N **1** *(of weather)* violence f **2** *(of meeting)* caractère m orageux; *(of crowd)* turbulence f, agitation f

temping ['tempɪŋ] N intérim m
▶▶ **t. agency** société f d'intérim

Templar ['templər] N *Hist* **(Knight) T.** Templier m, chevalier m du Temple

template ['templɪt] N **1** *(in metalworking), Carp etc* gabarit m, calibre m, patron m **2** *Comput (for keyboard)* réglette f, *(for program)* modèle m; *(for DTP document)* gabarit m

temple[1] ['temp(ə)l] N *Rel* temple m

temple[2] N *Anat* tempe f

tempo, *pl* **tempi** ['tempəʊ, -iː] N *Mus* tempo m; *Fig* **strikes that upset the t. of production** grèves qui perturbent le rythme de la production

temporal[1] ['tempər(ə)l] ADJ **1** *(power etc)* temporel **2** *Gram* temporel

temporal[2] ADJ *Anat (bone etc)* temporal, -aux

temporarily ['temp(ə)rərɪlɪ, tempə'reərɪlɪ] ADV temporairement; *(for the present time)* momentanément, temporairement; **we were t. delayed** nous avons été retardés quelques minutes

temporary ['temp(ə)rərɪ] ADJ *(office, entrance etc)* temporaire; *(hearing loss etc)* momentané, passager; *(work, employee)* intérimaire; **the improvement is only t.** l'amélioration n'est que passagère *ou* momentanée; **on a t. basis** temporairement; *(to work)* par intérim; **to exercise t. command** commander par intérim; **this will at least give you t. relief** cela vous soulagera pendant un moment; **t. appointment** poste m temporaire; *Admin* emploi m amovible; **t. job** emploi temporaire
▶▶ **t. contract** *(for employment)* contrat m de mission d'intérim, contrat temporaire; *Comput* **t. file** fichier m temporaire; *Law* **t. injunction** injonction f temporaire; **t. manager** directeur, -trice intérimaire; **t. replacement** suppléance f, *Am Law* **t. restraining order** injonction f du tribunal; **t. surface** *(of road)* revêtement m provisoire; **t. work** intérim m; **t. worker** intérimaire mf

temporize ['tempəraɪz] VI *Fml (seek to gain time)* temporiser, chercher à gagner du temps

tempt [tem(p)t] VT tenter; **to t. sb to do sth** inciter qn à faire qch; **to let oneself be tempted** se laisser tenter, céder à la tentation; **I'm tempted to try** je suis tenté *ou* j'ai envie d'essayer; **the fine weather tempted us to go out** le beau temps nous a donné envie de sortir; **to t. providence/fate** tenter la providence/le sort; **don't t. me!** ne me tente pas!

temptation [tem(p)'teɪʃən] N tentation f; **to throw** *or* **put t. in sb's way** exposer qn à la tentation; **to give in** *or* **yield to t.** succomber *ou* céder à la tentation; *Bible* **lead us not into t.** ne nous soumets pas à la tentation; **there's a great t. to say that …** on est très tenté de dire que …

tempter ['tem(p)tər] N tentateur m

tempting ['tem(p)tɪŋ] ADJ tentant, alléchant; *(meal)* appétissant

temptingly ['tem(p)tɪŋlɪ] ADV d'une manière tentante; **the grapes glistened t. in their bowl** les grappes dans le plat étaient brillantes et appétissantes; **the cool water beckoned t.** l'eau fraîche donnait envie de se baigner

temptress ['tem(p)trɪs] N *Lit, Hum* tentatrice f

ten [ten] N dix m; **number t.** le numéro dix; **some** *or* **about t. years ago** il y a une dizaine d'années; **three tens are thirty** trois fois dix font trente; **tens of thousands** des dizaines de milliers; **it's t. o'clock** il est dix heures; **to be t.** *(in age)* avoir dix ans; *Rugby* **t. metre line** ligne f des dix mètres; **they're t. a penny** il y en a à la pelle; **t. to one he'll mention it** je vous parie qu'il en parlera; **the top t.** *(in record charts)* palmarès m des dix meilleurs *ou* des dix meilleures ventes ◼ PRON dix; **about ten t.** ten une dizaine; **I need t.** *(of them)* il m'en faut dix, j'en ai besoin de dix ◼ ADJ dix; **t. people** dix personnes
▶▶ **the T. Commandments** les dix commandements mpl

tenable ['tenəb(ə)l] ADJ **1** *(position, fortress etc)* tenable; *(theory)* soutenable; *Mktg* **t. firm** entreprise f défendable **2** **appointment t. for three years** poste auquel on est nommé pour trois ans

tenacious [te'neɪʃəs] ADJ tenace; **t. memory** excellente mémoire f

tenaciously [tɪ'neɪʃəslɪ] ADV avec ténacité; *(stubbornly)* obstinément

tenacity, tenaciousness [tɪ'næsɪtɪ, tɪ-'neɪʃəsnɪs] N ténacité *f*; *(of memory)* sûreté *f*

tenancy ['tenənsɪ] N location *f*; **expiration of t.** expiration *f* de bail, échéance *f* de location; **during my t.** pendant la période de ma location

tenant ['tenənt] N locataire *mf*; **t. in possession, sitting t.** occupant, -ante

VT *(house etc)* occuper comme locataire; **only half the farms were still tenanted** il n'y avait de locataires que dans la moitié des fermes

▸▸**t. farmer** métayer, -ère; **t. farming** métayage *m*

tenantry ['tenəntrɪ] N, *no pl (tenants)* métayers *mpl*

tench [tenʃ] N *(fish)* tanche *f*

tend¹ [tend] VT *(sick person etc)* soigner; *(machine etc)* surveiller; *(sheep etc)* garder; *(garden, fire)* entretenir

▸ **tend to** VT INSEP *(look after)* s'occuper de

tend² VI **1** doctrine that tends towards socialism doctrine socialiste, doctrine qui penche vers le socialisme; **blue tending to green** bleu tirant sur le vert; **her tastes t. towards the exotic** elle a une attirance pour les choses exotiques; **I t. to(wards) the view that …** j'ai tendance à penser que …

2 to t. to do sth avoir tendance à faire qch; **to t. to skid** *(of car)* déraper facilement; **she tends to exaggerate** elle a tendance à exagérer; **we t. to think of man as being separate from nature** nous avons tendance à considérer que l'homme ne fait pas partie de la nature; **some people like that kind of film, but I t. not to** il y a des gens qui aiment ce genre de film, moi (je n'aime) pas trop

tendency ['tendənsɪ] N tendance *f* **(to** à**); t. to drink** penchant *m* pour la boisson; **he has artistic tendencies** il a des dons artistiques; **to have a t. to (do) sth** avoir (une) tendance à (faire) qch; **a growing t.** une tendance de plus en plus marquée

tendentious [ten'denʃəs] ADJ tendancieux

tendentiously [ten'denʃəslɪ] ADV tendancieusement

tendentiousness [ten'denʃəsnɪs] N caractère *m* tendancieux

tender¹ ['tendər] N *Naut (boat)* navire *m* annexe; *(for supplies)* ravitailleur *m*; *Rail* tender *m*

tender² ADJ **1** *(meat)* tendre; **to make meat t.** attendrir la viande **2** *(sensitive)* tendre, sensible; **t. conscience** conscience *f* délicate *ou* susceptible; **t. to the touch** sensible *ou* douloureux au toucher; **t. heart** cœur *m* tendre *ou* sensible; **to touch sb on a t. spot** toucher qn à un endroit sensible; *Fig* toucher le point sensible chez qn **3** *(plant etc)* délicat, fragile; *esp Lit, Hum* **a child of t. years** un(e) petit(e) enfant **4** *(affectionate) (person, sentiment etc)* tendre, affectueux; **they bade each other a t. farewell** ils se sont tendrement dit au revoir; **t. look** regard doux *ou* tendre; *Iron* **I leave him to your t. mercies** je l'abandonne à vos soins

tender³ N *Com* soumission *f*, offre *f*; **to invite tenders for a job, to put a job out to t.** mettre un travail en adjudication; **to make** *ou* **put in a t. for sth** soumissionner *ou* faire une soumission pour qch; **a call for t.** un appel d'offres; **by t.** par voie d'adjudication; *Law, Com* **legal t.** cours *m* légal, monnaie *f* libératoire; **to be legal t.** *(of money)* avoir cours, avoir force libératoire

VT *(one's services, money etc)* offrir; **to t. one's resignation** présenter sa démission; **to t. one's apologies** faire *ou* présenter ses excuses; *Law* **to t. money in discharge of**

debt faire une offre réelle; **please t. exact fare** veuillez avoir la monnaie exacte

VI *Com* **to t. for sth** soumissionner (pour) qch, faire une soumission pour qch; **to t. for a contract** soumissionner à une adjudication

▸▸**t. documents** documents *mpl* d'appel d'offres; **t. form** formule *f* de soumission; **t. insurance** assurance *f* offre; **t. price** prix *m* d'offre

tenderer ['tendərər] N *Com* soumissionnaire *mf*; **successful t.** adjudicataire *mf*

tenderfoot, *pl* **tenderfoots, tenderfeet** ['tendəfʊt(s), -fiːt] N *esp Am (in wild place)* nouveau venu *m*

tenderhearted [tendə'hɑːtɪd] ADJ au cœur tendre *ou* sensible; **to be too t.** avoir trop de cœur

tenderheartedness [tendə'hɑːtɪdnɪs] N compassion *f*, sensibilité *f*

tenderize ['tendəraɪz] VT *Culin (meat)* attendrir

tenderizer ['tendəraɪzər] N *Culin* attendrisseur *m*

tenderloin ['tendəlɔɪn] N *Culin (of beef etc)* filet *m*

tenderly ['tendəlɪ] ADV **1** *(to touch, hold sth)* doucement, délicatement **2** *(to look at, feel)* tendrement, avec tendresse

tenderness ['tendənɪs] N **1** *(of meat)* tendreté *f* **2** *(of plant)* délicatesse *f*, fragilité *f*, *(of conscience)* délicatesse *f* **3** *(affection)* tendresse *f*, affection *f* **(for** pour**)**

tendinitis [tendɪ'naɪtəs] N tendinite *f*

tendon ['tendən] N *Anat* tendon *m*

tendril ['tendrɪl] N *Bot* vrille *f*, cirre *m*

tenement ['tenɪmənt] N *(building)* immeuble *m* d'habitation, *Pej* vieil immeuble d'habitation en mauvais état

▸▸**t. building** immeuble d'habitation, *Pej* vieil immeuble d'habitation en mauvais état; **t. flat** appartement *m*, *Pej* appartement dans un vieil immeuble

tenet ['tenɪt, 'tiː-] N *(dogma)* doctrine *f*, dogme *m*; *(belief)* croyance *f*

tenfold ['tenfəʊld] ADJ décuple

ADV au décuple; **to increase t.** décupler

ten-gallon ADJ

▸▸**t. hat** = chapeau *m* de cowboy haut et à larges bords

Tenn *abbr* Tennessee

tenner ['tenər] N *Fam Br (ten-pound note)* billet *m* de dix livres; *(sum)* dix livres *fpl*; *Am (ten-dollar bill)* billet de dix dollars; **it cost a t.** ça a coûté dix livres

tennis ['tenɪs] N *Sport* **(lawn) t.** tennis *m*; **to play t.** jouer au tennis; **table t.** tennis de table; **deck t.** deck-tennis *m*; **(real** or **royal** or *Am* **court) t.** (jeu *m* de) paume *f*

▸▸**t. ball** balle *f* de tennis; **t. club** club *m* de tennis; **t. court** court *m* de tennis; *(in real tennis)* jeu de paume; **t. elbow** tennis-elbow *m*, synovite *f* du coude; **t. player** joueur, -euse de tennis; **t. racket, t. racquet** raquette *f* de tennis; **t. shoes** chaussures *fpl* de tennis, tennis *fpl ou mpl*

tenon ['tenən] N *Carp* tenon *m*

▸▸**t. saw** tenonneuse *f*

tenor ['tenər] N **1** *Mus (voice, singer)* ténor *m* **2** *(general sense) (of letter etc)* contenu *m*, sens *m* général **3** *Fin (of bill)* (terme *m* d')échéance *f*

▸▸**t. clef** clé *f* d'ut quatrième ligne; **t. sax(ophone)** saxo(phone) *m* ténor; **t. voice** voix *f* de ténor

tenpence ['tenpəns, -'pens] N *Br* (pièce *f* de) dix pence *mpl*

tenpenny ['tenpənɪ] ADJ *Br* de *ou* à dix pence; **t. stamp** timbre *m* de dix pence

tenpin ['tenpɪn] N quille *f*, *Am* **tenpins** *(game)* jeu *m* de quilles; *(in bowling alley)* bowling *m*

▸▸*Br* **t. bowling** jeu de quilles; *(in bowling alley)* bowling

tense¹ [tens] N *Gram* temps *m*; **verb in the present/future t.** verbe au (temps) présent/futur VOIR GRAMMAIRE A39–40; B30–2

tense² ADJ **1** *(nerves, situation, silence, moment etc)* tendu; *(muscle)* contracté, noué; **t. voice** voix *f* étranglée (par l'émotion); **to be t.** *(of person)* être tendu **2** *(cord etc)* tendu, raide

VT tendre; **he tensed himself as the door opened** il se raidit au moment où la porte s'ouvrit

VI se raidir

▸ **tense up** VT SEP, VI = **tense** VT, VI

tensely ['tenslɪ] ADV **he waited t. for the judge's decision** l'air tendu, il attendait la décision du juge; **we watched t. as he approached the door** nous le regardâmes s'approcher de la porte avec appréhension; **she spoke t.** on sentait la tension dans sa voix

tenseness ['tensnɪs] N **1** *(of nerves, situation etc)* tension *f* **2** *(of muscles etc)* contraction *f*

tensile ['tensaɪl] ADJ *(stretchable)* extensible, élastique; *(metal)* ductile

▸▸**t. load** charge *f* de traction; **t. strength** résistance *f* à la tension, limite *f* élastique à la tension; **t. stress** force *f* de tension

tension ['tenʃən] N **1** *(of mind, nerves)*, *Pol (in region etc)* tension *f* **2** *(of cord, muscular etc)* tension *f*; *Phys (of fluid)* tension, force *f* élastique; *Elec* tension, voltage *m*; **to keep a cable under t.** garder un câble sous tension **3** *Tech (stress)* (force *f* de) traction *f*; *(of spring)* tension *f*; **to be in t.** être en traction

▸▸**t. headache** mal *m* de tête dû à la tension nerveuse

tent [tent] N tente *f*, **bell t.** tente conique; **oxygen t.** tente à oxygène; **to pitch/strike tents** monter/démonter les tentes

▸▸**t. peg** piquet *m* de tente; **t. pole** mât *m* de tente

tentacle ['tentək(ə)l] N *Biol*, *Fig* tentacule *m*

tentative ['tentətɪv] ADJ *(hesitant)* hésitant; *(conclusion)* provisoire; **to make a t. move towards peace** faire un petit pas vers la paix; **t. offer** offre *f* préliminaire *ou* d'essai; **it was just a t. suggestion** ce n'était qu'une suggestion

tentatively ['tentətɪvlɪ] ADV à titre d'essai; *(hesitantly)* avec hésitation; *(to conclude)* provisoirement

tenterhooks ['tentəhʊks] N **to be on t.** être au supplice *ou* sur le gril *ou* sur des charbons ardents; **to keep sb on t.** faire languir qn, mettre qn sur des charbons ardents

tenth [tenθ] ADJ dixième

N **1** *(of month)* dix *m*; **(on) the t. (of May)** le dix (mai) **2** *(person, thing)* dixième *mf* **3** *(fraction)* dixième *m* **4** *Mus* (intervalle *m* de) dixième *f*

tenting ['tentɪŋ] N toile *f* de tente

tenuous ['tenjʊəs] ADJ *(argument, link etc)* ténu, faible

tenuously ['tenjʊəslɪ] ADV de façon ténue

tenuousness ['tenjʊəsnɪs] N *(of argument, link etc)* fragilité *f*

tenure ['tenjər] N **1** *Hist, Law (of property)* tenure *f*; **system of land t.** régime *m* foncier **2** *Law (period) (of office, property etc)* (période *f* de) jouissance *f ou* (d')occupation *f*; *(permanency of employment)* titularisation *f*; **during his t. of office** pendant qu'il exerçait ses fonctions

tepee ['tiːpiː] N tipi *m*, wigwam *m*

tepid ['tepɪd] ADJ *(water etc)* tiède; *(feeling, welcome etc)* tiède, mitigé

tepidly ['tepɪdlɪ] **ADV** mollement, de façon mitigée

tepidness ['tepɪdnɪs] **N** tiédeur *f*

tequila [tɪ'kiːlə] **N** tequila *f*

terabyte ['terəbaɪt] **N** *Comput* téraoctet *m*

tercentenary [tɜːsen'tiːnərɪ], **tercentennial** [tɜːsen'tenɪəl] **ADJ**, **N** tricentenaire *m*

tercet ['tɜːsɪt] **N** *(in prosody)* tercet *m*

TERM [tɜːm]

> **N** terme **1-6** ▪ conditions *(terms)* **4**
> ▪ clauses *(terms)* **4** ▪ période **5**
> ▪ durée **5** ▪ trimestre **5** ▪ fin **6**
> **VT** désigner ▪ qualifier

N 1 *(word, expression)* terme *m*; **technical/scientific t.** terme *ou* expression *f* technique/scientifique; **he spoke of him in the most flattering terms** il a parlé de lui en des termes les plus flatteurs; **I told her in no uncertain terms** je le lui ai dit carrément *ou* sans mâcher mes mots; **in terms of difficulty I'd say it was in the medium range** si on considère le degré de difficulté, je dirais que c'était moyennement difficile; **in terms of salary/pollution** du point de vue du salaire/de la pollution; **in terms of time, I think we're talking about twelve weeks** question temps, je pense qu'il faut compter douze semaines; **in layman's terms** pour parler clairement; **in financial terms** financièrement parlant, en matière de finance; **I was thinking more in terms of a family car/something under £50** je voyais plus une voiture du genre voiture familiale/quelque chose de moins de 50 livres; **in personal/political terms it was a disaster** d'un point de vue personnel/politique ça a été une catastrophe

2 *(relations)* **to be on good/bad terms with sb** être en bons/mauvais termes avec qn; **to be on friendly terms with sb** être en bons termes avec qn; **we remained on friendly terms** nos relations sont restées amicales; **to be on the best of terms with sb** être au mieux avec qn, être dans les meilleurs termes avec qn; **we're not on those kind of terms** nous ne nous connaissons pas aussi bien; **to come to terms with sth** accepter qch, se faire à qch

3 *(in logic)*, *Math* terme *m*; **to express one quantity in terms of another** exprimer une quantité en fonction d'une autre

4 *Com etc* **terms** *(conditions)* conditions *fpl*, *(of contract)* clauses *fpl*, termes *mpl*; **terms and conditions of a contract** conditions d'un contrat; **on these terms I accept** à ces conditions j'accepte; **make** *or* **name your own terms** fixez vos conditions; **under the terms and conditions of the contract** selon les termes du contrat; **to dictate terms** imposer ses conditions; **to come to** *or* **make terms** s'arranger *(with sb* avec qn); **weekly terms** *(in hotel etc)* pension *f* par semaine; **on easy terms** avec facilités de paiement; **not on any terms** à aucun prix

5 *(period)* terme *m*, période *f*, durée *f*, *Sch*, *Univ* trimestre *m*; *(of court)* session *f*; **to serve a t. of five years (in prison)** faire cinq ans de prison; **during her t. of** *or* **in office** *(of president, mayor etc)* pendant son mandat; *Com* **long-/short-t. transaction** opération *f* à long/court terme; **a long-t. policy** une politique à longue échéance; **in the long t.** à la longue; **in the short t.** à court terme; *Sch*, *Univ* **in t. time, during t.** pendant le trimestre; *Sch*, *Univ* **half t. (holiday)** congé *m* de mi-trimestre

6 *(limit)* terme *m*, fin *f*, *Com* *(of bill of exchange)* (terme d')échéance *f*; **to have reached (full) t.** *(of pregnancy)* être à terme; **to set** *or* **put a t. to sth** mettre fin *ou* un terme à qch

VT désigner, appeler; **critics termed the play a total disaster** les critiques ont qualifié la pièce d'échec complet

▸▸ *Fin* **t. bill** effet *m* à terme; *Fin* **terms of credit** conditions de crédit; *Fin* **t. day** *(jour m* du) terme; *Fin* **t. deposit** dépôt *m* à terme; *Fin* **t. draft** traite *f* à terme; *Fin* **terms of exchange** termes d'échange; *Fin* **t. insurance cover** couverture *f* à terme; *Fin* **t. loan** *(money lent)* prêt *m* à terme (fixe); *(money borrowed)* emprunt *m* à terme (fixe); *Am Sch, Univ* **t. paper** dissertation *f* trimestrielle; **terms of payment** conditions *ou* termes de paiement; **terms of reference** *(of commission etc)* attributions *fpl*, mandat *m*; *Econ* **terms of trade** termes de l'échange

termagant ['tɜːməgənt] **N** *Lit* mégère *f*, virago *f*

terminal ['tɜːmɪn(ə)l] **ADJ** *(phase, stage)* terminal, -aux; *(illness)* incurable; *Med* **I'm afraid it's t.** je crains que vous ne soyez/qu'il ne soit/*etc* condamné; *Fam* **t. boredom** ennui *m* mortel

N1 *Elec (of battery)* pôle *m* **2** *(rail, bus)* terminus *m*, gare *f* terminus; *(maritime)* gare maritime; *(for containers)* terminal *m*; *Aviat* **(air) t.** aérogare *f* **3** *Comput* (poste *m*) terminal *m*

▸▸ *Ins* **t. bonus** = bonus *m* versé au titulaire d'une assurance-vie, au terme de celle-ci; **t. building** *(at airport)* aérogare *f*; *Med* **t. case** malade *mf* en phase terminale; *Fin* **t. charges** charges *fpl* terminales; *Comput* **t. emulation** émulation *f* de terminal; *Comput* **t. emulator** émulateur *m* de terminal; *Acct* **t. loss** perte *f* finale; *St Exch* **t. market** marché *m* à terme; *Fin* **t. price** cours *m* du livrable; *Comput* **t. server** serveur *m* de terminaux; *Rail* **t. station** terminus *m*; *Elec* **t. voltage** tension *f* aux bornes

terminally ['tɜːmɪn(ə)lɪ] **ADV** *Med* **to be t. ill** être en phase terminale; **the t. ill** *(npl)* les malades *mpl* incurables *ou* condamnés

terminate ['tɜːmɪneɪt] **VT** *(employment, project, commitment)* mettre un terme à, mettre fin à; *(contract etc)* résilier; **the project was terminated in 1997** on a mis fin au projet en 1997; **to t. a pregnancy** *(of doctor)* interrompre une grossesse, pratiquer une IVG; *(of woman)* avoir une IVG; **to have one's pregnancy terminated** avoir une IVG

VI *(of word etc)* se terminer, finir *(in* en, par); *(of line etc)* se terminer, aboutir *(in, at* à); *(of train)* avoir son terminus *(at* à); **this train terminates here** terminus du train!

termination [tɜːmɪ'neɪʃən] **N1** *(of trial etc)* fin *f*, conclusion *f*; *(of relations, dealings etc)* cessation *f*; *Law (of obligation etc)* résolution *f*, résiliation *f*; **t. of pregnancy** interruption *f* (volontaire) de grossesse, IVG *f* **2** *Gram* terminaison *f*, désinence *f*

▸▸ **t. clause** clause *f* de résiliation

terminator ['tɜːmɪneɪtər] **N** *Comput* terminateur *m*

▸▸ *Agr* **t. gene** gène *m* terminator *ou* terminateur

terminological [tɜːmɪnə'lɒdʒɪk(ə)l] **ADJ** terminologique

terminologist [tɜːmɪ'nɒlədʒɪst] **N** terminologue *mf*

terminology [tɜːmɪ'nɒlədʒɪ] **N** terminologie *f*

terminus, *pl* **termini, terminuses** ['tɜːmɪnəs, -aɪ, -əsɪz] **N** *Rail etc* (gare *f*) terminus *m*

▸▸ **t. hotel** *(at train station)* hôtel *m* de gare

termite ['tɜːmaɪt] **N** *(insect)* termite *m*

tern [tɜːn] **N** *(bird)* sterne *f*; **arctic t.** sterne arctique

ternary ['tɜːnərɪ] **ADJ** *Chem*, *Math etc* ternaire

terrace ['terɪs] **N 1** *Constr*, *Geol*, *Agr* terrasse *f*, *Ftbl etc* **the terraces** les gradins *mpl* **2** *Br* **t.** *(of houses)* rangée *f* de maisons attenantes
VT *(garden etc)* disposer en terrasse(s); *(hillside etc)* terrasser

terraced ['terɪst] **ADJ** *(garden)* en terrasse; **t. hillsides** collines cultivées en terrasses
▸▸ *Br* **t. house** = maison *f* située dans une rangée de maisons attenantes et identiques; **t. houses** *(row)* rangée *f* de maisons attenantes

terracotta ['terə'kɒtə] **N** terre *f* cuite; *(colour)* ocre *m* foncé

terra firma ['terə'fɜːmə] **N** la terre ferme, *Fam* le plancher des vaches; **to be back on t. again** être de retour sur le plancher des vaches; *Fig (in known area etc)* se retrouver en terrain connu

terrain [tə'reɪn] **N** *Mil*, *Geog* terrain *m*

terrapin ['terəpɪn] **N** *(reptile)* tortue *f* d'eau douce

terrarium, *pl* **terraria, terrariums** [te-'reərɪəm, -ɪə, -ɪəmz] **N** terrarium *m*

terrestrial [tɪ'restrɪəl] **ADJ** *(globe, plant, life, TV programmes etc)* terrestre
N *(inhabitant of the Earth)* terrien, -ienne
▸▸ **t. broadcasting** diffusion *f* hertzienne *ou* terrestre; **t. channel** chaîne *f* hertzienne; **t. television** diffusion hertzienne *ou* terrestre; **the Cup Final will no longer be broadcast on t. television** la finale ne sera plus diffusée sur le réseau hertzien

terrible ['terɪb(ə)l] **ADJ** terrible; *(accident, crime, shock)* affreux, épouvantable; *(film, teacher etc)* nul; *(coffee, food etc)* infecte; *(injury)* très grave; **what a t. thing to say** c'est horrible de dire ça; **I'm t. at maths** je suis nul en math; **he's a t. talker** *(talks a lot)* c'est un sacré bavard; **going without a meal isn't so t.** ce n'est pas si terrible de sauter un repas

terribly ['terɪblɪ] **ADV 1** *(badly)* terriblement; *(to behave)* de manière atroce; **the economy has performed t.** les résultats économiques sont désastreux; **t. injured** très gravement blessé **2** *Fam (very)* très; **t. busy** très *ou* terriblement occupé; **t. worried** terriblement *ou* affreusement inquiet; **that's t. kind of you** vous êtes vraiment trop aimable; **he's t. keen to meet you** il a vraiment envie de te rencontrer; **not t. interesting** pas très intéressant; **are you interested? – not t.** ça vous intéresse? – pas vraiment

terrier ['terɪər] **N** *(dog)* (chien *m*) terrier *m*; *Fig* **he's a real t.** il n'abandonne jamais; **bull t.** bull-terrier *m*, *pl* bull-terriers

terrific [tə'rɪfɪk] **ADJ** *Fam (excellent)* génial, -aux; *(enormous)* énorme; **we had a t. time** c'était génial; **t.!** génial!; **a t. noise** un bruit énorme; **a t. pace** une allure vertigineuse

terrifically [tə'rɪfɪklɪ] **ADV** *Fam (very)* très; **it was t. hot** il faisait terriblement chaud

terrified ['terɪfaɪd] **ADJ** *(look, person)* terrifié; **to be t. of sb** avoir une peur bleue de qn; **they're t. of losing their jobs** ils tremblent à l'idée de perdre leur emploi; **to be t. (that)** être terrifié *ou* mort de peur (à l'idée que + *sub*)

terrify ['terɪfaɪ] **VT** terrifier, faire très peur à; **this remark terrified me** cette remarque m'a terrifié; **it terrifies me what he'll do next** je suis terrifié à la pensée de ce qu'il pourrait faire

terrifying ['terɪfaɪɪŋ] **ADJ** terrifiant, terrible, épouvantable

terrifyingly ['terɪfaɪɪŋlɪ] **ADV** *(difficult, dangerous)* épouvantablement; *(to scream)* d'une manière terrifiante; **to come t. close to death** passer à deux doigts de la mort, frôler la mort

terrine [te'riːn] **N** terrine *f*

territorial [terɪ'tɔːrɪəl] **ADJ 1** *(possessions,*

tax, claim etc) territorial, -aux **2 a t. animal** un animal qui a tendance à protéger son territoire; **gorillas are very t. creatures** les gorilles mettent toujours beaucoup d'acharnement à défendre leur territoire; **the sales director is highly t.** le directeur des ventes est prêt à tout pour défendre son territoire; **they're very t. about their part of the office** ils veulent que personne ne s'immisce dans leur partie du bureau

N *Br Mil* **T.** réserviste *m* volontaire

▶▶ *Br Mil* **T. Army** = armée *f* de réservistes volontaires; **t. waters** eaux *fpl* territoriales

territoriality [terɪtɔːrɪˈælɪtɪ] N territorialité *f*

territory ['terɪt(ə)rɪ] N **1** *(of state, animal)* territoire *m*; *Fig* **I'm afraid this isn't my t.** désolé, ce n'est pas mon domaine; *Fig* **this will be familiar t. for his readers** le lecteur se retrouvera en terrain familier

terror ['terər] N **1** *(fear)* terreur *f*, effroi *m*, épouvante *f*; **a look of t.** un regard épouvanté; **to be in (a state of) t.** être terrorisé; **to be in t. of one's life** craindre pour sa vie; **to go in t. of sb** avoir une peur bleue de qn; *Fam* **to have a holy t. of sth** craindre qch comme la peste; **a reign of t.** un régime de terreur; *Hist* **the T.** la Terreur; **t. campaign, campaign of t.** campagne *f* de terreur

2 *(person)* **he was the t. of the countryside** c'était la terreur du pays; *Fam* **she's a little** *or* **a holy t.** c'est un petit diable; *Fam* **he's a t. for being late** il est épouvantable avec sa manie d'être toujours en retard; *Fam* **he's a t. for the whisky/chocolate biscuits** c'est un fou de whisky/de petits gâteaux au chocolat

terrorism ['terərɪz(ə)m] N terrorisme *m*

terrorist ['terərɪst] N terroriste *mf*

ADJ terroriste

▶▶ **t. attack** attentat *m* (terroriste); **t. bombing** attentat à la bombe

terrorize ['terəraɪz] VT terroriser

terror-stricken, terror-struck ADJ *(expression, look)* de terreur; **to be t.** être saisi de terreur

terry ['terɪ] N *(fabric)* tissu *m* éponge

▶▶ **t. towel** serviette *f* éponge; **t. towelling** tissu éponge

terse [tɜːs] ADJ abrupt, brusque

tersely ['tɜːslɪ] ADV abruptement, brusquement

terseness ['tɜːsnɪs] N *(of reply etc)* brusquerie *f*, *(of style)* caractère *m* abrupt

tertiary ['tɜːʃ(ɪ)ərɪ] ADJ N tertiaire *m*

▶▶ **t. education** enseignement *m* du troisième cycle; **t. sector** secteur *m* tertiaire

Terylene® ['terɪliːn] N *Br Tex* tergal® *m*; **T. skirt** jupe en tergal

TESL ['tes(ə)l] N *(abbr* **Teaching English as a Second Language)** enseignement *m* de l'anglais deuxième langue

TESOL ['tesɒl] N *(abbr* **Teaching English to Speakers of Other Languages)** enseignement *m* de l'anglais langue étrangère

TESSA ['tesə] N *Br (abbr* **tax exempt special savings account)** plan *m* d'épargne exonéré d'impôts

┌─────────────────────────────┐
│ **TEST** [test]   │
│   │
│ N épreuve **1** ▪ test **1** ▪ essai **1** │
│ ▪ examen **2** ▪ interrogation **2** ▪ match │
│ international **3**   │
│ VT essayer ▪ tester ▪ vérifier ▪ analyser │
│ VI expérimenter ▪ se révéler │
└─────────────────────────────┘

N **1** *(trial, check etc)* épreuve *f*, *(scientific)* test *m*; **to put sth to the t.** mettre qch à l'épreuve *ou* à l'essai, éprouver qch; **to undergo a t.** subir une épreuve; **to pass** *or* **stand the t.** soutenir *ou* supporter l'épreuve; **method that has stood the t. of time** méthode *f*

éprouvée; **it was a t. of our friendship** ça a mis notre amitié à l'épreuve; **endurance t.** épreuve d'endurance; *Aut etc* **road t.** essai *m* sur route; **nuclear t.** essai nucléaire

2 *Sch, Med etc (examination)* examen *m*; **eye/blood t.** examen des yeux/du sang; *Sch* **French/maths t.** examen *ou* interrogation *f* de français/math; *Med etc* **blood t.** prise *f* de sang; *Aut* **driving t.** permis *m* de conduire; **hearing t.** examen de l'ouïe; *Cin etc* **screen t.** bout *m* d'essai

3 *Cr, Rugby (match)* match *m* international

VT *(try out) (car, computer system, product, method etc)* essayer, tester; *(weights and measures etc)* contrôler, vérifier; *(sb's sight)* examiner; *(procedure)* expérimenter; *(beam etc)* sonder; *(water etc)* analyser; **to t. sb's hearing** faire passer des tests auditifs à qn; **to t. sb's blood** faire une analyse de sang à qn; **to t. sb's fitness** tester l'endurance de qn; **to t. sb's knowledge** tester les connaissances de qn; *Sch* **to t. a class in algebra** faire faire un examen d'algèbre à une classe; *Med* **to t. sb for AIDS** faire subir le test de dépistage du SIDA à qn; **to t. an athlete for steroids** faire subir des tests à un athlète pour détecter l'usage de stéroïdes; **to t. a drug on sb/animals** expérimenter un médicament sur qn/des animaux

VI *(of scientist etc)* expérimenter; **to t. for AIDS/TB** procéder à un test de dépistage du SIDA/de la tuberculose; **she tested positive for AIDS** son test de dépistage du SIDA s'est révélé positif; *Sport* **he tested positive for banned substances** son contrôle antidopage s'est révélé positif; **to t. for alkaloids** faire la réaction des alcaloïdes; **one, two, testing** *(in soundcheck)* un, deux, essai

▶▶ **t. area** région *f* test; **t. ban** interdiction *f* des essais nucléaires; **t. ban treaty** traité *m* de prohibition des essais nucléaires; **t. bench** banc *m* d'essai; *Br TV* **t. card** mire *f*; *Law* **t. case** affaire *f* qui fait jurisprudence; *Aut* **t. centre** *(for repairs)* centre *m* d'essai; **t. certificate** certificat *m* d'essai; *TV* **t. chart** mire *f* (de réglage); *Mktg* **t. city** ville *f* test; **t. drive** essai *m* sur route; **to take a car for a t. drive** essayer une voiture; *Aviat* **t. flight** vol *m* d'essai; **t. market** marché-test *m*, *pl* marchés-tests, marché *m* témoin; *Cr, Rugby* **t. match** match *m* international; *Br Sch* **t. paper** *(questions)* sujets *mpl* d'examen; *(answers)* copie *f* d'examen; *Am TV* **t. pattern** mire *f* (de réglage); *Mus* **t. piece** morceau *m* imposé ou de concours; **t. pilot** pilote *m* d'essai; **t. run** essai *m*; **t. shot** lancement *m* d'essai; **t. site** site *m* témoin; *Aut* **t. track** piste *f* d'essai; **t. tube** éprouvette *f*

▶ **test out** VT SEP *(person, idea etc)* mettre à l'épreuve; **to t. out a scheme** essayer un projet; **to t. out an idea on sb** tester une idée sur qn

testament ['testəmənt] N **1** *(will)* testament *m*; **to make one's (last will and) t.** tester, faire son testament **2** *(tribute)* preuve *f*, témoignage *m*; **the victory was a t. to her bravery** cette victoire a été le témoignage de son courage **3** *Bible* **the Old/the New T.** l'Ancien/le Nouveau Testament *m*

testamentary [testəˈment(ə)rɪ] ADJ testamentaire

testate ['testeɪt] ADJ *Law* **to die t.** mourir en laissant un testament valable

testator [tesˈteɪtər], *f* **testatrix**, *pl* **testatrixes** [tesˈteɪtər, -ˈteɪtrɪks, -trɪsiːz, -trɪksɪz] N testateur, -trice

test-bed N banc *m* d'essai

test-drive VT *Aut* essayer

tester¹ ['testər] N **1** *(person)* contrôleur, -euse; *(device)* appareil *m* de contrôle **2** *(sample) (of cosmetic)* échantillon *m*

tester² N *(canopy over bed)* baldaquin *m*, ciel *m*

test-fly VT **to t. a plane** faire le vol d'essai d'un avion

testicle ['testɪk(ə)l] N testicule *m*

testify ['testɪfaɪ] VI *Law* témoigner; **to t. in sb's favour/against sb** témoigner en faveur de qn/contre qn; **to t. to a fact** *(of things)* témoigner d'un fait; *(of person)* attester *ou* affirmer un fait, témoigner d'un fait

VT **1** *(one's regret, faith etc)* témoigner **2** *Law* déclarer, affirmer sous serment

testily ['testɪlɪ] ADV d'un ton irrité

testimonial [testɪˈməʊnɪəl] N **1** *(character reference) (given by company, director)* références *fpl*; *(letter of recommendation)* lettre *f* de recommandation **2** *(tribute)* témoignage *m* d'estime; *Ftbl (match)* jubilé *m*

▶▶ *Mktg* **t. advertising** témoignage *m*, publicité *f* testimoniale; *Ftbl* **t. match** jubilé

testimony ['testɪmənɪ] N *(of senses etc)* témoignage *m*; *Law* attestation *f*, *(of witness)* déposition *f*; **to bear t. to sth** témoigner de qch, rendre témoignage de qch; **in t. whereof** en foi de quoi

testing ['testɪŋ] ADJ *(problem, time, experience etc)* difficile

N *(of machine, bridge etc)* essai *m*, épreuve *f*, *(of drug, cosmetic)* expérimentation *f*, **animal t.** expérimentation animale *ou* sur les animaux

▶▶ **t. laboratory** laboratoire *m* d'essai de produits

testis, *pl* **testes** ['testɪs, 'testiːz] N testicule *m*

test-market VT tester sur le marché

testosterone [tesˈtɒstərəʊn] N testostérone *f*

test-tube baby N bébé-éprouvette *m*, *pl* bébés-éprouvette

testy ['testɪ] ADJ irritable

tetanus ['tetənəs] N *Med* tétanos *m*

▶▶ **t. injection** piqûre *f* antitétanique

tetchily ['tetʃɪlɪ] ADV d'un ton irrité

tetchiness ['tetʃɪnɪs] N irritation *f*

tetchy ['tetʃɪ] ADJ irritable

tête-à-tête ['teɪtɑːˈteɪt] ADV tête-à-tête

N *(pl* **tête-à-têtes)** tête-à-tête *m inv*

tether ['teðər] N *(for tying horse etc)* longe *f*, attache *f*, *Fig* **to be at the end of one's t.** être à bout

VT *(horse etc)* attacher

tetrachloride [tetrəˈklɔːraɪd] N tétrachlorure *m*

tetragon ['tetrəgən] N quadrilatère *m*

tetragonal [teˈtrægən(ə)l] ADJ quadrilatère

tetrahedron [tetrəˈhiːdrən, -ˈhed-] N tétraèdre *m*

tetrameter [teˈtræmɪtər] N *(in poetry)* tétramètre *m*

Teutonic [tjuːˈtɒnɪk] ADJ teuton, teutonique; *Hist* **the T. Order (of Knights)** l'ordre *m* Teutonique

Tex *abbr* **Texas**

Texan ['teks(ə)n] ADJ texan

N Texan, -ane

Texas ['teksəs] N le Texas

Tex-Mex [teks'meks] ADJ tex-mex *inv*

text [tekst] N **1** *(of manuscript, author, in computing)* texte *m*; *(passage from Bible)* citation *f* tirée des Saintes Écritures; *Sch* **set texts** textes au programme **2** *(text message)* texto *m*, SMS *m*

VT *(send text message to)* envoyer un texto *ou* SMS à

VI *(send text messages)* envoyer des textos *ou* SMS

▶▶ **t. area** zone *f* de texte; *Comput* **t. block** bloc *m* de texte; **t. box** fenêtre *f* de saisie;

POSS ADJ (used instead of **thy** before a noun or adj beginning with a vowel or h mute) ton, f ta, pl tes

---

THING [θɪŋ]

chose **1, 3** ▪ truc **1** ▪ affaires (things) **1** ▪ vêtements (things) **1** ▪ être **2** ▪ créature **2** ▪ idée **3** ▪ mode **4**

N 1 chose f, Fam truc m; **a t. of beauty** une belle chose; **the things of this world** les choses de ce monde; **chocolate, sweets, and things (like that)** le chocolat, les bonbons, et autres choses de ce style; Fam **what's that t.?** qu'est-ce que c'est que ce machin-là?; Fam **where's that scraper t.?** où est le machin pour gratter?; **my things** (clothes etc) mes vêtements mpl; (belongings) mes affaires fpl; **winter things** (clothes) vêtements d'hiver; **bring along your swimming things** apportez vos affaires de bain; **to pack (up) one's things** faire ses valises; **I didn't bring a lot of things** (on holiday) je n'ai pas pris beaucoup d'affaires
2 Fam (person) (with adj expressing pity, contempt etc) être m, créature f; **poor t.!** le/la pauvre!; **you silly t.!** sot/sotte que tu es!; **poor little things!** pauvres petits!; **she's a dear old t.** c'est une petite vieille bien sympathique
3 (action, remark, fact etc) chose f; **that was a silly t. to do** ça, ce n'est pas très malin de ta/sa/etc part; **what a silly/nasty t. to say!** c'est vraiment stupide/méchant de dire ça ou une chose pareille; **the things you say!** les choses que tu peux dire parfois!; **how could you do such a t.?** comment avez-vous pu faire une chose pareille?; **how could you say such a t.!** comment avez-vous pu dire une chose pareille!; **did you ever hear of such a t.?** on n'a pas idée d'une chose pareille!; **you take things too seriously** vous prenez les choses trop au sérieux; **she gets things done** avec elle, le travail avance bien; **to think things over** réfléchir; **it's just one of those things** ce sont des choses qui arrivent; **it's a t. you need to give careful consideration to** c'est une chose à laquelle tu dois bien réfléchir; **to talk of one t. and another** parler de choses et d'autres; **it's been one t. after the other** (problems) on a eu des problèmes en cascade ou une cascade de problèmes; **what with one t. and another we haven't had time** on a été pris par plein de choses et on n'a pas eu le temps; **that's the very t.** c'est juste ce qu'il faut; **the t. is this** voici ce dont il s'agit; **the t. is, I haven't got any money** le problème, c'est que je n'ai pas d'argent; **the only t. left is to …** il ne reste plus qu'à …; **the important t. is that …** l'important c'est que …; **the t. to remember is that …** ce dont il faut se souvenir c'est que …; **that's quite another t.** ça, c'est tout autre chose; **neither one t. nor another** ni l'un(e) ni l'autre; **and another t.** en plus; Fam **he's on to a good t.** il est sur un bon filon ou un bon coup; **I don't know a t. about algebra** je n'y connais absolument rien en algèbre; **it doesn't mean a t. to me** (I don't understand it at all) je n'y comprends (absolument) rien; (it isn't at all familiar to me) ça ne me dit absolument rien; (it doesn't concern me at all) ça ne me concerne pas; **there isn't a t. we can do about it** il n'y a absolument rien que nous puissions y faire; **to know a t. or two** (to know a few tricks etc) avoir plus d'un tour dans son sac; (to be well informed) en savoir long; Fam **she's got a t. about French** (loves it) le français, c'est son truc; (hates it) le français, ce n'est pas son truc; Fam **he's got a t. about that, it's a t. with him** c'est son idée fixe; Fam **do your (own) t.!** fais comme il te plaira!; **things are going badly** ça va mal; **as things are** les choses étant comme elles

---

sont; Fam **how are things?, how's things?** comment ça va?
4 the latest t. in shoes la dernière mode en matière de chaussures; **it's the (very) latest t.** c'est tout ce qu'il y a de plus moderne; **he looks quite the t.** il est vraiment très chic; **the t. (to do)** (etiquette) l'usage m; **it's not the done t.** cela ne se fait pas
5 Fam (penis) machin m

thingummy, thingamy, thingumajig, thingumabob, thingy ['θɪŋəmɪ, -dʒɪg, -bɒb, 'θɪŋɪ] **N** Fam (object) truc m, machin m, bidule m; (person) machin m, machine f, trucmuche mf; **have you seen the t. for the food processor?** tu as vu le bitoniau du robot de cuisine?; **I saw t. who you used to work with last week** la semaine dernière, j'ai vu Machin-Chose avec qui tu travaillais dans le temps

---

THINK [θɪŋk]

N moment de réflexion
VI penser ▪ réfléchir
VT penser à **1** ▪ comprendre **1** ▪ s'imaginer **1** ▪ penser **2** ▪ croire **2, 3** ▪ supposer **2** ▪ juger **3** ▪ considérer **3**

N moment m de réflexion; **to have a t.** réfléchir; **what do you say? – I'll have a t. about it** qu'en dis-tu? – je vais réfléchir; Fam **you've got another t. coming!** tu peux toujours courir!
VI (pt, pp **thought** [θɔːt]) penser, réfléchir; **to t. aloud** penser tout haut; **to t. (long and) hard** bien réfléchir, Fam se creuser la tête; Fam **to t. big** être ambitieux; **I did it without thinking** je l'ai fait sans réfléchir ou sans y penser; **I'm sorry, I wasn't thinking** désolé, je l'ai fait/dit sans réfléchir; **I was so pressed for time that I wasn't even thinking** (during exam) j'étais tellement pris par le temps que j'écrivais n'importe quoi; **you just don't t., do you!** (are inconsiderate, careless etc) jamais tu ne réfléchis, hein!; **t. before you speak** réfléchissez avant de parler; **just t. a minute!** réfléchissez un peu!; **give me time to t.** laissez-moi une minute que je réfléchisse; **you t. too much** tu réfléchis trop; **to t. again** se raviser; **you can (just) t. again!** tu peux toujours courir!; **it makes you t.** ça vous fait réfléchir; **I'd t. twice about that, if I were you** j'y réfléchirais à deux fois si j'étais toi; **to t. on one's feet** savoir prendre des décisions rapidement

VT 1 (imagine, suppose) **what are you thinking?** à quoi penses-vous?; **I know what you're thinking** je sais ce que vous pensez ou ce que vous vous dites, je sais à quoi vous pensez; **I was just thinking 'I wonder where he is'** when … j'étais justement en train de me demander où il était lorsque …; **I (really) can't t. why/what/where …** je me demande bien pourquoi/ce que/où …; **I can't t. what you mean** je n'arrive pas à comprendre ou voir ce que vous voulez dire; **what will people t.?** que vont penser les gens?; **he thinks he knows everything** il s'imagine tout savoir; **one would have thought that …** on aurait pu croire que …; **anyone would t. she was asleep** on dirait qu'elle dort; **who'd have thought it!** qui l'eût cru?!; **just t.!** songez donc!; **to t. that he's only twenty!** et dire qu'il n'a que vingt ans!; **and to t. it used to cost just …!** quand je pense qu'avant ça ne coûtait que …; **t. what we could do with all that money!** pense ou songe à tout ce que nous pourrions faire avec tout cet argent!; **I have been thinking that …** l'idée m'est venue que …; esp Lit **I only thought to help you** ma seule pensée était de vous aider; **did you t. to bring any money?** avez-vous pensé ou songé à apporter de l'argent?; **to**

---

t. evil/kind thoughts avoir de sombres/douces pensées
2 (believe, have as opinion) **do you t. you could do it? – I t. I could** pensez-vous que cela vous serait possible? – je pense que oui; **it's better to get it over with, don't you t.?** il vaut mieux en finir, vous ne trouvez pas?; **I thought I heard her** j'ai cru l'entendre; **I thought it was all over** je croyais que tout était fini; **everyone asked him what he thought** chacun lui a demandé son avis; **what do you t., Jenny?** et toi, qu'en penses-tu, Jenny?; **well what do you t.? does it suit me?** alors, qu'est-ce que tu en penses, ça me va?; **I t. she's pretty/nice** je la trouve jolie/sympa; **everyone thought he was mad** on le tenait pour fou; **I rather t. it's going to rain** j'ai dans l'idée qu'il va pleuvoir; **it is thought that …** on suppose que … + ind; **I t. so** je pense que oui; **I don't t. so, I t. not** je pense que non; **that's what I t. (too)** c'est (aussi) mon impression; **so I thought, I thought so, I thought as much** c'est bien ce que je pensais; **I (should) hardly t. so** c'est peu probable; **I should t. so!** je crois bien!; **do you t. they'll agree? – I should t. so** croyez-vous qu'ils accepteront? – je pense que oui; **he's going to apologize – I should t. so (too)!** il va s'excuser – j'espère bien!; **he apologized – I should t. so (too)!** il s'est excusé – ce n'est pas trop tôt!; **I shouldn't t. so** je ne crois pas; Fam **that's what you t.!** c'est ce que tu crois!, tu te fais des idées! VOIR GRAMMAIRE A47–8
3 (judge) juger, considérer, croire; **if you t. it necessary to …** si vous jugez nécessaire de …; **I hardly t. it likely that …** il me semble peu probable que … + subj; **to t. fit or t. it proper to …** juger bon ou convenable de …; **you thought her (to be) a fool** vous l'avez prise pour une sotte; **they were thought to be rich** on les disait ou supposait riches; (they passed for rich) ils passaient pour (être) riches
4 (expect) **I little thought I would see him again** je ne m'attendais guère à le revoir
5 Fam **designers are thinking pink** le rose, c'est la couleur in chez les stylistes; **the company is thinking expansion** le maître mot dans la société, c'est expansion

▸ **think about VT INSEP 1** penser à; **what are you thinking about?** à quoi penses-tu?; **do you still t. about her?** pensez-vous encore à elle?; **he can't sleep for thinking about it** il perd le sommeil à force d'y penser, Fam il n'en dort plus; **that's worth thinking about** cela mérite réflexion; **quite cheap when you t. about it** plutôt bon marché quand on y pense
2 (consider) (proposal etc) réfléchir à; **what do you say? – I'll t. about it** qu'en dites-vous? – j'y songerai ou réfléchirai; **that will give them something to t. about** voilà qui va leur donner matière à réflexion; **to t. about doing sth** envisager de ou songer à faire qch
3 (take into account) penser à; **I've got my family/future to t. about** il faut que je pense à ma famille/mon avenir
4 (have opinion about) penser de; **what do you t. about him?** que pensez-vous de lui?; **what do you t. about it?** qu'en pensez-vous?

▸ **think back VI** repenser; **to t. back on past events** repenser à des événements passés; **when I t. back** quand j'y repense; **t. back to what you were doing in 1995** songez à ou rappelez-vous ce que vous faisiez en 1995; **thinking back, I suppose I never really liked him** réflexion faite, je crois que je ne l'ai jamais vraiment aimé

▸ **think of VT INSEP 1** (be attentive to) penser à, songer à; **to t. of others** penser aux autres; **I've got the children/the children's education to t. of** il faut que je songe aux enfants/à l'éducation des enfants; **I can't t. of everything!** je ne peux pas penser à tout!

2 *(reflect on)* penser à; **we're thinking of you** nous pensons à toi; **I was thinking of how much times have changed** je songeais combien les temps ont changé; **when I t. of what might have happened!** quand je pense à ce qui aurait pu arriver!; **it's rather silly, when you (come to) t. of it** c'est plutôt bête, quand on y pense; **come to t. of it, I did see her that night** maintenant que j'y pense, je l'ai vue cette nuit-là; **what am I thinking of?** où ai-je la tête?; **what were you thinking of, letting the child out on his own?** où avais-tu la tête, pour laisser cet enfant sortir seul?; **we wouldn't t. of letting our daughter travel alone** il ne nous viendrait pas à l'esprit de laisser notre fille voyager seule; **I couldn't t. of it!** c'est impossible!

3 *(recall, bring to mind) (name etc)* se rappeler (de); **I can't t. of their number at the moment** je n'arrive pas à me rappeler leur numéro là maintenant; **I can't t. of the right word** le mot juste m'échappe

4 *(imagine)* imaginer, se figurer; **just t. of it, a holiday in the Caribbean!** imagine, des vacances aux Caraïbes!; **and it weighs two tons, (just) t. of that!** et figure-toi que ça pèse deux tonnes!

5 *(have opinion about)* penser de; **what do you t. of him?** que penses-tu de lui?; **what do you t. of it?** qu'en pensez-vous?; **what do you t. of this picture?** que dites-vous de ce tableau?; **I don't t. much of the idea/her taste** je ne trouve pas que cette idée soit très bonne/qu'elle ait très bon goût; **to t. a lot of** *or* **highly of sb** avoir une haute opinion de qn; **to t. a great deal of oneself, to t. too much of oneself** avoir une haute idée de soi-même *ou* de sa personne; **to t. too much of sth** attacher trop d'importance à qch; **I told her what I thought of her** je lui ai dit son fait; **to t. well/badly of sb** avoir une bonne/mauvaise opinion de qn; **he is well thought of** il est bien vu *ou* considéré

6 to t. of doing sth envisager de *ou* songer à faire qch; **what were you thinking of giving her?** que pensais-tu lui donner?

7 *(have idea of)* imaginer, penser à, avoir l'idée de; *(solution)* imaginer; **the longest word I can t. of** le mot le plus long auquel je puisse penser; **I've thought of a way of persuading her** j'ai pensé à *ou* imaginé un moyen de la persuader; **try every method you can t. of** essayez toutes les méthodes que vous puissiez imaginer; **who thought of coming to this restaurant?** qui a eu l'idée de venir dans ce restaurant?; **why didn't you phone? – I didn't t. of it** pourquoi n'avez-vous pas téléphoné? – je n'y ai pas pensé; **who thought of the idea?** qui a eu cette idée?; **what a clever idea!, now why didn't I t. of that?** quelle idée géniale!, pourquoi n'y ai-je pas pensé *ou* songé?; **t. of a number** pensez à un chiffre; **I thought of him as being tall** je le voyais grand

▸**think out** VT SEP *(plan, solution)* imaginer; **he likes to t. things out for himself** il aime juger des choses par lui-même; **see if you can t. something out** essaie d'imaginer *ou* de trouver une solution; **well thought out plan** projet bien étudié; **carefully thought out answer** réponse bien pesée

▸**think over** VT SEP *(question etc)* réfléchir à; **I'll t. it over** j'y réfléchirai; **t. it over (carefully)** réfléchissez-y *ou* songez-y bien; **on thinking it over** réflexion faite, à la réflexion

▸**think through** VT SEP *(plan etc)* bien considérer; **I thought it through all night** j'y ai réfléchi toute la nuit; **the scheme has not been properly thought through** le plan n'a pas été considéré suffisamment en détail

▸**think up** VT SEP *(project, method)* imaginer; **who thought that idea up?** qui a eu cette idée?

thinkable ['θɪŋkəb(ə)l] ADJ concevable, imaginable; **is it t. that …?** peut-on imaginer que … + *sub* ?; **it is scarcely** *or* **barely t. that …** il est difficilement concevable *ou* imaginable que … + *sub*

thinker ['θɪŋkər] N penseur, -euse

thinking ['θɪŋkɪŋ] ADJ pensant, qui pense; **the paper for t. people** le journal pour les gens qui réfléchissent; **the t. man's pin-up** la pin-up des intellectuels; **any t. person would agree that …** n'importe qui réfléchissant un tant soit peu serait d'accord pour dire que …

N **1** *(process of thought)* pensée(s) *f(pl)*, réflexion(s) *f(pl)*; **to do some t.** réfléchir un peu; **he did some hard t.** il a sérieusement réfléchi; **we'd better do a bit of quick t.** nous ferions bien de réfléchir en vitesse; **to put on one's t. cap** cogiter; **good t.!** bien vu! **2** *(opinion)* opinion *f*, avis *m*; **to my (way of) t.** à mon avis; **I hope to bring you round to my way of t.** j'espère vous amener à mon opinion *ou* à mon point de vue; **she influenced the t. of a generation** elle a influencé la façon de penser de toute une génération

▸▸*Aut* **t. distance** temps *m* de réaction

think-tank N comité *m* *ou* groupe *m* d'experts

thin-lipped ADJ aux lèvres minces; **he was rather t.** *(displeased)* il avait les lèvres plutôt pincées

thinly ['θɪnlɪ] ADV *(in thin layers)* en couche(s) mince(s); *(in thin slices)* en tranches fines; **t. sown wheat** blé *m* clairsemé; **t. populated** peu peuplé; **t. clad** *(lightly)* légèrement vêtu; *(inadequately)* vêtu insuffisamment; **a t. veiled allusion** une allusion à peine voilée

thinner ['θɪnər] N *(for paint etc)* diluant *m*

thinness ['θɪnnɪs] N **1** *(of sheet of paper etc)* minceur *f*, *(of material etc)* légèreté *f*, *(of person)* minceur; *(excessive)* maigreur *f* **2** *(of liquid)* fluidité *f*, *(of air)* raréfaction *f*

thinning ['θɪnɪŋ] ADJ **his t. hair** ses cheveux qui commencent à se clairsemer

▸▸**t. agent** diluant *m*

thin-skinned ADJ *Fig (person)* susceptible, trop sensible

thin-sliced ADJ *(bread)* coupé en tranches fines, finement coupé

third [θɜːd] NUM ADJ, N *(day, floor etc)* troisième *mf*; **Edward the T.** Édouard III; **the t. of May** le trois mai; **on the t. of May** le trois mai; **every t. day** tous les trois jours; **we must find a t. way** il faut trouver une troisième voie

N **1** *(fraction)* tiers *m*; **to lose a t./two thirds of one's money** perdre le tiers/les deux tiers de son argent; **one t. full** plein au tiers **2** *Mus* tierce *f* **3** *Aut* **to go into t.** passer en troisième

▸▸**the t. age** le troisième âge; *Fam* **t. degree** interrogatoire *m* serré; **to give sb the t. degree** faire subir un interrogatoire serré à qn; *(treat roughly)* cuisiner qn; *Hist* **the T. Estate** le Tiers État; *Aut* **t. gear** troisième vitesse *f*, *(gearwheel)* pignon *m* de troisième; **t. party** tierce personne *f*, tiers *m*; **t. party cover** assurance *f* au tiers; **t. party fire and theft insurance** assurance au tiers vol et incendie; **t. party holder** tiers détenteur *m*; **t. party owner** tiers possesseur *m*; *Gram* **t. person** troisième personne *f*; **to act through a t. person** *(in negotiation etc)* passer par une tierce personne; *Fin* **t. quarter** *(of financial year)* troisième trimestre *m*; *Hist* **the T. Reich** le Troisième Reich; **the T. World** le tiers-monde

third-class ADJ *Br Univ (degree)* obtenu avec la mention passable

third-degree burn N *Med* brûlure *f* du troisième degré

third-generation ADJ *Tel* de troisième génération

thirdly ['θɜːdlɪ] ADV troisièmement, en troisième lieu

third-rate ADJ médiocre, de troisième ordre

thirst [θɜːst] N soif *f*; *Fig esp Lit* **the t. for** *or* **after knowledge** la soif de connaissances; **to satisfy one's t. for adventure** satisfaire sa soif d'aventures

VI *Arch, Lit* être altéré *ou* avide (**for** de); *Lit* **to t. for blood/revenge** être assoiffé de sang/de vengeance

thirstily ['θɜːstɪlɪ] ADV avidement

thirsty ['θɜːstɪ] ADJ *(person)* qui a soif; *(stronger)* assoiffé; *(earth etc)* desséché; *Fam (car)* qui consomme énormément; **to be** *or* **feel t.** avoir soif; **I'm t.** j'ai soif; **to make sb t.** donner soif à qn; *Fam* **all this talking is t. work** de parler autant, cela donne soif *ou* cela vous sèche le gosier; *Fig Lit* **t. for blood/ for riches** assoiffé *ou* altéré *ou* avide de sang/de richesses

thirteen [θɜːˈtiːn] NUM ADJ, N treize *m*; **she's t. (years old)** elle a treize ans; **at t. hundred hours** à treize heures

thirteenth [θɜːˈtiːnθ] NUM ADJ, N treizième *mf*; **(on) the thirteenth (of May)** le treize (mai); **Friday the t.** vendredi treize

N *(fraction)* treizième *m*

thirtieth ['θɜːtɪɪθ] NUM ADJ, N trentième *mf*; **(on) the t. (of June)** le trente (juin)

thirty ['θɜːtɪ] NUM ADJ, N trente *m*; **t.-three** trente-trois; **t.-first** trente et unième; **t.-second** trente-deuxième; **(on) the t.-first of May** le trente et un mai; **about t. guests** une trentaine d'invités; **to be t. (years old)** avoir trente ans; **the thirties** les années trente; **he leaves at two-t.** il part à deux heures trente

thirty-year rule N = loi *f* qui prescrit que, au bout de 30 ans, toute archive ou document secret tombe dans le domaine public

THIS [ðɪs] VOIR GRAMMAIRE A30-1; B14-15 DEM PRON *(pl* **these** [ðiːz]*)* **1** ceci, ce; **what's t.?, what are these?** qu'est-ce que c'est (que ceci *ou Fam* que ça?); **who's t.?** qui est-ce?; *Tel* **who is t.?** qui est à l'appareil?; **you'll be sorry for t.** vous le regretterez; **at t.** sur ce, là-dessus; **it ought to have happened before t.** cela aurait dû être fait depuis longtemps; **after t.** après cela, ensuite; **t. is curious** c'est curieux, voilà qui est curieux; **t. is what she told me** voici ce qu'elle m'a dit; **t. is Mr. Ford** je vous présente M. Ford; **t. are my children** voici mes enfants; **t. is where she lives** c'est ici qu'elle habite; **these are things we cannot do without** ce sont des choses dont on ne peut se passer; **listen to t.** écoutez bien ceci; **eat/drink some of t.** mangez-/ buvez-en un peu; **what's t. (that) I hear?** qu'est-ce que j'apprends?; **do it like t.** fais comme ceci; **what's all t.?** *(these objects)* qu'est-ce que c'est que tout ça?; *(what's happening?)* qu'est-ce qu'il y a?, qu'est-ce qui se passe?

2 *(opposed to that)* **will you have t. or that?** voulez-vous ceci ou cela?; *Fam* **they were talking about t. and that** ils parlaient de choses et d'autres

3 *(referring to sth already mentioned)* celui-ci, *f* celle-ci, *pl* ceux-ci, *f* celles-ci; **I prefer these to those** je préfère ceux-ci à ceux-là

DEM ADJ *(pl* **these***)* ce, *(before vowel or h mute)* cet, *f* cette, *pl* ces; *(for emphasis and in opposition to* **that, those***)* ce … -ci, cet … -ci, cette … -ci, *pl* ces … -ci; **t. book** ce livre(-ci); **these books** ces livres(-ci); **t. morning** ce matin; **t. afternoon** cet(te) après-midi; **t. week** cette semaine; **one of these days** un de ces jours; **(in) these days, in t. day and age** de nos jours; **by t. time** à l'heure qu'il est; **to run t. way and that** courir de-ci de-là; **he will tell you that in t. or that case you should …** il vous dira qu'en tel ou tel cas il faut …; **for t. reason …** voilà pourquoi …, pour cette raison …; *Fam* **t. here house** cette maison(-ci); *Fam* **I've known him these three years** je le connais depuis trois ans **DEM ADV** aussi … que ceci; **t. high, as high as t.** aussi haut que ceci *ou* que cela *ou* que ça; **t. far** jusqu'ici, jusque-là; **can you eat t. much?** pourras-tu manger tout cela?; **t. much is certain …** ceci au moins est sûr …

thistle ['θɪs(ə)l] **N** chardon *m*

thistledown ['θɪs(ə)ldaʊn] **N** duvet *m* de chardon

thither ['ðɪðər] **ADV** *Arch, Lit* là; *Lit* **to run hither and t.** courir çà et là

tho' [ðəʊ] **CONJ, ADV** *Fam, Lit* = **though**

thole, tholepin ['θəʊl(pɪn)] **N** *Naut* tolet *m*

thong [θɒŋ] **N 1** lanière *f* de cuir; *(of whip)* lanière; *Am, Austr* **a pair of thongs** *(sandals)* des tongs *fpl* **2** *(G-string)* string *m*

thoracic [θɔːˈræsɪk] **ADJ** thoracique

thorax, pl thoraces ['θɔːræks, θɔːˈreɪsiːz] **N** thorax *m*

thorn [θɔːn] **N 1** *Bot* épine *f*, *Fig* **to be a t. in sb's flesh** *or* **side** être un sujet continuel d'irritation pour qn **2** *(tree)* épine *f*

thornback ['θɔːnbæk] **N** *(fish)* raie *f* bouclée

thornbush ['θɔːnbʊʃ] **N** (arbrisseau *m*) épineux *m*

thornless ['θɔːnlɪs] **ADJ** sans épines

thorny ['θɔːnɪ] **ADJ** épineux; *Fig* **t. question** question *f* épineuse

thorough ['θʌrə] **ADJ** *(search etc)* minutieux; *(knowledge)* approfondi; *(understanding)* profond; *(job)* consciencieux; **to be t. in one's work** travailler consciencieusement; **to give a room a t. cleaning** nettoyer une pièce à fond; **it needs a t. revision** il/elle a besoin d'une révision en profondeur; **a t. scoundrel** un fieffé coquin; **to make a t. nuisance of oneself** se rendre complètement insupportable

thoroughbred ['θʌrəbred] **ADJ** *(cheval)* pur-sang *inv*; *(dog etc)* de race **N** *(horse)* pur-sang *m inv*; *(animal)* animal *m*, -aux de race; **she's a real t.** *(person)* elle a de la classe

thoroughfare ['θʌrəfeər] **N** voie *f* de communication; **busy t.** *(street)* rue *f* très passante; *(road)* importante voie de communication; **one of the main thoroughfares of the town** une des rues principales *ou* une des artères de la ville; **no t.** *(on sign)* *(no through road)* rue barrée; *(no access)* passage interdit (au public)

thoroughgoing ['θʌrəgəʊɪŋ] **ADJ** *(search, inspection etc)* minutieux; *(knowledge, revision etc)* approfondi; *(changes)* profond; *(reform)* en profondeur; **such a t. rogue as him** un fieffé coquin de cette espèce

thoroughly ['θʌrəlɪ] **ADV** *(to know language etc)* parfaitement; *(to know sth, to clean sth)* à fond; *(stupid)* complètement; **to be t. bored** s'ennuyer mortellement; **t. honest** d'une honnêteté à toute épreuve; **t. untrustworthy** totalement indigne de confiance

thoroughness ['θʌrənɪs] **N** *(of work)* minutie *f*, **the t. of his knowledge** ses connaissances très complètes

those *see* **that**

thou¹ [ðaʊ] **PERS PRON** *Bible, Arch (unstressed)* tu; *(stressed)* toi; **t. seest** tu vois; **t. art** tu es; **hearest t.?** entends-tu?; **t. and I** toi et moi

thou² [θaʊ] **N** *Fam (abbr* **thousand**) mille *m inv*

though [ðəʊ] **CONJ 1** *(in spite of the fact that)* quoique, bien que + *subj*, **t. she is poor she is generous** quoiqu'elle soit pauvre, elle est généreuse; **I respect him t.** je le respecte, bien qu'il ne me soit pas sympathique; **t. I am a father** tout père que je suis; **t. not handsome, he was attractive** sans être beau, il avait du charme; **I think I did quite well, t. I say so** *or* **it myself** je ne m'en suis pas mal sorti, si je peux me permettre de le dire **2** this statement, **terrible t. it be** cette déclaration, pour terrible qu'elle soit; **strange t. it may seem** si étrange que cela puisse sembler; **even t. you'll laugh at me** même si vous vous moquez de moi **3 as t.** comme si; **it looks as t. she's gone** il semble qu'elle soit partie; **as t. nothing had happened** comme si de rien n'était **ADV** cependant, pourtant; **it's not what I want** mais ce n'est pas ce que je veux; **I didn't mean it t.** mais je ne disais pas ça sérieusement; **he had promised to go, he didn't t.** il avait promis d'y aller, cependant, il n'en a rien fait; **did she t.!** elle a dit/fait cela?

thought¹ [θɔːt] **N 1** *(thinking)* pensée *f*, **contemporary t.** la pensée contemporaine; **capable of t.** capable de penser **2** *(idea)* pensée *f*, idée *f*; **he hasn't a t. in his head** il n'a pas une idée dans la tête; **happy t.** heureuse idée; **what a nice/kind t.!** quelle agréable/douce pensée!; **dark** *or* **gloomy thoughts** de sombres pensées; **that's** *or* **there's a t.** *(good idea)* ça, c'est une idée; **(that's true)** ça, c'est vrai; **now there's a t., why don't we …?** j'ai une idée, et si nous …?; *(sb else's thought)* ça c'est une bonne idée, et si nous …?; **it's quite a t.!** *(pleasant)* le rêve!; *(unpleasant)* quelle horreur!; **to read sb's thoughts** lire dans les pensées de qn; **the mere t. of it** rien que d'y penser; **have you ever given it a single t.?** y avez-vous jamais pensé?; **I didn't give it another t.** je n'y ai pas repensé; **what are your thoughts on the matter?** quelle est votre opinion sur ce sujet?; **to collect one's thoughts** rassembler ses idées; **her thoughts were elsewhere** son esprit était ailleurs **3** *(reflection)* réflexion *f*, considération *f*, *(meditation)* pensées *fpl*, rêverie *f*, méditation *f*, **after much t.** après mûre réflexion; **to give a great deal of t. to sth** réfléchir beaucoup à qch; **on second thoughts** réflexion faite, à la réflexion; **to be deep** *or* **lost in t.** être perdu *ou* absorbé dans ses pensées, être plongé dans ses réflexions **4** *(intention)* intention *f*, dessein *m*; **I had no t. of offending you** je n'avais pas l'intention de vous offenser; **you must give up all thought(s) of seeing him** il faut renoncer à le voir, il ne faut plus penser à le voir; **his one t. is to get money** il ne pense qu'à l'argent **5** *Old-fashioned Fam* **a t. too sweet** un rien trop sucré ▸▸ **t. reader** liseur, -euse de pensées

thought² **PT, PP** *see* **think**

thoughtful ['θɔːtfʊl] **ADJ 1** *(pensive)* *(person, expression)* pensif, méditatif; **to look t.** avoir l'air pensif **2** *(considerate)* *(person)* attentionné; **he was t. enough to warn me** il a eu la prévenance de m'avertir; **it was very t. of her to …** c'était très attentionné de sa part de …; **that wasn't very t.** ce n'était pas très gentil de sa/ta/*etc* part; **how t. (of you)!** comme c'est gentil (de ta part)!; **it was a very t. gesture (on his part)** c'était une belle preuve d'attention (de sa part); *Fml* **he was always t. of others' needs** il a toujours été très attentif aux besoins des autres

3 *(to which thought has been given)* *(analysis, book)* profond; **he gave me his usual t. advice** comme d'habitude, il m'a aidé avec ses sages conseils

thoughtfully ['θɔːtfʊlɪ] **ADV 1** *(pensively)* pensivement, d'un air pensif *ou* méditatif **2** *(considerately)* avec prévenance

thoughtfulness ['θɔːtfʊlnɪs] **N 1** *(pensiveness)* méditation *f* **2** *(consideration)* prévenance *f*

thoughtless ['θɔːtlɪs] **ADJ 1** *(ill-considered)* irréfléchi, étourdi; **t. action** acte *m* inconsidéré **2** *(inconsiderate)* **t. of others** qui manque d'égards *ou* de prévenance pour les autres; **that was t. of me** j'ai fait ça sans réfléchir; **it was very t. of you not to have phoned** ce n'était pas très gentil de ta part de ne pas téléphoner

thoughtlessly ['θɔːtlɪslɪ] **ADV 1** *(without thinking)* étourdiment, sans réfléchir **2** *(inconsiderately)* **to treat sb t.** manquer d'égards envers qn; **he very t. left it locked** il l'a laissé fermé sans se soucier des autres le moins du monde; **they t. took the whole lot** sans aucun égard, ils ont pris le tout

thoughtlessness ['θɔːtlɪsnɪs] **N 1** *(lack of forethought)* irréflexion *f*, étourderie *f* **2** *(lack of consideration)* manque *m* d'égards *ou* de prévenance

thought-out **ADJ** **well/poorly t. plan** projet bien/mal conçu; **carefully t. answer** réponse bien pesée; **this needs a carefully t. answer** il va falloir bien réfléchir avant de répondre

thought-provoking **ADJ** qui invite à la réflexion, qui donne à *ou* fait réfléchir

thousand ['θaʊz(ə)nd] VOIR GRAMMAIRE A12-13; B58-9 **NUM ADJ** mille *inv*; **a t. years** mille ans; **the year 4000 B.C.** l'an quatre mille av. J.-C.; *Law, Admin* **the year one t. nine hundred and thirty** l'an mil neuf cent trente; **about a t. men** un millier d'hommes; **three hundred t. people** trois cent mille personnes; *Fam* **I've got a t. and one things to ask you/to do** j'ai mille choses à vous demander/faire; **no, no, a t. times no!** non, non, et cent fois non! **N** mille *m inv*; **a t. mille; a. t. and one** mille un; **how many people were there? – about a t.** combien de gens étaient là? – un millier; **thousands of people** des milliers de gens; **in thousands** par milliers; **in hundreds of thousands** par centaines de mille; **she's one in a t.** c'est la femme entre mille ▸▸ **T. Island dressing** = sauce *f* à base de mayonnaise, de ketchup et de cornichons hachés

thousandfold ['θaʊz(ə)n(d)fəʊld] **ADJ** multiplié par mille **ADV** mille fois autant

thousandth ['θaʊz(ə)n(t)θ] **NUM ADJ, N** millième *f*

thraldom ['θrɔːldəm] **N** *Lit* esclavage *m*, assujetissement *m*, servitude *f*

thrall [θrɔːl] **N** *Lit* **kept in t.** maintenu en esclavage *m*

thrash [θræʃ] **VT** *(beat)* *(person, animal)* battre, rosser, rouer de coups; *(defeat heavily in game etc)* battre à plate(s) couture(s); **to t. sb soundly** donner une bonne raclée à qn; **to t. the water** donner des coups dans l'eau; **to t. one's arms and legs in the air** se débattre des mains et des pieds **VI** *(of water)* battre, clapoter *(against* contre); **the doctor was trying to avoid his thrashing limbs** le docteur essayait d'éviter ses coups de pieds et ses coups de poings **N 1** *Br Fam (party)* fiesta *f* **2** *(music)* thrash *m* (metal)

▸ **thrash about, thrash around VT SEP** to t.

one's arms and legs about se débattre des mains et des pieds
VI *(move furiously) (of person)* se débattre (des mains et des pieds); *(of fish)* remuer, se débattre; **the fish thrashed about in the net** le poisson se débattait dans le filet
▸ **thrash out VT SEP 1** *(discuss thoroughly)* discuter à fond; **to t. it out with sb** en débattre avec qn **2** *(reach) (solution, truth etc)* arriver à

thrashing ['θræʃɪŋ] **N** *(beating)* volée *f* (de coups), *Fam* raclée *f*, *Sport etc* défaite *f*; **to give sb a t.** donner une raclée à qn; **they were given a t. at the elections** ils ont pris une raclée aux élections; **to give one's opponent a t.** battre son adversaire à plate(s) couture(s)

thread [θred] **N 1** *(of cotton, nylon, silk etc)* fil *m*; **(length of) t.** *(of cotton, silk etc)* brin *m*, bout *m*; **gold t.** fil d'or; **button t.** fil à boutons; *Fig* **his life hung by a t.** sa vie ne tenait qu'à un fil; **to lose the t. of the conversation** perdre le fil de la conversation; **to gather up the threads of a story** retrouver le fil d'une histoire **2** *Tech (of screw, bolt etc)* filet *m*, filetage *m* **3** *Fam* **threads** *(clothes)* fringues *fpl* **4** *Comput* fil *m* de discussion
VT 1 *(needle, beads)* enfiler (**through sth** dans qch); **to t. one's way between the cars** se faufiler entre les voitures **2** *Tech (screw etc)* fileter; *(pipe, nut etc)* tarauder
VI 1 we threaded through the crowd nous nous sommes faufilés à travers la foule **2 to t. into sth** *(of screw etc)* se visser dans qch; **the tape threads through these holes** la bande passe par ces trous
▸▸ **t. mark** filigrane *m* *(des billets de banque)*

threadbare ['θredbeər] **ADJ** *(clothes etc)* râpé, élimé, usé jusqu'à la corde; *Fig (subject, argument, joke etc)* rebattu

threadworm ['θredwɜːm] **N** oxyure *m*

threat [θret] **N** menace *f*; **to make threats** faire des menaces; **to utter a t.** proférer une menace; **to make idle threats** lancer des menaces en l'air; **it was no idle t.** ce n'était pas une menace en l'air; **there is a t. of rain** il y a un risque de pluie; **to see sb/sth as a t.** considérer qn/qch comme une menace; **is that a t. or a promise?** est-ce qu'il faut que je m'en/qu'il s'en/*etc* réjouisse ou pas; **if we exist under the t. of nuclear war** si nous vivons sous la menace d'une guerre nucléaire

threaten ['θret(ə)n] **VT** *(person)* menacer; *Law (person)* intimider; **to t. sb with sth** menacer qn de qch; **(to be) threatened with sth** (être) menacé de qch; **a species threatened with extinction** une espèce en voie de disparition; **the threatened strike didn't come off** cette menace de grève n'a pas abouti; **the sky threatened rain** la pluie menaçait, le ciel était menaçant; **to t. to do sth** menacer de faire qch; **this situation threatens to become dangerous** cette situation menace de devenir dangereuse
VI a storm is threatening l'orage menace

threatening ['θret(ə)nɪŋ] **ADJ** *(tone, appearance)* menaçant; *(letter)* de menaces; *Law* d'intimidation; **the weather looks t.** le temps est menaçant; **t. language** menaces *fpl* (verbales)

threateningly ['θret(ə)nɪŋlɪ] **ADV** de manière menaçante

three [θriː] **N** trois *m*; **every t. months** tous les trois mois; **twenty-t.** vingt-trois; **t. and a half** trois et demi; **t. and t. are six** trois et trois font six; **to be t.** *(in age)* avoir trois ans; **it's t. o'clock** il est trois heures; **he leaves at t. thirty** *or* **at half past t.** il part à trois heures trente *ou* à trois heures et demie; **to come in t. by t.** *or* **in threes** entrer (trois) par trois; *Hist* **the Big T.** les Trois Grands *mpl* *(Roosevelt, Churchill et Staline)*; **t.-engine(d) aircraft** trimoteur *m*; **t.-pointed** à trois pointes; **t. sided** *or* **t. party conversations** conversations *fpl* tripartites; **t.-stranded rope** corde *f* à trois cordons
PRON trois; **t. is not enough** trois, ce n'est pas assez
ADJ trois; **t. people** trois personnes
▸▸ *Theat* **t. act play** pièce *f* en trois actes; **t. seater** triplace *m*; **t. star brandy** cognac *m* trois-étoiles; **t. star hotel** hôtel *m* trois-étoiles

three-button mouse N *Comput* souris *f* à trois boutons

three-colour(ed), *Am* **three-color(ed) ADJ** tricolore; *Phot* trichrome
▸▸ **t. printing** impression *f* en trois couleurs *ou* en trichromie, trichromie *f*; **t. process** trichromie

three-cornered ADJ triangulaire; **a t. discussion** un débat à trois
▸▸ **t. hat** tricorne *m*

three-course ADJ *(meal)* à trois plats

three-D ADJ *Fam* = **three-dimensional**
N in t. en trois dimensions

three-dimensional ADJ tridimensionnel

threefold ['θriːfəʊld] **ADJ** triple; **a t. increase in the membership figures** une augmentation au triple du nombre d'adhérents
ADV trois fois autant; **to increase t.** tripler

three-four ADJ
▸▸ *Mus* **t. time** trois-quatre *m inv*

3G [θriː'dʒiː] **ADJ** *Comput, Tel* 3G

three-handed ADJ *Cards etc* **t. game** partie *f* à trois

three-legged ADJ *(stool etc)* à trois pieds
▸▸ **t. race** = course *f* où les participants courent par deux, la jambe gauche de l'un attachée à la droite de l'autre

three-line whip N *Br Pol* = obligation *f* absolue faite aux députés de prendre part à un vote et de suivre les recommandations de leur parti

threepence ['θrep(ə)ns] **N** *Br* trois pence *mpl*

threepenny ['θrep(ə)nɪ] **ADJ** *Br* coûtant trois pence, à *ou* de trois pence
▸▸ *Hist* **t. bit** pièce *f* de trois pence

three-piece ADJ en trois pièces
▸▸ *Mus* **t. band** trio *m*; **t. suit** *(costume m)* trois-pièces *m inv*; *Br* **t. suite** salon *m* trois pièces *(canapé et deux fauteuils)*

three-pin ADJ
▸▸ **t. plug** prise *f* à trois fiches

three-ply ADJ *(wool etc)* à trois fils; *(rope)* à trois brins; *(tissues, toilet paper)* à trois épaisseurs

three-point ADJ
▸▸ *Aviat* **t. landing** atterrissage *m* trois points; *Aut* **t. seatbelt** ceinture *f* trois points; *Aut* **t. turn** demi-tour *m* en trois manœuvres, *pl* demi-tours

three-quarter N *Rugby* trois-quarts *m inv*
▸▸ *Rugby* **t. back** trois-quarts; **t. face portrait** portrait *m* de trois-quarts; **t. length coat** trois-quarts; *Rugby* **the t. line** la ligne des trois-quarts; *Aut* **t. vision** visibilité *f* de trois-quarts

three-ring ADJ
▸▸ *Am* **t. circus** = cirque *m* contenant trois arènes et montrant plusieurs numéros à la fois; *Fig* cirque, chantier *m*

threescore ['θriːskɔːr] **ADJ** *Arch, Lit* soixante; **t. (years) and ten** soixante-dix ans

threesome ['θriːsəm] **N** *(three people)* groupe *m* de trois personnes; *Golf* partie *f* à trois; **do you want to make up a t.?** *(in games)* veux-tu faire le troisième?; *(going out etc)* veux-tu te joindre à nous (deux)?;

we went as a t. nous y sommes allés à trois

three-speed ADJ à trois vitesses
▸▸ **t. gearbox** boîte *f* trois vitesses

three-storey(ed), *Am* **three-story, three-storied ADJ** *(house)* à trois étages

three-way ADJ *(division etc)* en trois; *(discussion etc)* à trois
▸▸ *Aut* **t. catalytic convertor** catalyseur *m* à trois voies; *Br Pol* **t. marginal** = circonscription *f* où trois candidats ont d'égales chances de succès

three-wheeled vehicle N trois-roues *m*

three-wheeler N *Aut* *(petite)* voiture *f* à trois roues; *(tricycle)* tricycle *m*

threnody ['θrenədɪ] **N** *Lit* thrène *m*, chant *m* funèbre

thresh [θreʃ] **VT** *(wheat)* battre; *Fig* **to t. the water** *(of ship's screw, of whale's tail etc)* battre l'eau

thresher ['θreʃər] **N** *(person)* batteur, -euse en grange; *(machine)* batteuse *f*

threshing ['θreʃɪŋ] **N** *(of wheat)* battage *m*
▸▸ **t. floor** aire *f* de battage; **t. machine** batteuse *f*

threshold ['θreʃəʊld] **N 1** *(of door etc)* seuil *m*, pas *m* de la porte; **on the t.** sur le seuil; *Fig* **on the t. of a great discovery** au seuil d'une grande découverte; **to cross the t.** franchir le seuil; *Fig* **to be on the t. of life** être au seuil de la vie **2** *Phys etc (of fission, reaction)* seuil *m*; **to have a low boredom t.** être prédisposé à l'ennui, s'ennuyer facilement; **to have a low/high pain t.** mal tolérer/bien tolérer la douleur
▸▸ *Br Econ* **t. agreement** accord *m* d'indexation des salaires sur les prix; *Physiol* **t. of audibility, t. of hearing** seuil d'audibilité; *Br Econ* **t. policy** politique *f* d'indexation des salaires sur les prix; *Fin* **t. price** prix *m* du seuil

threw **PT** *see* **throw VT**

thrice [θraɪs] **ADV** *Lit* trois fois

thrift [θrɪft] **N** économie *f*, épargne *f*
▸▸ *Am* **t. institution** caisse *f* d'épargne; *Am* **t. shop** = magasin *m* vendant des articles d'occasion au profit d'œuvres charitables

thriftily ['θrɪftɪlɪ] **ADV** avec économie; *(live)* frugalement

thriftiness ['θrɪftɪnɪs] **N** économie *f*, épargne *f*

thriftless ['θrɪftlɪs] **ADJ** *(spendthrift)* dépensier; *(improvident)* imprévoyant

thriftlessness ['θrɪftlɪsnɪs] **N** gaspillage *m*; *(improvidence)* imprévoyance *f*

thrifty ['θrɪftɪ] **ADJ** économe

thrill [θrɪl] **N** *(exciting feeling)* (vive) émotion *f*, *(trembling)* frisson *m*, tressaillement *m*; **t. of pleasure** frisson de plaisir; **the t. of riding a motorbike** le frisson que donne la moto; **to get a t. out of sth** se donner des sensations fortes avec qch; **it gave me quite a t.** ça m'a fait quelque chose; **all the thrills of the big wheel** tous les frissons que procure la grande roue; **all the thrills and spills of the circus** toutes les joies et tous les frissons que procure le cirque; *Fam* **go on, give us a t., let's see you dance!** allez, montre-nous ce que tu sais faire, danse!
VT *(of experience, thought, prospect)* exalter; *(of sb's touch)* faire frémir *ou* frissonner, donner des frissons à; *(of conjuror etc) (audience, children)* faire vibrer; **a novel/film that will t. you** un roman/film qui vous fera frémir; **he was absolutely thrilled with his present** son cadeau le transportait de joie *ou* le ravissait; **she's thrilled with her new car** elle est ravie de sa nouvelle voiture; **I'm thrilled for you** je suis très heureux pour vous; **to be thrilled at the sight of sth** être

fou de joie à la vue de qch; *Fam* **to be thrilled to bits** être fou de joie; **we were absolutely thrilled (Fam to bits) to hear your news/to have won the holiday** nous avons été ravis d'apprendre la nouvelle/d'avoir gagné les vacances

vi *esp Lit* tressaillir, frissonner (de joie)

thriller ['θrɪlər] **N** *(play, film, novel)* pièce f/ film m/roman m à suspense, thriller m

thrilling ['θrɪlɪŋ] **ADJ** passionnant; *(sight)* saisissant; *Sport* **t. finish** arrivée f palpitante; *Iron* **how t. for you!** c'est passionnant, ce qui t'arrive!

thrive [θraɪv] **vi** *(pt, pp* thrived [θraɪvd]; *Arch, Am pt* throve [θrəʊv]; *pp* thriven ['θrɪvn]) *(grow well) (of child, plant)* (bien) se développer; *(of adult)* bien se porter; *(of business etc)* bien marcher, bien aller; *(prosper) (of person)* prospérer; *(develop potential)* s'épanouir; **children who t. on milk** enfants à qui le lait profite bien; **plant that thrives in all soils** plante qui s'accommode de tous les sols; **to t. on danger** se nourrir du danger; **to t. on other people's misfortunes** se réjouir des malheurs d'autrui; **some people t. on stress** certaines personnes s'épanouissent dans le stress; **do I like it? I t. on it!** si j'aime ça? mais, j'adore!

thriving ['θraɪvɪŋ] **ADJ** *(physically) (plant)* vigoureux; *(person)* vigoureux, bien portant; *(prosperous) (person, business)* prospère, florissant

thro' [θru:] **PREP** *Fam* = **through**

throat [θrəʊt] **N** *Anat* gorge f, *(gullet)* gorge, gosier m; **the back of the t.** le fond de la gorge, l'arrière-gorge f, *pl* arrière-gorges; **to cut sb's t.** couper la gorge à qn; *Fig* **he's cutting his own t.** il travaille à sa propre ruine; *Com, Fig* **they're cutting each other's throats** ils se font une concurrence désastreuse; **to grab sb by the t.** attraper *ou* saisir qn à la gorge; **to have a sore t.** avoir mal à la gorge; **to clear one's t.** s'éclaircir la voix *ou* la gorge, se racler la gorge; *Fig Fam* **she's always ramming** *or* **shoving** *or* **forcing it down my t.** elle m'en rebat toujours les oreilles; *Fam* **there's no need to jump down my t.!** inutile de me rabrouer!; *Fam* **they're always at each other's throats** ils se battent continuellement; *Fam* **if you pour enough alcohol down his t., he'll tell you anything** si tu le fais boire suffisamment, il te dira tout ce que tu veux savoir; *Fam Hum* **my stomach thinks my t.'s cut** je crève la dalle

▸▸ **t. microphone** laryngophone m; *Med* **t. spray** insufflateur m

throatiness ['θrəʊtɪnɪs] **N** *(of voice)* qualité f gutturale

throaty ['θrəʊtɪ] **ADJ** *(voice, laugh)* guttural, -aux

throb [θrɒb] **N** *(of pulse, heart etc)* pulsation f, *(of engine)* vrombissement m; **the t. of the tom-toms** les vibrations fpl des tam-tams; **she felt a sudden t. of pain in her arm** soudain, elle ressentit un élancement dans le bras

vi *(-bb-)* *(of heart, pulse etc)* battre fort; *(of engine)* vrombir; *(of tom-toms)* vibrer; **a city throbbing with activity** une ville palpitante d'activité; **my finger is throbbing** j'ai des élancements dans le doigt, *Fam* mon doigt me lance; **my head is throbbing** j'ai une douleur lancinante dans la tête

throbbing ['θrɒbɪŋ] **ADJ** *(heart, pulse etc)* qui bat fort; *(engine)* vrombissant; *(pain)* lancinant; **the t. rhythm of the drums** les tambours qui battent fort *ou* qui vibrent

N *(of heart, pulse etc)* battement m (fort), pulsations fpl; *(of engine)* vrombissement m; *(of wound, infection etc)* élancements mpl

throes [θrəʊz] **NPL** **the t. of death** *or* **death t.** les affres fpl de la mort; *Fig* **the death t. of**

the old regime l'agonie f de l'ancien régime; **the company is in its death t.** l'entreprise est à l'agonie; **a country in the t. of revolution** un pays en proie à la révolution *ou* dans la tourmente de la révolution; *Fam* **we're in the t. of moving house** nous sommes en plein déménagement; *Fam* **don't disturb him while he's in the t. of writing** ne le dérange pas en pleine inspiration; **in the t. of a divorce** dans la tourmente d'un divorce

thrombosis, *pl* **thromboses** [θrɒm'bəʊsɪs, -iːz] **N** *Med* thrombose f, **coronary t.** infarctus m du myocarde

throne [θrəʊn] **N** trône m; *Fam (lavatory)* **on the t.** sur le trône; **to come to** *or* **ascend** *or* **Lit mount the t.** monter sur le trône; **the heir to the t.** l'héritier m au trône; **the power behind the t.** *(of king etc)*, *Fig* l'Éminence f grise

throneroom ['θrəʊnruːm] **N** salle f du trône; *Fam Hum* **in the t.** *(on the toilet)* sur le trône

throng [θrɒŋ] **N** foule f, **a t. of angels** une multitude d'anges

vi affluer; *(gather)* s'assembler en foule; **to t. to Paris/the main cities/the square** affluer à Paris/dans les grandes villes/sur la place; **to t. round sb** se presser autour de qn; **they thronged into the square** ils arrivèrent en foule sur la place

vt emplir; **the room was thronged with people** la pièce était bondée

thronging ['θrɒŋɪŋ] **ADJ** **a t. mass** une foule grouillante

throttle ['θrɒt(ə)l] **N** *Aut etc* étrangleur m, obturateur m, papillon m *(des gaz)*; *(on motorbike)* poignée f d'accélération; *(in plane)* commande f des gaz; *Tech (in steam engine)* régulateur m, prise f de vapeur; *Aut* **to open/to close the t.** ouvrir/fermer les gaz; **at full t.** à pleins gaz

vt *(strangle)*, *Fig* étrangler

▸▸ **t. cable** câble m d'accélération; **t. control, t. lever** *(on motorbike, speedboat, plane)* manette f des gaz

▸ **throttle back, throttle down** **vi** *(slow engine)* mettre le moteur au ralenti; *(cut, close off fuel)* couper *ou* fermer les gaz; **the pilot/rider gradually throttled back** le pilote/motard coupa les gaz progressivement **vt sep** *(engine)* mettre au ralenti

THROUGH [θruː]

| **PREP** à travers **1, 2** ▪ par **1, 3** ▪ dans **1** |
| ▪ pendant **2** ▪ par l'intermédiaire de **3** |
| **ADV** à travers **1** ▪ d'un bout à l'autre **2** |
| ▪ jusqu'au bout **2** |
| **ADJ** direct |

PREP 1 *(place)* à travers; **t. a hedge** au travers d'une haie; **to go t. sb's garden** passer par le jardin de qn; **I was wandering t. the garden/trees** j'errais dans le jardin/parmi les arbres; **to go t. a tunnel** passer dans un tunnel; **the nail/arrow went t. the wood/wall** le clou/la flèche traversa le bois/le mur; **the path goes** *or* **leads t. the forest** le sentier traverse la forêt; **I'm on my way t. Paris** je traverse Paris; **let's have dinner when I'm on my way t. Paris** on pourrait dîner ensemble pendant mon passage à Paris; **to look t. the window/a telescope/a hole** regarder par la fenêtre/dans un télescope/par un trou; **she came in t. the window** elle est entrée par la fenêtre; **to go t. someone's pockets** fouiller les poches de qn; *Aut* **to go t. a red light** brûler un feu (rouge); *Fam* **he's been t. it** *or* **t. a lot** il en a bavé, il en a vu de dures; **to speak t. one's nose** parler du nez; **she got t. her exam** elle a été reçue à son examen; *Fam* **to put sb t. it** rendre la vie dure à qn; **I'm halfway t. this book** j'ai lu la moitié de ce livre

2 *(time)* **all t. his life** durant *ou* pendant

toute sa vie; **t. the ages** à travers les âges; *esp Am* **Monday t. Friday** de lundi à vendredi, du lundi au vendredi

3 *(by means of)* **t. sb** par qn, par l'entremise *ou* l'intermédiaire de qn; **t. sth** par le *ou* au moyen de qch; *(as a result of)* à conséquence de qch, par suite de qch, à cause de qch; **to send sth t. the post** envoyer qch par la poste; **t. ignorance** par ignorance; **absent t. illness** absent par suite *ou* pour cause de maladie; **to act t. fear** agir sous le coup de la peur; **it's (all) t. me that he missed his train** c'est à cause de moi qu'il a manqué son train; **t. failing to lock the door ...** pour n'avoir pas fermé la porte à clé ...

4 *esp Am* **to be t. doing sth** avoir fini de faire qch; **are you t. telling me what to do?** tu as fini de me dire ce que j'ai à faire?

ADV 1 *(place)* à travers; **the water poured t.** l'eau coulait à travers; **the nail has come t.** le clou est passé à travers; **to let sb t.** laisser passer qn; **her trousers are t. at the knees** son pantalon est déchiré aux genoux; **he's t. in the living-room** il est de l'autre côté, dans le salon; **will you be t. tomorrow?** *(are you coming here?)* est-ce que tu viens demain?; **England are t. to the semi-final** l'Angleterre s'est qualifiée pour *ou* jouera la demi-finale; *Sport* **France are not t.** la France n'est pas qualifiée; **to be soaked t.** *(of person)* être trempé jusqu'aux os; *(of jacket etc)* être complètement trempé

2 *(from one end to the other)* d'un bout à l'autre; *(to the end)* jusqu'au bout, jusqu'à la fin; **to read a book (right) t.** lire un livre d'un bout à l'autre; **to see** *or* **carry sth t.** mener qch à bien; **I slept all night t.** j'ai dormi d'une traite cette nuit; **we'll stay t. until Friday** nous resterons jusqu'à vendredi; **I was aware all t. that ...** j'étais conscient tout du long de ce que ...; **we must go t. with it** il faut aller jusqu'au bout; **to be t. with sth** *(to have finished sth)* avoir fini qch; *(with scissors etc)* avoir fini avec qch; *(to have had enough of)* avoir (eu) assez de qch; **are you t. with your work?** avez-vous fini votre travail?; **I'm t. with you** je n'en ai fini avec toi; **we're t.** c'est fini entre nous; *esp Am* **to be t.** *(to have stopped talking etc)* avoir terminé *ou* fini; *Fam (to be done for)* être fichu

3 **to book t. to Paris** prendre un billet direct pour Paris; *Tel* **to get t. to sb** obtenir la communication avec qn; *Fam* **I can't get t. to him** *(make him understand)* je n'arrive pas à lui faire comprendre quoi que ce soit; *Tel* **I'll put you t. to the secretary** je vous passe la/le secrétaire; *Tel* **you're t.** vous avez la communication, vous êtes en ligne

4 **to be good/bad t. and t.** *(of person)* être foncièrement bon/mauvais; **to know sb t. and t.** connaître qn comme si on l'avait fait; **to know a district t. and t.** connaître un quartier comme sa poche

ADJ *(train, road, ticket)* direct; **no t. road** *(on sign)* voie f sans issue; **closed to t. traffic** *(on sign)* interdit aux non-résidents, riverains autorisés

▸▸ *Com* **t. bill** connaissement m direct; **t. carriage** transport m direct; **t. fare** tarif m direct; **t. freight** marchandises fpl en transit; **t. passenger** *(on same vehicle to final destination)* passager m 'direct'; **t. passenger to Paris** voyageur, -euse direct(e) pour Paris; **t. traffic** transit m; **t. train** train m direct

throughout [θruː'aʊt] **PREP** **t. the country** dans tout le pays; **t. the world** à travers le monde; **t. the year** pendant toute l'année; **t. her life** durant *ou* pendant toute sa vie

ADV *(place)* partout; *(time)* tout le temps; **the coat is lined t.** le manteau est entièrement doublé; **they remained loyal t.** ils sont restés loyaux du début à la fin

throughput ['θruːpʊt] **N** débit m

throughway ['θru:weɪ] N *Am* autoroute *f*

throve PT *see* **thrive**

THROW [θrəʊ]

| **N** | jet **1** ▪ lancement **1** ▪ lancer **1** |
| ▪ essai **1** ▪ tour **1** ▪ coup **1** |
| **VT** lancer **1** ▪ jeter **1** ▪ couvrir **1** |
| ▪ projeter **2** ▪ organiser **3** |
| ▪ déconcerter **8** |

N 1 *(action)* jet *m*, lancement *m*; *Sport (of javelin, discus etc)* lancer *m*; *(in wrestling) (of opponent)* mise *f* à terre; **his longest t. so far** son meilleur jet jusqu'à présent; **3 throws for 50p** *(at fair etc)* 3 essais *ou* tours pour 50 pence; **it's your t.** *(of javelin, dice etc)* à toi de lancer; **a t. of the dice** un coup de dés

2 *(of crankshaft)* maneton *m*, bras *m* de manivelle

3 *(cover)* jeté *m* de canapé/de fauteuil

VT *(pt* **threw** [θru:]; *pp* **thrown** [θrəʊn]*)* **1** *(ball etc)* lancer, jeter; *Sport (discus, javelin etc)* lancer; **to t. sth at sb/sth** lancer *ou* jeter qch à qn/qch; **to t. sth in sb's face** jeter qch à la figure de qn; *Fig* **don't t. that in my face** ne me faites pas de reproches à ce sujet; **to t. sb a kiss** envoyer un baiser à qn; **to t. the dice** jeter les dés; **to t. a five/a six** *(at dice)* avoir un cinq/six; **to t. a glance at sb** jeter un coup d'œil à *ou* sur qn; **to t. oneself forwards/backwards** se jeter en avant/arrière; **to t. oneself into sth** *(into river etc)* se jeter dans qch; *Fig (into undertaking)* se lancer à corps perdu dans qch; **to t. oneself on sb's mercy** s'en remettre à la merci de qn; *Fig* **she threw herself at him** *(in relationship)* elle s'est jetée à sa tête; **to t. temptation in sb's way** exposer qn à la tentation; **to t. the blame on sb** rejeter la faute sur qn; **to t. a sheet over sth** couvrir qch d'un drap; **to t. a shawl over one's shoulders** jeter un châle sur ses épaules; **to t. sb into prison** jeter *ou* mettre qn en prison; **to t. sb to the lions** jeter qn aux lions; **to t. into confusion** *(government, court, assembly)* semer la confusion au sein de; **to t. a switch** appuyer sur un interrupteur; **to t. open the door** ouvrir la porte toute grande; **to t. open one's house to sb** ouvrir sa maison à qn; **to t. sb out of work** mettre qn au chômage

2 *(image, shadow)* projeter (**on** sur); *Fig* **to t. light on the matter** éclairer la question

3 *Fam* **to t. a fit** piquer une crise; **to t. a party** organiser une soirée

4 *(opponent)* renverser; **to t. its rider** *(of horse)* désarçonner son cavalier; **to be thrown** *(of rider)* vider les arçons, être désarçonné

5 **to t. its skin** *(of reptile)* muer

6 *(of animals)* **to t. a litter** mettre bas

7 *Cer (pot)* tourner, façonner au tour

8 *Fam (disconcert)* déconcerter; **his question threw me for a moment** pendant un moment, je n'ai su que répondre (à sa question); **I was completely thrown** j'étais complètement déconcerté

9 *Sport Fam (deliberately lose) (match, race etc)* perdre délibérément

VI she can t. a hundred metres elle est capable de lancer à cent mètres; **I can't t. straight** je n'arrive pas à lancer droit

▸ **throw about, throw around** VT SEP jeter çà et là; *(scatter)* éparpiller, disséminer; **to a ball around** jouer à la balle; **to t. one's money about** *or* **around** gaspiller son argent; **to t. one's arms about** *or* **around** faire de grands gestes; **to t. oneself about** se démener; **to be thrown about** *(in vehicle etc)* être ballotté; **to like to t. one's weight around** aimer faire sentir sa force

▸ **throw aside** VT SEP *(throw to one side)* jeter sur le côté; *Fig (discard) (career, everything*

one's worked for etc*)* renoncer à; *(person)* rejeter, écarter; *(prejudices, fears, hatred etc)* se débarrasser de

▸ **throw away** VT SEP **1** *(discard)* jeter

2 *(waste)* gaspiller; **to t. away a chance** laisser passer une occasion; **to t. away one's life** *(waste)* gâcher sa vie; *(sacrifice for nothing)* se sacrifier inutilement; **don't t. yourself away on a waster like him** ne gâche pas ta vie pour un bon à rien pareil; **you're just throwing money away buying that stuff** tu gaspilles vraiment ton argent en achetant ce truc; **to t. away a line** *(of actor)* énoncer une phrase avec une indifférence calculée

▸ **throw back** VT SEP **1** *(return by throwing) (fish into water etc)* rejeter; *(ball etc)* renvoyer, relancer; *Fig* **to t. sth back in sb's face** jeter qch à la figure de qn

2 *(reflect) (of mirror) (image etc)* refléter, réfléchir; *(light, heat)* réverbérer

3 *(open forcefully) (shutters etc)* repousser

4 **to t. one's head back** rejeter la tête en arrière

5 *Fig* **to be thrown back upon sb/sth** être forcé de se rabattre sur qn/qch

▸ **throw down** VT SEP *(throw from height)* jeter *(du haut de qch)*; *(throw to the ground)* jeter à *ou* par terre; *(cast aside quickly)* jeter; *Cards* abattre; **to t. oneself down** se jeter sur le sol; **to t. down one's arms** jeter ses armes; *Fig (surrender)* se rendre; *Fam* **it's throwing it down!** *(raining)* qu'est-ce qui tombe!

▸ **throw in** VT SEP **1** *(throw into a place)* jeter dedans; *Ftbl* **to t. in the ball** remettre la balle en jeu; **to t. in one's hand** *ou* **one's cards** *(leave game)* abandonner *ou* quitter la partie; *Fig (admit defeat)* s'avouer vaincu; **to t. in the towel** *Boxing* jeter l'éponge; *Fig (admit defeat)* s'avouer vaincu, jeter l'éponge

2 *(add)* ajouter; *(give as extra)* donner en plus; **if you buy that table I'll t. in the bookcase** si vous achetez cette table, je vous donne la bibliothèque en supplément

3 *(remark, word)* placer

4 **to t. in one's lot with sb** partager le sort de qn

▸ **throw off** VT SEP **1** *(remove hastily) (one's clothes)* enlever *ou* ôter très rapidement; *(mask)* enlever d'un coup

2 *(get rid of) (cold etc)* guérir de; *(pursuer etc)* se débarrasser de; *(oppressive regime)* se libérer de; *(old image)* secouer, se débarrasser de

3 *(write hastily) (poem etc)* composer au pied levé

4 **to t. sb off his bicycle** faire tomber qn de sa bicyclette; **to t. off its rider** *(of horse)* désarçonner son cavalier

5 *(put off)* **to t. the dogs/the police off the scent** semer les chiens/la police

▸ **throw on** VT SEP *(put on hastily) (clothes)* mettre *ou* passer à la hâte; *(wood on fire)* jeter

▸ **throw out** VT SEP **1** *(eject)* jeter dehors; *(person) (from job, pub, nightclub)* mettre à la porte, mettre dehors; *(from school, private club, political party)* exclure

2 *(discard)* jeter *ou* mettre au rebut; *(reject) (bill etc)* rejeter, repousser; **the takeover will t. a lot of people out of work** le rachat va mettre beaucoup de monde au chômage

3 *(give out) (rays etc)* jeter, émettre; *(heat etc)* répandre; **to t. out roots** donner des racines

4 **to t. out one's chest** bomber la poitrine

5 *(challenge etc)* lancer; **to t. out a suggestion** émettre une proposition *(sans insister)*

6 *(disconcert) (speaker etc)* troubler, déconcerter; **to t. sb out in his calculations** tromper qn dans les calculs de qn

7 *Cr (batsman)* mettre hors jeu en lançant la balle sur le guichet

▸ **throw over** VT SEP *(friend etc)* abandonner; *(lover etc) Fam* lâcher, plaquer; **to t. sb over for sb else** laisser tomber qn pour qn d'autre

▸ **throw together** VT SEP **1** *Fam (make hurriedly) (meal)* préparer en vitesse

2 *(gather together hurriedly)* assembler à la hâte; **a few paintings/facts thrown together** quelques tableaux/faits assemblés à la hâte; **the film looks as if it's been thrown together** le film semble bâclé; **chance had thrown us together** le hasard nous avait réunis

▸ **throw up** VT SEP **1** *(throw upwards)* jeter en l'air; *(raise high) (hands etc)* lever haut, mettre haut; **to t. up one's hands in despair** lever les mains en l'air de désespoir

2 *Fam (vomit)* vomir, rendre

3 *(build hurriedly) (house etc)* construire à toute vitesse

4 *(abandon) (project etc)* renoncer à, abandonner; **to t. up one's job** quitter son emploi; **to feel like throwing everything up** avoir envie de tout plaquer

5 *(reveal)* révéler, indiquer; **recent events have thrown up anomalies in the law** les derniers événements ont révélé des anomalies dans la loi; **the discussion threw up some new ideas** la discussion a amené de nouvelles idées

VI *Fam (vomit)* vomir, rendre

---

throwaway ['θrəʊəweɪ] ADJ **1** *(disposable) (nappy, lighter)* à jeter, jetable **2 it was just a t. line** *or* **remark** il/elle/etc a dit ça comme ça **N** *esp Am Fam (leaflet)* prospectus *m*

throwback ['θrəʊbæk] N **1** *Biol* régression *f*; **he's a t. to his great-grandfather** il a hérité (des caractéristiques) de son arrière-grand-père **2** *Fig* retour *m* (en arrière); **it's a t. to the 16th century** c'est un retour au 16ème siècle

thrower ['θrəʊər] N *(of javelin, ball etc)* lanceur, -euse; **discus t.** discobole *m*

throw-in N *Ftbl, Rugby* remise *f* en jeu, touche *f*

throwing ['θrəʊɪŋ] N *(of projectile etc)* jet *m*, lancement *m*; *Sport (of discus etc)* lancer *m*

throw-outs NPL *Com* rebuts *mpl*

thru [θru:] PREP, ADV, ADJ *Am Fam* = **through**

thrum [θrʌm] VI **1** *(drum) (with fingers)* tambouriner **2** *(vibrate)* vrombir

thrush[1] [θrʌʃ] N *(bird)* grive *f*

thrush[2] N *Med* muguet *m*

thrust [θrʌst] N **1** *(push)* poussée *f*, *Fencing* coup *m* d'estoc; *Mil, Com etc Fig* poussée; **a bayonet t.** un coup de baïonnette; **with a single t. of his knife** d'un seul coup de couteau; *Fencing* **t. and parry** la botte et la parade; **the cut and t. of political debate** le jeu d'attaques et de ripostes des débats politiques **2** *(of argument)* the general *or* main t. of an argument l'idée générale d'une argumentation; **the argument has two main thrusts** l'argumentation a deux aspects principaux **3** *Tech* poussée *f*, butée *f*

VT *(pt, pp* **thrust***)* pousser (avec force); **to t. sth into sth** enfoncer *ou* fourrer qch dans qch; **to t. one's hands into one's pockets** fourrer *ou* plonger les mains dans ses poches; **to t. sb into a position of responsibility** être parachuté à un poste à responsabilités; **to t. oneself** *or* **one's way through the crowd** se frayer un chemin à travers la foule

VI to t. at sb *(with end of stick etc)* porter un coup à qn; *Fencing* porter un coup d'estoc à qn

▸ ▸ **t. washer** rondelle *f* de butée

▸ **thrust aside, thrust away** VT SEP *(reject)* repousser *ou* écarter d'un geste brusque;

Lit **to t. temptation aside** repousser *ou* écarter la tentation
▶ **thrust forward** VT SEP *(push forward)* pousser en avant; *Fig* **to t. oneself forward** se mettre en avant
▶ **thrust upon, thrust upon** VT SEP *(force on)* **to. t. sth on sb** forcer qn à accepter qch; **to t. an opinion on sb** imposer son opinion à qn; **the responsibility was t. upon me** on m'en a imposé la responsabilité; **and some have greatness t. upon them** et à certains la grandeur *ou* la noblesse s'impose; **to t. oneself (up)on sb** s'imposer à qn *ou* chez qn
▶ **thrust out** VT SEP *(one's arm, leg)* allonger brusquement; *(chest)* bomber; **he t. his head out of the car window** il passa brusquement la tête par la vitre de la voiture

thruster ['θrʌstər] N *Astronaut (rocket engine)* propulseur *m*

thrustful ['θrʌstfʊl] ADJ = **thrusting**

thrusting ['θrʌstɪŋ] ADJ *(dynamic)* entreprenant, dynamique

thruway ['θru:weɪ] N *Am* autoroute *f*

thud [θʌd] N bruit *m* sourd
VI **(-dd-)** tomber avec un bruit sourd; **his feet went thudding along the corridor** ses pas résonnaient sourdement dans le couloir; **my heart was thudding against my ribs** mon cœur cognait sourdement dans ma poitrine; **the missile thudded into its target** le projectile frappa sa cible avec un bruit sourd

thug [θʌg] N brute *f*

thumb [θʌm] N pouce *m*; *Fam* **he's all thumbs** il est maladroit; *Fig* **to be under sb's t.** être sous la domination de qn; **she's got him right under her t.** elle le mène à la baguette; *Fam* **to stick out like a sore t.** choquer la vue; *Fam* **thumbs up!** bravo!; *Fam* **to give the thumbs up/down to a proposal** accepter/rejeter une proposition
VT **1 to t. a book** feuilleter *ou* parcourir un livre; **well thumbed book** livre qui a beaucoup servi **2 to t. one's nose at sb** faire un pied de nez à qn **3** *Fam* **to t. a lift** *or* **ride** faire de l'auto-stop *ou* du stop; **I thumbed a lift with a Dutch motorist** un conducteur hollandais m'a pris en stop
VI **to t. through a book** feuilleter *ou* parcourir un livre
▶▶ **t. index** répertoire *m* à onglets

thumb-indexed ['θʌm'ɪndekst] ADJ *(edition etc)* à onglets

thumbmark ['θʌmmɑ:k] N marque *f* de pouce

thumbnail ['θʌmneɪl] N **1** ongle *m* du pouce **2** *Comput* vignette *f*
▶▶ **t. sketch** *(of plan)* aperçu *m*, croquis *m* rapide; *(of personality)* bref portrait *m*

thumbprint ['θʌmprɪnt] N empreinte *f* de pouce

thumbscrew ['θʌmskru:] N *Tech* vis *f* à oreilles; *(for torture)* = instrument *m* de torture utilisé pour écraser les pouces des prisonniers

thumbstall ['θʌmstɔ:l] N *Med* doigtier *m* pour pouce

thumbtack ['θʌmtæk] N *Am* punaise *f*

thump [θʌmp] N **1** *(sound)* bruit *m* sourd; **with a loud t.** avec un gros bruit sourd **2** *(blow with fist)* coup *m* de poing; **he's given himself a t. on the head** il s'est cogné la tête
VT *(person)* cogner; *(repeatedly)* bourrer de coups; *(table)* cogner sur; **don't t. it down like that, be careful!** *(put down heavily)* ne le cogne pas comme ça en le posant, fais attention!; **he thumped his fist on the table** il cogna du poing sur la table
VI *(on table etc)* cogner; **my heart was thumping** mon cœur battait la chamade;

the upstairs neighbours were thumping about les voisins d'en haut martelaient le sol; **stop thumping about!** vous voulez bien cesser ce boucan!
▶ **thump out** VT SEP *(play heavily)* **to t. out a tune** *(on piano)* marteler un air

thumping ['θʌmpɪŋ] ADJ *Fam* **a t. great …** un/une énorme …; **a t. headache** un mal de tête de tous les diables; **a t. big lie** un gros mensonge

thunder ['θʌndər] N tonnerre *m*; **clap of t.** coup *m* de tonnerre; **peal** *or* **roll of t.** roulement *m* *ou* grondement *m* *ou* coup de tonnerre; **there's t. in the air** le temps est à l'orage; **voice like t.** voix *f* tonnante *ou* tonitruante; **with a face like t.** le visage fulminant de colère; *Fig* **to steal sb's t.** couper ses effets à qn; *Old-fashioned* **what in t. do you think you're doing?** tonnerre de Dieu! mais qu'est-ce qui te prend?
VI **1** *Met (of guns, waves)* faire un bruit de tonnerre; **it's thundering** il tonne; **it's thundering and lightning** il y a du tonnerre et des éclairs **2** *(move noisily)* **the avalanche thundered down** l'avalanche dévala dans un bruit de tonnerre; **the train thundered past** le train passa dans un bruit de tonnerre; **lorries thundered through the village** des camions traversèrent le village dans un bruit de tonnerre **3** *(of speaker)* tonitruer, tonner; **to t. against sb/sth** tonner contre qn/qch; **he thundered about the need for greater vigilance** il tonnait *ou* tonitruait sur la nécessité d'une plus grande vigilance
VT *(order)* ordonner d'une voix tonitruante; **get out!, he thundered** dehors!, tonitrua-t-il *ou* dit-il d'une voix tonitruante

thunderbolt ['θʌndəbəʊlt] N coup *m* de foudre; *Fig (astounding event etc)* coup *m* d'éclat; *(piece of news)* nouvelle *f* foudroyante; **the news came like a t.** cette nouvelle m'a/t'a/l'a/*etc* stupéfait

thunderclap ['θʌndəklæp] N coup *m* de tonnerre

thundercloud ['θʌndəklaʊd] N nuage *m* orageux

thundering ['θʌnd(ə)rɪŋ] ADJ *(sound etc)* tonnant, tonitruant; **t. applause** tonnerre *m* d'applaudissements; **to be in a t. rage** être dans une colère noire; *Old-fashioned Fam* **what a t. nuisance!** que c'est embêtant!; *Old-fashioned Fam* **what a t. (great) lie!** quel mensonge énorme!

thunderous ['θʌnd(ə)rəs] ADJ *(voice etc)* tonnant, tonitruant; **t. applause** tonnerre *m* d'applaudissements, applaudissements *mpl* à tout rompre

thunderstorm ['θʌndəstɔ:m] N orage *m*

thunderstruck ['θʌndəstrʌk] ADJ abasourdi; **I was t. by the news** cette nouvelle m'a stupéfait *ou* stupéfié

thunderthighs ['θʌndəθaɪz] N *Fam Hum* = femme *f* aux grosses cuisses

thundery ['θʌndərɪ] ADJ *(sky)* orageux; *(weather)* orageux, d'orage; **the weather's t.** le temps est orageux *ou* à l'orage
▶▶ **t. shower** averse *f* accompagnée de tonnerre

Thur *abbr* **Thursday**

thurible ['θjʊərɪb(ə)l] N *Rel* encensoir *m*

Thurs *abbr* **Thursday**

Thursday ['θɜ:zdɪ] N jeudi *m*; **T. 5 May** jeudi 5 mai; **T. morning/evening** jeudi matin/soir; **it's T. today** nous sommes jeudi aujourd'hui; **he comes on Thursdays** il vient le jeudi; **he's coming on T.** il vient jeudi; **every T.** tous les jeudis; **Maundy T.** jeudi saint VOIR GRAMMAIRE A81–2; B61–2

thus [ðʌs] ADV **1** *esp Lit (in this way)* ainsi, de cette façon, de cette manière; **t. prepared** ainsi préparé, préparé de cette façon **2**

(therefore) ainsi, donc; **t., when he arrived** donc, lorsqu'il est arrivé **3 t. far** *(as far as this)* jusqu'ici; *(as far as that)* jusque-là; **t. much** autant que cela (et pas davantage)

thwack [θwæk] N *(blow)* coup *m*; *(with hand)* claque *f*, *Fam* taloche *f*; *(noise)* claquement *m*; **with a t.** avec un coup sec; **I gave myself a t. on the shin** je me suis donné un coup dans le tibia
VT *(hit hard) (ball, head)* frapper; *(slap)* gifler; **I thwacked my head on the beam** je me suis cogné la tête contre la poutre

thwart[1] [θwɔ:t, *Naut* θɔ:t] N *(in rowing boat)* banc *m* de nage

thwart[2] VT *(person)* contrarier; *(plot, scheme)* déjouer; **to be thwarted** *(of person)* essuyer un échec

thy [ðaɪ] POSS ADJ *(before a vowel* **thine***)* *Arch, Lit* ton, *f* ta, *pl* tes

thyme [taɪm] N *Bot, Culin* thym *m*; **wild t.** serpolet *m*

thymus ['θaɪməs] N *Anat* thymus *m*, glande *f* thymique

thyristor [θaɪ'rɪstər] N thyristor *m*

thyroid ['θaɪrɔɪd] ADJ, N thyroïde *f*

thyself [ðaɪ'self] PERS PRON *Arch, Lit* toi(-même); *(reflexive)* te

ti [ti:] N *Mus* si *m*

tiara [tɪ'ɑ:rə] N **1** diadème *m* **2** *Rel* tiare *f*

Tiber (the) [ðə'taɪbər] N le Tibre

Tiberius [taɪ'bɪərɪəs] N Tibère

Tibet [tɪ'bet] N Tibet *m*

Tibetan [tɪ'bet(ə)n] ADJ tibétain
N **1** Tibétain, -aine **2** *Ling* tibétain *m*

tibia ['tɪbɪə] N *Anat* tibia *m*

tic [tɪk] N *Med* tic *m*; **a nervous t.** un tic nerveux

tich [tɪtʃ] N *Br Fam* **a (little) t.** *(person)* un (petit) bout de chou

tichy ['tɪtʃɪ] ADJ *Br Fam* minuscule

tick[1] [tɪk] N **1** *(sound) (of clock)* tic-tac *m* **2** *Br Fam (moment)* instant *m*; **just a t.!, half a t.!** un instant!, une seconde!; **it'll only take me a couple of ticks** je vais faire ça en deux secondes **3** *(mark)* marque *f*, coche *f*; **to put a t. against a name** cocher un nom
VI **to t.** *(of clock)* faire tic-tac, tictaquer; **the minutes are ticking by** les minutes passent; *Fam* **I'd like to know what makes him t.** je voudrais bien savoir ce qui le motive
VT = **tick off 1**
▶▶ *St Exch* **t. size** échelon *m* de cotation
▶ **tick away** VI **time is ticking away** le temps passe
▶ **tick off** VT SEP **1** *(mark with tick) (article on list etc)* pointer; *(name)* cocher **2** *Br Fam (reprimand)* attraper, enguirlander; **to get ticked off** se faire rembarrer **3** *Am Fam (irritate)* **to t. sb off** embêter qn; **he's really ticked off** il est drôlement en rogne
▶ **tick over** VI *(of engine)* tourner au ralenti; **the engine is ticking over nicely** le moteur tourne bien; **my business is just ticking over** les affaires vont doucement; **business is ticking over nicely** les affaires tournent bien; **it keeps my brain ticking over** ça fait travailler ma cervelle

tick[2] N *(parasite) (on cattle etc)* tique *f*

tick[3] N *Br Fam (credit)* crédit *m*; **to buy** *or* **get sth on t.** acheter qch à crédit

tick[4] N *(mattress cover)* enveloppe *f*, housse *f* (à matelas)

ticker ['tɪkər] N **1** *Sl (watch)* montre *f*, *(clock)* pendule *f*; *(heart)* palpitant *m* **2** *St Exch* téléimprimeur *m*, téléscripteur *m*
▶▶ **t. tape** bande *f* de téléimprimeur; **to be given a t. tape welcome** être accueilli sous une pluie de serpentins

ticket ['tɪkɪt] N **1** *(railway, air, theatre, lottery* *etc*) billet *m*; *(underground, bus, for cloakroom etc)* ticket *m*; *Theat etc* **complimentary t.** billet de faveur; *Rail etc* **single t.** billet simple, (billet d')aller *m*; **return t.** billet d'aller-retour, aller-retour *m inv*; **left-luggage t., cloakroom t.** bulletin *m ou* ticket de consigne; **platform t.** ticket de quai; **season t.** carte *f* d'abonnement; **season-t. holder** abonné, -ée; *Aut Fam* **(parking) t.** P.V. *m inv*; papillon *m*; **to get a (parking) t.** attraper un P.V.; **t. holders only** *(on sign)* réservé aux personnes munies de billets

2 *Com* **(price) t.** étiquette *f*; **this doesn't have a t. on it** il n'y a pas de prix sur cet article

3 *esp Am Pol (list of candidates)* liste *f* des candidats; *Fam* **the Democratic t.** *(policies)* le programme du parti démocrate

4 *Naut Fam* **to get one's (master's) t.** passer (son brevet de) capitaine

5 *Fam* **it was just the t.!** voilà juste ce qu'il me fallait

VT (**ticketed**) *(goods)* étiqueter

▸▸ **t. agency** *Theat* agence *f* de spectacles; *Rail* agence de voyages; **t. barrier** portillon *m* automatique; *Rail* **t. collector** contrôleur, -euse, *Belg* accompagnateur, -trice de train; **t. desk** guichet *m*; *Br Rail* **t. inspector** contrôleur, -euse, *Belg* accompagnateur, -trice de train; **t. machine** distributeur *m* de tickets, billetterie *f* automatique; **t. office** bureau *m* de vente des billets, guichet *m*; **t. punch** *(of ticket inspector)* poinçon *m*; *(for use by passengers)* composteur *m*; *esp Am Pol* **t. splitting** panachage *m*; *Am* **t. taker** contrôleur, -euse; *Br* **t. tout** revendeur, -euse de billets *(au marché noir)*; **t. window** guichet *m*

ticketing ['tɪkɪtɪŋ] **N** *(issuing of tickets)* billetterie *f*

ticketless ['tɪkɪtləs] **ADJ** *(travel etc)* sans billet

ticking[1] ['tɪkɪŋ] **N** *(of clock)* tic-tac *m*

▸▸ *Br Fam* **t. off** engueulade *f*; **to get a t. off** (se) prendre un savon; **to give sb a t. off** passer un savon à qn

ticking[2] ['tɪkɪŋ] **N** *Tex* toile *f ou* coutil *m* à matelas

tickle ['tɪk(ə)l] **N** chatouillement *m*; **he gave her a t.** il lui a fait des chatouilles; **to have a t. in one's throat** avoir un chatouillement dans la gorge

VT 1 *(person)* chatouiller; *Fam (amuse)* amuser; **to t. the palate** *(of food, wine)* chatouiller le palais; *Fam* **to t. sb's fancy** faire envie à qn; *Fam* **to be tickled to death** *or* **tickled pink at** *or* **by sth** *(be amused)* s'amuser beaucoup de qch; *(be delighted)* être enchanté *ou* ravi de qch **2** *Fishing (trout)* pêcher à la main **3** *Hum* **to t. the ivories** pianoter, tapoter

VI **hey, that tickles!** eh, ça chatouille!; **you're tickling!** tu me chatouilles!

tickler ['tɪklər] **N** *esp Br Fam (problem)* os *m*; *(delicate subject)* sujet *m* délicat

tickling ['tɪklɪŋ] **ADJ** qui chatouille

N chatouillement *m*

ticklish ['tɪklɪʃ] **ADJ 1** *(person)* chatouilleux **2** *(touchy)* chatouilleux; *(subject, task etc)* délicat; **to be in a t. situation** se trouver dans une situation délicate

tickly ['tɪklɪ] **ADJ** *(blanket, pullover)* qui grattouille; *(cough)* irritant, d'irritation; **a t. throat** une irritation dans la gorge

ticktack ['tɪktæk] **N** *Br Horseracing* = signaux *mpl* utilisés entre les bookmakers

▸▸ **t. man** aide *m* de bookmaker (qui fait des signaux avec les bras)

tick-tack-toe N *Am* morpion *m*

tidal ['taɪd(ə)l] **ADJ 1** de la marée; *(energy etc)* marémoteur, -trice **2** *(river etc)* à marée

▸▸ **t. basin** bassin *m* à flot; **t. harbour** port *m* à *ou* de marée; **t. wave** raz-de-marée *m inv*; *Fig (of sympathy, enthusiasm, emotion)* vague *f*

---

tidbit ['tɪdbɪt] **N** *Am* = **titbit**

tiddler ['tɪdlər] **N** *Br Fam (small fish)* petit poisson *m*; *(minnow)* épinoche *f*, *(child)* bambin *m*, mioche *mf*

tiddl(e)y ['tɪdlɪ] **ADJ** *Br Fam* **1** *(small)* minuscule **2** *(drunk)* éméché

tiddlywinks ['tɪdlɪwɪŋks] **N** jeu *m* de puce

tide [taɪd] **N 1** marée *f*, **ebb t.** marée descendante, jusant *m*; **high/low t.** marée haute/basse; **neap t.** marée de morte-eau; **spring t.** grande marée, marée de vive eau; *Naut* **to go out with the t.** partir à la marée; **rise/fall of the t.** montée *f*/baisse *f* de l'eau; *also Fig* **against the t.** à contre-courant; *Fig* **the rising t. of discontent** la vague croissante du mécontentement; *Fig* **the t. of events** le cours des événements; *Fig* **when the t. of the battle turned** quand le cours de la bataille changea; *Fig* **the t. has turned** le vent a tourné

2 *Arch (season)* temps *m*, saison *f*

▸▸ **t. gate** porte *f* à flot; **t. race** courant *m* de marée rapide; **t. table** échelle *f ou* table *f* des marées, almanach *m* (des marées)

▸ **tide over VT SEP** aider à surmonter une difficulté, *Fam* dépanner; **can you lend me five pounds to t. me over till Monday?** pourrais-tu me prêter cinq livres pour me dépanner jusqu'à lundi?

tidemark ['taɪdmɑːk] **N 1** *(mark left by tide)* laisse *f* de haute mer **2** *Br Fam (line of dirt) (in bath etc)* ligne *f* de crasse

tidewater ['taɪdwɔːtər] **N** eau *f* de marée; *Am (coastal land)* côte *f*

tideway ['taɪdweɪ] **N** lit *m* de la marée

tidily ['taɪdɪlɪ] **ADV** avec ordre; *(dressed etc)* avec soin, soigneusement; **he puts everything away t. in a drawer at night** il range tout bien en ordre *ou* soigneusement dans un tiroir le soir

tidiness ['taɪdɪnɪs] **N** *(of room, files etc)* ordre *m*; *(of person)* goût *m* de l'ordre; *(in appearance, dress, of handwriting)* soin *m*

tidings ['taɪdɪŋz] **NPL** *Lit* nouvelle(s) *f(pl)*

tidy ['taɪdɪ] **ADJ 1** *(desk, room)* bien rangé, en ordre; *(handwriting)* net, soigné; *(hair)* soigné; **to have a t. mind** être méthodique, avoir l'esprit clair; **a clean and t. room** une pièce propre et nette; **he's very t.** *(in habits)* il est très ordonné; *(in appearance)* il est très soigné **2** *Fam (considerable)* assez considérable; *(profit)* joli petit; **a t. sum** une somme rondelette

N vide-poches *m inv*; **sink t.** coin *m* d'évier

VT *(room)* ranger, mettre de l'ordre dans; **to t. one's hair** s'arranger les cheveux

▸ **tidy away VT SEP** *(put away) (books etc)* ranger

▸ **tidy up VI** *(clear things away)* ranger

VT SEP *(room)* ranger, mettre de l'ordre dans; *(file, essay)* faire le ménage dans; **to t. things up** ranger; **to t. oneself up** faire un bout de toilette

tidy-out N nettoyage *m* par le vide

tidy-up N **to give a room a t.** ranger une pièce

TIE [taɪ]

N lien **1, 2** ■ attache **1** ■ cordon **2**		
■ cravate **3** ■ traverse **4** ■ match nul **6**		
VT nouer **1** ■ faire **1** ■ attacher **1**		
■ ligoter **1**		
VI être à égalité **1** ■ s'attacher **2**		

N 1 *(link)* lien *m*; **he has no ties to the place** il n'y a rien qui l'attache à cet endroit; **family ties** liens de famille; **ties of friendship** liens d'amitié

2 *(of rope, straw, wicker etc)* lien *m*; *(for plastic bag)* cordon *m*

---

3 *(neck tie)* cravate *f*; **bow t.** nœud *m* papillon; **black t.** *(on invitation)* = smoking *m*; **old school t.** = cravate *f* portée par les anciens élèves d'une école; **it's the old school t.** *(that's why he got the job etc)* ce sont les vieilles relations *ou* amitiés d'école

4 *Constr etc* crampon *m*; *Am Rail* traverse *f*

5 *Mus* liaison *f*

6 *Sport (match)* match *m* nul; *(competition)* = compétition *f* dont les gagnants sont ex æquo; **(cup) t.** *(match)* = match de coupe

VT *(pt, pp* **tied**, *prp* **tying**) **1** *(piece of string, neck tie etc)* nouer; *(knot)* faire; *(shoelace, hood strings)* attacher, nouer; *(dog to kennel etc)* attacher, ligoter; *(sb to post)* attacher, ligoter; **to t. sth to sth** attacher qch à qch; **to t. two things together** lier deux choses entre elles, attacher deux choses l'une à l'autre; *also Fig* **to t. sb's hands** lier les mains à qn; **to be tied hand and foot** être ligoté; **to have one's hands tied (behind one's back)** avoir les mains liées (derrière le dos); *Fig* **to have one's hands tied** avoir les mains liées, être pieds et poings liés

2 *(restrict)* **he was tied to his desk** il est resté rivé à son bureau; **the children kept her tied to the house** elle était clouée chez elle à cause des enfants; **she felt tied by her sense of duty** elle se sentait contrainte par son sens du devoir

3 *(link)* **to be tied to** avoir un lien avec

4 *Mus (two notes)* lier

VI 1 *Sport etc* être *ou* arriver à égalité (**with** avec); *(of candidates)* obtenir un nombre égal de suffrages; *Sch* **to t. for first place** être premier ex æquo (**with** avec)

2 *(apron, shoelace)* s'attacher, se nouer; **the dress ties at the back** la robe s'attache par derrière

▸▸ *Constr* **t. beam** longrine *f*; **t. clip** fixe-cravate *m*, *pl* fixe-cravates; **t. microphone** micro-cravate *m*, *pl* micros-cravates; **t. rack** porte-cravates *m inv*

▸ **tie back VT SEP** *(hair, curtains)* attacher (en arrière)

▸ **tie down VT SEP 1** *(prevent from moving by tying)* **to t. sb down** immobiliser qn en l'attachant; **to t. sth down** assujettir qch

2 *(restrict to certain conditions)* assujettir à certaines conditions; **children t. you down** les enfants représentent une contrainte; **this ticket doesn't t. you down to specific dates** ce billet vous laisse libre de changer vos dates de départ; **to t. sb down to facts** obliger qn à ne pas s'écarter des faits; **tied down to one's job** accaparé par son travail

▸ **tie in VI** *(correspond) (of facts, story)* concorder, cadrer, *Fam* coller (**with** avec); **the two versions don't t. in** les deux versions ne concordent *ou Fam* ne collent pas

VT to t. sth in with sth faire concorder *ou Fam* coller qch avec qch; **this sequence has to be tied in with the rest of the film** il faut qu'on intègre cette séquence au reste du film

▸ **tie on VT SEP 1** *(attach by tying) (label etc)* attacher avec une ficelle

2 *Am Fam* **to t. one on** *(get drunk)* prendre une cuite, se cuiter

▸ **tie up VT SEP 1** *(tie together) (parcel etc)* attacher, ficeler; *(hair)* nouer, attacher; *(top of bag)* lier, ficeler; *(injured arm etc)* bander, panser; **her hair was tied up with a ribbon** ses cheveux étaient attachés par un ruban; **there were various strands of the plot to t. up in the last episode** il y avait, dans l'histoire, beaucoup de péripéties qui demandaient une conclusion au dernier épisode

2 *(prevent from moving) (animal)* attacher; *(person)* ligoter; *(boat)* amarrer

3 *(prevent from being spent) (capital)* immobiliser; **my capital is tied up in stocks and shares** mon capital est immobilisé sous forme d'actions *ou* en actions guent très facilement; **to grow** *or* **get t. of doing sth** se lasser de faire qch; *Fam* **I'm t. of you** j'en ai assez de vous; **t. of arguing, he consented** de guerre lasse, il a donné son consentement; *Fam* **t. old carpet** vieux tapis *m* usé; **t. phrase** expression *f* usée; **in a t. voice** d'une voix lasse *ou* fatiguée

tiredly ['taɪədlɪ] ADV avec lassitude

tiredness ['taɪədnɪs] N fatigue *f, Med* asthénie *f*

tireless ['taɪəlɪs] ADJ *(worker, campaigner etc)* infatigable; *(efforts)* inlassable

tirelessly ['taɪəlɪslɪ] ADV infatigablement, inlassablement

tiresome ['taɪəsəm] ADJ *(boring)* assommant, ennuyeux; *(irritating, annoying)* fatigant, exaspérant; **how t.!** que c'est ennuyeux *ou* assommant!

Attention: ne pas confondre avec **tiring**, qui se rapporte le plus souvent à la fatigue physique.

tiring ['taɪərɪŋ] ADJ *(work, journey, day, person etc)* fatigant

Attention: ne pas confondre avec **tiresome**, qui signifie **ennuyeux**.

tiro, pl tiros, tiroes ['taɪrəʊ, -əʊz] N = **tyro**

'tis [tɪz] CONTR = **it is,** *see* **be**

tissue ['tɪʃuː] N **1** *Biol* tissu *m* **2** *(paper handkerchief)* mouchoir *m* en papier; *(paper)* papier *m* de soie; *Fig* **t. of lies** tissu de mensonges

▸▸ **t. paper** papier de soie

Note that the French word **tissu** also means **fabric**.

tiswas ['tɪzwɒz] N *Fam* = **tizzy**

tit¹ [tɪt] N *(bird)* mésange *f*; **blue t.** mésange bleue; **coal t.** mésange noire; **great t.** (mésange) charbonnière *f*

tit² N **t. for tat** un prêté pour un rendu; **to give sb t. for tat** rendre la pareille à qn; *(verbally)* répondre du tac au tac

tit³ N *Sl* **1** *(breast)* nichon *m*, téton *m*, néné *m*; **to get on sb's tits** *(annoy, irritate)* porter sur le système à qn **2** *(idiot)* imbécile *mf*; **I felt a right t.** je me suis senti vraiment bête, j'ai eu l'impression d'être un parfait imbécile

Titan ['taɪt(ə)n] N *Myth* Titan *m*; *Fig* **t.** titan *m*

titanic [taɪ'tænɪk] ADJ titanesque

titanium [taɪ'teɪnɪəm] N *Chem* titane *m*

titbit ['tɪtbɪt] N *(food)* morceau *m, pl* -aux, de choix; *(sweet)* friandise *f*; *(of gossip)* potin *m*

titch, titchy [tɪtʃ, 'tɪtʃɪ] *Br Fam* = **tich, tichy**

titfer ['tɪtfər] N *Old-fashioned Br Sl (hat)* galurin *m*, bitos *m*

tit-for-tat ADJ *(killing, expulsions etc)* fait en représailles *ou* en riposte

tithe [taɪð] N dîme *f*

▸▸ **t. barn** = grange *f* où l'on mettait les recettes de la dîme

Titian ['tɪʃɪən] N le Titien

ADJ *(hair)* acajou *inv*

titillate ['tɪtɪleɪt] VT *(readers, viewers)* émoustiller; *(senses)* émoustiller, titiller; *(palate)* chatouiller

VI *(of film, book etc)* titiller les sens

titillating ['tɪtɪleɪtɪŋ] ADJ titillant, émoustillant

titillation [tɪtɪ'leɪʃən] N titillation *f*

titivate ['tɪtɪveɪt] VT *Old-fashioned (person)* faire beau, pomponner; *(thing)* pomponner, bichonner; **to t. oneself** se faire beau, se pomponner

title ['taɪtl] N **1** *(of book, chapter)* titre *m*; *(of*

article, act) titre, intitulé *m*; **the story that gives the collection its t.** l'histoire qui donne son titre à la collection; **the t. is taken from …** le titre est tiré de …; **to publish fifty titles a year** publier cinquante titres par an **2** *(of person)* titre *m*; **to give sb a t.** donner un titre à qn, titrer qn; **to have a t.** *(of nobility)* avoir un titre de noblesse, être titré **3** *Sport* titre *m*; **to hold the t.** détenir le titre (de champion) **4** *Law (deed)* titre *m* (constitutif) de propriété, acte *m* de propriété; **t. to property** titre de propriété **5** *Cin, TV* **titles** *(credits)* générique *m*

VT *(book etc)* intituler

▸▸ *Comput* **t. bar** barre *f* de titre; *Law* **t. deed** titre (constitutif) de propriété, acte *m* de propriété; *Boxing* **t. fight** combat *m* comptant pour le titre; **non t. fight** combat ne comptant pas pour le titre; *Law* **t. holder** propriétaire *mf*; **t. music** musique *f* de générique; **t. page** page *f* de titre; **t. piece** *(of anthology)* conte *m*/morceau *m* qui donne son titre au recueil; *Theat* **t. rôle** rôle *m* qui donne son titre à la pièce; *Mus* **t. track** morceau *m* qui donne son titre à l'album

titled ['taɪtld] ADJ *(person)* titré; **to be t.** avoir un titre (de noblesse)

titleholder ['taɪtlhəʊldər] N *Sport* tenant, -ante du titre

titler ['taɪtlər] N *Cin* titreur, -euse

titmouse, pl titmice ['tɪtmaʊs, -maɪs] N *(bird)* mésange *f*

titrate ['taɪtreɪt] VT *Chem, Ind (solution)* titrer

titter ['tɪtər] N *(suppressed laughter)* rire *m* étouffé; *(nervous laughter)* petit rire nerveux *ou* bête

VI *(in suppressed way)* avoir un petit rire étouffé; *(laugh nervously)* rire nerveusement *ou* bêtement

tittering ['tɪtərɪŋ] N petits rires *mpl*

tittie ['tɪtɪ] N *Sl* = **titty**

tittle ['tɪt(ə)l] N = **jot**

tittle-tattle N *(gossip)* potins *mpl, Fam* cancans *mpl*

VI *(gossip)* *Fam* cancaner

titty ['tɪtɪ] N *Sl (breast)* nichon *m*; *Fig* **that's tough t., that's his tough t.** (c'est) tant pis pour lui

titular ['tɪtjʊlər] ADJ titulaire; *(function, office etc)* nominal, -aux; **t. possessions** terres *fpl* attachées à un titre

tizzy ['tɪzɪ] N *Fam* **to be in a t.** ne (pas) savoir où donner de la tête; **to get into a t.** se mettre dans tous ses états

T-junction N bifurcation *f* en T

TLC [tiːel'siː] N *(abbr* **tender loving care)** affection *f*

TNT [tiːen'tiː] N *(abbr* **trinitrotoluene)** TNT *m*

TO [tuː, *unstressed* tə]

PREP à **1, 2, 4–7, 9–11, 15** ▪ en **1, 4** ▪ vers **2** ▪ jusqu'à **5** ▪ sur **8** ▪ de **9** ▪ contre **11** | WITH THE INFINITIVE | pour **1** ▪ à **2**

PREP **1** à; **to go to church/to school** aller à l'église/à l'école; **what school do you go to?** à quelle école allez-vous?, *Fam* tu vas où à l'école?, tu es dans quelle école?; **I'm off to bed** je vais au lit *ou* me coucher; **I'm off to Paris** je pars pour Paris; **he went to France/to Japan** il est allé en France/au Japon; **she returned home to her family** elle est rentrée auprès de sa famille; **I am going to the grocer's** je vais chez l'épicier; **from town to town** de ville en ville; **flights to the Continent** vols à destination de l'Europe; **the road to London** la route de Londres; **a journey to Paris** un voyage à Paris; **the shortest way to the station** le plus court chemin pour aller à la gare

2 *(towards)* vers, à; **to the east** vers l'est; **to the trains** *(on sign)* accès aux quais; **to the right** à droite; **to the left** à gauche; **the rooms to the back** les chambres de derrière

3 *(next to)* **elbow to elbow** coude à coude; **I told him so to his face** je le lui ai dit en face; **to clasp sb to one's heart** serrer qn sur son cœur; **to fall to the ground** tomber à *ou* par terre

4 *(of time)* **from morning to night** du matin au soir; **from day to day** de jour en jour; **the day to day running of the school** l'administration de tous les jours de l'école; **ten minutes to six** six heures moins dix; **it's ten to** il est moins dix

5 *(until)* jusqu'à; **to this day** jusqu'à ce jour; **to count up to ten** compter jusqu'à dix; **moved to tears** ému (jusqu')aux larmes; **fight to the death** bataille *ou* combat à mort; **to a high degree** à un haut degré; **generous to a fault** généreux à l'excès; **accurate to a millimetre** exact au millimètre près; **a year to the day** un an jour pour jour; **to cut sth down to a minimum** réduire qch au minimum

6 *(purpose)* **to this end** à cet effet, dans ce but

7 *(result)* **to my despair** à mon grand désespoir; **to everyone's surprise** à la surprise de tous; **to put to flight** mettre en fuite; **to pull to pieces** mettre en pièces

8 **what tune is it sung to?** sur quel air cela se chante-t-il?

9 *(of)* **heir to sb/to an estate** héritier de qn/ d'une propriété; **ambassador to the King of Sweden** ambassadeur auprès du roi de Suède; **apprentice to a joiner** apprenti chez un menuisier; **the key to the door** la clef de la porte; **the answer to a question** la réponse à une question

10 *(in comparisons)* **superior to** supérieur à; **compared to this** comparé à *ou* en comparaison de celui-ci; **that's nothing to what I have seen** cela n'est rien à côté de ce que j'ai vu

11 *(expressing a proportion)* **three is to six as six is to twelve** trois est à six ce que six est à douze; **six votes to four** six voix pour quatre; **three goals to nil** trois buts à zéro; **to bet ten to one** parier dix contre un

12 **to all appearances** selon les apparences; **not to my taste** pas à mon goût; **to the best of my recollection** (pour) autant que je m'en souvienne

13 **to drink to sb** boire à la santé de qn

14 *(concerning)* **what did she say to my suggestion?** qu'est-ce qu'elle a dit de ma proposition?; **is that all there is to it?** c'est tout?; **there's nothing to it** *(it's easy)* c'est simple comme bonjour; **there's nothing** *or* **there isn't a lot to these cameras** ils ne sont pas bien compliqués, ces appareils-photos

15 *(used to form the dative)* à; **to give sth to sb** donner qch à qn; **he gave it to her** il le lui a donné; **who did you give it to?** à qui l'avez-vous donné?; **to speak to sb** parler à qn; *Fml* **to whom?** à qui?; **what's it to you?** qu'est-ce que ça peut te faire?; **to keep sth to oneself** garder qch pour soi; **he has been a father to me** il a été un père pour moi; **known to the ancients** connu des anciens

VOIR GRAMMAIRE A40–2; B35–7 *(with the infinitive)* **1** *(purpose, result)* pour; **he came to help me** il est venu (pour) m'aider; **we must eat (in order) to live** il faut manger pour vivre; **so to speak** pour ainsi dire; **born to rule** né pour régner; **happy to do it** heureux de le faire; **ready to listen** prêt à écouter; **old enough to go to school** en âge d'aller à l'école; **built to house 10 people** construit pour loger 10 personnes; **too hot to drink** trop chaud pour qu'on puisse le boire; **to hear her speak, you'd think she owned the place!** à l'entendre, on dirait que c'est elle le propriétaire des lieux!; **he left the house never to return to it again** il quitta la maison pour ne plus y revenir

2 I have a letter to write j'ai une lettre à écrire; **I have a lot to do** j'ai beaucoup à faire; **there was not a sound to be heard** on n'entendait pas le moindre bruit; **he isn't one to forget his friends** il n'est pas homme à oublier ses amis; **there's a tendency to forget that** on a tendance à l'oublier; **I have no desire to do that** je n'ai aucun désir de le faire

VOIR GRAMMAIRE A55

3 to lie is shameful, it is shameful to lie il est honteux de mentir; **to be or not to be** être ou ne pas être; **it is better to do nothing** il vaut mieux ne rien faire; **he learned to do it** il a appris à le faire; **I refuse to do it** je refuse de le faire

4 *(infinitive clause)* **I want him to know** je veux qu'il sache; **it seemed to grow** il/elle semblait grandir

5 *(in headline)* **a hundred employees to go** cent employés vont être mis au chômage; **Blair to meet Chirac** entretiens entre Messieurs Blair et Chirac

6 *(with ellipsis of verb)* **you ought to** vous devriez le faire; **I want to** j'ai envie de le faire; *(I would like to)* je voudrais bien; **take it, it would be absurd not to** prenez-le, ce serait absurde de ne pas le faire *ou* de ne manquer l'occasion; **we shall have to** il le faudra bien, nous serons bien obligés

ADV *(stressed)* **1 to pull the door to** fermer la porte; **to turn to** *ou* **set to with a will** se mettre résolument à l'ouvrage; **to come to** *(to one's senses)* reprendre connaissance

2 to go to and fro aller et venir; *(of shuttle bus etc)* faire la navette

toad [təʊd] **N 1** *(animal)* crapaud *m*; *Fam Pej, Hum (person)* crapule *f*; **you lying t.!** espèce de salaud de menteur! **2** *Br Culin* **t. in the hole** = saucisses *fpl* cuites au four dans de la pâte à crêpes

toadstool ['təʊdstuːl] **N** champignon *m* vénéneux

toady ['təʊdɪ] **N** lèche-bottes *mf inv*
VI to t. to sb lécher les bottes à qn

to-and-fro **ADJ t. movement** mouvement *m* de va-et-vient

toast [təʊst] **N 1** *(toasted bread)* pain *m* grillé, toast *m*; **piece** *or* **slice of t.** toast, tartine *f* grillée, rôtie *f*; **as warm as t.** bien chaud
2 *(tribute)* toast *m*; **to give** *or* **propose a t.** porter un toast; **to drink a t. to sb** boire à la santé de qn; **the t. was the future** on a porté un toast à l'avenir; **to be the t. of the town** être la célébrité de la ville
3 *Fam* **to be t.** *(in trouble)* être foutu; *(exhausted)* être naze *ou* crevé; **if Mum finds out, you're t.** si Maman s'en rend compte, t'es mort *ou* foutu!; **I can't drink any more or I'll be t. tomorrow** il faut que j'arrête de boire, sinon demain je serai dans le coaltar
VT 1 *(bread)* griller, faire griller; *Fam* **to t. one's feet (in front of the fire)** se rôtir les pieds (devant le feu); **toasted cheese** toast *m* au fromage; **toasted sandwich** sandwich *m* grillé
2 to t. sb porter un toast à (la santé de) qn, boire à la santé de qn
VI *(of bread)* griller; **it toasts well** ça fait du bon pain grillé
▸▸ **t. master** maître *m* de cérémonies, animateur *m* (de réception); *Br* **t. rack** porte-toasts *m inv*

toaster ['təʊstər] **N** grille-pain *m inv*; **sandwich t.** grill *m* (électrique)

toastie ['təʊstɪ] **N** *Fam* sandwich *m* grillé

toasting fork ['təʊstɪŋ] **N** fourchette *f* à rôties

toasty ['təʊstɪ] **N** *Fam* = toastie

tobacco, *pl* **tobaccos** [tə'bækəʊ, -əʊz] **N 1** tabac *m*; **chewing t.** tabac à chiquer *ou* mâcher; **t.-coloured** tabac *inv* **2** *(plant)* tabac *m*
▸▸ **t. plant** tabac; **t. pouch** blague *f* à tabac; **t. smoke** fumée *f* de tabac; **t. tin** boîte *f* à tabac, tabatière *f*

tobacconist [tə'bækənɪst] **N** *Br (person)* marchand, -ande de tabac, buraliste *mf*; **t.'s** *(shop)* (bureau *m ou* débit *m* de) tabac *m*
▸▸ **t.'s shop** (bureau *ou* débit de) tabac

Tobin tax ['təʊbɪn] **N** *Fin* taxe *f* Tobin

toboggan [tə'bɒgən] **N** *(for children)*, *Sport* luge *f*
VI *(of child)*, *Sport* faire de la luge; **to t. down a slope** descendre une pente en luge
▸▸ **t. run** piste *f* de luge

Note that the French word **toboggan** is a false friend. Its most common meaning is **slide** (in a playground).

tobogganing [tə'bɒgənɪŋ] **N** luge *f*; **to go t.** faire de la luge

toby jug ['təʊbɪ] **N** = pot *m* à bière décoratif *(en forme de gros bonhomme à tricorne)*

tocsin ['tɒksɪn] **N** tocsin *m*

tod [tɒd] **N** *Br Sl* **on my/his/etc t.** tout seul

today [tə'deɪ] **ADV** aujourd'hui; **it's a week ago t.** ça fait une semaine aujourd'hui; **t. week** aujourd'hui en huit; *Fam* **he's the kind who'll be here t. and gone tomorrow** *(in job, relationship etc)* c'est le genre de type qui ne peut pas se fixer; **a here t. and gone tomorrow fashion** une mode qui ne durera pas
N aujourd'hui *m*; **t.'s the day ...!** c'est aujourd'hui que ...!; **t.'s paper** le journal d'aujourd'hui *ou* du jour; **t.'s date/price** la date/le prix du jour; **t.'s date is ...** aujourd'hui, nous sommes le ...; **t.'s special** plat *m* du jour; **the young people of t.** les jeunes d'aujourd'hui

toddle ['tɒd(ə)l] **N** *Fam (short walk)* petite promenade *f*, balade *f*; **I'm going for a t.** je vais faire un tour, je vais me balader
VI 1 *(of young child)* marcher à petits pas chancelants; **she's just started toddling** elle commence à peine à marcher **2** *Fam (adult)* trottiner; **I'd better be toddling (along)** *(leaving)* il faut que j'y aille; **I'm just going to t. into town** je vais juste faire un tour en ville
▸ **toddle off VI** *Fam (leave)* partir, lever le camp

toddler ['tɒdlər] **N** enfant *mf* qui commence à marcher

toddy ['tɒdɪ] **N** grog *m*

todger ['tɒdʒər] **N** *Br Sl (penis)* chipolata *f*

to-die-for **ADJ** *Fam* de rêve

to-do **N** *Fam* remue-ménage *m inv*; **what a t.!** quelle histoire!; **there was a great t. about it** l'affaire a fait grand bruit

toe [təʊ] **N 1** *Anat* orteil *m*, doigt *m* de pied; **big/little t.** gros/petit orteil; **on the tips of one's toes** sur la pointe des pieds; **to tread** *or* **stand on sb's toes** marcher sur les pieds de qn; *Fig* **I hope I'm not treading on any toes** j'espère que je n'empiète pas sur les plates-bandes de personne; *Fig* **to be on one's toes** être en alerte, être vigilant; *Fig* **to keep people on their toes** faire en sorte que les gens restent vigilants **2** *(of shoe etc)* bout *m*, pointe *f*
VT 1 *Ftbl (ball)* frapper de la pointe du pied **2** *Sport* **to t. the line** *or* **the mark** s'aligner; *Fig* **to t. the line** obéir, s'exécuter; *Fig* **to t. the party line** s'aligner sur la position officielle du parti

toecap ['təʊkæp] **N** bout *m* rapporté

-toed [-təʊd] **SUFF two/three/etc-t.** à deux/trois/*etc* orteils; **square/pointed/etc-t.** *(shoes)* à bouts carrés/pointus/*etc*

toehold ['təʊhəʊld] **N** *(in climbing)* prise *f* de pied; *Fig* **to gain a t. in the market** mettre un pied sur le marché; **to maintain a t. on reality** garder un lien, si ténu soit-il, avec la réalité

toe-in **N** *Aut* pincement *m* des roues avant

toenail ['təʊneɪl] **N** ongle *m* d'orteil

toe-out **N** *Aut* ouverture *f*, pincement *m* négatif

toepiece ['təʊpiːs] **N** *(on ski)* butée *f*

toerag ['təʊræg] **N** *Br Sl* merdeux, -euse

toff [tɒf] **N** *Old-fashioned Br Fam* aristo *mf*; **the toffs** le gratin

toffee ['tɒfɪ] **N** caramel *m* au beurre; *Fam* **he can't sing for t.** il chante comme une casserole
▸▸ **t. apple** pomme *f* d'amour *(confiserie)*

toffee-nosed [-nəʊzd] **ADJ** *esp Br Fam* snob, snobinard

tofu ['təʊfuː] **N** tofu *m*

▸ **tog up, tog out** [tɒg] **VT SEP** *Fam (dress smartly)* fringuer; **to t. oneself up** bien se fringuer, se mettre sur son trente et un; **to be (all) togged up** *(dressed up)* être sur son trente et un; *(for tennis, football etc)* être en tenue

toga ['təʊgə] **N** *(garment)* toge *f*

together [tə'geðər] **ADV** ensemble; **to go** *or* **belong t.** aller ensemble; **we stand or fall t.** nous sommes tous solidaires; **t. with** *(as well as)* ainsi que; *(at the same time as)* en même temps que; **the Swedes objected t. with the French** les Suédois émirent une objection, de même que les Français; **to gather** *or* **collect** *or* **bring t.** réunir, rassembler; **to gather t.** *(come together)* se réunir, se rassembler; **to add t.** additionner; **to act t.** agir de concert; **to be t. again** *(of couple, partners)* être de nouveau ensemble; **to get t. again** *(of couple, partners)* se remettre ensemble; **the family will all be t. at Christmas** la famille sera réunie à Noël; **all t.** *(everybody gathered)* tous ensemble; *(at the same time)* tous à la fois; **all t. now!** *(sing)* tous en chœur maintenant!; **all t. now! – push!** tous ensemble maintenant! – poussez!; **all t. it cost us £480** l'ensemble nous a coûté 480 livres; **for hours t.** des heures durant, pendant des heures et des heures; *Fam* **she's really got it t.** *(in life)* elle sait ce qu'elle fait; *(in job etc)* elle domine son sujet; **I never thought he would get it t.** je n'aurais jamais pensé qu'il y arriverait
ADJ *Fam (person)* équilibré; **the band weren't very t.** *(didn't play in unison)* le groupe ne jouait pas vraiment ensemble

togetherness [tə'geðənɪs] **N** *(unity)* unité *f*, harmonie *f*; **the earlier feeling of t. had gone out of their relationship** le sentiment de former un couple uni qu'ils avaient éprouvé auparavant avait disparu; **the feeling of t. generated by a family Christmas** ce sentiment de chaleureuse communion que l'on ressent lors des Noëls passés en famille; **we all had a feeling of t. at the party conference** nous avons tous éprouvé un sentiment de cohésion lors du congrès du parti

toggle ['tɒg(ə)l] **N** *(on duffel coat etc)* olive *f*, barrette *f*
VI *Comput* basculer; **to t. between two applications** alterner entre deux applications; **to t. sth on/off** sélectionner/désélectionner qch
▸▸ *Comput* **t. key** touche *f* à bascule; **t. switch** *Elec* interrupteur *m* à bascule; *Comput* commande *f* à bascule

Togo ['təʊgəʊ] **N** Togo *m*

Togolese [təʊgə'liːz] **ADJ** togolais
N Togolais, -aise

togs [tɒgz] **NPL** *Fam (clothes)* fringues *fpl*, frusques *fpl*

toil [tɔɪl] N *Fml, Lit* dur labeur *m*, peine *f*; **a life of t. and trouble** une vie de douleur et de peine

▪ VI *(work hard)* travailler dur (**at** à), peiner (**at** sur); **to be toiling** *(having difficulty in race, finishing meal etc)* peiner; **I'm toiling to finish this drink as it is** j'ai déjà assez de mal à finir ce verre; **to t. up a hill** gravir péniblement une colline; **to t. on** *(continue work)* continuer péniblement son travail; *(continue journey)* continuer péniblement sa route

▪ VT **he toiled his way through a mass of papers** il a dû laborieusement lire tout un tas de documents

toiler ['tɔɪlər] N travailleur, -euse

toilet ['tɔɪlɪt] N **1** *(lavatory) (device)* cabinets *mpl*; *(room)* cabinet de toilette; **toilets** toilettes *fpl*; **to go to the t.** aller aux toilettes; **he's still in the t.** il est encore aux toilettes; **to throw sth down the t.** jeter qch dans les toilettes; *Fam* **to go down the t.** *(of plan, career, work)* être foutu en l'air; **that's our holidays down the t.!** on peut faire une croix sur nos vacances! **2** *Old-fashioned (washing and dressing)* toilette *f*; **to make** *or* **perform one's t.** faire sa toilette

▪▪ **t. block** bloc *m* sanitaire; **t. bowl** cuvette *f* (de W-C); **t. case** nécessaire *m ou* trousse *f* de toilette; **t. humour** humour *m* scatologique; **t. paper** papier *m* hygiénique; **t. roll** *(roll)* rouleau *m* de papier hygiénique; *(paper)* papier hygiénique; **t. seat** siège *m* des cabinets *ou* W-C *ou* toilettes; **t. soap** savon *m* de toilette; **t. table** (table *f* de) toilette, coiffeuse *f*; **t. tissue** papier hygiénique; **t. training** apprentissage *m* de la propreté *(pour un enfant)*; **t. water** eau *f* de toilette

toiletries ['tɔɪlɪtrɪz] NPL articles *mpl* de toilette

toilet-trained ADJ propre

toils [tɔɪlz] NPL *Lit, Fig (net)* filets *mpl*

toilsome ['tɔɪlsəm] ADJ *Lit* pénible

toing and froing [tu:ɪŋən'frəʊɪŋ] N va-et-vient *m*

Tokay [tə'kaɪ] N *(wine)* tokai *m*, tokaï *m*, to-kay *m*

toke [təʊk] *Sl* N *(of joint)* taffe *f*; **to take a t.** prendre une taffe

▪ VI **to t. on a joint** prendre une taffe d'un joint

token ['təʊk(ə)n] N **1** *(indication) (of identity, respect etc)* marque *f*, témoignage *m*; **in t.** *or* **as a t. of sincerity** en signe *ou* en témoignage de bonne foi; **by the same t.** *(therefore)* donc; *(equally)* pareillement; **a t. black person/t. woman** un noir/une femme qui est là pour la forme; *Mil etc* **a t. force** une force symbolique **2** *(disc etc) (for vending machine etc)* jeton *m*; **gift t.** bon *m* d'achat; **book t.** chèque-livre *m*, *pl* chèques-livres; **record t.** chèque-disque *m*, *pl* chèques-disques **3** *Old-fashioned (symbol)* signe *m*; **love t.** gage *m* d'amour

▪▪ **t. payment** paiement *m* symbolique *ou* d'avertissement; *Comput* **t. ring network** réseau *m* en anneau à jeton; **t. strike** grève *f* symbolique *ou* d'avertissement

tokenism ['təʊkənɪz(ə)m] N = pratique *f* qui consiste à nommer une ou deux personnes des minorités (femme, noir etc) pour donner l'impression d'une libéralisation; **the appointment of a woman to the board was nothing but t.** ils ont nommé une femme au conseil d'administration uniquement pour la forme

Tokyo ['təʊkɪəʊ] N Tokyo

told PT, PP *see* **tell**

Toledo [tɒ'leɪdəʊ] N Tolède

tolerable ['tɒlərəb(ə)l] ADJ **1** *(pain etc)* tolérable, supportable **2** *(acceptable)* passable; *(quite good)* assez bon; **we're in t. health** nous nous portons assez bien

tolerably ['tɒlərəblɪ] ADV passablement; **I'm t. well** je me porte assez bien; **it was t. well done** c'était assez bien fait

tolerance ['tɒlərəns] N **1** *(religious etc)* tolérance *f*; **to show great t.** faire preuve de beaucoup de tolérance *ou* d'une grande indulgence **2** *(for drug, alcohol)* tolérance *f* (**of, for** à); **increasing t.** *(to drug)* accoutumance *f* **3** *Tech etc* tolérance *f*, écart *m* admissible

tolerant ['tɒlərənt] ADJ **1** tolérant; *(parent etc)* tolérant, indulgent **2** *Med* **t. of a drug** *(patient)* qui tolère une drogue

tolerantly ['tɒlərəntlɪ] ADV avec tolérance; **to be t. disposed toward sb/sth** se montrer tolérant envers qn/qch

tolerate ['tɒləreɪt] VT **1** *(pain, contradiction etc)* tolérer, supporter; *(person, behaviour)* supporter; **I will not t. this behaviour** je ne supporterai pas une telle conduite **2** *Med (drug)* tolérer

toleration [tɒlə'reɪʃən] N tolérance *f*

toll¹ [təʊl] N **1** *(charge)* péage *m*, droit *m* de passage; *Fig* **to take its t.** *(of disease etc)* faire beaucoup de victimes; *(have severe effect)* laisser des traces (**of sb** sur qn); **accident that takes a heavy t. of human life** accident qui cause beaucoup de morts; **the years had taken their t.** *or* **a heavy t. on her health** sa santé s'était affaiblie avec le temps **2** *Am* **to call t. free** appeler gratuitement

▪▪ **t. bar** barrière *f* (de péage); **t. booth** poste *f* de péage; **t. bridge** pont *m* à péage; *Am Tel* **t. call** communication *f* interurbaine; **t. gate** barrière *f* (de péage); **t. house** péage; **t. road** route *f* à péage

toll² N *(of bell)* tintement *m*, son *m* (de cloche); *(for death)* glas *m*

▪ VT *(bell)* sonner; **the church clock tolled midday** l'horloge de l'église a sonné midi; **to t. sb's death** sonner le glas pour la mort de qn

▪ VI *(of bell)* tinter, sonner; *(for death)* sonner le glas; **to t. for the dead** sonner pour les morts

toll-free number N *Am* ≃ numéro *m* vert

tolling ['təʊlɪŋ] N *(of bell)* tintement *m*; *(for death)* glas *m*

tollway ['təʊlweɪ] N *Am* autoroute *f* à péage

Tom [tɒm] N Thomas, Tom; *Fam* **any T., Dick or Harry** n'importe qui, le premier venu

▪▪ **T. Thumb** le Petit Poucet

tom [tɒm] N *(cat)* matou *m*

▪▪ **t. cat** matou

tomahawk ['tɒməhɔːk] N hache *f* de guerre, tomahawk *m*

tomato, *pl* **tomatoes** [tə'mɑːtəʊ, -əʊz, *Am* tə'meɪtəʊ] N tomate *f*

▪▪ **t. juice** jus *m* de tomates; **t. ketchup** ketchup *m*; **t. purée** concentré *m ou* purée *f* de tomates; **t. sauce** sauce *f* tomate; *(ketchup)* ketchup

tomb [tuːm] N tombe *f*, tombeau *m*

tombac ['tɒmbæk] N *Metal* tombac *m*

tombola [tɒm'bəʊlə] N *Br* tombola *f*

tomboy ['tɒmbɔɪ] N garçon *m* manqué

tomboyish ['tɒmbɔɪɪʃ] ADJ *(behaviour etc)* de garçon manqué

tombstone ['tuːmstəʊn] N pierre *f* tombale

tomcat ['tɒmkæt] N matou *m*

▪ **tomcat around** VI *Am Fam* courir les filles

tome [təʊm] N *(volume)* tome *m*; *(large book)* gros livre *m*; *Fam (book)* bouquin *m*

tomfool [tɒm'fuːl] ADJ *Fam* idiot; **t. scheme** projet *m* insensé

tomfoolery [tɒm'fuːlərɪ] N *Fam* âneries *fpl*, bêtises *fpl*

tommy ['tɒmɪ] N *Br (soldier)* simple soldat *m* (de l'armée britannique), *Fam* troufion *m*

▪▪ *Mil* **T. gun** mitraillette *f*

tommyrot ['tɒmɪrɒt] N *Old-fashioned Fam* bêtises *fpl*, inepties *fpl*; **that's all t.** tout ça, c'est de la blague

tomography [tə'mɒgrəfɪ] N *Med* tomographie *f*

tomorrow [tə'mɒrəʊ] ADV demain; **t. morning** demain matin; **t. night** demain soir; **t. week** demain en huit

▪ N demain *m*; **the day after t.** après-demain; **t.'s breakfast** le petit déjeuner de demain; **who knows what t. holds?** qui sait ce que demain nous réserve?; **t. never comes** c'est maintenant ou jamais; **t. is another day** ça ira mieux demain; *Prov* **never put off till t. what you can do today** il ne faut pas remettre au lendemain ce qu'on peut faire le jour même; *Fam* **she was eating like there was no t.** elle mangeait comme si son dernier jour était arrivé; *Fig* **what will the world be like t.?** à quoi ressemblera le monde demain?; **the cities of t., t.'s cities** les villes de demain

tomtit ['tɒmtɪt] N *(bird)* mésange *f* bleue

tom-tom N tam-tam *m*, *pl* tam-tams

ton [tʌn] N **1** *(weight)* tonne *f*, *Br* **(long) t.** tonne longue (= 1016 kg); *Am* **(short** *or* **net) t.** tonne courte (= 907 kg); **metric t.** tonne (métrique) (= 1 000 kg); *Fam* **this suitcase weighs a t.** cette valise est rudement lourde *ou* pèse une tonne **2** *Fam Fig* **tons of ...** *(lots of)* des tonnes de ...; **we've tons of time** nous avons tout notre temps; **there's tons of it** il y en a des tas **3** *esp Br Sl (100 mph)* vitesse *f* de cent soixante à l'heure; *(score of 100)* cent *m*; *(£100)* cent livres *fpl*; **to do a t.** *(of vehicle, driver etc)* faire du cent soixante à l'heure

tonal ['təʊn(ə)l] ADJ tonal, -als

tonality [təʊ'nælɪtɪ] N tonalité *f*

tone [təʊn] N **1** *(sound)* son *m*; *(quality)* sonorité *f*; *(of voice, musical instrument)* timbre *m*; *Tel* **ringing t.** tonalité *f* d'appel; **record your message after the t.** laissez votre message après le bip sonore

2 *(sound of voice)* ton *m*, timbre *m*; **I knew by the t. of his voice** j'ai compris au ton *ou* timbre de sa voix; **in an impatient t.** avec impatience; **in an angry t. of voice** sur le ton de la colère; **I don't like your t. (of voice), don't take that t. with me** je vous prierai de ne pas me parler sur ce ton; **in a low t.** à voix basse; **to give a serious t. to a discussion** donner un ton sérieux à une discussion; **it was the t. of the letter I didn't like** c'est le ton de cette lettre qui ne m'a pas plu

3 *(in acoustics)*, *Mus* ton *m*; **whole t.** ton entier; **quarter t.** quart *m* de ton

4 *Art etc (of colour)* ton *m*, nuance *f*; *Phot (of print)* ton; **warm tones** tons chauds; *Art* **half t.** similigravure *f*, *Fam* simili *f*

5 *Ling* ton *m*, accent *m* tonique, accent *m* de hauteur

6 *Med (of muscles etc)* tonicité *f*, tonus *m*

▪ VT *(picture)* adoucir les tons de; *Phot (print)* virer; **toned paper** papier *m* teinté, papier crémé

▪▪ **t. arm** bras *m* de lecture; **t. control** bouton *m* de tonalité; *Ling* **t. language** langue *f* à tons; *Mus* **t. poem** poème *m* symphonique

▪ **tone down** VT SEP **1** *(make less bright) (colour etc)* adoucir, atténuer **2** *(moderate) (remarks etc)* modérer, adoucir; **the editor had to t. down the article** le rédacteur a dû atténuer les termes de l'article

▪ **tone in** VI *(of colour etc)* s'harmoniser (**with** avec)

▪ **tone up** VT SEP *(make stronger) (muscles)* tonifier

▪ VI *(become stronger) (of muscles)* se tonifier

▸**tone with** VT INSEP (match, nearly match) (of colour, wallpaper etc) s'harmoniser avec

tone-deaf ADJ incapable de reconnaître les notes; (not appreciating music) qui n'a aucun sens musical

tone-deafness N incapacité f à reconnaître les notes; (lack of musical appreciation) manque m de sens musical

toneless ['təʊnlɪs] ADJ (voice) blanc, f blanche, atone

tonelessly ['təʊnlɪslɪ] ADV (to say) d'une voix blanche ou atone

toner ['təʊnər] N 1 (cosmetic) lotion f tonique 2 (for photocopier, printer, fax) toner m, encre f; **t. cartridge** or **cassette** cartouche f de toner; **t. low warning** signal m de baisse du toner

Tonga ['tɒŋgə] N Tonga fpl

Tongan ['tɒŋgən] ADJ tongan
  N 1 Tonguien, -ienne 2 Ling tongan m

tongs [tɒŋz] NPL (pair of) t. pince(s) f(pl); (in glassmaking) morailles fpl; **fire t.** pincettes fpl; Culin **sugar t.** pince à sucre VOIR GRAMMAIRE A10

tongue [tʌŋ] N 1 Anat, Culin langue f; **to stick one's t. out** tirer la langue (at sb à qn); **the dog's t. was hanging out** le chien tirait la langue; **his t. was hanging out** (from thirst) il crevait de soif; (in expectation) il en bavait d'envie; **to have a ready** or **glib t.** avoir la langue déliée ou bien pendue; **hold your t.!** taisez-vous!; **to find one's t.** retrouver la parole ou sa langue; **have you lost your t.?** tu as perdu ta langue?; Fig **with one's t. in one's cheek** en plaisantant; **she was being t. in cheek** elle plaisantait; **it's hard to get your t. round these words** ces mots sont difficiles à prononcer 2 esp Lit (language) langue f, idiome m; **the German t.** la langue allemande; esp Bible **the gift of tongues** le don des langues 3 (of land, flame) langue f; (of shoe) patte f, languette f; (of bell) battant m; Mus (of oboe) anche f; Carp languette f
  VT Mus **to t. a passage** (on wind instrument) détacher les notes d'un passage avec la langue
  ▸▸ **t. twister** = mot m ou phrase f difficile à prononcer

tongue-and-groove Carp N (joint, edge) assemblage m à languette; (wood) lattes fpl à languette
  VT (boards, slats) pratiquer des languettes et des rainures sur

tongue-in-cheek ADJ (remark, article) fait pour plaisanter, ironique

tongue-lash VT tancer vertement

tongue-lashing N **to give sb a t.** tancer qn vertement

tongue-tied ADJ (with shyness etc) muet; (with surprise etc) interdit; **it's not like her to be t.** ça ne lui ressemble pas de rester sans rien dire

tonguing ['tʌŋɪŋ] N Mus (on wind instrument) coup m de langue

tonic ['tɒnɪk] ADJ 1 Med etc tonique, fortifiant 2 Gram (accent) tonique; Mus (note) tonique
  N 1 Med tonique m, remontant m, fortifiant m; Fig **to be a t. for sb** (of news etc) réconforter ou remonter qn; **he's a t.** il vous remonte le moral, il est stimulant 2 (drink) Schweppes® m; **gin and t.** gin-tonic m, pl gin-tonics 3 Mus tonique f
  ▸▸ Mus **t. solfa** solfège m; **t. water** ≃ Schweppes®

tonicity [təʊˈnɪsɪtɪ] N (of muscles etc) tonicité f

tonight [təˈnaɪt] ADV (evening) ce soir; (night) cette nuit
  N (evening) ce soir; (night) cette nuit; **t.'s main news** et voici les titres du journal ou de l'actualité

toning ['təʊnɪŋ] N Phot (of prints) virage m
  ▸▸ **t. down** (of colour, remarks) atténuation f, adoucissement m; **t. lotion** lotion f tonifiante

tonnage ['tʌnɪdʒ] N Naut tonnage m; **register(ed) t.** tonnage net
  ▸▸ **t. certificate** certificat m de jaugeage

tonne [tʌn] N tonne f (métrique)

tonneau cover ['tɒnəʊ] N Aut bâche f

tonsil ['tɒns(ə)l] N Anat amygdale f; **to have one's tonsils out** se faire opérer des amygdales; Fam Hum **to play t. hockey** se rouler des pelles ou des patins

tonsillectomy [tɒnsɪˈlektəmɪ] N amygdalectomie f

tonsillitis [tɒnsɪˈlaɪtɪs] N Med angine f, Spéc amygdalite f; **to have t.** avoir une angine ou Spéc amygdalite

tonsure ['tɒnʃər] N tonsure f
  VT (monk) tonsurer

tontine [tɒnˈtiːn] N (in insurance) tontine f

ton-up ADJ
  ▸▸ Old-fashioned Br Fam **t. boy** = fou m de moto

tonus ['təʊnəs] N Med tonicité f, tonus m

too [tuː] ADV 1 (excessively) trop; **it's t. difficult** c'est trop difficile; **t. difficult a job** un travail trop difficile; **t. many people** trop de gens; **t. far** trop loin; **to work t. much** or **t. hard** travailler trop, trop travailler; **50p t. much** 50p de trop; **this job's t. much for me** ce travail est au-dessus de mes forces; **I've listened to him t. long** je l'ai trop écouté; **I know her all** or **only t. well** je ne la connais que trop; **you're t. kind** vous êtes très ou trop gentil; **he's not t. well today** il ne va pas très bien aujourd'hui; Br Fam **t. right!** et comment!, vous l'avez dit! VOIR GRAMMAIRE A5
  2 (also) aussi, également; **you're coming t.** vous venez aussi; **she t. is a painter** elle aussi est peintre
  3 (moreover) en ou de plus; **30° in the shade and in September t.** 30° à l'ombre et en septembre en plus

toodle-oo, toodle-pip ['tuːd(ə)l'uː, -'pɪp] INT Old-fashioned Br Fam (goodbye) salut!

took PT see take VT, VI

tool [tuːl] N 1 (implement) outil m; (set of) **tools** outillage m; **garden** or **gardening tools** outils de jardinage; **power t.** outil à moteur; **you have to learn the tools of your trade** on ne peut pratiquer un métier sans apprentissage 2 Fig (means, instrument) instrument m; **to use sb as a t.** utiliser qn; **he was a mere t. in their hands** il n'était qu'un instrument entre leurs mains 3 Sl (penis) bite f
  VT 1 (leather, binding) ciseler; Tech (wrought iron) usiner, travailler; **tooled leather** cuir m repoussé 2 = **tool up** VT SEP 1
  ▸▸ **t. bag** sac m à outils; **t. holder** porte-outil m, porte-outil(s); **t. kit** trousse f à outils; **t. rack** râtelier m à outils; **t. set** jeu m d'outils, pl jeux d'outils; **t. shed** reserre f, remise f
▸**tool up** VT SEP 1 (equip with tools) (factory etc) outiller 2 Br Sl **to be tooled up** (carrying a weapon) être armé
  VI (become equipped with tools) s'outiller

toolbar N Comput barre f d'outils

toolbox ['tuːlbɒks] N boîte f ou coffre m à outils; Comput boîte à outils

tooling ['tuːlɪŋ] N (of leather, binding) ciselage m; Tech usinage m

tool-maker N fabricant m d'outils, outilleur m

toon [tuːn] N Am Fam (cartoon) dessin m animé

toot [tuːt] N 1 Naut coup m de sirène; Aut coup de klaxon; Aut **to give sb a t.** donner un coup de klaxon à qn, klaxonner qn 2 Sl (of cocaine) prise f de coke 3 Am Fam (drink-

ing spree) **to go on the t.** prendre une cuite
  VT 1 **to t. a horn/a trumpet** sonner du cor/de la trompette; Aut **to t. the horn** klaxonner; Aut Fam **to t. sb** klaxonner qn 2 Sl (cocaine) sniffer
  VI 1 (of person) sonner du cor; (of instrument) sonner; Aut (of driver) klaxonner 2 Sl (sniff cocaine) sniffer de la coke

tooth, pl **teeth** [tuːθ, tiːθ] N 1 dent f, (set of) **teeth** denture f, dentition f; **first** or **milk teeth** dents de lait; **buck teeth** dents proéminentes; (set of) **false teeth** dentier m, Fam râtelier m; **to have a fine set of teeth** avoir de belles dents; **to cut one's teeth** faire ou percer ses dents; Fig **to cut one's teeth on sth** se faire les dents sur qch; **to have a t. out** se faire arracher une dent; **to kick sb in the teeth** donner un coup de pied à qn dans les dents; Fig traiter qn avec mépris; **in the teeth of all opposition** malgré ou en dépit de toute opposition; **to show** or **bare one's teeth** montrer les dents; **armed to the teeth** armé jusqu'aux dents; **to give a law teeth** renforcer une loi; **to fight t. and nail** se battre bec et ongles; **a meal/book you can get your teeth into** un repas/livre consistant; Fam **a job you can get your teeth into** un boulot dans lequel on peut s'en donner à cœur joie; **I want to get my teeth into the problem** je veux m'attaquer à ce problème; **to grit one's teeth** serrer les dents; Fam **I'm fed up to the back teeth with it** j'en ai plein le dos de ce truc-là; Fam **she's a bit long in the t.** elle n'est plus toute jeune; Fam **I'm getting a bit long in the t. for that** je commence à me faire un peu trop vieux pour ça 2 (of saw, comb, cog) dent f, **teeth** (of wheel) denture f
  ▸▸ **t. decay** carie f dentaire; **the t. fairy** ≃ la petite souris; **t. glass, t. mug** verre m à dents; **t. powder** poudre f dentifrice

toothache ['tuːθeɪk] N mal m ou rage f de dents; **to have t.** avoir mal aux dents

toothbrush ['tuːθbrʌʃ] N brosse f à dents

toothed [tuːθt] ADJ 1 (animal) denté; (leaf etc) dentelé 2 Tech etc **t. belt** courroie f crantée; **t. wheel** roue f dentée

toothless ['tuːθlɪs] ADJ sans dents, édenté; Fig (law etc) qu'on n'a pas les moyens de faire respecter; **the committee has been criticized for being t.** on a reproché son impuissance à la commission

toothpaste ['tuːθpeɪst] N pâte f dentifrice, dentifrice m

toothpick ['tuːθpɪk] N cure-dent(s) m, pl cure-dents

toothsome ['tuːθsəm] ADJ (tasty) savoureux

toothy ['tuːθɪ] ADJ aux dents fpl saillantes, Pej aux dents de cheval; **to give a big t. grin** sourire à pleines dents
  ▸▸ **t. peg** (in children's language) dent f

tooting ['tuːtɪŋ] N Aut coups mpl de klaxon

tootle ['tuːt(ə)l] VI 1 Aut (toot) corner, klaxonner 2 Br Fam (go) (in car) rouler tranquillement; (on foot) se balader
▸**tootle along** VI Br Fam (go) aller tout tranquillement; **well, I'll t. along now** bon, je vais me mettre en route

toots [tʊts] N Fam (term of address) chéri, -ie

tootsy ['tʊtsɪ] N Fam (in children's language) (foot) peton m; (toe) doigt m de pied

---

TOP [tɒp]

N	haut **1, 3** ▪ sommet **1** ▪ cime **1**	
	▪ bout **1** ▪ surface **2** ▪ dessus **2, 3**	
	▪ couvercle **3** ▪ bouchon **3** ▪ capsule **3** ▪ corsage **3** ▪ toupie **8**	
ADJ	du dessus **1** ▪ du haut **1** ▪ d'en haut **1** ▪ dernier **1** ▪ premier **2**	
VT	surmonter **2** ▪ garnir **2** ▪ dépasser **3** ▪ être en tête de **5**	

N **1** *(highest point) (of tree, mountain)* haut *m*, sommet *m*, cime *f*, faîte *m*; *(of tower, head)* sommet; *(of page, map)* haut; *(end) (of table)* bout *m*; **he always sat at the t. of the table** à table, c'était toujours lui qui présidait; **to make it to the t.** *(in profession, sport, music etc)* se faire une place parmi les grands; **at the t. of the stairs** en haut de l'escalier; **at the t. of the street** au bout de la rue; **at the t. of the tree** en haut de l'arbre; *Fig* au sommet de sa profession; **it went right to the t.** *(of complaint, request etc)* cela est remonté jusqu'au sommet; *Sch* **to be (at) the t. of the class** être le premier/la première de la classe; **to be (at) the t. of the bill** *(of actor, singer etc)* être en haut de l'affiche; **from t. to bottom** de haut en bas; *(to search a flat etc)* de fond en comble; **from t. to toe** de la tête aux pieds; **to shout/sing at the t. of one's voice** crier/chanter à tue-tête; **to be on** *or* **at the t. of one's form** être *ou* se sentir en pleine forme; *Ir Fam* **(the) t. of the morning (to you)** bien le bonjour!; *Mil* **to go over the t.** (sortir des tranchées pour) aller à l'assaut; *Fam* **over the t.** *(overdone)* excessif; **I find her a bit over the t.** je trouve qu'elle exagère un peu; **turnip/carrot tops** fanes *fpl* de navets/de carottes
2 *(surface) (of table etc)* surface *f*, dessus *m*; *(of bus)* impériale *f*; **t. of the milk** crème *f* du lait
3 *(part) (of shoe)* dessus *m*; *(of box, pan etc)* couvercle *m*; *(of bottle etc)* bouchon *m*, capsule *f*; *(of pen etc)* capuchon *m*; *(of dress)* haut *m*, corsage *m*; *(separate garment)* haut; *Fam* **to blow one's t.** sortir de ses gonds
4 on t. of *(on)* sur; **on t. (of the pile)** sur le dessus (de la pile); **to put sth on t. of sth** mettre qch sur qch; **to put sth right on the t. of sth** mettre qch tout en haut de qch; **just put it on t.** mets-le sur le dessus; **a cake with a cherry on t.** un gâteau avec une cerise dessus; **to be on t.** *(be in control)* avoir le dessus; **to be on t. of the situation** maîtriser la situation; **you mustn't let things get on t. of you** il ne faut pas te laisser dépasser par les événements; **to come out on t.** prendre le dessus; **it's just one thing on t. of another** ça n'arrête jamais; **on t. of it all** et pour comble (de malheur), et en plus de tout cela; **to be** *or* **to feel on t. of the world** être *ou* se sentir en pleine forme
5 *Fam* **the tops** la crème, le gratin; **he's (the) tops!** c'est un as!; *Fam* **he's tops with me** pour moi, c'est le meilleur
6 the Big T. *(in circus)* le chapiteau
7 *Aut (gear)* vitesse *f* supérieure; **in t.** au rapport supérieur
8 (spinning *or* **peg) t.** *(toy)* toupie *f*
ADJ **1** *(highest)* du dessus, du haut, d'en haut; *(floor, stair)* dernier; **the t. people** *(prominent people)* les gens *mpl* en vue; *(in an organization)* les gros bonnets *mpl*; **all the t. people in New York eat there** c'est un restaurant où se retrouve toute l'élite new-yorkaise; *Fam* **to pay t. dollar for sth** dépenser beaucoup d'argent pour qch; **to be/to feel on t. form** être/se sentir en pleine forme; **t. shelf** étagère *f* du dessus *ou* du haut
2 *(best, major)* premier; **she got the t. mark** *or* **came t. in history** elle a eu la meilleure note en histoire; **the country's t. ten companies** les dix premières sociétés du pays; **one of the world's t. ten players** un des dix meilleurs joueurs mondiaux
VT **(-pp-) 1** *(remove top of) (tree, plant)* écimer; *(tree)* étêter; **to t. and tail carrots** retirer les fanes et couper les bouts des carottes
2 *(provide top for)* surmonter, couronner, coiffer (**with** de); *Culin (dessert etc)* garnir (**with** de); *Fig* **and to t. it all** et pour comble (de malheur), et en plus de tout cela
3 *(exceed)* excéder, dépasser; **the takings** **have topped a thousand pounds** les recettes dépassent mille livres; **to t. sb by a head** dépasser qn d'une tête
4 *(reach top of) (hill etc)* atteindre le sommet de
5 *(be at top of)* être en tête de; **to t. a list/a class** être à la tête d'une liste/de la classe; **topping the bill tonight we have ...** le clou de cette soirée est ...; **to t. the charts** *(of record, singer)* être à la première place *ou* en tête des hit-parades
6 *Golf (ball)* calotter
7 *Sl* **to t. oneself** *(commit suicide)* se foutre en l'air
▸▸ *Br* **t. boots** bottes *fpl* hautes; *Fam* **the t. brass** *(in army)* les officiers *mpl* supérieurs; *(in company etc)* les gros bonnets *mpl*; **t. coat** *(of paint)* dernière couche *f*; *Br* **t. copy** original *m*; *Fam* **t. dog** chef *m*; **to be t. dog** *(have the advantage)* avoir le dessus; *Br Aut* **t. gear** vitesse supérieure; **t. hat** *(chapeau m)* haut-de-forme *m*, *pl* hauts-de-forme; **t. pupil** premier, -ière de la classe; **t. rate** *(of tax)* taux *m* maximum; **t. security** sécurité *f* maximum; **he was given t. security** il a bénéficié du maximum de sécurité; **t. speed** vitesse maximum, vitesse de pointe; **to travel at t. speed** *(of plane, train etc)* aller à sa vitesse maximale; **car with a t. speed of 150 kph** voiture avec un plafond de 150 km/h; **t. table** *(at wedding)* table *f* d'honneur; **t. ten** = hit-parade *m* des dix meilleures ventes de disques pop et rock; **in the t. ten** au hit-parade; **t. twenty** = hit-parade des vingt meilleures ventes de disques pop et rock; **in the t. twenty** au hit-parade
▸ **top off** VT SEP *(complete) (evening)* couronner; **topped off with a cherry** garni d'une cerise
▸ **top out** *Br Constr* VT SEP *(building)* célébrer l'achèvement de la construction de
VI célébrer l'achèvement de la construction d'un immeuble
▸ **top up** VT SEP *(add more to) (glass etc)* remplir; *(mobile phone)* recharger le compte de; **to t. up one's life assurance premium** augmenter les versements de son assurance-vie; *Fam* **let me t. you up** vous en reprendrez bien un peu?; *Aut* **to t. up the battery/the oil/the tank/etc** ajouter de l'eau/de l'huile/ de l'essence/*etc*; **the government tops up the rest** *(pays the balance)* le gouvernement met l'argent qui manque *ou* rajoute la différence
VI *Aut (with oil)* ajouter de l'huile; *(with petrol)* faire le plein; *(add credit to one's mobile phone)* recharger son compte

topaz ['təʊpæz] N *(gem)* topaze *f*

top-bracket ADJ de première catégorie

topcoat ['tɒpkəʊt] N pardessus *m*, manteau *m*

top-down ADJ *(management)* contrôlé par le haut
▸▸ *Mktg* **t. forecasting** prévisions *fpl* hiérarchisées

top-drawer ADJ **1** *Old-fashioned Fam (upper class)* de la haute **2** = **top-flight**

top-dress VT *Agr* fumer en surface

tope [təʊp] VI *Old-fashioned Fam* boire, picoler

topee ['təʊpɪ] N casque *m* colonial

toper ['təʊpər] N *Old-fashioned Fam* picoleur, -euse

top-flight ADJ de premier ordre, excellent

top-heavy ADJ trop lourd du haut; *Naut (ship)* trop chargé dans les hauts; *Fig (organization)* dont les dirigeants sont trop nombreux

top-hole ADJ *Old-fashioned Br Fam* épatant, au poil

topi ['təʊpɪ] N = **topee**

topic ['tɒpɪk] N *(of text, discussion)* matière *f*, *(of conversation)* sujet *m*, thème *m*

topical ['tɒpɪk(ə)l] ADJ **1** *(question)* d'actualité; **matters of t. interest** des questions d'actualité; **it's very t.** c'est tout à fait d'actualité; **a few t. references in the text** quelques références à l'actualité dans le texte **2** *(index)* (organisé) par matières

topicality [tɒpɪ'kælɪtɪ] N actualité *f*

topically ['tɒpɪklɪ] ADV *(to write etc)* sur des thèmes d'actualité

topknot ['tɒpnɒt] N *(of bird)* huppe *f*, *(hair)* petit chignon *m*

topless ['tɒplɪs] ADJ *(dancer)* aux seins nus; **to go t.** *(of woman)* ne pas porter de haut
▸▸ **t. beach** plage *f* seins nus

top-level ADJ *(talks etc)* au plus haut niveau

topline ['tɒplaɪn] VT *Cin* jouer le rôle principal de

top-loader N *(washing machine)* machine *f* à laver à chargement par le haut

topmast ['tɒpməst] N *Naut* mât *m* de hune

topmost ['tɒpməʊst] ADJ le plus haut, le plus élevé

topnotch ['tɒpnɒtʃ] ADJ *Old-fashioned Fam* de premier ordre

top-of-the-range ADJ haut de gamme

topographer [tə'pɒgrəfər] N topographe *m*

topographic(al) [tɒpə'græfɪk, -ɪk(ə)l] ADJ topographique

topographically [tɒpə'græfɪklɪ] ADV topographiquement

topography [tɒ'pɒgrəfɪ] N topographie *f*

topologic(al) [tɒpə'lɒdʒɪk, -ɪk(ə)l] ADJ topologique

topology [tə'pɒlədʒɪ] N topologie *f*

-topped [-tɒpt] SUFF *Lit* **cloud-t. peaks** sommets couronnés de nuages; **ivory-t. walking stick** canne à pommeau d'ivoire

topper ['tɒpər] N *Fam (top hat)* haut-de-forme *m*, *pl* hauts-de-forme

topping ['tɒpɪŋ] ADJ *Old-fashioned Br Fam* excellent, formidable
N *Culin (for dessert, pizza etc)* garniture *f*, **ice-cream with raspberry t.** glace recouverte d'un coulis de framboises

topple ['tɒp(ə)l] VI *(fall)* tomber; *Fig (of government etc)* tomber; *(of share prices)* chuter; **he toppled into the pool/over the edge of the cliff** il a culbuté dans la piscine/par-dessus la falaise
VT faire tomber; *(building etc)* faire s'écrouler; *(government etc)* renverser
▸ **topple down, topple over** VI, VT SEP = **topple**

top-quality ADJ de qualité supérieure

top-rank(ing) ADJ haut placé; **t. civil servant** haut fonctionnaire *m*

tops [tɒps] ADV *Fam (at the most)* maxi; **it'll cost a fiver t.** ça coûtera cinq livres maxi *ou* à tout casser

topsail ['tɒps(ə)l] N *Naut* hunier *m*

top-secret ADJ *(information etc)* top secret, -ète

top-security ADJ
▸▸ **t. prison** prison *f* de haute sécurité; **t. wing** aile *f ou* quartier *m* de haute sécurité

top-shelf ADJ
▸▸ *Br* **t. magazine** revue *f* érotique

topside ['tɒpsaɪd] N **1** *Culin (of beef)* tende *f* de tranche **2** *Naut* **topsides** *(of ship)* accastillage *m*

topsoil ['tɒpsɔɪl] N *Agr* couche *f* arable

topsy-turvy [tɒpsɪ'tɜːvɪ] ADJ sens dessus dessous; **everything's t.** *(of organization etc)* c'est la confusion totale
ADV **the whole world's turned t.** c'est le monde à l'envers

top-up N *Aut* (remplissage *m* d')appoint *m*; *(for mobile phone)* rechargement *m*; **let me give you a t.** *(when serving drinks)* vous en reprendrez bien un peu?
▸▸ **t. card** *(for mobile phone)* recharge *f*; **t. fees** = frais *mpl* de scolarité complémentaires déterminés par chaque université, venant s'ajouter aux frais fixes payés par tous les étudiants britanniques; **t. finance** fonds *m* complémentaire; **t. loan** prêt *m* complémentaire

toque [təʊk] N *(hat)* toque *f*

tor [tɔːr] N *(hill)* pic *m*, butte *f* rocheuse

torch [tɔːtʃ] N **1** *(flame)* torche *f*, flambeau *m*; *Fig* **the t. of liberty** le flambeau de la liberté; *Fig* **to carry a t. for sb** avoir un faible pour qn; **to put sth to the t.** mettre le feu à qch **2** *(for welding)* chalumeau *m* **3** *Br* **(electric) t.** lampe *f* (électrique) (de poche), torche *f* électrique
▸▸ **t. song** chanson *f* d'amour triste

torchbearer ['tɔːtʃbeərər] N porte-flambeau *m inv*

torchlight ['tɔːtʃlaɪt] N lumière *f* de torche(s) *ou* de flambeau(x); *(of electric torch)* lumière d'une/de la torche (électrique); **by t.** à la lumière des torches *ou* des flambeaux/d'une torche électrique
▸▸ **t. procession** retraite *f* aux flambeaux

tore PT *see* tear[2]

toreador ['tɒrɪədɔːr] N toréador *m*, torero *m*

torment[1] ['tɔːment] N *esp Lit* tourment *m*, supplice *m*; **the torments of jealousy** les tourments de la jalousie; **he suffered torments** il souffrait le martyre; **to be in t.** être au supplice

torment[2] [tɔːˈment] VT *(cause suffering to)* *(person)* tourmenter, *(stronger)* torturer; *(pester)* *(person, animal etc)* harceler; **tormented with remorse** tourmenté par les remords, en proie aux remords; **tormented soul** âme *f* tourmentée

tormentor [tɔːˈmentər] N bourreau *m*

torn PP *see* tear[2]

tornado, *pl* **tornadoes** [tɔːˈneɪdəʊ, -əʊz] N tornade *f*

Toronto [təˈrɒntəʊ] N Toronto

torpedo, *pl* **torpedoes** [tɔːˈpiːdəʊ, -əʊz] N **1** *Naut etc* torpille *f* **2** *(fish)* (poisson *m*) torpille *f*
VT *(ship)*, *Fig (peace)* torpiller
▸▸ **t. boat** torpilleur *m*, vedette *f* lance-torpilles; **t. fish** (poisson) torpille *f*; **t. tube** tube *m* lance-torpilles

torpid ['tɔːpɪd] ADJ engourdi, torpide; **t. state** *(of animal)* engourdissement *m*

torpor ['tɔːpər], **torpidity** [tɔːˈpɪdɪtɪ] N torpeur *f*, engourdissement *m*

torque [tɔːk] N *Tech, Phys etc* moment *m* de torsion *ou* de rotation; *Aut* couple *m*, torque *m*; **starting t.** couple de *ou* au démarrage
▸▸ **t. converter** convertisseur *m* de couple; **t. plate** plateau *m* absorbeur de couple; **t. wrench** clé *f* dynamométrique

torqued [tɔːkt] ADJ *Am Fam* **1** *(angry)* furibard, furax **2** *(drunk)* bourré, fait

torrent ['tɒrənt] N torrent *m*; **it's raining in torrents** il pleut à torrents *ou* à verse; **t. of abuse/of tears** torrent *ou* déluge *m* d'injures/de larmes

torrential [tɒˈrenʃəl] ADJ torrentiel; **t. rain** pluie *f* diluvienne *ou* torrentielle

torrid ['tɒrɪd] ADJ *(heat, region, love affair)* torride

torsion ['tɔːʃən] N torsion *f*
▸▸ **t. bar** barre *f* de torsion

torso, *pl* **torsos** ['tɔːsəʊ, -əʊz] N *Anat, Art* torse *m*

tort [tɔːt] N *Law* acte *m* dommageable, préjudice *m*, délit *m* civil

tortoise ['tɔːtəs] N tortue *f* (terrestre)

tortoiseshell ['tɔːtəsʃel] N écaille *f* (de tortue); **t. comb** peigne *m* en écaille
▸▸ **t. cat** chat *m* écaille de tortue

tortuous ['tɔːtjʊəs] ADJ *(path, means)* tortueux; **to have a t. mind** avoir l'esprit tordu

tortuously ['tɔːtjʊəslɪ] ADV tortueusement

tortuousness ['tɔːtjʊəsnɪs] N *(of path, thinking etc)* caractère *m* tortueux

torture ['tɔːtʃər] N **1** torture *f*, **instruments of t.** instruments *mpl* de torture **2** *Fig (physical, mental pain)* torture *f*, supplice *m*; **wearing these shoes is t.** c'est un vrai supplice de porter ces chaussures
VT *(somebody)* torturer; *Fig (by making sb wait etc)* mettre au supplice; *Fig (text etc)* torturer; **tortured by remorse** torturé *ou* tenaillé par les remords
▸▸ **t. chamber** chambre *f* de torture; **t. victim** victime *f* de torture

torturer ['tɔːtʃərər] N tortionnaire *m*; *Hist* bourreau *m*

Tory ['tɔːrɪ] *Br Pol* N *(party member)* tory *m*; *(voter, supporter)* = partisan *m* du parti conservateur
ADJ tory, conservateur, -trice

Toryism ['tɔːrɪɪz(ə)m] N *Br Pol* torysme *m*

tosh [tɒʃ] N *Old-fashioned Br Fam* bêtises *fpl*, blague(s) *f(pl)*

toss [tɒs] N **1** *(of ball etc)* lancer *m*, lancement *m*; **it was decided by the t. of a coin** on a décidé cela (en tirant) à pile ou face; **to win/lose the t.** gagner/perdre à pile ou face; **to argue the t.** discuter inutilement *ou* pour rien **2** **t. of the head** brusque mouvement *m* de tête **3** *(fall)* **to take a t.** *(from horse etc)* faire une chute **4** *Br Sl* **he doesn't give a t.** **(what happens/etc)** il n'en a rien à fiche (de ce qui arrivera/etc); **who gives a t.?** qu'est-ce que ça peut foutre?
VT *(ball etc)* lancer, jeter en l'air; *(of bull)* *(person)* projeter en l'air; *(of sea etc)* secouer, ballotter; **to t. sth to sb** jeter qch à qn; **to t. sb in a blanket** faire sauter qn en l'air sur une couverture; **to t. a salad** remuer *ou* tourner *ou Fam* fatiguer une salade; **to t. a pancake** faire sauter une crêpe; **to t. a coin** jouer à pile ou face; **who's going to pay? – I'll t. you for it** qui va payer? – décidons-le à pile ou face; **to t. one's head** relever la tête avec dédain
VI **1** **to t. for sth** jouer qch à pile ou face **2** **to t. and turn in bed** se tourner et se retourner dans son lit **3** *(of waves)* s'agiter; **to t. on the waves** être ballotté par les flots; **to pitch and t.** *(of ship)* tanguer
▸ **toss about, toss around** VT SEP *(ball)* lancer, taper dans; *Fig Fam (idea)* étudier; **the ship, tossed about by the waves, …** le bateau, agité *ou* secoué *ou* ballotté par les vagues, …; **let's t. the idea around for a while** creusons un peu pour voir
▸ **toss across** VT SEP envoyer; **t. the newspaper across, will you?** envoie-moi le journal, s'il te plaît
▸ **toss away** VT SEP *(get rid of)* jeter
▸ **toss back** VT SEP *(ball)*, *Fig (report, proposal etc)* renvoyer; *(one's hair)* rejeter en arrière
▸ **toss off** VT SEP **1** *(drink quickly)* *(drink)* avaler d'un trait **2** *(complete quickly)* *(task, essay, article)* expédier **3** *Br Vulg (masturbate)* branler
VI *Br Vulg (masturbate)* se branler
▸ **toss out** VT SEP jeter; *Fam (rubbish)* balancer; **to t. sb out of a club** *(physically, cancel membership)* mettre qn à la porte *ou Fam* jeter qn d'un club
▸ **toss over** VT SEP = **toss across**
▸ **toss up** VT SEP *(throw up)* lancer, envoyer; **t. that brush up, will you** lance-moi *ou* envoie-moi la brosse, s'il te plaît; **to t. sth up**

into the air lancer *ou* envoyer qch en l'air
VI *(with coin)* tirer à pile ou face; **let's t. for it** jouons-le *ou* décidons-le à pile ou face

tosser ['tɒsər] N *Br Sl* connard *m*

tossing ['tɒsɪŋ] N *(of boat etc)* ballottement *m*

toss-up N **1** *(with coin)* coup *m* de pile ou face; **in the event of a tie the winner will be decided by a t.** en cas d'égalité, on tirera à pile ou face pour désigner le gagnant **2** *Fam* **in the end it was a t. between Majorca and Rhodes** finalement, nous avons dû choisir entre Majorque et Rhodes; **it's a t. which is best** il est impossible de dire quel est le meilleur; **I don't know, it's a t.** je ne sais pas, c'est kif-kif

tot [tɒt] N **1** *(child)* **(tiny) t.** tout(e) petit(e) enfant *mf*; **books for tiny tots** livres pour les tout-petits **2** *(small quantity)* *(of whisky etc)* (petite) goutte *f*
▸ **tot up** VT SEP *(add)* additionner; *(total)* faire le total de; **she has totted up 2,500 hours' flying time** elle totalise 2 500 heures de vol
VI *(of expenses etc)* s'élever (**to** à)

total ['təʊt(ə)l] ADJ total, -aux, global, -aux; **marketing the product accounts for 20% of the t. costs** le coût de commercialisation du produit revient à 20% du coût total; **t. failure** échec *m* complet; **t. guarantee** garantie *f* totale; **they were in t. ignorance of it** ils l'ignoraient complètement; **the t. population** la population totale; **t. receipts** total *m* des recettes; **t. sales** ventes *fpl* totales, chiffre *m* d'affaires global
N total *m*; *(sum of money)* montant *m*; **grand t.** total global; **there are a t. of thirteen inspectors in the whole country** au total, il y a treize inspecteurs dans tout le pays; **sum t.** somme *f* totale; **the t. amounts to £100** la somme *ou* le montant s'élève à 100 livres; **the t. payable** le total à payer; **a t. of 102 hours/people** un total de 102 heures/personnes; **in t.** au total
VT *(pt, pp* **totalled**, *Am* **totaled)** **1** *(add up)* *(expenditure)* additionner, totaliser **2** *(amount to)* se chiffrer à; **to t. £100** s'élever à *ou* se monter à 100 livres **3** *Am Fam (write off)* *(car)* bousiller, déglinguer, fusiller
▸▸ **t. amount** somme *f* totale *ou* globale, montant total; *Fin* **t. annual expenses** consommations *fpl* de l'exercice; *Fin* **t. assets** total de l'actif; *Fin* **t. asset value** valeur *f* de bilan; *Fin* **t. constructive loss** perte *f* totale; *Astron* **t. eclipse** éclipse *f* totale; *Com* **t. fixed cost** coût *m* fixe total; *Fin* **t. gross income** revenu *m* brut global; *Fin* **t. insured value** valeur *f* totale assurée; *Fin* **t. liabilities** total du passif; *Fin* **t. loss** perte totale; *Fin* **t. loss settlement** règlement *m* en perte totale; *Fin* **t. net income** revenu *m* net global; *Com* **t. quality control** contrôle *m* de la qualité totale; *Com* **t. quality management** qualité *f* totale; *Com* **t. unit cost** coût *m* complet unitaire; **t. war** guerre *f* totale

totalitarian [təʊtælɪˈteərɪən] ADJ *Pol* totalitaire

totalitarianism [təʊtælɪˈteərɪənɪz(ə)m] N *Pol* totalitarisme *m*

totality [təʊˈtælɪtɪ] N totalité *f*

totalizator ['təʊtəlaɪzeɪtər] N *Horseracing (for bets)* totalisateur *m*, totaliseur *m*

totalize ['təʊtəlaɪz] VT additionner, totaliser

totalling, *Am* **totaling** ['təʊtəlɪŋ] N chiffrage *m*

totally ['təʊtəlɪ] ADV totalement

tote[1] [təʊt] N *Horseracing Fam* = **totalizator**

tote[2] VT *esp Am (goods etc)* transporter; *(bag, gun)* porter
▸▸ **t. bag** grand sac *m*, fourre-tout *m inv*

totem ['təʊtəm] N totem *m*
▸▸ **t. pole** mât *m* totémique

totemic [təʊˈtemik] ADJ totémique

totemism [ˈtəʊtəmiz(ə)m] N totémisme m

t'other, tother [ˈtʌðər] ADJ, PRON Dial, Fam = the other

totter [ˈtɒtər] VI 1 (of person) chanceler, tituber; **to t. in/out** entrer/sortir d'un pas mal assuré ou chanceler 2 (of building, government) chanceler

tottering [ˈtɒtərɪŋ] ADJ (person) chancelant, titubant; (building, regime) chancelant; **t. steps** pas mpl chancelants ou mal assurés

tottery [ˈtɒtərɪ] ADJ chancelant

totty [ˈtɒtɪ] N Br Fam (attractive women) belles nanas fpl, belles gonzesses fpl; **he's at the beach checking out the t.** il est en train de mater les nanas sur la plage

toucan [ˈtuːkæn] N (bird) toucan m

TOUCH [tʌtʃ]

N	toucher **1, 2, 4** ▪ contact **1, 3, 6** ▪ touche **4, 7** ▪ soupçon **5** ▪ pointe **5**
VT	toucher **1, 3–5** ▪ toucher à **1** ▪ rivaliser avec **2** ▪ émouvoir **4**
VI	se toucher

N 1 (act of touching) toucher m, contact m; **I felt a t. on my arm** j'ai senti qu'on me touchait le bras; **the engine starts at the first t. of the starter** le moteur démarre du premier coup

2 (sense) toucher m; **hard/soft to the t.** dur/mou au toucher

3 (feel) contact m; **the cold t. of marble** le contact froid du marbre

4 (light blow) léger coup m; (with paintbrush) touche f; (with pencil) coup de crayon; **t. of or with a stick** léger coup de baguette; **to give one's horse a t. of the spurs** toucher son cheval de l'éperon; **to add a few touches to a picture** faire quelques retouches à un tableau; **to put the finishing touch(es) or to add the final t. to sth** mettre la dernière main à qch; **sculptor with a bold/light t.** sculpteur au ciseau hardi/délicat; **to have a light t.** (on piano) avoir un toucher délicat; (in cooking) avoir des doigts de fée; (in writing) avoir un style raffiné; **delicate t. (with or of the brush)** coup de pinceau délicat; Fig **there were some nice touches in the film** il y avait quelques notes bien vues dans le film; **he's lost his t.** il a perdu la main; **this house needs a woman's t.** il faut qu'une femme s'occupe de cette maison

5 (hint) pointe f, soupçon m; **t. of garlic** pointe ou soupçon d'ail; **a t. of bitterness** une pointe d'amertume; **there's a t. of colour in her cheeks** ses joues ont pris un peu de couleur; **the first touches of autumn** les premières teintes de l'automne; **a t. of originality** une note d'originalité; **to have a t. of flu** être un peu grippé

6 (communication) contact m; **to be in t. with sb** être ou se tenir en contact avec qn, être en rapport avec qn; **they're still in t.** ils ont maintenu le contact ou sont toujours en contact; **to get in t. with sb** joindre ou contacter qn, prendre contact ou se mettre en contact avec qn; **to get in t. with the police** prendre contact avec la police; **I'll be in t.** je vous ferai signe; **to put sb in t. with sb** mettre qn en relations ou en rapport avec qn; **to keep or stay in t. with sb** rester en contact avec qn; **keep in t.!** on reste en contact!; **to keep sb in t. with sth** tenir qn au courant de qch; **to be out of t. with foreign affairs** ne plus être au courant des affaires étrangères; **to be out of t. or to have lost t. with sb** ne plus être en contact avec qn; **to lose t. with reality** perdre le contact avec la réalité; **the President has lost t. with**

the electorate le Président a perdu le contact avec son électorat

7 Sport touche f; **kick into t.** envoi m en touche; Fig Fam **to kick a proposal into t.** mettre une proposition au placard; **the ball has gone into t.** le ballon est sorti en touche

8 Sl (financially) **to make a t.** taper quelqu'un; **easy or soft t.** (person) pigeon m; **I'm no easy or soft t.** il n'y a pas écrit 'pigeon' sur mon front

VT 1 (be in contact with) toucher; (finger, handle) toucher à; Fencing (one's opponent) toucher; **to t. sth with one's finger** toucher qch du doigt; **to t. sb on the shoulder** toucher qn à l'épaule; **to t. sb on the arm** toucher le bras à qn; **I never touched him!** (didn't hit) je ne l'ai même pas touché; **he touched his hat to me** il m'a salué en touchant son chapeau; **t. wood!** je touche/touchons du bois!; Fam **I wouldn't t. it with a bargepole or Am a ten foot pole** je ne voudrais pas y toucher, même avec des pincettes; Fam **I wouldn't t. him with a bargepole or Am a ten foot pole** je ne veux rien avoir à faire avec lui; **nobody will t. him these days** personne ne veut plus rien avoir à faire avec lui; **to t. (the) bottom** (of ship) toucher le fond; **he touched the bell** (pushed button) il a appuyé sur (le bouton de) la sonnette; **the curtains t. the floor** les rideaux descendent jusqu'au plancher; **the law can't t. her** la loi ne peut rien contre elle; **I never t. wine** je ne bois jamais de vin; **you haven't touched your meat!** tu n'as pas touché à ta viande!; **stains that other detergents won't t.** des taches contre lesquelles les autres détergents ne peuvent rien; **you haven't really touched the problem of ... in your essay** vous n'avez pas vraiment abordé le problème de ... dans votre essai; **if it's against the law, we won't t. it** si c'est illégal, nous ne nous en mêlerons pas

2 (rival) **when it comes to reliability, no other car can t. it** pour ce qui est de la fiabilité, aucune voiture ne peut l'égaler; **there's no one to t. him in comedy** il est sans égal dans les comédies; **there's only one other company that can t. them** il n'y a qu'une autre entreprise qui puisse rivaliser avec eux ou qui soit à leur niveau

3 (produce an effect on) (something) avoir un effet sur; **this quiet corner of the country was scarcely touched by the war** ce petit coin du pays n'a presque pas été touché par la guerre; **to t. sb on a raw or tender spot** toucher qn à un endroit sensible; **flowers touched by the frost** fleurs atteintes par la gelée

4 (move) (somebody) toucher, émouvoir; **to be touched by sb's kindness** être touché de ou par la bonté de qn

5 esp Fml (concern) (somebody) toucher, regarder; **the question touches you closely** la question vous touche de près

6 Fam **to t. sb for a fiver** taper qn de cinq livres

VI (of people, things) se toucher; **don't t.!** n'y touchez pas!; **please do not t.** (on notice) prière de ne pas toucher; **the two ships touched** les deux navires ont touché; Naut **to t. at a port** faire escale à un port

▸ ▸ Comput **t. pad** souris f tactile; **t. screen** écran m tactile; **t. screen computer** ordinateur m à écran tactile

▸ **touch down** VI 1 Rugby marquer un essai; Am Ftbl faire un touché-en-but, toucher dans les buts

2 Astronaut, Aviat (land) atterrir; (in mid-journey) faire escale

VT SEP (ball) Rugby plaquer au sol; Am Ftbl toucher dans les buts

▸ **touch off** VT SEP (detonate) (cannon etc) décharger; (mine) faire partir, faire exploser; (revolt, quarrel) déclencher

▸ **touch on** VT INSEP (make brief reference to) (subject) aborder; **her speech didn't even t. on this problem** elle n'a même pas abordé ou effleuré ce problème dans son discours

▸ **touch up** VT SEP 1 (add paint etc to) (painting) faire des retouches à; (colours of sth) aviver, rafraîchir; (story) enjoliver; (piece of work) retaper; **to t. up (the paint on) a window frame** etc donner un coup de pinceau à un châssis de fenêtre etc; **to t. up one's make-up** rafraîchir son maquillage; **to t. up a photograph** retoucher une photo

2 Br Sl (touch sexually) toucher, peloter

▸ **touch upon** VT INSEP = **touch on**

touch-and-go ADJ (affair) très risqué, hasardeux; **it's t. whether we'll have time** il n'est pas du tout sûr que nous ayons ou aurons le temps; **it's t. whether he'll live** il a une chance sur deux de s'en sortir; **right up to the minute they signed it was t.** jusqu'au moment où ils ont signé, rien n'était sûr

touchdown [ˈtʌtʃdaʊn] N 1 Rugby essai m; (in American football) touché-en-but m, pl touchés en-but, touché-à-terre m, pl touchés-à-terre 2 Astronaut, Aviat atterrissage m

touché [ˈtuːʃeɪ] INT touché!

touched [tʌtʃt] ADJ 1 (moved) touché, ému 2 Fam **t. (in the head)** toqué, timbré

touchiness [ˈtʌtʃɪnɪs] N susceptibilité f

touching [ˈtʌtʃɪŋ] ADJ (moving) touchant, émouvant

N **t. is not allowed, no t.!** il est défendu de toucher

PREP Fml concernant

touchingly [ˈtʌtʃɪŋlɪ] ADV d'une manière touchante ou émouvante

touch-judge N Rugby juge m de touche

touchline [ˈtʌtʃlaɪn] N Ftbl etc ligne f de touche

touch-sensitive ADJ Comput (screen etc) tactile; (key, switch) à effleurement

touchstone [ˈtʌtʃstəʊn] N pierre f de touche

touch-tone telephone N téléphone m à touches

touch-type VI taper au toucher

touch-typing N dactylographie f au toucher

touch-up N Phot retouche f

touchwood [ˈtʌtʃwʊd] N amadou m

touchy [ˈtʌtʃɪ] ADJ (person) susceptible (about sur); (subject) délicat; **to be t.** (of person) se froisser ou s'offusquer facilement; **she's very t. on that point** elle est très susceptible ou chatouilleuse là-dessus

touchy-feely [-ˈfiːlɪ] ADJ Pej qui affectionne les contacts physiques

tough [tʌf] ADJ 1 (meat etc) dur, coriace; (material, metal) dur, résistant

2 (resistant, strong) (person) fort, solide; **you have to be t. to ...** il faut être solide ou résistant ou Fam costaud pour ...; **to become t.** s'endurcir; Fam **a t. guy** un dur (à cuire); **as t. as old boots** coriace; (steak) dur comme de la semelle

3 (mentally) fort; (stubborn) opiniâtre; (strict) dur, sévère; **she's a t. customer** (not easy to deal with) elle n'est pas commode; (mentally resistant) c'est une dure (à cuire); **is he t. enough to be sales director?** a-t-il la force de caractère nécessaire à un directeur des ventes?; **we'll have to get t. with them** il faudra que nous nous montrions plus durs avec eux; Prov **when the going gets t., the t. get going** c'est dans les moments difficiles que les vrais hommes entrent en action

4 (difficult) (question, job, climb) dur, ardu; Hum **it's t. at the top** (in job etc) c'est dur au sommet; **it was a t. job** c'était une rude besogne; **to give sb a t. time** faire passer un

mauvais quart d'heure à qn; **they had a t. time when their parents died** ils en ont connu de dures quand leurs parents sont morts

5 *Fam (unfortunate)* dur; **that's t. on the rest of them** c'est dur pour ceux qui restent; **it's t. for him, great for us** c'est dur pour lui, mais génial pour nous; **well, isn't that just t.!** quel dommage!; **t. luck!** pas de chance!; **that's your t. luck!** ce n'est pas de chance pour toi, c'est tant pis pour toi

N voyou *m*

ADV *(to talk, act)* comme un dur

▸ **tough out** VT SEP *Fam* **t. it out** *(face up to sth)* faire front; *(endure sth)* tenir le coup

toughen ['tʌf(ə)n] VT durcir; *(person)* endurcir; **toughened glass** verre *m* trempé VI durcir; *(of person)* s'endurcir

▸ **toughen up** VT & VI = **toughen**

toughie ['tʌfɪ] N *Fam* **1** *(person)* dur *m* **2** *(question, problem)* casse-tête *f inv*; **question 5 was a real t.** la question 5 était une horreur

toughly ['tʌflɪ] ADV **1** *(to fight)* vigoureusement **2** *(to argue, refuse)* avec opiniâtreté; **a t. worded reply** une réponse très dure

toughness ['tʌfnɪs] N **1** *(of wood etc)* dureté *f*, résistance *f* **2** *(of person)* *(physical strength)* force *f*, solidité *f*; *(resistance to fatigue)* résistance *f*; *(mentally)* force de caractère; *(inflexibility)* ténacité *f*, opiniâtreté *f* **3** *(of task)* difficulté *f*

toupee ['tuːpeɪ] N postiche *m*

tour [tʊər] N **1** *(journey to different places)* voyage *m*; *(excursion)* excursion *f*, **conducted** *or* **guided t.** voyage organisé; *(of museum, city, factory etc)* visite *f* (guidée); **to go on a t. of the Highlands** partir en voyage dans les Highlands; **to go on a bus t. of Paris** faire une visite guidée de Paris en bus; **the PM was taken on a t. of the factory/hospital** le Premier Ministre a fait la visite de l'usine/l'hôpital; **would you like a t. of the garden?** voulez-vous que je vous fasse visiter le jardin?; **would you like a t. of the new offices?** aimeriez-vous visiter nos nouveaux bureaux?; **package t.,** *Am* **all-expense t.** voyage à forfait *ou* à prix forfaitaire; **cycle** *or* **cycling t.** excursion *ou* randonnée *f* à bicyclette; **walking t.** excursion *ou* randonnée à pied

2 *(by orchestra, theatre company etc)* tournée *f*, **during their European t.** *or* **t. of Europe** pendant leur tournée européenne *ou* en Europe; **concert t.** tournée de concerts; **to go on t.** partir en tournée; **to take a play on t.** jouer une pièce en tournée

VT **1** *(country)* voyager dans; *(hospital, factory etc)* visiter

2 *Mus, Theat* **to t. the provinces** *(of orchestra, company)* faire une tournée en province; *(of play)* passer en province

VI **1 we're just touring around** nous ne faisons que visiter la région; **we decided to t. through the Loire Valley** nous avons décidé de visiter la Vallée de la Loire

2 *(of orchestra, theatre company etc)* **we spend most of the year touring** nous passons la plus grande partie de l'année en tournée; **we go touring every summer** nous partons en tournée tous les étés

▸▸ **t. brochure** brochure *f ou* catalogue *m* de voyages; *Am* **t. conductor, t. director** *(courier)* accompagnateur, -trice; *Mil* **t. of duty** service *m*; **to do a t. of duty** servir; **t. de force** tour *m* de force; **t. group** groupe *m* (de touristes); **t. guide** *(person)* guide *mf*; *(book)* guide *m* touristique; **t. of inspection** tournée d'inspection; *Am* **t. leader, t. manager** accompagnateur, -trice; **t. operator** *(travel agency)* tour-opérateur *m*, *pl* tour-opérateurs, voyagiste *m*; *(bus company)* compagnie *f* de cars *(qui organise des voyages)*; **t. package** forfait *m* voyage

tourer ['tʊərər] N *(car)* voiture *f* de tourisme; *(cycle)* vélo *m* de randonnée

touring ['tʊərɪŋ] N **to do some t.** faire un circuit

ADJ **we had a t. holiday in the North of Italy** pour nos vacances nous avons visité le Nord de l'Italie

▸▸ **t. bike** vélo *m* de randonnée; **t. car** voiture *f* de tourisme; **t. caravan** caravane *f* de tourisme; *Theat* **t. company** *(permanently)* troupe *f* ambulante; *(temporarily)* troupe en tournée; **t. cycle** vélo de randonnée; **t. site** *(caravan site)* terrain *m* de caravaning

tourism ['tʊərɪz(ə)m] N tourisme *m*

tourism-generated [-dʒenəreɪtɪd] ADJ généré par le tourisme

tourist ['tʊərɪst] N touriste *mf*; **t. restaurant/pub** restaurant *m*/pub *m* pour touristes

▸▸ **t. agency** agence *f ou* bureau *m* de tourisme; **t. area** zone *f* touristique; **t. attraction** attraction *f ou* site *m* touristique; **t. board** comité *m* du tourisme; **t. centre** centre *m ou* ville *f* touristique; *Br* **t. class** classe *f* touriste; **t. destination** destination *f* touristique; **t. enclave** enclave *f* touristique; **t. guide** *(book)* guide *m* touristique; *(person)* guide *mf* (touristique); **t. industry** industrie *f* touristique, industrie du tourisme; **t. information centre** syndicat *m* d'initiative, office *m* du tourisme; **t. night** nuitée *f*; **t. route** itinéraire *m* touristique; **t. season** saison *f* touristique; **t. trade** tourisme *m*; **t. traffic** flot *m* des touristes; **t. trail** sentier *m* touristique; **t. trap** attrape-touristes *m inv*

touristic [tʊəˈrɪstɪk] ADJ touristique

touristy ['tʊərɪstɪ] ADJ *Fam Pej* (trop) touristique

tournament ['tʊənəmənt] N *Sport, Hist* tournoi *m*

tourniquet ['tʊənɪkeɪ] N *Med* garrot *m*

tousle ['taʊz(ə)l] VT *(sb's hair)* ébouriffer; **tousled hair** cheveux *mpl* ébouriffés

tout [taʊt] N **1** *(for hotels)* rabatteur, -euse; *(for shows etc)* racoleur *m*; *(of tickets)* revendeur, -euse de billets (au marché noir) **2** *(racing) t.* *(who sells tips)* vendeur, -euse de tuyaux; **according to the touts** d'après les gens qui s'y connaissent

VI **to t. for custom** racoler des clients

VT *(one's services)* offrir; **she had touted her article around all the newspapers** elle avait fait le tour de tous les journaux pour essayer de placer son article; **to t. a product (around)** faire l'article d'un produit; **to t. one's wares** vendre sa marchandise

tow[1] [təʊ] N *(act of towing)* **to give sb/sth a t.** remorquer qn/qch; **to take a car in t.** prendre une voiture en remorque; **to be taken in t.** se mettre en remorque; **to be on or in t.** être en remorque; *(of boat)* être à la traîne; *Fam* **he always has his family in t.** il trimbale toujours toute sa famille avec lui; *Fam* **with six assistants in t.** avec six assistants dans son sillage

VT *(boat, car)* remorquer; *(barge)* *(from towpath)* haler

▸▸ *Aut* **t. ball** rotule *f* d'attelage; **t. hook** croc *m* de remorque; **t. rope** câble *m* de remorquage; *Am* **t. truck** dépanneuse *f*, **t. weight** poids *m* remorqué

▸ **tow away** VT SEP remorquer, prendre en remorque; *(of police)* emmener à la fourrière; **you'll get towed away** tu vas te retrouver à la fourrière

tow[2] N *(fibres)* étoupe *f* (blanche), filasse *f*

towage ['təʊɪdʒ] N **1** *(act)* remorquage *m* **2** *(charge)* (frais *mpl* de) remorquage *m*

toward [təˈwɔːd, twɔːd] PREP *esp Am* = **towards**

towards [təˈwɔːdz, twɔːdz] PREP **1** *(of direction)* vers; **t. the town** vers la ville, du côté

de la ville; **he came t. me** il est venu vers moi; **it's out t. Versailles** c'est du côté de Versailles **2** *(of time)* vers; **t. evening** vers le soir; **t. the end of his life** vers *ou* sur la fin de sa vie **3** *(directed at)* *(of feelings, behaviour, attitude)* envers, à l'égard de; **her feelings t. me** ses sentiments envers *ou* pour moi, ses sentiments à mon égard; **they behaved strangely t. us** ils se sont conduits d'une manière étrange envers nous *ou* à notre égard **4** *(contributing to)* pour; **to save t. the children's education** économiser pour *ou* en vue de l'éducation des enfants; **to contribute (something) t. the cost of ...** participer à l'achat de ...; **would you like to give something t. it?** voulez-vous donner quelque chose?, voulez-vous participer?

towbar ['təʊbɑːr] N *Aut* timon *m* de remorque; *(of glider)* barre *f* de remorquage

towel ['taʊəl] N serviette *f* (de toilette); **hand t.** essuie-main(s) *m*, *pl* essuie-mains; *Fig* **to throw in the t.** jeter l'éponge; **roller t.** essuie-main(s) *(pour rouleau)*, serviette sans fin; **tea t., dish t.** torchon *m* (à vaisselle); **sanitary t.** serviette hygiénique *ou* périodique

VT (-ll-, *Am* -l-) essuyer *ou* frotter avec une serviette; **to t. oneself (dry)** *(after bath etc)* s'essuyer

▸▸ **t. rail** porte-serviettes *m inv*

towelhead ['taʊəlhed] N *Offensive Sl (Arab)* bougnoule *mf*

towelling, *Am* **toweling** ['taʊəlɪŋ] N *(fabric)* tissu-éponge *m*; **t. robe** peignoir *m* en tissu-éponge

tower ['taʊər] N **1** *Archit, Constr* tour *f*; **she's a t. of strength** c'est quelqu'un sur qui on peut compter en cas de problème, c'est quelqu'un de solide; **he is a t. of strength in the defence line** *(in football)* c'est le pilier de la défense; **church t.** clocher *m*; **clock t.** tour de l'horloge; *Tech* **water t.** château *m* d'eau; *Aviat* **control t.** tour de contrôle **2** *Comput* boîtier *m* vertical, tour *f* **3** *(for camera)* échafaudage *m* pour caméra

▸▸ **the T. of Babel** la tour de Babel; *Br* **t. block** tour d'habitation; **the T. of London** la Tour de Londres; *Comput* **t. system** système *m* à boîtier vertical, système à tour

▸ **tower above, tower over** VT INSEP *(be much higher than)* dominer, dépasser de beaucoup, être beaucoup plus grand que; *(in ability)* être bien meilleur que

towering ['taʊərɪŋ] ADJ *(building, cliff etc)* très haut, très grand; *(person)* très grand; *(ambitions)* sans bornes; **a t. great figure of a man** un géant; **in a t. rage** au paroxysme de la colère

towheaded ['təʊhedɪd] ADJ aux cheveux (blond) filasse

towing ['təʊɪŋ] N remorque *f*, remorquage *m*

▸▸ **t. rod** barre *f* de remorquage; **t. rope** câble *m* de remorquage; **t. weight** charge *f* remorquable

towline ['təʊlaɪn] N (câble *m* de) remorque *f*

town [taʊn] N **1** ville *f*; **fortified t.** place *f* forte; **the whole t. is talking about it** toute la ville en parle; **to go out on the t.** faire la bombe *ou* la noce **2** *(without article)* **to go into t.** aller *ou* se rendre à la *ou* en ville; **she's in t. shopping** elle est en train de faire ses courses en ville; **he's out of t.** il n'est pas en ville; **the best pizzas in t.** les meilleures pizzas de la ville; **man about t.** mondain *m*; *Fig Fam* **to go to t.** *(make great effort)* se mettre en quatre; *Fig Fam* **they really went to t.** *(on redecoration, doing a job etc)* ils ont vraiment mis le paquet; *(preparing a party etc)* ils ont vraiment fait les choses en grand; *Fig Fam* **I really went to t. on the third question** je me suis vraiment foulé pour la troisième question; *Fig Fam* **no need to go to t.**

on it ce n'est pas la peine de trop se fatiguer ► ► **t. centre** centre-ville *m*, *pl* centres-villes; *Hist* **t. clerk** secrétaire *mf* de mairie; **t. council** conseil *m* municipal; **t. and gown** = expression désignant collectivement les habitants et les étudiants de certaines villes universitaires et soulignant les différences de culture entre les deux milieux; **t. hall** hôtel *m* de ville, mairie *f*; **t. house** maison *f* en ville; (*aristocratic mansion*) ≃ hôtel particulier; *Am* (*semi-detached house*) maison mitoyenne (en ville); **t. house hotel** grande maison en ville aménagée en hôtel; **t. life** vie *f* urbaine; **t. planner** urbaniste *mf*; **t. planning** urbanisme *m*

townee, townie ['taʊnɪ] **N** *Fam* habitant, -ante de la ville

townsfolk ['taʊnzfəʊk] **NPL** habitants *mpl* ou gens *mpl* de la ville/des villes, citadins *mpl*

township ['taʊnʃɪp] **N 1** (*small town*) commune *f*, bourg *m* **2** *Admin Am* municipalité *f*, *Can* canton *m*; *Am* (*in New England*) commune *f* **3** (*in S Africa*) banlieue *f* noire

townsman, *pl* **townsmen** ['taʊnzmən] **N** habitant *m* de la ville, citadin *m*

townspeople ['taʊnzpi:p(ə)l] **NPL** habitants *mpl* ou gens *mpl* de la ville/des villes, citadins *mpl*

townswoman, *pl* **townswomen** ['taʊnzwʊmən, -wɪmɪn] **N** habitante *f* de la ville, citadine *f*

towpath ['təʊpɑːθ] **N** chemin *m* de halage

towrope ['təʊrəʊp] **N** (câble *m* de) remorque *f*

tow-start N to give sb a t. démarrer qn en remorque ► **vt** démarrer en remorque

toxaemia, *Am* **toxemia** [tɒkˈsiːmɪə] **N** *Med* toxémie *f*

toxic ['tɒksɪk] **ADJ** (*substance*) toxique ► ► *Med* **t. shock syndrome** syndrome *m* du choc toxique; **t. waste** déchets *mpl* toxiques

toxicologic(al) [tɒksɪkəˈlɒdʒɪk, -ɪk(ə)l] **ADJ** *Med* toxicologique

toxicologist [tɒksɪˈkɒlədʒɪst] **N** *Med* toxicologue *mf*

toxicology [tɒksɪˈkɒlədʒɪ] **N** *Med* toxicologie *f*

toxin ['tɒksɪn] **N** *Biol, Chem* toxine *f*

toy [tɔɪ] **N** jouet *m*; **he's like a child with a new t.** il est comme un enfant avec un nouveau jouet ► ► *Br Fam* **t. boy** jeune amant *m*; **she's got herself a t. boy** elle s'est déniché un petit jeune *ou* un jeune amant; **t. dog** chien *m* nain; **t. poodle** caniche *m* nain; **t. shop** magasin *m* de jouets; **t. soldier** soldat *m* de plomb; **t. trumpet** trompette *f* d'enfant ► **toy with vt insep** (*play with*) jouer avec; **to t. with one's food** jouer avec sa nourriture; **to t. with an idea** caresser une idée; **to t. with sb** s'amuser avec qn; **to t. with sb's affections** jouer avec le cœur de qn

tpi *Comput* (*abbr* **tracks per inch**) pistes *fpl* par pouce

TQC [tiːkjuːˈsiː] **N** (*abbr* **total quality control**) QG *f*

TQM [tiːkjuːˈem] **N** (*abbr* **total quality management**) gestion *f* de la QG

trace¹ [treɪs] **N 1** (*vestige*) trace *f*, vestige *m*; **they could find no t. of him** ils n'ont retrouvé aucune trace de lui; **there's not a t. of it** (*there's nothing left of it*) il n'en reste pas trace; **there's not a t. of your wallet anywhere in the house** ton portefeuille n'est nulle part dans la maison; **he has disappeared without t.** il a disparu sans laisser de trace; **the last remaining traces of an ancient civi-**

lization les derniers vestiges d'une civilisation ancienne
2 (*small amount*) trace *f*, quantité *f* infime; (*of irony, sarcasm*) soupçon *m*; **traces of cyanide/poison** des traces de cyanure/poison; **he said with a t. of amusement** dit-il, l'air légèrement amusé; **there was the t. of a smile on her face** il y avait l'ombre d'un sourire sur son visage
► **vt 1** (*outline*) (*plan, scheme etc*) exposer
2 (*draw*) (*plan, diagram*) tracer, faire le tracé de; (*copy*) (*drawing*) calquer; **to t. sth in the sand/dirt with a stick** dessiner qch dans le sable/la poussière avec un bâton
3 (*follow tracks of*) (*person, animal*) suivre la trace *ou* la piste de; (*locate*) (*lost property*) recouvrer; (*influence etc*) retracer, retrouver; **they traced him as far as Paris** *or* **to Paris** on a suivi sa piste jusqu'à Paris; **to t. the evil to its source** remonter à la source du mal
► ► **t. element** oligo-élément *m*, *pl* oligo-éléments
► **trace back vt sep** (*uncover origins of*) **to t. sth back to its source** remonter jusqu'à l'origine de qch; **to t. one's family back to William the Conqueror** faire remonter son arbre généalogique jusqu'à Guillaume le Conquérant
► **trace out vt sep** = **trace vt 1**

trace² **N** (*part of harness*) trait *m*; **in the traces** attelé; *Fig* **to kick over the traces** (*of person*) (*rebel*) ruer dans les brancards; (*break free*) s'émanciper

tracer ['treɪsər] **N** *Mil* ► ► **t. bullet** balle *f* traçante; **t. shell** traçant *m*

tracery ['treɪsərɪ] **N 1** *Archit* (*of rose window*) réseau *m*, remplage *m* **2** (*of leaf etc*) nervures *fpl*

trachea, *pl* **tracheae** [trəˈkiːə, -iːiː] **N** *Anat* trachée *f*

tracheal [trəˈkiːəl] **ADJ** *Anat* trachéal, -aux

tracheostomy [trækɪˈɒstəmɪ], **tracheotomy** [trækɪˈɒtəmɪ] **N** *Surg* trachéotomie *f*

trachoma [trəˈkəʊmə] **N** *Med* trachome *m*

tracing ['treɪsɪŋ] **N** (*copy*) calque *m* ► ► **t. paper** papier-calque *m inv*, papier *m* à décalquer

track [træk] **N 1** (*marks left*) (*of animal*) trace(s) *f(pl)*, piste *f*, foulées *fpl*; (*of person*) trace(s), piste; (*of wheel*) sillon *m*; **to follow in sb's tracks** suivre la voie tracée par qn; **to be on sb's t.** être sur la piste de qn; **to throw sb off the t.** dépister qn, *Fam* semer qn; *Fig Fam* **to be off the t.** divaguer; **to be on the right t.** être sur la (bonne) voie; *Fig* **to be on the wrong t.** (*in search, guess etc*) se fourvoyer, être sur la mauvaise piste; **to keep t. of sb/sth** suivre les progrès de qn/qch; **I've lost t. of her** je l'ai perdue de vue; **I've lost t. of all the times I've …** je ne compte plus les fois où j'ai …; *Fam* **to make tracks** (*leave*) partir, filer; **to stop in one's tracks** s'arrêter net; **to stop sb in his/her tracks** arrêter qn net
2 (*path*) piste *f*, chemin *m*, sentier *m*; *Rail* voie *f* (ferrée); **cycle t.** piste cyclable; *Sport* (*running*) **t.** piste; **the train left the t.** le train a déraillé; *Rail* **single-t./double-t. line** ligne *f* à une voie/à deux voies
3 (*in recording process, on disk*) piste *f*; (*song*) (*on record, CD etc*) morceau *m*; **sound t.** piste sonore; *Comput* **tracks per inch** pistes par pouce
4 (*of tracked vehicle*) chenille *f*
5 (*distance between wheels*) écartement *m* des roues, voie *f*
► **vt** (*animal, thief etc*) suivre à la piste, pister; (*fugitive*) traquer; (*missile*) suivre la trajectoire de
► **vi** (*of gear wheels etc*) être en alignement; (*of camera*) faire un travelling; **the band of**

rain that is tracking across the country le front de pluie qui se déplace à travers le pays
► ► *Aut* **t. arm** bras *m* de direction; *Sport* **t. event** épreuve *f* sur piste; *Sport* **t. and field events** épreuves *fpl* d'athlétisme; *Sport* **t. racing** courses *fpl* sur piste; *Sport, Fig* **t. record** (*past record, career to date*) antécédents *mpl*; (*list of achievements*) palmarès *m*; **he doesn't have a very good t. record for punctuality** il n'est pas réputé pour sa ponctualité; **in view of his t. record of getting home late every Friday night …** vu l'habitude qu'il a de rentrer tard tous les vendredis soirs …; **a company with a good/poor t. record in winning export orders** une entreprise avec un bon/mauvais palmarès sur le plan des commandes à l'exportation; **no wonder the insurance is high with your t. record!** pas étonnant que l'assurance soit chère avec ton palmarès!; **given the government's t. record in the field of cutting benefits** vu les antécédents du gouvernement en matière de réduction des prestations sociales; *Br Aut* **t. rod** biellette *f* de connexion; *Sport* **t. shoes** chaussures *fpl* de course; **t. vehicle** véhicule *m* chenillé
► **track down vt sep** (*discover*) (*criminal, prey etc*) dépister; (*information*) découvrir; (*missing object*) retrouver; **they tracked her down to her hideout** ils ont remonté sa trace *ou* sa piste jusqu'à sa cachette

trackball ['trækbɔːl] **N** *Comput* boule *f* de commande, trackball *m ou f*

tracked [trækt] **ADJ** (*vehicle*) chenillé

tracker ['trækər] **N 1** (*of game*) traqueur *m* **2** *TV* machiniste *m* de travelling
► ► **t. dog** chien *m* policier; *Fin* **t. fund** fonds *m* indiciel *ou* à gestion indicielle

tracking ['trækɪŋ] **N**
► ► **t. down** (*of criminal, cause etc*) dépistage *m*; *Cin, TV* **t. shot** traveling *m*, travelling *m*; *Astron* **t. station** station *f* d'observation; **t. systems** systèmes *mpl* de repérage et poursuite

tracklayer ['trækleɪər] **N** *Rail* (*person*) poseur *m* de voie

tracklaying ['trækleɪɪŋ] **N**
► ► **t. vehicle** véhicule *m* à chenilles

trackless ['træklɪs] **ADJ** (*place*) sans chemins, sans sentiers
► ► *Am* **t. trolley** trolleybus *m*

trackpad ['trækpæd] **N** *Comput* tablette *f* tactile

tracksuit ['træks(j)uːt] **N** *Sport* survêtement *m*

tract¹ [trækt] **N 1** (*of land*) étendue *f* **2** *Anat* (*respiratory, digestive*) appareil *m*

tract² **N** (*pamphlet*) brochure *f*, tract *m*

tractable ['træktəb(ə)l] **ADJ** (*person, character*) docile; (*material*) facile à ouvrer; **a t. problem** un problème que l'on peut résoudre

traction ['trækʃən] **N 1** *Tech* traction *f*, tirage *m* **2** *Med* traction *f*; **in t.** en traction
► ► **t. cable** câble *m* tracteur; *Aut* **t. control** contrôle *m* de traction; **t. engine** locomotive *f*; **t. wheels** roues *fpl* motrices

tractive ['træktɪv] **ADJ** tractif; (*force*) de traction

tractor ['træktər] **N** (*vehicle*) tracteur *m*; (*of lorry*) tracteur routier; **t.-drawn** tracté
► ► **t. driver** conducteur, -trice de tracteur; *Comput* **t. feed** dispositif *m* d'entraînement à picots; **t. holes** (*on tractor wheel*) trous *mpl* à ergots; **t. pin** (*in tractor wheel*) ergot *m* de tracteur; **t. wheel** (*on printer etc*) roue *f* d'entraînement

trad [træd] **N** *Br Mus Fam* jazz *m* traditionnel

tradable ['treɪdəb(ə)l] **ADJ** négociable

trade [treɪd] **N 1** *(commerce)* commerce *m*, affaires *fpl*, négoce *m*, échanges *mpl* commerciaux; *Am (commercial transaction)* transaction *f* (commerciale); *(swap)* échange *m*; **to do a t.** faire un échange; **(illicit) t.** trafic *m*; **to be in t.** être dans le commerce; **wholesale/retail t.** commerce de gros/de détail; **balance of t.** balance *f* commerciale; **the tea t.** le commerce du thé; **the t. in animal skins** le commerce des peaux; **it's good for t.** cela fait marcher le commerce; **we don't get much t. nowadays** les affaires ne marchent pas très bien ces temps-ci; **she's doing a roaring t.** elle fait des affaires en or; **he's t.** *(not old money)* c'est un nouveau-riche
2 *(profession)* métier *m*; *(as a body)* (corps *m* de) métier; **to be in the t.** être du métier; **to follow** *or* **carry on a t.** exercer un métier; **to learn a t.** apprendre un métier; **he's a plumber by t.** il est plombier de son état *ou* métier; **everyone to his t.** chacun son métier; **it's what we in the t. call a ...** c'est ce que, dans le métier, on appelle un ...; **the building t.** le bâtiment; **the publishing t.** l'édition *f*; **the printing t.** l'imprimerie *f*
VI 1 faire du commerce, commercer, faire le commerce *ou* le négoce (**in sth** de qch; **with sb** avec qn); **the company trades under the name of ...** l'entreprise opère sous le nom de ...; **he trades from a small stall in the market** il tient un petit étal au marché
2 *Am (to shop)* se ravitailler (**at, with** chez)
3 *St Exch (of shares)* s'échanger (**at** à)
VT 1 to t. sth for sth échanger *ou* troquer qch contre qch; **to t. places with sb** changer de place avec qn; **to t. insults/blows** échanger des insultes/coups
2 *St Exch* négocier
▶▶**t. advertising** publicité *f* auprès des intermédiaires; **t. agreement** accord *m* commercial; **t. allowance** remise *f* entre professionnels; **t. association** association *f* professionnelle; **t. ban** interdiction *f* de commerce; **t. barriers** barrières *fpl* douanières; **t. bill** effet *m* de commerce; **t. bloc** union *f* douanière; **t. body** syndicat *m* professionnel; **t. centre** place *f* commerciale; *Acct* **t. credit** crédit *m* fournisseur *ou* commercial; *Acct* **t. creditor** créancier, -ière d'exploitation; **t. cycle** cycle *m* de commercialisation; *Acct* **t. debtor** compte *m ou* créance *f* client; **t. deficit** balance *f* commerciale déficitaire, déficit *m* extérieur *ou* commercial; *Br* **the T. Descriptions Act** = loi *f* qui empêche la publicité mensongère; **t. directory** annuaire *m* de commerce; **t. discount** *(to customer)* escompte *m* commercial, escompte d'usage; *(to retailer)* escompte professionnel, remise professionnelle; **t. embargo** embargo *m* commercial; **t. exhibition** foire-exposition *f*, *pl* foires-expositions, exposition *f* commerciale; *Br* **t. fair** foire *f* commerciale, salon *m*; **t. gap** déficit *m* commercial; **t. journal** journal *m* professionnel, revue *f* professionnelle; **t. mission** mission *f* commerciale; **t. name** *(of product)* nom *m* de marque; *(of firm)* raison *f* commerciale; *Br Aut* **t. plate** plaque *f* d'immatriculation provisoire; **t. policy** politique *f* commerciale; **t. press** presse *f* spécialisée, presse professionnelle; **t. price** *Com* prix *m* marchand; *St Exch* prix de négociation; **t. promotion** promotion *f* auprès des intermédiaires; **t. publication** revue *f* spécialisée *ou* professionnelle; **t. references** références *fpl* commerciales; **t. register** registre *m* du commerce; **t. route** route *f* commerciale; **t. secret** secret *m* de fabrication; **t. show** salon *m* (professionnel); **t. ticket** avis *m* d'opéré, avis d'opération sur titres; **t. tribunal** tribunal *m* de commerce; *Br* **t. union** syndicat *m* (ouvrier); **she's very active in the t. union** c'est une syndicaliste militante; *Br* **t. union**

council conseil *m* syndical; *Br* **t. unionism** syndicalisme *m*; *Br* **t. unionist** (ouvrier, -ière) syndiqué(e); *Br* **t. union member** syndiqué, -ée; **t. war** guerre *f* commerciale; **t. wind** alizé *m*
▶ **trade down** **VI 1** *St Exch* acheter des valeurs basses **2** *(of car, home owner etc)* changer pour un modèle/un appartement/*etc* moins cher
▶ **trade in** **VT SEP** *(give in part exchange) (car etc)* donner en reprise
▶ **trade off** **VT SEP** **they have traded off quality against speed** ils ont fait primer la rapidité sur la qualité; **you can't ask me to t. off reputation against profit** vous ne pouvez pas me demander de choisir entre ma réputation et un profit; **you have to t. one thing off against another** il faut faire des choix
▶ **trade on** **VT INSEP** *(exploit) (sb's ignorance)* exploiter, tirer profit de
▶ **trade up** **VI 1** *St Exch* acheter des valeurs hautes **2** *(of car, home owner etc)* changer pour un modèle/un appartement/*etc* plus cher

tradeable ['treɪdəb(ə)l] **ADJ** négociable
traded option ['treɪdɪd] **N** *St Exch* option *f* négociable
trade-in **N** objet *m* donné en reprise; **will you take my old car as a t.?** est-ce que vous reprendrez ma vieille voiture?
▶▶**t. allowance** (valeur *f* de) reprise *f*; **t. facility** facilité *f* de reprise; **t. price** prix *m* à la reprise; **t. value** valeur *f* de reprise; **what's its t. value?** quelle est sa valeur de reprise?
trademark ['treɪdmɑːk] **N** marque *f* (de fabrique), marque de commerce; *Fig* **these close-up shots are her t.** ces gros-plans sont sa marque *ou* sa signature
▶▶**t. registration** dépôt *m* de marque
trade-off **N 1** *(compromise)* compromis *m*; **you're going to have a t. between speed and quality** si l'on va plus vite, ce sera au détriment de la qualité; **we do not believe there is a t. between ... and ...** nous ne croyons pas qu'il y ait incompatibilité entre ... et ... **2** *esp Am (exchange)* échange *m*
▶▶*Mktg* **t. analysis** analyse *f* conjointe
trader ['treɪdər] **N 1** *(person)* négociant, -ante, commerçant, -ante, marchand, -ande; *St Exch* opérateur *m*, spéculateur *m* **2** *(ship)* navire *m* marchand
trades [treɪdz] **NPL** *(winds)* (vents *mpl*) alizés *mpl*
tradesman, *pl* **tradesmen** ['treɪdzmən] **N** marchand *m*, fournisseur *m*; **tradesmen's entrance** entrée *f* des fournisseurs
trade-weighted index **N** *Econ* indice *m* pondéré par le commerce extérieur
trading ['treɪdɪŋ] **N** commerce *m*, négoce *m*
▶▶*Acct* **t. account** compte *m* d'exploitation générale; **t. bank** banque *f* commerciale; **t. capital** capital *m* engagé *ou* de roulement; **t. company** société *f* commerciale; *St Exch* **t. day** jour *m* de Bourse; *Br* **t. estate** zone *f* artisanale et commerciale; *St Exch* **t. floor** corbeille *f*, parquet *m*; **t. hours** heures *fpl* d'ouverture; *St Exch* horaires *mpl* des criées; *St Exch* **t. instrument** outil *m* de spéculation; **t. licence** carte *f* de commerçant; **t. loss** perte *f*; *St Exch* **t. member** intermédiaire *m* négociateur; *St Exch* **t. month** mois *m* d'échéance; *St Exch* **t. order** ordre *m* de négociation; **t. partners** partenaires *mpl* commerciaux; **France is our most important t. partner** la France est notre principal partenaire commercial; *Am* **t. post** *(store)* comptoir *m* commercial; *St Exch* parquet *m*, corbeille *f*; *Com* **t. profit** bénéfice(s) *m(pl)* d'exploitation; *Acct* **t. and profit and loss account** compte de résultat; *St Exch* **t. range** écart *m* de prix, fourchette *f* de cotation; **prices are stuck in a t. range** les prix ne varient pas beaucoup; *St Exch* **t. rate**

cours *m*; **t. results** résultats *mpl* de l'exercice; *St Exch* **t. room** salle *f* des changes *ou* des marchés; *St Exch* **t. session** séance *f* boursière; **t. stamp** timbre-prime *m*, *pl* timbres-prime(s), vignette-épargne *f*, *pl* vignettes-épargne; **t. standards** normes *fpl* de conformité; **t. year** année *f* d'exploitation, exercice *m*
tradition [trə'dɪʃən] **N** tradition *f*; **t. has it that ...** selon la tradition ...; **it has become a t.** c'est passé dans la tradition; **the t. is to ...** la tradition veut que l'on ... + *sub*
traditional [trə'dɪʃənəl] **ADJ** traditionnel
traditionalism [trə'dɪʃənəlɪz(ə)m] **N** traditionalisme *m*
traditionalist [trə'dɪʃənəlɪst] **ADJ, N** traditionaliste *mf*
traditionally [trə'dɪʃənəlɪ] **ADV** traditionnellement
traduce [trə'djuːs] **VT** *Fml, Lit* calomnier, diffamer
traffic ['træfɪk] **N 1** circulation *f*, trafic *m*; **heavy t.** circulation intense; **ocean t.** navigation *f* au long cours; **road t.** circulation routière; **rail(way) t.** trafic ferroviaire; **through t.** circulation directe; **southbound t. should avoid ...** les conducteurs se dirigeant vers le sud ont intérêt à éviter ...; *Fam* **go play in the t.!** va voir ailleurs si j'y suis! **2** *(movement of people)* passage *m*; *(on telephone network)* volume *m* de communications; *(on website)* trafic *m* **3** *Pej (trade)* trafic *m*
VT & VI *(pt, pp* **trafficked** ['træfɪkt]*)* *Pej* trafiquer (**in** de); *Fig* **reporters who t. in human misery** journalistes qui exploitent la misère humaine
▶▶*Mktg* **t. builder** *(product)* article *m* d'appel; **t. calming** contrôle *m* de la circulation; *Am* **t. circle** rond-point *m*, *pl* ronds-points, sens *m* giratoire; **t. cone** cône *m* de signalisation (pour la circulation routière); **t. control** régulation *f* de la circulation; *Aviat, Naut, Rail* contrôle *m* du trafic; *Am Fam* **t. cop** agent *m* de la circulation; **t. island** refuge *m*; *Br* **t. jam** embouteillage *m*, bouchon *m*; **t. lights,** *Am* **t. light** feu *m* de signalisation; **at the next t. lights** au(x) prochain(s) feu(x); **t. news** = informations *fpl* sur l'état de la circulation routière; **t. offence** infraction *f* au code de la route; **t. patrol** patrouille *f* de la circulation (routière); **t. police** *(for speeding, safety)* police *f* de la route; *(on point duty)* agents *mpl* de la circulation; **t. policeman** agent *m* de police; *(on point duty)* agent de la circulation; **t. pollution** pollution *f* automobile; *Radio* **t. programme** informations *fpl* routières; **t. regulations** règlements *mpl* sur la circulation; **t. sign** panneau *m* de signalisation, poteau *m* indicateur; **t. signals** feu de signalisation; *Br* **t. warden** contractuel, -elle
trafficator ['træfɪkeɪtər] **N** *Br Aut Old-fashioned* flèche *f* de direction
trafficker ['træfɪkər] **N** *Pej* trafiquant, -ante (**in** de, en); **drug t.** trafiquant de drogue
tragedian [trə'dʒiːdɪən] **N** *(dramatist)* auteur *m* tragique; *(actor)* tragédien *m*
tragedienne [trədʒiːdɪ'en] **N** *(actress)* tragédienne *f*
tragedy ['trædʒɪdɪ] **N** *(accident, disaster)*, *Theat* tragédie *f*; **to make a t. out of sth** prendre qch au tragique; **the t. of his death** sa mort tragique; **it will be a t. if ...** ce serait une tragédie *ou* un drame si ...; **the real t. was that ...** ce qu'il y avait de vraiment tragique, c'était que ...
tragic ['trædʒɪk] **ADJ** tragique; *Fam* **to put on a t. act** jouer la comédie pour se faire plaindre; **the t. side of the story is that ...** ce que cette histoire a de tragique c'est que ...; *Iron*

how t. for you! c'est bête ce qui t'arrive!; **t. dad in rescue bid** *(newspaper headline)* un père tente un sauvetage désespéré

▸▸**t. actor** tragédien *m*; **t. actress** tragédienne *f*

tragically ['trædʒɪklɪ] ADV tragiquement; **he died at a t. early age** c'est tragique qu'il soit mort si jeune

tragicomedy [trædʒɪ'kɒmɪdɪ] N tragi-comédie *f, pl* tragi-comédies

tragicomic(al) [trædʒɪ'kɒmɪk, -ɪk(ə)l] ADJ tragi-comique

trail [treɪl] N **1** *(of blood)* traînée *f; (of smoke)* panache *m; (of meteor)* queue *f; Mil (of gun carriage)* flèche *f,* crosse *f;* **a t. of broken promises** une série de promesses non tenues **2** *(marks left) (of animal, person)* piste *f,* trace *f; (of snail)* trace *f;* **to pick up the t.** *(of hounds)* retrouver la trace; **false t.** fausse piste; **to be on the t. of sb** être sur la piste de qn; **the criminals left with the police hot on their t.** les criminels sont partis avec la police sur leurs talons; **the t. was cold by then** la piste était déjà froide; **to leave a t. of destruction** tout détruire sur son passage **3** *(path)* sentier *m* (battu); *(in forest, cross-country skiing)* piste *f*

VT **1** *(pull) (something)* traîner après soi; *(of car etc) (caravan etc)* remorquer; *Fig* **to t. one's coat** se montrer délibérément provocateur **2** *(track) (animal, criminal)* traquer, pister, suivre à la piste; *(of crook) (victim)* suivre, filer **3** *Cin, TV* annoncer

VI **1** *(drag)* traîner; **your skirt is trailing (on the ground)** votre jupe traîne (par terre) **2** *(move slowly)* avancer lentement **3** *(of plant)* grimper, ramper **4** **to be trailing** *(be last)* être à la traîne; **our team is trailing at the bottom of the league** notre équipe se traîne en fin de classement

▸▸**t. bike** moto de cross; **t. mix** = mélange *m* de cacahuètes et de fruits secs; *Fishing* **t. net** traîne *f,* chalut *m,* traîneau *m*

▸**trail away** VI his voice trailed away in embarrassment il se tut, gêné; **her voice trailed away in the distance** sa voix se perdit dans le lointain

▸**trail behind** VI **1** *(linger)* traîner derrière (les autres), être à la traîne; *Fig (of team etc)* être en retard sur les autres **2** *(be towed)* se faire remorquer, être en remorque; **with a boat trailing behind** avec un bateau en remorque

▸**trail off** VI *(of voice)* diminuer jusqu'à s'éteindre; **her voice trails off** sa voix diminue jusqu'à devenir inaudible; **his voice trailed off in mid-sentence** il s'interrompit au milieu de sa phrase

trailblazer ['treɪlbleɪzər] N pionnier, -ière

trailblazing ['treɪlbleɪzɪŋ] ADJ *(work)* de pionnier, *(discovery)* qui ouvre la voie

trailer ['treɪlər] N **1** *Aut etc (behind vehicle)* remorque *f, Am (towed)* caravane *f, (mobile home)* camping-car *m, pl* camping-cars **2** *Cin, TV* bande-annonce *f, pl* bandes-annonces (**for** de)

▸▸*Am* **t. hitch** timon *m* de remorque; *Am* **t. park** = terrain *m* aménagé pour les camping-cars; *Am Fam Pej* **t. trash** prolos *mpl* (qui vivent dans des camping-cars)

trailer-truck N *Am* semi-remorque *f, pl* semi-remorques

trailing ['treɪlɪŋ] ADJ **1** *(skirt etc)* traînant **2** *(plant)* grimpant, rampant

▸▸*Aut* **t. arm** bras *m* tiré; *Aut* **t. brake shoe** segment *m* de frein secondaire; *Aviat* **t. edge** *(of wing)* bord *m* de fuite; *Mktg* **t. firm** entreprise *f* à la traîne; *Aut* **t. shoe** segment *m* secondaire; *Comput* **t. spaces** espaces *mpl* à droite; *Comput* **t. zeroes** zéros *mpl* à droite

train¹ [treɪn] N **1** *Rail* train *m; (underground)* rame *f,* **passenger/goods t.** train de voya-

geurs/de marchandises; **express t.** train express; **slow** *or* **stopping t.** train omnibus; **relief t.** train supplémentaire; **the 5 o'clock t.** le train de 5 heures; **the Cardiff t., the t. to Cardiff** le train de Cardiff; **she wasn't on the t.** elle n'était pas dans le train; **by t.** *(to travel)* par *ou* en chemin de fer, en train; **to the trains** *(on sign)* accès aux quais

2 *(of carriages, barges)* train *m,* convoi *m; (of events, circumstances)* succession *f,* série *f,* enchaînement *m; Min* traînée *f* (de poudre); **t. of thought** enchaînement d'idées; **to set** *or* **put sth in t.** mettre qch en route

3 *Tech (system of gears)* système *m* d'engrenages

4 *(retinue) (of prince etc)* suite *f,* cortège *m,* équipage *m; Mil* équipage, train *m;* **the evils that follow in the t. of war** les maux que la guerre engendre

5 *(of dress)* traîne *f,* queue *f; (of peacock)* queue

▸▸**t. bearer** demoiselle *f*/garçon *m* d'honneur; **t. journey** voyage *m* en *ou* par chemin de fer, voyage en train; **t. station** gare *f* (de chemin de fer)

train² VT **1** *(person)* former, instruire; *(animal)* dresser; *(character, mind)* former; *(ear)* exercer; *Sport (runner, racehorse etc)* entraîner; **he was trained at the Academy of Dramatic Art** il sort de l'Académie des Arts Dramatiques; **to t. sb for sth/to do sth** exercer qn à qch/à faire qch; **to t. sb in the use of a machine/weapon** apprendre à qn à se servir d'une machine/d'une arme; **to t. oneself to do sth** s'exercer à faire qch **2** *(in horticulture) (fruit tree, vine)* palisser, mettre en espalier **3** *(direct) (telescope, spotlight etc)* braquer, diriger (**on** sur); *Mil (gun)* pointer; *Naut (gun)* orienter, diriger

VI s'exercer; *Mil* faire l'exercice; *Sport* s'entraîner; **to t. for sth** s'exercer *ou* se préparer à qch; **to t. as a typist** suivre des cours de dactylographie; **she trained as a typist** elle est dactylographe de formation; **to t. as a ballet dancer** suivre une formation de danseur de ballet

▸**train up** VT SEP *(employees)* donner une formation complémentaire à

trained [treɪnd] ADJ *(person, worker etc)* formé; *(chien etc)* dressé; *(eye)* exercé; *Sport* entraîné; **highly/poorly t.** très bien/peu entraîné; **t. nurse** infirmière *f* diplômée; *Hum* **her husband is very well t.** *(does as he's told)* son mari est très bien dressé

trainee [treɪ'niː] N stagiaire *mf;* **t. manager, management t.** stagiaire de direction

traineeship [treɪ'niːʃɪp] N stage *m*

trainer ['treɪnər] N **1** *(person) (of animals)* dresseur *m, Sport, Horseracing (of athletes, football team, racehorses)* entraîneur *m; (for job)* formateur *m* **2** *(air-craft)* avion-école *f, pl* avions-écoles **3** **trainers** *(shoes)* chaussures *fpl* de sport

▸▸**t. aircraft** avion-école

training ['treɪnɪŋ] N **1** *(of person)* formation *f, Sport* entraînement *m; (of animal)* dressage *m;* **physical t.** éducation *f* physique; **vocational t.** formation professionnelle; **I'm a historian by t.** je suis historien de formation; *Fig* **it's good t. for when you're a parent** ça vous prépare pour quand vous aurez des enfants; *Mil* **military t.** instruction *f* militaire; *Sport* **to go into t.** s'entraîner; **to be in t.** *(being trained)* être à l'entraînement; *(fit)* être bien entraîné; **to be out of t.** ne plus être en forme **2** *(in horticulture) (of plant, fruit tree)* palissage *m; Mil (of gun)* orientation *f*

▸▸*Mil* **t. base** base *f* école; **t. centre** centre *m* de formation; **t. college** école *f* spécialisée *ou* professionnelle; **t. contract** contrat *m* d'apprentissage; **t. course** stage *m* (de formation); **t. manual** manuel *m* d'utilisation,

manuel d'instruction; **t. period** stage (de formation); **t. programme** programme *m* de formation; **t. scheme** plan *m* de formation; **t. session** entraînement *m; **t. ship** navire-école *m, pl* navires-écoles

trainload ['treɪnləʊd] N **t. of coal** train *m* chargé de houille; **t. of tourists** plein train de touristes; **they were arriving by the t.** ils arrivaient par trains entiers

trainspotter ['treɪnspɒtər] N = personne *f* dont le passe-temps est de noter les numéros des trains; *Fam* **he's a bit of a t.** il est vraiment ringard

trainspotting ['treɪnspɒtɪŋ] N = activité *f* consistant à repérer et répertorier les numéros des trains

traipse [treɪps] VI *Fam* **to t. through the streets** battre le pavé; **to t. around town** ça et là; **to t. around the shops** traîner dans les magasins; **we had to t. all the way back to ...** il a fallu qu'on se retape tout le trajet jusqu'à ...

trait [treɪt] N *(of character etc)* trait *m*

traitor ['treɪtər] N traître *m* (**to** à); **to turn t.** passer à l'ennemi, se vendre (à l'ennemi)

traitorous ['treɪt(ə)rəs] ADJ traître, *f* traîtresse, fourbe, perfide

traitorously ['treɪt(ə)rəslɪ] ADV traîtreusement

traitress ['treɪtrɪs] N *Old-fashioned* traîtresse *f*

trajectory [trə'dʒekt(ə)rɪ] N trajectoire *f, Fig (of company)* itinéraire *m*

TRAM [træm] N *(abbr* **transputer module)** module *m* de transputer

tram [træm] N *Br (vehicle)* tramway *m;* **to go by t.** aller en tramway

▸▸**t. driver** conducteur, -trice de tramway

tramcar ['træmkɑːr] N *Br Old-fashioned* tramway *m*

tramline ['træmlaɪn] N **1** *(route)* ligne *f* de tramways **2** **tramlines** *(track)* voie *f* de tramway; *Tennis* couloir *m; Sl (on arm)* traces *fpl* de piquouses

trammel ['træm(ə)l] *Lit* N *(hindrance)* **the trammels of routine** les entraves *fpl* de la routine

VT (**-ll-,** *Am* **-l-**) entraver, empêtrer; **trammelled by prejudices** entravé par les préjugés

tramp¹ [træmp] N **1** *(vagabond)* chemineau *m,* vagabond, -onde, clochard, -arde **2** *(sound)* bruit *m* de pas marqués; **I heard the (heavy) t. of the guard** j'ai entendu le pas lourd du gardien **3** *(walk)* promenade *f* à pied **4** *Fam Pej (promiscuous woman)* traînée *f*

VI **1** *(walk heavily)* marcher lourdement; **to t. on sth** piétiner *ou* écraser qch; **I wish you'd stop tramping on my foot!** j'aimerais bien que tu arrêtes de m'écraser le pied **2** *(travel on foot)* se promener *ou* voyager à pied; **to t. wearily along** suivre péniblement son chemin

VT **to t. the streets** battre le pavé; **to t. the country** parcourir le pays à pied

▸▸*Naut* **t. steamer** tramp *m*

tramp² N *Aut (of wheels)* rebondissement *m,* martèlement *m*

trample ['træmp(ə)l] VI **to t. on sth/sb** piétiner *ou* écraser qch/qn; **to t. on sb's feelings** fouler aux pieds les susceptibilités de qn

VT *(ground)* piétiner; **to t. sb/sth underfoot** piétiner qn/qch, fouler qn/qch aux pieds; *Fig* fouler qn/qch aux pieds; **to t. down the grass** fouler l'herbe; **the child was trampled to death (by the crowd)** l'enfant est mort piétiné (par la foule)

trampoline ['træmpəliːn] N *Gym etc* trampoline *m*

VI faire du trampoline

tramway ['træmweɪ] N rails mpl de tramway; (system) réseau m de tramway

trance [trɑːns] N Med (catalepsy) catalepsie f; (hypnotic) t. transe f, hypnose f; **to send** or **put sb into a t.** hypnotiser qn, mettre qn en transe; **to go into a t. (state)** (in spiritualism etc) se mettre en transe; **he's been wandering around in a t. ever since …** il erre en transe ou dans un état de transe depuis que …

tranche [trɑ̃ʃ] N Fin (of loan, payment, shares) tranche f

trank [træŋk], **trankie** ['træŋkɪ] N Fam tranquillisant m

tranny ['trænɪ] N **1** Old-fashioned esp Br Fam (transistor radio) transistor m **2** (transparency) diapositive f **3** Br Sl (transvestite) travelo m

tranquil ['træŋkwɪl] ADJ tranquille, serein, calme

tranquillity, Am **tranquility** [træŋ'kwɪlɪtɪ] N tranquillité f, calme m, sérénité f

tranquillize, Am **tranquilize** ['træŋkwɪlaɪz] VT (person, state of mind etc) tranquilliser, calmer, apaiser; (animal) anesthésier

tranquillizer, Am **tranquilizer** ['træŋkwɪlaɪzər] N Med etc tranquillisant m, calmant m; **to be on tranquillizers** être sous calmants

transact [træn'zækt] VT **to t. business with sb** faire des affaires avec qn; **the business was successfully transacted** la transaction ou l'affaire a été conclue à notre/sa/etc satisfaction

transaction [træn'zækʃən] N **1** (act of transacting) **open for the t. of business from …** ouvert au commerce à partir de … **2** (instance of transacting) opération f (commerciale); St Exch, Fin transaction f; **cash t.** opération ou marché m au comptant; **business transactions** affaires fpl, commerce m **3 transactions** (of learned society) mémoires mpl, procès verbaux mpl, comptes mpl rendus des séances
▸▸ St Exch **t. costs** frais mpl de Bourse

transalpine [trænz'ælpaɪn] ADJ transalpin

transatlantic [trænzət'læntɪk] ADJ transatlantique
▸▸ **t. carrier** transporteur m transatlantique

transaxle ['trænzæks(ə)l] N Aut boîte-pont f, pl boîtes-ponts

transceiver [træn'siːvər] N Radio émetteur-récepteur m, pl émetteurs-récepteurs

transcend [træn'send] VT **1** (go beyond) transcender, aller au delà de **2** (be superior to) surpasser

transcendence, transcendency [træn'sendəns(ɪ)] N Fml transcendance f

transcendent [træn'sendənt] ADJ transcendant

transcendental [trænsen'dent(ə)l] ADJ Phil transcendental, -aux

transcendentalism [trænsen'dentəlɪz(ə)m] N Phil transcendentalisme m

transcoder [trænz'kəʊdər] N transcodeur m

transcontinental [trænzkɒntɪ'nent(ə)l] ADJ transcontinental, -aux

transcribe [træns'kraɪb] VT **1** (write out) copier, transcrire; (shorthand) traduire; Acct **to t. entries** transcrire des écritures **2** Mus (piece of music for another instrument) transcrire **3** TV (record) enregistrer; (broadcast) retransmettre en différé

transcript ['trænskrɪpt] N transcription f, copie f; (of shorthand notes) traduction f; Am Scol, Univ livret m scolaire

transcription [træns'krɪpʃən] N **1** (written copy) = **transcript 2** Mus transcription f

transdermal [trænz'dɜːm(ə)l] ADJ transdermique
▸▸ **t. patch** timbre m autocollant transdermique

transducer [trænz'djuːsər] N transducteur m

transect [træn'sekt] VT couper transversalement

transept ['trænsept] N (of church) transept m; (arm of the) t. croisillon m

transfer¹ ['trænsfɜːr] N **1** (act) (of person, object, department etc) transfert m; (of employee etc) mutation f; Law (of right etc) transfert, transmission f; (of property) translation f, mutation; Banking etc (of money from one account to another) transfert, virement m; Fin (of shares) transfert; (disposal) (of assets, shares etc) cession f; Comput (of data) transfert; **t. of capital** transfert de capitaux; **t. of funds** virement de fonds, transfert de fonds; **t. of title** cession de titre; **t. to main airport** pré-acheminement m, pl pré-acheminements; **t. from main airport** post-acheminement m, pl post-acheminements; Br Sport **the new striker has asked for a t.** le nouveau buteur a demandé son transfert
2 (document) St Exch (feuille f de) transfert m; Law (deed of) **t.** acte m de cession **3** Cer, Sewing etc (design) décalque m **4** Can (ticket) correspondance f
▸▸ **t. advice** avis m de virement; Aut **t. box** boîte f de transfert; **t. bus** navette f; **t. cheque** chèque m de virement; **t. desk** (at airport) guichet m de transit; Acct **t. entry** article m de contre-passation; Ftbl etc **t. fee** (of player) prix m de transfert; Aut **t. gearbox** boîte f de transfert; Br **t. lounge** (at airport) salle f de transit; **t. order** ordre m ou mandat m de virement; **t. parameter** (in datacomms) paramètre m de transfert; Aviat **t. passengers** voyageurs mpl en transit; Pol **t. of power** passation f de pouvoir; Comput **t. rate** taux m de transfert; St Exch **t. register** registre m des transferts; Comput **t. speed** vitesse f de transfert; **t. tax** droits mpl de succession; (between living persons) droit de mutation; Can **t. ticket** correspondance f; **t. transport** transport m d'acheminement

transfer² [træns'fɜːr] (**-rr-**) VT **1** (something, somebody, from one place to another) transférer; (employee, soldier etc) muter; Law (rights etc) transmettre; (privilege etc) céder; (attention) déplacer (**to** sur); Banking etc (sum of money) virer; (dispose of) (assets, shares etc) céder; Acct (debt) transporter; Acct (entry) contre-passer; **to t. one's affections to another person** transférer son affection sur quelqu'un d'autre; **let's t. this desk into the blue room** mettons ce bureau dans la pièce bleue; **to t. a call** transférer un appel; Br Tel **transfer(red) charge call** communication f en PCV **2** Typ, Sewing etc (drawing) calquer, décalquer
VI **1** to **t. to a different department** (of person) être transféré dans un autre service; **to t. from one course to another** changer de cours; Ftbl **to t. to a different team** obtenir son transfert dans une autre équipe **2** (to change trains etc) changer; **to t. to a different plane** etc changer d'avion etc; **we then t. back to the train at …** puis on reprend le train à …

transferable [træns'fɜːrəb(ə)l] ADJ transmissible; Law (right, property) cessible, communicable, transférable; **non t.** (on ticket etc) non cessible; Fin **t. by endorsement** transmissible par endossement
▸▸ **t. credit** crédit m transférable; **t. document** document m transmissible; **t. letter of credit** crédit transférable; **t. securities** valeurs fpl négociables ou mobilières; **t. share** action f au porteur

transferee [trænsfə'riː] N cessionnaire mf

transference ['trænsfərəns] N transfert m; (thought) **t.** transmission f de pensée

transfiguration [trænsfɪgjʊ'reɪʃən] N transfiguration f

transfigure [træns'fɪgər] VT transfigurer; **her face was transfigured with happiness** la joie l'avait transfigurée

transfix [træns'fɪks] VT **1** (with lance etc) transpercer **2** Fig rendre immobile; **transfixed with fear** pétrifié ou cloué par la peur; **they were transfixed by the sight/her singing** (impressed) ils étaient hypnotisés par le spectacle/son chant

transform [træns'fɔːm] VT transformer (**into** en), métamorphoser; Elec (current) transformer

transformation [trænsfə'meɪʃən] N transformation f (**into** en); (of person) métamorphose f (**into** en)

transformational [trænsfə'meɪʃ(ə)nl] ADJ Ling transformationnel

transformer [træns'fɔːmər] N Elec transformateur m
▸▸ **t. station** station f de transformation

transfuse [træns'fjuːz] VT Med (blood) transfuser; Fig Lit **in a voice transfused with emotion** d'une voix emplie d'émotion

transfusion [træns'fjuːʒ(ə)n] N Med (blood) **t.** transfusion f de sang, transfusion sanguine; **to give sb a t.** faire une transfusion à qn

transgenic [trænz'dʒenɪk] ADJ transgénique

transgress [trænz'gres] Fml VT (law etc) transgresser, enfreindre
VI enfreindre la loi; (sin) pécher

transgression [trænz'greʃən] N Fml (of law etc) transgression f, infraction f (**of** à); (sin) péché m

transgressor [trænz'gresər] N Fml (of law etc) transgresseur m; (sinner) pécheur m, pécheresse f

tranship [træn'ʃɪp] VT (passengers, goods) transborder
VI changer de bateau

transhipment [træn'ʃɪpmənt] N transbordement m; **t. bill of lading** connaissement m de transbordement

transience ['trænzɪəns] N (of phenomenon etc) nature f passagère ou transitoire

transient ['trænzɪənt] ADJ transitoire; (happiness etc) passager, -ère; (beauty etc) éphémère; Am **t. visitor** client, -ente de passage
N Am client, -ente de passage

transire [træn'saɪər] N Com passavant m, laissez-passer m inv

transistor [træn'zɪstər] N Electron transistor m; (radio) transistor, poste m à transistors
▸▸ **t. radio, t. set** transistor, poste à transistors

transistorize [træn'zɪstəraɪz] VT transistoriser

transit ['trænsɪt] N **1** (of goods) transit m; **goods in t.** marchandises fpl en transit; **goods lost in t.** marchandises perdues en cours de route **2** (of people) (through country etc) voyage m **3** Astron (of planet over face of sun, heavenly body through meridian) passage m
▸▸ Com **t. bill** passavant m; **t. camp** camp m de transit; Astron **t. circle** cercle m méridien; Com **t. declaration** déclaration f de transit; Com **t. duty** droit m de transit; **t. hotel** hôtel m de passage ou de transit; **t. lounge** salle f de transit; **t. passenger** passager, -ère en transit; **t. visa** visa m de transit

transition [træn'zɪʃ(ə)n] N transition f; **t. from day to night/from fear to hope** passage *m* du jour à la nuit/de la crainte à l'espoir

▸▸ *Chem* **t. element** élément *m* de transition; **t. period** période *f* de transition, période transitoire

transitional [trænˈzɪʃ(ə)l] **ADJ** transitionnel, de transition; *Archit, Art* **t. style** style *m* de transition

transitive [ˈtrænzɪtɪv] *Gram* **ADJ** transitif **N** *(verb)* transitif *m*; **in the t.** à la forme transitive, transitivement

transitively [ˈtrænzɪtɪvlɪ] **ADV** *Gram* transitivement

transitory [ˈtrænsɪt(ə)rɪ] **ADJ** transitoire, passager, -ère; *(happiness, desire etc)* passager; *(glory etc)* de courte durée

translatable [trænsˈleɪtəb(ə)l] **ADJ** traduisible

translate [trænsˈleɪt] **VT 1** *(book etc)* traduire (**from** de; **into** en); **to t. words into action(s)** *or* **deeds** passer des paroles à l'acte; *Fam* **can you t. that (into plain English), please?** tu peux traduire (en langage de tous les jours), s'il te plaît; **we can now t. these figures into a graph** nous pouvons maintenant traduire ces chiffres en un graphe; **to t. a novel into film terms** adapter un roman à l'écran **2** *Rel (bishop)* transférer (**to** à); *Bible* **Enoch was translated (to heaven)** Énoch fut enlevé au ciel

VI *(of person)* faire de la traduction; *(of writing)* se traduire; **this expression translates literally as ...** la traduction littérale de cette expression est ...; **it doesn't really t. into film** cela se laisse difficilement adapter à l'écran; **how does that t. into economic reality?** comment est-ce que ça se traduit sur le plan économique?

translation [trænsˈleɪʃən] **N 1** *(of book etc)* traduction *f*; *Sch (Latin, Russian etc)* version *f*; *(of novel into film etc)* adaptation *f*; **a lot of the beauty is lost in t.** le texte perd beaucoup de sa beauté à la traduction; **a t. problem** un problème de traduction; **simultaneous t.** traduction simultanée **2** *Rel (of bishop)* translation *f*; *Bible* **(to heaven)** enlèvement *m* (au ciel)

▸▸ **t. agency** bureau *m ou* agence *f* de traduction; **t. company** cabinet *m ou* société *f* de traduction; *Comput* **t. table** table *f* de traduction

translator [trænsˈleɪtər] **N** traducteur, -trice

transliterate [trænzˈlɪtəreɪt] **VT** *(in different or phonetic characters)* translit(t)érer, transcrire

transliteration [trænzlɪtəˈreɪʃən] **N** *(in different or phonetic characters)* translit(t)ération *f*, transcription *f*

translucence [trænzˈluːsəns] **N** translucidité *f*

translucent [trænzˈluːsənt] **ADJ** translucide

transmigrate [trænzmaɪˈgreɪt] **VI** *(of people)* migrer; *(of soul)* transmigrer

transmigration [trænzmaɪˈgreɪʃən] **N** *(of people)* migration *f*; *(of soul)* transmigration *f*

transmissible [trænzˈmɪsɪb(ə)l] **ADJ** transmissible

transmission [trænzˈmɪʃən] **N 1** *Radio, TV, Phys (action)* transmission *f* **2** *(programme)* *TV* programme *m* télévisé; *Radio* programme radiodiffusé **3** *Aut* transmission *f*
▸▸ **t. brake** frein *m* sur transmission; **t. shaft** arbre *m* de transmission; **t. speed** vitesse *f* de transmission

transmit [trænzˈmɪt] **(-tt-)** **VT** *(disease, radio waves)* transmettre; *Radio, TV (programme)* diffuser; *Tech* **to t. a motion to sth** communiquer un mouvement à qch
VI *Radio, TV* émettre, diffuser

transmitter [trænzˈmɪtər] **N** *Tel etc* transmetteur *m*; *Radio, TV* (poste *m*) émetteur *m*, poste d'émission
▸▸ *Tel, Radio* **t. receiver** émetteur-récepteur *m*, *pl* émetteurs-récepteurs; *TV, Radio* **t. van** car *m* de transmission

transmogrify [trænzˈmɒgrɪfaɪ] **VT** *Hum* transformer, métamorphoser (**into** en)

transmutation [trænzmjuːˈteɪʃən] **N** *Fml* transmutation *f* (**into** en)

transmute [trænzˈmjuːt] **VT** transformer, changer (**into** en); *(in alchemy)* transmuer

transom [ˈtrænsəm] **N 1** *Archit (of window, door)* traverse *f*, linteau *m* **2** *Am (window over door)* imposte *f*

transparency [trænsˈpærənsɪ, -ˈpeər-] **N 1** *(quality)* transparence *f*; *(of water, excuse etc)* limpidité *f* **2** *(picture)* *Phot* diapositive *f*; *(for overhead projector)* transparent *m*; *Phot* **colour t.** diapositive en couleur

transparent [trænsˈpærənt, -ˈpeər-] **ADJ 1** *(glass etc)* transparent; *(eau, quartz etc)* limpide **2** *(obvious)* évident, clair, transparent

transparently [trænsˈpærəntlɪ, -ˈpeər-] **ADV** *(obviously)* de toute évidence; **that's t. obvious** c'est clair comme l'eau de roche

transpiration [trænspɪˈreɪʃən] **N** transpiration *f*

transpire [trænsˈpaɪər] **VI 1** *(turn out)* it **transpired that ...** il s'est avéré que ... **2** *(happen)* arriver, se passer **3** *Physiol, Bot* transpirer
VT *(of body, plant etc) (fluid)* exsuder; *(smell)* exhaler

> Note that the French verb **transpirer** is a false friend. Its most common meaning is **to sweat.**

transplant¹ [ˈtrænsplɑːnt, ˈtrɑː-] **N 1** *Surg (act of transplanting) (of organ)* transplantation *f*, greffe *f*; *(of skin)* greffe; *(transplanted organ etc)* transplant *m*, greffon *m*; **heart/ kidney/liver t.** greffe du cœur/rein/foie **2** *(in horticulture)* plant *m* repiqué

transplant² [trænsˈplɑːnt, ˈtrɑː-] **VT 1** *Surg (organ)* transplanter, greffer **2** *(population etc)* transplanter, transporter **3** *(in horticulture) (trees etc)* transplanter; *(plants)* repiquer

transplantation [trænsplɑːnˈteɪʃən, ˈtrɑː-] **N** transplantation *f*

transponder [trænsˈpɒndər] **N** transpondeur *m*

transport¹ [ˈtrænspɔːt] **N 1** *(of goods, passengers, troops etc)* transport *m*; **public t.** transports en commun; **road/rail t.** transport routier/ferroviaire **2** *(means of transport)* moyen *m* de transport; *(aircraft)* (avion *m* de) transport *m*; *(for cargo)* avion cargo; *Naut* **(troop) t.** (bâtiment *m* de) transport; *Fam* **have you got t.?** *(car)* est-ce que vous avez un moyen de transport? **3** *Lit (emotion)* **t. of joy** transports *mpl* de joie; **to go into a t. of joy** être transporté de joie
▸▸ **t. advertising** affichage *m* transport; **t. aircraft** (avion de) transport; *(for cargo)* avion cargo; **t. allowance** prime *f* de transport; *Br* **t. café** ≃ routier *m* *(restaurant)*; **t. company** entreprise *f ou* société *f* de transport; **t. costs** frais *mpl* de transport; **t. cover** garantie *f* transport; **t. document** titre *m ou* document *m* de transport; **t. facilities** moyens *mpl* de transport; **t. museum** musée *m* des transports; **t. plane** (avion de) transport; *(for cargo)* avion cargo; *Br* **t. police** = service *m* d'ordre des chemins de fer

transport² [trænsˈpɔːt] **VT 1** *(passengers, goods)* transporter; **to t. under armed guard** convoyer **2** *(usu passive)* *Lit* **to be transported with joy** être transporté de joie

transportable [trænsˈpɔːtəb(ə)l] **ADJ** transportable

transportation [trænspɔːˈteɪʃən] **N 1** transport *m*; *(means of transport)* moyen *m* de transport **2** *Law, Hist (to colonies)* transportation *f*
▸▸ *Am* **t. advertising** affichage *m* transport; *Am* **t. agreement** contrat *m* de transport; **t. company** société *f* de transport; *Am* **t. desk** *(in hotel)* bureau *m* de voyages; *Am* **t. insurance** assurance *f* transport

transporter [trænsˈpɔːtər] **N** *(vehicle)* transporteur *m*, transporteuse *f*; *(person)* entrepreneur *m* de transports; **car t.** *(lorry)* camion *m* pour transport d'automobiles; *Rail* wagon *m* transporteur de voitures

transpose [trænsˈpəʊz] **VT 1** *(words, terms of equation etc)* transposer **2** *Mus* transposer

transposition [trænspəˈzɪʃən] **N** *(of letters etc)*, *Mus* transposition *f*; *Typ* mastic *m*

transputer [trænsˈpjuːtər] **N** *Comput* transputeur *m*

transsexual [træn(z)ˈseksjʊəl] **ADJ, N** transsexuel, -elle

transship [træn(z)ˈʃɪp] = **tranship**

transshipment [træn(z)ˈʃɪpmənt] = **transhipment**

Trans-Siberian [træns-] **ADJ**
▸▸ **T. Railway** chemin *m* de fer transsibérien, Transsibérien *m*

transubstantiation [trænsəbstænʃɪˈeɪʃən] **N** *Rel* transsubstantiation *f*

Transvaal [ˈtrɑːnzvɑːl] **N** the Transvaal; **a T. farmer** un fermier transvaalien

transversal [trænzˈvɜːs(ə)l] **ADJ** transversal, -aux
N *Geom* transversale *f*

transversally [trænzˈvɜːsəlɪ] **ADV** transversalement

transverse [ˈtrænzvɜːs] **ADJ** *(section, muscle)* transversal; *Anat (colon)* transverse
▸▸ *Constr* **t. beam** traverse *f*; *Aut* **t. engine** moteur *m* transversal; *Geom* **t. line** transversale *f*

transversely [ˈtrænzvɜːslɪ] **ADV** *(mounted)* transversalement, en travers

transvestism [trænzˈvestɪz(ə)m] **N** tra(ns)vestisme *m*

transvestite [trænzˈvestaɪt] **N** travesti, -ie

trap [træp] **N 1** *(in hunting etc)* piège *m*; *(pit)* trappe *f*; *Fig* piège, ruse *f*, attrape *f*; **to set a t.** *(for animal)*, *Fig (for person)* dresser *ou* tendre un piège *(for* à*)*; **to catch an animal in a t.** prendre une bête au piège; **she's fallen into her own t.** elle est prise à son propre piège; **he fell into the t.** il s'y laissa prendre, il tomba dans le piège; **to walk** *or* **fall straight into the t.** tomber en plein dans le piège; *Mil* **tank t.** (obstacle *m*) antichar *m*; **radar** *or* **speed t.** zone *f* de contrôle de vitesse

2 *(trap door)* trappe *f*

3 *Sl (mouth)* gueule *f*; **shut your t.!** ta gueule!, la ferme!; **you would have to go and open your big t.!** il a fallu que tu ouvres ta grande gueule!

4 *Sport (for clay pigeons)* (projecteur *m*) ball-trap *m*, *pl* ball-traps; *(for live pigeons)* boîte *f* de lancement; *(in dog racing)* box *m* (de départ)

5 *Tech (for water, oil etc)* collecteur *m*; *(in plumbing)*, *Constr* siphon *m*

6 *(horse-drawn vehicle)* cabriolet *m*

7 *esp Am Mus* **traps** instruments *mpl* à percussion

VT **(-pp-) 1** *(animal, person)* prendre au piège, piéger; **to t. sb into saying sth** faire dire qch à qn en usant de ruse; **to t. sb into making a false move** piéger qn pour qu'il fasse un faux pas; **she trapped him into mar-**

riage elle l'a obligé à se marier avec elle en usant de ruse; **to t. one's finger in the door** se coincer le doigt dans la porte; **I was trapped in the lift for two hours** je suis resté coincé dans l'ascenseur pendant deux heures; **the climbers were trapped by an avalanche** les alpinistes ont été bloqués par une avalanche; **trapped by the flames** cerné par les flammes; **to feel trapped** *(in a relationship)* se sentir prisonnier *ou Fam* coincé **2** *(in pipe) (gas etc)* arrêter **3** *Sport (stop) (ball)* bloquer
VI *(set traps)* tendre des pièges, *Can* trapper
► ► **t. door** trappe

trapeze [trə'piːz] **N** trapèze *m*
► ► **t. artist** trapéziste *mf*

trapezium, *pl* **trapeziums, trapezia** [trə'piːzɪəm, -əmz, -ə] **N** *Geom* trapèze *m*

trapezoid ['træpɪzɔɪd] **N** *Geom* trapézoïde *m*

trapper ['træpər] **N** *(hunter)* trappeur *m*

trappings ['træpɪŋz] **NPL 1** *(of power, success etc)* signes *mpl* extérieurs, apparat *m*; **the t. of authority** les signes extérieurs de l'autorité **2** *(for horses)* harnachement *m*, caparaçon *m*

Trappist ['træpɪst] **ADJ, N** *Rel* trappiste *m*

trapshooting ['træpʃuːtɪŋ] **N** *Sport* ball-trap *m*

trash [træʃ] **N** *(worthless objects)* camelote *f*, *Am (refuse)* détritus *mpl*, déchets *mpl*, ordures *fpl*; *(people)* vermine *f*, racaille *f*, *(nonsense)* sottise *f*, *(literature)* littérature *f* de bas étage; *Comput* poubelle *f*, **the food was t.** la nourriture était très mauvaise; **she's t.** elle ne vaut rien; **those people are t.** c'est de la racaille, ces gens-là; **to talk a lot of t.** dire des tas d'imbécilités
► ► *Am* **t. can** poubelle *f*, boîte *f* à ordures; *Am Comput* **t. icon** icône *f* de la corbeille

trashed [træʃt] **ADJ** *Fam (drunk)* rond, fait, bourré; *(on drugs)* défoncé, raide

trashy ['træʃɪ] **ADJ** *(goods etc)* de pacotille; *(literature)* de bas étage

trauma, *pl* **traumas, traumata** ['trɔːmə, -əz, -ətə] **N** *Med, Psy* trauma *m*; *Med* traumatisme *m*

traumatic [trɔː'mætɪk] **ADJ** *Med* traumatique; *Fig (experience, journey, exam)* traumatisant

traumatism ['trɔːmətɪz(ə)m] **N** *Med* traumatisme *m*

traumatize ['trɔːmətaɪz] **VT** *Med, Fig* traumatiser

travail ['træveɪl] **N 1** *Lit (labour, hard work)* dur labeur *m* **2** *Arch, Lit (childbirth pains)* douleurs *fpl* de l'enfantement, travail *m*

travel ['træv(ə)l] **N 1** voyages *mpl*; **t. was slower in those days** on voyageait plus lentement à cette époque; **what do you spend on t. (to and from work)?** à combien vous reviennent vos déplacements (pour aller et revenir du travail)?; **when are you next off on your travels?** quand repartez-vous en voyage?; **I met him on my** *or* **in the course of my travels** j'ai fait sa connaissance au cours d'un de mes voyages **2** *Tech etc (of piston)* course *f*
VI **(-ll-,** *Am* **-l-) 1** *(journey)* voyager; *(journey around)* faire des voyages; *(of news)* circuler, se répandre; **he has travelled a great deal** *or* **widely** il a beaucoup voyagé; **to t. round the world** faire le tour du monde; **to t. all over the world** voyager partout dans le monde, courir le monde; **to t. through a country** *(visit all parts of)* parcourir un pays; *(on way to another destination)* traverser un pays; **light travels faster than sound** la lumière va *ou* se propage plus vite que le son; **news travels fast round here** les nouvelles vont vite par ici; **the train was travelling at**

150 km an hour le train roulait à 150 km à l'heure; **that's travelling!** *(is fast)* ça c'est de la vitesse!; **we were really travelling** nous allions très vite; **this wine won't t.** ce vin voyage mal
2 *Com* **to t. (for a firm)** voyager (pour une maison), représenter une maison); **to t. on business** voyager pour affaires; **to t. in wine** être représentant en vins
3 *Tech (of part)* se mouvoir, se déplacer; *(of electric current)* se déplacer
VT *(country)* parcourir; **to t. the length and breadth of the country** parcourir le pays de long en large; **I t. this road every day** je prends cette route tous les jours
► ► **t. agency** agence *f* de voyages; **t. agent** agent *m* de voyages; **t. agent's voucher** bon *m* d'agence *ou* d'échange, voucher *m*; **t. allowance** indemnité *f* de déplacement; **t. bag** sac *m* de voyage; *(guide)* guide *m* de voyage; **t. book** *(account)* récit *m* de voyages; *(guide)* guide *m* de voyage; **t. bureau** agence *f* de voyages; **t. company** voyagiste *m*; **t. directory** guide *m* de voyages; **t. documents** documents *mpl* de voyage; **t. expenses** frais *mpl* de déplacement; **t. firm** voyagiste *m*; *Am* **t. group charter** achat *m* de bloc-sièges; **t. guide** guide touristique; **t. insurance** assurance-voyage *f*, **t. literature** documentation *f* touristique; **t. medical insurance** assurance *f* médicale de voyage; *TV* **t. programme** émission *f* sur les voyages; **t. rug** plaid *m*; **t. trade** industrie *f* du voyage; **t. writer** auteur *m* de récits de voyage

travelator ['trævəleɪtər] **N** trottoir *m ou* tapis *m* roulant

travelled, *Am* **traveled** ['trævəld] **ADJ** **much** *or* **well t.** *(person)* qui a beaucoup voyagé; **much t.** *(road)* très fréquenté

traveller, *Am* **traveler** ['træv(ə)lər] **N** voyageur, -euse; *(salesperson)* représentant, -ante; *Br (living in caravan etc)* nomade *mf*, **I'm not a good t.** je supporte mal les voyages; **frequent t.** personne *f* qui est souvent en voyage

traveller's cheque, *Am* **traveler's check** **N** chèque *m* de voyage

travelling, *Am* **traveling** ['træv(ə)lɪŋ] **ADJ** *(circus)* ambulant, forain; *(preacher)* itinérant; *Tech (walkway etc)* roulant; *(crane)* mobile
N voyages *mpl*; **to do a lot of t.** beaucoup voyager; **there isn't a lot of t. in this job** on ne voyage pas beaucoup dans ce travail
► ► **t. clock** réveil *m* de voyage; **t. companion** compagnon *m* de voyage; **t. expenses** frais *mpl* de déplacement; **t. people** gens *mpl* du voyage; *Cin* **t. platform** travelling *m*; *Br* **t. rug** plaid *m*; **t. salesman** représentant *m ou* voyageur *m* de commerce; **t. scholarship** bourse *f* de voyage; *Cin* **t. shot** prise *f* de vue en travelling, plan *m* travelling; **t. show** *(at a fair)* spectacle *m* forain

travelogue, *Am* **travelog** ['trævəlɒg] **N** *(film)* documentaire *m* de voyage

travel-sick **ADJ** **she always gets t.** elle est toujours malade en voyage

travel-sickness **N** mal *m* des transports
► ► **t. pill** cachet *m* contre le mal des transports

travel-size **ADJ** *(shampoo etc)* de voyage

travelstained ['træv(ə)lsteɪnd] **ADJ** sali par le voyage

travel-weary **ADJ** fatigué par le(s) voyage(s)

traverse ['trævəs] **N 1** *Tech, Constr etc (of chassis, frame etc)* traverse *f*, entretoise *f* **2** *Geom* (ligne *f*) transversale *f*; *(in surveying)* cheminement *m* **3** *(in mountaineering, skiing) (across face of escarpment)* traversée *f*, vire *f*
VT *Lit (region, bridge, sea)* traverser

VI *(in mountaineering, skiing)* traverser, prendre une traverse; *(of horse)* se traverser

travesty ['trævəstɪ] **N** *(of play etc)* travestissement *m*; **a t. of the truth** un travestissement de la vérité; **it was a t. of justice** c'était une parodie de justice
VT *(story, figure etc)* parodier, travestir

trawl [trɔːl] **N 1** *Fishing (line)* palangre *f*, *(net)* chalut *m*, traille *f* **2** *Fig (search)* ratissage *m*
VI *Fishing* pêcher au chalut *ou* à la traille; *Fig* **to t. for business** aller à la pêche au client
VT *Fishing (net)* traîner; *(fish)* prendre à la traille *ou* au chalut; *Fig* **she trawled the small-ads for bargains** elle épluchait les petites annonces à la recherche de bonnes affaires; *Fig* **he trawled the singles bars** il écumait les bars pour célibataires
► ► *Fishing* **t. line** palangre *f*; **t. net** chalut, traille

trawler ['trɔːlər] **N 1** *Fishing (ship)* chalutier *m* **2** *(man)* pêcheur *m* au chalut, chalutier *m*

trawlerman, *pl* **trawlermen** ['trɔːləmən] **N** *Fishing* = **trawler 2**

trawling ['trɔːlɪŋ] **N** *Fishing* pêche *f* au chalut, chalutage *m*

tray [treɪ] **N 1** *(for carrying)* plateau *m*; *(of trunk etc)* casier *m*, châssis *m*; *(in office etc)* corbeille *f* (à correspondance); *(of printer)* bac *m*; *(for selling ice-cream etc)* éventaire *m*; **tea t.** plateau à thé; **to bring/take sth in on a t.** apporter/prendre qch sur un plateau; **a t. of sandwiches** un plateau de sandwiches; **in-t.** *(in office etc)* corbeille de la correspondance reçue; **out-t.** *(in office etc)* corbeille du courrier à expédier/des documents à classer **2** *Phot etc* cuvette *f*

traycloth ['treɪklɒθ] **N** napperon *m (de plateau)*

treacherous ['tretʃərəs] **ADJ** *(person, character)* traître, traîtresse, déloyal, -aux; *(action)* déloyal; *(roads, mountains, ice)* traître

treacherously ['tretʃərəslɪ] **ADV** *(act)* en traître, traîtreusement, perfidement; **we drove in t. bad conditions** nous avons conduit dans des conditions terriblement mauvaises; **it can get t. icy up there** il y a parfois un verglas traître par là-haut

treachery ['tretʃərɪ] **N** trahison *f*, perfidie *f*, **act of t.** trahison, perfidie

treacle ['triːk(ə)l] **N** mélasse *f*
► ► **t. tart** tarte *f* à la mélasse

treacly ['triːklɪ] **ADJ** *also Fig* sirupeux

tread [tred] **N 1** *(footstep)* pas *m*; *(sound)* bruit *m* de pas; **I heard his familiar t. on the path** j'ai entendu son pas familier sur le chemin; **heavy t.** pas lourd; *esp Lit* **to walk with measured t.** marcher à pas mesurés **2** *(of shoe)* semelle *f*, *(of stepladder etc)* échelon *m*; *Rail (of track)* surface *f ou* table *f* de roulement **3** *Aut (of tyre) (outer layer)* bande *f* de roulement, chape *f*, *(pattern)* sculpture *f*; **there isn't much t. left** *(on tyre)* le pneu est presque lisse; **the t. marks of a heavy vehicle on the sand** les empreintes *fpl* de pneus d'un véhicule lourd sur le sable
VI *(pt* **trod** [trɒd]; *pp* **trodden** ['trɒd(ə)n])* marcher; **to t. in/on sth** marcher dans/sur qch; **watch where you t.** regarde ou tu mets les pieds; *Fig* **we shall have to t. carefully** *or* **warily** il va falloir marcher sur des œufs *ou* faire très attention
VT 1 *(ground)* marcher sur; **to think that he has trodden this very soil!** quand je pense qu'il a foulé ce sol; **to t. sth underfoot** écraser qch du pied, fouler qch aux pieds; *Fig* **to t. sb underfoot** écraser qn; **don't t. it into the carpet!** ne marche pas dessus, ça va s'incruster dans la moquette!; **to t. mud/dirt into the carpet** mettre de la boue/de la terre

sur le tapis (avec ses chaussures); **well-trod-den path** chemin *m* battu; *(much used)* chemin *(très)* fréquenté; *Old-fashioned* **to t. a path** suivre un chemin; *Fig* **he trod the same path as his father before him** il a suivi la même voie que son père; **to t. grapes** fouler la vendange; **to t. water** *Swimming* flotter en remuant les jambes; *Fig* faire du surplace

2 *Orn (of male bird) (female bird)* couvrir, côcher

▸▸ *Aut* **t. plate** repose-pied *m, pl* repose-pieds; *Aut* **t. wear indicator** indicateur d'usure

▸ **tread down** VT SEP *(grass etc)* piétiner

treading ['tredɪŋ] N *(of grapes)* foulage *m*

treadle ['tred(ə)l] N *(of sewing machine etc)* pédale *f*

▸▸ **t. machine** machine *f* à pédale

treadmill ['tredmɪl] N *Hist (in prisons)* moulin *m* de discipline; *Fig (routine)* besogne *f* (quotidienne) ingrate; **the same old t.** le train-train quotidien

treason ['triːz(ə)n] N trahison *f*; **high t.** haute trahison

treasonable ['triːz(ə)nəb(ə)l] ADJ *(remarks etc)* traître, *f* traîtresse, perfide; *(act)* de trahison

treasure ['treʒər] N **1** trésor *m*; **art treasures** trésors *ou* richesses *fpl* artistiques **2** *Fig Fam (person)* trésor *m*; **my home help's a real t.** ma femme de ménage est une perle

VT *(person) (prize)* estimer; *(have affection for)* chérir; *(object, freedom)* tenir beaucoup à; *(advice)* faire beaucoup de cas de; *(memory)* chérir; **to t. sth in one's memory** garder précieusement le souvenir de qch

▸▸ **t. hunt** chasse *f* au trésor

treasure-house N *Old-fashioned* trésor *m*

treasurer ['treʒərər] N trésorier, -ière

treasure-trove N *Law* trésor *m* (qu'on a découvert); *Fig* **the museum is a real t.** le musée est une véritable caverne d'Ali-Baba; *Fig* **the book was a t. of anecdotes** le livre était une mine d'anecdotes

treasury ['treʒərɪ] N *(funds)* trésor *m* (public); *(place)* trésorerie *f*; *(of cathedral etc)* trésor; **the T.** *(government department)* ≃ ministère *m* des Finances

▸▸ *Fin* **t. bills, t. bonds** bons *mpl* du Trésor; *Com, Fin* **T. Department** Direction *f* du Trésor; *Br* **T. Minister** ≃ ministre *m* des Finances; *Fin* **T. note** billet *m* de trésorerie; *Am* **T. Secretary** ≃ ministre des Finances; *Fin* **T. swap** échange *m* cambiste; *Fin* **T. warrant** mandat *m* du Trésor

treat [triːt] N *(pleasure)* plaisir *m*; **these chocolates are a real t.** ces chocolats sont un véritable délice *ou* un vrai régal; **to give sb a t.** gâter qn; **to give oneself a t.** faire un petit extra, se faire plaisir; **it's my t.** *(I'm paying)* c'est moi qui paie; **it would be a great t. to go to the theatre** ce serait un véritable plaisir d'aller au théâtre; **it's a t. seeing you look so well!** c'est un plaisir de te voir aussi en forme!; **to have a t. in store for sb** avoir une surprise pour qn; **if you haven't seen the film yet you've got a t. in store** si tu n'as pas voir le film tu vas (l')adorer; *Fam* **to go down a t.** être très apprécié; **that whisky went down a t.!** ce whisky m'a fait du bien!; **it worked a t.** *(of plan)* ça a marché comme sur des roulettes; *(of machine, system)* ça a marché à merveille

VT **1** *(behave towards, use)* traiter; **to t. sb well** bien traiter qn; **to t. sb badly** mal traiter qn, ne pas bien traiter qn; **to t. sb/an animal roughly** malmener *ou* maltraiter qn/un animal; **my father still treats me like a child** mon père me traite encore comme un enfant; **he doesn't t. things seriously** il ne prend pas les choses au sérieux; **to t. sth as a joke** prendre qch comme une plaisan-

terie; **you t. this place like a hotel!** ce n'est pas un hôtel ici!

2 *(metal, paper etc)* traiter; *Med (patient, illness)* traiter; **to t. sb for rheumatism** soigner qn qui souffre de rhumatismes; **she was treated in hospital** elle a reçu des soins à l'hôpital; **to t. wood with creosote** traiter le bois à la créosote

3 *Liter, Mus etc (subject, theme)* traiter; **to t. a subject thoroughly/superficially** traiter un sujet à fond/de manière superficielle

4 to t. sb to sth offrir qch à qn; **to t. oneself to sth** s'offrir qch; **to t. sb to a night out at the theatre** inviter qn au théâtre; **I'll t. you to an ice-cream** je t'offre une glace; **to t. oneself to oysters** s'offrir des huîtres; **I'll t. you** *(pay for you)* je t'invite; *Iron* **he treated us to a fair old display of petulance** nous avons eu droit à une belle démonstration de mauvaise humeur

VI *Fml (negotiate)* **to t. with sb** traiter *ou* négocier avec qn; **to t. with the enemy** pactiser avec l'ennemi

▸ **treat of** VT INSEP *Fml (deal with)* traiter de

treatise ['triːtɪz] N traité *m* (**on** de)

treatment ['triːtmənt] N **1** *(of person)* traitement *m*; **to give special/preferential t. to sb** réserver un traitement spécial/un traitement de faveur à qn; **to receive good/bad t.** être bien/mal traité; *Fam* **to give sb the (full) t.** *(beat up)* rosser qn **2** *(of metal, paper etc)*, *Med* traitement *m* **3** *Liter, Mus etc (of subject, theme)* traitement *m*, façon *f* de traiter; **the subject is given fuller t. elsewhere** le sujet est traité à fond ailleurs **4** *Cin* traitement *m*

treaty ['triːtɪ] N **1** *(international) (peace, trade)* traité *m*; **T. on European Union** traité sur l'Union européenne **2** *(between individuals)* accord *m*; *(contract)* contrat *m*; **to sell sth by private t.** vendre qch de gré à gré *ou* à l'amiable

treble ['treb(ə)l] ADJ *(triple)* triple

ADV trois fois plus; **t. the number** le triple; **t. the amount** trois fois plus

N **1** *Mus (person, voice)* soprano *m* **2** *Electron* aigus *mpl*; **we could do with a bit more t.** il faudrait un peu plus d'aigus

VT *(value, number)* tripler

VI tripler

▸▸ *Mus* **t. clef** clef *f* de sol; **t. control** touche *f* de tonalité aiguë; *Aut* **t. seat** trois places *f*; *Mus* **t. voice** (voix *f* de) soprano

trebly ['treblɪ] ADV trois fois plus

tree [triː] N **1** arbre *m*; **fruit t.** arbre fruitier; **timber t.** arbre de haute futaie; *Fig* **to be at the top of the t.** être au sommet; *Fig* **to get to the top of the t.** arriver au sommet de sa profession; *Fig Fam* **to be up a (gum) t.** être dans une impasse *ou* dans le pétrin; *Fam* **to be out of one's t.** *(crazy)* débloquer; *(drunk)* être rond *ou* bourré; *(on drugs)* être défoncé *ou* raide; *Fam* **money doesn't grow on trees!** l'argent ne pousse pas sur les arbres; *Fam* **good handymen don't grow on trees** les bons hommes à tout faire ne courent pas les rues; *Bible* **the t. of life** l'arbre de vie

2 family t. arbre *m* généalogique

3 *Comput (of folders)* arborescence *f*

4 *Hist* **gallows t.** gibet *m*, potence *f*

5 (shoe) t. embauchoir *m* (pour chaussures)

VT *(chase up a tree) (animal, prey)* obliger à se réfugier sur un arbre

▸▸ **t. creeper** *(bird)* grimpereau *m* des bois; **t. diagram** organigramme *m*; **t. fern** fougère *f* arborescente; **t. frog** rainette *f*, *Pej* **t. hugger** écologiste *mf* fanatique; *Geog* **t. line** limite *f* des arbres; **above/below the t. line** au-dessus/en-dessous de la limite des arbres; **t. pipit** pipit *m* des arbres; *Comput* **t. structure** arborescence, structure *f* arborescente; **t. surgeon** arboriculteur, -trice (qui

s'occupe de soigner et d'élaguer les arbres); **t. trunk** tronc *m* d'arbre

treehouse ['triːhaʊs] N = cabane *f* construite dans un arbre

treeless ['triːlɪs] ADJ sans arbres

treetop ['triːtɒp] N cime *f* d'un/de l'arbre; *Aviat* **to skim the treetops** voler en rase-mottes

trefoil ['triːfɔɪl, 'tref-] N *Bot, Her etc* trèfle *m*

trek [trek] N *(hike)* marche *f*, **a long t.** *(especially on foot)* un trajet long et pénible; **it's quite a t. to the shops** ça fait une trotte pour aller jusqu'aux boutiques; **it's a long t. back up from the beach** le chemin est long et pénible pour remonter de la plage; *Hist* **the Great T.** le Grand Trek

VI (-kk-) *(make long journey)* faire un trajet long et pénible *(à pied)*; *(as holiday activity)* faire du trekking; *Fam* **to t. to the shops** aller jusqu'aux boutiques à pied; *Fam* **and I had to t. all the way back to the shops** et il a fallu que je me retape tout le trajet à pied jusqu'aux boutiques; **he trekked all over the country** il a sillonné le pays

trekking ['trekɪŋ] N *(as holiday activity)* randonnée *f*, trekking *m*; **a t. holiday in Nepal** des vacances *fpl* de trekking au Népal

trellis ['trelɪs] N treillis *m*, treillage *m*

VT **1** *(window etc)* treillisser, treillager **2** *(vine)* échalasser

▸▸ **t. window** fenêtre *f* treillissée

trelliswork ['trelɪswɜːk] N treillis *m*, treillage *m*

tremble ['tremb(ə)l] N tremblement *m*; **to be all of a t.** être tout tremblant

VI *(vibrate)* trembler; *(shiver)* trembler, frissonner; *(with emotion)* frémir; *(of voice)* trembler; **to t. like a leaf** trembler comme une feuille; **to t. with fear** trembler de peur; **where are they? – I t. to think!** où sont-ils? – je n'ose y penser!

trembling ['tremblɪŋ] ADJ tremblant

N tremblement *m*; *(of leaf)* frémissement *m*; **in fear and t.** tout tremblant

tremendous [trɪ'mendəs] ADJ **1** *(enormous)* immense, énorme; **there was a t. crowd** il y avait un monde fou; **a t. difference** une énorme différence; **a. t. lot of sth** une quantité énorme de qch **2** *Fam (excellent)* formidable; **thanks, that's t.** merci, c'est formidable

tremendously [trɪ'mendəslɪ] ADV *(enormously)* extrêmement; **it was t. successful** ce fut un grand succès

tremolo ['tremələʊ] N *Mus* trémolo *m*

tremor ['tremər] N **1** *(of emotion)* tremblement *m*, frémissement *m*; *(of fear)* frisson *m*; *Med* tremblement, trémulation *f* **2** *(of windows etc)* tremblement *m*; **earth t.** secousse *f* sismique

tremulous ['tremjʊləs] ADJ tremblotant, frémissant; *(smile)* timide, craintif; **to be t. with fear/emotion/joy** frémir de peur/émotion/joie; **t. voice** voix *f* tremblante *ou* chevrotante

tremulously ['tremjʊləslɪ] ADV en tremblant, en tremblotant; *(timidly)* timidement

trench [tren(t)ʃ] N **1** *Agr* tranchée *f*, fossé *m*; *(for draining)* rigole *f*; **water** *or* **irrigation t.** fossé d'irrigation **2** *Mil* tranchée *f*, **communication t.** boyau *m*, -aux

VT *(ground)* creuser un fossé *ou* une tranchée dans

VI creuser des fossés *ou* des tranchées

▸▸ **t. coat** trench-coat *m*, *pl* trench-coats; **t. plough** rigoleuse *f*; **t. warfare** guerre *f* de tranchées

trenchant ['tren(t)ʃənt] ADJ *(style, tone)* tranchant, net, incisif; *(reply, epigram)* mordant, caustique

trencher ['tren(t)ʃər] N *Hist* tranchoir *m*, tailloir *m*

trencherman, *pl* **trenchermen** ['tren(t)ʃəmən] N *Old-fashioned* gros mangeur *m*

trend [trend] N *(of public opinion etc)* tendance *f*, *(fashion)* mode *f*, *(direction)* direction *f*; **upward/downward t.** tendance à la hausse/la baisse; **to set** *or* **start a t.** lancer une mode; **a t. towards …** une tendance vers …; **current trends** tendances actuelles; **the general t. of the market** les tendances du marché; **if present trends continue** si les tendances actuelles se poursuivent ► vi se diriger, s'orienter (**to, towards** vers) ► *Mktg* **t. analysis** analyse *f* des tendances; *Mktg* **t. reversal** renversement *m* de tendance

trendiness ['trendɪnɪs] N *esp Br Fam* côté *m* branché *ou* à la mode; **the t. of his haircut/views** sa coupe/ses idées à la mode; **the t. of the decor** le décor branché

trendsetter ['trendsetər] N lanceur, -euse de modes *ou* de nouvelles tendances

trendsetting ['trendsetɪŋ] ADJ *(innovation, design etc)* qui lance une mode

trendspotter ['trendspɒtər] N = personne *f* employée par une société commerciale pour identifier les nouvelles tendances de la mode telles qu'elles apparaissent dans la rue, les bars, etc

trendy ['trendɪ] *esp Br Fam* ADJ *(clothes, person, views etc)* branché ► N *Pej (person)* personne *f* branchée

trepan [trɪ'pæn] *Surg* N trépan *m* ► VT (**-nn-**) trépaner

trepanning [trɪ'pænɪŋ] N *Surg* trépanation *f*

trepidation [trepɪ'deɪʃən] N *(anxiety)* agitation *f* nerveuse; **he stood there in t. before the headmaster** il se tenait tout tremblant devant le directeur de l'école; **he opened the letter with t.** il ouvrit la lettre en tremblant; **he picked up the phone and, not without t., dialled** il saisit l'écouteur et composa le numéro non sans nervosité

trespass ['trespəs] N **1** *Law (on property)* violation *f* de propriété **2** *Rel* offense *f*, péché *m*; **forgive us our trespasses** pardonne-nous nos offenses ► vi **1** *Law* **to t. (on sb's property)** entrer sans autorisation dans la propriété de qn; **please leave, you're trespassing** veuillez quitter les lieux, vous n'êtes pas autorisés à être ici; **to t. (up)on sb's rights** violer *ou* enfreindre les droits de qn; **I don't wish to t. on your time** je ne veux pas abuser de votre temps; **I don't wish to t. on your area of responsibility** je ne veux pas empiéter sur vos attributions **2** *Rel* pécher (**against** contre); **as we forgive those that t. against us** comme nous pardonnons à ceux qui nous ont offensés

---

Note that the French verb **trépasser** is a false friend and is never a translation for the English verb **to trespass**. It means **to die**.

---

trespasser ['trespəsər] N *Law (on sb's land)* intrus, -use *(dans une propriété privée)*; **trespassers will be prosecuted** *(on sign)* défense d'entrer sous peine d'amende

trespassing ['trespəsɪŋ] N *(on sb's land)* violation *f* de propriété (foncière); **no t.** *(on sign)* défense d'entrer

tress [tres] N boucle *f*, *(plait)* tresse *f*, *Lit* **tresses** *(of woman)* chevelure *f*, cheveux *mpl*

trestle ['tres(ə)l] N tréteau *m*, chevalet *m* ► **t. bridge** pont *m* sur chevalets; **t. table** table *f* à tréteaux

trews [tru:z] NPL *(trousers) Scot* pantalon *m* en tartan; *Br Fam* pantalon

triad ['traɪæd] N **1** *(group of three)* triade *f* **2** *(Chinese secret society)* triade *f* **3** *Chem* élément *m* trivalent **4** *Mus* accord *m* parfait ► *Mktg* **t. markets** marchés *mpl* de la triade

trial ['traɪəl] N **1** *Law (proceedings)* procès *m*; **to bring sb to t.** faire passer qn en jugement; **to be on t. for a crime/for one's life** passer en jugement pour un crime/pour un crime passible de la peine de mort; **they were sent for t.** ils furent renvoyés en jugement; **t. by jury** jugement *m* par jury; *Hist* **t. by combat** combat *m* judiciaire; **famous trials** causes *fpl* célèbres

2 *(test)* épreuve *f*, *(of instrument, vehicle etc)* essai *m* (technique); *Sport* match *m* de sélection; **t. of strength** épreuve de force; **to give sth a t.** faire l'essai de qch; **on t.** à l'essai; **to proceed by t. and error** procéder par tâtonnements *ou* par approximations successives; **sheepdog trials** concours *m* de chiens de berger; **speed t.** essai de vitesse

3 *(ordeal)* épreuve *f* (douloureuse); **that child is a great t. to his parents** cet enfant met ses parents au martyre; **despite the trials and tribulations** en dépit des caprices de la fortune; **after all your trials and tribulations** après tout ce que vous avez dû souffrir ► *Acct* **t. balance** balance *f* d'inventaire; *Fig* **t. balloon** ballon *m* d'essai; *Aviat* **t. flight** vol *m* d'essai; *Sport* **t. game** match *m* de sélection; **t. judge** ≃ juge *m* d'instance; **t. offer** offre *f* d'essai; *Mktg* **t. order** commande *f* d'essai; **t. period** période *f* d'essai; **to be on a t. period** *(of employee)* faire une période d'essai; **t. run** essai *m*; **to give sth a t. run** essayer qch, faire un essai avec qch; **t. separation** séparation *f* à l'essai

triangle ['traɪæŋg(ə)l] N **1** *Geom etc* triangle *m*; *Fam* **the eternal t.** l'éternel triangle **2** *Mus* triangle *m*; *(drawing instrument)* équerre *f* (en triangle) ► *Phys* **t. of forces** triangle *m* des forces

triangular [traɪ'æŋgjʊlər] ADJ *(shape etc)* triangulaire, en triangle; *(contest, relationship etc)* triangulaire

triangulate [traɪ'æŋgjʊleɪt] VT *(in surveying)* trianguler

triangulation [traɪæŋgjʊ'leɪʃən] N *(in surveying)* triangulation *f*

triathlon [traɪ'æθlɒn] N triathlon *m*

tribal ['traɪb(ə)l] ADJ *(society, warfare, system)* tribal, -aux *ou* -als; *(leader)* de tribu; *(people etc)* qui vit en tribus

tribalism ['traɪbəlɪz(ə)m] N tribalisme *m*

tribalistic [traɪbə'lɪstɪk] ADJ tribal, -aux *ou* -als

tri-band ['traɪ-] ADJ *Tel* triple bande

tribe [traɪb] N **1** tribu *f*, *Fig Fam* tribu, smala *f*; **the twelve tribes of Israel** les douze tribus d'Israël **2** *Biol* tribu *f*

tribesman, *pl* **tribesmen** ['traɪbzmən] N membre *m* d'une/de la tribu; **Bedouin t.** membre *m* d'une/de la tribu bédouine

tribulation [trɪbjʊ'leɪʃən] N *Fml* tribulations *fpl*; **I had no wish to add to her tribulations** je ne voulais pas ajouter à ses tourments

tribunal [tr(a)ɪ'bju:nəl] N tribunal *m*, -aux

tribune¹ ['trɪbju:n] N *(platform)*, *Fig* tribune *f*

tribune² N *(officer in ancient Rome etc)* tribun *m*

tributary ['trɪbjʊt(ə)rɪ] ADJ *(state)* tributaire; *(road)* secondaire ► N **1** *Geog (of river)* affluent *m* **2** *(person, country)* tributaire *m*

tribute ['trɪbju:t] N **1** *(homage)* tribut *m*, hommage *m*; **to pay (a) t. to sb** rendre hommage à qn; **it is a t. to her/his determina-** tion that the work was finished at all c'est grâce à elle/à sa détermination que le travail a été terminé; **to pay a last t. to sb** rendre à qn les derniers devoirs; **floral tributes** gerbes *fpl* et couronnes *fpl* (de fleurs) **2** *Hist (money)* tribut *m* ► *Hist* **t. money** tribut

trice [traɪs] N **in a t.** en un clin d'œil, en moins de rien

tricentenary, *esp Am* **tricentennial** [traɪsen'ti:nərɪ, -'tenɪəl] ADJ, N tricentenaire *m*

triceps ['traɪseps] N *Anat* triceps *m* ► **t. muscle** triceps

triceratops [traɪ'serətɒps] N tricératops *m*

trichinosis [trɪkɪ'nəʊsɪs] N *Med* trichinose *f*

trick [trɪk] N **1** *(ruse)* tour *m*, ruse *f*, *(dishonest)* supercherie *f*, *(practical joke)* farce *f*, tour; *(knack)* truc *m*; *(taught to animal, child etc)* tour d'adresse; *(of conjuror)* tour; **by a t. (to obtain sth)** par ruse; **to play a t. on sb** faire une farce *ou* une blague à qn; **my eyes must have been playing tricks on me** *or* **playing me tricks** mes yeux ont dû me jouer des tours, j'ai dû avoir la berlue; **t. of the light** effet *m* de lumière; **that was a nasty** *or* **mean** *or* **dirty t.** ça c'était un vilain tour!; **you've been up to your tricks again** vous avez encore fait des vôtres; **the car's up to its old tricks again** la voiture recommence à faire des siennes; **the tricks of the trade** les trucs *ou* les astuces *fpl* du métier; **that should do the t.** ça devrait faire l'affaire, ça devrait marcher; **he has the t. of always being in the right place at the right time** il a le chic pour être toujours au bon endroit au bon moment; **to teach a dog tricks** apprendre des tours à un chien; **card t.** tour de cartes; **conjuring t.** tour de prestidigitation *ou* de passe-passe; *Fam* **the whole bag of tricks** tout le bataclan, tout le tremblement; **she doesn't miss a t.** rien ne lui échappe; *Fam* **how's tricks?** *(how are you?)* comment vas-tu?; *(what's the news?)* quoi de neuf?

2 *Old-fashioned (mannerism)* manie *f*, *(habit)* habitude *f*; **he has a t. of repeating himself** il a la manie de se répéter

3 *Cards* pli *m*; **to take** *or* **make a t.** faire une levée *ou* un pli

4 *Sl (of prostitute)* passe *f*; **to turn a t.** faire une passe; **she's been turning tricks for years** ça fait des années qu'elle fait la pute ► VT *(person)* attraper, duper; **I've been tricked** j'ai été refait, je me suis fait avoir; **to t. sb into doing sth** amener qn à faire qch en usant de ruse; **you won't t. me into doing that again!** tu ne m'y reprendras pas!; **to t. sb out of sth** *(of opportunity etc)* frustrer qn de qch; *(of money etc)* escroquer qch à qn ► **t. cyclist** *(in circus)* cycliste *mf* acrobate; *Br Fam (psychiatrist)* psy *mf*; **t. photography** trucages *mpl*; **t. question** question-piège *f*, *pl* questions-pièges; **t. riding** *(on horseback)* voltige *f*

► **trick out** VT SEP *esp Lit (dress)* attifer (**in, with** de)

trickery ['trɪkərɪ] N tricherie *f*, duperie *f*, **piece of t.** supercherie *f*, **by t.** par ruse

trickiness ['trɪkɪnɪs] N *(of mechanism, situation)* difficulté *f*

trickle ['trɪk(ə)l] N *(of water etc)* filet *m*; **sales were down to a t.** il n'y avait presque plus de ventes; **emigration is down to a t.** l'émigration ne se fait plus qu'au compte-goutte; **we've had a slow but steady t. of contributions** les contributions nous arrivent assez lentement mais de manière régulière ► vi couler (goutte à goutte); **water was trickling down the wall** l'eau dégoulinait *ou* coulait le long du mur; **tears were trickling down her cheeks** les larmes coulaient le long de ses joues; **news is beginning to t.**

through *or* out from the devastated area on commence à recevoir peu à peu des nouvelles de la région sinistrée; **refugees are still trickling across the border** quelques rares réfugiés continuent à passer la frontière; **the ball just trickled into the hole** la balle a roulé tout doucement dans le trou; **the results began to t. in** les résultats commençaient à arriver lentement

vt *(liquid)* laisser goutter, laisser tomber goutte à goutte

▸▸ *Elec* **t. charger** chargeur *m* à régime lent; *Econ* **t.-down theory** = théorie *f* selon laquelle les richesses accumulées par un petit nombre bénéficieront à tous les membres de la société

trickster ['trɪkstər] **N** escroc *m*; **confidence t.** voleur, -euse à l'américaine

tricky ['trɪkɪ] **ADJ 1** *(difficult)* difficile; *(awkward)* compliqué, délicat **2** *(deceitful)* rusé; *Fam* **he's a t. customer** c'est un rusé *ou* un malin

tricolour, *Am* **tricolor** ['trɪkələr] **N** *(flag)* drapeau *m* tricolore *(principalement français ou irlandais)*

tricorn(e) ['traɪkɔːn] **ADJ** *(hat)* tricorne **N** tricorne *m*

tricuspid [traɪ'kʌspɪd] **ADJ** *Anat* tricuspide

tricycle ['traɪsɪk(ə)l] **N** tricycle *m*

trident ['traɪdənt] **N** trident *m*

tried [traɪd] **ADJ** **well t.** *(remedy)* éprouvé, qui a fait ses preuves; **t. and tested** *(formula)* éprouvé, qui a fait ses preuves; **t. and trusted** *(friend, employee)* sur qui l'on peut compter

triennial [traɪ'enɪəl] **ADJ** triennal, -aux; *(plant)* trisannuel

triennially [traɪ'enɪəlɪ] **ADV** tous les trois ans

trier ['traɪər] **N to be a t.** *(persevere)* faire des efforts, s'accrocher; **she might not be the best but she's a t.** ce n'est peut-être pas la meilleure mais elle est persévérante

trifle ['traɪf(ə)l] **N 1** *(insignificant thing)* broutille *f*, bagatelle *f*, vétille *f*; *(money)* petite somme *f* d'argent; *(object, gift)* bricole *f*; **to quarrel over a mere t.** se quereller pour un oui pour un non, se quereller sur des riens; **it was sold for a mere t.** on l'a vendu pour un rien **2 a t.** *(a little)* un tout petit peu, (un) tant soit peu; **a t. too wide/too short** un tantinet trop large/trop court **3** *Br Culin* = dessert *m* où alternent une couche de génoise imbibée d'alcool et de fruits en gelée et une couche de crème anglaise, le tout recouvert de Chantilly

▸ **trifle away** **vt sep** *(waste)* gaspiller; **to t. one's time away** gaspiller son temps

▸ **trifle with** **vt insep** *(affections etc)* jouer ou badiner avec; **she's not a woman to be trifled with** on ne joue pas *ou* ne plaisante pas avec elle; **to t. with one's food** manger du bout des dents, grignoter

trifling ['traɪflɪŋ] **ADJ** *(unimportant)* insignifiant, peu important; *(negligible)* négligeable; **t. incidents** menus incidents *mpl*; **that's a t. matter** ce n'est qu'une bagatelle; *Iron* **the t. sum of 10,000 euros** la bagatelle de 10 000 euros

triforium, *pl* **triforia** [traɪ'fɔːrɪəm, -ɪə] **N** triforium *m*

trigger ['trɪgər] **N** *(on gun)* détente *f*, gâchette *f*; *(on movie camera)*, *Tech* déclencheur *m*, poussoir *m* (à ressort); *Fig* catalyseur *m*; **to be quick on the t.,** *Fam* **to be t. happy** ne pas hésiter à tirer, *Fam* avoir la gâchette facile

vt *also Fig* déclencher

▸▸ **t. action** déclenchement *m*; **t. finger** index *m* *(avec lequel on appuie sur la gâchette)*; **my t. finger's itching** j'ai la gâchette qui me

démange; **t. mechanism** mécanisme *m* de déclenchement

▸ **trigger off** **vt sep** *Fig* = **trigger vt**

trigonometric(al) [trɪgənə'metrɪk, -ɪk(ə)l] **ADJ** trigonométrique

trigonometrically [trɪgənə'metrɪklɪ] **ADV** trigonométriquement

trigonometry [trɪgə'nɒmɪtrɪ] **N** trigonométrie *f*

trike [traɪk] **N** *(abbr* **tricycle)** tricycle *m*

trilateral [traɪ'læt(ə)rəl] **ADJ** trilatéral, -aux

trilby ['trɪlbɪ] **N** *Br* chapeau *m* mou, feutre *m*

▸▸ **t. hat** chapeau mou, feutre

trilingual [traɪ'lɪŋgw(ə)l] **ADJ** trilingue

trill [trɪl] **N 1** *Mus* trille *m* **2** *(of birds)* chant *m* perlé, trille *m* **3** *Ling* consonne *f* roulée

vi *Mus etc* faire des trilles

vt *Mus etc (note)* triller; *Ling* **trilled consonant** consonne *f* roulée; **I'm up here, trilled Penelope** je suis en haut, dit Pénélope d'une voix flûtée

trillion ['trɪljən] **N** VOIR GRAMMAIRE A76 **1** *Br* *(10¹⁸)* trillion *m* **2** *Am* *(10¹²)* billion *m*

trilogy ['trɪlədʒɪ] **N** trilogie *f*

trim [trɪm] **N 1** *(of hair etc)* coupe *f* d'entretien; **just a t.** *(said to hairdresser)* c'est simplement pour rafraîchir

2 in (good) t. en bon ordre; *(of person) (in good health)* en bonne santé; *(fit)* en (bonne) forme; **in fighting t.** prêt pour le combat

3 *Naut (of sails)* orientation *f*, **in t.** équilibré; **out of t.** déséquilibré

4 *(on car)* habillage *m*; **interior t.** garniture *f* intérieure; **seat t.** garniture *m* des sièges

5 *Sl (women)* nanas *fpl*, gonzesses *fpl*; **that's his new bit of t.** c'est sa nouvelle gonzesse

ADJ soigné; **a t. little yacht** un joli petit voilier; **to have a t. figure** *(of person)* avoir une silhouette svelte; **a t. little garden** un petit jardin coquet *ou* bien tenu

vt **(-mm-) 1** *(cut) (hedge, tree)* tailler; *(edge of book)* ébarber, rogner; *(beard etc)* tailler; *(sb's hair)* couper, rafraîchir; *Comput (database)* supprimer les espaces blancs inutiles de; **to t. (the wick of) a lamp** moucher une lampe; **to t. the budget** réduire le budget; *Culin* **to t. meat** habiller *ou* parer la viande **2** *(ship, plane)* équilibrer; *(load)* arrimer; *Naut (sails)* orienter

3 *Sewing etc (dress etc)* orner, garnir **(with** de); *(hat)* garnir; *Am (Christmas tree)* décorer; **trimmed with lace** garni de dentelles

▸ **trim away** **vt sep** *(excess growth, unnecessary details, verbiage)* élaguer

▸ **trim down** **vt sep** *(text, size of company, expenditure etc)* réduire

vi *(spend less)* réduire ses dépenses; *(shed staff)* réduire ses effectifs

▸ **trim off** **vt sep** *Culin etc (fat)* enlever; **to t. the fat off the meat** enlever le gras de la viande; *Fig* **they've trimmed £200 off the budget** ils ont réduit le budget de 200 livres; **I think we could t. a couple of hours off the journey** je pense que nous pourrions gagner environ deux heures sur le trajet

trimaran ['traɪməræn] **N** *Naut* trimaran *m*

trimester [tr(a)ɪ'mestər] **N** *esp Am* trimestre *m*

trimmer ['trɪmər] **N 1** *(machine) (for wood etc)* machine *f* à trancher; *(in papermaking, bookbinding etc)* massicot *m* **2** *Pej (opportunist)* opportuniste *mf*

trimming ['trɪmɪŋ] **N 1** *(cutting) (of hedges, trees)* taille *f*; *(of edges of book)* ébarbage *m*, rognage *m*; **trimmings** *(pieces) (of iron, wood, paper etc)* rognures *fpl*, ébarbures *fpl* **2** *(reduction) (of expenses etc)* réduction *f* **3** *(decoration) (of clothes, curtains etc)* garniture *f*, ornement *m*; **trimming(s)** *(on garment*

etc) passementerie *f*; *Br Culin* **(usual) trimmings** *(of dish)* accompagnements *mpl*, garniture; **roast beef and all the trimmings** du rosbif et tout ce qui l'accompagne; *Fig* **with all the trimmings** avec tout le tralala

trimness ['trɪmnɪs] **N** *(of person, thing)* air *m* soigné; *(of figure)* sveltesse *f*

Trinidad ['trɪnɪdæd] **N** (l'île de) la Trinité; **T. and Tobago** la Trinité-et-Tobago

Trinity ['trɪnɪtɪ] **N** *Rel* **the (Holy) T.** la (sainte) Trinité

▸▸ **T. Sunday** (la fête de) la Trinité; *Univ* **T. term** troisième trimestre *m* (universitaire) *(à Oxford, Cambridge et au Trinity College de Dublin)*

trinket ['trɪŋkɪt] **N** *(jewellery)* petit bijou *m* en toc; *(worthless object)* babiole *f*

trinomial [traɪ'nəumɪəl] **ADJ, N** *Math* trinôme *m*

trio, *pl* **trios** ['triːəu, -əuz] **N** *Mus etc* trio *m*

trip [trɪp] **N 1** *(journey)* voyage *m*; *(outing)* excursion *f*, business/honeymoon t. voyage d'affaires/de noces; **to go on a shopping t.** aller faire des courses; **the t. takes two hours** le trajet dure deux heures; **he's away on a t. to Italy** il est en voyage en Italie; **I'm afraid I'm going to have to make another t. to the loo** je crois que je vais devoir refaire un tour aux cabinets; **round t.** *(circular journey)* voyage circulaire; *Naut* croisière *f*, *(journey there and back)* voyage d'aller et retour; *Br Sch* **school t.** excursion scolaire; *(longer)* voyage scolaire; *Br Sch* **geography field t.** excursion d'études géographique; *(longer)* voyage d'études géographiques

2 *(drug)* **t.** voyage *m*, trip *m*; **to be on a t.** faire un voyage *ou* un trip, être en plein trip **3** *Sl (quantity of LSD)* dose *f* de LSD

4 *(stumble)* faux pas *m*

5 *Fam (experience)* **to be on a guilt t.** culpabiliser; **to be on a power t.** être en plein trip mégalo; **to be on an ego t.** se faire mousser

6 *Sport (foul)* croc-en-jambe *m*, *pl* crocs-en-jambe, croche-pied *m*, *pl* croche-pieds; **that was a t.!** il lui a fait un croc-en-jambe!

vi **(-pp-) 1** *(stumble)* trébucher, faire un faux pas; *(of horse)* broncher

2 *(step lightly)* aller d'un pas léger; **he tripped merrily into the room** il entra dans la pièce d'un pas léger

3 *Tech (of catch etc)* se déclencher; *(of part of mechanism)* basculer, culbuter

4 *Sl (on drugs)* faire un trip; **I was tripping at the time** j'étais en plein trip; **I don't know what he was tripping on** je ne sais pas ce qu'elle avait pris

5 to t. off the tongue *(of name, jingle etc)* bien couler; **her name doesn't exactly t. off the tongue** son nom n'est pas facile à prononcer

vt 1 = **trip up vt sep 1 2** *Tech (part of machine)* déclencher; *(lever etc)* culbuter **3** *Hum* **to t. the light fantastic** *(dance)* danser

▸▸ **t. computer** ordinateur *m* de bord; *Aut* **t. recorder** compteur *m* journalier, totalisateur *m* partiel; **t. wire** fil *m* tendu *(pour déclencher un mécanisme, pour faire tomber quelqu'un ou pour avertir de son arrivée)*

▸ **trip over** **vi** trébucher et tomber

vt insep *(something)* trébucher sur, buter contre; *Fig* **you can't go anywhere here without tripping over celebrities** par ici on ne peut pas faire un pas sans tomber sur une célébrité; **to t. over one's (own) feet** s'emmêler les pieds

▸ **trip up** **vt sep 1** *(cause to fall)* faire un croc-en-jambe *ou* un croche-pied à; *(of obstacle)* faire trébucher, faire tomber **2** *Fig (catch out)* démonter, désarçonner

vi 1 *(stumble)* trébucher, faire un faux pas; **to t. up over a word** trébucher sur un mot **2** *(make mistake)* faire une erreur; **the rob-**

bers/fugitives finally tripped up les vo-leurs/fugitifs ont fini par commettre une erreur; **that's where we tripped up** *(blundered)* c'est là que nous avons fait une gaffe

tripartite [traɪˈpɑːtaɪt] **ADJ** tripartite; *(divided into three)* divisé en trois, en trois parties

tripe [traɪp] **N** *Culin* tripes *fpl*; *Fam (nonsense)* bêtises *fpl*; *Fam* **that's all** *or* **a lot of t.** tout ça c'est des sottises

triphammer [ˈtrɪphæmər] **N** *Tech* marteau *m* à bascule *ou* à soulèvement

triphase [ˈtraɪfeɪz] **ADJ** *Elec (current)* triphasé

triphthong [ˈtrɪfθɒŋ] **N** triphtongue *f*

triplane [ˈtraɪpleɪn] **N** triplan *m*

triple [ˈtrɪp(ə)l] **ADJ** triple; *St Exch* **t. A rated** noté triple A
ADV t. the number/amount trois fois le nombre/la quantité
N triple *m*
VT & VI tripler
▸▸*Hist* **the T. Alliance** *(1668)* la Triple Alliance; *(1882-1914)* la Triple-Alliance, la Triplice; *St Exch* **t.-A rating** notation *f* AAA; *Med* **t. combination therapy** trithérapie *f*; **t. glazing** triple vitrage *m*; *Sport* **t. jump** triple saut *m*; *Med* **t. therapy** trithérapie *f*; *Mus* **t. time** mesure *f* ternaire *ou* à trois temps

triple-band **ADJ** *Tel* triple bande

triplet [ˈtrɪplɪt] **N** *(child)* triplé, -ée; *Mus* triolet *m*; *(in poetry)* tercet *m*

triplex [ˈtrɪpleks] **ADJ** *(planche)* de trois épaisseurs

triplicate¹ [ˈtrɪplɪkət] **ADJ t. copies** trois exemplaires *mpl*
N triple *m*, triplicata *m*; **in t.** en triple *ou* trois exemplaire(s); **invoice in t.** facture en triplicata *ou* en trois exemplaires

triplicate² [ˈtrɪplɪkeɪt] **VT** *Com (document)* rédiger en trois exemplaires

triply [ˈtrɪplɪ] **ADV** triplement

tripod [ˈtraɪpɒd] **N** trépied *m*

Tripoli [ˈtrɪpəlɪ] **N** Tripoli

tripos [ˈtraɪpɒs] **N** *Univ (at Cambridge)* = épreuves *fpl* pour l'obtention de la licence ès lettres/ès sciences

tripper [ˈtrɪpər] **N** *esp Br (person)* excursionniste *mf*; **they're (just) day trippers** ils sont (juste) venus passer la journée

trippy [ˈtrɪpɪ] **ADJ** *Fam* psychédélique

triptych [ˈtrɪptɪk] **N** *Art* triptyque *m*

trireme [ˈtraɪriːm] **N** trirème *f*, trière *f*

trisect [traɪˈsekt] **VT** *Geom etc (line, angle)* diviser *ou* couper en trois

trisomy [ˈtraɪsəʊmɪ] **N** *Med* trisomie *f*

trisyllabic [traɪsɪˈlæbɪk] **ADJ** *(in prosody)* tris(s)yllabe, tris(s)yllabique

trisyllable [traɪˈsɪləb(ə)l] **N** *(in prosody)* tris(s)yllabe *m*

trite [traɪt] **ADJ** banal, -als; *(theme)* rebattu; **t. remarks** banalités *fpl*, lieux *mpl* communs

tritely [ˈtraɪtlɪ] **ADV** banalement

triteness [ˈtraɪtnɪs] **N** banalité *f*

tritium [ˈtrɪtɪəm] **N** *Chem* tritium *m*

triton [ˈtraɪt(ə)n] **N** *(mollusc)*, *Myth* triton *m*

triturate [ˈtrɪtjəreɪt] **VT** *Tech* triturer, broyer

trituration [trɪtjəˈreɪʃən] **N** *Tech* trituration *f*

triumph [ˈtraɪəmf] **N** triomphe *m* (**over** sur); **to achieve great triumphs** remporter de grands succès; **she came home in t.** elle est rentrée triomphante chez elle; **a look of t.** un air triomphant; **the t. in his voice/eyes** le triomphe dans sa voix/ses yeux
VI triompher; **to t. over one's enemies** *(defeat)* triompher de ses ennemis

triumphal [traɪˈʌmf(ə)l] **ADJ** triomphal, -aux; **to get a t. reception** avoir une arrivée triomphale

triumphant [traɪˈʌmfənt] **ADJ** triomphant; *(success)* retentissant; **a t. expression** un air de triomphe; **to be t. over sb/sth** triompher de qn/qch

triumphantly [traɪˈʌmfəntlɪ] **ADV** *(to return etc)* en triomphe; *(to look at etc)* d'un air triomphant; *(to say)* d'un ton triomphant

triumvirate [traɪˈʌmvɪrɪt] **N** *Hist* triumvirat *m*; *Fig (of people)* trio *m*

triune [ˈtraɪjuːn] **ADJ** *Rel* d'une unité triple, en trois parties, trin

trivet [ˈtrɪvɪt] **N** *Culin* trépied *m*

trivia [ˈtrɪvɪə] **NPL** vétilles *fpl*, petits riens *mpl*; **to get bogged down in t.** s'embarrasser de futilités; **he has an amazing memory for t.** il a une mémoire remarquable pour les choses sans importance

trivial [ˈtrɪvɪəl] **ADJ 1** *(unimportant)* insignifiant, sans importance; **t. matter** bagatelle *f*, **t. offence** peccadille *f* **2** *(person)* superficiel, frivole; **he's just being t.** il plaisante **3** *(banal)* banal, -als, dépourvu d'originalité

> Note that the French word **trivial** is a false friend. It means **vulgar, coarse.**

triviality [trɪvɪˈælɪtɪ] **N 1** *(of loss, offence etc)* caractère *m* insignifiant; *(of remark etc)* banalité *f*, futilité *f* **2 to talk polite trivialities** dire des futilités *ou* des banalités pour être poli

trivialization [trɪvɪəlaɪˈzeɪʃən] **N** banalisation *f*

trivialize [ˈtrɪvɪəlaɪz] **VT** banaliser

trochaic [trəʊˈkeɪɪk] **ADJ, N** *(in prosody)* trochaïque *m*

trochee [ˈtrəʊkiː] **N** *(in prosody)* trochée *m*

trod **PT**, **trodden** **PP** *see* **tread**

trog [trɒg] **N** *Br Fam (ugly person)* mocheté *f*

trogloditic [trɒgləˈdɪtɪk] **ADJ** troglodytique

troglodyte [ˈtrɒglədaɪt] **N** troglodyte *m*

troika [ˈtrɔɪkə] **N** troïka *f*

troilism [ˈtrɔɪlɪz(ə)m] **N** amour *m ou* sexe *m* à trois

Trojan [ˈtrəʊdʒən] **ADJ** *Hist* troyen, de Troie
N *Hist* Troyen, -enne; **like a T.** *(to work)* sans relâche; *(to fight)* vaillamment
▸▸*Hist, Fig* **T. Horse** cheval *m* de Troie; **the T. War** la guerre de Troie

troll¹ [trəʊl] *Fishing* **N** cuiller *f*, *(of fishing rod)* moulinet *m*
VI to t. for pike pêcher le brochet à la cuiller

troll² **N** *Myth* troll *m*; *Br Fam (ugly person)* mocheté *f*

trollied [ˈtrɒlɪd] **ADJ** *Br Fam (drunk)* bourré, pété

trolley [ˈtrɒlɪ] **N 1** *Br (cart)* chariot *m*; *(two wheeled)* diable *m*; *(for luggage)* chariot à bagages; **(shopping) t.** *(in supermarket etc)* chariot, caddie *m*; **(dinner** *or* **tea) t.** table *f* roulante **2** *(wheel)* poulie *f* de) trolley *m*; *Fam* **he's off his t.** *(mad)* il débloque
▸▸*Am* **t. car** tramway *m*; *Br Fam Pej* **t. dolly** *(air hostess)* hôtesse *f* de l'air; **t. jack** cric *m* rouleur; **t. wheel** (poulie de) trolley

trolleybus [ˈtrɒlɪbʌs] **N** trolleybus *m*

trolling [ˈtrəʊlɪŋ] **N** *Fishing* pêche *f* à la cuiller

trollop [ˈtrɒləp] **N** *Old-fashioned, Hum* **1** *(dirty woman)* souillon *f* **2** *(promiscuous woman)* catin *f*, gourgandine *f*

trombone [trɒmˈbəʊn] **N** *Mus* trombone *m*

trombonist [trɒmˈbəʊnɪst] **N** tromboniste *mf*

troop [truːp] **N 1** *(of people)* groupe *m*, bande *f* **2** *Mil (unit) (of cavalry, tanks)* peloton *m*;

troops troupes *fpl*; **to raise troops** lever des troupes; **shock troops** troupes de choc **3** *(in scouting)* troupe *f*
VI to t. in/off/past entrer/partir/passer en groupe *ou* en bande
VT *esp Br Mil* **to t. the colour** faire le salut au drapeau
▸▸**t. carrier** *(ship)* transport *m* de troupes; *(plane)* avion *m* de transport militaire; *(vehicle)* véhicule *m* de transport de troupes; **t. train** train *m* militaire

trooper [ˈtruːpər] **N 1** *Mil (soldier)* cavalier *m*, soldat *m* de la cavalerie; *Am, Austr (mounted police officer)* membre *m* de la police montée; *(horse)* cheval *m* de cavalerie; *Am* **(state) t.** *(policeman)* = agent *m* de la police d'État; *Fam* **to swear like a t.** jurer comme un charretier **2** *Br* = **troopship**

trooping [ˈtruːpɪŋ] **N** *esp Br Mil* **t. (of) the colour** salut *m* au drapeau, présentation *f* du drapeau; *Br* **the T. of the Colour** = la parade militaire à l'occasion de l'anniversaire de la Reine

troopship [ˈtruːpʃɪp] **N** (navire *m* de) transport *m* de troupes

trophic [ˈtrɒfɪk] **ADJ** *Med* trophique

trophy [ˈtrəʊfɪ] **N** *(in hunting)*, *Sport, Fig* trophée *m*
▸▸*Hum Pej* **t. wife** = épouse *f* considérée comme un signe extérieur de réussite sociale

tropic [ˈtrɒpɪk] **N** *Astron, Geog* tropique *m*; **the tropics** les tropiques

tropical [ˈtrɒpɪk(ə)l] **ADJ** *(climate, heat, fish etc)* tropical, -aux; *(illness etc)* des tropiques; **it's absolutely t. in here!** il fait une chaleur torride ici!
▸▸**t. rain forest** forêt *f* tropicale humide

tropism [ˈtrəʊpɪz(ə)m] **N** *Biol* tropisme *m*

troposphere [ˈtrɒpəsfɪər] **N** *Met* troposphère *f*

Trot [trɒt] **N** *Pol Fam* trotskyste *mf*

trot [trɒt] **N 1** *Horseriding etc* trot *m*; **at a brisk t.** au grand trot; **to set off at a t.** partir au trot; *Fam* **they've had 22 wins on the t.** ils ont gagné vingt-deux fois à la file *ou* de suite; *Fam* **for five days on the t.** pendant cinq jours de suite; *Fam* **to keep sb on the t.** ne laisser aucun repos à qn **2** *Sl* **to have the trots** *(diarrhoea)* avoir la chiasse *ou* la courante
VI (**-tt-**) *Horseriding* trotter, aller au trot; *(of person)* trotter; *(of child)* trottiner; *Fam* **I must be trotting (along)** il faut que je file; *Fam* **I'll just t. up/down/along to the post office** je vais juste faire un saut à la poste; *Fam* **I'll just t. round to the shops** je vais faire quelques courses en vitesse; *Fam* **he trotted off down the road** il s'éloigna en trottinant dans la rue
VT *(horse)* faire trotter
▸ **trot out** **VT SEP** *Fam (produce) (excuses)* débiter; *(one's knowledge etc)* faire étalage de, débiter; *(old grievances)* rabâcher; **he can always t. out excuses** il est toujours prêt à débiter des excuses

troth [trəʊθ] **N** *Arch, Lit* foi *f*; **by my t.!** sur ma foi!

Trotskyism [ˈtrɒtskɪɪzm] **N** trotskisme *m*

Trotskyite [ˈtrɒtskɪaɪt] **ADJ, N** trotskyste *mf*

trotter [ˈtrɒtər] **N 1** *(horse)* cheval *m* de trot, trotteur, -euse **2** *Culin* **sheep's/pigs' trotters** pieds *mpl* de mouton/de porc **3** *Fam* **trotters** *(feet)* pieds *mpl*

trotting [ˈtrɒtɪŋ] **N** *Horseriding* trot *m*
▸▸**t. race** course *f* de trot (attelé)

troubadour [ˈtruːbədʊər] **N** *Liter* troubadour *m*

TROUBLE ['trʌb(ə)l]

> **N** ennuis **1** ▪ difficultés **1**
> ▪ problème(s) **1, 3** ▪ désordre **2**
> ▪ troubles **3** ▪ soucis **3**
> ▪ dérangement **4** ▪ peine **4** ▪ mal **4**
> **VT** inquiéter **1** ▪ faire souffrir **1**
> ▪ déranger **2**
> **VI** se déranger

N 1 (problem, difficulty) ennui m, difficulté f, problème m; **he told me his troubles** il m'a raconté ses malheurs ou ses problèmes; **her troubles are over** ses malheurs ou ses ennuis sont finis; **in one's time of t.** quand on a des ennuis; **money troubles** problèmes mpl d'argent; **what's the t.?** qu'est-ce qu'il y a?, quel est le problème?; **we must get to the root of the t.** il faut chercher la source du mal; **the t. is that ...** l'ennui ou le problème c'est que ...; **the t. with you** or **your t. is you don't think** ton problème ou le problème chez toi c'est que tu ne réfléchis pas; **the t. with these machines is (that) they're too complicated** le problème avec ces machines c'est qu'elles sont trop compliquées; **you'll have t. with him** il va vous causer des difficultés ou des ennuis; **did you have any t. finding the place?** est-ce que tu as eu du mal à trouver?; **this new machine's/system's more t. than it's worth** cette nouvelle machine/ce nouveau système pose plus de problèmes qu'elle/qu'il n'en résout; **this machine's been** or **given nothing but t.** cette machine ne m'a/ne nous a apporté que des problèmes; **to be in t.** avoir des ennuis ou des difficultés; **to get into t.** s'attirer des ennuis ou des désagréments; Fam (become pregnant) tomber enceinte; **to get into t. with the police** avoir affaire à la police; **to get sb into t., to make t. for sb** créer des ennuis à qn; Fam **to get a girl into t.** (make her pregnant) mettre une fille enceinte; **to get sb out of t.** tirer qn d'affaire; **to keep out of t.** éviter les ennuis; **to be looking** or **asking for t.** (cause problems for the future) se préparer des ennuis; **he was asking for t., the way he drank** il cherchait des ennuis, à boire autant; **are you looking for t.?** (said aggressively) tu cherches des ennuis?; **that's asking for t., not locking the door** ne pas verrouiller la porte, c'est tenter le diable; **to make** or **cause t.** semer la discorde; **to make t. for oneself** se créer des ennuis

2 (disorder, unrest) désordre m; **there was t. in the streets** il y a eu des violences dans la rue; **the Troubles** (in Northern Ireland) les troubles mpl; **there will be t.** il va y avoir du grabuge; **there'll be t. if he finds out** je vais/tu vas/on va/etc avoir des ennuis s'il s'en rend compte; Br Hum **there's t. at mill** la révolte gronde

3 (physical, medical, mechanical) **eye t.** affection f de l'œil; (sight disorder) troubles mpl de vision; **stomach t.** troubles digestifs; **to have heart t.** être malade du cœur; **to locate** or **trace the t.** (in machine, engine etc) trouver la source de la panne; **my eyes have been giving me some t.** mes yeux me donnent quelques soucis; **the car/engine hasn't given me any t.** je n'ai eu aucun problème avec la voiture/le moteur; Aut etc **engine t.** panne f de moteur; Fam **he's got woman/ she's got man t.** ça ne va pas très bien pour lui/elle côté cœur

4 (inconvenience) dérangement m, peine f, mal m; **to take the t. to do sth, to go to the t. of doing sth** prendre ou se donner la peine de faire qch; **to go to** or **put oneself to** or **to take a great deal of t.** se donner beaucoup de mal ou de peine; **it's not worth the t.** cela n'en vaut pas la peine; **nothing's too much t. for him** il est toujours prêt à aider les autres; **(it's) no t.** (ça ne pose) aucun problème; **if**

it's no t. si ça ne vous dérange pas; **they've gone to all that t. for nothing** ils se sont donné du mal pour rien

VT 1 (worry) inquiéter; Med affliger; **my back's been troubling me for years** ça fait des années que mon dos me fait souffrir ou que j'ai des douleurs dans le dos; **I'm troubled about his future** son avenir me préoccupe ou m'inquiète; **don't let it t. you!** que cela ne vous inquiète pas!, ne vous tourmentez pas à ce sujet!; **how long has this cough been troubling you?** depuis combien de temps souffrez-vous de cette toux?; **her conscience was troubling her** elle avait des problèmes de conscience

2 (disturb) déranger; **I'm sorry to t. you** excusez-moi de vous déranger; **could I t. you a minute?** excusez-moi, vous auriez une minute?; **may I t. you to shut the door?** cela vous dérangerait-il de fermer la porte?

VI don't t.!, you needn't t.! ne vous dérangez pas!; **he didn't even t. to ...** il n'a même pas pris la peine de ...

> ►►**t. spot** point m chaud ou de conflit

troubled ['trʌb(ə)ld] **ADJ** (worried) (look) inquiet, -ète; (period (of history) époque f troublée; **t. sleep** sommeil m agité; **he's got a t. conscience** il n'a pas la conscience tranquille

> ►► Fig **t. waters** eaux fpl troubles

trouble-free ADJ sans problèmes; **a t. holiday** des vacances qui se déroulent/se sont déroulées sans incidents ou sans anicroches

troublemaker ['trʌb(ə)meɪkər] **N** fauteur, -trice de troubles

troubleshooter ['trʌb(ə)lʃuːtər] **N** Pol, Ind etc médiateur, -trice, conciliateur, -trice; (for machinery etc) dépanneur m

troubleshooting ['trʌb(ə)lʃuːtɪŋ] **N** Pol, Ind etc médiation f, conciliation f, Comput dépannage m

> ►►**t. section** (in manual) section f de dépannage

troublesome ['trʌb(ə)lsəm] **ADJ** (problem, workforce, child etc) difficile; (rival) gênant; (cough) pénible

troubling ['trʌblɪŋ] **ADJ** inquiétant

troublous ['trʌbləs] **ADJ** Arch, Lit troublé, agité

trough [trɒf] **N 1** (feeding) t. auge f, mangeoire f; **drinking t.** abreuvoir m; Fig Fam **to have** or **get one's snout in the t.** avoir sa part du gâteau **2** Chem, Phys (for mercury, water) cuve f, cuvette f **3** Geol auge f **4** Phys, Math, Econ (of wave, graph, cycle) creux m; Met (barometric) dépression f, zone f dépressionnaire

trounce [traʊns] **VT** Sport (defeat heavily) écraser, battre à plate(s) couture(s)

trouncing [traʊnsɪŋ] **N** Sport (heavy defeat) défaite f écrasante; **Wales gave France a t.** le pays de Galles a battu la France à plate(s) couture(s)

troupe [truːp] **N** (of actors etc) troupe f

trouper ['truːpər] **N** Theat membre m d'une/ de la troupe; Fig **he's an old t.** c'est un vieux de la vieille; Fig **she's a real t.** elle s'y connaît

trousered ['traʊzəd] **ADJ** Br Fam (very drunk) rond comme une queue de pelle, plein

trouser ['traʊzər] **N**

> ►►**t. press** presse f à pantalons; **t. suit** tailleur-pantalon m, pl tailleurs-pantalons

trousers ['traʊzəz] **NPL** esp Br (pair of) t. pantalon m; Fam **she's the one who wears the t.** c'est elle qui porte la culotte; Fig Fam **to be caught with one's t. down** être pris au dépourvu; **short t.** shorts mpl; **when I was still in short t.** quand j'étais encore en culottes courtes VOIR GRAMMAIRE A10

trousseau ['truːsəʊ] **N** trousseau m

trout [traʊt] **N 1** (inv in pl) (fish) truite f **2** Fam (woman) old t. vieille bique f

> ►►**t. fishing** la pêche à la truite

trove [trəʊv] **N** = **treasure-trove**

trowel ['traʊəl] **N** Constr truelle f, (in gardening) déplantoir m; Fig Fam **to lay it on with a t.** en faire trop

Troy [trɔɪ] **N** Troie f

troy [trɔɪ] **N** (weight for gold, money) poids m troy

> ►►**t. ounce** once f troy (31,1g); **t. weight** poids troy

truancy ['truːənsɪ] **N** Sch absentéisme m scolaire

truant ['truːənt] **N** élève mf qui fait l'école buissonnière; **to play t.** faire l'école buissonnière

ADJ ATTRIB qui fait l'école buissonnière

Note that the French word **truand** is a false friend. It means **crook**.

truce [truːs] **N** trêve f, **to call a t.** demander une trêve; **let's call it a t.!** faisons une trêve!

truck¹ [trʌk] **N 1** (lorry) camion m; (big, HGV) poids m lourd; Min berline f, benne f, bac m; **fork-lift t.** chariot m élévateur à fourche; Am **wrecking t.** camion de dépannage, dépanneuse f **2** Rail (for freight) wagon m; **cattle t.** fourgon m à bestiaux

VT (goods) camionner, acheminer par camion

VI esp Am (drive a truck) être conducteur de camion, être camionneur; Fam **keep on trucking!** bon courage!

truck² **N 1** Fam (relations) (with sb) rapports mpl, relations fpl; **I'll have no t. with him** je ne veux rien avoir à faire avec lui **2** Am (vegetables) produits mpl maraîchers

> ►► Am **t. farmer** maraîcher, -ère; Am **t. garden** jardin m maraîcher; Am **t. gardener** maraîcher, -ère; Am **t. gardening** maraîchage m

truckdriver ['trʌkdraɪvər], **trucker** ['trʌkər] **N** esp Am camionneur m, routier m

trucking ['trʌkɪŋ] **N** Am camionnage m

> ►►**t. company** entreprise f de transports routiers

truckle ['trʌk(ə)l] **N** (of cheese) = petit fromage m rond

VI Lit ramper, s'abaisser (**to** devant)

> ►►**t. bed** m gigogne

truckstop ['trʌkstɒp] **N** esp Am café m de routiers, routier m

truculence ['trʌkjʊləns] **N** agressivité f

truculent ['trʌkjʊlənt] **ADJ** agressif

Note that the French word **truculent** is a false friend. It means **colourful** or **vivid**.

truculently ['trʌkjʊləntlɪ] **ADV** agressivement

trudge [trʌdʒ] **N** marche f pénible; **a long t.** un trajet long et pénible

VT they trudged the streets looking for a cheap hotel ils se traînaient péniblement à travers les rues à la recherche d'un petit hôtel bon marché

VI marcher lourdement ou péniblement, se traîner; **we trudged across the sodden fields** nous avancions avec peine à travers les champs détrempés; **I've been trudging around the shops all day** je me suis traîné péniblement dans les magasins toute la journée

► **trudge along VI** (walk heavily, with difficulty) cheminer ou avancer péniblement, se traîner

true [truː] **ADJ 1** (according with reality, not fictional) vrai; (accurate) exact; **t. account** récit m fidèle ou exact; **t. adventures** aventures *fpl* vécues; **it is t. that** … il est vrai que …; **if it were t. that** … s'il était vrai que … + *sub*; **to come t.** *(of wish etc)* se réaliser; **this also holds t. for** … il en est de même pour …; **how t.!, how very t.!** c'est bien vrai!; **that's all too t., I'm afraid** ce n'est que trop vrai, malheureusement; **I can't believe it's t.** je n'arrive pas à le croire; **it's getting late – t.** il se fait tard – tu as raison

2 *(genuine)* véritable; *(real)* vrai, réel; **t. repentance** repentir *m* sincère *ou* véritable; **her t. nature** son véritable caractère; **he's a t. Irishman** *(conforms to stereotype)* c'est bien un Irlandais; *(by birth)* c'est un Irlandais, un vrai; **to get a t. idea of the situation** se faire une idée juste de la situation

3 *Tech, Carp* juste, droit, rectiligne; **to make a piece t.** ajuster une pièce; **his aim was t.** *(was a good shot)* il était bon tireur; *(hit target)* il a visé juste; **the table isn't t.** la table n'est pas d'aplomb

4 *(faithful)* fidèle, loyal, -aux; **to be t. to a friend** être loyal envers *ou* fidèle à un ami; **to be t. to oneself** être fidèle à soi-même; **to be** *or* **remain t. to one's principles** être fidèle à ses principes; **to be t. to a promise** rester fidèle à une promesse; **t. to life** qui correspond bien à la réalité; **t. to form, he** … fidèle à lui-même, il …; **she was an accountant, and t. to type she** … elle était comptable, et bien entendu elle …; **t. friend** ami, -ie loyal(e), vrai(e) ami, -ie; **a jury of twelve good men and t.** un jury de douze citoyens de bonne renommée

5 *(voice, instrument)* juste

ADV 1 *Fam (truthfully)* **tell me t.** dis-moi la vérité **2** *(to sing, aim)* juste; **to run t.** *(of wheel)* tourner rond *ou* sans balourd

N *Tech etc* **out of t.** *(of vertical post, member etc)* hors d'aplomb; *(of horizontal post, member etc)* dénivelé; *(of axle etc)* faussé, dévoyé; *(of timber)* déjeté; *(of wheel)* désaxé

VT *(thing)* mettre bien en place

▸▸ **t. copy** copie *f* conforme; *Fin* **t. discount** escompte *m* en dedans; *Acct* **t. and fair view** *(of accounts)* image *f* fidèle; **t. love** *(feeling, person)* grand amour *m*; **t. north** vrai nord *m*, nord géographique; *Mktg* **t. sample** échantillon *m* représentatif

true-blue N *Br (Conservative)* Conservateur, -trice pur(e) et dur(e)

ADJ loyal, -aux, convaincu

trueborn ['tru:bɔ:n] **ADJ** *Old-fashioned* vrai, véritable; **a t. Englishman** un vrai Anglais d'Angleterre

true-false ADJ

▸▸ **t. questionnaire** questionnaire *m* auquel on répond par 'vrai' ou 'faux'

truffle ['trʌf(ə)l] **N** truffe *f*, *Br* (rum) **t.** *(sweet)* truffe au rhum

▸▸ **t. hound** chien *m* truffier

trug [trʌg] **N** *Br* panier *m* ou corbeille *f* de jardinier

truism ['tru:ɪz(ə)m] **N** truisme *m*, vérité *f* de La Palice, lapalissade *f*; **it is a t. that** … c'est un lieu commun de dire que …

truly ['tru:lɪ] **ADV 1** *(really, genuinely)* vraiment, véritablement; **a t. difficult situation** une situation vraiment difficile; **I am t. grateful to her** je lui suis sincèrement reconnaissant; **it's t. tragic** c'est vraiment tragique; **I t. believe that** … je crois vraiment *ou* sincèrement que …; **yours t.** *(letter ending)* ≃ je vous prie d'agréer *ou* de croire à mes sentiments distingués; *Fam* **yours t.** *(myself)* votre serviteur; *Fam* **meanwhile yours t. had left** entretemps mézigue *ou* votre serviteur était parti **2** *(in truth)* en vérité, à vrai dire; **(really and) t.?** vrai de vrai? **3** *(faithfully) (to serve sb)* fidèlement, loyalement

trump *Cards* **N** *Cards (card)* atout *m*; **spades**

are trumps c'est atout pique; **to play trumps** jouer l'atout; **to call no trumps** jouer sans atout; *Fig Fam* **she turned up trumps** elle a fait des miracles

VT *(card)* couper avec l'atout

▸▸ **t. card** atout; *Fig* **to play one's t. card** jouer son atout

▸ **trump up VT SEP** *(invent) (excuse)* inventer; **to t. up a charge against sb** fabriquer une accusation contre qn; **trumped-up story** histoire *f* inventée

trumpery ['trʌmpərɪ] **N** *(worthless objects)* camelote *f*, *(nonsense)* absurdités *mpl*

trumpet ['trʌmpɪt] **N** *Mus* trompette *f*, *Fig* **to blow one's own t.** chanter ses propres louanges

VI (-t-) trompeter, sonner de la trompette; *(of elephant)* barrir

VT *esp Lit (success)* claironner

▸▸ **t. blast, t. call** coup *m* ou sonnerie *f* de trompette; *Mil* **t. major** trompette-major *m*, *pl* trompettes-majors; **t. player** trompettiste *mf*, *(in band)* trompette

trumpeter ['trʌmpɪtər] **N** *Mil* trompette *m*; *Mus (by profession)* trompettiste *mf*

trumpeting ['trʌmpɪtɪŋ] **N** sonnerie *f* de trompette; *(of elephant)* barrissement *m*

truncate [trʌŋ'keɪt] **VT** *(body, text etc)* tronquer; *(meeting etc)* écourter

truncated [trʌŋ'keɪtɪd] **ADJ** *(body, text)* tronqué; *(meeting etc)* écourté

▸▸ *Geom* **t. cone** cône *m* tronqué

truncheon ['trʌn(t)ʃən] **N** matraque *f*, *(esp for directing traffic)* bâton *m*

VT matraquer

trundle ['trʌnd(ə)l] **VT** *(hoop etc)* faire rouler; *(wheelbarrow, hand cart)* pousser; **they trundled him in on his bed** ils l'ont fait entrer sur son lit à roulettes

VI *(of hoop etc)* rouler; *(of vehicle)* rouler péniblement; *(of cart)* rouler lourdement; **the project trundled on** le projet avançait péniblement

▸▸ **t. bed** lit *m* gigogne

▸ **trundle out VT SEP** *(old bicycle, theory etc)* ressortir

trunk [trʌŋk] **N 1** *(of tree, body, artery)* tronc *m*; *Archit (of column)* fût *m* **2** *(luggage)* malle *f* **3** *Am Aut* coffre *m* **4** *(of elephant)* trompe *f* **5** **trunks** *(for men, for swimming)* maillot *m* (de bain), slip *m* de bain

▸▸ *Br Tel Old-fashioned* **t. call** appel *m* interurbain; **t. line** *Rail* ligne *f* principale, grande ligne; *Tel* inter *m*; *Br* **t. road** (route *f*) nationale *f*

trunnion ['trʌnjən] **N** *Mil, Tech* tourillon *m*

truss [trʌs] **N 1** *Med* bandage *m* herniaire **2** *Constr (of beam etc)* armature *f*, *(for roof timbers, bridge)* ferme *f*, *(for vaulting)* cintre *m* **3** *(of flowers)* touffe *f*, *(of tomatoes)* grappe *f*

VT 1 *Constr, Tech (beam etc)* armer, renforcer **2** *Culin (fowl)* trousser, brider

▸ **truss up VT SEP** *(tie up) (person)* ligoter; **trussed up like a chicken** ficelé comme un poulet

trust [trʌst] **N 1** *(belief)* confiance *f* (in en); **to put one's t. in sb** mettre sa confiance en qn; **to put one's t. in sth** se reposer sur qch; **to betray sb's t.** trahir la confiance de qn; **I took what you said on t.** je t'ai cru sur parole, je t'ai fait confiance

2 *(responsibility)* responsabilité *f*, **to be in a position of t.** occuper un poste de confiance; **he placed his child in my t.** il m'a confié la garde de son enfant

3 *Law* fidéicommis *m*, fiducie *f*, **to hold in t.** tenir par fidéicommis; *(property etc)* administrer par fidéicommis; *Br* **National T.** = société *f* pour la conservation des sites et monuments

4 *Ind etc (group)* trust *m*; **brains t.** brain-

trust *m*, *pl* brain-trusts; *Fin* **(investment) t.** société *f* de placement(s); **unit t.** société d'investissement à capital variable

VT 1 *(believe in) (person)* faire confiance à, se fier à; *(something)* se fier à; **she's not to be trusted** on ne peut pas se fier à elle; **are the figures to be trusted?** est-ce que ces chiffres sont fiables?; **she's not to be trusted on the question of** … on ne peut pas lui faire confiance quand il s'agit de …; **I don't t. you with money** je ne te confierais pas mon argent; **you can't t. anyone nowadays** on ne peut faire confiance *ou* se fier à personne de nos jours; **I don't t. you with her!** je ne la laisserais pas seule avec toi!; **I couldn't t. myself not to say anything** je ne pourrais pas résister à l'envie de dire quelque chose; **to t. sb with sth** confier qch à qn; **to t. sb to do sth** laisser à qn le soin de faire qch; *Fam* **t. him to say that!** c'est bien de lui!; *Fam* **I've lost it – t. you!** je l'ai perdu – ça c'est tout toi! *ou* c'est typique de toi! *ou* ça ne m'étonne pas de toi!; **she won't t. him out of her sight** elle lui fait si peu confiance qu'elle ne le quitte pas des yeux; **to t. one's instincts** se fier à son instinct; **to t. sb's judgement** se fier au jugement de qn; *Fam* **I wouldn't t. her as far as I could throw her** je ne lui ferais pas confiance du tout; **there's no-one's judgement I t. as much as hers** je lui fais confiance comme à personne d'autre

2 *(entrust)* **to t. sth to sb** confier qch à qn

3 *esp Fml* **to t. (that)** … *(hope)* espérer que …; *(express wish that)* exprimer le vœu que … + *sub*; **I t. he is not ill** j'espère bien qu'il n'est pas malade

VI to t. to luck s'en remettre au hasard

▸▸ *Fin* **t. bank** banque *f* de gestion de patrimoine; *Fin* **t. company** société *f* fiduciaire; *Fin* **t. fund** fonds *m* en fidéicommis; *Pol* **t. territories** territoires *mpl* sous tutelle

▸ **trust in VT INSEP** *(put one's hopes in) (something)* mettre ses espérances *ou* son espoir en; **to t. in God** croire en Dieu; **I want someone I can t. in** *(have confidence in)* il me faut une personne de confiance

trustafarian [trʌstə'feərɪən] **N** *Br Fam* jeune personne *f* de milieu relativement aisé et de race blanche qui cultive une image rasta

trustbusting ['trʌstbʌstɪŋ] *Am* **N** démantèlement *m* des trusts

ADJ ATTRIB qui a trait au démantèlement des trusts

trusted ['trʌstɪd] **ADJ** *(person)* de confiance; **tried and t.** *(remedy, method)* éprouvé; *(friend)* fidèle, éprouvé

▸▸ *Comput* **t. third party** *(for Internet transactions)* tierce partie *f* de confiance

trustee [trʌs'tiː] **N 1** *Law* fidéicommissaire *m*, fiduciaire *m*; *(with powers of attorney)* mandataire *m* **2** *(of museum, charity, company, life assurance policy)* administrateur *m*; **board of trustees** conseil *m* d'administration

trusteeship [trʌs'tiːʃɪp] **N 1** *Law* fidéicommis *m* **2** *(of museum, charity etc)* fonction *f* d'administrateur **3** *Pol (of territory)* tutelle *f*

trustful ['trʌstfʊl] **ADJ** plein de confiance, confiant

trustfully ['trʌstfəlɪ] **ADV** avec confiance

trustfulness ['trʌstfʊlnɪs] **N** confiance *f*

trusting ['trʌstɪŋ] **ADJ** confiant; *(look)* plein de confiance; **you're far too t.** tu fais trop confiance aux gens; **it's very t. of you to lend it to them** tu leur fais drôlement confiance pour le leur prêter

trustingly ['trʌstɪŋlɪ] **ADV** avec confiance

trustworthiness ['trʌstwɜːðɪnɪs] **N** *(person)* loyauté *f*, honnêteté *f*; *(of testimony, account etc)* crédibilité *f*, véracité *f*

trustworthy ['trʌstwɜːðɪ] ADJ *(person)* digne de confiance; *(information)* digne de foi; *(testimony)* irrécusable; *(critic, guidebook etc)* très fiable

trusty ['trʌstɪ] ADJ *Arch, Lit* fidèle, loyal, -aux; *Hum* **my t. old typewriter** ma bonne vieille machine à écrire

truth [truːθ, *pl* truːðz] N vérité *f*; **in t.** en vérité; **the plain** *or* **honest t.** la pure vérité, la vérité pure et simple; **to speak** *or* **tell the t.** dire la vérité; **the t. (of the matter) is** *or* **to tell the t., I forgot it** pour dire la vérité *ou* à dire vrai je l'ai oublié; **... and that's the t.** ... et voilà la vérité; **there's some t. in what you say** il y a du vrai dans ce que vous dites; **there's not a word of t. in it** il n'y a pas un brin de vérité là-dedans; **I told him a few home truths** je lui ai dit son fait *ou* ses quatre vérités; *Law* **the t., the whole t., and nothing but the t.** la vérité, toute la vérité, rien que la vérité; *Prov* **t. will out** la vérité finit toujours par se faire jour; *Prov* **t. is the first casualty (of war)** toute guerre s'accompagne de son cortège de mensonges
▸▸ **t. drug** sérum *m* de vérité; **t. function** fonction *f* de vérité; **t. table** table *f ou* matrice *f* de vérité; **t. value** variable *f* 'vrai' *ou* 'faux'

truthful ['truːθfʊl] ADJ *(person)* sincère, honnête; *(account etc)* véridique; *(description, portrait etc)* fidèle; **to be t.** *(of person)* dire la vérité, être sincère *ou* honnête

truthfully ['truːθfʊlɪ] ADV *(to speak, answer, claim etc)* en disant la vérité; *(to portray etc)* fidèlement

truthfulness ['truːθfʊlnɪs] N *(of statement, claim etc)* véracité *f*; *(of portrait etc)* fidélité *f*

TRY [traɪ]

N	essai **1, 2** ▪ tentative **2**
VT	essayer **1–3** ▪ tenter **2** ▪ vérifier **4** ▪ juger **5** ▪ éprouver **6** ▪ mettre à l'épreuve **6**
VI	essayer ▪ faire des efforts

N **1** *(attempt)* essai *m*, tentative *f*; **to have a t. at doing sth** essayer de faire qch; **to have a t. at sth** s'essayer à qch; **I had a t. at skindiving** je me suis essayé à la plongée sous-marine; **let's have a t.!** essayons toujours!; **can I have a t.?** (est-ce que) je peux essayer?; **I think I'll have a t. for this job** je crois que je vais me présenter pour ce travail; **you've already had three tries** vous avez déjà essayé trois fois; **OK, you can have one more t.** bon d'accord, tu peux encore essayer une fois *ou* tu as encore un essai; **go on, give it a t.** *(activity)* allez, essaie; *(food)* allez, goûte; **at the first t.** du premier coup; **it won't be easy but it's worth a t.** ça ne va pas être facile mais ça vaut la peine *ou* le coup d'essayer; **worth a t.?** ça vaut le coup d'essayer?
2 *Rugby* essai *m*; **to score a t.** marquer un essai; **the t. scorer** celui qui a marqué l'essai; **France's leading t. scorer** celui qui a marqué le plus d'essais pour la France

VT *(pt, pp* tried [traɪd]) **1** *(sample)* essayer; **here, t. my pen** tenez, essayez avec mon stylo; **to t. a dish** goûter (à) un mets; **t. some** *(food)* goûtes-y; **I'll t. anything once** il faut tout essayer dans la vie
2 *(attempt to do)* essayer, tenter; **to t. an experiment** tenter une expérience; **to t. the door/the window** essayer (d'ouvrir) la porte/la fenêtre; **I'd like to see you t. it!** je voudrais bien t'y voir!
3 *(attempt) t.* **to do sth** essayer de faire qch; **she tried to smile** elle a essayé de sourire; **he was trying hard to keep back the tears** il s'efforçait de retenir ses larmes; **it's worth trying** cela vaut la peine d'essayer; *Fam* **to t. and do sth** tâcher *ou* essayer de

faire qch; *Fam* **t. and be nice to her** tâche d'être gentil avec elle; **to t. doing sth** essayer de faire qch; **t. (asking) Jane** demande à Jane; **have you tried the chemist's?** tu es allé voir à la pharmacie?; **I tried the number in the book but there was no reply** j'ai essayé le numéro de l'annuaire mais ça ne répondait pas VOIR GRAMMAIRE A43–4
4 *(check) (mechanism)* vérifier
5 *Law (case, person)* juger; *Am (of advocate) (case)* plaider; **to be tried for theft** passer en correctionnelle pour vol
6 *(test) (person)* éprouver, mettre à l'épreuve; *(sb's courage, sb's patience etc)* mettre à l'épreuve; **to t. one's strength against sb** se mesurer avec *ou* à qn; **a people sorely tried** une nation fort *ou* durement éprouvée; **to t. one's eyes (reading)** se fatiguer les yeux (à lire)
VI faire un effort *ou* des efforts; **to t. again** essayer de nouveau; **you must t. harder** il faut faire de plus grands efforts; **at least you tried** au moins tu as/auras essayé; **he didn't really t.** il n'a pas vraiment essayé; **you weren't really trying** tu n'as pas vraiment essayé; **go on then, t.!** alors vas-y, essaie!; **... and she wasn't even trying** ... et elle l'a fait sans le moindre effort; **just you t.!** essaie un peu pour voir!; **I'd like to see you t.!** *(answer to threat, challenge)* je voudrais bien t'y voir!
▸ **try for** VT INSEP *(attempt to obtain)* tâcher d'obtenir; **to t. for a job** poser sa candidature à un emploi; **he's trying for (a place at) music school** il essaie d'obtenir une place à l'école de musique; *Sport etc* **she's trying for the record** elle essaie de battre le record
▸ **try on** VT SEP **1** *(clothes etc)* essayer
2 *Fam* **to t. it on** tenter le coup (**with sb** avec qn); **they're just trying it on** ils bluffent, c'est du bluff; **you're (just) trying it on!** ça ne marche pas *ou* ne prend pas!; **she tried it on with my husband** *(attempted to seduce)* elle a essayé de séduire mon mari
▸ **try out** VT SEP *(test)* faire l'essai de; *(new procedure)* essayer, expérimenter; **to t. sth out on sb** essayer *ou* expérimenter qch sur qn; **they're trying him out in goal** ils l'essaient *ou* l'ont mis à l'essai comme gardien de but

trying ['traɪɪŋ] ADJ *(time, experience)* pénible, difficile; *(person)* pénible
N *Law (of case, person)* jugement *m*

try-on N *Br Fam* bluff *m*; **it's just a t.** c'est du bluff

try-out N *(of machine etc)* premier essai *m*, essai préliminaire; *Am Theat* audition *f*; *Sport* épreuve *f* de sélection; **to give sb/sth a t.** mettre qn à l'essai/essayer qch

tryst [trɪst] N *Lit* rendez-vous *m* amoureux

tsar [tsɑːr] N tsar *m*, czar *m*

tsarevitch ['tsɑːrəvɪtʃ] N tsarevitch *m*, czarévitch *m*

tsarina [tsɑːˈriːnə] N tsarine *f*, czarine *f*

tsarist ['tsɑːrɪst] ADJ, N tsariste *mf*

tsetse ['t(s)etsɪ] N (mouche *f*) tsé-tsé *f inv*
▸▸ **t. fly** (mouche) tsé-tsé

T-shirt N tee-shirt *m*

tsp *Culin (abbr* **teaspoon, teaspoonful**) cu. à c.; **2 t. sugar** *(in recipe)* 2 cu. à c. de sucre

TSS [tiːesˈes] N *(abbr* **toxic shock syndrome**) SCT *m*

T-stop N *Phot* diaphragme *m*

TT [tiːˈtiː] N **1** *Br Sport (abbr* **Tourist Trophy**) = course *f* motocycliste sur l'île de Man **2** *(abbr* **teetotal**) **I'm TT** je ne bois pas d'alcool

TTL [tiːtiːˈel] ADJ *Phot (abbr* **through the lens**) TTL

TTP [tiːtiːˈpiː] N *Comput (abbr* **trusted third party**) *(for Internet transactions)* TPC *f*

tub [tʌb] N **1** *(container)* baquet *m*, bac *m*; *(for flowers, shrubs)* bac, caisse *f*, *(for washing)* baquet; *(in washing machine)* cuve *f*, *(of ice-cream, cream etc)* pot *m*; *Br Fam* **a t. of lard** *(man)* un gros lard, un gros plein de soupe; *(woman)* une grosse dondon, une grosse vache **2** *(bathtub)* baignoire *f*; **a hot t.** *(bath)* un bain chaud **3** *Fam (boat)* **old t.** vieux rafiot *m*
▸▸ **t. chair** *(fauteuil m)* crapaud *m*

tuba ['tjuːbə] N *Mus* tuba *m*

tubby ['tʌbɪ] ADJ *Fam (person)* dodu, boulot, -otte

tube [tjuːb] N **1** *(of paint, toothpaste)* tube *m*; *(pipe)* tuyau *m*; *Med etc (for deep wound)* drain *m*; *Austr Fam (of beer)* boîte *f*, *Aut etc* **inner t.** *(of tyre)* chambre *f* à air; *Chem, Phys etc* **test t.** éprouvette *f*; **(Fallopian) tubes** trompes *fpl* (de Fallope); **(bronchial) tubes** bronches *fpl*; *Fam* **to have one's tubes tied** *(be sterilized)* se faire ligaturer les trompes; *Fam* **that's £500 down the tubes** voilà 500 livres de foutues en l'air; *Fam* **that's all our efforts (gone) down the tubes** et voilà tous nos efforts réduits à néant; *Fam* **he watched his marriage/life's work go down the tubes** il a vu son mariage/le travail de toute une vie tourner en eau de boudin **2** *Elec, Electron, TV etc (electronic, thermionic)* tube *m*; **cathode-ray t.** tube cathodique *ou* à rayons cathodiques; *esp Am Fam* **the t.** *(television)* la télé **3** *Br Fam* **the t.** *(London underground)* ≃ le métro
▸▸ *Br Fam* **t. station** ≃ station *f* de métro

tube-feeding N *Med* gavage *m*

tubeless ['tjuːblɪs] ADJ *(tyre)* sans chambre (à air)

tuber ['tjuːbər] N *(root)* racine *f* tubéreuse; *(on potato)* tubercule *m*

tubercle ['tjuːbɜːk(ə)l] N *Anat, Med, Bot* tubercule *m*

tubercular [tjuːˈbɜːkjʊlər] ADJ *Med, Bot* tuberculeux

tuberculin [tjuːˈbɜːkjʊlɪn] N *Med* tuberculine *f*
▸▸ **t. test** épreuve *f* de la tuberculinisation, tuberculino-diagnostic *m*

tuberculin-tested [-'testɪd] ADJ
▸▸ **t. milk** ≃ lait *m* certifié

tuberculosis [tjuːbɜːkjʊˈləʊsɪs] N *Med* tuberculose *f*

tuberculous [tjuːˈbɜːkjʊləs] ADJ *Med* tuberculeux

tubful ['tʌbfʊl] N cuvée *f*, plein baquet *m* (**of** de)

tubing ['tjuːbɪŋ] N *(no pl)* tubes *mpl*, *(pipework)* tuyauterie *f*; **rubber t.** tuyau(x) *m(pl)* en caoutchouc

tub-thumper [-θʌmpər] N *Fam* harangueur *m*

tubular ['tjuːbjʊlər] ADJ tubulaire
▸▸ *Mus* **t. bells** carillon *m* d'orchestre

TUC [tiːjuːˈsiː] N *Br Ind (abbr* **Trades Union Congress**) = confédération *f* des syndicats britanniques

tuck [tʌk] N **1** *Sewing* (petit) pli *m*, rempli *m*, plissé *m* **2** *Br Sch Fam (cakes, sweets)* gâteaux *mpl*, friandises *fpl*, sucreries *fpl*
VT **1** *Sewing (garment)* faire des plis à **2** *(fold)* replier **3** *(put)* mettre; **to t. one's legs under one** replier les jambes; **she tucked her arm in(to) mine** elle a passé son bras sous le mien; **he tucked his briefcase under his arm** il mit *ou* cala son porte-documents sous son bras; **to t. one's trousers into one's socks** mettre son pantalon dans ses chaussettes; **to t. a rug round sb** envelopper qn dans une couverture; **the bird tucked its head under its wing** l'oiseau a caché sa tête sous son aile; **she tucked her hair under her**

hat elle a glissé ses cheveux sous son chapeau

▶▶ *Br Sch* **t. box** gamelle *f (d'écolier); Br Sch* **t. shop** = petite boutique *f* où les écoliers achètent bonbons, gâteaux etc

▶ **tuck away** VT SEP *(put away)* ranger; *(hide)* cacher, mettre de côté; **he tucked it away in his bag** il l'a rangé dans son sac; **village tucked away in the valley** village blotti au fond de la vallée; **you are** *ou* **your house is a bit tucked away** vous êtes *ou* votre maison est un peu à l'écart; **to have some money tucked away** avoir de l'argent de côté; *Fam* **she really can t. it away!** *(eat a lot)* qu'est-ce qu'elle peut bouffer!; *Ftbl Fam* **he tucked it away nicely** *(scored)* il l'envoya dans les filets

▶ **tuck in** VT SEP *(put in, under)* rentrer; **to t. one's shirt in** rentrer sa chemise dans son pantalon; **to t. in the bedclothes** border le lit; **to t. sb in** border qn

VI *Fam (eat heartily)* manger à belles dents; **t. in!** allez-y!, mangez!

▶ **tuck into** VT INSEP *Fam (eat heartily) (meal)* manger de bon appétit, avaler; **here, t. into this** allez, attaque!

▶ **tuck up** VT SEP **1** *(one's skirt, sleeves)* relever, retrousser **2** *(somebody) (in bed)* border

tucker ['tʌkər] N **1** *Fam* **in one's best bib and t.** endimanché **2** *esp Austr Fam (food)* bouffe *f*

VT *esp Am Fam (tire out)* fatiguer; **tuckered (out)** épuisé, éreinté

tuck-in N *Fam* **to have a good t.** *(eating session)* s'envoyer un bon repas

Tudor ['tjuːdər] N **the Tudors** la maison des Tudors

ADJ des Tudors; *Archit* **T. house** maison *f* de style Tudor, maison élisabéthaine

▶▶ *Archit* **T. style** style *m* Tudor *ou* élisabéthain

Tue(s) *abbr* **Tuesday**

Tuesday ['tjuːzdɪ] N mardi *m*; **T. 30 April** mardi 30 avril; **T. morning/evening** mardi matin/soir; **it's T. today** nous sommes mardi aujourd'hui; **on Tuesdays** il vient le mardi; **she's coming on T.** elle vient mardi; **every T.** tous les mardis VOIR GRAMMAIRE A81–2; B61–2

tufa ['t(j)uːfə] N *Geol* tuf *m* calcaire

tuft [tʌft] N *(of grass, feathers, hair)* touffe *f*, *(small beard)* barbiche *f*, *(of bird)* huppe *f*, aigrette *f*, **t. of bristles** *(in brush)* loquet *m* de soies

tufted ['tʌftɪd] ADJ *(bird)* huppé

▶▶ **t. duck** *(fuligule f)* morillon *m*; **t. heron** héron *m* à aigrette, aigrette *f*

tug [tʌg] N **1** *(pull)* **to give sth a t.** tirer sur qch d'un coup sec; **to give a good t.** tirer fort; **he gave a t. at the bell** il a tiré *(sur)* la sonnette; **I felt a t. at my sleeve** j'ai senti qu'on me tirait par la manche; *Fig* **to feel a t. at one's heartstrings** avoir un serrement de cœur **2** *(boat)* remorqueur *m*

VI **(-gg-) to t. at** *(door, handle, sleeve, one's moustache)* tirer sur; *(sb's ear)* tirer

VT **1** *(door, handle, sleeve, one's moustache)* tirer sur; *(sb's ear)* tirer **2** *Naut (ship)* remorquer

▶▶ *Journ Fam* **t. of love** lutte *f* d'un couple pour la garde d'un/des enfant(s); **t. of war** *Sport* lutte *f* de traction à la corde; *Fig* lutte acharnée et prolongée

tugboat ['tʌgbəʊt] N remorqueur *m*

tuition [tjuː'ɪʃən] N instruction *f*, enseignement *m*; **maths t., t. in maths** enseignement en mathématiques; **private t.** leçons *fpl* particulières

tulip ['tjuːlɪp] N tulipe *f*

▶▶ **t. glass** *(verre m)* tulipe *f*; **t. tree** tulipier *m*

tulle [tjuːl] N *Tex* tulle *m*

---

tum [tʌm] N *(in children's language), Fam* ventre *m*

tumble ['tʌmb(ə)l] N *(fall)* chute *f*, *(head over heels)* culbute *f*; **to take a t.** tomber, faire la culbute; *(off horse, bike)* faire une chute; **she had a nasty t.** elle a fait une mauvaise chute; *Fig* **the party's popularity took a t.** le parti a beaucoup perdu de sa popularité; **prices have taken a bit of a t.** les prix ont chuté

VI *(fall)* tomber (par terre), faire une chute; *(head over heels)* culbuter, faire la culbute; *(of acrobat)* faire des culbutes; *Fig (of prices)* chuter; **to t. down the stairs** *(fall)* tomber dans les escaliers; *(rush)* descendre les escaliers quatre à quatre; **to t. into bed** se jeter dans son lit; **to t. out of bed** tomber du lit; **they were tumbling over one another** ils se bousculaient

VT **1 they tumbled the snowball down the hill** ils ont fait débouler la boule de neige dans la pente **2** *(clothes) (in tumble dryer)* mettre dans le sèche-linge **3** *Fam (make love to)* culbuter **4** *Fam (get wise to) (person)* démasquer

▶ **tumble about** VI *(of children, kittens)* gambader

▶ **tumble down** VI *(of wall etc)* s'écrouler; **the wall came tumbling down** le mur s'est écroulé; **building that is tumbling down** édifice qui s'écroule *ou* qui tombe en ruine

▶ **tumble out** VI **the suitcase came open and everything tumbled out** la valise s'est ouverte et tout est tombé par terre; **the van doors flew open and the children came tumbling out** les portes de la camionnette se sont ouvertes et les enfants se sont rués à l'extérieur

▶ **tumble to** VT INSEP *Fam (understand)* piger; **eventually she tumbled to it** elle a fini par piger

tumbledown ['tʌmb(ə)ldaʊn] ADJ *(house)* qui tombe en ruine(s)

tumble-drier N sèche-linge *m inv*

tumble-dry VT *(clothes)* faire sécher au sèche-linge

tumbler ['tʌmblər] N **1** *(glass)* verre *m (sans pied)* **2** *(of lock)* gorge *f*, *Elec (of switch etc)* culbuteur *m* **3** *(pigeon)* (pigeon *m*) culbutant *m* **4** *(toy)* poussa(h) *m* **5** *(acrobat)* acrobate *mf* **6** *(tumble-drier)* sèche-linge *m inv*

▶▶ **t. lock** serrure *f* à gorge(s); **t. pigeon** (pigeon *m*) culbutant

tumblerful ['tʌmbləfʊl] N plein verre *m* (**of** de)

tumbleweed ['tʌmb(ə)lwiːd] N herbes *fpl* roulées par le vent

tumbrel ['tʌmbrəl], **tumbril** ['tʌmbrɪl] N *Hist* charrette *f* (des condamnés)

tumefaction [tjuːmɪ'fækʃən] N tuméfaction *f*

tumefy ['tjuːmɪfaɪ] VT tuméfier

VI se tuméfier

tumescent [tjuː'mesənt] ADJ tumescent

tumid ['tjuːmɪd] ADJ **1** *Med* enflé, gonflé **2** *(style etc)* ronflant

tummy ['tʌmɪ] N *Fam* ventre *m*; **to have t. trouble** avoir l'estomac dérangé

▶▶ **t. ache** mal *m* de ventre; *Br* **t. button** nombril *m*

tumour, *Am* **tumor** ['tjuːmər] N *Med* tumeur *f*

tumult ['tjuːmʌlt] N tumulte *m*; *(of emotions)* trouble *m*, émoi *m*; **the t. of his emotions** son trouble; **to be in a t.** *(of person)* être en émoi; *(of country)* être agité; **her emotions were in a t.** elle était en émoi

tumultuous [tjɔ'mʌltjʊəs] ADJ tumultueux; **t. meeting** réunion *f* orageuse; **t. session** séance *f* mouvementée

tumultuously [tjɔ'mʌltjʊəslɪ] ADV tumultueusement

---

tumulus, *pl* **tumuli** ['tjuːmjʊləs, -aɪ] N tumulus *m*

tun [tʌn] N *(liquid measure)* tonneau *m*, fût *m*; *(vat) (in brewing)* cuve *f*

tuna ['tjuːnə] N *(fish)* thon *m*

tundra ['tʌndrə] N *Geog* toundra *f*

tune [tjuːn] N **1** *Mus (melody)* air *m*, mélodie *f*, *Fam* **give us a t.!** faites-nous un peu de musique!, jouez-nous un air!; **it's got no t.** il n'y a pas de mélodie; *Fig* **to call the t.** commander; **to the t. of the Marseillaise** sur l'air de la Marseillaise; *Fig* **to change one's t.** changer de discours; *Fig* **to be fined to the t. of £50** avoir une amende de 50 livres

2 the piano is in/out of t. le piano est accordé/désaccordé; **to get out of t.** se désaccorder; **to be out of t.** *(of singer, player)* chanter/jouer faux, détonner; **to sing in/out of t.** chanter juste/faux; **the trumpet isn't in t.** *or* **is out of t. with the other instruments** la trompette n'est pas en harmonie *ou* en accord avec les autres instruments; *Fig* **to be in t. with sb/with one's surroundings** être en harmonie avec qn/avec son milieu; *Fig* **the government's out of t. with public opinion** le gouvernement n'est pas en harmonie avec l'opinion publique; **perfectly in t.** *(of engine)* parfaitement réglé

VT **1** *Mus (instrument)* accorder; **to t. a string to …** accorder une corde sur …

2 *(radio)* régler; **to t. one's radio/TV to a station** régler son poste de radio/télévision sur une station/chaîne; *Radio, TV* **stay tuned (to this station/channel)** restez avec nous

3 *Aut etc (engine)* régler; **to be tuned** *(of engine)* être bien réglé

VI *Mus* **to t. to a note** s'accorder sur une note

▶ **tune in** VI *esp Radio* **don't forget to t. in again tomorrow** n'oubliez pas de nous rejoindre *ou* de vous mettre à l'écoute demain; **to t. in to a station/programme** se brancher sur *ou* mettre une station *ou* TV une chaîne/ une émission

▶ **tune up** VI *Mus (get in tune) (of orchestra)* s'accorder

VT SEP *Aut etc* = **tune** VT **3**

tuned-in [tjuːnd-] ADJ *Sl (aware)* branché; **she's very t. to other people's needs** elle est toujours consciente des besoins des gens

tuneful ['tjuːnfʊl] ADJ mélodieux, harmonieux

tunefully ['tjuːnfəlɪ] ADV mélodieusement

tunefulness ['tjuːnfʊlnɪs] N qualité *f* mélodieuse

tuneless ['tjuːnlɪs] ADJ *(unpleasant)* discordant; *(without melody)* sans mélodie

tuner ['tjuːnər] N **1** *Mus (person) (of pianos etc)* accordeur *m* **2** *Radio etc* tuner *m*, syntoniseur *m*

tune-up N *(of engine)* mise *f* au point

tungsten ['tʌŋstən] N *Chem* tungstène *m*

▶▶ **t. steel** acier *m* au tungstène

tungsten-halogen N tungstène-halogène *m*

▶▶ **t. lamp** lampe *f* tungstène-halogène, lampe au tungstène

tunic ['tjuːnɪk] N tunique *f*

tuning ['tjuːnɪŋ] N **1** *Mus* accord *m*; **fine t.** accord précis **2** *Aut etc* réglage *m*, *(re)*mise *f* au point **3** *Radio, TV* réglage *m*

▶▶ **t. fork** diapason *m*; **t. hammer** accordoir *m*, clef *f* d'accordeur

Tunisia [tjuːˈnɪzɪə] N Tunisie *f*

Tunisian [tjuːˈnɪzɪən] ADJ tunisien

N Tunisien, -ienne

tunnel ['tʌn(ə)l] N tunnel *m*; *(dug by mole etc)* galerie *f*, **to drive a t. through a mountain** percer un tunnel à travers *ou* sous une montagne; *Fig* **at last we can see (some** *or* **the) light at the end of the t.** enfin on voit le bout du tunnel; **is there light at the end of the t.?** est-ce qu'un jour on verra le bout du tunnel?; *Tech etc* **wind t.** tunnel aérodynamique, soufflerie *f* (aérodynamique)

VI (-ll-, *Am* -l-) creuser *ou* percer un tunnel; **to t. through into a hill** percer un tunnel à travers *ou* dans *ou* sous une colline; **rats had tunnelled under the foundations** des rats avaient creusé des galeries sous les fondations

VT to t. one's way out (of sth) creuser un tunnel pour s'échapper (de qch)

▸▸**t. net** verveux *m*; **t. vision** *Opt* rétrécissement *m* du champ visuel; *Fig* esprit *m* borné; *Fig* **to suffer from t. vision** avoir une vision limitée des choses, avoir des œillères

tunnelling, *Am* **tunneling** ['tʌn(ə)lɪŋ] **N** percement *m* d'un tunnel/de tunnels

▸▸**t. equipment** équipement *m* pour le percement d'un tunnel

tunny ['tʌnɪ] **N** thon *m*

▸▸**t. fish** thon

tuppence ['tʌp(ə)ns] **N** *Old-fashioned Br Fam* = **twopence**

tuppenny ['tʌpənɪ] **ADJ** *Old-fashioned Br Fam* = **twopenny; t. halfpenny** = **twopenny-halfpenny**

turban ['tɜːbən] **N** turban *m*

turbid ['tɜːbɪd] **ADJ 1** *(liquid)* trouble, bourbeux **2** *Fig Lit (thoughts)* embrouillé

turbidity [tɜːˈbɪdɪtɪ] **N** turbidité *f*

turbine ['tɜːbaɪn] **N** turbine *f*, **gas/steam t.** turbine à gaz/à vapeur

▸▸**t. engine** turbomoteur *m*

turbo ['tɜːbəʊ] **N** turbo *m*

▸▸*Comput* **t. button** bouton *m* de turbo; *Aut* **t. diesel** turbodiesel *m*; **t. diesel engine** moteur *m* turbodiesel

turbocharged ['tɜːbəʊtʃɑːdʒd] **ADJ** turbocompressé

▸▸**t. engine** moteur *m* turbocompressé

turbocharger ['tɜːbəʊtʃɑːdʒər] **N** turbocompresseur *m*, turbo *m*

turbocharging ['tɜːbəʊtʃɑːdʒɪŋ] **N** suralimentation *f* par turbocompresseur

turbo-electric **ADJ** turbo-électrique

turbofan ['tɜːbəʊfæn] **N** *Aviat* turboréacteur *m* à double flux

turbogenerator [tɜːbəʊˈdʒenəreɪtər] **N** *Elec* turbogénérateur *m*, turbogénératrice *f*

turbojet ['tɜːbəʊdʒet] **N** *(aircraft)* avion *m* à turbopropulseur; *(engine)* turboréacteur *m* *(à simple flux)*

▸▸**t. aircraft** avion à turbopropulseur; **t. engine** turboréacteur *(à simple flux)*

turbomarketing ['tɜːbəʊˈmɑːkɪtɪŋ] **N** *Mktg* turbo-marketing *m*

turboprop ['tɜːbəʊprɒp] **N** *(aircraft)* avion *m* à turbopropulseur; *(engine)* turbopropulseur *m*

▸▸**t. aircraft** avion à turbopropulseur; **t. engine** turbopropulseur

turbo-supercharger **N** turbocompresseur *m*

turbot ['tɜːbət] **N** *(fish)* turbot *m*

turbulence ['tɜːbjʊləns] **N** agitation *f*, *Met, Aviat* turbulences *fpl*

turbulent ['tɜːbjʊlənt] **ADJ** *(crowd)* agité, *Met, Aviat* turbulent

turbulently ['tɜːbjʊləntlɪ] **ADV** d'une manière turbulente

turd [tɜːd] **N** *Sl* **1** *(piece of excrement)* étron *m* **2** *(person)* con *m*, conne *f*

tureen [tjʊəˈriːn] **N** soupière *f*

turf *pl* **turves, turfs** [tɜːf, tɜːvz, tɜːfs] **N** *(grass-covered earth)* gazon *m*; *(piece)* motte *f* de

gazon; *Sl (territory)* territoire *m*; *Sl* **that's not my t.** c'est pas mon rayon; *Horseracing* **the t.** le turf, les courses *fpl* de chevaux

VT 1 *(area)* gazonner **2** *Br Fam (throw)* balancer

▸▸*Br Formal* **t. accountant** bookmaker *m*; **t. cutting** extraction *f* de la tourbe; **t. war** conflit *m* pour le contrôle d'un territoire

▸ **turf out** **VT SEP** *Br Fam (eject) (person)* virer; *(throw away) (thing)* foutre en l'air, bazarder; *(reject) (plan etc)* rejeter

▸ **turf over** **VT SEP** *(ground)* gazonner

turgid ['tɜːdʒɪd] **ADJ 1** *(swollen)* enflé, gonflé, *Lit* turgide **2** *(style etc)* boursouflé, ampoulé

turgidly ['tɜːdʒɪdlɪ] **ADV** *(written etc)* emphatiquement, pompeusement

Turin Shroud [tjʊəˈrɪn] **N the T.** le Saint-suaire

Turk [tɜːk] **N** Turc *m*, Turque *f*, *esp Pol* **young T.** jeune turc

Turkey ['tɜːkɪ] **N** Turquie *f*

turkey ['tɜːkɪ] **N 1** *(bird)* dindon *m*, dinde *f*, *Culin* dinde, dindonneau *m*; **hen t.** dinde **2** *esp Am Fam* **to talk t.** parler franchement; *Sl* **cold t.** état *m* de manque de drogue(s) **3** *esp Am Sl (failed play, film)* bide *m*, four *m*; *(ineffectual person)* abruti, -ie, crétin, -ine

▸▸**t. buzzard** vautour *m* aura; **t. cock** dindon *m*; *Fam Fig* crâneur, -euse

Turkish ['tɜːkɪʃ] **ADJ** turc, *f* turque

N *Ling* turc *m*

▸▸**T. bath** bain *m* turc; **T. delight** loukoum *m*; **T. towel** serviette éponge

Turkmenistan [tɜːkmenɪˈstɑːn] **N** le Turkménistan

turmeric ['tɜːmərɪk] **N** curcuma *m*

turmoil ['tɜːmɔɪl] **N** trouble *m*, tumulte *m*, agitation *f*, *(of rushing water)* remous *m*; **to be in a t.** *(of country, house)* être en ébullition; *(of person)* être agité; **the whole town is in (a) t.** toute la ville est agitée *ou* est en ébullition; **my mind was in a t.** la confusion régnait dans mon esprit

---

TURN [tɜːn]

N tour **1, 2, 5, 7** ▪ changement de direction **2** ▪ virage **2** ▪ tournant **2** ▪ tournure **2, 9** ▪ choc **3** ▪ crise **4** ▪ numéro **6** ▪ service **7**	
VT tourner **1–5, 8** ▪ retourner **2** ▪ diriger **4** ▪ changer **6** ▪ transformer **6** ▪ faire devenir **7**	
VI tourner **1, 4** ▪ se retourner **2, 3** ▪ se diriger **4** ▪ devenir **6**	

N 1 *(revolution) (of wheel)* tour *m*, révolution *f*; **with a t. of the wrist** avec un tour de poignet; **the meat is done to a t.** la viande est cuite à point

2 *(act of changing direction)* changement *m* de direction; *Ski* virage *m*; *(in path etc)* tournant *m*; *(of rope)* tour *m*; *(of spiral)* tour, spire *f*, *Aut* **the next t. on the left** la prochaine (rue/route) à gauche; *Aut* **no right/left t.** défense de tourner à droite/à gauche; **sharp t.** virage serré; **twists and turns** tours et détours *mpl*, *(of events)* tournure *f*, U **t.** demi-tour *m*, *pl* demi-tours; **three-point t.** demi-tour en trois manœuvres; *Fig* **at every t.** à tout bout de champ; **to take a tragic t.** *(of events)* tourner au tragique; **to take an unexpected t.** *(of events, conversation etc)* prendre une tournure que l'on n'aurait pas imaginée; **to take a t. for the better/worse** *(of situation etc)* s'améliorer/se détériorer; **the patient has taken a t. for the better/the worse** l'état du malade s'est amélioré/a empiré; **the t. of the tide** le changement *ou* renversement de la marée; *Fig* le renversement de tendances; **the milk is on the t.** le lait est en train de commencer à tourner; **at**

the t. of the century au tournant du siècle

3 *Fam (surprise, shock)* choc *m*, coup *m*; **it gave me quite a t.** ça m'a fait un coup; **you gave me such a t.!** vous m'avez fait une belle peur!

4 *Med Fam* **she had one of her turns** elle a eu une de ses crises *ou* attaques

5 *(short walk)* tour *m*, petite promenade *f*, **to take a t. in the garden** faire un tour *ou* quelques pas dans le jardin

6 *(at activity)* tour *m*; *Br Theat (in variety show etc)* numéro *m*; **whose t. is it?** c'est à qui le tour?; **it's your t.** *(in game)* c'est votre tour, c'est à vous (de jouer); **to take turns with sb** se relayer avec qn; **they take it in turns to drive** ils se relaient au volant; **each in (his) t., t. and t. about** chacun son tour; **to do sth t. and t. about** faire qch à tour de rôle; **in t.** *(alternately)* tour à tour, à tour de rôle; **they, in t., contributed food** pour leur part, ils donnèrent de la nourriture; **she was by turns optimistic and downcast** elle était tour à tour optimiste et déprimée; **to speak out of t.** parler mal à propos

7 *(service)* **to do sb a good t.** rendre (un) service à qn; **to do sb a bad t.** jouer un mauvais tour à qn; *Prov* **one good t. deserves another** à beau jeu beau retour, un service en vaut un autre

8 *Old-fashioned (purpose)* **it will serve my t.** cela fera mon affaire (pour le moment)

9 *(style etc)* **t. of mind** tournure *f* d'esprit; **humorous t. of mind** esprit *m* humoristique; **t. of phrase** tournure de phrase; **to have a good t. of speed** être rapide; *(of horse)* être capable de fournir un effort à grande allure

VT 1 *(wheel, handle etc)* (faire) tourner; *(steering wheel)* braquer; *(key in lock)* (faire) tourner, faire jouer; *Fig* **to t. the knife in the wound** retourner le fer *ou* le couteau dans la plaie

2 *(page etc)* tourner; *(mattress, hay etc)* retourner; **to t. a garment inside out** retourner un vêtement; **to t. everything upside down** mettre tout sens dessus dessous; *Fam* **he didn't t. a hair** il n'a pas bronché *ou* sourcillé; **the sight/story turned my stomach** ce spectacle/l'histoire m'a soulevé le cœur

3 *(direct)* **she turned her steps towards home** elle a dirigé ses pas vers la maison; **he never turned anyone from his door** il n'a jamais fermé sa porte à personne; **to t. one's thoughts to God** tourner ses pensées vers Dieu; **to t. one's attention to ...** tourner son attention vers *ou* sur ...; **to t. the conversation to ...** orienter la conversation vers ...

4 *(head)* tourner; *(gaze)* tourner, diriger *(towards* vers); **t. your face this way** regardez de ce côté; **t. your desk this way** tournez votre bureau dans cette direction

5 *(go round)* **to t. the corner** tourner au coin de la rue; *Fig* passer le moment critique; **she's turned forty** elle a quarante ans passés, elle a passé la quarantaine; **it's turned seven** il est sept heures passées

6 *(change)* transformer, changer *(into* en); **to t. water into wine** changer l'eau en vin; **his love has been turned to hate** son amour s'est changé *ou* s'est transformé en haine; **to t. a theatre into a cinema** convertir un théâtre en cinéma; **the witch turned him into a crow** la sorcière l'a transformé en corbeau; **we've turned the attic into a study** nous avons transformé *ou* converti le grenier en bureau

7 *(cause to become)* faire devenir; **the heat has turned the milk sour** la chaleur a fait tourner le lait; **autumn turns the leaves yellow** l'automne fait jaunir les feuilles; **to t. sth green/black** rendre qch vert/noir, verdir/noircir qch; **the blood turned the water red** le sang a rougi l'eau; **Angus MacKinnon, athlete turned journalist** Angus MacKinnon, athlète reconverti dans le journalisme; **success has turned her head** le succès lui a tourné la tête

8 *(make on lathe) (table leg etc)* tourner, façonner au tour; *Fig* **a well turned sentence** une phrase bien tournée; *Knitting* **to t. a heel** faire le talon

vi 1 *(rotate)* tourner; **to t. a complete circle** faire un tour complet; **the steering wheel won't t.** le volant ne tourne pas; **my head's turning** la tête me tourne

2 to toss and t. *(in bed)* se tourner et se retourner (dans son lit); **to t. upside down** se retourner

3 *(turn head, turn round)* se retourner; **he turned to look at the landscape** il s'est retourné pour regarder le paysage; **she turned to me – what do you think?** elle se tourna vers moi – qu'est-ce que tu en penses, toi?; *Mil* **right t.!** à droite!; **left t.!** à gauche!

4 *(change direction)* tourner, se diriger; **to t. to the right/the left** *(of person, path etc)* tourner à droite/à gauche; **he turned towards home** il s'est dirigé vers la maison; **the wind is turning** le vent tourne; **my thoughts often t. to this subject** mes réflexions se portent souvent sur ce sujet; **to t. to another subject** passer à une autre question; **the tide is turning** la marée change; **her luck has turned** sa chance a tourné

5 *(for help)* **to t. to sb** *(for help/advice)* s'adresser à qn (pour obtenir de l'aide/des conseils); **I didn't know who to t. to** je ne savais pas à qui m'adresser; **to t. to the dictionary** consulter le dictionnaire; **I don't know where** *or* **which way to t.** je ne sais pas à quel saint me vouer

6 *(change)* devenir, se transformer (**into** en); **caterpillars t. into butterflies** la chenille se métamorphose en papillon; **she's turned into a very hard-headed businesswoman** c'est devenue une femme d'affaires très réaliste; **everything he touches turns to gold** tout ce qu'il touche se change en or; **to t. (sour)** *(of milk)* tourner; *Fig* **to t. sour** tourner au vinaigre; **it's turning cold** il commence à faire froid; **the crowd turned nasty** la foule est devenue agressive; **the leaves are beginning to t.** les feuilles commencent à jaunir; **he turned red** il a rougi; **to t. red/blue** virer au rouge/bleu; **to t. sulky** devenir maussade; **to t. socialist** devenir socialiste

▸ **turn against vt insep** se retourner contre; **vt sep** *(make opposed to)* retourner contre; **she turns everyone against her** elle se met tout le monde à dos; **they turned his argument against him** ils ont retourné son argument contre lui

▸ **turn around vi, vt sep = turn round**

▸ **turn aside vi** se retourner; **to t. aside from the path of righteousness** se détourner du droit chemin

vt sep to t. aside a blow détourner *ou* faire dévier un coup

▸ **turn away vt sep 1** *(direct elsewhere) (head, gaze)* détourner; **police were turning drivers/people away (from the scene of the accident)** la police détournait *ou* écartait les automobilistes/les gens (du lieu de l'accident)

2 *(refuse entry, help etc to) (of hospital, hotel etc)* refuser; **to t. sb away in their hour of need** refuser de venir en aide à qn; *Theat etc* **to t. people away** refuser du monde; **we've been turning business away** nous avons refusé du travail

vi *(look away)* se détourner, détourner son regard; *(go away)* s'écarter; **to t. away from sb** *(turn one's back on)* tourner le dos à qn; *(abandon)* délaisser *ou* abandonner qn

▸ **turn back vi 1** *(return in same direction)* rebrousser chemin, faire demi-tour; *Fig*

there's no turning back now on ne peut plus faire marche arrière maintenant

2 *(in book)* **t. back to page …** revenez à la page …

vt sep 1 *(of person) (cause to return in same direction)* faire faire demi-tour à, faire revenir sur ses pas; **the refugees were turned back at the border** les réfugiés ont été refoulés à la frontière

2 *(fold) (sheets)* replier

3 *(adjust to earlier time) (watch etc)* retarder; **to t. the clocks back an hour** retarder les pendules d'une heure; *Fig* **you can't t. the clock back** on ne peut pas revenir en arrière *ou* revivre le passé

▸ **turn down vt sep 1** *(fold down) (collar)* rabattre; *(page of book)* plier, corner; **to t. down the bed** ouvrir le lit

2 *(reduce) (heat, sound etc)* baisser; **to t. down the TV/radio** baisser le son de la télé/radio

3 *(refuse, reject) (offer)* repousser, rejeter; *(candidate, claim etc)* refuser; **I've been turned down for that job** je n'ai pas été accepté pour cet emploi; **she turned me down flat** elle a refusé catégoriquement, *Fam* elle m'a envoyé promener; **they offered him a job but he turned them down** ils lui ont proposé un emploi mais il a rejeté leur offre

▸ **turn in vt sep 1 to t. one's toes** tourner les pieds en dedans

2 *Fam (hand in) (object)* rendre, rapporter *(à la police)*; *(betray to police) (person)* livrer *ou* vendre à la police

3 *Fam (give up) (one's job)* quitter, abandonner

4 *Sport, Theat* **to t. in a good score/performance** faire un bon score/une belle performance

vi 1 *(point inwards)* **his toes t. in** il a les pieds tournés en dedans

2 *(go through entrance off road etc)* **he turned in at the gate** arrivé à la porte, il est entré

3 *Fam* **I think I'll t. in (for the night)** *(go to bed)* je crois que je vais aller me pieuter

▸ **turn off vt sep 1** *(switch off) (water, tap, gas, electricity)* fermer; *(light, radio, TV etc)* éteindre

2 *Fam (take away enthusiasm from)* rebuter, refroidir; *(sexually)* couper l'envie à

vi 1 *(leave road, street)* changer de route; **I turned off to the left** j'ai pris (la route/la rue) à gauche, j'ai tourné à gauche; **he turned off onto the motorway** il s'est engagé sur l'autoroute

2 *(of heater etc)* se fermer

vt insep we turned off the main road nous avons quitté la grande route; **a small street turning off the High Street** une petite rue qui part de la rue principale

▸ **turn on vt sep 1** *(switch on) (water, tap, gas, electricity)* ouvrir; *(light, radio, TV etc)* allumer; **shall I t. on the light?** voulez-vous que j'allume?

2 *Fam (excite)* brancher; *(sexually)* exciter; **she turned me on to Zen Buddhism** elle m'a branché sur le bouddhisme zen

vt insep 1 *(attack physically or verbally)* s'attaquer à

2 *(depend on)* reposer sur, dépendre de; **everything turns on your answer** tout dépend de votre réponse

vi *(of heater etc)* se mettre en route *ou* en marche

▸ **turn out vt sep 1** *(eject)* mettre *ou Fam* flanquer à la porte; *(tenant)* déloger, évincer; *(cattle)* mettre au vert; *Naut (men)* réveiller; *Mil (troops)* alerter

2 *(empty) (pockets etc)* vider, retourner; *Culin (dessert etc)* démouler; **to t. out a drawer** *(empty)* vider un tiroir; *(empty and tidy)* mettre de l'ordre dans un tiroir; **to t. out a room** nettoyer une pièce à fond

3 *(switch off) (gas)* couper, éteindre; *(light)* éteindre

4 *(produce) (goods)* produire, fabriquer; **the factory turns them out by the thousand** l'usine en fabrique par milliers; **the sort of students that we aim to t. out here** le type d'étudiants que nous voulons former ici

5 well turned out *(person)* élégant, soigné

6 *(point outwards)* **to t. one's toes out** tourner les pieds en dehors

vi 1 *(attend) (to see parade, hear speech etc)* assister; *(of voters)* aller aux urnes; **the doctor/fire brigade had to t. out in the middle of the night** le docteur/les pompiers a/ont dû se déplacer au milieu de la nuit; **the whole town turned out to see it** toute la ville est allée le voir; **not many people turned out for his funeral/the march** il n'est pas venu beaucoup de monde à son enterrement/à la manifestation

2 *(point outwards)* **his toes t. out** il a les pieds tournés en dehors

3 *(end)* **to t. out well/badly** bien/mal tourner; **it'll t. out all right** ça s'arrangera; **how did the cake t. out?** le gâteau était-il réussi?; **I don't know how it will t. out** je ne sais pas comment cela finira; **as it turned out** en l'occurrence; **she's turned out (to be) beautiful** elle est devenue une belle femme/jeune fille

4 *(transpire)* **he turned out to be the son of an old friend of mine** il s'est trouvé qu'il était le fils d'un de mes anciens amis; **she turned out to be a real idiot** elle s'est avérée une vraie gourde; **it turns out that …** il se trouve que …; **as it turns out, we would have had time** en fait, nous aurions eu le temps

5 *Fam (get out of bed)* se lever, sortir du lit

▸ **turn over vt sep 1** *(turn)* retourner; *(page)* tourner; **to t. over the pages of a book** feuilleter un livre; **to t. over the body** over elle a retourné le corps; *Agr* **to t. over the soil** retourner la terre; **to t. an idea/a plan over (in one's mind)** retourner une idée/un projet dans sa tête; **if you want a bit of time to t. it over …** *(idea, offer etc)* si vous avez besoin d'un peu de temps pour y réfléchir …; *Fig* **to t. over a new leaf** tourner la page

2 *(surrender)* **to t. sth over to sb** remettre qch entre les mains de qn; **the thief was turned over to the police** on a remis le voleur entre les mains de la police

3 *(of business)* rapporter; **he must be turning over a good £1,000 a week** il doit gagner *ou Fam* se faire au moins 1 000 livres par semaine

4 *Sl (rob) (shop)* dévaliser; *(cheat)* rouler

vi 1 *(change position by turning)* se tourner, se retourner; **to t. over in bed** se retourner dans son lit; **to t. (right) over** *(of car etc)* capoter

2 *TV (change channel)* changer de chaîne

3 *(in reading)* tourner la page

4 *(of engine)* tourner au ralenti

▸ **turn round vi** *(rotate)* tourner; *(of crane etc)* tourner, pivoter; *(face other way) (of person)* se retourner; *(of vehicle)* tourner; *(abruptly)* faire volte-face; *(in one's opinions etc)* tourner casaque, virer de bord; **she turned round in her chair** elle se retourna sur sa chaise; **t. round and let me see your face** tournez-vous (un peu) que je voie votre visage; **he just turned round and hit me** tout d'un coup il s'est retourné et m'a frappé; **after eight years of marriage she turned round and said she was leaving** après huit années de mariage elle annonça soudain qu'elle partait

vt sep 1 *(move to face other way)* retourner; **she turned the chair round** elle retourna la chaise; **she turned the car round** elle a fait demi-tour

2 *(reverse) (bad situation)* renverser, retourner; **to t. the economy/a company round** re-

mettre l'économie/une entreprise sur pied **3** *Com (process, deal with) (order)* traiter, s'occuper de
VT INSEP *(go around) (corner)* tourner
▸ **turn up** **VI 1** *(arrive)* arriver, se présenter; **he turned up ten minutes late** il est arrivé *ou Fam* s'est amené dix minutes en retard; **she turned up at the party with a new boyfriend** elle est arrivée *ou Fam* a débarqué à la soirée avec un nouveau petit ami; **he'll t. up one of these days** il reparaîtra un de ces jours
2 I'm sure your keys will t. up *(be found)* je suis sûr qu'on retrouvera tes clés; **it's bound to t. up** il finira bien par réapparaître; **the pen turned up in his jacket** on a retrouvé le stylo dans sa veste; *Fig* **something is sure to t. up** il se présentera sûrement une occasion; **until something better turns up** en attendant mieux
3 *(turn upwards)* rebiquer; **her nose turns up** elle a le nez retroussé
VT SEP 1 *(fold upwards) (collar)* relever; *(sleeves, trouser legs)* retrousser; *(to shorten)* raccourcir en faisant un ourlet; **she turned her nose up at the job** elle a refusé l'emploi avec dédain; **don't t. your nose up like that** *(at food)* arrête de faire le dégoûté
2 *(uncover) (card)* retourner
3 *(find)* trouver; **the investigation has failed to t. up any new information** l'enquête n'a apporté aucun élément nouveau
4 *(increase, make louder etc)* augmenter; *(gas)* monter; **to t. the radio/radiator up** mettre la radio/le radiateur plus fort
5 *Br Sl* **t. it up!** *(stop that)* c'est fini, oui!

---

turnabout ['tɜːnəbaʊt] **N** retournement *m*, revirement *m*

turnaround ['tɜːnəraʊnd] **N** *(of situation, opinion)* retournement *m*, revirement *m*; *(of ship, aeroplane etc)* rotation *f*; *Com (of an order)* traitement *m*; *Com* **they offer a faster t.** leurs délais sont plus courts
▸▸ **t. time** *(for order)* délai *m* de livraison; *(of ferry, plane)* temps *m* de rotation

turncoat ['tɜːnkəʊt] **N** *Pol etc* renégat *m*

turndown ['tɜːndaʊn] **ADJ** *(collar etc)* rabattu
▸▸ **t. housekeeper** *(in hotel)* gouvernante *f* du soir

turned-up ['tɜːndʌp] **ADJ** *(collar etc)* relevé; *(nose)* retroussé

turner ['tɜːnər] **N** *Ind* tourneur *m*

turnery ['tɜːnərɪ] **N** atelier *m* de tourneur

turning ['tɜːnɪŋ] **N 1 the t. of the tide** le changement *ou* renversement de la marée; *Fig* le renversement de tendances **2** *(off road etc)* tournant *m*; **the first t. on the right** la première route/rue à droite; *Prov* **it's a long road that has no t.** après la pluie le beau temps **3** *(on lathe)* tournage *m*, travail *m* au tour
▸▸ *Br Aut* **t. circle** rayon *m* de braquage; **t. point** *(decisive moment)* moment *m* décisif; *(change)* tournant; **at the t. point of her career** au tournant de sa carrière

turnip ['tɜːnɪp] **N** *(plant, vegetable)* navet *m*; *Hum (pocket watch)* montre *f* de poche *ou* de gousset

turnkey ['tɜːnkiː] **N** *Arch (jailer)* geôlier, -ière
▸▸ **t. plant** usine *f* clés en main; **t. project** projet *m* clés en main; *Comput* **t. system** système *m* clés en main

turn-off **N 1** *(on motorway etc)* sortie *f*, embranchement *m*; **the Leeds t.** la sortie pour Leeds **2** *Sl* **it's a t.** *(boring)* c'est d'un ennui mortel; *(sexually)* c'est dégoûtant; **it's a t. for me** *(sexually)* cela me coupe l'envie

turn-of-the-century **ADJ** du début du siècle; **t. London** le Londres du début du siècle

turn-on **N** *Sl* **it's/he's a real t.** *(sexually)* c'est/il est vachement excitant; **is that a t.?** ça t'excite?

turnout ['tɜːnaʊt] **N 1** *(people present)* assistance *f*, *(at election)* (taux *m* de) participation *f*; **a good/poor t.** beaucoup/peu de monde; **there was a large** *or* **good t. at his funeral/the wedding/the meeting** il y avait beaucoup de monde à son enterrement/au mariage/à la réunion; **low turnouts at elections** faible participation *f* aux élections **2** *(cleaning) (of room etc)* nettoyage *m* à fond; **to give sth a good t.** nettoyer qch à fond **3** *Ind (production)* production *f*, rendement *m* **4** *(clothes)* tenue *f*

turnover ['tɜːnəʊvər] **N 1** *Fin* chiffre *m* d'affaires, *CA m*; **our annual t.** notre chiffre d'affaires annuel **2** *(of stock)* écoulement *m*, rotation *f*; **t. of capital** roulement *m* de capitaux; **the (staff) t. there is very high** le taux de renouvellement du personnel y est très élevé **3** *Culin* chausson *m*; **apple t.** chausson aux pommes
▸▸ *Com* **t. rate** taux *m* de rotation; *Fin* **t. tax** impôt *m* *ou* taxe *f* sur le chiffre d'affaires

turnpike ['tɜːnpaɪk] **N** *Am (road)* autoroute *f* (à péage); *Hist (barrier)* barrière *f* de péage

turnround ['tɜːnraʊnd] **N** *esp Br* = **turnaround**

turnstile ['tɜːnstaɪl] **N** tourniquet *m*

turntable ['tɜːnteɪb(ə)l] **N 1** *Rail* plaque *f* tournante; *Mil* plate-forme *f* tournante **2** *(of record player)* platine *f*

turn-up **N 1** *Br (on trousers)* revers *m* **2** *Fam* **what a t. (for the book)!** ça c'est une sacrée surprise!

turpentine ['tɜːp(ə)ntaɪn] **N** essence *f* de térébenthine
▸▸ **t. substitute** white-spirit *m*

turpitude ['tɜːpɪtjuːd] **N** *Fml* turpitude *f*

turps [tɜːps] **N** *Br Fam* essence *f* de térébenthine

turquoise ['tɜːkwɔɪz, -kwɑːz] **N 1** *(stone)* turquoise *f*; **t. necklace** collier *m* en turquoise **2** *(colour)* turquoise *m*
ADJ turquoise *inv*

turret ['tʌrɪt] **N** *Archit* tourelle *f*, *Mil, Naut* **(gun) t.** tourelle *f*

turreted ['tʌrɪtɪd] **ADJ** *Archit (castle)* à tourelles

turtle ['tɜːt(ə)l] **N** *(reptile)* tortue *f* de mer
ADV **to turn t.** *(of boat)* chavirer; *(of car)* capoter
▸▸ **t. dove** tourterelle *f* des bois; *Fig* **a pair of t. doves** *(lovers)* un couple d'amoureux *ou* de tourtereaux; **t. neck** col *m* montant; **t. neck(ed) sweater** pull *m* à col montant; *Culin* **t. soup** consommé *m* à la tortue

Tuscan ['tʌskən] **ADJ** *Geog, Archit* toscan
N 1 *(person)* Toscan, -ane **2** *Ling* toscan *m*

Tuscany ['tʌskənɪ] **N** Toscane *f*

tush[1] [tʌʃ] **INT** *Old-fashioned* bah!, tarata!

tush[2] [tʊʃ] **N** *esp Am Fam (buttocks)* derrière *m*

tusk [tʌsk] **N** *(of boar, elephant etc)* défense *f*

tusker ['tʌskər] **N** *(elephant)* pachyderme *m*

tussle ['tʌs(ə)l] **N** empoignade *f*, lutte *f* corps-à-corps; *Fig* lutte, bataille *f*; **to have a t.** en venir aux mains (**with sb** avec qn)
VI **to t. with sb** lutter avec qn; **to t. over sth** se disputer qch

tussock ['tʌsək] **N** touffe *f* d'herbe

tut [tʌt] **INT** **t. (tut)!** allons donc!
VI faire un bruit désapprobateur, émettre une exclamation désapprobatrice; **to t. t. at sb's behaviour** désapprouver la conduite de qn; **don't you t. t. at me!** je me passe de tes commentaires!

tutelage ['tjuːtɪlɪdʒ] **N** tutelle *f*; **to be under sb's t.** être sous la tutelle de qn

tutelar, tutelary ['tjuːtɪlər, -lərɪ] **ADJ** tutélaire

tutor ['tjuːtər] **N 1** *Br Univ* directeur, -trice d'études **2** **private t.** *(in individual subject)* professeur *m* particulier; *(employed on permanent basis)* précepteur *m*; **music t.** professeur de musique **3** *Scot Law (of minor etc)* tuteur, -trice
VT instruire; **to t. a child in French** donner à un enfant des leçons particulières de français

tutorial [tjuː'tɔːrɪəl] **ADJ** *(work etc)* de répétiteur; *Univ* **the t. system** = le système d'enseignement où les étudiant(e)s sont supervisé(e)s par un directeur d'études
N 1 *Br Univ* travaux *mpl* dirigés **2** *Comput* didacticiel *m*
▸▸ *Comput* **t. program** didacticiel

tutti-frutti ['tʊtɪ'frʊtɪ] **N** *Culin* plombières *f*

tutu ['tuːtuː] **N** *(garment)* tutu *m*

tu-whit tu-whoo [tʊ'wɪttə'wuː] **INT** hou hou!

tux [tʌks] **N** *esp Am Fam* smoking *m*

tuxedo [tʌk'siːdəʊ] **N** *esp Am* smoking *m*

TV[1] [tiː'viː] **N** *(abbr* **television)** télé *f*, TV *f*, *(television set)* poste *m* de télévision, téléviseur *m*
▸▸ **TV channel** chaîne *f* de télévision; **TV dinner** plateau-repas *m* surgelé, *pl* plateaux-repas surgelés; **TV lounge** salle *f* de télévision; **TV magazine** hebdo *m* télé; **TV movie** téléfilm *m*; **TV personality** vedette *f* télé; **TV programme** émission *f* de télévision; **TV screen** écran *m* de télévision; **TV set** poste de télévision, téléviseur; **TV station** station *f* de télévision

TV[2] **N** *Sl (abbr* **transvestite)** travelo *m*

TVP [tiːviː'piː] **N** *Culin (abbr* **textured vegetable protein)** protéine *f* végétale texturée

twaddle ['twɒd(ə)l] *Fam* **N** fadaises *fpl*, **to talk t.** dire *ou* débiter des balivernes *ou* des sottises
VI **to t. on about sth** débiter des sottises à propos de qch

twain [tweɪn] **ADJ, N** *Arch, Lit* deux *m*; *Hum* **and ne'er the t. shall meet** et ils resteront à jamais inconciliables

twang [twæŋ] **N 1** *(of bowstring)* bruit *m* sec; *(of guitar)* son *m* aigu **2** *(in voice)* **nasal t.** ton *m* nasillard, nasillement *m*; **to speak with a t.** nasiller, parler d'une voix nasillarde
VT *(drawn bowstring)* lâcher; *(strings etc)* faire vibrer; **to t. a guitar** gratter (une guitare)
VI 1 *(of string etc)* vibrer; **to t. on a guitar** gratter (une guitare) **2** *(speak with twang)* nasiller

'twas [twɒz] **CONTR** *Arch, Lit* = **it was**

twat [twæt] **N** *Br Sl* **1** *(vagina)* moule *f*, chatte *f* **2** *(idiot)* crétin, -ine

twatted ['twætəd] **ADJ** *Br Sl (drunk)* rond comme une queue de pelle, plein comme une barrique

tweak [twiːk] **N 1** *(twist)* **he gave her nose a t.** il lui a doucement tordu le nez **2** *(adjustment)* petite modification *f*; **to give sth a little t.** donner un petit coup à qch
VT 1 *(pinch)* pincer; *(twist)* tordre (avec les doigts); **to t. sb's ear** tirer l'oreille à qn **2** *(adjust) (engine)* régler; *(text)* apporter quelques petites modifications à

twee [twiː] **ADJ** *Br Fam Pej* mignard, gentillet

tweed [twiːd] **N** *Tex* tweed *m*; **t. jacket** veste *f* en *ou* de tweed; **tweeds** *(suit, outfit)* complet *m* *ou* costume *m* de *ou* en tweed

tweedy ['twiːdɪ] **ADJ** *(cloth)* qui tient du tweed; *Fam Pej (person)* qui affecte la tenue d'un propriétaire rural

'tween [twiːn] **PREP** *Arch, Lit* entre

'**tween decks** ['twiːndeks] *Naut* N faux-pont *m*, *pl* faux-ponts, entrepont *m*
  ADJ, ADV dans l'entrepont

tweet [twiːt] N *(of bird)* pépiement *m*, gazouillement *m*
  VI *(of bird)* pépier, gazouiller

tweeter ['twiːtər] N *(loudspeaker)* haut-parleur *m* aigu, *pl* haut-parleurs aigus, tweeter *m*

tweezers ['twiːzəz] NPL brucelles *fpl*, *(for hairs)* pince *f* à épiler VOIR GRAMMAIRE A10

twelfth [twelfθ] ADJ douzième; **Louis the T.** Louis XII
  N 1 *(of month)* douze *m*; **(on) the t. (of May)** le douze (mai) **2** *(person, thing)* douzième *mf* **3** *(fraction)* douzième *m*
  ▸▸ *Cr* **t. man** joueur *m* de réserve; **T. Night** la fête des Rois

twelve [twelv] ADJ, N douze *m*; **t. o'clock** *(midday)* midi *m*; *(midnight)* minuit *m*

twelvemonth ['twelvmʌnθ] N *Old-fashioned, Lit* année *f*

twelve-tone ADJ *Mus* dodécaphonique
  ▸▸ **t. system** dodécaphonisme *m*

twentieth ['twentɪɪθ] ADJ vingtième
  N 1 *(of month)* vingt *m*; **(on) the t. of June** le vingt juin **2** *(person, thing)* vingtième *mf* **3** *(fraction)* vingtième *m*

twenty ['twentɪ] ADJ, N vingt *m*; **t.-one** vingt et un; **t.-two** vingt-deux; **about t. people** une vingtaine de personnes; **the twenties** les années vingt; **to be in one's twenties** avoir entre vingt et trente ans; **we've been working t.-four hours a day** nous avons travaillé jour et nuit; *Fam* **t.-four/seven, 24/7** sans arrêt
  ▸▸ **t.-four-hour hotline** ligne *f* directe accessible 24 heures sur 24; **t.-four hour service** service *m* vingt-quatre heures sur vingt-quatre; **t.-t. vision** vue *f* parfaite; *Rugby* **t.-two metre line** ligne *f* des vingt-deux mètres

twerp [twɜːp] N *Br Fam* crétin, -ine

twice [twaɪs] ADV deux fois; **t. as big as sth** deux fois plus grand que qch; **t. as slow** deux fois plus lent; **t. over** à deux reprises; **to think t. before doing sth** y regarder ou réfléchir à deux fois avant de faire qch; **to think t. before saying sth** tourner sa langue sept fois dans la bouche avant de parler; **she didn't have to think t. before accepting** elle a accepté sans hésiter; **he didn't have to be asked t.** il ne se fit pas prier

twiddle ['twɪd(ə)l] *Fam* N **to give sth a t.** tourner qch
  VT jouer avec, tripoter; **to t. a knob** tourner un bouton; **to t. one's thumbs** se tourner les pouces; *Fig* **I've spent the whole day twiddling my thumbs** j'ai passé la journée à me tourner les pouces
  VI **to t. with sth** jouer avec ou tripoter qch

twig [twɪg] N brindille *f*
  VT & VI (**-gg-**) *Br Fam* piger; **I soon twigged his little game** je n'ai pas tardé à voir dans son jeu

twilight ['twaɪlaɪt] N crépuscule *m*, demi-jour *m*, *pl* demi-jours; **in the (evening) t.** au crépuscule, entre chien et loup, à la brune; *Fig* **in the t. of life** au crépuscule de la vie; **the t. hours** les heures *fpl* crépusculaires; *Fig* **the t. world of the paranormal** l'entre-deux-mondes *m* du paranormal
  ▸▸ **t. zone** *(in city)* quartier *m* délabré *(qui entoure un quartier commercial)*; *(in ocean)* zone *f* crépusculaire; *Fig* zone d'ombre, zone floue

twill [twɪl] N *Tex* (tissu *m*) croisé *m*, sergé *m*

'**twill** [twɪl] CONTR *Arch, Lit* = **it will**

twin [twɪn] N jumeau, -elle
  ADJ jumeau, jumelé

  VT (**-nn-**) *(towns)* jumeler; **Paisley is twinned with Furth** Paisley est jumelée avec Furth
  ▸▸ **t. beds** lits *m* jumeaux; *Obst* **t. birth** accouchement *m* de jumeaux; **t. brother** frère *m* jumeau; *Aut* **t. camshaft** double arbre *m* à cames; *Aut* **t. carburettor** carburateur *m* double-corps; **t. columns** colonnes *fpl* géminées; *Mktg* **t. plant** lot *m* de deux; **t. room** chambre *f* à deux lits; **t. sister** sœur *f* jumelle; **t. town** ville *f* jumelée *ou* jumelle; **Stirling's t. town is Villeneuve-d'Ascq** Stirling est jumelée avec Villeneuve-d'Ascq; *Aut* **t. turbo** double turbo *m*; *Aut* **t. tyres** pneus *mpl* jumelés

twin-bedded room [-bedɪd] N chambre *f* à lits jumeaux

twin-cam N *Aut* double arbre *m* à cames

twine [twaɪn] N *(string)* ficelle *f*
  VT *(threads)* tordre, tortiller; *(garland, fingers etc)* entrelacer
  VI **the road twined up the mountain** la route montait en lacets dans la montagne
  ▸ **twine about, twine around, twine round** VT SEP **to t. sth about** *or* **(a)round sth** enrouler qch autour de qch; **the honeysuckle had twined itself round the tree** le chèvrefeuille s'était enroulé autour de l'arbre
  VT INSEP s'enrouler *ou* s'enlacer autour de; **the ivy had twined around the tree** le lierre s'était enroulé autour de l'arbre

twin-engine(d) aircraft N avion *m* bimoteur

twinge [twɪn(d)ʒ] N *(of pain)* élancement *m*; *(of gout etc)* légère crise *f*; **t. of conscience** remords *m*; **my tooth/knee still gives the odd t.** ma dent/mon genou m'élance toujours de temps en temps

twining ['twaɪnɪŋ] ADJ *(plant, stem)* volubile

twinjet ['twɪndʒet] N biréacteur *m*

twinkle ['twɪŋk(ə)l] N *(of stars, distant lights)* scintillement *m*, clignotement *m*; *(of eyes)* pétillement *m*; **a mischievous t. in the eye** un éclair de malice dans les yeux; *Fam* **when you were just a t. in your father's eye** quand tu n'étais pas encore de ce monde; *(of light, star)* scintiller, étinceler, clignoter; *(of eyes)* pétiller; **her eyes twinkled with amusement/mischief** ses yeux pétillaient de rire/malice

twinkling ['twɪŋklɪŋ] ADJ *(star etc)* scintillant, étincelant, clignotant; **t. eyes** yeux *mpl* pétillants
  N scintillement *m*, étincellement *m*, clignotement *m*; **in the t. of an eye** en un clin d'œil

twinky ['twɪŋkɪ] N *Am Sl (homosexual)* homo *m*

twinning ['twɪnɪŋ] N *(of two towns etc)* jumelage *m*; **t. of companies** jumelage d'entreprises; **t. arrangements** arrangements *mpl* en vue d'un jumelage

twinset ['twɪnset] N *Br (garments)* twin-set *m*, *pl* twin-sets; **she's very t. and pearls** ≃ elle est très BCBG

twirl [twɜːl] N 1 *(movement)* tournoiement *m*; *(of dancer etc)* pirouette *f* **2** *(shape) (of smoke etc)* volute *f*, *Archit* enroulement *m*, volute *f*; *(of seashell)* spire *f*, *(in writing)* enjolivure *f* en spirale; *(in music)* fioriture *f*, **with a t. of cream on top** avec une spirale de crème dessus
  VT *(one's partner, lasso)* faire tournoyer; *(walking stick etc)* faire des moulinets avec; *(one's moustache)* tortiller
  VI *(turn round quickly)* se retourner d'un mouvement; *(when dancing)* tournoyer
  ▸ **twirl round** VT SEP = **twirl** VT
  VI se retourner brusquement; *(spin several times)* tournoyer

N tour **1** ▪ tournure **2** ▪ torsade **3** ▪ écheveau **3**	
VT tordre ▪ tortiller ▪ dénaturer ▪ altérer	
VI se tordre ▪ se tortiller ▪ serpenter	

N 1 *(act of twisting) (of lid, cap)* tour *m*; **with a t. of the wrist** en un tour de main; **give the lid another t.** donne encore un tour au couvercle
  2 *(of coil)* spire *f*, **twists and turns** *(of road)* tours et détours *mpl*, *(of events etc)* tournure *f*, **final t. in a story** tour *m* inattendu à la fin d'un récit; **this adds a new t. to events** ça donne une tournure inattendue aux événements; **that's a nice t.** *(in plot)* c'est bien trouvé; *(in story, anecdote)* c'est drôle, ça!; **by a t. of fate** par un coup du sort; *Br Fam* **to be round the t.** être fou *ou* cinglé; *Fam* **to get oneself into a t.** *(upset, nervous)* se mettre dans tous ses états
  3 *(of hair)* torsade *f*, tortillon *m*; *(of wool)* écheveau *m*; *(of paper)* tortillon *m*; **sweet in a t. of paper** bonbon dans une papillote; **a t. of lemon** une rondelle de citron; **t. of tobacco** morceau *m* de tabac
  4 *(dance)* twist *m*
  VT *(one's hair, rope etc)* tordre, tortiller; *Tex etc (thread)* retordre; *(sb's words, meaning of text)* dénaturer; *(truth, meaning of sth)* altérer; **to t. two wires together** torsader deux fils; **to t. one's ankle** se faire une entorse; *(less serious)* se fouler la cheville; **to t. sb's arm** tordre *ou* retourner le bras à qn; *Fig* exercer une pression sur qn; *Hum* **if you t. my arm** si tu insistes; **to t. one's knee** se déboîter le genou; *Fig* **to t. the knife in the wound** retourner le couteau dans la plaie
  VI se tordre; *(of worm etc)* se tortiller; *(of rope etc)* s'entortiller; *(spiral)* former une spirale; *(of smoke)* former des volutes; *(of road etc)* serpenter, faire des lacets, *(dance)* twister; **to t. and turn** *(of road etc)* serpenter
  ▸▸ **t. drill** foret *m* hélicoïdal; **t. grip** *(accelerator)* poignée *f* d'accélération; *(gear change)* poignée de changement de vitesses
  ▸ **twist off** VI *(of lid)* se dévisser
  VT SEP *(lid)* dévisser
  ▸ **twist round** VT SEP **1** *(wrap around)* **to t. sth round sth** enrouler *ou* entortiller qch autour de qch; *Fam* **he can t. her round his little finger** il la mène par le bout du nez
  2 she twisted her head round and stared at him elle tourna la tête et le fixa du regard
  VI *(turn)* se retourner; **to t. round in one's seat** se retourner sur son siège
  ▸ **twist up** VI *(of smoke)* s'élever en spirale
  2 VT SEP emmêler, entortiller; **to get all twisted up** *(of cables etc)* s'emmêler, s'entortiller

twisted ['twɪstɪd] ADJ **1** tordu; *(wire etc)* entortillé; *(tree)* tordu; *(limb)* tordu, contourné; **to get all t.** s'entortiller; **face t. with pain** traits *mpl* tordus par la douleur; **the t. wreckage of the plane/car** l'épave *f* enchevêtrée de l'avion/de la voiture **2** *Fig (disturbed) (person, character, logic, reasoning)* tordu; **to have a t. mind** avoir l'esprit tordu; **what a t. thing to do** il faut être tordu pour faire une chose pareille; **a t. way of looking at things** une façon tordue de voir les choses; **he's so bitter and t.** il est tellement amer et désabusé
  ▸▸ *Archit* **t. pillar** colonne *f* torse

twisted-pair cable N câble *m* en paire torsadée

twister ['twɪstər] N *Fam* **1** *Br (swindler)* escroc *m* **2** *esp Am (tornado)* tornade *f*

twisting ['twɪstɪŋ] ADJ *(path)* tortueux

twisty ['twɪstɪ] ADJ *(road etc)* tortueux

twit [twɪt] N *esp Br Fam* andouille *f*, imbécile *m*

VT (**-tt-**) *esp Lit* narguer, taquiner (**about** à propos de)

twitch [twɪtʃ] N **1** *(jerk)* petit coup *m* sec **2** *(tic) tic m*; *(of limb)* mouvement *m* convulsif

VT *(jerk)* tirer vivement, tirer d'un petit coup sec; **to t. its tail** *(of cat)* faire de petits mouvements de la queue

VI *(of face, limb)* se contracter nerveusement; *(of eyelid, lip)* trembler; *(of hands)* se crisper nerveusement

twitcher ['twɪtʃər] N *Br Fam* dingue *mf* d'ornithologie

twitter ['twɪtər] N **1** *(of birds)* gazouillement *m*, gazouillis *m* **2** *Fam* **to be in a t.** *(of person)* être tout en émoi *ou* dans tous ses états

VI *(of bird)* gazouiller; *Fig Pej (talk)* jacasser

twittering ['twɪtərɪŋ] ADJ *(bird)* gazouillant; *Fig Pej (person, voice etc)* piaillant

N gazouillement *m*; *Fig Pej (talk)* jacassement *m*

'twixt [twɪkst] PREP *Arch, Lit* entre

two [tuː] N deux *m*; **twenty-t.** vingt-deux; *Gym etc* **one, t.! one, t.!** une deux! une deux!; **no t. men are alike** il n'y a pas deux hommes qui se ressemblent; **to break/fold sth in t.** casser/plier qch en deux; **to walk in twos** *or* **t. by t.** marcher deux à deux *ou* (deux) par deux; *Fig* **to put t. and t. together** en tirer les conclusions (qui s'imposent), faire le rapprochement; *Fam* **that makes t. of us** on est deux; **t. fours are eight** deux fois quatre font huit; **it's t. o'clock** il est deux heures; **to be t.** *(in age)* avoir deux ans; **a mother of t.** la mère de deux enfants; **the t. of us/them** nous/eux deux; *Cards* **t. of spades** deux de pique; *Mus* **t. part song** chanson *f* à deux voix

PRON deux; **t. is not enough** deux, ce n'est pas assez

ADJ deux; **t. people** deux personnes

two-bit ADJ *Am Fam* de quatre sous; *(person)* à la noix

two-colour ADJ de deux couleurs, bicolore; *(print ribbon)* bicolore

▸▸ *Typ* **t. printing** impression *f* en deux couleurs *ou* en bichromie, bichromie *f*; *Typ* **t. process** bichromie *f*

two-dimensional ADJ bidimensionnel; *Fig Pej (character, film etc)* simpliste, superficiel

two-door ADJ *(car)* à deux portes

two-edged ADJ *(sword, argument)* à double tranchant; *(remark, answer etc)* ambigu, -uë

two-faced [-feɪst] ADJ hypocrite

twofer ['tuːfər] N *Am Fam* deux billets *mpl etc* vendus pour le prix d'un

twofold ['tuːfəʊld] ADJ double

ADV doublement; **kindness returned t.** bontés rendues au double

two-four ADJ

▸▸ *Mus* **t. time** mesure *f* à deux quatre; **in t. time** en deux quatre

two-handed ADJ *Cards (game)* qui se joue à deux

▸▸ *Tennis* **t. backhand** revers *m* à deux mains; **t. sword** épée *f* à deux mains, espadon *m*

two-headed ADJ bicéphale; *Her (eagle)* double, à deux têtes

two-horse ADJ *(carriage)* à deux chevaux; *Fig* **a t. race** une épreuve/élection qui ne comprend que deux concurrents

two-legged ADJ bipède

twonk [twɒŋk] N *Fam (fool)* andouille *f*, cruche *f*

two-part pricing N prix *mpl* à double détente

two-party ADJ *(system, politics etc)* bipartite

twopence ['tʌpəns] N *Br* deux pence *mpl*; *Fig Fam* **it isn't worth t.** ça ne vaut pas tripette

twopenny ['tʌp(ə)nɪ] ADJ *Br* à *ou* de deux pence; **a t. piece** une pièce de deux pence

twopenny-halfpenny ['tʌp(ə)nɪ'heɪpnɪ] ADJ *Br Fig Fam (person, ring etc)* à la noix, à la gomme

two-phase ADJ *Elec (current)* bi-phasé

two-piece ADJ *(suit, swimsuit)* deux pièces

N *(suit)* *(for woman)* deux-pièces *m inv*; *(for man)* costume *m* deux pièces; *(swimsuit)* deux-pièces

two-pin ADJ

▸▸ *Elec* **t. plug** prise *f* à deux fiches; **t. socket** prise à deux douilles

two-ply ADJ *(rope)* à deux brins; *(wool)* deux fils; *(tissue)* double épaisseur

two-seater N *(car)* voiture *f* à deux places; *(plane)* biplace *m*, avion *m* à deux places

two-sided ADJ *(contract, talks etc)* bilatéral, -aux

twosome ['tuːsəm] N **1** *(game)* jeu *m ou* partie *f* à deux joueurs; *(dance)* danse *f* à deux **2** *(pair)* paire *f*, *(of friends etc)* couple *m*; **let's just go as a t.** allons-y rien que tous les deux

two-speed ADJ *Pol (Europe)* à deux vitesses

▸▸ *Econ, Pol* **t. monetary union** union *f* monétaire à deux vitesses; *Aut* **t. wiper** essuie-glace *m* à deux vitesses, *pl* essuie-glaces

two-star ADJ **1** *(restaurant, hotel)* deux étoiles **2** *(petrol)* ordinaire

N *(petrol)* **five litres of t.** cinq litres d'(essence) ordinaire

two-step N *Mus* pas *m* de deux

two-stroke ADJ *(motorcycle)* à deux temps

▸▸ **t. engine** moteur *m* à deux temps; **t. mixture** *(mélange m)* deux-temps *m inv*

two-tier ADJ *(management structure)* à deux niveaux; *(education system, health service)* à deux vitesses

two-time VT *Fam* tromper; **she had been two-timing him with his best friend** elle le trompait avec son meilleur ami

two-timer N *Fam (husband, wife, lover)* personne *f* infidèle

two-timing ADJ *Fam* infidèle; **you t. bastard!** tu es un salaud fini!

two-tone ADJ *(paint, car)* deux tons; *(klaxon etc)* à deux tons

▸▸ **t. horn** avertisseur *m* deux tons; *Typ* **t. printing** bichromie *f*, impression *f* en deux couleurs

two-way ADJ *(street)* à double sens; *(mirror)* sans tain; *Elec (switch)* à deux directions; *Tel* bilatéral, -aux; **any relationship is a t. thing** *or* **street** toute relation ne peut exister que si elle est réciproque

▸▸ **t. converter** catalyseur *m* à deux voies; *Tel* **t. radio** émetteur-récepteur *m*, *pl* émetteurs-récepteurs; **t. trade** commerce *m* dans les deux sens

two-wheel drive N deux roues motrices *fpl*

two-wheeler N deux-roues *m inv*

tycoon [taɪ'kuːn] N *Fam* magnat *m*

tying up [taɪɪŋ] N *(of capital)* immobilisation *f*

tyke [taɪk] N *Fam* **1** *(dog)* cabot *m* **2** *(person)* salaud *m*; *(small child)* môme *mf*, *(mischievous child)* diablotin *m*

tympanum, *pl* **tympana, tympanums** ['tɪmpənəm, -ə, -əmz] N *Anat, Archit* tympan *m*

type [taɪp] N **1** *(class, sort, example)* type *m*,

genre *m*; **people/books of this t.** des personnes/des livres de ce genre; **people of every t.** des gens de toutes sortes; *Fam* **he's/she's not my t.** ce n'est pas mon genre; **she's not the t. to …** elle n'est pas du genre à …; *Fam* **he's an odd t.** *(person)* c'est un drôle de type VOIR GRAMMAIRE A13 **2** *Typ (letters)* caractères *mpl*; **to print in large t.** imprimer en gros caractères; **in t.** composé; **wait till you see it in t.** attend de le voir imprimé *ou* de voir ce que ça rend imprimé

VT 1 *(write on typewriter)* taper (à la machine), dactylographier **2** *Med* **to t. blood** déterminer un groupe sanguin

VI taper à la machine, dactylographier; **can you t.?** savez-vous taper à la machine?; **he types well** il tape bien

▸▸ *Biol* **t. genus** genre *m* type; **t. library** typothèque *f*

▸ **type in** VT SEP taper

▸ **type out** VT SEP taper à la machine

▸ **type up** VT SEP taper au propre

type-ahead N *Comput* frappe *f* en continu

▸▸ **t. buffer** zone *f* tampon de frappe en continu

typecase ['taɪpkeɪs] N *Typ* casse *f*

typecast ['taɪpkɑːst] VT *(pt, pp typecast)* *Theat, Cin (actor)* donner toujours les mêmes rôles à; **she was being t. as a dumb blonde** elle était cantonnée aux rôles de blondes écervelées; **he is always t. as a villain** on lui fait toujours jouer des rôles de bandit

typed [taɪpt] ADJ dactylographié, écrit à la machine

typeface ['taɪpfeɪs] N *(type family)* famille *f* de caractères; *(printing surface)* œil *m* (de caractère); **try another t.** essaie avec un autre caractère

typescript ['taɪpskrɪpt] N texte *m* dactylographié

typeset ['taɪpset] VT *(pt, pp typeset)* *Typ* composer; **t. by MWP** composition MWP

typesetter ['taɪpsetər] N *(person)* compositeur *m*; *(machine)* machine *f* à composer; *Comput (in DTP)* photocomposeuse *f*

typesetting ['taɪpsetɪŋ] N *Typ* composition *f*; **who did the t.?** qui a fait la composition?

▸▸ **t. machine** machine *f* à composer, composeuse *f*; **t. techniques** techniques *fpl* de composition

typesize ['taɪpsaɪz] N *(of text)* taille *f* des caractères

typewriter ['taɪpraɪtər] N machine *f* à écrire; **to write sth on a t.** écrire *ou* taper qch à la machine

▸▸ *Comput* **t. mode** mode *m* machine à écrire; **t. ribbon** ruban *m* de machine à écrire; *Br* **t. rubber** gomme *f* pour machine à écrire

typewriting ['taɪpraɪtɪŋ] N dactylographie *f*

typewritten ['taɪprɪt(ə)n] ADJ *(document etc)* écrit *ou* tapé à la machine, dactylographié

typhoid ['taɪfɔɪd] ADJ *Med (bacillus)* typhoïdique

N (fièvre *f*) typhoïde *f*

▸▸ **t. fever** (fièvre) typhoïde

typhoon [taɪ'fuːn] N *Met* typhon *m*

typhus ['taɪfəs] N *Med* typhus *m*

typical ['tɪpɪk(ə)l] ADJ typique (**of** de); **the t. Frenchman** le Français typique; **in a t. day you can earn £300** en une journée normale vous pouvez gagner 300 livres; *Fam* **isn't that** *or* **that's t.** c'est bien de lui/d'elle!; **t. man/woman!** c'est bien un homme/une femme!; **your letter took six days to get here – t.!** ta lettre a mis six jours pour arriver – ça c'est typique! *ou* ça ne m'étonne pas!

typically ['tɪpɪklɪ] ADV typiquement; **he's t. French** il est typiquement français; **the countryside is t. Mediterranean** le paysage est typiquement méditerranéen; **he made one of his t. obscure remarks** il a fait une de ses habituelles remarques obscures; **she was t. late** *(normally)* elle arrivait généralement en retard; *(as on other occasions)* conformément à son habitude elle était en retard; **she was t. rude, she was her t. rude self** comme à son habitude, elle a été très désagréable; **employees t. work a 40-hour week** les employés travaillent en moyenne 40 heures par semaine

typify ['tɪpɪfaɪ] VT *(of person) (officer etc)* personnifier; *(of specimen etc)* être caractéristique de

typing ['taɪpɪŋ] N dactylographie *f*, *Fam* dactylo *f*
▸▸ **t. error** faute *f* de frappe; **t. paper** papier *m* machine; **t. pool** bureau *m ou* pool *m* des

dactylos; **t. skills** compétences *fpl* en dactylographie; **t. speed** vitesse *f* de frappe

typist ['taɪpɪst] N *(copy)* **t.** dactylographe *mf*, *Fam* dactylo *mf*; **audio t.** dactylo audio-magnéto; **I'm no t.** je tape très mal; **t.'s error** faute *f* de frappe

typo ['taɪpəʊ] N *Typ Fam* coquille *f*, faute *f* de frappe

typographer [taɪ'pɒgrəfər] N typographe *mf*

typographic(al) [taɪpə'græfɪk, -ɪk(ə)l] ADJ typographique

typographically [taɪpə'græfɪklɪ] ADV typographiquement

typography [taɪ'pɒgrəfɪ] N typographie *f*

tyrannical [tɪ'rænɪk(ə)l] ADJ tyrannique

tyrannically ['tɪrænɪklɪ] ADV tyranniquement

tyrannize ['tɪrənaɪz] VT tyranniser

tyranny ['tɪrənɪ] N tyrannie *f*

tyrant ['taɪrənt] N tyran *m*

tyre ['taɪər] N *esp Br* pneu *m*, *pl* pneus
▸▸ **t. chain** chaîne *f* (de pneu); **t. iron, t. lever** démonte-pneu *m*, *pl* démonte-pneus; **t. marks** *(in mud, snow etc)* empreintes *fpl ou* traces *fpl* de pneu; **t. pressure** pression *f* des pneus; **t. pressure gauge** indicateur *m* de pression de pneu; **t. pump** pompe *f* (pour gonfler les pneus); **t. scrub** ripage *m* des pneus; **t. valve** valve *f* de gonflage; **t. wear** usure *f* des pneus

tyro ['taɪrəʊ] N novice *mf*, débutant, -ante

Tyrol (the) [ðɪ'rɒl] N le Tyrol

Tyrolean [tɪrə'liːən] ADJ tyrolien
▸▸ **T. hat** chapeau *m* tyrolien

tzar, tzarist *etc* = tsar, tsarist *etc*

T-zone N zones *fpl* grasses du visage *(front, nez, menton)*

U¹, u [ju:] N *(letter)* U, u *m*; **two u's** deux u; *Old-fashioned Fam* **U and non U** ce qui est bien *ou* comme il faut, et ce qui ne l'est pas

U² *Br Cin (abbr* **universal**) = désigne un film tous publics en Grande-Bretagne

UAE [ju:eɪˈiː] N *(abbr* **United Arab Emirates)** Émirats *mpl* arabes unis, EAU *mpl*

U-bend N **1** *(in pipe)* coude *m*; *(under sink)* siphon *m* **2** *Br (in road)* virage *m* en épingle à cheveux

UB40 [ju:biːˈfɔːtɪ] N *Br (abbr* **unemployment benefit form 40)** = carte *f* de pointage (de demandeur d'emploi); *(person)* chômeur, -euse

ubiquitous [ju:ˈbɪkwɪtəs] ADJ *(substance, theme, muzak)* omniprésent; *(person)* doué d'ubiquité; **the u. fast-food joint** l'inévitable fast-food

ubiquity [ju:ˈbɪkwɪtɪ] N omniprésence *f*, *(of person)* ubiquité *f*

U-boat N sous-marin *m* allemand, *pl* sous-marins allemands

U-bolt N étrier *m*

UCAS [ˈjuːkæs] N *Br (abbr* **Universities and Colleges Admissions Service)** = centre *m* national qui traite les demandes d'entrée à l'université

UCCA [ˈʌkə] N *Br Formerly (abbr* **Universities Central Council on Admissions)** = centre *m* national qui traitait les demandes d'entrée à l'université

UCITS [ju:siːˈaɪtiːˈes] N *Fin (abbr* **undertakings for collective investment in transferables)** OPCVM *m*

UDA [ju:di:ˈeɪ] N *Br Formerly (abbr* **Ulster Defence Association)** = groupement *m* paramilitaire protestant en Irlande du Nord

udder [ˈʌdər] N *(of cow etc)* mamelle *f*, pis *m*

UDI [ju:di:ˈaɪ] N *(abbr* **Unilateral Declaration of Independence)** déclaration *f* unilatérale d'indépendance

UDR [ju:di:ˈɑːr] N *Br Formerly (abbr* **Ulster Defence Regiment)** régiment *m* de réservistes de l'armée britannique en Irlande du Nord

UEFA [ju:ˈeɪfə] N *(abbr* **Union of European Football Associations)** UEFA *f*

UFO [ju:eˈfəʊ, ˈjuːfəʊ] N *(abbr* **unidentified flying object)** OVNI *m*

ufologist [ju:ˈfɒlədʒɪst] N spécialiste *mf* des ovnis

ufology [ju:ˈfɒlədʒɪ] N étude *f* des ovnis

Uganda [ju:ˈgændə] N Ouganda *m*

Ugandan [ju:ˈgændən] ADJ ougandais
▸ N Ougandais, -aise

ugh [ʌg] INT pouah!, beuh!

Ugli®, *pl* **Uglis, Uglies** [ˈʌglɪ, -ɪz] N *(fruit)* tangelo *m*

uglify [ˈʌglɪfaɪ] VT enlaidir

ugliness [ˈʌglɪnɪs] N laideur *f*

ugly [ˈʌglɪ] ADJ **1** *(in appearance etc) (per-* son) laid; *(building, furniture, pattern, hat, colour)* affreux, laid; *(word)* déplaisant; *(bruise, wound, scar)* vilain, méchant; **to grow u.** enlaidir; **an u. woman** un laideron, une femme laide; **she's as u. as sin** elle est laide comme les sept péchés capitaux *ou* comme un pou *ou* à faire peur **2** *Fig (threatening) (sky, look)* menaçant; *(incident, scene)* désagréable; *Fam* **an u. customer** un sale type; *Fam* **nationalism/racism reared its u. head** le nationalisme/racisme s'est réveillé; *Fam* **to cut up** *or* **turn u.** *(of person)* devenir agressif; **the situation was starting to turn u.** la situation commençait à mal tourner; **an u. rumour** un bruit sinistre
▸▸ **u. duckling** vilain petit canard *m*

UHF [ju:eɪtʃˈef] N *(abbr* **ultrahigh frequency)** UHF *f*

uh-huh INT **1** [ʌ'hʌ] *(agreeing, yes)* hmm hmm, oui oui **2** [ˈʌhʌ] *(disagreeing, no, don't)* tut-tut, non non

UHT [ju:eɪtʃˈti:] ADJ *(abbr* **ultra heat treated)**
▸▸ **U. milk** lait *m* UHT, lait longue conservation

UK [ju:ˈkeɪ] N *(abbr* **United Kingdom)** RU *m*, Royaume-Uni *m*; **UK sales/prices** ventes/prix au Royaume-Uni

Ukraine [ju:ˈkreɪn] N Ukraine *f*

Ukrainian [ju:ˈkreɪnɪən] ADJ ukrainien
▸ N **1** Ukrainien, -ienne **2** *Ling* ukrainien *m*

ukulele [ju:kəˈleɪlɪ] N *Mus* ukulélé *m*, guitare *f* hawaïenne

ulcer [ˈʌlsər] N *Med* ulcère *m*; *(in mouth)* aphte *m*; *Fig* plaie *f*; *(ugly building etc)* verrue *f*; **peptic u.** ulcère simple de l'estomac/du duodénum

ulcerate [ˈʌlsəreɪt] *Med* VT ulcérer; **ulcerated wound** blessure *f* ulcérée *ou* ulcéreuse
▸ VI s'ulcérer

ulceration [ʌlsəˈreɪʃən] N *Med* ulcération *f*

ulcerative [ˈʌls(ə)rətɪv] ADJ *Med* ulcératif

ulcerous [ˈʌls(ə)rəs] ADJ *Med* ulcéreux

ullage [ˈʌlɪdʒ] N *(in barrel)* creux *m* du tonneau

ulna [ˈʌlnə] N *Anat* cubitus *m*

Ulster [ˈʌlstər] N **1** Ulster *m* **2** **u.** *(coat)* ulster *m*

Ulsterman, *pl* **Ulstermen** [ˈʌlstəmən] N Ulstérien *m*

Ulsterwoman, *pl* **Ulsterwomen** [ˈʌlstəwʊmən, -wɪmɪn] N Ulstérienne *f*

ult [ʌlt] *Com Old-fashioned abbr* **ultimo**

ulterior [ʌlˈtɪərɪər] ADJ ultérieur
▸▸ **u. designs** desseins *mpl* secrets; **u. motive** arrière-pensée *f*, *pl* arrière-pensées; **without u. motive** sans arrière-pensée

ultimate [ˈʌltɪmət] ADJ **1** *(final)* final, -als, définitif; **the u. effect of an action** l'effet ultime d'une action; **the u. decision is his** c'est à lui qu'appartient la décision finale; **u. goal** but *m* final; **certain of u. success** certain du succès final; **the u. deterrent** l'arme *f* de dissuasion absolue; **they made the u. sacrifice** ils ont fait l'ultime sacrifice

2 *(basic, fundamental)* fondamental, -aux; **the u. constituents of matter** les constituants fondamentaux de la matière; **is this the u. physical particle?** est-ce la particule fondamentale?

3 *(supreme, best etc)* suprême, absolu; **the u. double-glazing/laser printer** le double vitrage/l'imprimante laser absolu(e); **the u. sound system** la meilleure sono qui soit; **that really is the u. cheek!** c'est vraiment le comble du culot!; **he really is the u. incompetent!** on ne fait pas plus incompétent que lui

4 *(furthest)* le plus lointain; **the u. ends of the universe** les limites externes de l'univers; **we traced our u. origins back to ...** nous avons établi nos origines les plus lointaines à ...
▸ N **1** *Rel, Phil* **the u.** *(the best)* l'absolu *m* **2** **the u.** *(the very best)* le fin du fin; **the u. in luxury** le summum du luxe; **it's the u. in vulgarity/bad taste** c'est le comble de la vulgarité/du mauvais goût
▸▸ *Mktg* **u. consumer** utilisateur, -trice final(e)

ultimately [ˈʌltɪmɪtlɪ] ADV **1** *(finally, in the end)* finalement; **the events which led u. to his downfall** les événements qui ont finalement conduit à sa chute **2** *(at bottom, basically)* en fin de compte; **u. it's the same thing** en fin de compte *ou* au fond c'est la même chose

ultimatum, *pl* **ultimatums, ultimata** [ʌltɪˈmeɪtəm, -təmz, -tə] N ultimatum *m*; **to deliver an u. to sb, to present sb with an u.** adresser un ultimatum à qn

ultimo [ˈʌltɪməʊ] ADV *Com Old-fashioned* du mois dernier; **on the tenth u.** le dix du mois dernier

ultra- [ˈʌltrə] PREF ultra-, hyper-

ultrafashionable [ˌʌltrəˈfæʃənəb(ə)l] ADJ à la pointe de la mode, *Fam* hyper-mode *inv*

ultrahigh [ˌʌltrəˈhaɪ] ADJ
▸▸ *Phys* **u. frequency** ondes *fpl* ultracourtes

ultraleft [ˌʌltrəˈleft] *Pol* ADJ d'extrême gauche
▸ N extrême gauche *f*

ultramarine [ˌʌltrəməˈriːn] ADJ, N (bleu *m* d')outremer *m*
▸▸ **u. blue** (bleu d')outremer

ultramodern [ˌʌltrəˈmɒd(ə)n] ADJ ultramoderne

ultramontane [ˌʌltrəˈmɒnteɪn] ADJ, N ultramontain, -aine

ultraright [ˌʌltrəˈraɪt] *Pol* ADJ d'extrême droite
▸ N extrême droite *f*

ultrasensitive [ˌʌltrəˈsensɪtɪv] **ADJ** ultrasensible

ultrashort [ˌʌltrəˈʃɔːt] **ADJ** *Phys* ultracourt

ultrasonic [ˌʌltrəˈsɒnɪk] **ADJ** ultrasonique; **u. alarm** alarme *f* à ultrasons
   N ultrasonics science *f* des ultrasons **VOIR GRAMMAIRE A10**

ultrasound [ˈʌltrəsaʊnd] **N** *Med* échographie *f*, ultrason *m*
   ►► **u. scan** échographie, ultrason

ultraviolet [ˌʌltrəˈvaɪələt] **ADJ** *Phys* ultraviolet
   ►► **u. rays** rayons *mpl* ultraviolets; *Med* **u. treatment** traitement *m* aux (rayons) ultraviolets

ultra vires [ˌʌltrəˈvaɪəriːz, ˌʊltrəˈviːreɪz] **ADJ, ADV** *Law* au delà de ses pouvoirs

ululate [ˈjuːljʊleɪt] **VI** *Fml* (of owl etc) ululer, huer; (of jackal etc) hurler; (of person, mourner) se lamenter

ululation [juːljʊˈleɪʃən] **N** *Fml* (of owl etc) ululation *f*, ululement *m*; (of jackal etc) hurlement *m*; (of person) lamentation *f*

Ulysses [ˈjuːlɪsiːz] **N** Ulysse *m*

um [ʌm] **INT** (hesitating in speaking) heu
   VI to um and err bafouiller

umber [ˈʌmbər] **N** *Art* terre *f* d'ombre *ou* de Sienne; **burnt u.** terre d'ombre brûlée
   ADJ couleur *inv* d'ombre

umbilical [ʌmˈbɪlɪk(ə)l, ˌʌmbɪˈlaɪk(ə)l] **ADJ** *Anat* ombilical, -aux
   ►► **u. cord** cordon *m* ombilical

umbilicus [ʌmˈbɪlɪkəs, ˌʌmbɪˈlaɪkəs] **N** *Anat* ombilic *m*, nombril *m*

umbrage [ˈʌmbrɪdʒ] **N** ombrage *m*, ressentiment *m*; **to take u. at sth** prendre ombrage de qch, se froisser de qch

umbrella [ʌmˈbrelə] **N 1** parapluie *m*; **to put up** *or* **open (up) one's u.** ouvrir son parapluie; **to put down** *or* **to fold (up) one's u.** fermer *ou* replier son parapluie; **beach u.** parasol *m* **2 under the u. of the United Nations** sous la protection des Nations Unies **3** *Mil, Aviat* **air** *or* **aerial u.** parapluie *m* aérien; **nuclear u.** parapluie nucléaire **4** (of jellyfish) ombrelle *f*
   ►► **u. committee** comité *m* de coordination; *Fin* **u. fund** fonds *m* de consolidation; **u. organization** organisation *f* qui en regroupe plusieurs autres; **u. stand** porte-parapluies *m inv*; *Mktg* **u. trademark** marque *f* ombrelle

> Note that the French word **ombrelle** is a false friend. It means **sunshade**.

Umbria [ˈʌmbrɪə] **N** Ombrie *f*

Umbrian [ˈʌmbrɪən] **N** Ombrien, -ienne
   ADJ ombrien

umlaut [ˈʊmlaʊt] **N** *Ling* **1** (vowel change) inflexion *f* vocalique, métaphonie *f* **2** (sign) tréma *m*

umph [hm] **INT** (disbelieving, not pleased) hum!, hmm!

umpire [ˈʌmpaɪər] *Sport etc* **N** arbitre *m*, juge *m*; **to be an u. at a match** arbitrer un match
   VT (match) arbitrer
   VI arbitrer (le/un match)

umpteen [ˌʌmpˈtiːn] **ADJ** *Fam* je ne sais combien de; **I've told you u. times not to …** je t'ai dit mille *ou* je ne sais combien de fois de ne pas …; **she's got u. books on Africa** elle a des tas de livres sur l'Afrique; **to have u. reasons for doing sth** avoir trente-six raisons de faire qch

umpteenth [ˌʌmpˈtiːnθ] **ADJ** *Fam* **that's the u. time I've told you** c'est la énième fois que je te le dis

UMTS [juːemtiːˈes] **N** *Tel* (abbr **Universal Mobile Telecommunications Services**) UMTS *m*

UN [juːˈen] **N** (abbr **United Nations**) ONU *f*, **UN troops/observers** soldats/observateurs de l'ONU

'un [ən] **PRON** *Sl* (one) **a little 'un** un petit, une petite; **he's a bad 'un** c'est un sale type

unabashed [ʌnəˈbæʃt] **ADJ** (person) aucunement déconcerté; **shocked at his u. confession of guilt** choqué de le voir avouer sa culpabilité sans aucune honte

unabashedly [ʌnəˈbæʃədlɪ] **ADV** (unashamedly) sans aucune honte; (without being discouraged) sans se laisser déconcentrer, sans se démonter

unabated [ʌnəˈbeɪtɪd] **ADJ** non diminué; **for three days the storm continued u.** pendant trois jours l'orage a continué sans répit; **the riots went on u.** les émeutes continuèrent sans faiblir; **the crowd continued to cheer with u. enthusiasm** la foule continuait à pousser des acclamations avec toujours autant d'enthousiasme

unabbreviated [ʌnəˈbriːvɪeɪtɪd] **ADJ** non abrégé

unable [ʌnˈeɪb(ə)l] **ADJ** incapable; **to be u. to do sth** ne pas pouvoir faire qch; (because of external factor) être dans l'impossibilité de faire qch, ne pas pouvoir faire qch; **he seems u. to understand you** il semble être incapable de vous comprendre; **we are u. to help you** nous ne sommes pas en mesure de vous aider; **I was u. to persuade him** je n'ai pas pu le persuader

unabridged [ʌnəˈbrɪdʒd] **ADJ** non abrégé, intégral, -aux; **u. edition** édition *f* intégrale; **u. text** texte *m* intégral

unabsorbed [ʌnəbˈzɔːbd] **ADJ**
   ►► *Fin* **u. cost** coût *m* non-absorbé

unaccented, unaccentuated [ʌnəkˈsentɪd, ʌnəkˈsentjʊeɪtɪd] **ADJ** *Ling* (syllable etc) non accentué, atone; *Mus* **u. beat** temps *m* faible

unacceptable [ʌnəkˈseptəb(ə)l] **ADJ** inacceptable; (theory) irrecevable; (behaviour) inadmissible; **these conditions are u. to us** nous ne pouvons pas accepter ces conditions; **it's quite u. for so many people to be homeless** il est tout à fait inacceptable *ou* inadmissible que tant de gens soient sans foyer

unacceptably [ʌnəkˈseptəblɪ] **ADV** **u. high level of** … un niveau inadmissible *ou* intolérable de …; **what they are, quite u., demanding is …** l'objet tout à fait inadmissible de leur demande est …

unaccommodating [ʌnəˈkɒmədeɪtɪŋ] **ADJ** (person) peu accommodant

unaccompanied [ʌnəˈkʌmp(ə)nɪd] **ADJ 1** (person, baggage) non accompagné **2** *Mus* sans accompagnement; **passage for u. violin** passage pour violon seul

unaccomplished [ʌnəˈkʌmplɪʃt] **ADJ 1** (not fulfilled, not completed) (ambition) non réalisé; (work) inachevé **2** (mediocre) (person, performance etc) médiocre

unaccountable [ʌnəˈkaʊntəb(ə)l] **ADJ 1** (inexplicable) inexplicable **2** (not accountable) **to be u. to sb** ne pas avoir à répondre devant qn

unaccountably [ʌnəˈkaʊntəblɪ] **ADV** inexpliquablement

unaccounted [ʌnəˈkaʊntɪd] **ADJ there are still several thousand soldiers who are u. for** il y a encore plusieurs milliers de soldats portés disparus; **these £10 are u. for in the balance sheet** ces 10 livres ne figurent pas au bilan; **five of the passengers are still u. for** on reste sans nouvelles de cinq passagers; **two books are still u. for** il manque toujours deux livres

unaccustomed [ʌnəˈkʌstəmd] **ADJ 1** inac-

coutumé, inhabituel **2** (person) **u. to sth/to doing sth** peu habitué à qch/à faire qch; **u. as I am to public speaking** n'ayant pas l'habitude de faire des discours

unacknowledged [ʌnəkˈnɒlɪdʒd] **ADJ 1** (child, talents) non reconnu; **to go u.** ne pas être reconnu **2** (quotation) dont on ne cite pas l'auteur **3** (letter) resté sans réponse; **you shouldn't let his letter go u.** tu ne devrais pas laisser sa lettre sans réponse

unacquainted [ʌnəˈkweɪntɪd] **ADJ to be u. with sb/sth** ne pas connaître qn/qch; **to be u. with a fact** ignorer un fait; **we are not u. with pressure** nous n'ignorons pas ce que c'est que le stress

unadapted [ʌnəˈdæptɪd] **ADJ** mal adapté, peu adapté (**to sth** à qch)

unaddressed [ʌnəˈdrest] **ADJ** (parcel etc) sans adresse, qui ne porte pas d'adresse

unadopted [ʌnəˈdɒptɪd] **ADJ** non adopté; **to remain u.** (of measure) rester en souffrance
   ►► *Br* **u. road** rue *f* non prise en charge par la municipalité

unadorned [ʌnəˈdɔːnd] **ADJ** sans ornement, sans fioritures; *esp Lit* **her u. beauty** sa beauté sans parure *ou* sans fard; **the u. truth** la vérité pure *ou* toute nue

unadulterated [ʌnəˈdʌltəreɪtɪd] **ADJ** pur, sans mélange; (wine) non frelaté; **u. joy** joie *f* sans mélange; **the u. truth** la vérité pure et simple; **u. by Western influences** non corrompu par les influences occidentales; **this is pure u. garbage!** ceci est purement et simplement de la foutaise!; **I've never heard such u. rot!** je n'ai jamais entendu de telles foutaises!

unadventurous [ʌnədˈventʃərəs] **ADJ** (life, person) peu aventureux; (style, performance, director, prose etc) peu audacieux, conventionnel; **we went to Spain again – that's very u. of you** nous sommes retournés en Espagne – ce n'est pas très aventureux de votre part

unadventurously [ʌnədˈventʃərəslɪ] **ADV** (produced, designed) peu audacieusement; (to decide, choose) sans prendre de risques; **we very u. chose beige carpets again** nous n'avons pas pris de risques et avons encore choisi des moquettes beiges

unadvertised [ʌnˈædvətaɪzd] **ADJ** (product, meeting etc) sans publicité; (action etc) discret, -ète

unadvisable [ʌnədˈvaɪzəb(ə)l] **ADJ** (action) peu recommandé, imprudent; **alcohol is u. for people suffering from heart complaints** l'alcool est à déconseiller aux cardiaques

unadvised [ʌnədˈvaɪzd] **ADJ** *esp Lit* (unwise) imprudent

unaesthetic [ʌniːsˈθetɪk] **ADJ** inesthétique

unaffected [ʌnəˈfektɪd] **ADJ 1** (without affectation) (person, behaviour) sans affectation, naturel, simple; (style) sans fioritures, simple; **u. joy** joie *f* qui n'a rien de simulé; **u. modesty** modestie *f* non simulée **2** (not touched) **to be u. by sth** (of person) ne pas être affecté par qch; (of thing) (by rain, cold, heat etc) ne pas être altéré par qch; **she remained u. by his tears** elle ne fut pas émue par ses larmes; **we were u. by the strike/recession** nous n'avons pas été affectés par la grève/récession; **there's snow everywhere, but the north-west is u.** il y a de la neige partout, mais le nord-ouest n'est pas touché
   ►► *Med* **u. carrier** porteur *m* sain

unaffectedly [ʌnəˈfektɪdlɪ] **ADV** (to behave, speak) simplement, sans affectation; (dressed) sobrement

unaffiliated [ʌnəˈfɪlɪeɪtɪd] **ADJ** non affilié (**to** à)

unaffordable [ʌnəˈfɔːdəb(ə)l] **ADJ** inabordable

unafraid [ʌnə'freɪd] ADJ sans peur

unaided [ʌn'eɪdɪd] ADV sans aide, sans assistance; **he did it u.** il l'a fait tout seul *ou* à lui seul

ADJ **by my own u. efforts** par mes propres moyens; **is this your own u. work?** est-ce que tu as travaillé tout seul?

unaired [ʌn'eəd] ADJ non aéré; *(opinions etc)* non exprimé

unalike [ʌnə'laɪk] ADJ dissemblable, différent; **they are not u.** ils se ressemblent un peu, ils ne sont pas totalement dissemblables

unalleviated [ʌnə'liːvɪeɪtɪd] ADJ sans répit; **u. boredom** ennui *f* mortel

unallocated [ʌn'æləkeɪtɪd] ADJ *(rooms, places)* non assigné; *(money, grants)* non alloué

unallotted [ʌnə'lɒtɪd] ADJ *St Exch (shares)* non réparti

unalloyed [ʌnə'lɔɪd] ADJ *Lit (happiness)* parfait

unalterable [ʌn'ɔːlt(ə)rəb(ə)l] ADJ immuable; *(character)* inaltérable

unalterably [ʌn'ɔːlt(ə)rəblɪ] ADV immuablement

unaltered [ʌn'ɔːltəd] ADJ inchangé; **let's leave it u.** n'y touchons pas

unambiguous [ʌnæm'bɪgjʊəs] ADJ non équivoque; *(reply)* sans ambiguïté; **what he meant was quite u.** il a été tout à fait clair; **u. terms** termes *mpl* tout à fait *ou* on ne peut plus clairs

unambiguously [ʌnæm'bɪgjʊəslɪ] ADV *(worded etc)* sans équivoque, sans ambiguïté; **he told us quite u. to** ... il nous a dit tout à fait clairement de ...

unambitious [ʌnæm'bɪʃəs] ADJ *(person, project etc)* sans ambition, peu ambitieux

un-American [ʌn-] ADJ contraire à l'esprit américain; *(in a damaging way)* antiaméricain; **he's so u.** ce n'est vraiment pas l'Américain type

unamused [ʌnə'mjuːzd] ADJ **she was distinctly u.** visiblement, cela ne l'amusait pas

unanimity [juːnə'nɪmɪtɪ] N unanimité *f*

unanimous [jʊ'nænɪməs] ADJ unanime; **they were u. in accusing him** ils étaient unanimes à l'accuser; **to reach a u. decision** se prononcer à l'unanimité; **u. vote** résolution *f* adoptée à l'unanimité

unanimously [jʊ'nænɪməslɪ] ADV à l'unanimité

unannounced [ʌnə'naʊnst] ADJ sans être annoncé; **he marched in u.** il est entré sans se faire annoncer

unanswerable [ʌn'ɑːns(ə)rəb(ə)l] ADJ *(argument)* incontestable, irréfutable; **u. question** question *f* à laquelle on ne peut pas répondre

unanswered [ʌn'ɑːnsəd] ADJ **1** *(letter, question)* sans réponse; **I had to leave two questions u.** j'ai dû laisser deux questions sans réponse; **our letter has remained u.** notre lettre est restée sans réponse **2** *(argument)* irréfuté

unapologetic [ʌnəpɒlə'dʒetɪk] ADJ **he's an u. royalist/admirer of Hitler** il ne se cache pas d'être royaliste/d'être un admirateur d'Hitler; **they're u. about it** ils estiment qu'il n'ont pas à s'excuser

unappealing [ʌnə'piːlɪŋ] ADJ peu attrayant

unappeased [ʌnə'piːzd] ADJ *Lit (hunger, desire, lust)* inassouvi

unappetizing [ʌn'æpɪtaɪzɪŋ] ADJ peu appétissant; **this dish looks really u.** ce plat n'est pas appétissant du tout

unappreciated [ʌnə'priːʃɪeɪtɪd] ADJ peu apprécié; *(difficulty, scope of task etc)* sous-

estimé; *(hard work, capability)* non reconnu; **her efforts go u.** le mal qu'elle se donne n'est pas apprécié à sa juste valeur

unappreciative [ʌnə'priːʃɪətɪv] ADJ *(audience)* insensible; *(report etc)* peu favorable; **she was very u. of everything we had done for her** elle ne montrait aucune gratitude après tout ce qu'on avait fait pour elle; **don't be so u.!** ne sois pas si ingrat!

unapproachable [ʌnə'prəʊtʃəb(ə)l] ADJ *(person, place)* inaccessible; **an u. sort of person** une personne d'un abord difficile

unappropriated [ʌnə'prəʊprɪeɪtɪd] ADJ *Fin (money)* inutilisé, disponible; *(profit)* non distribué

unarguable [ʌn'ɑːgjʊəb(ə)l] ADJ *(case, theory)* indéfendable

unarguably [ʌn'ɑːgjʊəblɪ] ADV *(indisputably)* incontestablement

unarmed [ʌn'ɑːmd] ADJ *(person)* non armé; **I am u.** je ne suis pas armé; **I'm not going in there u.** je n'entre pas là-dedans sans arme
▸ ▸ **u. combat** combat *m* à mains nues

unashamed [ʌnə'ʃeɪmd] ADJ *(delight, joy)* non déguisé; *(greed, hypocrisy)* flagrant; **to be u. about doing sth** ne pas avoir honte de faire qch; **his u. nationalism** son nationalisme éhonté; **with u. relief** avec un soulagement non dissimulé

unashamedly [ʌnə'ʃeɪmɪdlɪ] ADV sans honte; **George was u. in favour of the war** George se déclarait ouvertement en faveur de la guerre; **he was u. open about it all** il s'est exprimé sur cette affaire avec une franchise totale; **she was quite u. relieved about not having to** ... elle ne cacha pas son soulagement à l'idée de ne pas devoir ...; **he is u. outspoken in his support of** ... il affiche (tout à fait ouvertement) son soutien à ...

unasked [ʌn'ɑːskt] ADV *(to do sth)* spontanément; **she came to help us quite u.** elle est venue nous aider sans qu'on le lui ait demandé
ADJ **u. for** *(gift etc)* spontané, qu'on n'a pas demandé; *(unwanted) (advice)* non sollicité

unaspirated [ʌn'æspɪreɪtɪd] ADJ *Ling* non aspiré

unassailable [ʌnə'seɪləb(ə)l] ADJ *(fortress, position)* imprenable; *(conclusion, argument)* irréfutable; **his reputation is u.** il a une réputation à toute épreuve

unassigned [ʌnə'saɪnd] ADJ *(office, room) (for person)* non attribué; *(for purpose)* non affecté; *(task)* non assigné
▸ ▸ *Fin* **u. revenue** recettes *fpl* non gagées

unassimilated [ʌnə'sɪmɪleɪtɪd] ADJ inassimilé; **u. knowledge** connaissances *fpl* mal assimilées

unassisted [ʌnə'sɪstɪd] ADV sans aide, sans assistance; **he did it u.** il l'a fait tout seul
ADJ **by her own u. efforts** sans l'aide de personne

unassuming [ʌnə'sjuːmɪŋ] ADJ sans prétention(s), modeste

unassumingly [ʌnə'sjuːmɪŋlɪ] ADV modestement, avec modestie

unattached [ʌnə'tætʃt] ADJ **1** *(part, wire etc)* qui n'est pas attaché *(to* à) **2** *(journalist, group etc)* indépendant *(to* de); *Mil (officer)* disponible, en disponibilité **3** *(not married etc)* **to be u.** être libre *ou* sans attaches

unattainable [ʌnə'teɪnəb(ə)l] ADJ inaccessible *(by* à)

unattended [ʌnə'tendɪd] ADJ **1** *(shop, printer etc)* sans surveillance; **to leave one's car u.** laisser sa voiture sans surveillance; **do not leave your luggage u.** surveillez toujours vos bagages **2** *(person, child)* seul; **to leave a child u.** laisser un enfant sans surveillance; **don't leave the guests u. (to)** ne

négligez pas les invités, occupez-vous des invités; **the leaking pipe has gone u. (to) for months** ça fait des mois que le tuyau fuit et rien n'a été fait **3** *(queen etc)* sans escorte

unattractive [ʌnə'træktɪv] ADJ peu attrayant, sans attrait, peu séduisant; *(character)* peu sympathique; **extremely u.** pas du tout attrayant; **she is not u.** elle ne manque pas de charme

unaudited [ʌn'ɔːdɪtɪd] ADJ *(accounts)* non vérifié

unauthenticated [ʌnɔː'θentɪkeɪtɪd] ADJ dont l'authenticité n'est pas établie; *Law (document)* non légalisé

unauthorized [ʌn'ɔːθəraɪzd] ADJ non autorisé, sans autorisation; **no entry to u. persons, no u. access** *(sign)* accès interdit à toute personne étrangère au service
▸ ▸ *Comput* **u. access** accès *m* non autorisé

unavailability [ʌnəveɪlə'bɪlɪtɪ] N indisponibilité *f*

unavailable [ʌnə'veɪləb(ə)l] ADJ *(person, goods)* indisponible, pas disponible; *(sold out etc)* épuisé; **the minister was u. for comment** le ministre s'est refusé à tout commentaire

unavailing [ʌnə'veɪlɪŋ] ADJ inutile, vain; *(effort, attempt)* infructueux

unavailingly [ʌnə'veɪlɪŋlɪ] ADV inutilement, en vain

unavenged [ʌnə'vendʒd] ADV it won't go u. cela ne restera pas impuni; **the u. death of** ... la mort de ... qui n'a pas été vengée

unavoidable [ʌnə'vɔɪdəb(ə)l] ADJ inévitable; *(fate)* auquel on ne peut échapper; *(event)* qu'on ne peut prévenir; **my absence was u.** mon absence a été due à un cas de force majeure; **it is u. that** ... il est inévitable que ... + *sub*
▸ ▸ *Fin* **u. costs** coûts *mpl* induits

unavoidably [ʌnə'vɔɪdəblɪ] ADV inévitablement; **u. detained** retenu pour raison majeure

unaware [ʌnə'weər] ADJ ignorant, pas au courant *(of sth* de qch); **to be u. of sth** ignorer qch; **her husband was totally u. of what was going on** son mari ne se rendait absolument pas compte de ce qui se passait; **he was u. that he was being watched** il ne se rendait pas compte qu'on l'observait; **we are not u. of the need for reform** nous avons conscience de la nécessité d'une réforme; **is that so?, I was u. of that** ah oui?, je n'étais pas au courant; **you will surely not be u. of the importance of** ... l'importance de ... ne vous a certainement pas échappé; **if there are any other problems I am u. of them** s'il y a d'autres problèmes, je ne suis pas au courant; **he is sexually/politically u.** il vit dans un monde où la sexualité/la politique n'existe pas

unawares [ʌnə'weəz] ADV *(without realizing)* inconsciemment, sans s'en rendre compte; **to take** *or* **catch sb u.** *(by surprise)* prendre qn au dépourvu

unbalance [ʌn'bæləns] VT déséquilibrer; *(sb's mind)* déranger

unbalanced [ʌn'bælənst] ADJ **1** *(person, mind etc)* déséquilibré, dérangé **2** *(distribution)* inéquitable; *(reporting)* partial **3** *(steering)* mal équilibré **4** *Fin (account)* non soldé
▸ ▸ *Econ* **u. growth** croissance *f* déséquilibrée

unbandage [ʌn'bændɪdʒ] VT *(wound)* débander

unbankable [ʌn'bæŋkəbəl] ADJ *Fin (bill, paper)* non bancable

unbaptized [ʌnbæp'taɪzd] ADJ non baptisé

unbar [ʌn'bɑːr] VT *(door)* débarrer

unbearable [ʌn'beərəb(ə)l] ADJ insupportable, intolérable; **the children have been u. all day** les enfants ont été insupportables toute la journée; **in this heat, the office is u.** par cette chaleur le bureau n'est pas tenable

unbearably [ʌnˈbeərəblɪ] **ADV** **it was u. painful/hot** la douleur/chaleur était insupportable; **the last scene was u. moving** la dernière scène était d'une tristesse insupportable; **he's u. arrogant** son arrogance est insupportable

unbeatable [ʌnˈbiːtəb(ə)l] **ADJ** imbattable; *(army)* invincible; **we offer u. value** nous offrons de la qualité à des prix imbattables

unbeaten [ʌnˈbiːt(ə)n] **ADJ** *(champion, army)* invaincu; *(record)* qui n'a pas encore été battu

unbecoming [ʌnbɪˈkʌmɪŋ] **ADJ** inconvenant, malséant (**to** de la part de); *(garment)* peu seyant; *(facial hair)* peu esthétique; **it's u. of him to act in this manner** il lui sied mal d'agir de la sorte

unbeknown [ʌnbɪˈnəʊn] **ADV** **u. to me/her/ etc** à mon/son/*etc* insu; **to do sth u. to anyone** faire qch à l'insu de tous

unbeknownst [ʌnbɪˈnəʊnst] **ADV** *esp Am* = **unbeknown**

unbelief [ʌnbɪˈliːf] **N** incrédulité *f*; **he looked at me in u.** il me regarda avec incrédulité

unbelievable [ʌnbɪˈliːvəb(ə)l] **ADJ** incroyable; **it's u. that …** il est incroyable que … + *sub*

unbelievably [ʌnbɪˈliːvəblɪ] **ADV** incroyablement; **u. stupid** d'une sottise incroyable

unbeliever [ʌnbɪˈliːvər] **N** incrédule *mf*

unbelieving [ʌnbɪˈliːvɪŋ] **ADJ** incrédule

unbelievingly [ʌnbɪˈliːvɪŋlɪ] **ADV** *(to say, look)* d'une manière incrédule

unbend [ʌnˈbend] *(pt, pp unbent* [ʌnˈbent]) **VT** *(steel rod etc)* redresser; *(leg)* déplier **VI 1** *(relax)* devenir moins strict **2** *(straighten out)* se redresser; *(of limb)* se déplier

unbending [ʌnˈbendɪŋ] **ADJ** *(character)* inflexible, rigide; **u. attitude** attitude *f* intransigeante

unbias(s)ed [ʌnˈbaɪəst] **ADJ** impartial, -aux

unbidden [ʌnˈbɪd(ə)n] **ADV** *Old-fashioned* **to do sth u.** faire qch spontanément *ou* sans y avoir été invité

unbind [ʌnˈbaɪnd] **VT** *(pt, pp unbound* [ʌnˈbaʊnd]) **1** *(prisoner, hands)* délier **2** *(wound)* débander

unbleached [ʌnˈbliːtʃt] **ADJ 1** écru; **u. linen** toile *f* bise *ou* écrue **2** *(coffee filters, nappies etc)* sans chlore

unblemished [ʌnˈblemɪʃt] **ADJ** sans défaut; *(reputation)* sans tache

unblinking [ʌnˈblɪŋkɪŋ] **ADJ** *(person)* impassible; *(gaze, look)* fixe; **with u. eyes** sans ciller

unblock [ʌnˈblɒk] **VT** *(road, path)* dégager; *(pipe etc)* déboucher; *Comput* débloquer

unblushing [ʌnˈblʌʃɪŋ] **ADJ** sans vergogne, éhonté; **he remained u. as she declared her love** il écoutait sa déclaration d'amour sans rougir

unblushingly [ʌnˈblʌʃɪŋlɪ] **ADV** sans rougir

unbolt [ʌnˈbəʊlt] **VT** *(door)* déverrouiller; *(rail etc)* déboulonner

unbonded warehouse [ʌnˈbɒndɪd] **N** entrepôt *m* fictif

unborn [ˈʌnbɔːn] **ADJ** qui n'est pas (encore) né; **u. child** enfant *mf* à naître; **generations yet u.** [ʌnˈbɔːn] générations *fpl* à venir, générations futures

unbosom [ʌnˈbʊzəm] **VT** *Lit* **to u. oneself to sb** ouvrir son cœur à qn

unbound [ʌnˈbaʊnd] **ADJ** *(book)* non relié, broché; *(hands)* libre; *(prisoner)* pas attaché

unbounded [ʌnˈbaʊndɪd] **ADJ** sans bornes, illimité; *(ambition etc)* démesuré

unbowed [ʌnˈbaʊd] **ADJ** invaincu, insoumis; **bloody but u.** vaincu, mais non soumis

unbranded [ʌnˈbrændɪd] **ADJ** *Mktg* sans marque

unbreakable [ʌnˈbreɪkəb(ə)l] **ADJ** incassable; *(promise, rule etc)* sacré, inviolable; *Sport (record)* imbattable; *(habit)* immuable

unbreathable [ʌnˈbriːðəb(ə)l] **ADJ** *(air)* irrespirable

unbribable [ʌnˈbraɪbəb(ə)l] **ADJ** incorruptible

unbridled [ʌnˈbraɪd(ə)ld] **ADJ 1** *(passion, greed etc)* débridé, effréné; *(capitalism)* effréné **2** *(horse)* débridé, sans bride

unbroken [ʌnˈbrəʊk(ə)n] **ADJ 1** *(plate, chair etc)* non brisé, non cassé, intact **2** *(skin, seal etc)* intact; **u. spirit** optimisme *m* intact **3** *(promise)* inviolé; *(rules)* toujours observé *ou* respecté; **the peace remained u. for ten years** la paix n'a pas été troublée pendant dix ans; *Sport* **record still u.** record qui n'a pas été battu **4** *(silence, expanse of water, years of government etc)* ininterrompu; **u. sheet of ice** nappe de glace continue **5** *(horse)* non rompu, non dressé **6** *Agr* **u. ground** terre *f* vierge

unbrotherly [ʌnˈbrʌðəlɪ] **ADJ** peu fraternel

unbuckle [ʌnˈbʌk(ə)l] **VT** *(belt)* déboucler

unbudgeted [ʌnˈbʌdʒɪtɪd] **ADJ** non prévu au budget

unbuilt [ʌnˈbɪlt, ˈʌnbɪlt] **ADJ** **u. plot, plot of u. ground** terrain *m* vague *ou* non construit

unbundle [ʌnˈbʌnd(ə)l] **VT 1** *Am (itemize)* détailler **2** *Comput* décompresser

unbundling [ʌnˈbʌndlɪŋ] **N 1** *(of goods)* séparation *f* **2** *Comput* décompression *f*

unburden [ʌnˈbɜːd(ə)n] **VT** **to u. oneself** *or* **one's heart** s'épancher; **to u. oneself to sb** se confier à qn; **to u. oneself of a secret** se soulager du poids d'un secret; **to u. one's sorrows to sb** s'épancher auprès de qn

unburied [ʌnˈberɪd] **ADJ** non enterré

unbusinesslike [ʌnˈbɪznɪslaɪk] **ADJ** *(person)* peu commerçant, qui n'a pas le sens des affaires; *(procedure, handling)* peu professionnel; **to conduct one's affairs in an u. way** mal mener ses affaires

unbutton [ʌnˈbʌt(ə)n] **VT** *(one's coat etc)* déboutonner; **to come unbuttoned** se déboutonner

unbuttoned [ʌnˈbʌt(ə)nd] **ADJ** *Fam (relaxed)* décontracté

uncallable [ʌnˈkɔːləbəl] **ADJ** *Fin (capital)* non remboursable

uncalled [ʌnˈkɔːld] **ADJ** *Fin (capital)* non appelé

uncalled-for **ADJ** *(remark)* déplacé; *(rebuke)* immérité, injustifié; *(insult)* gratuit; **that was quite u.** c'était tout à fait injustifié

uncannily [ʌnˈkænɪlɪ] **ADV** étrangement, bizarrement

uncanny [ʌnˈkænɪ] **ADJ 1** *(strange, inexplicable)* étrange, mystérieux; **it's u. how he knows where I am** c'est vraiment étrange *ou* bizarre qu'il sache où je suis; **with u. accuracy** avec une exactitude surprenante **2** *(eerie)* inquiétant

uncared-for [ʌnˈkeəd-] **ADJ** négligé; **to leave a garden u.** laisser un jardin à l'abandon

uncaring [ʌnˈkeərɪŋ] **ADJ** qui ne se soucie pas (des autres), indifférent

uncarpeted [ʌnˈkɑːpɪtɪd] **ADJ** sans tapis, sans moquette

uncashed [ʌnˈkæʃt] **ADJ** non encaissé

uncatalogued [ʌnˈkætəlɒgd] **ADJ** qui n'est pas catalogué

unceasing [ʌnˈsiːsɪŋ] **ADJ** incessant, continuel; *(work)* assidu; *(effort)* soutenu

unceasingly [ʌnˈsiːsɪŋlɪ] **ADV** sans cesse, sans arrêt

uncensored [ʌnˈsensəd] **ADJ** *(scene, version etc)* non expurgé; *(version, edition)* intégral

unceremonious [ʌnserɪˈməʊnɪəs] **ADJ** **it resulted in his u. ejection from the hall** cela a eu pour conséquence qu'il s'est fait expulser de la salle sans cérémonie; **he was packed off in a very u. way to stay with his uncle in Australia** on l'a envoyé très cavalièrement *ou* sans aucune cérémonie chez son oncle en Australie; **after his u. departure from politics** après qu'il eut peu glorieusement abandonné la politique

unceremoniously [ʌnserɪˈməʊnɪəslɪ] **ADV** sans cérémonie, brusquement; **he was u. bundled into the police van** il fut embarqué dans le fourgon de police sans cérémonie

uncertain [ʌnˈsɜːt(ə)n] **ADJ** incertain; **it's u. who will win** on ne sait pas au juste qui gagnera; **I feel u. about him** j'ai des doutes à son sujet; **he told her in no u. terms** il lui dit sans mâcher ses mots; **to be u. what to do** ne pas savoir quoi faire; **I feel u. whether to trust him or not** je ne sais pas si je dois lui faire confiance

uncertainly [ʌnˈsɜːt(ə)nlɪ] **ADV** d'une façon incertaine; *(to look at sb)* d'un air un peu inquiet

uncertainty [ʌnˈsɜːt(ə)ntɪ] **N** incertitude *f*; **there is some u. about …** l'incertitude règne au sujet de …; **u. about** *or* **as to the future** incertitude quant à l'avenir; **to be in a state of u.** être dans l'incertitude; **to remove any u.** pour dissiper toute équivoque; **there's still some u. as to what was actually said** il reste quelque incertitude sur ce qui s'est réellement dit; **there are still too many uncertainties for my liking** il y a encore trop d'incertitudes à mon goût

uncertified [ʌnˈsɜːtɪfaɪd] **ADJ** non certifié

unchain [ʌnˈtʃeɪn] **VT** *(dog)* détacher; *(passions)* déchaîner

unchallengeable [ʌnˈtʃælɪndʒəb(ə)l] **ADJ** *(argument)* irréfutable; *(right)* incontestable; *(evidence, proof)* irrécusable; **to be in an u. position** *(of runner, team, politician etc)* être hors d'atteinte

unchallenged [ʌnˈtʃælɪndʒd] **ADJ 1** *(right)* indisputé, incontesté; **to let sth go** *or* **pass u.** *(statement)* ne pas relever qch; *(right)* ne pas contester qch; *(evidence)* ne pas récuser qch; **I can't let that go u.** je ne peux pas laisser passer cela; **to continue u.** continuer sans être contredit; *Sport* **his record stayed u. for several years** personne ne s'est attaqué à son record pendant plusieurs années **2** *Mil* **to let sb pass u.** laisser passer qn sans interpellation

unchangeable [ʌnˈtʃeɪndʒəb(ə)l] **ADJ** immuable

unchanged [ʌnˈtʃeɪndʒd] **ADJ** inchangé; *Med* **his condition remains u.** son état est stationnaire

unchanging [ʌnˈtʃeɪndʒɪŋ] **ADJ** immuable

uncharacteristic [ʌnkærəktəˈrɪstɪk] **ADJ** inhabituel; **it's u. of her** cela ne lui ressemble pas; **it's u. for her to make a mistake like that** ce n'est pas dans son habitude de faire une erreur pareille

uncharacteristically [ʌnkærəktəˈrɪstɪklɪ] **ADV** *(rude, late, reticent etc)* inhabituellement, anormalement; **u. (for him), he arrived late for the meeting** contrairement à son habitude, il arriva en retard à la réunion

uncharitable [ʌnˈtʃærɪtəb(ə)l] **ADJ** peu charitable; **that's rather u. of you** ce n'est pas très charitable de ta part

uncharted [ʌn'tʃɑːtɪd] ADJ *(unexplored)* in-exploré; *(not yet mapped)* non porté sur la carte; *Fig* **these are u. waters** *(of a science etc)* ce sont des domaines inexplorés

unchaste [ʌn'tʃeɪst] ADJ *esp Lit (person)* non chaste, impur; *(thoughts)* impur

unchastened [ʌn'tʃeɪs(ə)nd] ADJ *(person)* aucunement repentant, nullement assagi; **he was u. by his experience** son expérience n'a rien rabattu de ses prétentions

unchecked [ʌn'tʃekt] ADJ **1** *(not stopped)* *(advance)* sans (la moindre) opposition; *(passion)* effréné; *(anger)* non contenu; **we can't allow this abuse to go u.** nous ne pou-vons pas permettre que ces abus conti-nuent; **if AIDS were to spread u. …** si le sida se propageait sans qu'on lui oppose de résistance …; **the enemy advanced u.** l'en-nemi progressait sans rencontrer de résis-tance **2** *(not verified) (report, assessment)* non vérifié **3** **u. baggage** bagages *mpl* non-enregistrés

unchivalrous [ʌn'ʃɪvəlrəs] ADJ peu cour-tois

unchristian [ʌn'krɪstjən] ADJ peu chrétien; **that's very u. of you** ce sont là des paroles/ des pensées peu chrétiennes; *Fam* **at this u. hour** à cette heure indue

uncircumcised [ʌn'sɜːkəmsaɪzd] ADJ non circoncis

uncivil [ʌn'sɪv(ə)l] ADJ impoli

uncivilized [ʌn'sɪvɪlaɪzd] ADJ non civilisé, barbare; **at this u. hour** à cette heure indue; **it's very u. of you not to have any whisky in the flat!** ce n'est pas du tout civilisé de ta part de ne pas avoir une goutte de whisky chez toi!; **it's very u. of him to keep us wait-ing like this** ce n'est pas très correct de sa part de nous faire attendre comme ça

unclaimed [ʌn'kleɪmd] ADJ non réclamé; *(right)* non revendiqué; *(benefit)* non touché *ou* réclamé

unclasp [ʌn'klɑːsp] VT *(bracelet)* défaire; *(hand in handshake)* desserrer

unclassifiable [ʌn'klæsɪfaɪəb(ə)l] ADJ in-classable

unclassified [ʌn'klæsɪfaɪd] ADJ *(informa-tion)* non (classé), secret, -ète, non confi-dentiel

uncle ['ʌŋk(ə)l] N oncle *m*; *Fig* **rich u.** oncle d'Amérique; *Am Fam* **to cry u.** *(give up)* crier grâce
   ▸▸ **U. Sam** l'Oncle *m* Sam *(personnification des États-Unis)*; *Am Sl Pej* **U. Tom** = Noir *m* qui se comporte de façon obséquieuse avec les Blancs

unclean [ʌn'kliːn] ADJ *also Rel (thoughts etc)* impur; *Iron (cup etc)* souillé; **to feel u.** se sentir souillé

unclear [ʌn'klɪər] ADJ *(statement)* peu clair, vague; *(result)* incertain; *(prose, text)* obs-cur; **it's still u. what has happened** ce qui est arrivé n'est pas toujours très clair; **I'm u. about what is wanted** je ne suis pas sûr de ce qu'on demande

uncleared [ʌn'klɪəd] ADJ **1 u. ground** terrain *m* non défriché **2** *(debt)* non liquidé **3 u. goods** marchandises *fpl* non dédouanées **4** *(cheque)* non compensé, non crédité

unclench [ʌn'klen(t)ʃ] VT *(fist)* desserrer

unclimbable [ʌn'klaɪməb(ə)l] ADJ *(moun-tain)* impossible à escalader

unclimbed [ʌn'klaɪmd] ADJ *(mountain, peak)* invaincu *(par les alpinistes)*

uncloak [ʌn'kləʊk] VT *esp Lit (plans)* décou-vrir; *(impostor)* démasquer

unclog [ʌn'klɒg] VT *(-gg-)* *(machine)* déblo-quer; *(drain)* déboucher

unclothed [ʌn'kləʊðd] ADJ nu

unclouded [ʌn'klaʊdɪd] ADJ *(sky, future, bliss)* sans nuage(s); *(vision, liquid)* clair

uncluttered [ʌn'klʌtəd] ADJ **1** *(desk, room)* qui n'est pas encombré **2** *(style)* dépouillé; **an u. mind** un esprit clair

unco ['ʌŋkəʊ] ADV *Scot Arch* très

uncoil [ʌn'kɔɪl] VT dérouler; *Hum* **to u.** one-self from sb's arms se dégager (avec diffi-culté) des bras de qn
   VI *(of snake, rope)* **to u. (itself)** se dérouler

uncollectable [ʌnkə'lektəb(ə)l] ADJ *(tax)* non percevable

uncollected [ʌnkə'lektɪd] ADJ **1** *(luggage)* non réclamé **2 u. taxes** impôts *mpl* non perçus

uncoloured, *Am* **uncolored** [ʌn'kʌləd] ADJ non coloré; *Fig* **u. account of sth** rapport *m* impartial sur qch

uncombed [ʌn'kəʊmd] ADJ *(hair, wool)* non peigné

uncomely [ʌn'kʌmlɪ] ADJ peu joli

uncomfortable [ʌn'kʌmf(ə)təb(ə)l] ADJ **1** *(house, position etc)* inconfortable; *(arm-chair, garment)* peu confortable; **this is a ve-ry u. armchair** on est très mal (assis) dans ce fauteuil; **I'm in this bed** je ne suis pas bien dans ce lit; **I feel u. in this collar** je ne suis pas à l'aise avec ce col **2 to make things u. for sb** attirer *ou* créer des ennuis à qn **3 to feel** *or* **be u.** *(ill at ease)* être mal à l'aise; *(em-barrassed)* se sentir gêné; **to be** *or* **feel u. about sth** être mal à l'aise à propos de qch; **to make sb feel u.** mettre qn mal à l'aise; **I'd feel u. (about) asking my parents for money** ça me gênerait de demander de l'argent à mes parents; **it's a very u. feeling, knowing you could easily have been killed** c'est un sentiment très déplaisant de savoir que tu aurais très bien pu mourir; **there was an u. silence** il y eut un silence gêné

uncomfortably [ʌn'kʌmf(ə)təblɪ] ADV **1** *(be sitting)* inconfortablement; *(dressed)* de manière inconfortable; **it was u. stuffy in the plane** il y avait une atmosphère étouf-fante dans l'avion **2 to come u. close to sth** *(to bankruptcy, war, disaster etc)* s'approcher dangereusement de qch; **we came u. close to meeting them on holiday!** nous avons bien failli les rencontrer pendant les vacan-ces!; **I was u. aware of him watching me** j'étais désagréablement conscient du fait qu'il me regardait

uncommitted [ʌnkə'mɪtɪd] ADJ *(person)* non engagé; *(reserves, funds, troops)* non af-fecté; **we are u. to any course of action** nous sommes libres de tout engagement quant à la ligne de conduite à adopter; **to remain u.** ne pas s'engager

uncommon [ʌn'kɒmən] ADJ peu commun; **u. word** mot peu usité; **not u.** assez fréquent
   ADV *Arch Fam* singulièrement

uncommonly [ʌn'kɒmənlɪ] ADV **1 not u.** as-sez souvent **2** *Formal (very)* singulièrement; **u. good** excellent; **he took an u. long time over it** il a mis particulièrement longtemps à le faire

uncommunicative [ʌnkə'mjuːnɪkətɪv] ADJ peu communicatif, renfermé, taciturne; **he was very u. about it** il s'est montré très peu communicatif à ce sujet

uncomplaining [ʌnkəm'pleɪnɪŋ] ADJ qui ne se plaint pas, patient, résigné

uncomplainingly [ʌnkəm'pleɪnɪŋlɪ] ADV sans se plaindre

uncomplicated [ʌn'kɒmplɪkeɪtɪd] ADJ *(style, person)* simple; *(task)* facile

uncomplimentary [ʌnkɒmplɪ'ment(ə)rɪ] ADJ peu flatteur, -euse; **he was very u. about you** il ne s'est pas montré du tout flatteur à ton égard

uncomprehending [ʌnkɒmprɪ'hendɪŋ] ADJ *(person)* qui ne comprend pas; **to give sb an u. look** regarder qn sans comprendre; **in u. amazement** ahuri

uncomprehendingly [ʌnkɒmprɪ'hend-ɪŋlɪ] ADV sans comprendre

uncompromising [ʌn'kɒmprəmaɪzɪŋ] ADJ intransigeant; **a man of u. principles** un homme aux principes très stricts; **we took an u. stance on this** nous avons adopté une position inflexible à ce sujet; **u. honesty** honnêteté absolue; **our u. insistence on quality** notre intransigeance quant à la qualité

uncompromisingly [ʌn'kɒmprəmaɪzɪŋlɪ] ADV sans faire de concessions; **u. honest** d'une honnêteté absolue

unconcealed [ʌnkən'siːld] ADJ non dissi-mulé

unconcern [ʌnkən'sɜːn] N insouciance *f*, indifférence *f*; **to show u. in the face of danger** se montrer indifférent en face du danger

unconcerned [ʌnkən'sɜːnd] ADJ insou-ciant, indifférent; **u., he went on speaking** nullement troublé, il continua de parler; **they were quite u. about her well-being** ils ne se souciaient pas du tout de son bien-être; **he seems entirely u. about his results** il ne semble pas du tout s'inquiéter de ses résultats

unconcernedly [ʌnkən'sɜːnɪdlɪ] ADV d'un air indifférent, sans se (laisser) troubler

unconditional [ʌnkən'dɪʃənəl] ADJ incon-ditionnel, sans réserve
   ▸▸ *Law* **u. discharge** libération *f* incondi-tionnelle; **u. guarantee** garantie *f* incondi-tionnelle; *Fin* **u. order** ordre *m* (de payer) pur et simple; **u. surrender** reddition *f* inconditionnelle

unconditionally [ʌnkən'dɪʃənəlɪ] ADV in-conditionnellement; *(accept)* sans réserve; **to surrender u.** se rendre sans condition

unconfirmed [ʌnkən'fɜːmd] ADJ non confirmé; **the report remains u.** la nouvelle n'a pas encore été confirmée
   ▸▸ *Fin* **u. letter of credit** lettre *f* de crédit révocable

uncongenial [ʌnkən'dʒiːnɪəl] ADJ *(person)* peu sympathique, antipathique; *(climate)* peu favorable (**to** à); *(work, atmosphere)* peu agréable

unconnected [ʌnkə'nektɪd] ADJ *(facts etc)* sans rapport (**with** avec); **the two events are totally u.** les deux événements n'ont au-cun rapport entre eux; **this reaction was not u. with the recent …** cette réaction n'était pas sans rapport avec le récent …

unconquerable [ʌn'kɒŋkərəb(ə)l] ADJ *(en-emy)* invincible; *(courage)* indomptable; *(dif-ficulty)* insurmontable

unconquered [ʌn'kɒŋkəd] ADJ *(people, country)* qui n'a pas été conquis; *(peak)* in-vaincu, vierge

unconscionable [ʌn'kɒnʃənəb(ə)l] ADJ *Lit* déraisonnable, excessif; **to take an u. time doing sth** mettre un temps invraisemblable à faire qch

unconscious [ʌn'kɒnʃəs] ADJ **1** *Med* sans connaissance; **to become u.** perdre connaissance; **to knock sb u.** assommer qn **2** *(unaware) (movement etc)* inconscient; *(joke, insult)* involontaire; **to be u. of doing sth** ne pas se rendre compte qu'on fait qch; **to be u. of sth** ne pas avoir conscience de qch, ne pas se rendre compte de qch; **the u. mind** l'inconscient *m*
   N *Psy* **the u.** l'inconscient *m*

unconsciously [ʌn'kɒnʃəslɪ] ADV incons-ciemment, sans s'en rendre compte

unconsciousness [ʌnˈkɒnʃəsnɪs] N (*unawareness*), Med inconscience f

unconsecrated [ʌnˈkɒnsɪkreɪtɪd] ADJ non consacré

unconsidered [ʌnkənˈsɪdəd] ADJ (*remark, opinion*) inconsidéré

unconsolidated [ʌnkənˈsɒlɪdeɪtɪd] ADJ Fin (*debt*) non consolidé

unconstitutional [ʌnkɒnstɪˈtjuːʃən(ə)l] ADJ inconstitutionnel

unconstitutionally [ʌnkɒnstɪˈtjuːʃnəlɪ] ADV inconstitutionnellement

unconstrained [ʌnkənˈstreɪnd] ADJ 1 (*person*) sans contraintes, libre; **to be u. by convention** ne pas connaître les contraintes des conventions; (*consciously reject them*) faire fi des conventions 2 (*act*) spontané; (*passion, joy etc*) débordant; **u. laughter** hilarité f débordante

unconsummated [ʌnˈkɒnsəmeɪtɪd] ADJ (*marriage*) non consommé

uncontaminated [ʌnkənˈtæmɪneɪtɪd] ADJ (*by disease, radiation*), Fig non contaminé

uncontested [ʌnkənˈtestɪd] ADJ (*right*) incontesté; (*election, seat*) non disputé; **the championship has been** or **has gone u. for** ... le championnat n'a pas été disputé depuis ...

uncontrollable [ʌnkənˈtrəʊləb(ə)l] ADJ incontrôlable; (*movement, twitch*) incontrôlable, irrépressible; (*desire*) irrésistible, irrépressible; (*inflation*) irrésistible, incontrôlable; **u. laughter** fou rire m, rire irrépressible; **fits of u. temper** violents accès mpl de colère; **I felt an u. urge to** ... je me suis senti irrésistiblement poussé à ...

uncontrollably [ʌnkənˈtrəʊləblɪ] ADV **she sobbed/laughed/coughed u.** elle ne pouvait s'arrêter de sangloter/rire/tousser; **as inflation rises u.** alors que l'inflation augmente irrésistiblement; **she was u. jealous** elle était d'une jalousie maladive

uncontrolled [ʌnkənˈtrəʊld] ADJ (*anger, weeping, laughter*) incontrôlé; (*style*) débridé; **u. inflation** inflation f incontrôlée; **u. passions** passions fpl effrénées

uncontroversial [ʌnkɒntrəˈvɜːʃəl] ADJ (*subject*) qui ne soulève ou ne provoque pas de controverses

unconventional [ʌnkənˈvenʃənəl] ADJ peu conventionnel, non-conformiste

unconventionally [ʌnkənˈvenʃnəlɪ] ADV de manière peu conventionnelle

unconvinced [ʌnkənˈvɪnst] ADJ sceptique (**of** au sujet de); **I am still u.** je ne suis toujours pas convaincu

unconvincing [ʌnkənˈvɪnsɪŋ] ADJ (*evidence etc*) peu convaincant; (*excuse*) peu convaincant ou vraisemblable; **he was very u. as Tartuffe** il n'était pas convaincant du tout en Tartuffe

unconvincingly [ʌnkənˈvɪnsɪŋlɪ] ADV d'une manière peu convaincante

uncooked [ʌnˈkʊkt] ADJ non cuit

uncool [ʌnˈkuːl] ADJ Fam 1 (*unfashionable, unsophisticated*) ringard; **it's a really u. place** c'est nul comme endroit; **what an u. thing to do!** c'est vraiment nul de faire un truc pareil! 2 (*not allowed, not accepted*) mal vu; **I think it's a bit u. to smoke in here** je pense pas que ce soit permis de fumer ici 3 (*upset*) **she was a bit u. about me moving in with them** elle tenait pas trop à ce que je m'installe chez eux

uncooperative [ʌnkəʊˈɒp(ə)rətɪv] ADJ peu coopératif; **he's being very u.** il se montre très peu coopératif

uncooperatively [ʌnkəʊˈɒp(ə)rətɪvlɪ] ADV de manière peu coopérative

uncooperativeness [ʌnkəʊˈɒp(ə)rətɪvnɪs] N manque m de coopération

uncoordinated [ʌnkəʊˈɔːdɪneɪtɪd] ADJ (*manoeuvre, attack, undertaking, efforts*) qui manque de coordination ou d'organisation; (*movements*) désordonné; **to be u.** (*of person, dancer*) manquer de coordination

uncork [ʌnˈkɔːk] VT (*bottle*) déboucher; Fig (*pent-up emotions*) laisser libre cours à

uncorrected [ʌnkəˈrektɪd] ADJ (*exercise, proof*) non corrigé; (*error*) non rectifié ou corrigé; Phys **result u. for temperature/for pressure** résultat m brut

uncorroborated [ʌnkəˈrɒbəreɪtɪd] ADJ non corroboré

uncorrupted [ʌnkəˈrʌptɪd] ADJ (*person*) non corrompu

uncountable [ʌnˈkaʊntəb(ə)l] ADJ Gram indénombrable VOIR GRAMMAIRE A9–12

uncountably [ʌnˈkaʊntəblɪ] ADV Gram **nouns which can only be used u.** noms qu'on ne peut utiliser que de façon indénombrable

uncounted [ʌnˈkaʊntɪd] ADJ (*not counted*) non compté

uncouple [ʌnˈkʌp(ə)l] VT (*carriages, engine*) dételer, découpler

uncouth [ʌnˈkuːθ] ADJ (*person, behaviour*) grossier; **u. manners** manières fpl gauches ou frustes

uncover [ʌnˈkʌvər] VT 1 (*furniture, swimming pool*) découvrir; (*saucepan*) enlever le couvercle de 2 (*evidence, plot, conspiracy*) découvrir 3 Chess (*piece*) découvrir, dégarnir

uncovered [ʌnˈkʌvəd] ADJ 1 non couvert, découvert 2 Fin (*purchase, sale*) à découvert ▸▸ Fin **u. advance** avance f à découvert; Fin **u. balance** découvert m; **u. cheque** chèque m sans provision; St Exch **u. position** position f non couverte

uncreasable [ʌnˈkriːsəb(ə)l] ADJ (*fabric*) infroissable

uncritical [ʌnˈkrɪtɪk(ə)l] ADJ dépourvu de sens ou d'esprit critique; (*approach, acceptance*) sans discernement; (*audience*) peu exigeant; **to be u. of sb/sth** ne faire preuve d'aucun sens ou esprit critique à l'égard de qn/qch

uncross [ʌnˈkrɒs] VT (*legs*) décroiser

uncrossed [ʌnˈkrɒst] ADJ (*cheque*) non barré

uncrowded [ʌnˈkraʊdɪd] ADJ (*beaches*) presque vide; (*roads*) peu encombré; **I'd never seen Heathrow so u.** je n'avais jamais vu aussi peu de monde à Heathrow

uncrowned [ʌnˈkraʊnd] ADJ sans couronne; Fig **the u. king/queen of** ... le roi/la reine de ...

uncrunch [ʌnˈkrʌntʃ] VT Comput décompresser, décompacter

uncrushable [ʌnˈkrʌʃəb(ə)l] ADJ (*fabric*) infroissable

UNCTAD [ˈʌŋktæd] N (*abbr United Nations Conference on Trade and Development*) CNUCED f

unction [ˈʌŋkʃən] N 1 Rel onction f 2 = unctuousness

unctuous [ˈʌŋktjʊəs] ADJ mielleux, onctueux

unctuously [ˈʌŋktjʊəslɪ] ADV d'un air/d'un ton mielleux ou onctueux

unctuousness [ˈʌŋktjʊəsnɪs] N caractère m mielleux

uncultivated [ʌnˈkʌltɪveɪtɪd] ADJ (*land, person*) inculte

uncultured [ʌnˈkʌltʃəd] ADJ (*mind, person*) inculte; (*accent*) peu raffiné

uncurbed [ʌnˈkɜːbd] ADJ (*authority*) sans restriction; (*passion*) déchaîné; **if these tendencies are allowed to go u.** si on ne met pas un frein à ces tendances

uncurl [ʌnˈkɜːl] VT (*rope, wire*) dérouler; (*one's legs*) déplier; **to u. oneself** s'étirer VI (*of cat*) s'étirer; (*of snake*) se dérouler

uncut [ʌnˈkʌt] ADJ 1 (*hedge*) non coupé; (*diamond*) brut, non taillé 2 (*play, edition*) sans coupures, intégral, -aux; **u. version** (*of film*) version f longue

undamaged [ʌnˈdæmɪdʒd] ADJ non endommagé, intact; (*reputation*) intact

undamped, undampened [ʌnˈdæmpt, ʌnˈdæmpənd] ADJ (*courage*) non affaibli

undated [ʌnˈdeɪtɪd] ADJ non daté, sans date

undaunted [ʌnˈdɔːntɪd] ADJ **to be u. by sth** n'être aucunement intimidé ou aucunement ébranlé par qch; (*by difficulty*) n'être aucunement découragé par qch; **we carried on u.** nous avons continué sans nous laisser intimider ou décourager

undeceive [ʌndɪˈsiːv] VT Lit (*person*) détromper

undecided [ʌndɪˈsaɪdɪd] ADJ 1 (*question, problem*) non résolu; **that's still u.** aucune décision n'a encore été prise 2 (*person*) indécis; **to be u. about sth** être indécis à propos de qch; **he was u. whether he would go or not** il se demandait s'il irait ou non; **to be u. how to act** ne pas savoir comment agir

undeclared [ʌndɪˈkleəd] ADJ (*war, income*) non déclaré; (*love*) non avoué; **u. goods** (*at Customs*) marchandises fpl non déclarées

undefeated [ʌndɪˈfiːtɪd] ADJ invaincu

undefended [ʌndɪˈfendɪd] ADJ 1 Mil etc sans défense; (*goal*) non défendu; (*king at chess*) non protégé 2 Law (*defendant*) qui n'est pas représenté par un avocat; **u. case** débats mpl non contentieux; **u. suit** cause f où le défenseur s'abstient de plaider

undefiled [ʌndɪˈfaɪld] ADJ sans souillure, immaculé; **u. by any contact with Western society** non corrompu par la civilisation occidentale

undefinable [ʌndɪˈfaɪnəb(ə)l] ADJ indéfinissable

undefined [ʌndɪˈfaɪnd] ADJ (*term etc*) non défini; (*vague*) (*feeling etc*) indéterminé, vague

undelete [ʌndɪˈliːt] VT Comput restaurer

undelivered [ʌndɪˈlɪvəd] ADJ non livré, non remis; (*parcel*) en souffrance; **if u. return to sender** en cas de non-délivrance prière de retourner à l'expéditeur

undemanding [ʌndɪˈmɑːndɪŋ] ADJ (*job, book, person*) peu exigeant

undemocratic [ʌndeməˈkrætɪk] ADJ antidémocratique

undemonstrative [ʌndɪˈmɒnstrətɪv] ADJ (*person*) peu expansif, peu démonstratif

undeniable [ʌndɪˈnaɪəb(ə)l] ADJ indéniable, incontestable; (*evidence*) irrécusable; **of u. worth** d'une valeur indéniable

undeniably [ʌndɪˈnaɪəblɪ] ADV incontestablement; **an u. talented man** un homme d'un talent incontestable

undenominational [ʌndɪnɒmɪˈneɪʃənəl] ADJ non confessionnel

undependable [ʌndɪˈpendəb(ə)l] ADJ (*machine, trains, person*) peu fiable

UNDER [ˈʌndər]

PREP sous **1, 4, 6** ▪ au-dessous de **1** ▪ moins de **2** ▪ conformément à **3** ▪ en cours de **5**	
ADV au-dessous **1, 2**	

PREP 1 (*beneath*) sous, au-dessous de; **the dog is u. the table** le chien est sous la table;

u. water sous l'eau; **he hid u. it** il se cacha dessous; **you have to crawl u. it** il faut ramper dessous; **put it u. that** mettez-le là-dessous; **to wear a waistcoat u. one's jacket** porter un gilet sous son veston; **he pulled a stool out from u. the table** il a tiré un tabouret de sous la table; **visible u. the microscope** visible au microscope; *Agr* **field u. wheat** champ *m* mis en blé

2 *(less than)* **all their books were u. £5** tous leurs livres coûtaient moins de 5 livres; **salaries u. £10,000** salaires inférieurs à 10 000 livres; **he's u. thirty** il a moins de trente ans; **people u. thirty, the u. thirties** les moins de trente ans; **children u. ten** les enfants au-dessous de dix ans; **in u. ten minutes** en moins de dix minutes; **to speak u. one's breath** parler à mi-voix

3 *(according to)* **u. his father's will** d'après le testament de son père; **u. the terms of the agreement** d'après les termes de la convention; **u. the terms of the contract** conformément aux termes du contrat; *Com* **u. usual reserve** sauf bonne fin

4 *(under control of, subordinate to etc)* **to be u. sb** être sous les ordres de qn; **he had a hundred men u. him** il avait cent hommes sous ses ordres; **he has three sales teams u. him** il est responsable de trois équipes de ventes; **to be** *or* **to come u. the authority of the Home Office** relever du Ministère de l'Intérieur; **u. government control** soumis au contrôle de l'État; **u. Louis XIV** sous Louis XIV; **Britain u. Thatcher** la Grande-Bretagne sous Thatcher; **to study u. sb** étudier sous la direction de qn; **the orchestra, u. Alexander Gibson** l'orchestre, sous la direction d'Alexander Gibson; **she wrote it u. a pseudonym** elle l'a écrit sous un pseudonyme; **to be u. sentence of death** être condamné à mort; **to be u. orders to do sth** avoir reçu l'ordre de faire qch; **u. these conditions** dans ces conditions; **u. the circumstances** vu les circonstances

5 *(in the process of)* en cours de; **u. repair** en réparation; *Med* **u. observation** en observation; **to keep sb/sth u. observation** surveiller qn/qch; **u. construction** en construction; **the question is u. examination** la question est à l'étude

6 *(in list, directory etc)* **it's entered u. F** cela figure à la lettre F; **we're in the phone book u. Tomson** nous sommes dans l'annuaire sous le nom de Tomson; **are they u. decorators or painters?** sont-ils sous la rubrique décorateurs ou peintres?; **it's u. biology** *(in library etc)* c'est classé sous la rubrique biologie; **to look for/to file sth u.** *(the heading)* ... chercher/classer qch sous la rubrique ...

ADV 1 *(underneath)* (au-)dessous; **to stay u. for two minutes** *(underwater)* rester deux minutes sous l'eau; **to be u.** *(anaesthetic)* être sous anesthésiant; *Fam* **to get out from u.** *(from difficult situation)* se tirer d'affaire **2** *(less)* au-dessous; **children of seven years old and u.** des enfants de sept ans et moins

underachieve [ʌndərə'tʃiːv] VI ne pas obtenir les résultats escomptés

underachiever [ʌndərə'tʃiːvər] N = personne *f* qui n'obtient pas les résultats escomptés

under-age ADJ mineur
▸▸ **u. drinking** consommation *f* d'alcool par les mineurs

underarm [ʌndərɑːm] ADV *Cr, Tennis* **to bowl/to serve u.** lancer/servir la balle par en-dessous
ADJ **1** *Cr, Tennis (bowl, shot etc)* par en-dessous **2 u. deodorant** déodorant *m* pour les aisselles

underbelly [ʌndəbelɪ] N **1** *(of animal)* bas-ventre *m, pl* bas-ventres **2** *Fig* point *m* faible;

the soft u. of Europe le ventre mou de l'Europe

underbid [ʌndə'bɪd] *(pt* **underbid;** *pp* **underbid(den)** [-'bɪd((ə)n)]) VT *Com etc* **to u. sb** faire des soumissions *ou* offrir des conditions plus avantageuses que qn
VT & VI *Cards* **to u. (one's hand)** demander au-dessous de son jeu

underblanket [ʌndəblæŋkɪt] N = couverture *f* entre le matelas et le drap de dessous

underbody [ʌndəbɒdɪ] N *Aut* bas *m* de caisse

underborrow [ʌndə'bɒrəʊ] VI *Fin (of company)* ne pas emprunter assez

underborrowed [ʌndə'bɒrəʊd] ADJ *Fin (company)* sous-endetté

underborrowing [ʌndə'bɒrəʊɪŋ] N *Fin (of company)* sous-endettement *m*

underbrush [ʌndəbrʌʃ] N sous-bois *m*

undercapitalization [ʌndəkæpɪtəlaɪ'zeɪʃən] N *Econ* sous-capitalisation *f*

undercapitalized [ʌndə'kæpɪtəlaɪzd] ADJ *(industry)* sous-capitalisé

undercarriage [ʌndəkærɪdʒ] N *Aviat* train *m* d'atterrissage

undercharge [ʌndə'tʃɑːdʒ] VT **they undercharged him** on ne lui a pas fait payer assez; **they undercharged her** *or* **she was undercharged by £5** on aurait dû lui faire payer 5 livres de plus
VI demander trop peu *(for sth* pour qch*)*

underclass [ʌndəklɑːs] N *(of society)* sous-prolétariat *m*, quart-monde *m*

undercloth [ʌndəklɒθ] N *(on table)* sous-nappe *f, pl* sous-nappes

underclothes [ʌndəkləʊðz] NPL, **underclothing** [ʌndəkləʊðɪŋ] N sous-vêtements *mpl, (women's)* lingerie *f*, dessous *mpl*

undercoat [ʌndəkəʊt] N **1** *(of paint)* couche *f* de fond, première couche **2** *Am Aut* couche *f ou* revêtement *m* antirouille

undercoating [ʌndəkəʊtɪŋ] N = undercoat

underconsumption [ʌndəkən'sʌmpʃən] N *Econ* sous-consommation *f*

undercook [ʌndə'kʊk] VT ne pas assez cuire

under-correction N *Aut* sous-correction *f, pl* sous-corrections, correction *f* insuffisante

undercover [ʌndəkʌvər] ADJ secret, -ète, clandestin
ADV clandestinement
▸▸ **u. agent** agent *m* secret

undercurrent [ʌndəkʌrənt] N *(in sea)* courant *m* sous-marin; *Fig* **u. of discontent** vague *f* de fond de mécontentement; *Fig* **but there are undercurrents** *(in relationship etc)* mais il y a des tensions sous-jacentes

undercut [ʌndəkʌt] N *Culin* filet *m* (de bœuf)
VT *(pt, pp* **undercut;** *prp* **undercutting**) **1** *Sport (ball)* couper, lifter **2** *Com (competitor)* vendre moins cher que; *(prices)* casser

underdeveloped [ʌndədɪ'veləpt] ADJ **1** *Phot* insuffisamment développé **2** *(child)* retardé; *(muscle)* pas assez développé **3** *Econ (country)* sous-développé; *(area)* insuffisamment mis en valeur; *(resources)* sous-exploité

underdog [ʌndədɒg] N *Sport* outsider *m; (socially etc)* défavorisé, -ée; *Pol etc* **to side with the underdog(s)** prendre le parti des plus faibles; *Sport* **the underdogs won 5-2** ceux qui étaient donnés perdants à l'avance ont gagné 5 à 2

underdone [ʌndə'dʌn] ADJ *Culin (undercooked)* pas assez cuit; **I'd like my steak slightly u.** *(rare)* je voudrais mon steak légèrement saignant

underdrawers [ʌndədrɔːz] NPL *Am* caleçon *m* (d'homme)

underdressed [ʌndə'drest] ADJ **to be u.** *(not warm enough)* ne pas être assez habillé *ou* couvert; *(not formal enough)* ne pas être assez bien habillé

underemployed [ʌndərem'plɔɪd] ADJ *(person)* sous-employé; *(resources)* sous-exploité

underemployment [ʌndərem'plɔɪmənt] N *(of person)* sous-emploi *m*

underestimate[1], **underestimation** [ʌndər'estɪmɪt, -estɪ'meɪʃən] N sous-estimation *f, pl* sous-estimations

underestimate[2] [ʌndər'estɪmeɪt] VT *(expenses, person)* sous-estimer; *(difficulties, opponent)* méconnaître, mésestimer

underexpose [ʌndəreks'pəʊz] VT **1** *Phot (film)* sous-exposer **2** *(publicize insufficiently) (person, film, event)* faire insuffisamment la publicité de

underexposed [ʌndəreks'pəʊzd] ADJ *Phot* sous-exposé

underexposure [ʌndəreks'pəʊʒər] N **1** *Phot (of film)* sous-exposition *f* **2** *(to publicity)* manque *m* de publicité

underfed [ʌndə'fed] ADJ sous-alimenté, mal nourri

underfeeding [ʌndə'fiːdɪŋ] N sous-alimentation *f*

underfelt [ʌndəfelt] N *(for carpet)* thibaude *f*

underfinance [ʌndə'faɪnæns] VT financer insuffisamment

underfloor [ʌndəflɔːr] ADJ
▸▸ **u. heating** chauffage *m* par le sol

underfoot [ʌndə'fʊt] ADV sous les pieds; **it's wet u.** le sol est mouillé; **the snow crunched u.** la neige crissait sous les pieds; **to trample** *or* **tread sth u.** fouler qch aux pieds

underfunded [ʌndə'fʌndɪd] ADJ *(project etc)* insuffisamment financé

underfunding [ʌndə'fʌndɪŋ] N *(of industry)* insuffisance *f* de financement; **the project suffered from u.** le projet a souffert d'un financement insuffisant

undergardener N aide-jardinier *m, pl* aides-jardiniers

undergarment [ʌndəgɑːmənt] N sous-vêtement *m, pl* sous-vêtements

undergo [ʌndə'gəʊ] VT *(pt* **underwent** [-'went]; *pp* **undergone** [-'gɒn]) *(change)* passer par, subir; *(hardship, examination, operation)* subir; **to u. a complete change** subir une métamorphose complète; **undergoing repairs** en réparation; *Med* **to u. treatment** suivre un traitement

undergrad [ʌndə'græd] N *Fam* = undergraduate

undergraduate [ʌndə'grædjʊɪt] N étudiant, -ante *(qui prépare le DEUG/la licence)*; **in my u. days** lorsque j'étais étudiant; **u. life** la vie d'étudiant; **u. newspaper** journal étudiant

underground [ʌndəgraʊnd] ADV **1** *(in mine etc)* sous terre **2** *Fig (secretly)* clandestinement, secrètement; **to go u.** passer dans la clandestinité
ADJ **1** *(work)* sous terre; *(pipe, lake, cable)* souterrain; **u. workings** chantier *m* souterrain, travaux *mpl* souterrains **2** *Fig (clandestine) (organization, press)* clandestin, secret, -ète
N **1** *Br Rail* métro *m* **2** *(in occupied country etc)* **the u.** la résistance
▸▸ **u. economy** économie *f* souterraine; **u. gallery** souterrain *m*; **u. movement** mouvement *m* clandestin; *(in occupied country)* résistance *f*; **u. passage** souterrain; *Am Hist*

The U. Railroad *(network for escaping slaves)* = réseau *m* clandestin de libération des esclaves; **u. railway** métro *m*; **u. station** station *f* de métro; **u. train** rame *f* de métro

undergrowth ['ʌndəgrəʊθ] N broussailles *fpl*, sous-bois *m*

underhand ['ʌndəhænd] ADJ *(person)* sournois; **to behave in an u. way** agir en sousmain; **u. dealings** manœuvres *fpl* clandestines, *Fam* magouilles *fpl*

underhanded [ʌndə'hændɪd] ADJ **1** = **underhand 2** *Am (short of staff)* à court de personnel; *(short of workers)* à court de maind'œuvre

underhandedly [ʌndə'hændɪdlɪ] ADV en sous-main

underinsured [ʌndərɪn'ʃɔːd] ADJ sousassuré

underinvestment [ʌndərɪn'vestmənt] N insuffisance *f* d'investissement

underlay[1] ['ʌndəleɪ] N *(for carpet)* thibaude *f*, *(for tiling)* assise *f*

underlay[2] [ʌndə'leɪ] VT *(pt, pp* **underlaid** [-'leɪd]*)* **to u. sth with sth** mettre qch sous qch; **carpet underlaid with felt** moquette *f* sur thibaude

underlie [ʌndə'laɪ] VT *(pt* underlay [-'leɪ]; *pp* underlain [-'leɪn]; *prp* underlying [-'laɪɪŋ]*)* être à la base *ou* à l'origine de; **the reasons which underlay her decision** les raisons qui ont motivé sa décision

underline[1] ['ʌndəlaɪn] N souligné *m*

underline[2] [ʌndə'laɪn] VT *(word)* souligner; *Fig (fact)* souligner, appuyer sur, insister sur

underling ['ʌndəlɪŋ] N *Pej* subalterne *mf*, subordonné, -ée

underlining [ʌndə'laɪnɪŋ] N soulignement *m*, soulignage *m*

underlying [ʌndə'laɪɪŋ] ADJ *(rock, principles, causes etc)* sous-jacent
▸▸*Fin* **u. asset** actif *m* sous-jacent; *St Exch* **u. futures contract** contrat *m* à terme sous option; *Fin* **u. mortgage** hypothèque *f* sousjacente; *Fin* **u. security** titre *m* sous-jacent

undermanager ['ʌndəmænɪdʒər] N souschef *m*, *pl* sous-chefs, sous-directeur *m*, *pl* sous-directeurs

undermanned [ʌndə'mænd] ADJ à court de main-d'œuvre; **to be u.** manquer de main d'œuvre

undermanning [ʌndə'mænɪŋ] N manque *m ou* pénurie *f* de main-d'œuvre

undermentioned ['ʌndəmenʃənd] ADJ *Fml* (cité *ou* mentionné) ci-dessous; **the u. persons** les personnes dont les noms suivent

undermine [ʌndə'maɪn] VT **1** *(coast, wall)* miner, saper; *(of sea, river)* (cliffs, banks) affouiller; **foundations undermined by water** fondements minés par l'eau **2** *(principle, authority)* saper; *(sb's health)* miner; *(sb's confidence)* ébranler; **to u. the foundations of society** attaquer les bases de la société; **stop undermining me!** arrête de me faire du tort!

undermost ['ʌndəməʊst] ADJ **the u.** le plus bas, *f* la plus basse

underneath [ʌndə'niːθ] PREP au-dessous de, sous; **he pushed the letter u. the door** il a glissé la lettre sous la porte; **he pulled it (out) from u. the blanket** il l'a tiré de dessous la couverture
  ADV au-dessous, dessous; **he picked up the book and found the ticket u.** il a soulevé le livre et a trouvé le billet dessous
  N dessous *m*; **the u. of the box is black** le dessous de la boîte est noir
  ADJ de dessous, d'en dessous

undernourished [ʌndə'nʌrɪʃt] ADJ sousalimenté

undernourishment [ʌndə'nʌrɪʃmənt] N sous-alimentation *f*

underpaid [ʌndə'peɪd] ADJ *(work, worker)* sous-payé, sous-rémunéré

underpants ['ʌndəpænts] NPL *(for men)* slip *m*; **a pair of u.** un slip

underpart ['ʌndəpɑːt] N partie *f* inférieure

underpass ['ʌndəpɑːs] N *(for cars)* tunnel *m*; *(for pedestrians)* (passage *m*) souterrain *m*

underpay [ʌndə'peɪ] VT *(pt, pp* **underpaid** [-'peɪd]*)* *(worker etc)* sous-payer, sousrémunérer

underperform [ʌndəpə'fɔːm] VI *Fin (of shares, investment)* ne pas être performant

underpin [ʌndə'pɪn] VT *(-pp-)* *(wall)*, *Fig (theory)* étayer; *(organization)* être à la base de; **the principles which u. Marxism-Leninism** les principes de base du marxismeléninisme

underpinning [ʌndə'pɪnɪŋ] N étayage *m*; *(of organization, theory)* base *m*

underplay [ʌndə'pleɪ] VT **1** *(play down)* minimiser l'importance de **2** *Theat* **to u. a part** *(with subtlety)* jouer un rôle tout en nuances; *(with lack of force)* jouer un rôle de façon trop plate **3** *Fig* **to u. one's hand** ne pas être assez exigeant, ne pas demander assez; *(deliberately)* cacher son jeu

underpopulated [ʌndə'pɒpjʊleɪtɪd] ADJ sous-peuplé

underprice [ʌndə'praɪs] VT *(article)* mettre un prix trop bas à

underpriced [ʌndə'praɪst] ADJ très bon marché (par rapport à sa valeur réelle); **at £15.99 it's definitely u.** à 15,99 livres c'est vraiment donné

underpricing [ʌndə'praɪsɪŋ] N fixation *f* de prix trop bas

underprivileged [ʌndə'prɪvɪlɪdʒd] ADJ déshérité, défavorisé
  NPL **the u.** les défavorisés, les économiquement faibles

underproduce [ʌndəprə'djuːs] VI *Ind* être en situation de sous-production

underproduction [ʌndəprə'dʌkʃən] N *Ind* sous-production *f*

underproductive [ʌndəprə'dʌktɪv] ADJ *Ind* sous-productif

underqualified [ʌndə'kwɒlɪfaɪd] ADJ sous-qualifié

underrate [ʌndə'reɪt] VT *(opponent, difficulty, importance of sth)* sous-estimer

under-represent VT minimiser, ne pas donner assez d'importance à

under-representation N *esp Pol* sousreprésentation *f*

under-represented [-reprɪ'zentɪd] ADJ *esp Pol* sous-représenté

underscore[1] ['ʌndəskɔːr] N trait *m* de soulignement

underscore[2] [ʌndə'skɔːr] VT *(title etc)* souligner; *Fig (fact)* faire ressortir, mettre en évidence; *(importance of sth)* souligner

undersea ['ʌndəsiː] ADJ sous-marin

underseal ['ʌndəsiːl] *Br Aut* N couche *f* antirouille (pour dessous de châssis), couche anticorrosion
  VT **to u. (the chassis of) a car** traiter le châssis d'une voiture contre la rouille

undersecretary [ʌndə'sekrɪt(ə)rɪ] N soussecrétaire *mf*, *Br* **permanent u.** secrétaire *m* général *(d'un ministère)*

undersell [ʌndə'sel] VT *(pt, pp* undersold [-'səʊld]*)* *Com (competition etc)* vendre moins cher que; *(goods etc)* vendre au-dessous de sa valeur; *Fig* **don't u. yourself at the interview** essaie de bien te vendre lors de l'entretien; **she tends to u. herself** elle a ten-

dance à ne pas suffisamment se mettre en valeur

undersexed [ʌndə'sekst] ADJ de *ou* à faible libido; **he's u.** il a une faible libido

undersheet ['ʌndəʃiːt] N alaise *f*, alèse *f*

undershield ['ʌndəʃiːld] N *Aut* bouclier *m* inférieur

undershirt ['ʌndəʃɜːt] N *Am (for men)* maillot *m*

undershoot [ʌndə'ʃuːt] VT & VI *(pt, pp* undershot [-'ʃɒt]*)* *Aviat* **to u. (the runway)** se présenter *ou* atterrir trop court (sur la piste); *Fig* **to u. a production target** ne pas atteindre ses objectifs de production

underside ['ʌndəsaɪd] N dessous *m*

undersigned [ʌndə'saɪnd] ADJ, N soussigné, -ée; **I, the u.** je soussigné(e); **the u. declare that ...** les soussignés déclarent que ...

undersize(d) [ʌndə'saɪz(d)] ADJ de (trop) petite taille, trop petit

underskirt ['ʌndəskɜːt] N jupon *m*

underslung [ʌndə'slʌŋ] ADJ *Aut (chassis)* surbaissé; *(car)* à carrosserie surbaissée

understaffed [ʌndə'stɑːft] ADJ à court de personnel; **the office is u.** le bureau manque de personnel

understaffing [ʌndə'stɑːfɪŋ] N manque *m ou* pénurie *f* de personnel

understand [ʌndə'stænd] *(pt, pp* understood [-'stʊd]*)* VT **1** *(comprehend)* comprendre; **I don't u. French** je ne comprends pas le français; **he can't make himself understood in German** il ne peut pas se faire comprendre en allemand; **he understands business matters** il s'y connaît *ou* s'y entend en affaires; **this sentence can be understood in several ways** cette phrase peut s'interpréter de plusieurs façons; **no one understands me** personne ne me comprend; **to u. each other** *or* **one another** se comprendre; *(have same ideas etc)* s'entendre; **I quite u. that he must be tired** je comprends très bien qu'il soit fatigué; **I don't u. why he did it** je ne comprends pas pourquoi il l'a fait; **do you u. what he's talking about?** comprenez-vous quelque chose à ce qu'il raconte?; **what I can't u. is that ...** ce que je ne comprends pas, c'est que ... + *sub*; **I can u. your being angry** je comprends que vous soyez fâché; **I can't u. it** je ne (le) comprends pas; **I'm at a loss to u. it, I can't u. a word of it, I don't u. the first thing about it** je n'y comprends (absolument) rien; **(is that) understood?** (vous avez *ou* c'est bien) compris?, (c'est) entendu?; **that's easily understood** cela se comprend facilement

2 *(believe)* **I understood that I was to be paid for my work** j'ai cru comprendre que je devais être payé pour mon travail; **I u. (that) you're coming to work here** j'ai appris que vous veniez travailler ici; **he is understood to be abroad, it is understood that he is abroad** il serait à l'étranger; **it must be understood** *or* **you must u. that ...** il doit être (bien) entendu *ou* il faut (bien) comprendre que ...; **to give sb to u. that ...** laisser entendre à qn que ...; **I have made it understood** *or* **I have let it be understood that ...** j'ai laissé entendre que ...

3 *(sth implicit)* sous-entendre; **am I to u. that ...?** *(deduce)* dois-je en conclure que ...?; **in this sentence the verb is understood** dans cette phrase le verbe est sousentendu; **that's understood** cela va sans dire, cela va de soi

  VI comprendre; **now I u.!** je comprends *ou* j'y suis maintenant!; **you don't u.** vous n'y êtes pas; **do you u.?** vous comprenez?; **he left yesterday, I u.** il est parti hier, si j'ai bien compris *ou* si je ne me trompe (pas); **to u. about sth** comprendre qch

understandable [ʌndə'stændəb(ə)l] ADJ compréhensible; **that's u.** cela se comprend (facilement), c'est bien normal; **it's quite u. that she should be …** c'est tout à fait compréhensible qu'elle soit …

understandably [ʌndə'stændəblɪ] ADV naturellement, forcément; **he was u. disappointed** il était compréhensible qu'il soit déçu

understanding [ʌndə'stændɪŋ] ADJ compréhensif (**about sth** au sujet de qch); *(letter, words, smile)* plein de compréhension ▮ N 1 *(comprehension, conception)* compréhension *f*; **the age of u.** l'âge *m* de raison; **it's beyond all u.** c'est incompréhensible, c'est à n'y rien comprendre; **it's beyond my u.** cela dépasse mon entendement, je n'y comprends rien; **he showed great u.** *(sensitivity)* il s'est montré très compréhensif; **to be lacking in u. of a problem** ne pas bien comprendre un problème; **according to my u. of it** si j'ai bien compris; **my u. was that the venue would be paid for by the organizers** j'avais compris que les organisateurs paieraient pour la location des locaux **2** *(between nations etc)* entente *f*, accord *m*; *(agreement)* accord, arrangement *m*; **spirit of u.** esprit *m* d'entente; **they had an u., there was an u. between them** ils s'étaient arrangés entre eux; **to come to** *or* **to reach an u.** s'entendre *ou* s'arranger (**with sb** avec qn) **3** *(condition)* condition *f*; **on the u. that he gives it me back** à (la) condition qu'il me le rende; **on the firm u. that …** à la condition expresse que …

understandingly [ʌndə'stændɪŋlɪ] ADV *(to act)* avec compréhension

understate [ʌndə'steɪt] VT minimiser; *(problem etc)* ne pas insister sur; **understated** *(make-up etc)* discret, -ète; **the deliberately understated figures in the foreground** les silhouettes volontairement estompées au premier plan

understatement [ʌndə'steɪtmənt] N 1 euphémisme *m*; *Ling* litote *f*; **with typical British u.** avec un euphémisme typiquement britannique; **to say it's expensive is an u.** dire que c'est cher est un euphémisme; **that's an u. if I ever heard one!** c'est un des plus beaux euphémismes que j'aie jamais entendus; *Fam* **that's the u. of the year!** c'est le moins qu'on puisse dire! **2** *(low-key presentation) (of problem, distinction)* minimisation *f*

understeer [ʌndə'stɪər] VI sous-virer; **a car which understeers** une voiture sous-vireuse

understeer(ing) [ʌndə'stɪər(ɪŋ)] N sous-virage *m*, comportement *m* sous-vireur

understudy ['ʌndəstʌdɪ] *Theat* N doublure *f* ▮ VT *(actor)* doubler; *(role)* servir de doublure pour

undersubscribed [ʌndəsʌb'skraɪbd] ADJ *Fin, St Exch (issue, share)* non-souscrit

undertake [ʌndə'teɪk] VT *(pt* **undertook** [-'tʊk]; *pp* **undertaken** [-'teɪk(ə)n]) **1** *(journey etc)* entreprendre **2** *(task)* entreprendre; *(responsibility)* assumer; **to u. to do sth** s'engager à faire qch **3 to u. that …** garantir que … **4** *(vehicle)* doubler par l'intérieur

undertaker ['ʌndəteɪkər] N entrepreneur *m* des pompes funèbres; **the u.'s** les pompes funèbres

undertaking [ʌndə'teɪkɪŋ] N 1 *(enterprise)* entreprise *f*; **it's quite an u.** c'est toute une affaire; **the u. of this project meant that …** la mise en œuvre de ce projet signifiait que … **2** *(promise etc)* engagement *m*, promesse *f*; *Law* soumission *f*; **he gave an u. to do it** *or*

that he would do it il s'est engagé à *ou* il a promis de le faire; **I give you my solemn u. never to …** je vous promets solennellement de ne jamais …; **I can't give you that u.** je ne peux vous faire cette promesse **3** *(profession of undertaker)* métier *m* d'entrepreneur des pompes funèbres

undertax [ʌndə'tæks] VT *(something)* taxer insuffisamment; *(somebody)* ne pas faire payer assez d'impôts à

under-the-counter ADJ *(sales etc)* clandestin ▮ ADV clandestinement

undertone ['ʌndətəʊn] N 1 **in an u.** *(to talk)* à mi-voix, à voix basse **2 an u. of menace** une note de menace; **grey with blue undertones** gris nuancé de bleu

undertow ['ʌndətəʊ] N *(in water)* courant *m* (sous-marin) *(lorsqu'une vague se retire)*; *Fig* tension *f* sous-jacente

underuse[1] [ʌndə'juːs] N sous-utilisation *f*

underuse[2] [ʌndə'juːz] VT sous-utiliser

underutilization [ʌndəjuːtɪlaɪ'zeɪʃən] N *(of facilities, equipment)* sous-utilisation *f*

underutilize [ʌndə'juːtɪlaɪz] VT *(facilities, equipment)* sous-utiliser

undervalue [ʌndə'væljuː] VT *Com (goods)* sous-évaluer; *Fig* sous-estimer, mésestimer

undervest ['ʌndəvest] N *esp Br* = **vest**[1] **1**

underwater ADJ ['ʌndəwɔːtər] sous-marin ▮ ADV [ʌndə'wɔːtər] sous l'eau ▮▸ *Am St Exch* **u. option** option *f* à prix glissant à la baisse

underwear ['ʌndəweər] N sous-vêtements *mpl*, *(for women)* lingerie *f*, dessous *mpl*

underweight [ʌndə'weɪt] ADJ *(article)* d'un poids insuffisant; **to be u.** *(of person)* ne pas peser assez; **I'm ten lbs u.** ≃ il me manque cinq kilos, je devrais peser cinq kilos de plus

underwhelm [ʌndə'welm] VT *Hum* **your generosity underwhelms me** votre générosité me renverse; **he was obviously underwhelmed by his present** le cadeau l'avait laissé manifestement indifférent; **the critics were underwhelmed by his next film** son nouveau film fut accueilli avec un enthousiasme très relatif par la critique

underwired ['ʌndəwaɪəd] ADJ ▸▸ **u. bra** soutien-gorge *m* avec armature, *pl* soutiens-gorge

underworld ['ʌndəwɜːld] N 1 *Myth* **the u.** les enfers *mpl* **2** *(of criminals)* pègre *f*, milieu *m*

underwrite ['ʌndəraɪt] *(pt* **underwrote** [-rəʊt]; *pp* **underwritten** [-rɪt(ə)n]) VT *Fin (loan, new issue, policy, risk)* garantir, souscrire; **policy underwritten at Lloyd's** police garantie par Lloyd's

underwriter ['ʌndəraɪtər] N 1 *Fin* syndicataire *mf*, souscripteur *m*, garant *m*; **the underwriters** le syndicat de garantie **2** *(in insurance)* assureur *m*; **marine u.** assureur maritime ▸▸ *Fin* **u. agent** agent *m* souscripteur

underwriting ['ʌndəraɪtɪŋ] N *Fin (of issue, policy, risk)* garantie *f*, **marine u.** assurance *f* maritime ▸▸ *Fin* **u. agent** agent *m* souscripteur; **u. commission** commission *f* de garantie; **u. syndicate** syndicat *m* de prise ferme

undeserved [ʌndɪ'zɜːvd] ADJ *(praise, reproach)* immérité

undeservedly [ʌndɪ'zɜːvɪdlɪ] ADV à tort, injustement; *(be decorated etc)* sans l'avoir mérité

undeserving [ʌndɪ'zɜːvɪŋ] ADJ *(person)* sans mérite; *(cause etc)* peu méritoire; **u. of attention** indigne d'attention

undesirable [ʌndɪ'zaɪərəb(ə)l] ADJ indésirable; **an u. character** un personnage peu

recommandable; **to have an u. influence on sb** avoir une mauvaise influence sur qn; **if you think this is u.** si vous pensez que ce n'est pas souhaitable; **it is u. that he should be sent to an adult prison** il est inadmissible qu'on l'envoie dans une prison pour adultes ▮ N indésirable *mf*

undetected [ʌndɪ'tektɪd] ADJ non détecté, non décelé; **to go u.** passer inaperçu

undetermined [ʌndɪ'tɜːmɪnd] ADJ 1 *(quality, date)* indéterminé, incertain; *(issue)* non résolu, irrésolu **2** *(not resolute)* irrésolu, indécis

undeterred [ʌndɪ'tɜːd] ADJ **to carry on u.** continuer sans se laisser décourager (**by** par); **we remained u.** nous ne nous sommes pas laissé décourager; **u. by the weather, he went out for a walk** en dépit du mauvais temps, il est sorti se promener

undeveloped [ʌndɪ'veləpt] ADJ 1 *(ideas, suggestions)* non développé; *(land, resources)* inexploité, non exploité; *(mind)* non formé **2** *(film)* non développé

undeviating [ʌn'diːvɪeɪtɪŋ] ADJ *(course, path)* droit, direct; *(faithfulness)* qui ne se dément pas

undies ['ʌndɪz] NPL *Fam* lingerie *f*, dessous *mpl*

undifferentiated [ʌndɪfə'renʃɪeɪtɪd] ADJ indifférencié ▸▸ *Mktg* **u. marketing** marketing *m* indifférencié

undigested [ʌndɪ'dʒestɪd] ADJ *(food)* non digéré, mal digéré; *(facts)* mal assimilé

undignified [ʌn'dɪɡnɪfaɪd] ADJ peu digne, qui manque de dignité; **to be u.** manquer de dignité; **what an u. way to sit!** quelle manière peu élégante de s'asseoir!; **their business venture came to an u. end** leur entreprise a échoué de façon lamentable

undiluted [ʌndaɪ'luːtɪd] ADJ *(liquid)* non dilué; *(acid)* concentré; *(joy, delight, pleasure)* sans mélange

undiminished [ʌndɪ'mɪnɪʃt] ADJ non diminué, intact; **my respect for him remains u.** mon respect pour lui n'a pas diminué *ou* est resté intact; **thirty years later, the appeal of the film remains u.** trente ans plus tard, le film n'a rien perdu de son intérêt

undiplomatic [ʌndɪplə'mætɪk] ADJ peu diplomatique, peu diplomate

undiplomatically [ʌndɪplə'mætɪklɪ] ADV de manière peu diplomate *ou* peu diplomatique

undipped [ʌn'dɪpt] ADJ *Aut* **to drive with u. headlights** conduire en plein phares

undiscerning [ʌndɪ'sɜːnɪŋ] ADJ *(eater, wine-drinker)* peu raffiné, peu connaisseur, -euse; *(mind)* peu pénétrant; **to be u.** *(of person)* manquer de discernement

undischarged [ʌndɪs'tʃɑːdʒd] ADJ 1 *(debtor)* non libéré (d'une obligation); *(debt)* non liquidé **2** *(duty)* inaccompli ▸▸ *Law* **u. bankrupt** failli *m* non réhabilité

undisciplined [ʌn'dɪsɪplɪnd] ADJ indiscipliné

undisclosed [ʌndɪs'kləʊzd] ADJ non révélé ▸▸ *Com* **u. principal** acheteur *m* non identifié *ou* anonyme

undiscountable [ʌndɪs'kaʊntəb(ə)l] ADJ *Fin* inescomptable

undiscovered [ʌndɪs'kʌvəd] ADJ non découvert; **u. country** terre *f* inconnue; **the ruins of Troy went u. for centuries** l'emplacement des ruines de Troie est resté ignoré pendant des siècles

undiscriminating [ʌndɪs'krɪmɪneɪtɪŋ] ADJ sans discernement, qui manque de discernement

undiscriminatingly [ʌndɪs'krɪmɪneɪt-ɪŋlɪ] ADV sans discernement

undisguised [ʌndɪs'gaɪzd] ADJ non déguisé; *(feelings)* non dissimulé

undisguisedly [ʌndɪs'gaɪzɪdlɪ] ADV ouvertement

undismayed [ʌndɪs'meɪd] ADJ non découragé; **he was quite u. by the incident** l'incident ne l'a nullement découragé

undisputed [ʌndɪs'pjuːtɪd] ADJ *(champion)* incontesté, indiscuté; *(success, failure)* incontestable

undistinguished [ʌndɪs'tɪŋgwɪʃt] ADJ **1** médiocre; *(appearance)* peu distingué **2 the novel is u. by any great originality** ce roman n'a rien de particulièrement original

undistributed [ʌndɪs'trɪbjʊtɪd] ADJ *Fin (money, earnings, profit)* non distribué

undisturbed [ʌndɪs'tɜːbd] ADJ *(sleep)* paisible, calme; *(peace)* que rien ne vient troubler; *(papers)* non dérangé, non déplacé; **please leave us u. for fifteen minutes** veuillez ne pas nous déranger pendant quinze minutes; **she left his papers u.** elle n'a pas touché à ses papiers; **I could do with an u. night's sleep** une bonne nuit de sommeil me ferait du bien; **he was apparently u. by the news** la nouvelle ne l'a apparemment pas troublé

undivided [ʌndɪ'vaɪdɪd] ADJ non divisé; *(loyalties)* sans partage; **he gave her his u. attention/love** il lui a donné toute son attention/tout son amour

undo [ʌn'duː] *(pt* **undid** [-'dɪd]; *pp* **undone** [-'dʌn]) VT **1** *(piece of work)* défaire; **you can't u. the past** ce qui est fait est fait **2** *Comput (command)* annuler, défaire; **u. changes** annuler les révisions; **u. last** annuler dernière opération; **can't u.** impossible d'annuler **3** *(knot, button, knitting)* défaire; *(fastening)* ouvrir; *(screw)* desserrer; *(parcel)* défaire, déficeler; *(shoes)* délacer; *(one's dress)* dégrafer, déboutonner ▶ VI *(of dress etc)* se défaire
▸ ▸ *Comput* **u. command** commande *f* d'annulation

undocumented [ʌn'dɒkjʊmentɪd] ADJ *(subject, history etc)* sur lequel il n'existe pas de documentation

undoing [ʌn'duːɪŋ] N *(downfall)* ruine *f*, perte *f*; **that man will be her u.** cet homme la conduira à sa perte; **drink was his u.** l'alcool a causé sa perte

undomesticated [ʌndə'mestɪkeɪtɪd] ADJ **he's completely u.** il ne sait rien faire dans la maison

undone [ʌn'dʌn] ADJ **1** *(knot, button)* défait; **to come u.** *(of knot, button)* se défaire; *(of hair)* se dénouer; *(of screw)* se desserrer; *(of shoe)* se délacer; *(of dress)* se dégrafer; *(of seam)* se découdre, se défaire; *(of parcel)* se déficeler, se défaire **2** *Hum, Arch* **I am u.!** je suis perdu! **3** *(not finished, not done)* **we had to leave it u.** nous n'avons pas pu le terminer; *Lit* **we have left u. those things which we ought to have done** nous n'avons pas fait les choses que nous aurions dû faire

undoubted [ʌn'daʊtɪd] ADJ *(fact)* incontestable, indubitable

undoubtedly [ʌn'daʊtɪdlɪ] ADV indubitablement, incontestablement

undramatic [ʌndrə'mætɪk] ADJ *(lacking in interest)* pas très intéressant; **this seemingly u. incident ...** cet incident apparemment anodin ...

undrawn [ʌn'drɔːn] ADJ **the curtains were still u.** les rideaux n'étaient toujours pas tirés

undreamed-of, undreamt-of [ʌn'driːmd-ɒv, ʌn'dremtɒv] ADJ *(unsuspected)* insoupçonné; *(beyond one's dreams)* inimaginable

undress [ʌn'dres] VI se déshabiller
▶ VT déshabiller; **to get undressed** se déshabiller
▶ N **in a state of u.** en petite tenue

undressed [ʌn'drest] ADJ **1** *(without clothes)* déshabillé; *(in nightdress)* en déshabillé **2** *(cloth)* inapprêté; *(wood)* en grume; **u. stone** pierre *f* non taillée **3** *Culin (meat)* non accommodé; *(lobster)* nature *inv*; *(salad)* non assaisonné **4 u. wound** blessure *f* non pansée

undrinkable [ʌn'drɪŋkəb(ə)l] ADJ *(unpleasant)* imbuvable; *(harmful)* non potable

undubbed [ʌn'dʌbd] ADJ *Cin, TV* non doublé; **the u. version of the film** la version originale du film

undue [ʌn'djuː] ADJ **1** *(demand)* injustifiable **2** *(haste, optimism)* exagéré, excessif; **to pay u. attention to sb** s'empresser auprès de qn

undulate ['ʌndjʊleɪt] VI onduler, ondoyer

undulating ['ʌndjʊleɪtɪŋ] ADJ onduleux; *(wheat)* ondoyant; **u. country** pays *m* vallonné; **an u. walk** une démarche chaloupée

undulation [ʌndjʊ'leɪʃən] N ondulation *f*

unduly [ʌn'djuːlɪ] ADV *(excessively)* à l'excès, trop; **not u. expensive/concerned** pas excessivement cher/inquiet, -ète; **an u. high price** un prix excessif; **to be u. optimistic** faire preuve d'un optimisme peu justifié; **he worries u.** *or* **he's u. worried about his health** sa santé le préoccupe trop

undying [ʌn'daɪɪŋ] ADJ immortel; *(love)* éternel

unearned [ʌn'ɜːnd] ADJ **1** *(reward, punishment)* immérité **2** *(money)* qui ne provient pas du travail
▸ ▸ *Fin* **u. income** revenus *mpl* non professionnels, rentes *fpl*

unearth [ʌn'ɜːθ] VT **1** *(dig out of earth)* déterrer, exhumer **2** *(find) (old photograph, hat etc)* dénicher, *Fam* dégot(t)er; *(information)* découvrir, trouver; **wherever did you u. that?** où donc as-tu déniché ça?

unearthly [ʌn'ɜːθlɪ] ADJ **1** *(supernatural)* mystérieux; **an u. pallor** une pâleur mortelle **2** *Fam* **at an u. hour** à une heure impossible; **u. din** vacarme *m* de tous les diables; **for some u. reason** pour une raison absurde

unease [ʌn'iːz] N malaise *m*

uneasily [ʌn'iːzɪlɪ] ADV *(uncomfortably)* d'un air gêné; *(worriedly)* avec inquiétude; *(to sleep)* d'un sommeil agité; **the books were u. balanced on the edge of the shelf** les livres étaient en équilibre instable sur le bord de l'étagère

uneasy [ʌn'iːzɪ] ADJ *(ill at ease)* mal à l'aise, gêné; *(worried)* inquiet, -ète; *(sleep)* agité; **an u. truce** une trêve précaire *ou* incertaine; **there was an u. silence** il y a eu un silence gêné; **to be u.** être inquiet *ou* anxieux (**about** au sujet de); **to be u. in one's mind about sth** ne pas avoir l'esprit tranquille au sujet de qch; **I've just got an u. feeling that it won't work** j'ai justement la fâcheuse impression que ça ne marchera pas

uneatable [ʌn'iːtəb(ə)l] ADJ *(unpleasant to eat)* immangeable

uneaten [ʌn'iːt(ə)n] ADJ non mangé; **u. food** restes *mpl*

uneconomic [ʌniːkə'nɒmɪk] ADJ *(work)* pas rentable

uneconomical [ʌniːkə'nɒmɪk(ə)l] ADJ *(method, car)* peu économique; **it's u. to do it that way** ce n'est pas économique de faire ça

unedifying [ʌn'edɪfaɪɪŋ] ADJ peu édifiant

unedited [ʌn'edɪtɪd] ADJ *(text)* qui n'a pas été rédigé définitivement, à l'état brut; *(un-*

expurgated) intégral, -aux; *Comput (text)* non édité; *(film)* non monté; *(recording)* à l'état brut

uneducated [ʌn'edjʊkeɪtɪd] ADJ *(person)* sans instruction; *(speech, accent)* populaire; *(handwriting)* qui dénote un manque d'instruction

unelectable [ʌnɪ'lektəb(ə)l] ADJ inéligible

unemotional [ʌnɪ'məʊʃən(ə)l] ADJ *(person) (not feeling emotion)* peu émotif; *(not showing emotion)* impassible; *(reaction)* peu émotionnel; *(style)* neutre, dépourvu de passion; **he managed to stay quite u. about it** il a réussi à garder la tête froide

unemotionally [ʌnɪ'məʊʃən(ə)lɪ] ADV *(to react, look at things)* froidement

unemployable [ʌnɪm'plɔɪəb(ə)l] ADJ **I'm 65 but does that make me u.?** j'ai 65 ans mais est-ce que je suis inapte à travailler pour autant?; **he's u.** *(because of criminal record etc)* personne n'est prêt à l'employer

unemployed [ʌnɪm'plɔɪd] ADJ *(person)* au chômage, sans travail; **she was u. for months** elle est restée au chômage pendant des mois
▶ NPL **the u.** les chômeurs *mpl*
▸ ▸ *Fin* **u. capital** fonds *mpl* inactifs

unemployment [ʌnɪm'plɔɪmənt] N chômage *m*
▸ ▸ *Br Formerly* **u. benefit,** *Am* **u. compensation** allocation *f* (de) chômage; **u. contribution** cotisation *f* chômage; **u. figures** chiffres *mpl* du chômage; **u. fund** caisse *f* de chômage; **u. insurance** assurance *f* chômage; **u. rate** taux *m* de chômage; **u. trap** cercle *m* vicieux du chômage

unencumbered [ʌnɪn'kʌmbəd] ADJ non encombré (**by, with** de)
▸ ▸ *Law* **u. estate** propriété *f* franche d'hypothèques

unending [ʌn'endɪŋ] ADJ *(controversy, list of complaints etc)* interminable, qui n'en finit plus; *(bliss etc)* éternel

unendorsed [ʌnɪn'dɔːst] ADJ *Fin (cheque)* non endossé

unendurable [ʌnɪn'djʊərəb(ə)l] ADJ insupportable

unenforceable [ʌnɪn'fɔːsəb(ə)l] ADJ inapplicable

un-English [ʌn-] ADJ peu anglais; **he's very u.** ce n'est pas du tout l'Anglais type

unenlightened [ʌnɪn'laɪt(ə)nd] ADJ *(people)* ignorant; **an u. age** une époque où régnait l'ignorance; **I remained completely u.** je suis resté dans l'ignorance la plus totale

unenlightening [ʌnɪn'laɪtnɪŋ] ADJ *(comment)* qui jette peu de lumière (sur une question)

unenterprising [ʌn'entəpraɪzɪŋ] ADJ *(person)* peu entreprenant, qui manque d'initiative; *(plan)* qui manque d'audace; **that was very u. of you** vous avez vraiment manqué d'initiative, vous avez fait preuve d'une absence d'initiative totale

unenthusiastic [ʌnɪnθ(j)uːzɪ'æstɪk] ADJ peu enthousiaste; **he seems rather u. about it** ça n'a pas l'air de l'enthousiasmer

unenthusiastically [ʌnɪnθ(j)uːzɪ'æstɪklɪ] ADV sans enthousiasme

unenviable [ʌn'envɪəb(ə)l] ADJ peu enviable

unequal [ʌn'iːkwəl] ADJ **1** *(size, amount)* inégal, -aux; **an u. struggle** un combat inégal **2 he was u. to the task** il n'était pas à la hauteur de la tâche

unequalled [ʌn'iːkwəld] ADJ inégalé

unequally [ʌn'iːkwəlɪ] ADV inégalement

unequivocal [ʌnɪˈkwɪvək(ə)l] ADJ sans équivoque

unequivocally [ʌnɪˈkwɪvəklɪ] ADV sans équivoque

unerring [ʌnˈɜːrɪŋ] ADJ infaillible, sûr; **with u. aim, he hit the target** visant avec précision, il a touché la cible

unerringly [ʌnˈɜːrɪŋlɪ] ADV infailliblement

UNESCO [juːˈneskəʊ] N (abbr United Nations Educational, Scientific and Cultural Organization) UNESCO f

unescorted [ʌnɪˈskɔːtɪd] ADJ sans escorte

unessential [ʌnɪˈsenʃəl] ADJ non essentiel

unesthetic [ʌniːsˈθetɪk] ADJ Am = **unaesthetic**

unethical [ʌnˈeθɪk(ə)l] ADJ (behaviour) contraire à l'éthique

unethically [ʌnˈeθɪklɪ] ADV contrairement à l'éthique

uneven [ʌnˈiːv(ə)n] ADJ (not level, not regular) inégal, -aux; (terrain) accidenté; **the floorboards are u.** les lattes du plancher ne sont pas toutes au même niveau; **u. breathing** respiration f irrégulière; **u. temper** humeur f inégale

unevenly [ʌnˈiːv(ə)nlɪ] ADV inégalement; (to breathe) irrégulièrement; **the opponents were u. matched** les adversaires étaient de force inégale; **u. distributed load** charge f répartie inégalement

unevenness [ʌnˈiːv(ə)nnɪs] N inégalité f; (of breathing) irrégularité f

uneventful [ʌnɪˈventfʊl] ADJ (journey) sans incidents, calme; **u. life** vie f calme ou peu mouvementée

uneventfully [ʌnɪˈventfəlɪ] ADV **to pass u.** se passer sans incidents

unexceptionable [ʌnɪkˈsepʃənəb(ə)l] ADJ (behaviour) irréprochable; (person) tout à fait convenable

unexceptional [ʌnɪkˈsepʃən(ə)l] ADJ ordinaire, qui n'a rien d'exceptionnel

unexchangeable [ʌnɪksˈtʃeɪndʒəb(ə)l] ADJ inéchangeable; Fin (securities) impermutable, inéchangeable

unexciting [ʌnɪkˈsaɪtɪŋ] ADJ (tale, film, job) insipide, peu passionnant; (person) terne, insipide; (life) monotone; **u. day** (uneventful) journée f calme; (boring) journée ennuyeuse; **this restaurant serves very u. food** on sert des repas très ordinaires dans ce restaurant

unexpected [ʌnɪksˈpektɪd] ADJ (visitor, result, success) inattendu; (event) imprévu; (departure) inopiné; (help, happiness) inespéré; **u. meeting** rencontre f inopinée; **it was completely u.** on ne s'y attendait pas du tout; **this is all so u.!** tout est si inattendu! N **the u.** l'imprévu m

unexpectedly [ʌnɪksˈpektɪdlɪ] ADV de manière inattendue; **to arrive u.** arriver à l'improviste; **they won u.** on ne s'attendait pas à ce qu'ils gagnent; **he died u.** il est mort subitement

unexpired [ʌnɪksˈpaɪəd] ADJ (lease) non expiré; (passport, ticket) non périmé, encore valable

unexplained [ʌnɪksˈpleɪnd] ADJ inexpliqué

unexploded [ʌnɪksˈpləʊdɪd] ADJ (bomb) qui n'a pas explosé

unexploited [ʌnɪksˈplɔɪtɪd] ADJ inexploité

unexplored [ʌnɪksˈplɔːd] ADJ (country etc) inexploré

unexposed [ʌnɪksˈpəʊzd] ADJ 1 Phot (film) vierge 2 (criminal) non démasqué 3 **u. to the influences of the outside world ...** qui n'est pas en contact avec le monde extérieur ...; **u. to the influence of TV** qui n'est pas soumis à l'influence de la télévision

unexpressed [ʌnɪksˈprest] ADJ inexprimé

unexpurgated [ʌnˈekspɜːgeɪtɪd] ADJ (book, text) non expurgé; **u. edition** édition f intégrale

unfading [ʌnˈfeɪdɪŋ] ADJ (memory) ineffaçable, impérissable; (hope, love) impérissable

unfailing [ʌnˈfeɪlɪŋ] ADJ 1 (loyalty) à toute épreuve; (means, remedy) infaillible; (zeal) infatigable; (memory) sans défaillance; (kindness) inaltérable; (hope, courage) inébranlable; **to be u. in one's duty** ne jamais faillir à son devoir; **to have an u. ability to do sth** avoir le don de faire qch 2 (supply etc) inépuisable

unfailingly [ʌnˈfeɪlɪŋlɪ] ADV infailliblement, immanquablement

unfair [ʌnˈfeər] ADJ injuste (**to sb** envers qn); (deal, arrangement) peu équitable; **to be u. to sb** (of situation) défavoriser qn; **it's u.!** ce n'est pas juste!; **to have an u. advantage over everybody else** être injustement avantagé par rapport à tous les autres; **he has been put at an u. disadvantage** il a été désavantagé
▸▸ Com **u. competition** concurrence f déloyale; Ind **u. dismissal** licenciement m abusif

unfairly [ʌnˈfeəlɪ] ADV injustement, peu équitablement; (to play) déloyalement; **to be u. dismissed** être victime d'un licenciement abusif; **to act u.** se montrer injuste

unfairness [ʌnˈfeənɪs] N injustice f

unfaithful [ʌnˈfeɪθfʊl] ADJ 1 **to be u. to** (one's wife, husband) tromper, être infidèle à 2 (report) inexact, infidèle

unfaithfully [ʌnˈfeɪθfəlɪ] ADV (to betray, desert) de façon déloyale; **to act u. towards one's wife** se comporter de manière infidèle envers sa femme; **to report sth u.** faire un compte-rendu peu fidèle de qch

unfaithfulness [ʌnˈfeɪθfʊlnɪs] N infidélité f

unfaltering [ʌnˈfɔːltərɪŋ] ADJ sans défaillance; **u. steps** pas mpl assurés; **u. voice** voix f ferme

unfalteringly [ʌnˈfɔːltərɪŋlɪ] ADV sans faillir; (to speak) d'une voix ferme; (to walk) d'un pas bien assuré

unfamiliar [ʌnfəˈmɪliər] ADJ peu familier, peu connu; **to be u. with sth** ne pas connaître ou mal connaître qch, ne pas être au fait de qch; **I'm totally u. with this town** je ne connais pas du tout cette ville; **he is quite u. with this subject** il ne sait absolument rien sur ce sujet; **u. face** visage m inconnu; **the u. sounds of the language** les sonorités étranges de cette langue

unfamiliarity [ʌnfəmɪliˈærɪti] N 1 (of place) aspect m étrange 2 (lack of knowledge) ignorance f (**with** de); **because of my u. with the city/terrain** parce que je ne connaissais pas très bien la ville/le terrain

unfashionable [ʌnˈfæʃnəb(ə)l] ADJ (clothes) démodé, passé de mode; (restaurant, author) qui n'est pas ou plus à la mode; (ideas) démodé

unfashionably [ʌnˈfæʃ(ə)nəblɪ] ADV (to dress etc) sans se préoccuper de la mode

unfasten [ʌnˈfɑːs(ə)n] VT (garment, bracelet) défaire, dégrafer; (safety belt) défaire, détacher; (tie, knot) défaire; (door) ouvrir, déverrouiller; **to come unfastened** (of garment) se dégrafer; (unbuttoned) se déboutonner; (of knot) se défaire, se dénouer; (of belt) se détacher; **to u. sth from sth** détacher qch de qch
VT SE dégrafer; (of dress etc) se dégrafer

unfathomable [ʌnˈfæðəməb(ə)l] ADJ (abyss, mystery) insondable

unfathomed [ʌnˈfæðəmd] ADJ (abyss, mystery) insondé; **u. depths** profondeurs fpl inexplorées

unfavourable, Am **unfavorable** [ʌnˈfeɪv(ə)rəb(ə)l] ADJ défavorable, peu favorable (**to** à); (moment) peu propice, inopportun; (wind) contraire; (review) mauvais; (weather, report) défavorable; **to appear in an u. light** se montrer sous un jour défavorable

unfavourably, Am **unfavorably** [ʌnˈfeɪv(ə)rəblɪ] ADV défavorablement; **to be u. disposed towards sb/sth** être mal disposé envers qn/qch; **his work compares u. with his brother's** son travail supporte mal la comparaison avec celui de son frère

unfazed [ʌnˈfeɪzd] ADJ pas du tout impressionné

unfeeling [ʌnˈfiːlɪŋ] ADJ (person) insensible, dur

unfeelingly [ʌnˈfiːlɪŋlɪ] ADV (to act) sans pitié, impitoyablement; (to answer) durement, avec dureté

unfeigned [ʌnˈfeɪnd] ADJ non simulé, sincère

unfeignedly [ʌnˈfeɪnɪdlɪ] ADV sans simulation, sincèrement

unfeminine [ʌnˈfemɪnɪn] ADJ peu féminin

unfenced [ʌnˈfenst] ADJ (land etc) sans clôture

unfermented [ʌnfəˈmentɪd] ADJ non fermenté

unfertilized [ʌnˈfɜːtɪlaɪzd] ADJ (egg) non fécondé

unfettered [ʌnˈfetəd] ADJ sans entrave(s); (emotion) non refoulé

unfilial [ʌnˈfɪlɪəl] ADJ peu filial, -aux

unfinished [ʌnˈfɪnɪʃt] ADJ 1 (task, painting etc) inachevé; **to leave sth u.** laisser qch inachevé; **u. game** partie f interrompue; **to have some u. business** avoir quelques affaires à régler; (esp menacing) avoir des comptes à régler 2 Ind (article) semi-fini

unfit [ʌnˈfɪt] ADJ 1 (inappropriate) impropre, peu propre (**for** à); **u. for human consumption** impropre à la consommation; **u. to eat** non comestible; **u. to drink** (unpleasant) imbuvable; (harmful) non potable; **u. for publication** impubliable; **this house is u. for habitation** cette maison est inhabitable 2 (person) (not suitable) **u. for military service** inapte au service militaire; Mil **to be discharged as u.** être réformé; **she's u. for this type of job** elle n'est pas faite pour ce genre de travail; **to be u. to govern** ne pas être en état de gouverner 3 (physically) **to be u.** ne pas être en forme; **he's u. to travel** il n'est pas en état de voyager; **he is u. for duty** il n'est pas en état d'assurer ses fonctions

unfitness [ʌnˈfɪtnɪs] N 1 (unsuitability) u. **for sth/to do sth** inaptitude f à qch/à faire qch 2 (lack of fitness) mauvaise forme f

unfitted [ʌnˈfɪtɪd] ADJ **to be u. for sth** (of equipment) ne pas être adapté à qch; (of person) ne pas convenir à qch; (morally) être indigne de qch

unfitting [ʌnˈfɪtɪŋ] ADJ peu convenable; (remark) mal à propos, déplacé

unfittingly [ʌnˈfɪtɪŋlɪ] ADV (to behave etc) de manière peu convenable

unfix [ʌnˈfɪks] VT Mil **to u. bayonets** remettre la baïonnette

unflagging [ʌnˈflægɪŋ] ADJ (interest) soutenu; (vigour) inlassable; (optimism, courage) inébranlable

unflaggingly [ʌnˈflægɪŋlɪ] ADV inlassablement, infatigablement

unflappability [ʌnflæpəˈbɪlɪtɪ] N Fam imperturbabilité f

unflappable [ʌnˈflæpəb(ə)l] ADJ Fam imperturbable; **he is completely u.** il garde toujours son calme

unflattering [ʌnˈflætərɪŋ] ADJ peu flatteur (**to** pour); **her hat was most u.** son chapeau était loin de la mettre en valeur; **it shows him in an u. light** ça le montre sous un jour défavorable; **he was rather u. about your playing** il ne s'est pas montré très flatteur quant à votre jeu

unflatteringly [ʌnˈflætərɪŋlɪ] ADV d'une manière peu flatteuse

unfledged [ʌnˈfledʒd] ADJ **1** (bird) sans plumes **2** (person) sans expérience

unflinching [ʌnˈflɪnʃɪŋ] ADJ (person) qui ne bronche pas; (resolute) résolu; (resolve, courage) inébranlable

unflinchingly [ʌnˈflɪnʃɪŋlɪ] ADV sans broncher; (resolutely) résolument; **u. loyal** d'une loyauté à toute épreuve

unfold [ʌnˈfəʊld] VT **1** (newspaper, serviette) déplier; (map) déployer, déplier; **to u. one's arms** décroiser les bras **2** (reveal) (one's intentions, plan) révéler, exposer; (one's plans, secret) dévoiler
▸ VI se déployer, se dérouler; (of flower) s'ouvrir, s'épanouir; (of story, action) se dérouler

unforced [ʌnˈfɔːst] ADJ qui n'est pas forcé, spontané; **u. laugh** rire m franc
▸▸ Sport **u. error** faute f directe

unforeseeable [ʌnfɔːˈsiːəb(ə)l] ADJ imprévisible

unforeseen [ʌnfɔːˈsiːn] ADJ imprévu, inattendu; **unless something u. happens** sauf imprévu
▸▸ **u. circumstances** imprévus mpl; Law **force f majeure**; **u. expenses** dépenses fpl non prévues au budget

unforgettable [ʌnfəˈgetəb(ə)l] ADJ inoubliable

unforgivable [ʌnfəˈgɪvəb(ə)l] ADJ impardonnable, inexcusable; **it's u. of me** je suis impardonnable

unforgivably [ʌnfəˈgɪvəblɪ] ADV **he was u. rude** il s'est montré d'une impolitesse impardonnable

unforgiven [ʌnfəˈgɪv(ə)n] ADJ impardonné

unforgiving [ʌnfəˈgɪvɪŋ] ADJ implacable, impitoyable

unforgotten [ʌnfəˈgɒt(ə)n] ADJ inoublié

unformatted [ʌnˈfɔːmætɪd] ADJ (text) non mis en forme; Comput (disk) non formaté;
▸▸ Comput **u. capacity** (of disk) capacité f brute

unformed [ʌnˈfɔːmd] ADJ (bone) qui n'est pas (encore) formé; (mind) inculte; (idea) en gestation

unformulated [ʌnˈfɔːmjʊleɪtɪd] ADJ informulé

unforthcoming [ʌnfɔːθˈkʌmɪŋ] ADJ réservé; **to be u. about sth** être ou se montrer réticent au sujet de qch

unfortified [ʌnˈfɔːtɪfaɪd] ADJ non fortifié, sans fortifications

unfortunate [ʌnˈfɔːtjənɪt] ADJ **1** (unlucky) malchanceux; **he's been most u.** il n'a vraiment pas eu de chance; **the u. people whose houses were flooded** les malheureux dont les maisons ont été inondées **2** (accident, event) malheureux, malencontreux; (mistake) regrettable; **an u. state of affairs** une situation regrettable ou fâcheuse; **u. choice of words** choix de mots peu heureux; **in u. circumstances** dans des circonstances regrettables; **u. consequences** conséquences regrettables; **it's u. that she has to leave today** il est dommage qu'elle soit obligée de partir aujourd'hui; **how u.!** quel dommage!
▸ N malheureux, -euse; **the u.** les infortunés

mpl; **a poor u.** un pauvre malheureux, une pauvre malheureuse

unfortunately [ʌnˈfɔːtjənɪtlɪ] ADV malheureusement; **an u. worded statement** une déclaration formulée d'une façon regrettable; **u. for him** malheureusement pour lui

unfounded [ʌnˈfaʊndɪd] ADJ sans fondement; **u. criticism** critique f injustifiée; **u. rumour** bruit m dénué de tout fondement

unframed [ʌnˈfreɪmd] ADJ sans cadre

unfreeze [ʌnˈfriːz] (pt **unfroze** [ʌnˈfrəʊz]; pp **unfrozen** [ʌnˈfrəʊz(ə)n]) VT (de-ice) dégeler; Fin (credit) dégeler, débloquer
▸ VI dégeler

unfreezing [ʌnˈfriːzɪŋ] N (de-icing) dégel m; Fin (of credit) dégel, déblocage m

unfrequented [ʌnfrɪˈkwentɪd] ADJ peu fréquenté

unfriendliness [ʌnˈfrendlɪnɪs] N froideur f (**towards** envers, à l'égard de)

unfriendly [ʌnˈfrendlɪ] ADJ (person) peu sympathique; (tone, feeling) peu amical, -aux, inamical, -aux; **to be u. to(wards) sb** traiter qn avec froideur; **environmentally u.** nuisible à l'environnement; **u. reception** accueil m froid; **written in an u. style** écrit dans un style rébarbatif
▸▸ Mil **u. action** action f hostile

unfrock [ʌnˈfrɒk] VT (priest etc) défroquer

unfrozen [ʌnˈfrəʊz(ə)n] ADJ Fin (credit) dégelé, débloqué

unfruitful [ʌnˈfruːtfʊl] ADJ infructueux, vain

unfulfilled [ʌnfʊlˈfɪld] ADJ (duty) inaccompli; (promise) non tenu; (desire) non satisfait, inassouvi; (ambition) non réalisé; (prayer) inexaucé; **to feel u.** éprouver un sentiment d'insatisfaction

unfunded [ʌnˈfʌndɪd] ADJ sans subvention
▸▸ Fin **u. debt** dette f flottante ou non consolidée

unfunny [ʌnˈfʌnɪ] ADJ qui n'est pas drôle; **I find that distinctly u.** je ne trouve pas ça drôle du tout

unfurl [ʌnˈfɜːl] VT (sail, flag) déployer; (umbrella) ouvrir
▸ VI se déployer

unfurnished [ʌnˈfɜːnɪʃt] ADJ non meublé

ungainliness [ʌnˈgeɪnlɪnɪs] N gaucherie f

ungainly [ʌnˈgeɪnlɪ] ADJ gauche

ungallant [ʌnˈgælənt] ADJ peu galant, discourtois

ungeared [ʌnˈgɪəd] ADJ Fin sans endettement
▸▸ **u. balance sheet** bilan m sans emprunts ou à faible endettement

ungenerous [ʌnˈdʒen(ə)rəs] ADJ peu généreux; (remark) malveillant; **that was rather u. of you** ce n'était pas très généreux de ta part

ungentlemanly [ʌnˈdʒent(ə)lmənlɪ] ADJ peu galant, discourtois; **u. behaviour** manque m de savoir-vivre; Sport **u. conduct** manque de courtoisie

ungetatable [ʌngetˈætəb(ə)l] ADJ Fam inaccessible

ungird [ʌnˈgɜːd] VT (pt, pp **ungirt** [ʌnˈgɜːt]) (sword) détacher

unglazed [ʌnˈgleɪzd] ADJ **1** (window) sans vitres **2** (paper) mat, non glacé **3** Cer non verni, non émaillé; (brick) non vitrifié
▸▸ Cer **u. porcelain** biscuit m; Phot **u. print** épreuve f mate

ungodliness [ʌnˈgɒdlɪnɪs] N impiété f

ungodly [ʌnˈgɒdlɪ] ADJ **1** impie, irréligieux **2** Fam **an u. row** un bruit de tous les diables; **he got up at an u. hour** il s'est levé à une heure impossible ou indue

ungovernable [ʌnˈgʌv(ə)nəb(ə)l] ADJ **1** (people, country) ingouvernable **2** (desire, passion) irrésistible; **he has u. fits of temper** il a des accès de colère incontrôlables

ungraceful [ʌnˈgreɪsfʊl] ADJ sans grâce, gauche

ungracefully [ʌnˈgreɪsfəlɪ] ADV sans grâce, gauchement

ungracious [ʌnˈgreɪʃəs] ADJ peu élégant; **it would be u. of me to refuse** j'aurais mauvaise grâce à refuser

ungraciously [ʌnˈgreɪʃəslɪ] ADV (to refuse) de manière peu élégante; (to accept) de mauvaise grâce

ungraciousness [ʌnˈgreɪʃəsnɪs] N mauvaise grâce f

ungrammatical [ʌngrəˈmætɪk(ə)l] ADJ (grammaticalement) incorrect

ungrammatically [ʌngrəˈmætɪklɪ] ADV incorrectement

ungrateful [ʌnˈgreɪtfʊl] ADJ (person, response), Lit (task) ingrat; **to be u. to sb** être peu reconnaissant envers qn (**for sth** de qch), se montrer ingrat envers qn (**for sth** à propos de qch); **don't be so u.!** ne sois pas si ingrat!

ungratefully [ʌnˈgreɪtfəlɪ] ADV avec ingratitude

ungratefulness [ʌnˈgreɪtfʊlnɪs] N ingratitude f

ungratified [ʌnˈgrætɪfaɪd] ADJ (desire) inassouvi

ungrudging [ʌnˈgrʌdʒɪŋ] ADJ (assistance) donné de bon cœur; (admiration) (très) sincère

ungrudgingly [ʌnˈgrʌdʒɪŋlɪ] ADV de bon cœur, généreusement

unguarded [ʌnˈgɑːdɪd] ADJ **1** (not watched over) non gardé; (prisoner etc) sans surveillance; (town) sans défense; Sport **to leave the goal u.** laisser le but vide **2** (remark) inconsidéré, irréfléchi; **in an u. moment** dans un moment d'inattention **3** (mechanism) sans dispositif protecteur; (fire) sans garde-feu

unguent [ˈʌŋgwənt] N onguent m

ungulate [ˈʌŋgjʊleɪt] ADJ, N Zool ongulé m

unhallowed [ʌnˈhæləʊd] ADJ non béni, non consacré

unhampered [ʌnˈhæmpəd] ADJ non entravé (**by** par); (in one's movements) libre; **u. by regulations** sans être gêné par la réglementation

unhand [ʌnˈhænd] VT Arch, Hum lâcher; **u. me!** lâchez-moi!

unhappily [ʌnˈhæpɪlɪ] ADV **1** (unfortunately) malheureusement; **u. worded** rédigé de manière malheureuse ou maladroite **2** (sadly, miserably) tristement, d'un air triste; **to live u.** ne pas être heureux; **they're u. married** ils ne sont pas heureux en ménage

unhappiness [ʌnˈhæpɪnɪs] N chagrin m, tristesse f; **the u. of her childhood** son enfance malheureuse

unhappy [ʌnˈhæpɪ] ADJ **1** (sad) malheureux, triste; **to make sb u.** causer du chagrin à qn; (esp intentionally) rendre qn malheureux; **to be u. at leaving sb** être triste de quitter qn **2** (worried) inquiet, -ète; **I'm u. about leaving the house empty** je n'aime pas laisser ou ça m'inquiète de laisser la maison vide **3** (not pleased) pas satisfait; **to be u. with sb/sth** être mécontent de qn/qch; **we're u. with the quality** nous ne sommes pas satisfaits de la qualité **4** (remark) malheureux, malencontreux; **an u. state of affairs** une situation regrettable

unharmed [ʌnˈhɑːmd] ADJ (person) sain et sauf, f saine et sauve, indemne; (thing) intact, non endommagé; **to escape u.** s'en sortir indemne

unharness [ʌnˈhɑːnɪs] **VT** *(horse)* dételer

UNHCR [juːeneɪtʃsiːˈɑːr] **N** *(abbr* **United Nations High Commission for Refugees)** HCR *m*

unhealthiness [ʌnˈhelθɪnɪs] **N** *(of person)* mauvaise santé *f, (of air, place)* insalubrité *f, (of influence, relationship)* caractère *m* malsain

unhealthy [ʌnˈhelθɪ] **ADJ** *(person)* maladif; *(state of mind, influence, relationship)* malsain; *(air, place)* malsain, insalubre; **to have an u. fascination with death** avoir une fascination morbide pour la mort; **the car's sounding rather u.** la voiture fait un drôle de bruit; **u. curiosity** curiosité *f* morbide; *Fam* **it can be u. to ask too many questions** *(dangerous)* il peut être dangereux de poser trop de questions

unheard [ʌnˈhɜːd] **ADJ their screams went u.** personne n'a entendu leurs cris; **the opinions of the immigrant population go u.** personne ne tient compte des opinions des immigrés; **to condemn sb u.** condamner qn sans l'avoir entendu

unheard-of ADJ 1 *(incredible)* inouï; **that's u.!** c'est vraiment incroyable! **2** *(unknown)* inconnu; **it was u. in my day** de mon temps ça n'existait pas

unheated [ʌnˈhiːtɪd] **ADJ** non chauffé

unheeded [ʌnˈhiːdɪd] **ADJ his warning/advice went u.** on n'a pas tenu compte de son avertissement/ses conseils

unheeding [ʌnˈhiːdɪŋ] **ADJ to be u. of sb's advice** ne pas écouter les conseils de qn, ne pas tenir compte des conseils de qn

unhelpful [ʌnˈhelpfʊl] **ADJ** *(person)* peu serviable; *(criticism, advice)* peu utile; **that's rather u. of them** ce n'est pas très serviable de leur part; **don't be so u.!** tâche donc un peu de nous/m'*/etc* aider!

unhelpfully [ʌnˈhelpfəlɪ] **ADV** de façon peu serviable; **she u. suggested that I go and see a clairvoyant** elle n'a rien trouvé de mieux que de me conseiller d'aller voir un voyant; **someone very u. left the disk on a radiator** quelqu'un de très négligent a laissé la disquette sur un radiateur

unheralded [ʌnˈherəldɪd] **ADJ** *esp Lit* qui n'est pas annoncé; *(unexpected)* imprévu, inattendu

unhesitating [ʌnˈhezɪteɪtɪŋ] **ADJ** *(person)* qui n'hésite pas; **u. reply** réponse *f* immédiate *ou* prompte; **my u. reaction** ma réaction immédiate; **you can count on our u. support** vous pouvez compter sur notre soutien sans faille

unhesitatingly [ʌnˈhezɪteɪtɪŋlɪ] **ADV** sans hésiter, sans hésitation

unhindered [ʌnˈhɪndəd] **ADJ** sans obstacle; *(not disturbed)* sans être dérangé **(by** par); **to go u.** passer librement; **u. by all that luggage** être encombré par tous ces bagages; **u. by petty regulations** sans être gêné par des règlements tatillons; **u. by any moral scruples** nullement encombré de scrupules

unhinge [ʌnˈhɪndʒ] **VT** *(door etc)* enlever de ses gonds; *(sb's mind)* déranger, détraquer

unhinged [ʌnˈhɪndʒd] **ADJ** *(person)* dérangé

unhip [ʌnˈhɪp] **ADJ** *Fam* ringard

unhitch [ʌnˈhɪtʃ] **VT** détacher, décrocher; *(horse)* dételer

unholy [ʌnˈhəʊlɪ] **ADJ 1** *Rel (place etc)* profane; **u. thoughts** des pensées *fpl* coupables **2** *Fam (mess, mix-up etc)* épouvantable, affreux; **there was an u. row** il y a eu une dispute épouvantable

unhook [ʌnˈhʊk] **VT** *(picture)* décrocher;

(trailer) décrocher, dételer; *(garment)* dégrafer; **to come unhooked** *(of dress)* se dégrafer

VI *(picture)* se décrocher; *(dress)* se dégrafer

unhoped-for [ʌnˈhəʊpt-] **ADJ** inespéré

unhorse [ʌnˈhɔːs] **VT** désarçonner

unhurried [ʌnˈhʌrɪd] **ADJ** *(manner)* posé; **she gave an u. reply** elle a pris son temps pour répondre; **in an u. way** sans se presser

unhurt [ʌnˈhɜːt] **ADJ** *(person)* indemne, sain et sauf, *f* saine et sauve; **to escape u.** sortir indemne *ou* sain et sauf

unhygienic [ʌnhaɪˈdʒiːnɪk] **ADJ** non hygiénique; **it's u. to …** il est peu hygiénique de …, … est contraire à l'hygiène

uni [ˈjuːnɪ] **N** *Fam* **1** *Br (abbr* **university)** fac *f*; **he's doing law at u.** il fait une fac de droit **2** *Am (abbr* **uniform)** uniforme *m*

UNICEF [ˈjuːnɪsef] **N** *(abbr* **United Nations International Children's Emergency Fund)** UNICEF *m*, FISE *m*

unicellular [juːnɪˈseljʊlər] **ADJ** *Biol* unicellulaire

unicorn [ˈjuːnɪkɔːn] **N** *Myth* licorne *f*

unicycle [ˈjuːnɪsaɪk(ə)l] **N** monocycle *m*

unidentifiable [ʌnaɪˈdentɪfaɪəb(ə)l] **ADJ** non identifiable

unidentified [ʌnaɪˈdentɪfaɪd] **ADJ** non identifié

▸▸ **u. flying object** objet *m* volant non identifié

unidirectional [juːnɪd(a)ɪˈrekʃ(ə)l] **ADJ** *Phys etc* unidirectionnel

UNIDO [juːˈniːdəʊ] **N** *(abbr* **United Nations Industrial Development Organization)** UNIDO *f*

unification [juːnɪfɪˈkeɪʃən] **N** unification *f*

uniform [ˈjuːnɪfɔːm] **ADJ** *(colour, style)* uniforme; *(temperature)* constant; **these boxes are all of u. size** ces boîtes sont toutes de la même grandeur; **to make sth u.** uniformiser qch

N uniforme *m*; **in u.** en uniforme, en tenue; **out of u.** *Mil etc* en civil; *(air hostess etc)* sans son uniforme

▸▸ *Acct* **u. accounting** comptabilité *f* uniforme; *Com* **u. business rate** = taxe *f* assise sur la valeur des locaux commerciaux, ≃ taxe professionnelle; **u. rate** taux *m* uniforme

uniformed [ˈjuːnɪfɔːmd] **ADJ** en uniforme, en tenue; **the u. branch** = la police en uniforme

uniformity [juːnɪˈfɔːmɪtɪ] **N** *(of style)* uniformité *f, (of current)* constance *f*

uniformly [ˈjuːnɪfɔːmlɪ] **ADV** uniformément

unify [ˈjuːnɪfaɪ] **VT** unifier

VI s'unifier

unifying [ˈjuːnɪfaɪɪŋ] **ADJ** unificateur, -trice

unilateral [juːnɪˈlætərəl] **ADJ** unilatéral

▸▸ **u. disarmament** désarmement *m* unilatéral

unilaterally [juːnɪˈlætərəlɪ] **ADV** unilatéralement

unilingual [juːnɪˈlɪŋgwəl] **ADJ** unilingue

unimaginable [ʌnɪˈmædʒɪnəb(ə)l] **ADJ** inimaginable, inconcevable

unimaginably [ʌnɪˈmædʒɪnəblɪ] **ADJ** incroyablement

unimaginative [ʌnɪˈmædʒɪnətɪv] **ADJ** *(person)* qui manque d'imagination, peu imaginatif; *(cooking, solution, use of colours)* peu original, -aux; **they're very u. about their holidays** ils ne font preuve d'aucune imagination pour ce qui est de partir en vacances; **you're so u.** vous n'avez aucune imagination!

unimaginatively [ʌnɪˈmædʒɪnətɪvlɪ] **ADV**

sans imagination, d'une manière peu imaginative

unimaginativeness [ʌnɪˈmædʒɪnətɪvnɪs] **N** manque *m* d'imagination

unimpaired [ʌnɪmˈpeəd] **ADJ** *(health, hearing, force, quality)* intact; **his mind is u.** il conserve toute sa vigueur d'esprit

unimpeachable [ʌnɪmˈpiːtʃəb(ə)l] **ADJ** *(reputation)* inattaquable; *(evidence, witness)* irrécusable; *(conduct)* irréprochable; **of u. character** d'un caractère irréprochable; **I have it from an u. source** je le tiens de source sûre

unimpeded [ʌnɪmˈpiːdɪd] **ADJ** sans entrave; **u. by …** sans être entravé par …

unimportant [ʌnɪmˈpɔːtənt] **ADJ** sans importance; **it's quite u.** cela n'a pas la moindre importance; **it's u. what they think** leur opinion ne compte pas *ou* est sans importance

unimposing [ʌnɪmˈpəʊzɪŋ] **ADJ** *(air, aspect)* peu imposant, peu impressionnant

unimpressed [ʌnɪmˈprest] **ADJ** qui n'est pas impressionné, peu impressionné **(by** par); **I was u. by his speech** je n'ai pas été impressionné par son discours; **his colleagues were u. by his explanation** ses collègues n'ont pas été convaincus par son explication

unimpressive [ʌnɪmˈpresɪv] **ADJ** peu impressionnant; *(speech)* peu convaincant; **the countryside of the region is u.** la campagne de cette région n'a rien d'extraordinaire

uninflammable [ʌnɪnˈflæməb(ə)l] **ADJ** ininflammable

uninfluential [ʌnɪnflʊˈenʃəl] **ADJ** sans influence

uninformed [ʌnɪnˈfɔːmd] **ADJ** mal informé, mal renseigné **(about** sur); *(ignorant)* ignorant; *(mind)* inculte

uninhabitable [ʌnɪnˈhæbɪtəb(ə)l] **ADJ** inhabitable

uninhabited [ʌnɪnˈhæbɪtɪd] **ADJ** inhabité

uninhibited [ʌnɪnˈhɪbɪtɪd] **ADJ** *(person)* sans inhibitions, qui n'a pas d'inhibitions; *(emotion etc)* non refréné; **she's so u.** elle est si naturelle

uninitialized [ʌnɪˈnɪʃəlaɪzd] **ADJ** *Comput* non initialisé

uninitiated [ʌnɪˈnɪʃɪeɪtɪd] **ADJ** non initié **(in** à)

NPL the u. les profanes *mpl*, les non-initiés *mpl*

uninjured [ʌnˈɪndʒəd] **ADJ** indemne; **he was shaken but u. by the accident** il a été secoué par l'accident mais n'a pas été blessé

uninspired [ʌnɪnˈspaɪəd] **ADJ** *(person)* qui manque d'inspiration; *(architecture, suggestion, style)* banal, -als; **an u. performance** un spectacle peu passionnant

uninspiring [ʌnˈɪnspaɪrɪŋ] **ADJ** peu passionnant; **I find the prospect u.** l'idée ne m'inspire pas

uninstall [ʌnɪnˈstɔːl] **VT** *Comput* désinstaller, supprimer

uninsured [ʌnɪnˈʃʊəd] **ADJ** non assuré **(against** contre)

unintelligent [ʌnɪnˈtelɪdʒənt] **ADJ** inintelligent

unintelligible [ʌnɪnˈtelɪdʒɪb(ə)l] **ADJ** inintelligible

unintelligibly [ʌnɪnˈtelɪdʒɪblɪ] **ADV** inintelligiblement

unintended [ʌnɪnˈtendɪd] **ADJ** involontaire, non intentionnel; *(result)* inattendu; **the pun was quite u.** le calembour était tout à fait involontaire

unintentional [ʌnɪnˈtenʃ(ə)l] **ADJ** involontaire, non intentionnel; **it was quite u.** ce n'était pas fait exprès

unintentionally [ˌʌnɪnˈtenʃ(ə)nəlɪ] **ADV** involontairement; **(to annoy sb)** sans le vouloir; **he did it quite u.** il ne l'a pas fait exprès

uninterested [ʌnˈɪnt(ə)restɪd] **ADJ** indifférent (**in** à); **he was u. in what I was saying** il n'était pas intéressé par ce que je disais, ce que je disais ne l'intéressait pas

> Attention: ne pas confondre avec l'adjectif **disinterested**.

uninteresting [ʌnˈɪnt(ə)restɪŋ] **ADJ** inintéressant, sans intérêt

uninterrupted [ˌʌnɪntəˈrʌptɪd] **ADJ** ininterrompu, sans interruption; **u. correspondence** correspondance suivie

uninterruptedly [ˌʌnɪntəˈrʌptɪdlɪ] **ADV** sans interruption

uninvited [ˌʌnɪnˈvaɪtɪd] **ADJ** (intruder) intrus, -use; **u. guest** visiteur, -euse inattendu(e); **to come u.** venir sans invitation; **to do sth u.** faire qch sans y avoir été invité

uninviting [ˌʌnɪnˈvaɪtɪŋ] **ADJ** peu attirant, peu attrayant; (food) peu appétissant

union [ˈjuːnjən] **N 1** (joining, being joined) union f (**with** avec); esp Fml (marriage) union f, Fig **a u. of French and British skills** un mariage entre le savoir-faire français et britannique
2 (harmony) **in perfect u.** (to live together) en parfaite harmonie
3 **the (American) U.** les États-Unis mpl, l'Union f (américaine); **customs u.** union douanière
4 (trade union) syndicat m (ouvrier); **to join a u.** se syndiquer; **to form a u.** créer un syndicat; **non-u. workers** ouvriers, -ières non syndiqué(e)s; **unions and management** les syndicats et la direction, les partenaires sociaux; **increasing/decreasing u. membership** syndicalisation f croissante/décroissante
▸▸ Fam **u. bashing** critiques fpl constantes des syndicats; **u. branch** section f syndicale d'entreprise; **u. card** carte f syndicale; **u. demands** revendications fpl syndicales; **the U. Jack** l'Union Jack m (drapeau officiel du Royaume-Uni); **u. leader** responsable m ou dirigeant m syndical; **u. meeting** réunion f syndicale; **u. member** (in general) membre m d'un syndicat, syndiqué, -ée; (of particular union) membre du syndicat, syndiqué, -ée; **u. movement** mouvement m syndical; Tech **u. nut** écrou m de raccord; **u. regulations** règles fpl syndicales; **u. representative** délégué, -ée ou représentant, -ante syndical(e); Am **u. shop** atelier m d'ouvriers syndiqués, union shop m; Am **u. suit** combinaison f

unionism [ˈjuːnjənɪz(ə)m] **N 1** Ind syndicalisme m (ouvrier) **2** Pol unionisme m

unionist [ˈjuːnjənɪst] **N 1** Ind syndicaliste mf **2** Pol unioniste mf; **the U. party** le parti unioniste

unionize [ˈjuːnjənaɪz] **VT** (workers) syndiquer

uniparous [juːˈnɪpərəs] **ADJ** Biol unipare

unique [juːˈniːk] **ADJ 1** (sole) unique; **the sport is u. to this region** ce sport se joue exclusivement dans cette région, ce sport n'existe que dans cette région; **to be u. in doing sth** être le seul à faire qch; **you're not u.** ton cas n'est pas unique, tu n'es pas le seul **2** (exceptional) (offer, price) exceptionnel; (opportunity) unique, exceptionnel
▸▸ Mktg **u. proposition** proposition f unique; Mktg **u. selling point, u. selling proposition** proposition unique de vente

uniquely [juːˈniːklɪ] **ADV 1** (to correspond) exclusivement **2** (extremely) (suited, gifted)

exceptionnellement; **he is u. placed to get this information** il est exceptionnellement bien placé pour obtenir ce renseignement

uniqueness [juːˈniːknɪs] **N 1** caractère m unique; **that's his u. as an actor** c'est ce qui en fait un acteur à part **2** (exceptional nature) (of offer, price) caractère m exceptionnel

unisex [ˈjuːnɪseks] **ADJ** (hairdresser's, clothing) unisexe

unison [ˈjuːnɪs(ə)n] **N** Mus, Fig unisson m; **in u.** à l'unisson (**with** de); **they all replied in u.** ils ont tous répondu en même temps; **to act in u.** agir à l'unisson

unissued [ʌnˈɪʃuːd] **ADJ** St Exch (shares, share capital) non encore émis

unit [ˈjuːnɪt] **N 1** (measure) unité f, Math **units and tens** unités et dizaines; Com, Ind **each box contains a hundred units** chaque boîte contient cent unités; Tech **u. of energy/of work** unité d'énergie/de travail; **u. of velocity** unité de vitesse; Phys **u. of mass** unité de masse; Fin **monetary u.** unité monétaire; **standard u.** module m; **thermal u.** unité thermique
2 Admin (division) division f
3 (section, department) (in hospital) service m; (in school, university, company) groupe m, section f, Cin, TV (team) équipe f, Med **intensive care u.** centre m de soins intensifs; **X-ray u.** service m de radiologie
4 Mil (group) unité f, (fighting) u., Am (combat) u. unité de combat; **air force u.** unité ou groupe m de l'armée de l'air
5 Tech (element) unité f, élément m; **the engine forms a u. with the transmission** le moteur fait bloc avec la transmission; Comput **central processing u.** unité centrale; **input/ output u.** élément ou dispositif m (d')entrée-sortie; **(visual) display u.** console f de visualisation, visuel m; **(kitchen) u.** élément (de cuisine), placard m; **the knives are in the u. there** les couteaux sont dans ce placard
6 Austr (apartment) appartement m
▸▸ Fin **u. of account** unité f de compte; Tel **u. charge** taxe f unitaire; Constr **u. construction** préfabrication f, Com, Ind **u. cost** coût m unitaire; **u. furniture** mobilier m par éléments; Com, Ind **u. labour costs** coût unitaire de travail; **u. manager** directeur m de service; **u. price** prix m unitaire ou à l'unité; Br St Exch **u. trust** fonds m commun de placement, ≃ SICAV f

Unitarian [juːnɪˈteərɪən] **ADJ, N** Rel unitarien, -ienne, unitaire mf

Unitarianism [juːnɪˈteərɪənɪz(ə)m] **N** Rel unitarisme m

unitary [ˈjuːnɪt(ə)rɪ] **ADJ** (system etc) unitaire

unite [juːˈnaɪt] **VT 1** (join) unir; **to u. one country with another** unifier deux pays; **to u. idealism with common sense** allier l'idéalisme au bon sens; **he seemed to u. all the qualities one would wish for** il paraissait réunir toutes les qualités souhaitables **2** (unify) (people) mettre d'accord; (party) unifier; **if we stay united ...** si nous restons unis ...; **more unites us than separates us** ce qui nous unit est plus fort que ce qui nous divise; **common interests that u. two countries** intérêts communs qui unissent deux pays **3** Fml (marry) unir (en mariage)
VI s'allier (**with** avec); (of party, states) s'unifier; Chem (of atoms) s'unir, se combiner; **to u. against** s'unir contre; Pol (party) faire bloc contre; **to u. in doing sth** se mettre d'accord pour faire qch

united [juːˈnaɪtɪd] **ADJ** uni; (unified) unifié; **u. efforts** efforts conjugués; Prov **u. we stand, divided we fall** l'union fait la force; **to present a u. front** présenter un front uni

▸▸ **the U. Arab Emirates** les Émirats mpl arabes unis; **the U. Arab Republic** la République arabe unie; **the U. Kingdom** le Royaume-Uni; **the U. Nations** les Nations fpl unies; **the U. States** les États-Unis mpl

unity [ˈjuːnɪtɪ] **N 1** (oneness) unité f, national/political u. unité nationale/politique; Prov **u. is strength** l'union fait la force **2** (harmony) **there is no u.** in his work ses œuvres manquent d'unité ou d'harmonie; Theat **u. of time, place and action** unité de temps, de lieu et d'action

univ (abbr **university**) université f

univalent [juːnɪˈveɪlənt] **ADJ** Chem univalent

universal [juːnɪˈvɜːs(ə)l] **ADJ** universel; **he's a u. favourite** tout le monde l'aime; **this proposal met with u. rejection** la proposition a été unanimement rejetée; **to meet with u. agreement** faire l'unanimité; **to meet with u. acclaim** être applaudi par tout le monde
N Phil universel m
▸▸ **u. bar code** code-barres m, pl codesbarres; Tech **u. joint** (joint m de) cardan m; **u. product code** code-barres, pl codes-barres; **u. suffrage** suffrage m universel

universality [juːnɪvɜːˈsælɪtɪ] **N** universalité f

universalize [juːnɪˈvɜːsəlaɪz] **VT** universaliser

universally [juːnɪˈvɜːsəlɪ] **ADV** universellement

universe [ˈjuːnɪvɜːs] **N** univers m

university [juːnɪˈvɜːsɪtɪ] **N** université f, **to go to u.** aller à l'université; **he's been to u., he's had a u. education** il a fait des études supérieures; **to get a place at u.** être admis à l'université; **when I was at u.** quand j'étais à l'université; **London U.** l'université de Londres; Fig **the u. of life** l'école de la vie VOIR GRAMMAIRE A7
▸▸ **u. professor** professeur m d'université; **u. student** étudiant, -ante (à l'université), Belg, Suisse universitaire mf, **u. town** ville f universitaire

UNIX [ˈjuːnɪks] **N** Comput (abbr **Uniplexed Information and Computing System**) UNIX m; **U.-based** à base d'UNIX

unjust [ʌnˈdʒʌst] **ADJ** injuste (**to** envers, avec); **my suspicions were u.** mes soupçons n'étaient pas fondés

unjustifiable [ʌndʒʌstɪˈfaɪəb(ə)l] **ADJ** injustifiable

unjustifiably [ʌndʒʌstɪˈfaɪəblɪ] **ADV** sans justification

unjustified [ʌnˈdʒʌstɪfaɪd] **ADJ 1** (action etc) injustifié; **he was absolutely u. in doing that** ce qu'il a fait n'était absolument pas justifié **2** (text) non justifié

unjustly [ʌnˈdʒʌstlɪ] **ADV** injustement

unkempt [ʌnˈkem(p)t] **ADJ** (hair) mal peigné, hirsute; (beard) hirsute; (appearance) négligé; (person) (with regard to hair) dépeigné; (in appearance) débraillé; (garden) mal entretenu

unkind [ʌnˈkaɪnd] **ADJ** (person) dur, méchant; (less strong) peu aimable, pas gentil; (remark) méchant; **that's very u. of him** ce n'est pas du tout gentil de sa part; **to say u. things to sb** dire des méchancetés à qn; **to be u. to animals** être cruel avec les animaux; **to be u. to sb** être méchant envers ou avec qn; **it's u. to one's skin/hair** cela agresse la peau/les cheveux; Lit **the unkindest cut of all** la pire des trahisons

unkindly [ʌnˈkaɪndlɪ] **ADV** méchamment, durement; (less strong) peu aimablement; **to take u. to sth** mal accepter qch
ADJ (person) peu aimable, peu gentil

unkindness [ʌnˈkaɪndnɪs] **N** (of person)

manque *m* de gentillesse; *(stronger)* méchanceté *f*; *(of remark)* méchanceté; *(of climate)* rigueur *f*

unknot [ʌn'nɒt] **VT** (**-tt-**) dénouer

unknowing [ʌn'nəʊɪŋ] **ADJ** inconscient; **she was the u. cause of their quarrel** sans le savoir, elle était la cause de leur dispute

unknowingly [ʌn'nəʊɪŋlɪ] **ADV** inconsciemment, sans le savoir

unknown [ʌn'nəʊn] **ADJ** inconnu (**to** de); **u. person** inconnu, -ue; *Law* **verdict against person or persons u.** verdict contre inconnu; **this is a process u. to us,** this process is **u. to us** c'est un procédé qui nous est inconnu; **it is far from u. in our country** ceci est fort bien connu dans notre pays

ADV he did it u. to me il l'a fait à mon insu; **u. to us, the bus had already gone** nous ne le savions pas, mais le bus était déjà parti; **u. to everyone but her …** personne à part elle ne savait que …

N 1 *(person)* inconnu, -ue **2** *Math* inconnue *f* **3** the **u.** l'inconnu *m*

▸▸ *Math, Fig* **u. quantity** inconnue *f*; **he's an u. quantity** *(of uncertain value)* on ne sait pas ce qu'il vaut; *(unpredictable)* on ne sait pas ce qu'il pense; **the U. Soldier** le Soldat inconnu

unlace [ʌn'leɪs] **VT** *(one's shoes)* délacer, défaire

unladen [ʌn'leɪd(ə)n] **ADJ** *(ship, lorry)* sans charge

▸▸ **u. weight** poids *m* à vide

unladylike [ʌn'leɪdɪlaɪk] **ADJ** indigne d'une femme bien élevée, inélégant; *(manners)* peu distingué, inélégant; **it's u. to do that** une jeune femme qui se respecte ne fait pas cela

unlaid [ʌn'leɪd] **ADJ the table was still u.** la table n'était pas encore mise

unlamented [ʌnlə'mentɪd] **ADJ** non regretté; **he passed away u.** il est mort dans l'indifférence générale

unlatch [ʌn'lætʃ] **VT** *(door)* ouvrir
VI se déverrouiller

unlawful [ʌn'lɔːf(ʊ)l] **ADJ** *(possession, means, action)* illégal, -aux

▸▸ **u. arrest** arrestation *f* illégale; **u. detention** détention *f* abusive

unlawfully [ʌn'lɔːf(ʊ)lɪ] **ADV** illégalement

unleaded [ʌn'ledɪd] **ADJ** *(petrol)* sans plomb

N essence *f* sans plomb

unlearn [ʌn'lɜːn] **VT** (*pt, pp* **unlearnt** [-'lɜːnt], *occ* **unlearned** [-'lɜːnd]) désapprendre

unlearned [ʌn'lɜːnɪd] **ADJ** inculte

unleash [ʌn'liːʃ] **VT 1** *(dogs)* lâcher **2** *(force of army etc)* déchaîner; *(wave of repression)* provoquer, déclencher; **to u. a nuclear war** déclencher une guerre nucléaire; **to u. one's anger** déchaîner sa colère (**on sb** sur qn)

unleavened [ʌn'levənd] **ADJ** *(bread)* sans levain, azyme

unless [ʌn'les] **CONJ** à moins que + *subj*; **he will do nothing u. you ask him to** il ne fera rien à moins que vous ne lui demandiez; **I would always be back by 6.15, u. I was working late** je rentrais toujours à 6h 15 au plus tard, sauf quand je travaillais tard; **u. I'm mistaken** à moins que je (ne) me trompe; **will you do it? – not u. you pay me** le ferez-vous? – seulement si vous me payez; **there aren't any left, not u. you want this one** il n'y en a plus, à moins que vous ne vouliez celui-ci; **u. I hear to the contrary** sauf avis contraire; **u. otherwise stated** sauf indication contraire

unlettered [ʌn'letəd] **ADJ** *Lit* peu lettré, inculte

unliberated [ʌn'lɪbəreɪtɪd] **ADJ** *(woman)*

non libéré, non émancipé; **they're very u. here** les gens ne sont pas du tout émancipés ici

unlicensed [ʌn'laɪsənst] **ADJ 1** *(activity)* non autorisé, illicite; **u. taxi** taxi *m* qui opère sans licence **2** *(car)* ≃ sans vignette

▸▸ *Br* **u. premises** = établissement *m* non habilité à vendre des boissons alcoolisées

unlike [ʌn'laɪk] **ADJ** différent, dissemblable; **they're completely u.** ils ne se ressemblent pas du tout

PREP to be u. sb/sth être différent de qn/ qch; **he's not u. his sister** il ressemble assez à sa sœur; **a proposal not altogether u. yours** une proposition ne différant pas énormément de la vôtre; **he, u. his father** lui, à la différence de *ou* contrairement à son père; **it's u. him to do such a thing** cela ne lui ressemble pas de faire une chose pareille

unlik(e)able [ʌn'laɪkəb(ə)l] **ADJ** *(person)* antipathique, peu sympathique; *(thing)* peu agréable

unlikelihood, unlikeliness [ʌn'laɪklɪhʊd, -'laɪklɪnɪs] **N** improbabilité *f*

unlikely [ʌn'laɪklɪ] **ADJ** improbable, peu probable; *(explanation)* invraisemblable; **that's most** *or* **very** *or* **highly u.** c'est fort improbable; **it's not (at all) u.** c'est très probable, cela se pourrait bien; **it's u. to happen** il y a peu de chances pour que ça arrive; **in the u. event that they do come** au cas peu probable où ils viendraient vraiment; **he's u. to do it** il est peu probable qu'il le fasse; **he's an u. man for the job** il ne semble pas convenir pour ce travail; **we found the ring in a most u. place** nous avons retrouvé la bague dans un endroit auquel nous n'aurions jamais pensé; *Fam* **she wears the most u. clothes** elle s'habille d'une façon invraisemblable

unlimited [ʌn'lɪmɪtɪd] **ADJ** *(time)* illimité; *(patience)* sans borne(s); *(funds)* inépuisable; *Fin (cover)* sans limitation de somme; **u. buffet** buffet *m* à volonté; **there was u. coffee** il y avait du café à volonté; *Comput* **u. e-mail addresses** nombre *m* d'adresses électroniques illimité; **he has an u. fund of stories** il a un stock d'histoires inépuisable

▸▸ *Br Com* **u. company** société *f* à responsabilité illimitée *ou* infinie; *Br Com* **u. liability** responsabilité *f* illimitée; **u. mileage** *(of hired car)* ≃ kilométrage *m* illimité; **u. travel** *(with season ticket etc)* nombre *m* de voyages illimité

unlined [ʌn'laɪnd] **ADJ 1** *(face)* sans rides **2** *(paper)* non réglé **3** *(without lining)* non doublé

unlisted [ʌn'lɪstɪd] **ADJ** non répertorié; *Fin (share)* incoté; *(phone number)* qui n'est pas sur l'annuaire; **she was u. in the standard reference works** son nom ne figurait pas dans les livres de référence classiques

▸▸ *St Exch* **u. market** Bourse *f* coulisse; *St Exch* **u. securities market** marché *m* hors cote, second marché; *St Exch* **u. security** valeur *f* non cotée, valeur du second marché

unlit [ʌn'lɪt] **ADJ** non allumé; **the u. streets** les rues obscures

unload [ʌn'ləʊd] **VT 1** *(boat, car, goods)* décharger; *(from ship)* débarquer; *Fam (stolen goods)* fourguer; **to u. sth onto sb** fourguer qch à qn; *Fig* **to u. one's problems onto sb** se décharger de ses problèmes sur qn **2** *(gun, camera)* décharger

VI 1 *(of lorry, ship)* décharger **2** *Am Mktg (flood market)* inonder le marché

unloaded [ʌn'ləʊdɪd] **ADJ 1** *(lorry, ship)* *(with load removed)* déchargé; *(without a load)* non chargé, sans chargement **2** *(gun, camera)* non chargé; **don't worry, the gun's u.** n'aie pas peur, le fusil n'est pas chargé

unloading [ʌn'ləʊdɪŋ] **N** déchargement *m*; *(from ship)* débarquement *m*

▸▸ **u. dock** quai *m* de déchargement; **u. note,** u. permit permis *m* de débarquement; **u. platform** plate-forme *f* de déchargement, *pl* plates-formes de déchargement

unlock [ʌn'lɒk] **VT 1** *(door)* déverrouiller **2** *(secret)* révéler, découvrir **3** *(wheel, nut)* débloquer **4** *Comput (file, diskette, keyboard)* déverrouiller **5** **to u. the steering wheel** déverrouiller le système de blocage de la direction **6** *Fin (assets)* débloquer **7** *(mobile phone)* débloquer

VI se déverrouiller

unlocked [ʌn'lɒkt] **ADJ** *(door)* qui n'est pas fermé à clef

unlocking [ʌn'lɒkɪŋ] **N** *Aut, Comput* déverrouillage *m*

unlooked-for [ʌn'lʊkt-] **ADJ** imprévu

unloose(n) [ʌn'luːs(n)] **VT** *(bolt, screw, tie)* desserrer; **to u. one's grip** lâcher prise; **to u. sb's tongue** délier la langue à qn

unlov(e)able [ʌn'lʌvəb(ə)l] **ADJ** peu attachant

unloved [ʌn'lʌvd] **ADJ** mal-aimé; **to be feeling u.** ne pas se sentir aimé, se sentir mal-aimé

unlovely [ʌn'lʌvlɪ] **ADJ** *(person)* disgracieux; *(sight)* laid

unloving [ʌn'lʌvɪŋ] **ADJ** *(person)* peu affectueux, peu aimant; *(behaviour)* froid

unluckily [ʌn'lʌkɪlɪ] **ADV** malheureusement, par malheur; **u. for me** malheureusement pour moi

unlucky [ʌn'lʌkɪ] **ADJ 1** *(person)* malchanceux; **to be u.** ne pas avoir de chance; **talk about u.!** quelle malchance!; **you were u. not to have been chosen** tu n'as pas eu de chance de ne pas avoir été choisi; **to be u. in love** ne pas être heureux en amour; **it was u. for him that she arrived just at that moment** malheureusement pour lui, elle est arrivée à cet instant précis **2** *(coincidence, decision)* malheureux; **it had been an u. day** cela avait été un jour de malchance; **that's u.** ce n'est pas de chance **3** *(bringing bad luck) (number, colour etc)* qui porte malheur; **it's my u. colour** c'est la couleur qui me porte malheur; **don't walk under a ladder, it's u.** ne passez pas sous une échelle, ça porte malheur

unmade [ˈʌnmeɪd] **ADJ** qui n'est pas fait; *(bed)* défait; *(road)* non goudronné

unmade-up **ADJ** *(face)* non maquillé

unmake [ʌn'meɪk] **VT** (*pt, pp* **unmade** [-'meɪd]) défaire

unman [ʌn'mæn] **VT** (**-nn-**) *Lit (cause to lose courage)* décourager, démoraliser

unmanageable [ʌn'mænɪdʒəb(ə)l] **ADJ** *(person, child)* rebelle; *(horse)* indocile; *(vehicle, ship)* difficile à manœuvrer; *(large book etc)* difficile à manier, peu maniable; *(situation, problem)* ingérable; *(company)* impossible à diriger; **u. hair** cheveux difficiles à coiffer

unmanly [ʌn'mænlɪ] **ADJ 1** *(effeminate)* efféminé **2** *(cowardly)* lâche

unmanned [ʌn'mænd] **ADJ** *(ship, spaceship)* sans équipage; *Rail (level crossing)* automatique; **all of the ticket windows were u.** il n'y avait personne derrière les guichets; **the reception desk must never be left u.** il doit toujours y avoir quelqu'un au bureau de réception

▸▸ *Astronaut* **u. flight** vol *m* inhabité *ou* non habité

unmannerliness [ʌn'mænəlɪnɪs] **N** *Lit* manque *m* de savoir-vivre, impolitesse *f*

unmannerly [ʌn'mænəlɪ] **ADJ** *Lit (behaviour, person)* impoli

unmapped [ʌn'mæpt] ADJ u. territory territoire pour lequel il n'existe pas de carte

unmarked [ʌn'mɑːkt] ADJ 1 (no scratches etc) sans marque(s); (no stains etc) sans tache(s); u. (police) car voiture f (de police) banalisée; his body was bruised but his face was u. il avait des contusions sur le corps mais son visage était intact 2 Sport (player) démarqué 3 my essay was still u. ma dissertation n'était toujours pas corrigée

unmarketable [ʌn'mɑːkɪtəb(ə)l] ADJ invendable, non commercialisable

unmarriageable [ʌn'mærɪdʒəb(ə)l] ADJ immariable

unmarried [ʌn'mærɪd] ADJ non marié; he remained u. il est resté célibataire, il ne s'est jamais marié
▸▸ Old-fashioned u. mother mère f célibataire; u. state célibat m

unmask [ʌn'mɑːsk] VT démasquer; esp Lit (plot) dévoiler
VI se démasquer

unmatched [ʌn'mætʃt] ADJ (person, ability) sans égal, incomparable; she is u. as a novelist comme romancière, elle n'a pas sa pareille; he's u. for courage son courage est inégalé

unmentionable [ʌn'menʃənəb(ə)l] ADJ (event, thing) dont il ne faut pas parler; (word, name) qu'il ne faut pas prononcer
NPL Old-fashioned, Hum unmentionables sous-vêtements mpl

unmerciful [ʌn'mɜːsɪfʊl] ADJ impitoyable, sans pitié

unmercifully [ʌn'mɜːsɪfəlɪ] ADV impitoyablement, sans pitié

unmerited [ʌn'merɪtɪd] ADJ immérité

unmetered [ʌn'miːtəd] ADJ Comput (Internet access) illimité

unmethodical [ʌnmɪ'θɒdɪk(ə)l] ADJ peu méthodique

unmindful [ʌn'maɪndf(ʊ)l] ADJ esp Lit to be u. of sth être peu soucieux de qch; u. of one's own interests sans penser à ses propres intérêts

unmistakable [ʌnmɪs'teɪkəb(ə)l] ADJ (feeling) clair; (difference) marqué, manifeste; (person, building) que l'on ne peut pas confondre; (voice, style) reconnaissable entre mille, que l'on ne peut pas confondre; you'll see it all right, it's u. tu le verras sans problème, on ne peut pas le rater; the u. smell/symptom of … l'odeur/le symptôme caractéristique de …

unmistakably [ʌnmɪs'teɪkəblɪ] ADV clairement, nettement; the style is u. French le style est français, il n'y a pas à s'y tromper

unmitigated [ʌn'mɪtɪgeɪtɪd] ADJ (evil, horror, severity) total, -aux; (used as intensifier) (idiot, cock-up) véritable; the tedium was u. by even the slightest hint of humour l'ennui n'était même pas allégé par la moindre pointe d'humour; an u. lie un pur mensonge; an u. disaster un échec total

unmixed [ʌn'mɪkst] ADJ (joy) sans mélange

unmolested [ʌnmə'lestɪd] ADJ sans encombre; to leave sb u. (not bother) laisser qn en paix

unmortgaged [ʌn'mɔːgɪdʒd] ADJ non hypothéqué

unmotivated [ʌn'məʊtɪveɪtɪd] ADJ sans mobile; (person) non motivé; (without ambition) dépourvu d'ambition; his actions were u. by any desire for personal glory ses actes n'étaient pas motivés par un quelconque désir de gloire personnelle

unmounted [ʌn'maʊntɪd] ADJ 1 (gem) non serti; (photo) non encadré 2 (not on horseback) à pied

unmourned [ʌn'mɔːnd] ADJ non pleuré; he died u. personne n'a pleuré sa mort

unmoved [ʌn'muːvd] ADJ impassible; u. by sth aucunement ému de ou par qch; he remained u. by all our arguments, all our arguments left him quite u. tous nos arguments le laissaient indifférent ou froid

unmusical [ʌn'mjuːzɪk(ə)l] ADJ peu mélodieux; (person) peu musicien, -ienne; to my u. ear it sounds like … pour mon oreille peu musicienne ça ressemble à …

unnameable [ʌn'neɪməb(ə)l] ADJ innommable

unnamed [ʌn'neɪmd] ADJ (person) anonyme; (thing) innommé

unnatural [ʌn'nætʃərəl] ADJ 1 (not normal) anormal, -aux; (vice) contre nature; it's u. for him cela ne lui ressemble pas (to de) 2 (affected) (style, person) peu naturel, affecté; (laugh) forcé

unnaturally [ʌn'nætʃərəlɪ] ADV 1 (to develop etc) anormalement; she was u. shy elle était anormalement timide; not u. we turned the offer down comme on pouvait s'y attendre nous avons rejeté cette offre; not u. in the circumstances … ce qui est/était bien naturel étant donné les circonstances, … 2 (affectedly) (to speak) avec affectation; (to act, walk) peu naturellement; the text reads very u. ce texte est très forcé

unnavigable [ʌn'nævɪgəb(ə)l] ADJ non navigable

unnecessarily [ʌnnesɪ'serɪlɪ] ADV inutilement; you're being u. hard on yourself tu te fais du mal pour rien

unnecessary [ʌn'nesɪs(ə)rɪ] ADJ (costs, delay, trouble) inutile; it was quite u. of you to say that! tu n'avais vraiment pas besoin de dire cela!; it's u. to change it il n'est pas nécessaire ou ce n'est pas la peine ou il est inutile de le changer; it's totally u. for you to come too il est absolument inutile ou il n'est absolument pas nécessaire que tu viennes aussi

unneeded [ʌn'niːdɪd] ADJ inutile

unnegotiable [ʌnnə'gəʊʃəbəl] ADJ Fin (cheque, bill) non négociable

unneighbourly, Am **unneighborly** [ʌn'neɪbəlɪ] ADJ désobligeant; to behave in an u. manner manquer de respect envers ses voisins

unnerve [ʌn'nɜːv] VT (disconcert) déconcerter; to be unnerved by sb's presence se sentir déstabilisé ou troublé par la présence de qn

Note that the French verb **énerver** is a false friend. It means **to irritate** or **to make nervous**, depending on the context.

unnerving [ʌn'nɜːvɪŋ] ADJ déconcertant

unnervingly [ʌn'nɜːvɪŋlɪ] ADV he can be u. flippant il est parfois d'une désinvolture déconcertante; there was something u. peaceful about the village le calme du village avait quelque chose de troublant

unnoticed [ʌn'nəʊtɪst] ADJ inaperçu, inobservé; she left the party u. elle a quitté la soirée sans que personne ne s'en rende compte; to pass or go u. passer inaperçu; to let an insult pass u. ne pas relever une insulte

unnumbered [ʌn'nʌmbəd] ADJ 1 (page) non numéroté; (house) sans numéro 2 Lit (countless) innombrable

UNO ['juːnəʊ] N (abbr United Nations Organization) ONU f

unobjectionable [ʌnəb'dʒekʃənəb(ə)l] ADJ anodin; (person) anodin, inoffensif; it seems u. enough il n'y a rien à redire

unobservant [ʌnəb'zɜːvənt] ADJ to be u. ne pas être observateur, -trice; you're so u.! tu n'es vraiment pas observateur!

unobserved [ʌnəb'zɜːvd] ADJ (departure etc) inaperçu; he went out u. il est sorti sans que personne ne le voit

unobstructed [ʌnəb'strʌktɪd] ADJ (road) non encombré; they marched on u. to … ils ont poursuivi leur chemin sans rencontrer d'obstacles jusqu'à …; u. view vue dégagée ou libre

unobtainable [ʌnəb'teɪnəb(ə)l] ADJ impossible à obtenir, impossible à se procurer; Tel the number is u. le numéro n'est pas en service actuellement

unobtrusive [ʌnəb'truːsɪv] ADJ (person, building) discret, -ète; he always tried to remain u. il cherchait toujours à s'effacer

unobtrusively [ʌnəb'truːsɪvlɪ] ADV discrètement

unoccupied [ʌn'ɒkjʊpaɪd] ADJ 1 (not busy) inoccupé 2 (house) inoccupé, inhabité 3 Mil non occupé; the town was still u. la ville n'était toujours pas occupée 4 (table, seat) libre, disponible
▸▸ Mil u. zone zone f libre

unofficial [ʌnə'fɪʃəl] ADJ (meeting) non officiel; (information) officieux; in an u. capacity à titre officieux; from an u. source de source officieuse; it's still u. on ne l'a pas encore confirmé;
▸▸ Ind u. strike grève f sauvage

unofficially [ʌnə'fɪʃ(ə)lɪ] ADV non officiellement

unopened [ʌn'əʊpənd] ADJ non ouvert, qui n'a pas été ouvert

unopposed [ʌnə'pəʊzd] ADJ sans opposition; (to advance) sans rencontrer d'opposition ou de résistance; we cannot allow this sort of thing to go u. on ne peut pas laisser faire ce genre de choses; Parl the bill was given an u. second reading le projet de loi a été accepté sans opposition à la deuxième lecture
▸▸ Pol u. candidate candidat m unique

unorganized [ʌn'ɔːgənaɪzd] ADJ (event, group, person etc) non organisé; (disorganized) désorganisé
▸▸ Ind u. labour main-d'œuvre f non syndiquée

unoriginal [ʌnə'rɪdʒɪn(ə)l] ADJ sans originalité, peu original, -aux

unorthodox [ʌn'ɔːθədɒks] ADJ peu orthodoxe

unostentatious [ʌnɒsten'teɪʃəs] ADJ (person, behaviour, house, party) simple; (dress) sobre, simple

unostentatiously [ʌnɒsten'teɪʃəslɪ] ADV (to act) simplement; (dressed) simplement, sobrement

unostentatiousness [ʌnɒsten'teɪʃəsnɪs] N (of person, lifestyle, house etc) manque m d'ostentation, simplicité f

unpack [ʌn'pæk] VT (objects, books, boxes) déballer; (suitcase) défaire; (car) décharger
VI (after travelling) défaire sa valise; (after moving) déballer ou vider ses cartons

unpacking [ʌn'pækɪŋ] N (after moving house) déballage m; the u. didn't take long (after holiday) nous n'avons pas mis longtemps à défaire nos bagages

unpaid [ʌn'peɪd] ADJ 1 (work, person) non payé, bénévole; (post) non rétribué, non rémunéré 2 (bill) impayé; (debt) impayé, non acquitté; to leave an account u. laisser arrérager un compte 3 (money) non versé; the money is still u. l'argent n'a toujours pas été versé
ADV he refused to work u. il a refusé de travailler sans être payé; I'll work u. je vais travailler bénévolement
▸▸ u. bill impayé m; u. leave congé m sans solde

unpaid-up share N *Fin* action *f* non libérée

unpalatable [ʌnˈpælətəb(ə)l] ADJ **1** *(food)* peu appétissant **2** *Fig (truth, facts)* désagréable, dur à avaler

unparalleled [ʌnˈpærəleld] ADJ *(beauty)* incomparable, sans égal; *(action, event)* sans précédent

unpardonable [ʌnˈpɑːd(ə)nəb(ə)l] ADJ impardonnable, inexcusable

unpardonably [ʌnˈpɑːd(ə)nəblɪ] ADV de façon impardonnable; **she was u. late** elle est arrivée avec un retard impardonnable; **he was u. harsh** il a été d'une dureté impardonnable

unparliamentary [ʌnpɑːləˈment(ə)rɪ] ADJ *Parl (language, action)* contraire au règles du parlement

unpatented [ʌnˈpeɪtəntɪd, -ˈpæ-] ADJ non breveté

unpatriotic [ʌnpeɪtrɪˈɒtɪk, -pæ-] ADJ *(person)* peu patriote; *(action)* peu patriotique; **to be u.** *(of person)* être mauvais patriote

unpatriotically [ʌnpeɪtrɪˈɒtɪklɪ, -pæ-] ADV *(to act)* en mauvais patriote

unpaved [ʌnˈpeɪvd] ADJ non pavé, sans pavés

unperceived [ʌnpəˈsiːvd] ADJ non perçu

unperforated [ʌnˈpɜːfəreɪtɪd] ADJ sans perforations

unperson [ˈʌnpɜːsən] N *Pol* non-personne *f*, *pl* non-personnes

unperturbable [ʌnpəˈtɜːbəb(ə)l] ADJ imperturbable

unperturbed [ʌnpəˈtɜːbd] ADJ impassible; **to be u. by sth** ne pas se laisser perturber par qch

unpick [ʌnˈpɪk] VT *(seam, hem)* défaire; *(garment)* découdre

unpin [ʌnˈpɪn] VT (-nn-) ôter les épingles (**from** de)

unplaced [ʌnˈpleɪst] ADJ *(competitor)* non classé; *(horse etc)* non placé

unplanned [ʌnˈplænd] ADJ *(event)* imprévu; *(child)* non prévu

unplayable [ʌnˈpleɪəb(ə)l] ADJ **1** *Sport (pitch etc)* impraticable; *(service, shot etc)* injouable; **the ball was in an u. position** la balle n'était pas jouable **2** *Mus, Theat* injouable

unpleasant [ʌnˈplezənt] ADJ *(taste, smell)* désagréable; *(person, tone, manner)* désagréable, déplaisant; **to smell u.** sentir mauvais; **to taste u.** avoir mauvais goût; **to look u.** *(of thing, person)* être peu ragoûtant; **u. weather** mauvais temps *m*; **he made some u. remarks** il a dit des choses désobligeantes; **she was very u. with** *or* **to me** elle a été très désagréable avec moi; **things are getting rather u. between them** la situation est en train de se dégrader entre eux

unpleasantly [ʌnˈplezəntlɪ] ADV de façon désagréable; **the wine was u. sweet** le vin était trop sucré; **we had u. cold weather** il a fait vraiment trop froid

unpleasantness [ʌnˈplezəntnɪs] N **1** *(of person, thing)* caractère *m* désagréable; *(of place)* aspect *m* déplaisant; *(of food)* caractère peu appétissant **2** *(disagreement)* différend *m*; *(argument)* dispute *f*; **the will caused some u.** le testament a provoqué des disputes; **there was some u. between them** il y avait encore des tensions entre eux; **we managed to avoid any u.** nous avons réussi à éviter une dispute

unpleasing [ʌnˈpliːzɪŋ] ADJ déplaisant; **a not u. effect** un effet qui n'est pas désagréable

unpledged [ʌnˈpledʒd] ADJ
▸▸ *Fin* **u. revenue** recettes *fpl* non gagées

unplug [ʌnˈplʌg] VT (-gg-) **1** *(television etc)* débrancher **2** *(opening, pipe)* déboucher

unplumbed [ʌnˈplʌmd] ADJ *(depths, mystery, knowledge)* insondé

unpoetic(al) [ʌnpəʊˈetɪk, -ɪk(ə)l] ADJ peu poétique

unpolished [ʌnˈpɒlɪʃt] ADJ **1** *(surface)* non poli; *(stone)* brut; *(floor, furniture)* non ciré, non astiqué; *(shoes)* non ciré **2** *(person)* peu raffiné; *(style)* qui manque de raffinement

unpolluted [ʌnpəˈluːtɪd] ADJ non pollué

unpopular [ʌnˈpɒpjʊlər] ADJ *(decision, government)* impopulaire; **an u. make of car** une marque de voiture qui n'a pas de succès; **at school she had been an u. child** quand elle était à l'école les autres enfants ne l'aimaient pas beaucoup; **he makes himself u. with everybody** il se fait mal voir de tout le monde; **he's u. with his employees** ses employés ne l'aiment pas (beaucoup); **this decision was very u.** cette décision a été très mal accueillie *ou* très impopulaire

unpopularity [ʌnpɒpjʊˈlærɪtɪ] N impopularité *f*

unpopulated [ʌnˈpɒpjʊleɪtɪd] ADJ désert, non peuplé

unpractical [ʌnˈpræktɪk(ə)l] ADJ **1** *(person)* peu pratique; **he's completely u.** il n'a aucun sens pratique **2** *(plan)* irréalisable

unpractised, *Am* **unpracticed** [ʌnˈpræktɪst] ADJ inexpérimenté; **to be u. in the art of public speaking** ne pas avoir l'habitude de parler en public; **she's quite u. as a manager** elle n'a pas d'expérience en tant que directrice

unprecedented [ʌnˈpresɪdentɪd] ADJ *(decision)* sans précédent, exceptionnel; **this was quite u. in the continent's history** c'était du jamais vu dans l'histoire du continent

unpredictability [ʌnprɪdɪktəˈbɪlətɪ] N imprévisibilité *f*

unpredictable [ʌnprɪˈdɪktəb(ə)l] ADJ *(event, person, effect etc)* imprévisible; *(weather)* incertain

unprejudiced [ʌnˈpredʒʊdɪst] ADJ sans préjugés

unpremeditated [ʌnprɪˈmedɪteɪtɪd] ADJ *Law (offence)* non prémédité

unprepared [ʌnprɪˈpeəd] ADJ **1** *(food etc)* non préparé; *(speech)* improvisé, impromptu; **to find everything u.** ne rien trouver de prêt; **the hall was quite u. for the party** la salle n'était pas du tout prête pour la soirée **2** *(person)* **to be u. for sth** ne pas s'attendre à qch; **to go into an undertaking u.** faire qch sans être préparé; **I was quite u. for the exam** *(hadn't studied for it)* je n'étais pas du tout préparé à l'examen

unpreparedness [ʌnprɪˈpeədnɪs, -ˈpeərɪdnɪs] N impréparation *f* (**for** à)

unprepossessing [ʌnpriːpəˈzesɪŋ] ADJ *(person, building)* peu engageant; **a man of u. appearance** un homme à l'apparence peu engageante *ou* peu avenante

unpresentable [ʌnprɪˈzentəb(ə)l] ADJ pas présentable

unpretentious [ʌnprɪˈtenʃəs] ADJ *(person)* sans prétention, simple; *(tastes, house)* simple

unpretentiously [ʌnprɪˈtenʃəslɪ] ADV simplement

unpriced [ʌnˈpraɪst] ADJ *(article)* sans prix

unprincipled [ʌnˈprɪnsɪp(ə)ld] ADJ *(person)* dénué de principes, sans scrupules; *(behaviour)* sans scrupules; **what an u. thing to do** il ne faut vraiment pas avoir de scrupules pour faire une chose pareille

unprintable [ʌnˈprɪntəb(ə)l] ADJ impubliable; *Fig (comment, reply)* qu'on n'oserait

pas *ou* qu'on ne peut répéter; **what he actually said is u.** ce qu'il a vraiment dit n'est pas répétable

unprocessed [ʌnˈprəʊsest] ADJ *(film)* non développé

unproductive [ʌnprəˈdʌktɪv] ADJ *(method, capital)* improductif; *(land, conversation)* stérile; **an u. afternoon** une après-midi improductive

unprofessional [ʌnprəˈfeʃən(ə)l] ADJ *(person, action)* pas professionnel; **it looks u. not to ...** ça ne fait pas très professionnel de ne pas ...; **it's u. to leave a job unfinished** ce n'est pas professionnel de ne pas terminer un travail; **he's rather u. in his approach** il n'est pas très professionnel

unprofessionally [ʌnprəˈfeʃ(ə)nəlɪ] ADV *(to do job, work, carry out contract, behave)* de manière peu professionnelle; **he dealt with the whole situation rather u.** la façon dont il s'est occupé de l'affaire n'était pas très professionnelle

unprofitable [ʌnˈprɒfɪtəb(ə)l] ADJ *(operation, meeting)* peu fructueux; *(firm)* peu rentable; **we spent an u. morning/afternoon trying to ...** nous avons perdu la matinée/l'après-midi à essayer de ...

unprofitably [ʌnˈprɒfɪtəblɪ] ADV sans profit

Unprofor [ˈʌnprəfɔːr] N *(abbr* United Nations Protection Force) FORPRONU *f*

unpromising [ʌnˈprɒmɪsɪŋ] ADJ peu prometteur, -euse; **the weather looks u.** on dirait qu'il ne va pas faire beau; **that's an u. start** c'est un mauvais départ *ou* un départ qui augure mal de la suite

unprompted [ʌnˈprɒmptɪd] ADJ spontané; **that was quite u. by any self-interest** ce n'était motivé par aucun intérêt personnel

unpronounceable [ʌnprəˈnaʊnsəb(ə)l] ADJ imprononçable

unprotected [ʌnprəˈtektɪd] ADJ **1** *(undefended)* sans protection, sans défense; *(wood)* non traité; **u. wood will rot in this weather** si vous ne traitez pas le bois, il va pourrir avec le temps qu'il fait; **to have u. sex** avoir des rapports sexuels non protégés **2** *Tech (moving part, blade)* non protégé

unproved, **unproven** [ʌnˈpruːvd, -ˈpruːv(ə)n] ADJ non prouvé

unprovided-for [ʌnprəˈvaɪdɪd-] ADJ *(family)* sans ressources; *(eventuality)* non prévu; **he left his family u. in his will** il n'a rien laissé à sa famille dans son testament

unprovoked [ʌnprəˈvəʊkt] ADJ *(violence, criticism)* gratuit; **an u. attack** une agression gratuite

unpublicized [ʌnˈpʌblɪsaɪzd] ADJ non publié, inédit

unpublishable [ʌnˈpʌblɪʃəb(ə)l] ADJ impubliable

unpublished [ʌnˈpʌblɪʃt] ADJ inédit, non publié; **the u. facts** les faits qui n'ont pas été révélés au public

unpunctual [ʌnˈpʌŋktjʊəl] ADJ peu ponctuel, inexact

unpunctuality [ʌnpʌŋktjʊˈælɪtɪ] N manque *m* de ponctualité, inexactitude *f*

unpunished [ʌnˈpʌnɪʃt] ADJ *(crime, criminal)* impuni; **to go u.** rester impuni

unputdownable [ʌnpʊtˈdaʊnəb(ə)l] ADJ *Fam (book)* captivant, prenant; **I found it absolutely u.** je ne pouvais pas m'arrêter de lire

unqualified [ʌnˈkwɒlɪfaɪd] ADJ **1** *(person)* non qualifié; *(doctor, teacher)* non diplômé; **she's u. for the job** elle n'est pas qualifiée pour le poste; **to be u. to do sth** ne pas avoir la compétence nécessaire pour faire qch; **I'm quite u. to talk about it** je ne suis nullement qualifié pour en parler **2** *(unreserved)* *(accusation, support etc)* sans réserve; **to give sth one's u. support** soutenir qch complètement; **u. denial** dénégation *f* catégorique; **u. praise** éloges *mpl* sans réserve; **an u. disaster** un désastre sans nom; **it was an u. success** cela a été un succès formidable **3** *Gram (adjective)* non modifié

unquenchable [ʌn'kwenʃəb(ə)l] ADJ *(thirst, fire)* inextinguible; *(thirst, curiosity)* insatiable

unquenched [ʌn'kwenʃt] ADJ *(fire)* non éteint; *(thirst)* non étanché; *(desire, curiosity, passion)* inassouvi

unquestionable [ʌn'kwestjənəb(ə)l] ADJ indiscutable; *(right)* incontestable

unquestionably [ʌn'kwestjənəblɪ] ADV incontestablement, sans aucun doute

unquestioned [ʌn'kwestjənd] ADJ indiscuté, incontesté; **to let a statement pass** *or* **go u.** laisser passer une affirmation sans la relever

unquestioning [ʌn'kwestjənɪŋ] ADJ *(obedience)* aveugle; *(trust, loyalty)* absolu; **to be u. about sth** ne pas se poser de questions au sujet de qch

unquestioningly [ʌn'kwestjənɪŋlɪ] ADV aveuglément, sans se poser de question; **u. loyal** d'une loyauté absolue

unquiet [ʌn'kwaɪət] ADJ *esp Lit* inquiet, -ète; **u. times** époque *f* troublée

unquote ['ʌnkwəʊt] VI *(used only in imperative) (in quotation)* fermez les guillemets; *(in report)* fin de citation

unquoted [ʌn'kwəʊtɪd] ADJ *Fin (share)* incoté; *(company, securities)* non coté

unratified [ʌn'rætɪfaɪd] ADJ non ratifié

unravel [ʌn'ræv(ə)l] (-ll-, *Am* -l-) VT **1** *(fabric)* effiler, effilocher; *(knitting)* défaire; *(jumper, part of jumper)* détricoter **2** *(string)* démêler, débrouiller; *(plot)* dénouer, démêler; *(mystery)* débrouiller

VI **1 to u. (itself), to come unravelled** *(of cloth)* s'effiler, s'effilocher; *(of knitting)* se défaire; *(of jumper)* se détricoter; *(of rope)* se détordre; *Fig (of plan)* se désagréger **2** *(of facts, mystery)* s'éclaircir

unread [ʌn'red] ADJ qui n'a pas été lu; **to leave sth u.** ne pas lire qch; **he left the magazine on the table u.** il a laissé la revue sur la table sans l'avoir lue

unreadable [ʌn'riːdəb(ə)l] ADJ *(book, writing)*, *Comput* illisible

unreadiness [ʌn'redɪnɪs] N **1** *(lack of preparation)* manque *m* de préparation; **in a state of u.** sans être préparé **2** *(unwillingness)* **their u. to contribute** la mauvaise volonté qu'ils ont mise à contribuer; *(refusal)* leur refus *m* à contribuer

unready [ʌn'redɪ] ADJ **1** *(unprepared)* **to be u. for sth** ne pas être préparé pour qch **2** *(unwilling)* **to be u. to help** n'être pas prêt à aider; **she was u. to admit that she might be wrong** elle n'était pas prête à admettre qu'elle puisse avoir tort

unreal [ʌn'rɪəl] ADJ **1** irréel; **everything seemed u. to him** il avait l'impression de rêver **2** *Fam (very good, very bad, unbelievable) (action, situation)* dingue; *(person)* pas vrai

unrealistic [ʌnrɪə'lɪstɪk] ADJ irréaliste

unreality [ʌnrɪ'ælɪtɪ] N irréalité *f*

unrealizable [ʌnrɪə'laɪzəb(ə)l] ADJ irréalisable

unrealized [ʌn'rɪəlaɪzd] ADJ **1** *(hope, wish)* irréalisé **2** *Fin (capital)* non réalisé
▸▸ *Fin* **u. gain** gain *m* latent; **u. loss** perte *f* latente

unreasonable [ʌn'riːz(ə)nəb(ə)l] ADJ **1** *(person) (illogical)* déraisonnable; *(unfair)* injuste; **don't be u.!** sois raisonnable!; **you**

are being very u. tu es injuste; **they were quite u. in their demands** leurs exigences étaient tout à fait déraisonnables **2** *(assumption)* déraisonnable; *(demand)* immodéré; *(price)* excessif; **this would be a not u. assumption** cette supposition ne serait pas inacceptable; **surely it's not u. to expect that ...** on est bien en mesure de s'attendre à ce que ...; **at this u. hour** à cette heure indue

unreasonably [ʌn'riːz(ə)nəblɪ] ADV d'une manière peu raisonnable; **that's u. expensive** c'est excessivement cher; **they asked, and not altogether u., that ...** ils ont demandé, plutôt légitimement, que ...

unreasoning [ʌn'riːz(ə)nɪŋ] ADJ *(person)* qui ne raisonne pas; **u. hatred** haine *f* irraisonnée *ou* aveugle; **u. panic** peur *f* panique

unrecognizable [ʌnrekəg'naɪzəbl(ə)] ADJ méconnaissable

unrecognized [ʌn'rekəgnaɪzd] ADJ **1** *(not accepted) (government)* non reconnu; *(writer, talent etc)* méconnu; **her talent went u.** son talent n'a pas été reconnu *ou* est resté méconnu **2** *(by people in street etc)* **to go u.** ne pas être reconnu; **he mingled u. in the crowd** il s'est mêlé à la foule sans qu'on le reconnaisse
▸▸ *Comput* **u. command** commande *f* inconnue

unrecorded [ʌnrɪ'kɔːdɪd] ADJ **1** *(fact, comment)* non enregistré, non noté; **the details of the case went u.** il n'y a pas eu de trace écrite sur les détails de l'affaire **2** *(music, tape)* non enregistré; *(tape)* vierge

unrecoverable [ʌnrɪ'kʌvərəb(ə)l] ADJ **1** *Comput* irrécouvrable **2** *Fin (debt)* inexigible

unrecovered debt [ʌnrɪ'kʌvəd] N créance *f* impayée

unredeemed [ʌnrɪ'diːmd] ADJ **1** *(sinner)* non racheté; *(bad character)* non compensé (**by** par); **the film is u. by even a spark of humour** il n'y a même pas un soupçon d'humour pour racheter le film; **the town's ugliness is u. by any charm whatsoever** la ville n'a aucun charme quelconque qui puisse racheter sa laideur; **he led a life of u. evil** il a toujours vécu dans le mal **2** *(promise)* non rempli, non tenu **3** *(pawned object)* non dégagé **4** *Fin (loan)* non amorti, non remboursé; *(draft)* non honoré; *(mortgage)* non purgé; *(pledge)* non retiré

unreel [ʌn'riːl] VT *(film, cable)* dérouler
VI se dérouler

unrefined [ʌnrɪ'faɪnd] ADJ **1** *(sugar, petrol)* brut, non raffiné **2** *(person, taste)* peu raffiné, grossier; **u. manners** manières *fpl* frustes

unreformed [ʌnrɪ'fɔːmd] ADJ *(person)* qui ne s'est pas corrigé; *(law)* non amendé; **to remain u.** *(of person)* rester incorrigible

unrefreshed [ʌnrɪ'freʃt] ADJ encore fatigué, non reposé

unregistered [ʌn'redʒɪstəd] ADJ *(person)* non inscrit; *(luggage)* non enregistré; *(parcel)* non recommandé; *(car)* non immatriculé; *(birth)* non déclaré

unregretted [ʌnrɪ'gretɪd] ADJ que l'on ne regrette pas; **she died u.** personne n'a regretté sa mort

unrehearsed [ʌnrɪ'hɜːst] ADJ *(play)* joué sans répétitions; *(speech)* improvisé; **believe me, that was completely u.** crois-moi, ce n'était pas du tout prévu

unrelated [ʌnrɪ'leɪtɪd] ADJ **1** *(events)* sans rapport (**to** avec; **to each other** l'un avec l'autre); **these facts are totally u.** il n'y a aucun rapport entre ces faits **2** *(people)* **they are u.** il n'y a aucun lien de parenté entre eux

unrelenting [ʌnrɪ'lentɪŋ] ADJ *(struggle, criticism, efforts)* acharné; *(pain)* sans rémission; *(pressure, rain)* incessant; *(person,*

logic) implacable (**towards** à l'égard de); **he was u. in his insistence that I should ...** il insistait avec acharnement pour que je ... + *sub*; **he was u.** *(would not be persuaded, influenced)* il restait inflexible

unreliability [ʌnrɪlaɪə'bɪlɪtɪ] N *(of undertaking, person)* manque *m* de sérieux; *(of result)* inexactitude *f*; *(of machine, car, computer)* manque *m* de fiabilité

unreliable [ʌnrɪ'laɪəb(ə)l] ADJ *(person)* sur qui on ne peut pas compter; *(character)* instable; *(information, result, source)* douteux; *(machine, car, clock)* non fiable; **he's good but terribly u.** il est compétent mais on ne peut jamais compter sur lui

unrelieved [ʌnrɪ'liːvd] ADJ **1** *(unvarying) (monotony, ugliness, flatness)* uniforme; **she was dressed in u. black** elle était tout de noir vêtue; **u. boredom** ennui mortel; **vast expanses of grey, u. by any bright colour** de vastes étendues de gris qu'aucune couleur vive ne vient égayer **2** *(pain)* sans rémission, sans répit

unremarkable [ʌnrɪ'mɑːkəb(ə)l] ADJ *(person, film, food)* médiocre, quelconque

unremitting [ʌnrɪ'mɪtɪŋ] ADJ constant; **he was u. in his attentions** il était sans cesse plein d'attentions; **u. boredom** ennui mortel; **u. efforts** efforts soutenus

unremittingly [ʌnrɪ'mɪtɪŋlɪ] ADV sans cesse, inlassablement; *(to work)* sans relâche; **u. dull** d'un ennui mortel

unremunerative [ʌnrɪ'mjuːnərətɪv] ADJ peu rémunérateur, -trice

unrepealed [ʌnrɪ'piːld] ADJ *(law etc)* non abrogé

unrepeatable [ʌnrɪ'piːtəb(ə)l] ADJ **1** *(remark)* qu'on ne peut répéter, non répétable; **what he said was quite u.** ce qu'il a dit n'est pas répétable **2** *Com (price)* exceptionnel; *(offer)* unique, exceptionnel

unrepentant [ʌnrɪ'pentənt] ADJ impénitent; **to die u.** mourir dans le péché; **she was u. about what she had done** elle ne s'était pas repentie de ce qu'elle avait fait

unreported [ʌnrɪ'pɔːtɪd] ADJ *(accident, crime)* non signalé; **to go u.** *(of crime)* ne pas être signalé

unrepresentative [ʌnreprɪ'zentətɪv] ADJ peu représentatif; **it's completely u. of ...** ce n'est pas du tout représentatif de ...

unrepresented [ʌnreprɪ'zentɪd] ADJ non représenté; *(nation)* sans représentant, sans délégué

unrequited [ʌnrɪ'kwaɪtɪd] ADJ *(love, feelings)* non réciproque

unreserved [ʌnrɪ'zɜːvd] ADJ **1** *(outgoing) (person)* sans réserve **2** *(approval)* entier; **u. praise** éloges sans réserve; **to be u. in one's praise of sth** ne pas tarir d'éloges à propos de qch **3** *(unbooked) (seat, table)* non réservé

unreservedly [ʌnrɪ'zɜːvɪdlɪ] ADV sans réserve; **to trust sb u.** avoir pleine confiance en qn

unresisting [ʌnrɪ'zɪstɪŋ] ADJ soumis, docile

unresolved [ʌnrɪ'zɒlvd] ADJ **1** *(person)* irrésolu, indécis **2** *(problem etc)* non résolu

unresponsive [ʌnrɪ'spɒnsɪv] ADJ **1** *(engine)* qui manque de nervosité; *(steering)* qui ne répond pas bien; **u. to treatment** qui ne réagit pas au traitement; **she complains that her husband is u. in bed** elle se plaint du fait que son mari manque d'enthousiasme au lit **2** *(mentally) (to suggestion)* indifférent (**to** à); *(audience etc)* inerte, passif; **to be u. to sb's needs** ne pas répondre aux besoins de qn

unrest [ʌn'rest] N troubles *mpl*; **social u.** agitation *f* sociale; **labour** *or* **industrial u.** agitation ouvrière; **there was u. among the workers** il y avait de l'agitation parmi les ouvriers

unrestrained [ʌnrɪˈstreɪnd] **ADJ** non réprimé, effréné; **u. laughter** rires non réprimés

unrestrainedly [ʌnrɪˈstreɪnɪdlɪ] **ADV** librement, sans contrainte

unrestricted [ʌnrɪˈstrɪktɪd] **ADJ** sans restriction, illimité; *(power)* absolu; *(access)* libre; **u. by regulations** non réglementé

unrevealed [ʌnrɪˈviːld] **ADJ** non révélé

unrewarded [ʌnrɪˈwɔːdɪd] **ADJ** non récompensé; **they shouldn't go u.** on ne peut pas les laisser sans récompense

unrewarding [ʌnrɪˈwɔːdɪŋ] **ADJ 1** *(financially)* peu rémunérateur, -trice **2** *(intellectually etc)* *(job, subject etc)* ingrat

unrhythmical [ʌnˈrɪðmɪk(ə)l] **ADJ** *(person)* qui n'a pas le sens du rythme; *(music)* peu rythmé

unrig [ʌnˈrɪg] **VT (-gg-)** *Naut (ship)* dégréer

unrighteous [ʌnˈraɪtʃəs] **ADJ** *(person, action)* impie; *(life)* d'impiété
NPL the u. les impies *mpl*

unripe [ʌnˈraɪp] **ADJ** vert, qui n'est pas mûr; *(wheat)* en herbe

unrivalled, *Am* **unrivaled** [ʌnˈraɪv(ə)ld] **ADJ** sans rival, hors pair; **our goods are u.** nos articles sont sans concurrence

unroadworthy [ʌnˈrəʊdwɜːðɪ] **ADJ** *(vehicle)* qui n'est pas en état de rouler

unroll [ʌnˈrəʊl] **VT** *(map, cloth)* dérouler; *(banner)* déferler
VI se dérouler

unromantic [ʌnrəˈmæntɪk] **ADJ** peu romantique; **how very u. of you!** tu n'es vraiment pas romantique!, tu manques vraiment de romantisme!

unrope [ʌnˈrəʊp] **VI** *(in mountaineering)* se détacher (de la cordée)

unruffled [ʌnˈrʌf(ə)ld] **ADJ 1** *(person)* calme, serein; **u., he continued to speak** impassible, il a continué de parler **2** *(sea)* calme; *(hair, feathers)* lisse

unruled [ʌnˈruːld] **ADJ** *(paper)* non réglé, sans lignes

unruliness [ʌnˈruːlɪnɪs] **N** *(of child)* indiscipline *f*, turbulence *f*, *(of horse)* caractère *m* fougueux

unruly [ʌnˈruːlɪ] **ADJ** *(child)* indiscipliné, turbulent; *(horse)* fougueux; *(hair)* difficile à coiffer; **the crowd started getting u.** la foule commença à s'agiter

unsaddle [ʌnˈsæd(ə)l] **VT 1** *(horse)* desseller; *(donkey)* débâter **2** *(rider)* désarçonner

unsafe [ʌnˈseɪf] **ADJ 1** *(dangerous)* dangereux; *(bridge, structure)* peu sûr; *(chair, rope)* peu solide; *(undertaking)* hasardeux; **the chemicals are u. so close to the fire** il est dangereux de laisser ces produits chimiques si près du feu **2** *(in danger) (of person)* en danger; **it's u. to leave it near the fire** c'est dangereux de le laisser près du feu **2** *(in danger) (of person)* en danger; **to feel u.** ne pas se sentir en sécurité **3** *Law* douteux
▸▸**u. sex** rapports *mpl* non protégés

unsaid [ʌnˈsed] **ADJ to leave sth u.** passer qch sous silence; **there was a lot that was left u. between them** il y a eu beaucoup de non-dits entre eux; **it's better left u.** mieux vaut ne rien dire; **if you don't do as I say …, he muttered, and left the rest u.** si tu ne fais pas ce que je te demande …, murmura-t-il sans finir sa phrase

unsalaried [ʌnˈsælərɪd] **ADJ** *(position)* non rémunéré; *(person)* non salarié

unsaleable [ʌnˈseɪləb(ə)l] **ADJ** *(goods)* invendable

unsalted [ʌnˈsɔːltɪd] **ADJ** *(meat, fish)* sans sel
▸▸**u. butter** beurre *m* doux

unsatisfactorily [ʌnsætɪsˈfækt(ə)rɪlɪ] **ADV** d'une manière peu satisfaisante

unsatisfactory [ʌnsætɪsˈfækt(ə)rɪ] **ADJ** *(conclusion, explanation)* non satisfaisant; *(system)* défectueux; **if this item is u. in any way** si cet article ne vous donne pas satisfaction …; **this situation is most u.** cette situation n'est pas du tout satisfaisante

unsatisfied [ʌnˈsætɪsfaɪd] **ADJ 1** *(not content)* non satisfait **(with** de**) 2** *(not convinced)* **I was u. with her explanation** je n'étais pas satisfait de son explication **3** *(appetite)* non rassasié; *(desire, lust)* insatisfait, inassouvi; **the meal left us u.** le repas ne nous a pas rassasiés; **her desire for novelty was still u.** son désir de nouveauté restait inassouvi

unsatisfying [ʌnˈsætɪsfaɪɪŋ] **ADJ 1** *(novel, ending, explanation)* peu satisfaisant **2** *(meal etc)* insuffisant

unsavoury, *Am* **unsavory** [ʌnˈseɪv(ə)rɪ] **ADJ 1** *(smell)* désagréable; **the food looked rather u.** la nourriture n'était pas appétissante **2** *(person, district, bar, reputation)* louche; *(scandal, details)* abject; **there were some rather u. characters in the bar** il y avait des types plutôt louches dans le bar

unsay [ʌnˈseɪ] *(pt, pp* **unsaid** [ʌnˈsed]*)* **VT** rétracter, retirer; **you can't u. it** tu ne peux pas retirer ce que tu as dit; **what's said cannot be unsaid** ce qui est dit est dit

unscathed [ʌnˈskeɪðd] **ADJ** *(person)* indemne, sain et sauf; *(building)* intact; **she came through the trial with her reputation u.** sa réputation n'a pas souffert du procès

unscented [ʌnˈsentɪd] **ADJ** *(soap etc)* sans parfum, non parfumé

unscheduled [ʌnˈʃedjuːld] **ADJ** *(departure, meeting)* imprévu; *(plane, train)* supplémentaire; *(stop)* non prévu

unscholarly [ʌnˈskɒləlɪ] **ADJ** *(not appropriate for a scholar)* qui n'est pas digne d'un intellectuel; *(not written etc in a scholarly way)* peu académique

unschooled [ʌnˈskuːld] **ADJ 1** *Old-fashioned (person)* sans instruction; **he is u. in such matters** il est ignorant en la matière **2** *(horse)* non dressé

unscientific [ʌnsaɪənˈtɪfɪk] **ADJ** non scientifique; **isn't that rather u.?** ce n'est pas très scientifique; **that's very u.** ce n'est pas du tout scientifique

unscientifically [ʌnsaɪənˈtɪfɪklɪ] **ADV** peu scientifiquement

unscramble [ʌnˈskræmb(ə)l] **VT** déchiffrer; *Tel* désembrouiller

unscrambler [ʌnˈskræmblər] **N** *Tel* décodeur *m*

unscrambling [ʌnˈskræmblɪŋ] **N** *Tel* décodage *m*

unscrew [ʌnˈskruː] **VT** dévisser
VI se dévisser

unscripted [ʌnˈskrɪptɪd] **ADJ** *(dialogue in film)* improvisé; *(remark)* non préparé; **that was quite u.** c'était complètement improvisé

unscrupulous [ʌnˈskruːpjʊləs] **ADJ** *(person)* sans scrupules; *(dealings, methods etc)* peu scrupuleux

unscrupulously [ʌnˈskruːpjʊləslɪ] **ADV** *(to proceed, exploit)* sans scrupules

unscrupulousness [ʌnˈskruːpjʊləsnɪs] **N** *(of person)* absence *f* de scrupules; *(of dealings)* malhonnêteté *f*

unseal [ʌnˈsiːl] **VT** *(letter)* décacheter

unsealed [ʌnˈsiːld] **ADJ** *(letter)* décacheté

unseasonable [ʌnˈsiːz(ə)nəb(ə)l] **ADJ** *(fish, fruit)* hors de saison; **this weather's very u.** ce n'est pas un temps de saison

unseasonably [ʌnˈsiːz(ə)nəblɪ] **ADV it was u. warm/cold for the time of year** il faisait extrêmement chaud/froid pour la saison

unseasoned [ʌnˈsiːz(ə)nd] **ADJ** *(food)* non assaisonné; *(timber)* vert

unseat [ʌnˈsiːt] **VT 1** *(rider)* désarçonner **2** *Parl (MP)* faire perdre son siège à

unseaworthy [ʌnˈsiːwɜːðɪ] **N** *(ship)* innavigable

unsecured [ʌnsɪˈkjʊəd] **ADJ 1** *Fin (loan, overdraft)* non garanti **2** *(load)* mal attaché
▸▸*Fin* **u. advance** avance *f* à découvert; *Fin* **u. creditor** créancier, -ière ordinaire *ou* chirographaire; *Fin* **u. debenture** obligation *f* non garantie; *Fin* **u. debt** créance *f* chirographaire *ou* sans garantie

unseeded [ʌnˈsiːdɪd] **ADJ** *Tennis (player)* non classé

unseeing [ʌnˈsiːɪŋ] **ADJ to look at sb/sth with u. eyes** regarder qn/qch sans (le) voir

unseemliness [ʌnˈsiːmlɪnɪs] **N** *(of conduct)* inconvenance *f*

unseemly [ʌnˈsiːmlɪ] **ADJ** *(behaviour)* inconvenant

unseen [ʌnˈsiːn] **ADJ 1** *(hands, influence, force)* invisible; **u. by the guards they …** sans que les gardiens les voient, ils …; **to do sth u.** faire qch sans être vu; **to slip through u.** *(of person, mistake)* passer inaperçu **2 to buy sth (sight) u.** acheter qch sans l'avoir vu
N *Sch* version *f* non préparée
▸▸*Sch* **u. translation** version non préparée

unselfconscious [ʌnself'kɒnʃəs] **ADJ** *(charm)* naturel; *(laugh)* spontané; **he's got a big scar on his face but he's quite u. about it** il a une grande cicatrice sur le visage mais n'est pas complexé; **he's a very u. sort of person** c'est quelqu'un de très spontané *ou* naturel

unselfconsciously [ʌnself'kɒnʃəslɪ] **ADV** naturellement; *(to laugh)* de façon spontanée

unselfish [ʌnˈselfɪʃ] **ADJ** généreux; *(motive, gesture)* désintéressé; **one of the most u. people I've met** une des personnes les plus désintéressées que j'aie connues

unselfishly [ʌnˈselfɪʃlɪ] **ADV** généreusement; **he acted u. and put his own considerations last** il a agi avec désintéressement et a fait passer ses intérêts en dernier

unselfishness [ʌnˈselfɪʃnɪs] **N** générosité *f*, *(not putting self first)* désintéressement *m*

unsellable [ʌnˈseləb(ə)l] **ADJ** invendable

unsentimental [ʌnsentɪˈment(ə)l] **ADJ** peu sentimental, -aux; **the film remains u. throughout** le film ne verse jamais dans le mélo

unserviceable [ʌnˈsɜːvɪsəb(ə)l] **ADJ** inutilisable

unsettle [ʌnˈset(ə)l] **VT** *(sb's ideas)* ébranler; *(person) (less deeply)* troubler

unsettled [ʌnˈset(ə)ld] **ADJ 1** *(unstable, uncertain) (country)* troublé, instable; *(stock market)* instable; *(weather)* variable, changeant; *(mind)* inquiet, -ète, troublé; **I feel u. at the moment** je me sens perturbé en ce moment; **to have an u. stomach** avoir l'estomac un peu dérangé; **the u. state of the weather** l'incertitude *f* du temps **2** *(question, dispute)* irrésolu **3** *(bill)* impayé, non réglé **4** *(without settlers)* non colonisé

unsettling [ʌnˈsetlɪŋ] **ADJ** troublant, dérangeant

unsex [ʌnˈseks] **VT** *(man)* déviriliser; *(woman)* déféminiser

unshackle [ʌnˈʃæk(ə)l] **vt** (prisoner) ôter les fers à; Fig libérer

unshackled [ʌnˈʃæk(ə)ld] **ADJ** sans entraves, libre; **to be u. by convention** ne pas porter le poids des conventions

unshakeable [ʌnˈʃeɪkəb(ə)l] **ADJ** inébranlable

unshaken [ʌnˈʃeɪk(ə)n] **ADJ** (conviction) inébranlable; **his faith was u. by ...** sa foi restait inébranlable malgré ...; **he was u. by the news** la nouvelle ne l'a pas ébranlé

unshaven, unshaved [ʌnˈʃeɪv(ə)n, -ˈʃeɪvd] **ADJ** (chin, armpits, legs) non rasé; **he was u.** il n'était pas rasé

unsheathe [ʌnˈʃiːð] **vt** (sword etc) dégainer

unsheltered [ʌnˈʃeltəd] **ADJ** non abrité, non protégé (**from** contre)

unship [ʌnˈʃɪp] **vt** (-**pp**-) Naut décharger, débarquer

unshod [ʌnˈʃɒd] **ADJ 1** (person) sans chaussures; (having removed shoes) déchaussé **2** (horse) déferré

unsighted [ʌnˈsaɪtɪd] **ADJ 1** (not visible) invisible, qui n'est pas en vue; **he was u. by one of his own team** (not able to see clearly) un membre de son équipe lui bouchait la vue **2** (sightless) aveugle

unsightliness [ʌnˈsaɪtlɪnɪs] **N** laideur f

unsightly [ʌnˈsaɪtlɪ] **ADJ** laid; (scar) vilain; (hoardings, buildings) affreux

unsigned [ʌnˈsaɪnd] **ADJ** non signé, sans signature

unsinkable [ʌnˈsɪŋkəb(ə)l] **ADJ** insubmersible

unskilful, Am unskillful [ʌnˈskɪlf(ʊ)l] **ADJ** malhabile, maladroit (**at sth** à qch); **he's u. at convincing people** il ne sait pas convaincre les gens

unskilled [ʌnˈskɪld] **to be u. in** or **at doing sth** ne pas être doué pour ce qui est de faire qch
▸▸ **u. labour** main-d'œuvre f non spécialisée; **u. worker** ouvrier m non qualifié

unskimmed [ʌnˈskɪmd] **ADJ** (milk) entier

unslept-in [ʌnˈslept-] **ADJ** (bed) non défait

unsling [ʌnˈslɪŋ] **vt** (pt, pp **unslung** [-ˈslʌŋ]) dégréer; (hammock) décrocher; **to u. one's rifle** enlever son fusil de l'épaule

unsmiling [ʌnˈsmaɪlɪŋ] **ADJ** sérieux; **he stared at me u.** il me fixait sans sourire

unsmoked [ʌnˈsməʊkt] **ADJ** non fumé

unsociability [ʌnsəʊʃəˈbɪlɪtɪ], **unsociableness** [ʌnˈsəʊʃəblnɪs] **N** manque m de sociabilité

unsociable [ʌnˈsəʊʃəb(ə)l] **ADJ** sauvage, peu sociable

unsocial [ʌnˈsəʊʃəl] **ADJ 1 to work u. hours** travailler en-dehors des heures habituelles **2** = **unsociable**

unsold [ʌnˈsəʊld] **ADJ** invendu; **u. goods** invendus mpl; **the u. copies** les invendus mpl

unsoldierly [ʌnˈsəʊldʒəlɪ] **ADJ** peu militaire

unsolicited [ʌnsəˈlɪsɪtɪd] **ADJ** (comment) non sollicité; (contribution) volontaire; (application) spontané; **to do sth u.** faire qch spontanément
▸▸ **u. manuscript** manuscrit non commandé

unsolvable [ʌnˈsɒlvəb(ə)l] **ADJ** insoluble

unsolved [ʌnˈsɒlvd] **ADJ** (problem) non résolu

unsophisticated [ʌnsəˈfɪstɪkeɪtɪd] **ADJ** (person, tastes, pleasures) simple, non sophistiqué; (wine) sans prétention; (machine) non sophistiqué

unsound [ʌnˈsaʊnd] **ADJ 1** (kidney etc) malade; (foundations, bridge) en mauvais état; (timber) avarié; **his health was u.** il n'était pas

en bonne santé; **to be of u. mind** ne pas avoir toute sa raison **2** (theory, argument) mal fondé, peu solide; (decision, advice) peu judicieux; (investment) peu sûr, douteux; **it is financially u.** les finances ne sont pas saines; **I know it's (politically) u. to say so, but ...** je sais que cela va être mal vu de dire cela mais ...; **she regarded him as u. on social policy** elle considérait que ses vues en matière de politique sociale n'étaient pas orthodoxes; **he's still rather u. on the basics** ses bases ne sont pas encore très solides

unsparing [ʌnˈspeərɪŋ] **ADJ to be u. of one's time/with one's advice** ne pas être avare de son temps/de conseils; **to be u. in one's efforts** ne pas ménager ses efforts

unsparingly [ʌnˈspeərɪŋlɪ] **ADV** (to give, donate) sans compter, sans regarder à la dépense; (to work) sans ménager ses efforts

unspeakable [ʌnˈspiːkəb(ə)l] **ADJ 1** (bad) (conditions, state, pain) indicible; **it's u.!** c'est innommable ou inqualifiable!; **he's really u.!** il est au-dessous de tout! **2** (joy) indicible, ineffable

unspeakably [ʌnˈspiːkəblɪ] **ADV** indiciblement; **to behave u.** avoir une conduite inqualifiable; **u. bad** exécrable

unspecified [ʌnˈspesɪfaɪd] **ADJ** non spécifié; **certain u. persons** certaines personnes, dont on taira les noms

unspectacular [ʌnspekˈtækjʊlər] **ADJ** peu spectaculaire

unspent [ʌnˈspent] **ADJ** (money) non dépensé; (cartridge) qui n'a pas servi; **to vent one's u. rage on sb** se défouler sur qn

unspoilt [ʌnˈspɔɪlt] (occ **unspoiled** [ʌnˈspɔɪld]) **ADJ 1** (untouched) (countryside, view) intact; (tranquillity) parfait **2** (child) qui n'est pas gâté; **she's totally u.** ce n'est pas une enfant gâtée; **he was u. by his success** le succès ne lui a pas tourné la tête

unspoken [ʌnˈspəʊk(ə)n] **ADJ** (fear, thought, threat) inexprimé; (agreement) tacite; **her u. thought was that ...** intérieurement elle pensait que ...; **although his name remained u. ...** bien que son nom n'ait pas été prononcé ...

unsporting [ʌnˈspɔːtɪŋ], **unsportsmanlike** [ʌnˈspɔːtsmənlaɪk] **ADJ** peu sportif; **that's u.** ce n'est pas très sportif; **he was fined for u. behaviour** il a été pénalisé pour manque de sportivité

unstable [ʌnˈsteɪb(ə)l] **ADJ** instable
▸▸ Econ **u. equilibrium** équilibre m instable

unstained [ʌnˈsteɪnd] **ADJ 1** esp Lit (reputation) sans tache **2** (wood) non teinté

unstamped [ʌnˈstæmpt] **ADJ** (letter) sans timbre, non affranchi; Admin, Law (document) non estampillé

unstated [ʌnˈsteɪtɪd] **ADJ** inexprimé

unstatesmanlike [ʌnˈsteɪtsmənlaɪk] **ADJ** peu digne d'un homme d'État

unsteadily [ʌnˈstedɪlɪ] **ADV** (to walk) d'un pas chancelant, en titubant; (to hold sth) d'une main tremblante; (to write) d'une main tremblante

unsteadiness [ʌnˈstedɪnɪs] **ADJ** (of table, person) déséquilibre m; (of hand) manque m de sûreté; (of drunk person) démarche f chancelante; (of dollar etc) instabilité f

unsteady [ʌnˈstedɪ] **ADJ** (table) instable, branlant; (legs, footsteps, person) chancelant; (hand, voice) mal assuré; (position, foothold) mal assuré, incertain; (flame) tremblant, vacillant; (economy, the dollar etc) instable; (stock market) irrégulier; **to be u. on one's legs** or **feet** ne pas tenir très bien sur ses jambes

unsterilized [ʌnˈsterɪlaɪzd] **ADJ** non stérilisé

unstick [ʌnˈstɪk] **vt** (pt, pp **unstuck** [-ˈstʌk]) décoller

unstinted [ʌnˈstɪntɪd] **ADJ 1** (supplies) abondant, sans restriction **2** = **unstinting 2**

unstinting [ʌnˈstɪntɪŋ] **ADJ 1** (person) **to be u. in one's praise of sb/sth** ne pas tarir d'éloges au sujet de qn/qch; **to be u. in one's efforts to do sth** faire tous ses efforts pour faire qch **2** (compliments, support) sans réserve; (admiration) sans bornes; **u. efforts** efforts illimités; **to give u. praise** ne pas ménager ses louanges

unstintingly [ʌnˈstɪntɪŋlɪ] **ADV** généreusement; (to help, work) sans se ménager; **to praise sb u.** ne pas tarir d'éloges sur qn

unstitch [ʌnˈstɪtʃ] **vt** (seam) découdre; **to come unstitched** se découdre

unstop [ʌnˈstɒp] **vt** (-**pp**-) (remove stopper from) déboucher

unstoppable [ʌnˈstɒpəb(ə)l] **ADJ** (shot) imparable; **he's u. now** rien ne pourra l'arrêter désormais

unstressed [ʌnˈstrest] **ADJ** non accentué, atone

unstring [ʌnˈstrɪŋ] **vt** (pt, pp **unstrung** [-ˈstrʌŋ]) **1** (bow) débander; **to u. a violin** ôter les cordes d'un violon **2** (beads etc) ôter le fil de

unstructured [ʌnˈstrʌktʃəd] **ADJ** (activity) non structuré; (group) non organisé; Mktg (interview) non structuré, libre

unstuck [ʌnˈstʌk] **ADJ to come u.** se décoller; Fam (of person, plan) s'effondrer; Fam **that's where they came u.** c'est là qu'ils ont cafouillé

unstudied [ʌnˈstʌdɪd] **ADJ** spontané, naturel

unsubdued [ʌnsəbˈdjuːd] **ADJ** indompté

unsubmissive [ʌnsəbˈmɪsɪv] **ADJ** insoumis, rebelle

unsubscribe [ʌnsəbˈskraɪb] **vi** Comput (from ISP) résilier son abonnement; (from mailing list) se désinscrire

unsubscribed [ʌnsəbˈskraɪbd] **ADJ** Fin (capital) non souscrit

unsubsidized [ʌnˈsʌbsɪdaɪzd] **ADJ** non subventionné

unsubstantial [ʌnsəbˈstænʃəl] **ADJ** (meal) peu substantiel, peu nourrissant; (novel) creux

unsubstantiated [ʌnsəbˈstænʃɪeɪtɪd] **ADJ** (accusation) non prouvé; (rumour) non corroboré

unsubtle [ʌnˈsʌt(ə)l] **ADJ** peu subtil; **how could anyone be so u.!** comment peut-on manquer de subtilité à ce point!; **u. hints** allusions fpl lourdes

unsuccessful [ʌnsəkˈsesfʊl] **ADJ** (effort, attempt) vain, infructueux; (outcome, marriage) malheureux; **u. applications will not be acknowledged** nous ne répondrons pas aux personnes dont les candidatures n'ont pas été retenues; **your application has been u.** votre candidature n'a pas été retenue; **it was completely u.** cela a été un échec complet; **to be u.** (of person, plan, marriage) ne pas réussir; **she was u. in practically every undertaking she embarked on** elle échouait dans pratiquement tout ce qu'elle entreprenait; **the festival was u.** le festival a été un échec; **I've tried but have been u. up till now** j'ai essayé mais je n'ai pas réussi jusqu'à présent; **u. candidate** (at election) candidat non élu

unsuccessfully [ʌnsəkˈsesfəlɪ] **ADV** sans succès, en vain

unsuitability [ʌns(j)uːtəˈbɪlɪtɪ] **N** (of per-

son) inaptitude *f* (**for sth** à qch); *(of thing)* inadéquation *f* (**for sth** à qch); **the u. of the clothes he was wearing** les vêtements inadéquats qu'il portait

unsuitable [ʌn's(j)uːtəb(ə)l] **ADJ** *(tools)* impropre, mal adapté (**for** à); *(friend, people)* peu recommandable; *(music, choice of words)* déplacé; *(time)* inopportun; *(conditions, diet)* inadéquat, non approprié; *(clothes)* inadéquat; *(climate)* peu indiqué; *(couple, partners)* mal assorti; **this is an u. environment for a child** ce n'est pas un environnement approprié pour un enfant; **this is an u. time to bring the matter up** ce n'est pas le moment de parler de cela; **I thought Wednesday was u.** je pensais que mercredi ne vous/lui/*etc* convenait pas; **they're u. for each other** ils ne vont pas ensemble; **he's u. for her** ce n'est pas l'homme qu'il lui faut; **he's quite u. for the job** ce n'est pas la personne qu'il faut pour ce poste; **u. for the occasion** qui ne convient pas à la circonstance; **you have chosen a most u. time to ...** vous avez mal choisi le moment de ...; **the film is u. for children** ce n'est pas un film pour les enfants; **the climate is u. for wheat** le climat ne convient pas au blé

unsuitably [ʌn's(j)uːtəblɪ] **ADV** inadéquatement; *(to behave)* de façon inappropriée; **to be u. dressed** ne pas porter les vêtements qui conviennent; **they're u. matched** *(of couple)* ils sont mal assortis

unsuited [ʌn's(j)uːtɪd] **ADJ** *(person)* inapte (**for** *or* **to sth** à qch); *(material, clothes, equipment)* **she's clearly u. to this type of work** il est clair qu'elle n'est pas faite pour ce genre de travail; **they are u. (to each other)** ils sont mal assortis

unsullied [ʌn'sʌlɪd] **ADJ** sans tache; **her reputation was u. by ...** sa réputation n'a pas souffert de ...

unsung [ʌn'sʌŋ] **ADJ** *esp Lit (deed)* non célébré
▸▸ **u. hero** héros *m* méconnu

unsupervised [ʌn'suːpəvaɪzd] **ADJ** *(child)* non surveillé; **'u. minors not admitted'** 'interdit aux enfants non accompagnés'

unsupported [ʌnsə'pɔːtɪd] **ADJ 1** *(statement, charges)* sans preuves; **the theories were u. by any evidence** ces théories n'ont été étayées par aucune preuve **2** *(structure, wall)* sans support, sans appui; **to walk u.** marcher sans se faire aider; **he could walk u. by a stick** il marchait sans canne; **to leave one's family u.** ne pas subvenir aux besoins de sa famille; **more and more students are u. by the state** de plus en plus d'étudiants ne reçoivent pas d'aide de l'État

unsure [ʌn'ʃʊər] **ADJ** *(person)* incertain (**about** de); *(position)* peu sûr, précaire; **they were u. what to do next** ils n'étaient pas sûrs de savoir quoi faire après; **I was u. what she meant by this** je n'étais pas sûr de savoir ce qu'elle voulait dire par là; **to be u. of oneself** ne pas être sûr de soi; **I'm u. about it/him** j'ai des doutes là-dessus/en ce qui concerne

unsurpassable [ʌnsə'pɑːsəb(ə)l] **ADJ** insurpassable

unsurpassed [ʌnsə'pɑːst] **ADJ** sans égal

unsurprised [ʌnsə'praɪzd] **ADJ** non surpris; **I was u. by ...** je n'ai pas été surpris par ...

unsurprising [ʌnsə'praɪzɪŋ] **ADJ** peu surprenant

unsurprisingly [ʌnsə'praɪzɪŋlɪ] **ADV** u., **this suggestion was rejected** comme on pouvait s'y attendre, cette suggestion fut rejetée

unsuspected [ʌnsəs'pektɪd] **ADJ** insoupçonné (**by** de)

unsuspecting [ʌnsəs'pektɪŋ] **ADJ** qui ne se

doute de rien; *(by nature)* peu soupçonneux; **he's so u.** il est si peu soupçonneux; **when he later, all u., ...** quand plus tard, sans se douter de rien, il ...

unsuspicious [ʌnsəs'pɪʃəs] **ADJ** peu soupçonneux

unsustainable [ʌnsə'steɪnəb(ə)l] **ADJ** non viable

unsweetened [ʌn'swiːt(ə)nd] **ADJ** non sucré

unswerving [ʌn'swɜːvɪŋ] **ADJ** *(loyalty)* constant, ferme; **they have been u. in their support (for us)** ils nous ont prêté un appui constant

unswervingly [ʌn'swɜːvɪŋlɪ] **ADV** sans s'écarter du but; *(to maintain)* sans relâche; **u. loyal** d'une loyauté absolue

unsympathetic [ʌnsɪmpə'θetɪk] **ADJ 1** *(lacking understanding)* peu compatissant; **they were very u. about our problems** nos problèmes les laissaient complètement indifférents; **the idea met with an u. reception** l'idée a reçu un accueil plutôt froid; **he was generally u. to modern art** *(didn't like)* de manière générale il appréciait peu l'art moderne; *(made critical statements about)* il n'était pas généralement tendre avec l'art moderne **2** *(unlikeable)* antipathique; **I find the characters of this novel u.** les personnages de ce roman me sont peu sympathiques

unsympathetically [ʌnsɪmpə'θetɪklɪ] **ADV** froidement; **the novel/film was u. reviewed by the critics** les critiques n'ont pas été tendres avec le roman/le film

unsystematic [ʌnsɪstə'mætɪk] **ADJ** non systématique, sans méthode; **you're too u.** tu n'es pas assez méthodique

unsystematically [ʌnsɪstə'mætɪklɪ] **ADV** sans méthode

untainted [ʌn'teɪntɪd] **ADJ** *(person, judgment)* non corrompu; *(reputation)* sans tache

untalented [ʌn'tæləntɪd] **ADJ** peu doué

untam(e)able [ʌn'teɪməb(ə)l] **ADJ** *(animal, spirit)* indomptable

untamed [ʌn'teɪmd] **ADJ** *(animal, spirit, luxuriance)* indompté

untangle [ʌn'tæŋg(ə)l] **VT** *(wool, string, hair)* démêler; *(mystery)* éclaircir; *(sth complicated)* débrouiller

untapped [ʌn'tæpt] **ADJ** *(resources)* inexploité

untarnished [ʌn'tɑːnɪʃt] **ADJ** *(metal)*, Fig non terni, sans tache

untasted [ʌn'teɪstɪd] **ADJ** auquel on n'a pas goûté; **to send a dish away u.** renvoyer un plat sans y goûter

untaught [ʌn'tɔːt] **ADJ** *(person)* sans instruction; *(skill)* naturel

untaxable [ʌn'tæksəb(ə)l] **ADJ** non imposable

untaxed [ʌn'tækst] **ADJ** *(income)* exempt *ou* exempté d'impôts; *(product)* non imposé, non taxé; *(car)* ≃ sans vignette

unteachable [ʌn'tiːtʃəb(ə)l] **ADJ** *(person)* à qui l'on ne peut rien apprendre, incapable d'apprendre; *(subject, art)* impossible à enseigner

untenable [ʌn'tenəb(ə)l] **ADJ** *(position)* intenable; *(theory)* insoutenable

untenanted [ʌn'tenəntɪd] **ADJ** sans locataire(s); **these flats have been u. for years** ces appartements sont inoccupés depuis des années

untended [ʌn'tendɪd] **ADJ** *(sick person)* non soigné, sans soins; *(garden)* non entretenu

untested [ʌn'testɪd] **ADJ** inéprouvé, non prouvé; *(invention, drug)* non essayé; *(sample)* non analysé

unthinkable [ʌn'θɪŋkəb(ə)l] **ADJ** inconcevable, impensable; **it's u. that ...** il est inconcevable que ... + *sub*; **if the u. should happen** si l'inconcevable se produisait

unthinking [ʌn'θɪŋkɪŋ] **ADJ** *(person)* étourdi

unthinkingly [ʌn'θɪŋkɪŋlɪ] **ADV** *(to do sth)* sans réfléchir, étourdiment

unthought-of [ʌn'θɔːt-] **ADJ** auquel on n'a pas pensé

unthread [ʌn'θred] **VT** *(beads)* ôter le fil de

untidily [ʌn'taɪdɪlɪ] **ADV** en désordre; **she's always u. dressed** elle a toujours l'air débraillé

untidiness [ʌn'taɪdɪnɪs] **N** *(of room, appearance)* désordre *m*; *(of person) (characteristic)* manque *m* d'ordre

untidy [ʌn'taɪdɪ] **ADJ 1** *(room, desk)* en désordre, mal rangé; *(hair)* ébouriffé; *(writing)* brouillon; **u. appearance** tenue *f* débraillée; **his playing is u.** *(of musician)* son jeu manque de netteté; **he brings the novel to an u. end** il termine le roman d'une façon plutôt confuse; **an u. mind** un esprit brouillon; **his room/desk always gets u.** sa chambre/son bureau est toujours en désordre **2** *(person) (as characteristic)* désordonné, qui manque d'ordre; **he's such an u. sort of person** il est tellement désordonné

untie [ʌn'taɪ] **VT** *(pt, pp untied; prp untying)* *(shoelaces, ribbon)* défaire; *(knot)* dénouer; *(knot, parcel)* défaire, délier; *(parcel)* déficeler; *(one's hair, dog, boat)* détacher; **to u. itself, to come untied** *(of knot)* se défaire, se dénouer

until [ʌn'tɪl] **PREP** VOIR GRAMMAIRE A68; A73 **1** jusqu'à; **you have u. tomorrow to finish it** tu as jusqu'à demain pour le finir; **u. 2008** jusqu'en 2008; **u. now** jusqu'ici, jusque-là; **she didn't arrive u. yesterday** elle n'est arrivée qu'hier; **u. then we'll just have to make do** en attendant il va falloir se débrouiller; *Radio, TV* **u. tomorrow, I wish you a very good night** je vous souhaite une très bonne soirée, à demain

2 **not u. (after) eight o'clock** pas avant huit heures (passées); **not u. tomorrow** pas avant demain; **it wasn't u. after Easter that ...** ce n'est qu'après Pâques que ...; **I've never seen it u. now** c'est la première fois que je le vois

CONJ VOIR GRAMMAIRE A75 **1** jusqu'à ce que + *sub*; **u. all the windows are open** jusqu'à ce que toutes les fenêtres soient ouvertes; **we'll wait u. you're ready** nous attendrons que vous soyez prêt; **we waited u. the rain stopped** nous avons attendu jusqu'à ce que la pluie cesse; **wait u. the bus stops** attends que le bus soit arrêté; **he drank u. he was ill** il a bu jusqu'à s'en rendre malade; **we worked u. we dropped** nous avons travaillé jusqu'à n'en plus pouvoir; **he laughed u. he cried** il a pleuré de rire

2 **he won't come u. he's invited** il ne viendra pas avant d'être invité *ou* sans qu'on l'invite; **I won't leave him u. he's completely recovered** je ne le quitterai pas tant qu'il n'est pas tout à fait guéri; **don't do anything u. I say so** ne fais rien avant que je te le dise; **don't sign u. you've checked everything** ne signe rien avant d'avoir tout vérifié

untilled [ʌn'tɪld] **ADJ** non cultivé, non labouré

untimely [ʌn'taɪmlɪ] **ADJ** *(death)* prématuré; *(question, action)* inopportun, intempestif, mal à propos; **to come to an u. end** mourir avant l'âge

untiring [ʌn'taɪərɪŋ] **ADJ** infatigable, inlassable

untiringly [ʌn'taɪərɪŋlɪ] **ADV** infatigablement, inlassablement

unto ['ʌntʊ, 'ʌntə] PREP *Arch, Lit* to liken sth u. sth comparer qch à *ou* avec qch; *Bible* u. us a child is born un enfant nous est né; *Bible* and I say u. you ... en vérité je vous le dis ...; to turn u. sb se tourner vers qn

untold [ʌn'təʊld] ADJ *(riches)* immense, énorme; u. joy joie f indicible; u. suffering souffrances *fpl* inouïes

untouchable [ʌn'tʌtʃəb(ə)l] ADJ intouchable
N *(in India)* intouchable *mf*, paria *m*

untouched [ʌn'tʌtʃt] ADJ **1** *(by hand etc)* non touché; to be u. by the influence of ... ne pas avoir subi l'influence de ...; most of the city centre has remained u. une grande partie du centre ville est resté intact; u. by human hand *(food)* non manié; these artefacts have lain u. by human hand for thousands of years ces objets sont restés inconnus de l'homme pendant des milliers d'années **2** he'd left the meal u. il n'avait pas touché à son repas **3** *(safe) (person)* indemne, sain et sauf, f saine et sauve; *(thing)* intact **4** *(unmoved) (person)* indifférent, insensible (by à) **5** *(without equal)* sans égal, incomparable

untoward [ʌntə'wɔːd, *Am* ʌn'tɔːd] ADJ fâcheux; I hope nothing u. has happened j'espère qu'il n'est pas arrivé un malheur

untraceable [ʌn'treɪsəb(ə)l] ADJ introuvable

untrad(e)able [ʌn'treɪdəb(ə)l] ADJ *St Exch* incotable

untrained [ʌn'treɪnd] ADJ *(person)* qui n'a pas reçu de formation professionnelle; *(horse)* non dressé; u. ear oreille f inexercée

untrammelled [ʌn'træməld] ADJ non entravé (by par), libre (by de)

untransferable [ʌntræns'fɜːrəb(ə)l] ADJ non transmissible; *Law (right, property)* incessible

untranslatable [ʌntræns'leɪtəb(ə)l] ADJ intraduisible

untravelled [ʌn'trævəld] ADJ *(person)* qui n'a pas beaucoup voyagé; *(country)* inexploré, peu fréquenté; he's relatively u. il n'a pas beaucoup voyagé

untried [ʌn'traɪd] ADJ **1** *(not tried out)* qui n'a pas été essayé, non essayé **2** *(untested) (engine, system)* non testé; u. troops troupes qui n'ont pas encore combattu **3** *Law (prisoner, case)* qui n'a pas encore été jugé

untrodden [ʌn'trɒd(ə)n] ADJ *esp Lit (path)* peu fréquenté; *Fig* democracy remains for them an u. path ils n'ont jamais goûté à la démocratie; u. snow neige f immaculée *ou* vierge

untroubled [ʌn'trʌbəld] ADJ calme, tranquille; the markets have been u. by the interest rate rise les marchés n'ont pas été troublés par la hausse des taux d'intérêt; he seemed u. by the news la nouvelle ne semblait nullement le troubler

untrue [ʌn'truː] ADJ **1** *(incorrect)* faux, f fausse **2** *(unfaithful) (to wife, principles etc)* infidèle (to à); *(to comrades)* déloyal (to envers); to be u. to oneself trahir ses principes

untrustworthiness [ʌn'trʌstwɜːðɪnɪs] N *(of information, machine)* manque *m* de fiabilité; he was noted for his u. il avait la réputation de quelqu'un à qui on ne peut pas faire confiance

untrustworthy [ʌn'trʌstwɜːðɪ] ADJ *(person)* indigne de confiance; *(reference book, information)* peu fiable; *(evidence)* récusable

untruth [ʌn'truːθ, *pl* -'truːðz] N mensonge *m*; to tell an u. dire un mensonge

untruthful [ʌn'truːθfʊl] ADJ *(person)* men-

teur; *(story)* mensonger; he's an u. boy c'est un garçon qui ne dit jamais la vérité

untruthfully [ʌn'truːθfəlɪ] ADV de façon mensongère

untruthfulness [ʌn'truːθfʊlnɪs] N *(of evidence)* caractère *m* mensonger; he was notorious for his u. c'était un menteur notoire

untuned [ʌn'tjuːnd] ADJ *(instrument)* non accordé; *(engine)* qui n'est pas réglé

untuneful [ʌn'tjuːnfʊl] ADJ peu mélodieux

untutored [ʌn'tjuːtəd] ADJ *esp Lit (person)* peu instruit; *(mind, taste)* non formé

untwine [ʌn'twaɪn] VT détordre, détortiller

untwist [ʌn'twɪst] VT *(strands)* détordre, détortiller; *(jar lid etc)* dévisser; to u. itself, to come untwisted se détordre
VI se détordre

untypical [ʌn'tɪpɪk(ə)l] ADJ inhabituel; it's very u. of her c'est très inhabituel de sa part, cela ne lui ressemble pas

untypically [ʌn'tɪpɪk(ə)lɪ] ADJ inhabituellement

unusable [ʌn'juːzəb(ə)l] ADJ inutilisable

unused [ʌn'juːzd] ADJ **1** *(system, clothes etc)* dont on ne se sert pas; *(road)* pas fréquenté; *(talent)* non employé; *(building)* désaffecté; her talents had gone largely u. ses talents étaient restés inexploités; our nuclear weapons are still u. nos armes nucléaires n'ont encore jamais été utilisées **2** *(never yet used)* qui n'a jamais servi; *(clothes)* neuf **3** [ʌn'juːst] *(person)* peu habitué (to sth à qch); to be u. to doing sth ne pas avoir l'habitude de faire qch; I'm still u. to you being here je ne suis pas encore habitué à ce que tu sois là; we're not u. to it nous y sommes habitués

unusual [ʌn'juːʒʊəl] ADJ *(not common) (colour, style, design, thing to happen)* inhabituel, peu ordinaire; *(strange, out of the ordinary)* insolite; an u. case of ... un cas peu commun *ou* peu ordinaire de ...; an u. lapse une défaillance inhabituelle; a very u. exception une exception très inhabituelle; what do you think of my new haircut? – well, it's certainly u.! que penses-tu de ma nouvelle coupe de cheveux? – ah pour ça c'est original!; he has some rather u. tastes il a des goûts bizarres; it's u. for her not to notice these things c'est rare qu'elle ne remarque pas ces choses-là; you don't want a drink?, that's u. for you tu ne veux pas prendre un verre?, qu'est-ce qui t'arrive?; the sort of information which is u. in most dictionaries le genre d'information qu'on ne trouve habituellement pas dans les dictionnaires; it's u. to see him at the theatre il est rare qu'on le voie au théâtre; it's not u. ce n'est pas rare; nothing u. rien d'anormal; of u. interest d'un intérêt exceptionnel

unusually [ʌn'juːʒʊəlɪ] ADV inhabituellement; *(exceptionally)* exceptionnellement; u., this language ... chose inhabituelle, cette langue ...; she stayed u. quiet elle est restée inhabituellement calme; an u. stupid/clever man un homme d'une stupidité/intelligence exceptionnelle; u. tall exceptionnellement grand; it's very u. designed c'est conçu de manière très insolite *ou* inhabituelle; he was u. attentive contrairement à son habitude, il a été attentif

unutterable [ʌn'ʌt(ə)rəb(ə)l] ADJ *(misery, stupidity)* innommable; *(boredom)* incroyable

unutterably [ʌn'ʌt(ə)rəblɪ] ADV u. bored/miserable d'un ennui/dans une misère invraisemblable; u. stupid d'une stupidité innommable

unvaried [ʌn'veərɪd] ADJ *(landscape, life)* sans variété; *(diet)* qui manque de variété

unvarnished [ʌn'vɑːnɪʃt] ADJ *(surface)* non verni; *(pottery)* non vernissé; *Fig* the plain u. truth la vérité pure et simple

unvarying [ʌ'veərɪɪŋ] ADJ invariable, constant

unveil [ʌn'veɪl] VT *(statue, plaque etc)* inaugurer; *(new car etc)* présenter; *Fig (secret, plan)* dévoiler
VI se dévoiler

unveiled [ʌn'veɪld] ADJ sans voile

unveiling [ʌn'veɪlɪŋ] N *(of statue, plaque etc)* inauguration f, *(of new car etc)* présentation f
▸▸ u. ceremony (cérémonie f d')inauguration

unverifiable [ʌn'verɪfaɪəb(ə)l] ADJ invérifiable

unverified [ʌn'verɪfaɪd] ADJ non contrôlé, non vérifié

unversed [ʌn'vɜːst] ADJ peu versé (in dans)

unvoiced [ʌn'vɔɪst] ADJ **1** *(opinion)* non exprimé **2** *Ling (vowel, consonant)* sourd, muet

unwaged [ʌn'weɪdʒd] ADJ *(unpaid)* non rémunéré

unwanted [ʌn'wɒntɪd] ADJ non voulu; his help had been u. on n'avait pas voulu de son aide; to give away all one's u. books se débarrasser de tous les livres dont on n'a plus besoin; to be feeling u. *(in the way)* se sentir de trop; *(unloved)* se sentir mal-aimé; u. child enfant non désiré
▸▸ u. hair poils *mpl* superflus

unwarlike [ʌn'wɔːlaɪk] ADJ non belliqueux

unwarrantable [ʌn'wɒrəntəb(ə)l] ADJ injustifiable

unwarrantably [ʌn'wɒrəntəblɪ] ADV de manière injustifiable

unwarranted [ʌn'wɒrəntɪd] ADJ injustifié; u. familiarity familiarité indue u. insult insulte gratuite

unwary [ʌn'weərɪ] ADJ imprudent, imprévoyant; an u. reader un lecteur non averti
NPL the u. les imprudents *mpl*

unwashed [ʌn'wɒʃt] ADJ non lavé
NPL *Fam Hum* the great u. les prolétaires *mpl*, les prolos *mpl*

unwavering [ʌn'weɪvərɪŋ] ADJ constant; *(support, loyalty)* absolu; *(belief, conviction)* ferme; *(determination)* inébranlable; *(gaze)* soutenu

unwaveringly [ʌn'weɪvərɪŋlɪ] ADV *(to support, be in favour of)* résolument; *(to look at sb)* sans faiblir

unweaned [ʌn'wiːnd] ADJ *(child, kitten)* non sevré

unwearable [ʌn'weərəb(ə)l] ADJ *(garment)* immettable

unwearying [ʌn'wɪərɪɪŋ] ADJ inlassable, infatigable

unwed [ʌn'wed] ADJ *Old-fashioned, Lit* qui n'est pas marié; he remained u. il ne s'est jamais marié

unweighted [ʌn'weɪtɪd] ADJ *Econ (index)* non pondéré
▸▸ u. figures chiffres *mpl* bruts

unwelcome [ʌn'welkəm] ADJ *(visitor)* importun; *(news, development)* fâcheux; to feel u. ne pas se sentir le/la bienvenu(e); u. visit visite f importune a not u. visit une visite opportune; her news could not have been more u. les nouvelles qu'elle avait n'auraient pas pu être plus fâcheuses; to make sb feel u. faire sentir à qn qu'il n'est pas le bienvenu/qu'elle n'est pas la bienvenue; the extra £50 was not u. les 50 livres supplémentaires ne tombaient pas mal du tout

unwell [ʌn'wel] ADJ souffrant; are you feeling u.? êtes-vous souffrant?

unwholesome [ʌn'həʊlsəm] ADJ malsain;

Com **u. demand** *(for products)* demande *f* indésirable

unwieldy [ʌn'wiːldɪ] ADJ *(tool, object)* peu maniable, difficile à manier; *(method, approach)* trop complexe; *(system, bureaucracy)* lourd; *(person)* lourd et gauche

unwilling [ʌn'wɪlɪŋ] ADJ *(helper)* réticent; *(consent)* donné à contrecœur; **an u. accomplice** un complice malgré moi/lui/*etc*; **to be u. to do sth** être peu disposé à faire qch, ne pas vouloir faire qch; **I was u. that my wife should know** *or* **for my wife to know** je ne voulais pas que ma femme le sache

unwillingly [ʌn'wɪlɪŋlɪ] ADV à contrecœur

unwillingness [ʌn'wɪlɪŋnɪs] N réticence *f*; **they showed such an u. to accept the terms that …** ils ont été tellement réticents à accepter les conditions que …; **their u. to compromise on this issue made agreement impossible** leur refus du compromis sur ce point rendait tout accord impossible

unwind [ʌn'waɪnd] *(pt, pp* **unwound** [-'waʊnd])* VT dérouler; *(ball of wool)* défaire, dérouler ■ VI **1** *(unroll)* se dérouler; *(of ball of wool)* se défaire, se dérouler **2** *Fam (relax)* se détendre, se relaxer

unwise [ʌn'waɪz] ADJ *(person)* peu prudent, peu sage; *(action, investment)* peu judicieux; **that was very u. of you** c'était très imprudent de votre part

unwisely [ʌn'waɪzlɪ] ADV imprudemment

unwitting [ʌn'wɪtɪŋ] ADJ involontaire; **if I have caused you any u. offence** si je vous ai offensé sans le vouloir

unwittingly [ʌn'wɪtɪŋlɪ] ADV *(without realizing)* sans le savoir; *(without intending to)* involontairement

unwomanly [ʌn'wʊmənlɪ] ADJ peu féminin

unwonted [ʌn'wəʊntɪd] ADJ *esp Lit* inaccoutumé

unworkable [ʌn'wɜːkəb(ə)l] ADJ *(plan)* impraticable

unworldliness [ʌn'wɜːldlɪnɪs] N détachement *m* de ce monde; *(naivety)* simplicité *f*, candeur *f*

unworldly [ʌn'wɜːldlɪ] ADJ détaché de ce monde; *(naive)* simple, candide; *esp Lit (beauty)* qui n'est pas de ce monde, irréel

unworn [ʌn'wɔːn] ADJ *(clothes)* non porté; **these shoes look u.** on dirait que ces chaussures n'ont jamais été portées

unworthiness [ʌn'wɜːðɪnɪs] N indignité *f*

unworthy [ʌn'wɜːðɪ] ADJ indigne (**of sth/ sb** de qch/qn); **u. of notice** qui ne mérite pas qu'on y fasse attention; **that's u. of you** c'est indigne de vous

unwounded [ʌn'wuːndɪd] ADJ indemne; **to be u.** ne pas être blessé

unwrap [ʌn'ræp] VT *(-pp-)* *(parcel)* défaire; *(sweet, sandwich)* déballer; **to come unwrapped** *(of parcel)* se défaire

unwritten [ʌn'rɪt(ə)n] ADJ non écrit; *(tradition)* oral, -aux; *(agreement)* verbal, -aux; **it's an u. law in this office that …** dans ce bureau on respecte la convention selon laquelle …; **he had broken one of the u. laws of the gang** il n'avait pas respecté l'une des conventions du gang

unyielding [ʌn'jiːldɪŋ] ADJ *(material, surface)* qui ne cède pas, résistant; *(frozen ground)* dur; *(person, determination)* inébranlable, ferme; **u. grip** prise *f* de fer

unyoke [ʌn'jəʊk] VT dételer, découpler

unzip [ʌn'zɪp] *(-pp-)* VT **1** *(garment)* descendre la fermeture éclair® de; **will you u. me?** tu veux bien descendre *ou* défaire ma fermeture éclair? **2** *Comput* dézipper, décompresser

VI *(of garment)* **it unzips at the side** ça s'ouvre sur le côté

UP [juː'piː] N *Com (abbr* **unit price**) PU *m*

UP [ʌp] *(when* **up** *is an integral part of a verb eg* **come up, go up, get up, take up,** *the user should consult the verb in question)* ADV **1** *(at the top)* en haut; *(to the top)* vers le haut; **all the way up, the whole way up, right up (to the top)** *(of stairs, hill)* jusqu'en haut; **half way up** jusqu'à mi-hauteur; **to live three flights up** habiter *Br* au troisième *ou Am* au quatrième (étage); **to throw sth up in the air** jeter qch en l'air; **to put one's hand up** lever la main; **hands up!** haut les mains!; **what are you doing up there?** qu'est-ce que tu fais là-haut?; **up above** en haut; **up above sth** au-dessus de qch; **before the sun was up** avant le lever du soleil; **would you like the window up a bit?** *(in car)* veux-tu que je remonte un peu la vitre?; *Horseracing* **Comet with Thomas up** Comet monté par Thomas; **the river's up** la rivière est en crue; **to lay sth face up** mettre qch à l'endroit; **this side up** *(on packing case)* haut, dessus; **put it the other way up** retournez-le; **he's something quite high up in the civil service** il est haut placé dans l'administration; **to be up in arms** être en révolte; **up with …!** *(supporting)* vive …!

2 *(when travelling etc)* **to walk up and down** se promener de long en large; **to go up north** aller dans le nord; **to go up to London for the day** aller passer la journée à Londres; *Univ* **he's going up to Oxford** il va faire ses études à l'université d'Oxford; **up in London** à Londres; **up in Yorkshire** au nord dans le Yorkshire; *Univ* **up at Oxford** à l'université d'Oxford; **to come up before the judge** être cité devant les magistrats

3 *(and above)* **from £10 up** à partir de 10 livres; **suitable to children aged seven and up** convient aux enfants âgés de sept ans et plus; **all ranks from sergeant up** tous les rangs à partir de celui de sergent

4 *(on display, complete)* **to put up the results** afficher les résultats; **are the results up yet?** les résultats sont-ils déjà affichés?; **there's a big notice up at the station saying …** il y a un grand panneau à la gare disant …; **our curtains still aren't up** nous n'avons toujours pas accroché nos rideaux; **the new building is up** le nouveau bâtiment est terminé; **when the tent's up** quand la tente sera montée

5 *(for repair etc)* **this road's always up** cette route est toujours en réparation; **careful, we've got some of the floorboards up** attention au plancher, il manque des lattes; **when we've got the carpet up …** quand nous aurons enlevé la moquette …

6 *(higher)* **prices are 10% up on last year's** les prix ont augmenté de dix pour cent depuis l'année dernière; **petrol is up again** l'essence a encore augmenté; **the temperature is going up** la température monte; **business is looking up** les affaires sont à la hausse

7 *(ahead)* *Sport* **to be one goal up** mener par un but; *Golf* **to be one hole up** avoir un trou d'avance; **to be one up on sb** *(in point, score)* avoir un point d'avance sur qn; *Fig (have advantage)* avoir l'avantage sur qn; **his blood was up** le sang lui bouillait; **speak up!** parlez plus fort!

8 *(knowledgeable)* **to be well up in a subject** connaître un sujet à fond; **how well up are you in German?** tu t'y connais en allemand?

9 *(with proximity)* **lean it up against the wall** appuyez-le contre le mur; **they were standing close up to each other** ils se tenaient tout près l'un de l'autre; **to be up against difficulties** se heurter à des diffi-

cultés; *Fig Fam* **to be up against it** être dans le pétrin

10 *(out of bed)* debout, levé; **to be up late** veiller tard; **to be up all night** ne pas se coucher de la nuit; **isn't he up yet!** il n'est pas encore levé *ou* debout!; **I was up late this morning** je me suis levé tard ce matin; **he's always up and about by seven** il est toujours debout à sept heures; **to be up and about again** *(after illness)* être de nouveau sur pied

11 *Fam (wrong)* **what's up?** qu'est-ce qui se passe?, qu'y a-t-il?; **what's up with you/ him?** qu'est-ce qui te/lui prend?; **something's up** il y a quelque chose qui ne va pas; **there's something up with him** il y a quelque chose qui ne va pas chez lui; **there's something up with the TV** la télé débloque

12 *(finished)* **time is up** il est l'heure; **your time's up** c'est fini; **his time is up** *(of prisoner)* il a purgé sa peine; **his leave is up** sa permission est expirée; *Fam* **the game's up** *(we've been found out)* nous sommes faits; *(I've found you out)* vous êtes faits; *Fam* **I thought it was all up with me** j'ai cru que ma dernière heure était arrivée; *Fam* **it's all up with him** c'en est fait de lui, il a son compte

13 **up to** *(as far as)* jusqu'à; **to go up to sb** s'approcher de qn; **covered in mud up to the ears** couvert de boue jusqu'aux oreilles; **what page** *or* **where are you up to?** où en es-tu *ou* à quelle page en es-tu?; **we're up to page 50** nous en sommes à la page 50; **up to now, up to here** jusqu'ici, jusqu'alors, jusque-là; **up to £100 a week** jusqu'à 100 livres par semaine; **up to what age?** jusqu'à quel âge?

14 **up to** *(good enough for)* **to be up to one's job** être à la hauteur de sa tâche; **he's not up to it** il n'est pas capable de le faire; **he's not up to the journey** il n'est pas à même de faire le voyage; **I don't feel up to it** je ne m'en sens pas le courage; **I don't feel up to much** je ne me sens pas bien; **it's not up to much** ça ne vaut pas grand-chose

15 *esp Pej* **he's up to something** il mijote quelque chose; **what are the children up to?** que font les enfants?; **hey you, what do you think you're up to?** eh vous là-bas, qu'est-ce que vous fabriquez?; **what's that guy over there up to?** qu'est-ce qu'il fabrique, ce type là-bas?; **what's he up to with that ladder?** qu'est-ce qu'il a l'intention de faire *ou* qu'est-ce qu'il fabrique avec cette échelle?; **what are you up to with my girlfriend?** qu'est-ce que tu lui veux à ma copine?

16 *(to be decided by)* **what shall I do? – that's up to you** qu'est-ce que je fais? – c'est à toi de décider; **it's entirely up to you whether you go or not** il ne tient qu'à toi de rester ou de partir

17 *(be the responsibility of)* **it's up to him to do it** c'est à lui de le faire; **it's up to you to tell her** c'est à toi de lui dire

18 *(phrases)* **to be up and coming** *(person, team etc)* être plein d'avenir, prometteur; **to be up and running** *(of new machine etc)* être en service; *(of project)* être en route; **to get sth up and running** *(new machine)* mettre qch en service; *(project)* mettre qch en route ■ PREP **to go up the stairs** monter l'escalier; **to climb up a hill** monter *ou* grimper une colline; **to go up the street** remonter la rue; **further up the street** plus loin dans la rue; **they live further up the street** ils habitent plus loin *ou* plus haut dans cette rue; **the smoke went up my nose** la fumée m'est montée par le nez; **the gas goes up this pipe** le gaz monte par ce tuyau; **the cat is up that tree** le chat est *(perché)* sur cet arbre; **the cat went up a tree** le chat a grimpé à un arbre; **it's up river from here** c'est en amont d'ici; **to walk up and down the platform** aller et venir sur le quai; *(nervously etc)* arpenter le quai; **he lives up your way** il habite par chez vous *ou* du côté de chez vous; *Br Fam* **he's up the pub** il est au pub; *Br Fam* **I'm going up the shops** je vais faire un tour en courses; *Vulg* **up yours!** va te faire enculer!

ADJ *Comput* **up arrow** flèche *f* vers le haut; **up arrow key** touche *f* flèche vers le haut; **up escalator** escalator® *m* qui monte; **he ran down the up side** il est descendu en courant du côté où l'on est censé monter; *Rail* **up line** voie *f* en direction d'une grande gare; **up train** train *m* qui va dans une grande gare

N 1 ups and downs *(of life)* hauts et bas *mpl*, vicissitudes *fpl*; *(in politics)* avatars *mpl*; *Com (of market)* oscillations *fpl*; *(of terrain)* ondulations *fpl*; **life is full of ups and downs** la vie est faite de hauts et de bas

2 *Fam* **to be on the up and up** *(be honest)* être clair *ou* fiable; *Br (be improving)* être en train de monter *ou* de faire son chemin

VT **(-pp-) 1** *Fam (prices etc)* augmenter; **to up the stakes** *(at cards etc)*, *Fig* monter la mise; **to up sticks** plier bagages; **he just upped sticks and left** il a plié bagages et est parti

2 *(swans)* recenser

VI *Fam* **to up and leave** *or* **go** partir; **they upped and went** ils sont partis très soudainement; **one day he just upped and left her** un beau jour il l'a quittée sans crier gare; **he just upped and hit him** tout à coup il (s'est levé et) l'a frappé

up-and-coming **ADJ** *(person, economy, team)* qui est plein d'avenir, prometteur, -euse; *(town)* plein d'avenir

up-and-down **ADJ** **u. movement** mouvement *m* de haut en bas

up-and-over **ADJ**
  ▸▸ **u. door** porte *f* basculante *(d'un garage etc)*

up-and-under **N** *Rugby* up and under *m*

upbeat ['ʌpbiːt] **N** *Mus* levé *m*
  ADJ *Fam (optimistic, cheerful)* optimiste

upbraid [ʌp'breɪd] **VT** faire des reproches à, réprimander

upbringing ['ʌpbrɪŋɪŋ] **N** éducation *f*; **what sort of (an) u. has she had?** comment a-t-elle été élevée?, quelle éducation a-t-elle eu?

up-change **N** *(of gears)* passage *m* à la vitesse supérieure

upchuck ['ʌptʃʌk] **VT & VI** *esp Am Fam (vomit)* dégobiller

upcoming ['ʌpkʌmɪŋ] **ADJ** *Am* prochain

upcountry [ʌp'kʌntrɪ] *esp Am, Austr* **N** intérieur *m* *(du pays)*
  ADJ de l'intérieur *(du pays)*
  ADV **to go u.** aller vers l'intérieur

update¹ ['ʌpdeɪt] **N** mise *f* à jour; *Comput (of software package)* mise à jour, actualisation *f*; **to give sb an u. on sth** mettre qn au courant de qch; **a dictionary should have an u. at least every 5 years** un dictionnaire devrait être remis à jour au minimum tous les 5 ans

update² [ʌp'deɪt] **VT** *(file, record)* mettre à jour, actualiser; *(equipment etc)* moderniser; *(person)* mettre au courant; **could you u. me on what's been happening?** pourriez-vous me mettre au courant de ce qui s'est passé?; **it needs regular updating** une remise à jour régulière est nécessaire; **it hasn't been updated since 1973** il n'a pas été remis à jour depuis 1973

updating [ʌp'deɪtɪŋ] **N** mise *f* à jour

up-draught, *Am* **up-draft N** *Aviat* courant *m* d'air ascendant

upend [ʌp'end] **VT** *(thing)* mettre debout; **to u. sb** *(turn upside down)* mettre qn les pieds en l'air, mettre qn à l'envers

up-front **ADJ 1** *Fam (honest, frank)* franc, *f*

franche, direct *(about sth à propos de qch)* **2** *(payment)* à l'avance
  ADV *(to be paid etc)* à l'avance; **to ask for some of the cash u.** demander une avance

upgrade¹ ['ʌpgreɪd] **N 1** *Am (slope)* pente *f* ascendante; *(of railway line)* montée *f* **2** *Am* **to be on the u.** *(of prices)* monter; *(of business)* reprendre, se relever; *(of invalid)* être en voie de guérison **3** *Comput (of system)* augmentation *f* de puissance; *(for software)* mise *f* à jour, actualisation *f*, *(for hardware) (expansion)* extension *f*, *(new model, processor etc)* nouvelle version *f*
  ▸▸ *Comput* **u. kit** ensemble *m* de mise à niveau

upgrade² [ʌp'greɪd] **VT 1** *(improve) (product)* améliorer; *Comput (of user) (software)* se procurer la dernière version de; *(hardware) (expand)* ajouter une/des extension(s) à; *(buy new and better)* remplacer par une/des nouvelle(s) version(s); *(memory)* augmenter **2** *(raise to higher rank)* nommer à un niveau supérieur, surclasser; *(civil servant)* monter en grade
  VI *Comput (expand computer system)* ajouter une/des extension(s); *(buy newer and better model)* acquérir une/des nouvelle(s) version(s); **we've decided to u. to the GT model** nous avons décidé de passer à un modèle supérieur et d'acheter le GT

upgrad(e)ability [ʌpgreɪdə'bɪlɪtɪ] **N** possibilités *fpl* d'extension

upgrad(e)able [ʌp'greɪdəb(ə)l] **ADJ** *Comput (hardware, system)* évolutif; *(memory)* extensible; **u. architecture** architecture *f* évolutive

upgrading [ʌp'greɪdɪŋ] **N 1** *(of system)* amélioration *f*, *Comput (expansion)* ajout *m* d'une/de plusieurs extension(s) *(of à)*; *(replacement by newer and better)* acquisition *f* d'une/de nouvelle(s) version(s); *(of memory)* extension *f* **2** *(of person)* avancement *m*; **the u. of the polytechnic to university status** le reclassement de l'IUT au rang d'université

upheaval [ʌp'hiːv(ə)l] **N** bouleversement *m*; **political u.** agitation *f* politique; **an emotional u.** un bouleversement affectif; **moving house is such an u.** déménager est un tel bouleversement *ou* chamboulement; **the u. of moving office** le tumulte qu'entraîne un déménagement dans d'autres bureaux

uphill [ʌp'hɪl] **ADJ** *(road)* qui monte; *(struggle)* pénible, difficile; **it's u. all the way** ça monte tout le long du chemin; *Fig* c'est une lutte permanente
  ADV **to go u.** monter; **it's a good way u. from here** il faut monter pas mal pour y arriver; **to ski u.** skier en amont
  ▸▸ **u. ski** ski *m* amont

uphold [ʌp'həʊld] **VT** *(pt, pp* **upheld** [-'held]*)* soutenir; *(opinion, principle)* défendre; *Law (decision)* confirmer; **to u. the law** faire observer la loi

upholder [ʌp'həʊldər] **N** *(of cause)* défenseur *m*

upholster [ʌp'həʊlstər] **VT** *(pad)* capitonner, rembourrer; *(cover) (sofa etc)* tapisser, garnir *(with, in* de*)*

upholstered [ʌp'həʊlstəd] **ADJ** *(padded)* capitonné, rembourré; *(covered) (sofa)* tapissé, garni; **u. in velvet/leather** garni de velours/cuir; *Fam* **she's well u.** elle est bien rembourrée

upholsterer [ʌp'həʊlstərər] **N** tapissier *m* en ameublement

upholstery [ʌp'həʊlstərɪ] **N 1** *(padding) (of armchair etc)* capitonnage *m*, rembourrage *m*; *(covering)* garniture *f*, *(in car)* garniture intérieure; **leather u.** garniture en cuir **2** *(trade)* tapisserie *f* d'ameublement

UPI [juːpiːˈaɪ] **N** *(abbr* **United Press International***)* UPI *(agence de presse)*

upkeep ['ʌpkiːp] **N** *(of house, building, horse)* entretien *m*; **he paid nothing towards the u. of the children** il ne donnait pas d'argent pour subvenir aux besoins matériels des enfants

upland ['ʌplənd] **N** *(usu pl)* **the uplands** le haut pays, les hauteurs *fpl*
  ADJ *(village)* de montagne

uplift¹ ['ʌplɪft] **N** **(moral) u.** inspiration *f* *(morale)*
  ▸▸ **u. bra** soutien-gorge *m* de maintien, *pl* soutiens-gorge de maintien

uplift² [ʌp'lɪft] **VT 1** *(soul, heart)* élever **2** *Scot (collect)* récupérer

uplifted [ʌp'lɪftɪd] **ADJ 1** *(of hand)* levé **2** *(morally, spiritually)* élevé *(by sth* par qch*)*

uplifting [ʌp'lɪftɪŋ] **ADJ** *(experience, sermon etc)* édifiant

uplighter ['ʌplaɪtər] **N** = applique *f* ou lampadaire *m* diffusant la lumière vers le haut

uplink receiver ['ʌplɪŋk] **N** récepteur *m* de liaison terre/satellite

upload ['ʌpləʊd] **VT** *Comput* télécharger *(vers le serveur)*

up-market **ADJ** *(product)* haut de gamme; *(district, person, accent)* bourgeois
  ADV **to go u.** *(of company)* se mettre à faire du haut de gamme; *(of person)* prendre des goûts de luxe

upmost ['ʌpməʊst] **ADJ** = **uppermost 1**

upon [ə'pɒn] **PREP** **(on** and **upon** are interchangeable in meaning; in modern English **upon** is used more formally; in certain phrases, however, **upon** is preferable*)* sur; **u. my word!** ma parole!; **the enemy was u. us** l'ennemi nous attaquait; **I came u. it by accident** je l'ai trouvé par hasard; **you brought it u. yourself** ne t'en prends qu'à toi-même!
VOIR GRAMMAIRE A73

upper ['ʌpər] **ADJ 1** *(part, storey, deck, branch etc)* supérieur; **the u. atmosphere** les couches supérieures de l'atmosphère; **temperature in the u. twenties** température qui dépasse 25 degrés

2 *Geog* **the u. Rhine** le haut Rhin

3 the u. end of the table le bout de la table; **the u. echelons of the civil service** les plus hauts échelons de l'administration; **the u. classes** la haute société; **the u. middle classes** la haute bourgeoisie; **to gain the u. hand** prendre le dessus; **to let sb get the u. hand** laisser qn prendre le dessus, laisser qn dominer

4 *Mus (keyboard)* du côté droit; *(register)* aigu, -uë

N 1 *(of shoe)* empeigne *f*, *Fam* **to be down on one's uppers** être dans la gêne **2** *Sl (drug)* amphétamine *f*, amphé *f*
  ▸▸ *Anat* **u. arm** bras *m*; *Comput* **u. ASCII** ASCII *m* supérieur; **U. Canada** le haut Canada; *Theat* **u. circle** deuxième balcon *m*; *Fam* **u. crust** *(of society)* la haute, le dessus du panier, la crème; **U. Egypt** la Haute-Égypte; **the U. House** la Chambre haute; *(the House of Lords)* la Chambre des lords; **u. jaw** mâchoire *f* supérieure; **u. limit** plafond *m*; **u. lip** lèvre *f* supérieure; **u. reaches** *(of river)* amont *m*; *Br* **u. school** grandes classes *fpl*; *Br Sch* **u. sixth** terminale *f*

upper-case **ADJ** *Typ (letters)* majuscule

upper-class **ADJ** *(accent, person)* aristocratique; **to be very u.** être très aristocrate
  ▸▸ *Fam Pej* **u. twit** = aristocrate *m* bête et prétentieux

upper-crust **ADJ** *Fam (accent, person)* aristo, de la haute; **they're frightfully u.** ils sont très aristos

uppercut ['ʌpəkʌt] **N** *Boxing* uppercut *m*

uppermost ['ʌpəməʊst] ADJ **1** *(in position)* le plus haut, le plus élevé **2** *(in importance)* de la plus grande importance; **to be u.** tenir le premier rang; **the problem (which is) u. in our minds** le problème qui nous préoccupe au premier chef
▸ ADV en dessus

upping ['ʌpɪŋ] N **swan u.** recensement *m* des cygnes

uppity ['ʌpɪti], **uppish** ['ʌpɪʃ] ADJ *Fam* présomptueux, arrogant; **he's getting very u.** il se croit quelqu'un; **don't you get u. with me!** ne joue pas les arrogants avec moi!

upright ['ʌpraɪt] ADJ **1** *(line)* vertical, -aux; *(wall, writing)* droit **2** *(honest)* droit, honnête
▸ ADV debout; **to stand u.** se tenir droit; **sitting u. on his chair** assis droit sur sa chaise; **to put** *or* **stand sth u.** mettre qch debout *ou* d'aplomb
▸ N **1** *(of door, ladder etc)* montant *m*; *Ftbl* **the uprights** les montants de but **2** *(piano)* piano *m* droit
▸▸ **u. freezer** congélateur *m* armoire; **u. piano** piano droit

uprightly ['ʌpraɪtlɪ] ADV droitement, honnêtement

uprightness ['ʌpraɪtnɪs] N droiture *f*, honnêteté *f*

uprising ['ʌpraɪzɪŋ] N soulèvement *m*, insurrection *f*

uproar ['ʌprɔːr] N *(noise)* tapage *m*, vacarme *m*; *(protest)* tollé *m*; **the meeting finished in (an) u.** la réunion s'est terminée dans la confusion; **his suggestion caused an u.** *(shouting, protests)* sa suggestion a provoqué un tollé; **the recent u. in the press about ...** la tempête qui a récemment éclaté dans la presse au sujet de ...

uproarious [ʌp'rɔːrɪəs] ADJ *(noisy)* tumultueux; *(hilarious)* hilarant; **u. laughter** grands éclats de rire

uproariously [ʌp'rɔːrɪəslɪ] ADV **to laugh u.** rire à gorge déployée; **u. funny** désopilant

uproot [ʌp'ruːt] VT *(plant, evil)* déraciner, extirper; **to u. sb from his home** déraciner qn; **to feel uprooted** se sentir déraciné

UPS [juːpiːˈes] N *Comput (abbr* **uninterruptible power supply)** onduleur *m*

upsadaisy ['ʌpsədeɪzi] INT *Fam* hop là!

upset[1] ['ʌpset] N **1** *(disturbance)*, *Fig* bouleversement *m*; **the bad news caused quite an u.** les mauvaises nouvelles ont provoqué une grande consternation; **with the fewest possible number of upsets to our plans** avec le moins de bouleversements possibles dans nos projets; **he can't stand upsets in his routine** il ne supporte pas que sa routine soit dérangée; **have you had an u. with her?** *(difficulty, argument etc)* est-ce que tu t'es disputé *ou* as eu un problème avec elle?; **losing 25-3 was something of an u.** se faire battre 25 à 3 a été une sacrée déception; **after the u. at the last match** après la déception du dernier match; **that's going to cause a bit of an u.** cela va faire du bruit **2 to have a stomach u.** avoir une grippe intestinale

upset[2] [ʌp'set] VT *(pt, pp* **upset;** *prp* **upsetting) 1** *(knock over, spill)* renverser; *(boat)* (faire) chavirer **2** *(plans, schedule, calculations etc)* bouleverser, déranger **3** *(emotionally) (person)* faire de la peine à, blesser; *(of sight, news, death)* bouleverser; **don't mention that!, you'll u. her again** ne parle pas de ça!, tu vas encore la contrarier; **the least thing upsets him** il est très impressionnable; **don't u. yourself** arrête, tu te fais du mal **4** *(stomach)* déranger; *(digestion)* troubler

upset[3] *(before noun* ['ʌpset], *otherwise* [ʌp'set]) ADJ **1** *(sad)* triste; *(annoyed)* fâché, ennuyé; *(offended)* vexé, blessé; **she's u. because you called her names** elle est vexée parce que tu l'as insultée; **what are you so u. about?** qu'est-ce qui te met dans cet état?; **are you still u. or are we friends again?** est-ce que tu es toujours fâché ou sommes-nous amis à nouveau?; **we'd be u. too if we missed the deadline** nous serions très ennuyés si nous dépassions l'échéance; **you'd be u. too if you'd just paid ...** tu serais aussi fâché que moi si tu venais juste de payer ...; **I'm u. about losing it/her** ça me fait mal au cœur de le/la perdre; **she was clearly u. by the pictures** *(distraught, moved)* ces images l'avaient manifestement perturbée; **we're u. about losing the order** ça nous contrarie de perdre cette commande; **I'd be very u. if you didn't come** je serais très triste si tu ne venais pas; **he was so u. he couldn't speak** il était tellement bouleversé qu'il n'arrivait pas à parler; **come on now, there's nothing to be u. about** allons, il n'y a pas de quoi en faire un drame; **don't be** *or* **get u.** ne t'en fais pas **2** *(stomach)* dérangé
▸▸ *Am, Scot* **u. price** mise *f* à prix

upsetting [ʌp'setɪŋ] ADJ *(saddening)* attristant, affligeant; *(annoying)* contrariant, fâcheux; *(offending)* vexant, blessant; *(disturbing)* troublant; *(more seriously)* bouleversant; **I didn't find the experience in the least u.** l'expérience ne m'a pas du tout perturbé; **viewers might find some of these scenes u.** certaines des scènes qui vont suivre peuvent être de nature à perturber les téléspectateurs

upshift ['ʌpʃɪft] N *(of gears)* passage *m* à la vitesse supérieure

upshot ['ʌpʃɒt] N résultat *m*; **what will be the u. of it?** cela finira comment?; **the u. of it all was that he resigned** le résultat, c'est qu'il a donné sa démission

upside ['ʌpsaɪd] ADJ
▸▸ *St Exch* **u. potential** potentiel *m* de hausse; *St Exch* **u. risk** risque *f* de hausse

upside down ADV **1** à l'envers; *(person, animal)* la tête en bas; **to hold sth u.** tenir qch à l'envers; **to turn u.** se retourner **2** *(in disorder)* en désordre; **to turn everything u.** tout bouleverser, tout mettre sens dessus dessous
▸ ADJ renversé; **pineapple u. cake** gâteau *m* renversé à l'ananas

upstage [ʌp'steɪdʒ] ADJ *Theat* de l'arrière-scène
▸ ADV *Theat* à l'arrière-scène
▸ VT *(person)* éclipser

upstairs ['ʌpsteəz] ADV en haut; **he's u.** il est en haut; **she has a second living room u.** elle a un deuxième salon en haut *ou* à l'étage; **they live u. from us** ils habitent au-dessus de chez nous; **I'll take your things u.** je vais monter tes affaires; **to come/go u.** venir/monter à l'étage *ou* en haut; **he chased me u.** il m'a poursuivi dans les escaliers; *Fig Fam* **to kick sb u.** donner de l'avancement à qn pour s'en débarrasser; *Fam* **he hasn't got much u.** *(is not very clever)* il n'a pas grand-chose dans le crâne
▸ ADJ *(room)* d'en haut, du haut; **our u. neighbours** nos voisins du dessus; **we have an u. sitting room** nous avons un salon à l'étage
▸ N **(the) u.** les pièces *fpl* d'en haut; **the house has no u.** la maison n'a pas d'étage

upstanding [ʌp'stændɪŋ] ADJ **1** *(erect)* droit, qui se tient bien; **a fine u. young man** un jeune homme bien comme il faut **2** *(honest)* honnête **3** *Fml* **please be u. for the toast** veuillez vous lever pour porter le toast

upstart ['ʌpstɑːt] N parvenu, -ue

upstate ['ʌpsteɪt] *Am* ADJ du nord; **u. New York** la partie nord de l'État de New York
▸ ADV *(to go)* vers le nord

upstream ['ʌpstriːm] ADV **1** *(to be)* en amont *(* **from** de**) 2** *(to row etc)* en remontant le cou-rant, à contre-fil de l'eau; **the salmon swims u.** le saumon remonte la rivière
▸ ADJ d'amont

upstroke ['ʌpstrəʊk] N *(in writing)* délié *m*; *(of piston)* course *f* montante *ou* ascendante

upsurge ['ʌpsɜːdʒ] N *(of enthusiasm, hatred)* vague *f*; *(of activity, interest)* regain *m*; *(of inflation)* montée *f* soudaine

upswept ['ʌpswept] ADJ *Aut, Aviat* profilé; **u. hair(style)** coiffure *f* en hauteur

upswing ['ʌpswɪŋ] N **1** *(movement)* mouvement *m* ascendant **2** *(improvement)* amélioration *f* sensible; **business is on the u.** les affaires sont en train de redémarrer; **the economy is on the u.** il y a un redressement de l'économie

uptake ['ʌpteɪk] N **1** *Fam (understanding)* **to be quick on the u.** avoir l'esprit vif; **he's a bit slow on the u.** il est un peu lent à comprendre *ou* à la détente **2** *(taking up)*, *Biol* assimilation *f*; *Admin* **the u. of benefits** la proportion des gens qui font valoir leurs droits aux allocations

uptight [ʌp'taɪt] ADJ *Fam* **1** *(nervous)* nerveux, tendu; **he's u. about the exams/about meeting them** il est nerveux *ou* tendu à cause des examens/à l'idée de les rencontrer **2** *(inhibited)* coincé; *(on particular occasion)* crispé, mal à l'aise; **don't be so u., everyone else is enjoying themselves** ne sois pas aussi crispé, tout le monde s'amuse **3** *(conventional) (parents, attitude)* dur, strict **4** *Am Fam (excellent)* super, génial, -aux

up-to-date ADJ *(very recent)* récent; *(method, equipment, technology)* moderne, sophistiqué; *(person)* qui est dans le vent *ou* à la mode; *(information, views)* à jour; **to keep one's files/accounts u.** tenir ses fichiers/comptes à jour; **to bring sb u. on sth** mettre qn à jour sur qch; **to get the figures u.** mettre les chiffres à jour

up-to-the-minute ADJ *(news, information)* de dernière minute; *(style)* dernier cri *inv*

uptown ['ʌp'taʊn] *esp Am* ADV dans les quartiers résidentiels de la ville
▸ N les quartiers *mpl* résidentiels; **u. society** les milieux chics

upturn[1] ['ʌptɜːn] N amélioration *f*, *(in business, economy)* redressement *m*, reprise *f*

upturn[2] [ʌp'tɜːn] VT renverser

upturned ['ʌptɜːnd] ADJ **1** *(upside down)* *(boat, bowl)* renversé **2** *(nose)* retroussé; **he gazed down at her u. face** il contemplait son visage, qu'elle tenait levé vers lui

upward ['ʌpwəd] ADJ montant, ascendant; **their u. progress was halted by ...** leur ascension fut stoppée par ...; **u. tendency** *or* **movement** *(of prices etc)* tendance *f* à la hausse, mouvement de hausse; **u. movement** *(of piston)* mouvement *m* ascensionnel; **u. slope** pente *f* ascendante; **u. trend** tendance ascensionnelle
▸ ADV = **upwards**
▸▸ **u. mobility** ascension *f* sociale

upward-compatible ADJ *Comput* compatible vers le haut

upwardly ['ʌpwədlɪ] ADV **to be u. mobile** *(in society)* avoir la possibilité de s'élever dans la société; **the u. mobile** = les gens qui montent dans l'échelle sociale

upwards ['ʌpwədz] ADV *(to move, climb etc)* vers le haut; **to look u.** regarder en haut; **to put sth face u. on the table** mettre qch à l'endroit sur la table; **lying face u.** *(person)* couché sur le dos; **from £100 u.** à partir de 100 livres; **it costs u. of £100** ça coûte plus de 100 livres; **u. of 500 pupils** plus de 500 élèves; **children from ten (years) u.** des enfants à partir de dix ans; *Comput* **u. compatible** compatible avec les versions suivantes, compatible vers le haut

upwind ['ʌpwɪnd] **ADV** *(to sail)* contre le vent; *(to be)* contre le vent, au vent; **to be u. of an animal** être au vent d'un animal

Ural ['jʊərəl] **N the U. (river)** l'Oural *m*; **the U. mountains, the Urals** les monts *mpl* Oural, l'Oural

uranium [jʊ'reɪnɪəm] **N** *Chem* uranium *m*

Uranus [jʊ'reɪnəs, 'jʊərənəs] **N** *Astron* Uranus *f*; *Myth* Uranus *m*

urban ['ɜːbən] **ADJ** urbain
▸▸ **u. areas** agglomérations *fpl* urbaines; **u. clearway** rue *f* à stationnement interdit (en ville); *Aut* **u. cycle** cycle *m* urbain; **u. decay** dégradation *f* urbaine; **u. expressway** voie *f* rapide urbaine; *Aut* **u. fuel consumption** consommation *f* en ville; **u. guerilla** guerilla *f* des villes; **u. legend, u. myth** légende *f*, faux fait *m* divers; **u. planner** urbaniste *mf*; **u. renewal** rénovations *fpl* urbaines; **u. sprawl** étalement *m* urbain; **the u. sprawl of the London suburbs** la banlieue de Londres interminable

> Attention: ne pas confondre avec **urbane**.

urbane [ɜː'beɪn] **ADJ** *(person)* courtois, d'une politesse raffinée; *(wit, joke)* raffiné

> Attention: ne pas confondre avec **urban**.

urbanely [ɜː'beɪnlɪ] **ADV** courtoisement, avec urbanité

urbanism ['ɜːbənɪz(ə)m] **N** urbanisme *m*

urbanite ['ɜːbənaɪt] **N** *esp Am* citadin, -ine

urbanity [ɜː'bænɪtɪ] **N** urbanité *f*, courtoisie *f*

urbanization [ɜːbənaɪ'zeɪʃən] **N** urbanisation *f*

urbanize ['ɜːbənaɪz] **VT** urbaniser

urchin ['ɜːtʃɪn] **N** *(street)* **u.** galopin *m*; *esp Hum (child)* gamin, -ine

Urdu ['ʊədu:] **N** *Ling* ourdou *m*

urea [jʊ'ri:ə] **N** *Chem* urée *f*

ureter [jʊ'ri:tər] **N** *Anat* uretère *m*

urethra [jʊ'ri:θrə] **N** *Anat* urètre *m*

urge [ɜːdʒ] **N** *(desire)* envie *f*, *Psy* pulsion *f*; **to have an irresistible u. to do sth** avoir une envie irrésistible de faire qch; **to have a powerful u. to succeed** avoir très envie de réussir; **he's lost the u. to win** il a perdu l'envie *ou* la rage de gagner; **I had an u. to hit him** j'ai eu envie de le frapper; **I'll let you know if I ever get the u.** je te le dirai si j'en ai envie *ou* si ça me chante; *Fam* **when I get the u.** quand j'ai envie; *Fam* **the bottle's there, help yourself if you get the u.** la bouteille est là, servez-vous si ça vous dit
VT 1 *(try to persuade)* **to u. sb to do sth** conseiller vivement à qn de faire; **he urged me not to do it** il m'a vivement conseillé de ne pas le faire; **I urged him to accept** je lui ai vivement conseillé d'accepter; **they urged us to give up, but in vain** ils ont insisté pour que nous abandonnions, mais en vain
2 *(recommend earnestly)* **to u. caution** recommander *ou* conseiller la prudence; **to u. peace on the nations of the world** exhorter les nations du monde à la paix; **to u. that sth be done** recommander *ou* conseiller de faire qch
3 *(goad, encourage etc)* **to u. a horse forward** pousser un cheval; **he urged his men into battle** il poussa ses hommes dans la bataille
▸ **urge on VT SEP** *(person, team, runner)* encourager; *(horse)* pousser; **to u. sb on to do sth** pousser qn à faire qch

urgency ['ɜːdʒənsɪ] **N** urgence *f*; **it's a matter of u.** il y a urgence, c'est urgent; **could you do this as a matter of the utmost u.?** pourriez-vous faire ceci de toute urgence?; **there was a note of u. in her voice** il y avait

quelque chose de pressant dans sa voix; **what's all the u.?** qu'y a-t-il de si urgent?; **there's no u.** ce n'est pas urgent, il n'y a pas urgence; **he shows no sense of u.** il ne se presse pas

urgent ['ɜːdʒənt] **ADJ** *(need, case, delivery)* urgent; *(meeting, treatment, solution, tone)* d'urgence; **to be in u. need of sth** avoir un besoin pressant de qch; **I was in u. need of a drink** il me fallait absolument quelque chose à boire; **the matter is u.** c'est urgent; **this is u.** c'est une urgence, c'est urgent; **just how u. is it?** mais est-ce vraiment urgent?; **just how u. is it that you should be there tomorrow?** qu'y a-t-il de si urgent qui exige que tu y sois demain?; **the doctor had an u. call** le médecin a été appelé d'urgence; *Fml* **at their u. request** sur leurs instances pressantes

urgently ['ɜːdʒəntlɪ] **ADV** d'urgence; **a doctor is u. required** on demande un médecin d'urgence; **to press u. for sth** réclamer qch de façon urgente *ou* instamment; **they u. called a meeting** ils ont convoqué une réunion d'urgence

uric ['jʊərɪk] **ADJ** *(acid)* urique

urinal ['jʊərɪn(ə)l, jʊ'raɪn(ə)l] **N** urinoir *m*; **the urinals** l'urinoir

urinary ['jʊərɪnərɪ] **ADJ** *Anat* urinaire; **u. tract infection** infection *f* urinaire

urinate ['jʊərɪneɪt] **VI** uriner

urine ['jʊərɪn] **N** urine *f*, *Med* urines *fpl*
▸▸ **u. sample** échantillon *m* d'urine

URL [ju:ɑːr'el] **N** *Comput* (*abbr* **uniform resource locator**) (adresse *f*) URL *m*

urn [ɜːn] **N** urne *f*, *(tea)* **u.** fontaine *f* à thé

urogenital [jʊərəʊ'dʒenɪt(ə)l] **ADJ** *Anat* urogénital, -aux

urological [jʊərəʊ'lɒdʒɪk(ə)l] **ADJ** urologique

urologist [jʊ'rɒlədʒɪst] **N** urologue *mf*

urology [jʊ'rɒlədʒɪ] **N** *Med* urologie *f*

Ursa ['ɜːsə] **N**
▸▸ *Astron* **U. Major** la Grande Ourse; *Astron* **U. Minor** la Petite Ourse

urticaria [ɜːtɪ'keərɪə] **N** *Med* urticaire *f*

Uruguay ['jʊərəgwaɪ] **N** Uruguay *m*

Uruguayan [jʊərə'gwaɪən] **ADJ** uruguayen **N** Uruguayen, -enne

US [ju:'es] **N** (*abbr* **United States**) USA *mpl* **ADJ** *(forces, officials etc)* américain; **US dollar** dollar *m* américain

US PERS PRON OBJECTIVE CASE 1 *(unstressed)* [əs] nous; **he sees us** il nous voit; **in front of/behind us** devant/derrière nous; **he gave it to us** il nous l'a donné; **tell us** dis-nous; **he wrote us a letter** il nous a écrit une lettre; **he stayed with us a month** il est resté chez nous pendant un mois; **there are three of us** nous sommes trois; **those of us who were left ...** ceux d'entre nous qui restaient ...
VOIR GRAMMAIRE A27; B18–19 **2** *(stressed)* [ʌs] nous; **that concerns us alone** cela ne regarde que nous; **between them and us** entre eux et nous; **as for us Englishmen** quant à nous autres Anglais; **he couldn't believe that it was us** il ne pouvait pas croire que c'était nous **3** *Fam (me)* **let's have a look** fais-moi voir; **give us a bit** donnez-m'en un peu

USA [ju:es'eɪ] **N 1** (*abbr* **United States of America**) USA *mpl* **2** *abbr* **United States Army**

usable ['ju:zəb(ə)l] **ADJ** utilisable, employable

USAF [ju:eseɪ'ef] **N** *abbr* **United States Air Force**

usage ['ju:sɪdʒ] **N 1** *(use)* utilisation *f*, **the machine wasn't designed for such heavy u.** la machine n'avait pas été conçue pour une

utilisation aussi intensive; **this book has had some rough u.** ce livre a été maltraité **2** *(custom)* usage *m*; **an old u.** une vieille coutume; **sanctified by u.** consacré par l'usage **3** *Ling* usage *m*; **words in everyday u.** mots d'usage courant; **it's not in current u.** ce n'est pas dans l'usage courant; **a book on modern English u.** un livre sur les usages de l'anglais moderne; **it's not a u. I'm familiar with** ce n'est pas un usage que je connais

usance ['ju:səns] **N** *Banking, Fin (time limit)* usance *f*; **at thirty days' u.** à usance de trente jours
▸▸ **u. bill** effet *m* à usance

USB [ju:es'bi:] **N** *Comput* (*abbr* **universal serial bus**) norme *f* USB, port *m* série universel
▸▸ **U. cable** câble *m* USB; **U. port** port USB

USE¹ [ju:s]

> emploi **1** ▪ utilisation **1** ▪ usage **1, 2** ▪ utilité **3**

N 1 *(utilization)* emploi *m*, utilisation *f*; **the u. of steel in building** l'emploi de l'acier dans la construction; **one of the main uses of steel** un des principaux emplois de l'acier; **to make u. of sth** *(tool, equipment)* se servir de qch; *(word, material)* utiliser *ou* employer qch; **to make good u. of sth, to put sth to good u.** faire bon usage de qch; **I'll find a u. for it** ça peut servir; **a word in everyday u.** un mot d'usage courant; **the word is not in u.** any more ce mot ne s'emploie plus *ou* est désuet; **not in u., out of u.** *(on sign)* hors service; **for u. in case of fire** à employer en cas d'incendie; **for u. in schools** à l'usage des écoles; **directions** *or* **instructions for u.** mode *m* d'emploi; *Pharm* **for external u.** pour usage externe; **to improve with u.** s'améliorer à l'usage
2 *(ability to use)* jouissance *f*, usage *m*; *Law* usufruit *m*; **to have full u. of one's faculties** jouir de toutes ses facultés; **to lose the u. of a leg** perdre l'usage d'une jambe; **to have the u. of the bathroom** avoir le droit de se servir de la salle de bain; **you can have the u. of my car while I'm in London** tu pourras te servir de ma voiture pendant que je serai à Londres
3 *(usefulness)* utilité *f*, **to be of u.** être utile (**for sth** à qch); **can I be of any u. (to you)?** puis-je vous être utile à quelque chose?; **it's of no u. to me** je n'en ai pas besoin; **it's not much u.** cela ne sert pas à grand-chose; *Fam* **a fat lot of u. that'll be to you!** si tu crois que ça va t'avancer!; *Fam Iron* **you're a lot of u.!** je te remercie de ton aide!; *Fam* **he's no u.** c'est un incapable; **he's no u. in bed** au lit, il est nul; **to have no u. for sth** ne savoir que faire de qch; **I've no further u. for it** je n'en ai plus besoin; *Fam* **I have no u. for people like that** ces gens-là ne m'intéressent pas; **it was no u.** c'était inutile; **it's no u. discussing the question** inutile de discuter la question; **it's no u. crying** cela ne sert à rien de pleurer; **it's no u. my talking** ce que je dis ne sert à rien; **it's no use(, I can't do it)!** c'est peine perdue(, je ne peux pas le faire)!; **is it any u. writing to him?** est-ce que ça servirait à quelque chose de lui écrire?; **what u. would that be?** à quoi cela servirait-il?; **what's the u. of doing it/of going there?** à quoi bon le faire/y aller?; **what's the u.!, I give up!** à quoi bon! j'abandonne!
4 = usage

USE² [ju:z]

> se servir de **1, 3** ▪ utiliser **1** ▪ employer **1** ▪ consommer **3**

VT 1 *(object)* se servir de, utiliser; *(word)* employer, utiliser; **to be used for sth** servir à qch; **are you using this knife?** est-ce que tu te sers de ce couteau?; **I used the money to rebuild my garage** j'ai utilisé *ou* employé l'argent pour reconstruire mon garage; **the frying pan will last a long time if you u. it carefully** cette poêle à frire durera longtemps si vous en prenez soin; **do you mind if I u. the toilet?** puis-je utiliser vos toilettes?; **this word is no longer used** ce mot est désuet *ou* n'est plus usité; **the term is used more generally to refer to …** on utilise ce terme de manière plus générale pour désigner …; **word used figuratively** mot employé au (sens) figuré; **to u. one's intelligence/intuition** faire marcher son intelligence/intuition; **u. your head!** fais marcher ta cervelle!; **u. your eyes!** ouvrez les yeux!; **to u. force/violence** avoir recours à la force/la violence; **to u. diplomacy** user de diplomatie; **to u. discretion** agir avec discrétion; **to u. one's influence** user de son influence; **to u. every means (at one's disposal)** employer tous les moyens (à sa disposition); *Fam* **I could u. some coffee/a holiday** j'ai besoin d'un café/de vacances

2 *(exploit)* **I feel I've been used** j'ai l'impression qu'on se sert de moi; **she doesn't care about him, she's just using him** elle ne l'aime pas, elle ne fait que se servir de lui

3 *(consume) (petrol, electricity etc)* consommer; **we've been using too much electricity** nous avons consommé trop d'électricité

4 *Arch (treat)* **to u. sb well** bien traiter qn; **to u. sb badly** maltraiter qn; **he had a reputation for using his workers well** il avait la réputation de bien traiter ses employés.

V AUX [juːst] **when we were children we used to play together** quand nous étions enfants, nous jouions ensemble; **my father used to tell me that …** mon père me disait toujours que …; **it used to be a pleasant town to live in** c'était autrefois une ville agréable à habiter; **things aren't what they used to be** les choses ne sont plus ce qu'elles étaient; **she used not** *or* **usedn't to like oysters** avant, elle n'aimait pas les huîtres; **I used not to like him, I didn't u. to like him** avant, je ne l'aimais pas; **do you smoke? – I do now, but I didn't u.** est-ce que vous fumez? – je ne fumais pas mais je m'y suis mis; **do you smoke? – I used to** est-ce que vous fumez? – j'ai arrêté; **do you travel much? – I used to** voyagez beaucoup? – autrefois, oui VOIR GRAMMAIRE A61; B30

▸ **use up** VT SEP *(food, milk)* finir; *(funds, resources)* épuiser; *(energy)* dépenser la totalité de; *(paint, hot water, ideas, money, resources, time)* utiliser la totalité de; **she had used up all her strength** elle avait épuisé toutes ses forces; **u. up the leftovers to make soup** utiliser *ou* accommoder les restes pour faire un potage

> Note that the French verb **user** is a false friend. Its most common meaning is **to wear out**.

use-by date N date f limite de consommation

used ADJ **1** [juːzd] *(book, car, clothes)* d'occasion; *(worn)* usé, usagé; *(stamp)* oblitéré, qui a déjà servi; **hardly u.** presque neuf **2** [juːst] *(accustomed)* **u. to (doing) sth** habitué à (faire) qch; **to get u. to sth/sb** s'habituer *ou* se faire à qch/qn; **to get sb u. to sth** habituer qn à qch; **I'm not u. to it** je n'en ai pas l'habitude; **you'll get u. to it in time** vous vous y ferez à la longue; **I'm not u. to being spoken to like that!** je n'ai pas l'habitude qu'on me parle comme ça!

useful [ˈjuːsfʊl] ADJ **1** *(of use)* utile; **this book was very u. to me** ce livre m'a été très utile *ou* m'a rendu grand service; **it's u. to know** c'est bon à savoir; **it will come in very u.** cela

rendra bien service; **a u. man to know** une relation utile, un homme qu'il est bon d'avoir dans ses relations; **to make oneself u.** se rendre utile; *Iron* **that's u.!** formidable! **2** *(skilful)* **he plays a u. game of chess** il joue bien aux échecs; **to be u. with one's fists** savoir se servir de ses poings; **to be u. with a gun** savoir manier un fusil

▸▸ **u. life** *(of product)* vie f utile; **this machine has a u. life of ten years** cette machine a une durée de vie de dix ans

usefully [ˈjuːsfəlɪ] ADV utilement; **her time had been u. employed** elle s'était occupée utilement; **one might u. write a book on …** il serait fort utile qu'on écrive un livre sur …; **is there anything I can u. do?** puis-je faire quelque chose pour me rendre utile?

usefulness [ˈjuːsfʊlnɪs] N utilité f, **it has outlived its u.** cela ne sert plus à rien

useless [ˈjuːslɪs] ADJ **1** *(not useful)* inutile; *(unusable)* inutilisable; *(no good)* nul; *(remedy)* inefficace; **I hope I haven't been completely u. to you** j'espère que je ne t'ai pas été complètement inutile; **to be full of u. information** être riche en informations inutiles; **a map without a key is u.** une carte sans légende est inutilisable; *Fam* **to be worse than u.** *(of person)* être au-dessous de tout; *(of object)* ne rien valoir du tout, *Sl* ne pas valoir un pet de lapin

2 *(incompetent) (person)* bon à rien, incompétent, nul; **I'm u. at languages** je suis nul en langues; **he's u. in bed** au lit, il est nul; **a u. person** un bon à rien, f une bonne à rien

3 *(futile)* inutile; **it was u. to resist** il était inutile de résister; **it would be u. to make further requests** cela ne servirait à rien de faire d'autres demandes; **give up, it's u.!** laisse tomber, ça ne sert à rien!; **it's u. even trying to discuss it** ce n'est même pas la peine d'essayer d'en discuter

uselessly [ˈjuːslɪslɪ] ADV inutilement

uselessness [ˈjuːslɪsnɪs] N inutilité f, *(of person)* incompétence f, *(of remedy)* inefficacité f, **his general u.** sa nullité

Usenet [ˈjuːznet] N *Comput* Usenet m

user [ˈjuːzər] N *(of road, means of transport)* usager, -ère; *(of device, computer, dictionary)* utilisateur, -trice; *(of telephone)* abonné, -ée; **bus users** les usagers du bus

▸▸ *Comput* **u. group** club m d'utilisateurs; *Comput* **u. identification** identification f de l'utilisateur; *Comput* **u. identification code** code m d'identification de l'utilisateur; *Comput* **u. language** langage m utilisateur; *Comput* **u. manual** manuel m d'utilisation; *Comput* **u. name** nom m de l'utilisateur; *Comput* **u. network** réseau m d'utilisateurs; *Mktg* **u. panel** panel m d'utilisateurs; *Comput* **u. software** logiciel m utilisateur; *Comput* **u. support** assistance f à l'utilisateur

user-definable ADJ *Comput (characters, keys)* définissable par l'utilisateur

user-defined [-dɪˈfaɪnd] ADJ *Comput* défini par l'utilisateur

▸▸ **u. key** touche f personnalisée

user-friendliness N *(of software, computer)* convivialité f, *(of keyboard)* confort m d'emploi; *(of machine, dictionary, manual)* facilité f d'utilisation

user-friendly ADJ *(software, computer)* convivial, -aux; *(keyboard)* confortable, facile d'emploi; *(machine, technology, instruction manual, dictionary)* facile à utiliser

user-interface N *Comput etc* interface f utilisateur

user-programmable ADJ *Comput* programmable par l'utilisateur

user-specific ADJ spécifique à l'utilisateur

U-shaped ADJ en U; *Geog* **U-shaped valley** vallée f (à profil) en U

usher [ˈʌʃər] N *Law (in court)* (huissier m) audiencier m; *Theat, Cin* placeur m; *(at wedding)* garçon m d'honneur

VT I was ushered into the presence of the boss je fus introduit auprès du directeur; **they hastily ushered him away/out** ils le firent s'éloigner/sortir à la hâte

▸ **usher in** VT SEP introduire, faire entrer; **to u. in a new era** marquer le début d'une nouvelle époque

usherette [ʌʃəˈret] N *Theat, Cin* ouvreuse f

USM [juːesˈem] N **1** *(abbr* United States Mail) = service m des postes américain **2** *Mil abbr* United States Marines **3** *Fin abbr* United States Mint **4** *Fin (abbr* unlisted securities market) second marché m

USN [juːesˈen] N *(abbr* United States Navy) marine f nationale américaine

USP [juːesˈpiː] N *Mktg (abbr* unique selling point *or* proposition) proposition f unique de vente

USS [juːesˈes] N *(abbr* United States Ship) = initiales précédant le nom des navires américains; **U. Nimitz** le Nimitz

USSR [juːeses'ɑːr] N *Formerly (abbr* Union of Soviet Socialist Republics) URSS f

usual [ˈjuːʒʊəl] ADJ habituel; **at the u. time** à l'heure habituelle; **it's the u. practice** c'est la pratique courante; **I didn't get my u. bus this morning** je n'ai pas pris le bus que je prends d'habitude ce matin; **it wasn't the u. postman** ce n'était pas notre facteur habituel *ou Fam* de d'habitude; **u. time, u. place, OK?** même heure, même endroit, d'accord?; **she's back to her u. self again** elle a retrouvé la forme; **you're not your u. cheery self today** tu as perdu ton sourire aujourd'hui; **it's quite u. for that sort of thing to happen** ces choses-là arrivent fréquemment; **it's u. (for that to happen) with these machines** ça arrive fréquemment avec ces machines; **it's not u. to have to wait this long** d'habitude on n'attend pas aussi longtemps; **it's u. to pay in advance** il est d'usage de payer d'avance; **earlier/later than u.** plus tôt/plus tard que d'habitude; **more/less than u.** plus/moins que d'habitude; **as u., Fam as per u.,** comme d'habitude; **business as u.** *(on sign)* ouvert pendant les réparations; **despite recent events it was business as u.** malgré les récents événements, la vie continuait comme si de rien n'était

N *Fam (in bar)* **(are you having) your u.?** comme d'habitude?; **the u. please, Jim** comme d'habitude s'il te plaît, Jim

usually [ˈjuːʒʊ(ə)lɪ] ADV d'habitude, habituellement; **I u. get up at seven** d'habitude je me lève à sept heures, je me lève habituellement à sept heures; **he was more than u. polite** il s'est montré encore plus poli que d'habitude; **it's not u. that difficult** ce n'est pas aussi difficile que ça d'habitude *ou* habituellement; **she's not u. like that** d'habitude elle n'est pas comme ça

usufruct [ˈjuːzjʊfrʌkt] N *Law* usufruit m (**of** de)

usufructuary [juːzjʊˈfrʌktjərɪ] ADJ, N *Law* usufruitier, -ière

▸▸ **u. right** droit m usufructuaire

usurer [ˈjuːʒərər] N usurier, -ière

usurious [juːˈzjʊərɪəs] ADJ *(interest etc)* usuraire

usurp [juːˈzɜːp, -ˈsɜːp] VT *(throne, title)* usurper (**from** sur)

usurpation [juːzəˈpeɪʃən, -sɜː-] N usurpation f

usurper [jʊˈzɜːpər, -sɜː-] N usurpateur, -trice

usury [ˈjuːʒʊrɪ] N usure f, **that's u.!** c'est du vol!

Ut *abbr* Utah

utensil [juːˈtens(ə)l] N ustensile *m*; **(set of) kitchen utensils** batterie *f* de cuisine

uterine [ˈjuːtəraɪn] ADJ utérin

uterus [ˈjuːtərəs] N *Anat* utérus *m*

utilitarian [juːtɪlɪˈteərɪən] ADJ, N utilitaire *mf*

utilitarianism [juːtɪlɪˈteərɪənɪz(ə)m] N utilitarisme *m*

utility [juːˈtɪlɪtɪ] N **1** *(usefulness)* utilité *f* **2** **(public) utilities, utilities sector** secteur *m* des services, services *mpl* publics
▸▸ **u. car** voiture *f* utilitaire; **u. furniture** = meubles *mpl* fonctionnels et peu chers; *Sport* **u. player** joueur, -euse polyvalent(e); *Comput* **u. program** programme *m* (utilitaire), utilitaire *m*; **u. room** ≃ buanderie *f*; *Am St Exch* **u. stocks** valeurs *fpl* de services publics; **u. vehicle** véhicule *m* utilitaire

utilizable [juːtɪˈlaɪzəb(ə)l] ADJ utilisable

utilization [juːtɪl(a)ɪˈzeɪʃ(ə)n] N utilisation *f*, **better u. of resources** meilleure utilisation *ou* meilleur emploi des ressources

utilize [ˈjuːtɪlaɪz] VT utiliser, se servir de; *(take advantage of) (opportunity, situation)* tirer profit de

utmost [ˈʌtməʊst] ADJ **1** *(greatest)* **the u.** le plus grand; **the u. poverty** la misère la plus noire; **with the u. contempt** avec le plus grand mépris; **it is of the u. importance that he should be present** il est absolument essentiel qu'il soit présent; **with the u. ease** avec la plus grande facilité, avec une extrême facilité; **it was only with the u. difficulty that we were able to persuade them** nous avons eu toutes les peines du monde à les convaincre
2 *(furthest)* **the u. ends of the earth** les confins *mpl* *ou* les extrémités *fpl* de la terre
▸ N **1** **to live life to the u.** profiter pleinement de la vie; **to enjoy oneself to the u.** s'amuser au plus haut point; **to do sth to the u. of one's abilities** faire qch au maximum de ses capacités; **I'll help you to the u. of my ability** je ferai tout ce qui est en mon pouvoir pour vous aider; **to do one's u.** to achieve sth faire tout son possible pour arriver à qch; **she tried her u. to persuade him** elle a fait tout ce qu'elle a pu pour le persuader
2 **that's the u. we can offer** c'est le maximum que nous puissions offrir; **$50,000 at the u.** 50 000 dollars au grand maximum

Utopia [juːˈtəʊpɪə] N utopie *f*

Utopian [juːˈtəʊpɪən] ADJ utopique; **U. socialism** socialisme *m* utopique
▸ N utopiste *mf*

utter [ˈʌtər] ADJ complet, -ète, absolu; **he's an u. stranger to me** il m'est complètement étranger; **it's u. madness** c'est de la folie totale *ou* pure; **we were in u. darkness** nous étions dans l'obscurité totale; **u. boredom** ennui *m* mortel; **u. poverty** la misère la plus noire; *Br Fam* **u. rubbish** *(goods)* de la pure camelote; *(nonsense)* des absurdités; **what u. rubbish!** quel tas de sottises!; **he's an u. fool** il est complètement idiot; **to my u. horror** comble de l'horreur; **to her u. amazement** à sa plus grande stupéfaction
▸ VT **1** *(cry)* jeter, pousser; *(word)* prononcer, dire; *(curse)* lancer; **I didn't u. a word** je n'ai pas desserré les dents; **never u. his name in her presence** il ne faut jamais prononcer son nom devant elle; **if you u. another sound you're going straight to bed!** et si je t'entends encore une fois tu vas directement au lit! **2** *(lies)* débiter **3** *Fml (counterfeit money)* émettre, mettre en circulation

utterance [ˈʌtərəns] N **1** *(what is said)* paroles *fpl*, propos *mpl*, mots *mpl*; *Ling* énoncé *m*; **what was his last u.?** quels ont été ses derniers mots?; **they taped the child's first utterances** ils ont enregistré les premiers mots de l'enfant; **his recent utterances in the national press** ses récentes déclarations dans la presse nationale **2** *(expression) (of sound)* expression *f*, **on her u. of his name** au moment où elle prononça son nom; **to give u. to one's feelings/a thought** exprimer ses sentiments/une pensée

utterly [ˈʌtəlɪ] ADV complètement, absolument; **u. stupid** d'une bêtise extrême

uttermost [ˈʌtəməʊst] ADJ, N = **utmost**

U-tube N tube *m* en U

U-turn N **1** *Aut* demi-tour *m*, *pl* demi-tours; **to make a U. faire** (un) demi-tour; **no U-turns** *(sign)* défense de faire demi-tour **2** *Fig* volte-face *f inv*, revirement *m*; **the government were accused of making a U. on health policy** le gouvernement a été accusé de faire volte-face en matière de politique de santé

UV [juːˈviː] ADJ *(abbr* **ultra-violet)** UV

uvula, *pl* **uvulas, uvulae** [ˈjuːvjələ, -əs, -iː] N *Anat* uvule *f*, luette *f*

uvular [ˈjuːvjələr] ADJ uvulaire

uxorious [ʌkˈsɔːrɪəs] ADJ *Fml (husband)* soumis

uxoriousness [ʌkˈsɔːrɪəsnɪs] N *Fml (of husband)* soumission *f* à sa femme

Uzbekistan [ʊzbekɪˈstɑːn] N Ouzbékistan *m*

V¹, v¹ [viː] N (letter) V, v m; **two v's** deux v; **to fly in a V formation** (of birds) voler en formant un V

V² Elec (abbr **volt(s)**) V

v²1 (abbr **verse**) v. **2** Law, Sport abbr **versus 3** (abbr **very**) t.

Va abbr **Virginia**

V & A [viːənˈeɪ] N Br (abbr **Victoria and Albert Museum**) = musée m d'arts décoratifs, à Londres

vac [væk] N Br Univ, Sch Fam vacances fpl

vacancy [ˈveɪkənsɪ] N **1** (position) place f vacante, poste m vacant, vacance f; **we have a v. for ...** (job advert) nous recherchons ...; **to fill a v.** pourvoir un poste vacant; **v. on the board** siège m à pourvoir au conseil d'administration **2** (at hotel) chambre f libre; (at camp site) place f libre; **no vacancies** complet **3** (of expression) caractère m absent; **a look of sheer v.** un visage dénué de toute expression

Note that the French word **vacances** is a false friend. It means **holiday**.

vacant [ˈveɪkənt] ADJ **1** (empty) vide; (hotel room, seat, lavatory) libre; (flat) inoccupé; (official post) vacant, à pourvoir; **situations v.** (newspaper column) offres fpl d'emploi; **v. site** (for sale) terrain m à vendre **2** (mind) vide; (look) (absent-minded) distrait, vague, sans expression; (stupid) niais, stupide; **with a v. expression** le regard perdu **3** (time) libre
▸▸ Am **v. lot** terrain vague; Br **v. possession** libre possession f

vacantly [ˈveɪkəntlɪ] ADV (to gaze etc) (absentmindedly) d'un air distrait ou absent; (with lack of intelligence) d'un regard perdu; (stupidly) d'un air stupide

vacate [vəˈkeɪt] VT (seat, flat, hotel room, job) quitter; (room) libérer, quitter; Law **to v. the premises** vider les lieux

vacation [vəˈkeɪʃən] N **1** esp Am (holiday) vacances fpl; **during** or **in the v.** pendant les vacances; **we spent the v. travelling around Europe** nous avons voyagé en Europe pendant nos vacances; **to take a v.** prendre des vacances; **to be on v.** être en vacances **2** Br Univ (recess) vacances fpl, Law vacations fpl, vacances judiciaires; **over the v.** pendant les vacances **3** Fml (leaving) (of premises) évacuation f; **v. of office** démission f
▸ VI Am prendre ou passer ses vacances (**at, in** à, en)
▸▸ Am **v. center** club m de vacances; Am **v. home** résidence f secondaire; Am Admin **v. leave** congé m annuel; Am **v. resort** camp m de vacances; Am **v. work** travail m effectué pendant les vacances (par un étudiant)

vacationist, vacationer [veɪˈkeɪʃənɪst, -ər] N Am vacancier, -ière; (in summer) estivant, -ante

vaccinate [ˈvæksɪneɪt] VT Med vacciner (**against** contre); **to get vaccinated** se faire vacciner

vaccination [væksɪˈneɪʃən] N Med vaccination f; **smallpox v.** vaccination contre la variole

vaccine [ˈvæksiːn] N Med vaccin m

vaccinee [væksɪˈniː] N Am personne f vaccinée

vacillate [ˈvæsɪleɪt] VI hésiter (**between** entre)

vacillating [ˈvæsɪleɪtɪŋ] ADJ (undecided) irrésolu, indécis
▸ N (indecision) indécision f, irrésolution f

vacillation [væsɪˈleɪʃən] N indécision f

vacuity [væˈkjuːɪtɪ] N vacuité f; **vacuities** bêtises fpl, niaiseries fpl

vacuous [ˈvækjʊəs] ADJ (look) hébété, vide d'expression; (remark, laugh) niais, bête; (book, film) idiot; **he's completely v.** c'est un parfait idiot; **what an utterly v. thing to say** quelle niaiserie, quelle idiotie

vacuously [ˈvækjʊəslɪ] ADV bêtement

vacuousness [ˈvækjʊəsnɪs] N (of laugh) bêtise f, niaiserie f; (of remark, debate) vacuité f

vacuum, pl **vacua, vacuums** [ˈvækjʊm, -jʊə, -jʊmz] N **1** Phys vide m, vacuum m; Fig vide; **to produce** or **create a v.** faire le vide; **nature abhors a v.** la nature a horreur du vide; Fig **a cultural/political v.** un vide sur le plan culturel/politique; **to live in a v.** vivre en vase clos; **a v. of ideas** une pénurie d'idées **2** (machine) aspirateur m; **to give the carpet a v.** passer l'aspirateur sur la moquette **3** Aut (of venturi) dépression f
▸ VT (carpet) passer l'aspirateur sur; (room) passer l'aspirateur dans
▸▸ **v. advance** avance f à dépression; Am **v. bottle** (bouteille f) Thermos® f, **v. chamber** chambre f à dépression; **v. cleaner** aspirateur; Br **v. flask** (bouteille) Thermos®; **v. pack** emballage m sous vide; **v. pump** pompe f à vide; **v. tank** réservoir m à dépression; Am **v. tube** tube m électronique ou à vide

vacuuming [ˈvækjʊmɪŋ] N **to do the v.** passer l'aspirateur

vacuum-packed ADJ emballé sous vide

vade mecum [vɑːdɪˈmeɪkəm] N vade-mecum m inv, aide-mémoire m inv

vagabond [ˈvægəbɒnd] N vagabond, -onde
▸ ADJ vagabond, errant

vagary [ˈveɪgərɪ] N caprice m; **the vagaries of fashion/the weather** les caprices de la mode/du temps

vagina [vəˈdʒaɪnə] N Anat vagin m

vaginal [vəˈdʒaɪn(ə)l] ADJ Anat vaginal, -aux
▸▸ **v. discharge** pertes fpl blanches; **v. examination** examen m vaginal; **v. smear** frottis m vaginal; **to have a v. smear taken** se faire faire un frottis vaginal

vagrancy [ˈveɪgrənsɪ] N Law vagabondage m; **to be arrested for v.** être arrêté pour vagabondage

vagrant [ˈveɪgrənt] N vagabond, -onde
▸ ADJ errant

vague [veɪg] ADJ (person, look, reply) vague; (impression, memory) vague, imprécis, confus; (shape, outline) flou, imprécis; **to bear a v. resemblance to sb/sth** ressembler vaguement à qn/qch; **there's been some v. talk of ...** on a parlé vaguement de ...; **the conditions were left deliberately v.** les conditions ont été laissées délibérément vagues; **I haven't the vaguest idea** je n'en ai pas la moindre idée; **I had a v. idea that he was dead** j'avais vaguement l'idée qu'il était mort; **he was rather v. about the date** il s'est montré assez vague à propos de la date; **she was v. (about it)** elle est restée vague là-dessus

vaguely [ˈveɪglɪ] ADV (to look) d'un air vague; (to remember, express) vaguement, confusément; (to agree, resemble) vaguement; (slightly) légèrement; **to be v. reminiscent of ...** rappeler vaguement ...; **their music sounds v. like the Beatles** leur musique ressemble vaguement aux Beatles

vagueness [ˈveɪgnɪs] N caractère m vague, vague m, imprécision f; (of shape, outline, photograph) caractère flou; (of story, report, memory etc) manque m de précision

vain [veɪn] ADJ **1** (conceited) vaniteux, orgueilleux; **she was v. about her beauty** elle était fière de sa beauté **2** (unavailing) vain, inutile, stérile; **v. efforts** efforts mpl vains ou inutiles **v. promises** vaines promesses fpl, promesses vaines **3** (hope) vain; (pleasure) futile **4 in v.** en vain, vainement; **to labour in v.** travailler en vain, perdre sa peine; **her efforts were in v.** ses efforts ont été inutiles; **it was all in v.** c'était peine perdue; **to take God's name in v.** invoquer le nom de Dieu en vain; Fam **who's taking my name in v.?** qui est-ce qui parle de moi?

vainglorious [veɪnˈglɔːrɪəs] ADJ Fml vaniteux, orgueilleux

vaingloriously [veɪnˈglɔːrɪəslɪ] ADV Fml vaniteusement, orgueilleusement

vainglory [veɪnˈglɔːrɪ] N Fml vanité f, orgueil m

vainly [ˈveɪnlɪ] ADV **1** (uselessly) vainement, en vain **2** (conceitedly) vaniteusement, avec vanité

valance [ˈvæləns] N (on side of bed) frange f de lit; (for curtains) cantonnière f, lambrequin m; (on vehicle) tablier m, doublure f d'aile, bouclier m

valanced sheet [ˈvælənst] N housse f cache-sommier

vale [veɪl] N Arch, Lit vallée f, (small) vallon m; Fig **this v. of tears** cette vallée de larmes

valediction [vælɪˈdɪkʃən] N **1** (farewell)

adieu(x) *m(pl)* **2** *Am Univ, Sch* = **valedictory** N

valedictorian [vælɪdɪk'tɔ:rɪən] N *Am Univ, Sch* membre *m* d'une promotion qui prononce le discours d'adieu

valedictory [vælɪ'dɪktərɪ] ADJ *(address, dinner)* d'adieu
   N *Am Univ, Sch (at graduation)* discours *m* d'adieu

valence ['veɪləns] N *Am* = **valency**

valency ['veɪlənsɪ] N *Br Chem* valence *f*

valentine ['væləntaɪn] N **1** (St) Valentine's Day *(14 February)* la Saint-Valentin **2** *(card)* carte *f* de la Saint-Valentin; *(recipient of card)* = celui/celle qui reçoit une carte envoyée le jour de la Saint-Valentin; **will you be my v.?** = phrase *f* écrite sur les cartes de la Saint-Valentin pour exprimer ses sentiments amoureux à l'égard du/de la destinataire; **George is my v.** c'est George que j'aime
   ► ► **v. card** carte de la Saint-Valentin

valerian [və'leərɪən] N *Bot, Pharm* valériane *f*

valet ['væleɪ, 'vælɪt] N *(manservant)* valet *m* de chambre; *(in hotel)* = employé *m* qui s'occupe de l'entretien des vêtements des clients; *Am (who parks car)* = employé d'un hôtel ou d'un restaurant qui se charge de garer les voitures des clients
   VT *(valeted* ['vælɪtɪd]) **to v. a car** laver et nettoyer une voiture; **can I have my suit valeted?** puis-je faire nettoyer mon costume?;
valeting service *(for clothes)* service *m* de nettoyage des vêtements; *(for car)* service de lavage et de nettoyage
   ► ► **v. parking** *(sign)* service de voiturier; **v. service** *(in hotel)* pressing *m* de l'hôtel

valetudinarian [vælɪtjuː'neərɪən] ADJ, N valétudinaire *mf*

Valhalla [væl'hælə] N *Myth* Walhalla *m*

valiant ['vælɪənt] ADJ courageux, vaillant, valeureux; **to make a v. effort** faire un courageux effort (**to do** pour faire)

valiantly ['vælɪəntlɪ] ADV courageusement, vaillamment, valeureusement

valid ['vælɪd] ADJ *(contract, document etc)* valide, valable; *(passport)* en règle; *(reason, objection)* valable, recevable; **ticket v. for three months** billet bon pour trois mois; **no longer v.** *(ticket, passport etc)* périmé

> Note that the French word **valide** also means **able-bodied**.

validate ['vælɪdeɪt] VT **1** *(act, contract, ticket)* valider, rendre valable; *Am* **to v. an election** valider une élection **2** *(prove) (theory)* confirmer **3** *Comput* valider

validation [vælɪ'deɪʃən] N **1** *(of act, contract)* validation *f* **2** *(of theory)* confirmation *f* **3** *Comput* validation *f*

validator ['vælɪdeɪtər] N *(for tickets)* cachet *m*

validity [və'lɪdɪtɪ] N *(of contract, document)* validité *f*; *(of argument)* force *f*, justesse *f*; *(of claim)* bien-fondé *m*; **these objections have no v.** ces objections ne sont pas fondées

validly ['vælɪdlɪ] ADV validement, valablement

valise [və'liːs, -iːz] N *Old-fashioned (suitcase)* valise *f*, *(hand luggage)* sac *m* de voyage

Valium® ['vælɪəm] N Valium® *m*; **to be on V.** être sous Valium®; **the doctor has put her on V.** le docteur l'a mise au Valium®

Valkyrie ['vælkɪrɪ] N *Myth* Walkyrie *f*, Valkyrie *f*

valley ['vælɪ] N **1** vallée *f*, *(small)* vallon *m*; **the Rhone V.** la vallée du Rhône **2** *Constr* noue *f*, *(of roof)* cornière *f*

valor ['vælər] N *Am* = **valour**

valorization [vælərɑɪ'zeɪʃən] N valorisation *f*

valorize ['vælərɑɪz] VT *Com, Fin* valoriser

valorous ['vælərəs] ADJ *Fml* valeureux, vaillant

valour, *Am* **valor** ['vælər] N courage *m*, vaillance *f*, bravoure *f*; **to be decorated for v.** *(of soldier, police officer etc)* être décoré pour son courage

valuable ['væljʊəb(ə)l] ADJ *(help, time)* précieux; *(object)* précieux, de valeur, de prix; **v. gift** cadeau *m* de valeur; **nothing v. was taken** aucun objet de valeur n'a été volé; **she has given years of v. service** elle a donné des années de bons et loyaux services
   NPL **valuables** objets *mpl* de valeur

valuation [væljʊ'eɪʃən] N *Fin* **1** *(setting of value)* évaluation *f*, estimation *f*, appréciation *f*; *Law* prisée *f* et estimation; *(by expert)* expertise *f*, rapport *m* d'expertise; **to get a v. of sth** faire expertiser qch; **to make a v. of the goods** faire l'expertise des marchandises **2** *(value) (of painting, house)* valeur *f* estimée; **the v. on the house was £50,000** la valeur estimée de la maison était de 50000 livres; **to set too high/too low a v. on goods** surestimer/sous-estimer des marchandises; **to take** *or* **accept sb at his/her own v.** estimer qn selon l'opinion qu'il a de lui-même/qu'elle a d'elle-même
   ► ► *Fin* **v. charge** taxation *f* à la valeur

valuator ['væljʊeɪtər] N = **valuer**

value ['væljuː] N **1** *(worth)* valeur *f*; **to be of v.** *(of jewellery etc)* avoir de la valeur; **to go up/down in v.** prendre/perdre de la valeur; **of great v.** de grande *ou* haute valeur; **your help/contribution was of great v.** votre aide/contribution a été très précieuse; **she has been of great v. to the company** elle a apporté une contribution précieuse à l'entreprise; **to be of great sentimental v.** avoir une grande valeur sentimentale; **of little v.** de peu de valeur; **to be of little v.** être sans grande valeur; **her advice/help was of little v.** ses conseils n'ont/son aide n'a pas été très utile(s); **of no v.** sans valeur; **it is nothing of any v.** ce n'est rien qui ait une quelconque valeur; **to lose v.,** **to fall in v.** se dévaluer, s'avilir; *Fin* se dévaloriser; **loss of v., fall in v.** dévalorisation *f*; **to set a v. on sth** *(evaluate)* évaluer qch; *Com* attribuer une cote de valeur à qch; **to set a high/low v. on sth** attribuer une haute/faible valeur à qch; **to set too high a v. on sth** attacher trop de valeur *ou* de prix à qch, surestimer qch; **he sets a very high v. on her** il estime que c'est une personne d'une grande valeur; **goods to the v. of ten pounds** marchandises d'une valeur de dix livres; **what will this do to the v. of property?** quel effet est-ce que ça va avoir sur le prix de l'immobilier?; **commercial** *or* **market v.** *(worth)* valeur marchande; *(price)* cours *m*; **replacement v.** valeur de remplacement; **it's good v.** c'est très avantageux; **at £2 it's very good v.** à 2 livres, c'est une bonne affaire *ou* c'est intéressant; **v. for money** *(heading on restaurant or wine review)* rapport *m* qualité/prix; **to get (good) v. for one's money** en avoir pour son argent; **he gives you v. for money** il vous en donne pour votre argent; **it's (good) v. for money** ça vaut le coup, ce n'est pas cher; **the large size gives you better v. (for your money)** le grand format est plus avantageux

2 *Math, Mus, Ling* valeur *f*; **let y have the v. 15** soit y égale 15; **to give full v. to each word** donner du poids à chaque mot

3 **values** *(standards)* valeurs *fpl*; **sense of values** sens *m* des valeurs; **moral values** valeurs morales; **according to a set of values** selon certains principes

   VT **1** *(evaluate) (goods)* évaluer, estimer, apprécier; *Com (assess value of)* expertiser; *(property, painting)* faire l'expertise de; **to get sth valued** faire expertiser qch, faire évaluer qch; **to v. a house at £100,000** évaluer une maison à 100 000 livres; **they valued the company at \$10 billion** ils ont estimé la valeur de la société à 10 milliards de dollars **2** *(appreciate) (person, thing)* tenir à, faire grand cas de; **to v. sb as a friend** tenir à *ou* apprécier qn en tant qu'ami; **if you v. your life** si vous tenez à la vie
   ► ► *Fin* **v. analysis** analyse *f* de valeur; *Mktg* **v. brand** marque *f* de valeur; *Com* **v. chain** chaîne *f* de valeur; *Fin* **v. for collection** valeur à l'encaissement; *Fin* **v. date** date *f* de valeur; *Fin* **v. day** jour *m* de valeur; *Fin* **v. engineering** analyse de valeur; *Fin* **v. in exchange** valeur d'échange, contre-valeur *f*, *pl* contre-valeurs; **v. judgement** jugement *m* de valeur; **v. marketing** marketing *m* de la valeur; *Fin* **v. at maturity** valeur à l'échéance; *Fin* **v. for money audit** = estimation *f* des performances d'une société à but non lucratif ou d'un service gouvernemental; *Fin* **v. in use** valeur d'usage

value-add N valeur *f* ajoutée

value-added ADJ *Fin (product, service etc)* à valeur ajoutée; **high v. product** produit *m* à haute valeur ajoutée
   ► ► *Comput* **v. network** réseau *m* à valeur ajoutée; *Br* **v. tax** taxe *f* à la valeur ajoutée, taxe sur la valeur ajoutée

valued ['væljuːd] ADJ *(contribution)* précieux; *(colleague, employee)* estimé; **my v. friend, Mr Thomson** M. Thomson, dont l'amitié m'est si précieuse

valueless ['væljʊlɪs] ADJ sans valeur

> Attention: ne pas confondre avec **invaluable**, qui signifie **inestimable**.

valuer ['væljʊər] N *(of antique etc)* expert *m*; **official v.** commissaire-priseur *m*, *pl* commissaires-priseurs

valve [vælv] N *(in pipe, tube, air chamber)* valve *f*, *(in machine)* soupape *f*, valve; *Anat* valve; *(small)* valvule *f*; *Bot, Zool* valve; *Mus (of brass instrument)* piston *m*; *Elec (of radio)* lampe *f*, valve

valved [vælvd] ADJ *Tech* à valve(s), à soupape(s); *Mus (instrument)* à pistons

valvular ['vælvjʊlər] ADJ *Med* valvulaire

vamoose [və'muːs] VI *esp Am Fam* décamper, filer; **let's v.** filons, fichons le camp

vamp[1] [væmp] *Mus Fam* N accompagnement *m* improvisé
   VI *(improvise)* improviser (au piano)

vamp[2] *Old-fashioned Fam* N *(woman)* femme *f* fatale, vamp *f*
   VT *(of woman) (man)* vamper
   VI *(of woman)* jouer la femme fatale
   ► **vamp up** VT SEP *Fam (building)* retaper; *(story)* enjoliver, embellir

vampire ['væmpaɪər] N *(bat, monster)* vampire *m*; *(person)* vampire, sangsue *f*
   ► ► *Zool* **v. bat** vampire

vampiric [væm'pɪrɪk] ADJ vampirique

vampirism ['væmpaɪərɪz(ə)m] N vampirisme *m*

vampish ['væmpɪʃ] ADJ *Old-fashioned Fam (looks, dress)* de vamp, de femme fatale

VAN [væn] N *Comput (abbr* **value-added network)** réseau *m* à valeur ajoutée

van[1] [væn] N = **vanguard**

van[2] N **1** *Aut (large)* camion *m*, fourgon *m*; *Br (small)* camionnette *f*, fourgonnette *f*; **furniture** *or* **removal v.** camion de déménagement; **delivery v.** camion/camionnette de livraison; *Radio, TV* **outside broadcasting v.** car *m* de radio-reportage **2** *Br Rail* wagon *m*,

fourgon *m*; **luggage v.** fourgon à bagages
▸▸ *Am* **v. pool** = covoiturage *m* en minibus (*souvent aux frais de l'entreprise*)

van[3] N *esp Br Tennis* avantage *m*; **v. in/out** avantage dedans/dehors

vanadium [vəˈneɪdɪəm] N *Chem* vanadium *m*

vandal [ˈvænd(ə)l] N vandale *mf*

vandalism [ˈvændəlɪz(ə)m] N vandalisme *m*; **act of v.** acte *m* de vandalisme

vandalize [ˈvændəlaɪz] VT (*building, telephone etc*) saccager; **several pictures have been vandalized** plusieurs tableaux ont été mutilés (par des vandales)

vane [veɪn] N **1** (*for indicating wind direction*) girouette *f* **2** (*of windmill*) aile *f*, (*of turbine*) aube *f*, ailette *f*, palette *f*, (*of bomb, torpedo*) ailette *f*; **the vanes** (*of turbine*) l'aubage *m*

vanguard [ˈvænɡɑːd] N *Mil, Fig* avant-garde *f*, *Fig* **to be in the v. of a movement** être un des pionniers d'un mouvement; **to be in the v. of technological progress** être à la pointe du progrès technologique

vanilla [vəˈnɪlə] N vanille *f*; **flavoured with v.**, **v. flavoured** vanillé, (*parfumé*) à la vanille; **v. ice cream** crème *f* glacée à la vanille
▸▸ **v. essence**, **v. extract** extrait *m* de vanille; **v. plant** vanille, vanillier *m*; **v. pod** gousse *f* de vanille; **v. sugar** sucre *m* vanillé; *St Exch* **v. swap** swap *m* vanilla

vanillin [vəˈnɪlɪn] N *Chem* vanilline *f*

vanish [ˈvænɪʃ] VI disparaître; (*of visions, suspicions*) se dissiper, s'évanouir; (*of difficulties*) s'aplanir; **to make sth v.** faire disparaître qch; (*of magician*) escamoter qch, faire disparaître qch; **elephants are vanishing from the earth** les éléphants sont en voie de disparition; **to v. from sight** disparaître à la vue; **to v. without trace** disparaître sans laisser de trace; **to v. into thin air** se volatiliser; **he's vanished** il a disparu; *Fam* (*to avoid sth, sb*) il s'est éclipsé; **she saw her last hope** elle a vu s'évanouir son dernier espoir

vanishing [ˈvænɪʃɪŋ] ADJ *Fig* **to do a v. act** s'éclipser; **he's done his famous v. act again** le voilà qui s'est encore éclipsé
▸▸ *Old-fashioned* **v. cream** crème *f* de jour; **v. point** point *m* de fuite; *Fig* **profits have dwindled to v. point** les bénéfices se sont trouvés réduits à néant; **v. trick** tour *m* de passe-passe; *Fig* **he did a v. trick** (*disappeared*) il a disparu

vanity [ˈvænɪtɪ] N **1** (*conceit*) vanité *f*, orgueil *m*; **to do sth out of v.** faire qch par vanité *ou* pour la gloriole **2** *Lit* (*futility*) futilité *f*, *Bible* **all is v.** tout est vanité
▸▸ **v. bag** trousse *f* de toilette (*pour femme*); **v. case** mallette *f* de toilette, vanity-case *m*, *pl* vanity-cases; *Aut* **v. mirror** miroir *m* de courtoisie; *Am Aut* **v. plate** plaque *f* d'immatriculation personnalisée; **v. press** maison *f* d'édition à compte d'auteur; **v. publishing** publication *f* à compte d'auteur; **v. table** coiffeuse *f*, table *f* de toilette; **v. unit** = meuble *m* de salle de bains avec lavabo encastré

vanquish [ˈvæŋkwɪʃ] VT (*person, one's passions*) vaincre, triompher de

vanquisher [ˈvæŋkwɪʃər] N vainqueur *m*; **Alexander, the v. of the Persians** Alexandre, celui qui a triomphé des Perses

vantage [ˈvɑːntɪdʒ] N **1** (*point of*) **v.**, **v. point** (*place*) terrain *m* avantageux, position *f* avantageuse; **to take up a v. point** choisir une position avantageuse; **from our v. point we could see ...** de la position avantageuse où nous étions nous pouvions voir ...; *Fig* **from the v. point of the twentieth century, it is easy to ...** avec le recul qui

nous est possible au vingtième siècle, il est facile de ... **2** *Tennis* avantage *m*

Vanuatu [ˈvænuːætuː] N Vanuatu

vapid [ˈvæpɪd] ADJ (*conversation, remark*) fade, insipide; (*style*) fade, plat; (*person*) fade, terne

vapidity [vəˈpɪdɪtɪ] N (*of conversation*) fadeur *f*, insipidité *f*; (*of style*) platitude *f*; (*of person*) fadeur *f*

vapor [ˈveɪpər] N *Am* = **vapour**

vaporization [veɪpəraɪˈzeɪʃən] N vaporisation *f*

vaporize [ˈveɪpəraɪz] VT vaporiser; (*in science fiction*) pulvériser
VI se vaporiser, se gazéifier

vaporizer [ˈveɪpəraɪzər] N (*spray*) atomiseur *m*, vaporisateur *m*

vaporous [ˈveɪpərəs] ADJ *Fml* (*sky, style*) vaporeux

vapour, *Am* **vapor** [ˈveɪpər] N **1** vapeur *f* **2** *Med Old-fashioned* **to have the vapours** avoir des vapeurs
▸▸ *Constr* **v. barrier** coupe-vapeur *m inv*; **v. bath** bain *m* de vapeur; *Aviat* **v. trail** traînée *f* de condensation

variability [veərɪəˈbɪlɪtɪ] N (*of weather etc*) variabilité *f*, *Biol* (*of type*) inconstance *f*

variable [ˈveərɪəb(ə)l] ADJ (*weather, amounts etc*) variable; **rainfall is v. according to season** les précipitations varient selon les saisons; **the combinations are infinitely v.** les combinaisons peuvent varier à l'infini; **v. (at will)** réglable
N *Math, Comput* variable *f*, *Econ* **random v.** variable aléatoire
▸▸ *Fin* **v. costs** coûts *mpl* variables, frais *mpl* variables; *Banking* **v. interest rate** taux *m* d'intérêt variable; *Math* **v. quantity** quantité *f* variable; *Banking* **v. rate** taux variable; **v. star** étoile *f* variable

variable-income ADJ *Fin* (*bond, investment*) à revenu variable

variable-rate ADJ *Banking, Fin* (*interest*) variable; (*security*) à revenu variable

variable-yield ADJ *Fin* (*investments, securities*) à revenu variable

variably [ˈveərɪəblɪ] ADV variablement

variance [ˈveərɪəns] N **1** (*disagreement*) désaccord *m*, discordance *f*; **to be at v. with sb** être en désaccord *ou* en contradiction avec qn; **his views are totally at v. with mine** ses opinions sont totalement différentes des miennes; **historians are at v. on** this point les historiens diffèrent entre eux *ou* ne sont pas d'accord sur ce point; **this theory is at v. with the facts** cette théorie est incompatible *ou* en contradiction avec les faits **2** (*difference*) (*in temperature, volume etc*) variation *f*, *Chem, Math* variance *f*, *Acct* variance, écart *m*
▸▸ *Acct* **v. analysis** analyse *f* des écarts

variant [ˈveərɪənt] ADJ différent (**from** de); **a v. interpretation or reading** une interprétation *ou* lecture différente; **a v. spelling** une variante orthographique
N variante *f*

variation [veərɪˈeɪʃən] N **1** (*difference*) variation *f*; **there was very little v. in quality** la qualité variait très peu; **v. between two readings** (*using scientific instrument*) écart *m* entre deux lectures **2** (*different version*) variation *f*; **another v. on the same theme** une autre variation sur le même thème **3** *Mus* variation *f* (**on** sur); **theme and variations** thème *m* et variations

varicoloured, *Am* **varicolored** [ˈveərɪkʌləd] ADJ *Fml* aux couleurs variées, versicolore

varicose [ˈværɪkəʊs] ADJ *Med* variqueux
▸▸ **v. vein** varice *f*

varied [ˈveərɪd] ADJ **1** (*diverse*) varié **2** *Biol* (*in colour*) multicolore, versicolore

variegated [ˈveərɪɡeɪtɪd] ADJ **1** *Fml* (*diverse*) varié **2** (*multi-coloured*) bigarré, bariolé, versicolore; *Bot* panaché; **to become v.** (*of flower, leaf*) se panacher

variegation [veərɪˈɡeɪʃən] N (*in colour*) diversité *f* de couleurs, bigarrure *f*, *Bot* panachure *f*, diaprure *f*

varietal [vəˈraɪətəl] N (*wine*) monocru *m*

variety [vəˈraɪətɪ] N **1** (*diversity*) variété *f*, diversité *f*; **the hillocks give v. to the landscape** les petites collines accidentent le paysage; *Prov* **v. is the spice of life** il faut varier les plaisirs; (*a change is good*) le changement donne du piquant à la vie
2 (*assortment*) **a v. of patterns** un assortiment de modèles; **a large** *or* **wide v. of materials** (*in shop*) un grand *ou* vaste choix de tissus; **there is a v. of possible causes** il y a diverses causes possibles; **for a v. of reasons** pour un grand nombre de raisons diverses; **an astonishing v. of reasons was given** on a fourni des raisons incroyablement variées; **in a v. of ways** de diverses manières, diversement
3 *Bot* (*of flower etc*) variété *f*
4 (*sort*) type *m*
5 *Theat* variétés *fpl*; **to work in v.** travailler dans le monde des variétés
▸▸ **v. artist** artiste *mf* de variétés; *Am* **v. meat** abats *mpl*; **v. show** spectacle *m* de variétés; *Am* **v. store** grand magasin *m*; **v. theatre** théâtre *m* de variétés

variola [vəˈraɪələ] N *Med* variole *f*, petite vérole *f*

various [ˈveərɪəs] ADJ divers; **of v. kinds** de diverses sortes; **to talk about v. things** parler de chose(s) et d'autre(s) *ou* de choses diverses; **her skills are many and v.** ses aptitudes sont nombreuses et diverses; **known under v. names** connu sous des noms divers; **v. people saw it** plusieurs personnes l'ont vu; **for v. reasons** pour des raisons diverses; **there are v. reasons why you shouldn't go** tu ne dois pas y aller pour plusieurs raisons; **at v. times** à diverses reprises, en diverses occasions; **in v. ways** de diverses *ou* plusieurs manières, diversement

variously [ˈveərɪəslɪ] ADV diversement, de diverses *ou* plusieurs manières; **v. estimated at ...** estimé par diverses sources à ...; **she has v. been called ...** elle a été tour à tour surnommée ...

varlet [ˈvɑːlɪt] N *Arch* (*rascal*) coquin *m*, vaurien *m*

varmint [ˈvɑːmɪnt] N *esp Am* young **v.** petit polisson *m*

varnish [ˈvɑːnɪʃ] N vernis *m*; *esp Br* nail **v.** vernis à ongles; (**coat of**) **v.** (couche *f* de) vernis; **to give sth a v.** vernir qch
VT (*wood, painting*) vernir; **to v. one's nails** se mettre du vernis à ongles
▸▸ **v. remover** (*in painting*) décapant *m* pour vernis
▸ **varnish over** VT SEP vernir; *Fig* (*facts*) déguiser; (*incident*) passer sur; (*person's faults*) glisser sur, jeter un voile complaisant sur

varnisher [ˈvɑːnɪʃər] N vernisseur *m*

varnishing [ˈvɑːnɪʃɪŋ] N vernissage *m*
▸▸ *Art* **v. day** (jour *m* du) vernissage

varsity [ˈvɑːsɪtɪ] N **1** *Br Fam* université *f*, *Fam* fac *f*, **the V. match** le match entre Oxford et Cambridge **2** *Am Univ* (*team*) équipe *f* universitaire
ADJ universitaire

vary [ˈveərɪ] VT (*one's style, diet*) varier, diversifier; (*programme*) apporter de la variété à; **to v. one's methods** changer de méthodes; **to v. one's route** changer d'itinéraire de temps en temps

VI varier, changer; *Biol* s'écarter du type, présenter une variation; **the ingredients v. from place to place** les ingrédients varient d'un endroit à l'autre; **it varies with the weather** ça change en fonction du temps; **it varies** ça dépend; **to v. in quality/weight** varier en qualité/poids; **to v. from sth** s'écarter de *ou* différer de qch; **as to the date, authors v.** les auteurs ne sont pas d'accord *ou* varient quant à la date; **opinions v.** les avis sont partagés

varying ['veərɪɪŋ] **ADJ** qui varie, variable, changeant; **I've had v. reports about that restaurant** j'ai entendu des avis divergents sur ce restaurant; **they have v. opinions about this** leurs opinions divergent *ou* diffèrent sur ce point; **with v. results** avec des résultats plus ou moins satisfaisants; **with v. degrees of success** avec plus ou moins de succès

vascular ['væskjʊlər] **ADJ** *Biol* vasculaire

vascularization [væskjʊlərɑɪ'zeɪʃən] **N** *Med* vascularisation *f*

vas deferens [væz'defərenz] **N** *Anat* canal *m* déférent

vase [vɑːz, *Am* veɪz] **N** vase *m*; **flower v.** vase à fleurs

vasectomy [və'sektəmɪ] **N** *Surg* vasectomie *f*, **to have a v.** se faire faire une vasectomie

Vaseline® ['væsəliːn] **N** Vaseline® *f*

vasoconstricting [veɪzəʊkən'strɪktɪŋ] **ADJ** *Med* vasoconstricteur, -trice

vasoconstriction [veɪzəʊkən'strɪkʃən] **N** *Med* vasoconstriction *f*

vasoconstrictor [veɪzəʊkən'strɪktər] *Med* **N** vasoconstricteur *m*
ADJ vasoconstricteur, -trice

vasodilation [veɪzəʊdaɪ'leɪʃən] **N** *Med* vasodilatation *f*

vasodilator [veɪzəʊdaɪ'leɪtər] *Med* **N** vasodilatateur *m*
ADJ vasodilatateur, -trice

vasomotor [veɪzəʊməʊtər] **ADJ** *Anat* vasomoteur, -trice

vassal ['væs(ə)l] **ADJ** vassal
N vassal *m*
▸▸ **v. state** pays *m* vassal

vassalage ['væsəlɪdʒ] **N** *Hist* vassalité *f*, vasselage *m*; *Fig* sujétion *f*

vast [vɑːst] **ADJ** immense; **in the v. majority of cases** dans la très grande *ou* l'immense majorité des cas; **a v. number of people** un extrêmement grand nombre de gens; **a v. expanse of territory** une immense *ou* vaste étendue de territoire; **his v. knowledge** son immense savoir; **to spend a v. amount** *or* **v. sums (of money)** dépenser de grosses sommes d'argent; **at v. expense** à grands frais; **there's a v. difference between them** il y a une différence énorme entre eux

vastly ['vɑːstlɪ] **ADV** immensément; **to be v. knowledgeable about sth** avoir des connaissances très vastes *ou* très étendues sur qch; **v. different** extrêmement différent; **they're not v. different** ils ne sont pas très différents

vastness ['vɑːstnɪs] **N** immensité *f*

VAT [viːeɪ'tiː, væt] **N** *Br* (*abbr* **value added tax**) TVA *f*; **exclusive of** *or* **excluding V.** hors TVA; **subject to V.** soumis à la TVA; **V. exempt** exonéré de TVA; **to be V. registered** être assujetti à la TVA
▸▸ **V. credit** crédit *m* de TVA; **V. exemption** franchise *f* de TVA; *Br Fam* **V. man** = inspecteur *m* de la TVA; **V. rate** taux *m* de TVA; **V. rebate** décote *f* de TVA; **V. registration number** code *m* assujetti TVA; **V. return** déclaration *f* de TVA; **V. statement** état *m* TVA

vat [væt] **N** (*container*) cuve *f*, bac *m*
▸▸ **v. dye** matière *f* colorante insoluble

vatful ['vætfʊl] **N** (*quantity*) cuvée *f*

Vatican ['vætɪkən] **N the V.** le Vatican
▸▸ **the V. City** l'État *m* de la cité du Vatican, le Vatican; *Fam Hum* **V. roulette** = méthode *f* de contraception basée sur l'abstinence périodique

VAT-registered **ADJ** assujetti à la TVA

vaudeville ['vɔːdəvɪl] **N** *Am Theat* variétés *fpl*
▸▸ **v. artist** artiste *mf* de variétés; **v. show** spectacle *m* de variétés

vault[1] [vɔːlt, vɒlt] **N 1** *Archit* voûte *f*, **tunnel v.** voûte cylindrique; **fan v.** voûte en éventail; **ribbed v.** voûte d'ogives *ou* à nervures; *Fig* **the v. of heaven** la voûte céleste **2** (*underground*) (*of country house, castle*) cave *f*, (*of church, for burial*) caveau *m*; **family v.** caveau de famille; (*bank*) **v.** chambre *f* forte
VT *Archit* **to v. (over)** (*cellar*) voûter
VI *Archit* (*of roof*) former une voûte

vault[2] **N** *Gym* saut *m* (*en s'aidant d'une ou de deux mains*); (*on vaulting horse*) saut au cheval d'arçons; (*pole*) **v.** saut à la perche
VI (*jump*) sauter (*en s'aidant d'une ou de deux mains*); **he vaulted over the gate** il a sauté la barrière; **to v. into the saddle** sauter en selle
VT (*barrier*) sauter, franchir d'un saut (*en s'aidant d'une ou deux mains*)

vaulted ['vɔːltɪd, 'vɒl-] **ADJ** *Archit* voûté, en (forme de) voûte

vaulting[1] ['vɔːltɪŋ, 'vɒl-] **N** *Archit* voûte(s) *f(pl)*; **barrel v.** voûte(s) en berceau

vaulting[2] **N 1** *Archit* voûte *f*, voûtes *fpl* **2** *Sport* saut *m* à la perche
ADJ 1 *Sport* (*pole*) de saut **2** *Fig Lit* (*arrogance*) outrecuidant; (*ambition*) démesuré
▸▸ **v. horse** cheval-d'arçons *m inv*

vaunt [vɔːnt] **VT** se vanter de, se faire gloire de; **our most vaunted justice** notre justice tant vantée *ou* dont on fait tant l'éloge; *esp Lit* **the city vaunts a 13th century castle** la ville s'enorgueillit de son château du XIIIe siècle

VC [viː'siː] **N 1** *Br Mil* (*abbr* **Victoria Cross**) = la plus haute distinction britannique accordée pour récompenser le courage d'un militaire; **to be awarded the VC** recevoir la Victoria Cross; **John Smith VC** = John Smith, titulaire de la Victoria Cross **2** *Hist* *abbr* **Vietcong 3** *abbr* **vice chairman/chairwoman/chairperson** *abbr* **4** vice consul

V-chip ['viːtʃɪp] **N** *Comput, TV* puce *f* anti-violence

vCJD [viːsiːdʒeɪ'diː] **N** *Med* (*abbr* **new-variant Creutzfeldt-Jakob disease**) vMCJ *m*

VCR [viːsiː'ɑːr] **N** *esp Am* (*abbr* **video cassette recorder**) magnétoscope *m*

VCT [viːsiː'tiː] **N** *Fin* (*abbr* **venture capital trust**) FCPR *m*

VD [viː'diː] **N** *Med* (*abbr* **venereal disease**) maladie *f* vénérienne; **VD clinic** centre *m* de traitement des maladies vénériennes

VDT [viːdiː'tiː] **N** *Comput abbr Br* **visual** *or Am* **video display terminal**

VDU [viːdiː'juː] **N** *Comput* (*abbr* **visual display unit**) moniteur *m*
▸▸ *Comput* **V. operator** personne *f* travaillant sur écran

veal [viːl] **N** *Culin* veau *m*
▸▸ **v. cutlet** côtelette *f* de veau

vector ['vektər] **N** *Math, Phys, Med* vecteur *m*; **v.-borne disease** maladie *f* transmise par (agent) vecteur
▸▸ **v. function** fonction *f* vectorielle; *Comput* **v. generator** générateur *m* de vecteurs; *Comput* **v. graphics** image *f* vectorielle; **v. processing** traitement *m* de vecteurs, traitement vectoriel

vectored interrupt ['vektəd] **N** *Comput* interruption *f* vectorisée

vectorial [vek'tɔːrɪəl] **ADJ** *Math* vectoriel

vee engine [viː] **N** moteur *m* en V

veep [viːp] **N** *Am Fam* vice-président, -ente, *pl* vice-président(e)s

veer [vɪər] **N** (*of wind*) changement *m* de direction; (*of ship*) virement *m* de bord; *Fig* (*of opinion*) revirement *m*
VI (*of wind*) tourner; (*of ship*) virer de bord; (*of car, road*) tourner abruptement, virer; *Naut* **to v. off course** dévier du cap fixé, dévier de sa route; *Aut* **he veered to the right** il a viré à droite; **the car veered off the road** la voiture a fait une embardée et a quitté la route; *Fig* **the conversation veered towards politics** la conversation a tourné à la politique; **to v. between two extremes** alterner entre deux extrêmes
VT (*ship*) faire virer
▸ **veer round** **VI** (*of vehicle, person*) faire demi-tour; (*of wind*) changer de direction; *Fig* (*of person*) se ranger à l'opinion contraire

veg [vedʒ] *Fam* **NPL** *Br* légumes *mpl*; **meat and two v.** = plat *m* comportant de la viande et deux légumes (*typique de la gastronomie britannique traditionnelle*)
VI (*relax*) **to v. (out)** paresser

vegan ['viːgən] **N** végétalien, -ienne

veganism ['viːgənɪz(ə)m] **N** végétalisme *m*

vegeburger ['vedʒɪbɜːgər] **N** hamburger *m* végétarien

vegetable ['vedʒtəb(ə)l] **ADJ** végétal, -aux; **the v. kingdom** le règne végétal
N 1 *Culin* légume *m*; **to grow vegetables** cultiver *ou* faire pousser des légumes; **green vegetables** légumes verts; **early vegetables** primeurs *fpl*, *Fig* **the accident has left her a v.** l'accident l'a privée de toutes ses facultés **2** *Bot* végétal *m*
▸▸ **v. dish** plat *m* à légumes, légumier *m*; **v. garden** (jardin *m*) potager *m*; **v. knife** couteau *m* à légumes, éplucheur *m*; **v. marrow** courge *f*, **v. matter** matières *fpl* végétales; **v. oil** huile *f* végétale; **v. rack** casier *m* à légumes

vegetal ['vedʒɪt(ə)l] **ADJ** *Bot* végétal, -aux

vegetarian [vedʒɪ'teərɪən] **N** végétarien, -ienne; **to be a v.** être végétarien
ADJ végétarien

vegetarianism [vedʒɪ'teərɪənɪz(ə)m] **N** végétarisme *m*

Vegetarianism

Que ce soit pour des raisons éthiques, religieuses ou diététiques, le végétarisme s'est considérablement répandu au cours des dernières années en Grande-Bretagne – sensiblement plus que dans les autres pays européens ou aux États-Unis. Aujourd'hui, la majorité des restaurants proposent un menu avec un ou plusieurs plats sans viande, et lorsque l'on invite des gens à dîner, il est d'usage de s'enquérir s'ils sont végétariens ou non.

---

vegetate ['vedʒɪteɪt] **VI** *Pej* végéter; **to v. in an office** végéter *ou* moisir dans un bureau

vegetation [vedʒɪ'teɪʃən] **N** végétation *f*

vegetative ['vedʒɪtətɪv, -teɪtɪv] **ADJ** *also Fig* végétatif

veggie ['vedʒɪ] **N** *Fam* **1** (*vegetarian*) végétarien, -ienne **2** *esp Am* (*vegetable*) légume *m*

veggieburger ['vedʒɪbɜːgər] **N** = **vegeburger**

vehemence ['viːɪməns] **N** (*of orator*) véhémence *f*, **with all the v. of youth** avec l'ardeur de la jeunesse

vehement ['viːɪmənt] **ADJ** (*orator*) véhément; (*desire*) passionné; (*attack, effort, dislike*) violent; **she was most v. in her**

insistence elle a insisté avec une grande véhémence

vehemently ['viːɪməntlɪ] ADV avec véhémence; (to dislike) violemment; **to be v. opposed to sth** être fortement opposé à qch

vehicle ['viːɪk(ə)l] N **1** véhicule m; **heavy vehicles turning** (sign) passage d'engins; **v. emissions** gaz mpl d'échappement; **heavy goods v.** poids m lourd **2** Fig (of thought, for propaganda) véhicule m; **the newspaper as a v. for advertising** le journal comme moyen de publicité; **the play is merely a v. for his talents** la pièce n'est qu'un moyen de mettre ses talents en valeur **3** Pharm excipient m
▸▸**v. identification number** numéro m d'immatriculation; **v. registration document** carte f grise

vehicular [vɪ'hɪkjʊlər] ADJ des véhicules, des voitures
▸▸**v. access** accès m aux véhicules; **v. traffic** circulation f automobile

veil [veɪl] N (of nun, sign of mourning) voile m; (on hat) voilette f, Fig (of smoke, mist) voile; (of politeness, culture) vernis m; **bridal v.** voile de mariée; Rel **to take the v.** prendre le voile; Fig **to draw** or **throw a v. over sth** jeter un voile sur qch; **under a v. of secrecy** sous le voile du secret
VT (face, painting) voiler; (one's feelings, intentions) voiler, cacher, dissimuler; **their plans were veiled in secrecy** leurs plans étaient gardés secrets; **to v. oneself** se voiler; **to v. one's face** se voiler le visage

veiled [veɪld] ADJ voilé, couvert d'un voile; Fig voilé, caché, dissimulé; (comment, threat, allusion) voilé; **to express oneself in v. terms** s'exprimer en termes voilés; **a thinly v. reference to** une référence à peine voilée à; **thinly v. hostility** hostilité à peine déguisée

vein [veɪn] N **1** Anat veine f, Entom (of wing) nervure f, Bot (of leaf) nervure, veine; **he has noble blood in his veins** il a du sang bleu dans les veines **2** Geol, Min veine f, filon m; (in wood, marble) veine; Fig **a v. of melancholy/humour** une pointe de mélancolie/d'humour **3** Fig (manner, style) veine f, disposition f, humeur f; **the poetic v.** la veine poétique; **other remarks in the same v.** d'autres observations faites dans le même esprit

veined [veɪnd] ADJ (marble etc) veiné, à veines; Bot, Entom nervuré

veining ['veɪnɪŋ] N **1** (streaks) veinure f, marbrure f **2** Bot, Entom nervures fpl

velar ['viːlər] ADJ, N Ling vélaire f

Velcro® ['velkrəʊ] N (bande f) Velcro® m

veld(t) [velt] N veld(t) m

vellum ['veləm] N vélin m
▸▸**v. paper** papier m vélin

velocipede [vɪ'lɒsɪpiːd] N Hist vélocipède m

velocity [vɪ'lɒsɪtɪ] N vélocité f, vitesse f, Econ **v. of circulation** vitesse de circulation de la monnaie; Econ **v. of money** vitesse de circulation de la monnaie

velodrome ['viːlədrəʊm] N vélodrome m

velour(s) [və'lʊər] N Tex (velvet) velours m de laine; (felt) feutre m taupé

velum, pl **vela** ['viːləm, -ə] N Anat voile m du palais

velvet ['velvɪt] N **1** Tex velours m; **to have (a) skin like v.** avoir une peau de pêche; **as smooth as v.** (skin) doux comme du ou le velours; (drink) velouté; **black v.** (drink) = mélange m de champagne et de stout; Fig **to be on v.** jouer sur le velours; **to walk with a v. tread** marcher à pas de velours ou à pas feutrés; Fig **an iron hand in a v. glove** une main de fer dans un gant de velours **2** Am Fam (profit) bénef m; (easy money) argent m facile

▸▸Hist **the V. Revolution** la Révolution de Velours

velveteen [velvɪ'tiːn] N Tex veloutine f

velvety ['velvɪtɪ] ADJ (appearance, taste) velouté; (wine) velouté, qui a du velouté; (to the touch) velouteux, doux comme le velours

venal ['viːn(ə)l] ADJ vénal, -aux

venality [vɪ'nælɪtɪ] N vénalité f

vend [vend] VT esp Jur, Admin vendre; **machine that vends coffee** distributeur m automatique (payant) de café

vendee [ven'diː] N Law acquéreur m

vendetta [ven'detə] N vendetta f, **to wage a v. against sb** mener une vendetta contre qn

vending ['vendɪŋ] N Law vente f
▸▸**v. machine** distributeur m automatique

vendor ['vendɔːr] N **1** Com, Law (person) vendeur, -euse; Comput fournisseur m; **(street) v.** marchand m ambulant **2** (machine) distributeur m automatique (payant)
▸▸Fin, Law **v.'s lien** privilège m du vendeur; Fin, Law **v.'s shares** actions fpl d'apport ou de fondation

veneer [və'nɪər] N **1** (covering) placage m, revêtement m; (material) bois m de placage, bois à plaquer **2** Fig masque m, apparence f extérieure; (of culture) vernis m; **a v. of politeness/respectability** un vernis de politesse/respectabilité; **beneath the v. of politeness** sous le masque de politesse
VT (wood) plaquer (**with** avec)

venerable ['ven(ə)rəb(ə)l] ADJ (old man etc) vénérable

venerate ['venəreɪt] VT (somebody, something) vénérer

veneration [venə'reɪʃən] N vénération f (**for** pour); **to hold sb in v.** avoir de la vénération pour qn

venereal [vɪ'nɪərɪəl] ADJ Med vénérien
▸▸**v. disease** maladie f vénérienne

venereology [vɪnɪərɪ'ɒlədʒɪ] N Med vénéréologie f

Venetian [vɪ'niːʃən] ADJ vénitien
N Vénitien, -ienne
▸▸**V. blind** store m vénitien; **V. glass** verre m ou cristal m de Venise; **V. lace** point m de Venise

Venezuela [vene'zweɪlə] N Vénézuéla m

Venezuelan [vene'zweɪl(ə)n] ADJ vénézuélien
N Vénézuélien, -ienne

vengeance ['ven(d)ʒəns] N vengeance f, **to take v. on sb** se venger de qn; **to take v. for** tirer vengeance de; (person's death) venger; Fig Fam **with a v.** (to set to work) furieusement; (to start doing sth again) de plus belle; **to work with a v.** travailler d'arrache-pied; **the autumn set in with a v.** l'automne a fait une entrée en force; **she's back with a v.** elle fait un retour de force; **by then it was raining with a v.** à ce moment-là, la pluie tombait à torrents

vengeful ['ven(d)ʒfʊl] ADJ (person) vindicatif; (look) vengeur

vengefully ['ven(d)ʒfʊlɪ] ADV d'une manière vindicative

vengefulness ['ven(d)ʒfʊlnɪs] N (of action) caractère m vindicatif; (of person) esprit m de vengeance

venial ['viːnɪəl] ADJ **1** Rel (sin) véniel **2** (error) sans gravité, véniel

veniality [viːnɪ'ælɪtɪ] N caractère m véniel

Venice ['venɪs] N Venise f

venison ['venɪs(ə)n] N Culin venaison f, **haunch of v.** quartier m de chevreuil

venom ['venəm] N (poison), Fig venin m; **to say with v.** dire avec méchanceté ou malveillance

venomous ['venəməs] ADJ (snake, spider etc) venimeux; (plant) vénéneux; Fig (criticism) venimeux, envenimé; **a v. look** un regard venimeux; Fig **a v. tongue** une langue de vipère

venomously ['venəməslɪ] ADV avec venin ou méchanceté

venous ['viːnəs] ADJ (system, blood) veineux

vent[1] [vent] N **1** (for air, gas, liquid) orifice m, conduit m; (in chimney) conduit, tuyau m; (in volcano) cheminée f, (in barrel) trou m; (for ventilation) conduit d'aération; (of fish, bird) orifice anal **2** Fig **to give v. to one's grief/anger/indignation** donner libre cours à sa douleur/sa colère/son indignation; **to give v. to one's spleen** décharger sa bile
VT **1** (pipe) décharger, vider des gaz; (gas from pipe, steam from boiler) évacuer **2** Fig (one's anger) donner libre cours à, laisser éclater, exhaler; **to v. one's spleen/anger on sb** décharger sa bile/épancher sa colère sur qn
▸▸**v. pipe** évent m

vent[2] N (on jacket) fente f

ventilate ['ventɪleɪt] VT **1** (room) aérer, ventiler; (tunnel) ventiler; (mine) éventer **2** Fig (question, feelings) mettre au grand jour

ventilated ['ventɪleɪtɪd] ADJ **1** (aired) aéré **2** Br Fam (over-excited) **to get v. about sth** se mettre dans tous ses états à propos de qch

ventilation [ventɪ'leɪʃən] N (of room) aération f, ventilation f, (of mine) aérage m
▸▸Min **v. shaft** conduit m d'aération ou d'aérage; **v. system** système m d'aération ou de ventilation

ventilator ['ventɪleɪtər] N **1** Tech ventilateur m, aérateur m; Naut manche f à air **2** Med respirateur m, poumon m artificiel; **to be on a v.** être sur respirateur

venting screw ['ventɪŋ] N Aut vis f de mise à l'air libre ou de purge

ventral ['ventr(ə)l] ADJ Anat, Biol ventral, -aux
▸▸**v. fin** nageoire f pelvienne, nageoire abdominale

ventricle ['ventrɪk(ə)l] N Anat ventricule m

ventriloquism [ven'trɪləkwɪz(ə)m] N ventriloquie f

ventriloquist [ven'trɪləkwɪst] N ventriloque mf; **v.'s dummy** marionnette f de ventriloque

venture ['ventʃər] N **1** (risky undertaking) entreprise f hasardeuse ou risquée; **this v. into advertising/fiction** cette incursion dans la publicité/fiction; **desperate v.** tentative f désespérée **2** (business undertaking) entreprise f, **joint v.** (undertaking) entreprise commune; (company) société f en participation **3** Arch **at a v.** (at random) au hasard
VT (one's life, money) risquer, aventurer; **to v. to do sth** se hasarder à faire qch, se risquer à faire qch; **I v. to affirm he knew nothing about it** j'ose affirmer qu'il n'en savait rien; **to v. a remark** hasarder une remarque; **I ventured the remark that ...** je me suis hasardé à faire la remarque que ...; **to v. an opinion** se hasarder ou se risquer à donner une opinion; Prov **nothing ventured nothing gained** qui ne risque rien n'a rien
VI **to v. into unknown territory** s'aventurer en terre inconnue; **this is the first time he has ventured into historical fiction** c'est sa première incursion dans la fiction historique; **to v. out of doors** se risquer à sortir; **to v. too far** s'aventurer trop loin
▸ **venture forth, venture out** VI esp Lit (after illness, from hiding etc) s'aventurer à sortir; **they ventured forth into the unknown** ils s'aventurèrent dans l'inconnu; **they ventured forth on their quest for ...** ils partirent à la recherche de ...

▸▸ *Fin* **v. capital** capital-risque *m*; **v. capital company** société à capital-risque; **v. capital trust** fonds *m* commun de placement à risques; *Fin* **v. capitalist** pourvoyeur, -euse de capital-risque, spécialiste *mf* de la prise de risques *(dans la finance)*; *Br* **V. Scout** éclaireur *m (de grade supérieur)*

▸ **venture on, venture upon** VT INSEP se risquer à, se hasarder à

venturesome ['ventʃəsəm] ADJ **1** *(person)* aventureux, entreprenant **2** *(action)* risqué, hasardeux

venturi throat [ven'tjuːrɪ] N *Aut* col *m* du venturi

venue ['venjuː] N **1** *(hall)* salle *f*, *(for football match)* terrain *m*; **the v. for the concert will be the Albert Hall/Birmingham** le concert se déroulera à l'Albert Hall/Birmingham; **what is the v. for the match?** où est-ce que le match aura lieu?; **there has been a change of v.** ça n'a plus lieu au même endroit, ça se tiendra ailleurs **2** *Law* lieu *m* du jugement; **to change the v. of a trial** renvoyer une affaire devant une autre cour

> Note that the French word **venue** is a false friend and is never a translation for the English word **venue**. It means **coming, arrival**.

venule ['venjuːl] N *Anat* veinule *f*

Venus ['viːnəs] N *Astron, Myth* Vénus *f*
   ▸▸ *Bot* **V. flytrap** dionée *f*

veracious [vəˈreɪʃəs] ADJ *Fml (person, account)* véridique

veracity [vəˈræsɪtɪ], **veraciousness** [vəˈreɪʃəsnɪs] N *esp Fml (of person, report)* véracité *f*

veranda(h) [vəˈrændə] N *Archit* véranda *f*

verb [vɜːb] N *Gram* verbe *m* VOIR GRAMMAIRE A38–66; B24–53

verbal ['vɜːb(ə)l] ADJ *(agreement, promise)* verbal, -aux, oral, -aux; *(communication, skills)* verbal; *Fam* **to have v.** *Br* **diarrhoea** *or Am* **diarrhea** être atteint de diarrhée verbale N *Br Sl* **to give sb the v.** *(shout at sb)* engueuler qn; **they were given the v.** ils se sont fait engueuler
   ▸▸ **v. abuse** violence *f* verbale; **v. agreement** convention *f* verbale, accord *m* verbal; *Gram* **v. noun** nom *m* verbal

verbalize ['vɜːbəlaɪz] VT **1** *(idea)* exprimer par des mots; *Psy (experience)* verbaliser **2** *Gram (noun)* employer comme verbe

verbally ['vɜːbəlɪ] ADV **1** *(orally)* verbalement, oralement, de vive voix; **to be v. abused** se faire insulter verbalement; **to agree v. to do sth** se mettre d'accord verbalement pour faire qch **2** *(as a verb)* en tant que verbe

verbatim [vɜːˈbeɪtɪm] ADV mot à mot, textuellement; **to report a speech v.** rendre compte mot à mot d'un discours ADV exact, mot à mot; **to give a v. account of sth** faire un compte-rendu mot à mot de qch

verbena [vɜːˈbiːnə] N *Bot* verveine *f*, **lemon v.** citronnelle *f*

verbiage ['vɜːbɪɪdʒ] N verbiage *m*

verbose [vɜːˈbəʊs] ADJ *(writer, style)* verbeux, diffus, prolixe

verbosely [vɜːˈbəʊslɪ] ADV avec verbosité, verbeusement; **v. worded** verbeux

verbosity [vɜːˈbɒsɪtɪ] N verbosité *f*, prolixité *f*

verdant ['vɜːdənt] ADJ *Fml* vert, verdoyant

verdict ['vɜːdɪkt] N *Law* verdict *m*; **to bring in a v. of guilty/not guilty** rendre un verdict de culpabilité/de non-culpabilité; **to return a v.** prononcer *ou* rendre un verdict; **to reach a v.** conclure, décider; **the jury returned a v. of suicide** *(in coroner's court)* le jury

a conclu au suicide; **open v.** *(at inquest)* = jugement *m* qui ne formule aucune conclusion sur les circonstances dans lesquelles la mort a eu lieu **2** *Fig* jugement *m*, avis *m*; **to give one's v.** se prononcer (**on** sur); **what's your v.?** qu'est-ce que tu en penses?

verdigris ['vɜːdɪgrɪs] N vert-de-gris *m inv*

verdure ['vɜːdʒər] N *Lit (colour)* verdure *f*, *(foliage)* verdure, feuillage *m*

verge [vɜːdʒ] N **1** *Br Aut (of road)* bas-côté *m*, *pl* bas-côtés, accotement *m*; **sitting on the grass v. of the road** assis sur l'herbe du bord de la route; **soft verges** *(road sign)* accotement instable **2** *Fig* **on the v. of tears/disaster/a nervous breakdown** au bord des larmes/du désastre/de la crise de nerfs; **on the v. of death** à la frontière de la mort; **on the v. of ruin** à deux doigts de la ruine; **to be on the v. of doing sth** être sur le point de faire qch; **on the v. of manhood** au seuil de l'âge viril **3** *esp Lit (edge)* *(of river)* bord *m*; *(of forest)* orée *f*

▸ **verge on** VT INSEP confiner à, friser; **red verging on pink** rouge qui tire sur le rose; **he was verging on sixty/hysteria** il frisait la soixantaine/l'hystérie

verger ['vɜːdʒər] N *Br Rel* bedeau *m*

Vergil ['vɜːdʒɪl] N *Antiq, Liter* Virgile *m*

verifiable [verɪˈfaɪəb(ə)l] ADJ vérifiable

verification [verɪfɪˈkeɪʃən] N vérification *f*, **to produce evidence in v. of a theory** fournir des preuves qui confirment *ou* vérifient une théorie

verify ['verɪfaɪ] VT *(check, prove)* vérifier; *(confirm)* vérifier, confirmer; *(information, accounts)* vérifier, contrôler; **this verifies my suspicions/my fears** cela confirme mes soupçons/mes craintes; **I can v. that Gillian Love was present** je peux confirmer que Gillian Love était bien là

verily ['verɪlɪ] ADV *Bible, Arch* en vérité, vraiment

verisimilitude [verɪsɪˈmɪlɪtjuːd] N *Fml* vraisemblance *f*

veritable ['verɪtəb(ə)l] ADJ véritable, vrai; **this is a v. disaster** c'est un véritable *ou* vrai désastre

veritably ['verɪtəblɪ] ADV véritablement

verity ['verɪtɪ] N *Lit* vérité *f*, *Rel* **the (eternal) verities** les vérités éternelles

vermicelli [vɜːmɪˈtʃelɪ] N *Culin* vermicelle(s) *m(pl)*

vermicide ['vɜːmɪsaɪd] N *Pharm* vermicide *m*

vermiculite [vɜːˈmɪkjʊlaɪt] N vermiculite *f*

vermiform ['vɜːmɪfɔːm] ADJ vermiforme

vermifugal [vɜːmɪˈfjuːg(ə)l] ADJ vermifuge

vermifuge ['vɜːmɪfjuːdʒ] N vermifuge *m*

vermilion [vəˈmɪljən] N vermillon *m* ADJ (de) vermillon *inv*, vermeil, -eille

vermin ['vɜːmɪn] N *(inv in pl) (insects)*, *Fig* vermine *f*, *(rodents)* animaux *mpl* nuisibles VOIR GRAMMAIRE A11

verminous ['vɜːmɪnəs] ADJ *(covered with fleas, lice etc)* couvert de vermine; *Fig (dirty) (coat, flat)* miteux; *Fig* **you v. little creep!** espèce de vermine!

vermouth [vɜːˈmuːθ] N vermout(h) *m*

vernacular [vəˈnækjʊlər] ADJ **1** *Ling* vernaculaire, indigène **2** *Archit* local, -aux N **1** *(everyday speech)* langue *f* vulgaire; **in the v.** dans la langue vulgaire; **to translate the Bible into the v.** traduire la Bible dans la langue vulgaire **2** *(dialect)* langue *f* vernaculaire *ou* indigène **3** *Archit* style *m* local **4** *(jargon)* jargon *m*; **the sporting v.** le jargon sportif

vernal ['vɜːn(ə)l] ADJ *Liter* printanier
   ▸▸ **v. equinox** équinoxe *m* de printemps

Veronal® ['verən(ə)l] N *Pharm* véronal *m*

veronica [vəˈrɒnɪkə] N *Bot* véronique *f*

verruca, *pl* **verrucae** [veˈruːkə, -kiː] N verrue *f*

versant ['vɜːsənt] N *(of mountain)* versant *m*

versatile ['vɜːsətaɪl] ADJ **1** *(person)* aux talents variés, polyvalent; *(dress, jacket) (can be worn anywhere)* passe-partout; *(has detachable parts, is reversible etc)* polyvalent; *(tool, machine)* polyvalent, d'une grande souplesse d'emploi, universel; **a v. mind** un esprit souple *ou* universel **2** *Biol* versatile

> Note that the French word **versatile** is a false friend and is never a translation for the English word **versatile**. It means **fickle, changeable**.

versatility [vɜːsəˈtɪlɪtɪ] N **1** *(of person)* variété *f* de talents *ou* d'aptitudes; *(adaptability)* faculté *f* d'adaption; *(of mind)* souplesse *f*, universalité *f*, *(of tool, machine)* polyvalence *f*, grande souplesse d'emploi; **his v.** la variété de ses talents; **she has v. of mind** c'est un esprit universel **2** *Biol (of organ)* versatilité *f*

verse [vɜːs] N **1** *(poetry)* vers *mpl*; **free v.** vers libres; **light v.** poésie *f* légère **2** *(stanza) (of song)* couplet *m*; *(of poem, hymn)* strophe *f*, stance *f* **3** *(of Bible)* verset *m*

versed [vɜːst] ADJ versé (**in** en, dans); **v. in the arts** versé dans les arts; **to be well v. in mathematics** être fort instruit dans les mathématiques; **I am well v. in his ways** je le connais bien, je sais bien comment il est

versification [vɜːsɪfɪˈkeɪʃən] N **1** *(art)* versification *f* **2** *(metre) (of verse)* facture *f*, *(of author)* métrique *f*

versifier ['vɜːsɪfaɪər] N *Pej* versificateur *m*

versify ['vɜːsɪfaɪ] VT *(story etc)* versifier, mettre en vers VI versifier, faire des vers

version ['vɜːʃən] N **1** *(account) (of facts)* version *f*, **he gave us a very different v. of the affair** il nous a donné de cette affaire un récit très différent; **according to his v.** d'après sa version des faits; **her v. differs from mine** sa version des faits diffère de la mienne **2** *(variation) (of car, text, recipe)* version *f*, **the military v. of this aircraft** la version militaire de cet avion; **the TV v. of a novel** l'adaptation *f* d'un roman pour la télévision **3** *(translation)* version *f*, traduction *f*, **the English v. of the Bible** la version anglaise de la Bible

verso ['vɜːsəʊ] N **1** *(of page)* verso *m* **2** *(of medal)* revers *m*

versus ['vɜːsəs] PREP *Law, Sport* contre; *Sport* **Martin v. Thomas** Martin contre Thomas; *Fig* **the advantage of a higher salary v. the loss of security** l'avantage d'un salaire plus élevé en contrepartie d'une sécurité moindre; *Fig* **the relative merits of public v. private ownership** les avantages relatifs de la propriété de l'État par opposition à la propriété privée

vertebra, *pl* **vertebrae** ['vɜːtɪbrə, -iː] N vertèbre *f*

vertebral ['vɜːtɪbrəl] ADJ vertébral, -aux
   ▸▸ **v. column** colonne *f* vertébrale

vertebrate ['vɜːtɪbreɪt, -brɪt] ADJ *(animal)* vertébré; *(characteristic)* des vertébrés N vertébré *m*

vertex, *pl* **vertices** ['vɜːteks, -tɪsiːz] N **1** *Geom (of angle, curve)* sommet *m* **2** *Anat* vertex *m*

vertical ['vɜːtɪk(ə)l] ADJ vertical, -aux; **a v. cliff** une falaise à pic; **in a v. position** en position verticale, à la verticale; **a v. line** une ligne *f* verticale N *(line, position)* verticale *f*
   ▸▸ **v. elevation** altitude *f*, *Fin* **v. equity** équité *f* verticale; *TV* **v. hold** bouton *m* de

commande de synchronisme vertical; *Com* **v. integration** intégration *f* verticale; *Typ* **v. justification** justification *f* verticale; *Aviat* **v. landing** atterrissage *m* vertical; **v. marketing** marketing *m* vertical; *Fin* **v. spread** écart *m* vertical; *Aviat* **v. take-off** décollage *m* vertical

verticality [vɜːtɪˈkælɪtɪ] N verticalité *f*

vertically [ˈvɜːtɪklɪ] ADV verticalement, à la verticale; *Aviat* **to take off/land v.** décoller/ atterrir à la verticale

vertiginous [vɜːˈtɪdʒɪnəs] ADJ vertigineux

vertigo [ˈvɜːtɪɡəʊ] N *Med* vertige *m*; **to suffer from/get v.** avoir le vertige; **I had an attack of v.** j'ai été pris de vertige

verve [vɜːv] N verve *f*, brio *m*; **to play/act with v.** jouer avec verve *ou* brio

Very [ˈvɪərɪ] N
▸▸**V. light** fusée *f* éclairante; **V. pistol** pistolet *m* lance-fusées

VERY [ˈverɪ] ADV VOIR GRAMMAIRE A22–3 **1** *(extremely)* très; **v. good** *(adj phrase)* très bon, fort bon; *(adv phrase)* très bien, fort bien; **a v. good dictionary** un très *ou* fort bon dictionnaire; **v. good, captain** très bien, mon capitaine; **he is v. well known in Paris** il est très connu à Paris; **that's v. kind of you** c'est très gentil à vous; **you are v. kind** vous êtes bien bon; **so v. little** si peu; **there's v. little one can do to help** on ne peut pas faire grandchose pour aider; **I took only a v. little** j'en ai pris très peu; **it isn't so v. difficult** ce n'est pas tellement difficile, ce n'est pas si difficile que ça; **he was not v. pleased** il n'était pas très content; **v. (v.) few people** très (très) peu de gens; **are you hungry? – yes, v.** avezvous faim? – oui, très; **he wore a v. pleased expression** il avait l'air très satisfait; **I feel v. much better** je me sens beaucoup mieux; **it is v. much better to wait** il vaut bien mieux attendre; *Comput* **v. high level language** langage *m* très évolué; **v. large scale integration** intégration *f* à très grande échelle; *Rel* **the V. Reverend …** le très révérend …
2 *(emphatic use)* **the v. first** le tout premier; **we were the v. first to arrive** nous étions les tout premiers à arriver; **the v. last** le tout dernier; **the v. best** tout ce qu'il y a de mieux *ou* de meilleur; **at the v. most/least** tout au plus/au moins; **at the v. latest** au plus tard; **the v. same** exactement le même; **I v. nearly died** j'ai bien failli mourir; **it was the v. last thing I expected** c'était vraiment la dernière chose à laquelle je m'attendais; **the v. next day** dès le lendemain, le lendemain même; **in the v. front row** au tout premier rang; **a room of my v. own** une pièce rien qu'à moi; **it's my v. own** c'est à moi tout seul
ADJ **1** *(emphatic use)* même; **he lives in this v. house** il habite dans cette maison même; **sitting in this v. room** assis dans cette pièce même; **by its v. nature** par sa nature même; **you are the v. man I wanted to see** vous êtes justement l'homme que je voulais voir; **come here this v. minute!** venez ici à l'instant!; **this v. day** aujourd'hui même; **it was a year ago to the v. day** c'était il y a un an jour pour jour; **these are his v. words** ce sont là ses propres paroles; **at the v. beginning** au tout début; **he knows our v. thoughts** il connaît jusqu'à nos pensées; **the v. idea frightens me** cette pensée suffit à m'effrayer; **I shudder at the v. thought of it** je frémis rien que d'y penser
2 *Rel, Arch (real, true)* vrai, véritable
▸▸**v. high frequency** très haute fréquence *f*, *(gamme f des)* ondes *fpl* métriques; **v. low frequency** très basse fréquence *f*

VESA [ˈviːsə] N *Comput (abbr video electronics standard association)* VESA *m*

vesical [ˈvesɪk(ə)l] ADJ *Anat, Med* vésical, -aux

vesicle [ˈvesɪk(ə)l] N *Biol, Med* vésicule *f*

vesper [ˈvespər] N *Rel* **vespers** vêpres *fpl*; **to attend vespers** aller aux vêpres; **the v. bell** la cloche des vêpres *ou* du soir

vessel [ˈves(ə)l] N **1** *Naut* bateau *m*; *(large)* navire *m* **2** *(receptacle)* récipient *m*; *Phys* **communicating vessels** vases *mpl* communicants **3** *Anat, Bot* vaisseau *m*

vest[1] [vest] N **1** *Br (for men)* maillot *m* de corps; *(for women)* chemise *f*, *Can* camisole *f*; *(for baby)* brassière *f*; *Sport* maillot *m*; **string v.** gilet *m* en point noué *ou* en filet maille (aérée) **2** *Am (waistcoat)* gilet *m*

> Note that the French word **veste** is a false friend and is never a translation for the English word **vest**. It means **jacket**.

vest[2] VT **1** **to v. sb with authority** investir *ou* revêtir qn d'autorité; **to v. property in sb** assigner des biens à qn; **right vested in the Crown** droit dévolu à la Couronne; **by the authority vested in me** en vertu de l'autorité dont je suis investi; **authority vested in the people** autorité exercée par le peuple **2** *Rel (clothe) (dignitary, priest)* vêtir, revêtir

vestal virgin [ˈvest(ə)l] N *Antiq* vestale *f*

vested interest [ˈvestɪd] N intérêt *m*; *(person)* = personne *f* qui a un intérêt matériel; **to have a v. in sth** avoir des intérêts dans qch; **to have a v. in sth being done** avoir intérêt à ce que qch soit fait; **to have a v. in a business** avoir des capitaux investis dans une entreprise, être intéressé dans une entreprise; **I do have a v. in the play's success** j'ai intérêt à ce que la pièce soit un succès

vestibule [ˈvestɪbjuːl] N **1** *(in house, church)* vestibule *m*; *(in hotel)* vestibule, hall *m* d'entrée **2** *Am Rail* sas *m* **3** *Anat (of ear)* vestibule *m*

vestige [ˈvestɪdʒ] N **1** *(trace) (of civilization etc)* vestige *m*; **not a v. of …** *(truth, common sense)* pas une once de … **2** *Biol* organe *m* rudimentaire

vestigial [vesˈtɪdʒɪəl] ADJ **1** résiduel; **the v. remains of an abbey/a civilization** les vestiges d'une abbaye/d'une civilisation; **some v. sense of decency prevented him from doing it** le peu de décence qui lui restait l'a empêché de le faire **2** *Biol (organ)* rudimentaire

vestment [ˈvestmənt] N vêtement *m* (de cérémonie); *Rel* chasuble *f*, **(church) vestments** vêtements sacerdotaux

vest-pocket *Am* N poche *f* de gilet
ADJ *(book, object)* de poche; *Fig* minuscule, tout petit

vestry [ˈvestrɪ] N *Rel* **1** *(in church)* sacristie *f* **2** *(parish council)* conseil *m* paroissial

Vesuvius [vɪˈsuːvɪəs] N le Vésuve

vet[1] [vet] N vétérinaire *mf*; **to take an animal to the v.('s)** emmener un animal chez le vétérinaire

vet[2] VT (-tt-) *(person) (for security purposes)* effectuer un contrôle de sécurité sur; *(purchases, expenditure)* contrôler; *(candidate, proposal, decision) (examine)* examiner; *(approve)* approuver; **she's been positively vetted** le contrôle de sécurité dont elle a fait l'objet s'est avéré satisfaisant; **his mother vets his girlfriends** sa mère a un droit de regard sur ses petites amies

vet[3] N *Am Mil Fam (abbr* veteran*)* ancien combattant *m*

vetch [vetʃ] N *Bot* vesce *f*

veteran [ˈvet(ə)rən] N vétéran *m*, *Fam* vieux *m* de la vieille; *Mil* ancien combattant *m*; **a v. of the First World War, a First World War v.** un ancien combattant de la Première Guerre mondiale; **I have a real old v. of a typewriter** j'ai une machine à écrire, c'est une antiquité!
ADJ *(activist, opponent etc)* de longue date; *(sportsman, actor)* chevronné; **she is a v. campaigner for human rights** elle a fait campagne pour les droits de l'homme depuis très longtemps
▸▸**v. army** armée *f* de vétérans; *Br* **v. car** voiture *f* de collection *(normalement antérieure à 1905)*; **v. soldier** vieux soldat *m*

Veterans Day N *Am* ≃ l'Armistice *m*, *Can* ≃ le Jour du Souvenir

veterinarian [vet(ə)rɪˈneərɪən] N *esp Am* vétérinaire *mf*

veterinary [ˈvet(ə)rɪn(ə)rɪ] ADJ *(medicine, science)* vétérinaire; **she has a v. practice** elle a un cabinet de vétérinaire
▸▸*Br* **v. surgeon** vétérinaire *mf*

veto, *pl* **vetoes** [ˈviːtəʊ, -əʊz] N veto *m*; **right of v.** droit *m* de veto; **to have the right** *or* **power of v.** avoir le droit de veto; **to put a v. on sth** mettre *ou* opposer son veto à qch; **to use one's v.** exercer son droit de veto; *Comput* **put in v. mode** en mode sélectif
VT mettre *ou* opposer son veto à; **he vetoed it** il y a mis *ou* opposé son veto; **the spending was vetoed** cette dépense a été rejetée par véto

Vette [vet] N *Am Fam (Corvette®)* Corvette® *f*

vetting [ˈvetɪŋ] N *(examining) (of candidate, proposal, decision)* examen *m*; *(of purchases, expenditure)* contrôle *m*; *(security check)* contrôle de sécurité

vex [veks] VT ennuyer, fâcher, chagriner; **I was vexed by her attitude** son attitude m'ennuyait *ou* me chagrinait

> Note that the French verb **vexer** is a false friend. It means **to hurt somebody's feelings**.

vexation [vekˈseɪʃən] N **1** *(cause)* contrariété *f*, ennui *m* **2** *(sadness)* chagrin *m* **3** *(anger)* dépit *m*

vexatious [vekˈseɪʃəs] ADJ *esp Fml (person, thing)* contrariant, irritant, ennuyeux; *(circumstances)* fâcheux

vexed [vekst] ADJ **1** *(cross)* fâché, ennuyé, chagriné **2** **v. question** question *f* controversée *ou* très débattue *ou* non résolue; **it is a v. question whether …** c'est une question controversée de savoir si …

vexing [ˈveksɪŋ] ADJ contrariant, irritant, ennuyeux

VGA [viːdʒiːˈeɪ] N *Comput (abbr* video graphics adaptor*)* VGA *m*
▸▸**V. monitor** moniteur *m* VGA

VHF [viːeɪtʃˈef] ADJ *Radio, TV (abbr* very high frequency*)* VHF *f*; **to broadcast on V.** émettre en hyperfréquences
▸▸**V. radio** radio *f* en hyperfréquences

VHS [viːeɪtʃˈes] ADJ *TV (abbr* video home system*)* VHS *m*

via [ˈvaɪə, ˈviːə] PREP par; *(travelling)* par, via; **I found out v. Fiona/head office** j'ai découvert ça par l'intermédiaire de Fiona/du siège social

viability [vaɪəˈbɪlɪtɪ] N *(of foetus, seed, company etc)* viabilité *f*, *(of project etc)* viabilité, chances *fpl* de succès

viable [ˈvaɪəb(ə)l] ADJ *(foetus, seed, company etc)* viable; *(project etc)* viable, qui a des chances de réussir; **I can see no v. alternative** je ne vois pas d'autre moyen d'y parvenir

viaduct [ˈvaɪədʌkt] N viaduc *m*

Viagra® [vaɪˈægrə] N Viagra® *m*

vial [ˈvaɪəl] N *Fml* fiole *f*, *(for drugs)* ampoule *f*

viands [ˈvaɪəndz] NPL *Arch* aliments *mpl*

viaticum [vaɪˈætɪkəm] N *Rel* viatique *m*

vibes [vaɪbz] NPL *Fam* **1** *(atmosphere)* ambiance *f*; **the v. are good** ça marche, ça gaze; **this place gives me bad v.** cet endroit me fait un effet désagréable; **I get good v. from it** ça me branche; **I get good v. from him/her** il/elle me plaît; **I'm getting strange v. from him** je ne le sens pas très bien; **what sort of v. do you get from him?** comment tu le sens? **2** *Mus* vibraphone *m*

vibrancy ['vaɪbrənsɪ] N animation *f*, *(of colours, style)* vivacité *f*, *(of personality)* flamme *f*, fougue *f*

vibrant ['vaɪbrənt] ADJ **1** *(person, painting, description)* plein de vie; *(town, cultural scene, atmosphere)* très animé; *(style)* plein de vigueur; *(speech)* vibrant; *(new company)* très dynamique; **city v. with activity** ville palpitante d'activité **2** *(colour)* éclatant

vibraphone ['vaɪbrəfəʊn] N *Mus* vibraphone *m*

vibrate [vaɪ'breɪt] VI vibrer; *Phys* vibrer, osciller; **her voice vibrated with emotion** sa voix était vibrante d'émotion; **you're making the house v.** tu fais trembler les murs; **to v. with activity** vibrer d'activité
▸ VT faire vibrer

vibrating [vaɪ'breɪtɪŋ] ADJ vibrant
▸ ▸ **v. alert** *(on mobile phone)* vibration *f*

vibration [vaɪ'breɪʃən] N **1** vibration *f*, *Phys etc* oscillation *f*, pulsation *f* **2** *Fig Fam* **vibrations = vibes 1**

vibrato [vɪ'brɑːtəʊ] N *Mus* vibrato *m*

vibrator [vaɪ'breɪtər] N **1** *Elec* vibrateur *m*, vibreur *m* **2** *(for massage, also sexual)* vibromasseur *m*

vibratory [vaɪ'breɪtərɪ] ADJ *Phys etc* vibratoire

viburnum [vaɪ'bɜːnəm] N *Bot* viorne *f*

vicar ['vɪkər] N **1** *(in Church of England)* pasteur *m* **2** **the V. of Christ** le vicaire de Jésus-Christ
▸ ▸ **v. apostolic** vicaire *m* apostolique; **v. general** vicaire général

vicarage ['vɪkərɪdʒ] N *(in Church of England)* presbytère *m* *(d'un pasteur)*

vicarious [vaɪ'keərɪəs, vɪ-] ADJ **1** *(at second hand)* indirect; **to lead a v. existence** vivre par procuration; **to take v. pleasure in sth** retirer indirectement du plaisir de qch; **he gets a v. thrill from watching porn films** il trouve son plaisir à regarder des films pornographiques **2** *(power, authority)* délégué **3** *(punishment)* (fait) pour autrui; *(suffering, pain)* subi pour autrui

vicariously [vaɪ'keərɪəslɪ, vɪ-] ADV **1** *(on sb's behalf)* à la place d'un autre; *(indirectly)* indirectement; **to live v.** vivre par procuration **2** *(by delegation)* par délégation, par procuration

vice¹ [vaɪs] N *(immorality)* vice *m*; **to lead a life of v.** vivre dans le vice; **to sink into v.** sombrer dans le vice; **avarice is a v.** l'avarice est un vice; *Hum* **it's my only v.** c'est mon seul vice; **there's no v. in him** il n'est pas méchant
▸ ▸ **v. ring** organisation *f* criminelle *(impliquée dans la prostitution, le trafic de drogue/etc)*; **the V. Squad** la brigade mondaine ou des mœurs, *Fam* la Mondaine, *Fam* les Mœurs *fpl*

vice², *Am* **vise** N *Tech* étau *m*; **he had a grip like a v.** il avait une poigne de fer
▸ ▸ **v. jaw** mâchoire *f* d'étau

vice-admiral N vice-amiral *m* d'escadre, *pl* vice-amiraux d'escadre

vice-chairman, *pl* **vice-chairmen** N vice-président, *pl* vice-présidents

vice-chairmanship N vice-présidence *f*, *pl* vice-présidences

vice-chancellor N *Pol* vice-chancelier, *pl*

vice-chanceliers; *Br Univ* président *m* d'université

vice-chancellorship [vaɪs'tʃɑːnsələʃɪp] N *Pol* fonction *f* ou dignité *f* de vice-chancelier; *Br Univ* présidence *f* d'université

vice-consul N vice-consul *m*, *pl* vice-consuls

vice-consulate N *(post or premises)* vice-consulat *m*, *pl* vice-consulats

vicelike ['vaɪslaɪk] ADJ **held in a v. grip** serré dans une poigne de fer, serré comme dans un étau

vice-marshal N *Aviat* **air v.** général *m* de division aérienne

vice-presidency N vice-présidence *f*, *pl* vice-présidences; **a candidate for the v.** un candidat à la vice-présidence

vice-president N vice-président, *pl* vice-présidents

vice-presidential ADJ vice-présidentiel; **v. candidate** candidat *m* à la vice-présidence

viceroy ['vaɪsrɔɪ] N vice-roi *m*, *pl* vice-rois

vice versa ['vaɪsɪ'vɜːsə] ADV vice versa

vicinity [vɪ'sɪnɪtɪ] N **1** *(neighbourhood)* voisinage *m*; **in the v.** dans les alentours *ou* environs; **in the v. of Dover** à proximité de *ou* dans les environs de Douvres; **there was no-one in the immediate v.** il n'y avait personne dans le voisinage immédiat; **in the immediate v. of the factory** aux abords de l'usine; **in the v. of five thousand pounds** environ cinq mille livres, aux alentours de cinq mille livres **2** *Fml (nearness)* proximité *f* **(to** de**)**

vicious ['vɪʃəs] ADJ **1** *(harsh, violent)* rageur, violent; *(malicious)* méchant, haineux; *(struggle)* acharné; **v. blow/wind** coup *m*/vent *m* violent; **she has a v. tongue** c'est une mauvaise langue; **a v. attack** une attaque brutale; **to make a v. attack on sb's character** lancer une attaque haineuse contre la personne *ou* la réputation de qn; **v. gossip** méchants commérages *mpl* **2** *Old-fashioned, Lit (depraved)* vicieux, dépravé **3** *(horse, dog)* méchant
▸ ▸ **v. circle** cercle *m* vicieux

> Note that the French word **vicieux** is a false friend. It means **depraved** or **underhand**, depending on the context.

viciously ['vɪʃəslɪ] ADV *(violently)* violemment; *(maliciously)* méchamment, haineusement; *(to attack)*, *Fig* férocement

viciousness ['vɪʃəsnɪs] N *(of wind, blow)* violence *f*, *(of attack)* brutalité *f*, férocité *f*, *(of criticism)* méchanceté *f*

vicissitude [vɪ'sɪsɪtjuːd] N *Lit* vicissitude *f*

victim ['vɪktɪm] N *(of attack, murder etc)* victime *f*, *(of fire)* sinistré, -ée, incendié, -ée; *(of flood)* sinistré, -ée, inondé, -ée; *(of shipwreck etc)* sinistré, -ée; **to be sb's v.** être la victime de qn; **to be the v. of an attack** être victime d'une attaque; **the v. of sb's trickery** la dupe de la fourberie de qn; **v. of an accident, accident v.** accidenté, -ée; **to fall v. to sb's charm** succomber au charme de qn; **to fall v. to a disease** être frappé d'une maladie; **she was a** *or* **the v. of her own success** elle a été la victime de son propre succès

victimization [vɪktɪmaɪ'zeɪʃən] N brimades *fpl* **(of** sur, contre**)**; **this is management v.** c'est un traitement discriminatoire de la part de la direction; **it results in the v. of the lower paid** cela se traduit par la discrimination des petits salaires; **there will be no v. of workers who have gone on strike** les ouvriers qui se sont mis en grève ne souffriront aucune représaille

victimize ['vɪktɪmaɪz] VT **it victimizes the**

lower paid cela constitue un traitement discriminatoire à l'égard des petits salaires, ce sont les petits salaires qui en souffrent; **he felt that he was being victimized** il se croyait victime d'un traitement discriminatoire; **I'm being victimized** on s'en prend à moi; **strikers thought that they were being victimized** les grévistes se croyaient victimes de représailles

victimless ['vɪktɪmlɪs] ADJ
▸ ▸ **v. crime** délit *m* sans victime

victor ['vɪktər] N *Fml* vainqueur *m*; **to emerge the clear v.** sortir grand vainqueur

Victoria [vɪk'tɔːrɪə] N *(person)* **Queen V.** la reine Victoria
▸ ▸ *Mil* **V. Cross** Victoria Cross *f* *(en Grande-Bretagne, la plus haute décoration militaire)*; **V. Day** = fête *f* de Victoria *(jour férié en mai)*; **V. Falls** les chutes *fpl* Victoria

victoria [vɪk'tɔːrɪə] N *(plum)* = grosse prune *f* rouge
▸ ▸ **v. plum** = grosse prune rouge

Victorian [vɪk'tɔːrɪən] ADJ victorien, -ienne, du règne de la reine Victoria; *(values)* victorien
▸ N Victorien, -ienne

Victoriana [vɪktɔːrɪ'ɑːnə] N antiquités *fpl* de l'époque victorienne

victorious [vɪk'tɔːrɪəs] ADJ *(army, team etc)* victorieux, vainqueur; *(struggle, campaign)* victorieux; *(day etc)* de victoire; **to be v. over sb** remporter la victoire sur qn

victoriously [vɪk'tɔːrɪəslɪ] ADV victorieusement, en vainqueur

victory ['vɪktərɪ] N victoire *f*, **to claim v.** revendiquer la victoire; **to snatch v. from the jaws of defeat** arracher la victoire; **he described the decision as a v. for common sense** il a décrit la décision comme étant une victoire du bon sens; **to gain a** *or* **the v.** remporter la victoire **(over** sur**)**, être victorieux; **the Winged V. of Samothrace** la Victoire ailée de Samothrace
▸ ▸ **v. parade** défilé *m* de la victoire, défilé pour célébrer une victoire

victual ['vɪt(ə)l] (-ll-, *Am* -l-) VT *(ship, garrison)* ravitailler, approvisionner
▸ VI s'approvisionner, se ravitailler

victualler, *Am* **victualer** ['vɪtlər] N *Fml* fournisseur *m* de vivres; *Br Fml* **licensed v.** débitant *m* de boissons

victuals ['vɪt(ə)lz] NPL *Old-fashioned, Lit (food)* vivres *mpl*, victuailles *fpl*

vicuna [vɪ'kjuːnə] N *(animal, wool, cloth)* vigogne *f*

vid [vɪd] N *Fam (abbr* **video**) vidéo *f*, vidéocassette *f*

video ['vɪdɪəʊ] N *(medium)* vidéo *f*, *(cassette)* vidéocassette *f*, cassette *f* vidéo; *(recorder)* magnétoscope *m*; **a v. of the World Cup** une vidéo de la Coupe du Monde; **we've got a v. of the film** on a le film en vidéocassette; **to show a v.** passer une vidéo; **to have sth on v.** avoir qch sur vidéo; **they recorded the series on v.** ils ont enregistré le feuilleton au magnétoscope; **have you set the v.?** est-ce que tu as mis le magnétoscope en marche *ou* programmé le magnétoscope?; **the film went straight to v.** le film n'est jamais sorti en salle, il est sorti tout de suite sur cassette vidéo
▸ VT **1** *(record)* enregistrer (en vidéo), enregistrer sur magnétoscope, magnétoscoper **2** *(using camcorder)* filmer (à la caméra vidéo); **they didn't know they were being videoed** ils ne savaient pas qu'ils étaient filmés
▸ ▸ *Comput* **v. accelerator card** carte *f* vidéo accélératrice; **v. art** art *m* vidéo; *Comput* **v. board** carte vidéo; **v. camera** caméra *f* vidéo; *Comput* **v. card** carte vidéo; **v. cassette** vidéocassette *f*; **v. cassette recorder** magné-

toscope; **v. CD** vidéodisque *m*; **v. channel** canal *m* vidéo; **v. clip** clip *m*, vidéoclip *m*, clip vidéo; **v. club** club *m* vidéo; **v. conference** vidéoconférence *f*, visioconférence *f*; **v. conferencing** vidéoconférences; **v. controller** contrôleur *m* vidéo; **v. diary** journal *m* vidéo; *Am* **v. display terminal** console *f* de visualisation; **v. editing** montage *m* vidéo; **v. film** film *m* vidéo; **v. frequency** vidéofréquence *f*; **v. game** jeu *m* vidéo; **v. installation** installation *f* vidéo; **v. library** vidéothèque *f*; **v. link** liaison *f* vidéo; **v. machine** magnétoscope; **v. maker** vidéaste *mf*; **v. memory** mémoire *f* vidéo; *Br Fam* **v. nasty** = film vidéo à caractère violent et souvent pornographique; **v. player** magnétoscope *m*; **v. port** port *m* vidéo; **v. projector** vidéoprojecteur *m*; **v. prompter** télésouffleur *m*; **v. recorder** magnétoscope *m*; **v. recording** enregistrement *m* sur magnétoscope; **v. rights** droits *mpl* d'exploitation vidéo; **v. shop** ≃ vidéoclub *m*, *pl* vidéo-clubs; **v. signal** signal *m* vidéo

videodisc, Am videodisk ['vɪdɪəʊdɪsk] N disque *m* vidéo, vidéodisque *m*
▸▸ **v. player** lecteur *m* de vidéodisque

videogram ['vɪdɪəʊɡræm] N vidéogramme *m*

videographic ['vɪdɪəʊ'ɡræfɪk] ADJ vidéographique

video-on-demand N vidéo *f* à la demande

videophone ['vɪdɪəʊfəʊn] N vidéophone *m*, visiophone *m*

video-selling N *Mktg* vidéovente *f*

videoshopping ['vɪdɪəʊʃɒpɪŋ] N vidéoachat *m*

videotape ['vɪdɪəʊteɪp] N bande *f* vidéo
VT enregistrer sur magnétoscope

videotex ['vɪdɪəʊteks] N *Comput* vidéotex *m*

vie [vaɪ] VI (**vied** [vaɪd]; **vying** ['vaɪɪŋ]) rivaliser (**with sb** avec qn); **they are vying for the championship** ils se disputent le championnat; **to v. with each other in doing sth** rivaliser l'un avec l'autre/les uns avec les autres pour faire qch, faire qch à qui mieux mieux; **they v. with each other for cruelty** ils rivalisent de cruauté; **they were vying with one another to impress her** ils rivalisaient l'un avec l'autre pour la séduire

Vienna [vɪ'enə] N Vienne

Viennese [vɪə'niːz] ADJ viennois
N Viennois, -oise

Vietcong [vɪet'kɒŋ] N INV, ADJ Viêt-cong *mf*; **a prisoner of the V.** un prisonnier des Viêt-congs

Vietnam [vɪet'nɑːm, -'næm] N Vietnam *m*, Viêt Nam *m*

Vietnamese [vɪetnə'miːz] ADJ vietnamien
N **1** Vietnamien, -ienne **2** *Ling* vietnamien *m*

Viet Vet [vɪet'vet] N *Am Mil Fam* ancien *m* du Vietnam

VIEW [vjuː]

N	vue **1, 2** ▪ opinion **3**
VT	regarder **1** ▪ voir **2** ▪ considérer **3**
VI	regarder la télévision

N **1** (*sight*) vue *f* (**of** de); **exposed to/hidden from v.** exposé/caché aux regards; **to pass out of** *or* **be lost to v.** disparaître; **in v.** en vue; **in full v. of the crowd** sous les regards de la foule; **keep your hands in full v.** garde tes mains bien en vue; **they did it in full v. of the military guard** ils l'ont fait au nez et à la barbe de la sentinelle militaire; **at last a hotel came into v.** enfin j'ai/il a/*etc* aperçu un hôtel; **we were in v. of land** nous étions en vue de la terre; **to keep sth in v.** ne pas perdre qch de vue; **on v. (to the public)** (*of col-*

lection) ouvert au public; **famous people are permanently on v.** les gens célèbres sont en permanence exposés aux regards; **private v.** (*of exhibition etc*) avant-première *f*, *pl* avant-premières; (*of exhibition of paintings*) vernissage *m*; **field of v.** (*of telescope*) champ *m*; **angle of v.** angle *m* de champ
2 (*scene, prospect*) vue *f*, perspective *f*, (*photo etc*) vue; **a room with a v.** une chambre avec vue; **front v.** vue de face; **from here you have a good v. of the castle** d'ici on a une très belle vue du château; **you will get a better v. from here** vous verrez mieux d'ici; *Fig* **to take the long v.** adopter une perspective à long terme; *Archit* **front/back v.** élévation *f* du devant/du derrière; **sectional v.** vue en coupe, profil *m*
3 (*opinion*) opinion *f*, idée *f*, avis *m* (**about** au sujet de; **on** sur); **it's a widely-held v.** c'est une opinion très répandue; **point of v.** point *m* de vue; **to express a v.** exprimer une opinion *ou* un avis; **I support the v. that ...** je partage l'opinion selon laquelle ...; **to have very decided views on sth** avoir des idées très arrêtées sur qch; **what is your v. on the matter?** quelle est votre opinion sur la question?; **in my v.** à mon avis; **in the v. of many of our colleagues** de l'avis de nombreux de nos collègues; **our views differ** nos opinions diffèrent; **to share sb's views** partager les opinions de qn
4 (*intention*) **to have sth in v.** avoir qch en vue; **with this in v.** à cette fin; **they bought the house with a v. to letting it** ils ont acheté la maison en vue de *ou* dans le but de *ou* avec l'idée de la louer
5 (*prep phrase*) **in v. of what has happened** étant donné *ou* compte tenu de ce qui est arrivé; **in v. of these facts** compte tenu de ces faits; **in v. of the great heat** vu la grande chaleur
VT 1 (*look at, watch*) regarder; (*slides*) visionner; *TV* (*programme*) regarder; *Comput* (*codes*) visualiser; **when viewed from the outside** vu de l'extérieur
2 (*inspect*) inspecter, examiner; (*exhibition, paintings*) voir; (*house for sale*) visiter, voir
3 (*consider*) considérer, voir; (*prospect*) envisager; **viewed from a commercial perspective** *or* **standpoint, the proposal ...** d'un point de vue commercial, cette proposition ...; **how do you v. the situation?** comment voyez-vous la situation?; **when viewed in this light** vu sous cet angle; **to v. sth with horror/delight** envisager qch avec horreur/ravissement; **the proposal was viewed unfavourably by the authorities** la proposition était considérée d'un œil peu favorable par les autorités
VI *TV* regarder la télévision

viewable area ['vjuː:əbəl] ADJ *Comput* (*of monitor*) zone *f* d'affichage

viewdata® ['vjuː:deɪtə] N *Comput* vidéotex *m*

viewer ['vjuː:ər] N **1** *TV* téléspectateur, -trice; **I'm a regular v. of your programme** je suis un de vos fidèles téléspectateurs; **the programme has** *or* **attracts a lot of women viewers/young viewers** l'émission est beaucoup regardée par les femmes/les jeunes **2** *Phot* (*for slides*) visionneuse *f* **3** *Comput* (*program*) visualiseur *m*

viewership ['vjuː:əʃɪp] N *Am TV* public *m*

viewfinder ['vjuː:faɪndər] N *Phot* viseur *m*

viewing ['vjuː:ɪŋ] N **1** (*of exhibition, showhouse*) visite *f*, **open for v. from seven to nine** visites de sept à neuf heures; **v. is by arrangement with the owner** visite sur accord préalable du propriétaire **2** *TV* programme *m*, programmes *mpl*, émissions *fpl*; **we've got a good evening's v. tonight** il y a de bonnes choses à la télé ce soir; **this new pro-**

gramme is recommended v. cette nouvelle émission est à recommander; **the series makes for compulsive v.** c'est une série prenante *ou* captivante; **suitable for home v.** pour tout public; **the v. public** les téléspectateurs *mpl*
▸▸ *TV* **v. figures** taux *m ou* indice *m* d'écoute; *TV* **v. habits** habitudes *fpl* d'écoute; *TV* **v. hours** heures *fpl* d'écoute; **at peak v. hours** aux heures de grande écoute; *TV* **v. room** salle *f* de visionnage; *TV* **v. time** heures *fpl* de vision; **v. window** fenêtre *f* d'observation

viewpoint ['vjuːpɔɪnt] N **1** (*opinion*) point *m* de vue; **from the international v.** du point de vue international **2** (*lookout*) point *m* de vue

vigil ['vɪdʒɪl] N veille *f*, (*over sick person or corpse*) veillée *f*, *Rel* vigile *f*; **to keep v.** veiller

Note that the French word **vigile** is a false friend. Its most common meaning is **security guard**.

vigilance ['vɪdʒɪləns] N vigilance *f*
▸▸ *Am* **v. committee** groupe *m* d'autodéfense

vigilant ['vɪdʒɪlənt] ADJ vigilant; **under the v. eye of ...** sous l'œil vigilant de ...; **to be v. for sth** être à l'affût de qch; **to keep a v. watch over sth** surveiller qch avec vigilance

vigilante [vɪdʒɪ'læntɪ] N *Pej* membre *m* d'un groupe d'autodéfense
▸▸ **v. group** groupe *m* d'autodéfense

vigilant(e)ism [vɪdʒɪ'lænt(ɪ)ɪz(ə)m] N *esp Am Pej* = tendance *f* au développement de l'autodéfense ou des milices privées

vigilantly ['vɪdʒɪləntlɪ] ADV vigilamment, avec vigilance

vignette [vɪ'njet] N **1** (*illustration*) vignette *f*, (*portrait, photo*) buste *m* sur un fond dégradé; *Fig* **this ten-minute v. of city life** cet aperçu de dix minutes de la vie dans une grande ville **2** (*camera matte*) cache *m*

vigor ['vɪɡər] N *Am* = **vigour**

vigorous ['vɪɡərəs] ADJ **1** (*robust*) (*person, plant*) vigoureux; (*enthusiastic*) (*person*) enthousiaste **2** (*forceful*) (*opposition, campaign, support*) vigoureux, énergique; (*denial*) formel **3** (*energetic*) (*exercise*) énergique

vigorously ['vɪɡərəslɪ] ADV vigoureusement; **she v. denied the allegation** elle a vigoureusement nié

vigour, Am vigor ['vɪɡər] N **1** vigueur *f*, **to deny sth with great v.** nier qch vigoureusement; **the v. of youth** la sève de la jeunesse **2** *Am* **laws in v.** lois *fpl* en vigueur

Viking ['vaɪkɪŋ] *Hist* N Viking *mf*
ADJ viking
▸▸ **V. ship** drakkar *m*

vile [vaɪl] ADJ **1** (*nasty, unpleasant*) abominable, exécrable; **the soup was v.** la soupe était infecte; **he's in a v. temper** il est d'une humeur exécrable **2** (*base, despicable*) vil, infâme, ignoble; **to be v. to sb** être ignoble envers qn; **it was a v. thing to do/say** c'est ignoble d'avoir fait/dit ça; **a v. calumny** une calomnie infâme; **the vilest of men** le dernier des hommes

vilely ['vaɪllɪ] ADV **1** (*decorated etc*) d'une manière abominable *ou* exécrable **2** (*basely, despicably*) vilement, bassement; **to behave v. towards sb** se comporter d'une manière ignoble envers qn

vileness ['vaɪlnɪs] N **1** (*nastiness*) caractère *m* exécrable; **the v. of the weather** le temps abominable **2** (*baseness*) (*of person, feeling*) bassesse *f*, caractère *m* ignoble; **her v. towards her mother** la manière ignoble dont elle traite/traitait sa mère

vilification [vɪlɪfɪ'keɪʃən] N dénigrement m, diffamation f, calomnie f

vilify ['vɪlɪfaɪ] VT dénigrer, diffamer, calomnier; (reputation, name) salir

villa ['vɪlə] N (in country) maison f de campagne; (in town) pavillon m de banlieue; (at seaside, Roman) villa f; **to rent a v. in Spain** louer une villa en Espagne

village ['vɪlɪdʒ] N **1** village m; (large) bourg m; **I'm going into the v.** je vais au village; **the whole v. was talking about it** tout le village en parlait; **the v. church/grocer** l'église/l'épicier du village; **a v. inn** une auberge de campagne **2** Am (municipality) petite municipalité f
▸▸ Br **v. green** = pelouse f se trouvant au centre du village; **v. hall** salle f des fêtes; **v. idiot** idiot m du village

villager ['vɪlɪdʒər] N villageois, -oise

villain ['vɪlən] N (scoundrel) scélérat m; Br Fam (criminal) voyou m; Fam **you little v.!** petit garnement!, petit coquin!; Theat **the v. (of the piece)** le traître; Fig **so you're the v. of the piece!** alors c'est vous qui êtes responsable de tout ça!; Fig **why am I always the v. of the piece?** pourquoi est-ce que c'est toujours moi que l'on blâme?

villainous ['vɪlənəs] ADJ (behaviour, food etc) vil, infâme; (weather) exécrable; **he gave us a v. look** il nous a regardés d'un sale œil; **a v. deed** une infamie

villainously ['vɪlənəslɪ] ADV d'une manière infâme ou ignoble

villainy ['vɪlənɪ] N infamie f

villein ['vɪlən] N Hist vilain m, serf m

villus, pl **villi** ['vɪləs, -aɪ] N Anat villosité f

Vilnius ['vɪlnɪʌs] N Vilnious

vim [vɪm] N Fam vigueur f, énergie f; **full of v. (and vigour)** plein d'entrain; **put a bit more v. into it!** mets-y un peu plus d'entrain!

vinaigrette [vɪnɪ'gret] N Culin vinaigrette f

vindaloo [vɪndə'luː] N vindaloo m (plat indien très épicé)

vindicate ['vɪndɪkeɪt] VT (justify) (faith, claim, report) justifier; (exonerate) (person) disculper; (uphold) (what one has said) prouver; (report) appuyer; **I was vindicated by the official inquiry** l'enquête officielle m'a donné raison; **to v. one's rights** revendiquer ses droits, faire valoir son bon droit

vindication [vɪndɪ'keɪʃən] N justification f; **in v. of his conduct** pour justifier sa conduite, en justification de sa conduite; **this is a clear v. of our policy** cela démontre le bien-fondé de notre politique

vindicator ['vɪndɪkeɪtər] N défenseur m

vindictive [vɪn'dɪktɪv] ADJ (spiteful) vindicatif

vindictively [vɪn'dɪktɪvlɪ] ADV vindicativement; **he had quite v. made sure she would not get the job** par esprit de vengeance, il avait tout mis en œuvre pour qu'elle n'obtienne pas le poste

vindictiveness [vɪn'dɪktɪvnɪs] N (of reprisals, remarks) caractère m vindicatif; **the v. in her voice** son ton vindicatif; **she did it out of (sheer) v.** elle a fait cela par esprit de vengeance

vine [vaɪn] N **1** (grapevine) vigne f; Fig **to wither on the v.** ne pas aboutir **2** Am (climbing plant) plante f grimpante **3** Am Fam **vines** (clothes) fringues fpl
▸▸ **v. grower** viticulteur, -trice, vigneron, -onne; **v. growing** viticulture f; **v. harvest** vendange f, vendanges fpl

vinegar ['vɪnɪgər] N **1** (condiment) vinaigre m; **wine/cider v.** vinaigre de vin/de cidre; **tarragon v.** vinaigre à l'estragon **2** Am Fam (vitality) vigueur f, allant m

vinegary ['vɪnɪg(ə)rɪ] ADJ **1** (taste etc) de vinaigre; (sauce) vinaigré; **to turn v.** (of wine) tourner en vinaigre **2** Fam (tone) acerbe, aigre

vinery ['vaɪnərɪ] N (hothouse) serre f où l'on cultive la vigne

vineyard ['vɪnjəd] N (field) (champ m de) vigne f; (establishment) vignoble m; **the best vineyards** les meilleurs crus mpl

viniculture ['vɪnɪkʌltʃər] N viticulture f

vino ['viːnəʊ] N Fam (wine) pinard m

vinous ['vaɪnəs] ADJ vineux

vintage ['vɪntɪdʒ] N **1** (wine) vin m de cru; (year) cru m, millésime m; **this claret is an excellent v.** ce bordeaux est un très grand cru; **1982 was a good v.** 1982 a été un bonne année pour le vin; **a 1983 v.** un vin de 1983; **what v. is this wine?** quel est le millésime ou quelle est l'année de ce vin? **2** (period) époque f; **an old radio of pre-war v.** une vieille radio d'avant-guerre; **our parents are of the same v.** nos parents sont de la même génération
  ADJ **1** (wine) millésimé; (port) vieux **2** (old) ancien, antique **3** (classic, superior) classique; **the play is v. Shaw** la pièce est du meilleur Shaw
▸▸ Br **v. car** voiture f de collection (normalement construite entre 1919 et 1930); **v. year** (for wine) grand millésime m, grande année f, (for books, films) très bonne année f; **it's been a v. year for comedy** ça a été une excellente année pour ce qui est de la comédie

vintner ['vɪntnər] N Fml négociant m en vins

vinyl ['vaɪnɪl] N vinyle m; Mus Fam **the album is available on v. and CD** l'album existe sur vinyle et en CD
  ADJ (wallpaper, tiles, coat) de ou en vinyle; (paint) vinylique

viol ['vaɪəl] N Mus viole f; **bass v.** basse f de viole; Am (double bass) contrebasse f

viola[1] [vɪ'əʊlə] N Mus **1** (violin) alto m **2** (viol) viole f; **v. da gamba** viole de gambe
▸▸ **v. d'amore** viole d'amour; **v. player** altiste mf

viola[2] ['vaɪələ] N Bot **1** (genus) violacée f **2** (flower) violette f (de jardin)

violate ['vaɪəleɪt] VT **1** (disregard) violer; (sanctuary) violer, profaner; (rule) manquer à; (law) violer, enfreindre; (sb's trust) trahir; **to v. sb's privacy** faire intrusion auprès de qn **2** Old-fashioned (rape) violer, outrager

violation [vaɪə'leɪʃən] N (of oath, law, rights) violation f; (of sanctuary) viol m, profanation f; (of rule) manquement m, infraction f; (of order) infraction f; Am (traffic) **v.** infraction au code de la route; **v. of territorial waters** dépassement m des eaux territoriales; **v. of sb's privacy** intrusion f auprès de qn; **it's a v. of my privacy** c'est une intrusion; **v. of rights** abus m de droits; **in v. of the treaty, they ...** ils ont enfreint le traité et ...; **this is in v. of the treaty** c'est une violation du traité

violator ['vaɪəleɪtər] N **1** (of law) violateur, -trice **2** Old-fashioned (of woman) violateur m, violeur m

violence ['vaɪələns] N **1** (roughness) violence f; **v. on television** la violence à la télévision; **to use v.** user de violence; **to resort to v.** recourir ou en venir à la violence; Law **to commit acts of v.** se livrer à des voies de fait; **robbery with v.** vol m avec agression ou avec coups et blessures; **he had struck his victim with great v.** il avait frappé sa victime avec une grande violence; **to do v. to sth** (distort) faire violence à qch; **the translation does considerable v. to the original** la traduction dénature beaucoup le texte original **2** (intensity) violence f, intensité f; **she said, with some v.** dit-elle avec violence; **the v. of the impact** la violence du choc

violent ['vaɪələnt] ADJ **1** (fierce, rough) violent; (braking) brutal, -aux; **v. storm** orage m violent, tempête f; **to die a v. death** mourir de mort violente; **to be in a v. temper** être furieux; **to become v.** (of person) devenir violent ou agressif **2** (intense) violent, vif, fort; (coughing, fever, pain) violent; **v. colours** couleurs fpl criardes ou crues; **to take a v. dislike to sb** se prendre d'une aversion violente ou d'une vive aversion à l'égard de qn

violently ['vaɪələntlɪ] ADV **1** (fiercely, roughly) violemment, avec violence; (to die) de mort violente **2** (intensely) vivement, extrêmement; **his heart was beating v.** son cœur battait à se rompre; **after supper I became v. ill** après le souper j'ai été terriblement malade; **she was v. sick** elle a été prise de vomissements violents; **to fall v. in love with sb** tomber follement amoureux de qn

violet ['vaɪələt] N **1** (plant) violette f; Parma **v.** violette de Parme; Fig **shrinking v.** personne f timide; **she is no shrinking v.** elle est loin d'être timide **2** (colour) violet m
  ADJ violet

violin [vaɪə'lɪn] N violon m; **first v.** premier violon, violon principal
▸▸ **v. case** étui m à violon; **v. concerto** concerto m pour violon; **v. maker** luthier m

violinist [vaɪə'lɪnɪst] N violoniste mf

violoncellist [vaɪələn'tʃelɪst] N violoncelliste mf

violoncello [vaɪələn'tʃeləʊ] N violoncelle m

VIP [viːaɪ'piː] N (abbr very important person) personnage m de marque, VIP m inv; **to get the V. treatment** être traité comme un personnage de marque
▸▸ **V. guest** hôte m de marque; **V. list** liste f des VIP; **V. lounge** (in airport) = salon m d'accueil réservé aux personnages de marque

viper ['vaɪpər] N (snake), Fig vipère f; **to cherish a v. in one's bosom** réchauffer un serpent dans son sein
▸▸ Bot **v.'s bugloss** vipérin m

viperish ['vaɪpərɪʃ] ADJ vipérin, de vipère; (person) qui a une langue de vipère; Fig **v. tongue** langue f de vipère

virago [vɪ'rɑːgəʊ] N Pej virago f, mégère f

viral ['vaɪrəl] ADJ Med viral, -aux; **a v. infection** une infection virale
▸▸ Comput **v. marketing** marketing m viral

Virgil ['vɜːdʒɪl] N Antiq, Liter Virgile m

virgin ['vɜːdʒɪn] N vierge f, (man) puceau m; **he/she is a v.** il/elle est vierge; **the (Blessed) V.** la Sainte Vierge; Astron **the V.** la Vierge
  ADJ **1** (sexually) vierge **2** (forest, soil, wool) vierge; (fresh) virginal, -aux; **v. (olive) oil** huile f d'olives vierge
▸▸ Rel **the V. birth** l'Immaculée Conception f, **the V. Islands** les îles fpl Vierges; Hist **the V. Queen** (Elizabeth I) la Reine Vierge; **v. territory** territoire m vierge; Fig **this market is v. territory for the company** ce marché constitue un territoire vierge pour la société

virginal ['vɜːdʒɪn(ə)l] ADJ virginal, -aux, de vierge
  N Mus **virginal(s)**, **pair of virginals** virginal m

Virginia [və'dʒɪnɪə] N Geog la Virginie
▸▸ Bot **V. creeper** vigne f vierge; **V. tobacco** tabac m de Virginie, virginie m

virginity [və'dʒɪnɪtɪ] N virginité f; **to lose one's v.** perdre sa virginité; **to lose one's political/professional v.** perdre son innocence sur le terrain politique/professionnel

Virgo ['vɜːgəʊ] N *Astrol* Vierge f; **to be (a) V.** être (de la) Vierge

virile ['vɪraɪl, *Am* 'vɪrəl] ADJ viril

virility [vɪ'rɪlɪtɪ] N virilité f; **he's just trying to prove his v.** il essaye simplement de prouver sa virilité

virologist [vaɪ'rɒlədʒɪst] N virologiste mf, virologue mf

virology [vaɪ'rɒlədʒɪ] N virologie f

virtual ['vɜːtjʊəl] ADJ **1 it's a v. impossibility** c'est quasiment impossible; **he's a v. prisoner** il est quasiment prisonnier; **the v. extinction/monopoly** la quasi-extinction/le quasi-monopole; **he's the v. head of the business** c'est lui le vrai chef de la maison; **it was a v. failure** ce fut en fait un échec; **this was a v. admission of guilt** de fait c'était un aveu de culpabilité **2** *Phys, Comput* virtuel
▸▸ *Phys* **v. image** image f virtuelle; *Comput* **v. memory** mémoire f virtuelle; **v. reality** réalité f virtuelle; *Comput* **v. reality simulator** simulateur m de réalité virtuelle; *Comput* **v. storage** mémoire f virtuelle

virtually ['vɜːtjʊəlɪ] ADV virtuellement, pratiquement; **I'm v. certain of it** j'en suis virtuellement *ou* pratiquement certain; **v. all of them came** ils sont pratiquement tous venus

virtue ['vɜːtjuː] N **1** *(goodness, chastity)* vertu f; *Prov* **v. is its own reward** la vertu est sa propre récompense; **to make a v. of necessity** faire de nécessité vertu **2** *(advantage)* avantage m; **the hotel has the v. of being cheap** l'hôtel a l'avantage d'être bon marché; **there's no v. in just going faster** la rapidité n'a aucun mérite en soi **3** *(power)* vertu f; **the healing virtues of certain plants** les vertus curatives de certaines plantes **4 by** *or* **in v. of** en vertu de; **by v. of one's office** à titre d'office

virtuosity [vɜːtjʊ'ɒsɪtɪ] N *Mus etc* virtuosité f

virtuoso, *pl* **virtuosos, virtuosi** [vɜːtjʊ-'əʊzəʊ, -zəʊz, -ziː] N *Mus etc* virtuose mf; **he gave a v. performance** *(of musician, actor)* il a joué en virtuose

virtuous ['vɜːtjʊəs] ADJ vertueux; **to feel v. about doing sth** se sentir vertueux parce qu'on fait/a fait qch; **with that oh-so-v. look on his face** avec son (petit) air de sainte nitouche *ou* de ne pas y toucher; **there's no need to look so v.** ce n'est pas la peine de prendre ton air de petit saint

virtuously ['vɜːtjʊəslɪ] ADV vertueusement

virulence ['vɪr(j)ʊləns] N virulence f

virulent ['vɪr(j)ʊlənt] ADJ *(disease, prejudice)* virulent; *Fig (colour)* criard; **a particularly v. strain of flu** un type de grippe particulièrement violent; **to make a v. attack on sb** lancer une attaque virulente contre qn; **she was v. in her criticism of the system** elle était virulente dans sa critique du système

virulently ['vɪr(j)ʊləntlɪ] ADV avec virulence

virus, *pl* **viruses** ['vaɪrəs, -əsɪz] N **1** *Med* virus m; **there's a v. going round** il y a un virus qui sévit *ou* qui se promène; **I've got a v. of some kind** j'ai un virus quelconque; *Euph* **the v.** le sida **2** *Comput* virus m; **to disable a v.** désactiver un virus; **to write a v.** concevoir un virus
▸▸ *Comput* **v. attack** infection f virale; **v. author** créateur m de virus; **v. check** détection f de virus; **to run a v. check on a disk** faire tourner le programme détecteur de virus sur une disquette; **v. detection** détection f de virus; **v. detector** détecteur m de virus; **v. program** programme m virus

virus-free ADJ *Comput* dépourvu de virus

virus-infected ADJ *Comput* contaminé par un/des virus

Visa® ['viːzə] N
▸▸ **V. card** carte f Visa®

visa ['viːzə] N *(on passport, document)* visa m; **to apply for a v. for Poland** demander un visa pour la Pologne
VT (**visaed** ['viːzəd]) *(passport)* viser, apposer un visa à

visage ['vɪzɪdʒ] N *Fml* visage m, figure f

vis-à-vis ['viːzɑːviː] PREP *(compared with, in terms of)* par rapport à; *(about)* en ce qui concerne
N *(counterpart)* homologue mf

viscera ['vɪsərə] NPL *Anat* viscères mpl

visceral ['vɪsər(ə)l] ADJ *Anat, Fig* viscéral, -aux

viscid ['vɪsɪd] ADJ visqueux, gluant

viscidity [vɪ'sɪdɪtɪ] N viscosité f

viscose ['vɪskəʊs] N *Chem* viscose f

viscosity [vɪs'kɒsɪtɪ] N viscosité f

viscount ['vaɪkaʊnt] N vicomte m

viscountcy ['vaɪkaʊntsɪ] N vicomté f

viscountess ['vaɪkaʊntɪs] N vicomtesse f

viscounty ['vaɪkaʊntɪ] N vicomté f

viscous ['vɪskəs] ADJ visqueux
▸▸ *Tech* **v. coupling** visco-coupleur m, pl visco-coupleurs

vise [vaɪs] N *Am* = **vice²**

visibility [vɪzɪ'bɪlɪtɪ] N visibilité f; **good/bad v.** bonne/mauvaise visibilité; **v. was down to a few yards** la visibilité était réduite à quelques mètres; **v. is one hundred yards** la visibilité est de cent mètres; **the car has good front and rear v.** la voiture donne une bonne visibilité avant et arrière

visible ['vɪzɪb(ə)l] ADJ visible; **to become v.** apparaître; **the house was now v.** la maison était en vue; **v. to the naked eye** visible à l'œil nu; *Law* **to have no v. means of support** n'avoir aucun moyen apparent de subvenir à ses propres besoins; **with v. satisfaction** avec une satisfaction évidente
▸▸ *Econ* **v. assets** actif m corporel; *Com* **v. defect** défaut m apparent; *Econ* **v. earnings** gains mpl visibles; **v. horizon** horizon m

visibly ['vɪzɪblɪ] ADV visiblement, manifestement; *(to grow etc)* à vue d'œil; **she was v. moved** elle était visiblement émue

Visigoth ['vɪzɪgɒθ] N *Hist* Wisigoth, -othe

vision ['vɪʒən] N **1** *(sight)* vision f, vue f; **to have good/poor v.** avoir une bonne/une mauvaise vue; **the accident had impaired his v.** cet accident avait affaibli sa vue; **field/angle of v.** champ m/angle m visuel; *Med* **double v.** double vision, diplopie f
2 *Fig (foresight, imagination)* clairvoyance f, perspicacité f; **man/woman of v.** homme m/femme f d'une grande perspicacité *ou* qui voit loin dans l'avenir
3 *(dream)* vision f, *(apparition)* vision, apparition f, **to have** *or* **see visions** avoir des visions; **visions of wealth** visions de richesse(s); **to have visions of doing sth** se voir faire qch; **I had visions of having to walk all the way into town** je me suis vu devoir aller jusqu'en ville à pied; **I had visions of you in a police cell** je te voyais déjà dans une cellule de police; **she always had visions of owning her own business** elle avait toujours rêvé d'avoir sa propre entreprise
4 *TV* image f, **a temporary loss of v.** une perte momentanée de l'image
▸▸ **v. control** contrôle m de l'image; **v. mixer** *TV (equipment)* mixeur m, mélangeur m de signaux; *(person)* opérateur, -trice de mixage; *TV* **v. mixing** mixage m d'images

visionary ['vɪʒənərɪ] ADJ *(leader)* visionnaire
N visionnaire mf

visit ['vɪzɪt] N *(call, tour)* visite f, *(stay)* séjour m; *Comput (to Web page)* consultation f, *Am*

(talk) causerie f, causette f *(with sb* avec qn); **(social) v.** visite; **courtesy v.** visite de politesse; **I had a v. from your aunt last week** j'ai eu la visite de ta tante la semaine dernière; **to pay sb a v.** faire une visite à qn, rendre visite à qn; **to return sb's v.** rendre sa visite à qn; *Fam* **to pay a v.** *(go to lavatory)* aller au petit coin; **to be on a v.** *Br* to *or Am* **with friends** être en visite chez des amis; **I'm here on a v.** je suis ici en visite, je suis de passage ici; **the last time I made a v. to London** la dernière fois que je me suis rendu à Londres; **this is my first v. to your country** c'est la première fois que je viens dans votre pays; *Naut* **right of v. (and search)** *(at sea)* droit m de visite
VT **1** *(of doctor) (patient)* visiter; *(of representative) (customer)* passer chez; *Comput (Web page)* consulter; **to v. sb** *(call on)* rendre visite à qn; *(stay with)* faire un séjour chez qn; **we're visiting relatives** nous sommes en visite chez de la famille; **we visited the museums** nous avons visité les musées; **worth visiting** *(museum etc)* qui vaut la visite *ou* le détour **2** *Bible (punish) (person, sin)* punir; **to v. the sins of the fathers upon the children** punir les enfants pour les péchés des pères
VI **1** *(be on a visit)* être en visite; **I don't live here, I'm only visiting** je n'habite pas ici, je ne suis que de passage **2** *Am (talk)* **stay and v. a while** reste à bavarder un petit moment
▸ **visit with** VT INSEP *Am* **1** *(stay with)* être en visite chez **2** *(talk with)* bavarder avec

visitation [vɪzɪ'teɪʃən] N **1** *(official visit)* visite f, *(of bishop)* visite pastorale; **the restaurant had a v. from the Department of Health** le restaurant a eu une visite d'inspection du ministère de la Santé; *Hum* **we're having a v. from the managing director next week** le directeur général nous fait l'honneur de sa visite la semaine prochaine **2** *Rel* **(the Feast of) the V.** (la fête de) la Visitation; **v. (of God)** *(punishment)* châtiment m

visiting ['vɪzɪtɪŋ] ADJ *(circus, performers)* de passage; *(lecturer)* invité; *(birds)* de passage, migrateur, -trice; *Sport* **the v. team** les visiteurs mpl
N **to go v.** aller en visites
▸▸ *Br* **v. card** carte f de visite; *Am Fam* **v. fireman** visiteur m de marque; **v. hours** heures fpl de visite; **v. lecturer** *(who gives talks)* conférencier, -ière; *Am* **v. nurse** infirmier, -ère à domicile; *Univ* **v. professor** professeur m associé *ou* invité; *Law* **v. rights** *(of divorced parent)* droit m de visite

visitor ['vɪzɪtər] N **1** *(guest, tourist)* visiteur, -euse; *(in hospital, prison, museum etc)* visiteur, -euse; **an unexpected v.** un visiteur inattendu; **to have visitors** *(at the moment)* avoir du monde *ou* des invités *ou* de la visite; **I rarely have visitors** c'est rare que j'aie de la visite; **you have a v.** tu as de la visite; **London will have half a million visitors this summer** 500 000 personnes visiteront Londres cette été; **she is a frequent v. to our country** elle se rend régulièrement dans notre pays; **a v. from Mars** un voyageur venu de Mars; *Br* **health v.** infirmière f à domicile *ou* visiteuse **2** *(bird)* oiseau m migrateur; **this species is a winter v. to Britain** cette espèce vient passer l'hiver en Grande-Bretagne; **it's a rare v. to these shores** c'est une espèce que l'on voit rarement sous ces latitudes
▸▸ **visitors' book** *(at hotel)* registre m; *(at exhibition, tourist attraction)* livre m d'or; **v. centre** *(in park, at tourist attraction etc)* centre m d'accueil pour les visiteurs; *Br* **v.'s passport** = passeport m temporaire; **visitors' tax** taxe f de séjour

visor ['vaɪzər] N *(on helmet, cap)* visière f, **to raise/lower one's v.** soulever/baisser sa visière; *Aut* **sun v.** pare-soleil m inv

vista ['vɪstə] N vue f, perspective f, Fig perspective; Fig **to open up new vistas** ouvrir de nouvelles perspectives ou de nouveaux horizons

vistadome ['vɪstədəʊm] N Am Rail vistadôme m

visual ['vɪzjʊəl, 'vɪʒ-] ADJ visuel; **to have a v. memory** avoir une mémoire visuelle; **her comedy is very v.** son comique repose sur les effets visuels; **his fabrics have great v. appeal** ses tissus sont très attrayants visuellement
N (of design) maquette f, **visuals** (illustrative material) supports mpl visuels
▸▸ **v. aid** support m visuel; **v. arts** arts mpl visuels; **v. check** contrôle m visuel; Comput **v. display terminal, v. display unit** visuel m, écran m de visualisation; Cin, TV **v. effects** effets mpl spéciaux; Anat **v. nerve** nerf m optique; Mil, Naut **v. signal** signal m optique; Mil, Naut **v. signalling** signalisation f optique

visualization [vɪzjʊəlaɪ'zeɪʃən, vɪʒ-] N visualisation f

visualize ['vɪzjʊəlaɪz, 'vɪʒ-] VT (imagine) se représenter; (foresee) envisager; **she had difficulty visualizing him without his beard** elle avait du mal à se le représenter ou à l'imaginer sans sa barbe

visually ['vɪzjʊəlɪ, 'vɪʒ-] ADV visuellement; **v. handicapped** malvoyant; **the v. handicapped** les malvoyants mpl; **v. impaired** qui a des problèmes de vue; **the v. impaired** les personnes fpl qui ont des problèmes de vue

vital ['vaɪt(ə)l] ADJ 1 (essential to life) vital, -aux 2 (decisive, indispensable) essentiel, capital, -aux, vital, -aux; **it is v. that …** il est indispensable ou essentiel que … + subj; **to play a v. role** jouer un rôle capital; **a question of v. importance** une question d'une importance vitale ou capitale, une question de toute première importance 3 (full of life, vigorous) vigoureux, dynamique
N Anat etc **vitals** organes mpl vitaux
▸▸ **v. force** force f vitale; **v. functions** fonctions fpl vitales; **v. organ** organe vital; Med **v. signs** = température f, rythme m cardiaque et respiration f, **v. statistics** (demographic) statistiques fpl démographiques; Fam (of woman) mensurations fpl

vitality [vaɪ'tælɪtɪ] N (of organism) vitalité f, (of institution) vitalité, vigueur f, (of person, style) énergie f, vigueur; **I wish I had her v.** j'aimerais bien avoir son énergie

vitalize ['vaɪtəlaɪz] VT vitaliser, vivifier

vitally ['vaɪt(ə)lɪ] ADV **supplies are v. needed** on a un besoin vital de vivres; **v. important question** question d'une importance vitale ou de toute première importance; **it is v. important that …** il est essentiel ou il faut absolument que … + subj; **v. for the British, the European Commission has agreed** la Commission Européenne a accepté, ce qui est vital ou capital pour les Britanniques

vitamin ['vɪtəmɪn, Am 'vaɪ-] N Biol, Chem vitamine f, **v. C/D** vitamine C/D; **with added vitamins** vitaminé
▸▸ **v. deficiency** carence f vitaminique; (disease) avitaminose f, **v. pill** comprimé m de vitamines

vitiate ['vɪʃɪeɪt] VT 1 Fml (spoil, weaken) (blood, air) vicier 2 Law (contract) vicier

vitiation [vɪʃɪ'eɪʃən] N Fml viciation f

viticulture ['vɪtɪkʌltʃər] N viticulture f

vitreous ['vɪtrɪəs] ADJ 1 Chem, Geol vitreux 2 (enamel) vitrifié 3 Anat vitré
▸▸ **v. body** (in eye) corps m vitré; **v. enamel** émail m vitrifié; **v. humour** humeur f vitrée

vitrification [vɪtrɪfɪ'keɪʃən] N vitrification f

vitrified ['vɪtrɪfaɪd] ADJ vitrifié

vitrify ['vɪtrɪfaɪ] VT vitrifier
VI se vitrifier

vitriol ['vɪtrɪəl] N Chem, Fig vitriol m; **to throw v. at sb** lancer du vitriol sur qn, vitrioler qn; Fig **the v. of her remarks** la virulence ou l'acerbité de ses remarques; Fig **the article was sheer v.** c'était un article au vitriol

vitriolic [vɪtrɪ'ɒlɪk] ADJ (acid) vitriolique; Fig (attack, speech) au vitriol; **v. criticism** critique f mordante

vitriolize ['vɪtrɪəlaɪz] VT vitrioler

vituperate [vɪ'tjuːpəreɪt] VI Fml déblatérer, vitupérer (**against sb/sth** contre qn/qch)

vituperation [vɪtjuːpə'reɪʃən] N Fml vitupération f

vituperative [vɪ'tjuːpərətɪv] ADJ Fml injurieux

Vitus ['vaɪtəs] N Med Fam **Saint V.'s dance** danse f de Saint-Guy

viva[1] ['viːvə] INT, N (cry) vivat m

viva[2] ['vaɪvə] N Br Univ Fam = **viva voce** N

vivacious [vɪ'veɪʃəs] ADJ (esp woman, girl) vif, animé, enjoué; **she has a v. laugh** elle a un rire enjoué; **she is v.** elle a de la vivacité; **she was very v. yesterday evening** elle avait beaucoup d'entrain ou était très enjouée hier soir

vivaciously [vɪ'veɪʃəslɪ] ADV avec vivacité ou entrain; (to laugh) d'un air enjoué

vivacity [vɪ'væsɪtɪ] N vivacité f, entrain m; **the v. of her laugh** son rire enjoué

vivarium, pl **vivariums, vivaria** [vaɪ-'veərɪəm, -rəmz, -ɪə] N (for animals, plants) vivarium m

viva voce ['vaɪvə'vəʊsɪ] Br Univ N épreuve f orale, oral m; (for thesis) soutenance f de thèse
ADJ oral, -aux
ADV de vive voix, oralement

vivid ['vɪvɪd] ADJ (light, colour) vif, éclatant, brillant; (language, terms) vivant, coloré; (memory) très vif, très clair; **v. imagination** imagination f vive; **v. flash of lightning** éclair m aveuglant; **it left a v. impression on me** ça m'a laissé une forte impression; **I have a v. recollection of the scene** j'ai un souvenir très vif ou très net de la scène; **v. description of sth** description f vivante de qch

vividly ['vɪvɪdlɪ] ADV vivement, avec éclat; (to remember) nettement, clairement; **to describe sth v.** décrire qch d'une manière vivante ou sous de vives couleurs

vividness ['vɪvɪdnɪs] N (of light, colours) vivacité f, éclat m; (of memory) netteté f, **the v. of his style** la vigueur ou le pittoresque de son style

vivify ['vɪvɪfaɪ] VT Fml vivifier, (r)animer

viviparous [vɪ'vɪpərəs] ADJ Bot, Zool vivipare

vivisect [vɪvɪ'sekt, 'vɪvɪsekt] VT Fml pratiquer des vivisections sur

vivisection [vɪvɪ'sekʃən] N vivisection f, **the v. debate** le débat sur la vivisection

vivisectionist [vɪvɪ'sekʃənɪst] N (practitioner) personne f qui pratique la vivisection

vixen ['vɪks(ə)n] N (animal) renarde f, Pej (woman) mégère f

viz [vɪz] ADV (abbr **videlicet**) à savoir, c'est-à-dire

vizier [vɪ'zɪər] N Hist vizir m; **grand v.** grand vizir

vizor ['vaɪzər] N = **visor**

VJ [viː'dʒeɪ] N (abbr **video jockey**) présentateur, -trice de vidéoclips

VLF [viːel'ef] N Radio abbr **very low frequency**

VLSI [viːele'saɪ] N Comput abbr **very large scale integration**

V-neck N encolure f en V
ADJ à encolure en V

V-necked ADJ à encolure en V

vocab ['vəʊkæb] N Fam voca(bulaire) m

vocabulary [və'kæbjʊlərɪ] N 1 (glossary) vocabulaire m 2 (of person) vocabulaire m; (of language) vocabulaire, lexique m; **a large/small v.** un vocabulaire étendu/limité; **to enlarge one's v.** enrichir son vocabulaire
▸▸ **v. test** test m de vocabulaire

vocal ['vəʊk(ə)l] ADJ 1 Anat vocal, -aux; **the v. organs** les organes mpl vocaux 2 (music) vocal, -aux; (communication) verbal, -aux, oral, -aux 4 Fig (forthright) (person) qui se fait entendre; **to be v. in one's criticisms** faire clairement entendre ses critiques; **the most v. member of the audience** le membre de l'auditoire qui s'est fait le plus entendre; **he is very v. about …** il parle beaucoup de …, il se fait entendre souvent au sujet de … 5 (noisy) (assembly, meeting) bruyant 6 Ling (sound) vocalique; (consonant) voisé
N Ling son m vocal; Mus **vocals** chant m, partie f vocale; **on vocals** au chant
▸▸ **v. cords** cordes fpl vocales; **v. score** partition f chorale

vocalic [və'kælɪk] ADJ Ling vocalique

vocalist ['vəʊkəlɪst] N chanteur, -euse; **who was the v. on their first album?** qui chantait sur leur premier album?; **backing v.** choriste mf

vocalization [vəʊkəlaɪ'zeɪʃən] N Mus, Ling vocalisation f

vocalize ['vəʊkəlaɪz] VT 1 (articulate) (doubt, complaint) exprimer 2 Ling (consonant) vocaliser
VI Mus faire des vocalises, vocaliser

vocally ['vəʊkəlɪ] ADV vocalement, oralement; (to protest) à haute voix

vocation [vəʊ'keɪʃən] N vocation f, **to have a v.** avoir une vocation; **teaching is a v.** l'enseignement, c'est une vocation; **to miss one's v.** manquer sa vocation

vocational [vəʊ'keɪʃənəl] ADJ professionnel
▸▸ **v. course** (short) stage m de formation professionnelle; (longer) enseignement m professionnel; **v. guidance** conseiller d'orientation m; Am **v. guidance counselor** orienteur m professionnel; **v. qualification** qualification f professionnelle; **v. training** formation f professionnelle

vocative ['vɒkətɪv] Gram N vocatif m; **in the v.** au vocatif
ADJ **the v. case** le vocatif

vociferate [və'sɪfəreɪt] VI (protest) vociférer, crier (**against** contre)

vociferation [vəsɪfə'reɪʃən] N (protest) vocifération f, cri m

vociferous [və'sɪfərəs] ADJ vociférant, bruyant; **she was most v. in her opposition** elle s'y est opposée bruyamment

vociferously [vɒ'sɪfərəslɪ] ADV bruyamment; (to protest) à haute voix

VOD [viːəʊ'diː] N (abbr **video on demand**) vidéo f à la demande

vodka ['vɒdkə] N vodka f, **v. and orange** vodka-orange

vogue [vəʊg] N vogue f, mode f (**for** de); **in v.** en vogue, à la mode; **to come into v.** devenir à la mode; **out of v.** démodé; **v. word** mot m à la mode

voice [vɔɪs] N 1 (of person) voix f, **to raise/lower one's v.** hausser/baisser la voix; **to keep one's v. down** parler à voix basse; **his v. has broken** sa voix a mué; **his v. was breaking** (with emotion) sa voix se brisait; **in a low v.** à voix basse, à mi-voix; **he's got a deep v.** il a une voix grave; **to speak in a**

loud v. parler à haute voix *ou* à voix haute; **at the top of one's** v. à tue-tête; **to make one's** v. **heard** se faire entendre; **he likes the sound of his own** v. il aime à s'entendre parler; **she's not in (good)** v. *(of singer)* elle n'est pas en voix; **to lose one's** v. perdre sa voix **2** *Fig* a dissenting v. un protestataire; **hers was the only dissenting** v. elle était la seule à protester; **the** v. **of conscience/reason** la voix de la conscience/de la raison; **a little** v. **inside her told her it was wrong** *(her conscience told her)* une petite voix en elle lui dit que c'était mal; **the** v. **of the people** la voix du peuple; **with one** v. tout d'une voix, à l'unanimité; **to give** v. **to one's indignation** exprimer son indignation **3** *(right to express opinion)* voix f, suffrage m; **we have no** v. **in the matter** nous n'avons pas voix au chapitre; **proportional representation would give small parties a greater** v. la représentation proportionnelle donnerait davantage voix au chapitre aux petits partis
4 *Gram (of verb)* voix f, **in the active/passive** v. à la voix active/passive, à l'actif/au passif VOIR GRAMMAIRE A40; B39

▸ VT **1** *(opinion, one's anger etc)* exprimer; **to** v. **the general feeling** exprimer le sentiment général *ou* l'opinion générale **2** *Ling (consonant)* sonoriser

▸▸ v. **activation** commande f vocale; v. **box** larynx m; *Comput* v. **card** carte f vocale; *Comput* v. **chip** puce f de reconnaissance vocale; v. **coach** répétiteur m vocal; v. **dialling** *(on mobile phone)* numérotation f vocale; *Comput* v. **input** entrée f vocale; v. **mail** messagerie f vocale; V. **of America** = station f de radio américaine émettant dans le monde entier; *Comput* v. **recognition** reconnaissance f de la parole; *Comput* v. **recognition software** logiciel m de reconnaissance vocale; *Comput* v. **response** réponse f vocale; *Comput* v. **synthesizer** synthétiseur m de paroles; v. **test** audition f

voice-activated [-æktɪveɪtɪd] ADJ *(device)* commandé par la voix, à commande vocale

voiced [vɔɪst] ADJ *Ling (consonant)* sonore

-voiced [vɔɪst] SUFF **low/loud-v.** à la voix basse/forte

voiceless ['vɔɪslɪs] ADJ *Ling* sourd, non voisé

voice-over N *Cin, TV* voix f off, voix hors champ, voix en surimpression; **who did the** v.? qui a fait la voix off *ou* la voix hors champ?

void [vɔɪd] ADJ **1** v. **of** *(lacking in)* dépourvu *ou* dénué de; **the proposal is** v. **of reason** la proposition est dénuée *ou* dépourvue de raison **2** *Law (deed, contract)* **(null and)** v. nul; **to make** v. annuler, frapper de nullité **3** *Lit (empty)* vide

▸ N vide m; **to fill the** v. combler le vide; **the aching** v. **in his heart** le vide douloureux qu'il y avait dans son cœur

▸ VT **1** *Law (contract)* résoudre, annuler **2** *(one's bowels)* évacuer

voile [vɔɪl] N *Tex* voile m

vol 1 *Phys (abbr* **volume***)* vol **2** *(abbr* **volume***) (book in series)* tome, t

volatile ['vɒlətaɪl] ADJ **1** *(person)* versatile, inconstant; *(situation)* explosif; **she's been rather** v. **recently** elle est d'humeur assez changeante ces temps-ci **2** *(prices, market)* volatile **3** *Chem* volatil **4** *Comput (memory)* volatil

volatility [vɒlə'tɪlɪtɪ] N **1** *(of person)* inconstance f, caractère m changeant; *(of situation)* caractère explosif; *(of prices, market)* volatilité f; **the** v. **of her moods** ses changements d'humeur **2** *Chem* volatilité f

volatilize [vɒ'lætɪlaɪz] *Chem* VT *(liquid)* volatiliser

▸ VI se volatiliser

vol-au-vent ['vɒləʊvɒn] N *Culin* vol-au-vent m *inv*

volcanic [vɒl'kænɪk] ADJ *Geog, Fig* volcanique

volcano, *pl* **volcanoes** [vɒl'keɪnəʊ, -əʊz] N volcan m

vole [vəʊl] N *(animal)* campagnol m

volition [və'lɪʃən] N volition f, volonté f; **to do sth of one's own** v. faire qch de son propre gré

volley ['vɒlɪ] N **1** *(of gunfire)* volée f, salve f; *(of blows, stones etc)* volée, grêle f; *Fig (of insults)* volée, bordée f; **to fire** *or* **discharge a** v. tirer une volée *ou* une salve **2** *Sport (balle f prise de)* volée f; *Tennis* **half** v. demi-volée f, *pl* demi-volées

▸ VT **1** *Mil (projectiles)* tirer une volée *ou* une salve de **2** **to** v. **the ball** *Tennis* effectuer une volée; *Ftbl* reprendre la balle de volée; *Tennis* **to half** v. **the ball** effectuer une demi-volée

▸ VI **1** *(of guns)* partir ensemble **2** *Tennis* relancer la balle à la volée; **he is volleying extremely well** sa volée est superbe

volleyball ['vɒlɪbɔːl] N *Sport* volley-ball m, volley m

▸▸ v. **player** volleyeur, -euse

volt [vəʊlt] N *Elec* volt m

voltage ['vəʊltɪdʒ] N *Elec* tension f; **high/ low** v. haute/basse tension

voltaic [vɒl'teɪɪk] ADJ *Elec* voltaïque

volte-face ['vɒltfɑːs] N volte-face f *inv*; **to make a (complete)** v. faire volte-face

voltmeter ['vəʊltmiːtər] N *Elec* voltmètre m

volubility [vɒljʊ'bɪlɪtɪ] N volubilité f

voluble ['vɒljʊb(ə)l] ADJ voluble; **he was** v. **in his denials** il a nié avec volubilité; **to be a** v. **talker** parler avec beaucoup de volubilité

volubly ['vɒljʊblɪ] ADV avec volubilité

volume ['vɒljuːm] N **1** *(book)* volume m, tome m; v. **one** volume *ou* tome premier, premier volume; **work in six volumes, six-v. work** ouvrage m en six volumes; *Fig* **to speak volumes** *(of action, remark etc)* être révélateur **(about** de), en dire long **(about** sur) **2** *(amount)* volume m; v. **of business/sales** volume des affaires/des ventes; **volumes of smoke** nuages *mpl ou* tourbillons *mpl* de fumée; **volumes of water** flots *mpl ou* torrents *mpl* d'eau; **a huge** v. **of work** une énorme quantité de travail **3** *Mus, Radio, TV* volume m; **to turn the** v. **up/down** augmenter/diminuer le volume; *Radio* **at full** v. à fond, à plein volume; **turn the radio up full** v. mets la radio à fond

▸▸ *Radio, TV* v. **control** bouton m de réglage du volume; *Comput* v. **label** label m de volume; *Mktg* v. **mailing** multipostage m, publipostage m groupé

volumetric [vɒljʊ'metrɪk] ADJ *Chem, Phys* volumétrique

▸▸ v. **analysis** analyse f volumétrique

voluminous [və'luːmɪnəs] ADJ **1** *(correspondence, documentation)* volumineux; *(notes)* copieux; **in** v. **detail** en grands détails **2** *(jacket etc)* ample

voluminously [vɒ'luːmɪnəslɪ] ADV abondamment

voluntarily [vɒlʌn'teərɪlɪ] ADV **1** *(willingly)* volontairement, de son plein gré **2** *(unpaid)* bénévolement

voluntary ['vɒlənt(ə)rɪ] ADJ **1** *(freely given) (statement, donation, gift)* volontaire, spontané **2** *(unpaid) (help, service)* bénévole; **the shop is run on a** v. **basis** le personnel du magasin se compose de bénévoles, le magasin est tenu par des bénévoles **3** *(optional)* facultatif; **attendance on the course is purely** v. la participation au cours est facultative **4** *Physiol* volontaire

▸ N *Rel, Mus (on organ)* morceau m pour orgue; *(on trumpet)* morceau pour trompette

▸▸ *Com* v. **chain** chaîne f volontaire; v. **export restraint** autolimitation f des exportations; *Com* v. **group** groupe m volontaire; v. **organization** organisation f bénévole; *Br* v. **redundancy** départ m volontaire; *Com* v. **retailer chain** chaîne f volontaire de détaillants; v. **service** service m volontaire; v. **work** travail m bénévole, bénévolat m; v. **worker** bénévole mf

volunteer [vɒlən'tɪər] N **1** volontaire mf; **can I have a** v. **from the audience?** y a-t-il une personne dans la salle qui voudrait bien venir sur scène? **2** *(unpaid worker)* bénévole mf

▸ VT *(one's services)* offrir volontairement *ou* spontanément; *(information)* donner spontanément; **to** v. **advice** offrir des conseils; **she seemed unwilling to** v. **anything more than this** elle n'avait pas l'air de vouloir en dire plus; **'maybe I will' was as much as he would** v. pour toute réponse il déclara 'peut-être que oui'; **to** v. **to do sth** se porter volontaire *ou* se proposer pour faire qch; **I wish I'd never volunteered to help** si seulement je ne m'étais pas porté volontaire pour aider!; **he's always volunteering other people** il propose toujours les services des autres sans leur demander leur avis; **they volunteered their son to look after the neighbours' dog** ils ont proposé que leur fils s'occupe du chien des voisins

▸ VI se porter volontaire; *Mil* s'engager comme volontaire **(for** pour); *(for charitable work etc)* proposer ses services **(for** pour); **why don't you** v.? pourquoi est-ce que tu ne te portes pas volontaire?; *(as audience participant)* pourquoi est-ce que tu n'y vas pas?; **I wish I'd never volunteered for this** si seulement je ne m'étais pas porté volontaire!

▸▸ v. **army** armée f de volontaires; v. **service** service m volontaire

voluptuary [və'lʌptʊərɪ] N *esp Pej* voluptueux, -euse

voluptuous [və'lʌptjʊəs] ADJ **1** *(figure)* sensuel **2** *(pleasure)* voluptueux

voluptuously [və'lʌptʊəslɪ] ADV voluptueusement

voluptuousness [və'lʌptjʊəsnɪs] N **1** *(of figure)* sensualité f **2** *(of pleasure)* volupté f

vom [vɒm] *Fam* N *(vomit)* dégueulis m

▸ VI (**-mm-**) dégueuler, gerber

vomit ['vɒmɪt] N vomissure f, vomi m; **to choke on one's own** v. s'étouffer avec son propre vomi

▸ VT vomir; **to** v. **blood** vomir du sang; **he vomits everything he eats** il vomit *ou* rejette *ou* rend tout ce qu'il mange; **to** v. **(forth) smoke** *(of chimney)* vomir de la fumée

▸ VI vomir

vomiting ['vɒmɪtɪŋ] N vomissements *mpl*

voodoo ['vuːduː] N vaudou m

▸▸ v. **priest** prêtre m vaudou

voodooism ['vuːduːɪz(ə)m] N vaudou m

voracious [və'reɪʃəs, vɒ-] ADJ *(person, appetite)* vorace; *(hunger)* vorace, de loup; *(reader)* avide; **I was feeling quite** v. j'avais une faim de loup

voraciously [və'reɪʃəslɪ, vɒ-] ADV *(to eat)* voracement, avec voracité; *(to read)* avidement; **to be** v. **hungry** avoir une faim de loup

voracity [vɒ'ræsɪtɪ] N voracité f

vortex, *pl* **vortices, vortexes** ['vɔːteks, -ɪsiːz, -eksɪz] N *Lit (of dust, smoke)* tourbillon m; *(whirlpool)* gouffre m; *Fig* **the** v. **of politics** le tourbillon de la politique

votary ['vəʊtərɪ] N fervent, -ente **(of** de); *Rel* dévot, -ote **(of** à)

vote [vəʊt] N **1** *(by a group)* vote m, scrutin m;

(of individual) vote, voix *f*, suffrage *m*; *(right to vote)* droit *m* de vote; **v. by a show of hands** vote à main levée; **popular v.** consultation *f* populaire; **to put a question to the v.** soumettre une question au vote; **let's put it to the v.** votons; **to take the v.** procéder au scrutin; **to take a v. on sth** voter sur qch; **to give one's v. to sb** donner son vote *ou* sa voix à qn; **to count** *or* **tell the votes** compter les votes, dépouiller le scrutin; **they've got my v.** je vote pour eux; **can I count on your v.?** puis-je compter sur votre vote?; **to be elected by one v.** être élu à une voix de majorité; **the motion was adopted by six votes to two** la motion a été adoptée par six voix contre deux; **how many votes did she get?** combien de voix est-ce qu'elle a obtenu?; **to record** *or* **cast one's v.** voter; **the v. went against her** le vote a été en sa défaveur; **one man, one v.** suffrage universel; **to have the v.** avoir le droit de vote; **votes for women!** le droit de vote aux femmes!; **British women got the v. in 1928** les femmes britanniques ont obtenu le droit de vote en 1928; **the Republicans got 52% of the v.** les républicains ont remporté 52% du scrutin; **to increase one's (share of the) v.** obtenir de meilleurs résultats; **they increased their v. by 12%** ils ont amélioré leurs résultats de 12%; **to lose the trade union/black v.** perdre les suffrages des syndicalistes/des Noirs

2 *(of assembly)* motion *f*, résolution *f*; **v. of censure** *or* **no confidence** motion de censure; **v. of confidence** vote *m* de confiance; **to propose a v. of thanks** faire un discours de remerciement

VI voter **(for** pour; **against** contre); **to v. by (a) show of hands** voter à mains levées; **to v. in favour of a proposal** voter une proposition; **to v. Communist** voter communiste; **v. for Thomas!** votez Thomas!; *Fig* **to v. with one's feet** *(by leaving)* indiquer sa désapprobation en quittant les lieux; *(by not turning up)* indiquer sa désapprobation en ne venant pas

VT *(sum of money, credit)* voter; **to v. £50,000 for the victims of the disaster** voter 50 000 livres pour les sinistrés; **the senators voted themselves a pay rise** les sénateurs se sont voté une augmentation de salaire; **I v. (that) we go** je propose que nous y allions; **they voted the holiday a success** ils ont décidé d'un commun accord que les vacances avaient été une réussite

▸ **vote down** VT SEP *(motion)* rejeter; *(candidate)* *(not elect)* ne pas élire; *(not re-elect)* ne pas réélire

▸ **vote in** VT SEP *(candidate)* élire **(as** en tant que)

▸ **vote on** VT INSEP mettre au vote; **the Chairman refused to let them v. on it** le président a refusé de les laisser mettre la question au vote

▸ **vote out** VT SEP *(decision, bill etc)* rejeter; *(person)* ne pas réélire

▸ **vote through** VT SEP ratifier, approuver, accepter

vote-buying N achat *m* de voix *ou* de votes

vote-catcher N politique *f* électoraliste; **the government believes its new policy will be a v.** le gouvernement pense que sa nouvelle politique va lui rapporter des voix

vote-loser N = politique *f* peu populaire qui risque de faire perdre des voix; **his proposal to raise income tax is certain to be a v.** sa proposition d'augmenter l'impôt sur le revenu va très certainement lui faire perdre des voix

voter ['vəʊtər] N électeur, -trice, mandant,

-ante; **the voters** l'électorat *m*; **French voters go to the polls tomorrow** les Français vont aux urnes demain

▸▸ **v. apathy** apathie *f* électorale *ou* des électeurs; **v. registration** inscription *f* sur les listes électorales; **v. turnout** *(at election)* taux *m* de participation électorale

vote-selling N vente *f* de voix *ou* de votes

vote-trading N échange *m* de voix *ou* de votes

vote-winner N = politique *f* populaire permettant de remporter une victoire électorale; **Labour believes its plans to cut taxes were a v. at last year's elections** le Parti travailliste pense que c'est son intention de réduire les impôts qui lui a valu la victoire aux élections de l'année dernière

voting ['vəʊtɪŋ] ADJ *(assembly, member)* votant

N vote *m*; scrutin *m*; **result of the v.** résultat *m* du vote *ou* scrutin

▸▸ **v. behaviour** comportement *m* électoral; **v. booth** isoloir *m*; *Am* **v. machine** machine *f* pour enregistrer les votes; **v. method** méthode *f* électorale; **v. paper** bulletin *m* de vote; *Fin* **v. rights** droits *mpl* de vote; **v. shares** actions *fpl* donnant droit au vote

votive ['vəʊtɪv] ADJ votif

▸▸ **v. offering** ex-voto *m inv*

vouch [vaʊtʃ] VI **to v. for the truth of sth** témoigner de *ou* répondre de *ou* attester la vérité de qch; **to v. for sb** répondre de qn, se porter garant de qn; **I can v. for his honesty** je peux me porter garant de son honnêteté; **I can v. for the severity of the side effects** je peux témoigner de la sévérité des effets secondaires

voucher ['vaʊtʃər] N **1** *(receipt as proof of transaction)* pièce *f* justificative; *Com* pièce comptable **2** *(giving price reduction)* coupon *m*; *(to exchange for goods, service etc)* bon *m*; **(gift) v.** bon-cadeau *m*, *pl* bons-cadeaux; **luncheon v.** chèque-repas *m*, *pl* chèques-repas, chèque-restaurant *m*, *pl* chèques-restaurant

vouchsafe [vaʊtʃ'seɪf] VT *Fml* **to v. sb sth** accorder *ou* octroyer qch à qn; **to v. to do sth** *(condescend)* daigner faire qch

vow [vaʊ] N vœu *m*, serment *m*; **to take one's vows** prononcer *ou* faire ses vœux; **to make a v.** faire un vœu; **to do (to do** faire); **to take a v. of poverty** faire vœu de pauvreté; **to take a v. of silence** *(of monk etc)* faire vœu de silence; *(refuse to talk about sth)* promettre de ne rien dire; **to break a v.** rompre *ou* transgresser un vœu, rompre un serment; **to keep a v.** respecter un serment

VT vouer, jurer; **to v. obedience** jurer obéissance; **to v. revenge on sb** faire vœu de se venger sur qn; **to v. to do sth** faire vœu *ou* jurer de faire qch

vowel ['vaʊəl] N *Ling* voyelle *f*

▸▸ **v. shift** mutation *f* vocalique; **v. sound** son *m* vocalique

vox pop [vɒks] N forum *m* populaire; *(street interview)* micro-trottoir *m*, *pl* micros-trottoirs

voyage ['vɔɪɪdʒ] N traversée *f*; **a transatlantic v.** un voyage ou une traversée transatlantique; **to go on a v.** partir en voyage; **a round-the-world v.** un voyage autour du monde; **a v. to Jupiter** un voyage vers Jupiter

VI *Lit* voyager; **to v. across the ocean/the desert** traverser l'océan/le désert

voyager ['vɔɪɪdʒər] N *Lit* voyageur, -euse

voyeur [vwɑ:'jɜ:r] N voyeur, -euse

voyeurism [vwɑ:'jɜ:rɪz(ə)m] N voyeurisme *m*

voyeuristic [vwɑ:jɜ:'rɪstɪk] ADJ **to take a v. pleasure in sth** prendre un plaisir de voyeur à qch; **it's just v.** ce n'est que du voyeurisme

VP [vi:'pi:] N *abbr* **Vice-President**

VR [vi:'ɑ:r] *Br (abbr* **Victoria Regina)** la reine Victoria

VRAM ['vi:ræm] N *Comput (abbr* **volatile or video random access memory)** VRAM *f*

VRML [vi:ɑ:rem'el] N *Comput (abbr* **virtual reality modelling language)** VRML *m*

vs *(abbr* **versus)** contre

V-shaped ADJ en V

V-sign N **to give the V.** *(for victory, approval)* faire le V de la victoire; *Br* **to give sb the V.** *(as insult)* ≃ faire un bras d'honneur à qn

VSO [vi:es'əʊ] N *Br abbr* **Voluntary Service Overseas**

VT [vi:'ti:] N *(abbr* **videotape)** bande *f* vidéo; **VT editing** montage *m* vidéo

Vt *abbr* **Vermont**

VTOL [vi:ti:əʊ'el] N *(abbr* **vertical take-off and landing)** *(aircraft)* ADAV *m*; *(system)* décollage *m* et atterrissage *m* verticaux

VTR [vi:ti:'ɑ:r] N *(abbr* **videotape recorder)** magnétoscope *m*

vulcanite ['vʌlkənaɪt] N ébonite *f*

vulcanization [vʌlkənaɪ'zeɪʃən] N *Ind* vulcanisation *f*

vulcanize ['vʌlkənaɪz] VT *Ind (rubber)* vulcaniser

vulgar ['vʌlgər] ADJ **1** *(coarse)* vulgaire; **don't be v.!** ne sois pas vulgaire!; **to make v. remarks** dire des vulgarités *fpl*; **to be v. in one's speech** s'exprimer vulgairement **2** *Fml (widespread)* vulgaire, commun; **the v. tongue** la langue commune, la langue vulgaire

▸▸ **v. fraction** fraction *f* ordinaire; **V. Latin** latin *m* vulgaire

vulgarian [vʌl'geərɪən] N *(coarse person)* personne *f* vulgaire

vulgarism ['vʌlgərɪz(ə)m] N vulgarisme *m*; *(swearword)* vulgarité *f*, grossièreté *f*

vulgarity [vʌl'gærɪtɪ] N vulgarité *f*, grossièreté *f*

vulgarization [vʌlgəraɪ'zeɪʃən] N vulgarisation *f*

vulgarize ['vʌlgəraɪz] VT vulgariser; *Pej (one's style etc)* vulgariser, trivialiser

vulgarly ['vʌlgəlɪ] ADV *(coarsely)* vulgairement, grossièrement; *Fml (informally)* vulgairement

Vulgate ['vʌlgɪt, -eɪt] N *Rel* **the V.** la Vulgate

vulnerability [vʌln(ə)rə'bɪlɪtɪ] N vulnérabilité *f*

vulnerable ['vʌln(ə)rəb(ə)l] ADJ vulnérable; **he's at a v. age** il est à un âge vulnérable; **v. to criticism** sensible à la critique; **that's her v. spot** c'est son point faible *ou* son talon d'Achille; **the v. spot in our defences** le point faible de nos défenses; **this left them v. on their eastern border** cela les a laissés dans une position vulnérable sur leur frontière est

vulture ['vʌltʃər] N vautour *m*; *Fig* vautour, rapace *m*

vulva ['vʌlvə] N *Anat* vulve *f*

vulvitis [vʌl'vaɪtɪs] N *Med* vulvite *f*

VU meter [vju:] N *TV* vu-mètre *m*, *pl* vu-mètres

vv *abbr* **verses**

vying *see* **vie**

W¹, w [ˈdʌb(ə)ljuː] **N** *(letter)* W, w *m*; **two w's** deux w

W² 1 *Elec (abbr* **watt(s)**) W **2** *(abbr* **west**) O.

W3 [dʌb(ə)ljuːˈθriː] **N** *Comput (abbr* **World Wide Web**) W3 *m*, le Web *m*

WAAF [wæf] **N** *Mil (abbr* **Women's Auxiliary Air Force**) = groupe *m* de femmes, auxiliaires de l'armée de l'air britannique durant la Seconde Guerre mondiale

wack [wæk] **ADJ** *Am Fam (worthless)* nul, *f* nulle; *(mad)* cinglé, dingue; *(stupid)* débile

wack-job **N** *Am Fam* cinglé, -ée, dingue *mf*

wacko [ˈwækəʊ] *Fam* **N** cinglé, -ée, dingue *mf*
  ADJ cinglé, dingue

wacky [ˈwækɪ] **ADJ** *Fam (person, sense of humour)* farfelu; *(idea, film)* loufoque
  ► ► *Hum* **w. baccy** *(marijuana)* herbe *f*

wad [wɒd] **N 1** *(of cotton wool)* tampon *m*, bouchon *m*; *(of chewing gum)* boulette *f* **2** *(of bank notes)* liasse *f*, *(of forms, documents)* paquet *m*, pile *f*, tas *m*; *esp Am* **to shoot one's w.** *Fam (spend all one's money)* claquer tout son fric; *(Vulg (ejaculate)* décharger, envoyer la sauce *ou* la purée **3** *Mil (for cartridge)* bourre *f*
  VT (-dd-) 1 *Sewing* ouater, capitonner **2** *(paper)* faire un tampon de; **she wadded (up) the money and stuffed it in her pocket** elle plia les billets et les fourra dans sa poche
► **wad up** **VT SEP** = wad **VT**

wadding [ˈwɒdɪŋ] **N** *(material for clothes)* ouate *f*

waddle [ˈwɒd(ə)l] **N** dandinement *m*; **to walk with a w.** *(of person)* marcher en se dandinant
  VI se dandiner, marcher en se dandinant; **to w. along** avancer en se dandinant

wade [weɪd] **VI 1** *(in water)* **the only way to cross the river was by wading** la seule façon de traverser la rivière était à gué; **to w. across a stream** passer un cours d'eau à gué; **he waded out to the island** il est allé jusqu'à l'île à gué; **she waded into the river to rescue him** elle s'avança dans la rivière pour le sauver **2** *esp Am (paddle)* patauger dans l'eau
  VT *(stream)* passer à gué
► **wade in** **VI 1** *(go into water)* entrer dans l'eau **2** *Fig (to work, task)* s'y mettre; **when the fight started, everybody waded in** quand la bagarre a commencé tout le monde s'en est mêlé; **he always has to w. in with his opinion** il faut toujours qu'il donne son avis; **it would have been much better if you had let them sort it out themselves instead of wading in** tu aurais mieux fait de les laisser se débrouiller entre eux plutôt que de t'y mettre aussi
► **wade into** **VT INSEP** *Fig (attack) (person)* s'attaquer à, s'en prendre à; *(task)* s'attaquer à, se mettre à; **to w. into sb with one's fists**

attaquer qn à coups de poings; **when Anne insulted him, he waded into her** quand Anne l'a insulté, il lui a dit ses quatre vérités; **critics have waded into his latest film** la critique a démoli son dernier film
► **wade through** **VT INSEP** **to w. through mud** avancer *ou* marcher péniblement dans la boue; **to w. through piles of dirty clothing** *(walk through them)* se tailler un chemin à travers des piles de linge sale; *Fam (wash them)* venir à bout de piles de linge sale; *Fam* **I'm wading through his latest novel** j'avance péniblement dans son dernier roman; *Fam* **we spent two hours wading through the agenda** il nous a fallu deux heures pour venir à bout de l'ordre du jour

wader [ˈweɪdər] **N 1** *(bird)* échassier *m* **2 waders** *(boots)* cuissardes *fpl*, bottes *fpl* de pêcheur

wadi [ˈwɒdɪ] **N** *Geog* oued *m*

wading [ˈweɪdɪŋ] **N** *(in water)* marche *f* dans l'eau
  ► ► **w. bird** échassier *m*; *Am* **w. pool** *(in swimming pool)* petit bassin *m*; *(inflatable)* piscine *f* gonflable

wafer [ˈweɪfər] **N 1** *Culin* gaufrette *f*, *Rel* hostie *f* **2** *Electron (of silicon)* tranche *f*

wafer-thin **ADJ** *(slice)* mince comme du papier à cigarette *ou* comme une pelure d'oignon; *Fig (majority)* infime; **to cut sth w.** couper qch en tranches très fines

waffle¹ [ˈwɒf(ə)l] **N** *Culin* gaufre *f*
  ► ► **w. iron** gaufrier *m*

waffle² *Br Fam* **N** *(wordiness)* verbiage *m*; **a load of (pretentious) w.** beaucoup de blabla (prétentieux); **her speech was just the usual w.** son discours n'était que du verbiage, comme d'habitude
  VI parler pour ne rien dire; *(in writing)* faire du remplissage; **what did you say to that? – I just waffled** qu'est-ce que tu as répondu à ça? – j'ai baragouiné; **you won't get away with waffling in this interview** tu ne pourras pas te tirer de cet entretien en faisant du baratin *ou* en parlant dans le vague; **he just waffles on** (il n'a rien à dire mais) il ne sait pas s'arrêter

waft [wɑːft, wɒft] **N** *(of wind, perfume)* bouffée *f*
  VT *(of wind)* **to w. a sound/a scent through the air** porter *ou* transporter un son/un parfum dans les airs; **the music was wafted in by the breeze** la musique se faisait entendre, transportée par la brise
  VI *(of smell, sound)* être porté par le vent *ou* la brise; **the scent of roses wafted in through the window** le parfum des roses entrait par la fenêtre; **her voice wafted gently down the stairs** sa voix douce parvenait jusqu'en bas de l'escalier

wag¹ [wæg] **N** *(action)* agitation *f*, **with a w. of its tail** *(of dog)* en remuant *ou* en agitant la queue
  VT (-gg-) 1 *(finger)* agiter, remuer; **to w. its tail** *(of dog, bird)* remuer *ou* agiter la queue; **to w. one's finger at sb** menacer qn du doigt; **to w. one's head** hocher la tête **2** *Br Fam* **to w. it** *(play truant)* faire l'école buissonnière
  VI s'agiter, se remuer; **its tail was wagging** *(of dog)* sa queue frétillait *ou* remuait; **tongues are wagging** les langues vont bon train (**about** sur, au sujet de); **tongues were wagging about her behaviour** son comportement faisait jaser *ou* parler les gens; **if you carry on like this tongues will begin to w.** si tu continues comme ça, les gens vont jaser; **to set (people's) tongues wagging** faire jaser les gens

wag² **N** *Fam (person)* plaisantin *m*, farceur, -euse; **what w. left this here?** qui est le petit malin qui a laissé ça ici?

wage [weɪdʒ] **N** *(pay)* **wage(s)** paie *f*, salaire *m*; *(of domestic servant)* gages *mpl*; **basic w.** salaire de base; **living w.** minimum vital; **that's not even a living w.** c'est un salaire avec lequel on ne peut même pas vivre; **to get one's weekly w.** recevoir son salaire *ou* sa paie de la semaine, *Fam* toucher sa semaine; **to earn good wages** être bien payé; *Bible* **the wages of sin is death** la mort est le prix du péché VOIR GRAMMAIRE A11
  VT **to w. war** faire la guerre (**with, on, against** à); **to w. a campaign against smoking** mener une campagne anti-tabac; **to w. a campaign for peace/against homelessness** faire campagne pour la paix/pour les sans-abri
  ► ► **w. bargaining** négociations *fpl* salariales; **w. bill** masse *f* salariale, charges *fpl* salariales; **w. bracket** fourchette *f* de salaire; **w. ceiling** salaire plafonné; **w. claim** revendication *f* salariale; **w.-cost inflation** inflation *f* par les salaires; **w. cut** réduction *f* de salaire, réduction salariale; **w. deductions** retenues *fpl* salariales, retenues sur salaire; *Br* **w. differential** écart *m* salarial; **w. earner** salarié, -ée; **w. freeze** gel *m* ou blocage *m* des salaires; **w. increase** augmentation *f* de salaire; **w. inflation** inflation *f* des salaires; **wages ledger** grand livre *m* de paie, journal *m* de paie, journal des salaires; *Br* **w. packet** *(envelope)* paie en espèces; *(money)* paie, salaire; **wages policy** politique *f* des salaires; **w. and price spiral** spirale *f* des prix et des salaires; **w. rise** augmentation de salaire; **wages sheet** bordereau *m* de salaires; *Fam* **w. slave** = personne *f* qui dépend entièrement de son salaire pour vivre

wager [ˈweɪdʒər] *Old-fashioned, Fml* **N** pari *m*; **to lay** *or* **make a w.** faire un pari, parier; **he did it for a w.** il l'a fait pour tenir un pari
  VT *(sum of money)* parier; **to w. that ...** parier que ...; **to w. one's reputation** mettre sa réputation en jeu; **I'd w. my life on it** j'en mettrais ma main au feu

waggish [ˈwægɪʃ] **ADJ** *Old-fashioned Fam* facétieux, drôle; *(sense of humour)* blagueur

waggle ['wæg(ə)l] **VT & VI** remuer, bouger; **to w. one's eyebrows/ears** (faire) remuer ses sourcils/ses oreilles

Wag(g)on ['wægən] **N** Astron **the W.** la Grande Ourse

wag(g)on ['wægən] **N 1** (horse-drawn) chariot m; Am (child's toy) petit chariot **2** (truck) camionnette f, fourgon m; Am (**station**) **w.** break m; Am (**patrol**) **w.** voiture f cellulaire **3** Br Rail wagon m (de marchandises) **4** Fig (idiom) **to be on the w.** être au régime sec; **to fall off the w.** se remettre à boire ▸▸ **w. train** convoi m de chariots (en particulier de colons américains)

wag(g)oner ['wægənər] **N** roulier m, charretier m

wag(g)onette [wægə'net] **N** (carriage) break m attelé

wag(g)onload ['wægənləʊd] **N** (of hay etc) charretée f, Rail (charge f de) wagon m

Wagnerian [vɑːg'nɪərɪən] **ADJ, N** Mus wagnérien, -ienne

wagtail ['wægteɪl] **N** (bird) bergeronnette f, hochequeue m, lavandière f

wah-wah pedal ['wɑːwɑː] **N** Mus pédale f wah-wah ou wa-wa

waif [weɪf] **N** (child) enfant mf abandonné(e); (animal) animal m errant; **she looks like a w.** elle a l'air d'une petite malheureuse; **waifs and strays** miséreux mpl

waiflike ['weɪflaɪk] **ADJ** (appearance) maigrelet; **the w. look of some models** la maigreur famélique de certains mannequins

wail [weɪl] **N** cri m plaintif, plainte f, gémissement m; (of newborn baby) vagissement m; (of siren etc) hurlement m; **she heard a w. from upstairs, the baby had obviously woken up** elle entendit des pleurs venant d'en haut, manifestement, le bébé s'était réveillé; **a w. of complaint** un gémissement plaintif; **the child gave a w.** l'enfant se mit à hurler

VI gémir; (of newborn child) vagir; (of siren) hurler; **what's he wailing about now?** de quoi se plaint-il maintenant?; **to w. over sth** se lamenter sur qch, pleurer sur qch

wailing ['weɪlɪŋ] **ADJ** (person) gémissant; (sound) plaintif; **a w. saxophone** le son aigu d'un saxophone

N (of person) plaintes fpl, gémissements mpl; (of wind) gémissements, plainte f, (of siren) hurlement m, hurlements mpl ▸▸ **the W. Wall** le mur des Lamentations

wain [weɪn] **N** Arch, Lit charrette f, **hay w.** charrette à foin

wainscot ['weɪnskət] **N** lambris m, boiseries fpl

VT (-t(t)-) lambrisser

wainscot(t)ing ['weɪnskətɪŋ] **N 1** (material) lambris m, boiseries fpl **2** (action) lambrissage m

waist [weɪst] **N 1** (of person, garment) taille f, ceinture f, **down/up to the w.** jusqu'à la ceinture, jusqu'à mi-corps; **stripped to the w.** nu jusqu'à la ceinture, torse nu; **it's too tight at the w.** ça serre à la taille; **what w. are these trousers?** quel est le tour de taille de ce pantalon?; **to put one's arm round sb's w.** prendre qn par la taille **2** (of violin) partie f resserrée de la table; (of pipe) rétrécissement m **3** Naut (of ship) embelle f, passavant m ▸▸ **w. lock** (in wrestling) ceinture f, **w. measurement** tour m de taille

waistband ['weɪstbænd] **N** ceinture f

waistcoat ['weɪskəʊt] **N** Br gilet m

waist-deep **ADJ** (water) à hauteur de la taille; **the water was almost w.** l'eau arrivait à mi-corps; **to be w. in water** avoir de l'eau jusqu'à la taille ou jusqu'à mi-corps; Fig **I'm**

w. in work/files je croule sous le travail/les dossiers, je suis submergé de travail/dossiers

waisted ['weɪstɪd] **ADJ** (coat, jacket) cintré

waist-high **ADJ** (grass) à hauteur de la taille

waistline ['weɪstlaɪn] **N** Sewing taille f, **to watch one's** or **think of one's w.** surveiller sa ligne

WAIT [weɪt] **N 1** attente f, **it was quite a w.** il a fallu attendre très longtemps; **we had a long w.** nous avons dû attendre longtemps; **it was worth the w.** ça valait la peine d'attendre; **it will be a long w. before the next train** il va falloir attendre longtemps avant que le prochain train arrive; **to lie in w.** (ambush) se tenir en embuscade; **to lie in w. for sb** (ambush) attendre qn au passage; (of military, police) tendre un guet-apens à qn

2 Br Old-fashioned **waits** (door-to-door carol singers) chanteurs mpl de Noël

VI 1 attendre; **to w. for sb/sth** attendre qn/qch; **w. a moment/a minute/a bit** attendez un moment/un instant/un peu; **to w. for sth to be done** attendre que qch soit fait; **what are you waiting for?** qu'attendez-vous?; **we're waiting to be served** nous attendons qu'on nous serve ou qu'on s'occupe de nous; **to keep sb waiting** faire attendre qn; **w. until tomorrow** attendez jusqu'à demain; **I shall w. until she's ready** j'attendrai qu'elle soit prête; **(just) you w.!** (threat) attends un peu!, tu vas voir ce que tu vas voir!; **just w. till I tell you what's happened!** attends que je te dise ce qui s'est passé!; **w. for it!** (not yet, guess what) attends!; **I can't w. to …** j'ai hâte de …; **I can't w. to see him** je brûle d'impatience de le voir; **I can't w. for the weekend** vivement le weekend, j'ai hâte que le weekend arrive; **I can hardly w.** je meurs d'impatience; Iron je n'attends que ça, je brûle d'impatience; Com **repairs while you w.** réparations minute; Prov **everything comes to him** or **to he who waits** tout vient à point à qui sait attendre; **we must w. and see** il faudra voir; **w. and see!** attends voir!; **w.-and-see policy** politique f attentiste, attentisme m; **a w.-and-see approach** une approche attentiste

2 to w. at table servir (à table), faire le service

VT (opportunity, signal) attendre, guetter; **w. your turn!** attendez votre tour!; **don't w. dinner for me** ne m'attendez pas pour vous mettre à table

▸▸ Comput **w. loop** boucle f d'attente; Comput **w. state** état m d'attente

▸ **wait about VI** attendre; **don't keep me waiting about** ne me fais pas attendre

▸ **wait behind VI** rester; **could you w. behind?, there's something I'd like to ask you** est-ce que vous pourriez attendre?, j'aimerais vous demander quelque chose

▸ **wait in VI** (stay at home) rester à la maison; **to w. in for sb** rester à la maison pour attendre qn

▸ **wait on VT INSEP** (serve) servir; Am **to w. on table** servir (à table), faire le service; **to w. on sb hand and foot** être aux petits soins pour qn

VI (continue to wait) continuer à attendre

▸ **wait out VT SEP** (war, storm) attendre la fin de; **to w. it out** patienter

▸ **wait up VI 1** (not go to bed) ne pas aller se coucher, veiller, rester debout; **she always waited up until her daughter was home** elle attendait toujours que sa fille rentre pour se coucher; **I'll w. up for you** j'attendrai que tu arrives ou rentres avant d'aller me coucher; **I'll be late so don't w. up for me** je rentrerai tard, couche-toi sans m'attendre

2 Am (halt) attendre; **w. up, I can't walk as fast as you** attends-moi, je ne peux pas marcher aussi vite que toi

waiter ['weɪtər] **N** garçon m (de restaurant); **head w.** maître m d'hôtel; **w.!** s'il vous plaît, monsieur!

▸▸ **w. service** service m à table

waiting ['weɪtɪŋ] **N 1** attente f, **it's all the w. (that) I can't stand** ce que je ne supporte pas, c'est d'avoir à attendre tout le temps; Aut **no w.** stationnement interdit **2 w. at table** service m (à table)

ADJ (person, taxi) qui attend; **to play a w. game** Mil, Pol mener une politique d'attentisme; Fig jouer la montre, attendre son heure

▸▸ **w. chef** chef m serveur; **w. list** liste f d'attente; **there's a two-month w. list for an operation** il faut attendre deux mois pour une opération; **w. period** période f d'attente; **w. room** (in office, surgery, airport, station) salle f d'attente

waitlist ['weɪtlɪst] **VT** Am mettre sur la liste d'attente; **I'm waitlisted for the next flight** je suis sur la liste d'attente pour le prochain vol

waitperson ['weɪtpɜːs(ə)n] **N** Am (male) garçon m, serveur m; (female) serveuse f

waitress ['weɪtrɪs] **N** serveuse f, **w.!** s'il vous plaît, mademoiselle!

▸▸ **w. service** service m à table

waive [weɪv] **VT** (one's claims, rights) renoncer à, abandonner; (principle) déroger à; (condition, rule) ne pas insister sur; **on this occasion, I think we can w. the rules** pour cette fois, je crois que nous pouvons nous permettre d'ignorer le règlement

> Attention: ne pas confondre avec **to wave.**

waiver ['weɪvər] **N** Law **w. of a right** renonciation f à un droit; **w. of a claim** désistement m de revendication

wake¹ [weɪk] **N** Naut sillage m; Fig **in the w. of sth** à la suite de qch; **in the w. of the storm** à la suite de la tempête; **the war brought famine in its w.** la guerre a amené la famine dans son sillage; Fig **to follow in sb's w.** marcher sur les traces ou dans le sillage de qn; **Steven followed in his father's w. and became a lawyer** Steven a suivi l'exemple de son père et est devenu avocat; **since then many other countries have followed in our w.** depuis lors bon nombre d'autres pays nous ont suivis; **he left the other athletes trailing in his w.** il a laissé les autres athlètes à la traîne ou loin derrière lui

wake² **N** (vigil over body) veillée f de corps; **to have a w. for sb** organiser une veillée de commémoration en souvenir de qn; Fig **it is too soon to hold a w. for the ideal of European unity** il est encore trop tôt pour enterrer l'idéal de l'unité européenne

wake³ (pt **woke** [wəʊk], **waked** [weɪkt]; pp **woke, waked, woken** ['wəʊk(ə)n]) **VI** se réveiller; **to w. with a start** se réveiller en sursaut

VT (person) réveiller; (from inaction) tirer de sa torpeur; (emotion, memory) éveiller, ranimer; **w. me at six** réveillez-moi à six heures; **to be hard to w.** avoir le sommeil lourd; **to make enough noise to w. the dead** faire un bruit à réveiller les morts

▸ **wake up VI 1** (from sleep) se réveiller; **come on, w. up!** allons, réveillez-vous!; (be more alert) remuez-vous!, secouez-vous! **2** Fig (become aware) prendre conscience; **it took him a while to w. up to what was going on** il lui fallut un certain temps pour comprendre ou réaliser ce qui se passait; **she's gradually waking up to the truth** elle commence à voir les choses telles qu'elles sont; **come on, w. up!** enfin, ouvre les yeux!

VT SEP (person) (from sleep) réveiller; (from inaction) tirer de sa torpeur, secouer; Fig **this**

country needs waking up ce pays a besoin de se réveiller; *Fig* that woke her up to what was going on ça lui a ouvert les yeux sur ce qui se passait

wakeboard ['weɪkbɔːd] N monoski *m* nautique

wakeboarding ['weɪkbɔːdɪŋ] N monoski *m* nautique

wakeful ['weɪkfʊl] ADJ 1 *(not sleepy)* *(person)* éveillé, peu disposé à dormir; **to have a w. night** passer une nuit blanche 2 *(vigilant)* vigilant

wakefulness ['weɪkfʊlnɪs] N 1 *(insomnia)* insomnie *f* 2 *(vigilance)* vigilance *f*

waken ['weɪk(ə)n] VT 1 éveiller, réveiller; **noise fit to w. the dead** bruit à réveiller les morts 2 *(emotion)* réveiller, ranimer
VI *esp Lit* se réveiller, s'éveiller

wake-up ADJ
▸▸ **w. call** réveil *m* téléphonique; **to ask for a w. call** *(in hotel etc)* demander à être réveillé par téléphone

wakey-wakey ['weɪkɪ'weɪkɪ] INT *Fam* debout!, réveillez-vous!

waking ['weɪkɪŋ] N **between sleeping and w.** entre la veille et le sommeil; **w. hours** heures *fpl* de veille; **to spend (all) one's w. hours doing sth** passer tout son temps à faire qch

wale [weɪl] N *Fml (of whiplash)* marque *f*, trace *f*, zébrure *f*

Wales [weɪlz] N pays *m* de Galles; **New South W.** *(in Australia)* la Nouvelle-Galles du Sud

WALK [wɔːk]

N	marche **1** ▪ promenade **2, 5** ▪ démarche **3**
VI	marcher **1** ▪ aller à pied **2** ▪ se promener **2**
VT	accompagner **2** ▪ promener **3** ▪ faire marcher **3**

N 1 *(action)* marche *f*, **it's half an hour's w. from here** c'est à une demi-heure d'ici à pied *ou* une demi-heure de marche d'ici; **it's only a short w. (from here)** c'est à deux pas (d'ici) 2 *(stroll)* promenade *f* (à pied), tour *m*; **to go for a w.** (aller) se promener, faire un tour *ou* une promenade; **it's a lovely w. from here to the village** c'est une promenade très agréable d'ici jusqu'au village; **to take sb for a w.** emmener qn en promenade *ou* se promener; **to take the dog for a w.** sortir *ou* promener le chien; *Fam* **take a w.!** *(get lost!)* va te faire voir!, disparais!; *Fam* **it was a w. in the park** *(very easy)* c'était un jeu d'enfant 3 *(gait)* façon *f* de marcher, démarche *f*, allure *f*, **I know him by his w.** je le reconnais à sa démarche 4 *(speed)* **to go** *or* **move at a w.** aller *ou* avancer au pas; **to drop into a w.** *(of horse)* se mettre au pas; *(of person) (after running)* se remettre à marcher 5 *(path)* avenue *f*, promenade *f*, *(in garden)* allée *f*, **covered w.** allée couverte; *Archit* péristyle *m*, ambulatoire *m* 6 *Am (sidewalk)* trottoir *m*; *Am* **cross w.** passage *m* clouté (pour piétons) 7 *Fig* **w. of life** *(social class)* milieu *m*; **people from all walks of life** des gens de tous milieux

VI 1 *(move on foot)* marcher; **to w. on** *or* **in the road** marcher sur la chaussée; **to w. two paces forward** faire deux pas en avant; **to w. on all fours** marcher à quatre pattes; **is the baby walking yet?** est-ce que le bébé marche maintenant?; **to w. in one's sleep** *(be a sleepwalker)* être somnambule; **I'll w. a little way with you** je vais vous accompagner un bout de chemin; **I can't w. another step** je ne peux pas faire un pas de plus; **to w. with a**

limp boiter (en marchant); **he walks five kilometres every day** il fait cinq kilomètres à pied tous les jours; *Am* **w./don't w.** *(traffic sign)* (piétons) passez/attendez; **to w. up/down the street/the stairs** monter/descendre la rue/l'escalier; **to w. up and down** *(pace the floor)* se promener de long en large, faire les cent pas; **to w. up to sb** s'approcher de qn; **to w. across** *or* **over the street to speak to sb** traverser la rue pour parler à qn; **please w. in** entrez sans frapper; **to w. through the town/the crowd** traverser la ville/la foule à pied; *Fig* **you have to w. before you can run** chaque chose en son temps; *Fig* **to w. on water** marcher sur l'eau; **as far as the party faithful are concerned, he can w. on water** aux yeux des fidèles du parti, il est capable de miracles; *Fig* **to be walking on air** être aux anges

2 *(as opposed to riding, driving etc)* aller à pied; *(for exercise, pleasure)* se promener (à pied); **to w. home/back** rentrer/retourner à pied; **I missed the bus so I had to w.** j'ai raté le bus donc j'ai dû marcher; **w.!** *(don't run)* ne cours pas!

3 *(of horse, rider)* aller au pas 4 *(of ghost)* revenir 5 *Fam (disappear, be stolen) (of money, object)* disparaître; *(disappear) (of suspected criminal)* partir; **the money seems to have walked** l'argent semble s'être envolé

VT 1 *(move along)* **to w. the streets** *(wander)* courir les rues, battre le pavé; *(of prostitute)* faire le trottoir; **to w. one's beat** *or* **one's round** *(of policeman)* faire sa ronde; *Theat* **to w. the boards** être sur les planches; *Naut* **to w. the plank** subir le supplice de la planche; *Fam* **to w. it** gagner les doigts dans le nez

2 *(accompany)* **to w. sb home** raccompagner qn; **to w. sb to the bus stop** accompagner qn jusqu'à l'arrêt de bus; **he walked me halfway home** il m'a accompagné à pied jusqu'à mi-chemin

3 *(make move)* **John walked me off my feet in London** John m'a fait marcher pendant des kilomètres à Londres; **to w. a horse** *(lead along)* conduire *ou* promener un cheval (au pas); *(bring to a walk)* mettre un cheval au pas; **to w. the dog** promener *ou* sortir le chien; **the physio walked him up and down** le kiné l'aidait à faire quelques pas

▸ **walk away** VI s'en aller, partir; *Fig* **to w. away from trouble/a problem** éviter une situation difficile/un problème; *Fig* **to w. away from a situation** se distancier d'une situation; *Fig* **just w. away from it!** laisse tomber!; **you can't just w. away from it** tu ne peux pas te dérober comme ça

▸ **walk away with** VT INSEP *Fam* 1 *(take)* prendre; **I walked away with an antique dressing table for just thirty pounds** j'ai réussi à avoir une coiffeuse ancienne pour seulement trente livres; **he walked away with a small fine** il s'en est tiré avec une petite amende

2 *(steal)* faucher

3 *(win easily) (prize, nomination)* remporter haut la main

▸ **walk in on** VT INSEP *(disturb)* déranger; **she walked in on them having sex** elle est entrée sans prévenir et les a trouvés en train de faire l'amour

▸ **walk into** VT INSEP 1 *(enter) (room)* entrer dans; **to w. straight into a job** *(after leaving school etc)* trouver *ou* obtenir facilement un emploi

2 *(collide with) (person, thing)* rentrer dans; **he walked right into me/it** il m'est rentré en plein dedans/il est rentré en plein dedans

▸ **walk off** VI s'en aller, partir
VT SEP **to w. off one's lunch** faire une promenade pour digérer

▸ **walk off with** VT INSEP *Fam* = **walk away with**

▸ **walk on** VI 1 *(continue walking)* continuer à marcher

2 *Theat (have minor stage part)* figurer, faire *ou* remplir un rôle de figurant

▸ **walk out** VI sortir *(in a rage* en colère*)*; *(go on strike)* débrayer, se mettre en grève; **you can't just w. out as soon as things get a bit difficult** tu ne peux pas disparaître *ou* tout laisser tomber dès que les choses deviennent un peu difficiles; **to w. out on one's commitments** laisser tomber ses engagements, ne pas tenir ses engagements; **the delegates walked out of the meeting** les délégués ont quitté la réunion (en signe de protestation); *Fam* **to w. out on sb** *(desert)* abandonner qn, plaquer qn; *(leave in anger)* quitter qn en colère, partir en claquant la porte

▸ **walk over** VI INSEP *Fam (treat badly)* **to w. all over sb** marcher sur les pieds de qn; **you shouldn't let him/her/people w. all over you** tu ne devrais pas te laisser marcher sur les pieds

2 *Sport* **to w. over the course** inspecter le terrain *(avant l'épreuve)*

▸ **walk round** VT INSEP *(museum, shops etc)* faire le tour de

▸ **walk through** VT INSEP *(one's exams etc)* réussir sans effort, *Fam* réussir les doigts dans le nez

walkabout ['wɔːkəbaʊt] N *(of aborigines)* voyage *m* dans le désert; *Fig (of politician, celebrity)* bain *m* de foule; **to go w.** *(of aborigines)* aller faire un voyage dans le désert; *Fig Fam (disappear, be stolen) (of missing object, money etc)* disparaître, s'envoler; *Fig* **to go (on a) w.** *(of politician, celebrity)* prendre un bain de foule

walkaway ['wɔːkəweɪ] N *Am Sport, Fam* victoire *f* facile

'walk' button N *Comput* case *f* 'marche'

walker ['wɔːkər] N 1 *(person)*, *Sport* marcheur, -euse; *(for leisure)* promeneur, -euse; **I'm not much of a w.** je ne suis pas un grand marcheur; **he's a fast/slow w.** il marche vite/lentement 2 *(aid) (for infirm person)* déambulateur *m*; *(for baby)* trotte-bébé *m*, *pl* trotte-bébés, youpala *m*

walkie-talkie ['wɔːkɪ'tɔːkɪ] N *Radio* talkie-walkie *m*, *pl* talkies-walkies

walk-in ADJ *(safe, wardrobe)* de plain pied; **the flat is in w. condition** l'appartement est libre d'occupation
N *(customer in hotel)* client, -ente sans réservation; *esp Am (patient)* patient, -ente sans rendez-vous
▸▸ **w. cupboard** débarras *m*; *(for clothes)* dressing *m*; **w. fridge** armoire *f* réfrigérante

walking ['wɔːkɪŋ] ADJ *(clothes, shoes)* de marche; **at a w. pace** au pas; **to slow (down) to a w. pace** *(after running)* se remettre à marcher; **it's within w. distance** on peut aisément s'y rendre à pied; **it's not within w. distance** on ne peut pas s'y rendre à pied; **it's ten minutes' w. distance** c'est à dix minutes à pied; **a w. holiday in the Vosges** un séjour de randonnée dans les Vosges; **we went on a w. tour of the Alps** nous avons fait de la randonnée dans les Alpes; **that man's a w. disaster area!** ce type est une catastrophe ambulante!; **she's a w. dictionary/encyclopedia** c'est un dictionnaire/une encyclopédie ambulant(e); *Am Fam* **to give sb their w. orders** *or* **papers** *(employee)* mettre *ou* flanquer qn à la porte, renvoyer qn; *(lover etc)* plaquer qn
N marche *f* (à pied), promenade *f*, promenades *fpl*, *(hiking)* randonnée *f*, *Sport* marche (athlétique); **w. is the best form of exercise** la marche est le meilleur des exercices; **two hours' w.** deux heures de marche *ou* de promenade; **I like w.** j'aime bien marcher

▸▸**w. frame** déambulateur *m*; **w. race** épreuve *f* de marche; **w. shoes** chaussures *fpl* de marche; **w. stick** canne *f*; *Mil* **w. wounded** blessés *mpl* en état de marcher

walking-out dress N *Mil* tenue *f* de ville

Walkman® ['wɔːkmən] N *(personal stereo)* Walkman® *m*, baladeur *m*

walk-on N *Theat (part)* rôle *m* de figurant
ADJ *Aviat etc (flight, service)* = pour lequel il n'est pas nécessaire d'effectuer de réservation
▸▸*Theat* **w. part** rôle *m* de figurant

walkout ['wɔːkaʊt] N *(going on strike)* débrayage *m*, mise *f* en grève; *(from meeting)* départ *m* (en signe de protestation); **to cause a w.** *(at meeting etc)* provoquer le départ d'un groupe *ou* d'une faction (en signe de protestation); **they staged a w. when their demands were refused** *(went on strike)* ils se sont mis en grève quand leurs revendications ont été refusées

walkover ['wɔːkəʊvər] N *Sport, Fam* victoire *f* facile; **it was a w.!** c'était facile *ou Fam* fastoche!

walk-through N *Theat* répétition *f* (technique)

walk-up N *(apartment)* = appartement *m ou* bureau *m* situé dans un immeuble sans ascenseur; *(building)* = immeuble *m* sans ascenseur; **they live in a third-floor w.** ils habitent un troisième étage sans ascenseur
ADJ *(apartment)* situé dans un immeuble sans ascenseur; *(building)* sans ascenseur

walkway ['wɔːkweɪ] N allée *f* (couverte), passage *m* (couvert); **(moving) w.** tapis *m* roulant

wall [wɔːl] N **1** *(of house etc)* mur *m*; *(of town, city)* murs *mpl* (d'enceinte), remparts *mpl*; *(for fortification)* muraille *f*; *(of blood cell, abdomen, cave, tunnel etc)* paroi *f*; **to live outside the city walls** vivre à l'extérieur des remparts; **only the rich lived within the walls of the city** seuls les riches vivaient intra-muros; **to leave only the four walls standing** ne laisser que les quatre murs; **between these four walls** entre ces quatre murs; **what I say now must not go beyond these four walls** ce que je vais vous dire maintenant ne doit pas sortir d'ici; **the Great W. of China** la grande muraille de Chine
2 *(of tyre)* flanc *m*
3 *Fig (of ice)* muraille *f*; *(of fire)* rideau *m*, mur *m*; *(of silence)* mur; *(of policemen)* barrage *m*; **a w. of flame** un mur de flammes; **to break down a w. of silence** abattre un mur de silence; **to come up against a blank** *or* **brick w.** se heurter à un mur; **to have one's back to the w.** avoir le dos au mur, être dans une situation désespérée; **to drive** *or* **push sb to the w.** acculer qn, mettre qn au pied du mur; **to go to the w.** *(go bankrupt)* faire faillite; **the weakest always go(es) to the w.** le plus faible est toujours battu; **to bang** *or* **beat one's head against a (brick) w.** se cogner la tête contre les murs; *Fam* **you might as well talk to a brick w.** autant parler à un mur; *Fam* **to drive** *or* **send sb up the w.** rendre qn dingue; **people like him should be put (up) against the w. (and shot)** les gens comme lui méritent la peine de mort
VT murer, entourer de murs
▸▸**w. bars** espalier *m* (pour exercices); **w. bracket** support *m* mural; **w. clock** pendule *f* murale; **w. cupboard** placard *m* mural; **w. lamp** applique *f* murale, lampe *f* murale; **w. map** carte *f* murale; **w. painting** peinture *f* murale; **W. Street** Wall Street
▸ **wall in** VT SEP murer, entourer de murs; **the park was walled in on all four sides by giant buildings** le parc était bordé sur les quatre côtés par des immeubles gigantesques; **he felt walled in by the surrounding moun-**

tains il se sentait prisonnier des montagnes qui l'entouraient
▸ **wall off** VT SEP séparer par un mur; **part of the garden was walled off from the rest** une partie du jardin était isolée du reste par un mur
▸ **wall up** VT SEP *(window, door)* murer, condamner; *Hist (prisoner)* emmurer

wallaby ['wɒləbɪ] N *(animal)* wallaby *m*

wallah ['wɒlə] N *(in India)* employé *m*, garçon *m*; *Fam* **tea w.** préposé *m* au thé; **punkah-w.** tireur *m* de panka

wallchart ['wɔːltʃɑːt] N affiche *f*, panneau *m* mural

wallcovering ['wɔːlkʌvərɪŋ] N tapisserie *f*, revêtement *m* mural

walled [wɔːld] ADJ *(garden)* clos
▸▸**w. city** ville *f* fortifiée

wallet ['wɒlɪt] N portefeuille *m*

wall-eyed ADJ *(person, fish) (with large amount of white showing)* aux yeux globuleux; *(person) (with squint)* à strabisme divergent

wallflower ['wɔːlflaʊər] N *(plant)* giroflée *f* jaune; *Fig* **to be a w.** *(at a dance)* faire tapisserie

walling up ['wɔːlɪŋ] N *(of window)* murage *m*

wall-mounted ADJ *(clock, telephone)* mural, -aux

Walloon [wɒ'luːn] ADJ wallon
N **1** Wallon, -onne **2** *Ling* wallon *m*

wallop ['wɒləp] N **1** *Fam (blow)* gros coup *m*; *(spanking)* fessée *f*; **I'll give you a w. in a minute** je vais te coller une beigne dans une minute; **she gave him a real w. across the face** elle lui a flanqué une sacrée beigne; **give it a w. with the hammer** mets-y un coup de marteau; **to pack quite a w.** *(of boxer etc)* frapper dur; *(of drink)* être fort, arracher **2** *Br Sl (beer)* bière *f*
VT *Fam (person) (one blow)* filer un gnon à; *(several blows)* battre, flanquer une raclée à; *Sport (defeat)* battre à plate(s) couture(s); **to w. the ball** *(with bat, hand)* frapper dans la balle; **she walloped him over the head with the rolling pin** elle lui donna un grand coup sur la tête avec le rouleau à pâtisserie; **w. it with the hammer** tape dessus à coup(s) de marteau; **and w.! it crashed to the ground!** et paf! il est tombé par terre!

walloping ['wɒləpɪŋ] *Fam* ADJ énorme; **a w. great lie** un gros *ou* énorme mensonge
N rossée *f*; **to give sb a w.** rosser qn; *Sport* battre qn à plate(s) couture(s); **he got a w. from his mother** il s'est fait coller une raclée par sa mère; *Sport* **we gave them a w. they'll never forget** on leur a flanqué une pâtée qu'ils ne sont pas près d'oublier

wallow ['wɒləʊ] N *(pool etc)* trou *m* bourbeux, mare *f* bourbeuse; **there's nothing like a w. in a warm bath to unwind** rien de tel qu'un bon bain pour se détendre; **to have a w. in the mud** se vautrer dans la boue; **we all enjoy a good w. in nostalgia** tout le monde aime se laisser aller à la nostalgie de temps en temps
VI *(of animal)* se vautrer; *(of ship)* être ballotté (par les flots); **to w. in self-pity** s'apitoyer sur son propre sort; **to w. in a bath** se prélasser dans un bain; **to be wallowing in luxury** baigner dans le luxe; **to w. in sin/nostalgia** se complaire dans le péché/la nostalgie

wallpaper ['wɔːlpeɪpər] N *also Comput* papier *m* peint
VT *(room)* tapisser
▸▸**w. paste** colle *f* badigeon

wallpapering ['wɔːlpeɪpərɪŋ] N **w. is easy** poser du papier peint est facile
▸▸**w. brush** *(for applying paste)* pinceau *m*

à encoller le papier peint; *(for smoothing paper)* balai *m* de colleur

wall-to-wall ADJ *(widespread, complete)* **the room was w. with people** la pièce était bondée; *Fig* **w. coverage** *(of event)* couverture *f* complète; **the sort of party where you get w. trendies** le genre de soirée bourrée de gens branchés
▸▸**w. carpet** moquette *f*; **w. carpeting** moquette *f*; **all the rooms have w. carpeting** toutes les pièces ont de la moquette

wally ['wɒlɪ] N *Br Fam (idiot)* andouille *f*, imbécile *mf*; **I felt a bit of a w.** je me suis senti un peu idiot; **he looked a real** *or* **right w.** il avait vraiment l'air d'un imbécile

walnut ['wɔːlnʌt] N **1** *(fruit)* noix *f*; **w. cake** gâteau *m* aux noix; **w. stain** brou *m* de noix **2** *(tree, wood)* noyer *m*; **w. desk** bureau *m* en noyer
▸▸**w. oil** huile *f* de noix; **w. tree** noyer

walrus ['wɔːlrəs] N *(animal)* morse *m*; **w. moustache** moustache *f* à la gauloise

Walter Mitty [wɔːltə'mɪtɪ] ADJ **to be a W. character, to live in a W. world** vivre dans un monde imaginaire

waltz [wɔːls] N valse *f*; **to play a w.** jouer une valse; **to dance a w.** danser une valse, valser; **may I have this w.?** voulez-vous danser cette valse avec moi?
VI valser; **to w. with sb** faire valser qn; *Fig* **to w. into a room** faire irruption dans une pièce; **she waltzed through the interview** elle a passé son entretien brillamment *ou Fam* les doigts dans le nez
▸ **waltz off** VI *Fam (leave)* partir, s'en aller; **to w. off with first prize** remporter le premier prix haut la main

waltzer ['wɔːlsər] N *(dancer)* valseur, -euse

wampum ['wɒmpəm] N **1** *(beads)* wampum *m (ceintures faites de coquillages servant de monnaie à certaines tribus indiennes en Amérique du Nord)* **2** *Am Fam (money)* pognon *m*, fric *m*

WAN [wæn] N *Comput (abbr wide area network)* réseau *m* longue distance

wan [wɒn] ADJ *Lit (person) (pale)* pâle, blême, blafard; *(sad)* triste; *(smile)* pâle, faible; *(light, star)* pâle

wand [wɒnd] N **1** *(magic)* baguette *f* **2** *(for bar codes)* lecteur *m* de codes barres

wander ['wɒndər] N balade *f*; **to go for a w. in the woods** aller se promener dans les bois, faire une balade dans les bois
VI **1** *(roam, stray)* errer, se promener au hasard; **we weren't allowed to w. too far from the path** nous n'avions pas le droit de nous aventurer trop loin du chemin; **don't w. too far, the bus will be here in ten minutes** ne t'éloigne pas trop, le bus sera là dans dix minutes; **they were allowed to w. wherever they wanted** ils avaient le droit d'aller là où ils voulaient; **they wandered round the town, soaking up the atmosphere** ils flânèrent dans la ville, s'imprégnant de l'atmosphère; **to w. about the house** errer dans la maison; **to w. (about) aimlessly** errer sans but; **to w. about the world** rouler sa bosse (un peu partout); **his eyes wandered over the scene** ses regards se promenaient sur cette scène
2 *(verbally)* radoter; **to w. (in one's mind)** divaguer; **to w. from the subject** sortir du sujet, digresser; **my thoughts were wandering** j'avais l'esprit ailleurs, j'étais ailleurs; **to let one's thoughts w.** laisser vaguer ses pensées; **his mind wanders at times** *or* **is apt to w.** il a des absences
3 *Fam (go)* **I think I'll be wandering off now** je crois que je vais y aller *ou* me mettre en route maintenant; **I'll just w. down to the beach later** j'irai faire un tour *ou* je descen-

drai à la plage plus tard; **could you w. round to the post office for me?** pourriez-vous passer à la poste pour moi?; **he just wandered in to the office at about 10.30** il est tranquillement arrivé au bureau à 10h30; **shall we start wandering back then?** alors, on prend doucement le chemin du retour?

VT to w. the streets traîner dans les rues; **to w. the world** courir le monde; **to w. the hills** se balader dans les collines

wanderer ['wɒndərər] N vagabond, -onde; **the w. returns!** voilà un revenant!

wandering ['wɒndərɪŋ] ADJ **1** (person) errant, vagabond; (tribe) nomade **2** (distracted) (mind, thoughts, attention) distrait, vagabond **3** (confused) (mind, person) qui divague, qui délire; (thoughts) incohérent
▸▸ Fam **w. hands** mains fpl baladeuses; **the W. Jew** le Juif errant; **w. minstrels** ménestrels mpl

wanderings ['wɒndərɪŋz] NPL **1** (roaming) pérégrinations fpl **2** (mental) **in his w.** dans ses divagations

wanderlust ['wɒndəlʌst] N désir m de voyager, passion f des voyages

wane [weɪn] N **to be on the w.** (of moon) décroître; (of person, civilization) être à ou sur son déclin; (of popularity, enthusiasm) diminuer; (of beauty) être sur le retour; (of career) être sur la pente descendante, décliner; Fig **his star is on the w.** son étoile pâlit
VI (of moon) décroître, décliner; (of beauty) se fâner; (of enthusiasm) s'affaiblir, s'attiédir; (of popularity, power, influence) diminuer; Fig **his star/his glory is waning** son étoile pâlit/sa gloire diminue

wangle ['wæŋɡ(ə)l] Fam N combine f, embrouille f, truc m
VT (get) carotter, resquiller; **I wangled myself a trip to Rome** je me suis débrouillé pour obtenir un voyage à Rome; **I'll w. it somehow** je me débrouillerai; **he wangled his way onto the delegation/into the hall** il réussit à s'immiscer dans la délégation/à s'introduire dans le hall; **could you w. me a ticket?** est-ce que tu pourrais m'avoir un ticket?; **how did you w. that?** comment est-ce que tu as arrangé ça?

wangler ['wæŋɡlər] N Fam resquilleur, -euse

wangling ['wæŋɡlɪŋ] N Fam resquillage m, carottage m; **with a bit of w. I managed to get myself a ticket** j'ai eu mon ticket en faisant marcher le système D; **it just needs a bit of w.** il suffit de resquiller un peu

waning ['weɪnɪŋ] ADJ (moon) décroissant, à son déclin; (interest, power) qui diminue; (empire) sur son déclin, en déclin; **his w. influence** son influence déclinante ou décroissante; **his w. enthusiasm** son enthousiasme en baisse
N (of moon) décroissement m; (of interest, power) diminution f; (of empire) déclin m

wank [wæŋk] Br Vulg N **1** (masturbation) branlette f; **to have a w.** se branler, se faire une branlette; **to give sb a w.** branler qn **2** Fig (nonsense) conneries fpl; **he was talking a load of w.** il disait beaucoup de conneries
VI (masturbate) se branler
▸ **wank off** Br Vulg VI se branler
VT SEP **to w. oneself off** se branler; **to w. sb off** branler qn

wankel engine ['wæŋk(ə)l] N Aut moteur m wankel

wanker ['wæŋkər] N Br Vulg connard m

wankered ['wæŋkəd] ADJ Br Vulg (drunk) rond comme une queue de pelle, fin plein

wanky ['wæŋkɪ] ADJ Br Vulg (stupid) débile, con; **he's OK but all his friends are a bit w.** lui, ça va, mais tous ses copains son assez cons

wanly ['wɒnlɪ] ADV (to shine) faiblement; (to smile) tristement

wanna ['wɒnə] CONTR Fam = want to, see want

wannabe ['wɒnəbiː] N esp Am Fam = personne f rêvant de devenir célèbre, riche etc (mais qui n'en a pas l'étoffe); **the disco was full of J-Lo wannabes** la discothèque était pleine de clones de J-Lo; **they're just a bunch of wannabes** ce n'est qu'un tas de rêveurs (qui n'arriveront jamais nulle part)

wanness ['wɒnnɪs] N pâleur f

WANT	['wɒnt]	
N	besoin **1, 2**	▪ manque **2, 3**
VT	vouloir **1**	▪ avoir besoin de **2**
	▪ demander **2**	▪ chercher **2**
VI	manquer	

N **1** (need) besoin m; **to minister** or **attend to sb's wants** pourvoir aux besoins de qn; **my wants are few** j'ai peu de besoins
2 (poverty) misère f, besoin m; **to be in w.** être dans le besoin ou la gêne; **war on w.** lutte f contre la misère
3 (lack) manque m, défaut m; **there was no w. of volunteers** on ne manquait pas de volontaires; **to be in w. of sth** avoir besoin de qch; **w. of imagination/respect** manque d'imagination/de respect; **for w. of sth** faute de qch, à défaut de qch; **it was not for w. of trying** ce n'est pas faute d'avoir essayé; **for w. of foresight** par manque de prévoyance; **for w. of something better** faute de mieux; **for w. of something better to do** faute d'avoir quelque chose de mieux à faire; **for w. of a better word** faute d'un mot plus approprié; Prov **for w. of a nail the shoe was lost, for w. of a shoe the horse was lost** faute d'un point Martin perdit son âne
VT **1** (desire) vouloir; **she knows what she wants** elle sait ce qu'elle veut; **the more you get the more you w.** plus on en a, plus on en veut; **do you w. any?** en voulez-vous?; **is that all you w.?** est-ce tout ce que vous voulez?; **what more do you w.?** que voulez-vous de plus?; **what** or **how much do you w. for this armchair?** combien vendez-vous ce fauteuil?, combien voulez-vous pour ce fauteuil?; Iron **you don't w. much, do you!** tu es bien exigeant!; **you're wanted** on vous demande; **you're wanted on the phone** on vous demande au téléphone; **the boss wants you (in his office)** le patron veut te voir (dans son bureau); **we're not wanted here** nous sommes de trop ici; **people like you are not wanted round here** on ne veut pas de gens comme vous par ici; **they don't w. (to have) me** ils ne veulent pas de moi; **what does he w. with me?** que me veut-il?; **what does he w. me for?** qu'est-ce qu'il me veut?; **to w. sth from sb** vouloir qch de qn; **what do you w. from her?** que voulez-vous d'elle?; **to w. to do sth** vouloir faire qch; **I w. to tell you that ...** je voudrais vous dire que ...; **I w. to see the manager** je veux voir le directeur; **there's someone here who wants to see the manager** il y a quelqu'un qui veut voir ou qui demande le directeur; **he could have done it if he had wanted to** il aurait pu le faire s'il l'avait voulu; **don't come if you don't w. to** or **unless you w. to** ne venez pas si ça ne vous dit pas; **I don't w. it known** je ne veux pas que cela se sache; **what do you w. done?** que désirez-vous qu'on fasse?; **I don't w. you turning everything upside down** je ne veux pas que vous mettiez tout sens dessus dessous; **I don't w. any fuss** je ne veux pas d'histoires; **I've had enough criticism from you, I w. no more of it!** j'ai eu assez de critiques de ta part, ça suffit!
2 (need) (of person) avoir besoin de; (of

thing) exiger, réclamer, demander; **you w. good eyesight to be a pilot** il faut avoir une bonne vue pour être pilote; **that child wants taking down a peg or two** cet enfant a besoin d'être remis à sa place; **it wants a bit more red to make it the same shade** il faut un peu plus de rouge pour obtenir le même ton; **to w. rest** avoir besoin de repos; **it's a situation that wants careful handling** cette situation demande du tact ou qu'on ait du tact; **I shall w. you** j'aurai besoin de vous; **have you everything you w.?** avez-vous tout ce qu'il vous faut?; **we've more than we w.** nous en avons plus qu'il n'en faut; **you shall have as much as you w.** vous en aurez autant que vous voudrez; **I've had all I want(ed)** j'en ai eu assez; **the goods can be supplied as (and when) they are wanted** on peut fournir les articles au fur et à mesure des besoins; **that's the very thing I w., that's just what I w.** c'est juste ce qu'il me faut, cela fera parfaitement mon affaire; **I have the very thing you w.** j'ai juste ce qu'il vous faut; **the very man we w.** l'homme de la circonstance; **what does she w. with a house?** qu'est-ce qu'elle veut faire d'une maison?; **wanted, a good cook** (advertisement) on demande ou recherche une bonne cuisinière; **he's wanted by the police** il est recherché par la police; **your hair wants cutting** tu as besoin de te faire couper les cheveux, tu devrais te faire couper les cheveux; **the lawn wants cutting** la pelouse a besoin d'être tondue; **the plants w. watering about once a week** il faut arroser les plantes environ une fois par semaine
3 (giving advice, instructions) **you w. to be on your guard** il faut vous méfier; **you w. to be careful with him** il faut que tu fasses attention avec lui
VI (be lacking) manquer (for de); **to w. for nothing** ne manquer de rien; **her family will see to it that she doesn't w. (for anything)** sa famille veillera à ce qu'elle ne manque de rien
▸▸ Am **w. ad** petite annonce f
▸ **want in** VI Fam (of cat, dog) vouloir entrer; Fig (want to be part of sth) vouloir être inclus; **Big Vern wants in on the deal** Big Vern veut être sur le coup
▸ **want out** VI Fam (of cat, dog) vouloir sortir; Fig (no longer want to be part of sth) vouloir retirer ses cartes du jeu; **this has gone far enough, I w. out!** c'est allé trop loin, je laisse tomber!

wanted ['wɒntɪd] ADJ (desired) désiré, voulu; (child) désiré; (criminal) recherché par la police; **'w. for murder'** 'recherché pour meurtre'; **a w. poster** un avis de recherche; **to feel w.** se sentir apprécié
▸▸ **w. notice** avis m de recherche

wanting ['wɒntɪŋ] ADJ **1** (missing) **to be w.** faire défaut; **there is something w.** le compte n'y est pas **2 to be w. in sth** (of person) manquer de qch; **to be w. in intelligence** être peu intelligent; **he's not w. in intelligence** il n'est pas bête; Lit **to be found w.** se trouver en défaut; **he was tried and found w.** il a été mis à l'épreuve et cela n'a pas été concluant

wanton ['wɒntən] ADJ **1** (action, cruelty) gratuit, sans motif; (destroyer) vicieux **2** Old-fashioned (licentious) (person, behaviour) licencieux, impudique
N Old-fashioned (woman) femme f légère; (man) libertin m

wantonly ['wɒntənlɪ] ADV **1** (to injure, insult) sans motif **2** Old-fashioned (licentiously) de façon dévergondée

wantonness ['wɒntənnɪs] N **1** (of insult etc) gratuité f **2** Old-fashioned (licentiousness) libertinage m

WAP [wæp] N Tel (abbr **wireless applications protocol**) WAP m
▸▸ **W. phone** téléphone f WAP

wapiti ['wɒpɪtɪ] N (deer) wapiti m

War abbr Warwickshire

war [wɔːr] N **1** guerre f; **a state of w. now exists** l'état de guerre est déclaré (**between** entre); **in (time of) w.** en temps de guerre; **w. establishment** or **strength** effectif(s) m(pl) de guerre; **to set a unit on a w. footing** mettre une unité sur pied de guerre; **preparations for w.** préparatifs mpl de guerre; Lit **to let loose the dogs of w.** déchaîner les fureurs de la guerre; **to start a w.** déclencher une guerre; **to be at w. with a country** être en (état de) guerre avec un pays; **to make** or **wage w. on** or **against a country** faire la guerre à ou contre un pays; **to go to w.** se mettre en guerre (**over a territory** pour un territoire); Fig Fam **you look as if you've been in the wars** te voilà dans un drôle d'état; **the American Civil W.**, Am **the W. Between the States** la guerre de Sécession; **the Great W.** (1914-1918) la Grande Guerre **2** Fig guerre f, lutte f; **w. of nerves** guerre des nerfs; **class w.** lutte des classes; Econ **price w.** guerre des prix; **w. of words** dispute f, altercation f; **to wage w. on** or **against sb/sth** faire la guerre à ou contre qn/à qch, lutter ou militer contre qn/qch; **the w. on drugs** la lutte contre la drogue
VI (-rr-) **to w. against sb/sth** mener une campagne contre qn/qch, lutter contre qn/qch
▸▸ **w. cemetery** cimetière m militaire; **w. chest** caisse f spéciale; **w. correspondent** correspondant, -ante de guerre; **w. crimes** crimes mpl de guerre; also Fig **w. cry** cri m de guerre; **w. dance** danse f de guerre ou guerrière; **the w. effort** l'effort m de guerre; **w. film** film m de guerre; **w. game** Mil (simulated battle with maps) kriegspiel m, wargame m; (manoeuvres) manœuvres fpl militaires; (game) wargame; **w. grave** = tombeau m d'un soldat tombé au champ d'honneur; **w. hero** héros m de guerre; **w. memorial** monument m aux morts; Formerly **the W. Office** = ancien nom du ministère de la Défense britannique; **w. paint** (of Amerindian) peinture f de guerre; Hum (of woman) maquillage m; **w. risk** (in insurance) risques mpl de guerre; **w. widow** veuve f de guerre; **w. zone** zone f de guerre

warble ['wɔːb(ə)l] N (of bird) gazouillement m, gazouillis m
VI (of bird) gazouiller; (of lark) grisoller; Fig (of person) chanter
VT Fig (of person) (song) roucouler

warbler ['wɔːblər] N (bird) fauvette f

warbling ['wɔːblɪŋ] ADJ (bird) gazouillant; (sound) mélodieux
N = **warble** N

ward [wɔːd] N **1** (person) pupille mf; (guardianship) tutelle f; **to be in w.** être sous tutelle judiciaire **2** Med salle f d'hôpital; **which w. is she in?** dans quelle salle est-elle?; **to walk the wards** (of medical student) assister aux leçons cliniques **3** Pol (electoral division) circonscription f électorale
▸▸ Law **w. of court** pupille mf sous tutelle judiciaire; **to be made a w. of court** être placé sous tutelle judiciaire
▸ **ward off** VT SEP (blow) parer, écarter; (danger) détourner, écarter; (illness, accusations) éviter

warden ['wɔːd(ə)n] N (of institution, hostel, prison) directeur, -trice; (of national park) gardien, -ienne; Br **Lord W. of the Cinque Ports** gouverneur m des Cinq Ports

warder ['wɔːdər] N Br (in prison) gardien, -ienne

wardress ['wɔːdrɪs] N Br (in prison) gardienne f

wardrobe ['wɔːdrəʊb] N **1** (cupboard) armoire f, garde-robe f, pl garde-robes **2** (clothes) (ensemble m de) vêtements mpl, garde-robe f; **Miss Smith's w. by ...** (on film credits) les costumes de Miss Smith ont été fournis par ...; **to have a large w.** avoir une garde-robe importante; **she brought half her w. with her** elle a emporté la moitié de sa garde-robe **3** Theat **to work in w.** être costumier, f costumière, s'occuper des costumes
▸▸ **w. drawer** tiroir m d'armoire; **w. mirror** miroir m d'armoire; **w. mistress** costumière f; **w. trunk** malle f (penderie)

wardroom ['wɔːdruːm] N Naut carré m des officiers

wardship ['wɔːdʃɪp] N tutelle f

ware [weər] N **1** (manufactured articles) articles mpl; **aluminium w.** ustensiles mpl en aluminium; **cast-iron w.** poterie f en fonte **2** wares (goods for sale) marchandise(s) f(pl); Lit **to cry one's wares** faire l'article de ou vanter sa marchandise

warehouse¹ ['weəhaʊs] N entrepôt m, dépôt m de marchandises; (for furniture) garde-meuble m, pl garde-meubles; **bonded w.** entrepôt de la douane; Com **ex w.** sortie f d'entrepôt
▸▸ Com **w. charges** frais mpl d'entreposage; Com **w. club** club m de gros; **w. manager** responsable mf d'entrepôt; **w. party** = soirée f house dans un local désaffecté; Com **w. warrant** certificat m d'entreposage

warehouse² ['weəhaʊz] VT entreposer, mettre en entrepôt

warehouseman, pl **warehousemen** ['weəhaʊsmən] N magasinier m, entrepositaire m, manutentionnaire m

warehousing ['weəhaʊzɪŋ] N (of goods) entreposage m; (of shares) parcage m
▸▸ **w. company** société f d'entrepôts; **w. costs** frais mpl d'entreposage

warfare ['wɔːfeər] N guerre f

warhead ['wɔːhed] N ogive f, (on torpedo) cône m de charge

warhorse ['wɔːhɔːs] N **1** (person) an old w. Mil un vieux soldat; Pol un vétéran de la politique **2** Hist (horse) destrier m, cheval m de bataille **3** Mktg cheval m de bataille

warily ['weərɪlɪ] ADV avec précaution; **the soldiers advanced w. through the forest** les soldats avançaient avec prudence dans la forêt; **they eyed him w. as he continued his explanation** ils le regardaient avec méfiance alors qu'il poursuivait son explication

wariness ['weərɪnɪs] N circonspection f, prudence f; **his w. of computers** sa réticence envers l'informatique

warlike ['wɔːlaɪk] ADJ (appearance, bearing) guerrier; (people) belliqueux

warlock ['wɔːlɒk] N sorcier m, magicien m

warlord ['wɔːlɔːd] N seigneur m de la guerre; **the local w.** le chef militaire local

warm [wɔːm] ADJ **1** (garment, colour etc) chaud; (iron, oven) assez chaud; **to be w.** (of water) être chaud; (of person) avoir chaud; **come inside, it's lovely and w.** viens à l'intérieur, il fait bon; **the water's only just w.** l'eau est à peine chaude; **to get w.** (of person, room) se réchauffer; (of water) chauffer; **the radiator was getting warmer** le radiateur commençait à chauffer; **you're getting warmer** (in guessing game etc) tu chauffes; **you're really w.** (in guessing game etc) tu brûles; **make sure you keep w.** ne prends pas froid; **to keep a dish w.** garder un plat au chaud; Fig **to keep a place w. for sb** (job) garder un emploi pour qn; **I'll do it once the**

w. weather is here je le ferai quand il commencera à faire chaud; **it's getting warmer** (of weather) il commence à faire plus chaud; **it's w. work** c'est une besogne qui donne soif; Fig **to make things** or **it w. for sb** mener la vie dure à qn, en faire voir de toutes les couleurs à qn; Fig **things were getting a bit too w.** (dangerous) ça commençait à chauffer
2 (enthusiastic, kind) chaleureux; **w. heart** cœur généreux; **w. smile** sourire accueillant; **to meet with a w. reception** être accueilli chaleureusement; **w. welcome** accueil chaleureux; **to give sb a w. welcome** accueillir qn chaleureusement
N **to have a w.** se réchauffer; **come into the w.** viens au chaud; **to give sb a w.** réchauffer qch; **to give one's hands a w. at the fire** se réchauffer les mains près du feu
VT (faire) chauffer; **to w. oneself by the fire/in the sun** se chauffer près du feu/au soleil; **wine/news that warms the heart** vin/nouvelle qui réchauffe le cœur; **that will w. the cockles of your heart** voilà qui vous réchauffera; **it warms the cockles of my heart to see ...** ça me réchauffe le cœur de voir ...
VI (se) chauffer, s'échauffer, se réchauffer; Fig **to w. to sb** (commencer à) ressentir de la sympathie pour qn; **I didn't w. to him** il ne m'a pas plu; **they warmed to one another immediately** ils se sont pris de sympathie immédiatement; **to w. to an idea** se laisser séduire par une idée; **to w. to one's theme** bien entrer dans son sujet
▸▸ Met **w. front** front m chaud; Comput **w. start** redémarrage m à chaud
▸ **warm over** VT SEP **1** esp Am (soup etc) (faire) réchauffer **2** Fig (novel etc) réchauffer
▸ **warm up** VI **1** (of weather) faire plus chaud; Fig (of party, audience) s'animer; (of discussion) s'échauffer, s'animer **2** (of dancer, musician, orchestra), Sport s'échauffer; (of engine, radio) se mettre en route
VT SEP (thing) faire chauffer; (person) réchauffer; Fig (party) animer; Aut **to w. up the engine** (faire) chauffer le moteur; **to w. up the soup** (faire) réchauffer le potage; Fig **to w. an audience up** chauffer le public, mettre un public en train

warm-blooded ADJ (animal) à sang chaud; Fig (person) passionné, ardent

warm-hearted [-'hɑːtɪd] ADJ (person, welcome) chaleureux; **we were given a very w. welcome** nous fûmes chaleureusement accueillis; **she is very w.** elle a un grand cœur

warm-heartedly [-'hɑːtɪdlɪ] ADV chaleureusement, avec chaleur

warming ['wɔːmɪŋ] ADJ (drink) qui réchauffe; (thought) qui réchauffe le cœur, réconfortant
N chauffage m
▸▸ **w. pan** bassinoire f; **w. up** (of food) réchauffage m; Sport échauffement m

warmly ['wɔːmlɪ] ADV **1** (dressed) chaudement **2** (to applaud) chaudement; (to recommend) vivement, chaudement; (to welcome, thank sb) chaleureusement; **his suggestion was not w. received** sa proposition n'a pas été chaudement accueillie; **the film was w. received by the critics** le film a été accueilli par la critique avec enthousiasme

warmonger ['wɔːmʌŋgər] N belliciste mf

warmongering ['wɔːmʌŋg(ə)rɪŋ] N bellicisme m, propagande f de guerre

warmth [wɔːmθ] N **1** (of sun, fire) chaleur f; **we huddled together for w.** nous nous sommes blottis les uns contre les autres pour nous tenir chaud **2** (enthusiasm) ardeur f, chaleur f; (of welcome) cordialité f, chaleur; **to receive sth with w.** (idea, proposal) accueillir qch avec enthousiasme **3** (anger) emportement *m*, vivacité *f*, ... she said with some w. ... dit-elle d'un ton vif

warm-up N **1** *(of dancer, musician, orchestra)*, *Sport* échauffement *m*; **to do a w.** s'échauffer; **they get a ten-minute w.** ils ont dix minutes d'échauffement **2** come and have a w. by the fire viens te réchauffer auprès du feu

▸▸ **w. exercises** exercices *mpl* d'échauffement; **w. man** personne *f* chargée de chauffer la salle; **w. match** match *m* préparatoire *ou* d'entraînement; *esp Am* **w. suit** survêtement *m*

warn [wɔːn] VT **1** *(caution)* avertir, prévenir (**that** que); **he warned me not to do it** il m'a déconseillé de le faire; **to w. sb about** *or* **against sth** mettre qn en garde contre qch; **to w. sb about** *or* **against doing sth** conseiller à qn de ne pas faire qch; **he warned her against going**, **he warned her not to go** il lui a conseillé (fortement) de ne pas y aller; **to w. sb of a danger** avertir qn d'un danger; **they warned me about you** on m'avait mis en garde contre toi, on m'avait prévenu à ton égard; *Hum* **my parents warned me about people like you!** mes parents m'avaient bien dit de me méfier des gens comme toi!; **you have been warned!** vous voilà averti *ou* prévenu!; **I'm warning you for the last time** je te préviens pour la dernière fois; **I shan't w. you again** tenez-vous-le pour dit

2 *(alert, inform)* informer, donner l'éveil à; **she had been warned in advance** elle était prévenue; **to w. the police** alerter la police

VI **he warned of possibly serious consequences** il évoqua les graves conséquences possibles

▸ **warn off** VT SEP **1** *(tell to leave)* **he warned them off his land** il leur demanda instamment de quitter ses terres; **the signs are meant to w. people off** les panneaux sont là pour interdire aux gens d'entrer **2** *(advise against)* **to w. sb off sth** déconseiller qch à qn; **to w. sb off drink/smoking** déconseiller l'alcool/la cigarette à qn; **to w. sb off doing sth** déconseiller à qn de faire qch

warning ['wɔːnɪŋ] N **1** *(caution)* avertissement *m*; *(alarm)* alerte *f*; **to give sb a w.** mettre qn en garde; **this is your last w.** *(to child)* c'est la dernière fois que je te le dis; *(to worker)* c'est votre dernier avertissement; **in spite of repeated warnings** malgré de nombreux avertissements; **to sound a note of w.** recommander la prudence; **he was let off with a w.** il en a été quitte pour un avertissement; **let this be a w. to you** que cela vous serve de leçon *ou* d'exemple *ou* d'avertissement; **she gave him a w. glance** elle lui lança un regard d'avertissement *ou* pour l'avertir

2 *(advance notice)* avis *m*, préavis *m*; **we only received a few days' w.** nous n'avons été prévenus que quelques jours à l'avance; **she didn't give him much w.** elle l'a prévenu assez tard; **I'm giving you fair w.** vous voilà averti!; **without w.** sans préavis, sans déclaration préalable; **he just left without w.** il est parti sans crier gare; **it just broke down without w.** elle est tombée en panne d'un seul coup; *Ind* **strike w.** préavis de grève

▸▸ **w. beep** signal *m* sonore; **w. bell** sonnette *f* *ou* sonnerie *f* d'alarme; **w. buzzer** avertisseur *m* sonore; **w. device** avertisseur *m*; **w. light** voyant *m* (avertisseur), avertisseur lumineux; *Comput* **w. message** message *m* d'avertissement; *Naut*, *Fig* **w. shot** coup *m* de semonce, avertissement; *Fig* **to fire a w. shot** tirer sur le signal d'alarme; **w. sign** panneau *m* avertisseur; **w. signal** signal *m* d'alarme *ou* d'alerte; *Aut* signal de détresse; *Ind* **w. strike** grève *f* d'avertissement; **w. system** système *m* *ou* dispositif *m* d'alarme; *Br Aut* **w. triangle** triangle *m* de signalisation

warp [wɔːp] N **1** *(distortion)* *(of plank)* voilure *f*, gauchissement *m*; *(in time)* brèche *f* **2** *Tex* chaîne *f*, *(for tapestry)* lisse *f*, lice *f*

▸ VT *(distort)* *(wood, metal sheet)* gauchir, voiler; *Fig* *(mind, character, person)* pervertir; *(judgement)* fausser

▸ VI *(of cupboard door etc)* se déformer, gauchir; *(of timber)* se voiler, gauchir; *(of sheet metal)* (se) gondoler

warpath ['wɔːpɑːθ] N **to be on the w.** *(of Amerindian etc)* être sur le sentier de la guerre; *Fig* en vouloir à tout le monde; *Fig* **the boss is on the w.** le patron est d'une humeur massacrante

warped [wɔːpt] ADJ *(wood)* gauchi, voilé; *Fig* *(mind, person)* perverti; *(judgement)* faussé; **that's a very w. way of thinking** c'est une drôle de manière de voir les choses; **w. sense of humour** sens de l'humour tordu; **you must be a bit w. if you think that's funny!** tu dois être un peu tordu pour trouver ça drôle!

warping ['wɔːpɪŋ] N *(of plank)* gauchissement *m*; *(of metal sheet)* gondolement *m*; *(of wheel)* voilure *f*, voilement *m*

warplane ['wɔːpleɪn] N avion *m* de guerre

warrant ['wɒrənt] N **1** *Com* *(guarantee)* garantie *f*, *Fin* bon *m* de souscription d'actions, *Obsa* *m inv* **2** *Law* mandat *m*, ordre *m*; *Admin* mandat; **w. of arrest** mandat d'arrêt *ou* d'arrestation; **there's a w. out against him** *or* **for his arrest** il est sous le coup d'un mandat d'arrêt; **warehouse w.** certificat *m* d'entrepôt, warrant *m*, warrant cédule *f*; **w. for payment** ordonnance *f* de paiement; **travel w.** feuille *f* de route

▸ VT *(justify)* justifier; **nothing can w. such conduct** rien ne justifie une pareille conduite, rien ne peut excuser une telle conduite; **his performance warranted better** sa prestation méritait mieux **2** *(guarantee)* *(something)* garantir, répondre de; *Old-fashioned* **it won't happen again, I w. you!** cela n'arrivera pas deux fois, je vous le promets! **3** *Com* warranter

▸▸ **w. officer** adjudant *m* *(auxiliaire d'un officier)*

warrantable ['wɒrəntəb(ə)l] ADJ *(justifiable)* justifiable

warrantee [wɒrən'tiː] N receveur, -euse d'une/de la garantie

warrantor ['wɒrəntɔ:r] N *Law* garant, -ante

warranty ['wɒrəntɪ] N *Com* garantie *f*, **under w.** sous garantie; **is it still under w.?** est-ce que c'est encore sous garantie?; **the iron has a one-year w.** le fer à repasser est garanti un an; **breach of w.** rupture *f* de garantie

▸▸ **w. certificate** certificat *m* de garantie

warren ['wɒrən] N *(of rabbit)* garenne *f*, clapier *m*; *Fig* labyrinthe *m*, dédale *m*

warring ['wɔːrɪŋ] ADJ *(countries)* en guerre; *Fig* *(ideologies)* en conflit; **w. factions within the Labour Party** des factions adverses au sein du Labour Party

warrior ['wɒrɪər] N guerrier, -ière

Warsaw ['wɔːsɔː] N Varsovie

▸▸ **the W. Pact** le pacte de Varsovie; **the W. Pact nations** les nations *fpl* du pacte de Varsovie

war-scarred [-skɑːd] ADJ *(city, country)* dévasté par la guerre

warship ['wɔːʃɪp] N navire *m* *ou* vaisseau *m* de guerre

wart [wɔːt] N verrue *f*; **a biography of Charles de Gaulle, warts and all** une biographie de Charles de Gaulle écrite sans complaisance *ou* qui ne fait pas de cadeaux; **she'll have to accept him as he is, warts and all** il faudra qu'elle l'accepte comme il est, avec tous ses défauts

warthog ['wɔːthɒg] N phacochère *m*

wartime ['wɔːtaɪm] N temps *m* de guerre; **in w.** en temps de guerre

▸▸ **w. rations** rations *fpl* de guerre

warty ['wɔːtɪ] ADJ couvert de verrues, verruqueux

wary ['weərɪ] ADJ avisé, prudent, circonspect; **to be w. of sb/sth** se méfier de qn/qch; **I'm still w. about signing it** j'hésite encore à le signer; **to keep a w. eye on sb** surveiller qn de près

was PT *see* **be**

Wash *abbr* **Washington**

WASH [wɒʃ] N **1** *(action)* lavage *m*; **to have a w.** se laver; **give your face a w.** lave-toi le visage; **to have a w. and brush up** faire un brin de toilette; **to give sth a w.** laver qch

2 *(laundry)* lessive *f*, blanchissage *m*; **to send clothes to the w.** donner du linge à laver *ou* à blanchir; **to do the w.** faire la lessive; **your jeans are in the w.** *(being washed)* ton jean est au lavage; **it'll come out in the w.** *(be removed)* ça partira au lavage; *Fig* **it will all come out in the w.** *(become known)* ça finira par se savoir; *(be all right)* ça finira par s'arranger

3 *Med* *(for wounds)* lotion *f*, *(for plants)* lessive *f* *(insecticide)*; *(against mildew)* bouillie *f*

4 *Art* *(of water colour, Indian ink)* lavis *m*; **colour w.** *(for walls)* badigeon *m*

5 *(of waves, ship)* remous *m*

▸ VT **1** *(clean)* *(car, clothes, plate, etc)* laver; **w. in cool/hot water** à laver à l'eau tiède/chaude; **hand w. only** laver à la main seulement; **to w. sth in cold water** laver qch à l'eau froide; **to w. oneself** se laver; **to w. one's face/hands/hair** se laver le visage/les mains/les cheveux; *Br Euph* **would you like to w. your hands?** *(go to lavatory)* voulez-vous que je vous montre où est la salle de bain?; *Fig* **to w. one's hands of sb/sth** se laver les mains de qn/qch; *Fig* **I w. my hands of the affair** je me lave les mains de cette affaire; *Rel* **to be washed of one's sins** être lavé de ses péchés

2 *Med* *(wound)* nettoyer

3 *Ind* *(mineral, coal)* laver; *(gas)* épurer

4 *Art* *(drawing)* laver; **to w. the walls** *(paint)* badigeonner les murs *(with* de*)*

5 *(of sea)* *(shore)* baigner; **to w. sb/sth ashore** rejeter qn/qch sur le rivage; **he was washed overboard** il fut emporté par une vague

▸ VI **1** *(wash oneself)* se laver; **material that washes well** tissu qui se lave bien; **you w. and I'll dry** *(doing dishes)* tu laves et j'essuie; *Br Fam* **that won't w.!** ça ne prend pas!, ça ne marche pas!

2 **the waves washed against the cliff** les vagues baignaient la falaise

▸▸ *Art* **w. drawing** dessin *m* au lavis

▸ **wash away** VT SEP **1** *(remove by washing)* faire partir; **to w. one's sins away** se laver de ses péchés

2 *(of rain, flood etc)* **the flood washed away part of the river bank** l'inondation a érodé une partie de la berge; **the village was washed away by the flood** le village a été emporté par l'inondation; **heavy rains had washed away the topsoil** des pluies abondantes avaient entraîné la terre; **washed away by the tide** emporté *ou* enlevé par la mer

▸ VI *(of mark, stain)* s'en aller *ou* partir au lavage

▸ **wash down** VT SEP **1** *(walls, car)* laver à grande eau

2 *(help to swallow)* *(pill)* faire descendre; **to w. down one's dinner with a glass of beer** boire un verre de bière en dînant

▸ **wash off** VT SEP *(remove by washing)* enlever, faire partir

VI *(of mud, dirt)* s'en aller *ou* partir au lavage

▶ **wash out** VT SEP **1** *(remove by washing)* *(stain)* enlever

2 *(clean) (cup, bottle)* laver, rincer, nettoyer; **to w. out a few clothes** *or* **things** faire une petite lessive; *Fig* **to be completely washed out** *(tired)* être complètement lessivé *ou* vanné *ou* à plat

3 *Art (colour)* dégrader; **washed out** *(of colour, material)* délavé, déteint

4 *Min* **to w. out the gold** extraire l'or

5 *(of football match etc)* **to be washed out** être annulé à cause de la pluie

6 *Geol* éroder

VI *(of stain, colour)* partir au lavage; **it will w. out** ça partira au lavage

▶ **wash over** VT INSEP *(of waves)* balayer; *Fig (have no effect on)* ne faire aucun effet à; **anything I say just washes over her** rien de ce que je lui dis ne lui fait le moindre effet

▶ **wash up** VT SEP **1** *Br* **to w. up the dishes** laver *ou* faire la vaisselle

2 *(of sea)* rejeter sur le rivage; **wreckage washed up by the sea** débris rejetés par la mer

VI **1** *Br (do dishes)* faire la vaisselle

2 *Am (have a wash)* se débarbouiller

3 *Fig (end up) (of person)* finir, échouer; **he washed up in Australia** il a échoué en Australie

washable ['wɒʃəb(ə)l] ADJ lavable

wash-and-wear ADJ lavé-repassé

washbasin ['wɒʃbeɪs(ə)n] N lavabo *m*

washboard ['wɒʃbɔːd] N planche *f* à laver

washbowl ['wɒʃbəʊl] N lavabo *m; (large)* bassine *f*

washcloth ['wɒʃklɒθ] N *Br (for washing dishes)* lavette *f, Am (face cloth)* = gant *m* de toilette

washday ['wɒʃdeɪ] N jour *m* de la lessive

washed-out ['wɒʃd-] ADJ *(faded)* délavé; *Fig (tired)* lessivé

washed-up ADJ *Fig Fam* **to be (all) w.** *(of person)* être fini *ou Fam* fichu; *(of plan)* être tombé à l'eau; **he's all w.** c'est un homme fini *ou* liquidé; **he's all w. as a boxer** il est fini comme boxeur

washer[1] ['wɒʃər] N **1** *(person)* laveur, -euse **2** *Fam (machine) (for clothes)* machine *f* à laver; *(for dishes)* lave-vaisselle *m inv*

▶▶ *Aut* **w. bottle** réservoir *m* de lave-glace

washer[2] N *Tech* rondelle *f*, bague *f;* **the tap needs a new w.** il faut changer la bague du robinet

washer-dryer N machine *f* à laver séchante

washer-up, *pl* **washers-up, washer-upper,** *pl* **washer-uppers** N *Br Fam* laveur, -euse de vaisselle; *(in restaurant)* plongeur, -euse

washerwoman, *pl* **washerwomen** ['wɒʃəwʊmən, -wɪmɪn] N blanchisseuse *f*

wash-hand basin N lavabo *m*

washing ['wɒʃɪŋ] N **1** *(action) (of car, wall etc)* lavage *m; (of clothes) (at laundry)* blanchissage *m; (of one's body)* toilette *f, Rel (of feet, hands)* lavement *m;* **to do the w.** faire la lessive; **Monday is w. day** le lundi est le jour de la lessive **2** *(dirty clothes)* linge *m* à laver; *(clean clothes)* linge lavé

▶▶ **w. machine** machine *f* à laver, lave-linge *m inv;* **w. powder** lessive *f ou* détergent *m* *(en poudre);* **w. soda** cristaux *mpl* de soude

Washington ['wɒʃɪŋtən] N **1** *(state)* **W. (State)** l'État *m* de Washington **2** *(town)* **W. (DC)** Washington

washing-up N *Br* vaisselle *f;* **to do the w.** faire la vaisselle; *(in restaurant)* faire la plonge

▶▶ **w. bowl** cuvette *f*, bassine *f; Br* **w. liquid**

produit *m* pour la vaisselle, liquide *m* vaisselle; **w. water** eau *f* de vaisselle

washleather ['wɒʃleðər] N peau *f* de chamois

washout ['wɒʃaʊt] N *Fam (failure)* fiasco *m; (person)* raté, -ée, zéro *m;* **the whole thing's a w.** c'est une perte sèche

washrag ['wɒʃræg] N *Am* ≃ gant *m* de toilette

washroom ['wɒʃruːm] N **1** *esp Am (lavatory in hotel etc)* toilettes *fpl;* **where's the w.?** où sont les toilettes? **2** *(with toilets, washbasins etc)* salle *f* d'eau, cabinet *m* de toilette

washstand ['wɒʃstænd] N *(table)* table *f* de toilette; *Am (washbasin)* lavabo *m*

washtub ['wɒʃtʌb] N *(for clothes)* baquet *m* (à lessive)

washup ['wɒʃʌp] N **1** *Med Fam (before operating)* stérilisation *f* des mains **2** *Am* **to have a w.** se laver (les mains et la figure), se débarbouiller

wash-wipe N *Aut* lavage-balayage *m*

wasn't ['wɒz(ə)nt] CONTR = **was not,** *see* **be**

Wasp [wɒsp] N *Am esp Pej (abbr* **White Anglo-Saxon Protestant)** = Américain *m* blanc protestant d'origine anglo-saxonne

wasp [wɒsp] N *(insect)* guêpe *f*, **wasps' nest** guêpier *m;* **to have a w. waist** avoir une taille de guêpe

waspish ['wɒspɪʃ] ADJ méchant, acerbe; *(tone)* hargneux

waspishly ['wɒspɪʃlɪ] ADV *(to do)* d'une manière acerbe; *(to say)* avec hargne

wassail ['wɒseɪl] VI *Lit* chanter des chants de Noël; **to go wassailing** aller de maison en maison en chantant des chants de Noël

wastage ['weɪstɪdʒ] N **1** *(loss)* gaspillage *m; (of heat)* déperdition *f*, perte *f*, *Com (in shipping)* freinte *f* **2** *(what is wasted)* déchets *mpl*, rebuts *mpl;* **buy enough material to allow for w.** achetez suffisamment de tissu pour compenser les pertes **3** *(reduction of workforce)* départ *m* d'employés; **we hope to achieve this by natural w.** nous pensons y parvenir grâce à des départs volontaires

waste [weɪst] ADJ **1** *(uncultivated) (ground)* en friche; *(region)* désert, désolé; **to lay w.** *(country)* dévaster, ravager, piller

2 *(product)* non utilisé, perdu

N **1** *(of money, effort)* gaspillage *m;* **it's a terrible w. of food** c'est un terrible gâchis *ou* gaspillage de nourriture; **it's a w. of their skills** c'est gaspiller leurs talents; **w. of time** perte *f* de temps; **it's a w. of time** c'est du temps perdu; **it's a w. of time trying to convince her** je perds mon/tu perds ton/*etc* temps à essayer de la convaincre; **that film is a real w. of time** ce film ne vaut rien, ce film est nul; *Fam* **he's a w. of space** il est nul; **to go to w.** *(of food, talent)* se perdre; *(of land, garden)* partir à l'abandon

2 *(rubbish)* déchets *mpl*, *(household waste)* ordures *fpl* ménagères; *Min* déblais *mpl*

3 *(desert)* région *f* inculte, désert *m;* **the wastes of the Sahara** les étendues désertes du Sahara

VT **1** *(squander) (stocks, money)* gaspiller; *(paper)* gâcher; *(fortune)* dissiper, dilapider; *(time)* perdre, gaspiller; *(opportunity)* rater, manquer; **she felt that she had wasted her youth** *(misspent)* elle avait l'impression d'avoir gâché sa jeunesse; **nothing is wasted** rien ne se perd; **I hate wasting food** j'ai horreur de gâcher la nourriture; **to w. one's life** gâcher sa vie; **she's wasted in that job** cet emploi est bien au-dessous de ses capacités; **to w. one's words** *or* **breath** parler en pure perte; **don't w. your breath on him** ne perds pas ta salive, il ne vaut pas; **you're wasting your breath, he won't understand** ne gaspille pas ta salive pour rien, il ne

comprend pas; **you're wasting your energy** vous vous dépensez inutilement; **I haven't any time to w. on him** je n'ai pas de temps à perdre sur lui; **we're wasting time** nous perdons notre temps; **we've already wasted too much time on this** nous avons déjà perdu trop de temps là-dessus; **to w. no time doing sth** ne pas perdre de temps pour faire qch; *Fam* **you didn't w. any time, did you!** tu n'as pas perdu de temps, hein?; **that would be wasted on me** ce serait trop beau pour moi; **expensive wine is wasted on me** *(not appreciated by)* je suis incapable d'apprécier le bon vin; **a beautiful house like that is wasted on such people** une belle maison comme ça, c'est trop beau pour des gens pareils; **the joke was wasted on him** il n'a pas compris la plaisanterie; *Prov* **w. not, want not** qui épargne gagne

2 *(consume) (person)* consumer, épuiser, faire dépérir; *(body, limb)* décharner, atrophier; **her body was wasted by disease** son corps était décharné par la maladie

3 *Sl (murder)* tuer; *(attack)* casser la gueule à, démonter le portrait à; **to w. sb's face** casser *ou* défoncer la gueule à qn, faire une tête au carré à qn

▶▶ **w. collection** ramassage *m* des ordures; **w. disposal** élimination *f ou* destruction *f* des déchets *ou* des ordures; **w. disposal site** dépôt *m* d'ordures; **w. disposal unit** broyeur *m* d'ordures; **w. ground** terre *f* inculte *ou* en friche; *(in town)* terrain *m* vague; **w. heat** chaleur *f* perdue; **w. heat recovery** récupération *f* de la chaleur perdue; **w. land** terre inculte *ou* en friche; *(in town)* terrain vague; **w. pipe** (tuyau *m* de) vidange *f*, **w. products** déchets; **w. water** *(domestic)* eaux *fpl* usées; *Ind* eaux résiduaires *ou* usées; **w. water treatment** traitement *m* des eaux usées

▶ **waste away** VI *(of person)* dépérir, s'affaiblir

wastebasket ['weɪstbɑːskɪt] N *esp Am* corbeille *f* (à papier); *Comput* corbeille *f*

▶▶ *Comput* **w. icon** icône *f* de la corbeille

wastebin ['weɪstbɪn] N corbeille *f* à papier

wasted ['weɪstɪd] ADJ *(sick person, body)* affaibli, amaigri; *(through drug use)* dévasté, ravagé; *(limb)* atrophié **2** *(money)* gaspillé; *(effort)* inutile; *(opportunity)* perdu; **it was a w. journey** c'était un voyage pour rien; **w. life** vie gaspillée; **w. time** temps perdu **3** *Fam (drunk)* pété, bourré; *(on drugs)* défoncé, raide

wasteful ['weɪstfʊl] ADJ *(person)* gaspilleur, -euse; *(expense)* excessif; *(process)* peu économique; **w. practices** gaspillage *m;* **don't be so w. with the hot water!** ne gaspillez pas l'eau chaude!; **it is w. of human resources** c'est gaspiller les ressources humaines

wastefully ['weɪstfəlɪ] ADV prodigalement, avec prodigalité; **to spend money w.** gaspiller son argent

wastefulness ['weɪstfʊlnɪs] N gaspillage *m*

wasteland ['weɪstlænd] N *(desert)* région *f* inculte, désert *m; (in city)* terrain *m* vague; *Fig* désert; **an industrial/cultural w.** un désert industriel/culturel

wastepaper ['weɪstpeɪpər] N vieux papiers *mpl*

▶▶ **w. basket** corbeille *f* à papier

waster ['weɪstər] N **1** *(wasteful person)* gaspilleur, -euse; **time w.** fainéant, -ante **2** *(good for nothing)* bon *m*/bonne *f* à rien

wasting ['weɪstɪŋ] N **1** *(of resources, time)* gaspillage *m* **2** *(of body)* dépérissement *m*, amaigrissement *m; (of limb)* atrophie *f, Med* **w. of muscle** fonte *f* musculaire

▶▶ *Acct* **w. asset** actif *m* qui se déprécie; **w. away** *(of body)* dépérissement, amaigrissement; *(of limb)* atrophie; **w. disease** maladie *f* qui ronge

wastrel ['weɪstrəl] N *(useless person)* vaurien, -ienne, bon *m*/bonne *f* à rien

WATCH [wɒtʃ]

| **N** garde **1** ▪ surveillance **1** |
| **VI** regarder **1** ▪ veiller **2** |
| **VT** observer **1** ▪ regarder **1, 2** ▪ faire attention à **3** ▪ surveiller **4** |

N 1 *(observation)* garde *f*, surveillance *f*; **to keep w.** monter la garde; **to keep a close w. on** *or* **over sb** surveiller qn de près; **to put** *or* **set a w. on sb** faire surveiller qn; **to be on the w. for sb** épier *ou* guetter qn
2 *(timepiece)* montre *f*; **it's six o'clock by my w.** il est six heures à ma montre
3 *Naut (shift)* quart *m*; *(men)* bordée *f*; **to be on w.** être de quart; **the officer of the w.** l'officier *m* du quart
4 *Hist (guard)* **the w.** la garde, le guet
5 *(vigil)* veille *f*; *Lit* **in the watches of the night** pendant les heures de veille; **to keep w. at sb's bedside** veiller au chevet de qn
VI 1 *(look on)* regarder; **they watched helplessly as the wall came tumbling down** ils regardaient, impuissants, le mur qui s'écroulait; **they're watching to see if you make a mistake** ils surveillent pour voir si tu fais une erreur
2 *(keep vigil)* veiller; **to w. by a sick person** veiller auprès d'un malade
VT 1 *(observe)* observer, regarder attentivement; **I'm not going to stand back and w. him make a fool of himself** je ne vais pas juste le regarder se ridiculiser; **I want to w. what happens when you tell him the news** je veux voir ce qui se passe quand tu lui annonceras la nouvelle; **to w. sb closely** ne pas quitter qn des yeux; *(of police, secret service)* surveiller qn de près; **to have sb watched** faire surveiller qn; **we are being watched** on nous observe; **to w. birds** observer les oiseaux; **you're not doing it properly, w. me** tu t'y prends mal, regarde-moi faire; *Prov* **a watched pot never boils** plus on désire une chose plus elle se fait attendre
2 *(look at, monitor)* regarder; **I watched her working** je la regardais travailler; **to w. television** regarder la télévision; **is there anything worth watching on TV?** est-ce qu'il y a quelque chose de bien (à regarder) à la télévision?; **to w. a football match** *(attend)* assister à un match de football; *(on television)* regarder un match de football; **to w. the course of events/sb's career** suivre le cours des événements/la carrière de qn; *Pej* **to w. the clock** avoir les yeux rivés *ou* fixés sur l'heure; **to w. the world go by** regarder passer la foule VOIR GRAMMAIRE A41; B35
3 *(be careful of)* faire attention à; **we shall have to w. the expenses** il nous faudra faire attention aux dépenses; **we'll have to w. the time** *(so as not to be late)* il va falloir que nous fassions attention à l'heure; **w. what you say about ...** fais attention à ce que tu dis au sujet de ...; **w. you don't say anything stupid** fais attention à ne pas dire quelque chose de stupide; **w. where you're going!** *(or you'll fall)* regarde où tu vas!; *(or you'll bump into somebody)* regarde devant toi!; **w. your language!** surveille ton langage!; **to w. one's weight** surveiller sa ligne; **w. the step!** *(fais)* attention à la marche!; **w. your step!** *(don't fall)* fais attention de ne pas tomber!; *(step carefully)* fais attention où tu mets les pieds!; *(be careful)* fais attention!; *Fam* **w. it!** fais gaffe!
4 *(keep an eye on)* (children, luggage etc) surveiller; **our neighbour is watching the flat while we're away** notre voisin s'occupe de notre appartement pendant que nous sommes en voyage
5 *(be mindful of)* **to w. one's opportunity/time** guetter l'occasion/le moment propice

▸▸ **w. chain** chaîne *f* de montre; **w. night** nuit *f* de la Saint-Sylvestre; **w. night service** messe *f* (de minuit) de la Saint-Sylvestre; **w. pocket** gousset *m*; *Comput* **w. pointer** pointeur-montre *m*, *pl* pointeurs-montres; **w. spring** ressort *m* de montre
▸ **watch for** VT INSEP **something to w. for this month is the London marathon** la chose à ne pas rater ce mois, c'est le marathon de Londres; **w. for the moment when he realizes she may be the killer** regarde bien la scène où il comprend qu'elle est peut-être l'assassin
▸ **watch out** VI faire attention; **you'd better w. out, the boss knows** tu devrais te méfier, le patron est au courant; **w. out!** attention!, prenez garde!
▸ **watch out for** VT INSEP **1** *(look for)* **ask the garage to w. out for a decent second-hand car** demande au garage d'essayer de trouver une bonne voiture d'occasion; **w. out for trouble when Fred gets out of prison** méfiez-vous quand Fred sortira de prison
2 *Am (take care of) (person)* s'occuper de
3 *(keep watch) (for return of)* attendre; *(for approach of)* guetter
4 *(be careful of)* faire attention à; **w. out for Ronnie!** gare à Ronnie!
▸ **watch over** VT INSEP *(guard, protect)* (person) veiller sur; *(person's interest, welfare)* veiller à

watchband ['wɒtʃbænd] N bracelet *m* de montre
watchdog ['wɒtʃdɒg] N chien *m* de garde; *Fig (person)* contrôleur *m*; *(organization)* organisme *m* de surveillance *ou* de contrôle; **(consumer) w.** protecteur *m* des intérêts du consommateur; *(organization)* organisme protégeant les intérêts du consommateur; **the committee acts as w. on environmental issues** le comité veille aux problèmes d'environnement
▸▸ *Comput* **w. program** programme *m* sentinelle
watcher ['wɒtʃər] N *(of political etc scene)* observateur, -trice; **Downing Street/Kremlin watchers** les observateurs de Downing Street/du Kremlin
watchful ['wɒtʃfʊl] ADJ vigilant, alerte, attentif; **to be w.** être sur ses gardes; **to keep a w. eye on** *or* **over sb** surveiller qn de près; **under the w. eye of his grandmother** sous l'œil vigilant de sa grand-mère; **we're keeping a w. eye on the situation** nous suivons la situation de près; **to be w. of sb** observer *ou* épier qn d'un œil méfiant *ou* jaloux
watchfully ['wɒtʃfəlɪ] ADV avec vigilance, d'un œil attentif
watching brief ['wɒtʃɪŋ] N **to have a w.** avoir un mandat de contrôle
watchmaker ['wɒtʃmeɪkər] N horloger, -ère
watchmaking ['wɒtʃmeɪkɪŋ] N horlogerie *f*
watchman, *pl* **watchmen** ['wɒtʃmən] N gardien *m*
watchstrap ['wɒtʃstræp] N bracelet *m* de montre
watchtower ['wɒtʃtaʊər] N tour *f* d'observation *ou* de guet; *(in prison camp)* mirador *m*
watchword ['wɒtʃwɜːd] N mot *m* de passe; *(slogan)* mot d'ordre
water ['wɔːtər] N **1** eau *f*, **is the w. safe to drink?** est-ce que l'eau est potable?; **to take** *or* **drink the waters** *(mineral springs)* prendre les eaux, faire une cure; *Fig* **to get into hot w.** se mettre dans de mauvais draps; **to drink a glass of cold w.** boire un verre d'eau fraîche; *Fig* **to pour cold w. on a scheme** se montrer très négatif à l'égard d'un projet; **to**

put w. in one's wine couper son vin d'eau; **the wine flowed like w.** le vin a coulé à flots; *Fig* **to spend money like w.** jeter l'argent par les fenêtres; *Prov* **you can lead a horse to w. but you cannot make him drink** on ne saurait faire boire un âne qui n'a pas soif; *Fig* **to hold w.** *(of argument etc)* tenir debout; **my shoes let in w.** mes chaussures prennent l'eau; **to take w. on** *(of ship)* embarquer son eau, faire de l'eau; **the waters of the Danube** les eaux du Danube; **to feel like a fish out of w.** se sentir perdu *ou* hors de son élément; *Prov* **still waters run deep** il faut se méfier de l'eau qui dort; **the steeple of the church was all that remained above w.** seul le clocher de l'église était hors de *ou* au-dessus de l'eau; **to keep oneself** *or* **one's head above w.** se maintenir à la surface *ou* sur l'eau; *Fig* garder la tête hors de l'eau; *(financially)* faire face à ses engagements; **by w.** en bateau; *(to transport goods)* par voie d'eau; **under w.** *(land, roots)* inondé; *(submarine)* en plongée; *(to swim)* sous l'eau; *Fig* **that's all w. under the bridge now** c'est du passé tout ça; *Fig* **a lot of w. has flowed under the bridge since then** il y a de l'eau qui a coulé sous les ponts depuis; **she's a real w. baby** c'est un vrai petit poisson; **high/low w.** marée *f* haute/basse; *Chem* **w. soluble** hydrosoluble; **hot w. bottle** bouillotte *f*
2 *Med* **w. on the brain** hydrocéphalie *f*; **w. on the knee** hydarthrose *f* du genou, épanchement *m* de synovie; *Obst* **breaking of the waters** perte *f* des eaux; **her waters have broken** elle a perdu les eaux; **to pass** *or* **make w.** uriner
3 *(of diamond)* **a diamond of the first w.** un diamant de première eau; *Old-fashioned Fig* **a villain of the first w.** une canaille de premier ordre
VT 1 *(plant, garden)* arroser; **an area watered by many rivers** une région arrosée par de nombreuses rivières
2 *(liquid)* diluer, délayer; **to w. one's wine** couper son vin
3 *(animals)* faire boire, donner à boire à, abreuver
VI *(of eyes)* pleurer, larmoyer; **it makes my mouth w.** cela me fait venir l'eau à la bouche
▸▸ **w. bed** lit *m* à matelas d'eau; **w. bird** oiseau *m* aquatique; **w. birth** accouchement *m* sous l'eau; *Br* **w. biscuit** = biscuit *m* salé croquant; **w. blister** ampoule *f*, *Spec* phlyctène *f*; *Br Admin* **w. board** service *m* des eaux; *Entom* **w. boatman** notonecte *f*, **w. bottle** bouteille *f* d'eau; *(soldier's, worker's)* bidon *m* à eau; *(in leather)* gourde *f*; **w. buffalo** *(in India)* buffle *m* d'Inde; *(in Malaysia)* karbau *m*, kérabau *m*; *(in Asia)* buffle d'Asie; **w. butt** citerne *f* (à eau de pluie); **w. cannon** canon *m* à eau; **w. carrier** *(container)* bidon à eau; *(person)* porteur, -euse d'eau; **w. chestnut** châtaigne *f* d'eau; **w. chute** *(in swimming-pool)* toboggan *m*; *Old-fashioned* **w. closet** W.C. *mpl*, toilettes *fpl*, cabinets *mpl*; **w. cooler** distributeur *m* d'eau fraîche; *TV Fam* **w. cooler show** = émission *f* dont tout le monde parle; **w. cooling** refroidissement *m* par eau; *Am* **w. cracker** = biscuit salé croquant; **w. cures** thermalisme *m*, cures *fpl* thermales; **w. damage** dégâts *mpl* des eaux; **w. gun** pistolet *m* à eau; **w. hammer** *(in pipes)* cognements *mpl* dans la canalisation; **w. heater** chauffe-eau *m inv*; **w. hen** poule *f* d'eau; **w. hole** *(for animals)* mare *f*, *Br* **w. ice** sorbet *m*; **w. jacket** chemise *f* d'eau; *Aut* **w. jet** gicleur *m* d'eau; **w. jump** brook *m*; **w. level** *(of river, sea)* niveau *m* de l'eau; *(in tank)* niveau d'eau; *Bot* **w. lily** nénuphar *m*; **w. line** ligne *f* de flottaison; **w. main** conduite *f* d'eau; **w. mattress** matelas *m* à eau; **w. meadow** prairie *f* (souvent inondée); **w. meter** compteur *m* d'eau; **w. mill** moulin *m* à eau; **w. park** parc *m* aquatique; **w. pipe**

Constr conduite *ou* canalisation *f* d'eau; *(hookah)* narguilé *m*; **w. pistol** pistolet *m* à eau; **w. plant** plante *f* aquatique; **w. polo** water-polo *m*; **w. power** énergie *f* hydraulique, houille *f* blanche; **w. pump** pompe *f* à eau; *Zool* **w. rat** rat *m* d'eau; *Br* **w. rate** taxe *f* sur l'eau; **w. shortage** pénurie *f* d'eau; **w. ski** ski *m* nautique; **w. skiing** ski nautique; *Zool* **w. snail** hélice *f* aquatique; **w. sports** *(water skiing, windsurfing etc)* sports *mpl* nautiques; *Vulg* = pratique *f* sexuelle qui consiste à uriner sur son ou sa partenaire; *Myth* **w. sprite** ondin, -ine; **w. supply** *(for campers, troops)* provision *f* d'eau; *(to house)* alimentation *f* en eau; *(to area, town)* distribution *f* des eaux, approvisionnement *m* en eau; **w. table** niveau *m* de la nappe phréatique; **w. tank** réservoir *m* d'eau, citerne *f*; **w. tower** château *m* d'eau; **w. transport** transport *m* par voie d'eau; **w. wheel** roue *f* à eau, roue hydraulique; **w. wings** *(for swimming)* flotteurs *mpl*
▶ **water down** VT SEP **1** *(liquid)* diluer, délayer **2** *Fig (expression, remark, accusation)* atténuer; **to w. down one's claims** en rabattre, mettre de l'eau dans son vin; **to w. down an article** rendre un article moins virulent; **a watered-down version of sth** une version édulcorée de qch

waterborne ['wɔːtəbɔːn] ADJ **1** *(vessel)* à flot, flottant **2** *(goods)* transporté par voie d'eau **3** *(disease)* d'origine hydrique

watercolour, *Am* **watercolor** ['wɔːtəkʌlər] N *(picture)* aquarelle *f*, *(paint)* couleur *f* pour aquarelle, peinture *f* à l'eau; **to paint in watercolours** faire de l'aquarelle
▶▶ **w. artist** aquarelliste *mf*

water-cooled [-kuːld] ADJ refroidi par eau
▶▶ **w. engine** moteur *m* à refroidissement d'eau

watercourse ['wɔːtəkɔːs] N cours *m* d'eau

watercress ['wɔːtəkres] N *Bot, Culin* cresson *m* de fontaine

watered ['wɔːtəd] ADJ
▶▶ *Tex* **w. silk** soie *f* moirée; *Fin* **w. stock** titres *mpl* dilués

waterfall ['wɔːtəfɔːl] N chute *f* d'eau, cascade *f*

Waterford crystal ['wɔːtəfəd] N = cristal *m* fabriqué à Waterford en Irlande

waterfowl ['wɔːtəfaʊl] N **1** *(bird)* oiseau *m* aquatique **2** *(no pl) (birds)* gibier *m* d'eau, sauvagine *f*

waterfront ['wɔːtəfrʌnt] N *(seafront)* front *m* de l'eau; *(at harbour)* quais *mpl*; **on the w.** *(on seafront)* face à la mer; *(at harbour)* sur les quais

wateriness ['wɔːtərɪnɪs] N *(of soup, sth boiled)* insipidité *f*, fadeur *f*; *(of colour)* ton *m* délavé

watering ['wɔːtərɪŋ] N **1** *(of plant)* arrosage *m*; *(of fields)* irrigation *f* **2** *(of animals)* abreuvage *m* **3** *(of eyes)* larmoiement *m* **4** *Tex (of silk)* moirage *m*
▶▶ **w. can** arrosoir *m*; **w. hole** *(for animals)* point *m* d'eau; *Fam Hum (pub)* troquet *m*; *Fam* **this was my favourite w. hole** c'est là que j'allais régulièrement me rincer le gosier; **w. place** *(waterhole)* point d'eau; *Br (spa)* station *f* thermale; *Br (seaside resort)* station balnéaire

waterlogged ['wɔːtəlɒɡd] ADJ *(boat, carpet)* plein d'eau; *(wood)* imprégné d'eau; *(shoes, clothes)* trempé; *(land)* détrempé, imbibé d'eau; *(subsoil)* détrempé

Waterloo [wɔːtə'luː] N **the Battle of W.** la bataille de Waterloo; *Fig* **to meet one's W.** *(come up against unresolvable situation)* avoir son compte; *(come up against unbeatable opponent)* trouver son maître; **it's like W. station here** *(noisy and busy)* c'est une vraie maison de fous ici

watermark ['wɔːtəmɑːk] N **1** *Naut (for high or low water)* laisse *f* **2** *(on paper, bank note)* filigrane *m*
VT filigraner

watermelon ['wɔːtəmelən] N pastèque *f*, melon *m* d'eau

waterproof ['wɔːtəpruːf] ADJ *(clothing, material)* imperméable; *(watch, container, seal)* étanche; **w. sheet** bâche *f* étanche
N imperméable *m*; **waterproofs** vêtements *mpl* imperméables
VT imperméabiliser

waterproofing ['wɔːtəpruːfɪŋ] N *(action)* imperméabilisation *f*, *(substance)* imperméabilisant *m*

water-repellent ADJ imperméable, hydrofuge; *(product, spray)* imperméabilisant
N imperméabilisant *m*

water-resistant ADJ qui résiste à l'eau, résistant à l'eau

watershed ['wɔːtəʃed] N **1** *Geog (line)* ligne *f* de partage des eaux; *Am (area)* bassin *m* hydrographique **2** *Fig* point *m* décisif, tournant *m*; *TV* **the (nine o'clock) w.** = l'heure *f* après laquelle l'émission de programmes destinés aux adultes est autorisée; **at this w. in her life** à ce moment critique de sa vie; **the decision proved to be a w.** la décision s'est avérée marquer un grand tournant

waterside ['wɔːtəsaɪd] N bord *m* de l'eau
ADJ *(house, path)* au bord de l'eau; *(flower)* du bord de l'eau; **w. residents** riverains *mpl*
▶▶ *Am* **w. workers** dockers *mpl*

waterspout ['wɔːtəspaʊt] N **1** *Met* trombe *f* **2** *(pipe)* tuyau *m*, descente *f* (d'eau)

watertight ['wɔːtətaɪt] ADJ **1** étanche (à l'eau); **to be w.** *(keep water in)* retenir l'eau **2** *Fig (alibi)* en béton; *(argument, reasoning)* inattaquable, indiscutable
▶▶ *Naut* **w. bulkhead** cloison *f* étanche

waterway ['wɔːtəweɪ] N voie *f* navigable

waterworks ['wɔːtəwɜːks] NPL **1** *(establishment)* usine *f* de distribution d'eau **2** *Br Fam (urinary system)* voies *fpl* urinaires; **he's having a bit of trouble with his w.** il a des problèmes de vessie **3** *Fam* **to turn on the w.** *(start to cry)* se mettre à pleurer, ouvrir la fontaine

watery ['wɔːtərɪ] ADJ **1** *(surroundings, world)* aquatique; *(ground, soil)* détrempé, saturé d'eau; **the sailors found a w. grave** les marins ont été ensevelis par les eaux **2** *(eyes)* larmoyant, humide **3** *(coffee, tea)* trop léger; *(soup)* trop liquide; *(milk)* qui a trop d'eau; *(vegetables, beer)* insipide; *(taste)* fade, insipide **4** *(light, sun, smile)* faible; *(colour)* délavé, pâle; *(sky)* chargé de pluie; **she gave a w. smile** elle sourit à travers ses larmes

watt [wɒt] N *Elec* watt *m*

wattage ['wɒtɪdʒ] N *Elec* puissance *f* ou consommation *f* en watts

watt-hour N *Elec* wattheure *m*

wattle¹ ['wɒt(ə)l] N **1** **w.-and-daub wall** mur *m* en clayonnage revêtu de boue *ou* d'argile **2** *Austr (tree)* acacia *m*

wattle² N *(of bird)* caroncule *f*, *(of fish)* barbillon *m*

wave [weɪv] N **1** *Naut* vague *f*, lame *f*, *Fig* vague; **the pain came in waves** la douleur venait par vagues; *Art* **new w.** nouvelle vague; **w. of crime/refugees/enthusiasm** vague de criminalité/de réfugiés/d'enthousiasme; **w. of anger** bouffée *f* de colère; **a w. of bitterness swept over her** un flot d'amertume l'envahit; *Fam* **to make waves** *(cause trouble)* créer des remous
2 *Phys (electric, magnetic)* onde *f*, **radio waves** ondes radio; **long waves** grandes ondes; **medium/short waves** ondes moyennes/courtes

3 *(in hair)* ondulation *f*, **to have a natural w. (in one's hair)** avoir les cheveux qui ondulent naturellement; **her hair fell in waves to her waist** ses cheveux ondulaient jusqu'à sa taille
4 *(movement)* balancement *m*, ondoiement *m*; *(of hand, hat)* geste *m*, signe *m*; **with a w. of his hand** d'un geste *ou* d'un signe de la main; **the Queen gave them a w. from the car** la Reine les salua de la main depuis la voiture; **with a w. of her magic wand** d'un coup de baguette magique
VI **1** *(of person)* faire signe; *(of flag)* flotter (au vent); *(of corn, grass, plume)* ondoyer, onduler; **to w. to sb** *(signal to)* faire signe à qn; *(greet)* saluer qn de la main; **the kids went to the window to w.** *(goodbye/hello)* les gosses sont allés à la fenêtre pour faire au revoir/bonjour de la main; **the President stepped onto the balcony to w. to the crowd** le président est sorti sur le balcon pour saluer la foule; **he waved to us as he left** il nous fit au revoir de la main en partant; **I waved to him to stop** je lui ai fait signe d'arrêter
2 my hair waves naturally mes cheveux ondulent naturellement
VT **1** *(arm, handkerchief)* agiter; *(umbrella, walking stick)* brandir; **to w. a flag** agiter un drapeau; **to w. one's hand** faire signe de la main; **to w. one's arms about** agiter les bras; **stop waving that gun about** cesse d'agiter ce pistolet dans tous les sens; **to w. a magic wand** agiter une baguette magique; *Fig* **to do sth by waving a magic wand** faire qch d'un coup de baguette magique; **to w. goodbye to sb** agiter la main en signe d'adieu à (l'adresse de) qn, faire au revoir de la main à qn; **w. Mummy goodbye** fais au revoir à maman; *Fig* **you can w. your money goodbye** tu peux abandonner tout espoir de récupérer ton argent
2 *(hair)* **to have one's hair waved** se faire faire une mise en plis
▶▶ **w. machine** machine *f* à vagues; **w. power** énergie *f* des vagues
▶ **wave aside** VT SEP **to w. sb aside** faire signe à qn de s'écarter; **to w. aside an objection** écarter une objection
▶ **wave down** VT SEP **to w. a car/sb down** faire signe à une voiture/qn de s'arrêter
▶ **wave on** VT SEP **to w. a car on** faire signe à une voiture de continuer; **he waved us on** de la main il nous a fait signe de continuer

> Attention: ne pas confondre avec **to waive**.

waveband ['weɪvbænd] N *Radio* gamme *f* d'ondes, plage *f* (d'ondes)

wavelength ['weɪvleŋθ] N *Radio, Fig* longueur *f* d'onde; *Fig* **we weren't on the same w.** nous n'étions pas sur la même longueur d'onde

waver ['weɪvər] VI *(falter) (of person)* vaciller; *(of voice)* trembler; *(of courage)* faiblir; *(of gaze)* flotter; *(of troops)* fléchir; *(of flame)* vaciller; **they never wavered in their support, their support never wavered** leur soutien n'a jamais faibli; **to w. in one's resolution** chanceler dans sa résolution; **the price wavered around the £46 per kilo mark** le prix tournait autour des 46 livres le kilo; **to w. between** hésiter entre; **to w. over** hésiter sur; **they wavered over whether to tell their parents** ils se demandèrent s'ils allaient en parler à leurs parents

waverer ['weɪvərər] N indécis, -ise

wavering ['weɪvərɪŋ] ADJ *(person, mind)* irrésolu, indécis, vacillant; *(voice)* tremblant; *(courage)* faiblissant; *(flame)* vacillant, tremblotant; **their w. resolution** leur détermination chancelante

N (of person) hésitation f, irrésolution f, (of voice) tremblement m, (of courage) défaillance f, (of flame) tremblement, vacillement m

waviness ['weivinis] N (of surface) caractère m onduleux ou ondulé; (of hair) ondulations fpl naturelles

waving ['weiviŋ] ADJ (fields, corn) ondulant, ondoyant

wavy ['weivi] ADJ (line, surface, hair) ondulé

wax¹ [wæks] N cire f, (for skis) fart m, (in ears) cérumen m; (paraffin) w. cire (minérale), paraffine f, to mould sb like w. façonner ou former (le caractère de) qn comme de la cire

VT 1 (floor, furniture) cirer, encaustiquer; (furniture) astiquer; Ski farter 2 (in order to remove hairs) épiler (à la cire); to w. one's legs s'épiler les jambes (à la cire)

▶▶ Am w. beans haricots mpl beurre; w. crayon crayon m gras; w. museum musée m de cire

wax² VI 1 (of the moon) croître; to w. and wane croître et décroître 2 esp Fml (be, become) to w. eloquent in support of sth déployer toute son éloquence en faveur de qch; he waxed indignant il s'indigna; to w. lyrical/poetical devenir lyrique/poétique (about à propos de)

waxed [wækst] ADJ (floor, tablecloth) ciré; (thread) poissé; (moustache) gominé

▶▶ w. cotton coton m ciré, w. jacket veste f en toile huilée

waxen ['wæks(ə)n] ADJ 1 (candle, figure) de cire, en cire 2 (face, complexion) cireux

waxing¹ ['wæksiŋ] N (of floor, furniture) cirage m, encaustiquage m; (of skis) fartage m

waxing² N (of moon) croissance f 2 Aut (of diesel) paraffinage m

waxwing ['wækswiŋ] N (bird) jaseur m

waxwork ['wækswɜːk] N (object) objet m de ou en cire; (statue of person) statue f de cire

waxworks ['wækswɜːks] N musée m de cire

waxy ['wæksi] ADJ (texture, complexion) cireux; (potato) ferme, pas farineux

WAY [wei]

| ▪ rue 1 ▪ chemin 1–3 ▪ route 2 |
| ▪ direction 4 ▪ sens 4 ▪ moyen 5 |
| ▪ façon 6 ▪ manière 6 ▪ égard 7 |
| ▪ état 10 |

N 1 (street) rue f, (path) chemin m; over or across the w. de l'autre côté du chemin ou de la rue; the house/the people over or across the w. la maison/les gens d'en face 2 (route) chemin m; the w. to the station le chemin qui mène ou qui conduit à la gare, le chemin de la gare; to show sb the w. montrer la route ou le chemin à qn; to ask one's w. demander son chemin; to lose one's w. s'égarer, se perdre; that's the w. to ruin c'est le chemin de la ruine; the right w. le bon chemin, la bonne route; to go the wrong w. se tromper de chemin, faire fausse route; to go the nearest or shortest w. prendre le plus court chemin; to know one's w. about a place connaître un endroit; you'll soon find your w. about tu trouveras bientôt ton chemin tout seul; Fig he knows his w. about or around il sait se débrouiller, il est débrouillard; to prepare the w. préparer la voie; on the w. en cours de route, en chemin, chemin faisant; to stop on the w. s'arrêter en chemin; to start on one's w. se mettre en route; to be on one's or the w. to Paris être en route pour Paris; on my or the w. home en revenant chez moi, en rentrant; I must be on my w. je dois partir; I'm on my w. (coming) j'arrive; (going) je pars; he's well on the w. to doing it il est en bonne voie de le faire; the building is well on the w. to completion l'édifice est bien avancé; Fam there's a baby on the w. elle attend un bébé; to lead the w. être à la tête de la recherche; to lead the w. in research être à la pointe de la recherche; to lead the w. in fighting inflation être le chef de file dans la lutte contre l'inflation; to go the w. of all things or of all flesh aller où va toute chose, mourir; we went our separate ways nous avons suivi chacun notre chemin; to go one's own w. (follow own wishes) faire à sa guise; (differ from others) faire bande à part, suivre son chemin; to go out of one's w. s'écarter de son chemin, dévier de sa route, faire un détour; Fig to go out of one's w. to oblige sb se donner de la peine pour être agréable à qn; the w. to a man's heart is through his stomach = pour conquérir le cœur d'un homme, il faut lui faire de bons petits plats; the village is rather out of the w. le village est un peu isolé; that's nothing out of the w. rien d'extraordinaire à cela; Rel the W. of the Cross le chemin de la Croix; w. in entrée f, w. out sortie f, to find a w. out/in trouver moyen de sortir/d'entrer; w. through passage m; to find a w. out of a deadlock trouver une issue à une impasse; to find a w. out of a problem trouver une solution à un problème; to leave sb a w. out laisser à qn le moyen de sortir d'une difficulté; easy w. out solution f de facilité; to find one's w. to a place se rendre quelque part; can you find your w. there? est-ce que tu sais y aller tout seul?; I can't find my w. back to the hotel je n'arrive pas à retrouver l'hôtel; can you find your w. out? vous connaissez le chemin pour sortir?; I can find my own w. out (out of house etc) je trouverai mon chemin; however did it find its w. into print? comment en est-on venu à l'imprimer?; she made her w. to the door/the bar elle se dirigea vers la porte/se rendit au bar; to make one's w. towards sb se diriger vers qn; to make or work or push one's w. through the crowd se frayer un chemin à travers la foule; she made her w. into the house elle a pénétré dans la maison; to make one's w. back/out/home revenir/sortir/rentrer; how to make one's w. (in the world) comment réussir; to work one's w. up s'élever (à force de travail); to pay one's w. (of company) se suffire; (contribute to expenses) payer sa part; to see one's w. (clear) to doing sth être à même de faire qch; couldn't you see your w. (clear) to doing it? ne trouveriez-vous pas moyen de le faire?; to stand in sb's w. être dans le chemin de qn, barrer le passage à qn; I don't wish to stand in the w. of your happiness je ne voudrais pas faire obstacle à votre bonheur; to stand in the w. of a scheme s'opposer à un projet; the obstacles that stand in our w. les obstacles qui se dressent sur notre chemin; to put difficulties in sb's w. opposer ou créer des difficultés à qn; to get in one another's w. se gêner (les autres); work gets in the w. of my social life le travail m'empêche de sortir autant que je voudrais; to be in sb's w. gêner qn; this table is in the w. cette table gêne le passage ou est encombrante; you're in the w. tu gênes le passage; Fig tu gênes, tu me/nous/etc déranges; to get out of the w. (to let sb pass) se ranger, s'ôter du chemin, s'écarter; (get) out of the w.! poussez-vous!, ôtez-vous de là ou de mon chemin!; to get out of sb's w. s'ôter ou s'écarter du chemin de qn; Fig (in relationship) laisser le champ libre à qn; to get sb out of the w. se débarrasser de qn, écarter ou éloigner qn; to get sth out of the w. enlever ou pousser qch; Fig let's get the subject of holidays out of the w. first réglons d'abord la question des vacances; to keep out of the w. se tenir à l'écart; to keep out of sb's w. éviter qn; to make w. for sb laisser passer qn, faire place à qn; clear the w.! poussez-vous!; the agreement will clear the w. for the company's expansion l'accord déblaiera le terrain pour permettre l'expansion de la société; Fig the w. is clear la voie est libre; he is retiring to make w. for a younger man il prend sa retraite pour céder la place à un plus jeune; the cinema is going to be demolished to make w. for a supermarket le cinéma va être démoli et sera remplacé par un supermarché

3 (distance) to go a little w. or part of the w. with sb faire un bout de chemin avec qn; all the w. tout le long du chemin; (to the end) jusqu'au bout; he talked the entire or whole w. il a parlé pendant tout le trajet; Fam to go the whole w. or all the w. (sexually) aller jusqu'au bout; Fig I'm with you all the w. (agree) je suis tout à fait d'accord (avec toi); I flew most of the w. j'ai fait la plupart du voyage en avion; I've come a long w. j'ai fait un long voyage, j'arrive de loin; Fig she's come a long w. (been successful) elle a bien réussi (dans la vie); Fig she'll go a long w. elle ira loin; it's a long w. to London, London's a long w. from here Londres est bien loin d'ici; it's a long w. from Paris to Rome la route est longue de Paris à Rome; to have a long w. to go avoir un long chemin à faire; a little or short w. off à peu de distance; it's only a short w. (off) c'est assez proche; Christmas is still a long w. off Noël est encore loin; a little understanding goes a long w. un peu de compréhension facilite bien les choses; a little of it goes a long w. (it's very economical, strong-tasting) il en faut très peu; I like it but a little goes a long w. (of rich food) j'aime ça mais à petites doses; a little of him goes a long w. on en a vite assez de lui; you can make a little meat go a long w. by doing this utilisez au mieux un petit morceau de viande en faisant ceci; to make one's money go a long w. savoir ménager ses sous; by a long w. de beaucoup; not by a long w. il s'en faut de beaucoup; you're a long w. out or out by a long w. vous êtes loin du compte, vous vous trompez de beaucoup

4 (direction) côté m, direction f, sens m; which w. is the wind blowing? d'où vient ou souffle le vent?; which w. does the tap turn? dans quel sens faut-il tourner le robinet?; Fig so that's the w. the wind's blowing! ça se passe donc comme ça!; this w. de ce côté-ci, par ici; that w. de ce côté-là, par là; (step) this w.! venez ou passez par ici!; is this the w.? c'est par ici?; which w. is the library from here? par où faut-il passer pour aller à la bibliothèque?; which w. did you come? par où êtes-vous venu?; which w. did she go? par où est-elle passée?; which w. do we go? de quel côté ou par où allonsnous?; this w. and that de-ci de-là, de tous (les) côtés; he didn't know which w. to look il ne savait pas où regarder; to look the other w. détourner les yeux; I've nothing to say one w. or the other je n'ai rien à dire pour ou contre; they set off, each going his own w. ils sont partis chacun de leur côté; I'm going your w. je vais de votre côté; the next time you're that w. la prochaine fois que vous passerez par là; Fam down our w. chez nous; Fam she lives out Hampstead w. elle habite du côté de Hampstead; if the chance comes your w. si l'occasion se présente à vous; that works both ways ça vaut ou marche dans les deux sens; Fig Fam to swing both ways (be bisexual) être ou marcher à voile et à vapeur; the wrong w. à contre-sens; Fig Fam to rub sb up the wrong w. prendre qn à rebrousse-poil; the wrong w. up sens dessus dessous, à l'envers; to hold sth (the) right w. up tenir qch dans le bon sens; to split a sum of money three ways partager une somme en trois; Am every which w. dans tous les sens

5 *(means)* moyen *m*; **to find a w. of doing sth** trouver (le) moyen de faire qch; *Admin* **ways and means** voies et moyens; **there are ways and means** il y a des moyens; *Parl* **Committee of Ways and Means** Commission *f* du Budget

6 *(manner)* façon *f*, manière *f*; **in this w.** de cette façon; **in a friendly w.** amicalement; *(to treat sb)* en ami; **speaking in a general w.** (parlant) d'une façon générale; **in such a w. as to ...** de façon à ..., de telle sorte que ...; *Fam* **no w.!** jamais de la vie!, pas question!, *Fam* des clous!; *Fam* **there's no w. he'll ...** il est absolument impossible qu'il ... + *subj*, *Fam* **there's no w. that's Jeanne Moreau!** tu rigoles?, ce n'est pas Jeanne Moreau!; **without in any w. wishing to criticize** sans aucunement vouloir critiquer; **either w.** *(whatever you decide)* quoi que tu décides; *(whatever happens)* quoi qu'il arrive; **that's the w.!** ça y est!, voilà!, à la bonne heure!; **in such and such a w.** de telle et telle façon; **to go** *or* **set about it the right w.** s'y prendre de la bonne manière *ou* comme il faut; **you're going the right w. to make her angry** ça, c'est la meilleure manière de la mettre en colère; **the best w. is to say nothing** le mieux est de ne rien dire; **in one w. or another** d'une façon ou d'une autre; **there are no two ways about it** il n'y a pas à discuter; **we can't go on in the same old w.** nous ne pouvons pas (toujours) continuer comme ça; **I don't like the w. things are going** je n'aime pas la tournure que prennent les choses; **they'll never finish it the w. things are going** ils n'en finiront jamais, au train où vont les choses; **w. of doing sth** manière *ou* façon de faire qch; **w. of speaking/writing** façon de parler/d'écrire; **w. of living** style *m* de vie; **her w. of looking at things** sa manière de voir (les choses); **it isn't what he says, it's the w. he says it** ce n'est pas ce qu'il dit mais la manière dont il le dit; **I don't like the w. you talk to her** je n'aime pas la manière dont tu lui parles; **to my w. of thinking** selon moi, à mon sens; **that's not my w. (of doing things)** ce n'est pas mon genre, ce n'est pas ma façon de faire; **that's her w.** c'est sa façon de faire; **that's always the w. when you're in a hurry** c'est toujours comme ça quand on est pressé; **that's always the w. with him** il est toujours comme ça, c'est toujours comme ça avec lui; **to do things in one's own w.** faire les choses à sa façon *ou* à sa manière; **to have a w. of one's own** *or* **one's own w. of doing sth** avoir une façon à soi de faire qch, avoir sa méthode pour faire qch; **he's a genius in his w.** c'est un génie dans son genre; **she does what she can for them in her small w.** elle les aide dans la mesure de ses moyens; **the restaurant is doing quite well in a small w.** le restaurant marche bien à son échelle; **he started out in a small w.** *(of businessman)* il a commencé petit; **one's ways** *(behaviour)* ses manières; **you'll soon get into our ways** vous vous ferez bientôt à nos habitudes; **engaging ways** petites façons engageantes; **I know his little ways** je connais ses petites manies; **to get** *or* **fall into the w. of doing sth** *(through habit)* prendre l'habitude de faire qch, s'habituer à faire qch; *(through practice)* apprendre à faire qch; **you'll get into the w. of it** vous vous y ferez; **that's one w. of looking at it!** c'est une façon de voir!; **he has a w. with children** il sait s'y prendre avec les enfants; **to have one's (own) w.** en faire à sa tête; **to get one's (own) w.** arriver à ses fins; **she wants her (own) w.** elle veut n'en faire qu'à sa tête; **if I had my w.** si on me laissait faire; **have it your (own) w.** *(do as you like)* faites ce que vous voulez *ou* à votre guise; *(if you insist)* soit; **she had it all her (own) w.** elle a fait exactement ce qu'elle a voulu;

you can't have it both ways on ne peut pas avoir le beurre et l'argent du beurre; *Old-fashioned, Hum* **he had his w. with her** *(sexually)* il a obtenu ses faveurs

7 *(respect)* égard *m*; **in many ways** à bien des égards; **in some ways** à certains points de vue; **in every w.** sous tous les rapports, en tous points; **in one w.** d'un certain point de vue; **you're right in a w.** d'une certaine manière vous avez raison; **in no w.** en aucune façon, nullement; **she is in no w.** *or* **not in any w. to blame** elle n'est aucunement *ou* elle n'est en aucune façon responsable; **this should in no w. be regarded as a victory** cela ne doit en aucune façon être considéré comme une victoire

8 *(sphere)* **I met him in the ordinary w. of business** je l'ai rencontré dans le courant de mes affaires

9 *(progress) Naut* erre *f*; **to get under w.** *(of person)* se mettre en route; *(of ship)* appareiller; *(of meeting)* commencer; *(of campaign etc)* démarrer; **the ship was under w.** le navire était en marche *ou* en route; **an important experiment is under w.** une expérience importante est en cours; **the project is well under w.** le projet est bien avancé

10 *(state, condition)* état *m*; **to be in a good/bad w.** être bien/mal en point; **things seem in a bad w.** les choses ont l'air d'aller mal; **his business is in a bad w.** ses affaires vont mal *ou* péniclitent; **to be in a fair w. to do sth** être en bonne voie de *ou* en (bonne) passe de faire qch; **to put sb in the w. of earning a few pounds** donner à qn l'occasion de gagner quelques livres

11 by the w., ... au fait ..., à propos ...; **to mention sth by the w.** mentionner qch en passant *ou* incidemment; **(let it be said) by the w.** soit dit en passant; **all this is by the w.** tout ceci est entre parenthèses; **by the w., did you see him yesterday?** à propos, l'avez-vous vu hier?; **by w. of** *(via)* par, via; *(with the intention of)* à titre de; **by w. of introduction/warning** à titre d'introduction/d'avertissement; **he asked after her dog by w. of changing the conversation** il a demandé des nouvelles de son chien, histoire de changer de sujet; **what do you have by w. of** *or* **in the w. of fruit?** qu'est-ce que vous avez comme fruits?

▸ *ADV Fam (a lot)* très; **w. ahead** très avancé (**of** sur); **he is w. crazy** il est vachement atteint; **it was w. back in the twenties** cela remonte aux années vingt; **Mary and I go w. back** *or* **are friends from w. back** Mary et moi sommes amies de longue date; **w. down south** là-bas dans le sud; **to be w. out** *(mistaken) (of person)* faire une grosse erreur, se tromper sérieusement; **your guess was w. out** vous étiez très loin de la vérité; **it's w. more than I can afford** c'est beaucoup plus que je ne peux payer

▸ ▸ *Am* **w. station** *Rail* petite gare *f*, *Fig* étape *f*, *Am Rail* **w. train** (train *m*) omnibus *m*

waybill ['weɪbɪl] N *Com* feuille *f* de route, connaissement *m*, bulletin *m ou* bordereau *m* d'expédition

wayfarer ['weɪfeərər] N voyageur, -euse (à pied)

wayfaring ['weɪfeərɪŋ] N voyages *mpl* (à pied)
▸ *ADJ* voyageur; **a w. life** une vie de voyages; **w. man** voyageur *m* (à pied)

waylay [weɪ'leɪ] VT *(pt, pp* **waylaid** [weɪ-'leɪd]**) 1** *(attack)* attaquer, agresser; **to be waylaid** se faire agresser **2** *(in order to speak to)* arrêter au passage

way-out *ADJ* **1** *Fam (weird, eccentric)* dingue **2** *Old-fashioned Sl (great)* géant

wayside ['weɪsaɪd] N bord *m* de la route; **to fall by the w.** *(not keep up)* rester en chemin;

(become dishonest), Hum s'écarter du droit chemin
▸ *ADJ* au bord de la route; **a w. inn** une auberge au bord de la route; **w. flowers** les fleurs qui bordent la route

wayward ['weɪwəd] *ADJ* capricieux; **to be w.** *(of person)* n'en faire qu'à sa tête

waywardness ['weɪwədnɪs] N caractère *m* difficile; **a certain w. became apparent in his character** il est apparu comme quelqu'un qui n'en faisait qu'à sa tête

wazz [wæz] *Br Sl* N **to have a w.** *(urinate)* faire la petite commission; **to go for a w.** aller faire la petite commission
▸ *VI (urinate)* faire la petite commission

wazzock ['wæzək] N *Br Sl* andouille *f*, cloche *f*

WC [dʌb(ə)lju:'si:] N *(abbr* water closet) WC *mpl*; **where is the WC?** où sont les WC?

we [wi:] PERS PRON PL *VOIR GRAMMAIRE A27–8* **1** *(unstressed)* nous; **we were playing** nous jouions; **here we are!** nous voilà!; **we both thank you** nous vous remercions tous (les) deux

2 *(stressed)* nous; **we are English, they are French** nous, nous sommes anglais, eux, ils sont français; **you don't think that we did it!** vous ne pensez pas que c'est nous qui l'avons fait?; **we English** nous autres Anglais **3** *(indefinite)* on; **how are we this morning, Mrs Smith?** comment ça va ce matin, Mme Smith?; **as we say in England** comme on dit en Angleterre; **we all make mistakes sometimes** tout le monde peut se tromper *VOIR GRAMMAIRE A28* **4** *(plural of majesty, editorial* we) nous; **we are convinced that ...** nous sommes convaincus que ...

w/e *(abbr* **week ending)** semaine se terminant

weak [wi:k] *ADJ* **1** *(person, currency)* faible; *(in character)* faible (mentalement), mou, molle; *(health)* fragile, délicat; *(body)* fragile; *(argument)* faible, peu convaincant; *(style)* mou; *(decision)* qui dénote de la faiblesse; **to grow w.** *(of person)* s'affaiblir, faiblir; **to be w. in body** être physiquement faible; **to have a w. heart** avoir le cœur faible; **to have a w. (eye)sight** avoir une mauvaise vue; **to have a w. stomach** avoir un estomac délicat; **w. with hunger** affaibli par la faim; **to feel as w. as a kitten** se sentir mou comme une chiffe; *Fam* **to be w. in the head** être faible d'esprit; *Fam* **you must be w. in the head if you believe that** tu dois être dérangé pour croire ça; *Old-fashioned* **the weaker sex** le sexe faible; **in a w. moment** dans un moment de faiblesse; **his w. side** *or* **spot** son point faible; **to find sb's w. spot** trouver le point faible de qn; **she gave a w. smile** elle a eu un faible sourire; **the weaker pupils** les élèves moins doués; **to be w. in French** être faible en français; **the play is w. in character analysis** la pièce est faible du point de vue de l'analyse des personnages; **to have a w. chin/mouth** avoir le menton fuyant/la bouche tombante; **I feel all w. at the knees** j'ai les jambes en coton; **he makes me go all w. at the knees** j'ai les jambes en coton rien que de le voir; *Mus* **w. beat** temps *m* faible; *Radio* **w. signal** signal *m* faible

2 *(solution)* dilué, étendu; *(tea, coffee)* léger; *Aut* **w. mixture** mélange *m* pauvre

3 *Gram (verb)* faible; *Ling (syllable)* non accentué

weaken ['wi:k(ə)n] VT affaiblir; *(foundations of house)* miner; *Aut* **to w. the mixture** appauvrir le mélange
▸ *VI (of person, authority, argument)* s'affaiblir, faiblir; *(of sound)* fléchir; *(of currency)* s'affaiblir; **don't w.** ne faiblis pas; **her courage weakened** son courage a fléchi *ou* faibli;

the pound has weakened against the dollar la livre est en baisse par rapport au dollar

weakening ['wi:k(ə)nɪŋ] ADJ *(makes lose strength)* affaiblissant; *(losing strength)* faiblissant

N affaiblissement *m*; *(of will, resistance)* fléchissement *m*; *(of current, currency)* affaiblissement, fléchissement

weakhearted [wi:k'hɑ:tɪd] ADJ sans courage

weak-kneed [-'ni:d] ADJ *Fig (person)* lâche, mou, *f* molle; *(decision)* lâche

weakling ['wi:klɪŋ] N *(morally)* mauviette *f*, faible *mf*; *(physically)* gringalet *m*

weakly ['wi:klɪ] ADJ *(person)* débile, chétif
ADV **1** *(lacking strength)* faiblement **2** *(lacking energy)* sans énergie, mollement; **she protested w.** elle protesta mollement

weak-minded ADJ **1** *(unintelligent)* faible d'esprit **2** *(lacking character)* irrésolu, indécis, qui manque de résolution

weakness ['wi:knɪs] N **1** *(of body, character, link, argument)* faiblesse *f*, *Aut (of mixture)* pauvreté *f* **2** *(fault)* point *m* faible; **we all have our own weaknesses** nous avons tous nos faiblesses; **to have a w. for sth/sb** *(like)* avoir un faible pour qch/qn

weak-willed [-'wɪld] ADJ faible, sans volonté

weal[1] [wi:l] N *(from whip)* marque *f ou* trace *f* de coup

weal[2] N *Arch* **the common w.** le bien commun

wealth [welθ] N **1** *(riches)* richesse(s) *f(pl)*; **he was a man of great w.** il était très riche **2** *(abundance) (of details etc)* abondance *f*, profusion *f*; **a w. of information** une mine d'informations; **this job offers a w. of opportunity for travel** cet emploi offre de nombreuses occasions de voyage; **she has had a w. of opportunities to prove it** elle a eu une quantité d'occasions de le prouver
▸▸ **w. creation** création *f* de richesses; *Fin* **w. tax** impôt *m* de solidarité sur la fortune

wealth-creating [-krɪ'eɪtɪŋ] ADJ générateur, -trice de richesses

wealthy ['welθɪ] ADJ riche, opulent; **a w. heiress** une riche héritière
NPL **the w.** les riches *mpl*

wean [wi:n] VT *(baby)* sevrer; *Fig* **youngsters today are being weaned on computers** les jeunes d'aujourd'hui sont nourris d'informatique; **she had been weaned on Mozart** elle a grandi sur les airs de Mozart; *Fig* **to w. sb from** *or* **off a bad habit** détacher *ou* détourner qn d'une mauvaise habitude; *Fig* **he was trying to w. himself off cigarettes** il essayait de se passer peu à peu de la cigarette

weaner ['wi:nər] N *(pig)* = porcelet *m* venant d'être sevré et pesant moins de 40 kg

weaning ['wi:nɪŋ] N sevrage *m*

weapon ['wepən] N *Mil, Fig* arme *f*; **the carrying of weapons is illegal** le port d'armes est prohibé; **he was carrying a w.** il avait une arme sur lui; *Fig* **it is an important w. in the fight against inflation** c'est une arme importante dans la lutte contre l'inflation
▸▸ **weapons inspection** inspecteur *m* du désarmement; **weapons inspector** inspecteur *m* du désarmement; **weapons of mass destruction** armes de destruction massive

weaponry ['wepənrɪ] N *(weapons)* armes *fpl*, armement *m*

WEAR [weər]

N usure **2** ▪ usage **2**	
VT porter **1** ▪ avoir **1** ▪ user **2**	

N **1** *(clothing)* vêtements *mpl*; **children's w.** vêtements pour enfants; **for country w.** pour la campagne

2 *(use, deterioration)* usure *f*, détérioration *f* *(par usure)*; *(of machine)* fatigue *f*, *(of road)* dégradation *f*; **to stand hard** *or* **heavy w.** *(of material)* être d'un bon usage; **those shoes still have some w. in them** ces chaussures sont toujours mettables; **my shoes are showing signs of w.** mes chaussures commencent à s'user; **you'll get lots of w. out of it** *(it will last for a long time)* vous le porterez longtemps; *(it is versatile, can be worn often)* vous le porterez beaucoup; **they get very heavy w.** *(of shoes etc)* ils ont la vie dure; **w. and tear** usure *f*, fair *or* normal w. and tear usure normale; **living in the big city puts a lot of w. and tear on people** les grandes villes sont une source de stress pour leurs habitants; **to be the worse for w.** *(of garment, sofa etc)* être usé *ou* défraîchi; *(of machine)* être abîmé; *Fig (of person) (tired)* être épuisé; *(bruised)* être amoché; *(hung over)* avoir la gueule de bois; **the next morning he was looking a bit the worse for w.** le lendemain matin il avait l'air plutôt en travers

VT *(pt* **wore** [wɔːr]; *pp* **worn** [wɔːn]) **1** *(garment, glasses, watch, beard etc) (have on)* porter; *(put on)* mettre; *(look, smile)* avoir; **he was wearing glasses/his new jacket** il portait des lunettes/sa nouvelle veste; **w. your glasses/your new jacket** mets tes lunettes/ta nouvelle veste; **she wasn't wearing make-up** elle ne s'était pas maquillée; **she never wears make-up** elle ne se maquille pas; **she was wearing eye-shadow/lipstick** elle avait de l'ombre à paupières/du rouge à lèvres; **I never w. eye-shadow/lipstick** je ne mets jamais d'ombre à paupières/de rouge à lèvres; **his face wore a smile** il souriait; **his face wore a dubious look** son visage affichait un air dubitatif, il avait un air dubitatif; **skirts are being worn long this year** les jupes sont longues cette année; **to w. black** porter du noir; **I've nothing (fit) to w.** je n'ai rien à me mettre, je n'ai rien de mettable; **he was wearing his slippers** il était en pantoufles; **to w. one's hair long** avoir les cheveux longs; **to w. one's hair in pigtails/in a bun** porter des nattes/un chignon; **you must w. your seat belt** tu dois attacher ta ceinture de sécurité; **she wears her age well** elle porte bien son âge; *Br Fig Fam* **they won't w. it** ça ne marchera pas avec eux; *Br Fig Fam* **she won't w. that argument** on ne lui fera pas avaler cet argument

2 *(use, rub down)* user; **to w. holes in sth** faire des trous à qch (à force d'usage); **to w. a hole/a track in sth** faire un trou/creuser un sillon dans qch; **the water had worn grooves in the rock** l'eau avait creusé des rigoles dans le rocher; **worn with anxiety** usé par les soucis; **the surface has been worn smooth** la surface est devenue lisse (à force d'usure); **to be worn to a shadow** *(of person)* ne plus être que l'ombre de soi-même; **to w. a surface flat** araser une surface; **a path had been worn across the lawn** des centaines d'allées et venues avaient fait un chemin dans la pelouse

VI **1** *(become rubbed etc)* s'user; **to w. smooth** *(of stone)* devenir lisse (par frottement); **my patience is wearing thin** je suis bientôt à bout de patience; **his jokes are wearing a bit thin** ça commence à bien faire avec ses blagues

2 *(last)* **to w. well** *(of material)* être de bon usage, faire bon usage; *Fam (of person)* bien porter son âge; **jeans w. well** *(look good after much use)* les jeans vieillissent bien; **this coat has worn well** ce manteau m'a bien servi *ou* m'a fait de l'usage; **the film has not worn well** le film n'a pas bien vieilli; **it will w. for ever** c'est inusable

3 to w. to a close *or* **an end** toucher à sa fin
▸ **wear away** VT SEP user, ronger; **much of**

the detail has been worn away les détails ont été en grande partie effacés; **the pattern on the carpet has been worn away** le motif du tapis s'est effacé
VI *(of material)* s'user; *(of pattern)* s'effacer; **the stone has worn away** la pierre s'est érodée
▸ **wear down** VT SEP user; **to w. one's heels down** user ses talons; **to w. down the enemy's resistance** user *ou* épuiser peu à peu la résistance de l'ennemi; *Fig* **to w. sb down** faire céder qn, *Fam* avoir qn à l'usure
VI s'user
▸ **wear off** VI **1** *(be removed) (of colour, pattern)* s'effacer, disparaître
2 *(decrease) (of pain)* se calmer; *(of anaesthetic)* cesser de faire effet; **the novelty soon wore off** l'attrait de la nouveauté a vite passé; **it'll w. off** ça passera
▸ **wear on** VI *(of time)* s'écouler (lentement), avancer (lentement); **as the evening wore on** à mesure que la soirée avançait
▸ **wear out** VT SEP **1** *(one's clothes etc)* user **2** *(exhaust) (person, sb's patience)* épuiser; **I'm worn out** je suis crevé; **to w. oneself out** s'user, s'épuiser; **to w. oneself out with work** se tuer au travail *ou* à travailler
VI **1** *(of material)* s'user; **this material will never w. out** ce tissu ne s'use pas *ou* est inusable
2 *(of patience)* s'épuiser

wearable ['weərəb(ə)l] ADJ *(garment)* mettable

wearer ['weərər] N **a jacket that is too heavy for the w.** une veste trop lourde à porter; **designed with the w.'s comfort in mind** conçu pour le confort de celui qui le portera

wearily ['wɪərɪlɪ] ADV **1** *(to smile etc)* d'un air las, avec lassitude; *(to answer)* d'un ton las **2** *(to walk etc)* péniblement

weariness ['wɪərɪnɪs] N **1** *(tiredness)* fatigue *f*, lassitude *f*; **a general air of w. has settled over the country** un sentiment général de morosité s'est emparé du pays **2** *(discontent)* ennui *m*, lassitude *f*

wearing ['weərɪŋ] ADJ fatigant, lassant; *(stronger)* épuisant; **their company is rather w.** je trouve leur présence assez pénible; **a very w. day** une journée très fatigante

wearisome ['wɪərɪs(ə)m] ADJ fatigant, ennuyeux; **his w. insistence on …** sa façon pénible d'insister sur …

weary ['wɪərɪ] ADJ **1** *(tired) (physically)* fatigué, las, *f* lasse; *(mentally)* las, dégoûté *(of* de); **in their present w. state** dans l'état de fatigue où ils sont pour le moment; **he had grown w. of listening to their complaints** il s'était lassé de les écouter se plaindre; **to feel w.** se sentir las; **to look w.** avoir l'air fatigué; **to be w. of war/solitude** être las de la guerre/de la solitude; **to be w. of life** être dégoûté de la vie; **to grow w. of waiting** se lasser d'attendre; **a w. smile** un sourire las
2 *(tiring)* fatigant, ennuyeux; **a w. day** une journée fatigante; **it was a w. climb** la montée était pénible
VI se lasser, se fatiguer *(of* de); **to w. of doing sth** se lasser de faire qch
VT lasser, fatiguer; **he wearies me with all his complaints** je suis las de l'entendre se plaindre, il me lasse avec ses plaintes

wearying ['wɪərɪɪŋ] ADJ fatigant, ennuyeux; **I find her quite w.** je la trouve très pénible; **I find it very w.** cela me fatigue beaucoup

weasel ['wi:z(ə)l] N *(animal)* belette *f*, *Fig Fam (person)* personne *f* sournoise
▸▸ *Fam* **w. words** paroles *fpl* ambiguës
▸ **weasel out** VI *Fam* **to w. out of an obligation** se débrouiller pour éviter une obligation; **you're not going to w. out of it this time!** tu ne vas pas te défiler cette fois!

weather ['weðər] N temps *m*; **in all weathers** par tous les temps; **in (the) hot/cold w.** par temps chaud/froid; **the w. is settled, we're in for a spell of fine w.** le temps est au beau; **we had good w. for the time of year** nous avons eu du beau temps pour la saison; **what kind of w. did you have on your holiday?** quel temps avez-vous eu pendant vos vacances?; **what's the w. like?** quel temps fait-il?; **in spite of bad w.** en dépit du mauvais temps; **in this** *or* **such w.** par un temps pareil; **w. permitting** si le temps le permet; *Fig* **to make heavy w. (of doing sth)** *(make a fuss)* faire un tas d'histoires (pour faire qch); *(find difficulty)* avoir toutes les peines du monde (à faire qch); **to make heavy w.** *(of ship)* bourlinguer; *Fig* **to keep one's w. eye open** veiller au grain; *Fig* **to be under the w.** *(ill)* ne pas se sentir bien, ne pas être très bien; *(depressed)* être déprimé SEE GRAMMAR B29

VT **the rocks had been weathered by wind and rain** le vent et la pluie avaient érodé les rochers; *Naut* **to w. a storm** étaler une tempête; *Fig* **to w. the storm** tenir le coup; *Pol* tenir le coup, surmonter la crise

VI *(of rock)* s'éroder; *(of copper)* se couvrir de patine, se patiner; *(fade) (of paintwork, stonework etc)* vieillir; **the brickwork has weathered to a pleasant shade of pink** la brique a pris une jolie couleur rose avec le temps; **a stone that weathers well** une pierre qui supporte bien le passage du temps; *Fig* **he has weathered well** il a bien vieilli; **the theory has weathered well** la théorie a bien résisté au temps

▸▸ **w. bulletin** bulletin *m* météorologique; **w. chart** carte *f* météorologique; **w. forecast** prévisions *fpl* météorologiques, météo *f*; **what's the w. forecast for tomorrow?** quelle est la météo pour demain?; **w. map** carte *f* météorologique; **w. report** bulletin météorologique; **w. satellite** satellite *m* météorologique; **w. ship** navire *m* météorologique; **w. side** *(of house etc)* côté exposé au vent; *Naut* bord du vent; **w. station** station *f ou* observatoire *m* météorologique; **w. strip** *(for door, window)* bourrelet *m* isolant, calfeutrage *m*; **w. vane** girouette *f*; **w. warning** alerte *f* météorologique; **to issue a w. warning** lancer une alerte météorologique

weatherbeaten ['weðəbiːt(ə)n] ADJ *(person, face)* hâlé, basané; *(cliffs, rocks, castle)* battu par le vent et la pluie

weatherboarding ['weðəbɔːdɪŋ] N *Constr* planches *fpl* à recouvrement

weatherbound ['weðəbaʊnd] ADJ retenu *ou* arrêté par le mauvais temps

weathercock ['weðəkɒk] N *(on roof)*, *Fig* girouette *f*

weathergirl ['weðəgɜːl] N présentatrice *f* de météo

weathering ['weðərɪŋ] N *(of rocks)* érosion *f*; *(fading) (of paintwork, stonework)* vieillissement *m*

weatherman, *pl* **weathermen** ['weðəmæn, -men] N *TV, Radio* monsieur *m* météo; **what did the w. say?** qu'est-ce qu'ils ont dit à la météo?

weatherproof ['weðəpruːf] ADJ *(paint, coating)* résistant à l'eau; *(fabric)* imperméable; *(windows, house)* étanche; *(equipment, machinery)* qui résiste aux intempéries

VT *(fabric)* imperméabiliser; *(house)* rendre étanche

weatherstrip ['weðəstrɪp] VT *(window)* calfeutrer

weave [wiːv] N *Tex (pattern)* tissage *m*; **a tight/loose w.** un tissage serré/lâche

VT *(pt* **wove** [wəʊv]; *pp* **woven** ['wəʊv(ə)n]) *Tex* tisser; *(garland, basket)* tresser; *(strands,* *small branches)* entrelacer; **to w. yarn into cloth** tisser du fil; **to w. a garland out of flowers** tresser une guirlande de fleurs; *Fig* **skilfully woven plot** intrigue bien tissée *ou Fam* ficelée; **to w. a spell** composer un charme; **to w. one's way through sth** se faufiler entre *ou* parmi qch; **she weaves the various strands of the story into a satisfying whole** elle tisse les différents fils de l'histoire en un tout satisfaisant; **political elements have been woven into the plot** des éléments politiques ont été introduits dans *ou* intégrés à l'intrigue

VI *Tex* tisser **2** *Fig* **to w. through the traffic** se frayer un chemin parmi les voitures; **to w. in and out of the crowd** se faufiler dans la foule *ou* parmi la foule **3** *Fam* **to get weaving** *(start)* s'y mettre; **get weaving!** vas-y!

weaver ['wiːvər] N *Tex* tisserand, -ande, tisseur, -euse

weaver(bird) ['wiːvə(bɜːd)] N tisserin *m*

weaving ['wiːvɪŋ] N *Tex* tissage *m*

Web [web] N *Comput* **the W.** le Web, la Toile

▸▸ **W. address** adresse *f* de site Internet; **W. authoring** création *f* de pages Web; **W. authoring tool** outil *m* de création de pages Web; **W. browser** navigateur *m*, logiciel *m* de navigation; **W. designer** concepteur, -trice de sites Web; **W. forum** forum *m* Internet; **W. hosting** hébergement *m* de sites Web; **W. master** Webmaster *m*, Webmestre *m*, responsable *mf* de site Web; **W. page** page *f* Web; **W. phone** téléphone *m* par Internet; **W. publishing** édition *f* sur le Web; **W. server** serveur *m* Web; **W. site** site *m* Web, site Internet; **W. space** espace *m* Web; **W. streaming** streaming *m*

web [web] N **1** *(fabric)* tissu *m* **2** *(of spider)* toile *f* **3** *Fig (of lies)* tissu *m*; *(of intrigue)* réseau *m* **4** *Biol (on feet) (of duck, frog)* palmure *f*; *(of human)* palmature *f* **5** *Typ* bande *f* de papier continue

webbed [webd] ADJ palmé; **to have w. feet or toes** *(duck, frog)* avoir les pattes palmées; *(human)* avoir une palmature

webbing ['webɪŋ] N **1** *(of chair, bed etc)* sangles *fpl* **2** *(fabric)* toile *f* à sangles **3** *Biol* palmure *f* **4** *Mil* sangles *fpl*

webcam ['webkæm] N caméra *f* Internet

webcast ['webkɑːst] N webcast *m*
VT diffuser sur Internet

webcaster ['webkɑːstər] N diffuseur *m* sur Internet

webcasting ['webkɑːstɪŋ] N webcasting *m*

web-footed, web-toed ADJ palmipède, aux pieds palmés

weblog ['weblɒg] N *Comput* weblog *m*

web-offset printing N impression *f* (offset) continue

webzine ['webziːn] N webzine *m*

Wed *abbr* **Wednesday**

wed [wed] *(pt, pp* **wedded,** *occ* **wed**; *prp* **wedding)** VT **1** *(get married to)* épouser; *Fig* **to be wedded to one's work** faire passer son travail avant tout; **they're wedded to the idea of …** ils tiennent absolument à l'idée de …; **the fate of the project was wedded to that of the Chairman** la destinée du projet était liée à celle du Président **2** *(of priest) (couple)* marier; **he wanted to see all his daughters w. before he died** il voulait voir toutes ses filles mariées avant sa mort
VI se marier

we'd [wiːd] CONTR **1** = **we had,** *see* **have**
2 = **we would,** *see* **would**

wedded ['wedɪd] ADJ *(person)* marié; **my (lawful) w. wife/husband** mon épouse/époux légitime; **w. bliss** bonheur *m* conjugal

wedding ['wedɪŋ] N mariage *m*, noces *fpl*; **I've been invited to a w.** j'ai été invité à un mariage; **the w. guests** les invités *mpl* (au mariage)

▸▸ **w. anniversary** anniversaire *m* de mariage; **w. band** alliance *f*; **w. breakfast** repas *m* de noces; **w. cake** gâteau *m* de noces, ≃ pièce *f* montée; **w. day** jour *m* du mariage; **on my w. day** le jour de mon mariage; **w. dress** robe *f* de mariée; **w. invitation** invitation *f* de mariage; **w. list** liste *f* de mariage; **w. march** marche *f* nuptiale; **w. night** nuit *f* de noces; **w. planner** organisateur, -trice de mariages; **w. present** cadeau *m* de mariage; **w. ring** alliance *f*; *Fam Hum* **w. tackle** *(man's genitals)* bijoux *mpl* de famille

wedge [wedʒ] N **1** *Tech (for keeping sth in place)* cale *f*; *(for cutting wood)* coin *m*; **to drive in a w.** enfoncer un coin; *Fig* **it has driven a w. between them** ça a mis une distance entre eux; *Fig* **it's the thin end of the w.** c'est s'engager sur une mauvaise pente; **w.-heeled shoes** chaussures *f* à semelles compensées **2** *w.* **of cake** morceau *m* de (triangulaire) de gâteau, part *f* (de gâteau); **a w. of cheese** un morceau de fromage **3** *Br Sl (money)* fric *m*, flouze *m*, pognon *m*
VT *Tech* coincer; **to w. a door open** maintenir une porte ouverte avec une cale; **to w. a piece of paper in a crack** coincer *ou* enfoncer un bout de papier dans une fente; **I was wedged (in) between two large women** je me suis trouvé coincé entre deux grosses femmes

wedge-shaped ADJ en (forme de) coin; **a w. piece of cheese/land** un triangle de fromage/de terre

wedgie ['wedʒɪ] N *Fam* **to have a w.** avoir le slip coincé entre les fesses; **to give sb a w.** = remonter brusquement le slip de quelqu'un pour le lui coincer entre les fesses

wedlock ['wedlɒk] N *Law* mariage *m*; **to be born out of w.** être un enfant illégitime

Wednesday ['wenzdɪ] N mercredi *m*; **W. 9 September** mercredi 9 septembre; **W. morning/evening** mercredi matin/soir; **it's W. today** nous sommes mercredi aujourd'hui; **on Wednesdays** le mercredi; **they're coming on W.** ils viennent mercredi; **every W.** tous les mercredis VOIR GRAMMAIRE A81–2; B61–2

wee¹ [wiː] ADJ *esp Scot Fam* petit; **a w. bit** un petit peu; **a w. drop of whisky** un doigt *ou* une larme de whisky

wee² N, VI *Br Fam* = **wee-wee**

weed [wiːd] N **1** *(in garden)* mauvaise herbe *f*; **the garden was overgrown with weeds** le jardin était envahi par les mauvaises herbes **2** *Old-fashioned Fam* **the w.** *(tobacco)* le tabac; **to give up the w.** arrêter de fumer **3** *Fam (marijuana)* marijuana *f*, herbe *f* **4** *Pej (person) (in build)* personne *f* chétive, gringalet *m*; *(in character)* mauviette *f*, **don't be such a w.!** arrête de faire la mauviette!
VT *(garden)* désherber; *(path)* arracher les mauvaises herbes de
VI arracher *ou* enlever les mauvaises herbes; *(with hoe)* sarcler

▸ **weed out** VT SEP *Fig (weak candidates)* éliminer; **to w. out the bad (from the good)** éliminer *ou* rejeter ce qui est de mauvaise qualité

weeding ['wiːdɪŋ] N désherbage *m*; *(with hoe)* sarclage *m*

weedkiller ['wiːdkɪlər] N herbicide *m*, désherbant *m*

weeds [wiːdz] NPL *Old-fashioned (widow's)* vêtements *mpl* de deuil

weedy ['wiːdɪ] ADJ **1** *(garden etc)* couvert de mauvaises herbes **2** *Pej (person, arms)* malingre, chétif **3** *(feeble) (sound of instrument)* faible

weegie ['wiːdʒɪ] *Br Fam Pej* **N** habitant, -ante de Glasgow
ADJ de Glasgow

week [wiːk] **N** semaine *f*; **what day of the w. is it?** quel jour de la semaine sommes-nous?; **next/last w.** la semaine prochaine/dernière; **the w. before last** pas la semaine dernière, celle d'avant; **the w. after next** pas la semaine prochaine, celle d'après; **w. in w. out** toutes les semaines que Dieu nous envoie; **I haven't seen her for** *or* **in weeks** ça fait des semaines que je ne l'ai pas vue, je ne l'ai pas vue depuis des semaines; *Rel* **Holy W.** la semaine sainte; **once/twice a w.** une/deux fois par semaine; **every w.** tous les huit jours; **within a w.** sous huitaine; **a w. from now, today w., in a w.'s time** aujourd'hui en huit, dans une huitaine; **tomorrow/Tuesday w.** demain/mardi en huit; **yesterday w.** il y a eu hier huit jours; **in a w. or so** dans une huitaine; **it'll take a w. to get there** il faudra une semaine pour arriver là-bas; **in six weeks' time** dans six semaines; **a w. ago today** il y a (aujourd'hui) huit jours; **I'm taking a w.'s holiday** *or* **a w. off** je vais prendre huit jours de congé; *Ind etc* **forty-hour w.** semaine de quarante heures; **a w.'s wages** le salaire d'une semaine, une semaine de salaire; *Fam* une semaine; **this dress cost me a w.'s wages** cette robe m'a coûté une semaine de salaire; **to be paid by the w.** être payé à la semaine

weekday ['wiːkdeɪ] **N** jour *m* ouvrable; **on weekdays** en semaine; **weekdays only** en semaine uniquement, tous les jours sauf samedi et dimanche

weekend [wiːk'end] **N** week-end *m*, *pl* week-ends, *Can* fin *f* de semaine; **to have one's weekends free** être libre le week-end; **have a good w.!** bon week-end!, *Can* bonne fin de semaine!; **I'll do it at** *or esp Am* **on the w.** je le ferai pendant ce week-end; *Br* **what do you do at the weekend(s)?**, *esp Am* **what do you do (on) weekends?** qu'est-ce que vous faites le week-end?; **what are you doing at the w.?** qu'est-ce que vous faites ce week-end?; **to make a w. visit to relations** rendre visite à la famille pendant le week-end
VI passer le week-end *ou Can* la fin de semaine
▸ ▸ **w. break** = séjour *m* d'un week-end; **w. cottage** maison *f* secondaire *ou* de campagne *(où on passe le week-end)*; *Br Rail* **w. return** = billet *m* aller-retour valable du vendredi au dimanche soir

weekender [wiːk'endər] **N** = personne *f* en voyage pour le week-end; **they're weekenders** ils viennent/vont y passer le week-end

weekly ['wiːklɪ] **ADJ** *(magazine, visit, payment)* hebdomadaire; *(pay)* de la semaine; *(tenant)* à la semaine; **these incidents were an almost w. occurrence** ces incidents avaient lieu presque chaque semaine
N *(journal m/revue f)* hebdomadaire *m*; **the weeklies** la presse hebdomadaire
ADV *(every week)* toutes les semaines, tous les huit jours, chaque semaine; **twice w.** deux fois par semaine; **to be paid w.** être payé à la semaine

weeknight ['wiːknaɪt] **N** soir *m* de semaine; **at seven on weeknights** à sept heures les soirs de semaine; **I'm not letting you go to a party on a w.** je ne vais pas te permettre d'aller à une soirée pendant la semaine

weenie ['wiːnɪ] *N Am* = **wiener**

weeny ['wiːnɪ] **ADJ** *Fam* minuscule

weeny-bopper [-bɒpər] **N** *Fam* = très jeune fan *f* de musique pop

weep [wiːp] **N to have a good w.** pleurer un bon coup; **a good w. would help you** pleure un bon coup, ça ira mieux; **to have a little w.** verser quelques larmes
VI *(pt, pp* **wept** [wept]*)* **1** *(of person)* pleurer; **to w. bitterly** pleurer à chaudes larmes; **to w. for joy** pleurer de joie; **to w. for sb** *(mourn)* pleurer (la mort de) qn; *(feel sorry for)* pleurer sur le sort de qn; **to w. for one's lost youth** pleurer sa jeunesse perdue; **it's enough to make you w.** c'est à faire pleurer; **I could have wept to see it** j'en aurais pleuré (en le voyant) **2** *(of wall, rock)* suinter, suer; *(of sore)* couler, exsuder; **the smoke was making my eyes w.** la fumée me faisait pleurer les yeux
VT to w. tears of joy pleurer de joie; **to w. one's heart** *or* **one's eyes out** pleurer à chaudes larmes

weeping ['wiːpɪŋ] **ADJ 1** *(child)* qui pleure **2** *Med (eczema)* suintant
N *(of person)* pleurs *mpl*, larmes *fpl*; **we could hear w. from the next room** on pouvait entendre quelqu'un qui pleurait dans la pièce d'à côté; **the sound of w.** des pleurs; **a fit of w.** une crise de larmes
▸ ▸ **w. willow** saule *m* pleureur

weepy ['wiːpɪ] *Fam* **ADJ 1** *(book, film)* larmoyant, mélo; **there's a w. bit coming next** il y a un passage mélo après **2 to feel w.** avoir envie de pleurer; **it makes me go all w.** ça me fait pleurer
N *(book, film)* mélo *m*, livre *m*/film *m* à faire pleurer dans les chaumières

weevil ['wiːvɪl] **N** *(beetle)* charançon *m*

wee-wee *Br Fam* **N** *(in children's language)* pipi *m*; **to have a w.** faire pipi; **do you want to go w.?** tu veux faire pipi?
VI faire pipi

WEF [dʌb(ə)ljuːiː'ef] **N** *(abbr* **World Economic Forum**) Forum *m* mondial de l'économie

weft [weft] **N** *Tex* trame *f*

weigh [weɪ] **VT 1** *(package etc)* peser; **to w. sth in one's hand** soupeser qch; **to w. oneself** se peser **2** *(consider) (one's words)* peser, mesurer, ménager; **to w. sth in one's mind** considérer qch; **to w. the consequences** calculer les conséquences (**of sth** de qch); **to w. the pros and (the) cons** peser le pour et le contre; **to w. the risks/the evidence** évaluer les risques/les preuves; **to w. one thing against another** mettre deux choses en balance **3** *Naut* **to w. anchor** lever l'ancre, appareiller
VI 1 *(of person, parcel etc)* peser; **it weighs two kilos** ça pèse deux kilos; *Fam* **this case weighs a ton** cette valise pèse une tonne; **how much do you w.?** combien est-ce que tu pèses? **2 it's weighing on my mind** cela me trouble *ou* me tracasse; **it weighed heavy on his conscience** cela pesait sur sa conscience **3** *(have influence)* **her qualifications weighed in her favour** ses qualifications ont fait pencher la balance en sa faveur *ou* ont joué en sa faveur; **his past record weighed against him** son passé a joué en sa défaveur
▸ **weigh down VT SEP** surcharger; **in order to w. the body down** pour alourdir le corps; **branch weighed down with fruit** branche surchargée de fruits; *Fig* **weighed down by** *or* **with heavy responsibilities** accablé de grosses responsabilités; *Fig* **to be weighed down by** *or* **with grief** être accablé par la tristesse
▸ **weigh in VI 1** *(of jockey, boxer) (before race or match)* se faire peser; **he weighed in at 75 kilos** il faisait 75 kilos à la pesée **2** *Fam (enter fight, debate)* intervenir; **to w. in (with an argument)** intervenir (en présentant un argument)
▸ **weigh out VT SEP** peser; **w. out 200 grams of flour for me** pèse-moi 200 grammes de farine
▸ **weigh up VT SEP to w. up the situation** peser la situation; **to w. sb up** *(their character)* estimer la valeur de qn; *(their intentions)* estimer les intentions de qn; **to w. up one's chances of doing sth** calculer ses chances de faire qch; **to w. up the advantages and disadvantages of sth** peser le pour et le contre de qch

weighbridge ['weɪbrɪdʒ] **N** pont-bascule *m*, *pl* ponts-bascules

weigh-in **N** *Boxing, Horseracing* pesée *f*

weighing ['weɪɪŋ] **N** pesage *m*
▸ ▸ **w. in** *(of jockey, boxer)* pesage; **w.-in room** pesage; **w. machine** *(for people)* balance *f*, *(for loads)* bascule *f*

weight [weɪt] **N 1** *(of person, parcel etc)* poids *m*; **to feel the w. of sth** *(in hand)* soupeser qch; **that case must be quite a w.** cette valise doit être drôlement lourde; **to sell by w.** vendre au poids; **to give short w.** tricher sur le poids; **it's ten pounds in w.** cela pèse dix livres; **it's twice the w. of the other one** ça pèse deux fois plus que l'autre; **they're the same w.** ils font le même poids; **it's worth its w. in gold** cela vaut son pesant d'or; **what a w.!** que ça pèse lourd!, que c'est lourd!; **to lose w.** perdre du poids; **to gain** *or* **put on w.** prendre du poids; **to watch one's w.** surveiller son poids; **to have a w. problem** avoir un problème de poids; **to be a w. watcher** surveiller son poids; *Fig* **to pull one's w.** y mettre du sien; *Fig* **you're not pulling your w.** tu ne fais pas assez d'effort; *Horseracing* **to carry w.** être handicapé **2** *(for weighing)* poids *m*; **set of weights** série *f* de poids; **weights and measures** poids et mesures *fpl* **3** *(object) (of clock)* poids *m*; *(for fishing net)* lest *m*; **don't lift any heavy weights** ne soulève pas de poids trop lourds **4** *(load)* charge *f*; **this pillar bears the w. of the whole building** cette colonne soutient tout le bâtiment; **to give way under the w. of sth** fléchir sous le poids de qch; **he feels the w. of his responsibilities** ses responsabilités lui pèsent; **that is** *or* **takes a w. off my mind** cela me soulage, ça m'ôte un poids; *Fam* **I'm going to take the w. off my feet for a bit** je vais me reposer un peu **5** *(of blow)* force *f*; **his blow had no w. behind it** son coup était sans force; **you'll feel the w. of my hand, my lad!** tu vas recevoir une claque, mon gars! **6** *Fig (importance)* importance *f*; **to give w. to an argument** donner du poids à un argument; **what he says carries w.** sa parole a du poids *ou* de l'autorité; **she doesn't carry much w. with the committee** elle n'a pas beaucoup d'influence auprès du comité; **the w. of the evidence was against him** les témoignages pesaient contre lui; **he threw his w. behind the other candidate** il a soutenu l'autre candidat à fond; *Fam* **to throw one's w. about** *or* **around** faire l'important; **they won the battle by sheer w. of numbers** ils ont gagné la bataille parce qu'ils avaient l'avantage numérique
VT 1 *(fix a weight to)* attacher un poids à; *(net, rope)* lester, plomber; *(walking stick)* plomber **2** *Econ (index, average etc)* pondérer; *Fig* **the circumstances are weighted in his favour** les circonstances pèsent en sa faveur *ou* lui sont favorables; **the electoral system is weighted against small parties** le système électoral défavorise les petits partis
▸ ▸ **w. allowance** *(in aeroplane)* poids *m* de bagages autorisé; **w. charge** taxation *f* au poids; **w. loss** perte *f* de poids; **w. training** entraînement *m* aux haltères; **to do w. training** faire des haltères

▶ **weight down** VT SEP *(hold down)* retenir *ou* maintenir avec un poids; **the body had been weighted down with stones** le corps avait été alourdi de pierres

weighted ['weɪtɪd] ADJ **1** *(with a weight)* chargé d'un poids; *(balloon)* lesté; *(walking stick)* plombé **2** *(average, index)* pondéré

▶▶ *Fin* **w. average** moyenne *f* pondérée; *Acct* **w. average cost** coût *m* moyen pondéré; *Mktg* **w. distribution** distribution *f* valeur

weightily ['weɪtɪlɪ] ADV *(to reason)* puissamment, avec force

weighting ['weɪtɪŋ] N *Econ (of index etc)* pondération *f*, coefficient *m*; *Admin* **London w.** indemnité *f* de résidence à Londres

weightless ['weɪtlɪs] ADJ *Astronaut* en état d'apesanteur

▶▶ **w. conditions** état *m* d'apesanteur

weightlessness ['weɪtlɪsnɪs] N *Astronaut* apesanteur *f*

weightlifter ['weɪtlɪftər] N haltérophile *mf*

weightlifting ['weɪtlɪftɪŋ] N haltérophilie *f*

weighty ['weɪtɪ] ADJ **1** *(heavy)* pesant, (très) lourd **2** *Fig (motive)* grave, important, sérieux; *(reasoning)* puissant, d'un grand poids; *(argument)* de poids

weir [wɪər] N *(across river etc)* barrage *m*

weird [wɪəd] ADJ **1** *(eerie)* mystérieux, inquiétant **2** *(odd)* étrange, bizarre; **he went a bit w. after his parents died** il est devenu un peu bizarre après la mort de ses parents; **that's w.** c'est bizarre

▶ **weird out** VT SEP *Am Fam* faire flipper

weirdie ['wɪədɪ] N *Fam* = **weirdo**

weirdly ['wɪədlɪ] ADV *(oddly)* étrangement, bizarrement

weirdness ['wɪədnɪs] N *(oddness) (of person, clothing)* caractère *m* étrange *ou* bizarre

weirdo, weirdy ['wɪədəʊ, -dɪ] N *Fam* excentrique *mf*, drôle d'oiseau *m*; *(frightening etc)* type *m* bizarre

WELCOME ['welkəm] ADJ **1** *(person)* bienvenu; **to make sb w.** faire bon accueil à qn; **you're always w.** vous êtes toujours le bienvenu; **any friend of Bob's is always w. here** les amis de Bob sont toujours les bienvenus ici; **I did not feel w.** je ne me suis pas senti le bienvenu; **the card is w. in over 1,000 outlets** la carte est acceptée dans plus de 1000 points de vente; **w.!** soyez le bienvenu!; **w. to England!** bienvenue en Angleterre!; **w. back!** nous sommes heureux de vous revoir!; *Radio, TV (after commercial)* re-bonjour!/re-bonsoir!; **w. home!** bienvenue à la maison!

2 *(agreeable)* agréable; **a w. cup of coffee** une bonne tasse de café; **this is a very w. development** c'est un grand progrès; **this is w. news** je me réjouis/nous nous réjouissons de cette nouvelle; **the hotel was a w. sight** on a aperçu l'hôtel avec plaisir; **that would be most w.** *(coffee, brandy, sandwich)* ça me ferait le plus grand bien; **this cheque is most w.** ce chèque est vraiment bienvenu *ou* tombe à merveille; **a w. change** un changement opportun; **the laid-back atmosphere of Somerset made a w. change from London** l'atmosphère détendue de Somerset nous changeait en bien de Londres

3 *(free)* **to be w. to do sth** être le bienvenu à faire qch; **you're w. to ask any questions** vos questions seront les bienvenues; **anybody is w. to attend** c'est ouvert à tous; **you're w. to borrow any of my books** ma bibliothèque est à votre disposition; **they're w. to stay with us** ils peuvent venir chez nous; **you're w. to it** je t'en prie (ne te gêne pas); *Iron* je te le/la laisse; **you're w. to try** libre à vous d'essayer; **you're w.!** *(on being thanked)* je vous en prie!, de rien!, ce n'est rien!; **tell her she's w.** dis-lui que ce n'est rien

N accueil *m*; **we were given a wonderful w.** nous avons été merveilleusement bien accueillis; **the whole town prepared a w. for him** la ville entière se préparait à l'accueillir; **to extend a w. to sb** souhaiter la bienvenue à qn; **to give sb a warm w.** faire un accueil chaleureux à qn; **he gave us a very poor or cold w.** il nous a reçus froidement, il nous a mal reçus; **w. bouquet** bouquet *m* d'accueil; **w. drink** cocktail *m* de bienvenue, pot *m* d'accueil

VT **1** *(person) (wish welcome)* souhaiter la bienvenue à; *(greet)* faire bon accueil à, bien accueillir, accueillir *ou* recevoir avec plaisir; **to w. the/an opportunity to do sth** se réjouir de *ou* saluer l'occasion de faire qch; **I w. every chance of getting out of the house** je suis content de sortir de la maison chaque fois que c'est possible; **his efforts weren't welcomed** ses efforts ont reçu peu d'encouragement; *Radio, TV* **I am pleased to w. back Billy Bragg** j'ai le plaisir d'accueillir à nouveau Billy Bragg

2 *(receive)* accueillir; **to w. sb warmly** faire un accueil chaleureux à qn; **the announcement was welcomed with indifference** la nouvelle a été accueillie avec indifférence

▶▶ **w. committee** comité *m* d'accueil; **w. mat** paillasson *m*; *Fig* **they put out the w. mat for him** ils l'ont accueilli à bras ouverts; **w. pack** *(at conference, in hotel)* documentation *f (remise à l'accueil)*; **w. reception** réception *f* de bienvenue

welcoming ['welkəmɪŋ] ADJ *(smile, person, atmosphere)* accueillant; *(speech, committee)* d'accueil

weld [weld] N *(joint)* soudure *f*

VT **to w. (together)** *(pieces of metal)* souder; *(pieces of plastic)* unir à chaud; *Fig* **to w. employees into a team** réunir des employés en une équipe bien soudée; **he has welded his players into a formidable unit** il a soudé ses joueurs pour former une équipe formidable

▶▶ **w. spot** point *m* de soudure

welder ['weldər] N soudeur, -euse; **w.'s mask** masque *m* protecteur pour la soudure

welding ['weldɪŋ] N soudure *f*, soudage *m*; **arc w.** soudure à l'arc

▶▶ **w. torch** chalumeau *m*

welfare ['welfeər] N **1** *(wellbeing)* bien-être *m*; **to have sb's w. at heart** avoir à cœur le bonheur *ou* le bien-être de qn; **the w. of the nation** le bien public **2** *Am (social security)* aide *f* sociale; **to be on w.** toucher les allocations; **the w. lines are lengthening** la masse des gens qui touchent le chômage augmente; **to stand in the w. line** recevoir les allocations chômage

▶▶ *Am* **w. benefits** avantages *mpl* sociaux; **w. centre** ≃ centre *m* d'assistance sociale; *Am* **w. check** *(chèque m d')* allocations *fpl*; **the W. State** *(concept)* l'État *m* providence; **w. work** travail *m* social; **w. worker** assistant, -ante social(e)

well¹ [wel] N **1** *(of water, oil)* puits *m*; **we get our water from a w.** notre eau vient d'un puits; **to drive/sink a w.** forer/creuser un puits **2** *(shaft) (for lift)* puits *m*, cage *f*, *(stairwell)* cage, jour *m*; *(sump)* fond *m* de carter; *(on fishing boat)* vivier *m*, réservoir *m*; *Br Law* **the w. of the court** le barreau; *Culin* **make a w. in the flour** faire une fontaine dans la farine **3** *Arch (spring)* source *f*, fontaine *f*

▶▶ **w. digger** puisatier *m*

WELL² [wel] *(comp* **better**; *superl* **best)** ADJ **1** *(in good health)* **to be w.** être bien portant *ou* en bonne santé, se porter *ou* aller bien; **to sound w.** avoir l'air en forme; **are you okay?, you don't sound very w.** ça va?, tu n'as pas l'air bien; **how are you? – w., thank you** comment allez-vous? – bien, merci; **he's not very w.** il n'est pas très bien; **to get w.** guérir, se rétablir, se remettre; **you look w.** tu as l'air en forme; **he's not a w. man** il ne se porte pas bien, il n'a pas une bonne santé

2 it is w. to ... *(advisable)* il est opportun de ...; **it would be w. to ...** il serait bon *ou* utile *ou* recommandable de ...; **it would be w. not to mention it again** il vaudrait mieux ne plus en reparler; **it would be just as w. if you were present** ce serait mieux si vous étiez présent, vous feriez mieux d'être présent; **it is just as w. we did leave without her** c'est aussi bien que nous soyons partis sans elle; **it might be as w. to ...** il faudrait peut-être ..., il serait peut-être bon de ...; **it was w. for him that nobody saw him** heureusement pour lui que personne ne l'a vu; *Prov* **all's w. that ends w.** tout est bien qui finit bien; **all's w.!** tout va bien!; **that's all very w., but ...** c'est bien beau *ou* joli, tout ça, mais ...; **it is all very w. for you to say that** tu peux bien dire ça, toi; **w. and good!** soit!, bon!; **that's all very w. and good, but ...** c'est très bien, tout ça, mais ...

ADV **1** *(satisfactorily etc)* bien; **to work w.** bien travailler; **to do as w. as one can** faire de son mieux; **this boy will do w.** ce garçon ira loin; **to be doing w.** *(after operation etc)* aller bien; **mother and baby are both doing w.** la mère et l'enfant se portent bien; **w. done!** bravo!, très bien!; **w. played!** bien joué!; **the government hasn't come out of it very w.** le gouvernement n'en est pas sorti grandi; **to do oneself w.** *(indulge oneself)* bien se soigner; *(in restaurant etc)* bien manger (et bien boire); **it wouldn't look w. if we refused** si on refusait cela ferait mauvaise impression; **you would do w. to be quiet (about it)** vous feriez bien *ou* le mieux serait de vous taire; **I know her w.** je la connais bien; **I know only too w. what patience it needs** je ne sais que trop quelle patience cela exige; **I can't very w. do it** il ne m'est guère possible de le faire; **he apologized, as w. he might** il s'est excusé, ce qui était la moindre des choses; **one might as w. say that black is white** autant dire que blanc est noir; **you might as w. stay** *(there's no point in going now)* tu ferais aussi bien de rester; **I might (just) as w. do it myself** je ferais aussi bien de le faire moi-même; **very w.!** *(OK)* (très) bien!, entendu!; **everyone speaks w. of him** tout le monde dit du bien de lui; **she is very w. thought of** on pense beaucoup de bien d'elle; **to do w. by sb** se montrer généreux envers qn; **he meant w.** il voulait bien faire; **he means w.** ses intentions sont bonnes; **you're w. out of it** soyez heureux d'en être quitte; **the fête went off w.** la fête s'est bien passée; *Arch* **w. met!** heureuse rencontre!, vous arrivez bien à propos!

2 *(intensive)* bien; **it is w. known that ...** tout le monde sait que ...; **it's w. worth trying** cela vaut bien la peine *ou Fam* le coup d'essayer; **she's w. able to look after herself** elle est tout à fait capable de se débrouiller toute seule; **I can w. believe it** je veux bien le croire; **I am w. aware of that** j'en suis bien conscient; **we'll be w. away by the time she wakes up** nous serons déjà loin quand elle se réveillera; *Br Fam* **w. away** *(drunk)* parti; **it's w. after six** il est six heures bien sonnées; **buy your tickets w. ahead of time or w. in advance** achetez vos billets bien à l'avance; **he's w. over fifty** il a largement dépassé la cinquantaine; **to be w. up in a subject** bien posséder un sujet; **leave w. enough alone** ne t'en mêle pas; *Br Fam* **w. and truly** bel et bien; *Hum* **w. padded or upholstered** *(plump)* bien rembourré

3 pretty w. all presque tout; **it's pretty w.**

finished c'est presque *ou* pratiquement terminé; *Fam* **it serves him damn w.** *or* **jolly w. right!** il l'a bien cherché *ou* mérité!, c'est bien fait pour lui!

4 as w. *(also)* aussi; **take me as w.** emmenez-moi aussi; **I need some as w.** il m'en faut également; **as w. as** *(in addition to)* de même que, comme, ainsi que; **by day as w. as by night** de jour comme de nuit, le jour comme la nuit

5 *(introducing remark)* eh bien, donc; *(exclamatory)* ça alors!, pas possible!; **w., as I was telling you** eh bien *ou* donc comme je vous disais; **w., who was it?** eh bien, qui était-ce?; **w., here we are (at last)!** enfin nous voilà!; **you told her?, (oh** *or* **ah) w.!** vous le lui avez dit?, eh bien!; **w., w.!** *(expressing resignation)* tant pis!, que voulez-vous!; *(surprise)* tiens, tiens!; **w. then** eh bien, alors; **w. I never!** ça alors!; **w., that's life!** c'est la vie!; **w. then, why worry about it?** eh bien *ou* alors, pourquoi se faire du mauvais sang?

▶ **1 the w. and the sick** *(pl)* les bien portants *mpl* et les malades

▶ **2 to wish sb w.** vouloir du bien à qn; *(in attitude)* être bien disposé envers qn

▶ **well out** vi *(of liquid)* jaillir
▶ **well over** vi *(of tears)* jaillir
▶ **well up** vi *(of water, spring)* jaillir, *Lit* monter; **tears welled up in her eyes** les larmes lui sont montées aux yeux

we'll [wi:l] CONTR **1** = **we shall,** *see* **shall 2** = **we will,** *see* **will²**

well-adjusted ADJ équilibré

well-advised [-əd'vaizd] ADJ sage, prudent, judicieux; **you would be w. to say yes** tu aurais (tout) intérêt à dire oui; **it was not very w. of you to annoy her like that** ce n'était pas très malin de l'ennuyer comme ça

well-appointed ADJ *(house)* bien aménagé

well-argued [-'ɑ:gju:d] ADJ bien argumenté

well-attended [-ə'tendɪd] ADJ bien suivi; **the classes were not w.** les cours étaient peu suivis

well-balanced ADJ *(person, debate)* équilibré; *(coverage)* impartial, -aux; **I think she's fairly w.** je pense qu'elle est plutôt bien équilibrée

well-behaved ADJ *(child)* sage; *(animal)* bien dressé

wellbeing ['welbi:ɪŋ] N bien-être *m*; **physical and moral w.** santé *f* physique et morale

well-born ADJ de bonne famille; **she was not sufficiently w. to marry him** elle n'était pas assez bien née pour l'épouser

well-bred [-bred] ADJ *(polite)* bien élevé; *(of good family)* de bonne famille

well-built ADJ *(building)* bien construit, solide; *(machine, car)* de bonne fabrication; *(person)* solide, bien bâti

well-chilled [-tʃɪld] ADJ *(wine)* frais, *f* fraîche

well-chosen ADJ bien choisi; **a few w. words** quelques mots bien choisis

well-connected ADJ **to be w.** avoir des relations

well-defined [-dɪ'faɪnd] ADJ bien défini

well-developed [-dɪ'veləpt] ADJ développé

well-disposed ADJ *(person)* bien disposé (**towards** envers)

well-documented [-'dɒkjʊmentɪd] ADJ bien documenté

well-done [-dʌn] ADJ *Culin* bien cuit

well-dressed [-drest] ADJ bien habillé

well-earned ADJ bien mérité

well-educated ADJ instruit, cultivé

well-endowed [-ən'daʊd] ADJ *(physically) (man)* bien monté; *(woman)* bien roulé

well-equipped ADJ bien équipé

well-established ADJ bien implanté

well-fed ADJ bien nourri

well-fixed ADJ *Am Fam* riche

well-founded [-'faʊndɪd] ADJ *(suspicion)* fondé

well-groomed ADJ *(person)* soigné; *(horse)* bien pansé

well-grounded ADJ fondé

wellhead ['welhed] N *Petr* tête *f* de puits

well-heeled [-hi:ld] ADJ *Fam* riche, cossu

well-hung ADJ *Sl (man)* bien monté

wellied ['welɪd] ADJ *Br Fam (drunk)* bourré comme un coing, rond comme une queue de pelle

well-in ADJ *Fam* **1** *Br* **to be w. with sb** être bien avec qn **2** *Austr (rich)* riche

well-informed ADJ *(about specific event etc)* informé; *(generally) (person, mind)* au courant; **to be w. on a subject** bien posséder un sujet

wellington ['welɪŋtən] N *Br (boot)* botte *f* en caoutchouc
▶▶ **w. boot** botte en caoutchouc

well-intentioned [-ɪn'tenʃənd] ADJ bien intentionné

well-judged [-dʒʌdʒd] ADJ judicieux; *(shot, pass)* bien visé, bien vu

well-kept ADJ *(garden)* bien (entre)tenu, soigné; *(hands)* soigné; *(secret)* bien gardé

well-known ADJ (bien) connu, célèbre; *(expert)* réputé; **a w. liar** un fameux menteur; **it is w. that ...** il est bien connu que ...

well-liked [-laɪkt] ADJ apprécié

well-loved [-lʌvd] ADJ très aimé

well-made ADJ *(furniture)* bien fait, de fabrication soignée; *(garment)* de coupe soignée; *(play)* bien construit

well-mannered ADJ poli, bien élevé

well-matched [-mætʃt] ADJ *(couple)* bien assorti; *(teams)* de force égale; **Bob can't possibly be as boring as Sarah – oh yes he is, they're very w.** Bob ne peut pas être aussi ennuyeux que Sarah – et pourtant si, ils se sont bien trouvés

well-meaning ADJ *(person)* bien intentionné; *(remark)* fait avec les meilleures intentions; **she's very w.** elle est pleine de bonnes intentions

well-nigh ADV presque, pratiquement; **it's w. impossible** c'est presque *ou* quasi impossible

well-off ADJ riche; **to be very w.** avoir de la fortune, *Fam* avoir de quoi; **you don't know when you're w.** vous ne connaissez pas votre bonheur; **to be w. for books/cupboards/ paper** avoir beaucoup de livres/placards/ papier
NPL **the w.** les riches *mpl*

well-oiled ADJ *Fig Fam (drunk)* soûl, parti

well-paid ADJ bien payé, bien rétribué

well-preserved ADJ bien conservé; *Fig* **she's w.** elle est bien conservée

well-proportioned ADJ bien proportionné

well-read [-red] ADJ *(person)* instruit, cultivé

well-respected ADJ respecté

well-rounded ADJ *(education, course etc)* complet

well-spent ADJ *(money, time)* bien utilisé, bien employé; **it was time w.** je n'ai/il n'a/ *etc* pas perdu mon/son/*etc* temps; **I'm not sure this is time w.** je crains que ça ne soit une perte de temps

well-spoken ADJ qui parle bien

well-stacked [-stækt] ADJ *Sl (woman)* bien balancé, bien roulé, bien foutu; **she's w.!** il y a du monde au balcon!

well-stocked [-stɒkt] ADJ *(shop)* bien approvisionné

well-thought-of ADJ apprécié

well-thought-out ADJ *(plan etc)* bien pensé

well-thumbed [-θʌmbd] ADJ *(book, magazine)* qui a fait de l'usage, écorné

well-timed [-taɪmd] ADJ opportun, bien calculé

well-to-do ADJ aisé, riche, cossu
NPL **the w.** les riches *mpl*, les fortunés *mpl*

well-tried ADJ *(remedy)* éprouvé, qui a fait ses preuves

well-trodden [-'trɒdən] ADJ **a w. path** un chemin très fréquenté; *Fig* **a w. path to fame** une voie très fréquentée qui mène vers la célébrité

well-turned [-tɜ:nd] ADJ *(speech)* bien tourné; *(ankle)* galbé

well-versed ADJ versé (**in** dans)

wellwisher ['welwɪʃər] N *(of cause etc)* partisan, -ane; **a w.** *(at end of anonymous letter)* un ami qui vous veut du bien; **surrounded by wellwishers** entouré d'admirateurs

well-woman clinic N clinique *f* pour femmes; *(session)* consultations *fpl* dans la clinique pour femmes

well-worn ADJ *(garment)* très usé; *(argument)* rebattu, usé jusqu'à la corde

well-written ADJ bien écrit

welly ['welɪ] N *Br Fam (boot)* botte *f* en caoutchouc; **to give it some w.** mettre le paquet; **he really gave the ball some w.** il a tapé dans le ballon de toutes ses forces

Welsh [welʃ] ADJ gallois, du pays de Galles
N **1 the W.** *(pl)* les Gallois *mpl* **2** *Ling* gallois *m*
▶▶ **the Welsh Assembly** l'Assemblée *f* du pays de Galles; **W. dresser** vaisselier *m*; **W. rabbit** ≃ croque-monsieur *m inv*; **W. rarebit** ≃ croque-monsieur

Welsh Assembly
L'assemblée nationale du pays de Galles fut établie dans le cadre de la décentralisation engagée par le gouvernement travailliste et fut inaugurée à Cardiff en mai 1999. Les soixante membres de l'assemblée forment le "Welsh Cabinet" et siègent sous la houlette du "First Secretary" qui représente les intérêts gallois au parlement de Westminster. L'assemblée nationale du pays de Galles, la première depuis six siècles, a toutefois moins de pouvoirs que le parlement écossais mis en place en même temps.

▶ **welsh on** VT INSEP *Fam* **to welsh on sb** faire faux bond à qn; **to welsh on a bet** ne pas tenir un pari

Welshman, *pl* **Welshmen** ['welʃmən] N Gallois *m*

Welshwoman, *pl* **Welshwomen** ['welʃ- wʊmən, -wɪmɪn] N Galloise *f*

welt [welt] N **1** *(of shoe)* trépointe *f* **2** *(left by blow)* marque *f ou* trace *f* de coup

welter¹ ['weltər] N **a w. of** *(details, statistics)* une pléthore de; *(forms)* une masse de; **a w. of blood and guts** une marée de sang

welter² VI *Lit (in mud)* se vautrer, se rouler; *(in blood)* nager, baigner

welterweight ['weltəweɪt] N *Boxing* poids *m* mi-moyen, poids welter; **to fight as** *or* **at w.** boxer dans la catégorie des poids welters
▶▶ **w. match** match *m* de poids welters

wen [wen] N *Med* kyste *m* sébacé, *Fam* loupe *f*

wench [wentʃ] N **1** *Hum Fam (young woman)* (jeune) fille *f*, jeune femme *f*; **great strapping w.** grande gaillarde *f* **2** *Arch* **(serving) w.** *(in inn)* serveuse *f*; **kitchen w.** fille *f* de cuisine

   VI *Arch, Hum* **to go wenching** courir le jupon

wencher ['wentʃər] N *Arch, Hum* coureur *m* de jupons

wend [wend] VT **to w. one's way** se diriger, s'acheminer (**to** vers); **to w. one's way homeward** prendre le chemin du retour

Wendy house® ['wendɪ] N *Br* = maison *f* en modèle réduit pour enfants

Wensleydale ['wenzlɪdeɪl] N = fromage *m* anglais à pâte dure originaire de Wensleydale

went PT see **go**

wept PT, PP see **weep**

were PT see **be**

we're [wɪər] CONTR = we are, see **be**

weren't [wɜːnt] CONTR = were not, see **be**

werewolf, *pl* **werewolves** ['wɪəwʊlf, -wʊlvz] N *Myth* loup-garou *m*, *pl* loups-garous

Wesleyan ['weslɪən] ADJ, N wesleyen, -enne

west [west] N ouest *m*; **the house faces the w.** la maison est exposée à l'ouest; **on the w., to the w.** à l'ouest (**of** de); **the W.** *(the Occident)* l'Occident *m*, les pays *mpl* occidentaux; *(in United States)* l'Ouest *m* (*États situés à l'ouest du Mississippi*); *Am* **the Far W.** le Far-West; *Am* **the Mid W.** les États de la Prairie

   ADV à l'ouest; **to travel w.** voyager vers l'ouest; *Old-fashioned Fam (die)* casser sa pipe, passer l'arme à gauche; *Fam* **there's another plate gone w.!** encore une assiette de cassée!

   ADJ ouest *inv*; *(wind)* d'ouest; *(wall, window)* qui fait face *ou* qui est exposé à l'ouest; **the w. coast** la côte ouest

   ▸▸ **W. Africa** Afrique *f* occidentale; **the W. Bank** la Cisjordanie; *Formerly* **W. Berlin** Berlin *m* Ouest; **the W. Coast** la côte ouest *(des États-Unis)*; **the W. Country** = le sud-ouest de l'Angleterre (Cornouailles, Devon et Somerset); *Br* **W. End** *(in general)* quartiers *mpl* ouest; *(of London)* West End *m (centre touristique et commercial de la ville de Londres connu pour ses théâtres)*; **in the W. End** dans le West End; *Formerly* **W. Germany** Allemagne *f* de l'Ouest; **the W. Indies** Antilles *fpl*; **W. Point** = importante école *f* militaire américaine; *Am* **the W. Side** les quartiers *mpl* ouest de New York

westbound ['westbaʊnd] ADJ *(traffic)* en direction de l'ouest; *(lane, carriageway)* de l'ouest; *(road)* qui va vers l'ouest; **w. traffic is subject to delays** la circulation est ralentie dans le sens ouest; **there's a jam on the w. carriageway** il y a un bouchon en direction de l'ouest

westerly ['westəlɪ] ADJ *(wind)* d'ouest, qui vient de l'ouest; *(current)* qui se dirige vers l'ouest; **w. point** point *m* situé à *ou* vers l'ouest

   ADV vers l'ouest

   N vent *m* d'ouest

western ['westən] ADJ ouest *inv*, de l'ouest; *(wind)* d'ouest; *esp Pol* occidental, -aux; *Pol* **the W. powers** les puissances occidentales

   N *Cin* western *m*; *(novel)* roman-western *m*, *pl* romans-westerns

   ▸▸ **W. Australia** l'Australie-Occidentale *f*; **W. Europe** Europe *f* occidentale; **W. Isles** Hébrides *fpl*; *Sport* **w. roll** rouleau *m* costal

Westerner ['westənər] N **1** *Pol* occidental, -aux **2** *Geog* habitant, -ante de l'ouest

westernization [westənaɪ'zeɪʃən] N occidentalisation *f*

westernize ['westənaɪz] VT *(people)* occidentaliser; **to become westernized** s'occidentaliser

Westminster ['westmɪnstər] N Westminster *(siège du gouvernement britannique)*

Westminster

C'est dans ce quartier que se trouvent le Parlement et le palais de Buckingham. Le nom de "Westminster" est également employé pour désigner le Parlement lui-même.

---

westward ['westwəd] ADJ vers l'ouest, en direction de l'ouest

   ADV = **westwards**

westwards ['westwədz] ADV vers l'ouest, en direction de l'ouest

wet [wet] ADJ *(comp* **wetter**; *superl* **wettest)* **1** *(soaked)* mouillé; *(damp)* humide; *(weather)* pluvieux; **to get w.** se mouiller; **to get one's feet w.** se mouiller les pieds; **to be w. through** *or* **w. to the skin** être trempé *ou* mouillé jusqu'aux os; **her cheeks were w. with tears** ses joues étaient baignées de larmes; **the ink/paint was still w.** l'encre/la peinture n'était pas encore sèche; *Fig* **he's (still) w. behind the ears** il manque de maturité, il n'est pas mûr; **when you're a bit less w. behind the ears** quand tu seras un peu plus mûr; **three w. days** trois jours de pluie; **the wettest summer on record** l'été le plus humide dont on se souvienne; **when it's w.** *(raining)* quand il pleut; **the w. season** la saison des pluies; **a w.-look hairstyle** une coiffure à l'aspect mouillé; **a w.-look coat** un manteau moiré *ou* brillant; **w. paint** *(notice)* peinture fraîche

   2 *Br Fam (silly)* bête, idiot; *(excuse)* faible; *(weak, pathetic)* lamentable; *Pol* modéré; **don't be so w.!** *(stupid)* ne sois pas si bête!; *(lacking in physical courage)* du nerf!; **he thinks it's w. to discuss emotions** il trouve ça mièvre de parler des sentiments

   3 *(allowing alcohol sales) (country, state)* qui permet la vente des boissons alcoolisées

   N **1** *(dampness)* humidité *f*

   2 *(rain)* pluie *f*; *Austr* **the w.** *(season)* la saison des pluies; **to go out in the w.** sortir sous la pluie

   3 *Br Pol Fam* modéré, -ée

   VT (**-tt-**) mouiller, humecter; *(sponge)* imbiber; *(pastry)* mouiller; *(clay)* humidifier, mouiller; **to w. the bed** *(of child)* faire pipi au lit; **to w. one's pants** *or* **oneself** mouiller sa culotte, faire pipi dans sa culotte; *Fig Fam* pisser dans sa culotte; *Hum Fam* **to w. one's whistle** se rincer *ou* s'humecter le gosier; *Fig Fam* **we'll have to w. the baby's head** il faudra qu'on arrose la naissance du bébé

   ▸▸ *Fam* **w. blanket** rabat-joie *m inv*; *Elec* **w. cell** pile *f* à élément humide; **w. dock** bassin *m* à flot; **w. dream** éjaculation *f ou* pollution *f* nocturne; **w. fish** poisson *m* frais; **w. lease** *(for aircraft)* location *f* d'avion avec équipage; **w. nurse** nourrice *f*; **w. rot** moisissure *f* humide; **w. suit** combinaison *f ou* ensemble *m* de plongée

wetback ['wetbæk] N *Am Pej* = ouvrier *m* agricole mexicain entré illégalement aux États-Unis

wether ['weðər] N *(ram)* bélier *m* châtré

wetlands ['wetləndz] NPL marais *mpl*

wetness ['wetnɪs] N humidité *f*; **renowned for the w. of its climate** connu pour son climat pluvieux

wetting ['wetɪŋ] N **to get a w.** se faire mouiller; **w. the bed can be a sign that …** l'incontinence nocturne peut indiquer que …

   ▸▸ *Chem* **w. agent** (agent *m*) mouillant *m*

wet-weather tyre N pneu *m* pluie

WEU [dʌb(ə)ljuːiːˈjuː] N *Pol (abbr* **Western European Union)** UEO *f*

we've [wiːv] CONTR = we have, see **have**

WFP [dʌb(ə)ljuːefˈpiː] N *(abbr* **World Food Programme)** PAM *m*

whack [wæk] *Fam* N **1** *(blow) (with stick)* coup *m* retentissant *ou* bien appliqué; *(with hand)* claque *f*, taloche *f*; **to give sb a w.** donner un grand coup à qn; *Fig* **to have a w. at doing sth** *(try)* essayer de faire qch; **to have a whack** tenter le coup

   2 *(share)* part *f*; **all I want is a fair w.** tout ce que je veux, c'est ma part; **he didn't get his w.** il n'a pas eu sa part; **you're already earning (the) top w. for this job** tu gagnes déjà le maximum pour ce travail; **we can offer you £50,000, top w.** *(no more)* nous pouvons vous offrir 50 000 livres, dernier prix *ou* grand maximum

   INT v'lan!, vlan!

   VT **1** *(hit) (person) (one blow)* filer un gnon à; *(several blows)* battre, *Fam* cogner; *(ball) (of tennis player, golf player)* donner un grand coup dans; *(of football player)* donner un grand coup de pied dans; **to w. sb over the head** frapper qn sur la tête; **to w. sb with a stick/ruler** donner un coup de bâton/de règle à qn; **Pele whacked the ball into the net** Pele a envoyé le ballon d'un grand coup de pied dans le filet

   2 *Sport (defeat) (one's opponents)* battre à plate(s) couture(s), piler

   VI **to w. at sth with a stick** donner un coup de bâton à qch

   ▸ **whack off** VI *Sl (masturbate)* se branler

whacked [wækt] ADJ *Br Fam (exhausted)* vanné, crevé

whacker ['wækər] N *Fam* **1** *(large thing)* **what a w.!, isn't it a w.!** *(piece of meat, vegetable, fish)* quel morceau!, c'est un sacré morceau!; **he's got a w. of a nose** il a un nez énorme **2** *Old-fashioned (lie)* gros mensonge *m*

whacking ['wækɪŋ] *Fam* ADJ énorme

   ADV vachement; **a w. great dog** un chien énorme; **a w. great lie** un gros mensonge

   N **1** *(beating)* rossée *f*, raclée *f*; **his father gave him a w.** son père lui a donné une raclée **2** *Sport (defeat)* **we gave them a w.** on leur a mis la pâtée

whacko ['wækəʊ] ADJ *Fam* = **wacky**

   INT *Old-fashioned Br Sl* magnifique!

whacky ['wækɪ] ADJ *esp Am Fam* = **wacky**

whale [weɪl] N **1** baleine *f*; **blue w.** baleine bleue; **white w.** bél(o)uga *m* **2** *Fam* **we had a w. of a time** on s'est drôlement bien amusé

   VI pêcher la baleine, aller à la pêche à la baleine

   ▸▸ **w. calf** baleineau *m*; **w. hunter** baleinier *m*; **w. oil** huile *f* de baleine

whaleboat ['weɪlbəʊt] N baleinier *m*

whalebone ['weɪlbəʊn] N *(in corset)* busc *m*, baleine *f*

whaler ['weɪlər] N *(person, vessel)* baleinier *m*

whaling ['weɪlɪŋ] N pêche *f ou* chasse *f* à la baleine

   ▸▸ **w. ship** baleinier *m*

wham ['wæm] *Fam* INT v'lan!, vlan!

   VI (**-mm-**) rentrer (**into** dans); **the ball whammed into the back of the net** le ballon a filé dans les buts; **her fist whammed into his face** son poing s'est écrasé sur son visage; **she whammed into the wall** elle s'est écrasée contre le mur; **the car whammed into the lamppost** la voiture est rentrée dans le réverbère

   VT enfoncer; **to w. the ball into the net** envoyer le ballon dans le filet à toute volée

wharf, pl **wharfs, wharves** [wɔːf, -s, wɔːvz] N quai m; Com ex **w.** à prendre sur quai

wharfage [ˈwɔːfɪdʒ] N droits mpl de quai ou de bassin

WHAT [wɒt]

> **ADJ** quel **2, 3**
> **PRON** ce qui **1, 3** ▪ ce que **1, 3** ▪ qu'est-ce qui **1** ▪ qu'est-ce que **2** ▪ que **2** ▪ quoi **2** ▪ combien **2** ▪ comment **2**

ADJ 1 (rel) he took **w.** little I had left il m'a pris le peu qui me restait; **I'll give you w. money I have** je vais vous donner ce que j'ai comme argent **VOIR GRAMMAIRE A33**

2 (interr direct or indirect) quel, quelle, pl quels, quelles; **w. time is it?** quelle heure est-il?; **w. date is it (today)?** quelle est la date (d'aujourd'hui)?; **tell me w. books you want** dites-moi quels livres vous désirez; **w. right has she to give orders?** de quel droit donne-t-elle des ordres?; **w. good** or **use is this?** à quoi ça sert?; **w. sort of (a) book is it?** quelle sorte de livre est-ce?; **w. colour/ size is it?** c'est de quelle couleur/de quelle taille? **VOIR GRAMMAIRE A31–2; B16**

3 (exclamatory) **w. an idea!** quelle idée!; **a fool he is!** qu'il est bête!, comme il est bête!; **w. a fuss about nothing!** voilà bien du bruit pour rien!; **w. a question!** quelle question!; **w. a man!** quel homme!; **w. a pity!** quel dommage!; **w. a (long) time you're taking to get dressed!** qu'est-ce que vous êtes long à vous habiller!; **w. a lot of people!** que de gens!, que de monde! **VOIR GRAMMAIRE A5; B17**

PRON 1 (rel) (subject) ce qui; (object) ce que; **w. is done cannot be undone** ce qui est fait est fait; **I don't know w. has happened** je ne sais pas ce qui est arrivé; **I like a detective story** moi, ce que j'aime, ce sont les romans policiers; **w. is most remarkable is that …** ce qu'il y a de plus remarquable c'est que …; **this is w. it's all about** voici ce dont il s'agit; **but that's not w. I said** mais ce n'est pas ce que j'ai dit; **come w. may** advienne que pourra; **he never talks about w. he has gone through** il ne parle jamais de ce qu'il a enduré; **w. with golf and tennis I have no time to write** entre le golf et le tennis je n'ai pas le temps d'écrire; **SI to give sb w. for** (scold) passer un savon à qn; (beat) flanquer une bonne raclée à qn **SEE GRAMMAR B23**

2 (interr direct) (subject) (object) ce qui; (object) qu'est-ce que, que, quoi; **w. has happened?** qu'est-ce qui est arrivé?; **w.'s happening?** que se passe-t-il?; Fam **w.'s up?** comment ça va?; **w. do you want?** qu'est-ce que vous voulez?; **w. on earth are you doing here?** qu'est-ce que vous pouvez bien faire ici?; **w. is it?** (identify it) qu'est-ce?, qu'est-ce que c'est?; (what is wrong) qu'est-ce qu'il y a?; **w.'s that?** (identify it) qu'est-ce que c'est que ça?; (what did you say) quoi?; **w.'s that you're telling me?** qu'est-ce que vous me dites?; **w. will become of her?** que deviendra-t-elle?; **w.'s the matter?** qu'est-ce qu'il y a?, qu'y a-t-il?; **w.'s the date (today)?** quel jour sommes-nous?; **w.'s her address?** quelle est son adresse?; **w.'s his name?** quel est son nom?, comment s'appelle-t-il?; **w.'s that to you?** qu'est-ce que cela vous fait?, est-ce que ça vous regarde?; **w. is she to you that you're so concerned about her?** il faut qu'elle soit bien importante pour toi pour que tu sois aussi inquiet à son sujet; **w. is there to see in this town?** qu'y a-t-il à voir dans cette ville?; **w.'s the good** or **the use?** à quoi bon?; **w.'s to be done?** que faire?; **w. did I tell you?** qu'est-ce que je vous avais dit?, je vous l'avais bien dit!; **w. will people say?** que dira-t-on?, que vont dire les gens?; **w.'s the French for 'dog'?** comment dit-on

'dog' en français?; **w. else could bring me here?** quoi d'autre pourrait me faire venir ici?; **w. could be more beautiful?** quoi de plus beau?; **w. do seven and eight make?** combien font sept plus huit?; **w. is the rent?** à combien s'élève le loyer?; **w. do I owe you?** qu'est-ce que je vous dois?; (in shop) c'est combien?, ça fait combien?; **w. is he like?** comment est-il?; **w. do you take me for?** pour qui me prenez-vous?; **w.'s it made of?** en quoi est-ce que c'est fait?, c'est fait en quoi?; **w. are you thinking of?** à quoi pensez-vous?; **w. were you thinking of, letting her go out on her own?** qu'est-ce qui t'a pris de la laisser sortir toute seule?; **w. about the ten pounds I lent you?** et les dix livres que je vous ai prêtées?; **w. about a game of bridge?** si on faisait une partie de bridge?; **w. about you?** et vous?; **w. about that coffee?** et ce café?; **w.'s that for?** à quoi cela sert-il?, à quoi ça sert?; **w. did he do that for?** pourquoi a-t-il fait cela?; **w. for?** pourquoi?; **w. on earth for?** mais pourquoi donc?; **and w. if she hears about it?** et si elle l'apprend?; **w. then?** et après?; Fam **so w.?** et alors?; Fam **d'you think I'm mad or w.?** tu crois que je suis fou ou quoi?; **w. did you say?** vous disiez?, pardon?; **w. of it?** qu'est-ce que cela fait?, eh bien, et après?; **well, w. of it?** et bien?, et après? **VOIR GRAMMAIRE A31–2; B17**

3 (indirect) (subject) ce qui; (object) ce que; **tell me w.'s happened** dites-moi ce qui s'est passé; **I don't know w. you want** je ne sais pas ce que vous désirez; **he didn't know w. to say/do** il ne savait que dire/faire; **there were books and I don't know w.** il y avait des livres et je ne sais quoi d'autre ou encore; Fam **paper, pens, pencils, and w. not** or **and w. have you** du papier, des stylos, des crayons et d'autres choses encore ou et je ne sais quoi encore; **tell me w. you're crying for** dites-moi pourquoi vous pleurez; **tell me w.'s to be done** dis-moi ce qu'il y a à faire; **I'll tell you w.** je vais vous dire, écoutez; **he knows w.'s w.** (in a subject) il s'y connaît; **I've still to find out w.'s w.** (how things work etc) il faut que je trouve comment ça marche; (what the situation is) il faut que je me mette au courant de la situation; **I'll show him w.'s w.!** je vais lui montrer de quel bois je me chauffe!

4 (exclamatory) **w. she has suffered!** ce qu'elle a souffert!; **w. next (I ask myself)!** ça par exemple!, et puis quoi encore!; **w.! you can't come!** comment! vous ne pouvez pas venir!; **w.! no eggs!** quoi! pas d'œufs!; Old-fashioned Fam **nice girl, w.!** joli brin de fille, hein!

what-d'ye-call-her [ˈwɒtdjəkɔːlər] N Fam (person) Machine f

what-d'ye-call-him [ˈwɒtdjəkɔːlɪm] N Fam (person) Machin m

what-d'ye-call-it [ˈwɒtdjəkɔːlɪt] N Fam (thing) machin m, truc m

whate'er [wɒtˈeər] PRON Lit = whatever

whatever [wɒtˈevər] **VOIR GRAMMAIRE A32; A33**
PRON 1 (rel) (subject) tout ce qui; (object) tout ce que; **w. you like** tout ce qui vous plaira, tout ce que vous voudrez

2 (no matter what) quoi que + sub; **w. it is** or **may be** quoi que ce soit; **w. happens, keep calm** quoi qu'il survienne, restez calme; **he shall have w. he wants** quoi qu'il désire, il l'aura; **w. she says** or **may say** en dépit de ce qu'elle dit; **use w. you can find** utilise ce que tu trouveras; **w. can she have said to make him so angry?** qu'est-ce qu'elle a bien pu dire pour le mettre dans une telle colère?

3 Fam **pens, pencils, paper and w.** des stylos, des crayons, du papier et tout ce que vous voulez; **… or w.** (something similar) … ou quelque chose de ce genre; (anything you like) … ou tout ce que vous voulez

ADJ 1 (no matter what) **w.** price they are asking quel que soit le prix qu'ils demandent; **w. mistakes I (may) have made** quelles que soient les erreurs que j'ai faites

2 (emphatic) **under any pretext w.** sous quelque prétexte que ce soit; **no hope w.** pas le moindre espoir, pas l'ombre d'un espoir; **is there any hope w.?** y a-t-il l'ombre d'un espoir?; **none w.** pas un seul; **nothing w.** absolument rien

what-ho INT Br Old-fashioned **1** eh bien!, tiens! **2** (greeting) bonjour!, salut!

whatnot [ˈwɒtnɒt] N **1** (for ornaments) étagère f **2** Fam (thing) machin m, truc m; (person) chose mf, machin m, machine f **3** Fam **… and w.** … et ainsi de suite, … et tout ce qui s'ensuit; **there was champagne, caviar and w.** il y avait du champagne, du caviar et tout le tralala

what's-her-name, what's-his-name, what's-its-name [ˈwɒtsə-, -ɪz-, -ɪtsneɪm] N = **what-d'ye-call-her, what-d'ye-call-him, what-d'ye-call-it**

whatsit [ˈwɒtsɪt] N Fam machin m, truc m

whatsoever [wɒtsəʊˈevər] PRON Lit **w. it may be** quoi que ce soit
ADJ (emphatic) = **whatever** ADJ **2**

wheat [wiːt] N blé m, froment m; **to plant land with w.** mettre une terre en blé; Agr, Fig **to separate the w. from the chaff** séparer le bon grain de l'ivraie
▸ **w. field** champ m de blé

wheatear [ˈwiːtɪər] N (bird) traquet m (motteux), cul-blanc m, pl culs-blancs

wheaten [ˈwiːt(ə)n] ADJ (bread) de froment, de blé

wheatgerm [ˈwiːtdʒɜːm] N germes mpl de blé

wheatmeal [ˈwiːtmiːl] N farine f grossière, grosse farine de froment
▸ **w. bread** pain m de froment

wheatsheaf [ˈwiːtʃiːf] N gerbe f de blé

wheedle [ˈwiːd(ə)l] VT **1** to **w. sb into doing sth** faire faire qch à qn à force de cajoleries; **she wheedled me into agreeing** elle m'a cajolé tant et si bien que j'ai fini par accepter **2** to **w. sth out of sb** obtenir ou soutirer qch de qn par des cajoleries; **he wheedled his way into the old lady's confidence** il s'est assuré la confiance de la vieille dame à force de cajoleries

wheedling [ˈwiːd(ə)lɪŋ] ADJ (manner etc) enjôleur, cajoleur; **a w. voice** une voix pateline
N cajoleries fpl

wheel [wiːl] N **1** (on car, printer etc) roue f, (small) roulette f, **on wheels** sur roues/roulettes; Br **meals on wheels** = repas mpl livrés à domicile (aux personnes âgées etc); Fam **my wheels** (my car) ma bagnole; Fig **the fifth w.** la cinquième roue du carrosse; Am Fam **to feel like a fifth w.** être la cinquième roue du carrosse; Aviat **landing wheels** roues (du train) d'atterrissage; Aviat **nose w.** roue (d'atterrisseur) avant; **the wheels (of mechanism, watch)** les rouages mpl; Fig **the wheels of government** les rouages du gouvernement; Fig **there are wheels within wheels** c'est une affaire très compliquée ou dont il faut connaître les dessous, c'est plus compliqué que cela n'en a l'air; Fig **the w. has come full circle** la boucle est bouclée; Hist **to condemn a criminal to the w.** condamner un criminel à la roue; Hist **to break sb on the w.** rouer qn; Fig **big w.** (at fair) grande roue; Am Fam (important person) gros bonnet m, huile f; **the w. of fortune** la roue de la fortune

2 (for steering) Aut volant m (de direction); Naut roue f du gouvernail, barre f, **to be at the w.** Aut être au volant; Naut tenir la barre *ou* le gouvernail; *Fig* tenir la barre; **the man at the w.** *Aut* le conducteur, l'homme au volant; *Naut* l'homme de barre; *Fig* l'homme qui mène la barque, *Fam* le grand patron; **do you want to take a turn at the w.?** tu veux me remplacer au volant?; *Naut* tu veux me remplacer à la barre?

3 *Mil etc (movement)* (mouvement *m* de) conversion *f*; **left/right w.** conversion à gauche/à droite

VT *(barrow, bicycle)* pousser; **to w. sth in a barrow** transporter qch en brouette; **to w. a child in a pram** promener un enfant dans son landau

VI 1 *(circle) (of birds)* tournoyer; *(of plane)* tourner **2** *Mil* opérer *ou* effectuer une conversion; **left w.!** par file à gauche, gauche! **3** *Fam* **to w. and deal** brasser des affaires (plus ou moins louches); **after spending the whole week wheeling and dealing** après une semaine complète de tractations

▸▸ *Aut* **w. alignment** parallélisme *m* des roues; *Aut* **w. arch** passage *m* de roue; *Aut* **w. bolt** boulon *m* de roue; **w. brace** clef *f* en croix; *Aut* **w. chain** chaîne *f* (de pneu); *Aut* **w. cover** enjoliveur *m*; *Aut* **w. cylinder** cylindre *m* de roue; *Aut* **w. disc** enjoliveur; *Aut* **w. hop** rebond *m* des roues; *Aut* **w. lock(-up)** blocage *m* des roues; *Aut* **w. nut** écrou *m* de roue; *Aut* **w. rim** jante *f* de roue; *Aut* **w. shimmy** phénomène *m* de shimmy; *Aut* **w. spin** patinage *m* de roues; *Aut* **w. track** alignement *m* des roues; *Aut* **w. trim** enjoliveur de roues; *Aut* **w. wobble** flottement *m* des roues

▸ **wheel about, wheel around VI 1** *(turn)* faire demi-tour *ou* se retourner (brusquement); **she wheeled around to face him** elle s'est retournée brusquement pour lui faire face **2** *(circle)* tourner en rond *ou* en cercle, tournoyer; **vultures wheeling about in the sky** des vautours qui tournoient dans le ciel **VT SEP** *(turn)* tourner; *(dancing partner)* faire tourner

▸ **wheel in VT SEP 1** *(in wheelchair)* faire entrer en fauteuil roulant **2** *Br Fam (show in)* faire entrer; **w. him in as soon as he arrives** faites-le entrer dès qu'il arrive

▸ **wheel round VI, VT SEP** = **wheel about**

wheelbarrow ['wiːlbærəʊ] **N** brouette *f*

wheelbase ['wiːlbeɪs] **N** *Aut* empattement *m*

wheelchair ['wiːltʃeər] **N** fauteuil *m* roulant; **she'll be in a w. for the rest of her life** elle sera dans un fauteuil roulant pour le reste de ses jours; **access is difficult for people in wheelchairs** l'accès est difficile pour les personnes en fauteuil roulant

▸▸ **w. access** accès *m* aux handicapés

wheelclamp ['wiːlklæmp] *Aut* **N** sabot *m* de Denver

VT mettre un sabot de Denver à; **I got wheelclamped last week** je me suis pris un sabot la semaine dernière

wheeled [wiːld] **ADJ** à roues; *(on castors)* à roulettes

-wheeled [-wiːld] **SUFF** **two/three-w.** à deux/trois roues

-wheeler [-'wiːlər] **SUFF** **two/three-w.** voiture *f*/bicyclette *f* à deux/trois roues, véhicule *m* à deux/trois roues

wheeler-dealer **N** *Fam* brasseur *m* d'affaires, *Pej* magouilleur, -euse

wheelhouse ['wiːlhaʊs] **N** *Naut* abri *m* de navigation

wheelie ['wiːlɪ] **N** *Br Fam* **to do a w.** = rouler sur la roue arrière d'une bicyclette *ou* d'une moto

wheeling ['wiːlɪŋ] **N 1** *(of birds etc)* tournoiement *m* **2 w. and dealing** brassage *m* d'affaires, *Pej* tractations *fpl*, magouilles *fpl*

wheelmouse ['wiːlmaʊs] **N** *Comput* souris *f* à molette

wheelwright ['wiːlraɪt] **N** charron *m*

wheeze [wiːz] **N 1** *(noise)* respiration *f* sifflante **2** *Br Fam (trick)* ruse *f*, truc *m*; **a good w.** une bonne astuce, une bonne combine **VI** respirer péniblement

wheezing ['wiːzɪŋ] **N** *(of person)* respiration *f* difficile; *Med* sibilance *f* respiratoire

wheezy ['wiːzɪ] **ADJ** *(person, voice)* asthmatique, poussif; **she's still a little bit w. after her cold** elle a encore un peu de mal à respirer après son rhume; *Fig* **a w. old barrel organ** un vieil orgue de Barbarie asthmatique

whelk [welk] **N** buccin *m*

whelp [welp] **N** *(dog)* jeune chien *m*, chiot *m*; *(of big cat)* petit *m*; *Old-fashioned Fam (youth)* garnement *m*

VI *(of animals)* mettre bas

WHEN [wen]

ADV	quand **1** ▪ où **2**
CONJ	quand **1, 2** ▪ lorsque **1** ▪ alors que **3**
PRON	quand **1**

ADV 1 *(interr)* quand; **w. will you come?** quand viendrez-vous?; **w. will the wedding be?** à quand le mariage?; **w. ever** *or* **w. on earth will he come?** quand donc *ou* quand diable viendra-t-il?; *Fam* **say w.!** *(when pouring drink)* dites-moi stop!

2 *(rel)* **the day w. I first met her** le jour où je l'ai rencontrée pour la première fois; **one day w. I was on duty** un jour que j'étais de service; **at the very time w. ...** au moment même où ..., alors même que ...

CONJ VOIR GRAMMAIRE A75; B31–2 **1** *(at the time that)* quand, lorsque; **w. I came into the room** quand *ou* lorsque je suis entré dans la pièce; **w. I think of what she must have suffered!** quand je pense à ce qu'elle a dû souffrir!; **I get very irritated w. talking to her** je m'énerve chaque fois que je lui parle; *Culin* **w. cool, turn out onto a dish** une fois refroidi, démouler sur un plat

2 *(at which time)* **the prince will arrive on the 10th, w. he will open the new university** le prince arrivera le dix et inaugurera la nouvelle université; **I had just gone to bed w. the phone rang** je venais de me mettre au lit quand le téléphone sonna

3 *(though)* **he walked there w. he could have taken the car** il y est allé à pied, alors qu'il aurait pu prendre la voiture

4 *(since)* **what's the good of telling you w. you won't listen to me?** à quoi bon vous le dire puisque vous ne voulez pas m'écouter?

PRON 1 *(interr)* **until w. can you stay?** jusqu'à quand pouvez-vous rester?; **since w. have you been living in Paris?** depuis quand habitez-vous Paris?; *Iron* **since w. have you been interested in opera?** depuis quand est-ce que tu t'intéresses à l'opéra?

2 *(rel)* **since w. I have always bought a car of that make** depuis lors je n'achète que des voitures de cette marque; **until w. I shall stay in Paris** d'ici là je reste à Paris

N **the w. and the how of it** quand et comment cela s'est-il passé/se passera-t-il

whence [wens] **ADV** *Arch, Lit* d'où; **no one knows w. he comes** personne ne sait d'où il vient; **w. I conclude that ...** d'où je conclus que ...

whenever, *Lit* **whene'er** [wen'evər, -'eər] **CONJ, ADV** VOIR GRAMMAIRE A75 **1** *(every time)* toutes les fois *ou* chaque fois que; **w. I see it I think of you** chaque fois que je le vois je pense à vous; **I go w. I can** j'y vais aussi souvent que possible **2** *(any time)* à n'importe quel moment; **come w. you like** venez quand vous voudrez *ou* à n'importe quel

---

moment; **Sunday, Monday or w.** dimanche, lundi, ou n'importe quel jour; **next month or w.** le mois prochain ou n'importe quand **3** *(interr)* quand; **w. did you find (the) time to do all that?** quand avez-vous trouvé le temps de faire tout cela?

WHERE [weər]

INTERR ADV	où **1**
CONJ	où ▪ là où ▪ là que

INTERR ADV 1 *(in what place or direction)* où; **w. am I?** où suis-je?; **tell me w. she is** dites-moi où elle est; **w. did you put it?** où l'avez-vous mis?; **w. are you going to?** où allez-vous?; **w. does he come from?** d'où vient-il?; **w. have you got to?, w. are you?** *(in work, book etc)* où en êtes-vous?; *(when looking for someone)* où êtes-vous passé?, où êtes-vous?; **w. should I be if I had followed your advice?** qu'est-ce que je serais devenu si j'avais suivi vos conseils?

2 w. is the use *or* **the good of it?** à quoi bon (faire) cela?

REL CONJ, REL ADV *(in, at, to the place which)* (là) où; **I'll stay w. I am** je resterai (là) où je suis; **go w. you like** allez où vous voudrez; **that's w. we've got to** voilà où nous sommes; **that is w. you are mistaken** c'est là que vous vous trompez, voilà où vous vous trompez; **he came to (the place) w. I was fishing** il est venu à l'endroit où je pêchais; **I can see it from w. we are** je le vois d'où nous sommes; **delete w. inapplicable** *(on form)* rayer les mentions inutiles; **the house w. I was born** la maison où *ou* dans laquelle je suis né; **they went to Paris, w. they stayed a week** ils sont allés à Paris et y sont restés huit jours VOIR GRAMMAIRE A75

N the w. and the when le lieu et la date/l'heure

whereabouts ADV [weərə'baʊts] où; **do you know w. the town hall is?** savez-vous de quel côté se trouve l'hôtel de ville?; **w. in France do you live?** où est-ce que tu habites en France?

NPL ['weərəbaʊts] **nobody knows her w., her w. are unknown** personne ne sait où elle est; **we are still unsure of his exact w.** on ignore encore le lieu où il se trouve exactement; **the precise w. of the control centre** le lieu précis où se trouve le centre de contrôle

whereafter [weər'rɑːftər] **REL ADV** *Arch, Lit* après quoi, à la suite de quoi

whereas [weər'ræz] **CONJ 1** *Law etc (introducing preamble)* attendu que, vu que, puisque **2** *(on the other hand)* alors que, tandis que

whereat [weər'ræt] **ADV, CONJ** *Arch, Lit* à quoi, sur quoi; **w. he replied that ...** (ce) à quoi il a répondu que ...

whereby [weər'baɪ] **ADV** *Arch, Fml* par quoi, par quel moyen; **we have a situation here w. ...** nous sommes ici en présence d'une situation dans laquelle ...; **a scheme w. we can ...** un plan par lequel nous pouvons ...

wherefore [weəfɔːr] **ADV** *Arch, Lit* **1** *(interr)* pourquoi, pour quelle raison **2** *(rel)* donc, pour cette raison

N the why and the w. le pourquoi et le comment

wherein [weər'ɪn] **ADV** *Arch, Lit* en quoi; **w. the difficulty lies** où se trouve la difficulté

whereof [weər'ɒv] **ADV** *Arch, Lit (interr)* en quoi, de quoi; *(rel)* dont; **a matter w. I know nothing** une affaire dont j'ignore tout

whereon [weər'ɒn] **ADV** *Arch, Lit* sur lequel; **the day w. ...** le jour où ...; **w. he left us** sur quoi il nous a quittés

wheresoever, wheresoe'er [weəsəʊ'evər, -'eər] **ADV, CONJ** *esp Lit* = **wherever**

whereupon [weərə'pɒn] ADV, CONJ *Lit (at which point)* sur quoi, après quoi; **w. he left us** sur quoi il nous a quittés

wherever [weə'revər] CONJ, ADV VOIR GRAMMAIRE A75 **1** *(every place)* partout où, n'importe où; **I shall remember it w. I go** où que j'aille, je m'en souviendrai; **I'll go w. you want (me to)** j'irai partout où vous voudrez (que j'aille); **w. possible** partout où cela est possible; *Fam* **at home, in the office or w.** à la maison, au bureau ou n'importe où **2** *(whichever place)* **w. they come from** d'où qu'ils viennent; **he comes from Glossop, w. that may be** il est originaire d'un bled qui s'appelle Glossop, et ne me demandez pas où cela se trouve **3** *(interr)* où; **w. can he be?** où peut-il bien être?

wherewithal ['weərwɪðɔːl] N **the w.** l'argent *m*, le nécessaire, les moyens *mpl*; **I haven't the w. to buy it** je n'ai pas de quoi l'acheter

whet [wet] VT (**-tt-**) **1** *(sharpen) (tool, blade)* aiguiser, affûter, repasser **2** *(stimulate) (appetite)* stimuler, aiguiser; **the weekend break in Florence had whetted her appetite for travel** ce week-end à Florence lui avait donné soif de voyages

whether ['weðər] CONJ VOIR GRAMMAIRE A74 **1** *(indirect question)* si; **I don't know w. it's true** je ne sais pas si c'est vrai; **it's doubtful** *or* **uncertain w. ...** il est douteux *ou* peu certain que ... + *subj*; **I doubt w. he'll come** je doute qu'il vienne; **I want to know w. ... or w. ...** je voudrais savoir si ... ou si ...; **it depends on w. you're in a hurry or not** cela dépend (de) si vous êtes pressé ou non **2** *(conditional)* **w. it rains or (whether it) snows, he always goes out** qu'il pleuve ou qu'il neige, il sort toujours; **w. she comes or not we shall leave** qu'elle vienne ou non *ou* qu'elle vienne ou qu'elle ne vienne pas, nous partirons; **w. or not this is true** qu'il en soit ainsi ou non; **everyone, w. rich or poor, needs it** chacun, qu'il soit riche ou pauvre, en a besoin; **you'll listen to me w. you like it or not** tu vas m'écouter, que tu le veuilles ou non; **w. he likes it or not** que cela lui plaise ou non

whetstone ['wetstəʊn] N pierre *f* à aiguiser *ou* à repasser

whew [hjuː] INT **1** *(relief, fatigue)* ouf! **2** *(astonishment)* mon Dieu!

whey [weɪ] N petit-lait *m*, *pl* petits-laits

WHICH [wɪtʃ] VOIR GRAMMAIRE A31–2

ADJ	quel **1** ▪ lequel **2**
PRON	lequel **1, 3** ▪ qui **2** ▪ que **2** ▪ ce qui **2** ▪ ce que **2**

ADJ 1 *(interr)* quel, *f* quelle, *pl* quels, quelles; **w. colour do you like best?** quelle couleur aimez-vous le mieux?; **w. way do we go?** par où allons-nous?; **w. way is the wind blowing?** d'où vient le vent?; **w. one?** lequel?, laquelle?; **w. ones?** lesquels?, lesquelles?; **I know w. one you want** je sais lequel vous désirez VOIR GRAMMAIRE A31–2; B16 **2** *(rel)* lequel, laquelle, *pl* lesquels, lesquelles; **he stayed here two weeks, during w. time he never left the house** il est resté ici deux semaines, et pendant (tout) ce temps il n'a pas quitté la maison; **she came at noon, at w. time I'm usually in the garden** elle est venue à midi, heure à laquelle je suis habituellement au jardin VOIR GRAMMAIRE A33

PRON 1 *(interr)* lequel, laquelle, *pl* lesquels, lesquelles; **w. have you chosen?** lequel/laquelle/lesquels/lesquelles avez-vous choisi(e)(s)?; **w. of you?** lequel d'entre vous?; **w. of the two (girls) is the prettier?** laquelle des deux (filles) est la plus jolie?; **w. would you rather have?** lequel préfériez-vous

(avoir)?; **I can never tell w. is w.** je ne sais jamais les distinguer, je ne sais jamais lequel est l'un et lequel est l'autre; **I don't know w. to choose** je ne sais (pas) lequel choisir; **I don't mind w.** n'importe (lequel) SEE GRAMMAR B17 **2** *(rel) (subject)* qui; *(object)* que; *(referring to whole clause) (subject)* ce qui; *(object)* ce que; **the house w. is for sale** la maison qui est à vendre; **the book w. I bought yesterday** le livre que j'ai acheté hier; **he looked like a retired colonel, w. in fact he was** il avait l'air d'un colonel en retraite, ce qu'il était en effet; **she was back in London, w. I didn't know** elle était de retour à Londres, fait que *ou* ce que j'ignorais VOIR GRAMMAIRE A32–3; B22–3 **3** *(with prepositions)* lequel, laquelle, *pl* lesquels, lesquelles; **to w., at w.** auquel, à laquelle, *pl* auxquels, auxquelles; **of w., from w.** duquel, de laquelle, *pl* desquels, desquelles; **the house of w. I am speaking** la maison dont je parle; **the countries to w. we are going** *or* **w. we're going to** les pays où nous allons; **the pen with w. I'm writing, the pen w. I'm writing with** le stylo avec lequel j'écris; **the town in w. we live, the town w. we live in** la ville où nous habitons *ou* que nous habitons *ou* dans laquelle nous habitons; **he insists that actors should have talent, in w. he is right** il exige que les acteurs aient du talent, (ce) en quoi il a raison; **there are no trains on Sunday, w. I hadn't thought of** il n'y a pas de trains le dimanche, ce à quoi je n'avais pas pensé; **after w. he went out** après quoi il est sorti

whichever [wɪtʃ'evər] VOIR GRAMMAIRE A33 PRON **1** *(any) (subject)* celui qui, *f* celle qui, *pl* ceux qui, celles qui; *(object)* celui *etc* que; **take w. you like best** prenez celui que vous préférez; **w. of you comes in first** celui (d'entre vous) qui arrive le premier; **the 30th or the last Friday in the month, w. comes first** le 30 ou le dernier vendredi du mois, suivant lequel de ces deux jours survient le premier **2** *(no matter which)* **w. of the measures they adopt ...** *(one)* quelle que soit la mesure qu'ils adoptent ..., quelque mesure qu'ils adoptent ..., qu'ils adoptent une mesure ou une autre ..., ils peuvent adopter n'importe quelle mesure ...; *(more than one)* quelles que soient les mesures qu'ils adoptent ..., quelques mesures qu'ils adoptent ..., ils peuvent adopter n'importe quelles mesures ...; **w. you choose, you will have a good bargain** quel que soit celui/quelle que soit celle/*etc* que vous choisissiez *ou* vous pouvez choisir n'importe lequel/laquelle/*etc*, vous ferez une bonne affaire **3** *(interr)* lequel, laquelle, *pl* lesquels, lesquelles; **w. shall I choose?** lequel vais-je choisir? VOIR GRAMMAIRE A32 **ADJ 1** *(the one/ones which)* **buy w. model is cheapest** achète le modèle qui est le moins cher(, peu importe lequel); **take w. ties you prefer** prends les cravates que tu préfères (, peu importe lesquelles); **I'll have w. cake Mary doesn't want** je prendrai le gâteau que Mary ne veut pas; **you should write to w. organization you think best** vous devriez écrire à l'organisme qui vous paraît le meilleur **2** *(no matter which)* **w. candidate wins the election, he will have to ...** quel que soit le candidat qui remporte l'élection, il lui faudra ...; **w. road you take, it'll take you two hours** quelle que soit la route que tu prennes *ou* quelque route tu prennes *ou* que tu prennes une route ou une autre *ou* tu peux prendre n'importe quelle route, tu mettras deux heures; **in w. company you work ...** quelle que soit l'entreprise dans laquelle tu travailles ..., dans quelque entre-

prise que tu travailles ..., que tu travailles dans une entreprise ou dans une autre ..., tu peux travailler dans n'importe quelle entreprise ...; **w. way you turn ...** de quelque côté que vous vous tourniez ..., que vous vous tourniez d'un côté ou d'un autre ..., vous pouvez vous tourner de n'importe quel côté ...

whiff [wɪf] N *(smell) (of wine, socks, incense etc)* odeur *f*; *Fig* **a w. of scandal** un parfum de scandale; **to catch a w. of sth** *(smell)* sentir qch; *Fig (hear rumours about)* avoir vent de qch; **he had caught a w. of something suspicious** il avait senti que quelque chose de louche était dans l'air; **there mustn't be the slightest w. of suspicion that I'm involved** rien ne doit laisser penser que je suis impliqué; *Fam* **what a w.!** *(bad smell)* qu'est-ce que ça pue!

whiffy ['wɪfɪ] ADJ *Br Fam* puant, qui pue; **the dog's a bit w.** ce chien sent fort; **it's a bit w. in here, don't you think?** ça schlingue par ici, tu ne trouves pas?

Whig [wɪg] N *Pol, Hist* whig *m*

while [waɪl] N **1** *(time)* (espace *m* de) temps *m*; **a short w.** un petit moment; **some w. later** *(soon after)* un moment plus tard; *(longer)* quelque temps plus tard; **after a w.** au bout de quelque temps, quelque temps après; **after a little w., a little w. later** peu de temps après; **for a (short) w.** pendant un moment; **in a short** *or* **little w.** sous peu, avant peu; **a short** *or* **little w. ago** il y a peu de temps; **a long w.** longtemps; **a long w. ago** il y a longtemps; **a good w.** pas mal de temps; **it lasted a good w.** ça a duré un bon moment; **it will be a good w. before you see him again** vous ne le reverrez pas de si tôt; **it will take me quite a w.** cela me prendra un certain temps *ou* pas mal de temps; **it took me a w. to realize what she meant** j'ai mis un certain temps à comprendre ce qu'elle voulait dire; **stay a little w. longer** restez encore un peu; **all the w.** tout le temps; **once in a w.** de temps en temps, de temps à autre; *Arch* **the w.** en attendant, pendant ce temps

2 to be worth (one's) w. valoir la peine, *Fam* valoir le coup; **it's not worth our w. waiting** cela ne vaut pas *ou* ce n'est pas la peine que nous attendions; **it is perhaps worth w. pointing out that ...** cela vaut peut-être la peine de faire remarquer que ...; **I'll make it worth your w.** vous serez bien récompensé de votre peine

CONJ **1** *(during the time that)* pendant que, tandis que; **don't speak w. the performance is in progress** ne parlez pas pendant le spectacle; **he drowned w. he was having a bath** il s'est noyé en prenant un bain; **w. (he was) here** pendant qu'il était ici; **w. in Paris** pendant mon/son/*etc* séjour à Paris; **w. reading I fell asleep** tout en lisant, je me suis endormi; **w. this was going on** sur ces entrefaites; **w. you're at** *or* **about it, could you photocopy this too?** pendant que tu y es, peux-tu aussi me photocopier cela? VOIR GRAMMAIRE B31–2 **2** *(as long as)* tant que **3** *(although)* quoique + *subj*, bien que + *subj*; **w. I admit it's difficult** quoique j'admette que c'est difficile **4** *(whereas)* tandis que; **one of the sisters was in white, w. the other was all in black** une des sœurs était vêtue de blanc, tandis que l'autre était tout en noir

▶ **while away** VT SEP *(time)* faire passer, tuer; *(hour)* tuer; **we whiled away the hours by playing cards** on faisait passer le temps en jouant aux cartes; **I played patience to w. away the time** j'ai fait des réussites pour m'occuper

whilst [waɪlst] CONJ *esp Br* = **while**

whim [wɪm] N caprice *m*, fantaisie *f*, lubie *f*;

passing w. toquade *f*; **to do sth on a w.** faire qch sur un coup de tête; **it was just a w.** ce n'était qu'un caprice; **it was a sudden w. of his** c'était un de ses caprices; **she indulges his every w.** elle lui passe tous ses caprices

whimper ['wɪmpər] **N** *(crying)* pleurniche-rie *f*, pleurnichement *m*; *(of dog)* petit cri *m* plaintif; *Fig (complaint)* geignement *m*, plainte *f*; **without so much as a w.** sans se plaindre

VI *(of person)* pleurnicher, geindre; *(of dog)* pousser de petits cris plaintifs; **the dog's whimpering to be let in** le chien gémit pour qu'on le laisse entrer

whimpering ['wɪmpərɪŋ] **ADJ** pleurni-cheur, gémissant; *(dog)* qui pousse de petits cris plaintifs

N *(crying)* pleurnichement *m*, pleurniche-ries *fpl*; *(of dog)* petits cris *mpl* plaintifs; *Fig (complaints)* plaintes *fpl*

whimsey ['wɪmzɪ] **N** = whimsy

whimsical ['wɪmzɪk(ə)l] **ADJ** *(person)* ca-pricieux, fantasque; *(playful)* malicieux; *(behaviour, sense of humour, story, remark)* farfelu; *(smile)* malicieux

whimsicality [wɪmzɪ'kælɪtɪ] **N** *(of person)* caractère *m* capricieux *ou* fantasque; *(play-fulness)* malice *f*; *(of behaviour, sense of hu-mour, story, remark)* caractère farfelu

whimsically ['wɪmzɪklɪ] **ADV** *(capriciously)* capricieusement; *(playfully)* malicieuse-ment; *(directed, written)* de façon farfelue; *(to smile)* malicieusement

whimsy ['wɪmzɪ] **N 1** *(capricious idea)* fan-taisie *f*; **she dismissed the idea as a mere piece of w.** elle rejeta cette idée qui lui parut de la plus haute fantaisie **2** *(playfulness)* ma-lice *f*

whin [wɪn] **N** *(plant)* ajonc *m*, genêt *m* épineux

whine [waɪn] **N 1** *(crying) (of child)* gémisse-ment *m*; *(of dog)* gémissement *m*, geigne-ment *m* **2** *(of engine etc)* bruit *m* strident

VI 1 *(cry) (of child)* pleurnicher; *(of person, dog)* gémir; *(in pain etc)* geindre **2** *(com-plain)* se plaindre; **she's always whining about something** elle est toujours en train de se lamenter à propos d'une chose ou d'une autre; **you've nothing to w. about** il n'y a pas de quoi vous plaindre; **stop whi-ning!** assez de jérémiades!

whinge [wɪndʒ] *Fam* **N** *(complaint)* plainte *f*, **to have a w. about sth** se plaindre (à pro-pos) de qch

VI 1 *(cry) (of child)* pleurnicher, gémir **2** *(complain)* se plaindre; **stop whingeing!** as-sez de jérémiades!; *Austr* **a whingeing pom** un Anglais qui se plaint toujours

whinger ['wɪndʒər] **N** *Fam* geignard, -arde

whining ['waɪnɪŋ] **ADJ** *(voice)* geignard; *(child)* pleurnicheur; *(tone)* plaintif

N 1 *(of person, dog)* gémissement *m*; *(in pain etc)* geignement *m* **2** *(complaining)* jé-rémiades *fpl*, plaintes *fpl*; **stop your w.!** as-sez de jérémiades!; **I've had enough of his w.** j'en ai assez de ses jérémiades

whinny ['wɪnɪ] **N** *(of horse)* hennissement *m*

VI *(of horse)* hennir; *Fig (of person)* brailler

whinnying ['wɪnɪɪŋ] **ADJ a w. laugh** un rire qui ressemble à un hennissement; **he gave a w. laugh** il se mit à rire en hennissant

whiny ['waɪnɪ] **ADJ** pleurnichard

whip [wɪp] **N 1** *(lash)* fouet *m*; *Fig Fam* **to give sb a fair crack of the w.** donner toutes ses chances à qn; *Fig Fam* **to get a fair crack of the w.** avoir toutes ses chances; *Fig* **to have** *or* **hold the w. hand** avoir l'avantage, avoir le dessus; *Fig* **to have the w. hand over sb** avoir barre(s) sur qn

2 *Parl (person)* chef *m* de file, whip *m*; *(or-*

der) appel *m* aux membres d'un groupe

3 *(movement) (of cable etc)* mouvement *m* brusque

4 *Culin* mousse *f*, **strawberry/raspberry w.** mousse aux fraises/framboises

VT (-pp-) **1** *(horse)* fouetter; *(child)* donner le fouet à; *Culin (egg whites)* battre en neige; *(cream)* fouetter, battre; **to w. a top** fouetter ou faire aller un sabot; **whipped cream** crème fouettée; *Fig* **he whipped the crowd into a frenzy with his speech** son discours rendit la foule frénétique; **the rain was whipping the window panes** la pluie fouet-tait *ou* cinglait les vitres

2 *Fam (defeat)* battre à plate(s) couture(s); **I know when I'm whipped** je sais quand dé-clarer forfait

3 *Sewing* **to w. a seam** surjeter une couture, faire un surjet

4 *Fam (move quickly)* **she whipped it out of sight** elle l'a caché d'un mouvement rapide; **she's been whipped into hospital** elle a été transportée à l'hôpital de toute urgence

5 *Fam (steal)* faucher, piquer; **someone's whipped my wallet** on m'a piqué mon porte-feuille

VI fouetter; **the rain was whipping against the panes** la pluie fouettait *ou* cinglait les vi-tres

▸ **whip away VT SEP** *Fam (remove quickly)* enlever brusquement *ou* d'un geste rapide

▸ **whip back VI** *Fam (return)* retourner rapi-dement; **w. back and get it** retournez-y en vitesse le chercher

▸ **whip in VI** *Fam (go in, drop in)* **I'll just w. in and buy some bread** je vais juste passer acheter du pain

VT SEP *(of huntsman)* rassembler

▸ **whip off VT SEP** *Fam (remove) (clothes)* ôter *ou* enlever rapidement, se débarrasser de

▸ **whip out** *Fam* **VT SEP** *(extract)* sortir rapide-ment; **he whipped out a revolver** il a sorti brusquement un revolver; **to w. out sb's ap-pendix** enlever l'appendice de qn

VI *(go out)* sortir en vitesse; **I'm just whip-ping out to the library** je file à la biblio-thèque

▸ **whip round VI** *Fam* **1** *(turn)* se retourner vi-vement **2** *(go quickly)* **w. round to the chem-ist's for me** fais un saut à la pharmacie pour moi

▸ **whip up VT SEP 1** *(arouse) (horse)* toucher (du fouet); *Fig* **to w. up an audience** galvani-ser *ou* exalter un public **2** *Parl (summon) (members of party)* faire passer un appel ur-gent à; **to w. up support for sth** susciter un soutien en faveur de qch **3** *Culin (egg whites)* battre en neige; *(cream)* battre, fouetter; *Fam* **I'll w. you up something to eat** je vais te préparer *ou* te faire quelque chose à man-ger en vitesse; *Fam* **I'll see what I can w. up** je vais voir ce que je peux préparer en vitesse

whipcord ['wɪpkɔːd] **N 1** *(on whip)* mèche *f* de fouet **2** *Tex* whipcord *m*; **w. trousers** pan-talon *m* en whipcord

whiplash ['wɪplæʃ] **N 1** *(stroke of whip)* coup *m* de fouet; *Fig* **tongue like a w.** langue cinglante **2** *Med (injury)* coup *m* du lapin, *Spec* syndrome *m* cervical traumatique

▸▸ *Med* **w. effect** effet *m* du coup du lapin; *Med* **w. injury** coup du lapin, *Spec* syndrome cervical traumatique

whipper-in [wɪpər-] **N** *(of hounds)* piqueur *m*

whippersnapper ['wɪpəsnæpər] **N** *Fam* petit malin *m*

whippet ['wɪpɪt] **N** *(dog)* whippet *m*

whipping ['wɪpɪŋ] **N** correction; **to give sb a w.** donner une correction à qn

▸▸ **w. boy** bouc *m* émissaire; **w. cream** ≃ crème *f* fraîche (à fouetter)

whippoorwill ['wɪpʊwɪl] **N** *Am (bird)* en-

goulevent *m* de Virginie, *Can* engoulevent bois-pourri

whipround ['wɪpraʊnd] **N** *Br Fam* quête *f*, collecte *f*; **to have a w. for sb** organiser une collecte pour qn

whir [wɜːr] **N, VI** = **whirr**

whirl [wɜːl] **N** *(of wheel)* mouvement *m* gira-toire; *(of leaves, dust)* tourbillon *m*, tournoie-ment *m*; *Fig Fam* **would you like to give it a w.?** tu veux essayer?; *Fig Fam* **I'll have a w. at it** je vais tenter le coup; **a w. of activity** un tourbillon d'activités; **my head's in a w.** la tête me tourne; **the social w.** les tourbillons de la vie mondaine

VI *(of dead leaves etc)* tourbillonner, tour-noyer; *(of propeller etc)* tourner; *(of top)* tournoyer; **whirling dervish** derviche *m* tourneur; **my head's whirling** la tête me tourne; **the thoughts that were whirling through my head** les pensées qui tourbil-lonnaient dans ma tête

VT *(dead leaves etc)* faire tournoyer, faire tourbillonner; **to w. sb/sth around** *(of per-son)* faire tournoyer qn/qch autour de soi; **he whirled her onto the dance floor** il l'a en-traînée en tournoyant sur la piste de danse

▸ **whirl along VI** filer à toute vitesse *ou* à toute allure

VT SEP entraîner à toute vitesse *ou* à fond de train; **the train whirled us along** le train nous emportait à grande allure

▸ **whirl round VI** *(of person)* se retourner brusquement; *(of dancer)* pirouetter; *(of leaves)* tourbillonner, tournoyer; **she whir-led round and round in the middle of the dance floor** elle tournait et tournait au mi-lieu de la piste de danse

VT SEP **to w. sb round** faire tournoyer qn

whirligig ['wɜːlɪgɪg] **N** *(top)* tourniquet *m*; *(merry-go-round)* manège *m* de chevaux de bois

whirlpool ['wɜːlpuːl] **N** tourbillon *m* (d'eau), gouffre *m*; *Fig* **a w. of violence** un tourbillon de violence

▸▸ **w. bath** bain *m* à remous, Jacuzzi® *m*

whirlwind ['wɜːlwɪnd] **N** tourbillon *m* (de vent), trombe *f* (de vent); **to come in like a w.** entrer comme une tornade

▸▸ **w. romance** aventure *f* enivrante; **w. tour** visite *f* éclair

whirlybird ['wɜːlɪbɜːd] **N** *Old-fashioned Fam (helicopter)* hélico *m*

whirr [wɜːr] **N** *(of machines)* ronflement *m*, ronronnement *m*; *(of propeller etc)* vrombis-sement *m*

VI *(of machinery etc)* ronfler, ronronner; *(of propeller)* vrombir

whisk [wɪsk] **N 1** *(for beating eggs)* fouet *m*, batteur *m* **2** *(action)* **give the eggs a w.** bat-tre les œufs; **a w. of the tail/the duster** un coup de queue/de chiffon

VT 1 to w. its tail *(of cow etc)* agiter sa queue; **to w. a duster over the table** donner un coup de chiffon sur la table **2** *(move quickly)* **he was whisked to hospital** il a été trans-porté à l'hôpital de toute urgence; **she whis-ked it out of sight** elle l'a caché d'un mouvement rapide **3** *Culin (eggs)* battre; *(cream)* fouetter

VI **she whisked past me** elle est passée de-vant moi comme un éclair

▸ **whisk away, whisk off VT SEP** *(thing)* enle-ver d'un geste rapide; *(person)* emporter très rapidement; **to w. away a fly** chasser une mouche; **the president was whisked away in a helicopter** le président a été emmené à toute vitesse en hélicoptère; **he was whis-ked away to hospital in an ambulance** il a été transporté de toute urgence en ambu-lance à l'hôpital

▸ **whisk up VT SEP** *Culin (eggs)* battre; *(cream)* fouetter

whisker ['wɪskər] N whiskers *(of man) (side whiskers)* favoris *mpl*; *(moustache)* moustache *f*, *(beard)* barbe *f*, *(of cat, mouse etc)* moustache(s) *f(pl)*; *Sport Fig* **to win by a w.** gagner d'un poil *ou* de justesse; *Fig* **to escape death by a w.** frôler la mort, échapper de justesse à la mort

whiskered ['wɪskəd] ADJ *(man)* qui porte des favoris

whisky, *Ir, Am* **whiskey** ['wɪskɪ] N whisky *m*; **two whiskies** deux whiskies; **a w. and soda** un whisky soda; **w. on the rocks** whisky avec des glaçons, *Can* whisky sur glace *ou* aux glaçons
▸▸ **w. company** société *f* de fabrication de whisky; **w. distillery** distillerie *f* de whisky; **w. glass** verre *m* à whisky; **w. mac** = boisson *f* à base de whisky et d'alcool au gingembre; **w. sour** = cocktail *m* à base de whisky et de jus de citron

whisper ['wɪspər] N **1** *(of person speaking)* chuchotement *m*; *esp Lit (of wind in leaves)* bruissement *m*; **to speak in a w.** *or* **in whispers** chuchoter, parler en chuchotant; **to say sth in a w.** chuchoter qch, dire qch tout bas; **... she said in a loud w.** ... chuchota-t-elle assez fort **2** *(rumour)* rumeur *f*, bruit *m*; **I've heard whispers** *or* **a w. that ...** j'ai entendu dire que ...; **and remember, not a w. of it to anyone!** et souviens-toi, pas un mot à qui que ce soit!
VI *(of person speaking)* chuchoter, parler bas; *esp Lit (of wind in leaves)* bruire; **to w. to sb** chuchoter à l'oreille de qn, parler à voix basse à qn; **stop whispering, Evans!** ça suffit les messes basses, Evans!
VT **1 to w. sth to sb** chuchoter qch à qn, dire qch à voix basse à qn; **what were you whispering to her?** qu'est-ce que tu lui disais à l'oreille?; **whispered conversation** conversation à voix basse **2** *(as rumour)* **it is being whispered that ...** le bruit court que ..., on dit que ...

whispering ['wɪspərɪŋ] N **1** *(of person speaking)* chuchotement *m*; *esp Lit (of wind)* bruissement *m*; **stop that w.!** ça suffit les messes basses! **2** *Pej (rumours)* rumeur *f*
▸▸ **w. campaign** campagne *f* de diffamation; *Archit* **w. gallery** galerie *f* à écho

whist [wɪst] N *Cards* whist *m*; **to have a game of w.** faire une partie de whist; **to play w.** jouer au whist
▸▸ **w. drive** tournoi *m* de whist; **w. player** joueur, -euse de whist

whistle ['wɪs(ə)l] N **1** *(noise)* sifflement *m*; *(blow on a whistle)* coup *m* de sifflet; **she gave a w. of surprise** elle a sifflé de surprise; *Sport* **final w.** coup de sifflet final **2** *(object)* sifflet *m*; **to blow a w.** donner un coup de sifflet; *Sport* **to blow the w. for a foul/for half-time** siffler une faute/la mi-temps; *Fig Fam* **to blow the w. on sth** révéler *ou* dévoiler qch; *Fig Fam* **to blow the w. on sb** dénoncer qn; *Fig Fam* **who blew the w.?** qui a vendu la mèche?
VI *(of person, bird, wind etc)* siffler; *(on whistle)* donner un coup de sifflet; **she whistled in surprise** elle a sifflé de surprise; **the bullet whistled past his ear** la balle a passé en sifflant tout près de son oreille; *Fig* **to w. in the dark** essayer de se rassurer; **to w. for one's dog/a taxi** siffler son chien/un taxi; *Fig Fam* **he can w. for his money** il peut courir après son argent; *Fig Fam* **you can w. for it!** tu peux toujours courir!
VT *(tune)* siffler, siffloter; *Sport* **to w. half-time** siffler la mi-temps
▸ **whistle up** VT SEP *Fam* **I'll w. up a few friends to help us** je vais trouver quelques amis pour nous aider; **can you w. up some more sandwiches?** peux-tu nous avoir *ou* dégoter quelques sandwichs?

whistle-blower N *Fig Fam* personne *f* qui vend la mèche; **we need a few more whistle-blowers like her** il faudrait d'autres personnes comme elle pour tirer sur la sonnette d'alarme

whistler ['wɪslər] N **1** *(person)* siffleur, -euse **2** *(bird)* oiseau *m* siffleur **3** *(animal)* siffleur *m*, marmotte *f* canadienne, *Can* siffleux *m*

whistle-stop N **1** *Am Rail* arrêt *m* facultatif **2** *(town)* village *m* perdu
ADJ **she made a w. tour of Europe** elle a fait une tournée rapide en Europe
VI *Am Pol* = faire une tournée électorale en passant par des petites villes
▸▸ **w. town** village perdu

whistling ['wɪslɪŋ] N sifflement *m*

Whit [wɪt] N Pentecôte *f*
▸▸ **W. Monday** lundi *m* de Pentecôte; **W. Sunday** dimanche *m* de Pentecôte

whit [wɪt] N *(usu in neg)* brin *m*; **it won't make a w. of difference** ça ne changera rien à rien; **it doesn't matter a w.** ça n'a aucune espèce d'importance; **she doesn't care a w. about him or anyone else** elle se fiche de lui comme de l'an quarante; **he's not a w. the better for it** il ne s'en porte nullement mieux; **I don't care a w.** je m'en moque comme de ma première chemise *ou* comme de l'an quarante

white [waɪt] ADJ blanc, *f* blanche; **as w. as snow** blanc comme la neige; **we had a w. Christmas** on a eu de la neige à Noël; **to turn** *or* **go w.** *(of face)* devenir blanc *ou* pâle *ou* blême; *(of hair)* blanchir; **he's going w.** *(hair)* il commence à blanchir; **he went w. overnight** ses cheveux sont devenus blancs du jour au lendemain; **w. with fear** blanc de peur; **w. as a ghost/sheet** pâle comme la mort/un linge; *Fig* **whiter than w.** *(person)* blanc comme neige; **do you take your coffee w.?** tu prends du lait dans ton café?; **a w. man** un Blanc; **the w. man's burden** = obligation *f* pour les blancs d'assurer l'instruction des habitants noirs de leurs colonies
N **1** *(colour)* blanc *m*; **dressed in w.** habillé en blanc *ou* de blanc; **whites** *(linen)* blanc; *Sport* tenue *f* de sport blanche; **wash your whites with Jizmo** lavez votre linge avec Jizmo **2** *(person)* blanc *m*, blanche *f* **3** *(of egg, eyes)* blanc *m*
VT *Rel, Fig* **whited sepulchre** sépulcre *m* blanchi
▸▸ **w. alloy** métal *m* blanc; **w. ant** fourmi *f* blanche, termite *m*; **w. blood cell** globule *m* blanc, leucocyte *m*; **w. chocolate** chocolat *m* blanc; **w. coat** blouse *f* blanche; *Med Fam* **w.-coat syndrome** syndrome *m* de la blouse blanche; **w. coffee** café *m* au lait; *Astron* **w. dwarf** naine *f* blanche; **w. elephant** *(useless construction)* = réalisation *f* de prestige dont l'utilité ne justifie pas le coût; **the fear is that the new museum will turn out to be another w. elephant** on craint que le nouveau musée ne soit une nouvelle construction coûteuse et peu utile; *Br* **w. elephant stall** *(at fair, jumble sale)* stand *m* de bibelots; *Naut* **w. ensign** pavillon *m* blanc; *Hist* **w. feather** = symbole *m* de lâcheté; *Br* **w. fish** poisson *m* à chair blanche; **w. flag** drapeau *m* blanc; **w. flour** farine *f* de ménage; **w. gold** or *m* blanc; **w. goods** *(household equipment)* appareils *mpl* ménagers; *(linen)* linge *m* de maison, blanc; **w. hope** espoir *m*; **w. horses** *(waves)* moutons *mpl*; **the W. House** la Maison-Blanche; *Fig* **w. knight** sauveur *m*, chevalier *m* blanc; **w. lie** pieux mensonge *m*; *Fam* **w. lightning** tord-boyaux *m inv* *(distillé illégalement)*; **w. magic** magie *f* blanche; **w. meat** viande *f* blanche; *(of poultry)* blanc; **w. metal** métal blanc; *Br* **w. meter heating** = système *m* de chauffage permettant d'ac-

cumuler la chaleur pendant les heures creuses; **w. noise** bruit *m* de fond; *Am* **W. Out®** correcteur *m* liquide; *Br* **w. paper** *(government report)* livre *m* blanc; **w. pepper** poivre *m* blanc; *Culin* **w. pudding** boudin *m* blanc; **W. Russia** Russie *f* Blanche; *Am* **w. sale** promotion *f* sur le blanc; **w. sauce** sauce *f* blanche; **w. shark** requin *m* blanc; **w. slavery** traite *f* des blanches; **w. space** *(on page)* espace *m* blanc; **w. spirit** white-spirit *m*; **w. stick** *(of blind person)* canne *f* blanche; **w. supremacist** partisan, -ane de la suprématie (de la race) blanche; **w. supremacy** suprématie *f* (de la race) blanche; *Aviat Sl* **w. tail** = avion *m* n'appartenant encore à aucune compagnie aérienne; **w. tie** *(formal clothes)* habit *m*; *(on invitation)* ≃ tenue de soirée exigée; *Pej* **w. trash** Blancs *mpl* pauvres; **w. water** eau *f* vive; **w. wedding** mariage *m* en blanc; **she's having a w. wedding** elle se marie en blanc; **w. whale** bélouga *m*, béluga *m*
▸ **white out** VT SEP *(delete)* masquer au vernis correcteur blanc

whitebait ['waɪtbeɪt] N *(fish)* blanchaille *f*, **a dish of w.** un plat de friture

whiteboard ['waɪtbɔːd] N tableau *m* blanc

whitebread ['waɪtbred] ADJ *Am Pej* conventionnel

whitecaps ['waɪtkæps] NPL *(waves)* moutons *mpl*

white-collar ADJ
▸▸ **w. crime** délits *mpl* financiers; **w. union** syndicat *m* d'employés de bureau; **w. worker** employé *m* de bureau, col *m* blanc

white-faced [-'feɪst] ADJ au visage pâle

whitefish ['waɪtfɪʃ] N corégone *m*

white-haired ADJ aux cheveux blancs
▸▸ *Am Fig* **w. boy** chouchou *m*

Whitehall ['waɪthɔːl] N *(British government)* l'Administration *f* britannique

> **Whitehall**
> De nombreux services gouvernementaux ont leurs bureaux dans cette rue londonienne dont le nom est souvent employé pour désigner le gouvernement lui-même.

white-headed ADJ **1** *(animal)* à tête blanche **2** *(person)* aux cheveux blancs
▸▸ *Am Fig* **w. boy** chouchou *m*

white-hot ADJ chauffé *ou* porté à blanc

white-knuckle ADJ *Fam* **I'm a w. flyer** j'ai la trouille en avion; **a w. ride** *(at fair etc)* un manège terrifiant

white-livered [-lɪvəd] ADJ *Fig (person)* poltron

whiten ['waɪt(ə)n] VT **1** *(hair, linen, shoes)* blanchir **2** *(with whitewash)* blanchir à la chaux, badigeonner de chaux
VI blanchir; *(with fear etc)* pâlir, blêmir

whiteness ['waɪtnɪs] N *(of snow, skin)* blancheur *f*, *(of face)* pâleur *f*

white-on-black N *Typ* noir au blanc *m*

whiteout ['waɪtaʊt] N visibilité *f* nulle (à cause de la neige); **in w. conditions** dans des conditions de visibilité nulle

white-slaver N personne *f* qui se livre à la traite des blanches

whitethorn ['waɪtθɔːn] N *(tree)* aubépine *f*

whitethroat ['waɪtθrəʊt] N *(bird)* fauvette *f* grisette

whitewall ['waɪtwɔːl] N **w. (tyre** *or Am* **tire)** pneu *m* à flanc blanc

whitewash ['waɪtwɒʃ] N **1** *(paint)* blanc *m ou* lait *m* de chaux, badigeon *m* à la chaux; **to give a wall a coat of w.** badigeonner un mur (à la chaux) **2** *Fig (dishonest exonera-*

tion) blanchiment *m*; **a w. (job)** une opération de blanchiment **3** *Sport Fam* défaite *f* à zéro, raclée *f*

VT 1 *(paint)* peindre *ou* blanchir à la chaux, badigeonner en blanc **2** *Fig (exonerate dishonestly)* blanchir; *(events, episode)* maquiller **3** *Sport Fam (one's opponents)* battre à plate couture, donner une raclée à

whitewashing ['waɪtwɒʃɪŋ] **N 1** *(painting)* peinture *f* à la chaux, badigeonnage *m* **2** *Fig (of sb's reputation)* blanchiment *m*

whitewood ['waɪtwʊd] **N** bois *m* blanc

whitey ['waɪtɪ] **N** *Am Pej* blanc *m*, blanche *f*; *(npl)* les blancs

whither ['wɪðər] **ADV, CONJ** *Arch, Lit* **1** *(interr)* où, vers quel lieu; **w. Britain?** où va la Grande-Bretagne? **2** *(rel)* (là) où; **I shall go w. fate leads me** j'irai là où me mènera le destin

whiting ['waɪtɪŋ] **N** *(fish)* merlan *m*

whitish ['waɪtɪʃ] **ADJ** blanchâtre

whitlow ['wɪtləʊ] **N** *Med* panaris *m*

Whitney system ['wɪtnɪ] **N** *(in hotel)* planning *m* Whitney

Whitsun(tide) ['wɪtsən(taɪd)] **N** (la fête *ou* la saison de) la Pentecôte

whittle ['wɪt(ə)l] **VT** *(stick)* tailler (au couteau)

▸ **whittle away VT SEP** *(one's capital)* rogner, manger; *(resistance)* faire tomber petit à petit; **our capital/lead has been whittled away** notre capital/avance a été réduit(e) à presque rien

▸ **whittle down VT SEP** *(one's capital)* rogner, manger; **we've whittled down the number of candidates** nous avons réduit le nombre des candidats; **can you w. it down by another 5%?** peux-tu le réduire d'encore 5%?

Whitworth thread ['wɪtwəθ] **N** *Tech* filetage *m* Whitworth

whizz [wɪz] **INT** pan!

N 1 *(of bullet)* sifflement *m* **2** *Fam (expert)* as *m*, crack *m* (**at** en); **he's a real w. in the kitchen** il cuisine comme un chef; **she's a real w. with computers** c'est un as en informatique **3** *Br Sl (amphetamines)* amphés *fpl*, amphets *fpl* **4** *Am Sl* **to take a w.** *(urinate)* faire pipi

VI 1 *(of bullet etc)* siffler **2** *Fam (move quickly)* **we were whizzing along at top speed** on fonçait; **the cars whizzed past** les voitures passaient à toute allure; **she whizzed back into the house to get some money** elle retourna dare-dare à la maison chercher de l'argent

▸▸ *Fam* **w. kid** jeune prodige *m*

▸ **whizz by VI** *Fam (of traffic)* passer à toute vitesse; *(of holiday, time etc)* passer à toute vitesse, filer

▸ **whizz through VT INSEP** *Fam (work)* faire à toute vitesse; *(meal)* avaler; *(book)* lire à toute vitesse

WHO [dʌb(ə)lju:eɪtʃ'əʊ] **N** *(abbr* **World Health Organization)** OMS *f*

who [hu:] **PRON 1** *(interr) (subject)* qui, qui est-ce qui; *(object)* qui, qui est-ce que; **w. is it?** qui est-ce?; **w. with?** avec qui?; **w. is that woman?** qui est cette femme?; **w. on earth told you that?** qui diable vous a dit cela?; *Tel* **w.'s speaking?** qui est à l'appareil?; *Tel* **may I ask w.'s speaking?** *(when taking call for another)* c'est de la part de qui?; **w. is this?** *(on telephone)* qui êtes-vous?; **w. did you say?** qui ça?; **w. does he think he is?** pour qui se prend-il?; **w. of us can still remember it?** qui parmi nous *ou* lesquels d'entre nous se le rappelle(nt) encore?; **w. do you want?** qui voulez-vous?; **w. were you talking to?** à qui parliez-vous?; **to know w.'s w.** *(the right people)* avoir des relations; **you'll soon find out w.'s w.** *(who people are)*

tu connaîtras très vite tout le monde; **tell me w.'s w.** dites-moi qui est qui VOIR GRAMMAIRE A31; B17

2 *(rel)* qui; *(to avoid ambiguity), Fml* lequel, laquelle, *pl* lesquels, lesquelles; *(independent rel)* (celui/celle/etc) qui; **the friends w. came yesterday** les amis qui sont venus hier; **Louise's father, w. is very rich** le père de Louise, qui *ou Fml* lequel est très riche; **deny it w. will** le nie qui voudra VOIR GRAMMAIRE A32–3; B22–3

whoa [wəʊ] **INT** *(to horse)* ho!, holà!; *Fam (to person)* doucement!, attendez!

whodun(n)it [hu:'dʌnɪt] **N** *Fam (novel)* roman *m* policier; *(film)* film *m* policier

whoever [hu:'evər] **PRON 1** *(anyone that)* celui/celle/etc qui, quiconque; **w. finds it may keep it** celui qui le trouvera pourra le garder **2** *(no matter who)* qui que + *subj*; **w. you are, speak!** qui que vous soyez, parlez!; **w. wrote that letter** qui que ce soit qui ait écrit cette lettre; *Fam* **... or w.** ... ou qui que ce soit; **w. she marries** qui que ce soit qu'elle épousera, celui qu'elle épousera; **w. you like** qui vous voudrez VOIR GRAMMAIRE A33 **3** *(intensive)* **w. can that be at this time of night?** qui cela peut-il bien être à cette heure tardive? VOIR GRAMMAIRE A32

whole [həʊl] **ADJ 1** *(entire)* entier, complet, -ète; **cook the fish w.** faites cuire le poisson entier; **he swallowed it w.** *(food)* il l'a avalé sans le mâcher; *Fig* il a pris ça pour de l'argent comptant; **a w. loaf** un pain entier; **to tell the w. truth** dire toute la vérité; **the w. world** le monde entier; **do you have to tell the w. world?** est-ce que tu tiens à ce que le monde le sache?; **to last a w. week** durer toute une semaine; **I never saw her the w. evening** je ne l'ai pas vue de (toute) la soirée; **w. families died of it** des familles entières en sont mortes; *Fam* **to go the w. hog** aller jusqu'au bout; **they went the w. hog for the party** ils n'ont pas fait les choses à moitié pour la fête VOIR GRAMMAIRE A36

2 *(emphatic)* tout, entier, tout entier; **I don't think it will make a w. lot of difference** je ne pense pas que ça fasse une énorme différence; **we've had a w. heap of problems** nous avons eu tout un tas de problèmes; **the w. lot of you** vous tous; **there's still a w. lot left** il en reste encore plein; **for a w. lot of reasons** pour tout un tas de raisons **3** *(intact) (thing)* intact; *Bible* **his hand was made w.** sa main fut guérie

N tout *m*, totalité *f*, ensemble *m*; **the w. of the school** l'école entière, toute l'école; **nearly the w. of our resources** la presque totalité de nos ressources; **he spent the w. of that year in London** il a passé toute cette année-là à Londres; **the w. amounts to ...** le total se monte à ...; **to buy/sell sth as a w.** acheter/vendre qch en bloc; **taken as a w.** pris dans sa totalité; **on the w.** dans l'ensemble; **the w. is greater than the sum of its parts** le tout est plus grand que la somme des parties

▸▸ **w. milk** lait *m* entier; *Math* **w. number** *(integer)* nombre *m* entier

wholefood ['həʊlfu:d] **N** aliments *mpl* complets; **w. shop** magasin *m* diététique

wholehearted [həʊl'hɑ:tɪd] **ADJ** *(enthusiasm, support etc)* sans réserve; *(laugh)* qui vient du cœur; **she was less than w. in her endorsement of him** elle ne l'approuvait qu'à moitié; **a w. admirer** un admirateur inconditionnel; **she had never really been w. in her commitment to Europe** elle n'a jamais été convaincue à 100% par l'Europe

wholeheartedly [həʊl'hɑ:tɪdlɪ] **ADV** de bon *ou* de grand *ou* de tout cœur; *(to agree)* de tout cœur; **to support sb w.** soutenir qn sans réserve *ou* inconditionnellement; **I admire you w.** je vous admire sans réserve

wholemeal ['həʊlmi:l] **ADJ** *Br (bread, flour)* complet, -ète

wholeness ['həʊlnɪs] **N** intégralité *f*, intégrité *f*

wholesale ['həʊlseɪl] **N** (vente *f* en) gros *m*; **w. and retail** gros et détail

ADJ 1 *Com* de gros, en gros **2** *Fig* **by w. borrowing** en empruntant de tous côtés; **a w. slaughter** un massacre, une tuerie en masse

ADV 1 **to sell/buy w.** vendre/acheter en gros; **I can get it for you w.** je peux vous l'avoir au prix de gros **2** *Fig* en masse, en bloc; **communities have been destroyed w.** des communautés entières ont été détruites

▸▸ *Fin* **w. bank** banque *f* de gros; **w. co-operative** coopérative *f* d'achats; **w. customer** client, -ente qui achète en gros; **w. dealer** grossiste *mf*, commerçant, -ante en gros; **w. distribution** distribution *f* en gros; **w. goods** marchandises *fpl* de gros; *Banking* **w. market** marché *m* de gré à gré entre banques; **w. merchant** grossiste, commerçant, -ante en gros; **w. price** prix *m* de gros; **w. price index** indice *m* des prix de gros; **w. trade** commerce *m* de gros; **w. trader** grossiste

wholesaler ['həʊlseɪlər] **N** grossiste *mf*, commerçant, -ante en gros

▸▸ **w. margin** marge *f* du grossiste

wholesaling ['həʊlseɪlɪŋ] **N** vente *f* en gros

wholesome ['həʊlsəm] **ADJ** *(food)* sain; *(air, climate)* salubre; *(person, appearance)* comme il faut; **a very w. young man** un petit jeune homme propre sur lui; **she has a w. appearance** elle a l'air rangé, elle a l'air (bien) comme il faut

wholesomeness ['həʊlsəmnɪs] **N** *(of food)* nature *f* saine; *(of air)* salubrité *f*; **the w. of her appearance** son côté rangé *ou* (bien) comme il faut

wholewheat ['həʊlwi:t] **ADJ** *Am (bread, flour)* complet(ète)

wholly ['həʊllɪ] **ADV** tout à fait, complètement, entièrement

wholly-owned subsidiary **N** *Com* filiale *f* à 100%

whom [hu:m] **PRON** *(objective case)* often *Fml* **1** *(interr)* qui, qui est-ce que; **w. did you see?** qui avez-vous vu?, qui est-ce que vous avez vu?; **to w./of w. are you speaking?** à qui/de qui parlez-vous?; **I don't know to w. to turn** je ne sais à qui m'adresser VOIR GRAMMAIRE A31; B17 **2** *(rel) (direct object)* que, lequel, laquelle, *pl* lesquels, lesquelles; *(indirect object and after prep)* qui; **the woman w. you saw** la femme que vous avez vue; **somebody to w. he could talk** quelqu'un à qui il pouvait parler; **the friend of w. I speak** l'ami dont je parle; **these two men, both of w. were quite young** ces deux hommes, qui l'un et l'autre étaient tout jeunes VOIR GRAMMAIRE A32; B22 **3** *(independent rel)* celui/celle/etc que, qui; **those w. the gods love die young** qui est aimé des dieux meurt jeune

whomsoever [hu:msəʊ'evər] **PRON** *Fml* **1** *(any person whom)* celui (quel qu'il soit) que; **w. they choose** celui qu'ils choisiront **2** *(no matter whom)* qui que ce soit que

whoop **N 1** [wu:p] *(shout)* cri *m* (de joie); *Am (of owl)* (h)ululement *m*; *esp Am Iron* **big w.!** la belle affaire! **2** [hu:p] *Med (in whooping cough)* quinte *f*

VI 1 [wu:p] *(shout)* crier, pousser des cris (de joie); *Am (of owl)* (h)ululer; *Fam* **to w. it up** *(have good time, celebrate)* faire la noce **2** [hu:p] *Med* = tousser convulsivement à cause d'une coqueluche; **she's been whooping all night** elle a eu des quintes de toux toute la nuit

whoopee [wʊ'pi:] **INT** youpi

['wʊpi:] **N** *Old-fashioned Fam* **to make w.**

(enjoy oneself) faire la noce *ou* la bombe; *(sexually)* faire l'amour

whooper ['hu:pər] N
▸▸**w. swan** cygne *m* chanteur *ou* sauvage

whooping cough ['hu:pɪŋ] N coqueluche *f*

whoops [wʊps] INT houp-là!

whop [wɒp] VT (**-pp-**) *Fam* **1** *(hit)* battre, rosser **2** *(defeat)* battre à plates coutures, massacrer

whopper ['wɒpər] N *Fam* **1** *(huge thing)* quelque chose de colossal *ou* d'énorme; **a w. of a fish** un poisson énorme *ou* maous(se); **it's a real w.!** il est énorme! **2** *(lie)* énorme *ou* gros mensonge *m*

whopping ['wɒpɪŋ] *Fam* ADJ énorme; **it costs a w. £3,000** ça coûte la coquette somme de trois mille livres
ADV **a w. great lie** un mensonge énorme; **that was a w. huge mistake!** c'était une sacrée bourde!

whore [hɔ:r] N prostituée *f*, *Sl* putain *f*
VI *Old-fashioned, Lit (of man)* **to w., to go whoring** fréquenter les prostituées

whorehouse ['hɔ:haʊs] N *Fam* bordel *m*

whoremonger ['hɔ:mʌŋgər] N *Arch* habitué *m* des lieux de débauche; **he was a w.** il fréquentait les filles de petite vertu

whoring ['hɔ:rɪŋ] N *Old-fashioned, Lit* **1** *(by woman)* prostitution *f* **2** *(by man)* **because of all his w.** parce qu'il n'arrêtait pas de fréquenter les prostituées

whorl [wɜ:l] N **1** *Bot* verticille *m* **2** *(turn of spiral)* spire *f*, volute *f*, *(of shell)* spire, enroulement *m*; *(of fingerprint)* sillon *m*

whorled [wɜ:ld] ADJ *(flower)* verticillé *m*; *(shell)* convoluté

whortleberry ['wɜ:t(ə)lberɪ] N *(fruit)* airelle *f* myrtille *f*

whose [hu:z] POSS PRON **1** *(interr)* de qui; *(ownership)* à qui; **w. are these gloves?** à qui sont ces gants?; **w. daughter are you?** de qui êtes-vous la fille?; **w. fault is it?** à qui la faute?; **w. book did you borrow?** à qui avez-vous emprunté un livre?; **w. is this?** à qui est-ce? VOIR GRAMMAIRE A31 **2** *(rel)* dont; *(after prep)* de qui, duquel, de laquelle, *pl* desquels, desquelles; **the pupil w. work I showed you** l'élève dont je vous ai montré le travail; **the man to w. wife I gave the money** l'homme à la femme de qui *ou* duquel j'ai donné l'argent VOIR GRAMMAIRE A33; B23

whosoever [hu:səʊ'evər] PRON *Arch, Fml =* **whoever**

Who's Who N *Br* ≃ Bottin *m* mondain

why [waɪ] ADV, CONJ **1** *(interr)* pourquoi, pour quelle raison; **w. (ever) didn't you say so?** pourquoi ne l'avez-vous pas dit?; **w. not?** pourquoi pas?; **w. not agree?** pourquoi ne pas accepter?; **w. bother?** à quoi bon (s'en donner la peine)?; **w. get angry?** à quoi bon se mettre en colère? VOIR GRAMMAIRE A41

2 *(rel)* pourquoi; **that is (the reason) w. ...** voilà pourquoi ..., c'est pourquoi ...; **w. he should always be late I do not understand** qu'il soit toujours en retard, je ne me l'explique pas; **I'll tell you w.** je vais vous dire pourquoi
N *(pl* **whys**) pourquoi *m*, raison *f*; **I like to know the whys and wherefores of things** j'aime connaître le pourquoi et le comment des choses
INT **1** *(surprise)* **w., it's David!** tiens, mais c'est David!; **w., you're not afraid, are you?** vous n'avez tout de même pas peur, si? **2** *(protest)* **w., it's simple** allons, c'est simple; **w., what's the harm?** mais quel mal y a-t-il? **3** *(hesitation)* **w., I really don't know** vraiment *ou* franchement je ne sais pas

4 *(introducing consequence)* **if this doesn't do, w. we must try something else** si ceci ne réussit pas, alors *ou* eh bien il faudra essayer autre chose

WI [dʌb(ə)lju:'aɪ] N **1** *Br abbr* **Women's Institute 2** *abbr* **West Indies**

wick [wɪk] N **1** *(of lamp, candle)* mèche *f* **2** *Br Sl* **she gets on my w.** elle me tape sur les nerfs; **it gets on my w. that he's always there** ça me tape sur les nerfs qu'il soit toujours là

wicked ['wɪkɪd] ADJ **1** *(evil)* mauvais, méchant; *(crime)* atroce, affreux; **what a w. thing to do!** qu'est-ce que c'est méchant!; **a w. lie** un affreux mensonge; *Fam* **you w. little thing!** *(to child)* petit vilain!/petite vilaine!

2 *Fig (dreadful) (weather)* affreux, atroce; *(pain)* cruel, atroce; **he's got a w. temper** il a très mauvais caractère; **it's w. to waste so much food** c'est un crime de gaspiller tant de nourriture; **they're asking a w. price for their house** ils ont mis leur maison en vente à un prix exorbitant; **it's a w. shame that ...** il est scandaleux que ... + *sub*
3 *Fig (mischievous)* malicieux, espiègle
4 *Sl (good)* génial, -aux, super; **she makes a w. curry** elle fait un curry d'enfer
NPL **the w.** les méchants *mpl*; *Hum* **(there's) no rest for the w.** pas de répit pour les braves

wickedly ['wɪkɪdlɪ] ADV **1** *(evilly)* méchamment **2** *Fig (extremely)* terriblement, affreusement; **w. expensive** hors de prix; **w. funny** à mourir de rire; **she makes a w. good curry** elle fait un curry d'enfer **3** *(mischievously)* malicieusement; **she was smiling w.** elle souriait d'un air malicieux

wickedness ['wɪkɪdnɪs] N méchanceté *f*, perversité *f*, *(of crime)* atrocité *f*

wicker ['wɪkər] N osier *m*; **a w. basket/chair** un panier/une chaise en osier

wickerwork ['wɪkəwɜ:k] N *(material)* osier *m*; *(objects)* vannerie *f*, **is the chair made of w.?** est-ce que la chaise est en osier?; **they sell w.** ils vendent de la vannerie

wicket ['wɪkɪt] N **1** *(beside large door etc)* *(door)* porte *f* à piétons; *(gate)* petite porte à claire-voie **2** *Am (in bank, post office etc)* guichet *m* **3** *Cr (sticks)* guichet *m*; *(area)* terrain *m* entre les guichets; **to take/lose a w.** prendre/perdre un guichet; **to keep w.** garder les guichets
▸▸**w. door** porte à piétons; **w. gate** petite porte à claire-voie

wicketkeeper ['wɪkɪtki:pər] N *Cr* gardien *m* de guichet

widdle ['wɪdəl] *Br Fam* N **to have a w.** *(urinate)* faire pipi
VI faire pipi

wide [waɪd] ADJ **1** *(broad) (road, river)* large; *(desert, ocean)* vaste; *(garment)* ample, large; **the road gets wider after the village** la route s'élargit après le village; **to be five metres w.** faire cinq mètres de large *ou* de largeur; **how w. is the room?** quelle est la largeur de la pièce?, combien est-ce que la pièce fait de large?; **to travel the w. world** parcourir le vaste monde; **in the whole w. world** dans le monde entier; **to give a w. yawn** bâiller en ouvrant largement la bouche; *Phot* **w. angle of view** grand angle de champ

2 *(extensive) (range, experience, knowledge)* étendu, vaste, ample; *(influence)* répandu; **there is a w. difference between ...** il y a une grande différence entre ...; **in a wider sense** dans un sens plus large, par extension; **in the widest sense of the word** dans l'acception la plus large du mot
3 *Br Fam (cocky)* culotté, gonflé
ADV **1** *(far)* loin; **w. apart** espacé; **with one's**

legs w. apart les jambes très écartées
2 *(to open etc)* largement, grandement; **to fling the door open w.** *or* **w. open** ouvrir la porte toute grande; **w.-open door** porte toute grande ouverte; **to open one's eyes w.** ouvrir les yeux tout grands; **to be w. awake** être largement *ou* bien éveillé; *Fig* avoir l'esprit vif; *Boxing* **to leave oneself w. open** se découvrir; *Fig* **to leave oneself w. open to criticism** prêter le flanc à *ou* s'exposer à la critique; **this town is w. open (to attack)** cette ville est très exposée (aux attaques); *Aut* **to take a bend w.** prendre un virage large
3 *(to fall, shoot)* loin du but; **w. of the mark** *(far from target)* loin du but; *(far from truth)* loin de la réalité *ou* de la vérité
N *Cr* balle *f* écartée *ou* qui passe hors de la portée du batteur
▸▸*Comput* **w. area network** réseau *m* longue distance; *Br Fam Pej* **w. boy** escroc *m*, fricoteur *m*; *Aut* **w. load** *(notice on vehicle) =* convoi exceptionnel; *Cin, TV* **w. shot** plan *m* d'ensemble

wide-angle ADJ
▸▸**w. lens** grand-angle *m*, *pl* grands-angles, grand-angulaire *m*, *pl* grands-angulaires; *Cin, TV* **w. shot** panoramique *m*

wide-body ADJ
▸▸*Aviat* **w. aircraft** avion *m* à fuselage élargi, gros-porteur *m*, *pl* gros-porteurs

wide-eyed ADJ les yeux grands ouverts, les yeux écarquillés; **he looked at me in w. amazement** il m'a regardé avec des yeux grands comme des soucoupes, il m'a regardé les yeux écarquillés

widely ['waɪdlɪ] ADV **1** *(extensively)* largement; **she has travelled w.** elle a beaucoup voyagé; **it is w. thought** *or* **believed that ...** on pense couramment *ou* communément que ...; **w. known** très connu, connu partout; **w. different versions of what happened** des versions très différentes des événements **2** *(broadly)* **to smile w.** faire un grand sourire; **to yawn w.** bâiller profondément; **the houses were w. scattered/spaced** les maisons étaient très dispersées/espacées

widely-read [-red] ADJ **to be w.** *(of person)* avoir beaucoup lu; *(of author)* avoir un public très étendu; *(of book, newspaper)* être très lu; **the Bible remains the most w. of all books** la Bible demeure le livre le plus lu

widen ['waɪd(ə)n] VT **1** *(road, channel, garment, hole)* élargir **2** *(influence, limits of sth)* étendre
VI **1** s'élargir; **the breach is widening** la rupture s'accentue **2** *(of influence)* s'étendre
▸ **widen out** VI *(of road, river, valley)* s'élargir

wideness ['waɪdnɪs] N largeur *f*

widening ['waɪd(ə)nɪŋ] N **1** *(of road, channel)* élargissement *m* **2** *(of influence)* extension *f*

widescreen ['waɪdskri:n] N grand écran *m*
▸▸**w. television** téléviseur *m* grand écran

widespread ['waɪdspred] ADJ *(belief, poverty)* répandu; **w. damage** des dégâts importants; **w. opinion** opinion largement répandue *ou* généralement admise

widgeon ['wɪdʒən] N *(bird)* canard *m* siffleur

widget ['wɪdʒɪt] N *Br Fam* truc *m*

widow ['wɪdəʊ] N *also Typ* veuve *f*; **she was left a w. at (the age of) thirty** elle a été veuve à l'âge de trente ans; *Fam* **golf w.** *=* femme *f* délaissée par son mari qui joue constamment au golf
VT **to be widowed** *(of man)* devenir veuf; *(of woman)* devenir veuve
▸▸*Bible Fig* **w.'s mite** denier *m* de la veuve; **w.'s peak** *=* ligne *f* de cheveux sur le front en

forme de v; **w.'s pension** allocation *f* veuvage; **w.'s weeds** deuil *m* de veuve

widowed ['wɪdəʊd] ADJ *(man)* veuf; *(woman)* veuve; **his w. mother** sa mère qui est/était veuve

widower ['wɪdəʊər] N veuf *m*

widowhood ['wɪdəʊhʊd] N veuvage *m*

width [wɪdθ] N **1** *(of road, chest)* largeur *f*, *(of garment)* ampleur *f*, *(of tyre)* grosseur *f*, *(of cloth, wallpaper)* lé *m*, laize *f*, largeur *f*, *Typ (of letter)* chasse *f*; **to be three metres in w.** avoir trois mètres de large **2** *(of knowledge)*, *Mktg (of product range)* largeur *f* **3** *(of swimming pool)* largeur *f*; **to swim six widths (of the pool)** nager six largeurs

widthways ['wɪdθweɪz], **widthwise** ['wɪdθwaɪz] ADV dans la largeur, en largeur

wield [wiːld] VT **1** *(handle) (sword, pen)* manier; *Fig (power, influence)* exercer **2** *(brandish) (weapon, stick)* brandir

Wiener ['viːnər] N
▸▸ *Culin* **W. schnitzel** escalope *f* viennoise

wiener ['wiːnər] N *Am* **1** saucisse *f* de Francfort **2** *Sl (penis)* zizi *m*
▸▸ **w. roast** barbecue *m* de saucisses de Francfort

wife, *pl* **wives** [waɪf, waɪvz] N **1** femme *f* (mariée); *esp Admin* épouse *f*; **Mr Martin and his w.** M. Martin et sa femme; **she was his second w.** c'était sa deuxième femme; **the baker's w.** *(who is also a baker)* la boulangère; *(who is not a baker)* la femme du boulanger; *Br Fam* **the w.** ma/ta/*etc* moitié **2** *Arch (woman)* femme *f*

wifely ['waɪflɪ] ADJ de bonne épouse

wife-swapping [-swɒpɪŋ] N échangisme *m*
▸▸ **w. party** soirée *f* échangiste

wig [wɪg] N *(full length)* perruque *f*, *(hairpiece)* postiche *m*; *Br (for lawyers)* perruque; **she's wearing a w.** elle porte une perruque
▸ **wig out** VI *Am Fam (get angry)* piquer une crise, péter les plombs; *(go mad)* devenir cinglé, perdre la boule; *(get excited)* devenir dingue

wigeon ['wɪdʒən] N *(bird)* canard *m* siffleur

wigged [wɪgd] ADJ *(judge etc)* à perruque

wigging ['wɪgɪŋ] N *Old-fashioned Br Fam* réprimande *f*; **to give sb a good w.** attraper qn; **to get a good w.** se faire passer un savon

wiggle ['wɪg(ə)l] N *(of body etc)* tortillement *m*; **to give sth a w.** agiter *ou* remuer qch; **she gave her hips a seductive w.** elle marchait en tortillant les fesses
VT agiter, remuer; **he wiggled his backside** il remuait du derrière; **to w. one's toes** remuer ses orteils; **to w. one's hips** tortiller des hanches
VI *(of person, snake)* se remuer, se tortiller; *(of fish)* frétiller; **stop wiggling!** arrête de te tortiller!; *Fig* **to try to w. out of it** chercher une échappatoire

wiggly ['wɪglɪ] ADJ *Fam (snake etc)* qui se remue *ou* se tortille; **a w. line** un trait ondulé

wiggy ['wɪgɪ] ADJ *Am Fam (mad)* cinglé, tapé; *(eccentric)* loufoque, allumé

wigmaker ['wɪgmeɪkər] N perruquier, -ière

wigwam ['wɪgwæm] N wigwam *m*

wilco ['wɪlkəʊ] INT *esp Radio* j'exécute

WILD [waɪld] ADJ **1** *(animal, plant)* sauvage; **w. and woolly** *(untamed)* frustre, rustre; *(not thought out)* irréfléchi; *Fig* **w. horses wouldn't drag it out of me** rien au monde ne me le ferait dire; *Pol* extrémiste *m*; *Fig* **to sow one's w. oats** jeter sa gourme
2 *(wind)* furieux, violent; **the weather's been pretty w.** les éléments se sont déchaînés; *Naut* **in w. weather** par gros temps;

w. sea mer agitée; **a w. (and stormy) night** une nuit de tempête
3 *(unrestrained) (person)* dissipé, dissolu; *(adolescent)* indiscipliné; *(behaviour)* déréglé; *(idea)* délirant, abracadabrant; *(project)* insensé, extravagant; *(party)* fou, *f* folle, déchaîné; **he's got some pretty w. friends** certains de ses amis sont de vrais casse-cou; **what a w. thing to do!** quelle inconscience!; **I'm worried by all his w. talk** tous ses propos irréfléchis m'inquiètent; **having so much money is beyond my wildest dreams** même dans mes rêves les plus fous je n'aurais jamais espéré posséder autant d'argent; **to make a w. rush at sth** se ruer sur qch; **w. applause** applaudissements frénétiques; **w. eyes** yeux égarés; **w. enthusiasm** enthousiasme délirant *ou* débordant; **w. with joy/rage** fou de joie/rage; **it makes me w. to think that …** j'enrage *ou* cela me met en rage quand je pense que …; **to drive sb w.** mettre qn en fureur; **w. promises** promesses extravagantes *ou* insensées; **w. rumour** bruit extravagant *ou* sans fondation
4 *(random)* **it was just a w. guess** c'était un coup au hasard; **to make a w. guess (at the answer)** répondre à tout hasard *ou* à l'aveuglette; **some of the estimates were pretty w.** certaines des estimations étaient complètement à côté
5 *Cards* libre; **the joker is w.** le joker peut être joué n'importe quand
6 *Fam (enthusiastic)* **to be w. about sb/sth** être emballé par qn/qch, être dingue de qn/qch; **I'm not w. about it** ça ne m'emballe pas
ADV **to grow w.** *(of plant)* pousser à l'état sauvage; **to run w.** *(of children)* mener une vie sans discipline; *(of hooligans)* se livrer à des actes de violence; *(of escaped bull etc)* s'emballer; *(of garden)* être laissé à l'abandon, être abandonné; **their children are allowed to run w.** leurs enfants peuvent faire tout et n'importe quoi
N **in the w.** *(of animal)* à l'état sauvage; **the call of the w.** l'appel de la nature; **in the wilds** dans une région sauvage *ou* déserte; **he lives in the wilds of Africa/Ealing** il habite au fin fond de l'Afrique/d'Ealing
VI *Am Sl* = effectuer, en bande, des actes de violence extrême contre des personnes
▸▸ **w. card** *(in card games)* joker *m*; *Comput* joker; *Sport (player)* = sportif *m* invité à participer à une compétition sans s'être qualifié; *(in American football)* = équipe *f* qualifiée pour la finale sans pour autant avoir remporté sa poule; *Comput* **w. card character** caractère *m* joker; **w. cherry** *(fruit)* merise *f*, *(tree)* merisier *m*; **w. dog** chien *m* sauvage; **w. flowers** fleurs *fpl* des champs *ou* sauvages; **w. goose** oie *f* sauvage; **w. man** *(savage)* sauvage *m*; *Culin* **w. rice** zizania *m*, riz *m* sauvage; **W. West** Far West *m*

wildcard ['waɪldkɑːd] N *Comput* joker *m*
▸▸ **w. character** caractère *m* joker

wildcat ['waɪldkæt] N **1** *(animal)* chat *m* sauvage; *Fig* **she's a w.** c'est une tigresse **2** *Am Petr (well)* forage *m* d'exploration **3** *Mktg (product)* dilemme *m*
ADJ *(imprudent, ill-considered)* aléatoire, hasardeux
VI *Am Petr* faire un forage d'exploration
▸▸ **w. strike** grève *f* sauvage; *Am Petr* **w. well** forage d'exploration

wildcatter ['waɪldkætər] N *Am Petr (company)* entrepreneur *m* de forage d'exploration; *(driller)* ouvrier *m* qui effectue des forages d'exploration

wildebeest ['wɪldɪbiːst, 'vɪl-] N *(animal)* gnou *m*

wilder ['waɪldər] N *Am Sl* = membre *m* d'une bande de jeunes voyous effectuant des actes de violence extrême contre des personnes

wilderness ['wɪldənɪs] N **1** *(desert)* désert *m*; **an economic w.** un désert économique; **a voice in the w.** une voix qui prêche dans le désert; *Fig* **to be in the w.** *(of politician, party)* faire sa traversée du désert; *Fig* **during his w. years** pendant sa traversée du désert; **the party believes that the w. years may be about to end** le parti pense que sa traversée du désert touche à sa fin **2** *(overgrown garden)* jungle *f*; **the garden is turning into a w.** le jardin est en train de se transformer en jungle

wildfire ['waɪldfaɪər] N **to spread like w.** *(of news)* se répandre comme une traînée de poudre; *(of disease)* se propager très rapidement

wildfowl ['waɪldfaʊl] N gibier *m* d'eau, sauvagine *f*

wild-goose chase N fausse piste *f*; **the search for the information was a real w.** on a cherché en vain les renseignements; **I've been on a w. round town trying to get the fabric** j'ai couru toute la ville pour rien à la recherche du tissu; **to go on a w.** faire fausse piste; **to send sb on a w.** mettre qn sur une fausse piste

wilding ['waɪldɪŋ] N *Am Sl* = actes *mpl* de violence extrême effectués par une bande de voyous contre des personnes

wildlife ['waɪldlaɪf] N *(wild animals)* faune *f*, *(wild animals and plants)* la faune et la flore
▸▸ **w. park** réserve *f* naturelle; **w. programme** émission *f* sur la nature; **w. reserve** réserve animale; **w. sanctuary** réserve animale

wildly ['waɪldlɪ] ADV **1** *(without control) (to behave)* sans contraintes; *(to cheer)* frénétiquement; *(to applaud)* à tout rompre; **to talk w.** dire des folies; **to talk w. of suicide** tenir des propos insensés de suicide; **the children had been behaving w. all afternoon** les enfants ont été intenables toute l'après-midi; **to rush about w.** courir comme un fou; **her heart was beating w.** son cœur battait à tout rompre; **prices have been fluctuating w.** les prix ont subi des fluctuations violentes
2 *(at random) (to answer, guess)* au hasard, au petit bonheur; **by now it was clear that he was guessing w.** il était clair qu'il répondait au hasard; **to hit out w.** lancer des coups au hasard
3 *(as intensifier) (expensive, funny etc)* extrêmement; **w. inaccurate** dramatiquement inexact; **w. happy** follement heureux, aux anges; **to be w. excited** être surexcité; **it's not w. encouraging** ça n'est pas franchement encourageant; **w. exaggerated** follement exagéré; **I'm not w. enthusiastic about it** je ne suis pas franchement emballé

wildness ['waɪldnɪs] N **1** *(of country, animal)* état *m* sauvage; *(of region)* état inculte **2** *(of wind, waves)* fureur *f*, violence *f*, *(of storm)* violence **3** *(of applause)* frénésie *f*, *(of ideas, words)* extravagance *f*

wiles [waɪlz] NPL ruses *fpl*, artifices *mpl*; **he used all of his w. to persuade her** il l'a persuadée à force de ruse(s) *ou* d'artifice(s); **to fall victim to sb's w.** succomber aux séductions de qn

wilful, *Am* **willful** ['wɪlfʊl] ADJ **1** *(stubborn)* obstiné, entêté, volontaire **2** *(deliberate)* délibéré, intentionnel, volontaire; *Law* **w. murder** homicide *m* volontaire *ou* prémédité; **w. damage** bris *m*, dommage *m* délibéré; **with w. intent** délibérément

wilfully, *Am* **willfully** ['wɪlfəlɪ] ADV **1** *(stubbornly)* obstinément, avec entêtement; **she has behaved quite w. over this issue** elle n'en a fait qu'à sa tête pour cette question **2** *(deliberately)* délibérément; **are you being w. obtuse?** est-ce que tu fais exprès de faire l'idiot?

wilfulness, *Am* **willfulness** ['wɪlfʊlnɪs] **N1** *(stubbornness)* obstination *f*, entêtement *m*; **the sheer w. of his refusal** son refus obstiné *ou* entêté **2** *(deliberateness)* caractère *m* délibéré

wiliness ['waɪlɪnɪs] **N** astuce *f*, caractère *m* rusé

WILL¹ [wɪl] **N1** *(faculty, determination)* volonté *f*; **to have a strong/weak w.** avoir beaucoup/peu de volonté; **w. of iron, iron w.** volonté de fer; **he has a w. of his own** il sait ce qu'il veut, il est volontaire; **strength of w.** force *f* de volonté; **the w. to live** la volonté de survivre; **she seems to have lost the w. to live** elle semble avoir perdu sa volonté de vivre; **good/ill w.** bienveillance *f*/malveillance *f*; **to show good w.** faire preuve de bonne volonté; **I bear her no ill w.** *(have no wish for revenge)* je ne lui en veux pas; *(do not dislike her)* je ne lui veux aucun mal; **to work with a w.** travailler de bon cœur *ou* avec détermination; **with the best w. in the world** avec la meilleure volonté du monde; *Prov* **where there's a w. there's a way** vouloir c'est pouvoir

2 *(desire, wish)* volonté *f*, désir *m*; **the w. of the people** la volonté du peuple; **to impose one's w. on sb** imposer sa volonté à qn; **at w.** *(to choose, fire)* à volonté; *(to depart etc)* quand on veut; **free w.** libre arbitre *m*; **to do sth of one's own free w.** faire qch de son plein gré; **to do sth against one's w.** faire qch contre son gré *ou* à contrecœur; *Bible* **Thy w. be done** que ta volonté soit faite

3 *Law* testament *m*; **the last w. and testament of …** les dernières volontés de …; **to make one's w.** faire son testament; **to mention sb in one's w.** mettre *ou* coucher qn sur son testament

VT (**-ll-**) **1 to w. sb to do** *or* **into doing sth** faire faire qch à qn (par la volonté), souhaiter ardemment que qn fasse qch; *(by hypnotism)* suggestionner à qn de faire qch; **the crowd was willing him to win** la foule voulait absolument qu'il gagne; **she was willing her child to live** elle souhaitait de toutes ses forces que son enfant survive; **you can't just w. these things to happen** on ne peut pas faire arriver ces choses par un simple acte de volonté; **to w. oneself to do sth** faire un effort de volonté pour faire qch; *Arch, Lit* **God so willed it** Dieu l'a voulu ainsi

2 *Law* *(leave in one's will)* **to w. sth** léguer qch, disposer de qch par testament; **to w. sth to sb** léguer qch à qn

WILL² MODAL AUX V VOIR GRAMMAIRE A57–8 (**I will, you/he/we/***etc* **will;** *Arch* **thou wilt;** *pt, cond* **would** [wʊd], **I will, he will** *etc are often contracted into* **I'll** [aɪl], **he'll** [hiːl] *etc*; **would, they would** *etc to* **I'd** [aɪd], **they'd** [ðeɪd] *etc*; **will not** *and* **would not** *to* **won't** [wəʊnt], **wouldn't** ['wʊd(ə)nt]) **1** *(expressing future)* **I'll do it tomorrow** je le ferai demain; **he won't do it again** il ne le fera plus; **w. he be there? – he w.** y sera-t-il? – oui (il y sera); **w. he be there? – no, he won't** y sera-t-il? – non (il n'y sera pas); **but I'll starve! – no, you won't** mais je vais mourir de faim! – mais non!; **you won't forget, w. you?** vous n'oublierez pas, hein?; **you'll write to me, won't you?** vous m'écrirez, n'est-ce pas?; **we w. be there** nous serons là; **Mr Long w. explain the situation to you** *(immediate future)* M. Long va vous expliquer la situation VOIR GRAMMAIRE A50–1

2 *(consent)* **I w. not do it** je refuse de le faire; **I w. not have that said of me** je ne veux pas qu'on dise cela de moi; *Fam* **w. do!** d'accord!; **the engine won't start** le moteur ne veut pas

démarrer; **it won't open** ça ne s'ouvre pas, ça ne veut pas s'ouvrir; **just wait a moment, w. you?** pouvez-vous attendre un instant?; *(emphatic)* voulez-vous bien attendre un instant?; **won't you sit down?** asseyez-vous, je vous en prie

3 *(emphatic)* **accidents will happen** on ne peut pas éviter les accidents; **she will go out in spite of her cold** elle persiste à sortir malgré son rhume; **he will get in my way** il est toujours dans mon chemin; **the doctor will have his little joke** il aime (à) plaisanter, le docteur; **I will not have it!** je ne permettrai pas cela!; **will you be quiet!** voulez-vous bien vous taire!

4 *(habit)* **this hen will lay up to six eggs a week** cette poule pond jusqu'à six œufs par semaine

5 *(conjecture)* **you'll be tired** vous devez être fatigué

6 *(wish)* vouloir; **do as you w.** faites comme vous voudrez; **say what you w., you won't be believed** quoi que vous disiez, on ne vous croira pas

7 *(injunction)* **you'll be here at three** soyez ici à trois heures

willful *etc Am* = **wilful** *etc*

William the Conqueror ['wɪlɪəm] **N** Guillaume le Conquérant

willie ['wɪlɪ] **N** *Br Fam (penis)* zizi *m*

willies ['wɪlɪz] **NPL** *Fam* **to have the w.** avoir le trac *ou* la frousse; **this place gives me the w.** cet endroit me fiche la frousse *ou* me donne les chocottes; **I had a bad case of the w.** j'avais une frousse incroyable

willing ['wɪlɪŋ] **ADJ 1** *(compliant)* de bonne volonté, bien disposé; *Fig* **w. horse** bonne poire **2** *(ready)* **to be w. to do sth** bien vouloir faire qch, être disposé à faire qch; **w. to help** prêt à rendre service, serviable; **she's always w. to lend a hand** elle est toujours prête à rendre service; **I am more than w. to come with you** je ne demande pas mieux que de vous accompagner; **I am w. and able to help them** je peux les aider et je le ferai très volontiers; **she wasn't very w. to tell me what had happened** elle ne tenait pas vraiment à me dire ce qui s'est passé; **w. or not** bon gré mal gré; **God w.** s'il plaît à Dieu; *Fam* **to show w.** faire preuve de bonne volonté

willingly ['wɪlɪŋlɪ] **ADV 1** *(voluntarily)* volontairement; **he came along quite w.** il est venu de son plein gré; **she had not gone there w.** elle n'y était pas allée de son plein gré **2** *(with pleasure)* volontiers, avec plaisir

willingness ['wɪlɪŋnɪs] **N 1** *(compliance)* bonne volonté *f*; **with the utmost w.** de très bon cœur **2** *(readiness)* empressement *m* (**to do sth** à faire qch)

will-o'-the-wisp [wɪləðə'wɪsp] **N** *also Fig* feu *m* follet

willow ['wɪləʊ] **N 1** *(tree)* saule *m* **2** *Cr Old-fashioned Fam* **the w.** la batte
▸▸**w. pattern** = motif *m* de céramique; **w. pattern plates** des assiettes *fpl* à motifs chinois; **w. tree** saule

willowy ['wɪləʊɪ] **ADJ** *(person)* souple, svelte, élancé

willpower ['wɪlpaʊər] **N** volonté *f*; **through w. alone** par ma/sa/*etc* seule volonté; **lack of w.** manque *m* de volonté

willy ['wɪlɪ] **N** = **willie**

willy-nilly [-'nɪlɪ] **ADV 1** *(without order, randomly)* au hasard; **the editor just altered a few words w.** le rédacteur a simplement changé quelques mots au hasard **2** *(willingly or not)* bon gré mal gré

wilt¹ [wɪlt] **VI 1** *(of plant)* se flétrir, se faner **2** *Fig (of person) (with heat, fatigue)* dépérir, languir; *(at reproach)* perdre contenance;

(lose courage) se dégonfler; **I'm beginning to w.** *(become tired)* je commence à fatiguer; **he tends to w. under pressure** il ne résiste pas à la pression
VT *(of heat) (flowers)* faner, dessécher

wilt² *see* **will²**

Wilts *abbr* Wiltshire

wily ['waɪlɪ] **ADJ** rusé, astucieux, malin, *f* -igne, roublard; **he's a w. old bird** *or* **fox** c'est un vieux roublard

wimp [wɪmp] **N** *Fam* poule *f* mouillée, mauviette *f*
▸**wimp out VI** *Fam* se dégonfler; **he wimped out of the fight** il s'est dégonflé au dernier moment et a refusé de se battre; **he wimped out of telling her the truth** finalement il a eu la trouille de lui dire la vérité

wimpish ['wɪmpɪʃ], **wimpy** ['wɪmpɪ] **ADJ** *Fam (behaviour, attitude)* de poule mouillée, de mauviette; **you didn't go because it was raining?, how w.!** tu n'y es pas allé à cause de la pluie?, quelle mauviette!

wimple ['wɪmp(ə)l] **N** *(worn by nun)* guimpe *f*

win [wɪn] **N** *Sport etc* victoire *f*; **to have three wins in succession** emporter trois victoires consécutives; **to back a horse for a w.** jouer un cheval gagnant

VT *(pt, pp* **won** [wʌn]; *prp* **winning) 1** *(be successful in) (battle, race, bet)* gagner; **to w. an election** remporter une élection; **to w. an argument** avoir le dessus dans une discussion; *Fam* **you can't w. them all, you w. some you lose some** on ne peut pas toujours gagner

2 *(obtain) (prize)* remporter, gagner; **to w. a contract** remporter un marché; **I won 500 pounds off him at poker** j'ai gagné 500 livres en jouant au poker contre lui; **the Greens have won ten seats** les Verts ont gagné dix sièges; **they won the seat from Labour** ils ont enlevé le siège aux Travaillistes

3 *(acquire) (popularity, sb's good will)* acquérir; *(sb's attention)* captiver; *(sb's confidence)* gagner; **to w. fame** trouver la gloire; **she was desperate to w. his favour** elle cherchait désespérément à attirer ses bonnes grâces; **to w. a reputation for sth** se faire une réputation de qch; **to w. the right to do sth** obtenir le droit de faire qch; **to w. sb's love** se faire aimer de qn; **to w. recognition** parvenir à être reconnu; **he has finally won recognition for his work** son travail a finalement été reconnu; **she was gradually winning recognition as a talented young poet** elle commençait à se faire connaître en tant que jeune poète; **you've just won yourself a friend** tu viens juste de te faire un ami; **how to w. friends and influence people** comment se faire des amis et influencer les gens; **to w. sb away from sth** détourner *ou* détacher qn de qch; **she won her way to the top of her profession** elle a réussi à atteindre le sommet de sa profession

VI gagner; *Sport* **to w. by a length** gagner d'une longueur; **to back a horse to w.** jouer un cheval gagnant; *Fam* **you (just) can't w.** j'aurai/tu auras/*etc* toujours tort; *Fam* **to w. hands down** gagner les doigts dans le nez *ou* les mains dans les poches; **w. or lose, I'm sure I'll enjoy this match** que je gagne ou que je perde je suis certain que je vais m'amuser pendant ce match
▸**win back VT SEP** *(territory, championship)* reprendre (**from** à), reconquérir (**from** sur); *(esteem, friendship)* reconquérir; *(money)* regagner
▸**win out VI** *(succeed)* y arriver, réussir
▸**win over, win round VT SEP** I think we should manage to w. her over *or* round in the end je pense qu'on devrait finir par la

persuader; **to w. sb round** *or* **over to one's position** gagner qn à sa cause; **see whether you can w. him over** essayez de le persuader de se mettre avec nous; **I won him round to my point of view** j'ai réussi à le rallier à mon point de vue

▸ **win through** VI *(succeed)* y arriver, réussir; *Sport* **to w. through to the second round** passer le premier tour

wince [wɪns] N *(of pain etc)* crispation f
VI *(with pain)* tressaillir; *(with embarrassment)* se crisper; **the remark made him w.** il s'est crispé en entendant cette remarque

winceyette [wɪnsɪ'et] N *Br Tex* flanelle f de coton

winch [wɪntʃ] N treuil m; *(on boat)* winch m
▸ **winch in** VT SEP amener *ou* rentrer à l'aide d'un treuil
▸ **winch up** VT SEP soulever *ou* hisser *ou* monter à l'aide d'un treuil; **the crew were winched up by helicopter** l'équipage a été hissé à l'aide d'un hélicoptère *ou* a été hélitreuillé

wind¹ [wɪnd] N **1** *(air)* vent m; **strong winds** vents forts *ou* violents; **there's quite a w.** il y a beaucoup de vent; *Naut* **to sail against the w.** avoir le vent debout; *Naut* **to sail or run before the w.** avoir *ou* être vent arrière; *Naut* **to sail with w. and tide** avoir vent et marée; **in the teeth of the w.** contre le vent; **to sail into the w.** venir *ou* aller au lof; *Fig* **to sail close to the w.** jouer un jeu dangereux; *(when telling joke)* friser l'indécence; *(in business dealings)* friser la malhonnêteté; *Fig* **my friends are all scattered to the four winds** mes amis sont dispersés aux quatre coins du monde; *Fig* **to throw caution to the w.** oublier toute prudence; *Fig* **to see or find out which way the w. blows** voir d'où vient le vent; *Fig* **there's something in the w.** il se prépare *ou* se mijote quelque chose; *Fig* **a w.** *or* **the winds of change** un vent de changement; *Fig* **to go like the w.** aller comme le vent; *Old-fashioned Fam* **to raise the w.** rassembler des fonds; *Fig Fam* **to put the w. up sb** faire une peur bleue à qn; *Fig Fam* **to have** *or* **get the w. up** avoir le trac *ou* la frousse; *(stronger)* avoir une peur bleue; *Fig* **to take the w. out of sb's sails** déjouer les projets de qn, couper l'herbe sous le pied à qn
2 *(scent)* vent m; *Fig* **to get w. of sth** avoir vent de qch
3 *Med (flatulence)* vent(s) m(pl), flatuosité f; **to break w.** lâcher un vent; **to have w.** avoir des gaz; **beans give you w.** les haricots donnent des gaz; **the baby's got w.** le bébé n'a pas fait son rot; **to get the baby's w. up** faire faire son rot au bébé; *Fam* **to be full of w.** *(useless talk)* parler à tort et à travers *ou* pour ne rien dire; *(boastful talk)* être vantard
4 *(breath)* souffle m, respiration f; **let me get my w.** laissez-moi souffler *ou* reprendre mon souffle
5 *Mus* **the w.** *(in orchestra)* les instruments mpl à vent
6 *Ind* vent m, air m *ou* vent de soufflerie
VT *(of blow)* **(person)** couper la respiration *ou* le souffle à; *(of race)* **(person, horse)** essouffler; *(baby)* faire faire son rot à; **I was badly winded** *(by blow)* j'avais le souffle coupé; *(by race)* j'étais très essoufflé
▸▸ *Mus* **w. chest** *(of organ)* laie f, sommier m; **w. chimes** carillon m éolien; **w. energy** énergie f éolienne; **w. ensemble** ensemble m d'instruments à vent; **w. farm** parc m d'éoliennes; **w. gag** *(on microphone)* anti-vent m, pl anti-vents; **w. gauge** anémomètre m; *Aviat* **w. indicator** indicateur m de direction du vent; *Mus* **w. instrument** instrument m à vent; *Theat* **w. machine** machine f à souffler le vent; *Aut* **w. noise** bruit m aérodynamique; **w. power** énergie du vent *ou* éo-

lienne; **w. pump** éolienne f; *Aut* **w. roar** bruit m du vent; *Aviat* **w. sleeve** manche f à air; **w. tunnel** tunnel m aérodynamique; **w. turbine** éolienne f

wind² [waɪnd] N **to give the clock a w.** remonter la pendule
VI *(pt, pp* **wound** [waʊnd]*)* tourner; *(of path, river)* serpenter; *(of staircase)* monter en colimaçon; **the road winds up/down the hill** le chemin monte/descend en serpentant
VT **1** *(roll)* enrouler; *Tex (thread, silk)* dévider; **to w. wool into a ball** enrouler de la laine (pour en faire une pelote); **to w. cotton on a reel** bobiner du coton; *Fishing* **to w. in the line** ramener la ligne; **to w. a bobbin** enrouler le fil sur une bobine; *Elec* **to w. a dynamo** armer une dynamo **2** *(clock)* remonter **3** *(handle)* tourner
▸ **wind down** VT SEP **1** *(car window)* baisser **2** *(reduce)* réduire progressivement *ou* graduellement
VI **1** *(of party, meeting etc)* tirer à sa fin; **the party didn't begin to w. down until nearly 4 am** la fête n'a commencé à diminuer en intensité que vers 4 heures du matin **2** *Fam (relax)* décompresser, se détendre
▸ **wind round** VT SEP enrouler autour de; **to w. a scarf round one's neck** enrouler une écharpe autour de son cou; **she wound her arms round the child** elle a entouré l'enfant de ses bras
VT INSEP *(of thread)* s'enrouler autour de
▸ **wind up** VT SEP **1** *(car window)* remonter **2** *(rope etc)* enrouler **3** *(clock)* remonter; *(spring)* bander; *Fig* **to be all wound up** *(of person)* être excité *ou* énervé **4** *(end)* finir, terminer; *Com (company)* liquider, dissoudre; *(account)* régler, clôturer; **she wound up her speech by announcing that ...** elle a terminé son discours en annonçant que ...; **she winds up the book with a chapter on ...** elle boucle son livre par un chapitre sur ... **5** *Br Fam (tease)* faire marcher; **they're only winding you up** ils te font marcher, ils essaient seulement de te mettre en boîte; **don't you know when you're being wound up?** tu ne te rends même pas compte quand on te fait marcher *ou* quand on essaie de te mettre en boîte? **6** *Br Fam (irritate)* foutre en rogne
VI **1** *(end speech etc)* conclure **2** *Fam (end up)* **he'll w. up in prison** il finira en prison; **we usually w. up back at my place** généralement nous finissons chez moi; **we wound up working for the same company** nous nous sommes retrouvés à travailler pour la même société

windbag [wɪndbæg] N *Fam* moulin m à paroles; **what a w.!** quel bavard!

windblown [wɪndbləʊn] ADJ *(hair)* ébouriffé par le vent; *(trees)* fouetté *ou* cinglé par le vent

wind-borne ADJ porté par le vent

windbreak [wɪndbreɪk] N brise-vent m inv

windcheater [wɪndtʃiːtər] N *(jacket)* blouson m, *Can* coupe-vent m inv

wind-chill ADJ
▸▸ **w. factor** facteur m d'abaissement de la température provoqué par le vent

winder [waɪndər] N **1** *(device) Tex* bobinoir m, dévidoir m; *(on clock, watch)* remontoir m **2** *Aut (on car door)* lève-glace m inv **3** *(person), Tex* bobineur, -euse, dévideur, -euse; *(of clocks)* remonteur, -euse

windfall [wɪndfɔːl] N **1** *(in garden, orchard etc)* fruit m abattu par le vent, fruit tombé **2** *Fig* aubaine f, bonne fortune f; *(legacy)* héritage m inattendu; **I've had a bit of a w. from my aunt** j'ai eu la chance d'hériter d'un peu d'argent de ma tante
▸▸ **w. profits** bénéfices mpl exceptionnels; **w. tax** impôt m sur les bénéfices exceptionnels

winding [waɪndɪŋ] ADJ *(road, street)* tortueux, sinueux; *(river)* sinueux; *(staircase)* en hélice, en colimaçon
N **1** *(process)* enroulement m; *Elec (wire)* bobinage m, enroulement m, enroulement m **2** *(in a river)* méandres mpl, coudes mpl; *(in a road)* zigzags mpl
▸▸ **w. gear** *(of lift)* treuil m; *Mining* appareils mpl *ou* machine f d'extraction; **w. sheet** linceul m

winding-up N *(of business etc)* liquidation f, dissolution f; *(of speech)* fin f, conclusion f; *(of account)* clôture f

windjammer [wɪndʒæmər] N *Naut* grand voilier m

windlass [wɪndləs] N treuil m

windmill [wɪndmɪl] N moulin m à vent; *Fig* **to tilt at windmills** se battre contre des moulins à vent

window [wɪndəʊ] N **1** *(of house etc)* fenêtre f; **to look in at/out of the w.** regarder par/à la fenêtre; **to break a w.** casser une vitre *ou* un carreau; *Fig Fam* **to throw money out of the w.** jeter l'argent par les fenêtres; *Fig Fam* **that's my holiday out of the w.** voilà mes vacances fichues en l'air; **that's her chances of qualifying out of the w.** voilà ses chances de qualification qui partent en fumée; *Fig* **a w. on sth** un aperçu de qch; **w. of opportunity** ouverture f
2 *Comput* fenêtre f
3 *(of ticket office)* guichet m
4 *(of shop)* vitrine f, devanture f
5 *(of car, train)* vitre f, glace f
6 *(on envelope)* fenêtre f
▸▸ **w. box** jardinière f; **w. cleaner** *(person)* laveur, -euse de vitres *ou* de carreaux; *(substance)* nettoyant m pour vitres; **w. display** étalage m; **w. envelope** enveloppe f à fenêtre; **w. frame** châssis m de fenêtre; **w. ledge** *(inside)* appui m de fenêtre; *(outside)* rebord m de fenêtre; **w. seat** *(in room)* banquette f sous la fenêtre; *(in train, plane)* place f côté fenêtre; **w. tab** *(on suspension file)* onglet m à fenêtre; *Aut* **w. winder** lève-vitre m, pl lève-vitres

window-dress VT *(accounts, balance sheet)* camoufler, habiller

window-dresser N étalagiste mf

window-dressing N *(art m de l')* étalage m; *Fig* façade f, décor m de théâtre, camouflage m; **w. of a balance sheet** habillage m *ou* camouflage de bilan; **no amount of w. can hide the fact that the party is in crisis** rien ne pourra camoufler l'état de crise dans lequel se trouve le parti; *Fig* **it's just w.** ce n'est qu'une façade

windowing [wɪndəʊɪŋ] N *Comput* fenêtrage m

windowless [wɪndəʊlɪs] ADJ sans fenêtres

windowpane [wɪndəʊpeɪn] N vitre f, carreau m

window-shop VI faire du lèche-vitrines; **to w. for a coat** faire du lèche-vitrines pour trouver un manteau

window-shopper N personne f qui fait du lèche-vitrines; **the streets were full of window-shoppers** les rues étaient pleines de gens en train de faire du lèche-vitrines

window-shopping N lèche-vitrines m; **to go w.** faire du lèche-vitrines

windowsill [wɪndəʊsɪl] N *(outside)* rebord m de fenêtre; *(inside)* appui m *ou* tablette f de fenêtre

windpipe [wɪndpaɪp] N *Anat* trachée f

wind-pollinated [-pɒlɪneɪtɪd] ADJ pollinisé par le vent

wind-pollination N pollinisation f par le vent

windscreen ['wɪndskriːn] N *Br Aut* pare-brise *m inv*
  ▶▶**w. cleaner** lave-glace *m, pl* lave-glaces; **w. washer** lave-glace; **w. wiper** essuie-glace *m, pl* essuie-glaces

windshield ['wɪndʃiːld] N *Am* = windscreen

windsock ['wɪndsɒk] N *Aviat* manche *f* à air, *Sl* biroute *f*

windstorm ['wɪndstɔːm] N tempête *f* de vent

windsurf ['wɪndsɜːf] VI faire de la planche à voile

windsurfer ['wɪndsɜːfər] N *Sport* **1** *(board)* planche *f* à voile **2** *(person)* véliplanchiste *mf*

windsurfing ['wɪndsɜːfɪŋ] N *(sport)* planche *f* à voile; **to go w.** faire de la planche à voile

windswept ['wɪndswept] ADJ *(place)* balayé par le vent; *(hair)* ébouriffé par le vent; **you're looking very w.** tu as l'air tout ébouriffé par le vent

wind-up ['waɪnd-] N *Br Fam* **is this a w.?** tu me fais marcher?

windward ['wɪndwəd] ADJ au vent
  ADV contre le vent; **to sail w.** avoir le vent debout
  N côté *m* au vent; **lying to (the) w. of …** situé au vent de …
  ▶▶**the W. Islands** les îles *fpl* du Vent

windy[1] ['wɪndɪ] ADJ **1** *(day)* de grand vent; **it's very w.** il fait beaucoup de vent; **March is usually a w. month** en général il y a du vent au mois de mars **2** *(place)* balayé par le vent, exposé au vent *ou* aux quatre vents; **the W. City** = surnom donné à Chicago **3** *Old-fashioned Br Fam* **to be w.** *(afraid)* avoir le trac *ou* la frousse

windy[2] ['waɪndɪ] ADJ *(road etc)* sinueux

wine [waɪn] N **1** vin *m*; **a bottle/glass of w.** une bouteille/un verre de vin; **red/white w.** vin rouge/blanc; **the wines of Spain** les vins espagnols; **wines and spirits** *(shop sign)* vins et spiritueux **2** *(colour)* lie *f* de vin
  VT **to w. and dine sb** fêter qn
  ▶▶**w. bar** bistrot *m*; **w. box** Cubitainer® *m*; **w. cellar** cave *f* (à vin), cellier *m*; **w. cooler** *(container)* seau *m* à rafraîchir (le vin); *Am (drink)* = mélange *m* de vin, de jus de fruit et d'eau gazeuse; **w. list** carte *f* des vins; **w. merchant** *(shopkeeper)* marchand, -ande de vin(s); *(wholesaler)* négociant, -ante en vin(s); **w. rack** casier *m* à vin; **w. route** route *f* des vins; *Am* **w. steward** sommelier *m*; **w. tasting** dégustation *f* (de vins); **w. vinegar** vinaigre *m* de vin; **w. waiter** sommelier

wine-coloured, *Am* **wine-colored** ADJ lie de vin *inv*

wineglass ['waɪnglɑːs] N verre *m* à vin

winepress ['waɪnpres] N pressoir *m*

wing [wɪŋ] N **1** *(of bird, insect, plane)* aile *f*, *Fig* **to take sb under one's w.** prendre qn sous son aile *ou* sous sa protection; *Lit* **fear lent him wings** la peur lui donnait des ailes; **to shoot a bird on the w.** tirer un oiseau au vol *ou* à la volée; **to be on the w.** *(of bird)* voler; **to take w.** s'envoler, prendre son vol *ou* son essor; *Fig* **to spread** *or* **stretch one's wings** élargir son horizon; *Fig* **on a w. and a prayer** Dieu sait comment; *Aviat* **wings** *(insignia)* insigne *m* de pilote
  2 *(of building)* aile *f*; *(of hospital)* pavillon *m*; *(of door)* battant *m*; *Theat* **the wings** la coulisse, les coulisses; **to be standing** *or* **waiting in the wings** *Theat* attendre dans les coulisses; *Fig* rester dans les coulisses
  3 *Mil (of army)* aile *f*, flanc *m*; *Sport* aile; *(player)* ailier *m*; **the w. halves** les demis *mpl* aile; **she plays on the w.** elle est ailier;

Pol **the left w. of the party** l'aile gauche du parti
  4 *(of nut)* oreille *f*, ailette *f*
  5 *Br (of car)* aile *f*
  6 *Mil, Aviat (unit)* escadre *f* aérienne; *Am* brigade *f* aérienne
  VT **1** *(injure)* *(bird)* frapper *ou* blesser à l'aile; **I've winged him** je lui ai mis du plomb dans l'aile
  2 *Fam* **to w. it** improviser
  3 **to w. its/one's way towards** *(of bird)*, *Fig (of person)* voler vers; **my report should be winging its way towards you now** mon rapport devrait te parvenir incessamment sous peu
  ▶▶**w. chair** bergère *f* à oreilles; **w. collar** col *m* cassé; **w. commander** ≃ lieutenant-colonel *m, pl* lieutenants-colonels; **w. flap** *(of plane)* volet *m*; **w. forward** *(in rugby)* ailier *m*; **w. mirror** rétroviseur *m* extérieur; **w. nut** papillon *m*, écrou *m* à ailettes; *Rugby* **w. threequarter** trois-quarts aile *m*

wingding ['wɪŋdɪŋ] N *Am Fam (party)* fête *f*, bringue *f*

winged [wɪŋd, *Lit* often 'wɪŋɪd]
  ADJ *(possessing wings)* ailé
  ▶▶*Lit* **w. words** paroles *fpl* ailées

-winged [wɪŋd] SUFF **red/white/etc-w.** aux ailes rouges/blanches/etc

winger ['wɪŋər] N *Ftbl, Rugby* ailier *m*

wingless ['wɪŋlɪs] ADJ sans ailes, aptère

wingspan ['wɪŋspæn], **wingspread** ['wɪŋspred] N *(of bird, plane)* envergure *f*, **the eagle has a w. of two metres** l'aigle a une envergure de deux mètres

wink [wɪŋk] N clignement *m* d'œil, clin *m* d'œil; **to give sb a w.** faire un clin d'œil à qn; **with a w.** en clignant de l'œil; *Fig Fam* **to tip sb the w.** prévenir *ou* avertir qn *(about* de); **I didn't sleep a w.** *or* **didn't get a w. of sleep all night** je n'ai pas fermé l'œil *ou* dormi de la nuit; **it was all over in the w. of an eye** tout était fait en un clin d'œil; **a nod's as good as a w. to him** il comprend à demi-mot
  VI cligner de l'œil *ou* des yeux; *(of star, light)* clignoter; **it's as easy as winking** c'est simple comme bonjour
  VT **she winked an eye** elle a fait un clin d'œil
  ▶ **wink at** VT INSEP *(person)* faire un clin d'œil à; *Fig (abuse, illegal practice)* fermer les yeux sur

winker ['wɪŋkər] N *Br Aut Fam* clignotant *m*

winking ['wɪŋkɪŋ] ADJ *(light)* clignotant

winkle ['wɪŋk(ə)l] N **1** *(mollusc)* bigorneau *m* **2** *Fam (penis)* zizi *m*
  ▶▶*Br Fam* **w. pickers** chaussures *fpl* à bout pointu
  ▶ **winkle out** VT SEP *Br Fam (something)* extraire; **I finally winkled the information out of him** j'ai fini par lui tirer les vers du nez; **it's no good trying to w. any money out of me** ce n'est pas la peine d'essayer de me soutirer de l'argent

winner ['wɪnər] N **1** *(person)* vainqueur *m*, gagnant, -ante; *(horse)* cheval *m* gagnant; **the w. of the big prize** *(in lottery)* le gagnant du gros lot; **to back a w.** *Horseracing* jouer un cheval gagnant; *Fig* jouer gagnant, bien miser; **every one's a w.!** *(at fair, in raffle etc)* à tous les coups (l')on gagne! **2** *Fig (successful novel, play)* roman *m*/pièce *f* à grand succès; **this book will be a w.** ce livre a un succès assuré; **to be onto a w.** jouer gagnant *ou* la bonne carte

winning ['wɪnɪŋ] ADJ **1** *(victorious)* gagnant; **the w. side** les vainqueurs *mpl*; **to be on a w. streak** remporter victoire sur victoire; **w. number** *(in lottery)* numéro *m* gagnant *ou* sortant **2** *(attractive)* attrayant, séduisant; *(smile)* engageant, charmant;

that child has a w. way with her cette enfant est très gracieuse
  N **1** *(of sth)* acquisition *f* **2** *(usu pl)* **winnings** *(at races etc)* gains *mpl*
  ▶▶**w. post** poteau *m* d'arrivée; **he was first past the w. post** il est arrivé premier

winnow ['wɪnəʊ] VT *Agr (grain)* vanner; **to w. the chaff from the grain** séparer le bon grain de l'ivraie; *Fig* **to w. the evidence** passer les témoignages au crible *ou* au peigne fin

winnowing ['wɪnəʊɪŋ] N *Agr* vannage *m*; *Fig* examen *m* minutieux; **winnowings** *(of grain)* vannure *f*
  ▶▶**w. basket** van *m*

wino ['waɪnəʊ] N *Fam* ivrogne *mf*, soûlard, -arde

winsome ['wɪnsəm] ADJ charmant, séduisant

winsomely ['wɪnsəmlɪ] ADV d'une manière séduisante, de façon charmante

winter ['wɪntər] N hiver *m*; **in w.** en hiver; **she was born in the w. of 1946** elle est née pendant l'hiver 1946; **a cold w.'s day** une froide journée d'hiver; *Lit* **he has seen sixty winters** il compte soixante hivers VOIR GRAMMAIRE A7
  VI *(of people)* passer l'hiver (**at** à); *(of cattle)* hiverner
  VT *(livestock)* hiverner
  ▶▶**w. clothing** vêtements *mpl* d'hiver; **w. corn** semis *m* d'hiver; **w. garden** *(conservatory)* jardin *m* d'hiver; **w. holiday** vacances *fpl* d'hiver; **the W. Olympics** les jeux *mpl* Olympiques d'hiver; **w. quarters** quartiers *mpl* d'hiver; **w. resort** station *f* de sports d'hiver; **w. season** saison *f* d'hiver; **w. solstice** solstice *m* d'hiver; **w. sports** sports *mpl* d'hiver

winter-flowering ADJ *(plant)* hibernal, -aux, hiémal, -aux

wintergreen ['wɪntəgriːn] N *(plant)* gaulthérie *f*

winterize ['wɪntəraɪz] VT *esp Am (car, house etc)* mettre en état pour passer l'hiver, *Can* hivériser

wintertime ['wɪntətaɪm], *Lit* **wintertide** [-taɪd] N hiver *m*

winterweight ['wɪntəweɪt] ADJ *(coat etc)* d'hiver

wint(e)ry ['wɪnt(ə)rɪ] ADJ hivernal, -aux; *Fig (smile, look)* glacial, -aux; **it's quite w. this morning** c'est presque un jour d'hiver, ce matin; **because of the w. conditions** parce qu'il fait/faisait un temps d'hiver

WIP [dʌb(ə)ljuːaɪˈpiː] N *Acct (abbr* **work in progress)** travail *m* en cours, encours *m* de production de biens

wipe [waɪp] N **1** *(action)* *(with cloth, handkerchief, sponge)* coup *m* de torchon/de mouchoir/d'éponge; **to give sth a w. (over/round)** essuyer qch, donner un coup de torchon/d'éponge à qch **2** *(moist tissue)* lingette *f* **3** *TV, Cin* volet *m*
  VT **1** *(table, plate)* essuyer; **to w. one's face/hands/eyes** s'essuyer la figure/les mains/les yeux; **to w. oneself, to w. one's bottom** s'essuyer les fesses, se torcher; *Vulg* **it's not fit to w. your arse with** c'est de la merde; *Fig Fam* **we wiped the floor with them** nous n'en avons fait qu'une bouchée **2** *(erase recording etc from)* effacer; **the tape has been wiped** la bande a été effacée
  VI **1** *(when washing up, dusting)* essuyer **2** **the windscreen wiper isn't wiping** l'essuie-glace ne marche pas
  ▶ **wipe away** VT SEP *(tears)* essuyer; *(mark)* enlever, ôter; *Fig (memories)* effacer
  ▶ **wipe off** VT SEP **1** *(splash)* enlever, essuyer **2** *(sth from blackboard)* effacer; *(marks)* enlever; *Fam* **that'll w. the smile off his face** ça

va lui enlever le sourire; *Fam* **w. that smile off your face!** arrête de sourire comme ça!; **to w. a town off the map** *or* **off the face of the earth** rayer une ville de la carte **3** *Fin (debt)* annuler; **several millions of pounds were wiped off the value of shares** la valeur des actions a baissé de plusieurs millions de livres

VI *(of stain etc)* s'enlever

▸ **wipe out** **VT SEP 1** *(bath etc)* nettoyer **2** *(debt)* liquider, amortir; **his gambling debts wiped out his entire fortune** ses dettes de jeu ont eu raison de toute sa fortune; **many small traders were wiped out in the recession** de nombreux petits commerçants ont été balayés par la récession **3** *(memory, one's past)* effacer **4** *(army)* exterminer; **whole families were wiped out by the disease** des familles entières ont été exterminées par la maladie; **the fire wiped out the whole district** l'incendie a détruit tout le quartier **5** *Fam (exhaust)* lessiver; **I feel wiped out after interviewing so many people** ça m'a crevé *ou* lessivé de faire passer tous ces entretiens

▸ **wipe up** **VT SEP** *(dirt)* nettoyer, enlever; *(liquid)* essuyer; *(dishes)* essuyer
VI essuyer la vaisselle

wiped [waɪpt] **ADJ** *Fam (exhausted)* lessivé, crevé

wiper ['waɪpər] **N** *Aut (for windscreen)* essuie-glace *m*, *pl* essuie-glaces
▸▸ **w. blade** balai *m* d'essuie-glace

wiping out ['waɪpɪŋ] **N 1** *(of debt)* liquidation *f*, amortissement *m* **2** *(of memory)* effacement *m*

wire ['waɪər] **N 1** fil *m* métallique, fil de fer; *Elec* fil (électrique); **cheese w.** fil à couper le beurre; **the high w.** *(in circus)* la corde raide; *Fig* **to get one's wires crossed** mal se comprendre; *esp Am Fam* **to pull the wires** tirer les ficelles, faire jouer ses pistons **2** *esp Am (finishing line)* ligne *f* d'arrivée; *Fig* **down to the w.** jusqu'à la dernière minute; **to get an application in under the w.** soumettre une demande juste à temps; *Fig* **to (just) get in under the w.** *(of application etc)* arriver de justesse **3** *Fam (hidden microphone)* **he agreed to wear a w.** il accepta de porter un micro **4** *Old-fashioned (telegram)* télégramme *m*
VT 1 *(fix with wire)* attacher avec du fil de fer; *(jaw)* mettre en place avec du fil de fer; *(flowers etc)* monter sur fil de fer; *(close off with wire) (opening)* grillager; **wired glass** verre armé **2** *Elec (house)* faire l'installation électrique de; **to w. a hall for sound** sonoriser une salle **3** *esp Am Fam (police officer)* munir d'un micro **4** *(send telegram to)* envoyer un télégramme à; *(message)* télégraphier; **he wired that he would arrive at twelve** il a télégraphié qu'il arriverait à midi
▸▸ **w. brush** brosse *f* métallique; *Mil* **w. entanglements** barbelés *mpl*; **w. fence** clôture *f* en fil de fer; **w. mesh** grillage *m*, treillis *m* métallique; **w. netting** grillage, treillis métallique; **w. rope** câble *m* métallique; *Am* **w. service** agence *f* de presse *(envoyant des dépêches télégraphiques)*; *Aut* **w. wheel** roue *f* avec jante à rayons; **w. wool** éponge *f* métallique

▸ **wire into** **VT INSEP** *Fam* **he wired into his colleagues about their failure to keep him informed** il est rentré dans ses collègues en leur reprochant leur mauvaise communication avec lui; **they wired into the food as if they hadn't eaten for days** ils ont attaqué la nourriture comme s'ils n'avaient pas mangé depuis des jours; **they got wired into the backlog of work** ils ont attaqué le *ou* se sont attelés au travail en retard

▸ **wire up** **VT SEP** *Comput, Elec (devices)* brancher (**to** sur); *(put electronic bugs in) (room)* installer des micros dans

wirecutter ['waɪəkʌtər] **N** coupe-fil *m inv*; **(pair of) wirecutters** pince(s) *f(pl)* coupante(s)

wired ['waɪəd] **ADJ** *Fam (highly strung)* sur les nerfs, à cran; *(after taking drugs)* défoncé *(après avoir pris de la cocaïne ou des amphétamines)*

wire-haired **ADJ** *(terrier)* à poil dur

wireless ['waɪəlɪs] **ADJ** sans fil
N *Br Old-fashioned* T.S.F. *f*, poste *m* de T.S.F., radio *f*; **they communicated by w.** ils communiquaient par radio
▸▸ *Comput* **w. keyboard** clavier *m* sans fil; *Comput* **w. mouse** souris *f* sans fil; **w. network** réseau *m* sans fil; **w. network card** carte *f* de réseau sans fil; *Br Old-fashioned* **w. set** T.S.F., poste de T.S.F.

wirepuller ['waɪəpʊlər] **N** *esp Am Fam* personne *f* qui a du piston

wirepulling ['waɪəpʊlɪŋ] **N** *esp Am Fam* intrigues *fpl*; **a bit of w. would help his cousin get the job** un peu de piston pourrait aider son cousin à avoir le poste

wiretap ['waɪətæp] **N** **they've put a w. on him** *or* **his telephone** on a mis sa ligne sur écoute
VT *(telephone line)* mettre sur écoute

wiretapping ['waɪətæpɪŋ] **N** mise *f* sur écoute d'une ligne téléphonique

wireworm ['waɪəwɜːm] **N** *(pest)* larve *f* de taupin; *(millipede)* iule *m*

wiring ['waɪərɪŋ] **N** installation *f* électrique; **the house needs new w.** il faut refaire l'installation électrique *ou* l'électricité dans la maison
▸▸ **w. diagram** schéma *m* de branchement, schéma de câblage

wiry ['waɪərɪ] **ADJ 1** *(hair)* raide **2** *(person)* vigoureux, (sec et) nerveux

Wis *abbr* Wisconsin

wisdom ['wɪzdəm] **N** *(knowledge)* sagesse *f*, *(advisability)* sagesse, prudence *f*; **the received** *or* **conventional w.** l'opinion communément admise; **to question the w. of a decision** mettre en cause la sagesse d'une décision
▸▸ **w. tooth** dent *f* de sagesse

wise¹ [waɪz] **ADJ** *(knowledgeable)* sage; *(advisable)* prudent; **a w. man** un sage; **the Three W. Men** les (Rois) Mages *mpl*; **to get** *or* **grow wise(r)** *(learn more)* s'assagir; *(gain experience)* acquérir de l'expérience; **it wouldn't be w. to do it** ça ne serait pas sage *ou* prudent (de le faire); **w. after the event** sage après coup; **everyone can be w. after the event** c'est facile d'avoir raison après coup; **I'm no wiser than you** je n'en sais pas plus long que vous; **she's none** *or* **not any the wiser (for it)** elle n'est pas plus avancée; **without anyone being (any) the wiser** à l'insu de tout le monde, sans que personne ne sache; **no one will be any the wiser** personne n'en saura rien; *Fam* **to get w. to a fact** se rendre compte d'un fait; *Fam* **to get w. to sb** se rendre compte de *ou* réaliser ce que qn fait; *Fam* **I'm w. to his tricks** je connais ses combines; *Fam* **to put sb w. to sth** avertir qn de qch; *Fam* **to put sb w. to sb** prévenir qn contre qn
▸▸ *Fam* **w. guy** malin, -igne; **don't be a w. guy!** ne fais pas le malin!

▸ **wise up** *esp Am Fam* **VT SEP** mettre au courant; **w. me up about it** mets-moi au courant
VI **to w. up to sb** se rendre compte du petit jeu de qn; **to w. up to the fact that …** se rendre compte du fait que …; **w. up!** ouvre les yeux!

wise² **N** *Lit (way)* manière *f*, façon *f*; **in no w.**

en aucune manière *ou* façon, nullement, aucunement

-wise [waɪz] **SUFF 1** *(indicating direction)* dans le sens de …; **lengthw.** dans le sens de la longueur **2** *Fam (with reference to)* en ce qui concerne …, du point de vue de …, côté …; **healthw.** en ce qui concerne la santé, côté santé; **salaryw.** en ce qui concerne le salaire, côté salaire VOIR GRAMMAIRE A20

wiseacre ['waɪzeɪkər] **N** *(person who wants to seem wise)* petit malin *m*

wiseass ['waɪzæs] **N** *Am Sl* je-sais-tout *mf inv*

wisecrack ['waɪzkræk] *Fam* **N** vanne *f*, blague *f*; **to make a w.** faire *ou* lancer une vanne; **I don't want any more wisecracks** je ne veux plus entendre une seule vanne
VI sortir une/des vanne(s), faire de l'esprit

wisecracking ['waɪzkrækɪŋ] **ADJ** *Fam* blagueur

wisely ['waɪzlɪ] **ADV 1** sagement, prudemment
2 **to shake one's head w.** secouer la tête d'un air entendu

WISH [wɪʃ]

N désir **1** ▪ vœu **2** ▪ souhait **2**				
▪ amitiés **3**				
VI vouloir ▪ souhaiter				
VT vouloir **1, 2** ▪ souhaiter **1–3**				

N 1 *(desire)* désir *m*; **I have no w. to go/to see it** je n'ai pas envie d'y aller/de le voir; **I have no w. to offend you, but …** je n'ai aucune envie de le blesser, mais …; **to express a w. to do sth** exprimer le désir de faire qch; **the w. to please** le désir de plaire; **by my father's w.** sur le désir de mon père; *Hum* **your w. is my command** vos désirs sont des ordres; **it was done against** *or* **contrary to my wishes** cela s'est fait à l'encontre de mon désir *ou* contre mon gré; **to make a w.** faire un vœu; **your w. will come true** ton vœu se réalisera **2** *(what is desired)* **you shall have your w.** votre vœu sera exaucé; **his great w. was to see his son become president** son plus grand souhait *ou* désir était de voir son fils président **3** *(greeting)* **they send you their best wishes** ils te font leurs amitiés; **please give your parents my best wishes** *(said verbally)* fais toutes mes amitiés à tes parents; *(in writing)* transmets mes meilleures pensées à tes parents; **with best wishes** *(at end of letter)* (bien) amicalement; **with best wishes for a speedy recovery** avec tous mes/nos meilleurs vœux de prompt rétablissement; **to send all good wishes to sb** présenter ses souhaits à qn
VI **to w. for sth** désirer *ou* vouloir *ou* souhaiter qch; **to w. for happiness/peace** désirer *ou* souhaiter le bonheur/la paix; **to have everything one can** *or* **could w. for** avoir tout pour être heureux; **I couldn't w. for anything better** je ne pourrais désirer mieux; **what more can** *or* **could you w. for?** que souhaiter de plus?; **as you w.** comme vous voulez
VT 1 *(want)* vouloir; **to w. to do sth** désirer *ou* vouloir faire qch; **I w. it to be done** je désire *ou* je veux que cela soit fait; **I w. them to be here tomorrow** je désire *ou* je souhaite qu'ils soient là demain; **it is to be wished that …** il est à souhaiter que …
2 *(want sth impossible, unlikely)* **I w. I were a bird!** je voudrais être un oiseau!; **I w. I were in your place** je voudrais bien être à votre place; **I w. I had seen it!** j'aurais bien voulu voir cela!, si seulement j'avais pu le voir!; **I w. I hadn't left so early** je regrette d'être parti si tôt, si seulement je n'étais pas parti si tôt; I

w. she would come j'aimerais bien qu'elle vienne; **how I w. I could (do it)!** si seulement je pouvais (le faire)!; **I w. he wouldn't say things like that!** il ne pourrait pas éviter de dire des choses pareilles!; **w. you were here!** *(on postcard)* je pense à vous

3 *(have feelings towards, greet)* **he wishes me well** il est bien disposé envers moi; **he wishes nobody ill** il ne veut de mal à personne; **w. me luck** souhaite-moi bonne chance; **to w. sb a pleasant journey** souhaiter bon voyage à qn; **to w. sb goodnight** souhaiter bonne nuit à qn, dire bonsoir à qn; *Iron* **I w. you joy of it** je te souhaite bien du plaisir

▸▸ *Psy* **w. fulfilment** accomplissement *m* d'un désir

▸ **wish away** VT SEP faire disparaître comme par enchantement; **you can't w. your problems away** tu ne vas pas te débarrasser de tes problèmes d'un coup de baguette magique; **to w. one's life away** souhaiter que sa vie soit différente

▸ **wish on** VT SEP **to w. sth on sb** obliger qn à accepter qch; **it was wished on me by my boss** j'ai été obligé de l'accepter à cause de mon patron, mon patron m'a obligé à l'accepter; **the boss wished his son on the head of marketing** le patron a imposé son fils au directeur du marketing; **I wouldn't w. this on my worst enemy** je ne souhaiterais pas cela à mon pire ennemi; **it's not an experience I would w. on anyone** c'est une expérience que je ne souhaiterais à personne; **can we w. the children on you for the day?** est-ce qu'on peut vous laisser les enfants pour la journée?

wishbone ['wɪʃbəʊn] N fourchette *f*, bréchet *m*; *esp Am (on surfboard)* wishbone *m*; **to pull a w. with sb** = faire un vœu avec qn en essayant de casser le bréchet du poulet

▸▸ *Aut* **w. suspension** suspension *f* triangulée

wishful thinking ['wɪʃfʊl] N **that's a bit of w.** c'est prendre ses désirs pour des réalités

wishy-washy ['wɪʃɪwɒʃɪ] ADJ *Fam (style)* fade, insipide; *(person)* indécis; *(compromise)* insatisfaisant; **a w. liberal** un libéral mou

wisp [wɪsp] N *(strand) (of straw, wool)* brin *m*; **w. of smoke** trainée *f* de fumée; **w. of hair** mèche *f* de cheveux; **a little w. of a girl** un tout petit bout de fille; **a w. of cloud** un filet de nuage

wispy ['wɪspɪ] ADJ *(beard, hair)* fin; *(cloud)* vaporeux

wisteria [wɪs'tɪərɪə] N *(plant)* glycine *f*

wistful ['wɪstfʊl] ADJ nostalgique; *(look, air, smile)* mélancolique; **he sounded w. when he spoke of her** il parlait d'elle avec une nuance de regret dans la voix

wistfully ['wɪstfəlɪ] ADV avec nostalgie, avec regret; **she looked w. at the children playing in the street** *(wanting to join them)* elle regardait avec envie les enfants qui jouaient dans la rue; *(thinking of the baby she never had)* elle regardait avec regret les enfants qui jouaient dans la rue

wit[1] [wɪt] N **1** *(intelligence) (often pl)* esprit *m*, entendement *m*, intelligence *f*; **he hasn't the w. to see it** il n'est pas assez intelligent pour s'en apercevoir; **he didn't have the w. to come and tell me** il n'a pas eu la présence d'esprit de me le dire; **he hasn't the w. he was born with!** il n'a pas inventé la poudre!; **to have quick wits** avoir l'esprit vif; **to have lost one's wits** avoir perdu l'esprit *ou* la raison; **to collect** *or* **gather one's wits** se ressaisir, reprendre ses esprits; **to have/keep one's wits about one** avoir/conserver toute sa présence d'esprit; **you need your wits about you in this job** il faut avoir de la présence d'esprit dans ce métier; **she has all her wits about her** c'est une maligne *ou* une fine; **to be at one's w.'s end** ne plus savoir que faire; **to have** *or* **engage in a battle of wits** jouer au plus fin; **to live by one's wits** vivre d'expédients; **to scare sb out of his/her wits** faire une peur bleue à qn; **to put one's wits to work on a problem** s'attaquer à un problème

2 *(humour)* esprit *m*, vivacité *f* d'esprit; **in a speech full of his usual w.** dans un de ses discours très spirituels; **flash of w.** trait *m* d'esprit; **sparkling with w.** étincelant d'esprit

3 *(person)* bel esprit *m*, homme *m*/femme *f* d'esprit; **what a w.!** toujours le mot pour rire!

wit[2] ADV *Law* **to w.** à savoir …, c'est-à-dire …

witch [wɪtʃ] N sorcière *f*, *Fig Pej* garce *f*, chameau *m*; **old w.** vieille sorcière

▸▸ **w. doctor** sorcier *m* guérisseur; **w. hazel** *(plant)* hamamélis *m*

witchcraft ['wɪtʃkrɑːft] N sorcellerie *f*, **to practise w.** pratiquer la sorcellerie

witchery ['wɪtʃərɪ] N **1** *(practice)* ensorcellement *m*, enchantement *m* **2** *(influence, charm)* envoûtement *m*, fascination *f*

witch-hunt N *Pol* chasse *f* aux sorcières

witch-hunting N *Pol* chasse *f* aux sorcières

witching ['wɪtʃɪŋ] ADJ *Lit, Hum* **the w. hour** minuit *m*, l'heure *f* du crime

WITH [wɪð]

▪ avec **1, 3, 5** ▪ à **2** ▪ chez **1, 3** ▪ de **5**	

PREP **1** *(expressing accompaniment)* avec; **to travel/work w. sb** voyager/travailler avec qn; **he is staying w. friends** il est chez des amis; **to mingle w. the crowd** se mêler à la foule; **I have nobody to go out w.** je n'ai personne avec qui sortir; **here I am w. nobody to talk to** me voilà sans personne à qui parler; **I'll be w. you in a moment** je serai à vous dans un instant; **some cheese to eat w. it** du fromage pour manger avec; **this is a problem that will always be w. us** ce problème sera toujours d'actualité; **she came in w. a suitcase** elle est entrée avec une valise; **I'm sorry I don't have a handkerchief w. me** je suis désolé, je n'ai pas de mouchoir; **do you have a pencil w. you?** avez-vous un crayon sur vous?; **to leave a child w. sb** laisser un enfant à la garde de qn; **the decision rests** *or* **lies w. you** c'est à vous de décider; **what will happen to her w. both her parents dead?** *(now that they are dead)* que va-t-elle devenir maintenant que son père et sa mère sont morts?

2 *(having)*; **a knife w. a silver handle** un couteau à manche d'argent; **a girl w. blue eyes** une jeune fille aux yeux bleus; **a child w. a cold** un enfant enrhumé; **w. his/her hat on** le chapeau sur la tête; **w. his (over)coat on** en pardessus; **w. your intelligence you'll easily guess what followed** intelligent comme vous l'êtes vous devinerez facilement la suite; *Arch* **w. child** *(of woman)* enceinte

3 *(expressing association)* avec; **to correspond w. sb** correspondre avec qn; **to have to do w. sb** avoir à faire avec qn; **to have nothing to do w. sb** n'avoir rien à faire avec qn; **to part w. sth** se dessaisir *ou* se défaire de qch; **the next move is w. him** c'est à lui d'agir maintenant; **w. him all men are equal** tous les hommes sont égaux à ses yeux *ou* pour lui; **to be patient w. sb** être patient avec qn; **to be honest w. oneself** être honnête envers *ou* avec soi-même; **it's a habit w. me** c'est une habitude chez moi; **to use one's influence w. sb** agir auprès de qn; **all is well w. her** elle va bien; **I sympathize w. you** je vous plains; **I don't agree w. you** je ne suis pas d'accord avec vous; **I'm w. you** *(I support you)* je suis de votre côté; *(I understand)* je vous suis, je comprends; **I'm not w. you** *(I don't understand)* je ne (vous) suis pas, je ne comprends pas; *Fam* **to be w. it** *(fashionable)* être à la page *ou* dans le vent; *Fam* **I'm not w. it today** je n'y suis pas aujourd'hui; **to rise w. the lark** se lever au chant du coq; **w. these words/w. that he dismissed me** sur ces mots/là-dessus, il m'a congédié; **she said this w. a smile** elle a dit ça avec un sourire *ou* en souriant; **w. a cry** en poussant un cri; **to compete w. sb** concourir avec qn; **to fight w. sb** se battre contre *ou* avec qn; *Fam* **get w. it** *(become alert)* réveille-toi; *(realize what's happening)* ouvre les yeux

4 *(despite)* malgré; **w. all his faults** malgré tous ses défauts; **w. the best will in the world** avec la meilleure volonté du monde

5 *(expressing instrument, agent)* **to cut sth w. a knife** couper qch avec un couteau *ou* au couteau; **to walk w. (the aid of) a stick** marcher avec une canne; **to fight w. swords** se battre à l'épée; **to take sth w. both hands** prendre qch à deux mains; **to strike w. all one's might** frapper de toutes ses forces; **to tremble w. rage** trembler de rage; **to be stiff w. cold** être engourdi par le froid; **to be ill w. measles** avoir la rougeole; **to fill a vase w. water** remplir un vase d'eau; **lorry loaded w. timber** camion chargé de bois; **it's pouring w. rain** il pleut à verse

6 *(forming adv phrase)* **to work w. a will** travailler avec courage *ou* ardeur; **to receive/welcome sb w. open arms** recevoir/accueillir qn à bras ouverts; **w. all due respect** avec tout le respect que je vous dois; **w. your permission** avec votre permission; **w. this object (in view)** dans ce but; **I say it w. regret** je le dis à regret; **w. a few exceptions** à part quelques exceptions, quelques exceptions mises à part; **away w. care!** plus de soucis!, ça suffit, les soucis!; **down w. the police!** à bas les flics!; *Fam* **to hell w. him!** qu'il aille au diable!, qu'il aille se faire voir!

withal [wɪ'ðɔːl] ADV *Arch* de plus

withdraw [wɪð'drɔː] *(pt* **withdrew** [-'druː]; *pp* **withdrawn** [-'drɔːn]) VT **1** *(one's hand, support)* retirer; **the government has withdrawn funding from the project** le gouvernement a arrêté de financer le projet **2** *(troops)* retirer **3** *(money)* retirer; **to w. coins from circulation** retirer des pièces de la circulation, démonétiser des pièces **4** *(offer, remark, candidacy)* retirer; *(promise)* retirer, revenir sur; *(claim)* renoncer à; **to w. a charge** se rétracter; **to w. an order** *Com* annuler une commande; *Admin* rapporter un décret; *Law* **to w. one's action** retirer sa plainte; *Fml* **to w. one's labour** faire la grève; **the right to w. one's labour** le droit de grève VI **1** *(also after sex act)* retirer *(* **from** *de)*; **he withdrew ten paces** il a reculé de dix pas; **to w. in favour of sb** *(of candidate)* se désister en faveur de qn; **to w. into oneself** se replier sur soi-même; **to w. into silence** se renfermer dans le silence **2** *Mil* se retirer

withdrawal [wɪð'drɔː(ə)l] N **1** *(of one's troops)* retrait *m*; *(by troops)* retraite *f*; **to make a w.** *(of troops)* se retirer, battre en retraite; *Fig* **to make a w. from one's position** battre en retraite

2 *Banking* retrait *m*; **cash w.** retraite *m* en espèces; **to make a w.** faire un retrait; **w. of capital** retrait de fonds; **w. from circulation** démonétisation *f*

3 *Psy* repli *m* sur soi; *(from drugs)* (état *m* ou

crise *f* de) manque *m*; **the boy is showing signs of w.** le jeune garçon présente des signes de repli sur lui-même

4 *(of decree, order)* rappel *m*; *(of promise, accusation)* rétractation *f*; *(of complaint)* retrait *m*; **w. of a candidate** désistement *m* d'un candidat

5 *(after sex act)* retrait *m*

▸▸*Banking* **w. limit** plafond *m* (d'autorisation) de retrait; **w. method** *(of contraception)* coït *m* interrompu; *Banking* **w. notice** avis *m* de retrait; *Banking* **w. slip** bordereau *m* de retrait; **w. symptoms** symptômes *mpl* de manque; **to suffer w. symptoms** *(of alcoholic, drug addict)* être en manque; *Fig* se sentir perdu

withdrawn [wɪð'drɔːn] **ADJ** *(reserved)* replié sur soi-même

wither ['wɪðər] **VI** *(of plant)* se dessécher, se flétrir, se faner; *(of limb)* s'atrophier; *Fig (of beauty)* passer, (se) faner; *(of hope)* s'évanouir; *(of person, company)* dépérir; **without the steel industry the region will simply w. and die** sans l'industrie sidérurgique, la région va mourir lentement; **the party gradually withered and died** le parti s'est peu à peu éteint

VT *(of wind, heat) (plant)* dessécher, flétrir, faner; *(limb)* atrophier; *Fig* **to w. sb with a look** foudroyer qn du regard

▸ **wither away**, **wither up** **VI** = wither

withered ['wɪðəd] **ADJ 1** *(plant)* desséché, flétri, fané; *(face, cheek)* fané, flétri; **he was old and w.** il était vieux et complètement desséché **2** *(arm)* atrophié

withering ['wɪðərɪŋ] **ADJ** *(heat)* qui dessèche, qui flétrit; *Fig (look)* foudroyant; *(tone)* de mépris; **w. sarcasm** sarcasme cinglant; **to give sb a w. look** foudroyer qn du regard

witheringly ['wɪðərɪŋlɪ] **ADV** *(to look at)* avec mépris; *(to say)* d'un ton méprisant

withers ['wɪðəz] **NPL** *(of horse)* garrot *m*

withershins ['wɪðəʃɪnz] **ADV** *Scot* à contresens

withhold [wɪð'həʊld] **VT** *(pt, pp* withheld [-'held])* **1** *(not give) (consent, help)* refuser; *(money)* retenir; *(taxes)* prélever; **to w. recognition of a country** ne pas reconnaître un pays **2** *(suppress) (fact etc)* taire, supprimer; *(information)* retenir, bloquer; **I managed to w. my indignation/laughter** j'ai réussi à contenir mon indignation/rire; **to w. the truth from sb** cacher la vérité à qn **3** *Law (property)* détenir

withholding [wɪð'həʊldɪŋ] **N 1** *(of help, aid, loan)* refus *m*; *(of taxes)* prélèvement *m*, retenue *f* **2** *(of information, facts)* rétention *f*

within [wɪð'ɪn] **ADV** from w. de l'intérieur; **seen from w.** vu de l'intérieur *ou* du dedans; **staff required, apply w.** *(notice in shop window)* on recherche du personnel, se présenter à l'intérieur

PREP 1 *(not beyond)* **w. reason** dans des limites raisonnables; **to keep w. the law** rester dans (les limites de) la légalité; **it is quite w. the realms of possibility** c'est dans les limites du possible; **to keep** *or* **live w. one's income** vivre selon ses moyens; **w. sight** en vue; **to keep sb/sth w. sight** avoir qn/qch à portée de vue; **to be w. sight of the shore** avoir la côte en vue; **w. call** à portée de (la) voix; **w. two miles of the town** à moins de deux milles de la ville; **w. a radius of ten kilometres** dans un rayon de dix kilomètres; **I live w. walking distance of the office** je peux aller au travail à pied; **is it w. walking distance?** est-ce qu'on peut y aller à pied?; **we were w. an inch of death** nous étions à deux doigts de la mort

2 *(in expressions of time)* **w. an hour** en moins d'une heure; **it will be ready w. an** *or* **the hour** ça sera prêt d'ici une heure; **w. a**

week *(in the space of)* en moins d'une semaine; *(by the time a week has passed)* d'ici une semaine; **w. the week** avant la fin de la semaine, dans la semaine; **w. a year of his death** *(after he died)* moins d'un an après sa mort; *(before he died)* moins d'un an avant sa mort; **w. the next week** dans le courant de la semaine prochaine; **w. the next five years, w. five years from now** d'ici cinq ans; **w. the required time** dans le délai prescrit; **w. twenty-four hours** dans les vingt-quatre heures; **w. ten days of receipt of your order** dans un délai de dix jours à compter de la réception de votre commande; **w. a short time** *(soon)* à court délai; *(soon after)* peu de temps après; **her time was w. a few seconds of the world record** son temps était à quelques secondes du record du monde

3 *Old-fashioned, Lit (inside)* à l'intérieur de, en dedans de; **w. these four walls** entre ces quatre murs; **the enemy is w. our frontiers** l'ennemi est dans nos frontières; **a voice w. me** une voix intérieure

without [wɪð'aʊt] **PREP 1** sans; **she did it w. asking/being asked** elle l'a fait sans demander/sans qu'on le lui demande; **to be w. a care in the world** n'avoir aucun souci; **w. a tail/coat/hope** sans queue/manteau/espoir; **to be w. food** manquer de nourriture; **he came back w. any money** il est revenu sans argent; **w. any difficulty** sans aucune difficulté; **the rumour is w. foundation** la rumeur est dénuée de fondement *ou* n'est pas fondée; **not w. difficulty** non sans difficulté; **w. end** sans fin; **he passed by w. seeing me/being seen** il est passé sans me voir/être vu; **it goes w. saying that ...** il va sans dire *ou* de soi que ...; **can you do it w. her knowing about it?** pouvez-vous le faire sans qu'elle le sache?; **they are w. any knowledge of French** ils n'ont aucune connaissance du français; **to do** *or* **go w. sth** se passer de qch; **I don't want her to go w. anything** je ne veux pas qu'elle manque de quoi que ce soit; **w. so much as saying goodbye/asking permission** sans même dire au revoir/demander la permission **2** *Arch (outside)* en dehors de

ADV *Arch* à l'extérieur, au dehors; **from w.** de l'extérieur; **seen from w.** vu de l'extérieur *ou* du dehors

with-pack premium **N** *Mktg* prime *f* directe

with-profits **ADJ** *Fin (pension fund)* avec participation aux bénéfices

withstand [wɪð'stænd] **VT** *(pt, pp* withstood [-'stʊd])* *(person, pain, pressure)* résister à; **to w. the heat** supporter la chaleur; *Mil etc* **to w. an attack** soutenir une attaque

withy ['wɪðɪ] **N** brin *m ou* lien *m* d'osier

witless ['wɪtlɪs] **ADJ** stupide, sot, *f* sotte; *Fam* **to scare sb w.** faire une peur bleue à qn

witness ['wɪtnɪs] **N 1** *(person)* témoin *m*; *(to will)* témoin testamentaire; **will you act as a w. at our wedding?** est-ce que vous voulez bien être témoin à notre mariage?; **I gave my name as a w.** j'ai donné mon nom en tant que témoin; *Law* **w. to a document** *or* **a deed** témoin instrumentaire, témoin à un acte; *Law* **to call sb as w.** citer qn comme témoin; *Law* **w. for the defence/prosecution** témoin à décharge/charge

2 *(testimony)* témoignage *m*; **to give w. on behalf of the accused** rendre témoignage pour l'accusé, témoigner en faveur de l'accusé; **to bear w. to sth** rendre *ou* porter témoignage de qch, témoigner de qch, attester qch; **this situation bears w. to the need to ...** cette situation témoigne de la nécessité de ...; *Rel* **to bear false w.** porter un faux témoignage; **I call you to w.** j'en appelle à votre témoignage

VT *(scene)* être spectateur *ou* témoin de; *(interview etc)* assister à; *Law (deed)* attester; *Law (signature)* certifier; **I witnessed the whole thing** j'ai assisté à tout ce qui s'est passé; **this house has witnessed many deaths** cette maison a vu de nombreux décès; **we are witnessing a historic event** nous assistons à un événement historique; **he had witnessed the entire scene from his window** il avait vu *ou* assisté à toute la scène depuis sa fenêtre; **never in my entire life have I witnessed such stupidity** je n'ai jamais, de ma vie entière, vu une telle stupidité

VI *Law* **to w. to sth** témoigner de qch; **to w. against/for sb** témoigner contre/en faveur de qn

▸▸*Br* **w. box** barre *f* des témoins

-witted [-'wɪtɪd] **SUFF** slow/quick/*etc*-w. qui a l'esprit lent/vif/*etc*

witter ['wɪtər] **VI** *Br Fam* **to w. (on)** parler interminablement, parler pour ne rien dire; **to w. (on) about sth** parler interminablement de qch; **what's he wittering (on) about now?** qu'est-ce qu'il est encore en train de raconter?

wittering ['wɪtərɪŋ] **N** *Br Fam* bavardage *m*; **his constant w. gets on my nerves** son papotage me tape sur les nerfs

witticism ['wɪtɪsɪz(ə)m] **N** mot *m* d'esprit, bon mot

wittily ['wɪtɪlɪ] **ADV** spirituellement, avec esprit

wittiness ['wɪtɪnɪs] **N** *(of remark etc)* esprit *m*, sel *m*

wittingly ['wɪtɪŋlɪ] **ADV** *(intentionally)* sciemment, en connaissance de cause, intentionnellement

witty ['wɪtɪ] **ADJ** spirituel, plein d'esprit

wizard ['wɪzəd] **N 1** sorcier *m*, magicien *m*; *Fig* génie *m*; **he's a real w. with figures/computers** c'est un as des chiffres/des ordinateurs; **to be a financial w.** avoir le génie de la finance *ou* des affaires; **she's a w. on the violin** c'est une violoniste géniale *ou* de génie; **to be a w. with a sewing needle** avoir des doigts de fée (pour la couture) **2** *Comput* assistant *m*

ADJ *Old-fashioned Br Fam* épatant, excellent

wizardry ['wɪzədrɪ] **N** sorcellerie *f*, magie *f*; *Fig* génie *m*, habileté *f*; **her financial w.** son talent génial en matière de finance; **that was sheer w. with the ball** c'était un jeu purement et simplement génial

wizened ['wɪzənd] **ADJ** ratatiné; *(cheeks)* parcheminé; *(apple)* ratatiné, ridé; **to become w.** *(of person, apple)* se ratatiner; *(of skin)* se parcheminer

wk *abbr* week

WO [dʌb(ə)ljuː'əʊ] **N** *Br Mil abbr* warrant officer

wo(a) ['wəʊ(ə)] **INT** *(to horse)* ho!, holà!

woad [wəʊd] **N** guède *f*

wobble ['wɒb(ə)l] **N 1** *(swaying)* **the chair/desk has got a bit of a w.** la chaise/le bureau est légèrement bancal(e) *ou* branlant(e); **there is a slight w. in the front wheel of the bike** la roue avant du vélo a un léger jeu; *Aut* **front-wheel w.** shimmy *m* **2** *(of voice)* tremblement *m*

VI 1 *(sway) (of flame)* vaciller, osciller; *(of jelly, thighs etc)* trembler; *(of table)* branler; *(of person)* chanceler; *(of building, tooth)* bouger; *(of wheel)* avoir du jeu **2** *(of voice etc)* trembler, chevroter **3** *Fam (hesitate)* hésiter

wobbly ['wɒblɪ] **ADJ 1** *(table, chair)* branlant; *(flame)* vacillant; *(person)* chancelant; **the whole structure is slightly w.** toute la structure bouge légèrement; **my legs** *or* **I feel w.** j'ai les jambes en coton; *Fam* **I'm a**

bit w. on irregular verbs je ne maîtrise pas vraiment les verbes irréguliers **2** *(voice etc)* chevrotant, tremblotant

N *Br Fam* **to throw a w.** piquer une *ou* sa crise

wodge [wɒdʒ] **N** *Br Fam (of bread)* gros morceau *m*; *(of money)* gros paquet *m*; **a huge w. of time** un bon bout de temps

woe [wəʊ] **N** *Lit* malheur *m*, chagrin *m*, peine *f*; **to tell a tale of w.** raconter ses malheurs; **to recount one's woes** égrener ses malheurs; **w. is me!** pauvre de moi!, malheureux que je suis!; **w. betide you if you're late** malheur à toi si tu es en retard

woebegone ['wəʊbɪgɒn] **ADJ** *(look, face)* désolé, abattu; **to look w.** avoir l'air désolé

woeful ['wəʊfʊl] **ADJ 1** *(bad)* déplorable, mauvais; **w. standard of workmanship** qualité *f* de travail déplorable **2** *Lit (look)* affligé, malheureux; *(news)* attristant, affligeant; **the Knight of the W. Countenance** le chevalier à la Triste Figure

woefully ['wəʊfəlɪ] **ADV 1** *(bad, ill-equipped, inadequate etc)* terriblement; *(low)* déplorablement; **a w. inadequate husband** un très mauvais mari **2** *(to say, look at)* tristement

wog [wɒg] **N** *Br Offensive Sl* métèque *m*

wok [wɒk] **N** wok *m*, poêle *f* chinoise

wold [wəʊld] **N** *Geog* plateau *m*

wolf, *pl* **wolves** [wʊlf, wʊlvz] **N 1** loup *m*; **she w.** louve *f*; **to be as hungry as a w.** avoir une faim de loup; *Fig* **that will keep the w. from the door** cela vous/nous/*etc* mettra à l'abri du besoin; *Fig* **to throw sb to the wolves** sacrifier qn; **a w. in sheep's clothing** un loup déguisé en agneau; **to cry w.** crier au loup **2** *Fam (womanizer)* coureur *m* de jupons

▸▸ *Old-fashioned Br Fam* **W. Cub** *(scout)* louveteau *m*; **w. whistle** sifflement *m (au passage d'une femme)*

▸ **wolf down** **VT SEP** engloutir, dévorer

wolfhound ['wʊlfhaʊnd] **N** chien-loup *m*, *pl* chiens-loups; **Irish w.** lévrier *m* d'Irlande

wolfish ['wʊlfɪʃ] **ADJ** de loup; *(appetite)* vorace; **a w. grin** un sourire aux dents longues

wolfram ['wʊlfrəm] **N** *Miner* wolfram *m*

wolfsbane ['wʊlfsbeɪn] **N** *(plant)* aconit *m*

wolf-whistle **VT & VI** siffler; **to get wolf-whistled** se faire siffler

wolverine ['wʊlvəriːn] **N** glouton *m*

woman, *pl* **women** ['wʊmən, 'wɪmɪn] **N** VOIR GRAMMAIRE A13 femme *f*; **an old w.** une vieille femme, *Pej* une vieille; *Fam (man)* un chipoteur; **the other w.** l'autre femme; **they have a w. in to do the cleaning** ils ont quelqu'un qui vient faire le ménage; **she's his w.** c'est sa compagne; **he's got women all over the place** il a des maîtresses partout; *Old-fashioned Fam* **the little w.** *(my wife)* ma femme; *Fam* **get in the car, w.!** allez femme, en voiture!; **to run after women** courir le jupon; **a w.'s place is in the home** une femme doit rester à la maison; *Prov* **a w.'s work is never done** = les femmes sont constamment occupées (à la maison); **the women's movement**, *Fam* **women's lib** le Mouvement pour la libération de la femme; *Fam Pej* **women's libber** féministe *f*, *Journ* **women's page** page *f* des lectrices; **women's magazines** magazines féminins, revues féminines; **women's problems** ennuis *ou* problèmes de femmes *ou* féminins; **women's refuge, women's shelter** centre *m* d'accueil pour les femmes

▸▸ **w. artist** femme *f* peintre; **w. doctor** (femme) médecin *m*; **w. driver** conductrice *f*; **it was a w. driver** c'était une femme qui conduisait; **w. friend** amie *f*

womanhater ['wʊmənheɪtər] **N** misogyne *m*

womanhood ['wʊmənhʊd] **N** féminité *f*; **to grow to w.** devenir femme

womanish ['wʊmənɪʃ] **ADJ** *Pej (characteristic of a woman)* de femme; *(man)* efféminé

womanize ['wʊmənaɪz] **VI** courir les femmes, courir le jupon

womanizer ['wʊmənaɪzər] **N** coureur *m* (de femmes)

womanizing ['wʊmənaɪzɪŋ] **N** aventures *fpl*; **she was fed up with his w.** elle en avait assez qu'il coure le jupon

womankind ['wʊmənkaɪnd] **N** *(no pl)* les femmes *fpl*

womanliness ['wʊmənlɪnɪs] **N** féminité *f*

womanly ['wʊmənlɪ] **ADJ** féminin

womb [wuːm] **N** *Anat* utérus *m*; **the child she carried in her w.** l'enfant qu'elle portait dans son ventre *ou* *Lit* sein; **while still in his mother's w.** quand il était encore dans le ventre de sa mère

wombat ['wɒmbæt] **N** wombat *m*, phascolome *m*

women ['wɪmɪn] **NPL** *see* **woman**

womenfolk ['wɪmɪnfəʊk] **N** *(no pl)* les femmes *fpl*; **the settlers brought their w.** les colons ont amené leurs femmes et leurs filles

won **PT**, **PP** *see* **win**[2]

wonder ['wʌndər] **N 1** *(miracle)* merveille *f*, miracle *m*, prodige *m*; **to work** *or* **do wonders** faire des merveilles *ou* des miracles; **the seven wonders of the world** les sept merveilles du monde; **one of the wonders of the world** une des merveilles du monde; **it's a w. (that) he hasn't lost it** c'est un miracle qu'il ne l'ait pas perdu; **no** *or* **little** *or* **small w. that the plan failed** il n'est guère *ou* pas étonnant que le projet n'ait pas réussi; **she's angry and no** *or* **little w.** elle est en colère et ce n'est pas étonnant; **a nine-day(s') w.** la merveille d'un jour; **w. cure** traitement *m* miracle; **w. drug** remède *m* miracle

2 *(astonishment)* étonnement *m*, surprise *f*; *(admiration)* émerveillement *m*, admiration *f*; **in w.** émerveillé; **to look at sb in w.** regarder qn avec émerveillement; **to fill sb with w.** émerveiller qn; **an expression** *or* **look of w.** un air émerveillé, une expression d'émerveillement; **I looked at it with a sense of w.** je l'ai regardé, émerveillé; **he has no sense of w.** il n'a aucune capacité d'émerveillement

VI *(be amazed)* s'étonner, s'émerveiller (**at** de); *Iron* **I really w. at you sometimes!** tu me surprendras toujours!; **I w. at how he manages to do it** je suis étonné par sa façon de s'y prendre; **I w. about her sometimes** je me pose des questions à son sujet parfois; **I was wondering about buying a new car** je songeais à acheter une nouvelle voiture; **I don't w. at it** cela ne m'étonne pas *ou* ne me surprend pas; **it's not to be wondered at that she left** il n'est pas étonnant qu'elle soit partie, rien d'étonnant à ce qu'elle soit partie

VT 1 *(be amazed)* **to w. that ...** s'étonner que ... + *sub*; **I w. that nobody thought of it before** je m'étonne que personne n'y ait pensé avant; **can you w. that he refused?** comment s'étonner qu'il ait refusé?

2 *(ask oneself)* se demander; **I w.** *(if he/she/etc will do that)* je ne le demande; **one wonders!** c'est à se demander!; **it makes you w. how safe these power stations are** on en vient à se demander si ces centrales électriques sont vraiment sûres; **I w. whether he'll come** je me demande s'il va vouloir bien venir; **one wonders whether ...** c'est à se demander si ...; **I shouldn't w. if he were already married** cela ne m'étonnerait pas *ou* ne me surprendrait pas qu'il soit

déjà marié; **she knows a lot more, I shouldn't w.** cela ne m'étonnerait pas qu'elle en sache beaucoup plus long que ça; **I w. who invented that** je suis curieux de savoir qui a inventé cela; **I w. why!** je voudrais bien savoir pourquoi!; **their son will help them – I w.!** leur fils leur viendra en aide – vous croyez?; **I was wondering if you were free tonight** je me demandais si vous étiez libre ce soir; **oh, I just wondered** *(answering question 'why do you ask?')* oh, pour rien, comme ça; **I was just wondering where you'd got to** j'étais en train de me demander où tu étais

Wonderbra® ['wʌndəbrɑː] **N** Wonderbra® *m*

wonderful ['wʌndəfʊl] **ADJ** merveilleux, prodigieux, admirable; *(film, book)* remarquable, formidable; **it's w. weather** il fait un temps fantastique; **a w. meal** un excellent *ou* délicieux repas; **she's a w. mother** c'est une mère merveilleuse; **she's a w. person** elle est fantastique; **it was w.!** c'était merveilleux *ou* magnifique!; **we had a w. time** nous nous sommes très bien amusés

wonderfully ['wʌndəfʊlɪ] **ADV** merveilleusement; **he sings w.** il chante merveilleusement *ou* remarquablement (bien); **it was w. hot** il faisait délicieusement chaud; **w. well** merveilleusement bien, à merveille; **a w. good book** un livre absolument génial; **we had some w. good food** nous avons très bien mangé

wondering ['wʌndərɪŋ] **ADJ** *(amazed)* étonné, émerveillé; **the child's w. eyes** les yeux émerveillés de l'enfant

wonderingly ['wʌndərɪŋlɪ] **ADV** avec étonnement, d'un air étonné

wonderland ['wʌndəlænd] **N** pays *m* des merveilles; **Alice in W.** Alice au Pays des Merveilles

wonderment ['wʌndəmənt] **N** *Lit* émerveillement *m*; **she looked at him with** *or* **in w.** elle l'a regardé avec émerveillement

wondrous ['wʌndrəs] *Arch, Lit* **ADJ** merveilleux

ADV merveilleusement

wondrously ['wʌndrəslɪ] **ADV** *Arch, Lit* merveilleusement

wonga ['wɒŋgə] **N** *Br Fam (money)* fric *m*, flouze *m*, pognon *m*

wonk [wɒŋk] **N** *Am (student)* bûcheur, -euse; *(intellectual, expert)* intello *mf* (qui n'intéresse qu'à sa discipline)

wonky ['wɒŋkɪ] **ADJ** *Br Fam (machine)* détraqué, déglingué; *(gadget, zip, switch etc)* qui débloque; *(collar, picture etc)* de travers; *(wardrobe, shelves)* branlant; *(one leg short)* *(chair, table)* boiteux; *(idea)* fumeux; **to feel w.** *(of person)* se sentir patraque; **this sentence is a bit w.** il y a quelque chose qui cloche dans cette phrase; **my grammar's a bit w.** ma grammaire cloche un peu; **the floorboards are a bit w.** le plancher n'est pas dans un état merveilleux

wont [wəʊnt] *Lit* **ADJ** **to be w. to do sth** avoir coutume *ou* l'habitude de faire qch; **he is w. to panic** il a tendance à paniquer, il panique facilement

N coutume *f*, habitude *f*; **according to his w., as is/was his w.** selon sa coutume, à *ou* selon *ou* suivant son habitude

won't [wəʊnt] **CONTR** = **will not**, *see* **will**[2]

wonted ['wəʊntɪd] **ADJ** *Lit* habituel, accoutumé

woo [wuː] **VT 1** *Fig (potential employee, supporter, company)* courtiser; *(fame)* rechercher; **they wooed voters with promises of reforms** *(tried to attract)* ils ont essayé d'attirer les électeurs avec des promesses de réforme; *(succeeded in attracting)* ils se sont assuré les voix des électeurs avec des promesses de réforme; **they wooed him away from their rivals by promising him more money** ils lui ont fait quitter leurs concurrents en lui promettant plus d'argent **2** *Arch, Lit (court) (woman)* faire la cour à, courtiser

wood [wʊd] **N 1** *(group of trees)* bois *m*; **a walk in the woods** une promenade en forêt; *Fig* **you can't see the w. for the trees** les arbres cachent la forêt; **his problem is that he can't see the w. for the trees** son problème, c'est que les arbres lui cachent la forêt; *Fig* **we're not out of the w. yet** nous ne sommes pas encore tirés d'affaire

2 *(material)* bois *m*; **made of w.** fait de bois, en bois; *Fig* **touch w.!**, *Am* **knock on w.!** touchons du bois!; *Am* **to put the w. to sb** *Fam (beat up)* tabasser qn; *(defeat)* battre qn à plates coutures; *Vulg (have sex with)* tringler qn; *Vulg* **to get w.** *(erection)* bander

3 *(in wine making)* le tonneau, le fût; **wine in the w.** vin *m* en tonneau *ou* en fût; **beer (drawn) from the w.** bière tirée au fût **4** *Golf* bois *m*; **a number 4 w.** un bois numéro 4

5 *(in game of bowls)* boule *f*

6 *Mus* = **woodwind**

▸▸**w. alcohol** esprit-de-bois *m*, alcool *m* méthylique; *Bot* **w. anemone** anémone *f* des bois; **w. ash** cendre *f* de bois; **w. block** planche *f*, bois; **w. carver** sculpteur *m* sur bois; **w. carving** sculpture *f* sur bois; **w. chisel** ciseau *m* à bois; **w. fire** feu *m* de bois; **w. nymph** nymphe *f* des bois, dryade *f*; **w. panelling** boiserie *f*; *Orn* **w. pigeon** ramier *m*; **w. pulp** pâte *f* à papier; **w. stove** poêle *m* à bois

woodbine [wʊdbaɪn] **N** *(honeysuckle)* chèvrefeuille *m* des bois; *Am (Virginia creeper)* vigne *f* vierge

woodchuck [wʊdtʃʌk] **N** marmotte *f* d'Amérique

woodcock [wʊdkɒk] **N** *(usu inv in pl)* bécasse *f* (des bois)

woodcraft [wʊdkrɑːft] **N 1** *(knowledge of forest)* connaissance *f* de la forêt **2** *(woodwork)* (pratique *f* du) travail *m* sur bois

woodcut [wʊdkʌt] **N** gravure *f* sur bois

woodcutter [wʊdkʌtər] **N** bûcheron *m*

woodcutting [wʊdkʌtɪŋ] **N 1** *Art (process, object)* gravure *f* sur bois **2** *(in forest)* abattage *m* du bois

wooded [wʊdɪd] **ADJ** boisé; **densely w.** très boisé

wooden [wʊd(ə)n] **ADJ 1** *(made of wood)* de bois, en bois; **the W. Horse of Troy** le cheval de Troie **2** *Fig (movement, manner)* raide, gauche; *(look)* impassible; *(performance, actor)* peu naturel; **w. smile** sourire *m* forcé

▸▸*Fam Hum* **w. overcoat** *(coffin)* costume *m* de sapin; **w. pallet** palette *f* en bois; **w. spoon** cuillère *f* en bois; *Fig* prix *m* de consolation

wooden-headed **ADJ** *Fam (stupid)* stupide, bouché

woodenness [wʊdənnɪs] **N** *Fig (of manner)* raideur *f*; *(of actor, performance)* manque *m* de naturel

woodfree [wʊdfriː] **ADJ** *(paper)* sans bois

woodie [wʊdɪ] **N** *Am Sl (erection)* érection *f*, bandaison *f*; **to have a w.** bander

woodland [wʊdlənd] **N** région *f* boisée, bois *mpl*

ADJ *(fauna)* des bois; **w. scenery** paysage *m* boisé

woodlark [wʊdlɑːk] **N** alouette *f* des bois

woodlouse, *pl* **woodlice** [wʊdlaʊs, -laɪs] **N** cloporte *m*

woodman, *pl* **woodmen** [wʊdmən] **N** *(logger)* bûcheron *m*

woodpecker [wʊdpekər] **N** pic *m*

woodpile [wʊdpaɪl] **N** tas *m ou* monceau *m* de bois

woodshed [wʊdʃed] **N** remise *f* à bois; *Fig* **there's something nasty in the w.** il se passe du vilain

woodsman, *pl* **woodsmen** [wʊdzmən] **N** *esp Am (hunter)* chasseur *m* (en forêt); *(for skins)* trappeur *m*; *(in forestry)* forestier *m*

woodstack [wʊdstæk] **N** = **woodpile**

woodwind [wʊdwɪnd] **N** *Mus (single instrument)* bois *m*; *(family of instruments)* bois *mpl*

▸▸**w. instrument** bois; **w. section** bois

woodwork [wʊdwɜːk] **N 1** *(action)* travail *m* du bois; *(smaller scale)* menuiserie *f*, ébénisterie *f*, *(school subject)* menuiserie **2** *(carved wood)* bois *m* travaillé; *(ornamental)* boiserie *f*, *(structural)* charpente *f*; **that's a fine piece of w.** c'est de la belle menuiserie; *Fig Pej* **to come out of the w.** sortir d'on ne sait où; *Sport* **to hit the w.** heurter les bois

woodworm [wʊdwɜːm] **N** ver *m* à bois; **this table's got w.** cette table est vermoulue; **it's full of w.** c'est rongé par les vers

woody [wʊdɪ] **ADJ 1** *(countryside)* boisé **2** *Bot* ligneux **3** *(smell, texture)* de bois

wooer [wuːər] **N** *Old-fashioned, Lit* prétendant *m*

woof¹ [wʊf] **N** *(of dog)* aboiement *m*; **the doggie goes w. (w.)** *(in children's language)* le toutou fait oua-oua

VI 1 *(of dog)* aboyer, faire oua-oua **2** *Am Sl (boast, bluff)* frimer, flamber

woof² [wuːf] **N** *Tex* trame *f*

woofer [wuːfər] **N** *(in stereo equipment)* haut-parleur *m* de basses, *pl* hauts-parleurs de basses, boomer *m*, woofer *m*

woofter [wʊftər] **N** *Br Offensive Sl (homosexual)* tante *f*, tapette *f*

wool [wʊl] **N 1** *(material)* laine *f*, **pure** *or* **w. suit** complet *m* pure laine; **a ball of w.** une pelote de laine; *Fig* **to pull the w. over sb's eyes** jeter de la poudre aux yeux de qn; *Fig* **you can't pull the w. over my eyes** tu ne peux pas me faire croire n'importe quoi **2** *(of animal)* pelage *m* **3** *Tech* **steel** *or* **wire w.** paille *f* de fer

ADJ 1 *(made of wool) (cloth)* de laine; *(socks, dress)* en laine **2** *(relating to wool)* **the w. industry** l'industrie *f* lainière; **the w. trade** le commerce des laines; **w. shop** magasin *m* de laines

woolen, wooly *etc Am* = **woollen, woolly** *etc*

woolgathering [wʊlgæð(ə)rɪŋ] **N** *Fam* **1** *(daydreaming)* rêvasserie *f* **2** *(used as a verb)* **to be w.** rêvasser, être dans les nuages; **he's always w.** il a toujours l'esprit ailleurs, il est toujours ailleurs

woollen, *Am* **woolen** [wʊlən] **ADJ** *(dress etc)* en laine; **w. materials** laines *fpl*, lainages *mpl*

NPL woollens lainages *mpl*

woolliness, *Am* **wooliness** [wʊlɪnɪs] **N 1** *(of reasoning, style)* imprécision *f*, *(of ideas)* caractère *m* confus; *(of outline)* manque *m* de netteté, flou *m* **2** *(resemblance to wool)* nature *f* laineuse (**of** de)

woolly, *Am* **wooly** [wʊlɪ] **ADJ 1** *(resembling wool)* laineux, de laine; **w. clouds** nuages ouatés; **w. hair** cheveux crépus **2** *Fig (vague)* peu net; *(outline)* flou; **w. ideas** idées vagues *ou* nébuleuses; **w.-minded** aux idées imprécises *ou* vagues; **w. style** style qui manque de précision; **a w. liberal** un libéral aux idées vagues

N *Fam (garment)* tricot *m*, laine *f*; **winter woollies** vêtements chauds d'hiver

Woolsack [wʊlsæk] **N** *Br Parl* **the W.** = le siège du Lord Chancellor (à la Chambre des Lords)

woozy [wuːzɪ] **ADJ** *Fam (person)* dans les vapes, patraque; **I feel a bit w.** je me sens un peu patraque, je me sens tout chose

wop [wɒp] **N** *Offensive Sl* macaroni *m*, rital *m*

Worcs *abbr* **Worcestershire**

WORD [wɜːd]

N	mot **1, 5, 9** ▪ nouvelle **3** ▪ parole **4, 7** ▪ ordre **6**
VT	formuler

N 1 mot *m*; **w. for w.** *(to repeat sth)* mot pour mot; *(to translate sth)* mot à mot, textuellement; **in a w.** en un mot, (en) bref; **in a w., no** en un mot, non; **in a few words** en quelques mots; **in other words** en d'autres termes, autrement dit; **those were her very words** ce sont ses propres mots; **I told him what I thought of him in so many words** je lui ai dit clairement ce que je pensais de lui; **did she say you could take it? – well, not in so many words** est-ce qu'elle a dit que tu pouvais le prendre? – eh bien, pas exactement; **in the strict sense of the w.** au sens strict du mot; **he doesn't know a w. of German** il ne sait pas un mot d'allemand; **'robbery' would be a better w. for it** 'vol' serait un mot plus approprié; **'bad' isn't the w. for it** 'mauvais' n'est pas le mot; **that's the wrong** *or* **not the right w. (for it)** ce n'est pas le mot qui convient; **there's a w. for it in Russian** il y a un mot pour exprimer cela en russe; **the Spanish w. for 'mouse'** 'mouse' en espagnol; **he was reserved – that's one w. for it!** il était réservé – c'est le moins qu'on puisse dire!; **there's a w. for people like you, it's 'thief'** les gens dans ton genre, on les appelle des voleurs; **she used a less flattering w.** elle a utilisé un terme moins flatteur; **what's the w. I'm looking for?** quel est le mot que je cherche?; **there's no other w. for it** il n'y a pas d'autre mot; **the spoken/ written w.** la parole/les écrits *mpl*; **in the words of Voltaire** selon (l'expression de) Voltaire, comme l'a dit Voltaire; **that is your w., not mine** c'est toi qui as dit cela, pas moi; **in your own words** selon tes propres mots; **a 600-w. article** un article de 600 mots; **I can't put it into words** je n'arrive pas à l'exprimer par des mots; **he's a man of few words** c'est un homme qui parle peu *ou* qui ne parle pas beaucoup; **I can't get a w. out of her** je ne peux pas en tirer un mot; **I couldn't get a w. in (edgeways)** je n'ai pas pu placer un mot; **he didn't say a w.** il n'a rien dit, il n'a pas soufflé mot; **not a w.!** pas un mot!, bouche cousue!; **without a w.** sans mot dire; **with these words, he went** sur ces mots *ou* là-dessus, il est parti; **words fail me!** j'en perds la parole!; **too ridiculous for words** d'un ridicule sans nom; *Am Fam* **w. (up)!** *(I agree)* parfaitement!; *(it's true)* sans dec!; **too stupid for words** d'une bêtise indicible; **too beautiful for words** d'une beauté ineffable; **fine words, but we'll see if their actions match them** belles paroles, mais nous verrons si l'on peut en dire de même de leurs actes; **kind words** des mots aimables; **words per minute** *(of printer, typist)* mots par minute; **to be w. perfect** *(of actor)* savoir son rôle sur le bout du doigt

2 *(remarks, conversation)* **may I have a w. with you?, I'd like a w. with you** puis-je vous parler un instant?; **I'll have a w. with her about it** je lui en toucherai deux mots; **I have been asked to say a few words of introduction** on m'a demandé de dire quelques mots d'introduction; **you're putting words into my mouth** vous me faites dire des choses que je ne veux pas dire; **you've taken the**

words (right) out of my mouth tu me l'as retiré de la bouche; **to put in a good w. for sb** dire *ou* glisser un mot en faveur de qn; **he never has a good w. for anyone** il ne peut pas s'empêcher de dire du mal des gens; **a w. in/out of season** un conseil opportun/inopportun; **a w. of warning** une mise en garde; **I gave him a w. of warning** je l'ai mis en garde; **can I offer you a w. (or two) of advice?** puis-je vous donner un petit conseil?; **they had few words of comfort for her** ils ne lui ont pas dit grand-chose pour la consoler; **a w. of sympathy** un mot de condoléances

3 *(no pl) (message)* nouvelle *f*, *(official etc)* avis *m*, déclaration *f*; **to send sb w. of sth** faire part à qn de qch; *(officially, formally)* faire savoir qch à qn; **they sent w. that …** ils ont fait savoir que …; **we received w. that … **on nous a apporté la nouvelle que …; **have you had any w. yet?** *(of how they are etc)* est-ce que tu as eu des nouvelles?; **there's (been) no w. from Moscow** on n'a pas de nouvelles de Moscou; **by w. of mouth** *(to tell somebody something)* verbalement; *(to spread) (of rumours)* de bouche à oreille; **w.-of-mouth advertising** publicité *f* de bouche à oreille; **the w. is that he's retiring** on raconte qu'il va prendre sa retraite; **the w. on the street is that the Mafia did it** le bruit court que c'est la Mafia qui l'a fait; **she left w. with George for them to join her** a demandé à George de leur dire de la rejoindre

4 *(promise)* parole *f*; **one's w. of honour** sa parole d'honneur; **to give sb one's w.** donner sa parole à qn; **to keep one's w.** tenir (sa) parole; **to break one's w.** manquer à sa parole; **to go back on one's w.** revenir sur sa parole; **I give you my w., (you can) take my w. for it** je vous en donne ma parole, je vous en réponds; **I'll take your w. for it** je vous crois sur parole, je m'en rapporte à vous; **we've only got her w. for it** du moins, c'est ce qu'elle nous a dit; **it's your w. against his** c'est votre parole contre la sienne; **he's a man of his w.** c'est un homme de parole; **she's as good as her w.** elle tient parole; **she was better than her w.** elle a fait mieux que tenir ses promesses; **his w. is as good as his bond** sa parole vaut sa signature; **they took her at her w.** ils l'ont prise au mot; **we will hold you to your w.** nous vous obligerons à tenir parole; **my w.!** ma parole!

5 to have words with sb *(argue)* se disputer *ou* se quereller avec qn; **they had words** ils ont eu des mots

6 *(order)* **w. of command** ordre *m*; **to give the w. to do sth** *(give order)* donner l'ordre de faire qch; *(give signal)* donner le signal de faire qch; **if you want any more paper just say the w.** si tu veux encore du papier, dis-le

7 *Rel* **the w. of God** la parole de Dieu; **the W.** *(Christ)* le Verbe; **to spread the w.** *(proselytize)* annoncer la bonne parole

8 *Comput* mot *m*

9 words *(lyrics)* paroles *fpl*; **words and music by Ian Smith** paroles *fpl* et musique *f* par Ian Smith; **listen to the words** écoute les paroles

vt *(document etc)* formuler, rédiger; *(comment)* formuler, exprimer; **it could have been better worded** il aurait/tu aurais/*etc* pu mieux le formuler; **be careful how you w. it** fais attention à la manière dont tu le formules; **a cleverly worded contract** un contrat habilement formulé

▸ ▸ **w. association** association *f* d'idées par les mots; *Typ* **w. break** césure *f*; *Comput* **w. count** nombre *m* des mots; **to do a w. count** compter les mots; **w. count facility** fonction *f* de comptage de mots; **w. group** groupe *m* de mots, membre *m* de phrase; **w. list** liste *f*

de mots; *(content of dictionary)* nomenclature *f*, **w. order** ordre *m* des mots; **w. picture** description *f* imagée *ou* pittoresque; *(of person)* portrait *m* en prose; **w. processing** traitement *m* de texte; **w. processor** logiciel *m* de traitement de texte; *Typ* **w. split** coupure *f* de mot

wordbook [ˈwɜːdbʊk] **N** vocabulaire *m*, lexique *m*

wordiness [ˈwɜːdɪnɪs] **N** verbosité *f*, prolixité *f*

wording [ˈwɜːdɪŋ] **N 1** *(choice of words) (of article, document)* formulation *f*, (choix *m* de) termes *mpl*; *(of problem)* énoncé *m*; *(of banker's draft, bill of exchange)* libellé *m*; **the w. was ambiguous** les termes étaient ambigus, la formulation était ambiguë; **it is important to get the w. right** il est important de choisir les termes appropriés **2** *(action) (of document)* rédaction *f*

wordless [ˈwɜːdlɪs] **ADJ** *esp Lit* sans paroles, muet

wordlessly [ˈwɜːdlɪslɪ] **ADV** sans dire un mot

word-process **VT** réaliser par traitement de texte; **word-processed text** texte *m* écrit au traitement de texte
  VI travailler sur traitement de texte

wordsmith [ˈwɜːdsmɪθ] **N he's a real w.** il sait manier les mots

wordwrap [ˈwɜːdræp] **N** *Comput* passage *m* automatique à la ligne suivante

wordy [ˈwɜːdɪ] **ADJ** verbeux, prolixe, diffus

wore **PT** *see* **wear**

WORK [wɜːk]

| **N** travail **1, 2, 4, 5** ▪ besogne **2** ▪ œuvre **3** ▪ ouvrage **3** ▪ emploi **4** ▪ usine **5** ▪ travaux **6, 7** ▪ mécanisme **8** |
| **VI** travailler **1, 2** ▪ fonctionner **3** ▪ marcher **3, 4** |
| **VT** faire travailler **1** ▪ faire marcher **2** ▪ travailler **5** ▪ exploiter **5** |

N 1 *(labour)* travail *m*, -aux; **to be at w.** être au travail; **they are at w. on a new book** ils sont en train de travailler à un nouveau livre; **the forces at w.** les forces en jeu; **there are evil forces at w.** des forces maléfiques sont à l'œuvre; **to be hard at w.** être en plein travail; **he was hard at w. gardening** il était en plein jardinage; **to start w., to set** *or* **get to w.** se mettre au travail; **they set to w. digging the hole** ils se sont mis à creuser le trou; **they put him to w. in the kitchen** ils l'ont mis au travail dans la cuisine; **she was set to w. cataloguing the collection** on lui a donné pour tâche de répertorier la collection; **to stop w.** cesser le travail; *(for the day)* suspendre le travail; **w. in progress** *Acct* produits *mpl* en cours; *(actual work)* travaux en cours

2 *(task)* travail *m*, -aux, ouvrage *m*, besogne *f*, tâche *f*; **I've (got) w. to do** j'ai (du travail) à faire; **to have too much w. to do** avoir trop de travail à faire; **to get through a lot of w.** abattre de la besogne; **to give sb some w. to do** donner du travail à faire à qn; **there's a lot of w. to be done** il y a beaucoup (de travail) à faire; **it will take a lot of w. to make a team out of them** ça va être un drôle de travail de faire d'eux une équipe; **she put a lot of w. into her exams** elle a beaucoup travaillé à ses examens; **they're doing some w. for an American firm** *(of subcontractor)* ils travaillent pour une firme américaine; **very little w. has been done on this disease** peu de travail a été effectué sur cette maladie; **let's get down to w.!** mettons-nous au travail!; **a fine piece of w.** un beau travail; **the brandy had**

done its w. l'eau-de-vie avait fait son effet; **I'll have my w. cut out to finish in time** je vais en baver pour finir à l'heure; **you'll have your w. cut out with him** il vous donnera du fil à retordre; **he made quick w. of the ironing** il est rapidement venu à bout du repassage; **to make w. for sb** compliquer la vie à qn; **day's w.** (travail d'une) journée *f*; **it's all in a day's w.** ça n'a rien d'exceptionnel; **good w.!** bien fait!; **it was thirsty w.** c'était un travail qui donnait soif; **the w. of a professional** le travail *ou* l'œuvre *f* d'un professionnel; **this break-in is the w. of a professional** cette effraction est l'œuvre d'un professionnel

3 *(product, achievement)* ouvrage *m*, œuvre *f*; **the works of God** les œuvres de Dieu; **good works** bonnes œuvres; **the (complete) works of Shakespeare** les œuvres *ou* l'œuvre *m ou* f de Shakespeare; **a w. of art/genius** une œuvre d'art/de génie; **his early works** ses premières œuvres; **w. of fiction** ouvrage de fiction; **is this all your own w.?** est-ce que vous avez fait ça tout seul?; **her w. sells well** ses ouvrages se vendent bien; **very detailed/delicate w.** *(embroidery, carving etc)* ouvrage très détaillé/délicat

4 *(employment)* travail *m*, emploi *m*; **I need w.** il me faut du travail; **what kind of w. are you looking for?** quel genre de travail recherchez-vous?; **cleaning w.** nettoyage *m*; **I'm looking for translation w.** je cherche du travail dans la traduction; **office w.** travail de bureau; **manual w.** travail manuel; **skilled w.** travail qualifié; **the factory will provide w. for a hundred people** l'usine fournira du travail à cent personnes; **to be off w.** ne pas travailler *(parce qu'on est malade)*; **to be out of w.** *(unemployed)* être en *ou* au chômage; **she's not in w. at the moment** elle ne travaille pas en ce moment; *Fam* **nice w. if you can get it** il y en a qui ne s'embêtent pas!; *Br Fam* **he's a nasty bit** *or* **piece of w.** c'est un sale type; *Br Fam* **their daughter is a nasty bit** *or* **piece of w.** leur fille est une sale gosse

5 *(workplace)* (lieu *m* de) travail *m*; **works** *(factory)* usine *f*; **he's not at w. today** il ne travaille pas aujourd'hui; **on my way to w.** en allant travailler *ou* au travail; **someone at w. told me** quelqu'un au travail me l'a dit; **someone from w.** quelqu'un du travail; **someone from your w. called** quelqu'un de ton travail a appelé; **works council** comité *m* d'entreprise; **works outing** sortie *f* annuelle des employés *ou* des ouvriers

6 *Mil (usu pl)* **works** ouvrages *mpl*, travaux *mpl*; **field works** travaux de campagne

7 *Constr (usu pl)* **works** travaux *mpl*; **public works** travaux publics; **road works ahead!** attention travaux!; *Am* **w. zone!** travaux!, chantier!

8 *(mechanism) (usu pl)* **works** *(of watch etc)* rouages *mpl*, mécanisme *m*

9 *Fam* **they had eggs, bacon, toast, the works** ils avaient des œufs, du bacon, du pain grillé, tout, quoi!; *Fam* **the whole works** tout le bataclan, tout le tralala; **in his autobiography we are given the full works** *(full details of life)* son autobiographie nous livre tous les dessous de sa vie; **I treated myself to the full works at the beauty parlour** je me suis payé une séance de luxe chez l'esthéticienne; *Sl* **to give sb the works** *(beating)* passer qn à tabac; *(luxury treatment)* jouer le grand jeu à qn; *esp Am Fam* **to shoot the works** *(spend all one's money)* claquer tout son fric; **to be in the works** *(in preparation)* être en cours

VI 1 *(of person)* travailler; *(for good of other people)* œuvrer; **to w. hard** travailler dur; **to w. like a slave** *or* **a dog** *or* **a Trojan** *or* **a beaver** travailler comme un forçat *ou* comme un bœuf; **to w. a 40-hour week** faire une semaine de 40 heures; **to w. long hours** faire de grandes journées de travail; *Ind* **to w. to rule** faire la grève du zèle; **to w. in leather/ brass** travailler dans le cuir/cuivre; **she works in publishing** elle travaille dans l'édition; **to w. on** *ou* **for a newspaper** collaborer à un journal; **to w. for a good cause** travailler pour une bonne cause; **he worked with the poor and the sick** il travaillait avec les pauvres et les malades; **the city council, working to improve the quality of life** le conseil municipal, à l'œuvre pour l'amélioration de la qualité de la vie; **all her life she worked for peace/to bring the two countries together** toute sa vie elle a œuvré pour la paix/pour unir les deux pays; **we are working towards a peaceful solution** nous œuvrons en vue d'une solution pacifique; **to w. against sb** intriguer *ou* travailler contre qn; **their earlier popularity was now working against them** leur popularité des débuts jouait maintenant en leur défaveur; **let your body weight w. for you rather than against you** laisse ton poids jouer en ta faveur plutôt que contre toi; **her age worked in her favour** son âge a joué en sa faveur; **working from the principle that …** partant du principe que …; **I am working on the assumption that you can type** je pars du principe que vous savez taper à la machine

2 *(be employed)* travailler, avoir un emploi; **who do you w. for?** chez qui est-ce que vous travaillez?; **she works for Smith and Wilson** elle travaille chez Smith and Wilson; **she works for the water board** elle travaille au service des eaux

3 *(function) (of machine, system)* fonctionner, marcher; **the pump isn't working** la pompe ne marche *ou* ne fonctionne pas; **the lift isn't working** l'ascenseur est hors de service *ou* est en panne; **the system works well** le système fonctionne bien; **I can't get this machine to w.** je n'arrive pas à faire marcher cette machine; **they soon got** *or* **had it working** ils sont vite parvenus à le faire fonctionner; **can you show me how the photocopier works?** est-ce que tu peux me faire voir comment marche la photocopieuse?; **it works like this, here's how it works** *(of machine, system)* cela marche de la façon suivante, voilà comment ça marche; **it works both ways** ça marche dans les deux sens; **to w. as sth** *(serve the function of)* faire office de qch; **high unemployment works as a brake on wage claims** le taux élevé de chômage freine la hausse des salaires; **the clock works off electricity** la pendule marche à l'électricité; **these tools w. by compressed air** ces outils sont actionnés par *ou* marchent à l'air comprimé

4 *(have effect, succeed) (of drug, cleaning product)* faire effet; *(of plan, method)* marcher, y faire; *(of yeast)* fermenter; **the drug works in most cases** le médicament fait de l'effet dans la plupart des cas; **rubbing the stain won't w.** frotter la tache ne servira à rien; **she tried everything she could think of but nothing worked** elle a essayé tout ce à quoi elle pouvait penser mais rien n'a marché; **this isn't working** ça ne marche pas; **his plan didn't w.** son projet a échoué *ou* n'a pas réussi; **that/flattery won't w. with me** ça/la flatterie ne prend pas avec moi

5 *(of face, features)* remuer, s'agiter

6 *(move)* **to w. upstream** remonter le courant; **a band of rain working across the country** un front de pluie qui traverse le pays; **the infection has worked downwards** l'infection a progressé vers le bas; **I knew what he was trying to w. round to** je savais où il voulait en venir; **he finally worked round to asking her out** il l'a finalement invitée à sortir; **I haven't done it yet but I'm working round to it** je ne l'ai pas encore fait,

mais je vais m'en occuper; **to w. loose** *(of nut etc)* se desserrer

VT 1 *(person, horse etc)* faire travailler; **he works his employees/himself very hard** il exige beaucoup de travail de son personnel/lui-même; **to w. oneself to death** se tuer à force de travailler; **don't w. yourself to death!** ne va pas te tuer à la tâche *ou* à l'ouvrage!; *Iron* ne te fais pas trop mal, surtout!

2 *(operate) (machine etc)* faire travailler, faire fonctionner, faire marcher; **it is worked by steam/electricity** cela marche à la vapeur/à l'électricité

3 *(bring about) (miracle, cure)* opérer; *(change)* amener; **the beauty of the place was beginning to w. its magic on her** la beauté de l'endroit commençait à exercer sa magie sur elle; **the destruction wrought by the fire** la dévastation causée par l'incendie; **I'll w. it** *or* **things so that they pay in advance** je ferai de sorte qu'ils paient à l'avance; **his keys had worked a hole in his pocket** ses clefs avaient fini par faire un trou dans sa poche

4 *(move)* **to w. one's hands free** parvenir à dégager ses mains; **she worked the ropes loose** elle a réussi à desserrer les cordes petit à petit; **to w. one's way down/up** descendre/monter petit à petit *ou* avec précaution; **his hand worked its way up my leg** sa main remontait progressivement sur ma jambe; **he worked his way towards her** il s'est avancé vers elle petit à petit; **they worked their way through the crowd** ils se sont frayé un chemin à travers la foule; **they worked their way through the list** ils ont traité chaque élément de la liste tour à tour; **we're working our way through the French subjunctive** nous sommes en train d'étudier le subjonctif en français; **he's worked his way through the whole grant** il a épuisé toute la subvention; **they have worked themselves into a corner** ils se sont mis dans une impasse

5 *(mine, quarry)* exploiter; *(land)* travailler; *Com* **to w. the south-east** *(of representative)* couvrir le sud-est

6 *Naut* **to w. one's passage** payer son passage par son travail; **he worked his passage to Rio** il a payé son passage à Rio en travaillant; **to w. one's way through university** *(of student)* travailler pour payer ses études

7 *Sewing (design, initials)* broder; **the flowers are worked in silk** les fleurs sont brodées en soie

▸ **w. area** *(in school, home)* coin *m* de travail; *Comput* zone *f* de travail; *Comput* **w. file** fichier *m* de travail; **w. group** groupe *m* de travail; **w. permit** permis *m* de travail; **w. rate** cadence *f* *ou* rythme *m* de travail; **w. standard** norme *f* de travail

▸ **work in** VT SEP *(include, introduce) (incident in novel etc)* introduire; *(mix in)* incorporer, mélanger; **to w. in a reference to unemployment** faire une allusion au chômage; **to w. the other ingredients in** incorporer les autres ingrédients

▸ **work into** VT SEP gently **w. the cream into your hands** massez-vous les mains pour faire pénétrer la crème; **w. the dye into the surface of the leather** faites pénétrer la teinture dans le cuir; **he worked several references to her into his speech** il a glissé plusieurs allusions à elle dans son discours; **she worked the clay into the shape of a giraffe** elle modela l'argile pour en faire une girafe; **his oratory had them worked into a frenzy** sa virulence oratoire les avait rendus frénétiques; **it takes a while to w. yourself into the right frame of mind** il faut un certain temps pour se mettre dans le bon état d'esprit

▸ **work off** VT SEP *(one's anger, bad mood)*

évacuer (**by doing** en faisant); **to w. off one's anger on sb** passer sa colère sur qn; **I want to w. off some fat** je veux perdre du poids

▸ **work on** VI *(continue to work)* continuer à travailler

VT INSEP **1** *(be involved in)* travailler à *ou* sur; **he's working on an edition of Hamlet** il travaille à *ou* prépare une édition de Hamlet; **we're working on it** nous travaillons là-dessus; **a detective is working on this case** un détective est sur cette affaire; **he's been working on his breaststroke/emotional problems** il a travaillé sa brasse/essayé de résoudre ses problèmes sentimentaux

2 *(use as basis)* **have you any data to w. on?** avez-vous des données sur lesquelles vous fonder?

3 *(somebody) (persuade)* influencer, agir sur (l'esprit de); *(attempt to persuade)* travailler

▸ **work out** VT SEP **1** *(calculate) (cost, distance, sum)* calculer; **from this information, w. out the answer** à partir de cette information, déduisez la réponse; **it took me ages to w. out the right answer** j'ai mis un temps fou pour trouver la réponse exacte; **to w. out the total** faire la somme; **I w. it out at £22** d'après mes calculs, ça fait 22 livres; **the dog had worked out how to open the door** le chien avait compris comment ouvrir la porte; **he's a strange person – I'd worked that out!** il est bizarre – je m'en étais rendu compte!; **well, you can w. it out for yourself** alors, pas besoin que je te fasse un dessin

2 *(devise) (way of doing sth)* trouver, mettre au point; *(scientific method etc)* élaborer

3 *(resolve) (problem)* résoudre; **we must try to w. out our differences** nous devons essayer de résoudre nos désaccords; **I'm sure we can w. this thing out** *(your problem)* je suis sûr que nous pouvons arranger ça; *(our argument)* je suis sûr que nous finirons par nous mettre d'accord

4 *(understand)* comprendre; **I can't w. her out** je n'arrive pas à la comprendre; **she couldn't w. it out** elle n'y comprenait rien

5 *(of mine, seam)* **to be worked out** être épuisé

VI **1** *(be resolved)* **I wonder how it will all w. out** je me demande comment cela finira *ou* va finir; **it** *or* **things worked out very well for me** ça a *ou* les choses ont très bien marché pour moi; **it worked out well** *or* **all right for us** ça s'est bien passé pour nous, les choses ont bien tourné pour nous; **but it didn't w. out that way** mais il en a été tout autrement; **it worked out badly for them** les choses ont mal tourné pour eux

2 *(succeed) (of marriage, arrangement)* marcher; **they started a business together, but it didn't w. out** ils ont monté une affaire ensemble, mais ça n'a pas marché; **I don't like my job, but things may w. out** je n'aime pas mon travail, mais ça va peut-être s'arranger; **how is the new system working out?** est-ce que le nouveau système marche?; **are things working out for you OK?** est-ce que ça se passe bien pour toi?; **how's the new manager working out?** comment est-ce que le nouveau directeur se débrouille?

3 *(amount to)* **how much does it all w. out at?** ça fait combien en tout?; **the cost works out at £150 a head** cela fait 150 livres par personne; **it'll w. out more expensive like that** ça reviendra plus cher comme ça

4 *Sport* s'entraîner

▸ **work up** VT SEP **1** *(develop)* **to w. up an appetite** s'ouvrir l'appétit; **I can't w. up much enthusiasm/interest for the idea** j'ai du mal à m'enthousiasmer pour/à m'intéresser à cette idée

2 *(arouse)* **he worked the crowd up into a frenzy** il a rendu la foule frénétique; **she**

had worked herself up into a dreadful rage elle s'était mise dans une rage terrible; **to get worked up** (upset) se rendre malade (**about** au sujet de); (angry) se fâcher (**about** au sujet de); (excited) se mettre dans tous ses états (**about** au sujet de); **he's all worked up** il est dans tous ses états; **I'm too worked up to do it now** je suis trop énervé ou trop à cran pour le faire maintenant VI (of skirt) remonter

▸ **work up to** VT INSEP (move towards) (something) avancer par degrés à; **what are you working up to?** où voulez-vous en venir?; **he was working up to a discussion of his salary** il amenait progressivement la discussion sur le sujet de son salaire; **the symphony was working up to its finale** la symphonie allait crescendo, annonçant le finale

workability [wɜːkəˈbɪlɪtɪ] N Tech maniabilité f

workable [ˈwɜːkəb(ə)l] ADJ **1** Tech (material) maniable **2** (mine) exploitable **3** (project) réalisable, possible; **it isn't a w. proposition** ce n'est pas une proposition réalisable

workaday [ˈwɜːkədeɪ] ADJ (clothes, routine) de tous les jours; (man) ordinaire, banal, -als; (incident) courant, banal; **the w. world of the office** la routine du bureau

workaholic [wɜːkəˈhɒlɪk] N Fam bourreau m de travail

workbag [ˈwɜːkbæg] N Sewing sac m à ouvrage

workbasket [ˈwɜːkbɑːskɪt] N Sewing corbeille f à ouvrage

workbench [ˈwɜːkbentʃ] N établi m

workbook [ˈwɜːkbʊk] N cahier m d'exercices

workbox [ˈwɜːkbɒks] N Sewing boîte f à ouvrage

workday [ˈwɜːkdeɪ] N (weekday) jour m ouvrable; (day of work) journée f de travail

worker [ˈwɜːkər] N **1** travailleur, -euse; Ind ouvrier, -ière; **hard w.** travailleur assidu; **to be a hard w.** être un bon travailleur; **Workers of the world unite!** travailleurs de tous les pays, unissez-vous!; **the workers** (as opposed to management) le personnel; **workers and management** partenaires mpl sociaux; **workers' control** autogestion f **2** Entom ouvrière f

▸▸ Entom **w. ant** (fourmi m) ouvrière; Entom **w. bee** (abeille f) ouvrière; **w. director** = ouvrier qui fait partie du conseil d'administration; **w. participation** participation f ouvrière

worker-priest N prêtre-ouvrier m, pl prêtres-ouvriers

workfare [ˈwɜːkfeə(r)] N Pol = principe m selon lequel les bénéficiaires de l'allocation de chômage doivent fournir un travail en échange

workflow [ˈwɜːkfləʊ] N rythme m de travail ▸▸ **w. schedule** plan m de travail

workforce [ˈwɜːkfɔːs] N main-d'œuvre f, (non-industrial) personnel m

workhorse [ˈwɜːkhɔːs] N cheval m de labour; Fig **to be a w.** travailler comme un cheval ou une bête; **she's a willing w.** elle est toujours prête à faire n'importe quelle tâche

workhouse [ˈwɜːkhaʊs] N **1** Hist (for the poor) asile m des pauvres **2** Am Old-fashioned (prison) maison f de correction

workie [ˈwɜːkɪ] N Br Fam ouvrier m

working [ˈwɜːkɪŋ] ADJ **1** (person) qui travaille; (population) actif; **he's very hard-w.** il est très travailleur, il travaille très dur **2** (day, hours) **w. day** journée f de travail; Admin jour m ouvrable; **the w. week** la semaine de travail; **throughout her w. life** tout

au long de sa vie active ou de sa vie professionnelle

3 (machine etc) qui fonctionne; **in w. order** en état de fonctionnement ou marche; **to be in good w. order** bien fonctionner; **w. parts of a machine** mécanisme m d'une machine **4** (clothes, conditions) de travail; **the two leaders have a good w. relationship** les deux dirigeants ont une bonne relation de travail; **a relaxed w. environment** un milieu professionnel détendu

5 **w. agreement** modus vivendi m; **to have a w. knowledge of French/the law** posséder une connaissance suffisante du français/du droit

N **1** (work) travail m; **w. at home** le travail à domicile

2 (of mine, forest) exploitation f; Min **workings** chantiers mpl d'exploitation; **old mine workings** anciens chantiers d'exploitation d'une mine

3 (operation) (of machine etc) manœuvre f **4** (mechanism) (usu pl) **workings** mécanisme m, rouages mpl; (of organization, system) rouages; **I can't fathom the workings of her mind** je ne comprends pas ce qui se passe dans sa tête

▸▸ Fin **w. account** compte m d'exploitation; Acct **w. assets** actif m circulant; Fin **w. capital** fonds mpl de roulement, capital m de roulement; Fin **w. capital cycle** cycle m du besoin en fonds de roulement; Fin **w. capital fund** compte d'avances; **the w. class** la classe ouvrière; **the w. classes** la classe ouvrière; **w. copy** (of document, text) copie f de travail; Comput **w. file** fichier m de travail; **w. girl** (prostitute) professionnelle f, **w. lunch** déjeuner m d'affaires ou de travail; **w. majority** majorité f suffisante; Br **w. men's club** = club m pour ouvriers; **w. model** modèle m qui fonctionne; **w. mother** mère f de famille qui travaille; Math **w. out** (of problem) résolution f, **w. party** (committee for study) groupe m de travail; (for enquiry) commission f d'enquête; (group of prisoners, soldiers) groupe de travail; **w. speed** vitesse f de régime; **w. theory** théorie f qui donne des résultats; **w. title** titre m provisoire; **w. woman** (worker) ouvrière f, employée f, (woman with job) femme f qui travaille

working-class ADJ (family etc) ouvrier; (accent) prolétaire; Fam prolo; **he's very w.** il fait très prolétaire

workload [ˈwɜːkləʊd] N quantité f de travail; **to have a heavy w.** avoir beaucoup de travail

workman, pl **workmen** [ˈwɜːkmən] N ouvrier m; **he's a good/bad w.** c'est un bon/mauvais ouvrier; Prov **a bad w. always blames his tools** les mauvais ouvriers ont toujours de mauvais outils; **workmen's compensation** indemnité f d'invalidité (pour les ouvriers)

workmanlike [ˈwɜːkmənlaɪk] ADJ (job) bien fait, de professionnel; **to do sth in a w. manner** faire qch de façon professionnelle; **w. performance** représentation f honnête

workmanship [ˈwɜːkmənʃɪp] N (of sth made) travail m; (of clothes) façon f, **sound w.** fabrication ou exécution soignée; **fine (piece of) w.** beau travail; **the w. on this furniture is superb** ce meuble est fait de façon superbe; **poor w.** travail de mauvaise qualité; **he was famous for his w.** il était connu pour la finesse de son travail; **Swiss w. is second to none** la fabrication suisse est la meilleure du monde; **you don't get any w. these days** la qualité n'est plus ce qu'elle était

workmate [ˈwɜːkmeɪt] N esp Br collègue mf de travail

work-out N Sport séance f d'entraînement

workpeople [ˈwɜːkpiːp(ə)l] NPL ouvriers mpl

workplace [ˈwɜːkpleɪs] N lieu m de travail

workroom [ˈwɜːkruːm] N atelier m ou salle f de travail

workshare [ˈwɜːkʃeər] N travail m en temps partagé; (person) travailleur, -euse en temps partagé; **workshares are becoming more common** le partage du travail devient de plus en plus courant

worksharing [ˈwɜːkʃeərɪŋ] N partage m du travail; **we have a w. arrangement** nous avons un système de partage du travail; **w. is becoming popular** le partage du travail est de plus en plus courant

workshop [ˈwɜːkʃɒp] N atelier m; **a music/ an acting w.** un atelier de musique/de théâtre

workshy [ˈwɜːkʃaɪ] ADJ fainéant; **to be w.** bouder ou renâcler à la besogne

workspace [ˈwɜːkspeɪs] N Comput espace m de travail

workstation [ˈwɜːksteɪʃən] N Comput station f ou poste m de travail

worktable [ˈwɜːkteɪb(ə)l] N table f de travail; Sewing table à ouvrage

worktop [ˈwɜːktɒp] N (in kitchen) plan m de travail

work-to-rule N Ind grève f du zèle; **to operate a w.** faire une grève du zèle

workweek [ˈwɜːkwiːk] N esp Am semaine f de travail; **a four-day w.** une semaine (de travail) de quatre jours; **the forty-hour w.** la semaine de quarante heures

WORLD [wɜːld] N **1** monde m; **in this w.** en ce monde; **the other** or **next w., the w. to come** l'autre monde; Rel **the w., the flesh and the devil** le monde, la chair et le diable; **he's not long for this w.** il n'en a pas pour longtemps à vivre; **to bring a child into the w.** (of mother, midwife, doctor) mettre un enfant au monde; **she came into the w. on 22nd May 1973** elle est venue au monde le 22 mai 1973; **he wants the best of both worlds** il veut tout avoir; **the end of the w.** la fin du monde; Fam **it's not the end of the w.** ce n'est pas la fin du monde, ce n'est pas une catastrophe; Rel **w. without end** pour les siècles des siècles; **the whole w.** le monde entier; **there isn't a nicer spot in the whole w.** il n'y a pas d'endroit plus agréable au monde; **to be alone in the w.** être seul au monde; **you're not the only person in the w.!** tu n'es pas seul au monde!; **the happiest man in the w.** l'homme le plus heureux du monde; **he's the w.'s worst letter-writer** il n'y a pas pire correspondant que lui au monde; **you're the w.'s worst!** il n'y a pas pire que toi!; **she lives in a w. of her own** elle vit dans un monde à part; **you live in a dream** or **fantasy w.** tu vis dans un monde imaginaire; **the w. we live in is not like that** le monde dans lequel nous vivons n'est pas comme ça; **it's a different w. up north** c'est complètement différent au nord; **the book takes us into a w. of corruption and intrigue** le livre nous entraîne dans un monde de corruption et d'intrigues; Fam **it's out of this w.** c'est (quelque chose d')extraordinaire ou épatant; Fam **it was out of this w.** (of experience, holiday etc) c'était fabuleux; Fam **the mountains were out of this w.** les montagnes étaient d'une beauté extraordinaire; **what in the w. is the matter with you?** que pouvez-vous bien avoir?; **where in the w. is that?** où est-ce que ça peut bien être?; **I wouldn't do it for (anything in) the w.** je ne le ferais pour rien au monde; **nothing in the w. could make me leave** rien au monde ne pourrait me faire partir; **what I want most of all in the w. is for you to be happy** ce que je souhaite le plus au monde, c'est que tu sois heureux; **it's**

been happening ever since the w. began ça se passe comme ça depuis que le monde est monde; **to go round the w.** faire le tour du monde; **round-the-w. trip** or **tour** voyage m autour du monde; **he has seen the w.** il a vu du pays; **map of the w.** carte f du monde; (in two hemispheres) mappemonde f, **(all) the w. over, all over the w.** dans le monde entier; **people are the same the w. over** les gens sont partout pareils; **to the end of the w.** jusqu'au bout du monde; **it's a small w.!** (que) le monde est petit!; **the Old/New W.** l'ancien/le nouveau monde; **the ancient** or **classical w.** l'antiquité f, **the English-speaking w.** le monde anglophone; **the richest nation in the w.** la nation la plus riche au monde

2 (society) monde m; **it's the way of the w.** ainsi va le monde; **what is the w. coming to?** où allons-nous?; **man of the w.** homme m qui connaît la vie ou qui a l'expérience du monde; **she doesn't care what the w. thinks** elle se moque de ce que les gens pensent; **he's gone up in the w.** il a fait du chemin; **to come down in the w.** déchoir; **all the w. knows** c'est bien connu, tout le monde le sait; Fam **the w. and his wife seemed to be there** tout le monde sans exception semblait être présent; **the singer had the w. at her feet** la chanteuse avait tout le monde à ses pieds

3 (circle, field) **the w. of literature** or **of letters, the literary w.** le milieu ou monde littéraire; **the theatrical w.** le milieu ou monde du théâtre

4 (great deal) **that will do you a w. of good** cela vous fera le plus grand bien; **there's a w. of difference between …** il y a une différence énorme entre …; **their opinions are worlds apart** leurs opinions sont totalement différentes; **she thinks the w. of him** elle l'admire énormément; **she means the w. to them** elle compte énormément à leurs yeux; **I'd give the w. to know what he's thinking** je donnerais n'importe quoi pour savoir ce qu'il pense; **they kept on talking, for all the w. as if nothing had happened** ils ont continué à parler comme s'il ne s'était rien passé

▶▶**the W. Bank** la Banque mondiale; **w. champion** champion m du monde; **w. championship** championnat m du monde; **the W. Cup** la Coupe du monde; **w. domination** domination f du monde; **they have w. domination in gymnastics** ils dominent le monde de la gymnastique; **W. Economic Forum** Forum m économique mondial; **W. Fair** exposition f universelle; **W. Food Programme** Programme m alimentaire mondial; **the W. Health Organization** l'Organisation f mondiale de la santé; **w. history** histoire f universelle; **w. map** carte du monde; (in two hemispheres) mappemonde; Com **w. market** marché m mondial ou international; **w. opinion** l'opinion internationale; **w. politics** politique f mondiale; **w. power** puissance f mondiale; **w. record** record m mondial; Fin **w. reserves** réserves fpl mondiales; **w. rights** droits mpl d'exploitation pour le monde entier; **the W. Series** = le championnat américain de baseball; Radio **the W. Service** = service m étranger de la BBC; **w. television** mondovision f, **w. trade** commerce m international; **the W. Trade Organization** l'Organisation mondiale du commerce; **w. tour** voyage autour du monde; **w. war** guerre f mondiale; Comput **the W. Wide Web** le World Wide Web

world-beater N a **w.** le meilleur/la meilleure du monde, le leader mondial; **we've got a real w. here** c'est le nouveau leader mondial

world-beating [-biːtɪŋ] ADJ meilleur du monde; **of w. quality** d'une qualité inéga-

lée; **the new w. X52** le X52, nouveau leader mondial

world-famous ADJ de renommée mondiale, célèbre dans le monde entier

worldliness ['wɜːldlɪnɪs] N **1** (knowledge of world) connaissance f du monde; **there was an air of w. about her** elle avait l'air de quelqu'un qui a l'expérience du monde **2** (materialism) matérialisme m, attachement m aux biens de ce monde

worldly ['wɜːldlɪ] ADJ **1** (of this world) de ce monde, matériel; **all his w. goods** toute sa fortune; **he's a child in w. matters** il n'a aucune expérience du monde; **w. pleasures** les plaisirs de ce monde; **w. wisdom** la sagesse du monde ou du siècle **2** (knowledgeable) qui a l'expérience du monde, qui connaît le monde; **she was very w. for one so young** elle avait une bien grande expérience du monde pour quelqu'un d'aussi jeune **3** (materialistic) matérialiste

worldly-wise ADJ qui a l'expérience du monde, qui connaît le monde; **with a w. air** avec l'air de quelqu'un qui connaît le monde

world-weary ADJ las, f lasse de ce monde

worldwide ['wɜːldwaɪd] ADJ mondial, -aux ADV dans le monde entier; **the Olympics are watched w.** on regarde les Jeux Olympiques dans le monde entier

▶▶**w. rights** droits mpl d'exploitation pour le monde entier

WORM [wɜːm] Comput (abbr **write once read many times**) WORM

worm [wɜːm] N **1** ver m; (maggot) asticot m; Fig **the w. has turned** j'en ai/elle en a/etc assez de se laisser mener par le bout du nez; Fig **even a w. will turn** il y a une limite à tout; **he's a w.** c'est un minable; **w.'s-eye view** (from below) perspective f vue d'en bas; (from lowly position) perspective au ras des pâquerettes; Cin, Phot, TV contre-plongée f, pl contre-plongées; **to get a w.'s-eye view of the theatre/catering industry** voir le monde du théâtre/de la restauration au ras des pâquerettes ou d'un point de vue restreint; Fig **the w. in the bud** le ver dans le fruit; Fam **that's opening a real can of worms** nous allons nous fourrer dans un véritable guêpier; Med, Vet **to have worms** avoir des vers; Fam **to be food for worms** bouffer les pissenlits par la racine; **meal w.** ver de farine

2 Tech (of screw) filet m; **w. and roller steering** direction f à vis et galet

3 Comput (invasive program) ver m

VT **1** he wormed himself or his way along the tunnel il a avancé dans le tunnel en rampant ou en se tortillant; **to w. one's way out of/into sth** se faufiler hors de/dans qch; Fig **I'd like to see her w. her way out of that one** j'aimerais bien voir comment elle va s'en tirer; **to w. oneself into sb's favour/confidence** s'insinuer dans les bonnes grâces de qn/la confiance de qn; **to w. a secret out of sb** tirer un secret de qn, arracher un secret à qn; **I'll w. it out of him** je saurai lui tirer les vers du nez

2 Vet **to w. a dog** débarrasser un chien de ses vers

▶▶ Tech **w. drive** transmission f par vis sans fin; Tech **w. gear** engrenage m de vis sans fin; **w. powder** poudre f à vers, poudre f vermifuge; **w. tablets** comprimés mpl vermifuges

wormcast ['wɜːmkɑːst] N déjection f de ver de terre

wormeaten ['wɜːmiːtən] ADJ (wood) vermoulu; (fruit) véreux; Fig (hat, slippers) miteux

wormhole ['wɜːmhəʊl] N (in wood, ground) trou m de ver; (in cloth, wood) piqûre f (de ver)

wormwood ['wɜːmwʊd] N Bot armoise f (amère); Lit **life to him was gall and w.** la vie pour lui n'était qu'amertume et dégoût

wormy ['wɜːmɪ] ADJ (furniture) infesté ou plein de vers; (fruit) véreux; (wood, cloth) piqué des vers

worn [wɔːn] PP see **wear**
ADJ **1** (weary) las, f lasse; **w. with anxiety** usé par les soucis **2** (with use) (shoes, edges etc) usé

worried ['wʌrɪd] ADJ **1** (look, expression, letter) inquiet, -ète; (person) tracassé, soucieux; **I'm w. about this** cela m'inquiète ou me tracasse; **he was w. by these developments** ces développements l'inquiétaient; **she's w. about the car** elle est inquiète au sujet de la voiture; **they're w. sick about her** ils sont malades d'inquiétude à son sujet; **he looks w.** il a l'air préoccupé ou soucieux **2** (weaker sense) **I was w. it would be the wrong size** j'avais peur que ce ne soit pas la bonne taille

worriedly ['wʌrɪdlɪ] ADV avec inquiétude

worrier ['wʌrɪər] N anxieux, -ieuse; **he's such a w.** il se fait tellement de soucis; **don't be such a w.** arrête de t'inquiéter comme ça

worrisome ['wʌrɪsəm] ADJ tracassant, inquiétant

worry ['wʌrɪ] N souci m, tracas m; **financial worries** soucis d'argent; **it's causing me a lot of w.** cela m'inquiète beaucoup; **that's the least of my worries** c'est le moindre ou le dernier de mes soucis; Fam **what's your w.?** qu'est-ce qui ne va pas?; Austr Fam **no worries!** pas de problème!

VT **1** (cause anxiety to) inquiéter; **these events worried her greatly** ces événements l'ont beaucoup inquiétée; **that boiler worries me, suppose it blows up?** la chaudière m'inquiète, si elle explosait?; **Janet worries me sometimes, she's not like other little girls** Janet m'inquiète parfois, elle n'est pas comme les autres petites filles; **something is worrying her** il y a quelque chose qui la préoccupe ou qui la travaille; **tell me what's worrying you** dites-moi ce qui vous préoccupe; **it doesn't w. me what other people think** je ne me soucie pas de ce que les autres pensent; **it worried him that he was getting older** le fait de vieillir le préoccupait; **it doesn't seem to w. you if other people get hurt** que d'autres souffrent ne semble pas te préoccuper; **doesn't it w. you, your daughter being out this late?** ça ne vous inquiète pas que votre fille ne soit pas rentrée à cette heure tardive?; **it doesn't w. her who she upsets** elle ne se préoccupe pas des gens qu'elle froisse; **it worries me to think of them all on their own** ça m'inquiète de penser qu'ils sont tous seuls; **to w. oneself sick** or **to death about sb/sth** se rendre malade d'inquiétude ou mourir d'inquiétude au sujet de qn/qch

2 (bother, disturb) ennuyer; **he doesn't want to be worried with these minor details** il ne veut pas être embêté par ces petits détails; **don't w. him about it, I'll do it** ne l'ennuie pas avec ça, je m'en occuperai; **don't w. yourself about it** ne t'embête pas avec ça; **don't you w. your pretty little head about it** ne te fais pas de soucis, mignonne!

3 (of dog, wolf) (harass) (sheep) attaquer, harceler; (bite) secouer entre ses dents

VI se tracasser, s'inquiéter, se faire du souci ou de la bile ou du mauvais sang; **don't tell them, they'll only w.** ne le leur dis pas, ça ne fera que les inquiéter; **don't (you) w.! not to w.!** ne vous tracassez ou inquiétez pas!, ne vous en faites pas!; **sorry, I forgot the milk – don't w. (about it)** je suis désolée, j'ai oublié le lait – ne vous inquiétez pas (pour ça); **not to w.! it'll wash out** ce n'est rien, ça partira au lavage; **don't (you) w. about me** ne t'inquiète pas pour moi; **there's plenty more beer, don't you w.** il reste plein de bière, ne t'en fais pas; **you'll find out soon enough,** don't you w. vous n'allez pas tarder à le savoir, ne vous en faites pas; **there's** or **it's nothing to w. about** il n'y a pas de quoi se faire du souci; **it's only a scratch, nothing to w. about** ce n'est qu'une égratignure, pas de quoi s'inquiéter; **what's the use of worrying?** à quoi bon se tourmenter?; Fam **I should w.!** ce n'est pas mon affaire!

▸▸ **w. beads** ≃ komboloï m (pour s'occuper les mains)

worryguts ['wʌrɪgʌts] N Br Fam bileux, -euse; **don't be such a w.** arrête de te tracasser autant

worrying ['wʌrɪɪŋ] ADJ tracassant, inquiétant

N tracas m, tourment m, inquiétude f; **all this w. will get you nowhere** à quoi bon se tourmenter?

worrywart ['wʌrɪwɔːt] N Am Fam = **worryguts**

WORSE [wɜːs]

ADJ	pire ▪ plus mauvais ▪ plus mal
N	pire
ADV	plus mal

ADJ (comp of bad) pire, plus mauvais (than que); **I'm a w. player than he is** or **him** or Fml **he** je joue plus mal que lui; **your problems are w. than ours** vos problèmes sont pires que les nôtres; **the situation was w. than (it had been) before** la situation était pire qu'avant; **there's nothing w. than arriving too early** il n'y a rien de pire que d'arriver trop tôt; **you're bad at French but he's w.** tu es mauvais en français mais il est plus mauvais que toi; **in w. condition** dans un plus mauvais état; **this is getting w. and w.** c'est ou ça va de mal en pis; **how are things? – no w. than before** comment ça va? – pas plus mal qu'avant; **things could be w.** ça pourrait être pire; **you're only making things** or **matters w.** vous ne faites qu'aggraver les choses; **to make things** or **matters w. ...** par ou pour surcroît de malheur ...; **it'll just make it w. if you tell them** ça ne va faire qu'empirer les choses si tu le leur dis; **you'll only make matters w. for yourself by offending them** tu ne feras qu'aggraver ton cas en les blessant; **it will be even w. for them if she finds out** ça va être encore pire pour eux si elle l'apprend; **it might** or **could have been w.** ça aurait pu être pire; **he escaped with nothing w. than a fright** il en fut quitte pour la peur; **what is w. ...** ce qui est plus grave ...; **to go from bad to w.** aller de mal en pis; **to get w.** (deteriorate) s'altérer; (of illness) s'aggraver, empirer; **the situation is getting w.** la situation s'aggrave; **his memory's got a lot w.** sa mémoire s'est beaucoup amoindrie; **how do you feel today? – w.** comment ça va aujourd'hui? – pire; **things will get w. before they get better** les choses vont empirer avant de s'améliorer; **I'm none the w. for it** je ne m'en trouve pas plus mal; **they were none the w. for their experience** ils ne s'en sont pas trouvés plus mal pour autant; **I think none the w. of him because he accepted** ce n'est pas parce qu'il a accepté que j'ai une moins bonne opinion de lui; **so much the w. for them!** tant pis pour eux!; **she was the w. for drink** elle était éméchée; **a sofa somewhat the w. for wear** un sofa un peu défraîchi; **he was rather the w. for wear** il était en mauvais état; **she was looking the w. for w.** elle avait l'air en travers; Fam **w. things happen at sea** ce n'est pas la fin du monde; **w. luck!** hélas!

N **there was w. to follow** or **to come** le pire était encore à venir; **I have seen w.** j'en ai vu bien d'autres, j'ai vu pire; **to change for the w.** s'altérer; **a change for the w.** un changement en mal; **he has taken a sudden turn for**

the w. son état s'est subitement aggravé

ADV (comp of badly) plus mal, Lit pis; **w. still** pire encore; **you could do (a lot) w.** (than accept offer) ce n'est vraiment pas si mal; (than marry him or her) tu aurais pu tomber plus mal; **he could do w. than accept their offer** il pouvait faire pire que d'accepter leur proposition; **to think w. of sb for doing sth** estimer qn moins pour avoir fait qch; **I don't think any w. of her for it** je n'ai pas une plus mauvaise opinion d'elle pour autant; **he is w. off than before** (in worse situation) sa situation a empiré; (even poorer) il est encore plus pauvre qu'avant; **the noise went on w. than ever** le vacarme a repris de plus belle

worsen ['wɜːs(ə)n] VT (situation) empirer; (crisis, infection, bad mood) aggraver; (relations, driving conditions) rendre plus difficile

VI (of situation) empirer, devenir pire; (of health) s'aggraver, empirer; **the situation has since worsened** la situation a empiré depuis; **the worsening situation** la situation qui est en train de s'aggraver; **her worsening memory** sa mémoire faiblissante

worsening ['wɜːs(ə)nɪŋ] N aggravation f

Worship ['wɜːʃɪp] N esp Br (title) **His W. the Mayor** monsieur le maire; **yes, your W.** oui, Votre Honneur

worship ['wɜːʃɪp] N **1** Rel culte m; **divine w.** le culte divin; **hours of w.** heures fpl des offices; **place of w.** lieu m consacré au culte; **to be an object of w.** être un objet d'adoration **2** (love, adoration) adoration f

VT (-pp-) **1** Rel (god, idol) rendre ou vouer un culte à, adorer; **to w. the golden calf** adorer le veau d'or **2** (love, adore) adorer, vouer un culte à; **she worshipped her mother** elle adorait sa mère; **he worships Elvis Presley** il voue un culte à Elvis Presley; **he worships the ground she walks on** il vénère jusqu'au sol qu'elle foule; **to w. money** vouer un culte à l'argent

VI **the church where his family has worshipped for years** l'église où sa famille fait ses dévotions depuis des années; **where does he w.?** à quelle église/à quel temple/à quelle synagogue/à quelle mosquée va-t-il?

worshipful ['wɜːʃɪpfʊl] ADJ esp Br honorable (titre des membres des Corporations de Londres, des juges de paix)

worshipper ['wɜːʃɪpər] N adorateur, -trice; **the worshippers** (in church) les fidèles mpl

WORST [wɜːst]

ADJ	le pire ▪ le plus mauvais
N	le pire
ADV	le plus mal

ADJ (superl of bad) (le) pire, (le) plus mauvais; **that was his w. mistake** c'était sa plus grave erreur; **his w. enemy** son pire ennemi; **you're your own w. enemy** tu es ton plus grand ennemi; **the w. thing about it was the heat** le pire c'était la chaleur; **the w. weather was in the south** c'était dans le sud qu'il faisait le plus mauvais temps; **the w. possible situation** la pire situation possible

N **the w. that could happen** le pire ou la pire chose qui puisse arriver; **the w. of it is that ...** le pire c'est que ...; **that's the w. of cheap shoes** c'est l'inconvénient des chaussures bon marché; **when things are at their** or **the w.** quand les choses vont au plus mal; **to get the w. of it** (in a fight) avoir le dessous; **he's prepared for the w.** il s'attend au pire; **at the w., if it comes to the w., if the w. comes to the w.** au pire; **if it comes to the w., we can always take the train** dans le pire des cas, nous pouvons toujours prendre le train; **at the w. there's still the possibility of finding another actor** au pire, il y a tou-

jours la possibilité de trouver un autre acteur; **the w. is yet to come** on n'a pas encore vu le pire, et ce n'est pas fini; **do your w.!** allez-y!, essayez toujours!; **the w. is over** le plus mauvais moment est passé; **the w. of the storm is over** le plus fort de l'orage est passé; **the w. has happened!** c'est la catastrophe!; **and that's not the w. of it!** et ce n'est pas le pire!, et il y a pire encore!; **I'm at my w. in the morning** le matin est mon plus mauvais moment de la journée; **you haven't seen her at her w.** tu ne l'as pas vue dans ses mauvais moments; **even at her w. she is still a brilliant player** même quand elle joue mal, elle reste une joueuse fantastique

ADV (superl of badly) (le) plus mal, Lit (le) pis; **out of all of us I played w.** j'ai joué le plus mal de nous tous; **that frightened me w. of all** c'est ce qui m'a fait le plus peur; **the w. possible situation** la pire situation possible; **the elderly are the w. off** les personnes âgées sont les plus mal loties; **they are the w. paid** ce sont les plus mal payés; **the w. dressed men in Europe** les hommes les plus mal habillés d'Europe

VT Old-fashioned battre, vaincre, défaire; **to be worsted** avoir le dessous

worst-case ADJ **w. scenario** scénario m catastrophe; **what's the w. scenario?** quel est le pire qui puisse se produire?

worsted ['wʊstɪd] N Tex laine f peignée, peigné m

WORTH [wɜːθ] ADJ **1** (having a value of) valant; **to be w. ...** valoir ...; **to be w. a lot of money** (of thing) valoir cher, avoir beaucoup de valeur; (of person) être riche; **this ring is w. $500** cette bague vaut 500 dollars; **how much** or **what is this painting w.?** combien vaut ce tableau?; **it's not w. anything** cela ne vaut pas quatre sous; **the house isn't w. what they paid for it** la maison ne vaut pas le prix qu'ils ont payé pour l'avoir; **this cheque/contract isn't w. the paper it's printed on** ce chèque/contrat n'a aucune valeur; **she's w. ten of you** elle en vaut dix comme toi; **to be w. nothing** ne rien valoir; **what is the euro w.?** combien vaut l'euro?; **it's not w. much** cela ne vaut pas grand-chose; **to be w. sth to sb** valoir qch pour qn; **this old book is w. a lot to me** ce vieux livre a beaucoup de valeur pour moi; **what's my silence w. to you?** tu donnerais combien pour que je me taise?; **whatever it may be w.** quoi que cela vaille; **I'll tell you this for what it's w.** je vous dis ça pour ce que ça vaut; **she's a lawyer, for what that's w.** elle est avocate, pour ce que cela vaut; **for what it's w., I think they're wrong** pensez-en ce que vous voulez mais je crois qu'ils ont tort; **that's my advice, for what it's w.** c'est mon conseil, il vaut ce qu'il vaut; **it would be as much as my life is w.** ce serait risquer ma vie; **it would be more than my job's w.** ça me coûterait mon emploi, Fig **it's not w. the candle** le jeu ne vaut pas la chandelle

2 (meriting) **it's not w. the trouble** cela ne ou n'en vaut pas la peine; **is it w. while?, is it w. it?** cela (en) vaut-il la peine?; **it's not w. my/your/etc while doing it** ça ne vaut pas la peine que je le fasse/tu le fasses/etc; **it isn't w. it** ça ne vaut pas le coup; **don't get upset, he isn't w. it** ne te rends pas malade, il n'en vaut pas la peine; **you're w. it** tu en vaux la peine; **this novel is not w. reading** ce roman ne vaut pas la peine ou ne mérite pas d'être lu; **it's so late, it's not w. going** il est si tard, ça ne vaut pas la peine ou Fam le coup d'y aller; **something w. having** une chose précieuse; **without you, life wouldn't be w. living** sans toi, la vie ne vaudrait pas la peine d'être vécue; **your life won't be w. living** (if you get on the wrong side of him etc) ça sera invivable pour toi; **it's the only thing that makes their lives w. living** c'est la seule chose qui donne de la valeur à leur vie; **it's w. thinking about** cela mérite réflexion; **it's w. knowing** c'est bon à savoir; **the castle is w. a visit** le château vaut la visite; **your friendship/opinion is w. a lot to me** ton amitié/ton opinion représente beaucoup pour moi

3 *(having money)* **he's w. millions** il est riche à millions; **that is all I am w.** voilà toute ma fortune; *Fig* **he was pulling for all he was w.** il tirait de toutes ses forces

N valeur *f*; **of great/little/no w.** de grande/ de peu de/d'aucune valeur; **give me £40 w. of petrol** donnez-moi (pour) 40 livres d'essence; **to have/want one's money's w.** en avoir/en vouloir pour son argent; **a day's w. of food/water** un jour de vivres/d'eau; **an hour's w. of my time** une heure de mon temps; **she has no sense of her own w.** elle n'est pas consciente de sa propre valeur

---

worthily ['wɜːðɪlɪ] **ADV** *(to live)* dignement, honorablement; *(to donate, sacrifice)* honorablement

worthiness ['wɜːðɪnɪs] **N** mérite *m*

worthless ['wɜːθlɪs] **ADJ 1** *(object)* sans valeur, qui ne vaut rien **2** **he's completely w.** c'est un vaurien

> Attention: ne pas confondre avec l'adjectif **priceless**, qui signifie **inestimable**.

worthlessness ['wɜːθlɪsnɪs] **N 1** *(of object)* peu *m* de valeur **2** *(of person)* nature *f* méprisable

worthwhile [wɜːθ'waɪl] **ADJ** qui en vaut la peine *ou Fam* le coup; **at last I've found a w. job** j'ai enfin trouvé un poste qui me donne satisfaction; **she didn't think it w. replacing the van** elle ne pensait pas que cela valait la peine de remplacer la camionnette

worthy ['wɜːðɪ] **ADJ 1** *(distinguished, meriting respect)* digne; **a w. man** un homme respectable *ou* estimable; **a w. life** une vie honorable *ou* vertueuse **2 w. of** *(deserving, meriting)* digne de; **surely my letter was at least w. of an answer?** ma lettre méritait quand même une réponse, non?; **w. of respect** digne de respect; **you're not w. of your father** tu n'es pas digne de ton père; **her remarks are w. of contempt** ses remarques sont dignes de mépris; **he is a w. winner** il a mérité sa victoire; **to be w. to do sth** être digne de faire qch; **I am not w. to kiss your hand** je ne suis pas digne de baiser ta main; **it is w. of note that …** il est à noter que …; **the town has no museum w. of the name** la ville n'a aucun musée digne de ce nom

N *(of place)* personnage *m*; *Hum* **the village worthies** les notables *mpl* du village

wotcher ['wɒtʃər] **INT** *Br Fam* salut!

[wʊd] **MODAL AUX V** VOIR GRAMMAIRE A57–8 (**I would, they would** *etc are often contracted to* **I'd** [aɪd], **they'd** [ðeɪd] *etc*; **would not** *to* **wouldn't** ['wʊd(ə)nt]) **1** *(expressing future)* **she told me she w. be there** elle m'a dit qu'elle serait là

2 *(consent)* **I wouldn't do it for anything** je ne le ferais pour rien au monde; **w. you pass the mustard please?** voudriez-vous bien me passer la moutarde?; **the wound wouldn't heal** la blessure ne voulait pas se cicatriser, la blessure ne se cicatrisait pas

3 *(emphatic)* **I quite forgot! – you** would! j'ai oublié! – c'est bien de vous! *ou* ça ne m'étonne pas de vous!; **you** would **insist on going** évidemment, il a fallu que tu insistes pour y aller; *Fam* **I wouldn't know** *(I don't know)* je ne saurais dire

4 *(habit)* **she w. often return home exhausted** elle rentrait souvent très fatiguée

5 *(conjecture)* **w. that be your cousin you have in mind?** c'est à votre cousin que vous pensez?; **that w. be your job, am I right?** et ce serait toi qui t'occuperais de cela, non?

6 *(wish)* vouloir; **what w. you have me do?** que voulez-vous que je fasse?; **he w. if he could** il le ferait s'il le pouvait; *Lit* **w. (that) I were a bird!** je voudrais être un oiseau!; **w. to God it wasn't true!** plût à Dieu que cela ne fût pas vrai!

7 *(conditional)* **she w. come if you invited her** elle viendrait si vous l'invitiez; **had he** *or* **if he had let go, he w. have fallen** s'il avait lâché prise il serait tombé VOIR GRAMMAIRE A52–3; B34

would-be **ADJ** prétendu; *Pej* soi-disant; *(housebuyer, student)* potentiel; *(musician, actor)* en herbe; **troops seized the w. assassin** les militaires ont attrapé l'assassin avant qu'il ne commette le crime; **the w. burglar was tied up to a chair** le cambrioleur, pris sur le fait, était attaché à une chaise

wound [wuːnd] **N 1** *Med* blessure *f*, **bullet w.** blessure par balle **2** *Fig* plaie *f*; **to reopen a w.** *or* **an old w.** rouvrir une plaie; **to rub salt in the w.** retourner le fer *ou* le couteau dans la plaie

VT blesser; **to be badly wounded** être gravement blessé; **wounded in the shoulder** blessé *ou* atteint à l'épaule **2** *Fig (of accusation etc)* blesser; **to w. sb's pride** blesser qn dans son amour-propre; **to w. sb's feelings** blesser les susceptibilités de qn, froisser *ou* heurter qn; **my feelings were wounded** j'ai été froissé *ou* heurté

VI causer une blessure

wound [waʊnd] **PT, PP** *see* **wind**

wounded ['wuːndɪd] **ADJ 1** blessé; **the w. man** le blessé **2** *Fig (feelings, pride)* blessé **NPL** **the w.** les blessés *mpl*

wounding ['wuːndɪŋ] **ADJ** blessant; **he found it w. to his pride** cela a blessé son amour-propre

wove **PT** *see* **weave**

woven **PP** *see* **weave**

wow [waʊ] **INT** oh là là!

N *(success)* succès *m* fou; **it's a w.** c'est sensationnel; **this is a w. of a show** c'est un spectacle sensationnel

VT emballer

wow **N** *(in sound system)* pleurage *m*

WP [dʌb(ə)lju:'pi:] **N** *Comput* **1** *abbr* **word processing 2** *abbr* **word processor**

wp *(abbr* **weather permitting)** si le temps le permet

WPC [dʌb(ə)lju:pi:'si:] **N** *Br (abbr* **woman police constable)** femme-agent *f*, *pl* femmes-agents

wpm [dʌb(ə)lju:pi:'em] *(abbr* **words per minute)** mots par minute

WRAC [ræk] **N** *Br (abbr* **Women's Royal Army Corps)** ≃ AFAT

wrack [ræk] **N** *(seaweed)* varec(h) *m*

wrack **N** = **rack**

WRAF [ræf] **N** *Br Mil (abbr* **Women's Royal Air Force)** = section *f* féminine de l'armée de l'air britannique

wraith [reɪθ] **N** apparition *f*

wraithlike ['reɪθlaɪk] **ADJ** *(appearance)* semblable à une apparition *ou* un spectre, spectral

wrangle ['ræŋɡ(ə)l] **N** dispute *f*, querelle *f*

VI se disputer, se quereller, se chamailler (**over** à propos de)

VT *Am (livestock)* garder

wrangler ['ræŋɡlər] **N 1** *(quarreller)* querelleur, -euse **2** *Am (cowboy)* cowboy *m* **3** *Cin (animal trainer)* animalier *m*

wrangling ['ræŋɡlɪŋ] **N** *(quarrelling)* disputes *fpl*, querelles *fpl*; **there has been a lot of**

w. over who to give the job to il y a eu beaucoup de querelles pour décider à qui donner le poste

wrap [ræp] **N** *(blanket) (for journey)* couverture *f*, *(shawl)* châle *m*; *(cloak)* pèlerine *f*, manteau *m*; *Fig* **to keep sth under wraps** garder qch secret; *Fig* **the wraps were taken off the new car today** la voiture a été montrée au public pour la première fois aujourd'hui; **it's a w.!** *Cin* c'est dans la boîte!; *Fam (it's complete)* ça y est, c'est fini!

VT (**-pp-**) envelopper, emballer; **to w. sth in paper** envelopper *ou* empaqueter qch dans du papier; **the cheese was wrapped in plastic** le fromage était emballé *ou* enveloppé sous plastique; **would you like it wrapped?** *(of gift)* c'est pour offrir?; **to w. a baby in a shawl** emmitoufler un bébé dans un châle; *Fig* **wrapped in mystery** enveloppé *ou* entouré de mystère

VI 1 *Comput (of lines)* se boucler **2** *Cin* finir de tourner

▸ **wrap round** **VT SEP** **to w. sth round sth** enrouler *ou* entortiller qch autour de qch; **w. this blanket round you/your shoulders** enroule cette couverture autour de toi/de tes épaules; **he wrapped the bandage round my finger** il a enroulé le bandage autour de mon doigt; **the cable wrapped itself round the …** le câble s'est enroulé autour du …; *Fam* **he wrapped his car round a tree** il a encadré un arbre

▸ **wrap up** **VT SEP 1** *(parcel, present)* envelopper; **to w. sth up in sth** envelopper qch dans qch; **w. yourself up well** *(dress warmly)* emmitoufle-toi bien; **wrapped up** *(person)* emmitouflé **2** *Fig* **to be wrapped up in sth** *(absorbed)* être uniquement préoccupé de qch; **he is wrapped up in his work** il est entièrement absorbé par son travail; **she is too wrapped up in herself/in her own problems** elle est trop préoccupée par elle-même/par ses propres problèmes; **they are wrapped up in each other** ils sont uniquement préoccupés l'un par l'autre **3** *Fam (bring to an end)* *(deal, negotiations, discussion)* conclure; **well that about wraps it up for today** voilà, c'est à peu près tout pour aujourd'hui

VI 1 *(put on warm clothes)* (bien) s'emmitoufler **2** *Br Fam (stop talking)* se taire; **w. up!** ferme-la!, écrase!

wraparound ['ræpəraʊnd] **N** = **wrapround**

▸▸ **w. bumper** pare-chocs *m* enveloppant; **w. sunglasses** lunettes *fpl* panoramiques

wrapover ['ræpəʊvər] **N** *(skirt)* jupe *f* portefeuille

ADJ *(dress, skirt etc)* portefeuille *inv*

wrapped [ræpt] **ADJ** *(bread, sweets etc)* emballé

wrapper ['ræpər] **N 1** *(packaging)* (papier *m* d')emballage *m*; *(of sweet)* papier; *(of cigar)* emballage; **her pocket was full of old sweet wrappers** sa poche était pleine de vieux papiers de bonbons **2** *(of book)* couverture *f*, couvre-livre *m*, *pl* couvre-livres; *(to protect jacket)* liseuse *f*, *(of newspaper being mailed)* bande *f* **3** *Old-fashioned (dressing gown)* saut-de-lit *m*, *pl* sauts-de-lit

wrapping ['ræpɪŋ] **N** *(material)* emballage *m*

▸▸ **w. paper** *(for gift)* papier *m* cadeau; *(for parcel)* papier d'emballage

wrapround ['ræpraʊnd] **N** *(in word processing)* bouclage *m*, renouement *m* (des mots)

▸▸ *Aut* **w. rear window** lunette *f* arrière panoramique; **w. windscreen** pare-brise *m* panoramique

wrath [rɒθ] **N** *Lit* courroux *m*; **the w. of God** la colère de Dieu

wrathful ['rɒθful] **ADJ** *Lit* courroucé, en colère

wreak [riːk] **VT** *(havoc)* entraîner; **to w. (one's) vengeance upon sb** exercer *ou* assouvir sa vengeance sur qn; **the hurricane**

wreaked terrible destruction on the island l'ouragan a entraîné de terribles destructions sur l'île

wreath [ri:θ, *pl* ri:ðz, ri:θs] **N 1** *(of flowers)* couronne *f*, guirlande *f*; **(funeral) w.** couronne mortuaire; **w. of poppies** couronne de coquelicots; **he laid a w. on her grave** il a déposé une couronne sur sa tombe **2** *(of smoke, mist)* volute *f*

wreathe [ri:ð] **VT 1** *(encircle)* enguirlander; *(sb's head)* couronner; **the mountain was wreathed with mist** la montagne était entourée de brouillard; **her face was wreathed in smiles** son visage était rayonnant **2** *(entwine) (flowers)* enrouler (**round** autour de) **VI** *(of smoke)* tourbillonner

wreck [rek] **N 1** *(ship)* navire *m* naufragé, épave *f*, *(car, lorry, train, plane)* voiture *f*/camion *m*/train *m*/avion *m* accidenté(e), épave; **my car's a total w.** ma voiture est bonne pour la casse; **the burnt-out w. of a bus** les restes calcinés d'un bus; **human wrecks** épaves (humaines); *Fig* **to be a physical/nervous w.** avoir la santé détraquée/ les nerfs détraqués; **the man's an emotional w.** le type est une loque, au niveau émotionnel; *Fig* **after two hours with those kids I was a total w.** après deux heures avec ces gamins j'étais complètement épuisé **2** *(destruction) (of ship)* naufrage *m*; **to be saved from the w.** échapper au naufrage **VT 1** *(ship)* faire faire naufrage à, causer le naufrage de; **to be wrecked** *(of ship, person)* faire naufrage; **the ship was wrecked on these rocks** le bateau a fait naufrage sur ces rochers **2** *(car)* démolir; *(building)* démolir, détruire; **vandals have wrecked the building/train** les vandales ont abîmé le bâtiment/le train; **to w. one's health** se ruiner la santé **3** *Fig (undertaking)* faire échouer, saboter; *(person's hopes)* détruire, ruiner, briser; *(chances)* ruiner; **to w. sb's plans** faire échouer les projets de qn; **to w. sb's marriage** ruiner *ou* détruire le mariage de qn; **this defeat has wrecked the team's chances** cette défaite a anéanti les chances de l'équipe; **the accident wrecked her hopes** l'accident a anéanti ses espoirs; **you wrecked his life/career** tu as brisé sa vie/sa carrière

wreckage ['rekɪdʒ] **N** *(no pl) (of ship)* épave *f*, *(of aircraft, train, car)* débris *mpl*; **piece of w.** épave; **documents were found in the w.** on a trouvé des documents parmi les débris; *Fig* **she hoped to salvage something from the w. of her career** elle espérait sauver quelque chose de ce qui restait de sa carrière

wrecked [rekt] **ADJ** *Fam (drunk)* bourré, pété; *(on drugs)* défoncé, raide; *(exhausted)* crevé, claqué

wrecker ['rekər] **N 1** *Constr (of buildings)* démolisseur *m* **2** *(salvager)* sauveteur *m* d'épaves **3** *Am Aut (vehicle)* dépanneuse *f*, camion *m* de dépannage; *(person)* dépanneur *m* **4** *Hist (person who causes shipwrecks)* naufrageur *m*, pilleur *m* d'épave

wrecking truck, wrecking car ['rekɪŋ] **N** *Am* camion *m* de dépannage, dépanneuse *f*

Wren [ren] **N** *Br Fam* = membre *m* du Women's Royal Naval Service; **the Wrens** = section *f* féminine de la marine britannique

wren [ren] **N** troglodyte *m*

wrench [rentʃ] **N 1** *(twist)* mouvement *m* violent de torsion; **to give sth a w.** tordre qch violemment; **he gave his ankle a w.** il s'est fait une entorse; *(less serious)* il s'est foulé la cheville **2** *Fig (emotional)* **the separation was a terrible w.** la séparation fut un déchirement affreux; **it will be a w. to leave the old house** il m'en/nous en/*etc* coûtera de quitter la vieille maison **3** *(tool)* clef *f*; **adjustable w.** clef à ouverture variable, clef universelle

VT *(twist)* tordre *ou* tourner violemment; **to w. one's ankle/shoulder** se fouler la cheville/l'épaule; **to w. the lid open** forcer le couvercle; **to w. off/out** arracher *ou* enlever (avec un violent effort de torsion); **to w. sth (away) from sb** arracher qch à qn; **she wrenched herself free** d'une secousse elle se dégagea; *Fig* **nothing could w. her away from her book** rien ne pouvait l'arracher à son livre

wrest [rest] **VT** arracher (**from** à); **she wrested the knife from him** *or* **his grip** elle lui a arraché le couteau; **to w. a confession from sb** arracher un aveu à qn; **we could w. no meaning from the coded message** nous n'avons pu tirer aucun sens du message codé; **I managed to w. her attention away from the tennis** j'ai réussi à l'arracher au tennis qui occupait toute son attention

wrestle ['res(ə)l] **VI 1** *(physically)* lutter (**with** avec, contre); **to w. together** lutter, se prendre corps à corps; **the two men wrestled briefly** les deux hommes ont brièvement lutté; *Fig* **to w. with one's umbrella** se (dé)battre avec son parapluie; *Fig* **he wrestled with the zip/knot in the darkness** il s'est débattu avec la fermeture éclair®/le nœud dans le noir **2** *Fig* **to w. with** *(difficulties, temptation)* lutter contre; *(adversity)* être aux prises avec; *(problem)* s'attaquer à; **they've been wrestling with the problem for years** ils sont aux prises avec ce problème depuis des années; **to w. with one's conscience** être aux prises avec sa conscience **VT** lutter avec *ou* contre; **he wrestled his attacker to the ground** il a jeté son attaquant au sol dans la lutte

N *(fight)*, *Fig* lutte *f* (corps à corps), corps à corps *m* (**with** contre); **after a w. with the knot, she was free** après s'être débattue avec le nœud, elle était libre; *Fig* **after a w. with his conscience, he agreed** après une lutte avec sa conscience, il a accepté
▸ **wrestle down VT SEP** *(one's opponent)* terrasser *(à la lutte)*

wrestler ['reslər] **N** lutteur, -euse

wrestling ['reslɪŋ] **N** lutte *f*, *(professional)* catch *m*; **Sumo w.** lutte *f* Sumo
▸▸ **w. match** match *m* de catch

wretch [retʃ] **N 1** *(pitiable person)* malheureux, -euse; **poor w.** pauvre diable *m*; *(despicable person)* misérable *mf*; **you w.!** misérable!; **you little w.!** petit fripon!

wretched ['retʃɪd] **ADJ 1** *(miserable)* misérable; **to feel w.** *(ill)* être mal en train; *(depressed)* avoir le cafard; *(guilty)* s'en vouloir; **to lead a w. existence** mener une existence misérable; **to be in w. poverty** être dans une misère affreuse **2** *(bad, pitiful)* pitoyable, lamentable; *(meal)* triste, pauvre; **the animal/house was in a w. state** l'animal/la maison était dans un état lamentable; **this coffee is w. stuff!** ce café est abominable; **what w. weather!** quel temps abominable!, quel temps de chien!; **it's a w. business** c'est une affaire *ou* une histoire lamentable; **she's a w. singer** c'est une piètre chanteuse; **w. hovel** taudis *m* **3** *(despicable)* misérable; **it was a w. thing to do/say** c'est immonde d'avoir fait/dit ça **4** *Fam (expressing anger, contempt etc)* fichu, *Old-fashioned* damné, sacré; **I can't find that w. umbrella** je ne retrouve pas ce fichu parapluie

wretchedly ['retʃɪdlɪ] **ADV 1** *(as intensifier)* *(cold, poor, unhappy)* terriblement, affreusement; **to be w. poor** être dans une misère affreuse; **to be w. ill** être malade à faire pitié **2** *(in an unhappy fashion)* de façon pitoyable, pitoyablement

wretchedness ['retʃɪdnɪs] **N 1** *(misfortune)* misère *f* **2** *(sadness)* tristesse *f* **3** *(of clothes, living conditions)* extrême pauvreté *f*

wriggle ['rɪg(ə)l] **N** tortillement *m* du corps;

to give a w. se tortiller, se trémousser **VI 1** *(of worm, person)* se tortiller; *(of fish)* frétiller; **stop wriggling!** arrête de t'agiter!; **to w. through a hedge** se faufiler à travers une haie (en se tortillant); **to w. into the sweater** il a réussi à enfiler le pull en se tortillant; **to w. free** se libérer en se faufilant **2** *Fig* **to w. out of a difficulty** se tirer d'affaire; **I'd like to see him w. out of this one!** j'aimerais savoir comment il va s'en sortir!; **w. out of that one if you can!** à toi de t'en sortir!; **to try to w. out of it** chercher une échappatoire; **he tried to w. out of his promise** il a essayé de se dégager de sa promesse

VT *(fingers)* tortiller; *(legs)* agiter; **she wriggled her way along the tunnel** elle s'est faufilée le long du tunnel; *Fig* **to w. one's way out of a situation/a problem/a commitment** se dérober devant *ou* se dégager d'une situation/d'un problème/d'un engagement; *Fig* **I'd like to see him w. his way out of that!** j'aimerais bien voir comment il va se sortir de cette situation!

wriggler ['rɪglər] **N** **he's a terrible w.** il gigote tout le temps

wriggling ['rɪg(ə)lɪŋ] **ADJ** = **wriggly**
N tortillement *m*; **a w. movement** un tortillement

wriggly ['rɪglɪ] **ADJ** *(person)* qui gigote; **the children started getting w.** les enfants commençaient à gigoter; **the fish was wet and w.** le poisson était humide et frétillant; **a w. worm** un ver qui se tortille

wring [rɪŋ] **N** **to give the clothes a w.** tordre le linge; *(by machine)* essorer le linge; **he gave my hand a w.** il m'a donné une vigoureuse poignée de main

VT *(pt, pp wrung* [rʌŋ]*)* tordre; *(washing)* tordre; *(by machine)* essorer; **do not w.** *(on garment label)* ne pas essorer; **to w. sb's hand** serrer (longuement) la main de qn; **to w. one's hands (in despair)** se tordre les mains (de désespoir); **to w. a bird's neck** tordre le cou à une volaille; *Fam* **I'd like to w. his neck** j'ai envie de lui tordre le cou; **to w. a secret from sb** arracher un secret à qn; **to w. money from sb** arracher *ou* extorquer de l'argent à qn; **to w. tears from sb** arracher des larmes à qn; **to w. the last drop of pathos from a situation** extraire la dernière goutte de pathos d'une situation
▸ **wring out VT SEP** *(washing)* tordre; *(by machine)* essorer; **to w. the water out** *(from clothes)* exprimer l'eau; **to feel wrung out** se sentir lessivé *ou* moulu

wringer ['rɪŋər] **N** essoreuse *f* (à rouleaux); **he put the clothes through the w.** il passa les vêtements à l'essoreuse; *Fig Fam* **to put sb through the w.** faire passer un mauvais quart d'heure à qn

wringing ['rɪŋɪŋ] **ADJ** **w. (wet)** *(clothes)* complètement trempé; *(person)* complètement trempé, trempé jusqu'aux os; **the shirt was w. with sweat** la chemise était trempée de sueur

N *(of washing)* tordage *m*; *(by machine)* essorage *m*; **she told us the news, with much w. of hands** elle nous a annoncé la nouvelle, en se tordant les mains

wrinkle ['rɪŋk(ə)l] **N 1** *(on skin)* ride *f*, *(in cloth, paper, carpet)* faux pli *m* **2** *Old-fashioned Fam (tip)* renseignement *m* utile, tuyau *m*

VT *(skin)* rider, plisser; *(dress)* froisser, chiffonner, faire des plis à; **to w. one's forehead** froncer les sourcils; **to w. one's nose** froncer le nez; **her stockings were wrinkled** ses bas faisaient des plis

VI *(of skin)* se rider, se plisser; *(of dress)* se plisser, faire des plis; *(of fruit)* se rider, se ratatiner

wrinkled ['rɪŋk(ə)ld] **ADJ** *(forehead)* plissé;

(skin) ridé; *(dress)* froissé, chiffonné; *(fruit)* ridé, ratatiné; **a w. old man** un vieil homme (tout) fripé

wrinkly ['rɪŋklɪ] ADJ *(skin) (after bath)* fripé; *(with old age)* ridé, fripé; *(blouse)* froissé; **to go all w.** *(of fruit)* se ratatiner; *(of skin, fingers)* se friper, devenir tout fripé
N *esp Br Fam Pej, Hum (old person)* croulant, -ante

wrist [rɪst] N *(of hand, dress etc)* poignet *m*
▸▸ *Comput* **w. rest** repose-poignets *m inv*

wristband ['rɪstbænd] N **1** *(on shirt)* poignet *m*, manchette *f* **2** *(sweatband)* bracelet *m* en éponge; *Gym (of leather)* bracelet de force (en cuir) **3** *(of watch)* bracelet *m*

wristbone ['rɪstbəʊn] N *Anat* os *m* du carpe

wristlet ['rɪstlɪt] N bracelet *m*

wristlock ['rɪstlɒk] N *(in wrestling)* clef *f* de poignet; **to put a w. on sb** faire une clef de poignet à qn

wristwatch ['rɪstwɒtʃ] N montre-bracelet *f*, *pl* montres-bracelets, bracelet-montre *m*, *pl* bracelets-montres

writ[1] [rɪt] N *Law* acte *m* judiciaire, mandat *m*, ordonnance *f*, *(summons)* assignation *f*, **to serve a w. on sb, to issue a w. against sb** assigner qn (en justice); **his w. no longer runs in this part of the country** cette région n'est plus sous son pouvoir; *Rel* **Holy W.** les saintes Écritures *fpl*, l'Écriture sainte
▸▸ **w. of attachment** ordonnance de saisie; **w. of possession** envoi *m* en possession

writ[2] PP *see* **write**

WRITE [raɪt] *(pt* **wrote** [rəʊt]*; pp* **written** ['rɪt(ə)n]*, Arch* **writ** [rɪt]*)* VT **1** *(one's name, novel, letter, piece of music etc)* écrire; *(article)* rédiger; *(cheque)* faire, écrire; *Com* libeller; **can I w. you a cheque for it?** est-ce que je peux vous faire un chèque?; **w. the answer in the space provided** écrivez la réponse dans l'espace réservé à cet effet; **that was not written by me** cela n'est pas écrit de ma main; **do you w. it with a capital?** ça s'écrit avec une majuscule?, ça prend une majuscule?, tu l'écris avec une majuscule?; **the paper is written all over** la feuille est couverte d'écritures; **embarrassment was written all over her (face)** la gêne se lisait sur son visage; **his guilt was written on his face** sa culpabilité se lisait sur son visage; *Fam* **he's got journalist written all over him** on voit tout de suite que c'est un journaliste; *Fig* **writ large** *(obvious)* écrit en gros, écrit en grosses lettres; **this is Conservative policy writ large** c'est la politique conservatrice tout crachée; **it is written that …** il est écrit que …; *Comput* **to w. sth to disk** écrire qch sur disque
2 *esp Am (write a letter to)* écrire à; **I wrote them to complain** je leur ai écrit pour me plaindre
VI écrire; **w. and tell me what you think** écris-moi pour me dire ce que tu en penses; **she writes well** *(of author)* elle écrit bien; *(expresses herself well in writing)* elle a un beau style; *(has good handwriting)* elle a une belle écriture; **he can w. in Italian** il sait écrire l'italien; **they can read and w.** ils savent lire et écrire; **please w. in black ink** prière d'écrire en noir; **this pen won't w.** ce stylo ne marche pas *ou* n'écrit pas; **she writes** *(is an author)* elle écrit; **to w. for children** écrire des livres pour enfants; **to w. for a paper** écrire dans *ou* collaborer à un journal; **he writes on** *or* **about gardening** il écrit des articles sur le jardinage; **to w. to sb** écrire à qn; **I wrote (to them) to complain** je leur ai écrit pour me plaindre; **we still w.** *(to each other)* nous nous écrivons toujours; **he writes home regularly** il écrit à sa famille régulièrement; *Fig* **that's nothing to w. home about** il n'y a pas de quoi s'en relever la

nuit *ou* s'extasier; **w. for our catalogue/more information** nous écrire pour obtenir un catalogue/plus d'informations
▸▸ *Comput* **w. access** accès *m* en écriture; *Comput* **w. area** zone *f* d'écriture; *Comput* **w. density** densité *f* d'écriture; *Tech* **w. head** tête *f* d'enregistrement; *Comput* **w. protection** protection *f* contre l'écriture *ou* en écriture; *Comput* **w. speed** vitesse *f* d'écriture
▸ **write away for** VT INSEP écrire pour demander; **w. away for a free sample** écrire pour obtenir un échantillon gratuit
▸ **write back** VI écrire pour répondre; **she wrote back to say that …** elle a répondu (à la lettre) pour dire que …
▸ **write down** VT SEP **1** *(in order to remember)* noter; *(one's name)* écrire; **to w. down one's thoughts/ideas** mettre ses pensées/ses idées par écrit
2 *Fin (capital)* réduire; *Acct* déprécier
▸ **write in** VT SEP *(enter in writing) (correction)* insérer; **w. in the correct answer** mettez *ou* écrivez la bonne réponse; *Am* **to w. in a complaint** envoyer une plainte à la direction; *Am Pol* **to w. sb in** inscrire qn
VI *(send letter)* écrire; **many (of our) viewers wrote in with suggestions** de nombreux téléspectateurs nous ont envoyé leurs suggestions; **to w. in for** *(catalogue, free gift etc)* demander par courrier
▸ **write off** VT SEP **1** *Fin (capital)* réduire, amortir; *(debt)* amortir; **to w. £1000 off for wear and tear** déduire 1000 livres pour l'usure; *Com* **to w. off a bad debt** défalquer une mauvaise créance, passer une créance aux profits et pertes
2 *Br Fam* **my car was written off** ma voiture était bonne pour la casse; *Br* **she wrote off her father's car** elle a bousillé la voiture de son père; *Fam* **the critics wrote the play off** les critiques ont démoli la pièce; **they had written her off as a has-been** ils l'avaient cataloguée comme une ringarde
VI *(send letter)* écrire; **to w. off for a catalogue** demander *ou* commander un catalogue par courrier
▸ **write out** VT SEP **1** *(write in full)* transcrire; *(copy)* mettre au net; **w. this out neatly** écris *ou* recopie cela au propre; **to w. sth out in full** écrire qch en toutes lettres
2 *(write) (cheque)* faire; *Med (prescription)* rédiger
3 *TV, Radio (remove from script) (character)* supprimer (le rôle de)
▸ **write up** VT SEP **1** *(prepare) (news item, report)* écrire, rédiger; **w. up your notes** mettez vos notes au propre
2 *(praise)* faire l'éloge de
3 *(update) (diary, accounts)* mettre à jour
4 *Fin (capital, stocks)* augmenter; *Acct (asset)* revaloriser

write-back N *Acct* **w. of provisions** reprises *fpl* sur provisions

write-down N *Fin* dépréciation *f*

write-off N **1** *Acct* annulation *f* par écrit; **w. of expenditure** amortissement *m* de dépenses **2** *(car)* épave *f*; *Fam (project etc)* perte *f* sèche; **my car was a (complete) w.** ma voiture a été complètement détruite *ou* n'était plus qu'une épave

write-protect VT *Comput* protéger contre l'écriture

write-protected ADJ *Comput* protégé en écriture

writer ['raɪtər] N **1** *(professional)* écrivain *m*; *(of novel, scenario, letter etc)* auteur *m* *(of* de); **woman w.** femme *f* écrivain; **w.'s block** vertige *m* de la page blanche; **w.'s cramp** crampe *f* des écrivains; **the present w., the w.** *(of this letter)* celui qui écrit, l'auteur *(de cette lettre)*; **I'm not a good letter w.** *(I don't write often)* la correspondance n'est

pas mon fort; *(I don't write well)* je n'ai pas la plume facile; **to be a good/bad w.** bien/mal écrire **2** *Scot Law* notaire *m*; **W. to the Signet** ≃ avoué *m*

writer-director N *Cin, TV* auteur-réalisateur, -trice, *pl* auteurs-réalisateurs, -trices

write-up N **1** *Journ* article *m*; **the play got a good w.** la pièce a eu une bonne critique **2** *Fin (of stock)* augmentation *f* de la valeur comptable

writhe [raɪð] VI *(of person)* se contorsionner; *(with pain)* se tordre; *(of snakes, worms)* grouiller; **to w. in agony** se tordre dans des souffrances atroces; **the remark made him w.** *(with shame, embarrassment)* en entendant la remarque, il ne savait plus où se mettre; *(with indignation, anger)* en entendant la remarque, il s'est raidi d'indignation/de colère; **the memory still makes me w. with embarrassment** ce souvenir me fait encore rougir

writing ['raɪtɪŋ] N **1** *(action)* écriture *f*; **the art of w.** l'art de l'écriture; **I'm very bad about letter w.** je suis très mauvais correspondant; **at the time of w.** au moment où j'écris/il écrit/*etc*; *Journ* à l'heure où nous rédigeons ceci; **that's my w.** *(handwriting)* c'est mon écriture; **his w. is bad** *(illegible)* il écrit mal; *Fig* **the w. is on the wall** la catastrophe est imminente; **the w. was on the wall for the Roman Empire** la fin de l'empire romain était imminente; **I could see the w. on the wall** je savais à quoi m'attendre; **in w.** *(to put sth, answer)* par écrit; **I won't be satisfied until I see it in w.** je ne serai pas satisfait tant que ce ne sera pas écrit noir sur blanc; **can I have that in w.?** est-ce que vous pouvez me mettre cela par écrit?; **to commit the facts to w.** consigner les faits par écrit; **to take up w.** *(of author)* commencer à écrire **2** *(work)* littérature *f*, œuvre *f* littéraire; **the writings of an author** les écrits *mpl ou* l'œuvre *m* d'un auteur; **selected writings** morceaux *mpl* choisis; **a fine piece of w.** *(passage)* un beau passage; *(book, article)* quelque chose de très bien écrit **3** *(style)* style *m*; **his w. has matured** son style a mûri
▸▸ **w. case** nécessaire *m* de correspondance; **w. desk** secrétaire *m (meuble)*; *Acct* **w. off** *(of debt)* amortissement *m*; **w. pad** bloc-notes *m*, *pl* bloc-notes; **w. paper** papier *m* à lettres; **w. table** secrétaire *(meuble)*

written ['rɪt(ə)n] PP *see* **write**
ADJ écrit; *(in writing)* par écrit; **w. confirmation** confirmation *f* écrite *ou* par écrit; **the w. word** le mot écrit; **w. consent** consentement *m* par écrit; **w. law** loi *f* écrite; *Sch etc* **w. examination** épreuve *f* écrite

written-down cost, written-down value N *Fin* valeur *f* amortie

WRNS [renz] N *Br Mil (abbr* **Women's Royal Naval Service)** = section *f* féminine de la marine britannique

WRONG [rɒŋ]

ADJ	mauvais **1, 2** ▪ faux **2** ▪ mal **1, 2, 4, 5** ▪ tort **2**	
N	mal **1** ▪ tort **2, 3**	
ADV	mal **1, 2**	
VT	faire du tort à	

ADJ **1** *(morally bad) (judgement etc)* mauvais; **it is w. to steal, stealing is w.** c'est mal de voler; **it was w. of you not to tell me!** c'était très mal de votre part de ne pas me'n parler!; **it is w. for people to have to pay for hospital care** il n'est pas normal que les gens doivent payer les soins hospitaliers; **it's w. that they should suffer because of other people's incompetence** il n'est pas normal qu'ils pâtissent de l'incompétence des autres
2 *(incorrect, mistaken)* faux, *f* fausse; *(atti-*

tude, sort, key, bus, road) mauvais; *(answer)* mauvais, incorrect; **my watch is w.** ma montre n'est pas à l'heure; **w. use of a word** emploi abusif d'un mot; **don't get the w. idea** ne te fais pas de fausses idées; **his ideas are all w.** il a des idées tout de travers; **to be in the w. place** ne pas être à sa place; **to drive on the w. side of the road** conduire du mauvais côté de la route; *Fig* **to get out of bed on the w. side** se lever du pied gauche; *esp Br Fig* **to get on the w. side of sb** se faire mal voir de qn; **your sock is the w. side out** ta chaussette est à l'envers; **to be (the) w. side up** être à l'envers; **to be on the w. side of forty** avoir (dé)passé la quarantaine; **to take the w. train** se tromper de train; *also Fig* **to back the w. horse** miser sur le mauvais cheval; **to take the w. road** se tromper de chemin *ou* de direction; **this is the w. road for Munich** ce n'est pas la bonne route pour aller à Munich; **she gave me the w. address** elle ne m'a pas donné la bonne adresse, elle m'a donné une mauvaise adresse; **to put sb on the w. track** mettre qn sur une fausse piste; **to be on the w. scent** *or* **track** suivre une mauvaise piste, faire fausse piste; **you've got the w. man, Jack Taylor isn't a murderer** vous faites erreur, Jack Taylor n'est pas un meurtrier; **to come at the w. time** venir à un mauvais moment *ou* mal à propos; **to do/say the w. thing** commettre un impair, dire/faire ce qu'il ne faut pas, *Fam* faire une gaffe, mettre les pieds dans le plat; **I'm the w. person to ask** il ne faut pas me demander ça à moi; **you're talking to the w. person** *(ask sb else)* ce n'est pas à moi qu'il faut demander ça; *Tel* **w. number** mauvais numéro *m*; **to dial the w. number** composer un mauvais numéro; **I think you've got the w. number** je crois que vous n'avez pas le bon numéro; **it was the w. number** *(I didn't dial correctly)* ce n'était pas le bon numéro; **who was that? – nobody, it was a w. number** qui était-ce? – personne, c'était une erreur de numéro *ou* un mauvais numéro; *Mus* **w. note** fausse note; *Fig* **her speech hit the w. note** son discours n'était pas dans la note

3 to be w. *(of person)* avoir tort, se tromper, être dans l'erreur; **they were w. to assume** *or* **in assuming that …** ils ont eu tort de supposer que …; **that's just where you are w.** c'est justement ce qui vous trompe, c'est justement là que vous vous trompez; **to be w. about sb/sth** se tromper sur le compte de qn/sur qch; **you were w. about the price** tu avais tort en ce qui concerne le prix; **I was w. about her** je me suis trompé sur son compte *ou* sur elle; **you were w. to contradict him** vous avez eu tort de le contredire

4 we went the w. way nous nous sommes trompés de chemin; **I was sent the w. way** on m'a mal dirigé; **if you want to impress him you're going the w. way about it!** si tu veux l'impressionner tu t'y prends mal!; **you're setting about it in the w. way** vous vous y prenez mal *ou* de travers; **to take sth the w. way** prendre quelque chose à contrepied; **it went down the w. way** *(of food)* je l'ai/il l'a/*etc* avalé de travers; **to stroke a cat the w. way** caresser un chat à rebrousse-poil

5 *(amiss)* **what's w.?** qu'est-ce qui ne va pas?; **is there something** *or* **anything w.?** quelque chose ne va pas?; **what's w. with you?** qu'avez-vous?, qu'est-ce qui ne va pas?; **what's w. with these people?** *(that they don't understand)* qu'est-ce qu'ils ont qui ne va pas, ces gens?; **there's something w. with me** *(ill)* j'ai quelque chose qui ne va pas; **there must be something w. with me** *(that people don't like me)* il doit y avoir quelque chose qui ne va pas chez moi; *Fam* **he's w. in the head** il a quelque chose qui ne

tourne pas rond dans sa tête, il est un peu timbré; **there was something w. with our car** nous avons eu des ennuis avec la voiture; **there's nothing w. with the engine** le moteur fonctionne normalement; **there's something w. somewhere** il y a quelque chose qui cloche *ou* qui ne tourne pas rond; **I hope there's nothing w.** j'espère qu'il n'est rien arrivé; *Fam* **what's w. with that?** qu'avez-vous à redire à cela?; **there's nothing w. about wanting a holiday without the kids** il n'y a pas de mal à vouloir des vacances sans les enfants; **what's w. with going to France?** quel mal y a-t-il à aller en France?; **what's w. with my idea?** qu'est-ce qu'elle a qui ne va pas, mon idée?

N 1 *(immoral action)* mal *m*; **to know right from w.** distinguer le bien du mal; **in her eyes he can do no w.** il trouve toujours grâce à ses yeux; **the president can do no w.** le président ne peut pas mal faire

2 *(unjust action)* tort *m*, injustice *f*; **to right a w.** réparer une injustice; **two wrongs do not make a right** on ne répare pas le mal par le mal; **to do sb w., to do w. to sb** faire tort à qn; **you do her great w. in accusing her of not caring** tu lui as fait beaucoup de tort en l'accusant de s'en moquer

3 *(mistake)* **to be in the w.** *(because of an action)* être dans son tort; *(be mistaken)* avoir tort; **to put sb in the w.** mettre qn dans son tort

ADV 1 *(morally)* mal; **you did w.** vous avez mal agi

2 *(incorrectly)* mal, incorrectement; **to guess w.** mal deviner; **you've added it up w.** vous avez mal calculé; **you have spelt my name w.** vous avez mal orthographié mon nom; **she got the time/address/name w.** *(was mistaken about)* elle s'est trompée d'heure/d'adresse/ de nom; *(misunderstood)* elle a mal compris l'heure/l'adresse/le nom; *Fam* **don't get me w., I'm not saying …** comprenez-moi bien, je ne dis pas …; *Fam* **you've got me w.** vous m'avez mal compris; *esp Am* **to get in w. with sb** se faire mal voir de qn

3 to go w. *(of mechanism)* se dérégler, se dérégler, se détraquer; *(of business)* aller mal, aller de travers; *(mistake route)* se tromper de chemin; *Fig* se fourvoyer, faire fausse route; *(go morally astray)* se dévoyer, mal tourner; *(be mistaken)* se tromper, commettre une erreur; **then things started to go terribly w.** et puis les choses ont commencé à aller très mal; **his son went w.** son fils a mal tourné; **we went w. at that crossroads** nous nous sommes trompés à ce carrefour; **it's at the end of this road, you can't go w.** c'est au bout de cette route, vous ne pouvez pas vous tromper; **where I went w. was in being too kind to him** là où j'ai commis une erreur, c'est en me montrant trop gentil avec lui; **you can't go w. buying secondhand** vous ne faites pas d'erreur en achetant d'occasion, vous faites forcément le bon choix en achetant d'occasion; **the clock's gone w. again** la pendule s'est déréglée encore une fois; **something went w. with the lighting** nous avons/il y a/*etc* eu un problème avec l'éclairage; **all our plans went w.** tous nos projets ont échoué; **things have gone w.** les choses ont mal tourné; **she used to be a normal, happy little girl, but something went w.** c'était une petite fille normale et heureuse mais quelque chose a mal tourné; **the space flight went disastrously w.** le vol spatial a tourné à la catastrophe

VT faire (du) tort à, léser, être injuste pour *ou* envers; **he feels wronged** il se sent lésé

wrongdoer ['rɒŋduːər] **N 1** *(of immoral action)* auteur *m* d'une injustice; **they did not**

regard themselves as wrongdoers ils ne se considéraient pas comme coupables **2** *(of illegal action)* malfaiteur *m*

wrongdoing ['rɒŋduːɪŋ] **N 1** *(immoral action)* (*usu pl*) méfaits *mpl* **2** *(illegal action)* infraction *f* à la loi

wrong-foot **VT** *Sport* prendre à contrepied; *Fig* prendre à l'improviste *ou* au dépourvu *ou* au pied levé

wrongful ['rɒŋfʊl] **ADJ** *(unjust)* injuste; *(unjustified)* injustifié; *(illegal)* illégal, -aux, illicite ▸▸ *Law* **w. arrest** arrestation *f* arbitraire; *Ind* **w. dismissal** renvoi *m* injustifié; **w. imprisonment** emprisonnement *m* injustifié

wrongfully ['rɒŋfəlɪ] **ADV** injustement, à tort, de façon arbitraire

wrong-headed **ADJ** buté

wrongly ['rɒŋlɪ] **ADV 1** *(unjustly)* à tort, à faux; **I've been w. accused** on m'a accusé injustement *ou* à tort *ou* à faux; **rightly or w.** à tort ou à raison **2** *(incorrectly)* mal, incorrectement; **to choose w.** mal choisir

wrongness ['rɒŋnɪs] **N 1** *(incorrectness)* erreur *f*, inexactitude *f* **2** *(injustice)* *(of accusation etc)* injustice *f*

wrote **PT** *see* **write**

wrought [rɔːt] **PT, PP** *see* **work**
ADJ *(silver, gold)* travaillé, ouvragé, façonné; *(metal)* ouvré, forgé; *Fig* **finely w. phrase** phrase finement ciselée
▸▸ **w. iron** fer *m* forgé

wrought-iron **ADJ** en fer forgé

wrought-up **ADJ** *(nervous, anxious)* anxieux; *(angry, upset)* en colère, dans tous ses états; **there's no need to get so w. about it!** pas la peine de vous faire de soucis pour ça!; **she's still pretty w. over her son's death** elle est encore très affectée par la mort de son fils

WRVS [dʌb(ə)ljuːɑːrviː'es] **N** *Br abbr* **Women's Royal Voluntary Service**

wry [raɪ] **ADJ** *(comp* **wrier, wryer***)* *(smile, comment)* ironique; *(humour)* pince-sans-rire; **to pull a w. face** faire la grimace; **she's w. but never bitter** elle est désabusée mais jamais amère

wryly ['raɪlɪ] **ADV** *(to remark etc)* avec ironie; **to smile w.** avoir un sourire ironique; **her w. observed portrait** son portrait ironique

wt *(abbr* **weight***)* p.

WTO [dʌb(ə)ljuːtiː'əʊ] **N** *(abbr* **World Trade Organization***)* OMC *f*

wulfenite ['wʊlfənaɪt] **N** wulfénite *f*

wunderkind ['wʌndəkɪnd, 'vʊndəkɪnt] **N** enfant *mf* prodige

wuss [wʊs] **N** *Fam* mauviette *f*, lavette *f*

wussy ['wʊsɪ] *Fam* **N** mauviette *f*, lavette *f*
ADJ mou, *f* molle, mollasson

WVa *abbr* **West Virginia**

WW *abbr* **World War**

WWF [dʌb(ə)ljuːdʌb(ə)lju:'ef] **N** *(abbr* **World Wildlife Fund, Worldwide Fund for Nature***)* WWF *m*

WWW [dʌb(ə)lju:dʌb(ə)lju:'dʌb(ə)lju:] **N** *Comput (abbr* **World Wide Web***)* WWW *m*, W3 *m*

wych-elm [wɪtʃ-] **N** orme *m* blanc *ou* de(s) montagne(s)

wynd [waɪnd] **N** *Scot* venelle *f*

Wyo *abbr* **Wyoming**

WYSIWYG ['wɪzɪwɪg] **N** *Comput (abbr* **what you see is what you get***)* tel écran-tel écrit *m*, tel-tel *m*, Wysiwyg *m*
▸▸ **W. display** affichage *m* tel écran-tel écrit *ou* tel-tel *ou* Wysiwyg

X, x [eks] N *(letter)* X, x *m*; **X marks the spot** l'endroit est marqué d'une croix; **for x number of years** pendant x années
▶▶ *Cin Formerly* **X (certificate) film** = film *m* interdit aux moins de 18 ans; **the film was an X** le film a été interdit aux moins de 18 ans; *Biol* **X chromosome** chromosome *m* x

x-axis N *Math* axe *m* des X, abscisse *f*

X-Dax ['eksdæks] N *St Exch* **the X-Dax (index)** le X-Dax, l'indice *m* X-Dax

xenon ['zenɒn] N *Chem* xénon *m*

xenophobe ['zenəfəʊb] N xénophobe *mf*

xenophobia [zenə'fəʊbɪə] N xénophobie *f*

xenophobic [zenə'fəʊbɪk] ADJ xénophobe

xerography [zɪə'rɒgrəfɪ] N xérographie *f*

Xerox® ['zɪərɒks] N photocopie *f* ▶ VT photocopier

Xetra-Dax ['ekstrədæks] N *St Exch* **the X. index** l'indice *m* Xetra-Dax

XL ['ek'sel] *(abbr* **extra large**) XL

Xmas ['krɪsməs, 'eksməs] N *(abbr* **Christmas**) Noël *m*

XML [eksem'el] N *Comput (abbr* **Extensible Markup Language**) XML *m*

X-rated ADJ *Cin Formerly* interdit aux moins de 18 ans; *Fig* obscène, indécent

X-ray N **1** *(radiation)* rayon *m* X; *Fig Fam* **you must have X. eyes!** tu es médium! **2** *(picture)* radio *f*; *Med* **to have/take an X.** passer/faire une radio
▶ VT *Med (person, chest)* radiographier; **to be**

X-rayed se faire radiographier, *Fam* passer à la radio
▶▶ *Med* **x. diagnosis** radiodiagnostic *m*; **X. machine** machine *f* à rayon X; *Med* **x. photograph** radiographie *f*, radio *f*; **X. photography** radiographie, radio; **X. therapy** radiothérapie *f*; *Med* **x. unit** service *m* de radiologie

xylograph ['zaɪləʊgrɑːf] N xylographie *f*

xylographic [zaɪləʊ'græfɪk] ADJ xylographique

xylography [zaɪ'lɒgrəfɪ] N xylographie *f*

xylophone ['zaɪləfəʊn] N *Mus* xylophone *m*

xylophonist [zaɪ'lɒfənɪst] N *Mus* joueur, -euse de xylophone

Y, y [waɪ] N (letter) Y, y m, i m grec; **two y's** deux y
  ▸▸ *Biol* **Y chromosome** chromosome m y

Y2K [waɪtuːˈkeɪ] ADJ (abbr **year 2000**) de l'an 2000; **Y. compliant** or **compatible** conforme à l'an 2000

yacht [jɒt] N yacht m; **(sailing) y.** voilier m; **racing y.** yacht de course
  VI faire de la voile
  ▸▸ **y. club** yacht-club m, pl yacht-clubs; **y. race** régate f

yachting [ˈjɒtɪŋ] N voile f, **to go y.** faire de la voile;
  ▸▸ **y. cap** casquette f de yachtman

yachtsman, pl **yachtsmen** [ˈjɒtsmən] N yacht(s)man m, pl yacht(s)men; (in yacht race) régatier m; (for amusement) plaisancier m; **round-the-world y.** navigateur m qui fait/a fait/etc le tour du monde

yachtswoman, pl **yachtswomen** [ˈjɒtswʊmən, -wɪmɪn] N yacht(s)woman f, pl yacht(s)women; (in yacht race) régatière f, (for amusement) plaisancière f, **round-the-world y.** navigatrice f qui fait/a fait/etc le tour du monde

yack [jæk] Fam N jacasserie f, **to have a y. about sth/sb** jacasser au sujet de qch/qn; **it's ages since we've had a really good y.** ça fait longtemps qu'on ne s'est pas taillé une bonne bavette
  VI jacasser; **it's y., y., y. all day long!** elle n'arrête/ils n'arrêtent/etc pas de jacasser toute la journée!

yackety-yack [ˈjækətɪ-] ADV Fam **to go y.** jacasser

yah [jɑː] INT (in affirmation) oui (évidemment)
  N Fam (loud upper-class person) bourge mf

yahoo [jəˈhuː] N Fam brute f

yak [jæk] N (animal) ya(c)k m

yak² N, VI Fam = yack

yam [jæm] N (plant, tuber) igname f

yammer [ˈjæmər] Fam N boucan m; **a terrible y. of voices** un brouhaha terrible
  VI (complain) pleurnicher, geindre; **what's he yammering on about?** (going on about) qu'est-ce qu'il raconte?

yang [jæŋ] N Phil yang m

Yank, Yankee [jæŋk, ˈjæŋkɪ] Fam N **1** (from the US) Ricain, -aine, Amerloque mf, Yankee mf **2** Am esp Pej (from the Northern US) = habitant, -ante des États du Nord
  ADJ **1** (from the US) ricain, amerloque **2** Am esp Pej (from the Northern US) qui habite les États du Nord

yank [jæŋk] Fam N **to give sth a y.** tirer qch un bon coup; **she gave his hair a y.** elle lui a tiré les cheveux; Vulg **to have a y.** (masturbate) se tirer sur l'élastique, se taper sur la colonne
  VT tirer (d'un coup sec); **to y. the door open**

ouvrir la porte d'un coup sec; **to y. sth loose/out/off** arracher qch d'un coup sec; **to y. out a tooth** arracher une dent (d'un seul coup); Fam **to y. sb's chain** (tease) faire marcher qn
  VI Vulg (masturbate) se tirer sur l'élastique, se taper sur la colonne

yap [jæp] N **1** (of dog) jappement m **2** Fam (mouth) clapet m, gueule f, **shut your y.!** ferme ton clapet!, la ferme! **3** Am Fam (idiot) andouille f, truffe f, (country bumpkin) pécore mf, péquenaud, -aude
  VI (-pp-) **1** (of dog) japper **2** Fig Fam (of person) jacasser; **the shop assistants were yapping away instead of serving** les vendeuses jacassaient au lieu de servir la clientèle; **what's he yapping on about now?** qu'est-ce qu'il est encore en train de raconter?

yapping [ˈjæpɪŋ] ADJ (dog) jappeur
  N (no pl) (of dog) jappement m; **I wish that dog would stop its y.!** si ce chien pouvait arrêter ses jappements! **2** Fig Fam (of person) jacasseries fpl

yappy [ˈjæpɪ] ADJ Fam (dog) jappeur

yard¹ [jɑːd] N **1** (measurement) yard m (0,914m); Can verge f; **square y.** yard carré (0,836m²); Fig **his face was a y. long** il faisait une tête de trois pieds de long; Fig **yards of statistics, statistics by the y.** des statistiques à n'en plus finir **2** Naut (spar) vergue f

yard² N **1** (of house, farm, stable etc) cour f, Am (garden) jardin m; Sch cour, préau m; Austr (cattle enclosure) parc m à bétail ou à bestiaux **2** Ind (for working) chantier m; **timber** or **lumber y.** chantier de bois; **builder's y.** chantier (de construction); Naut **repair y.** chantier de radoub; **(ship) y.** chantier naval; **naval (dock)yard, Am navy y.** chantier naval de l'État, arsenal m maritime ou de la marine **3** (for storage) dépôt m de marchandises **4** Br Fam **the Y.** (Scotland Yard) ≃ la Sûreté
  ▸▸ Am **y. sale** vide-greniers m inv; **y. work** jardinage m

yardage [ˈjɑːdɪdʒ] N ≃ métrage m

yardarm [ˈjɑːdɑːm] N Naut bout m de vergue

yardie [ˈjɑːdɪ] N Fam = membre m d'une organisation criminelle fondée en Jamaïque

yardman [ˈjɑːdmæn] N Am jardinier m

yardstick [ˈjɑːdstɪk] N (ruler) yard m; Fig (standard of comparison) critère m, point m de référence; Fig **to measure others by one's own y.** mesurer les autres selon ses propres valeurs

yarmulka [ˈjɑːməlkə] N (Jewish skullcap) kippa f

yarn [jɑːn] N **1** Tex fil m; (cotton) filé m **2** Fam (unbelievable story) histoire f à dormir debout; (long story) longue histoire; **to spin a y.** raconter une histoire à dormir debout
  VI Fam débiter des histoires, bavasser

yarrow [ˈjærəʊ] N (plant) achillée f, millefeuille f

yashmak [ˈjæʃmæk] N (Muslim veil) litham m

yaw [jɔː] N Naut embardée f, Aviat (mouvement m de) lacet m
  VI Naut faire une embardée; Aviat faire un (mouvement de) lacet

yawl [jɔːl] N Naut (sailing vessel) sloop m, yawl m; (small boat) yole f

yawn [jɔːn] N **1** bâillement m; **to give a y.** bâiller; **to let out a y.** laisser échapper un bâillement **2** Fig (boring thing) plaie f, **the book/film is one long y.** le livre/film est ennuyeux à mourir
  VI **1** (with tiredness etc) bâiller (**with** de) **2** Fig (of chasm etc) être béant, béer; **the gulf yawned at his feet** le gouffre s'ouvrait ou béait à ses pieds
  VT Fam **to y. one's head off** bâiller à se décrocher la mâchoire

yawning [ˈjɔːnɪŋ] ADJ **1** (person) qui bâille **2** Fig (chasm) béant, ouvert; (difference, gap) énorme
  N bâillement m

yaws [jɔːz] NPL Med pian m

y-axis N Math axe m des Y ou des ordonnées

yay [jeɪ] N Am Sl (cocaine) coco f, neige f

yd N (abbr **yard**) yard m (0,914m)

ye¹ [jiː] DEF ART Arch, Hum le, la, les; **Ye Olde Shoppe** la Vieille Boutique

ye² PERS PRON **1** pl Arch, Lit vous; **seek and ye shall find** cherchez et vous trouverez; Fam **ye gods!** grand Dieu! **2** sing Fam, Dial tu, vous; **how d'ye do?** comment vas-tu?, comment allez-vous?

yea [jeɪ] ADV Bible, Lit **1** (yes) oui **2** (truly, indeed) en vérité
  N oui m; Am Pol **yeas and nays** voix fpl pour et contre

yeah [jeə] ADV Fam ouais; **oh y.?** (in disbelief, challenging) vraiment?, ah ouais?; **y. y.!, y., right!** (in disbelief) ouais, c'est ça!

year [jɪər] N SEE GRAMMAR B61 **1** an m, année f, **in the y.** (Arch of our Lord or of grace) 1850 en l'an ou en l'année (du Seigneur ou de grâce) 1850; **a ticket valid for one year** or **a y.** un billet valable (pour) un an; **I've known him for ten years** je le connais depuis dix ans; Hist **the Thirty Years' War** la Guerre de Trente Ans; **sentenced to ten years' imprisonment** condamné à dix ans de prison; **he got five years** (prison sentence) il en a pris pour cinq ans; **a y.'s work/salary** un an de travail/de salaire; **a y. last/next September** il y a eu/il y aura un an en septembre; **it will be a y. in April** (answering question 'how long?') ça va faire un an en avril; **we're going/we went to Greece this y.** nous allons/nous sommes allés en Grèce cette année; **last y.** l'an dernier, l'année dernière; **next y.** l'an prochain, l'année prochaine; **this day next y.** dans un an jour pour jour; **every y.** tous les ans, chaque année, *Fml* annuellement; **twice a y.** deux fois par an; **to earn £10,000 a y.** gagner 10 000 livres par an; **a y.-old child, a one-y.-old (child)** un enfant (âgé) d'un an; **to be ten years old** avoir dix ans; *Fml* **she's in her eightieth y.** elle est dans sa quatre-vingtième année; **new y.** nouvel an; **we'll see you in the new y.** nous vous verrons au début de l'année prochaine; **New Y.'s Day** le jour de l'An, le 1er de l'An; *Am* **New Y.'s** (*New Year's Day*) le jour de l'An, le 1er de l'An; (*New Year's Eve*) le 31 décembre, la Saint-Sylvestre; **Happy New Y.!** bonne année!; **to see the old y. out** *or* **the new y. in** faire la veillée *ou* le réveillon de la Saint-Sylvestre, réveillonner; **for many long years** pendant de longues années; **for many years now we have been promised a new road** ça fait maintenant de nombreuses années qu'on nous promet une nouvelle route; **all (the) y. round** (pendant) toute l'année; **y. in (and) y. out** une année après l'autre; **y. by y.** d'année en année; **over the years** au fil des ans *ou* années; **in the early years of the century/their marriage** au cours des premières années de ce siècle/de leur mariage; **years ago** il y a bien des années; **this is where I met him, all those years ago** c'est ici que je l'ai rencontré il y a tant d'années; **it's years since I saw him, I haven't seen him for** *or* **in years** (*for many years*) ça fait des années que je ne l'ai pas vu, je ne l'ai pas vu depuis des années; *Fam* (*for a long time*) il y a une éternité que je ne l'ai vu; **it seemed like years rather than hours** les heures m'ont semblé des années; **years and years** des années et des années; **the best years of our lives** les plus belles années de notre vie; **from his earliest years** dès son plus jeune âge; **to be old for one's years** (*of child*) être précoce; (*of adult*) faire plus vieux que son âge; **to be young for one's years** faire jeune pour son âge; **to be getting on in years** prendre de l'âge; **advanced in years** âgé; **smoking can take years off your life** fumer peut raccourcir la durée de votre vie; *Fam* **those kids have taken years off my life!** ces gamins m'ont fait prendre dix ans d'un coup!; **working there put years on him** le fait de travailler là l'a vieilli; **that dress takes years off her** cette robe la fait paraître des années plus jeune *ou* la rajeunit beaucoup; **calendar** *or* **civil y.** année civile; **financial** *or* **fiscal** *or* **tax y.** année budgétaire, exercice *m* (financier); **leap y.** année bissextile; *Astron* **light y.** année-lumière *f*, *pl* années-lumière, année de lumière; **school y.** année scolaire; **solar/lunar y.** année solaire/lunaire

2 (*at school, university etc*) année *f*; **third-y. student** étudiant, -ante de troisième année; **he was in my y.** (*at school*) il était dans ma classe; (*at university*) il est de ma promotion; **she was in the y. above/below me** elle était dans la classe au-dessus/en dessous de la mienne

3 (*of wine*) millésime *m*, année *f*, **a good y. for claret** une bonne année *ou* un bon millésime pour le bordeaux rouge; *Fig* **it was a good y. for apples/French cinema** ça a été une bonne année pour les pommes/le cinéma français

4 *Comput* **y. 2000 compatible** *or* **compliant** conforme à l'an 2000

▸▸*Fin* **y. of assessment** année *f* d'imposition; *Fin* **y. end** fin *f* d'exercice

When translating the word **year**, note that the French words **an** and **année** are not interchangeable. **Année** is used when the emphasis is on duration, while in cases where it is preceded by a number, **year** is usually translated by **an**.

yearbook ['jɪəbʊk] N annuaire *m*, almanach *m*

year-end N *Acct* de fin d'exercice;
▸▸**y. accounts** compte *m* de résultats; **y. audit** vérification *f* comptable de fin d'exercice; **y. closing of accounts** clôture *f* annuelle des livres; **y. loss** perte *f* de fin d'exercice; **y. profits** bénéfices *mpl* de fin d'exercice

yearling ['jɪəlɪŋ] N (*in general*) animal *m* d'un an; (*horse*) poulain *m* d'un an; (*thoroughbred*) yearling *m*
ADJ d'un an

yearlong ['jɪəlɒŋ] ADJ qui dure/a duré un an *ou* toute l'année; **they had a y. wait** ils ont attendu une année entière *ou* toute une année

yearly ['jɪəlɪ] ADJ annuel
ADV (*once a year*) annuellement, une fois par an; (*every year*) annuellement, tous les ans
N (*publication*) publication *f* annuelle

yearn [jɜːn] VI **to y. for** *or* **after sb/sth** languir après qn/qch; **they y. for their own country** ils ont la nostalgie de leur propre pays; **to y. to do sth** brûler de faire qch

yearning ['jɜːnɪŋ] N désir *m* (**for** de); **he felt a great y. to ...** il ressentait un désir ardent de ...

yearningly ['jɜːnɪŋlɪ] ADV avec un désir ardent

year-round ADJ ininterrompu; **California enjoys y. sun** en Californie il y a du soleil toute l'année

yeast [jiːst] N levure *f*, **brewer's y.** levure de bière

yeasty ['jiːstɪ] ADJ de levure

yell [jel] N **1** hurlement *m*, grand cri *m*; **to give a y.** pousser un grand cri *ou* un hurlement; **yells of laughter** hurlements de rire **2** *Am* (*organized shout*) (*of students etc*) cri *m* de guerre *ou* de bataille
VI hurler, crier à tue-tête; **to y. at sb** hurler après qn; **to y. with pain/laughter** hurler de douleur/de rire
VT **y. (out)** (*song*) hurler, beugler; (*order*) hurler, *Fam* gueuler

yelling ['jelɪŋ] N hurlements *mpl*; **there was a lot of y. going on next door** ça hurlait *ou Fam* gueulait pas mal à côté

yellow ['jeləʊ] ADJ **1** (*in colour*) jaune; **to turn** *or* **go y.** jaunir **2** *Fam* (*cowardly*) trouillard, lâche; **he says you're y.!** il dit que tu n'es qu'un trouillard *ou* un lâche!; **to turn** *or* **go y.** se dégonfler; **to have a y. streak** être un peu trouillard sur les bords
N **1** (*colour*) jaune *m* **2** (*yolk*) jaune *m* (d'œuf)
VT & VI jaunir; **papers yellowed with age** papiers jaunis par le temps
▸▸**y. card** (*in football, rugby*) carton *m* jaune; *Belg* carte *f* jaune; **y. fever** fièvre *f* jaune; *Am* **y. light** feu *m* orange; **y. line** bande *f* jaune; *Br* **to park on a double y. line** = se garer sur une zone de stationnement interdit; **y. metal** (*brass*) cuivre *m* jaune, laiton *m*; (*gold*) métal *m* jaune, or *m*; **Y. Pages®** Pages *fpl* jaunes; *Old-fashioned* **y. peril** péril *m* jaune

Yellow lines

En Grande-Bretagne, une ligne jaune parallèle au trottoir signifie "arrêt autorisé réglementé"; une double ligne jaune signifie "stationnement interdit".

yellowbelly ['jeləʊbelɪ] N *Fam* (*coward*) froussard, -arde, trouillard, -arde

yellowhammer ['jeləʊhæmər] N (*bird*) bruant *m* jaune

yellowish ['jeləʊɪʃ] ADJ jaunet, -ette, *Pej* jaunâtre

yellowness ['jeləʊnɪs] N **1** (*colour*) ton *m* jaune, teinte *f* jaune; (*of person*) teint *m* jaune; **judging by the y. of her skin** à en juger par son teint jaune **2** (*cowardice*) lâcheté *f*

yelp [jelp] N jappement *m*, glapissement *m*; **to let out a y.** laisser échapper un jappement *ou* un glapissement
VI japper, glapir; **to y. with pain** gémir de douleur

yelping ['jelpɪŋ] N (*no pl*) jappements *mpl*, glapissements *mpl*

Yemen (the) [ðə'jemən] N le Yémen

Yemeni(te) ['jemənɪ, -aɪt] ADJ yéménique, yéménite
N Yéménite *mf*

yen [jen] N (*currency*) yen *m*

yen [jen] N (*desire*) envie *f*; **to have a y. for sth/to do sth** avoir envie de qch/de faire qch

yeoman, *pl* **yeomen** ['jəʊmən] N **1** *Hist* (*small freeholder*) franc-tenancier *m*, *pl* francs-tenanciers; *Fig* **to do y. service** rendre des services inestimables **2** *Br Mil, Hist* soldat *m* du yeomanry; **Y. of the Guard** = hallebardier *m* à la Tour de Londres

yeomanry ['jəʊmənrɪ] N (*no pl*) **1** *Hist* (*small freeholders*) francs-tenanciers *mpl* **2** *Br Mil, Hist* = corps *m* de cavalerie composé de volontaires

yep [jep] ADV *esp Am Fam* ouais

yes [jes] ADV **1** oui; (*contradicting negation*) si; **to answer y. or no** répondre par oui ou (par) non; **to say y.** dire oui, dire que oui; **y., certainly!, oh y.!** mais oui!; **are you hungry? – y. (I am)** avez-vous faim? – oui; **you didn't hear me? – y., I did** vous ne m'avez pas entendu? – (mais) si; **would you like some cake? – y. please** *or esp Am* **thanks** est-ce que vous voulez du gâteau? – oui, s'il vous plaît; **could I have a glass of water? – y., of course** est-ce que je pourrais avoir un verre d'eau? – oui, bien sûr; **y. sir/madam** (*I'm coming*) voilà, monsieur/madame; *Mktg* **y./no question** (*in survey*) question *f* fermée SEE GRAMMAR B64 **2** (*interrogatively*) **y.?** (*are you sure*) vraiment?; (*go on*) et puis après?; (*to sb waiting to speak*) oui?, vous désirez?
N (*pl* **yeses** ['jesɪz]) oui *m inv*; **an emphatic y.** un oui énergique

yes-man, *pl* **yes-men** ['jesmæn, -men] N *Fam* béni-oui-oui *m inv*

yesterday ['jestəd(e)ɪ] ADV, N hier *m*; **the day before y.** avant-hier; **a week ago y.** il y a eu hier huit jours; **y. week, a week (from) y.** d'hier en huit; **y.'s paper/milk** le journal/le lait d'hier; **y. morning/evening** hier matin/soir; **I can remember it as clearly as if it had happened y.** je m'en souviens comme si c'était hier; *Pej* **y.'s men/designers** les hommes/designers qui appartiennent au passé; **y.'s heroes** les héros *mpl* de jadis; *Lit* **our yesterdays** les jours *mpl* d'autrefois *ou* d'antan

yesteryear ['jestəjɪər] N *Lit* **of y.** d'antan; **the snows of y.** les neiges *fpl* d'antan

yet [jet] ADV **1** (*still*) encore; **we've got ten minutes y.** nous avons encore dix minutes; **jobs y. to be done** tâches encore à faire; **y. again** encore une fois; **y. more** encore plus; **y. greater advantages** des avantages encore plus grands; **y. another mistake** encore une erreur; **y. one more** encore un(e) autre
2 (*in neg phrases*) encore; (*in questions*) (*already*) déjà; **I haven't finished y.** je n'ai pas encore fini; **we're not ready y.** nous ne sommes pas encore prêts; **have they decided y.?** est-ce qu'ils ont déjà décidé?; **are you ready y.?** tu es prêt?; **not y.** pas encore; **don't go y.** ne partez pas encore; **it will not happen just y.** cela n'arrivera pas tout de suite; **we're not going just y.** nous ne partons pas tout de suite; **as y. nothing has been done** jusqu'à

présent *ou* jusqu'ici rien n'a été fait; **not as y.** pas encore; **as y. unexplored jungle** jungle pas encore explorée

3 *(in spite of everything)* malgré tout; **I shall catch him y.!** je finirai bien par l'attraper!; **I'll do it y.!** j'y arriverai!

4 *Old-fashioned (even)* **not finished nor y.** started pas achevé ni même commencé **conj** néanmoins, cependant, tout de même; **and y. I like him** et cependant *ou* et malgré tout *ou* néanmoins il me plaît, mais il me plaît tout de même

yeti ['jetɪ] N yeti *m*

yew [ju:] N *(tree)* if *m*; *(wood)* (bois *m* d')if

Y-fronts® ['waɪ'frʌnts] NPL slip *m* ouvert

YHA [waɪeɪtʃ'eɪ] N *(abbr* **Youth Hostels Association)** FUAJ *f*

Yid [jɪd] N *Offensive Sl* youpin, -ine

Yiddish ['jɪdɪʃ] ADJ, N *Ling* yiddish *m*

yield [ji:ld] N **1** *(of field, machine)* rendement *m*; *(of fruit tree, capital outlay, land etc)* rapport *m*; *(of mine)* production *f*, produit *m*, débit *m*; **this tree gives a better/poor y.** cet arbre donne un meilleur/un faible rapport **2** *Fin (from investments)* rapport *m*, rendement *m*; *(profit)* bénéfice *m*, bénéfices *mpl*; *(from tax)* recette *f*, rapport; **the y. on these shares is large** ces actions rapportent beaucoup

vt **1** *(give)* rapporter, produire, donner; **shares that y. high interest** actions à gros rendement; **to y. a profit** rapporter *ou* dégager un bénéfice; **these remarks y. an insight into his motives** ces remarques donnent une idée de ses motifs; **further investigations yielded no new information** des recherches supplémentaires n'ont fourni aucune information nouvelle

2 *(concede)* *(fortress to enemy, right etc)* céder; **to y. ground** céder du terrain; **to y. a point to sb** céder à qn sur un point; *also Sport* concéder un point à qn; *Lit* **to y. (up) the ghost** *or* **one's soul** rendre l'âme

vi **1** *(surrender)* céder **(to** à); *(of army, enemy)* se rendre; **to y. to force** céder devant la force; **to y. to reason** se rendre à la raison; **we shall not y. to threats** nous ne céderons pas aux menaces; **I had to y. to them on that point** j'ai dû leur céder sur ce point; **to y. to temptation** succomber *ou* céder à la tentation; **to y. to sb's wishes** consentir *ou* céder aux désirs de qn

2 *(of rope etc)* céder; *(of beam etc)* s'affaisser, fléchir; **the plank yielded under our weight** la planche a manqué *ou* cédé sous notre poids

3 *Am Aut* **y.!** *(on sign)* vous n'avez pas la priorité!

▸▸ *Fin* **y. capacity** productivité *f*; **y. curve** courbe *f* des taux; *Fin* **y. gap** prime *f* de risque

yielding ['ji:ldɪŋ] ADJ **1** *(person)* facile, complaisant, accommodant; **the management hasn't been very y.** la direction n'a pas été très accommodante **2** *(substance)* souple, élastique, flexible

yikes [jaɪks] INT *Fam* mince!

yin [jɪn] N *Phil* yin *m*; **y. and yang** le yin et le yang

yippee [jɪ'pi:] INT *Fam* hourra!, bravo!

Y-junction N fourche *f*

YMCA [waɪemsi:'eɪ] N *(abbr* **Young Men's Christian Association)** Union *f* chrétienne de jeunes gens

yo [jəʊ] INT hé!, eh!

yob [jɒb], **yobbo** ['jɒbəʊ] N *Br Fam* voyou *m*, loubar(d) *m*; **the y. culture that prevails in this country today** l'aggressivité et l'anti-intellectualisme qui règnent aujourd'hui dans notre pays

yobbish ['jɒbɪʃ] ADJ *Br Fam* de voyou; **it**

makes you look y. ça te donne l'air d'un voyou; **don't be so y.** arrête de jouer les voyous

yodel ['jəʊd(ə)l] *Mus* N (chant *m* à la) tyrolienne *f*

▸ vi **(-ll-,** *Am* **-l-)** jodler, iodler

yod(el)ler, *Am* **yodler, yodeler** ['jəʊd(ə)lər] N jodleur, -euse, iodleur, -euse

yoga ['jəʊgə] N yoga *m*

yoghurt, yoghourt ['jɒgət, 'jəʊ-] N yaourt *m*, yog(h)urt *m*

▸▸ **y. drink** yaourt à boire

yogi ['jəʊgɪ] N yogi *m*

yogurt ['jɒgət, 'jəʊ-] N = **yoghurt**

yoke [jəʊk] N **1** *(for ox), Fig* joug *m*; *Fig* **the y. of convention** le joug des conventions; *Fig* **to throw off the y.** secouer le joug, s'affranchir du joug **2** *(for carrying)* palanche *f* **3** *Sewing* empiècement *m* **4** *Elec (of dynamo)* carcasse *f*, bâti *m*

▸ vt **1** *(oxen)* accoupler, atteler **(to the plough** à la charrue); *Fig* lier; *Fig* **to y. together** *(in marriage)* unir **2** *Tech (pieces of equipment)* accoupler

yokel ['jəʊk(ə)l] N *Pej* rustre *m*, campagnard, -arde

yolk [jəʊk] N **1** *Culin (of egg)* jaune *m*; **take the y. of an egg** prenez un jaune d'œuf **2** *Biol* vitellus *m*; **y. bag** *or* **sac** membrane *f* vitelline

Yom Kippur [jɒmkɪ'pʊər] N *Rel* Yom Kippour *m*

yomp [jɒmp] vi *Mil* crapahuter; **a group of hikers was yomping towards us** un groupe de marcheurs se dirigeait vers nous avec tout leur chargement

yon [jɒn] ADJ, ADV *Arch, Dial* = **yonder**

yonder ['jɒndər] *Lit* ADV **(down/over) y.** là-bas

ADJ **ce** … **-là, cette** … **-là,** *pl* **ces** … **-là; y. elms** ces ormes là-bas, ces ormes-là

yonks [jɒŋks] NPL *Fam* une éternité; **we've been waiting for y.** ça fait une éternité qu'on attend; **I haven't been there in y.** ça fait une paye que je n'y suis pas allé; **that was y. ago** ça fait une paye

yoohoo ['ju:hu:] INT ohé!

yore [jɔ:r] N *Arch, Lit* **of y.** (d')autrefois, d'antan; **in days of y.** au temps jadis, autrefois

Yorkshire ['jɔ:kʃɪər] N le Yorkshire

▸▸ **Y. pudding** = crêpe *f* épaisse salée traditionnellement servie avec du rôti de bœuf; **Y. terrier** yorkshire-terrier *m*, *pl* yorkshire-terriers, yorkshire *m*

Yoruba ['jɒrubə] N **1** *(person)* Yor(o)uba *mf* **2** *Ling* yor(o)uba

ADJ yor(o)uba

you [ju:] PERS PRON SEE GRAMMAR B67 **1** *(subject)* sing, *pl* vous; *sing (when addressing relatives, intimate friends, children, animals, deities)* tu; **y. are very kind** vous êtes/tu es bien aimable(s); **how are y.?** comment allez-vous?/vas-tu?; **there y. are** *(here's what you wanted, it's done, see what I mean)* et voilà; *(I was looking/waiting for you)* vous/te voilà; **y. all know who I mean** vous savez tous de qui je veux parler VOIR GRAMMAIRE A27-9; A43; B18-21

2 *(as object of verb)* vous/te, *pl* vous; **I hope to see y. tomorrow** j'espère vous/te voir demain; **I'll give y. some** je vous en/t'en donnerai; **I told y. so!** je vous/te l'avais bien dit! SEE GRAMMAR B18-19

3 *(after preposition)* vous/toi, *pl* vous; **between y. and me** *(when confiding)* entre vous et moi/entre toi et moi, entre nous soit dit; **I gave them to y.** je te/vous les ai donnés; **away with y.!** allez-vous-en!/va-t'en!; **all of y.** vous tous; **to/for y. and yours** à/pour toi et les tiens/vous et les vôtres; **now there's a**

singer for y.! ah, voilà un chanteur!; **now there's a typical politician for y.** voilà un politicien type; **now there's manners for y.!** ça au moins c'est quelqu'un de bien élevé/ce sont des gens bien élevés!; *Iron* en voilà des manières!

4 *(stressed)* vous/toi, *pl* vous; **y. and I will go by train** vous et moi/toi et moi nous irons par le train; **is that y.?** c'est vous/toi?; **oh, it's y.** ah, c'est vous/toi; **I am older than y.** je suis plus âgé que vous/que toi; **if I were y.** (si j'étais) à votre/ta place; **hey! y. there!** eh! dites donc, là-bas!; **poor old y.!** mon pauvre vieux!, ma pauvre vieille!; **silly/lucky (old) y.!** quel gros bêta/veinard tu fais!; *Fam* **that jacket/job wasn't y.** cette veste/ce travail n'était pas ton style!; **y. two are very different** vous êtes très différents tous les deux; **y. four! come with me** vous quatre! venez avec moi; **where are y. two going?** où est-ce que vous allez, tous les deux?; **how long have y. two been married?** cela fait combien de temps que vous êtes mariés tous les deux?

5 *(in the imperative)* **don't y. cry!** ne pleure pas!; **don't y. dare!** ne t'avise surtout pas de faire ça!; **y. sit down and eat your lunch!** toi, assieds-toi et mange ton déjeuner!; **never y. mind!** ne t'occupe pas de ça, toi!; **now you tell a joke** à ton tour *ou* à toi de raconter une blague maintenant; **don't you start!** ne commence pas, toi!, ne t'y mets pas, toi!; **just y. try!** essaye un peu pour voir!

6 *(in apposition)* **y. lawyers/Englishmen** vous autres avocats/Anglais; *Fam* **y. lot** vous; **y. idiot(, y.)!** idiot que tu es!, espèce d'idiot!; **y. darling(, y.)!** tu es un amour!

7 *(indefinite)* on; **y. never can tell** on ne sait jamais; **the joy y. feel when** … la joie qu'on ressent quand …; **exercise is good for y.** (prendre de) l'exercice est bon pour la santé VOIR GRAMMAIRE A29; B16

you-all [j(ə)'ɑ:l] PERS PRON *Am Fam (used in Southern US)* vous tous; *(speaking to one person)* vous

you'd [ju:d] CONTR **1** = **you had,** *see* **have 2** = **you would,** *see* **will²**

you-know-who N qui-vous-savez *mf*; **yesterday I had a telephone call from y.** hier, j'ai reçu un coup de téléphone de qui-vous-savez

you'll [ju:l] CONTR **1** = **you will,** *see* **will²** **2** = **you shall,** *see* **shall**

young [jʌŋ] ADJ **1** *(person, animal)* jeune; *(baby animal)* petit; **younger** plus jeune; **younger son/daughter** fils cadet/fille cadette; **my younger brother** mon frère cadet; **the youngest** le/la plus jeune, le cadet/la cadette; **this is my youngest, Vicki** voici ma cadette *ou* ma dernière, Vicki; **he's younger than me** *or* **I (am)** il est plus jeune *ou* moins âgé que moi, il est mon cadet; **she's two years younger than me** elle est plus jeune que moi *ou* elle est ma cadette de deux ans; **they wanted someone younger** ils voulaient quelqu'un de plus jeune; **when I was twenty years younger** quand j'avais vingt ans de moins; **if I were twenty years younger!** si j'avais vingt ans de moins!; **you're only y. once** on n'est jeune qu'une fois, la jeunesse ne dure qu'un temps; **she's too y. for alcohol/to get married** elle est trop jeune pour boire de l'alcool/se marier; **don't be too hard on him, he's only y.** ne sois pas trop sévère avec lui, il est encore bien jeune; **I am not as y. as I used to be** je n'ai plus mes jambes de vingt ans; **y. man** jeune homme; **y. woman** jeune femme; **now you listen to me, y. man/woman** écoute-moi un peu jeune homme/ma petite dame; **he's her y. man** c'est son petit ami; **a y. couple/mother** un jeune couple/une jeune mère; **a y. family** des enfants en bas âge; **y. people** jeunes gens *mpl*, jeunes *mpl*; **Pliny the Younger** Pline le Jeune; **the younger generation** la jeune génération; **in his younger days** dans son jeune temps, dans sa jeunesse; **in my young(er) days** dans ma jeunesse; **a y. country/company** un pays/une société de création récente; **a y. wine** un vin vert; **the night is y.!** j'ai/nous avons toute la soirée devant moi/nous!

2 *(youthful)* jeune; **y. for his age** *or* **years** jeune pour son âge; **y. in spirit** *or* **at heart** jeune d'esprit; **to grow** *or* **get y. again, to grow younger** rajeunir; **you look younger than ever!** tu parais plus jeune que jamais!; **she's a y. forty** elle ne fait pas ses quarante ans; **thirty's still y.!** trente ans c'est encore jeune!

N 1 *(people)* **the y.** les jeunes (gens) *mpl*, la jeunesse; **books for the y.** livres pour la jeunesse; **it appeals to y. and old alike** ça plaît aux jeunes comme aux moins jeunes

2 an animal and its y. un animal et ses petits; **a mare with y.** *(pregnant)* une jument pleine

▸▸ *Br Pol* **Y. Conservatives** jeunes conservateurs *mpl*; **Y. Liberals** jeunes libéraux *mpl*; *Br* **Y. Offenders' Institution** = centre *m* de détention pour mineurs

youngish ['jʌŋɪʃ] ADJ assez jeune; *Fam* jeunet, -ette; **he's a y. fifty** il ne fait pas tout à fait ses cinquante ans

youngster ['jʌŋstər] N **1** *(young person)* jeune *mf*, jeune personne *f* **2** *(child)* petit, -ite, *Fam* gosse *mf*

your [jɔːr] POSS ADJ **1** *sing, pl* votre, *pl* vos; *sing (when addressing relatives, intimate friends, children, animals, deities)* ton, ta, *pl* tes; **y. friends** vos/tes ami(e)s; **y. house** votre/ta maison; **y. father and mother** votre père et votre mère/ton père et ta mère; *(formal)* vos père et mère; **the most recent of y. books, y. most recent book** votre/ton livre le plus récent; **have you hurt y. hand?** vous vous êtes/tu t'es fait mal à la main?; **turn y. head(s)** tourne(z) la tête; **y. turn!** *(to play etc)* à vous/toi!; **I like y. London buses** j'aime bien les bus que vous avez à Londres; **I object to y. visiting the children** je m'oppose à ce que tu rendes visite aux enfants VOIR GRAMMAIRE A30; B21

2 *(indefinite)* son, sa, *pl* ses; **you cannot alter y. nature** on ne peut pas changer son caractère

3 *Fam* **y. (typical** *or* **average) Frenchman** le Français moyen; **of course, y. kings and queens don't do that** bien sûr, les rois et les reines ne font pas ça

4 *(in titles)* **Y. Highness** Votre Majesté *(à un roi, une reine, un prince ou une princesse)*; **Y. Holiness** Très Saint Père; **Y. Honour** Votre Honneur; **Y. Majesty** Votre Majesté *(à un roi ou une reine uniquement)*

you're [jɔːr] CONTR = **you are,** see **be**

yours [jɔːz] POSS PRON SING, PL VOIR GRAMMAIRE A30; B21–2 **1** le vôtre, la vôtre, *pl* les vôtres; *sing (when addressing relatives, intimate friends, children)* le tien, la tienne, *pl* les tiens, les tiennes; **this is y.** ceci est à vous/à toi, c'est le vôtre/le tien; **these are y.** ceux-ci sont à toi/à vous, ceux-ci sont les tiens/les vôtres;

you and y. vous et les vôtres/toi et les tiens; **the bathroom's all y.** la salle de bains est libre maintenant; **can I use your telephone? – it's all y.** est-ce que je peux utiliser ton téléphone? – vas-y; *Com, Fml* **in reply to y. of the 14th November** en réponse à votre lettre en date du 14 novembre; **y. is a nation of travellers** vous êtes une nation de voyageurs; **y. was no easy task** ta tâche n'était pas facile; **he is a friend of y.** c'est un de vos/tes amis, c'est un ami à vous/toi; **that's no business of y.** cela ne vous/te regarde pas, ce n'est pas votre/ton affaire; *Pej* **that dog of y. votre/ton sacré** *ou* fichu *ou* foutu chien **2** *(in letter)* **y., Peter** ≃ bien à vous *ou* à bientôt, Peter; **y. sincerely, y. faithfully** *(in letters)* ≃ je vous prie d'agréer, Madame/Monsieur, l'expression de mes sentiments distingués

yourself [jɔːˈself], *pl* **yourselves** [jɔːˈselvz] PERS PRON VOIR GRAMMAIRE A29–30 **1** *(emphatic) sing, pl* vous-même(s); *sing (when addressing relatives, intimate friends, children, deities)* toi-même; **you said y.** *or* **you y. said it was cheap** tu as dit toi-même/vous avez dit vous-même que ce n'était pas cher; **tell her y.** dis-lui toi-même/dites-lui vous-même; **you don't look quite y.** vous avez/tu as l'air mal en train; **just be y.** contente-toi d'être toi-même/contentez-vous d'être vous-même

2 *(reflexive)* vous/te, *pl* vous; **are you enjoying y.?** tu t'amuses/vous vous amusez bien?; **have you hurt y.?** vous êtes-vous/tu t'es fait mal?; **I see you've got y. a wife/you've bought y. a car** je vois que tu t'es trouvé une femme/que tu t'es acheté une voiture; *Fam* **have y. a good time** amuse-toi bien; **and you call y. a Christian/socialist!** et vous vous dites/tu te dis chrétien/socialiste! SEE GRAMMAR B28

3 *(after preposition)* **see for y.** vois toi-même/voyez vous-même; **see for yourselves** voyez vous-mêmes; **tell us something about y.** parle-nous de toi/parlez-nous de vous; **what about y.?** et toi/vous?; **speak for y.!** parle pour toi!/parlez pour vous!; **keep it for y.** garde-le pour toi/gardez-le pour vous; **do you live by y.?** vous vivez/tu vis (tout) seul?; **did you do this by y.?** est-ce que vous avez/tu as fait ça tout seul?; **among yourselves** *(reciprocal)* entre vous

4 *(used impersonally)* soi-même; *(reflexive)* se; **you have to do it y.** il faut le faire soi-même; **you can't take y. too seriously** il ne faut pas se prendre trop au sérieux

youth [juːθ, *pl* juːðz] N VOIR GRAMMAIRE A11 **1** *(no pl) (period)* jeunesse *f*, jeune âge *m*; **in his early y.** dans sa première jeunesse; **she is not in the first flush of y.,** she is past her first y. elle n'est pas de la première jeunesse; **lost y.** jeunesse perdue; *Myth* **the fountain of Y.** la Fontaine de Jouvence; **y. will have its way** *or* **its fling** il faut que jeunesse se passe **2** *(male teenager)* jeune homme *m*, adolescent *m* **3** *(no pl) (young people) (of village etc)* jeunes gens *mpl*, jeunesse *f*; **inner-city y.** la jeunesse des quartiers déshérités; **the y. of today** la jeunesse *ou* les jeunes d'aujourd'hui

▸▸ *Br* **y. club** ≃ maison *f* des jeunes; **y.**

culture culture *f* des jeunes; **y. fare** tarif *m* jeune; **y. hostel** auberge *f* de jeunesse; **Y. Hostels Association** association *f* des auberges de jeunesse; *Mktg* **y. market** marché *m* de la jeunesse; *Mktg* **y. marketing** marketing *m* de la classe des jeunes, marketing des juniors; **y. orchestra** orchestre *m* de jeunes

youthful ['juːθfʊl] ADJ **1** *(person, face, fashion etc)* jeune; **to look y.** avoir l'air jeune; **y. good looks** *(of men)* air *m* de jeune homme; **he is a y. fifty-two** il est jeune pour ses cinquante-deux ans **2** *(error)* de jeunesse; *(enthusiasm, impetuousness)* juvénile

youthfulness ['juːθfʊlnɪs] N jeunesse *f*; *(youthful appearance)* air *m* de jeunesse, air jeune

you've [juːv] CONTR = **you have,** see **have**

yowl [jaʊl] N *(of dog)* hurlement *m*; *(of cat)* miaulement *m*; **there was a y. of protest/pain from him** il a émis un cri de protestation/douleur

VI *(of dog, person)* hurler; *(of cat)* miauler

yo-yo® ['jəʊjəʊ] N **1** yo-yo® *m inv*; *Fam* **he was jumping up and down like a y.** il sautait sur place comme s'il était monté sur un ressort; *Fam* **I've been up and down the stairs like a y. all day** je n'ai pas arrêté de monter et de descendre l'escalier toute la journée **2** *Am Fam (fool)* abruti, -ie

yr *(abbr* **year)** a.

YTS [waɪtiːˈes] N *Br (abbr* **Youth Training Scheme)** *(person)* TUC *mf*; *(job)* TUC *m*

yuan [juːˈæn] N INV yuan *m*

yucca ['jʌkə] N *(plant)* yucca *m*; **a y. plant** un yucca

yuck [jʌk] INT *Fam* pouah!, berk!

yucky ['jʌkɪ] ADJ *Fam* dégoûtant; **to feel y.** *(not well)* se sentir patraque

Yugoslav ['juːgəʊslɑːv] ADJ yougoslave
N Yougoslave *mf*

Yugoslavia [juːgəʊˈslɑːvɪə] N *Formerly* Yougoslavie *f*; **the ex-Y.** l'ex-Yougoslavie

Yugoslavian [juːgəʊˈslɑːvɪən] ADJ *Formerly* yougoslave

yule [juːl] N *Arch, Lit* Noël *m*
▸▸ **y. log** bûche *f* de Noël

yuletide ['juːltaɪd] N *Arch, Lit* période *f* de Noël; **y. festivities** fêtes *fpl* de Noël

yummy ['jʌmɪ] ADJ *Fam* délicieux; *(person)* sexy *inv*; **y.!** miam-miam!

yum-yum [jʌmˈjʌm] INT *Fam* miam-miam!

yup [jʌp] ADV *Am Fam* ouais

yuppie ['jʌpɪ] N *usu Pej (abbr* **young upwardly mobile professional)** yuppie *mf*, ≃ jeune cadre *m* dynamique
ADJ *(club)* pour jeunes cadres dynamiques; *(lifestyle, neighbourhood)* de yuppies
▸▸ **y. flu** encéphalomyélite *f* myalgique

yuppify ['jʌpɪfaɪ] VT *Fam* rendre chic et branché; **the area/pub has become rather yuppified** ce quartier/pub est plein de yuppies maintenant

YWCA [waɪdʌb(ə)ljuːsiːˈeɪ] N *(abbr* **Young Women's Christian Association)** Union *f* chrétienne de jeunes femmes

Z, z [zed, *Am* zi:] N *(letter)* Z, z *m*; **two z's** deux z

Zaire [zɑːˈɪər] N Zaïre *m*

Zairean [zɑːˈɪərɪən] ADJ zaïrois N Zaïrois, -oise

Zambezi (the) [ðəzæmˈbiːzɪ] N le Zambèze

Zambia [ˈzæmbɪə] N Zambie *f*

Zambian [ˈzæmbɪən] ADJ zambien N Zambien, -ienne

zaniness [ˈzeɪnɪnɪs] N *Fam* loufoquerie *f*

zany [ˈzeɪnɪ] ADJ *Fam* loufoque

zap [zæp] *Fam* INT *(esp in comic books)* paf! N *(energy)* punch *m*; **to be full of z.** avoir une pêche d'enfer VT **1** *(destroy, stun, disable) (with ray gun, by bombing etc)* détruire; *(person)* éliminer **2** *(put, send)* **z. it in the microwave** balance-le au micro-ondes; **we'll z. it across to you by courier** on vous l'enverra *ou* expédiera vite fait par courrier; **they zapped him off to the TV studios** ils l'ont emmené vite fait *ou* sur les chapeaux de roues aux studios de la télé **3** *Comput (delete)* effacer **4** *(hit)* donner un coup à, cogner VI **1** *(change channel on TV)* zapper, *Can* pitonner **2** *(move fast)* **he's been zapping in and out of his office all morning** il n'arrête pas d'entrer et de sortir de son bureau depuis ce matin; **the project's really zapping along** le projet avance vraiment à fond de train; **z., z. and it's done!** tac tac et c'est fini!
▸ **zap up** VT SEP *Fam (make more exciting)* **to z. up one's style** rendre son style plus coloré *ou* vivant; **to z. up the colour scheme** *(in house etc)* rehausser les couleurs

zapped [zæpt] ADJ *Fam (exhausted)* crevé, claqué

zapper [ˈzæpər] N *Fam (for TV)* télécommande *f*

zapping [ˈzæpɪŋ] N *(changing TV channels)* zapping *m*

zappy [ˈzæpɪ] ADJ *Fam (fast) (car, computer)* rapide; *(stylish, punchy) (prose, manager, style)* énergique, qui a du punch

ZBB [zedbiːˈbiː, *Am* zi:bi:ˈbi:] N *Fin (abbr* **zero-base budgeting)** BBZ *m*

Z chart N tableau *m* en Z

zeal [zi:l] N zèle *m*, ardeur *f*; *(religious)* zèle *m*, ferveur *f*; **to show excessive z.** faire preuve d'un zèle excessif

zealot [ˈzelət] N **1** *Bible, Hist* Z. zélote *mf* **2** *Fig* fanatique *mf*, *Lit* zélateur, -trice (**for** de)

zealotry [ˈzelətrɪ] N fanatisme *m*, ferveur *f*

zealous [ˈzeləs] ADJ zélé; *(campaigner, advocate)* fervent; **z. to do sth** empressé de faire qch; **to be z. in doing sth** faire qch avec zèle

zealously [ˈzeləslɪ] ADV avec zèle

zebra [ˈzebrə, ˈziːbrə] N **1** *(animal)* zèbre *m* **2** *Am Sl (in American football)* arbitre *m*

▸▸ *Br* **z. crossing** passage *m* clouté *ou* pour piétons

zebu [ˈziːbuː] N *(animal)* zébu *m*

zed [zed] N *Br (letter)* z *m*

zeds [zedz] NPL *Fam (sleep)* **to catch some z.** faire un roupillon

zee [zi:] N *Am (letter)* z *m*
▸▸ **z. chart** tableau *m* en Z

zees [zi:z] NPL *Am Fam (sleep)* **to catch some z.** faire un roupillon

Zen [zen] N zen *m*
ADJ zen *inv*
▸▸ **Z. Buddhism** le bouddhisme zen, les préceptes *mpl* du zen; **Z. Buddhist** bouddhiste *mf* zen

zenith [ˈzenɪθ] N *Astron, Fig* zénith *m*; *Fig* **at the z. of his fame** à l'apogée *ou* au sommet de sa gloire

zephyr [ˈzefər] N *Lit* zéphyr *m*

zeppelin [ˈzepəlɪn] N *Aviat, Hist* zeppelin *m*

zero [ˈzɪərəʊ] N *Math, Comput* zéro *m*; **z. point two (0.2)** zéro virgule deux (0,2); *Comput* **with z. wait states** sans état d'attente; **the thermometer is at z./four below z.** le thermomètre est à zéro/à quatre au-dessous de zéro; **the temperature fell below z.** la température est tombée au-dessous de zéro; **exports are down to z.** les exportations sont tombées à zéro; **I'd put your chances at z.** je dirais que tes chances sont nulles VOIR GRAMMAIRE A77
ADJ *Fam* **he's got z. intelligence/charm** il n'a aucun(e) intelligence/charme
VT *(instrument etc)* (re)mettre à zéro
▸▸ **z. altitude** altitude *f* zéro; *Fin* **z. coupon bond** obligation *f* à coupon zéro; *Mktg* **z. defects** zéro défaut *m*; *Mktg* **z. defects purchasing** achats *mpl* de qualité à 100%, achats zéro défaut; **z. gravity** apesanteur *f*; **z. hour** heure *f* H; **z. growth** croissance *f* zéro; *Pol* **the z. option** l'option *f* zéro; **z. point** *(on graduated scale)* zéro; **z. rating** imposition *f* nulle **z. tolerance** = politique *f* d'intransigeance à l'égard de toute infraction à la loi ou au règlement
▸ **zero in** VT SEP *Mil (gun)* régler le tir de
VI *(of missile etc)* se régler sur une/la cible
▸ **zero in on** VT INSEP *Mil (target)* régler le tir sur; *(of missile etc)* se régler sur; *Fig (concentrate on) (subject, problem)* se concentrer sur; *(identify)* aller droit sur; **they zeroed in on the one weak point of the argument** ils ont été droit sur le seul point faible de l'argument

zero-base budgeting N *Fin* budget *m* base zéro, budgétisation *f* base zéro

zeroed [ˈzɪərəʊd] ADJ *(milometer)* à zéro

zeroing [ˈzɪərəʊɪŋ] N *Comput* initialisation *f* du compteur

zero-rated ADJ *(without VAT)* exempt *ou* exonéré de TVA; **in Britain, books are z. en** Grande-Bretagne, les livres sont exempts *ou* exonérés de TVA

zero-rating N franchise *f* de TVA, taux *m* zéro, taux nul

zest [zest] N **1** *(enjoyment)* enthousiasme *m*, entrain *m*; *(in speaking)* verve *f*; **with z.** *(to fight etc)* avec élan, avec entrain; *(to eat)* avec appétit, de bon appétit; **her z. for life** sa joie de vivre **2** *(interest)* saveur *f*, goût *m*; **to add z. to the adventure** donner du piquant à l'aventure **3** *(of orange, lemon)* zeste *m*

zestful [ˈzestfʊl] ADJ *(person)* plein d'enthousiasme *ou* d'entrain; *(in speaking)* plein de verve; *(approach)* enthousiaste; *(performance)* plein de vie

zeugma [ˈzjuːgmə] N zeugma *m*, zeugme *m*

zigzag [ˈzɪgzæg] N *(in design)* zigzag *m*; *(on road)* lacet *m*
ADJ *(path, line)* en zigzag; *(pattern)* à zigzag *ou* zigzags; **the path follows a z. course across the fields** le chemin traverse les champs en zigzaguant
ADV en zigzag
VI (**-gg-**) *(of road, line)* zigzaguer, faire des zigzags

zigzagging [ˈzɪgzægɪŋ] N zigzags *mpl*

zilch [zɪltʃ] N *Sl* zéro *m*, que dalle

zillion [ˈzɪljən] N *Fam* des millions *mpl* (et des millions)

Zimbabwe [zɪmˈbɑːbweɪ] N Zimbabwe *m*

Zimbabwean [zɪmˈbɑːbweɪən] ADJ zimbabwéen N Zimbabwéen, -éenne

Zimmer® [ˈzɪmər] N Z.® *(frame)* déambulateur *m*

zinc [zɪŋk] N zinc *m*
▸▸ **z. ointment** pommade *f* à l'oxyde de zinc; **z. oxide** oxyde *m* de zinc; **z. white** blanc *m* de zinc, oxyde de zinc

zincblende [ˈzɪŋkblend] N *Miner* blende *f*

zing [zɪŋ] *Fam* N **1** *(zest)* punch *m* **2** *(sound)* sifflement *m*
VI *(of projectile)* siffler, passer dans un sifflement; **the bullet zinged past me** la balle est passée à côté de moi dans un sifflement
VT *Am (tease)* vanner, chambrer

zinnia [ˈzɪnɪə] N *(flower)* zinnia *m*

Zion [ˈzaɪən] N Sion *m*

Zionism [ˈzaɪənɪz(ə)m] N *Pol* sionisme *m*

Zionist [ˈzaɪənɪst] ADJ, N *Pol* sioniste *mf*

zip [zɪp] N **1** fermeture *f* éclair®, fermeture à glissière, *Belg* tirette *f* **2** *Fam (vigour)* énergie *f*, vitesse *f*; **put some z. into it!** mets-y du nerf!; **your style needs more z.** ton style a besoin d'un peu plus de punch **3** *(of bullet)* sifflement *m*
VI (**-pp-**) *(like bullet)* siffler; **to z. past** *(of car etc)* passer en trombe
VT **1** *Comput* zipper, compresser **2** *Sl* **z. it!** la ferme!, ferme ton clapet!

▸▸ *Am* **z. code** code *m* postal; *Br* **z. fastener** fermeture éclair®, fermeture à glissière, *Belg* tirette; *Comput* **z. file** fichier *m* zippé; *Am Fam* **z. gun** pistolet *m* rudimentaire *(à ressort)*

▸ **zip along** **vi** foncer, aller à fond de train

▸ **zip in** **vt sep** *(lining)* attacher à l'aide d'une fermeture éclair® *ou* à glissière
vi s'attacher à l'aide d'une fermeture éclair® *ou* à glissière

▸ **zip into** **vt insep** **to z. into the chemist's** faire un saut à la pharmacie
vt sep **they zipped themselves into their sleeping bags** ils ont fermé leurs sacs de couchage; **to z. oneself into one's tent/overalls** fermer la fermeture éclair® de sa tente/combinaison; **she zipped the baby into his anorak** elle a enfilé le bébé dans son anorak et a fermé la fermeture éclair®

▸ **zip on** **vt sep** attacher à l'aide d'une fermeture éclair® *ou* à glissière
vi s'attacher à l'aide d'une fermeture éclair®

▸ **zip through** **vt insep** *Fam (do quickly)* faire à toute vitesse; *(read quickly)* lire à toute vitesse

▸ **zip up** **vt sep** *(clothes)* remonter *ou* fermer la fermeture éclair® *ou* à glissière de; **z. me up** remonte ma fermeture
vi **1** *(clothes)* se fermer à l'aide d'une fermeture éclair® *ou* à glissière **2** *Sl* **z. up!** la ferme!, ferme ton clapet!

Zip® disk **n** *Comput* cartouche *f* Zip®

Zip® drive **n** *Comput* lecteur *m* Zip®

zipper [ˈzɪpər] **n** *esp Am* fermeture *f* éclair® *inv* *ou* à glissière, *Belg* tirette *f*
▸▸ **z. bag** (sac *m*) fourre-tout *m* *inv* à fermeture éclair® *ou* à glissière

zipping [ˈzɪpɪŋ] **n** *(with tape)* avance *f* rapide

zippy [ˈzɪpɪ] **adj** *Fam* plein d'énergie *ou* d'entrain *ou* de punch; **a z. little car** une petite voiture nerveuse; **look z.!** grouille-toi!

zircon [ˈzɜːkɒn] **n** *Miner* zircon *m*

zit [zɪt] **n** *Am Fam (pimple)* bouton *m*

zither [ˈzɪðər] **n** *Mus* cithare *f*

zizz [zɪz] **n** *Br Fam* somme *m*; **to have a z.** faire un petit somme

zodiac [ˈzəʊdɪæk] **n** *Astrol* zodiaque *m*; **the signs of the z.** les signes *mpl* du zodiaque

zodiacal [zəʊˈdaɪək(ə)l] **adj** zodiacal, -aux

zombi(e) [ˈzɒmbɪ] **n** *Rel, Fig* zombi *m*; **he walks about like a z.** il a tout le temps l'air abruti *ou* l'air d'un zombi; **I feel like a z.** je me sens complètement abruti

zonal [ˈzəʊn(ə)l] **adj** zonal, -aux

zone [zəʊn] **n** **1** zone *f*, *Admin* **no parking z.** zone d'interdiction de stationner; **parking meter z.** ≃ zone bleue; *Mil* **battle/war z.** zone de l'avant/de guerre; **danger z.** zone dangereuse; **z. of vision** *(when driving)* périmètre *m* de vision **2** *Am (postal delivery)* **z.** zone *f* (de distribution) postale **3** *Am Sl* **to be in a z.** *(dazed)* être dans le coaltar; *(after taking drugs)* être raide, planer; *Sport* **to be in the z.** être au top de sa forme
vt *(town etc)* répartir en zones

zoning [ˈzəʊnɪŋ] **n** répartition *f* en zones; *(in town planning)* zonage *m*

zonked (out) [zɒŋkt(ˈaʊt)] **adj** *Sl (drugged)* défoncé; *(drunk)* pété, bourré; *(exhausted)* crevé, vanné

zoo [zuː] **n** jardin *m* zoologique, *Fam* zoo *m*

zookeeper [ˈzuːkiːpər] **n** gardien, -ienne de zoo

zoological [zəʊəˈlɒdʒɪk(ə)l, zuː-] **adj** zoologique
▸▸ **z. gardens** jardin *m* *ou* parc *m* zoologique

zoologist [zəʊˈɒlədʒɪst, zuː-] **n** zoologiste *mf*

zoology [zəʊˈɒlədʒɪ, zuː-] **n** zoologie *f*

zoom [zuːm] **n** **1** *(noise)* bourdonnement *m*; *(louder)* vrombissement *m* **2** *Cin, TV (lens, effect)* zoom *m*
vi **1** **to z. along** *or* **past/through** passer/traverser en trombe *ou* comme une flèche; **the cars are zooming along the road** les voitures passent en trombe sur la route; **children were zooming around on skateboards** des enfants passaient à toute vitesse sur des planches à roulettes **2** *Aviat (climb steeply)* monter en chandelle
▸▸ *Comput* **z. box** case *f* zoom; **z. lens** zoom

▸ **zoom in** **vi** *Cin, TV* faire un zoom; **the camera zoomed in on the laughing children** la caméra a fait un zoom sur les enfants en train de rire

▸ **zoom off** **vi** déguerpir, partir en vitesse; **they're zooming off on holiday tomorrow** ils filent en vacances demain

▸ **zoom out** **vi** *Cin, TV* faire un zoom arrière

▸ **zoom up** **vi** *(of plane)* monter en chandelle; *(of rocket etc)* s'élever; *(of hit record etc)* monter comme une flèche; *(of prices etc)* monter en flèche

zooming [ˈzuːmɪŋ] **n** *Phot* changement *m* de focale

zoophyte [ˈzəʊəfaɪt] **n** *Biol* zoophyte *m*

zooted [ˈzuːtɪd] **adj** *Am Fam (drunk)* bourré, pété; *(on drugs)* raide, défoncé

zoot suit [ˈzuːtsuːt] **n** = costume *m* tapageur des années 40, rembourré aux épaules

zounds [zaʊndz] **int** *Arch* morbleu!, sacrebleu!

zowie [ˈzaʊɪ] **int** *Am Fam* oh là là!, la vache!

zucchini [zuːˈkiːnɪ, zuː-] **n** *Am* courgette *f*

Zulu [ˈzuːluː] **adj** zoulou
n **1** Zoulou, -oue **2** *Ling* zoulou *m*

Zululand [ˈzuːluːlænd] **n** Zoulouland *m*

zwieback [ˈzwiːbæk] **n** *Am* biscotte *f*

zygote [ˈzaɪɡəʊt] **n** *Biol* zygote *m*

200 EXPRESSIONS ANGLAISES À CONNAÎTRE

L'amour et l'affection

she is the apple of his eye
il tient à elle comme à la prunelle de ses yeux

> ✋ L'expression anglaise est toujours au singulier (the apple of his/her eye) et s'applique toujours à une personne, jamais à une chose.

to sweep somebody off their feet
faire perdre la tête à quelqu'un

to carry a torch for someone
avoir un faible pour quelqu'un

to fall head over heels for someone
tomber follement amoureux de quelqu'un

Aimer/ne pas aimer

to be in someone's good books
être dans les petits papiers de quelqu'un

to have been bitten by the bug
avoir la folie de quelque chose

to get on like a house on fire
s'entendre à merveille

to turn one's nose up at something
dédaigner quelque chose

to give someone the cold shoulder
snober quelqu'un

to make someone's toes curl
donner des frissons de plaisir à quelqu'un

to ruffle someone's feathers
froisser quelqu'un

to get up someone's nose
taper sur les nerfs à quelqu'un

to look daggers at someone
foudroyer quelqu'un du regard

S'amuser

to let one's hair down
se détendre, se laisser aller

> ✋ Cette expression fait référence au fait qu'autrefois les femmes ne laissaient retomber leurs cheveux que dans l'intimité.

to have a blast
s'éclater

to paint the town red
faire la noce

to be out on the tiles
sortir faire la bringue

> ✋ L'expression compare ceux qui sortent s'amuser aux chats qui se promènent sur les toits la nuit.

Le bonheur

to be on top of the world
être en pleine forme

to be walking on air
to be on cloud nine
to be over the moon
être ravi, être aux anges

La tristesse

with one's heart in one's boots
complètement abattu

to hit rock bottom
toucher le fond

to be down in the mouth
être déprimé

to be in the doldrums
avoir le moral à zéro

 Le terme "doldrums" désigne la zone des calmes équatoriaux, où les vents sont faibles et où les bateaux à voiles ont donc du mal à avancer.

La colère

to hit the ceiling
péter les plombs

to go off at the deep end
piquer une crise

to blow one's top
sortir de ses gonds

to go ballistic
piquer une crise

to be like a red rag to a bull to somebody
avoir le don de mettre quelqu'un hors de soi

to get hot under the collar
se mettre en rogne

to be at the end of one's tether
être à bout

 Littéralement: avoir atteint le bout de sa longe. Quand l'herbe à portée de l'animal attaché est épuisée, il tire sur sa longe pour tenter de brouter plus loin.

Attention: cette expression n'est pas l'équivalent du français "être au bout du rouleau".

La mauvaise humeur

to be like a bear with a sore head
être d'humeur massacrante

to get out of bed on the wrong side
se lever du pied gauche

Les critiques

to drive a coach and horses through something
tailler quelque chose en pièces

to haul someone over the coals
démolir quelqu'un (en le critiquant)

the pot calling the kettle black
l'hôpital qui se moque de la charité

to give someone the rough side of one's tongue
parler brutalement à quelqu'un

to cut someone down to size
remettre quelqu'un à sa place

to pick holes in something
relever des erreurs dans quelque chose

to take a pot shot at someone
lancer une critique à quelqu'un

Les réprimandes

to throw the book at someone
passer un savon à quelqu'un

 L'expression fait référence au code pénal.

to send someone away with a flea in their ear
envoyer quelqu'un promener

to bite someone's head off
rembarrer quelqu'un

to jump down someone's throat
rabrouer quelqu'un

to have someone's guts for garters
massacrer quelqu'un

 Cette expression s'emploie toujours sous forme de menace.

to get it in the neck
en prendre pour son grade

La peur

to brick it
avoir les jetons

to get cold feet
avoir la frousse

to scare the pants off someone
faire une peur bleue à quelqu'un

to have one's heart in one's mouth
avoir le cœur qui bat la chamade

to get the wind up
avoir une peur bleue

Les opinions

to nail one's colours to the mast
afficher ses opinions

Au cours d'une bataille navale, un navire voulant abandonner le combat descendait jadis son pavillon en signe de défaite. Impossible de déclarer forfait lorsque le pavillon est cloué au mât.

to get on one's soapbox
haranguer les foules

Littéralement: monter sur sa caisse à savon (soapbox), c'est-à-dire sur une tribune improvisée, pour faire un discours.

to be in bed with someone
être allié avec quelqu'un de façon officieuse

to see eye to eye (with someone)
voir les choses du même œil (que quelqu'un)

to vote with one's feet
indiquer sa désapprobation en quittant les lieux

to change horses in midstream
se raviser en cours de route

to stick to one's guns
rester sur ses positions, tenir bon

L'expression fait référence au soldat qui continue à tirer au lieu de s'enfuir devant l'ennemi.

to stick one's oar in
mettre son grain de sel

Contrôle et manipulation

to have someone eating out of one's hand
faire faire ce qu'on veut à quelqu'un

to wrap someone round one's little finger
faire ce qu'on veut de quelqu'un

to be in the saddle
tenir les rênes

to run a tight ship
mener tout le monde à la baguette

to twist someone's arm
exercer une pression sur quelqu'un

La tromperie

a wolf in sheep's clothing
un loup déguisé en agneau

to lead someone up the garden path
duper quelqu'un, faire marcher quelqu'un

to sell someone down the river
trahir quelqu'un, vendre quelqu'un

Cette expression idiomatique fait allusion aux esclaves que l'on transportait sur le Mississippi jusqu'aux marchés aux esclaves de la Nouvelle-Orléans.

to pull the wool over someone's eyes
faire croire n'importe quoi à quelqu'un

"The wool" était une perruque portée autrefois par les riches. Un voleur ou un plaisantin pouvait les désorienter en tirant la perruque sur leur visage.

L'âge

to have been around the block a few times
ne plus être de la première jeunesse

to be over the hill
commencer à se faire vieux

to be as old as the hills
dater de Mathusalem

to be long in the tooth
ne plus être tout jeune

On peut estimer l'âge d'un cheval à la longueur de ses dents. En général, plus les dents sont longues, plus le cheval est âgé.

L'entraide

to bend over backwards
se mettre en quatre

to give someone a hand
donner un coup de main à quelqu'un

to get someone off the hook
tirer quelqu'un d'affaire

to give someone a leg up
donner un coup de pouce à quelqu'un

L'apparence

to look like death warmed up
avoir une mine de déterré

to be knee-high to a grasshopper
être haut comme trois pommes

to look like something the cat brought in
être en piteux état

to look like a million dollars
être superbe

L'argent

to be made of money
être plein aux as, rouler sur l'or

to bring home the bacon
faire bouillir la marmite

to laugh all the way to the bank
s'en mettre plein les poches

to cost an arm and a leg
coûter les yeux de la tête

to pay through the nose for something
payer quelque chose les yeux de la tête

it's daylight robbery
c'est du vol organisé

to cut corners
faire des économies exagérées

to push the boat out
ne pas regarder à la dépense

to throw money around
jeter l'argent par les fenêtres

to go Dutch
payer chacun sa part

to take someone to the cleaners
nettoyer quelqu'un, plumer quelqu'un

Boisson et ivresse

to drink like a fish
boire comme un trou

to be on the wagon
être au régime sec

> À l'origine, cette expression d'origine américaine était "on the water wagon", terme qui désignait le chariot qui transportait la citerne d'eau.

to wet one's whistle
se rincer le gosier

to be three sheets to the wind
avoir du vent dans les voiles

La prise de risques

a leap in the dark
un saut dans l'inconnu

to sail close to the wind
jouer un jeu dangereux

> Si on navigue au plus près, c'est-à dire presque contre le vent, le bateau risque de chavirer.

better the devil you know
mieux vaut se contenter de ce que l'on a plutôt que de risquer de trouver pire

> L'expression anglaise est la forme tronquée du proverbe "better the devil you know than the devil you don't know": mieux vaut un danger que l'on connaît qu'un danger que l'on ne connaît pas.

on a wing and a prayer
Dieu sait comment

> Il s'agit d'une référence à une chanson des années 40 à propos d'un pilote d'avion.

to dice with death
risquer sa vie

to go out on a limb
prendre des risques

> Dans cette expression, l'image est celle d'une personne s'aventurant sur une branche d'arbre.

to skate on thin ice
toucher à un sujet délicat

to stick one's neck out
prendre des risques

avoir le cafard
to feel down

avoir une tête d'enterrement
to look sombre

avoir le moral à zéro
to be feeling down in the dumps

Laughter

s'en payer une tranche
to have the time of one's life

se fendre la pipe
to split one's sides (laughing)

être plié en deux
to be doubled up with laughter

rire comme un bossu/comme une baleine
to laugh one's head off

> It is believed that 'rire comme une baleine' (to laugh like a whale) might have derived from 'se tordre comme une baleine de parapluie retourné', playing on the words 'se tordre' which means both 'to bend' and 'to laugh' (in colloquial language), and 'baleine', which of course means 'whale', but which also means 'umbrella rib'.

rire à s'en décrocher la mâchoire
to split one's sides (laughing)

Madness

il ne tourne pas rond
he's not all there

travailler du chapeau
to have a screw loose

avoir un petit vélo dans la tête
to be off one's rocker

perdre la boule
to go round the bend

être marteau
to be nuts

être tombé sur la tête
to have a screw loose

avoir une araignée au plafond
to have bats in the belfry

être timbré
to be cracked

Stupidity

il n'a pas inventé l'eau chaude/la poudre
he'll never set the Thames on fire

être bête à manger du foin
to be as thick as two short planks

> This expression plays on the two meanings of the word 'bête'; as a noun it means 'animal' but as an adjective it means 'stupid'.

être bête comme ses pieds
to be unbelievably stupid

raisonner comme un tambour
to talk through one's hat

> This expression plays on the verbs 'raisonner' (to think) and 'résonner' (to echo). The hollowness of the drum (tambour) also suggests a person of little intelligence.

avoir une case de vide
to have a screw loose

avoir une cervelle de moineau
to be feather-brained

être dur à la détente
to be slow on the uptake

 The image is that of a weapon that is difficult to fire because of a stiff trigger.

Hunger and eating

avoir l'estomac dans les talons
to be ravenous

avoir les crocs
to be famished

avoir la dalle
to be hungry

avoir une faim de loup
to be ravenous

avoir les dents du fond qui baignent
to have stuffed oneself

tu as les yeux plus grands que le ventre
your eyes are bigger than your belly

manger sur le pouce
to have a quick snack

Drinking

boire comme un trou
to drink like a fish

avoir la gueule de bois
to be hungover

avoir du vent dans les voiles
to be three sheets to the wind

 This expression likens the teetering drunkard to a ship that is buffeted by the wind.

lever le coude
to booze

ne pas sucer que de la glace
to drink like a fish

Doing things easily

ce n'est pas la mer à boire
it's no big deal

c'est du gâteau
it's a piece of cake

faire quelque chose les doigts dans le nez
to do something very easily

ce n'est pas le bout du monde
it's no big deal

 Do not confuse with the expression 'ce n'est pas la fin du monde', which means 'it isn't the end of the world'.

c'est simple comme bonjour
it's as easy as pie

Leaving

prendre ses jambes à son cou
to take to one's heels

mettre les bouts/les voiles
to skedaddle

prendre le large
to clear off

prendre la poudre d'escampette
to make off

 The word 'escampette' only occurs in this expression and derives from 'escamper', an old French verb which means 'to flee'.

se faire la malle
to clear off

filer à l'anglaise
to sneak off, to take French leave

 Interestingly, but unsurprisingly, the French and the English credit each other with this type of rude behaviour.

prendre ses cliques et ses claques
to pack one's bags and go

Work and effort

mettre la main à la pâte
to lend a hand

 In this expression the word 'pâte' refers to the dough prepared and kneaded by bakers.

retrousser ses manches
to roll up one's sleeves

en mettre un coup
to pull out all the stops

mettre les bouchées doubles
to really get a move on

être un bourreau de travail
to be a workaholic

un travail de Romain
a Herculean task

se mettre en quatre pour faire quelque chose
to do one's utmost to do something

faire des pieds et des mains pour faire quelque chose
to move heaven and earth to do something

Laziness

avoir les côtes en long
to be bone-idle

 Literally, this expression means 'to have vertical ribs', a condition that would make it impossible to bend over and do any kind of physical work.

se tourner les pouces
to twiddle one's thumbs

peigner la girafe
to do damn all

ne pas se fouler la rate
not to strain oneself

les avoir palmées
to be a complete layabout

 This expression means 'to have webbed hands', a condition that would, obviously, make work somewhat difficult.

avoir un poil dans la main
to be workshy

Success

marcher comme sur des roulettes
to be going very smoothly

casser la baraque
to bring the house down

faire un malheur
to be a sensation

avoir le vent en poupe
to have the wind in one's sails

Failure

battre de l'aile
to be in a bad way

faire chou blanc
to draw a blank

tomber à l'eau
to fall through

s'en aller en eau de boudin
to go down the drain

rester le bec dans l'eau
to be left high and dry

c'est la fin des haricots
we've had it now

 It is believed that this expression came to describe a hopeless situation because beans used to be the main staple of a soldier's diet and running out of beans was therefore considered a disaster.

Money

ne pas attacher son chien avec des saucisses
to be tight with one's money

Obviously, using link sausage as a lead for one's dog would be a sign that one doesn't care too much about money.

être près de ses sous
to be a penny-pincher

avoir des oursins dans le porte-monnaie
to be tight-fisted

Literally, 'to have sea urchins in one's purse'. The idea is that someone does not want to put his hand into his purse because the spikes of the sea urchins might hurt him.

coûter les yeux de la tête/la peau des fesses
to cost an arm and a leg

jeter l'argent par les fenêtres
to throw money down the drain

l'argent lui fond entre les doigts
money runs through his fingers

être un panier percé
to be a spendthrift

plaie d'argent n'est pas mortelle
money isn't everything

être plein aux as
to be rolling in it

rouler sur l'or
to be rolling in money

tirer le diable par la queue
to be hard up

mener la vie de château
to lead a life of luxury

s'en mettre plein les poches
to make a packet

un chèque en bois
a rubber cheque

être sans un radis
to be stony broke

être raide (comme un passe-lacets)
to be stony broke

être sur la paille
to be on one's uppers

plumer quelqu'un
to fleece somebody

Death

casser sa pipe
to kick the bucket

passer l'arme à gauche
to snuff it

The expression 'passer l'arme à gauche' meaning 'to die' comes from military terminology, referring to the position in which soldiers hold their weapons when they stand at ease; this is because in French the expression for 'to stand at ease' is 'être au repos' which can also mean 'to be at rest', ie dead.

manger les pissenlits par la racine
to be pushing up the daisies

lâcher la rampe
to kick the bucket

GRAMMAIRE ANGLAISE

ENGLISH GRAMMAR

TABLE DES MATIÈRES

1 GLOSSAIRE DES TERMES GRAMMATICAUX

ABSTRAIT
Un nom abstrait est un nom qui ne désigne pas un objet physique ou une personne, mais une qualité ou un concept. *Bonheur*, *vie*, *longueur*, ou en anglais kindness (*gentillesse*), love (*amour*), etc. sont des exemples de noms abstraits.

ACTIF
La voix active (ou l'actif) correspond aux phrases dont le sujet est considéré comme agissant, par exemple *mon père lave la voiture*. Elle s'oppose à la forme passive : *la voiture est lavée par mon père*. Voir PASSIF.

ADJECTIF
Mot adjoint au nom pour le décrire ou le déterminer. Parmi les adjectifs, on distingue les adjectifs qualificatifs (*une petite maison*), les adjectifs démonstratifs (*cette maison*), les adjectifs possessifs (*ma maison*), etc.

ADJECTIF SUBSTANTIVÉ
C'est un adjectif employé comme nom. Par exemple les adjectifs *jeune*, *réel*, *virtuel*, etc. peuvent aussi s'employer comme noms : *les jeunes, le réel, le virtuel*. De même en anglais, the blind (*les aveugles*), the homeless (*les sans-abri*), etc.

ADVERBE
Les adverbes accompagnent le plus souvent un verbe pour ajouter une information supplémentaire en indiquant comment l'action est accomplie (adverbe de manière), **quand**, **où** et **avec quelle intensité** l'action est accomplie (adverbes de temps, de lieu et d'intensité), etc. Certains adverbes peuvent aussi s'employer avec un adjectif ou un autre adverbe (par exemple *une fille très mignonne*, *il y va trop souvent*).

ANTÉCÉDENT
Mot auquel renvoie un pronom. Par exemple, dans *je connais l'homme qui a fait ça*, *l'homme* est l'antécédent du pronom relatif *qui*.

APPOSITION
On dit qu'un mot ou une proposition est en apposition par rapport à un autre mot ou une autre proposition lorsque l'un ou l'autre est placé directement après le nom ou la proposition, sans y être relié par aucun mot (par exemple *M. Duclos, notre directeur, a téléphoné ce matin*).

ARTICLE DÉFINI
Les articles définis sont *le, la, les* en français. Ils correspondent tous à the en anglais.

ARTICLE INDÉFINI
Les articles indéfinis sont *un, une* (et *des* au pluriel) en français. Ils correspondent à a (ou an devant une voyelle ou un h muet) en anglais.

ASPECT
L'aspect correspond à la manière dont on envisage l'action exprimée par le verbe : dans sa durée, son déroulement, son achèvement, etc. On distingue en anglais l'aspect simple, l'aspect progressif (ou continu) et le "perfect".

Voir FORME PROGRESSIVE et PERFECT.

ATTRIBUT
Nom ou, le plus souvent, adjectif, relié au sujet ou au complément d'objet par le verbe *être* ou un autre verbe d'état. Par exemple, **I am** tired (*je suis fatigué*), **it seems** interesting (*cela semble intéressant*). Voir aussi ÉPITHÈTE.

AUXILIAIRE
Les auxiliaires sont employés pour former les temps composés d'autres verbes, par exemple dans **he has** gone (*il est parti*), l'auxiliaire employé est have (et *être* en français). En anglais, on distingue les auxiliaires ordinaires (have, be, do) et les auxiliaires modaux (can, could, may, etc.). Voir MODAL.

CARDINAL
Les nombres cardinaux sont *un, deux, trois*, etc. Ils expriment la quantité. On les oppose aux nombres ordinaux. Voir ORDINAL.

COLLECTIF
Un collectif est un mot qui est au singulier mais qui désigne un groupe de gens ou de choses. Par exemple, crowd (*foule*), flock (*troupeau*) et fleet (*flotte*) sont des noms collectifs.

COMPARATIF
Le comparatif des adjectifs et des adverbes permet d'établir une comparaison entre deux personnes, deux choses ou deux actions. En français, on emploie *plus... que* (comparatif de supériorité), *moins... que* (comparatif d'infériorité) et *aussi... que* (comparatif d'égalité).

COMPLÉMENT D'OBJECT DIRECT
Groupe nominal qui accompagne un verbe (= verbe transitif direct), sans préposition entre les deux. Par exemple, *j'ai rencontré un ami*. Les pronoms peuvent aussi s'employer comme compléments d'objet direct : *je l'ai rencontré*.

COMPLÉMENT D'OBJECT INDIRECT
Groupe nominal ou pronom qui suit un verbe (= verbe transitif indirect), normalement séparé de ce dernier par une préposition (en général à en français) : *je parle à mon ami*. Vous noterez qu'en français comme en anglais, on omet souvent la préposition devant un pronom. Par exemple, dans *je lui ai envoyé un cadeau*, *lui* est l'équivalent de à *lui* : c'est le complément d'objet indirect. De même, him correspond à to him dans la phrase équivalente anglaise **I sent** him a present.

CONDITIONNEL
Mode verbal employé pour exprimer ce que quelqu'un ferait ou ce qui arriverait si une condition était remplie, par exemple *il viendrait s'il le pouvait ; la chaise se serait cassée s'il s'était assis dessus.*

CONJONCTION
Les conjonctions sont des mots qui relient deux mots ou propositions. On distingue les conjonctions de coordination, comme *et, ou, or*, et les conjonctions de subordination comme *parce que, après que, bien que*, qui introduisent une proposition subordonnée. Voir SUBORDONNÉE.

CONTINU
Voir FORME PROGRESSIVE.

DÉMONSTRATIF
Les adjectifs démonstratifs (*ce, cette, ces*, etc.) et les pronoms démonstratifs (*celui-ci, celui-là*, etc.) s'emploient pour désigner une personne ou un objet bien précis.

DÉNOMBRABLE Un nom est dénombrable s'il peut avoir un pluriel et si on peut l'employer avec un article indéfini. Par exemple **house** (*maison*), **car** (*voiture*), **dog** (*chien*). On les oppose aux noms indénombrables. Voir INDÉNOMBRABLE.

ÉPITHÈTE Adjectif ou nom qui n'est pas relié au nom par un verbe, par opposition à l'attribut. Par exemple, **an interesting film** (*un film intéressant*). Voir aussi ATTRIBUT.

FORME PROGRESSIVE La forme progressive (ou forme continue) d'un verbe exprime l'action dans sa durée. Elle se forme avec to be + participe présent : **I am thinking** (*je pense*), **he has been writing all day** (*il a passé la journée à écrire*), **will she be staying with us?** (*est-ce qu'elle va loger chez nous ?*).

GÉNITIF Le génitif anglais (ou cas possessif) permet d'exprimer l'appartenance ou la dépendance. Il se forme avec 's après un nom singulier (**my father's car** *la voiture de mon père*) et simplement avec l'apostrophe après un nom pluriel (**my parents' car**, *la voiture de mes parents*).

GÉRONDIF Le gérondif anglais est une forme verbale ayant une fonction nominale. On l'appelle aussi "verbe substantivé". Il se forme en ajoutant la terminaison -ing au radical du verbe. Par exemple, **skiing is fun** (*c'est amusant de faire du ski*). Il peut aussi être précédé d'une préposition : **I'm fed up with waiting** (*j'en ai assez d'attendre*). Attention à ne pas le confondre avec le participe présent anglais qui se forme de la même manière.

IDIOMATIQUE Se dit d'un emploi ou d'une expression propres à une langue donnée et qui ne peuvent donc pas se traduire mot à mot dans une autre langue. Par exemple, **he thinks he's the cat's whiskers** correspond en français à *il se croit sorti de la cuisse de Jupiter*.

IMPÉRATIF Mode qui permet d'exprimer un ordre (*va-t'en, tais-toi !*) ou de faire des suggestions (*allons-y*).

INDÉFINI Les pronoms et les adjectifs indéfinis sont des mots qui ne se rapportent pas à des personnes ou des choses précises (par exemple *chaque, quelqu'un*, etc.).

INDÉNOMBRABLE Les indénombrables sont des noms qui n'ont pas de pluriel et ne peuvent normalement pas être précédés de l'article indéfini ou d'un adjectif cardinal. Par exemple *le beurre, la paresse* en français, et **advice** (*conseil*), **travel** (*voyage*) en anglais. On les oppose aux noms dénombrables. Voir DÉNOMBRABLE.

INDICATIF Mode qui permet de décrire l'action ou l'état de manière neutre : *j'aime, il est venu, nous essayons*. Il s'oppose au subjonctif, au conditionnel et à l'impératif.

INFINITIF Forme de base du verbe qui ne porte pas d'indication de personne et qui, en anglais, peut être précédée ou non de to. Le verbe à l'infinitif employé sans to s'appelle le "radical". Par exemple, **to eat** ou **eat** (*manger*).

INTERROGATIF Les pronoms interrogatifs sont employés pour formuler une question. Il peut s'agir d'une question directe (*quand arriveras-tu ?*) ou d'une question indirecte (*je ne sais pas quand il arrivera*). Voir QUESTION.

INTRANSITIF Se dit d'un verbe qui n'a pas de complément d'objet et dont l'action se limite au sujet, par opposition à un verbe transitif. Par exemple, *marcher* est un verbe intransitif. Voir TRANSITIF.

MODAL Les auxiliaires modaux permettent de modifier un verbe en exprimant différentes notions : la capacité, la possibilité, l'obligation, etc. Les auxiliaires modaux anglais sont **can/could, may/might, must/had to, shall/should, will/would, ought to**. On trouve aussi les "semi-auxiliaires" : **used to, dare** et **need**. Une des caractéristiques des auxiliaires modaux est que, aux formes interrogative et négative, ils se construisent sans do.

MODE Le mode représente l'attitude du sujet parlant vis-à-vis de l'action dont il est question dans la phrase. Voir aussi INDICATIF, SUBJONCTIF, CONDITIONNEL, IMPÉRATIF.

NOM Un nom (ou substantif) est un mot qui sert à désigner une chose, un être animé, un lieu ou des idées abstraites. Par exemple *passeport, chat, magasin, vie*. On distingue aussi les dénombrables, les indénombrables et les collectifs. Voir DÉNOMBRABLE, INDÉNOMBRABLE et COLLECTIF.

NOM COMPOSÉ Nom formé de deux mots distincts ou plus, comme *ouvre-boîte* et *tiroir-caisse* en français, ou **table napkins** (*serviettes de table*) et **mother-in-law** (*belle-mère*) en anglais.

NOMBRE Le nombre d'un nom indique si celui-ci est **singulier** ou **pluriel**. Un nom singulier fait référence à une seule chose ou à une seule personne (*train, garçon*), et un nom pluriel à plusieurs (*trains, garçons*).

OBJET DIRECT Voir COMPLÉMENT.

OBJET INDIRECT Voir COMPLÉMENT.

ORDINAL Les nombres ordinaux sont *premier, deuxième, troisième*, etc. Ils expriment l'ordre, le classement. On les oppose aux nombres cardinaux. Voir CARDINAL.

PARTICIPE PASSÉ Forme verbale qui se place après l'auxiliaire pour former les temps composés (*il a mangé, ils sont arrivés*) ou la voix passive (*la maison vient d'être vendue*). Le participe passé anglais se forme en ajoutant la terminaison -d ou -ed au radical (participes passés réguliers) et s'emploie après l'auxiliaire have, pour former le "perfect" et après l'auxiliaire be dans les phrases au passif. Voir PASSIF et PERFECT. Pour la liste des participes passés irréguliers, voir pp. A63-5.

PARTICIPE PRÉSENT Le participe présent en anglais est la forme verbale qui se termine en -ing. Il permet par exemple d'exprimer la manière : **they went running out of the house** (*ils sont partis de la maison en courant*). Il sert aussi à former l'aspect progressif. Voir FORME PROGRESSIVE.

PARTITIF En français, l'article partitif *de* (ou *du*, *de la*) permet de désigner une partie par rapport à un tout qu'on ne peut pas dénombrer. Par exemple, *j'ai de l'argent*, *il nous faut du bois*, etc.

PASSIF Un verbe est au passif ou à la voix passive lorsque le sujet n'accomplit pas l'action mais la subit. En français, le passif se forme avec le verbe être + participe passé du verbe, par exemple, *il est aimé*, *les tickets sont vendus à l'entrée*, etc. En anglais, la voix passive se forme avec le verbe **to be** + participe passé du verbe, par exemple **he was rewarded** (*il fut récompensé*). Voir ACTIF.

PAST PERFECT Voir PERFECT.

PERFECT C'est l'aspect qui permet d'exprimer une action accomplie dans le passé ayant des conséquences au moment de l'énonciation ou une action commencée dans le passé et qui se poursuit dans le présent. Il se forme avec **to have** + participe passé. On distingue le "present perfect", comme dans **I have arrived** (*je suis arrivé*) ou **I have seen** (*j'ai vu*), et le "past perfect" (ou "pluperfect") comme dans **I had arrived** (*j'étais arrivé*) ou **I had seen** (*j'avais vu*).

PLUPERFECT Voir PERFECT.

POSSESSIF Les adjectifs et les pronoms possessifs s'emploient pour indiquer la possession ou l'appartenance. Ce sont des mots comme *mon/le mien*, *ton/le tien*, *notre/le nôtre*, etc.

PRÉPOSITION Les prépositions introduisent le complément d'un nom, d'un verbe, d'un adjectif ou d'un adverbe. Ce sont des mots tels que *avec*, *dans*, *vers*, *à*, etc. Ils sont normalement suivis d'un nom ou d'un pronom.

PRESENT PERFECT Voir PERFECT.

PRINCIPALE Au sein d'une phrase, la proposition principale est celle dont dépendent les autres propositions (dites subordonnées). Par exemple *il a dit* dans *il a dit qu'il viendrait*. Voir SUBORDONNÉE.

PRONOM Mot qui remplace un nom. Les principales catégories de pronoms sont les :
* pronoms personnels (*je, me, moi, tu, te, toi*, etc.)
* pronoms démonstratifs (*celui-ci, celui-là*, etc.)
* pronoms relatifs (*qui, que*, etc.)
* pronoms interrogatifs (*qui ?, quoi ?, lequel ?*, etc.)
* pronoms possessifs (*le mien, le tien*, etc.)
* pronoms réfléchis (*me, te, se*, etc.)
* pronoms indéfinis (*quelque chose, tout*, etc.)

PROPOSITION Une proposition est un groupe de mots qui contient au moins un sujet et un verbe : *il chante* est une proposition. Une phrase peut être composée de plusieurs propositions : *il chante | quand il prend sa douche | et qu'il est content*.

QUESTION Il existe deux types de questions : les questions au style **direct**, qui sont retranscrites telles qu'elles ont été posées, avec un point d'interrogation (par exemple, *quand viendra-t-il ?*) ; les questions au style **indirect**, qui sont introduites par une proposition et ne nécessitent pas de point d'interrogation (par exemple, *je me demande quand il viendra*).

RADICAL Voir INFINITIF.

RÉFLÉCHI Les verbes réfléchis "renvoient" l'action sur le sujet (par exemple *je me suis habillé*). En anglais, on emploie les pronoms réfléchis **myself, yourself**, etc. : **enjoy yourself** (*amuse-toi bien*). Les verbes réfléchis sont moins nombreux en anglais qu'en français.

SUBJONCTIF Mode employé pour exprimer un souhait, un doute ou une possibilité, etc. Par exemple, le verbe *venir* est au subjonctif dans la phrase *il se peut qu'il vienne*. En anglais, on le trouve notamment dans les propositions conditionnelles (**if I were you, I would tell him** *si j'étais toi, je lui dirais*) mais de manière générale, son emploi n'est pas très courant.

SUBORDONNÉE Au sein d'une phrase, la subordonnée est une proposition qui dépend de la proposition principale. Sans cette dernière, la subordonnée ne formerait pas une phrase complète du point de vue syntaxique. Par exemple, dans *il a dit qu'il viendrait*, *qu'il viendrait* est la proposition subordonnée.

SUBSTANTIF Voir NOM.

SUPERLATIF C'est le degré le plus élevé de la comparaison. On distingue d'une part le superlatif relatif qui se construit en français avec *le plus...*, *le moins...*, et d'autre part le superlatif absolu (*très sympathique*).

TEMPS COMPOSÉ Les temps composés sont des temps verbaux formés de plus d'un élément. En anglais, ils se forment avec l'**auxiliaire** + **participe présent** ou **passé** du verbe conjugué. Par exemple **I am reading** (*je suis en train de lire*), **he has gone** (*il est parti*).

TRANSITIF Se dit d'un verbe qui se construit avec un complément d'objet. Les verbes transitifs s'opposent aux verbes intransitifs. Les verbes transitifs directs régissent leur complément (complément d'objet direct) sans intermédiaire ; c'est le cas de *manger*. Les verbes transitifs indirects régissent leur complément (complément d'objet indirect) par l'intermédiaire d'une préposition ; par exemple, *parler à*. Voir INTRANSITIF.

VERBE COMPOSÉ Les verbes composés anglais ou verbes à particules (en anglais "phrasal verbs") sont des verbes dont le sens n'équivaut pas forcément à la somme du sens des deux éléments qui les composent. Par exemple, **run up** peut avoir le sens de "monter en courant" ou de "laisser s'accumuler" (**I've run up a huge overdraft** *j'ai un découvert énorme*). Les verbes composés forment donc un tout ; la particule est indispensable, elle permet de modifier le sens du verbe principal.

2 LES ARTICLES

A LES FORMES

a) L'article indéfini "un/une" se traduit par **a** devant une consonne et **an** devant une voyelle :

a **cat**	un chat
a **dog**	un chien
an **owl**	une chouette
an **umbrella**	un parapluie

Il est cependant important de se souvenir que l'on emploie **a/an** selon que l'initiale du mot qui suit se prononce comme une voyelle ou non. Ainsi, le "h" muet des trois mots suivants (ainsi que ceux de la même famille) est précédé de **an** :

an **hour** ['aʊə(r)]	une heure
an **heir** [eə(r)]	un héritier
an **honest man** ['ɒnɪst]	un honnête homme

Il en est de même pour les abréviations commençant phonétiquement par une voyelle :

an **MP** ['em'piː]	un député

En revanche, la diphtongue se prononçant "iou" et qui s'écrit "eu" ou "u" est précédée de **a** :

a **university** ['juːnɪ'vɜːsəti]	une université
a **eucalyptus tree** ['juːkə'lɪptəs]	un eucalyptus
a **union** ['juːnjən]	un syndicat

Avec le mot **hotel**, on peut employer **a** ou **an**, bien qu'à l'oral on préfère l'emploi de **a**. Les deux formes de l'article indéfini sont également possibles devant les adjectifs **historic** et **historical**, même si à l'écrit ou dans un style littéraire on dira plutôt **an historic**.

b) L'article défini "le/la/les" se traduit toujours par **the** :

the **cat**	le chat
the **owl**	la chouette
the **holidays**	les vacances

On peut prononcer le e de **the** un peu comme un "i" français lorsque le mot qui suit commence phonétiquement par une voyelle (voir a) ci-dessus), comme pour **the owl**, ou lorsqu'il est accentué :

he's definitely the man for the job
voilà vraiment l'homme qu'il faut pour ce travail

B LA POSITION DE L'ARTICLE

L'article précède le nom et tout adjectif (avec ou sans adverbe) placé devant un nom :

a **good book**/the **good book**
un bon livre/le bon livre

a **very good book**/the **very good book**
un très bon livre/le très bon livre

Cependant **all** et **both** précèdent l'article défini :

they drank **all the wine**
ils ont bu tout le vin

both the men (= both **men**) were guilty
les deux hommes étaient tous les deux coupables

L'adverbe **rather** peut se placer avant ou après l'article, sans qu'il y ait de différence de sens :

it was **rather** a **good play**/a **rather good play**
c'était une assez bonne pièce

that was a **rather unfortunate remark**/**rather an unfortunate remark**
c'était une remarque plutôt malencontreuse

À la différence de **rather**, l'adverbe **quite** ne signifie pas la même chose lorsqu'il est placé avant ou après l'article. Il a le même sens que **rather** (*assez*) quand il précède l'article, mais il signifie "complètement", "tout à fait", quand il se trouve entre l'article et l'adjectif. Comparez :

it was **quite** a **good play**
c'était une assez bonne pièce

that would be a **quite useless task**
ce serait une tâche tout à fait inutile

Les adverbes **too**, **so** et **as** précèdent l'adjectif et l'article indéfini. On a donc la construction **too/so/as** + adjectif + article + nom :

if that is **not too great a favour to ask**
si ce n'est pas trop vous demander

never have I seen **so boring a film**
je n'ai jamais vu de film aussi ennuyeux

I have never seen **as fine an actor as Olivier**
je n'ai jamais vu d'acteur aussi bon qu'Olivier

On peut aussi trouver **many a** (*plus d'un*), **such a** (*un tel*) et **what a** (*quel !*) :

many a man would do the same
plus d'un homme ferait la même chose

she's **such a fool**	**what a joke!**
elle est tellement idiote	*quelle blague !*

Remarquez qu'avec **such** l'adjectif suit l'article indéfini, tandis qu'avec **so** il le précède (voir aussi ci-dessus) :

I have never seen **such a beautiful painting**
je n'ai jamais vu une peinture aussi belle

I have never seen **so beautiful a painting**
je n'ai jamais vu une peinture aussi belle

Half (*la moitié de*) aussi précède en général l'article :

half the world knows about this
presque tout le monde est au courant

I'll be back in **half an hour**
je reviens dans une demi-heure

Lorsque **half** fait partie d'un nom composé (half-bottle, half-brother, etc.), l'article se place bien sûr en premier :

why don't you buy a **half-bottle of rum?**
pourquoi tu n'achètes pas une demi-bouteille de rhum ?

Comparez avec :

he drank **half a bottle of rum**
il a bu la moitié d'une bouteille de rhum

C L'EMPLOI DES ARTICLES

1 L'article indéfini (a, an)

L'article indéfini ne s'emploie normalement que pour les noms dénombrables, bien que la distinction "dénombrable/indénombrable" ne soit pas toujours évidente, comme nous le verrons p. A9.

a) Devant un nom générique, pour faire référence à une catégorie ou à une espèce :

a **mouse is smaller than a rat**
une souris est plus petite qu'un rat

A mouse et **a rat** représentent les souris et les rats en général. Avec une légère différence de sens, l'article défini peut aussi s'employer devant un terme générique. Voir 2b).

Remarquez que le terme générique **man** représentant l'humanité (à la différence de **a man** = "un homme", "une personne de sexe masculin") ne prend pas d'article :

this could be considered **man's greatest achievement**
on pourrait considérer ça comme le plus grand exploit de l'homme

b) Avec des noms attributs du sujet ou dans des appositions, ou bien après as (en particulier avec des noms de métiers, à la différence du français) :

he is a hairdresser
il est coiffeur

she has become a Member of Parliament
elle est devenue députée

John McIntyre, a journalist with over twenty years' experience, seems the best candidate for the job
John McIntyre, journaliste ayant plus de vingt ans d'expérience, semble être le meilleur candidat pour ce travail

her brother, a retired police officer, was able to give her advice on making her home more secure
son frère, policier à la retraite, a pu la conseiller sur la manière de rendre sa maison plus sûre

he used to work as a skipper
il travaillait comme capitaine

L'article indéfini s'emploie lorsque le nom fait partie d'un groupe. S'il n'y a pas d'appartenance à un groupe, on omet l'article, comme dans l'exemple suivant, où la personne mentionnée est unique :

she is now Duchess of York
elle est maintenant duchesse d'York

Professor Draper, head of the English department
le professeur Draper, chef du département d'anglais

Si on a une liste de mots en apposition, on peut omettre l'article :

Olivia Ford, actress, charity worker and campaigner, died yesterday after a long illness
Olivia Ford, actrice, bénévole et militante, est morte hier après une longue maladie

Mais on emploiera l'article défini the pour une personne célèbre (ou pour distinguer deux personnes ayant le même nom) :

Nicole Kidman, the actress
Nicole Kidman, l'actrice

c) Comme préposition :

L'article indéfini peut s'employer dans le sens de "par", comme dans les exemples suivants :

the haddock is £6 a kilo
le haddock est à 6 livres le kilo

take two tablets twice a day
prenez deux comprimés deux fois par jour

d) Avec little (*peu de* + indénombrable) et few (*peu de* + dénombrable) :

L'article indéfini qui accompagne ces deux mots indique un sens positif (*un peu de*). Employés seuls, little et few ont un sens négatif :

she needs a little attention (= some attention)
elle a besoin d'un peu d'attention

she needs little attention (= hardly any attention)
elle a besoin de peu d'attention

they have a few paintings (= some)
ils ont quelques tableaux

they have few paintings (= hardly any)
ils ont peu de tableaux

Only a little/only a few signifient plus ou moins la même chose que little/few, qui sont moins courants :

I have only a little coffee left (= hardly any)
il ne me reste presque plus de café

I can afford only a few books (= hardly any)
je ne peux me permettre d'acheter que quelques livres

Remarquez aussi l'expression a good few, qui équivaut à "pas mal de" en français :

there are a good few miles to go yet
il y a encore pas mal de kilomètres à faire

he's had a good few to drink
il a pas mal bu

2 L'article défini (the)

a) L'article défini s'emploie avec des noms dénombrables et des noms indénombrables :

the butter *(indénombrable)*	*le beurre*
the cup *(sing. dénombrable)*	*la tasse*
the cups *(pl. dénombrable)*	*les tasses*

b) Comme l'article indéfini, l'article défini peut s'employer devant un nom générique. Il semble alors plus scientifique :

the mouse is smaller than the rat (comparez avec 1a) ci-dessus)
la souris est plus petite que le rat

when was the potato first introduced to Europe?
quand est-ce que la pomme de terre fut introduite en Europe pour la première fois ?

c) Si un groupe prépositionnel est placé après le nom et qu'il a pour fonction de définir de manière précise le nom auquel on fait référence, il faut employer l'article défini. Cet article désigne alors un objet ou une personne en particulier :

she has just met the man of her dreams
elle vient juste de rencontrer l'homme de sa vie

the money from my parents hasn't arrived yet
l'argent que mes parents m'ont envoyé n'est pas encore arrivé

Si par contre le groupe prépositionnel sert à décrire le nom de manière générale et que la phrase exprime un fait général, on omet normalement l'article. Comparez l'exemple qui suit avec le dernier des exemples précédents :

I often receive money from my parents
je reçois souvent de l'argent de mes parents

knowledge of a second language would be an advantage
la connaissance d'une deuxième langue serait un avantage

presence of mind is what he needs
ce qu'il lui faut, c'est de la présence d'esprit

Dans la phrase :

the presence of mind that she showed was extraordinary
la présence d'esprit dont elle a fait preuve était extraordinaire

l'emploi de the est obligatoire car la proposition relative (that she showed) permet de faire référence à un exemple de présence d'esprit bien précis.

Cependant, quand le complément du nom introduit par of sert à la fois à définir et à décrire le nom, on emploie l'article défini :

the women of Paris (= women from Paris, in general)
les femmes de Paris

the children of such families (= children from such families)
les enfants de telles familles

d) L'omission de l'article défini :

À la différence du français, l'omission de l'article défini en anglais est très fréquente. Ainsi, un grand nombre de noms ne sont pas précédés de l'article s'ils font référence à une fonction ou à des caractéristiques générales, plutôt qu'à l'objet. On n'emploie pas l'article défini pour :

i) les institutions, par exemple :

church	*l'église*
prison	*la prison*
college	*l'établissement d'enseignement supérieur*

school	*l'école*
court	*le tribunal*
university	*l'université*
hospital	*l'hôpital*

Exemples:

do you go to church?
tu vas à la messe ?, tu es pratiquant ?

she's in hospital/in prison   **Tom is at university**
elle est à l'hôpital/en prison   *Tom est à l'université*

aren't you going to school today?
tu ne vas pas à l'école aujourd'hui ?

Cependant, en anglais américain, on préfère l'emploi de l'article défini devant hospital :

Caroline is back in the hospital
Caroline est de retour à l'hôpital

Si le nom fait référence au bâtiment plutôt qu'à sa fonction, on emploie alors the :

walk up to the church and turn right
allez jusqu'à l'église, puis tournez à droite

the taxi stopped at the school
le taxi s'est arrêté devant l'école

The s'emploie aussi pour désigner un nom défini ou précisé par le contexte :

at the university where his father studied
à l'université où son père a étudié

she's at the university
elle est à l'université (dans cette ville, etc.)

Pour faire référence à l'institution en général, on emploie l'article :

the Church was against it
l'Église était contre

ii)   les moyens de transport précédés de by :

we always go by bus/car/boat/train/plane
nous partons toujours en bus/en voiture/en bateau/en train/en avion

iii)   les repas :

can you meet me before lunch?
tu peux me voir avant le déjeuner ?

buy some chicken for dinner, will you?
tu veux bien acheter du poulet pour le dîner ?

Mais si l'on fait référence à une occasion précise, on emploie l'article. Ainsi, il y a une différence entre :

I enjoy lunch   et :   **I enjoyed the lunch**
j'aime le déjeuner   *j'ai apprécié ce déjeuner*

Dans le premier cas, on fait référence au plaisir de manger à midi ; dans le second cas, on parle d'un repas particulier.

iv)   les moments de la journée et de la nuit, après une préposition autre que in et during :

I don't like going out at night
je n'aime pas sortir le soir/la nuit

these animals can often be seen after dusk
on peut souvent voir ces animaux après le crépuscule

they go to bed around midnight
ils vont se coucher vers minuit

mais :

see you in the morning!
à demain matin !

if you feel peckish during the day, have an apple
si tu as un petit creux dans la journée, mange une pomme

v)   les saisons, en particulier pour exprimer un contraste par rapport à une autre saison plutôt que pour faire référence à une période de l'année. Ainsi :

spring is here! (winter is over)
le printemps est là ! (l'hiver est fini)

it's like winter today
on se croirait en hiver aujourd'hui

mais :

the winter was spent at expensive ski resorts
on passait l'hiver dans des stations de ski de luxe

he needed the summer to recover
il avait besoin de l'été pour récupérer

Après in, on emploie parfois l'article défini, avec très peu de différence de sens entre les deux cas :

most leaves turn yellow in (the) autumn
la plupart des feuilles deviennent jaunes en automne

En anglais américain, on préfère l'emploi de the.

vi)   les expressions de temps avec next et last :

Si de telles expressions sont envisagées par rapport au présent, on n'emploie normalement pas l'article :

can we meet next week?
est-ce qu'on peut se voir la semaine prochaine ?

he was drunk last night
il était soûl hier soir

Dans les autres cas, on emploie l'article :

we arrived on 31 March and the next day was spent relaxing by the pool
nous sommes arrivés le 31 mars et on a passé le jour suivant à se relaxer près de la piscine

vii)   les noms abstraits :

a talk about politics
un discours sur la politique

a study of human relationships
une étude sur les relations humaines

suspicion is a terrible thing
le soupçon est quelque chose de terrible

Mais, bien sûr, lorsque le mot est précisé, on emploie l'article (voir 2c) ci-dessus) :

the politics of disarmament
la politique de désarmement

viii)   certaines maladies :

he has diabetes   **I've got jaundice**
il a du diabète   *j'ai la jaunisse*

Cependant, pour certaines maladies courantes, on peut employer l'article dans un anglais un peu plus familier :

she has (the) flu   **he's got (the) measles**
elle a la grippe   *il a la rougeole*

ix)   les noms de couleurs :

red is my favourite colour
le rouge est ma couleur préférée

x)   les noms de matériaux, d'aliments, de boissons, de corps chimiques, etc. :

concrete is used less nowadays
on utilise moins le béton de nos jours

oxygen is crucial to life
l'oxygène est indispensable à la vie

I prefer gold jewellery
je préfère les bijoux en or

xi) les noms de langues (qui prennent des majuscules en anglais) et de matières scolaires :

German is harder than English
l'allemand est plus difficile que l'anglais

I hate maths
je déteste les maths

xii) les noms pluriels pris dans un sens général :

he loves antiques
il adore les antiquités

he's frightened of dogs
il a peur des chiens

e) L'article défini n'est normalement pas employé lorsque l'on fait référence à des noms de pays, de comtés, d'États :

| Switzerland | *la Suisse* | Sussex | *le Sussex* |
| England | *l'Angleterre* | Texas | *le Texas* |

he went to South America
il est parti en Amérique du Sud

I live in France
j'habite en France

i) mais il existe quelques exceptions :

(the) Yemen *le Yémen* (the) Sudan *le Soudan*
(the) Gambia *la Gambie* (the) Lebanon *le Liban*

Et l'on emploie l'article lorsque le nom du pays est qualifié :

the Republic of Ireland
la République d'Irlande

the People's Republic of China
la République populaire de Chine

ii) les noms de lieux au pluriel prennent l'article :

the Philippines	*les Philippines*
the Azores	*les Açores*
the Shetlands	*les Shetlands*
the Midlands	*les Midlands*
the Netherlands	*les Pays-Bas*
the United States	*les États-Unis*
the Borders	*la région des Borders*

iii) les fleuves, les rivières et les océans prennent l'article :

the Thames *la Tamise* the Pacific *le Pacifique*
the Danube *le Danube* the Atlantic *l'Atlantique*

iv) les noms de régions prennent l'article :

the Tyrol *le Tyrol* the Ruhr *la Ruhr*
the Orient *l'Orient* the Crimea *la Crimée*
the City (of London)
la Cité de Londres

v) les noms de montagnes et de lacs ne prennent pas l'article :

Ben Nevis *le Ben Nevis* K2 *le K2*
Loch Ness *le loch Ness* Lake Tahoe *le lac Tahoe*

Mais les chaînes de montagnes sont précédées de l'article :

the Himalayas *l'Himalaya* the Alps *les Alpes*

Cependant, il existe des exceptions :

the Matterhorn *le mont Cervin* the Eiger *l'Eiger*

vi) les noms de rues, de parcs, de places, etc. ne prennent normalement pas l'article :

they met in Hyde Park
ils se sont rencontrés à Hyde Park

he lives in Wilton Street
il habite Wilton Street

there was a concert in Trafalgar Square
il y avait un concert à Trafalgar Square

Mais il existe des exceptions où l'article fait partie intégrante du nom :

the Strand *le Strand*

Et parfois on trouve des exceptions fondées sur un usage purement local :

the Edgware Road *l'Edgware Road*

f) On omet l'article dans les **énumérations** (même à deux termes) :

the boys and girls
les garçons et les filles

the hammers, nails and screwdrivers
les marteaux, les clous et les tournevis

g) Les noms d'hôtels, de pubs, de restaurants, de théâtres, de cinémas, de musées sont normalement précédés de the :

the Caledonian (Hotel)	the Red Lion
the Copper Kettle	the Old Vic
the Odeon	the Tate (Gallery)

h) On trouve l'article défini dans les titres de journaux (the Observer, the Independent, the Guardian, etc.) et de quelques magazines (the Spectator, the Economist, etc.)

Cependant, la plupart des magazines ne sont pas précédés de l'article : FHM, Vanity Fair, Punch, Private Eye, etc.

i) Les instruments de musique :

L'article défini s'emploie lorsqu'on fait référence à une aptitude :

she plays the clarinet
elle joue de la clarinette

Cependant, lorsqu'on fait référence à une occasion précise plutôt qu'à une aptitude d'ordre général, on omet l'article :

in this piece he plays bass guitar
il joue de la basse dans ce morceau

j) Les noms de titres sont normalement précédés de l'article défini :

the Queen *la reine*
the President *le président*

Cependant, on omet l'article défini lorsque le titre est suivi du nom de la personne :

Doctor MacPherson *le docteur MacPherson*
Queen Elizabeth *la reine Élisabeth*
Prime Minister Churchill *le Premier ministre Churchill*

Remarquez :

Christ *le Christ*

k) L'omission de l'article défini pour produire un effet particulier :

i) dans des phrases auxquelles on veut donner de l'importance ou dans un jargon :

all pupils will assemble in hall
tous les élèves se rassembleront dans le hall

the number of delegates at conference
le nombre des délégués à la conférence

ii) dans les gros titres de journaux (omission aussi de l'article indéfini a/an) :

Attempt To Break Record Fails
La tentative de pulvériser le record échoue

New Conference Centre Planned
Projet pour un nouveau Palais des Congrès

iii) dans les instructions (omission aussi de l'article indéfini a/an) :

break glass in emergency
casser la vitre en cas d'urgence

Pour la traduction de l'article partitif, voir some, any, no et none pp. A34-5. Pour les articles employés avec les parties du corps, voir p. A30.

3 LES NOMS

A LES TYPES DE NOMS

Les noms anglais n'ont pas de genre grammatical ("le" et "la" se disent the).

1 Les noms concrets et les noms abstraits

On peut classer les noms de différentes manières. On peut ainsi les diviser en noms concrets, c'est-à-dire des noms qui font référence à des êtres animés ou à des choses, comme **woman** (femme), **cat** (chat) et **stone** (pierre), et en noms abstraits, c'est-à-dire des noms qui expriment des concepts, des caractéristiques ou des activités : **love** (l'amour), **ugliness** (la laideur), **classification** (la classification).

Un grand nombre de noms abstraits se forment en ajoutant une terminaison (suffixe) à un adjectif, à un nom ou à un verbe. Cependant, beaucoup de noms abstraits ne prennent pas cette terminaison. C'est le cas, par exemple, de **love** (l'amour), **hate** (la haine), **concept** (le concept). Voici quelques terminaisons de noms abstraits couramment employées (certaines peuvent aussi s'employer pour des noms concrets).

a) *Les noms abstraits formés à partir d'autres noms*

-age	percent + -age	percentage	*pourcentage*
-cy	democrat + -cy	democracy	*démocratie*
-dom	martyr + -dom	martyrdom	*martyre*
-hood	child + -hood	childhood	*enfance*
-ism	alcohol + -ism	alcoholism	*alcoolisme*
-ry	chemist + -ry	chemistry	*chimie*

b) *Les noms abstraits formés à partir d'adjectifs*

-age	short + -age	shortage	*pénurie*
-cy	bankrupt + -cy	bankruptcy	*faillite*
	normal + -cy	normalcy (*Am*)	*normalité*
-hood	likely + -hood	likelihood	*probabilité*
-ism	social + -ism	socialism	*socialisme*
-ity	normal + -ity	normality	*normalité*
-ness	kind + -ness	kindness	*gentillesse*

c) *Les noms abstraits formés à partir de verbes*

-age	break + -age	breakage	*rupture*
-al	arrive + -al	arrival	*arrivée*
-ance	utter + -ance	utterance	*déclaration*
-(at)ion	starve + -ation	starvation	*famine*
	operate + -ion	operation	*opération*
-ing	voir le gérondif, p. A43		
-ment	treat + -ment	treatment	*traitement*

Remarquez que la terminaison du nom, de l'adjectif ou du verbe doit parfois subir quelques changements avant l'ajout du suffixe (**likely → likelihood, arrive → arrival**, etc.). Voir chapitre 19, p. A79

2 Les noms communs et les noms propres

On peut aussi classer les substantifs en noms communs et en noms propres, ces derniers faisant référence à des noms de personnes ou à des noms géographiques, de jours et de mois. Ils s'écrivent avec une majuscule.

COMMUNS		PROPRES	
cup	*tasse*	**Peter**	*Pierre*
palace	*palais*	**China**	*la Chine*
cheese	*fromage*	**Wednesday**	*mercredi*
time	*le temps*	**August**	*août*
love	*l'amour*	**Christmas**	*Noël*

3 Les noms dénombrables et les noms indénombrables

Une classification, déterminante pour l'absence ou la présence de l'article indéfini, permet de distinguer les noms dénombrables et les noms indénombrables. Un nom dénombrable à part entière peut, bien sûr, être considéré comme une "unité" (c'est-à-dire qu'il peut être précédé de l'article indéfini ou de tout adjectif numéral), et doit avoir une forme au singulier et au pluriel (il peut être précédé de **these/few/many**, etc.). Les noms indénombrables à part entière ne sont quant à eux ni au singulier, ni au pluriel, puisque par définition on ne peut les compter, bien qu'ils soient suivis d'un verbe au singulier (ils peuvent être précédés de **this/little/much**, etc.). On dit qu'ils représentent une "totalité" :

DÉNOMBRABLES		
a/one pen/three pens	*un crayon/trois crayons*
a/one coat/three coats	*un manteau/trois manteaux*
a/one horse/three horses	*un cheval/trois chevaux*
a/one child/three children	*un enfant/trois enfants*

INDÉNOMBRABLES			
furniture	*les/des meubles*	**rubbish**	*les/des ordures*
spaghetti	*les/des spaghettis*	**information**	*les/des informations*
spinach	*les/des épinards*	**news**	*les/des nouvelles*
fish	*les/des poissons*	**progress**	*les/des progrès*
fruit	*les/des fruits*	**violence**	*la violence*

Lorsque l'on veut faire référence à une unité de chacun de ces noms indénombrables, il faut faire précéder le nom indénombrable d'un autre nom qui soit dénombrable. Ainsi on emploie, par exemple, **piece** pour indiquer une ou plusieurs unités :

a piece of furniture/two pieces of furniture
un meuble/deux meubles

De même, on dira **an act of violence** (*un acte de violence*), **an item of news** (*une nouvelle*), **a strand of spaghetti** (*un spaghetti*), où **act**, **item** et **strand** sont des dénombrables tout à fait normaux. Le dénombrable qui accompagne **cattle** est **head**, qui ne prend jamais de -s dans ce sens : **ten head of cattle** (*dix têtes de bétail*).

Voici d'autres exemples de noms indénombrables à part entière : **baggage** (*les bagages*), **luggage** (*les bagages*), **garbage** (*les ordures*), **advice** (*les conseils*).

Pour **accommodation**, voir p. A11.

a) *Les noms pouvant être dénombrables ou indénombrables*

i) Certains noms peuvent être dénombrables ou indénombrables, suivant que leur sens fait référence à une "unité" ou une "totalité". De tels noms font souvent référence à la nourriture ou aux matériaux :

DÉNOMBRABLES	INDÉNOMBRABLES
that sheep has only one lamb	**we had lamb for dinner**
ce mouton n'a qu'un agneau	*nous avons eu de l'agneau au dîner*

would you like a glass of
 wine?
prendrez-vous un verre de vin ?

the table is made of glass
c'est une table en verre

he bought a paper
il a acheté un journal

I need some wrapping
 paper
il me faut du papier cadeau

she's a beauty
c'est une beauté

beauty is only skin-deep
la beauté n'est pas tout

ii) Comme en français, les noms indénombrables deviennent dénombrables lorsqu'ils signifient "un verre de", "une variété de", etc. :

I'd like a coffee
je voudrais un café

two white wines, **please**
deux vins blancs, s'il vous plaît

Britain has a large selection of cheeses
la Grande-Bretagne a une grande variété de fromages

a **very good** beer
une très bonne bière

iii) Certains noms habituellement indénombrables peuvent s'employer au pluriel dans quelques expressions figées et idiomatiques :

EMPLOI NORMAL

EMPLOI PARTICULIER

my shoes let in water
mes chaussures prennent l'eau

the boat has just entered
 Japanese waters
*le bateau vient d'entrer dans
 les eaux (territoriales)
 japonaises*

it's beautiful weather
il fait beau

in all weathers
par tous les temps

iv) Certains noms abstraits indénombrables (**indignation, hate, anger**, etc.) sont précédés de l'article indéfini lorsqu'ils sont accompagnés d'un adjectif ou d'un groupe adjectival qui permet de qualifier et de spécifier le nom :

he expressed an indignation so intense **that people
 were taken aback**
*il exprima une indignation si véhémente que les gens en
 furent stupéfaits*

b) *Les noms en -ics*

Lorsque ces noms sont considérés comme des concepts abstraits, ils sont indénombrables et suivis d'un verbe au singulier :

economics is a difficult subject
l'économie est une matière difficile

En revanche, on préférera un verbe au pluriel lorsque le nom en -ics est utilisé dans un sens concret, et non plus de manière générale :

the economics of the project are to be considered
il faut considérer l'aspect financier du projet

what are your politics?
quelles sont vos opinions politiques ?

c) *Les indénombrables se terminant par -s*

Certains noms se terminant par ce qui semble être le -s du pluriel sont indénombrables. C'est le cas des noms en -ics que nous venons de voir, mais aussi du mot **news** (*nouvelles*), des maladies telles que **measles** (*rougeole*), **mumps** (*oreillons*), **rickets** (*rachitisme*), **shingles** (*zona*) et de quelques noms de jeux tels que **billiards** (*billard*), **bowls** (*boules*), **darts** (*fléchettes*), **dominoes** (*dominos*), **draughts** (*Br*) ou **checkers** (*Am*) (*dames*) :

the news hasn't arrived yet
la nouvelle n'est pas encore arrivée

mumps is **not a life-threatening disease**
les oreillons ne sont pas une maladie mortelle

darts is **still played in many pubs**
on joue encore aux fléchettes dans beaucoup de pubs

d) *Noms de "paires"*

Certains noms au pluriel faisant référence à des objets composés de deux parties identiques n'ont pas de forme au singulier et doivent être précédés de a pair of si l'on veut mettre l'accent sur leur nombre :

a pair of trousers
un pantalon

two pairs of trousers
deux pantalons

this is a nice pair of trousers
c'est un beau pantalon

those are nice trousers
c'est un beau pantalon

de même :

bellows *soufflet*
binoculars *jumelles*
breeches *culotte*
glasses *lunettes*
knickers *culotte, slip*
pants *culotte (Br), pantalon (Am)*
pincers *tenailles*
pliers *pinces, tenailles*

pyjamas ou pajamas *(Am)
 pyjama*
scissors *ciseaux*
shears *cisailles*
shorts *short*
spectacles *lunettes*
tights *bas*
tongs *fer à friser*
tweezers *pince à épiler*

e) *Noms habituellement employés au pluriel*

i) arms *armes*
arrears *arriéré(s)*
auspices *auspices*
banns *bans (de mariage)*
clothes *vêtements*
customs *douane(s)*
dregs *la lie*
earnings *revenus*
entrails *entrailles*
goods *biens, marchandise(s)*
greens *légumes verts*
guts *(Fam) boyaux, courage*
lodgings *logement(s)*
looks *apparence(s)*
manners *manières*
means *moyens (financiers)*

odds *chances, cote (d'un
 cheval, etc.)*
outskirts *environs, ban-
 lieue(s)*
pains *peine, effort*
premises *locaux*
quarters *résidence(s)*
remains *restes*
riches *richesse(s)*
spirits *humeur, alcool*
(soap) suds *mousse (de
 savon)*
surroundings *environs,
 cadre*
tropics *tropiques*
valuables *objets de valeur*

Ces noms sont normalement accompagnés d'un verbe au pluriel.

Quelques noms doivent se mettre au singulier dans certains contextes et au pluriel dans d'autres. Le changement de nombre apporte des nuances différentes mais le sens de base reste le même :

contents (*le contenu*) mais content (*la quantité qui peut être contenue*) :

show me the contents of your bag
montrez-moi le contenu de votre sac

spinach has a high iron content
les épinards contiennent beaucoup de fer

funds (*des fonds*) mais fund (*un fonds*) :

I'm a bit short of funds
je n'ai pas beaucoup d'argent

we started a church roof repair fund
*nous avons commencé à faire une collecte pour réparer le
 toit de l'église*

thanks (*les remerciements*) : vous noterez la possibilité d'employer l'article indéfini devant un adjectif (pas de singulier dans ce cas) :

a very special thanks to our sponsor
un grand merci à notre sponsor

wages (*le salaire, la paie*) : souvent au singulier aussi, particulièrement lorsqu'il est précédé d'un adjectif :

all we want is a decent wage
tout ce que nous voulons, c'est un salaire correct

accommodations (*l'hébergement*) est employé en anglais américain. En anglais britannique, on emploie **accommodation** comme indénombrable pour désigner un logement.

ii) Quelques noms pluriels ne portent jamais la marque du pluriel :

cattle *bétail*   police *police, policiers*
clergy *(membres du) clergé*   vermin *vermine, parasites*
livestock *(têtes de) bétail*

Mais même **clergy** et **police** peuvent parfois être accompagnés d'un article indéfini, s'ils sont qualifiés par un adjectif, par un groupe prépositionnel ou par une proposition relative. Dans de tels cas, il existe une différence de sens importante entre **clergymen** (*ecclésiastiques*) et **body of clergymen** (*ensemble du clergé*), et **policemen** (*policiers*) et **police force** (*la police*). Comparez :

seventy-five clergy were present
soixante-quinze membres du clergé étaient présents

the problem is whether the country needs a clergy with such old-fashioned views
le problème est de savoir si le pays a besoin d'un clergé aux idées aussi dépassées

at least thirty police were needed for that task
on a eu besoin d'au moins trente policiers pour cette tâche

the country had a semi-military police
le pays avait une police semi-militaire

Le nom pluriel **folk** (*gens, personnes*) ne prend normalement pas de -s en anglais britannique :

some folk just don't know how to behave
certaines personnes ne savent pas se tenir

Dans un registre plus familier, on pourrait également employer **folks** dans l'exemple ci-dessus. **Folks** désigne aussi familièrement "la famille", "les parents" (**my folks are from Chicago** *ma famille est de Chicago*).

f) *Les noms collectifs*

i) Ce sont des noms qui, au singulier, désignent un groupe de personnes ou de choses. Ils sont accompagnés d'un verbe au singulier quand le nom désigne un ensemble, ou d'un verbe au pluriel si l'on désire mettre l'accent sur les membres du groupe :

the jury is one of the safeguards of our legal system (*sing*)
le jury est garant de notre système législatif

the jury have returned their verdict (*pl*)
le jury a rendu son verdict

Les pronoms et les adjectifs possessifs s'accordent normalement en nombre avec le verbe (voir **their** dans l'exemple ci-dessus).

L'emploi du verbe au pluriel est plus répandu en anglais britannique qu'en anglais américain.

Les mots suivants sont des exemples typiques de noms collectifs :

army	*armée*	government	*gouvernement*
audience	*public*	group	*groupe*
choir	*chorale*	majority	*majorité*
chorus	*chœur*	minority	*minorité*
class	*classe*	orchestra	*orchestre*

committee	*comité*	Parliament	*Parlement*
enemy	*ennemi*	proletariat	*prolétariat*
family	*famille*	public	*public*
firm	*firme*	team	*équipe*
gang	*gang*		

(younger/older) generation
(*jeune/ancienne*) *génération*

● Les mots **crew** (*équipage*), **staff** (*personnel*), **people** (*peuple*) sont souvent des noms collectifs, comme dans :

the crew is excellent (*sing*)
l'équipage est excellent

the crew have all enjoyed themselves (*pl*)
l'équipage s'est bien amusé

the staff of that school has a good record (*sing*)
le personnel de cette école a obtenu de bons résultats

the staff don't always behave themselves (*pl*)
le personnel ne se conduit pas toujours bien

it is difficult to imagine a people that has suffered more (*sing*)
il est difficile d'imaginer un peuple qui ait plus souffert

the people have not voted against the re-introduction of capital punishment (*pl*)
le peuple n'a pas voté contre le rétablissement de la peine capitale

Ces trois mots diffèrent des autres noms collectifs par le fait qu'ils peuvent être des dénombrables à part entière, avec ou sans la terminaison -s au pluriel, suivant leur sens. Si le pluriel est en -s, il est le même que le pluriel en -s d'autres noms collectifs : **five crews/staffs/peoples** (*nations*)/**armies/governments**, etc.

Cependant, le pluriel sans -s fait référence à des membres individuels :

the captain had to manage with only fifteen crew
le capitaine a dû se débrouiller avec seulement quinze membres d'équipage

the English Department had to get rid of five staff
le département d'anglais a dû renvoyer cinq personnes

he spoke to six people about it
il a parlé à six personnes à ce sujet

On peut tout aussi bien dire **crew members, staff members** ou **members of staff** au pluriel.

Pour **clergy** et **police**, voir e) ii) ci-dessus.

● Youth (*la jeunesse, les jeunes*) peut être suivi aussi bien d'un verbe au singulier que d'un verbe au pluriel :

our country's youth has/have little to look forward to
la jeunesse de notre pays a peu de perspectives d'avenir

mais il est dénombrable dans le sens de "jeune homme" :

they arrested a youth/two youths
ils ont arrêté un jeune/deux jeunes

● Le nom pluriel **media** (*les médias, la presse*) se comporte comme un nom collectif. Il s'emploie très souvent au singulier, mais il peut aussi être suivi du pluriel :

the media follows/follow her everywhere
les journalistes la suivent partout

Le mot **data** (*données*), du latin **datum** (*sing*), peut s'utiliser au pluriel (**these data are**...) mais il est très souvent employé comme indénombrable (**this/much/little data is**...) : on considère que les données forment un tout. On devra donc utiliser le terme **piece** pour dissocier les données (**seven pieces of data**).

ii) Les pays :

Les noms de nations faisant référence à une équipe (sportive) sont normalement accompagnés d'un verbe au pluriel en anglais britannique :

France have beaten England
la France a battu l'Angleterre

bien que le singulier et le pluriel soient tout aussi corrects.

Remarquez que les noms de pays au pluriel sont suivis d'un verbe au singulier :

the United States exerts a great influence on the world political stage
les États-Unis exercent une grande influence sur la scène politique internationale

Il en est de même pour **the Bahamas, the Philippines,** etc.

B LES FORMES DU PLURIEL

1 Les pluriels en -(e)s

a) La marque du pluriel est normalement -(e)s en anglais :

soup	→	soups	*soupe*
peg	→	pegs	*pince à linge*
bus	→	buses	*bus*
quiz	→	quizzes	*jeu télévisé*
bush	→	bushes	*buisson*
match	→	matches	*allumette*
page	→	pages	*page*

-es s'emploie pour des mots en -s, -x, -z, -ch ou -sh. On le prononce alors /ɪz/.

Remarquez que les noms de famille au pluriel prennent -(e)s en anglais, alors qu'ils sont invariables en français :

the Smiths
les Smith

b) Pour les noms se terminant par une consonne + -y, le -y se transforme en -ies :

lady	→	ladies	*dame, demoiselle*
fairy	→	fairies	*fée*

Mais les noms qui se terminent par une voyelle + -y ont un pluriel régulier en -s :

trolley	→	trolleys	*chariot*

Pour plus de détails, voir le chapitre 19, p. A79.

c) Les noms en -o prennent parfois un -s, parfois -es au pluriel. Il est difficile d'établir des règles précises dans ce cas ; toutefois, on peut dire que l'on ajoute seulement un -s si :

le -o suit une autre voyelle : embryo → **embryos** (*embryons*), studio → **studios** (*studios*)

le nom est une abréviation : photo → **photos**, piano → **pianos** (de pianoforte)

Dans d'autres cas, il est difficile de généraliser, bien que l'on puisse observer une préférence pour le -s avec des mots qui ont encore une connotation étrangère pour les Britanniques :

avec -es : echo, cargo (*cargaison*), hero, mosquito (*moustique*), Negro, potato (*pomme de terre*), tomato, torpedo (*torpille*)

avec -s : canto (*chant*), memento, proviso (*stipulation*), quarto, solo, zero, zoo

avec -s ou -es : banjo, buffalo (*buffle*), commando,

flamingo (*flamand rose*), motto, volcano

d) Pour certains noms en -f(e), le -f se transforme en -ve au pluriel :

calf	→	calves	*veau*

Il en est de même pour :

elf	*elfe*	self	*soi*
half	*moitié*	sheaf	*gerbe*
knife	*couteau*	shelf	*étagère*
leaf	*feuille d'arbre*	thief	*voleur*
life	*vie*	wife	*épouse*
loaf	*pain*	wolf	*loup*

Certains peuvent avoir un pluriel en -ves ou en -s :

dwarf	→	dwarfs/dwarves	*nain*
hoof	→	hoofs/hooves	*sabot*
scarf	→	scarfs/scarves	*écharpe*
wharf	→	wharfs/wharves	*quai*

Un grand nombre de ces mots conservent le -f :

belief	→	beliefs	*croyance*

Il en est de même pour :

chief	*chef*	roof	*toit*
cliff	*falaise*	safe	*coffre-fort*
proof	*preuve*	sniff	*reniflement, etc.*

e) Quelques mots français se terminant avec un -s muet au singulier ne changent pas leur pluriel à l'écrit ; on ajoute cependant le son /z/ au pluriel à l'oral : corps (*sing* [kɔː(r)], *pl* [kɔːz]).

f) Les mots français en -eu ou -eau prennent un -s ou un -x (que l'on prononce tous les deux /z/), par exemple :

adieu, bureau, tableau

gateau prend normalement un -x.

g) Les noms d'animaux

Certains noms d'animaux, notamment les noms de poissons, se comportent (presque toujours) comme les noms mentionnés dans la section 3a) ci-dessous, c'est-à-dire qu'ils ne prennent pas la marque du pluriel :

cod	*morue*	salmon	*saumon*
hake	*colin*	trout	*truite*
herring	*hareng*	deer	*cerf*
mackerel	*maquereau*	sheep	*mouton*
pike	*brochet*	grouse	*coq de bruyère*

D'autres noms d'animaux au pluriel prennent un -s dans certains cas et n'en prennent pas dans d'autres. Dans le contexte de la chasse, on omet souvent le -s. Comparez :

these antelopes have just been bought by the zoo
le zoo vient juste d'acheter ces antilopes

they went to Africa to shoot antelope
ils sont allés en Afrique pour chasser l'antilope

Il en est de même pour :

buffalo	*buffle*	fowl	*volaille*
giraffe	*girafe*	partridge	*perdrix*
lion	*lion*	pheasant	*faisan*
duck	*canard*	et bien d'autres	

Le pluriel régulier de fish est fish, mais fishes s'emploie pour faire référence à des espèces de poissons (**cod and haddock are two different fishes that can be found in British waters**).

h) Les adjectifs numéraux

i) hundred (*cent*), thousand (*mille*), million, dozen (*douzaine*), score (*vingt*) et gross (*douze douzaines*) n'ont pas de pluriel en -s lorsqu'ils sont précédés d'un autre adjectif numéral. Remarquez la différence de construction avec le français pour "million", "milliard" et "douzaine" :

five hundred/thousand/million people
cinq cents personnes/cinq mille personnes/cinq millions de personnes

two dozen eggs
deux douzaines d'œufs

we'll order three gross
nous en commanderons trente-six douzaines

mais :

there were hundreds/thousands/millions of them
il y en avait des centaines/milliers/millions

I've told you dozens of times
je te l'ai dit des dizaines de fois

Peter and Kate have scores of friends
Peter et Kate ont des tas d'amis

ii) Les unités de mesure **foot** et **pound** peuvent être soit au pluriel, soit au singulier :

Kate is five foot/feet eight
Kate mesure un mètre soixante-douze

that comes to three pound(s) fifty
ça fait trois livres cinquante

2 Les pluriels avec un changement de voyelle

Il existe un petit groupe de mots dont le pluriel se forme au moyen d'un changement de voyelle :

foot	→	feet	*pied*
goose	→	geese	*oie*
louse	→	lice	*pou*
man	→	men [men]	*homme*
mouse	→	mice	*souris*
tooth	→	teeth	*dent*
woman	→	women ['wɪmɪn]	*femme*

3 Les pluriels invariables

a) singulier et pluriel sans -s :

aircraft (*avion*), counsel (*avocat*), offspring (*progéniture*), quid (*Fam livre sterling*), par exemple :

we saw a few aircraft   **these are my offspring**
nous avons vu quelques avions   *c'est ma progéniture*

both counsel asked for an adjournment
les deux avocats ont demandé un renvoi

this will cost you ten quid
ça te coûtera cent livres

Les mots kind, sort, type (*genre, sorte, type*), apparaissant dans une phrase du type these/those + nom + of, ne prennent souvent pas de -s :

these kind of people always complain
ce genre de personne se plaint toujours

she always wears those sort of clothes
elle porte toujours ce genre de vêtements

b) singulier et pluriel en -s :

barracks	*caserne*	means*	*moyen*
crossroads	*carrefour*	series	*série*
gallows	*potence*	shambles	*désordre*
headquarters	*quartier général*	species	*espèce*
		works	*usine*
innings	*tour de batte*		

*Comparez avec means (= moyens financiers) p. A10.

Voici quelques exemples :

every means was tried to improve matters
on a usé de tous les moyens pour améliorer les choses

this is a dreadful shambles
c'est un désordre abominable

they have built a new gasworks north of here
ils ont construit une nouvelle usine à gaz au nord d'ici

Certains de ces noms, en particulier **barracks, gallows, headquarters, works** peuvent aussi s'employer dans un sens singulier avec un verbe au pluriel :

these are the new steelworks
c'est la nouvelle aciérie

On fait référence ici à une seule usine.

c) dice et pence

Dice, pluriel irrégulier de die (*dé*), est également devenu le terme communément employé au singulier, die ne s'utilisant plus que dans les expressions idiomatiques telles que the die is cast (*les dés sont jetés*) ou straight as a die (*d'une grande honnêteté, franc comme l'or*). On a donc, avec dice, la même forme au singulier et au pluriel :

he threw the dice
il a lancé le dé ou les dés

Lorsque l'on parle de la monnaie et de la valeur de l'argent, le pluriel de penny est irrégulier (pence). Par ailleurs, il n'est pas rare d'entendre one pence plutôt que one penny quand on parle du coût de quelque chose. Cependant, lorsque l'on désigne une pièce d'un penny (ou d'un cent aux États-Unis), le pluriel est régulier :

these are 18th-century pennies
ce sont des pennies du XVIIIe siècle

4 Les pluriels en -en

Il n'en existe que trois, et un seul est commun :

child	→	children	*enfant*

Les autres sont :

ox	→	oxen	*bœuf*
brother	→	brethren	*frère*

ce dernier faisant référence aux membres d'une congrégation religieuse, comme dans :

our Catholic brethren from other countries
nos frères catholiques d'autres pays

Le pluriel normal de brother est brothers.

5 Les pluriels en -a ou -s

Ce sont des noms latins au singulier en -um ou des noms grecs au singulier en -on. Beaucoup d'entre eux ont un pluriel en -s, en particulier s'ils sont employés couramment, par exemple :

museum (*musée*), stadium (*stade*), demon, electron

Certains, souvent employés dans un langage scientifique et dont le singulier est -um/-on, ont un pluriel en -a, par exemple :

an addendum   *un addenda (ou addendum)*

numerous addenda   *de nombreux addenda*

De même, on a bacterium (*bactérie*), curriculum (*programme d'étude*), erratum, ovum (*ovule*), criterion (*critère*), phenomenon

Certains mots acceptent les deux formes du pluriel (en -s et en -a) :

memorandum, millennium (*millénaire*), symposium, automaton (*automate*)

Le pluriel de medium est toujours mediums lorsque ce mot fait référence à un extralucide. Lorsqu'il signifie "moyen", le pluriel est media ou mediums.

Pour media et data, voir p. A11.

6 Les pluriels en -e ou -s

Ces noms sont latins ou grecs et ont une terminaison en -a au singulier. Ceux qui sont fréquemment employés ont un pluriel en -s, comme **arena** et **drama**. Les noms plus techniques ou scientifiques ont tendance à avoir un pluriel en -e (on obtient alors la terminaison -ae prononcée /iː/ ou /aɪ/ selon le mot), par exemple **alumna** (*ancienne élève ou étudiante*) et **larva**.

La terminaison de certains noms varie selon leur sens et le contexte. Ainsi, **antenna** prend toujours un -e lorsqu'il fait référence aux insectes, mais un -s lorsqu'il signifie "antenne de télévision" en américain. Il en est de même pour **formula** qui prend un -e ou -s lorsqu'il s'agit d'une formule de chimie, de mathématiques, etc., mais qui a toujours un pluriel en -s quand le terme désigne une expression.

7 Les pluriels en -i ou -s (mots italiens)

Quelques mots empruntés à l'italien, notamment **libretto**, **tempo** et **virtuoso**, peuvent conserver leur pluriel italien en -i /iː/ ou prendre le -s du pluriel régulier anglais.

Vous noterez que **confetti**, **graffiti**, **macaroni**, **ravioli**, **spaghetti**, etc. sont indénombrables, c'est-à-dire qu'ils sont suivis d'un verbe au singulier.

8 Les pluriels en -i ou -es (mots latins)

Ceux qui sont courants prennent normalement la terminaison -es au pluriel, comme :

> **campus**, **chorus** (*refrain, chœur*), **virus**

Ceux qui appartiennent au langage plus érudit gardent en général leur pluriel latin en -i (que l'on prononce /iː/ ou /aɪ/ selon le mot) comme par exemple :

> **alumnus** (*ancien élève ou étudiant*), **bacillus** (*bacille*), **stimulus** (*stimulant, stimulus*).

D'autres prennent les deux formes au pluriel : **cactus**, **fungus** (*champignon, fongus*), **nucleus** (*noyau*), **syllabus** (*programme d'enseignement*). Il en est de même pour les noms grecs latinisés : **hippopotamus** et **papyrus**.

Le pluriel de **genius** est **geniuses** au sens de "personne extrêmement intelligente", mais **genii** lorsqu'il signifie "(bon/mauvais) esprit".

9 Les pluriels des noms en -ex ou -ix

Ces noms latins peuvent conserver leur pluriel d'origine, leur singulier en -ex/-ix se transforme alors en -ices au pluriel, ou bien ils prennent -es, par exemple :

> **index** → **indices** ou **indexes**

Il en est de même pour **appendix**, **matrix**, **vortex**.

Mais remarquez que **appendixes** est le seul pluriel pour la partie du corps, tandis que **appendixes** et **appendices** peuvent s'employer pour désigner les parties d'un livre ou d'une thèse.

10 Le pluriel des noms grecs en -is

La terminaison -is /ɪs/ de ces mots se transforme en -es /iːz/ au pluriel, par exemple :

an analy**sis**	*une analyse*
different analy**ses**	*différentes analyses*

Il en est de même pour : **axis**, **basis**, **crisis**, **diagnosis**, **hypothesis**, **oasis**, **parenthesis**, **synopsis**, **thesis**.

Mais remarquez : **metropolis** → **metropolises**

11 Les pluriels en -im ou -s

Les mots hébreux **kibbutz**, **cherub** (*chérubin*) et **seraph** (*séraphin*) peuvent prendre soit -(e)s (pluriel régulier), soit -im au pluriel.

12 Les pluriels des noms composés

a) *Le pluriel porte sur le deuxième élément*

Lorsque le deuxième élément est un nom (et qu'il n'est pas précédé d'une préposition) :

lip balms (*baumes pour les lèvres*), **lion cubs** (*lionceaux*), **pencil sharpeners** (*taille-crayon*), **table napkins** (*serviettes de table*), **road users** (*usagers de la route*), etc.

et lorsque le mot composé est formé d'un verbe + adverbe :

lay-bys (*aires de stationnement*), **lie-ins** (*grasses matinées*), **sit-ins**, **stand-bys**, **tip-offs** (*tuyaux*)

Remarquez que les noms de mesures se terminant par -ful peuvent avoir un -s à la fin de l'un ou l'autre de leurs éléments : **spoonfuls** ou **spoonsful**.

b) *Le pluriel porte sur le premier élément*

Lorsque le deuxième élément est un groupe prépositionnel :

editors-in-chief	*rédacteurs en chef*
fathers-in-law*	*beaux-pères*
aides-de-camp	*aides de camp*
men-of-war	*bâtiments de guerre*

*Remarquez que **law** se met au pluriel dans l'expression familière **in-laws**, forme abrégée de **parents-in-law** (**my in-laws are coming this weekend** *mes beaux-parents viennent ce week-end*).

Mais si le premier élément ne désigne pas une personne, on place le -s sur le dernier élément, comme dans :

will-o'-the-wisps	**jack-in-the-boxes**
feux follets	*diables à ressort*

Les noms composés formés d'un nom (dérivé d'un verbe) et d'un adverbe prennent eux aussi un -s à la fin du premier élément (à la différence de ceux composés d'un verbe + adverbe, voir a) ci-dessus) :

hangers-on	**passers-by**
parasites	*passants*

Les noms composés avec -to-be prennent un -s à la fin du premier élément :

brides-to-be	**mothers-to-be**
futures mariées	*futures mamans*

Le premier élément porte aussi la marque du pluriel si le second élément est un adjectif :

Lords temporal and spiritual
membres laïques et ecclésiastiques de la Chambre des lords

Mais beaucoup peuvent aussi porter la marque du pluriel sur le deuxième élément (ce qui est de plus en plus courant) :

attorneys general ou **attorney generals**
directors general ou **director generals**
poets laureate ou **poet laureates**
courts-martial ou **court-martials**

C USAGE : PLURIEL OU SINGULIER ?

a) *Le pluriel distributif*

i) type 1, dans un groupe nominal

Dans la plupart des cas, l'anglais préfère le pluriel :

between the ages of 30 and 45
entre l'âge de 30 et 45 ans

the reigns of Henry VIII and Elizabeth I
*le règne d'Henri VIII et celui d'Élisabeth Ire*

ii) type 2, dans une proposition

En anglais, lorsque le sujet d'une phrase est pluriel, on a très souvent un pluriel dans la proposition complément d'objet, contrairement au français :

cats seem to spend their lives **sleeping**
les chats semblent passer leur vie à dormir

many people are unhappy about their careers
beaucoup de gens ne sont pas satisfaits de leur carrière

they both broke their legs
ils se sont tous les deux cassé la jambe

we took off our coats
nous avons enlevé notre manteau

we changed our minds
nous avons changé d'avis

Dans certaines expressions, on peut employer soit le pluriel avec un adjectif possessif, soit le singulier avec l'article défini :

they were up to their waists/the waist **in water**
l'eau leur arrivait à la ceinture

they were up to their necks/the neck **in debt**
ils étaient endettés jusqu'au cou

b) *Le complément du nom placé avant ou après le nom*

i) Lorsqu'un nom est suivi d'un complément du nom au pluriel, ce dernier est toujours singulier devant le nom car il a valeur d'adjectif (voir p. A17) :

a collection of bottles → **a bottle collection**
une collection de bouteilles

ii) En anglais, il est possible de mettre des compléments du nom commençant par un nombre en position adjectivale. Dans ce cas-là, le nom qui fait partie du syntagme adjectival ne prend pas de -s et les différents termes doivent être séparés par un trait d'union :

a girl of eight (= eight years old) → **an eight-**year**-old**
une fille de huit ans **girl**

a baby of twelve months → **a twelve-**month**-old**
un bébé de douze mois **baby**

Cette construction est très courante et, dans certains cas, l'emploi d'un complément du nom avec of ne semblerait pas naturel. On dira par exemple :

a thirty-minute **talk**
un exposé de trente minutes

a two-week **holiday**
deux semaines de vacances

a two-mile **walk**
une promenade de trois kilomètres

Comparez aussi avec l'emploi du génitif expliqué au paragraphe D 2b).

D LE GÉNITIF

1 Les formes

a) Le génitif singulier se forme en ajoutant -'s après le nom du "possesseur" :

the cat's **tail**   *la queue du chat*

et le génitif pluriel en ajoutant seulement l'apostrophe au pluriel :

the cats' **tails**   *la queue des chats*

Il y a souvent confusion au sujet de la position de l'apostrophe. Comparez ces deux exemples :

the boy's **school**   *l'école du garçon*
the boys' **school**   *l'école de garçons*

Dans le premier exemple, boy est au singulier, on parle donc de l'école d'un garçon en particulier. Dans le deuxième exemple, le nom boys est au pluriel, on parle donc de l'école de garçons en général.

Si le pluriel ne se termine pas en -s, le génitif pluriel se forme avec -'s comme le singulier :

the men's **toilet**   *les toilettes pour hommes*
the children's **room**   *la chambre des enfants*

b) Cas particuliers

i) La forme du génitif des noms propres se terminant par -s varie en fonction de la longueur et de l'accentuation des mots. Les noms d'une ou deux syllabes prennent 's (prononcé /ɪz/) :

Dickens's (ou Dickens') **novels**
les romans de Dickens

Ross's/James's/Thomas's **car**
la voiture de Ross/James/Thomas

Les noms de plus de deux syllabes et ceux qui se terminent par le son /iːz/ ne prennent que l'apostrophe :

Hercules' **labours** ['hɜːkjʊliːz] Socrates' **wife** ['sɒkrətiːz]
les travaux d'Hercule   *l'épouse de Socrate*

Mais les noms de plus de deux syllabes accentués sur l'avant-dernière syllabe (la pénultième) prennent -'s :

Dionysus's **mother** ['daɪə'naɪsəsɪz]
la mère de Dionysos

Ce sont là les règles de base, mais le génitif des noms propres dépend aussi de l'usage.

ii) Avant le mot sake (*amour de/nom de*), le génitif singulier n'est normalement indiqué que par l'apostrophe avec des noms communs se terminant par -s :

for goodness' **sake!** (mais **for** God's/Christ's/heaven's **sake!**)
pour l'amour du ciel ou *de Dieu !*

for politeness' **sake**
par politesse

c) Pour les types de noms composés mentionnés au paragraphe B 12 du génitif au deuxième élément, même si c'est le premier élément qui porte la marque du pluriel -s :

I met the editor-in-chief's **wife**
j'ai rencontré la femme du rédacteur en chef

my parents-in-law's **house is huge**
la maison de mes beaux-parents est immense

2 Le génitif avec of

a) *Les êtres animés (personnes, animaux)*

Le génitif est très courant avec les personnes :

John's **car**   my mother's **ring**
la voiture de John   *la bague de ma mère*

L'emploi de la préposition of ne semblerait pas naturel dans ces deux exemples.

Avec les animaux, on peut employer le génitif ou la construction avec of :

the wings of an insect/an insect's wings
les ailes d'un insecte

the movements of the worm/the worm's movements
les mouvements du ver de terre

b) *Les objets inanimés, les concepts, etc.*

La construction normale se forme avec **of** :

the pages of the book
les pages du livre

the roof of the car
le toit de la voiture

Cependant, souvenez-vous qu'en anglais on utilise très souvent la forme composée :

the laptop screen
l'écran de l'ordinateur portable

Le génitif est également possible avec certains noms :

the mind's ability to forget
la capacité de l'esprit à oublier

the nation's strength lies in its young people
ce sont les jeunes qui font la force du pays

en particulier si de tels noms font référence à des lieux ou à des institutions :

England's heritage (= the heritage of England)
l'héritage de l'Angleterre

the University's catering facilities (= the catering facilities of the University)
le service de restauration de l'université

Les noms faisant référence au temps et à la valeur de l'argent sont souvent accompagnés du génitif :

today's menu
le menu du jour

two months' work
deux mois de travail

you've had your money's worth
tu en as eu pour ton argent

Comparez ce dernier exemple avec l'emploi de la structure adjectivale expliqué au paragraphe C b) ii).

Les mesures de distances sont parfois au génitif, en particulier dans des expressions figées :

a stone's throw (away)
à deux pas (d'ici)

at arm's length
à distance

3 Le génitif sans nom

a) Si le nom déterminé par le génitif a déjà été mentionné ou si le contexte est assez clair, on n'est pas obligé de le rajouter :

it's not my father's car, it's my mother's
ce n'est pas la voiture de mon père, c'est celle de ma mère

On omet aussi le nom après le génitif lorsqu'il est sous-entendu. C'est le cas des noms de lieux :

at the baker's (= baker's shop)
chez le boulanger

at Alex's (= at Alex's place)
chez Alex

b) Le "double génitif" (c'est-à-dire la construction avec **of** et le génitif dans la même phrase) est fréquent si le génitif fait référence à une personne bien définie. Mais le premier nom est normalement précédé d'un article indéfini, d'un pronom indéfini ou d'un adjectif numéral :

they are relatives of Karen's
ils font partie de la famille de Karen

he's a friend of Peter's
c'est un ami de Peter

he's an acquaintance of my father's
c'est une connaissance de mon père

he's an uncle of Mrs Pitt's
c'est un oncle de Mme Pitt

Un pronom démonstratif peut parfois précéder le premier nom. Ceci implique un certain degré de familiarité :

that car of your father's, how much does he want for it?
cette voiture, ton père, combien est-ce qu'il la vend ?

L'article défini ne peut normalement pas s'employer avec le pre-mier nom, à moins qu'une proposition relative (ou autre déter-minatif) ne suive le génitif :

the poem of Larkin's we read yesterday is lovely
le poème de Larkin que nous avons lu hier est très joli

this is the only poem of Larkin's to have moved me
c'est le seul poème de Larkin qui m'ait ému

c) On trouve souvent le "groupe génitif" dans deux types de cons-tructions : (1) nom + déterminatif introduit par une préposi-tion, et (2) noms reliés par **and**. Dans de telles combinaisons, on peut ajouter le **-'s** au dernier élément :

John and Kate's new house
la nouvelle maison de John et de Kate

the head of department's office
le bureau du chef de service

an hour and a half's work
un travail d'une heure et demie

the Queen of Holland's yacht
le yacht de la reine de Hollande

Si le nom du possesseur est au pluriel, on emploie normalement la construction avec **of** :

the regalia of the Queens of Holland
les insignes royaux des reines de Hollande

Cependant, si les deux noms ne forment pas une unité, ils pren-nent chacun la marque du génitif **-'s** :

Shakespeare's and Marlowe's plays
les pièces de Shakespeare et de Marlowe

E LE FÉMININ

En anglais, on trouve énormément de noms communs qui s'em-ploient à la fois pour un homme et pour une femme :

artist	*artiste*	neighbour	*voisin(e)*
banker	*banquier(-ère)*	novelist	*romancier(-ère)*
cousin	*cousin(e)*	teacher	*enseignant(e)*
friend	*ami(e)*	zoologist	*zoologiste*
lawyer	*avocat(e)*	etc.	

Mais il existe certains cas où l'on emploie différentes terminaisons pour déterminer le genre d'un nom :

MASCULIN			FÉMININ	
actor	*acteur*	→	actress	*actrice*
duke	*duc*	→	duchess	*duchesse*
god	*dieu*	→	goddess	*déesse*
hero	*héros*	→	heroine	*héroïne*
prince	*prince*	→	princess	*princesse*
widower	*veuf*	→	widow	*veuve*
businessman	*homme d'affaires*	→	businesswoman	*femme d'affaires*

Mais on peut aussi dire **she is a good actor** (*c'est une très bonne actrice*), ou bien **she was the hero of the day** (*ce fut l'héroïne du jour*).

On utilise aussi des termes complètement différents pour distinguer le féminin du masculin : **son/daughter** (*fils/fille*), **bull/cow** (*tau-reau/vache*), etc.

Pour les noms qui ont normalement la même forme au masculin et au féminin, il est possible de rajouter les adjectifs **male/female** ou les noms **man/woman** si l'on veut absolument identifier le sexe d'une personne :

a female friend	*une amie*	**a male friend**	*un ami*
a female student	*une étudiante*	**a male student**	*un étudiant*
		a woman doctor	*une femme médecin*
a man doctor	*un médecin*		

Mais attention, cet emploi est maintenant considéré comme extrême-ment sexiste. Il est préférable d'employer le mot neutre **person**, qui s'utilise aussi lorsque l'on ne connaît pas le sexe de la personne en question :

a chairman/chairwoman → a chairperson un(e) président(e)

a salesman/saleswoman → a salesperson un(e) représentant(e) de commerce

a spokesman/spokeswoman → a spokesperson un porte-parole

4 LES ADJECTIFS

! Les adjectifs anglais ne s'accordent jamais avec le nom.

L'adjectif se place toujours devant le nom, en dehors de certaines exceptions (voir 2b) et c) ci-dessous).

1 Épithète et attribut

Les termes "épithète" et "attribut" font référence à la position de l'adjectif par rapport au nom. Si l'adjectif est placé devant le nom, il est épithète (**this old car** *cette vieille voiture*). S'il est placé après le verbe, il est attribut (**this car is old** *cette voiture est vieille*).

Certains adjectifs (ou certains sens d'un adjectif) sont uniquement épithètes, alors que d'autres ne peuvent être qu'attributs.

a) *Épithète seulement*

i) Certains adjectifs ayant un rapport très étroit avec le nom auquel ils se rapportent dans des constructions toutes faites sont uniquement épithètes. Par exemple :

he's a moral philosopher
c'est un philosophe spécialiste en éthique

ii) Les participes passés sont parfois employés comme adjectifs épithètes :

a disabled toilet (= toilet for disabled people)
des toilettes pour handicapés

iii) On emploie très souvent en anglais des noms faisant fonction d'adjectifs :

a logistics problem
un problème de logistique

a polystyrene container   a cardboard box
un emballage en polystyrène   une boîte en carton

a foreign affairs correspondent
un correspondant à l'étranger

Pour l'emploi des compléments du nom en position adjectivale, voir aussi p. A15.

b) *Attribut seulement*

Les adjectifs qui sont uniquement attributs qualifient généralement une condition physique ou un état mental, comme **afraid** (*effrayé*), **ashamed** (*honteux*), **faint** (*prêt à s'évanouir*), **fond** (*attaché*), **poorly** (*souffrant*), **(un)well** (*en mauvaise/bonne santé*) :

the children need not feel ashamed
les enfants ne doivent pas avoir honte

my uncle is fond of me   the girl is afraid
mon oncle m'aime beaucoup   la fille a peur

he suddenly felt faint
tout à coup, il se sentit mal ou il fut pris d'un malaise

our mother has been unwell for some time
cela fait quelque temps que notre mère est souffrante

Mais remarquez l'expression suivante construite avec une épithète :

he's not a well man
il ne se porte pas bien du tout

2 La position de l'adjectif

a) Si plus d'un adjectif précède le nom, celui ou ceux qui peuvent être aussi attributs se placent en premier. Les adjectifs uniquement épithètes ont un rapport trop étroit avec le nom pour qu'un autre mot puisse se placer entre eux et le nom :

he is a young parliamentary candidate
c'est un jeune candidat parlementaire

they have employed a conscientious social worker
ils ont employé une assistante sociale consciencieuse

a big old red brick house
une grande et vieille maison de brique rouge

Remarquez que les adjectifs **old** et **little** changent de sens selon leur position. Lorsqu'ils sont employés au sens propre, c'est-à-dire qu'ils signifient respectivement "vieux" et "petit", ils peuvent se placer devant un autre adjectif (et pourraient aussi être attributs) :

I'll just wear my old black shoes
je vais mettre mes vieilles chaussures noires

pass me that little black notebook
passe-moi ce petit cahier noir

Mais lorsque l'adjectif **little** signifie "petit" dans le sens de "plus jeune", il ne peut pas être séparé du nom par un autre adjectif car il forme une unité sémantique (**little brother**). De même, **old** et **little** employés au sens figuré dans des expressions marquant l'affection doivent précéder le nom. Dans les exemples suivants, **little** et **old** ne peuvent être qu'épithètes :

my greedy little brother ate all the ice cream
mon petit frère, gourmand comme tout, a mangé toute la glace

you poor old thing!   you poor little thing!
mon pauvre vieux !   mon pauvre petit !

b) L'adjectif peut parfois se mettre en apposition, c'est-à-dire directement après le nom sans qu'un verbe soit nécessaire. La fonction et l'emploi de ces adjectifs (et toute qualification supplémentaire éventuelle) sont similaires à ceux des propositions relatives :

this is a custom peculiar to Britain
c'est une coutume propre à la Grande-Bretagne

this is a man confident of success
c'est un homme sûr de réussir

Seuls les adjectifs qui s'emploient aussi comme attributs (après un verbe) peuvent se mettre en apposition. La mise en apposition est fréquente lorsque les adjectifs sont suivis d'un groupe prépositionnel, comme on le voit dans les exemples ci-dessus. Mais on trouve aussi des adjectifs en apposition employés dans un but emphatique, toujours employés par deux et plus :

her expression, cold and untrusting, spoke volumes
l'expression de son visage, froide et méfiante, en disait long

the building, tall and imposing, was visible from almost anywhere in the city
cet édifice, haut et imposant, se voyait pratiquement de n'importe quel endroit en ville

Il est à noter que l'emploi des adjectifs entre virgules est assez rare en anglais, contrairement au français.

La mise en apposition de l'adjectif est également possible après des mots imprécis comme **things** et **matters**. Cependant, cet emploi est assez rare et souvent littéraire :

his interest in matters linguistic
son intérêt pour tout ce qui touche à la linguistique

she has an abhorrence of things English
elle a horreur de tout ce qui est anglais

Enfin, les adjectifs en -able ou -ible peuvent se mettre après le nom, surtout si celui-ci est précédé de only (*seul, unique*) ou d'un superlatif :

he's the only person responsible
c'est la seule personne responsable

they committed the worst atrocities imaginable
ils commirent les pires atrocités imaginables

this is the most inexpensive model available
c'est le modèle disponible le moins cher

c) Certains adjectifs d'origine française ou latine se placent après le nom auquel ils se rapportent, comme en français, et dans des expressions toutes faites comme :

devil incarnate *diable incarné*
letters patent *lettres patentes*
lion rampant *lion rampant*
Lords Spiritual = *membres ecclésiastiques de la Chambre des lords*
Lords Temporal = *membres laïques de la Chambre des lords*
poet laureate *le poète lauréat*
the Princess Royal *la Princesse Royale*

3 Les adjectifs employés comme noms

a) Les adjectifs peuvent s'employer comme noms. Cet emploi concerne en général les concepts et les classes ou groupes de gens (en général ou dans un contexte particulier) :

i) Classes ou groupes de gens :

she gives money to the homeless **every month**
elle donne de l'argent tous les mois aux sans-abri

the government must do more to help the poor
le gouvernement doit faire davantage pour aider les pauvres

he does charity work for the blind
il fait du bénévolat pour les aveugles

a game suitable for young **and** old **alike**
un jeu pour les jeunes et les moins jeunes

Remarquez qu'en anglais ces mots ont un sens de pluriel collectif (voir p. A11). Pour désigner une personne dans un groupe, on ajoute man, woman, person, etc. :

a blind woman   **three deaf people**
une aveugle   *trois sourds*

ii) Concepts abstraits :

it's not always easy to distinguish the true **from the false**
il n'est pas toujours facile de distinguer le vrai du faux

Cet emploi est néanmoins assez rare.

b) Normalement, un adjectif ne peut pas remplacer un nom singulier dénombrable. Dans ce cas, il est nécessaire d'employer one (mais voir aussi One, pp. A37-8) :

I don't like the striped shirt; I prefer the plain **one**
je n'aime pas la chemise à rayures, je préfère l'unie

of all the applicants, the French **one was the best**
de tous les candidats, le Français était le meilleur

Cependant, il existe un certain nombre de participes passés que l'on peut utiliser (avec l'article défini) à la place d'un nom dénombrable. Par exemple :

the accused   **the deceased**
l'accusé/les accusés   *le mort/les morts*

the accused's family was with him in court
la famille de l'accusé était avec lui au tribunal

the deceased's possessions were sold
les biens du mort furent vendus

Ces adjectifs substantivés ne prennent pas de -s au pluriel.

c) Pour les exemples au pluriel en a), on n'ajoutait pas de -s à l'adjectif. Mais il arrive parfois que la conversion d'un adjectif en nom soit totale et que l'adjectif prenne un -s au pluriel :

the Blacks **against the** Whites **in South Africa**
les Noirs contre les Blancs en Afrique du Sud

the Reds
les rouges (les communistes)

here come the newlyweds
voilà les jeunes mariés

put all the empties **in a box**
mets toutes les bouteilles vides dans un carton

d) Nationalités

i) En anglais, les adjectifs et les noms désignant la nationalité prennent une majuscule (ainsi que les noms de langues) :

an American car   **an American**
une voiture américaine *un Américain*

ii) On peut classer les nationalités en quatre groupes, selon la forme de l'adjectif et du nom :

GROUPE 1	adjectif ordinaire
GROUPE 2	adjectif et nom identiques (se terminant par -ese et -s)
GROUPE 3	comme le groupe 2, mais le nom prend un -s au pluriel (adjectifs se terminant par -an, -i, etc.)
GROUPE 4	adjectif et nom différents (mais au pluriel, le nom + -s est aussi possible)

GROUPE 1

adjectif :   **English literature**
                  la littérature anglaise

employé comme nom lorsqu'il se réfère à une nation :

the English **are rather reserved**
les Anglais sont plutôt réservés

Les adjectifs du Groupe 1 ne peuvent pas s'utiliser comme noms pour faire référence à des individus. Dans ce cas, il faut ajouter la terminaison -man (ou -woman) :

we spoke to two Englishmen/Englishwomen
nous avons parlé à deux Anglais/Anglaises

De même pour :

Dutch	*hollandais*	Irish	*irlandais*
French	*français*	Welsh	*gallois*

GROUPE 2

adjectif :   **Japanese art**
                  l'art japonais

employé comme nom lorsqu'il se réfère à une nation :

the Japanese **are famous for their technology**
les Japonais sont célèbres pour leur technologie

et lorsqu'il se réfère à des individus (sans -s au pluriel) :

their new au pair is a Japanese
leur nouvelle fille au pair est japonaise

I've got six Japanese **in my class**
il y a six Japonais dans ma classe

De même pour :

Burmese	*birman*	Swiss	*suisse*
Chinese	*chinois*	Vietnamese	*vietnamien*
Portuguese	*portugais*		

GROUPE 3

adjectif : **German institutions**
les institutions allemandes

employé comme nom (avec un -s au pluriel) lorsqu'il fait référence à une nation :

the Germans produce some fine cars
les Allemands produisent de belles voitures

et lorsqu'il se réfère à des individus (avec un -s au pluriel) :

he was having a conversation with a German
il était en conversation avec un Allemand

we met quite a few Germans on our holiday
nous avons rencontré un bon nombre d'Allemands pendant nos vacances

De même, ceux qui se terminent en -an, par exemple :

African	*africain*	European	*européen*
American	*américain*	Hungarian	*hongrois*
Asian	*asiatique*	Indian	*indien*
Australian	*australien*	Iranian	*iranien*
Belgian	*belge*	Italian	*italien*
Brazilian	*brésilien*	Norwegian	*norvégien*
Canadian	*canadien*	Russian	*russe*

(mais notez que **Arabian** (*arabe*) appartient au Groupe 4 ci-dessous)
et ceux qui se terminent en -i :

Bangladeshi	*bangladais*	Israeli	*israélien*
Iraqi	*iraquien*	Pakistani	*pakistanais*

On trouve aussi dans ce groupe :

Cypriot	*chypriote*	Greek	*grec*
Czech	*tchèque*		

GROUPE 4

adjectif : **Danish furniture**
les meubles danois

employé comme nom lorsqu'il fait référence à une nation :

the Danish enjoy good food
les Danois apprécient la bonne chère

Mais il y a un nom différent qui peut aussi être utilisé pour faire référence à la nation :

the Danes enjoy good food
les Danois apprécient la bonne chère

et qui est la seule forme admise pour désigner les individus :

I met a Dane on the bus
j'ai fait la connaissance d'un Danois dans le bus

there were two Danes in the cast
il y avait deux Danois parmi les acteurs

De même pour :

British/Briton	*Britannique*	Spanish/Spaniard	*Espagnol*
Finnish/Finn	*Finlandais*	Polish/Pole	*Polonais*
Polish/Pole	*Polonais*	Swedish/Swede	*Suédois*

Cas particulier : **Arabian, Arabic** et **Arab**

L'adjectif courant est **Arabian** (**The Arabian Nights** *les Mille et Une Nuits*) sauf si l'on parle de la langue ou des chiffres :

do you speak Arabic?
est-ce que vous parlez arabe ?

this figure should be written in Arabic numerals, not Roman ones
ce nombre devrait être écrit en chiffres arabes, et non en chiffres romains

Arab est employé pour désigner les individus des pays de culture arabe, sauf si **Saudi** le précède. Dans ce cas, on emploie

Saudi Arabian ou **Saudi** :

he's worked a lot with Arabs
il a beaucoup travaillé avec des Arabes

the hotel has been hired by Saudi Arabians (ou Saudis)
l'hôtel a été loué par des Saoudiens

iii) Remarques sur **Scottish, Scots** et **Scotch** (*écossais*) :

Aujourd'hui, **Scotch** est rarement utilisé, sauf dans des locutions (concernant souvent la nourriture ou les boissons), telles que **Scotch egg** (= œuf dur entouré de chair à saucisse et enrobé de chapelure), **Scotch whisky, Scotch broth** (= soupe écossaise à base de légumes et d'orge perlée) et **Scotch terrier.**

Dans les autres cas, on utilise normalement l'adjectif **Scottish** comme dans a **Scottish bar** (*un bar écossais*), **Scottish football supporters** (*supporters de football écossais*), même si **Scots** est parfois utilisé pour les personnes : a **Scots lawyer** (*un avocat écossais*). On distingue aussi le **Scottish English** (= l'anglais parlé avec un accent écossais) du **Scots** (= le dialecte écossais).

Pour désigner la nation, on emploie **the Scots** (*les Écossais*) (parfois **the Scottish**). L'individu est a **Scot** (au pluriel **Scots**) ou a **Scotsman/Scotswoman** (au pluriel **Scotsmen/Scotswomen**).

5 LES ADVERBES

Par adverbe, on entend un seul mot (par exemple **happily**) et par groupe adverbial ou proposition adverbiale, on entend un groupe de mots ayant une fonction adverbiale (par exemple **in a friendly way**).

A LES DIFFÉRENTS TYPES

On peut classer les adverbes en différentes catégories, selon leur forme ou leur sens.

a) *Forme*

On distingue deux sortes d'adverbes suivant leur forme : les adverbes "en tant que tels" et les adverbes "dérivés".

Les adverbes dérivés sont ceux qui dérivent de mots issus d'une autre catégorie grammaticale et auxquels on ajoute une terminaison particulière (voir B) :

happily *heureusement*, de l'adjectif **happy**
hourly *par heure*, du nom **hour** ou de l'adjectif **hourly**
moneywise *en ce qui concerne l'argent*, du nom **money**

Parmi les adverbes en tant que tels, on trouve :

here	*ici*	often	*souvent*
there	*là-bas*	never	*jamais*
now	*maintenant*	soon	*bientôt*
then	*alors*	very	*très*

b) *Sens*

Les adverbes peuvent se diviser en divers types selon leur sens. Les adverbes suivants sont particulièrement courants :

i) Adverbes de temps :

now (*maintenant*), **then** (*alors*), **once** (*une fois*), **soon** (*bientôt*), **always** (*toujours*), **briefly** (*brièvement*)

I saw her once
je l'ai vue une fois

you always say that
tu dis toujours ça

ii) Adverbes de lieu :

here (*ici*), **there** (*là-bas*), **everywhere** (*partout*), **up** (*en haut*), **down** (*en bas*), **back** (*derrière*)

come here
viens ici

iii) Adverbes de manière :

well (*bien*), **clumsily** (*maladroitement*), **beautifully** (*merveilleusement*), **etc.**

what's worth doing is worth doing well
ce qui vaut la peine d'être fait vaut la peine d'être bien fait

iv) Adverbes d'intensité :

rather (*plutôt*), **quite** (*assez*), **very** (*très*), **hardly** (*à peine*), **extremely** (*extrêmement*)

this gravy is rather good
cette sauce est plutôt bonne

B LES DIFFÉRENTES FORMES

a) *Les adverbes en -ly*

On ajoute normalement cette terminaison directement à l'adjectif :

sweet → **sweetly**
gentil *gentiment*

Mais si l'adjectif se termine en -ic, on ajoute -ally :

intrinsic → **intrinsically** **drastic** → **drastically**
intrinsèque *intrinsèquement* *radical* → *radicalement*

Les seules exceptions sont :

public → **publicly**
public *publiquement*

politic → **politicly** (*rarement employé*)
judicieux *judicieusement*

Pour les changements orthographiques (comme dans **happy** → **happily** ou **noble** → **nobly**), voir p. A79.

Remarquez que l'on prononce toujours la voyelle -e (c'est-à-dire le son /ɪ/) de -ed à l'intérieur d'un adverbe, qu'on la prononce dans l'adjectif correspondant ou pas :

assured [ə'ʃʊəd] → **assuredly** [ə'ʃʊərɪdlɪ]
assuré *assurément*

offhanded [ɒf'hændɪd] → **offhandedly** [ɒf'hændɪdlɪ]
désinvolte *avec désinvolture*

b) *Même forme que l'adjectif*

Certains adverbes ont la même forme que l'adjectif correspondant, par exemple :

in the far distance (*adj*)
tout au loin

you don't have to go far (*adv*)
tu n'as pas besoin d'aller très loin

Voir la liste d'adverbes et les exemples donnés dans la section C, 2 de ce chapitre.

c) *-wise*

On peut ajouter le suffixe -wise à des noms pour former un adverbe qui a le sens général de "en ce qui concerne" (quel que soit le nom) :

how's he feeling? – do you mean mentally or healthwise?
comment se sent-il ? – tu veux dire mentalement ou côté santé ?

Bien que cette construction soit très courante, elle a tendance à être plus employée à l'oral qu'à l'écrit, et elle n'est pas toujours

considérée comme particulièrement élégante :

things are going quite well schedule-wise
les choses se passent assez bien en ce qui concerne nos prévisions

we're not really short of anything furniture-wise
nous ne manquons pas de grand-chose côté meubles

the town's quite good restaurant-wise
la ville a pas mal de restaurants

C L'EMPLOI

1 Fonctions de l'adverbe et des constructions adverbiales

Les adverbes et les groupes adverbiaux s'emploient pour modifier :

a) des verbes :

he spoke well
il a bien parlé

he spoke in a loud voice
il a parlé à haute voix

b) des adjectifs :

that's awfully nice of you
c'est vraiment gentil à vous

this isn't good enough
ça n'est pas assez bien

c) d'autres adverbes :

she didn't sing well enough
elle n'a pas assez bien chanté

it happened extremely quickly
ça s'est passé extrêmement vite

(Remarquez que **enough** suit l'adjectif ou l'adverbe qu'il modifie ; voir 3d) vi) p. A23)

d) des noms :

this is rather a mess
c'est plutôt en désordre

he's quite a hero
c'est un vrai héros

e) toute la phrase :

fortunately they accepted the verdict
par bonheur, ils ont accepté le verdict

amazingly enough, it was true
aussi incroyable que cela puisse paraître, c'était vrai

2 Les adverbes ayant la même forme que l'adjectif

Parmi ceux-ci on trouve :

far (*lointain – loin*) (voir B, b) ci-dessus), **fast** (*rapide – vite*), **hard** (*dur, difficile – dur*), **little** (*petit – peu*), **long** (*long – longtemps*), **early** (*matinal, en avance – tôt*), **only** (*seul – seulement*)

et un certain nombre en -ly dérivés de noms (faisant souvent référence au temps), par exemple :

daily (*quotidien – tous les jours*), **monthly** (*mensuel – tous les mois*), **weekly** (*hebdomadaire – toutes les semaines*), **deathly** (*cadavérique – comme la mort*), **leisurely** (*tranquille – sans se presser*)

ADJECTIF	ADVERBE
this is a fast train *c'est un train rapide*	**you're driving too fast** *vous roulez trop vite*
it's a hard question *c'est une question difficile*	**he worked hard** *il a travaillé dur*
he bought a little house *il a acheté une petite maison*	**little do you care!** *ça t'importe peu !*
she was wearing a long dress *elle portait une longue robe*	**have you been here long?** *tu es là depuis longtemps ?*
you'll have to catch the early plane *il faudra que tu prennes le premier avion*	**they arrived early** *ils sont arrivés tôt*

she's an only child
elle est fille unique

I've only got two tickets
je n'ai que deux billets

do you get a daily newspaper?
vous achetez un quotidien ?

there's a flight twice daily
il y a un vol deux fois par jour

you'll receive this in monthly instalments
vous le recevrez en versements mensuels

the list will be updated monthly
la liste sera mise à jour tous les mois

a deathly silence fell on the spectators
un silence de mort s'abattit sur les spectateurs

she was deathly pale
elle avait le teint blafard

we took a leisurely stroll after lunch
nous sommes allés faire une petite balade tranquille après manger

we spent a month travelling leisurely through the Loire Valley
nous avons passé un mois à voyager tranquillement dans la vallée de la Loire

3 La position de l'adverbe

! En anglais, l'adverbe ne peut pas se placer entre le verbe et le complément. On dira toujours :

they speak English well (*et jamais* they speak well English)
ils parlent bien anglais

Il faut donc faire attention à ne pas garder systématiquement la structure française. Lorsqu'il peut se placer au milieu d'une phrase, l'adverbe anglais se mettra toujours **devant** le verbe (ou entre l'auxiliaire et le verbe principal pour les temps composés) :

we often go to the cinema (*et jamais* we go often to the cinema)
on va souvent au cinéma

Certains adverbes peuvent se placer au début, au milieu ou à la fin de la phrase, alors que le choix est beaucoup plus restreint pour d'autres. Vous trouverez ci-dessous les différentes positions possibles des adverbes les plus courants.

a) *Les adverbes de temps*

i) S'ils font référence à un moment précis, on les place en début ou en fin de phrase (et non au milieu) :

tonight the shops close at 8
ce soir, les magasins ferment à 8 heures

I'll come and see you tomorrow
je viendrai te voir demain

Mais l'adverbe now est possible aux trois endroits dans la phrase car il peut aussi précéder le verbe :

I now see the point
je vois maintenant ce que vous voulez dire

ii) Si l'on fait référence à un moment imprécis, l'adverbe peut aussi se placer avant le verbe principal :

we soon got to know him
on a vite appris à le connaître

we have often talked about it
on en a souvent parlé

they have frequently discussed such matters
ils ont fréquemment discuté de tels sujets

Remarquez que les adverbes de fréquence never et always se placent toujours avant le verbe :

I always buy my shirts here
j'achète toujours mes chemises ici

we'll never know the truth
on ne connaîtra jamais la vérité

Mais les adverbes de fréquence se placent normalement après le verbe **to be** :

he's never late
il n'est jamais en retard

he was frequently in trouble with the police
il avait souvent des ennuis avec la police

S'il y a plus d'un auxiliaire, ces adverbes peuvent se mettre entre les deux auxiliaires ou devant le verbe principal :

she has frequently been/has been frequently visited by distant relatives
des parents lointains lui ont fréquemment rendu visite

b) *Les adverbes de lieu*

Ils ne peuvent pas se mettre au milieu de la phrase (entre le sujet et le verbe). Ils se placent en général en fin de phrase, c'est-à-dire qu'ils suivent le verbe (et le complément d'objet) :

they travelled everywhere
ils ont voyagé partout

I saw you there
je vous ai vu là-bas

he's doing some gardening outside
il est en train de jardiner dehors

Mais remarquez la position en début de phrase devant be, come et go :

there's the postman
voilà le facteur

here are your books
voici tes livres

here comes the bus
voilà le bus qui arrive

et devant des pronoms personnels avec ces mêmes verbes :

there he is
le voilà

here she comes
la voilà (qui arrive)

c) *Les adverbes de manière*

i) La position d'un adverbe de manière ne change pas le sens général de la phrase, sauf dans les cas où l'adverbe peut modifier le verbe ou la phrase entière (voir iv) ci-dessous). On peut souvent le placer où l'on veut, suivant les nuances ou le ton que l'on souhaite donner à la phrase. Néanmoins, la position en début de phrase est assez rare (voir iii) ci-dessous) :

they stealthily crept upstairs
they crept stealthily upstairs
they crept upstairs stealthily
ils ont monté les escaliers furtivement

stealthily, they crept upstairs
furtivement, ils ont monté les escaliers

she carefully examined the report
she examined the report carefully
elle examina le rapport avec attention

Mais, lorsque l'adverbe donne une information importante dans le contexte, il se met en fin de phrase. Comparez :

I quickly packed my bags and left
j'ai fait mes valises en vitesse et je suis parti

I packed my bags quickly, that's why I forgot my passport
j'ai fait mes valises en vitesse, voilà pourquoi j'ai oublié mon passeport

Dans la phrase suivante, une seule position est possible car l'adverbe constitue l'information générale :

they fought the war intelligently
ils ont mené la guerre avec intelligence

A21

ii) Si le complément d'objet direct est extrêmement long, on évite de placer l'adverbe en fin de phrase :

she carefully **examined the report sent to her by the Minister**
elle examina attentivement le rapport envoyé par le ministre

iii) La position en tête de phrase est très descriptive et emphatique :

clumsily, **he made his way towards the door**
maladroitement, il se dirigea vers la porte

iv) Les adverbes de manière modifiant les phrases ou seulement les verbes :

Suivant la place qu'il a dans la phrase, l'adverbe va modifier la phrase entière ou bien le verbe seul. Comparez les phrases suivantes :

she spoke wisely **at the meeting**
elle a parlé avec sagesse durant la réunion

she wisely **spoke at the meeting**
elle a eu la sagesse de parler à la réunion

Voici des exemples analogues :

she spoke naturally **and fluently** (*modifie le verbe*)
elle parla avec naturel et aisance

she naturally **assumed it was right** (*modifie la phrase*)
elle supposa naturellement que c'était vrai

naturally, **she assumed it was right** (*modifie la phrase*)
naturellement, elle supposa que c'était vrai

she understood it clearly (*modifie le verbe*)
elle l'a bien compris

she clearly **understood it** (*modifie la phrase ou le verbe*)
de toute évidence, elle l'a compris
elle l'a bien compris

clearly, **she understood it** (*modifie la phrase*)
de toute évidence, elle l'a compris

Le mot enough peut aussi s'employer après un adverbe pour marquer le fait que l'adverbe est employé pour modifier la phrase :

funnily (enough), **they both spoke at the meeting**
aussi drôle que cela puisse paraître, ils ont tous les deux parlé lors de la réunion

d) *Les adverbes d'intensité*

i) Si les adverbes d'intensité modifient d'autres adverbes, des adjectifs ou des noms, ils viendront se placer juste devant ces mots :

she played extremely **well**
elle a joué extrêmement bien

it's too **difficult to define**   it's rather **a shame**
c'est trop difficile à définir   *c'est bien dommage*

Remarquez que les adverbes tels que well et badly, qui permettent d'évaluer la qualité de quelque chose, se placent toujours en fin de phrase :

she plays tennis **badly**
elle joue mal au tennis

sauf dans les tournures passives où l'adverbe viendra se placer entre l'auxiliaire to be et le verbe principal :

the bridge was badly **built**
le pont a été mal construit

ii) Sinon, les adverbes d'intensité (ainsi que ceux qui permettent d'attirer l'attention sur un élément de la phrase : just,

also, only, etc.) précèdent normalement le verbe principal :

we very much **enjoyed your book**
nous avons beaucoup apprécié votre livre

I could hardly **remember a thing**
je ne me souvenais de presque rien

we just **want to know the time of departure**
nous voulons juste connaître l'heure du départ

they also **went to France last year**
ils sont aussi allés en France l'année dernière

Mais contrairement à also, l'adverbe too suit normalement les mots qu'il modifie et peut donc se placer aussi en fin de phrase :

you too **should go and see the exhibition**
toi aussi, tu devrais aller voir cette exposition

you should go and see that exhibition too
tu devrais aussi aller voir cette exposition

iii) Only (*seulement*)

Only est en général placé avant le verbe, mais il peut aussi se mettre en début de phrase lorsqu'il fait référence au sujet :

only James **came to visit her in hospital**
seul James est venu la voir à l'hôpital

Cet adverbe pose rarement problème à l'oral, car le contexte, l'accentuation et l'intonation permettent de déduire son sens :

(a) Jayne only **saw Gillian today**
Jayne a seulement vu Gillian aujourd'hui
(mais elle ne lui a pas parlé)

(b) Jayne only **saw Gillian today**
Jayne n'a vu que Gillian aujourd'hui
(elle n'a vu personne d'autre)

(c) Jayne only **saw Gillian today**
Jayne n'a vu Gillian qu'aujourd'hui
(elle l'a vue seulement aujourd'hui)

Mais de telles différences sont difficiles à cerner à l'écrit, à moins que le contexte ne soit bien clair. Ainsi, dans l'exemple (b) à l'écrit, on changerait la place de l'adverbe de la façon suivante :

Jayne saw only **Gillian today**
Jayne n'a vu que Gillian aujourd'hui

et (c) deviendrait :

it was only **today that Jayne saw Gillian**
ce n'est qu'aujourd'hui que Jayne a vu Gillian

Pour l'exemple (a), on écrirait probablement le mot accentué en italique :

Jayne only *saw* **Gillian today**
Jayne n'a fait que voir Gillian aujourd'hui

iv) Very ou much ? (*très/beaucoup*)

● Devant des adjectifs dans leur forme de base, on emploie very :

these are very **nice**
ils sont très beaux

ainsi que devant des superlatifs en -est :

these are the very **nicest flowers I've seen**
ce sont les plus belles fleurs que j'aie jamais vues

Cependant, dans la construction au superlatif qui suit, much s'emploie devant le the du superlatif :

this is much the best **example in the book**
c'est de loin le meilleur exemple du livre

Pour le superlatif, voir le chapitre 6, pp. A24-7.

● Le comparatif est accompagné de **much** :

she's much taller **than you**
elle est bien plus grande que toi

she's much more **particular**
elle est beaucoup plus pointilleuse

Pour le comparatif, voir le chapitre 6, pp. A24-7.

● Il en est de même avec les adverbes :

you do it very well, but I do it much **better**
tu le fais très bien, mais je le fais bien mieux

● Les verbes sont accompagnés de **much** (qui est lui-même modifié par **very**) :

I love you very much
je t'aime énormément

● Avant les participes passés :

S'ils ont la fonction d'adjectif, on emploie **very** :

they were very **offended   I'm** very **tired**
ils étaient extrêmement vexés   je suis très fatigué

we're very **interested in this house**
nous sommes très intéressés par cette maison

I'm very **pleased to meet you**
je suis très heureux de faire votre connaissance

these suitcases are looking very **used**
ces valises ont l'air très usées

Mais s'ils ne sont pas considérés comme adjectifs en tant que tels, ou s'ils gardent leur fonction verbale, on emploie alors **much**, et non **very** :

these suitcases haven't been much **used**
ces valises n'ont pas été très utilisées

he has been much **maligned**
on l'a beaucoup calomnié

this has been much **spoken about**
on en a beaucoup parlé

his new house is much **admired by people round here**
les gens du coin ont beaucoup d'admiration pour sa nouvelle maison

Dans un langage légèrement familier, on préfère employer a lot à la place de **much**, en particulier à la forme affirmative (a lot se met après le verbe) :

these have been used a lot
ceux-ci ont été beaucoup utilisés

v) **All** (*tout*)

All peut s'employer comme adverbe d'intensité et signifie alors "tout", "complètement". Il peut se placer devant un adjectif, un participe passé, un adverbe ou un groupe prépositionnel :

she was all **alone** (*+ adjectif*)
elle était toute seule

he was all **covered in mud** (*+ participe passé*)
il était tout couvert de boue

that's what I've been saying all **along** (*+ adverbe*)
c'est ce que je dis depuis le début

I forgot all **about the meeting** (*+ préposition*)
j'ai complètement oublié qu'il y avait une réunion

et devant des comparatifs :

I've stopped smoking and feel all **the better for it**
j'ai arrêté de fumer et je me sens tellement mieux

it makes her all **the more interesting**
ça la rend encore plus intéressante

vi) **Enough** (*assez*)

Lorsqu'il est employé comme adverbe, **enough** se place après l'adjectif :

he isn't big enough **for that yet**
il n'est pas encore assez grand pour ça

On l'emploie aussi après un nom employé comme adjectif attribut :

he isn't man enough **for the job**
il n'a pas la carrure suffisante pour ce travail

Remarquez que **enough** peut séparer l'adjectif du nom :

it's a decent enough **town**
c'est pas mal comme ville

e) *Les adverbes modifiant toute la phrase*

i) Tout comme la plupart des adverbes de manière (voir c) i) ci-dessus), ces adverbes peuvent se placer à différents endroits dans la phrase, selon l'importance que l'on veut leur donner :

fortunately, **he stopped in time**
heureusement, il s'est arrêté à temps

he fortunately **stopped in time**
il s'est heureusement arrêté à temps

he stopped in time, fortunately
il s'est arrêté à temps, heureusement

ii) Les adverbes **probably**, **certainly** et **definitely** se placent presque toujours au milieu de la phrase (juste avant le verbe) :

he'll probably **come later**
il va probablement venir plus tard

I definitely **saw him yesterday**
je suis sûre de l'avoir vu hier

Mais **surely** et **perhaps** se mettent habituellement en début de phrase :

surely **you must be joking!   perhaps he'll come**
vous plaisantez, j'espère ?   il va peut-être venir

f) *La place de l'adverbe de négation* not

i) Not précède le groupe adverbial qu'il modifie :

is he here? – not **yet**
est-ce qu'il est là ? – pas encore

do you mind? – not **at all**
ça ne te dérange pas ? – pas du tout

he speaks not **only English, but also French**
il parle non seulement anglais, mais aussi français

he lives not **far from here**
il n'habite pas loin d'ici

Dans l'exemple suivant, c'est **absolutely** (*absolument*) qui qualifie **not**, et non le contraire :

have you said something to her? – absolutely **not**
tu lui as dit quelque chose ? – absolument pas

ii) Not suit le verbe to be :

he is not **hungry**
il n'a pas faim

iii) À la forme négative, on ajoute not après l'auxiliaire ou -n't directement à l'auxiliaire. Not (ou -n't) se met normalment après le premier auxiliaire :

he does not/doesn't smoke
il ne fume pas

they would not/wouldn't have seen her
ils ne l'auraient pas vue

Mais dans des questions, la forme complète de not suit le sujet, tandis que -n't le précède, puisqu'il est lié à l'auxiliaire :

did they not go there last year?
didn't they go there last year?
n'y sont-ils pas allés l'an dernier ?

have they not already been there?
haven't they already been there?
ne sont-ils pas déjà allés là-bas ?

iv) En anglais américain, not peut précéder un subjonctif :

it is important that he not be informed of this
il est important qu'il n'en soit pas informé

v) Remarquez aussi les emplois suivants :

did you do it? – not me *(Fam)*
c'est toi qui l'as fait ? – non, c'est pas moi

will she come? – I hope not
est-ce qu'elle viendra ? – j'espère que non

Ici not est la négation de will come (I hope she won't come *j'espère qu'elle ne viendra pas*). Pour cet emploi de not avec hope, voir p. A38.

g) *L'emploi de* some/any, something/anything *comme adverbes*

i) Some est utilisé comme adverbe :

devant des nombres = "à peu près", "autour de" :

some fifty people were present
il y avait une cinquantaine de personnes présentes

avec more :

talk to me some more
parle-moi encore un peu

seul, en anglais américain :

we talked some
on a un peu parlé

ii) Any est utilisé comme adverbe devant les comparatifs :

he isn't any less of a friend in spite of this
malgré cela, il n'en est pas moins mon ami

I refuse to discuss this any further
je refuse de continuer cette discussion

iii) Something et anything sont aussi employés comme adverbes devant like. Something a alors le sens de "plutôt" ou "environ" et anything le sens de "rien" :

it looks something like a Picasso
ça ressemble à du Picasso

something like fifty or sixty people were present
il y avait environ cinquante à soixante personnes présentes

it wasn't anything like I had imagined
ça n'avait rien à voir avec ce que j'avais imaginé

On entend parfois des expressions dans lesquelles something est utilisé comme adverbe d'intensité. Il s'agit là d'un emploi régional ou familier, grammaticalement incorrect :

it hurts something awful!
ça fait vachement mal !

she fancies him something rotten
elle est dingue de lui

Pour l'emploi de some/any comme adjectifs ou pronoms indéfinis et de something/anything comme pronoms, voir pp. A34-5.

h) *L'emploi de* no *et* none *comme adverbes*

i) No est adverbe lorsqu'il est employé devant un comparatif :

he earns no more than £15,000 a year
il ne gagne pas plus de 15 000 livres par an

ii) None est aussi adverbe devant the + comparatif :

she's none the worse for her adventure
son aventure ne lui a pas fait de mal

he's taken some medicine but is feeling none the better
il a pris des médicaments, mais il ne se sent pas mieux pour autant

after his explanation we were all none the wiser
malgré ses explications, nous n'étions pas plus avancés

Dans ce dernier exemple, on aurait aussi pu dire : **none of us was any the wiser after his explanation** (voir g) ii) ci-dessus).

Pour l'emploi de no comme adjectif et de none comme pronom, voir p. A35.

i) *L'emploi de* either, neither *et* nor *comme adverbes*

i) L'adverbe either n'est utilisé que dans des propositions négatives. Dans les phrases affirmatives, on emploiera too (voir d) ii) p. A22) :

I can't do it either   **I can do it too**
je ne peux pas le faire non plus   *je peux le faire aussi*

ii) Les adverbes neither et nor sont utilisés dans les propositions qui suivent les propositions négatives. Attention à l'inversion sujet-auxiliaire :

I can't swim and neither/nor can she
je ne sais pas nager, et elle non plus

I can't swim – neither/nor can I *(ou* me neither *dans un style familier)*
je ne sais pas nager – moi non plus

I don't like coffee, nor do I like tea
je n'aime pas le café et je n'aime pas le thé non plus

I don't like coffee, (and) nor/neither does she
je n'aime pas le café, et elle non plus

Voir aussi **Les conjonctions**, p. A74, ainsi que **Les pronoms et les adjectifs indéfinis**, p. A37.

6   LA COMPARAISON

1   Les formes

Le comparatif et le superlatif des adjectifs et des adverbes se forment de la même manière.

a) Il existe trois degrés de comparaison : **le positif** (forme de base), **le comparatif** et **le superlatif** :

sweet	**beautiful**	(positif)
doux	*beau*	

sweeter   more **beautiful**   (comparatif)
plus doux   *plus beau*

sweetest   the most **beautiful** (superlatif)
le plus doux   *le plus beau*

Pour les changements orthographiques résultant de l'addition de -er, -est (happy - happier ou big - bigger), voir pp. A79-80.

b) -er/-est ou more/most ?

  i) Plus l'adjectif est court, plus il est probable que son comparatif et son superlatif se forment en ajoutant -er et -est. Ceci concerne tout particulièrement les adjectifs monosyllabiques, comme keen, fine, late, wide, neat, etc. Des adjectifs très courants tels que big ou fast prennent toujours la forme -er/-est. Il en est de même pour les adverbes qui ont la même forme que l'adjectif correspondant (voir pp. A20-1) :

    a faster car *(adj)*
    une voiture plus rapide

    I can run faster than you think *(adv)*
    je peux courir plus vite que tu ne crois

    if he could just work a little harder! *(adv)*
    si seulement il pouvait travailler un peu plus !

    Si les adjectifs ont deux syllabes, on trouve les formes -er/-est et more/most, les suffixes -er/-est étant particulièrement courants avec les adjectifs qui se terminent en -y, -le, -ow, -er :

    noisy :   **this is the noisiest pub I've ever seen**
           c'est le pub le plus bruyant que j'aie jamais vu

    feeble : **this is the feeblest excuse I've heard**
           c'est la plus mauvaise excuse que j'aie entendue

    shallow : **the stream is shallower up there**
           le ruisseau est moins profond en amont

    clever : **she's the cleverest of them all**
           c'est la plus intelligente de tous ou de toutes

    Les adjectifs formés à partir d'autres adjectifs dissyllabiques peuvent prendre -er/-est ou s'employer avec more/most :

    she's unhappier than she has ever been
    elle est plus malheureuse que jamais

    he's got the untidiest room in the whole house
    il a la chambre la plus mal rangée de toute la maison

  ii) Les adjectifs de plus de deux syllabes s'utilisent avec more au comparatif et the most au superlatif :

    this is the most idiotic thing I ever heard!
    c'est la chose la plus idiote que j'aie entendue !

    I prefer a more traditional Christmas
    je préfère un Noël plus traditionnel

    she's getting more and more predictable
    il devient de plus en plus facile de deviner ce qu'elle va faire

  iii) Les adjectifs formés à partir de participes passés s'emploient avec more et the most :

    she's more gifted than her sister
    elle est plus douée que sa sœur

    the most advanced students
    les étudiants les plus avancés

    that's the most bored I've ever been!
    je ne me suis jamais autant ennuyé !

    Tired peut prendre les terminaisons -er/-est.

  iv) Les adverbes formés à partir de l'adjectif + -ly ont un comparatif et un superlatif construits avec more et the most :

the most recently published works in this field
les ouvrages publiés le plus récemment dans ce domaine

Mais early, qui n'est pas dérivé d'un adjectif sans -ly, prend -er/-est. Il a la même forme que l'adjectif et se comporte donc de la même manière (voir l'explication concernant les adjectifs dissyllabiques, b) ii) ci-dessus) :

we arrived earlier than we expected
nous sommes arrivés plus tôt que prévu

  v) Si la comparaison se fait entre deux adjectifs (comme choix de mots), on ne peut employer que more :

    this sauce is more sweet than sour
    cette sauce est plus douce qu'aigre

c) Les comparatifs et superlatifs irréguliers

    Quelques adjectifs et adverbes ont un comparatif et un superlatif irréguliers.

bad *(adj)*	**worse**	**the worst**
mauvais	*pire*	*le pire*
badly *(adv)*	**worse**	**the worst**
mal	*pire*	*le pire*
far *(adj)*	**further/farther**	**the furthest/the farthest**
éloigné, lointain	*plus éloigné*	*le plus éloigné*
far *(adv)*	**further/farther**	**the furthest/the farthest**
loin	*plus loin*	*le plus loin*
good *(adj)*	**better**	**the best**
bon	*meilleur*	*le meilleur*
well *(adv)*	**better**	**the best**
bien	*meilleur*	*le meilleur*
little *(adj)*	**less/lesser**	**the least**
peu de, petit	*moins de/moindre*	*le moins de/moindre*
little *(adv)*	**less**	**the least**
peu	*moins*	*le moins*
many *(adj)*	**more**	**the most**
beaucoup de	*plus de*	*le plus de*
much *(adv ou adj*)*	**more**	**the most**
beaucoup (de)	*plus (de)*	*le plus (de)*

*much peut être adjectif avec les indénombrables (voir p. A35) et dans les structures interrogatives ou négatives (**there isn't much cake left** *il ne reste pas beaucoup de gâteau*). Le contraire de much est l'adjectif little.

Le comparatif régulier de late (*tard*) est later (*plus tard*) et le superlatif, the latest (*le plus récent*). Remarquez aussi que late possède un comparatif et un superlatif irréguliers avec des significations différentes : latter (*le second*) et the last (*le dernier*).

De même, old (*vieux*) possède un comparatif et un superlatif réguliers, older (*plus vieux*) et the oldest (*le plus vieux*), ainsi qu'une forme irrégulière : elder (*plus vieux*) et the eldest (*aîné*).

Pour les différences d'usage entre the latest et the last, the oldest et the eldest, further/the furthest et farther/the farthest, voir les cas particuliers p. A26.

Pour l'emploi du comparatif et du superlatif (et les variantes), voir ci-dessous et pp. A22-3.

d) Le comparatif d'égalité

    On forme le comparatif d'égalité avec la construction as... as :

    he's as funny as his father
    il est aussi drôle que son père

e) Les comparatifs d'infériorité et superlatifs d'infériorité

Le comparatif d'infériorité se forme avec less... than, et le superlatif d'infériorité avec the least + adjectif :

he's less successful than his brother
il a moins de succès que son frère

he is the least successful of the three brothers
c'est celui des trois frères qui a le moins de succès

On peut également exprimer l'infériorité en employant le comparatif d'inégalité, not as/so... as :

he's not as/so successful as his brother
il n'a pas autant de succès que son frère

Remarquez que so ne peut être utilisé qu'à la forme négative.

f) "plus/moins..., plus/moins..."

Pour traduire la tournure française "plus/moins..., plus/moins..." l'anglais utilise le comparatif précédé de the :

the hotter it gets, the less I want to work
plus il fait chaud, moins j'ai envie de travailler

the less I see of him the better!
moins je le vois, mieux je me porte !

Remarquez les expressions proverbiales :

the more the merrier	**the sooner the better**
plus on est de fous, plus on rit	*le plus tôt sera le mieux*

2 L'emploi

a) Dans les comparaisons, than se traduit par "que" :

it's hotter here than in Spain
il fait plus chaud ici qu'en Espagne

b) Le comparatif est employé quand deux personnes ou deux choses sont comparées :

of the two, she is the cleverer
des deux, elle est la plus intelligente

Dans l'anglais parlé d'aujourd'hui, certains emploient aussi le superlatif :

of the two, she is the cleverest
des deux, elle est la plus intelligente

sauf, bien sûr, quand than suit (she is cleverer than her brother *elle est plus intelligente que son frère*).

c) Quand plus de deux personnes ou choses sont comparées, on emploie le superlatif :

she is the cleverest in the class
c'est la plus intelligente de la classe

d) Dans certains cas, le comparatif est employé non pas pour marquer le degré, mais le contraste. Cela s'applique surtout pour les adjectifs qui n'ont pas de forme de base :

former/latter	inner/outer
premier/dernier	*intérieur/extérieur*
upper/lower	lesser/greater
supérieur/inférieur	*petit/grand*

Ces adjectifs, dans ce sens, sont toujours épithètes.

e) Le superlatif absolu :

Il permet de renforcer un adjectif, et non de comparer des choses ou des personnes. On emploie normalement most au lieu de -est, même avec des adjectifs monosyllabiques (cet emploi de most fait partie d'un registre soutenu ou littéraire) :

this is most kind!
c'est très gentil !

I thought his lecture was most interesting
j'ai trouvé que sa conférence était des plus intéressantes

Mais on peut également employer un superlatif en -est comme épithète :

she was rather plain but had the sweetest smile
elle n'était pas très jolie, mais elle avait un sourire magnifique

please accept my warmest congratulations!
veuillez accepter mes plus chaleureuses félicitations !

3 Cas particuliers

a) Further/the furthest et farther/the farthest

Further est d'un usage plus courant que farther quand on fait référence à la distance (et lorsqu'il est employé comme adverbe) :

this is the furthest (farthest) point
c'est le point le plus éloigné

(En tant qu'adverbe : I can't go any further (farther) *je ne peux pas aller plus loin*)

Si on fait référence au temps ou à un nombre, on ne peut employer que further :

any further misdemeanours and you're out
une autre incartade et tu sors

this must be delayed until a further meeting
ceci doit être reporté à un prochain meeting

anything further can be discussed tomorrow
pour le reste, on verra demain

et comme adverbe :

don't try my patience any further
n'abuse pas de ma patience

the police want to question him further
la police veut encore l'interroger

b) Later/latest et latter/last

Later et latest font référence au temps, latter et last à un ordre, à une série :

(a) **his latest book is on war poetry**
son dernier livre en date est sur la poésie en temps de guerre

(b) **his last book was on war poetry**
son dernier livre était sur la poésie en temps de guerre

Latest en (a) a le sens de "le plus récent", alors que last en (b) fait référence au dernier d'une série de livres.

Pour latter, voir **Les nombres**, p. A77. Notez, de plus, que latter sous-entend une division en deux, comme dans the latter part of the century (*la deuxième moitié du siècle*).

c) Less/lesser

Less est quantitatif, the lesser est qualitatif :

use less butter	**the lesser of two evils**
prenez moins de beurre	*le moindre mal*

it'll take less time if you go by train
vous mettrez moins de temps en train

there's a lesser degree of irony in this novel
il y a moins d'ironie dans ce roman

d) Older/oldest et elder/eldest

Elder et eldest ne font en général référence qu'aux liens familiaux :

this is my elder/eldest brother
c'est mon frère aîné

bien que older puisse aussi s'utiliser dans ce contexte. Si than (*que*) suit, seul older est possible :

my brother is older than I am
mon frère est plus vieux que moi

Remarquez l'emploi de elder comme nom :

listen to your elders
écoute tes aînés

the elders **of the tribe**
les anciens de la tribu

she is my elder by two years
elle est mon aînée de deux ans

7 LES PRONOMS PERSONNELS

	SINGULIER	**PLURIEL**
1ère	**I/me**	**we/us**
2ème	**you**	**you**
3ème	**he/him, she/her, it**	**they/them**

Voir p. A78 pour l'ordre des pronoms personnels dans une phrase.
Dans le tableau ci-dessus, la première forme de chaque paire est la forme du sujet, la seconde étant celle des autres emplois :

she's not here yet (*sujet*)
elle n'est pas encore là

Jane didn't see her (*complément d'objet direct*)
Jane ne l'a pas vue

Jane wrote her **a letter** (*complément d'objet indirect*)
Jane lui a écrit une lettre

it's her!   **with/for** her
c'est elle !   *avec/pour elle*

You correspond, en français, à toutes les formes de la deuxième personne du singulier et du pluriel (*tu, toi, te, vous*)

a) *Pronoms sujets ou pronoms compléments ?*

   i) Les pronoms **I, you, he, she, it, we, they** s'utilisent comme sujets :

       my wife and I are always there
       ma femme et moi, nous sommes toujours là

       Mais on entend parfois à l'oral des phrases incorrectes où le pronom complément est employé à la place du pronom sujet :

       me and my wife are always there (*Fam*)

       Mais, de manière générale, on utilise souvent en anglais le pronom complément (**me, you, him, her, it, us, them**) là où en français on utilise les pronoms "moi", "toi", etc. :

       who is it? – it's me   **who did it? – me** (ou **I did**)
       qui est-ce ? – c'est moi   *qui a fait cela ? – moi*

       Cependant, si une proposition relative suit, il est assez courant d'utiliser la forme sujet, à condition que le pronom relatif fasse fonction de sujet. Ainsi, on dira :

       it was I who did it ou : **it was me that did it** (*Fam*)
                                       c'est moi qui l'ai fait

       mais toujours :   **it was me (that) you spoke to**
                                c'est à moi que vous avez parlé

       Comme en français, le pronom complément s'utilise après une préposition :

       we have a long day in front of us
       nous avons une longue journée devant nous

       have you got any cash on you?
       avez-vous du liquide sur vous ?

he has his whole life before him
il a toute la vie devant lui

   ii) On place généralement le pronom complément après **than** et **as** (si aucun verbe ne suit) :

        she's not as good as him, but she's better than me
        elle n'est pas aussi bonne que lui, mais elle est meilleure que moi

        mais si un verbe suit, c'est le pronom sujet qui doit être employé :

        she's not as good as he is, but she's better than I am
        elle n'est pas aussi bonne que lui, mais elle est meilleure que moi

        Cependant, dans un style plus soutenu, le pronom sujet peut être placé en position finale après **than** et **as**, et surtout après **than** :

        he is a better player than I
        il joue mieux que moi

b) *Omission du pronom sujet*

   On omet bien sûr les pronoms sujets à l'impératif :

   don't say a word!
   ne dis rien !

   Mais on peut les utiliser pour renforcer le sens de l'impératif (par exemple, pour proférer une menace) :

   don't you say a word!
   je t'interdis de dire quoi que ce soit !

c) *He, she ou it ?*

   Le pronom **it** s'emploie pour désigner des choses et des animaux alors que les pronoms **he** (**him, his**) ou **she** (**her**) s'emploient pour des personnes. Cependant, **he** (**him, his**) ou **she** (**her**) peuvent s'utiliser à la place de **it** dans des cas bien particuliers :

   i) Les animaux :

       On emploie **it** lorsque l'on parle d'un animal en général (c'est-à-dire de l'espèce), et **he/she** quand on connaît bien l'animal dont il est question :

       have you seen the cat? — I think she's gone out
       est-ce que tu as vu la chatte ? – je crois qu'elle est sortie

       the dog is hungry, would you mind feeding him?
       le chien a faim, est-ce que tu veux bien lui donner à manger ?

   ii) Les moyens de transport :

        Le pronom qui s'utilise habituellement pour désigner un moyen de transport est **it** :

        where's the car? – it's in the driveway
        où est la voiture ? – elle est dans l'allée

        this ship is larger than that one, and it has two funnels
        ce bateau est plus grand que celui-là, et il a deux cheminées

        Cependant, on peut trouver parfois le pronom féminin pour une voiture. Par cet emploi, le locuteur montre qu'il est attaché à sa voiture :

        she's been a long way, this old car
        elle en a fait du chemin, cette vieille voiture

        Il arrive aussi que le féminin soit employé pour un bateau, dans un style très soutenu ou littéraire :

        I saw the QE2 when she first sailed
        j'ai vu le Queen Elizabeth II lors de sa première sortie en mer

iii) Les pays :

On emploie pratiquement toujours it pour les pays, mais on peut trouver aussi le pronom féminin (emploi rare et littéraire) :

Denmark will remember those who died for her
le Danemark se souviendra de ceux qui sont morts pour lui

d) It *sans référence*

i) Comme en français, on peut utiliser en anglais le pronom impersonnel it pour parler du temps, donner des jugements, décrire des situations, etc. :

it's raining	**it's freezing in here**
il pleut	*on se gèle ici*
it's wrong to steal	**what's it like outside today?**
il ne faut pas voler	*il fait quel temps dehors aujourd'hui ?*
it's very cosy here	**it's clear that they don't like it**
c'est très confortable ici	*il est clair que ça ne leur plaît pas*

it's not easy to raise that sort of money
ce n'est pas facile de trouver une telle somme d'argent

it looks as if they've left
on dirait qu'ils sont partis

Et aussi pour faire référence à un point précis dans l'espace ou dans le temps :

it's ten o'clock	**it's 10th June**
il est dix heures	*c'est le 10 juin*
it's time to go	**it's at least three miles**
il est temps de partir	*ça fait au moins cinq kilomètres*

Mais si on évoque la durée, on emploie there :

there's still time to put things right
il reste du temps pour arranger les choses

Remarquez aussi la phrase it says (on dit, il est dit) pour faire référence à un texte :

it says in today's newspaper that they're getting divorced
on dit dans le journal d'aujourd'hui qu'ils vont divorcer

ii) It peut aussi être utilisé de façon impersonnelle, surtout dans des expressions toutes faites :

that's it! (= that's right)	**beat it!** *(Fam)*
c'est ça !	*va-t'en !*
she thinks she's it *(Fam)*	**she has it in for him** *(Fam)*
elle s'y croit	*elle a une dent contre lui*

e) *Emploi collectif*

You, **we** et **they** sont souvent employés de façon collective pour désigner les gens en général. Le pronom they exclut normalement le locuteur :

you don't see many phone boxes any more
on ne voit plus beaucoup de cabines téléphoniques

I'm afraid we simply don't treat animals very well
j'ai bien peur qu'on ne traite pas très bien les animaux

they say he won the lottery
il paraît qu'il a gagné au loto

i) You est employé pour faire une remarque sur une situation :

you never can find one when you need one
on n'en trouve jamais quand on en a besoin

you never can be too careful
on n'est jamais trop prudent

ii) You est également employé pour donner des instructions :

you first crack the eggs into a bowl
cassez d'abord les œufs dans un saladier

you must look both ways before crossing
il faut regarder des deux côtés avant de traverser

Pour l'emploi de one, voir h) ci-dessous.

f) *Un emploi particulier de* we

We s'utilise parfois à la place de la deuxième personne du singulier et du pluriel (= *tu*, *vous*) et équivaut au "nous" de condescendance ou ironique :

have we all done our homework, class?
alors, on a tous fait ses devoirs ?

how are we feeling today, then?
eh bien, comment allons-nous aujourd'hui ?

g) *Emploi de* they

i) L'emploi de they collectif est devenu très courant, pour renvoyer à somebody, someone, anybody, anyone, everybody, everyone, nobody, no one. Le they collectif évite le he or she maladroit (parfois écrit s/he).

Certains considèrent malheureux l'emploi de he seul comme pronom collectif signifiant "les gens". Le they (their, them(selves)) collectif est maintenant courant dans l'anglais parlé et parfois écrit (même si on ne fait référence qu'à un sexe) et offre un moyen pratique d'éviter de s'exprimer d'une façon qui pourrait être jugée sexiste :

if anybody has anything against it, they should say so
si certains sont contre, qu'ils le disent

everybody grabbed their possessions and ran
tout le monde a ramassé ses affaires et s'est enfui

somebody has left their bike right outside the door
quelqu'un a laissé son vélo juste devant la porte

Cet emploi est de plus en plus courant avec des noms précédés any, some ou no.

some person or other has tampered with my files – they'll be sorry
quelqu'un a touché à mes dossiers sans permission – il va le regretter

no child is allowed to leave until they have been seen by a doctor
aucun enfant ne pourra sortir avant d'avoir été examiné par un médecin

Pour l'emploi de one, voir h) ci-dessous.

ii) They est employé pour faire référence à une (ou plusieurs) personne(s) que l'on ne connaît pas, mais qui représente(nt) l'autorité, le pouvoir, le savoir :

they're going to have to close the factory
ils vont devoir fermer l'usine

they should be able to repair it
ils devraient pouvoir le réparer

they will be able to tell you at the advice centre
on pourra vous renseigner au bureau d'information

when you earn a bit of money they always find a way of taking it off you
quand on gagne un peu d'argent, ils trouvent toujours moyen pour vous en prélever

h) *Le pronom personnel indéfini* one

One peut s'employer comme sujet et comme complément d'objet. La forme possessive est one's et la forme réfléchie, oneself. L'emploi de one est soutenu ; ce pronom ne s'utilise que très rarement aujourd'hui.

i) Si **one** est pris dans un sens collectif, le locuteur s'inclut dans "les gens en général" :

well, what can one do?
eh bien, qu'est-ce qu'on peut faire ?

one is not supposed to do that
on n'est pas censé faire ça

Il est à noter qu'en anglais américain, le pronom masculin de la troisième personne peut suivre **one** :

one shouldn't take risks if he can avoid it
on ne devrait pas prendre de risques si on peut l'éviter

One offre un moyen pratique d'éviter les erreurs d'interprétation de **you**. En effet, l'emploi collectif **you** est parfois source d'ambiguïté. Dans la phrase suivante par exemple, on ne sait pas si **you** est utilisé de manière générale ou s'il renvoie à l'interlocuteur :

you need to be ruthless if you want to get anywhere in this world
tu dois être impitoyable si tu veux réussir dans la vie

Pour être plus précis, un locuteur désirant énoncer une généralité, et non pas faire référence à un individu en particulier, préférera utiliser la phrase suivante :

one needs to be ruthless if one wants to get anywhere in this world
il faut être impitoyable si l'on veut réussir dans la vie

ii) L'emploi de **one** pour la première personne, c'est-à-dire à la place de **I** (*je*) ou **we** (*nous*), est maintenant considéré comme un style précieux :

seeing such misery has taught one to appreciate how lucky one is in one's own country
le spectacle de tant de misère nous a appris à apprécier la chance que nous avons dans notre pays

i) **It** ou **so** ?

Pour l'emploi de **so** comme pronom, voir p. A38.

Le pronom personnel **it** ne s'utilise pas de la même manière que **so**. Comparez :

(a) I can't believe he said it
je n'arrive pas à croire qu'il l'ait dit

(b) you'll do it because I said so
tu vas le faire parce que je l'ai dit

En (a), le pronom **it** est un complément d'objet ; il renvoie à quelque chose de très précis. En (b), **so** est plus vague ; il renvoie au **fait** que le locuteur l'ait dit.

8 LES PRONOMS RÉFLÉCHIS

	SINGULIER	PLURIEL
1ère	**myself** (*moi-même*)	**ourselves**
2ème	**yourself**	**yourselves**
3ème	**himself, herself, itself, oneself**	**themselves**

a) *Employés comme attributs, compléments d'objet direct, compléments d'objet indirect et après des prépositions pour renvoyer au sujet*

I am not myself today (*attribut*)
je ne me sens pas bien aujourd'hui

she has burnt herself (*complément d'objet direct*)
elle s'est brûlée

we gave ourselves a treat (*complément d'objet indirect*)
on s'est fait plaisir

why are you talking to yourself? (*après une préposition*)
pourquoi est-ce que tu parles tout seul ?

b) *Emploi d'intensité*

Lorsque le locuteur souhaite donner une certaine intensité à ce dont il parle, il emploie souvent un pronom réfléchi :

you're quite well-off now, aren't you? – you haven't done so badly yourself
tu es plutôt riche maintenant, n'est-ce pas ? – tu ne t'es pas si mal débrouillé non plus

only they themselves know whether it is the right thing to do
eux seuls savent si c'est la bonne chose à faire

get me a beer, will you? – get it yourself
tu vas me chercher une bière, s'il te plaît ? – va te la chercher toi-même

La position du pronom réfléchi peut modifier le sens de la phrase :

the Queen wanted to speak to him herself
la Reine a voulu lui parler elle-même

mais :

the Queen herself wanted to speak to him
la Reine elle-même a voulu lui parler (c'est-à-dire la Reine en personne)

c) *Après* as, like, than *et* and

Après ces mots, il n'est pas rare de voir les pronoms réfléchis utilisés à la place des pronoms personnels car on hésite parfois entre la forme sujet et la forme complément (voir **Les pronoms personnels** p. A27). Mais cet emploi est familier et grammaticalement incorrect :

he's not quite as old as myself
il n'est pas aussi âgé que moi

like yourself, I also have a few family problems
comme vous, j'ai aussi quelques problèmes familiaux

d) *Verbes réfléchis*

i) Quelques rares verbes ne sont que réfléchis, par exemple :

absent oneself *s'absenter*   **ingratiate oneself** *se faire*
avail oneself of *utiliser*   *bien voir*
demean oneself *s'abaisser*   **perjure oneself** *se parjurer*
                                        pride oneself *se fier*

ii) D'autres ont des significations totalement différentes lorsqu'ils sont réfléchis et lorsqu'ils ne le sont pas :

he applied for the post
il a posé sa candidature pour le poste

he should apply himself more to his studies
il devrait se consacrer davantage à ses études

the jury acquitted him at the trial
le jury l'a acquitté au procès

he acquitted himself well in the recent championships
il s'en est bien sorti lors des récents championnats

iii) Et il existe plusieurs verbes dont le sens demeure le même, que le verbe soit réfléchi ou non :

they always behave (themselves) in public
ils se conduisent toujours bien en public

we found it very difficult to adjust (ourselves) to the humid climate
nous avons trouvé très difficile de nous adapter au climat humide

Notez que l'élément réfléchi peut ajouter la notion de détermination. Comparez :

(a) he proved to be useful
il a fini par être utile

(b) he'll have to prove himself more useful if he wants to keep his job
il va falloir qu'il se montre plus utile s'il veut garder son travail

(c) the crowd pushed forward
la foule avançait

(d) the crowd pushed itself forward
la foule s'avançait

Dans l'exemple (d), il y a plus de détermination que dans l'exemple (c).

9 LES POSSESSIFS

a) *Forme et emploi des possessifs*

LES ADJECTIFS POSSESSIFS

	SINGULIER	PLURIEL
1ère	my (mon, ma, mes)	our (notre, nos)
2ème	your (ton, ta, tes ; votre, vos)	your (votre, vos)
3ème	his (son, sa, ses)	their (leur, leurs)
	her (son, sa, ses)	
	its (son, sa, ses)	

LES PRONOMS POSSESSIFS

	SINGULIER	PLURIEL
1ère	mine (le mien, etc.)	ours
2ème	yours	yours
3ème	his, hers, its	theirs

! Il existe trois formes à la troisième personne du singulier ; on les utilise selon que le possesseur est de sexe masculin ou féminin ou qu'il est neutre. Il est important de se souvenir qu'il n'y a pas de genres grammaticaux en anglais et que le choix entre his/her dépend uniquement du sexe du possesseur. Pour les objets et les animaux, on emploie its (voir ci-dessous) :

who is that man? — what is his name?
qui est cet homme ? — *quel est son nom ?*

who is that woman? — what is her name?
qui est cette femme ? — *quel est son nom ?*

what street is this? — what is its name?
quelle est cette rue ? — *quel est son nom ?*

Dans les cas particuliers où he/she désignent des animaux ou des objets (voir **Les pronoms personnels** p. A27), on emploie les possessifs correspondants :

our dog's hurt his/its paw — the lion is hunting its prey
notre chien s'est fait mal à la patte — *le lion chasse sa proie*

Les pronoms possessifs anglais ne permettent pas de distinguer le nombre du nom auquel ils renvoient (la forme du pronom est la même, que l'antécédent soit singulier ou pluriel). Cette infor-

mation nous est donnée par les pronoms personnels, les verbes qui suivent ou le contexte. Par ailleurs, si l'on veut traduire la phrase anglaise, il est nécessaire de connaître l'antécédent pour savoir le genre que l'on doit utiliser en français :

mine is this one
le mien/la mienne, c'est celui-ci/celle-ci

mine are these ones
les miens/les miennes, ce sont ceux-là/celles-là

ours is much younger (= our daughter)
la nôtre est beaucoup plus jeune

ours are much younger (= our children)
les nôtres sont beaucoup plus jeunes

they've bought their tickets *(adj)*/they've bought theirs *(pron)*
ils ont acheté leur(s) billet(s)/ils ont acheté le(s) leur(s)

Dans ce dernier exemple, la phrase anglaise ne permet pas de savoir s'ils ont acheté un billet chacun ou plusieurs. Seul le contexte peut nous renseigner. Cet emploi du pluriel distributif après l'adjectif possessif anglais est expliqué pp. A14-15.

Remarquez le "double génitif" (voir p. A16) avec les pronoms possessifs :

he's an old friend of mine
c'est un vieil ami à moi ou *un de mes vieux amis*

that mother of hers is driving me mad
sa mère me rend fou

b) *Adjectif possessif ou article ?*

L'adjectif possessif anglais correspond très souvent en français à l'article défini, notamment lorsque l'on parle d'une partie du corps ou d'un vêtement :

he put his hands behind his back — my head is spinning
il a mis les mains derrière le dos — *j'ai la tête qui tourne*

she's broken her leg
elle s'est cassé la jambe

what have you got in your pockets?
qu'est-ce que tu as dans les poches ?

En général, on emploie l'article défini après une préposition (bien que l'adjectif possessif soit aussi possible) :

he grabbed her by the hair
il l'a attrapée par les cheveux

he was punched on the nose
il a reçu un coup de poing dans le nez

Mais si le mot est qualifié par un adjectif, on emploiera l'adjectif possessif à la place de l'article :

he grabbed her by her long hair
il l'a attrapée par ses longs cheveux

Voir aussi "le pluriel distributif" pp. A14-15.

10 LES DÉMONSTRATIFS

SINGULIER	PLURIEL
this, that	these, those

Les formes sont les mêmes pour l'adjectif démonstratif (*ce, cette, ces*, etc.) et le pronom démonstratif (*celui-ci, celle-ci, celle-là*, etc.).

a) **This et these** renvoient à quelque chose qui se trouve près du locuteur, ou qui a un rapport immédiat avec le locuteur, alors que that et those ont un rapport plus distant avec lui :

(a) this pen is mine; that one is yours
   ce crayon-ci est à moi ; celui-là est à toi

(b) that pen is mine; this one is yours
   ce crayon-là est à moi ; celui-ci est à toi

En (a), le crayon mentionné en premier se trouve plus près du locuteur que l'autre crayon ; en (b), c'est le contraire.

De même au téléphone :

hi, this is Christine, is that Joanna?
bonjour, c'est Christine, c'est Joanna à l'appareil ?

La distinction entre this/these et that/those se fait aussi en fonction de la distance dans le temps :

honestly, teenagers these days!
vraiment, les adolescents d'aujourd'hui !

in those days it wasn't possible
à cette époque-là, ce n'était pas possible

Remarquez que la même phrase peut prendre un sens différent selon le démonstratif employé :

(a) this is what I want you to do
   voici ce que je veux que tu fasses

(b) that's what I want you to do
   c'est ça que je veux que tu fasses

En (a), le locuteur est sur le point de dire à l'interlocuteur ce dont il s'agit, tandis qu'en (b) l'explication vient juste d'être mentionnée.

Quand ils sont pronoms, les démonstratifs ne renvoient jamais à des personnes, sauf dans les phrases où ils sont sujets (this is Carla *c'est Carla*) et dans les questions (who is this? *qui est-ce ?*).

b) This/these *indéfinis*

L'emploi de this/these comme pronoms indéfinis est très courant en anglais familier, quand on raconte une histoire ou une blague par exemple :

the other day these guys came up to me...
l'autre jour, des types se sont approchés de moi...

this Irishman was sitting in a pub when...
un Irlandais était assis dans un pub quand...

c) That/this *adverbes*

That/this sont souvent utilisés comme adverbes, dans un sens proche de so (*si*), avant un adjectif ou un autre adverbe :

I like a red carpet but not one that red
j'aime bien les tapis rouges, mais pas aussi rouges que ça

I don't like doing it that/this often
je n'aime pas le faire si souvent

now that we've come this far, we might as well press on
maintenant qu'on en est là, autant continuer

I don't want that/this much to eat!
je ne veux pas manger autant que ça !

she doesn't want to marry him, she's not that stupid
elle ne veut pas se marier avec lui, elle n'est pas si stupide

11 LES INTERROGATIFS

Les interrogatifs anglais sont :

who/whom/whose, which, what et toutes les formes composées avec le suffixe -ever, par exemple : whichever.

Les interrogatifs peuvent s'employer comme pronoms ou comme adjectifs (sauf who et whom qui ne s'emploient que comme pronoms) :

which do you want? *(pron)* *lequel veux-tu ?*	which flavour do you want? *(adj)* *quel parfum veux-tu ?*

Remarquez qu'ils sont invariables. Le premier exemple pourrait tout aussi bien se traduire par "laquelle/lesquels/lesquelles veux-tu ?"

a) Who *et* whom

Who et whom sont toujours des pronoms (c'est-à-dire qu'ils ne sont jamais suivis par un nom) et ils renvoient à des personnes :

who are you?
qui êtes-vous ?

to whom were your remarks addressed?
à qui s'adressaient vos remarques ?

Whom est utilisé dans un style soutenu, lorsqu'il est complément d'objet (direct ou indirect) ou qu'il suit une préposition :

whom did she embrace?
qui a-t-elle embrassé ?

to whom did he give his permission?
à qui a-t-il donné la permission ?

I demanded to know to whom he had spoken
ou :
I demanded to know whom he had spoken to
j'ai exigé de savoir à qui il avait parlé

En anglais parlé d'aujourd'hui, on utilise en général who (au lieu de whom) pour toutes les fonctions grammaticales. Whom reste obligatoire lorsqu'il est placé directement après une préposition, même si ce genre de tournure ne s'emploie plus tellement à l'oral. Par exemple :

who did you see at the party?
tu as vu qui à la soirée ?

I want to know who you spoke to just now
I want to know to whom you spoke just now *(style soutenu)*
je veux savoir avec qui tu étais en train de parler

b) Whose

C'est la forme au génitif de who. Il peut être pronom ou adjectif :

whose are these bags? *(pron)* *à qui sont ces sacs ?*	whose bags are these? *(adj)* *ce sont les sacs de qui ?*

c) Which/what

Au contraire de who(m), which peut être adjectif ou pronom, et peut renvoyer à une personne ou à un objet :

which actor do you mean? *(adj)* *de quel acteur parles-tu ?*	which album do you prefer? *(adj)* *quel album tu préfères ?*

which of the actors do you mean? *(pron)*
duquel des acteurs parles-tu ?

of these two albums, which do you prefer? *(pron)*
de ces deux albums, lequel tu préfères ?

La différence entre which et who/what est que which est restrictif : il invite celui à qui on parle à faire un choix parmi un certain nombre de choses précises.

Comparez :

what would you like to drink?
qu'est-ce que tu veux boire ?

I've got coffee or tea, which would you like?
j'ai du café ou du thé, qu'est-ce que tu veux ?

Si l'objet du choix n'est pas identifié avant la question, on ne peut employer que **what** :

what would you like to drink? I've got beer, red wine or mineral water
qu'est-ce que tu veux boire ? j'ai de la bière, du vin rouge ou de l'eau minérale

d) **What**

Lorsqu'il est **pronom**, what ne renvoie jamais à une personne :

what's this book?　　　**don't ask me what I did**
qu'est-ce que c'est que ce livre ?　*ne me demande pas ce que j'ai fait*

Lorsqu'il est **adjectif**, what peut renvoyer à une personne, à un animal ou à une chose :

what child does not like sweets?
quel enfant n'aime pas les bonbons ?

what kind of soap do you use?
quelle sorte de savon utilisez-vous ?

Pour la différence entre which et what, voir c) ci-dessus.

Remarquez l'emploi de what dans les exclamations :

what awful weather!　　　**what a dreadful day!**
quel temps affreux !　　　*quelle journée épouvantable !*

what must they think!
qu'est-ce qu'ils doivent penser !

e) *Avec -ever*

Le suffixe -ever exprime la surprise, la confusion ou la gêne, l'agacement :

whatever do you mean? *(confusion ou gêne)*
qu'est-ce que tu veux dire ?

whoever would have thought that? *(surprise)*
qui donc aurait pu penser cela ?

whatever did you do that for? *(agacement)*
pourquoi donc as-tu fait ça ?

12 LES RELATIFS

Les relatifs anglais sont :
who/whom/whose, which, what, that et toutes les formes composées avec le suffixe -ever, par exemple : whichever.

Les pronoms relatifs (sauf what) ont en général un antécédent auquel ils se rapportent.

Dans :

she spoke to the man who/that sat beside her
elle a parlé à l'homme qui était assis à côté d'elle

who/that est le pronom relatif et the man, l'antécédent.

a) *Déterminative et explicative*

Une proposition relative peut être déterminative ou explicative.

Si elle est déterminative, elle est nécessaire au sens de la phrase complète par le lien qui l'unit à l'antécédent ; elle restreint le sens de l'antécédent :

that's the man who asked to see you
c'est l'homme qui a demandé à vous voir

Si elle est explicative, elle a un rapport moins étroit avec l'antécédent et son rôle est similaire à celui d'une parenthèse. Par exemple :

Janice, who came to see us yesterday, told us she was expecting a baby
Janice, qui est venue nous voir hier, nous a annoncé qu'elle attendait un enfant

Au contraire des propositions déterminatives, les propositions explicatives doivent être précédées d'une virgule. Cependant, la virgule est souvent oubliée, ce qui entraîne parfois une ambiguïté au niveau du sens de la phrase. Ainsi, la proposition de l'exemple suivant :

he helped the woman who had cried out
il aida la femme qui avait appelé au secours

peut être soit déterminative (= il aida la femme qui avait appelé au secours et non celle qui ne l'avait pas fait), soit explicative (= il aida la femme (qui, par ailleurs, avait appelé au secours)).

! Le pronom relatif that est uniquement employé dans des propositions relatives déterminatives. Who et which peuvent être utilisés dans les deux cas.

b) **Who/whom/that**

Who ou that sont utilisés comme pronoms sujets (*qui*) :

the woman who/that called was his sister
la femme qui a appelé était sa sœur

Who(m) ou that sont utilisés comme compléments (*que*) :

the man who(m)/that she rescued was a tourist
l'homme qu'elle a sauvé était un touriste

Whom est utilisé dans un style plus soutenu (voir **Les interrogatifs**, p. A31)

c) **Who/which/that**

i) **Who/that**

Ces formes renvoient à des personnes ou, dans certains cas, à des animaux (voir **Les pronoms personnels** p. A27) :

we ignored the people who/that were late
nous n'avons pas tenu compte des gens qui étaient en retard

our cat, who is two years old, keeps sharpening his claws on the curtains
notre chat, qui a deux ans, n'arrête pas de faire ses griffes sur les rideaux

Remarquez que seul who, et non that, peut être employé dans le second exemple, qui est une proposition relative explicative, voir b) ci-dessus.

Pour les noms collectifs (voir p. A11), on emploie who ou that si l'on veut leur donner un caractère individuel. Mais si l'on considère le groupe de manière moins personnelle, on emploie which ou that :

the crowd who/that had gathered were in great spirits *(aspect personnalisé)*
la foule qui s'était rassemblée était très enthousiaste

the crowd which/that had gathered was enormous *(aspect collectif)*
la foule qui s'était rassemblée était énorme

ii) **Which/that**

Which ou that renvoient à des objets, des concepts, etc. :

the car **which/that** drove into me
la voiture qui m'est rentrée dedans

the disks **which/that** I sent you
les disquettes que je t'ai envoyées

! Bien que les pronoms personnels puissent être utilisés pour des moyens de transport, comme on l'a vu p. A27, cette personnalisation ne s'applique pas aux pronoms relatifs, c'est-à-dire que **who** ne pourra jamais renvoyer à des véhicules, etc.

d) **Whose**

La forme au génitif **whose** renvoie à des personnes et à des animaux, mais elle est aussi souvent employée, à la place de **of which**, pour un objet ou une chose :

this is the girl **whose** mother has just won the lottery
c'est la fille dont la mère vient juste de gagner au loto

that's that new machine **whose** cover is damaged
c'est la nouvelle machine dont le couvercle est abîmé

the department, **whose** staff are all over 50, is likely to be closed down
ce service, dont tout le personnel a plus de 50 ans, risque de fermer

the vehicles, the state **of which** left a good deal to be desired, had been in use throughout the year
les véhicules, dont l'état laissait à désirer, avaient été en service pendant toute l'année

e) **Which**

i) **Which** ne renvoie jamais aux personnes, mais toujours aux objets, aux idées, etc. :

I received quite a few books for Christmas, **which** I still haven't read
j'ai reçu un bon nombre de livres pour Noël, que je n'ai pas encore lus

Mais il peut renvoyer à une caractéristique d'une personne :

she complains that her husband is a bit insensitive, **which** in fact he is
elle se plaint que son mari est un peu insensible, ce qui d'ailleurs est vrai

ii) On ne trouve **which** utilisé comme adjectif qu'après une préposition ou lorsque son antécédent est une chose. L'emploi de **which** comme adjectif est d'un style soutenu et littéraire, surtout quand il n'est pas accompagné d'une préposition :

he returned to Nottingham, in **which** city he was born and bred
il revint à Nottingham, ville dans laquelle il avait grandi

he rarely spoke in public, **which** fact only added to his obscurity
il parlait très peu en public, particularité qui contribuait à le laisser dans l'ombre

f) **What**

i) **What** est le seul relatif qui ne prend pas d'antécédent. Il peut être pronom ou adjectif. Quand il est pronom, il fait normalement référence à une chose et a souvent le sens de **that which** (*ce qui/que*), ou au pluriel, de **the things which** (*les choses qui/que*) :

show me **what** did the damage
montre-moi ce qui a causé les dégâts

Quand il est adjectif, il peut renvoyer à une personne ou à une chose, et il correspond à **the** + nom + **who/which** :

show me **what** damage was done
montre-moi quels dégâts ont été faits

with **what** volunteers they could find, they set off for the summit
avec les volontaires qu'ils ont pu trouver, ils sont partis à la conquête du sommet

what money they had left, they spent on drink
l'argent qu'il leur restait, ils le dépensèrent en alcool

ii) **What** ou **which** ?

Seul **which** peut renvoyer à une proposition complète alors que **what** n'a pas d'antécédent. Mais le pronom **what** peut annoncer ou introduire une proposition sujet ou complément :

she left the baby unattended, **which** was a silly thing to do
elle a laissé le bébé tout seul, ce qui était inconscient de sa part

what you need is a hot bath *(proposition sujet)*
ce qu'il vous faut, c'est un bon bain chaud

she has **what** it takes to succeed *(proposition complément)*
elle a ce qu'il faut pour réussir

g) *Avec* **-ever**

Au contraire des pronoms interrogatifs (voir p. A32), **-ever** n'exprime pas la surprise, la confusion ou l'agacement quand il est associé à un relatif ; il permet seulement de les renforcer dans le sens de **no matter who/which/what** (*qui/quoi que ce soit*) :

take **whichever** tool is best *(adj)*
prends l'outil qui convient le mieux

take **whichever** is best *(pron)*
prends celui qui convient le mieux

I'll do it **whatever** happens *(pron)*
je le ferai quoi qu'il arrive

do **whatever** you like *(pron)*
fais ce que tu veux

whatever problems we may have to face, we'll solve them *(adj)*
quels que soient les problèmes que nous ayons à affronter, nous les résoudrons

h) *Omission du relatif*

Le pronom relatif peut être omis (ce qui est très souvent le cas à l'oral) dans les propositions relatives déterminatives, sauf s'il est sujet ou s'il est précédé d'une préposition :

these are the things **(which/that)** we have to do
ce sont les choses que nous devons faire

I saw the boy **(who/that)** you met last night
j'ai vu le garçon que tu as rencontré hier soir

is this the sales assistant **(who/that)** you spoke to?
est-ce à cette vendeuse que tu as parlé ?

who's the girl **(who/that)** you came to the party with?
qui est la fille avec qui tu es venu à la soirée ?

Remarquez que la construction assez soutenue :

who are the people **with whom** you are doing business?
qui sont les gens avec qui vous travaillez ?

peut être évitée si l'on change de place la préposition (**with**) :

who are the people you are doing business **with**?

13 LES PRONOMS ET LES ADJECTIFS INDÉFINIS

a) Some *et* any

i) Some et any s'emploient avec des indénombrables et des noms pluriels. Avec les noms dénombrables singuliers, on emploiera l'article indéfini a (**do you have** a **car?** *est-ce que tu as une voiture ?*). Some et any peuvent être pronoms ou adjectifs :

I have some **money** *(adj)*   **I have** some *(pron)*
j'ai de l'argent   *j'en ai*

do you have any **friends?**   **do you have** any? *(pron)*
(adj)   *en avez-vous ?*
est-ce que vous avez des amis ?

Les formes composées avec les suffixes -body, -one, -thing sont toujours des pronoms :

did you speak to anybody?   **tell me** something
as-tu parlé à quelqu'un ?   *dis-moi quelque chose*

ii) Some/any comme adjectifs :

De manière générale, some s'emploie dans les phrases affirmatives et any dans les propositions négatives, interrogatives et conditionnelles :

I have some **money**   **I haven't got** any **money**
j'ai de l'argent   *je n'ai pas d'argent*

have you got any **money?**
est-ce que tu as de l'argent ?

if you've got any **money, could you lend it to me?**
si tu as de l'argent, tu peux m'en prêter ?

Any s'utilise aussi dans les phrases affirmatives qui ont un sens négatif (c'est-à-dire avec des adverbes, des prépositions ou des verbes négatifs) :

I've got hardly any **money**
je n'ai presque pas d'argent

you never **asked me for** any **help**
tu ne m'as jamais demandé de t'aider

I can do it without any **difficulty**
je peux le faire sans aucune difficulté

the noise outside prevented me **from doing** any **work**
le bruit qu'il y avait dehors m'a empêché de travailler

ou lorsqu'il a le sens de "n'importe quel" :

you can choose any **number**
tu peux choisir n'importe quel nombre

La différence entre some et any est souvent subtile. Some est aussi très fréquent dans les propositions interrogatives et conditionnelles ; le locuteur sous-entend alors quelque chose de légèrement différent.

Comparez :

(a) **shall I buy** some **wine for dinner?**
dois-je acheter du vin pour le dîner ?

(b) **will you give** some **money to the kids?**
tu veux bien donner un peu d'argent aux enfants ?

(c) **if there's** some **chocolate left, can I have it?**
s'il reste du chocolat, est-ce que je peux le manger ?

(d) **have we got** any **wine in the house?**
est-ce qu'on a du vin à la maison ?

(e) **did you take** any **money from my purse?**
est-ce que tu as pris de l'argent dans mon porte-monnaie ?

(f) **if there was** any **chocolate left, he would have eaten it**
s'il restait du chocolat, il l'aurait mangé

En (a)-(c), some veut dire "un peu de" ou "quelques", alors qu'en (d)-(f), any signifie "du tout". On a tendance à employer some dans les phrases interrogatives ou conditionnelles lorsqu'on attend une réponse positive de la part de l'interlocuteur, ou lorsqu'on veut l'encourager à dire "oui".

iii) Some/any comme pronoms et leurs composés :

Comparez :

(a) **has she written** any? (any = **books, chapters,** etc.)
est-ce qu'elle en a déjà écrit ?

(b) **has she written** anything?
est-ce qu'elle a déjà écrit quelque chose ?

En (a), le nom auquel any fait référence est sous-entendu et a été évoqué un peu plus tôt, tandis qu'en (b) anything est plus vague ; il ne renvoie à rien de spécifique.

Les pronoms some et any peuvent renvoyer à des noms indénombrables :

I've run out of coffee, have you got any?
je n'ai plus de café, tu en as ?

Remarquez que some est pronom quand il a le sens de "certains" :

some **say it wasn't an accident**
certains disent que ce n'était pas un accident

iv) Some(thing)/any(thing) + of + nom :

Some et any suivis d'une locution commençant par of ont un sens quantitatif, alors que something et anything suivis d'une locution commençant par of sont qualitatifs. Comparez :

(a) **give me** some of **that cheese**
donne-moi un peu de ce fromage

(b) **he hasn't got** any of **her qualities**
il n'a aucune de ses qualités

(c) **there is** something of **the artist in her**
il y a quelque chose d'artistique chez elle

(d) **he hasn't got** anything of **her qualities**
il n'a en rien ses qualités

En (a) et (b), some et any signifient "une part de", "un peu de", alors qu'en (c) et (d) ils ont le sens de "quelque chose dans la manière de" ou "quelque chose qui relève de".

Remarquez que la construction any of + nom ou pronom au pluriel peut être suivie d'un verbe au singulier ou au pluriel, si une ou plusieurs personnes sont sous-entendues :

if any of **your friends** wants **the ticket, phone me**
si un de tes amis veut le billet, appelle-moi

if any of **your friends** want **to come, they're welcome**
si certains de tes amis veulent venir, ils sont les bienvenus

v) Some = "un(e) certain(e)" :

On a vu plus haut (en ii) ci-dessus) que some est utilisé dans un contexte positif avec des noms au pluriel (**would you like** some **biscuits?**) ou des noms indénombrables (**he stayed here for** some **time**). Lorsqu'il est placé devant un nom dénombrable au singulier, il fait référence à quelqu'un ou quelque chose que l'on ne connaît pas et veut souvent dire "un certain" :

some person **(or other) must have taken it**
quelqu'un l'aura pris

some fool **left the door open**
un imbécile a laissé la porte ouverte

he's gone to some town **in the north**
il est parti dans une ville quelque part dans le nord

come and see me some day
il faudra que tu viennes me voir un jour

Comparez avec l'emploi de any + nom dénombrable singulier (= n'importe quel) :

come and see me any day
viens me voir n'importe quel jour

vi) Some = "un mauvais" ou "un bon" :

En anglais familier, on utilise souvent some pour exprimer soit son mépris, son irritation, soit son admiration :

some husband **you are, forgetting my birthday like that!**
quel mauvais mari tu fais, oublier mon anniversaire, quand même !

this really is some party!
c'est vraiment une soirée excellente !

Pour l'emploi de some/any, something/anything comme adverbes, voir p. A24.

b) Many et much

Many et much s'emploient surtout dans les phrases interrogatives ou négatives. Dans les phrases affirmatives, ils permettent de créer un style un peu plus soutenu que a lot of ou lots of.

On emploie many avec des noms pluriels dénombrables et much avec des indénombrables :

ii) Many/much comme adjectifs :

how many students **came?**
combien d'étudiants sont venus ?

she got cards from all her many admirers
elle a reçu des cartes de ses nombreux admirateurs

there isn't much money **left**
il ne reste pas beaucoup d'argent

we don't have much time
on n'a pas beaucoup de temps

iii) Many/much comme pronoms :

many **of the audience** were children
il y avait beaucoup d'enfants dans l'assistance

we can only fit in so many
nous n'avons de place que pour un certain nombre de personnes

we spent much **of the time** arguing
on a passé la plupart du temps à se disputer

he didn't have much **to say on the subject**
il n'avait pas grand-chose à dire à ce sujet

Pour l'emploi de much comme adverbe, voir pp. A22-3.

c) No et none

No et none ont le même sens que not any, mais ils permettent parfois d'insister davantage ou de formuler une phrase de manière plus soutenue :

he doesn't have any **money**
il n'a pas d'argent

he has no **money**
il n'a pas d'argent

he doesn't have any **left**
il n'en a plus

he has none **left**
il n'en a plus

i) No est un adjectif :

he has no **house,** no **money,** no **friends**
il n'a pas de maison, pas d'argent, pas d'amis

ii) None est un pronom :

do you have any cigarettes? – no, I've none **left**
est-ce que vous avez des cigarettes ? – non, je n'en ai plus

I tried on a lot of jumpers but none **(of them) fitted**
j'ai essayé beaucoup de pulls, mais aucun ne m'allait

Remarquez qu'une phrase comme **I have** none (*je n'en ai pas*) est plus soutenue que celle employée couramment, **I don't have** any.

Quand on fait référence à des gens, none **of them/us/you** (*aucun d'eux/de nous/de vous*) est plus courant que none (*aucun, personne*) à l'oral :

none **of us knew where he had filed it**
aucun de nous ne savait où il l'avait classé

I waited for them for hours, but none **of them came**
je les ai attendus pendant des heures, mais aucun d'eux n'est venu

many have set out to climb this mountain but none **have ever returned**
nombreux sont ceux qui sont partis à la conquête de cette montagne, mais aucun n'en est jamais revenu

Quand on veut donner à une phrase un ton emphatique, on peut employer la construction not one :

not one **(of them) was able to tell me the answer!**
pas un seul (d'entre eux) n'a été capable de me répondre !

iii) None : singulier ou pluriel ?

Le sens littéral de none étant no one (*pas un*), le verbe qui suit doit toujours être au singulier :

none **of them** has **seen it before**
aucun d'eux ne l'a jamais vu

Cependant, on rencontre parfois le pluriel (none **of them** have **seen it before**), mais il s'agit là d'un usage incorrect.

Pour l'emploi de no et none comme adverbes, voir p. A24.

d) Every et each

i) Each (*chaque*) peut être pronom ou adjectif ; every (*tout*) est toujours adjectif. Ils font tous les deux uniquement référence à des noms dénombrables :

each **child was given a Christmas present** (*adj*)
on a donné un cadeau de Noël à chaque enfant

each **of them was given a Christmas present** (*pron*)
on a donné un cadeau de Noël à chacun d'eux

each **was given a Christmas present** (*pron*)
on a donné un cadeau de Noël à chacun

every **child was given a Christmas present** (*adj*)
on a donné un cadeau de Noël à tous les enfants

Every renvoie à la totalité des enfants (il n'y a pas d'exception) alors que each permet de les individualiser. Dans les exemples avec each, on insiste davantage sur le fait qu'ils ont reçu un cadeau "les uns après les autres". Every est plus général ; il désigne "tous les enfants".

Remarquez que every peut être précédé d'un génitif ou d'un adjectif possessif :

Wendy's every move was commented on
on commenta chacun des faits et gestes de Wendy

her every move was commented on
on commenta chacun de ses faits et gestes

et notez son emploi avec les nombres et avant other :

she goes to the dentist every three months
elle va chez le dentiste tous les trois mois

I call my parents every two days
j'appelle mes parents tous les deux jours

every other day something goes wrong
un jour sur deux, il y a quelque chose qui ne va pas

Dans la plupart des cas, every two et every other sont interchangeables. Mais every two insiste davantage sur la régularité des faits (expression prise au sens littéral), tandis que every other peut avoir soit le sens de "tous les deux (jours, etc.)", soit un sens plus vague, comme dans le dernier exemple ci-dessus dans lequel every other day signifie "souvent" et ne doit pas être pris au sens littéral de "un jour sur deux".

Remarquez aussi son emploi adverbial :

every now and then
every now and again
every so often
de temps en temps

ii) Everybody/everyone et everything sont des pronoms et sont toujours suivis d'un verbe au singulier mais, comme les autres pronoms indéfinis, everybody peut être suivi de they, them(selves) ou their (voir **Les pronoms personnels**, p. A28).

e) All

i) All peut être adjectif ou pronom ; il renvoie à des noms dénombrables et indénombrables. Remarquez que, lorsqu'un article défini, un pronom personnel ou un adjectif démonstratif ou possessif est utilisé, il se place entre all et le nom :

all expenses will be reimbursed
tous les frais seront remboursés

I want all the/those/their biscuits
je veux tous les/ces/leurs biscuits

all his energy was spent
il a dépensé toute son énergie

I want them all/all of them   **I want it all/all of it**
je les veux tous   *je le veux en entier*

ii) All et everything :

La différence entre ces deux pronoms est souvent assez subtile. Remarquez que all that, employé en début de phrase, signifie "la seule chose qui/que". Seul all peut renvoyer à des noms indénombrables.

we ate everything that was on the table
nous avons mangé tout ce qui était sur la table

all that was on the table was a single vase
il n'y avait qu'un vase sur la table

did you eat the ice-cream? – not all of it
as-tu mangé la glace ? – pas tout

they believed everything/all he said
ils croyaient tout ce qu'il disait

did he say anything? – all that he said was 'do nothing'
est-ce qu'il a dit quelque chose ? – tout ce qu'il a dit, c'est "ne faites rien"

iii) All et whole :

La différence principale entre all et l'adjectif whole réside dans le fait que whole insiste davantage sur le nom qu'il qualifie, en apportant souvent une nuance différente au niveau du sens :

he ate all (of) the cake   **he ate the whole cake**
il a mangé tout le gâteau   *il a mangé le gâteau en entier*

don't interrupt me all the time
ne m'interromps pas tout le temps

she said nothing the whole time we were there
elle n'a rien dit tout le temps que nous étions là

All the time exprime la répétition tandis que the whole time insiste sur la durée.

Mais whole s'emploie uniquement devant les noms dénombrables :

the whole town/all the town (*dénombrable*)
toute la ville

all the butter (*indénombrable*)
tout le beurre

Remarquez que whole ne s'emploie pas avec un nom au pluriel. On emploie par exemple :

he read all the books in their entirety
il a lu tous les livres en entier

Pour l'emploi de all en tant qu'adverbe, voir p. A23.

f) Other(s) *et* another

i) Another, qui peut être adjectif ou pronom, s'emploie uniquement pour les noms singuliers dénombrables. Seul l'adjectif other peut être suivi d'un nom pluriel ; others est toujours pronom (d'un antécédent au pluriel) :

I want another hamburger (*adj*)/**I want another** (*pron*)
je veux un autre hamburger/j'en veux un autre

other children get more money (*adj*)
les autres enfants ont plus d'argent

I like these colours – don't you like the others? (*pron*)
j'aime ces couleurs – tu n'aimes pas les autres ?

ii) Avec la construction nom + than, on peut placer other avant ou après le nom :

there are difficulties other than those mentioned by the government
there are other difficulties than those mentioned by the government
il y a d'autres difficultés que celles qui sont mentionnées par le gouvernement

Mais other est toujours placé après none :

who should arrive? none other than the Prime Minister himself
et qui est arrivé ? le Premier ministre en personne

iii) On utilise parfois no other à la place de not another :

he has no other coat/he doesn't have another coat (*adj*)
il n'a pas d'autre manteau

for this reason, if for no other/if not for another *(pron)*
pour cette raison, à défaut d'une autre

iv) Remarquez la construction avec some et ses composés, quand some veut dire "un(e) certain(e)..." (comparez avec a) v) ci-dessus). On ajoute or other pour intensifier le caractère vague de ce dont on parle :

he married some girl or other from the Bahamas
il s'est marié avec une fille des Bahamas

somebody or other must have betrayed her
quelqu'un a dû la trahir

we'll get there somehow or other *(emploi adverbial)*
on y arrivera d'une manière ou d'une autre

v) Avec one :

One... another et one... the other ont en général la même signification :

one day after another went by
one day after the other went by
les jours se sont écoulés petit à petit

Mais si l'on ne fait référence qu'à deux choses ou à deux personnes, on préférera employer one... the other :

the two brothers worked well together: one would sweep the yard while the other chopped the wood
les deux frères travaillaient bien ensemble : l'un balayait la cour pendant que l'autre coupait le bois

Cependant, si le second élément est précédé d'une préposition, comme dans le premier exemple, on peut aussi employer one... another :

they would sit there and repeat, one after another, every single word of the lesson
ils s'asseyaient là et répétaient, l'un après l'autre, chaque mot de la leçon

On trouve aussi parfois la combinaison the one... the other, qui aurait pu être employée dans l'exemple des deux frères ci-dessus.

Dans la locution on the one hand... on the other hand..., l'article est obligatoire devant one :

on the one hand, you'd earn less, on the other hand, your job satisfaction would be greater
d'un côté tu gagnerais moins d'argent, mais de l'autre, tu aurais une plus grande satisfaction professionnelle

g) Either et neither

i) Either a souvent le sens de "l'un ou l'autre" en parlant de deux choses ou de deux personnes (on utilisera any s'il y en a plus de deux). Il peut être adjectif ou pronom :

you can take either route *(adj)*
tu peux prendre l'un ou l'autre de ces chemins

either bus will get you there *(adj)*
les deux bus y vont

you can take either *(pron)*
vous pouvez prendre l'un ou l'autre/n'importe lequel (des deux)

Either employé comme adjectif peut aussi vouloir dire "chaque" ou "les deux" :

there were candles at either end of the table
il y avait des bougies aux deux bouts/à chaque bout de la table

Cependant, il est parfois préférable d'éviter cet emploi de either dans le sens de each et both, car il peut être ambigu :

vehicles may be parked on either side of the road
il est possible de se garer des deux côtés de la rue
ou *il est possible de se garer d'un côté*

ii) Neither est la forme négative de either :

neither bag is big enough *(adj)*
aucun des deux sacs n'est assez grand

which do you prefer? — neither! *(pron)*
lequel des deux préfères-tu ? — ni l'un ni l'autre !

iii) On emploie toujours un verbe au singulier après either et neither suivis de of + nom pluriel :

neither of the boys is likely to have done it
il est peu probable que l'un des deux garçons l'ait fait

either of the boys is likely to have done it
il est probable que l'un des deux garçons l'ait fait

Pour l'emploi de either et neither comme adverbe, voir p. A24.

h) Both

Both fait référence à deux choses ou à deux personnes et signifie "l'un et l'autre", "les deux". Il est soit adjectif, soit pronom, et comme pour all, il peut être suivi d'un adjectif démonstratif ou possessif, d'un pronom personnel, d'un article défini :

I like both jackets	I like both those/of those jackets
j'aime ces deux vestes	*j'aime l'une et l'autre de ces vestes*
I love both my parents	I love both (of them)/them both
j'aime mon père et ma mère	*je les aime tous les deux*

both (the/of the) versions are correct
les deux versions sont correctes

i) One

i) Ce pronom est employé dans le sens de "une seule chose/personne" en référence à ce qui a été évoqué dans une phrase ou une proposition précédente :

I love dogs but I've never owned one
j'aime bien les chiens mais je n'en ai jamais eu

he's got a lot of cousins, but I've only got one
il a beaucoup de cousins, mais moi, je n'en ai qu'un

his case is a sad one
son cas est triste

this solution is one of considerable ingenuity
c'est une solution remarquablement ingénieuse

Il peut aussi être employé au pluriel (ones) :

she goes to a lot of restaurants, especially Italian ones
elle va dans beaucoup de restaurants différents, notamment dans les restaurants italiens

ii) L'emploi restrictif

The one s'emploie lorsque l'on fait un choix parmi un certain nombre de choses précises et signifie alors "celui que/qui", etc. :

which cat do you prefer? – the white one
quel chat préférez-vous ? – le blanc

I prefer the pen you gave me to the one my mother gave me
je préfère le stylo que vous m'avez donné à celui que ma mère m'a donné

these are the ones I meant
ce sont celles dont je parlais

these burgers are better than the ones you make
ces hamburgers sont meilleurs que ceux que tu fais

iii) Comme le montre le premier exemple du ii) ci-dessus,

one(s) s'emploie en général après des adjectifs qui font référence à des noms dénombrables :

I asked for a large whisky and he gave me a small one
je lui ai demandé un grand whisky, et il m'en a donné un petit

which shoes do you want? the grey ones?
quelles chaussures voulez-vous ? les grises ?

Cependant, si deux adjectifs opposés se suivent, on peut parfois se dispenser d'utiliser one(s) :

I drink a lot of wine, both red and white
je bois beaucoup de vin, aussi bien du rouge que du blanc

she stood by him in good times and bad
elle est restée à ses côtés dans les bons et les mauvais moments

today I wish to talk about two kinds of climate, the temperate and the tropical
je vais vous parler aujourd'hui de deux sortes de climats, le climat tempéré et le climat tropical

Si aucun nom n'a été mentionné de manière précise et que seul un terme général est sous-entendu (men, etc.), l'adjectif fonctionne comme un nom, et one(s) n'a pas besoin d'être employé. On remarque notamment cette absence de one(s) dans les expressions idiomatiques :

the survival of the fittest   **fortune favours** the brave
la persistance du plus apte   *la chance sourit aux braves*

Il est évident que one ne peut pas renvoyer à un nom indénombrable :

do you want white sugar or brown?
voulez-vous du sucre blanc ou du roux ?

iv) One est parfois employé dans un sens proche de "quelqu'un" ou "une personne", comme dans :

I'm not one for big parties
je ne raffole pas des grandes fêtes

I'm not one to complain
je ne suis pas du genre à me plaindre

v) One pris dans un sens collectif, voir pp. A28-9.

j) **So**

So est un pronom quand il renvoie à une affirmation ou à une question ; il permet d'éviter de répéter les termes venant d'être énoncés et remplace donc une proposition relative introduite par that :

did she manage to escape? – I believe so (= I believe that she managed to escaped)
est-elle parvenue à s'échapper ? – je crois bien que oui

has he left? – it seems so (= it seems that he has left)
il est parti ? – on dirait bien

I knew it would happen, I told you so (= I told you that it would happen)
je savais bien que ça arriverait, je te l'avais dit

So ne s'utilise qu'après certains verbes dont les plus courants sont : appear, believe, expect, guess, hope, imagine, seem, reckon, suppose, think.

Remarquez que ces verbes peuvent se construire de deux manières différentes à la forme négative (verbe à la forme négative + so ; verbe à la forme affirmative + not), sauf pour hope et guess qui n'acceptent que la structure avec not. Par ailleurs, cet emploi de not est beaucoup moins courant avec les verbes think, believe et seem :

I believe so
je crois (que oui)

I don't believe so (= I believe not, *plus soutenu*)
je ne crois pas

I think so
je pense (que oui)

I don't think so (= I think not, *plus soutenu*)
je ne pense pas

I hope so
j'espère bien

I hope not
j'espère que non

14 LES VERBES

A LES DIFFÉRENTS TYPES

On peut distinguer trois types de verbes : les verbes réguliers, les verbes irréguliers et les auxiliaires.

1 Les verbes réguliers

Ces verbes forment leur prétérit et leur participe passé en ajoutant -(e)d au radical du verbe :

		PRÉTÉRIT	PARTICIPE PASSÉ
seem	*sembler*	**seemed**	**seemed** [siːmd]
kiss	*embrasser*	**kissed**	**kissed** [kɪst]
plant	*planter*	**planted**	**planted** ['plɑːntɪd]
manage	*diriger*	**managed**	**managed** ['mænɪdʒd]

Pour les modifications orthographiques, voir p. A79.

2 Les verbes irréguliers

Les verbes irréguliers se caractérisent par leurs formes particulières au prétérit et au participe passé, qui font apparaître parfois un changement de voyelle :

parler	speak, spoke, spoken	*gâter*	spoil, spoilt, spoilt
voir	see, saw, seen	*couper*	cut, cut, cut
aller	go, went, gone		

Vous trouverez la liste des verbes irréguliers pp. A63-5.

3 Les auxiliaires

Un auxiliaire modifie le verbe principal de la phrase. Dans he can sing (*il sait chanter*), l'auxiliaire est can et le verbe principal est sing. On fait la distinction entre les auxiliaires "ordinaires" et les auxiliaires modaux.

a) Les **auxiliaires ordinaires** sont be, have et do.

On les appelle "ordinaires" parce qu'ils fonctionnent aussi comme verbes à part entière, signifiant alors *être* (be), *avoir* (have) et *faire* (do) :

he does not sing (does = auxiliaire, sing = verbe principal)
il ne chante pas

he does the washing up (does = verbe principal)
il fait la vaisselle

Voir aussi les sections 9, 17 et 23 de la partie C de ce chapitre.

b) Les **auxiliaires modaux** sont appelés ainsi car ils remplacent le mode du subjonctif dans de nombreux cas (voir p. A53). En voici la liste :

can - could	pouvoir (capacité)
may - might	pouvoir (possibilité - permission)
shall - should	futur - conditionnel, devoir (moral), conseil, etc.
will - would	futur - conditionnel, ordre, etc.
must	devoir (obligation)
ought to	devoir (moral)

Les auxiliaires modaux peuvent s'employer seuls lorsque le verbe ordinaire est sous-entendu :

can you come at 8 p.m.? – yes, I can
est-ce que tu peux venir à 20 heures ? – oui

Pour l'emploi des auxiliaires modaux, voir pp. A57-61.

B LES FORMES

1 L'infinitif

On distingue l'infinitif complet (avec to) et l'infinitif sans to :

he is trying to sing
il essaie de chanter

he can sing
il sait chanter

Dans ces deux phrases le mot sing est à l'infinitif.

Pour l'infinitif passé et la voix passive, voir sections 7 et 9 ci-dessous.

2 Le participe présent

Il se forme à partir du radical + -ing :

they were whispering
ils murmuraient

Le participe présent sert notamment à former l'aspect progressif. Pour son emploi, voir pp. A44-5. Pour les modifications orthographiques, voir p. A79.

3 Le participe passé

Le participe passé des verbes réguliers est identique à leur prétérit (radical du verbe + -ed) :

they have watched it on TV
ils l'ont regardé à la télé

Les verbes irréguliers ont un grand nombre de formes différentes au participe passé. Voir A2 ci-dessus, ainsi que la liste des verbes irréguliers pp. A63-5.

Pour l'emploi du participe passé, voir p. A46.

4 Le gérondif

Le gérondif, comme le participe présent, se forme à partir du radical + -ing. Il a une fonction nominale :

I like picking strawberries
j'aime cueillir les fraises

sailing is a very popular sport in Greece
la voile est un sport très populaire en Grèce

Pour l'emploi du gérondif, voir p. A43. Pour la comparaison entre le gérondif et le participe présent, voir pp. A45-6.

5 Le présent

À la 3ème personne du singulier, il se construit avec le radical + -(e)s (pour les modifications orthographiques, voir p. A79). La forme du verbe au présent est la même pour toutes les autres personnes :

	Singulier		
1ère	**I**	**sing**	*je chante*
2ème	**you**	**sing**	*tu chantes*
3ème	**he/she/it**	**sings**	*il/elle chante*
	Pluriel		
1ère	**we**	**sing**	*nous chantons*
2ème	**you**	**sing**	*vous chantez*
3ème	**they**	**sing**	*ils/elles chantent*

Les auxiliaires modaux ne changent pas de forme à la 3ème personne du singulier. Il en est de même pour les verbes dare et need lorsqu'ils sont employés comme auxiliaires :

he may come
il se peut qu'il vienne

how dare he come here!
comment ose-t-il venir ici !

Les auxiliaires ordinaires ont des formes irrégulières, voir la liste p. A66. Pour dare et need, voir p. A61.

6 Le prétérit

Le prétérit des verbes réguliers est identique à leur participe passé (radical du verbe + -ed) :

they kicked the ball
ils ont donné un coup de pied dans le ballon

Pour les verbes irréguliers et les auxiliaires, voir A2 et 3 ci-dessus, ainsi que la liste des verbes irréguliers et des auxiliaires pp. A63-6. La forme du verbe est la même à toutes les personnes :

		RÉGULIER (*embrasser*)	IRRÉGULIER (*chanter*)	AUXILIAIRE (*pouvoir*)
	Singulier			
1ère	I	kissed	sang	could
2ème	you	kissed	sang	could
3ème	he/she/it	kissed	sang	could
	Pluriel			
1ère	we	kissed	sang	could
2ème	you	kissed	sang	could
3ème	they	kissed	sang	could

7 Les temps et les aspects

La plupart des temps peuvent avoir différents aspects, considérant un événement dans le temps de trois manières différentes. On distingue donc l'aspect simple, l'aspect progressif (ou continu) et le perfect (ou passé).

La forme progressive, qui exprime l'action dans sa durée, se construit avec l'auxiliaire be + participe présent.

Le perfect, qui exprime une action accomplie ou une action du passé ayant des conséquences au moment de l'énonciation, se forme avec l'auxiliaire have + participe passé.

Pour la conjugaison des auxiliaires be et have, voir p. A66.

Dans la liste ci-dessous les traductions sont données à titre indicatif :

infinitif	**(to) watch** (*regarder*)
infinitif progressif	**(to) be watching** (*être en train de regarder*)
infinitif passé	**(to) have watched** (*avoir regardé*)
infinitif passé progressif	**(to) have been watching** (*avoir été en train de regarder*)
présent simple	**(I/you/he, etc.) watch(es)** (*je/tu/il, etc. regarde(s)*)
présent progressif	**" am/are/is watching** (*" suis/es/est, etc. en train de regarder*)
passé simple (ou prétérit)	**" watched** (*je regardai, etc.*)
passé progressif	**" was/were watching** (*j'étais, etc. en train de regarder*)
present perfect	**" have/has watched** (*j'ai regardé, etc.*)
present perfect progressif	**" have/has been watching** (*j'ai, etc. été en train de regarder*)
past perfect	**" had watched** (*j'avais regardé, etc.*)
past perfect progressif	**" had been watching** (*j'avais, etc. été en train de regarder*)
futur simple	**" will watch** (*je regarderai, etc.*)
futur progressif	**" will be watching** (*je serai, etc. en train de regarder*)
futur antérieur	**" will have watched** (*j'aurai, etc. regardé*)

futur antérieur progressif	" will have been watching *(j'aurai, etc. été en train de regarder)*
conditionnel présent	" would watch *(je regarderais, etc.)*
conditionnel présent progressif	" would be watching *(je serais, etc. en train de regarder)*
conditionnel passé	" would have watched *(j'aurais, etc. regardé)*
conditionnel passé progressif	" would have been watching *(j'aurais, etc. été en train de regarder)*

8 Les modes

Les modes font référence à l'attitude d'une personne par rapport aux propos qu'elle rapporte. Il existe quatre modes :

● l'**indicatif** pour exprimer des faits réels

● le **subjonctif** pour exprimer un souhait, une incertitude ou une possibilité, etc.

● le **conditionnel** pour exprimer l'éventualité ou le résultat d'une condition

● l'**impératif** pour exprimer des ordres et des suggestions.

La seule différence de forme entre l'indicatif et le subjonctif réside dans la présence de -(e)s à la 3ème personne du singulier au présent de l'indicatif :

> **God save the Queen!**
> *vive la reine !*

Le subjonctif de **to be** est **be** à toutes les personnes du présent et **were** à toutes les personnes du passé :

> **they are welcome to attend, whether they be members or not**
> *ils peuvent venir, qu'ils soient membres ou pas*

> **if I were you, I'd leave him**
> *si j'étais toi, je le quitterais*

Le conditionnel se forme généralement avec l'auxiliaire **would** dans la proposition principale (voir aussi l'exemple précédent) :

> **if I had a car, I would go and visit her more often**
> *si j'avais une voiture, j'irais la voir plus souvent*

Comme le montre cet exemple, c'est souvent le subjonctif passé que l'on trouve dans la proposition subordonnée. Mais il est possible d'employer d'autres temps. Voir pp. A52-3.

Pour le mode impératif, on emploie le radical du verbe seul :

> **give it to me!**   **somebody go and get it!**
> *donne-le-moi !*   *que quelqu'un aille le chercher !*

9 Les voix (actif et passif)

Les deux "voix" sont la voix active et la voix passive. À la voix active, le sujet accomplit l'action :

> **the new members signed the contract**
> *les nouveaux membres ont signé le contrat*

À la voix passive, le sujet subit l'action :

> **the contract was signed by the new members**
> *le contrat a été signé par les nouveaux membres*

La voix passive est plus courante en anglais qu'en français.

Le passif se forme avec l'auxiliaire **be** + participe passé (pour la conjugaison de **be**, voir p. A66) :

infinitif	(to) be watched *(être regardé)*
infinitif passé	(to) have been watched *(avoir été regardé)*
infinitif progressif	(to) be being watched *(être en train d'être regardé)*

présent simple	am/are/is watched *(suis/es/est, etc. regardé)*
présent progressif	am/are/is being watched *(suis/es/est, etc. en train d'être regardé)*
passé simple (ou prétérit)	was/were watched *(étais, etc. regardé)*
passé progressif	was/were being watched *(étais, etc. en train d'être regardé)*
present perfect	have/has been watched *(ai, etc. été regardé)*
present perfect progressif	have/has been being watched *(ai, etc. été en train d'être regardé)*
past perfect	had been watched *(avais, etc. été regardé)*
past perfect progressif	had been being watched *(avais, etc. été en train d'être regardé)*
futur simple	will be watched *(serai, etc. regardé)*
futur progressif	will be being watched *(serai, etc. en train d'être regardé)*
futur antérieur	will have been watched *(aurai, etc. été regardé)*
conditionnel présent	would be watched *(serais, etc. regardé)*
conditionnel présent progressif	would be being watched *(serais, etc. en train d'être regardé)*
conditionnel passé	would have been watched *(aurais, etc. été regardé)*

Quelques exemples :

> **it was hidden under some old papers**
> *il était caché sous de vieux papiers*

> **it was thought to have been hidden by the Romans**
> *on pensait qu'il avait été caché par les Romains*

> **it had deliberately been hidden by his assistant**
> *il avait délibérément été caché par son assistant*

> **you'll be closely watched**
> *tu seras surveillé de près*

> **the programme will have been watched by ten million viewers in total**
> *l'émission aura été regardée en tout par dix millions de téléspectateurs*

> **if he had made any comment it would have been ignored**
> *s'il avait fait des commentaires, ils n'en auraient pas tenu compte*

Le passif de l'infinitif progressif est plutôt rare. Il en est de même pour le passif du present perfect progressif :

> **he may have been being operated on by then**
> *il était peut-être en train de se faire opérer à ce moment-là*

C EMPLOIS

1 L'infinitif

a) *L'infinitif sans* to

i)   Après l'auxiliaire **do** et les auxiliaires modaux :

I don't know — I must go
je ne sais pas — *il faut que je m'en aille*

ii) Après dare et need lorsqu'ils sont employés comme auxiliaires (voir p. A61) :

how dare you talk to me like that!
comment oses-tu me parler ainsi !

you needn't talk to me like that
tu n'as pas besoin de me parler comme ça

iii) Après had better et had best (ou would best en anglais américain) :

you'd better apologize
tu ferais mieux de t'excuser

you'd best ask the manager
tu ferais mieux de demander au directeur

iv) Dans la construction complément d'objet direct : nom/pronom + infinitif. Comparez avec b) ii) ci-dessous :

● Après let (*laisser*), make (*faire*) et have (*faire* dans ce cas) dans les tournures anglaises qui signifient "laisser faire" ou "faire faire" (voir aussi pp. A56-7) :

we let him smoke — I made him turn round
nous l'avons laissé fumer — *je l'ai fait se retourner*

we had him say a few words
nous lui avons fait dire quelques mots

● Après les verbes de perception feel (*sentir*), hear (*entendre*), see (*voir*), watch (*regarder*) :

I felt the floor tremble — they saw him die
j'ai senti trembler le sol — *ils l'ont vu mourir*

we heard her tell the manager
on l'a entendue le dire au directeur

we watched the train approach the platform
on a regardé le train s'approcher du quai

Pour feel (*penser, avoir l'impression que*), voir b) ii) ci-dessous.

Remarquez que ces verbes peuvent aussi être suivis du participe présent qui met l'accent sur la durée de l'action :

I felt her creeping up behind me
je sentais qu'elle s'approchait de moi à pas de loup

we heard her crying bitterly in the next room
nous l'avons entendue pleurer amèrement dans l'autre pièce

she saw smoke coming from the house
elle a vu de la fumée venir de la maison

they watched him slowly dying
ils l'ont vu mourir petit à petit

● On peut trouver les deux formes de l'infinitif après help :

we helped him (to) move house
nous l'avons aidé à déménager

Pour les constructions passives correspondantes employées avec ces verbes, voir b) ii) ci-dessous.

v) Après why ou why not :

why stay indoors in this lovely weather?
pourquoi rester à l'intérieur par ce beau temps ?

why not try our cream cakes?
pourquoi ne pas essayer nos gâteaux à la crème ?

b) *L'infinitif avec* to

i) L'infinitif avec to peut s'employer comme sujet, comme attribut ou comme complément d'objet direct. La phrase

suivante contient les trois emplois (dans cet ordre) :

to die is to cease to exist
mourir, c'est cesser d'exister

ii) Comme complément d'objet direct, comparez avec a) iv) ci-dessus.

● Après des verbes exprimant un désir ou une antipathie, en particulier want (*vouloir*), wish (*souhaiter*), like (*aimer*), prefer (*préférer*), hate (*détester*, ici *ne pas vouloir*) :

I want you to remember this
je veux que tu t'en souviennes

we wish you to leave
nous souhaitons que vous partiez

we would like you to come with us
nous aimerions que vous veniez avec nous

we prefer your cousin to stay here
nous préférons que ton cousin reste ici

I would hate you to think I was avoiding you
je ne voudrais pas vous donner l'impression que je cherchais à vous éviter

● Dans un niveau de langue assez soutenu, on trouve souvent to be et to have après des verbes exprimant une opinion, un jugement, une supposition ou une affirmation :

we believe this to be a mistake
nous pensons qu'il s'agit d'une erreur

we believe this to have some serious consequences
nous pensons que cela va avoir de graves conséquences

we considered/judged it to be of little use
nous considérions/jugions cela peu utile

I felt/knew it to be true
j'avais l'impression/je savais que c'était vrai

he maintained these accusations to be false
il soutenait que ces accusations étaient fausses

En anglais plus courant, on préférera une simple proposition relative, introduite ou non par that :

we believe (that) this is a mistake
nous croyons que c'est une erreur

I know (that) it's true
je sais que c'est vrai

he maintained that these accusations were false
il a soutenu que ces accusations étaient fausses

● Dans la construction passive correspondante, on emploie l'infinitif complet :

this was believed to be a mistake
on pensait que c'était une erreur

● Remarquez l'expression courante be said to, pour laquelle il n'existe pas d'équivalent à la voix active en anglais :

it is said to be true — he's said to be rich
il paraît que c'est vrai — *il paraît qu'il est riche*

this hotel is said to have the most beautiful gardens
il paraît que cet hôtel a des jardins absolument magnifiques

● La forme to + infinitif doit aussi être employée dans des constructions passives avec les verbes mentionnés en a) iv) ci-dessus :

she was made to do it
on l'a forcée à le faire

the aircraft was seen to crash just after take-off
on a vu l'avion s'écraser juste après le décollage

iii) Employé après des noms, des pronoms et des adjectifs :

he has a tendency to forget things
il a tendance à tout oublier

there are things to be done
il y a des choses à faire

we shall remember this in years to come
on se rappellera cela pendant des années

we were afraid to ask
nous avions peur de demander

this game is easy to understand
ce jeu est facile à comprendre

there is that to take into consideration
il y a ça à prendre en considération

pleased to meet you!
heureux de faire votre connaissance !

De telles constructions sont particulièrement courantes après des superlatifs et après only :

this is the latest book to appear on the subject
c'est le livre le plus récent qui soit paru sur ce sujet

she's the only person to have got near him
elle est la seule personne à avoir pu l'approcher

iv) Correspondant à une proposition subordonnée :

● Pour exprimer le but ou la conséquence (l'infinitif pouvant être précédé de in order ou so as (but) ou only (conséquence) pour souligner ses propos) :

he left early to/in order to/so as to get a good seat for the performance
il est parti tôt pour/afin d'être bien placé au spectacle

they arrived (only) to find an empty house
à leur arrivée, la maison était vide

● Dans des propositions interrogatives indirectes :

tell me what to do
dis-moi ce que je dois faire

I didn't know where to look
je ne savais pas où regarder

we didn't know who to ask
nous ne savions pas à qui demander

we weren't sure whether to tell him or not
nous ne savions pas si nous devions le lui dire ou non

● Pour exprimer le temps ou la circonstance :

I shudder to think of it (= ... when I think of it)
j'en tremble rien que d'y penser

to hear him speak, one would think he positively hates women (= when one hears him speak...)
à l'entendre parler, on dirait vraiment qu'il déteste les femmes

v) Dans des exclamations :

to think she married him!
et dire qu'elle l'a épousé !

vi) Dans des phrases elliptiques exprimant des événements à venir. Cet emploi de l'infinitif est courant dans le langage journalistique :

Blair to Make Speech on Iraq
Blair doit s'exprimer sur l'Irak

Chirac to Visit Disaster Zone
Chirac doit se rendre dans la zone sinistrée

vii) On peut aussi trouver l'infinitif avec césure : un adverbe vient s'intercaler entre to et le radical du verbe. Cette forme est devenue très courante, mais peu appréciée de beaucoup, qui soutiennent qu'il ne faut jamais séparer to du radical :

nobody will ever be able to fully comprehend his philosophy
personne ne sera jamais capable de comprendre complètement sa philosophie

Comparez les deux exemples suivants :

the way out of this is to really try and persuade him
le moyen de s'en sortir, c'est de vraiment essayer de le persuader

the way out of this is really to try and persuade him
le moyen de s'en sortir, c'est en fait d'essayer de le persuader

Dans le premier exemple, l'adverbe really signifie "beaucoup" et il renforce try, tandis que dans le deuxième exemple, il signifie "en fait" et modifie toute la phrase.

viii) On emploie souvent to sans le radical du verbe dans une répétition, plutôt que l'infinitif complet :

why haven't you tidied your room? I told you to
pourquoi n'as-tu pas rangé ta chambre ? je t'ai dit de le faire

I did it because she encouraged me to
je l'ai fait parce qu'elle m'y a encouragé

ix) Dans la construction for + nom/pronom + infinitif avec to :

it took an hour for the taxi to get to the station
le taxi a mis une heure pour aller jusqu'à la gare

there's no need for you to worry
il n'y a aucune raison de vous inquiéter

he waited for her to finish
il attendit qu'elle ait fini

Cette construction grammaticale et idiomatique exprime souvent la condition, le but ou encore la circonstance, et peut même être sujet de la phrase :

for the university to function properly, more money is needed
afin que l'université fonctionne bien, il faut plus d'argent

for me to say nothing would be admitting defeat (*sujet*)
ne rien dire serait admettre ma défaite

for a man to get custody of his children used to be difficult (*sujet*)
à l'époque, il était difficile pour un homme d'obtenir la garde de ses enfants

x) En anglais parlé, on remplace très souvent le to de l'infinitif par and après des verbes tels que try, go, come ou stay :

try and be there around 6 (= try to be there around 6)
essaie d'arriver vers 18 heures

Cette structure avec try ne peut s'employer qu'à l'infinitif, alors qu'il est possible d'utiliser les verbes suivants au passé ou à la 3ème personne du présent :

you should go and see this film (= you should go to see this film)
tu devrais aller voir ce film

he went and saw it
il est allé le voir

he goes and sees her every week
il va la voir toutes les semaines

come and have dinner with us (= come to have dinner with us)
viens manger avec nous un soir

he usually comes and has dinner with us on Sundays
en général, il vient manger avec nous tous les dimanches soir

he came and had dinner with us yesterday
il est venu manger avec nous hier soir

2 Le gérondif

Le gérondif (ou verbe substantivé) possède des caractéristiques propres aux noms et aux verbes.

a) *Caractéristiques nominales*

i) Un gérondif peut être sujet, attribut ou complément d'objet :

surfing is difficult *(sujet)*
le surf, c'est difficile

that's cheating *(attribut)*
c'est de la triche

I love reading *(complément)*
j'adore lire

Comme on l'a vu, ce sont là des fonctions communes à l'infinitif (voir p. A41) ; pour les différences d'emploi, voir section 4 ci-dessous.

ii) Il peut être placé après une préposition (contrairement à l'infinitif) :

he's thought of leaving
il a pensé partir

his back hurt from lifting heavy boxes
il avait mal au dos après avoir soulevé de gros cartons

iii) Il peut être précédé d'un article puis suivi d'un groupe prépositionnel (c'est-à-dire introduit par **of**) :

the timing of his remarks was unfortunate
il a mal choisi son moment pour faire des remarques

Et il peut être modifié par un adjectif ou un possessif :

careless writing leaves a bad impression
une écriture peu soignée fait mauvaise impression

the soprano's singing was wonderful
le chant du soprano était magnifique

do you remember his trying to persuade her?
tu te souviens qu'il a essayé de la persuader ?

b) *Caractéristiques verbales*

i) Un gérondif peut avoir un sujet :

the thought of John doing that is absurd
penser que John ait pu faire ça est absurde

ii) Il peut être suivi d'un complément d'objet ou d'un attribut :

hitting the wing mirror was unavoidable
nous n'avons pas pu éviter le rétroviseur

becoming an expert took him more than twenty years
il lui a fallu plus de vingt ans pour devenir expert en la matière

iii) Il peut être modifié par un adverbe :

she was afraid of totally disillusioning him
elle avait peur de lui faire perdre toutes ses illusions

3 Le possessif et le gérondif

Devant un gérondif, il n'est pas rare d'hésiter entre l'emploi d'une forme complément ou celui d'une forme possessive :

do you remember him/his trying to persuade her?
tu te souviens qu'il a essayé de la persuader ?

Les deux formes sont ici correctes. Mais il existe parfois des différences d'emploi entre les deux. Il convient de noter les exemples suivants :

a) *Le gérondif sujet ou attribut*

Dans ce cas, on emploie normalement le possessif (un adjectif possessif ou le génitif) :

your trying to persuade me will get you nowhere
tu auras beau essayer, tu n'arriveras pas à me convaincre

it was John's insisting that we went there that saved the situation
c'est grâce à l'insistance de John qui voulait que nous y allions que la situation fut sauvée

b) *Le gérondif complément ou placé après une préposition*

Dans ce cas, il est possible d'employer soit un nom/pronom complément d'objet direct, soit la forme possessive :

you don't mind me/my turning up so late, do you?
ça ne te dérange pas que j'arrive si tard, n'est-ce pas ?

they spoke at great length about him/his being elected president
ils parlèrent longtemps de son élection comme président

they spoke at great length about Richard/Richard's being elected president
ils parlèrent longtemps de l'élection de Richard comme président

Remarquez que l'emploi du possessif est plus soutenu que celui du nom/pronom complément. On aura donc tendance à employer la forme complément à l'oral ou dans un style plus familier :

they laughed their heads off at him falling into the river
ils riaient à n'en plus pouvoir parce qu'il était tombé dans la rivière

On a également plus tendance à employer le possessif devant le gérondif en anglais américain qu'en anglais britannique.

Pour la comparaison entre le gérondif et le participe présent et les ambiguïtés éventuelles, voir section 6, p. A45.

c) *Le facteur d'emphase*

Si le sujet du gérondif est accentué, on préférera l'emploi de la forme complément à celui de la forme possessive :

just to think of HIM marrying Karen!
que ce soit lui qui épouse Karen, je n'arrive pas à le croire !

4 Comparaison entre le gérondif et l'infinitif

a) *Emploi identique*

On a vu que l'infinitif et le gérondif ont des caractéristiques nominales du fait qu'ils peuvent fonctionner comme sujet, complément d'objet ou attribut. Il y a donc souvent peu ou pas de différence de sens entre les deux :

we can't bear seeing you like this
we can't bear to see you like this
nous ne supportons pas de te voir comme ça

I prefer being called by my first name
I prefer to be called by my first name
je préfère qu'on m'appelle par mon prénom

En anglais américain, l'infinitif est souvent utilisé là où en anglais britannique on emploierait un gérondif :

I like cooking *(Br)*
I like to cook *(Am)*
j'aime faire la cuisine

b) *Différents sens*

i) Quand le verbe **try** signifie simplement "essayer", on peut souvent employer l'infinitif ou le gérondif :

I tried to make a chocolate cake, but it wasn't very good
I tried making a chocolate cake, but it wasn't very good
j'ai essayé de faire un gâteau au chocolat, mais il n'était pas très bon

Mais ces formes verbales ne sont pas toujours interchangeables. Lorsque **try** a le sens de "faire un effort, essayer quelque chose de difficile", on emploie l'infinitif :

I really tried to understand
j'ai vraiment cherché à comprendre

Si try a le sens de "tenter quelque chose pour voir ce qui va se passer", on emploie le gérondif :

I tried sending her a letter of apology, but it didn't work
j'ai essayé de lui envoyer une lettre pour m'excuser, mais ça n'a pas marché

ii) Après **forget** (*oublier*) et **remember** (*se souvenir*), l'in-finitif fait référence au futur, le gérondif au passé :

I won't forget to ask her to dinner (*dans le futur*)
je n'oublierai pas de l'inviter à dîner

I won't forget asking her to dinner (*dans le passé*)
je n'oublierai pas que je l'ai invitée à dîner

will she remember to meet me? (*dans le futur*)
est-ce qu'elle se souviendra de notre rendez-vous ?

will she remember meeting me? (*dans le passé*)
est-ce qu'elle se souviendra d'avoir fait ma connaissance ?

iii) Vous verrez dans le point c) ci-dessous une liste de verbes après lesquels l'infinitif et le gérondif sont employés comme compléments d'objet direct. Il en est de même pour le gérondif dans la phrase suivante :

I stopped looking at her
je me suis arrêté de la regarder

Mais l'infinitif n'est pas complément d'objet direct dans :

I stopped to look at her
je me suis arrêté pour la regarder

Ici, l'infinitif fonctionne comme un complément circonstan-ciel de but, ce qui explique la différence considérable de sens entre les deux phrases. La différence est la même entre les deux exemples suivants :

he was too busy talking to her
il était trop occupé à lui parler

he was too busy to talk to her
il était trop occupé pour lui parler

iv) Il est aussi important de faire la distinction entre **to**, mar-que de l'infinitif, et **to**, préposition. Après une préposition, on trouvera toujours le gérondif :

I'm tired of watching television
j'en ai assez de regarder la télévision

what do you think about getting a loan?
qu'est-ce que tu dirais de faire un emprunt ?

Ceci, bien sûr, concerne aussi la préposition **to** :

they are committed to implementing the plan
ils se sont engagés à réaliser le projet

we're looking forward to receiving your letter
nous attendons votre lettre avec impatience

they object to working overtime
ils ne sont pas d'accord pour faire des heures supplémen-taires

we're not used to getting up at this hour
nous ne sommes pas habitués à nous lever à cette heure-ci

c) *L'infinitif seulement ou le gérondif seulement*

i) L'infinitif seulement :

Certains verbes ne peuvent être suivis que de l'infinitif, par exemple : **demand** (*exiger*), **deserve** (*mériter*), **expect** (*s'attendre à*), **hope** (*espérer*), **want** (*vouloir*), **wish** (*souhaiter*) :

I want/wish to leave   **he deserves to be punished**
je veux/souhaite partir   *il mérite d'être puni*

we hope to be back by five
nous espérons être de retour vers cinq heures

ii) Le gérondif seulement :

D'autres verbes ne sont suivis que du gérondif, par exemple : **avoid** (*éviter*), **consider** (*considérer*), **dislike** (*ne pas aimer*), **enjoy** (*apprécier*), **finish** (*finir*), **keep** (*conti-nuer*), **mind** (*déranger, gêner*), **practise** (*faire, prati-quer*), **risk** (*risquer*) :

he avoided answering my questions
il évitait de répondre à mes questions

will you consider taking some time off work?
est-ce que vous songez à prendre des congés ?

I dislike flying
je n'aime pas prendre l'avion

we enjoy having friends round to dinner
nous aimons recevoir des amis pour le dîner

she finished writing her e-mail
elle a fini d'écrire son e-mail

they keep teasing him
ils n'arrêtent pas de le taquiner

do you mind going out when the weather's cold?
est-ce que cela vous ennuie de sortir quand il fait froid ?

you must practise playing the piano more often
tu dois travailler ton piano plus souvent

I don't want to risk upsetting Jennifer
je ne veux pas risquer de contrarier Jennifer

Il faut noter aussi que l'adjectif **worth** et la préposition **like** ne peuvent être suivis que du gérondif :

that suggestion is worth considering
cette proposition vaut la peine d'être examinée

that's just like wishing for the moon
c'est comme si je demandais la lune

5 Le participe présent

Le participe présent s'emploie comme forme verbale ou comme adjectif.

a) *Comme forme verbale*

i) Le participe présent s'emploie après **be** pour former l'aspect progressif :

he is/was/has been/had been running
il court/courait/a couru/avait couru

ii) Le participe présent s'emploie souvent pour former une proposition relative elliptique (sans pronom relatif et sans auxiliaire) :

I saw the people coming out of the theatre (= who were coming)
j'ai vu les gens qui sortaient du théâtre

iii) Le participe présent peut avoir pour sujet celui de la propo-sition principale. Dans ce cas, il est précédé d'une virgule. Le participe présent peut s'employer après une proposition principale au présent ou au passé :

she turned towards the man, looking pleasantly sur-prised
elle se tourna vers l'homme, l'air agréablement surpris

Dans cet exemple, le sujet de **looking** est **she** ; mais si l'on omet la virgule, le sujet de **looking** est **the man**, et la phrase appartient alors au type ii) ci-dessus (= **the man who is/was looking pleasantly surprised**).

Ce participe présent peut précéder son sujet :

looking pleasantly **surprised**, she **turned towards the man**
l'air agréablement surpris, elle se tourna vers l'homme

La proposition introduite par un participe présent équivaut souvent à une proposition subordonnée de cause, de condition ou de temps :

living alone, she often feels uneasy at night (= because/since/as she lives alone…)
vivant seule, elle est souvent inquiète le soir

it might be more expensive, **living alone** (= …if you lived alone)
ce doit être plus cher de vivre seul

driving along, I suddenly saw him standing at the side of the road (= as/while I was driving along…)
j'étais en train de conduire, quand soudain je l'ai vu sur le bord de la route

Mais il correspond aussi parfois à une proposition indépendante :

she walked away from him, **shouting** that she never wanted to see him again (= and (she) shouted that…)
elle est partie en criant qu'elle ne voulait plus jamais le revoir

living in London, he is an artist who has organized many cultural events (= he lives in London and (he) is…)
vivant à Londres, c'est un artiste qui a organisé de nombreuses manifestations culturelles

Dans tous ces exemples, le sujet du participe est le même que celui de la proposition principale. Comparez avec les exemples du point v) ci-dessous dans lesquels le participe présent a son propre sujet.

iv) Le participe présent "non rattaché" :

Un participe présent est considéré comme "non rattaché" si son sujet est différent de celui du verbe de la proposition principale :

coming down the staircase carrying an umbrella, one of the cats tripped him up
un des chats le fit trébucher alors qu'il descendait l'escalier, un parapluie à la main

Dans cet exemple, on peut facilement deviner que le sujet de coming est en fait le complément d'objet de la principale (him). Mais il est préférable d'éviter cette structure de phrase grammaticalement incorrecte et souvent source d'ambiguïté.

L'emploi du participe présent est toutefois normal et très courant lorsqu'un sujet indéfini est sous-entendu, comme le we indéfini ou le "on" français. On trouve surtout cet emploi dans des expressions figées :

generally speaking, British cooking is much better than it used to be
d'une manière générale, la cuisine britannique s'est beaucoup améliorée

judging by the way she dresses, she must have a lot of confidence
à voir ou à en juger par sa façon de s'habiller, elle doit avoir une grande confiance en elle

v) Comme en français, le sujet du participe (différent de celui de la principale) peut le précéder dans ce qu'on appelle la "construction absolue". La proposition contenant le participe présent équivaut là aussi à une proposition subordon-

née causale (voir iii) ci-dessus) :

the lift **being out of order**, we had to use the stairs
l'ascenseur étant en panne, nous avons dû monter par les escaliers

she being the hostess, any kind of criticism was out of the question
étant donné que c'était elle qui recevait, il était hors de question de faire quelque critique que ce soit

b) *Comme adjectif*

she has always been a **loving** child
elle a toujours été une enfant aimante

her appearance is **striking**
elle a une allure frappante

she finds Steven very **charming**
elle trouve Steven très charmant

De cette fonction adjectivale dérive la fonction adverbiale :

he is **strikingly** handsome
il est d'une beauté saisissante

Remarquez que cette structure est bien plus courante en anglais qu'en français :

a **self-adjusting** mechanism
un mécanisme à autoréglage

the **falling** birth rate   **increasing** sales
le taux de natalité en baisse   *des ventes en hausse*

6 Comparaison entre le participe présent et le gérondif

a) *Ambiguïté*

La phrase suivante peut se comprendre de deux manières différentes :

I hate | people | trying **to get in without paying**
je déteste les gens qui essaient d'entrer sans payer

Si trying est un gérondif, le sens de la phrase est : I hate the fact that (some) people try to get in without paying (*je n'aime pas le fait que certaines personnes essaient d'entrer sans payer*). Grammaticalement, on pourrait couper la phrase au niveau de la barre bleue.

Si c'est un participe présent, le sens devient : I hate people who try to get in without paying (*je n'aime pas les gens qui essaient d'entrer sans payer*). Grammaticalement, on pourrait couper la phrase au niveau de la barre noire.

Mais si la forme en -ing est précédée d'un adjectif possessif, il ne peut s'agir que d'un gérondif (voir p. A43) :

I hate **their** trying **to get in without paying**
je n'aime pas qu'ils essaient d'entrer sans payer

De même, dans la phrase suivante, la forme en -ing ne peut être qu'un gérondif ; sa fonction nominale entraîne un verbe au singulier :

children suffering like that **is** on our conscience (= the suffering of children)
la souffrance de ces enfants pèse sur notre conscience

Au contraire, le pluriel de la phrase suivante montre que suffering est un participe présent :

children suffering like that **are** on our conscience (= children who suffer)
les enfants qui souffrent comme cela pèsent sur notre conscience

b) *Accentuation*

Quand un gérondif modifie un nom, seul le gérondif est accentué dans le discours, et non le nom :

a **living** room [ə ˈlɪvɪŋ rʊm]   a **walking** stick [ə ˈwɔːkɪŋ stɪk]
un salon   *une canne*

Mais quand l'élément modificateur est un participe présent, celui-ci et le nom sont accentués de la même manière :

a living animal [ə 'lɪvɪŋ 'ænɪml]
un animal vivant

the walking wounded [ðə 'wɔːkɪŋ 'wuːndɪd]
les blessés qui peuvent encore marcher

Remarquez que ces deux derniers adjectifs sont des participes présents car "l'action" est accompli par le nom ("un animal qui vit", etc.), ce qui n'est pas le cas des deux premiers adjectifs. Ces derniers sont des gérondifs : ils qualifient les noms en indiquant leur rôle (= "une pièce pour vivre", "un bâton pour marcher").

7 Le participe passé

Parmi les emplois suivants, beaucoup peuvent être comparés avec ceux du participe présent. Voir 5 pp. A44-5.

a) *Comme forme verbale*

i) Le participe passé s'emploie après l'auxiliaire **have** pour former le present perfect et le past perfect :

he has/had arrived
il est/était arrivé

et après l'auxiliaire **be** pour former la voix passive :

she is/was admired
elle est/était admirée

et avec les deux auxiliaires pour former le passif au present perfect et au past perfect :

she has/had been admired
elle a/avait été admirée

ii) Le participe passé est souvent employé pour former une proposition relative elliptique (sans pronom relatif et sans auxiliaire) :

they go to all the concerts given by the local orchestra (= **which are given**)
ils vont à tous les concerts donnés par l'orchestre local

they went to all the concerts given by the local orchestra (= **which were/had been given**)
ils sont allés à tous les concerts donnés par l'orchestre local

Il peut aussi avoir la fonction de subordonnée de cause, de condition ou de temps. Des conjonctions (en particulier **if** et **when**), non obligatoires en début de phrase, permettent de rendre le sens plus explicite :

watched over by her family, **Monica felt safe but unhappy** (= **because/since/as she was watched over**...)
surveillée par sa famille, Monica se sentait en sécurité, mais malheureuse

(if) treated with care, CDs should last indefinitely
si l'on en prend soin, les CD ne s'usent jamais

CDs should last indefinitely if treated with care
les CD ne s'usent jamais si l'on en prend soin

(when) asked why, he refused to answer
quand on lui demanda pourquoi, il refusa de répondre

he refused to answer when asked why
il refusa de répondre lorsqu'on lui demanda pourquoi

Ou il peut avoir valeur de proposition indépendante :

born in Aberdeen, he now lives in Perth with his wife (= **he was born in Aberdeen and he now lives**...)
né à Aberdeen, il habite maintenant à Perth avec sa femme

iii) On trouve parfois des phrases avec un participe passé non rattaché au sujet de la phrase (appelé en anglais **dangling**

participle). Cependant, il est préférable d'éviter cette structure de phrase grammaticalement incorrecte et qui donne souvent lieu à des ambiguïtés (voir 5a) iv) p. A45) :

told to cancel the meeting, his project was never discussed

On pourrait exprimer ceci de manière plus élégante :

his project was never discussed as he was told to cancel the meeting
son projet ne fut jamais examiné car on lui demanda d'annuler la réunion

iv) Dans la "construction absolue", le participe passé a son propre sujet et il équivaut à une proposition subordonnée (voir 5a) v) p. A45) :

the problems solved, they went their separate ways (= **when the problems were solved**...)
les problèmes résolus, ils sont partis chacun de leur côté

that done, he left (= **once that was done**...)
une fois que ce fut terminé, il est parti

b) *Comme adjectif*

the defeated army retreated	**I am very tired**
l'armée vaincue battit en retraite	*je suis très fatigué*

Remarquez que l'on peut placer l'adverbe **very** avant un participe passé adjectif. Lorsque l'on insiste plus sur le caractère verbal du participe passé, on emploie **much**, et non **very** :

I am much obliged
je vous suis très obligé

Pour la différence d'emploi entre **very** et **much**, voir pp. A22-3.

Lorsque **aged** (*âgé*), **beloved** (*bien-aimé*), **blessed** (*sacré*), **cursed** (*maudit*) et **learned** (*érudit*) sont des adjectifs épithètes, on prononce normalement -ed /ɪd/. Mais lorsque ce sont des verbes, on adopte la prononciation régulière /d/ ou /t/ :

he has aged [eɪdʒd]	**a man aged 50** [eɪdʒd]
il a vieilli	*un homme âgé de 50 ans*

mais :

an aged man ['eɪdʒɪd]
un homme âgé

La prononciation /ɪd/ est toutefois rare et littéraire.

8 Les questions

a) *Phrases complètes*

i) On emploie l'auxiliaire **do** pour former les questions à moins que la phrase ne contienne un autre auxiliaire (**have**, **will**, etc.), auquel cas l'auxiliaire précède le sujet, ou que le sujet ne soit un pronom interrogatif. **Do** se met au présent ou au passé, et le verbe principal est à l'infinitif. Le sujet se place entre l'auxiliaire et le verbe :

he always arrives late	→	**does he always arrive late?**
il arrive toujours en retard		*est-ce qu'il arrive toujours en retard ?*
she often goes there	→	**does she go there often?**
elle y va souvent		*est-ce qu'elle y va souvent ?*
he saw her	→	**did he see her?**
il l'a vue		*est-ce qu'il l'a vue ?*
you said that...	→	**what did you say?**
tu as dit que...		*qu'est-ce que tu as dit ?*

how do we get to Oxford Street from here?
comment fait-on pour aller d'ici à Oxford Street ?

Quand d'autres auxiliaires sont employés, ce sont eux qui précèdent le sujet :

they are trying to... → are they trying **to call us?**
ils essaient de... *est-ce qu'ils essaient de nous appeler ?*

he's taking her to... → **where** is he taking **her?**
il l'emmène à... *où est-ce qu'il l'emmène ?*

they've seen us → have they seen **us?**
ils nous ont vus *est-ce qu'ils nous ont vus ?*

you'll help us → will you help **us?**
tu nous aideras *tu pourras nous aider ?*

you can come at eight → can you come **at eight?**
tu peux venir à huit heures *est-ce que tu peux venir à huit heures ?*

Quand on a un pronom interrogatif sujet et qu'il n'y a pas d'auxiliaire existant, la question se forme sans l'auxiliaire do :

who said that? **what** happened?
qui a dit ça ? *qu'est-ce qui s'est passé ?*

Pour dare et need, voir p. A61. Pour have, voir pp. A55-7.

ii) En anglais parlé, où l'on distingue une proposition interrogative d'une proposition affirmative par l'intonation, on peut employer l'ordre des mots d'une affirmative dans une interrogative (emploi moins fréquent en anglais, qu'en français) :

you just left him standing there?
tu l'as laissé planté là ?

Dans des propositions interrogatives indirectes, l'ordre des mots est identique à celui de la proposition affirmative directe. Mais attention à la concordance des temps :

when are you leaving? *(style direct)*
quand est-ce que tu pars ?

he asked her **when she was leaving** *(style indirect)*
il lui a demandé quand elle partait

b) *Les question-tags*

Le question-tag, équivalent du "n'est-ce pas ?" français, est une tournure interrogative très courante en anglais, qui se place en fin de phrase et qui permet généralement de demander confirmation. Il se compose d'un pronom personnel et d'un auxiliaire.

i) Une proposition affirmative est suivie d'un tag à la forme négative et vice versa :

you can see it, **can't you?** you can't see it, **can you?**
tu le vois, n'est-ce pas ? est-ce que tu peux le voir ?

Lorsqu'un tag est emphatique, c'est-à-dire lorsqu'il sert à renforcer le sens de la phrase principale plutôt qu'à poser une question ou demander confirmation, on emploie un tag à la forme affirmative après une proposition affirmative :

so you've seen a ghost, **have you?** *(incrédulité ou ironie)*
alors comme ça, tu as vu un fantôme ?

you think that's fair, **do you?** *(ressentiment)*
tu crois que c'est juste, hein ?

you've bought a new car, **have you?** *(surprise ou intérêt)*
alors, tu as acheté une nouvelle voiture ?

ii) Le question-tag reprend le temps employé dans la principale. Si la proposition précédente est au présent simple ou au prétérit, et donc sans auxiliaire, on utilisera do dans le question-tag :

you want to meet him, **don't you?** *(présent)*
tu veux le rencontrer, n'est-ce pas ?

you wanted to meet him, **didn't you?** *(passé)*
tu voulais le rencontrer, n'est-ce pas ?

you'll want to meet him, **won't you?** *(futur)*
tu voudras le rencontrer, n'est-ce pas ?

iii) Si, comme dans ce dernier exemple, la proposition qui précède est régie par un auxiliaire, il faut le répéter dans le tag :

you have seen it before, **haven't you?**
tu l'as déjà vu, n'est-ce pas ?

they aren't sold yet, **are they?**
ils n'ont quand même pas déjà été vendus ?

you will help me, **won't you?**
tu m'aideras, n'est-ce pas ?

I shouldn't say anything to him, **should I?**
je ne devrais rien lui dire, n'est-ce pas ?

iv) Lorsque le tag suit un impératif, on emploie un auxiliaire à la forme affirmative (en particulier will/would). Ces tags permettent souvent de nuancer l'impératif, d'éviter un ton trop sec :

leave the cat alone, **will you?**
laisse le chat tranquille, tu veux ?

take this to Jackie, **would you?**
tu veux bien apporter ça à Jackie ?

La forme négative won't indique une invitation :

help yourselves to drinks, **won't you?**
servez-vous à boire, je vous en prie

9 Les négations

a) *La négation des formes conjuguées*

i) On emploie l'auxiliaire do avec not pour former la négation, à moins que la proposition ne contienne un autre auxiliaire (should, will, etc.). En anglais, on utilise pratiquement tout le temps les formes contractées (don't, won't, can't, etc.), mais elle doivent toutefois être évitées dans un style soutenu à l'écrit :

we accept traveller's cheques → we **do not/don't** accept traveller's
nous acceptons les chèques cheques
de voyage *nous n'acceptons pas les chèques de voyage*

Lorsque l'on a déjà un auxiliaire, on doit le reprendre à la forme négative :

he should come → he should **not/shouldn't** come
il devrait venir *il ne devrait pas venir*

ii) Dans une question négative, not se place après le sujet, à moins que la forme contractée ne soit utilisée :

do they **not** accept traveller's cheques?
don't they **accept traveller's cheques?**
ils n'acceptent pas les chèques de voyage ?

should you **not** try his office number?
shouldn't you **try his office number?**
ne devrais-tu pas essayer son numéro au bureau ?

iii) Les verbes exprimant un point de vue believe, suppose, think, etc. sont normalement à la forme négative, même si la négation porte logiquement sur le verbe dans la proposition complément d'objet :

I don't believe **we have met**
je ne crois pas que nous nous soyons déjà rencontrés

I don't suppose **you could lend me a fiver?**
ça t'embêterait de me prêter un billet de 5 livres ?

I didn't think **these papers were yours**
je ne pensais pas que ces papiers étaient à toi

mais hope est plus logique :

I hope **it** won't give **me a headache**
j'espère que ça ne me donnera pas mal à la tête

et il n'est pas accompagné de do lorsqu'il est employé seul :

is she ill? – I hope not
elle est malade ? – j'espère que non

De nombreuses formes sont possibles pour des réponses courtes avec des verbes tels que believe, suppose et think :

will she marry him?
va-t-elle l'épouser ?

I don't believe/think so *(couramment employé)*
je ne crois pas/ne pense pas

I believe/think not *(moins courant, plus soigné)*

I don't suppose so *(couramment employé)*

I suppose not *(couramment employé)*

Voir aussi p. A38.

b) *La négation des infinitifs et des gérondifs*

On forme la négation des infinitifs et des gérondifs en plaçant not devant :

we tried **not to upset her**
nous avons essayé de ne pas la contrarier

I want you to think seriously about **not going**
je veux que tu songes sérieusement à ne pas partir

not eating **enough fruit is a cause of vitamin deficiency**
ne pas manger assez de fruits peut entraîner une carence en vitamines

L'exemple avec l'infinitif ci-dessus a bien sûr un sens différent de la phrase suivante, où c'est try qui est à la forme négative :

we didn't try to upset her
nous n'avons pas essayé de la contrarier

Remarquez l'expression idiomatique not to worry = don't worry :

I won't manage to finish it by tomorrow – not to worry
je n'arriverai pas à terminer avant demain – ce n'est pas grave

c) *La négation des impératifs*

i)   La négation des impératifs se forme avec l'auxiliaire do. Do not a pour forme contractée don't :

don't worry   don't be **silly**
ne t'inquiète pas   *ne sois pas bête*

L'emploi de la forme complète do not est courant dans les déclarations officielles, dans les modes d'emploi, sur les panneaux, etc. :

do not fill in **this part of the form**
ne pas remplir cette partie du formulaire

do not feed **the animals**
prière de ne pas donner à manger aux animaux

do not exceed **the stated dose**
ne pas dépasser la dose prescrite

La forme complète s'emploie aussi à l'oral pour rendre un impératif plus emphatique :

I'll say it again: do not touch!
je te le redis encore : ne touche pas !

Dans la forme de l'impératif let's, employée pour des suggestions, l'ordre des mots est le suivant :

don't let's **wait any longer**
n'attendons pas plus longtemps

Mais cette tournure est assez rare. On emploiera normalement :

let's not wait **any longer**
n'attendons pas plus longtemps

ii) On peut également exprimer la négation à l'impératif en employant uniquement not après le verbe. Cette structure, soutenue et littéraire, peut aussi s'employer sur un ton humoristique :

worry not, **I'll be back soon**
ne t'inquiète pas, je reviendrai bientôt

fear not, **the situation is under control**
n'aie pas peur, je maîtrise la situation

d)   Never

L'adjectif négatif never n'est normalement pas accompagné de do :

we never accept **traveller's cheques**
nous n'acceptons jamais les chèques de voyage

I never said **a word**
je n'ai rien dit

On trouve l'auxiliaire do après never uniquement lorsque l'on veut insister sur le verbe (pour l'emploi de do comme auxiliaire emphatique, voir p. A57) :

you never did like **my cooking, did you?**
tu n'as jamais aimé ma cuisine, hein ?

Si never est en début de phrase, on emploiera do avec une inversion sujet-auxiliaire (style soutenu) :

never did **it taste so good!**
ça n'a jamais été aussi bon !

never did **their courage waver**
à aucun moment leur courage n'a faibli

Dans le premier de ces deux exemples, la phrase est plus une exclamation qu'une négation, et dans la seconde, le style est poétique ou rhétorique.

Cette inversion est possible avec d'autres adverbes négatifs (voir p. A78).

e)   *La traduction des formes négatives françaises*

i)   ne... jamais

he never speaks **to me**
he doesn't ever speak **to me**
il ne me parle jamais

ii) ne... rien

I saw nothing
I didn't see anything
je n'ai rien vu

iii) ne... personne

she agrees with nobody/no-one
she doesn't agree with anybody/anyone
elle n'est d'accord avec personne

iv) ne... plus

I don't smoke any more/any longer
I no longer smoke
je ne fume plus

words which are no longer used
words which aren't used any longer
des mots qui ne sont plus employés

Voir aussi le chapitre **Les adverbes**, pp. A23-4.

10 Pour exprimer le présent

On peut exprimer le présent de différentes façons selon que l'on fait référence à des événements habituels et d'ordre général, ou à des événements précis, et selon que l'on considère ces événement précis comme des actions en cours ou des événements ponctuels. Cette section décrit les emplois des formes verbales appropriées.

a) *Le présent simple*

i) Pour des événements habituels ou d'ordre général, ou pour des vérités universelles :

I get up **at seven o'clock every morning**
je me lève à sept heures tous les matins

she teaches **French at the local school**
elle enseigne le français dans l'école du quartier

the earth revolves **round the sun**
la terre tourne autour du soleil

ii) Avec des verbes qui n'impliquent pas d'idée de progression dans le temps. Ces verbes, parfois appelés "verbes statiques", expriment souvent un sentiment, une opinion, ou font référence aux sens :

I (dis)like/love/hate/want **that girl**
j'aime (je n'aime pas)/j'adore/je déteste/je veux cette fille

I believe/suppose/think **you're right**
je crois/suppose/pense que vous avez raison

we hear/see/feel **the world around us**
nous entendons/voyons/sentons le monde qui nous entoure

it tastes **good/it** smells **good**
c'est bon/ça sent bon

Remarquez que ces verbes statiques peuvent devenir des "verbes dynamiques", si l'on considère l'action dans son déroulement ou dans sa durée. Dans de tels cas, on emploie le présent progressif (voir b) ci-dessous) :

what are **you** thinking **about?**
à quoi penses-tu ?

how are **you** feeling **today?**
comment vous sentez-vous aujourd'hui ?

we're tasting **the wine to see if it's all right**
nous goûtons le vin pour voir s'il est bon

b) *Le présent progressif*

i) Le présent progressif est employé avec des verbes dynamiques, c'est-à-dire des verbes qui renvoient à des événements en cours et normalement temporaires :

don't interrupt while I'm talking to somebody else
ne m'interromps pas quand je parle à quelqu'un d'autre

please be quiet; I'm watching a good programme
tais-toi, s'il te plaît ; je suis en train de regarder une émission intéressante

he's trying to get the car to start
il essaie de faire démarrer la voiture

not now, I'm thinking
pas maintenant, je réfléchis

Comparez :

I live **in London** (*présent simple*)
je vis à Londres

I'm living in London (*présent progressif*)
je vis à Londres (maintenant)

La deuxième phrase implique que le locuteur n'est pas installé à Londres de façon permanente et définitive ; ce n'est que temporaire.

ii) Les adverbes de fréquence s'emploient généralement avec le présent simple :

he always goes **to bed after midnight**
il se couche toujours après minuit

Mais on trouve parfois ces adverbes employés avec le présent progressif. Cet aspect sous-entend que l'action ou le fait en question se produit souvent, mais de manière inattendue ou non intentionnelle. Dans l'exemple suivant, on ne peut employer que le présent progressif avec **forever** :

John is forever forgetting **his car keys**
John oublie toujours ses clés de voiture

Comparez les deux phrases suivantes :

he always meets **her in this pub**
il la retrouve ou rejoint toujours dans ce pub

he's always meeting **her in this pub**
il la rencontre ou croise toujours dans ce pub

Dans le premier exemple, l'aspect simple permet de décrire quelque chose de prévu (= ils se donnent toujours rendez-vous dans ce pub). L'aspect progressif du deuxième exemple permet de deviner qu'il s'agit du verbe **meet** employé dans le sens de "rencontrer par hasard".

Mais dans certains cas, il n'y a pas de différence de sens entre l'aspect simple et l'aspect progressif :

you always say **that!**   **he** always criticizes **me**
you're always saying **that!**   **he's** always criticizing **me**
tu dis toujours ça !   *il me critique tout le temps*

11 Pour exprimer le passé

a) *Le prétérit*

On emploie le prétérit lorsque l'on veut mettre l'accent sur l'accomplissement d'une action qui s'est déroulée à un moment précis, souvent indiqué par un adverbe :

he caught **the train yesterday**
il a pris le train hier

he didn't say **a word at the meeting**
il n'a pas dit un mot pendant la réunion

she sang **at the Lyric Opera only a few times**
elle ne chanta/n'a chanté à l'Opéra qu'en de rares occasions

Pour les verbes irréguliers au prétérit, voir la liste pp. A63-5.

b) Used to/would

Lorsque l'on souhaite faire référence à un événement habituel dans le passé, on emploie souvent **used to** ou **would** :

on Sundays we used to go **to my grandmother's**
on Sundays we would go **to my grandmother's**
le dimanche, on allait chez ma grand-mère

Pour cet emploi de l'auxiliaire **would**, voir p. A57. Pour l'emploi de **used to** et la distinction que l'on peut faire entre les deux, voir p. A61.

c) *Le passé progressif*

Ce temps permet d'insister sur la continuité d'une action ou d'un événement :

what were **you** doing **last night when I called?**
qu'est-ce que tu faisais hier soir quand j'ai appelé ?

sorry, could you say that again? I wasn't listening
pardon, est-ce que tu peux répéter ? je n'écoutais pas

she was watching **her favourite programme when the phone rang**
elle était en train de regarder son émission préférée quand le téléphone a sonné

I was having **dinner when he came home**
j'étais en train de dîner quand il est arrivé à la maison

Le passé simple et le passé progressif sont souvent employés pour mettre en valeur le lien qui existe entre deux faits du passé. Le passé progressif s'emploie pour des événements servant de toile de fond à d'autres événements de courte durée, pour lesquels on préfère l'aspect simple. Dans le dernier exemple ci-dessus, une action ponctuelle (he came home) s'oppose à une action qui dure (I was having dinner). Comparez avec cette phrase :

I had **dinner when he** was **coming home**
j'ai dîné pendant qu'il rentrait à la maison

Le sens est différent : l'action qui dure se trouve dans la proposition subordonnée (he was coming home). La proposition principale (I had dinner) fait référence à quelque chose qui a lieu à un moment précis pendant le déroulement d'une action plus longue.

d) *Le present perfect (progressif)*

On emploie le present perfect pour des actions du passé ou des événements qui ont un lien avec le présent :

she has **read a lot of books to prepare for this exam**
(c'est-à-dire qu'elle est prête)
elle a lu beaucoup de livres pour préparer cet examen

Comparez le present perfect avec le prétérit dans les phrases qui suivent :

have you heard **the news this morning?** (c'est encore la matinée)
tu as entendu les informations ce matin ?

did you hear **the news this morning?** (c'est maintenant l'après-midi ou le soir)
tu as entendu les informations ce matin ?

he has **just arrived** (il est là maintenant)
il vient d'arriver

he arrived **a moment ago** (accent sur le moment du passé)
il est arrivé il y a un instant

Mrs Smith has **died** (elle est morte maintenant)
Mme Smith est morte

Mrs Smith died **a rich woman** (au moment où elle est morte, elle était riche)
Mme Smith est morte riche

Pour insister sur le fait qu'une action est continue, on peut employer l'aspect progressif :

I've been living **in this city for ten years**
cela fait dix ans que je vis dans cette ville

Cependant, on peut également employer ici la forme simple dans le même sens :

I've lived **in this city for ten years**

Remarquez que "depuis" se traduit par for devant un nombre, c'est-à-dire lorsqu'il s'agit d'une période de temps, mais par since lorsque l'on fait référence à un moment précis dans le temps. Par ailleurs, le present perfect employé avec for et since se traduit en général par un présent en français :

I've been living **here** since **1991**
je vis ici depuis 1991

I've been waiting **for three hours/since 5 o'clock**
j'attends depuis trois heures (durée)/depuis 17 heures

e) *Le past perfect (progressif)*

Le past perfect permet de décrire des actions et des événements passés survenus avant d'autres événements passés. Il exprime un passé par rapport à un autre passé. Comparez avec le prétérit :

she had **left when I arrived** (past perfect)
elle était partie lorsque je suis arrivé

she left **when I arrived** (prétérit)
elle est partie lorsque je suis arrivé

L'aspect progressif permet d'insister sur la durée de l'action :

she had been trying **to contact me for hours when I finally turned up**
cela faisait des heures qu'elle essayait de me contacter lorsque je suis enfin arrivé

I had been meaning **to contact him for ages**
cela faisait très longtemps que j'avais l'intention de le contacter

Pour le past perfect dans les propositions conditionnelles, voir p. A53.

12 Pour exprimer le futur

a) Will *et* shall

i) Pour exprimer le futur à la 1ère personne du singulier ou du pluriel, on emploie will ou shall devant le verbe. L'emploi de shall est néanmoins peu fréquent. Will et shall se contractent en 'll, et will not/shall not en won't/shan't :

I will/I'll/I shall **inform Mr Thompson of her decision**
je ferai part de sa décision à M. Thompson

we won't/shan't **be long**
nous n'en avons pas pour longtemps

ii) Aux autres personnes, on emploie will :

he will/he'll **get angry if you tell him this**
il va se mettre en colère si tu lui dis cela

you will/you'll **be surprised when you see him**
vous serez surpris quand vous le verrez

! Remarquez qu'après when l'anglais emploie un présent pour faire référence au futur, comme dans l'exemple ci-dessus. Ceci s'applique aussi pour d'autres conjonctions de temps, par exemple :

I'll do it **as soon as** I get **home**
je le ferai dès que j'arriverai à la maison

it'll be easy **once** you get **there**
une fois que tu seras arrivé là-bas, ce sera facile

while **you're in London you should visit the British Museum**
pendant que vous serez à Londres, vous devriez visiter le British Museum

iii) Si le locuteur exprime une intention à la 2ème ou 3ème personne (souvent une promesse ou une menace), on rencontre alors parfois shall, mais cet emploi est aujourd'hui bien moins courant que celui de will :

you shall **get what I promised you**
tu auras ce que je t'ai promis

they shall **pay for this!**
ils vont me le payer !

Si le futur dépend de l'intention ou de la volonté d'une personne autre que le locuteur, on emploie will ('ll) :

he will/he'll **do it, I'm sure**
il le fera, j'en suis sûr

iv) On emploie shall pour faire des propositions, des suggestions :

shall **we go?**   shall **I do it for you?**
on y va ?   *tu veux que je te le fasse ?*

Will ne pourrait pas s'employer dans ces deux exemples.

v) On emploie will pour demander à quelqu'un de faire quelque chose :

will you please put your cigarette out?
pouvez-vous éteindre votre cigarette, s'il vous plaît ?

ou pour donner des ordres :

you'll be here at three
soyez ici à trois heures

vi) Pour exprimer l'avenir immédiat, on préférera l'emploi de will à celui de shall. La forme contractée est ici très courante :

leave that, I'll do it   try some, you'll like it
laisse, je vais le faire   goûte, tu vas aimer

I'll have a beer, please
je prendrai une bière, s'il vous plaît

b) *Le futur progressif*

i) Will et shall peuvent être suivis de la forme progressive (be + forme en -ing) si le locuteur veut insister sur la continuité de l'action, sur le fait que l'action sera en cours à un moment précis du futur :

this time next Saturday I'll be sunbathing
samedi prochain à cette heure-ci, je serai en train de me faire bronzer

I'll be marking essays and you'll be looking after the baby
je corrigerai les dissertations et tu t'occuperas du bébé

ii) La forme progressive s'emploie aussi pour indiquer un arrangement préalable :

she'll be giving two concerts in London next week (= she is due to give...)
elle donnera deux concerts à Londres la semaine prochaine

iii) Le futur progressif permet également de formuler des questions sur un ton plus poli, moins direct. Par ailleurs, il y a parfois des nuances différentes entre le futur simple et le futur progressif. Comparez aussi les exemples suivants :

will you speak to him about it? *(simple)*
tu lui en parleras ?

will you be speaking to him about it? *(progressif)*
tu comptes lui en parler ?

L'emploi de la forme progressive dans le second exemple indique que le locuteur ne fait pas une demande directe (comme dans le premier exemple), mais qu'il demande simplement et objectivement si la personne à laquelle il s'adresse a l'intention de "lui en parler".

c) Be going to

i) Il n'y a souvent aucune différence entre be going to et will :

I wonder if this engine is ever going to start (= ... will ever start)
je me demande si le moteur va finir par démarrer

you're going to just love it (= you'll just love it)
tu vas adorer ça

what's he going to do about it? (= what'll he do about it?)
qu'est-ce qu'il a l'intention de faire ?

ii) Be going to est plus courant que will ou shall pour indiquer une intention :

we're going to sell the house after all
en fin de compte, nous allons vendre la maison

he's going to sue us
il va nous intenter un procès

I'm going to go to London tomorrow
je vais aller à Londres demain

iii) On préférera employer be going to plutôt que will lorsque les raisons justifiant les prévisions sont directement liées au présent :

it's going to rain (look at those clouds)
il va pleuvoir (regarde ces nuages)

I know what you're going to say (it's written all over your face)
je sais ce que tu vas dire (ça se lit sur ton visage)

d) *Le présent simple*

i) Comme en français, le présent simple peut exprimer le futur lorsque l'on fait référence à un programme établi, à un événement prévu, à un horaire, etc. :

when does university start?
quand a lieu la rentrée universitaire ?

classes start on 6 October
les cours reprennent le 6 octobre

the train for London leaves at 11 a.m.
le train qui va à Londres part à 11 heures

ii) Lorsque la proposition principale est au futur, on emploie le présent simple dans les propositions subordonnées temporelles (voir a) iii) ci-dessus) ou conditionnelles :

you'll like him when you see him
il te plaira quand tu le verras

if he turns up, will you speak to him?
tu lui en parleras s'il vient ?

Ne confondez pas les propositions de ce type commençant par when et if et les propositions interrogatives indirectes. Dans ces dernières, la forme du verbe est la même que celle du verbe de l'interrogation directe correspondante ; il est donc possible d'employer le futur :

when will they be here? → **I know when they'll be here**
quand vont-ils arriver ?   *je sais quand ils vont arriver*

will she be there?   → **I wonder if she'll be there**
est-ce qu'elle y sera ?   *je me demande si elle y sera*

e) *Le présent progressif*

i) Le présent progressif s'emploie souvent de façon semblable à be going to pour exprimer une intention :

I'm taking this book with me (= I'm going to take...)
j'emporte ce livre (= je vais emporter...)

what are you doing over Christmas? (= what are you going to do...) *qu'est-ce que tu fais à Noël ? (= qu'est-ce que tu vas faire... ?)*

ii) Le présent progressif peut aussi être employé pour faire référence à un événement organisé ou prévu dans le futur, son emploi étant alors similaire à celui du futur progressif ou du présent simple :

she's giving two concerts in London next week
elle donne deux concerts à Londres la semaine prochaine

the train for London is leaving soon
le train pour Londres part bientôt

f) Be to

On emploie souvent be to pour faire référence à des projets d'avenir spécifiques, en particulier des projets qui dépendent de la décision d'autres personnes :

the President is to visit the disaster zone (pour le style journalistique, voir aussi p. A42)
le président doit se rendre dans la zone sinistrée

we are to be there by ten o'clock (soutenu)
nous devons y être pour dix heures

g) **Be about to**

Be about to exprime le futur très proche :

you are about to meet a great artist
vous êtes sur le point de rencontrer un grand artiste

please take your seats, the play is about to start
veuillez vous asseoir, la pièce va maintenant commencer

Be about to peut aussi s'employer pour exprimer les intentions futures d'une personne :

I'm not about to sign a contract like that!
je ne signerai pas un tel contrat !

h) *Le futur antérieur (progressif)*

On emploie le futur antérieur pour faire référence à une action qui s'achèvera avant une autre action dans le futur :

by the time we get there he will already have left
le temps que nous arrivions, il sera déjà parti

by then we'll have been working on this project for five years (forme progressive)
nous aurons alors travaillé pendant cinq ans sur ce projet

On emploie aussi le futur antérieur pour exprimer des suppositions quant au présent ou au passé :

I expect you'll have been wondering why I asked you here
je suppose que vous vous êtes demandé pourquoi je vous ai convoqué

13 Pour exprimer la condition

Dans les phrases conditionnelles, on exprime la condition dans une proposition subordonnée placée avant ou après la proposition principale et commençant normalement par if :

if the train is late, we'll miss our plane
si le train a du retard, nous raterons notre avion

we'll miss our plane if the train is late
nous raterons notre avion si le train a du retard

Pour les conditions négatives, on emploie parfois unless + forme affirmative (*si... ne, à moins que*) :

unless the train is on time, we'll miss our plane
if the train isn't on time, we'll miss our plane
si le train n'est pas à l'heure, nous raterons notre avion

Étant donné que l'action de la principale dépend de la condition de la subordonnée, cette action doit être au futur (pour les exceptions voir a) i) ci-dessous).

La forme des verbes varie selon le temps auquel ils font référence et selon le degré de probabilité de la condition.

a) *Pour faire référence au présent/futur*

   i) Possibilité vraisemblable :

     Le verbe de la proposition subordonnée est au présent ou au present perfect. La proposition principale comprend la construction will + infinitif (quelquefois shall + infinitif à la 1ère personne) :

     if you see her, you will not recognize her
     si tu la vois, tu ne la reconnaîtras pas

     if you are sitting comfortably, we will begin
     si vous êtes assis confortablement, nous allons commencer

     if you have completed the forms, I will send them off
     si vous avez rempli les formulaires, je les enverrai

     if he comes back, I shall ask him to leave
     s'il revient, je lui demanderai de partir

     Il y a trois exceptions importantes :

● Si le verbe de la principale est aussi au présent, on sousentend une conséquence logique, un résultat automatique ou habituel. Dans ces phrases, if a presque le sens de when(ever) (*quand, à chaque fois que*) :

if the sun shines, people look happier
quand le soleil brille, les gens ont l'air plus heureux

if you're happy, I'm happy
si ça te va, ça me va

if you don't increase your bid, you don't get the house
si vous n'offrez pas plus, vous n'aurez pas la maison

● Lorsque will est aussi employé dans la subordonnée, le locuteur fait alors référence à la bonne volonté d'une personne ou à son intention de faire quelque chose :

if you will be kind enough to stop singing, we will/shall be able to get some sleep
si vous vouliez bien arrêter de chanter, que nous puissions dormir

if you will insist on driving home, you'll have to stay on soft drinks all night
si tu tiens vraiment à rentrer à la maison en voiture, il faudra ne pas boire de toute la soirée

Lorsque cette forme est employée pour demander à quelqu'un de faire quelque chose, on peut rendre la phrase plus polie en employant would :

if you would be kind enough to stop singing, we would/should be able to get some sleep
si vous aviez la bonté d'arrêter de chanter, nous pourrions dormir

● Lorsque l'on emploie should dans la subordonnée (à toutes les personnes), on sous-entend que la condition est moins probable, qu'elle a moins de chance de se réaliser. Ces propositions avec should sont souvent suivies de l'impératif, comme c'est le cas dans les deux premiers exemples :

if you should see him, ask him to call
au cas où vous le verriez, demandez-lui de m'appeler

if he should turn up, please tell him I want to see him
si jamais il vient, dis-lui que je veux le voir, s'il te plaît

if they should attack you, you will have to fight them
s'ils en venaient à vous attaquer, il vous faudrait vous défendre

Dans un style légèrement plus soutenu, on peut omettre if et faire commencer la phrase par should avec une inversion sujet-auxiliaire :

should the matter arise again, telephone me at once
si le problème devait se présenter de nouveau, téléphonezmoi immédiatement

  ii) Possibilité peu probable ou irréelle :

    L'expression "possibilité peu probable ou irréelle" signifie que l'on s'attend à ce que la condition ne se réalise pas ou qu'on l'oppose à des faits connus. Le verbe de la proposition subordonnée est au passé ; la principale comprend la construction would + infinitif (ou aussi should + infinitif à la 1ère personne) :

    if you saw her, you would not recognize her
    si tu la voyais, tu ne la reconnaîtrais pas

    if she had a car, she would visit you more often
    si elle avait une voiture, elle viendrait te voir plus souvent

if I won that amount of money, I would/should just
spend it all
si je gagnais une telle somme d'argent, je dépenserais tout

if the lift was working properly, there would not be
so many complaints
*si l'ascenseur marchait correctement, il n'y aurait pas
autant de plaintes*

Néanmoins, ce type de phrase n'exprime pas toujours une
possibilité peu probable ou irréelle. Elle présente souvent peu
de différence avec la construction du type a) i) ci-dessus :

if you worked harder, you would pass the exam
if you work harder, you will pass the exam
si tu travaillais davantage, tu réussirais ton examen

L'emploi du passé peut donner à la phrase un ton un peu
plus amical, moins direct et plus poli.

b) *Pour faire référence au passé*

   i) Dans ce cas-là, la condition ne s'est pas réalisée puisque ce
qui est exprimé dans la subordonnée ne s'est pas produit.
Le verbe de la subordonnée est au past perfect ; la principale comprend la construction would + infinitif passé (ou
aussi should + infinitif passé à la 1ère personne) :

if you had seen her, you would not have recognized
her
si tu l'avais vue, tu ne l'aurais pas reconnue

if I had been there, I would/should have ignored him
si j'avais été là, j'aurais fait semblant de ne pas le voir

Dans un style légèrement plus soutenu, on peut omettre if
et faire commencer la phrase par had avec une inversion
sujet-auxiliaire:

had I been there, I would/should have ignored him

  ii) Exceptions :

● Si la proposition principale fait référence à la non-réalisation
dans le présent d'une condition dans le passé, on peut aussi
employer would + infinitif :

if I had studied harder, I would be an engineer
today
si j'avais étudié davantage, je serais ingénieur maintenant

● On emploie le passé dans les deux propositions si, comme
c'est le cas en a) i) ci-dessus, on sous-entend une conséquence logique, un résultat automatique ou habituel (if =
when(ever)) :

if people got ill in those days, they often died
*si les gens tombaient malades à cette époque-là, ils
mouraient souvent*

if they tried to stand up to the boss, they were fired
s'ils essayaient de tenir tête au patron, ils étaient virés

● Si la condition est censée s'être réalisée, les restrictions
quant à la concordance des temps indiquées en a) et b) ci-
dessus ne s'appliquent plus. Dans ce cas-là, if signifie souvent "comme" ou "puisque". Remarquez, par exemple, la
diversité des formes verbales employées dans les propositions
principales qui suivent les propositions subordonnées (qui
sont toutes au passé) :

if he was rude to you, why did you not walk out?
*s'il a été grossier avec toi, pourquoi est-ce que tu n'es pas
parti ?*

if he was rude to you, why have you still kept in
touch?
if he was rude to you, why do you still keep in touch?
*s'il a été grossier avec toi, pourquoi est-ce que tu es
resté/restes en contact avec lui ?*

if he told you that, he was wrong
s'il t'a dit ça, il a eu tort

if he told you that, he is a fool
s'il t'a dit ça, c'est un imbécile

if he told you that, he has broken his promise
s'il t'a dit ça, il a manqué à sa promesse

14 Le subjonctif

Par opposition à l'indicatif, qui est le mode du réel, le subjonctif est
le mode du non-réel, exprimant le souhait, l'espoir, la possibilité, etc.
(Voir Les modes p. A40).

Le présent du subjonctif est identique par sa forme à l'infinitif (sans
to) aux trois personnes du singulier et du pluriel. Autrement dit, la
seule différence entre les formes du présent du subjonctif et celles du
présent de l'indicatif est l'omission du -s à la 3ème personne du singulier.

L'imparfait du subjonctif (ou subjonctif passé) est identique par sa
forme au prétérit, sauf pour le verbe to be qui devient were à la
1ère et 3ème personne du singulier. Cependant, dans le langage de
tous les jours, on emploie de préférence was (voir aussi b) vi) ci-
dessous).

a) *Le subjonctif dans les propositions principales*

    Cet emploi du subjonctif est limité à des locutions fixes et
idiomatiques exprimant, par exemple, l'espoir ou le souhait :

God save the Queen!   long live the King!
vive la Reine !   *vive le Roi !*

Heaven be praised!
Dieu soit loué !

b) *Le subjonctif dans les propositions subordonnées*

   i) Dans les propositions conditionnelles, le subjonctif passé est
très courant (voir 13a) ii) ci-dessus). L'emploi du présent
du subjonctif appartient à un niveau de langue très soutenu
ou à un style littéraire :

if this be true, old hopes are born anew *(littéraire)*
si c'était vrai, tous les espoirs renaîtraient

if this were/was true, I'd be so happy *(courant)*
si c'était vrai, je serais vraiment contente

On trouve aussi le subjonctif présent dans l'expression consacrée if need be *(s'il le faut, si besoin est)* :

if need be, we can sell the furniture
s'il le faut, nous pouvons vendre les meubles

Remarquez aussi l'emploi du subjonctif présent dans les
tournures concessives, avec l'inversion sujet-verbe :

they are all interrogated, be they friend or foe *(littéraire)*
ils sont tous interrogés, qu'ils soient amis ou ennemis

  ii) Les propositions comparatives, introduites par as if ou as
though, contiennent souvent, mais pas dans tous les cas,
un subjonctif passé :

he treats me as if I was/were a child
il me traite comme si j'étais un gamin

  iii) Le subjonctif passé est employé après if only et dans les
propositions compléments d'objet direct qui suivent wish et
had rather. Toutes ces propositions expriment le souhait
ou le désir :

if only we had a bigger house, life would be perfect
*si seulement nous avions une maison plus grande, tout
serait parfait*

are you going abroad this year? – I wish I were/was
*est-ce que tu pars à l'étranger cette année ? – si seulement
je pouvais !*

where's your passport? – I wish I knew
où est ton passeport ? – si je le savais !

do you want me to tell you? – I'd rather you didn't
tu veux que je te le dise ? – je n'aime mieux pas !

iv) Dans un langage soutenu ou juridique, on rencontre parfois le présent du subjonctif dans les propositions compléments d'objet direct qui suivent les expressions impersonnelles ("il est souhaitable", "il est important", etc.) ou les verbes indiquant une suggestion ou un souhait :

it is important that he take steps immediately
il est important qu'il prenne immédiatement des mesures

it is imperative that this matter be discussed further
il est impératif de discuter davantage de cette affaire

we propose that the clause be extended to cover such eventualities
nous proposons que la clause soit élargie pour couvrir ces éventualités

Dans ces propositions, le subjonctif est d'un emploi plus courant en anglais américain qu'en anglais britannique et il n'est pas rare de le rencontrer en dehors du langage des négociations ou du langage juridique. En anglais britannique, on préférera l'emploi de should + infinitif :

we suggest that the system (should) be changed
nous suggérons que le système soit changé

I am adamant that this (should) be put to the vote
j'insiste pour que cela soit soumis au vote

it is vital that he (should) start as soon as possible
il est primordial qu'il commence aussi vite que possible

v) On emploie aussi le subjonctif passé après it's time, lorsque le locuteur veut insister sur le fait que quelque chose devrait être fait :

it's time we spoke to him
il est temps que nous lui parlions

it's high time they stopped that
il est grand temps qu'ils arrêtent

Comparez avec l'emploi de l'infinitif qui ne fait qu'exprimer l'opportunité du moment :

it's time to speak to him about it
c'est le moment de lui en parler

vi) If I was/if I were

Les confusions sont fréquentes quant à l'emploi correct de if I was/if I were.

Lorsque la condition à laquelle on fait référence n'est en aucun cas une condition irréelle, on ne peut employer que if I was :

if I was mistaken about it then I can only apologize
si je me suis trompé, eh bien je ne peux que m'excuser

Le locuteur ne met pas en cause le fait qu'il se soit trompé. Comparez avec la phrase suivante :

if I were mistaken about it, surely I would have realized
si je m'étais trompé, je m'en serais certainement aperçu

Ici, le locuteur émet un doute quant à la réalité de l'erreur, d'où l'emploi du subjonctif were. Mais dans un niveau de langue moins soutenu, on pourrait également employer was dans cette phrase.

15 Un emploi particulier du passé

Nous avons vu dans les sections 13 et 14 comment le subjonctif passé peut faire référence au présent dans des propositions condition-

nelles ou autres. Outre ces emplois du subjonctif passé, le passé peut faire référence au présent dans les propositions principales exprimant une attitude plus hésitante et donc plus polie et respectueuse. Ainsi :

did you want to see me?
vous vouliez me voir ?

est plus poli ou moins direct que :

do you want to see me?
vous voulez me voir ?

Remarquez aussi l'emploi du passé progressif dans l'expression I was wondering, qui permet de demander quelque chose de manière plus polie :

I was wondering if you could help me do this (= I wonder if you could help me do this)
est-ce que vous pourriez m'aider à faire cela ?

L'expression I was hoping, qui permet aussi de formuler indirectement et poliment une requête, n'a pas de construction correspondante au présent :

I was hoping you could help me
est-ce que vous pourriez m'aider ?

16 La voix passive

Pour les différences de forme entre la voix active et la voix passive, voir p. A40.

a) *Le passif direct et le passif indirect*

Dans la phrase à la voix active :

they sent him another bill
ils lui ont envoyé une autre facture

another bill est le complément d'objet direct et him, le complément d'objet indirect. Si dans une construction correspondante à la voix passive, le complément d'objet direct de la phrase à la voix active devient le sujet de la phrase à la voix passive, on a alors un "passif direct" :

another bill was sent to him
une autre facture lui a été envoyée

Un "passif indirect" aurait pour sujet le complément d'objet indirect de la phrase à la voix active :

he was sent another bill
on lui a envoyé une autre facture

b) *Le passif d'état et le passif d'action*

Dans la phrase suivante, le verbe exprime un état :

the shop is closed
la boutique est fermée

tandis que, dans l'exemple suivant, il exprime une action :

the shop is closed by the manager at the end of the day
la boutique est fermée par le gérant à la fin de la journée

Dans la première phrase, le verbe est appelé "verbe d'état" ; dans la deuxième phrase, il est appelé "verbe d'action". C'est le contexte qui nous renseigne et non la forme. La forme du verbe reste la même. L'absence de formes distinctes peut parfois donner lieu à des ambiguïtés, comme par exemple :

his neck was broken when they lifted him

Cette phrase signifie soit "son cou était cassé quand ils l'ont soulevé" (passif d'état), soit "son cou s'est cassé quand ils l'ont soulevé" (passif d'action). Cependant, si l'on souhaite insister sur le passif d'action (souvent plus vivant), on peut employer get comme auxiliaire à la place de be, notamment dans le langage courant :

his neck got broken when they lifted him
il a eu le cou cassé quand ils l'ont soulevé

they finally got caught
ils ont fini par se faire prendre

On peut aussi employer le verbe have pour exprimer un passif d'action :

he had his neck broken when they lifted him
il a eu le cou cassé quand ils l'ont soulevé

they've had their house burgled three times
ils se sont fait cambrioler trois fois

c) *Voix passive ou voix active ?*

i) Si la personne qui fait l'action est moins importante que l'action elle-même, on préfère souvent la voix passive à la voix active :

his invitation was refused
son invitation a été refusée

Ici, d'après le locuteur, l'identité de la personne qui refuse l'invitation n'a pas d'importance. Ce qui est important, c'est le fait qu'elle ait été refusée.

Dans certains cas, notamment dans le domaine scientifique, on emploie de très nombreuses tournures passives parce que l'on considère que mentionner l'agent ou celui qui fait l'action manque d'objectivité :

the experiment was conducted in darkness (*objectivité*)
l'expérience a été effectuée dans le noir

I conducted the experiment in darkness (*subjectivité*)
j'ai effectué l'expérience dans le noir

ii) De nombreux verbes peuvent également s'employer à la voix active, tout en ayant un sens passif :

the theatre runs at a profit (= the theatre is run at a profit)
le théâtre fait des bénéfices

her eyes filled with tears (= her eyes were filled with tears)
elle avait les larmes aux yeux

Dans ces deux exemples, on pourrait tout aussi bien employer les formes passives données entre parenthèses. Mais certains verbes intransitifs à sens passif ne peuvent pas s'employer d'une autre manière :

a cloth which feels soft   **it flies beautifully**
un tissu qui est doux au toucher   *il se pilote très bien*

silk blouses do not wash well
les chemisiers en soie ne se lavent pas bien

this essay reads better than your last one
cette dissertation se lit mieux que la dernière que vous avez écrite

where is the film showing?   **he photographs well**
dans quel cinéma passe ce film ?   *il est photogénique*

iii) On trouve également des infinitifs à sens passif dans les constructions du type there is + nom/pronom + infinitif :

when we get home there'll be suitcases to unpack
quand nous rentrerons à la maison, il y aura les valises à défaire

there was plenty to eat
il y avait beaucoup de choses à manger

have you got anything to wash?
est-ce que tu as quelque chose à laver ?

Dans certains cas, on peut employer indifféremment l'infinitif actif ou l'infinitif passif :

there's nothing else to say/to be said
il n'y a rien d'autre à dire

is there anything to gain/to be gained from it?
est-ce qu'il y a quelque chose à y gagner ?

there is work to do/to be done
il y a du travail à faire

Mais lorsque ces constructions suivent les pronoms some-thing, anything, nothing, il peut y avoir une différence entre l'infinitif actif (à sens passif) et l'infinitif passif de do. Comparez par exemple :

there is always something to do
on trouve toujours à s'occuper

there is always something to be done
il y a toujours du travail à faire

iv) "On"

Le passif est bien plus employé en anglais qu'en français. Le français préfère souvent une construction avec le pronom personnel indéfini "on" :

he was spotted leaving the bar
on l'a vu sortir du bar

that's already been done
on l'a déjà fait/ça a déjà été fait

I hadn't been told that
on ne m'avait pas dit ça

17 Be, have, do

a) **Be**

i) Be s'emploie comme auxiliaire avec le participe passé pour former le passif (voir p. A40 et section 16 ci-dessus). Be peut parfois remplacer have en tant qu'auxiliaire pour l'aspect "perfect" (ou passé), comme dans :

are you finished? (= have you finished?)
est-ce que tu as fini ?

his voice is gone (= his voice has gone)
il a une extinction de voix

Dans ces cas-là, on insiste particulièrement sur l'état présent plutôt que sur l'action.

ii) Comme les autres auxiliaires modaux, be n'est pas accompagné de do dans les négations et les interrogations (he isn't Spanish, is he Spanish?, etc.). Mais lorsque be se comporte comme un verbe indépendant et non pas comme un auxiliaire, on emploie do dans les impératifs à la forme négative :

don't be silly
ne dis pas n'importe quoi

iii) Lorsque be est un verbe ordinaire, et non un auxiliaire, il ne s'emploie à l'aspect progressif que lorsqu'il fait uniquement référence au comportement. Comparez :

you are funny   **you are being funny**
tu es drôle (= de nature)   *tu es drôle* (= en ce moment)

he is annoying   **he is being annoying**
il est énervant   *il devient énervant*

b) **Have**

i) Have est employé avec le participe passé pour former l'aspect "perfect" (voir p. A39).

En tant que verbe ordinaire, il permet parfois d'exprimer une activité, quelque chose dont on fait l'expérience (des difficultés, etc.) ou des impressions que l'on ressent, comme dans les expressions idiomatiques :

to have dinner   **to have a shower**
dîner   *prendre une douche*

to have a chat   **to have a good time**
bavarder   *s'amuser*

to have difficulty (doing something)
avoir du mal (à faire quelque chose)

Lorsque have n'exprime pas une activité, il fait normalement référence à la possession, à un état ou à quelque chose de prévu :

to have a farm
avoir une ferme

to have an appointment
avoir un rendez-vous

to have toothache
avoir mal aux dents

to have time (for something/to do something)
avoir le temps (pour quelque chose/de faire quelque chose)

On désignera le verbe have sous le nom de have 1 lorsque son emploi correspond aux exemples du premier type et de have 2 lorsqu'il est employé comme dans les exemples du deuxième type.

ii) Have 1 :

● Il se comporte comme les verbes ordinaires normaux dans les interrogations et dans les négations (ainsi que dans les question-tags), c'est-à-dire qu'il est accompagné de do :

did you have the day off yesterday?
est-ce que tu étais en congé hier ?

we don't have fun any more
on ne s'amuse plus tellement maintenant

we had a marvellous time, didn't we?
nous avons vraiment passé un très bon moment, n'est-ce pas ?

● Il peut s'employer à l'aspect progressif :

he telephoned as we were having lunch
il a téléphoné pendant que nous déjeunions

I'm having problems with Carol these days
j'ai des problèmes avec Carol en ce moment

iii) Have 2 :

● Au lieu de have 2, l'anglais britannique emploie souvent have got, notamment à l'oral, et surtout au présent :

he has/he has got/he's got a large garden
il a un grand jardin

Au passé, on emploie normalement had ou used to have, cette dernière forme insistant davantage sur l'idée de possession, sur la répétition ou l'habitude :

they all had flu in July last year
ils ont tous eu la grippe en juillet l'année dernière

he had/used to have a large garden once
autrefois, il avait un grand jardin

we had/used to have lots of problems in those days
à cette époque-là, nous avions beaucoup de problèmes

● Dans les interrogations, le sujet et have peuvent être inversés :

have you any other children?
avez-vous d'autres enfants ?

Dans les négations, not peut s'employer sans do :

he hasn't a garden
il n'a pas de jardin

On considère parfois ces phrases comme appartenant à un niveau de langue plutôt soutenu, et dans le langage de tous les jours, on préfère employer have... got ou une construction avec do :

have you got/do you have any other children?
he hasn't got/doesn't have a garden

La tournure en do, qui était avant un emploi exclusivement américain, est maintenant très courante, notamment lorsque l'on fait référence à quelque chose d'habituel, de permanent. Comparez :

have you got/do you have any sweets?
est-ce que tu as des bonbons ?

do you always have sweets in the cupboard?
est-ce que tu as toujours des bonbons dans ton placard ?

De même :

have you got/do you have a pain in your chest?
est-ce que vous ressentez une douleur dans la poitrine ?

do you frequently have a pain in your chest?
est-ce que vous ressentez souvent une douleur dans la poitrine ?

Remarquez aussi que les deux auxiliaires sont possibles dans les réponses à la forme négative :

have you a minute? – no, I haven't
have you a minute? – no, I don't
tu as une minute ? – non

Dans les question-tags après have, on peut employer have ou do puisque, comme nous l'avons vu, have peut s'employer avec ou sans do dans les interrogations. Do est particulièrement courant au passé, mais on le trouve aussi au présent :

he has a dog, hasn't/doesn't he?
il a un chien, n'est-ce pas ?

they had a large garden once, hadn't they/didn't they?
ils avaient un grand jardin autrefois, n'est-ce pas ?

Mais après have got, on ne peut employer que have dans les questions-tags :

he's got a dog, hasn't he?
il a un chien, n'est-ce pas ?

● On ne peut employer l'aspect progressif avec have 2 que lorsqu'on fait référence au futur. Ainsi :

they are having a baby

ne signifie en aucun cas "ils ont un bébé", mais "ils vont avoir un bébé".

iv) L'emploi causatif de have :

Le verbe have est employé dans la construction du type "faire faire quelque chose", qui se forme avec have + complément d'objet direct + participe passé. Par exemple :

they're having a conservatory built
ils se font construire une véranda

could you have these photocopied?
est-ce que vous pouvez faire photocopier cela ?

I'll have it done immediately
je vais le faire faire immédiatement

we'll have to have it fixed
il va falloir que nous le fassions réparer

Remarquez que get peut s'employer à la place de have dans tous ces exemples.

Cette construction n'a pas toujours le sens littéral de "faire faire quelque chose". Dans l'exemple suivant, la construction signifie simplement "demandez-lui d'entrer" :

Mr Braithwaite is here – ah, have him come in
M. Braithwaite est là – ah, faites-le entrer

On emploie aussi **have** ou **get** + infinitif pour dire "faire faire quelque chose à quelqu'un" :

I'll have the kitchen send it up to your room, madam
I'll get the kitchen to send it up to your room, madam
je vais demander à la cuisine de vous le monter dans votre chambre, madame

Notez que l'infinitif après **have** est employé sans **to**, ce qui n'est pas le cas de **get**.

v) Constructions à la voix passive :

Le verbe **have** s'emploie aussi pour former un type de construction passive, notamment lorsque l'on sous-entend que le sujet de la phrase a souffert d'une manière ou d'une autre (voir aussi 16b) :

he's had all his money stolen
il s'est fait voler tout son argent

c) **Do**

Nous avons vu l'emploi de **do** dans les interrogations et les négations dans les sections 8 et 9 de ce chapitre. Pour son emploi dans les autres cas d'inversion, voir **La structure de la phrase**, p. A78.

i) **Do** emphatique :

Dans les phrases qui ne sont ni interrogatives ni négatives, on peut marquer l'emphase en employant l'auxiliaire **do** (que l'on accentue à l'oral) devant le verbe principal :

oh, I do like your new jacket!
oh, j'aime beaucoup ta nouvelle veste !

do try to keep still !
essaye de rester tranquille !

he doesn't know any German but he does know a few words of French
il ne comprend pas l'allemand, mais par contre il connaît quelques mots de français

I didn't manage to get tickets for Saturday night, but I did get some for Monday
je n'ai pas réussi à avoir de billets pour samedi soir, mais j'en ai pris pour lundi

Et le verbe ordinaire **do** (*faire*) peut s'employer avec **do** en tant qu'auxiliaire emphatique. Mais cette construction, qui n'est pas très élégante, est assez rare :

we don't do everything but what we do do, we do well
nous ne faisons pas tout, mais ce que nous faisons, nous le faisons bien

ii) **Do** pour remplacer le verbe :

L'auxiliaire **do** peut s'employer seul lorsque le verbe principal a déjà été énoncé. On pourrait répéter à la place le verbe principal précédé de l'auxiliaire (voir l'emploi emphatique ci-dessus) ou parfois sans l'auxiliaire :

she never drinks! – oh yes, she does (= oh yes, she does drink)
elle ne boit jamais ! – bien sûr que si !

can I help myself to another cream cake? – please do (= please do help yourself)
est-ce que je peux avoir un autre gâteau à la crème ? – mais je vous en prie !

do you both agree? – I do, but she doesn't (= I agree, but she doesn't)
vous êtes tous les deux d'accord ? – moi oui, mais pas elle

Voir aussi la section traitant des question-tags (p. A47).

18 Les auxiliaires modaux

Ce sont les auxiliaires **will–would, shall–should, can–could, may–might, must–had to, ought to**.

a) Will–would

Les formes négatives contractées sont **won't–wouldn't**.

i) Pour l'emploi du futur, voir pp. A50-2.

ii) Pour les phrases au conditionnel, voir pp. A52-3.

iii) Pour donner des ordres, exprimer l'obligation ou la détermination :

you will do as you are told!   will you stop that!
tu feras ce qu'on te dit !   arrête ça !

new recruits will report to headquarters on Tuesday
les jeunes recrues se présenteront au quartier général mardi

I will not stand for this!   I will be obeyed!
je ne le supporterai pas !   je veux qu'on m'obéisse !

Dans ces phrases, **will** apporte des nuances différentes ; il fait plus qu'exprimer un simple futur.

iv) Pour faire appel, sur un ton plutôt cérémonieux, aux souvenirs ou aux connaissances de quelqu'un :

you will recall last week's discussion about the purchase of a computer
vous vous souvenez certainement de notre discussion de la semaine dernière concernant l'achat d'un ordinateur

you will all know that the company has just been sold
vous savez certainement tous que l'entreprise vient d'être vendue

v) Pour faire des suppositions :

there's the telephone, Mary! – oh, that will be John
le téléphone sonne, Mary ! – oh, ça doit être John

they'll be there by now
ils doivent être arrivés maintenant

how old is he now? – he'll be about 45
quel âge a-t-il maintenant ? – il doit avoir à peu près 45 ans

vi) Pour insister sur la notion de capacité, d'inclination naturelle ou inhérente, d'habitude ou de comportement caractéristique :

cork will float on water   the car won't start
le liège flotte sur l'eau   la voiture ne veut pas démarrer

the Arts Centre will hold about 300 people
le centre culturel peut contenir environ 300 personnes

John will sit playing quietly on his own for hours
John peut rester tranquillement assis à jouer tout seul pendant des heures

it's so annoying, he will keep interrupting! (accent sur **will** à l'oral)
c'est énervant, il n'arrête pas de m'interrompre !

De même **would**, pour faire référence au passé :

when he was little, John would sit playing quietly on his own for hours
quand il était petit, John restait tranquillement assis à jouer tout seul pendant des heures

she created a scene in public – she would!
elle a fait une scène en public – c'est bien elle !

vii) Pour poser des questions ou proposer quelque chose de manière légèrement soutenue :

will you have another cake? – thank you, I will
voulez-vous un autre gâteau ? – oui, merci, je veux bien

won't you try some of these?
vous ne voulez pas y goûter ?

viii) Pour demander à quelqu'un de faire quelque chose :

will you move your car, please?
est-ce que vous pouvez déplacer votre voiture, s'il vous plaît ?

On peut poser la même question de façon légèrement plus polie et moins directe avec **would** :

would you move your car, please?
est-ce que vous pourriez déplacer votre voiture, s'il vous plaît ?

b) **Shall–should**

Les formes négatives contractées sont **shan't–shouldn't**.

i) Pour **shall** exprimant le futur, voir pp. A50-2.

ii) Pour les phrases au conditionnel, voir pp. A52-3.

iii) Pour **should**, équivalent du subjonctif, voir p. A54.

iv) Dans le langage juridique ou officiel, **shall** (uniquement) s'emploie fréquemment pour exprimer une obligation. Ce sens de **shall** est très semblable à celui de **must** (voir p. A60) :

the committee shall consist of six members
le comité sera constitué de six membres

the contract shall be subject to English law
le contrat sera régi par la loi anglaise

v) Pour exprimer une obligation, souvent morale (uniquement **should**) :

you should lose some weight
tu devrais perdre du poids

he shouldn't be allowed to
il ne devrait pas y être autorisé

you really should see this film
tu devrais essayer de voir ce film

something was not quite as it should be
il y avait quelque chose qui n'allait pas

what do you think I should do?
à ton avis, qu'est-ce que je devrais faire ?

vi) Pour exprimer la déduction, la probabilité (uniquement **should**) :

it's ten o'clock, they should be back any minute
il est dix heures, ils devraient rentrer d'un moment à l'autre

John should have put up those shelves by now
John devrait maintenant avoir fini d'installer ces étagères

are they there? – I don't know, but they should be
ils sont là ? – je ne sais pas, mais ils devraient

vii) Pour donner son avis de manière hésitante (uniquement **should**) :

I should just like to say that...
j'aimerais simplement dire que...

I should hardly call him a great intellectual but...
je ne dirais pas vraiment que c'est un grand intellectuel, mais...

will he agree? – I shouldn't think so
est-ce qu'il sera d'accord ? – je ne pense pas

viii) **Should** est souvent employé pour faire référence à la notion (par opposition à la réalité concrète) d'une action. Cet emploi de **should** est parfois qualifié de "putatif" :

that she should want to take early retirement is quite understandable
il est tout à fait compréhensible qu'elle veuille prendre sa retraite anticipée

Comparez ce dernier exemple avec :

it is quite understandable that she wanted to take early retirement
il est tout à fait compréhensible qu'elle ait voulu prendre sa retraite anticipée

Dans le premier cas, la proposition subordonnée est au présent. Dans le second cas, elle est au passé.

Il est important de remarquer que ce **should** est neutre pour ce qui est du temps. Le premier exemple pourrait tout aussi bien faire référence au passé (she has taken early retirement) ou au futur (she will be taking early retirement) suivant le contexte. Le second exemple ne peut bien sûr que faire référence au passé.

L'emploi putatif peut être comparé à l'emploi de **should** après les tournures impersonnelles ou les verbes indiquant la suggestion, le souhait ou l'ordre, dont il est question dans la section sur le subjonctif, p. A54.

Dans l'exemple ci-dessus, l'emploi putatif de **should** est apparu dans une proposition subordonnée, mais on le trouve aussi dans des propositions principales, qui expriment souvent l'agacement, la surprise, etc. :

where have I put my glasses? – how should I know?
où est-ce que j'ai mis mes lunettes ? – comment veux-tu que je le sache ?

as we were sitting there, who should walk by but George!
nous étions assis là, et devine qui est passé ?... George !

c) **Can–could**

Les formes négatives contractées sont **can't–couldn't**. La forme négative non contractée de **can** est **cannot**.

i) Pour exprimer la capacité, le fait de pouvoir faire quelque chose (= be able to) :

I can't afford it   **I can swim**
je ne peux pas me le permettre   *je sais nager*

when I was young, I could swim for hours
quand j'étais jeune, je pouvais nager pendant des heures

Ce dernier exemple est au passé. Cependant, dans les propositions conditionnelles, **could** + infinitif fait référence au présent et au futur (comparez avec **would** dans la section 13 p. A53) :

you could do a lot better if you'd only try
tu pourrais faire bien mieux si seulement tu faisais un effort

Be able to (*pouvoir, être capable de*) permet d'exprimer la capacité à d'autres temps :

I'll be able to tell you the answer tomorrow
je pourrai te donner la réponse demain

I've never been able to understand her
je n'ai jamais pu la comprendre

ii) Pour demander ou donner la permission :

can/could I have a sweet?   **you can come with me**
je peux avoir un bonbon ?   *tu peux venir avec moi*

Remarquez que **could** fait autant référence au présent ou au futur que **can** lorsque l'on demande la permission de faire quelque chose. La seule différence réside dans le fait que **could** est un peu plus poli.

Mais could peut s'employer pour exprimer une permission dans un contexte au passé :

for some reason we couldn't smoke in the waiting room before, but now we can
pour une raison que j'ignore, on ne pouvait pas fumer avant dans le salon, mais maintenant on peut

Be allowed to (*pouvoir, être autorisé à*) permet d'exprimer la permission à tous les temps :

we weren't allowed to smoke in the lounge
nous n'avions pas le droit de fumer dans le salon

will they be allowed to change the rules?
est-ce qu'ils auront le droit de changer les règles ?

Lorsqu'ils signifient "avoir le droit de", may est plus poli et plus soutenu que can (voir d) i) ci-dessous).

iii) Pour exprimer la possibilité :

what shall we do tonight? – we can/could watch a film
qu'est-ce qu'on va faire ce soir ? – on pourrait regarder un film

Là encore, remarquez que could ne fait pas référence au passé, mais au présent ou au futur. Pour faire référence au passé, on doit employer could + infinitif passé :

instead of going out, we could have watched a DVD
au lieu de sortir, nous aurions pu regarder un DVD

I could have (could've) gone there if I'd wanted to, but I didn't
j'aurais pu y aller si j'avais voulu, mais je n'en avais pas envie

Could et may sont parfois interchangeables lorsqu'ils expriment la possibilité, l'éventualité :

you could/may be right
vous avez peut-être raison

Mais il existe parfois une différence importante entre can et may : can indique souvent une conséquence logique ou un simple fait, tandis que may exprime l'incertitude, le hasard ou la probabilité d'un événement :

(a) **your comments can be overheard**
on peut entendre vos remarques

(b) **your comments may be overheard**
on pourrait entendre vos remarques

En (a), il est possible d'entendre les remarques (parce qu'elles sont faites à voix haute, par exemple), mais cela ne signifie pas forcément que quelqu'un les entendra. En (b), il existe une probabilité, une chance que les remarques soient réellement entendues.

La différence est la même dans les propositions à la forme négative :

he can't have heard us (= it is impossible for him to have heard us)
il ne peut pas nous avoir entendus

he may not have heard us (= it is possible that he did not hear us)
il se peut qu'il ne nous ait pas entendus

iv) Pour faire des suggestions (uniquement could) :

you could try a supermarket
tu peux essayer d'aller voir au supermarché

they could always sell their second house
ils peuvent toujours vendre leur maison secondaire

v) Pour faire des reproches (uniquement could) :

you could have let us know!
tu aurais pu nous le dire !

he could have warned us!
il aurait pu nous prévenir !

d) May–might

La forme négative contractée mayn't exprimant la "permission négative" (= l'interdiction) n'est pas très courante. On emploie à la place may not ou must not/mustn't ou encore can't. La forme négative contractée de might est mightn't, mais elle ne s'emploie pas pour exprimer l'interdiction.

i) Pour demander ou donner la permission (ou exprimer l'interdiction) :

you may sit down
vous pouvez vous asseoir

may I open a window? – no, you may not!
est-ce que je peux ouvrir une fenêtre ? – non, pas question !

Comparez avec can dans c) ii) ci-dessus. May est plus soutenu que can.

Remarquez que l'on emploie may not dans les réponses aux questions commençant par l'auxiliaire may (voir le dernier exemple ci-dessus), mais que dans les simples phrases négatives, on emploiera en général must not/mustn't :

you must not/mustn't open the windows in here
tu ne dois pas ouvrir les fenêtres ici

L'emploi de might pour exprimer la permission est plus poli que can, could ou may :

I wonder if I might have another glass of wine
pourrais-je avoir un autre verre de vin, s'il vous plaît ?

might I suggest we adjourn the meeting?
puis-je suggérer que nous ajournions la réunion ?

Notez que might fait référence au présent et au futur. Il s'utilise très rarement au passé lorsqu'il est employé dans une proposition principale. Comparez :

he then asked if he might smoke (*emploi soutenu de* might *dans la proposition subordonnée*)

he then asked if he was allowed to smoke
il a alors demandé s'il pouvait fumer

et : **he wasn't allowed to smoke**
il n'avait pas le droit de fumer, il ne pouvait pas fumer

On ne peut pas employer might dans le dernier exemple. Might ne s'emploie dans une proposition principale au passé que dans certaines tournures de phrase, par exemple après l'adverbe nor (attention à l'inversion sujet-auxiliaire après cet adverbe ; voir aussi p. A78) :

in those days we were told not to drink; nor might we smoke or be out after 10 o'clock
à cette époque, nous n'avions pas le droit de boire, pas plus que de fumer ou de rentrer après dix heures

Une manière plus courante et moins littéraire de formuler cette phrase serait :

in those days we were told not to drink; nor were we allowed to smoke or be out after 10 o'clock

ii) Pour exprimer la possibilité :

it may/might rain   **they may/might be right**
il va peut-être pleuvoir   *il se peut qu'ils aient raison*

it may not/mightn't be so easy as you think
ce ne sera peut-être pas aussi facile que vous le pensez

she may/might have left already
elle est peut-être déjà partie

Might exprime généralement une possibilité moins forte.

iii) Pour exprimer la surprise, l'amusement ou l'agacement, comme dans les tournures idiomatiques suivantes :

and who may/might **you be?**
à qui ai-je l'honneur ?

and who may/might **you be to give out orders?**
et pour qui est-ce que tu te prends pour donner des ordres ?

iv) Pour formuler des suggestions (uniquement might) :

you might **help me dry the dishes**
tu pourrais m'aider à essuyer la vaisselle

well, you might **at least try!**
tu pourrais au moins essayer, enfin !

you might **have a look at chapter 2 for next Wednesday**
vous voudrez bien lire le chapitre 2 pour mercredi prochain

he might **be a little less abrupt**
il pourrait être un peu moins brusque

v) Pour faire des reproches (uniquement might) :

you might **have warned us what would happen!**
vous auriez pu nous prévenir de ce qui allait se produire !

he might **have tried to stop it!**
il aurait pu essayer d'arrêter cela !

vi) Pour exprimer des souhaits :

may **the best man win!**
que le meilleur gagne !

may **you be forgiven for telling such lies!**
que le bon Dieu te pardonne de tels mensonges !

might **I be struck dumb if I tell a lie!**
que le diable m'emporte si je mens !

Attention à bien respecter l'ordre des mots : auxiliaire-sujet-verbe.

Cet usage est normalement réservé à des expressions consacrées (comme dans les deux premiers exemples) ou considérées comme étant d'un style quelque peu ampoulé ou littéraire (comme dans le dernier).

e) **Must–had to**

La forme négative contractée de must est mustn't. Pour les formes contractées de have, voir p. A66.

i) Pour exprimer l'obligation :

you must **try harder**
il faut que tu fasses un effort

I must **stop spending so much money**
je dois arrêter de dépenser autant d'argent

Au passé, on utilise had to. On ne peut employer must qu'au discours indirect passé, mais même dans ce cas, had to est beaucoup plus courant :

you said the other day that you had to/must **clean out the garden shed**
tu as dit l'autre jour qu'il fallait que tu nettoies la cabane du jardin

Au présent, on peut aussi employer have to, ou dans un style plus familier have got to. La différence entre must et have (got) to réside généralement dans le fait que must exprime des sentiments personnels d'obligation ou de contrainte tandis que have (got) to est plus souvent employé lorsqu'une obligation extérieure est sous-entendue. Comparez :

I must **go to the dentist (= I have toothache, etc.)**
il faut que j'aille chez le dentiste (= j'ai mal aux dents, etc.)

I have (got) to go to the dentist (= I have an appointment)
je dois aller chez le dentiste (= j'ai rendez-vous)

ii) Pour exprimer l'interdiction ou l'absence d'obligation (formes négatives) :

On ne peut employer must not/mustn't que pour exprimer l'interdiction (= "une obligation de ne pas faire quelque chose") :

we mustn't **park the car here (= we're not allowed to park here)**
nous ne devons pas nous garer ici (= nous n'avons pas le droit de nous garer ici)

you mustn't **take so many pills (= do not take so many pills)**
il ne faut pas que tu prennes autant de comprimés

Don't have to ou haven't got to sont employés pour indiquer, non pas l'interdiction, mais l'absence d'obligation, c'est-à-dire qu'il n'est pas nécessaire ou obligatoire de faire quelque chose :

we don't have to **park here, we could always drive a little further**
nous ne sommes pas obligés de nous garer ici, nous pouvons aller un peu plus loin

you don't have to **take so many pills (= you needn't take…)**
tu n'as pas besoin de prendre autant de comprimés

we haven't got to **be there before nine**
nous n'avons pas besoin d'y être avant neuf heures

iii) Pour exprimer la déduction, la probabilité :

if they're over 65, they must **be entitled to benefits**
s'ils ont plus de 65 ans, ils doivent avoir droit à des prestations

they must **have been surprised to see you**
ils ont dû être surpris de te voir

hello, you must **be Susan**   **you** must **be joking!**
bonjour, vous devez être Susan   *tu veux rire !*

Have to s'emploie aussi souvent dans ce sens :

you have to **be kidding!**
tu veux rire !

de même que have got to, notamment en anglais britannique :

well if she said so, it's got to be true (it's = it has)
si elle l'a dit, c'est que c'est vrai

À la forme négative, on emploie can :

he can't **be that old!**
il ne peut pas être si vieux que ça !

f) **Ought to**

La forme négative contractée est oughtn't to. L'infinitif placé après ought est précédé de to, contrairement aux autres auxiliaires modaux.

i) Pour exprimer l'obligation :

Ought to a le même sens que should lorsqu'ils expriment l'obligation :

I ought to **be going now**
il faudrait que je m'en aille maintenant

I know I really ought to, **but I don't want to**
je sais bien que je devrais, mais je n'en ai pas envie

you oughtn't to **speak to her like that**
tu ne devrais pas lui parler de cette façon

Mais ought to est moins fort que must dans ce sens.
Comparez :

I must/have to avoid fatty foods (*obligation ferme ou nécessité*)
je dois éviter les matières grasses

I ought to avoid fatty foods (*obligation moins stricte*)
je devrais éviter les matières grasses

Should remplace normalement ought to dans les questions :

should you visit your mother every Sunday?
est-ce que tu dois aller voir ta mère tous les dimanches ?

ii) Pour exprimer la déduction, la probabilité :

they ought to have reached the summit by now
ils devraient maintenant avoir atteint le sommet

£20 ought to be enough
20 livres, ça devrait suffire

Comparez ought to et must exprimant la probabilité :

if they have three cars and a holiday home in France, they must be rich (*déduction logique*)
s'ils ont trois voitures et une résidence secondaire en France, ils doivent être riches

if they have three cars and a holiday home in France, they ought to be happy (*prévision ou probabilité logique – ou obligation morale*)
s'ils ont trois voitures et une résidence secondaire en France, ils devraient être heureux

g) **Used to**

Used to (pour exprimer une habitude ou un fait durable dans le passé) peut être considéré comme une sorte de semi-auxiliaire, puisque l'emploi de do est normalement facultatif dans les phrases interrogatives et négatives (même s'il est en fait rarement omis) :

he used not to visit us so often (*très rare*)
he didn't use to visit us so often (*emploi habituel*)
(autrefois), il ne venait pas nous voir aussi souvent

À la forme interrogative, la forme sans do est possible, mais elle ne s'emploie jamais à l'oral et que très rarement à l'écrit :

used you to live abroad? (*très rare*)
did you use to live abroad? (*emploi habituel*)
est-ce que vous habitiez à l'étranger (autrefois) ?

On emploie souvent never à la place de not :

he never used to visit us so often
(autrefois), il ne venait pas nous voir aussi souvent

Comme used to, would peut exprimer une action habituelle dans le passé (voir a) vi) ci-dessus) :

he used to/would visit us every week
avant, il venait nous voir toutes les semaines

La différence entre les deux est que used to peut s'utiliser à la fois pour des actions habituelles et pour des faits ou des situations dans le passé, tandis que would ne s'emploie que pour des actions habituelles et répétitives, des comportements typiques ou caractéristiques. On ne pourrait donc pas employer would dans les phrases suivantes car il s'agit de faits, et non d'actions :

John used to play badminton when he was younger
John jouait au badminton lorsqu'il était plus jeune

I used to live abroad
autrefois, je vivais à l'étranger

do you smoke? – I used to
est-ce que tu fumes ? – plus maintenant

19 Dare, need

Ces verbes peuvent se comporter soit comme des verbes ordinaires, soit comme des auxiliaires modaux. Lorsqu'ils sont auxiliaires :

● ils ne prennent pas de -s à la troisième personne du singulier du présent

● on n'emploie pas do dans les phrases interrogatives ou négatives

● s'ils sont suivis d'un infinitif, celui-ci n'est pas précédé de to.

a) *Comme verbes ordinaires*

nobody dares to contradict her
personne n'ose la contredire

he didn't dare to speak
il n'osait pas parler/il n'a pas osé parler

does he really dare to talk openly about it?
est-ce qu'il ose vraiment en parler ouvertement ?

all he needs to do now is buy the tickets
tout ce qu'il a à faire maintenant, c'est d'acheter les billets

you don't need to pay for them now
ce n'est pas la peine que tu les paies maintenant

does he really need all this money?
est-ce qu'il a vraiment besoin de tout cet argent ?

Cependant, dare peut avoir des caractéristiques à la fois du verbe ordinaire (par exemple avec do dans les phrases interrogatives ou négatives) et de l'auxiliaire (suivi d'un infinitif sans to) :

does he really dare talk openly about it?
est-ce qu'il ose vraiment en parler ouvertement ?

mais on doit employer l'infinitif avec to après le participe présent :

not daring to speak to her, he quietly left the room
n'osant pas lui parler, il sortit de la pièce silencieusement

Dans les propositions principales à la forme affirmative (c'est-à-dire les propositions principales qui ne sont ni interrogatives ni négatives), need se comporte toujours comme un verbe ordinaire :

I need to go to the dentist
il faut que j'aille chez le dentiste

b) *Comme auxiliaires modaux*

this is as much as I dare spend on it
je ne peux pas me permettre de dépenser plus

he dared not speak
il n'osait pas parler/il n'a pas osé parler

dare he talk openly about it?
est-ce qu'il ose en parler ouvertement ?

all he need do now is buy the tickets
tout ce qu'il a à faire maintenant, c'est d'acheter les billets

you needn't pay for them right now
ce n'est pas la peine que tu les paies maintenant

need I pay for this now?
est-ce qu'il faut que je paie ça maintenant ?

Notez l'expression idiomatique I dare say (= *probablement*) :

I dare say he'll forget
je suppose qu'il va oublier

is it going to rain, do you think? – I dare say it will
est-ce que tu crois qu'il va pleuvoir ? – probablement

20 Les verbes composés

Les verbes composés ou verbes à particules (phrasal verbs) sont une spécificité de la langue anglaise, une structure verbale réputée difficile. Les verbes composés forment un tout ; la particule est indispensable, elle permet de modifier le sens du verbe principal.

a) *Les verbes composés inséparables*

i) Il est important de faire la distinction entre un "verbe + préposition introduisant un complément", (a) et (c) ci-dessous, et un "verbe composé + complément d'objet direct", (b) et (d). Dans ce dernier cas, la préposition fonctionne comme une particule faisant partie intégrante du verbe. Comparez les deux phrases :

(a) **they** | danced | after **dinner** *(sujet | verbe |*
complément de temps)
ils ont dansé après le dîner

(b) **they** | looked after | **the child** *(sujet | verbe |*
complément d'objet direct)
ils se sont occupés de l'enfant

La structure de ces deux phrases n'est pas la même. Les deux mots look after forment une seule unité verbale (comparez avec they nursed the child *ils ont soigné l'enfant*), ce qui n'est pas le cas pour danced after : after dinner est un complément de temps introduit par une préposition distincte du verbe, tandis qu'en (b), the child est le complément d'objet direct de look after. Grammaticalement, on pourrait couper les phrases au niveau des barres verticales.

On observe la même différence dans les deux exemples suivants :

(c) **they** | went | through **Germany**
ils sont passés par l'Allemagne

(d) **they** | went through | **the accounts**
ils ont examiné la comptabilité

ii) Look after et go through *(examiner)* sont des verbes composés inséparables : le complément d'objet direct vient après la particule ; il ne peut jamais séparer le verbe de la particule. Ces verbes sont très souvent idiomatiques, c'est-à-dire qu'on ne peut pas les traduire littéralement car leur sens n'équivaut pas forcément à la somme du sens des deux éléments qui les composent. Voici d'autres exemples :

go by *(suivre des instructions)*

pick on *(chercher querelle à, s'en prendre à)*

get at *(Fam)* *(attaquer ; graisser la patte à)*

you can't do your own thing; you have to go by **the book**
tu ne peux pas faire ce que tu veux ; il faut agir selon les règles

the teacher's always picking on **him**
le professeur s'en prend toujours à lui

my mother is always getting at **me**
ma mère est toujours sur mon dos

I'm sure the jury have been got at
je suis sûr qu'on a graissé la patte au jury

iii) Puisque les verbes composés sont suivis d'un complément d'objet direct, ils admettent l'emploi des pronoms interrogatifs compléments who(m) et what (voir **Les interrogatifs**, pp. A31-2) :

they looked after the girl → who(m) **did they** look
ils se sont occupés de **after?**
la petite fille *de qui se sont-ils occupés ?*

they went through the → what **did they** go
accounts **through?**
ils ont examiné la *qu'est-ce qu'ils ont examiné ?*
comptabilité

the police officer grappled→ who(m) **did he** grapple
with the thug **with?**
l'agent de police a lutté *avec qui a-t-il lutté ?*
avec le voyou

Mais on ne pourrait pas former des phrases interrogatives commençant par where, when, how avec des verbes com-

posés, car ces adverbes permettent de poser une question sur un complément circonstanciel introduit par une préposition, et non sur un complément d'objet direct. Les verbes suivants ne sont donc pas des verbes composés :

they went through Germany → where **did they go?**
ils sont passés par l'Allemagne *par où est-ce qu'ils sont*
passés ?

they danced after dinner → when **did they dance?**
ils ont dansé après le dîner *quand ont-ils dansé ?*

they worked with great care → how **did they work?**
ils ont travaillé avec beaucoup *comment ont-ils tra-*
de soin *vaillé ?*

Les particules des verbes inséparables précèdent les pronoms relatifs, ce qui n'est jamais le cas des verbes composés séparables (pour les verbes séparables, voir b) ci-dessous) :

this is a man on whom **you can** rely
c'est un homme sur lequel vous pouvez compter

iv) Un verbe composé étant considéré comme une seule unité, on peut souvent l'employer dans une construction passive :

the child has been looked after **very well indeed**
on s'est vraiment très bien occupé de l'enfant

the accounts have been gone through
la comptabilité a été examinée

do you feel you're being got at?
est-ce que tu as l'impression que tout le monde est après toi ?

v) Certains verbes transitifs inséparables sont composés de trois mots, c.-à-d. qu'ils ont deux particules, par exemple :

come up with *(trouver, concocter)*

Avec ces verbes, le complément d'objet ne peut jamais séparer le verbe et ses particules (on ne peut PAS dire : **have you come it up with?**). Le complément d'objet direct doit toujours suivre la dernière particule.

we've come up with **a great solution**
nous avons trouvé une solution idéale

Les deux particules ne peuvent pas non plus précéder un pronom relatif. Ainsi, on mettra toujours les particules à la fin de la proposition :

is there anything else (which) **you can** come up **with?**
est-ce que tu peux trouver quelque chose d'autre ?

Autres exemples de verbes composés à deux particules :

make off with *(voler, partir avec)*
live up to *(se montrer à la hauteur de)*
stand up for *(défendre, prendre le parti de)*
crack down on *(sévir contre)*

somebody made off with **her suitcase**
quelqu'un est parti avec sa valise

it was difficult for him to live up to **this reputation**
il lui était difficile d'être à la hauteur de cette réputation

why didn't you stand up for **me if you knew I was right?**
pourquoi est-ce que tu n'as pas pris mon parti si tu savais que j'avais raison ?

the police are cracking down on **petty criminals**
la police est en train de sévir contre les délinquants

b) *Les verbes composés séparables*

i) Au contraire des verbes composés inséparables, les verbes composés séparables peuvent admettre un complément d'objet direct avant la particule (entre le verbe et la particule) ou après :

turn down the television	look up these words
turn the television down	look these words up
baisse la télévision	*cherche ces mots (dans le dictionnaire)*

have you switched on the computer?
have you switched the computer on?
est-ce que tu as allumé l'ordinateur ?

have you tried on any of your new clothes?
have you tried any of your new clothes on?
est-ce que tu as essayé quelques-uns de tes nouveaux vêtements ?

Si le complément d'objet direct est un pronom, on doit placer la particule après celui-ci :

look them up	turn it down	switch it on
cherche-les	*baisse-la*	*allume-le*

ii) Tandis que les verbes composés inséparables sont toujours transitifs (lorsqu'on les considère comme unités complètes), certains verbes composés séparables sont toujours transitifs et d'autres peuvent être transitifs ou intransitifs :

back up (*soutenir – seulement transitif*) :
he always backs her up
il la soutient toujours

call back (*rappeler – transitif*) :
he said he'll call you back later
il a dit qu'il te rappellerait plus tard

call back (*rappeler – intransitif*) :
can you call back later?
est-ce que vous pouvez rappeler plus tard ?

iii) Comme de nombreux verbes composés inséparables (voir a) ii) ci-dessus), les verbes composés séparables sont très idiomatiques :

square up (*régler – des dettes, etc.*)
bring round (*faire reprendre connaissance à ; convertir à un point de vue*)
set back (*Fam*) (*coûter – de l'argent à quelqu'un*) :

if you pay now, we can square up later
si tu payes maintenant, on réglera nos comptes plus tard

give him a brandy; that'll bring him round
donne-lui un cognac pour qu'il reprenne ses esprits

do you think anything will bring him round to our point of view?
est-ce que tu crois qu'on pourrait l'amener à penser comme nous ?

that car must have set you back at least £25,000
cette voiture doit vous avoir coûté au moins 25 000 livres

c) *Les verbes composés seulement intransitifs*

Il y a aussi des verbes composés intransitifs, qui ne sont bien entendu jamais séparables puisque, par définition, ils n'appellent pas de complément d'objet direct :

he got off at Victoria Station
il descendit à la gare Victoria

do you mind if I listen in while you talk?
ça vous dérange si j'écoute votre conversation ?

the entire species is on the verge of dying out
l'espèce entière est sur le point de disparaître

À la différence des verbes composés inséparables, ces verbes n'ont jamais de forme passive.

21 Le temps au discours indirect

Le discours indirect permet de rapporter les paroles de quelqu'un. La concordance des temps en anglais dans le dis-

cours indirect a les mêmes caractéristiques qu'en français :

Henry said/had said, "I am unhappy" (*direct*)
Henry a dit/avait dit : "je suis malheureux"

Henry said/had said (that) he was unhappy (*indirect*)
Henry a dit/avait dit qu'il était malheureux

22 Liste des verbes irréguliers

Les américanismes sont indiqués par *. Les formes peu courantes, archaïques ou littéraires sont données entre parenthèses. Les traductions ci-dessous ne sont pas restrictives et ne donnent qu'un des sens de base.

INFINITIF		PRÉTÉRIT	PARTICIPE PASSÉ
abide	supporter	(abode) [1]	abided
arise	surgir	arose	arisen
awake	s'éveiller	awoke, awaked	awoken, (awaked)
bear	porter	bore	borne [2]
beat	battre	beat	beaten [3]
become	devenir	became	become
befall	arriver	befell	befallen
beget	engendrer	begot	begotten
begin	commencer	began	begun
behold	apercevoir	beheld	beheld
bend	courber	bent	bent [4]
bereave	priver	bereaved	bereft [5]
beseech	implorer	besought	besought
bestride	chevaucher	bestrode	bestridden
bet	parier	bet, betted	bet, betted
bid	offrir	bid	bid
bid	commander	bade	bidden
bind	attacher	bound	bound
bite	mordre	bit	bitten
bleed	saigner	bled	bled
blow	souffler	blew	blown
break	casser	broke	broken [6]
breed	élever	bred	bred
bring	apporter	brought	brought
broadcast	diffuser	broadcast	broadcast
build	construire	built	built
burn	brûler	burnt, burned	burnt, burned
burst	éclater	burst	burst
buy	acheter	bought	bought
cast	jeter	cast	cast
catch	attraper	caught	caught
chide	gronder	chid, chided	chid, (chidden), chided
choose	choisir	chose	chosen
cleave	fendre	clove, cleft	cloven, cleft [7]
cleave	adhérer	cleaved, (clave)	cleaved
cling	s'accrocher à	clung	clung
clothe	habiller	clothed, (clad)	clothed, (clad)
come	venir	came	come
cost	coûter	cost	cost
creep	ramper	crept	crept
crow	chanter	crowed, (crew)	crowed
cut	couper	cut	cut
dare	oser	dared, (durst)	dared, (durst)
deal	traiter	dealt	dealt

A63

INFINITIF		PRÉTÉRIT	PARTICIPE PASSÉ	INFINITIF		PRÉTÉRIT	PARTICIPE PASSÉ
dig	fouiller	dug	dug	let	laisser	let	let
dive	plonger	dived, dove*	dived	lie	coucher	lay	lain
draw	dessiner, tirer	drew	drawn	light	allumer	lit, lighted	lit, lighted [14]
dream	rêver	dreamt, dreamed	dreamt, dreamed	lose	perdre	lost	lost
				make	faire	made	made
drink	boire	drank	drunk [8]	mean	signifier	meant	meant
drive	conduire	drove	driven	meet	rencontrer	met	met
dwell	demeurer	dwelt, dwelled	dwelt, dwelled	melt	fondre	melted	melted, molten [15]
eat	manger	ate	eaten	mow	faucher	mowed	mown, mowed
fall	tomber	fell	fallen				
feed	nourrir	fed	fed	pay	payer	paid	paid
feel	sentir	felt	felt	plead	plaider	pled*, pleaded	pled*, pleaded [16]
fight	battre	fought	fought				
find	trouver	found	found	put	poser	put	put
fit	aller à	fit*, fitted	fit*, fitted	quit	quitter	quit, (quitted)	quit, (quitted) [17]
flee	s'envoler	fled	fled				
fling	lancer	flung	flung	read	lire	read	read
fly	voler	flew	flown	rend	déchirer	rent	rent
forbear	s'abstenir	forbore	forborne	rid	débarrasser	rid, (ridded)	rid
forbid	interdire	forbad(e)	forbidden	ride	monter à	rode	ridden
forget	oublier	forgot	forgotten	ring	sonner	rang	rung
forgive	pardonner	forgave	forgiven	rise	se lever	rose	risen
forsake	abandonner	forsook	forsaken	run	courir	ran	run
freeze	geler	froze	frozen	saw	scier	sawed	sawn, sawed
get	obtenir	got	got, gotten* [9]				
				say	dire	said	said
gild	dorer	gilt, gilded	gilt, gilded [10]	see	voir	saw	seen
gird	ceindre	girt, girded	girt, girded [10]	seek	chercher	sought	sought
give	donner	gave	given	sell	vendre	sold	sold
go	aller	went	gone	send	envoyer	sent	sent
grind	grincer	ground	ground	set	mettre	set	set
grow	pousser	grew	grown	sew	coudre	sewed	sewn, sewed
hang	accrocher, suspendre	hung, hanged [11]	hung, hanged [11]				
hear	entendre	heard	heard	shake	secouer	shook	shaken
heave	lever	hove, heaved [12]	hove, heaved [12]	shear	tondre	sheared	shorn, sheared [18]
hew	tailler	hewed	hewn, hewed	shed	perdre	shed	shed
				shine	briller	shone [19]	shone [19]
hide	cacher	hid	hidden	shoe	chausser	shod, shoed	shod, shoed [20]
hit	frapper	hit	hit				
hold	tenir	held	held	shoot	abattre, tirer	shot	shot
hurt	blesser	hurt	hurt	show	montrer	showed	shown, showed
keep	garder	kept	kept				
kneel	s'agenouiller	knelt, kneeled	knelt, kneeled	shrink	rétrécir	shrank, shrunk	shrunk, shrunken [21]
knit	tricoter	knit, knitted [13]	knit, knitted [13]	shut	fermer	shut	shut
				sing	chanter	sang	sung
know	savoir, connaître	knew	known	sink	couler	sank	sunk, sunken [22]
lay	coucher	laid	laid	sit	s'asseoir	sat	sat
lead	mener	led	led	slay	tuer	slew	slain
lean	s'appuyer	leant, leaned	leant, leaned	sleep	dormir	slept	slept
				slide	glisser	slid	slid
leap	sauter	leapt, leaped	leapt, leaped	sling	lancer	slung	slung
				slink	se glisser furtivement	slunk	slunk
learn	apprendre	learnt, learned	learnt, learned	slit	fendre	slit	slit
leave	laisser	left	left	smell	sentir	smelt, smelled	smelt, smelled
lend	prêter	lent	lent				

INFINITIF		PRÉTÉRIT	PARTICIPE PASSÉ
smite	frapper	smote	smitten [23]
sneak	se faufiler, se glisser	snuck*, sneaked	snuck*, sneaked
sow	semer	sowed	sown, sowed
speak	parler	spoke	spoken
speed	aller vite	sped, speeded	sped, speeded
spell	écrire	spelt, spelled	spelt, spelled
spend	dépenser	spent	spent
spill	renverser	spilt, spilled	spilt, spilled
spin	filer	spun	spun
spit	cracher	spat, spit*	spat, spit*
split	se briser	split	split
spoil	abîmer	spoilt, spoiled	spoilt, spoiled
spread	étendre	spread	spread
spring	bondir	sprang	sprung
stand	se tenir	stood	stood
steal	voler	stole	stolen
stick	enfoncer, coller	stuck	stuck
sting	piquer	stung	stung
stink	puer	stank	stunk
strew	répandre	strewed	strewn, strewed
stride	marcher à grands pas	strode	stridden
strike	frapper	struck	struck, stricken [24]
string	enfiler	strung	strung
strive	s'efforcer	strove	striven
swear	jurer	swore	sworn
sweat	suer	sweat*, sweated	sweat*, sweated
sweep	balayer	swept	swept
swell	gonfler	swelled	swollen, swelled [25]
swim	nager	swam	swum
swing	se balancer	swung	swung
take	prendre	took	taken
teach	enseigner	taught	taught
tear	déchirer	tore	torn
tell	dire	told	told
think	penser	thought	thought
thrive	fleurir	thrived, (throve)	thrived, (thriven)
throw	jeter	threw	thrown
thrust	pousser	thrust	thrust
tread	marcher	trod	trodden
understand	comprendre	understood	understood
undertake	s'engager	undertook	undertaken
wake	se réveiller	woke, waked	woken, waked
wear	porter	wore	worn
weave	tisser	wove [26]	woven [26]
weep	pleurer	wept	wept
wet	mouiller	wet*, wetted [27]	wet*, wetted [27]

INFINITIF		PRÉTÉRIT	PARTICIPE PASSÉ
win	gagner	won	won
wind	remonter	wound	wound
wring	tordre	wrung	wrung
write	écrire	wrote	written

1 Régulier dans la construction abide by *se conformer à, suivre* : **they abided by the rules.**

2 Mais born au passif = *né* ou comme adjectif : **he was born in France; a born gentleman.**

3 Remarquez la forme familière **this has me beat/you have me beat there** *cela me dépasse/tu m'as posé une colle* et **beat** dans le sens de "très fatigué, épuisé" : **I'm (dead) beat.**

4 Remarquez la phrase **on one's bended knees** *à genoux.*

5 Mais bereaved dans le sens de "endeuillé", comme dans **the bereaved received no compensation** *la famille du disparu ne reçut aucune indemnité.* Comparez : **he was bereft of speech** *il en perdit la parole.*

6 Mais broke quand il s'agit d'un adjectif = *fauché* : **I'm broke.**

7 Cleft n'est employé qu'avec le sens de "coupé en deux". Remarquez cleft **palate** *palais fendu* et **to be caught in a cleft stick** *être dans une impasse,* mais **cloven foot/hoof** *sabot fendu.*

8 Quand il s'agit d'un adjectif épithète (placé devant le nom) désignant une personne, il est possible d'employer drunken (**a lot of drunk(en) people** *beaucoup de gens ivres*). Mais il doit toujours être employé devant les noms de choses, d'objets inanimés, etc. (drunken **parties** *des soirées bien arrosées*).

9 Mais **have got to** s'emploie aussi en américain avec le sens de "devoir, être obligé de" : **I've got to go** *je dois y aller.* Comparez avec : **she has gotten into a bit of a mess** *elle s'est fourrée dans le pétrin.*

10 Les formes du participe passé gilt et girt s'emploient comme adjectifs épithètes : gilt **mirrors** *des miroirs dorés,* **a flower-girt grave** *une tombe entourée de fleurs* (mais toujours gilded **youth** *la jeunesse dorée,* où gilded est employé au sens figuré).

11 Régulier quand il signifie *pendre quelqu'un.*

12 Hove est utilisé dans le domaine nautique comme dans l'expression heave into sight (*poindre à l'horizon*), également employée au sens figuré : **and suddenly, she hove into sight** *et tout à coup, elle apparut.*

13 Irrégulier quand il a le sens de "unir" (**a close-knit family** *une famille unie*), mais régulier lorsqu'il a le sens de "fabriquer en laine" et quand il fait référence aux os (= *se souder*).

14 Lorsque le participe passé est employé comme adjectif épithète, on préfère souvent lighted à lit : **a lighted candle** *une bougie allumée* (mais : **the candle is lit** *la bougie est allumée,* **she has lit a candle** *elle a allumé une bougie*). Dans les noms composés, on emploie généralement lit : **well-lit streets** *des rues bien éclairées.* Au sens figuré (avec up), c'est uniquement lit qui est employé au prétérit et au participe passé : **her face lit up when she saw me** *son visage s'illumina lorsqu'elle me vit.*

15 On emploie molten uniquement comme adjectif épithète, et seulement lorsqu'il signifie "fondu à très haute température", par exemple : molten **lead** *du plomb fondu* (mais melted **butter** *du beurre fondu*).

16 En anglais d'Écosse et en américain, on emploie pled au passé et au participe passé.

17 En américain, les formes régulières ne sont pas employées, et elles sont de plus en plus rares en anglais britannique.

18 Le participe passé est normalement shorn devant un nom

(newly-shorn **lambs** *des agneaux tout juste tondus*) et toujours dans l'expression **to be shorn of** *être privé de* : **shorn of his riches he was nothing** *privé de ses richesses, il n'était plus rien.*

19 Mais régulier quand il a le sens de "cirer, astiquer" en américain.

20 Quand il est adjectif, on n'emploie que **shod** : **a well-**shod **foot** *un pied bien chaussé.*

21 Shrunken n'est employé que lorsqu'il est adjectif : **shrunken limbs/her face was** shrunken *des membres rabougris/son visage était ratatiné.*

22 Sunken ne s'emploie que comme adjectif : **sunken eyes** *des yeux enfoncés.*

23 Verbe archaïque dont le participe passé smitten s'emploie encore comme adjectif : **he's completely** smitten **with her** *il est complètement fou d'elle.*

24 Stricken n'est utilisé qu'au sens figuré (stricken **with grief** *accablé par le chagrin*). Il est très courant dans les noms composés (*accablé par*) : **poverty-**stricken, **fever-**stricken, **grief-**stricken, **horror-**stricken (aussi horror-**struck**), **terror-**stricken (aussi terror-**struck**), mais on dit toujours **thunder-**struck *abasourdi.*

C'est aussi un emploi américain : **the remark was** stricken **from the record** *la remarque a été rayée du procès-verbal.*

25 Swollen est plus courant que swelled comme verbe (**her face has** swollen *son visage a gonflé*) et comme adjectif (**her face is swollen/a swollen face**). **To have a** swollen **head** (*avoir la grosse tête*) devient **to have a** swelled **head** en américain.

26 Mais il est régulier lorsqu'il a le sens de "se faufiler" : **the motorbike** weaved **through the traffic** *la moto se faufila entre les voitures.*

27 Mais irrégulier aussi en anglais britannique lorsqu'il a le sens suivant : **he** wet **his bed** *il a fait pipi au lit.*

23 Les formes des auxiliaires be, have, do

BE

	PRÉSENT	PRÉTÉRIT	PARTICIPE PASSÉ
1ère	I am	I was	been
2ème	you are	you were	
3ème	he/she/it is	he/she/it was	
1ère	we are	we were	
2ème	you are	you were	
3ème	they are	they were	

Formes contractées avec le sujet :

I'm = I am
you're = you are
he's/John's = he is/John is
we're/you're/they're = we are/you are/they are

Formes contractées avec not :

aren't I? (questions seulement) = am I not?
you/we/they aren't = you/we/they are not
he isn't = he is not
I/he wasn't = I/he was not
you/we/they weren't = you/we/they were not

On a aussi : I'm not ; you're not, etc.

Pour le subjonctif, voir pp. A53-4.

HAVE

	PRÉSENT	PRÉTÉRIT	PARTICIPE PASSÉ
1ère	I have	I had	had
2ème	you have	you had	
3ème	he/she/it has	he/she/it had	
1ère	we have	we had	
2ème	you have	you had	
3ème	they have	they had	

Formes contractées avec le sujet :
I've/you've/we've/they've = I have, etc.
he's = he has
I'd/you'd/he'd/we'd/they'd = I had, etc.

Vous noterez que he's/she's ne sont normalement pas contractés lorsqu'ils sont employés comme verbes en tant que tels, et non comme auxiliaires, au présent :

I've **two cars**   he has **two cars**
j'ai deux voitures   *il a deux voitures*

Formes contractées avec not :

haven't = have not
hasn't = has not
hadn't = had not

DO

	PRÉSENT	PRÉTÉRIT	PARTICIPE PASSÉ
1ère	I do	I did	done
2ème	you do	you did	
3ème	he/she/it does	he/she/it did	
1ère	we do	we did	
2ème	you do	you did	
3ème	they do	they did	

Formes contractées avec not :

don't = do not
doesn't = does not
didn't = did not

15 LES PRÉPOSITIONS

1 Les prépositions servent à relier grammaticalement ou sémantiquement les noms ou pronoms devant lesquels elles sont placées, à un autre élément de la phrase. Elles permettent d'exprimer des relations de temps, de lieu, de provenance, de possession, etc.

after (*après*)	**I'll see you** after **the show** *je te verrai après le spectacle*
on (*sur*)	**the keys are** on **the table** *les clefs sont sur la table*
from (*de*)	**I have just arrived** from **London** *j'arrive juste de Londres*
of (*de*)	**would you like a cup** of **tea?** *est-ce que tu veux une tasse de thé ?*

Cependant, dans certaines constructions les prépositions anglaises peuvent se placer en fin de proposition :

the people I came here with
les gens avec lesquels je suis venu

something I had never dreamed of
quelque chose dont je n'avais jamais rêvé

Voir aussi **Les verbes composés**, pp. A61-3, ainsi que **Les interrogatifs** et **Les relatifs**, pp. A31-3.

2 Voici une liste des prépositions les plus couramment employées. La plupart des prépositions ayant différents sens et emplois, seuls les usages les plus importants et ceux particulièrement intéressants ou susceptibles de poser problème sont mentionnés ci-dessous.

ABOUT ET AROUND

i) dans les environs, dans tous les sens :

Il n'y a souvent pas de différence entre about et around, bien qu'en anglais américain on préfère around :

they walked about/around town
ils se sont promenés dans la ville

he must be about/around somewhere
il doit être dans les parages

the dog was racing about/around in the garden
le chien courait dans tous les sens dans le jardin

ii) au coin, autour de :

he lives just around the corner
il habite au coin de la rue

when I arrived they were all seated around the table
quand je suis arrivé, ils étaient tous assis autour de la table

iii) environ, à peu près :

I have about £15 on me
j'ai environ quinze livres sur moi

he's about/around your age
il a à peu près votre âge

iv) au sujet de, sur (seulement about) :

what's the book about? – it's a story about nature
de quoi parle le livre ? – c'est une histoire sur la nature

v) sur le point de (seulement about) :

I was just about to leave
j'allais partir/j'étais sur le point de partir

what were you about to say?
qu'est-ce que vous alliez dire ?

ABOVE

Above exprime normalement le fait d'être "situé au-dessus de" dans un sens purement physique :

the shirts had been placed in the wardrobe above the socks
les chemises avaient été placées dans l'armoire au-dessus des chaussettes

Il y a en général peu de différence entre above et over lorsque ce dernier signifie "au-dessus de" :

he has a lovely mirror above/over the mantelpiece
il a un très joli miroir au-dessus de la cheminée

mais contrairement à over, above ne peut pas avoir le sens de "sur" :

he flung his coat over a chair
il a jeté son manteau sur une chaise

ACROSS

i) d'un côté à l'autre :

he swam across the lake
il a traversé le lac à la nage

ii) de l'autre côté de :

we live across the street from them
nous habitons en face de chez eux

iii) à travers :

the study of literature across cultures
l'étude de la littérature à travers différentes cultures

Across et over ont souvent un sens très proche, mais across a tendance à indiquer une dimension horizontale (sur la largeur de) :

he laid out his suit across the bed
il étendit son costume en travers du lit

AFTER

i) après (dans le temps et dans l'espace) :

I'll call him after breakfast
je l'appellerai après le petit déjeuner

the shopping centre is just after the church
le centre commercial est juste après l'église

ii) après, derrière :

close the door after you
fermez la porte après vous

iii) à la recherche de (toujours utilisé avec le verbe to be) :

the police are after him
il est recherché par la police

she's after a full-time job
elle cherche un travail à temps plein

iv) After peut être employé comme particule de verbes composés (voir p. A62), par exemple dans la construction to ask after. Remarquez dans ce cas, les différences d'emploi entre les verbes to ask after et to ask for, qui peuvent avoir un sens similaire ou complètement différent :

he asked after you
il m'a demandé de tes nouvelles

he asked for you
il a demandé à te parler

tell him I'm asking for him
dis-lui bonjour de ma part

v) Dans un sens temporel, on pourrait comparer after et since. La différence entre les deux apparaît dans l'emploi des temps : prétérit (after) et present perfect (since). Comparez :

he wasn't well after his journey
il ne se sentait pas très bien après son voyage

he hasn't been well since his journey
il ne se sent pas très bien depuis son voyage

AGAINST

i) contre (pour indiquer une position ou un choc) :

he leant his bike against the wall
il appuya son vélo contre le mur

he knocked his head against the wall
il s'est cogné la tête contre le mur

ii) en sens inverse :

we're sailing against the current
nous naviguons à contre-courant

iii) contre, à l'encontre de (pour indiquer l'opposition ou une opinion contraire) :

it's against the law
c'est illégal ou contraire à la loi

they voted against it
ils ont voté contre

iv) contre, sur (pour indiquer un contraste) :

he stood against the light
il était à contre-jour

she was silhouetted against the snow
sa silhouette se découpait sur la neige

v) contre (pour un match, une guerre, etc.) :

United against Everton
United contre Everton

they fought against them
ils ont combattu contre eux

vi) contre (pour indiquer une mesure de précaution ou de protection) :

our car is insured against accidents
notre voiture est assurée contre les accidents

his coat protected him against the cold
son manteau le protégeait du froid

AMONG(ST)

au milieu de, parmi, entre (voir aussi **between**) :

she was lost among the crowd
elle était perdue dans la foule

I count her among my friends
je la compte parmi mes amis

she said, among other things, that she would be late
elle a dit, entre autres, qu'elle serait en retard

share out the sweets among the children
partagez les bonbons entre les enfants

AT

i) à (pour faire référence à un point précis dans le temps et dans l'espace) :

I'm meeting him at six o'clock
je dois le retrouver à six heures

I like studying at night
j'aime étudier la nuit

they waited at the bus stop
ils attendaient à l'arrêt de bus

he was sitting at the table
il était assis à table

Pour les noms de villes, on utilise habituellement la préposition **in**, sauf dans certains cas particulier. Dans l'exemple suivant, les villes sont des étapes sur un itinéraire.

the train stops at Dundee, Edinburgh and York
le train s'arrête à Dundee, Édimbourg et York

ii) à l'âge de :

he started working at 15
il a commencé à travailler à (l'âge de) 15 ans

iii) vers, dans la direction de :

look at this!
regarde ça!

he shot at the rabbit
il a tiré sur le lapin

iv) à (pour indiquer une activité) :

my parents are at work
mes parents sont au travail

v) à (pour indiquer un prix, une vitesse, une température, un taux, etc.) :

it's a bargain at £5
à 5 livres, c'est une bonne affaire

he drove at 50 mph
il faisait du 80 (à l'heure)

the temperature stands at 30°
la température est de 30 °

vi) en (pour introduire le complément d'un adjectif) :

he's hopeless at maths
il est nul en maths

BEFORE

i) avant, auparavant :

be there before six o'clock
sois là avant six heures

before that, she was a teacher
auparavant, elle était professeur

I saw him the day before yesterday
je l'ai vu avant-hier

Dans le sens temporel de **before**, comparez son emploi et celui de **until** avec des verbes à la forme négative. **Before** signifie

"plus tôt que" et **until** "jusqu'à (un certain temps)" :

(a) you will not get the letter before Monday
tu ne recevras pas la lettre avant lundi

(b) you will not get the letter until Monday
tu ne recevras pas la lettre avant lundi

En (a), la lettre arrivera lundi ou n'importe quel jour après lundi (mais pas avant); en (b), la lettre arrivera lundi.

ii) avant (dans un ordre de préférence) :

her name came before mine in the list
son nom était avant le mien sur la liste

iii) devant (dans l'espace et au sens figuré) :

the accident happened before my very eyes
l'accident s'est déroulé sous mes propres yeux

we have a difficult task before us
nous avons une tâche difficile devant nous

iv) devant, en présence de :

he said it before witnesses
il l'a dit devant ou en présence de témoins

Lorsque la préposition **before** est employée pour indiquer la position au sens littéral, on peut la remplacer par **in front of**, qui est plus courant et moins soutenu que **before** :

he was standing in front of the judge in the queue
il se tenait devant le juge dans la file

Mais lorsque **before** n'est pas pris au sens littéral, il n'est pas possible d'employer **in front of** :

he was brought before the judge
il a été amené à comparaître devant le juge

BELOW

i) au-dessous de, en dessous de, sous :

he lives in the flat below ours
il habite dans l'appartement au-dessous ou en dessous du nôtre

there was a feeling of anxiety lying below the surface
on sentait une angoisse sous-jacente

ii) au-dessous de, inférieur à :

his grades are below average
ses notes sont au-dessous de la moyenne

En général, **below** est le contraire de **above** (*au-dessus de*), et **under** (*sous*) est le contraire de **over** ou **on** (*sur*). Mais remarquez l'emploi de **below** dans le sens de "en aval", et non de "au-dessous de" :

he was sitting under the bridge
il était assis sous le pont

below the bridge the water gets deeper
en aval du pont, l'eau est plus profonde

BESIDE

i) à côté de, près de :

come and sit beside me
viens t'asseoir à côté de moi

ii) par rapport à, comparé à :

these results don't look very good beside last year's
ces résultats n'ont pas l'air très bons par rapport à ceux de l'année dernière

iii) à part, excepté :

other people beside ourselves might need it
d'autres (personnes) que nous pourraient en avoir besoin

iv) être loin de (au sens figuré) :

that is beside the point
cela n'a rien à voir (avec l'affaire en question)

BESIDES

en plus de, à part :

there were three guests there besides him and me
il y avait trois invités à part lui et moi

BETWEEN

i) entre (dans le temps et dans l'espace) :

I'll be home between six and seven
je serai à la maison entre six et sept heures

the crowd stood between him and the door
la foule le séparait de la porte

Remarquez que between ne s'emploie qu'avec deux éléments. Lorsque l'on veut désigner plus de deux éléments, on emploiera among(st) :

he sat between John and Joan   he sat among(st) his
il était assis entre John et Joan   friends
il était assis parmi ses amis

ii) entre (pour une tranche d'âge, une fourchette, etc.) :

the theatre company is for children between the ages
of 8 and 12
c'est une troupe de théâtre pour enfants de 8 à 12 ans

iii) entre (pour indiquer une relation entre deux personnes/choses) :

it's a half-hour drive between home and the office
il y a une demi-heure de route entre la maison et le bureau

he felt things weren't right between them
il sentait que ça n'allait pas entre eux

iv) entre (pour indiquer un choix, une alternative) :

I had to choose between going with them and staying
at home
il fallait que je choisisse entre les accompagner et rester à la maison

v) entre (pour indiquer le partage) :

they shared the cake between them
ils se sont partagé le gâteau

BUT

Lorsqu'il est employé comme préposition, but signifie "sauf", "à part". Il se place généralement après des pronoms indéfinis ou interrogatifs, ou des adverbes comme anywhere, where, etc. :

she wouldn't see anyone but her lawyer
elle ne voulait voir personne sauf ou à part son avocat

where but in America could you find such a gadget?
il n'y a qu'en Amérique qu'on trouve un tel gadget

Dans la plupart des cas, on peut employer except à la place de but :

nobody but/except you would think of that
personne à part toi ne penserait à ça

where else but/except in France would you...?
où, sinon en France, est-ce qu'on pourrait... ?

BY

i) près de, à côté de, devant :

he was sitting by the table
il était assis près de la table

she parked her car by the kerb
elle gara sa voiture au bord du trottoir

I drive by the school every day
je passe (en voiture) devant l'école tous les jours

ii) par :

she left by the back door
elle est partie par la porte de derrière

iii) par, en (pour indiquer le moyen de paiement, de communication, de transport) (comme en français, le nom qui suit ne prend pas d'article) :

to pay by cheque   by letter/phone
payer par chèque   *par courrier/téléphone*

to go by bus/car/plane/train
aller en autobus/voiture/avion/train

iv) par (au passif pour introduire le complément d'agent) :

the house was surrounded by   I was shocked by his
police   reaction
la police a cerné la maison   *sa réaction m'a choqué*

v) en (avec un participe présent) :

he learned to cook by watching his mother
il a appris à faire la cuisine en regardant sa mère

vi) avant, pas plus tard que :

be there by six o'clock
sois là avant ou pour six heures

Comparez avec at qui s'emploie pour faire référence à un point précis dans le temps :

be there at six o'clock
sois là à six heures

vii) selon, d'après :

it's 6:15 by my watch
il est 6 h 15 à ma montre

viii) de (en ce qui concerne) :

he's an actor by profession
il est acteur de profession

Remarquez aussi les verbes composés to live by et to live on. To live by signifie "gagner sa vie d'une occupation", tandis que to live on signifie "vivre avec un revenu de" ou "se nourrir de". L'emploi de by insiste sur le moyen :

he lives by acting in commercials
il gagne sa vie en jouant dans des pubs

he lives on fruit
il se nourrit de fruits

he lives by his pen   he lives on £100 a month
il vit de sa plume   *il vit avec 100 livres par mois*

To live by signifie aussi "vivre selon les règles de" :

it is difficult to live by such a set of doctrines
il est difficile de vivre en appliquant un tel ensemble de doctrines

ix) à, par, en (pour indiquer la fréquence, le taux, la vitesse, etc.) :

little by little   day by day   year by year
peu à peu   *jour par jour ou*   *d'année en année*
                    de jour en jour

DURING

pendant, au cours de (voir aussi for) :

they met during the war
ils se sont rencontrés pendant la guerre

EXCEPT

sauf (voir aussi but) :

everybody was there except him
tout le monde était là sauf lui

FOR

i) pour (pour indiquer un but, une fonction) :

we were in Vienna for work
nous étions à Vienne pour le travail

ii) pour, à l'intention de :

these flowers are for her
ces fleurs sont pour elle

iii) pour, dans la direction de :

they left for Spain
ils sont partis pour l'Espagne

iv) à :

for rent　　　　　　　**for sale**
à louer　　　　　　　　*à vendre*

v) pour, pendant (pour une période dans le futur ou dans le passé) ; depuis (pour une action qui n'est pas encore terminée) :

they're going away for the weekend
ils partent pour le week-end

I lived there for one month
j'y ai vécu pendant un mois

I've been playing tennis for years
je joue au tennis depuis des années

Pour la différence de temps entre l'anglais et le français dans ce dernier exemple, voir l'emploi du present perfect p. A50.

Lorsque for est employé comme préposition de temps, il est utile de la comparer à during (*pendant*) et in (*en*). For insiste sur l'idée de durée (pendant combien de temps ?), tandis que during indique la période au cours de laquelle des actions se produisent (quand ?) :

he let the cat out for the night
il a fait sortir le chat pour la nuit

he let the cat out during the night
il a fait sortir le chat pendant/dans la nuit

On peut aussi comparer for (utilisé pour indiquer une durée) à in, qui signifie "dans une période" :

I haven't seen her for five years
je ne l'ai pas vue depuis cinq ans

he didn't see her once in five years
il ne l'a pas vue une seule fois en cinq ans

Cependant, on pourrait maintenant aussi employer in dans le premier exemple :

I haven't seen her in five years
ça fait cinq ans que je ne l'ai pas vue

Pour l'emploi de for/since avec des expressions de temps, voir p. A50.

vi) pendant (pour indiquer la distance) :

we walked for several miles
nous avons marché pendant plusieurs kilomètres

vii) For s'utilise également dans des constructions avec des verbes à l'infinitif :

it's not for him to decide
il ne lui appartient pas ou ce n'est pas à lui de décider

FROM

i) de, à partir de, depuis (pour indiquer la provenance ou un point de départ, dans l'espace et dans le temps) :

her parents came from France
ses parents venaient de France

she was unhappy from her first day at boarding school
elle a été malheureuse dès son premier jour à l'internat

the price has gone up from 50 pence to 60 pence
le prix a augmenté de 50 pence à 60 pence

ii) de (pour indiquer la cause) :

she died from multiple injuries
elle n'a pas survécu à ses blessures multiples

iii) de (pour indiquer un endroit) :

from the top of the hill you can see the whole city
du haut de la colline on voit toute la ville

iv) après l'adjectif different (on trouve parfois different suivi de to, mais cette construction est incorrecte) :

yours is different from mine
le tien est différent du mien

what he just said is different from what he had said before
ce qu'il vient de dire est différent de ce qu'il avait dit auparavant

En anglais américain, on emploie **different than.**

IN FRONT OF

devant (voir aussi before) :

she was sitting in front of the TV
elle était assise devant la télé

IN

(voir aussi at et for)

i) dans (pour indiquer un lieu, un moment précis dans le temps, etc.) :

what have you got in your pockets?
qu'est-ce que tu as dans tes poches ?

we swam in the sea
nous nous sommes baignés dans la mer

throw the letter in the bin
jette la lettre à la poubelle

I'll be back in five minutes
je reviens dans cinq minutes

she could see a reflection in the mirror
elle voyait un reflet dans la glace

ii) à (avec des noms de villes) :

he lives in Paris
il habite à Paris

iii) en (avec les pays, les vêtements, les saisons, les années ; pour indiquer la durée, le moyen, etc.) :

they live in Spain
ils habitent en Espagne

he was in a suit
il était en costume

in (the) spring/summer/autumn/winter
au printemps, en été/automne/hiver

he cooked the meal in ten minutes
il prépara le repas en dix minutes

she paid in cash
elle a payé en liquide

he writes in English
il écrit en anglais

iv) à, en (pour faire référence à des institutions) :

he spent five years in prison
il a passé cinq ans en prison

she's in hospital
elle est à l'hôpital

he teaches in a language school
il enseigne dans une école de langues

INTO

(voir aussi in)

i) dans (pour indiquer une direction, un mouvement) :

come into my office
venez dans mon bureau

On emploie donc into après un verbe de mouvement et in simplement pour indiquer l'endroit :

he was sitting in the living room
il était assis dans la salle de séjour

he went into the living room
il est entré dans la salle de séjour

Ainsi, lorsque le verbe to be a le même sens que to go, on pourra employer la préposition into :

you've been in the bathroom for an hour
tu es dans la salle de bains depuis une heure

have you been into/in the bathroom yet?
est-ce que tu es allé dans la salle de bains ?

ii) dans, contre (pour indiquer une collision) :

the truck ran into the wall
le camion est rentré dans le mur

iii) en (pour indiquer un changement, une transformation) :

he's grown into a man
c'est un homme maintenant

iv) dans (pour donner une indication de temps) :

we worked well into the night
nous avons travaillé (jusque) tard dans la nuit

v) avec le verbe to be dans le sens de "bien aimer" *(Fam)* :

he's into fast cars at the moment
il est branché voitures de sport en ce moment

OF

i) de (pour indiquer la quantité, la possession, etc.) :

he bought a pound of onions
il a acheté une livre d'oignons

there are six of us *(et jamais* **we are six***)*
nous sommes six

I need a map of Spain **he's a friend of mine**
il me faut une carte d'Espagne *c'est un ami à moi*

ii) de (pour exprimer une attitude, une émotion ou pour décrire une qualité) :

I'm proud of it **he is a man of courage**
j'en suis fier *c'est un homme de courage*

iii) de (pour indiquer la cause) :

he never thought about the consequence of his actions
il n'a pas pensé à la conséquence de ses actes

iv) de (pour indiquer un moment précis dans l'espace ou dans le temps) :

it was the happiest day of his life
c'était le plus beau jour de sa vie

there was a cat in the middle of the road
il y avait un chat au milieu de la chaussée

OFF

i) de (pour indiquer un mouvement) :

he fell off his chair
il est tombé de sa chaise

ii) de (pour quelque chose que l'on enlève) :

I've stripped the wallpaper off the walls
j'ai décollé le papier peint des murs

iii) de (pour indiquer la provenance) :

a cool breeze off the sea
une brise fraîche venant du large

iv) pour indiquer un lieu :

just off Oxford Street there's a pretty little square
à deux pas d'Oxford Street il y a une petite place ravissante

v) pour indiquer l'absence de quelque chose ou de quelqu'un:

you need a few days off work
vous avez besoin de quelques jours de congé

Mr Dale is off work today
M. Dale est absent aujourd'hui

ON

(voir aussi by et upon)

i) sur (pour indiquer une position, un lieu, etc.) :

the vase is on the shelf **they live on a farm**
le vase est sur l'étagère *ils habitent une ferme*

the child fell on the floor **I'm on the bus/train**
l'enfant est tombé par terre *je suis dans le bus/train*

Pour indiquer un lieu, on peut employer in à la place de on si l'idée d'intérieur domine :

it's often cold in British trains
il fait souvent froid dans les trains britanniques

ii) sur, à propos de, au sujet de :

I watched a film on the French Revolution
j'ai regardé un film sur la Révolution française

we all agree on that point
nous sommes tous d'accord sur ce point

Remarquez que on (au sujet de, sur) peut être plus technique, plus académique que about :

he gave a paper on Verdi and Shakespeare
il a fait un exposé sur Verdi et Shakespeare

a book on English history
un livre sur l'histoire anglaise

iii) selon :

everyone will be judged on their merits
chacun sera jugé selon ses mérites

iv) à (pour un moyen, une source d'énergie, la simultanéité de deux événements, etc.) :

he came on foot **it runs on electricity**
il est venu à pied *ça marche à l'électricité*

he'll deal with it on his return **who's on bass?**
il s'en occupera à son retour *qui est à la basse ?*

v) à (pour les moyens de communication) :

it's the first time she's been on television
c'est la première fois qu'elle passe à la télévision

I heard it on the radio **he's on the phone**
je l'ai entendu à la radio *il est au téléphone*

vi) par (pour indiquer une cause) :

I shall refuse on principle
je refuserai par principe

vii) pour indiquer une activité, un intérêt :

they went on safari
ils ont fait un safari

he's good on music
il a de bonnes connaissances côté musique

Remarquez que la préposition on dans ce dernier exemple n'a pas le même sens que la préposition at. La phrase **he's good at music** implique qu'il sait bien jouer d'un instrument.

viii) devant les jours de la semaine :

can you come on Saturday?
tu peux venir samedi ?

ix) en (avec un participe présent) :

she cried on hearing the news
elle a pleuré en apprenant la nouvelle

OPPOSITE

en face de :

they live just opposite
ils habitent juste en face

Lorsqu'il indique une position, il peut toujours être accompagné de to :

the house opposite (to) ours is being pulled down
on est en train de démolir la maison en face de la nôtre

Mais il est impossible d'utiliser to dans la phrase suivante :

she played opposite Richard Burton in many films
elle fut la partenaire de Richard Burton dans de nombreux films

OUTSIDE

dehors, en dehors de, à l'extérieur de :

nobody is allowed outside (of) the house
personne n'a le droit de quitter la maison

Remarquez que outside est souvent accompagné de of en anglais américain (ce qui est peu fréquent en anglais britannique).

En outre, il peut parfois avoir le sens de "devant" :

they met outside the cathedral
ils se sont retrouvés devant la cathédrale

OVER

(voir aussi above et across)

i) au-dessus de :

they live over the shop
ils habitent au-dessus du magasin

ii) sur, par-dessus :

she wore a cardigan over her dress
elle portait un gilet par-dessus sa robe

he was watching me over his newspaper
il m'observait par-dessus son journal

iii) plus de (avec un nombre) :

he must be over thirty
il doit avoir plus de trente ans

iv) au sujet de:

they disagree over the working conditions
ils ont un conflit portant sur les conditions de travail

OWING TO

en raison de, à cause de, grâce à :

this was owing to his alertness of mind
c'était grâce à sa vivacité d'esprit

owing to bad weather they arrived late
ils sont arrivés en retard à cause du mauvais temps

SINCE

depuis (voir aussi after) :

he has been talking about it since yesterday
il en parle depuis hier

Remarquez également la préposition ever since (depuis) :

ever since that day he's been afraid of dogs
depuis ce jour-là, il a peur des chiens

TILL

jusqu'à (+ complément de temps) (voir until)

TO

(voir aussi for et until)

i) à, jusqu'à, en, pour (pour indiquer une direction, un lieu, une période, etc.) :

what's the best way to the station?
quel est le meilleur chemin pour aller à la gare ?

I'm off to Paris
je pars à/pour Paris

I will be away from Tuesday night to Thursday morning
je serai absent du mardi soir (jusqu')au jeudi matin

ii) jusqu'à (pour un niveau, un âge, un montant, etc.) :

the snow came (up) to her knees
la neige lui arrivait aux genoux

it's accurate to the millimetre
c'est exact au millimètre près

iii) avant (pour une date, etc.) :

there's only two weeks to Christmas
il ne reste que deux semaines avant Noël

iv) pour (pour indiquer une intention) :

I did it to annoy her
je l'ai fait exprès pour l'énerver

v) pour (pour indiquer un avis, une opinion) :

it sounds suspicious to me
cela me semble bizarre

to be honest, I don't think he will come
pour être franc, je ne crois pas qu'il viendra

vi) pour, contre, dans, etc. (pour indiquer la composition, la proportion) :

use one cup of sugar to every three cups of fruit
mettez une tasse de sucre pour trois tasses de fruits

the vote was 6 to 3
il y avait 6 voix contre 3

vii) à (pour indiquer la comparaison) :

they often compare his work to Coppola's
on a souvent comparé ses films à ceux de Coppola

that's nothing (compared) to what I've seen
ce n'est rien à côté de ce que j'ai vu

viii) de (dans le sens de of ou for) :

here is the key to the front door
voici la clé de la porte d'entrée

her husband is the French ambassador to Algeria
son mari est l'ambassadeur français en Algérie

Pour l'emploi de l'infinitif avec to, voir pp. A41-2.

TOWARD(S)

i) dans la direction de, vers :

he turned towards her
il s'est tourné vers elle

ii) envers (pour faire référence à une attitude) :

she's very hostile towards me
elle est très hostile à mon égard

iii) pour (en contribution à) :

I'll give you something towards your expenses
je vous donnerai quelque chose pour payer une partie de vos frais

Toward s'emploie normalement en anglais américain et towards en anglais britannique.

UNDER

(voir aussi **below**)

i)   sous :

the newspaper was under the chair
le journal était sous la chaise

ii)   moins de, au-dessous de :

everything is under £5
tout est à moins de 5 livres

iii) dans (pour indiquer une condition ou des circonstances particulières) :

she was murdered under strange circumstances
elle a été tuée dans d'étranges circonstances

iv)   en cours de :

this building is under construction
cet immeuble est en cours de construction

UNTIL

jusqu'à (+ complément de temps) (voir aussi **before**)

she was here (up) until February
elle a été ici jusqu'en février

On peut aussi employer **until** après la préposition **from**. Comparez avec l'emploi de **from... to** ; la différence est la même qu'en français (*à/jusqu'à*) :

the shop is closed from 1 to 2 p.m.
le magasin ferme de 13 heures à 14 heures

last night I worked from eight until/till midnight
hier soir j'ai travaillé de huit heures jusqu'à minuit

Il n'y a pas de différence de sens entre **until** et **till**.

UPON

(voir aussi **on**)

La préposition **upon** a le même sens que **on**, mais elle fait partie d'un niveau de langue plus soutenu.

i)   sur :

she had a sad look upon her face
elle avait l'air triste

ii)   contre :

attacks upon old people are on the increase
les agressions contre les personnes âgées sont de plus en plus fréquentes

iii) lorsque, en (avec un participe présent) :

upon hearing the news, he rang home
lorsqu'il a appris la nouvelle, il a appelé chez lui

WITH

i)   avec :

she filled the vase with water
elle a rempli le vase d'eau

stop fighting with your brother
arrête de te battre avec ton frère

she went out with her friend
elle est sortie avec son amie

he spoke with ease
il s'exprima avec aisance

ii)   à :

a boy with green eyes
un garçon aux yeux verts

iii) chez :

I'm staying with friends
je loge chez des amis

isn't he with Ford anymore?
ne travaille-t-il plus chez Ford ?

iv)   de (dans des expressions idiomatiques) :

he was white with fear
il était blanc de peur

I was sick with worry
j'étais malade d'inquiétude

WITHOUT

sans :

we couldn't have done it without you
on n'aurait pas pu le faire sans vous

I knocked without getting a reply
j'ai frappé sans obtenir de réponse

16 LES CONJONCTIONS

Les conjonctions sont des mots qui servent à relier deux mots ou deux propositions. On distingue deux types de conjonctions :

Les **conjonctions de coordination** relient des mots ou des propositions qui ont une même fonction. Elles servent à marquer l'union (**and**), l'opposition (**but**), l'alternative (**or**), la négation (**nor**), etc.

Les **conjonctions de subordination** relient des propositions qui **dépendent** d'autres mots ou propositions. Elles servent à marquer la cause (**because**), la comparaison (**as if**), la concession (**although**), le lieu (**where**), etc.

Voir aussi **La structure de la phrase**, pp. A78-9.

1   Les conjonctions de coordination

Elles peuvent être simples :

and *et*   **but** *mais*   **or** *ou/ni*   **nor** *ni*

ou corrélatives :

both... and *à la fois... et*
either... or *ou... ou, soit... soit, ni... ni (avec une négation)*
neither... nor *ni... ni*
not only... but also *non seulement... mais aussi*

a)   *Exemples de conjonctions de coordination simples*

i)   **And** peut relier deux noms, deux adjectifs, deux adverbes, deux verbes ou deux propositions :

she's old and fragile
elle est âgée et frêle

you need butter and flour
tu as besoin de beurre et de farine

she spoke naturally and fluently
elle parla avec naturel et aisance

they ate and drank a great deal
ils ont beaucoup mangé et beaucoup bu

they finished their work and then went out to dinner
ils ont terminé leur travail et puis ils sont sortis dîner

ii)   **But** et **or** offrent les mêmes possibilités de combinaison que **and**, par exemple :

he came home tired but happy
il est rentré fatigué mais heureux

I can go today or tomorrow
je peux y aller aujourd'hui ou demain

iii) **Nor** s'emploie devant le second élément (ou le troisième, etc.) lorsque la proposition principale est à la forme négative :

I don't eat sweets, nor chocolate, nor any kind of sugary thing
je ne mange pas de bonbons, ni de chocolat, ni aucunes sucreries

On peut aussi employer *or* dans cette même construction :

I don't eat sweets, or chocolate, or any kind of sugary thing

b) *Exemples de conjonctions de coordination corrélatives*

i) **Both... and** permettent de relier deux noms, deux adjectifs ou deux verbes :

you need both butter and flour
vous avez besoin de beurre et de farine

she's both old and fragile
elle est (à la fois) âgée et frêle

the film made me both laugh and cry
le film m'a fait à la fois rire et pleurer

ii) De manière générale, on emploiera **either... or** dans les phrases affirmatives et **neither... nor** lorsque le sens est négatif :

you need either butter or margarine
tu as besoin soit de beurre, soit de margarine

they're either very rich or very stupid
ils sont soit très riches, soit très bêtes

she was travelling either to or from Aberdeen
elle allait à Aberdeen ou bien elle en revenait

I have neither the time nor the inclination to do it
je n'ai ni le temps ni l'envie de le faire

she neither drinks nor smokes
elle ne boit ni ne fume

Mais on peut aussi employer **either... or** dans une phrase négative. Dans ce cas-là, il ne faut pas oublier le *not* de la négation :

I've not met either him or his brother
je n'ai rencontré ni lui ni son frère

iii) Si **(n)either... (n)or** relient deux noms, le verbe s'accorde en nombre avec le nom le plus proche du verbe :

either the turntable or the speakers have to be replaced
either the speakers or the turntable has to be replaced
il faut remplacer soit les enceintes, soit la platine

Lorsque les deux noms ou pronoms sont singuliers, le verbe qui suit doit se mettre au singulier (même si l'on trouve parfois un verbe au pluriel dans un langage familier et incorrect) :

neither he nor his wife has ever spoken to me
ni lui ni sa femme ne m'ont jamais adressé la parole

iv) **Not only... but also**

she plays not only the guitar, but also the piano
elle joue non seulement de la guitare, mais aussi du piano

Remarquez aussi l'emploi avec l'adverbe *too* :

she's not only bright, she's funny too
elle est non seulement intelligente, mais en plus elle est drôle

c) *Les différents emplois de* or

i) *Or* peut exprimer l'alternative ou avoir un sens exclusif :

he lives in Liverpool or Manchester, I can't remember which
il habite à Liverpool ou à Manchester, je ne me souviens plus exactement

ii) Il sert aussi à relier deux synonymes :

bovine spongiform encephalopathy, or BSE
l'encéphalite spongiforme bovine, ou ESB

iii) Il peut avoir le sens de "sinon" lorsqu'il relie deux propositions :

apologize to her, or she'll never speak to you again
excuse-toi auprès d'elle, ou elle ne te parlera plus jamais

2 Les conjonctions de subordination

Il existe un grand nombre de conjonctions de subordination. Certaines sont simples :

because *parce que*	so that *si bien que*
although *bien que*	when *quand* etc.

D'autres sont corrélatives :

as... as *aussi... que*
more... than *plus... que*
so... that *afin... que* etc.

a) *Introduisant une proposition substantive*

Les propositions substantives ont la même fonction dans la phrase que les noms ou pronoms et les groupes nominaux :

(a) I told him that they had done it
je lui ai dit qu'ils l'avaient fait

(b) I told him the facts
je lui ai dit les faits

En (a), le complément d'objet direct de *told* est une proposition substantive, alors qu'en (b) c'est un groupe nominal.

Les conjonctions qui introduisent des propositions substantives sont :

that *que*   whether *si (+ choix)*   if *si*   how *comment*

That peut être omis si la proposition subordonnée est le complément d'objet direct de la phrase, mais jamais si elle en est le sujet :

he said (that) he wanted to see me *(complément d'objet)*
il a dit qu'il voulait me voir

that such films can be made is unbelievable *(sujet)*
que l'on puisse faire de tels films est incroyable

he asked me if/whether I had any money *(complément d'objet)*
il m'a demandé si j'avais de l'argent (ou pas)

whether I have any money or not is none of your business *(sujet)*
que j'aie de l'argent ou non, ça ne te regarde pas

he told us how he had seen his child being born *(complément d'objet)*
il nous a raconté qu'il avait vu naître son enfant

how it's done is immaterial *(sujet)*
la manière dont c'est fait est sans importance

Cet emploi de *if*, *whether* et *how* est différent de celui décrit ci-dessous, où ces conjonctions ont pour rôle d'introduire un groupe adverbial (voir ci-dessous).

b) *Introduisant une proposition adverbiale*

Voir aussi **Les adverbes**, p. A19.

Il existe un grand nombre de conjonctions qui introduisent des propositions adverbiales. On peut trouver des noms qui servent de conjonctions :

he arrived the minute the clock struck twelve (= *when*, conjonction de temps)
il est arrivé à la minute où la pendule sonnait midi

he didn't explain it the way you did (= *how*, conjonction de manière)
il ne l'a pas expliqué de la manière dont tu l'as fait

ou des participes passés ou présents :

provided you keep quiet, you can stay (= if, *conjonction de condition*)
du moment que tu restes sage, tu peux rester

he's doing well considering he's been here for only a week (= although/even if, *conjonction de concession*)
il se débrouille bien si l'on considère qu'il n'est ici que depuis une semaine

Voici les principales conjonctions adverbiales :

i) Conjonctions de temps :

after *après que*	**until** *jusqu'à ce que*
as *alors que*	**when** *lorsque*
before *avant que*	**whenever** *chaque fois que*
since *depuis que*	**while** *tandis que*

L'idée de futur dans les subordonnées introduites par l'une de ces conjonctions est exprimée par un présent en anglais (voir p. A51).

he came back after the show had finished
il est revenu après que le spectacle fut fini

the phone rang as he was having a bath
le téléphone a sonné alors qu'il prenait son bain

before you sit down, you must see the bedroom
avant que tu ne t'asseyes, il faut que tu voies la chambre

they've been crying (ever) since their parents left
ils pleurent depuis que/le moment où leurs parents sont partis

he talked non-stop until it was time to go home
il n'a pas arrêté de parler jusqu'à ce qu'il fût l'heure de partir

when he's ready we'll be able to get going at last
(*présent dans la subordonnée*)
quand il sera prêt, on pourra enfin se mettre en route

whenever we go on a picnic, it rains
chaque fois qu'on part en pique-nique, il pleut

will you go and see him while you're in Barcelona?
(*présent dans la subordonnée*)
est-ce que vous irez le voir quand vous serez à Barcelone ?

ii) Conjonctions de lieu :

where *où*	
wherever *où que, partout où*	

plant them where there is a lot of shade
plante-les là où il y a beaucoup d'ombre

wherever you go it's the same thing
où que vous alliez c'est la même chose

wherever we went, he complained about the food
partout où on est allés, il s'est plaint de la nourriture

iii) Conjonctions de manière, de comparaison ou d'intensité :

as *comme*	**how** *comment, comme*
as if *comme si*	**however** *de quelque*
as though *comme si*	*manière que*

he does it as he's always done it
il le fait comme il l'a toujours fait

he behaved as if/as though there was (were) something wrong
il s'est comporté comme s'il y avait quelque chose qui n'allait pas

tell me how you do it
dites-moi comment vous faites

you can pay how you want
tu peux payer comme tu veux

it'll be fine, however you do it
de quelque manière que vous le fassiez, ça ira

iv) Conjonctions de cause :

as étant donné que	**for** *car, parce que*
because *parce que*	**since** *puisque*

as there was nothing in the fridge, we went out to eat
comme il n'y avait rien dans le frigo, nous sommes sortis dîner

he came because it was his duty
il est venu parce que c'était son devoir

I was surprised when he arrived punctually, for he was usually late (*soutenu*)
je fus surpris de le voir arriver à l'heure, car il était souvent en retard

since you've been so kind to me, I want to give you a present
puisque tu as été si gentil avec moi, je veux te faire un cadeau

v) Conjonctions de concession :

(al)though *bien que*	**even though** *bien que*
even if *même si*	**whether** *que*

although I've never liked him, I do respect him
bien que je ne l'aie jamais aimé, je le respecte

you can stay, even if you haven't been invited
tu peux rester, même si tu n'as pas été invité

even though she explained it in detail, I couldn't understand
bien qu'elle l'ait expliqué en détail, je n'ai pas réussi à comprendre

I'm going whether you like it or not
je vais y aller que ça te plaise ou non

vi) Conjonctions de but :

in order to *afin de*	
lest *de peur/crainte que/de*	
so that *afin que*	

they went to the stage door in order to get a glimpse of him
ils sont allés à l'entrée des artistes afin de pouvoir l'apercevoir

he did it so that she would be happy
il l'a fait afin qu'elle soit heureuse

they whispered lest the children should hear
ils parlèrent à voix basse de peur que les enfants ne les entendent

Remarquez que lest a tendance à être employé dans un style littéraire. Il est possible d'employer so that... not à la place :

they whispered so that the children wouldn't hear
ils parlèrent à voix basse afin que les enfants ne les entendent pas

vii) Conjonctions de conséquence :

so that *si bien que, de façon à ce que*

she didn't eat enough, so that in the end she fell ill
elle ne mangeait pas assez, si bien qu'elle a fini par tomber malade

viii) Conjonctions de condition :

if *si*	
so/as long as *à condition que, pourvu que*	
unless *à moins que*	

if he comes, we'll ask him
s'il vient, on lui demandera

you can have it as long as you give me it back
vous pouvez le prendre à condition que vous me le rendiez

tell me, unless you don't want to
dis-le-moi, à moins que tu ne le veuilles pas

c) But *comme conjonction de subordination*

i) L'emploi de but comme conjonction de subordination signifiant "sans que" (après les adverbes négatifs never, barely, hardly, etc.) est d'un style soutenu et littéraire :

she never hears his name but she starts to weep
elle ne peut entendre son nom sans verser des larmes

barely/hardly a day goes by but he receives another invitation
il ne se passe pas un jour sans qu'il reçoive une nouvelle invitation

ii) But peut aussi s'employer comme conjonction de subordination devant that après certains noms précédés de no :

there's no doubt (but) that he's responsible
il n'y a aucun doute que c'est lui le responsable

d) *Introduisant des propositions comparatives*

Les propositions subordonnées comparatives ne modifient pas d'autres propositions (comme le font les propositions adverbiales). Elles modifient des éléments de la proposition : groupes nominaux, adverbiaux et adjectivaux.

Les conjonctions comparatives sont corrélatives (comparez avec les conjonctions de coordination, p. A73) :

more... than *plus... que*
less... than *moins... que*
as... as *autant/aussi... que*

i) Modifiant un nom :

we invited more people than we had planned to
nous avons invité plus de gens que prévu

he has as much money as we do
il a autant d'argent que nous

ii) Modifiant un adjectif :

it was less interesting than we'd thought
c'était moins intéressant que nous n'avions pensé

it was as interesting as we thought
c'était aussi intéressant que nous le pensions

iii) Modifiant un adverbe :

she paints better than she sculpts
elle peint mieux qu'elle ne sculpte

she sang as well as she could
elle chanta aussi bien qu'elle put

Remarquez l'absence de négation dans les exemples anglais.

Voir aussi **La comparaison**, pp. A24-7.

17 LES NOMBRES

1 Les nombres cardinaux et les nombres ordinaux

CARDINAUX		ORDINAUX	
1	one	1st	first
2	two	2nd	second
3	three	3rd	third
4	four	4th	fourth
5	five	5th	fifth
6	six	6th	sixth
7	seven	7th	seventh
8	eight	8th	eighth
9	nine	9th	ninth
10	ten	10th	tenth
11	eleven	11th	eleventh
12	twelve	12th	twelfth
13	thirteen	13th	thirteenth
14	fourteen	14th	fourteenth
15	fifteen	15th	fifteenth
16	sixteen	16th	sixteenth
17	seventeen	17th	seventeenth
18	eighteen	18th	eighteenth
19	nineteen	19th	nineteenth
20	twenty	20th	twentieth
21	twenty-one	21st	twenty-first
30	thirty	30th	thirtieth
40	forty	40th	fortieth
50	fifty	50th	fiftieth
60	sixty	60th	sixtieth
70	seventy	70th	seventieth
80	eighty	80th	eightieth
90	ninety	90th	ninetieth
100	a/one hundred	100th	(one) hundredth
101	a/one hundred and one	101st	(one) hundred and first
200	two hundred	200th	two hundredth
1,000	a/one thousand	1,000th	(one) thousandth
1,345	a/one thousand, three hundred and forty-five	1,345th	one thousand, three hundred and forty-fifth

1,000,000	a/one million	millionth
1,000,000,000 (10^9)	a/one billion	billionth
1,000,000,000,000 (10^{12})	a/one trillion	trillionth

Remarquez qu'en anglais britannique a thousand million était autrefois 10^9 (un milliard), a billion 10^{12} et a trillion 10^{18}. Aujourd'hui, on n'emploie que les valeurs données dans la liste, qui étaient à l'origine américaines.

Remarquez également l'emploi de la virgule pour indiquer les milliers, là où en français on a un espace.

2 Les fractions

a) *Les fractions ordinaires*

Comme en français, on écrit les fractions avec un nombre cardinal (ou parfois a à la place de one) + un nombre ordinal :

$1/5$ = **a/one fifth** *un cinquième*
$3/8$ = **three eighths** *trois huitièmes*
$3\ 4/9$ = **three and four ninths** *trois exposant quatre neuvièmes*
$1/2$ = **a/one half** *un demi*
$1/4$ = **a quarter** *un quart*
$3/4$ = **three quarters** *trois quarts*
$1\ 1/4$ **hours** = **an/one hour and a quarter** ou **one and a quarter hours** *(une heure et quart)*

Voir aussi **Les expressions de temps**, p. A80.

Remarquez que le -s est maintenu lorsque les fractions sont employées comme adjectifs :

they had a two-thirds majority
ils ont eu une majorité de deux tiers

L'emploi des fractions ordinaires est très courant en anglais.

b) *Les nombres décimaux*

Alors que dans les autres pays européens on utilise une virgule pour les nombres décimaux, les anglophones se servent du point :

25.5 = twenty-five point five

Les décimales sont énumérées une à une après le point :

25.552 = twenty-five point five five two

3 Nought, zero, 0, nil

a) *Anglais britannique*

i) **Nought** et **zero** sont utilisés pour le chiffre 0. Dans les calculs, on emploie habituellement **nought** :

add another nought (ou **zero**) **to that number**
ajoute un autre zéro à ce chiffre

put down nought and carry one
je pose zéro et je retiens un

0.6 = nought point six ou **zero point six**
zéro virgule six

ii) Pour un nombre sur une échelle, on préfère **zero** :

it's freezing, it's 10 below zero
il gèle, il fait moins 10

De même, on emploiera **zero** en anglais scientifique ou économique, dans le sens de **nothing** (*rien*) :

given zero conductivity
étant donné une conductivité de zéro

a country striving for zero inflation
un pays qui se bat pour atteindre une inflation zéro

production was soon reduced to zero (ou **nil**)
la production fut rapidement réduite à zéro/à néant

iii) Pour les numéros de téléphone, on prononce le chiffre comme la lettre o, mais on emploie aussi maintenant **zero** (voir le point 4 ci-dessous).

iv) **Nil** est toujours utilisé pour les points ou les scores :

Arsenal won four nil/by four goals to nil (= 4-0)
Arsenal a gagné quatre zéro/quatre buts à zéro

sauf au tennis, où l'on utilise **love** :

Hewitt leads forty-love
Hewitt mène quarante zéro

b) *Anglais américain*

Zero s'utilise dans presque tous les cas :

how many zeros are there in a billion?
combien y a-t-il de zéros dans un milliard ?

my telephone number is 721002 (= **seven two one zero zero two**)

Chicago Cubs zero – Detroit Tigers six (*au base-ball*)

Cependant, on utilise toujours le mot **love** au tennis.

4 Les numéros de téléphone

Les numéros de téléphone se lisent chiffre par chiffre :

1567 = one five six seven
40032 = four zero zero three two (*Am, Br*) **four double 'o' three two** (*Br*)

Remarquez l'emploi de **double** en anglais britannique lorsqu'on a deux chiffres identiques. Cependant, cet emploi n'est pas systématique ; on peut aussi répéter les deux chiffres.

À l'écrit, on regroupe normalement les chiffres en fonction des différents codes régionaux. À l'oral, on marquera une pause après chaque groupe de chiffres :

0141-221-5266 = 'o' one four one – double two one ou **two two one – five two double six** ou **six six**

5 Les adresses

En Amérique du Nord, les numéros de rue à quatre chiffres se lisent comme les dates (voir **Les expressions de temps**, p. A81), c'est-à-dire deux par deux :

3445 Sherbrooke Street = thirty-four forty-five

6 Les opérations

Il existe plusieurs façons d'exprimer les opérations arithmétiques. Voici les plus courantes :

12 + 19 = 31
twelve plus nineteen is/equals thirty-one

19 – 7 = 12
nineteen minus seven is/equals twelve
seven from nineteen is/leaves twelve
nineteen take away seven is/leaves twelve (*emploi enfantin*)

2 x 5 = 10
twice five is ten
two fives are ten

4 x 5 = 20
four times five is/equals twenty
four fives are twenty

36 x 41 = 1476
thirty-six times forty-one is/equals one thousand four hundred and seventy-six
thirty-six multiplied by forty-one is/equals one thousand four hundred and seventy-six

10 ÷ 2 = 5
ten divided by two is/equals five
two into ten goes five (*emploi plus familier*)

7 L'emploi du pluriel

Pour **hundred, thousand, million** (**billion, trillion**) avec ou sans **-s**, voir **Les noms**, pp. A12-13.

Voici quelques exemples où l'on utilise le pluriel :

there were tens of thousands of refugees
il y avait des dizaines de milliers de réfugiés

she's now in her eighties
elle est maintenant octogénaire (elle a entre 80 et 90 ans)

in the 1950s (= **nineteen fifties**) ou **in the 50s** (= **fifties**)
dans les années cinquante

Voir aussi p. A81.

8 The former et the latter

Au lieu d'employer **the first**, on emploie **the former** si l'on fait référence à une personne/chose parmi deux qui viennent juste d'être énoncées ; et **the latter** (au lieu de **the last**) quand on fait référence à la dernière de deux personnes/choses :

Lauren and Alison are both good candidates for the job, but the former is more experienced than the latter
Lauren et Alison sont de bonnes candidates pour ce poste, mais la première a plus d'expérience que la seconde

De ces expressions, **the latter** est la plus souvent utilisée, et elle peut aussi renvoyer à la dernière chose d'une énumération qui comprend plus de deux éléments :

Spain, Italy, Greece: of these countries the latter is still the most interesting as regards...
l'Espagne, l'Italie, la Grèce : de tous ces pays, le dernier est le plus intéressant en ce qui concerne...

The former/the latter peuvent avoir une fonction adjectivale, c'est-à-dire qu'ils peuvent en effet être suivis d'un nom :

of dogs and cats, the former animal makes a better pet
du chien ou du chat, c'est le premier qui est le meilleur animal domestique

9 Once et twice

Once signifie "une fois" et **twice**, "deux fois". **Thrice** (*trois fois*) est archaïque :

I've been there once before
j'y suis déjà allé une fois

I've only seen her twice
je ne l'ai vue que deux fois

18 LA STRUCTURE DE LA PHRASE

1 Le sujet

En général, le sujet précède l'auxiliaire et le verbe :

I can swim
je sais nager

L'inversion du sujet et du verbe a lieu dans les cas suivants (s'il y a plus d'un auxiliaire, seul le premier auxiliaire précède le sujet) :

a) dans les questions :

may I?
puis-je ?

(when) can you come?
(quand) peux-tu venir ?

would you have liked to come with us?
tu aurais aimé venir avec nous ?

b) dans les propositions conditionnelles, lorsque if est omis :

had I got there in time, she'd still be alive
si j'étais arrivé à temps, elle serait encore en vie

should that be true, I'd be most surprised
si c'était vrai, je serais vraiment surpris

c) quand la phrase commence avec un mot dont le sens est négatif (comme never, seldom) :

I can't swim – nor/neither can I
je ne sais pas nager – moi non plus

never did I think this would happen
je n'aurais jamais pensé que cela arriverait

little did I think this would happen
je ne me doutais pas du tout que cela arriverait

hardly had he entered the room, when the phone rang
à peine était-il entré dans la pièce que le téléphone sonna

seldom have I enjoyed a meal so much
j'ai rarement autant apprécié un repas

Mais après nevertheless/nonetheless et only, qui renvoient à la proposition précédente, il n'y a pas d'inversion :

I know he's not very nice, nevertheless/nonetheless he should **be invited**
je sais bien qu'il n'est pas très sympa, mais on devrait quand même l'inviter

we'd like you to come, only we haven't got **enough room**
nous aimerions que vous veniez, mais nous n'avons pas assez de place

d) souvent quand une phrase commence avec un adverbe d'intensité :

so marvellously did he play that it brought tears to my eyes
il a joué tellement bien que j'en avais les larmes aux yeux

only too well do I remember those words
je m'en souviens trop bien, de ces paroles

e) parfois lorsque la phrase commence par un complément circonstanciel ou un complément d'objet indirect et que l'on veut insister sur le sujet ou le complément d'objet (le verbe étant moins important) :

in that year came the announcement that the space shuttle would be launched
cette année-là fut annoncé le lancement de la navette spatiale

on the stage stood the three main actors
sur la scène se tenaient les trois acteurs principaux

to his brave efforts do we owe our happiness *(littéraire)*
c'est à son grand courage que nous devons notre bonheur

Remarquez aussi que l'on peut placer out, in, etc. devant le verbe pour insister ou donner un effet stylistique dans une narration. Il s'agit là d'un emploi assez courant :

a big black car pulled up and out jumped Margot
une grosse voiture noire s'arrêta et Margot en sortit avec précipitation

out came a scream so horrible that it made my hair stand on end
on entendit tout à coup un cri si horrible que j'en eus la chair de poule

Le pronom se place avant le verbe :

in you go!
entre !

out you get!
sors !

f) après so placé en position initiale (= aussi) :

I'm hungry – so am I
j'ai faim – moi aussi

g) au discours direct :

Après le discours direct, le verbe de parole précède parfois son sujet, surtout si celui-ci est un nom (plus le nom ou le groupe nominal est important, plus on aura tendance à inverser l'ordre des mots) :

"you're late again", said John/John said
"tu es encore en retard", dit John

"you're late again!", boomed the furious sergeant/the furious sergeant boomed
"tu es encore en retard", hurla le sergent, furieux

Mais il n'y a pas d'inversion du sujet avec les temps composés :

"you're late again", John had said
"tu es encore en retard", avait dit John

Si le sujet est un pronom, il se met normalement avant le verbe :

"you're late again", he said
"tu es encore en retard", dit-il

Le verbe précède le pronom lorsqu'une proposition relative suit ou lorsque l'on veut donner un ton humoristique à la phrase :

"you're late again", said I, who **had been waiting for at least two hours**
"tu es encore en retard", ai-je dit ; ça faisait au moins deux heures que j'attendais

S'il y a un adverbe, l'inversion est moins courante, mais possible :

"you're back again", said John tentatively/John said tentatively
"tu es de retour", fit John d'un ton hésitant

Mais s'il y a un complément d'objet, après ask ou tell par exemple, on ne fait pas l'inversion :

"she's late again", John told the waiting guests
"elle est encore en retard", dit John aux invités qui attendaient

2 Le complément d'objet

a) Le complément d'objet suit normalement le verbe, mais il est en position initiale dans les cas suivants :

i) dans les questions qui commencent par un pronom interrogatif complément d'objet :

who(m) did you meet?
qui as-tu rencontré ?

ii) dans les propositions subordonnées interrogatives et relatives (les pronoms étant compléments d'objet) :

please ask him what he thinks
demande-lui, s'il te plaît, ce qu'il en pense

he brought back what she'd given him
il a ramené ce qu'elle lui avait donné

iii) pour renforcer un complément d'objet, surtout quand celui-ci est that :

that I couldn't put up with
cela, je ne pouvais pas l'accepter

that I don't know
ça, je ne sais pas

but his sort I don't like **at all**
son genre, je ne l'aime pas du tout

b) L'ordre des compléments d'objet direct et indirect

i) Le complément d'objet indirect précède le complément d'objet direct quand celui-ci est un nom (ice-cream), que le complément indirect soit un pronom ou un nom (him, the children) :

she gave him an ice-cream
elle lui a donné une glace

she gave the children some ice-cream
elle a donné de la glace aux enfants

Mais si le complément d'objet indirect est introduit par une préposition, il vient se placer après le complément d'objet direct :

she gave some ice-cream to the children
elle a donné de la glace aux enfants

ii) Quand les deux compléments sont des pronoms, le complément d'objet indirect précède le complément d'objet direct :

he wouldn't sell me them
il ne voulait pas me les vendre

would you give me one?
tu veux bien m'en donner un ?

could you please send her these?
eh bien, dis-le-leur

well, tell them that, **then**
tu peux les lui envoyer, s'il te plaît ?

Mais les phrases où l'on emploie le pronom personnel it après les verbes give, lend, etc. peuvent se construire des deux manières suivantes :

could you give him it **when you see him?**
could you give it to him **when you see him?**
tu veux bien le lui donner quand tu le verras ?

Avec la préposition to, l'ordre des mots est semblable à celui de l'exemple ci-dessus :

he wouldn't sell them to me
il ne voulait pas me les vendre

would you give one to me?
tu veux bien m'en donner un ?

19 LES CHANGEMENTS ORTHOGRAPHIQUES

1 y devient i

Un y placé après une **consonne** se change en i devant les terminaisons suivantes :

-able, -ed, -er *(adjectifs ou noms)*
-est, -es *(noms et verbes)*
-ly et -ness

ply	→	plies, pliable
cry	→	cried, cries, crier
happy	→	happier, happiest, happily, happiness

Exceptions :

shyly (*timidement*) et slyly (*sournoisement*) (on évite d'employer slily qui est rare). Par contre, drily est plus courant que dryly.

Les noms propres qui se terminent en -y prennent seulement -s :

there were two Henrys **at the party**
il y avait deux Henri à la soirée

Les composés en -by prennent -s :

standbys *remplaçants*

On trouve aussi parmi les exceptions les noms dyer (*teinturier*) et parfois flyer (*aviateur*) (aussi flier).

Mais y précédé d'une voyelle ne change pas et la terminaison des noms ou des verbes est -s au lieu de -es :

play	→	plays, playable, player
coy	→	coyer, coyest, coyly, coyness

Mais remarquez les verbes irréguliers :

lay	→	laid	say →	said
pay	→	paid		

ainsi que les adverbes formés à partir des adjectifs :

day	→	daily	gay →	gaily (aussi gayly).

2 ie devient y

Ce changement a lieu devant -ing :

die	→	dying	lie →	lying

3 Chute de la voyelle finale -e

On enlève normalement le -e si l'on ajoute une syllabe commençant par une voyelle :

love	→	loving, lovable	stone →	stony

Exceptions :

Parmi les exceptions principales, on peut citer :

matey *copain*
likeable *aimable*
mileage *distance parcourue en miles*
dyeing *teinture* (à ne pas confondre avec dying = *mourir*)
hoeing *binage*
swingeing *énorme* (à ne pas confondre avec swinging = *dans le vent*)

Si le mot se termine en -ce ou en -ge, alors le -e est maintenu devant -a et -o :

irreplaceable, changeable, outrageous

Si la syllabe suivante commence par une consonne, on conserve normalement le -e :

love	→	lovely	bore →	boredom

Mais là encore, il existe des exceptions importantes, notamment :

argue	→	argument	true →	truly
due	→	duly	whole →	wholly

4 -our ou -or

Quand on ajoute un suffixe à certains mots se terminant par -our, le -u tombe :

humour	→	humorist	vigour →	vigorous

Mais l'exception importante concerne le mot colour :

colour	→	colourful, colourlessness, colourist

En anglais américain, la terminaison -our devient -or. On aura donc toujours -or pour les noms avec ou sans suffixe :

humor	→	humorist
vigor	→	vigorous
color	→	colorful, etc.

5 Doublement des consonnes

Après une voyelle courte accentuée, on double la consonne finale lorsqu'elle est placée devant -er, -est, -ed, -ing :

big [bɪg]	→	bigger, biggest
fit [fɪt]	→	fitter, fittest, fitted, fitting
begin [bɪˈgɪn]	→	beginner, beginning

On double aussi le -r dans les mots qui se terminent par -ur ou -er (voyelles longues accentuées) :

blur [blɜː(r)]	→	blu**rr**ed, blu**rr**ing
occur [əˈkɜː(r)]	→	occu**rr**ed, occu**rr**ing
refer [rɪˈfɜː(r)]	→	refe**rr**ed, refe**rr**ing

Mais on ne double pas la consonne dans les monosyllabes à voyelle longue ou à diphtongue (= voyelle qui change de timbre au cours de son émission) :

keep [kiːp]	→	kee**p**er, kee**p**ing
cure [kjʊə(r)]	→	cu**r**ed, cu**r**ing

et dans les dissyllabes accentués sur la première syllabe :

vomit [ˈvɒmɪt]	→	vomi**t**ed, vomi**t**ing

En anglais britannique, le -l est doublé même dans une syllabe non accentuée :

revel [ˈrevəl]	→	reve**ll**ed, reve**ll**er, reve**ll**ing
travel [ˈtrævəl]	→	trave**ll**ed, trave**ll**er, trave**ll**ing

Mais ce doublement n'a pas lieu en anglais américain :

travel	→	trave**l**ed, trave**l**er, trave**l**ing

Remarquez aussi :

kidnap [ˈkɪdnæp]	→	kidna**pp**ed, kidna**pp**er (*Br*)
kidnap	→	kidna**p**ed, kidna**p**er (*Am*)

6 c devient ck

Le -c final d'un mot devient -ck devant -ed, -er, -ing :

frolic	→	froli**ck**ed, froli**ck**ing
picnic	→	picni**ck**ed, picni**ck**er, picni**ck**ing

7 Anglais américain

En plus des variantes américaines données en 4 et 5 ci-dessus, il faut noter les différences suivantes entre l'orthographe britannique et l'orthographe américaine :

a) Anglais britannique -gue, anglais américain -g :

catalo**gue** (*Br*) – catalo**g** (*Am*)

b) Anglais britannique -tre, anglais américain -ter :

cen**tre** (*Br*) – cen**ter** (*Am*)

me**tre** (*Br*) – me**ter** (*Am*)

c) Anglais britannique -nce, anglais américain -nse :

defe**nce** (*Br*) – defe**nse** (*Am*)

offe**nce** (*Br*) – offe**nse** (*Am*)

prete**nce** (*Br*) – prete**nse** (*Am*)

d) Quelques mots qui s'écrivent différemment :

Br	Am
cheque	check
pyjamas	pajamas
practise (*pratiquer*)	practice (le nom se termine en -ce des deux côtés de l'Atlantique)
programme	program (de même en anglais britannique dans le domaine de l'informatique)
tyre (*pneu*)	tire

20 LES EXPRESSIONS DE TEMPS

A L'HEURE

what's the time?, what time is it?	what time do you make it?
quelle heure est-il ?	*quelle heure avez-vous ?*

a) *Les heures*

it's one/two (o'clock)	it's 12 (o'clock)/midnight
il est une heure/deux heures	*il est minuit*

it's 12 (o'clock)/noon/12 noon/midday
il est midi

b) *Les demi-heures*

it's half past one, it's one thirty (*Am*), it's half one (*Fam*)
il est une heure et demie

it's half past midnight	it's half past twelve
il est minuit et demi	*il est midi/minuit et demi*

On peut ajouter in the afternoon et at night soit pour insister, soit pour éviter toute ambiguïté lorsque le contexte ne permet pas de savoir s'il s'agit de "midi" ou "minuit" :

it was half past twelve in the at afternoon	it was half past twelve night
il est midi et demi	*il est minuit et demi*

c) *Les quarts d'heure*

it's (a) quarter past two	at (a) quarter to two
il est deux heures et quart	*à deux heures moins le quart*

d) *Les minutes*

it's twenty-three minutes past four (= 4.23)
il est quatre heures vingt-trois

it's twenty to five (= 4.40)
il est cinq heures moins vingt

En anglais américain, on emploie after au lieu de past (it's twenty after five *il est cinq heures vingt*) et of au lieu de to (it's twenty of five *il est cinq heures moins vingt*).

e) **a.m.** *et* **p.m.**

a.m.	p.m.
du matin	*de l'après-midi/du soir*
it's 6.50 a.m.	it's 7.10 p.m.
il est 6 h 50	*il est 7 h 10 (du soir)/19 h 10*

A.m. et p.m. s'utilisent surtout lorsque le contexte ne permet pas de savoir s'il s'agit du matin ou de l'après-midi/du soir et que l'on veut éviter toute ambiguïté.

Les expressions du type "quinze heures" (à la place de "trois heures") ne s'emploient pas en anglais de tous les jours. Cependant, on les rencontre parfois dans les horaires et dans le langage militaire (souvent suivis de hours) :

fifteen hundred hours	fifteen thirty hours
quinze heures	*quinze heures trente*

'o' five hundred hours
cinq heures du matin

L'emploi de 'o', pour désigner le zéro devant le chiffre, est uniquement militaire. Dans les horaires, on emploiera simplement **five hundred hours**.

Pour les moyens de transport, on peut aussi dire :

we took the sixteen-twenty **to Brighton**
nous avons pris le train de 16 h 20 pour Brighton

Remarquez les abréviations : 7.15 = 7 h 15.

B LA DATE

1 Les mois, les jours et les saisons

Les jours et les mois prennent une majuscule en anglais.

a) *Les mois* (the months)

January	*janvier*	July	*juillet*
February	*février*	August	*août*
March	*mars*	September	*septembre*
April	*avril*	October	*octobre*
May	*mai*	November	*novembre*
June	*juin*	December	*décembre*

b) *Les jours de la semaine* (the days of the week)

Monday	*lundi*	Friday	*vendredi*
Tuesday	*mardi*	Saturday	*samedi*
Wednesday	*mercredi*	Sunday	*dimanche*
Thursday	*jeudi*		

c) *Les saisons* (the seasons)

spring	*le printemps*	autumn	*l'automne*
summer	*l'été*	winter	*l'hiver*

En anglais américain, "l'automne" se dit aussi **fall**. Pour l'emploi de l'article, voir p. A7.

2 Les dates

a) *Les années*

Pour lire les années, on sépare les deux premiers chiffres des deux derniers :

1945 (19|45) = nineteen forty-five (littéralement *dix-neuf, quarante-cinq*)

L'emploi de **hundred** est possible, mais plus rare ; il s'utilisera dans un style très soutenu :

1945 = nineteen hundred and forty-five (*dix-neuf cent quarante-cinq*)

Mais les dates suivantes se disent pratiquement toujours de la même manière :

811* = eight hundred and eleven
1026 = ten twenty-six
1000* = one thousand
2000* = two thousand
2005 = two thousand and five

*Pour les années qui précèdent l'an 1000, ainsi que pour l'an 1000 et l'an 2000, on ajoute en général **the year** devant l'année (= the year 2000).

b) *Les jours et les mois*

En anglais, on emploie souvent les nombres ordinaux pour les dates (contrairement au français) :

14th July (qui se dit **"the fourteenth of July"**)
le 14 juillet

2nd November (qui se dit **"the second of November"**)
le 2 novembre

I wrote to you on 3rd March (qui se dit **"on the third of March"**)
je vous ai écrit le 3 mars

Mais il y a en fait différentes manières d'écrire la date :

12(th) May   **May 12(th)**

L'emploi du nombre cardinal est beaucoup plus courant que celui du nombre ordinal en anglais américain. En anglais britannique, il est aussi parfaitement possible d'employer le nombre cardinal.

En anglais américain, on omet pratiquement tout le temps le **the** à l'oral quand on commence par le mois :

May 12 se dit **May twelfth/May twelve**

En anglais britannique, on écrit les dates en mettant le jour en premier (comme en français), alors que c'est l'inverse en anglais américain :

10/4/92 = 10th April 1992, anglais britannique
4/10/92 = 10th April 1992, anglais américain (**10/4/92** = **4th October 1992** en américain)

Pour les nombres ordinaux, voir **Les nombres** p. A76.

C EXPRESSIONS IDIOMATIQUES

at 5 o'clock	*à cinq heures*
at about 11 o'clock	*à onze heures environ*
at about midnight	*vers minuit*
at about 10 o'clock	*vers (les) dix heures*
it's past six o'clock	*il est six heures passées*
at exactly four o'clock	*à quatre heures précises/ pile*
on the stroke of three	*sur le coup de trois heures*
from 9 o'clock onwards	*à partir de neuf heures*
shortly before seven	*peu avant sept heures*
shortly after seven	*peu après sept heures*
it's late	*il est tard*
he's late	*il est en retard*
the train is twenty minutes late	*le train a vingt minutes de retard*
my watch is six minutes slow	*ma montre retarde de six minutes*
my watch is six minutes fast	*ma montre avance de six minutes*
one day/morning/evening	*un jour/matin/soir*
this evening, tonight	*ce soir*
tomorrow evening, tomorrow night	*demain soir*
yesterday evening, last night	*hier soir*
Saturday evening, Saturday night	*samedi soir*
I'm going out on Saturday night ou evening	*je sors samedi soir*
on Saturday evening	*dans la soirée de samedi*
during Saturday night	*dans la nuit de samedi (à dimanche)*
tomorrow morning	*demain matin*
yesterday morning	*hier matin*
Monday morning	*lundi matin*
I'm going (on) Monday morning	*j'y vais lundi matin*
the next day	*le lendemain*
the next morning	*le lendemain matin*
a week on Monday, Monday week	*lundi en huit*
a fortnight on Monday	*lundi en quinze*
next week	*la semaine prochaine*
this (coming) week	*la semaine qui vient*
last week	*la semaine dernière*
I saw him the other Saturday	*je l'ai vu l'autre samedi*
I'm starting on Monday	*je commence lundi*
he comes on Mondays, he comes on a Monday	*il vient le lundi*
come one Monday	*viens un lundi*
he comes in the afternoon(s)	*il vient l'après-midi*
come one afternoon	*viens un après-midi*

every other Monday, every second Monday	*un lundi sur deux*
every Saturday	*tous les samedis*
every Saturday evening ou night	*tous les samedis soir*
I spent the whole Sunday doing the cleaning	*j'ai passé tout mon dimanche à faire le ménage*
all her Sundays	*tous ses dimanches*
in the early afternoon/evening	*en début d'après-midi/de soirée*
I'll phone him first thing in the morning	*je lui téléphonerai à la première heure demain matin*
in the middle of June, mid-June	*au milieu du mois de juin, (à la) mi-juin*
in the middle of winter, mid-winter	*au milieu de l'hiver*
I've a meeting late morning	*j'ai une réunion à la fin de la matinée ou en fin de matinée*

at the end of winter	*à la fin de l'hiver*
we'll talk about it again at the end of January	*on en reparlera fin janvier ou à la fin du mois de janvier*
what day is it today?	*quel jour sommes-nous aujourd'hui ?*
what's the date?	*le combien sommes-nous ?*
it's the third of April	*c'est le trois avril*
in February	*au mois de/en février*
in 1996	*en 1996*
in the summer of 1996, in summer 1996	*l'été 1996*
in the sixties, in the 60s, in the 1960s	*dans les années soixante*
in the early/late sixties	*au début/à la fin des années soixante*
in the seventeenth century in the 17th C	*au dix-septième siècle au XVIIᵉ s.*

FRENCH GRAMMAR

GRAMMAIRE FRANÇAISE

CONTENTS

GLOSSARY OF GRAMMATICAL TERMS

ADJECTIVE
An adjective provides supplementary information about a noun, describing what something is like, eg *a small house, a red car, an interesting pastime.*

ADVERB
Adverbs are normally used with a verb to add extra information by indicating **how** the action is done (adverbs of manner), **when**, **where** or **with how much intensity** the action is done (adverbs of time, place and intensity), or **to what extent** the action is done (adverbs of quantity). Adverbs may also be used with an adjective or another adverb, eg *a very attractive girl, very well.*

AGREEMENT
In French, words such as adjectives, articles and pronouns must agree in number and gender with the noun or pronoun to which they refer. This means that their spelling changes according to the **number** of the noun (singular or plural) and according to its **gender** (masculine or feminine).

ANTECEDENT
The antecedent of a relative pronoun is the word or words to which the relative pronoun refers. The antecedent is usually found directly before the relative pronoun, eg in the sentence *I know the man who did this, the man* is the antecedent of *who.*

APPOSITION
A word or a clause is said to be in apposition to another when it is placed directly after it without any joining word, eg *Mr Jones, our bank manager, rang today.*

ARTICLE
See DEFINITE ARTICLE, INDEFINITE ARTICLE and PARTITIVE ARTICLE.

ASPIRATE H
If a word begins with an aspirate h in French, it means that there is no liaison between it and the word preceding it, eg in **les haricots** the s of **les** is not pronounced. Similarly, there is no contraction in spelling, eg **la haine** and not **l'haine**. See SILENT H.

AUXILIARY
The French auxiliary verbs are **avoir** (*to have*) and **être** (*to be*). They are used to make up the first part of compound tenses, the second part being a past participle, eg *j'ai mangé, il est allé.*

CARDINAL
Cardinal numbers are numbers such as *one, two, ten, fourteen*, as opposed to ORDINAL numbers, eg *first, second.*

CLAUSE
A clause is a group of words which contains at least a subject and a verb: *he said* is a clause. A clause often contains more than this basic information, eg *he said this to her yesterday.* Sentences can be made up of several clauses, eg *he said/he'd call me/if he were free.* See SENTENCE.

COMPARATIVE
The comparative forms of adjectives and adverbs allow two things, persons or actions to be compared. In English, *more ... than, ...er than, less ... than* and *as ... as* are used for comparison.

COMPOUND
Compound tenses are verb tenses consisting of more than one element. In French, the compound tenses of a verb are formed by the auxiliary verb and the past participle: *j'ai visité, il est venu.*

CONDITIONAL
This mood is used to describe what someone would do, or something that would happen if a condition were fulfilled, eg *I would come if I were well; the chair would have broken if he had sat on it.*

CONJUGATION
The conjugation of a verb is the set of different forms taken in the particular tenses of that verb.

CONJUNCTION
Conjunctions are used to link different clauses. They may be coordinating or subordinating. Coordinating conjunctions are words like *and, but, or*; subordinating conjunctions are words like *because, after, although.*

DEFINITE ARTICLE
The definite article is *the* in English and *le, la* and *les* in French.

DEMONSTRATIVE
Demonstrative adjectives such as *this, that, these* and pronouns such as *this one, that one* are used to point out a particular person or object.

DIRECT OBJECT
A direct object is a noun or a pronoun which in English follows a verb without any linking preposition, eg *I met a friend.*

ELISION
Elision consists in replacing the last letter of certain words (*le, la, je, me, te, se, de, que*) with an apostrophe before a word starting with a vowel or a silent h, eg *l'eau, l'homme, j'aime.*

ENDING
The ending of a verb is determined by the person (1st/2nd/3rd) and number (singular/plural) of its subject. In French, most tenses have six different endings. See PERSON and NUMBER.

EXCLAMATION
An exclamation is a word or sentence used to express surprise or wonder, eg *what!, how!, how lucky!, what a nice day!*

FEMININE
See GENDER.

GENDER
The gender of a noun indicates whether the noun is masculine or feminine (all French nouns are either masculine or feminine).

IDIOMATIC EXPRESSIONS
Idiomatic expressions (or idioms) are expressions which cannot normally be translated word for word. For example, *it's raining cats and dogs* is translated by *il pleut des cordes.*

IMPERATIVE
This mood is used for giving orders, eg *eat!, don't go!*

INDEFINITE
Indefinite pronouns and adjectives are words that do not refer to a definite person or object, eg *each, someone, every.*

INDEFINITE ARTICLE
The indefinite article is *a* in English and *un, une* and *des* in French.

INDICATIVE
The indicative is the normal form of a verb as in *I like, he came, we are trying.* It is opposed to the subjunctive, conditional and imperative.

INDIRECT OBJECT
An indirect object is a pronoun or noun which follows a verb indirectly, with a linking preposition (usually *to*), eg *I spoke to my friend/him.*

INFINITIVE
The infinitive is the basic form of the verb as found in dictionaries. Thus *to eat, to finish, to take* are infinitives. In French, the infinitive is recognizable by its ending (*-er, -ir* or *-re*, eg *manger, finir, prendre*).

INTERROGATIVE
Interrogative words are used to ask a question. This may be a direct question (*when will you arrive?*) or an indirect question (*I don't know when he'll arrive*). See QUESTION.

MASCULINE
See GENDER.

MOOD This is the name given to the four main areas within which a verb is conjugated. See INDICATIVE, SUBJUNCTIVE, CONDITIONAL, IMPERATIVE.

NOUN A noun is a word or group of words which refers to a living creature, a thing, a place or an abstract idea, eg *postman, cat, shop, passport, life.*

NUMBER The number of a noun indicates whether the noun is singular or plural. A singular noun refers to one single person or thing, eg *boy, train* and a plural noun to more than one, eg *boys, trains.*

ORDINAL Ordinal numbers are *first, second, third, fourth* and all other numbers which end in -th. In French, all ordinal numbers, except for *premier* (first) and *second* (second), end in -ième.

PARTITIVE ARTICLE The partitive articles are *some* and *any* in English and *du, de la, de l'* and *des* (as in *du pain, de la confiture, de l'eau, des bananes*) in French.

PASSIVE A verb is used in the passive when the subject of the verb does not perform the action but is subjected to it. The passive is formed with the verb *to be* and the past participle of the verb, eg *he was rewarded.*

PAST PARTICIPLE The past participle of a verb is the form which is used after *to have* in English, eg *I have eaten, I have said, you have tried.*

PERSON In any tense, there are three persons in the singular (1st: *I ...* , 2nd: *you ...* , 3rd: *he/she ...*), and three in the plural (1st: *we ...* , 2nd: *you ...* , 3rd: *they ...*). See also ENDING.

PERSONAL PRONOUNS Personal pronouns stand for a noun. They usually accompany a verb and can be either the subject (*I, you, he/she/it, we, they*) or the object of the verb (*me, you, him/her/it, us, them*).

PLURAL See NUMBER.

POSSESSIVE Possessive adjectives and pronouns are used to indicate possession or ownership. They are words like *my/mine, your/yours, our/ours.*

PREPOSITION Prepositions are words such as *with, in, to, at.* They are followed by a noun or a pronoun.

PRESENT PARTICIPLE The present participle is the verb form which ends in -ing in English and -ant in French.

PRONOUN This is a word which stands for a noun. The main categories of pronouns are:

* Relative pronouns (eg *who, which, that*)

* Interrogative pronouns (eg *who?, what?, which?*)

* Demonstrative pronouns (eg *this, that, these*)

* Possessive pronouns (eg *mine, yours, his*)

* Personal pronouns (eg *you, him, us*)

* Reflexive pronouns (eg *myself, himself*)

* Indefinite pronouns (eg *something, all*)

QUESTION There are two question forms: **direct** questions stand on their own and require a question mark at the end, eg *when will he come?*; **indirect** questions are introduced by a clause and require no question mark, eg *I wonder when he will come.*

REFLEXIVE Reflexive verbs 'reflect' the action back onto the subject, eg *I dressed myself.* They are always found with a reflexive pronoun and are much more common in French than in English.

SENTENCE A sentence is a group of words made up of one or more clauses (see CLAUSE) and which makes a complete grammatical structure. The end of a sentence is indicated by a punctuation mark (usually a full stop, a question mark or an exclamation mark).

SILENT H The term 'silent h' is actually misleading since an h is never pronounced in French. The point is that when a silent h occurs, any preceding vowel is not pronounced either. For example, the h in *j'habite* is silent (note the *j'*). The h in *je hurle*, however, is **aspirate**, and so there is no contraction in spelling.

SIMPLE TENSE Simple tenses are tenses in which the verb consists of one word only, eg *j'habite, Maurice partira.*

SINGULAR See NUMBER.

SUBJECT The subject of a verb is the noun or pronoun which performs the action. In the sentences, *the train left early* and *she bought a record*, the train and she are the subjects.

SUBJUNCTIVE The subjunctive is a verb form which is rarely used in English, eg *if I were you, God save the Queen*, but common in French.

SUPERLATIVE The superlative is the form of an adjective or an adverb which, in English, is marked by *the most ...* , *the ...est* or *the least ...*

TENSE Verbs are used in tenses, which tell us whether an action takes place in the present, the past or the future.

VERB A verb is a word which describes the performance of an action, eg *to sing, to work, to watch* or the existence of a state, eg *to be, to have, to hope.*

2 ARTICLES

A THE DEFINITE ARTICLE

1 Forms

In English, there is only one form of the definite article: **the**. In French, there are three forms, depending on the gender and number of the noun following the article:

- with a masculine singular noun: le ⎱
- with a feminine singular noun: la ⎰ the
- with a plural noun (masc or fem): les

MASC SING	FEM SING	PLURAL
le **chauffeur**	la **secrétaire**	les **étudiants**
the driver	*the secretary*	*the students*
le **salon**	la **cuisine**	les **chambres**
the living-room	*the kitchen*	*the bedrooms*

Note: le and la both change to l' before a vowel or a silent h:

	MASCULINE	FEMININE
BEFORE VOWEL	l'**avion**	l'**odeur**
	the plane	*the smell*
BEFORE SILENT H	l'**homme**	l'**hôtesse**
	the man	*the hostess*

Pronunciation: the s of les is pronounced z when the noun following it begins with a vowel or a silent h.

2 Forms with the prepositions 'à' and 'de'

When the definite article is used with à or de, the following spelling changes take place:

a) with à (to, at)

à + le   →   au
à + les   →   aux

à + la and à + l' do not change

au restaurant
at/to the restaurant

aux enfants
to the children

à la plage
at/to the beach

à l'aéroport
at/to the airport

Pronunciation: the x of aux is pronounced z when the noun following it begins with a vowel or a silent h.

b) with de (of, from)

de + le   →   du
de + les   →   des

de + la and de + l' do not change

du directeur
of/from the manager

des chômeurs
of/from the unemployed

de la région
of/from the area

de l'usine
of/from the factory

Pronunciation: the s of des is pronounced z when the noun following it begins with a vowel or a silent h.

3 Use

As in English, the definite article is used when referring to a particular person or thing, or particular persons or things:

les amis dont je t'ai parlé
the friends I told you about

le café est prêt
the coffee is ready

However, the definite article is used far more frequently in French than in English. It is used in particular in the following cases where English uses no article:

a) when the noun is used in a general sense

   i) to refer to all things of a kind:

vous acceptez les chèques?
do you take cheques?

le sucre est mauvais pour les dents
sugar is bad for the teeth

   ii) to refer to abstract things:

le travail et les loisirs
work and leisure

la musique classique
classical music

   iii) when stating likes and dislikes:

j'aime la viande mais je préfère le poisson
I like meat, but I prefer fish

je déteste les tomates
I hate tomatoes

b) with geographical names

   i) continents, countries and areas:

le Canada	**la France**	**l'Europe**
Canada	*France*	*Europe*
la Bretagne	**l'Afrique**	**les États-Unis**
Brittany	*Africa*	*the United States*

But: the article la is omitted with the prepositions en and de when used with feminine country names:

j'habite en France
I live in France

il vient d'Italie
he comes from Italy

With masculine country names, the corresponding prepositions à and de follow the normal rules:

j'habite au Portugal/aux États-Unis
I live in Portugal/in the United States

je viens du Japon/des Pays-Bas
I come from Japan/the Netherlands

A very few country names do not require an article, eg Panamá, Cuba, Taïwan, Singapour.

   ii) mountains, lakes and rivers:

le mont Everest
Mount Everest

le lac de Genève
Lake Geneva

c) with names of seasons

l'automne	*autumn/Am fall*
l'hiver	*winter*
le printemps	*spring*
l'été	*summer*

But: **en automne/été/hiver**
in autumn/summer/winter

au printemps
in spring

un jour d'été
a summer's day

d) with names of languages

j'apprends le français
I'm learning French

But: **ce film est en anglais**
this film is in English

e) with parts of the body

j'ai les cheveux roux
I've got red hair

ouvrez la bouche
open your mouth

les mains en l'air!
hands up!

l'homme à la barbe noire
the man with the black beard

f) with names following an adjective

le petit Pierre
little Pierre

la pauvre Isabelle
poor Isabelle

g) with titles

le docteur Coste
Doctor Coste

le commandant Cousteau
Captain Cousteau

h) with days of the week to express regular occurrences

que fais-tu le samedi?
what do you do on Saturdays?

le docteur reçoit le lundi et le vendredi
the doctor sees patients on Mondays and Fridays

i) with names of subjects or leisure activities

les maths
maths

l'histoire et la géographie
history and geography

la natation, la lecture, le football
swimming, reading, football

j) in expressions of price, quantity etc

c'est combien le kilo/la douzaine/la bouteille?
how much is it for a kilo/dozen/bottle?

B THE INDEFINITE ARTICLE

1 Forms

In French, there are three forms of the indefinite article, depending on the number and gender of the noun it accompanies:

- with a masculine singular noun: un   *a*
- with a feminine singular noun: une   *a*
- with a plural noun (masc or fem):   des   *some*

Note: des is often not translated in English:

il y a des nuages dans le ciel
there are clouds in the sky

2 Use

a) On the whole, the French indefinite article is used in the same way as its English equivalent:

un homme	**une femme**	**des hommes/femmes**
a man	*a woman*	*(some) men/women*
un livre	**une tasse**	**des livres/tasses**
a book	*a cup*	*(some) books/cups*

b) However, the English indefinite article is not always translated in French:

i) when stating someone's profession or occupation:

mon père est architecte
my father is an architect

elle est médecin
she is a doctor

Note, however, that the article is used after c'est, c'était etc:

c'est un acteur célèbre
he's a famous actor

ce sont des fraises
these are strawberries

ii) with nouns in apposition:

Madame Leclerc, employée de bureau
Mrs Leclerc, an office worker

iii) after quel in exclamations:

quel dommage! **quelle surprise!**
what a pity! *what a surprise!*

c) In negative sentences, de (or d') is used instead of un, une, des:

je n'ai pas d'amis **je n'ai plus de voiture**
I don't have any friends *I don't have a car any more*

d) In French (but not in English), the indefinite article is used with abstract nouns followed by an adjective:

avec une patience remarquable
with remarkable patience

elle a fait des progrès étonnants
she's made amazing progress

Note, however, that the article is not used when there is no adjective:

avec plaisir **sans hésitation**
with pleasure *without hesitation*

C THE PARTITIVE ARTICLE

1 Forms

There are three forms of the French partitive article, which corresponds to 'some'/'any' in English:

- with a masculine singular noun: **du**
- with a feminine singular noun: **de la**
- with plural nouns (masc or fem): **des**

du vin	**de la bière**	**des fruits**
some wine	*some beer*	*some fruit*

Note that de l' is used in front of masculine or feminine singular nouns beginning with a vowel or a silent h:

de l'argent	**de l'eau**	**de l'helium**
some money	*some water*	*some helium*

2 Use

a) On the whole, the French partitive article is used as in English.

However, English tends to omit the partitive article where French does not:

achète du pain **vous avez du beurre?**
buy (some) bread *do you have (any) butter?*

je voudrais de la viande **tu veux de la soupe?**
I'd like some meat *do you want (any) soup?*

tu dois manger des légumes **as-tu acheté des poires?**
you must eat (some) vegetables *did you buy any pears?*

b) The partitive article is replaced by de (or d') in the following cases:

i) in negative expressions:

il n'y a plus de café **je n'ai pas de frères**
there isn't any coffee left *I don't have any brothers*

nous n'avons plus d'argent **je n'ai pas d'enfants**
we don't have any money left *I don't have any children*

Note, however, that when the clause is introduced by c'est, il est etc, the partitive article remains:

ce n'est pas du cuir, c'est du plastique
it's not leather, it's plastic

ii) after expressions of quantity (see also p B60):

il boit trop de café **il gagne assez d'argent**
he drinks too much coffee *he earns enough money*

iii) after avoir besoin de:

j'ai besoin d'argent **tu as besoin de timbres?**
I need (some) money *do you need (any) stamps?*

iv) where an adjective is followed by a plural noun:

de petites villes **d'énormes mensonges**
(some) small towns *outrageous lies*

Note, however, that if the adjective comes after the noun, des does not change:

des résultats encourageants
encouraging results

3 Partitive or definite article?

When no article is used in English, it is not always clear which is the right article in French: le/la/les or du/de la/des.

If some/any can be inserted before the English noun, the French partitive article should be used. But if the noun is used in a general sense and inserting some/any in front of the English noun does not make sense, the definite article must be used:

did you buy fish? (ie any fish)
tu as acheté du poisson?

yes, I did; I like fish (ie fish in general)
oui; j'aime le poisson

3 NOUNS

A noun is a word or group of words which refers to a person, an animal, a thing, a place or an abstract idea.

A GENDER

All French nouns are either masculine or feminine; there is no neuter as in English. Though no absolute rule can be stated, the gender can often be determined either by the meaning or the ending of the noun.

1 Masculine

a) *by meaning*

i) words referring to men and male animals:

un homme	le boucher	le tigre
a man	*the butcher*	*the tiger*

ii) names of common trees and shrubs:

le chêne	le sapin	le laurier
the oak	*the fir tree*	*the laurel*

iii) days, months, seasons:

lundi	mars	le printemps
Monday	*March*	*spring*

iv) languages:

le français	le polonais	le russe
French	*Polish*	*Russian*

v) rivers and countries not ending in a silent e:

le Nil	le Portugal	le Danemark
the Nile	*Portugal*	*Denmark*

Note, however, that there are exceptions to this rule:

le Danube	le Rhône	le Mexique
the Danube	*the Rhone*	*Mexico*

b) *by ending*

-acle **le spectacle** (*show*)
But: **une débâcle** (*shambles*)

-age **le fromage** (*cheese*)
But: **la cage** (*cage*), **une image** (*picture*), **la nage** (*swimming*), **la page** (*page*), **la plage** (*beach*), **la rage** (*rage, rabies*)

-é **le marché** (*market*)
But: nouns ending in -té and -tié are usually feminine (see 2b)

-eau **le chapeau** (*hat*)
But: **l'eau** (*water*), **la peau** (*skin*)

-ège **le piège** (*trap*), **le collège** (*secondary school*)

-ème **le thème** (*theme, topic*)
But: **la crème** (*cream*)

-isme, -asme **le communisme** (*communism*), **le tourisme** (*tourism*), **l'enthousiasme** (*enthusiasm*)

-o **le numéro** (*the number*)
But: **la dynamo** (*dynamo*) and most abbreviated expressions: **une auto** (*car*), **la météo** (*weather forecast*), **la photo** (*photograph*), **la radio** (*radio*), **la sténo** (*shorthand*), **la stéréo** (*stereo*)

Nouns ending in a consonant are usually *masculine.*

Notable exceptions are:

i) most nouns ending in -tion, -sion, -ation, -aison, -ison

ii) most abstract nouns ending in -eur (see 2b)

iii) the following nouns ending in a consonant:

la clef (*key*)	la nef (*nave*)
la soif (*thirst*)	la faim (*hunger*)
la fin (*end*)	la façon (*manner*)
la leçon (*lesson*)	la boisson (*drink*)
la moisson (*harvest*)	la rançon (*ransom*)
la mer (*sea*)	la cuiller (*spoon*)
la chair (*flesh*)	la basse-cour (*farmyard*)
la cour (*yard*)	la tour (*tower*)
la brebis (*ewe*)	une fois (*once*)
la vis (*screw*)	la souris (*mouse*)
la part (*share*)	la plupart (*majority, most*)
la dent (*tooth*)	la dot (*dowry*)

la forêt (*forest*)	la jument (*mare*)
la mort (*death*)	la nuit (*night*)
la croix (*cross*)	la noix (*nut*)
la paix (*peace*)	la perdrix (*partridge*)
la toux (*cough*)	la voix (*voice*)

2 Feminine

a) *by meaning*

i) words referring to women and female animals:

la mère	la bonne	la génisse
the mother	*the maid*	*the heifer*

ii) names of rivers and countries ending with a silent e:

la Seine	la Russie	la Belgique
the Seine	*Russia*	*Belgium*

iii) saints' days and festivals:

la Toussaint	la Pentecôte
All Saints' Day	*Whitsun*

Note, however, that **Noël** (*Christmas*) is masculine except when used with the definite article: **à la Noël** (*at Christmas*)

b) *by ending*

-ace **la place** (*square, seat*)
But: **un espace** (*space*)

-ade **la salade** (*salad*)
But: **le grade** (*degree, rank*), **le stade** (*stadium*)

-ance, -anse **la puissance** (*power*), **la danse** (*dancing*)

-ée **la soirée** (*evening*), **la journée** (*day*)
But: **le musée** (*museum*), **le lycée** (*secondary school*)

-ence, -ense **une évidence** (*evidence*), **la défense** (*defence*)
But: **le silence** (*silence*)

-ère **la lumière** (*light*)
But: **le mystère** (*mystery*), **le caractère** (*character*)

-eur **la peur** (*fear*)
But: **le bonheur** (*happiness*), **le chœur** (*choir*), **le cœur** (*heart*), **un honneur** (*honour*), **le labeur** (*toil*), **le malheur** (*misfortune*)

-ie **la pluie** (*rain*)
But: **le génie** (*genius*), **un incendie** (*fire*), **le parapluie** (*umbrella*)

-ière **la bière** (*beer*)
But: **le cimetière** (*cemetery*)

-oire **la gloire** (*glory*)
But: **le laboratoire** (*laboratory*), **le pourboire** (*tip*)

-tion, -sion, -ation, -aison, -ison **la fiction** (*fiction*), **la nation** (*nation*), **la raison** (*reason*), **la prison** (*prison*)

-té **la bonté** (*goodness*)
But: **le côté** (*side*), **le comté** (*county*), **le traité** (*treaty*), **le pâté** (*pâté*)

-tié **la moitié** (*half*), **la pitié** (*pity*)

Most nouns ending in a silent e following two consonants are feminine:

la botte (*boot*), **la couronne** (*crown*), **la terre** (*earth*), **la masse** (*mass*), **la lutte** (*struggle*)

But: **le verre** (*glass*), **le parterre** (*flower-bed*), **le tonnerre** (*thunder*), **un intervalle** (*interval*), **le carrosse** (*carriage*)

3 Difficulties

a) Some nouns may have either gender depending on the sex of the person to whom they refer:

un artiste	une artiste
a (male) artist	*a (female) artist*

le Russe	la Russe
the Russian (man)	*the Russian (woman)*

similarly:

un aide/une aide	an assistant
un camarade/une camarade	a friend
un domestique/une domestique	a servant
un enfant/une enfant	a child
un malade/une malade	a patient
un propriétaire/une propriétaire	an owner

b) Others have only one gender for both sexes:

un ange	un amateur	un auteur
an angel	*an amateur*	*an author*
une connaissance	une dupe	un écrivain
an acquaintance	*a dupe*	*a writer*
une personne	le médecin	le peintre
a person	*the doctor*	*the painter*
la recrue	le sculpteur	la sentinelle
the recruit	*the sculptor (sculptress)*	*the sentry*
le témoin	la victime	la vedette
the witness	*the victim*	*the (film) star*

Note, however, that modern French tends to use feminine forms for many different functions. La ministre, la juge and la professeur can now be commonly found in the press, and new forms such as une écrivaine have also begun to appear.

c) The following nouns change meaning according to gender:

	MASCULINE	FEMININE
aide	male assistant	assistance, female assistant
crêpe	mourning band	pancake
critique	critic	criticism
faux	forgery	scythe
livre	book	pound
manche	handle	sleeve
manœuvre	labourer	manoeuvre
mémoire	memorandum	memory
mode	method, way	fashion
mort	dead man	death
moule	mould	mussel
page	pageboy	page
pendule	pendulum	clock
physique	physique	physics
poêle	stove	frying pan
poste	post (job), set	post office
somme	nap	sum
tour	trick, tour	tower
trompette	trumpeter	trumpet
vapeur	steamer	steam
vase	vase	silt
voile	veil	sail

d) A few words vary in gender according to their usage. The plural noun gens is regarded as feminine when it follows an adjective, and masculine when it precedes it:

de bonnes gens	**des** gens **ennuyeux**
good people	*boring people*

amour, délice and orgue are masculine when used in the singular and feminine when used in the plural:

un **amour de** jeunesse	des **amours** maheureuses
an old flame	*unhappy love affairs*
un **délice** inoubliable	des **délices** infinies
an unforgettable delight	*infinite delights*
un **orgue** électrique	les **grandes** orgues
an electric organ	*the great organ*

e) City names

Some city names are traditionally feminine:

La Rochelle	La Haye	Alger la Blanche
La Rochelle	*The Hague*	*Algiers, the white city*

Others are masculine in everyday usage:

le Paris **des années 30**	le Londres **de mon souvenir**
Paris in the 30s	*the London I remember*
le vieux Nice	Berlin **fut totalement** détruit
old Nice	*Berlin was completely destroyed*

In literary French, however, city names are feminine:

Caen **fut prise après de terribles bombardements**
Caen was taken after a terrible bombardment

B THE FORMATION OF FEMININES

The feminine of nouns may be formed in the following ways:

1 By adding an e to the masculine form:

un ami	une amie
a (male) friend	*a (female) friend*
un Hollandais	une Hollandaise
a Dutchman	*a Dutch woman*

Note that nouns which end in -e in the masculine form do not change:

un élève	une élève
a (male) pupil	*a (female) pupil*

Note also that the addition of an e often entails an alteration of the masculine form:

i) nouns ending in -t and -n double the final consonant:

le chien	la chienne *(dog/bitch)*
le chat	la chatte *(cat)*

ii) nouns ending in -er add a grave accent to the e immediately preceding the r:

un ouvrier une ouvrière *(workman/female worker)*

iii) nouns ending in -eur change into -euse:

le vendeur la vendeuse *(male/female shop assistant)*

However, a few nouns ending in -eur change into -eresse:

le pécheur la pécheresse *(sinner)*

iv) nouns ending in -teur change into -teuse or -trice according to the following guidelines:

if the stem of the word is also that of a present participle the feminine form ends in -euse:

le chanteur la chanteuse *(male/female singer)*

if the stem is not that of a present participle, the feminine form ends in -trice:

le lecteur la lectrice *(male/female reader)*

v) nouns ending in -f change into -ve:

le veuf la veuve *(widower/widow)*

vi) nouns ending in -x change into -se:

un époux une épouse *(husband/wife)*

vii) nouns ending in -eau change into -elle:

le jumeau la jumelle *(male/female twin)*

2 By using a different word (as in English):

le beau-fils	la belle-fille *(son-/daughter-in-law)*
le beau-père	la belle-mère *(father-/mother-in-law)*
le bélier	la brebis *(ram/ewe)*

le bœuf	la vache	*(ox/cow)*
le canard	la cane	*(drake/duck)*
le cheval	la jument	*(horse/mare)*
le cerf	la biche	*(stag/hind)*
le coq	la poule	*(cock/hen)*
le fils	la fille	*(son/daughter)*
le frère	la sœur	*(brother/sister)*
un homme	une femme	*(man/woman)*
un jars	une oie	*(gander/goose)*
le mâle	la femelle	*(male/female)*
le neveu	la nièce	*(nephew/niece)*
un oncle	une tante	*(uncle/aunt)*
le parrain	la marraine	*(godfather/godmother)*
le père	la mère	*(father/mother)*
le porc	la truie	*(pig/sow)*
le roi	la reine	*(king/queen)*

3 By adding the word femme (or femelle for animals):

une femme médecin *(doctor)*
un perroquet femelle *(female parrot)*

4 *Irregular feminine forms*

un abbé	une abbesse	*(abbot/abbess)*
un âne	une ânesse	*(donkey)*
le comte	la comtesse	*(count/countess)*
le dieu	la déesse	*(god/goddess)*
le duc	la duchesse	*(duke/duchess)*
un Esquimau	une Esquimaude	*(Eskimo)*
le fou	la folle	*(madman/mad woman)*
un Grec	une Grecque	*(Greek)*
un héros	une héroïne	*(hero/heroine)*
un hôte	une hôtesse	*(host/hostess)*
le maître	la maîtresse	*(master/mistress)*
le prêtre	la prêtresse	*(priest/priestess)*
le prince	la princesse	*(prince/princess)*
le tigre	la tigresse	*(tiger/tigress)*
le Turc	la Turque	*(Turk)*
le vieux	la vieille	*(old man/old woman)*

C THE FORMATION OF PLURALS

1 Most nouns form their plural by adding s to the singular:

le vin	les vins	*wine*
un étudiant	des étudiants	*student*

2 Nouns ending in -s, -x or -z remain unchanged:

le bras	les bras	*arm*
la voix	les voix	*voice*
le nez	les nez	*nose*

3 Nouns ending in -au, -eau and -eu add x to the singular:

le tuyau	les tuyaux	*drainpipe*
le bateau	les bateaux	*boat*
le jeu	les jeux	*game*

But: le landau | les landaus | *pram*
le bleu | les bleus | *bruise*
le pneu | les pneus | *tyre*

4 Nouns ending in -al change to -aux:

le journal | les journaux | *newspaper*

But: le bal | les bals | *dance*
le carnaval | les carnavals | *carnival*
le festival | les festivals | *festival*

5 Nouns ending in -ail change to -aux:

le bail	les baux	*lease*
le travail	les travaux	*work*
le vitrail	les vitraux	*stained-glass window*

But: le détail | les détails | *detail*
l'épouvantail | les épouvantails | *scarecrow*
l'éventail | les éventails | *fan*

le rail | les rails | *rail*

6 Nouns ending in -ou:

a) Seven nouns ending in -ou add x in the plural:

le bijou	les bijoux	*jewel*
le caillou	les cailloux	*pebble*
le chou	les choux	*cabbage*
le genou	les genoux	*knee*
le hibou	les hiboux	*owl*
le joujou	les joujoux	*toy*
le pou	les poux	*louse*

b) Other nouns ending in -ou add s:

le clou | les clous | *nail*

7 Plural of compound nouns:

Each noun ought to be checked individually in a dictionary:

eg | le chou-fleur | les choux-fleurs | *cauliflower*
le beau-père | les beaux-pères | *father-in-law*

But: un essuie-glace | des essuie-glaces | *windscreen wiper*
le tire-bouchon | les tire-bouchons | *corkscrew*

8 Irregular plurals:

un œil	des yeux	*eye*
le ciel	les cieux	*sky*
Monsieur	Messieurs	*Mr*
Madame	Mesdames	*Mrs*
Mademoiselle	Mesdemoiselles	*Miss*

9 Collective nouns:

a) Some nouns are singular in French but plural in English:

le bétail	*cattle*
la recette	*takings*
la police	*police*

la police a arrêté certains grévistes
the police have arrested some strikers

b) Others are plural in French but singular in English:

le nouvelles	*news*
les capitaux	*capital*
les cheveux	*hair*

les nouvelles sont bonnes
the news is good

10 Proper nouns:

a) Ordinary family names are invariable:

j'ai rencontré les Leblanc
I met the Leblancs

b) Historical names add -s:

les Stuarts | les Bourbons | les Tudors
the Stuarts | *the Bourbons* | *the Tudors*

4 ADJECTIVES

Adjectives usually accompany a noun (or a pronoun) and provide extra information about what someone or something is like:

une grande ville
a large city

un film intéressant
an interesting film

elle est espagnole
she is Spanish

c'était ennuyeux
it was boring

A AGREEMENT OF ADJECTIVES

In French, adjectives agree in number and gender with the noun or pronoun to which they refer. Therefore French adjectives have four different forms which are determined by the noun they accompany:

- masculine singular (basic form, found in the dictionary)
- feminine singular
- masculine plural
- feminine plural

un passeport vert	**une voiture** verte
a green passport	*a green car*
des gants verts	**des chaussettes** vertes
green gloves	*green socks*

Note that if two singular words share the same adjective, the adjective will be in the plural:

un foulard et un bonnet rouges
a red scarf and (a red) hat

If one of these words is feminine and the other masculine, the adjective will be in the masculine plural:

une robe et un manteau noirs
a black dress and (a black) coat

B FEMININE FORMS OF ADJECTIVES

1 General rule

Add the letter e to the masculine singular form:

MASCULINE	FEMININE
grand	grande
amusant	amusante
anglais	anglaise
bronzé	bronzée

un livre amusant	**une histoire** amusante
an amusing book	*an amusing story*
il est bronzé	**elle est** bronzée
he is suntanned	*she is suntanned*

2 Adjectives already ending in -e

These do not change:

MASCULINE	FEMININE
rouge	rouge
jeune	jeune
malade	malade

mon père est malade	**ma mère est** malade
my father is ill	*my mother is ill*

3 Others

The spelling of some adjectives changes when the e is added:

a) The following masculine endings generally double the final consonant before adding e:

MASCULINE ENDING	FEMININE ENDING
-el	-elle
-eil	-eille
-en	-enne
-on	-onne
-as	-asse
-et	-ette

MASCULINE		FEMININE
réel	*(real)*	réelle
cruel	*(cruel)*	cruelle
pareil	*(similar)*	pareille
ancien	*(old)*	ancienne
italien	*(Italian)*	italienne
bon	*(good)*	bonne
gras	*(greasy)*	grasse
bas	*(low)*	basse

muet	*(dumb)*	muette
net	*(clear)*	nette
un problème actuel		**la vie** actuelle
a topical problem		*present-day life*
un bon conseil		**c'est une bonne recette**
good advice		*it's a good recipe*

Note, however, that the feminine ending of some common adjectives in -et is -ète instead of -ette:

MASCULINE		FEMININE
complet	*(complete)*	complète
incomplet	*(incomplete)*	incomplète
concret	*(concrete)*	concrète
discret	*(discreet)*	discrète
inquiet	*(worried)*	inquiète
secret	*(secret)*	secrète

b) MASCULINE IN -er — FEMININE IN -ère

cher	*(dear)*	chère
fier	*(proud)*	fière
dernier	*(last)*	dernière

c) MASCULINE IN -x — FEMININE IN -se

heureux	*(happy)*	heureuse
malheureux	*(unhappy)*	malheureuse
sérieux	*(serious)*	sérieuse
jaloux	*(jealous)*	jalouse

But:

doux	*(soft)*	douce
faux	*(false)*	fausse
roux	*(red-haired)*	rousse
vieux	*(old)*	vieille

d) MASCULINE IN -eur — FEMININE IN -euse

menteur	*(lying)*	menteuse
trompeur	*(deceitful)*	trompeuse

This rule, however, applies only when the stem of the adjective is also the stem of a present participle (eg mentant, trompant). The following five adjectives simply add an e to the feminine, -eur becoming -eure:

MASCULINE		FEMININE
extérieur	*(external)*	extérieure
intérieur	*(internal)*	intérieure
inférieur	*(inferior)*	inférieure
supérieur	*(superior)*	supérieure
meilleur	*(better)*	meilleure

The feminine ending of the remaining adjectives in -teur is -trice:

MASCULINE		FEMININE
protecteur	*(protective)*	protectrice
destructeur	*(destructive)*	destructrice

e) MASCULINE IN -f — FEMININE IN -ve

neuf	*(new)*	neuve
vif	*(lively)*	vive
naïf	*(naive)*	naïve
actif	*(active)*	active
passif	*(passive)*	passive
positif	*(positive)*	positive
bref	*(brief)*	brève *(note the è)*

f) MASCULINE IN -c — FEMININE IN -che or -que

blanc	*(white)*	blanche
franc	*(frank)*	franche
sec	*(dry)*	sèche *(note the è)*
public	*(public)*	publique
turc	*(Turkish)*	turque
grec	*(Greek)*	grecque *(note the c)*

g) The following five common adjectives have an irregular feminine form and two forms for the masculine singular; the second masculine form, based on the feminine form, is used before words starting with a vowel or a silent h:

MASCULINE	FEMININE	MASCULINE 2
beau (beautiful)	belle	bel
nouveau (new)	nouvelle	nouvel
vieux (old)	vieille	vieil
fou (mad)	folle	fol
mou (soft)	molle	mol

un beau lac a beautiful lake	une belle vue a beautiful view	un bel enfant a beautiful child
un nouveau disque a new record	la nouvelle année the new year	un nouvel ami a new friend
un vieux tableau an old painting	la vieille ville the old town	un vieil homme an old man

h) Other irregular feminines:

MASCULINE		FEMININE
favori	(favourite)	favorite
gentil	(nice)	gentille
nul	(no)	nulle
frais	(fresh)	fraîche
malin	(shrewd)	maligne
sot	(foolish)	sotte
long	(long)	longue
aigu	(sharp)	aiguë
ambigu	(ambiguous)	ambiguë
chic	(elegant)	chic
châtain	(chestnut)	châtain

C PLURALS OF ADJECTIVES

1 General rule

The masculine and feminine plural of adjectives is formed by adding an s to the singular form:

un vélo neuf a new bike	des vélos neufs new bikes
une belle fleur a beautiful flower	de belles fleurs beautiful flowers
le livre intéressant the interesting book	les livres intéressants the interesting books

2 Adjectives ending in -s or -x

If the masculine singular ends in -s or -x, the plural form does not take an s:

il est heureux he's happy	ils sont heureux they are happy
un touriste anglais an English tourist	des touristes anglais English tourists

3 Others

A few masculine plurals are irregular (the feminine plurals are all regular):

a)

SINGULAR IN -al		PLURAL IN -aux
normal	(normal)	normaux
brutal	(brutal)	brutaux
loyal	(loyal)	loyaux
But: fatal	(fatal)	fatals
natal	(native)	natals
naval	(naval)	navals

Note that the adjective final (final) has two masculine plural forms: finals and finaux.

b)

SINGULAR IN -eau		PLURAL IN -eaux
beau	(beautiful)	beaux
nouveau	(new)	nouveaux

D POSITION OF ADJECTIVES

1 Unlike English adjectives, French adjectives usually follow the noun:

un métier intéressant an interesting job	des parents modernes modern parents

Adjectives of colour and nationality always follow the noun:

des chaussures rouges red shoes	le drapeau britannique the British flag

2 However, the following common adjectives generally come before the noun:

beau	beautiful
bon	good
court	short
gentil	nice
grand	big, tall
gros	fat
haut	high
jeune	young
joli	pretty
long	long
mauvais	bad
méchant	nasty, naughty
meilleur	better
moindre	lesser, least
petit	small
pire	worse
vieux	old
vilain	nasty, ugly

3 Some adjectives have a different meaning according to their position:

	BEFORE NOUN	AFTER NOUN
ancien	former	ancient
brave	good	brave
certain	some	sure
cher	dear	expensive
dernier	last (final)	last (latest)
grand	great (people only)	big, tall
même	same	very
pauvre	poor (pitiable)	poor (not rich)
propre	own	clean
seul	single, only	alone, lonely
simple	mere	simple
vrai	real	true

mon ancien métier my former job	un tableau ancien an old painting
un brave type a nice fellow	un homme brave a brave man
un certain charme a certain charm	un fait certain a definite fact
chère Brigitte dear Brigitte	un cadeau cher an expensive present
la dernière séance the last performance	le mois dernier last month
une grande vedette a great star	un homme assez grand a fairly tall man
le même endroit the same place	la vérité même the truth itself
mon pauvre ami! my poor friend!	des gens pauvres poor people
mon propre frère my own brother	une chambre propre a clean room

mon seul **espoir**	**un homme** seul
my only hope	*a lonely man*
un simple **employé**	**des goûts** simples
an ordinary employee	*simple tastes*
un vrai **casse-pieds**	**une histoire** vraie
a real bore	*a true story*

If a noun is accompanied by several adjectives, the same rules apply to each of them:

le bon vieux **temps**
the good old days

un joli **foulard** rouge
a pretty red scarf

E COMPARATIVE AND SUPERLATIVE OF ADJECTIVES

Persons or things can be compared by using:

1. *the comparative form of the adjective:*

   more ... than
   ...er than
   less ... than
   not as ... as
   as ... as

2. *the superlative form of the adjective:*

   the most ...
   the ...est
   the least ...

1 The comparative

The French comparative is formed as follows:

plus ... (que)	plus **long**	plus **cher**
more ... (than)	*longer*	*more expensive*
... er (than)		
moins ... (que)	moins **long**	moins **récent**
less ... (than)	*less long*	*less recent*
not as ... (as)		
aussi ... (que)	aussi **bon**	aussi **important**
as ... (as)	*as good*	*as important*

une plus grande **maison**
a larger house

un village plus ancien
an older village

le football est-il plus populaire **que le rugby?**
is football more popular than rugby?

ces gants sont moins chauds **que les autres**
these gloves are less warm than the other ones

elle est beaucoup/bien moins **patiente** que lui
she's far less patient than he is

le problème de la pollution est tout aussi **grave**
the pollution problem is just as serious

2 The superlative

a) *Formation*

le/la/les plus ...	*the most ... , the ...est*
le/la/les moins ...	*the least ...*

le plus grand **pays**	la plus grande **ville**
the largest country	*the largest city*
les plus grands **acteurs**	les plus grandes **voitures**
the greatest actors	*the largest cars*

b) *Word order*

   i) The normal rules governing word order of adjectives apply. When a superlative adjective comes after the noun, the article is used twice, before the noun and before the adjective:

   le plat le plus **délicieux**
   the most delicious dish

   l'histoire la plus **passionnante**
   the most exciting story

   ii) When a possessive adjective is used, there are two possible constructions, depending on the position of the adjective:

   ma plus forte **matière**
   my best subject

   or: **mon besoin** le plus **urgent est de trouver un emploi**
   my most urgent need is to find a job

c) 'in' is normally translated by **de**:

   la plus jolie maison du **quartier/de la** ville
   the prettiest house in the area/town

   le restaurant le plus cher **de France**
   the most expensive restaurant in France

   Note that verbs following the superlative usually take the subjunctive (see p B33).

3 Irregular comparatives and superlatives

ADJECTIVE	COMPARATIVE	SUPERLATIVE
bon	meilleur	le meilleur
good	*better*	*best*
mauvais	pire	le pire
bad	plus mauvais	le plus mauvais
	worse	*the worst*
petit	moindre	le moindre
small	plus petit	le plus petit
	smaller, lesser	*the smallest, the least*

Note that **pire** and **le pire** are, strictly speaking, the correct comparative and superlative forms of **mauvais**. **Plus mauvais** and **le plus mauvais** can also be found in everyday French, however, with a slight difference in meaning: **pire** and **le pire** express the absolute (ie one cannot conceive of a worse example of ...) while **plus mauvais** and **le plus mauvais** indicate a comparison of a lesser degree:

il n'y a pas de pire **professeur que lui**
he is the worst teacher of all

c'est la pire **chose qui pouvait lui arriver**
it's the worst thing that could happen to him

ma note est plus mauvaise **que la tienne**
my mark is worse than yours

c'est le plus mauvais **élève de la classe**
he's the worst pupil in the class

Note, too, that **moindre** usually means 'less in importance', and **plus petit** 'less in size':

le moindre **de mes soucis**
the least of my worries

elle est plus petite **que moi**
she is smaller than I (am)

F ADJECTIVES OF NATIONALITY

1 French, unlike English, does not use capital letters for adjectives of nationality. Only nouns indicating nationality are written with a capital letter in French:

une voiture anglaise	**une Anglaise**
an English car	*an English woman*

2 An adjective of nationality in English is sometimes best translated by a genitive construction in French:

l'ambassade de France	**l'équipe de France de rugby**
the French embassy	*the French rugby team*
l'équipe de Nantes	**l'équipe de Glasgow**
the Nantes team	*the Glasgow or Glaswegian team*

le championnat de France
the French league

la Coupe de France de football
the French football cup

la Grand Prix du Brésil
the Brazilian Grand Prix

la terre de France
French soil

la couronne de France
*the French crown, the crown
of France*

les côtes de France
the French coastline

une grammaire de l'anglais
an English grammar

5 ADVERBS

Adverbs are normally used with a verb to express:

how		ADVERBS OF
how		manner
when		time
where	an action is done	place
with how much		intensity
intensity		
to what extent		quantity

A ADVERBS OF MANNER

These are usually formed by adding -ment to the adjective (like -ly
in English):

1 If the adjective ends in a consonant, -ment is added to its feminine form:

ADJECTIVE	ADVERB
(masc, fem)	
doux, douce *(soft)*	doucement *(softly)*
franc, franche *(frank)*	franchement *(frankly)*
final, finale *(final)*	finalement *(finally)*

2 If the adjective ends in a vowel, -ment is added to its masculine
form:

ADJECTIVE	ADVERB
absolu *(absolute)*	absolument *(absolutely)*
désespéré *(desperate)*	désespérément *(desperately)*
vrai *(true)*	vraiment *(truly)*
simple *(simple)*	simplement *(simply)*

But: gai *(cheerful)* gaiement *or*
gaîment *(cheerfully)*

nouveau *(new)* nouvellement *(newly)*
fou *(mad)* follement *(madly)*

3 Many adverbs have irregular forms:

a) Some change the e of the feminine form of the adjective to é
before adding -ment:

ADJECTIVE	ADVERB
commun *(common)*	communément *(commonly)*
précis *(precise)*	précisément *(precisely)*
profond *(deep)*	profondément *(deeply)*
énorme *(enormous)*	énormément *(enormously)*
aveugle *(blind)*	aveuglément *(blindly)*

b) Adjectives which end in -ent and -ant change to -emment
and -amment. Note that both endings are pronounced like
amant:

ADJECTIVE	ADVERB
prudent *(careful)*	prudemment *(carefully)*
évident *(obvious)*	évidemment *(obviously)*
brillant *(brilliant)*	brillamment *(brilliantly)*

But: lent *(slow)* lentement *(slowly)*

4 Some adverbs are completely irregular, including some of the
most commonly used ones:

ADJECTIVE	ADVERB
bon *(good)*	bien *(well)*
bref *(brief)*	brièvement *(briefly)*
gentil *(kind)*	gentiment *(kindly)*
mauvais *(bad)*	mal *(badly)*
meilleur *(better)*	mieux *(better)*

5 Some adjectives are also used as adverbs in certain set expressions:

parler bas/haut *or* fort	to speak softly/loudly
coûter/payer cher	to cost/pay a lot
s'arrêter net	to stop short
couper court	to cut short
voir clair	to see clearly
marcher droit	to walk straight
travailler dur	to work hard
chanter faux/juste	to sing off key/in tune
sentir mauvais/bon	to smell bad/good
refuser net	to refuse point blank

6 After verbs relating to saying something or looking at something
in French an adverbial phrase is often preferred to an adverb:

'tu m'écriras?' dit-il d'une voix triste
'will you write to me?' he said sadly

elle nous a regardés d'un air dédaigneux
she looked at us disdainfully

7 English adverbs may be expressed in French by a preposition
followed by a noun:

sans soin	carelessly
avec fierté	proudly
avec amour	lovingly

B ADVERBS OF TIME

These are not usually formed from adjectives. The commonest ones
are the following:

alors	then
après	afterwards
aujourd'hui	today
aussitôt	at once
bientôt	soon
d'abord	first
déjà	already
demain	tomorrow
encore	still, again
pas encore	not yet
enfin	at last, finally
hier	yesterday
parfois	sometimes
rarement	seldom
souvent	often
tard	late
tôt	early
toujours	always
tout de suite	immediately

c'est déjà Noël!
it's Christmas already!

tu as déjà essayé?
have you tried before?

il mange encore!
he's still eating!

elle n'est pas encore
arrivée
she hasn't arrived yet

C ADVERBS OF PLACE

Like adverbs of time, these are not usually formed from adjectives. The commonest ones are the following:

ailleurs	somewhere else, elsewhere
ici	here
là	there
loin	far away
dessus	on top, on it
au-dessus	over, above
dessous	underneath
au-dessous	below
dedans	inside
dehors	outside
devant	in front, ahead
derrière	behind
partout	everywhere

ne restez pas dehors!
don't stay outside!

mon nom est marqué dessus
my name is written on it

qu'est-ce qu'il y a dedans?
what's inside?

passez devant
go in front

D ADVERBS OF INTENSITY AND QUANTITY

These may be used with a verb, an adjective or another adverb. The commonest ones are the following:

à peine	hardly
assez	enough, quite
autant	as much/many
beaucoup	a lot, much/many
combien	how much/many
comme	how
moins	less
plus	more
presque	nearly
peu	little
seulement	only
si	so
tant	so much/many
tellement	so much/many
très	very
trop	too, too much/many
un peu	a little

vous avez assez bu!
you've had enough to drink!

il ne fait pas assez chaud
it's not warm enough

nous avons beaucoup ri
we laughed a lot

comme c'est amusant!
how funny!

je vais un peu mieux
I'm feeling a little better

c'est si fatigant!
it's so tiring!

elle parle trop
she talks too much

il est très timide
he's very shy

Note that all of these adverbs, except à peine, comme, presque, si, très and seulement, may be followed by de and a noun to express a quantity (see p B60).

E POSITION OF ADVERBS

1 Adverbs usually follow verbs:

je vais rarement au théâtre
I seldom go to the theatre

comme vous conduisez prudemment
you do drive carefully!

2 With compound tenses, shorter adverbs usually come between the auxiliary and the past participle:

j'ai enfin terminé
I have finished at last

il me l'a déjà dit
he's already told me

nous y sommes souvent allés
we've often gone there

elle avait beaucoup souffert
she had suffered a lot

3 Adverbs of place and many adverbs of time, however, follow the past participle:

je l'ai rencontré hier
I met him yesterday

elle avait cherché partout
she had looked everywhere

mettez-le dehors
put it outside

tu t'es couché tard?
did you go to bed late?

4 Adverbs usually come before adjectives or other adverbs, as in English:

très rarement
very seldom

trop vite
too quickly

elle est vraiment belle
she is really beautiful

F COMPARATIVE AND SUPERLATIVE OF ADVERBS

1 The comparative and superlative of adverbs are formed in the same way as those of adjectives:

ADVERB	COMPARATIVE	SUPERLATIVE
souvent *often*	plus souvent (que) *more often (than)*	le plus souvent *(the) most often*
	moins souvent (que) *less often (than)* *not as often (as)*	le moins souvent *(the) least often*
	aussi souvent (que) *as often (as)*	

Note that the superlative of the adverb always takes the masculine singular article le:

je le vois plus souvent qu'avant
I see him more often than I used to

il conduit moins prudemment que moi
he drives less carefully than I do
he doesn't drive as carefully as I do

c'est lui qui conduit le moins prudemment
he's the one who drives the least carefully

je sais cuisiner aussi bien que toi!
I can cook as well as you!

Note:

a) 'as ... as possible' is translated either by aussi ... que possible or by le plus ... possible:

as far as possible

aussi loin que possible
le plus loin possible

b) after a negative, aussi is often replaced by si:

pas si vite!
not so fast!

c) In French, the idea of 'not so', 'not as' is often expressed by moins *(less)*:

parle moins fort!
don't talk so loud!

2 Irregular comparatives and superlatives

ADVERB	COMPARATIVE	SUPERLATIVE
beaucoup *much, a lot*	plus *more*	le plus *(the) most*

bien	mieux	le mieux
well	*better*	*(the) best*

mal	pis	le pis
	plus mal	le plus mal
badly	*worse*	*(the) worst*

peu	moins	le moins
little	*less*	*(the) least*

il est mieux payé que moi
he is better paid than me

c'est lui le mieux payé
he's the best paid

Note:

a) mieux/le mieux must not be confused with meilleur/le meilleur which are adjectives, used in front of a noun.

elle chante mieux que toi
she sings better than you (do)

c'est elle qui chante le mieux
she sings best

elle est meilleure chanteuse que toi
she is a better singer than you

c'est la meilleure chanteuse
she is the best singer

b) pis/le pis are only found in certain set expressions or in literary French:

tant pis
too bad

de mal en pis
from bad to worse

il n'y a rien de pis que cela
there is nothing worse than that

on en dit pis que pendre
nobody has a good word to say about it

6 PRONOUNS AND CORRESPONDING ADJECTIVES

A DEMONSTRATIVES

1 Demonstrative adjectives

a) *CE*

ce is often used to point out a particular person or thing, or persons or things. It is followed by the noun to which it refers and agrees in number and gender with that noun:

●	with a masculine singular noun:	ce (cet)	*this/that*
●	with a feminine singular noun:	cette	*this/that*
●	with a plural noun (masc or fem):	ces	*these/those*

ce roman m'a beaucoup plu   **il a neigé ce matin**
I really liked this novel   *it snowed this morning*

cette chanson m'énerve   **cette fois, c'est fini!**
that song gets on my nerves   *this time, it's over!*

tu trouves que ces lunettes me vont bien?
do you think these glasses suit me?

cet is used instead of ce in front of a masculine singular word that begins with a vowel or a silent h:

cet été   **cet hôtel**
this summer   *that hotel*

b) *-CI and -LÀ*

French does not have separate words to distinguish between 'this' and 'that'. However, when a particular emphasis is being placed on a person or object, or when a contrast is being made between persons or objects, -ci and -là are added to the noun:

-ci translates the idea of   *this/these*
-là translates the idea of   *that/those*

je suis très occupé ces jours-ci
I'm very busy these days

que faisiez-vous ce soir-là?
what were you doing that evening?

tu préfères cette robe-ci ou cette robe-là?
do you prefer this dress or that dress?

2 Demonstrative pronouns

Demonstrative pronouns are used instead of a noun with ce/cette/ces. They are:

celui, celle, ceux, celles
ce
ceci, cela, ça

a) *CELUI*

celui agrees in number and gender with the noun it refers to. It has four different forms:

	MASCULINE	FEMININE
SINGULAR	celui	celle
PLURAL	ceux	celles

celui, celle, ceux and celles cannot be used on their own. They are used:

● with -ci or -là, for emphasis or for contrast:

celui-ci	celle-ci	*this (one)*
celui-là	celle-là	*that (one)*
ceux-ci	celles-ci	*these (ones)*
ceux-là	celles-là	*those (ones)*

j'aime bien ce maillot mais celui-là est moins cher
I like this swimsuit, but that one is cheaper

je voudrais ces fleurs – lesquelles? celles-ci ou celles-là?
I'd like these flowers – which ones? these or those?

● with de + noun, to express possession:

je préfère mon ordinateur à celui de Jean-Claude
I prefer my computer to Jean-Claude's

range ta chambre plutôt que celle de ta sœur
tidy your own bedroom rather than your sister's

mes parents sont moins sévères que ceux de Nicole
my parents aren't as strict as Nicole's

les douches municipales sont mieux que celles du camping
the public showers are better than those at the campsite

● with the relative pronouns qui, que, dont to introduce a relative clause (for use of these relative pronouns, see p B22).

celui/celle/ceux/celles qui	*the one(s) who/which*
celui/celle/ceux/celles que	*the one(s) whom/which*
celui/celle/ceux/celles dont	*the one(s) of which/whose*

lequel est ton père? celui qui a une moustache?
which one is your father? the one with the moustache?

regarde cette voiture! celle qui est garée au coin
look at that car! the one which is parked at the corner

deux filles, celles qu'il avait rencontrées la veille
two girls, the ones he had met the day before

voilà mon copain, celui dont je t'ai parlé l'autre jour
here's my friend, the one I told you about the other day

b) *CE*

ce (meaning 'it' or 'that') is normally used with the verb être:

c'est	**ce serait**	**c'était**
it's/that's	*it/that would be*	*it/that was*

Note that ce changes to c' before an e or an é.

● with a noun or pronoun, ce is used to identify people or things, or to emphasize them; it is translated in a variety of ways:

qu'est-ce que c'est? – c'est mon billet d'avion
what's that? – it's my plane ticket

qui est-ce? – c'est moi	**ce doit être lui**
who is it? – it's me	*that must be him*
c'est un artiste bien connu	**c'était une bonne idée**
he's a well-known artist	*it was a good idea*
ce sont mes amis	**c'est la dernière fois!**
they're my friends	*it's the last time!*
c'est elle qui l'a fait	**c'est celui que j'ai vu**
she's the one who did it	*he's the one I saw*
ce sont des gens sympathiques	**ce ne sont pas mes chaussures**
they're nice people	*those aren't my shoes*

● before an adjective, ce is used to refer to an idea, an event or a fact which has already been mentioned; it does not refer to any specific noun:

c'était formidable	**ce serait amusant**
it was great	*it would be funny*
oui, c'est vrai	**c'est sûr?**
yes, that's true	*is that definite?*
ce n'est pas grave	**c'est bon à entendre**
it doesn't matter or it's not serious	*that's good to hear*
c'est exact!	**c'est rare qu'il pleuve en juin**
that's right!	*it doesn't often rain in June*

Note that the translation of it is an area of some difficulty for students of French, as it is sometimes translated by ce and sometimes by il/elle; see p B66 for further information.

c) *CECI, CELA, ÇA*

ceci (this), cela (that) and ça (that) are used to refer to an idea, an event, a fact or an object. They never refer to a particular noun already mentioned.

non, je n'aime pas ça!	**ah, bon? cela m'étonne**
no, I don't like that!	*really? that surprises me*
ça, c'est un acteur!	**souvenez-vous de ceci**
that's what I call an actor!	*remember this*
ça m'est égal	**cela ne vous regarde pas**
I don't mind	*that's none of your business*
buvez ceci, ça vous fera du bien	
drink this, it'll do you good	
ça alors!	
well, really!	
cela s'appelle comment, en anglais?	
what do you call this in English?	

Note that ceci is not very common in French; cela and ça are often used to translate 'this' as well as 'that'; ça is used far more frequently than cela in spoken French.

B INDEFINITE ADJECTIVES AND PRONOUNS

1 Indefinite adjectives

They are:

MASCULINE	FEMININE	
autre(s)	autre(s)	*other*
certain(s)	certaine(s)	*certain*
chaque	chaque	*each, every*
même(s)	même(s)	*same*
plusieurs	plusieurs	*several*
quelque(s)	quelque(s)	*some*
tel(s)	telle(s)	*such*
tout (tous)	toute(s)	*all, every*

Note that, when used as indefinite adjectives, all the above adjectives are placed before the nouns to which they refer. Certain and même can be found after the noun but they will then have a different meaning (see p B10).

a) *CHAQUE and PLUSIEURS*

chaque (each) is always singular, plusieurs (several) always plural; the feminine form is the same as the masculine form:

j'y vais chaque jour	**chaque personne**
I go there every day	*each person*
plusieurs années	**il a plusieurs amis**
several years	*he's got several friends*

b) *AUTRE, MÊME and QUELQUE*

autre (other), même (same) and quelque (some) agree in number with the noun that follows; the feminine is the same as the masculine:

je voudrais un autre café	**d'autres couleurs**
I'd like another coffee	*other colours*
la même taille	**les mêmes touristes**
the same size	*the same tourists*
quelque temps après	**à quelques kilomètres**
some time later	*a few kilometres away*

c) *CERTAIN, TEL and TOUT*

certain (certain, some), tel (such) and tout (all) agree in number and gender with the noun; they have four different forms:

un certain charme	**une certaine dame**
a certain charm	*a certain lady*
à certains moments	**certaines personnes**
at (certain) times	*some people*
un tel homme	**une telle aventure**
such a man	*such an adventure*
de tels avantages	**de telles difficultés**
such advantages	*such difficulties*

quoi! tu as mangé tout le fromage et tous les fruits?
what! you've eaten all the cheese and all the fruit?

toute la journée	**toutes mes matières**
all day long	*all my subjects*

Note:
i) tel: the position of the article un/une with tel is not the same as in English: un tel homme = *such a man*.

ii) tel cannot qualify another adjective; when it is used as an adverb, 'such' is translated by si or tellement:

c'était un si bon repas/un repas tellement bon!
it was such a good meal!

iii) tous les/toutes les are often translated by 'every':

tous les jours	**toutes les places**
every day	*all seats, every seat*

2 Indefinite pronouns

a) These are:

MASCULINE	FEMININE	
aucun	aucune	*none, not any*
autre(s)	autre(s)	*another one, other ones*
certains	certaine(s)	*certain, some*
chacun	chacune	*each one, every one*
on		*everyone, one, someone, you, they, people, we*
personne		*nobody*
plusieurs	plusieurs	*several (ones)*
quelque chose		*something, anything*
quelqu'un		*someone*
quelques-uns	quelques-unes	*some, a few*
rien		*nothing*
tout (tous)	toute(s)	*everything, every one, all*

pas celui-là, l'autre
not that one, the other one

où sont les autres?
where are the others?

certains disent que …
some say that …

personne n'est venu
no one came

qui est là? – personne
who's there? – nobody

qu'as-tu? – rien
what's wrong? – nothing

plusieurs d'entre eux
several of them

chacun pour soi!
every man for himself!

il manque quelque chose?
is anything missing?

dis quelque chose!
say something!

quelqu'un l'a averti
someone warned him

il y a quelqu'un?
is anyone in?

j'ai tout oublié
I've forgotten everything

c'est tout, merci
that's all, thanks

elles sont toutes arrivées
they've all arrived

allons-y tous ensemble
let's all go together

b) Points to note

i) aucun(e), personne and rien: these can be used on their own, but they are more often used with a verb and the negative word ne (see negative expressions, pp B62-3):

personne n'habite ici
no one lives here

il n'y a rien à manger
there's nothing to eat

ii) aucun(e), un(e) autre, d'autres, certain(e)s, plusieurs and quelques-un(e)s: when these pronouns are used as direct objects, the pronoun en must be used before the verb:

je n'en ai lu aucun
I haven't read any (of them)

donne-m'en une autre
give me another one

j'en ai vu d'autres qui étaient moins chers
I saw other ones which were cheaper

j'en connais certains
I know some of them

il y en a plusieurs
there are several

tu m'en donnes quelques-uns?
will you give me a few?

achètes-en quelques-unes
buy a few

iii) personne, quelque chose, rien, plusieurs: when these are followed by an adjective, the preposition de (or d') must be used in front of the adjective:

il n'y a personne de libre
there's no one available

quelque chose de mieux
something better

il y en avait plusieurs de cassés
several of them were broken

rien de grave
nothing serious

iv) autre is commonly used in the following expressions:

quelqu'un d'autre
someone else

quelque chose d'autre
something else

rien d'autre
nothing else

c) *ON*

This pronoun is used in a variety of ways in French. It can mean:

i) *one/you/they/people* in a general sense:

en France, on roule à droite
in France, they drive on the right

on ne sait jamais
you/one never know(s)

on ne doit pas mentir
you shouldn't lie

ii) *someone* (an undefined person)

In this sense, on is often translated by the passive (see p B39):

on me l'a déjà dit
someone's already told me / I've already been told

on vous l'apportera
someone will bring it to you / it will be brought to you

iii) *we*

In spoken French, on is frequently used instead of nous; although it refers to a plural subject, it is followed by the third person singular:

qu'est-ce qu'on fait?
what shall we do?

fais vite, on t'attend!
hurry up, we're waiting for you!

Note that in compound tenses with the auxiliary être, the agreement of the past participle with on is optional:

on est allé au cinéma
on est allés au cinéma
we went to the cinema

on est rentré en taxi
on est rentrées en taxi
we went home by taxi

C INTERROGATIVE AND EXCLAMATORY ADJECTIVES AND PRONOUNS

1 The interrogative adjective QUEL?

a) Forms

quel *(which, what)* agrees in number and gender with the noun it refers to. It has four forms:

- with a masculine singular noun: quel?
- with a feminine singular noun: quelle?
- with a masculine plural noun: quels?
- with a feminine plural noun: quelles?

b) Direct questions:

quel est votre passe-temps favori?
what's your favourite pastime?

quelle heure est-il?
what time is it?

quels jours as-tu de libres?
which days have you got free?

quelles affaires comptes-tu prendre avec toi?
what/which things do you intend to take with you?

c) Indirect questions:

je ne sais pas quel CD choisir
I don't know which CD to choose

il se demande quelle veste lui va le mieux
he's wondering which jacket suits him best

2 The exclamatory adjective QUEL!

quel! has the same forms as the interrogative adjective quel?:

quel dommage!
what a pity!

quelle belle maison!
what a beautiful house!

quels imbéciles!
what idiots!

quelles jolies chaussures!
what lovely shoes!

3 Interrogative pronouns

These are:

lequel/laquelle/ lesquels/lesquelles?	*which (one(s))?*
qui?	*who?/whom?*
que?	*what?*
quoi?	*what?*
ce qui	*what*
ce que	*what*

ce qui and ce que are used only in indirect questions; all other interrogative pronouns can be used both in direct and indirect questions.

a) *LEQUEL?*

i) forms

lequel *(which?, which one?)* agrees in gender and in number with the noun it stands for:

● with a masculine singular noun: **lequel?** *which (one)?*
● with a feminine singular noun: **laquelle?** *which (one)?*
● with a masculine plural noun: **lesquels?** *which (ones)?*
● with a feminine plural noun: **lesquelles?** *which (ones)?*

After the prepositions à and de, the following changes occur:

à + lequel?	→	auquel?
à + lesquels?	→	auxquels?
à + lesquelles?	→	auxquelles?

de + lequel?	→	duquel?
de + lesquels?	→	desquels?
de + lesquelles?	→	desquelles?

Note that à/de + **laquelle?** do not contract.

ii) direct questions:

je cherche un hôtel; lequel recommandez-vous?
I'm looking for a hotel; which one do you recommend?

nous avons plusieurs couleurs; vous préférez laquelle?
we have several colours; which one do you prefer?

lesquels de ces livres sont à toi?
which of these books are yours?

je voudrais essayer ces chaussures – lesquelles?
I would like to try these shoes on – which ones?

iii) indirect questions:

demande-lui lequel de ces ordinateurs est le moins cher
ask him/her which (one) of these computers is the cheapest

c'est dans une de ces rues mais je ne sais plus laquelle
it's in one of these streets, but I can't remember which one

b) *QUI?*

qui *(who?, whom?)* is used to refer to people; it can be both subject and object and can be used after a preposition:

qui t'a accompagné?
who came/went with you?

qui as-tu appelé?
who did you call?

tu y vas avec qui?
who are you going with?

c'est pour qui?
who is it for?

pour qui vous prenez-vous?
who do you think you are?

à qui l'as-tu donné?
who did you give it to?

Note that qui does not contract to qu' before a vowel or a silent h:

qui est-ce qu'elle attend?
who is she waiting for?

qui? can be replaced by **qui est-ce qui?** (subject) or **qui est-ce que?** (object) in direct questions:

qui est-ce qui veut du café?
who wants coffee?

qui est-ce que tu as vu?
who did you see?

avec qui est-ce que tu sors ce soir?
who are you going out with tonight?

Note, however, that qui cannot be replaced by **qui est-ce qui** or **qui est-ce que** in indirect questions:

j'aimerais savoir qui vous a dit ça
I'd like to know who told you that

elle se demandait de qui étaient les fleurs
she was wondering who the flowers were from

For more details on the use of qui/que as relative pronouns, see p B22.

c) *QUE?*

que *(what?)* is used to refer to things. It is only used in direct questions, is always a direct object and cannot be used after prepositions:

que désirez-vous?
what do you wish?

qu'a-t-il dit?
what did he say?

que? is rather formal and is usually replaced by **qu'est-ce qui?** or **qu'est-ce que?** in spoken French.

Note that que becomes qu' before a vowel or a silent h.

d) *QU'EST-CE QUI?*

qu'est-ce qui? *(what?)* is used as the subject of a verb; it cannot refer to a person:

qu'est-ce qui t'est arrivé?
what happened to you?

qu'est-ce qui la fait rire?
what makes her laugh?

e) *QU'EST-CE QUE?*

qu'est-ce que? *(what?)* replaces que? as the object of a verb; it becomes qu'est-ce qu' before a vowel or a silent h:

qu'est-ce que tu aimes lire?
what do you like reading?

qu'est-ce qu'il va faire pendant les vacances?
what's he going to do during the holidays?

f) *QUOI?*

quoi? *(what?)* refers to things; it is used:

i) instead of que or qu'est-ce que after a preposition:

à quoi penses-tu?
what are you thinking about?

dans quoi l'as-tu mis?
what did you put it in?

ii) in indirect questions:

demandez-lui de quoi il a besoin
ask him what he needs

je ne sais pas à quoi ça sert
I don't know what it's for

g) *CE QUI, CE QUE*

ce qui and ce que *(what)* are only used in indirect questions; they replace qu'est-ce qui and (qu'est-ce) que.

They are used in the same way as the relative pronouns ce qui and ce que (see p B23).

i) ce qui is used as the subject of the verb in the indirect question (ce qui is the subject of s'est passé in the following example):

nous ne saurons jamais ce qui s'est passé
we'll never know what happened

ii) ce que (ce qu' before a vowel or a silent h) is used as the object of the verb in the indirect question (ce que is the object of il faisait in the following example):

je n'ai pas remarqué ce qu'il faisait
I didn't notice what he was doing

D PERSONAL PRONOUNS

There are four categories of personal pronouns:

- subject pronouns
- object pronouns
- disjunctive pronouns
- reflexive pronouns

For reflexive pronouns, see p B28.

1 Subject pronouns

PERSON	SINGULAR		PLURAL	
1st	je (j')	I	nous	we
2nd	tu	you	vous	you
3rd	il	he, it	ils	they
	elle	she, it	elles	they
	on	one, we, they		

Note:

a) je changes to j' before a vowel or a silent h:

j'ai honte
I'm ashamed

j'adore les frites
I love chips

j'habite en Écosse
I live in Scotland

b) tu and vous

vous can be plural or singular; it is used when speaking to more than one person (plural), or to a stranger or an older person (singular):

pourriez-vous m'indiquer la gare?
could you show me the way to the station?

vous venez, les gars?
are you coming, guys?

tu is used when speaking to a friend, a relative, a younger person, or someone else you know well:

tu viens, Marc?
are you coming, Marc?

c) il/ils, elle/elles may refer to people, animals or things, and must be of the same gender as the noun they replace:

ton stylo? il est là
your pen? there it is

ta montre? elle est là
your watch? there it is

tes gants? ils sont là
your gloves? there they are

tes lunettes? elles sont là
your glasses? there they are

When referring to several nouns of different genders, French uses the masculine plural ils:

j'ai trouvé dans mon sac un stylo et une montre. Ils ne m'appartiennent pas
I found a pen and a watch in my bag. They don't belong to me

d) on: see p B16.

2 Object pronouns

There are three types of object pronouns:

- direct object pronouns
- indirect object pronouns
- the pronouns en and y

a) *Forms*

	PERSON	DIRECT	INDIRECT
SING	1st	me (m') *me*	me (m') *(to) me*
	2nd	te (t') *you*	te (t') *(to) you*
	3rd	le (l') *him, it*	lui *(to) him*
		la (l') *her, it*	lui *(to) her*
PLUR	1st	nous *us*	nous *(to) us*
	2nd	vous *you*	vous *(to) you*
	3rd	les *them*	leur *(to) them*

Note:

i) me, te, le and la change to m', t' and l' before a vowel or a silent h:

il m'énerve!
he gets on my nerves!

je m'habituerai à lui
I'll get used to him

ii) te and vous: the same distinction should be made as between the subject pronouns tu and vous (see D 1b).

iii) le is sometimes used in an impersonal sense to refer to a fact, a statement or an idea which has already been expressed; it is usually not translated in English:

j'irai aux États-Unis un jour; en tout cas je l'espère
I'll go to the States one day; I hope so anyway

elle a eu un bébé – je le sais, elle me l'a dit
she's had a baby – I know, she told me

iv) when used as an indirect object pronoun, lui can be masculine or feminine:

pose-lui la question
ask him/her the question

j'ai décidé de lui offrir un cadeau
I've decided to give him/her a present

v) when they are used with imperatives, moi and toi are used instead of me and te, except when en follows:

écris-moi bientôt
write to me soon

donne m'en
give me some

b) *Position*

In French, object pronouns come immediately before the verb they refer to. With a compound tense, they come before the auxiliary:

on t'attendra ici
we'll wait for you here

je l'ai rencontrée en ville
I met her in town

Note that when there are two verbs, the pronoun comes immediately before the verb to which it refers:

j'aimerais lui demander
I'd like to ask him/her

tu l'as entendu chanter?
have you heard him sing?

In positive commands (the affirmative imperative) the pronoun follows the verb and is joined to it by a hyphen:

regarde-les!
look at them!

parle-lui!
speak to him/her!

dis-nous ce qui s'est passé
tell us what happened

c) *Direct pronouns and indirect pronouns*

i) Direct object pronouns replace a noun which directly follows the verb. They answer the question 'who(m)?' or 'what?'

WHO(M) did you see?
qui as-tu vu?
I saw my friend; I saw him
j'ai vu mon ami; je l'ai vu

tu me connais
you know me
j'aime le voir danser
I like to see him dance

je les ai trouvés
I found them
ne nous ennuie pas!
don't bother us!

ii) Indirect object pronouns replace a noun which follows the verb with a linking preposition (usually à, to whom?). They answer the question 'who to?'

WHO did you speak to?
à qui as-tu parlé?
I spoke to Marc; I spoke to him
j'ai parlé à Marc; je lui ai parlé

elle lui a menti
she lied to him/her
je te donne ce CD
I'm giving this CD to you

je ne leur parle plus
I'm not talking to them any more

iii) le/la/les or lui/leur?

Direct pronouns differ from indirect pronouns only in the 3rd person and great care must be taken to use the correct one.

English indirect object pronouns often look like direct objects; this becomes obvious when the object is placed at the end of the clause, after a linking preposition:

I showed him your photo = I showed your photo to him
je lui ai montré ta photo

This is particularly the case with the following verbs:

acheter	to buy	**offrir**	to offer, to give
donner	to give	**prêter**	to lend
montrer	to show	**vendre**	to sell

je lui ai acheté un livre
I bought him/her a book
= I bought a book for him/her
ne leur prête pas mes affaires
don't lend them my things
= don't lend my things to them

Some verbs take a direct object in English and an indirect object in French (see p B53):

je ne lui ai rien dit
I didn't tell him/her anything
je leur demanderai
I'll ask them

tu lui ressembles
you look like him/her
téléphone-leur
phone them

Some verbs take a direct object in French and an indirect object in English (see p B53):

je l'attends
I'm waiting for him/her
écoutez-les!
listen to them!

d) *Order of object pronouns*

When several object pronouns are used together, they come in the following order:

i) Before the verb:

1	me	te	nous	vous
2	le	la	les	
3		lui	leur	

il me l'a donné
he gave it to me
je vais vous les envoyer
I'll send them to you

ne la leur vends pas
don't sell it to them
je le lui ai acheté
I bought it for him/her

ii) After the verb:

With a positive command (the affirmative imperative), the

order is as follows:

1		le	la		les	
2	moi (m')	toi (t')		nous	vous	
3		lui		leur		

apporte-les-moi!
bring them to me!
prête-la-nous!
lend it to us!

dites-le-lui!
tell him/her!
rends-la-leur!
give it back to them!

3 The pronoun EN

a) *Use*

en is used instead of de + noun. Since de has a variety of meanings, en can be used in a number of ways:

i) It means 'of it/them', but also 'with it/them', 'about it/them', 'from it/there', 'out of it/there':

tu es sûr du prix? – j'en suis sûr
are you sure of the price? – I'm sure of it

je suis content de ce cadeau; j'en suis content
I'm pleased with this present; I'm pleased with it

elle est folle des animaux; elle en est folle
she's crazy about animals; she's crazy about them

il est descendu du train; il en est descendu
he got off the train; he got off it

il revient de Paris; il en revient
he's coming back from Paris; he's coming back from there

ii) Verbal constructions

Particular care should be taken with verbs and expressions which are followed by de + noun. Since de is not always translated in the same way, en may have a number of meanings:

il a envie de ce livre; il en a envie
he wants this book; he wants it

je te remercie de ton aide; je t'en remercie
thank you for your help; thank you for it

tu as besoin de ces papiers? tu en as besoin?
do you need these papers? do you need them?

elle a peur des chiens; elle en a peur
she's afraid of dogs; she's afraid of them

tu te souviens de ce film? tu t'en souviens?
do you remember this film? do you remember it?

iii) 'some'/'any'

en replaces the partitive article (du, de la, des) + noun; it means 'some'/'any':

tu veux du café? – non, je n'en veux pas
do you want (any) coffee? – no, I don't want any

j'achète des fruits? – non, j'en ai chez moi
shall I buy (some) fruit? – no, I've got some at home

il y a de la place? – en voilà là-bas
is there any room? – there's some over there

iv) Expressions of quantity

en must be used with expressions of quantity not followed by a noun. It replaces de + noun and means 'of it/them', but is seldom translated in English:

tu as pris assez d'argent? tu en as pris assez?
did you take enough money? did you take enough?

vous avez combien de frères? – j'en ai deux
how many brothers do you have? – I've got two

j'ai fini mes cigarettes; je vais en acheter un paquet
I've finished my cigarettes; I'm going to buy a packet

b) *Position*

Like object pronouns, en comes immediately before the verb, except with positive commands (the affirmative imperative), where it comes after the verb and is linked to it by a hyphen:

j'en veux un kilo
I want a kilo (of it/them)

j'en ai marre!
I'm fed up (with it)!

prends-en assez!
take enough (of it/them)!

laisses-en aux autres!
leave some for the others!

When used in conjunction with other object pronouns, it always comes last:

ne m'en parlez pas!
don't tell me about it!

je vous en donnerai
I'll give you some

prête-lui-en!
lend him/her some!

gardez-nous-en!
keep some for us!

4 The pronoun Y

a) *Use*

y is used instead of à + noun, but never refers to a person. It is used:

i) As the indirect object of a verb. Since the preposition à is translated in a variety of ways in English, y may have various meanings (*it, of it/them, about it/them* etc):

tu joues au tennis? – non, j'y joue rarement
do you play tennis? – no, I seldom play (it)

je pense à mon pays natal; j'y pense souvent
I'm thinking about my home country; I often think about it

il s'intéresse à la photo; il s'y intéresse
he's interested in photography; he's interested in it

ii) To mean 'there':

j'ai passé deux jours à Londres; j'y ai passé deux jours
I spent two days in London; I spent two days there

il est allé en Grèce; il y est allé
he went to Greece; he went there

Note that y must always be used with the verb aller (to go) when the place is not mentioned in the clause. It is often not translated in English:

comment vas-tu à l'école? – j'y vais en bus
how do you get to school? – I go (there) by bus

allons-y!
let's go!

on y va demain
we're going (there) tomorrow

iii) To replace the prepositions en, dans, sur + noun; y then means 'there', 'in it/them', 'on it/them':

je voudrais vivre en France; je voudrais y vivre
I'd like to live in France; I'd like to live there

je les ai mis dans ma poche; je les y ai mis
I put them in my pocket; I put them there

sur la table? – non, je ne l'y vois pas
on the table? no, I don't see it there

b) *Position*

Like other object pronouns, y comes immediately before the verb, except with a positive command (the affirmative imperative), where it must follow the verb:

j'y réfléchirai
I'll think about it

il s'y est habitué
he got used to it

pensez-y!
think about it!

n'y allez pas!
don't go!

When used with other object pronouns, y comes last:

il va nous y rencontrer
he'll meet us there

je l'y ai vu hier
I saw him there yesterday

5 Disjunctive pronouns

a) *Forms*

PERSON	SINGULAR	PLURAL
1st	moi	nous
	me	*us*
2nd	toi	vous
	you	*you*
3rd (masculine)	lui	eux
	him	*them*
(feminine)	elle	elles
	her	*them*
(impersonal)	soi	
	oneself	

Note:

i) toi/vous: the same difference should be made as between tu and vous (see p B18).

ii) soi is used in an impersonal, general sense to refer to indefinite pronouns and adjectives (on, chacun, tout le monde, personne, chaque etc); it is mainly found in set phrases, such as:

chacun pour soi
every man for himself

cela va de soi
that goes without saying

b) *Use*

Disjunctive pronouns, also called emphatic pronouns, are used instead of object pronouns when referring to persons in the following cases:

i) In answer to a question, alone or in a phrase without a verb:

qui est là? – moi
who's there? – me

j'ai aimé ce film; et toi?
I liked that film; did you?

qui préfères-tu, lui ou elle? – elle, bien sûr
who do you prefer, him or her? – her, of course

ii) After c'est/ce sont, c'était/c'étaient etc:

ouvrez, c'est moi!
open up, it's me!

non, ce n'était pas lui
no, it wasn't him

iii) After a preposition:

vous allez chez lui?
are you going to his place?

tu y vas avec elle?
are you going with her?

regarde devant toi!
look in front of you!

oh, c'est pour moi?
oh, is that for me?

iv) With verbal constructions. Special care should be taken when the verb is followed by a preposition:

tu peux compter sur moi
you can count on me

quoi! tu as peur de lui?
what! you're afraid of him?

il m'a parlé de toi
he told me about you

je pense souvent à vous
I often think about you

Note that emphatic pronouns are only used when referring to people. In other cases y or en must be used.

v) For emphasis, particularly when two pronouns are contrasted. The unstressed subject pronoun is usually included:

vous, vous m'énervez!
you get on my nerves!

lui, il joue bien; elle, non
he plays well; she doesn't

moi, je n'aime pas l'hiver
I don't like winter

eux, ils sont partis
they've left

vi) In the case of multiple subjects (two pronouns or one pronoun and one noun):

lui et son frère sont dans l'équipe
he and his brother are in the team

ma famille et moi allons très bien
my family and I are very well

vii) As the second element of a comparison:

il est plus sympa que toi
he is nicer than you

elle chante mieux que lui
she sings better than he does

viii) Before a relative pronoun:

c'est lui que j'aime
he's the one I love

c'est toi qui l'as dit
you're the one who said it

lui qui n'aime pas le vin blanc en a bu six verres
he who doesn't like white wine had six glasses

ix) With -même(s) *(-self, -selves)*, aussi *(too)*, seul *(alone)*:

faites-le vous-mêmes
do it yourselves

j'irai moi-même
I'll go myself

lui aussi est parti
he too went away

elle seule le sait
she alone knows

x) To replace a possessive pronoun (see E2):

c'est le mien; il est à moi
it's mine; it belongs to me

cette valise n'est pas à lui?
doesn't that suitcase belong to him?

E POSSESSIVE ADJECTIVES AND PRONOUNS

1 Possessive adjectives

a) *Forms*

Possessive adjectives always come before their related noun. Like other adjectives, they agree in gender and number with the noun; the masculine and feminine plural forms are identical:

SINGULAR MASC	FEM	PLURAL (MASC AND FEM)	
mon	ma	mes	*my*
ton	ta	tes	*your*
son	sa	ses	*his/her/its/ one's*
notre	notre	nos	*our*
votre	votre	vos	*your*
leur	leur	leurs	*their*

j'ai mis mon argent et mes affaires dans mon sac
I've put my money and my things in my bag

comment va ton frère? et ta sœur? et tes parents?
how's your brother? and your sister? and your parents?

notre rue est assez calme
our street is fairly quiet

ce sont vos amis
they're your friends

Note that mon/ton/son are used instead of ma/ta/sa when the next word starts with a vowel or silent h:

mon ancienne maison
my old house

ton amie Christine
your friend Christine

son haleine sentait l'alcool
his/her breath smelled of alcohol

b) *Use*

i) The possessive adjective is repeated before each noun and agrees in number and gender with it:

mon père et ma mère sont sortis
my mother and father have gone out

ii) son/sa/ses

son, sa and ses can all mean 'his', 'her' or 'its'. In French, the form of the adjective is determined by the gender and number of the noun that follows, and not by the possessor:

il m'a prêté sa mobylette et son casque
he lent me his moped and his helmet

elle s'entend bien avec sa mère mais pas avec son père
she gets on well with her mother, but not with her father

elle vit pour son travail; lui pour ses enfants
she lives for her job; he lives for his children

iii) ton/ta/tes and votre/vos

The two sets of words for 'your', ton/ta/tes and votre/vos, correspond to the two different forms of tu and vous; they must not be used together with the same person:

tu as parlé à ton patron?
have you spoken to your boss?

Monsieur, vous oubliez votre parapluie!
excuse me, sir, you've forgotten your umbrella!

iv) In French, the possessive adjective is replaced by the definite article (le/la/les) with the following:

● parts of the body:

il s'est essuyé les mains
he wiped his hands

elle a haussé les épaules
she shrugged (her shoulders)

● descriptive phrases at the end of a clause, where English adds 'with':

il marchait lentement, les mains dans les poches
he was walking slowly, with his hands in his pockets

elle l'a regardé partir, les larmes aux yeux
she watched him leave with tears in her eyes

2 Possessive pronouns

SINGULAR MASC	FEM	PLURAL (MASC AND FEM)	
le mien	la mienne	les mien(ne)s	*mine*
le tien	la tienne	les tien(ne)s	*yours*
le sien	la sienne	les sien(ne)s	*his/hers/its*
le nôtre	la nôtre	les nôtres	*ours*
le vôtre	la vôtre	les vôtres	*yours*
le leur	la leur	les leurs	*theirs*

Possessive pronouns are used instead of a possessive adjective + noun. They agree in gender and in number with the noun they stand for, and not with the possessor (it is particularly important to remember this when translating 'his' and 'hers'):

j'aime bien ton appartement mais je préfère le mien
I quite like your flat, but I prefer mine

on prend quelle voiture? la mienne ou la tienne?
which car shall we take? mine or yours?

comment sont vos profs? les nôtres sont sympas
what are your teachers like? ours are nice

j'avais mon passeport mais Brigitte avait oublié le sien
I had my passport, but Brigitte had forgotten hers

j'ai gardé ma moto mais Paul a vendu la sienne
I've kept my motorbike but Paul has sold his

à or de + possessive pronoun

The prepositions à and de combine with the articles le and les in the usual way:

à + le mien	→	au mien
à + les miens	→	aux miens
à + les miennes	→	aux miennes
de + le mien	→	du mien
de + les miens	→	des miens
de + les miennes	→	des miennes

demande à tes parents, j'ai déjà parlé aux miens
ask your parents, I've already spoken to mine

leur appartement ressemble beaucoup au nôtre
their flat is very similar to ours

j'aime bien les chiens mais j'ai peur du tien
I like dogs, but I'm afraid of yours

Note that after the verb être, the possessive pronoun is often replaced by à + emphatic pronoun (see p B21):

à qui est cette écharpe? – elle est à moi
whose scarf is this? – it's mine

ce livre est à toi? – non, il est à elle
is this book yours? – no, it's hers

c'est à qui? à vous ou à lui?
whose is this? yours or his?

F RELATIVE PRONOUNS

1 Definition

Relative pronouns are words which introduce a relative clause. In the sentence:

I bought the book which you recommended

'which' is the relative pronoun, 'which you recommended' is the relative clause and 'the book' is the antecedent (ie the noun to which the relative pronoun refers).

2 Form

Relative pronouns are:

qui	*who/which*	lequel	*which*
que	*who(m)/which*	dont	*of which/whose*
quoi	*what*	ce qui	*what*
où	*where*	ce que	*what*

qui, que, quoi, lequel, ce qui and ce que can also be used as interrogative pronouns (see p B17) and must not be confused with them.

3 Use

a) QUI

qui is used as the subject of a relative clause. It means:

i) 'who', 'that' (referring to people):

est-ce que tu connais le monsieur qui habite ici?
do you know the man who lives here?

ce n'est pas lui qui a menti
he's not the one who lied

ii) 'which', 'that' (referring to things):

tu as pris le journal qui était sur la télé?
did you take the paper which/that was on the TV?

b) QUE

que (which contracts to qu' before a vowel or a silent h) is used as the object of a relative clause; it is often not translated. It means:

i) 'who(m)', 'that' (referring to people):

la fille que j'aime ne m'aime pas
the girl (that) I love doesn't love me

ii) 'which', 'that' (referring to things):

j'ai perdu le briquet qu'il m'a offert
I've lost the lighter (which/that) he gave me

c) QUI or QUE?

qui (subject) and que (object) are translated by the same words in English (who, which, that). To use the correct pronoun in French, it is essential to know whether a relative pronoun is the object or the subject of the relative clause:

i) when the verb of the relative clause has its own subject, the object pronoun que must be used:

c'est un passe-temps que j'adore
it's a pastime (that) I love (the subject of 'adore' is 'je')

ii) otherwise the relative pronoun is the subject of the verb in the relative clause and the subject pronoun qui must be used:

j'ai trouvé un manteau qui me plaît
I've found a coat that I like (the subject of 'plaît' is 'qui')

d) LEQUEL

i) *forms*

lequel (which) has four different forms, as it must agree with the noun to which it refers:

	SINGULAR	PLURAL	
MASCULINE	lequel	lesquels	} which
FEMININE	laquelle	lesquelles	

lequel etc combines with the prepositions à and de as follows:

à + lequel	→	auquel
à + lesquels	→	auxquels
à + lesquelles	→	auxquelles
de + lequel	→	duquel
de + lesquels	→	desquels
de + lesquelles	→	desquelles

à + laquelle and de + laquelle do not change.

quels sont les sports auxquels tu t'intéresses?
what sports are you interested in?

voilà le village près duquel on campait
here's the village which we camped near

ii) qui or lequel with a preposition

When a relative pronoun follows a preposition, the pronoun used is either qui or lequel. In English, the relative pronoun is seldom used and the preposition is frequently placed after the verb or at the end of the sentence.

qui is generally used after a preposition when referring to people:

où est la fille avec qui je dansais?
where's the girl I was dancing with?

montre-moi la personnne à qui tu as vendu ton vélo
show me the person you sold your bike to

lequel is often used after a preposition when referring to things:

l'immeuble dans lequel j'habite est très moderne
the building (which) I live in is very modern

je ne reconnais pas la voiture avec laquelle il est venu
I don't recognize the car (which) he came in

lequel is also used when referring to persons after the prepositions entre (between) and parmi (among):

elle observait les invités parmi lesquels elle ne reconnaissait personne
she was watching the guests, none of whom she recognized

il y avait deux candidats, entre lesquels nous avons dû choisir
there were two candidates, between whom we had to choose

e) DONT

dont is frequently used instead of de qui, duquel etc. It means:

i) of which/of whom:

un métier dont il est fier
a job (which) he is proud of

Care must be taken with verbs that are normally followed by de + object: de is not always translated by 'of' in English, and is sometimes not translated at all (see section on verbal constructions p B53):

voilà les choses dont j'ai besoin
here are the things (which) I need

les gens dont tu parles ne m'intéressent pas
I'm not interested in the people you're talking about

l'enfant dont elle s'occupe n'est pas le sien
the child she is looking after is not hers

ii) whose

dont is also used to translate the English pronoun 'whose'. In French, the construction of the clause that follows dont differs from English in two ways:

the noun which follows dont is used with the definite article (le, la, les, l'):

mon copain, dont le père a eu un accident
my friend, whose father had an accident

the word order in French is dont + subject + verb + object:

je te présente Hélène, dont tu connais déjà le frère
this is Hélène, whose brother you already know

c'était dans une petite rue dont j'ai oublié le nom
it was in a small street the name of which I've forgotten

Note that dont cannot be used after a preposition:

une jolie maison, près de laquelle il y a un petit lac
a pretty house, next to which there is a small lake

f) OÙ

i) où generally means 'where':

l'hôtel où on a logé était très confortable
the hotel where we stayed was very comfortable

ii) où often replaces a preposition + lequel, and means 'in/to/on/at which' etc:

c'est la maison où je suis né
that's the house in which/where I was born

une soirée où il a invité tous ses amis
a party to which he invited all his friends

iii) où is also used to translate 'when' after a noun referring to time:

le jour où   la fois où   le moment où
the day when   the time when   the moment when

tu te rappelles le soir où on a raté le dernier métro?
do you remember the evening when we missed the last train?

le jour où j'ai eu mon permis de conduire
the day when I got my driving licence

g) CE QUI, CE QUE

ce is used before qui and que when the relative pronoun does not refer to a specific noun. Both ce qui and ce que mean 'that which', 'the thing which', and are usually translated by 'what':

i) ce qui

ce qui is followed by a verb without a subject (qui is the subject):

ce qui s'est passé ne vous regarde pas
what happened is none of your business

ce qui m'étonne, c'est sa patience
what surprises me is his patience

Note that in French, this structure requires a comma between the two clauses, and the second clause must be introduced by c'est/c'était/ce sera depending on the tense being used.

ii) ce que

ce que (ce qu' before a vowel or a silent h) is followed by a verb with its own subject (que is the object):

fais ce que tu veux   c'est ce qu'il a dit?
do what you want   is that what he said?

ce que vous me demandez est impossible
what you're asking me is impossible

iii) tout ce qui/que

tout is used in front of ce qui/que in the sense of 'all that', 'everything that':

c'est tout ce que je veux   tout ce que tu as fait
that's all I want   everything you did

tu n'as pas eu de mal; c'est tout ce qui compte
you weren't hurt; that's all that matters

iv) ce qui/que are often used in indirect questions (see p B17):

je ne sais pas ce qu'ils vont dire
I don't know what they'll say

v) when referring to a previous clause, ce qui and ce que are translated by 'which':

elle est en retard, ce qui arrive souvent
she's late, which happens often

vi) ce qui/que are used with a preposition; ce qui is used as the subject of the verb in the relative clause and ce que is used as the object of the verb in the relative clause:

ce n'est pas étonnant, après ce qui nous est arrivé
it's not surprising, after what happened to us

il y a du vrai dans ce que vous dites
there is some truth in what you say

When a preposition is required by the verb in the relative clause, eg penser à, s'expliquer sur, quoi is used instead of ce que and comes after the preposition:

c'est ce à quoi je pensais
that's what I was thinking about

voici ce sur quoi il devra s'expliquer
this is what he'll have to explain

ce dont is used instead of de + ce que when de is the preposition required by the verb in the relative clause, eg avoir peur de, avoir besoin de:

c'est ce dont j'avais peur
that's what I was afraid of

tu as trouvé ce dont tu avais besoin?
did you find what you needed?

7 VERBS

A REGULAR CONJUGATIONS

1 Conjugations

There are three main conjugations in French, which are determined by the infinitive endings. The first conjugation verbs, by far the largest category, end in -er, eg **aimer** and will be referred to as -er verbs; the second conjugation verbs end in -ir, eg **finir** and will be referred to as -ir verbs; the third conjugation verbs, the smallest category, end in -re, eg **vendre** and will be referred to as -re verbs.

2 Simple tenses

The simple tenses in French are:

- present
- imperfect
- future
- conditional
- past historic
- present subjunctive
- imperfect subjunctive

For the use of the different tenses, see pp B30-2.

3 Formation of tenses

The tenses are formed by adding the following endings to the stem of the verb (usually the stem of the infinitive) as set out in the following section:

a) PRESENT: stem of the infinitive + the following endings:

-er verbs	-ir verbs	-re verbs
-e, -es, -e,	-is, -is, -it,	-s, -s, ø,
-ons, -ez, -ent	-issons, -issez, -issent	-ons, -ez, -ent

AIMER	FINIR	VENDRE
j'aime	je finis	je vends
tu aimes	tu finis	tu vends
il aime	il finit	il vend
elle aime	elle finit	elle vend
nous aimons	nous finissons	nous vendons
vous aimez	vous finissez	vous vendez
ils aiment	ils finissent	ils vendent
elles aiment	elles finissent	elles vendent

b) IMPERFECT: stem of the first person plural of the present indicative (ie the 'nous' form minus -ons) + the following endings:

-ais, -ais, -ait, -ions, -iez, -aient

j'aimais	je finissais	je vendais
tu aimais	tu finissais	tu vendais
il aimait	il finissait	il vendait
elle aimait	elle finissait	elle vendait
nous aimions	nous finissions	nous vendions
vous aimiez	vous finissiez	vous vendiez
ils aimaient	ils finissaient	ils vendaient
elles aimaient	elles finissaient	elles vendaient

Note that the only irregular imperfect is **être: j'étais** etc.

c) FUTURE: infinitive + the following endings:

-ai, -as, -a, -ons, -ez, -ont

Note that verbs ending in -re drop the final e of the infinitive.

j'aimerai	je finirai	je vendrai
tu aimeras	tu finiras	tu vendras
il aimera	il finira	il vendra
elle aimera	elle finira	elle vendra
nous aimerons	nous finirons	nous vendrons
vous aimerez	vous finirez	vous vendrez
ils aimeront	ils finiront	ils vendront
elles aimeront	elles finiront	elles vendront

d) CONDITIONAL: infinitive + the following endings:

-ais, -ais, -ait, -ions, -iez, -aient

Note that verbs ending in -re drop the final e of the infinitive.

j'aimerais	je finirais	je vendrais
tu aimerais	tu finirais	tu vendrais
il aimerait	il finirait	il vendrait
elle aimerait	elle finirait	elle vendrait
nous aimerions	nous finirions	nous vendrions
vous aimeriez	vous finiriez	vous vendriez
ils aimeraient	ils finiraient	ils vendraient
elles aimeraient	elles finiraient	elles vendraient

e) PAST HISTORIC: stem of the infinitive + the following endings:

-er verbs	-ir verbs	-re verbs
-ai, -as, -a,	-is, -is, -it,	-is, -is, -it,
-âmes, -âtes,	-îmes, -îtes,	-îmes, -îtes,
-èrent	-irent	-irent

j'aimai	je finis	je vendis
tu aimas	tu finis	tu vendis
il aima	il finit	il vendit
elle aima	elle finit	elle vendit
nous aimâmes	nous finîmes	nous vendîmes
vous aimâtes	vous finîtes	vous vendîtes
ils aimèrent	ils finirent	ils vendirent
elles aimèrent	elles finirent	elles vendirent

f) PRESENT SUBJUNCTIVE: stem of the first person plural of the present indicative (ie the 'nous' form minus -ons) + the following endings:

-e, -es, -e, -ions, -iez, -ent

j'aime	je finisse	je vende
tu aimes	tu finisses	tu vendes
il aime	il finisse	il vende
elle aime	elle finisse	elle vende
nous aimions	nous finissions	nous vendions
vous aimiez	vous finissiez	vous vendiez
ils aiment	ils finissent	ils vendent
elles aiment	elles finissent	elles vendent

g) IMPERFECT SUBJUNCTIVE: stem of the first person singular of the past historic + the following endings:

-er verbs	-ir verbs	-re verbs
-asse, -asses, -ât,	-isse, -isses, -ît,	-isse, -isses, -ît,
-assions, -assiez,	-issions, -issiez,	-issions, -issiez,
-assent	-issent	-issent

j'aimasse	je finisse	je vendisse
tu aimasses	tu finisses	tu vendisses
il aimât	il finît	il vendît
elle aimât	elle finît	elle vendît
nous aimassions	nous finissions	nous vendissions
vous aimassiez	vous finissiez	vous vendissiez
ils aimassent	ils finissent	ils vendissent
elles aimassent	elles finissent	elles vendissent

B STANDARD SPELLING IRREGULARITIES

Spelling irregularities affect only -er verbs.

1 Verbs ending in -cer and -ger

a) Verbs ending in -cer require a cedilla under the c (ç) before an a or an o to preserve the soft sound of the c: eg **commencer** *(to begin)*; **il commença** *(he began)*.

b) Verbs ending in **-ger** require an **-e** after the **g** before an **a** or an **o** to preserve the soft sound of the **g**: eg **manger** *(to eat)*; **je mangeais** *(I was eating)*.

Changes to **-cer** and **-ger** verbs occur in the following tenses: present, imperfect, past historic, imperfect subjunctive and present participle.

COMMENCER	MANGER
PRESENT	
je commence	je mange
tu commences	tu manges
il commence	il mange
elle commence	elle mange
nous commençons	nous mangeons
vous commencez	vous mangez
ils commencent	ils mangent
elles commencent	elles mangent
IMPERFECT	
je commençais	je mangeais
tu commençais	tu mangeais
il commençait	il mangeait
elle commençait	elle mangeait
nous commencions	nous mangions
vous commenciez	vous mangiez
ils commençaient	ils mangeaient
elles commençaient	elles mangeaient
PAST HISTORIC	
je commençai	je mangeai
tu commenças	tu mangeas
il commença	il mangea
elle commença	elle mangea
nous commençâmes	nous mangeâmes
vous commençâtes	vous mangeâtes
ils commencèrent	ils mangèrent
elles commencèrent	elles mangèrent
IMPERFECT SUBJUNCTIVE	
je commençasse	je mangeasse
tu commençasses	tu mangeasses
il commençât	il mangeât
elle commençât	elle mangeât
nous commençassions	nous mangeassions
vous commençassiez	vous mangeassiez
ils commençassent	ils mangeassent
elles commençassent	elles mangeassent
PRESENT PARTICIPLE	
commençant	mangeant

2 Verbs with other **-er** endings

a) *Verbs ending in* -eler

Verbs ending in **-eler** double the **l** before a silent **e** (ie before **-e**, **-es**, **-ent** of the present indicative and subjunctive, and throughout the future and present conditional): eg **appeler** *(to call)*.

PRESENT INDICATIVE	PRESENT SUBJUNCTIVE
j'appelle	j'appelle
tu appelles	tu appelles
il appelle	il appelle
elle appelle	elle appelle
nous appelons	nous appelions
vous appelez	vous appeliez
ils appellent	ils appellent
elles appellent	elles appellent
FUTURE	**CONDITIONAL**
j'appellerai	j'appellerais
tu appelleras	tu appellerais
il appellera	il appellerait
elle appellera	elle appellerait
nous appellerons	nous appellerions
vous appellerez	vous appelleriez
ils appelleront	ils appelleraient
elles appelleront	elles appelleraient

Note, however, that some verbs in **-eler**, including the following, are conjugated like **acheter** (see p B26):

celer	to conceal
congeler	to (deep-)freeze
déceler	to detect, to reveal
dégeler	to defrost
geler	to freeze
harceler	to harass
marteler	to hammer
modeler	to model
peler	to peel

b) *Verbs ending in* -eter

Verbs ending in **-eter** double the **t** before a silent **e** (ie before **-e**, **-es**, **-ent** of the present indicative and subjunctive, and throughout the future and conditional): eg **jeter** *(to throw)*.

PRESENT INDICATIVE	PRESENT SUBJUNCTIVE
je jette	je jette
tu jettes	tu jettes
il jette	il jette
elle jette	elle jette
nous jetons	nous jetions
vous jetez	vous jetiez
ils jettent	ils jettent
elles jettent	elles jettent
FUTURE	**CONDITIONAL**
je jetterai	je jetterais
tu jetteras	tu jetterais
il jettera	il jetterait
elle jettera	elle jetterait
nous jetterons	nous jetterions
vous jetterez	vous jetteriez
ils jetteront	ils jetteraient
elles jetteront	elles jetteraient

Note, however, that some verbs in **-eter**, including the following, are conjugated like **acheter** (see p B26):

crocheter	to pick (lock)
fureter	to ferret about
haleter	to pant
racheter	to buy back

c) *Verbs ending in* -oyer *and* -uyer

In verbs ending in **-oyer** and **-uyer** the **y** changes to **i** before a silent **e** (ie before **-e**, **-es**, **-ent** of the present indicative and subjunctive, and throughout the future and conditional): eg **employer** *(to use)* and **ennuyer** *(to bore)*.

PRESENT INDICATIVE	PRESENT SUBJUNCTIVE
j'emploie	j'emploie
tu emploies	tu emploies
il emploie	il emploie
elle emploie	elle emploie
nous employons	nous employions
vous employez	vous employiez
ils emploient	ils emploient
elles emploient	elles emploient
FUTURE	**CONDITIONAL**
j'emploierai	j'emploierais
tu emploieras	tu emploierais
il emploiera	il emploierait
elle emploiera	elle emploierait
nous emploierons	nous emploierions
vous emploierez	vous emploieriez
ils emploieront	ils emploieraient
elles emploieront	elles emploieraient

Note that **envoyer** *(to send)* and **renvoyer** *(to dismiss)* have an irregular future and conditional: **j'enverrai**, **j'enverrais**; **je** renverrai, je renverrais.

d) *Verbs ending in -ayer*

In verbs ending in -ayer, eg **balayer** *(to sweep)*, **payer** *(to pay)*, **essayer** *(to try)*, the change from y to i is optional:

eg	je balaie	or	je balaye
	je paie	or	je paye
	j'essaie	or	j'essaye

e) *Verbs in e- + consonant + -er*

Verbs like **acheter, enlever, mener, peser** change the (last) e of the stem to è before a silent e (ie before -e, -es, -ent of the present indicative and subjunctive and throughout the future and conditional):

PRESENT INDICATIVE	PRESENT SUBJUNCTIVE
j'achète	j'achète
tu achètes	tu achètes
il achète	il achète
elle achète	elle achète
nous achetons	nous achetions
vous achetez	vous achetiez
ils achètent	ils achètent
elles achètent	elles achètent

FUTURE	CONDITIONAL
j'achèterai	j'achèterais
tu achèteras	tu achèterais
il achètera	il achèterait
elle achètera	elle achèterait
nous achèterons	nous achèterions
vous achèterez	vous achèteriez
ils achèteront	ils achèteraient
elles achèteront	elles achèteraient

Verbs conjugated like **acheter** include:

achever *to complete*	haleter *to pant*
amener *to bring*	harceler *to harass*
celer *to conceal*	lever *to lift*
crever *to burst*	marteler *to hammer*
crocheter *to pick (lock)*	mener *to lead*
élever *to raise*	modeler *to model*
emmener *to take away*	peler *to peel*
enlever *to remove*	peser *to weigh*
étiqueter *to label*	se promener *to go for a*
fureter *to ferret about*	*walk*
geler *to freeze*	semer *to sow*
	soulever *to lift*

f) *Verbs in é- + consonant + -er*

Verbs like **espérer** *(to hope)* change é to è before a silent e in the present indicative and subjunctive. Note, however, that in the future and conditional é is retained.

PRESENT INDICATIVE	PRESENT SUBJUNCTIVE
j'espère	j'espère
tu espères	tu espères
il espère	il espère
elle espère	elle espère
nous espérons	nous espérions
vous espérez	vous espériez
ils espèrent	ils espèrent
elles espèrent	elles espèrent

FUTURE	CONDITIONAL
j'espérerai	j'espérerais
tu espéreras	tu espérerais
il espérera	il espérerait
elle espérera	elle espérerait
nous espérerons	nous espérerions
vous espérerez	vous espéreriez
ils espéreront	ils espéreraient
elles espéreront	elles espéreraient

Verbs conjugated like **espérer** include verbs in -éder, -érer, -éter etc:

accéder	*to accede to*
céder	*to yield*
célébrer	*to celebrate*
compléter	*to complete*
considérer	*to consider*
décéder	*to die*
digérer	*to digest*
gérer	*to manage*
inquiéter	*to worry*
libérer	*to free*
opérer	*to operate*
pénétrer	*to penetrate*
persévérer	*to persevere*
posséder	*to possess*
précéder	*to precede*
préférer	*to prefer*
protéger	*to protect*
récupérer	*to recover*
refréner	*to curb*
régler	*to rule*
régner	*to reign*
répéter	*to repeat, to rehearse*
révéler	*to reveal*
sécher	*to dry*
succéder	*to succeed*
suggérer	*to suggest*
tolérer	*to tolerate*

C AUXILIARIES AND THE FORMATION OF COMPOUND TENSES

1 Formation

a) The two auxiliary verbs avoir and être are used with the past participle of a verb to form compound tenses.

b) *The past participle*

The regular past participle is formed by taking the stem of the infinitive and adding the following endings:

-er	-ir	-re
aim(er) + é	fin(ir) + i	vend(re) + u
aimé	fini	vendu

For the agreement of past participles see p B38.

c) *Compound tenses*

In French there are seven compound tenses: perfect, pluperfect, future perfect, past conditional (conditional perfect), past anterior, perfect subjunctive, pluperfect subjunctive.

2 Verbs conjugated with AVOIR

PERFECT	PLUPERFECT
present of avoir + past participle	imperfect of avoir + past participle
j'ai aimé	j'avais aimé
tu as aimé	tu avais aimé
il a aimé	il avait aimé
elle a aimé	elle avait aimé
nous avons aimé	nous avions aimé
vous avez aimé	vous aviez aimé
ils ont aimé	ils avaient aimé
elles ont aimé	elles avaient aimé

FUTURE PERFECT	PAST CONDITIONAL
future of avoir + past participle	conditional of avoir + past participle
j'aurai aimé	j'aurais aimé
tu auras aimé	tu aurais aimé
il aura aimé	il aurait aimé
elle aura aimé	elle aurait aimé

nous aurons aimé
vous aurez aimé
ils auront aimé
elles auront aimé

nous aurions aimé
vous auriez aimé
ils auraient aimé
elles auraient aimé

nous soyons arrivé(e)s
vous soyez arrivé(e)(s)
ils soient arrivés
elles soient arrivées

nous fussions arrivé(e)s
vous fussiez arrivé(e)(s)
ils fussent arrivés
elles fussent arrivées

PAST ANTERIOR

past historic of avoir +
past participle

j'eus aimé
tu eus aimé
il eut aimé
elle eut aimé
nous eûmes aimé
vous eûtes aimé
ils eurent aimé
elles eurent aimé

PERFECT SUBJUNCTIVE

present subjunctive of
avoir + past participle

j'aie aimé
tu aies aimé
il ait aimé
elle ait aimé
nous ayons aimé
vous ayez aimé
ils aient aimé
elles aient aimé

PLUPERFECT SUBJUNCTIVE

imperfect subjunctive of
avoir + past participle

j'eusse aimé
tu eusses aimé
il eût aimé
elle eût aimé
nous eussions aimé
vous eussiez aimé
ils eussent aimé
elles eussent aimé

3 Verbs conjugated with ÊTRE

PERFECT

present of être +
past participle

je suis arrivé(e)
tu es arrivé(e)
il est arrivé
elle est arrivée
nous sommes arrivé(e)s
vous êtes arrivé(e)(s)
ils sont arrivés
elles sont arrivées

FUTURE PERFECT

future of être +
past participle

je serai arrivé(e)
tu seras arrivé(e)
il sera arrivé
elle sera arrivée
nous serons arrivé(e)s
vous serez arrivé(e)(s)
ils seront arrivés
elles seront arrivées

PAST ANTERIOR

past historic of être +
past participle

je fus arrivé(e)
tu fus arrivé(e)
il fut arrivé
elle fut arrivée
nous fûmes arrivé(e)s
vous fûtes arrivé(e)(s)
ils furent arrivés
elles furent arrivées

PERFECT SUBJUNCTIVE

present subjunctive of
être + past participle

je sois arrivé(e)
tu sois arrivé(e)
il soit arrivé
elle soit arrivée

PLUPERFECT

imperfect of être +
past participle

j'étais arrivé(e)
tu étais arrivé(e)
il était arrivé
elle était arrivée
nous étions arrivé(e)s
vous étiez arrivé(e)(s)
ils étaient arrivés
elles étaient arrivées

PAST CONDITIONAL

conditional of être +
past participle

je serais arrivé(e)
tu serais arrivé(e)
il serait arrivé
elle serait arrivée
nous serions arrivé(e)s
vous seriez arrivé(e)(s)
ils seraient arrivés
elles seraient arrivées

PLUPERFECT SUBJUNCTIVE

imperfect subjunctive of
être + past participle

je fusse arrivé(e)
tu fusses arrivé(e)
il fût arrivé
elle fût arrivée

4 AVOIR or ÊTRE?

a) *Verbs conjugated with* avoir

The compound tenses of most verbs are formed with avoir:

j'ai marqué un but
I scored a goal

elle a dansé toute la nuit
she danced all night

b) *Verbs conjugated with* être

i) all reflexive verbs (see p B28):

je me suis baigné
I had a bath

ii) the following verbs (mainly of motion):

aller	*to go*
arriver	*to arrive*
descendre	*to go/come down*
entrer	*to go/come in*
monter	*to go/come up*
mourir	*to die*
naître	*to be born*
partir	*to leave*
passer	*to go through, to drop in*
rester	*to remain*
retourner	*to return*
sortir	*to go/come out*
tomber	*to fall*
venir	*to come*

and most of their compounds:

revenir	*to come back*
devenir	*to become*
parvenir	*to reach, to manage to*
rentrer	*to return home*
remonter	*to go up again*
redescendre	*to go down again*

Note, however, that prévenir *(to warn)* and subvenir *(to provide for)* are conjugated with avoir:

je t'avais prévenu!
I did warn you!

elle avait subvenu à toutes les dépenses
she met all the expenses

Note too that passer can also be conjugated with avoir:

il a passé par Paris
he went via Paris

Some of the verbs listed above can take a direct object. In such cases they are conjugated with avoir and will have a different meaning:

descendre	*to take/bring down, to go down (the stairs, a slope)*
monter	*to take/bring up, to go up (the stairs, a slope)*
rentrer	*to take/bring/put in*
retourner	*to turn over*
sortir	*to take/bring out*

les élèves sont sortis à midi
the pupils came out at midday

les élèves ont sorti leurs livres
the pupils took out their books

elle n'est pas encore descendue
she hasn't come down yet

elle a descendu un vieux tableau du grenier
she brought an old painting down from the loft

elle a descendu l'escalier
she came down the stairs

les prisonniers sont montés sur le toit
the prisoners climbed on to the roof

le garçon a monté les bouteilles de vin de la cave
the waiter brought the bottles of wine up from the cellar

nous sommes rentrés tard
we got home late

j'ai rentré la voiture dans le garage
I put the car in the garage

je serais retourné à Paris
I would have returned to Paris

le jardinier a retourné le sol
the gardener turned over the soil

ils sont sortis de la piscine
they got out of the swimming pool

il a sorti les mains de ses poches
he took his hands out of his pockets

D REFLEXIVE VERBS

1 Definition

Reflexive verbs are so called because they 'reflect' the action back onto the subject. Reflexive verbs are always accompanied by a reflexive pronoun, eg in the following sentence:

I look at myself in the mirror

'myself' is the reflexive pronoun.

je lave la voiture	**je me lave**
I'm washing the car	*I'm washing myself*
j'ai couché le bébé	**je me suis couché**
I put the baby to bed	*I went to bed (I put myself to bed)*

2 Reflexive pronouns

They are:

PERSON	SINGULAR	PLURAL
1st	me (m') *myself*	nous *ourselves*
2nd	te (t') *yourself*	vous *yourself/selves*
3rd	se (s') *himself, herself, itself, oneself*	se (s') *themselves*

Note:

a) m', t' and s' are used instead of me, te and se in front of a vowel or a silent h:

tu t'amuses? – non, je m'ennuie
are you enjoying yourself? – no, I'm bored

il s'habille dans la salle de bain
he gets dressed in the bathroom

b) French reflexive pronouns are often not translated in English:

je me demande si ...	**ils se moquent de moi**
I wonder if ...	*they're making fun of me*

c) Plural reflexive pronouns can also be used to express reciprocal actions; in this case they are translated by 'each other' or 'one another':

nous nous détestons	**ils ne se parlent pas**
we hate one another	*they're not talking to each other*

d) se can mean 'ourselves' or 'each other' when it is used with the pronoun on meaning 'we' (see p B16):

on s'est perdu	**on se connaît**
we got lost	*we know each other*

3 Position of reflexive pronouns

Reflexive pronouns are placed immediately before the verb, except in positive commands, where they follow the verb and are linked to it by a hyphen:

tu te dépêches?	**dépêchons-nous!**
will you hurry up?	*let's hurry!*
ne t'inquiète pas	**ne vous fiez pas à lui**
don't worry	*don't trust him*

Note that reflexive pronouns change to emphatic (disjunctive) pronouns in positive commands:

elle doit se reposer	**repose-toi**
she needs to rest	*have a rest*

4 Conjugation of reflexive verbs

a) *Simple tenses*

These are conjugated in the same way as non-reflexive verbs, except that a reflexive pronoun is used.

b) *Compound tenses*

These are conjugated using the auxiliary être followed by the past participle of the verb.

A full conjugation table is given on p B47.

5 Agreement of the past participle

a) In most cases, the reflexive pronoun is a direct object and the past participle of the verb agrees in number and in gender with the reflexive pronoun:

il s'est trompé	**elle s'est endormie**
he made a mistake	*she fell asleep*
ils se sont excusés	**elles se sont assises**
they apologized	*they sat down*

b) When the reflexive pronoun is used as an indirect object, the past participle does not change:

nous nous sommes écrit	**elle se l'est acheté**
we wrote to each other	*she bought it for herself*
elles se sont parlé	**les années se sont succédé**
they spoke to each other	*one year followed another*

When the reflexive verb has a direct object, the reflexive pronoun is the indirect object of the reflexive verb and the past participle does not agree with it:

Caroline s'est tordu la cheville
Caroline sprained her ankle

vous vous êtes lavé les mains, les filles?
did you wash your hands, girls?

elles se sont égratigné les genoux
they scratched their knees

6 Common reflexive verbs

s'en aller *to go away*	**s'éloigner (de)** *to move away (from)*	**se moquer de** *to laugh at*
s'amuser *to have fun*	**s'endormir** *to fall asleep*	**s'occuper de** *to take care of*
s'appeler *to be called*	**s'ennuyer** *to be bored*	**se passer** *to happen*
s'approcher (de) *to come near*	**s'étonner (de)** *to be surprised (at)*	**se passer de** *to do without*
s'arrêter *to stop*	**s'excuser (de)** *to apologize (for)*	**se promener** *to go for a walk*
s'asseoir *to sit down*	**se fâcher** *to get angry/fall out*	**se rappeler** *to remember*

s'attendre à	**s'écrier**	**se raser**
to expect	*to cry out/exclaim*	*to shave*
se baigner	**s'habiller**	**se renseigner**
to have a bath	*to get dressed*	*to make enquiries*
se battre	**se hâter**	**se ressembler**
to fight	*to hurry*	*to look alike*
se blesser	**s'inquiéter**	**se retourner**
to hurt oneself	*to worry*	*to turn round*
se coucher	**s'installer**	**se réveiller**
to go to bed	*to settle down*	*to wake up*
se débarrasser de	**se laver**	**se sauver**
to get rid of	*to wash*	*to run away*
se demander	**se lever**	**se souvenir (de)**
to wonder	*to get up*	*to remember*
se dépêcher	**se mêler de**	**se taire**
to hurry	*to meddle with*	*to be/keep quiet*
se déshabiller	**se mettre à**	**se tromper**
to undress	*to start*	*to be mistaken*
se diriger vers	**se mettre en route**	**se trouver**
to move towards	*to set off*	*to be (situated)*

E IMPERSONAL VERBS

1 Conjugation

Impersonal verbs are used only in the third person singular and in the infinitive. The subject is always the impersonal pronoun il (= it).

il neige	**il y a du brouillard**
it's snowing	*it's foggy*

2 List of impersonal verbs

a) *verbs describing the weather:*

i) **faire + adjective:**

il fait beau/chaud	**il fait frais/froid**
it's fine/warm	*it's cool/cold*
il fera beau demain	**il va faire très froid**
the weather will be good tomorrow	*it will be very cold*

ii) **faire + noun:**

il fait beau temps	**il fait mauvais temps**
the weather is nice	*the weather is bad*
il fait jour	**il fait nuit**
it's daylight	*it's dark*

iii) other impersonal verbs and verbs used impersonally to describe the weather:

il gèle	**(geler)**	*it's freezing*
il grêle	**(grêler)**	*it's hailing*
il neige	**(neiger)**	*it's snowing*
il pleut	**(pleuvoir)**	*it's raining*
il tonne	**(tonner)**	*there's thunder*

Note that some of these verbs may be used personally:

je gèle	*I'm freezing*

iv) **il y a + noun:**

il y a des nuages	*it's cloudy*
il y a du brouillard	*it's foggy*
il y a du verglas	*it's icy*

b) être

i) **il est + noun:**

il est cinq heures	**il était une fois un géant**
it's five o'clock	*once upon a time there was a giant*

ii) **il est + adjective + de + infinitive:**

il est difficile de	*it's difficult to*
il est facile de	*it's easy to*
il est nécessaire de	*it's necessary to*
il est inutile de	*it's useless to*
il est possible de	*it's possible to*
il est difficile d'en parler	
it's difficult to talk about it	

Note that the indirect object pronoun in French corresponds to the English 'for me', 'for him' etc:

il m'est difficile d'en parler
it's difficult for me to talk about it

iii) **il est + adjective + que:**

il est douteux que	*it's doubtful that*
il est évident que	*it's clear that*
il est possible que	*it's possible that*
il est probable que	*it's probable that*
il est peu probable que	*it's unlikely that*
il est vrai que	*it's true that*

Note that que may be followed by the indicative or the subjunctive (see p B32):

il est probable qu'il ne viendra pas
he probably won't come

il est peu probable qu'il vienne
it's unlikely that he'll come

c) arriver, se passer *(to happen)*

il est arrivé une chose curieuse	**que se passe-t-il?**
a strange thing happened	*what's happening?*

d) exister *(to exist)*, rester *(to remain)*, manquer *(to be missing)*

il existe trois exemplaires de ce livre
there are three copies of this book

il me restait un euro	**il me manque 4 euros**
I had one euro left	*I am 4 euros short*

e) paraître, sembler *(to seem)*

il paraîtrait/semblerait qu'il ait changé d'avis
it would appear that he has changed his mind

il paraît qu'il va se marier
it seems he's going to get married

il me semble que le professeur s'est trompé
it seems to me that the teacher has made a mistake

f) other common impersonal verbs

i) s'agir de *(to be a matter of)* may be followed by a noun, a pronoun or an infinitive:

il s'agit de ton avenir	**de quoi s'agit-il?**
it's about your future	*what's it about?*
il s'agit de trouver le coupable	
we must find the culprit	

ii) falloir *(to be necessary)* may be followed by a noun, an infinitive or the subjunctive:

il faut deux heures pour aller à Paris
it takes two hours to get to Paris

il me faut plus de temps
I need more time

il faudra rentrer plus tôt ce soir
we'll have to come home earlier tonight

il faut que tu parles à Papa
you have to speak to Dad

iii) **suffire** *(to be enough)* may be followed by a noun, an infinitive or the subjunctive:

il suffit de peu de choses pour être heureux
it doesn't take much to be happy

il suffit de passer le pont
you just have to cross the bridge

il suffira qu'ils te donnent le numéro de téléphone
they will only have to give you the telephone number

iv) **valoir mieux** *(to be better)* may be followed by an infinitive or the subjunctive:

il vaudrait mieux prendre le car
it would be better to take the coach

il vaut mieux que vous ne sortiez pas seule le soir
you'd better not go out alone at night

F TENSES

For the formation of the different tenses, see pp B24 and B26-8.

Note that French has no continuous tenses (as in 'I am eating', 'I was going', 'I will be arriving'). The 'be' and '-ing' parts of English continuous tenses are not translated as separate words. Instead, the equivalent tense is used in French:

| **je mange** | **je mangerai** |
| *I am eating* | *I will be eating* |

1 PRESENT

The present is used to describe what someone does/something that happens regularly, or what someone is doing/something that is happening at the time of speaking.

a) *regular actions*

il travaille dans un bureau
he works in an office

je lis rarement le journal
I seldom read the paper

b) *continuous actions*

ne le dérangez pas, il travaille
don't disturb him, he's working

je ne peux pas venir, je garde mon petit frère
I can't come, I'm looking after my little brother

Note that the continuous nature of the action can also be expressed by using the phrase **être en train de** *(to be in the process of)* + infinitive:

je suis en train de cuisiner
I'm (busy) cooking

c) *immediate future*

je pars demain
I'm leaving tomorrow

However, the present cannot be used after **quand** and other conjunctions of time when the future is implied (see p B31):

je le ferai quand j'aurai le temps
I'll do it when I have the time

d) *general truths*

la vie est dure
life is hard

2 IMPERFECT

The imperfect is a past tense used to express what someone was doing or what someone used to do, or to describe something in the past. The imperfect refers particularly to something that continued over a period of time, as opposed to something that happened at a specific point in time.

a) *continuous actions*

The imperfect describes an action that was happening, often

when something else took place:

il prenait un bain quand le téléphone a sonné
he was having a bath when the phone rang

excuse-moi, je pensais à autre chose
I'm sorry, I was thinking of something else

Note that the continuous nature of the action can be emphasized by using **être en train de** + infinitive:

j'étais en train de faire le ménage
I was (busy) doing the housework

b) *regular actions in the past*

je le voyais souvent quand il habitait dans le quartier
I used to see him often when he lived in this area

quand il était plus jeune il voyageait beaucoup
when he was younger he used to travel a lot

c) *description in the past*

il faisait beau ce jour-là	**c'était formidable!**
the weather was good that day	*it was great!*
elle portait une robe bleue	**elle donnait sur la rue**
she wore a blue dress	*it looked onto the street*

3 PERFECT

The perfect tense is a compound past tense, used to express single actions which have been completed. What someone did, has done or has been doing, or something that has happened or has been happening are all expressed using the perfect tense:

je l'ai envoyé lundi	**on est sorti hier soir**
I sent it on Monday	*we went out last night*
tu t'es bien amusé?	**je ne l'ai pas vu de toute la journée**
did you have a good time?	*I haven't seen him all day*
j'ai lu toute la journée	**tu as déjà mangé?**
I've been reading all day	*have you eaten?*

In English, the simple past ('did', 'went', 'prepared') is used to describe both single and repeated actions in the past. In French, the perfect only describes single actions in the past, while repeated actions are expressed by the imperfect (they are sometimes signposted by 'used to'). Thus 'I went' should be translated 'j'allais' or 'je suis allé' depending on the nature of the action:

après dîner, je suis allé en ville
after dinner I went into town

l'an dernier, j'allais plus souvent au théâtre
last year I went to the theatre more often

4 PAST HISTORIC

This tense is used in the same way as the perfect tense, to describe a single, completed action in the past (what someone did or something that happened). It is a literary tense, not common in everyday spoken French; it is found mainly as a narrative tense in written form:

le piéton ne vit pas arriver la voiture
the pedestrian didn't see the car coming

5 PLUPERFECT

This compound tense is used to express what someone had done/had been doing or something that had happened or had been happening:

il n'avait pas voulu aller avec eux
he hadn't wanted to go with them

elle était essoufflée parce qu'elle avait couru
she was out of breath because she'd been running

However, the pluperfect is not used as in English with **depuis** *(for, since)*, or with **venir de** + infinitive *(to have just done something)*. For details see p B31:

il neigeait depuis une semaine
it had been snowing for a week

les pompiers venaient d'arriver
the firemen had just arrived

6 FUTURE

This tense is used to express what someone will do or will be doing or something that will happen or will be happening:

je ferai la vaisselle demain   **j'arriverai tard**
I'll do the dishes tomorrow   *I'll be arriving late*

Note that the future and not the present, as in English, is used in time clauses introduced by quand *(when)* or other conjunctions of time where the future is implied (see section 11):

il viendra quand il le pourra
he'll come when he can

French makes frequent use of aller + infinitive *(to be about to do something)* to express the immediate future:

je vais vous expliquer ce qui s'est passé
I'll explain (to you) what happened

il va déménager la semaine prochaine
he's moving house next week

7 FUTURE PERFECT

This compound tense is used to describe what someone will have done or will have been doing in the future or to describe something that will have happened in the future:

j'aurai bientôt fini
I will soon have finished

In particular, it is used instead of the English perfect in time clauses introduced by quand or other conjunctions of time where the future is implied (see section 11):

appelle-moi quand tu auras fini
call me when you've finished

on rentrera dès qu'on aura fait les courses
we'll come back as soon as we've done the shopping

8 PAST ANTERIOR

This tense is used instead of the pluperfect to express an action that preceded another action in the past (ie a past in the past). It is usually introduced by a conjunction of time (translated by 'when', 'as soon as', 'after' etc) and the main verb is in the past historic:

il se coucha dès qu'ils furent partis
he went to bed as soon as they'd left

à peine eut-elle raccroché que le téléphone sonna
she'd hardly hung up when the telephone rang

9 Use of tenses with 'depuis' (for, since)

a) The present must be used instead of the perfect to describe actions which started in the past and are still continuing:

il habite ici depuis trois ans
he's been living here for three years

elle t'attend depuis ce matin
she's been waiting for you since this morning

Note, however, that the perfect, not the present, is used when the clause is negative or when the action has been completed:

il n'a pas pris de vacances depuis longtemps
he hasn't taken any holidays for a long time

j'ai fini depuis un bon moment
I've been finished for quite a while

Note:

i)   il y a ... que or voilà ... que are also used with the present tense to translate 'for':

it's been ringing for ten minutes
ça sonne depuis dix minutes
il y a dix minutes que ça sonne
voilà dix minutes que ça sonne

ii) depuis que is used when 'since' introduces a clause, ie when there is a verb following depuis:

elle dort depuis que vous êtes partis
she's been sleeping since you left

iii) Do not confuse depuis *(for, since)* and pendant *(for, during)*: depuis refers to the starting point of an action which is still going on and pendant refers to the duration of an action which is over and is used with the perfect:

il vit ici depuis deux mois
he's been living here for two months

il a vécu ici pendant deux mois
he lived here for two months

b) The imperfect must be used instead of the pluperfect to describe an action which had started in the past and was still going on at a given time:

elle le connaissait depuis son enfance
she had known him since her childhood

il attendait depuis trois heures quand on est arrivé
he had been waiting for three hours when we arrived

Note, however, that if the sentence is negative or if the action has been completed, the pluperfect and not the imperfect is used:

je n'étais pas allé au théâtre depuis des années
I hadn't been to the theatre for years

il était parti depuis peu
he'd been gone for a short while

Note:

i)   il y avait ... que + imperfect is also used to translate 'for':

she'd been living alone for a long time
elle habitait seule depuis longtemps
il y avait longtemps qu'elle habitait seule

ii) depuis que is used when 'since' introduces a clause; if it describes an action which was still going on at the time, it can be followed by the imperfect, otherwise it is followed by the pluperfect:

il pleuvait depuis que nous étions en vacances
it had been raining since we had been on holiday

il pleuvait depuis que nous étions arrivés
it had been raining since we arrived

iii) Do not confuse depuis and pendant: depuis refers to the starting point of an action which is still going on and pendant refers to the duration of an action which is over; pendant is used with the pluperfect:

j'y travaillais depuis un an
I had been working there for a year

j'y avais travaillé pendant un an
I had worked there for a year

10 Use of tenses with 'venir de'

venir de + infinitive means 'to have just done'.

a) If it describes something that has just happened, it is used in the present instead of the perfect:

l'avion vient d'arriver   **je viens de te le dire!**
the plane has just arrived   *I've just told you!*

b) If it describes something that had just happened, it is used in the imperfect instead of the pluperfect:

le film venait de commencer   **je venais de rentrer**
the film had just started   *I'd just got home*

11 Use of tenses after conjunctions of time

quand	when
tant que	as long as
dès/aussitôt que	as soon as
lorsque	when
pendant que	while

Verbs which follow these conjunctions must be used in the following tenses:

a) future instead of present:

je te téléphonerai quand je serai prêt
I'll phone you when I'm ready

elle ira le voir dès qu'elle le pourra
she'll go to see him as soon as she can

b) future perfect instead of perfect when the future is implied:

on rentrera dès qu'on aura fini les courses
we'll come back as soon as we've done the shopping

je t'appellerai dès qu'il sera arrivé
I'll call you as soon as he's arrived

c) conditional present/perfect instead of perfect/pluperfect in indirect speech:

il a dit qu'il sortirait quand il aurait fini
he said that he would come out when he had finished

For the tenses of the subjunctive and conditional, see G1 and G3.

G MOODS

1 THE SUBJUNCTIVE

In everyday spoken French, the only two subjunctive tenses that are used are the present and the perfect. The imperfect and the pluperfect subjunctive are found mainly in literature or in texts of a formal nature.

The subjunctive is always preceded by the conjunction **que** and is used in subordinate clauses when the subject of the subordinate clause is different from the subject of the main verb.

Some clauses introduced by **que** take the indicative. The subjunctive must be used after the following:

a) Verbs of emotion:

être content que	to be pleased that
être désolé que	to be sorry that
être étonné que	to be surprised that
être heureux que	to be happy that
être surpris que	to be surprised that
être triste que	to be sad that
avoir peur que ... ne	to be afraid/to fear that
craindre que ... ne	to be afraid/to fear that
regretter que	to be sorry that

ils étaient contents que j'aille les voir
they were pleased (that) I went to visit them

je serais très étonné qu'il mente
I would be very surprised if he was lying

je regrette que tu ne puisses pas y aller
I'm sorry (that) you can't go

Note that **ne** is used after several verbs in the subjunctive mood but it does not have a negative meaning in itself and is not translated in English:

je crains que l'avion ne soit en retard
I'm afraid (that) the plane will be late

j'ai bien peur qu'il ne soit déjà trop tard
I'm very much afraid (that) it's already too late

pour éviter que la situation ne s'aggrave
to prevent the situation from getting any worse

b) Verbs of wishing and willing:

aimer que	to like
désirer que	to wish (that)
préférer que	to prefer (that)
souhaiter que	to wish (that)
vouloir que	to want

Note that in English, such verbs are often used in the following type of construction: verb of willing + object + infinitive (eg I'd

like you to listen); this type of construction is impossible in French, where a subjunctive clause has to be used:

je souhaite que tu réussisses
I hope you will succeed

il aimerait que je lui écrive plus souvent
he'd like me to write to him more often

voulez-vous que je vous y amène en voiture?
would you like me to drive you there?

préférez-vous que je rappelle demain?
would you rather I called back tomorrow?

c) Impersonal constructions (expressing necessity, possibility, doubt, denial, preference):

il faut que	it is necessary (that) (must)
il est nécessaire que	it is necessary that (must)
il est important que	it is important (that)
il est possible que	it is possible that (may)
il se peut que	it is possible that (may)
il est impossible que	it is impossible (that) (can't)
il est douteux que	it is doubtful whether
il est peu probable que	it is unlikely that
il semble que	it seems (that)
il est préférable que	it is preferable (that)
il vaut mieux que	it is better (that) (had better)
c'est dommage que	it is a pity (that)

Note that these expressions may be used in any appropriate tense:

il faut absolument que je le leur dise
I simply must tell them

il était important que tu le saches
it was important that you should know

il se pourrait qu'elle change d'avis
she might change her mind

il est peu probable qu'ils s'y intéressent
they're unlikely to be interested in that

il semble qu'elle ait raison
she appears to be right

il vaudrait mieux que tu ne promettes rien
you'd better not promise anything

c'est dommage que vous vous soyez manqués
it's a pity you missed each other

d) Some verbs and impersonal constructions expressing doubt or uncertainty (mainly used negatively or interrogatively):

douter que	to doubt (that)
(ne pas) croire que	(not) to believe (that)
(ne pas) penser que	(not) to think (that)
(ne pas) être sûr que	(not) to be sure that
il n'est pas certain que	it isn't certain that
il n'est pas évident que	it isn't obvious that
il n'est pas sûr que	it isn't certain that
il n'est pas vrai que	it isn't true that

je doute fort qu'il veuille t'aider
I very much doubt whether he'll want to help you

croyez-vous qu'il y ait des places libres?
do you think there are any seats available?

on n'était pas sûr que ce soit le bon endroit
we weren't sure that it was the right place

il n'était pas certain qu'elle puisse gagner
it wasn't certain whether she could win

e) attendre que (to wait until someone does something or something happens, to wait for someone to do something or for something to happen):

attendons qu'il revienne
let's wait until he comes back

f) Some subordinating conjunctions:

bien que	although
quoique	although
sans que	without
pour que	so that
afin que	so that
à condition que	provided that
pourvu que	provided that
jusqu'à ce que	until
en attendant que	until
avant que ... (ne)	before
à moins que ... (ne)	unless
de peur que ... ne	for fear that
de crainte que ... ne	for fear that
de sorte que	so that
de façon que	so that
de manière que	so that

Note that when ne is shown in brackets, it may follow the conjunction, although it is seldom used in spoken French; it does not have a negative meaning, and is not translated in English.

il est allé travailler bien qu'il soit malade
he went to work although he was ill

elle est entrée sans que je la voie
she came in without me seeing her

voilà de l'argent pour que tu puisses aller au cinéma
here's some money so that you can go to the cinema

d'accord, pourvu que tu me promettes de ne pas le répéter
all right, as long as you promise not to tell anyone

tu l'as revu avant qu'il (ne) parte?
did you see him again before he left?

je le ferai demain, à moins que ce (ne) soit urgent
I'll do it tomorrow, unless it's urgent

elle n'a pas fait de bruit de peur qu'il ne se réveille
she didn't make any noise in case he woke

parle moins fort de sorte qu'elle ne nous entende pas
talk more quietly so that she doesn't hear us

Note that when de façon/manière que *(so that)* expresses a result, as opposed to a purpose, the indicative is used instead of the subjunctive:

il a fait du bruit de sorte qu'elle l'a entendu
he made some noise, and as a result she heard him

g) A superlative or adjectives like premier *(first)*, dernier *(last)*, seul *(only)* followed by qui or que:

c'était le coureur le plus rapide que j'aie jamais vu
he was the fastest runner I ever saw

Note, however, that the indicative is used with a statement of fact rather than the expression of an opinion:

c'est lui qui me l'a dit
it was he who told me

h) Negative and indefinite pronouns (eg rien, personne, quelqu'un) followed by qui or que:

je ne connais personne qui fasse aussi bien les crêpes
I don't know anyone who can make such good crêpes

il n'y a aucune chance qu'il réussisse
he hasn't got a chance of succeeding

ils cherchent quelqu'un qui puisse garder le bébé
they're looking for someone who can look after the baby

2 AVOIDING THE SUBJUNCTIVE

Note, however, that the subjunctive is not used if the verbs in both clauses have the same subject. The infinitive will be used in the subordinate clause instead, sometimes introduced by a preposition (à or de) (see pp B35-7).

a) **de** + infinitive replaces the subjunctive after:

i) verbs of emotion:

j'ai été étonné d'apprendre la nouvelle
I was surprised to hear the news

il regrette de ne pas être arrivé plus tôt
he's sorry he didn't arrive earlier

tu as peur de ne pas avoir assez d'argent?
are you worried you won't have enough money?

ii) **attendre** *(to wait)* and **douter** *(to doubt)*:

j'attendrai d'avoir bu mon café
I'll wait until I've drunk my coffee

iii) most impersonal constructions:

il serait préférable de les en informer tout de suite
it would be better to let them know immediately

il est indispensable de parler une langue étrangère
it's essential to be able to speak a foreign language

iv) most conjunctions:

il est resté dans la voiture afin de ne pas se mouiller
he stayed in the car so as not to get wet

j'ai lu avant de m'endormir
I read before falling asleep

tu peux sortir à condition de rentrer avant minuit
you can go out, as long as you're back before midnight

b) **à** + infinitive replaces the subjunctive after:

i) **de façon/manière**

mets la liste sur la table de manière à ne pas l'oublier
put the list on the table so that you won't forget it

ii) **premier, seul, dernier**

il a été le seul à s'excuser
he was the only one who apologized

c) The infinitive without any linking preposition replaces the subjunctive after:

i) verbs of wishing and willing:

je voudrais sortir avec toi
I'd like to go out with you

ii) **il faut, il vaut mieux**:

il vous faudra prendre des chèques de voyage
you'll have to take some traveller's cheques

il lui a fallu recommencer à zéro
he had to start all over again

il vaudrait mieux lui apporter des fleurs que des bonbons
it would be better to take her flowers than sweets

Note that il faut + infinitive is used to state a generality. If one particular person etc is the subject of the action, an indirect object is used:

il faut réserver à l'avance
you have to book in advance

il lui faut se dépêcher
he has to hurry

iii) verbs of thinking:

je ne crois pas le connaître
I don't think I know him

tu penses être chez toi à cinq heures?
do you think you'll be home at five?

iv) **pour** and **sans**:

le car est reparti sans nous attendre
the coach left without waiting for us

j'économise pour pouvoir **acheter une moto**
I'm saving up to buy a motorbike

3 THE CONDITIONAL

a) *The conditional present*

i) The conditional present is used to describe what someone would do or would be doing, or what would happen (if something else were to happen):

si j'avais de l'argent, je ferais **le tour du monde**
if I had money, I would travel around the world

Note that when the main verb is in the conditional present, the verb after si is in the imperfect.

ii) It is also used in indirect questions or reported speech instead of the future:

il ne m'a pas dit s'il viendrait
he didn't tell me whether he would come

b) *The conditional perfect (or past conditional)*

The conditional perfect or past conditional is used to express what someone would have done or would have been doing or what would have happened:

si j'avais su, je n'aurais rien dit
if I had known, I wouldn't have said anything

qu'aurais-je fait **sans toi?**
what would I have done without you?

Note that if the main verb is in the conditional perfect, the verb introduced by si is in the pluperfect.

c) *Tenses after si*

The tense of the verb introduced by si is determined by the tense of the verb in the main clause:

MAIN VERB		VERB FOLLOWING 'SI'
conditional present	→	imperfect
conditional perfect	→	pluperfect

je te le dirais **si je le** savais
I would tell you if I knew

je te l'aurais dit **si je l'**avais su
I would have told you if I had known

The conditional and the future should never be used with si unless si means 'whether' (ie when it introduces an indirect question):

je me demande si j'y serais arrivé **sans toi**
I wonder if I would have managed without you

4 THE IMPERATIVE

a) *Definition*

The imperative is used to give commands or polite instructions, or to make requests or suggestions; these can be positive ('do!') or negative ('don't!'):

mange ta soupe!   **n'aie pas peur!**
eat your soup!   *don't be afraid!*

partons!   **entrez!**
let's go!   *come in!*

faites attention!   **n'hésitez pas!**
be careful!   *don't hesitate!*

tournez à droite à la poste
turn right at the post office

b) *Forms*

The imperative has only three forms, which are the same as the tu, nous and vous forms of the present tense, but without the subject pronoun:

	-ER VERBS	-IR VERBS	-RE VERBS
'tu' form:	regarde *watch*	choisis *choose*	attends *wait*
'nous' form:	regardons *let's watch*	choisissons *let's choose*	attendons *let's wait*
'vous' form:	regardez *watch*	choisissez *choose*	attendez *wait*

Note:

i) The -s of the tu form of -er verbs is dropped, except when y or en follow the verb:

parle-lui!   **parles-en avec lui**
speak to him!   *speak to him about it*

achète du sucre!   **achètes-en un kilo**
buy some sugar!   *buy a kilo (of it)*

ii) The distinction between the subject pronouns tu and vous (see p B18) applies to the tu and vous forms of the imperative:

prends ta sœur avec toi
take your sister with you

prenez le plat du jour, Monsieur; c'est du poulet rôti
have today's special, sir; it's roast chicken

ouvrez vos livres à la page 24
open your books at page 24

c) *Negative commands*

In negative commands, the verb is placed between ne and pas (or the second part of other negative expressions):

ne fais pas ça!   **ne dites rien!**
don't do that!   *don't say anything!*

d) *Imperative with object pronouns*

In positive commands, object pronouns come after the verb and are attached to it by a hyphen. In negative commands, they come before the verb (see pp B18-20):

dites-moi ce qui s'est passé   **attendons-les!**
tell me what happened   *let's wait for them*

prends-en bien soin, ne l'abîme pas!
take good care of it, don't damage it!

ne le leur dis pas!   **ne les écoutez pas**
don't tell them (that)!   *don't listen to them*

e) *Imperative of reflexive verbs*

The position of the reflexive pronoun of reflexive verbs is the same as that of object pronouns:

tais-toi!   **levez-vous!**
be quiet!   *get up!*

méfiez-vous de lui   **arrêtons-nous ici**
don't trust him   *let's stop here*

ne nous plaignons pas   **ne t'approche pas plus!**
let's not complain   *don't come any closer!*

f) *Alternatives to the imperative*

i) infinitive

the infinitive is often used instead of the imperative in written instructions and in recipes:

s'adresser au concierge   **ne pas fumer**
see the caretaker   *no smoking*

verser le lait et bien mélanger
pour in the milk and mix well

ii) subjunctive

as the imperative has no third person (singular or plural), que + subjunctive is used for giving orders in the third person:

Jacques s'est trompé
Jacques made a mistake

Marie s'était levée tard
Marie had got up late

ils se sont disputés?
did they have an argument?

elles se sont vues
they saw each other

Michèle et Marie, vous vous êtes habillées?
Michèle and Marie, have you got dressed yet?

Note, however, that the past participle does not agree when the reflexive pronoun is an indirect object:

elles se sont écrit
they wrote to each other

elle s'est lavé les cheveux
she washed her hair

ils se sont serré la main
they shook hands

J THE PASSIVE

1 Formation

The passive is used when the subject does not perform the action, but is subjected to it, eg:

the house has been sold   he was made redundant

Passive tenses are formed with the corresponding tense of the verb être ('to be', as in English), followed by the past participle of the verb, eg:

j'ai été invité
I was invited

The past participle must agree with its subject, eg:

il sera puni
he will be punished

elle a été renvoyée
she has been dismissed

ils seront déçus
they will be disappointed

elles ont été vues
they were seen

2 Avoidance of the passive

The passive is far less common in French than in English. In particular, an indirect object cannot become the subject of a sentence in French; the following sentence, where 'he' is an indirect object, has no equivalent in French:

he was given a book (ie a book was given to him)

In general, French tries to avoid the passive wherever possible. This can be done in several ways.

a) *By using the pronoun* on

on m'a volé mon portefeuille
my wallet has been stolen

on construit une nouvelle piscine
a new swimming pool is being built

en France, on boit beaucoup de vin
a lot of wine is drunk in France

b) *By making the agent the subject of the verb*

If the agent, that is the real subject, is mentioned in English, it can become the subject of the French verb:

la nouvelle va les surprendre
they will be surprised by the news

mon correspondant m'a invité
I've been invited by my penfriend

mon cadeau te plaît?
are you pleased with my present?

c) *By using a reflexive verb*

Reflexive forms can be created for a large number of verbs, particularly in the third person:

elle s'appelle Anne
she is called Anne

ton absence va se remarquer
your absence will be noticed

ce plat se mange froid
this dish is eaten cold

cela ne se fait pas ici
that isn't done here

d) *By using se faire + infinitive (when the subject is a person)*

il s'est fait renverser par une voiture
he was run over by a car

je me suis fait couper les cheveux
I've had my hair cut

3 Conjugation

For the complete conjugation of a verb in the passive, see être aimé *(to be loved)* p B41.

K MODAL AUXILIARY VERBS

The modal auxiliary verbs are always followed by the infinitive. They express an obligation, a probability, an intention, a possibility or a wish rather than a fact.

The five modal auxiliary verbs are: devoir, pouvoir, savoir, vouloir and falloir.

1 Devoir (for conjugation see p B44) is used to express the following:

a) *obligation*

nous devons arriver à temps
we must arrive in time

nous avions dû partir
we had (had) to go

demain tu devras prendre le bus
tomorrow you'll have to take the bus

j'ai dû avouer que j'avais tort
I had to admit that I was wrong

In the conditional, devoir may be used for advice, ie to express what should be done (conditional present) or should have been done (conditional past):

vous devriez travailler davantage
you ought to/should work harder

tu ne devrais pas marcher sur l'herbe
you shouldn't walk on the grass

tu aurais dû tout avouer
you should have admitted everything

tu n'aurais pas dû manger ces champignons
you shouldn't have eaten those mushrooms

Note that the French infinitive is translated by a past participle in English: manger = eaten.

b) *probability*

il doit être en train de dormir
he must be sleeping (he's probably sleeping)

j'ai dû me tromper de chemin
I must have taken the wrong road

Note that in a past narrative sequence in the distant past, 'must have' is translated by a pluperfect in French:

il dit qu'il avait dû se tromper de chemin
he said he must have taken the wrong road

c) *intention, expectation*

je dois aller chez le dentiste
I am supposed to go to the dentist

le train doit arriver à 19h30
the train is due to arrive at 7.30 p.m.

2 Pouvoir (for conjugation see p B48) is used to express the following:

a) *capacity/ability*

il peut rester plusieurs jours sans dormir
he can go without sleep for several days

cette voiture peut faire du 150
this car can go up to 93 mph

il était si faible qu'il ne pouvait pas sortir de son lit
he was so weak that he couldn't get out of bed

b) *permission*

puis-je entrer?
may I come in?

puis-je vous offrir du thé?
may I offer you some tea?

c) *possibility*

cela peut arriver
it can happen

ça peut n'avoir aucune importance
it might not be at all important

Note that **pouvoir** + the infinitive is usually replaced by **peut-être** + the finite tense, eg **il s'est peut-être trompé de livres** *(he may have taken the wrong books)*.

In the conditional, **pouvoir** is used to express something that could or might be (conditional present) or that could or might have been (conditional past):

tu pourrais t'excuser
you might apologize

j'aurais pu vous prêter mon téléphone portable
I could have lent you my mobile phone

Note that with verbs of perception, eg **entendre** *(to hear)*, **sentir** *(to feel, to smell)*, **voir** *(to see)*, **pouvoir** is often omitted.

j'entendais le bruit des vagues
I could hear the sound of the waves

3 **Savoir** (for conjugation see p B49) is used to express 'to know how to':

je sais/savais conduire une moto
I can/used to be able to ride a motorbike

elle sait parler plusieurs langues
she can speak several languages

4 **Vouloir** (for conjugation see p B51) is used to express the following:

a) *desire*

je veux partir
I want to go

voulez-vous danser avec moi?
will you dance with me?

b) *wish*

je voudrais être riche
I wish I were rich

je voudrais trouver un travail intéressant
I'd like to find an interesting job

j'aurais voulu te donner un coup de poing
I would have liked to punch you

c) *intention*

il a voulu sauter par la fenêtre
he tried to jump out of the window

Note that **veuillez**, the imperative of **vouloir**, is used as a polite form to express a request *('would you please ... ')*:

veuillez ne pas déranger
please do not disturb

5 **Falloir** (for conjugation see p B46) is used to express necessity:

il faut manger pour vivre
you must eat to live

il faudrait y aller tout de suite
we should go right away

il aurait fallu apporter des sandwichs
we should have brought sandwiches

Note that some of the above verbs can also be used without infinitive constructions in which case they have a different meaning, eg **devoir** = *to owe*, **savoir** = *to know*.

je te dois 20 euros
I owe you 20 euros

elle le sait par cœur
she knows it by heart

L CONJUGATION TABLES

The following verbs provide the main patterns of conjugation including the conjugation of the most common irregular verbs. They are arranged in alphabetical order:

-er verb (see p B24)	AIMER
-ir verb (see p B24)	FINIR
-re verb (see p B24)	VENDRE
Reflexive verb (see pp B28-9)	SE MÉFIER
Verb with auxiliary être (see p B27)	ARRIVER
Verb in the passive (see p B39)	ÊTRE AIMÉ
Auxiliaries (see pp B26-8)	AVOIR
	ÊTRE
Verb in -eler/-eter (see p B25)	APPELER
Verb in -e + consonant + er (see p B26)	ACHETER
Verb in é + consonant + er (see p B26)	ESPÉRER
Modal auxiliaries (see p B39)	DEVOIR
	POUVOIR
	SAVOIR
	VOULOIR
	FALLOIR
Irregular verbs	ALLER
	CONDUIRE
	CONNAÎTRE
	CROIRE
	DIRE
	DORMIR
	ÉCRIRE
	FAIRE
	METTRE
	OUVRIR
	PRENDRE
	RECEVOIR
	TENIR
	VENIR
	VIVRE
	VOIR

ACHETER   *to buy*

PRESENT	IMPERFECT	FUTURE	SUBJUNCTIVE	IMPERATIVE
j'achète	j'achetais	j'achèterai	**PRESENT**	achète
tu achètes	tu achetais	tu achèteras	j'achète	achetons
il achète	il achetait	il achètera	tu achètes	achetez
nous achetons	nous achetions	nous achèterons	il achète	
vous achetez	vous achetiez	vous achèterez	nous achetions	
ils achètent	ils achetaient	ils achèteront	vous achetiez	
			ils achètent	**INFINITIVE**

PAST HISTORIC	PERFECT	PLUPERFECT	IMPERFECT	PRESENT
j'achetai	j'ai acheté	j'avais acheté	j'achetasse	acheter
tu achetas	tu as acheté	tu avais acheté	tu achetasses	
il acheta	il a acheté	il avait acheté	il achetât	**PAST**
nous achetâmes	nous avons acheté	nous avions acheté	nous achetassions	avoir acheté
vous achetâtes	vous avez acheté	vous aviez acheté	vous achetassiez	
ils achetèrent	ils ont acheté	ils avaient acheté	ils achetassent	
	CONDITIONAL		PERFECT	PARTICIPLE

PAST ANTERIOR	PRESENT	PAST	PERFECT	PARTICIPLE
j'eus acheté etc	j'achèterais	j'aurais acheté	j'aie acheté	**PRESENT**
	tu achèterais	tu aurais acheté	tu aies acheté	achetant
	il achèterait	il aurait acheté	il ait acheté	
	nous achèterions	nous aurions acheté	nous ayons acheté	**PAST**
FUTURE PERFECT	vous achèteriez	vous auriez acheté	vous ayez acheté	acheté
j'aurai acheté etc	ils achèteraient	ils auraient acheté	ils aient acheté	

AIMER   *to like/to love*

PRESENT	IMPERFECT	FUTURE	SUBJUNCTIVE	IMPERATIVE
j'aime	j'aimais	j'aimerai	**PRESENT**	aime
tu aimes	tu aimais	tu aimeras	j'aime	aimons
il aime	il aimait	il aimera	tu aimes	aimez
nous aimons	nous aimions	nous aimerons	il aime	
vous aimez	vous aimiez	vous aimerez	nous aimions	
ils aiment	ils aimaient	ils aimeront	vous aimiez	
			ils aiment	**INFINITIVE**

PAST HISTORIC	PERFECT	PLUPERFECT	IMPERFECT	PRESENT
j'aimai	j'ai aimé	j'avais aimé	j'aimasse	aimer
tu aimas	tu as aimé	tu avais aimé	tu aimasses	
il aima	il a aimé	il avait aimé	il aimât	**PAST**
nous aimâmes	nous avons aimé	nous avions aimé	nous aimassions	avoir aimé
vous aimâtes	vous avez aimé	vous aviez aimé	vous aimassiez	
ils aimèrent	ils ont aimé	ils avaient aimé	ils aimassent	
	CONDITIONAL		PERFECT	PARTICIPLE

PAST ANTERIOR	PRESENT	PAST	PERFECT	PARTICIPLE
j'eus aimé etc	j'aimerais	j'aurais aimé	j'aie aimé	**PRESENT**
	tu aimerais	tu aurais aimé	tu aies aimé	aimant
	il aimerait	il aurait aimé	il ait aimé	
	nous aimerions	nous aurions aimé	nous ayons aimé	**PAST**
FUTURE PERFECT	vous aimeriez	vous auriez aimé	vous ayez aimé	aimé
j'aurai aimé etc	ils aimeraient	ils auraient aimé	ils aient aimé	

ÊTRE AIMÉ   *to be loved*

PRESENT	IMPERFECT	FUTURE	SUBJUNCTIVE	IMPERATIVE
je suis aimé(e)	j'étais aimé(e)	je serai aimé(e)	**PRESENT**	sois aimé(e)
tu es aimé(e)	tu étais aimé(e)	tu seras aimé(e)	je sois aimé(e)	soyons aimé(e)s
il (elle) est aimé(e)	il (elle) était aimé(e)	il (elle) sera aimé(e)	tu sois aimé(e)	soyez aimé(e)(s)
nous sommes aimé(e)s	nous étions aimé(e)s	nous serons aimé(e)s	il (elle) soit aimé(e)	
vous êtes aimé(e)(s)	vous étiez aimé(e)(s)	vous serez aimé(e)(s)	nous soyons aimé(e)s	
ils (elles) sont aimé(e)s	ils (elles) étaient aimé(e)s	ils seront aimé(e)s	vous soyez aimé(e)(s)	
			ils (elles) soient aimé(e)s	**INFINITIVE**

PAST HISTORIC	PERFECT	PLUPERFECT	IMPERFECT	PRESENT
je fus aimé(e)	j'ai été aimé(e)	j'avais été aimé(e)	je fusse aimé(e)	être aimé(e)(s)
tu fus aimé(e)	tu as été aimé(e)	tu avais été aimé(e)	tu fusses aimé(e)	
il (elle) fut aimé(e)	il (elle) a été aimé(e)	il (elle) avait été aimé(e)	il (elle) fût aimé(e)	**PAST**
nous fûmes aimé(e)s	nous avons été aimé(e)s	nous avions été aimé(e)s	nous fussions aimé(e)s	avoir été aimé(e)(s)
vous fûtes aimé(e)(s)	vous avez été aimé(e)(s)	vous aviez été aimé(e)(s)	vous fussiez	
ils (elles) furent aimé(e)s	ils (elles) ont été aimé(e)s	ils (elles) avaient été aimé(e)s	ils (elles) fussent aimé(e)s	
	CONDITIONAL		PERFECT	PARTICIPLE

PAST ANTERIOR	PRESENT	PAST	PERFECT	PARTICIPLE
j'eus été aimé(e) etc	je serais aimé(e)	j'aurais été aimé(e)	j'aie été aimé(e)	**PRESENT**
	tu serais aimé(e)	tu aurais été aimé(e)	tu aies été aimé(e)	étant aimé(e)(s)
	il (elle) serait aimé(e)	il (elle) aurait été aimé(e)	il (elle) ait été aimé(e)	
	nous serions aimé(e)s	nous aurions été aimé(e)s	nous ayons été aimé(e)s	**PAST**
FUTURE PERFECT	vous seriez aimé(e)(s)	vous auriez été aimé(e)(s)	vous ayez été aimé(e)(s)	été aimé(e)(s)
j'aurai été aimé(e) etc	ils (elles) seraient aimé(e)s	ils (elles) auraient été aimé(e)s	ils (elles) aient été aimé(e)s	

ALLER — *to go*

PRESENT	IMPERFECT	FUTURE	SUBJUNCTIVE	IMPERATIVE
je vais	j'allais	j'irai	**PRESENT**	va
tu vas	tu allais	tu iras	j'aille	allons
il va	il allait	il ira	tu ailles	allez
nous allons	nous allions	nous irons	il aille	
vous allez	vous alliez	vous irez	nous allions	
ils vont	ils allaient	ils iront	vous alliez	
			ils aillent	

PAST HISTORIC	PERFECT	PLUPERFECT	IMPERFECT	INFINITIVE
j'allai	je suis allé(e)	j'étais allé(e)	j'allasse	**PRESENT**
tu allas	tu es allé(e)	tu étais allé(e)	tu allasses	aller
il alla	il (elle) est allé(e)	il (elle) était allé(e)	il allât	
nous allâmes	nous sommes allé(e)s	nous étions allé(e)s	nous allassions	**PAST**
vous allâtes	vous êtes allé(e)(s)	vous étiez allé(e)(s)	vous allassiez	être allé(e)(s)
ils allèrent	ils (elles) sont allé(e)s	ils (elles) étaient allé(e)s	ils allassent	

	CONDITIONAL		PERFECT	PARTICIPLE
PAST ANTERIOR	PRESENT	PAST	je sois allé	**PRESENT**
je fus allé(e) etc	j'irais	je serais allé(e)	tu sois allé(e)	allant
	tu irais	tu serais allé(e)	il (elle) soit allé(e)	
	il irait	il (elle) serait allé(e)	nous soyons allé(e)s	**PAST**
	nous irions	nous serions allé(e)s	vous soyez allé(e)(s)	allé
FUTURE PERFECT	vous iriez	vous seriez allé(e)(s)	ils (elles) soient allé(e)s	
je serai allé(e) etc	ils iraient	ils (elles) seraient allé(e)s		

APPELER — *to call*

PRESENT	IMPERFECT	FUTURE	SUBJUNCTIVE	IMPERATIVE
j'appelle	j'appelais	j'appellerai	**PRESENT**	appelle
tu appelles	tu appelais	tu appelleras	j'appelle	appelons
il appelle	il appelait	il appellera	tu appelles	appelez
nous appelons	nous appelions	nous appellerons	il appelle	
vous appelez	vous appeliez	vous appellerez	nous appelions	
ils appellent	ils appelaient	ils appelleront	vous appeliez	
			ils appellent	

PAST HISTORIC	PERFECT	PLUPERFECT	IMPERFECT	INFINITIVE
j'appelai	j'ai appelé	j'avais appelé	j'appelasse	**PRESENT**
tu appelas	tu as appelé	tu avais appelé	tu appelasses	appeler
il appela	il a appelé	il avait appelé	il appelât	
nous appelâmes	nous avons appelé	nous avions appelé	nous appelassions	**PAST**
vous appelâtes	vous avez appelé	vous aviez appelé	vous appelassiez	avoir appelé
ils appelèrent	ils ont appelé	ils avaient appelé	ils appelassent	

	CONDITIONAL		PERFECT	PARTICIPLE
PAST ANTERIOR	PRESENT	PAST	j'aie appelé	**PRESENT**
j'eus appelé etc	j'appellerais	j'aurais appelé	tu aies appelé	appelant
	tu appellerais	tu aurais appelé	il ait appelé	
	il appellerait	il aurait appelé	nous ayons appelé	**PAST**
	nous appellerions	nous aurions appelé	vous ayez appelé	appelé
FUTURE PERFECT	vous appelleriez	vous auriez appelé	ils aient appelé	
j'aurai appelé etc	ils appelleraient	ils auraient appelé		

ARRIVER — *to arrive/to happen*

PRESENT	IMPERFECT	FUTURE	SUBJUNCTIVE	IMPERATIVE
j'arrive	j'arrivais	j'arriverai	**PRESENT**	arrive
tu arrives	tu arrivais	tu arriveras	j'arrive	arrivons
il arrive	il arrivait	il arrivera	tu arrives	arrivez
nous arrivons	nous arrivions	nous arriverons	il arrive	
vous arrivez	vous arriviez	vous arriverez	nous arrivions	
ils arrivent	ils arrivaient	ils arriveront	vous arriviez	
			ils arrivent	

PAST HISTORIC	PERFECT	PLUPERFECT	IMPERFECT	INFINITIVE
j'arrivai	je suis arrivé(e)	j'étais arrivé(e)	j'arrivasse	**PRESENT**
tu arrivas	tu es arrivé(e)	tu étais arrivé(e)	tu arrivasses	arriver
il arriva	il (elle) est arrivé(e)	il (elle) était arrivé(e)	il arrivât	
nous arrivâmes	nous sommes arrivé(e)s	nous étions arrivé(e)s	nous arrivassions	**PAST**
vous arrivâtes	vous êtes arrivé(e)(s)	vous étiez arrivé(e)(s)	vous arrivassiez	être arrivé(e)(s)
ils arrivèrent	ils (elles) sont arrivé(e)s	ils (elles) étaient arrivé(e)s	ils arrivassent	

	CONDITIONAL		PERFECT	PARTICIPLE
PAST ANTERIOR	PRESENT	PAST	je sois arrivé(e)	**PRESENT**
je fus arrivé(e) etc	j'arriverais	je serais arrivé(e)	tu sois arrivé(e)	arrivant
	tu arriverais	tu serais arrivé(e)	il (elle) soit arrivé(e)	
	il arriverait	il (elle) serait arrivé(e)	nous soyons arrivé(e)s	**PAST**
	nous arriverions	nous serions arrivé(e)s	vous soyez arrivé(e)(s)	arrivé
FUTURE PERFECT	vous arriveriez	vous seriez arrivé(e)(s)	ils (elles) soient arrivé(e)s	
je serai arrivé(e) etc	ils arriveraient	ils (elles) seraient arrivé(e)s		

AVOIR — *to have*

PRESENT	IMPERFECT	FUTURE	SUBJUNCTIVE	IMPERATIVE
j'ai	j'avais	j'aurai	**PRESENT**	aie
tu as	tu avais	tu auras	j'aie	ayons
il a	il avait	il aura	tu aies	ayez
nous avons	nous avions	nous aurons	il ait	
vous avez	vous aviez	vous aurez	nous ayons	
ils ont	ils avaient	ils auront	vous ayez	
			ils aient	
PAST HISTORIC	**PERFECT**	**PLUPERFECT**	**IMPERFECT**	**INFINITIVE**
j'eus	j'ai eu	j'avais eu	j'eusse	**PRESENT**
tu eus	tu as eu	tu avais eu	tu eusses	avoir
il eut	il a eu	il avait eu	il eût	
nous eûmes	nous avons eu	nous avions eu	nous eussions	**PAST**
vous eûtes	vous avez eu	vous aviez eu	vous eussiez	avoir eu
ils eurent	ils ont eu	ils avaient eu	ils eussent	
	CONDITIONAL		**PERFECT**	*PARTICIPLE*
PAST ANTERIOR	**PRESENT**	**PAST**	j'aie eu	**PRESENT**
j'eus eu etc	j'aurais	j'aurais eu	tu aies eu	ayant
	tu aurais	tu aurais eu	il ait eu	
	il aurait	il aurait eu	nous ayons eu	**PAST**
	nous aurions	nous aurions eu	vous ayez eu	eu
FUTURE PERFECT	vous auriez	vous auriez eu	ils aient eu	
j'aurai eu etc	ils auraient	ils auraient eu		

CONDUIRE — *to lead/to drive*

PRESENT	IMPERFECT	FUTURE	SUBJUNCTIVE	IMPERATIVE
je conduis	je conduisais	je conduirai	**PRESENT**	conduis
tu conduis	tu conduisais	tu conduiras	je conduise	conduisons
il conduit	il conduisait	il conduira	tu conduises	conduisez
nous conduisons	nous conduisions	nous conduirons	il conduise	
vous conduisez	vous conduisiez	vous conduirez	nous conduisions	
ils conduisent	ils conduisaient	ils conduiront	vous conduisiez	
			ils conduisent	
PAST HISTORIC	**PERFECT**	**PLUPERFECT**	**IMPERFECT**	**INFINITIVE**
je conduisis	j'ai conduit	j'avais conduit	je conduisisse	**PRESENT**
tu conduisis	tu as conduit	tu avais conduit	tu conduisisses	conduire
il conduisit	il a conduit	il avait conduit	il conduisît	
nous conduisîmes	nous avons conduit	nous avions conduit	nous conduisissions	**PAST**
vous conduisîtes	vous avez conduit	vous aviez conduit	vous conduisissiez	avoir conduit
ils conduisirent	ils ont conduit	ils avaient conduit	ils conduisissent	
	CONDITIONAL		**PERFECT**	*PARTICIPLE*
PAST ANTERIOR	**PRESENT**	**PAST**	j'aie conduit	**PRESENT**
j'eus conduit etc	je conduirais	j'aurais conduit	tu aies conduit	conduisant
	tu conduirais	tu aurais conduit	il ait conduit	
	il conduirait	il aurait conduit	nous ayons conduit	**PAST**
	nous conduirions	nous aurions conduit	vous ayez conduit	conduit
FUTURE PERFECT	vous conduiriez	vous auriez conduit	ils aient conduit	
j'aurai conduit etc	ils conduiraient	ils auraient conduit		

CONNAÎTRE — *to know*

PRESENT	IMPERFECT	FUTURE	SUBJUNCTIVE	IMPERATIVE
je connais	je connaissais	je connaîtrai	**PRESENT**	connais
tu connais	tu connaissais	tu connaîtras	je connaisse	connaissons
il connaît	il connaissait	il connaîtra	tu connaisses	connaissez
nous connaissons	nous connaissions	nous connaîtrons	il connaisse	
vous connaissez	vous connaissiez	vous connaîtrez	nous connaissions	
ils connaissent	ils connaissaient	ils connaîtront	vous connaissiez	
			ils connaissent	
PAST HISTORIC	**PERFECT**	**PLUPERFECT**	**IMPERFECT**	**INFINITIVE**
je connus	j'ai connu	j'avais connu	je connusse	**PRESENT**
tu connus	tu as connu	tu avais connu	tu connusses	connaître
il connut	il a connu	il avait connu	il connût	
nous connûmes	nous avons connu	nous avions connu	nous connussions	**PAST**
vous connûtes	vous avez connu	vous aviez connu	vous connussiez	avoir connu
ils connurent	ils ont connu	ils avaient connu	ils connussent	
	CONDITIONAL		**PERFECT**	*PARTICIPLE*
PAST ANTERIOR	**PRESENT**	**PAST**	j'aie connu	**PRESENT**
j'eus connu etc	je connaîtrais	j'aurais connu	tu aies connu	connaissant
	tu connaîtrais	tu aurais connu	il ait connu	
	il connaîtrait	il aurait connu	nous ayons connu	**PAST**
	nous connaîtrions	nous aurions connu	vous ayez connu	connu
FUTURE PERFECT	vous connaîtriez	vous auriez connu	ils aient connu	
j'aurai connu etc	ils connaîtraient	ils auraient connu		

CROIRE   *to believe*

PRESENT	IMPERFECT	FUTURE	SUBJUNCTIVE	IMPERATIVE
je crois	je croyais	je croirai	**PRESENT**	crois
tu crois	tu croyais	tu croiras	je croie	croyons
il croit	il croyait	il croira	tu croies	croyez
nous croyons	nous croyions	nous croirons	il croie	
vous croyez	vous croyiez	vous croirez	nous croyions	
ils croient	ils croyaient	ils croiront	vous croyiez	
			ils croient	

PAST HISTORIC	PERFECT	PLUPERFECT	IMPERFECT	INFINITIVE
je crus	j'ai cru	j'avais cru	je crusse	**PRESENT**
tu crus	tu as cru	tu avais cru	tu crusses	croire
il crut	il a cru	il avait cru	il crût	
nous crûmes	nous avons cru	nous avions cru	nous crussions	**PAST**
vous crûtes	vous avez cru	vous aviez cru	vous crussiez	avoir cru
ils crurent	ils ont cru	ils avaient cru	ils crussent	
	CONDITIONAL		**PERFECT**	*PARTICIPLE*
PAST ANTERIOR	**PRESENT**	**PAST**	j'aie cru	**PRESENT**
j'eus cru etc	je croirais	j'aurais cru	tu aies cru	croyant
	tu croirais	tu aurais cru	il ait cru	
	il croirait	il aurait cru	nous ayons cru	**PAST**
	nous croirions	nous aurions cru	vous ayez cru	cru
FUTURE PERFECT	vous croiriez	vous auriez cru	ils aient cru	
j'aurai cru etc	ils croiraient	ils auraient cru		

DEVOIR   *to owe/to have to*

PRESENT	IMPERFECT	FUTURE	SUBJUNCTIVE	IMPERATIVE
je dois	je devais	je devrai	**PRESENT**	dois
tu dois	tu devais	tu devras	je doive	devons
il doit	il devait	il devra	tu doives	devez
nous devons	nous devions	nous devrons	il doive	
vous devez	vous deviez	vous devrez	nous devions	
ils doivent	ils devaient	ils devront	vous deviez	
			ils doivent	

PAST HISTORIC	PERFECT	PLUPERFECT	IMPERFECT	INFINITIVE
je dus	j'ai dû	j'avais dû	je dusse	**PRESENT**
tu dus	tu as dû	tu avais dû	tu dusses	devoir
il dut	il a dû	il avait dû	il dût	
nous dûmes	nous avons dû	nous avions dû	nous dussions	**PAST**
vous dûtes	vous avez dû	vous aviez dû	vous dussiez	avoir dû
ils durent	ils ont dû	ils avaient dû	ils dussent	
	CONDITIONAL		**PERFECT**	*PARTICIPLE*
PAST ANTERIOR	**PRESENT**	**PAST**	j'aie dû	**PRESENT**
j'eus dû etc	je devrais	j'aurais dû	tu aies dû	devant
	tu devrais	tu aurais dû	il ait dû	
	il devrait	il aurait dû	nous ayons dû	**PAST**
	nous devrions	nous aurions dû	vous ayez dû	dû (due, dus)
FUTURE PERFECT	vous devriez	vous auriez dû	ils aient dû	
j'aurai dû	ils devraient	ils auraient dû		

DIRE   *to say*

PRESENT	IMPERFECT	FUTURE	SUBJUNCTIVE	IMPERATIVE
je dis	je disais	je dirai	**PRESENT**	dis
tu dis	tu disais	tu diras	je dise	disons
il dit	il disait	il dira tu dises	tu dises	dites
nous disons	nous disions	nous dirons	il dise	
vous dites	vous disiez	vous direz	nous disions	
ils disent	ils disaient	ils diront	vous disiez	
			ils disent	

PAST HISTORIC	PERFECT	PLUPERFECT	IMPERFECT	INFINITIVE
je dis	j'ai dit	j'avais dit	je disse	**PRESENT**
tu dis	tu as dit	tu avais dit	tu disses	dire
il dit	il a dit	il avait dit	il dît	
nous dîmes	nous avons dit	nous avions dit	nous dissions	**PAST**
vous dîtes	vous avez dit	vous aviez dit	vous dissiez	avoir dit
ils dirent	ils ont dit	ils avaient dit	ils dissent	
	CONDITIONAL		**PERFECT**	*PARTICIPLE*
PAST ANTERIOR	**PRESENT**	**PAST**	j'aie dit	**PRESENT**
j'eus dit etc	je dirais	j'aurais dit	tu aies dit	disant
	tu dirais	tu aurais dit	il ait dit	
	il dirait	il aurait dit	nous ayons dit	**PAST**
	nous dirions	nous aurions dit	vous ayez dit	dit
FUTURE PERFECT	vous diriez	vous auriez dit	ils aient dit	
j'aurai dit etc	ils diraient	ils auraient dit		

DORMIR — *to sleep*

PRESENT	IMPERFECT	FUTURE	SUBJUNCTIVE	IMPERATIVE
je dors	je dormais	je dormirai	**PRESENT**	dors
tu dors	tu dormais	tu dormiras	je dorme	dormons
il dort	il dormait	il dormira	tu dormes	dormez
nous dormons	nous dormions	nous dormirons	il dorme	
vous dormez	vous dormiez	vous dormirez	nous dormions	
ils dorment	ils dormaient	ils dormiront	vous dormiez	
			ils dorment	

PAST HISTORIC	PERFECT	PLUPERFECT	IMPERFECT	INFINITIVE
je dormis	j'ai dormi	j'avais dormi	je dormisse	**PRESENT**
tu dormis	tu as dormi	tu avais dormi	tu dormisses	dormir
il dormit	il a dormi	il avait dormi	il dormît	
nous dormîmes	nous avons dormi	nous avions dormi	nous dormissions	**PAST**
vous dormîtes	vous avez dormi	vous aviez dormi	vous dormissiez	avoir dormi
ils dormirent	ils ont dormi	ils avaient dormi	ils dormissent	
	CONDITIONAL		PERFECT	*PARTICIPLE*
PAST ANTERIOR	PRESENT	PAST	j'aie dormi	**PRESENT**
j'eus dormi etc	je dormirais	j'aurais dormi	tu aies dormi	dormant
	tu dormirais	tu aurais dormi	il ait dormi	
	il dormirait	il aurait dormi	nous ayons dormi	**PAST**
	nous dormirions	nous aurions dormi	vous ayez dormi	dormi
FUTURE PERFECT	vous dormiriez	vous auriez dormi	ils aient dormi	
j'aurai dormi etc	ils dormiraient	ils auraient dormi		

ÉCRIRE — *to write*

PRESENT	IMPERFECT	FUTURE	SUBJUNCTIVE	IMPERATIVE
j'écris	j'écrivais	j'écrirai	**PRESENT**	écris
tu écris	tu écrivais	tu écriras	j'écrive	écrivons
il écrit	il écrivait	il écrira	tu écrives	écrivez
nous écrivons	nous écrivions	nous écrirons	il écrive	
vous écrivez	vous écriviez	vous écrirez	nous écrivions	
ils écrivent	ils écrivaient	ils écriront	vous écriviez	
			ils écrivent	

PAST HISTORIC	PERFECT	PLUPERFECT	IMPERFECT	INFINITIVE
j'écrivis	j'ai écrit	j'avais écrit	j'écrivisse	**PRESENT**
tu écrivis	tu as écrit	tu avais écrit	tu écrivisses	écrire
il écrivit	il a écrit	il avait écrit	il écrivît	
nous écrivîmes	nous avons écrit	nous avions écrit	nous écrivissions	**PAST**
vous écrivîtes	vous avez écrit	vous aviez écrit	vous écrivissiez	avoir écrit
ils écrivirent	ils ont écrit	ils avaient écrit	ils écrivissent	
	CONDITIONAL		PERFECT	*PARTICIPLE*
PAST ANTERIOR	PRESENT	PAST	j'aie écrit	**PRESENT**
j'eus écrit etc	j'écrirais	j'aurais écrit	tu aies écrit	écrivant
	tu écrirais	tu aurais écrit	il ait écrit	
	il écrirait	il aurait écrit	nous ayons écrit	**PAST**
	nous écririons	nous aurions écrit	vous ayez écrit	écrit
FUTURE PERFECT	vous écririez	vous auriez écrit	ils aient écrit	
j'aurai écrit etc	ils écriraient	ils auraient écrit		

ESPÉRER — *to hope*

PRESENT	IMPERFECT	FUTURE	SUBJUNCTIVE	IMPERATIVE
j'espère	j'espérais	j'espérerai	**PRESENT**	espère
tu espères	tu espérais	tu espéreras	j'espère	espérons
il espère	il espérait	il espérera	tu espères	espérez
nous espérons	nous espérions	nous espérerons	il espère	
vous espérez	vous espériez	vous espérerez	nous espérions	
ils espèrent	ils espéraient	ils espéreront	vous espériez	
			ils espèrent	

PAST HISTORIC	PERFECT	PLUPERFECT	IMPERFECT	INFINITIVE
j'espérai	j'ai espéré	j'avais espéré	j'espérasse	**PRESENT**
tu espéras	tu as espéré	tu avais espéré	tu espérasses	espérer
il espéra	il a espéré	il avait espéré	il espérât	
nous espérâmes	nous avons espéré	nous avions espéré	nous espérassions	**PAST**
vous espérâtes	vous avez espéré	vous aviez espéré	vous espérassiez	avoir espéré
ils espérèrent	ils ont espéré	ils avaient espéré	ils espérassent	
	CONDITIONAL		PERFECT	*PARTICIPLE*
PAST ANTERIOR	PRESENT	PAST	j'aie espéré	**PRESENT**
j'eus espéré etc	j'espérerais	j'aurais espéré	tu aies espéré	espérant
	tu espérerais	tu aurais espéré	il ait espéré	
	il espérerait	il aurait espéré	nous ayons espéré	**PAST**
	nous espérerions	nous aurions espéré	vous ayez espéré	espéré
FUTURE PERFECT	vous espéreriez	vous auriez espéré	ils aient espéré	
j'aurai espéré etc	ils espéreraient	ils auraient espéré		

ÊTRE — *to be*

PRESENT	IMPERFECT	FUTURE	SUBJUNCTIVE	IMPERATIVE
je suis	j'étais	je serai	**PRESENT**	sois
tu es	tu étais	tu seras	je sois	soyons
il est	il était	il sera	tu sois	soyez
nous sommes	nous étions	nous serons	il soit	
vous êtes	vous étiez	vous serez	nous soyons	
ils sont	ils étaient	ils seront	vous soyez	
			ils soient	

PAST HISTORIC	PERFECT	PLUPERFECT	IMPERFECT	INFINITIVE
je fus	j'ai été	j'avais été	je fusse	**PRESENT**
tu fus	tu as été	tu avais été	tu fusses	être
il fut	il a été	il avait été	il fût	
nous fûmes	nous avons été	nous avions été	nous fussions	**PAST**
vous fûtes	vous avez été	vous aviez été	vous fussiez	avoir été
ils furent	ils ont été	ils avaient été	ils fussent	

	CONDITIONAL		PERFECT	PARTICIPLE
PAST ANTERIOR	**PRESENT**	**PAST**	j'aie été	**PRESENT**
j'eus été etc	je serais	j'aurais été	tu aies été	étant
	tu serais	tu aurais été	il ait été	
	il serait	il aurait été	nous ayons été	**PAST**
	nous serions	nous aurions été	vous ayez été	été
FUTURE PERFECT	vous seriez	vous auriez été	ils aient été	
j'aurai été etc	ils seraient	ils auraient été		

FAIRE — *to do/to make*

PRESENT	IMPERFECT	FUTURE	SUBJUNCTIVE	IMPERATIVE
je fais	je faisais	je ferai	**PRESENT**	fais
tu fais	tu faisais	tu feras	je fasse	faisons
il fait	il faisait	il fera	tu fasses	faites
nous faisons	nous faisions	nous ferons	il fasse	
vous faites	vous faisiez	vous ferez	nous fassions	
ils font	ils faisaient	ils feront	vous fassiez	
			ils fassent	

PAST HISTORIC	PERFECT	PLUPERFECT	IMPERFECT	INFINITIVE
je fis	j'ai fait	j'avais fait	je fisse	**PRESENT**
tu fis	tu as fait	tu avais fait	tu fisses	faire
il fit	il a fait	il avait fait	il fît	
nous fîmes	nous avons fait	nous avions fait	nous fissions	**PAST**
vous fîtes	vous avez fait	vous aviez fait	vous fissiez	avoir fait
ils firent	ils ont fait	ils avaient fait	ils fissent	

	CONDITIONAL		PERFECT	PARTICIPLE
PAST ANTERIOR	**PRESENT**	**PAST**	j'aie fait	**PRESENT**
j'eus fait etc	je ferais	j'aurais fait	tu aies fait	faisant
	tu ferais	tu aurais fait	il ait fait	
	il ferait	il aurait fait	nous ayons fait	**PAST**
	nous ferions	nous aurions fait	vous ayez fait	fait
FUTURE PERFECT	vous feriez	vous auriez fait	ils aient fait	
j'aurai fait etc	ils feraient	ils auraient fait		

FALLOIR — *to be necessary*

PRESENT	IMPERFECT	FUTURE	SUBJUNCTIVE	IMPERATIVE
il faut	il fallait	il faudra	**PRESENT**	
			il faille	

PAST HISTORIC	PERFECT	PLUPERFECT	IMPERFECT	INFINITIVE
il fallut	il a fallu	il avait fallu	il fallût	**PRESENT**
				falloir
				PAST
				avoir fallu

	CONDITIONAL		PERFECT	PARTICIPLE
PAST ANTERIOR	**PRESENT**	**PAST**	il ait fallu	**PRESENT**
il eut fallu	il faudrait	il aurait fallu		

FUTURE PERFECT				**PAST**
il aura fallu				fallu

among		**chez les Écossais** *among the Scots*
about		**ce qui m'énerve chez toi, c'est** *what annoys me about you is …*
in		**chez Sartre** *in Sartre's work*

CONTRE

against	(place)	**contre le mur** *against the wall*
with	(after verb)	**je suis fâché contre elle** *I'm angry with her*
for		**elle a échangé un billet contre des pièces** *she changed a note for coins*

DANS

in	(position)	**dans ma serviette** *in my briefcase*
	(time)	**je pars dans deux jours** *I'm leaving in two days' time*
	(idiom)	**dans l'attente de vous voir** *looking forward to seeing you*
from	(removal)	**prendre quelque chose dans l'armoire** *to take something from the cupboard*
on	(position)	**dans le train** *on the train*
out of	(idiom)	**boire dans un verre** *to drink out of a glass*

DE

from	(place)	**je suis venu de Glasgow** *I have come from Glasgow*
	(date)	**du 5 février au 10 mars** *from 5 February to 10 March*
		d'un week-end à l'autre *from one weekend to another*
of	(adjectival)	**un cri de triomphe** *a shout of triumph*
	(contents)	**une tasse de café** *a cup of coffee*
	(cause)	**mourir de faim** *to die of hunger*
	(measurement)	**long de 3 mètres** *3 metres long*
	(time)	**ma montre retarde de 10 minutes** *my watch is 10 minutes slow*
	(price)	**le montant est de 20 euros** *the total is 20 euros*
	(possessive)	**la père de mon ami** *my friend's father*
	(adjectival)	**les vacances de Pâques** *the Easter holidays*
	(after 'quelque chose')	**quelque chose de bon** *something good*
	(after 'rien')	**rien de nouveau** *nothing new*
	(after 'personne')	**personne d'autre** *nobody else*
	(quantity)	**beaucoup de, peu de** *many, few*
by	(idiom)	**je le connais de vue** *I know him by sight*

in	(manner)	**de cette façon** *in this way*
	(after superlatives)	**la plus haute montagne d'Écosse** *the highest mountain in Scotland*
on	(position)	**de ce côté** *on this side*
than	(comparative)	**moins de 2 euros** *less than 2 euros*
		plus de 3 litres *more than 3 litres*
to	(after adjectives)	**ravi de vous voir** *delighted to see you*
		il est facile de se tromper *it is easy to make a mistake*
	(after verbs)	**s'efforcer de** *to try to*
with	(cause)	**tomber de fatigue** *to drop with exhaustion*

DEPUIS

for	(time)	**j'étudie le français depuis 3 ans** *I have been studying French for 3 years*
		j'étudiais le français depuis 3 ans *I had been studying French for 3 years*
		je n'y ai pas joué depuis des années *I haven't played for years*
from	(place)	**depuis ma fenêtre, je vois la mer** *from my window I can see the sea*
	(time)	**depuis le matin jusqu'au soir** *from morning till evening*
since		**depuis dimanche** *since Sunday*

DERRIÈRE

behind	(place)	**derrière la maison** *behind the house*

DÈS

from	(time)	**dès six heures** *from six o'clock onwards*
		dès 1934 *as far back as 1934*
		dès le début *from the beginning*
		dès maintenant *from now on*
	(place)	**dès Édimbourg** *from (the moment of leaving) Edinburgh*

DEVANT

in front of	(place)	**devant l'école** *in front of the school*
before	(place)	**sur la table devant eux** *on the table before them*

EN

in	(place)	**être en ville** *to be in town*
		en Angleterre *in England*

	(colour)	**un mur peint en jaune** *a wall painted yellow*
	(material)	**une montre en or** *a gold watch*
by	(means)	**en auto/en avion** *by car/by plane*
	(dates, seasons)	**en quelle année?** *in what year?*
		en 2004 *in 2004*
		en été *in the summer*
		en juillet *in July*
	(dress)	**en jupe** *in a skirt*
	(language)	**en chinois** *in Chinese*
	(time)	**j'ai fait mes devoirs en 20 minutes** *I did my homework in 20 minutes*
like, as		**il s'est habillé en femme** *he dressed as a woman*
on	(idiom)	**en vacances** *on holiday*
		en moyenne *on average*
	(+ present participle)	**en faisant** *on/while/by doing*

Note that en is not used with the definite article except in certain expressions: **en l'an 2020** *(in the year 2020)*, **en l'honneur de** *(in honour of)* and **en la présence de** *(in the presence of)*.

EN TANT QUE

as/in one's capacity as	**en tant que professeur** *as a teacher*

ENTRE

among		**être entre amis** *to be among friends*
between	(place)	**entre Londres et Paris** *between London and Paris*
	(time)	**entre 6 et 10 heures** *between 6 and 10 o'clock*
	(idiom)	**entre nous** *between you and me*
in	(punctuation)	**entre guillemets** *in inverted commas*
		entre parenthèses *in brackets*

D'ENTRE

of/from among	**certains d'entre eux** *some of them*

ENVERS

to/towards	**être bien disposé envers quelqu'un** *to be well-disposed towards someone*

HORS DE

out of	**hors de danger** *out of danger*

JUSQUE

up to/as far as	(place)	**jusqu'à la frontière espagnole** *as far as the Spanish border*
	(time)	**jusqu'ici** *up to now*
		jusque-là *up till then*
till		**jusqu'à demain** *till tomorrow*

MALGRÉ

in spite of	**malgré la chaleur** *in spite of the heat*

PAR

by	(agent)	**la décision fut prise par le président** *the decision was made by the President*
	(means of transport)	**par le train** *by train*
	(distributive)	**trois fois par semaine** *three times a week*
		deux par deux *two by two*
	(place)	**par ici/là** *this/that way*
in/on	(weather)	**par un temps pareil** *in such weather*
		par un beau jour d'hiver *on a beautiful winter's day*
through/ out of	(place)	**regarder par la fenêtre** *to look out of the window*
		jette-le par la fenêtre *throw it out of the window*
to/on		**tomber par terre** *to fall to the ground*
		étendu par terre *lying on the ground*
	(+ infinitive)	**commencer/finir par faire** *to begin/end by doing*

PARMI

among	**parmi mes ennemis** *among my enemies*

PENDANT

for	(time)	**il l'avait fait pendant 5 ans** *he had done it for 5 years*
during		**pendant l'été** *during the summer*

POUR

for		**ce livre est pour vous** *this book is for you*
		mourir pour la patrie *to die for one's country*
	(purpose)	**c'est pour cela que je suis venu** *that's why I've come*
	(emphatic)	**pour moi, cet argument ne tient pas** *if you ask me, this argument isn't valid*
	(time)	**j'en ai pour une heure** *it'll take me an hour*

je suis en vacances pour 2 semaines
I'm on holiday for 2 weeks

(**pour** stresses intention and future time: see **depuis** and **pendant**, pp B55 and B56)

	(idiom)	**c'est bon pour la santé** *it's good for your health*
to	(+ infinitive)	**il était trop paresseux pour réussir ses examens** *he was too lazy to pass his exams*

PRÈS DE

near	(place)	**près du marché** *near the market*
nearly	(time)	**il est près de minuit** *it's nearly midnight*
	(quantity)	**près de cinquante** *nearly fifty*

QUANT À

as for	**quant à moi** *as for me*

SANS

without	(+ noun)	**sans espoir** *without hope*
	(+ pronoun)	**je n'irai pas sans vous** *I won't go without you*
	(+ infinitive)	**sans parler** *without speaking*
		sans s'arrêter *without stopping*

SAUF

except for	**ils sont tous partis, sauf John** *everyone left except John*
barring	**sauf accidents/sauf imprévu** *barring accidents/the unexpected*

SELON

according to	**selon le président** *according to the President*
	selon moi *in my opinion*

SOUS

under	(physical)	**sous la table** *under the table*
	(governed by)	**sous Élisabeth II** *under Elizabeth II*
in	(weather)	**sous la pluie** *in the rain*
	(idiom)	**sous peu** *before long/shortly*
		sous la main *to hand*
		sous tous rapports *in all respects*
		sous mes yeux *before my eyes*

SUR

on/upon	(place)	**le chat est sur le toit** *the cat's on the roof*
off		**je l'ai pris sur l'étagère** *I took it off the shelf*

out of	(proportion)	**neuf sur dix** *nine out of ten*
		une semaine sur trois *one week in three*
over	(place)	**le pont sur la Loire** *the bridge over the Loire*
		l'emporter sur quelqu'un *to prevail over someone*
about	(idiom)	**une enquête sur ...** *an enquiry about ...*
at		**sur ces paroles** *at these words*
		sur ce, il est sorti *at this he went out*
by		**quatre mètres sur cinq** *four metres by five*
in		**sur un ton amer** *in a bitter tone (of voice)*

VERS

towards	(place)	**vers le nord** *towards the north*
	(time)	**vers la fin du match** *towards the end of the match*
about	(time)	**vers 10 heures** *about 10 o'clock*

VOICI/VOILÀ

here	**le voici qui vient** *here he comes*
there	**voilà où il demeure** *that's where he lives*

9 CONJUNCTIONS

Conjunctions are words or expressions which link words, phrases or clauses. They fall into two categories, coordinating conjunctions and subordinating conjunctions:

A COORDINATING CONJUNCTIONS

1 Definition

These link two similar words or groups of words, eg nouns, pronouns, adjectives, adverbs, prepositions, phrases or clauses. The principal coordinating conjunctions (or adverbs used as conjunctions) are:

et *and*	**mais** *but*	**ou** *or*
ou bien *or (else)*	**soit** *either*	**ni** *neither*
alors *then*	**aussi** *therefore*	**donc** *then, therefore*
puis *then (next)*	**car** *for (because)*	**or** *now*
cependant *however*	**néanmoins** *nevertheless*	**pourtant** *yet, however*
toutefois *however*		

il est malade mais il ne veut pas aller au lit
he's ill but he won't go to bed

il faisait beau alors il est allé se promener
it was nice weather so he went for a walk

2 Repetition

a) Some coordinating conjunctions are repeated:

soit ... soit ...   *either ... or ...*
ou (bien) ... ou (bien) ... *either ... or ...*

prenez soit l'un soit l'autre
take one or the other

soit tu viens avec nous, soit tu restes ici mais tu te décides
either you come with us or you stay here, but you have to decide

ou tu t'habitues ou tu démissionnes
either you get used to it or you resign

ni ... ni ...   *neither ... nor ...*

le vieillard n'avait ni amis ni argent
the old man had neither friends nor money

b) et and ou can be repeated in texts of a literary nature:

et ... et ...   *both ... and ...*
ou ... ou ...   *either ... or ...*

elle ne cessa et de crier et de pleurer
she didn't stop shouting and crying

ou c'est lui ou c'est moi !
it's either him or me!

3 Aussi

aussi means 'therefore' only when placed before the verb. The subject pronoun is placed after the verb (see p B62).

il pleuvait, aussi Pascal n'est-il pas sorti
it was raining, so Pascal didn't go out

When aussi follows the verb it means 'also':

j'ai aussi emporté des pulls, au cas où
I also brought some jumpers, just in case

B SUBORDINATING CONJUNCTIONS

These join a subordinate clause to another clause, usually a main clause. The principal subordinating conjunctions are:

comme	*as*	parce que	*because*
puisque	*since*	ainsi que	*(just) as*
à mesure que	*as*	tant que	*as long as*
avant que	*before*	après que	*after*
jusqu'à ce que	*until*	depuis que	*since*
pendant que	*while*	tandis que	*whereas*
si	*if*	à moins que	*unless*
pourvu que	*provided that*	quoique	*although*
bien que	*although*	quand	*when*
lorsque	*when*	dès que	*as soon as*
aussitôt que	*as soon as*	pour que	*in order that*
afin que	*so that*	de sorte que	*so that*
de façon que	*so that*	de peur que (+ ne)	*for fear that, lest*

Note that some subordinating conjunctions require the subjunctive (see p B33).

C QUE

1 Coordinating (see pp B11 and B13-14)

que is a coordinating conjunction when used in comparisons:

il est plus fort que moi
he is stronger than I

elle est plus courageuse que tu ne crois
she's braver than you think

2 Subordinating

a) *meaning 'that':*

elle dit qu'elle l'a vu je pense que tu as raison
she says she has seen him *I think you're right*

il faut que tu viennes il paraît qu'elle a gagné
you'll have to come   *it seems she's won*

b) *replacing another conjunction:*

When a conjunction introduces more than one verb, que usually replaces the second subordinating conjunction and any subsequent ones to avoid repetition:

comme il était tard et que j'étais fatigué, je suis rentré
as it was late and I was tired, I went home

s'il fait beau et que tu es libre, nous irons à la piscine
if the weather's nice and you're free, we'll go to the swimming pool

nous sortirons lorsque nous aurons déjeuné et que tu te seras reposé
we'll go out when we've had lunch and you've had a rest

10 NUMBERS AND QUANTITY

A CARDINAL NUMBERS

0	zéro	40	quarante
1	un (une)	50	cinquante
2	deux	60	soixante
3	trois	70	soixante-dix
4	quatre	71	soixante et onze
5	cinq	72	soixante-douze
6	six	80	quatre-vingt(s)
7	sept	90	quatre-vingt-dix
8	huit	99	quatre-vingt-dix-neuf
9	neuf	100	cent
10	dix	101	cent un(e)
11	onze	102	cent deux
12	douze	121	cent vingt et un(e)
13	treize	122	cent vingt-deux
14	quatorze	200	deux cents
15	quinze	201	deux cent un(e)
16	seize	1000	mille
17	dix-sept	1988	mille neuf cent
18	dix-huit		quatre-vingt-huit
19	dix-neuf	2000	deux mille
20	vingt	10 000	dix mille
30	trente	1 000 000	un million

Note:

a) un is the only cardinal number which agrees with the noun in gender:

un kilo   une pomme
a kilo   *an apple*

b) hyphens are used in compound numbers between 17 and 99 except where et is used (this also applies to compound numbers after 100: cent vingt-trois 123).

c) cent and mille are not preceded by un as in English (one hundred).

d) vingt and cent multiplied by a number take an s when they are not followed by another number.

il a quatre-vingts ans
he's eighty

elle a remporté quatre-vingt-deux victoires
she has notched up eighty-two wins

c'est une civilisation vieille de huit cents ans
it's a civilization which is eight hundred years old

ce livre compte trois cent cinq pages
this book has three hundred and five pages

e) mille is invariable.

trente mille personnes ont assisté à la rencontre
thirty thousand people went to the match

B ORDINAL NUMBERS

		abbreviation
1st	premier/première	1er/1ère
2nd	deuxième/second	2^e
3rd	troisième	3^e
4th	quatrième	4^e
5th	cinquième	5^e
6th	sixième	6^e
7th	septième	7^e
8th	huitième	8^e
9th	neuvième	9^e
10th	dixième	10^e
11th	onzième	11^e
12th	douzième	12^e
13th	treizième	13^e
14th	quatorzième	14^e
15th	quinzième	15^e
16th	seizième	16^e
17th	dix-septième	17^e
18th	dix-huitième	18^e
19th	dix-neuvième	19^e
20th	vingtième	20^e
21st	vingt et unième	21^e
22nd	vingt-deuxième	22^e
30th	trentième	30^e
100th	centième	100^e
101st	cent unième	101^e
200th	deux centième	200^e
1000th	millième	1000^e
10,000th	dix millième	10 000^e

Note:

a) ordinal numbers are formed by adding -ième to cardinal numbers, except for premier and second; cinq, neuf and numbers ending in e undergo slight changes: cinquième, neuvième, onzième, douzième etc.

b) ordinal numbers agree with the noun in gender and number:

le Premier ministre
the Prime Minister

la première fleur
du printemps
the first flower of spring

c) there is no elision with huitième and onzième:

le huitième jour
the eighth day

du onzième candidat
of the eleventh candidate

d) cardinal numbers are used for monarchs, except for 'first':

Charles deux
Charles II

Charles premier
Charles I

C FRACTIONS AND PROPORTIONS

1 Fractions

Fractions are expressed as in English: cardinal followed by ordinal:

deux cinquièmes
two fifths

But: ¼ un quart

½ un demi, une demie

⅓ un tiers

¾ trois quarts

2 Decimals

The English decimal point is conveyed by a comma in French:

un virgule huit (1,8)
one point eight (1.8)

3 Approximate numbers

une huitaine
about eight

une dizaine
about ten

une trentaine
some thirty

une centaine
about a hundred

But: un millier
about a thousand

Note that de is used when the approximate number is followed by a noun:

une vingtaine d'enfants
about twenty children

4 Arithmetic

Addition:	deux plus quatre	2 + 4
Subtraction:	cinq moins deux	5 - 2
Multiplication:	trois fois cinq	3 x 5
Division:	six divisé par deux	6 ÷ 2
Square:	deux au carré	2^2
Power:	deux puissance six	2^6

D MEASUREMENTS AND PRICES

1 Measurements

a) *Dimensions*

long(ue)/de longueur/de long	long
profond(e)/de profondeur/de profond	deep
épais(se)/d'épaisseur	thick
haut(e)/de hauteur/de haut	high

la salle de classe est longue de 12 mètres
la salle de classe a/fait 12 mètres de longueur/de long
the classroom is 12 metres long

ma chambre fait quatre mètres sur trois
my bedroom is about four metres by three

b) *Distance*

à quelle distance sommes-nous de la gare?
how far are we from the station?

nous sommes à deux kilomètres de la gare
we are two kilometres from the station

combien y a-t-il d'ici à Blois?
how far is it to Blois?

2 Price

ce pull m'a coûté 50 euros
this sweater cost me 50 euros

j'ai payé ce pull 50 euros
I paid 50 euros for this sweater

des pommes à 2 euros le kilo
apples at 2 euros a kilo

du vin blanc à 5 euros la bouteille
white wine at 5 euros a bottle

cela fait/revient à 6 euros
that comes to 6 euros

ils coûtent 4 euros pièce
they cost 4 euros each

E EXPRESSIONS OF QUANTITY

Quantity may be expressed by an adverb of quantity, eg 'a lot', 'too much' or by a noun which names the actual quantity involved, eg 'a bottle', 'a dozen'.

1 Expression of quantity + 'de' + noun

Before a noun, adverbs and other expressions of quantity are followed by **de** (**d'** before a vowel or a silent **h**) and never by **du, de la** or **des**, except for **bien des** and **la plupart du/des**:

assez de enough	**autant de** as much/many
beaucoup de a lot of/much/many	**combien de** how much/many
moins de less/fewer	**plus de** more
peu de little/few	**un peu de** a little
tant de so much/many	**tellement de** so much/many
bien du/de la/des many/a lot of	**la plupart du/de la/des** most
trop de too much/many	

il y a assez de fromage?
is there enough cheese?

autant de gens
as many people

je n'ai pas beaucoup de temps
I haven't got much time

il y a combien de pièces?
how many rooms are there?

j'ai mis moins de temps que lui
I took less time than him

mange plus de légumes!
eat more vegetables!

peu de gens le savent
not many people know that

tu veux un peu de pain?
would you like a little bread?

il y a tant d'années
so many years ago

j'ai tellement de travail
I've got so much work

bien des gens
a good many people

la plupart des Français
most French people

tu as bien de la patience
you have a lot of patience

il y a trop de voitures
there are too many cars

2 Noun expressing quantity + 'de' + noun

une boîte de a box/tin/can/jar of	**une bouteille de** a bottle of
une bouchée de a mouthful of (food)	**une cuillerée de** a spoonful of
une douzaine de a dozen	**une gorgée de** a mouthful of (drink)
un kilo de a kilo of	**un litre de** a litre of
une livre de a pound of	**un morceau de** a piece of
un paquet de a packet of	**une paire de** a pair of
une part de a share/helping of	**une tasse de** a cup of
une tranche de a slice of	**un verre de** a glass of

je voudrais une boîte de thon et un litre de lait
I'd like a tin of tuna and a litre of milk

il y a une boîte de limonade dans le frigo
there's a can of lemonade in the fridge

j'ai pris deux parts de choucroute
I took two helpings of sauerkraut

il a mangé une douzaine d'œufs et six morceaux de poulet
he ate a dozen eggs and six pieces of chicken

3 Expressions of quantity used without a noun

When an expression of quantity is not followed by a noun, **de** is replaced by the pronoun **en** (see pp B19-20):

il y avait beaucoup de neige; il y en avait beaucoup
there was a lot of snow; there was a lot (of it)

elle a mangé trop de chocolats; elle en a trop mangé
she's eaten too many chocolates; she's eaten too many (of them)

11 EXPRESSIONS OF TIME

A THE TIME

quelle heure est-il?	*what time is it?*

a) *Full hours*

il est midi/minuit *it is 12 noon or midday/ midnight*	**il est une heure** *it is 1 o'clock*

b) *Half-hours*

il est minuit et demi(e) *it is 12.30 a.m.*	**il est midi et demi(e)** *it is 12.30 p.m.*
il est une heure et demie *it is 1.30*	

c) *Quarter-hours*

il est deux heures un/ et quart *it is a quarter past two*	**il est deux heures moins le quart** *it is a quarter to two*

d) *Minutes*

il est quatre heures vingt-trois *it is 23 minutes past 4*	**il est cinq heures moins vingt** *it is 20 to 5*

Note that **minutes** is usually omitted; **heures** is never omitted.

e) *A.m. and p.m.*

du matin *a.m., in the morning*	**de l'après-midi/du soir** *p.m., in the evening*

il est sept heures moins dix du soir
t is 7.10 p.m. or in the evening

il est sept heures dix du matin
it is 6.50 a.m. or in the morning

The 24-hour clock is commonly used:

dix heures trente *10.30 a.m.*	**quatorze heures trente-cinq** *2.35 p.m.*

dix-neuf heures dix
7.10 p.m.

Note that times are often abbreviated as follows:

dix-neuf heures dix	**19h10**

B THE DATE

1 Names of months, days and seasons

a) *Months*

janvier	*January*
février	*February*

mars	March
avril	April
mai	May
juin	June
juillet	July
août	August
septembre	September
octobre	October
novembre	November
décembre	December

b) *Days of the week*

lundi	Monday
mardi	Tuesday
mercredi	Wednesday
jeudi	Thursday
vendredi	Friday
samedi	Saturday
dimanche	Sunday

c) *Seasons*

le printemps	spring
l'été	summer
l'automne	autumn
l'hiver	winter

For prepositions used with the seasons see p B4.

Note that in French, months and days are masculine and do not have a capital letter unless they begin a sentence.

2 Dates

a) Cardinals (eg **deux, trois**) are used for the dates of the month except the first:

le quatorze juillet   **le deux novembre**
the fourteenth of July   *the second of November*

But: **le premier février**
the first of February

The definite article is used as in English; French does not use prepositions ('on' and 'of' in English):

je vous ai écrit le trois mars
I wrote to you on the third of March

b) **mil** *(a thousand)* is used instead of **mille** in dates from 1001 onwards:

mil neuf cent quatre-vingt sept
nineteen hundred and eighty-seven

l'an deux mil deux
the year two thousand and two

3 Année, journée, matinée, soirée

Année, journée, matinée, soirée (the feminine forms of **an, jour, matin** and **soir**) are usually found in the following cases:

a) *when duration is implied:*

pendant une année	*for a (whole) year*
toute la journée	*all day long, the whole day*
dans la matinée	*in the (course of the) morning*
passer une soirée	*to spend an evening*
l'année scolaire/universitaire	*the school/academic year*

b) *with an ordinal number or an indefinite expression:*

la deuxième année	*the second year*
dans sa vingtième année	*in his twentieth year*
plusieurs/quelques années	*several/a few years*
bien des/de nombreuses années	*many years*
environ une année	*about a year*

c) *with an adjective:*

de bonnes/mauvaises années	*good/bad years*

C IDIOMATIC EXPRESSIONS

à cinq heures	at five o'clock
à onze heures environ	(at) about eleven o'clock
vers minuit	(at) about midnight
vers (les) dix heures	(at) about ten o'clock
il est six heures passées	it's past six o'clock
à quatre heures précises ou pile	at exactly four o'clock
sur le coup de trois heures	on the stroke of three
à partir de neuf heures	from nine o'clock onwards
peu avant sept heures	shortly before seven
peu après sept heures	shortly after seven
tôt ou tard	sooner or later
au plus tôt	at the earliest
au plus tard	at the latest
il est tard	it is late
il est en retard	he is late
il se lève tard	he gets up late
il est arrivé en retard	he arrived late
le train a vingt minutes de retard	the train is twenty minutes late
ma montre retarde de six minutes	my watch is six minutes slow
ma montre avance de six minutes	my watch is six minutes fast
ce soir	this evening, tonight
demain soir	tomorrow evening, tomorrow night
hier soir	yesterday evening, last night
samedi soir	Saturday evening
je sors samedi soir	I'm going out on Saturday night or evening
dans la soirée de samedi	on Saturday evening
dans la nuit de samedi (à dimanche)	during Saturday night
demain matin	tomorrow morning
hier matin	yesterday morning
lundi matin	Monday morning
j'y vais lundi matin	I'm going there on Monday morning
demain en huit	tomorrow week
le lendemain	the next day
le lendemain matin	the next morning
hier matin	yesterday morning
la semaine dernière	last week
la semaine prochaine	next week
la semaine qui vient	this coming week
je l'ai vu l'autre samedi	I saw him the other Saturday
lundi	on Monday
le lundi	on Mondays
je commence lundi	I'm starting (on) Monday
il vient le lundi	he comes on Mondays, he comes on a Monday
vient un lundi	come one Monday
un lundi sur deux	every other Monday, every second Monday
tous les lundis	every Monday
tous les lundis soirs	every Monday evening or night
tous mes lundis	all my Mondays
lundi en huit	a week on Monday, Monday week
lundi en quinze	a fortnight on Monday
il y a trois semaines	three weeks ago
il vient l'après-midi	he comes in the afternoon(s)
viens un après-midi	come one afternoon
une demi-heure	a half-hour, half an hour
un quart d'heure	a quarter of an hour
trois quarts d'heure	three quarters of an hour
passer son temps (à faire)	to spend one's time (doing)
perdre son temps	to waste one's time
de temps en temps	from time to time

de temps à autre	from time to time
dans les temps	on time
au début de l'après-midi/ de la soirée, en début d'après-midi/de soirée	in the early afternoon/ evening
je te téléphonerai en début de matinée	I'll phone you first thing in the morning
au début du mois	at the beginning of the month
j'ai une réunion au milieu de la matinée ou en milieu de matinée	have a meeting mid-morning
au milieu (du mois) de juin, (à la) mi-juin	in the middle of June, mid-June
au milieu de l'hiver	in the middle of winter, midwinter
j'ai une réunion à la fin de la matinée ou en fin de matinée	I have a meeting late morning
à la fin de l'hiver	at the end of the winter
on en reparlera fin janvier ou à la fin du mois de janvier	we'll talk about it again at the end of January
quel jour sommes-nous aujourd'hui?	what day is it today?
le combien sommes-nous aujourd'hui?	what's the date today?, what's today's date?
nous sommes/c'est le trois avril	it's the third of April
aujourd'hui nous sommes samedi	today is Saturday, it's Saturday today
vendredi 11 janvier 2004	Friday, 11 January 2004
nous nous sommes vus le vendredi 11 janvier	we saw each other on Friday, 11th January
le vendredi treize juillet	Friday the thirteenth of July
en février/au mois de février	in February/in the month of February
en février 2004	in February 2004
l'été 2004	in the summer of 2004, in summer 2004
en 2004	in 2004
dans les années soixante	in the sixties, in the 60s, in the 1960s
au début/à la fin des années soixante	in the early/late sixties
au dix-septième siècle	in the seventeenth century
au XVIIᵉ	in the 17th century
le jour de l'An	New Year's Day
avoir treize ans	to be thirteen (years old)
être âgé de quatorze ans	to be fourteen (years old)
elle fête ses vingt ans	she's celebrating her twentieth birthday
elle a une vingtaine d'années	she's around twenty (years old)
un plan quinquennal	a five-year plan
une année bissextile	a leap year
une année civile	a calendar year
une année-lumière	a light year

12 THE SENTENCE

A WORD ORDER

Word order is usually the same in French as in English, except in the following cases:

1 Adjectives

Many French adjectives follow the noun (see p B10):

de l'argent suisse
(some) Swiss money

j'ai les yeux bleus
I've got blue eyes

2 Adverbs

In simple tenses, adverbs usually follow the verb (see p B13):

j'y vais rarement
I seldom go there

il fera bientôt nuit
it will soon be dark

3 Object pronouns

Object pronouns usually come before the verb (see p B18):

je t'attendrai
I'll wait for you

il la lui a vendue
he sold it to him

4 Noun phrases

Noun phrases are formed differently in French (see p B67):

une chemise en coton
a cotton shirt

le père de mon copain
my friend's father

5 Exclamations

The word order is not affected after que or comme (unlike after 'how' in English):

que tu es bête!
you are silly!
(how silly you are!)

qu'il fait froid!
it's so cold!

comme il chante mal!
he sings so badly!

comme c'est beau!
that's so beautiful!

6 DONT

dont must be followed by the subject of the clause it introduces; compare:

l'ami dont j'ai perdu l'adresse
the friend whose address I lost

l'ami dont l'adresse a changé
the friend whose address has changed

7 Inversion

In certain cases, the subject of a French clause is placed after the verb. Word order is effectively that of an interrogative sentence (see pp B63-4). This occurs:

a) *after the following, when they occur at the beginning of a clause:*

à peine	aussi	peut-être
hardly	*therefore*	*maybe, perhaps*

à peine Alain était-il sorti qu'il a commencé à pleuvoir
Alain had barely gone out when it started raining

il y avait une grève du métro, aussi a-t-il pris un taxi
there was an underground strike, so he took a taxi

peut-être vont-ils téléphoner plus tard
maybe they'll phone later

But: **Alain était à peine sorti qu'il a commencé à pleuvoir**
ils vont peut-être téléphoner plus tard

b) *when a verb of saying follows direct speech:*

'si tu veux,' a répondu Marie
'if you want,' Marie replied

'attention!' a-t-elle crié
'watch out!' she shouted

'j'espère que non,' dit-il
'I hope not,' he said

'répondez!' ordonna-t-il
'answer!' he ordered

B NEGATIVE EXPRESSIONS

1 Main negative words

a)
ne ... pas	not
ne ... point	not (literary)
ne ... plus	no more/longer, not ... any more
ne ... jamais	never
ne ... rien	nothing, not ... anything
ne ... guère	hardly

b)
ne ... personne	nobody, no one, not ... anyone
ne ... que	only
ne ... ni (ni ... ni)	neither ... nor

ne ... aucun(e)	no, not any, none
ne ... nul(le)	no
ne ... nulle part	nowhere, not ... anywhere

Note:

i) ne becomes n' before a vowel or a silent h.

ii) aucun and nul, like other adjectives and pronouns, agree with the word they refer to; they are used only in the singular.

2 Position of negative expressions

a) *with simple tenses and with the imperative*

Negative words enclose the verb: ne comes before the verb, and the second part of the negative expression comes after the verb:

je ne la connais pas
I don't know her

n'insistez pas!
don't insist!

je n'ai plus d'argent
I haven't any money left

tu ne le sauras jamais
you'll never know

ne dis rien
don't say anything

il n'y a personne
no one's here

je n'avais que 3 euros
I only had 3 euros

il n'est nulle part
it isn't anywhere

tu n'as aucun sens de l'humour
you have no sense of humour

il n'est ni bête ni crédule
he's neither stupid nor gullible

b) *with compound tenses*

With ne ... pas and the other expressions in list 1a), the word order is: ne + auxiliary + pas + past participle:

il n'est pas revenu
he didn't come back

je n'ai plus essayé
I didn't try any more

je n'avais jamais vu Paris
I had never seen Paris

on n'a rien fait
we haven't done anything

With ne ... personne and the other expressions in list 1b), the word order is: ne + auxiliary + past participle + personne/que/ni etc:

il ne l'a dit à personne
he didn't tell anyone

tu n'en as acheté qu'un?
did you only buy one?

je n'en ai aimé aucun
I didn't like any of them

il n'est allé nulle part
he hasn't gone anywhere

c) *with the infinitive*

i) ne ... pas and the other expressions in list 1a) are placed together before the verb:

je préfère ne pas y aller
I'd rather not go

essaye de ne rien perdre
try not to lose anything

ii) ne ... personne and the other expressions in list 1b) enclose the infinitive:

il a été surpris de ne voir personne
he was surprised not to see anybody

j'ai décidé de n'en acheter aucun
I decided not to buy any of them

d) *at the beginning of a sentence*

When personne, rien, aucun and ni ... ni ... begin a sentence, they are followed by ne:

personne ne le sait
nobody knows

rien n'a changé
nothing has changed

ni Paul ni Simone ne sont venus
neither Paul nor Simone came

aucun secours n'est arrivé
no help arrived

3 Combination of negative expressions

Negative expressions can be combined:

ne ... plus jamais	
ne ... plus rien	ne ... jamais rien
ne ... plus personne	ne ... jamais personne
ne ... plus ni ... ni	ne ... jamais ni ... ni
ne ... plus que	ne ... jamais que

on ne l'a plus jamais revu
we never saw him again

il n'y a plus rien
there isn't anything left

plus personne ne viendra
no one will come any more

tu ne dis jamais rien
you never say anything

je ne bois jamais que de l'eau
I only ever drink water

je ne vois jamais personne
I never see anybody

je ne pardonnerai jamais ni n'oublierai
I will never forgive nor forget

4 Negative expressions without a verb

a) pas

pas *(not)* is the most common of all negatives; it is frequently used without a verb:

tu l'aimes? – pas beaucoup
do you like it? – not much

ah non, pas lui!
oh no, not him!

non merci, pas pour moi
no thanks, not for me

un roman pas très long
not a very long novel

lui, il viendra, mais pas moi
he will come, but I won't

j'aime ça; pas toi?
I like that; don't you?

b) ne

ne is not used when there is no verb:

qui a crié? – personne
who shouted? – nobody

jamais de la vie!
not on your life!

rien! je ne veux rien!
nothing! I want nothing!

rien du tout
nothing at all

c) non

non *(no)* is always used without a verb:

tu aimes la natation? – non, pas du tout
do you like swimming? – no, not at all

tu viens, oui ou non? – je crois que non
are you coming, yes or no? – I don't think so

Note that non plus means 'neither':

je ne le crois pas – moi non plus
I don't believe him – neither do I

je n'ai rien mangé – nous non plus
I haven't eaten anything – neither have we

C DIRECT AND INDIRECT QUESTIONS

1 Direct questions

There are three ways of forming direct questions in French:

a) *subject + verb (+ question word)*

The word order remains the same as in statements (subject + verb) but the intonation changes: the voice is raised at the end of the sentence. This is by far the most common question form in conversational French:

tu l'as acheté où?
where did you buy it?

je peux téléphoner d'ici?
can I phone from here?

vous prendrez quel train?
which train will you take?

tu me fais confiance?
do you trust me?

c'était comment?
what was it like?

la gare est près d'ici?
is the station near here?

le train part à quelle heure?
what time does the train leave?

cette robe me va?
does this dress suit me?

b) *(question word)* + est-ce que + *subject* + *verb*

This question form is also very common in conversation:

qu'est-ce que tu as?
what's the matter with you?

est-ce qu'il est là?
is he in?

est-ce que ton ami s'est amusé?
did your friend have a good time?

où est-ce que vous avez mal?
where does it hurt?

c) *inversion*

This question form is the most formal of the three, and the least commonly used in conversation:

i) If the subject is a pronoun, the word order is as follows:

(question word) + verb + hyphen + subject

où allez-vous?
where are you going?

voulez-vous commander?
do you wish to order?

quand est-il arrivé?
when did he arrive?

avez-vous bien dormi?
did you sleep well?

ii) If the subject is a noun, a pronoun referring to the noun is inserted after the verb, and linked to it with a hyphen:

(question word) + noun subject + verb + hyphen + pronoun

où ton père travaillait-il?
where did your father work?

Nicole en veut-elle?
does Nicole want any?

iii) -t- is inserted before il and elle when the verb ends in a vowel:

comment va-t-il voyager?
how will he travel?

aime-t-elle le café?
does she like coffee?

pourquoi a-t-il refusé?
why did he refuse?

Marie viendra-t-elle?
will Marie be coming?

Note that when a question word is used, modern French will often just invert the verb and the noun subject, without adding a pronoun; no hyphen is then necessary:

où travaille ton père?
where does your father work?

2 Indirect questions

a) *Definition*

Indirect questions follow a verb and are introduced by an interrogative word, eg:

ask him when he will arrive   *I don't know why he did it*

b) *Word order*

i) The word order is usually the same as in statements: question word + subject + verb:

je ne sais pas s'il voudra
I don't know if he'll want to

dis-moi où tu l'as mis
tell me where you put it

il n'a pas dit quand il appellerait
he didn't say when he would phone

ii) If the subject is a noun, the verb and subject are sometimes inverted:

demande-leur où est le camping
ask them where the campsite is

But: **je ne comprends pas comment l'accident s'est produit**
I don't understand how the accident happened

il ne savait pas pourquoi elle avait l'air triste
he didn't know why she looked sad

3 Translation of English question tags

Examples of question tags are: isn't it? aren't you? doesn't he? won't they? haven't you? is it? did you? and so on. Question tags are not used in French as often as they are in English. Some of them can, however, be translated in the following ways:

a) **n'est-ce pas?**

n'est-ce pas? is used at the end of a sentence when confirmation of a statement is expected:

c'était très intéressant, n'est-ce pas?
it was very interesting, wasn't it?

tu voudrais partir en vacances, n'est-ce pas?
you'd like to go on holiday, wouldn't you?

vous n'arriverez pas trop tard, n'est-ce pas?
you won't be arriving too late, will you?

b) **hein?** *and* **non?**

In conversation **hein?** and **non?** are often used after affirmative statements instead of **n'est-ce pas:**

il fait beau, hein?
the weather's nice, isn't it?

il est amusant, non?
he's funny, isn't he?

D ANSWERS ('YES' AND 'NO')

1 OUI, SI and NON

a) **oui** and **si** mean 'yes' and are equivalent to longer affirmative answers such as 'yes, it is', 'yes, I will', 'yes, he has' etc:

tu m'écriras? – oui, bien sûr!
will you write to me? – (yes) of course I will

b) **non** means 'no' and is equivalent to longer negative answers such as 'no, it isn't', 'no, I didn't' etc:

c'était bien? – non, on s'est ennuyé
was it good? – no, it wasn't, we were bored

2 OUI or SI?

oui and **si** both mean 'yes', but **oui** is used to answer an affirmative question, and **si** to contradict a negative question:

cette place est libre? – oui
is this seat free? – yes (it is)

tu n'aimes pas lire? – si, bien sûr!
don't you like reading? – yes, of course (I do)

13 TRANSLATION PROBLEMS

A GENERAL TRANSLATION PROBLEMS

1 French words not translated in English

Some French words are not translated in English, particularly:

a) *Articles*

Definite and indefinite articles are not always translated (see pp B3-5):

dans la société moderne
in modern society

les gens en ont assez!
people have had enough!

ah non! encore du riz! je déteste le riz!
oh no! rice again! I hate rice!

b) que

que meaning 'that' as a conjunction (see p B58) or
'that'/'which'/'whom' as a relative pronoun (see p B22) cannot
be omitted in French:

j'espère que tu vas mieux   elle pense que c'est vrai
I hope you're better   *she thinks it's true*

celui que j'ai vu   c'est un pays que j'aime
the one I saw   *it's a country I like*

c) *Prepositions*

Some French verbs are followed by a preposition (+ indirect
object) when their English equivalent takes a direct object without a preposition (see p B53):

elle a téléphoné au médecin   tu l'as dit à ton père?
she phoned the doctor   *did you tell your father?*

d) le

When le *(it)* is used in an impersonal sense (see p B18), it is
not translated:

oui, je le sais   dis-le-lui
yes, I know   *tell him*

2 English words not translated in French

Some English words are not translated in French, for example:

a) *Prepositions*

i) with verbs which take an indirect object in English, but a
direct object in French (see p B53):

tu l'as payé combien?   écoutez cette chanson
how much did you pay for it?   *listen to this song*

ii) in certain expressions (see p B61):

je viendrai te voir lundi soir
I'll come and see you on Monday night

b) *'can'*

'can' + verb of hearing or seeing (see pp B39-40):

je ne vois rien!   tu entends la musique?
I can't see anything!   *can you hear the music?*

3 Other differences

a) *English phrasal verbs*

Phrasal verbs are verbs which, when followed by a preposition,
take on a different meaning, eg 'to give up', 'to walk out'. They
do not exist in French and are translated by simple verbs or by
expressions:

to give up   to run away   to run across
abandonner   s'enfuir   traverser en
                                    courant

b) *English possessive adjectives*

English possessive adjectives (my, your etc) are translated by the
French definite article (le/la/les) when parts of the body are
mentioned (see p B21):

brush your teeth   *he hurt his foot*
brosse-toi les dents   il s'est fait mal au pied

c) *'from'*

'from' is translated by à with verbs referring to taking something
away (see p B53):

he hid it from his parents   borrow some from your dad
il l'a caché à ses parents   empruntes-en à ton père

B SPECIFIC TRANSLATION PROBLEMS

1 Words ending in -ing

The English verbal form ending in **-ing** is translated in a number of
ways in French:

a) *by the appropriate French tense* (see p B30):

he's speaking *(present tense)*   il parle
he was speaking *(imperfect)*   il parlait
he will be speaking *(future)*   il parlera
he has been speaking *(perfect)*   il a parlé
he had been speaking *(pluperfect)*   il avait parlé
he would be speaking *(conditional)* il parlerait

b) *by a French present participle* (see p B37)

i) as an adjective:

un livre amusant   c'est effrayant
a funny book   *it's frightening*

ii) as a verb, with en (while/on/by doing something; see p
B38):

'ça ne fait rien', dit-il en souriant
'it doesn't matter', he said smiling

j'ai vu mes copains en sortant du lycée
I saw my friends when I was coming out of school

Note, however, that en + present participle cannot be used
when the two verbs have different subjects, eg:

I saw my brother coming out of school
j'ai vu mon frère sortir du lycée/qui sortait du lycée

c) *by a present infinitive* (see pp B35-7):

i) after a preposition:

au lieu de rire   avant de traverser
instead of laughing   *before crossing*

ii) after verbs of perception:

je l'ai entendu appeler   je l'ai vue entrer
I heard him calling   *I saw her going in*

iii) after verbs of liking and disliking:

j'adore faire du camping   tu aimes lire?
I love camping   *do you like reading?*

iv) after verbs followed by à or de:

tu passes tout ton temps à ne rien faire
you spend all your time doing nothing

il a commencé à neiger   continuez à travailler
it started snowing   *go on working*

tu as envie de sortir?   il doit finir de manger
do you feel like going out?   *he must finish eating*

v) when an English verb in **-ing** is the subject of another verb:

attendre serait inutile   écrire est une corvée!
waiting would be pointless   *writing is a real chore!*

vi) when an English verb in **-ing** follows 'is' or 'was' etc:

mon passe-temps favori, c'est de lire
my favourite pastime is reading

d) *by a perfect infinitive* (see p B37)

i) after après *(after)*:

j'ai pris une douche après avoir nettoyé ma chambre
I had a shower after cleaning my room

ii) after certain verbs:

regretter	remercier de	se souvenir de
to regret	to thank for	to remember

j'ai regretté de leur en avoir parlé
I regretted speaking to them about it

il m'a remercié d'être allé le chercher
he thanked me for going to pick him up

e) *by a noun*

particularly when referring to sports, activities, hobbies etc:

le ski	**la natation**	**l'équitation**
skiing	swimming	horse-riding
la voile	**le patinage**	**le canoë**
sailing	skating	canoeing
la lecture	**la planche à voile**	**la cuisine**
reading	windsurfing	cooking
la boxe	**la lutte**	**la marche à pied**
boxing	wrestling	walking

2 IT IS (IT'S)

'it is' (it's) can be translated in three ways in French:

a) il *or* elle (see p B18)

il or elle are used with the verb être to translate 'it is', 'it was' etc (+ adjective) when referring to a particular masculine or feminine noun (a thing, a place etc):

merci de ta carte; elle était très amusante
thanks for your card; it was very funny

regarde ce blouson; il n'est vraiment pas cher
look at this jacket; it really isn't that expensive

b) ce (see p B15)

ce (c' before a vowel) is used with the verb être to translate 'it is', 'it was' etc in two cases:

i) If être is followed by a word which is not an adjective on its own, ie by a noun, a pronoun, an expression of place etc:

c'était ta voix	**c'est une grande maison**
it was your voice	*it's a big house*
c'est moi! c'est Claude!	**c'est le tien?**
it's me! it's Claude!	*is it yours?*
c'est en France que tu vas?	**c'est pour lundi**
is it France you're going to?	*it's for Monday*

ii) If être is followed by an adjective which refers to something previously mentioned, such as an idea, an event or a fact, but not to a specific noun:

l'homme n'ira jamais sur Saturne; ce n'est pas possible
Man will never go to Saturn; it's not possible

j'ai passé mes vacances en Italie; c'était formidable!
I spent my holidays in Italy; it was great!

oh, je m'excuse! – ce n'est pas grave
oh, I'm sorry! – it's all right

c) il (see pp B29-30)

il is used to translate 'it is', 'it was' etc in three cases:

i) With être followed by an adjective + de or que, ie referring to something that follows, but not to a specific noun:

il est impossible de connaître l'avenir
it's impossible to know the future

il est évident que tu ne me crois pas
it's obvious you don't believe me

ii) To describe the weather (see p B29):

il y a du vent	**il faisait très froid**
it's windy	*it was very cold*

iii) With être to tell the time and in phrases relating to the time of day, or in such expressions as il est temps de (it's time to):

il est deux heures du matin	**il est tard!**
it's two in the morning	*it's late!*

il est temps de partir
it's time to go

Note that with other expressions of time, c'est is used:

c'est lundi ou mardi aujourd'hui?	**c'était l'été**
is it Monday or Tuesday today?	*it was summer*

3 TO BE

Although 'to be' is usually translated by être, it can also be translated in the following ways:

a) avoir

i) avoir is used instead of être in many set expressions:

avoir faim/soif	*to be hungry/thirsty*
avoir chaud/froid	*to be warm/cold*
avoir peur/honte	*to be afraid/ashamed*
avoir tort/raison	*to be wrong/right*

ii) avoir is also used for age:

quel âge as-tu?	**j'ai vingt-cinq ans**
how old are you?	*I'm twenty-five*

b) aller

aller is used for describing health:

je vais mieux	**tout le monde va bien**
I am/feel better	*everyone's fine*

c) faire

faire is used in many expressions to describe the weather (see p B29):

il fait beau	**il fera chaud**
the weather's nice	*it will be hot*

Note that il y a can also be used to describe the weather, but only before du/de la/des:

il y a du vent/des nuages/de la tempête
it's windy/cloudy/stormy

d) *untranslated*

'to be' is not translated when it is the first part of an English continuous tense; instead, the appropriate tense is used in French (see p B30):

I'm having a bath	*he was driving slowly*
je prends un bain	**il conduisait lentement**

4 ANY

'any' can be translated in three different ways:

a) du/de la/des *or* de (see p B5)

The partitive article is used with a noun in negative and interrogative sentences:

il ne mange jamais de viande	**tu veux du pain?**
he never eats meat	*do you want any bread?*

b) en (see pp B19-20)

en is used to translate 'any' when it occurs without a noun in negative and interrogative sentences:

je n'**en** ai pas
I haven't got any

il **en** reste?
is there any left?

c) n'importe quel(le)/quel(le)s *or* tout(e)/tou(te)s

these are used to translate 'any' (and 'every') when they mean 'no matter which':

il pourrait arriver à n'importe quel **moment**
he could arrive any time

prends n'importe quelle **couleur, je les aime toutes**
take any colour, I like them all

5 ANYONE, ANYTHING, ANYWHERE

Like 'any', these can be translated in different ways:

a) *in interrogative sentences:*

il y a **quelqu'un?**
is anyone in?

tu l'as vu **quelque part?**
did you see it anywhere?

il a dit **quelque chose?**
did he say anything?

b) *in negative sentences:*

il n'y a **personne**
there isn't anyone

je ne le vois **nulle part**
I can't see it anywhere

je n'ai **rien** fait
I didn't do anything

c) *in the sense of 'any' (and 'every'), 'no matter which':*

n'importe qui **peut le faire**
anyone can do that

il croit **n'importe quoi**
he believes anything

j'irai **n'importe où**
I'll go anywhere

n'importe quand
anytime

6 YOU, YOUR, YOURS, YOURSELF

French has two separate sets of words to translate 'you', 'your', 'yours', 'yourself':

● tu, te (t'), toi, ton/ta/tes, le tien etc

● vous, votre/vos, le vôtre etc

For their respective meanings and uses, see pp B18, B20-1.

a) tu *etc*

tu, te, ton etc correspond to the tu form of the verb (second person singular) and are used when speaking to one person you know well (a friend, a relative) or to someone younger. They represent the familiar form of address:

si **tu viens au concert avec ton copain, je t'achète deux places; une pour toi et une pour lui**
if you're coming to the concert with your boyfriend, I'll get you two tickets; one for you and one for him

b) vous *etc*

vous, vos etc correspond to the vous form of the verb (second person plural) and are used:

i) when speaking to more than one person:

dépêchez-vous, les gars! Vous allez manquer le train
hurry up, boys! You'll miss the train

ii) when speaking to one person you do not know well or to someone older. They represent the formal or polite form of address:

je regrette, Monsieur, mais vous ne pouvez pas garder votre chien avec vous dans ce restaurant
I'm sorry, sir, but you can't keep your dog with you in this restaurant

c) when speaking or writing to one person, you must not mix words from both sets, but decide whether you are being formal or familiar, and use the same form of address throughout:

**Cher Michel,
Merci pour ta lettre. Comment vas-tu? ...**
*Dear Michel,
Thanks for your letter. How are you? ...*

**Monsieur,
Pourriez-vous me réserver une chambre dans votre hôtel pour le 8 juin?**
*Dear Sir,
Could you book a room for me in your hotel for 8th June?*

vous etc and tu etc can only be used together when vous is plural (ie when it refers to more than one person):

tu sais, Jean, toi et ta sœur, vous vous ressemblez
you know, Jean, you and your sister look like each other

7 Noun phrases

A noun phrase is a combination of two nouns used together to name things or people. In English, the first of these nouns is used to describe the second one, eg 'a love story'. In French, however, the position of the two nouns is reversed, so that the describing noun comes second and is linked to the first one by the preposition de (or d'):

une histoire **d'amour**
a love story

une feuille **d'impôts**
a tax form

un magasin **de disques**
a record shop

un acteur **de cinéma**
a film actor

un arrêt **d'autobus**
a bus stop

un film **d'aventure**
an adventure film

un coup **de soleil**
sunstroke

une boule **de neige**
a snowball

un roman **de science-fiction**
a science-fiction novel

un match **de football**
a football match

le château **d'Édimbourg**
Edinburgh castle

un conte **de fées**
a fairy tale

un joueur **de rugby**
a rugby player

un employé **de bureau**
an office worker

Note that when the describing noun refers to a type of material, the preposition en is often used instead of de:

un pull **en laine**
a woollen jumper

un pantalon **en cuir**
leather trousers

une bague **en or**
a gold ring

un sac **en plastique**
a plastic bag

8 Possession

In English, possession is often expressed by using a noun phrase and tagging '**s** at the end of the first word, eg:

my friend's cat

This is translated in French by: object + de + possessor:

le chat de mon ami

Note the use of the article le/la/les.

le fiancé **de ma sœur**
my sister's fiancé

les amis **de Claire**
Claire's friends

les événements **de la semaine dernière**
last week's events

When '**s** is used to refer to someone's house or shop etc, it is translated by the preposition chez:

je téléphone de **chez Paul**
I'm telephoning from Paul's (house)

chez le dentiste
at/to the dentist's

FRANÇAIS–ANGLAIS

FRENCH–ENGLISH

A, a [ɑ] NM *(lettre)* A, a; **connaître un sujet de A (jusqu')à Z** to know a subject inside out *or* from A to Z *or* from beginning to end; **prouver qch par A plus B** to prove sth in a logical *or* scientific fashion

A [a]

to **1, 3, 5, 9, 11, 13, 14** ▪ at **1–3, 8, 10** ▪ in **2, 9** ▪ by **4, 8** ▪ from **5** ▪ with **6, 8** ▪ for **7, 10, 11** ▪ on **8, 9** ▪ + infinitif **12**	

PRÉP SEE GRAMMAR B54 *(contracts with the article* **le** *into* **au**, *with the article* **les** *into* **aux**) **1** *(direction)* **il est venu à moi** he came (up) to me; **revenir à la surface** to come back (up) to the surface, to resurface; **aller à l'église/au collège/au cinéma/au marché** to go to church/to school/to the cinema/to the market; **se mettre** *ou* **s'asseoir au piano** to sit down at the piano; **monter au premier étage** to go up to the first floor; **partir à la recherche de ses ancêtres** to begin a search for one's ancestors; **de Paris à Lyon** from Paris to Lyons; **se rendre au Japon/aux Antilles/à la Guadeloupe/à Terre-Neuve** to travel to Japan/to the West Indies/to Guadeloupe/to Newfoundland; **au lit!** off to bed!; **au feu!** fire!; **au voleur!** stop thief!; **courir à sa perte** to head for disaster; **(de) vingt à trente personnes** between twenty and thirty people **2** *(position)* **au coin de la rue** at the corner of the street, at the street corner; **vivre à Montpellier/à la campagne** to live in Montpellier/in the country; **à l'horizon** on the horizon; **à la page deux** on page two; **à l'ombre** in the shade; **au grenier** in the attic; **à la maison** at home; **au théâtre** at the theatre; **au Canada** in Canada; **aux États-Unis** in the United States; **à la Jamaïque** in Jamaica; **à Cuba** in Cuba; **à Paris** in Paris; **se tenir à la fenêtre** to stand at the window; **à 2 kilomètres d'ici** 2 kilometres (away) from here; **avoir mal aux dents/yeux/pieds/au ventre** to have toothache/sore eyes/sore feet/stomachache; **à la télévision/à la radio** on (the) television/on the radio; **le sourire aux lèvres** with a smile on his/her/*etc* lips; **un livre à la main** with a book in his/her/*etc* hand; **au fond** basically, fundamentally; **au fond, il n'est pas méchant** deep down, he's not a bad person **3** *(dans le temps)* **du matin au soir** from morning to *or* till night; **remettre une affaire à plus tard** to put something off (until later), to postpone something; **à jamais** for ever; **à demain!/mardi!** see you tomorrow!/on Tuesday!; **du lundi au vendredi** from Monday to Friday, *Am* Monday to *or* thru Friday; **je serai chez elle de lundi à vendredi** I'll be at her house from Monday to Friday; **il sera là à 8 heures/à la tombée de la nuit/au petit matin** he'll be there at 8 o'clock/at nightfall/in the early hours; **à temps** on time; **à un certain moment** at some moment; **au prin-**temps in (the) spring; **le 2 au soir** on the evening of the 2nd; **à Noël** at Christmas; **au revoir** goodbye (for now); **à ces mots** at these words; **au premier mot** at the first word; **à première vue** on first sight; **à mon arrivée** on my arrival; **à deux heures** at two o'clock; **à toute heure du jour et de la nuit** at all hours of the day and night; **au vingtième siècle** in the twentieth century; **à l'avenir** in (the) future; **à l'aube** at dawn **4** *(distribution)* **faire du 10 litres aux 100 (km)** to do 100 kilometres on 10 litres; **faire du 90 km à l'heure** to do 90 km an *or* per hour; **payé au mois/au forfait** paid monthly *or* by the month/at a fixed rate; **travailler à la pièce** to do piecework; **vendre des oranges à la pièce** to sell oranges separately *or* individually; **vendre des huîtres à la douzaine** to sell oysters by the dozen; **entrer deux à deux** to come in two by two; **se battre d'homme à homme** to fight man to man; *Tennis* **quinze à** fifteen all; **monter l'escalier quatre à quatre** to go upstairs four (steps) at a time; **peu à peu, petit à petit** little by little, gradually **5** *(avec complément d'objet indirect)* **attacher un cheval à un arbre** to tie a horse to a tree; **aspirer au calme** to long for peace and quiet; **échapper à qch** to escape from sth; *Fig* **avoir un fil à la patte** to be tied down; **attacher de l'importance à qch** to attach importance to sth; **s'adresser à qn** to address sb, to speak to sb; **lettre ouverte à …** open letter to …; **donner qch à qn** to give sth to sb, to give sb sth; **parler à qn** to speak to sb; **dire qch à qn** to say sth to sb, to tell sb sth; **penser à qn/qch** to think of *or* about sb/sth; **s'habituer à qch** to become used to sth; **à quoi cela sert-il?** what's that used for?; *(quel intérêt?)* what's the good of that?; **survivre à qn/qch** to survive *or* outlive sb/sth; **prendre qn à témoin** to call sb to witness *or* as a witness; **s'opposer à qch** to oppose sth; **résister à qn/qch** to resist sb/sth; **cacher/voler qch à qn** to hide/steal sth from sb; **prendre qch à qn** to take sth from sb; **boire à (même) la bouteille** to drink (straight) from the bottle; **faire faire qch à qn** to make sb do sth, to get sb to do sth; **faire savoir qch à qn** to tell sb about sth, to inform sb of sth; **laisser croire à qn que …** to let sb think *or* believe that …; **c'est à vous de décider** it's for you *or* up to you to decide; **c'est à vous** *(de jouer etc)* it's your turn; *Radio* **à vous** over (to you); **la parole est à M. Dupont** Mr Dupont will now speak; **c'est aimable à vous d'être venu** it's kind *or* good of you to have come **6** *(possession, attributs etc)* **ce livre est à Paul** this book is Paul's, this is Paul's book, this book belongs to Paul; **un ami à moi** a friend of mine; *Fam* **la sœur à Anne** Anne's sister; **enfant aux yeux bleus** child with blue eyes, blue-eyed child; **homme à barbe noire** man with a black beard; **une expression** bien à Anne a typically Anne expression; **chambre à deux lits** room with twin beds; **voiture à toit ouvrant** car with a sunroof **7** *(destination, usage)* for; **affaire à suivre** something worth watching *or* keeping an eye on; **c'est à voir** it remains to be seen; **bon à jeter** fit for the dustbin; **une machine à coudre** a sewing machine; **j'ai une veste à nettoyer** I have a jacket to be cleaned; *(c'est moi qui vais le faire)* I have a jacket to clean; **j'ai une lettre à écrire** I have a letter to write; **je voudrais quelque chose à boire** I'd like something to drink; **maison à vendre** house for sale; **tasse à thé** teacup; **brosse à dents** toothbrush; **moulin à vent** windmill; **moulin à café** coffee grinder; **pompe à vélo** bicycle pump; **poudre à récurer** scouring powder; **pompe à eau** water pump SEE GRAMMAR B36 **8** *(manière)* **à pied** on foot; **écrire à la machine** to type; **montre à quartz** quartz watch; **ça fonctionne à l'électricité** it runs on electricity; **à la main** by hand; **fait à la main** handmade; **peint à la main** hand-painted; **jouer un air au violon** to play a tune on the violin; **arriver à l'improviste** to arrive unexpectedly; **à toute allure** at top speed; **à ce rythme, nous y sommes encore demain** the way we're going *or* at this rate, we'll still be at it tomorrow; **recevoir qn à bras ouverts** to receive sb with open arms; **cuisine à l'huile** cooking with oil; **à l'espagnole** in the Spanish manner *or* way; **un repas à l'anglaise** a typical(ly) English meal; *Fam* **encore une histoire à la Marie** another one of Marie's typical stories; **manger à sa faim** to eat one's fill; *(autant que possible)* to eat as much as one can; **faire qch à sa manière** *ou* **façon** to do sth (in) one's own way; **nous l'avons fait à trois** there were three of us doing it; **se mettre à plusieurs pour faire qch** to team up *or* to get together with several people to do sth; *Sport* **rugby à quinze/treize** Rugby Union/League **9 à mon avis** in my opinion; **à ce qu'il dit** according to him *or* what he says, from what he says; **au reste** moreover, besides; **à cette condition** on this condition; **cela se fera à une seule condition** that will be done on one condition; **à la demande générale** by popular request; **à ma grande surprise** to my great surprise **10** *(expression du prix)* **vendre qch à dix euros le kilo** to sell sth for *or* at ten euros a kilo; **à quel prix vendez-vous cela?** how much are you asking for that?; **un timbre à deux euros** a two-euro stamp; **à ce prix, on ne peut pas se plaindre** at that price, you can't complain **11** *(après adjectif)* **indispensable à qn/qch** indispensable *or* essential to sb/for sth; **parallèle à** parallel to; **hostile à** hostile to; **utile à** useful for **12** *(avec le verbe à l'infinitif)* **penser à faire qch** *(envisager)* to think of doing sth; *(se souvenir)* to remember to do sth; **songer à faire**

qch to dream of or about doing sth; **consentir à faire qch** to consent or agree to do sth; **encourager qn à faire qch** to encourage sb to do sth; **c'est à refaire** it will have to be done again; **il me reste à faire une dissertation de philo** I still have to do a philosophy essay; **il ne me reste qu'à vous remercier** it only remains for me to thank you; **commencer à faire qch** to begin to do sth, to start doing sth; **apprendre à lire** to learn to read SEE GRAMMAR B33; B36

13 (conséquence) **laid à faire peur** frightfully ugly; **s'ennuyer à mourir** to be bored to death; **c'était à mourir de rire** it was hilarious; **jolie à croquer** pretty as a picture; **il est à croquer dans son petit costume de marin** he looks good enough to eat in his little sailor suit; **c'est à se demander si elle sait de quoi elle parle** you begin to wonder if she knows what she's talking about; **geler à pierre fendre** to freeze hard; **à quoi bon le lui dire?** what's the good or use of telling him/her?

14 je suis prêt à vous écouter I'm willing to listen to you; **facile à comprendre** easy to understand; **il est homme à se défendre** he's the kind of man who will hit back; **elle est à plaindre** she is or deserves to be pitied; **être le seul à faire qch** to be the only one to do sth; **le troisième à arriver** the third to arrive

15 à partager les mêmes périls, ils ont appris à s'estimer by or through sharing the same dangers, they gained respect for each other; **à rouler trop vite, tu vas finir par avoir un accident** if you go on driving too fast, you're going to end up having an accident; **à en juger par ...** judging by ..., to judge by ...; **à les en croire** according to them, if we are to believe them

AA [aa] NF Banque, Bourse (notation) AA AA (rating), double-A rating

AAA [aaa] NF Banque, Bourse (notation) A. AAA (rating), triple-A rating

A3 [atrwa] NM A3

A4 [akatr] NM A4

abaissant [abɛsɑ̃] ADJ degrading

abaisse [abɛs] NF Culin thinly rolled pastry

abaisse-langue NM INV Méd spatula, tongue depressor

abaissement [abɛsmɑ̃] NM **1** (d'un store etc) lowering, pulling down; (du niveau d'un fleuve etc) lowering **2** (chute) fall; (du sol, d'un bâtiment) subsidence, sinking; (de la température, des prix) fall, drop; (des prix) reduction **3** Litt (humiliation) abasement, humiliation

abaisser [abese] VT **1** to lower; (store) to pull down; (pont-levis) to let down; **a. son regard** to look down; **a. un mur** to pull down a wall **2** (prix) to lower; (prix, coût, pression etc) to reduce **3** Litt (humilier) to humble, to abase **4** Math **a. une perpendiculaire à une ligne** to drop a perpendicular to a line; **a. le chiffre des dizaines** (dans une division) to bring down the figure in the tens column **5** Culin **a. une pâte** to roll out pastry

▸ VPR **s'abaisser 1** to fall away, to dip, to slope down, to go down; (s'effondrer) to subside; **la fenêtre s'abaisse quand on appuie sur ce bouton** the window slides down when you press this button **2** (chuter) to drop, to fall **3 s'a. jusqu'à faire qch** (consentir) to stoop so low as to do sth; (d'une personne orgueilleuse) to condescend to do sth; **s'a. à des compromissions** to stoop to compromise **4 s'a. devant Dieu** to humble oneself before God

abaisseur [abɛsœr] NM Anat depressor
▸ ADJ Élec (transformateur) step-down

abandon [abɑ̃dɔ̃] NM **1** (de biens) surrender; (de droits) renunciation, surrender; Fin **a. de**

créances debt forgiveness; **faire a. de qch à qn** to make over or relinquish or surrender sth to sb

2 Sport (au cours d'une épreuve) retirement, withdrawal; (avant la course) withdrawal

3 Jur (d'enfants) desertion, abandonment; (de fonction) desertion, dereliction; **a. du domicile conjugal** desertion

4 (état) neglect; **finir sa vie dans l'a.** to end one's life alone; **à l'a.** (jardin) (completely) neglected; Naut adrift, derelict

5 (détente) lack of restraint; **parler avec un complet a.** to speak quite freely or without restraint; **dans un moment d'a.** in a moment of abandon or freedom

6 Ordinat abort

7 Bourse **a. de l'option, a. de prime** relinquishment or abandonment of the option

abandonné, -ée [abɑ̃dɔne] ADJ (personne) abandoned, deserted; (air) untidy; **navire a. en mer** derelict; **maison abandonnée** deserted house

abandonner [abɑ̃dɔne] VT **1** (personne) to desert, to abandon, Litt to forsake; Naut **a. un homme** to maroon a man; Naut **a. le bâtiment** to abandon ship; Aviat **a. le bord** ou **un avion en vol** to bale out; Mil **a. son poste** to desert one's post

2 (délaisser) (voiture) to abandon; (village) to abandon, to desert; **mes forces m'abandonnent** my strength is failing me

3 (renoncer à) (quelque chose) to surrender, to renounce, to give up; **a. la course** to abandon or withdraw from the race; **a. un projet** to abandon a project; **il a abandonné les études à quatorze ans** he dropped out (of school) when he was fourteen; **a. la partie** to throw in one's hand; **a. sa part d'héritage** (à sa sœur) to forgo one's share of an inheritance (in favour of one's sister); **a. ses prétentions** to renounce or surrender one's claims

4 Ordinat to abort

5 Bourse **a. l'option** ou **la prime** to relinquish or abandon or surrender the option

▸ VI to give up; Sport to give up, to retire; Fam **c'est trop dur, j'abandonne** it's too hard, I give up

▸ VPR **s'abandonner 1** (se laisser aller) to let oneself go, Fml to be unconstrained; **s'a. au chagrin** to give oneself up to or to abandon oneself to grief; **s'a. au sommeil** to abandon oneself to sleep **2** (s'en remettre à) **s'a. à son sort** to resign oneself to one's fate **3** (se confier) to open up

abaque [abak] NM **1** (boulier) abacus, counting frame **2** Math chart, graph **3** Archit abacus

abasourdir [abazurdir] VT to deafen; Fig to astound, to stun; Fig **nous sommes restés abasourdis par la nouvelle** we were flabbergasted or astounded or stunned by the news

abasourdissant [abazurdisɑ̃] ADJ (bruit) deafening; Fig (nouvelle) stunning, astounding

abasourdissement [abazurdismɑ̃] NM bewilderment, stupefaction

abat [aba] NM **1** Arch slaughter **2 pluie d'a.** sudden shower

▸ NMPL **abats** offal, Am variety meat; (de volaille) giblets

abâtardi [abatardi] ADJ degenerate

abâtardir [abatardir] VT (espèce) to cause to degenerate; (qualité) to debase

▸ VPR **s'abâtardir** to degenerate, to deteriorate

abâtardissement [abatardismɑ̃] NM degeneracy

abat-jour NM INV lampshade; Fig **mettre la main en a.** to shade one's eyes with one's hand

abattage [abataʒ] NM **1** (de bâtiments) knocking down, pulling down; (d'arbres etc) felling, cutting down, clearing; Min cutting, working; Min **face d'a.** working face; Naut **a. en carène** careening; **avoir de l'a.** Vieilli to be full of energy; Fig (d'un acteur, d'un politicien etc) to have charisma **2** (d'animal) slaughtering, killing; **grand a. de gibier** heavy bag of game **3** Com **vente à l'a.** sale at knock-down prices

abattant [abatɑ̃] ADJ **siège a.** tip-up seat
▸ NM (d'un comptoir, d'une table) flap

abattement [abatmɑ̃] NM **1** (physique) exhaustion, Fml prostration **2** (moral) despondency, dejection, depression, low spirits **3** Fin (d'impôts) **a. fiscal** tax allowance; **a. forfaitaire** fixed-rate rebate

---

Il faut noter que le nom anglais **abatement** est un faux ami. Il signifie **apaisement**.

---

abatteur, -euse [abatœr, -øz] N **1 a. de besogne** hard worker, Fam slogger **2** (d'arbres) feller **3** (d'animaux) slaughterer

abattis [abati] NM **1** (des arbres) felling, clearing **2** Région heap of felled trees; **a. de maisons** heap of fallen houses

▸ NMPL **1** Culin giblets **2** Arg limbs, hands and feet; **si tu viens te battre avec moi, commence par numéroter tes a.!** if you're going to pick a fight with me, you can say your prayers right now!

abattoir [abatwar] NM slaughterhouse, abattoir; Fig **envoyer des hommes à l'a.** to send men to the slaughter or to be slaughtered or butchered

abattre [abatr] (conj like **battre**) VT **1** (faire tomber) to knock down, to throw down, to pull down; (régime) to overthrow; **a. son rival** to floor or fell one's opponent, to knock down one's opponent; **a. une maison/un mur** to pull or knock down a house/a wall; **a. de la besogne** to get through a lot of work **2** (arbres) to fell, to cut down, to clear; **a. du minerai** to break down or to stope ore

3 (tuer) (personne, cochon, bœuf) to slaughter, to kill; (animal malade ou dangereux) to destroy; Arg (personne) to bump off; **a. un avion** to bring down or shoot down an aircraft; **c'est un homme à a.** this man is on the hit-list

4 (poussière, vent) to lay; Prov **petite pluie abat grand vent** a soft answer will turn away wrath

5 (du vent) (arbre) to blow down; (blé) to flatten; Naut **a. navire en carène** to careen a ship

6 Fig (fatiguer) (de la chaleur) to drain of energy; (d'une maladie) to lay low

7 (démoraliser) to dishearten, to depress; **ne vous laissez pas a.!** keep your chin or spirits up!; **cette nouvelle l'a profondément abattu** this news has really crushed or demoralized him

8 Cartes **a. ses cartes** ou **son jeu** to lay one's cards on the table, to lay down one's hand; Fig to lay one's cards on the table

9 Naut to pay off

▸ VPR **s'abattre 1** (tomber) to fall, to crash down, to collapse; **le pilier s'abattit** the pillar came crashing down **2 s'a. sur qch** to pounce on sth; (d'un oiseau) to swoop down on(to) sth; **les précipitations qui se sont abattues sur la région** the torrential rain which has been falling on the region; **les injures n'ont pas cessé de s'a. sur l'orateur** insults rained down constantly on the speaker; **le malheur s'abattra sur toi et ta descendance!** misfortune will descend upon you and your offspring!

abattu [abaty] ADJ dejected, dispirited, low-spirited; **a. par la chaleur** limp with the heat;

a. par l'échec depressed *or* demoralized by the failure; **visage a.** drawn face
　NM fusil à l'a. uncocked rifle

abbatial, -iale, -iaux, -iales [abasjal, -jo] **ADJ** *terres abbatiales* abbey lands; **église abbatiale** abbey (church)
　NF abbatiale abbey (church)

abbaye [abei] **NF** abbey

abbé [abe] **NM 1** *(supérieur d'une abbaye)* abbot **2** *(prêtre)* j'en parlerai à monsieur l'a. I'll mention it to the priest; **(Monsieur) l'a. Constantin** Father Constantin

abbesse [abɛs] **NF** abbess

abc [abese] **NM INV 1** *(livre pour apprendre à lire)* ABC, alphabet (book); *(livre scolaire)* primer **2** *Fig (d'une science)* rudiments; **apprendre l'a. du métier** to learn the rudiments *or* basics of the job

abcès [apsɛ] **NM** abscess; **a. à la gencive** gumboil; *Fig* **crever** *ou* **vider l'a.** to resolve the situation

abdication [abdikasjɔ̃] **NF** *(d'un monarque, d'une autorité, de droits)* abdication; *(d'une autorité, de droits)* renunciation, surrender

abdiquer [abdike] **VT** *(trône, autorité)* to abdicate; *(droits etc)* to renounce, to surrender
　VI to abdicate

abdomen [abdɔmɛn] **NM** *Anat* abdomen

abdominal, -ale, -aux, -ales [abdɔminal, -o] **ADJ** abdominal
　NMPL abdominaux abdominal *or* stomach muscles; **faire des abdominaux** to do exercises for the stomach muscles

abdos [abdo] **NMPL** *Fam* stomach muscles; **faire des a.** to do exercises for the stomach muscles

abducteur [abdyktœr] *Anat* **ADJ** *(muscle)* abductor
　NM abductor muscle

abécédaire [abesedɛr] **ADJ** *Vieilli* alphabetical
　NM ABC, alphabet book

abeille [abɛj] **NF** *(insecte)* bee; **a. mâle** drone; **a. mère** queen bee; **nid d'abeilles** bees' nest, honeycomb; *Aut* **radiateur nid d'abeilles** honeycomb radiator; *Fam* **elle ne cesse de travailler, c'est une vraie petite a.** she never stops working, she's a real busy bee; *très Fam* **avoir les abeilles** to be hacked off *or* cheesed off
　►**a. domestique** hive *or* honey bee; **a. neutre** *ou* **ouvrière** worker (bee)

aber [abɛr] **NM** *Géog* deep estuary

aberrant [abɛrɑ̃] **ADJ 1** *Biol* aberrant **2** *(absurde) (comportement)* aberrant, illogical; *(remarque)* nonsensical; **avoir une conduite aberrante** to behave illogically; **c'est a.!** it's absurd!

aberration [abɛrasjɔ̃] **NF** *(de l'esprit, du comportement), Astron, Biol, Math, Opt* aberration; **a. chromosomique** chromosome abnormality; **dans un moment d'a.** in a moment of aberration; **c'est une a.!** it's absurd!

abêtir [abetir] **VT a. qn** to make sb stupid; **la télévision abêtit les enfants** television deadens *or* stultifies children's minds
　VI to addle the brain
　VPR s'abêtir to grow *or* become stupid

abêtissant [abetisɑ̃] **ADJ** mind-destroying, mindless

abhorrer [abɔre] **VT** *Litt* to abhor, to loathe

abîme [abim] **NM 1** *(de l'océan)* abyss, chasm, depth(s); *Fig* gulf; *Géol* swallowhole; **les abîmes de l'océan** the ocean depths; *Fig* **un a. nous sépare** we are separated by a gulf, there is a gulf between us; **plonger dans les abîmes de l'angoisse** to plunge into the depths of anguish; *Fig* **le livre est un a. d'ennui** this book is extremely boring *or* deadly dull; *Fig* **un a. de science** a person of im-

mense learning; *(qui peut fournir beaucoup de renseignements)* a mine of information; *Litt* **les abîmes de l'histoire** the earliest beginnings of history, the mists of time **2** *(moral)* despair; **il est au bord de l'a.** he is on the brink *or* verge of depression *or* despair **3** *(financier)* ruin; **courir à l'a.** to be on the road to ruin, to be heading for ruin

abîmer [abime] **VT** *(objet)* to spoil, to damage; *Fam (personne)* to injure; **livre abîmé par la pluie** book spoilt by the rain; **a. ses affaires** to damage one's belongings; **abîmé en cours de transit** damaged in transit; *Fam* **se faire a. (le portrait)** to get beaten up *or* knocked about
　VPR s'abîmer 1 *Litt* **s'a. dans les flots** to sink, *Litt* to be engulfed by *or* swallowed up by the sea; *Fig* **s'a. dans la douleur/dans ses pensées** to be sunk in grief/lost in thought **2** *(d'un fruit)* to spoil, to go bad; *(de chaussures)* to wear out; **s'a. facilement** not to wear well **3** **s'a. la santé** to damage one's health; **tu t'abîmes les yeux** you're ruining your eyes *or* eyesight

abject [abʒɛkt] **ADJ** *Litt (pauvreté)* abject; *Péj (personne, comportement)* mean, contemptible, despicable

abjectement [abʒɛktəmɑ̃] **ADV** *Litt* abjectly; *Péj* contemptibly, despicably

abjection [abʒɛksjɔ̃] **NF** *Litt* abjectness, abjection; **se conduire avec a.** to behave abjectly

abjuration [abʒyrasjɔ̃] **NF** abjuration; *(d'un serment)* renunciation; *(d'une menace, d'une hérésie)* recantation

abjurer [abʒyre] **VT** to abjure, to forswear; *(serment)* to renounce; *(hérésie)* to recant; *(insulte, confession)* to retract

ablatif, -ive [ablatif, -iv] *Gram* **ADJ** ablative
　NM ablative case; **à l'a.** in the ablative; **a. absolu** ablative absolute

ablation [ablasjɔ̃] **NF** ablation; *Méd* **a. des amygdales** removal of the tonsils, tonsillectomy

ablette [ablɛt] **NF** *(poisson)* bleak

ablution [ablysjɔ̃] **NF** washing, *Fml* ablution; *Fam* **faire ses ablutions** to wash, *Hum* to perform one's ablutions

abnégation [abnegasjɔ̃] **NF** abnegation, self-sacrifice

aboi [abwa] **NM** *Chasse* bay; **aux abois** *(cerf, ennemi)* at bay; *Fig (dans un état désespéré)* hard-pressed, with one's back to *or* against the wall; *Fig* **ils sont aux abois** they are in desperate *or* dire straits

aboiement [abwamɑ̃] **NM** *(d'un chien)* barking; *(des chiens de la meute)* baying; **il fit entendre un a. timide** he gave a timid little bark; **les aboiements de votre chien** your dog's barking; *Fig Péj* **les aboiements de la presse** the rantings of the press

abolir [abɔlir] **VT** to abolish, to suppress; *(dette etc)* to cancel; **le téléphone abolit les distances** the telephone makes distances irrelevant

abolissement [abɔlismɑ̃] **NM**, **abolition** [abɔlisjɔ̃] **NF** abolition, suppression; *(d'un décret)* repeal, annulment; **l'a. de l'esclavage** the abolition of slavery

abolitionnisme [abɔlisjɔnism] **NM** *Hist* abolitionism

abolitionniste [abɔlisjɔnist] **ADJ, N** *Hist* abolitionist

abominable [abɔminabl] **ADJ** abominable, foul; *(crime)* heinous; *(odeur)* foul; **une fin** *ou* **mort a.** a horrible death; **l'a. homme des neiges** the abominable snowman; **temps a.** abominable *or* filthy weather

abominablement [abɔminabləmɑ̃] **ADV** abominably

abomination [abɔminasjɔ̃] **NF 1** abomination, abhorrence; **avoir qn/qch en a.** to loathe sb/sth **2** *(chose atroce)* abomination; **ne l'écoute pas, elle ne dit que des abominations** don't listen to her, she has a foul tongue; **ce café est une a.** this coffee is abominable; **c'est une a.!** it's abominable!, it's atrocious!

abominer [abɔmine] **VT** to abominate, to loathe

abondamment [abɔ̃damɑ̃] **ADV** abundantly, plentifully, copiously; **manger/boire a.** to eat/drink in copious amounts; **se servir a. de pain/dans la caisse du magasin** to help oneself to plenty of bread/from the till; **il a plu a. toute la nuit** it rained heavily all night; **peu a.** scantily; **dossier a. documenté** well-researched file; **se documenter a.** to gather large amounts of information *or* material; **parler a.** to talk a great deal

abondance [abɔ̃dɑ̃s] **NF 1** *(profusion)* abundance, plenty; **on trouve des pommes en a. sur le marché** there is an abundant *or* a plentiful supply of apples on the market; **il y a une a. de fautes** there are numerous mistakes; **une a. de fruits** an abundance of fruit; **corne d'a.** cornucopia, horn of plenty **2** *(d'informations, de détails)* wealth; **vivre dans l'a.** to live in affluence; **parler avec a.** to speak volubly; *Litt* **parler d'a.** to speak off the cuff, to speak extempore

abondant [abɔ̃dɑ̃] **ADJ** abundant, copious, plentiful; *(style, vocabulaire)* rich; *(feuillage)* luxuriant; *(repas)* copious, hearty; *(excuses, saignement)* profuse; *(pluie)* heavy; **une chevelure abondante** a thick head of hair; **chevelure peu abondante** thin hair; **une récolte peu abondante** a poor *or* scanty harvest; **elle m'a donné d'abondants conseils** she gave me a great deal of advice

abondement [abɔ̃dmɑ̃] **NM** *Fin* = employer's contribution to company savings scheme

abonder [abɔ̃de] **VI 1** *(foisonner)* to be plentiful, to abound (**en** in); **le raisin abonde cet automne** the grapes are plentiful this autumn **2** **rivière qui abonde de** *ou* **en poissons** river that abounds in fish; **votre texte abonde en images** your text abounds *or* is rich in imagery; **a. de biens** to be blessed with riches **3** **a. dans le sens de qn** to be entirely of sb's opinion, to agree entirely *or* thoroughly with sb

abonné, -ée [abɔne] **N** *(à un journal etc)* subscriber; *Rail, Théâtre* season-ticket holder; *Admin* **abonnés du gaz/de l'électricité** gas/electricity consumers; *Tél* **il n'y a pas d'a. au numéro que vous avez demandé** = the number you have dialled has not been recognized; **a. numérique** digital subscriber
　ADJ *(à un journal)* subscribing; *Rail, Théâtre* holding a season ticket; **les membres abonnés au théâtre** members holding a season ticket for the theatre; *Admin* **être a. au téléphone/gaz** to be a telephone subscriber/gas consumer; *Fig* **j'ai l'habitude de ce genre d'ennui, j'y suis a.!** I'm used to this kind of problem, it's the story of my life!

abonnement [abɔnmɑ̃] **NM 1** *(à un journal etc)* subscription; **prendre un a. au Figaro** to subscribe to *or* take out a subscription to the Figaro; **sur a.** on subscription **2** *Admin* **a. au téléphone** (telephone) line rental; **a. à un service en ligne** on-line subscription; *Rail, Théâtre* **(carte d')a.** season ticket; **a. collectif** group subscription; **a. saisonnier** season ticket; **prendre un a.** to take out a season ticket

abonner [abɔne] **VT** *(à une revue etc)* to take out a subscription for; **être abonné à qch** to subscribe to sth, to have a subscription to sth; **je vais vous a. à cette revue** I'll take out a subscription to that magazine for you

▪ **VPR s'abonner 1 s'a. à une revue** to take out a subscription to a magazine **2** *Rail, Théâtre* to take out a season ticket; *Admin* **s'a. au téléphone** to be a telephone subscriber

abord [abɔr] **NM 1** *(à terre)* access, approach; **île d'un a. difficile** island that is difficult to approach; *Fig* **un auteur d'un a. difficile** an author who is difficult to get to grips with *or* not very accessible **2 abords** approaches (**d'un endroit** to a place); *(d'une ville)* outskirts **3** *(façon d'accueillir)* approachability; **être d'un a. rude/chaleureux** to have a rough/welcoming manner (with people); **être d'un a. facile/difficile** to be approachable/unapproachable

▪ **ADV d'a., tout d'a.** at first, to begin with; *(tout de suite)* straight away, at once; *(première-ment)* first, in the first place, first and foremost; **dès l'a.** from the (very) first, from the outset; **au premier a., de prime a.** at first sight; **d'a., elle ne dit jamais merci** for a start, she never says thank you; **toi, d'a., je ne te parle plus!** I'm not talking to you, so there!

abordable [abɔrdabl] **ADJ 1** *(piste d'atterris-sage etc)* easy to land on; *(côte, rivage)* easy to approach; *(lieu)* easily accessible **2** *(prix)* reasonable, affordable; **vos prix ne sont pas abordables** your prices are unreasonable **3** *(personne)* approachable; **peu a.** aloof, stan-doffish; *(grincheux)* grumpy

abordage [abɔrdaʒ] **NM** *Naut* **1** *(manœuvre de guerre)* boarding; **monter** *ou* **sauter à l'a. (d'un navire)** to board a ship; **à l'a.!** get ready to board! **2** *(collision)* **il y a eu un a. causé par le brouillard** two ships collided in the fog **3** *(pour attaquer) (autre bateau)* boarding; *(pour s'amarrer)* coming along-side

aborder [abɔrde] **VI** *Naut* to land, to make land; *(dans un port)* to berth; *Vieilli* **a. à un port** to reach a port

▪ **VT 1** *(personne)* to accost; **se faire a. dans la rue** to be approached in the street **2** *(ques-tion, difficulté)* to tackle **3** *Naut (navire dans un combat)* to board, to grapple; *(se mettre côte à côte de) (bateau)* to come alongside **4** *Naut (rentrer en collision avec) (bateau)* to collide with *or* run foul of *or* run down

aborigène [abɔriʒɛn] **ADJ** native, indige-nous (**de** to); *(relatif aux peuplades austra-liennes)* Aboriginal

▪ **N** *(d'un pays)* native; **les aborigènes d'Aus-tralie** the (Australian) Aborigines

abortif, -ive [abɔrtif, -iv] **ADJ 1** abortive **2** *Méd* **pilule abortive** abortion pill; *Jur* **ma-nœuvres abortives** (procuring of) abortion ▪ **NM** *Méd* abortifacient

aboucher [abuʃe] **VT 1** *(faire rencontrer) (personnes)* to put in touch *or* contact **2** *Tech* **a. le tuyau au robinet** to connect the pipe (up) to the tap

▪ **VPR s'aboucher 1** *(rencontrer)* **s'a. avec qn** to get in touch with sb, to contact sb **2** *Tech* **le tuyau s'abouche sur l'aspirateur** the tube is connected *or* connects to the vacuum cleaner

Aboukir [abukir] **N** Ab(o)ukir; *Hist* **la bataille d'A.** the battle of the Nile

abouler [abule] *Arg* **VT** to bring; *(donner)* to hand over; **aboule ça ici!** bring it here!, hand it over!

▪ **VPR s'abouler** *(arriver)* to turn up, to show up

about [abu] **NM** *Tech* butt

abouter [abute] **VT** *Tech (poutres etc)* to join end to end, to butt(-joint)

aboutir [abutir] **VI 1 a. à qch** *(mener à) (d'un chemin, escalier)* to lead to sth, to lead; *(de diffé-rentes directions)* to converge on sth, to lead

to sth; *Fig (d'une tentative, d'efforts)* to result in sth; **n'a. à rien** *(d'un projet)* to come to nothing, *Fam* to go up in smoke; **leur raison-nement aboutit à une évidence** their rea-soning leads to an obvious conclusion; **pour a. aux fins que nous poursuivons** to at-tain the end (which) we have in view; **a. dans un champ/sur la place du village** *(d'une per-sonne)* to end up in a field/in *or* at the village square; *Fig* **j'ai abouti à la conclusion que ...** I finally concluded that ...; *Fig* **nous n'avons abouti à aucun résultat** in the end, we didn't get any result **2** *(d'un projet etc)* to succeed; **ne pas a.** to fail, to fall through; **faire a. qch** to bring sth to a successful conclusion

aboutissants [abutisɑ̃] **NMPL connaître les tenants et les a. d'une affaire** to know the ins and outs of an affair, to know all there is to know about an affair

aboutissement [abutismɑ̃] **NM** *(d'un effort etc)* result, outcome

aboyer [abwaje] **VI** *(j'aboie, j'aboierai) (d'un chien)* to bark; *(chien de meute)* to bay; *Fig* **a. après qn** to shout *or* yell at sb

aboyeur, -euse [abwajœr, -øz] **ADJ** *(chien)* barking
▪ **N** *Fam* tout, *Am* barker
▪ **NM** *(oiseau)* sandpiper

abracadabra [abrakadabra] **NM** abraca-dabra

abracadabrant [abrakadabrɑ̃] **ADJ** *Fam (his-toire)* cock-and-bull

abraser [abraze] **VT** *Tech* to abrade

abrasif, -ive [abrazif, -iv] **ADJ, NM** *Tech* abrasive

abrasion [abrazjɔ̃] **NF** *Tech* abrasion; *Géol* **a. de la roche par l'eau** abrasion of the rock by the water

abrégé [abreʒe] **NM** précis, summary; *(d'un roman)* abridg(e)ment; *(d'une thèse)* abs-tract; **a. d'histoire de France** short history of France; **a. de philosophie** short guide to phi-losophy; **voici les faits en a.** here are the facts in a few words *or* in brief; **en a.** in abridg-ed *or* abbreviated form; **écrire en a.** to write in abbreviated form

abrègement [abrɛʒmɑ̃] **NM 1** *(d'un discours etc)* summarizing; *(d'une syllabe)* shorten-ing; **a. d'un délai** shortening of the amount of time allowed for sth **2** *(texte)* summary, précis; *(d'un roman)* abridg(e)ment; *(d'un mot)* abbreviation; **a. (d'un ouvrage)** abridg-ed edition (of a work)

abréger [abreʒe] *(j'abrège, n. abrégeons; j'abrégerai)* **VT 1** *(vie, travail etc)* to shorten, to cut short; **pour a. votre attente** so as not to keep you waiting **2** *(article)* to abridge, to cut down; *(mot)* to abbreviate
▪ **VI** to be brief; **pour a.** to be brief, to cut it short; *Fam* **allez, abrège!** come on, get *or* come to the point!

abreuvement [abrœvmɑ̃] **NM** *(des anima-ux)* watering

abreuver [abrœve] **VT 1** *(chevaux, bétail etc)* to water **2** *(pré etc)* to flood, to irrigate; *(pompe)* to prime; *(tonneau)* to season; **l'Égypte est abreuvée par le Nil** Egypt is watered by the Nile; *Fig* **a. qn d'injures** to shower *or* cover sb with insults, to heap in-sults on sb; *Fig* **les téléspectateurs sont abreuvés de publicité** the viewers are swamped *or* bombarded with advertising
▪ **VPR s'abreuver** *(d'un cheval)* to drink; *Fam (d'une personne)* to knock it back

abreuvoir [abrœvwar] **NM** *(dans un cours d'eau, une mare)* watering place; *(baquet)* drinking trough; **mener les chevaux à l'a.** to lead the horses to water

abréviation [abrevjasjɔ̃] **NF** abbreviation

abri [abri] **NM** shelter, cover; *(écran, para-vent)* screen; *(pour les plantes)* (tent) cloche;

a. à outils/à vélos tool/bike shed; **a. public** public shelter; **a. de sous-marins** submarine pen; **a. bétonné** bunker; **a. sous roche** rock shelter; **famille sans a.** homeless family; **à l'a.** sheltered, under shelter, under cover; **mettre qch à l'a.** to shelter *or* screen sth; **se mettre à l'a.** to take shelter; **à l'a. de qch** sheltered *or* screened from sth; **se mettre à l'a. de la pluie** to (take) shelter from the rain; **se mettre à l'a.** to shelter in the doorway; **a. contre le vent** windscreen; *Fig* **à l'a. de toute suspicion** free from (all) suspi-cion; *Fig* **personne n'est à l'a. d'une erreur** anybody can make a mistake; **il sera tou-jours à l'a. du besoin** he will always be pro-tected from hardship, he will never experience hardship; *Naut* **à l'a. de la côte** under the lee of the shore

▪ ▸ **a. antinucléaire** (nuclear) bunker; **a. fis-cal** tax shelter; **a. souterrain** air-raid shelter

Abribus® [abribys] **NM** bus shelter

abricot [abriko] **NM** apricot
▪ **ADJ INV** apricot-coloured

abricoté [abrikɔte] **ADJ** apricot-flavoured

abricotier [abrikɔtje] **NM** apricot tree

abricotine [abrikɔtin] **NF** *Suisse* apricot brandy

abrier (s') [sabrije] **VPR** *Can* to wrap up (well)

abri-garage, *pl* **abris-garages NM** carport

abriter [abrite] **VT 1** *(protéger)* to shelter, to screen, to shield, to protect; *(yeux)* to shade; **a. ses yeux du soleil** to shade one's eyes from the sun; **cet auvent nous abrite des regards indiscrets** the awning shields us from prying eyes **2** *(héberger)* to house; **cet hôtel peut a. cent personnes** the hotel can accommodate a hundred people

▪ **VPR s'abriter** *(de la pluie)* to (take) shelter (**de** from); *(des tirs)* to take cover; **s'a. der-rière qn** to shelter behind sb; *Fig* **il s'abrite derrière le règlement** he shelters *or* hides behind the rules

abrivent [abrivɑ̃] **NM** windbreak

abrogation [abrɔgasjɔ̃] **NF** *(de la loi etc)* abrogation, rescinding, repeal

abrogeable [abrɔʒabl] **ADJ** repealable

abroger [abrɔʒe] **VT** *(j'abrogeai(s); n. abro-geons) (loi etc)* to abrogate, to rescind, to repeal

abrupt [abrypt] **ADJ 1** *(rocher, pente)* sheer, steep **2** *Fig (manière)* abrupt, blunt; **répon-dre d'un ton a.** to give an abrupt *or* short answer, to answer abruptly *or* shortly
▪ **NM** steep slope

abruptement [abryptəmɑ̃] **ADV 1** steeply, abruptly **2** *Fig* abruptly

abruti, -ie [abryti] **ADJ 1** stupefied, dazed; *(par la chaleur)* exhausted; **j'étais complète-ment a. après cette séance** my mind *or* brain was totally dead after that session; **a. par l'alcool** stupefied *or* sodden with drink **2** *Fam* stupid, idiotic, moronic; **avoir un air a.** to look stupid *or* moronic
▪ **N** *Fam* idiot, fool

abrutir [abrytir] **VT 1** *(abêtir) (personne)* to exhaust; **ce travail m'abrutit** this work's addling my brain; **la chaleur m'abrutissait** my brain couldn't work in that heat; **je suis abruti de travail** my brain's dead from too much work **2** *(de l'alcool etc)* to stupefy; **les buveurs, que l'alcool abrutit** drinkers, whose minds are (being) numbed *or* dead-ened by alcohol

▪ **VPR s'abrutir 1** *(se fatiguer)* **s'a. de travail/de discussions** to work oneself to the point of exhaustion/to wear oneself out with discus-sion **2** *(devenir stupide)* to become dazed *or* stupefied; **on s'abrutit à trop regarder la té-lévision** too much television addles the brain

abrutissant [abrytisã] ADJ **1** *(fatigant)* exhausting, wearing; *(bruit)* deafening **2** *(abêtissant)* mind-destroying

abrutissement [abrytismã] NM *(abêtissement)* **a. de qn** reducing of sb to a mindless state; **propagande qui cause l'a. des masses** propaganda that stops people thinking for themselves

ABS [abeɛs] NM *Aut (abrév* **Antiblockiersystem) système A.** ABS

abscisse [apsis] NF abscissa

abscons [apskɔ̃] ADJ *Péj* obscure, abstruse

absence [apsɑ̃s] NF **1** *(de personne)* absence; **en** *ou* **pendant mon a.** in *or* during my absence, when I am/was/*etc* away; **en l'a. de ma secrétaire** while *or* when my secretary is away; **nous avons regretté votre a.** we were sorry that you weren't with us; **nous regrettons tous les jours son a.** *(d'un mort)* we miss him every day; **briller par son a.** to be conspicuous by one's absence; **a. de l'école** non-attendance at *or* absence from school; **comment expliquez-vous toutes ces absences?** how do you explain all these absences? **2** *(manque)* (de meubles, de principes, du père etc)* lack; **a. de demande** absence *or* lack of demand; **a. de goût** lack of taste, tastelessness; **a. d'imagination** lack of imagination; **a. d'esprit** absent-mindedness; **j'ai eu une a. d'esprit et j'ai oublié ...** I absent-mindedly forgot ...; **il a des absences** he's apt to be absent-minded, he has *or* is prone to memory lapses; **dans un moment d'a.** in a moment of absent-mindedness, in an absent-minded moment; *(de négligence, de manque d'attention)* without thinking **3** *Méd* **a. (épileptique)** petit mal fit ▸▸ *Mil etc* **a. illégale** absence without leave; **a. non rémunérée** unpaid leave; **a. rémunérée** paid leave

absent, -ente [apsɑ̃, -ɑ̃t] ADJ **1** absent, away; **il est a. de Paris en ce moment** he isn't in Paris at the moment; **quand ma femme est absente** when my wife's away; *Mil* **a. sans permission** absent without leave, AWOL **2** *(qui n'existe pas)* absent, missing; **une déclaration d'où tout humour était a.** a statement totally lacking in humour; **chez cet animal, les dents sont absentes** this animal has no teeth **3** *(distrait, rêveur)* absent; **son esprit est a.** his mind is far away, *Fam* he's miles away; **il avait un air a.** he was miles away

N *(d'une réunion etc)* absentee; **les Russes ont été les grands absents lors de la Coupe du monde** the Russians were the most notable absentees from the World Cup; *Prov* **les absents ont toujours tort** it's always the people who are not there that get blamed; **il ne faut pas dire du mal des absents** you shouldn't say bad things about people when they're not there to defend themselves

absentéisme [apsɑ̃teism] NM absenteeism

absentéiste [apsɑ̃teist] ADJ (regularly) absent; **propriétaire a.** absentee landlord
N (regular) absentee

absenter (s') [sapsɑ̃te] VPR *(de chez soi)* to go away; *(de l'école)* to stay away; **je ne me suis pas absentée de toute la journée** I haven't been out all day; **il a dû s'a. pour quelques heures** he had to go somewhere for a few hours, *Fam* he had to pop out for a few hours; **son mari s'absente beaucoup** her husband is away a lot

absidal, -ale, -aux, -ales [apsidal, -o] ADJ apsidal

abside [apsid] NF *Archit* apse

absidiole [apsidjɔl] NF *Archit* apsidal chapel

absinthe [apsɛ̃t] NF **1** *(boisson)* absinthe **2** *(plante)* wormwood

absolu [apsɔly] ADJ **1** absolute; **zéro a.** abso-

lute zero; **poser une règle absolue** to lay down a hard-and-fast rule; **refus a.** flat refusal; **majorité absolue** absolute majority
2 *(total)* absolute; **nous sommes dans l'impossibilité absolue de vous donner des réponses définitives** we are quite unable to give you any definite answers; **pouvoir a.** absolute power; **caractère a.** autocratic nature; **liberté absolue** absolute *or* total freedom
3 *(ton, voix)* peremptory
4 *Gram* absolute
NM *Phil* **l'a.** the absolute; **juger qch dans l'a.** to judge sth in the absolute *or* out of context

absolument [apsɔlymã] ADV **1** *(complètement)* absolutely; **a.!** absolutely!; **a. pas!** absolutely not!; **a. rien** nothing whatsoever
2 *(strictement) (parler)* peremptorily; **c'est a. défendu** it is absolutely *or* strictly forbidden; **je le veux a.** I insist on it; **nier a. qch** to deny sth flatly
3 *(sans faute)* simply, absolutely; **vous devez a. y aller!** you simply *or* absolutely must go!
4 *(sans limite)* **régner a.** to reign as an absolute monarch; **a. parlant** speaking generally
5 *Gram* absolutely

absolution [apsɔlysjɔ̃] NF **1** *Rel* absolution **2** *Jur* discharge, acquittal

absolutisme [apsɔlytism] NM *Pol* absolutism

absorbant [apsɔrbã] ADJ **1** *(matériau, qualités)* absorbent **2** *(livre, tâche)* absorbing, engrossing

absorber [apsɔrbe] VT **1** *(d'une éponge etc) (eau etc)* to absorb, to soak up; *Chimie (gaz)* to occlude; **le noir absorbe la lumière** black absorbs light
2 *(nourriture)* to consume; *(boisson)* to drink; *(médicament)* to take; *Écon* **la multinationale va a. cette entreprise** the multinational is going to take over *or Fam* swallow up the firm; **les travaux ont absorbé toutes mes économies** the repairs have used up all my savings
3 *(d'une lecture)* to absorb, to engross; **son travail l'absorbe** he/she is completely wrapped up in his/her work; **cette pensée m'absorbe complètement** I think about it constantly; **être absorbé dans ses pensées** to be lost in thought
VPR **s'absorber** to become absorbed *or* engrossed **(dans** in); **s'a. dans la lecture d'un livre** to be absorbed *or* lost in a book

absorption [apsɔrpsjɔ̃] NF absorption; **a. de médicaments** (the) taking of medicines; *Écon* **a. d'une petite société par une grosse** the takeover of a small company by a large one

absorption-fusion, *pl* **absorptions-fusions** NF *Écon* merger

absoudre [apsudr] VT *(prp* absolvant; *pp* absous, *f* absoute; *pr ind* j'absous, il absout, n. absolvons, ils absolvent; *pr sub* j'absolve; *p hist & fu* j'absoudrai) **1 a. qn de qch** to forgive sb sth; *Rel* **a. qn de ses péchés** to absolve sb from his sins, to forgive sb his sins; *Rel* **je vous absous** I absolve you **2** *Jur (personne)* to absolve, to acquit

abstenir (s') [sapstənir] VPR *(conj like* tenir) to stand aside *or* aloof; *Pol* to abstain (from voting); **s'a. de qch** to abstain from sth, to forgo sth; **s'a. de faire qch** to refrain *or* abstain from doing sth; **s'a. de commentaires** to refrain from comment; **s'a. de manger du chocolat/de boire de l'alcool** to keep off chocolate/alcohol; **dans le doute, abstiens-toi** when in doubt, don't

abstention [apstɑ̃sjɔ̃] NF abstention (**de** from)

abstentionnisme [apstɑ̃sjɔnism] NM *Pol (de vote etc)* abstention

abstentionniste [apstɑ̃sjɔnist] N *Pol* abstainer; **le nombre des abstentionnistes** the number of abstentions

abstinence [apstinɑ̃s] NF abstinence; *(qualité d'une personne)* abstemiousness; *Rel* **jour d'a.** day of abstinence; **faire a. le vendredi** to abstain from eating meat on Fridays; **a. (sexuelle)** (sexual) abstinence

abstinent, -ente [apstinɑ̃, -ɑ̃t] ADJ abstemious
N abstainer; *(qui ne boit pas d'alcool)* teetotaller; *Rel* person who practises abstinence

abstraction [apstraksjɔ̃] NF **1** *Phil* abstraction; **un esprit capable d'a.** a mind capable of abstract thought **2 faire a. de qch** to disregard sth; **a. faite du style** style apart **3** *(idée abstraite)* abstract idea, abstraction; **se perdre dans des abstractions** to lose oneself in abstractions

abstraire [apstrɛr] *(conj like* traire) VT to separate, to isolate; *Phil* to abstract
VPR **s'abstraire** **s'a. dans qch** to become engrossed in sth

abstrait [apstrɛ] ADJ *(idée, art etc)* abstract; *(question)* abstruse, deep
NM **1** *(abstraction)* abstract, abstraction; **dans l'a.** in the abstract, in theory **2** *Beaux-Arts* abstract art; *(artiste)* abstract artist; *(tableau)* abstract (painting)

abstraitement [apstrɛtmã] ADV **1** *(en théorie)* in the abstract; **parler a.** to talk in the abstract *or* in abstract terms **2** *(distraitement)* abstractedly, absentmindedly

abstrus [apstry] ADJ abstruse, recondite

absurde [apsyrd] ADJ absurd, preposterous; **votre conduite est totalement a.!** your behaviour is totally preposterous!; **elle est complètement a.** she's completely ridiculous
NM absurdity; *Phil* the absurd; **réduire une théorie à l'a.** to reduce a theory ad absurdum; *Phil* **démonstration par l'a.** reductio ad absurdum; **l'a. de la situation** the absurdity *or* absurdness of the situation, the absurd thing about the situation; **le théâtre de l'a.** the theatre of the absurd

absurdement [apsyrdəmã] ADV absurdly, preposterously

absurdité [apsyrdite] NF **1** *(caractère absurde)* absurdity, preposterousness; **l'a. de l'existence** the absurdity of existence **2** *(chose absurde)* piece of nonsense; **cette réaction est une a.** this reaction is completely absurd; **dire des absurdités** to talk nonsense

abus [aby] NM **1** *(mauvais emploi)* abuse, misuse (**de** of); *(excès)* overindulgence (**de** in); **l'a. de médicaments** the misuse of pharmaceutical drugs; **l'a. de boissons** alcohol abuse; **faire a. de qch** to indulge too freely in sth; **faire a. de son autorité** to abuse one's authority; **employer un terme par a.** to misuse a term
2 *Jur (de droits)* violation; **a. de confiance** breach of trust; **a. d'autorité/de pouvoir** abuse *or* misuse of (one's) authority/power; **a. de biens sociaux** misuse of a company's assets; **a. de droits sociaux** misappropriation of corporate funds
3 *(pratique)* abuse, corrupt practice; **un écrivain connu pour ses a. de langage** a writer known for his abuse of the language *or Fam* for murdering the language; **réformer un a.** to remedy an abuse; **je ne supporte plus ses a.!** I can't stand his/her outrageous behaviour any longer!; **faire quelques a.** to overdo it, to overindulge; *Fam* **il y a de l'a.!** that's going too far!

abuser [abyze] VI **a. de qch** to misuse sth; *(exploiter)* to take (unfair) advantage of sth; **vous abusez de vos forces** you're overtaxing yourself; **a. du tabac** to smoke too much; **il ne faut pas a. des bonnes choses** good things should be enjoyed in moderation, enough is as good as a feast; **a. de l'amabilité de qn** to impose on sb *or* on sb's kindness; **a. de la confiance de qn** to abuse sb's confidence; **j'abuse de votre temps** I am taking up too much of your time; **n'abusez point** be moderate; **je ne voudrais pas a., j'ai peur d'a.** I don't want to cause you any inconvenience; **c'est un peu fort, elle abuse!** she's going a bit (too) far!; **vous abusez!** that's a bit much!; **a. de qn** to sexually abuse sb

vt to deceive; **il ne nous abusera pas par de belles paroles** he will not deceive us with fine words

vpr s'abuser to be mistaken; **je vous ai déjà rencontré, si je ne m'abuse** I've met you before, if I'm not mistaken

> Il fait noter que le verbe anglais **to abuse** ne s'emploie jamais dans le sens d'**exagérer**.

abusif, -ive [abyzif, -iv] **ADJ 1** *(emploi d'un mot)* incorrect; **il serait a. de l'affirmer** it would be an exaggeration to say that **2** *(excessif)* excessive; **emploi a. de la force** excessive *or* unwarranted use of force; **mère abusive** possessive *or* domineering mother

abusivement [abyzivmɑ̃] **ADV** incorrectly, wrongly; **employer un mot a.** to use a word incorrectly *or* wrongly; **elle a profité a. de la situation** she took unfair advantage of the situation

abuter [abyte] **vt a. un camion à un quai** to back a lorry against a platform

abyme [abim] **NM tableau/film/pièce avec structure en a.** painting within a painting/film within a film/play within a play

abyssal, -ale, -aux, -ales [abisal, -o] **ADJ** *(faune etc)* abyssal; *Fig (profondeurs)* unfathomable; **les fosses abyssales** the troughs of the ocean depths

abysse [abis] **NM** *Géog* abyssal zone; *Fig* **les abysses du désespoir** the depths of despair

Abyssinie [abisini] **NF** Abyssinia

abyssinien, -ienne [abisinjɛ̃, -jɛn] **ADJ** Abyssinian

N A. Abyssinian

A.C. [ase] *abrév* **appellation contrôlée**

acabit [akabi] **NM** *Péj* **ils sont du même a.** they're tarred with the same brush; **je me méfie des gens de cet a.** I don't trust people like that; **des drogués, des dealers et autres paumés de cet a.** drug addicts, dealers and other dropouts of the same type

acacia [akasja] **NM** *(arbre)* **a. vrai** acacia; *(robinier)* **a. vulgaire, faux a.** locust tree, false acacia

académicien, -ienne [akademisjɛ̃, -jɛn] **N** *(membre d'une académie)* academician; *(membre de l'Académie française)* member of the Académie française

académie [akademi] **NF 1** *(des lettres, des sciences, d'art)* society; **l'A. française** the French Academy **2** *(école)* school, academy; **a. de musique** music school, school of music; **a. de danse** dancing school; **a. de dessin** school of art, art school **3** *Admin (en France)* educational district **4** *(de Platon etc)* academy **5** *(étude)* nude

> ### Académie française
> The Académie was originally a group of men of letters who were encouraged by Cardinal Richelieu in 1635 to become an official body. Consisting of forty distinguished writers ("les Quarante" or "les Immortels"), the Académie's chief task was, and is, to produce a definitive dictionary and to be the ultimate authority in matters concerning the French language.

académique [akademik] **ADJ 1** academic; **les palmes académiques** = insignia of decoration granted by the French Ministry of Education; **séance a.** sitting *or* meeting of an Academy; **occuper un fauteuil a.** *(de l'Académie française)* to be a member of the Académie française; *Littér Péj* **style a.** pedantic style; **débat a.** academic discussion **2** *Admin* **inspection a.** board of school inspectors **3** *Beaux-Arts* **figure a.** nude **4** *Belg, Suisse, Can Univ* **l'année a.** the academic year

académisme [akademism] **NM** *Beaux-Arts Péj* academicism

Acadie [akadi] **NF** *Hist* Acadia

acadien, -ienne [akadjɛ̃, -jɛn] **ADJ** Acadian
NM *Ling* Acadian
N A. Acadian

acajou [akaʒu] **NM 1** mahogany; **table en a.** mahogany table **2 noix d'a.** cashew nut; **a. à noix** cashew nut tree
ADJ INV reddish-brown, auburn

acanthe [akɑ̃t] **NF** *Bot, Archit* acanthus

a cappella [akapɛla] **ADV** *Mus* a cappella; **chanter a c.** to sing a cappella

acariâtre [akarjatr] **ADJ** bad-tempered, cantankerous; **être d'humeur a.** to be bad-tempered

acarien [akarjɛ̃] **NM** *(insecte)* dust mite

accablant [akablɑ̃] **ADJ 1** *(malchance, témoignage, responsabilités)* overwhelming; *(chaleur)* overpowering, oppressive **2** *(témoignage)* damning

accablé [akable] **ADJ** *(de travail etc)* overwhelmed; *(de peine)* overcome, weighed down; **a. de fatigue** overwhelmed with fatigue; **a. par la chaleur** overwhelmed *or* overcome by the heat; **a. de dettes** burdened with debt

accablement [akabləmɑ̃] **NM** dejection, despondency, depression

accabler [akable] **vt 1** to overpower, to overwhelm; **être accablé de douleur** to be grief-stricken; **il m'accable de travail** he piles work on me; **il m'accable de questions** he bombards me with questions; **a. qn d'injures** to heap abuse on sb; **elle nous accable de recommandations** she heaps advice on us **2** *(fournir des preuves contre)* to damn

accalmie [akalmi] **NF** lull; **dans un moment d'a.** in a calm moment, in a moment of respite

accaparant [akaparɑ̃] **ADJ** demanding; **un emploi a.** a demanding job; **leurs enfants sont très accaparants** their children take up a lot of their time

accaparement [akaparmɑ̃] **NM** monopolizing; *(des stocks)* buying up; *(des marchandises)* cornering

accaparer [akapare] **vt** *(stocks)* to buy up; *(marchandises)* to corner, to hoard; *(pouvoir)* to seize; **a. le marché de l'automobile** to corner the automobile market; **a. la conversation** to monopolize the conversation; **a. les meilleures places** to secure *or* corner the best seats; **son travail l'accapare trop** his/her work takes up too much of his/her time; **je ne voudrais pas vous a. toute la soirée** I don't want to monopolize you for the whole evening

accapareur, -euse [akaparœr, -øz] **N** *(de nourriture etc)* buyer-up; *(société)* monopolist, *Péj* grabber
ADJ *(personne)* possessive

accastillage [akastijaʒ] **NM** *Naut (d'un navire)* fittings

accastiller [akastije] **vt** *Naut (navire)* to fit out

accédant, -e [aksedɑ̃, -ɑ̃t] **N a. à la propriété** first-time buyer, new home owner

accéder [aksede] **vi** (**j'accède, n. accédons;** **j'accéderai**) **1** *(atteindre)* to have access (**à** to); **on accède à la porte par un escalier** a flight of steps leads to the door; *Ordinat* **a. à un programme** to access a program **2** *(accepter)* to comply, to agree; **a. à une requête** to comply with a request; **a. à une condition** to agree *or* assent to a condition **3** *(parvenir)* to accede; **a. à de hautes responsabilités** to acquire important responsibilities; **a. à un poste important** to obtain *or* to get an important job; **a. au trône** to accede to the throne; **a. à la propriété** *(d'un appartement, d'une maison)* to be a first-time buyer; **pour permettre aux jeunes ménages d'a. à la propriété** to allow young couples to buy their first home

accélérateur, -trice [akseleratœr, -tris] **ADJ** accelerating
NM *Aut, Ordinat* accelerator; *Nucl* **a. de particules** particle accelerator; **a. d'électrons** betatron; *Aut* **appuyer sur l'a.** to accelerate; *Ordinat* **a. graphique** graphic(s) accelerator

accélération [akselerasjɔ̃] **NF** acceleration; *(du travail)* speeding up; **a. de la pesanteur** gravitational acceleration; *Aut* **pédale d'a.** accelerator (pedal); *Aut* **en a. partielle** part-throttle; **avoir une bonne a.** to have good acceleration

accéléré [akselere] **ADJ** quick, fast, rapid; *(mouvement)* accelerated; **un cours a.** a crash course
NM *Cin, TV* accelerated motion, time lapse

accélérer [akselere] (**j'accélère, n. accélérons; j'accélérerai**) **vt** to accelerate, to speed up; **a. le mouvement** to speed up
vi **dépêche-toi, accélère!** hurry up, get a move on!; *Aut* **passe en seconde et accélère** go into second and accelerate; **a. à vide** to rev the engine
vpr s'accélérer to accelerate, to speed up; *(du pouls)* to go faster, to speed up

accent [aksɑ̃] **NM 1** *(phonétique)* accent, stress; **a. d'intensité** *ou* **tonique** tonic accent **2** *Gram* accent; **a. aigu/grave** acute/grave (accent); **e a. circonflexe** e circumflex **3** *(prononciation)* accent; **parler le français avec un a. anglais** to speak French with an English accent; **il n'a pas l'a.** *ou* **d'a.** he doesn't have an accent **4** *(inflexion)* tone of voice; *Fig* **son récit a l'a. de la vérité** his account rings true; *Ling* **a. de phrase** sentence stress; *Fig* **mettre l'a. sur la présentation du produit** to put the emphasis on *or* to emphasize the presentation of the product **5 les accents du désespoir** the accents of despair; **il parlait avec des accents de rage/de terreur dans la voix** his voice was angry/terror-stricken; **les accents de la Marseillaise** the strains of the Marseillaise

accentuation [aksɑ̃tɥasjɔ̃] **NF 1** *(des syllabes etc)* stressing; **les règles de l'a. espagnole** the stress rules in Spanish **2** *Gram* accentuation, placing of the grammatical accents; **faire les fautes d'a.** to put accents in the wrong place **3** *(d'un phénomène)* growth

accentué [aksɑ̃tɥe] **ADJ** stressed, accented; *Fig* pronounced, marked; **traits fortement accentués** pronounced *or* strongly marked features; **les traits accentués par la fatigue** features drawn with fatigue

accentuer [aksɑ̃tɥe] **vt 1** *(syllabes etc)* to stress; **syllabe non accentuée** unstressed syllable **2** *Gram* **a. une voyelle** to mark a vowel with an accent **3** *Fig* to emphasize, to accentuate; **son conseil/cet incident n'a fait qu'a. leurs problèmes** his advice/this incident has only added to their problems; **a. le chômage** to increase *or* add to unemployment

VPR s'accentuer to become more pronounced or marked

acceptabilité [aksɛptabilite] **NF** Gram acceptability; Mktg a. de la marque brand acceptability

acceptable [aksɛptabl] **ADJ 1** acceptable (à to); **offre a.** reasonable offer **2** (voiture, maison, machine) in fair condition; (performance) reasonably good

acceptablement [aksɛptabləmɑ̃] **ADV** acceptably, in an acceptable manner

acceptant, -ante [aksɛptɑ̃, -ɑ̃t] **ADJ, N** Com, Jur acceptant

acceptation [aksɛptasjɔ̃] **NF** acceptance; **a. sous condition** conditional acceptance; **sous réserve d'a. du dossier** subject to a favourable report; Fin **a. bancaire** banker's acceptance

accepter [aksɛpte] **VT** to accept; (défi) to take up; (pari) to take on; (chèque, effet) to accept, to sign, to honour; **il n'accepte pas l'échec/la difficulté** he refuses to acknowledge failure/the existence of problems; **elle n'arrive pas à a. le mariage de sa fille** she can't come to terms with her daughter's marriage; **je n'accepte pas votre conduite d'hier soir** I find your behaviour last night unacceptable; **je n'accepte pas cette théorie** I don't accept that theory, I don't agree with that theory; **a. de faire qch** to agree to do sth; **elle n'accepte pas que son mari soit au chômage** she can't or won't accept the fact that her husband is unemployed; **a. qn comme ou pour arbitre** to accept sb as an arbitrator; **il a été accepté dans la famille** he was accepted into the family; **acceptez-vous Gérard Manvussat pour époux?** ≃ do you take this man, Gérard Manvussat, as your lawfully wedded husband?

accepteur [aksɛptœr] **NM 1** Com (d'une facture) acceptor, drawee **2** Chimie, Électron acceptor

acception [aksɛpsjɔ̃] **NF** Fml **1** (d'un mot etc) meaning, sense, Fml acceptation **2 sans a. de race/de sexe** (dans une offre d'emploi) open to candidates of all races/of both sexes, irrespective of race/sex

accès [aksɛ] **NM 1** (approche) access, approach; **les a. de la gare** the station approaches, the approaches to the station; **le refuge est facile d'a.** the shelter is easily accessible or easy to reach; **avoir a. à qch** to have access to sth; **donner a. à qch** to give access or to lead to sth; **ce diplôme donne a. à toute une gamme de professions passionnantes** this diploma opens the door to a wide range of exciting professions; **trouver a. auprès de qn** to be admitted to sb's presence; **être d'a. facile/difficile** (d'une personne) to be approachable/unapproachable; (d'un auteur, d'un livre etc) to be accessible/not very accessible; **facile/difficile d'a.** (lieu) easy/hard to reach, easy/hard to get to; **l'a. à la profession de médecin devient de plus en plus difficile** entry into the medical profession is becoming more and more difficult; **l'a. au statut de membre de l'Union européenne** entry into the European Union; Rail **a. aux quais** to the trains **2** (poussée) fit, attack, outburst; **a. de fièvre** attack or bout of fever; **des a. de toux** fits of coughing, coughing fits; **a. de faiblesse** fainting fit; **a. d'enthousiasme** burst or fit of enthusiasm; **a. de tristesse/découragement** wave of sadness/discouragement; **a. de colère/folie** fit of anger/madness; **travailler par a.** to work by or in fits and starts **3** Ordinat access; (à une page Web) hit; **avoir a. à** to be able to access; **code d'a.** access code; **à a. multiple** multi-access; **temps d'a.** access time; **a. aléatoire** random access; **a. au bus local** local bus access; **a. commuté, a.**

par ligne commutée dial-up access; **a. direct à la mémoire** direct memory access; **a. à distance** remote access; **a. en écriture** write access; **a. rapide** high-speed access, fast access; **a. sécurisé par mot de passe** password-protected access; **a. sélectif** selective access; **a. séquentiel** sequential access; **a. au système** system access

accessibilité [aksɛsibilite] **NF** accessibility

accessible [aksɛsibl] **ADJ 1** (où l'on peut arriver) accessible; **séminaire a. à tous les licenciés** seminar open to all graduates; **endroit a.** accessible place, place that can be reached easily; **parc a. à tous** park open to everybody; Fig **les prix sont très accessibles** the prices are within everyone's reach, the prices are very affordable; **un livre tout à fait a.** a very accessible book **2** (personne) approachable; **a. à la pitié** open to pity; **a. à la flatterie** susceptible to flattery

accession [aksɛsjɔ̃] **NF 1** (au pouvoir etc) accession; **faciliter l'a. des femmes à la politique** to make it easier for women to enter politics; **a. à la propriété** home ownership; **l'a. à la propriété est rendue possible à tous** home ownership is within everyone's reach; **a. au trône** accession to the throne; **l'a. du pays à l'indépendance a eu lieu en 1968** the country became independent or gained independence in 1968; **a. au statut de membre de l'Union européenne** entry into the European Union **2** (à un contrat, un parti) adherence, adhesion

accessit [aksɛsit] **NM** (dans un examen) honourable mention; **remporter un a. en musique** to get an honourable mention in music

accessoire [aksɛswar] **ADJ** accessory; Compta (frais) incidental; **jouer un rôle a.** to play a subordinate role; **c'est un détail a.** it's an incidental detail
NM 1 (objet) accessory, Fml appurtenance; **voiture vendue sans accessoires** car sold without accessories; **chapeau et accessoires coordonnés** hat and matching accessories; **a. d'objectif** lens attachment; Ordinat **a. de bureau** desk accessory **2** Théâtre etc **accessoires** properties, Fam props; **magasin des accessoires** property room **3** (ce qui est accessoire) (minor) details; **on s'occupera de l'a. plus tard** we'll take care of the (minor) details later

accessoirement [aksɛswarmɑ̃] **ADV** (si besoin est) if necessary, if need be; **je m'occupe a. de la comptabilité** I look after the accounts in addition to my main duties

accessoiriser [aksɛswarize] **VT** (vêtements etc) to accessorize

accessoiriste [aksɛswarist] **N** Théâtre etc props (man, f woman), property man, f mistress; TV props buyer

accident [aksidɑ̃] **NM 1** (événement imprévisible) accident; (contretemps) mishap; **je l'ai retrouvé par a.** I found it by accident, I found it accidentally; **nous sommes arrivés sans a.** we arrived safely or safe and sound; **la cérémonie s'est déroulée sans a.** the ceremony went off without a hitch
2 (collision, malheur) crash, accident; **a. de chemin de fer** railway accident; **a. d'avion** plane or air crash; **a. de voiture** car accident or crash; **a. de la route** road accident, car crash; **a. de la circulation** traffic accident; **a. mortel** fatal accident, fatality; **être victime d'un a.** to meet with an accident
3 Méd **a. cardiaque** cardiac arrest, heart attack; **a. vasculaire** vascular accident
4 Mus accidental
5 a. de terrain unevenness or irregularity of the ground
▶▶ **a. de parcours** hitch; Fig **son échec n'est qu'un a. de parcours** his failure is just a tem-

porary hitch or setback; **a. du travail** industrial accident, accident in the workplace

accidenté, -ée [aksidɑ̃te] **ADJ 1** (terrain) uneven, broken **2 voiture accidentée** damaged car
N victim of an accident; **les accidentés** the injured, the casualties; **accidentés de la route** road accident victims; **les accidentés du travail** victims of industrial accidents

accidentel, -elle [aksidɑ̃tɛl] **ADJ 1** (imprévu) accidental; **une rencontre accidentelle** a chance or an accidental meeting; **je le rencontrai de façon purement accidentelle** I met him quite by accident; **mort accidentelle** (dans un accident) accidental death **2** Mus **signes accidentels** accidentals; (armature constante) key signature

accidentellement [aksidɑ̃tɛlmɑ̃] **ADV** accidentally; (mourir) in an accident, as a or the result of an accident

accidenter [aksidɑ̃te] **VT** (voiture) to damage, Fam to prang

accidentologie [aksidɑ̃tɔlɔʒi] **NF** study of road accidents

accidentologue [aksidɑ̃tɔlɔg] **N** accident researcher, person who specializes in the study of road accidents

acclamation [aklamasjɔ̃] **NF** acclamation, cheering; **les acclamations de la foule** the cheers or acclamations of the crowd; **discours salué d'acclamations** speech greeted with cheers; **elle fut élue par a.** she was elected by acclamation

acclamer [aklame] **VT** (personne, discours) to acclaim, to cheer; (en tapant dans les mains) to applaud; (saluer qn, discours) to greet with cheers; **a. qn empereur** to acclaim sb emperor

acclimatable [aklimatabl] **ADJ** acclimatizable, Am acclimatable

acclimatation [aklimatasjɔ̃] **NF** acclimatization, Am acclimation; **jardin d'a.** zoological gardens

acclimatement [aklimatmɑ̃] **NM** acclimatization, Am acclimation

acclimater [aklimate] **VT** to acclimatize, Am to acclimate (à to); Fig (usages) to introduce
VPR s'acclimater to become or get acclimatized or Am acclimated

accointance [akwɛ̃tɑ̃s] **NF** Péj accointances dealings, relations; **avoir des accointances dans le milieu des affaires** to have contacts in the business world

accointer (s') [sakwɛ̃te] **VPR** Péj Vieilli **s'a. avec qn** to take up with sb

accolade [akɔlad] **NF 1** (embrassade) (formal) embrace; **donner/recevoir l'a.** to embrace/to be embraced **2** Hist accolade; **recevoir l'a.** ≃ to be knighted **3** Mus brace; Typ curly bracket, brace **4** Archit **(arc en) a.** ogee arch

accolement [akɔlmɑ̃] **NM** joining, bracketing

accoler [akɔle] **VT 1** (joindre côte à côte) to join side by side, to couple; Typ to brace, to bracket; **le nom de l'épouse est accolé à celui du mari** the wife's surname is joined or added to that of the husband; **accolé aux murs** built on the walls **2** (vigne) to tie up
VPR s'accoler (de plantes) to intertwine, to cling

accommodant [akɔmɔdɑ̃] **ADJ** accommodating; **a. en affaires** easy to do business with

accommodation [akɔmɔdasjɔ̃] **NF 1** (adaptation) adapting; **a. d'une pièce aux usages d'un bureau** adaptation or conversion of a room for office use **2** Physiol (des yeux) accommodation

accommodement [akɔmɔdmɑ̃] **NM**

compromise, arrangement, agreement; **en venir à un a.** to come to a compromise *or* arrangement, to come to terms (**avec** with); **politique d'a.** give-and-take policy; *Com* **a. avec ses créanciers** composition with one's creditors

accommoder [akɔmɔde] VT **1** *Culin (nourriture)* to prepare; **a. les restes** to use up the leftovers; **a. une salade** to dress a salad **2 a. qch à qch** to fit *or* adapt sth to sth; **a. une pièce à un usage particulier** to adapt a room to *or* for a particular purpose; *Opt* **a. l'objectif sur l'infini** to set *or* adjust the lens to infinity

VI *Opt* to focus

VPR **s'accommoder 1** *Litt* **s'a. à qch** to adapt to sth; **il s'accommode à toutes les circonstances** he's very adaptable; **je m'accommode à tout** anything will do for me **2 s'a. de qch** to make the best of sth, to put up with sth; **il vous faudra vous a. de cette pièce pour dormir** you'll have to make do with sleeping in this room **3 s'a. avec qn** to come to an agreement with sb; *(par un compromis)* to compromise with sb; *(créancier)* to compound with sb **4** *Arch (dans un fauteuil etc)* to make oneself comfortable, to settle down

Il faut noter que le verbe anglais **to accommodate** est un faux ami. Il ne signifie jamais **accommoder**.

accompagnateur, -trice [akɔ̃paɲatœr, -tris] N **1** *Mus* accompanist **2** *(d'un voyage organisé)* courier, tour guide, tour leader; *(de sortie scolaire)* accompanying adult **3** *Belg Rail* **a. de train** ticket inspector

accompagnement [akɔ̃paɲmɑ̃] NM **1** *Mus* accompaniment; **chanter sans a.** to sing unaccompanied **2** *Mil etc* close support; **tir d'a.** supporting fire; *Aviat* **chasseur d'a.** escort fighter **3** *Culin (servi avec la viande etc)* accompaniment, trimmings; **qu'y a-t-il comme a.?** what does it come with?, what is it served with?; **servi avec des frites en a.** served with chips

accompagner [akɔ̃paɲe] VT **1** *(venir avec, aller avec) (personne)* to go *or* come with, *surtout Fml* to accompany; **il est arrivé accompagné de ses amis** he arrived with his friends; **accompagné de sa secrétaire** accompanied by his secretary; **est-ce que tu vas m'a.?** are you coming with me?; **a. qn jusqu'à la gare** to see sb to the station; **a. qn un bout de chemin** to go part of the way with sb; **l'angoisse qui accompagne ses pensées** the anguish which accompanies his thoughts **2** *(escorter)* to escort; *(groupe de touristes)* to act as courier *or* tour guide to; *(groupe d'enfants)* to accompany; **accessible aux enfants accompagnés uniquement** children must be accompanied by an adult **3** *Mus* **a. qn au piano** to accompany sb on the piano **4** *(ajouter à)* **il a accompagné ses mots d'un sourire** he said it with a smile; **il a accompagné le bouquet de fleurs d'une carte** he enclosed a card with the bouquet of flowers; *Culin* **a. une viande de pommes de terre** to serve potatoes with meat

VPR **s'accompagner 1** *Mus* **elle s'accompagne elle-même** she plays her own accompaniment **2** *Culin (avec des légumes etc)* to be served; **le porc s'accompagne bien de pommes** apples go well with pork **3** *(advenir en même temps que)* to be accompanied by, to come with; **ces maux de tête s'accompagnent souvent de saignements de nez** these headaches are often accompanied by nosebleeds

accompli [akɔ̃pli] ADJ *(musicien, linguiste, menteur etc)* accomplished; **fait a.** fait accompli, accomplished fact; **on le mit devant le fait a.** he was presented with a fait accompli; **il a quarante ans accomplis** he's turned forty; **à quarante ans accomplis, il serait temps que tu prennes une décision** now you've turned forty, it's time you made a decision

accomplir [akɔ̃plir] VT **1** *(but etc)* to accomplish, to achieve; *(tâche)* to carry out; *(formalités)* to go through; *(souhait, promesse)* to fulfil; **a. son devoir** to perform one's duty **2** *(apprentissage etc)* to complete, to finish; **c'est une mauvaise action que tu as accomplie là** it was very wrong of you to do that; **a. un geste** to make a gesture

VPR **s'accomplir 1** to be realized, to come true; **notre souhait s'est accompli** our wish came true; *Rel* **que la volonté du Seigneur s'accomplisse** the Lord's will be done

accomplissement [akɔ̃plismɑ̃] NM **1** *(d'une tâche, d'une fonction)* accomplishment, performance, carrying out; *(d'un souhait)* fulfilment; **c'était l'a. de plusieurs années de travail** it was the result of several years' work **2** *(d'un apprentissage)* completion

accord [akɔr] NM **1** *(traité)* agreement; *(non formel)* understanding; *(transaction commerciale)* bargain; *(pour résoudre un conflit)* settlement; **conclure un a.** to enter into an agreement; **a. de principe** agreement in principle; **arriver** *ou* **parvenir à un a.** to come to an agreement, to reach (an) agreement; **un a. est intervenu d'après lequel ...** an agreement has been reached by which ...

2 *(entente)* agreement (**sur** on); **vivre en** *ou* **de bon a.** to live in harmony; **l'a. parfait qui règne entre nous deux** the perfect harmony between us; **être en a. avec la nature** to be in harmony *or* at one with nature; **vivre en a. avec ses principes** to live by one's principles; **être en a. avec soi-même** to be true to oneself; **en a. avec qn** in agreement with sb; **mettre d'a. deux points de vue** to reconcile two points of view; **se mettre d'a.** *ou* **tomber d'a. avec qn** to come to an agreement with sb; **être d'a. avec qn** to agree with sb; **les témoins ne sont pas d'a.** the witnesses disagree *or* differ; **mes comptes sont d'a.** my accounts balance; **tout est d'a.** everything is settled *or* arranged; **c'est d'a., d'a.!** all right!, OK!; **d'un commun a.** by common consent, by mutual agreement

3 *(autorisation)* consent; **il a donné son a.** he gave his consent; **la décision doit être prise en a. avec les différents intéressés** the decision must be made with the agreement *or* the consent of the different parties involved

4 *Gram* agreement, concordance (**avec** with); **l'a. de l'adjectif avec le nom** the agreement of the adjective with the noun; **les règles d'a.** the rules of agreement

5 *Mus* chord; **a. parfait** common chord; **faux a.** discord; **a. arpégé** *ou* **brisé** *ou* **figuré** broken chord; **a. de sensible** dominant seventh (chord)

6 *(réglage)* *Mus* pitch; *Tech* tuning; *Mus* **tenir l'a.** *(d'un piano etc)* to keep *or* stay in tune

▸▸ *Com* **a. d'achat et de vente** buy-sell agreement; *Électron* **a. d'antenne** alignment input; *Com, Pol* **a. d'association** partnership agreement; *Com, Pol* **a. bilatéral** bilateral agreement; *Com* **a. de clearing** clearing agreement; *Com* **a. commercial** trade agreement; *Com, Pol* **a. de compensation** offset agreement; *Com, Pol* **a. de coopération** cooperation agreement; *Com* **a. de crédit** credit agreement; *Com* **a. de distribution exclusive** exclusive distribution agreement; *Com* **a. d'exclusivité** exclusivity arrangement; *Com* **a. de franchise** franchise agreement; **A. général sur les tarifs et le commerce** General Agreement on Tariffs

and Trade; **accords d'Helsinki** Helsinki Agreement *or* Accord; *Com* **a. de libre-échange** Free Trade Agreement; *Com* **A. de libre-échange nord-américain** North American Free Trade Agreement; *Com* **a. de licence** licensing agreement; *UE* **A. monétaire européen** European monetary agreement; *Com* **a. multilatéral** multilateral agreement; *Com* **a. multilatéral sur l'investissement** multilateral investment agreement; *Com* **a. de partenariat** partnership agreement; *UE* **a. de préadhésion** pre-accession agreement; *Radio* **a. précis** fine tuning; *Com* **a. de représentation** agency agreement; *Com* **a. de reprise** buyback arrangement; **a. salarial** pay *or* wage agreement; **a. verbal** verbal agreement

accordage [akɔrdaʒ], **accordement** [akɔrdəmɑ̃] *Mus* tuning

accord-cadre, *pl* **accords-cadres** NM outline agreement

accordéon [akɔrdeɔ̃] NM accordion; **a. à touches** *ou* **à boutons/diatonique** piano/diatonic accordion; *Fig* **en a.** *(chaussettes)* wrinkled, coming down; **plissé** *ou* **plissage a.** accordion pleats; *Fig* **voiture en a.** concertinaed car

accordéoniste [akɔrdeɔnist] N accordionist, accordion player

accorder [akɔrde] VT **1** *(ennemis)* to reconcile

2 *Gram* **a. le verbe avec le sujet** to make the verb agree with the subject

3 *Mus (instrument de musique)* to tune; **a. les violons au ton du piano** to tune the violins to the pitch of the piano; *Fig* **il faudrait a. vos violons** *(de deux personnes ou plus)* you'd better get your story straight

4 *(faveur, pardon etc)* to grant; *(découvert bancaire)* to allow, to give; *(prêt)* to authorize, to extend; **a. des dommages-intérêts** to award damages; **a. un escompte** to allow a discount; *Com* **a. une licence à qn** to license sb; **pouvez-vous m'a. quelques minutes?** can you spare me a few minutes?; **je n'ai pas essayé très longtemps, je vous l'accorde** I didn't try for very long, I grant you *or* I admit; **je t'accorde qu'il a tout pour plaire** he's very attractive, I('ll) grant you that; **a. à qn de faire qch** to give sb permission to do sth; **elle accorde la plus grande importance à ce travail** she attaches the greatest importance to this job; **il n'accorde pas la moindre valeur à ce que je dis** he doesn't attach the slightest value to anything I say; **c'est à peine s'il m'a accordé un regard** he barely glanced my way; **on m'a accordé huit jours de congé** I have been given a week's leave

5 *(harmoniser)* to match (up)

VPR **s'accorder 1** *(se mettre d'accord) (sur quelque chose)* to agree, to come to an agreement (**avec qn** with sb); **s'a. sur le prix** to agree (on) the price; **s'a. à** *ou* **pour faire qch** to agree to do sth; **on s'accorde à penser que la maladie sera curable d'ici là** there is a general belief *or* it is generally believed that the disease will be curable by then; **tout le monde s'accorde à dire qu'elle est stupide** everyone agrees that she's stupid

2 *(s'entendre)* to get on (**avec qn** with sb); **ils s'accordent mal** they don't get on (at all) well; **ils s'accordent très bien** they get on very well (together)

3 *(aller avec, correspondre)* to correspond; *(de couleurs etc)* to harmonize; *(de chiffres)* to tally; *(de témoignages)* to square; *(d'un projet)* to fit in (**avec** with); **cette action ne s'accorde pas avec son caractère** this action is not in keeping *or* in line with his/her character; **cela ne s'accorde pas avec mes idées** it doesn't fit in with my ideas; *Com* **faire a. les livres** to agree the books; **il faut que la pratique s'accorde avec la théorie** the practice

should correspond to *or* with the theory; **cette ceinture s'accorde à toutes les tenues** this belt goes with *or* can be worn with everything
4 *Gram* to agree; **le verbe s'accorde avec le sujet** the verb agrees with the subject
5 *(se donner)* to allow *or* grant oneself; **s'a. dix minutes de repos** to allow *or* give oneself ten minutes' rest

accordeur [akɔrdœr] NM (piano) tuner

accordoir [akɔrdwar] NM (piano) tuning key

accort [akɔr] ADJ *Litt* winsome

accostable [akɔstabl] ADJ *Naut* **plage a.** beach suitable for mooring

accostage [akɔstaʒ] NM **1** *Fam (de personne)* accosting **2** *Naut (du quai)* drawing alongside **3** *Astronaut* docking

accoster [akɔste] VT **1** *(personne)* to go *or* come up to, to accost; *(pour l'agresser)* to accost **2** *Naut* **a. un bateau le long du quai** to bring a boat alongside (the quay); **le bateau nous a accostés** the boat came alongside us VI *Naut (navire)* to come on board; *(d'un navire)* to berth, to dock; *Astronaut* to dock

accotement [akɔtmɑ̃] NM **1** *(de la route)* verge, *Am* berm; **a. non stabilisé** soft verge *or* shoulder **2** *Rail* shoulder

accoter [akɔte] VT to lean (**contre** against); *(navire, mur etc)* to shore up; **accoté contre qch** leaning against sth; **a. une échelle à** *ou* **contre un mur** to lean a ladder against a wall VPR **s'accoter** to lean; **s'a. à** *ou* **contre un mur** to lean against a wall

accotoir [akɔtwar] NM armrest, elbow rest; *(pour la tête)* headrest

accouchée [akuʃe] NF mother *(of newborn child)*; *Méd* **salle des accouchées** maternity ward

accouchement [akuʃmɑ̃] NM childbirth; **elle a eu un a. difficile** she had a difficult birth; **ce médecin fait plusieurs accouchements par jour** this doctor carries out *or* performs several deliveries a day; **on a dû provoquer l'a.** she had to be induced; *Fig* **il a enfin fini son texte, ce fut un véritable a.!** he really laboured to finish his text!
▸▸ **a. aux forceps** forceps delivery; **a. avant terme** premature delivery *or* birth; **a. naturel** natural childbirth; **a. prématuré** premature delivery *or* birth; **a. sans douleur** natural childbirth; **cours d'a. sans douleur** natural childbirth classes; **a. à terme** full-term delivery

accoucher [akuʃe] VI **1** to give birth; **a. d'un garçon** to give birth to a boy; **elle doit a. dans un mois** her baby's due in a month's time; **a. chez soi** to have a home birth *or* confinement **2** *Fam* **mais accouche donc!** come on, out with it! *or* spit it out!; **il a accouché de ce recueil de nouvelles** he has laboured to produce this collection of short stories
VT to deliver

accoucheur, -euse [akuʃœr, -øz] N *(médecin)* obstetrician
NF **accoucheuse** *(sage-femme)* midwife

accouder (s') [sakude] VPR to lean on one's elbow(s); **s'a. à la fenêtre** to lean out of the window; **s'a. sur son bureau** to be sitting with one's elbows on one's desk, to lean (one's elbows) on one's desk

accoudoir [akudwar] NM **1** *(de fauteuil)* armrest, elbow rest **2** *Archit* balustrade

accouple [akupl] NF leash

accouplement [akupləmɑ̃] NM **1** coupling, join(ing), link(ing); *Élec* connecting; *(de bœufs)* yoking **2** *(d'animaux)* pairing, mating
▸▸ *Aviat* **a. bendix** bendix drive; *Tech* **a. à débrayage** disengaging gear, clutch coupling; *Aut* **a. direct** direct drive; *Aut* **a. à glissement** slip clutch; *Aviat* **a. à griffe(s)** dog clutch, coupling

accoupler [akuple] VT **1** *(unir par deux)* to couple, to join; *(pièces)* to couple (up); *Élec (batteries etc)* to connect, to group; *(bœufs)* to yoke; **a. un moteur à une batterie** to connect an engine up to a battery **2** *(animaux)* to mate
VPR **s'accoupler** to mate, to pair; *(avoir des relations sexuelles)* to copulate

accourir [akurir] VI *(conj like* courir; *aux* avoir *or* être*)* to run (up), to rush up; **à mes cris, ils ont accouru** *ou* **sont accourus** they came running when they heard my cries; **ils ont accouru** *ou* **sont accourus à mon secours** they ran *or* came running to help me

accoutrement [akutrəmɑ̃] NM *Péj* dress, garb, *Fam* get-up

accoutrer [akutre] VT *souvent Péj* to rig out (**de** in); **accoutré d'une vieille capote** rigged out in an old army greatcoat; **tu ne peux pas l'a. ainsi, il est ridicule!** you can't rig him out like that, it looks ridiculous!
VPR **s'accoutrer** to rig oneself out (**de** in)

accoutumance [akutymɑ̃s] NF **1** *(adaptation)* familiarization (**à** with); *(à la douleur etc)* inurement (**à** to); *Méd* **a. (à une drogue)** tolerance (to a drug); **l'effet d'a. des drogues dures** the habit-forming effect of hard drugs **2** *Litt (habitude)* habit, usage

accoutumé [akutyme] ADJ usual, habitual; **à l'heure accoutumée** at the usual time
ADV **à l'accoutumée** usually; **il est arrivé à huit heures comme à l'accoutumée** he arrived at eight o'clock as usual

accoutumer [akutyme] VT **a. qn à qch** to accustom sb to sth, to get sb used to sth; **être accoutumé à qch** to be accustomed *or* used to sth
VPR **s'accoutumer** **s'a. à** to get *or* become used *or* accustomed to; **s'a. à la fatigue** to become accustomed *or* used *or* hardened to fatigue; **je ne peux pas m'y a.** I can't get used to it

accouvage [akuvaʒ] NM artificial incubation

accréditation [akreditasjɔ̃] NF *(d'un ambassadeur, d'un journaliste)* accreditation, accrediting

accrédité, -ée [akredite] ADJ of good standing, accredited; **notre représentant a.** our authorized representative
N **agent**; *Fin* beneficiary, payee

accréditer [akredite] VT **1** *(ambassadeur, journaliste)* to accredit; *(dans le générique d'un film etc)* to acknowledge; **je suis accrédité pour mener les négociations** I have been appointed to lead the negotiations; *Fin* **a. un client** to open an account for a client; *Fin* **être accrédité auprès d'une banque** to have credit facilities at a bank **2** *(rendre plausible)* to substantiate, to give credence to; **cette rumeur est accréditée par ses dernières actions** this rumour is substantiated *or* backed up by his latest actions
VPR **s'accréditer** *(d'une rumeur etc)* to gain ground, to spread

accréditif [akreditif] NM credential; *(lettre de crédit)* letter of credit

accro [akro] *Fam* ADJ *(à la drogue, à une activité)* *Fig* addicted (**à** to), hooked (**à** on); **il va à tous les matchs de foot, il est a.** he goes to all the football matches, he's a real addict
N *(à une activité)* addict

accroc [akro] NM **1** *(dans les vêtements etc)* tear, *Fml* rent **2** *Fig* hitch, difficulty, snag; **la cérémonie s'est déroulée sans a.** the ceremony went off without a hitch; **faire un a. à sa réputation** to spoil one's reputation, *Fam* to blot one's copybook

accrochage [akrɔʃaʒ] NM **1** *Aut* minor accident; *Boxe* clinch **2** *Rail* hitching on, coupling **3** *(d'un tableau etc)* hanging (up); *(dans* un musée) (small) exhibition **4** *Radio (d'une station)* picking up **5** *(dispute)* altercation, squabble; *Mil* brush, skirmish

accroche [akrɔʃ] NF *(titre d'appel)* blurb; *(verbale)* striking (publicity) slogan, catch phrase

accroche-casseroles [akrɔʃkasrɔl] NM INV saucepan rack

accroche-cœur, *pl* **accroche-cœurs** NM kiss curl; **se faire des accroche-cœurs** to put one's hair into kiss curls

accrocher [akrɔʃe] VT **1** *(retenir)* to hook, to catch; **a. un asticot à son hameçon** to attach a maggot to one's fishing hook; **a. sa robe à des ronces** to catch one's dress on brambles; *Aut* **il a accroché mon pare-chocs** he caught *or* hit my bumper; **titre qui accroche le lecteur** striking *or* eye-catching title; **vitrine qui accroche le regard** eye-catching window display; *Fam* **a. qn** to buttonhole *or* corner sb
2 *Rail (wagon)* to hitch on, to couple
3 *(navire)* to grapple
4 *(suspendre)* to hang up; *Constr (porte)* to hang; **a. son manteau** to hang up one's coat; *Fig* **il faut avoir le cœur bien accroché** you need a strong stomach *or* strong nerves; *Arg* **a. sa montre** to put one's watch in hock, to pop one's watch
5 *Radio* **a. une station** to tune in to a station
VI *(aux vêtements etc)* to stick, to catch; *Fig* **les négociations ont accroché** there has been a hitch in the negotiations; **ça ne marche pas très bien entre eux, ça accroche souvent** things aren't very good between them, they argue a lot; **ça n'a pas du tout accroché** *(entre deux personnes)* they didn't get on, *Fam* they didn't click
VPR **s'accrocher 1 s'a. à qn/qch** to hold on to sb/sth; *(ne pas lâcher)*, *Fig* to cling on to sb/sth; **accroche-toi à la rampe** hold on tight *or* hang on to the handrail; *Fig* **elle s'accroche à lui, il est son seul espoir** she's clinging to him as her only hope; *Fig* **s'a. à des illusions** to cling to illusions; *Fig* **Fam accroche-toi, tu n'as pas tout entendu!** brace yourself, you haven't heard everything yet!
2 *(se fixer)* **ça s'accroche au mur par un clou** you fasten *or* attach it to the wall with a nail
3 *(tenir)* to stick at it, *Fam* to hang in there
4 *Boxe* to clinch; *Fig* **les deux voitures se sont accrochées** the two cars clipped each other
5 *Fam (se disputer)* to have a row; **s'a. avec qn** to have a row with sb, to clash with sb
6 *Fam* **tu peux te l'a.!** you can kiss goodbye to that!, you've had it!

accrocheur, -euse [akrɔʃœr, -øz] ADJ **1** *(tenace)* tenacious, stubborn **2** *(titre, slogan etc)* eye-catching, catchy
N **c'est un a.** he's a fighter

accroire [akrwar] VT **faire a. à qn que ...** to make sb believe that ...; **elle veut nous en faire a.** *(abuser de notre crédulité)* she's trying to fool us; *(se faire valoir)* she's trying to impress us

accroissement [akrwasmɑ̃] NM **1** increase (**de** in); **les nouveaux équipements ont permis un a. de la productivité** the new equipment has led to an increase in productivity; **taux d'a.** rate of increase; *Math* **a. d'une fonction** increment of a function; *Fin* **a. global net** aggregate net increment **2** *(d'une plante etc)* growth

accroître [akrwatr] *(prp* accroissant; *pp* accru; *pr ind* j'accrois, il accroît, n. accroissons, ils accroissent; *impf* j'accroissais; *p hist* j'accrus; *fu* j'accroîtrai*)* VT to increase, to enlarge, to add to; *(réputation)* to enhance
VPR **s'accroître** to increase, to grow

accroupir (s') [sakrupir] VPR to squat

(down), to crouch (down); **accroupi** squatting, crouching

accroupissement [akrupismɑ̃] NM crouching, squatting

accru [akry] NM *Bot* sucker

accu [aky] NM *Élec* battery; *Fig* **recharger ses accus** to recharge one's batteries

accueil [akœj] NM *(façon d'accueillir)* reception, welcome, greeting; *(lieu)* reception; **tenir l'a.** to be on reception; **hôtesse d'a.** receptionist; **centre d'a.** reception centre; **passez à l'a.** go to the reception desk, go to reception; **a. handicapés** services for the disabled; **faire bon a. à qn/qch** to welcome sb *or* give sb a warm welcome/to welcome sth; **faire mauvais a. à qn** to give sb a cool reception; **ils ont fait un a. très mitigé à notre proposition** they gave our proposal a very mixed reception; **a. hostile** *ou* **défavorable** hostile reception; **discours/cérémonie d'a.** welcoming speech/ceremony; *Com* **faire (bon) a. à une traite** to honour a bill

accueillant [akœjɑ̃] ADJ welcoming

accueillir [akœjir] VT *(conj like cueillir)* *(personne, nouvelle idée)* to receive, to greet; **(bien) a. qn** to welcome sb, to give sb a warm welcome; **mal a. qn** to give sb a bad reception; **a. qn à bras ouverts** to welcome sb with open arms; **cet hôtel peut a. jusqu'à 500 visiteurs** the hotel can accommodate up to 500 visitors; **j'ai un ami qui pourrait vous a. pendant un certain temps** I have a friend who could put you up for a while; **se faire a. par des volées de pierre** to be greeted with *or* by volleys of stones; **le film a été mal accueilli par le public** the film got a bad reception from the public; *Com* **a. une traite** to meet *or* honour a bill

acculer [akyle] VT *(personne)* to drive back (**contre** against); *(animal)* to bring to bay *or* to a stand; *Fig (personne)* to drive to the wall; *Fig* **être acculé aux aveux/à la ruine** to be forced into a confession/into bankruptcy

acculturation [akyltyrasjɔ̃] NF acculturation

accumulateur [akymylatœr] NM *Élec* battery, accumulator; *Aut* **a. de carburant** fuel accumulator

accumulation [akymylasjɔ̃] NF **1** *(action)* accumulation; *(d'énergie)* storage; *(d'argent)* hoarding; *(de dettes)* accumulation; *(en magasin)* stockpiling; *Fin* **a. de capital** capital accumulation; **a. des intérêts** accrual of interest; **chauffage par a.** storage heating; **chauffage à a. nocturne** (night) storage heating **2** *(stock)* accumulation; *(d'argent, de nourriture)* hoard; *(d'objets)* collection; *(d'erreurs)* series

accumuler [akymyle] VT to accumulate, to amass; *(nourriture, argent)* to hoard; *(dettes)* to accumulate; *(énergie)* to accumulate, to store; *(entasser)* to heap up, to pile up; *(en magasin)* to stockpile; **a. les médailles** to accumulate medals; **intérêts accumulés** accrued interest; **a. les preuves/renseignements** to gather evidence/information; **a. les gaffes/erreurs** to make a series of blunders/mistakes; **quand je suis fatigué, j'accumule les erreurs** I make lots of mistakes when I'm tired; *Fam* **tu les accumules!** you're making quite a habit of it!

VPR **s'accumuler** to accumulate; *(de nuages)* to gather, to build up; *Fin (des intérêts)* to accrue; *(des dettes)* to accumulate, to pile up; **les plaintes s'accumulent sur mon bureau** complaints are piling up on my desk; **les preuves s'accumulent contre elle** the evidence is building up against her

accusateur, -trice [akyzatœr, -tris] ADJ *(regard, doigt)* accusing, *Fml* accusatory; *(preuve)* incriminating; **j'ai pointé vers lui un**

index **a.** I pointed an accusing finger at him N accuser; *(d'un officiel)* impeacher, arraigner; *Hist* **a. public** public prosecutor

accusatif [akyzatif] NM *Gram* accusative (case); **mot à l'a.** word in the accusative

accusation [akyzasjɔ̃] NF **1** *(condamnation)* accusation; **lancer** *ou* **porter une a. contre qn** to bring an accusation against sb **2** *Jur* **mettre qn en a.** to commit sb for trial; **quels sont les chefs** *ou* **les sujets d'a.?** what are the charges? **3** *Pol* impeachment, arraignment; **faire une a. contre la politique extérieure actuelle** to deliver an indictment against current foreign policy

accusé, -ée [akyze] ADJ *(trait etc)* prominent, pronounced, bold; *(baisse, hausse)* sharp; **rides très accusées** very deep wrinkles

N *(d'un crime)* accused; *(au tribunal)* defendant, prisoner at the bar

NM **a. de réception** *(pour une lettre)* acknowledgement (of receipt); *(d'un colis)* receipt; *Ordinat* acknowledge, acknowledgement, confirmation page

accuser [akyze] VT **1** *(incriminer)* to accuse; **a. qn de (faire) qch** to accuse sb of (doing) sth; **on l'accuse de meurtre** he is (being) accused of murder; *Fig* **a. le sort** to blame fate **2** *(tendance, baisse etc)* to show; **paroles qui accusent une grande ignorance** words that betray *or* show *or* reveal great ignorance; **la Bourse accuse une forte baisse** the Stock Market is registering big losses; **elle accuse trente ans** she looks (at least) thirty; **il commence à a. son âge** he's starting to look his age; **il accuse le coup** *Boxe* he's feeling that one; *Fig* he's obviously shaken **3** *(faire ressortir)* to define, to show up, to accentuate; **esquisse qui accuse tous les muscles** sketch that brings out every muscle; **le temps a accusé son avarice** he has got meaner with time

4 a. réception de qch to acknowledge (receipt of) sth

VPR **s'accuser 1** *(se rendre coupable)* to admit, to confess; **il s'est accusé du crime pour protéger son frère** he confessed to the crime to protect his brother **2** *(se renforcer)* to become more pronounced *or* marked

acerbe [asɛrb] ADJ sharp, harsh, acerbic; **réprimande a.** sharp reprimand; **discussion a.** ill-tempered discussion; **parler d'un ton a.** to speak sharply

acéré [asere] ADJ *(lame etc)* sharp; *Fig (remarque)* cutting, scathing; **langue acérée** sharp tongue; **il écrit des satires d'une plume acérée** he writes satire with a scathing pen

acérer [asere] VT (**j'acère; j'acérerai**) *(rare)* to sharpen, to give a keen edge to

acériculteur, -trice [aserikyltœr] N *Can* maple syrup and sugar producer

acériculture [aserikyltyr] NF *Can* production of maple syrup and sugar

acétate [asetat] NM *Chimie* acetate; **a. de cuivre** copper acetate; *Tex* **a. de cellulose** cellulose acetate

acétique [asetik] ADJ *Chimie* acetic; **odeur a.** vinegary smell

acétocellulose [asetɔselyloz] NF *Chimie* cellulose acetate

acétone [asetɔn] NF *Chimie* acetone

acétylène [asetilɛn] NM *Chimie* acetylene; **lampe à a.** acetylene lamp *or Am* torch

acétylsalicylique [asetilsalisilik] ADJ *Pharm* **acide a.** acetylsalicylic acid

ACF [aseɛf] NM *(abrév* **Automobile Club de France** *)* = automobile association of France

achalandage [aʃalɑ̃daʒ] NM *Jur, Com* custom, customers, clientele; *(fonds de commerce)* goodwill

achalandé [aʃalɑ̃de] ADJ **bien a.** well-stocked; *Vieilli (ayant nombreux clients)* with a large clientele; **mal a.** *Vieilli (ayant peu de clients)* with a small clientele; *(mal approvisionné)* poorly-stocked

achalander [aʃalɑ̃de] VT *Fam (magasin)* to stock

achaler [aʃale] VT *Can* to annoy, to bother

achards [aʃar] NMPL *Culin* relish

acharné [aʃarne] ADJ *(enragé, furieux) (lutte)* desperate, bitter; *(concurrence)* cut-throat; *(travail)* relentless; *(joueur)* inveterate; **meute acharnée à la poursuite** pack in hot *or* eager pursuit; **hommes acharnés les uns contre les autres** men fighting desperately against each other; **ils sont acharnés à se faire du mal** they're bent on hurting each other, they're desperately trying to hurt each other

acharnement [aʃarnəmɑ̃] NM relentlessness; **a. au** *ou* **pour le travail** passion for work; **avec a.** relentlessly; **se battre avec a.** to fight tooth and nail; *Pharm* **a. thérapeutique** = use of intensive medication to keep a person alive

acharner [aʃarne] VPR **s'acharner s'a. après** *ou* **contre** *ou* **sur qn** *(persécuter)* to be always after sb; **le meurtrier s'est acharné sur sa victime** the murderer savaged his victim; **les examinateurs se sont acharnés sur le candidat** the examiners really stuck the knife into the candidate; **pourquoi t'acharnes-tu à essayer de le lui faire comprendre?** why are you so determined to try to make him understand?; **le malheur s'acharne après lui** he is dogged by misfortune; **s'a. à** *ou* **sur qch** to work desperately hard at sth, to slave (away) at sth; **il s'acharne à vous nuire** he is set on harming you; **elle ne se décourage pas, elle s'acharne** she doesn't let herself be discouraged, she just keeps at it *or Fam* keeps plugging away

VT *Vieilli* **a. la meute après une bête** to set the pack on (the track of) a quarry; **a. un chien** to flesh *or* blood a hound

achat [aʃa] NM **1** *(action)* purchase, buying; **faire un a.** to make a purchase, to buy something; **faire l'a. de qch** to buy sth; **aller faire ses achats** to go shopping; **pouvoir d'a.** purchasing power; **prix d'a.** purchase price; **centrale d'a.** central purchasing office; *Can* **agent d'a.** procurement officer **2** *(ce qu'on a acheté)* purchase; **ses achats** one's shopping, *surtout Fml* one's purchases; **tu me montres tes achats?** show me what you've bought

▸ ▸ **a. au comptant** *ou* **contre espèces** *ou* **en espèces** cash purchase; **a. à crédit** purchase on credit, credit purchase; **a. de droits** rights buying; **a. d'espace** media buying; **a. impulsif** impulse buy; **achats institutionnels** institutional buying; *Com* **a. juste à temps** just-in-time purchasing; **a. non prémédité** impulse buy; **a. renouvelé** repeat purchase; **a. spontané** impulse buy; *Com* **a. de système** systems buying; *Fin* **a. à terme** forward purchase; **achats centralisés** centralized purchasing; *Mktg* **achats comparatifs** comparison shopping; **achats directs** direct purchasing; **achats à domicile** teleshopping; **achats hors taxes** tax-free shopping; **achats regroupés** one-stop buying *or* shopping; **achats spéculatifs** speculative buying; *Bourse* **a. à terme** forward buying

acheminement [aʃminmɑ̃] NM **1** *(progrès)* step, progress (**à, vers** towards) **2** *(de marchandises, paquets)* forwarding, shipment; **l'a. des marchandises se fait par Calais** the goods are routed through Calais; **a. du courrier** mail delivery *or* handling

acheminer [aʃmine] VT **1** *(conduire) (personne)* to set on his way (**sur, vers** towards)

2 *(marchandises etc)* to dispatch, to convey, to forward (**sur, vers** to); *(courrier)* to handle
  VPR s'acheminer s'a. vers to set out for, to make one's way towards; **s'a. vers le succès** to be heading for success; **nous nous acheminons vers de grands changements structurels** we are moving towards great structural changes

acheter [aʃte] (**j'achète, n. achetons; j'achèterai**) **VT 1 a. qch** to buy sth, *Fml* to purchase sth; **a. qch à qn** to buy sth from sb; **a. qch à** *ou* **pour qn** to buy sth for sb; **je vais lui a. un livre** I'm going to buy him/her a book; **a. en gros/au détail** to buy wholesale/retail; **a. qch par correspondance** to buy sth by mail order; **a. qch à crédit /au comptant** to buy sth on credit/for cash; **a. qch à tempérament** to buy sth on hire purchase *or Am* on the installment plan; *Fin* **à terme** to buy forward; **j'ai acheté ce livre 10 euros** I bought this book for 10 euros; **je ne l'ai pas acheté cher** I didn't pay much for it *or* a high price for it; **a. qch (à) bon marché** to buy sth cheap; *Fig* **a. qch chèrement** to pay a high price for sth; *Fig* **c'est une façon bien basse d'a. votre pardon** it's a very low way of buying forgiveness; **a. chat en poche** to buy a pig in a poke
  2 *Fam (personne)* to bribe, to buy off; **a. la complicité de qn** to buy sb's silence; **se faire a.** to be bribed
  VPR s'acheter ça s'achète en pharmacie you can buy it there in any pharmacy; **ces choses-là ne s'achètent pas** such things cannot be bought *or* are not for sale; *Fig* **s'a. une conduite** to turn over a new leaf

acheteur, -euse [aʃtœr, -øz] **N** buyer, purchaser; *Jur* vendee; *Com* **elle est acheteuse pour Prisunic®** she is a buyer for Prisunic®; *Mktg* **a. impulsif** impulsive buyer, impulse buyer; **a. industriel** business buyer; **je suis a.!** I'm in the market!, I'm interested!

achevé [aʃve] **ADJ** *(artiste, style etc)* accomplished; *(travail)* perfect; *(perfection)* absolute; **il est d'un ridicule a.** he's utterly ridiculous; *Fam* **sot a.** utter *or* absolute fool; **menteur a.** *(accompli)* consummate *or* accomplished liar; *(sans honte)* out and out liar

achèvement [aʃevmɑ̃] **NM** *(de travaux)* completion, finishing; **date d'a.** target *or* completion date

> Il faut noter que le nom anglais **achievement** est un faux ami. Il signifie **réussite**.

achever [aʃve] (**j'achève, n. achevons; j'achèverai**) **VT 1** *(finir) (discours)* to end, to conclude; *(travail etc)* to finish (off), to complete; **laisse-lui le temps d'a. sa phrase** let him finish what he's saying; **toutes nos peines sont loin d'être achevées** our troubles are all far from over; **avant d'a. ma lettre** before closing *or* finishing my letter; **a. ses jours** *ou* **sa vie** to end one's days; **a. de faire qch** to finish doing sth; **achève de boire ton café** drink up *or* finish your coffee
  2 *(mettre à mort) (personne)* to finish off; *(animal)* to put out of its misery *or* out of pain; *Fam* **cette grosse perte l'a achevé** this heavy loss was the end of him; *Fam* **ça m'a achevé** that really finished me (off)
  VPR s'achever 1 *(finir)* to draw to a close, to end; **c'est ainsi que l'histoire s'achève** that's how the story finishes *or* ends; **le jour s'acheva tristement** the day closed *or* ended sadly *or* on a sad note **2** *(d'un travail)* to reach completion

> Il faut noter que le verbe anglais **to achieve** est un faux ami. Il ne signifie jamais **achever**.

achigan [aʃigɑ̃] **NM** *Can (poisson)* (black) bass

Achille [aʃil] **N** Achilles

achoper [aʃɔpe] **VI** *Can Fig* **a. sur qch** to stumble over sth

achoppement [aʃɔpmɑ̃] **NM** *Litt* obstacle, difficulty; **pierre d'a.** stumbling block

achopper [aʃɔpe] **VI c'est là que ça achoppe** that's the stumbling block; **a. au problème de …** to come to grief over the problem of …; **a. sur un mot** to stumble over a word

achromatique [akrɔmatik] **ADJ** achromatic

achrome [akrom] **ADJ** *Phot* achromous, achromatous

acide [asid] **ADJ** acid(ic); *(au goût)* tart, sour; *Fig (personne)* witty; *Fig (propos, remarques)* acid, cutting; **une pomme a.** a sour apple; *Biol* **milieu a.** acidic environment; **savon a.** acidic soap
  NM *(drogue), Chimie* acid; **a. désoxyribonucléique** deoxyribonucleic acid; **a. folique** folic acid; **a. gras** fatty acid

acidificateur [asidifikatœr] **NM** acidifier, acidifying agent

acidification [asidifikasjɔ̃] **NF** acidification

acidifier [asidifje] **VT** to acidify
  VPR s'acidifier to become acid, to turn sour

acidité [asidite] **NF** acidity; *(d'une pomme etc)* sourness, tartness; *Fig (d'un commentaire)* wittiness; *Chimie* **l'a. d'une solution** the acidity of a solution; *Méd* **a. gastrique** acid stomach, hyperacidity

acidose [asidoz] **NF** *Méd* acidosis

acidulé [asidyle] **ADJ** acidulous; **bonbons acidulés** acid drops

acier [asje] **NM** steel; **lame d'a.** *ou* **en a.** steel blade; **a. au chrome/au nickel** chrome/nickel steel; *Fig* **avoir un moral d'a.** to be very resilient, *Fam* to be a tough cookie; *Fig* **regard d'a.** steely look
  ▸▸ **a. au carbone** carbon steel; **a. cémenté** case-hardened steel; **a. embouti** pressed steel; **a. galvanisé** galvanized steel; **a. inoxydable** stainless steel; **a. à ressort** spring steel; **a. trempé** hardened *or* tempered steel

aciérie [asjeri] **NF** steel works

aciériste [asjerist] **N** steel maker *or* manufacturer

acmé [akme] **NM** *ou* **NF** *Litt* acme, peak; *Méd* crisis

acné [akne] **NF** acne; **a. juvénile** *ou* **vulgaire** teenage acne; **avoir de l'a.** to have *or* suffer from acne; **traitement contre l'a.** acne treatment

acolyte [akɔlit] **NM 1** *Péj* confederate, accomplice **2** *Rel* acolyte

acompte [akɔ̃t] **NM** instalment, *Am* installment; *(avance, premier versement)* payment on account, down payment; **payer par acomptes** to pay by *or* in instalments; **recevoir un a.** to receive something on account; **verser un a.** to make a down payment; **a. de** *ou* **sur dividende** interim dividend; *Fin* **a. provisionnel** interim payment; **a. mensuel** monthly instalment, monthly payment; **recevoir un a. sur son salaire** to receive an advance on one's salary; *Fig* **j'ai pris un petit a.** I had a little taster

aconit [akɔnit] **NM** *(plante)* aconite

a contrario [akɔ̃trarjo] **ADV** **raisonnement a c.** converse reasoning

acoquiner (s') [sakɔkine] **VPR** *Péj* to team up, to fall in (**avec** with)

Açores [asɔr] **NFPL** **les A.** the Azores

à-côté, *pl* **à-côtés** [akote] **NM 1** *(verbal)* aside **2** *(élément secondaire)* **les à-côtés d'une question** the side issues of a question; **les à-côtés de l'histoire** sidelights on history **3** *Fam (financier etc)* extra; **il a quelques à-côtés** he makes a bit on the side

à-coup, *pl* **à-coups** [aku] **NM** jerk, jolt, jar,

shock; *Élec* surge (of current); **il y eut des à-coups au départ de la voiture** the car jerked *or* jolted as it set off; **il travaille par à-coups** he works by *or* in fits and starts; *Aut* **le moteur a des à-coups** the engine judders; **sans à-coups** smoothly

acousticien, -ienne [akustisjɛ̃, -jɛn] **N** acoustician

acoustique [akustik] **ADJ** acoustic; **cornet a.** ear trumpet; **tuyau a.** speaking tube; **voûte a.** whispering gallery; **les phénomènes acoustiques** acoustics
  NF *Phys* acoustics; **a. d'une salle** acoustics of a hall; **avoir une bonne/mauvaise a.** to have good/bad acoustics

acquéreur [akerœr] **NM** purchaser, buyer; *Jur* vendee; **notre voiture n'a pas trouvé a.** we couldn't find a buyer for our car

acquérir [akerir] (*prp* **acquérant;** *pp* **acquis;** *pr ind* **j'acquiers, il acquiert, n. acquérons, ils acquièrent;** *pr sub* **j'acquière, n. acquérions;** *impf* **j'acquérais;** *p hist* **j'acquis;** *fu* **j'acquerrai**) **VT 1** *(obtenir)* to acquire, to obtain, to get; *(habitude)* to get into; *(expérience, confiance)* to acquire, to gain; **nous avons acquis la certitude de son innocence** we have established beyond doubt that he/she is innocent; **l'expérience acquise au long d'une carrière** the experience gained in the course of one's career; **a. de mauvaises habitudes** to get into bad habits; *Prov* **un bien en acquiert un autre** money attracts money
  2 *(prendre)* to acquire; **a. de la valeur** to go up *or* increase in value
  3 *(devenir propriétaire de)* to acquire; *(acheter)* to purchase, to buy; **a. une terre d'un voisin** to purchase *or* buy land from a neighbour; **a. un bien par héritage** to come into *or* to inherit some property
  4 **a. qch à qn** to bring sth to sb, to bring sb sth
  VPR s'acquérir 1 *(se prendre)* **cette habitude s'acquiert facilement** it's easy to get into the habit; **une fortune peut s'a. de différentes manières** there are different ways of making one's fortune **2** *(s'attirer)* to win, to gain

acquêt [akɛ] **NM** *Jur* acquisition; *(fortuit)* windfall; **communauté réduite aux acquêts** = marriage settlement whereby only goods acquired since the marriage are deemed to be held in common

acquiescement [akjɛsmɑ̃] **NM** acquiescence; *Jur* **a. licite/conditionnel** lawful/conditional consent; **hocher la tête en signe d'a.** to nod one's agreement

acquiescer [akjese] **VI** (**j'acquiesçai(s); n. acquiesçons**) **a. à qch** *(se résigner)* to acquiesce in sth; *(consentir)* to agree *or* assent to sth; **a. d'un signe de tête** to agree with a nod of the head, to nod one's approval; **elle a acquiescé d'un sourire** she gave a smile of agreement, she smiled her agreement; *Jur* **a. à un acte** to consent (fully) to an act

acquis [aki] **ADJ** *(savoir, caractères etc)* acquired; **fait a.** established *or* accepted fact; **tenir pour a.** to take for granted; **son aide nous est acquise** we can take it for granted that he will help us; **droits a.** vested interests; **cela est a.** that's been established; **ce droit lui est a.** he/she has an established right in this respect; **je vous suis tout a.** I entirely agree
  NM *(connaissances)* knowledge; *(réussite)* attainments, achievements; **a. sociaux** social benefits that have been won

acquisitif, -ive [akizitif, -iv] **ADJ** *Jur* acquisitive

acquisition [akizisjɔ̃] **NF 1** *(fait)* acquisition; **faire l'a. de qch** *(entrer en possession de)* to acquire sth; *(acheter)* to purchase sth **2** *(bien acquis)* acquisition; *(bien acheté)* purchase; **c'est ma dernière a.** it's my latest acquisition

3 *UE* **a. intracommunautaire** intra-Community acquisition

acquit [aki] NM **1** *Com* receipt; **donner a. de qch** to give a receipt for sth; **pour a.** received (with thanks), paid; **a. de douane** customs receipt; **a. de paiement** receipt; **a. de transit** transshipment note **2** *(d'un navire)* clearance **3** *(d'une promesse)* discharge, release; **par a. de conscience** to ease one's conscience, to put one's mind at rest; **faire qch par manière d'a.** to do sth as a matter of form **4** *Jur* **sentence** *ou* **ordonnance d'a.** order of acquittal

acquit-à-caution, *pl* **acquits-à-caution** [akiakosjɔ̃] NM bond note

acquittement [akitmɑ̃] NM **1** *(d'une dette etc)* discharge, payment; *(d'effet)* acquittal **2** *Jur* acquittal; **verdict d'a.** verdict of not guilty

acquitter [akite] VT **1 a. qn** *(d'une obligation etc)* to release sb **2** *Jur* **a. un accusé** to acquit *or* discharge a defendant **3** *(obligation)* to fulfil; *(dette)* to discharge, to pay off; *(chèque)* to endorse **4** *(facture)* to receipt, to pay ▸VPR **s'acquitter s'a. d'une obligation/d'un devoir** to fulfil *or* carry out *or* discharge an obligation/a duty; **s'a. de son devoir** to do one's duty; **s'a. d'une facture** to pay a bill; **comment pourrai-je m'a. envers vous?** how can I repay you?

acre [akr] NF *Hist* acre
NM *Can* acre

âcre [akr] ADJ *(goût)* bitter; *(odeur)* pungent, acrid; *Fig (souvenir)* bitter; *(propos, humeur)* caustic

âcreté [ɑkrəte] NF *(d'un goût)* bitterness; *(d'une odeur)* pungency; *Fig (de la jalousie, la douleur)* bitterness; *(de propos)* caustic nature

acrimonie [akrimɔni] NF *(mauvaise humeur)* acrimony; *(d'un discours, d'une querelle)* acrimoniousness, bitterness

acrimonieux, -ieuse [akrimɔnjø, -jøz] ADJ *(mots, querelle etc)* acrimonious, bitter

acrobate [akrɔbat] N acrobat; *Fig* **c'est un a.** he can wriggle out of anything
NM *(mammifère)* flying squirrel

acrobatie [akrɔbasi] NF **1** *(art)* acrobatics; **numéro** *ou* **tour d'a.** acrobatic feat; **faire des acrobaties** to do *or* perform acrobatics; **a. aérienne** stunt flying, aerobatics **2** *Fig (virtuosité)* clever trick; **a. intellectuelle** intellectual acrobatics; **il s'en sortira par une a.** he'll wriggle out of it somehow

acrobatique [akrɔbatik] ADJ acrobatic

acronyme [akrɔnim] NM *Ling* acronym

acropole [akrɔpɔl] NF acropolis; **l'A.** the Acropolis

acrostiche [akrɔstiʃ] NM acrostic

acrylique [akrilik] ADJ *Chimie, Tex* acrylic
NM *Tex* acrylic; **pull en a.** acrylic pullover

ACT [asete] NM *(abrév* **arbre à cames en tête)** ohc

acte [akt] NM **1** *(action)* action, act, deed; **moins de paroles, des actes!** let's have less talk and more action!; **a. de courage** act of bravery *or* courage, brave *or* courageous act *or* action; **faire a. de bonne volonté** to show willing *or* good will; **faire a. d'autorité** to use *or* exercise one's authority; **passer aux actes** to take action; **il menace de se suicider, j'ai peur qu'il passe aux actes** I'm scared that he'll carry out his threats of suicide; **faire a. de présence** to put in an appearance; **faire a. de candidature à un emploi** to submit an application *or* to apply for a job; **faire a. de souverain** to exercise the royal prerogative; **faire a. d'héritier** to come forward as an heir; **a. de terrorisme** act of terrorism; **a. de guerre** act of war; **être facturé à l'a.** to be billed on a usage basis

2 *Jur* instrument; *(establishing ownership)* deed, title; **a. authentique** *ou* **notarié, a. sur papier timbré** deed executed and authenticated by a notary; **dont a.** duly noted *or* acknowledged **3** *(certificat)* record; **prendre a. de qch** to record *or* note *or* take a note of *or* set down sth; *Fml* **nous prenons a. de votre candidature** we acknowledge your application; **donner a. de qch** to grant sth, to admit sth **4** **actes** *(de procès etc)* records; *(d'un organisme scientifique etc)* transactions; *(d'un colloque)* proceedings **5** *Théâtre* act; **tragédie en trois actes** three-act tragedy, tragedy in three acts; **dans le second a.** in the second act
▸▸*Jur* **a. d'accusation** bill of indictment, charges; *Bible* **Actes des Apôtres** Acts of the Apostles; *Jur* **a. d'association** partnership deed; *Jur* **a. de cession** deed *or* certificate of transfer; *Rel* **a. de contrition** act of contrition; **a. de décès** death certificate; *Jur* **a. de dernière volonté** last will and testament; **a. d'état civil** = certificate of birth/marriage/death; *Rel* **a. de foi** act of faith; *Jur* **a. hypothécaire** mortgage deed; *Jur* **a. judiciaire** writ; **a. de mariage** marriage certificate; **a. médical** medical treatment; **a. de naissance** birth certificate; *Jur* **a. notarié** notarized deed; *Jur* **a. de propriété** title deed; *Jur* **a. sous seing privé** private agreement; **a. unique européen** Single European Act; *Jur* **a. de vente** bill of sale, deed of sale

acter [akte] VT *Belg (noter)* to take a note of, to note; *Jur* to record

acteur, -trice [aktœr, -tris] N **1** *Théâtre, Cin* actor, *f* actress; **a. de cinéma** screen actor, movie *or Br* film actor; **se faire a.** to go on the stage; **a. comique** comic actor; **a. de composition** feature player; **a. de théâtre** stage actor; **a. à transformations** quick-change artist; **a. virtuel** virtual-reality actor, *Fam* synthespian **2** *(d'un événement)* participant; *(sur le marché)* player; **les différents acteurs de la négociation** the different participants in *or* parties involved in the negotiation; **a. économique** economic agent *or* player; **a. du marché** market participant, market player; **les acteurs sociaux** = employers, workers and trade unions

actif, -ive [aktif, -iv] ADJ **1** *(défenseur, participation), Gram (verbe, voix)* active; *(substance etc)* potent, active; **le principe a. d'un produit** the active ingredient of a product; *Écon* **population active** labour force; **femme active** working woman; *Mil* **armée active** regular army; **service a.** (active) service; **citoyen a.** person with the right to vote **2** *(personne)* active; **sa grand-mère est très active pour son âge** his grandmother is very sprightly for her age; **faire un commerce a.** to do brisk trade **3** *Com, Jur* **dettes actives** accounts receivable **4** *Ordinat (fichier, fenêtre)* active; **rendre a.** *(unité etc)* to activate
NM **1** *Com* assets; *(moyens financiers)* credit (account); **mettre qch à l'a. de qn** to credit sb with sth; *Fig* **il faut mettre sa patience à son a.** you have to give him credit for patience; *Fig* **avoir plusieurs prix à son a.** to have several prizes to one's name *or* credit; *Fig* **avoir plusieurs infractions à son a.** to have several offences to one's name **2** *Gram* **verbe à l'a.** verb in the active voice
VOIR GRAMMAIRE A40
N active person; **c'est un a.** he likes to do things, he's a doer
▸▸*Compta* **a. brut** gross assets; **a. circulant** circulating *or* floating *or* current assets; **a. corporel** tangible asset; **a. disponible** liquide available assets; **a. fictif** fictitious asset; **a. immobilisé** fixed *or* capital asset; **a.**

incorporel intangible asset; **a. liquide** liquid assets; **a. net** net assets *or* worth; **a. réel** real assets; **a. de roulement** current assets; **a. sous-jacent** underlying asset; **a. soustractif** depreciated credit balance; **a. stable** fixed *or* long-term asset

action [aksjɔ̃] NF **1** *(acte)* action, act; **l'a. de marcher** the act of walking; **commettre** *ou* **faire une a. insensée** to commit a senseless act; **commettre** *ou* **faire une bonne/mauvaise a.** to do a good/bad deed; **a. d'éclat** brilliant feat
2 *(influence, effet) (d'une substance)* action, effect; **a. sur qch** action *or* effect on sth; **ce désherbant n'a aucune a. sur le liseron** this weedkiller has no effect on bindweed; **exercer une a. sur qn** to have influence over sb; **sans a.** ineffectual, ineffective; **a. de l'eau** effect of water; **par l'a. personnelle d'un membre du club** through the personal intervention of a club member
3 *(activité) (d'une machine etc)* action, motion, working, functioning; **entrer en a.** *(d'une loi etc)* to come into force *or* effect; *Pol* **recourir à l'a. directe** to resort to direct action; **hors d'a.** out of action; **développer son champ d'a.** to expand one's sphere of activity *or* field of operations, to expand the scope of one's activities; **homme d'a.** man of action, action man; **passer à l'a.** to take action, to act; **mettre qch en a.** to set sth in motion, to put sth into operation
4 *(d'un orateur etc)* action, gesture
5 *(intrigue)* action; *(d'une pièce, d'un roman)* plot; **scène qui retarde l'a.** scene that delays the action; **un film d'a.** action-packed movie; *(genre)* action movie; *TV, Cin* **a.!** action!; **l'a. se déroule à Prague** the action is set in Prague
6 *Fin* share; *(document)* share certificate; **actions** shares, *esp Am* stock; **avoir des actions dans** to have shares *or* a shareholding in; **détenir des actions d'une société** to have shares in a company; **compagnie par actions** joint-stock company; **hausse/baisse des actions** rise/fall in the value of shares; *Fig* **les actions du ministre montent/baissent** the minister's stock is rising/falling
7 *Jur* action, lawsuit, trial; **intenter une a. judiciaire** *ou* **en justice** to take legal action; **mener une a. contre qch** to take action against sth; *(pour de l'argent)* to sue sb; **a. en divorce** divorce suit
8 *Mil* action, fight, engagement; **dans le feu de l'a.** *(pendant la guerre)* in the heat of battle; *Fig* in the heat of the moment
9 *Suisse (vente promotionnelle)* **acheter qch en a.** to buy sth on special offer; **acheter une a.** to buy something on special offer
▸▸*Fin* **a. d'attribution** bonus share; *Fin* **a. de capitalisation** capital share; *Fin* **a. cotée (en Bourse)** quoted share; *Fin* **a. de distribution** income share; *Fin* **a. gratuite** bonus share; *Fin* **a. de jouissance** dividend share; *Ordinat* **a. logique** logical operation; *Fin* **a. nominative** bearer registered share; *Fin* **a. ordinaire** ordinary share, *Am* common stock; *Fin* **a. au porteur** bearer stock share; *Fin* **a. privilégiée** preference share, *Am* preferred stock; *Mktg* **a. de stimulation** sales stimulation campaign; *Mktg* **a. de vente** sales campaign *or* drive *or* action

actionnaire [aksjɔnɛr] N *Fin* shareholder, *Am* stockholder; **a. majoritaire/minoritaire** majority/minority shareholder, *Am* majority/minority stockholder; **a. de référence** major shareholder *or Am* stockholder

actionnariat [aksjɔnarja] NM *Fin* shareholding; **a. intermédiaire** nominee shareholding; **a. ouvrier** workers' shareholding, worker share ownership

actionnement [aksjɔnmɑ̃] NM activation; **a. à distance** remote-control operation

actionner [aksjɔne] **VT 1** *(mettre en marche)* to start up, to turn on; *(faire fonctionner)* to operate, to drive, to run; *Tech* to actuate; **actionné à la main** hand operated; **a. les freins** to put on *or* apply the brakes **2** *Jur* to sue, to bring an action against; **a. qn en dommages-intérêts** to sue sb for damages

actionneur [aksjɔnœr] **NM** *Tech* actuator

activation [aktivasjɔ̃] **NF** activation

activé [aktive] **ADJ** *Chimie* activated; *Ordinat* active

activement [aktivmɑ̃] **ADV** actively, briskly, busily; **prendre a. qch en charge** to take an active responsibility for sth; **s'occuper a. de qch** to be actively engaged in sth; **vivre a.** to lead an active life

activer [aktive] **VT 1** *(presser)* to stimulate, to rouse; *(accélérer)* to speed up; *(feu)* to stoke; **a. un ouvrage** to press on with *or* to speed up a piece of work; *Fam* **activez!** get a move on! **2** *Chimie, Nucl etc* to activate **3** *Ordinat* to activate; **a. une option** to select an option
VPR s'activer to be busy, to busy oneself, to bustle about; **s'a.** to get on *or* press on (**à qch** with sth)

activisme [aktivism] **NM** *Pol* activism

activiste [aktivist] **ADJ, N** *Pol* activist

activité [aktivite] **NF** activity; *(d'une substance)* potency; **l'a. d'une ville** the (amount of) activity in a city; **elle déploie une grande a. au travail** she invests a lot of energy in her work; **maintenir l'a. industrielle** to keep industry going; **une région reconnue pour son a.** a region known for its industrial/cultural/*etc* activity; **en a.** in action, in operation, in progress; *(personne)* working, employed; **en pleine a.** *(entreprise)* in full operation *or* production, fully operational; *(personne)* very busy; *(secteur économique, hôtel etc)* very busy, bustling; **un moment de grande a.** a very busy time; **marché sans a.** dull market; **l'usine est en a.** the factory is working *or* is in production; **volcan en a.** active volcano; **le temps d'a. d'un employé** the length of (active) service of an employee; **être en a. (de service)** to be on active duty *or* on the active list; **je ne connais pas ses activités** I know nothing about his activities; **le centre de jeunes propose les activités suivantes** the following activities are available at the youth centre
▸ ▸ **a. économique** economic activity; **a. de plein air** outdoor activity; **a. professionnelle** occupation; **a. solaire** solar activity; **a. sportive** sport, sporting activity; *Scol etc* **activités dirigées** project work, projects

actrice [aktris] **NF** actress *(voir aussi* **acteur 1**)

actuaire [aktɥer] **N** actuary

actualisation [aktɥalizasjɔ̃] **NF 1** *(de textes etc)* updating, update **2** *Écon* discounting; **taux d'a.** rate of discount **3** *Phil* actualization **4** *Ordinat* refresh

actualiser [aktɥalize] **VT 1** *(texte, méthode de travail)* to update **2** *Écon* to discount **3** *Phil* **a. qch** to turn sth into a reality, to actualize sth **4** *Ordinat* to refresh
VPR s'actualiser 1 *(se moderniser)* to become more up to date **2** *Phil* to become a reality, to come into being

actualité [aktɥalite] **NF 1** topicality; **l'a., les questions d'a.** current affairs; **l'a. politique française** the current French political scene; **cette question est toujours d'a.** this is still a topical question; **question d'une a. brûlante** burning question; **les actualités** *(dans la presse)* current events *or* affairs; *TV, Radio* news; **il est passé aux actualités** he was on the news; **actualités filmées** newsreel; **actualités télévisées** television news **2** *Phil* actuality, reality

actuariat [aktɥarja] **NM** actuarial profession

actuariel, -ielle [aktɥarjɛl] **ADJ** actuarial

actuel, -elle [aktɥɛl] **ADJ** present, current; **le gouvernement a.** the present government; **l'état a. du pays** the present *or* current state of the country; **valeur actuelle** present *or* current value; **à l'heure actuelle** at the present time; **dans la situation actuelle** as things are *or* stand at the moment; **cette question est toujours actuelle** this is still a topical question, the question is still relevant today

> Il faut noter que l'adjectif anglais **actual** est un faux ami. Il ne signifie jamais **actuel**.

actuellement [aktɥɛlmɑ̃] **ADV** now, at present, currently, at the present time

> Il faut noter que l'adverbe anglais **actually** est un faux ami. Il signifie **en fait**.

acuité [akɥite] **NF** *(de la douleur etc)* acuteness, sharpness, keenness; *(d'un argument)* sharpness; **il a analysé le problème avec une a. remarquable** his analysis of the problem was remarkably shrewd; **a. d'un son** high pitch of a sound; **a. visuelle** keenness of vision *or* eyesight; **a. intellectuelle** sharpness of intellect

acuponcteur, -trice, acupuncteur, **-trice** [akypɔ̃ktœr, -tris] **N** *Méd* acupuncturist

acuponcture, acupuncture [akypɔ̃ktyr] **NF** *Méd* acupuncture; **se soigner à l'a.** to have acupuncture treatment

acutangle [akytɑ̃gl] **ADJ** *Math* acute-angled

ADAC [adak] **NM** *(abrév* avion à décollage et atterrissage courts) STOL

adage [adaʒ] **NM** adage, (common) saying; **selon l'a.** as the saying goes

adagio [adadʒjo] **ADV, NM** *Mus* adagio

Adam [adɑ̃] **N** Adam; *Fam* **en costume d'A.** in one's birthday suit; **pomme d'A.** Adam's apple

adaptabilité [adaptabilite] **NF** adaptability (**à** to)

adaptable [adaptabl] **ADJ** adaptable

adaptateur, -trice [adaptatœr, -tris] **NM 1** *Élec, Tech, Phot, Ordinat* adapter; **a. (secteur)** (mains) adapter; *Ordinat* **a. graphique amélioré** enhanced graphics adapter, EGA; *Phot* **a. graphique couleur** colour graphics adapter; **a. femelle/mâle** female to male adapter; **a. vidéo** video adapter **2** *Radio* convertor
N *(d'un roman pour le cinéma etc)* adapter

adaptation [adaptasjɔ̃] **NF 1** adaptation (**à** to); **faire un effort d'a.** to make an effort to adapt; **faculté d'a.** adaptability **2** *TV, Cin, Théâtre* adaptation; **a. d'une nouvelle au théâtre/pour la télévision** adaptation of a short story for the stage/for television; *TV, Cin* **a. à l'écran** screen adaptation; *TV* **a. en feuilleton** *(d'un roman etc)* serialization; **faire une nouvelle a. de 'Macbeth'** to do a new adaptation of 'Macbeth'; **a. théâtrale** stage adaptation

adapter [adapte] **VT 1 a. qch à qch** to adapt sth to sth; **a. un règlement à un cas personnel** to adapt a rule to (fit) individual circumstances; **est-ce vraiment adapté à la situation?** is it really suitable for the situation?; **a. un tube à un autre** to make one tube fit another **2** *TV, Cin, Théâtre* **a. un roman à la scène** to adapt a novel for the stage; *TV* **a. en feuilleton** to serialize
VPR s'adapter to adapt; **la prise s'adapte à toutes les télévisions** the plug fits all types of television; **s'a. aux conditions nouvelles** to adapt (oneself) *or* adjust to new conditions; **il sait s'a.** he's very adaptable *or* flexible

ADAV [adav] **NM** *(abrév* avion à décollage et atterrissage verticaux) VTOL

addenda [adɛ̃da] **NM INV** addendum (**à** to)
VOIR GRAMMAIRE A13

additif, -ive [aditif, -iv] **ADJ** additive
NM 1 supplement, addition; *(à un texte)* additional clause; **a. à un budget** addition to a budget **2** *Chimie etc* additive; **sans additifs** additive free; **a. antidétonant** anti-knock additive; **a. antigivre** antifreeze additive; **a. anti-mousse** anti-foam additive; **a. antioxydant** oxidation inhibitor; **a. détergent** detergent additive

addition [adisjɔ̃] **NF 1** *(fait d'ajouter)* addition, adding (to); *(pour faire un total)* adding up; **apprendre à faire les additions** to learn how to do addition *or* how to add up; **faire l'a. des chiffres** to add up *or* *Fam* tot up the figures; **l'a. d'un paragraphe à un texte** the addition *or* adding of a paragraph to a text; **l'a. de thym améliorera le ragoût** adding some thyme will improve the stew **2** *(extension)* addition, extension; **faire une a. à une maison** to build an extension to a house; **en a. à** in addition to **3** *Math* addition SEE GRAMMAR A77; B59 **4** *(au restaurant etc)* bill, *Am* check **5** *Typ* note

additionnel, -elle [adisjɔnɛl] **ADJ** additional, extra; *Ordinat* add-on

additionner [adisjɔne] **VT** to add (up), *Fam* to tot up; **a. un alcool d'un peu d'eau** to add a little water to a drink; **lait additionné d'eau** watered down milk; **café additionné d'eau-de-vie** coffee laced with spirits
VI to add (up)
VPR s'additionner to add up; **aux longues heures de travail s'additionnent celles passées dans le métro** along with the long working hours, there are those spent on the underground *or* *Am* subway

additionneur [adisjɔnœr] **NM** *Ordinat* adder

additionneuse [adisjɔnøz] **NF** adding machine, adder

adducteur, -trice [adyktœr, -tris] **ADJ** *Anat etc* adducent; **canal a.** feeder canal
NM 1 *Anat* adductor **2** *Constr* supply main

adduction [adyksjɔ̃] **NF 1** *Anat* adduction **2** *Tech* admission, intake; *Constr* **a. d'eau** canalization; **adductions d'eau** water supply

adénoïde [adenɔid] **ADJ** *Méd* **végétations adénoïdes** adenoids

adénopathie [adenɔpati] **NF** adenopathy

adent [adɑ̃] **NM** *Menuis* dovetail

adepte [adɛpt] **N 1** *(partisan)* follower, adherent; **un a. de la non-violence** a supporter of non-violence; **les adeptes de la marche à pied** walking enthusiasts; **a. du cinéma** film fan *or* buff; **a. des ordinateurs** computer buff; **c'est une a. du ski** she loves skiing; **faire des adeptes** to attract followers *or* a following **2** *(rare) (personne initiée)* adept, initiate

adéquat [adekwa] **ADJ** *(personne, lieu, expression, méthode)* appropriate, suitable; *(montant, quantité)* adequate

adéquation [adekwasjɔ̃] **NF** appropriateness, suitability; *Fin* **a. des fonds propres** capital adequacy; **l'a. entre l'offre et la demande favorise la stabilité des prix** the balance between supply and demand encourages stable prices

adhérence [aderɑ̃s] **NF** adhesion, adherence; **a. des pneus (à la route)** grip of the tyres (on the road); **cette voiture a une excellente a. à la route** this car has excellent road-holding

adhérent, -ente [aderɑ̃, -ɑ̃t] **ADJ** *(substance, propriétés)* adhesive
N member; **a. d'un parti** member of a party;

(partisan) supporter of a party; **carte d'a.** membership card

adhérer [adere] **VI** (**j'adhère, n. adhérons; j'adhérerai**) **1** to adhere, to stick (**à** to); **a. à la route** *(des pneus)* to grip the road **2** *(à une opinion, un idéal etc)* to adhere, to hold, to subscribe (**à** to) **3** *(s'inscrire)* **a. (à un parti)** to join (a party)

adhésif, -ive [adezif, -iv] **ADJ** adhesive, sticky; **pansement a.** sticking plaster; **papier a.** sticky(-backed) paper
NM adhesive

adhésion [adezjɔ̃] **NF 1** *(fait de coller)* adhesion, sticking; *(des pneus)* grip(ping), road-holding; **force d'a.** adhesiveness **2** *(accord)* agreement, approval; **donner son a. à un projet** to support *or* give one's support to a plan **3** *(inscription)* adhesion, adherence (**à** to); *(d'un parti)* membership; **après leur a. à l'UE** after joining the EU; **le nombre des adhésions augmente** the number of new members is increasing

ad hoc [adɔk] **ADJ, ADV** ad hoc

adieu, *pl* **-eux** [adjø] **INT 1** *Arch* goodbye!, *Arch* farewell!; **dire a. à qn** to say goodbye to sb; *Fig Fam* **dire a. à qch** to kiss sth goodbye, to say goodbye to sth **2** *Région (bonjour)* hello!, hi!; **allez a., à demain!** bye then, see you tomorrow!
NM farewell; **des adieux déchirants/émouvants** heart-rending/emotional farewells *or* partings; **faire ses adieux** to make one's farewells, to say one's goodbyes; **faire ses adieux à qn** to say goodbye to sb; **faire ses adieux à la scène** to make one's final appearance on stage; **baiser d'a.** goodbye kiss; *(à tout jamais)* parting *or* farewell kiss

adipeux, -euse [adipø, -øz] **ADJ** *(tissu etc)* adipose, fatty; **un visage pâle et a.** a pale, bloated face

adiposité [adipozite] **NF** adiposity

adjacent [adʒasɑ̃] **ADJ** adjacent (**à** to); *Math* **angles adjacents** adjacent angles

adjectif, -ive [adʒɛktif, -iv] **ADJ** *(expression, locution etc)* adjectival
NM adjective; **a. attribut** predicative adjective; **a. épithète** attributive adjective; **a. déterminatif** determiner; **a. verbal** present participle; **a. substantivé** adjective used as a noun SEE GRAMMAR A17–19; B8–12

adjectival, -ale, -aux, -ales [adʒɛktival, -o] **ADJ** adjectival

adjectiver [adʒɛktive] **VT** to use as an adjective

adjoindre [adʒwɛ̃dr] *(conj like* **joindre**) **VT 1 a. qch à qch** to unite *or* associate sth with sth; **a. un mode d'emploi à un appareil** to include *or* enclose an instruction booklet with an appliance **2 a. qn à qn** to give sb to sb as an assistant; **a. qn à un comité** to add sb to a committee
VPR s'adjoindre *(assistant)* to engage, to take on; **s'a. à d'autres** to join (in) with others

adjoint, -ointe [adʒwɛ̃, -wɛ̃t] **ADJ** assistant, deputy; *(directeur etc)* associate; *Can* **Sous-ministre a.** Assistant Deputy Minister
N assistant; **a. au maire** deputy mayor

adjonction [adʒɔ̃ksjɔ̃] **NF 1** *(fait d'ajouter)* adding, addition; **produit sans a. de sucre** product with no added sugar **2** *(élément adjoint)* *(à un texte etc)* addition; *(d'un hôpital)* annexe

adjudant [adʒydɑ̃] **NM 1** *Mil* warrant officer class II, *Am* warrant officer (junior grade); **a.-chef** warrant officer class I, *Am* chief warrant officer; **(capitaine) a.-major** adjutant, *Am* executive officer **2** *(oiseau)* adjutant bird

adjudicataire [adʒydikatɛr] **N** *(à un contrat)* successful tenderer; *(aux enchères)* highest bidder, purchaser; **être l'a.** to be awarded the contract

adjudicateur, -trice [adʒydikatœr, -tris] **N** adjudicator; *(d'un contrat etc)* awarder

adjudication [adʒydikasjɔ̃] **NF** adjudication, allocation; *(d'un contrat)* award; *(vente aux enchères)* selling *or* sale by auction; **mettre qch en a.** *(marché administratif)* to invite tenders for sth; *(aux enchères)* to put sth up for (sale by) auction; **a. forcée** compulsory sale

adjuger [adʒyʒe] (**j'adjugeai(s); n. adjugeons**) **VT a. qch à qn** to award sth to sb; *(allouer)* to allocate sth to sb; *(aux enchères)* to knock sth down to sb; **une fois! deux fois! trois fois! adjugé! vendu!** going! going! gone!
VPR s'adjuger s'a. qch to appropriate sth, to take possession of sth; **elle s'est adjugé la plus belle part** she took the biggest share for herself

adjuration [adʒyrasjɔ̃] **NF** entreaty, plea

adjurer [adʒyre] **VT a. qn de faire qch** to implore *or* entreat sb to do sth

adjuvant [adʒyvɑ̃] **NM 1** *Méd* adjuvant **2** *Chimie, Tech* additive (**de** to); *Pétr* dope **3** *Fig* stimulus

ADM [adeɛm] **NFPL** *(abrév* **armes de destruction massive**) weapons of mass destruction, WMD

admettre [admɛtr] **VT** *(conj like* **mettre**) **1** *(accueillir)* **a. qn** to admit sb, to let sb in; **les chiens ne sont pas admis** *(sur la porte d'un magasin etc)* no dogs allowed; **a. qn chez soi** to let sb into one's house; **être admis à un club** to be admitted to a club; **être admis à l'université** to be accepted for university; **être admis à un examen** to pass an examination; *Bourse* **a. une société à la cote** to list a company
2 *(accepter)* **a. qn à siéger** to admit sb as a (new) member; **a. qch** to admit *or* admit of *or* permit sth; **je n'admets pas qu'on me mente** I won't tolerate being lied to; **il n'admet pas mes explications** he doesn't *or* won't accept my explanations; **elle n'admet pas la discussion** she won't allow *or* permit any discussion; **cette règle n'admet aucune exception** the rule admits of *or* allows no exceptions, there can be no exceptions to the rule; **l'usage admis** the accepted custom; **non, cela je ne l'admets pas!** no, I don't agree with that!; **cela je ne l'admettrai pas** I won't allow it, I'm not having it
3 *(reconnaître)* to admit, to acknowledge; **il admet que c'est vrai** he admits *or* acknowledges that it is true; **admettons que j'aie tort** assuming *or* supposing (that) I'm wrong
4 *Jur* **a. un appel** to grant leave to appeal
5 *(laisser entrer)* *(vapeur, pétrole)* to let in; **l'essence est admise dans le moteur par ce conduit** the petrol enters the engine through this pipe

administrateur, -trice [administratœr, -tris] **N 1** administrator; **a. foncier** land agent; *(qui vend des maisons, des appartements)* estate agent **2** *(d'une société, d'une banque etc)* director **3** *(de fondation)* trustee
▸▸ **a. délégué** executive director; **a. judiciaire** official receiver; *TV, Cin* **a. de la production** production accountant; *Ordinat* **a. de réseau** network manager; *Ordinat* **a. de serveur** server administrator; **a. du système** systems administrator

administratif, -ive [administratif, -iv] **ADJ** administrative
N administrative worker; **les administratifs** the administrative staff

administration [administrasjɔ̃] **NF 1** *(d'affaires etc)* administration, direction, management; *(d'un pays)* governing, **conseil d'a.** board of directors; **elle a confié à des collaborateurs** she entrusted the handling of her business to colleagues;

mauvaise a. *(d'une société)* mismanagement **2** *(ensemble des directeurs)* board of directors; *(d'une institution)* governing body; **l'a. est en délibération** the board is meeting **3** *(service public)* government service; *(fonctionnaires)* authorities, officials; **l'a. publique, l'A.** ≃ the Civil Service; **entrer dans l'a.** ≃ to become a civil servant; **travailler dans l'a.** ≃ to work in the Civil Service
▸▸ **a. communale** local government; **a. des Douanes** Customs and Excise; **l'a. des Eaux et Forêts** *Br* ≃ the Forestry and Wildlife Commission; **a. fiscale** tax authorities; **a. locale** local authority; **a. municipale** local government; **a. du personnel** personnel management; **a. portuaire** port authorities; **a. privée** private administration; *Ordinat* **a. de réseau** network management; **a. des ventes** sales management

administrativement [administrativmɑ̃] **ADV** administratively

administré, -ée [administre] **N** citizen

administrer [administre] **VT 1** *(affaire, propriété)* to administer, to manage; *(affaire)* to conduct; *(pays)* to govern **2** *(justice)* to dispense; *Rel (sacrements)* to administer; **a. un malade** to administer *or* give the last rites to a sick person; **a. un remède à un malade** to administer medication to a patient; **je vais lui a. une bonne correction** I'm going to give him/her a good hiding **3** *Jur* **a. des preuves** to produce proofs

admirable [admirabl] **ADJ** admirable; *(très bon)* *(cuisinière, père de famille)* wonderful; **elle a été a. de courage/volonté** she showed admirable courage/willpower

admirablement [admirabləmɑ̃] **ADV** admirably; *(très bien)* *(chanter, cuisiner)* wonderfully; **ça fonctionne a. bien** it's working perfectly

admirateur, -trice [admiratœr, -tris] **N** admirer; *(d'une vedette de variété etc)* fan

admiratif, -ive [admiratif, -iv] **ADJ** *(geste etc)* admiring

admiration [admirasjɔ̃] **NF** admiration; **avoir de l'a. pour qn** to admire sb, to be full of *or* filled with admiration for sb; **être en a. devant qch** to be filled with admiration for sth; **il est en a. devant sa fille** he is full of *or* filled with admiration for his daughter; **tomber en a.** to be filled with admiration for; **tu fais l'a. de plus d'un** many people admire you; **cette peinture a fait l'a. de tout le monde** this painting was admired by everybody; **soulever l'a. de qn** to be admired by sb

admirer [admire] **VT** to admire; **admiré de tous** admired by all; *Iron* **j'admire la légèreté avec laquelle tu parles de la famine dans ton pays!** I admire the way you speak so casually about famine in your country!

admis, -ise [admi, -iz] **ADJ 1** *(reçu)* accepted **2** *(autorisé à entrer)* admitted, allowed (in) **3** *(accepté)* allowed, acceptable; **c'est chose communément admise ici** it's a widely accepted fact here; **c'est l'opinion communément admise** it's the commonly held opinion **4** **il a été a. à passer les épreuves à la session de septembre** *(autorisé à)* he was allowed *or* permitted to take the tests in September
N *Univ (à un examen)* successful candidate

admissibilité [admisibilite] **NF** admissibility; *(à un emploi)* eligibility; *Scol* **épreuves d'a. (à l'examen oral)** written examinations (to gain admission to the oral examination)

admissible [admisibl] **ADJ** *(excuse, preuve, conduite)* admissible, allowable; *Jur (preuve)* admissible; **a. à un emploi** eligible for a job; *Scol* **(candidats) admissibles** candidates who have qualified for the oral examination

admission [admisjɔ̃] **NF 1** admission (**à,**

dans to); **l'a. des pays de l'Est dans l'Union européenne** the entry or admission of Eastern European countries into the European Union; **demande d'a. dans un club** club membership application; **a. à un club** admission to a club; **cotisation d'a.** entrance or admission fee

2 Com (de marchandises) entry; **a. en franchise** duty-free entry; **a. temporaire** temporary entry

3 (entrée) Tech intake; Aut induction; (temps moteur) induction or intake stroke; **période d'a.** induction stroke; **soupape d'a.** inlet valve

4 Bourse **a. à la cote** admission to quotation; **faire une demande d'a. à la cote** to seek admission to quotation

5 Univ pass; **le nombre des admissions à un concours** the number of passes or successful candidates at a competitive examination; **il a eu son a. à Centrale** he was accepted into Centrale

admixtion [admiksjɔ̃] NF admixture (à with)
admonestation [admɔnɛstasjɔ̃] NF admonishing
admonester [admɔnɛste] VT to admonish
admonition [admɔnisjɔ̃] NF admonition
ADN [adeɛn] NM (abrév acide désoxyribonucléique) DNA
ado [ado] N Fam (adolescent) teenager; **magazine/club/musique pour ados** teenage magazine/club/music
adobe [adɔb] NM (brique, maison) adobe
adolescence [adɔlesɑ̃s] NF adolescence; **pendant l'a.** during adolescence or one's teenage years or one's teens
adolescent, -ente [adɔlesɑ̃, -ɑ̃t] ADJ adolescent, teenage
N adolescent, teenager
adon [adɔ̃] NM Can Fam coincidence
Adonis [adɔnis] N Myth Adonis
adonis [adɔnis] NM **1** (bel homme) Adonis; **je ne suis pas vraiment un a.!** I'm no Adonis!, I'm no oil painting! **2** (insecte) adonis
adonner [adɔne] V IMPERS Can to suit, to be convenient; **viens me voir quand ça t'adonnera** come and see me whenever it suits you
VI Can **a. avec qch** (vêtements etc) to go with sth
VPR **s'adonner s'a. à qch** to give oneself up to sth; **s'a. à l'étude** to devote oneself to study; **s'a. à une profession** to take up a profession; **s'a. à la boisson** to take to drink; **s'a. à une vie de plaisirs** to abandon oneself to a life of pleasure
adoptant, -ante [adɔptɑ̃, -ɑ̃t] ADJ adoptive
N adoptive parent
adopté, -ée [adɔpte] ADJ adopted
N adopted child
adopter [adɔpte] VT **1** (prendre sous sa tutelle) (enfant) to adopt; Fig **nous l'avons adopté comme un fils** we treated him like a son **2** (accepter) **a. qn pour ami** to choose sb as a friend, to befriend sb; **il a très vite été adopté par ses nouveaux collègues** he was very quickly accepted by his new colleagues **3** (choisir) (produit) to adopt; (nom) to adopt, to assume; (cause) to adopt, to take up, to embrace; **a. un produit comme norme** to standardize on a product **4** (approuver, voter) **a. un projet de loi/une résolution** to adopt or pass or carry a bill/a resolution; **adopté à l'unanimité** carried unanimously
adopteur [adɔptœr] NM Mktg (d'un produit) adopter; **a. précoce** early adopter
adoptif, -ive [adɔptif, -iv] ADJ (enfant, pays) adopted; (parent) adoptive
adoption [adɔpsjɔ̃] NF (d'un enfant, d'une proposition, d'une idée, d'une mode) adop-

tion; **procédure d'a.** adoption procedure; Parl (d'un projet de loi) adoption, carrying; **mon pays d'a.** my country of adoption, my adopted country
adorable [adɔrabl] ADJ adorable, charming; **vous êtes a. dans cette robe** you look charming in that dress
adorablement [adɔrabləmɑ̃] ADV adorably
adorateur, -trice [adɔratœr, -tris] N **1** (d'une religion) worshipper **2** (d'un chanteur) ardent admirer, fan; (d'une femme) admirer
adoration [adɔrasjɔ̃] NF **1** (d'une divinité) adoration, worship **2** (attachement très profond) profound admiration (de for); **vouer une véritable a. à qn** to nurse a feeling of adoration for sb; **être en a. devant son bébé** to worship one's baby
adorer [adɔre] VT **1** (divinité) to adore, to worship **2** (personne, chose) to love; (plus fort) to adore; (star du cinéma, petit ami etc) to idolize; Euph **Joseph Beuys?, bof, je n'adore pas** Joseph Beuys?, well, I wouldn't call him my favourite; **j'adore monter à cheval** I adore or love riding
VPR **s'adorer** to adore each other
adossé [adose] ADJ **1** (dos contre dos) back to back **2 a. à qch** (personne) with one's back against sth, leaning against sth; (édifice etc) backed on to sth
adosser [adose] VT **1 a. deux choses** to place two things back to back **2 a. qch à** ou **contre qch** to place or lean or rest sth (with its back) against sth; **a. une chaise à qch** to put a chair with its back against sth
VPR **s'adosser s'a. à** ou **contre qch** to lean (up) against sth; **le village s'adosse à la colline** the village is built against the hillside
adouber [adube] VT **1** Échecs (pièce) to adjust **2** Arch (chevalier) to dub
adoucir [adusir] VT **1** (voix, eau, tissu, peau) to soften; (contraste, couleur) to tone down; (lumière) to subdue; (boisson, goût) to sweeten; **sa nouvelle coiffure adoucit son expression** her new haircut softens her face **2** (tempérer) (douleur, chagrin etc) to alleviate, to relieve, to ease; **a. une situation tendue** to ease or alleviate a tense situation; Prov **la musique adoucit les mœurs** music hath charms to soothe the savage breast **3** (personne) to pacify, to mollify **4** (surface, bois etc) to smooth, to soften; (angle) to smooth off; (verre) to (rough-)polish **5** Métal to temper; (fonte de fer) to soften
VPR **s'adoucir 1** (d'une voix) to grow softer, to soften, to mellow **2** (du temps) to get or grow milder **3** (de la douleur) to decrease **4** (du caractère) to mellow; **il s'est adouci avec l'âge** he has mellowed with age; **ce cognac s'adoucit avec le temps** this brandy mellows with age
adoucissage [adusisaʒ] NM **1** Métal tempering; (de fonte de fer) softening **2** (de glace, de marbre) polishing **3** (des couleurs) toning down
adoucissant [adusisɑ̃] ADJ softening; **crème adoucissante pour les mains** hand cream; **produit a. pour le linge** fabric softener
NM (pour le linge) fabric softener
adoucissement [adusismɑ̃] NM **1** (de la voix etc) softening; (du caractère) calming; (de la température) rise; **on prévoit un a.** milder weather is forecast **2** (de la douleur etc) alleviation **3** (de surfaces, d'angles) smoothing **4** sweetening; (de l'eau) (water) softening **5** Métal annealing
adoucisseur [adusisœr] NM (water) softener
ad patres [adpatrɛs] ADV **envoyer qn a.** to send sb to meet his maker
ad(r). abrév adresse
adrénaline [adrenalin] NF Méd adrenalin(e)

adressable [adrɛsabl] ADJ Ordinat addressable
adressage [adrɛsaʒ] NM Ordinat addressing; **mode d'a.** address mode; **a. direct** direct addressing
adresse [adrɛs] NF **1** address; **nom, profession et a.** name, address and occupation; **nous avons échangé nos adresses** we exchanged addresses; **a. personnelle** home address; **a. au bureau** office address; **a. de facturation** invoicing address, address for invoicing; **a. de livraison** delivery address; (d'objets volumineux) shipping address; **a. du siège social** head office or registered office address; **carnet d'adresses** address book; **changer d'a.** to change one's address; **faire son changement d'a.** (à la poste) to have one's mail redirected; Fig **tu te trompes d'a.** you've come to the wrong person, you're knocking at the wrong door; **il m'a donné une bonne a.** (de restaurant, de magasin etc) he recommended a good restaurant/shop/etc; **inconnu à cette a.** not known at this address; Fig **une observation à votre a.** (intention) a remark aimed at or meant for you; **je l'ai dit à l'a. de ceux qui …** I said it for the benefit of those who … VOIR GRAMMAIRE A77 **2** (dans une assemblée) (formal) address **3** (habileté) skill, dexterity; (savoir faire) diplomacy; **jongler avec a.** to juggle skilfully or with dexterity; **faire des tours d'a.** to perform tricks; **dénué d'a.** bungling; **il lui faudra une sacrée a. pour se tirer de cette situation** he'll have to be damn clever to get out of this situation **4** Ordinat address; **a. absolue** absolute or specific address; Can **a. de courriel** e-mail address; **a. électronique** e-mail address; **a. Internet** Internet or web address; **a. IP** IP address; **a. de mémoire** memory address; **a. URL** URL; **a. virtuelle** virtual address
adresser [adrese] VT **1** (lettre etc) to address; **la lettre lui fut adressée dans sa résidence d'été** the letter was addressed to (him at) his summer residence; **lettre mal adressée** incorrectly addressed letter **2** (envoyer) to send or to refer (**qn à qn** sb to sb); **on m'a adressé à vous** (par le biais d'un médecin etc) I have been recommended to come and see you, I have been referred to you; **le médecin m'a adressé à un spécialiste** the doctor sent or referred me to a specialist **3** (remarques etc) to address, to aim; **a. des remerciements à qn** to deliver thanks to sb; **cette remarque était adressée à Martin** this remark was aimed at or meant for Martin; **a. un sourire à qn** to smile at sb; **elle ne m'adresse plus la parole depuis notre dispute** she hasn't spoken to me since our argument
VPR **s'adresser s'a. à qn** (d'une remarque, recommandation etc) to apply to sb; (d'une personne) to speak to sb; **s'a. ici** apply within; (pour des renseignements) enquire within; **adressez-vous à l'agent** ask the policeman; **s'a. à l'imagination/au bon sens de qn** to appeal to sb's imagination/common sense; **le livre s'adresse aux enfants** the book is aimed at children
Adriatique [adriatik] ADJ Adriatic
NF **l'A.** the Adriatic
Adrien [adriɛ̃] N Adrian; (en histoire romaine) Hadrian
adroit [adrwa] ADJ **1** (habile) dexterous, deft; **être a. de ses mains** to be clever or good with one's hands **2** (réponse, diplomate) shrewd, clever, skilful, Am skillful; **il le lui a annoncé de but en blanc, ce qui n'est pas très a.** he informed him quite bluntly, which wasn't very tactful; **phrase adroite** neatly turned phrase, neat turn of phrase
adroitement [adrwatmɑ̃] ADV (fabriqué)

skilfully, *Am* skillfully, cleverly; *(juger)* shrewdly; *(finir un discours etc)* neatly; **se défendre a.** to defend oneself skilfully *or* adroitly

adr. tél. *abrév* **adresse télégraphique**

ADSL [adeesɛl] NF *(abrév* **Asynchronous Digital Subscriber Line)** ADSL

adsorber [atsɔrbe] VT *Phys, Biol* to adsorb

adsorption [atsɔrpsjɔ̃] NF *Phys, Biol* adsorption

adulateur, -trice [adylatœr, -tris] N *Litt* adulator; *(flatteur)* sycophant

adulation [adylasjɔ̃] NF *Arch* adulation, flattery *(de* of); *Péj* sycophancy

aduler [adyle] VT to idolize

adulte [adylt] ADJ *(personne)* adult, grown-up; *(plante, animal)* mature, fully grown; **l'âge a.** adulthood; **atteindre l'âge a.** to reach adulthood; **à l'âge a.** when fully grown; **ça n'est pas très a., cette réaction** that is not a very mature way to react
 N adult, grown-up

adultère [adyltɛr] ADJ adulterous
 N adulterer, *f* adulteress
 NM *(infidélité)* adultery; **commettre un a.** to commit adultery; **pour cause d'a.** for reasons of adultery, on grounds of adultery

adultérin [adylterɛ̃] ADJ *Jur* **enfant a.** child conceived in adultery, adulterine child

ad valorem [advalɔrɛm] ADJ, ADV ad valorem

advenir [advǝnir] V IMPERS *(conj like* venir) to occur, to happen, *Litt* to befall, to chance; **or, il advint que …** now it came to pass that …; **quoi qu'il advienne** no matter what happens; **advienne que pourra** come what may

adventice [advɑ̃tis] ADJ *(imprévu)* adventitious; *(sans cause ou but précis)* casual

adventif, -ive [advɑ̃tif, -iv] ADJ *Bot (racine etc)* adventitious; *Géol (cône)* parasitic

adverbe [adverb] NM adverb; **a. de manière/ de temps** adverb of manner/time SEE GRAMMAR A19–24; B12–14

adverbial, -iale, -iaux, -iales [adverbjal, -jo] ADJ adverbial; **locution adverbiale** adverbial phrase

adversaire [adverser] N adversary, opponent; *(dans un conflit, une guerre)* enemy

adverse [advers] ADJ *(hostile)* adverse, unfavourable, *Am* unfavorable; **fortune a.** bad luck; **critique a.** unfavourable criticism; *Jur* **la partie a.** the opposing party, the other side; *Sport* **le camp a.** the opposing side

adversité [adversite] NF *Litt* **1** *(sort)* adversity, adverse circumstances **2** *(malheur)* misfortune, trial; **lutter contre l'a.** to fight in the face of adversity

advertorial [advertɔrjal] NM *Journ* advertorial

ad vitam aeternam [advitametɛrnam] ADV *Fam* from here to eternity, till kingdom come

AELE [aǝlǝ] NF *(abrév* **Association européenne de libre-échange)** EFTA

aérage [aera3] NM **1** *(d'une pièce etc)* ventilation, airing **2** *(de l'eau)* aeration

aérateur [aeratœr] NM ventilator, (air) vent

aération [aerasjɔ̃] NF = **aérage**

aéré [aere] ADJ airy, well-ventilated

aérer [aere] *(j'aère, n. aérons; j'aérerai)* VT **1** *(mine)* to ventilate; *(pièce, linge)* to air **2** *(eau)* to aerate **3** *(rendre moins dense) (texte, exposé etc)* to lighten
 VPR **s'aérer** to get some fresh air; **avoir besoin de s'a.** to need some fresh air *or* a breath of fresh air

aérien, -ienne [aerjɛ̃, -jɛn] ADJ **1** air; *(plante, racine)* aerial; *(phénomène etc)* atmospheric; *Mil* **les forces aériennes** the air force; **défense/attaque aérienne** air defence/raid; *Aviat* **compagnie aérienne** airline; **poste aérienne** airmail; **expédier par fret a.** to airfreight **2** *(texture etc)* (light and) airy; *(grâce, allure, démarche etc)* light, floating; **marcher d'un pas a.** to have a spring in one's step **3** *(câble etc)* overhead; *(voie ferrée)* elevated

aérium [aerjɔm] NM (open-air) sanatorium

aéro- [aerɔ, -o] PRÉF aero-

aérobic [aerobik] NM aerobics; **professeur/ cours d'a.** aerobics teacher/class; **faire de l'a.** to do aerobics

aérobie [aerobi] ADJ aerobic

aérocâble [aerokɑbl] NM cableway

aéro-club, *pl* **aéro-clubs** NM flying *or* aero club

aérodrome [aerodrom] NM aerodrome, airfield, *Am* airdrome

aérodynamique [aerodinamik] ADJ aerodynamic; *(forme, voiture)* streamlined
 NF aerodynamics

aérodynamisme [aerodinamism] NM aerodynamics

aérodyne [aerodin] NM aerodyne

aérofrein [aerofrɛ̃] NM *Aviat* air brake

aérogare [aerogar] NF air terminal, terminal building

aérogastrie [aerogastri] NF *Méd* aerogastria

aéroglisseur [aeroglisœr] NM hovercraft

aérogramme [aerogram] NM airmail letter

aérographe [aerograf] NM airbrush; **retoucher qch à l'a.** to airbrush sth; **ajouter/effacer qch à l'a.** to airbrush sth in/out

aérologie [aerolɔ3i] NF aerology

aéromodélisme [aeromɔdelism] NM model aircraft making

aéromoteur [aeromɔtœr] NM wind engine

aéronaute [aeronot] N aeronaut

aéronautique [aeronotik] ADJ aeronautic(al)
 NF aeronautics; **ingénieur d'a.** aeronautical engineer

aéronaval, -ale, -als, -ales [aeronaval] ADJ *(forces etc)* air and sea
 NF **l'Aéronavale** *Br* ≃ the Fleet Air Arm, *Am* ≃ the Naval Air Service

aéronef [aeronɛf] NM aircraft; *(dirigeable)* airship

aérophagie [aerofa3i] NF **avoir** *ou* **faire de l'a.** to suffer from flatulence

aérophotographie [aerofotografi] NF aerial photography

aéroplane [aeroplan] NM *Vieilli* aeroplane, *Am* airplane

aéropoint [aeropwɛ̃] NM *Aviat* ≃ airmile; **accumuler des aéropoints** to collect airmiles

aéroport [aeropɔr] NM airport; **a. de destination** airport of destination, destination airport; **a. de départ** airport of departure, departure airport; **a. de déroutement** diverting airport; **a. de remplacement** alternative airport; **Aéroports de Paris** Paris Airports Authority

aéroporté [aeropɔrte] ADJ airborne

aéroportuaire [aeropɔrtɥer] ADJ *(équipement, installations etc)* airport

aéropostal, -ale, -aux, -ales [aeropɔstal, -o] ADJ airmail
 NF *Hist* **l'Aéropostale** the (French) airmail service

aérosol [aerosɔl] NM aerosol; **vendu en a.** sold in aerosol *or* spray form
 ADJ INV aerosol; **bombe a.** aerosol (can)

aérospatial, -iale, -iaux, -iales [aerospasjal, -jo] ADJ *(équipement etc)* aerospace

aérostat [aerosta] NM balloon, aerostat

aérostatique [aerostatik] ADJ aerostatic
 NF aerostatics

aérostier [aerostje] NM balloonist

Aérotrain® [aerotrɛ̃] NM hovertrain

aérotransporté [aerotrɑ̃spɔrte] ADJ *(marchandises, passagers, troupes)* airborne

AF *abrév* **1** allocations familiales **2** Air France

AFB [aɛfbe] NF *(abrév* **Association française des banques)** = French Bankers' Association

affabilité [afabilite] NF graciousness, affability *(avec, envers* to, towards); **être d'une grande a.** to be very gracious *or* affable

affable [afabl] ADJ gracious, affable *(envers, avec* to, towards, with)

affablement [afabləmɑ̃] ADV graciously, affably

affabulateur, -trice [afabylatœr, -tris] ADJ **qu'est-ce que tu peux être a.** you're too fond of telling tall stories
 N fibber, storyteller

affabulation [afabylasjɔ̃] NF fabrication(s), distortion(s); **les résultats publiés ne sont qu'une a.** the published results are pure invention

affabuler [afabyle] VI to invent things, to make things up

affacturage [afaktyra3] NM *Com* factoring

affactureur [afaktyrœr] NM *Com* factor

affadir [afadir] VT *(nourriture etc)* to make insipid *or* tasteless; *(couleur, style, personnalité etc)* to make dull *or* uninteresting
 VPR **s'affadir** *(nourriture etc)* to become insipid; *(couleur, style, personnalité etc)* to become dull *or* uninteresting

affaiblir [afeblir] VT **1** *(réduire)* to lessen, to reduce; **l'usage a affaibli le sens du mot** the meaning of the word has become weakened through overuse; **a. le courage de qn** to dampen sb's courage; *Phot* **a. un cliché** to reduce (the contrasts of) a negative **2** *(d'une maladie)* to weaken, *Fml* to enfeeble, to debilitate; **affaibli par la maladie** weakened by illness
 VPR **s'affaiblir 1** *(devenir faible)* to grow *or* become weak(er) *or* feeble(r), to lose one's strength; *(d'un son)* to become *or* grow fainter; **ma vue s'affaiblit rapidement** my eyesight is deteriorating *or* failing rapidly; **mes forces s'affaiblissaient** my strength was failing; **la tempête s'affaiblit** the storm is abating **2** *(s'atténuer)* **le sens du mot s'affaiblit au XVIe siècle** the word took on a weaker meaning in the 16th century

affaiblissement [afeblismɑ̃] NM **1** weakening; *(de la force etc)* diminution; *(du sens d'un mot)* weakening; *TV (de signaux)* attenuation; **a. de la lumière** dimming (of the light) **2** *(faiblesse)* weakness; *Méd* debility

affaiblisseur [afeblisœr] NM *Phot* reducer

affaire [afer] NF **1** business, concern; **ce n'est pas votre a.** it's not your business, it's none of your business; **occupez-vous de vos affaires** mind your own business; **ça, c'est mon a.** that's my business; *(je m'en occupe)* (you can) leave that to me; **mettre le nez dans les affaires de qn** to stick one's nose into sb's business; **mettre de l'ordre dans ses affaires** to put one's affairs in order; **ce n'est pas l'a. de tout le monde** not everybody can do that; **c'est l'a. d'un médecin** it's a case for a doctor; **a. d'argent** money matter; **a. de cœur** love affair; **a. d'honneur** duel; **a. de conscience** matter of conscience; **a. difficile** difficult question *or* matter; **c'est (une) a. de goût** it's a matter *or* question of taste; **ce n'est que l'a. d'un instant** it won't take a minute; **ça, c'est une autre a.** that's another question *or* another matter; **avoir a. à** to deal with; **nous avons eu a. à un homme charmant** we were dealt with by a charming man; **s'il continue à mentir, il aura a. à moi!** if he keeps on lying, he'll have me to contend with *or* me to answer to!

2 *(compte)* **ça fait mon a.** that's just what I need *or* what I was looking for; **cela ne fera pas l'a.** that won't do; **il fera votre a.** he's just the man for you; **cela devrait tout à fait faire mon a.** that should do the trick; **faire son a. à qn** *Fam* to give sb what he deserves *or* what he's asking for *or* what was coming to him; *Arg (le tuer)* to do sb in, to bump sb off **3** *(ennui)* (difficult *or* serious) business; **c'est une a. de pots-de-vin qui a fait la une des journaux** it's a case of bribery which made the headlines; **c'est une sale/drôle a.** it's a nasty/funny business; **il cherche à étouffer l'a.** he's trying to hush up the whole affair; **ce n'est pas une petite a., c'est toute une a.** it's quite a business; **je n'en fais pas une a.** I'm not making an issue of it; **en voilà une a.!** here's a nice mess *or* a nice kettle of fish!; *(ce n'était pas la peine)* it's a lot of fuss about nothing!; **la belle a.!** is that all?, so what?; **se tirer d'a.** to get out of a difficulty; **tirer qn d'a.** to get sb out of trouble *or* out of the woods; **les médecins vont pouvoir le tirer d'a.** the doctors will be able to pull him through; **se faire une a. de qch** to get all worked up about sth; *Pol* **l'a. de Suez** the Suez crisis; **l'a. est encore chaude** *(toute la presse en parle)* it's still very much in the news, it's still hot news **4** *(transaction)* (business) transaction, deal; *(achat à bon marché)* bargain; **une bonne/mauvaise a.** a good/bad deal; **on fait des affaires dans ce magasin** you get good bargains in this shop; **être dur en affaires** *(homme)* to be a hard-headed businessman; *(femme)* to be a hard-headed businesswoman; **ils font des affaires en or** they're coining it, they're making money hand over fist, they're raking it in; **faire a. avec qn** to do a deal with sb; **faire des affaires avec qn** to do business with sb; **il est sur une a. avec le Mozambique** he's doing a deal with Mozambique; **chiffre d'affaires** turnover; **homme d'affaires** businessman; *(d'un sportif etc)* business manager; **femme d'affaires** businesswoman; **voyage d'affaires** business trip; **déjeuner d'affaires** business *or* working lunch; **droit des affaires** corporate law; **avocat d'affaires** corporate lawyer **5** **les affaires** business; **être dans les affaires** to be a businessman/businesswoman; **comment vont les affaires?** how's business?; **parler affaires** to talk business *or* *Fam* shop; **les affaires sont les affaires (et on ne fait de cadeaux à personne)** business is business (and nobody gets any favours *or* anything for nothing) **6** *(entreprise)* firm, business; **une grosse a.** a large firm **7** **affaires** *(effets personnels)* things, possessions, belongings; **tu peux mettre tes affaires dans le vestibule** you can put your things in the hall; **ranger ses affaires** to put one's things away, to tidy up one's things; **mettre de l'ordre dans ses affaires** to tidy up; **mets tes petites affaires dans ce sac** put your small things in this bag; *Hum* **il est en train de préparer ses petites affaires** he's sorting out his bits and pieces **8** *Pol* **les affaires de l'État** affairs of state; **ce n'est pas une a. d'État** it's of no great importance; **on ne va pas en faire une a. d'État** we're not going to make a big issue of it; **le ministère des Affaires étrangères** *Br* ≃ the Foreign (and Commonwealth) Office, *Am* ≃ the State Department; **ministre des Affaires étrangères** *Br* ≃ Foreign (and Commonwealth) Secretary, *Am* ≃ Secretary of State; *Can* **Ministère des Affaires extérieures** External Affairs Department

affairé [afere] ADJ busy; **ils entraient et sortaient d'un air a.** they were bustling in and out; **être a. à faire qch** to be busy doing sth

affairement [afermɑ̃] NM bustle, bustling activity

affairer (s') [safere] VPR to be busy, to busy oneself; **s'a. autour de qn** to fuss (a)round sb; **s'a. à tout remettre en place** to be busy tidying up

affairisme [aferism] NM *Péj* wheeling and dealing

affairiste [aferist] N *Péj* wheeler-dealer; **ce n'est qu'un a.** he thinks of nothing but making money *or* getting rich *or* *Am* making a fast buck

affaissement [afɛsmɑ̃] NM **1** *(de terrain)* subsidence, sinking; *(d'une fondation)* settling; *(du plancher, d'une poutre)* sagging; **il y a eu un a. de terrain** there was (land) subsidence **2** *(accablement)* depression, dejection, despondency; *Méd* prostration, collapse; **l'a. de l'enthousiasme** the waning of enthusiasm; **l'a. du moral** the collapse of morale

affaisser (s') [safɛse] VPR **1** *(du terrain)* to subside; *(d'une poutre, d'un fauteuil etc)* to sag **2** *(tomber, s'écrouler) (dans une chaise)* to sink down *or* back; *(de fatigue etc)* to collapse **3** *Fig Litt (décliner)* to decline, to sink; **il s'affaisse de jour en jour** he is declining *or* sinking day by day

affaler [afale] VT *(objet)* to lower; *Naut* **a. la voile** to lower the sail; **affale!** lower away!
▸ VPR **s'affaler** to collapse; **s'a. par terre** to sink to the ground; **s'a. dans un fauteuil** to sink *or* *Fam* flop into an armchair

affamé, -ée [afame] ADJ hungry, *Fam* starving, ravenous, famished; *(mourant de faim)* starving; **regarder qch d'un œil a.** to look hungrily at sth; *Fig* **être a. de succès/d'argent** to be hungry for success/money
▸ N **les affamés** the hungry, the starving

affamer [afame] VT to starve

affectation [afɛktasjɔ̃] NF **1** *Péj (pose)* affectation, affectedness; *(simulacre)* pretence, affectation; **parler avec a.** to speak affectedly; **être sans a.** to be without affectation, to be unaffected; **sans a.** *(dire etc qch)* without affectation, unaffectedly; **avec une a. de générosité** with a show of generosity **2** *(fait de désigner)* assignment, allocation, allotment; **l'a. de subventions à une association** the allocation of subsidies to an association; **a. des places** seating plan **3** *Mil etc* assignment, posting; **avoir une** *ou* **être en a. spéciale** ≃ to be in a reserved occupation **4** *Ordinat (de touche)* assignment; **a. de mémoire** memory allocation
▸▸ **affectations budgétaires** budget appropriations; **a. de fonds** appropriation of funds; **a. hypothécaire** mortgage charge

affecté [afɛkte] ADJ *Péj (personne, manière)* affected

affecter [afɛkte] VT **1** *(destiner)* to assign (à to), to allocate, to earmark; **a. des fonds à** to allocate funds to **2** *(désigner) (employé)* to assign, to appoint; *Mil (soldat, détachement)* to detail, to post, to draft; *Naut* **être affecté à un navire** to be posted to a ship **3** *(feindre)* to feign, to affect; **a. de faire qch** to pretend to do sth; **a. la désinvolture la plus complète** to feign *or* affect an extremely offhand attitude **4** *(toucher) (personne)* to affect, to move; **vivement affecté par la nouvelle** greatly moved by the news **5** *(agir sur) (carrière, santé etc)* to affect, to have an effect on; **la grève a affecté plusieurs usines** the strike has affected *or* hit several factories; **les pluies qui affectent le nord de l'Europe** the rain affecting *or* over northern Europe

6 *(prendre) (forme, couleur etc)* to assume, to take on
▸ VPR **s'affecter** to be troubled *or* unsettled; **elle s'affecte de la moindre dispute** she is upset by the slightest argument

affectif, -ive [afɛktif, -iv] ADJ emotional, *Spéc* affective; **sa vie affective** his emotional life

affection [afɛksjɔ̃] NF **1** *(attachement)* affection, fondness, liking (**pour** for); **une preuve d'a.** a show of affection; **en manque d'a.** in need of affection; **prendre qn en a.** to become attached to *or* fond of sb; **terme d'a.** term of affection; **avoir de l'a. pour qn** to feel *or* have affection for sb, to be fond of sb; **avec a.** affectionately **2** *Méd* disease, complaint, ailment; **a. cutanée** skin disorder *or* complaint

affectionné [afɛksjɔne] ADJ affectionate, loving; **votre cousin(e) affectionné(e)** *(dans une lettre)* your affectionate cousin

affectionner [afɛksjɔne] VT *(ami, connaissance etc)* to be attached to, to be fond of; *(chiens etc)* to like; **affectionné de tous loved by all**; **le genre de petits plats qu'il affectionne** the type of food he likes *or* is fond of

affectivité [afɛktivite] NF affectivity

affectueusement [afɛktɥøzmɑ̃] ADV affectionately; **a. à tous** *(dans une lettre)* love to all

affectueux, -euse [afɛktɥø, -øz] ADJ affectionate, loving

afférent [aferɑ̃] ADJ **1** *Jur* **la part afférente à** the portion accruing to **2** **a. à** *(concernant)* relating to, relevant to, pertaining to **3** *Méd* afferent

affermage [afɛrmaʒ] NM **1** *(d'un bien rural)* tenant farming **2** *(d'un emplacement publicitaire)* contracting

affermer [afɛrme] VT *(ferme etc)* to lease, to rent; *(terre etc)* to take on lease; *(emplacement publicitaire)* to contract for

affermir [afɛrmir] VT **1** *(fondations etc)* to strengthen, to make firm; **crème pouvant a. les chairs** toning *or* firming cream **2** *(pouvoir, croyance)* to strengthen, to consolidate; *(santé)* to improve; **a. sa voix** to strengthen one's voice; **a. qn dans sa position** to strengthen *or* consolidate sb in his/her position
▸ VPR **s'affermir** to become stronger, to strengthen; *(du ciment)* to harden; *(des chairs, des muscles)* to firm up

affermissement [afɛrmismɑ̃] NM strengthening; *(du pouvoir etc)* consolidation; *(d'un ciment)* hardening; *(des chairs, des muscles)* firming up

affichage [afiʃaʒ] NM **1** *(pose d'affiches)* billsticking, billposting; **a. interdit** stick *or* *Am* post no bills; **tableau** *ou* **panneau d'a.** notice board, *Am* bulletin board; *(dans aéroport, gare)* arrivals and departures (board) **2** *Ordinat* display; **horloge/montre à a. digital** *ou* **numérique** digital clock/watch **3** *Cin* billing **4** *Aviat* visual indicator
▸▸ *Ordinat* **a. couleur** colour display; **a. à cristaux liquides** liquid crystal display; **a. digital** digital display *or* readout; **a. dynamique** *(publicité)* mobile advertising; *Ordinat* **a. graphique** graphics display; *Ordinat* **a. inversé** reverse video; **a. mobile** *(publicité)* mobile advertising; *Ordinat* **a. non entrelacé** non-interlaced display; *Ordinat* **a. numérique** digital display; *Ordinat* **a. à plasma** plasma display; **a. des prix** price display; **a. routier** *(publicité)* roadside advertising; *Ordinat* **a. rural** *(publicité)* rural advertising; *Ordinat* **a. tel écran-tel écrit, a. tel-tel** WYSIWYG; *Ordinat* **a. TFT** TFT display; **a. transport** *(publicité)* public transport advertising, transportation advertising; **a. urbain** *(publi-*

cité) urban (poster) advertising; *Ordinat* **a. vectoriel** vector graphics

affiche [afiʃ] NF poster, bill; *(de protestation)* placard; *(de publicité)* advertisement; **colleur d'affiches** billsticker, bill poster; **a. à la main** handbill; **a. électorale** election poster; **affiches publicitaires** advertisements; **a. de théâtre** playbill; **être à l'a.** *(de spectacle)* to be on, to be showing; **les pièces à l'a.** the plays now on *or* now showing; **la pièce a tenu l'a.** *ou* est restée à l'a. **pendant deux ans** the play ran for two years; **tenir longtemps l'a.** to have a long run; **qui tient l'a.** long-running; **mettre à l'a.** to put on, to stage; **quitter l'a.** to close; **être en tête d'a.** to be top of the bill, to have top billing

afficher [afiʃe] VT **1** *(annonce, affiche)* to stick (up), to post (up); *(prix)* to display; **a. une vente** to advertise a sale, *Am* to post a sale; **défense d'a.** stick *or Am* post no bills; **a. complet** *(d'un spectacle)* to be sold out **2** *(montrer, étaler)* to parade, to show off, to flaunt, to make a display of; *(mépris, indifférence)* to put on; **a. son savoir** to air *or* flaunt one's knowledge; **a. son ignorance** to display *or* expose *or* betray one's ignorance; **a. sa pauvreté** to plead poverty; **derrière cette nonchalance affichée** behind this outwardly casual air; **a. son nouvel amant** to flaunt *or* parade one's latest lover; *Com* **a. un déficit/un excédent** to show a deficit/a surplus **3** *Ordinat (message)* to display; *(fichiers, articles)* to show; **l'écran affiche ...** the on-screen message appears ..., the screen displays the message ...

VPR **s'afficher 1** *(d'une personne)* **elle s'affiche avec un homme plus âgé qu'elle** she's flaunting herself with an older man **2** *(sur un écran)* to be displayed **3** *Fam (se ridiculiser)* to make an idiot of oneself; **il a fait tomber ses lunettes dans le bol de punch; je te dis pas comment il s'est affiché!** his glasses fell off into the punch bowl, what an idiot he made of himself!

affichette [afiʃet] NF small poster *or* advertisement

afficheur [afiʃœr] NM **1** *(colleur d'affiches)* billsticker, billposter; *(entreprise d'affichage)* poster advertising company **2** *Ordinat* VDU, visual display unit; **a. LCD** LCD display; **a. à cristaux liquides** liquid crystal display

affichiste [afiʃist] N poster designer

affidavit [afidavit] NM *Jur* affidavit

affidé, -ée [afide] N *Péj* accomplice

affilage [afilaʒ] NM sharpening, whetting

affilée (d') [dafile] ADV **cinq heures d'a.** five hours at a stretch *or* at a time *or* on end; **lire vingt chapitres d'a.** to read twenty chapters in one go *or* straight off *or* at one sitting

affiler [afile] VT *(lame etc)* to sharpen, to whet, to put an edge on; *Fig* **avoir la langue bien affilée** *(être méchant)* to have a sharp *or* wicked tongue

affiliation [afiljasjɔ̃] NF affiliation; **demander son a. à un club** to apply for membership to a club; **l'a. d'un membre à un club** a member's affiliation to a club

affilié, -ée [afilje] ADJ affiliated
N affiliated member

affilier [afilje] VT to affiliate (**à** to, with)
VPR **s'affilier** to join; *(d'une organisation)* to become affiliated; **s'a. à un parti** to join a party

affin [afɛ̃] ADJ *Ling* related, cognate; *Math* affine

affinage [afinaʒ] NM *Métal* refining; *(de l'acier, du fer)* smelting; *(du vin, du fromage)* maturing

affinement [afinmɑ̃] NM refinement

affiner [afine] VT **1** *(purifier)* to improve, to refine, to make better; *(fer, or)* to refine; *(fromage etc)* to ripen, to mature **2** *(intelligence)* to sharpen; *(goût, plaisir etc)* to refine; **ces livres ont affiné son jugement** these books have sharpened his judgment

VPR **s'affiner 1** *(d'une personne)* to become more refined; *(des traits)* to become finer; *(de l'intelligence)* to become sharper; **elle s'est affinée en suivant un nouveau régime** she has lost weight *or* slimmed down on her new diet **2** *(du fromage etc)* to ripen, to mature

affinité [afinite] NF **1** *(entre personnes)* affinity (**entre** between); *(physique)* resemblance; *(de caractère)* similarity of character; **nous avons une grande a. de goûts** we have many tastes in common **2** *Chimie* attraction; **a. pour un corps** affinity for a body

affirmatif, -ive [afirmatif, -iv] ADJ **1** affirmative, positive; **réponse affirmative** affirmative answer, answer in the affirmative; **signe a.** nod (of agreement); **faire un signe a. de la tête** to nod in agreement **2** *(personne)* assertive, positive; **il a été très a.** he was very definite
NF **l'affirmative** the affirmative; **dans l'affirmative** if so, if the answer is yes, if you can; **répondre par l'affirmative** to answer in the affirmative, to say *or* answer yes
INT affirmative

affirmation [afirmasjɔ̃] NF affirmation, assurance, assertion, statement; **a. trop générale** sweeping statement; **a. de soi** self-assertion; **a. de la personnalité** assertion of one's personality
▶▶ *Jur* **a. de créance** proof of debt; **a. sous serment** affidavit; *(lors d'un procès etc)* statement on oath

affirmativement [afirmativmɑ̃] ADV in the affirmative

affirmer [afirme] VT **1** *(soutenir)* to maintain; **il affirme vous connaître** he maintains that he knows you; **je ne peux rien a.** I can't say anything for certain; **je n'affirmerais pas que ...** I wouldn't swear to it that ...; **a. qch sous serment** to state sth on oath *or* on affidavit **2** *(manifester, prouver)* to assert; **a. son autorité** to assert one's authority, to make one's authority felt; **a. son amitié** to declare one's friendship
VPR **s'affirmer 1** *(s'exprimer pleinement)* *(d'une personne)* to assert oneself **2** *(se révéler)* **son talent s'affirme peu à peu** his/her talent is gradually expressing itself *or* becoming apparent; **beaucoup de vos observations se sont affirmées justes** many of your observations have proved correct *or* have been confirmed; **cet ordinateur s'est affirmé le plus performant de tous** this computer has established itself as the best performer

affleurement [aflœrmɑ̃] NM *Géol* outcrop

affleurer [aflœre] VT *(bois de charpente etc)* to bring to the same level, to make flush; **a. à qch** to be level *or* even *or* flush with sth
VI *aussi Fig* to float *or* rise to the surface; *Géol (d'un filon)* to outcrop; *Fig* **l'espace d'une seconde il laissa a. ses sentiments** for a second he let his feelings show through

affliction [afliksjɔ̃] NF affliction, sorrow; **plongé dans l'a.** deeply distressed

affligé, -ée [afliʒe] ADJ **1** *(atteint)* afflicted, troubled (**de** with) **2** *(peiné)* grieved, distressed
N **les affligés** the afflicted

affligeant [afliʒɑ̃] ADJ *(nouvelle, vision)* distressing, painful; **manque d'imagination a.** pitiful *or* appalling lack of imagination

affliger [afliʒe] *(j'affligeai(s); n. affligeons)* VT **1** *(atteindre)* to afflict (**de** with); **région que le choléra afflige** area afflicted with cholera; **la nature l'a affligé d'un grand nez** nature has cursed him with a big nose **2** *(peiner)* to pain, to distress, to grieve; **la nouvelle l'a profondément affligé** the news deeply distressed him *or* caused him great distress
VPR **s'affliger** to be grieved *or* distressed (**de qch** about sth); **ne vous affligez pas ainsi** don't take it so much to heart

affluence [aflyɑ̃s] NF *(de personnes)* crowd; *(de marchandises)* abundance; **heures d'a.** *(transports)* rush hours; *(dans les magasins etc)* peak hours

affluent [aflyɑ̃] NM *(d'une rivière)* tributary

affluer [aflye] VI *(d'un liquide)* to flow (**vers** towards; **dans** into); *(du sang)* to rush, to flow (**à** to); **a. à** *ou* **dans un endroit** to crowd *or* flock to a place

afflux [afly] NM *Méd etc (de sang)* rush; *Élec (de courant)* surge; *(de visiteurs)* crowd; *Compta* **a. de capitaux** inflow *or* influx of capital, capital inflow

affolant [afɔlɑ̃] ADJ *(spectacle, nouvelle)* distressing, horrifying; *Fam* **c'est a.** *(ce qu'elle a grandi etc)* it's frightening *or* incredible

affolé [afɔle] ADJ **1** demented, frantic, panic-stricken; **il était a.** he was scared out of his wits **2** *Tech (aiguille du compas)* spinning, crazy

affolement [afɔlmɑ̃] NM **1** *(de personne)* panic, *Fam* flap; **voyons, pas d'a.** come on, there's no need to panic; **dans un moment d'a.** in a moment of panic, in a panic-stricken moment **2** *(d'une aiguille magnétique)* perturbation, unsteadiness, spinning **3** *(d'un moteur, d'une hélice etc)* racing; *(d'une poulie etc)* disconnecting

affoler [afɔle] VT **1** *(personne)* to madden, to drive crazy *or* to distraction; *(foule)* to throw into a panic **2** *(aiguille de compas)* to disturb, to perturb
VPR **s'affoler 1** *(paniquer)* to panic, to get in(to) a panic, *Fam* to lose one's head; **s'a. pour un rien** to get into a flap about nothing **2** *(d'une aiguille de compas)* to spin **3** *(d'une machine)* to begin to race

affouiller [afuje] VT *(de l'eau)* *(rive, fondation etc)* to undermine, to erode, to wash away, to lay bare

affranchi, -ie [afrɑ̃ʃi] ADJ **1** *(esclave)* free(d), emancipated; *Fig* **un esprit a.** an open mind; **un esprit a. des préjugés** a mind free from prejudice **2** *(lettre)* stamped, with a stamp on; **lettre bien/mal affranchie** letter with/without enough stamps on it
N **1** *(esclave)* emancipated slave **2** *(marginal)* free spirit

affranchir [afrɑ̃ʃir] VT **1** *(esclave etc)* to free, to set free, to emancipate; **a. qn/qch de qch** to free *or* release sb/sth from sth; **par son attitude très cordiale, il nous a affranchis de toute gêne** his friendly attitude ensured that we didn't feel in the least awkward **2** *(envoi)* to pay the postage on; *(tamponner)* *(lettre)* to frank, to stamp; **colis affranchi** pre-paid parcel; **machine à a. (les lettres)** franking machine, franker **3** *Cartes (couleur)* to unblock **4** *Fam (renseigner)* **a. qn** to put sb in the picture
VPR **s'affranchir s'a. du joug** to cast off the yoke; **s'a. d'une habitude** to break (oneself of) a habit; **s'a. d'idées préconçues** to rid oneself of preconceived ideas

affranchissement [afrɑ̃ʃismɑ̃] NM **1** *(d'un esclave etc)* emancipation, setting free **2** *(de lettre)* prepayment; *(fait de tamponner)* stamping, franking; *(montant payé) (de lettre, de paquet etc)* postage, carriage; **tarif d'a.** postage rate

affranchisseuse [afrɑ̃ʃisøz] NF franking machine, franker

affres [afr] NFPL *Litt* (*angoisse*) (spasm of) anguish; (*du doute etc*) agonies, horrors; **a. de la mort** death throes; **a. de la faim** pangs of hunger, hunger pangs; **découvrir toutes les a. de l'humiliation** to discover the agonies of humiliation

affrètement [afretmɑ̃] NM charter, *Fml* affreightment; **a. au voyage** trip charter; **a. à temps** time charter

affréter [afrete] VT (**j'affrète, n. affrétons; j'affréterai**) (*navire, avion*) to charter

affréteur [afretœr] NM *Naut* charterer; *Aut* **a. routier** road haulier

affreusement [afrøzmɑ̃] ADV (*en retard*) terribly, frightfully; (*blessé, torturé*) horribly; (*défiguré*) horribly, shockingly; **je suis a. coiffée** my hair's a mess; **il parle a. mal l'anglais** his English is awful

affreux, -euse [afrø, -øz] ADJ **1** (*laid*) horrible, hideous, dreadful, ghastly; **un visage a.** a horrible *or* hideous face; **il est a.** he's terribly *or* horribly ugly; **un a. petit chapeau / chien** a horrible *or* an ugly little hat/dog **2** (*atroce*) (*nouvelles, pauvreté, crime etc*) awful, horrible, dreadful, shocking **3** *Fam* (*détestable*) awful, dreadful; **mal de tête a.** splitting headache; **qu'est-ce que ça a augmenté, c'est a.!** it's dreadful *or* shocking how the price has gone up!; **c'est a. ce qu'il y a comme monde!** it's dreadfully *or* awfully busy!; **ce gamin est un a. jojo** that child is a (frightful) little horror; **temps a.** filthy *or* shocking weather
▸ N **1** *Mil Fam* white mercenary (*usually in Africa*) **2** *Fam* (*vilain personnage*) **c'est un a.** he's a nasty piece of work

affriander [afrijɑ̃de] VT *Litt* to entice, to allure

affriolant [afrijɔlɑ̃] ADJ (*décolleté, vêtement*) alluring, tantalizing; **ce travail n'a rien d'a.** it's not the world's most exciting job

affrioler [afrijɔle] VT to excite, to tempt

affriquée [afrike] NF *Ling* affricate (consonant)

affront [afrɔ̃] NM affront, insult, *Fam* slap in the face; **subir un a.** to be affronted *or* insulted; **faire** *ou* **infliger un a. à qn** to affront *or* insult sb; (*snober qn*) to snub sb; **doubler ses torts d'un a.** to add insult to injury

affrontement [afrɔ̃tmɑ̃] NM **1** (*de l'ennemi, du danger etc*) confrontation, confronting, clash; **l'a. de deux personnalités différentes** the clash *or* conflict of two different personalities **2** (*de deux choses*) joining edge to edge; *Chir* bringing into apposition

affronter [afrɔ̃te] VT **1** (*personne, chose*) to face, to confront, to brave, to tackle; **a. une épreuve avec courage** to face *or* meet an ordeal bravely; **a. la colère de qn** to brave the wrath of sb **2** (*mettre de front*) (*plaques de métal etc*) to bring together; *Chir* to bring into apposition **3** *Sport* to meet, to clash with
▸ VPR **s'affronter** (*d'ennemis etc*) to clash, to confront each other; *Sport* (*de deux équipes, joueurs etc*) to meet, to clash; **leurs personnalités s'affrontent constamment** their personalities clash constantly; **deux thèses s'affrontent** there are two conflicting theories

affubler [afyble] *Péj* VT **a. qn de qch** to dress sb up in sth, to deck *or* rig sb out in sth; **elle m'affublait toujours des pires guenilles** she always made me wear the most awful old rags
▸ VPR **s'affubler** to rig *or* deck oneself out, to get oneself up (**de** in); **il s'affuble souvent des vêtements les plus ridicules** he often gets himself all rigged out in the most ridiculous clothes

affût [afy] NM **1** (*guet*) hiding place; (*pour observatoire d'oiseaux etc*) hide; **chasse au cerf à l'a.** deer stalking; **être** *ou* **se mettre à l'a. de** (*personne*) to lie in wait for; (*être vigilant*) (*vis-à-vis de qn, qch*) to be on the watch *or* lookout for; *Fig* **être à l'a. de qch** to be on the lookout for sth **2** *Mil* carriage; (*d'un télescope etc*) mounting

affûtage [afytaʒ] NM **1** (*d'outils*) sharpening, grinding; (*d'une scie*) setting **2** set of bench tools

affûter [afyte] VT (*outil*) to grind, to sharpen, to whet; (*scie*) to set; *Fig* (*esprit*) to sharpen; *Courses de chevaux* **a. un cheval** to bring a horse to the top of its form

affûteur [afytœr] NM (tool) grinder, sharpener; (*de scies*) setter

affûteuse [afytøz] NF grinding machine

afghan, -ane [afgɑ̃, -an] ADJ Afghan
▸ N **A.** Afghan
▸ NM *Ling* Afghan

Afghanistan [afganistɑ̃] NM Afghanistan

aficionado, -os [afisjɔnado, -os] NM aficionado; **les aficionados du vélo** cycling enthusiasts

afin [afɛ̃] ADV **1 a. de faire qch** (in order) to, so as to do sth **2 a. que** + *sub* so that, in order that, *Fml, Litt* that; **a. que les autres puissent le voir** so that the others may see it SEE GRAMMAR A74; B58

AFNOR [afnɔr] NF (*abrév* **Association française de normalisation**) French industrial standards authority, *Br* ≃ BSI, *Am* ≃ ANSI

à-fond, *pl* **à-fonds** [afɔ̃] NM *Belg* **faire un à.** to down one's drink in one
▸ NMPL *Suisse* **à-fonds** spring-cleaning; **faire les à-fonds** to spring-clean, to do the spring-cleaning

a fortiori [afɔrsjɔri] ADV a fortiori, all the more so

AF-P [aɛfpe] NF *abrév* **Agence France-Presse**

AFPA [afpa] NF *abrév* **Association pour la formation professionnelle des adultes**

AFR [aɛfer] NF *abrév* **allocation de formation reclassement**

africain, -aine [afrikɛ̃, -ɛn] ADJ African
▸ N **A.** African

africanisation [afrikanizasjɔ̃] NF *Pol* Africanization

africaniser [afrikanize] VT to Africanize
▸ VPR **s'africaniser** to become Africanized

africaniste [afrikanist] N student of African races and languages

afrikaans [afrikɑ̃s] NM *Ling* Afrikaans

Afrikander [afrikɑ̃der] N Afrikaner

Afrique [afrik] NF Africa; **l'A. du Nord** North Africa; **l'A. du Sud** South Africa

afro [afro] ADJ (*coupe de cheveux*) Afro; **avoir une coiffure a.** to have an Afro; **à l'a.** Afro (style); **les cheveux à l'a.** Afro hair

afro-américain, -aine, *pl* **afro-américains, -aines** ADJ Afro-American, Black American
▸ N **A.** Afro-American, Black American

afro-asiatique, *pl* **afro-asiatiques** ADJ Afro-Asian
▸ N **A.** Afro-Asian

afro-cubain, -aine, *pl* **afro-cubains, -aines** ADJ Afro-Cuban
▸ N **A.** Afro-Cuban

after-shave [aftœrʃɛv] NM INV aftershave
▸ ADJ INV **lotion a.** aftershave (lotion)

A.G. [aʒe] *abrév* **assemblée générale**

agaçant [agasɑ̃] ADJ annoying, irritating, aggravating

agacement [agasmɑ̃] NM irritation, annoyance; **dire/témoigner son a.** to express/show one's annoyance *or* irritation

agacer [agase] VT (**j'agaçai(s); n. agaçons**) **1** (*dents*) to set on edge; (*nerfs*) to grate on, to set on edge **2** (*énerver*) **a. qn** to annoy sb, to irritate sb, to aggravate sb, to get on sb's nerves; **ça m'agace de t'entendre dire encore la même chose** it annoys me *or* gets on my nerves to hear you saying the same thing again; **a. un chien** to tease a dog; **il m'agace avec ses questions** he's getting on my nerves, asking all those questions; **elle m'agace, avec sa façon de faire l'enfant tout le temps** she gets on my nerves, the way she acts so childishly all the time

agaceries [agasri] NFPL charms, wiles; **faire des a.** to use one's charm(s) *or* wiles

agaceur, -euse [agasœr, -øz] ADJ *Can* irritating, annoying; **ce qu'il peut être a.!** he can be so annoying!

agapanthe [agapɑ̃t] NF *Bot* agapanthus

agape [agap] NF *Hum* agapes feast, spread; **nous allons faire des agapes chez Jeannot** we're going to have a real feast *or Fam* slap-up meal at Jeannot's

agar-agar, *pl* **agars-agars** [agaragar] NM agar-agar

agaric [agarik] NM (*champignon*) agaric

agate [agat] NF **1** *Minér* agate; **a. noire** *ou* **d'Islande** obsidian; **a. onyx** sardonyx **2** (*bille*) glass marble

agave, agavé [agav, agave] NM (*plante*) agave; **a. d'Amérique** American aloe, sisal-hemp

AGC [aʒese] NM *Phot* (*abrév* **adaptateur graphique couleur**) CGA

AGE [aʒeə] NF (*abrév* **assemblée générale extraordinaire**) EGM

âge [aʒ] NM **1** (*d'une personne*) age; **quel â. avez-vous?** how old are you?; **quand j'avais votre â.** when I was your age; **à ton â., je travaillais** when I was your age, I was working; **à ton â., on ne pleure plus** you're old enough now not to cry, at your age, you shouldn't be crying; **nous avons le même â., nous sommes du même â.** we are the same age; **à l'â. de six ans** at the age of six; **quel â. lui donnez-vous?** how old do you think he is *or* would you say he was?; **on ne lui donne pas du tout son â.** he doesn't look his age at all; **je ne sais pas quel â. lui donner** I don't know how old he can be; **accuser** *ou* **faire son â.** to look one's age; **dès son â. le plus tendre** *ou* **dès son plus jeune â.** from his/her earliest years; **un homme d'un certain â.** a middle-aged man; **en dépit de son grand â.** in spite of his/her great age; **mourir à un grand â.** *ou* **à un â. avancé** *ou* **à un bel â.** to die at a ripe old age; **un homme d'un grand â.** a very old man; **faire plus jeune que son â.** to look younger than one really is, not to look one's age; **il n'a pas d'â., on ne peut pas dire quel â. il a** it is difficult to tell how old he is; **être d'â. légal** to be of age; **être en â. de faire qch, être d'â. à faire qch** to be old enough to do sth; **j'ai passé l'â. de ce genre de choses** I've grown out of that kind of thing; **fréquenter des gens de son â.** to see people of one's own age; **ce n'est plus de mon â.** I'm too old for that type of thing; **être en â. de se marier** to be old enough *or* of an age to marry; **un whisky de 15 ans d'â.** a 15-year-old whisky; **hors d'â.** (*cheval*) aged; **le bas â.** infancy; **enfant en bas â.** infant; **le premier â.** childhood; (*tout premier*) infancy; **couches premier/deuxième â.** nappies for children up to 12 months old/between 12 and 18 months old; **le bel â.** youth; **l'â. ingrat** the awkward *or* difficult age; **sans â.** ageless; **avoir l'â. de raison** to have reached the age of reason; **l'â. d'homme** manhood; **l'â. adulte** adulthood; **être d'â. mûr** *ou* **entre deux âges** *ou* **d'un certain â.** to be middle-aged; **elle est bien pour son â.** she's marvellous for her age; **les maux qui viennent avec**

l'â. the aches and pains that come with old age; **un homme d'â.** an old man; **le troisième â.** retirement age; *(personnes)* the over-sixties; **les gens du troisième â.** the elderly, senior citizens, *Am* golden agers; **à l'â. que j'ai, à mon â.** at my age, at my time of life; **mourir avant l'â.** to die before one's time, to die young; **â. mental** mental age; **avoir un â. mental de six ans** to have a mental age of six; *Fig* **être dans** *ou* **à la fleur de l'â.** to be in the bloom *or* flower of youth; *Fig* **être dans la force de l'â.** to be in one's prime *or* the prime of life; *Fig* **le retour d'â.** the change of life **2** *(génération)* generation; **d'â. en â.** from generation to generation **3** *Hist* age, period, epoch; *Archéol* **l'â. de (la) pierre** the Stone Age; **l'â. de la pierre taillée** the Palaeolithic age; **l'â. de la pierre polie** the Neolithic age; **l'â. de** *ou* **du bronze** the Bronze Age; **l'â. de** *ou* **du fer** the Iron Age; *Hist* **le Moyen Â.** the Middle Ages; **costumes du Moyen Â.** medi(a)eval costumes; *Myth* **l'â. d'or** the golden age; **l'â. d'or du cinéma muet** the golden age of silent movies; **c'est une tradition qui est venue du fond des âges** it's a tradition which has come down through the ages

âgé [aʒe] **ADJ 1** *(qui a tel âge)* old, aged; **â. de dix ans** ten years old, ten years of age, aged ten; **je suis plus/moins â. que vous** I am older/younger than you **2** *(vieux)* old; *Litt* aged ['eidʒid]; **assez â.** elderly; **les personnes âgées** old *or* elderly people, senior citizens

Aged [aʒed] **NF** *abrév* **allocation de garde d'enfant à domicile**

agence [aʒãs] **NF 1** agency, bureau; **a. d'intérim** temping agency; **a. de publicité/de traduction** advertising/translation agency; **a. de renseignement(s)** information bureau; **a. de placement** employment agency *or* bureau; **a. de presse** press *or* news agency; **a. commerciale** *(d'agence de voyages etc)* public sales office; **a. conseil en communication** public relations *or* PR consultancy; *Com* **a. de distribution physique** physical distribution agency; **A. France-Presse** Agence France-Presse *(French national news agency)*; **a. maritime** shipping agency, forwarding agency; **Agence nationale pour l'emploi** *Br* ≃ Jobcentre, *Can* ≃ CEC; **a. de notation** credit rating agency, *Am* credit bureau; **a. de promotion des ventes** sales promotion agency; **a. de réceptif** ground handling agency, ground operator; **a. de réservation** booking agency; **a. de voyages de discompte** discount travel agency, bucket shop; **a. distributrice** *(d'agence de voyages)* retail travel agency; **a. photographique** photographic agency; **a. réceptive** ground handling agency; **a. de presse de télévision** television news agency; **a. de tourisme** *ou* **de voyages** travel agency *or* agent's; **a. immobilière** estate agent's *or* agency; **a. de recouvrements** debt collection agency **2** *(de banque)* branch office; **a. bancaire** bank branch

agencé [aʒãse] **ADJ** *Suisse (cuisine)* fitted

agencement [aʒãsmã] **NM 1** arrangement; *(des pièces d'une machine etc)* fitting (together); *(d'une maison, d'une radio, d'un embrayage etc)* layout; **a. de l'intrigue** *(d'un roman etc)* construction of the plot; **l'a. d'un spectacle** the way a show is put together **2 agencements** fixtures, fittings

agencer [aʒãse] **VT** (**j'agençai(s); n. agençons**) *(maison etc)* to lay out, to design; *(pièces de machine etc)* to fit (together), to adjust; **local bien agencé** well-designed premises; **phrases mal agencées** badly constructed sentences

VPR s'agencer to be laid out; **les parties du discours s'agencent bien/mal** the different

parts of the speech go/don't hang well together

agencier [aʒãsje] **NM** *Journ* news agency journalist

agenda [aʒɛ̃da] **NM** *(pour noter des rendez-vous, journal)* diary; *Ordinat* organizer, planner; **a. de poche/de bureau** pocket/desk diary; **a. organisateur** personal organizer, Filofax®; **a. de réservation** book *or* hotel register, reservations book; **a. électronique** personal organizer, electronic organizer

> Il faut noter que le nom anglais **agenda** est un faux ami. Il signifie **ordre du jour**.

agender [aʒãde] **VT** *Suisse (rendez-vous, date)* to note down (in a diary *or Am* notebook)

agenouiller (s') [saʒnuje] **VPR** to kneel (down); **s'a. devant un autel** to kneel at *or* before an altar

agenouilloir [aʒnujwar] **NM** prie-dieu; *(coussin)* hassock; *(planche)* kneeling bench

agent [aʒã] **NM 1** *(facteur)* agent, agency, medium; **a. économique/atmosphérique** economic/atmospheric factor; **a. chimique** chemical agent; **a. monétaire** circulating medium **2** *Gram* agent; **complément d'a. agent 3** *(personne)* agent; **un a. de la CIA** CIA agent; **a. (de police)** police officer *or* constable; **a. de la circulation** traffic policeman; **pardon, monsieur l'a.** excuse me, officer
▸ ▸ *Com* **a. d'affaires** business agent; *Com* **a. agréé** registered agent; **a. d'ambiance** = policeman assigned to patrol in dangerous areas; **a. d'assurance(s)** insurance broker *or* agent; **a. de change** *Fin* stockbroker, exchange broker; *Com* **a.** mercantile broker; *Com* **a. autorisé** authorized representative; *Com* **a. commercial** sales agent, sales representative, sales rep; *Com* **a. commissionnaire** commission agent; *Com* **a. de contact** contact; *Com* **a. direct** commission agent; *Com* **a. de distribution à l'export** export distribution agent; **a. en douanes** customs broker; **a. double** double agent; *Com* **a. exclusif** sole agent; *Com* **a. exportateur** export agent; *Com* **a. de fret** freight forwarder, forwarding agent; **a. du fisc** tax official; *Com* **a. général** agent; **a. immobilier** estate agent; *Com* **a. importateur** importer; *Com* **a. indépendant** free agent; *Com* **a. intermédiaire** agent middleman; **a. de liaison** *Com* contact; *Mil* liaison officer; *Com* **a. lié** tied agent; *Com* **a. de ligne** forwarding agent; **a. littéraire** literary agent; **a. de maîtrise** foreman; *Com* **a. mandataire** authorized representative; **a. maritime** shipping agent; **a. publicitaire, a. de publicité** advertising agent, publicity agent; **a. de réceptif** ground handling agent; **a. de recouvrements** debt collector; **a. de réservation** reservation agent; **a. secret** secret agent; **a. de sécurité** security officer; *Com* **a. technico-commercial** sales technician; **a. de transmission** runner, dispatch rider, messenger; **a. du trésor** government broker; **a. de voyages** travel agent

AGETAC [aʒetak] **NM** *(abrév* **Accord général sur les tarifs et le commerce)** GATT

aggiornamento [a(d)ʒjornamento] **NM** adaptation to new circumstances; **le parti doit faire son a.** the party has to move with the times

agglomérant [aglɔmerã] **ADJ** *(matériau)* binding
NM binding material, binder

agglomérat [aglɔmera] **NM** agglomerate

agglomération [aglɔmerasjɔ̃] **NF 1** *(de ville)* agglomeration, built-up area; **vitesse limi-**

tée dans les agglomérations speed restriction in built-up areas; **les grandes agglomérations** the great urban centres; **l'a. lyonnaise/parisienne** Lyons/Paris and its suburbs; **l'a. londonienne** Greater London **2** *(de fuel etc)* caking

aggloméré [aglɔmere] **ADJ** conglomerate; **panneau de fibres agglomérées** fibreboard
NM 1 *Géol, Constr* conglomerate **2** *(briquette)* compressed fuel, briquette **3** *(de bois)* fibreboard; **a. de liège** agglomerated cork

agglomérer [aglɔmere] **(j'agglomère, n. agglomérons; j'agglomérerai) VT** to agglomerate; **toute la population est agglomérée dans le …** the entire population is packed together in the …
VPR s'agglomérer to agglomerate; *(d'un mélange, de substances différentes)* to cohere, to bind; *(de fuel etc)* to cake; **les populations pauvres s'agglomèrent dans les favelas** the poor population is packed together in the shanty towns

agglutinant [aglytinã] **ADJ 1** *(adhésif)* agglutinant, adhesive **2** *Ling (langues)* agglutinative
NM *(de conglomérats)* bond

agglutination [aglytinasjɔ̃] **NF 1** *(action)* agglutination, caking; *(d'un mélange, de substances différentes)* binding **2** *(de microbes)* clump **3** *Ling* **phénomène d'a.** agglutination

agglutiner [aglytine] **VT** to agglutinate; *(mélange etc)* to bind
VPR s'agglutiner 1 *(de personnes)* to congregate, to gather **2** *Méd (des bords d'une plaie)* to join, to unite

aggravant [agravã] **ADJ** *Méd, Jur etc (symptôme, circonstances)* aggravating

aggravation [agravasjɔ̃] **NF 1** *(d'une maladie etc)* aggravation; *(du temps, d'un conflit etc)* worsening **2** *(d'une peine)* increase

aggraver [agrave] **VT 1** *(maladie, crime)* to worsen, to make worse, to aggravate; **pour a. les choses** to make matters worse **2** *(peine)* to increase, to augment; *(difficultés, imposition)* to increase
VPR s'aggraver to worsen, to become worse, to deteriorate; **la situation s'aggrave de jour en jour** the situation is getting *or* becoming worse by the day; **son état s'est aggravé** his condition has deteriorated, he has taken a turn for the worse; **les choses s'aggravent** things are getting worse

agile [aʒil] **ADJ** *aussi Fig* agile, nimble; *(démarche)* nimble; **elle est a. de ses doigts** she has nimble fingers

agilement [aʒilmã] **ADV** agilely, nimbly

agilité [aʒilite] **NF** *(physique, mentale)* agility; **a. d'un raisonnement** agility of an argument

agios [aʒjo] **NMPL** *Fin* premium; *(dans un échange de devises)* agio; *(quand on est à découvert)* bank charges; *(d'un emprunt)* interest payments

agiotage [aʒjɔtaʒ] **NM** *Bourse* stock jobbing, agiotage; *(truquage)* rigging the market; *(en prenant des risques financiers)* speculating, gambling

agioter [aʒjɔte] **VI** *Bourse* to speculate, to gamble

agioteur, -euse [aʒjɔtœr, -øz] **N** *Bourse* speculator, gambler

agir [aʒir] **VI 1** *(faire quelque chose)* to act; **a. de soi-même** to act on one's own initiative; **a. sur le conseil de qn** to act on sb's advice; **maintenant agissons** now let's get going, now let's get down to it; **il est temps d'a.** it's time to take action *or* to act; **faire a. qn** to get sb to act *or* to take action; **je vais a. en votre faveur (auprès du ministre)** I am going to intervene on your behalf (with the minister); **faire a. qch** to set sth going *or* working, to put sth in motion; **a. en connaisseur** to know what one is doing; **a. en sage** to act wisely; **bien/mal a. envers qn** to act *or* behave well/badly towards sb; **je n'aime pas sa façon** *ou* **manière d'a.** I don't like the way he goes about things; **est-ce ainsi que vous agissez envers moi?** is this how you treat me?

2 *(produire un effet)* to act, to operate, to take effect; **médicament qui agit vite** quick-acting medicine, medicine that acts *or* takes effect quickly; **a. sur qch** to act on sth; **les mauvaises conditions de travail finissent par a. sur le moral/la santé** bad working conditions will end up affecting one's morale/health; **a. sur qn** to exercise an influence on sb; **a. sur les sentiments de qn** to work on sb's feelings; *Bourse* **a. sur le marché** to rig the market

3 *Jur* **a. au nom de qn** to act on behalf of sb; **a. civilement contre qn** to sue sb; **a. au criminel/civil** to prosecute/to sue

v IMPERS s'agir (de) SEE GRAMMAR B29 **1** *(être question de)* **de quoi s'agit-il?** what's the matter?, what's it all about?, *Fam* what's up?; **il ne veut pas me dire de quoi il s'agit** he won't tell me what the matter is; **je ne sais pas vraiment de quoi il s'agit** I don't really know what it's about; **l'affaire dont il s'agit** the matter in hand; **il ne s'agit pas d'argent** it's not a question of money; **il ne s'agit pas de cela** that is not the question *or* not the point, that's neither here nor there; **il s'agit de lui** it concerns him, it is about him; **quand il s'agit d'aider, il est toujours occupé!** when it comes to helping, he always seems to be busy!; **s'agissant de …** as for …, as far as … is concerned

2 *(falloir)* to be a question of …; **il ne s'agit que de les rendre heureux** it is only a question of making them happy; **il s'agirait de savoir si …** the question is whether …; **il s'agirait de se dépêcher** we've got to hurry; *(c'est notre dernière chance)* it's a case of now or never; **il s'agit de savoir ce que tu veux!** make up your mind!

âgisme [aʒism] NM agism

agissant [aʒisɑ̃] ADJ effective, efficient; **un remède a.** an effective remedy

agissements [aʒismɑ̃] NMPL *souvent Péj* dealings, manoeuvres, machinations

agitateur, -trice [aʒitatœr, -tris] N *Pol* agitator

NM **1** *Chimie* stirring *or* glass rod **2** *(appareil)* stirring machine, agitator, mixer

agitation [aʒitasjɔ̃] NF **1** *(de la mer)* roughness, choppiness **2** *(inquiétude)* agitation; *(bougeotte)* restlessness, agitation, fidgeting; *(excitation)* excitement; *Pol* unrest; *Psy* *(state of)* perturbation *or* disturbance; **l'a. de la ville** the bustle of the city; **ville en pleine a.** bustling town; **il l'a trouvée dans un état de grande a.** he found her greatly excited; **cette nouvelle a provoqué l'a. des esprits** the news greatly upset *or* worried people; **l'a. ouvrière** (labour) unrest; **a. sociale** civil commotion

agité, -ée [aʒite] ADJ **1** *(mer)* choppy, rough; *(ciel)* wild **2** *Méd (patient)* feverish, restless; *(nuit)* restless, sleepless; *(sommeil)* broken, fitful **3** *(foule)* agitated, tumultuous; *(personne)* restless, excited, fidgety; *(esprit)* perturbed, troubled; *(époque)* unsettled; **vie agitée** hectic life

N restless *or* unsettled person; *Méd* **pavillon des agités** security wing, wing for dangerous patients; *Fam Hum* **a. du bocal** nutter, *Am* wacko

agiter [aʒite] VT **1** *(mouchoir, drapeau, bras)* to wave; *(bouteille)* to shake; *(aile, éventail)*

to flutter; *(du vent) (arbre, branches)* to sway; *(mer)* to rouse; *(mélange)* to stir; *(air)* to fan; **a. la queue** *(d'un chien)* to wag its tail; *(d'un cheval)* to flick its tail; **a. avant usage/de consommer** shake before use

2 *(inquiéter)* to perturb, to trouble; *(malade)* to agitate, to excite; **cette nouvelle risque de l'a. encore plus** this news could upset him even more; **malade agité par la fièvre** patient restless with fever; **elle est agitée par cette rencontre** the meeting has upset her *or* has got her (all) worked up; **a. le peuple** *ou* **les masses** to stir up the masses

3 *(idée)* to discuss, to debate

VPR s'agiter 1 to be agitated; *(s'affairer)* to bustle around; **s'a. dans l'eau** to splash about in the water; **s'a. dans son sommeil** to toss (about) *or* thrash around in one's sleep

2 *(s'énerver)* to become agitated *or* excited, to get upset *or* worked up; *(de la mer)* to get rough; **il ne faut pas que le malade s'agite** care should be taken not to upset *or* excite the patient

agit-prop [aʒitprɔp] NF INV agit-prop

agneau, -eaux [aɲo] NM lamb; **(peau d')a.** lambskin; **laine d'a.** lamb's wool; *Fig* **c'est un a.** he is as meek as a lamb; *Fig* **mon a.** my (pet) lamb; **doux comme un a.** as gentle as a lamb; *Rel* **l'A. sans tache** the Lamb (of God); *Culin* **côtelette d'a.** lamb chop; *Culin* **gigot d'a.** leg of lamb

agnelage [aɲəlaʒ] NM **1** *(mise à bas)* lambing **2** *(saison)* lambing season

agneler [aɲəle] VI **(elle agnèle; elle agnèlera)** to lamb

agnelet [aɲəlɛ] NM lambkin, young lamb

agneline [aɲəlin] NF lamb's wool

agnelle [aɲɛl] NF ewe lamb

agnosticisme [agnɔstisism] NM agnosticism

agnostique [agnɔstik] ADJ, N agnostic

agonie [agɔni] NF death agony *or* struggle, pangs of death; **être à l'a.** to be at one's last gasp *or* at death's door; *Fig* to be suffering agonies; **lente a.** lingering death; *Fig* **l'a. d'un régime** the death throes of a regime

> Il faut noter que le nom anglais **agony** est un faux ami. Il signifie **douleur atroce** ou **angoisse**, selon le contexte.

agonir [agɔnir] VT **a. qn d'injures/d'insultes** to heap insults *or* abuse on sb, to hurl insults *or* abuse at sb; **se faire a.** to be loudly insulted *or* abused

agonisant, -ante [agɔnizɑ̃, -ɑ̃t] ADJ dying, in the throes of death; **de sa voix agonisante** with his dying breath; *Fig* **un règne a.** a reign in its dying moments *or* death throes

N dying person; **prières pour les agonisants** prayers for the dying

agoniser [agɔnize] VI to be dying *or* at the point of death; *Fig (d'une entreprise)* to be on its last legs

> Il faut noter que le verbe anglais **to agonize** est un faux ami. Il signifie **se tourmenter**.

agoraphobe [agɔrafɔb] ADJ, N *Méd* agoraphobic

agoraphobie [agɔrafɔbi] NF *Méd* agoraphobia; **souffrir d'a.** to be agoraphobic

agrafage [agrafaʒ] NM fastening; *(de feuilles de papier)* stapling; *(d'un objet sur un établi etc)* clamping; *Tech* dowelling; *(de vêtements)* fastening, hooking

agrafe [agraf] NF **1** fastener; *(d'une médaille, d'un album)* clasp; *(d'une sangle)* buckle; *(de bureau)* staple; *Chir etc* suture clip; **a. de diamants** diamond clasp; **agrafes et portes (de couturière)** hooks and eyes; *Com* **a. antivol**

anti-theft *or* security tag **2** *Constr* clamp, cleat, cramp iron **3** *(d'une fenêtre etc)* hasp, catch **4** *Archit (d'une voûte)* keystone

agrafer [agrafe] VT **1** *(accrocher)* to fasten, to clip together; *(avec une agrafeuse)* to staple; *(robe)* to hook up; *(ceinture)* to buckle; **j'ai tellement grossi que je n'arrive plus à a. mes vêtements!** I've put on so much weight that I can't do up *or* fasten my clothes!; *Fam* **aide-moi à a. ma robe!** do me up! **2** *Constr* to clamp, to cramp **3** *Fam (de la police) (arrêter)* to nab, to nick; **il va finir par se faire a.** he's going to end up getting nabbed *or* nicked

agrafeuse [agraføz] NF stapler

agraire [agrɛr] ADJ agrarian; **réforme a.** land reform; **mesures agraires** land measures; *Jur* **loi a.** land act

agrammatical, -ale, -aux, -ales [agramatikal, -o] ADJ *Ling* ungrammatical

agrandir [agrɑ̃dir] VT **1** *(rendre plus grand)* to make larger, to enlarge; *(photographie etc)* to enlarge; *(sur écran)* to magnify; *(fenêtre)* to maximize; *(influence, cercle de relations)* to increase, to extend; **a. une maison/un appartement** to extend a house/flat; **a. qch en long/en large** to lengthen/widen sth

2 *(faire paraître plus grand)* to make appear larger, to magnify; **ce papier peint agrandit la pièce** this wallpaper makes the room look larger

3 *(développer) (affaire)* to expand

4 *(esprit etc)* to uplift

VPR **s'agrandir** *(devenir plus grand)* to grow larger; *(en quantité)* to become greater, to increase; *(prendre du volume)* to expand; **nous allons nous a.** we are going to enlarge our premises; **elle veut s'a.** *(dans son appartement)* she wants more space

agrandissement [agrɑ̃dismɑ̃] NM **1** *(extension)* enlargement, extension, expansion; **a. en long/en large** lengthening/widening; **travaux d'a.** extension work **2** *(d'une entreprise etc)* extension; *(d'un holding etc)* increase **3** *Phot* enlargement

agrandisseur [agrɑ̃disœr] NM *Phot* enlarger

agrarien, -ienne [agrarjɛ̃, -jɛn] ADJ, N *Pol* agrarian

agréable [agreabl] ADJ pleasant, agreeable; *(apparence, arrangement)* pleasing; *(manière etc)* nice, pleasant; **un jeune homme très a.** a very pleasant *or* nice young man; **se rendre a. à qn** to be pleasant to sb; **a. au goût** pleasant to the taste; **a. à voir** pleasing to the eye; **peu a.** disagreeable

NM **joindre l'utile à l'a.** to combine business with pleasure

N **faire l'a.** to make oneself pleasant (**auprès de** to)

agréablement [agreabləmɑ̃] ADV pleasantly, agreeably; **nous avons été a. surpris par ta décision** we were pleasantly surprised by your decision

agréé [agree] ADJ *(échantillon etc)* approved; *Com* recognized, authorized; *Can* **comptable a.** chartered *or* *Am* certified accountant

agréer [agree] VT *(fournisseur, équipement)* to approve; **a. un contrat** to approve an agreement; **veuillez a. l'assurance de mes salutations distinguées** *(dans une lettre) (à une personne dont on connaît le nom)* yours sincerely; *(à une personne dont on ne connaît pas le nom)* yours faithfully

VI to please; **si cela vous agrée** if that suits you

agrég [agreg] NF *Univ Fam* = **agrégation 1**

agrégat [agrega] NM aggregate

agrégatif, -ive [agregatif, -iv] N agrégation exam candidate

agrégation [agregasjɔ̃] NF **1** *Univ* **(concours**

de) l'a. = competitive examination for posts on the teaching staff of lycées and universities **2** *Constr* aggregation, binding; **matière d'a.** *(pour une route etc)* binding material

Agrégation

This is a prestigious professional qualification for teachers in France. Those who pass the challenging competitive exam for the "agrég" become teachers in secondary education or universities and are entitled to higher pay and a less onerous timetable than those who have passed the **CAPES** (*see box at this entry*).

agrégé, -ée [agreʒe] *Univ* **ADJ** = who has passed the agrégation examination
N = graduate who has passed the agrégation examination

agréger [agreʒe] **VT 1** *(rassembler)* **les cristaux agrégés dans la roche** the crystals incorporated in the rock **2** *(admettre) (société)* to incorporate; *(individu)* to admit
VPR s'agréger 1 to combine, to merge **2 s'a. à un groupe** to join a group

agrément [agremã] **NM 1** *(plaisir)* pleasure, amusement; **voyage d'a.** pleasure trip; **arts d'a.** amateur artistic pursuits; **livres d'a.** light reading
2 *(charme)* attractiveness, pleasantness, charm; **une ville sans a.** an unattractive town; **agréments** *(d'un lieu)* amenities; *(d'une personne)* charm
3 *Mus* **notes d'a.** grace notes
4 *(accord)* approval, consent; **nous avons besoin de l'a. de la Sécurité sociale pour commencer à vous soigner** the Social Security must give us their approval or consent before we can begin to treat you
5 *Com (d'agence de voyages)* agency appointment; *(garantie financière)* bonding scheme

> Il faut noter que le nom anglais **agreement** est un faux ami. Il signifie **accord**.

agrémenter [agremãte] **VT** to ornament, to decorate; *(robe etc)* to trim; **texte agrémenté de citations** text laced with quotations

agrès [agrɛ] **NMPL 1** *Naut* tackle **2** *Sport* (gymnastics) apparatus; **faire des a.** to do exercises on the apparatus

agresser [agrese] **VT** to attack (without provocation), to assault; *(yeux, tympans)* to assault; **le soleil agresse la peau** the sun damages the skin or has a damaging effect on the skin; **se faire a.** to be attacked; *(dans un lieu public et pour son argent)* to be mugged; **arrête de m'a., ce n'est pas de ma faute!** stop being so aggressive towards me, it's not my fault!; *Fam* **ne te sens pas agressé** don't think you're being got at

agresseur [agresœr] **NM** attacker, aggressor, assailant

agressif, -ive [agresif, -iv] **ADJ** *(ton, personne, couleur etc)* aggressive

agression [agresjõ] **NF 1** *(agressivité)* aggression **2** *(acte) (sur un passant etc)* mugging *(de* of); *(d'un pays)* act of aggression *(de* against); **ce genre de publicité est une véritable a.** this kind of advertising is extremely aggressive; **être victime d'une a.** to be attacked; *(dans un lieu public et pour son argent)* to be mugged; **a. de la peau par les intempéries** damaging effects of bad weather on the skin; **le bruit est une réelle a.** noise is a real act of aggression; **les agressions de la vie moderne** the stresses of modern life

agressivement [agresivmã] **ADV** aggressively

agressivité [agresivite] **NF** aggressiveness

agreste [agrɛst] **ADJ** *Litt* **1** rustic; *(site)* rural **2** *(personne, manières)* uncouth

agricole [agrikɔl] **ADJ** *(produit, nation etc)* agricultural; **comice(s) agricole(s)** agricultural show; **exploitation a.** *(ferme)* farm; **petite exploitation a.** small farm, smallholding; **travail a.** farmwork, farming; **ouvrier a.** farm worker or hand; **la population a.** the farming population

agriculteur, -trice [agrikyltœr, -tris] **N** farmer

agriculture [agrikyltyr] **NF** agriculture, farming

agripper [agripe] **VT** *(personne, objet)* to clutch (at), to grip; *(saisir) (objet)* to seize (hold of)
VPR s'agripper to cling; **il s'agrippait au bord de la fenêtre** he was clinging to the windowsill

agritourisme [agriturism] **NM** agritourism

agro [agrɔ] **NM** *Fam abrév* **Institut national agronomique**

agro-alimentaire [agroalimãter] **ADJ** *(industrie, secteur)* food-processing
NM food-processing industry, agribusiness

agrochimie [agroʃimi] **NF** agrochemistry

agrochimiste [agroʃimist] **N** agrochemist

agronome [agrɔnɔm] **N** agronomist, agricultural economist; **ingénieur a.** agricultural engineer or scientist

agronomie [agrɔnɔmi] **NF** agronomy; *Écon* agronomics

agronomique [agrɔnɔmik] **ADJ** agronomic(al); **l'Institut national a.** = (university level) college for students of agronomics

agrume [agrym] **NM** citrus fruit

agrumicole [agrymikɔl] **ADJ** citrus fruit-producing

aguerrir [agerir] **VT** *(personne)* to harden, to toughen; *(troupes)* to train (for battle)
VPR s'aguerrir s'a. à *ou* **contre qch** to become hardened to sth; *(apprendre à accepter, se débrouiller)* to learn to take sth in one's stride; **ça va te permettre de t'a.** *(d'aller en pension etc)* it will toughen you up a bit

aguets [agɛ] **NMPL aux a.** on the watch, on the lookout; **être** *ou* **se tenir aux a.** to be on the watch or on the lookout; **avoir l'oreille aux a.** to keep one's ears open

aguichant [agiʃã] **ADJ** seductive, provocative

aguiche [agiʃ] **NF** *(publicité)* teaser

aguicher [agiʃe] **VT** to excite, to arouse, *Fam* to lead on

aguicheur, -euse [agiʃœr, -øz] **ADJ** seductive, provocative; **une fillette aguicheuse** a little tease, a nymphet
NF aguicheuse provocative woman, tease

Ah *(abrév* **ampère-heure)** Ah

ah [ɑ] **INT** ah!; *(exprimant la surprise)* oh!; **ah, que c'est beau!** isn't it beautiful!; **ah oui!** well yes, of course!; **ah ça non/oui!** certainly not/certainly!; *Iron* **ah ah! je savais bien que tu me cachais quelque chose!** aha! I knew that you were hiding something from me!
NM INV pousser des oh et des ah to ooh and ah

ahaner [aane] **VI** *Litt* to puff and pant

ahuri, -ie [ayri] **ADJ** *(regard)* astounded; *(personne)* stupefied, *Fam* flabbergasted; **avoir l'air a.** to look astounded or stupefied
N idiot, numbskull

ahurir [ayrir] **VT** to astound, to stupefy

ahurissant [ayrisã] **ADJ** astounding, incredible, stupefying; *Fam* **il a un culot a.** he's got one hell of a cheek

ahurissement [ayrismã] **NM** stupefaction; **il ne revient pas de son a.** he can't get over it

aï [ai] **NM** *(mammifère)* three-toed sloth

AIDA [aida] **NM** *Mktg (abrév* **attention-intérêt-désir-action)** AIDA

aide¹ [ɛd] **NF** help, assistance; *(humanitaire)* aid; **j'ai dû lui demander de l'a.** I had to ask him for help; **appeler à l'a.** to call for help; **donner son a. à qn** to help sb; **venir en a. à qn, apporter son a. à qn** to help sb, to come to sb's assistance or aid; **recourir à l'a. d'un médecin** to call in a doctor; **à l'a.!** help!; **à l'a. de qch** with the help or assistance of sth; **avec l'a. de qn** with the help or assistance of sb; **faire qch sans a.** to do sth without help or on one's own
▸▸ *Ordinat* **a. à la césure** hyphenation help; *Ordinat* **a. contextuelle** context-sensitive help; *Écon* **a. au développement** foreign aid (to developing countries); **a. de l'État** = national assistance; **a. financière** financial aide or assistance; *Compta* **a. fiscale** tax credit; **a. gouvernementale** government aid; **a. judiciaire** legal aid; *Ordinat* **a. en ligne** online help; **a. au logement** accommodation allowance; **a. publique au développement** official development assistance; **a. au retour** = voluntary repatriation allowances for immigrant workers leaving France; **a. sociale** *Br* social security, *Am* welfare

aide² **N** assistant, helper; *Naut* mate; *(de géomètre)* chainman
▸▸ *Mil* **a. de camp** aide-de-camp; **a. de cuisine** assistant cook, kitchen hand; **a. familiale** *ou* **maternelle** mother's help; **a. de laboratoire** laboratory assistant; **a. ménagère** home help

aidé [ede] **ADJ 1** *(assisté)* **elle n'est pas très aidée** she doesn't have much help (around the house); **elle est très aidée par cette femme** she gets a lot of help from this woman **2** *Admin* **contrat a.** = employment contract whereby part of an employee's salary is paid by the state **3** *Fig* **il n'est pas très a.** *(pas très intelligent)* he's not very smart, he's a bit of a dimwit

aide-comptable, *pl* **aides-comptables** **N** assistant accountant, accounts clerk

aide-cuisinier, *pl* **aides-cuisiniers** **N** kitchen assistant

aide-éducateur, *pl* **aides-éducateurs** **N** = in the French educational system, assistant helping with pupil activities and supervision

aide-électricien, *pl* **aides-électriciens** **NM** *Cin, TV* best boy

aide-gouvernante, *pl* **aides-gouvernantes** **NF** assistant housekeeper

aide-mécanicien, *pl* **aides-mécaniciens** **NM** garage hand

aide-mémoire **NM INV** aide-memoire; *TV* prompt card; *Ordinat* quick reference guide; **j'ai besoin d'un a.** I need something to jog my memory

aide-monteur *pl* **aides-monteurs** **NM** *Cin, TV* assistant film editor

aide-opérateur *pl* **aides-opérateurs** **NM** *Cin, TV* assistant cameraman

aider [ede] **VT** to help, to assist, to aid; **attends, je vais t'a.** hold on, I'll help you or I'll give you a hand; **que puis-je faire pour vous a.?** how may I help you?; **je me suis fait a. par un ami** I got a friend to help me or to give me a hand; **tu ne peux pas t'occuper de ta maison toute seule, fais-toi a.** you can't look after the house on your own, get some help or get someone to help you; **a. qn à faire qch** to help sb to do sth; **a. qn à monter/descendre/entrer/sortir** to help sb up/down/in/out; **a. qn à mettre/ôter son pardessus** to help sb on/off with his/her coat; **Dieu aidant** with God's help; *Iron* **tu veux que je t'aide?** stop that VOIR GRAMMAIRE A41

VI a. à qch to contribute to(wards) sth; **elle n'aide jamais!** she never helps (out), she never lends a hand

VPR s'aider 1 *Prov* **aide-toi et le ciel t'aidera** God helps those who help themselves; **il faut s'a. les uns les autres** we must help one another **2 s'a. de qch** to make use of sth; **s'a. d'un dictionnaire** to consult a dictionary; **marcher en s'aidant d'une canne/de béquilles** to walk with the aid of a stick/crutches

aide-serveur, *pl* **aides-serveurs NM** waiter's assistant, *Am* busboy

aide-soignant, -ante, *pl* **aides-soignants, -antes N** nursing auxiliary, auxiliary nurse

aïe [aj] **INT** *(cri de douleur)* ow!, ouch!; *Fig* **a.! j'ai fait une gaffe!** oh no *or* oh dear, I've put my foot in it!; **a. a. a.!** boy oh boy!

AIEA [aiəa] **NF** *Nucl (abrév* **Agence internationale de l'énergie atomique)** IAEA

aïeul, -eule [ajœl, ajø] **N 1** *(pl* **aïeux)** *(ancêtre)* ancestor; *Fam* **mes aïeux!** goodness me! **2** *Vieilli (pl* **aïeuls)** grandfather, *f* grandmother

aigle [ɛgl] **NM 1** *(oiseau)* eagle; **a. royal** *ou* **fauve** *ou* **doré** golden eagle; **grand a. des mers** erne, sea eagle; *Fig* **un œil d'a.** a keen *or* penetrating glance; *Fig* **avoir un œil d'a.** to be eagle-eyed; **nez en bec d'a.** hook *or* aquiline nose **2** *Fig* genius, mastermind; **ce n'est pas un a.** he's no genius **3** *(lutrin)* lectern **4** *(poisson)* **a. de mer** eagle ray **5** *(en patinage)* **grand a.** spread-eagle

NF 1 *Hér* eagle; **a. de sable éployée** eagle displayed sable; **double a., a. à deux têtes** double-headed eagle **2** *Mil* eagle, standard; **les aigles romaines** the Roman eagles; **l'a. impériale (des armées napoléoniennes)** the imperial eagle

aiglefin [ɛgləfɛ̃] **NM** *(poisson)* haddock

aiglette [ɛglɛt] **NF** *Hér* eaglet

aiglon, -onne [ɛglɔ̃, -ɔn] **N** *(oiseau)* eaglet, young eagle; *Hist* **L'A.** Napoleon II

aigre [ɛgr] **ADJ** *(goût etc)* sour, sharp, acid, tart; *(lait)* sour; *Fig (propos)* cutting; *(personne)* sour; *(éprouvant du ressentiment)* bitter; *(vent, froid)* bitter; *(son)* harsh, shrill; **parler d'un ton a.** to speak sharply

NM tourner à l'a. *(d'un aliment etc)* to turn sour; *Fig (d'une discussion)* to turn nasty

aigre-doux, -douce *pl* **aigres-doux, -douces ADJ** *(sauce)* sweet and sour; *Fig (remarque)* snide, *Fam* catty

aigrefin [ɛgrəfɛ̃] **NM** *Péj* swindler, *(financial)* shark

aigrelet, -ette [ɛgrəlɛ, -ɛt] **ADJ** *(vin, goût)* (rather) sour; *(son, voix)* harsh, reedy

aigrement [ɛgrəmɑ̃] **ADV** acrimoniously, bitterly

aigrette [ɛgrɛt] **NF 1** *(d'un héron)* aigrette; *(d'un perroquet etc)* crest; *(d'une chouette)* horn; *(de cheveux, de fourrure)* tuft **2** *(panache)* aigrette, plume; **a. de diamants** spray of diamonds **3** *Bot* egret; *(du maïs)* tassel **4** *Élec (décharge)* aigrette, brush **5** *(oiseau)* egret

aigreur [ɛgrœr] **NF 1** *(d'un goût)* sourness, tartness, acidity; *Fig (du tempérament)* sourness; *(d'une remarque)* sharpness, bitterness; **il en parle encore avec a.** he's still very bitter about it **2** *Méd* **aigreurs (d'estomac)** acidity, excess stomach acid

aigri [ɛgri] **ADJ** embittered, soured

aigrir [ɛgrir] **VT a. qch** to turn sth sour; *Fig* **a. qn** to embitter sb, to make sb bitter

VI to turn *or* grow sour; *(du lait)* to turn

VPR s'aigrir *(devenir acide)* to turn sour; *Fig* **son caractère s'est aigri** he has become embittered

aigu, -uë [egy] **ADJ 1** *(douleur)* acute, sharp; *(curiosité)* intense; *(conflit, jalousie)* bitter; *(regard)* penetrating; *(esprit, sensation, intelligence)* keen, sharp; **elle a un sens a. du rôle de chacun** she has a keen sense of what everybody's role should be **2** *(instrument)* sharp, pointed; *(dans le réglage de la tonalité)* treble; *Math* **angle a.** acute angle **3** *(son)* shrill, sharp, high-pitched **4** *Gram* **accent a.** acute (accent)

NM les aigus the treble; **il y a trop d'aigus** the treble is too high

aigue-marine, *pl* **aigues-marines** [ɛgmarin] **NF** aquamarine

aiguillage [eguijaʒ] **NM 1** *Rail (manœuvre)* switching *or* shifting of points; *(d'un train)* shunting; **poste d'a.** signal box **2** *Rail (appareil)* points, *Am* switches; **a. à deux voies** two-way switch **3** *Fig* orientation; **faire une erreur d'a.** to take the wrong turning *or* course

aiguille [eguij] **NF 1** needle; **a. à coudre/repriser/tricoter** sewing/darning/knitting needle; **travail à l'a.** needlework; **a. à passer** *ou* **à lacet** bodkin; *Méd* **a. hypodermique** hypodermic needle; *Fig* **chercher une a. dans une botte de foin** to look for a needle in a haystack; *Fig* **de fil en a. nous en sommes venus à parler de notre enfance** one thing led to another and we got talking about our childhood

2 *Ordinat* pin; **imprimante à aiguilles** 24-pin printer

3 a. de glace icicle; *Géol* **a. (rocheuse)** needle; *(d'un sommet)* spine; **a. de pin** pine needle; **a. de mer** *(poisson)* pipe fish, garfish; **a. à tracer** scriber; **a. de graveur** etching needle

4 *Rail* tongue rail, point rail, blade; **a. de raccordement** points, *Am* switches

5 *(d'un obélisque, d'un pic etc)* needle, point; *(d'une église)* (church) spire

6 *(de boussole, de compteur de vitesse etc)* needle; *(d'une montre, d'une horloge)* hand; **petite a.** hour hand; **grande a.** minute hand; **a. trotteuse** second hand

aiguillée [eguije] **NF** (short) piece of thread

aiguiller [eguije] **VT** *Rail (train)* to shunt, *Am* to switch; *Fig* **a. la police sur une fausse piste** to put the police on a false scent; *Fig* **on l'a aiguillé vers la profession de banquier** he was steered into banking; *Fig* **il a été mal aiguillé dans ses études** he was badly advised about his studies; *Fig* **a. ses recherches vers un certain domaine** to orient(ate) *or* direct one's research towards a particular field

aiguilleur [eguijœr] **NM** *Rail* pointsman, *Am* switchman; *Aviat* **a. du ciel** air traffic controller

aiguillon [eguijɔ̃] **NM 1** *(pique-bœuf)* goad; *Fig* incentive, spur, stimulus; *Fig* **sa remarque me fut l'effet d'un a.** his/her remark spurred me on **2** *Bot* prickle, thorn; *(d'une guêpe)* sting

aiguillonner [eguijɔne] **VT** *(bœufs)* to goad; *Fig (personne) (de la jalousie, de l'ambition)* to spur on; *(d'une personne)* to urge on; *Fig* **l'appât du gain l'aiguillonne** the lure of money spurs him on

aiguisé [egize] **ADJ** *(couteau)* sharp; *Fig (appétit, intérêt)* keen

aiguiser [egize] **VT 1** *(couteau etc)* to sharpen, to put an edge on, to grind; *(scie, rasoir)* to set; *(faux)* to whet; *(outil)* to sharpen to a point **2** *Fig (curiosité, jalousie)* to arouse; *(appétit)* to whet; *(intelligence)* to sharpen

aiguiseur, -euse [egizœr, -øz] **N** *(d'outils etc)* grinder, sharpener

aiguisoir [egizwar] **NM** *(outil)* (knife) sharpener, steel; *(pierre à aiguiser)* whetstone

aïkido [ajkido] **NM** *Sport* aikido; **faire de l'a.** to do aikido

ail, *pl* **ails** [aj] *Vieilli* **aulx** [o] **NM 1** *Culin* garlic; **une gousse d'a.** a clove of garlic; **un bulbe** *ou* *Fam* **une tête d'a.** a head of garlic **2** *(plante)* allium

aile [ɛl] **NF 1** *(d'oiseau, de papillon etc)* wing; *(de manchot)* flipper; **battre des ailes** to beat *or* flap its wings; **battre de l'a.** *(d'un oiseau)* to flutter; *Fig (d'une personne)* to be flustered *or* embarrassed; **l'entreprise bat de l'a.** the firm is struggling (to survive) *or* is in a bad way; **avoir du plomb dans l'a., en avoir dans l'a.** *(d'un oiseau)* to be winged; *Fig (d'une personne)* to be hard hit; *Fig* **la théorie a du plomb dans l'a.** the theory doesn't stand up; *Fig* **la peur nous donnait des ailes** fear lent us wings; *Fig* **voler de ses propres ailes** to stand on one's own (two) feet; *Fig* **vouloir voler avant d'avoir ses ailes** to want to run before one can walk; *Fig* **rogner les ailes à qn** to clip sb's wings; *Fig Fam* **avoir un coup dans l'a.** to have had a bit too much to drink; *Fig* **prendre qn sous son a.** to take sb under one's wing; *Fig* **travailler sous l'a. d'un grand professeur** to be the protégé of an eminent professor

2 *Aut* wing, *Am* fender; *(d'un bâtiment, de la scène)* wing; *(d'une armée)* wing, flank; *(d'un moulin)* sail; *(d'un sémaphore)* arm; *(d'une hélice, d'une turbine)* blade; *(d'une oreille)* helix; *(du nez)* wing; *(d'une poutre)* flange

3 *Aviat* wing, aerofoil, *Am* airfoil; **a. courbe** cambered wing; **a. en flèche** swept-back wing; **a. à fente** slotted wing; **a. en delta** delta wing; **a. cantilever, a. en porte à faux** cantilever wing

4 *Rugby, Ftbl* wing; **les demi ailes** the wing halves; **jouer trois quarts a.** to play wing three-quarters; **à l'a. gauche** on the left wing

5 *Sport* **a. volante** *ou* **libre** *(sport)* hang-gliding; *(objet)* hang-glider; **faire de l'a. volante** to hang-glide, to go hang-gliding

ailé [ele] **ADJ** winged, feathered, *Spéc* alate

aileron [ɛlrɔ̃] **NM 1** *(d'oiseau)* pinion; *(de requin etc)* fin **2** *Aviat* aileron **3** *Aviat etc* fin; **a. stabilisateur** stabilizer fin; **stabilisateur à a.** fin stabilizer **4** *Aut* wing, *Am* fender; *(de voiture de course)* aerofoil; **a. arrière** rear wing **5** *(de roue à eau)* paddle board **6** *(d'un sous-marin)* fin keel; *(d'une planche à voile)* skeg

ailette [ɛlɛt] **NF 1** *(d'un radiateur)* radiating plate, fin; *Aut* **a. de refroidissement** cooling fin; **tube à ailettes** fanned *or* gilled tube **2** *(d'une pièce de machine)* lug, tenon; *(d'un coquillage)* stud; **vis à ailettes** wing nut, thumbscrew **3** *(d'une torpille, d'un éventail, d'un ventilateur etc)* vane; *(d'une bombe, d'une missile)* wing, fin; *(d'un avion)* fin; *(d'une turbine)* blade; **à ailettes** *(roue etc)* bladed; *(bombe, missile)* winged

ailier [elje] **NM** *Sport* winger

ailler [aje] **VT** *Culin* to add garlic to

ailleurs [ajœr] **ADV 1** *(à un autre endroit)* elsewhere, somewhere else; **elle vient d'a.** she's not from here, she's not from these parts; **c'est dit a. dans le texte** it's mentioned somewhere else in the text; **on a dû passer par a.** we had to come a different way; *Fig* **être a.** to be miles away; **partout a.** everywhere else; *(n'importe où)* anywhere else; **nulle part a.** nowhere else; **vous mangerez ici comme nulle part a.** you'll eat better here than you will anywhere else; *Fam* **va voir a. si j'y suis** take a walk *or* hike

2 d'a. besides, anyway, *surtout Fml* moreover; *(quoi qu'il en soit)* however; *(au fait)* come to that, for that matter; **j'avais quelque chose à te dire à ce sujet** by the way, I had something to tell you about this

3 par a. in other respects; *(par qn d'autre etc)* from another source; *(d'ailleurs)* moreover

NM il avait quitté son pays en quête d'un a. où la vie serait meilleure he had left his country in search of a better life elsewhere *or* somewhere else

ailloli [ajɔli] **NM** = aïoli

aimable [ɛmabl] **ADJ 1** *(gentil)* kind, pleasant, agreeable; **vous êtes bien a., c'est très a. de votre part** it's very kind of you, it's very good of you; **peu a.** disagreeable; *(remerciements, propos etc)* ungracious; **échanger quelques mots aimables avec qn** to exchange a few kind words with sb **2** *Arch (que l'on peut aimer facilement)* lovable, attractive

aimablement [ɛmabləmɑ̃] **ADV** kindly, pleasantly

aimant¹ [ɛmɑ̃] **NM** magnet; **a. supraconducteur** superconducting magnet

aimant² [ɛmɑ̃] **ADJ** *(parent etc)* loving

aimantation [ɛmɑ̃tasjɔ̃] **NF** magnetization

aimanter [ɛmɑ̃te] **VT** to magnetize

aimer [eme] **VT 1** *(d'amour)* to love; **a. qn (d'amour)** to love sb, to be in love with sb; **tu crois qu'il m'aime?** do you think he loves me?
2 *(apprécier, avoir de l'affection pour) (personne, chose)* to like, to be fond of; **il te téléphone encore, ouh, je n'aime pas ça!** he's calling you again, oh I don't like that at all!; **elle n'aime pas la viande crue** she doesn't like raw meat; **a. qn d'amitié** to be good friends with sb; **je n'aime guère Pierre** I don't like Pierre very much, I don't care for Pierre very much; **j'aime beaucoup Pierre** I like Pierre very much, I'm very fond of Pierre; **j'aime beaucoup la musique** I'm very fond of music; **je t'aime bien** I like you a lot; **se faire a. de qn** to win sb's affection; **plante qui aime un sol calcaire** plant that likes a chalky soil; **tu sais que nous n'aimons pas ce genre de choses** you know we don't like that sort of thing; **a. (à) faire qch** to like doing sth; **j'aurais aimé le voir** I would like to have seen him; *Prov* **qui m'aime aime mon chien** love me, love my dog; **je vais prendre un pot – qui m'aime me suive!** I'm going for a drink – anyone want to join me?; **j'aime autant le cidre que le vin** I like cider just as much as wine; **j'aime(rais) autant rester ici** I would just as soon stay here (**que de … as …**); **j'aime autant qu'il ne m'attende pas** I would just as soon he didn't wait for me; **a. mieux** to prefer; **ah, j'aime mieux ça, j'ai cru que tu avais oublié de les inviter** that's just as well, I thought you'd forgotten to invite them; **j'aime** *ou* **j'aimerais mieux rester ici** I would rather *or* sooner stay here; *Fam* **j'aime mieux pas** I'd rather not

VPR s'aimer 1 *(être attaché par amour)* to love each other, to be in love (with each other); *(avoir des relations sexuelles)* to make love; **ils s'aiment** they are in love (with each other) **2** *(être fier de soi)* to think a lot of oneself; *(à une occasion particulière)* to be pleased with oneself; **je ne m'aime pas dans cette veste** *(ne me plais pas)* I don't like myself in this jacket

aine [ɛn] **NF** *Anat* groin

aîné, -ée [ene] **ADJ** *(de deux personnes)* elder; *(de plus que deux personnes)* eldest; **mon frère a.** my elder brother; *(plus de deux frères)* my eldest brother; **la branche aînée de la famille** the elder *or* senior branch of the family VOIR GRAMMAIRE A26–7

N elder *or* eldest (child); **l'a. ne va pas encore à l'école** the eldest doesn't go to school yet; **nos aînés** our elders; **il est mon a.** he is older than me; **il est mon a. de deux ans** he is two years older than me

aînesse [enɛs] **NF** **droit d'a.** law of primogeniture

ainsi [ɛ̃si] **ADV 1** *(de cette façon)* like this, like that, in this *or* that way, *Fml* thus; **c'est a. que commence la chanson** the song starts like this, this is how the song starts; **c'est a. qu'il est devenu soldat** and that is *or* was how he became a soldier; **s'il en est a.** if that is the case, if (it is) so; **puisqu'il en est a., je n'ai plus rien à dire** under the circumstances, I have nothing more to say; **les choses étant a.** if that's the way *or* how things are; **et a. de suite** and so on, and so forth; **pour a. dire** so to speak, as it were; **a. soit-il** so be it; *Rel* amen; **a. donc** so; **a. donc tu nous quittes** so you're leaving us then?
2 *(par exemple)* for example, for instance; **il m'arrive des aventures, a., l'autre jour …** things happen to me, for instance, the other day …

CONJ 1 so; **a. vous ne venez pas?** so you're not coming? **2** as well as, and; **cette règle a. que la suivante me paraît** *ou* **paraissent inutile(s)** this rule, as well as *or* and the next, seems to me to be unnecessary

AIO [aio] **NM** *Mktg (abrév* **activités, intérêts et opinions)** AIO

aïoli [ajɔli] **NM** *Culin* garlic mayonnaise

AIR [ɛr] **NM 1** *(gaz)* air, atmosphere; **une bouffée d'a. pur** a breath of fresh air; *Fig* **cette discussion a été comme une bouffée d'a. pur** this discussion has been like a breath of fresh air; **privé d'a., sans a.** airless; **cela manque d'a. ici** it's stuffy in here; **j'ouvre la porte pour faire de l'a.** I'll open the door to let some air in; **l'a. de la mer/des montagnes** (the) sea/mountain air; **donner de l'a. à** *(pièce)* to ventilate, to air; *(personne)* to give some (fresh) air; **à a. conditionné** air conditioned; **avoir l'a. conditionné** to have air conditioning; **sortir prendre l'a.** to go out for some fresh air; *Fig* **vivre de l'a. du temps** to live on *(next to)* nothing *or* on fresh air; **ne pas laisser à l'a.** not to be exposed to the air; **allez, de l'a.!** go on, clear off!; **au grand a., en plein a., à l'a. libre** in the fresh air, in the open air; **vie au grand a.** open-air life; **vie de plein a.** outdoor life; **concert en plein a.** open-air concert; **libre comme l'a.** free as a bird; *Typ* **donner de l'a. à la composition** to lead out *or* space out the type
2 *(ciel)* **l'a.** the air; **la conquête de l'a.** the conquest of the air; **prendre l'a.** *(d'un avion)* to take off; **la navette spatiale s'éleva dans les airs** the space shuttle rose into the air; **tenir l'a.** to keep flying; *(être en état de voler)* to be airworthy; **ministère de l'A.** = ministry responsible for air defence; **Armée de l'A.** Air Force; **École de l'A.** = training college for the French air force, *Br* ≃ RAF College, *Am* ≃ USAF Academy; **hôtesse de l'a.** air hostess; **jouer les filles de l'a.** to vanish into thin air; **mal de l'a.** air sickness; **en l'a.** in the air; **regarder en l'a.** to look up; *Fig* **être en l'a.** *(en désordre)* to be in a mess; **il a mis toute la maison/mon bureau en l'a.** he made an awful mess of the house/my office; *Fig* **ficher qch en l'a.** to mess sth up; **mes projets sont fichus en l'a. à cause de lui** my plans have all gone up in smoke because of him; *Fig* **elle veut tout envoyer** *ou Fam* **foutre en l'a.** she wants to throw it all up *or Fam* chuck *or* jack it all in; *Fig* **paroles en l'a.** idle talk; *Fig* **parler en l'a.** to talk wildly *or* rashly; *Fig* **j'ai dit ça en l'a.** I was talking off the top of my head; *Fig* **c'est une tête en l'a.** he's got his head in the clouds
3 *Fig (atmosphère)* **elle est passée prendre l'a. de l'atelier** she looked in at the workshop to see how things were; **changer d'a.** to have a change of scene; **il y a quelque chose dans l'a.** there's something in the air *or* wind, there's something brewing; **il y a de la dispute/de l'orage dans l'a.** there's an argument/a storm brewing; **c'est dans l'a. du**

temps *(de se préoccuper de l'environnement etc)* it's the in thing
4 *(vent)* wind; **courant d'a.** draught; **il ne fait pas d'a.** there's not a breath of air
5 *(allure)* appearance, look; **avoir bon** *ou* **grand a.** *(d'une personne)* to look distinguished; *(d'une robe etc)* to be smart; *(être seyant)* to be becoming; **a. de famille** family likeness; **un jeune homme à l. très comme il faut** a very respectable-looking young man; **avoir un faux a. de …** to have a vague *or* slight resemblance to …, to look vaguely like …; **il a un drôle d'a.** he looks odd *or* funny; **cette fillette a un petit a. malin** that little girl looks very mischievous; **la ville a un a. de fête** the town is looking festive, the town has a festive look about it; **elle, avec son a. de ne pas y toucher** her, with her innocent look; **se donner** *ou* **prendre des airs** to give oneself *or* to put on airs, to (try to) look important; **prendre des airs entendus** to have a knowing look; **ne prends pas tes grands airs!** don't get on your high horse!
6 **avoir l'a.** to look, to seem; **avoir l'a. fatigué/déçu/de s'ennuyer/d'être intéressé** to look tired/disappointed/bored/interested; **sa voiture a l'a. ancienne** his car looks old; **Marie a l'a. contente** Marie looks happy; *Fam* **avoir l'a. fin** to look daft; **il a l'a. d'un étranger** he looks like a foreigner; **ils ont l'a. d'avoir peur** they look as if they're afraid; **tu as l'a. de ne pas comprendre le problème** you look as if you don't understand the problem; **cela en a tout l'a.** it looks like it; **n'avoir l'a. de rien** *(d'une personne)* to seem *or* appear insignificant, to seem *or* appear of no importance; *(d'une maison etc)* to be unpretentious, to look nothing much (from the outside); *(d'un travail)* to look (deceptively) easy; **il n'a l'a. de rien, mais il est d'une force extraordinaire** he doesn't look much, but he's unbelievably strong; **le temps a l'a. d'être à la pluie** it looks like rain
7 *Mus* tune, air, melody; **un a. à la mode** a popular tune; **a. varié** theme with variations; **un a. d'opéra** an (operatic) aria
8 *Équitation* **les airs du manège** the paces of a horse

▸▸ **a. comprimé** compressed air; **a. liquide** liquid air; **a. recyclé** recirculated air; **a. refroidi** cooled air

airain [ɛrɛ̃] **NM** *(cuivre et étain)* bronze; *(cuivre et zinc)* brass; *Écon* **la loi d'a.** (Lassalle's) iron law of wages

air-air [ɛrɛr] **ADJ INV** *Mil* air-to-air; **missile a.** air-to-air missile

Air Bag® [ɛrbag] **NM 1** *(dispositif)* Airbag® **2** *Fam* **air bags** *(seins)* tits, jugs

Airbus® [ɛrbys] **NM** *Aviat* Airbus®

aire [ɛr] **NF 1** *(surface plane)* (plane) surface; *(plancher)* floor; *(d'un pont)* roadway, floor; **a. (d'une orange)** threshing floor **2** *(d'un champ, d'un triangle, d'un bâtiment etc)* area; *Fig* **a. d'influence** sphere of influence; **a. linguistique** linguistic region; *Géog* **a. de drainage** drainage area, basin **3** *(d'un aigle)* eyrie **4** *Naut* **les aires de vent** the points of the compass

▸▸ *Aviat* **a. d'atterrissage** landing area; *Géog* **a. continentale** continental shield; **a. de dédouanement** customs clearance area; **a. de jeux** play area; *Astronaut* **a. de lancement** launching site; **a. de lavage** *Aut* car wash, washing bay, *Am* wash rack; *Aviat* washdown; *Aviat* **a. de manœuvre** apron; **a. de pique-nique** picnic site *or* area; **a. de repos** *(sur l'autoroute)* parking *or* picnic area; **a. de services (principale)** service area; *(panneau indicateur)* services; **a. de stationnement** *Aviat* tarmac, apron; *Aut* parking area, lay-by

airedale [ɛrdɛl] **NM** Airedale (terrier)

airelle [ɛrɛl] NF (*plante*) a. **myrtille** blueberry, bilberry; a. **coussinette** cranberry

air-sol [ɛrsɔl] ADJ INV *Mil* air-to-ground; **missile a.** air-to-ground missile

ais [ɛ] NM *Typ* wetting board; (*en reliure*) press board

aisance [ɛzɑ̃s] NF 1 (*facilité*) ease; (*de mouvement etc*) freedom; **faire qch avec a.** to do sth easily *or* with ease; **donner de l'a. à qch** to ease sth; **parler** *ou* **s'exprimer avec a.** to speak *or* express oneself with great ease *or* facility; **jouir de l'a., être dans l'a.** to be well off *or* comfortably off; **vivre dans l'a.** to live comfortably 2 **fosse d'aisances** cesspool; *Vieilli* **lieu** *ou* **cabinet d'aisances** public convenience *or* lavatory
▸▸ *Jur* **a. de voirie** easement

aise [ɛz] NF ease, comfort; **être à l'a.** *ou* **à son a.** (*bien installé*) to be comfortable; (*avoir beaucoup de place*) to have (elbow) room; (*financièrement*) to be well off; **tu serais plus à l'a. si tu lui en parlais une bonne fois pour toutes** you'd feel more comfortable *or* more at ease if you told him once and for all; **tu seras bien plus à l'a. dans cette pièce** you'll be much more comfortable in this room; **on tient à l'a. à six dans cette voiture** this car holds six comfortably; *Fam* **à l'a.!** easy!, no problem!, it's a piece of cake *or Br* a doddle!; **à ton a.!** suit yourself!; **ne pas être à son a., se sentir mal à l'a.** to feel awkward, to feel uncomfortable; (*physiquement*) to feel indisposed *or* off colour; **être (très) à l'a.** to be relaxed; **je l'ai mis à l'a. en l'appelant Roger** I put him at his ease by calling him Roger; *Iron* **elle peut en parler à son a.!** it's easy (enough) *or* it's all right for her to talk!; **mettez-vous à votre a.** make yourself comfortable; **il en prend à son a. avec ses collègues** he takes his colleagues for granted; **faire qch à son a.** to do sth at one's own convenience; **aimer ses aises** to like one's comforts; **il prend ses aises** he makes himself at home; *Fam* **et lui il se tournait les pouces, à l'a., Blaise!** and there he was, twiddling his thumbs without a care in the world!
ADJ *Litt* **je suis bien** *ou* **tout a. de l'entendre parler ainsi** I'm delighted to hear him talk this way

aisé [eze] ADJ 1 (*manière*) easy, free; (*vêtement, situation*) comfortable; (*personne*) (*financièrement*) comfortably off, well-to-do, *Fam* well heeled; **parler d'un ton a.** to speak in a natural way 2 (*tâche*) easy

aisément [ezemɑ̃] ADV (*facilement*) easily, readily

aisselle [ɛsɛl] NF 1 *Anat* armpit 2 *Bot* axilla

AITA [aitea] NF (*abrév* **Association internationale des transports aériens**) IATA

Aix-la-Chapelle [ɛkslaʃapɛl] N Aachen, Aix-la-Chapelle

ajiste [aʒist] N (*youth*) hosteller

ajointer [aʒwɛ̃te] VT to join up; (*planches, tuyaux etc*) to fit end to end

ajonc [aʒɔ̃] NM (*plante*) furze, gorse

ajour [aʒur] NM (*laissant passer la lumière*) opening, hole, orifice; (*en sculpture etc*) (ornamental) perforation, openwork; *Couture* **ajours** hemstitching; (*dans une dentelle etc*) openwork

ajouré [aʒure] ADJ perforated; (*motif*) openwork; **travail a.** *Menuis* fretwork; *Couture* drawn-thread work

ajourer [aʒure] VT 1 (*pour laisser passer la lumière*) to pierce an opening; **a. une mansarde** to make a window in an attic 2 (*d'un ornement*) to perforate, to pierce; *Couture* to hemstitch

ajournement [aʒurnəmɑ̃] NM 1 (*d'une réunion*) postponement; (*après le début de la séance*) adjournment; *Scol* (*d'un candidat*)

referring; *Mil* (*d'un conscrit*) deferment 2 *Jur* writ of summons (to appear), subpoena

ajourner [aʒurne] VT 1 (*réunion, décision, voyage etc*) to postpone, to put off, to defer; (*après le début de la séance*) to adjourn; (*projet*) to delay; *Pol* (*projet de loi*) to table; *Scol* (*candidat*) to refer; *Mil* (*conscrit*) to grant deferment to 2 *Jur* (*personne*) to subpoena

ajout [aʒu] NM (*à un texte*) addition; (*à un bâtiment*) extension; *Mktg* **a. à la gamme** range addition; *Mktg* **a. à la ligne** line addition; *Ordinat* **a. de mémoire** memory upgrade

ajoute [aʒut] NF *Belg* (*ajout*) addition

ajouté [aʒute] NM (*à un manuscrit, un contrat*) addition

ajouter [aʒute] VT 1 to add; *Ordinat* (*à une base de données*) to append; **a. qch à qch** to add sth to sth; **sans a. que …** not to mention the fact that …; **a. aux embarras de qn** to add to sb's difficulties; **'venez aussi,' ajouta-t-il** 'you come too,' he added; **nous devons a. que …** it should also be stated that …; **je dois a. qu'il m'a été très utile** I must add *or* I must also say that he has been very useful to me 2 **a. foi à qch** to believe sth, to have faith in sth
VI **a. à** to add to
VPR **s'ajouter** to be added (**à** to); **à ceci viennent s'a. les frais de déplacement** on top of this there are travel expenses (to be added)

ajustable [aʒystabl] ADJ adjustable

ajustage [aʒystaʒ] NM 1 (*d'une robe etc*) fitting 2 (*d'une machine*) assembly; **atelier d'a.** fitting shop; **a. mécanique** machining 3 fit; **a. serré** tight fit; **a. lâche** *ou* **à jeu** loose fit

ajustement [aʒystəmɑ̃] NM 1 (*d'un appareil, des prix etc*) adjusting, adjustment; (*fait de régler*) arrangement; **a. des salaires** wage adjustment; *Com* **a. fret** bunker adjustment factor; **a. saisonnier** seasonal adjustment; *Mktg* **a. stratégique** strategic *or* marketing fit 2 **ajustements** fittings

ajuster [aʒyste] VT (*appareil, outil*) to adjust; (*monter*) (*machine*) to set up; (*pièce*) to gauge; (*salaire, prix, monnaie*) to adjust; **nous ajustons la moquette aux dimensions de la pièce** we're altering the carpet to fit the dimensions of the room; **a. le tir** to aim; **feu bien ajusté** well aimed fire; **a. son coup** to have a precise target (in mind); **a. qch à qch** to fit *or* adjust *or* adapt sth to sth; **on a fait a. la veste à la taille de ma sœur** we had the jacket altered to fit my sister; **veste (bien) ajustée** close- *or* tight-fitting jacket; **a. son chapeau devant le miroir** to adjust one's hat in front of the mirror; *Fam* **comme vous voilà ajusté!** what a sight you look!; **a. la théorie à la pratique** to adapt the theory to the practice
VPR **s'ajuster** 1 (*de personne*) to straighten one's clothes, to tidy oneself up 2 **l'embout s'ajuste sur le tuyau** the nozzle fits the pipe; **cette clef s'ajuste à chacune des serrures** this key fits each of the locks

ajusteur [aʒystœr] NM **a. sur métaux, a. mécanicien** (metal) fitter, filer, bench hand; **a. de tubes (de chaudières)** tube setter

alacrité [alakrite] NF *Litt* liveliness, alacrity

Aladin [aladɛ̃] N Aladdin

alaire [alɛr] ADJ *Aviat* **charge a.** wing load(-ing); **surface a.** wing area

alaise [alɛz] NF drawsheet

alambic [alɑ̃bik] NM *Chimie, Ind* still; **passer qch par** *ou* **à l'a.** to distil *or Am* distill sth

alambiqué [alɑ̃bike] ADJ (*texte*) abstruse, overcomplicated; (*esprit*) oversubtle; (*explication, système etc*) convoluted, involved

alangui [alɑ̃gi] ADJ languid

alanguir [alɑ̃gir] VT to make languid; (*affaiblir*) to enfeeble, to make feeble; **la chaleur**

alanguit les ouvriers the heat is making the workers lethargic *or* listless
VPR **s'alanguir** to grow languid, to flag, to droop, to wilt

alanguissement [alɑ̃gismɑ̃] NM languor

alarmant [alarmɑ̃] ADJ alarming, frightening; **son état est a.** his condition is giving serious cause for concern

alarme [alarm] NF (*alerte*) alarm; **donner/sonner l'a.** to give/sound the alarm; **signal d'a.** alarm; *Rail* **tirer la sonnette d'a.** to pull the communication cord; *Fig* **à la prochaine a., il faudra vous amener à l'hôpital** if there's another scare *or* alarm, you'll have to be taken to hospital; *Fig* **une fausse a.** a false alarm; **état d'a.** state of alarm
▸▸ **a. antivol** anti-theft alarm; **a. incendie** fire alarm; **a. lumineuse** warning light; *Aut* **a. périmétrique** perimeter alarm; **a. sonore** beep; **a. télécommandée** remote-control alarm; **a. à ultrasons** ultrasonic alarm

alarmer [alarme] VT to alarm, to frighten; (*d'un bruit*) to startle; **la nouvelle ne nous a pas alarmés** we were not alarmed at *or* by the news
VPR **s'alarmer** to take fright; **il s'alarme pour un rien** the least thing frightens him; **il n'y a pas lieu de s'a.** there is no cause for alarm *or* concern

alarmisme [alarmism] NM alarmism

alarmiste [alarmist] ADJ alarmist; **la presse a.** the sensational press
N alarmist

Alaska [alaska] NM Alaska; **en A.** in Alaska

albanais, -aise [albanɛ, -ɛz] ADJ Albanian
NM *Ling* Albanian
N **A.** Albanian

Albanie [albani] NF Albania

albanophone [albanɔfɔn] ADJ (*communauté, populations*) Albanian-speaking
N Albanian speaker

albâtre [albɑtr] NM alabaster; **peau d'a.** alabaster skin, skin like alabaster

albatros [albatrɔs] NM (*oiseau*) albatross

albigeois, -oise [albiʒwa, -waz] NPL *Hist* **les A.** the Albigenses, the Albigensians

albinisme [albinism] NM albinism

albinos [albinos] ADJ INV albino; **un lapin a.** an albino rabbit
N INV albino

Albion [albjɔ̃] NF *Hist* Albion, Britain; *Litt* **la perfide A.** perfidious Albion

album [albɔm] NM 1 *Phot, Mus etc* album; **a. de timbres/de photos** stamp/photo album 2 *Ordinat* (*sur Macintosh*) scrapbook

albumen [albymɛn] NM *Biol* albumen

albumine [albymin] NF *Chimie* albumin

alcali [alkali] NM *Chimie* alkali

alcalin [alkalɛ̃] ADJ *Chimie* alkaline

alcaloïde [alkalɔid] NM *Chimie* alkaloid

alchimie [alʃimi] NF alchemy

alchimiste [alʃimist] NM alchemist

alcolo [alkɔlo] N *Fam* = **alcoolo**

alcool [alkɔl] NM 1 alcohol; **lampe à a.** spirit lamp, *Am* alcohol lamp 2 (*boisson*) alcohol; (*whisky, eau-de-vie etc*) spirits, hard liquor, *Fam* the hard stuff; **je ne bois jamais d'a.** I don't drink (anything alcoholic); **il ne tient pas l'a.** he can't hold his drink; **l'a. au volant accroît considérablement les risques d'accidents** drink-driving greatly increases the risk of accidents; **a. de poire** pear brandy; **vous prendrez bien un petit a.?** would you like a liqueur or a brandy or something?
▸▸ **a. à 90°** surgical spirit, *Am* rubbing alcohol; **a. absolu** pure *or* absolute alcohol; **a. blanc** (*kirsch etc*) clear spirits; **a. à brûler** methylated spirits; *Ind* **a. dénaturé** methylated spirits; **a. éthylique** ethyl alcohol

alcoolémie [alkɔlemi] NF *Méd* presence of alcohol in the blood; **taux d'a.** level of alcohol in the blood

alcoolique [alkɔlik] ADJ alcoholic ▸ N alcoholic; **être un a.** to be an alcoholic

alcoolisation [alkɔlizasjɔ̃] NF alcoholization

alcoolisé [alkɔlize] ADJ *(boisson)* alcoholic

alcooliser [alkɔlize] VT *(vin)* to fortify ▸ VPR **s'alcooliser** to drink too much, to get drunk

alcoolisme [alkɔlism] NM alcoholism

alcoolo [alkɔlo] N *Fam* alcoholic, drunk

alcoologie [alkɔlɔʒi] NF *Méd* alcohology

alcoologue [alkɔlɔg] N *Méd* alcohologist

alcoomètre [alkɔmɛtr] NM alcohol(o)meter

Alcootest® [alkɔtɛst] NM breathalyser test; **faire passer** *ou* **subir un A. à un conducteur** to breathalyse *or* breath-test a motorist

alcôve [alkov] NF alcove; **a. de dortoir** cubicle; **secrets d'a.** pillow talk

aldéhyde [aldeid] NM *Chimie* aldehyde; **a. formique** formaldehyde

al dente [aldɛnte] ADJ *Culin (pâtes)* al dente

aldin [aldɛ̃] ADJ *Typ (édition, caractère)* Aldine

ALE [aɛlə] NF *(abrév* **Association de libre-échange)** FTA

ale [ɛl] NF (light) ale

aléa [alea] NM risk, hazard, chance; **l'affaire présente trop d'aléas** it's too risky a business; **les aléas de la vie** the hazards of life

aléatoire [aleatwar] ADJ *(échantillon)* random; *(résultat)* unpredictable, chancy, uncertain; *Jur (contrat etc)* aleatory; *Math* **fonction/variable a.** random function/variable; *Ordinat* **accès a.** random access

alémanique [alemanik] ADJ *Ling* **Suisse a.** German-speaking Switzerland

ALENA [alena] NM *(abrév* **Accord de libre-échange nord-américain)** NAFTA

alène [alɛn] NF awl; **a. plate** bradawl

alentour [alɑ̃tur] ADV around, round about; **les villages a.** the surrounding *or* neighbouring villages; **le pays d'a.** the surrounding *or* neighbouring countryside

▸ NMPL **alentours** surroundings, vicinity; **aux alentours de la ville/300 euros** in the vicinity of the town/300 euros; **il n'y avait personne aux alentours** there was no one around *or* in the vicinity; **il est arrivé aux alentours de midi** he arrived (some time) around midday

aléoute [aleut], **aléoutien, -ienne** [aleusjɛ̃, -jɛn] ADJ Aleutian; **les (îles) Aléoutiennes** the Aleutian Islands ▸ N A. Aleut(ian)

alerte[1] [alɛrt] NF alarm; **donner/sonner l'a.** to give/sound the alarm; **fausse a.** false alarm; **a. (aérienne)** air-raid warning; **à la première a.** as soon as the alarm goes; **en cas d'a.** if the alarm sounds; **état d'a.** state of alert; **l'état d'a. est déclaré** a state of alert has been declared; **être en a.** to be on the alert; *Mil* **fin d'a.** all clear; *Aviat* **a. en piste** scramble; **côte d'a.** danger level; **l'a. fut chaude** it was a narrow escape; *Méd* **nous avons eu une a. en septembre** we had a warning sign *or* a scare in September ▸ INT look out!, *Arch* to arms!

▸▸ **a. à la bombe** bomb scare; **a. rouge** red alert

alerte[2] ADJ **1** alert; *(démarche)* brisk; *(personne)* sprightly, alert; **style a.** *(écrit)* lively style; **il est paralysé mais son esprit est très a.** he's paralysed but his mind is (still) very alert **2** *Arch* vigilant, watchful

alerter [alɛrte] VT *(troupes, opinion publique etc)* to alert; **a. qn sur qch** to alert sb to sth

alésage [alezaʒ] NM *Métal* **1** *(opération)* boring (out); *(d'un cylindre)* reaming **2** *(diamètre) (d'un canon de fusil)* bore; *(d'un moteur à combustion)* bore; *(d'un cylindre etc)* internal diameter

alèse [alɛz] NF *Méd* drawsheet, undersheet

aléser [aleze] VT *Métal* to bore (out); *(élargir)* to ream

aléseuse [alezøz] NF *Métal* borer; *(pour élargir)* reamer

alester [aleste], **alestir** [alestir] VT *Naut (gréement)* to trim up, to tidy up

alevin [alvɛ̃] NM alevin, fry, young fish

alevinage [alvinaʒ] NM *(d'une rivière etc)* stocking with young fish

aleviner [alvine] VT to stock a river with young fish

alevinier [alvinje] NM, **alevinière** [alvinjer] NF breeding pond, nursery

Alexandre [alɛksɑ̃dr] N **A. le Grand** Alexander the Great

Alexandrie [alɛksɑ̃dri] N Alexandria

alexandrin [alɛksɑ̃drɛ̃, -in] ADJ **1** *Littér* alexandrine; **poème en vers alexandrins** poem in alexandrine verse *or* in alexandrines **2** *Géog* Alexandrian; *Fig* **des discussions alexandrines** convoluted discussions ▸ NM *Littér* alexandrine (verse)

alexie [alɛksi] NF *Méd* word blindness, alexia

alezan [alzɑ̃, -an] ADJ *(cheval)* chestnut ▸ NM **a. châtain** chestnut sorrel; **a. roux** red bay

alfa [alfa] NM *Bot* esparto (grass); **papier d'a.** esparto paper; **tiré sur a.** printed on esparto paper

algarade [algarad] NF row, quarrel; **nous avons eu une a.** we've had a row

algèbre [alʒɛbr] NF algebra; **a. booléenne** Boolean algebra; **résoudre un problème par l'a.** to solve a problem algebraically; *Fig* **c'est de l'a. pour moi** it's all Greek to me

algébrique [alʒebrik] ADJ algebraic

Alger [alʒe] N Algiers; *Hist* (the Department of) Alger

Algérie [alʒeri] NF Algeria; **en A.** in Algeria

algérien, -ienne [alʒerjɛ̃, -jɛn] ADJ Algerian ▸ N A. Algerian

algérois, -oise [alʒerwa, -waz] ADJ of *or* from Algiers ▸ N A. inhabitant *or* native of Algiers

algie [alʒi] NF ache, pain

algol [algɔl] NM *Ordinat* ALGOL

algonkien, -ienne [algɔ̃kjɛ̃, -jɛn] *Géol* ADJ Algonkian ▸ NM Algonkian

algonquin, -ine [algɔ̃kɛ̃, -in] ADJ *(peuple)* Algonquin ▸ NM Algonquian ▸ N A. Algonquin

algorithme [algɔritm] NM *Math, Ordinat* algorithm; *Ordinat* **a. de chiffrement** coding *or* encryption algorithm; *Ordinat* **a. de tri** sorting algorithm

algorithmique [algɔritmik] ADJ *Math, Ordinat* algorithmic

algothérapie [algɔterapi] NF = alternative medicine based on marine plant extracts

algue [alg] NF *(piece of)* seaweed, *Spéc* alga; **algues** seaweed, *Spéc* algae

alias [aljas] NM *Ordinat (de courrier électronique, de bureau)* alias ▸ ADV alias, otherwise *or* also known as; *Ordinat* alias; **Joe Balance, a. le Braqueur** Joe Balance, alias *or* aka the Robber

aliassage [aljasaʒ] NM *Ordinat* aliasing

alibi [alibi] NM alibi; **il a invoqué un a. absurde pour justifier son absence** he gave an absurd alibi to explain his absence

alicament [alikamɑ̃] NM nutraceutical

aliénable [aljenabl] ADJ *Jur* alienable, transferable

aliénant [aljenɑ̃] ADJ alienating

aliénation [aljenasjɔ̃] NF **1** *(de l'esprit)* alienation; **conditions d'a.** alienating conditions; *Psy* **a. mentale** insanity **2** *Jur (des droits, de biens etc)* alienation, transfer; *(de liberté)* loss

aliéné, -ée [aljene] *Psy* ADJ mad, insane ▸ N insane person; **les aliénés** the insane; **hospice d'aliénés** mental hospital

aliéner [aljene] (**j'aliène; n. aliénerons**) VT **1** *(sentiments etc)* to alienate, to estrange; **ce commentaire vous a aliéné la sympathie de l'auditoire** that comment lost you the audience's sympathy; **ces conditions de vie ne peuvent qu'a. les jeunes** such living conditions can only alienate young people **2** *Jur (biens, droits etc)* to alienate, to transfer; **a. sa liberté** to give up one's freedom **3** *(psychisme)* to derange, to unhinge ▸ VPR **s'aliéner** *(objet)* to lose; *(personne)* to alienate (oneself from); **s'a. la sympathie de l'électorat** to lose the goodwill of the electorate; **s'a. un ami** to alienate a friend; **s'a. l'amitié de qn** to lose sb's friendship; **s'a. par le travail** to be alienated by work

aliéniste [aljenist] N *Méd* alienist

alignement [alin(ə)mɑ̃] NM **1** *(opération)* alignment, aligning; *Mil (d'une ligne)* dressing; *Compta (d'un compte etc)* making up, balancing; *(de son, image)* tracking; **être dans l'a.** to be in a line; **maison frappée d'a.** house scheduled for realignment; **se mettre à l'a.** to fall into line, to line up; *Mil* **à droite a.!** right dress!; *Écon* **a. monétaire** alignment of currencies; *Com* **a. des prix** alignment of prices, price alignment; **l'a. des salaires sur le coût de la vie** bringing salaries into line with the cost of living; *Pol* **l'a. du parti sur la politique des États-Unis** the party's alignment with US policy **2** *(d'un mur etc)* alignment, line; **un a. de menhirs** a line of menhirs; *Constr* **déborder** *ou* **dépasser l'a.** to project beyond the building line; **prendre des alignements** to get one's bearings **3** *Rail (ligne droite)* straight stretch **4** *Ordinat* alignment

aligner [aline] VT **1** *(mettre en ligne)* to align, to line up, to put in a line; *(arranger)* to lay out; *Mil* to dress (a line); *Compta (compte)* to balance; **a. un terrain** to mark out a plot of ground); *Typ* **a. des caractères** to align *or* range type; *Pol* **a. sa politique sur celle des États voisins** to fall into line with the policy of neighbouring states; *Écon* **a. une monnaie** to align a currency; **les petits commerçants ne peuvent pas a. leurs prix sur ceux des grandes surfaces** small shopkeepers can't bring their prices into line with those of hypermarkets **2** *(dire, faire à la suite) (arguments)* to marshal; **a. des phrases** to string sentences together; **je passe ma journée à a. des chiffres** I spend my day producing lists of figures; *Fam* **les a.** *(payer)* to pay up, to cough up **3** *Fam (réprimander)* **a. qn** to tell sb off; **il s'est fait a. par un flic en moto** a motorcycle cop slapped a fine on him **4** *Ordinat* to align ▸ VPR **s'aligner 1** *(se mettre en ligne) (enfants)* to line up; *Mil (soldats)* to dress **2** *(d'un pays, d'une personne)* to fall into line; *Pol (sur un pays, une politique)* to align oneself (sur in); *Arg* **tu peux toujours t'a.!** *(tu n'es pas à la hauteur)* just you try it!

aliment [alimɑ̃] NM **1** food; **a. pauvre/riche** food that is low/high in nutritional value; **des aliments en conserve/surgelés** tinned/frozen food; **a. périssable** perishable food;

Physiol a. **complet** complete food; *Fig* **cette histoire a servi d'a. à la presse** the press made a meal out of the story **2** *Jur* **aliments** alimony

alimentaire [alimɑ̃tɛr] ADJ **1** *(denrée, plante etc)* nutritious; **produits alimentaires** food, foodstuffs; **conserves alimentaires** tinned *or* canned food(s); **régime a.** diet; *Admin, Hist* **carte a.** ration card; **surveiller son bol a.** to watch what one eats; **mauvaises habitudes alimentaires** bad eating habits **2** *Jur* **pension** *ou* **provision a.** alimony, maintenance; **payer** *ou* **verser une pension a.** to pay alimony *or* maintenance; **il est en retard dans le paiement de la pension a.** he's late with his *or* the alimony; *Fig* **travail** *ou* **occupation a.** job that keeps body and soul together **3** *Physiol* **canal** *ou* **tube a.** alimentary canal; **pompe a.** feed pump

alimentation [alimɑ̃tasjɔ̃] NF **1** *(régime alimentaire)* food, nourishment; *Biol* nutrition; **avoir une a. équilibrée** to have a balanced diet; **a. défectueuse** malnutrition; **surveillez votre a.** watch what you eat, watch your diet; **article d'a.** foodstuff; **(magasin d')a.** grocer's shop; **(rayon d')a.** grocery department, food counter
2 *(action) (de plantes, d'animaux etc)* feeding; *(de ville, de marché etc)* supply; **l'a. d'une ville en eau** the water supply to a town
3 *Tech (d'une chaudière etc)* feed(ing); *(d'un fusil)* feed mechanism; *(en électricité)* power supply; **pompe d'a.** feed pump; **a. par pesanteur** *ou* **par gravité** gravity feed; *Aut* **a. par injection** fuel injection; *Élec* **bloc d'a.** power supply; **câble** *ou* **fil d'a.** feeder; **a. papier** *(d'une imprimante)* sheetfeed, paper feed; **a. feuille à feuille** *ou* **page par page** *(d'une imprimante)* cut sheet *or* single sheet feed; *Ordinat* **a. ininterruptible** uninterruptible power supply

alimenter [alimɑ̃te] VT *(personne)* to feed, to nourish; *(marché)* to supply with food; *(chaudière)* to feed; **ruisseaux qui alimentent une rivière** streams that feed a river; *Élec* **a. une usine en courant** to supply a factory with power; *Fig* **a. la curiosité de qn** to feed sb's curiosity; *Fig* **a. la conversation par des anecdotes** to keep the conversation going with anecdotes; *Fig* **ces petits incidents risquent d'a. la discorde entre elles** these little incidents are likely to fuel the discord between them; **a. un compte** to pay money into an account
VPR s'alimenter to eat; *(d'un malade)* to take (solid) food

alinéa [alinea] NM *Typ* **1** *(renfoncement)* paragraph indent, indent; **mettre à l'a., faire un a.** to indent; **a. négatif** hanging indent **2** *(texte)* paragraph, *Fam* para; **sans a.** full-out

alité [alite] ADJ confined to (one's) bed, *Fam* laid up; *(infirme)* bedridden

alitement [alitmɑ̃] NM confinement to bed; **trois jours d'a.** three days in bed

aliter [alite] VT **a. qn** to confine sb to bed, to keep sb in bed
VPR s'aliter *(se mettre au lit)* to take to one's bed

alizé [alize] ADJ, NM **les (vents) alizés** the trade winds

Allah [ala] N Allah

allaitant [alɛtɑ̃] ADJ suckling, nursing; **mère allaitante** nursing mother

allaitement [alɛtmɑ̃] NM feeding, nursing, suckling; **a. au biberon** bottle-feeding; **a. mixte** mixed feeding; **a. naturel** breastfeeding; **durant l'a.** during breastfeeding

allaiter [alete] VT *(enfant)* to breastfeed, to nurse; *(enfant, petit)* to suckle

allant [alɑ̃] ADJ *(personne)* active, busy, live-

ly; *(personne âgée)* active, mobile, able to move *or* walk about
NM initiative, drive, energy; **avoir de l'a., être plein d'a.** to be full of go *or* (drive and) energy; **elle travaille avec a.** she works energetically *or* with gusto

alléchant [aleʃɑ̃] ADJ *(offre, plat)* attractive, alluring, enticing, tempting; *(odeur etc)* appetizing

allécher [aleʃe] VT **(j'allèche, n. alléchons; j'allécherai)** to attract, to entice, to tempt, to allure; **j'étais alléché par cette proposition** I was tempted by the proposal

allée [ale] NF **1** *(dans un jardin, menant à une maison)* path; *(permettant le passage de voitures)* drive; *(entre deux immeubles)* passage, alley; *(dans une ville)* street, avenue; *(longée d'arbres)* walk; **a. (cavalière)** bridle path; **a. de circulation** *(d'un magasin)* aisle **2** **allées et venues** coming(s) and going(s), running about; **j'ai dû faire de nombreuses allées et venues pour obtenir ce visa** I had to run all over the place to get this visa; **qu'est-ce que signifient ces allées et venues à cette heure tardive?** what's the meaning of all these comings and goings at this time of night?

allégation [alegasjɔ̃] NF allegation

allégé [aleʒe] ADJ *(yaourt, chips)* low-fat, diet; *(confiture)* low-sugar

allège [alɛʒ] NF **1** *Naut* lighter, hopper, barge; *Com* **frais d'a.** lighterage; **franco a.** free over side **2** *(de fenêtre)* window breast, (window)sill

allégeance [aleʒɑ̃s] NF **1** *(nationalité)* nationality; **avoir la double a.** to have dual nationality **2** *Arch* **serment d'a.** oath of allegiance; **faire a. à …** to pledge one's allegiance to … **3** *Naut* handicap

allégement, allègement [aleʒmɑ̃] NM **1** *(d'impôts, charges etc)* reduction; **a. fiscal** tax relief **2** *(de véhicule, fardeau)* lightening

alléger [aleʒe] VT **(j'allège, n. allégeons; j'allégeai(s); j'allégerai)** **1** *(impôts, charges etc)* to reduce; *(douleur, chagrin)* to alleviate, to relieve, to soothe **2** *(véhicule, fardeau etc)* to lighten; *(poutres de charpente etc)* to ease the strain on; *Scol* **a. un programme scolaire** to lighten a school syllabus **3** *Tech (objet)* to reduce the volume of; *(bois)* to plane down; *(métal)* to file down, to fine down

allégorie [alegɔri] NF allegory; **par a.** allegorically

allégorique [alegɔrik] ADJ allegorical

allégoriquement [alegɔrikmɑ̃] ADV allegorically

allègre [alɛgr] ADJ lively, jolly, cheerful; *(musique)* lively; **parler d'un ton a.** to speak cheerfully *or* light-heartedly; **caractère a.** cheerful disposition; **avoir le cœur a.** to be light-hearted; **marcher d'un pas a.** to walk with a spring in one's step

allègrement [alɛgrəmɑ̃] ADV cheerfully; *Iron* blithely; *(marcher)* with a spring in one's step; **il s'est a. moqué de nous** he has been quite blithely making fools of us

allégresse [alegrɛs] NF joy, cheerfulness, liveliness; **plein d'a.** full of joy; **a. générale** general rejoicing; **cris d'a.** cries of joy

allegretto [alegretto] ADV, NM *Mus* allegretto

allegro [alegro] ADV, NM *Mus* allegro

alléguer [alege] VT **(j'allègue, n. alléguons; j'alléguerai)** **1** *(invoquer)* to allege, to plead; **a. l'ignorance** to plead ignorance; **a. une excuse/une raison** to put forward *or* offer *or* give an excuse/a reason; **a. comme raison que le temps manquait** to give lack of time as one's reason; **il allégua que personne ne l'avait informé de ce projet** he alleged that

no one had informed him of the plan **2** *(auteur, texte etc)* to cite, to quote

alléluia [aleluja] INT, NM *Rel* alleluia, hallelujah

Allemagne [alman] NF Germany; *Anciennement* **l'A. de l'ouest/de l'est** West/East Germany; *Anciennement* **les deux Allemagnes** the two Germanies; **l'ambassadeur d'A.** the German ambassador

allemand, -ande [almɑ̃, -ɑ̃d] ADJ German; **la langue allemande** the German language, German
NM *Ling* German, the German language
N **A.** German; *Anciennement* **A. de l'Est/de l'Ouest** East/West German
NF **allemande** *Mus* allemande

ALLER¹ [ale]

VI to go **1, 2, 4, 6, 7, 9, 13, 15** ■ to go + *adv* **3** ■ *future tense* **14** ■ to walk **2** ■ to lead **4** ■ to work **7** ■ to fit *(aller à)* **8, 11** ■ to suit *(aller à)* **11** ■ to match *(aller avec)* **12** ■ to go well with *(aller avec)* **12** ■ *interjection* **16**
VPR to go away **1** ■ to come off **3**

VI *(prp* allant; *pp* allé; *pr ind* je vais *(Arch, Région* je vas), tu vas, il va, n. allons, v. allez, ils vont; *pr sub* j'aille, n. allions, ils aillent; *imp* va (vas-y), allons, allez; *impf* j'allais; *p hist* j'allai; *fu* j'irai; the aux is être) **1** *(se rendre)* to go; **a. à Paris** to go to Paris; **navire allant à Bordeaux** ship bound for Bordeaux; **a. chez le coiffeur/médecin/au marché** to go to the hairdresser's/to the doctor/to the market; **a. en course/à la chasse/à la pêche/à cheval/en voiture/au galop/au trot** *voir ces mots*; **a. aux champignons** to go mushroom-picking; **on va sur Lyon** we're going to *or* as far as Lyons; **a. de ville en ville** to go from town to town; **a. devant/derrière/à côté de qn** to go in front of/behind/beside sb; **a. chez qn** to go to sb's house, to call on *or* visit sb, to go and see sb; **je vais chez lui pour dîner ce soir** I'm going to his house for dinner this evening; **je vais chez ma grand-mère quand je suis à Paris** I call on *or* visit my grandmother whenever I'm in Paris; **nous allons toujours chez Maxim's** we always go to Maxim's; **a. jusqu'à qch/qn** to go as far as sth/to go up to sb; **qui va là?** who goes there?; **ne faire qu'a. et venir** to be always on the go *or* on the move; **je n'ai fait qu'a. et venir ce matin pour obtenir les papiers** I did nothing but run all over the place this morning to get the papers; **je ne ferai qu'a. et revenir** I shall come straight back; **où allons-nous?** where are we going?; *Fig (qu'est-ce qu'on va devenir?)* what are things coming to?; *Fam* **où tu vas?** are you mad?, have you got a screw loose?, *Br* are you off your head?; **je suis allé aux nouvelles** I went to find out what was happening; **il va sur ses quarante ans** he is getting on for forty, he is nearly forty (years old); **il ira loin** he will go far *or* will distinguish himself; **insulter un agent de police? ça peut a. loin, ça** insulting a policeman can have serious consequences; **vous allez trop loin** you're going too far; **vous n'irez pas loin avec 50 euros** 50 euros won't get you very far, you won't get very far on 50 euros; **soyez tranquille, cela n'ira pas plus loin** don't worry, it won't go any further; **cette vieille voiture n'ira pas loin** this old car won't get very far; **a. jusqu'au bout** to see it through; *(avoir des rapports sexuels)* to go the whole way; **nous irons jusqu'au bout** we shall carry on to the end; **a. au fond des choses** to get to the bottom of things; **décontractez-vous, laissez-vous a.** relax, let yourself go; **il faut apprendre à laisser a. les choses** you must learn to let things take their course; **reprends-toi, tu ne dois pas te lais-**

ser a. pull yourself together, you mustn't let yourself go; **se laisser a. à la tendresse/à de meilleurs sentiments** to give way to tenderness/better feelings; **sa remarque m'est allée droit au cœur** his remark went straight to my heart; **l'eau va jusqu'à la taille** the water is waist-deep; **l'eau lui allait jusqu'à la taille** the water came up to his/her waist; **ses cheveux vont jusqu'à la taille** her hair goes down to her waist, she has waist-length hair

2 (*se déplacer*) to go, to move; (*à pied*) to walk; **on y va à pied** we're walking there; **a. en vélo/voiture/avion/bateau** to go by bike/car/plane/boat; **on va à la catastrophe** we're heading for disaster; **j'y suis allé très lentement** I went very slowly; **j'y suis allé en deux heures** it took me two hours to get there

3 (*with adv*) **a. bon train** to go at a good pace; **a. grand train** to race along; **la voiture va vite** the car goes fast

4 (*mener*) to lead, to go; **chemin qui va à la gare** road leading to the station; *Prov* **tous les chemins vont à Rome** all roads lead to Rome

5 (*être conçu pour*) **ces ciseaux vont bien pour couper les roses** these scissors are good for cutting roses; **plat qui va au feu** *ou* **allant au feu** *ou* **au four** fireproof *or* ovenproof dish

6 (*marcher*) (*bien, mal*) to go; **tout va bien** everything is going well *or* is fine; **tout va mal** things are going badly, things aren't going at all well; **non, ça ne va pas du tout** (*ce n'est pas ce que j'ai demandé*) no, that won't do at all; **ça va!** (*d'accord*) OK!; **ça va, ça va, on te pardonne** OK, OK, you're forgiven; *Fam* **non, mais ça va pas (la tête)?!** are you crazy?!, what's wrong with you?!; **ça ira!** we'll/I'll/*etc* manage!; **ça va comme ça** it's all right *or* it's fine *or* that will do (as it is); **merci, ça va comme ça, j'ai eu assez à manger** that will do *or* that's fine, thanks, I've had enough to eat; **faire a.** to get by, to struggle along; **ça n'irait pas du tout** that would never do; **ça va a. mal si tu me mens** if you've been lying to me, there'll be trouble; **il y a quelque chose qui ne va pas** there's something wrong; **tout a l'air d'a. bien entre eux** everything seems to be fine between them; **je vous en offre 100 euros, ça va?** I'll give you 100 euros for it, OK?; **ça va tout seul** it's a piece of cake; **cela ne va pas tout seul** it's not (that) easy, it's not an easy job

7 (*d'un appareil, d'une horloge etc*) to go, to work, to run; **la pendule va bien/mal** the clock is/isn't working (properly); **quand le bâtiment va, tout va** what's good for the construction industry is good for us all; **les affaires vont/ne vont pas** business is good/slack; **faire a. un commerce** to run a business; **tout va comme sur des roulettes** everything is going like clockwork

8 (*être de la bonne taille etc*) to fit; **ce veston ne va pas bien** this jacket doesn't fit well

9 (*tenir*) **c'est trop grand pour a. dans le panier** it's too big to go *or* get *or* fit into the basket; **je ne sais pas où vont les assiettes** I don't know where the plates go

10 (*se porter*) **comment allez-vous?** how are you?; **je vais bien**, *Fam* **ça va** I'm well, I'm all right, I'm fine; **cela va mieux** I'm better; **cela ne va pas** I'm not feeling very well

11 a. à qn (*de couleurs etc*) to suit sb; (*de vêtements*) to fit sb; (*de climat, de denrées*) to agree with sb; (*d'un projet etc*) to suit sb; **cela vous va comme un gant** (*d'une robe etc*) it fits you like a glove; (*d'une situation etc*) it suits you down to the ground; **cette robe te va mal** (*elle te grossit*) that dress doesn't suit you; **la chemise ne me va pas** (*elle est trop petite*) the shirt doesn't fit me; **ça me va!** (*d'accord*) agreed!, done!; **ça te va bien de**

me conseiller you're a fine one to give me advice

12 (*être assorti*) **a. avec qch** (*de couleurs etc*) to go well with sth, to match sth; **a. (bien) ensemble** to go well together; **chaussettes qui ne vont pas ensemble** odd socks

13 (*aller + inf*) **a. voir qn** to go and *or* to see sb, to call on sb; **a. trouver qn** to go and find sb; **va voir si quelqu'un n'a pas sonné à la porte** go and see if that was someone ringing the doorbell; **a. se promener** to go for a walk; **va donc le lui dire!** go and tell him then!; **n'allez pas vous imaginer que ...** don't imagine that ..., don't go imagining that ..., don't get it into your head that ...; **allez donc savoir!** how are you (supposed) to know?; *Fam* **allez vous faire voir!** go to hell!

14 (*utilisé comme auxiliaire*) to be going, to be about (to do sth); **il va s'en occuper** he is going to see about it, he'll deal with it; **je vais te dire quelque chose** let me tell you something; **je sais ce que tu vas me dire** I know what you're about to tell me; **il va venir** he'll be coming; **je vais devoir prendre une décision** I'm going to have to make a decision; **il va pouvoir acheter la voiture dont il rêve** he's going to be able to buy the car of his dreams; **elle allait tout avouer** she was about to confess everything; **sa santé va (en) empirant** his/her health is steadily deteriorating

15 (*avec 'y'*) **j'y vais!, on y va!** coming!; **j'y vais** (*ouvrir la porte*) I'll get it; **est-ce comme ça que vous y allez?** is that how you go about it *or* do it?; **allez-y doucement!** easy *or* gently (does it)!; **il y va fort** he's going a bit too far, he's going a bit over the top; **y a. de tout son cœur** to put one's heart and soul into it; **y a. carrément** *ou* **franchement** to make no bones about it; **vas-y, dis-moi ce que tu as à dire!** go on then, say what you've got to say!; **maintenant allons-y!** now (let's get down) to it!; **allons-y!** well, here goes!; **vas-y!/allez-y!** go!, on you go!; (*au travail etc*) get on with it!; (*pose-moi ces questions*) fire away!; *Fam* **y a. de qch** to lay *or* stake sth; **il y est allé de ses économies** he staked his savings; **y a. de son reste** to stake one's all; **y a. de sa personne** to take a hand in it oneself, *Fam* to do one's bit; **il y est allé de son histoire/sa petite chanson** he gave us his story/little song

16 (*interjection*) **allons, dépêchez-vous!** come on, hurry up!; **allez, s'il te plaît, viens avec moi!** oh go on, come with me, please!; **allons donc!** (*c'est vrai?*) (well I) never!; **allez, je vous écoute** go ahead, I'm listening; **allez, c'est oublié** don't worry, it's all forgotten; **allons bon!** there now!; (*exprimant de l'irritation*) oh no!; **allons, sois un peu raisonnable!** come on now, be reasonable!; **allons, allons, calme-toi** come on now, calm down; **va pour une soirée au cinéma** OK then, a night out at the cinema it is; **allez, allez, débarrasse la table!** come on *or* along (now), clear the table!; *Fam* **va donc, eh patate!** if you don't like it, you can lump it!; **va donc eh, vieux crétin!** get lost, you idiot!

VPR s'en aller (*pr ind* **je m'en vais**; *imp* **va-t'en, allons-nous-en, allez-vous-en, ne t'en va pas, ne nous en allons pas**; *perf* **je m'en suis allé(e), nous nous en sommes allé(e)s**) **1** (*partir*) to go away, to leave; **les voisins s'en vont** the neighbours are moving; **s'en a. en vacances** to go away on holiday; **elle s'en est allée** *ou Fam* **s'est en allée assez satisfaite** she went away fairly satisfied; **allez-vous-en!** go away!; **allons-nous-en!** let's go!; **s'en a. en fumée** to go up in smoke; **demain, je m'en vais** I'm off, see you tomorrow; **il faut que je m'en aille** I must be going; **ses forces s'en allaient** his strength was failing **2** (*mourir*) to pass away, to die; **le malade s'en va** the patient is sinking (fast)

3 (*disparaître*) **les taches ne veulent pas s'en a.** the stains won't come off *or* out

4 (*+ inf*) **s'en a. faire qch** to go off and *or* to do sth; **je m'en vais lui dire ce que je pense** I'm going to tell him exactly what I think; **va savoir s'il ne ment pas!** how am I/are we/*etc* supposed to know if he's telling the truth or not?; **je m'en vais vous raconter ça** I'll tell you all about it

V IMPERS il va sans dire *ou* **il va de soi que ...** it stands to reason *or* it goes without saying that ...; **il va sans dire qu'elle a refusé** it goes without saying that she refused, needless to say, she refused; **il en va de même pour lui/moi** it's the same with him/me; **il n'en va pas de même pour eux** things are different for them; **il en va de sa réputation** his reputation is at stake; **il y va de vingt mille euros** it's a matter of twenty thousand euros; **il y allait de sa vie** it was a matter of life and death (for him), his life was at stake; **il y va de sa place** his job is at stake; **il y va de votre santé** your health is at risk, you're risking your health

aller² NM going; (*d'un aller retour*) outward journey; **a. retour, voyage d'a. (et) retour** round trip, return journey, journey there and back; *Naut* voyage out and home; **billet a. retour** return ticket, *Am* round-trip ticket; *Fam* **un a.** a single ticket, *Am* a one-way ticket; **deux allers et un a. retour pour Marseille, s'il vous plaît** two singles and a return to Marseilles, please; *Bourse* **a. et retour** bed and breakfasting; **à l'a.** on the way there; **je me suis arrêté en route à l'a.** I stopped on my *or* the way (there); **cargaison d'a.** outward cargo; *Sport* **match a.** away match; **a. retour du piston** up and down stroke; *Fam* **si tu continues, tu vas recevoir un a. et retour dont tu te souviendras** if you carry on, you'll get a clip round the ear that you won't forget in a hurry

allergène [alɛrʒɛn] NM *Méd* allergen

allergénique [alɛrʒenik] ADJ *Méd* allergenic

allergie [alɛrʒi] NF *Méd* allergy; **avoir** *ou* **faire une a. au poil de chat** to have an allergy *or* to be allergic to cat hair; *Fig* **elle a fini par faire** *ou* **avoir une véritable a. au travail** she eventually became completely allergic to work

allergique [alɛrʒik] ADJ *Méd* allergic (**à** to); *Fig* **il est a. aux maths** he's allergic to maths

allergologiste [alɛrgɔlɔʒist], **allergologue** [alɛrgɔlɔg] N *Méd* allergist

alliage [aljaʒ] NM *Métal* alloy; **sans a.** pure, unalloyed; *Fig* **un a. d'idées fausses** a mishmash *or* hotchpotch of mistaken ideas

alliance [aljɑ̃s] NF **1** (*entente*) alliance; (*d'un couple*) marriage, union; **conclure une a.** to enter into *or* forge an alliance; **faire a. avec/contre qn** to ally *or* team up with/against sb; **entrer par a. dans une famille** to marry into a family; **faire a. avec une autre famille** to be joined to another family by marriage; **parent par a.** relation by marriage; **traité d'a.** treaty of alliance; *Mktg* **a. de marques** co-branding **2** (*bague*) wedding ring **3** (*combinaison*) (*de parfums etc*) combination; **une a. de termes très réussie** a very effective juxtaposition of terms; **a. de mots** (*figure de style*) oxymoron

---

Alliance française

In many respects, the activities of the Alliance française are similar to those of the British Council, although it is a private body. It organizes classes in French language and civilization and has branches all over the world.

allié, -ée [alje] ADJ **1** *(nation etc)* allied **2** *(dans une famille)* related by marriage; **être bien a.** to be well connected
▪ N ally; *(de famille)* relation by marriage; *(moins précis)* family connection; **invitation lancée aux parents et alliés** invitation sent out to immediate family and close relatives; **il est d'accord avec nous, c'est un a.** he agrees with us, he's on our side; *Hist* **les Alliés** the Allies

allier [alje] *(impf, pr sub* **n. alliions, v. alliiez)** VT **1** *(unir)* to ally, to unite; **intérêts communs qui allient deux pays** common interests that unite two countries; **a. une famille à** *ou* **avec une autre** to unite one family with another by marriage **2** *(métaux)* to alloy, to mix; *(couleurs)* to harmonize, to blend, to match; *(qualités, mots etc)* to combine (**à** with); **a. l'intelligence à la beauté** to combine intelligence and beauty
▪ VPR **s'allier 1** *(s'unir)* to form an alliance, to become allies, to ally (**avec qn** with sb); **s'a. à une famille** to marry into a family; **s'a. contre qn/qch** to unite against sb/sth **2** *(de liquides)* to mix; *(de métaux)* to alloy; *(de couleurs)* to harmonize, to blend; *(de goûts, de qualités)* to combine

alligator [aligatɔr] NM alligator

allitératif, -ive [aliteratif, -iv] ADJ alliterative

allitération [aliterasjɔ̃] NF alliteration; **a. en s** alliteration of (the letter) s

allô, allo [alo] INT *Tél* hello!

alloc [alɔk] NF *Fam* benefit; **les allocs** *(allocations familiales)* child benefit

allocataire [alɔkater] N beneficiary; *(à la Sécurité sociale etc)* claimant, recipient

allocation [alɔkasjɔ̃] NF **1** *(d'argent, de terres, de marchandises etc)* allocation, granting; *Fin (de titres etc)* allotment, allocation **2** *(prestation financière)* allowance, grant; **elle touche les allocations (familiales)** she gets child benefit
▪▸▸ **a. (de) chômage** unemployment benefit; **a. de garde d'enfant à domicile** = allowance paid to working parents who employ a childminder at home; **a. (de) logement** housing benefit, *Am* rent subsidy; **a. (de) maternité** maternity benefit; **allocations familiales** child benefit, family allowance(s), *Am* dependents' allowances; **a. de formation reclassement** = allowance paid to employees requiring further training or new qualifications; **a. de parent isolé** = allowance paid to single parents; **a. de rentrée scolaire** = allowance paid to parents to help cover costs incurred at the start of the school year; **a. de solidarité spécifique** = allowance paid to long-term unemployed people who are no longer entitled to unemployment benefit; **a. vieillesse** old-age pension

allocution [alɔkysjɔ̃] NF **1** short speech, address; **prononcer une a.** to make a speech **2** *Rel, Jur (par un évêque, un juge aux jurés)* charge

allogène [alɔʒɛn] ADJ *(population etc)* non-indigenous, non-native

allogreffe [alɔgrɛf] NF *Chir* allograft, homograft

allonge [alɔ̃ʒ] NF **1** *(d'une table)* (extension) leaf; *(d'un tuyau, d'une cornue etc)* extension; *(de machine)* coupling rod; **mettre une a. à qch** to put an extension to sth, to lengthen sth; **a. de tige** extension rod; **a. de boucher** meathook **2** *Boxe* reach; **il a une bonne a.** he has a long reach

allongé, -ée [alɔ̃ʒe] ADJ long; *(forme, silhouette)* elongated; **avoir le visage a.** to have a long face; *Méd* **les malades allongés** recumbent patients; *Anat* **la moelle allongée** the medulla oblongata; *Sport* **coup a.** follow through
▪ N *Méd* recumbent patient

allongement [alɔ̃ʒmɑ̃] NM **1** *(d'un canal etc)* lengthening, extension; *(d'une robe)* lengthening; *(de métaux etc)* elongation, strain; *Mil (des tirs)* lifting **2** *(de temps)* protraction, extension; **a. de la journée de travail** lengthening *or* extension of the working day; **a. de l'espérance de vie des femmes** increase in women's life expectancy **3** *Aviat (des ailes)* aspect ratio

allonger [alɔ̃ʒe] *(j'allongeai(s); n. allongeons)* VT **1** *(rendre plus long)* to lengthen; *(forme, silhouette)* to elongate; *(vêtement)* to let down; *Mil (tirs)* to lift; **cette robe allonge votre silhouette** this dress makes you look taller; *Culin* **a. la sauce** to thin (down) the sauce; *Fig* to spin it out
2 *(bras)* to stretch out; *(cou)* to crane; **a. le pas** to quicken one's pace *or* step(s); *Sport* **a. l'allure** to increase the pace
3 a. un malade to lay a sick person down; *Fam* **a. qn** to knock sb down, to floor sb; **a. un coup à qn** to aim a blow at sb; *Fam* **je lui ai allongé une gifle dont il se souviendra** I gave him a slap he'll remember for a long time; *Fam* **a. l'argent** *(payer)* to hand over *or* fork out the money
4 *(conversation, période, délai etc)* to protract, to prolong
▪ VPR **s'allonger 1** *(des jours etc)* to grow longer, to lengthen; *(d'un enfant)* to get taller, to grow; **elle a changé de corps, elle commence à s'a.** her body has changed, she's starting to stretch out
2 *(se coucher)* to stretch (oneself) out, to lie down
▪ VI to extend; *Sport* **le peloton des coureurs allonge derrière** the field is strung out behind; **les jours commencent à a.** the days are starting to get longer, the days are drawing out

allopathe [alɔpat] *Méd* ADJ allopathic
▪ N allopath, allopathist

allopathie [alɔpati] NF *Méd* allopathy

allouer [alwe] VT *Admin (salaire, pension, etc)* to award, to grant; *(actions, rations etc)* to allocate, to apportion; **on lui a alloué un délai supplémentaire de deux jours** he was granted *or* allowed a two-day extension; **a. une dépense/un budget** to allow *or* pass an item of expenditure/a budget; *Jur* **a. une somme à qn à titre de dommages-intérêts** to award sb damages; **pendant le temps alloué** *(faire qch)* within the allotted time, within the time allowed

allouf [aluf] NF match *(for lighting fire)*

allumage [alymaʒ] NM *(d'une lampe, d'un feu)* lighting; *(d'une lampe électrique)* switching on; *(d'un moteur à combustion)* ignition; *(d'une mine)* firing; *Aut* **a. par bobine batterie** battery-coil ignition; **a. par compression** compression ignition; **a. à déclenchement statique** breakerless ignition; **a. défectueux** misfiring; **a. électronique** electronic *or* breakerless ignition; **a. par magnéto haute tension** high-tension magneto ignition; **a. prématuré** pre-ignition; **a. sans rupteur** breakerless ignition; **a. à rupteur transistorisé** transistorized ignition; **a. statique** breakerless ignition; **a. transistorisé** transistorized ignition

allumé, -ée [alyme] ADJ **1** alight, burning; *(d'un haut fourneau)* in blast **2** *Fam (ivre)* tiddly, tipsy **3** *Fam (dingue)* crazy, off one's head *or* rocker
▪ N *Fam* nutcase, nutter

allume-cigare, *pl* **allume-cigares** [alymsigar] NM cigar lighter

allume-gaz [alymgaz] NM INV *(pour cuisinière)* gas lighter

allumer [alyme] VT **1** *(lampe à pétrole, feu, pipe)* to light; *(lampe, télévision, électricité)* to switch on, to turn on; *Ordinat* to power up; **tu pourrais a. la chambre?** could you switch on *or* turn on *or* put on the light in the bedroom?; **veux-tu a. la lumière?** will you switch on *or* turn on *or* put on the lights?; **a. une pompe** to prime a pump
2 *Fig (passions, personnes)* to inflame, to excite, to stir up; **a. l'imagination** to fire the imagination; **elle allume les hommes** she excites men, she turns men on; **se faire a.** *(séduire)* to get aroused, *Fam* to get turned on; *(reprendre)* to get a ticking *or* telling off; *(tuer)* to get bumped off
▪ VPR **s'allumer** *(de la lumière)* to come on; *Fig (des yeux)* to light up; *Ordinat* to power up; **ça ne s'allume pas** the light's not working; **où est-ce que ça s'allume?** where does it switch *or* turn on?; **ça s'allume et ça s'éteint** the light's going on and off; **s'a. prématurément** *(d'un moteur)* to backfire
▪ VI to switch on *or* turn on *or* put on the light(s)

allumette [alymɛt] NF **1** match; **a. de sûreté** safety match; **pochette/boîte d'allumettes** book/box of matches; **frotter une a.** to strike a match; *Fam* **des jambes comme des allumettes** legs like matchsticks **2** *Culin* **a. au fromage** cheese straw; **pommes allumettes** thinly cut chips

allumeur [alymœr] NM **1** *(appareil)* lighter, igniting device; *(de moteur)* distributor; *Aut* **a.-distributeur** distributor unit **2** *Arch* lighter, igniter; **a. de réverbère** lamplighter

allumeuse [alymøz] NF *Fam (femme séductrice)* tease

allure [alyr] NF **1** *(vitesse)* pace, speed; **marcher à (une) vive a.** to walk at a brisk pace; **à toute a.** at full *or* top speed; *Sport* at full stretch; **pleine a.** maximum speed
2 *(démarche)* walk, gait; *(manière de se tenir)* bearing, appearance; **allures d'un cheval** paces of a horse; **cela lui donne une belle a.** that makes her look nice
3 *(manière de se présenter)* manner; *(manière d'agir)* way(s) of doing things; *(d'une personne, d'événements etc)* appearance, look; **il prend** *ou* **se donne des allures de roi quand il est en visite** he acts *or* behaves like royalty when he's visiting; **elle/la voiture a de l'a.** she's/the car's got (real) style; **l'a. des affaires** the way things are going; **prendre bonne a.** to look promising, to look well
4 *(d'un fourneau, d'un moteur etc)* working; **a. régulière** smooth running; **a. de marche** rating; **a. normale** normal speed; **a. économique de croisière** cruising speed

> Il faut noter que le nom anglais **allure** est un faux ami. Il signifie **attrait**.

allusif, -ive [alyzif, -iv] ADJ allusive; **sois moins a.!** be more specific!

allusion [alyzjɔ̃] NF allusion (**à** to); *Péj* innuendo; **faire a. à qn/qch** to refer to *or* to allude to *or* to make an allusion to sb/sth; **c'est à vous que s'adresse cette a.** that's a dig at you, that's meant for you; **cette a. m'échappe** I can't see what he's/she's/you're/etc getting at

allusivement [alyzivmɑ̃] ADV allusively

alluvial, -iale, -iaux, -iales [alyvjal, -jo] ADJ *Géol* alluvial

alluvions [alyvjɔ̃] NFPL *Géol* alluvium

alma mater [almamatɛr] N *Belg, Can, Suisse* Alma Mater; **l'université de Genève est mon a.** Geneva University is my Alma Mater

almanach [almana] NM *(calendrier)* almanac, yearbook

aloès [alɔɛs] NM *(plante)* aloe; *Pharm* **amer d'a.** bitter aloes

aloi [alwa] NM **1** *(de chose, de personne)* de bon a. genuine; une plaisanterie de mauvais a. an unsavoury joke, a joke in bad taste; des résultats de mauvais a. unpromising results; un succès de bon a. a well-deserved *or* worthy success **2** *(titre)* = proportion of precious metal in an alloy

alopécie [alɔpesi] NF *Méd* alopecia

alors [alɔr] ADV **1** *(à cette époque-là) (dans le passé)* then, at that time, at the time; *(dans le futur)* then; elle était a. institutrice she was a teacher then *or* at the time; a. nous nous marierons then we'll get married; que faisiez-vous a.? what were you doing then *or* at the time?; jusqu'a. until then; la vie d'a. life then *or* in those days; le ministre d'a. the minister at the time, the then minister

2 *(dans ce cas)* (well) then, in that case, in such a case; s'il mourait, a., elle devrait reprendre son travail if he died, then she would have to go back to work; a. vous viendrez? well then, you're coming?; et (puis) a.?, a. quoi? and what then?; *(qu'est-ce que ça peut faire?)* so what?; *Fam* non mais a., pour qui te prends-tu? really!, just who do you think you are?; je ne suis pas le banquier de tout le monde, non mais a.! honestly! I'm not made of money, you know!; a., tu viens? are you coming then?; merde a.! shit!; a. ... right ..., now then ...; a. Sophie, tu es prête? OK *or* right Sophie, are you ready?, are you ready then, Sophie?

3 *(donc)* therefore, so; il n'était pas là, a. je suis revenu he wasn't there, so I came back CONJ a. (même) que (at the very time) when, even when; *(bien que)* even though; vous dépensez, a. qu'il faudrait économiser you're spending, when you should be saving; a. même que je le pourrais even though I could

alouette [alwɛt] NF **1** *(oiseau)* lark; a. des champs skylark; a. des bois woodlark; a. de mer summer snipe, sea lark, dunlin **2** *Culin* a. sans tête veal olive

alourdi [alurdi] ADJ heavy, dull; a. de sommeil drowsy; a. par le sommeil heavy with sleep; style a. par trop de tournures compliquées style weighed down by too many complicated expressions; *Fin* le marché est a. the market is dull

alourdir [alurdir] VT **1** *(rendre plus lourd) (objet)* to make heavy; *(personne, objet)* to weigh down; *Fig (sens)* to dull; *(phrase)* to make cumbersome *or* unwieldy; les abus de toutes sortes ont alourdi ses traits overindulgence has thickened his features **2** *(alourdir) (charges, impôts)* to increase VPR s'alourdir to grow *or* become heavy

alourdissement [alurdismɑ̃] NM (process of) growing heavy; *(des membres etc)* growing heaviness; *(des sens)* dulling; sensation d'a. feeling of heaviness

aloyau, -aux [alwajo] NM *Culin (de bœuf)* sirloin; bifteck d'a. T-bone (steak)

alpaga [alpaga] NM *Zool, Tex* alpaca

alpage [alpaʒ] NM *(pâturage)* alp, mountain pasture; *(droit) (dans les pâturages)* right of pasture; *(saison)* = season spent by livestock in mountain pastures

alpaguer [alpage] VT *Fam* to nab, to collar; se faire a. par la police to get nabbed *or* collared by the police

alpe [alp] NF **1** *Région (pâturage)* alp, mountain pasture **2** les Alpes the Alps; les Alpes suisses the Swiss Alps; cor des Alpes alpenhorn

alper [alpe] VI *Suisse* = to move cattle up to higher mountain pastures at the beginning of summer

alpestre [alpɛstr] ADJ *(paysage, climat etc)* alpine; plante a. alpine (plant)

alpha [alfa] NM **1** *(lettre de l'alphabet grec)*

alpha; *Fig* l'a. et l'oméga alpha and omega, the beginning and the end; *Fig* connaître l'a. et l'oméga de qch to know sth from beginning to end **2** *(particule, rayons, radiation)* alpha

alphabet [alfabɛ] NM **1** alphabet; apprendre son a. à un enfant to teach a child the alphabet **2** *Scol* spelling book

alphabétique [alfabetik] ADJ alphabetical; par ordre a. in alphabetical order, alphabetically; classer qch par ordre a. to put sth in alphabetical order, to alphabetize sth; index a. index in alphabetical order

alphabétiquement [alfabetikmɑ̃] ADV alphabetically

alphabétisation [alfabetizasjɔ̃] NF l'a. de la population teaching the population to read and write; taux d'a. literacy rate

alphabétiser [alfabetize] VT to teach to read and write

alpha-hydroxy-acide [alfaidrɔksiasid] NM alpha hydroxy acid

alphanumérique [alfanymerik] ADJ alphanumeric

Alphapage® [alfapaʒ] NM bleeper

alpha-test, *pl* **alpha-tests** NM *Ordinat* alpha test; **alpha-tests** alpha testing

alpin [alpɛ̃] ADJ *(plante, chasseurs)* alpine; la chaîne alpine, le massif a. the Alps; ski a. downhill skiing

alpinisme [alpinism] NM *Sport* mountaineering, climbing; faire de l'a. to go mountaineering *or* climbing

alpiniste [alpinist] N mountaineer, climber

Alsace [alzas] NF Alsace

alsacien, -ienne [alzasjɛ̃, -jɛn] ADJ from Alsace, Alsatian

NM *Ling* Alsatian (dialect)

N A. inhabitant of Alsace, Alsatian

altérable [alterabl] ADJ liable to deterioration; marchandise a. perishable goods

altéragène [alteraʒɛn] ADJ *(substance)* harmful to the environment, noxious

altérant [alterɑ̃] ADJ thirst-producing, thirst-making

altération [alterasjɔ̃] NF **1** change (for the worse); *(de la santé etc) (par un agent extérieur)* impairment; *(de denrées, de la santé etc)* deterioration; *Ordinat (de fichier)* corruption; a. de la voix breaking of the voice **2** *(falsification) (de monnaie, document etc)* falsification; *(de denrées)* adulteration; *(de texte)* garbling; *(de faits)* misrepresentation **3** *Mus* sharp/flat sign, inflection; *(dans le courant du morceau)* accidental **4** *(soif)* great thirst

altercation [alterkasjɔ̃] NF altercation, dispute; avoir une a. avec qn to have a quarrel *or* a row with sb

altéré [altere] ADJ **1** *(couleur)* faded; *(visage)* drawn, haggard; voix altérée par l'émotion voice strained *or* faltering with emotion; les faits sont altérés the facts have been distorted **2** *Ordinat* corrupt **3** *Litt (assoiffé)* thirsty; a. de sang thirsting for blood, bloodthirsty; être a. de pouvoir to thirst *or* hunger for power

alter ego [alterego] NM INV alter ego

altérer [altere] (j'altère, n. altérons; j'altérerai) VT **1** *(détériorer)* to change (for the worse); *(viande, vin)*, *Fig (tempérament)* to spoil, to taint; *(vin, alimentation)* to adulterate; *(santé)* to impair **2** *Ordinat* to corrupt **3** *(fausser) (dispositif)* to tamper with; *(document)* to falsify; *(texte, histoire)* to garble; *(monnaie)* to falsify; a. la vérité to twist the truth **4** *Mus* a. une note to inflect a note **5** a. qn to make sb thirsty

VPR s'altérer to deteriorate; *(de couleurs)* to fade; *Ordinat* to go corrupt

altérité [alterite] NF *Phil* otherness

altermondialisation [altermɔ̃djalizasjɔ̃] NF ethical globalization

alternance [alternɑ̃s] NF **1** *(des saisons, des feuilles etc)* alternation; a. des cultures crop rotation; en a. alternately; nous venons en a. un jour sur deux we come on alternate days; formation en a. = training given partly in an educational institution and partly in the workplace **2** *Pol (des membres du gouvernement)* alternation; a. du pouvoir changeover of political power; pratiquer l'a. to take turns running a country **3** *Élec* alternation; redresseur à deux alternances full-wave rectifier

alternateur [alternatœr] NM *Élec* alternating-current generator, alternator

alternatif, -ive [alternatif, -iv] ADJ **1** *(successif, périodique)* alternative **2** *Élec (courant)* alternating; *(moteur, scie, mouvement)* reciprocating **3** *(projet, médecine etc)* alternative

NF **alternative 1** *(succession)* alternation, succession; des alternatives de lumière et d'obscurité alternation(s) of light and shade **2** *(choix)* alternative, option, choice; vous pouvez accepter ou refuser, voilà l'alternative take it or leave it, there's no other choice; être dans une alternative to have to choose one way or the other; alternatives économiques economic alternatives; l'alternative verte *ou* écologique the green alternative *or* option

alternativement [alternativmɑ̃] ADV alternately, in turn

alterne [altern] ADJ *(feuilles, angles etc)* alternate

alterner [alterne] VI **1** *(se succéder)* to alternate **2** *(avec qn)* to take turns, to take it in turns *(pour* to + *inf)*; ils alternent pour veiller they take it in turns to sit up; a. à la surveillance to take (it in) turns to keep watch VT *(cultures)* to rotate

altesse [altɛs] NF highness; son A. impériale His/Her Imperial Highness

altier, -ière [altje, -jɛr] ADJ *(ton, port)* haughty, proud, arrogant

altimètre [altimetr] NM altimeter, altitude indicator; *Aviat* a. à contact altitude switch

altiport [altipɔr] NM high altitude airport

altiste [altist] N *Mus* viola player

altitraceur [altitrasœr] NM altitude recorder

altitude [altityd] NF altitude; à basse/haute a. at low/high altitude; à 100 mètres d'a. at an altitude of 100 metres; en a. at (a high) altitude; *Aviat* prendre de l'a. to climb; vol à haute a. altitude flight; a. limite ceiling; *Méd* cure d'a. high-altitude treatment; mal d'a. altitude sickness; ivresse d'a. altitude narcosis

alto [alto] NM *Mus* **1** alto, counter-tenor (voice) **2** *(instrument à cordes)* viola; *(saxophone)* alto

altocumulus [altɔkymylys] NM INV *Météo* altocumulus

altostratus [altɔstratys] NM INV *Météo* altostratus

altruisme [altrɥism] NM altruism

altruiste [altrɥist] ADJ altruistic

N altruist

Altuglas® [altyglas] NM = thick form of Perspex®

alumine [alymin] NF *Chimie* alumina, aluminium oxide

aluminé [alymine] ADJ aluminized

aluminium [alyminjɔm] NM aluminium, *Am* aluminum; sulfate d'a. aluminium sulphate

alun [alœ̃] NM alum; pierre d'a. styptic pencil

alunir [alynir] VI to land on the moon

alunissage [alynisaʒ] NM moon landing

alvéolaire [alveɔlɛr] ADJ cellular; (motif) honeycomb; (nerf, veine, consonne) alveolar

alvéole [alveɔl] NF 1 (pulmonaire) alveolus; (de cire d'abeilles etc) cell; (d'un bureau etc) pigeonhole; (d'un revolver) chamber; **alvéoles pulmonaires** alveoli of the lungs 2 (de dent) socket; (de diamant) socket, seat(ing) 3 (de pierre etc) cavity, pit; Élec **alvéoles d'un grillage** interstices of an accumulator grid 4 Mil gun pit

alvéolé [alveɔle] ADJ honeycomb(ed), Spéc alveolate; **carton a.** corrugated cardboard

AM [aɛm] NF 1 (abrév **assurance maladie**) health insurance 2 (abrév **amplitude modulation**) AM

amabilité [amabilite] NF friendliness, amiability; (bonté) kindness; **dans un ton plein d'a.** in a friendly tone (of voice); **auriez-vous l'a. de me dire …?** would you be good or kind enough to tell me …?; **faites mes amabilités à …** give my kindest regards to …

amadou [amadu] NM tinder

amadouement [amadumɑ̃] NM (fait d'enjôler) wheedling, coaxing; (apaisement) softening

amadouer [amadwe] VT (enjôler, gagner) to coax, to wheedle, to persuade; (apaiser) to soften; **elle essaie de l'a. pour qu'il accepte** she's trying to coax or to wheedle him into accepting

amagnétique [amaɲetik] ADJ non-magnetic

amaigrir [amɛgrir] VT 1 to make thin; **la maladie l'a amaigri** his illness has made him lose weight 2 Agr (sol) to impoverish 3 Constr (colonne, poutre etc) to thin down, to reduce
▪ VPR **s'amaigrir** to grow thin, to lose weight

amaigrissant [amɛgrisɑ̃] ADJ (régime) slimming

amaigrissement [amɛgrismɑ̃] NM 1 (non volontaire) weight loss, growing thin; (volontaire) slimming; **cure d'a.** slimming cure 2 (dans l'épaisseur) reducing; (d'une poutre etc) thinning down

amalgamation [amalgamasjɔ̃] NF amalgamation

amalgame [amalgam] NM 1 (dentaire), Chimie amalgam; Fig confusion; **il est tentant de faire l'a. de ces deux idées** these two ideas are easily confused 2 (alliage) mixture

amalgamer [amalgame] VT 1 (or, argent), Élec (plaque de zinc) to amalgamate 2 (banques, sociétés etc) to amalgamate, to merge; **il a tendance à a. les deux partis** (il ne voit pas la différence) he tends to get confused between the two parties; (il les considère comme un seul parti) he tends to think of the two parties as one
▪ VPR **s'amalgamer** to merge, to amalgamate

amanché [amɑ̃ʃe] ADJ Can **mal a.** badly dressed

amande [amɑ̃d] NF (fruit) almond; (dans un noyau d'abricot etc) kernel; **amandes amères/douces** bitter/sweet almonds; **amandes pilées** ground almonds; **pâte d'amandes** almond paste; Fig **les yeux en a.** almond(-shaped) eyes

amandier [amɑ̃dje] NM (arbre) almond tree

amanite [amanit] NF (champignon) **a. phalloïde** death cap; **a. tue-mouches** fly agaric

amant, -ante [amɑ̃, -ɑ̃t] N lover; **a. de la nature** nature-lover
▪ NM lover; **prendre un a.** to take a lover

amarante [amarɑ̃t] NF (fleur) amarant(h); **a. commune** ou **à fleurs en queue** love-lies-bleeding

amariner [amarine] VT Naut 1 (navire enne-mi) to man 2 (homme, équipage) to accustom to life at sea
▪ VPR **s'amariner** to find or get one's sea legs

amarrage [amaraʒ] NM Naut 1 mooring, fastening; (lieu) berth, moorings; **droits d'a.** berthing dues 2 **faire un a. sur une corde** to lash a rope

amarre [amar] NF 1 (mooring) rope; (d'avant) painter; **navire sur ses amarres** ship at her moorings; **rompre ses amarres** (d'un navire) to break adrift, to break its moorings; **larguer les amarres** to cast off; Fig to break one's moorings 2 (câble) cable, hawser; **a. de retenue** guy

amarrer [amare] VT Naut etc 1 (navire etc) to make fast, to moor; **navire amarré à quai** boat berthed or lying at the quay 2 (cordage, chaîne) to make fast 3 (haussières etc) to seize, to lash

amaryllis [amarilis] NF (fleur) amaryllis; **a. belle-dame** belladonna lily

amas [ama] NM 1 (tas) heap, pile, accumulation; **des a. de glace** packs of ice; Anat **a. graisseux** lump of fat 2 Astron cluster, constellation; **a. globulaire** globular cluster 3 (de cristal) colony 4 Min lode

amasser [amase] VT 1 (amonceler) to amass, to heap up, to pile up 2 (de l'argent) to hoard (up); **a. une belle somme** to amass a tidy sum 3 (rassembler) to collect; (troupes etc) to gather together
▪ VPR **s'amasser** to build up, to pile up; **une foule s'amassait** a crowd was gathering; **les preuves s'amassent contre vous** the evidence is building up or piling up against you

amateur [amatœr] NM 1 (passionné) lover; **a. de vieux meubles/de vieilles photos** lover of old furniture/old photos; **a. d'art** art lover; **a. d'oiseaux** bird fancier; **édition d'a.** collector's or booklover's edition; **a. de cinéma** film buff; **être a. de qch** to be fond of or to have a taste for sth 2 (dans une vente) bidder; **est-ce qu'il y a des amateurs?** any takers? 3 (non-professionnel) amateur; **photographe/théâtre a.** amateur photographer/theatre; **elle joue bien pour un a.** she plays well for an amateur; Sport **championnat d'amateurs** amateur championship; **faire qch en a.** to do sth as a hobby, to dabble in sth; **il fait de la photo en a.** he's an amateur photographer; **travail d'a.** work done by an amateur; Péj amateurish work

amateurisme [amatœrism] NM Sport etc amateurism; Péj amateurishness, amateurism

amazone [amazon] NF 1 Myth Amazon 2 l'A. the (river) Amazon 3 (cavalière) horsewoman; **monter en a.** to ride side-saddle 4 (jupe) riding habit

Amazonie [amazɔni] NF Amazonia

ambages [ɑ̃baʒ] NFPL (seulement dans l'expression) **parler sans a.** to speak plainly, not to beat about the bush; **il me l'a dit sans a.** he told me quite plainly or without beating about the bush

ambassade [ɑ̃basad] NF 1 (mission) embassy; (moins importante) mission; **envoyer une a. extraordinaire** to send a special mission; **être envoyé en a. auprès de qn** to be sent on a mission to sb 2 (édifice) embassy; (personnel) ambassador's staff, embassy; **l'a. de France/du Canada** the French/Canadian embassy; **a. de Tunisie en France** the Tunisian embassy in France; **obtenir une a.** to be appointed ambassador

ambassadeur [ɑ̃basadœr] NM ambassador; (représentant) envoy; **a. extraordinaire** ambassador extraordinary; **l'a. de Grande-Bretagne** the British ambassador; **a. auprès du roi/de la reine d'Angleterre** Ambassador to or at the Court of St James; Fig **l'a. de la poé-** sie indienne the ambassador of Indian poetry; Fig **vous êtes les ambassadeurs de votre pays** you are ambassadors for your country

ambassadorial, -iale, -iaux, -iales [ɑ̃basadɔrjal, -jo] ADJ ambassadorial

ambassadrice [ɑ̃basadris] NF 1 (diplomate) (woman) ambassador; Fig ambassadress 2 (femme de l'ambassadeur) ambassador's wife

ambiance [ɑ̃bjɑ̃s] NF (environnement) surroundings, environment; (atmosphère) atmosphere, ambiance; Cin room tone; **une a. de travail** a working atmosphere; **l'a. au travail** the atmosphere at work; **musique d'a.** atmospheric music, Péj Muzak®; **régulateur d'a.** thermostat; Fin **l'a. générale** the prevailing tone; Fam **il y a de l'a. ici** there's a cheerful or good atmosphere here; **il y a beaucoup d'a.** it's very lively, there's a very good atmosphere; **mettre de l'a.** to liven things up, to create a good atmosphere

ambiant [ɑ̃bjɑ̃] ADJ (atmosphère etc) surrounding; Cin ambient; **milieu a.** environment; **température ambiante** room temperature; Tech ambient temperature

ambidextre [ɑ̃bidɛkstr] ADJ ambidextrous

ambigu, -uë [ɑ̃bigy] ADJ ambiguous

ambiguïté [ɑ̃biguite] NF ambiguity; **répondre sans a.** to give an unambiguous or unequivocal answer

ambigument [ɑ̃bigymɑ̃] ADV ambiguously

ambitieusement [ɑ̃bisjøzmɑ̃] ADV ambitiously; Péj pretentiously

ambitieux, -ieuse [ɑ̃bisjø, -jøz] ADJ ambitious
▪ N ambitious person; Péj careerist

ambition [ɑ̃bisjɔ̃] NF ambition (**de faire** to do); **elle manque d'a.** she lacks ambition; **être dévoré par l'a.** to be consumed with ambition; **un homme sans a.** an unambitious man; **mettre toute son a. à un travail** to put everything one has into a piece of work, Fam to give it one's all; **avoir de l'a.** to have ambition, to be ambitious

ambitionner [ɑ̃bisjɔne] VT to set one's heart on (**qch** sth; **de faire qch** doing sth)

ambivalence [ɑ̃bivalɑ̃s] NF ambivalence

ambivalent [ɑ̃bivalɑ̃] ADJ ambivalent

amble [ɑ̃bl] NM Équitation amble, pace, Am single-foot; **a. rompu** rack; **aller l'a.** to amble

ambler [ɑ̃ble] VI (d'un cheval etc) to amble (along)

ambre [ɑ̃br] NM 1 **a. gris** ambergris; **pomme d'a.** pomander 2 **a. jaune** (yellow) amber; **un collier en a.** an amber necklace
▪ ADJ INV amber

ambré [ɑ̃bre] ADJ 1 perfumed with amber(-gris) 2 amber-coloured, Am -colored; (complexion, couleur) warm; **un vin a.** an amber-coloured wine

ambroisie [ɑ̃brwazi] NF ambrosia; Fig **c'est de l'a.!** it's like nectar!

ambulance [ɑ̃bylɑ̃s] NF ambulance; Fig **il a assez souffert sans que les médias s'y mettent, on ne tire pas sur une a.** he's suffered enough without the media having a go at him, you shouldn't kick a man when he's down; **il faut soutenir l'ONU au lieu de la critiquer, on ne tire pas sur une a.** the UN should be supported instead of criticized, one shouldn't make a difficult situation worse

ambulancier, -ière [ɑ̃bylɑ̃sje, -jɛr] N ambulance man, f ambulance woman; (conducteur) ambulance driver

ambulant [ɑ̃bylɑ̃] ADJ itinerant, travelling; **épicier a.** mobile grocer; **comédiens ambulants** strolling players; **marchand a.** itinerant dealer, hawker; **cirque a.** travelling circus; Méd **érysipèle a.** migrant erysipelas;

Fam **c'est un cadavre a.** he's a walking corpse, he looks like death warmed up; **c'est un dictionnaire a.** he's a walking dictionary **NM** *Admin (de taxes, de douanes etc)* itinerant collector

ambulatoire [ɑ̃bylatwar] **ADJ** ambulatory; *Méd* **malade a.** out-patient; **(fièvre) typhoïde a.** ambulant typhoid; **traitement a.** outpatient treatment

AME [aɛmə] **NM** *(abrév* **Accord monétaire européen)** EMA

âme [ɑm] **NF 1** *Rel, Phil* soul; *(motif) (d'une entreprise)* inspiration, soul, life; **se donner corps et â. à qch** to give oneself body and soul to sth; **rendre l'â.** to give up the ghost; **de toute mon â.** with all my heart; **elle a l'â. d'une artiste** she has the soul of an artist; **il est peintre dans l'â.** he's a painter through and through *or* to the core; **il jouait de la flûte avec â.** he played the flute with great feeling; **une déclaration sans â.** an unfeeling *or* a soulless declaration; **Dieu ait son â.** God rest his soul; **les âmes en peine** the souls in Purgatory; **aller comme une â. en peine** to wander around like a lost soul; **avoir l'â. chevillée au corps** to have nine lives; **chercher la paix de l'â.** to seek spiritual peace; **â. sœur** kindred soul *or* spirit, soul mate; **en mon â. et conscience** to the best of my knowledge and belief; **cet homme est d'une grandeur d'â.** extraordinaire that man has an extraordinary nobility of spirit; **état d'â.** state of mind, mood; **elle était l'â. de notre organisation** she was the heart and soul of our organization

2 *(personne)* **une bonne â.** a well-meaning person, a good soul; **ne pas rencontrer â. qui vive** not to meet a (living) soul; **un hameau de 50 âmes** a hamlet of some 50 inhabitants; *Iron* **il y a toujours de bonnes âmes pour conseiller quand c'est trop tard!** there are always plenty of people ready with helpful advice when it's too late!; **c'est une â. généreuse** he has great generosity of spirit; **je connais quelques grandes âmes** I know a few high-minded people; **avoir charge d'âmes** *Rel* to have the cure of souls; *(d'enfants, de passagers etc)* to have lives in one's care

3 *(d'un fusil, d'une pompe)* bore; *(d'une statue, d'un câble)* core; *(d'une poutre de bois ou métallique)* web; *(de rail)* centre rib; *Aviat (des ailes)* web; *Mus (d'un violon)* sound post

améliorable [ameljɔrabl] **ADJ** capable of being improved, improvable; **le système est a.** the system could be improved

améliorant [ameljɔrɑ̃] **ADJ** *Agr* soil-improving; **culture** *ou* **plante améliorante** cover crop

amélioration [ameljɔrasjɔ̃] **NF 1** improvement, change for the better; *Ordinat (d'image, de qualité)* enhancement; **on note une nette a. dans les relations des deux pays** there has been a distinct improvement in the relations between the two countries; **l'a. de son état de santé** the improvement in his condition; **il y a de l'a.** there's some improvement; **il y a de l'a. dans les affaires** business is improving; **faire des améliorations dans qch** to make improvements to sth; **travaux d'a.** improvements; *Mktg* **a. du produit** product augmentation *or* improvement **2** *Jur (de biens etc)* appreciation

amélioré [ameljɔre] **ADJ** improved; *(modèle, version)* enhanced; **un petit mousseux a.** a very good quality sparkling wine

améliorer [ameljɔre] **VT 1** *(propriété, sol, traduction etc)* to improve; *(service, chambre d'hôtel)* to upgrade; **a. son état** to improve one's situation **2** *Ordinat (logiciel)* to upgrade; *(image, qualité)* to enhance

VPR s'améliorer to get better, to improve; **sa**

---

santé/le temps s'améliore his health/the weather is improving; **ça ne s'améliore pas** it's not getting any better

amen [amen] **NM INVAR** amen; *Fig* **il s'attend à ce que je dise a. à tout ce qu'il dit!** he expects me to agree with everything he says!

aménagement [amenaʒmɑ̃] **NM 1** *(disposition)* arrangement, layout; *Can* **a. paysager** open-plan offices

2 aménagements fittings, fixtures, installations; *Naut, Aviat* accommodation, berthing; **les nouveaux aménagements dans un quartier** new developments in a district

3 *(action)* equipping, arranging; *(d'un navire)* fitting out; **a. d'une usine** equipping *or* fitting out of a factory

4 *Écon, Admin* **a. urbain et rural** town and country planning; *Écon, Admin* **a. du territoire** regional development, physical planning; **a. forestier** forest management

5 *(amendement)* adjustment; **un a. dans un contrat** an adjustment to a contract; **a. fiscal** tax adjustment

6 *Ordinat* housekeeping

aménager [amenaʒe] **VT** (**j'aménageai(s); n. aménageons**) **1** *(maison, navire etc)* to fit out; **étable aménagée** converted cowshed; **a. une cuisine en salle à manger** to convert a kitchen into a dining room; **a. une douche dans une salle de gymnastique** to install *or Am* instal a shower in a gym; **route aménagée** made-up road; **a. un emploi du temps** to adjust a timetable **2** *(ville)* to plan; *(approvisionnement etc)* to divide, to distribute; **a. une forêt** to manage a forest

amende [amɑ̃d] **NF 1** fine, penalty; **mettre une a. à qn** to fine sb; **être condamné à l'a.** *ou* **à une a.** to be fined; *Fam* **mettre qn à l'a.** to fine sb; **200 euros d'a.** a 200 euro fine; **défense d'entrer sous peine d'a.** trespassers will be prosecuted; **a. fiscale** tax penalty; **a. pour stationnement interdit** parking fine; **a. immédiate** on-the-spot fine **2 faire a. honorable** to make amends

amendement [amɑ̃dmɑ̃] **NM 1** *(du sol etc)* improvement **2** *(engrais)* (soil) conditioner **3** *Pol (à un projet de loi etc)* amendment; *(clause)* additional clause; **proposer un a.** to move an amendment (**à qch** to sth); **a. constitutionnel** constitutional amendment; **a. européen** European amendment

amender [amɑ̃de] **VT 1** to make better; *(sol etc)* to improve **2** *Pol etc (projet de loi etc)* to amend **3** *Suisse (infliger une amende à)* to fine **VPR s'amender** to turn over a new leaf

amène [amɛn] **ADJ** pleasing, agreeable; **peu a.** unpleasant, disagreeable

amenée [amne] **NF 1** tuyau *ou* conduite d'a. *Constr* branch pipe; *(d'eau)* supply pipe; *Élec* lead **2** *(d'air)* inlet, intake

amener [amne] (**j'amène, n. amenons; j'amènerai**) **VT 1** *(personne)* to bring; *Mil (réserves etc)* to bring up; *(eau, gaz etc)* to lay on; **amenez votre ami/chien avec vous** bring your friend/dog (with you); **quel bon vent vous amène?** what brings you here?; **les oléoducs amènent le pétrole à la raffinerie** the pipelines carry the oil to the refinery; *Culin* **a. l'eau à ébullition** to bring the water to the boil; **a. qn à faire qch** to get *or* induce sb to do sth; **et ceci nous amène à parler de la ponctualité** which brings us to the question of punctuality; **a. qn à son opinion** to bring sb round to one's point of view; **a. un sujet** to bring up *or* raise a subject; **a. la conversation sur un sujet** to bring the conversation round to a subject; **un bon auteur sait a. le dénouement de son récit** a good author knows how to bring his story to a conclusion; **a. une querelle** to bring about *or* lead to a quarrel; **a. une mode** to bring in a fashion

---

2 *Naut (signal)* to haul down; *(couleurs)* to strike; *(bateau, drapeau, voile)* to lower

3 *(tirer à soi)* to draw in, to bring in; **le pêcheur amène les filets** the fisherman draws in the nets

VPR s'amener *Fam* to turn up; **amène-toi ici!** come (over) here!

> Do not confuse **amener** and **apporter**. The former should be used with animate objects and the latter with inanimate objects.

aménité [amenite] **NF 1** *(de manières, d'un accueil etc)* charm, graciousness; *(de style)* charm, grace; **nous avons été traités sans a.** we were treated ungraciously **2** *Iron* **aménités** insults, uncomplimentary remarks

aménorrhée [amenɔre] **NF** *Méd* amenorrhoea

amenuisement [amənɥizmɑ̃] **NM** *(des ressources)* diminishing, dwindling; *(des espoirs)* dwindling

amenuiser [amənɥize] **VT** to reduce, to thin (down), to whittle down; **a. ses économies/ ses réserves** to whittle down one's savings/ supplies

VPR s'amenuiser *(d'une valeur)* to decline; *(de l'espoir, des chances)* to fade; *(économies, provisions)* to dwindle, to run low

amer¹, -ère [amɛr] **ADJ** *(goût)*, *Fig (souvenirs, personne)* bitter

NM *(boisson)* bitters

amer² **NM** *Naut* seamark, landmark

amèrement [amɛrmɑ̃] **ADV** bitterly

américain, -aine [amerikɛ̃, -ɛn] **ADJ** American; **cuisine américaine** = kitchen with a bar separating the cooking and eating areas

N A. American

NM 1 *Ling* American (English) **2** *Belg Culin Fam (steak tartare)* steak tartare

NF américaine 1 *Culin* **homard à l'américaine** lobster américaine **2** *Cyclisme* track relay (race) **3** *Aut* American car

américanisation [amerikanizasjɔ̃] **NF** Americanization

américaniser [amerikanize] **VT** to Americanize

VPR s'américaniser to become Americanized

américanisme [amerikanism] **NM** *Ling* Americanism

américaniste [amerikanist] **N** specialist in American studies

amérindien, -ienne [amerɛ̃djɛ̃, -jɛn] **ADJ** Amerindian, American Indian

N A. Amerindian, American Indian

Amérique [amerik] **NF** America; **l'A. du Nord/du Sud** North/South America; **l'A. latine** Latin America; **l'A. centrale** Central America; **les Amériques** the Americas

Amerlo(t) [amerlo], **Amerloque** [amerlɔk] **N** *Fam* Yank

amerrir [amerir] **VI 1** *Aviat* to land on the sea, to make a sea landing **2** *(d'un vaisseau spatial)* to splash down

amerrissage [amerisaʒ] **NM** *Aviat* landing on the sea, sea landing; *(d'un vaisseau spatial)* splashdown; *Aviat* **a. forcé** ditching

amertume [amɛrtym] **NF** bitterness

améthyste [ametist] **NF** amethyst

ameublement [amœbləmɑ̃] **NM 1** *(action de meubler)* furnishing **2** *(meubles)* set *or* suite of furniture; **un a. très simple** very simple furniture; **magasin d'a.** furniture store; **tissu d'a.** furnishing fabric

ameublir [amœblir] **VT 1** *Agr (sol)* to loosen, to break up **2** *Jur (biens immobiliers)* to convert into personalty, to bring into the communal estate

ameublissement [amœblismɑ̃] NM **1** *Agr (du sol)* loosening, breaking up **2** *Jur (biens immobiliers)* conversion into personalty, inclusion in the communal estate

ameuter [amøte] VT **1** *(gens)* to bring out; **a. une foule** to draw a crowd; **elle va a. tout le voisinage si elle continue à hurler comme ça!** she'll have the whole neighbourhood out if she carries on shouting like that! **2** *(chiens)* to form into a pack, to pack
▶ VPR **s'ameuter** to form a mob

AMI [aɛmi] NM *(abrév* **accord multilatéral sur l'investissement***)* MAI

ami, -ie [ami] N friend; **un de mes meilleurs amis** one of my best friends; **a. intime** close friend; **a. d'enfance** childhood friend; **un a. de la maison** a friend of the family; **en a.** as a friend; **mon a.** *(entre amis)* my dear fellow; *(entre époux)* my dear; **mon amie** my dear, my love; **être sans amis** to be friendless, to have no friends; **faire a.-a.** *(de deux personnes)* to decide to be pals; *(se réconcilier)* to make up **(avec** with); **les amis de mes amis sont mes amis** any friend of yours/his/*etc* is a friend of mine; **son a.** her boyfriend; *(amant)* her lover; *Fam* **sa petite amie** his girlfriend; **son amie** *(sa maîtresse)* his mistress; **eh l'a.! viens donc m'aider!** hey, you (over) there, come and give me a hand!; **un a. des arts** a patron of the arts; **les amis de la nature/des bêtes** nature/animal lovers; *Ling* **faux amis** false friends, faux amis; *Géog* **les îles des Amis** the Friendly Islands, Tonga; **Société des Amis** Society of Friends, Quakers
▶ ADJ friendly (**de** to); *(vent)* favourable; **un visage a.** a friendly face; **peuple a.** ally, friendly state

amiable [amjabl] ADJ *Jur* friendly, conciliatory, amicable; **partage a.** amicable sharing arrangement; **a. compositeur** arbitrator
▶ ADV **à l'a.** amicably; *Jur* **arranger une affaire à l'a.** to settle a difference out of court; **s'arranger à l'a.** to settle out of court; **divorce à l'a.** no-fault divorce; **arrangement à l'a.** amicable arrangement; **vente à l'a.** private sale, sale by private contract

amiante [amjɑ̃t] NM *Minér* asbestos; **plaque d'a.** asbestos mat; **fibres d'a.** asbestos fibres

amibe [amib] NF amoeba, *Am* ameba

amibiase [amibjaz] NF *Méd* amoebiasis, *Am* amebiasis

amibien, -ienne [amibjɛ̃, -jɛn] ADJ *Méd* amoebic, *Am* amebic; **dysenterie amibienne** amoebic dysentery

amical, -ale, -aux, -ales [amikal, -o] ADJ *(conseil, ton etc)* friendly; *(relations)* amicable; **être a. avec qn** to be friendly towards sb; **peu a.** unfriendly; *Sport* **match a.** friendly (match); **association amicale** association
▶ NF **amicale** association; *Br Scol* old-boys'/-girls' *or* former pupils' association; *Am Univ* alumni association

amicalement [amikalmɑ̃] ADV in a friendly way; **discuter a.** to have a friendly chat; **bien a. à vous** *(dans une lettre)* yours (ever)

amide [amid] NM *Chimie* amide

amidon [amidɔ̃] NM starch

amidonnage [amidɔnaʒ] NM starching

amidonner [amidɔne] VT to starch

amieuter(s') [samjøte] VPR *Can* to improve, to get better

amigne [amiɲ] NM *Suisse* = grape variety from the Valais canton, and white wine produced from these grapes

amincir [amɛ̃sir] VT to make thinner; *(bois)* to fine down, to thin down; *(métal)* to machine down; **cette robe t'amincit** that dress makes you look thinner *or* slimmer
▶ VPR **s'amincir** to get thinner
▶ VI to get slimmer

amincissant [amɛ̃sisɑ̃] ADJ slimming; **régime a.** (slimmer's *or* slimming) diet

amincissement [amɛ̃sismɑ̃] NM *(de choses)* thinning down; *(du métal)* machining down; *(d'une personne)* growing thinner *or* slimmer; **a. rapide** rapid loss of weight

amine [amin] NF *Chimie, Pharm* **a. de réveil** amphetamine

aminé [amine] ADJ *Chimie* **acide a.** amino acid

aminoacide [aminoasid] NM *Chimie* amino acid

amiral, -ale, -aux, -ales [amiral, -o] ADJ **vaisseau a.** *(en mer)* flagship; *(dans un port)* guardship
▶ NM **1** *Mil* admiral, flag officer; **a. de la flotte** admiral of the fleet **2** *(coquillage)* admiral shell

amirale [amiral] NF admiral's wife

amirauté [amirote] NF **1** *Mil* Admiralty; **conseil d'a.** *Br* ≃ Admiralty Board; *Jur* High Court of Admiralty **2 îles de l'A.** the Admiralty Islands; **île de l'A.** *(Colombie-Britannique)* Admiralty Island

amitié [amitje] NF **1** *(sentiment)* friendship; **éprouver de l'a. ou un sentiment d'a. pour ou envers qn** to have friendly feelings towards sb; **étroite a.** close friendship; **concevoir de l'a. pour qn, prendre qn en a.** to take a liking to sb, to take to sb; **se lier d'a. avec qn** to make friends with sb, to become friendly with sb; **par a.** out of friendship; **une très ancienne a.** a long-standing friendship; **a. particulière** homosexual relationship; *Pol* **l'a. qui existe entre nos deux pays** the friendship between our two countries **2** *(marque)* kindness, favour; **faites-moi l'a. de le lui dire** do me the favour of telling him so; **mes amitiés à votre sœur** my best wishes to your sister; **sincères amitiés de ...** best wishes from ...

amitieux, -euse [amitjø, -øz] ADJ *Belg* friendly, affectionate

ammoniac, -iaque [amɔnjak] *Chimie* ADJ **gaz a.** ammonia; **sel a.** sal ammoniac
▶ NM ammonia

ammoniacal, -ale, -aux, -ales [amɔnjakal, -o] ADJ *Chimie* of ammonia

ammoniaque [amɔnjak] NF *Chimie* ammonia

ammoniaqué [amɔnjake] ADJ ammoniated

ammonite [amɔnit] NF *(fossile)* ammonite

amnésie [amnezi] NF *Méd* amnesia; **souffrir d'a.** to have amnesia

amnésique [amnezik] *Méd* ADJ amnesic; **être a.** to have amnesia
▶ N amnesia case, amnesiac

amniocentèse [amnjosɛ̃tez, amnjosātez] NF *Méd* amniocentesis; **se faire faire une a.** to have an amniocentesis

amnioscopie [amnjoskɔpi] NF *Méd* amnioscopy

amniotique [amnjɔtik] NF *Physiol* amniotic; **liquide a.** amniotic fluid

amnistie [amnisti] NF amnesty; **accorder une a.** to grant an amnesty

> **Amnistie**
> Parking fines as well as some prison sentences are traditionally waived by the French president immediately after a presidential election. The latter is known as "la grâce présidentielle".

amnistier [amnistje] VT *(pr sub, impf* n. **amnistiions, v. amnistiiez***)* to grant amnesty to, to pardon

amocher [amɔʃe] *Arg* VT **a. qn** to knock *or* bash sb about, to beat sb up; **la voiture est sérieusement amochée** the car's really been bashed up, the car's (in) one hell of a mess; **se faire a.** to get bashed up *or* beaten up
▶ VPR **s'amocher elle s'est bien amochée en tombant** she smashed herself up when she fell

amoindrir [amwɛ̃drir] VT to decrease, to lessen, to diminish; *(affaiblir)* to weaken; *(mal)* to mitigate; *(déconsidérer) (personne)* to belittle; **la fièvre amoindrit ses forces** the fever is sapping his strength; **a. la puissance de qn** to curtail sb's power
▶ VPR **s'amoindrir** to diminish, to grow less

amoindrissement [amwɛ̃drismɑ̃] NM lessening, decrease, diminution

amollir [amɔlir] VT *(substance etc)* to soften; **pareille chaleur m'amollit** heat like this makes me feel weak
▶ VPR **s'amollir** to soften, to become soft; *(du courage etc)* to flag, to weaken

amollissement [amɔlismɑ̃] NM *(du courage etc)* softening, weakening, flagging; **pareille chaleur entraîne l'a. général** heat like this makes everyone feel weak

amonceler [amɔ̃sle] *(j'amoncelle, n. amoncelons; j'amoncellerai)* VT to pile up, to heap up, to accumulate, to amass; **a. des preuves** to pile up *or* amass evidence
▶ VPR **s'amonceler** to pile up, to accumulate

amoncellement [amɔ̃sɛlmɑ̃] NM **1** *(action)* heaping (up), piling (up), accumulation; *(des nuages)* banking up **2** *(pile)* heap, pile; **a. de neige** covering of snow

amont [amɔ̃] NM **1** *(d'une rivière)* upper waters, upstream side; **en a., vers l'a.** upstream, up river; **la Seine en a. de Paris** the Seine above Paris; **vent d'a.** off-shore wind; **le ski a.** the uphill ski **2** *Com* **activités d'a.** upstream activities; **en a.** upstream

amoral, -ale, -aux, -ales [amɔral, -o] ADJ amoral

amoralité [amɔralite] NF amorality

amorçage [amɔrsaʒ] NM **1** *(d'une pompe, d'un moteur, d'une cartouche etc)* priming; *(d'un champ magnétique)* building up; *Ordinat* booting; *Méd (du sommeil)* induction; **le système d'a. d'une bombe** the detonating system of a bomb **2** *(d'un crochet, d'un cordage)* baiting

amorce [amɔrs] NF **1** beginning; *(d'une route etc en travaux)* initial section; **a. de négociations** preliminary talks **2** *(détonateur)* primer, fuse, detonator; *(d'une petite arme)* percussion *or* cartridge cap; *Élec* fuse; *(d'une pompe)* priming; *(d'une soudure)* scarf; **pistolet à amorces** cap gun **3** *Pêche* bait **4** *Cin* leader

amorcer [amɔrse] *(j'amorçai(s); n. amorçons)* VT **1** *(bâtiment, route, attaque, discours etc)* to begin, to start; **a. des négociations** to initiate negotiations **2** *Ordinat* to boot (up); **a. de nouveau** to reboot **3** *(pompe)* to prime, to fetch; *(coquillage)* to cap; *Élec (dynamo)* to start, to excite; *(arc)* to strike; *(soudure)* to scarf; *(bombe)* to fuse **4** *(cordage, piège etc)* to bait **5** *Vieilli (animal, personne)* to entice
▶ VPR **s'amorcer** to begin; *Ordinat* to boot (up); **une baisse des cours s'amorce** stocks and shares are showing a downward trend

amorçoir [amɔrswar] NM **1** *Pêche* groundbaiting appliance **2** *(vrille)* auger, twist bit, boring bit

amorphe [amɔrf] ADJ **1** *Chimie, Minér, Biol* amorphous **2** *(sans énergie)* lifeless, apathetic; **cette chaleur me rend totalement a.** this heat is making me lethargic *or* listless

amorti [amɔrti] ADJ **1** *Phys (vague)* damped **2** **marteau a.** cushioned hammer **3** *Fin (bien)* depreciated; *(capital)* amortized
▶ NM *Tennis etc* drop shot; *Ftbl* trap

amortir [amɔrtir] **VT 1** *(bruit)* to deaden, to muffle; *(lumière)* to subdue; *(douleur)* to dull; *(ardeur)* to damp; *(passion)* to damp, to cool; *(couleur)* to tone down; *(chute)* to break; *(choc)* to absorb, to deaden; *(coup)* to break the force of; *Ftbl (ballon)* to trap; *Tennis (balle)* to kill; *Aut (secousses)* to damp **2** *Fin (rembourser) (dette, prêt)* to redeem, to pay off, to amortize; *Compta* to write off, to amortize **3** *Fin (rentabiliser)* **il a amorti sa nouvelle voiture en six mois** he recouped the cost of his new car in six months; **le matériel a été amorti dès la première année** the equipment paid for itself by the end of the first year **4** *Phys (oscillations)* to damp down *or* out **5** *Constr* to slack, to slake (lime)

▪ VPR s'amortir 1 *(dépenses, investissement etc)* to pay for itself **2** *(de bruits etc)* to fade, to die down

amorti-sacrifice, *pl* **amortis-sacrifices NM** *Sport* squeeze-bunt

amortissable [amɔrtisabl] **ADJ** *Fin* redeemable

amortissant [amɔrtisɑ̃] **ADJ** *Aut* shock-absorbent

amortissement [amɔrtismɑ̃] **NM 1** *Fin (d'une dette)* redemption, paying off, liquidation; **l'a. est plus rapide** *(d'une voiture)* it pays for itself faster; **fonds** *ou* **caisse d'a.** sinking fund; *Compta* **a.-dépenses** amortization *or* write-off of expenditure **2** *Compta (perte de valeur)* depreciation; **provision pour a.** depreciation allowance; **a. dégressif** accelerated depreciation; **a. dérogatoire** excess tax depreciation over normal; **a. linéaire** straightline depreciation; **amortissements cumulés** cumulative depreciation; **amortissements différés** deferred depreciation **3** *(d'une chute)* breaking; *(d'un choc)* absorption; *Aut* damping; *(du son)* deadening

amortisseur [amɔrtisœr] **NM 1** *Aut etc* shock absorber, *Am* snubber; **a. de commande sur carburateur** carburettor damper; **a. de vibrations** vibration damper; **a. hydraulique** hydraulic shock absorber, hydraulic damper; **a. à gaz** gas strut; **a. hydro-élastique** hydroelastic displacer unit **2** *Tech* **a. à moulinet** air brake; **a. pneumatique** air cushion **3** *Élec* damper

amour [amur] **NM** *(f in pl)* **1** *(sentiment)* love; **aimer qn d'a.** to be in love with sb; **ils filent le parfait a.** they are completely in love (with each other); **l'a. d'une mère** a mother's love; **l'a. maternel/paternel/filial** a mother's/father's/child's love; **l'a. du prochain** love of one's neighbour; **avec a.** lovingly; *(traiter, soigner)* with loving care; **a. platonique** platonic love; **s'aimer d'a. platonique** to love each other platonically; **l'a. libre** free love; **elle est folle d'a. pour lui** she's madly in love with him; **a. intéressé** cupboard love; **alors, c'est le grand a.?** so, it's true love then?; *Fam* so, it's the real thing then?; **chanson d'a.** love song; **enfant de l'a.** love child; **se marier par a.** to marry for love; **faire qch par a.** to do sth out of love; **mariage d'a.** love match; **roman/film d'a.** romantic novel/film; **histoire d'a.** love story; *Fig* **c'est une véritable histoire d'a. qui me lie à cette ville** I have a love affair with this city; **faire l'a.** to make love (**avec** with); **l'a. de Dieu** the love of God; **pour l'a. du Ciel, tiens-toi bien!** for heaven's sake, sit up straight!; *Can* **être/tomber en amour (avec qn)** to be/fall in love (with sb) **2 amours** *(vie amoureuse)* love life; **les premières amours** first love, calf love; **à tes amours!** *(en buvant)* your health!, cheers!; *(à qn qui éternue)* bless you!; **où en sont tes amours?** how's your love life? **3** *(personne)* **mon a.** my love, my darling; **une de mes anciennes amours** an old flame

of mine; **les voitures sont ses seul(e)s amours** cars are his/her sole passion **4 A.** Cupid, Eros, the god of Love; **beau comme l'A.** handsome as a Greek god; **quel a. d'enfant!** what an adorable child!; **tu es un a.!** you('re an) angel!; **sois un a.!** be a dear!, be an angel!; **tu serais un a. si tu voulais me chercher mes cigarettes** be an angel and fetch me my cigarettes; **un a. d'histoire** a very sweet story **5** *(goût)* **l'a. (pour qch)** love (of sth), passion (for sth); **l'a. de la nature** love of nature; **l'a. de la justice** passion for justice; **faire qch avec a.** to do sth lovingly *or* with love

▪ NMPL *Suisse (vin)* **les amours** = the last drops of wine in a bottle

amouracher (s') [samuraʃe] **VPR s'a. de qn** to become infatuated with sb

amourette [amuret] **NF 1** *(entre deux personnes)* little fling **2** *Culin* **amourettes** marrowbone jelly

amoureusement [amurøzmɑ̃] **ADV** *(avec tendresse)* lovingly; *(avec passion)* amorously

amoureux, -euse [amurø, -øz] **ADJ 1** *(soin, regard, geste)* loving; **vie amoureuse** love life; **tomber a.** to fall in love; **être a. de qn** to be in love with sb; *Fig* **il est a. de cette petite maison** he's in love with this little house; **être a. de qch** to be a lover of sth; **je suis a. de cette région** I love that part of the country; **je suis a. de la nature** I'm a nature-lover **2** *(passionné) (regard, geste)* amorous

▪ N lover, man/woman in love; **pour les a. de la nature** for nature-lovers *or* lovers of nature; **c'est mon a.** he's my boyfriend

amour-propre [amurprɔpr] **NM** *(dignité)* self-respect, pride; **il n'a aucun a.** he has no self-respect *or* pride; **blesser l'a. de qn** to hurt *or* wound sb's pride; **elle est blessée dans son a.** her pride is hurt; **pétri d'a.** eaten up with conceit

amovible [amɔvibl] **ADJ 1** detachable; *Ordinat (disque dur)* removable; **siège a.** sliding seat **2** *Jur (fonctionnaire)* removable; **fonction a.** = office that may be withdrawn from the holder (and given to another person)

ampérage [ɑ̃peraʒ] **NM** *Élec* amperage

ampère [ɑ̃per] **NM** *Élec* ampere

ampère-heure, *pl* **ampères-heures NM** ampere-hour

ampèremètre [ɑ̃permetr] **NM** *Élec* ammeter

amphé [ɑ̃fe] **NF** *Fam (amphétamine)* speed

amphétamine [ɑ̃fetamin] **NF** amphetamine

amphi [ɑ̃fi] **NM** *Univ Fam (salle)* lecture hall; *(cours)* lecture

amphibie [ɑ̃fibi] **ADJ** *Biol (plante, animal)* amphibious; **appareil** *ou* **voiture a.** amphibian; *Mil* **opération a.** combined operation **▪ NM** *(véhicule etc)*, *Biol* amphibian

amphibiens [ɑ̃fibjɛ̃] **NMPL** *Zool* amphibians, Amphibia

amphithéâtre [ɑ̃fiteatr] **NM 1** *Univ* lecture hall **2** *Théâtre* gallery, *Fam* the gods **3** *Archit* amphitheatre, *Am* amphitheater; **en a.** in tiers, tier upon tier

amphore [ɑ̃fɔr] **NF** jar; *Archéol* amphora

ample [ɑ̃pl] **ADJ 1** *(robe, jupe etc)* full **2** *(magasin, théâtre etc)* roomy, spacious **3** *(récit)* full; *(approvisionnement)* plentiful, ample; **jusqu'à plus a. informé** until fuller *or* more information is available; **le sujet est a.** the subject is a wide one; **je vais vous donner de plus amples détails** I will give you fuller *or* more details

amplement [ɑ̃pləmɑ̃] **ADV** amply, fully; **nous avons a. le temps** we have plenty of time; **je vous ai a. servi** I have given you

plenty; **il nous a a. renseigné/conseillé** he has given us plenty of information/advice; **c'est a. suffisant** it's more than enough

ampleur [ɑ̃plœr] **NF 1** *(d'un vêtement)* width, fullness; *(de la voix)* volume, fullness; **ça manque un peu d'a. au bras** it's not quite full enough in the arm **2** *(importance)* scale, extent; **le mouvement politique prend de l'a.** the (political) movement is growing in size *or* is taking on new dimensions; **devant l'a. du désastre** in view of the extent *or* the scope of the disaster; *Mktg* **a. de gamme** breadth of range; *Mktg* **a. de la ligne de produits** product-line length

ampli [ɑ̃pli] **NM** *Fam* amplifier

amplificateur, -trice [ɑ̃plifikatœr, -tris] **ADJ** *Radio etc* amplifying; *Opt* magnifying **▪ NM** amplifier; **a. de puissance** power amplifier

amplification [ɑ̃plifikasjɔ̃] **NF 1** *(d'un sujet)* amplification, development; *(d'un mouvement politique, phénomène)* growth; *(exagération)* exaggeration **2** *Radio etc* amplification; *Opt* magnification

amplifier [ɑ̃plifje] *(impf, pr sub* **n. amplifiions, v. amplifiiez)* **VT 1** *(bruit, son, idée etc)* to amplify; *(histoire)* to embroider on; *(scandale)* to magnify, to blow up; **a. les échanges commerciaux** to increase trade **2** *Opt* to magnify; *Élec* to amplify

▪ VPR s'amplifier *(en taille, en étendue etc)* to grow; **le bruit s'amplifie** the noise is growing *or* getting louder; **les revendications ouvrières s'amplifient** the workers' demands are increasing, the workers are increasing their demands

ampliforme [ɑ̃plifɔrm] **ADJ** *(soutien-gorge)* padded

amplitude [ɑ̃plityd] **NF 1** *(d'une oscillation)* amplitude; *Radio* **modulation d'a.** amplitude modulation **2** *(variation)* range; **a. thermique** temperature range **3** *Litt (de l'espace etc)* amplitude, vastness; *(d'un désastre, d'une catastrophe)* magnitude, scale

ampoule [ɑ̃pul] **NF 1** *(d'une lampe électrique)* (light) bulb; *(d'un thermomètre)* bulb; *(d'un Thermos®)* container; **une a. de 75 watts** a 75 watt bulb; **a. à baïonnette/vis** bayonet/screw-in (light) bulb; *Aut* **a. de détection de chaleur** heat-sensing bulb; *Phot* **a. de flash** flashbulb, flashlight **2** *(de la peau, du métal etc)* blister; *Hum* **il ne risque pas de se faire des ampoules** he's not going to die of exhaustion **3** *(fiole)* phial

ampoulé [ɑ̃pule] **ADJ** *Péj (discours)* inflated, bombastic

amputation [ɑ̃pytasjɔ̃] **NF 1** *(d'un membre etc)* amputation **2** *Fig (d'un livre etc)* cutting down; *(d'une revendication)* reduction; **cet article a subi de sérieuses amputations** this article has been drastically cut; **c'est une sérieuse a. à sa fortune** it has cut into his fortune

amputé, -ée [ɑ̃pyte] **N** amputee

amputer [ɑ̃pyte] **VT 1** *(membre)* to amputate; **il fut amputé du bras gauche** his left arm was amputated **2** *Fig (article etc)* to cut down; *(revendication)* to cut, to reduce (**de** by); **a. un capital** to make inroads into one's/sb's capital

amulette [amylet] **NF** amulet, charm

amusant [amyzɑ̃] **ADJ** amusing, funny; *(divertissant)* entertaining; **comme c'est a., je n'avais pas remarqué ...** that's funny, I hadn't noticed ...; **je ne trouve pas ça très a.** I don't find that very funny *or* amusing, *Hum* I am not amused; **c'était très a.** it was great fun

▪ NM **le plus a., c'est que ...** the funniest *or* most amusing thing is that ...; **l'a. de l'histoire** the amusing part of the story, what was funny *or* amusing about the story

amuse-gueule [amyzgœl] NM INV cocktail snack, nibble; *Fig* appetizer

amusement [amyzmɑ̃] NM amusement; **avoir besoin d'a.** to need amusement *or* entertainment; **faire qch pour son a.** to do sth for one's own amusement; *Iron* **tu parles d'un a.!** what fun!

amuser [amyze] VT to amuse; *(divertir)* to entertain; **l'histoire m'a beaucoup amusé** I found the story really funny; *(divertissante)* I found the story really entertaining; **en attendant, il faut a. la salle** in the meantime, we must keep the audience amused; **si tu penses que ça m'amuse!** if you think I enjoy (doing) it!; **tu crois que ça m'amuse, ce genre de situations?** do you think I enjoy this kind of situation?; **ah ça t'amuse, toi!** you think that's funny, do you?; **fais-le si ça t'amuse** do it if it amuses you; **il avait un regard amusé quand il nous a dit bonjour** he looked amused *or* as if something was amusing him when he said hello to us

VPR **s'amuser** *(se distraire)* to enjoy oneself, to have a good time; **je ne me suis jamais aussi bien amusé** I've had the time of my life; **les enfants s'amusent dans le jardin** the children are playing in the garden; **amusez-vous bien!** have fun!, enjoy yourselves!; **s'a. aux dépens de qn** to amuse oneself at sb's expense; **s'a. avec qn** to have fun with sb; **s'a. de qn/de qch** to make fun of sb/sth; **s'a. à faire qch** to have fun doing sth; **faire qch pour s'a.** to do sth for fun *or* for the fun of it; *Fam* **ne t'amuse pas à recommencer** don't you dare do that again; **si tu crois que je vais m'a. à faire ça** if you think I've nothing better to do than that; **nous n'avons pas le temps de nous a. en chemin/à faire ça** we can't afford to waste time on the way/doing that

---

> Il faut noter que le verbe anglais **to amuse oneself** est un faux ami. Il signifie **s'occuper, passer le temps**.

---

amusette [amyzɛt] NF **1** *Vieilli* pastime, diversion **2** *Belg* frivolous person

amuseur, -euse [amyzœr, -øz] N entertainer

amygdale [ami(g)dal] NF tonsil; **inflammation des amygdales** tonsillitis; **se faire opérer des amygdales** to have one's tonsils out; *Fam* **se sucer les amygdales** to snog (furiously)

amygdalectomie [ami(g)dalɛktɔmi] NF *Chir* tonsillectomy

amygdalite [ami(g)dalit] NF *Méd* tonsillitis; **faire une a.** to have tonsillitis

an [ɑ̃] NM year; **tous les trois ans** every three years; **dans trois ans** in three years' time, three years from now; **l'an passé** *ou* **dernier** last year; **l'an prochain** next year; **par an** per year; *Fin* per annum; **j'ai deux semaines de vacances par an** I have two weeks' holiday per *or* a year; **deux fois par an** twice a year; **un prêt sur vingt ans** a loan over twenty years; **tous les ans** every year; **avoir dix ans** to be ten (years old); *(d'une machine)* to be ten years old; **je gagne tant par an** I earn so much a year; **ami de vingt ans** friend of twenty years' standing; **bon an, mal an** on average over the years; **le jour** *ou* **le premier de l'an, le Nouvel An** New Year's day; **l'an II de la République** Year Two of the Republic; **en l'an 2005** in the year 2005; **je m'en moque comme de l'an 40** I couldn't give a damn about it, I couldn't care less

anabaptisme [anabatism] NM Anabaptism

anabaptiste [anabatist] ADJ, N Anabaptist

anabolisant [anabɔlizɑ̃] NM *Méd* anabolic steroid
   ADJ anabolic

anabolisme [anabɔlism] NM *Méd* anabolism

anacarde [anakard] NM cashew nut

anacardier [anakardje] NM cashew tree

anachorète [anakɔrɛt] NM recluse; *Rel* anchorite; *Fig* **il mène une vie d'a.** he lives the life of a recluse

anachronique [anakrɔnik] ADJ anachronistic

anachronisme [anakrɔnism] NM anachronism

anacoluthe [anakɔlyt] NF anacoluthia

anaconda [anakɔ̃da] NM anaconda

anaérobie [anaerɔbi] ADJ anaerobic

anagrammatique [anagramatik] ADJ anagrammatic(al)

anagramme [anagram] NF anagram

ANAH [ana] NF (*abrév* **Agence nationale pour l'amélioration de l'habitat**) = housing department

anal, -ale, -aux, -ales [anal, -o] ADJ *Anat, Psy* anal

analeptique [analɛptik] ADJ, NM *Pharm* analeptic

analgésie [analʒezi] NF *Méd* analgesia

analgésique [analʒezik] ADJ, NM *Pharm* analgesic

anallergique [analɛrʒik] ADJ *(produit cosmétique)* hypoallergenic

analogie [analɔʒi] NF analogy; **raisonner par a.** to argue from analogy; **par a. avec** by analogy with

analogique [analɔʒik] ADJ **1** analogical; **dictionnaire a.** analogical dictionary **2** *Électron* analogue, *Am* analog; **calculatrice a.** analog computer; **montre a.** analogue watch

analogue [analɔg] ADJ analogous (**à** to, **with**), similar (**à** to); **dans des conditions analogues** in similar conditions
   NM analogue, *Am* analog, parallel; **ce mot anglais n'a pas d'a. en français** this English word has no equivalent in French

analphabète [analfabɛt] ADJ, N illiterate (person)

analphabétisme [analfabetism] NM illiteracy

analysable [analizabl] ADJ analysable, *surtout Am* analyzable

analyse [analiz] NF **1** *(étude)* analysis; **en dernière a.** in the last *or* final analysis, when all is said and done, all things considered; **avoir l'esprit d'a.** to have an analytical mind; **faire l'a. de qch** to analyse sth; **roman/film d'a.** psychological novel/film; **a. de la situation** situation(al) VOIR GRAMMAIRE A14

   2 *Méd* test; **laboratoire d'analyses** pathology laboratory; **a. de sang/d'urine** blood/urine test; **faire des analyses de sang** to undergo blood tests

   3 *Psy* (psycho)analysis; **être en a.** to be in analysis; **commencer/finir son a.** to begin *or* go into analysis/to finish *or* come out of analysis

   ▶▶ *Mktg* **a. des attraits et des atouts** opportunity and issue analysis; *TV, Radio* **a. de l'audience** audience research *or* analysis; **a. des besoins** needs analysis; **a. du chemin critique** critical path analysis; **a. des coûts** cost analysis; **a. de coût et d'efficacité** cost-effectiveness; **a. coût-profit** cost-benefit analysis; **a. de la demande** demand analysis; **a. de données** data analysis; **a. des écarts** variance analysis; *Écon* **a. économique** economic analysis; *Ordinat* **a. factorielle** factor analysis; **a. fonctionnelle** systems analysis; *Mktg* **a. des forces et faiblesses** strengths and weaknesses analysis; *Mktg* **a. des forces, faiblesses, opportunités et menaces** SWOT analysis; *Ling* **a. grammaticale** parsing; *Ling* **faire l'a. grammaticale d'une phrase** to parse a sentence; *Math* **a. infinitésimale** *(différentielle et intégrale)* cal-

culus; *Ling* **a. logique** analysis; *Ling* **faire l'a. logique d'une phrase** to analyse a sentence; **a. du marché** market analysis; **a. des médias** media analysis; *Mktg* **a. d'un modèle de décision en arborescence** decision-tree analysis; *Ordinat* **a. numérique** numerical analysis; *Mktg* **a. des opportunités et des menaces** opportunity and threat analysis; *Ordinat* **a. organique** systems design; *Ordinat* **a. des performances du système** system evaluation; **a. de portefeuille** portfolio analysis; **a. prévisionnelle** predictive analysis; **a. qualitative** qualitative analysis; *Chimie* **a. quantitative** quantitative analysis; **a. du rendement** rate-of-return analysis; **a. des risques** risk analysis; **a. par secteur d'activité** segment reporting; **a. par segment** cluster analysis; **a. de séries temporelles** time-series analysis; **a. statistique** statistical analysis; **a. du style de vie** lifestyle analysis; *Ordinat* **a. syntaxique** parsing; **a. de système, a. systémique** systems analysis; **a. du ton de la voix** voice pitch analysis; **a. de la valeur** value analysis; **a. de la valeur perçue** perceived value analysis; **a. vectorielle** vector analysis; **a. des ventes** sales analysis; **a. volumétrique** volumetric analysis

analyser [analize] VT **1** *(faits etc)* to analyse, *esp Am* to analyze; *Méd (sang, urine etc)* to test; *Ordinat* to parse; *Ling* **a. une phrase** *Gram* to parse a sentence; *(en propositions)* to analyse a sentence **2** *Psy* to (psycho)analyse; **se faire a.** to be (psycho)analysed
   VPR **s'analyser** to analyse one's feelings; **elle s'analyse trop** she goes in for too much self-analysis

analyseur [analizœr] NM analyser, *surtout Am* analyzer; *TV* scanner; *Ordinat* **a. syntaxique** parser; *Ordinat* **a. logique** logic analyzer

analyste [analist] N *Ordinat etc* analyst; *Psy* (psycho)analyst; **être un bon a. de ses sentiments** to be good at analysing one's feelings; *Mktg* **a. du marché** market analyst; **a. des médias** media analyst; *Mktg* **a. mercaticien** marketing analyst; *Fin* **a. en placements financiers** investment analyst

analyste-programmeur, *pl* **analystes-programmeurs** NM *Ordinat* systems analyst

analytique [analitik] ADJ analytical; **géométrie a.** analytic geometry; **un esprit a.** an analytical mind; *Psy* **suivre un traitement a.** to have psychoanalytical treatment
   NF analytics

analytiquement [analitikmɑ̃] ADV analytically

anamnèse [anamnɛz] NF *Méd* anamnesis

anamorphique [anamɔrfik] ADJ *Cin, TV* anamorphic

anamorphose [anamɔrfoz] NF anamorphosis

ananas [anana(s)] NM *(fruit)* pineapple; *(plante)* pineapple plant; **serre à a.** pinery; **a. frais/en conserve** fresh/tinned *or* canned pineapple

anaphore [anafɔr] NF anaphora

anaphorique [anafɔrik] ADJ anaphoric

anaphylactique [anafilaktik] ADJ anaphylactic; **choc a.** anaphylactic shock

anar [anar] N *Fam* = anarchiste

anarchie [anarʃi] NF *Pol, Fig* anarchy

anarchique [anarʃik] ADJ *(comportement)* anarchic(al); *(philosophie, système)* anarchistic

anarchiquement [anarʃikmɑ̃] ADV anarchically, in an anarchic(al) manner; *Fig* chaotically, in a chaotic manner

anarchisant [anarʃizɑ̃] ADJ with anarchist tendencies *or* leanings

anarchisme [anarʃism] NM anarchism

anarchiste [anarʃist] *Pol* **ADJ** anarchist; *Fig* chaotic, disorderly; *(personne)* rebellious, non-conformist
  N anarchist; *Fig* rebel, non-conformist

anarcho-syndicaliste, *pl* **anarcho-syndicalistes** [anarkosɛ̃dikalist] **N** anarchosyndicalist

anathématiser [anatematize] **VT** to curse, *Fml* to anathematize

anathème [anatɛm] **NM** anathema

anatife [anatif] **NM** *(crustacé)* barnacle

anatomie [anatɔmi] **NF** anatomy; *Méd* **a. pathologique** morbid anatomy; *Fam* **une belle a.** a great body; **pièce d'a.** anatomical figure; **avoir une a. d'athlète** to have the body of an athlete

anatomique [anatɔmik] **ADJ** anatomical

anatomiquement [anatɔmikmɑ̃] **ADV** anatomically

anatomiste [anatɔmist] **N** anatomist

ancestral, -ale, -aux, -ales [ɑ̃sɛstral, -o] **ADJ** ancestral

ancêtre [ɑ̃sɛtr] **NM** ancestor; *Fam (vieillard)* old man; **la maison de ses ancêtres** his family home; *(château etc)* his ancestral home; **être sur les traces de ses ancêtres** to be tracking down one's ancestors; **nos ancêtres les Gaulois** our ancestors *or* forefathers the Gauls; **Bartok est l'a. de la musique contemporaine** Bartok is the father of contemporary music; **c'est l'a. de la vidéo** it's the forerunner of the video

anche [ɑ̃ʃ] **NF** *Mus (de hautbois, de clarinette etc)* reed, tongue; **jeu d'anches** *(d'un orgue)* reed-stop

anchois [ɑ̃ʃwa] **NM** *(poisson)* anchovy; **a. de Norvège** sprat; **beurre d'a./sauce aux a.** anchovy paste/sauce; **filets d'a.** anchovy fillets; *Fam* **serrés comme des a.** packed like sardines

ancien, -ienne [ɑ̃sjɛ̃, -jɛn] **ADJ** SEE GRAMMAR B10 **1** *(vieux)* ancient, old, antique; **monument a.** ancient monument; **meubles anciens** antique furniture; **anciens meubles** old furniture
  2 *Hist* ancient, old(en), early, bygone, past; **les peuples anciens** people of antiquity; **le grec a.** ancient *or* classical Greek; **dans l'a. temps** in the old(en) days, in bygone days, in days gone by; **l'A. Testament** the Old Testament; **c'est de l'histoire ancienne** *(c'est oublié)* that's ancient history
  3 *(révolu) (professeur, élève etc)* former, old, ex-; *(avant) (voiture, maison etc)* old; **a. président** former *or* past president; **a. élève** *(d'une école)* old pupil, old boy; *Am Univ* alumnus; **je suis un de vos anciens élèves** I'm a former pupil of yours; **anciens combattants** ex-servicemen, *Am* veterans; **mon a. époux** my ex-husband; **c'est un a. boxeur** he's a former boxer, he used to be a boxer
  4 *(capitaine, officier etc)* senior; **je suis plus a. que vous dans la profession** I've been in the profession longer than you; **il est votre a.** he is senior to you
  NM 1 *Hist* **les anciens** the ancients
  2 *Rel, Pol* elder; **les anciens du village** the older inhabitants of the village; **les anciens de la tribu** the elders of the tribe; **respecter les anciens** to respect one's elders; *Fam* **l'a.** *(père)* the old man
  3 **aimer l'a.** *(meubles)* to like antique furniture *or* antiques; *(architecture)* to like old buildings
  4 *Vieilli (de scouts)* patrol leader
  N *(par l'expérience)* **c'est une ancienne dans la maison** she's been with the firm a long time; **les anciens de l'entreprise** the company's long-time *or* long-serving employees

> Il faut noter que le mot anglais **ancient** est un faux ami. Il correspond au français **antique.**

anciennement [ɑ̃sjɛnmɑ̃] **ADV** formerly

ancienneté [ɑ̃sjɛnte] **NF 1** *(d'un monument, d'une race etc)* age, antiquity; **de toute a.** from time immemorial **2** *(par l'expérience)* seniority, length of service; **a. de grade** seniority in rank; **avoir 15 ans d'a. dans une entreprise** to have 15 years' service with a firm; **avancer à l'a.** to be promoted by seniority; **il a plus d'a. que moi** he's been with the company longer than I have

ancillaire [ɑ̃silɛr] **ADJ** ancillary; **amours ancillaires** love affairs with a servant/servants

ancolie [ɑ̃kɔli] **NF** *(fleur)* aquilegia, columbine

ancrage [ɑ̃kraʒ] **NM 1** *Naut* anchoring; *(attache)* anchorage; **(droits d')a.** anchorage dues **2** *Constr etc (action)* anchoring, anchorage, fixing; *(d'un mur)* bracing, staying; *(dispositif)* wall tie; **plaque/tige d'a.** plate/tie; **point d'a.** *(d'un câble)* cable anchorage; *Fig* base; *Fig* **ce studio à Londres est son point d'a., c'est à partir de là qu'il rayonne** this studio in London is his base for touring around; *Fig* **l'a. de nouvelles idées** the taking root of new ideas **3** *Ordinat* justification; **a. à droite/gauche** right/left justification

ancre [ɑ̃kr] **NF 1** anchor; **a. de veille** sheet anchor; **lever l'a.** to weigh anchor; *Fig Fam (partir)* to get moving, to hit the road; **jeter l'a.** to anchor; *Fig* to settle down; *Aviat* **a. de ballon** balloon anchor, grapnel; *Naut Arch* **a. de miséricorde** sheet anchor **2** *Constr etc (d'un mur, d'un fourneau etc)* anchor, cramp iron, tie (plate); *(d'une chaudière)* brace, stay **3** *Ordinat* anchor

ancrer [ɑ̃kre] **VT 1** *(navire, montgolfière)* to anchor; *Fig* **il faut lui a. cette idée dans la tête** we/you/*etc* have to get that into his head; *Fig* **je ne sais pas qui lui a ancré cette idée dans la tête, mais il n'en démord pas** I don't know who put that idea in his head, but he won't let go of it; **cette idée est profondément ancrée en lui** this idea is firmly rooted in his mind **2** *Constr (cheminée, moteur, chaudière etc)* to brace, to tie, to stay, to anchor
  VPR **s'ancrer** *(d'anémone de mer etc)* to attach itself; *Fig (d'une idée, d'un concept)* to stick, to become rooted; *Fig* **elle a décidé de s'a. dans cette région** she has decided to put down roots in the region; *Fig* **je m'ancrais dans mon intention première** I stuck fast to my original intention; *Fig* **celui en qui s'ancre la foi …** he whose faith is steadfast …

andain [ɑ̃dɛ̃] **NM** swathe

andalou, -ouse [ɑ̃dalu, -uz] **ADJ** Andalusian
  NM 1 *Ling* Andalusian (dialect) **2** *(cheval)* Andalusian horse
  N A. Andalusian

Andalousie [ɑ̃daluzi] **NF** Andalusia

andante [ɑ̃dɑ̃t(e)] **ADV, NM** *Mus* andante

andantino [ɑ̃dɑ̃tino] **ADV, NM** *Mus* andantino

Andes [ɑ̃d] **NFPL** **les A.** the Andes; **la Cordillère des A.** the Andean *or* the Great Cordillera

andin [ɑ̃dɛ̃] **ADJ** Andean

andorran, -ane [ɑ̃dɔrɑ̃, -an] **ADJ** Andorran
  N A. Andorran

Andorre [ɑ̃dɔr] **N** Andorra; **le val/la principauté d'A.** the Vale/Principality of Andorra

andouille [ɑ̃duj] **NF 1** *Culin* chitterlings sausage **2** *Fam (imbécile)* fool, twit; **faire l'a.** to play the fool

andouiller [ɑ̃duje] **NM** *(d'un cervidé)* antler

andouillette [ɑ̃dujɛt] **NF** *Culin* = small chitterlings sausage (for frying)

androgène [ɑ̃drɔʒɛn] **ADJ** androgenic
  NM androgen, male hormone

androgyne [ɑ̃drɔʒin] **ADJ** androgynous
  N androgyne

androïde [ɑ̃drɔid] **NM** android

andrologie [ɑ̃drɔlɔʒi] **NF** andrology

andrologue [ɑ̃drɔlɔg] **NM** andrologist

Andromaque [ɑ̃drɔmak] **N** Andromache

Andromède [ɑ̃drɔmɛd] **N** Andromeda

andropause [ɑ̃drɔpoz] **NF** male menopause

âne [ɑn] **NM 1** donkey, *Litt, Vieilli* ass; **â. mâle** jackass; **promenade à dos d'â.** donkey ride; **se promener à dos d'â.** to go for a donkey ride; *Prov* **on ne saurait faire boire un â. qui n'a pas soif** you may lead a horse to water but you cannot make him drink; **être comme l'â. de Buridan** to be unable to make up one's mind between two things; *Fig* **le coup de pied de l'â.** the final insult, the last straw **2** *Fam (idiot)* ass; *(ignare)* dunce; **bonnet d'â.** dunce's cap; **espèce d'â. bâté!** stupid ass!

anéantir [aneɑ̃tir] **VT** to annihilate; **a. les espérances de qn** to dash sb's hopes, to put an end to sb's hopes; *Fig* **la nouvelle l'a anéantie** she was staggered by the news
  VPR **s'anéantir 1** *(disparaître) (d'espoir, de chances de succès)* to be dashed **2** *Rel (devant Dieu)* to humble *or* abase oneself

anéantissement [aneɑ̃tismɑ̃] **NM 1** *(de l'espoir etc)* destruction; *(d'un empire etc)* annihilation, destruction; **l'a. de l'individu/de la personnalité** the annihilation of the individual/the personality **2** *(abattement)* **dans un état d'a. total** completely shattered

anecdote [anɛkdɔt] **NF** anecdote

anecdotique [anɛkdɔtik] **ADJ** anecdotal

anémie [anemi] **NF** *Méd* anaemia, *Am* anemia; **faire de l'a.** to have anaemia; **a. pernicieuse** pernicious anaemia; *Fig* **l'a. d'un secteur** the enfeebled state of an industrial sector

anémier [anemje] **VT** **a. qn** to make sb anaemic *or Am* anemic; *Fig* **la crise a anémié la sidérurgie** the crisis has severely weakened the steel industry
  VPR **s'anémier** to become anaemic *or Am* anemic; *Fig* **un secteur qui s'anémie** an industrial sector that is falling into decline

anémique [anemik] **ADJ** *(personne)* anaemic, *Am* anemic; *Fig* feeble, weak

anémomètre [anemɔmɛtr] **NM** anemometer, wind gauge; **a. badin** airspeed indicator

anémone [anemɔn] **NF** anemone; **a. sylvie** wood anemone; **a. de mer** sea anemone

ânerie [ɑnri] **NF** *Fam* **1** *(stupidité, bêtise)* stupidity; **il est d'une â.!** what an idiot!; **quelle â.!** *(ta décision etc)* how idiotic! **2** *(action, propos)* **je crois que je viens de dire/faire une â.** I think I've just said/done something silly; **faire des âneries** to make an ass *or* a fool of oneself; **dire des âneries** to talk tripe *or* rubbish

anéroïde [anerɔid] **ADJ** *Météo (baromètre)* aneroid

ânesse [ɑnɛs] **NF** she ass, jenny; **lait d'â.** ass's milk

anesthésiant [anɛstezjɑ̃] **ADJ, NM** *Méd* anaesthetic, *Am* anesthetic

anesthésie [anɛstezi] **NF** *Méd* anaesthesia, *Am* anesthesia; **a. générale/locale** general/local anaesthetic; **on va vous faire une a. locale/générale** we're going to give you a local/general anaesthetic; **mettre un malade sous a.** to anaesthetize a patient, to put a patient under anaesthetic; **elle est encore sous a.** she's still under (the) anaesthetic

anesthésier [anɛstezje] **VT** *Méd* to anaesthetize, *Am* to anesthetize; *Fig (crainte)* to deaden; *(opinion publique)* to anaesthetize

anesthésiologie [anɛstezjɔlɔʒi] **NF** *Méd* anaesthetics, *Am* anesthesiology

anesthésique [anɛstezik] ADJ, NM *Méd* anaesthetic, *Am* anesthetic

anesthésiste [anɛstezist] N *Méd (médecin)* anaesthetist, *Am* anesthetologist; *Am (infirmière)* anesthetist

aneth [anɛt] NM *(plante)* dill

anévrisme, anévrysme [anevrism] NM *Méd* aneurism, aneurysm

anfractuosité [ãfraktɥozite] NF crevice, crack

ange [ãʒ] NM *Rel* angel; **un visage d'a.** an angelic face; *Beaux-Arts* **a. joufflu** chubby little cherub; **être le bon a. de qn** to be sb's good angel; **être le mauvais a. de qn** to be a bad influence on sb; **être aux anges** to be in seventh heaven, to be walking on air; **rire aux anges** to smile contentedly; *Fam* **faiseuse d'anges** backstreet abortionist; *Fam* **un a. passe** silence is wonderful; **un a. passa** there was a sudden silence in the conversation; *Fig* **discuter du sexe des anges** to talk round in circles; **oui, mon a.** yes (my) angel; **tu es un a.** you're an angel; **tu serais un a. si tu allais me chercher mes cigarettes** be an angel and fetch me my cigarettes; **beau comme un a.** pretty as a picture; **sage comme un a.** (as) good as gold; **une patience d'a.** the patience of a saint; **une douceur d'a.** angelic sweetness
▸▸ **a. déchu** fallen angel; **a. gardien** guardian angel; *Iron* bodyguard; *Vieilli* **a. tutélaire** guardian angel

angéiologie [ãʒejoloʒi] NF *Méd* angiology

angélique [ãʒelik] ADJ angelic(al); *Rel* **la salutation a.** the Hail Mary; **être d'une patience a.** to have the patience of a saint
NF *Culin* angelica

angélisme [ãʒelism] NM saintliness

angelot [ãʒlo] NM **1** little angel, cherub **2** *(poisson)* monkfish, angel fish *or* ray *or* shark

angélus [ãʒelys] NM *Rel* angelus (bell)

angevin, -ine [ãʒvɛ̃, -in] ADJ Angevin, (of *or* from) Angers/Anjou
N **A.** Angevin, person from Angers/Anjou

angine [ãʒin] NF *Méd* sore throat, *Fam* strep throat; *(des amygdales)* tonsillitis; **avoir une a.** to have a sore throat/to have tonsillitis; **a. de poitrine** angina (pectoris)

angiogenèse [ãʒjoʒənɛz] NF *Méd* angiogenesis

angiographie [ãʒjografi] NF *Méd* angiography

angiome [ãʒjom] NM *Méd* angioma

angioplastie [ãʒjoplasti] NF *Méd* angioplasty

anglais, -aise [ãglɛ, -ɛz] ADJ English; *(incorrect au sens strict) (armée, marchandises etc)* British
NM English (language); **l'a.** correct the King's *or* Queen's English; **a. britannique/américain** British/American English
N **A.** Englishman, *f* Englishwoman; *(incorrect au sens strict)* Briton; **les A.** the English; *(incorrect au sens strict)* the British; **les A. ont débarqué**, *Can* **j'ai la visite des A.** I have my period
NF **anglaise** *Culin* **pommes de terre à l'anglaise** boiled potatoes
NFPL **anglaises** ringlets

angle [ãgl] NM **1** *(d'un mur, d'une pièce etc)* corner, angle; **la maison qui fait l'a. appartient à mon oncle** the house on the corner belongs to my uncle; **armoire d'a.** corner cupboard; **l'a. de la rue** the street corner; **à l'a. du chemin** at the bend of the road; **l'a. de la table** the corner of the table; *Fig* **arrondir les angles** to smooth things over; **c'est toujours elle qui arrondit les angles** she's always the one who smooths things over

2 *(point de vue)* angle, point of view; **nous ne voyons pas les choses sous le même a.** we don't see things from the same angle *or* in the same way; **sous cet a.-là** from that angle, from that point of view; **vu sous cet a.** seen from that angle; **a. d'attaque** *(d'un sujet)* line of attack, approach

3 *Géom* angle; **a. aigu/obtus** acute/obtuse angle; **a. plat/droit** straight angle/right angle; **les rues se coupent à angles droits** the roads cross at right angles; **former un a. avec qch** to be at right angles to sth

4 *Menuis etc* **abattre les angles de qch** to chamfer sth; **soudure d'a.** fillet weld; **roue d'a.** bevel wheel, mitre wheel; **a. oblique** bevel rule, mitre square; **engrenage d'a.** bevel gear; **fer d'a.** angle iron

5 *(d'un outil)* edge; **à angles vifs** with sharp edges
▸▸ *Aut* **a. de braquage** turning circle; **a. de cap** track course; *Aut* **a. de chasse** caster angle; *Aviat* **a. critique** stalling angle; *Opt* **a. d'incidence** angle of incidence; *Mil* **a. de mire** angle of sight; **a. mort** *(au tir)* dead angle; *(dans un rétroviseur etc)* blind spot; *TV, Cin* **a. plongée** high angle; *TV, Cin* **a. de prise de vue** shooting *or* camera angle; *Opt* **a. de réfraction** angle of refraction; *TV, Cin* **a. de vue** angle of view

angledozer [ãgledozɛr] NM angledozer

Angleterre [ãglətɛr] NF England; *(incorrect au sens strict)* Britain; *Hist* **la bataille d'A.** the Battle of Britain; *Couture* **point d'A.** Brussels (bobbin) lace

anglican, -ane [ãglikã, -an] *Rel* ADJ Anglican; **l'Église anglicane** the Church of England, the Anglican Church
N Anglican

anglicanisme [ãglikanism] NM *Rel* Anglicanism

anglicisant, -ante [ãglisizã, -ãt] N student of English, English scholar

angliciser [ãglisize] VT *(mot etc)* to anglicize
VPR **s'angliciser** to become anglicized

anglicisme [ãglisism] NM *Ling* Anglicism

angliciste [ãglisist] N *(étudiant)* student of English; *(spécialiste)* specialist in English, Anglicist

anglo- [ãglo] PRÉF Anglo-

anglo-américain, -aine, *pl* **anglo-américains, -aines** ADJ Anglo-American
NM *Ling* American English
N **A.** Anglo-American

anglo-catholique, *pl* **anglo-catholiques** *Rel* ADJ Anglo-Catholic
N Anglo-Catholic

anglo-irlandais, -aise, *pl* **anglo-irlandais, -aises** ADJ Anglo-Irish; **l'Accord a.** the Anglo-Irish Agreement
N **A.** Anglo-Irishman, -woman

anglomane [ãgloman] N anglomaniac

anglomanie [ãglomani] NF anglomania

anglo-normand, -ande, *pl* **anglo-normands, -andes** ADJ **1** **les îles Anglo-Normandes** the Channel Islands **2** *Hist* Anglo-Norman
NM *Ling* Anglo-Norman

anglophile [ãglofil] ADJ anglophile, pro-English
N anglophile

anglophilie [ãglofili] NF anglophilia

anglophobe [ãglofɔb] ADJ anglophobic
N anglophobe

anglophobie [ãglofɔbi] NF anglophobia

anglophone [ãglofɔn] ADJ English-speaking, *Can* anglophone
N English-speaking person, *Can* Anglophone

anglo-saxon, -onne, *pl* **anglo-saxons, -onnes** [ãglosaksɔ̃, -ɔn] ADJ Anglo-Saxon; **les pays anglo-saxons** the English-speaking countries
NM *Ling* Anglo-Saxon
N **A.** English speaker; *Hist* Anglo-Saxon

> **Anglo-saxon**
> Note that the adjective "anglo-saxon" and the noun "Anglo-Saxon" are often used in French to refer to British and American people, culture, customs etc: "la musique anglo-saxonne", "la littérature anglo-saxonne".

angoissant [ãgwasã] ADJ *(nouvelles)* distressing; *(attente)* agonizing; *(film, livre)* frightening; *(moment)* tense, anxious; *(situation, expérience)* alarming; **le fait d'être au chômage peut être très a.** being out of work can be very distressing

angoisse [ãgwas] NF anguish, distress; *(douleur)* agony; *Méd* **une crise d'a.** an anxiety attack; **les angoisses de la mort** the pangs of death; **vivre dans l'a. de la mort** to live in fear of dying; **considérer qch avec a.** *(à l'avenir)* to dread sth; *(au passé)* to look back on sth with anguish; *Fam* **c'est l'a.!, bonjour l'a.!** what a pain *or* drag *or* bummer!

angoissé [ãgwase] ADJ distressed, anxious; **j'étais a.** my heart was in my mouth
N anxious person

angoisser [ãgwase] VT **a. qn** to fill sb with anxiety *or* distress *or* anguish; *Fam* **ça m'angoisse d'entrer dans un supermarché seul avec lui** I can't face going into a supermarket/being alone with him; **ce n'est tout de même pas ça qui t'angoisse!** you're not getting all worked up over a thing like that, are you?
VI *Fam* to worry, to get worked up; **j'angoisse à mort** I'm worried to death, I'm worried stiff
VPR **s'angoisser** to get anxious, *Fam* to get worked up; **elle s'angoisse pour un rien** she gets worked up over nothing

Angola [ãgola] NM Angola

angolais, -aise [ãgolɛ, -ɛz], **angolan, -ane** [ãgolã, -an] ADJ Angolan
N **A.** Angolan

angora [ãgora] ADJ *(souvent inv) (laine, pull)* angora; **poil de chèvre a.** mohair
NM **1** *(lapin)* angora rabbit; *(chat)* Persian cat; *(chèvre)* angora **2** *Tex* angora (wool)

angstrœm, angström [ãgstrœm] NM *Phys* angström

anguille [ãgij] NF *(poisson)* eel; **a. de mer** conger eel; *Fig* **il y a a. sous roche** there's something fishy going on, I smell a rat; *Fam* **elle a filé comme une a.** she ran off like greased lightning; **être souple comme une a.** to be (as) flexible as rubber, to be made of rubber

angulaire [ãgylɛr] ADJ angular; *Constr* **pierre a.** cornerstone; *Fig* **la pierre a. d'une théorie/de la société** the cornerstone of a theory/of society
NM *Phot* **grand a.** wide-angle lens

anguleux, -euse [ãgylø, -øz] ADJ *(visage, silhouette etc)* angular, bony; *(contours etc)* rough, rugged; *Fig* **caractère a.** awkward disposition

anicroche [anikrɔʃ] NF difficulty, hitch, snag; **se passer sans a.** to go smoothly *or* without a hitch

aniline [anilin] NF *Chimie* aniline

animal, -ale, -aux, -ales [animal, -o] NM animal; **société protectrice des animaux** society for the prevention of cruelty to animals; **a. domestique** pet; **l'homme est un a. social** man is a social animal; **il en a de la chance, cet a.-là!** what a lucky beggar!; **c'est un drôle d'a.** he's a funny old beggar; *Fam*

quel a.! what a brute!, what a beast!; **espèce d'a.!** you pig! VOIR GRAMMAIRE A12; A15; A27

ADJ 1 *(règne, question etc)* animal; **chaleur animale** animal warmth **2** *(instinct etc)* animal; **avoir une confiance animale en qn** to trust sb instinctively

animalerie [animalri] NF animal room; *(bâtiment séparé)* animal house

animalier [animalje] **ADJ** *(peinture etc)* animal; **peintre a.** animal painter
NM **1** *(peintre)* painter *or* sculptor of animals **2** *(dans un laboratoire)* animal keeper

animalité [animalite] NF animality, animal nature; *(des êtres humains)* animal side

animateur, -trice [animatœr, -tris] ADJ *(énergie, pouvoir)* life-giving
N **1** *Radio, TV* presenter; *(d'émission de variétés)* host, compère, MC, *Am* emcee; *(de jeu télévisé ou radiophonique)* quiz *or* question master; *Radio* presenter, radio personality; *(d'une émission de musique pop)* disc jockey, DJ, deejay; *(d'un débat)* moderator **2** *(sur un bateau)* entertainments officer; *(de centre aéré)* organizer; **l'animatrice d'un centre de jeunes** the organizer *or* youth leader of a youth club; *Mktg* **a. d'une réunion de groupe** group discussion moderator **3** *Cin* animator **4** *(personne qui a de l'entrain)* stimulating person; **il a d'excellents talents d'a.** he's extremely good at livening things up
▸▸**a. socioculturel** = community worker in social and cultural activities; **a. sportif** sports presenter; *TV* **a. vedette** star presenter; **a. des ventes** marketing executive

animation [animasjɔ̃] NF **1** *(vie)* animation, liveliness; **l'a. des rues** the bustle in the streets; **mettre de l'a. dans une soirée** to liven up a party; **il parle avec beaucoup d'a.** he speaks with great animation; **ville pleine d'a.** town full of life; *Fin* **a. du marché** buoyancy of the market; *Com* **a. des ventes** sales drive *or* promotion **2** *(divertissements)* activities; **faire de l'a.** to organize activities in a community **3** *Cin* animation; **film d'a.** animated film; **a. de photos** photo-animation; **a. par ordinateur** computer animation **4** *Météo* **a. satellite** satellite picture

animatique [animatik] NF *Ordinat* animation; *TV, Cin* animatic

animé [anime] ADJ **1** *(personne, discussion etc)* animated, spirited, lively; *(agité)* *(discussion)* heated; *(rue, quartier etc)* busy, bustling; *Fin* **marché a.** brisk *or* buoyant market **2** *Cin* **dessin a.** cartoon

animer [anime] VT **1** *(stimuler)* *(personne, chose)* to animate, to give life to; **la passion du travail l'anime** he is driven by his passion for work; **animé par un nouvel espoir** buoyed up with new hope
2 *(mener, diriger)* to move, to propel; *(discussion)* to lead, to conduct; *(entreprise)* to lead, to mastermind; *(machine)* to drive; **animé d'un sentiment de jalousie** prompted by feelings of jealousy; **animé de bonnes intentions** motivated by good intentions
3 *(rendre plus vivant)* *(conversation)* to enliven; *(quartier, pièce)* to liven up; *(pièce)* to brighten up
4 *Cin* to animate; *TV, Radio* **a. une émission** to present a programme
VPR **s'animer** to come to life; **la conversation s'animait** the conversation was getting more lively *or* was warming up; **la ville s'anime avec le marché** the town comes to life on market day; **la rue s'anime le soir** the street wakes up at night; **son visage s'anima** his face lit up; **les esprits s'animent, il va y avoir de la bagarre** people are getting worked up, there's going to be trouble

animisme [animism] NM animism

animiste [animist] ADJ, N animist

animosité [animozite] NF animosity (**contre** for, towards), hostility (**contre** towards); **être plein d'a. envers** *ou* **contre** *ou* **pour qn** to feel great hostility towards sb; **avoir de l'a. contre** *ou* **pour qn** to feel animosity towards sb; **garder de l'a. contre qn** to nurse a grudge against sb; **agir par a.** to act out of spite

anion [anjɔ̃] NM *Phys* anion

anis [ani(s)] NM *(plante)* anise; *(boisson)* **(si-rop d')a.** aniseed cordial; *Culin* **(graine d')a.** aniseed; **à l'a.** aniseed-flavoured

aniser [anize] VT *Culin* to flavour with aniseed

anisette [anizɛt] NF anisette

ankylose [ākiloz] NF stiffness; *Méd* ankylosis; **une sorte d'a. gagne peu à peu tous ses membres** his limbs are gradually stiffening up

ankyloser [ākiloze] VT *Méd* to ankylose; **être ankylosé** to be stiff
VPR **s'ankyloser** to become *or* get stiff; *Fig (dans un métier etc)* to get into a rut

annal, -ale, -aux, -ales [anal, -o] ADJ *Jur* valid for one year; **location annale** yearly letting

annales [anal] NFPL annals, (public) records; **les a. du crime** the annals of crime; **les a. du bac** = past examination papers (with annotations); **a. de géographie/littéraires** geographical/literary review; *Fig* **ça restera dans les a.** it will go down in (the annals of) history

annamite [anamit] ADJ Annamese, Annamite
NM *Ling* Annamese
N **A.** person from Annam

anneau, -eaux [ano] NM **1** *(cercle, bague)* ring; **a. de rideau** curtain ring; **avoir des petits anneaux d'or aux oreilles** to have little gold rings in one's ears; **toutes ses clés sont sur un même a.** *(d'un porte-clés)* all his keys are on the same ring; *Gym* **les anneaux** the rings; *Gym* **exercices aux anneaux** ring exercises; **jeu des anneaux** hoop-la
2 *Bot* annulus
3 *(de chaîne)* link; *(de cheveux)* ringlet, curl; *(d'un serpent)* coil; *(d'une clé)* bow
4 *Tech* ring, collar; *(d'un moyeu etc)* hoop; *(d'un cordage)* sling; **a. brisé** key *or* split ring; **a. à fiche** ring-bolt, eye-bolt; *Aut* **a. de retenue de charge** load restraining eye
5 *Naut* **a. de port** = berth with facilities for hooking up to land-based power and water supplies
▸▸**a. épiscopal** episcopal *or* bishop's ring; **a. nuptial** *ou* **de mariage** wedding ring; *Astron* **a. de Saturne** ring of Saturn

année [ane] NF SEE GRAMMAR B61 year; **Bonne A.!** Happy New Year!; **fin d'a.** end of the year; **une a. de vacances** a year's holiday; **payer à l'a.** to pay by the year; **a. après a.** year after year; **d'a. en a.** year by year; **une a. après l'autre** year in year out; **nous nous connaissons depuis bien des années** we've known each other for years; **il y a des années que je ne l'ai pas vue** I haven't seen her for years; **les années 80** the eighties, the 80s; **en quelle a. Charlemagne a-t-il été couronné?** in what year was Charlemagne crowned?; **l'a. prochaine/dernière** next/last year; **pendant les années de guerre/d'occupation** during the war years/the years of occupation; **quelle est son a. de naissance?** what year was he/she born?; **elle entre dans sa trentième a.** she'll be thirty (on her) next birthday; *Univ* **entrer en troisième a. de médecine** to go into one's third year of medicine; *Univ* **les classes de deuxième a.** the second year students, *Am* the sophomores
▸▸**a. bissextile** leap year; **a. budgétaire** financial year; **a. civile** calendar year; **a. comptable** accounting *or* financial year, *Am* fiscal year; **a. fiscale** tax year; **a. d'imposition** year of assessment

année-lumière, *pl* **années-lumière** NF light year; **à des années-lumière** *(étoile etc)* light years away; *Fig* **nous sommes à des années-lumière l'un de l'autre** we're light years away from each other, we're worlds apart

annelé [anle] ADJ *(colonne, ver etc)* ringed

annexe [anɛks] NF **1** *(bâtiment)* annex(e); *(de ferme, château)* outbuilding **2** *(de projet de loi)* rider; *(de loi)* schedule; *(de livre, rapport)* appendix; *(de lettre)* enclosure; **en a. à ma lettre** enclosed with my letter; **en a., veuillez trouver …** please find enclosed …; **annexes** *Compta* notes to the accounts; *(d'un livre)* back matter, appendices **3** *Rel* chapel of ease **4** *(d'un État)* dependency **5** *Naut (d'un bateau)* dinghy
ADJ **établissement a.** annex(e); **lettre a.** covering letter; **industries annexes** subsidiary industries; **revenus annexes** supplementary income

annexer [anɛkse] VT **1** *Pol (territoire)* to annex **2** *(document etc)* to append, to attach; **pièces annexées** *(à une lettre)* enclosures
VPR **s'annexer s'a. qch** to acquire sth for oneself; **il s'est annexé la meilleure place** he grabbed the best seat for himself

annexion [anɛksjɔ̃] NF annexation

Annibal [anibal] N *Antiq* Hannibal

annihilation [aniilasjɔ̃] NF annihilation; *(des efforts, effets etc)* destruction

annihiler [aniile] VT **1** *(armée etc)* to annihilate, to destroy; *(efforts, travail etc)* to destroy; **toute forme d'agressivité l'annihile** he goes to pieces when faced with any form of aggressive behaviour **2** *Jur* to annul, to cancel

anniversaire [aniverser] ADJ *(cérémonie)* anniversary; **la date a.** *(de la Libération etc)* the anniversary
NM *(d'une naissance)* birthday; *(d'une victoire, d'une mort etc)* anniversary; *(d'un mariage)* (wedding) anniversary; **le cinquantième a. de leur mariage** their fiftieth wedding anniversary; **c'est mon a.** it's my birthday; **mon vingtième a., l'a. de mes vingt ans** my twentieth birthday; **bon a.!** happy birthday!; **gâteau/carte d'a.** birthday cake/card

> Attention: ne pas confondre **anniversary** et **birthday** lorsqu'on traduit **anniversaire**. **Birthday** s'utilise pour l'anniversaire d'une personne et **anniversary** pour celui d'un événement.

annonce [anɔ̃s] NF **1** announcement; *(surtout par écrit)* notification, notice; *Cartes* declaration, bid; *Fig* sign, indication; *Rel* **faire l'a. d'un mariage** to publish the banns; **faire une a.** to make an announcement; **les annonces de la semaine** the weekly notices; *Fig* **le retour des hirondelles est l'a. du printemps** it's a sign of spring when the swallows return; *TV, Radio* **a. de continuité** continuity announcement; *TV* **a. de programme** programme trail **2** *(de publicité etc)* advertisement; **passer une (petite) a. dans un journal/sur Minitel®** to put an ad(vert) in a newspaper/on Minitel®; **petites annonces** classified advertisements, small ads; **annonces classées** classified ads

annoncer [anɔ̃se] (j'annonçai(s); n. annonçons) VT **1** *(déclarer)* to announce, to give notice of; **a. une mauvaise nouvelle à qn** to break bad news to sb; **a. ses fiançailles en public** to announce one's engagement publicly
2 *(dans journal)* *(soldes etc)* to advertise
3 *(indiquer)* to promise, to foretell, to herald; **tout semble a. le succès** everything

points to success; **cela n'annonce rien de bon** it looks unpromising, no *or* nothing good will come of that; **l'hirondelle annonce le printemps** the swallow is a sign that spring is on its way, the swallow heralds the approach of spring

4 a. qn to show sb in; *(lors d'une occasion officielle)* to announce sb; **se faire a.** to give one's name

VPR s'annoncer 1 *(prévenir de sa visite)* to give notice of one's arrival **2** *(se présenter)* *(de la situation)* **cela s'annonce bien** it looks promising; **cela s'annonce mal** it looks unpromising, no good *or* nothing good will come of that; **l'avènement de la démocratie s'annonce partout en Europe** there are signs all over Europe of the advent of democracy **3** *Suisse (se présenter, s'adresser à)* to go, to report; **annoncez-vous à la réception** report to reception

annonceur, -euse [anɔ̃sœr, -øz] **N** *Radio, TV (speaker)* announcer
NM *(de publicité)* advertiser

annonciateur, -trice [anɔ̃sjatœr, -tris] **ADJ** **signes annonciateurs du printemps** signs that spring is on the way, signs that herald the approach of spring

annonciation [anɔ̃sjasjɔ̃] **NF** *Rel* annunciation; **fête de l'A.** Feast of the Annunciation, Lady Day

annotateur, -trice [anɔtatœr, -tris] **N** *(d'un texte etc)* annotator, commentator

annotation [anɔtasjɔ̃] **NF 1** *(action)* annotating, making notes **2** *(note)* annotation, note; **faire des annotations dans un texte** to annotate a text

annoter [anɔte] **VT** *(texte)* to annotate; *(livre)* to write notes in; *(épreuves)* to mark up

annuaire [anɥɛr] **NM** annual; *(d'un organisme international)* yearbook; *Ordinat* directory; **l'a. du téléphone** *ou* **téléphonique** the telephone directory, *Fam* the phone book; **je suis dans l'a.** I'm in the book; **je ne suis pas dans l'a., je suis sur la liste rouge** I'm not in the (phone) book, I'm ex-directory; **a. du commerce** trade directory; **a. papier** printed directory; **a. électronique** electronic directory; **a. des marées** tide table; **l'A. militaire** the Army list, *Am* the Army Register; **l'A. de la Marine** the Navy List; **a. de l'université** university calendar

annualisation [anɥalizasjɔ̃] **NF** annualization; **l'a. du temps de travail permettra de répondre à une demande saisonnière** calculating working hours across the year will enable us to meet seasonal demand

annualiser [anɥalize] **VT** to annualize

annuel, -elle [anɥɛl] **ADJ** annual, yearly; **budget a.** annual budget; **chiffre d'affaires a.** annual *or* yearly turnover; **congé a.** annual leave; **plante annuelle** annual; **rente annuelle** annuity; **magistrature annuelle** = judicial office held only for one year

annuellement [anɥɛlmɑ̃] **ADV** annually, yearly

annuitaire [anɥitɛr] **ADJ** *Compta, Fin (dette)* redeemable by yearly payments

annuité [anɥite] **NF 1** *(dans le remboursement d'un emprunt)* annual instalment *or Am* installment *or* repayment; *Compta* **a. constante** *(de remboursement)* fixed annual payment; *Compta* **a. d'amortissement** annual depreciation *or* writedown **2** *Can, Suisse (rente)* annuity

annulaire [anɥlɛr] **ADJ** annular, ring-shaped
NM ring finger, third finger

annulation [anylasjɔ̃] **NF 1** *(d'un contrat, d'une commande, de vacances etc)* cancelling, cancellation; *Jur etc (d'un mariage)* annulment; *(d'un jugement)* quashing, setting aside; *(d'un acte judiciaire)* annulment, re-

peal; *(d'un contrat)* voidance; *(d'un testament)* setting aside; *Com* **a. rétroactive** retroactive cancellation; **a. de dernière minute** late cancellation **2** *Ordinat* deletion; **a. d'entrée** *(commande)* cancel entry; **a. des révisions** *(commande)* undo changes

annuler [anyle] **VT 1** *(contrat, commande etc)* to cancel; *(dette)* to cancel, to write off; *(marché)* to call off; *Jur (mariage)* to annul; *(loi, jugement)* to render void, to repeal, to rescind; *(testament)* to set aside; **a. un ordre de grève** to call off a strike **2** *Banque (chèque etc)* to cancel **3** *(remplacer)* to supersede, to cancel; **ce catalogue annule les précédents** this catalogue supersedes all previous issues **4** *Ordinat* to cancel; *(opération)* to undo; **a. les révisions** *(commande)* undo changes **5** *Ftbl (but)* to disallow
VPR s'annuler to cancel each other out

anoblir [anɔblir] **VT a. qn** to ennoble sb, to raise sb to the peerage

> Do not confuse with **ennoblir**, which means **to elevate morally**.

anoblissement [anɔblismɑ̃] **NM** ennoblement (**de** of); **lettres d'a.** letters patent of nobility

anode [anɔd] **NF** *Élec* anode

anodin [anɔdɛ̃] **ADJ** harmless, innocuous; *(blessure, changement)* slight, minor; *(infection)* mild; **cette remarque n'était pas anodine** this remark was not as innocent as it might seem; **une personne tout à fait anodine** a totally insignificant person; *Méd* **remèdes anodins** painkillers; *Fig* **moyen/remède a.** ineffective method/remedy; **mensonge a.** white lie

anodique [anɔdik] **ADJ** *Élec* anodic, anodal; *(courant)* anode

anomalie [anɔmali] **NF** *Gram, Astron, Biol* anomaly; *Méd* disorder; **si vous remarquez la moindre a. dans la comptabilité** if you should notice the slightest irregularity in the accounting; **il y a une a. dans le fonctionnement de la machine** the machine has a malfunction

ânon [anɔ̃] **NM** little donkey; *(très jeune)* baby donkey

ânonnement [anɔnmɑ̃] **NM** mumbling, faltering tone

ânonner [anɔne] **VT** *(paroles)* to stumble *or* blunder through; **â. une récitation** to recite sth falteringly
VI to mumble

anonymat [anɔnima] **NM** anonymity; **garder l'a.** to remain anonymous; **faire qch dans l'a. le plus complet** to do sth anonymously

anonyme [anɔnim] **ADJ** *(écrivain, lettre etc)* anonymous; *Fig (décor, intérieur)* impersonal, anonymous

anonymement [anɔnimmɑ̃] **ADV** anonymously

anophèle [anɔfɛl] **NM** *Zool* anopheles mosquito

anorak [anɔrak] **NM** anorak

anorexie [anɔrɛksi] **NF** *Méd* anorexia; **a. mentale** anorexia nervosa; **faire de l'a.** to suffer from anorexia

anorexique [anɔrɛksik] **ADJ, N** *Méd* anorexic

anormal, -ale, -aux, -ales [anɔrmal, -o] **ADJ 1** *(non-conforme)* abnormal; **personne d'une maigreur anormale** abnormally thin person; **évolution anormale d'une maladie** unexpected development of an illness; **enfants anormaux** *(en intelligence)* educationally subnormal children; **il fait un temps a.** the weather is abnormal, *Fam* the weather is all wrong for this time of year; **il fait une chaleur anormale** it's abnormally hot **2** *(injuste)* unjust, unfair; **il est a. que ... + sub** it

is unfair that ... **3** *(extraordinaire)* extraordinary; **ce qu'il y a d'a., c'est que ...** the strange *or* extraordinary thing is that ...
N *Méd, Psy* mentally defective person; *Fam* **c'est un a.** he's round the bend
NM l'a., c'est que ... *(injuste)* what's unjust is that ...; *(extraordinaire)* what's unusual is that ...

anormalement [anɔrmalmɑ̃] **ADV** abnormally

anormalité [anɔrmalite] **NF** abnormality

ANPE [aɛnpeø] **NF** *(abrév* **Agence nationale pour l'emploi)** *Br* ≃ Jobcentre, *Can* ≃ CEC; **être à l'A.** ≃ to be registered with the Jobcentre

ANRS [aɛnɛrɛs] **NF** *(abrév* **Agence nationale de recherches sur le sida)** Aids research institute

anse [ɑ̃s] **NF 1** *(d'une cruche, d'un panier)* handle; *(d'un cadenas)* shackle; *Fig* **faire danser** *ou* **valser l'a. du panier** *(d'un domestique etc)* to fiddle the books; *Archit* **voûte en a. de panier** basket-handle arch; *Fig* **faire le pot** *ou* **le panier à deux anses** to have someone on each arm **2** *(d'une corde etc)* loop, bight; *Anat* loop; **a. à vis** screw eye (bolt) **3** *Géog* cove

antagonique [ɑ̃tagɔnik] **ADJ** *(forces, personnes etc)* antagonistic; *(intérêts, influences)* conflicting

antagonisme [ɑ̃tagɔnism] **NM** *(de personne)* antagonism; *Physiol* antagonism

antagoniste [ɑ̃tagɔnist] **ADJ** antagonistic, opposed; **avoir des positions antagonistes** to have opposing *or* conflicting opinions; **les partis antagonistes** the opposing parties; **force a.** antagonistic force; *(de contrôle)* controlling force, countercheck; *Anat* **muscles antagonistes** antagonists; **couple a.** opposing couple
N antagonist, opponent

antalgique [ɑ̃talʒik] **ADJ, NM** *Pharm* analgesic

antan [ɑ̃tɑ̃] **ADV** *Arch, Litt* **d'a.** of yesteryear; **où sont les neiges d'a.?** where are the snows of yesteryear?

antarctique [ɑ̃tarktik] *Géog* **ADJ** Antarctic; **cercle a.** Antarctic circle
NM l'A. Antarctica, the Antarctic; **une expédition dans l'A.** an Antarctic expedition

anté- [ɑ̃te] **PRÉF** ante-, pre-

antécédence [ɑ̃tesedɑ̃s] **NF** *Phil, Géog* antecedence

antécédent [ɑ̃tesedɑ̃] **ADJ** previous, antecedent, anterior (**à** to)
NM *Ling, Phil* antecedent SEE GRAMMAR A32–3; B22–3
NMPL antécédents previous history, past record, *Fml* antecedents; **antécédents médicaux** medical history; **il y a des antécédents cancéreux dans ma famille** my family has a history of cancer; **avoir de bons/mauvais antécédents** to have a good/bad record

antéchrist [ɑ̃tekrist] **NM** antichrist

antédiluvien, -ienne [ɑ̃tedilyvjɛ̃, -jɛn] **ADJ** antediluvian; *Fam* **ma télévision est antédiluvienne** my television is an antique; *Fam* **c'est une relation antédiluvienne** I've known him/her for donkey's years

antémémoire [ɑ̃tememwar] **NF** *Ordinat* cache (memory); **mettre en a.** to cache

anténatal, -ale, -aux, -ales [ɑ̃tenatal, -o] **ADJ** *Méd* antenatal

antenne [ɑ̃tɛn] **NF** VOIR GRAMMAIRE A14 **1** *Radio* aerial, antenna; *(d'un satellite, d'un robot)* antenna; **a. de télévision** television aerial; **à l'a.** on-air; **être à l'a.** to be on the air; **on est à l'a. dans cinq minutes** we'll be on the air in five minutes; **prendre/garder l'a.** to go/stay on the air; **passer à l'a.** *(d'une émission)* to be broadcast *or* televised;

(d'une personne) to be on television/radio; **rendre l'a.** *(d'un présentateur etc)* to go back, to return (to the studio/*etc*); **je dois rendre l'a.** I have to hand over now; **je vous passe l'a., à vous l'a.!** (I'll hand) over to you; **hors a.** off-air; **déclarer hors a. que ...** to declare off the air that ...; **sur notre a.** *Radio* on this station; *TV* on this channel

2 *(d'un insecte)* antenna, feeler; *Fig* **avoir des antennes** to have a sixth sense, to be perceptive, to pick up on things; *Fig* **avoir ses antennes quelque part** to have one's feelers out, to have informers

3 *Mil* **a. chirurgicale** advanced surgical unit **4** *(de société)* branch

▸▸ **a. en cadre** loop aerial; *TV* **a. collective** shared aerial; *Aut* **a. électrique** electric aerial; **a. d'émission** broadcast antenna; **a. fermée** loop aerial; *Aut* **a. manuelle** manual aerial; **a. parabolique** (satellite) dish, *Am* dish antenna; *Aviat* **a. pendante** trailing aerial; **a. de réception** receiver aerial, receiving aerial *or* antenna; **a. satellite** satellite antenna; **a. téléscopique** telescopic mast; **a. terrestre** ground antenna; **a. en V** rabbit's ears

antépénultième [ɑ̃tepenyltjɛm] ADJ antepenultimate, third (from) last

antérieur [ɑ̃terjœr] ADJ**1** *(période)* former; *(date)* earlier; *(année)* previous; *(engagement)* prior; **tous ces événements sont antérieurs à la révolution** all these events took place before the revolution; **cela est a. à ma naissance** that was before I was born; **a. au mariage** premarital; **dans une vie antérieure** in a previous life *or* existence; *Gram* **futur a.** future perfect VOIR GRAMMAIRE A52; *Gram* **passé a.** past anterior SEE GRAMMAR B31 **2** *(muscle)* anterior; *(membre etc)* fore; *(mur, voyelle etc)* front

antérieurement [ɑ̃terjœrmɑ̃] ADV previously, earlier; **cela s'est passé a. à notre rencontre** that happened before we met

antériorité [ɑ̃terjɔrite] NF precedence; *Gram* anteriority

anthère [ɑ̃tɛr] NF *Bot* anther

anthologie [ɑ̃tɔlɔʒi] NF anthology

anthracite [ɑ̃trasit] NM **1** *Minér* anthracite **2** *(couleur)* charcoal grey

ADJ INV charcoal grey

anthrax [ɑ̃traks] NM *Méd* carbuncle; **a. malin** anthrax

anthropique [ɑ̃trɔpik] ADJ anthropogenic

anthropocentrique [ɑ̃trɔpɔsɑ̃trik] ADJ anthropocentric

anthropocentrisme [ɑ̃trɔpɔsɑ̃trism] NM anthropocentrism

anthropoïde [ɑ̃trɔpɔid] ADJ anthropoid NM anthropoid ape

anthropologie [ɑ̃trɔpɔlɔʒi] NF anthropology

anthropologique [ɑ̃trɔpɔlɔʒik] ADJ anthropological

anthropologiste [ɑ̃trɔpɔlɔʒist], **anthropologue** [ɑ̃trɔpɔlɔg] N anthropologist

anthropométrie [ɑ̃trɔpɔmetri] NF anthropometry

anthropométrique [ɑ̃trɔpɔmetrik] ADJ anthropometric(al); *Admin* **service a.** criminal anthropometry department, *Br* ≃ Criminal Records Office; **fiche a.** = record containing fingerprints and details of height, weight etc

anthropomorphe [ɑ̃trɔpɔmɔrf] ADJ anthropomorphic

anthropomorphisme [ɑ̃trɔpɔmɔrfism] NM anthropomorphism

anthropophage [ɑ̃trɔpɔfaʒ] ADJ cannibalistic, man-eating N cannibal

anthropophagie [ɑ̃trɔpɔfaʒi] NF cannibalism

anti¹ [ɑ̃ti] PRÉF anti-

anti² PRÉF ante-

antiacnéique [ɑ̃tiakneik] ADJ *(médicament, crème, traitement)* anti-acne

antiadhésif [ɑ̃tiadezif] ADJ *(revêtement etc)* nonstick

NM antiadhesive; **casserole recouverte d'un a.** nonstick saucepan

antiaérien, -ienne [ɑ̃tiaerjɛ̃, -jɛn] ADJ *(arme, défense)* anti-aircraft; **abri a.** air-raid shelter

anti-âge ADJ INV *(traitement, crème)* anti-ageing

antialcoolique [ɑ̃tialkɔlik] ADJ *(ligue etc)* temperance

antialcoolisme [ɑ̃tialkɔlism] NM temperance, teetotalism

anti-aliassage [ɑ̃tialjasaʒ] NM *Ordinat* anti-aliasing

antiallergique [ɑ̃tialɛrʒik] ADJ hypoallergenic

antiasthénique [ɑ̃tiastenik] ADJ *Méd* antiasthenic

antiatomique [ɑ̃tiatɔmik] ADJ antinuclear; **abri a.** fall-out shelter; **manifestation a.** ban-the-bomb *or* anti-nuclear demonstration

antibactérien [ɑ̃tibakterjɛ̃] ADJ antibacterial NM antibacterial product

antibalistique [ɑ̃tibalistik] ADJ *(missile)* antiballistic

antibiogramme [ɑ̃tibjɔgram] NM *Méd* antibiogram

antibiotique [ɑ̃tibjɔtik] *Pharm* ADJ antibiotic; **un traitement a.** a course of antibiotics NM antibiotic; **être sous antibiotiques** to be on antibiotics

antiblocage [ɑ̃tiblɔkaʒ] NM *Aut* **a. de freins** anti-lock braking system, anti-lock brakes; **a. des roues** anti-lock brakes

antibrouillage [ɑ̃tibrujaʒ] NM *Radio etc* anti-jamming

antibrouillard [ɑ̃tibrujar] ADJ, NM *Aut* **(phare) a.** fog lamp

antibruit [ɑ̃tibrɥi] ADJ INV *(mur)* soundproof; **lutte a.** noise abatement campaign

antibuée [ɑ̃tibɥe] ADJ, NM *Aut* **(dispositif) a.** demister

anticalcaire [ɑ̃tikalker] NM *(qui empêche les dépôts)* scale preventer; *(qui détartre)* scale remover

anticancéreux, -euse [ɑ̃tikɑ̃serø, -øz] ADJ **centre/sérum a.** cancer hospital/serum

anticasseurs [ɑ̃tikasœr] ADJ INV *Pol* **Loi a.** = law banning violent behaviour during demonstrations

anticathode [ɑ̃tikatɔd] NF anticathode

antichambre [ɑ̃tiʃɑ̃br] NF waiting room, antechamber; **pilier d'a.** *(d'un ministre etc)* hanger-on; **faire a.** to hang around in the waiting room; *Fig* to wait patiently to see sb

antichar [ɑ̃tiʃar] *Mil* ADJ anti-tank NM anti-tank device

antichoc [ɑ̃tiʃɔk] ADJ INV shock-proof; *Méd* **traitement a.** anti-shock treatment

antichute [ɑ̃tiʃyt] ADJ **traitement a.** treatment to stop hair loss

anticipatif, -ive [ɑ̃tisipatif, -iv] ADJ anticipatory, anticipative; **paiement a.** prepayment

anticipation [ɑ̃tisipasjɔ̃] NF anticipation; **payer par a.** to pay in advance; **demander l'a. d'un paiement** to ask for payment in advance; **littérature d'a.** science fiction; **film d'a.** science-fiction film

anticipé [ɑ̃tisipe] ADJ *(paiement)* advance;

(départ, retour) early; **prendre sa retraite anticipée** to take early retirement; **avec mes remerciements anticipés** thanking you in advance

anticiper [ɑ̃tisipe] VT to forecast; *(réaction, réponse)* to anticipate; *(action)* to forestall; **plaisir anticipé** anticipated pleasure; **j'anticipais déjà le pire** I was expecting the worst; *Fin* **dividende anticipé** advance dividend; **remboursement anticipé** redemption before due date; **a. un paiement** to pay in advance

VI to anticipate, to look *or* think ahead; *Sport etc* to anticipate one's opponent's moves; **n'anticipons pas** let's not look *or* think too far ahead; **a. sur les événements** to anticipate events; **je ne voudrais pas a. sur ce qui sera dit plus tard** I don't wish to anticipate *or* guess what will be said later; **a. sur ses revenus** to spend one's income in advance

anticlérical, -ale, -aux, -ales [ɑ̃tiklerikal, -o] ADJ, N anticlerical

anticléricalisme [ɑ̃tiklerikalism] NM anticlericalism

anticlinal, -aux [ɑ̃tiklinal, -o] NM *Géol* anticline

anticoagulant [ɑ̃tikoagylɑ̃] ADJ, NM *Pharm* anticoagulant

anticolonialisme [ɑ̃tikɔlɔnjalism] NM anticolonialism

anticolonialiste [ɑ̃tikɔlɔnjalist] ADJ anticolonialist

anticommercial, -iale, -iaux, -iales [ɑ̃tikɔmɛrsjal, -jo] ADJ *(attitude, pratique)* unbusinesslike

anticommunisme [ɑ̃tikɔmynism] NM *Pol* anticommunism; **faire de l'a. primaire** to be a dyed-in-the-wool anticommunist

anticommuniste [ɑ̃tikɔmynist] ADJ, N *Pol* anticommunist

anticonceptionnel, -elle [ɑ̃tikɔ̃sɛpsjɔnɛl] ADJ *(pilule)* contraceptive; *(mesures etc)* contraceptive, birth-control

anticonformisme [ɑ̃tikɔ̃fɔrmism] NM nonconformism; **faire de l'a.** to be a nonconformist

anticonformiste [ɑ̃tikɔ̃fɔrmist] ADJ, N nonconformist

anticonstitutionnel, -elle [ɑ̃tikɔ̃stitysjɔnɛl] ADJ anticonstitutional, unconstitutional

anticonstitutionnellement [ɑ̃tikɔ̃stitysjɔnɛlmɑ̃] ADV unconstitutionally

anticorps [ɑ̃tikɔr] NM antibody; **a. monoclonal** monoclonal antibody

anti-corrosion ADJ corrosion-resistant

anti-crevaison ADJ *Aut (pneu)* run-flat

anticyclique [ɑ̃tisiklik] ADJ anticyclic

anticyclonal, -ale, -aux, -ales [ɑ̃tisiklɔnal, -o] ADJ *Météo* anticyclonic; **aire anticyclonale** high-pressure area

anticyclone [ɑ̃tisiklon] *Météo* NM anticyclone ADJ **abri a.** cyclone cellar

anticyclonique [ɑ̃tisiklɔnik] ADJ *Météo* anticyclonic

antidate [ɑ̃tidat] NF antedate

antidater [ɑ̃tidate] VT to backdate; *(contrat etc)* to antedate

antidéflagrant [ɑ̃tideflagrɑ̃] ADJ explosion-proof

antidémarrage [ɑ̃tidemaraʒ] NM *Aut* engine immobilizer; **a. codé** (security-coded) immobilizer

antidémocratique [ɑ̃tidemɔkratik] ADJ antidemocratic, undemocratic

antidépresseur [ɑ̃tidepresœr] ADJ, NM antidepressant

antidérapant [ɑ̃tiderapɑ̃] *Aut* ADJ *(pneu, route)* non-skid; *(semelle, tapis)* non-slip
NM *(pneu)* non-skid tyre; *(revêtement)* non-slip coating

antidétonant [ɑ̃tidetɔnɑ̃] ADJ, NM anti-knock

antidiphtérique [ɑ̃tidifterik] ADJ vaccin a. diphtheria vaccine

antidiscriminatoire [ɑ̃tidiskriminatwar] ADJ *(mesures, politique)* anti-discriminatory

antidopage [ɑ̃tidɔpaʒ] NM, **antidoping** [ɑ̃tidɔpiŋ] NM *Sport* **contrôle a.** drug(s) test; **être positif au contrôle a.** to fail a drugs test

antidote [ɑ̃tidɔt] NM *Méd, Fig* antidote (**contre** for)

antidumping [ɑ̃tidœmpiŋ] ADJ *(loi, législation)* anti-dumping

anti-éblouissant ADJ *Aut (phares)* anti-dazzle

antiéconomique [ɑ̃tiekɔnɔmik] ADJ *(mesure)* uneconomic

antiémétique [ɑ̃tiemetik] ADJ, NM *Méd* antiemetic

antiémeute [ɑ̃tiemøt] ADJ antiriot

antienne [ɑ̃tjɛn] NF antiphon; *Fig* **c'est toujours la même a.** he says that all the time, it's always the same old tune; *Fig* **chanter toujours la même a.** to be always harping on the same subject

antiesclavagisme [ɑ̃tiɛsklavaʒism] NM *Pol* anti-slavery movement, abolitionism

antiesclavagiste [ɑ̃tiɛsklavaʒist] ADJ anti-slavery, abolitionist
N person opposed to slavery, abolitionist

antifading [ɑ̃tifadiŋ] NM INV automatic volume control

antifasciste [ɑ̃tifasist, -ʃist] ADJ, N *Pol* anti-fascist

antifongique [ɑ̃tifɔ̃ʒik] ADJ *Méd* fungicidal
NM fungicide

anti-friction NM INV babbit, bearing *or* white metal

anti-g [ɑ̃tiʒe] ADJ INV *Aviat* **vêtement ou combinaison a.** (anti) G suit

antigang [ɑ̃tigɑ̃g] ADJ **brigade a.** = police squad concerned with combating terrorism and organized crime

antigaz [ɑ̃tigaz] ADJ anti-gas

antigel [ɑ̃tiʒɛl] NM antifreeze

antigène [ɑ̃tiʒɛn] NM *Méd* antigen

antigivre [ɑ̃tiʒivr] ADJ *Aviat* anti-icing; *Aut* de-icing
NM *Aviat* anti-icer; *Aut* de-icer

antiglisse [ɑ̃tiglis] ADJ INV **vêtements/tissu a.** non-slip clothing/material

antigrippal, -ale, -aux, -ales [ɑ̃tigripal, -o] ADJ *(médicament, remède etc)* anti-flu

antihalo [ɑ̃tialo] NM *Phot* anti-halo

antihéros [ɑ̃tiero] NM antihero

antihistaminique [ɑ̃tiistaminik] ADJ, NM *Méd* antihistamine

antihygiénique [ɑ̃tiiʒjenik] ADJ unhygienic, insanitary

anti-inflammatoire ADJ *Méd* anti-inflammatory

anti-inflationniste ADJ *Écon* anti-inflation(ary)

antillais, -aise [ɑ̃tijɛ, -ɛz] ADJ West Indian
N A. West Indian

Antilles [ɑ̃tij] NFPL **les A.** the (French) West Indies; **la mer des A.** the Caribbean (Sea)

antilog [ɑ̃tilɔg] NM *Math Fam* antilog

antilogarithme [ɑ̃tilɔgaritm] NM *Math* antilogarithm

antilope [ɑ̃tilɔp] NF antelope VOIR GRAMMAIRE A12

antimagnétique [ɑ̃timaɲetik] ADJ antimagnetic

antimatière [ɑ̃timatjɛr] NF antimatter

antimilitarisme [ɑ̃timilitarism] NM antimilitarism

antimilitariste [ɑ̃timilitarist] ADJ, N antimilitarist

antimissile [ɑ̃timisil] ADJ anti-missile; **missile a.** anti-missile missile

antimite(s) [ɑ̃timit] ADJ *(vêtement)* mothproof; *(produit)* moth-repellent; **bombe a.** mothkiller
NM antimite mothkiller, moth-repellent

antimoine [ɑ̃timwan] NM *Chimie* antimony

antimonarchique [ɑ̃timɔnarʃik] ADJ antimonarchic(al)

antimonarchisme [ɑ̃timɔnarʃism] NM antimonarchism

antimonarchiste [ɑ̃timɔnarʃist] N antimonarchist

antimondialisation [ɑ̃timɔ̃djalizasjɔ̃] NF antiglobalization

antimondialiste [ɑ̃timɔ̃djalist] ADJ antiglobalist
N *(personne)* antiglobalist

anti-mousse ADJ INV *(pouvoir, agent)* antifoam

antimycosique [ɑ̃timikɔzik] ADJ, NM *Méd* antimycotic

antinazi, -ie [ɑ̃tinazi] ADJ, N anti-Nazi

antinévralgique [ɑ̃tinevralʒik] ADJ, NM *Pharm* antineuralgic

antinomie [ɑ̃tinɔmi] NF antinomy

antinomique [ɑ̃tinɔmik] ADJ antinomic

antinucléaire [ɑ̃tinykleɛr] ADJ anti-nuclear

Antiope ® [ɑ̃tjɔp] NM *TV* = information system available via the French television network, *Br* ≃ Teletext®

antioxydant [ɑ̃tiɔksidɑ̃] NM anti-oxidant

anti-paludéen, -enne *Pharm* ADJ anti-malarial
NM antimalarial (drug)

antipaludique [ɑ̃tipalydik] *Pharm* ADJ antimalaria(l)
NM antimalarial (drug)

antipape [ɑ̃tipap] NM *Hist, Rel* antipope

antiparasitage [ɑ̃tiparazitaʒ] NM *Radio, Élec* suppression

antiparasite [ɑ̃tiparazit] *Radio, Aut etc* NM suppressor, interference eliminator
ADJ **dispositif a.** suppressor, interference eliminator

antiparlementaire [ɑ̃tiparləmɑ̃tɛr] ADJ *Pol* antiparliamentary

antiparlementarisme [ɑ̃tiparləmɑ̃tarism] NM antiparliamentarianism

antipathie [ɑ̃tipati] NF antipathy; **avoir ou éprouver de l'a. pour qn** to have antipathy for *or* feel antipathy towards sb; **éprouver une grande a. pour qn** to have great antipathy for *or* feel great antipathy towards sb

antipathique [ɑ̃tipatik] ADJ unpleasant; **je le trouve très a.** I don't like him at all; **je ne le trouve pas du tout a.** I quite like him

antipelliculaire [ɑ̃tipelikylɛr] ADJ **shampooing a.** (anti-)dandruff shampoo

antipersonnel [ɑ̃tipɛrsɔnɛl] ADJ INV *Mil* antipersonnel

antiphone [ɑ̃tifɔn] NM *Rel* antiphon

antiphrase [ɑ̃tifraz] NF *Ling* antiphrasis; **dire qch par a.** to say sth ironically

antipodal, -ale, -aux, -ales [ɑ̃tipɔdal, -o] ADJ antipodean

antipode [ɑ̃tipɔd] NM *Géog* antipodes; **la Nouvelle-Zélande est l'a. ou aux antipodes de la France** New Zealand is on the other side of the world from France; **aux antipodes** at *or* in the antipodes; *Fig* diametrically opposed, poles apart; *Fig* **son opinion est à l'a. ou aux antipodes de la mienne** his opinion is quite the opposite of mine *or* is poles apart from mine

antipoétique [ɑ̃tipɔetik] ADJ unpoetic

antipoison [ɑ̃tipwazɔ̃] ADJ *Méd* **centre a.** poisons unit

antipoliomyélite [ɑ̃tipɔljɔmjelit] ADJ **vaccination a.** polio vaccination

antipollution [ɑ̃tipɔlysjɔ̃] ADJ INV *(mesures)* anti-pollution

antiprogressif, -ive [ɑ̃tiprɔgrɛsif, -iv] ADJ reactionary

antiprotectionniste [ɑ̃tiprɔtɛksjɔnist] ADJ *(ligne d'action)* free-trade
N antiprotectionist, free trader

antipsychiatrie [ɑ̃tipsikjatri] NF antipsychiatry

antipyrétique [ɑ̃tipiretik] ADJ, NM *Méd* antipyretic, antifebrile

antipyrine [ɑ̃tipirin] NF *Méd* antipyrine

antiquaille [ɑ̃tikaj] NF *Péj* worthless old junk

antiquaire [ɑ̃tikɛr] N antique dealer

antique [ɑ̃tik] ADJ old, ancient; *(mobilier)* antique, *Péj* old-fashioned, antiquated; **la Grèce a.** ancient *or* classical Greece
NM 1 *(art)* art from the antiquity; *(objets d'art de l'Antiquité)* works of art from the antiquity 2 **l'a.** the antique, classical antiquity 3 *Typ* antique

antiquité [ɑ̃tikite] NF 1 *(ancienneté)* antiquity 2 *(temps anciens)* ancient times, antiquity; **ça remonte à la plus haute a.** that goes back *or* dates back to time immemorial; **connu de toute a.** known (about) since time immemorial 3 *Hist* **l'a. grecque** ancient Greek civilization 4 **antiquités** *(meubles etc anciens)* antiques; **magasin d'antiquités** antique shop 5 **les antiquités** the works of classical antiquity

antirabique [ɑ̃tirabik] ADJ *Méd (vaccin)* anti-rabies

antirachitique [ɑ̃tiraʃitik] ADJ *Méd* antirachitic

antiracisme [ɑ̃tirasism] NM antiracialism, anti-racism

antiraciste [ɑ̃tirasist] ADJ, N antiracist, antiracialist

antiradar [ɑ̃tiradar] ADJ anti-radar
NM anti-radar device

antireflet [ɑ̃tirəflɛ] ADJ INV nonreflective; *Ordinat* non-reflecting, antiglare

antiréglementaire [ɑ̃tiregləmɑ̃tɛr] ADJ against regulations

antireligieux, -ieuse [ɑ̃tirəliʒjø, -jøz] ADJ antireligious

antirépublicain, -aine [ɑ̃tirepyblikɛ̃, -ɛn] ADJ, N antirepublican

antirétroviral, -ale, -aux, -ales [ɑ̃tiretroviral, -o] ADJ *(molécule, traitement)* antiretroviral

antirévolutionnaire [ɑ̃tirevɔlysjɔnɛr] ADJ, N antirevolutionary

antirides [ɑ̃tirid] ADJ INV *(crème)* anti-wrinkle

anti-roman, pl anti-romans NM *Littér* anti-novel

antirouille [ɑ̃tiruj] NM rust preventive
ADJ INV *(métal)* rustproof, non-rusting; *(produit, traitement)* rust-preventing

antiroulis [ɑ̃tiruli] NM *Naut, Aviat* (gyro) stabilizer; *Aut* anti-roll bar

anti-scintillements ADJ *Ordinat* flicker-free

antiscorbutique [ɑ̃tiskɔrbytik] ADJ, NM *Pharm* antiscorbutic

antisèche [ɑ̃tisɛʃ] NF *Fam* crib sheet

antiségrégationniste [ɑ̃tisegregasjɔnist] ADJ, N antisegregationist

antisémite [ɑ̃tisemit] ADJ anti-semitic N anti-semite

antisémitique [ɑ̃tisemitik] ADJ anti-semitic

antisémitisme [ɑ̃tisemitism] NM anti-semitism

antisepsie [ɑ̃tisɛpsi] NF *Méd* antisepsis

antiseptique [ɑ̃tisɛptik] ADJ, NM *Méd* antiseptic

antisérum [ɑ̃tiserɔm] NM *Méd* antiserum

antisionisme [ɑ̃tizjɔnism] NM anti-Zionism

antisioniste [ɑ̃tizjɔnist] ADJ, N anti-Zionist

antisocial, -iale, -iaux, -iales [ɑ̃tisɔsjal, -jo] ADJ antisocial

antisolaire [ɑ̃tisɔlɛr] ADJ sun-reflective

anti-sous-marin ADJ *Mil* anti-submarine

antisoviétique [ɑ̃tisɔvjetik] ADJ anti-Soviet

antispasmodique [ɑ̃tispasmɔdik] ADJ, NM *Pharm* antispasmodic

antisportif, -ive [ɑ̃tispɔrtif, -iv] ADJ *(opposé au sport)* anti-sport; *(contraire à l'esprit du sport)* unsportsmanlike, unsporting

antistrophe [ɑ̃tistrɔf] NF antistrophe

antisudoral, -aux [ɑ̃tisydɔral, -o] ADJ, NM antiperspirant

antitabac [ɑ̃titaba] ADJ INV *(lutte, campagne)* anti-smoking

antiterroriste [ɑ̃titɛrɔrist] ADJ anti-terrorist, anti-terrorism

antitétanique [ɑ̃titetanik] *Méd* ADJ antitetanus NM antitetanus serum

antithèse [ɑ̃titɛz] NF antithesis; *Fig* **je suis l'a. de ma sœur** I'm the opposite of my sister

antithétique [ɑ̃titetik] ADJ antithetic(al)

antitoxine [ɑ̃titɔksin] NF *Méd* antitoxin

antitoxique [ɑ̃titɔksik] ADJ *Méd* antitoxic

antitrust [ɑ̃titrœst] ADJ INV anti-monopoly, antitrust; **lois a.** anti-monopoly *or* antitrust laws

antituberculeux, -euse [ɑ̃titybɛrkylø, -øz] ADJ *Méd* antitubercular; **centre a.** tuberculosis centre

antitussif, -ive [ɑ̃titysif, -iv] ADJ, NM *Méd* **sirop a.** cough mixture *or* syrup *or* medicine

antivariolique [ɑ̃tivarjɔlik] ADJ *Méd* **vaccin a.** smallpox vaccine

antivénérien [ɑ̃tivenerjɛ̃] ADJ *Méd* antivenereal

antivenimeux, -euse [ɑ̃tivənimø, -øz] ADJ antivenin

anti-vent, *pl* **anti-vents** NM *(pour microphone)* wind gag

antivieillissement [ɑ̃tivjɛjismɑ̃] NM *(produit qui ralentit le vieillissement)* anti-ageing product; **traitement a.** anti-ageing treatment

antiviral, -ale, -aux, -ales [ɑ̃tiviral, -o] ADJ *Méd* antivirus

antivirus [ɑ̃tivirys] NM antivirus

antivivisection(n)iste [ɑ̃tivivisɛksjɔnist] N antivivisectionist ADJ antivivisection(ist); **société a.** antivivisection society

antivol [ɑ̃tivɔl] ADJ INV *(équipement)* anti-theft; *(serrure)* thief-proof; *Aut* **alarme a.** car alarm NM *(pour les cycles)* lock; *(pour les voitures)* steering lock; *Aut* **a. de direction** steering column lock; *Aut* **a.-contact** ignition lock

antonomase [ɑ̃tɔnɔmaz] NF *Litt* antonomasia

antonyme [ɑ̃tɔnim] ADJ antonymous NM antonym

antre [ɑ̃tr] NM **1** *(caverne)* cave, cavern; *(d'animaux, de brigands)*, *Fig (d'une personne)* den, lair; **un a. de voleurs** a den of thieves **2** *Anat* antrum, sinus

anurie [anyri] NF *Méd* anuria

anus [anys] NM *Anat* anus; *Chir* **a. artificiel** colostomy

Anvers [ɑ̃vɛr(s)] N Antwerp

anversois, -oise [ɑ̃vɛrswa, -waz] ADJ of/from Antwerp N A. *(natif)* native of Antwerp; *(habitant)* inhabitant of Antwerp

anxiété [ɑ̃ksjete] NF anxiety; **éprouver de l'a.** to feel anxious; **avec a.** anxiously

anxieusement [ɑ̃ksjøzmɑ̃] ADV anxiously

anxieux, -ieuse [ɑ̃ksjø, -jøz] ADJ **1** *(inquiet)* anxious, uneasy **2 a. de faire qch** anxious *or* impatient to do sth; **il est a. de partir** he's anxious *or* impatient to leave N worrier

anxiogène [ɑ̃ksjɔʒɛn] ADJ causing anxiety

anxiolytique [ɑ̃ksjɔlitik] ADJ anxiolitic NM tranquillizer

AOC [aose] NF *(abrév* **appellation d'origine contrôlée)** = guarantee of quality

aorte [aɔrt] NF *Anat* aorta

aortique [aɔrtik] ADJ *Anat* aortic, aortal

août [u(t)] NM August; **en a., au mois d'a.** in (the month of) August; **le premier/le sept a.** (on) the first/the seventh of August, *Am* (on) August the first/the seventh; **le quinze a.** the Assumption, Assumption Day; **à la mi-a.** in mid-August SEE GRAMMAR A81–2; B60–2

aoûtat [auta] NM harvest mite, *Am* chigger

aoûtien, -ienne [ausjɛ̃, -jɛn] N August holidaymaker *or Am* vacationer

apache [apaʃ] NM **A.** Apache

apaisant [apɛzɑ̃] ADJ *(geste, paroles)* appeasing; *(nouvelles, effet etc)* soothing, calming

apaisement [apɛzmɑ̃] NM *(d'une personne en colère, des dieux)* appeasement, appeasing; *(d'une personne en colère ou inquiète)* calming (down); *(de la douleur)* alleviation; **donner des apaisements à qn** *(paroles)* to give (re)assurance to sb, to (re)assure sb

apaiser [apeze] VT *(personne en colère, dieux)* to appease, to pacify; *(personne en colère ou inquiète)* to calm (down); *(douleur, enfant)* to soothe; *(faim)* to appease, to satisfy; *(soif)* to quench; *(craintes)* to calm, to allay VPR **s'apaiser** *(d'une personne)* to calm down; *(du vent)* to drop, to subside; *(de la douleur, des craintes)* to subside; **la foule s'apaisait** the crowd was calming down *or* becoming quieter

apanage [apanaʒ] NM prerogative; **elle croit avoir l'a. de la sagesse** she thinks she has a monopoly on wisdom

aparté [aparte] NM **1** *Théâtre* aside, stage whisper; **en a.** aside, in a stage whisper **2** *(entre deux personnes)* private conversation; **en a.** in private, as an aside; **il le lui a dit en a.** he took him/her aside *or* to one side to tell him/her

apartheid [aparted] NM apartheid

apathie [apati] NF apathy, listlessness; **le malade est dans une a. totale** the patient is completely listless; **il sombra dans une complète a.** he sank into a state of complete apathy

apathique [apatik] ADJ apathetic, listless

apatride [apatrid] ADJ stateless N *Jur* stateless person

apatridie [apatridi] NF *Jur* statelessness

APE [apeə] NF *(abrév* **Assemblée parlementaire européenne)** EP

APEC [apɛk] NF *(abrév* **Association pour l'emploi des cadres)** = agency providing information on recruitment and training opportunities for professionals

Apennins [apenɛ̃] NMPL Apennines

aperception [apɛrsɛpsjɔ̃] NF *Phil* apperception

apercevoir [apɛrsəvwar] *(prp* apercevant; *pp* aperçu; *pr ind* j'aperçois, n. apercevons, ils aperçoivent; *pr subj* j'aperçoive, n. apercevions; *impf* j'apercevais; *p hist* j'aperçus; *fu* j'apercevrai) VT to perceive, to see; *(soudain, rapidement) (personne, chose)* to catch sight of, to catch a glimpse of; **je n'ai fait que l'a.** I only caught a glimpse of him/her; **elle cherche à ne pas laisser a. sa fatigue** she's trying not to let her tiredness show; **je commence à a. ses raisons** I'm starting to see his reasons; **si on y pense bien, on aperçoit des difficultés** if you think about it, you start to see difficulties VPR **s'apercevoir 1** *(être visible)* to be noticeable; **cela ne s'aperçoit pas** it isn't visible *or* noticeable **2** *(comprendre, réaliser)* **s'a. de qch** to realize *or* notice sth, to become aware *or* conscious of sth; **il s'est aperçu qu'il n'avait pas ses clés** he realized that he hadn't got his keys with him; **sans s'en a.** without being aware of it, without noticing it **3** *(se voir) (de deux personnes)* to catch a glimpse of each other; *(soi-même)* to catch sight of oneself

aperçu [apɛrsy] NM **1** *(coup d'œil)* glimpse; **a. sur la campagne** glimpse of the countryside **2** *(idée générale)* general idea, outline, summary; **par a.** at a rough estimate; **ça te donnera un a. du travail à faire** that'll give you an idea of the work to be done; *Ordinat* **a. avant impression** print preview **3** *(intuition)* insight *(sur* into)

apériodique [aperjɔdik] ADJ *Élec* aperiodic

apéritif [aperitif] NM aperitif; **viens prendre l'a. chez moi demain soir** come round and have an early evening drink tomorrow ADJ *Litt (promenade etc)* pre-prandial

---

Apéritif

In France, the "apéritif", or "apéro", is an informal social ritual. It is quite usual to invite people for before-dinner drinks without actually providing dinner, or to arrange to meet someone in a café "pour l'apéritif" before going out for a meal.

---

apéro [apero] NM *Fam* = **apéritif**

aperture [apɛrtyr] NF *Ling* aperture

apesanteur [apəzɑ̃tœr] NF weightlessness; **en état d'a.** in weightless conditions

à-peu-près NM INV approximation, rough estimate, guess; **calculer une somme par à.** to make a rough calculation; **il y a trop d'à. dans votre exposé** there is too much woolliness in your report

apeuré [apœre, -øre] ADJ scared, frightened

apeurer [apœre] VT to frighten, to scare

APEX [apɛks] NM *(ticket)* APEX

apex [apɛks] NM apex

aphasie [afazi] NF *Méd* aphasia

aphasique [afazik] *Méd* ADJ aphasi(a)c N aphasic

aphis [afis] NM aphis, greenfly

aphone [afɔn] ADJ *Méd* voiceless; **elle était a. pour avoir trop crié** she'd lost her voice through shouting too much

aphonie [afɔni] NF *Méd* loss of voice; **être atteint d'a.** to have lost one's voice

aphorisme [afɔrism] NM aphorism; *Péj* **s'exprimer par aphorismes** to speak in platitudes

aphrodisiaque [afrɔdizjak] ADJ, NM *Pharm* aphrodisiac

aphte [aft(ə)] NM *Méd* mouth ulcer

aphteux, -euse [aftø, -øz] ADJ *Méd, Vét* fièvre aphteuse foot-and-mouth disease

API [apei] NF *abrév* allocation de parent isolé

à-pic [apik] NM INV cliff, bluff

apicole [apikɔl] ADJ apiarian; **exploitation a.** honey farm

apiculteur, -trice [apikyltœr, -tris] N beekeeper, apiarist

apiculture [apikyltyr] NF beekeeping, apiculture

apitoiement [apitwamã] NM pity, compassion; **porté à l'a.** compassionate; **pas d'a.!** *(à mon égard)* don't commiserate (with me)!, don't be sympathetic!; **leurs apitoiements** their pity *or* compassion

apitoyer [apitwaje] (**j'apitoie, n. apitoyons; j'apitoierai**) VT **a. qn** to move sb (to pity), to incite sb to pity
▶ VPR **s'apitoyer s'a. sur qn** to pity sb, to feel pity for sb; **s'a. sur (le sort de) qn** to commiserate with sb; **s'a. sur soi-même** *ou* **sur son sort** to feel sorry for oneself; **ça ne sert à rien de s'a. sur soi-même** feeling sorry for yourself/himself/*etc* won't help, self-pity won't help

ap. J.-C. = apr. J.-C.

APL [apeɛl] NF (*abrév* Aide personnalisée au logement) ≃ housing benefit

aplanir [aplanir] VT *(surface)* to flatten, to smooth; *(bois)* to plane; *(métal)* to planish; *(route etc)* to level; *(imperfections)* to smooth out; *Fig (difficultés)* to iron out; *Fig (conflit)* to settle
▶ VPR **s'aplanir** *(du sol)* to become level; **les problèmes se sont aplanis d'eux-mêmes** the problems have ironed *or* smoothed themselves out

aplanissement [aplanismã] NM *(du sol)* levelling; *(des difficultés)* ironing out

aplat [apla] NM *Ordinat* solid (figure)

aplati [aplati] ADJ **1** flattened, flat; *(nez)* flat **2** *(sphère etc)* oblate

aplatir [aplatir] VT *(objet)* to flatten, to make flat; *(angle)* to blunt; *Métal (rivet)* to clench; *(tête de rivet)* to hammer down; **a. au fer** to press; **a. qch à coups de marteau** to hammer sth flat; *Fig Fam* **a. qn** *(casser la figure à qn)* to flatten sb; **il l'a aplati d'un coup de poing** he knocked him down *or* flattened him with one punch
▶ VI *Rugby* to score a try, to touch down
▶ VPR **s'aplatir** *(de coiffure)* to go flat; *(d'un chapeau)* to get flattened; **s'a. par terre** to lie down flat on the ground; *Fam (tomber)* to come a cropper; **s'a. contre un mur** to flatten oneself against a wall; *Fig* **s'a. devant qn** to grovel to sb

aplatissage [aplatisaʒ] NM *Tech* pressing; *(d'une surface, d'une couture)* flattening; *(d'un rivet)* hammering down

aplatissement [aplatismã] NM **1** flatness; **l'a. de la Terre aux pôles** the flattening of the earth at the poles **2** *Fig (abaissement)* grovelling

aplomb [aplõ] NM **1** perpendicularity; **d'a.** upright, vertical(ly), plumb; **mets la bouteille d'a., elle va tomber** straighten up the bottle, it's going to fall; **les étagères ne sont pas d'a.** the shelves are out of plumb *or* off plumb; **bien d'a. sur ses pieds** steady on one's feet; *Fig Fam* **je ne suis pas d'a. aujourd'hui** I'm out of sorts *or* off colour today; *Fig* **voilà qui vous remettra d'a.** that will revive you, *Fam* that will buck you up; *Fig* **il me faut deux mille euros pour me remettre d'a.** I need two thousand euros to set me back on my feet; **hors d'a.** out of plumb, out of true; **à l'a. de qch** straight above/below sth; *Tech* plumb with sth **2** *(assurance)* (self-)assurance, coolness; **perdre son a.** to lose one's self-assurance; *Péj* **avoir l'a. de dire/de faire**

qch to have the cheek *or* nerve to say/do sth; **il ne manque pas d'a.** he's got a nerve *or* a cheek

aplomber [aplõbe] *Can* VT *(verticalement)* to make straight; *(horizontalement)* to make level
▶ VPR **s'aplomber** to straighten up

apnée [apne] NF *Méd* apnoea, *Am* apnea; **plongée en a.** apnoea diving, breath-holding diving; **plonger en a.** to dive without breathing apparatus

apnéiste [apneist] N apnoea diver, breath-holding diver

apocalypse [apɔkalips] NF apocalypse, revelation; *Bible* **l'A.** the Book of Revelation, the Apocalypse; **les quatre cavaliers de l'A.** the four horsemen of the Apocalypse; *Fig* **vision d'a.** apocalyptic vision; *Fig* **un paysage d'a.** a post-holocaust landscape

apocalyptique [apɔkaliptik] ADJ apocalyptic(al); *Fig* **silence/paysage a.** doom-laden silence/post-holocaust landscape

apocope [apɔkɔp] NF *Ling* apocope

apocryphe [apɔkrif] ADJ apocryphal, *Péj* of doubtful authenticity
NMPL *Bible* **les Apocryphes** the Apocrypha

apogée [apɔʒe] NM *Astron* apogee; **la lune est à son a.** the moon is at its apogee; *Fig* **à l'a. de sa gloire** at the height of one's fame; *Fig* **être à l'a. de sa carrière** to be at the height *or* pinnacle of one's career; *Fig* **atteindre son a.** to reach one's peak

apolitique [apɔlitik] ADJ apolitical

apolitisme [apɔlitism] NM apolitical attitude

Apollon [apɔlõ] N *Myth* Apollo; *Beaux-Arts* **A. du Belvédère** Apollo Belvedere

apollon [apɔlõ] NM *Fig* Adonis, Greek god; **ce n'est pas vraiment un a.!** he's no Adonis!, he's no oil painting!

apologétique [apɔlɔʒetik] ADJ apologetic
NF *Rel* apologetics

apologie [apɔlɔʒi] NF *(défense)* apologia *(de* for), defence; *(éloge)* encomium, eulogy; **faire l'a. de qn/qch** to justify *or* defend sb/sth; *(louer)* to eulogize sb/sth

> Il faut noter que le nom anglais **apology** est un faux ami. Il signifie **excuses**.

apologiste [apɔlɔʒist] N apologist

apologue [apɔlɔg] NM apologue

apophyse [apɔfiz] NF *Phys* apophysis

apoplectique [apɔplɛktik] ADJ, N *Méd* apoplectic

apoplexie [apɔplɛksi] NF *Méd* apoplexy; **attaque d'a.** apoplectic seizure, stroke

apostasie [apɔstazi] NF *Rel* apostasy; **faire acte d'a.** to apostatize, to become an apostate; *Fig* to renounce one's party *or* principles, to desert the cause

apostasier [apɔstazje] VI *(pr sub, impf n. apostasiions, v. apostasiiez)* to apostatize, to become an apostate; *Fig* to renounce one's party *or* principles, to desert the cause

apostat, -ate [apɔsta, -at] ADJ apostate, renegade; **curé a.** renegade priest
N apostate; *Fig* **ce politicien est un a.** that politician has renounced his principles

a posteriori [apɔsterjɔri] ADV with hindsight, after the event; *Phil* a posteriori; **a. je me suis rendu compte que c'était moi qui avais raison** with hindsight, I realized that I was right
ADJ INV **méthode a.** a posteriori method

apostolat [apɔstɔla] NM *Rel* apostolate; *Fig* **cette profession est un a.** this job is a real vocation

apostolique [apɔstɔlik] ADJ *(temps, église etc)* apostolic; **vicaire a.** vicar apostolic; **pères apostoliques** apostolic fathers

apostrophe[1] [apɔstrɔf] NF **1** *Ling, Gram* apostrophe; **mot mis en a.** word used in apostrophe; **le vocatif est le cas de l'a.** the vocative is the case of direct address **2** *(interpellation)* reproach, reprimand; **les apostrophes des conducteurs énervés** the rude remarks of angry motorists

apostrophe[2] *Gram (signe)* apostrophe; **s apostrophe** s apostrophe

apostropher [apɔstrɔfe] VT **a. qn** *(pour attirer l'attention)* to shout to sb; *(être impoli envers sb)* to address sb rudely, to shout at sb
▶ VPR **s'apostropher** to shout at one another; **les supporters des équipes de foot s'apostrophent** the football supporters hurl abuse at each other

apothéose [apɔteoz] NF **1** apotheosis, deification; *Fig (consécration)* crowning moment *or* glory; **cette promotion est l'a. de sa carrière** this promotion is the crowning moment of his/her career; **l'a. du cinéma français** the supreme achievement *or* the crowning glory of French cinema; **finir en a.** to end in triumph **2** *Théâtre* grand finale

apothicaire [apɔtikɛr] NM *Vieilli* apothecary; *Fig* **tenir des comptes d'a.** to know where every penny goes

apôtre [apotr] NM apostle; *Fig* **se faire l'a. du recyclage** to become an advocate of recycling; *Fig* **il fait toujours le bon a.** he always puts on such a saintly air

Appalaches [apalaʃ] NMPL **les (monts) A.** the Appalachian Mountains, the Appalachians

appalachien, -ienne [apalaʃjɛ̃, -jɛn] ADJ Appalachian; **relief a.** Appalachian relief

apparaître [aparɛtr] *(conj like* **paraître**; *the auxiliary is* **être**, *sometimes* **avoir**) VI **1** *(devenir visible)* to appear; **il lui est apparu en rêve** he came *or* appeared to her in a dream; **a. à travers le brouillard** to loom out of the fog; **un spectre lui était apparu** a ghost had appeared to him **2** *(se révéler)* to become evident *or* apparent; **cette décision m'est apparue évidente** it seemed the obvious decision **3** *(sembler)* **le projet lui apparaissait impossible** the plan seemed impossible to him; **il m'apparaît comme le seul capable d'y parvenir** he seems to me to be the only person capable of doing it
VI IMPERS **il apparaît que vous avez été souvent absent** it appears that you have frequently been absent; **selon les statistiques, il apparaîtrait que ...** according to the statistics, it would appear that ...

apparat [apara] NM pomp, show, display; **tenue d'a.** ceremonial dress; **en grand a.** with great pomp and ceremony; **dîner d'a.** banquet; **discours d'a.** ceremonial speech; **lettres d'a.** illuminated letters

apparatchik [aparatʃik] NM apparatchik

apparaux [aparo] NMPL **1** *Naut* tackle, gear; **les gros a.** the purchase **2** *Gym* apparatus

appareil [aparɛj] NM **1** *(instrument)* apparatus, equipment; *Ind (sing or pl)* plant; **appareils ménagers** household appliances; **appareils de laboratoire** laboratory apparatus; **a. auxiliaire** *ou* **de secours** stand-by equipment; **a. de pêche** fishing tackle; *Min* **a. de forage** drilling rig; **a. d'enregistrement** recorder; **a. de lecture** *(de microfilm)* reader; *Tech* **a. de levage** lifting tackle; *Cin* **a. de projection** film projector; **a. à gaz** gas appliance; *Rail* **a. de voie** switch gear; **a. de prothèse** prosthesis, artificial limb/*etc*; **a. (dentaire)** *(correctif)* brace; *(dentier)* dentures; **a. à sous** slot machine, fruit machine, one-armed bandit
2 *Tél* telephone; **Marcelline à l'a.** Marcelline speaking *or* here; **qui est à l'a.?** who's speaking?; **a. mains libres** free-hands device

3 *Aviat* aircraft, plane; **a. de chasse** fighter; **a. d'école** training aircraft, trainer **4** *Phot* **a. (photographique), a. photo** camera; **a. photo numérique** digital camera; **a. reflex** reflex camera **5** *(administration etc)* bodies, authorities; **mettre en jeu l'a. de la justice** to put the machinery of the law in motion; **l'a. du parti** the party machine *or* apparatus; *Ind* **a. de production** production facilities; **a. commercial** commercial structure **6** *Méd* dressing; *(pour fracture)* splint, plaster **7** *Anat* system, apparatus; **a. digestif** digestive system; **a. respiratoire** respiratory system **8** *Constr (de pierres)* height; *(agencement)* bond; **assise de grand a.** course of large stones **9** *(d'un texte)* **a. critique** critical apparatus **10** *Litt* display, magnificence, pomp; *Fig* **dans le plus simple a.** in the nude

appareillage [apaʀɛjaʒ] NM **1** *Naut* getting under way, weighing (anchor), setting sail **2** *(matériel)* fittings, equipment, accessories; *Ind* plant; **a. électrique** electrical equipment **3** *(d'un atelier etc)* installation, fitting (up), setting up **4** *Constr (de pierres, de briques)* bonding

appareillement [apaʀɛjmɑ̃] NM *(d'animaux pour la reproduction)* pairing, mating; *(de bœufs)* pairing

appareiller [apaʀeje] VT **1** *Naut* **a. un navire** to rig a boat out **2** *Constr (pierres, briques)* to bond **3** *(filet)* to spread **4** *(atelier etc)* to install, to fit up *or* out **5** *Méd (handicapé)* to fit up; **a. un sourd** to fit a deaf person with a hearing aid **6** *(assortir)* **a. une lampe** to find a match for a lamp
  ▸ VI *Naut* to get under way

appareilleur [apaʀɛjœʀ] NM *(de pierres etc)* trimmer, fitter, dresser; *Constr* foreman mason

apparemment [apaʀamɑ̃] ADV apparently; **a. tout allait bien** everything seemed to be going well

apparence [apaʀɑ̃s] NF **1** *(air, aspect extérieur)* appearance, look; **cette maison/voiture a une belle a.** this house/car looks nice; **donner une belle a. à sa maison en la repeignant** to make one's house look nice by repainting it; **quelque a. de (la) vérité** some semblance of truth; **un homme à l'a. négligée/soignée** an untidy-looking *or* an unkempt(-looking) man/a tidy-looking *or* a neat(-looking) man; **selon toute a.** to all appearances; **contre toute a.** against all expectations **2** *(aspect trompeur)* **il ne faut pas se fier aux apparences** appearances can be deceptive; **prendre l'a. pour réalité** to confuse appearance with reality; **sous de fausses apparences** under false pretences; **sous une a. de douceur se cache une grande fermeté** beneath a mild-mannered exterior there lies great strength of will; **il a l'air gentil, mais ce n'est qu'une (fausse) a.** he seems nice, but it's only a façade; **il ne faut pas juger sur les apparences** you shouldn't judge by *or* on appearance(s) (alone); **il ne faut pas s'arrêter à l'a.** you should look beyond the façade; **en a.** outwardly, on the surface; **plus difficile en a. qu'en réalité** less difficult than it looks; **pour sauver les apparences** for the sake of appearances; *(pour éviter une humiliation)* to save face **3** *(trace)* semblance, vestige; **elle n'a plus la moindre a. de respect pour lui** she no longer has the slightest vestige of respect for him

apparent [apaʀɑ̃] ADJ **1** *(visible)* visible, apparent; **peu a.** hardly noticeable; **sans raison apparente** for no apparent reason **2** *(prétendu)* apparent, not real; **c'est la raison apparente, mais la vérité est autre** that's the ostensible reason, but the truth is quite different; **mouvement a. du soleil** apparent movement of the sun; **sous cette apparente bonté se cache un grand égoïsme** beneath that kind exterior there lies great selfishness; **piété apparente** outward piety **3** *Jur* **héritier a.** heir apparent

apparenté [apaʀɑ̃te] ADJ **1** *(par le mariage)* related; *(qui a des liens avec)* related, connected; **bien a.** well connected **2** *Pol* **candidat a. au Parti socialiste** = candidate who, though not a member of the Socialist Party, can count on its support in an election **3** *Chimie* **éléments apparentés** related *or* affinitive elements

apparentement [apaʀɑ̃təmɑ̃] NM *Pol* = practice of forming electoral alliances (under proportional representation)

apparenter (s') [sapaʀɑ̃te] VPR **1** to marry (à une famille into a family) **2** *Pol* to form an alliance (à with) **3** *Fig* to have sth in common (à with); **les deux tendances s'apparentent en de nombreux points** the two trends have many things in common

apparier [apaʀje] *(impf & pr sub n.* **appariions,** v. **appariiez)** VT **1** *(oiseaux pour la reproduction)* to couple, to pair, to mate **2** *(chaussettes, chevaux etc)* to match, to pair; *(adversaires)* to pair off
  ▸ VPR **s'apparier** *(des oiseaux)* to mate

appariteur [apaʀitœʀ] NM *(d'université)* mace bearer

apparition [apaʀisjɔ̃] NF **1** appearance; *(d'une fièvre)* outbreak; **l'a. des boutons/des symptômes** the appearance of the spots/symptoms; **faire une courte a.** *(d'une personne)* to make a brief appearance; **brève a.** *(à l'écran)* short *or* cameo appearance, cameo; **la star a finalement fait son a. vers 18 heures** the star finally appeared *or* made his/her appearance around 6 o'clock **2** *(de fantôme)* apparition; *(d'un ange)* appearance; **avoir des apparitions** to see things

appartement [apaʀtəmɑ̃] NM **1** flat, *Am* apartment; *(dans un hôtel etc)* suite, set of rooms; **a. de passage** pied-à-terre; **a. de fonction** company flat; **a. témoin** show flat, *Am* model apartment; **vivre en a.** to live in a flat; **plantes d'a.** indoor *or* house *or* pot plants **2** *(dans un château etc)* **les grands appartements** the state apartments

appartenance [apaʀtənɑ̃s] NF **1 a. à qch** (the fact of) belonging to sth *or* being part of sth; *Math* **a. à un ensemble** membership of a set; **a. à un parti** membership of a party **2 appartenances** *(d'une maison, d'un château)* appurtenances

appartenir [apaʀtəniʀ] *(conj like* **tenir)** VI **1** *(être la possession de)* to belong (à to), to be owned (à by); **cette maison lui appartient en propre** this house is his own personal property **2** *(dépendre)* **pour des raisons qui t'appartiennent** for your own private reasons; **cela n'appartient pas à mes fonctions** this does not come within the scope of my duties **3** *(par famille etc)* **a. à qch** to be part of sth, to belong to sth, to be a member of sth; *Math* **a. à un ensemble** to be a member of a set; **elle appartient à une famille très riche** she comes from a very wealthy family
  ▸ VPR **s'appartenir** **je ne m'appartiens pas** I'm not my own master; *(je n'ai pas de temps à moi)* I've no time to call my own
  ▸ V IMPERS **à tous ceux qu'il appartient** to all whom it may concern; **il appartient au comité de prendre la décision** it is for the committee *or* up to the committee to decide, the decision lies with the committee; **il ne m'appartient pas de le critiquer** it is not for me to criticize him; *Iron* **il vous appartient**

bien de me critiquer you're a fine one to criticize me

appas [apɑ] NMPL *Litt* charms

appât [apɑ] NM **1** *(de pêche)* bait; *Fig (du succès)* lure; **a. de fond** ground bait; **mettre l'a. à la ligne** to bait the line; **mordre à l'a.** *(d'un poisson)*, *Fig (d'une personne)* to rise to the bait; *Fig* **animé par l'a. du gain** driven by the lure of money **2** *(pour la volaille)* soft food

appâter [apɑte] VT **1** *(poissons, oiseaux etc)* to lure with bait; *Fig (personne)* to entice; *Fig* **a. qn par des promesses** to entice sb with promises **2** *(hameçon etc)* to bait **3** *Vieilli (volaille)* to force-feed

appauvrir [apovʀiʀ] VT to impoverish; *Méd* **a. le sang** to thin the blood; **a. la constitution de qn** to weaken sb's constitution
  ▸ VPR **s'appauvrir** to grow poorer; *(du sol)* to lose its fertility, to become impoverished; **la langue risque de s'a.** there is a risk that the language will become impoverished

appauvrissement [apovʀismɑ̃] NM *(d'un pays, du sol etc)* impoverishment; *(d'une race)* degeneration; *(de la santé, des stocks)* deterioration; *(du sang)* thinning; *(d'une entreprise)* decline in the financial position

appeau, *pl* **appeaux** [apo] NM bird call; *Fig* **servir d'a. à qn** to act as a decoy for sb

appel [apɛl] NM **1** *(invitation, sollicitation)* appeal; *(d'un spécialiste etc)* calling in; **faire a. à qn** to call on sb; *(faire venir) (plombier etc)* to send for sb; **faire a. à la générosité de qn** to appeal to sb's generosity; **cette formation fait a. à des connaissances commerciales** this training course calls for *or* requires some knowledge of business; **faire a. à tout son courage** to summon up all one's courage; **il faut faire a. à vos souvenirs** you have to search your memory; **l'a. à la révolte** the call to revolt; **l'a. du Général de Gaulle** General de Gaulle's appeal *or* call to the French nation; **Radio nous lançons un a. à tous les automobilistes sur la R.N. 7** here is a message for all motorists on the RN 7 **2** *Jur* appeal (at law); **avis d'a.** notice of appeal; **Cour d'a.** Court of Appeal; **faire a. d'une décision** to appeal (against) a decision; **juger en a. (d'une décision)** to hear an appeal (from a decision); **casser un jugement en a.** to quash a sentence on appeal; **jugement sans a.** final judgment; *Fig* **c'est ce que j'ai décidé, et c'est sans a.** that's my decision and it's final *or Fam* that's that **3** *(attirance)* call; *(voix)* voice; **l'a. du printemps** the call of spring; **l'a. du large** ou **de la mer** the call of the sea; **l'a. de la nature** the call of the wild; **l'a. de la conscience** the voice of conscience **4** *(cri)* call, shout; **cri d'a.** call for help; **entendre un a. au secours** to hear a cry for help; **a. d'incendie** fire alarm; **accourir à un a.** to run in answer to sb's call; *Fig* **il m'a fait un a. du regard pour que je lui vienne en aide** his eyes pleaded with me to help; *Fig* **faire un a. du coude à qn** *(pour attirer son attention sur qch)* to nudge sb; *Aut* **faire un a. de phares** to flash one's headlights (à qn at sb) **5** *Fin* **faire un a. de fonds** to call up capital; *Com* **faire un a. d'offres** to invite bids *or* tenders; **a. de couverture** ou **de garantie** ou **de marge** margin call; *Mktg* **a. à froid** cold call; *Com* **produit d'a.** loss leader **6** *Mil* **l'a. aux armes** the call to arms; **devancer l'a.** to join up before being enlisted; **a. de mobilisation** mobilization order **7** *Tél* **touche d'a.** call key; **signal d'a.** call waiting service; **numéro d'a.** (telephone) number; **a. téléphonique** (tele)phone call; **a. de réveil** wake-up *or* alarm call; *Vieilli* **a. interurbain** trunk call, long-distance call;

a. matinal early morning call; **a. national** national call; **a. gratuit** freecall; *Mktg* **a. à froid** cold call; **il y a eu un a. pour vous** there was a (telephone) call for you; **a. avec préavis** person to person call; *Radio* **indicatif d'a.** call sign

8 *Aviat* **a. particulier** selective calling

9 *(pour vérifier)*, *Scol* roll call, register; **faire l'a. (des écoliers)** to take *or* call the register; **répondre à l'a.** to be present; **feuille/cahier d'a.** roll, register; *Mil* **l'a. du soir** tattoo; **manquant à l'a.** missing

10 *Tech* **a. d'air** intake of air; **vitesse d'a.** inflow; **a. d'un aimant** pull of a magnet; **le moteur part au premier a.** the engine starts at the first touch of the switch

11 *Typ* **a. de note** footnote reference, superior figure

12 *Sport* take-off; **quel est le pied d'a.?** which is the take-off foot?; **un bon coup d'a. sur le tremplin** a good kick off from the springboard

13 *(signal)* signal, call; **l'a. à la prière** (Muslim) call to prayer

14 *Ordinat* call; *(de commande)* selection; **a. automatique** automatic dial

appelant, -ante [aplɑ̃, -ɑ̃t] ADJ *Jur (partie etc)* appealing

N 1 *Jur* appellant (against a judgment); **se porter a.** to appeal **2** *Tél* caller

appelé [aple] NM **1** *Mil* conscript; *Fig* **il y a beaucoup d'appelés, mais peu d'élus** many are called, but few are chosen **2** *Tél* party called

appeler [aple] (**j'appelle, n. appelons; j'appellerai**) VT **1** *(personne, chien)* to call (to); *(taxi)* to call, to hail; **a. au secours** to call for help; **a. qn dans la rue** to call to sb in the street; **a. qn de la main** *ou* **du geste** to beckon (to) sb; **les noms sont appelés un à un** the names are called out one by one; *Jur* **a. une cause** to call (out) a case

2 *Tél* **a. qn (au téléphone)** to ring sb (up), to call sb; **a. Paris** to call Paris; **a. un taxi/un médecin** to phone for a taxi/a doctor

3 *(convoquer)* to call in, to send for, to summon; *Jur* **a. qn (en justice)** to summon(s) sb; *(poursuivre)* to sue sb; **a. qn à témoin** to call sb to witness; **a. les pompiers** to call the fire brigade; **faire a. un médecin** to call in *or* send for a doctor; **a. l'ascenseur** to call the lift; **elle a été appelée auprès de son père mourant** she was called to her dying father's bedside; *Mil* **a. qn sous les drapeaux** to call sb up, to conscript sb; *aussi Hum* **le devoir t'appelle** duty calls; *Fin* **capital appelé** called-up capital

4 a. qn à *(fonction etc)* to appoint *or* assign sb to; **être appelé à qch** to be destined for sth; **cette technique est appelée à se développer partout dans le monde** the technique is destined *or* set to spread throughout the world; **son courage l'appelle à ce genre d'action** his courage inspires him to that kind of action; **il fut appelé à travailler à l'étranger** he was called to work overseas

5 *(donner un nom à)* to call; **nous l'avons appelé David** we have called him David; **tu l'appelles par son prénom?** do you call him by his first name?; **j'appelle cela une bêtise** I call that *or* that's what I call a stupid mistake; **voilà ce que j'appelle un homme** now that's what I call a man; **vous appelez cela danser?** (do) you call that dancing?; **a. un chat un chat, a. les choses par leur nom** to call a spade a spade

6 *(demander, réclamer)* to call for; *(critique)* to invite; **ce problème appelle une solution immédiate** the problem calls for an immediate solution; **a. qn à faire qch** to call on *or* invite sb to do sth; **je vous appelle tous à y réfléchir** I call on *or* invite you all to think about it

7 *(entraîner)* to provoke, to arouse, to attract; *Prov* **un malheur en appelle un autre** misfortunes never come singly; **la violence appelle la violence** violence breeds *or* begets violence

8 *Ordinat (fichier)* to call up

VI 1 *(crier)* to call, to shout; **il arrive qu'il appelle la nuit** he sometimes calls out *or* shouts out in the night; **elle appelait à l'aide** *ou* **au secours** she was calling *or* shouting for help; **si tu as un problème, tu appelles** if you have a problem, just shout

2 *Tél* to call, to phone; **laisse-la a. la première** wait for her to call *or* phone you

3 en a. à qn to appeal to sb; **j'en appelle à votre bon sens** I appeal to your common sense; **j'en appelle de votre décision** I challenge your decision; *Jur* **a. d'un jugement** to appeal against a sentence; **en a.** to appeal

VPR s'appeler 1 *(avoir pour nom)* to be called; **comment vous appelez-vous?** what is your name?; **je m'appelle David** my name is David; **cela s'appelle un plaqueminier** it's called a persimmon; *Fam* **voilà qui s'appelle pleuvoir!** it's raining with a vengeance!; **nous nous appelons par nos prénoms** we call each other by our first names, we're on first-name terms

2 *Tél (entre plusieurs individus)* **alors, on s'appelle, hein?** talk to you on the phone

---

Il faut noter que le verbe anglais **to appeal** est un faux ami. Il ne signifie jamais **appeler**.

---

appellation [apelasjɔ̃] NF name; *(de produit)* designation, *Fml* appellation; **vin sans a.** non-vintage wine; **a. injurieuse** abusive term

▸▸ **a. contrôlée** *(de vin)* guaranteed vintage; **a. d'origine** designation *or* label of origin

appendice [apɛ̃dis] NM VOIR GRAMMAIRE A14 **1** *Anat* appendix; *Zool, Bot* appendage; **se faire enlever l'a.** to have one's appendix out; *Hum* **quel a. nasal!** what a conk *or* hooter! **2** *(d'un livre)* appendix, supplement **3** *Vieilli (d'un bâtiment)* annex(e) **4** *(d'un ballon)* neck

appendicectomie [apɛ̃disɛktɔmi] NF *Chir* append(ic)ectomy

appendicite [apɛ̃disit] NF *Méd* appendicitis; **crise d'a.** appendicitis; **a. chronique** grumbling appendix; **se faire opérer de l'a.** to have an operation for appendicitis, to have one's appendix out

appentis [apɑ̃ti] NM *Constr (bâtiment)* lean-to; *(toit)* lean-to, sloping roof; *(remise)* outhouse, shed

appesantir [apəzɑ̃tir] VT *(rendre moins agile)* to slow down, to weigh down; **l'âge a appesanti sa démarche** old age has slowed his step; **paupières appesanties par le sommeil** eyes heavy with sleep

VPR s'appesantir to grow heavier; **son pas s'appesantit avec la fatigue** his step grew slower *or* heavier through fatigue; *Fig* **la main de fer de l'Inquisition s'appesantit sur ...** the iron fist of the Inquisition weighed down on ...; *Fig* **la nuit s'appesantit sur la ville** black night fell over the town; *Fig* **s'a. sur un sujet** to dwell on a subject; *Fig Fam* **pas la peine de s'a., passons à autre chose** there's no point in dwelling on it, let's get on to something else

appesantissement [apəzɑ̃tismɑ̃] NM *(de la marche, des recherches)* slowing (down); *(des pas)* (growing) heaviness

appétence [apetɑ̃s] NF *Litt* penchant, partiality; **une a. d'aventure** a penchant for adventure

appétissant [apetisɑ̃] ADJ *(nourriture)* appetizing, tempting; *Fig (femme)* alluring

appétit [apeti] NM **1** *(de nourriture)* appetite; **couper l'a. à qn** to spoil *or* take away sb's appetite; **donner de l'a. à qn** to give sb an appetite; **mettre qn en a.** to give sb an appetite; **manger de bon a.** *ou* **avec a.** to eat heartily *or* with relish, *Fam* to tuck in; **avoir un a. d'oiseau** to have a small *or* poor appetite, to peck at one's food; **avoir bon** *ou* **un gros a.** to have a hearty appetite; **bon a.!** enjoy your meal!, bon appetit!; **manger sans a.** *(sans plaisir)* not to enjoy one's food; *(picorer)* to pick at one's food; **je n'ai plus d'a.** I've lost my appetite, I'm off my food; *Prov* **l'a. vient en mangeant** only when you start eating do you realize you're hungry; *Fig* **the more you get the more you want 2** *(désir)* desire, craving (de for); **a. sexuel** sexual desire; **a. du gain** craving for money; **l'a. de la connaissance** a thirst *or* hunger for knowledge

applaudimètre [aplodimɛtr] NM clapometer

applaudir [aplodir] VT to applaud; **se faire a. à tout rompre** to get tremendous applause, to bring the house down; *Fig* **je vous applaudis de tout cœur** I congratulate you with all my heart

VI to applaud, to clap; **a. à tout rompre** to applaud *or* clap thunderously; *Fig* **nous applaudissons à la reprise des relations entre nos deux pays** we welcome the resumption of relations between our two countries; *Fig* **a. à une décision/un changement** to applaud *or* welcome a decision/a change

VPR s'applaudir s'a. (d'avoir fait qch) to congratulate oneself, to pat oneself on the back (for having done sth)

applaudissement [aplodismɑ̃] NM *(souvent pl)* **1** applause, clapping; **un tonnerre** *ou* **une tempête d'applaudissements** thunderous applause; **soulever des applaudissements** to be applauded **2** *Litt* approval

applicable [aplikabl] ADJ applicable; **cette règle est a. à tous les cas** this rule applies to all cases; **a. à partir du 1er janvier** to take effect from 1 January

applicateur [aplikatœr] NM *(dispositif)* applicator; **tampon avec a.** applicator tampon

ADJ **pinceau a.** applicator

application [aplikasjɔ̃] NF **1** *(de peinture etc)* application, applying; **première a. de peinture** first coat of paint; *Couture* **broderie d'a.** appliqué (work); **bois d'a.** veneer

2 *(d'un règlement)* application; *(de la loi)* enforcement; **mettre une théorie en a.** to put a theory into practice; **mettre une loi en a.** to enforce *or* implement a law; **entrer en a.** to come into force; **a. d'une somme d'argent à un projet** use of a sum of money for a project; **en a. de ce décret** in pursuance of this decree; *Mil etc* **école d'a.** school of instruction

3 *(débouché)* application; *(de la matière première)* use

4 *(assiduité)* application (to one's work), industriousness; **travailler avec a.** to apply oneself to one's work, to work diligently

5 *Ordinat* **a. bureautique** business application; **a. phare** killer app; **a. en service** current application; **a. graphique** graphics application; **logiciel d'a.** application software

applique [aplik] NF **1** *(lampe)* wall light **2** *Couture* appliquéd ornament

appliqué [aplike] ADJ **1** *(personne)* hardworking, diligent; *(écriture)* careful **2** *(sciences)* applied; **informatique appliquée à la gestion** computer technology applied to management

appliquer [aplike] VT **1** *(mettre)* to apply (sur to); **a. une couche de peinture sur qch** to put a coat of paint on sth, *surtout Fml* to apply a coat of paint to sth; **a. une oreille au mur** to put one's ear to the wall, to listen through the wall; **un coup bien appliqué** a well-planted or well-aimed blow; **elle lui fit une bise bien appliquée** she planted a kiss on his cheek

2 (mettre en œuvre) to apply; (peine) to enforce; (sanctions, règlement, mesures) to enforce, to apply; (idée, réforme) to put into practice, to implement; (recette, méthode) to use; **a. une loi à un cas particulier** to apply a law to a particular case; **a. (les dispositions de) la loi** to apply the law; **a. un traitement à une maladie** to apply a treatment to an illness; **a. une recette particulière** to use a particular recipe; Jur **a. le maximum de la peine** to impose the maximum penalty

3 (concentrer) to apply; **a. toute son attention à un problème** to devote or apply all one's attention to a problem; **a. son esprit à ses études** to apply one's mind to one's studies

VPR s'appliquer 1 (se concentrer) to apply oneself, to take pains; **elle doit s'a. davantage** she has to apply herself more; **s'a. à qch** to apply oneself to sth, to take pains over sth; **il s'applique à vérifier toutes les dates** he's taking pains to check all the dates; **elle s'applique à me contredire** she is making a point of contradicting me; **il s'applique à apprendre le français** he is making a serious effort to learn French

2 (d'un règlement etc) to apply (à to); **à qui s'applique cette remarque?** who is that remark intended for?; **le règlement s'applique pour tous** the rule applies to everybody

3 (se placer) to be applied; **le cataplasme s'applique directement sur la peau** the poultice should be applied directly (on)to the skin

appoint [apwɛ̃] NM **1** Com, Fin exact money or change; **faire l'a.** (ajouter le reste) to make up the full amount, to give the exact change; (donner la somme exacte) to pay the exact amount; **ressources d'a.** additional (sources of) income; **ce travail à mi-temps lui fait un petit a.** this part-time job brings him a little extra income; **chauffage/éclairage d'a.** additional heating/lighting; **siège d'a.** extra chair; **un travail d'a.** a second job **2** (contribution) contribution; **apporter son a. à qch** to contribute to sth, to take part in sth

appointements [apwɛ̃tmɑ̃] NMPL salary; **toucher ses a.** to draw one's salary

Il faut noter que le nom anglais **appointment** est un faux ami. Il signifie **rendez-vous** ou **nomination**, selon le contexte.

appointer [apwɛte] VT **1** (payer) (personne) to pay (a salary to); **être appointé à la semaine** to be paid weekly or by the week **2** (crayon etc) to sharpen

appondre [apɔ̃dr] VT Suisse to join (together)

appontage [apɔ̃taʒ] NM (d'un porte-avions) landing (on an aircraft carrier); **officier d'a.** landing officer; **crosse** ou **crochet d'a.** arrester hook

appontement [apɔ̃tmɑ̃] NM Naut (de bois) jetty, pier, landing stage

apponter [apɔ̃te] VI (sur un porte-avions) to land (on an aircraft carrier)

apport [apɔr] NM **1** (fait d'apporter) contribution, contributing; Écon inflow, influx; **a. de capitaux** contribution of capital; Compta **a. en capital** capital contribution; Compta **a. en numéraire** cash contribution; **a. d'argent frais** injection of new money; Compta **apports libérés** fully paid-up capital; **capital d'a.** initial capital; **actions d'a.** founder's or promoter's shares; **l'a. du tourisme dans une région** the financial contribution made by tourism to a region; **sans a. extérieur,**

nous étions perdus without outside (financial) help, we'd have been ruined; Jur **a. de pièces** (dans une enquête) deposit(ing) of documents; Jur **biens d'a.** estate brought in by husband/wife on marriage; **a. en communauté** = goods contributed by husband and wife to the joint estate; **terres d'a.** earthworks; **l'a. de la civilisation grecque** the contribution made by Greek civilization

2 (contribution) contribution; Fin initial share; **un a. en nature** a contribution in kind; **les fruits donnent un a. de vitamines indispensable** fruit provides essential vitamins; **l'a. en vitamines du foie** the vitamins provided by liver, the vitamins present in liver; Agr **un gros a. d'engrais** a heavy dressing of manure; **a. de chaleur, a. calorifique** heat supply or input

3 Tech coating, layer, deposit

▸▸Jur **a. dotal** dowry, marriage portion

apporter [apɔrte] VT **1** to bring (**qch à qn** sth to sb); **je t'ai apporté la cassette vidéo** I've brought you the video; **si tu vas la voir, apporte-lui des fleurs** if you go to see her, take her some flowers; Fin **a. des capitaux** to bring in capital

2 a. du soin/un grand intérêt à faire qch to do sth carefully/with great interest

3 (donner) (bonheur, soulagement etc) to bring; **cette démonstration n'apporte aucune preuve supplémentaire** this demonstration gives or provides no additional proof; **cette expérience lui a beaucoup apporté** the experience has been very beneficial for him; **qu'est-ce que ça peut t'a.?** what good can that do you?; **notre relation ne m'apporte plus rien** I'm not getting anything out of our relationship any more, our relationship doesn't do anything for me any more; **tu ne m'apportes plus rien** you've got nothing to offer me any more, I've outgrown you; **ce travail ne m'apporte pas grand-chose** I don't get very much out of this work **4** (changements etc) to cause, to bring about; **ce que l'avenir apportera** what the future has in store

Do not confuse **apporter** and **amener**. The former should be used with inanimate objects and the latter with animate objects.

apposer [apoze] VT to place, to put, Fml to affix; **a. une affiche sur un mur** to stick a poster on a wall; Jur **a. les scellés** (pour interdire tout accès) to affix the seals; **a. sa signature à** to put one's signature to; Jur **a. sa signature à un acte** to append or affix one's signature to a deed; **a. une clause à un acte** to insert a clause in or add a clause to an act

apposition [apozisjɔ̃] NF **1** Admin (d'un sceau, de scellés, de signature etc) affixing, appending **2** Gram apposition; **mot en a.** word in apposition SEE GRAMMAR A6; B5

appréciable [apresjabl] ADJ **1** (par les sens) perceptible **2** (évolution, changement etc) appreciable, noticeable; **une différence à peine a.** a barely perceptible difference; **la différence est difficilement a.** it's difficult to tell the difference **3** (non négligeable) considerable, appreciable (usu attrib); **à une distance a.** at an appreciable or considerable distance **4** (louable) (motivations) praiseworthy; **ses qualités de dirigeant ont été fort appréciables** his leadership qualities were greatly appreciated; **le changement de temps est tout à fait a.** (bienvenu) the change in the weather is very welcome

appréciateur, -trice [apresjatœr, -tris] N appreciator (**de** of); Com etc appraiser, valuer; **a. du talent** person who recognizes talent, good judge of talent

appréciatif, -ive [apresjatif, -iv] ADJ (re-

gard, silence) appreciative; Com **devis a.** estimate

appréciation [apresjasjɔ̃] NF **1** (évaluation) valuation, estimation, estimate; (d'une distance) judging; **faire l'a. des marchandises** to value or to make a valuation of goods; **a. des risques** risk assessment **2** (opinion) judgment, opinion; (d'une œuvre d'art, d'un repas etc) appreciation; **les appréciations sont notées dans la marge** the comments are in the margin; **je laisse cette tapisserie/ce problème à votre a.** I'll leave you to form an opinion on this piece of tapestry/this problem **3** (augmentation de valeur) appreciation, rise in value; **a. monétaire** currency appreciation

apprécier [apresje] (pr sub, impf n. **appréciions,** v. **appréciiez**) VT **1** (évaluer) to appraise; (peinture etc) to estimate the value of, to value; **tu ne l'apprécies pas à sa juste valeur** you don't appreciate his/her true worth

2 (déterminer) to determine; (approximativement) (température, son) to estimate; (distance) to judge; (différences, nuances) to appreciate, to judge

3 (aimer) to appreciate; **un bon repas entre amis, voilà ce que j'apprécie le plus** having a good meal with friends is what I enjoy doing most or is what I like most; **je n'apprécie pas ce genre de plaisanterie** I don't appreciate or I don't much care for that kind of joke; **elle ne l'apprécie pas du tout** she doesn't like him at all; **elle l'apprécie, sans plus** she just likes him; (ils ne sont pas amants) she's just good friends with him

VI Fam **elle n'a pas apprécié** she didn't or pleased

VPR s'apprécier 1 (de personnes) to like each other

2 (de monnaie) to appreciate; **l'euro s'est apprécié par rapport au dollar** the euro has risen against the dollar

appréhender [apreɑ̃de] VT **1** Jur **a. qn (au corps)** to arrest or apprehend sb **2** (craindre) to dread, to fear; **j'appréhende de rentrer** ou **le retour** I'm dreading going back; **j'appréhende toujours un peu les voyages en avion** I'm always a bit apprehensive about travelling by air **3** (notion) to grasp

VI to be apprehensive

appréhensif, -ive [apreɑ̃sif, -iv] ADJ apprehensive

appréhension [apreɑ̃sjɔ̃] NF **1** (crainte) apprehension (**de** of); **avoir des appréhensions** to be apprehensive **2** (d'une notion) grasp

apprenant, -ante [aprənɑ̃, -ɑ̃t] N learner

apprendre [aprɑ̃dr] (conj like **prendre**) VT **1** (leçon, commerce, langue, méthode etc) to learn; **il n'a jamais rien appris à l'école** he didn't learn a thing at school

2 (nouvelles etc) to learn, to hear (of), to get to know of; **comment l'avez-vous appris?** how did you hear or find out?; **nous l'avons appris à la radio/aux informations** we heard it on the radio/on the news; **j'ai appris que tu allais te marier** I've heard that you're getting married; **je l'ai appris de bonne source** I have it on good authority

3 (enseigner) **a. qch à qn** to teach sb sth; **a. à qn à faire qch** to teach or show sb how to do sth; **il m'a tout appris** he taught me everything I know

4 (informer) **a. qch à qn** to inform sb of sth, to tell sb sth; Fam **vous ne m'apprenez rien!** you're telling me!, you're not telling me anything new!; **il faut tout lui a., il ne sait rien** he has to be told everything, he hasn't a clue

VI to learn; **a. facilement** to find learning easy; **a. vite/lentement** to be a fast/slow learner; **a. à faire qch** to learn how to do sth; **a. à lire/skier** to learn to read/(how) to ski; *Prov* **on apprend à tout âge** it is never too late to learn, you're never too old to learn; *Fam* **je vous apprendrai à me parler de la sorte!** I'll teach you to speak to me like that!; *Fam* **ça vous apprendra!** serve(s) you right!, that'll teach you!; *Fam* **je vais lui a. à vivre** I'm going to teach him a few manners

VPR **s'apprendre ça s'apprend vite** it's easy to learn, it can be learned quickly; **le chinois ne s'apprend pas facilement** it isn't easy to learn Chinese

apprenti, -ie [aprɑ̃ti] N apprentice; *Jur* articled clerk; **une apprentie couturière** an apprentice dressmaker; **a. menuisier** carpenter's apprentice; **je ne suis qu'un a.** I'm only a beginner *or* a novice

▸▸ **a. conducteur** learner (driver); **a. sorcier** sorcerer's apprentice; *Fig* **cesse donc de jouer les apprentis sorciers!** stop meddling with things that you know nothing about!

apprentissage [aprɑ̃tisaʒ] NM training; *(chez un artisan)* apprenticeship; **centre d'a.** training school; **contrat d'a.** contract of apprenticeship; **mettre qn en a. chez un patron** to apprentice sb to an employer; **être en a. chez qn** to be apprenticed to sb; **faire l'a. de la vie** to gain some experience of life, *Fam* to go through the university of life; **faire l'a. de la douleur** to become acquainted with grief

apprêt [apre] NM 1 *(opération) (de tissus, de cuirs etc)* dressing, finishing 2 *(substance) (de tissu etc)* finish, dress; *(de peinture)* primer, size; **a. anti-corrosion** anti-corrosion primer 3 *(affectation)* affectation, affectedness; **style sans a.** unaffected style

apprêtage [apretaʒ] NM *Tech* 1 *(de tissu)* dressing, finishing 2 *(de peinture)* priming, sizing

apprêté [aprete] ADJ 1 *(style, attitude etc)* affected, stiff; **coiffure apprêtée** fussy hairstyle 2 **papier a.** glossy paper

apprêter [aprete] VT 1 *(repas etc)* to prepare; **a. un enfant** to get a child ready, to dress a child; **les femmes apprêtent la mariée** the women help the bride to dress *or* get ready 2 *(tissus etc)* to dress, to finish, to stiffen; *(cuir)* to finish 3 *(surface)* to prime

VPR **s'apprêter** *(s'habiller)* to get dressed; *(se donner un coup de peigne etc)* to tidy oneself (up); **s'a. à faire qch** to be getting ready *or* preparing to do sth, to be on the point of doing sth

apprivoisable [aprivwazabl(ə)] ADJ tameable

apprivoisé [aprivwaze] ADJ tame

apprivoisement [aprivwazmɑ̃] NM taming, domestication

apprivoiser [aprivwaze] VT *(animal)* to tame; *Fig (personne)* to win over; *Fig* **je veux a. cette peur** I want to conquer this fear

VPR **s'apprivoiser** *(d'un animal)* to become domesticated *or* tame; *Fig (d'une personne)* to become more sociable; *Fig Litt* **s'a. à une idée** to get used to *or* come round to an idea

approbateur, -trice [aprobatœr, -tris], **approbatif, -ive** [aprobatif, -iv] ADJ *(geste, sourire etc)* approving; **regard a.** look of approval

approbation [aprobasjɔ̃] NF approval *(de qch* of sth); *(de documents officiels, de comptes rendus)* certifying, approval; **donner son a. à qch** to give one's approval to sth, to approve sth; **le film a reçu l'a. du public** the film was well received by the public; **a. tacite** tacit approval; **votre conduite est digne d'a.** your behaviour is commendable; **cette étude mérite l'a. de tous** this study merits general approval; *Com* **pour a.** for approval; **a. des comptes** approval of the accounts

approchable [aprɔʃabl] ADJ *(endroit, personne)* approachable, accessible; **le refuge n'est pas a. en voiture** the shelter is not accessible *or* cannot be reached by car; **elle n'est pas a. aujourd'hui** *(elle est de mauvaise humeur)* she's not very approachable today

approchant [aprɔʃɑ̃] ADJ similar, approximate *(*de to); **offre approchante** near offer; **je n'ai jamais rien vu d'a.** I've never seen anything like it *or* anything approaching it; **voilà ce qu'il a dit, ou quelque chose d'a.** that is what he said, or something like it; **je cherche qch d'a.** I'm looking for something similar

ADV *Suisse* about, around; **gagner a. cinq mille francs** *ou* **cinq mille francs a.** to earn about five thousand francs

approche [aprɔʃ] NF 1 approach; **l'a. de l'hiver** the approach of winter; **à l'a. de la vieillesse** as old age draws/drew near; **aux approches de la trentaine** as you/etc near *or* approach thirty; **à son a.** as he came up, as he approached; **d'une a. difficile** *(lieu)* hard to get to, not easily accessible; *(personne)* unapproachable; *(livre etc)* hard to understand; **à l'a. de la difficulté, elle abandonne** she gives up whenever a difficulty arises; **un homme d'a. facile** an approachable man

2 *(manière d'aborder)* **une nouvelle a. du problème** a new approach to the problem; **travail d'a.** manoeuvre, *Am* maneuver; **cette étude a nécessité un long travail d'a.** the study required a great deal of preliminary work; *Mktg* **a. bayésienne** Bayesian theory; *Aviat* **a. à vue** visual approach; **chasse à l'a.** deerstalking

3 *(environs)* **les approches d'une ville** the approaches of a town; **aux approches du village** on the outskirts of the village

4 *Typ (faute)* = extra space wrongly inserted between two letters; *(signe)* close-up sign *or* mark

5 *Zool* mating

approché [aprɔʃe] ADJ *(résultat, valeur)* approximate

approcher [aprɔʃe] VT 1 *(personne, objet)* to approach, to come near, to come close to; **a. qch de qn/qch** to bring *or* draw sth near (to) sb/sth; **approchez votre chaise** pull up your chair; **a. sa chaise de la lampe** to move one's chair nearer the lamp; **ne m'approchez pas** don't come near me; **elle approche les plus grands noms du spectacle** she rubs shoulders with the biggest names in showbusiness; **a. des lions d'assez près** to get quite close to some lions; **on ne peut pas l'a.** you can never see him; *(parce qu'il ne le veut pas)* you can't get near him, he's unapproachable; **le président? on ne peut pas l'a. comme ça!** you can't just walk up to the president!

2 *(faire des démarches auprès de) (personne)* to approach; **il a été approché par diverses sociétés** he was approached by various companies

VI 1 to approach, to draw near(er), to come nearer; **l'heure** *ou* **le moment approche** it will soon be time; **la nuit approchait** night was falling, it was beginning to get dark; **faites-le a.** ask him to come closer; **approche! je vais te montrer quelque chose!** come (over) here! I've something to show you!; **a. de qn/qch** to approach sb/sth; **nous approchons de Paris** we are approaching *or* getting near Paris; **a. du but** to be nearing one's goal; **il approche de la trentaine** he's getting on for *or* nearing *or* approaching thirty; **nous approchions alors les 200 km/heure** we were going at almost 200 km an hour

2 **a. de qch** to be *or* to come close to sth; **ça en approche** it's close, it's getting close (to it); **son art approche de la perfection** his

art comes close to perfection; **tu approches de la vérité** you're getting close to the truth; **son comportement approche de la folie** his behaviour borders on insanity

3 *Zool* to mate

VPR **s'approcher** to come *or* go closer *or* nearer, to draw near(er), to approach; **je n'ai pas pu m'a. de la scène, il y avait trop de monde** I couldn't get near the stage, there were too many people; **je me suis approché pour voir** I went closer to have a look; **s'a. de qn/qch** to come *or* go up to sb/sth; **ne t'approche pas du chien** don't go near the dog; **il faut t'a.!, viens!** come on!, come closer!; **le navire s'approchait de la terre** the ship was nearing land; **s'a. de la perfection** to be almost perfect, to be close to perfection

approfondi [aprɔfɔ̃di] ADJ *(recherche)* elaborate, detailed, extensive; *(enquête)* detailed, in-depth; *(connaissances)* thorough, in-depth

approfondir [aprɔfɔ̃dir] VT 1 *(lit de la rivière etc)* to deepen, to excavate 2 *(examiner) (problème)* to go deeply *or* thoroughly into; *(sujet)* to study thoroughly; **a. une affaire** to get to the root of a matter; **sans a. la question** *ou* **le sujet** without going into too much detail; **laisse-moi le temps d'a. la question** give me time to examine the question in detail

VPR **s'approfondir** to become deeper, to deepen

approfondissement [aprɔfɔ̃dismɑ̃] NM 1 *(d'un canal etc)* deepening, excavating, excavation 2 *(d'une question)* in-depth analysis; *(d'une étude)* further development

appropriation [aprɔprijasjɔ̃] NF 1 *(de biens etc)* appropriation; **a. par violence** forcible seizure; **a. de fonds** embezzlement, misappropriation of funds 2 *Arch, Belg* cleaning, tidying up

approprié [aprɔprije] ADJ appropriate (à for)

approprier [aprɔprije] *(pr sub, impf* n. **appropriions,** v. **appropriiez)** VT 1 *(adapter)* **a. qch** to arrange sth, to suit sth; **a. qch à qch** to adapt sth to sth; **a. son style à un public** to adapt one's style to an audience 2 *Arch, Belg (nettoyer)* to clean; *(ranger)* to tidy

VPR **s'approprier** 1 *(s'adjuger)* **s'a. qch** to appropriate sth 2 *(s'adapter)* **s'a. à qch** to be suitable *or* appropriate for sth, to be in keeping with sth, to suit sth; **cette musique s'approprie à la situation** this music is suitable for the occasion

approuver [apruve] VT **a. qch** to approve of sth; **a. qch de la tête** to nod approval; **a. qn** to agree with sb; **a. qn de faire/d'avoir fait qch** to think sb is right for doing/having done sth; **elle approuve tout ce qu'il dit/fait** she agrees with everything he says/does; **nous vous approuvons dans votre choix** we approve of your choice; **a. qch officiellement** to agree formally to sth; *Com* **a. une facture** to pass an invoice; **a. un contrat** to ratify a contract; *Com* **a. et contre-argumenter** to agree and counter; *Admin* **a. une nomination** to confirm an appointment; **a. un appel** to endorse an appeal; **lu et approuvé** read and approved; **lessive approuvée par un grand nombre de fabriquants** washing powder recommended by a large number of manufacturers; *Méd* **médicament approuvé** approved drug *or* medicine

approvisionné [aprɔvizjɔne] ADJ stocked, supplied *(*de, en with); **bien a.** well-stocked; **magasin bien/mal a. en ...** shop with a good/poor stock of ...

approvisionnement [aprɔvizjɔnmɑ̃] NM 1 *(ravitaillement) (d'une ville, d'une armée)* supplying; *(d'une personne)* catering; *(d'un magasin)* stocking; **l'a. de la ville en produits frais** the supply(ing) of fresh produce to the town **2** *(provisions)* supply, stock, provisions; **faire un a. de qch** to stock up with sth

approvisionner [aprɔvizjɔne] **VT 1** *(ravitailler, fournir)* to supply (**en** with); *(personne)* to cater for; *(magasin)* to stock; **a. une île en produits frais** to supply an island with fresh produce **2** *Banque* **a. son compte** to pay money into one's account; **son compte en banque n'est plus approvisionné** his bank account is no longer in credit

VPR s'approvisionner to lay in provisions, to get a stock *or* a supply (**en** of); **s'a. chez qn** to get one's supplies from sb; *(d'une ménagère etc)* to shop at sb's; **s'a. au marché** to shop *or* to do one's shopping *or* to buy one's provisions at the market; **s'a. en qch** to stock up on sth

approximatif, -ive [aprɔksimatif, -iv] **ADJ** *(calcul, estimation)* approximate, rough; **ce chiffre est très a.** this figure is only a rough estimate; **nous nous sommes exprimés dans un anglais a.** we expressed ourselves in broken English

approximation [aprɔksimasjɔ̃] **NF** approximation, rough estimate; *Math* approximation

approximativement [aprɔksimativmɑ̃] **ADV** approximately, roughly; **dans une heure a.** in an hour or so

appt *abrév* **appartement**

appui [apɥi] **NM 1** *(support)* support, prop; *Archit* balustrade; **mur d'a.** supporting *or* retaining wall; **barre d'a.** handrail; **point d'a.** *(d'un levier)* fulcrum; *Mil (d'opérations)* base; **à hauteur d'a.** elbow high; **mettre un a. à un mur** to shore up a wall; **prendre a. sur qch** to be supported by *or* on sth; *(d'une personne)* to support oneself on sth; **prendre a. sur le pied gauche** *(pour sauter)* to take off from the left foot; **a. de fenêtre** window ledge *or* sill; **a. de porte** door sill
2 *(aide)* support, backing; **a. moral** moral support; **a. financier** (financial) backing; **la société ne bénéficie pas d'un a. financier suffisant** the company does not have sufficient financial backing; **prêter son a. à qn** to support *or* lend support to sb, to back sb up; **vous avez mon a.** you have my support *or* backing; **être sans appui(s)** to be friendless; **avoir des appuis en haut lieu** to have friends in high places; **à l'a.** *(de qch)* in support; **à l'a., il me montra tes lettres** to support *or* to back up what he said, he showed me your letters; **avec preuves à l'a.** with supporting evidence; **à l'a. d'un témoignage** in support of testimony
3 *Mil* **a. direct** close *or Am* direct support; **tir d'a.** covering fire; **a. tactique/aérien** tactical/air support
4 *Ordinat* **a. droite** flush right; **texte en a. droite** right justified text

appui-bras, *pl* **appuis-bras NM** armrest

appuie- [apɥi] *(compound nouns of which the first element is **appui-** have an alternative form **appuie-**, in which case they are invariable)*

appui-jambes, *pl* **appuis-jambes NM** leg rest

appui-nuque, *pl* **appuis-nuque NM** headrest

appui-queue, *pl* **appuis-queue NM** *Billard* (cue) rest, *Fam* jigger

appui-tête, *pl* **appuis-tête NM** headrest, head restraint

appuyé [apɥije] **ADJ** *(plaisanterie, ironie)* laboured, *Am* labored, heavy; **regard a.** (fixed) stare; **il lui lançait des regards appuyés** he stared at him intently

appuyer [apɥije] (**j'appuie,** n. **appuyons;** **j'appuierai**) **VT 1** *(mettre contre)* to lean, to rest (**qch contre qch** sth against sth); **a. sa**

tête contre la fenêtre to lean one's head against the window; **a. sa tête sur l'épaule de qn** to rest one's head on sb's shoulder; *Fig* **a. son opinion sur qch** to base one's opinion on sth; *Fig* **théorie appuyée sur des faits** theory supported by facts
2 *(exercer une pression sur)* **a. qch sur qch** to press sth on sth; **a. son pied sur la pédale de frein** to put one's foot on the brake; *Fig* **a. son regard sur qn** to stare intently at sb
3 *(mur, solive etc)* to support, to prop (up)
4 *Fig (soutenir)* **a. une pétition** to support a petition (**par** by); **a. une proposition** to second a proposal; **a. un candidat** to back *or* support a candidate; **a. la demande de qn** to support sb's request; **a. qn financièrement** to back sb (financially), to give sb financial backing

VI 1 *(reposer)* to bear (**sur** on); **poutre qui appuie sur deux montants** beam resting *or* bearing on two uprights
2 *(presser)* to depress; **a. sur la valise pour la fermer** to press down on the suitcase to close it; **a. sur le point sensible** to press the sore spot; **a. sur son stylo** to press on one's pen; **a. sur le bouton** to press the button; *Aut Fam* **a. sur le champignon** *(accélérer)* to step on it, to put one's foot down; **a. sur une syllabe** to stress a syllable; *Mus* **a. sur une note** to hold a note; **a. sur l'urgence d'un problème** to stress the urgency of a problem; *Fam* **inutile d'a. là-dessus, on a compris** you don't need to keep going on about it, we understand; **appuyez à droite à la sortie du village** bear right as you leave the village

VPR s'appuyer 1 *(reposer)* **s'a. sur** *ou* **contre** *ou* **à qch** to lean *or* rest on *or* against sth; **s'a. sur** *ou* **contre le bras de qn** to lean on sb's arm; **s'a. sur qn** to lean on sb; *Fig* to lean *or* to rely *or* depend on sb; **s'a. sur son expérience pour conseiller qn** to draw on *or* to use one's experience to advise sb; **ses recherches s'appuient sur des découvertes récentes** his research is based on recent discoveries
2 *Fam* **s'a. une corvée** to be lumbered with a chore; **c'est toujours moi qui m'appuie la vaisselle!** it's always me who gets lumbered with the dishes!; **s'a. un bon dîner/un gentil petit voyage** to treat oneself to *or* stand oneself a good dinner/a nice little trip

âpre [apr] **ADJ 1** *(aigre)* rough, harsh; **voix â.** rasping voice; **goût â.** sour taste; **vin â.** rough wine **2** *(temps, vent)* raw **3** *(dégoût)* bitter, biting, sharp; *(ironie)* scathing **4** *(lutte)* bitter **5** *(concurrence etc)* keen; **homme â. (au gain)** grasping man; **être â. au gain** to be grasping *or* money-grabbing

âprement [aprəmɑ̃] **ADV** *(défendu)* fiercely; *(se disputer)* violently

après [aprɛ] **PRÉP 1** *(dans le temps, dans l'espace)* after; **il est arrivé a. moi** he arrived after me; **a. tout** after all; **fermé a. 20 heures** closed from 8 o'clock (onwards); **a. bien des discussions, nous avons décidé de …** after a great deal of discussion, we decided to …; **jour a. jour** day after day; **a. vous, monsieur/madame!** after you!; **et a. cela, madame?** *(au restaurant)* and to follow, madam?; **a. quoi** after which; **je suis** *ou* **viens a. lui** I am *or* come after him; **tourner à droite a. la poste** turn right just past the post office; *Fam* **courir a. qn** to run after sb; **les chiens risquent de nous courir a.** the dogs might run after us; *Fig Fam* **ces garçons qui te courent a.** those boys who are (always) chasing (after) you; *Fig Fam* **tout le monde leur court a.** everybody runs after them; **jurer/maugréer a. qn** to swear/grumble at sb; **il est toujours a. moi** he's always nagging at me *or* getting at me; *Fam* **en**

avoir a. qn to have it in for sb; **les jeux passent a. le travail** work comes before play; **ça passe a. tout le reste** everything else comes first
2 d'a. according to; **d'a. ce qu'elle a dit** going by *or* according to what she said; **d'a. l'horloge, il est trois heures** according to the clock, it's three; **peint d'a. nature** painted from life; **paysage d'a. Turner** landscape after Turner; **texte d'a. Cicéron** text adapted from Cicero; **d'a. l'article 12** under article 12; **d'a. vos instructions** in accordance with your instructions
3 (+ *inf*) **a. avoir dîné** after dinner; **a. manger** after eating

ADV afterwards, later; **parlez d'abord, je parlerai a.** you speak first, I'll speak afterwards; **six semaines a.** six weeks later; **les vacances, ça passe a.** holidays are not a priority; **avec lui, la famille, ça passe a.** his family takes second place; **le jour (d')a.** the next *or* following day, the day after; **la page d'a.** the next *or* following page; **nous eûmes des huîtres, et a. du saumon** we had oysters, followed by salmon; **et a.?** what then?; **et a., qu'est-ce qu'il a dit?** and then what did he say?; *Fam* **eh bien, et puis a.?** well, what of it?, what about it?, so what?

CONJ a. que after, when; **a. que je fus** *ou Fam* **sois parti** after I had gone; *Vieilli* **a. que j'aurai fini** when I have finished

après- [aprɛ] **PRÉF** post-…; **la période de l'a.-soixante-huit** the period after 1968, the post-1968 period; **le Moscou de l'a.-Gorbatchev** Moscow in the post-Gorbachev era; **les jeunes de l'a.-sida** the post-Aids generation

après-demain ADV the day after tomorrow

après-dîner, *pl* **après-dîners NM** evening; **discours d'a.** after-dinner speech

après-guerre, *pl* **après-guerres NM** postwar period

après-midi NM INV OU NF INV afternoon; **trois heures de l'a.** three (o'clock) in the afternoon, three pm

après-rasage, *pl* **après-rasages ADJ INV** lotion **a.** aftershave (lotion)
NM aftershave

après-ski NM INV *(chaussure)* snowboot

> Il faut noter que le nom anglais **après-ski** est un faux ami. Il désigne les activités récréatives auxquelles on se livre après une séance de ski.

après-vente ADJ INV *Com* **service a.** after-sales service

âpreté [aprəte] **NF 1** *(du vin, de la voix, de l'hiver etc)* roughness, harshness; *(du froid)* sharpness; *(d'un fruit)* sourness, tartness **2** *(du ton etc)* bitterness; *(des reproches)* sharpness, bitterness; *(de la concurrence)* fierceness

a priori [apriɔri] **ADJ INV** a priori; **raisonnement a.** a priori reasoning
ADV a priori; **a. ça me paraît possible** in principle, I think it's possible
NM INV preconception, apriorism; **avoir des a. (contre/en faveur de qch)** to be biased *or* prejudiced (against/in favour of sth); **être sans a p.** to be impartial

apr. J.-C. *(abrév* **après Jésus-Christ)** AD

à-propos NM *(d'une expression etc)* aptness, appropriateness, relevance; **avoir l'esprit d'à.** to have presence of mind; **répondre avec à.** to give a suitable *or* an appropriate reply; **il fait des commentaires sans le moindre à.** he makes comments that aren't the slightest bit relevant; **votre observation manque d'à.** your remark is not to the point *or* is irrelevant; **son manque d'à. lui jouera des tours** the fact that he always does/says the wrong thing is going to cause him problems

apte [apt] **ADJ** a. à faire qch/à qch fit or suited or qualified to do sth/for sth; **peu a. (à faire qch)** unsuitable, ill-equipped (to do sth); **a. à accomplir une tâche** well-suited or qualified to carry out a task; **a. à naviguer** seaworthy; *Mil* **a. au service** fit for military service; *Jur* **a. à hériter** entitled to inherit

aptère [apter] **ADJ** wingless; *Beaux-Arts* **victoire a.** wingless victory

aptéryx [apteriks] **NM** *(oiseau)* kiwi

aptitude [aptityd] **NF 1** *(capacité)* aptitude, ability (**à, pour** to); **il a des aptitudes manuelles** he's good with his hands; **avoir des aptitudes intellectuelles** to have intellectual skills; **avoir une a. pour qch** *(être doué)* to have a gift for sth; **test d'a.** aptitude test; **certificat d'a. professionnelle** = vocational training certificate **2** *Jur* capacity

apurement [apyrmã] **NM 1** *(d'un compte)* auditing, agreeing **2** *(d'une dette, du passif)* discharge

apurer [apyre] **VT 1** *(comptes)* to audit **2** *(dette, passif)* to discharge

aquaculteur, -trice [akwakyltœr, -tris] **N** fish farmer

aquaculture [akwakyltyr] **NF** aquaculture; *(de poissons)* fish farming

aquaplanage [akwaplanaʒ] **NM** *Aut* aquaplaning

aquaplane [akwaplan] **NM** *Sport* aquaplaning; *(planche)* aquaplane

aquaplaning [akwaplaniŋ] **NM** *Aut* = **aquaplanage**

aquaplaniste [akwaplanist] **N** *Sport* aquaplaner

aquarelle [akwarɛl] **NF** *Beaux-Arts* watercolour, *Am* watercolor; **peindre à l'a.** to paint in watercolours; **une a. de Matisse** a watercolour by Matisse, a Matisse watercolour

aquarelliste [akwarɛlist] **N** watercolourist, *Am* watercolorist

aquarium [akwarjɔm] **NM** aquarium; **a. d'eau de mer** oceanarium

aquatinte [akwatɛ̃t] **NF** aquatint

aquatique [akwatik] **ADJ 1** *(oiseau, plante, sport)* aquatic **2** *(sol)* marshy, watery

aqueduc [ak(ə)dyk] **NM 1** *(construction)* aqueduct **2** *Anat* aqueduct, canal

aqueux, -euse [akø, -øz] **ADJ 1** *(boisson, fruit etc)* watery; *(sol)* waterlogged **2** *Anat, Chimie etc* aqueous, water; **humeur aqueuse** aqueous humour

à quia [akɥija] **ADV** *Litt* **être à.** to be at a loss for words or a reply; **mettre qn à.** to render sb speechless, to nonplus sb

aquiculture [akɥikyltyr] **NF** = **aquaculture**

aquifère [akɥifɛr] **ADJ** *Géol* **nappe a.** aquifer

aquilin [akilɛ̃, -in] **ADJ** *(profil etc)* aquiline; **nez a.** aquiline or hook or Roman nose

aquilon [akilɔ̃] **NM** north wind

Aquin [akɛ̃] **N** **Saint Thomas d'A.** St Thomas Aquinas

aquitain, -aine [akitɛ̃, -ɛn] **ADJ** of or from Aquitaine

N A. *(natif)* native of Aquitaine; *(habitant)* inhabitant of Aquitaine

Aquitaine [akitɛn] **NF** *Hist* (province of) Aquitaine; **bassin d'A.** Basin of Aquitaine

A.R. *(abrév* **aller retour)** return

ara [ara] **NM** *(oiseau)* macaw

arabe [arab] VOIR GRAMMAIRE A19 **ADJ** *(monde, littérature, pays)* Arab, Arabic; *(chiffres, langue etc)* Arabic; *(cheval)* Arab; *(coutumes, civilisation etc)* Arabian, Arabic

NM *Ling* Arabic

N A. Arab

arabesque [arabɛsk] **ADJ** *(architecture etc)* arabesque, Arabian

NF *(danse, ornement)* arabesque; **la fumée monte en arabesques** the smoke curls up

arabica [arabika] **NM** *(café)* arabica

Arabie [arabi] **NF** Arabia; **A. saoudite** Saudi Arabia; **le désert d'A.** the Arabian desert

arabique [arabik] **ADJ** **gomme a.** gum arabic

arabisant, -ante [arabizã, -ãt] **N** Arabic scholar, Arabist

arabisation [arabizasjɔ̃] **NF** Arabization

arabiser [arabize] **VT** to Arabize

arable [arabl] **ADJ** *(terre etc)* arable

arabophone [arabɔfɔn] **ADJ** Arabic-speaking

N Arabic speaker

arachide [araʃid] **NF** *(plante)* peanut, groundnut, *Br Fam* monkey nut; **huile d'a.** groundnut oil; **beurre d'a.** peanut butter

arachnéen, -enne [araknee, -ɛn] **ADJ** *(de l'araignée)* of spiders; *Litt* **légèreté arachnéenne** gossamer lightness; **être d'une légèreté arachnéenne** to be as light as thistledown

arachnides [araknid] **NMPL** *Zool* Arachnida

arachnoïde [araknɔid] **NF** *Anat* arachnoid *(membrane)*

araignée [areɲe] **NF 1** spider; **toile d'a.** cobweb, spider's web; *Fam* **avoir une a. au plafond** to have a screw loose, to have bats in the belfry; *Fig* **a. du matin, chagrin, a. du soir, espoir** = seeing a spider in the morning will bring bad luck, seeing one in the evening will bring good luck **2** *Ordinat* spider

▸▸ *Zool* **a. d'eau** water spider; **a. de mer** *(crustacé)* spider crab; *(poisson)* weever *(fish)*

araire [arɛr] **NM** *Agr* swing or ard plough

araméen, -enne [aramee, -ɛn] **ADJ, NM** *Ling* Aramaic

arasé [araze] **ADJ** flush; **armoire arasée** built-in cupboard

araser [araze] **VT 1** *Constr* **a. un mur** to level (off) a wall; **a. deux pierres** to make two stones flush; **a. une planche** to plane a plank down **2** *Géol (roche)* to erode, to weather

aratoire [aratwar] **ADJ** *(outils, instruments)* agricultural

araucaria [arokarja] **NM** *(arbre)* araucaria, monkey puzzle (tree)

arbalète [arbalɛt] **NF** crossbow

arbalétrier [arbaletrije] **NM 1** *Constr (d'un toit etc)* principal rafter **2** *(soldat)* crossbowman

arbitrage [arbitraʒ] **NM 1** *Sport (au tennis)* umpiring; *(au football)* refereeing; *(dans un conflit social)* arbitration; **conseil d'a.** *(dans un conflit social)* conciliation or arbitration board; **soumettre un litige à l'a. d'un tiers** to take a dispute to arbitration by a third party; *Sport* **erreur d'a.** mistake by the referee or umpire **2** *Banque etc* arbitrage

▸▸ a. de change arbitration of exchange; *Bourse* **a. en reports** jobbing in contango(e)s

arbitragiste [arbitraʒist] **N** *Bourse* arbitrager

arbitraire [arbitrɛr] **ADJ 1** *(nom, choix etc)* arbitrary; *(punition etc)* discretionary **2** *(gouvernement, pouvoir, action etc)* arbitrary, despotic, high-handed; *(ordre)* arbitrary

NM arbitrariness, arbitrary nature; **laisser qch à l'a. de qn** to leave sth to sb's discretion

arbitrairement [arbitrɛrmã] **ADV** arbitrarily

arbitral, -ale, -aux, -ales [arbitral, -o] **ADJ** *Jur* arbitration; **tribunal a.** tribunal, court of arbitration; **solution arbitrale, règlement a.** settlement by arbitration; **commission arbitrale** board of referees

arbitre [arbitr] **NM 1** *Jur* arbitrator, referee, adjudicator **2** *Sport* referee; *Tennis* umpire; **a. de touche** *Ftbl* linesman; *Rugby* touch judge **3** *Fig (de la mode, dans une dispute etc)* arbiter **4** *Phil* **libre a.** free will

▸▸ a. rapporteur *(dans un conflit commercial)* arbitrator

arbitrer [arbitre] **VT 1** *Jur* to arbitrate **2** *Sport (match de football)* to referee; *(match de tennis)* to umpire **3** *Bourse* **a. des valeurs** to do arbitrage trading

arboré [arbɔre] **ADJ** planted with trees

arborer [arbɔre] **VT 1** *(dresser)* to raise, to erect, to set up; *(drapeau)* to hoist; *Naut (mât)* to step; **a. l'étendard de la révolte** to raise the standard of revolt **2** *(porter, exhiber)* **a. une cravate rouge/une rose à la boutonnière** to wear or sport a red tie/a rose in one's buttonhole; **elle arbore un sourire triomphant** she is wearing a triumphant smile; **a. un air de mépris** to affect an air of disdain; **a. certaines idées** to parade certain ideas

arborescence [arbɔresãs] **NF 1** *Bot* arborescence **2** *Ordinat (structure)* tree diagram or structure, directory structure; *(chemin)* directory path; **a. des répertoires** directory tree

arborescent [arbɔresã] **ADJ 1** *Bot* arborescent; **fougère arborescente** tree fern **2** *Math, Ordinat* **structure arborescente** tree diagram or structure, directory structure

arborétum [arbɔretɔm] **NM** *Bot* arboretum

arboricole [arbɔrikɔl] **ADJ 1** *(technique etc)* arboricultural **2** *(animal)* tree-dwelling, arboreal

arboriculteur, -trice [arbɔrikyltœr, -tris] **N** nurseryman, nurserywoman

arboriculture [arbɔrikyltyr] **NF** arboriculture; **a. fruitière** fruit growing

arborisation [arbɔrizasjɔ̃] **NF** *(de cristaux)* arborization; *(du givre sur les vitres)* tree-like markings

arborisé [arbɔrize] **ADJ 1** *Minér* dendritic **2** *Suisse (boisé)* planted with trees

arbouse [arbuz] **NF** arbutus berry

arbousier [arbuzje] **NM** *(arbre)* arbutus; **a. commun** strawberry tree

arbre [arbr] **NM 1** *(végétal)* tree; **jeune a.** sapling; **a. fruitier** fruit tree; **arbres d'agrément** ornamental trees; **a. à feuille(s) caduque(s)** deciduous tree; **a. résineux** softwood (tree); **a. feuillu** hardwood (tree); **a. vert** evergreen (tree); *Fig* **faire l'a. fourchu** to do a headstand *(with one's legs apart)*; *Prov* **entre l'a. et l'écorce, il ne faut point mettre le doigt** don't get involved in other people's affairs; *Fig* **les arbres cachent la forêt** you can't see the wood for the trees; *Fig* **les arbres lui cachent la forêt** he can't see the wood for the trees; *Fig* **couper l'a. pour avoir le fruit** to kill the goose that lays the golden egg SEE GRAMMAR B6

2 *Ordinat* tree; *Math, Ordinat* **structure en a.** tree diagram

3 *Tech* shaft, spindle, axle; *(d'horloge etc)* arbor

▸▸ a. d'accouplement coupling shaft; *Aut* **a. arrière** back axle shaft; **a. à cames** camshaft; *Aut* **a. à cames en tête** overhead camshaft; **a. à caoutchouc** rubber tree; **a. à cardan** ou **de cardan(s)** cardan shaft; **a. coudé** ou **vilebrequin, a.-manivelle** crankshaft; **a. creux** hollow spindle, tubular shaft; **l'a. de la Croix**

the Rood; **a. de culbuteur** rocker shaft; *Mktg* **a. de décision** decision tree; *Aut* **a. de distribution** distributor shaft, camshaft; *Aut* **a. d'entrée** input *or* primary shaft; **a. d'entraînement** drive shaft; *Aut* **a. d'essieu** axle shaft; **a. à excentrique(s)**, **a. excentré** *ou* **excentrique** eccentric shaft; **a. fou** loose shaft; **a. généalogique** family tree; **faire son a. généalogique** to trace one's family tree; **a. de l'hélice**, **a. porte-hélice** propeller shaft; *Élec* **a. d'induit** armature shaft; *Aut* **a. intermédiaire** layshaft, countershaft; **a. de Jessé** tree of Jesse; **a. de Judée** Judas tree; **a. de la liberté** tree of liberty; **a. moteur** *ou* **de commande** main *or* driving shaft; **a. de Noël** Christmas tree; **a. à pain** bread(fruit) tree; **a. de plein vent** standard; *Aut* **a. de pompe** pump shaft; *Aut* **a. primaire** primary *or* input shaft; *Aut* **a. principal** mainshaft, third motion shaft; *Aut* **a. de renvoi** layshaft; *Anat* **a. respiratoire** respiratory system; *Aut* **a. de roue** axle shaft; *Aut* **a. secondaire** secondary shaft, layshaft; *Aut* **a. de sortie** output shaft; **a. de tour** lathe spindle, mandrel; **a. de transmission** line shaft; *Aut* propeller *or* transmission shaft, propshaft; **a. de vie** tree of life

arbrisseau, -eaux [arbriso] NM shrub; **plantation d'arbrisseaux** shrubbery

arbuste [arbyst] NM bush, shrub; **plantation d'arbustes** shrubbery

arc [ark] NM **1** *(arme)* bow; **tir à l'a.** archery; **tirer à l'a.** to do archery; **tu sais tirer à l'a.?** can you use a bow and arrow?; **à la portée de l'a.** within bowshot; **corde de l'a.** bowstring; *Fig* **avoir plusieurs cordes à son a.** to have more than one string to one's bow; **ressort à a.** bow spring; **scie à a.** bow saw **2** *Archit, Anat* arch; **l'a. des sourcils/de l'aorte** the arch of the eyebrows/of the aorta; **a. dentaire** dental arch **3** *Géom* **a. de cercle** arc of a circle; **assis en a. de cercle** sitting in a semicircle **4** *Élec* **a. voltaïque** voltaic arc; **a. électrique** electric arc; **soudure en a.** arc welding; **lampe à a.** arc lamp ▸▸ **a. brisé** *ou* **aigu** gothic arch; **a. en fer à cheval** horseshoe arch; **a. en plein cintre**, **a. roman** semicircular arch; **a. de triomphe** triumphal arch

arcade [arkad] NF **1** *Archit* archway; **a. feinte** blind arch; **arcades** arcade; **se promener sous les arcades** to walk through the arcade **2** *Anat* **a. dentaire/orbitaire** dental/orbital arch; **a. sourcilière** the arch of the eyebrows **3** *Suisse (local commercial)* shop, store

arcadé [arkade] ADJ *(allée, promenade etc)* arcaded

arcane [arkan] NM mystery; **les arcanes de la politique/du pouvoir** the arcane mysteries of politics/of power

arcature [arkatyr] NF *Archit* arcature, blind arcade

arc-boutant, pl arcs-boutants [arkbutɑ̃] NM **1** *Archit* flying buttress **2** *Constr* abutment pier

arc-bouter [arkbute] VT **1** *(mur)* to buttress, to support with flying buttresses **2** *(étayer)* *(mur etc)* to prop up, to shore up ▸ VPR **s'arc-bouter** to brace oneself; **s'a. sur ses jambes** to brace one's legs

arc-doubleau, pl arcs-doubleaux [arkdublo] NM *Archit* transverse rib

arceau, -eaux [arso] NM **1** *(d'une voûte)* arch **2** *(croquet)* hoop; *Méd* (bed)-cradle; *Aut* **a. de sécurité** roll bar, roll-over framework

arc-en-ciel, pl arcs-en-ciel [arkɑ̃sjɛl] NM rainbow

archaïque [arkaik] ADJ *(style, expression etc)* archaic

archaïsant [arkaizɑ̃] ADJ archaistic

archaïsme [arkaism] NM archaism

archange [arkɑ̃ʒ] NM archangel

arche¹ [arʃ] NF *Rel* ark; **l'a. de Noé** Noah's ark; **l'a. d'alliance**, **l'a. sainte** the Ark of the Covenant

arche² NF *(d'un pont etc)* arch; *Géol* **a. naturelle** natural arc

archéologie [arkeɔlɔʒi] NF arch(a)eology

archéologique [arkeɔlɔʒik] ADJ arch(a)eological

archéologue [arkeɔlɔg] N arch(a)eologist

archer [arʃe] NM archer, bowman

archet [arʃɛ] NM **1** *(de violon etc)* bow; **scie à a.** bow saw; **avoir un bon coup d'a.** *(d'un violoniste)* to be a good violinist; *(d'un violoncelliste)* to be a good cellist **2** *Rail* pantograph

archétypal, -ale, -aux, -ales [arketipal, -o] ADJ archetypal

archétype [arketip] ADJ archetypal NM archetype, prototype; **c'est l'a. du père de famille** he is the archetypal father figure

archevêché [arʃəveʃe] NM **1** *(territoire)* archbishopric, archdiocese **2** *(fonction)* archbishopric **3** *(résidence)* archbishop's palace

archevêque [arʃəvɛk] NM archbishop

archiconnu [arʃikɔny] ADJ *Fam* very well known; **c'est a.** everybody knows that

archicube [arʃikyb] NM *Scol Fam* graduate of the École normale supérieure

archidiacre [arʃidjakr] NM *Rel* archdeacon

archidiocèse [arʃidiɔsɛz] NM *Rel* archdiocese, archbishopric

archiduc [arʃidyk] NM archduke

archiduchesse [arʃidyʃɛs] NF archduchess

Archie [arʃi] NM *Ordinat* Archie

archiépiscopal, -ale, -aux, -ales [arʃiepiskɔpal, -o] ADJ archiepiscopal

archiépiscopat [arʃiepiskɔpa] NM archiepiscopate, archiepiscopacy

archifaux, -fausse [arʃifo, -fos] ADJ *Fam* dead wrong

Archimède [arʃimɛd] N *Hist* Archimedes; *Phys* **le principe d'A.** Archimedes' principle; *Tech* **vis d'A.** Archimedean screw

archimillionnaire [arʃimiljɔnɛr] ADJ, N *Fam* multimillionaire

archipel [arʃipɛl] NM *Géog* archipelago

archisec, -sèche [arʃisɛk, -sɛʃ] ADJ *Fam* bone-dry

archisecret, -ète [arʃisəkrɛ, -ɛt] ADJ *Fam* top secret, hush-hush

architecte [arʃitɛkt] N *(d'un immeuble)*, *Fig (d'une réforme)* architect; **a. paysagiste** landscape architect; **a. naval** naval architect; *Ordinat* **a. de réseaux** network architect; **a. urbaniste** town planner

architectonique [arʃitɛktɔnik] ADJ architectonic NF architectonics

architectural, -ale, -aux, -ales [arʃitɛktyral, -o] ADJ architectural

architecture [arʃitɛktyr] NF *(d'une ville, d'un ordinateur etc)* architecture; **a. navale/industrielle/religieuse** naval/industrial/religious architecture; **cette maison a une très belle a.** this house is beautifully designed; *Fig* **l'a. du corps** the way the body is designed, the structure of the body; *Ordinat* **a. client-serveur** client-server architecture; *Ordinat* **a. évolutive** upgradable architecture; *Ordinat* **a. à micro-canaux** microchannel architecture

architecturer [arʃitɛktyre] VT *(discours, roman, texte)* to structure; *Ordinat* **architecturé autour de …** with its architecture built around …

architrave [arʃitrav] NF *Archit* architrave

archivage [arʃivaʒ] NM archiving, filing

archive [arʃiv] NF *Ordinat* archive

archiver [arʃive] VT to archive, to file

archives [arʃiv] NFPL archives, records; **exemplaire des a.** file copy; **les a. nationales** ≃ the (Public) Record Office; **a. audiovisuelles/sonores** audiovisual/sound archives; **a. de coupures de presse** cuttings library; **a. photographiques** photographic archives; *Fam* **ça restera dans les a.** that'll go down in history, wonders will never cease

archiviste [arʃivist] N archivist; *(fonction publique)* keeper of public records; *Com etc* clerk (in charge of records), filing clerk

arçon [arsɔ̃] NM **1** *(de selle)* saddle bow; **vider les arçons** to fall off one's horse; **être ferme sur ses arçons** to be steady in the saddle; *Fig Vieilli Fam* to have fixed opinions; *Gym* **cheval d'arçons** (vaulting) horse **2** *Tex* bow

arçonner [arsɔne] VT *Tex (coton, laine etc)* to card *or* clean with a bow

arctique [arktik] ADJ arctic; **cercle a.** Arctic Circle NM **l'A.** the Arctic

ardemment [ardamɑ̃] ADV *(aimer)* ardently, passionately; *(travailler)* enthusiastically, eagerly; **désirer qch a.** to crave sth; **désirer a. faire qch** to yearn to do sth

Ardennes [arden] NFPL **les A.** the Ardennes; **la Bataille des A.** the Battle of the Bulge

ardent [ardɑ̃] ADJ **1** *(feu etc)* burning hot, scorching, blazing; **soleil a.** scorching *or* blazing sun; **soif ardente** raging thirst; **cheveux d'un blond/roux a.** strawberry *or* reddish blond/fiery red hair; **rouge a.** fiery red **2** *(passionné)* fiery, passionate, ardent; **désir a.** burning desire; **jeune homme a.** hot-blooded *or* passionate young man; **ardente conviction** deep-seated conviction; **j'en ai l'ardente conviction** I am firmly convinced of it; **socialiste a.** red-hot Socialist; **a. sportif** keen sportsman **3** *(vif) (intérêt)* keen; *(imagination)* vivid; *(curiosité)* burning; *Fam (lutte)* fierce; **être dans une colère ardente** to be in a furious rage

ardeur [ardœr] NF **1** *(du soleil, du feu etc)* heat **2** *(enthousiasme)* eagerness, ardour, *Am* ardor, fervour, *Am* fervor; **cheval plein d'a.** high-spirited *or* high-mettled horse; **travailler avec a.** to work hard *or* enthusiastically; **soutenir son opinion avec a.** to argue one's case with passion *or* passionately; **modère tes ardeurs!** calm down!, don't get excited!; **les ardeurs de la passion** the heat of passion; **son a. à lire** his passion for reading

ardoise [ardwaz] NF **1** *Minér* slate; **(feuille d')a.** slate; **maison au toit d'ardoises** house with a slate roof; **couvrir un toit d'a.** to slate a roof **2** **a. (à écrire)** (writing) slate; *Fam (compte)* bill, cost; **crayon d'a.** slate pencil; *Fam* **mets ça sur mon a.** put it on my slate *or* bill *or* tab; *Fam* **il a des ardoises dans tous les bars de la ville** he owes money in all the bars in town; *Fam* **j'ai quelques ardoises a régler** I've got a few bills to pay; *TV, Cin* **a. d'identification** identifying head slate; *Ordinat* **a. électronique** notepad computer ADJ **(couleur) gris a.** slate grey (colour)

ardoisé [ardwaze] ADJ slate-colour(ed), bluish-grey

ardoisier, -ière [ardwazje, -jɛr] ADJ slaty; **schiste a.** slate clay, shale NM *(exploitant)* owner of a slate quarry; *(ouvrier)* slate worker *or* quarryman NF **ardoisière** slate quarry

ardt *abrév* arrondissement

ardu [ardy] ADJ **1** *(tâche etc)* difficult, hard, arduous **2** *Rare (pente etc)* steep

are [ar] NM *Agr* are (= 100 *square metres*)

arec [arɛk] NM **1** areca palm (tree) **2 (noix d').** areca *or* betel nut

areligieux, -ieuse [arəliʒjø, -jøz] ADJ not religious

aréna [arena] NF *Can* arena

arène [arɛn] NF **1** (*d'amphithéâtre*) arena; (*de tauromachie*) bullring; **les arènes d'Arles** the amphitheatre of Arles; *Fig* **descendre dans l'a.** to enter the ring *or* the fray, to take up the challenge; *Fig* **l'a. politique** the political arena **2** *Arch, Litt* sand

arénicole [arenikɔl] ADJ that lives in sand

aréole [areɔl] NF *Anat, Bot, Méd* areola

aréomètre [areɔmɛtr] NM hydrometer

aréométrie [areɔmetri] NF hydrometry

aréopage [areɔpaʒ] NM *Fig* learned gathering *or* assembly

arête [arɛt] NF **1** (*de poisson*) (fish) bone; **c'est du poisson pané, garanti sans arêtes** it's breaded fish, guaranteed boneless; **enlever toutes les arêtes d'un poisson** to bone a fish; **poisson plein d'arêtes** bony fish; **grande a.** (*d'un poisson*) backbone; **dessin en a. de hareng** *ou Archit* **de poisson** herringbone pattern **2** (*du nez*) bridge **3** *Constr etc* line; **a. d'un comble** hip of a roof; **pierre d'a.** quoin stone; **a. de voûte** groin **4** *Aviat* **dorsale** (*du fuselage*) dorsal fin **5** *Géog* ridge **6** (*de graminées etc*) beard **7** (*de la lame d'une épée, d'une baïonnette*) ridge, rib

argent [arʒɑ̃] NM **1** (*métal*) silver; **vaisselle d'a.** (silver) plate; **couverts en a.** silver cutlery; **a. en feuille** silver foil, silver leaf; **bijoux en a.** silver jewellery; *Prov* **la parole est d'a., le silence est d'or** speech is silver, silence is golden; *Sport* **gagner la médaille d'a.** to win the silver (medal); *Fig* **cheveux d'a.** silvery(-grey) hair; **reflets d'a. sur le lac** silvery glints on the lake
2 *Fin* money; **avoir de l'a.** (*être riche*) to have money; (*sur soi*) to have some money; *Compta* **a. en caisse** cash in hand; (*recettes*) takings; **payer a. comptant** to pay (in) cash; *Fam* **se faire un a. fou** to make lots *or* loads of money; **placer son a.** to invest one's money; **les puissances de l'a.** the rich and powerful; **a. à bon marché** cheap money; *Fig* **l'a. lui fond entre les mains** money just slips through his fingers; **elle le fait pour l'a.** she does it for the money; **attendre une rentrée d'a.** to be waiting for money to come in; *Fig* **jeter de l'a. par les fenêtres** to throw money down the drain, to throw money away; **en avoir pour son a.** to have *or* get one's money's worth, to get good value for (one's) money; *Fig* **plaie d'a. n'est pas mortelle** money isn't everything, it's only money; *Fig* **prendre tout pour a. comptant** to take everything at face value; **le temps, c'est de l'a.** time is money
▸▸**a. électronique** e-cash, electronic money; **a. liquide** cash (in hand), ready money *or* cash; **a. de poche** pocket money; **a. à vue** call money

argenté [arʒɑ̃te] ADJ **1** (*couleur*) silver, silvery; **gris a.** silver-grey; **reflet a.** silvery glint, glint of silver; **renard a.** silver fox **2** (*plaqué, couvert*) silver-plated **3** *Fam* (*riche*) well-heeled, loaded; **je ne suis pas très a. en ce moment** I'm not in funds at the moment, I'm a bit hard up at the moment, I'm a bit strapped at the moment

argenter [arʒɑ̃te] VT to silver(-plate); *Fig* **la lune argente le lac de ses reflets** the moon gives the lake a silvery sheen

argenterie [arʒɑ̃tri] NF (silver) plate, silverware

argenteur [arʒɑ̃tœr] NM silverer, silver plater

argentier [arʒɑ̃tje] NM **1** (*meuble*) silver ca-

binet **2** *Hist* = superintendent of the Royal Household **3** *Fam* **le Grand a.** (*ministre*) the Finance Minister

argentin[1] [arʒɑ̃tɛ̃] ADJ (*voix, rire, vagues*) silvery; (*cloche*) tinkling

argentin[2]**, -ine** [arʒɑ̃tɛ̃, -in] ADJ Argentinian, Argentine; **la République Argentine** Argentina, the Argentine (Republic)
▸N **A.** Argentinian, Argentine
▸NF **l'Argentine** Argentina, the Argentine (Republic)

argile [arʒil] NF clay; **a. à blocaux** boulder clay; **a. schisteuse** shale; **traitement par l'a.** mud-pack treatment; **masque d'a.** mud-pack; **a. cuite** terracotta, earthenware; *Fig* **une statue** *ou* **un colosse aux pieds d'a.** an idol with feet of clay

argileux, -euse [arʒilø, -øz] ADJ clayey

argon [argɔ̃] NM *Chimie* argon

argonaute [argɔnot] NM **1** *Myth, Fig* Argonaut **2** (*mollusque*) argonaut, paper nautilus

argot [argo] NM slang; **parler a.** to talk (in) slang; **mot d'a.** slang word; **l'a. (parisien)** Paris(ian) slang; **a. des voleurs** thieves' cant; **a. du milieu** underworld slang; **a. scolaire** school slang

> **Argot**
> This term can refer both to "la langue verte" (the slang of the underworld) or the jargon of particular social or professional groups (such as butchers, soldiers, students etc). Some "argot" has evolved from being part of the secret language of a select group to becoming part of everyday speech, while other terms have become obsolete, supplanted by **verlan** (*see box at this entry*), the slang used by young people in the suburbs of big cities.

argotique [argɔtik] ADJ (*langue*) slangy; **expression a.** (*propre à un milieu*) cant phrase; (*familière*) slang expression

argotisme [argɔtism] NM slang expression

arguer [arg(ɥ)e] (**j'argue** [ʒargy] *or* [nuzargyjɔ̃]) VT **1** *Litt* to infer, to assert, to deduce; **que peut-il a. de ce fait?** what can he deduce *or* infer from this fact?, what conclusion(s) can he draw from this fact?; **il argue qu'on ne l'avait pas prévenu** his excuse is that he was not informed **2** *Jur* **a. une pièce de faux** to assert a deed to be forged
▸VI **a. de qch** to give sth as a reason; **elle argua du manque d'informations fournies** she argued that insufficient information had been provided

argument [argymɑ̃] NM **1** (*démonstration*) argument; **tirer a. de qch** to use sth as an argument; **a. de vente** selling point; **arguments de vente** sales pitch **2** (*d'un livre etc*) outline, summary; (*d'un article, d'un film*) synopsis **3** *Math* argument

argumentaire [argymɑ̃tɛr] NM (sales) blurb; *Com* **rédiger un a.** to draw up a list of selling points; **l'a. est très convaincant** the sales pitch is very convincing

argumentateur, -trice [argymɑ̃tatœr, -tris] *Péj* ADJ argumentative
▸N arguer

argumentation [argymɑ̃tasjɔ̃] NF **1** argument; **une a. serrée** a series of closely argued points **2** *Com* sales pitch

argumenter [argymɑ̃te] VI to argue (**contre** against); *Fam* to be argumentative; **on ne peut pas a. de ce fait** you can't base an argument on that fact; **discours/démonstration bien argumenté(e)** well-argued speech/demonstration

Argus [argys] NM **1** *Myth* Argus **2 l'A. (de l'Automobile)** = guide to used car prices; **être/**

ne plus être coté à l'**A.** to be listed/not be listed any more in the guide to used car prices; **acheter/vendre qch à l'A.** to buy/sell sth for the book price

argutie [argysi] NF quibble; **mettre fin à des arguties** to stop quibbling

aria [arja] NF *Mus* aria

aride [arid] ADJ (*pays, sujet*) arid, dry, barren; (*œuvre*) dry; (*cœur*) unfeeling; **une imagination a.** an unfertile imagination

aridité [aridite] NF aridity, aridness, barrenness; **l'a. d'un sujet** the dryness *or* aridity of a topic

arien, -ienne [arjɛ̃, -jɛn] ADJ Aryan
▸N **A.** Aryan

ariette [arjɛt] NF *Mus* arietta, ariette

aristo [aristo] N *Fam* nob, toff

aristocrate [aristokrat] N aristocrat

aristocratie [aristokrasi] NF aristocracy

aristocratique [aristokratik] ADJ aristocratic

Aristote [aristɔt] N *Phil* Aristotle; **la logique d'A.** Aristotelian logic

aristotélicien, -ienne [aristɔtelisjɛ̃, -jɛn] ADJ, N *Phil* Aristotelian

arithméticien, -ienne [aritmetisjɛ̃, -jɛn] N arithmetician

arithmétique [aritmetik] ADJ arithmetical
▸NF **1** (*matière, calculs*) arithmetic; **a. en virgule fixe** fixed point arithmetic; **a. en virgule flottante** floating point arithmetic SEE GRAMMAR A77; B59 **2** (*livre*) arithmetic book

arlequin [arləkɛ̃] NM *Théâtre* Harlequin; **habillé en a.** in Harlequin costume; **manteau d'a.** proscenium arch

arlequinade [arləkinad] NF *Théâtre* harlequinade; *Fig* (piece of) buffoonery

arlésien, -ienne [arlezjɛ̃, -jɛn] ADJ Arlesian, of *or* from Arles
▸N **A.** (*natif*) native of Arles; (*habitant*) inhabitant of Arles; *Fig* **c'est l'Arlésienne!** (*d'une femme*) does this girl really exist?; (*d'un homme*) does this man really exist?

armada [armada] NF *Hist* armada; **l'Invincible A.** the Invincible Armada; *Fig Fam* **une a. de photographes** an army of photographers

armagnac [armaɲak] NM Armagnac

armailli [armaji] NM *Suisse* shepherd

armateur [armatœr] NM *Naut* (*d'un navire, d'une expédition*) fitter-out; (*propriétaire*) shipowner

armature [armatyr] NF **1** (*dans le béton*) reinforcement; (*d'une poutre etc*) truss; (*d'une fenêtre etc*) frame, brace; (*d'un soutien-gorge*) underwired bra; *Fig* **l'a. de nos principes moraux** the basis *or* the underpinnings of our moral principles **2** (*d'un câble électrique*) armouring, sheathing **3** *Élec* (*d'un aimant, d'une petite dynamo, d'un magnétophone*) armature; (*d'un condensateur*) plate; **a. de soupape/de pompe** valve/pump gear **4** *Mus* key signature

arme [arm] NF **1** arm, weapon; (*en escrime*) sword; **salle d'armes** armoury; (*d'escrime*) fencing school; **l'a. du crime** the murder weapon; **port d'a.** carrying of weapons; **porter une a. sur soi** to carry a weapon; **prendre le pouvoir par les armes** to take power by force; **nation en** *ou* **sous les armes** nation in arms; **prendre les armes** to take up arms, to rise up in arms (**contre** against); *Mil* to parade under arms; **déposer les armes** to lay down one's arms, to surrender; **porter les armes** to be a soldier; *Mil* **aux armes!** to arms!, guard turn out!; **le métier** *ou* **la carrière des armes** the military profession, soldiering; **suspension d'armes** cessation of hostilities; **frères d'armes** brothers in arms; **place d'ar-**

mes parade ground; **passer qn par les armes** to send sb to the firing squad; **sans armes** unarmed; *Fig* **passer l'a. à gauche** to snuff it, to kick the bucket; *(dans un accident)* to cop it; *Fig* **il fait ses premières armes** he's earning his spurs; *Fig* **fournir des armes à qn** to provide sb with ammunition; *Fig* **le cynisme est son a. favorite** cynicism is his favourite weapon; *Fig* **l'indépendance est une a. à double tranchant** independence is a two-edged sword; *Fig* **la télévision est l'a. absolue des politiciens** television is the politician's ultimate weapon; *Fig* **à armes égales** on equal terms; *Fig* **avec armes et bagages** (with) bag and baggage

2 *(section de l'armée)* arm, branch, service; **a. de l'infanterie** infantry; **douze mille hommes de toutes armes** twelve thousand men of all arms *or* services

3 *Hér* armes (coat of) arms

▶▶ **a. atomique** atomic weapon; **a. biologique** biological weapon; **a. blanche** knife; **combat à l'a. blanche** knife fight; **a. chimique** chemical weapon; **armes classiques** conventional weapons; **armes conventionnelles** conventional weapons; **armes de destruction massive** weapons of mass destruction; **a. de dissuasion** deterrent; **a. à feu** firearm; **a. non classique** non-conventional weapon, advanced weapon; **a. non conventionnelle** non-conventional weapon, advanced weapon; **a. nucléaire** nuclear weapon; **armes portatives** small arms; **armes traditionnelles** conventional weapons

armé [arme] ADJ **1** armed; **troupe armée** body of troops; **vol à main armée** hold-up, armed robbery; **animal a. de piquants/d'une carapace** animal with spines/a shell; **a. d'une canne/d'un dictionnaire/d'un guide touristique** armed with a stick/a dictionary/a guidebook; **a. jusqu'aux dents** armed to the teeth; **sortir a. de chez soi** to go out carrying a weapon; *Fig* **être bien/mal a. pour partir dans la vie** to be well/badly equipped to make one's way in the world; *Fig* **mes enfants partiront armés dans le monde du travail** my children will be well qualified to find a job **2** *(renforcé)* fortified, strengthened; **poutre armée** trussed beam; **béton a.** reinforced concrete; **verre a.** wired glass **3** *(arme à feu)* cocked; **pistolet à demi a.** pistol at half cock

NM **à l'a.** *(arme à feu)* cocked

armée [arme] NF **1** *Mil* army; **partir à l'a.** to join the army; *(pour faire son service militaire)* to start one's military service; **a. de métier** professional *or* regular army; **a. d'occupation** army of occupation; **lever une a.** to raise an army; **a. permanente** standing army; **a. régulière** *ou* **active** regular army; **l'a. de terre** the army, the land forces; **l'a. de l'air** the air force; **l'a. de mer** the navy, the naval forces; **a. de secours** relieving army; **les armées alliées** the allied armies *or* forces; **être dans l'a.** to be in the army; **la 8ème a.** the 8th army; **le Dieu des armées** the Lord of Hosts; **groupe d'a.** army group VOIR GRAMMAIRE A11 **2** **l'A. du salut** the Salvation Army **3** *(foule)* **quelle a. d'incapables!** what a shower (of incompetents)!; **toute une a. de fonctionnaires** a whole army of officials; **une a. d'insectes ravageurs** an army of marauding insects

armement [arməmã] NM **1** *(d'une armée)* *(action)* arming, equipping; *(équipement)* armament, equipment; *(armes)* **armements** armaments, weaponry; **officier d'a.** ordnance officer; **vente d'armements** sale of arms; **la vente d'armements a diminué** arms sales have decreased; **réduction des armements** arms reduction; **course aux armements** arms race

2 *(d'une poutre etc)* strengthening, bracing; *(d'un câble etc)* sheathing

3 *Naut (action)* commissioning, fitting out; *(équipement)* equipment, gear, stores; **mettre un navire en a.** to put a ship in commission; **port d'a.** port of registry

4 *(en personnel)* manning

5 *Com (profession)* merchant shipping

6 *(d'un fusil)* loading; *(d'un fusible)* arming; *(d'un appareil photo etc)* setting; *(d'une arme à feu chargée)* cocking; *(d'une machine etc)* mounting, fitting up

Arménie [armeni] NF Armenia

arménien, -ienne [armenjɛ̃, -jɛn] ADJ Armenian

NM *Ling* Armenian

N **A.** Armenian

armer [arme] VT **1** *(munir d'armes) (soldats)* to arm (**de** with); **je sors toujours armé** I always carry a weapon when I go out; *Fig* **a. qn contre les difficultés de la vie** to equip sb to deal with the difficulties of life; *Fig* **il est armé d'un solide bagage universitaire** he's equipped with a good university education; *Fig* **cette position l'arme de tous les pouvoirs** this job puts him in a position of real power

2 *(ville)* to fortify; *(solive)* to strengthen, to brace; *(dynamo)* to wind; *(câble)* to sheathe, to armour; **a. du béton** to reinforce concrete **3** *Naut (navire)* to equip, to fit out, to commission; *(bateau etc)* to man; *(cabestan)* to rig; **a. les avirons** to ship the oars **4** *(fusible)* to arm; *(appareil)* to set; *(arme à feu)* to cock; *(canons, pompe)* to man; *(machine, artillerie)* to mount; *(machine)* to fit up; **a. son appareil photo** to set one's camera **5** *Hist* **a. qn chevalier** to knight sb **6** *Mus* **a. la clef** *(d'un morceau de musique)* to put the key signature

VI *Naut* **le navire arme à Brest** the ship is being commissioned at Brest; **a. sur un navire** to serve on a vessel

VPR **s'armer** to arm oneself; *Fig* **je me suis armé de mon livre préféré pour attendre** I armed myself with my favourite book to read while I waited; *Fig* **s'a. de courage/de patience** to summon up (one's) courage/patience

armistice [armistis] NM armistice; *(temporaire)* truce; **journée** *ou* **anniversaire de l'A.** Armistice Day, Remembrance Day, *Am* Veterans' Day

armoire [armwar] NF *(placard)* cupboard, *surtout Am* closet; *(pour les vêtements)* wardrobe, *surtout Am* closet; **a. à linge** linen cupboard; **a. à provisions** store cupboard; **a. à pharmacie** medicine chest *or* cabinet; **a. frigorifique** cold store; **a. de toilette** *ou* **de salle de bain** bathroom cabinet; **a. ignifugée** fireproof cabinet; **a. à fournitures** stationery supplies cupboard; **a. de cuisine** kitchen cupboard; **a. normande** large wardrobe; **a. à glace** mirrored wardrobe; *Fig Hum* **c'est une a. à glace** he's built like a tank

armoiries [armwari] NFPL *Hér* (coat of) arms, armorial bearings

armorial, -iale, -iaux, -iales [armɔrjal, -jo] ADJ armorial

armoricain, -aine [armɔrikɛ̃, -ɛn] ADJ Armorican; **massif a.** Armorican massif

N *Hist* **A.** Armorican, ancient Breton

Armorique [armɔrik] NF Armorica

armoriste [armɔrist] NM heraldic artist

armure [armyr] NF **1** *(cuirasse etc)* armour; *(d'animaux)* defence; **a. complète** suit of armour; **a. d'un navire de guerre** armour (plating) of a warship; *Fig* **cette insolence est une a., elle s'en protège** she uses insolence as a defence mechanism **2** *Tex* weave, pattern, design; **a. toile** plain weave **3** *Élec (d'une dynamo)* pole piece, armouring; *(d'un câble)* sheathing **4** *Mus* key signature

armurier [armyrje] NM **1** *(fabricant etc)* arms manufacturer; *(de pistolets etc)* gunsmith; *(vendeur)* gun dealer **2** *Mil etc* armourer

ARN [aɛrɛn] NM *(abrév* **acide ribonucléique***)* RNA

arnaque [arnak] NF *Fam* swindle, rip-off; **attention à l'a.!** be careful you don't get ripped off!; **c'est de l'a.!** what a rip-off!

arnaquer [arnake] VT *Fam* to cheat, to swindle, to rip off; **se faire a.** to get ripped off

arnaqueur, -euse [arnakœr, -øz] N *Fam* swindler, rip-off merchant

arnica [arnika] NF *Bot, Pharm* arnica

arobase [arɔbaz] NF at-sign

aromate [arɔmat] NM *(herbe)* herb; *(épice)* spice

aromathérapie [arɔmaterapi] NF *Méd* aromatherapy

aromatique [arɔmatik] ADJ **1** aromatic; *(saveur)* spicy; **plantes aromatiques** aromatic plants **2** *Chimie* **carbures aromatiques** aromatics

aromatisation [arɔmatizasjɔ̃] NF *Chimie* aromatization

aromatiser [arɔmatize] VT **1** *Culin* to flavour, *Am* to flavor; **aromatisé à la vanille** vanilla-flavoured **2** *Chimie* to aromatize

arome, arôme [arom] NM aroma; *(goût)* flavour, *Am* flavor; **crème glacée, a. vanille** vanilla flavour ice cream

aronde [arɔ̃d] NF *Menuis* queue d'a. dovetail; **assembler qch en queue d'a.** to dovetail sth

arpège [arpɛʒ] NM *Mus* arpeggio

arpéger [arpeʒe] VT *Mus* **a. un accord** to play a chord in *or* as an arpeggio

arpent [arpã] NM *Hist* arpent (= one acre)

arpentage [arpãtaʒ] NM surveying, land measuring; **faire l'a. d'un terrain** to measure a piece of ground

arpenter [arpãte] VT **1** *(terre)* to survey, to measure **2** *(parcourir rapidement)* **a. le terrain** to stride over the ground; **il arpentait le quai** he was pacing up and down the platform

arpenteur [arpãtœr] NM (land) surveyor

arpion [arpjɔ̃] NM *Arg (pied)* hoof; *(orteil)* toe; **tu vas quand même pas te laisser marcher sur les arpions par ce minable?** you're not going to let that pathetic specimen walk all over you, surely?

arqué [arke] ADJ arched, curved; *(poutre etc)* cambered; *(nez)* high-bridged; *(cheval)* bandy-legged; **jambes arquées** bow legs

arquebuse [arkəbyz] NF (h)arquebus

arquebusier [arkəbyzje] NM *(soldat)* (h)arquebusier

arquer [arke] VT *(bois, fer etc)* to bend, to arch, to curve; *(surface)* to camber; **a. le dos** to arch one's back

VI **1** *(fléchir)* to bend, to sag, to buckle **2** *Fam (marcher)* to walk; **je ne pouvais plus a.** *(j'étais épuisé)* I couldn't walk another step, I couldn't put one foot in front of the other

VPR **s'arquer** to bend, to become bent *or* arched

arr *abrév* = **arrt**

arrachage [araʃaʒ] NM *(des plantes etc)* pulling up, uprooting; *(des pommes de terre)* lifting; *(d'une dent, d'un clou etc)* pulling out, extraction; *(en imprimerie)* picking

arraché [araʃe] NM *Sport (en haltérophilie)* snatch; *Fig* **obtenir un accord à l'a.** to obtain a deal after much effort; *Fig* **gagner à l'a.** to snatch a victory

arrache-agrafes [araʃagraf] NM INV staple remover

arrache-clou, *pl* **arrache-clous** [araʃklu] NM claw hammer

arrachement [araʃmã] NM **1** (d'un arbre etc) uprooting **2** Fig (déchirure) wrench; **l'a. du départ** the wrench of leaving; **nous ne pouvons quitter Paris sans a.** it will be a wrench leaving Paris **3** Constr toothing **4** (en mécanique) tearing, wrenching, stripping; **effort d'a.** wrenching force **5** Méd etc wrench

arrache-moyeu, pl **arrache-moyeux** [araʃmwajø] NM Aut **a. universel** universal hub puller

arrache-pied (d') [daraʃpje] ADV without interruption, relentlessly; **travailler d'a.** to work steadily; (excessivement) to slave away

arracher [araʃe] VT **1** (enlever) to pull out; (arbre) to pull up, to uproot; (pommes de terre) to lift; Fig (argent, promesse, secret) to extract (**de** from); (dent) to extract, to pull out; (affiche) to tear down, to pull down; **a. qch à qn/des mains de qn** to snatch sth from sb/from sb's hands; Fig **on est quand même parvenu à lui a. quelques paroles** we did manage to get a few words out of him; Fig **nous sommes parvenus à lui a. cet aveu** we managed to extract that confession from him; **se faire a. une dent** to have a tooth extracted or out; **a. les yeux à qn** to tear sb's eyes out; Fig **j'avais envie de lui a. les yeux** I wanted to strangle him; Fig **il faut a. son masque** we/they/etc must unmask him

2 (déchirer) **cela m'arrache le cœur** it breaks my heart; très Fam **la tequila pure, ça arrache la gueule!** pure tequila will blow your head off!; très Fam **ça t'arracherait la gueule de dire merci/de t'excuser** it wouldn't kill you to say thanks/to apologize

3 Fig (personne) **a. qn de son foyer** (armée d'occupation, police) to drag or uproot sb from his home; **a. qn à la mort** to snatch or rescue sb from the jaws of death; **a. qn au sommeil** to rouse sb from (his) sleep; **la sonnerie du réveil m'a arraché du lit** the alarm dragged me out of bed; **a. qn à son travail/à la télé** to tear or drag sb away from his work/the TV

VI **1** Arg (alcool fort, piment) **ça arrache!** that's dynamite!

2 Can **en a.** to have difficulties

VPR **s'arracher** (se déchirer) Fig **je n'y comprends rien, je m'arrache les cheveux!** I don't understand it at all, I'm tearing my hair out!; Fig **c'est à s'a. les cheveux!** it's enough to make you tear your hair out!; Fig **tout le monde la demande, on se l'arrache** she's very much in demand, they're even fighting over her; **on se l'arrache** (d'un livre etc) copies are being snatched up; Fig **impossible de m'a. de ce pays** I could never tear myself away from this country; Fig **s'a. à sa rêverie** to wake from one's daydream; Arg **alors, on s'arrache?** time to go?

arrache-roulement, pl **arrache-roulements** [araʃrulmã] NM Aut **a. universel** universal bearing puller

arracheur, -euse [araʃœr, -øz] N (de pommes de terre etc) lifter; Fig **mentir comme un a. de dents** to lie through one's teeth

NF Agr **arracheuse** (outil) grubbing plough, grubber; (de pommes de terre) (potato) lifter; (de betteraves) (beet) puller

arrachoir [araʃwar] NM Agr (de pommes de terre) (potato) lifter; (de betteraves) (beet) puller

arraisonnement [arɛzɔnmã] NM Naut (d'un navire) boarding; **a. de la patente (d'un navire)** examination of the bill of health, sanitary report

arraisonner [arɛzɔne] Naut VT **a. un navire** to hail a vessel; (l'aborder) to stop and examine a ship

VI **a. avec les autorités du port** to report to the port authorities

arrangeant [arãʒã, -ãt] ADJ accommodating, helpful

arrangement [arãʒmã] NM **1** (fait d'arranger) arranging, putting in order; (manière d'être arrangé) (du mobilier etc) arrangement; **l'a. des fleurs dans un vase** the arrangement of flowers in a vase; **l'a. de ses cheveux demande un soin constant** his hairstyle demands constant attention; **l'a. des mots dans une phrase** the word order in a sentence **2** Mus **a. pour violon** arrangement for violin **3** (accord) agreement, settlement; (officieux) understanding; **mal prendre ses arrangements** to arrange or plan things badly; **sauf a. contraire** unless otherwise agreed; **essayer de trouver un a. financier avec son banquier** to try to come to (some kind of) an arrangement with one's banker; Jur **a. à l'amiable** out of court settlement

arranger [arãʒe] (j'**arrangeais;** n. **arrangeons**) VT **1** (meubles etc) to arrange; (livres, pièce) to put in order; (pièce) to tidy (up); (cravate etc) to straighten; Fam **le voilà bien arrangé!** what a mess he looks!; **ils l'ont drôlement arrangé, il a des bleus partout** they've given him a good going over, he's covered in bruises; **a. qn de la belle manière** (physiquement, en dire du mal) to have a go at sb; Fam **on vous a arrangé** (volé) you've been had or done, you've been ripped off; **voilà un bouge où on vous arrange le client** it's a rip-off joint; Arg **se faire a.** (tuer) to get bumped off

2 (voiture, montre etc) to repair, to overhaul; (montre) to mend; **je vais t'a. ça** I'll fix it for you

3 (concert etc) to arrange, to organize; **a. qch d'avance** to arrange or plan sth in advance; **il arrange bien sa vie** he's got his life well organized; **je vous ai arrangé un entretien avec lui** I've arranged a meeting with him for you; **ne t'en fais pas, j'ai tout arrangé** don't worry, I've made all the arrangements

4 (conflit etc) to settle; **je vais essayer d'a. les choses** I'll try to put things right; **cela n'arrangera rien** that won't (be much) help; **cela n'arrange pas nos affaires** that's no good (to us), that doesn't help (us)

5 (plaire à, satisfaire) (personne) to suit, to be convenient for; **ça t'arrangerait que je vienne te chercher?** would it suit you or would it be convenient if I came to collect you?; **faire qch pour a. qn** to do sth to help sb; **on ne peut pas a. tout le monde** you can't please everybody; **tu ne fais que ce qui t'arrange** you only do what suits you; **ça t'arrange?** does that suit you?

6 Mus (morceau pour violon etc) to arrange

VPR **s'arranger 1** (s'organiser etc) to manage; **si vous pouvez vous a. pour le voir** if you can manage to see him or make the time to see him; **arrangez-vous pour être là** make sure you're there; Fam **je ne sais pas comment tu t'arranges, mais tu es toujours en retard** I don't know how you manage it, but you're always late

2 (se contenter) **il s'arrange de tout** he's very adaptable; **s'a. d'un vieux lit** to make do with an old bed

3 (sa tenue, son apparence) to tidy oneself up; **tu as vu comment tu t'es arrangé!** have you seen the state you're in?!

4 (se mettre d'accord) **s'a. avec qn** to come to an agreement or to terms with sb; **arrange-toi avec elle, elle peut peut-être te prêter sa voiture** sort things out with her, maybe she can lend you her car; **arrangez-vous** settle it among yourselves; **on s'est arrangé à l'amiable** we came to an amicable arrangement or agreement

5 (s'améliorer) to work out; **cela s'arrangera** things will turn out all right; **cela s'arrangera**

tout seul that will sort itself out; **ça ne s'arrange pas!** it's not getting any better!; **elle ne fait rien pour s'a.** she doesn't do anything to make the most of herself; **ça n'a pas l'air de s'a. entre eux** things don't seem to have got any better between them

arrangeur, -euse [arãʒœr, -øz] N Mus arranger

arrérages [areraʒ] NMPL **1** (de salaires, du loyer etc) arrears **2** (intérêt) back interest; **coupon d'a.** interest or dividend warrant

arrestation [arɛstasjɔ̃] NF arrest; **procéder à l'a. de qn** to arrest sb; **mettre qn en état d'a.** to place sb under arrest; **en état d'a.** under arrest; **a. préventive/provisoire** custodial/conditional arrest

arrêt [arɛ] NM **1** (interruption) stop, stoppage, stopping; **a. de travail** (grève) stoppage; (congé) sick leave; (certificat) doctor's or medical certificate; **être en a. de travail** to be on sick leave; **a. maladie** sick leave; **être en a. maladie** to be on sick leave; **véhicule à l'a.** stationary vehicle; **a. d'urgence** emergency stop; **point d'a.** stopping place or point; Mus (pendant une pause) pause; **faire un a. au cours de son voyage** to break one's journey, to stop over; **nous avons fait plusieurs arrêts pendant le voyage** we made several stops during the journey; **a. en cours de route** break of journey, stopover; **trajet sans a.** non-stop journey; **New York est un a. obligatoire** New York is an absolute must; **il neige sans a. depuis mercredi** it's been snowing non-stop or continuously since Wednesday; **la machine tombe sans a. en panne** the machine is constantly or continually breaking down; **c'est ce que je lui dis sans a.** that's what I tell him over and over again; **dix minutes d'a.** ten minutes' stop; (pour café, repos etc) ten minutes' break; **temps d'a.** pause, halt; **chien d'a.** setter, pointer; Fig **rester** ou **tomber en a. devant qn/qch** to stop and stare at sb/sth; **marquer un temps d'a.** to pause, to halt, to mark time; **a. de paiement** stoppage of payment(s); **a. des comptes** closing (off) the accounts; Méd **a. du cœur** heart failure; **a. (inopiné)** breakdown; Radio, TV **a. d'émission** break in transmission; Ordinat **a. de fin de session** shutdown; TV, Cin **a. sur image** freeze frame, stop frame; **faire un a. sur image** to freeze a frame; Ordinat **a. anormal du système** system crash; Ordinat **a. de défilement** scroll lock; Ordinat **a. de l'impression** (commande) stop printing

2 (de bus etc) **a. de bus** bus stop; **a. facultatif** request stop; **ne pas descendre avant l'a.** do not get off before the bus/train/etc has come to a complete stop; **le train est sans a. jusqu'à l'aéroport** the train goes non-stop to the airport

3 (d'une porte etc) stop, catch; (d'un verrou) tumbler; **cran d'a.** safety catch; **a. de pied** toeclip

4 Jur (prononcé par la cour d'assises, cour d'appel ou cour de cassation) judgment, adjudication; **prononcer** ou **rendre un a.** to pronounce or deliver judgment; **a. par défaut** judgment by default; **a. de défense** stay of execution; **a. de mort** death sentence; Fig **les arrêts de la Providence** the decrees of Providence; Fig **les arrêts de la mode** the dictates of fashion

5 (arrestation) arrest; **ordre** ou **mandat d'a. (d'une personne)** warrant for the arrest; **mettre un officier aux arrêts** to put an officer under arrest; **arrêts à la chambre, arrêts domestiques** house arrest; **être en maison d'a.** to be in prison, to be under or to be held in detention

6 (saisie) seizure, impounding, attachment; **faire a. sur des marchandises** to impound or seize goods

7 *Ftbl* tackle; *Rugby* **a. de volée** mark; **faire un a. de volée** to make a mark **8** *Naut (d'un navire)* detention

arrêt-court, *pl* **arrêts-courts** [arɛkur] NM *Can Sport* shortstop

arrêté [arete] ADJ **1** *(idées etc)* fixed, decided; **homme aux opinions arrêtées** dogmatic man, man with set ideas; *(décidé)* man with decided views; **c'est une chose arrêtée** it's already been decided; **dessein a.** settled design **2** *Sport* **départ a.** standing start
  NM **1** *Admin* decision, order, decree; **a. ministériel** departmental order (signed by a minister); **a. municipal** by-law; **a. préfectoral** by-law; **a. d'exécution** = decree providing for the enforcement of a law **2** *Com* **a. de compte(s)** closing off of an account

arrêter [arete] VT **1** *(stopper) (personne)* to stop; *(véhicule)* to bring to a stop or to a standstill; *(appareil)* to turn off; *(fuite)* to stem; *Ordinat* to halt; *(système)* to shut down; **là je vous arrête, je ne suis pas d'accord!** stop right there, I don't agree!; **tu pourrais m'a. au bureau de tabac?** could you drop me off at the tobacconist's?; **a. un cheval** to pull up a horse; **rien ne l'arrêtera** nothing will stop him, he will stop at nothing; **quel obstacle vous arrête?** what's stopping you?; **a. le vent** to break (the force of) the wind; *Aut* **a. le moteur** to switch off the engine; **a. la croissance** to arrest growth; **le brouillard/la neige a complètement arrêté toute circulation** fog/snow has brought traffic to a (complete) standstill; *Ftbl* **a. un tir** to save or stop a shot; **a. le gibier** *(d'un chien)* to point game
  2 *(fixer) (volet, planche etc)* to fix, to fasten, to secure; *Fig* **a. l'attention** to draw or catch attention; *Fig* **je voudrais a. votre attention sur ce point** I'd like to draw your attention to this point; *Fig* **ce détail arrêta mon attention** this detail caught my attention; *Couture* **a. un point** to fasten off a stitch; *Tricot* **a. les mailles** to cast off
  3 *(criminel)* to arrest, to seize; *(contrebande, livres etc)* to seize; **l'assassin n'a pas encore été arrêté** the murderer is still at large
  4 *(déterminer)* to decide; **a. un jour** to fix or appoint a day; **la date n'a pas encore été arrêtée** the date has not yet been decided on or fixed; **a. un prix** to fix a price; **a. un programme/un projet** to draw up a programme/plan; **il a été arrêté que la séance débuterait à 14 heures** it has been decided that the meeting will begin at 2 o'clock; **a. un marché** to close a deal
  5 *Com (compte)* to make up, to close (off)
  VI to stop, to halt; **dites au chauffeur d'a. devant l'hôtel de ville** tell the driver to stop at or in front of the town hall; **elle n'arrête jamais de parler** she never stops talking; **elle est toujours occupée à laver, elle n'arrête pas** she's always washing something or other, she never stops; **arrête!, arrêtez!** stop (it)! that's enough!
  VPR **s'arrêter 1** *(s'immobiliser)* to stop, to come to a stop or a standstill; *(d'un corps mobile)* to come to rest; *Ordinat (système)* to shut down; **s'a. court** to stop short; **ma montre s'est arrêtée** my watch has stopped; **la voiture s'est arrêtée** the car stopped or pulled up; *(en s'approchant)* the car drew up; **s'a. en route** to break one's journey; **nous nous sommes arrêtés dans un village pittoresque** we stopped in a picturesque village; **s'a. chez qn** to call at sb's house/*etc*; **passer sans s'a.** to pass without stopping
  2 *(cesser)* to stop; **la pluie va s'a.** the rain will stop or it will stop raining soon; **s'a. de faire qch** to stop doing sth; **s'a. de fumer** to give up smoking
  3 *(faire attention à)* to fix one's attention (**à**

qch on sth), to dwell, to insist (**à qch** on sth); **il ne faut pas s'a. aux apparences** one should not go by appearances

arrhes [ar] NFPL deposit; **verser des a.** to pay a deposit; **stipulation d'a.** = right to annul a sale by paying a fine

arriération [arjerasjɔ̃] NF *Psy* **a. mentale** retardation; *(d'un enfant etc)* backwardness

arrière [arjɛr] ADV **1 en a.** *(à une certaine distance)* behind; **rester en a.** *(ne pas aller, sortir)* to remain or stay behind; *(en se promenant avec d'autres personnes)* to lag behind; *Naut* **avoir le vent en a.** to have the wind astern; **en a. de qn/qch** behind sb/sth; **il est resté en a. de sa classe** he stayed at the bottom of the class; **en a. de son siècle** *ou* **de son temps** behind the times
  2 *(en retard)* **locataire en a. pour ses loyers** tenant in arrears with his/her rent
  3 *(derrière)* backwards; **a.!** (stand) back!; **a., Satan!** get thee behind me, Satan!; **cheveux en a.** hair brushed or combed back, hair swept back; **revenir en a.** to come back; *Fig* **j'ai l'impression de revenir en a., c'est tout à fait comme dans mon enfance** I feel like I've gone or stepped back in time, it's exactly how it was in my childhood; **pencher la tête en a.** to lean one's head back; **retourner en a.** to go or turn back; *Fig* **il faut remonter loin en a. pour trouver une épidémie de ce genre** you have to go back a long way (in history) to find such an epidemic; *Fig* **vous revenez en a., nous avons déjà parlé de ça** you're going (back) over previous ground, we've already talked about or covered that; *Fig* **pas la peine de revenir en a., c'est oublié** there's no point in looking back, it's all been forgotten; **regarder en a.** to look back; *Naut* **en a. (à) toute (vitesse)!** full speed astern!
  ADJ INV back; **faire marche a.** to reverse, to back; *Naut* **faire marche** *ou* **machine a.** to go astern; *Fig* to back down, to backtrack; *Aut* **où est la marche a.?** where is reverse (gear)?; *Aut* **essieu a.** back or rear axle; **lunette a.** rear window; **feu a.** rear light; **à moteur a.** rear-engined; **siège** *ou* **banquette a.** *(d'une voiture)* back seat; *Couture* **point a.** backstitch
  NM **1** *(d'une maison etc)* back, back part, rear; *Aut* tail; **assis à l'a. de la voiture** sitting in the back of the car; *Aut* **un modèle tout à l'a.** a rear-engined model
  2 *Naut (d'un navire)* stern; **vers l'a.** aft; **sur l'a.** astern; **aller à l'a.** to go aft
  3 *Mil* **l'a.** the rear; *Fig* **protéger ses arrières** to protect one's rear, to leave oneself a way out
  4 *Ftbl* (full) back; *Rugby* full back; *Ftbl* **a. gauche** left back; **à l'a.** at full back

arriéré, -ée [arjere] ADJ **1** *(dû)* late, behind, in arrears; **paiement a.** overdue or outstanding payment **2** *(dépassé, démodé)* **être a.** *(d'une personne)* to be behind the times; **idées arriérées** old-fashioned ideas; *Écon* **pays arriérés** underdeveloped or backward countries **3** *(attardé) (enfant)* backward
  NM *(d'un compte etc)* arrears; *(de travail, d'une correspondance etc)* backlog; **a. du loyer** rent arrears, arrears of rent; **a. d'impôts** tax arrears, back taxes; **il y a un a. de 5000 euros** 5,000 euros are still outstanding; **avoir des arriérés** to be in arrears; *Mil* **a. de solde** back pay; **a. de permissions** accumulated leave
  N backward or retarded person

arrière-ban, *pl* **arrière-bans** NM *Fig* **tout le monde était là, le ban et l'a.** they were all there, the world and his wife; **le ban et l'a. de LVMH** the entire LVMH clan

arrière-bassin, *pl* **arrière-bassins** NM inner dock

arrière-bouche, *pl* **arrière-bouches** NF back of the mouth, *Spéc* fauces

arrière-boutique, *pl* **arrière-boutiques** NF back shop, *Am* back store

arrière-cour, *pl* **arrière-cours** NF backyard

arrière-cuisine, *pl* **arrière-cuisines** NF scullery, back kitchen

arrière-défense, *pl* **arrière-défenses** NF *Ftbl* (the) back four (defence), the backs

arrière-fond, *pl* **arrière-fonds** NM innermost depth(s)

arrière-garde, *pl* **arrière-gardes** NF *Mil* rearguard; *Naut* rear squadron; *Fig* **c'est un professeur d'a.** he's a teacher of the old guard

arrière-gorge, *pl* **arrière-gorges** NF back of the throat; **voix d'a.** throaty voice

arrière-goût, *pl* **arrière-goûts** NM *aussi Fig* aftertaste (**de** of); **ce vin a un a. de fruit** this wine leaves a fruity aftertaste

arrière-grand-mère, *pl* **arrière-grands-mères** NF great-grandmother

arrière-grand-oncle [arjɛrgrɑ̃tɔ̃kl], *pl* **arrière-grands-oncles** [arjɛrgrɑ̃zɔ̃kl] NM great-great-uncle

arrière-grand-père, *pl* **arrière-grands-pères** NM great-grandfather

arrière-grands-parents NMPL great-grandparents

arrière-grand-tante, *pl* **arrière-grands-tantes** NF great-great-aunt

arrière-main, *pl* **arrière-mains** NM *Tennis etc* **(coup d')a.** backhand (stroke)
  NF *(d'un cheval)* (hind)quarters

arrière-neveu, *pl* **arrière-neveux** NM great-nephew

arrière-nièce, *pl* **arrière-nièces** NF great-niece

arrière-pays NM INV hinterland

arrière-pensée, *pl* **arrière-pensées** NF ulterior motive

arrière-petite-fille, *pl* **arrière-petites-filles** NF great-granddaughter

arrière-petite-nièce, *pl* **arrière-petites-nièces** NF great-great-niece

arrière-petit-fils, *pl* **arrière-petits-fils** NM great-grandson

arrière-petit-neveu, *pl* **arrière-petits-neveux** NM great-great-nephew

arrière-petits-enfants [arjɛrpətizɑ̃fɑ̃] NMPL great-grandchildren

arrière-plan, *pl* **arrière-plans** NM *aussi Ordinat* background; **à l'a.** in the background; *(derrière, en arrière)* at the back; *Théâtre* upstage; *Fig* **ce projet est passé à l'a.** this plan has been put on the back burner; *Fig* **mettre qch à l'a.** to put sth on the back burner; *Fig* **rester à l'a.** to remain in the background; **se trouver relégué à l'a.** to be pushed into the background; *Théâtre, Fig* to be upstaged

arrière-pont, *pl* **arrière-ponts** NM *Naut* afterdeck

arrière-port, *pl* **arrière-ports** NM inner harbour

arriérer [arjere] (**j'arrière,** n. **arriérons; j'arriérerai**) VT *(paiement etc)* to postpone, to delay, to defer
  VPR **s'arriérer** to fall into arrears

arrière-saison, *pl* **arrière-saisons** NF **1** late season, late autumn or *Am* fall **2** *Agr* **les pêches sont chères dans l'a.** peaches are expensive at the end of the season

arrière-salle, *pl* **arrière-salles** NF back room

arrière-train, *pl* **arrière-trains** NM *(d'un animal)* (hind)quarters; *Fam (d'une personne)* rump, rear

arrimage [arimaʒ] NM *Naut etc* **1** (*du chargement d'un navire etc*) stowing; **bois d'a.** dunnage **2** (*chargement*) stowage **3** (*d'une navette spatiale*) docking

arrimer [arime] VT **1** *Naut etc* (*cargaison etc*) to stow **2** (*fixer*) to secure *or* fasten; **a. un chargement sur le toit d'une voiture** to secure *or* fasten a load to the roof of a car ▪ VI *Astronaut* to dock

arrimeur [arimœr] NM *Naut* stevedore

arrivage [arivaʒ] NM (*de marchandises*) consignment; **nous attendons un a. (de produits) venant de France** we're expecting a consignment *or* delivery from France; *Iron, Péj* **t'as vu le nouvel a.?** (*vacanciers etc*) have you seen the new arrivals *or* the new lot?; *Fin* **a. de fonds de l'étranger** accession of funds from abroad

arrivant, -ante [arivã, -ãt] N arrival; **le dernier a.** the last person to arrive; **les nouveaux arrivants** the new arrivals, the newcomers

arrivé, -ée [arive] ADJ **être a.** (*socialement*) to have made it in society; **il fait très quadragénaire a.** he looks a real forty-something nouveau riche
▪ N (*personne*) **un nouvel a.** a newcomer, a new arrival; **le dernier a.** the last (person) to arrive; **le dernier a. a un gage!** = last one there's a cissy!

arrivée [arive] NF **1** (*de personne etc*) arrival, coming; (*d'une situation, d'une nouvelle étape*) advent; **on attend son a. pour la semaine prochaine** he/she is expected to arrive next week; **depuis son a. au pouvoir** since his coming to power; **depuis son a. à la direction** since he joined the management; **a. matinale** early morning arrival; **a. tardive** late arrival; **à mon a.** when I arrived; **arrivées** arrivals; **tableau des arrivées** arrivals board; **heures d'a.** (*du courrier*) times of delivery; **l'a. du printemps** the coming *or* arrival *or* onset of spring; **l'a. de nouveaux produits sur le marché** the arrival of new products onto the market **2** *Tech* inlet; (*pour la vapeur etc*) intake, admission; **a. (d'huile)** (oil) feed; *Aut* **a. d'essence** petrol inlet; *Aut* **a. de carburant** fuel inlet **3** *Sport* (winning) post, finish; **ligne d'a.** finishing line

arriver [arive] VI (*aux* être) **1** (*parvenir à destination*) to arrive, to come; (*dans un hôtel*) to arrive, to check in; **a. en voiture** to come by car; **a. par le train/le bateau** to come by train/boat; **il est arrivé en courant** he came running up; **il arrive de voyage** he is just back from a journey; **a. chez soi** to arrive home, or to be get home; **a. à temps** to arrive *or* to be on *or* in time; **a. en retard** to be late; **a. le premier** to be the first to arrive, to come *or* be first; **a. dans les premiers** to be among the first to finish; **le printemps est arrivé!** spring is here!, spring has arrived!; **l'avion devait a. à midi** the plane was due at midday; **j'arrive!** (I'm) coming!, I'll be with you in a moment!, I'll be right there!; **c'est à cette heure-là que tu arrives?** and what time do you call this to be turning up?; **arrive (vite)!** hurry up!; **nous sommes presque arrivés** we're almost there; **mangeons, ça la fera peut-être a.** let's start eating, maybe that'll make her come
2 a. à un endroit to reach *or* get to *or* arrive at a place; **a. à quai** to berth, to dock; **a. à bon port** to arrive safely; **le paquet m'est arrivé trop tard** the parcel reached me too late; **l'eau m'arrive aux chevilles** the water comes up to my ankles; **ma fille m'arrive déjà à l'épaule** my daughter comes up to my shoulder already; **ses cheveux lui arrivent aux épaules** her hair comes down to her shoulders *or* is shoulder-length; **le bruit arrivait jusqu'à ma chambre** the noise reached

my bedroom; *Fig* **elle ne lui arrive pas à la cheville** she's not in the same class as him, he's head and shoulders above her
3 j'en étais arrivé là quand … I had got to that point when …; **j'en arrive à me demander s'il n'est pas stupide** I'm beginning to wonder whether he's stupid or something; *Fam* **si c'est pas malheureux d'en a. là!** it's such a pity to be reduced to that!, what a pity it's come to that!; **en a. aux coups** to come to blows
4 (*socialement*) to succeed; **c'est un homme qui arrivera** he is a man who will succeed *or* get on *or* do well
5 (*parvenir à un but*) to succeed; **a. à ses fins** to succeed in one's aims *or* plans; **avec du courage on arrive à tout** with courage one can achieve anything; **a. à faire qch** to succeed in doing sth; **je n'arrive pas à le faire toute seule** I can't do *or* manage it on my own; **pour a. à le lui faire accepter, tu devras être patient** to get him to accept it, you'll just have to be patient; **je n'arrive pas à y croire** I just can't believe it; **j'arrive au même résultat que tout à l'heure** I get the same result as before; *Fig* **a. à la vérité** to arrive at *or* get at the truth; *Fig* **a. au fait** to come to the point; **et pour ma voiture? – j'y arrive** what about my car? – I'm (just) coming to that; **tu n'y arriveras pas!** you'll never do it!; **comment y a.?** how can it be done?; **tu n'arriveras jamais à rien!** you'll never amount to anything!, you'll never get anywhere in life!; *Fam* **tu y arrives?** can you do *or* manage *or* get *or* make it?; **a. à échéance** to fall due; (*d'un bail*) to expire; (*d'un prêt*) to mature
6 (*se produire*) to happen, to occur; **ça t'est déjà arrivé?** has that ever happened to you (before)?; **cela arrive tous les jours** it happens every day; *Prov* **un malheur n'arrive jamais seul** misfortunes never come singly; **ça n'arrive qu'aux autres** it's something that happens to other people; **cela ne nous arrivera jamais** it will never happen to us; **cela n'arrive qu'à nous!** just our luck!; **il lui est arrivé un accident** he had an accident; **je ne voudrais pas qu'il lui arrive quelque chose** I don't want anything to happen to him; **cela arrive à tout le monde** it can happen to anyone; **quoi qu'il arrive** whatever happens, whatever may happen, come what may; **devine ce qu'il m'arrive!** guess what!, guess what's happened (to me)!; **mais qu'est-ce qu'il t'arrive en ce moment?** what's wrong with you at the moment?; **il m'arrive souvent d'oublier** I often forget, I'm apt to forget; **il nous arrive rarement d'aller au restaurant** we rarely go to restaurants; **il pourrait a. qu'il se trompe** he might have made a mistake, it could be that he's made a mistake; **s'il vous arrivait de la voir, dites-le-lui** if you (should) happen to see her, tell her SEE GRAMMAR B29

arrivisme [arivism] NM *Péj* pushiness, ambitiousness

arriviste [arivist] N *Péj* careerist

arrogance [arɔgãs] NF arrogance; **parler avec a.** to speak arrogantly

arrogant, -ante [arɔgã, -ãt] ADJ arrogant, overbearing
▪ N arrogant person

arroger (s') [sarɔʒe] VPR (**je m'arrogeai(s); n. n. arrogeons**) **s'a. un droit/un privilège** to assume *or* claim a right/a privilege

arrondi [arɔdi] ADJ **1** rounded, round; **visage a.** round face; **chiffre a.** rounded-off number **2** *Ling* **voyelle arrondie** rounded vowel
▪ NM **1** roundness, rounded form; (*d'une bordure etc*) round-off; *Aviat* fillet, fillet radius; **l'a. du visage** the round shape *or* roundness of the face **2** *Aviat* flare out; **atterrissage avec a.** flared landing **3** (*d'une jupe*) hemline

arrondir [arɔdir] VT **1 a. qch** to round sth (off), to make sth round; **la grossesse commence à a. son ventre** her pregnancy is beginning to make her stomach swell; **cette coupe de cheveux arrondit ton visage** that haircut makes your face look round(er); **a. une jupe** to level a skirt; **a. son bras** to flex one's (arm) muscles; **les yeux arrondis par l'étonnement** in wide-eyed astonishment; *Fig* **a. les angles** to smooth down the rough edges, to smooth things over
2 *Ling* **a. une voyelle** to round a vowel
3 *Fin etc* (*vers le haut*) to round up; (*vers le bas*) to round down; **a. sa fortune** to amass a considerable sum of money; *Fam* **a. ses fins de mois** to supplement one's income; **a. une somme/un poids** to round off a sum/a weight; **vous pouvez a. à 200 euros** you can round it up to 200 euros; **a. à l'euro supérieur/inférieur** to round up/down to the nearest euro; **a. son champ** to add to *or* to round off one's land; *Math* **a. un résultat** to correct a result (to the nearest whole number *or* to so many decimal places)
4 *Naut* **a. un cap** to round *or* double a cape
5 *Aviat* (*avant l'atterrissage*) to flare out
▪ VPR **s'arrondir** to become rounded; (*du visage*) to round out, to fill out; **pendant la grossesse, elle s'est arrondie** she swelled up during her pregnancy; **son visage s'est arrondi** his face has become round(er) *or* has filled out; **sa fortune s'arrondit** his fortune is growing

arrondissement [arɔdismã] NM **1** *Admin* (à Paris, Marseille, Lyon) = administrative district **2** (*d'un territoire etc*) rounding (off)

> ### Arrondissement
> In Paris, Lyons and Marseilles, the number of the "arrondissement" corresponds to the last two figures in a postcode: thus, you can tell from the postcode 75012 that it refers to the 12th arrondissement of Paris.

arrosage [arozaʒ] NM **1** (*des plantes*) watering; (*d'une pelouse etc*) sprinkling, spraying; *Culin* (*de la pâte etc*) wetting, moistening; *Fam* **un bon a.** a good soaking; **a. des rues** watering of the streets; **voiture d'a.** water cart; **tuyau d'a.** hose **2** (*publicité*) bombardment, flood; **l'a. continuel par les médias** the constant media bombardment **3** (*d'un pré*) irrigation **4** (*du vin etc*) watering, diluting **5** *Mil* heavy bombing *or* shelling

arroser [aroze] VT **1** (*rues, plantes*) to water; (*pelouse*) to sprinkle, to spray; *Culin* **a. un rôti** to baste a joint; *Fam* **j'ai été bien arrosé** I got soaking wet; **vous allez vous faire a.** you're going to get soaked; **ville très peu arrosée** town with little rainfall; **repas (abondamment) arrosé de vin** meal washed down with (plenty of) wine; **café arrosé** laced coffee; *Vieilli* **visage arrosé de larmes** face bathed in tears
2 a. une prairie to irrigate a meadow; **rivière qui arrose une région** river that waters a district; **la Seine arrose Paris** the Seine flows through Paris
3 (*vin, lait*) to water down, to dilute
4 (*de la publicité*) to bombard
5 *Mil* **a. une ville** to bomb *or* shell a town; **a. des troupes de projectiles** to spray the troops with missiles
6 *Fig Fam* (*soudoyer*) **a. qn pour obtenir qch de lui** to grease sb's palm to get sth from him; **on a dû l'a. pour qu'il accepte** we had to bribe him into accepting
▪ VPR **s'arroser 1 ça ne s'arrose pas** (*plante*) it doesn't need watering **2 ça s'arrose!** that calls for a drink!

arroseur [arozœr] NM (*appareil*) sprinkler;

Fig **c'est (le gag de) l'a. arrosé** the boot's on the other foot

arroseuse [aʁozøz] NF *(de rue)* water(ing) cart, street sprinkler

arrosoir [aʁozwaʁ] NM watering can

arrt *abrév* arrondissement

ARS [aɛʁɛs] NF *abrév* allocation de rentrée scolaire

arsenal, -aux [aʁsənal, -o] NM **1** *Mil* arsenal; **a. maritime** *ou* **de la marine** naval dockyard **2** *(dépôt d'armes)* **a. d'artillerie** gun factory; **découverte d'un a. chez un particulier** discovery of an arsenal of weapons in sb's house **3** *Fam (attirail)* gear, paraphernalia; **un a. d'outils** a whole range of tools; **il emporta son a. de drogues** he took his whole stock of drugs with him; **l'a. des lois** the weight of the law

arsenic [aʁsənik] NM *Chimie* arsenic

art [aʁ] NM **1** *(technique)* art, craft; **l'a. militaire** *ou* **de la guerre** the art of war; **l'a. oratoire** (the art of) public speaking; **l'a. culinaire** the art of (good) cooking; **dans les règles de l'a.** by the book, according to the rules
2 *(esthétique)* art; **l'a. pour l'a.** art for art's sake; **pour l'amour de l'a.** for art's sake; **a. égyptien/italien** Egyptian/Italian art; **l'a. antique/baroque/de la Renaissance** antique/baroque/Renaissance art; **musée d'a. contemporain** museum of modern art; **beaux-arts** fine arts; *Beaux-Arts, Fig* **œuvre d'a.** work of art; **l'a. poétique** poetics; **ville d'a.** city of artistic interest; **livre d'a.** art book; **histoire de l'a.** history of art; **c'est du grand a.!** it's a work of art!
3 le septième/le huitième/le neuvième a. cinema/television/cartoons; **cinéma d'a. et d'essai** art cinema
4 *(savoir-faire)* **l'a. de ...** the art of ...; **elle a l'a. des soirées réussies** she's got a flair *or* a knack for organizing successful parties; **les Français ont l'a. de vivre** French people know how to live *or* how to enjoy life; **il a l'a. et la manière pour parler aux femmes** he has a way with women; *Fam* **il a l'a. de m'énerver** he's got a gift for getting up my nose
5 *(adresse)* skill; **faire qch avec a.** to do sth skilfully
6 *Can Scol* **maître ès arts** Master of Arts
7 *Constr* **travaux** *ou* **ouvrages d'a.** civil engineering structures *or* works
▸▸**a. déco** art deco; **a. dramatique** dramatic art; **a. du feu** ceramics; **a. nouveau** art nouveau; **l'a. sacré** *ou* **religieux** religious art; **arts décoratifs** decorative arts; **arts graphiques** graphic arts; **arts martiaux** martial arts; **arts plastiques** fine arts; **a. vidéo** video art

Arte [aʁte] N = French-German cultural TV channel

artefact [aʁtefakt] NM artefact, artifact

artère [aʁtɛʁ] NF **1** *Anat* artery; **a. aorte** aorta; **a. pulmonaire** pulmonary artery; **on a l'âge de ses artères** you're as old as you feel **2** *Fig* artery; *(route etc)* main highway, arterial road; *(en ville)* main thoroughfare

artériel, -ielle [aʁteʁjɛl] ADJ *Physiol* arterial; **tension artérielle** blood pressure

artériole [aʁteʁjɔl] NF *Anat* arteriole

artériosclérose [aʁteʁjɔskleʁoz] NF *Méd* arteriosclerosis, hardening of the arteries

artésien, -ienne [aʁtezjɛ̃, -jɛn] ADJ *(puits)* Artesian

arthrite [aʁtʁit] NF *Méd* arthritis; **a. sèche** *ou* **déformante** rheumatoid arthritis

arthritique [aʁtʁitik] *Méd* ADJ arthritic; N arthritic (patient), sufferer from arthritis

arthro- [aʁtʁo] PRÉF arthro-

arthropode [aʁtʁɔpɔd] NM arthropod

arthrose [aʁtʁoz] NF *Méd* osteoarthritis

Arthur [aʁtyʁ] N *Fam* **je vais me faire appeler A.!** I'll catch it!

artichaut [aʁtiʃo] NM *(légume)* globe artichoke; *Culin* **fonds d'artichauts** artichoke hearts; *Fig* **c'est un cœur d'a.** he/she flits from one affair to another

artiche [aʁtiʃ] NM *Fam* dough, bread, *Br* dosh, *Am* bucks

article [aʁtikl] NM **1** *Com* article, commodity; **articles** goods, wares; **articles de luxe** luxury goods; **a. en réclame** special offer; **nous ne suivons** *ou* **faisons plus cet a.** we don't stock that item any more; **articles de voyage** travel goods; **articles de ménage** household requisites; **articles de bureau** office supplies; **articles de toilette** toiletries; **articles pour hommes/femmes** menswear/ladies' wear; **a. bas de gamme** bottom of the range item; **a. démarqué** markdown; **a. haut de gamme** top of the range item; **a. de marque** branded article; **a. à forte rotation** fast mover; **articles de consommation** consumables, consumer goods; **faire l'a.** to make a sales pitch; *Mktg* **a. d'appel** traffic builder; *Mktg* **a. de caisse** check-out display item
2 *(d'une facture etc)* item; *(de compte)* entry; **articles divers** sundries
3 *(dans un journal etc)* article; **a. de journal** newspaper article; *Journ* **a. de tête** editorial, leader, leading article; **un a. de dictionnaire** a dictionary entry; *Journ* **a. clé en main** rip 'n' read article; *Journ* **a. d'appel** lead(ing) story; *Journ* **a. de fond** feature (article); *Journ* **a. nécrologique** obituary; *Journ* **a. principal** lead(ing) story, main feature
4 *(d'un traité etc)* article, clause; *(sujet)* point; **il est très ferme sur cet a.** he's very strict about that *or* on that point; **a. de foi** article of faith
5 *(point critique)* critical point; **ce qu'il a dit à l'a. de la mort** what he said just before he died; **être à l'a. de la mort** to be at the point of death
6 *Entom* joint
7 *Gram* **a. défini/indéfini** definite/indefinite article SEE GRAMMAR A5–8; B3–5
8 *Ordinat (dans base de données)* record; *(commande)* command; **a. 'annuler'** undo command; **a. contrasté** highlighted command; **a. de menu** command, menu item

articulaire [aʁtikylɛʁ] ADJ *Anat* articular, articulatory; *Méd* **rhumatisme a.** rheumatoid arthritis

articulation [aʁtikylasjɔ̃] NF **1** *Anat etc* joint, *Spéc* articulation; *Bot* node; *Anat* **a. du doigt** knuckle; **a. à** *ou* **par emboîtement** ball-and-socket joint **2** *Tech* connection, joint; **accouplement à a.** jointed coupling; **a. à rotule** ball-and-socket joint **3** *(prononciation)* articulation **4** *(organisation)* **l'a. des idées d'un texte** the structuring of ideas in a text **5** *Jur (des faits)* numeration

articulé [aʁtikyle] ADJ **1** articulate(d), jointed; *(membre, articulation etc)* hinged; **poupée articulée** doll with movable joints; *Tech* **courroie articulée** chain *or* link belt **2** *Ling (discours)* articulate

articuler [aʁtikyle] VT **1** *(assembler)* to articulate, to hinge, to link, to joint; **a. des idées dans un texte** to organize ideas in a text **2** *Ling* to articulate; *Fig (dire)* **il n'a même pas pu a. son nom, tant il était terrorisé** he was so afraid, he couldn't even say his own name **3** *Jur (faits)* to enumerate, to set forth; *(fait)* to state clearly *or* definitely
VPR **s'articuler** to be joined together; **la façon dont les os s'articulent** the way the bones are joined together; **ces deux parties s'articulent assez bien** the two parts of the text hang together well; **son raisonnement s'articule autour d'un point central** his argu-

ment is based on a central point; *Ling* **le j espagnol s'articule dans le fond de la gorge** the Spanish j is pronounced in the back of the throat
VI to articulate; **mal a.** to mumble; **articule!** speak clearly!, *Fml* articulate!

artifice [aʁtifis] NM **1** *(ruse)* trick, contrivance; **user de tous les artifices pour ...** to resort to every trick (in the book) in order to ...; **les artifices de la toilette** the little tricks women use to make themselves (look) beautiful **2** *(pyrotechnique)* **pièce d'a.** firework

artificialité [aʁtifisjalite] NF artificiality

artificiel, -ielle [aʁtifisjɛl] ADJ **1** *(non naturel)* *(lumière, fleurs, goût etc)* artificial; *(lac)* artificial, man-made; *(perle etc)* imitation; *(dent etc)* false; *Fig (personne)* artificial, false; **jambe artificielle** artificial leg; **colorant a.** artificial colouring; **rire a.** forced laugh **2** *(arbitraire)* arbitrary; **classification artificielle** arbitrary classification

artificiellement [aʁtifisjɛlmɑ̃] ADV artificially; *(arbitrairement)* arbitrarily

artificier [aʁtifisje] NM *(fabricant)* firework manufacturer; *(dans un feu d'artifice)* master of ceremonies

artificieusement [aʁtifisjøzmɑ̃] ADV *Litt* deceitfully, craftily

artificieux, -ieuse [aʁtifisjø, -jøz] ADJ *Litt* deceitful, wily

artillerie [aʁtijʁi] NF **1** artillery, ordnance; **a. de campagne** field artillery; **a. légère/lourde** light/heavy artillery; **a. navale** naval artillery; **a. motorisée** motorized artillery; **a. antichars,** *Belg* **a. anti-blindés** anti-tank artillery; **a. antiaérienne** anti-aircraft artillery; **a. d'assaut** assault artillery *or* guns; **tir d'a.** artillery fire; **pièce d'a.** artillery cannon; *Aut* **roue type a.** artillery type wheel **2** *(collectif)* gunnery

artilleur [aʁtijœʁ] NM artilleryman, gunner

artimon [aʁtimɔ̃] NM *Naut* **(mât d')a.** mizzenmast; **voile d'a.** mizzen (sail); **a. de cape** storm mizzen

artisan, -ane [aʁtizɑ̃, -an] N artisan, craftsman, *f* craftswoman; *Fig* **il est l'a. de sa réussite** he brought about his own success, he's the author *or* architect of his own success

artisanal, -ale, -aux, -ales [aʁtizanal, -o] ADJ **métier a.** craft; **production artisanale** small-scale production (by craftsmen); **magasin a.** craft shop; **poterie artisanale** handmade pottery; **fait de façon artisanale** made in the traditional way; **leur maison d'édition est restée très artisanale** their publishing house has remained very small-scale

artisanalement [aʁtizanalmɑ̃] ADV **fait a.** hand-crafted, made by craftsmen

artisanat [aʁtizana] NM *(profession)* craft industry; **l'a. indigène** the native craftsmen; **encourager l'a.** to encourage small-scale industry *or* the craft industries; **a. d'art** arts and crafts; **produits d'a. régional** local handicrafts

artiste [aʁtist] N **1** *(esprit créatif)* artist; *Fig* **avoir une sensibilité d'a.** to have an artistic temperament, to be artistic; **c'est un a., il a une mentalité d'a.** he's a real eccentric; *Fig* **eh l'a.! viens par là!** hey, smarty pants! come over here! **2** *Théâtre, Mus* performer; *Théâtre* actor, *f* actress; *(chanteur)* singer; *(danseur)* dancer; **a. peintre** painter; **représentation** *ou* **vue d'a.** artist's impression; **entrée des artistes** stage door
ADJ *(tempérament, style)* artistic; **se donner un genre a.** to try to look all arty

> Il faut noter que le terme anglais **artist** désigne un peintre, un dessinateur ou un sculpteur.

artistement [artistəmā] ADV artistically

artistique [artistik] ADJ artistic

artistiquement [artistikmā] ADV artistically

arum [arɔm] NM *(fleur)* arum

arvine [arvin] NF *Suisse* = grape variety from the Valais canton, and white wine produced from these grapes

aryen, -enne [arjɛ̃, -ɛn] ADJ Aryan
N A. Aryan

AS *abrév* assurances sociales

as [ɑs] NM **1** *Cartes etc* ace; **amener deux as** to throw two aces; **as de pique** ace of spades; *Culin Fam (dans la volaille)* parson's nose; *Fig Fam* **être ficelé** *ou* **fichu comme l'as de pique** to be dressed any old how; *Fig Fam* **être coiffé comme l'as de pique** to have hair like a bird's nest; *Arg Fig* **être aux as** *ou* **plein aux as** to be rolling (in it); *Fam* **ma prime est passée à l'as** my bonus never materialized; *Fam* **les vacances sont passées à l'as** that's the holidays out of the window **2** *(dominos)* one; **l'as blanc** one blank **3** *Fam (champion)* ace; *(aux jeux)* crack player, star; **au tennis c'est un as** he's an ace at tennis; **as du volant** *ou* **de la route** crack (racing) driver, ace driver; **Pierre c'est un as, il sait tout faire** Pierre's ace, he can do anything

a/s *(abrév* **aux soins de***)* c/o

asbeste [azbɛst] NM *Minér* asbestos

asbestose [azbɛstoz] NF *Méd* asbestosis

ASBL [aɛsbeɛl] NF *(abrév* **association sans but lucratif)** non-profit-making organization, *Am* not-for-profit organization

ascendance [asɑ̃dɑ̃s] NF **1** *Astron* ascent **2** *(de famille etc)* ancestry; **l'une et l'autre famille avaient une a. canadienne** both families were of Canadian ancestry *or* descent; **a. maternelle** ancestry on his/her/*etc* mother's side; **être d'a. noble** to be of noble ancestry **3** *Phys* **a. thermique** thermal (current)

ascendant [asɑ̃dɑ̃] ADJ *(mouvement, courant, échelle, série)* ascending; *(mouvement etc)* upward; *Aviat* **vol a.** climbing flight; **course ascendante** *(d'un piston)* up stroke; **tuyau a.** standpipe
▸ NM **1** *Astron etc* ascendant; **astre qui est à l'a.** star in the ascendant **2** *(influence)* ascendancy, influence; **avoir de l'a. sur qn** to have influence over sb; **elle subit l'a. de son mari** she's dominated by her husband **3** **ascendants** *(famille)* ancestry **4** *Astrol* rising sign; **Verseau a. Cancer** Aquarius with Cancer as his rising sign *or* with Cancer in the ascendant

ascenseur [asɑ̃sœr] NM **1** lift, *Am* elevator; **a. de marchandises** goods hoist; **a. de service** service lift; **a. à bagages** baggage lift; **a. à tous les étages** lift to all floors; **a. à sas** canal lift; *Fig* **renvoyer l'a.** to return the favour **2** *Ordinat* scroll box

ascension [asɑ̃sjɔ̃] NF **1** *(montée, escalade)* ascent; *Aviat* climb; **faire l'a. d'une montagne** to climb a mountain; **une a. facile** an easy climb; **l'a. du mont Blanc** the climbing *or* ascent of Mont Blanc; *Aviat* **angle d'a.** climbing angle; *Aviat* **a. verticale** vertical climb; *Astron* right ascension; *Rel* **fête** *ou* **jeudi de l'A.** Ascension Day; **l'île de l'A.** Ascension Island **2** *Astron* **a. d'un astre** ascension of a star; **a. verticale** right ascension **3** *Fig* progress, ascent, rise; **l'a. professionnelle de qn** sb's climb up the professional ladder; **l'a. de Bonaparte** the rise of Bonaparte

ascensionnel, -elle [asɑ̃sjɔnɛl] ADJ *(mouvement)* upward; *Aviat* **force ascensionnelle** lifting power, lift; **vitesse ascensionnelle** rate of climb, climbing speed; **mouvement a.** upstroke; *Sport* **parachutisme a.** parascending

ascensionner [asɑ̃sjɔne] VI to climb

ascensionniste [asɑ̃sjɔnist] N climber, mountaineer

ascèse [asɛz] NF asceticism; **mener une vie d'a.** to live an ascetic life

ascète [asɛt] N ascetic

ascétique [asetik] ADJ ascetic; **vie a.** ascetic life

ascétisme [asetism] NM asceticism

ASCII [aski] NM *Ordinat (abrév* **American Standard Code for Information Interchange)** ASCII; **A. inférieur** lower ASCII; **A. supérieur** upper ASCII

ascorbique [askɔrbik] ADJ *(acide)* ascorbic

asdic [asdik] NM *Naut (abrév* **Allied Submarine Detection Investigation Committee)** ASDIC

ASE [aɛsə] NF *(abrév* **Agence spatiale européenne)** ESA

asepsie, aseptie [asɛpsi] NF *Méd* asepsis

aseptique [asɛptik] ADJ *Méd* aseptic

aseptisation [asɛptizasjɔ̃] NF *(d'une blessure, d'un pansement)* sterilization, asepsis; *(d'une pièce)* disinfection

aseptiser [asɛptize] VT *Méd (blessure)* to sterilize; *(pièce)* to disinfect; *Fig Péj* **un univers aseptisé** a sterile *or* sanitized environment

asexué [asɛksɥe], **asexuel, -elle** [asɛksɥɛl] ADJ *Biol* asexual

asiatique [azjatik] ADJ Asian, Asiatic; **grippe a.** Asian flu
N A. Asian, Asiatic

Il faut noter qu'en anglais britannique le nom **Asian** désigne le plus souvent une personne originaire du sous-continent indien.

Asie [azi] NF Asia; **l'A. Mineure** Asia Minor; **A. du Sud-Est** South-East Asia

asile [azil] NM **1** *Jur* sanctuary; **droit d'a.** right of sanctuary; **a. politique/diplomatique** political/diplomatic asylum; **demander l'a. politique** to ask for political asylum **2** *(abri)* shelter, refuge, retreat; **lieu d'a.** (place of) refuge; **sans a.** without refuge; **a. des pauvres** ≃ workhouse; **a. de nuit** night shelter, *Fam* dosshouse; **a. des marins** sailors' home; **a. (d'aliénés)** mental hospital, *Vieilli* lunatic asylum; *Fam* **il faut le mettre à l'a.!** he belongs in the loony bin *or* at the funny farm!, he ought to be locked away!; *Litt* **a. de paix** haven of peace; **le dernier a.** the grave **3** *Mktg (document publicitaire)* stuffer, insert

asinien, -ienne [azinjɛ̃, -jɛn] ADJ asinine

asocial, -iale, -iaux, -iales [asɔsjal, -jo] ADJ maladjusted
▸ N misfit, maladjusted person

asparagus [asparagys] NM asparagus fern

aspartam(e) [aspartam] NM aspartame

aspect [aspɛ] NM **1** *(vue)* sight, *Fml* aspect **2** *(air)* appearance, look; **avoir un a. imposant** to look imposing; **je n'aime pas l'a. de cette affaire** I don't like the look of the thing; **un**

démon qui pouvait prendre tous les aspects a demon who could take on any appearance **3** *(angle)* angle, point of view; **considérer une affaire sous tous ses aspects** to look at a problem from every angle *or* from all points of view; **vu sous cet a.** seen from this angle *or* point of view **4** *Astrol (des étoiles)* aspect, relative positions **5** *Gram* aspect; **a. perfectif** perfective VOIR GRAMMAIRE A39

asperge [aspɛrʒ] NF **1** *(plante)* asparagus; **a. plumeuse** asparagus fern; **une botte d'asperges** a bunch of asparagus; **pointe** *ou* **tête d'a.** asparagus tip; **plant d'asperges** asparagus bed **2** *Fam (personne)* beanpole

asperger [aspɛrʒe] VT *(j'aspergeai(s);* n. **aspergeons)** *(linge etc)* to sprinkle with water; **a. qn d'eau bénite** to sprinkle sb with holy water; **une voiture nous a aspergés d'eau** a (passing) car sprayed us with water; **se faire a.** to get splashed

aspergès [aspɛrʒɛs] NM *Rel* **1** *(goupillon)* aspergillum, holy-water sprinkler **2** *(rite)* asperges

aspérité [asperite] NF **1** *(d'une surface etc)* unevenness, ruggedness, roughness **2** *(d'un caractère, d'une voix)* asperity, harshness, sharpness

asperme [aspɛrm] ADJ *Bot* seedless

aspersion [aspɛrsjɔ̃] NF sprinkling; *Agr* drench

aspersoir [aspɛrswar] NM **1** *Rel* aspergillum **2** *(d'un arrosoir)* rose

asphaltage [asfaltaʒ] NM *Constr etc* asphalting

asphalte [asfalt] NM *Minér* asphalt; **a. minéral** pitch, bitumen; **route en a.** asphalt road; *Fam* **arpenter l'a.** to pace up and down the streets

asphalter [asfalte] VT *(route etc)* to asphalt

asphodèle [asfɔdɛl] NM *(plante)* asphodel; **a. rameux** branched lily, king's rod; **a. blanc** king's spear

asphyxiant [asfiksjɑ̃] ADJ **1** asphyxiating, suffocating; **gaz a.** poison gas **2** *Fig (atmosphère etc)* stifling, suffocating

asphyxie [asfiksi] NF asphyxia, asphyxiation, suffocation; *Min etc* gassing; **mourir d'a.** *ou* **par a.** to die of asphyxiation; *Fig* **a. économique** economic strangulation

asphyxié [asfiksje] ADJ *(personne)* asphyxiated, suffocated; *Min etc* gassed; **mourir a.** to die of asphyxiation

asphyxier [asfiksje] *(pr sub, impf n.* **asphyxiions,** *v.* **asphyxiiez)** VT to asphyxiate, to suffocate; *Min etc* to gas; *Fig* **elle se sent asphyxiée par sa famille** she feels suffocated *or* stifled by her family
▸ VPR **s'asphyxier** *(accidentellement)* to be asphyxiated, to suffocate; *(au gaz)* to be gassed; *(pour se suicider)* to suffocate oneself; *(au gaz)* to gas oneself

aspic [aspik] NM **1** *(serpent)* asp **2** *Culin* aspic

aspidistra [aspidistra] NM *(plante)* aspidistra

aspirant, -ante [aspirɑ̃, -ɑ̃t] ADJ sucking; **pompe aspirante** suction pump; **ventilateur a.** suction fan; **course aspirante** induction *or* admission stroke
▸ N candidate (**au** for)
▸ NM *Naut* midshipman; *Mil* officer cadet; *Naut* **a. pilote** apprentice pilot

aspirateur, -trice [aspiratœr, -tris] ADJ aspiratory; *(mécanisme)* suction
▸ NM *(pour la maison)* vacuum (cleaner), Hoover®; *Chimie, Ind, Méd (de gaz, d'air)* exhauster, aspirator; **passer l'a. dans la maison** to vacuum(-clean) *or* hoover the house; **passer une pièce/moquette à l'a.** to vacuum(-clean) *or* hoover a room/rug; **un coup d'a.** a quick once-over with the vacuum (cleaner)

or Hoover®; **a. à céréales** grain elevator; **a. de buées** extractor fan

aspiration [aspirasjɔ̃] NF **1** Physiol inhaling (of air into the lungs), Spéc inspiration; Tech (d'eau dans pompe etc) suction, sucking up; Aut aspiration; **Aut à a. naturelle** naturally aspirated, unblown; **ventilateur à a.** exhaust fan; (d'un moteur à combustion interne) admission, induction; **clapet d'a.** intake valve **2** (désir, ambition) aspiration, yearning (**à**, **vers** for, after); **aspirations à la scène** ambitions to go on the stage **3** Ling aspiration

aspiré [aspire] ADJ Ling aspirate(d)

aspirée [aspire] NF Ling aspirate

aspirer [aspire] VI **1** (inspirer) to breathe in, to inhale **2** (ambitionner) to aspire (**à** to); **a. à la gloire/la célébrité** to aspire to glory/fame; **a. à un poste** to covet a post; **a. à faire qch** to long to do sth; **elle aspire à devenir actrice** she longs to become an actress
▸ VT **1** (air, parfum etc) to inhale, to breathe (in); (poudre etc) to sniff up **2** (eau etc) (d'une pompe) to suck up, to suck in, to draw (up) **3** Ling (un son) to aspirate, to breathe; **l'h est aspiré en allemand** the h is aspirated in German

aspirine [aspirin] NF Pharm aspirin; **un cachet d'a.** an aspirin; **prenez deux aspirines** take two aspirin(s)

aspiro-batteur, pl **aspiro-batteurs** [aspirobatœr] NM beating vacuum cleaner

ASS [aɛsɛs] NF abrév **allocation de solidarité spécifique**

assagir [asaʒir] VT to quieten down; **le mariage l'a assagi** marriage has calmed him down; **voilà qui l'assagira** that will knock some sense into him; **le temps assagit les passions** passions will cool with time
▸ VPR **s'assagir** to settle down

assagissement [asaʒismɑ̃] NM quietening (down), calming (down); (des esprits) calming (down)

assaillant, -ante [asajɑ̃, -ɑ̃t] N assailant, attacker

assaillir [asajir] VT (prp **assaillant**; pp **assailli**; pr ind **j'assaille, n. assaillons, ils assaillent**; impf **j'assaillais**; p hist **j'assaillis**; fu **j'assaillirai**) to assault, to attack; Fig (de difficultés, remords etc) to beset; **à mon retour, j'ai été assailli de questions** when I came back, I was bombarded with questions

assainir [asenir] VT (maison, murs) to clean up; (atmosphère etc) to cleanse, to purify; (étable) to clean, to disinfect; (marais) to drain; (ville) to improve the sanitation of; (monnaie, marché etc) to stabilize; Compta (bilan) to balance; **a. les finances/l'administration** to reorganize finance/administration; **a. une rivière** to clean up a river
▸ VPR **s'assainir** (d'atmosphère), Fig (de marché) to become healthier; Fig **la situation s'est assainie** the situation has improved

assainissant [asenisɑ̃] ADJ cleansing, purifying

assainissement [asenismɑ̃] NM (d'atmosphère) cleansing, purifying; (de terrain) drainage; (de ville) improving of the sanitation; Fin stabilization; **a. monétaire** stabilization of the currency; **travaux d'a.** drainage work

assaisonnement [asɛzɔnmɑ̃] NM **1** (de plat) seasoning, flavouring; (de salade) dressing; **je n'aime pas ce plat, l'a. est trop fade** I don't like this dish, it's under-seasoned **2** (aromate etc) seasoning, flavouring

assaisonner [asɛzɔne] VT **1** Culin to season, to flavour (**de** with); (salade) to dress; Fig Fam **se faire a.** (réprimander) to get a good telling-off; **le président a vraiment été assai-**

sonné dans le journal de ce matin the president really got it in the paper this morning **2** Fam (faire payer plus) to rip off; **je me suis fait assaisonner** I got ripped off

assassin, -ine [asasɛ̃, -in] NM murderer, f murderess; (d'une personnalité politique etc) assassin; **à l'a.!** murder!; **l'a. est Madame Duval** the murderer is Mrs Duval
▸ ADJ **1** (horde etc) murderous **2** Fig (sourire) provocative, bewitching; **elle lance des œillades assassines à tous les hommes** she's always making eyes at men

assassinat [asasina] NM murder; (d'une personnalité politique etc) assassination; Jur premeditated murder, Am murder in the first degree

assassiner [asasine] VT to murder; (homme politique etc) to assassinate; Fam (chanson etc) to murder; Fig **si je rentre en retard, je vais me faire a. par mes parents** if I get home late, my parents will murder me; Fig **je ne vais pas vous a., c'est seulement 10 euros** I'm not going to charge you the earth, it's only 10 euros

assaut [aso] NM **1** (attaque) assault, attack; surtout Mil charge, onslaught; **canon d'a.** assault gun; **troupes d'a.** assault or storm troops; **a. à la baïonnette** bayonet charge; **donner l'a. à** to storm, to launch an attack on; Fig **partir à l'a. du mont Blanc/d'une entreprise** to set out to conquer Mont Blanc/to take over a firm; **les meilleures places ont été prises d'a.** everybody made a rush for the best seats; **les assauts répétés d'une maladie** the repeated attacks or onslaughts of a disease **2** (combat) match, bout; **a. de lutte** wrestling bout; **a. de boxe** boxing match; **faire a. d'élégance/de zèle/de courtoisie** to (try to) outdo each other in elegance/zeal/politeness

assèchement [asɛʃmɑ̃] NM (de route) drying; (de terrain, mare etc) draining, drainage; (de mine) pumping dry

assécher [aseʃe] (j'assèche, n. asséchons; j'assécherai) VT to dry; (marais etc) to drain; (mine etc) to pump dry or out
▸ VPR **s'assécher** to become dry, to dry up

ASSEDIC [asedik] NFPL (abrév **Associations pour l'emploi dans l'industrie et le commerce**) = French unemployment benefits department, Br ≃ Unemployment Benefit Office, Am Unemployment Office; **toucher les A.** to get unemployment benefit; **faire un dossier aux A.** to apply for unemployment benefit

assemblage [asɑ̃blaʒ] NM **1** (de personnes) gathering; (d'objets) collection, combination; **a. de circonstances** combination of circumstances **2** (d'éléments de machine etc) assembling, assembly; Menuis joint, joining; Couture sewing together; Tricot making up; (de feuillets) gathering, collating **3** (structure) assembly; **un a. de tiges métalliques** an assembly or structure of metal shafts; **a. à queue d'aronde** dovetail joint; **a. par vis/à rivets** screw/rivet assembly; **a. à tenon et mortaise** mortise-and-tenon joint **4** Ordinat **programme d'a.** assembler **5** Élec connection; **a. en quantité** parallel connection **6** (par soudure) bond

assemblée [asɑ̃ble] NF **1** (réunion) assembly; (plus petite) meeting; **se réunir en a.** to assemble (for a meeting) **2** Pol **A. nationale** National Assembly, Br ≃ House of Commons, Am ≃ House of Representatives; **A. parlementaire européenne** European Parliamentary Assembly **3** (foule) gathering; **une nombreuse a.** a large gathering; **l'a. des fidèles** the congregation
▸▸ **a. des actionnaires** shareholders' meeting; **a. annuelle/extraordinaire** annual/extraordinary general meeting; **a. générale**

annual general meeting; **a. générale d'actionnaires** general meeting of shareholders; **a. générale annuelle** annual general meeting; **a. générale extraordinaire** extraordinary general meeting; **a. générale ordinaire** annual general meeting

---

Assemblée nationale

The French parliament has two chambers: the National Assembly and the Senate. The members of the National Assembly (the "députés") are elected in the "élections législatives" held every five years.

---

assembler [asɑ̃ble] VT **1** to assemble; (personnes) to call together, to assemble; (comité etc) to convene; (ingrédients, idées, ce dont on a besoin etc) to collect, to gather (together); Naut **a. l'équipage** to muster the crew **2** (machine, meuble en kit etc) to assemble, to put or fit together; (documents) to collate; (feuillets) to collate, to gather **3** Menuis, Tech etc to join (up), to joint; **a. deux morceaux à plat** to butt-joint two pieces; **a. deux pièces par soudure/collage** to weld/glue two parts together **4** Ordinat (programme) to assemble; (modules) to link **5** Élec (cellules) to connect, to join up
▸ VPR **s'assembler** to assemble, to meet, to gather; (d'une foule) to gather; **s'a. devant un spectacle insolite** to gather in front of an unusual sight; **les membres s'assemblent deux fois par an** the members meet twice a year; Prov **qui se ressemble s'assemble** birds of a feather flock together

assembleur, -euse [asɑ̃blœr, -øz] N assembler; (de machines etc) fitter
▸ NF **assembleuse** (machine) gatherer
▸ NM Ordinat assembler

asséner [asene] VT (j'assène, n. assénons; j'assénerai) (coup) to strike; **coup bien asséné** telling or well-aimed blow; **a. une réplique** to answer back like a shot; **la façon dont la propagande est assénée** the way propaganda is thrust at you; **on nous assène des publicités toute la journée** we are bombarded with adverts all day long; **c'est là qu'il lui a asséné l'argument final** that's when he hurled the final argument at him

assentiment [asɑ̃timɑ̃] NM assent, consent, agreement; **donner/refuser son a.** (**à qch**) to give/withhold one's assent (to sth); **avoir l'a. de tous** to be supported unanimously; **sourire d'a.** smile of agreement

asseoir [aswar] (prp **asseyant**; pp **assis**; pr ind **j'assieds** [asje], **il assied, n. asseyons, ils asseyent** or **j'assois, il assoit, ils assoient**; pr sub **j'asseye, n. asseyions** or **j'assoie**; imp **assieds, asseyons, asseyez**; impf **j'asseyais** or **j'assoyais**; p hist **j'assis**; impf sub **j'assisse**; fu **j'assiérai** or **j'assoirai**) VT **1** (installer) to seat, to sit; **asseyez-le sur le gazon** sit him down on the grass; **faire a. qn** to ask sb to sit down or to take a seat
2 (fondations etc) to place, to lay; **a. une pierre** to bed a stone; **a. une statue sur un piédestal** to stand a statue on a pedestal; **a. une tente/un camp** to pitch a tent/(a) camp; Fig **a. son autorité/sa réputation** to establish one's authority/reputation; Fig **a. une théorie sur des résultats scientifiques** to base a theory on scientific results; Fin **a. l'impôt sur le revenu** to base taxation on income
3 Fam (étonner) to amaze, to stagger; **ça m'assoit complètement de voir qu'il réussit aussi vite** I'm staggered to see him succeeding so quickly
▸ VPR **s'asseoir** to sit (down); **asseyez-vous** (à de nombreuses personnes) sit down, be seated; (à une ou deux personnes) sit down, have or take a seat; **asseyez-vous, je vous en prie** please sit down or take a seat; **vous**

permettez que je m'asseye *ou* m'assoie? may I sit down?; **s'a. sur une chaise/dans un fauteuil** to sit on a chair/in an armchair; **s'a. (sur son séant)** *(d'une position allongée)* to sit up; *Fig Fam* **s'a. sur qn** to ignore sb; *Fig Fam* **les ordres du patron, moi, je m'assois dessus!** I don't give a damn about the boss's orders!

assermentation [asɛrmɑ̃tasjɔ̃] NF *Can, Suisse* swearing in, taking of an oath

assermenté [asɛrmɑ̃te] ADJ sworn (in); *(témoin etc)* on oath; **fonctionnaire a.** sworn official; *Hist* **(prêtre) non a.** non-juring (priest)

assermenter [asɛrmɑ̃te] VT *(personne)* to swear in; *(témoin etc)* to administer the oath to

assertion [asɛrsjɔ̃] NF assertion

asservi [asɛrvi] ADJ *(appareil)* servo; **moteur a.** servomotor

asservir [asɛrvir] VT 1 *(assujettir)* to enslave, to subjugate, to subdue; *(nation)* to reduce to slavery; **a. ses instincts** to control one's instincts, to keep one's instincts under control; **être asservi à la mode** to be a slave to fashion 2 *(de mécanisme de commande etc) (pièce)* to control
▪ VPR **s'asservir** to submit, to bow (**à** to)

asservissant [asɛrvisɑ̃] ADJ enslaving; **avoir un emploi a.** to be a slave to one's job

asservissement [asɛrvismɑ̃] NM 1 *(assujettissement) (d'un pays)* subjection (**à** to), reduction to slavery, enslavement; *(envers qn de plus fort)* subservience; **vivre dans l'a. des médias** to believe everything the newspapers and television say 2 *Tech* control; *(de mécanisme)* servo control

assesseur [asesœr] NM 1 *Jur (juge)* **a.** *(auprès d'un magistrat etc)* assessor 2 **être secondé par ses assesseurs** to be supported by one's assistants

assez [ase] ADV 1 *(suffisamment)* enough; **vous travaillez bien a.** you work quite enough; **elle parle a. bien l'anglais pour ce poste** she speaks English well enough for the job; **(c'est) a. parlé!** that's enough talking!; **nous sommes a. de trois, nous n'avons pas besoin de toi** three's enough, we don't need you; **il est a. bête pour le croire!** he's stupid enough to believe her!; **il n'est pas a. bête pour dire oui** he's not so stupid as to say yes; **être a. près pour voir** to be near enough to see; **il n'avait pas a. pour vivre/pour acheter des cigarettes** he hadn't enough to live on/enough (money) to buy cigarettes; **a.! c'est enough!, stop!; a.! je ne veux plus t'entendre!** that's enough! I don't want to hear another sound out of you!; **j'en ai a.!** I've had enough (of it)!, I'm sick *or* tired of it!, I'm fed up!; **en voilà a. (sur ce sujet)!** that's enough (about that)!; **c'en est a.!** that's enough of that!; **j'en ai plus qu'a. de ses sautes d'humeur!** I've had more than enough of his moods VOIR GRAMMAIRE A23
2 a. de (+ *n*) enough; **il y a a. de pain pour tous** there's enough bread for everybody; **avez-vous a. d'argent?** have you enough money?; **a. de promesses! des actes!** enough (of) promises! let's see some action! **3** *(plutôt)* quite, rather, fairly; **elle est a. jolie** she's quite pretty; **je suis a. de votre avis** I'm rather inclined to agree with you; **je suis a. content de ma carrière** I'm quite *or* fairly happy with my career; **arriver a. tard** to arrive rather *or* fairly late; **j'ai dû attendre a. longtemps** I had to wait quite a long time; **il parle a. peu** he doesn't talk much VOIR GRAMMAIRE A5

assidu [asidy] ADJ assiduous; *(employé, élève etc)* industrious, hard-working; *(soin, attention)* constant; *(visiteur)* regular, constant; **efforts assidus** untiring efforts; **travailleur a.** hard worker; **présence assidue aux cours** regular attendance at classes; **le médecin est a. auprès de ses malades** the doc-

tor takes good care of *or* is very attentive to his patients; **faire une cour assidue à qn** to court sb persistently; *Vieilli* **un amoureux a.** a persistent suitor

assiduité [asidɥite] NF 1 assiduity, perseverance; *Scol etc* regular attendance; **a. à (faire) qch** assiduity in (doing) sth; **a. au travail** devotion to work 2 *(fréquence)* constant attention(s), constant care; **fréquenter qn avec a.** to be a frequent visitor at sb's house 3 **il la poursuit de ses assiduités depuis des années** he's been forcing his attentions on her for years

assidûment [asidymɑ̃] ADV assiduously, unremittingly; *(fréquenter un lieu)* regularly; **il y travaille** he is hard at work on it

assiégé, -ée [asjeʒe] ADJ besieged
NPL **les assiégés** the besieged

assiégeant, -ante [asjeʒɑ̃, -ɑ̃t] ADJ *(armée etc)* besieging
N besieger

assiéger [asjeʒe] VT (**assiégeant; j'assiège, n. assiégeons; j'assiégerai**) *(ville, château)* to besiege, to lay siege to; *(personne)* to surround, to crowd round; *Fig* **les journalistes ont assiégé l'hôtel** journalists besieged *or* laid siege to the hotel; *Fig* **assiégé par l'inondation** hemmed in by flood water; *Fig* **la ville est assiégée par les touristes** the town is overrun with *or* by tourists; *Fig* **a. qn de demandes** to pester sb with requests

assiette [asjɛt] NF 1 *(vaisselle)* plate; **manger dans une a.** to eat off *or* from a plate; **ne mange pas avec le nez dans ton a.** don't eat like that with your nose right in your plate 2 *(fondation) (de bâtiment etc)* situation, site; *(de camp)* disposition; *(du terrain)* lie; *(de pierre, poutre etc)* set; *(d'un impôt, d'un taux)* base; *(d'une route)* foundation, bottom, bed 3 *(d'un cavalier)* seat; *(de bateau)* trim; *Aviat, Naut* **angle d'a.** trim angle; **avoir une bonne a.** *Équitation* to have a good seat; *Naut* to be in good trim; *Fam* **ne pas être dans son a.** to be out of sorts *or* off colour *or* under the weather; **prendre son a.** *(de fondation, canon etc)* to set, to settle, to bed down
▸▸ *Culin* **a. anglaise** assorted cold meat(s), cold cuts; *Fam* **a. au beurre** cushy job; **a. des coupes** felling plan; **a. creuse** soup dish; **a. à dessert** dessert plate; **a. fiscale, a. de l'impôt** tax base; **a. plate** dinner plate; *Belg* **a. profonde** soup dish; **a. à soupe** soup dish *or* plate

assiettée [asjete] NF plate(ful)

assignable [asiɲabl] ADJ *(limite)* assignable; *(cause, raison)* ascribable, attributable

assignataire [asiɲatɛr] ADJ **banque a.** warrant bank

assignation [asiɲasjɔ̃] NF 1 *Fin (de parts, fonds)* assignment, transfer (**à** to); *Bourse* exercise notice 2 *Jur (action)* serving of a writ *or* summons *or* process; *(acte)* (writ of) summons, subpoena; **signifier** *ou* **faire** *ou* **donner** *ou* **envoyer une a.** to serve a writ on, to issue a summons to; *(témoin)* to subpoena
▸▸ **a. à comparaître** summons; **a. à résidence** house arrest

assigner [asiɲe] VT 1 to assign; *(heure etc)* to fix, to appoint; *(cause)* to attribute, to ascribe (**à** to); **a. une tâche à qn** to assign *or* allot a job to sb; **a. une somme à un paiement** to earmark a sum for a payment, to allocate a sum to a payment; **a. une dépense sur le trésor public** to charge an expense to public funds 2 *Jur (témoin etc)* to summon, to cite; **a. qn en justice** *(de la cour)* to issue a writ against sb; *(d'un demandeur)* to have a writ issued against sb; *(d'un huissier)* to serve a writ on sb; **a. qn à résidence** to place sb under house arrest

assimilable [asimilabl] ADJ 1 *(absorbable) (connaissances, aliment)* easily assimilated *or* absorbed; **population très a.** population that assimilates *or* integrates easily 2 *(comparable)* **une maladie a. à une autre** an illness comparable to another

assimilation [asimilasjɔ̃] NF 1 *(absorption, Fig)* assimilation; **l'a. chlorophyllienne** photosynthesis; *Ling* **a. de phonèmes** assimilation of phonemes; **politique d'a.** policy of assimilation 2 *(comparaison)* comparison

assimilé [asimile] ADJ 1 *(immigrés etc)* assimilated 2 *(de même nature)* related; **le sucre et produits assimilés** sugar and related products 3 *Mil, Naut* **être a. à ...** to rank as *or* with ..., to be ranked as ...; **a. au grade de capitaine** ranking *or* ranked as a captain
NM *Journ* = press employee entitled to carry a press card; **cadres et assimilés** executives and their equivalents; **officiers et assimilés** officers and equivalent

assimiler [asimile] VT 1 *(absorber) (aliment)*, *Fig (connaissances, immigrés etc)* to assimilate 2 *(comparer)* to assimilate, to compare (**à** to, with); **a. qch à** to class sth as, to put sth in the same category as
▪ VPR **s'assimiler 1** *(des aliments etc)* to be assimilated; *(d'immigrants etc)* to assimilate, to become assimilated; **ces minéraux s'assimilent facilement** these minerals are easily assimilated 2 *(être comparable)* to be comparable (**à** to)

assis [asi] ADJ sitting, seated; **nous étions a. auprès du feu** we were sitting *or* seated round the fire; *Fig Fam* **en rester a.** to be flabbergasted; *Fig* **il a une situation bien assise** he has a secure job; *Rail, Théâtre etc* **places assises** seats; **il n'y a plus de places assises** standing room only; *Jur* **la magistrature assise** the Bench

Assise [asiz] N Assisi; **St François d'A.** St Francis of Assisi

assise [asiz] NF 1 *(des fondations)* bed; *(de moteur etc)* bed(plate); *Géol* bed, stratum; *Fig (d'un raisonnement, d'une théorie)* basis, foundation; **ajuster l'a. d'une soupape** to seat a valve 2 *Constr (de maçonnerie)* course; *(de ciment)* layer 3 *Jur* **les assises** the assizes; **cour d'assises** Assize Court; **être envoyé devant la cour d'assises** to be committed for trial; **avocat d'assises** criminal lawyer 4 **assises** *(d'un congrès)* sittings; *(d'un syndicat)* conference; **tenir ses assises** *(d'un parti)* to hold a conference; *(d'un club)* to hold a general meeting

assistanat [asistana] NM 1 *(aide)* aid 2 *Univ* assistantship

assistance [asistɑ̃s] NF 1 *(assemblée)* audience; *Sport* spectators; *(lors d'une manifestation etc)* onlookers; *Rel* congregation; **je demande un peu de calme à l'a.** could the audience please be quiet; **y a-t-il un médecin dans l'a.?** is there a doctor in the house? 2 *(aide)* assistance, help, aid; **demander l'a. de qn** to ask for sb's assistance *or* help; **prêter (son) a.** to assist; **faire qch sans a.** to do sth unaided *or* without help 3 **elle est à l'A. (publique) depuis l'âge de trois ans** she's been in care since she was three; **les enfants de l'A. (publique)** children in care 4 *(de magistrat, prêtre)* presence, attendance
▸▸ **a. dépannage** roadside assistance; *Aut* **a. des freins** power braking; **a. judiciaire** *ou* **juridique** legal aid; *Com* **a. maritime** salvage; **a. médicale** *(à un pays du tiers-monde)* medical aid *or* assistance; *Méd* **a. respiratoire** artificial respiration; **a. sanitaire** medical care; **a. sociale** welfare work; **a. technique** *(à un pays du tiers-monde)* technical aid *or* assistance; *Ordinat* technical assistance; **a.**

technique aux véhicules roadside assistance; *Ordinat* a. à l'utilisateur user support

assistant, -ante [asistɑ̃, -ɑ̃t] N **1** *(aide)* assistant; *(à l'école)* language assistant; *Univ (de travaux pratiques)* demonstrator, laboratory assistant; **l'a. du metteur en scène** assistant producer; **maître a.** ≃ senior lecturer, *Am* assistant professor **2 assistants** members of the audience; *Sport* spectators ▸▸ *TV, Cin* **a. cadreur, a. cameraman** assistant cameraman; **a. du chef de cuisine** sous chef; **a. de direction** personal assistant, PA; *Ordinat* **a. numérique** personal digital assistant, PDA; **a. opérateur** camera assistant; **a. personnel** personal assistant; **a. de production** production *or* producer's assistant, PA; *TV, Cin* **a. réalisateur** assistant director; **assistante sociale** social worker, welfare worker *or* officer; *(à l'hôpital)* medical social worker

assisté [asiste] ADJ **1** *Admin (personne)* on social security; **enfants assistés** children in care **2** *Aut* **freins assistés** power-assisted brakes; **direction assistée** power steering **3** *Ordinat* **a. par ordinateur** *(enseignement, fabrication etc)* computer-aided *or*-assisted ▸ N person on social security; *Péj* person living on hand-outs; **avoir une mentalité d'a.** to expect everything to be handed to one on a plate

assister [asiste] VI **a. à qch** to be (present) at sth; *(cérémonie)* to attend sth; **je ne peux pas vous répondre, je n'ai pas assisté à la scène** I can't give you an answer, I wasn't at the scene
▸ VT *(personne)* to help, to assist; *(soutenir financièrement)* to help (financially); **dans cette entreprise, je ne me sens pas assisté du tout** I don't feel I'm getting any help in this company at all; **tu devrais te faire a.** you ought to get help, you ought to get somebody to help you; **a. qn de ses conseils** to give sb some helpful advice; **prêtre assisté de deux enfants de chœur** priest attended by two altar boys

> Il faut noter que le verbe anglais **to assist** n'a jamais le sens d'**être présent** (à un événement).

associatif, -ive [asɔsjatif, -iv] ADJ *Math* **loi associative** associative law; **mouvement a.** association; **mémoire associative** involuntary memory

association [asɔsjasjɔ̃] NF **1** *(groupe, société)* society, association; *Com* partnership **2** *(réunion) (de mots, d'idées)* association; **cette a. a été très bénéfique pour les deux entreprises** this association has been very beneficial for both companies; **a. capital-travail** profit-share scheme; **l'a. de ces deux aliments** the combination of these two foods ▸▸ **a. d'automobilistes** motoring organization; **a. de bienfaisance** charity, charitable organization *or* institution; **a. à but non lucratif** non-profit-making *or Am* not-for-profit organization; **a. commerciale** trade association; **a. de consommateurs** consumer association; **a. de défense des consommateurs** consumer protection association; **A. européenne de libre-échange** European Free Trade Association; **A. française des banques** French Bankers' Association; **A. internationale des transports aériens** International Air Transport Association; **a. loi 1901** = type of non-profit-making organization; *Jur* **a. de malfaiteurs** conspiracy; **a. de parents d'élèves** parent-teacher association; **a. professionnelle** trade association; **a. sportive** sports club; **a. syndicale** trade union; **a. d'utilité publique** public utility

associé, -ée [asɔsje] ADJ associated; *surtout*

Fin, Bourse joint; *Fin* **porteurs** *ou* **souscripteurs associés** joint holders (of stock); *Admin* **territoires associés** associated territories
▸ N associate, honorary member; *Com* partner, business associate; **a. gérant** active partner; **a. principal** senior partner; **a. commandité** active partner; **a. commanditaire** sleeping partner; **a. en second** junior partner

associer [asɔsje] *(pr sub, impf* n. **associions,** v. **associiez)** VT **1** *(joindre, lier)* to associate, to unite, to join; **comment peux-tu a. deux thèses aussi différentes?** how can you compare two such different theories?; **a. les travailleurs aux profits de leur entreprise** to allow workers to share in their firm's profits; **il a associé son frère à son expédition** he brought his brother in on his expedition; **son entreprise est associée au projet** his company is taking part in the project
2 *(mentalement)* to associate; **j'ai toujours associé la neige à Noël** I've always associated snow with Christmas; **a. des idées** to associate ideas
▸ VPR **s'associer 1 s'a. à qch** to share *or* participate *or* join in sth; **s'a. à un voyage** to come *or* go along on a trip; **je m'associe à votre douleur** I share (in) your grief; **s'a. à un crime** to be a party to a crime
2 s'a. à *ou* **avec qn** *(dans une lutte etc)* to join forces with sb; *Com etc* to enter into partnership with sb; **s'a. qn** to take sb on as a partner; **les deux pays se sont associés** the two countries have joined forces
3 *(s'allier)* to combine; **les deux parfums s'associent merveilleusement bien** these two fragrances combine wonderfully *or* go wonderfully well together

assoiffant [aswafɑ̃] ADJ *(travail)* thirsty

assoiffé [aswafe] ADJ thirsty; *Fig* **a. de sang** bloodthirsty; *Fig* **a. de savoir/de vengeance** thirsty *or* hungry for knowledge/revenge

assoiffer [aswafe] VT to make thirsty

assolement [asɔlmɑ̃] NM *Agr (des cultures)* rotation; **a. triennal** three course system

assoler [asɔle] VT *Agr* to rotate

assombrir [asɔ̃bʀiʀ] VT to darken, to obscure; *Fig* to cast a shadow over; **cette triste nouvelle a assombri le repas** the sad news cast a shadow over the meal; **nous avons passé des vacances merveilleuses sans rien qui vienne les a.** nothing spoiled *or* marred our wonderful holidays; **ciel assombri** cloudy *or* overcast sky; **visage assombri** gloomy face
▸ VPR **s'assombrir** *(du ciel)* to become dark; *(du ciel, d'un visage)* to cloud over; **il s'assombrit en me voyant** he glowered when he saw me

assombrissement [asɔ̃bʀismɑ̃] NM *(du ciel, de l'humeur)* darkening, clouding over; *(d'une pièce)* darkening

assommant [asɔmɑ̃] ADJ *Fam* boring, tedious, deadly dull; **il est a., cet enfant-là!** that child is a real pain!

assommer [asɔme] VT **1 a. un bœuf** to fell an ox; **a. qn** *(l'étourdir)* to knock sb senseless, to stun sb; *Fig* **arrête ou je t'assomme!** stop that or I'll knock your block off!; **la chaleur m'assomme** the heat's overpowering **2** *Fam (ennuyer)* to bore (to death); *(harceler)* to pester; **tu m'assommes à toujours demander la même chose** you're getting on my nerves always asking the same thing

assommeur, -euse [asɔmœʀ, -øz] N slaughterer

assommoir [asɔmwaʀ] NM **1** *(arme)* club, bludgeon; *(plus petit)* cosh, *Am* blackjack; *Fam* **porter un coup d'a. à qn** to deal sb a knock-out blow **2** *(bar)* dive

assomption [asɔ̃psjɔ̃] NF **1** *Rel* **(fête de) l'A. (de la Vierge Marie)** (feast of) the Assumption (of the Blessed Virgin) **2** *Géog* **A.** Asunción **3** *(hypothèse)* assumption

---

Assomption

The Feast of the Assumption, on the 15th of August, is a Catholic feast day and an important holiday in France.

---

assonance [asɔnɑ̃s] NF *Ling* assonance

assorti [asɔʀti] ADJ **1** *(en harmonie)* matched, matching; **bien a.** well-matched; **couple mal a.** ill-matched *or* ill-assorted couple; **couleurs assorties** colours that match, matching colours; **pull avec jupe assortie** jumper with matching skirt **2** *(bonbons, clous etc)* assorted, mixed; **fromages assortis** choice of cheeses; *(au restaurant)* cheese board *or* platter **3 bien a.** *(magasin etc)* well-stocked **4** *(accompagné)* **a. de** accompanied by, along with; **une peine de prison, assortie d'une amende de 2000 euros** a prison sentence, accompanied by a fine of 2,000 euros; **un accord a. de plusieurs conditions** an agreement with several conditions

assortiment [asɔʀtimɑ̃] NM **1** *(ensemble) (de marchandises etc)* assortment, variety, collection; *(d'outils)* set; *(de produits)* mix, selection; **ample a. d'échantillons** wide range of patterns; **a. de charcuterie** assorted cold meats **2** *(action)* matching; **a. parfait de couleurs** perfect match(ing) of colours

assortir [asɔʀtiʀ] *(j'assortis, n. assortissons)* VT **1** *(couleurs etc)* to match; **a. les accessoires à sa robe** to match one's accessories to *or* with one's dress; **elle n'a pas su a. les invités** she didn't manage to choose a good mix of guests; **nos mentalités sont bien/mal assorties** we think/don't think the same way **2** *Com* to restock
▸ VPR **s'assortir 1** *(être en harmonie)* to match, to blend, to go well together; **la ceinture s'assortit à la robe** the belt goes well with the dress **2** *(s'accompagner)* **le texte s'assortit d'illustrations** the text is accompanied with *or* by illustrations

assoupi [asupi] ADJ dozing, *Fml* somnolent; *(volcan, passion)* dormant

assoupir [asupiʀ] VT *(personne)* to make drowsy *or* sleepy, to send to sleep; *(la douleur, les sens)* to calm, to deaden, to dull; **a. une dispute** to calm a dispute
▸ VPR **s'assoupir** to drop off to sleep, to doze off; *(de la douleur, du chagrin)* to die down

assoupissant [asupisɑ̃] ADJ soporific

assoupissement [asupismɑ̃] NM *(somnolence)* drowsiness

assouplir [asupliʀ] VT to soften; *(cuir)* to make supple; *Fig (réglementation, règlement)* to relax, to make less strict; **cette lessive va a. votre linge** this washing powder will make your clothes feel soft; *Fig* **cela va finir par a. son caractère** it'll eventually make him more flexible
▸ VPR **s'assouplir** *(du cuir, d'une personne)* to become supple; *(du caractère)* to become more flexible; **s'a. les muscles** to limber up

assouplissant [asuplisɑ̃] ADJ **liquide a. (pour le linge)** fabric softener
▸ NM fabric softener

assouplissement [asuplismɑ̃] NM softening; *Fig (de la réglementation, des contrôles)* relaxing; **exercices d'a., assouplissements** limbering-up exercises; **a. du crédit** easing of credit

assouplisseur [asuplisœʀ] NM (fabric) softener

assourdir [asuʀdiʀ] VT **1** *(personne)* to make deaf, to deafen **2** *(son)* to deaden, to muffle; *(tambour, cloche, oreilles)* to muffle; *(violon)*

to mute; *Ling (consonne)* to unvoice **3** *(lumière, couleur)* to soften, to subdue, to tone down
▪ **VPR s'assourdir** *Ling* to become unvoiced *or* voiceless

assourdissant [asurdisɑ̃] **ADJ** *(bruit etc)* deafening

assourdissement [asurdismɑ̃] **NM** *(de personne) (processus)* deafening; *(résultat)* temporary deafness; *(de son)* deadening; *(de tambour)* muffling; *Ling (de consonne)* unvoicing

assouvir [asuvir] **VT** *(faim, désir)* to satisfy, to appease, to assuage; **a. sa soif** to quench one's thirst; **a. sa curiosité** to satisfy one's curiosity
▪ **VPR s'assouvir** *(faim)* to be satisfied *or* assuaged; *(passions)* to be assuaged

assouvissement [asuvismɑ̃] **NM** *(de la faim, du désir etc)* satisfying, satisfaction; *(de la soif)* quenching; **un sentiment d'a.** a feeling of satisfaction, a satisfied feeling

assuétude [asɥetyd] **NF** *Méd* addiction

assujetti, -ie [asyʒeti] **ADJ** *(peuple)* subject, subjugated *(à* to); **tous les citoyens sont assujettis à l'impôt** all citizens are subject *or* liable to tax
▪ **N** person liable for tax

assujettir [asyʒetir] **VT 1** *(province etc)* to subdue, to subjugate **2** *(personne)* to subject, to make liable *(à* to); **a. qn à faire qch** to compel *or* oblige sb to do sth; **a. une population à des lois** to subject a population to laws; **a. une population à l'impôt** to make a population liable for tax **3** *(objet)* to fix, to fasten *(à* to), to make secure; **les planches sont assujetties par des clous** the planks are held in place with nails
▪ **VPR s'assujettir** to submit *(à* to)

assujettissant [asyʒetisɑ̃] **ADJ** *(travail)* exacting, demanding

assujettissement [asyʒetismɑ̃] **NM 1** *(action)* subjection, subjugation **2** *(état)* subjection, subservience *(à* to) **3** *(contrainte)* tie **4** *(à l'impôt)* liability *(à* for)

assumer [asyme] **VT 1** *(droit, responsabilité etc)* to assume, to take on, to take upon oneself; **a. les frais** to meet the costs *or* expenses, to bear the costs; **a. un risque** to take a risk; **a. un poste** to hold a post; **a. son service** to take up one's duties **2** *(accepter) (conséquences)* to bear, to take on board
▪ **VI** *Fam* **il va falloir que tu assumes** you'll have to live with it
▪ **VPR s'assumer** to come to terms with oneself

> Il faut noter que le verbe anglais **to assume** est un faux ami. Il signifie le plus souvent **supposer**.

assurable [asyrabl] **ADJ** insurable

assurance [asyrɑ̃s] **NF 1** *(confiance)* (self-)assurance, (self-) confidence; **parler avec a.** to speak confidently *or* with confidence; **perdre son a.** to lose one's self-assurance; **vous pouvez l'acheter en toute a.** you can buy it with complete confidence **2** *(garantie)* security, pledge; **elle vivait dans l'a. de la réussite** she was assured of success; **je vous donne l'a. que tout sera fait d'ici demain** I assure you *or* I guarantee (you) that everything will be done by tomorrow; **demander/recevoir des assurances** to ask for/to receive assurance; **recevez l'a. de mes sentiments distingués** *(dans une lettre)* yours faithfully **3** *Com* insurance; **police d'a.** insurance policy; **prime d'a.** insurance premium; **compagnie** *ou* **société d'assurances** insurance company; **agent d'assurance(s)** insurance agent; **courtier d'assurance(s)** insurance

broker; *Fam* **je vais écrire à mon a.** I'll write to my insurance company; **contracter une a.** to take out insurance, to take out an insurance policy
4 *(en alpinisme)* **(point d')a.** *(d'alpiniste)* belay
▪▪ **a.-accident, a. contre les accidents** accident insurance; **a. 'ad valorem'** replacement value insurance; **a. automobile** car *or* motor insurance; **a. bagage(s)** baggage insurance; *Suisse Aut* **a. casco** comprehensive *or* all-risks insurance; *Com* **a. catalogue coface** standard export guarantee insurance; **a. catalogue évolutif** upgradable standard insurance; **a. chômage** *(payée par le patron et le salarié)* ≃ unemployment insurance; *(reçue par le chômeur)* ≃ unemployment benefit(s); **a. collective** group insurance; **a. confiscation** confiscation insurance; **a. contre les accidents du travail** employers' liability insurance; **a. crédit** credit *or* loan insurance; **a. décès-invalidité** whole life and disability insurance; **a. dépannage** car breakdown and recovery insurance; **a. foire** exhibition insurance; **a. garantie constructeur** manufacturer's guarantee insurance; **a.-incendie, a. contre l'incendie** fire insurance; **a. invalidité** ≃ disability pension; **a. maintenance étendue** extended maintenance insurance; **a. maintenance visite** call-out maintenance insurance; **a. maladie** health insurance; **a. maritime** marine insurance; **a. maternité** ≃ maternity benefit(s); **a. médicale** medical insurance; **a. multirisque** comprehensive insurance; **a. offre** tender insurance; **a. offre coface** Export Credit Guarantee tender insurance; **a. panne mécanique** mechanical breakdown insurance; **a. perte de l'exploitation** insurance for loss of trade; **a. de portefeuille** portfolio insurance; **a. prospection** market exploration insurance; **a. responsabilité civile** public liability insurance; **a. responsabilité produit** product liability insurance; *Admin* **assurances sociales** ≃ national insurance; **a. au tiers** third-party insurance; **a. tous risques** comprehensive *or* all-risks insurance; **a. tous risques chantiers** comprehensive site insurance; **a. transport** transportation insurance; **a. vacances** holiday insurance; **a. vieillesse** ≃ retirement pension; *Suisse* **a. vieillesse et survivants** = Swiss pension scheme; **a. sur la vie, a.-vie** life insurance, *Br* life assurance; **prendre une a.-vie** to take out life insurance; **a. vol** theft insurance

assuré, -ée [asyre] **ADJ 1** *(plein d'assurance) (pas, voix etc)* firm, sure; *(air, personne)* assured, confident; **voix mal assurée** unsteady *or* quavering voice; **d'une main assurée** with a steady hand **2** *(certain) (remède)* certain; *(retraite)* secure, safe; **il n'y a encore rien d'a.** there is nothing fixed yet; **tenez pour a. qu'il vous écrira** rest assured that he will write to you; **la victoire est assurée** we/they/*etc* are certain of victory
▪ **N** **l'a.** the policy holder, the insured; *Admin* **les assurés sociaux** ≃ national insurance contributors, those who pay national insurance

assurément [asyremɑ̃] **ADV** assuredly, surely, undoubtedly, certainly; **il le fera a.** he's certain to do it; **a. non!** certainly not!; **oui, a.!** yes, of course!

assurer [asyre] **VT 1** *(immobiliser)* to make firm *or* steady; *(attacher)* to fix, to secure, to fasten; *(échelle)* to steady; *(mur)* to prop up; *(corde)* to make fast; *(alpiniste)* to belay; **a. qn sec** to give sb a tight rope; **a. ses arrières** *Mil* to protect one's rear; *Fig* to protect oneself against any eventuality; **a. la sécurité d'un pays** to make a country secure; **a. sa fortune** to consolidate one's fortune

2 *(se charger de)* to look after; **le courrier littéraire sera assuré par M. Leclerc** the literary column will be looked after by Mr Leclerc; **la France assure le rapatriement des touristes** the French government is repatriating the tourists; **un service régulier est assuré entre Paris et Londres** there is a regular service between Paris and London; **la sécurité est assurée par des soldats de métier** professional soldiers are providing the security cover *or* are responsible for security; **la secrétaire assurera la permanence de neuf heures à midi** the secretary will be there from nine till twelve; **a. la défense de qn** to defend sb; **a. une rente à qn** to settle an annuity on sb
3 *(garantir)* to ensure, to guarantee; **cette formation vous assure un avenir brillant** this type of training will ensure *or* guarantee you a brilliant future; **ma retraite m'assure de quoi vivre** my pension gives me enough to live on; **ce but assure la victoire des Allemands** this goal assures the Germans of victory; **a. une créance** to stand security for *or* to guarantee a debt
4 *(certifier)* **a. qch à qn, a. qn de qch** to assure sb of sth; **il m'a assuré qu'il voulait bien le faire** he assured me that he was willing to do it; **il m'a assuré de son amitié** he assured me of his friendship; **c'est bien vrai, je te l'assure** *ou Fam* **je t'assure** it's quite true, I (can) assure you; **je t'assure que ce n'est pas amusant** I (can) assure you it's not funny; **il vient de nous a. de sa participation** he's just assured us that he will be taking part
5 *(par contrat d'assurance)* **a. qn** to insure sb; **se faire a. sur la vie** to take out a life insurance (policy); **a. un immeuble contre l'incendie** to insure a building against fire; **êtes-vous assuré?** are you insured?; **a. qch pour deux millions d'euros** to insure sth for two million euros
▪ **VI** *Fam* to cope well; **j'assure pas du tout en maths** I'm hopeless at maths, I'm no good at maths; **elle assure, cette nana, avec les mecs** she has a real way with the men, that girl; **t'as pas amené les sandwichs? vraiment, t'assure pas!** didn't you bring the sandwiches? honestly, you're hopeless!; **ça assure!** brilliant!, wicked!; **a. comme une bête** to do brilliantly; *Fam* **à l'entretien, j'ai assuré un max** I did brilliantly at the interview
▪ **VPR s'assurer 1** *(vérifier)* **s'a. de qch** to make sure *or* certain of sth; **je vais m'en a.** *(le vérifier)* I'll check; *(faire en sorte que ça soit fait)* I'll make sure of it; **assurez-vous que c'est encore possible** make sure *or* check that it's still possible; **s'a. du transport** to make sure one has transport; **il faut que nous nous assurions de la véracité de ses dires** we must ensure that he is speaking the truth
2 *(par contrat d'assurance)* to take out insurance, to insure oneself (**contre** against); **s'a. au tiers/sur la vie** to take out third-party/life insurance
3 *(se pourvoir)* **tu aurais dû t'a. de l'aide** you should have got help; **s'a. la collaboration de qn** to secure sb's collaboration; **s'a. du silence de qn** to secure sb's silence; **les Allemands se sont assuré la victoire** the Germans have ensured themselves of victory
4 *(s'affermir)* to settle oneself firmly; *(d'un alpiniste)* to belay oneself; **s'a. sur ses pieds** to steady oneself on one's feet

assureur [asyrœr] **NM** underwriter; *(agent)* insurance agent; *(compagnie)* insurance company; *(courtier)* insurance broker

assureur-conseil, *pl* **assureurs-conseils** **NM** insurance adviser

Assyrie [asiri] **NF** Assyria

assyrien, -ienne [asirjɛ̃, -jɛn] **ADJ** Assyrian
▪ **NM** *Ling* (ancient) Assyrian
▪ **N A.** Assyrian

aster [aster] NM aster; **a. de Chine** China aster; **a. œil-du-Christ** Michaelmas daisy, *Am* aster

astérisque [asterisk] NM *Typ* asterisk

astéroïde [asteroid] NM *Astron* asteroid

asthénie [asteni] NF *Méd* tiredness, *Spéc* asthenia

asthmatique [asmatik] ADJ, N *Méd* asthmatic

asthme [asm] NM *Méd* asthma; **être atteint d'a., avoir** *ou* **faire de l'a.** to suffer from *or* to have asthma; **crise d'a.** attack of asthma, asthma attack

asticot [astiko] NM maggot; *Fam (type)* bloke, geezer

asticoter [astikɔte] VT *Fam* to needle, to bug, to bait

astigmate [astigmat] ADJ, N *Méd, Opt* astigmatic

astigmatisme [astigmatism] NM *Méd, Opt* astigmatism

astiquage [astikaʒ] NM polishing

astiquer [astike] VT *(maison)* to clean; *(sol)* to polish; *(casserole)* to scour

astragale [astragal] NM **1** *Anat* ankle bone **2** *Archit (de colonne etc)* astragal

astrakan [astrakɑ̃] NM astrakhan (fur); **manteau d'a.** astrakhan coat

astral, -ale, -aux, -ales [astral, -o] ADJ *(influence, corps etc)* astral; **esprits astraux** astral spirits; **thème a.** (astrological) star chart

astre [astr] NM star, heavenly body; **contempler les astres** to look at the stars, to stargaze; **consulter les astres** to consult the stars; **beau comme un a.** (as) handsome as a Greek god; **né sous un a. favorable** born under a lucky star

astreignant [astrɛɲɑ̃] ADJ exacting, demanding

astreindre [astrɛ̃dr] *(prp* **astreignant;** *pp* **astreint;** *prind* **j'astreins, il astreint,** *n.* **astreignons;** *impf* **j'astreignais;** *p hist* **j'astreignis;** *fu* **j'astreindrai)** VT to compel, to oblige (**à faire qch** to do sth), to tie down (**à un devoir** to a duty); **astreint au service militaire** liable for military service

VPR **s'astreindre s'a. à un régime sévère** to keep to a strict diet; **s'a. à faire du sport** to force oneself to do sport

astreinte [astrɛ̃t] NF obligation; **les astreintes de la vie moderne** the pressures of modern life

astringence [astrɛ̃ʒɑ̃s] NF astringency

astringent [astrɛ̃ʒɑ̃] ADJ, NM astringent

astro- [astrɔ] PRÉF astro-

astrolabe [astrɔlab] NM spacelab

astrologie [astrɔlɔʒi] NF astrology

astrologique [astrɔlɔʒik] ADJ astrological

astrologue [astrɔlɔg] N astrologer

astronaute [astrɔnot] N astronaut

astronautique [astrɔnotik] NF astronautics

astronef [astrɔnɛf] NM spaceship

astronome [astrɔnɔm] N astronomer

astronomie [astrɔnɔmi] NF astronomy

astronomique [astrɔnɔmik] ADJ *Astron, Fig* astronomical; **heure a.** sidereal time; *Fig Fam* **pratiquer des prix astronomiques** *(d'un magasin)* to charge astronomical prices

astronomiquement [astrɔnɔmikmɑ̃] ADV astronomically

astrophysicien, -ienne [astrɔfizisjɛ̃, -jɛn] N astrophysicist

astrophysique [astrɔfizik] ADJ astrophysical
NF astrophysics VOIR GRAMMAIRE A10

astuce [astys] NF **1** *(finesse)* astuteness, shrewdness; **elle a répondu avec beaucoup**

d'a. she answered very astutely *or* shrewdly; **c'est un enfant plein d'a.** he/she is a very sharp child **2** *(truc)* trick; *(conseil)* tip; **il doit y avoir une a.** there must be a trick to it; **l'a., c'est de ne pas pointer en sortant** the trick is not to clock off when you leave; **les astuces du métier** the tricks of the trade; **a. du vendeur** sales acumen; **Windows® XP: 50 astuces** Windows® XP: 50 tips **3** *(plaisanterie)* witticism; *(jeu de mots)* pun; **je ne saisis pas l'a.** I don't get it

astucieusement [astysjøzmɑ̃] ADV astutely, shrewdly; **il a arrangé sa petite chambre très a.** he has arranged his little room very cleverly

astucieux, -ieuse [astysjø, -jøz] ADJ *(personne, comportement)* astute, shrewd, clever; *(solution, méthode)* clever, cunning; **réponse astucieuse** crafty *or* clever answer

asymétrie [asimetri] NF asymmetry

asymétrique [asimetrik] ADJ asymmetrical

asymptomatique [asɛ̃ptɔmatik] ADJ *Méd (maladie)* asymptomatic; **porteur a.** carrier without symptoms

asymptote [asɛ̃ptɔt] NF *Math* asymptote

asynchrone [asɛ̃kron] ADJ *Ordinat* asynchronous

asyntaxique [asɛ̃taksik] ADJ *Gram* asyntactic

atavique [atavik] ADJ atavistic; *Biol* **retour a.** throwback

atavisme [atavism] NM atavism; **faire qch par a.** to do sth because it's in one's genes

atchoum [atʃum] INT *(éternuement)* atishoo!

atelier [atəlje] NM **1** *(work)*shop; *(dans une maison)* workroom; *(d'artiste)* studio; **a. de réparations** repair shop; *Tech* **a. de montage** *ou* **d'assemblage** assembly shop; **a. d'ajustage** fitting shop; **a. de constructions mécaniques** machine shop; **a. de tissage** weaving shed; **a. de constructions navales** shipyard; *Aut* **a. de carrosserie** bodyshop; *Aut* **a. de peinture** paint shop; *TV, Cin* **a. de décors** scenic workshop; *TV, Cin* **a. de production** production workshop, graphics studio; *Ordinat* **a. de flashage** bromide bureau; **chef d'a.** foreman; **il est devenu contremaître après cinq ans d'a.** he became a foreman after five years on the factory *or* shop floor; **camion a.** repair van **2** *(ensemble du personnel d'un atelier)* staff **3** *(groupe de travail)* (work-)group; **les enfants travaillent en ateliers de trois** the children work in groups of three **4** *(loge maçonnique)* lodge

atemporel, -elle [atɑ̃pɔrɛl] ADJ timeless

atermoiement [atɛrmwamɑ̃] NM **1** *Com, Jur* = arrangement with creditors for extension of time for payment; **a. d'une lettre de change** renewal of a bill **2** *Fam* **atermoiements** delays, procrastination, shillyshally(-ing); **après mille atermoiements, elle a dit oui** after much shillyshallying, she said yes; **sans atermoiements** without a moment's hesitation

atermoyer [atɛrmwaje] VI to procrastinate

ATF [ateɛf] NM *Bourse (abrév* **accord de taux futur)** forward rate agreement, future rate agreement

athée [ate] ADJ *(personne, argument)* atheistical
N atheist

athéisme [ateism] NM atheism

athénée [atene] NM **1** Athenaeum **2** *Belg* (state) secondary school

Athènes [atɛn] N Athens

athénien, -ienne [atenjɛ̃, -jɛn] ADJ Athenian
N **A.** Athenian; *Hum* **et c'est là que les Athéniens s'atteignirent** and at that point things started to get rather complicated

athlète [atlɛt] N athlete; **avoir un corps d'a.** to have the body of an athlete *or* an athletic body

athlétique [atletik] ADJ athletic

athlétiquement [atletikmɑ̃] ADV athletically

athlétisme [atletism] NM athletics, track and field; **épreuves d'a.** athletic events, track and field events

Atlantide [atlɑ̃tid] NF Atlantis

atlantique [atlɑ̃tik] ADJ Atlantic; **l'océan A.** the Atlantic (Ocean)
NM **l'A.** the Atlantic (Ocean); **Organisation du traité de l'A. Nord** North Atlantic Treaty Organization

atlas [atlas] NM **1** *(recueil de cartes)* atlas **2** *Myth, Géog* **A.** Atlas **3** *Anat* atlas

atmosphère [atmosfɛr] NF **1** atmosphere; **humidité de l'a.** atmospheric humidity; *Fig* **vivre dans l'a. de qn** to breathe the same air as sb; *Fig* **une a. de vacances** a holiday atmosphere *or* feeling; *Fig* **avoir besoin de changer d'a.** to need a change of atmosphere *or* scene(ry) **2** *Phys (unité)* atmosphere

atmosphérique [atmosferik] ADJ atmospheric; *Radio* **parasites atmosphériques** atmospherics; **perturbations atmosphériques** atmospheric disturbances

atoca [atɔka] NM *Can (plante)* cranberry

atoll [atɔl] NM *Géog* atoll

atome [atom] NM particle, bit; *Phys* atom; **atomes de poussière** specks of dust; *Fig* **avoir des atomes crochus avec qn** to hit it off with sb, to get on very well with sb; *Fig* **nous n'avons aucun a. crochu** we have nothing in common; *Fig* **pas un a. de vérité** not an ounce *or* iota of truth

atome-gramme, *pl* **atomes-grammes** NM *Phys* gram-atom

atomicité [atomisite] NF *Chimie* atomicity

atomique [atomik] ADJ *(théorie, poids etc)* atomic; **masse a.** atomic mass; **nombre** *ou* **numéro a.** atomic number; **sciences atomiques** atomics; **bombe a.** atom(ic) bomb; **guerre a.** atomic war(fare); **énergie a.** atomic energy; **sous-marin à propulseur** *ou* **propulsion a.** nuclear(-powered *or* -propelled) submarine; **pile a.** atomic reactor; **centre a.** atomic research station; **usine a.** atomic energy plant; **l'époque a.** the nuclear *or* atomic age; **Commissariat à l'énergie a.** *Br* ≃ Atomic Energy Authority, *Am* ≃ Atomic Energy Commission

atomisation [atomizasjɔ̃] NF atomization; *Pol Péj* **a. du pouvoir** dispersal of power

atomisé, -ée [atomize] N victim of a nuclear attack
ADJ *Aut* atomized

atomiser [atomize] VT **1** *(pulvériser)* to atomize; **a. de l'eau sur les fleurs** to mist the flowers **2** *Mil* to destroy with nuclear warheads, *Fam* to nuke; *(à la bombe)* to drop a nuclear bomb on; *Fig* to smash to smithereens

atomiseur [atomizœr] NM atomizer, spray; *Aut* atomizer; *(injecteur)* sprayer; **parfum en a.** spray perfume

atomisme [atomism] NM *Phil* atomism

atomiste [atomist] N **1** *Phys* nuclear *or* atomic physicist **2** *Phil* atomist

atomistique [atomistik] NF nucleonics, nuclear engineering, atomic science
ADJ atomic; *Phil* **théorie a.** atomistic theory

atonal, -ale, -aux, -ales [atonal, -o] ADJ *(musique)* atonal

atonalité [atonalite] NF atonality

atone [aton] ADJ **1** *(regard)* dull, vacant, lacklustre; **un individu a.** a lacklustre individual **2** *Méd* atonic **3** *Ling* unstressed, unaccented

atonie [atɔni] NF **1** *(mollesse)* lethargy, listlessness, lack of vitality **2** *Méd* poor physical condition, *Spéc* atony

atours [atur] NMPL adornments, finery; **parée de ses plus beaux a.** in all her finery

atout [atu] NM **1** *Cartes* trump; *Fig* asset, advantage; **a. maître** master trump; **a. carreau** diamonds are trumps; **jouer a.** to play a trump, to play trumps; *Cartes, Fig* **avoir tous les atouts dans son jeu** to hold all the winning cards; *Fig* **ce candidat a des atouts** this candidate has a lot going for him; *Fig* **c'est un a. que de savoir l'anglais** a knowledge of English is an asset **2** *Fam (coup)* clout, thump; **prendre un a.** to get clouted *or* thumped

atoxique [atɔksik] ADJ *Biol* non-poisonous, non-toxic

âtre [ɑtr] NM **1** *(cheminée)* fireplace, hearth; **au coin de l'â.** by *or* round the fireplace **2** *Ind (de forge etc)* hearth; *(du forgeron)* (blacksmith's) forge

atriqué [atrike] ADJ *Can* **mal a.** badly dressed

atroce [atrɔs] ADJ *(crime etc)* atrocious, heinous; *(terrible)* dreadful, horrible; **douleur a.** excruciating *or* agonizing pain; **j'avais une peur a. de le rencontrer** I dreaded meeting him; **d'une laideur a.** hideously ugly; **une odeur a.** a foul *or* an awful *or* a horrible smell; **il fait un temps a.** the weather is shocking *or* dreadful; **elle a fait un a. cauchemar** she had an awful nightmare

atrocement [atrɔsmɑ̃] ADV *(cruellement)* atrociously, shockingly; *(horriblement)* dreadfully, awfully, horribly, terribly; **elle a été a. torturée** she was hideously tortured; **elle a a. mal** she's in dreadful *or* terrible pain; **ça sentait a. mauvais** it smelled awful *or* horrible; **il a fait a. froid** it was dreadfully cold

atrocité [atrɔsite] NF **1** *(cruauté)* atrociousness; *(d'un crime)* atrocity; **leurs exactions sont d'une a. indescriptible** their acts of violence are indescribably atrocious **2** *(acte)* atrocity; **les atrocités commises pendant la guerre** the atrocities committed during the war; *Fam* **on m'a raconté des atrocités sur votre compte** I have been hearing dreadful things about you; *Fam* **ce tableau est une a.** this picture is a real horror *or* an atrocity

atrophie [atrɔfi] NF *Méd (d'un membre, du foie)* atrophy; **a. intellectuelle** intellectual atrophy

atrophié [atrɔfje] ADJ *(foie, intelligence)* atrophied; *(membre)* wasted, withered

atrophier [atrɔfje] VT *(membre, intelligence)* to atrophy
▪ VPR **s'atrophier** *(d'un membre)* to wither away; *Fig (de l'intelligence)* to atrophy

atropine [atrɔpin] NF *Chimie* atropin(e)

attabler (s') [satable] VPR to sit down at the (dinner *etc*) table; **veuillez vous a. pour que nous commencions à dîner** please sit down at the table so that we can begin to eat

attachant [ataʃɑ̃] ADJ **1** *(livre)* captivating **2** *(personnalité)* engaging, attractive

attache [ataʃ] NF **1** *(fixation)* point d'a. connection; **pièce d'a.** fastening; **rivets d'a.** jointing rivets; *Naut* **droit d'a.** mooring right; **droits d'a.** *(frais)* mooring dues, moorage; **port d'a.** home port, port of registry; *Fig* home base; **borne d'a.** *Naut* bollard; *Élec* terminal

2 *(lien)* tie, fastener, fastening; *(pour réparer la porcelaine)* rivet; *Élec* (wire) clamp; *(sur les vêtements)* loop, tab; **a. de diamants** diamond clasp; *Rail* **a. de rail** rail fastening; **a. de bureau** clip; *Fig* **nos attaches dans ce pays** our close ties *or* links with this country;

Fig **sans attaches** unattached, unconnected; *Fig* **je n'avais plus aucune a. dans cette ville** there was nothing to keep me in the town; *Fig* **j'ai gardé beaucoup d'attaches en France** I have kept many ties with France

3 *Anat (de muscle)* origin, attachment; **a. de la main/du pied** wrist/ankle joint; **avoir les attaches fines** to have delicate wrists and ankles

4 *Constr etc* connection, bond, brace; *(de poutre en béton armé)* binder

5 *Bot* tendril

attaché, -ée [ataʃe] ADJ **1** *(enchaîné)* fastened, tied up; *(chien)* chained up; **on l'a laissé a. au radiateur pendant une semaine** he was left tied (up) to the radiator for a week **2** *(lié affectivement)* attached; **être a. à qn/qch** to be attached *or* devoted to sb/sth; **être très a. à une région/à ses responsabilités** to be very attached to a region/very devoted to one's duties **3** *(dépendant)* linked, attached; **les avantages attachés à une fonction** the benefits going with a post; **mon bonheur est a. au vôtre** my happiness is bound up with yours; *Bourse* **coupon a.** cum dividend

N **attaché**; **a. militaire** military attaché; **a. commercial** *(d'une ambassade)* commercial attaché; *(d'une entreprise)* sales representative; **a. de presse** press attaché *or* officer; **a. d'administration** junior civil servant

attaché-case, *pl* **attachés-cases** [ataʃekɛs] NM attaché case

attachement [ataʃmɑ̃] NM **1** *(pour quelqu'un, quelque chose)* attachment (**pour** to), affection (**pour** for) **2** *Constr* = daily statement of work carried out and expenses incurred **3** *Mktg* **a. à la marque** brand bonding

attacher [ataʃe] VT **1** *(fixer, enchaîner)* to attach, to fasten (**qch à qch** sth to sth); *(avec ficelle, corde)* to tie (up), to do up; *(avec une chaîne)* to chain (up); **a. un cheval** to tie up *or* tether a horse; **a. qch avec une boucle** to buckle sth; **a. qch avec des clous/épingles** to nail/pin sth on; **a. deux choses avec des clous/épingles** to nail/pin two things together; **a. ses cheveux avec un ruban** to tie a ribbon in one's hair; **a. ses cheveux** to tie one's hair back; **a. une étiquette à un paquet** to stick a label on a parcel; **il faut bien a. le paquet** you should tie up the parcel securely; **a. un prisonnier au poteau** to tie a prisoner to the stake; **attachez vos ceintures** fasten your seat belts; **tu peux m'a. ma robe?** can you fasten my dress?, can you do up my dress?, can you do me up?; **a. ses lacets** *ou* **chaussures** to do up *or* tie (up) *or* fasten one's shoelaces

2 *(accorder)* **a. de l'importance à qch** to attach importance to sth; **a. du prix** *ou* **de la valeur à** to attach great value to; **a. une signification à un fait/un acte** to read into a fact/an act

3 a. un nouveau secrétaire à une ambassade to attach a new secretary to an embassy; **ce domestique est attaché au service de la famille depuis cinquante ans** this servant has been in the family's employment for fifty years

4 *(lier sentimentalement)* to attach; **ce qui m'attache à lui** what attaches me to him; **tout ce qui nous attache à la vie** everything we hold dear in life

5 a. ses yeux *ou* **ses regards sur** to fix one's eyes on

▪ VI *Culin Fam* **les pommes de terre ont attaché** the potatoes have stuck (to the pan); **casserole qui n'attache pas** non-stick saucepan

▪ VPR **s'attacher 1** *(d'une chose)* to cling, to stick (**à** to); *(ne pas s'enlever)* to be attached *or* stuck (**à** to); *(avec une agrafe etc)* to be fastened (**à** to); *(avec ficelle, corde etc)* to be tied

(à on, to); **les manifestants se sont attachés aux grilles avec des menottes et des chaînes** the protesters handcuffed and chained themselves to the railings; **la sangsue s'attacha à son mollet** the leech clung *or* stuck to his calf; **le lierre s'attache aux arbres** ivy clings to trees; **collier qui s'attache avec une agrafe** necklace that fastens with a clip; **la jupe s'attache par derrière** the skirt fastens (up) *or* does up at the back; *Fig* **s'a. aux pas de qn** to follow sb closely

2 *(se lier sentimentalement)* **tu t'attaches trop aux gens que tu rencontres** you get too attached to the people you meet; **elle s'est beaucoup attachée à cette vieille dame** she has got *or* become very attached to that old lady; **s'a. à qn** to become *or* grow fond of *or* attached to sb; **s'a. à une région** to become attached to a region; **je ne veux pas m'a.** I don't want to tie myself down *or* get involved *or* commit myself; **elle sait s'a. ses élèves** she knows how to gain her pupils' affection

3 *(se concentrer sur)* **s'a. aux faits** to stick to the facts; **ce n'est pas la peine de s'a. aux détails** there's no point getting caught up in details; **s'a. à une tâche** to apply oneself to a job; **s'a. à qch** to pay particular attention to sth; **s'a. à bien faire son travail** to take particular care over one's work; **s'a. à l'honnêteté/l'éducation** to attach great importance to *or* to set great store by honesty/education

attaquable [atakabl] ADJ **1** *Mil* open to attack, attackable **2** *(fait, opinion etc)* contestable; *(testament etc)* open to attack

attaquant, -ante [atakɑ̃, -ɑ̃t] ADJ attacking
N assailant, attacker; *Sport* striker

attaque [atak] NF **1** *Mil etc* attack, assault; *(d'une voiture, d'un train etc)* hold-up (**de** of); **à l'a.!** attack!; **a. concertée** concerted attack; **reprise d'a.** renewed attack; **corps d'a.** attacking party; *aussi Fig* **passer à l'a.** to go on to the offensive; *Fig* **il a attendu de la connaître un peu mieux pour passer à l'a.** he waited until he knew her a bit better before he moved in for the kill; **repasser à l'a.** to return to the attack; **monter une a.** to mount an attack; **a. frontale** *ou* **de front** frontal *or* head-on attack; **subir une a.** to be attacked; *Fig* **les attaques de la presse** attacks by the press; *Fig* **diriger de violentes attaques contre qn** to attack sb violently; **a. de côté** flank attack; **a. latérale** flank attack; **a. par encerclement** encirclement attack

2 *Sport* attack; *(à l'aviron)* catch; *Cartes* lead **3 d'a.** vigorously; **se sentir d'a.** to feel in good shape, *Am* to feel bright-eyed and bushy-tailed; **se sentir d'a. pour faire qch** to feel up to *or* ready to do sth; **être d'a.** *(en pleine forme)* to be on top form; **il est toujours d'a.** he is still going strong; **il n'est plus assez d'a. pour faire de longues marches** he's no longer up to going for long walks

4 *Méd (de maladie douloureuse)* attack; *(de fièvre, grippe)* bout; **a. d'épilepsie** epileptic fit; **a. d'apoplexie** (apoplectic) stroke; **a. de nerfs** fit of hysterics; **une a.** *(crise cardiaque)* a heart attack

5 *Tech* **a. directe** *(de moteur)* direct drive; **pignon d'a.** driving pinion; *Aviat, Naut* **bord d'a.** *(d'aile, d'hélice)* leading edge; **angle d'a.** leading angle

6 *(d'un article)* intro; *Mus (d'un instrument)* entry; *(d'une note)* attack; **chef d'a.** *(de l'orchestre)* first violin, leader

▸ ▸ *Aviat* **a. aérienne** air raid *or* strike; **a. à la bombe** bomb attack, bombing; **a. à main armée** armed robbery

attaquer [atake] VT **1** *(personne, ennemi, place forte etc)* to attack; *(personne, ennemi)* to set upon, to assault; *(de l'acide) (métal)* to attack, to eat into, to corrode; *Mil* **a. de front** to make *or* to launch a frontal attack on; **at-**

taquez! engage!; être attaqué par les moustiques to be attacked by mosquitoes; a. qn à coup de poings to lay into sb, to go for sb with one's fists; *Fig* a. les abus/les préjugés to attack injustice/prejudices; *Fig* a. qn sur un sujet to tackle sb on a subject; *Jur* a. (la validité d')un testament to contest a will; *Jur* a. qn en justice to prosecute sb, to bring an action against sb; *Fig* a. la réputation/ l'honneur de qn to attack sb's reputation/ honour; *Méd* le poumon droit est attaqué the right lung is affected

2 *(repas, sujet, travail etc)* to tackle, to get to work on; nous attaquons demain l'ascension du mont Blanc tomorrow we('ll) attack or tackle Mont Blanc; attaquons le repas avant que ça ne refroidisse let's tuck in or get stuck in before it gets cold

3 *Mus (note)* to attack; *(morceau)* to strike up; bien a. la note to hit the note well or clearly

vi 1 to attack; qui a attaqué le premier? *(à deux enfants qui se battent)* who started it?; *Mktg* a. de front to launch a frontal attack; *Mktg* a. latéralement to launch a flank attack **2** *Mus* a. faux to hit the wrong note **3** *Cartes* a. trèfle/de la reine to lead clubs/ the queen **4** *(d'acides etc)* to corrode

vpr s'attaquer s'a. à qn/qch to attack or make an attack on or tackle sb/sth; elle s'attaque à tout le monde she's always having a go at people; s'a. à une difficulté/un problème to grapple with or to tackle a difficulty/a problem

attardé, -ée [atarde] **ADJ 1** il ne restait plus que quelques passants attardés there were only a few people out late; il profite de la pénombre pour attaquer les promeneurs attardés he takes advantage of the dim light to attack people who are out walking late **2** *(dans le temps)* behind the times; ma grand-mère est complètement attardée my grandmother is completely behind the times or old-fashioned; idées *ou* conceptions attardées old-fashioned or outmoded ideas **3** *Psy (mentalement) (enfant)* (mentally) retarded

N 1 *Psy* a. (mental) (mentally) retarded person **2** *(dans une course etc)* les attardés the laggards, those that bring up the rear

attarder [atarde] **VT** to keep late, to delay; une crevaison nous a attardés we were delayed by a puncture

vpr s'attarder to linger, to loiter; *(en se promenant)* to lag behind, to dawdle; s'a. en route to dawdle on the way; ne nous attardons pas let's not linger, *Fam* let's not hang about; nous nous sommes attardés chez nos amis we stayed on late at our friends' house; elle s'est attardée au travail she stayed late at work; s'a. pour regarder le paysage to linger to look at the scenery; s'a. à qch to linger over sth; *Péj* to waste one's time on sth; ne nous attardons pas sur ce point let's not dwell on this point; inutile de s'a. là-dessus there's no point in dwelling on it

atteindre [atɛ̃dr] *(prp* atteignant; *pp* atteint; *pr ind* j'atteins, il atteint, *n.* atteignons; *impf* j'atteignais; *p hist* j'atteignis; *fu* j'atteindrai)* **VT 1** *(parvenir à)* to reach, *Fml* to attain; a. la ville to reach the town, to get to the town; a. la plus haute étagère to reach the top shelf; je ne peux pas l'a. I can't reach it; a. qn to catch sb up; a. l'ennemi to catch up with the enemy; a. son but to attain or achieve one's aim; a. l'âge de soixante ans to reach the age of sixty

2 *(s'élever à)* to reach; le nombre des participants atteint le millier the number of participants is nearing or reaching the thousand mark; très peu de montagnes at-

teignent 8000 mètres very few mountains reach (a height of) 8,000 metres; la pollution atteint la cote d'alerte pollution is reaching danger level; a. un prix élevé to reach or fetch a high price

3 *(toucher)* to hit, to reach; a. le but to hit the target or the mark; ne pas a. le but to fall short of the mark; a. une couche pétrolifère to strike oil; être atteint (par une balle) à la jambe to be shot in the leg; être atteint d'une maladie to be struck down by a disease; *(d'arbres etc)* to be attacked by a disease; le poumon est atteint the lung is affected; un malade très atteint a seriously ill patient; *Fam* il est complètement atteint *(fou)* he's completely cracked or potty; *Fig* tu peux le lui dire, mais cela ne l'atteint pas you can tell him, but it doesn't have any effect; *Fig* rien ne l'atteint nothing affects him, he's impervious to everything; *Fig* elle est atteinte dans son amour-propre her pride has been wounded or hurt; *Fig* une perte qui m'a profondément atteinte a loss which affected me very badly

vi a. à qch to reach or attain sth; a. à son but to achieve one's aim; son travail atteint à la perfection his work is close to or is nearing perfection

atteinte [atɛ̃t] **NF 1** *(portée)* reach; hors d'a. *(fuyard etc)* beyond reach, out of reach; *Fig* sa réputation est hors d'a. his reputation is beyond attack or is unassailable; se dérober *ou* se soustraire à l'a. de la loi to circumvent or get round or *Fam* dodge the law; *(s'échapper)* to get out of the clutches of the law

2 *(attaque)* blow, stroke, attack; légère a. au bras slight blow on the arm; les premières atteintes d'une maladie the first attacks of an illness; a. au crédit de qn blow to sb's credit; porter a. à l'autorité de qn to undermine sb's authority; a. portée aux privilèges breach of privilege; porter a. aux intérêts de qn to interfere with sb's interests, to affect sb's interests; je considère que c'est une a. à mon honneur I consider it an attack on or a blow to my honour; porter a. à la réputation de qn to damage sb's reputation

attelage [atlaʒ] **NM 1** *(action d'atteler)* harnessing; *(de bœufs)* yoking; *Constr etc* attachment; *(de remorques etc)* tying, fastening; *(avec un crochet)* hooking on; *Rail* coupling; *Astronaut* l'a. d'engins spatiaux the docking of spacecraft **2** *(animaux)* team; *(de chevaux)* pair; *(de bœufs)* yoke; *(voiture)* carriage (and horses)

atteler [atle] *(j'attelle, n. attelons; j'attellerai)* **VT 1** *(chevaux etc)* to harness; *(bœufs)* to yoke; *Fig* toujours attelé à son travail always hard at work or hard at it **2** a. une voiture to attach horses to a carriage; voiture attelée de quatre chevaux carriage drawn by four horses; *Sport* course de trot attelé trotting race; *Rail* a. des wagons to couple (up) wagons

vpr s'atteler le gouvernement doit s'a. au problème du chômage the government must tackle the problem of unemployment; s'a. à une tâche/un travail to buckle down or get down to a task/a job; je m'y attelle tous les jours I force myself to do it every day

attelle [atɛl] **NF** *Méd* splint

attenant [at(ə)nɑ̃] **ADJ** adjacent (à to), adjoining, bordering; deux chemins attenants two intersecting paths

attendre [atɑ̃dr] **VT** to wait for; *Fml, Litt* to await; qu'attendez-vous? what are you waiting for?; le déjeuner nous attend lunch is ready; une surprise vous attend there's a surprise in store for you, you've got a surprise waiting for you; l'avenir nous attend the future lies before us; j'attends midi pour lui téléphoner I'll wait until twelve o'clock before I telephone him; aller a. qn à la gare

to go to meet or to go and meet sb at the station; a. la fin de l'histoire to wait for or until the end of the story; il se fait a. he's keeping us waiting; la réponse ne s'est pas fait a. the reply wasn't long in coming; tu t'es fait a.! and about time too!; nous n'attendions que toi now you're here, we can start/go/*etc*; on l'attend la semaine prochaine he is expected next week; je l'attends d'un moment à l'autre I'm expecting him any minute now; nous l'attendions tous avec impatience we were all looking forward to seeing him; nous attendons les résultats avec impatience we can't wait to get the results; j'attends des explications I'm waiting for an explanation; je n'en attends rien de bon I'm not expecting anything good to come of it; a. un bébé, *Belg* a. famille to be expecting (a baby); attendez voir just wait, wait and see; *(laissez-moi réfléchir)* let me see; on ne t'attendait plus we'd given up on you; qu'attend-il de moi? what does he want or expect from me?; elle n'attend que ça that's (just) what she wants or is waiting for; je n'attends qu'une chose, les vacances I (just) can't wait for the holidays to begin; a. que qn fasse qch to wait for sb to do sth; j'attendrai (jusqu'à ce) qu'il soit prêt I shall wait until he's ready; *Fig* a. qn au tournant to be waiting to catch sb out; a. son tour to wait one's turn; qu'est-ce que tu attends pour aller porter plainte? what are you waiting for? go and complain

vi 1 to wait; perdre son temps à a. to waste one's time waiting; désolé de vous avoir fait a. sorry to have kept you waiting; le train n'attendra pas the train won't wait; j'attends de voir pour juger I'll wait and see before I pass judgment; a. de faire qch to wait (until it is time) to do sth; attendons jusqu'à demain let's wait until tomorrow; *Fam* on ne va pas a. 107 ans we're not going to wait forever; *Iron* j'ai failli a.! nice of you to turn up!; attends un peu que je t'attrape! just you wait till I catch you!; attendez (donc)! hang or hold on!, wait (a bit)!, just a moment or a minute!; sans plus a. without further ado; *Prov* tout vient à point à qui sait a. everything comes to him who waits; il vaut mieux a. encore un peu it would be better to wait a bit longer; a. une heure to wait (for) an hour; il ne perd rien pour a. he's got it coming to him; un plat qui n'attend pas a dish that won't wait, a dish you have to eat straight away

2 *Fam* a. après qn/qch to wait for or to need sb/sth; porte-lui ce livre, il attend après take this book to him, he is waiting for it

3 en attendant meanwhile, in the meantime; un remplaçant va arriver mais, en attendant, c'est nous qui devons tout faire a replacement will arrive, but in the meantime we have to do everything; en attendant son arrivée until he arrives, while waiting for him to arrive; en attendant de vous voir until I/we/*etc* see you; il te dit peut-être qu'il t'aime, mais en attendant il vit avec une autre maybe he does say he loves you, but he's living with somebody else in the meantime

vpr s'attendre s'a. à qch to expect sth; il ne faut pas s'a. à des miracles you can't expect miracles; il faut s'a. à tout one must be prepared or ready for anything; a. m'y attendais I expected as much; il fallait s'y a. it was only to be expected; je m'attendais à ce que tu me le dises I was expecting you to tell me; je ne m'attendais pas à ça I wasn't expecting or hadn't expected that

> Il faut noter que le verbe anglais **to attend** est un faux ami. Il signifie le plus souvent **être présent, assister à.**

attendri [atɑ̃dri] **ADJ** regard a. fond or tender look

attendrir [atɑ̃drir] **VT 1** *(le cœur de qn)* to soften; *(personne)* to move, to touch; **cela attendrirait un cœur de pierre** it would melt a heart of stone; **s'il espère m'a. avec ses cadeaux, il se trompe** if he's hoping to soften me up with his presents, he's got another think coming **2** *(viande)* to make tender, to tenderize
▸ **VPR s'attendrir** to be moved *or* touched; **les médecins ne peuvent se permettre de s'a.** doctors cannot allow themselves to get emotionally involved; **s'a. sur qch** to be moved (to tears) *or* touched by sth; **s'a. sur un bébé** to gush over a baby; **s'a. sur soi-même** *ou* **sur son propre sort** to feel sorry for oneself; **il s'attendrit facilement** he is very emotional

attendrissant [atɑ̃drisɑ̃] **ADJ** moving, touching; **sa crédulité est attendrissante** his/her naivety is touching

attendrissement [atɑ̃drismɑ̃] **NM** tenderness; **allons, pas d'a.!** come on, let's not get emotional!; **larmes d'a.** tender tears of emotion

attendrisseur [atɑ̃drisœr] **NM** (meat) tenderizer

attendu [atɑ̃dy] **ADJ** expected; **le jour tant a. est arrivé** the long-awaited *or* much-awaited day arrived; **le train est a. pour cinq heures** the train is expected at five o'clock
▸ **PRÉP** *(les circonstances)* considering; *(les événements)* owing to; *(ses services)* in consideration of; **a. son attitude envers moi** considering *or* in view of his attitude towards me
▸ **CONJ a. que** + *ind* considering that, seeing that; *Jur* whereas

attentat [atɑ̃ta] **NM** attack; **a. contre la vie de qn** attempted murder on sb, attempt on sb's life; *Pol* assassination attempt on sb; **victime d'un a.** victim of an attack
▸▸ **a. à la liberté** violation *or* infringement of liberty; *Jur* **a. aux mœurs** indecent behaviour, public indecency; **a. à la pudeur** indecent assault; **a. à la sûreté de l'État** high treason

attentatoire [atɑ̃tatwar] **ADJ** *Jur* **action a. à l'autorité** action that is a challenge to *or* in contempt of authority; **mesure a. à la liberté** measure that constitutes an infringement of *or* an attack on liberty

attente [atɑ̃t] **NF 1** *(fait d'attendre)* waiting; *(période)* wait; **je ne supporte plus cette a. !** can't stand this waiting any longer; **vous devez compter une a. de quatre heures** you should expect a four-hour wait; **être dans l'a. de qch** to be waiting for sth; **salle d'a.** waiting room; **rester en a.** to be held over; **liste d'a.** waiting list; *Br* **file d'a.** queue, *Am* line; *Ordinat* **liste de fichiers à imprimer en a.** print queue; *Mil* **combat d'a.** delaying action; *Chir* **ligature d'a.** temporary ligature; *Aviat* **circuit d'a.** holding pattern, stack **2** *(espoir)* expectation(s), anticipation; **contre toute a.** contrary to all expectations; **remplir l'a. de qn, répondre à l'a. de qn** to come up *or* live up to sb's expectations; **dans l'a. de votre réponse/de vous rencontrer** *(dans une lettre)* awaiting your reply/looking forward to meeting you

attenter [atɑ̃te] **VI** to make an attempt (**à** on, against); **a. à la vie de qn** to make an attempt on sb's life; **a. à ses jours** to attempt suicide; **a. à la liberté de qn** to infringe upon sb's liberty

attentif, -ive [atɑ̃tif, -iv] **ADJ 1** *(en alerte)* **soyez attentifs!** pay attention!; **il n'est pas a.** he doesn't pay attention; **être (très) a. aux autres** to be (very) attentive to others; **écouter d'un air a./d'une oreille attentive** to listen attentively; **être a. à qch** to look after sth, to see to sth; **être a. à ses intérêts** to look after one's (own) interests; **être a. à sa santé** to look after oneself *or* one's health; **a. aux prix** price-conscious **2** *(appliqué)* careful; **examen a.** careful examination

attention [atɑ̃sjɔ̃] **NF 1** attention; **appliquer toute son a. à qch** to devote one's undivided attention to sth; **faute d'a.** through not paying attention; **faire un effort d'a.** to try to be more attentive, to try to concentrate; **écouter avec a.** to listen attentively; **porter ou tourner ou diriger son a. vers ou sur qch** to turn one's attention to sth; **attirer l'a.** *(d'un objet ou d'un fait)* to attract attention; **c'est ce détail qui a attiré mon a.** it's this detail which attracted *or* caught my attention; **attirer l'a. de qn sur qch** to draw sb's attention to sth; **puis-je avoir votre a., s'il vous plaît** (may I have) your attention, please; **faire a. à sa santé** to take care of one's health; **ne faire aucune a. à qn/qch, ne pas prêter la moindre a. à qn/qch** to take no *or* to take not the slightest notice of sb/sth; **il a fait très a. de ne pas la blesser** he took great care not to hurt her; **(faites) a.!** take care!, look out!, watch it!; **a. à la peinture** mind the paint; *(écriteau)* wet paint; *Rail* **a. à la fermeture des portières!, a. au départ!** ≃ stand clear of the doors!, mind the doors!; **a. au train** beware of (the) trains!; **a., verglas** caution, ice; **a. aux travaux** caution, road works ahead; **il a une petite amie/une bagnole, a. les yeux!** you should see his girlfriend/car!, his girlfriend/car is an absolute *Br* cracker *or Am* crackerjack; **faites a. à ou de ne pas vous perdre** be careful not to get lost; **faites a. (à ce) que personne ne sorte** take care *or* be sure that no one leaves (the house); **à l'a. de Marie Berne** for the attention of Marie Berne **2** *(amabilité)* attention(s), consideration; **être plein d'attention(s) envers qn** to be full of consideration for sb, to be very attentive towards sb; **il a eu l'a. de m'avertir** he was considerate enough to warn me

attentionné [atɑ̃sjɔne] **ADJ** attentive; **être a. envers qn** to be full of consideration for sb, to be very attentive towards sb

attentisme [atɑ̃tism] **NM** wait-and-see policy

attentiste [atɑ̃tist] **ADJ** *(politique)* wait-and-see
▸ **N** advocate of a wait-and-see policy

attentivement [atɑ̃tivmɑ̃] **ADV** attentively, carefully; *(regarder)* closely

atténuant [atenɥɑ̃] **ADJ** *Jur (circonstances)* mitigating, extenuating

atténuateur [atenɥatœr] **NM** attenuator

atténuation [atenɥasjɔ̃] **NF 1** diminishing, reducing, lessening; *(de lumière)* dimming, subduing; *(de couleur)* toning down; *(d'une chute)* breaking; *(d'un châtiment, d'une sentence)* mitigation, reduction; *(de la douleur)* easing, relief **2** *Phot (de négatif)* reduction; *(des contrastes)* softening **3** *(d'un crime)* extenuation

atténué [atenɥe] **ADJ** attenuated, diminished; *Jur* **responsabilité atténuée** diminished responsibility

atténuer [atenɥe] **VT 1** to diminish, to reduce, to lessen; *(couleur)* to tone down; *(lumière)* to dim, to subdue; *(châtiment, conséquences)* to mitigate; *(douleur)* to ease, to relieve; **a. une chute** to break a fall **2** *Phot (négatif etc)* to reduce; *(contrastes)* to soften, to tone down **3** *(offense)* to extenuate; *(crime etc)* to make less serious; **sa situation n'atténue en rien la gravité de ce qu'il a fait** his situation in no way lessens *or* reduces the seriousness of what he has done
▸ **VPR s'atténuer** to lessen; *(de la lumière)* to fade

atterrant [aterɑ̃] **ADJ** overwhelming; *(nouvelle)* shattering

atterrer [atere] **VT** to appal; **sa naïveté m'atterre** I am appalled *or* staggered by his/her naivety; **ils se regardent atterrés** they look at each other aghast

atterrir [aterir] **VI 1** *Naut (voir la terre)* to make *or* sight land, to make a landfall; *(toucher le fond)* to ground, to run ashore **2** *Aviat* to land; **l'avion a dû a. en catastrophe** the aeroplane had to make an emergency landing; **a. trop court** to undershoot; **a. trop long** to overshoot; **a. brutalement** to crash (land), to make a rough *or* bumpy landing; *Fam* **a. dans un bar/dans un fossé/à l'hôpital** to land up *or* end up *or* finish up in a bar/a ditch/hospital; *Fam* **atterris, mon vieux!** you dozy thing!

atterrissage [aterisaʒ] **NM 1** *Aviat* landing, touchdown; *Fig Fam* **elle a cru qu'il l'aimait et l'a. a été difficile** she thought he loved her but she came down to earth with a bump; **a. trop long** overshoot; **a. trop court** undershoot; **a. forcé** forced landing; **a. à vue** visual landing; **a. aux instruments** instrument landing; **a. sans visibilité** blind landing; **a. brutal** rough *or* bumpy landing; **a. en catastrophe** emergency landing; **terrain d'a.** *(ensemble des pistes)* landing strip *or* field; **pont d'a.** *(de porte-avions)* landing deck; **a. en douceur** soft landing **2** *Naut* making (the) land, landfall; *(en touchant le fond)* grounding, running ashore **3** *Tél (de câble marin)* landing

attestation [atestasjɔ̃] **NF** *(action)* attestation; *(certificat)* certificate; **demander l'a. du professeur** to ask for a reference from the teacher; **a. du médecin/de l'employeur** doctor's/employer's certificate; **a. d'assurance** certificate of insurance; **a. de rejet** *(de chèque)* notification of returned cheque; *Jur* **a. du titre** warranty of title; **a. sous serment** *ou* **sur l'honneur** affidavit

attester [ateste] **VT 1** **a. qch** to attest *or* certify sth, to testify to sth; *(la réputation de qn)* to vouch for sth; *(sortie d'argent)* to confirm sth; **a. que qch est vrai** to attest *or* certify that sth is true; **c'est un fait attesté** it is an established fact, it is beyond doubt; **sa réponse atteste sa mauvaise foi** his reply bears witness to *or* demonstrates his bad faith; **nous pensons tous qu'il a menti et la bande enregistrée en atteste** we all think he lied and the tape recording proves it; *Ling* **forme attestée** attested form; **ce mot n'est attesté dans aucun dictionnaire** this word isn't attested *or* doesn't occur in any dictionary **2** *(prendre à témoin)* **a. qn** to call sb to witness (**de qch** to sth); **a. l'autorité de qn en faveur d'une affirmation** to advance a statement on the authority of sb

attiédir [atjedir] **VT** *(eau chaude etc)* to cool; *(eau froide)* to warm, to take the chill off; *Fig* **a. les passions de qn** to calm *or* cool sb's passions
▸ **VPR s'attiédir** *(de l'eau chaude)* to cool down, to become tepid *or* lukewarm; *(de l'eau froide)* to warm up; *Fig (des passions)* to cool

attiédissement [atjedismɑ̃] **NM** *(de l'eau chaude)* cooling down; *(de l'eau froide)* warming up; *Fig (des passions)* cooling

attifer [atife] **VT** *Fam* to rig out, to get up, to deck out (**de** in); **elle est toujours attifée de manière impossible** she's always rigged out in the most ridiculous fashion; **elle attife ses enfants n'importe comment** she dresses her children any old how; **comme te voilà attifé!** what a sight he looks!
▸ **VPR s'attifer** **elle s'attife toujours bizarrement** she's always wearing strange rig-outs

attiger [atiʒe] **VI** (**j'attigeais; n. attigeons**) *Arg Vieilli (exagérer)* to go over the top, to go too far; **tu attiges!** come off it!

attique [atik] ADJ *Antiq* Attic, Athenian
NM **1** *Archit (étage)* attic **2** *Suisse* **appartement en a.** top-floor flat

attirail [atiraj] NM **1** equipment, gear; *(d'outils etc)* set; *(de cuisine)* utensils; *(de jardin)* tools; **a. de pêche** fishing tackle **2** *Fam* paraphernalia; **avant d'acheter la moto, il s'est acheté tout l'a.** before buying the motorbike, he bought himself all the right gear; **elle est arrivée avec tout un a. de photographe** she arrived with a lot of photographer's paraphernalia

attirance [atirãs] NF attraction (**vers** to); *(du plaisir, d'un endroit etc)* lure, fascination; **éprouver de l'a. pour qn** to be drawn or attracted to sb; **je n'ai aucune a. vers** ou **pour les mathématiques** maths does not appeal to me in the least

attirant [atirã] ADJ attractive; *(force etc)* drawing; *(manières, sourire)* alluring, engaging

attirer [atire] VT **1** *(d'un aimant, du soleil etc)* to attract, to draw; **quelque chose les attire l'un vers l'autre** something draws them together, there is some kind of attraction between them; **ce qui m'attire dans ce projet** what attracts me or what I find attractive about this project; **je ne sais pas ce qui m'attire en** ou **chez elle** I don't know what attracts me to her; **la Grèce, ça ne vous attire pas?** doesn't Greece appeal to you?; **sa pièce attire un grand public** his play draws a large audience; **a. qn dans un coin** to draw or take sb into a corner; **a. qch à** ou **sur qn** to bring sth on sb; **cela risque de vous a. des ennuis/des ennemis** that may cause you problems/make enemies for you; **avec ton insolence, tu vas nous a. des ennuis** your insolence is going to cause us problems; **a. la colère de qn sur qn** to bring down sb's wrath on sb; **je voudrais a. votre attention sur ce point** I'd like to draw your attention to this point; **c'est vraiment quelqu'un qui attire la sympathie** he/she is someone who gains a lot of sympathy; **son roman a attiré de violentes critiques** his novel has come in for or has attracted harsh criticism; **affiche qui attire les regards** eye-catching poster
2 *(séduire)* to attract; **elle attire les hommes d'un certain âge/paumés** she attracts middle-aged men/losers; **a. qn dans un piège** to lure sb into a trap; **a. qn par des promesses** to entice sb with promises
VPR **s'attirer 1** *(mutuellement)* to attract each other; **ils s'attirent** they're attracted to each other; **les contraires s'attirent** opposites attract (each other)
2 *(sur soi)* **s'a. des critiques/des éloges** to come in for criticism/praise; **je me suis attiré la colère de mon père** I incurred my father's anger; **il s'est attiré la reconnaissance du patron** he earned his boss's gratitude; **s'a. des sympathies/des ennemis** to gain sympathy/to make enemies

attiser [atize] VT **1** *(feu)* to stir (up), to poke; *Ind etc* to stoke **2** *Fig (désir, mécontentement)* to fan the flames of, to fuel; **a. les haines/le racisme** to stir up hatred/racism

attitré [atitre] ADJ *(chargé d'une fonction)* appointed, recognized; *(journaliste)* accredited; **fournisseurs attitrés de Sa Majesté** purveyors by appointment to His/Her Majesty; *(habituel)* **mon marchand de légumes a.** my usual or regular greengrocer; **mon fauteuil a.** my chair, the chair I sit in

attitrer [atitre] VT *(ambassadeur)* to appoint

attitude [atityd] NF **1** *(disposition)* attitude; **a. hostile/intransigeante** hostile/uncompromising attitude (**envers, à l'égard de, pour, en face de** towards); **quelle est votre a. vis-à-vis de ce problème?** what is your stance or position on this problem?, how

do you stand on this problem? **2** *(conduite)* attitude; **je n'aime pas son a.** I don't like his attitude; **tu as eu une a. déplorable au cours de cette réunion** you behaved appallingly during the meeting, your behaviour during the meeting was appalling; **ce n'est qu'une a.** it's only an act or a pose **3** *(port)* attitude; **il prit une a. décontractée** he struck a casual pose

attouchement [atuʃmã] NM **1** *(pour guérir)* laying on of hands **2** *(sexuel)* **se livrer à des attouchements sur qn** to fondle sb; *Jur* to interfere with sb

attractif, -ive [atraktif, -iv] ADJ *Phys (pouvoir)* attractive, drawing; *(force)* gravitational **2** *Fig (prix, vertu)* attractive

attraction [atraksjõ] NF **1** *(d'un aimant etc)* attraction, pull; *Phys* **a. universelle** gravitation; **a. moléculaire** molecular attraction **2** *(d'un endroit, d'une personne etc)* attraction; **l'a. de deux personnes l'une pour l'autre** the attraction between two people; **exercer une a. sur qn** to attract sb; **l'a. qui me porte vers cet endroit** the attraction this place has for me; **les automobiles allemandes suscitent une a. très marquée chez les Britanniques** German cars are very popular with the British **3** *(de cabaret)* number; *Fam* **c'est la grosse a.** he/she is the big attraction **4** **attractions** attractions; *(à la foire)* sideshows; *Théâtre* variety show; *(au restaurant)* cabaret show; **parc d'attractions** amusement park; **les attractions passent à 21 heures** the show starts at 9 o'clock; **a. touristique** tourist or visitor attraction

attrait [atrɛ] NM **1** *(chose)* attraction, lure; *(état)* attractiveness; *(de la jeunesse etc)* charm; **l'a. de la mer** the call of the sea; **a. touristique** *(charme)* tourist appeal; **l'a. de l'aventure** the lure of adventure; **les attraits d'une carrière dans le commerce** the attraction of a business career; *Mktg* **a. commercial** market appeal; **dépourvu d'a.** unattractive, devoid of attraction; **ressentir de l'a. pour qn** to feel attracted by sb **2 attraits** *(d'une femme)* charms

attrapade [atrapad] NF, **attrapage** [atrapaʒ] NM *Fam* **1** *(dispute)* quarrel, set-to **2** *(réprimande)* ticking-off, telling-off; **j'ai eu droit à un(e) bon(ne) a.** I got a right telling-off

attrape [atrap] NF **1** *(farce)* trick, hoax; **faire une a. à qn** to play a trick or a practical joke on sb; *(tromper)* to take sb in; **c'est une a.** there's a catch in it; **magasin de farces et attrapes** joke shop **2** *Arch (à oiseaux etc)* trap, gin snare

attrape-couillon, *pl* **attrape-couillon(s)** NM *Fam* gimmick

attrape-mouche, *pl* **attrape-mouches** NM **1** *(piège)* flypaper **2** *(fleur)* Venus flytrap, Venus's flytrap

attrape-nigaud, *pl* **attrape-nigauds** NM trick

attraper [atrape] VT **1** *(capturer)* *(personne, animal)* to catch
2 *(saisir)* *(ballon, voleur etc)* to catch; *(se saisir de)* to grab; **les voleurs se sont fait a.** the thieves were caught; **attention je te t'attrape!** if I catch you, there'll be trouble!; **il l'attrapa par le poignet** he grabbed or caught her (by the) wrist; **tu peux m'a. le torchon?** could you grab that cloth for me?; **a. un autobus/un train** to catch a bus/a train; **je n'ai pu a. que quelques secondes/bribes de leur conversation** I could only catch a few seconds/snatches of their conversation
3 *(prendre, contracter)* **a. froid** to catch a chill; **a. un bon coup de soleil** to get badly sunburned; **a. un rhume** to catch (a) cold; **j'ai attrapé mal à la tête** I've got a headache; **a. mal** to catch a cold; **en a. pour dix ans** to get ten years' (imprisonment); *Aut etc* **a. une**

contravention to get a ticket, to pick up a ticket; **a. un accent** to pick up an accent
4 *(tromper)* **a. qn** to trick or cheat sb, to take sb in; **là, vous êtes bien attrapé** you fell for it hook, line and sinker or good and proper
5 *(surprendre)* to catch; *Fam* **a. qn à faire qch** to catch sb doing sth; **et méfie-toi, si je t'y attrape encore une fois …!** don't let me catch you (at it) again, or else …!; **a. qn sur le fait** to catch sb in the act, to catch sb red-handed
6 *Fam (gronder)* **a. qn** to scold sb, to give sb a good talking to; **se faire a.** to get told off, to catch it
VPR **s'attraper 1** *(d'une maladie etc)* to be caught; **le sida ne s'attrape pas par la salive** you can't catch AIDS through saliva; **ça s'attrape facilement** it's very catching **2** *(se disputer)* to scold each other

attrape-touristes NM INV *Fam* tourist trap

attrayant [atrɛjã] ADJ attractive, appealing; **peu a.** unattractive

attribuable [atribɥabl] ADJ attributable, ascribable (**à** to)

attribuer [atribɥe] VT **1** *(allouer)* to assign, to allot (**à** to), to confer (**à** (up)on); *(prix, récompense)* to award; *Fin (actions)* to allot; *Ordinat (mémoire)* to allocate; **a. des rôles** ou **des fonctions** to allocate duties (**à** to); *Théâtre* **a. un rôle à qn** to cast sb for a part; **a. le rôle de Cyrano à qn** to cast sb as Cyrano **2** *(fait, livre etc)* to attribute, to ascribe (**à** to); *(crime, erreur)* to blame (**à** on); *(de l'importance à qch)* to attach; **on attribue l'incendie à une inattention** the fire has been blamed on carelessness; **ne m'attribue pas des motivations qui sont les tiennes** don't project your motives onto me; **a. un projet à qn** to give sb the credit for a plan; **tableau attribué à Hogarth** painting attributed to Hogarth
VPR **s'attribuer** *(un devoir)* to take upon oneself; **s'a. qch** to claim or lay claim to sth; **il s'est attribué tout le mérite** he claimed or took all the credit

attribut [atriby] [VOIR GRAMMAIRE A17] NM attribute; *Mktg* **a. du produit** product attribute; *Ordinat* **a. de fichier** file attribute; *Ordinat* **a. de mise en forme** formatting parameter
ADJ *Gram* attributive; **nom a.** attributive noun

attribution [atribysjõ] NF **1** assigning, attribution, attributing (**à** to); *(des tâches)* allocation, allocating; *(de bourses d'étude etc)* awarding; *Théâtre (des rôles)* casting; *Fin (d'actions)* allotment; *(d'un salaire, d'une prime)* assigning, allocation; *Bourse* **actions d'a.** bonus shares; **avis d'a.** letter of allotment; **a. (d'essence/de sucre)** quota, ration (of petrol/sugar); **attributions** prerogative, competence, powers; *(de fonction)* duties, functions, responsibilities; **cela entre dans ses attributions** this comes within his competence or is part of his duties **2** *(d'une œuvre)* attribution; **l'a. de cette œuvre à Maillol est inexacte** this work is wrongly attributed to Maillol **3** *Gram* **complément d'a.** indirect object

attriqué [atrike] ADJ *Can* **mal a.** badly dressed

attristant [atristã] ADJ *(nouvelle etc)* saddening, depressing

attristé [atriste] ADJ *(visage)* sad; *(regard)* sorrowful; **contempler qch d'un œil a.** to gaze sadly at sth

attrister [atriste] VT to sadden, to grieve; **cette décision m'attriste** I am saddened by this decision; **cela m'attriste de voir …** it makes me sad or saddens me to see …
VPR **s'attrister** to be sad (**de qch** about sth); **je m'attriste de les voir si démunis** I'm sad or saddened to see them so helpless

attroupement [atrupmã] NM *(de manife-*

stants etc) crowd; *Jur* unlawful *or* riotous assembly; **leur éclat dans la rue a provoqué un a.** their scene in the street drew a crowd; **la loi contre les attroupements** ≃ the Riot Act; **un a. pacifique** a peaceful assembly

attrouper [atʁupe] **VT** *(foule etc)* to gather together; **arrêtez de crier, vous allez a. les passants** stop shouting, you'll draw a crowd

VPR s'attrouper to gather, to assemble; **les manifestants s'attroupaient** the demonstrators were gathering

atypique [atipik] **ADJ** atypical

au [o] *voir* **à**

aubade [obad] **NF** dawn serenade; **donner l'a. à qn** to serenade sb

aubaine [obɛn] **NF 1** *(chance etc)* windfall, godsend; **c'était vraiment une a. de vendre ton salon à ce prix-là** it was a real godsend to be able to sell your suite for that price; **profiter de l'a.** to take advantage of one's good luck; **quelle a.!** what a stroke of luck! **2** *Can (occasion)* bargain, good buy

aube¹ [ob] **NF 1** *(matin)* dawn; **à l'a. (du jour)** at dawn, at daybreak; **partir dès l'a.** to leave at dawn; *Fig* **l'a. de la civilisation** the dawn of civilization **2** *Rel* alb

aube² **NF 1** *Naut (de roue)* paddle, blade; **roue à aubes** paddle (wheel); **vapeur à roue à aubes** paddleboat **2** *(de turbine)* blade, vane; *(de ventilateur)* vane

aubépine [obepin] **NF** *(arbuste)* hawthorn, may (tree); **fleurs d'a.** may (blossom)

aubère [obɛʁ] **ADJ** red roan
NM red roan (horse)

auberge [obɛʁʒ] **NF** inn; **a. rurale** *ou* **de campagne** country inn; **tenir a.** to keep an inn; *Fig* **c'est un peu une a. espagnole** what you get out of it depends on what you put in; **a. de jeunesse** youth hostel; **il prend notre maison pour une a.** he treats our house like a hotel; *Fig Fam* **on n'est pas sorti de l'a.** we're not out of the wood(s) yet

aubergine [obɛʁʒin] **NF 1** *(plante)* aubergine, *Am* eggplant **2** *Fig Fam Vieilli (contractuelle)* (female) traffic warden
ADJ INV aubergine

aubergiste [obɛʁʒist] **N** innkeeper

aubette [obɛt] **NF** *surtout Belg* newspaper kiosk; *(Abribus®)* bus shelter

aubriétie [obʁiesi] **NF** *(plante)* aubrietia

auburn [obœʁn] **ADJ INV** auburn

AUCUN, -UNE [okœ̃, -yn] **PRON** *SEE GRAMMAR A35; B16; B63* **1** *(avec négation exprimée ou sous-entendue, accompagné de 'ne' ou 'sans')* *(être humain)* no one, nobody; *(chose)* none, not any; **lequel des deux veux-tu? – a.** which of the two do you want? – neither; **je ne me fie à a. d'entre eux** I don't trust any of them; **a. (des deux) ne viendra** neither (of them) will come; **de tous ces élèves, a. n'a répondu** not one of these pupils answered **2** *(avec négation implicite)* **de tous vos soi-disant amis, a. interviendra-t-il?** will any of your so-called friends intervene? **3** *(positif)* anyone; **il travaille plus qu'a.** he works more than anyone (else) **4** *Litt* **d'aucuns** some people; **d'aucuns prétendent qu'il est encore en vie** there are some who maintain that he is still alive
ADJ 1 *(positif, interrogatif)* any; **un des plus beaux livres qui aient été écrits sur a. sujet** one of the finest books written on any subject; **plus rapide qu'a. autre coureur** faster than any other runner; **avez-vous aucune intention de le faire?** have you any intention of doing it?
2 *(négatif)* no, not any; **je n'ai aucune idée** I don't have any idea, I have no idea; **sans aucune exception** without any exception; **le fait n'a aucune importance** the fact is of no importance; **oui, sans a. doute** yes, without

a *or* any doubt; **en aucune façon je ne l'aiderai** I will not help him in any way (at all); **sans mentionner a. nom** mentioning no names, without mentioning any names; **réparer qch sans a. mal** to repair sth with no difficulty at all *or* without any difficulty at all; **il n'a jamais fait a. mal à personne** he never did anyone any harm

aucunement [okynmɑ̃] **ADV** in no way, not at all, by no means, not in the slightest, not in the least; **je n'en suis a. étonné** I am not the slightest surprised; **je ne la connais a.** I don't know her at all; **je ne m'attendais a. à ce qu'il vînt** I never expected him to come

audace [odas] **NF 1** *(courage, assurance)* audacity, boldness, daring; **il faut beaucoup d'a. pour le faire/réussir** you need to be very bold *or* very daring to do it/to succeed **2** *(culot)* audacity, impudence; **vous avez l'a. de me dire cela!** you have the audacity *or* impudence *or* cheek *or* nerve to tell me that!; **ah! tu ne manques pas d'a.!** you've got the cheek of the Devil! **3** *(action audacieuse)* **elle est jeune, elle a toutes les audaces** she is young and daring; **une a. de style** daring, conventionality of style, stylistic daring

audacieusement [odasjøzmɑ̃] **ADV 1** *(avec courage)* audaciously, boldly, daringly; **elle a. demandé un rendez-vous avec le grand patron** she boldly requested a meeting with the big boss **2** *(avec culot)* impudently

audacieux, -ieuse [odasjø, -jøz] **ADJ 1** *(courageux)* audacious, bold, daring; **il fait des harmonies de couleurs très audacieuses** he uses very bold combinations of colour **2** *(culotté)* impudent; *(mensonge etc)* brazen

au-deçà *Arch* **ADV** on this side
PRÉP a. de on this side of

au-dedans **ADV** inside
PRÉP a. de inside, within

au-dehors **ADV** outside
PRÉP a. de outside, beyond

au-delà **ADV** beyond; **il est très connu dans la région et même a.** he is very well-known in the region and even further afield; **jusqu'à une certaine somme, mais pas a.** up to a certain sum, but no further
NM l'a. the next world, the hereafter
PRÉP a. de beyond, on the other side of; **n'allez pas a. de 100 euros** don't go above *or* beyond 100 euros

au-dessous [odəsu, otsu] **ADV** below, underneath; **sur la table et a.** on the table and under it; **les locataires a.** the tenants below *or* downstairs; **les enfants âgés de sept ans et a.** children of seven (years) and under; **on en trouve à 10 euros et même a.** you can get them for 10 euros or even less; **musique transposée deux tons a.** music transposed two tones lower *or* two tones down
PRÉP a. de below, under; **50 kilomètres a. Paris** 50 kilometres south of Paris; **a. du genou** below the knee; **les locataires a. de nous** the tenants below *or* underneath us; **15 degrés a. de zéro** 15 degrees below zero; **a. de la moyenne/du pair** below average/par; *Litt* **il est a. de lui de se plaindre** it is beneath him to complain; **a. de cinq ans** under five (years) of age); **quantités a. de 30 kilos** quantities of less than 30 kilos; **a. de 100 euros** less than *or* below 100 euros; **acheter qch a. de sa valeur** to buy sth for less than it is worth; **son travail était a. de mon attente** his work fell short of what I expected; **je suis a. de la tâche** I'm not up to the job; **être a. de tout** to be beneath contempt
VOIR GRAMMAIRE A68

au-dessus [odəsy, otsy] **ADV** above; **une terrasse avec une marquise a.** a terrace with an awning over it *or* above (it); **la salle de bains est a.** the bathroom is upstairs; **1000 euros et a.** 1,000 euros and up(wards); **la qualité**

a. the next grade up; **tout ce qui est a. est bien meilleur** everything up-market of this is a lot better; **musique transposée un ton a.** music transposed a tone higher *or* up a tone
PRÉP a. de above; **le château est situé a. du village** the castle stands above the village; **il a son nom a. de la porte** his name is above *or* over the door; **les avions volaient a. de nos têtes** the planes were flying overhead; **l'eau leur montait jusqu'a. des genoux** the water came up above their knees; **2 degrés a. de zéro** 2 degrees above zero; **a. de 50 euros** more than 50 euros, over 50 euros; **50 kilomètres a. de Paris** 50 kilometres north of Paris; **a. de la moyenne** above average; **a. de cinq ans** over five (years of age); **le colonel est a. du commandant** a colonel is higher than a major; **la tâche est a. de leurs forces** the job is too much for them *or* is beyond them; **vivre a. de ses moyens** to live beyond one's means; **je suis a. de ça** I'm above that, I wouldn't stoop to that *VOIR GRAMMAIRE A67*

au-devant [odvɑ̃] *(utilisé uniquement dans les propositions telles que aller ou courir ou se jeter ou se précipiter au-devant)* **ADV** **quand il y a du danger, je vais a.** when there is danger ahead, I go to meet it; **quand je prévois une objection, je vais a.** when I anticipate an objection, I take steps in advance
PRÉP aller/courir a. de qn to go/run to meet sb; **aller a. des désirs de qn** to anticipate sb's wishes; **aller a. d'un danger** to anticipate a danger; **aller a. d'un complot** to forestall a plot; **aller a. du danger/d'une défaite** to court danger/failure

audibilité [odibilite] **NF** audibility

audible [odibl] **ADJ** audible

audience [odjɑ̃s] **NF 1** *Jur* hearing, session, court; **plaider en pleine a.** *ou* **en a. publique** to plead in open court; **a. à huis clos** hearing in camera; **tenir a.** to hold a court *or* a sitting; **l'a. est suspendue** the case is adjourned; **a. est reprise** the case is resumed **2** *(intérêt du public)* following; **ce cinéaste a trouvé a. auprès des jeunes** this film-maker has gained a following among young people **3** *Mktg (public)* audience; **a. captive** captive audience; **a.-cible** target audience; **a. cumulée** cumulative audience (size); **a. télévisuelle** television audience; **a. utile** *(d'un support, d'un média)* addressable audience; **a. utile nette** *(d'un support, d'un média)* net addressable audience reached **4** *(entrevue)* audience, hearing; **recevoir qn sur lettre d'a.** to interview sb by appointment; **tenir une a.** *(roi)* to hold an audience; **donner une a. à qn** to grant sb an audience

> Do not confuse with **auditoire**.

audiencier [odjɑ̃sje] **NM** *Jur* **huissier a.** court crier, usher

Audimat® [odimat] **NM** *(appareil)* = device installed in homes for calculating television audience ratings; *(résultats)* audience ratings, audience viewing figures; **cette émission a un bon A.** this programme attracts a large audience

audimètre [odimɛtʁ] **NM** audiometer, people meter, setmeter

audimétrie [odimetʁi] **NF** = calculation of audience ratings

audio [odjo] **ADJ** audio

audiocassette [odjokasɛt] **NF** (audio) cassette

audioconférence [odjokɔ̃feʁɑ̃s] **NF** audio-conference; **a. multipoint** multipoint audio-conference; **a. point à point** point-to-point audioconference

audiofréquence [odjofʁekɑ̃s] **NF** audio-frequency

audiomètre [odjometr] NM audiometer

audionumérique [odjonymerik] ADJ digital audio; **disque a.** compact disc; **a. DAB** digital audio broadcasting, DAB

audio-oral, -ale, -aux, -ales [odjooral, -o] ADJ (méthode, exercice) audio

audiophone [odjofon] NM **1** (de malentendant) hearing aid **2** (lors d'une visite de musée) audiophone

audioprothésiste [odjoprotezist] N hearing-aid specialist

audiotypie [odjotipi] NF audiotyping

audiotypiste [odjotipist] N audiotypist

audio(-)visuel, -elle [odjovizyɛl] ADJ **1** Scol etc (méthodes etc) audiovisual **2** TV, Radio television and radio
NM **1** Scol etc audiovisual aids **2** TV, Radio television and radio

audiphone [odifon] NM Tél = pre-recorded telephone message service

audit [odit] NM audit; **cabinet d'a.** firm of auditors; **être chargé de l'a. d'une société** to audit a company; **a. social** = management consultancy report; **a. de diagnostic** diagnostic audit; **a. de qualité** quality audit; **a. de vente** sales audit; Mktg **a. des détaillants** retail audit; **a. marketing** ou **mercatique** marketing audit; **a. consommateur** consumer audit; **a. opérationnel** operational audit

auditer [odite] VT (entreprise) to audit

auditeur, -trice [oditœr, -tris] N **1** listener; **les auditeurs** the audience; Radio, TV **programme des auditeurs** request programme; Univ **suivre un cours en a. libre** = to follow a university course without being officially registered as a student, Am to audit a course **2** Admin **a. à la Cour des comptes** = Commissioner of Audit **3** (chargé de l'audit) auditor; **a. mercatique** marketing auditor; **a. externe/interne** external/internal auditor

auditif, -ive [oditif, -iv] ADJ (nerf) auditory; **avoir des problèmes auditifs** to have hearing problems; **prothèse** ou **aide auditive** hearing aid; **mémoire auditive** aural memory

audition [odisjɔ̃] NF **1** (de chanteur etc) audition; **passer une a.** to have an audition; **faire passer une a. à qn** to audition sb **2** (écoute) hearing; **juger d'un opéra à la première a.** to judge an opera at the first hearing **3** Jur **a. des témoins** hearing or examination of the witnesses; **nouvelle a.** rehearing **4** (concert) **a. de piano** (private) piano recital

auditionner [odisjone] VT **1** Théâtre to audition **2** Jur to hear
VI Théâtre etc to have an audition, to audition (**pour un rôle** for a part)

auditoire [oditwar] NM **1** audience **2** Jur court; Belg, Suisse auditorium, lecture hall

> Do not confuse with the French noun **audience**.

auditorium [oditorjom] NM auditorium; Radio, TV (broadcasting, television) studio; **a. d'enregistrement** sound studio

auge [oʒ] NF **1** (pour animaux) trough; **a. d'écurie** manger; Fam **amène ton a.!** (assiette) pass me your plate **2** (pour mener l'eau au moulin) flume, channel **3** (d'un concasseur) hopper

auget [oʒɛ] NM **1** (small) trough; (d'une cage d'oiseau) seed or water trough **2** (de roue à eau) bucket; **roue à augets** bucket or overshot wheel

augmentation [ogmɑ̃tasjɔ̃] NF **1** increase, growth; Admin (de salaire) increment; **a. des dépenses/du chômage/de la consommation** increase in expenditure/unemployment/consumption; **a. de salaire** (pay-)rise, rise or increase in wages, Am raise; **a. de bé-**néfices** earnings growth; **a. du capital** increase in capital; **demander une a.** to ask for a (pay-)rise or Am a raise; **a. de prix** price increase; **a. du prix de vente** mark-up; **être en a.** to be rising, to be on the increase; **les chiffres du chômage sont en nette a.** there is a marked increase in the unemployment figures
2 Ordinat **a. de puissance** upgrade, upgrading
3 Mus augmentation
4 Tricot **faire une a.** to make a stitch, to make one

augmenter [ogmɑ̃te] VT to increase; **a. la durée de cuisson** to increase the cooking time; **édition augmentée** enlarged edition; **a. une douleur** to aggravate a pain; **cela risque d'a. sa colère** that is liable to make him/her even more angry; **a. le prix de qch** to put up or increase or raise the price of sth; **a. qn** to raise or increase sb's salary or wages
VI **1** to increase; **la criminalité augmente** crime is increasing or on the increase; **empêcher les frais d'a.** to keep expenses down; **tout augmente!** everything's going up!; **le prix a augmenté de 10% par rapport à l'année dernière** the price is up 10% on last year; **la douleur augmente** the pain is worsening; **la chaleur augmente** it is getting hotter; **un conflit qui va en augmentant** an escalating conflict
2 Tricot to make a stitch, to make one; **a. de deux mailles au commencement du rang suivant** increase two at the beginning of the next row
3 Mus **en augmentant** crescendo
VPR **s'augmenter** **notre société s'est augmentée d'une nouvelle part de capital/de trois nouveaux cadres/de filiales à l'étranger** our firm has acquired new capital/three new managers/branches abroad

augure [ogyr] NM **1** Antiq (devin) augur; **consulter les augures** to consult the oracle; **le Collège des augures** the College of Augurs **2** (présage) augury, omen; **de bon a.** auspicious; **ce beau temps me paraît de bon a.** this nice weather seems to be a good omen; **de mauvais a.** ominous; **prendre les augures** to take the auguries; Fig **oiseau de mauvais a.** bird of ill omen

augurer [ogyre] VT to augur, to forecast; **a. l'avenir** to forecast or foresee the future; **a. bien/mal de qch** to bode well/not to bode well for sth, to augur well/ill for sth; **une querelle le premier jour, voilà qui augure mal de leur mariage** a quarrel on the first day doesn't bode well for their marriage; **que peut-on a. de cette rencontre prochaine?** what does this next meeting hold in store?; **je n'augure rien de bon de tout cela** I don't see any good coming of all this

Auguste [ogyst] NM **1** Hist Augustus; **le siècle d'A.** the Augustan Age **2** l'a. (au cirque) the clown

auguste [ogyst] ADJ august, majestic; **une a. assemblée** an august or illustrious assembly

Augustin [ogystɛ̃] ADJ Rel Augustinian
NM **1** Augustine **2** Rel Augustinian (friar); **les Augustins** the Augustin friars

augustinien, -ienne [ogystinjɛ̃, -jɛn] ADJ Phil Augustinian

auj abrév aujourd'hui

aujourd'hui [oʒurdɥi] ADV **1** (ce jour) today; **quel jour sommes-nous a.?** what day is it today, what's today?; **c'est a. le cinq/dimanche** today is the fifth/Sunday, it's the fifth/Sunday; **le journal d'a.** today's paper; **ce sera tout pour a.** that's all for today; **(d')a. en huit/en quinze** a week/two weeks today, Br today week/fortnight; **il y a a. huit jours** a week ago today; **ce n'est pas d'a. que je la**

connais I have known her for a long time; Fam **c'est pour a. ou pour demain?** I/we haven't got all day!; Belg **a. matin** this morning; Belg **a. soir** this evening, tonight
2 (à l'heure actuelle) nowadays, these days; **les jeunes gens d'a.** (the) young people (of) today; **l'Europe d'a.** modern-day or present-day Europe, the Europe of today

aula [ola] NF Suisse (dans une école) (conference) hall

aulne [on] NM (arbre) alder

aulx voir ail

aumône [omon] NF alms; **demander l'a.** to beg or ask for charity; **faire l'a. à qn** to give money to sb; **donner qch en a. à qn** to give sb sth out of charity; **réduit à l'a.** reduced to begging; Fig **faire l'a. d'un regard à qn** to spare sb a glance, to condescend or deign to look at sb

aumônier [omonje] NM chaplain; **a. militaire** army chaplain

aune[1] [on] NM (arbre) alder

aune[2] NF Arch ell (= 1.188 m); Vieilli Fig **figure longue d'une a.** face as long as a fiddle

auparavant [oparavɑ̃] ADV before(hand), previously; **a., il faut s'assurer de …** first, we/you must make sure of …; **l'année a.** the preceding year, the year before; **comme a.** as before; **mais a. nous devons parler** but we must have a talk first or beforehand

auprès de [oprɛ də] PRÉP **1** (près de) close to, (close) by, beside, near; **tout auprès de qn/qch** close to or beside sb/sth; **il a toujours une garde-malade auprès de lui** he always has a nurse with him or at hand
2 (indiquant une relation) **agir auprès de qn** to use one's influence with sb; **se renseigner auprès de qn** to ask sb; **se renseigner auprès d'un service** to enquire at a department; **être bien auprès de qn** to be in favour with sb, to be in sb's good books; **trouver grâce auprès de qn** to be in favour with sb, to find favour with sb; **je sais que je passe pour un idiot auprès d'eux** I know that they take me for an idiot; **ambassadeur auprès du roi de Suède** ambassador to the King of Sweden; **avocat auprès du tribunal** advocate attached to the tribunal
3 (comparé à) compared with, in comparison with, next to

auquel [okɛl] voir lequel

aura [ora] NF aura; Méd **a. épileptique** epileptic aura

auréole [oreol] NF **1** (de saint, de la lune) halo; (du soleil) corona; Fig **il pare son épouse d'une a.** he puts his wife on a pedestal; **entouré de l'a. de la gloire/réussite** bathed in glory/flushed with success **2** (trace) ring, mark; **le tableau a laissé une a. sur le mur** the picture has left a ring on the wall; **son matelas est couvert d'auréoles** his mattress is covered in dirty marks; **détachant qui ne laisse pas d'a.** stain remover that doesn't leave rings

auréoler [oreole] VT (d'un peintre) to surround with a halo; Fig to exalt, to glorify; **elle est auréolée de génie** she positively radiates genius
VPR **s'auréoler** to be crowned (**de** with)

auréomycine [oreomisin] NF Méd aureomycin

auriculaire [orikylɛr] ADJ (confession etc) auricular; Anat **appendice a.** auricular appendix; Mil etc **protecteur a.** ear protector
NM little finger

auricule [orikyl] NF **1** Anat (du cœur) auricle; **a. de l'oreille** lower lobe of the ear **2** Bot, Zool auricula, auricle; (de mollusque) auricula

auriculothérapie [orikyloterapi] NF Méd aural acupuncture

aurifère [ɔrifɛr] ADJ gold-bearing; **champ** *ou* **gisement a.** goldfield

aurifier [ɔrifje] VT *(une dent)* to put a gold filling in

Aurigny [ɔriɲi] NM Alderney; **vache d'A.** Alderney (cow)

auriol [ɔrjɔl] NM *(oiseau)* oriole

aurique [ɔrik] ADJ *Naut* **voile a.** gaffsail; **gréement a.** gaff rig; **à gréement a.** gaff-rigged

aurochs [ɔrɔks] NM aurochs, wild ox

aurore [ɔrɔr] NF **1** dawn, daybreak, break of day; **aux aurores** at the crack of dawn; **l'a. commence à paraître** *ou* **à poindre** dawn is breaking; *Fig* **l'a. de la civilisation** the dawn of civilization **2** *(papillon)* orange tip
  ADJ INV *(saffron or* golden) yellow
  ▸▸ **a. australe** aurora australis, southern lights; **a. boréale** aurora borealis, northern lights; **a. polaire** aurora polaris, polar light

auscultation [ɔskyltasjɔ̃] NF *Méd* auscultation

ausculter [ɔskylte] VT *Méd (patient etc)* to auscultate, to sound

auspices [ɔspis] NMPL **1** *(présage)* auspice, omen; **mauvais a.** ill *or* bad omen; **l'année commence sous d'heureux/de fâcheux a.** the year begins auspiciously/inauspiciously **2** *(appui)* **sous les a. de qn** under the auspices of sb

aussi [osi] ADV **1** *(également)* also, too; **c'est a. ce que je pense** that's what I think too; **vous venez a.** you are coming too; **elle fait du grec, et a. du latin** she's doing Greek, and Latin too; **je suis fatigué – toi a.?** I'm tired – you too?; **gardez a. ceux-là** keep those too, keep those as well; **moi a.** me too, so am I/so can I/so do I/so shall I/so did I/so was I/*etc*; **et moi a. je suis peintre** I'm a painter too *or* as well; **j'écoute le classique a. bien que du jazz** I listen to classical music as well as jazz, I listen to (both) classical music and jazz
  2 *(tellement)* so; **après avoir attendu a. longtemps** after waiting so long *or* for such a long time; **je ne pensais pas que tu étais a. sensible** I didn't think you were so *or* that sensitive; **une a. bonne affaire, ça ne se manque pas** a deal as good as that shouldn't be passed up; **un homme a. travailleur que vous** a man as hardworking as you; **d'a. belles journées** such nice days; **avez-vous jamais entendu une symphonie a. bizarre?** have you ever heard such a peculiar symphony? VOIR GRAMMAIRE A5
  3 *(dans les phrases comparatives)* as; **pas a. gros que** not so big as, not as big as; **il est a. grand que son frère** he is as tall as his brother; **tout a. au sud/à l'est que Paris** as far south/east as Paris; **ma méthode est tout a. bonne que la vôtre** my method is just *or* every bit as good as yours; **on pourrait a. bien rester là ce soir** we might as well stay here this evening; **je le connais a. peu que son frère** I don't know him any better than I know his brother
  4 *(quelque)* however; **a. bizarre que cela soit/semble** however odd it may be/seem, (as) strange as it my be/seem
  CONJ therefore, consequently, so; **la vie est chère ici, a. nous devons** *ou* **devons-nous économiser** the cost of living is high here, so we have to economize; **il ne regarde pas où il met les pieds, a. il tombe tout le temps** he doesn't watch where he's going, so he falls over all the time; *Fam* **a. c'est ta faute** after all, it's your fault SEE GRAMMAR B57; B62

aussitôt [osito] ADV immediately, straight away, at once; **a. dit, a. fait** no sooner said than done; **a. l'argent reçu, je vous paierai** as soon as I get the money, I will pay you; **a. après** immediately after; **a. après son retour,**

je suis parti as soon or the minute he returned, I left
  CONJ **a. que** + *ind* as soon as; **il se repentit de ses paroles a. qu'il les eut prononcées** he regretted his words as soon as he had said them; **a. que le train est parti, je me suis aperçu que ...** no sooner had the train left than I realized ... SEE GRAMMAR B31–2

austère [ostɛr] ADJ *(vie)* austere; *(jeûne)* strict; *(style)* severe, austere; *(expression)* stern; *(robe)* plain, severe

austèrement [ostɛrmɑ̃] ADV austerely; **elle s'habille a.** she dresses very austerely *or* plainly

austérité [osterite] NF **1** austerity; **vivre dans l'a.** to live in austerity; **la période d'a.** the days of austerity; **mesures d'a.** austerity measures **2 austérités** asceticism, mortification of the flesh

austral, -ale, -als *ou* **-aux, -ales** [ostral, -o] ADJ *(hémisphère)* southern

Australasie [ostralazi] NF Australasia

australasien, -ienne [ostralazjɛ̃, -jɛn] ADJ Australasian
  N **A.** Australasian

Australie [ostrali] NF Australia

australien, -ienne [ostraljɛ̃, -jɛn] ADJ Australian
  N **A.** Australian

austro-hongrois, -oise, *pl* **austro-hongrois, -oises** [ostroɔ̃grwa, -waz] *Hist* ADJ Austro-Hungarian
  N **A.** Austro-Hungarian

AUTANT [otɑ̃] ADV **1** *(intensité)* **je ne savais pas qu'il avait a. souffert** I did not know he had suffered so *or* as much; **je ne le savais pas a. respecté** I did not know he was so greatly respected; **travailles-tu toujours a.?** *(qu'aujourd'hui)* do you always work so *or* as or this hard?; *(qu'avant)* are you working as hard as ever?; **a. en emporte le vent** it's all idle talk; **a. vous l'aimez, a. il vous hait** he hates you as much as you love him; **tout a.** quite as much; **il m'en veut, mais je lui en veux tout a.** he's angry with me, but I'm just as angry with him; **encore a.** as much again
  2 *(quantité)* **tout a.** quite as much; *(de choses individuelles)* quite as many; **encore a.** as much/many again; **je n'en ai pas assez, remettez m'en encore a.** I don't have enough, give me as much/many again *or* the same again; **tous les salariés ont été augmentés d'a.** all the employees received the same pay rise, everybody's salary went up by the same amount; **le coût de la vie a augmenté de 5%, mais les salaires n'ont pas augmenté d'a.** the cost of living has increased by 5%, but salaries have not risen accordingly *or* have not risen in line; **a. pour moi!** I stand corrected!
  3 *(de même)* the same, likewise; **on ne peut pas en dire a. de tout le monde** you can't say as much *or* the same for everybody; **essaie un peu d'en faire a.** try to do the same; **peux-tu en dire a.?** can you say as much?
  4 ils disent qu'ils réfléchissent, a. dire qu'ils ont accepté they say they're thinking about it, in other words they've accepted; **j'aime a. vous dire que je n'apprécie pas vos manières!** I don't mind telling you that I don't care for your manners!; **j'aime a. vous le dire tout de suite** I might as well tell you right away; **j'aimerais a. aller au cinéma** I would just as soon go to the cinema; **a. le faire tout de suite** better do it right away; **a. ne rien faire du tout** we might as well do nothing at all; **a. rester ici** we may as well stay here; **a. dire que ...** one might as well say that ...; **a. dire que c'était difficile/que je n'étais pas content** as you can imagine, it was difficult/I wasn't happy
  5 a. que as much as; *(de choses in-*

dividuelles) as many as; **a. que possible** as far as possible; **sois à l'heure a. que possible** do your best to be on time; **faites a. que vous pourrez** do as much as you can; **(pour) a. que je sache** as far as I know, to the best of my knowledge; **j'en sais a. que toi** your guess is as good as mine, I know as much (about it) as you do; **c'est a. ta faute que la mienne** it is as much your fault as mine, you're as much to blame as I am; **il est a. à craindre qu'elle** he is as much to be feared as she is; *Fam* **ça qu'autre chose** it's all the same to me; **a. que j'en puis(se) juger** as far as I can judge; **pour a. qu'il est en mon pouvoir** to the best of my ability; **a. que faire se peut** as much as possible, as much as can be; **je me suis dépêché a. que faire se peut** I hurried as fast as I could
  6 a. de as much, so much; *(de choses individuelles)* as many, so many; **a. de filles que de garçons** as many girls as boys; **ils ont a. de terrain/d'amis que vous** they have as much land/as many friends as you; *Litt* **ce sont a. de (voleurs/etc)** they are nothing better than (a pack of thieves/etc); **ce sera a. de moins à payer** it will be so much the less to pay; **c'est a. de gagné** that's so much gained, that's so much to the good
  7 d'a. (plus) que especially *or* particularly since; **d'a. plus/moins (que)** all the more/less (because); **j'en suis surpris, d'a. plus qu'au fond il est honnête** I am all the more surprised because basically he is honest; **elle travaille d'a. mieux qu'elle se sait surveillée** she works all the better for knowing that someone's keeping an eye on her; **cela vous sera d'a. plus facile que vous êtes jeune** it will be all the easier for you since you are young
  8 pour a. for all that; **j'ai plus de travail, mais ce n'est pas pour a. que j'ai plus d'argent** just because I have more work doesn't mean that I have more money; **elle est très riche, elle n'est pas plus heureuse pour a.** she's very rich, but she isn't any the happier for it *or* but that doesn't mean she's any the happier; **elle ne s'en fait pas pour a.** she doesn't worry about it

autarcie [otarsi] NF *Pol* autarky; **une communauté qui vit en a.** a self-sufficient community

autarcique [otarsik] ADJ *Pol* autarkic

autel [otɛl] NM *aussi Fig* altar; **maître a.** high altar; **a. latéral** side altar; **nappe d'a.** altar cloth; **pierre d'a.** altar stone *or* table; **tableau d'a.** altarpiece; **conduire sa fille à l'a.** to give one's daughter away (in marriage); **suivre qn à l'a.** to walk up the aisle with sb, to marry sb

auteur [otœr] NM **1** *(de livre)* author, writer; *(de chanson)* composer; *(de tableau)* painter; **droit d'a.** copyright; **droits d'a.** royalties; **un droit d'a. de 10%** a 10% royalty; *Fig* **citer ses auteurs** to quote one's authorities **2** *(responsable)* author; *(d'un crime)* perpetrator; *(d'un projet)* promoter, sponsor; *Jur* principal; **a. d'un accident** party at fault in an accident; *Fig* **être l'a. de la ruine de qn** to be the cause of sb's downfall; **qui est l'a. de cette plaisanterie?** whose idea was that joke?; *Hum* **je vous présente l'a. de mes jours** this is my beloved father/mother

auteur-compositeur, *pl* **auteurs-compositeurs** NM songwriter

authenticité [otãtisite] NF authenticity; **on conteste l'a. de ce tableau** the authenticity of this painting is in doubt

authentification [otãtifikasjɔ̃] NF authentication; **cachet d'a.** approved stamp

authentifier [otãtifje] VT to authenticate

authentique [otãtik] ADJ authentic, genuine; **c'est un fait a.** it's a true fact; **bourgo-**

gne a. genuine Burgundy; *Jur* **acte a.** instrument drawn up by a solicitor; **copie a.** certified copy; *Fam* **je ne te mens pas, c'est a.! c'est ce qu'il a dit!** I'm not lying to you, it's true! that's what he said!

authentiquement [otɑ̃tikmɑ̃] ADV authentically, genuinely

authentiquer [otɑ̃tike] VT *Vieilli (document etc)* to authenticate, to certify, to legalize

autisme [otism] NM *Psy* autism

autiste [otist] ADJ, N *Psy* autistic

autistique [otistik] ADJ *Psy* autistic

auto [oto] NF (motor)car; **les autos tamponneuses** Dodgems®, bumper cars; **jouer avec des petites autos** to play with toy cars
ADJ INV **assurance a.** car insurance; **budget a.** car budget

auto- PRÉF auto-, self-

auto-accusation, *pl* **auto-accusations** NF self-accusation

auto-adhésif, -ive ADJ self-adhesive; **bande auto-adhésive** adhesive tape

auto-allumage, *pl* **auto-allumages** NM running-on, self-ignition, post-ignition

auto-amorçage, *pl* **auto-amorçages** NM automatic *or* self priming

auto-antigène, *pl* **auto-antigènes** NM *Physiol* autoantigen

autoberge [otobɛrʒ] NF = highway running along a river embankment

autobiographie [otobjɔgrafi] NF autobiography

autobiographique [otobjɔgrafik] ADJ autobiographical

autobronzant [otobrɔ̃zɑ̃] ADJ self-tanning NM self-tanning cream; *Fam* fake tan

autobus [otobys] NM bus

autocar [otokar] NM coach, bus; **a. de luxe** luxury coach

autocariste [otokarist] NM coach tour operator

autocassable [otokasabl] ADJ **ampoule a.** easy-to-open *or* break-open phial

autocélébrer (s') [sotoselebre] VPR to sing one's own praises

autocensure NF self-censorship; **faire de l'a.** to practise self-censorship

autocensurer (s') [sotosɑ̃syre] VPR to practise self-censorship

autochenille [otoʃnij] NF half-track vehicle

autochrome [otokrom] ADJ *(pellicule, film)* colour

autochtone [otɔkton] ADJ aboriginal, *Can* native; *Géol* **terrain a.** autochthonous rock N native, *Admin* non-alien, *Spéc* autochthon; *Can* **Conseil national des autochtones du Canada** Native Council of Canada; *Hum* **les autochtones ne sont pas très accueillants** the natives aren't very friendly

autocinétique [otosinetik] ADJ autokinetic

autoclave [otoklav] ADJ hermetically sealed, pressure-sealed; **marmite a.** autoclave, digester
NM 1 *Chimie, Ind* autoclave, digester 2 *Méd* sterilizer 3 *Culin Vieilli* pressure cooker

autocode [otokɔd] NM *Ordinat* assembly language

autocollant [otokɔlɑ̃] ADJ self-adhesive; *(enveloppe)* self-sealing NM sticker

autocommutateur [otokɔmytatœr] NM *Ordinat* autoswitch; **a. privé** PBX, private branch exchange

autoconduction [otokɔ̃dyksjɔ̃] NF *Électron* mutual induction

autoconsommation [otokɔ̃sɔmasjɔ̃] NF subsistence farming; **économie d'a.** subsistence economy

autocopiant [otokɔpjɑ̃] ADJ self-copying

autocopie [otokɔpi] NF *(de documents)* duplicating

autocopier [otokɔpje] VT *(pr sub, impf* n. **autocopiions, v. autocopiiez)** to duplicate

autocorrecteur [otokɔrɛktœr] ADJ *Ordinat* self-correcting

autocorrection [otokɔrɛksjɔ̃] NF self-correction; **faire de l'a.** to do one's own correction

autocouchette ADJ INV **train a.** = car-sleeper train

autocrate [otokrat] N *Pol* autocrat

autocratie [otokrasi] NF *Pol* autocracy

autocratique [otokratik] ADJ autocratic

autocratiquement [otokratikmɑ̃] ADV autocratically

autocritique [otokritik] NF self-criticism; **faire son a.** to criticize oneself

autocuiseur [otokɥizœr] NM pressure cooker

autodafé [otodafe] NM *Hist* auto-da-fé; **faire un a. de livres rares** to burn rare books

autodébrayage [otodebrejaʒ] NM *Aut* automatic clutch

autodéfense [otodefɑ̃s] NF self-defence

autodestructeur, -trice [otodɛstryktœr, -tris] ADJ self-destructive

autodestruction [otodɛstryksjɔ̃] NF self-destruction

autodétermination [otodetɛrminasjɔ̃] NF *Pol* self-determination

autodidacte [otodidakt] ADJ self-taught, self-educated N autodidact

autodrome [otodrom] NM motor-racing track; *(pour les essais)* car-testing track

auto-école, *pl* **auto-écoles** NF school of motoring, driving school

autoérotique [otoerɔtik] ADJ *Psy* auto-erotic

autoérotisme [otoerɔtism] NM *Psy* auto-eroticism

autofécondation [otofekɔ̃dasjɔ̃] NF *Bot* self-pollination

autofiction [otofiksjɔ̃] NF autofiction

autofinancé [otofinɑ̃se] ADJ *Fin* financed from cashflow

autofinancement [otofinɑ̃smɑ̃] NM *Fin* self-financing, financing from cashflow

autofinancer (s') [sotofinɑ̃se] VPR *Fin* to be self-financing

autofocus [otofɔkys] *Phot* NM autofocus ADJ autofocus; **appareil a.** autofocus camera

autogène [otoʒɛn] ADJ 1 *Physiol* **faire du training a.** to learn how to relax 2 *Tech* **soudure a.** autogenous weld

autogenèse [otoʒənɛz] NF *Biol* autogenesis

autogéré [otoʒere] ADJ self-managed

autogestion [otoʒɛstjɔ̃] NF self-management

autogestionnaire [otoʒɛstjɔnɛr] ADJ self-managing

autogire [otoʒir] NM *Aviat* autogyro

autograissage [otogrɛsaʒ] NM *Tech* self-lubrication

autograisseur, -euse [otogrɛsœr, -øz] ADJ *(roulement, palier etc)* self-lubricating

autographe [otograf] ADJ autograph; *(lettre etc)* handwritten NM autograph

autogreffe [otogrɛf] NF *Chir* autograft

autoguidage [otogidaʒ] NM **(retour par) a.** homing; **cellule d'a.** homing eye

autoguidé [otogide] ADJ *(missile)* self-directional, homing

auto-immun ADJ *Méd* autoimmune

auto-immunisation, *pl* **auto-immunisations** NF *Méd* autoimmunization

auto-induction, *pl* **auto-inductions** NF *Électron* self-induction

auto-intoxication, *pl* **auto-intoxications** NF autointoxication, autotoxaemia

autolimitation [otolimitasjɔ̃] NF setting of voluntary limits

autolimiter [otolimite] VT to set voluntary limits to; **les Japonais autolimitent leurs exportations de voitures** the Japanese set voluntary limits to their car exports

autolubrifiant [otolybrifjɑ̃] ADJ self-lubricating

autolubrification [otolybrifikasjɔ̃] NF self-lubrication

autolyse [otoliz] NF autolysis

auto-marché, *pl* **auto-marchés** NM car mart

automate [otomat] NM **1** automaton, robot; **marcher comme un a.** to walk like a robot; **vivre comme un a.** to live like an automaton VOIR GRAMMAIRE A13 **2** *Suisse (distributeur)* vending machine; *(distributeur de billets)* cash dispenser

automation [otomasjɔ̃] NF automation

automatique [otomatik] ADJ *(action)* automatic; *(appareil)* self-acting; **'attention à la fermeture a. des portières'** 'danger, automatically closing doors'; **à mise en marche a.** self-starting; **réflexe a.** automatic reflex; *Méd* involuntary reflex; **payer l'électricité par prélèvement a.** to pay one's electricity bill by direct debit; *Fam* **votre dossier est envoyé à Paris, c'est a.** your file has been sent to Paris, that's the usual procedure; **il va vouloir te voir, c'est a.** he'll want to see you, it's a dead cert
NM **1** *(téléphone)* direct dialling **2** *(pistolet)* automatic
NF **1** *Tech* automatics, automation **2** *Aut* automatic

automatiquement [otomatikmɑ̃] ADV automatically; **votre nom est inséré a. dans le fichier** your name is automatically entered in the file; *Fam* **si vous ne payez pas vos impôts, vous agissez a. contre la loi** by not paying your tax you are automatically breaking the law

automatisable [otomatizabl] ADJ automatable

automatisation [otomatizasjɔ̃] NF automation

automatiser [otomatize] VT to automate

automatisme [otomatism] NM **1** *Physiol, Méd* automatism; **agir par a.** to act automatically; **fermer la porte à double tour est devenu un a.** double-locking the door has become automatic **2** *(fonctionnement)* automatic working *or* functioning **3** *(dispositif)* automatic device

automédication [otomedikasjɔ̃] NF self-medication

automitrailleuse [otomitrajøz] NF armoured car

automnal, -ale, -aux, -ales [otɔ(m)nal, -o] ADJ autumnal

automne [otɔn] NM VOIR GRAMMAIRE A7 autumn, *Am* fall; **l'équinoxe d'a.** the autumnal equinox; **en a., à l'a.** in autumn; **une soirée d'a.** an autumn evening; *Fig* **à l'a. de sa vie** in the autumn of his/her life

automobile [otomɔbil] ADJ **1** *(à moteur)* self-propelling, automotive; **voiture a.** motor vehicle; **canot a.** motor boat **2** *(relatif à la voiture)* **club a.** automobile club; **assurance a.** car *or* motor insurance; **industrie a.** automobile *or* car industry; **accessoires automobiles** car accessories

NF (motor)car, *Am* automobile; *Mil* a. **blindée** armoured car; **salon de l'a.** motor show; **l'a. marche bien en France** the car industry is doing well in France

automobilisme [otomɔbilism] NM motoring

automobiliste [otomɔbilist] N motorist

automoteur, -trice [otomɔtœr, -tris] ADJ *(véhicule)* self-propelling, automotive; *(valve etc)* self-acting; **train a.** multiple unit (Diesel) train
▪ NF **automotrice** railcar
▪ NM *Naut* self-propelled barge

automutilation [otomytilasjɔ̃] NF self-mutilation

autoneige [otonɛʒ] NF *Can* snowmobile

autonettoyant [otonetwajɑ̃] ADJ **four a.** self-cleaning oven

autonome [otonɔm] ADJ autonomous, self-governing; *(État, région etc)* independent; *(appareil)* self-contained; *(personne)* self-sufficient; *Ordinat* **calculateur a.** standalone (computer)

autonomie [otonɔmi] NF **1** *Pol* autonomy, self-government **2** *(de personne)* self-sufficiency; **ma fille veut avoir son a.** my daughter wants her independence **3** *Aviat* cruising radius, range; *(de voiture)* range; **l'avion a deux heures/800 km d'a.** the aircraft has a range of two hours/800 km **4** *(de batterie)* battery life, life; *(d'un téléphone portable)* talktime

autonomiste [otonɔmist] N *Pol* autonomist

autopalpation [otopalpasjɔ̃] NF *Méd* self-examination

auto-patrouille, *pl* **auto-patrouilles** NF *Can* police car

autopont [otopɔ̃] NM flyover

autoportant [otopɔrtɑ̃], **autoporteur¹, -euse** [otopɔrtœr, -øz] ADJ *Archit* self-supporting

autoporteur² ADJ *Aut* integral, integrated; *(carrosserie)* frameless

autoportrait [otopɔrtrɛ] NM self-portrait

autopropulsé [otopropylse] ADJ self-propelled

autopropulsion [otopropylsjɔ̃] NF self-propulsion

autopsie [otopsi] NF autopsy; **a. (cadavérique)** postmortem (examination); **pratiquer une a.** to carry out a postmortem (examination); *Fig* **faire l'a. d'une œuvre** to examine a work critically

autopsier [otopsje] VT to perform a postmortem (examination) on, to autopsy

autopunition [otopynisjɔ̃] NF *Psy* self-punishment

autoradio [otoradjo] NM car radio

autorafraîchissement [otorafrɛʃismɑ̃] NM *Ordinat* auto-refresh

autorail [otoraj] NM railcar

auto-régénérateur, -trice [otorezeneratœr, -tris] ADJ *Nucl (réacteur etc)* breeder

autoréglage [otoreglaʒ] NM *Tech* self-regulation

autorégulateur, -trice [otoregylatœr, -tris] ADJ self-regulating
▪ NM self-acting regulator

autorégulation [otoregylasjɔ̃] NF self-regulation

autoreverse [otorəvɛrs] ADJ **appareil a.** auto-reverse
▪ NM auto-reverse

autorisation [otorizasjɔ̃] NF **1** authorization, authority, permission; **donner à qn l'a. de faire qch** to authorize sb to do sth, to give sb permission to do sth; **demander l'a. de faire qch** to ask permission to do sth; *surtout*

Mil, Admin etc to request authority to do sth; **je n'ai pas eu l'a. de sortir ce soir** I didn't get permission to go out tonight; **il nous manque encore l'a. du conseil municipal pour ouvrir le restaurant** we still need the council's authorization to open the restaurant; **avoir l'a. de bâtir** to have planning permission **2** *(document)* licence; **montrez-moi votre a.** show me your permit
▸▸ *Ordinat* **a. d'accès** access authorization; **a. de crédit** credit line; **a. de découvert** overdraft facility; **a. de dédouanement** customs clearance authorization; *TV, Cin* **a. d'exploitation** rights; **a. d'exporter** export permit; **a. de prélèvement** direct debit mandate; *Admin* **a. de sortie du territoire** = parental authorization for a minor to travel abroad; *Aviat* **a. de vol** flight clearance

autorisé [otorize] ADJ **1** *(qualifié)* authorized; **tenir qch d'une source autorisée** to have sth from an authoritative source; **les milieux autorisés** (the) official circles **2** *(permis)* permitted, permissible, allowed; **tournure autorisée par l'usage** turn of phrase sanctioned *or* hallowed by usage; **il se croit tout a.** he thinks he can get away with anything **3** *(étalon)* approved

autoriser [otorize] VT **1 a. qn à faire qch** to authorize *or* permit sb to do sth, to give sb the authority to do sth; **je vous autorise à sortir de table** you may have my permission to leave the table; **l'alcool ne lui est pas autorisé** he/she is not allowed (to drink) alcohol; **a. la pêche** to allow fishing **2** *(justifier) (une action)* to justify, to authorize, to sanction; **ces découvertes autorisent à penser que ...** these discoveries entitle us to believe that ...; **rien ne nous autorise à le croire** nothing entitles us to believe that
▪ VPR **s'autoriser je m'autorise de ces résultats pour ...** on the basis of these results, I feel entitled to ...

autoritaire [otoriter] ADJ authoritarian

autoritairement [otoritermɑ̃] ADV authoritatively, *Péj* in an authoritarian manner

autoritarisme [otoritarism] NM authoritarianism

autorité [otorite] NF **1** *(domination)* authority; **exercer son a. sur qn** to exercise authority over sb; **il n'a aucune a. sur ses élèves** he can't keep order *or* he has no control over his pupils; **a. parentale** parental authority; **être sous l'a. de qn** to be under sb's authority; **il veut tout emporter d'a.** he wants his own way in everything, *Fam* he wants to run the whole show; **agir de pleine a.** to act with full powers; **faire qch d'a.** to do sth on one's own (responsibility), to take it upon oneself to do sth; **de sa propre a.** on one's own authority; **territoire soumis à l'a. de ...** area within the jurisdiction of ...; *Jur* **l'a. de la loi** the force of the law
2 *(poids)* authority; **avoir de l'a. sur qn** to have influence *or* authority over sb; **faire a. en qch** to be an authority on sth; **il fait a. en matière de physique nucléaire** he is an authority on nuclear physics; **ce livre fait a. dans le milieu** this book is taken as the authority here; *Jur* **cas d'espèce qui font a.** leading cases; **parler avec a.** to speak authoritatively *or* with authority
3 *(gouvernement)* **l'a.** the authorities; **les représentants de l'a.** the representatives of authority; **l'a. fiscale** the tax authorities; **les autorités** the authorities, the powers that be; **les autorités locales/religieuses** the local/religious authorities; **autorités portuaires** port authorities
4 *(personne)* **citer une a.** to quote an authority; **c'est une a., elle est très écoutée** she's an authority, people take a lot of notice of what she says

autoroute [otorut] NF **1** *Aut* motorway, *Am* freeway, *Am* thruway; **prendre l'a.** to take the motorway; **a. à péage** toll motorway, *Am* turnpike (road) **2** *Ordinat* **a. de l'information** information (super)highway; **a. interactive** interactive highway; **a. électronique** electronic highway, superhighway

autoroutier, -ière [otorutje, -jɛr] ADJ **système a.** motorway *or Am* freeway system *or* network

autosatisfaction [otosatisfaksjɔ̃] NF self-satisfaction

auto-stop NM hitchhiking, *Fam* hitching; **faire de l'a.** to hitchhike, *Fam* to hitch, to thumb a lift; **prendre qn en a.** to pick up a hitchhiker; **je ne voyage qu'en a.** I hitchhike everywhere I go; **faire le tour de l'Europe en a.** to hitchhike around Europe

auto-stoppeur, -euse, *pl* **auto-stoppeurs, -euses** N hitchhiker, *Fam* hitcher

autosuffisance [otosyfizɑ̃s] NF *Écon* self-sufficiency

autosuggestion [otosygʒɛstjɔ̃] NF auto-suggestion

autotest [ototɛst] NM *Ordinat* self-test

autotester (s') [ototɛste] VPR *Ordinat* to self-test, to auto-test

autour¹ [otur] ADV around; **une ville avec des murs tout a.** a town with walls all around it
▪ PRÉP **a. de** around, *surtout Br* round, about; **nous nous sommes assis a. de la table** we sat down round the table; **discuter qch a. d'un verre** to discuss sth over a drink; **enrouler qch a. de son cou** to coil sth round one's neck; **ce qui se passe a. de nous** what is going on around *or* round about us; *Fam* **il a a. de vingt ans** he is (somewhere) about twenty, he's twentyish; **tourner a. de la question** *ou* **du pot** to beat about the bush; **tout a. de ... all around ...** VOIR GRAMMAIRE A67

autour² NM *(oiseau)* **a. (des palombes)** goshawk

autovaccin [otovaksɛ̃] NM *Méd* autovaccine

AUTRE [otr] VOIR GRAMMAIRE A36–7; B15–16

ADJ other **1, 4** ▪ another **1, 3, 4**
▪ something else *(autre chose)* **5**
PRON another **2–4, 6–8** ▪ both *(l'un et l'autre)* **4** ▪ either *(l'un ou l'autre)* **5, 6**
▪ each other *(l'un l'autre)* **7** ▪ else **9, 10**

ADJ 1 other; **l'a. côté** the other side; **une a. semaine/un a. jour** another week/another day; **une a. fois** another time; **toute a. femme aurait agi de la même façon** any other woman would have acted in the same way; **les choux et autres légumes** cabbages and (all) other vegetables; **des choux et d'autres légumes** cabbages and some other vegetables; **tous les autres verbes que ceux en -er** all verbs other than those in -er; **je ne pourrai pas y aller, entre autres raisons je suis à court d'argent** I can't go, for one thing I'm short of money; **l'a. monde** the next world; **sans faire d'a. observation** without making any further observation; **sans a. perte de temps** without further loss of time; **l'a. lundi** the other Monday; *(prochain)* Monday week; **je l'ai vu l'a. jour/soir** I saw him the other day/evening

2 vous autres hommes, vous êtes seuls coupables it is you men alone who are to blame; **nous autres Anglais** we English (people); **vous autres** you others, all of you; **eh, vous autres! venez par ici!** hey, you lot! come over here!

3 *(second)* **il se croit un a. Napoléon** he thinks he is a second *or* another Napoleon; **mon frère, c'est un a. moi-même** my brother is just another me

4 *(différent)* other, different; **donnez-moi un**

a. torchon give me another cloth; *Prov* **autres temps, autres mœurs** other days, other ways; **il est a. que je ne le pensais** he is different from what I thought; **elle est devenue a.** she has changed, she has become different; **cela a fait de lui un a. homme** it made a new man of him; **une tout a. femme** quite a different woman; **j'ai des idées autres** I have different ideas, my ideas are different; **être d'une a. opinion** to think otherwise *or* differently

5 a. chose *(en plus)* something else; *(en remplacement)* something different; **j'ai a. chose d'important à vous dire** I have something else of importance to tell you; **avez-vous a. chose à faire?** have you anything else to do?; **ce qu'il éprouve pour elle, ce n'est pas a. chose que de l'amour** what he feels for her is nothing other than love; *Fam* **a. chose, ma mère est partie hier** not only that, but my mother left yesterday; **c'est tout a. chose!** that's quite a different thing!; **une chose est de parler, a. chose est d'agir** it's one thing to talk, it's another to act; **a. part** somewhere else

PRON 1 les défauts des autres the failings of others; **d'autres vous diront que ...** others *or* other people will tell you that ...; **tous les autres sont là** all the others are there; **encore un a.** one more, another (one); **encore bien d'autres** many more besides

2 cela peut arriver d'un jour à l'a. it may happen any day; **je l'attends d'un moment à l'a.** I expect him/her any moment; **je le vois de temps à a.** I see him from time to time *or* now and again *or* now and then; **un jour ou l'a.** one day or another, one of these days; **d'un bout à l'a.** from one end to the other, from start to finish, from end to end; **il a menti d'un bout à l'a.** he lied from start to finish

3 la science est une chose, l'art en est une a. science is one thing, art is another; **il parle d'une façon et agit d'une a.** he says one thing and does another

4 l'un et l'a. both; **les uns et les autres** *(tout le monde)* all (and sundry), one and all; *(deux groupes)* both parties; **il a parlé aux uns et aux autres** he spoke to them all; **l'un et l'a. ont été punis** both were punished; **il passe son temps chez l'un ou l'a.** he spends his time with one friend or another

5 l'un ou l'a. either; **c'est l'un ou l'a.!** it's either or!, it's one thing or the other!; **c'est tout l'un ou tout l'a.** there is no happy medium, it's either one extreme or the other; **ni l'un ni l'a.** neither; **ni l'un ni l'a. ne sont venus** neither of them came; **je ne les connais ni l'un ni l'a.** I don't know either of them; **je n'ai vu ni les uns ni les autres** I didn't see any of them

6 l'un ..., l'a. ... one ..., the other ...; **l'un dit ceci, l'a. dit cela** one says this and the other says that; **les uns ..., les autres ...** some ..., others ..., some ..., some ...; **ils s'en allèrent, les uns par ci, les autres par là** they went off, some one way, some another; **sans prendre parti ni pour les uns ni pour les autres** without taking either side; **l'un ne va pas sans l'a.** you can't have one without the other, the two go hand in hand; **qui voit l'un voit l'a.** there's no difference between them, you can't tell the two apart; **l'un vaut l'a.** there's no difference between them, the one's just as good/bad as the other

7 l'un l'a. each other, one another; **on va s'aider l'un l'a.** we'll help each other; **elles se moquent les unes des autres** they make fun of each other; **vivre l'un pour l'a.** to live for each other; **aller l'un à côté de l'a.** to walk side by side; **ils dépendent l'un de l'a.** they depend on each other; **l'un auprès de l'a., auprès l'un de l'a.** near each other, near one another

8 l'un dans l'a., il se fait mille euros with one

thing and another, he earns a thousand euros; **une année dans l'a.** taking one year with another

9 d'a. else; **il y a quelque chose d'a. dans la boîte?** – **non, rien d'a.** is there anything else in the box? – no, nothing else; **il n'y en a pas d'a.** there's no other; **parler de choses et d'autres** to talk about this and that; **personne d'a. ne le sait** nobody else knows; **quelqu'un d'a.** somebody else; **je ne demande rien d'a.** I don't ask for anything more, I ask for nothing more; **c'est de la stupidité et rien d'a.** it's stupidity and nothing else, it's nothing but stupidity, it's sheer stupidity; **que pouvait-il faire d'a.?** what else could he do?; **que pouvaient-ils faire d'a. que de l'inviter?** what else could they do but invite him/her?; **qui d'a. que lui aurait pu le faire?** who else (but him) could have done it?; **(dites cela) à d'autres!** who do you think you're kidding?, get away!; *Fam* **j'en ai vu bien d'autres** I've been through worse than that

10 *(personne)* someone *or* somebody else; **adressez-vous à un a.** ask someone else *or* somebody else; **je l'ai pris pour un a.** I mistook him for someone else; **c'était un touriste comme un a.** he was just an ordinary tourist; **c'est une raison comme une a.** it's as good a reason as any; **c'est un homme pas comme les autres** he is not like other men; **peut m'importe ce que pensent les autres** I don't care what anyone else thinks *or* what other people think; *Fam* **comme dit l'a.** as the saying goes, as they say; *Fam* **dis donc! t'as vu l'a.?** God! did you see him/her there?; *Fam* **l'a. qui fait encore son cirque!** and that one making his/her usual scene!; **il n'est pas plus bête qu'un a.** he is no more stupid than anyone else; **nul a. ne l'a vu** no one else *or* nobody else saw him; **tout a. le comprendrait** anyone else would understand it; **il y avait des Écossais, entre autres** there were some Scots, among others

autrefois [otrəfwa] ADV formerly, in the past; *(à une époque particulière)* once; **c'est ce qu'on faisait a. à la maison, avant l'accident** that's what we used to do at home, before the accident; **a., il était plus bavard he** was more talkative before *or* in the past, he used to be more talkative; **il y avait a. un roi** once upon a time there was a king; **c'était l'usage a.** it was the custom in former times *or* in olden days; **d'a.** of long ago; **sa vie d'a.** his past life; **les hommes d'a.** men of old *or* of olden times; **des chants d'a.** old-time songs

autrement [otrəmã] ADV 1 *(différemment)* otherwise, differently; **il me l'a raconté a. que vous** the way he told it was different from the way you told it; **faisons a.** let's do *or* set about it (in) another way; **Alain, a. appelé Jojo** Alain, otherwise known as Jojo; **le bouton d'or, a. appelé ...** the buttercup, otherwise known as ..., the buttercup, *or* ...; **a. dit** in other words, put differently; **tu ne viendras pas demain? a. dit, tu ne veux plus me voir!** so you're not coming tomorrow? in other words, you don't want to see me any more!; **il ne put faire a. que d'obéir** he had no alternative but to obey; **à chaque fois que je le vois, je pleure, je n'arrive pas à faire a.** every time I see him I cry, I can't help myself; *Fam* **pas moyen de faire a.** there's no alternative, there's no other way; **pas moyen de faire a. que de l'emmener** there's no alternative *or* there's nothing else to do *or* nothing else for it but to take him along

2 *(plus)* (far) more; **elle est a. intelligente** she is far more intelligent, she is more intelligent by far; **c'est bien a. sérieux** that is far more serious

3 *(sinon)* otherwise, or (else); **venez demain, a. il sera trop tard** come tomorrow,

otherwise it will be too late; **explique-lui, a. elle n'arrivera pas à le faire** explain it to her, otherwise *or* or (else) she won't be able to do it; **les verres n'étaient pas propres, a. c'était pas mal** the glasses weren't clean, but otherwise it wasn't bad

4 pas a. not particularly; **cela ne me surprend pas a.** that does not particularly surprise me

Autriche [otriʃ] NF Austria

autrichien, -ienne [otriʃjɛ̃, -jɛn] ADJ Austrian

N A. Austrian

autruche [otryʃ] NF *(oiseau)* ostrich; **œuf d'a.** ostrich egg; **chaussures/sac en a.** ostrich-skin shoes/handbag; *Fig Fam* **avoir un estomac d'a.** to have a cast-iron stomach; *Fig* **pratiquer la politique de l'a., faire l'a.** to bury one's head in the sand

autrui [otrui] PRON INDÉF others, other people; **convoiter le bien d'a.** to covet one's neighbour's property; **ne fais pas à a. ce que tu ne voudrais pas qu'on te fît** do as you would be done by

auvent [ovã] NM 1 porch roof; **un toit en a.** a sloping roof; **s'abriter sous l'a.** to shelter in the porch 2 *(de tente)* canopy, awning 3 *Ind (au-dessus de l'âtre etc)* hood; *Aut* **auvents de capot** bonnet louvres

auvergnat, -ate [overɲa, -at] ADJ of Auvergne

NM *Ling* Auvergne dialect

N A. *(natif)* native of Auvergne; *(habitant)* inhabitant of Auvergne

aux [o] *voir* à

auxiliaire [oksiljɛr, o-] ADJ *(verbe, troupes etc)* auxiliary; **machine a.** auxiliary engine; **bureau a.** sub-office; **services auxiliaires de l'armée** non-combatant services; **maître a.** supply teacher

N *(aide)* auxiliary, helper, assistant; *Admin* temporary civil servant; *(aux PTT)* non-permanent employee; *Com* facilitator; **c'est un a. précieux** he's a valuable helper

NM 1 *Naut* auxiliary cruiser **2** *Aviat, Naut* **les auxiliaires** the auxiliary engines **3** *Mil* **auxiliaires** auxiliaries **4** *Gram* auxiliary verb SEE GRAMMAR A38–9; A55–61; B26–8

▶▶ a. familiale ≃ mother's help; **a. de justice** representative of the law; **a. médical** medical auxiliary

auxquels [okɛl] *voir* **lequel**

AV *(abrév* **avant)** front

av. *abrév* **avenue**

avachi [avaʃi] ADJ 1 *(vêtements, bottes etc) (déformé par l'usage)* out of shape, shapeless; **elle traîne toujours son vieux manteau tout a.** she wears her shapeless old coat everywhere she goes 2 *(posture)* sloppy; *(personne, muscles)* flabby; **être a. dans un fauteuil** to be slumped in an armchair

avachir [avaʃir] VT 1 *(vêtements etc)* to make shapeless; *(cuir)* to soften 2 *(personne, muscles)* to make flabby; **la chaleur m'avachit** the heat makes me feel quite limp *or* floppy

VPR s'avachir 1 *(du cuir)* to soften, to become soft; *(des vêtements)* to become shapeless, to lose its shape **2** *(de personne)* to become flabby; *(se laisser aller)* to let oneself go, to go to seed; **s'a. dans un fauteuil** to flop into an armchair

avachissement [avaʃismã] NM *(de cuir)* softening; *(des vêtements)* losing shape; *(de posture)* sloppiness; *(de personne, muscles)* flabbiness

aval¹, -als [aval] NM *Fin (d'un effet de commerce)* endorsement; **a. bancaire** bank guarantee, aval; **pour a.** for approval; **donner son a. à un billet** to endorse *or* back a bill; **donneur d'a.** guarantor, backer; *Fig* **donner son a. à un projet** to give a project one's backing or support

aval² NM **1** downstream side; **les villages d'a.** the villages downstream; **canal d'a.** (d'écluse) tail race; **porte d'a.** tail or aft gate; **en a.** downstream, downriver; Rail down the line; **en a. du village/du torrent** downstream of the village/torrent; **le ski a.** the downhill ski **2** Com **stade a.** (de la production) downstream; **en a.** downstream **3** Tél down side

avalanche [avalɑ̃ʃ] NF avalanche; **a. de pierres** avalanche of stones; **a. boueuse** avalanche of mud; **couloir d'a.** avalanche corridor; **a. électronique/ionique** avalanche of electrons/ions; Fig **a. d'injures/de compliments** shower of insults/compliments; Fig **ce fut une a. de lettres** letters came pouring in, there was a flood of letters

avalancheux, -euse [avalɑ̃ʃø, -øz] ADJ prone to avalanches; **couloir a.** avalanche corridor

avaler [avale] VT **1** (absorber) to swallow (down); **a. son repas sans mâcher** to swallow down one's meal without chewing it; **a. son repas** to bolt one's meal; **j'avale mon repas et j'arrive** I'll just get my food down, then I'll be along; **a. son vin d'un trait** to swallow one's wine in one gulp; **j'ai avalé de travers** it went down the wrong way; **a. qch tout rond** to swallow sth whole; **je meurs de faim, je n'ai rien avalé depuis hier** I'm starving, I haven't had a thing to eat since yesterday; Fig **a. ses mots** to swallow one's words; **a. la fumée** to inhale; Fig **j'ai cru qu'elle allait m'a. tout cru** I thought she was going to bite my head off; **a. une carte de crédit** (d'un distributeur automatique) to eat or swallow a credit card; **je préfère a. ma salive et penser à autre chose** I prefer to grin and bear it and think of something else; **on dirait qu'il a avalé son parapluie!** he's as stiff as a poker!; **a. les kilomètres** to eat up the miles; **il a avalé 'Vol de Nuit' en une soirée** he read or devoured 'Vol de Nuit' in an evening

2 Fig **a. le morceau** ou **la pilule** to take one's medicine or one's punishment; **celle-là est dure à a.** that's a tall story, I can hardly swallow that; **tu auras du mal à leur faire a. ça** you'll have a job getting them to swallow that; **on peut lui faire a. n'importe quoi, il est tellement naïf** he's so naive he'll swallow anything; Fam **tu as avalé ta langue?** have you lost your tongue?, has the cat got your tongue?; Fam **a. son acte de naissance** to kick the bucket, to pop one's clogs

VI to swallow; Fam **qu'est-ce qu'il avale!** he doesn't half put it away!

avaleur [avalœr] NM **a. de sabres** sword-swallower

avaliser [avalize] VT Fin to avalize; Com (effet de commerce) to endorse, to back; (signature) to guarantee; Fig **a. un projet** to back a project

avaliste [avalist] NM Jur endorser, guarantor, backer

à-valoir NM INV (paiement) advance

AVANCE [avɑ̃s] NF **1** (marche) advance; **l'a. d'une armée/d'un mouvement indépendantiste** the advance of an army/of an independence movement; **l'a. rapide de l'indice du coût de la vie** the rapid rise or climb of the cost of living index; Élec **a. d'une magnéto** magneto lead; **a. rapide** (sur magnétophone) fast-forwarding; **mettre une cassette en a. rapide** to fast-forward a cassette, to put a cassette on fast forward

2 (dans le temps, l'espace, avantage) lead; **avoir de l'a. sur qn** to be ahead of sb; **avoir une a. de 2 minutes/2 km** to have a 2-minute/2-km lead; **avoir 2 minutes/2 km d'a. sur qn** to have a 2-minute/2-km lead over sb; (en début de course) to have a 2-minute/

2-km head start on sb; Sport **un trou/but/set d'a.** one hole/goal/set up; **j'ai fini le projet avec deux jours d'a. sur le programme** I finished the project two days ahead of schedule; **j'ai fini le contrôle avec un quart d'heure d'a.** I finished the test a quarter of an hour ahead of time; **arriver avec cinq minutes d'a.** to arrive five minutes early; **il vaut toujours mieux arriver à la gare avec quelques minutes d'a.** it's always better to arrive at the station a few minutes early or with a few minutes to spare; **nous avons pris de l'a. sur nos poursuivants/concurrents** we've pulled away from our pursuers/competitors; **accentuer/conserver/perdre son a. sur qn** to increase/maintain/lose one's lead over sb; Sport **donner de l'a. à qn** to give sb a head start; **je vais le laisser prendre de l'a. dans la ligne droite** I'll let him get ahead in the straight; **grâce à l'a. acquise pendant les deux premières heures de la course** thanks to the lead he/she/etc established or built up during the first two hours of the race; **Paris-St-Germain cherche à préserver son a. au classement** Paris-St-Germain are trying to hold on to or maintain their lead in the league; **l'a. des Français au niveau de la recherche** the French lead in the sphere of research; **une mauvaise gestion peut nous faire perdre notre a.** we may lose our lead through bad management; Fam **la belle a.!** much good that will do/did/is doing you!

3 Tech (d'un outil) feed movement, travel; **mécanisme d'a.** feed mechanism

4 Aut **a. à l'allumage** ignition advance; **mettre de l'a. à l'allumage** to advance the ignition; **réduire l'a.** to retard the ignition; **levier d'a.** ignition lever; **a. à l'échappement** exhaust lead

5 Fin **a.** (de fonds) advance; **a. à découvert** unsecured or uncovered advance; **a. en devises** foreign currency loan; **a. en numéraire** cash advance; **a. de trésorerie** cash advance; **par a., à titre d'a.** as an advance; **faire une a. de mille euros à qn** to give sb an advance of a thousand euros; **demander une a. sur salaire** to ask for an advance on one's salary; **faire les avances d'une entreprise** to advance funds for an enterprise; Cin **a. sur recette(s)** (d'acteur) advance payment; (de metteur en scène) = money invested in the production of a film, to be recouped from the box office takings

6 **faire des avances à qn** to approach sb; (sexuellement) to make advances to sb; **ne réponds jamais aux avances de ce monsieur!** don't ever respond to that man's advances!

7 Suisse **faire de l'a.** (prendre de l'avance) (sur un travail, des devoirs, etc) to get ahead (sur in, with)

8 Ordinat **a. automatique** automatic feed

9 **d'a., à l'a., par a.** in advance; **payer qn d'a.** ou **à l'a.** to pay sb in advance; **payable à l'a.** payable in advance; **retenir** ou **louer une place huit jours à l'a.** to book a seat a week in advance; **et pourtant, je les ai prévenus deux mois à l'a.** I did warn them two months in advance or beforehand; **entrer à l'école primaire avec un an d'a.** to go to primary school a year early; Scol **avoir un an d'a.** to be a year ahead; **je vous remercie d'a., par a., merci** (dans une lettre) thanking you in advance or in anticipation; **je m'en réjouis d'a.** I'm greatly looking forward to it; **je savourais à l'a. le plaisir de …** I was relishing (in anticipation) the thought of …, I was relishing the prospect of …

10 **en a.** early; **je suis en a. d'une demi-heure** I am half an hour early; **je suis arrivé très en a.** I arrived very early; **elle sait déjà lire, elle est très en a. pour son âge** she can already read, she's very advanced for her age; **être en a. sur son temps** to be ahead of

one's time; **la moisson est en a. cette année** the harvest is early this year; Fam **je vous préviens, nous ne sommes pas en a.!** I'm warning you, we're not exactly running on time!

avancé [avɑ̃se] ADJ **1** (dans l'espace) advanced; **position avancée** advanced or forward position; Rail **signal a.** distant signal; **j'étais trop a. sur ma route pour pouvoir faire demi-tour** I had gone too far along the road to be able to turn back

2 (précoce) forward; **les pommiers sont bien avancés cette année** the apple trees are early this year; **c'est un esprit a.** he's a progressive thinker; **élève a.** pupil ahead of his class; **opinions avancées** advanced or progressive ideas

3 (dans le temps) **à une heure avancée de la nuit** late in the night, well on in the night; **à une heure peu avancée** quite early on; Can **heure avancée** daylight saving time; **l'été est bien a.** summer is well advanced; **à un âge a.** late in life, at an advanced age

4 (fruit) overripe; **viande avancée** rotten meat

5 (presque à terme) (far) advanced; **à un stade a. du projet** at an advanced stage in the project; **je ne suis pas assez a. dans mon travail pour pouvoir sortir ce soir** I'm not far enough ahead with my work to be able to go out tonight; Fam **vous voilà bien a.!** a lot of good that's done you!; **tu es bien a. maintenant que tu l'as renvoyé: tu n'as personne pour le remplacer!** a lot of good it's done you firing him, you've got no one to replace him!; **vous n'en êtes pas plus a.** you're no further forward

avancée [avɑ̃se] NF **1** (saillie) bulge, projection, protuberance; Constr **a. du toit** eaves **2** (de la mer, du désert), Fig (des nationalistes etc) advance **3** (d'une ligne de pêche) leader, trace

avancement [avɑ̃smɑ̃] NM **1** (mouvement) advancing, putting forward **2** Ordinat etc **a. automatique** automatic feed; **a. ligne par ligne** line feed; **a. du papier** paper feed; **a. par friction** friction feed **3** (de projet) advancement, furtherance; **état d'a. des travaux** progress report **4** (promotion) advancement; **a. à l'ancienneté** promotion by seniority; **avoir** ou **obtenir de l'a.** to be promoted **5** (progrès) advance(ment), progress; **l'a. des sciences** the advance or progress of science **6** Jur **a. d'hoirie** = part of inheritance given in advance

AVANCER [avɑ̃se] (**j'avançai(s); n. avançons**)

VT to move forward **1** ▪ to put forward **2** ▪ to bring forward **3** ▪ to lend **4** ▪ to further **5**	
VI to move forward **1** ▪ to advance **1, 3** ▪ to progress **2** ▪ to be fast **4** ▪ to jut out **5**	
VPR to move forward **1** ▪ to make headway **2** ▪ to jut out **4**	

VT **1** (mettre en avant) to move forward; (la main) to stretch out, to hold out; **avance un peu ton pied, tu écrases la queue du chien** move your foot (forward) a bit, you're crushing the dog's tail; **a. sa chaise pour mieux voir** to pull up or forward one's chair to see better; **il avança son verre** he held out his glass; **elle avança son petit visage vers moi** she moved her little face towards me; **a. une voiture jusqu'au portail** to drive a car up to the door; Fml, Hum **l'automobile de Monsieur est avancée** Sir's carriage awaits; Fam **laisse-moi t'a. jusqu'au métro** let me take you as far as the underground; Échecs **a. un pion** to advance a pawn

2 Fig **a. une proposition** to put forward or advance a proposal; **a. ses raisons** to produce *or* set out one's reasons; **comment peut-il prouver ce qu'il avance?** how can he prove his assertion?; **comme l'ont avancé certains chercheurs ...** as some researchers have proposed ...

3 *(dans le temps)* to bring forward; **la réunion a été avancée du 14 au 7** the meeting has been brought forward from the 14th to the 7th; **a. l'heure du dîner** to put dinner forward; **a. une montre d'une heure** to put a watch forward one hour

4 a. de l'argent à qn to advance money to sb; *(prêter)* to lend sb money; **tu peux m'a. (l'argent de) mon train?** could you lend me my train fare?

5 *(promouvoir)* to further; **être avancé** to be promoted, to get promotion; **a. ses recherches** to push on with *or* get ahead with one's research; **a. une plante** to bring on *or* force a plant; **est-ce que ça t'avancerait si je faisais les courses?** would it help you along if I did the shopping?; **à quoi cela vous avancera-t-il?** what good will that do you?, how much better (off) will you be for it?; **ça ne t'avancera à rien de te mettre en colère** losing your temper won't get you anywhere; **je lui ai posé des questions, mais ses réponses ne m'ont pas beaucoup avancé** I asked him some questions, but his answers got me no further forward *or* left me none the wiser

vi 1 *(aller de l'avant)* to move *or* go forward; *(d'un bateau)* to make headway; *(d'une armée)* to advance; **a. à grands pas** to stride along; **a. à pas de loup** to creep along; **a. à tâtons** to feel *or* grope one's way; **a. d'un pas** to take a *or* one step forward; **avancez vers moi** come towards me; **chaque année, la mer avance un peu plus sur notre terrain** each year, the sea encroaches a little further on our land; **faire a. qn** to help sb along; *(en le poussant)* to push sb along; **faire a. une chaise roulante** to push a wheelchair; *Mil* **faire a. les troupes** to advance the troops, to move the troops forward; **faire a. sa voiture jusqu'à la porte** to drive one's car up to the door; **vous ne pouvez pas a., s'il vous plaît?** je ne peux pas passer could you move, please? I can't get past; **tu n'avances pas assez vite, on ne sera jamais à l'heure** you're not going fast enough, we'll never be on time; **allez avance! on va être en retard** come on, move! we're going to be late; **aux heures de pointe, on n'avance pas sur cette route** during the rush hours, you can't move on this road; **nous n'avancions pas d'un centimètre** we weren't moving an inch; **nous avancions péniblement dans les marais** we struggled our way through the swamp; **le vieil homme avançait en traînant les pieds** the old man shuffled along

2 *(faire des progrès)* to progress, to get on; **le travail avance** the work is progressing *or* getting on *or* coming along; **depuis sa démission, ça n'avance plus** since he/she resigned, things have been at a standstill *or* have ground to a halt; *Fam* **alors, ça avance?** so how's it coming along?; **je n'avance pas dans mon livre** I'm not making any headway with this book; **mon livre n'avance pas du tout** my book isn't coming along at all; **on sentait en lui le désir de faire a. les choses** you could tell he wanted to get things moving (along); **faire a. la cause de la démocratie** to advance the cause of democracy, to further democracy; **faire a. la science** to bring about scientific progress; **a. en âge** to be getting on; **la nuit avance** it's getting late; **la matinée avançait péniblement** the morning was dragging on *or* wore on

3 *(dans une carrière etc)* to advance; **a. en grade** to get promoted; *Mil* to rise in rank

4 *(dans le temps)* *(d'une montre)* to be fast; **l'horloge avance** the clock is fast; **montre qui avance d'une minute par jour** watch that

gains a minute a day; **vous avancez de dix minutes** your watch is ten minutes fast

5 *(de promontoire, toit etc)* to jut out, to project, to protrude; **les rochers avançaient sur la mer** the rocks jutted out into the sea; **le balcon avançait sur la baie** the balcony jutted out over the bay

VPR s'avancer 1 *(aller devant)* to move forward; **s'a. vers qch** to make one's way *or* to head towards sth; **s'a. d'un pas** to take a *or* one step forward; **avance-toi si tu veux voir** move forward if you want to see; **s'a. péniblement** to drag oneself along

2 *(dans une tâche)* to make headway; **elle en a profité pour s'a. dans son travail** she made use of this to get ahead in her work

3 *Fig* **il s'est trop avancé pour reculer** he has gone too far to take it back; **elle refuse de s'a. sur ce point** she won't be drawn on this matter; **je crois que je me suis trop avancé en disant que mes parents leur prêteraient leur maison** I think I went too far when I said my parents would lend them their house; **tu t'avances un peu en disant que je vais avoir ce boulot** you're getting ahead of yourself a bit in saying that I'm going to get this job

4 *(de promontoire)* to jut out; **une langue de terre s'avance dans la mer** a strip of land juts out *or* runs out into the sea

avanie [avani] **NF** *Litt* snub; **subir** *ou* **essuyer une a.** to be snubbed

AVANT [avɑ̃]

PRÉP	before **1–6** ▪ by **1** ▪ within **1** ▪ until **4, 5** ▪ by the time **5**
ADV	before **1, 2** ▪ beforehand **1** ▪ far **3** ▪ late **4**
ADJ INV	front
NM	front **1, 3** ▪ forward **1**

PRÉP SEE GRAMMAR A68; B54 **1** *(dans le temps)* before; **venez a. midi** come before twelve o'clock; **il sera ici a. une heure** he will be here by one o'clock; *(dans moins d'une heure)* he will be here within an *or* the hour; **je le verrai a. quinze jours** I shall see him within *or* in less than a fortnight; **pas a. lundi** not before Monday; **pas a. de nombreuses années** not for many years to come; **il a terminé la course a. moi** he finished the race before me *or* ahead of me; **a. son arrivée** before he arrives/arrived, before his arrival; **juste a. la pluie** just before it started to rain, just before the rain started; **800 a. Jésus-Christ** 800 BC; **a. imposition** *ou* **impôt** before tax

2 *(dans l'espace)* before; **la maison est a. la boucherie** the house is before the butcher's; **l'article se place a. le nom** the article is placed before the noun *or* in front of the noun

3 *(priorité)* **a. la ceinture noire, il y a la ceinture bleue** the blue belt comes before the black belt; **mettre** *ou* **faire passer la santé a. le reste** to put one's health above *or* before all else; **pour lui, la famille passe a. tout** for him, (the) family comes first; **a. tout** first of all, above all; **a. toute chose** before anything else, in the first place; **a. tout, il faut que tu sois satisfait** above all (else) *or* first and foremost, we want you to be satisfied

4 a. de faire before doing; **je vous reverrai a. de partir** I shall see you before I leave; **ne fais rien a. d'être tout à fait sûr** do not do anything until you are quite certain; **lave-toi les mains a. de manger** wash your hands before eating *or* you eat; *Litt* **a. que de mourir** before dying

5 je vous reverrai a. que vous (ne) partiez I shall see you again before you leave; **je serai parti a. que vous ayez fini** I shall be gone by the time (that) you have finished; **ne partez pas a. qu'on vous le dise** don't go until you are told; *Fam* **celle-là, a. qu'elle arrive!** the

time it takes (for) her to get here!

6 il est à quelques mètres en a. de nous he's a few metres in front of us; **en a. du village se trouvait une petite église** there was a little church just before the village; *Litt* **avec rien que la mort en a. de nous** with nothing but death awaiting *or* before us

ADV 1 *(auparavant)* before; *(par rapport à un événement futur)* beforehand; **a. j'avais les cheveux longs** I used to have long hair; **a. je voulais être prof** I wanted to be a teacher before, I used to want to be a teacher; **il était arrivé quelques mois a.** he had arrived some months before *or* earlier; **réfléchis a., tu parleras après** think first, speak later; **on commencera mardi, que tout le monde ait lu la pièce a.** we'll start on Tuesday, (so) everyone make sure you've read the play beforehand; **tu ferais mieux de téléphoner a.** you'd better phone beforehand; **du pain comme on le faisait a.** bread the way they used to make it; **bien/peu a.** well/shortly before; **juste a.** just before; **il l'a mentionné a. dans la préface** he mentioned it before *or* earlier in the preface; **le jour d'a., tout était calme** the day before, everything was quiet

2 *(dans l'espace)* **n'allez pas jusqu'à l'église, sa maison est a.** don't go as far as the church, his house is before (you come to) it

3 *(loin)* far, deep; **pénétrer très a. dans les terres** to penetrate far inland; **le harpon pénétra très a. dans les chairs** the harpoon sank deep into the flesh; *Fig* **tu t'es engagé trop a.** you've got too involved, you're in too deep; **on l'a empêché de pousser plus a. son enquête** he was prevented from taking his investigation(s) any further

4 *(tard)* far, late; **très a. dans la journée** very late in the day; *Litt* **on dut attendre fort a. dans le siècle la diffusion du vaccin** vaccinations did not become readily available until well on into the century

5 en a. in front, ahead; *Mil* **en a.!** forward!; *Mil* **en a., marche!** forward march!; **en a. toute!** *Naut* full steam ahead!; *Fig* forward march!; **en a. la musique!** (on y va) let's be off!; *(ça recommence)* here we go again!; **il est parti en a. pour reconnaître le chemin** he set off ahead to reconnoitre the route; **envoyer qn en a.** to send sb ahead *or* on (in front); **aller en a.** to go to the front; **elle marche toujours quelques mètres en a.** she always walks a few yards in front *or* ahead; **se pencher en a.** to lean forward(s); **tomber en a.** to fall forwards; **faire deux pas en a.** to take two steps forward, to move forward two steps; *Fig* **mettre qn en a.** to push sb forward; *Fig* **mettre le règlement/la loi en a.** to hide behind the rule book *or* the law; *Fig* **mettre en a. une question** to bring up a question

ADJ INV front; **la partie a. du navire** the fore part of the ship; **roue a.** front wheel; *Aut* **à traction a.** with front-wheel drive

NM 1 *Aut, Rail, Aviat* front; *Naut* bow; *(de piston)* crank end; **l'a. de la voiture est complètement défoncé** the front of the car is completely smashed in; **les enfants ne doivent pas s'asseoir à l'a.** children may not sit in (the) front; **tu seras mieux à l'a.** you'll be better in (the) front; **le logement de l'équipage est à l'a.** the crew's quarters are forward; *Naut* **présenter l'a. à la lame** to be head to sea; **aborder un navire par l'a.** to collide with a ship head on; **par tribord a.** on the starboard bow; **sur ou à l'a. du mât** before the mast; **aller de l'a.** to go *or* forge ahead; *Fig* **lui, au moins, il allait de l'a.** at least he always forged ahead

2 *Ftbl etc* forward; **la ligne des avants** the forward line; *Rugby* **a. de deuxième ligne** second-row forward, lock (forward); **il joue a.** he plays up front

3 *Mil* **l'a.** the front

avantage [avɑ̃taʒ] NM **1** (*profit*) advantage; **a. pécuniaire** monetary gain; **a. en nature** benefit in kind, *Fam* perk; **avantages acquis** long-service benefits; **a. concurrentiel** competitive advantage; **avantages et coûts comparatifs** comparative advantages and costs; **a. fiscal** tax benefit, tax incentive; **a. matériel/personnel** material/personal gain; **avantages sociaux** social security benefits; **il ne m'en revient aucun a.** I'm not getting any advantage *or* benefit from it; **être à l'a. de qn** to be to sb's advantage; **la situation tourne à votre a.** the situation is turning to your advantage; **et voilà que Vincent cherche encore à tirer a. de la situation** there's Vincent trying to turn the situation to his advantage again; **trouver de l'a. à faire qch** to find it an advantage *or* advantageous to do sth

2 (*atout*) advantage; **présenter un a.** to have an advantage; **cette solution a l'a. d'être rapide et efficace** this solution has the advantage of being quick and effective; **les avantages que vous procure un appartement en ville** the benefits *or* advantages gained from having a flat in town; **posséder un ordinateur est un a. certain** owning a computer is a definite advantage; **sa connaissance du français lui est un a. précieux** his knowledge of French is a great asset to him; **avoir un a. sur qn** to have an advantage over sb; **avoir (sur qn) l'a. du nombre/de l'âge** to have the advantage of number/age (over sb)

3 *Jur* gift, donation; **à titre d'a.** as a gift

4 *Sp, Tennis, Fig* advantage; **donner l'a. à qn** to give sb a head start; **je vais lui donner l'a. dans la ligne droite** I'll let him go in front of me in the straight; **c'est tout à ton a. d'être arrivé en avance** it's to your advantage that you arrived early; **il a changé à son a.** he has changed for the better; **s'habiller à son a.** to dress to one's best advantage; **paraître à son a.** (*physiquement*) to look one's best; (*à un entretien*) to be at one's best; **il est à son a. en uniforme** he looks his best in uniform; **parler à l'a. de qn** to speak in sb's favour; **avoir l'a. sur qn** to have the advantage of *or* over sb; **prendre l'a.** *Sport* to go into the lead; (*sur un marché*) to become the leader; **conserver l'a.** *Sport* to stay in the lead; (*sur un marché*) to hold onto one's lead; **prendre l'a. sur qn** to take the lead over sb; **il a l'a.** the odds are in his favour; *Tennis* **a. (au) service** (*Mauresmo au service*) advantage Mauresmo; *Tennis* **a. dehors** (*Pierce au service, Mauresmo en face*) advantage Mauresmo; *Tennis* **a. Williams** advantage Williams

5 **il y a a. à** + *inf* it is best to, it is worth one's while to + *inf*; **il y aura a. à ce que vous soyez présent** it will be a good thing *or* just as well if you are present; **tu aurais a. à être poli la prochaine fois** you would do well to be polite next time

6 *Fml* **à quoi dois-je l'a. de votre venue?** to what do I owe the honour of your visit?; **je n'ai pas l'a. de vous connaître** I have not had the honour of making your acquaintance

avantagé [avɑ̃taʒe] ADJ **être fort a. par rapport aux autres** to enjoy many advantages over others; **a. par la nature** (*physiquement*) well endowed; *Péj* **la pauvre, elle n'a pas été avantagée par la nature!** the poor thing, nature hasn't been too kind to her!; *Sport* **joueur a.** player who has been given a start

avantager [avɑ̃taʒe] VT (**j'avantageai(s); n. avantageons**) **1** (*favoriser*) to favour, to give an advantage to; **ton expérience t'avantage par rapport aux autres candidats** your experience gives you an advantage over the other candidates; **son bégaiement ne l'avantage pas** his stammer doesn't help

him **2** (*physiquement*) **l'uniforme l'avantage** he looks his best in uniform; **cette coiffure ne l'avantage vraiment pas** that hairstyle really doesn't flatter her

avantageusement [avɑ̃taʒøzmɑ̃] ADV advantageously, to advantage; **elle sait mettre a. son décolleté en valeur** she knows how to show off her cleavage to advantage; **parler de qn a.** to speak favourably of sb

avantageux, -euse [avɑ̃taʒø, -øz] ADJ **1** (*intéressant*) advantageous, favourable; (*bon marché*) good value; *Com* **prix a.** reasonable price **2** (*flatteur*) **parler de qn en termes a.** to speak favourably of sb; **robe avantageuse** becoming dress; **portrait a.** flattering portrait **3** **poitrine avantageuse** well-developed bust **4** *Péj* (*vaniteux*) conceited, vain; **prendre un ton a.** to adopt a superior tone

avant-aile, *pl* **avant-ailes** NM *Rugby* wing-forward, flanker

avant-bassin, *pl* **avant-bassins** NM *Naut* outer basin, dock

avant-bras NM INV *Anat* forearm

avant-cale, *pl* **avant-cales** NF *Naut* fore hold

avant-centre, *pl* **avants-centres** NM *Ftbl* centre forward

avant-corps NM INV *Archit* (*d'un bâtiment*) projecting part

avant-cour, *pl* **avant-cours** NF *Archit* forecourt

avant-coureur, *pl* **avant-coureurs** NM forerunner, precursor; *Mil* scout

ADJ (*symptôme*) warning; **choc a. (de séisme)** preliminary tremor; **les signes avant-coureurs du changement** the harbingers of change

avant-dernier, -ière, *pl* **avant-derniers, -ières** ADJ last but one, second (to) last, *Fml* penultimate; **l'avant-dernière fois** the time before last

N last but one, second (to) last, next to last

avant-garde, *pl* **avant-gardes** NM **1** *Mil* advance(d) guard; **détachement d'a.** advance(d) party **2 hommes d'a.** men in the van, pioneers; *Pol* **les éléments d'a.** the avant-garde; **livre d'a.** avant-garde book; **les découvertes de l'a.** the discoveries of the avant-garde; **technique d'a.** avant-garde technique; **être à l'a. de la mode/du progrès** to be in the vanguard *or* at the forefront of fashion/progress

avant-gardisme, *pl* **avant-gardismes** [avɑ̃gardism] NM avant-gardism

avant-gardiste, *pl* **avant-gardistes** [avɑ̃gardist] ADJ avant-garde
N avant-gardiste

avant-goût, *pl* **avant-goûts** NM foretaste, anticipation, first impression; **cela m'a donné un a. de ce qu'allait être ma vie/mon travail** it gave me a taste *or* foretaste of my life to come/of what my work would be like

avant-guerre, *pl* **avant-guerres** NM OU NF pre-war period; **la mode d'a.** pre-war fashion

avant-hier [avɑ̃tjɛr] ADV the day before yesterday; **a. au soir** the night *or* evening before last

avant-main, *pl* **avant-mains** NM **1** (*de cheval*) forequarters, forehand **2** *Tennis* **coup d'a.** forehand (stroke)

avant-midi [avɑ̃midi] NM OU NF INV *Belg, Can* morning

avant-plan, *pl* **avant-plans** NM *Beaux-Arts, Phot etc* foreground

avant-pont, *pl* **avant-ponts** NM *Naut* foredeck

avant-port, *pl* **avant-ports** NM *Naut* outer harbour

avant-poste, *pl* **avant-postes** NM *Mil* outpost

avant-première, *pl* **avant-premières** NF private view *or* viewing, preview; *Théâtre* dress rehearsal; **présenté en a.** (*film, pièce etc*) previewed, given an advanced showing

avant-programme, *pl* **avant-programmes** NM (*d'un festival*) synopsis of events

avant-propos NM INV (*de livre*) preface, foreword; *Fig* **après quelques a.** after a few preliminary remarks; **en a. à cette conférence** before the lecture gets underway, as a prelude to this lecture

avant-scène, *pl* **avant-scènes** NF *Théâtre* **1** *Antiq* proscenium, apron, forestage **2** (*loge d'*)**a.** stage box

avant-spectacle, *pl* **avant-spectacles** NM pre-show performance; **en a.** as a curtain-raiser

avant-titre, *pl* **avant-titres** NM (*d'un livre*) half-title

avant-toit, *pl* **avant-toits** NM eaves; **comble avec a.** umbrella roof

avant-train, *pl* **avant-trains** NM **1** *Aut* front-axle unit **2** (*d'une charrue*) wheels **3** *Mil* limber

avant-veille, *pl* **avant-veilles** NF two days before; **l'a. de Noël** two days before Christmas

avare [avar] ADJ **1** (*mesquin*) mean, miserly, *Fam* tight **2 il n'est pas a. de compliments** he's generous *or* lavish with his compliments; **il n'est pas a. de ses conseils** he's only too happy to offer advice
N miser

avarice [avaris] NF avarice, miserliness; **au diable l'a.!** you can't take it with you!, to hell with the expense!

avaricieux, -ieuse [avarisjø, -jøz] ADJ miserly, avaricious, *Fam* stingy
N miser, skinflint; **un vieil a.** an old miser

avarie [avari] NF **1** (*à un bateau, moteur etc*) damage; **subir une a.** to be damaged; **faire subir une a. à qch** to damage sth **2 déclaration d'avaries** (ship's) protest; **avaries matérielles de mer** damage done by sea water **3 avaries-frais** average; **règlement d'avaries** adjustment of average; **répartiteur d'avaries** average adjuster

avarié [avarje] ADJ (*marchandises etc*) damaged, spoiled; (*viande, poisson etc*) rotten

avarier [avarje] (*pr sub, impf n. avariions, v. avariiez*) VT (*marchandises etc*) to damage
VPR **s'avarier** (*nourriture etc*) to go off, to go bad, to rot; (*denrées non comestibles*) to be damaged

avatar [avatar] NM **1** (*transformation*) transformation, change, metamorphosis; **avatars (de la vie politique etc)** ups and downs, vicissitudes **2** (*mésaventure*) mishap, misadventure **3** (*incarnation*) avatar, incarnation **4** *Ordinat* avatar

Ave [ave] NM Ave; **l'A. Maria** the Hail Mary

AVEC [avɛk]

PRÉP	with **1–5, 7–9** ▪ in spite of **5** ▪ to **8**

PRÉP **1** with; **je vous ai vu a. lui** I saw you with him; **je crois a. vous que …** like you, I believe that …; **le public est a. nous** the public is with *or* behind us; **a. qui viendras-tu?** who are you coming with?, *Fml* with whom are you coming?; **être bien/mal a. qn** to be getting on well/badly with sb; **un pavillon a. garage** a detached house with a garage; **elle ressemble à sa sœur, a. des traits plus réguliers** she is like her sister, but with more regular features

2 (*manière*) **a. enthousiasme/tristesse** enthusiastically/sadly, with enthusiasm/sadness; **a. beaucoup de gentillesse** very kindly, with great kindness; **a. beaucoup de franchise** very candidly; **elle danse a. beaucoup de grâce** she dances very gracefully; **c'est a. émotion que j'accepte le poste** I'm thrilled to accept the job; **mots dits a. colère** words spoken in anger

3 (*simultanéité*) **la capacité pulmonaire diminue a. l'âge** lung capacity decreases with age; **l'oxygène se raréfie a. l'altitude** air becomes thinner with altitude; **cela viendra a. le temps** that will come in *or* with time; **il se lève a. le soleil** he gets up at sunrise; **il est arrivé a. la nuit** he arrived when it was getting dark, he arrived at nightfall; **le paysage change a. les saisons** the countryside changes with the seasons

4 (*à cause de*) **a. tous les ennuis qu'il a eus, il ne sait plus où donner de la tête** with all the problems he's had, he doesn't know whether he's coming or going; **a. cette sécheresse, rien ne pousse** nothing will grow with this drought; **impossible de sortir a. cette pluie/ce temps** it's impossible to go out in *or* with this rain/weather

5 (*malgré*) **a. tous ses défauts, il a quand même réussi à se faire accepter** with or in spite of all his faults, he has still managed to become accepted; **a. tout le respect que je vous dois** with all due respect

6 (*moyen*) **a. l'aide de qn** with sb's help; **ouvrir une porte a. une clef** to open a door with a key; **a. 2000 euros par mois, on s'en sort très bien** you can get by *or* manage perfectly well on *or* with 2,000 euros per month; **je fais toujours mes devoirs a. de la musique** I always have music on when I'm doing my homework; **aujourd'hui, on va faire notre gymnastique a. de la musique** today we're going to do our gymnastics to music; **je m'endors mieux a. de la musique** I fall asleep more quickly with music on; **je préfère travailler a. la lumière du jour** I prefer to work in daylight; **j'ai eu un accident a. cet avion** I had an accident in this plane

7 (*contre*) **lutter a. qch** to struggle with sth; **se battre a. qn** to fight (with) sb

8 (*à l'égard de*) **elle est toujours gentille a. moi/les enfants** she's always nice to me/children; **c'est un amour a. sa femme** he's a darling to his wife; **être dur a. qn** to be hard on sb; **être franc a. qn** to be frank with sb

9 (*en ce qui concerne*) **a. elle, on ne sait jamais** you never can tell with her; **a. toi, c'est toujours pareil** it's always the same with you, it's always the same old story with you; **tu sais bien qu'a. lui on peut avoir confiance** you know that he can be trusted; **a. le caractère qu'elle a** with her character; *Fam* **il nous embête a. ses problèmes de famille!** he's driving us mad with all his family problems!

10 *Fam* **elle est grande, mince, athlétique, et sympa a. ça** she's tall, slim, athletic, and what's more, she's nice; **et a. (tout) ça, il n'est pas content!** and he still isn't happy!; **... et ne me dis pas a. (tout) ça qu'il n'a pas triché!** ... and don't tell me after all that that he didn't cheat!; **et a. cela** *ou* **ceci, madame?** anything else, madam?

11 **d'a.** from; **distinguer** *ou* **séparer le bon d'a. le mauvais** to distinguish (the) good from (the) bad; **divorcer d'a. sa femme** to divorce one's wife

▸ ADV *Fam* with it; with them; **il a pris la caisse et s'est sauvé a.** he ran off with the takings; **j'espérais qu'il laisserait sa femme à la maison, malheureusement, il est venu a.** I was hoping he'd leave his wife at home, unfortunately he brought her with him; **nous n'avions qu'un vieux tourne-disque, il a bien fallu faire a.** we only had an old record player so we had to make do (with it); *Région* **tu viens a.?** are you coming too?

aveline [avlin] NF (*fruit*) hazel nut, cob (nut)

avelinier [avlinje] NM (*arbre*) hazel

aven [aven] NM *Géol* swallowhole

avenant [avnɑ̃] ADJ (*personne, manières etc*) pleasant, gracious

▸ NM **1 à l'a.** in keeping, correspondingly; **ils se sont conduits à l'a.** they acted accordingly; **le bâtiment est beau et le jardin est à l'a.** the building is beautiful and the garden is in keeping with it **2** (*de traité*) codicil **3** (*de police d'assurance*) additional clause, endorsement **4** (*de verdict*) rider

avènement [avɛnmɑ̃] NM **1** (*du Christ etc*) advent; (*d'un messie*) coming; **depuis l'a. de l'automobile** since the advent of the (motor)car **2** (*accession*) advent, coming, arrival; **a. au trône** accession to the throne

avenir[1] [av(ə)nir] NM future; **qu'est-ce que l'a. nous réserve?** what does the future hold for us?, what has the future in store for us?; **prédire l'a.** to predict the future; **jeune homme d'un grand a.** *ou* **de beaucoup d'a.** young man with a great future ahead of him; **c'est un homme d'a.** he's an up-and-coming man *or* a man with a (promising) future; *Sport* **un joueur d'a.** a coming player; **un métier d'a.** a career with good prospects; **un avocat d'a.** a lawyer with a great future (ahead of him), an up-and-coming lawyer; **situation sans a.** job with no future *or* prospects, dead-end job; **assurer l'a. de qn** to make provision for sb; **dans l'a.** in the future, at some future date; **dans un a. très prochain** in the very near *or* in the immediate future; **à l'a., je serai plus circonspect** in future, I shall be more cautious

avenir[2] NM INV *Jur* (*à l'avocat de la partie adverse*) writ of summons; **signifier un a. à la partie adverse** to serve a writ on the other party

Avent [avɑ̃] NM *Rel* Advent

aventure [avɑ̃tyr] NF **1** adventure; **tu ne peux pas savoir l'a. qui m'est encore arrivée** you can't imagine the adventure I've just had *or* what's just happened to me; **homme d'aventures** adventurous man, adventurer; **film d'aventures** adventure film; **a. effrayante** terrifying experience; **pour trouver des fruits en hiver, c'est tout une a.** it's quite a business *or Fam* a heck of a job finding fruit in winter

2 (*liaison*) (love) affair; **il collectionne les aventures (amoureuses)** he has one affair after another **3 l'a.** chance, luck; **tenter l'a.** to try one's luck; **vie d'a.** life of adventure; **l'a. est au coin de la rue** the unexpected is always round the corner; **à l'a.** at random; **aller** *ou* **errer à l'a.** to wander about aimlessly; **partir à l'a.** to set off in search of adventure; **vivre à l'a.** to live in a happy-go-lucky fashion; *Litt* **par a., d'a.** by chance

4 la bonne a. fortune-telling; **dire** *ou* **tirer la bonne a. à qn** to tell sb's fortune; **diseuse de bonne a.** fortune teller

aventuré [avɑ̃tyre] ADJ risky, chancy

aventurer [avɑ̃tyre] VT (*sa vie etc*) to risk; **a. une grosse somme d'argent** to risk *or* venture a large sum of money

▸ VPR **s'aventurer** to venture (**dans** into); **s'a. en pays inconnu** to venture into an unknown country; *Fig* **s'a. en terrain glissant** to venture into dangerous territory; **je ne m'aventurerai pas à dire que ...** I won't go so far as to say ...

aventureusement [avɑ̃tyrøzmɑ̃] ADV adventurously

aventureux, -euse [avɑ̃tyrø, -øz] ADJ adventurous; **homme a. au jeu** reckless gambler; **projet a.** hazardous *or* risky plan

aventurier, -ière [avɑ̃tyrje, -jɛr] N adventurer, *f* adventuress

aventurisme [avɑ̃tyrism] NM *Pol* adventurism

avenue [avny] NF (*de ville*) avenue; (*menant à une maison*) drive(way); **les avenues du pouvoir** the paths to power

avéré [avere] ADJ (*fait*) recognized, established; **ennemi a.** avowed enemy; **marxistes avérés** professed Marxists; **il est a. que ...** it is confirmed that ...

avérer [avere] (j'avère, n. avérons; j'avérerai) VT *Jur Vieilli* (*fait*) to aver

▸ VPR **s'avérer** to be proved (correct), to be confirmed; **elle s'est avérée indispensable dans l'équipe** she's proved to be *or* turned out to be an essential member of the team; **il s'est avéré que ...** it's turned out that ..., as it's turned out, ...

avers [aver] NM (*de monnaie*) obverse

averse [avers] NF sudden shower, downpour; **essuyer une a.** to be caught in a shower; *Fig* **une a. de félicitations** a flood *or* stream of congratulations

aversion [aversjɔ̃] NF aversion (**pour** to, for), dislike (**pour** for, of); **avoir une a. pour** *ou* **contre qn** to have an aversion to *or* for sb, to have a dislike for sb; **prendre qn en a.** to take a dislike to sb

averti [averti] ADJ (*bien informé*) (well-)informed; (*expérimenté*) experienced; **un homme a.** an experienced man, an expert; *Prov* **un homme a. en vaut deux** forewarned is forearmed; **a. de qch** aware *or* warned of sth; **se tenir pour a.** to take a warning; **vous voilà a.!** I give you fair warning!, don't say I haven't warned you!

avertir [avertir] VT **a. qn de qch** to inform sb of sth; **a. qn du danger d'une situation** to warn *or* tell sb of *or* about the danger(s) of a situation; **je l'en avais averti** I had warned him of *or* against it; **je vous en avertis!** I give you fair warning!; **je vais me mettre en colère, je t'avertis!** I'm going to get angry, I'm warning you!; *Ordinat* **a. de la réception de** to acknowledge

> Il faut noter que le verbe anglais **to advertise** est un faux ami. Il ne signifie jamais **avertir**.

avertissement [avertismɑ̃] NM **1** (*avis préalable*) warning; **renvoyer qn sans a. préalable** to discharge sb at a moment's notice; **lettre envoyée à titre d'a.** letter sent as a reminder; (*avis*) warning letter **2** (*réprimande*) warning, reprimand; *Sport* (*de l'arbitre*) warning, caution **3** (*signal*) danger signal *or* sign, warning signal; **a. de tempête** gale warning; **a. (au lecteur)** foreword (to book); *Ordinat* **a. de réception** (*de message*) acknowledgement; *Ordinat* **a. à réception d'un courrier** mail received message **4** *Jur* billet d'a. summons to appear before a magistrate **5** *Admin* demand note

> Il faut noter que le nom anglais **advertisement** est un faux ami. Il signifie **publicité** ou **annonce**, selon le contexte.

avertisseur, -euse [avertisœr, -øz] NM **1** (*dispositif*) warning signal, alarm; *Aut* horn; *Ind* hooter; *Rail* signal; **a. d'incendie** fire alarm; **a. sonore** warning buzzer; (*Klaxon®*) horn; **avertisseurs sonores interdits après 22.00 heures** no sounding of horns after 10 p.m.; *Aut* **a. de marche arrière** reversing beeper; *Aut* **a. deux tons** two-tone horn; **a. lumineux** warning light; **a. optique** warning light **2** *Théâtre* callboy

▸ ADJ **signal a.** warning signal

aveu, -eux [avø] NM **1** (*confession*) confession, acknowledgement; *Jur* admission; **faire l'a. d'une erreur** to own up *or* confess to a mistake; **passer aux aveux** to make a confession; **faire des aveux complets** to make a full confession; **de son a. même, il est ruiné** on his own admission, he's bankrupt; **je dois vous faire un a., je n'y étais pas non plus** I must confess or admit, I wasn't there either, I have to tell you, I wasn't there either; **arracher des aveux à un accusé** to drag or wring or wrest a confession out of or from a defendant; **il est certain, de l'a. de tout le monde, que ...** it is commonly acknowledged that ... **2** Jur consent, authorization; **obtenir l'a. de qn pour faire qch** to obtain sb's consent to do sth **3** Hist recognition between a vassal and his overlord; **homme sans a.** vagabond, vagrant

aveuglant [avœglɑ̃] **ADJ** blinding, dazzling; Fig **une évidence/preuve aveuglante** a glaringly or patently or blindingly obvious fact/proof

aveugle [avœgl] **ADJ 1** (atteint de cécité) blind; **devenir a.** to go blind; **a. d'un œil** blind in one eye; **être a. de naissance, naître a.** to be born blind, to be blind from birth; Opt **point a.** blind spot **2** Archit Fig **fenêtre/arcade a.** blind window/arch; **mur a.** blind wall; Tech **écrou a.** blind nut; **trou a.** dead hole; **bout a. (d'un tuyau)** blind end **3** (haine) blind, unreasoning; (confiance) implicit; **avoir une confiance a. en qn** to trust sb implicitly or unreservedly; **obéissance a.** blind or unquestioning obedience; **son amour pour elle le rend a.** he's blinded by his love for her

N blind man, f blind woman; **les aveugles** the blind; Fig **suivre qn en a.** to follow sb blindly; Vieilli **aller à l'a.** to grope one's way

aveuglement [avœgləmɑ̃] **NM 1** (moral, mental) blindness; **l'a. de la passion/de la colère** the blindness of passion/of anger **2** Arch blinding; **depuis son a.** since his blindness

aveuglément [avœglemɑ̃] **ADV** blindly; **obéir a.** to obey blindly

aveugle-né, -née, pl **aveugles-nés, -nées** **ADJ** (homme, femme) blind from birth
N congenitally blind person, person blind from birth

aveugler [avœgle] **VT 1** (rendre aveugle) to blind **2** (de la lumière etc) to blind, to dazzle; Fig **aveuglé par la colère** blind with rage; Fig **son amour pour elle l'aveugle** he's blinded by his love for her **3** Naut **a. une voie d'eau** to stop a leak **4** (boucher) to plug, to stop (up), to block up; **a. une fenêtre** to wall up or block a window
VPR s'aveugler Fig to be blind, to shut one's eyes (sur qch to sth); **il ne faut pas t'a., ça ne sera pas facile** don't delude yourself or Fam kid yourself, it won't be easy; **s'a. sur les défauts de qn** to shut one's eyes or turn a blind eye to sb's faults

aveuglette (à l') [alavœglɛt] **ADV** blindly; **aller à l'a.** to feel or grope one's way; **avancer à l'a. vers qch** to feel or grope one's way to(-wards) sth; Fig **choisir qch à l'a.** to choose sth at random or in the dark or blindly; **lancer des coups à l'a.** to hit out blindly; Aviat **voler à l'a.** to fly blind

aveulir [avølir] **VT** Litt to enervate; (sentiments) to deaden
VPR s'aveulir to be effete

aveulissement [avølismɑ̃] **NM** effeteness

aviaire [avjɛr] **ADJ** **peste a.** fowl plague or pest

aviateur, -trice [avjatœr, -tris] **N** aviator

aviation [avjasjɔ̃] **NF 1** (activité) flying, aviation; **aimer l'a.** to like flying; **il fait de l'a. le week-end** he goes flying at the weekends; **école d'a.** flying school, school of aviation **2** (secteur) aviation; **a. civile/commerciale** civil/commercial aviation; **a. de tourisme** ci-

vil aviation; **champ** ou **terrain d'a.** airfield; **usine d'a.** aircraft factory; **compagnie d'a.** airline **3** Mil air force; **base d'a.** air base

avicole [avikɔl] **ADJ** **élevage a.** (activité) poultry farming; (établissement) poultry farm

aviculteur, -trice [avikyltœr, -tris] **N** poultry farmer

aviculture [avikyltyr] **NF 1** (d'oiseaux) aviculture **2** (de volailles) poultry farming

avide [avid] **ADJ 1** (passionné) eager, avid, greedy; **a. de qch** (âpre) greedy for sth; (plein d'enthousiasme) eager for sth; **espérances avides** eager hopes; **a. de sang** bloodthirsty; **a. de tout savoir** eager for knowledge **2** Péj greedy, covetous (**de** of); (mains, nature) grasping

avidement [avidmɑ̃] **ADV** greedily, hungrily; **écouter a.** to listen eagerly or avidly

avidité [avidite] **NF** avidity, greed(iness); (de nourriture) greed, gluttony; **manger avec a.** to eat greedily; **écouter avec a.** to listen eagerly or avidly

Avignon [aviɲɔ̃] **NF** Géog Avignon; **à** ou **en Avignon** in Avignon; Théâtre **le festival d'Avignon** the Avignon festival

---

Le festival d'Avignon

Founded by Jean Vilar in 1947 and held every summer in Avignon in the South of France, this arts festival is a showcase for new theatre and dance performances: "La pièce sera donnée d'abord en Avignon". Along with the programme of official shows ("le in") performed in prestigious venues such as the Court of Honour of the "Palais des Papes", a programme comprising numerous fringe shows, referred to as "le off", has also been performed since the 1970s.

---

avili [avili] **ADJ 1** (personne) degraded, debased, demeaned **2** Com (monnaie, système monétaire) debased; (biens) depreciated

avilir [avilir] **VT 1** (dégrader) to degrade, to debase, to lower **2** Com (monnaie, prix etc) to depreciate, to lower, to bring down
VPR s'avilir 1 (d'une personne) to lower or demean oneself **2** (de biens) to depreciate, to come down (in value)

avilissant [avilisɑ̃] **ADJ** debasing, degrading

avilissement [avilismɑ̃] **NM 1** (dégradation) debasement, degradation **2** Com depreciation; (de prix) fall

aviné [avine] **ADJ** (attrib) intoxicated, inebriated; **haleine avinée** breath reeking of wine

aviner [avine] **VT** (tonneau) to impregnate with wine

avion [avjɔ̃] **NM** aeroplane, aircraft, plane, Am airplane; **j'ai fait une partie du trajet en a.** I flew part of the way; **par a.** (by) airmail; **voyager en a.** to travel by plane or air, to fly; **prendre l'a. pour aller à Londres** to get or take the plane to London, to fly to London; **accident d'a.** plane crash; **détournement d'a.** hijacking, hijack, skyjacking
▸ ▸ **a. d'attaque au sol** ground attack aircraft; **a. bimoteur** twin-engine aircraft; **a. de bombardement** bomber; **a. charter** charter plane; **a. de chasse** fighter (plane); **a. commercial** commercial aircraft; **a. à décollage et atterrissage courts** short take-off and landing aircraft; **a. à décollage et atterrissage verticaux** vertical take-off and landing aircraft; **a. furtif** stealth bomber; **a. à géométrie variable** swing-wing aircraft; **a. gros porteur** jumbo jet, wide bodied aircraft; **a. à hélices** prop jet; **a. de ligne** airliner, passenger aircraft; **a. mixte** passenger

and cargo plane; **a. moyen porteur** regular bodied aircraft; **a. de pénétration** intruder; **a. petit porteur** narrow bodied aircraft; **a. ravitailleur** tanker; **a. à réaction** jet, jet plane, jet aircraft; **a. de reconnaissance** reconnaissance aircraft; **a. supersonique** supersonic aircraft; **a. de tourisme** private aircraft; **a. transbordeur** air ferry; **a. de transport** transport aircraft

avion-cargo, pl **avions-cargos** **NM** freight plane, cargo plane

avion-citerne, pl **avions-citernes** **NM** Aviat tanker (aircraft)

avion-école, pl **avions-écoles** [avjɔ̃ekɔl] **NM** trainer, training aircraft

avion-espion, pl **avions-espions** [avjɔ̃-ɛspjɔ̃] **NM** spy plane

avionique [avjɔnik] **NF** Aviat avionics

avionneur [avjɔnœr] **NM 1** (concepteur) airframe designer **2** (constructeur) airframe manufacturer

avion-suicide, pl **avions-suicides** **NM** suicide plane

avion-taxi, pl **avions-taxis** **NM** air taxi, taxiplane

aviron [avirɔ̃] **NM 1** (rame) oar, Can (canoe) paddle; **a. de couple** scull; **avirons de couple** ou **accouplés** double-banked oars; **avirons de** ou **en pointe** single-banked oars; **a. de galère** sweep; **les avirons dans l'eau!** hold water!; **engager son a.** to catch a crab; **coup d'a.** stroke **2** Sport **l'a.** rowing; **cercles d'a.** rowing clubs; **faire de l'a.** to row

avironner [avirɔne] **VI** Can (en canoë) to paddle

avis [avi] **NM 1** (opinion) opinion, judg(e)ment; **a. d'expert** expert advice or opinion; **exprimer** ou **émettre un a.** to express a view or an opinion; **être du même a. que qn** to be of the same opinion as sb; **ne pas être du même a. que qn** to disagree with sb; **sauf meilleur a., je crois que ...** with all due deference, I think that ...; Prov **deux a. valent mieux qu'un** two heads are better than one; **à** ou **selon mon a.** in my opinion; **à mon humble a. ...** in my humble opinion ...; Fam **on ne t'a pas demandé ton a.!** nobody asked you!, mind your own business!, nobody asked your opinion!; **de l'a. de tous** in the opinion or judgment of all; **on dit qu'il est généreux, mais ce n'est pas l'a. de tout le monde** he's said to be generous, but not everyone would agree with that; **je suis tout à fait de votre a.** I entirely agree with you; **j'ai changé d'a.** I have changed my mind; Hum **elle change d'a. comme de chemise** she changes her mind like she changes her underwear; **être d'a. de faire qch** to be of a mind to do sth; **êtes-vous d'a. de rester ici?** are you for staying here?

2 (conseil) advice; **donner des a. à qn sur qch** to give sb some advice on or about sth; **prendre** ou **demander l'a. de qn** to ask sb's advice

3 (avertissement) notice, announcement; **a. (au public)** public notice, notice (to the public); **donner a. de qch** to give notice of sth; **donner a. à qn de qch** to advise sb of sth; aussi Iron **a. aux amateurs!** any takers?; **a. par écrit** notice in writing; **jusqu'à nouvel a.** until further notice, until you hear further; **à moins d'a. contraire** unless I/you/etc hear to the contrary; Com **note** ou **lettre d'a.** advice note; **suivant a.** as per advice
▸ ▸ Bourse **a. d'attribution** allotment letter; **a. de la banque** bank notification or advice; **a. de crédit** credit advice; **a. de débit** debit advice; Com **a. de domiciliation** domiciliation advice; Journ **a. éditorial** editorial opinion; Bourse **a. d'exécution** contract note; **a. d'expédition** (de marchandises) dispatch or consignment note; **a. d'expédition stan-**

dard *(de marchandises)* standard shipping note; **a. d'imposition** tax assessment; **a. de licenciement** redundancy notice; **a. de livraison** delivery note; **a. de paiement** payment advice; **a. de prélèvement** direct debit advice; **a. de réception** acknowledgement (of receipt); **a. de rejet** *(de chèque)* notice of returned cheque; *Banque* **a. de virement** (bank) transfer advice

avisé [avize] ADJ sensible, wise, prudent; **être trop a. pour faire qch** to be too sensible *or* cautious *or* wary to do sth; **il est trop a. pour …** he knows better than to …; **acheteur a.** discriminating purchaser; **bien a.** well-advised; **mesures mal avisées** ill-advised measures; **tu serais mal a. de …** you'd be ill-advised to …

aviser [avize] VT **1** *(informer)* to inform, to notify, to advise; **a. qn de qch** to inform *or* warn *or Com* advise sb of sth; **a. qn de faire qch** to give sb notice to do sth; **a. qn que … +** *ind* to warn sb that … **2** *Arch, Litt (entrevoir)* to perceive, to catch a glimpse of

VI **a. à** *(situation etc)* to decide what to do about, to see about *or* to; **vous ferez bien d'y a.** you had better look into it; **a. à faire qch** to see about doing sth; **a. à ce que qch se fasse** to take steps to have sth done; **il est temps d'a.** it is time to decide *or* to make up one's mind; **j'aviserai en temps voulu** I'll see to that when it's necessary

VPR **s'aviser 1 s'a. de qch** to think of sth; **il ne s'avise de rien** he's not aware of anything; **s'a. que** to notice that, to become aware that, to realize that **2 s'a. de faire qch** to take it upon oneself to do sth; **ne vous en avisez pas!** don't dare to do such a thing!, don't you dare!, you'd better not!; **et ne t'avise pas de recommencer!** don't (you) dare start again!

aviso [avizo] NM *Naut* sloop; **a.-torpilleur** torpedo gunboat; **a. d'escorte** corvette; **canonnière-a.** gunboat

avitaminose [avitaminoz] NF vitamin deficiency, avitaminosis

aviver [avive] VT **1** *(couleurs)* to brighten; *(image)* to touch up; *(plaie, blessure)* to irritate; *(passion)* to excite, to stir up; *(feu)* to fan, to revive, to stir up; *(appétit)* to sharpen; *(querelle)* to stir up; **a. d'anciennes rancunes** to revive ancient grudges **2** *(ferronnerie)* to burnish; *(marbre)* to polish **3** *(surfaces à souder)* to clean up **4** *(outil etc)* to put a keen edge on, to whet

VPR **s'aviver** *(souvenirs, controverse etc)* to be stirred up, to be revived; *(couleur)* to become brighter

av. J.-C. *(abrév* **avant Jésus-Christ)** BC

avocat¹, -ate [avɔka, -at] N **1** *Jur* lawyer, *surtout Am* attorney; *(à la barre) Br* barrister, *Am* trial lawyer *or* attorney; **plaider par a.** to be represented by counsel; **elle est a.** *ou* **avocate** she's a lawyer **2** *Fig* advocate; **a. du diable** devil's advocate

▸▸ **a. conseil** legal adviser; **a. consultant** counsel in chamber; **a. général** assistant public prosecutor (in a court of appeal)

avocat² NM *(fruit)* avocado (pear)

avocat-avoué, *pl* **avocats-avoués** NM ≃ attorney

avocatier [avɔkatje] NM *(arbre)* avocado (tree)

avocette [avɔset] NF *(oiseau)* avocet

avoine [avwan] NF **1** oats; **a. commune** common oats; **farine d'a.** oatmeal; **flocons d'a.** porridge oats; **bouillie d'a.** (oatmeal) porridge; **galette d'a.** oatcake **2** *Arg (argent)* dough, *Br* dosh

AVOIR¹ [avwar] *(prp* **ayant**; *pp* **eu**; *pr ind* **j'ai, tu as, il a, n. avons, v. avez, ils ont;** *pr sub* **j'aie, tu aies, il ait, n. ayons, v. ayez, ils aient;** *imp* **aie, ayons, ayez;** *impf* **j'avais;** *p hist* **j'eus,**

tu eus, il eut, n. eûmes, v. eûtes, ils eurent; *impf sub* **j'eusse;** *fu* **j'aurai;** *avoir is the auxiliary of all transitive and of many intransitive verbs)*

| VT to have 1, 2, 4, 7, 10 ▪ to get 2, 5 ▪ to be 3, 8 ▪ to hit 5 ▪ to make 6 ▪ to give 6 |
| V IMPERS to be 1, 4 |
| V AUX to have |

VT VOIR GRAMMAIRE A55-7 **1** *(maison, télévision, sœur, enfant, animal domestique)* to have; **tu ne veux pas a. d'enfants?** do you not want to have children?; **elle vient d'a. un enfant** she's just had a child; **quel diplôme avez-vous?** what degree have you got?, what degree do you have?; **il donnerait tout ce qu'il a pour …** he'd give everything he's got *or* he has to …; **on a 4 heures d'anglais par semaine** we have *or* we've got 4 hours (of) English a week; *Fam* **faut que j'y aille, j'ai math!** I've got to go, I've got maths!; **j'ai Monsieur Lê comme professeur de math** I've (got) Mr Lê for maths; **j'ai Bill pour ami/voisin** Bill is a friend/neighbour of mine; **a. un entretien/une dispute/une conversation avec qn** to have an interview/an argument/a conversation with sb; **j'ai rendez-vous chez le médecin** I have *or* I've got a doctor's appointment; **a. des amis à dîner** to have friends to *or* for dinner; **je te rappelle que nous avons des amis à dîner ce soir** remember we're having friends to *or* for dinner tonight; **as-tu de quoi manger/vivre?** have you (got) enough to eat/live on?, do you have enough to eat/live on?; **ça coûte cher d'a. une voiture** it's expensive to run a car; **qu'est-ce que vous avez là?** what have you (got) there?; **c'est un joli collier que vous avez là** that's a pretty necklace you have *or* you've got there; **il a encore son père** his father is still alive, he's still got his father; **Dieu ait son âme** God rest his/her soul

2 *(obtenir)* to get; **j'ai eu sa réponse ce matin** I had *or* got his answer this morning; **pourriez-vous m'a. ce renseignement?** could you get that information for me?; **j'ai eu du mal à a. Paris/le numéro** *(au téléphone)* I've had trouble getting (through to) Paris/the number; **c'est lui que j'ai eu au téléphone hier** he's the one I talked to *or* had on the phone yesterday; **j'ai bien eu mon train ce matin** I caught my train all right this morning; **j'ai eu ce réfrigérateur à bon marché** I got *or* bought this refrigerator cheap; **celui-là, je l'aime et je l'aurai!** *(je le séduirai)* I love that man and I'll get him! *or* I'm going to have him!

3 *(mesure, âge)* **a. dix ans** to be ten (years old); **le mur a trois mètres de haut** the wall is three metres high; **a. plusieurs centaines de mètres de profondeur/de longueur/de largeur** to be several hundred metres deep/long/broad

4 *(dans les descriptions physiques et morales)* to have; **a. les yeux bleus** to have blue eyes; **a. de grandes mains/de beaux yeux** to have big hands/beautiful eyes; **a. les cheveux longs** to have long hair; **je commence à a. des cheveux blancs** I'm starting to get a few grey hairs; **a. du charme** to have charm, to be full of charm; **elle a du talent** she has (got) talent; **il a beaucoup d'ambition** he's got a lot of ambition; **elle a beaucoup d'humour** she has (got) a good sense of humour; **elle avait un foulard sur les cheveux** she had a scarf in her hair; **elle avait une jolie robe bleue** she had a pretty blue dress on; **il avait un bébé dans les bras** he had a baby in his arms

5 *(toucher)* to hit, to get; *Fam (duper)* to take for a ride, to con; *Fam (cible)* I think I hit *or* got it; **on les aura!** we'll get them!; **il finira par se faire a.** *(par la po-*

lice) he'll end up getting done (by the police); **on l'a eu!** *(dupé)* he's been had!, he's been taken for a ride!; **je t'ai eu!** got you!; **tu m'as bien eu cette fois-ci!** you really got me that time!, I really fell for it that time!; **se faire a.** to be had, to be taken for a ride; **je veux acheter une voiture d'occasion, mais je ne veux pas me faire a.** I want to buy a second-hand car, but I don't want to get ripped off *or* done *or* conned; **je me suis fait a. de 50 euros** I got done out of 50 euros

6 *(faire)* **il eut un mouvement brusque** he made a sudden movement; **il eut un sourire** he gave a smile; **il eut un cri de surprise** he gave a cry of surprise; **il eut un petit rire moqueur** he gave a mocking little laugh; **il eut un regard étrange** he gave a strange look

7 *(souffrir de)* to have; **a. un rhume/la grippe/le hoquet** to have a cold/(the) flu/(the) hiccups; **a. du diabète/du cholestérol** to have diabetes/excess cholesterol; **a. mal au cœur** to feel sick; **a. de la fièvre** to have a *or* be running a temperature; **a. la rougeole** to have measles

8 *(éprouver)* **qu'avez-vous?, qu'est-ce que vous avez?** what's wrong *or* the matter *or* up (with you)?; **je ne sais pas ce que j'ai, je ne me sens pas bien du tout** I don't know what's wrong *or* the matter with me, I don't feel at all well; **mais qu'est-ce qu'elle a, cette auto?** what's wrong *or* the matter with this car?; **qu'est-ce que tu as? – j'ai que je suis en colère!** what's wrong with you? – I'm angry, that's what's wrong with me!; **mais qu'est-ce qu'elle a à râler tout le temps?** what's the matter with her, moaning all the time?; **a. de la peine** to be upset; **a. des soucis** to be worried; **a. des doutes** to have misgivings; **a. des remords** to feel remorse

9 *(après en)* **nous en avons pour deux heures** it will take us two hours, we'll be two hours; **j'en ai pour une minute** I won't be a minute; **tu en auras pour combien de temps?** how long will you be?, how long will it take you?; **j'en ai assez, je n'en veux plus** I've had enough, I don't want any more; **j'en ai assez** *ou Fam* **marre** *ou Fam* **ras le bol** I've had enough *or Fam* I've had it up to here *or Fam* I'm sick (to the back teeth) of it; **j'en ai eu pour 100 euros** *(c'est le prix)* it cost me 100 euros; *(en quantité)* I had 100 euros' worth; **en a. contre** *ou* **après qn** to have it in for sb

10 a. qch à faire to have sth to do; **pourquoi tu t'en vas? – parce que j'ai à faire** why are you leaving? – because I have things to do; **je n'ai rien à faire** I have nothing to do; **j'ai à travailler** I've work to do; **vous n'avez pas à vous inquiéter** you have no need to worry; **tu n'as pas à te mêler de cette histoire** you shouldn't get mixed up in this matter; **je n'ai que faire de cela** I don't need that

11 *for the verbal phrases* **a. affaire, faim, froid, pitié, raison** *etc, see under these words* SEE GRAMMAR B66

V IMPERS **il y a 1** *(être présent)* **il y a un problème** there is a problem; **il y a des problèmes** there are problems; **qu'est-ce qu'il peut (bien) y a. dans ce tiroir?** I wonder what's in this drawer; **qu'est-ce qu'il y a à voir?** what is there to see?; **combien y a-t-il de blessés?** how many wounded are there?; **il n'y a qu'un** there is only one; **il n'y en aura pas assez pour tout le monde** there won't be enough for everyone; **il n'y en a que pour elle** she gets all the attention; **un homme comme il y en a peu** a man in a million; **une petite fille tout ce qu'il y a de gentil** the nicest little girl you've ever seen; **il y a du soleil aujourd'hui** it's sunny today, the sun is shining today; **il n'y a pas de quoi!** please don't mention it!, you're welcome!; *Fam* **quand (il) y en a pour deux, (il) y en a pour trois** there's more than enough to go round; *Fam* **quand (il n')y en a plus, (il) y en** a encore there'll be plenty more when that's finished; *(comme on apporte encore de la nourriture)* as soon as one lot is finished, another one is on its way; **il y a hôpital et hôpital!** there are hospitals and hospitals!; **il y en a qui disent que ...** there are people who say that ..., some people say that ...; **il y en a un qui va être surpris** someone is in for a surprise; **il n'y a que lui qui ... + subj** he's the only one who ..., it's only him that ...; **il n'y a qu'à demander** you only have to ask, just ask; **il n'y a pas à hésiter, il faut lui parler** there's no point in hanging about, I/you/we/*etc* have to talk to him; *Fam* **il n'y a pas à dire, tu es plus fort que moi** there's no denying it *or* there's no question, you're stronger than I am; **à l'entendre, y'a qu'à faire ceci, y'a qu'à faire cela, c'est trop simple** listening to him and his just do this, just do that, it's all too easy

2 *(se passer)* **il doit y a. quelque chose** there must be something wrong; **qu'y a-t-il à présent?** what now?; **qu'est-ce qu'il y a?** what's the matter?, what's up?; **il y a qu'on t'attendait hier** we were expecting you yesterday, that's what's wrong *or* that's what's the matter

3 *(temps)* **il y a deux ans** two years ago; **il y avait six mois que j'attendais** I had been waiting for six months; **il y a des années qu'on ne s'est pas vus** we haven't seen each other for years; *Fam* **il y a une éternité** ages ago

4 *(distance)* **combien y a-t-il d'ici à Londres?** how far is it (from here) to London?; **il y a 5 km d'ici à Londres** it's 5 km (from here) to London

V **AUX** **j'ai fini** I have *or* I've finished; **j'ai fini ce matin** I finished this morning; **je n'ai pas compris** I did not *or* didn't understand; **je l'ai déjà vu** I have already seen him, I have seen him before; **l'avez-vous lu?** have you read it?; **je l'ai vu/vue hier** I saw him/her yesterday; **attendez que nous ayons fini** wait until we've finished; **j'ai eu vingt ans hier** I was twenty yesterday; **j'ai eu bientôt fini de m'habiller** I (had) soon finished dressing; **quand il eut** *ou* **a eu fini de parler** when he had finished speaking; **j'aurai bientôt fini** I shall soon have finished **SEE GRAMMAR B26–8; B38**

avoir² **NM** *(biens)* property, possessions; *(de société)* assets *pl*, *(capital)* capital; *(sur compte)* credit; *(attestation de crédit)* credit note; **a. de compte** account credit; **a. en banque** bank credit; *Compta* **a.-client** customer credit; *Compta* **a.-fournisseur** supplier credit; **a. en devises** foreign currency holding; **a. disponible** liquid assets; **a. fiscal** tax credit; **tout mon a.** all I possess *or* have; *Com* **doit et a.** debit and credit; **obtenir un a.** to be given credit, to obtain *or* to get credit; **je ne peux pas vous rembourser, mais je peux vous faire un a.** I can't give you your money back, but I can give you a credit note

avoirdupoi(d)s [avwardypwa] **NM** avoirdupois

avoisinant [avwazinã] **ADJ** neighbouring, nearby; **il a cinquante ans ou un âge a.** he's fifty or thereabout(s); **il a volé une somme avoisinante de 500 euros** he has stolen a sum of around 500 euros *or* close to 500 euros

avoisiner [avwazine] **VT** **a. qch** to be near *or* close to *or* adjacent to sth, to border on sth; **il a volé une somme avoisinant les 500 euros** he has stolen a sum of around 500 euros *or* close to 500 euros; **cela avoisine la malhonnêteté** it's bordering on dishonesty

avortement [avɔrtəmã] **NM** **1** *(chez une femme)* **a. spontané** miscarriage; **a. provoqué** abortion; **a. thérapeutique** termination *or* abortion (for medical reasons) **2** *(chez un animal)* casting **3** *Fig (de projet etc)* failure, falling through

avorter [avɔrte] **VI** **1** *(d'une femme)* *(faire une fausse couche)* to miscarry; **elle veut a.** she wants (to have) an abortion; **faire a. qn** to give sb an abortion; *(d'une injection etc)* to induce a miscarriage in sb **2** *(d'un animal)* to cast **3** *Bot* to develop imperfectly, to fail to ripen, to abort; **arbres avortés** stunted trees **4** *Fig* **projet qui a avorté** plan that fell through

VT *(médecin)* to abort; **se faire a.** to have an abortion

avorteur, -euse [avɔrtœr, -øz] **N** abortionist

avorton [avɔrtɔ̃] **NM** *(personne, animal)* runt; *(plante)* stunted plant; *Péj* **espèce d'a.!** you little shrimp *or* squirt!

avouable [avwabl] **ADJ** *(fait, motif)* avowable; **c'est un métier plus a.** it's a more respectable trade

avoué¹ [avwe] **NM** *Jur Br* ≃ solicitor, *Am* ≃ attorney

avoué² **ADJ** **1** *(fait)* acknowledged, admitted **2** *(auteur, partisan)* confessed; **il est le père a. de cette petite fille** he admits he's the father of this little girl **3** *(but)* ostensible; **il est allé là-bas dans le but a. de se venger** he went there ostensibly *or* supposedly for revenge

avouer [avwe] **VT** *(faute etc)* to confess, to admit, to own up to; **elle ne veut pas a. que c'est elle qui a pris l'argent** she won't admit that she took the money; **elle avoue avoir trente ans** she admits to being thirty; **ceci me surprend, je l'avoue** this surprises me, I must confess *or* admit *or* say; **il faut bien a. que c'est lui qui avait raison** it must be admitted *or* said that he was right; **a. avoir fait qch** to confess *or* to own up to having done sth

VI to confess

VPR **s'avouer** to admit (to being + *adj*); **s'a. coupable** to admit one's guilt; **s'a. vaincu** to acknowledge oneself beaten, to acknowledge defeat

avril [avril] **NM** April; **en a.** in April; **au mois d'a.** in the month of April; **pluie d'a.** April showers; **le sept a.** (on) the seventh of April, (on) April (the) seventh; **le premier a.** *(jour des farceurs)*, April Fools' Day; **poisson d'a.!** April fool! **SEE GRAMMAR A81–2; B60–2**

AVS [aveɛs] **NF** *Suisse (abrév* **assurance vieillesse et survivants)** = Swiss pension scheme

avunculaire [avõkylɛr] **ADJ** avuncular

axe [aks] **NM** **1** *Géom (de plante, de la terre, d'ellipse etc)* axis; **grand/petit a.** major/minor axis; **a. de rotation** axis of rotation; *Constr* **a. d'une route/d'un pont** centre line of a road/bridge; *Aut* **a. routier** trunk road; **les grands axes de la circulation** trunk *or* major roads; *Fig* **les grands axes de sa politique** the main thrust of his policy; *Math* **a. des x/des y** x-axis/y-axis; **a. des abscisses/des ordonnées** x-/y-axis; **axes de coordonnées** co-ordinate axes; *Tech* **axes principaux d'un corps** principal axes of a body; **cristal à deux axes** biaxial crystal **VOIR GRAMMAIRE A14**

2 *Tech etc* axle, spindle, pin; *(de roue de vélo)* axle (pin); **a. de pompe** pump spindle; **a. d'une grue** pin of a crane; **a. du piston** *(d'un moteur)* gudgeon pin; *Aut* **a. de fusée** king pin; **a. transversal** cross-shaft; **a. roulis** roll axis

3 *Hist* axis; **les Puissances de l'A.** the Axis powers

4 *Mil* **a. de progression** main direction of advance; **a. (principal) de ravitaillement** main line of supply, main supply route

5 *Aviat* **a. de sustentation** lift axis; **a. de descente** glide path, line of descent; **a. balisé** radio range course; **a. balisé d'atterrissage** radio landing beam; **a. de référence** datum line

axer [akse] **VT** to centre, *Am* to center; **être**

axé sur *ou* autour de to centre on; **sa philosophie est axée sur le don de soi** his philosophy is centred *or* based on self-denial; **toute sa vie est axée là-dessus** it's his whole life, his whole life revolves around it; **il a toujours été axé sur le travail/l'argent** he has always been work-oriented/money-oriented; **il a toujours été axé sur la religion/la recherche du plaisir** for him, everything has always revolved around religion/pleasure-seeking; **une visite touristique axée sur ...** a guided tour focusing on ...; **axé sur le profit** profit-oriented; **l'expansion de la compagnie sera axée sur ...** the central thrust of company expansion will be ...

axial, -iale, -iaux, -iales [aksjal, -jo] **ADJ** *(ligne, plan)* axial; **effort de compression axiale** collapsible load; *Géol* **plan a.** axial plane; **éclairage a.** *(des rues)* central overhead lighting

axillaire [aksilɛr] **ADJ** *Anat, Bot* axillary

axiomatique [aksjɔmatik] **ADJ** axiomatic

axiome [aksjom] **NM** axiom

axis [aksis] **NM** *Anat* axis

ayant cause, *pl* **ayants cause** [ɛjã koz] **NM** *Jur (bénéficiaire de testament)* legal successor, successor in title, legatee; *(bénéficiaire de cadeau)* donee; *(bénéficiaire de transfert)* assignee; *(acheteur)* vendee; *(agent désigné)* executor, trustee

ayant-compte, *pl* **ayants-comptes** **NM** *Banque* account holder

ayant droit, *pl* **ayants droit** [ɛjãdrwa] **NM** *Jur* eligible party, entitled beneficiary

ayatollah [ajatɔla] **NM** ayatollah

azalée [azale] **NF** *(plante)* azalea

Azerbaïdjan [azɛrbajdʒã] **NM** Azerbaijan

azerbaïdjanais, -aise [azɛrbajdʒanɛ, -ɛz] **ADJ** Azerbaijani **N A.** Azerbaijani

azéri, -ie [azeri] **ADJ** Azeri **NM** *Ling* Azerbaijani **N A.** Azeri

azimut [azimyt] **NM** *Astron etc* azimuth; *Naut etc* **prendre un a.** to take a bearing; *Fam* **dans tous les azimuts** everywhere, all over the place; *Fig Fam* **y aller tous azimuts** to go flat out *or* all out, to go at it hammer and tongs; *Fig* **une campagne électorale tous azimuts** an all-out electoral campaign

azimutal, -ale, -aux, -ales [azimytal, -o] **ADJ** azimuth(al); **cercle a.** azimuth circle; **compas a.** azimuth compass

azimuté [azimyte] **ADJ** *Fam* crazy, round the bend

azotate [azɔtat] **NM** *Chimie* nitrate; **a. de potasse** nitre, saltpetre

azote [azɔt] **NM** *Chimie* nitrogen

azoté [azɔte] **ADJ** nitrogenous; **engrais azotés** nitrate fertilizers, nitrates

azoter [azɔte] **VT** to nitrogenize

azotique [azɔtik] **ADJ** *Chimie* nitric

azotite [azɔtit] **NM** *Chimie* nitrite

AZT® [azɛdte] **NM** *Pharm (abrév* **azidothymidine)** AZT

aztèque [aztɛk] **ADJ** Aztec **N A.** Aztec

azur [azyr] **NM** **1** *(couleur)* azure, sky-blue **2** *Géog* **la Côte d'A.** the French Riviera **3** *Litt* **l'a.** *(le ciel)* the sky **4** *Hér* **champ d'a.** field azure **5** **pierre d'a.** lapis lazuli **6** *Com (pour linge)* blue

azuré [azyre] **ADJ** **1** (sky-)blue, azure **2** *Litt* tinged with blue

azurer [azyre] **VT** **1** *(linge etc)* to blue **2** *Litt* to tinge with blue

azyme [azim] **ADJ** **pain a.** unleavened bread **NM** *Rel* **fête des Azymes** feast of unleavened bread, Passover

B, b [be] NM **1** *(lettre)* B, b **2** *Chimie (symbole du bore)* B

B.A. [bea] NF *(abrév* **bonne action**) good deed; **faire sa/une B.A.** to do one's good deed for the day/a good deed

baba[1] [baba] NM *Culin* **b. au rhum** (rum) baba; *Fam* **elle l'a eu dans le b.** she came unstuck

baba[2] ADJ INV *Fam* dumbfounded, flabbergasted; **j'en suis resté b.** I was absolutely flabbergasted; **j'en suis complètement b.** I'm absolutely flabbergasted

b.a.-ba [beaba] NM *Fam* ABC, *Am* ABCs, rudiments; **je ne connais que le b. de la comptabilité** I only know the rudiments of accountancy; **c'est le b. de la physique quantique** *(livre)* it's the idiot's guide to quantum physics

baba cool N hippie

Babel [babɛl] N Babel; **la tour de B.** the Tower of Babel; *Fig* **c'est une vraie tour de B.** you hear every language under the sun there

babeleer [babəlɛr] NM *Belg Fam* chatterbox

babeurre [babœr] NM buttermilk

babil [babi(l)] NM *(d'un enfant)* prattle, prattling; *(des oiseaux)* twittering; *(d'un ruisseau)* babbling

babillage [babijaʒ] NM **1** = **babil 2** *Psy* lallation

babillard, -arde [babijar, -ard] ADJ *(personne)* chattering; *(enfant)* prattling; *(bébé)* babbling; *Fig* **ruisseau b.** babbling brook
N *(personne)* chatterbox
NM **1** *Can Scol* flannel board **2** *Ordinat* bulletin board, BBS

babillement [babijmā] NM = **babil**

babiller [babije] VI *(d'une personne)* to chatter; *(d'un enfant)* to prattle; *(d'un ruisseau)* to babble; *(d'un oiseau)* to twitter

babines [babin] NFPL *Zool* chops; *Fam (d'une personne)* chops, lips; **s'essuyer les b.** to wipe one's chops *or* lips; **d'avance, je m'en lèche les b.** my mouth's watering in anticipation

babiole [babjɔl] NF **1** *(bibelot)* knick-knack, trinket **2** *(incident)* trifle

bâbord [babɔr] NM *Naut* port (side); **la barre à b. toute!, b. toute!** hard a-port!; **la terre par b.!** land on the port side!; **aviron de b.** stroke side-oar

babouche [babuʃ] NF Turkish slipper

babouin [babwɛ̃] NM baboon

baboune [babun] NF *Can Fam* **faire la b.** to sulk

baby [bebi] ADJ INV **taille b.** baby-size(d); **whisky b.** small whisky
NM small whisky

baby-boom, *pl* **baby-booms** NM baby boom; **enfants du b.** baby-boomers

baby-foot [babifut] NM INV table football; *(table)* football table

---

Babylone [babilɔn] N *Antiq* Babylon

Babylonie [babilɔni] NF *Antiq* Babylonia

babylonien, -ienne [babilɔnjɛ̃, -jɛn] *Antiq* ADJ Babylonian
N B. Babylonian

babyphone [babifɔn] NM baby monitor

baby-sitter, *pl* **baby-sitters** [bebisitœr, babi-] N baby-sitter

baby-sitting [bebisitiŋ, babi-] NM baby-sitting; **faire du b.** to baby-sit

bac[1] [bak] NM **1** *(bateau)* ferry (boat); **b. à piétons** passenger ferry; **passer qn dans un b.** to ferry sb across; *Jur* **droit de b.** ferry (right) **2** *(récipient) (pour liquides)* tank, vat; *(d'une cellule électrique)* pot; *(d'un accumulateur, pour la nourriture etc)* box, container; *(de mineur)* truck, tub; *(d'imprimeur, de photographe)* tray
▸ ▸ **Ordinat b. d'alimentation** sheet feed; *Aut* **b. à cartes** map pocket; **b. à correspondance** correspondence tray; **b. à douche** shower tray; *Ordinat* **b. feuille à feuille** cut sheet feeder; *Ordinat* **b. de feuilles** paper tray; **b. à glace** ice tray; **b. introducteur** *(de feuillets)* sheet feed; **b. à laver** wash tub; **b. à légumes** salad drawer *or* crisper; *Belg* **b. à ordures** *Br* dustbin, *Am* garbage *or* trash *or* ash can; **b. de ou à papier** *(d'imprimante)* paper tray; **b. de papier A4** A4 paper tray; *Aut* **b. de rangement** stowage bin; **b. roulant** file trolley; **b. à sable** sandpit

bac[2] NM *Fam* = secondary school examination qualifying for entry to university, *Br* ≃ A levels, *Am* ≃ high school diploma; *Scot* ≃ Scottish Higher Certificate of Education; *Ir* ≃ School Leaving Certificate; **passer le b.** to take *or Br* sit one's baccalauréat; **préparer le b.** to study for one's baccalauréat; **b. + 3** *(dans une annonce)* three years of higher education required

baccalauréat [bakalɔrea] NM **1** = secondary school examination qualifying for entry to university, *Br* ≃ A levels, *Am* ≃ high school diploma; *Scot* ≃ Scottish Higher Certificate of Education; *Ir* ≃ School Leaving Certificate **2** *Anciennement* **b. en droit** = degree granted when a student has passed his first two examinations for the Licence en Droit **3** *Can Univ* bachelor's degree; **b. ès arts/ès sciences** Bachelor of Arts/Science

---

Baccalauréat

The "baccalauréat", or "bac", is taken by pupils who have completed their final year at the "lycée"; successful candidates may go to university. Depending on which subjects pupils choose to study at "lycée", they prepare for a "baccalauréat général", "technologique" (vocational) or "professionnel" (vocational and including professional training). Since the last major reform, in 1995, there have been three main types of "baccalauréat général", each corresponding to a specific field: "bac L" (arts subjects), "bac ES" (economics and social studies) and "bac S" (sciences).

---

baccara(t)[1] [bakara] NM *Cartes* baccarat

baccarat[2] NM *(cristal)* Baccarat crystal

bacchanale [bakanal] NF **1** *(orgie)* orgy; *(débauche)* drunken revel; *(danse)* bacchanalian dance **2** *Antiq* **les bacchanales** the bacchanalia

bacchante [bakāt] NF **1** *Antiq* bacchante **2** *Fam* **bacchantes** moustache

bâche [baʃ] NF **1** *Tech (réservoir)* tank, cistern **2** *(serre)* forcing frame **3** *(toile)* tarpaulin, canvas cover; **b. de campement** ground sheet
▸ ▸ **b. d'alimentation** feed tank; **b. goudronnée** tarpaulin

bachelier, -ière [baʃəlje, -jɛr] N *Scol* student who has passed the baccalauréat

bâcher [baʃe] VT **b. qch** to cover sth (with a tarpaulin)
VPR **se bâcher** *Fam* to hit the sack *or* the hay

bachi-bouzouk, *pl* **bachi-bouzouks** [baʃibuzuk] NM *Hist* Bashi-Bazouk; *Fam* **espèce de b.!** you crackpot!

bachique [baʃik] ADJ Bacchic; **scène b.** bacchanalian scene; **chanson b.** drinking song

bachot[1] [baʃo] NM *Naut* skiff, wherry

bachot[2] NM *Fam* = **baccalauréat; boîte à b.** crammer

bachotage [baʃotaʒ] NM *Scol Fam* cramming, *Br* swotting; **faire du b.** to do some cramming

bachoter [baʃote] VI *Scol Fam* to cram, *Br* swot

bachoteur, -euse [baʃotœr, -øz] N *Scol Fam* student cramming *or Br* swotting for an exam

bacillaire [basiler] ADJ bacillary
N tubercular patient

bacille [basil] NM **1** *Biol* bacillus VOIR GRAMMAIRE A14 **2** *(insecte)* stick insect

bacillose [basiloz] NF *Méd* bacillosis, bacillus infection; **b. pulmonaire** pulmonary tuberculosis

background [bakgrawnd] NM background

back-office, *pl* **back-offices** [bakɔfis] NM *Banque* back office

bâclage [baklaʒ] NM *Fam (d'un travail)* botching (up)

bâcle [bakl] NF *(d'une porte, fenêtre)* bar

bâclé [bakle] ADJ *(travail etc)* botched (up), slapdash

bâcler [bakle] VT **1** *Fam (travail)* to botch (up); **b. sa toilette** to give oneself a quick wash **2** *Arch (porte, fenêtre)* to bar
VI to do a botched job

bacon [bekɔn] NM *Culin* bacon; **œufs au b.** bacon and eggs

bactéricide [bakterisid] ADJ bactericidal ■ NM bactericide

bactérie [bakteri] NF bacterium, *pl* -ia

bactérien, -ienne [bakterjɛ̃, -jɛn] ADJ bacterial

bactériologie [bakterjɔlɔʒi] NF bacteriology

bactériologique [bakterjɔlɔʒik] ADJ bacteriological; **guerre b.** bacteriological *or* germ warfare

bactériologiste [bakterjɔlɔʒist], **bactériologue** [bakterjɔlɔg] N bacteriologist

bactériophage [bakterjɔfaʒ] NM bacteriophage

badaboum [badabum] INT *Fam* **et b., il est tombé** he fell down, crash, bang, wallop

badaud, -aude [bado, -od] ADJ gawping, *Am* rubbernecking ■ N **1** *(promeneur)* stroller; *(curieux)* gawper, *Am* rubberneck **2** *Ordinat (sur Internet)* lurker

badauder [badode] VI *Vieilli (se promener)* to stroll about (idly); *(regarder)* to gawp, *Am* to rubberneck

baderne [badɛrn] NF *Fam Péj* **une (vieille) b.** an old fogey, an old fossil, an old stick-in-the-mud

badge [badʒ] NM badge, *Am* button; *(pour scouts)* badge

badigeon [badiʒɔ̃] NM *(pour les murs etc)* (colour)wash, distemper; **b. à la chaux** whitewash; *Méd* **faire un b. de teinture d'iode sur une blessure** to paint a wound with tincture of iodine

badigeonnage [badiʒɔnaʒ] NM **1** *(de mur etc)* colourwashing, distempering; *(à la chaux)* whitewashing **2** *Méd (avec de l'iode etc)* painting

badigeonner [badiʒɔne] VT **1 b. une surface de qch** to daub a surface with sth; **b. un mur en blanc/en couleur** to whitewash/to colourwash a wall, to distemper a wall; **b. la tourte de jaune d'œuf** to brush the pie with egg yolk **2** *Méd* to paint (**d'iode, à l'iode** with iodine)

badin¹ [badɛ̃] ADJ playful, light-hearted

badin² NM *Aviat* airspeed indicator

badinage [badinaʒ] NM banter, jesting; **sur un ton de b.** in a bantering *or* playful tone

badine [badin] NF cane, switch

badiner [badine] VI to jest, to joke; **b. de tout** to turn everything into a joke; **on ne badine pas avec l'amour** love is not something to be trifled with; **il ne faut pas b. avec ce genre de choses** these things are no laughing matter; **il ne badine pas avec la ponctualité** he's very strict about *or* he's a real stickler for punctuality

badinerie [badinri] NF jest

bad-lands [badlãds] NFPL badlands

badminton [badmintɔn] NM *Sport* badminton

bâdrant [bɑdrɑ̃] ADJ *Can* bothersome

bâdrer [bɑdre] VT *Can Fam* **b. qn** to bug sb, *Am* to give sb a pain (in the neck)

baffe [baf] NF *Fam (gifle)* slap, clout, clip on the ear; **recevoir/donner une paire de baffes** to get/give a couple of slaps; **tu veux une b. ou quoi?** do you want a clip on the ear?

baffer [bafe] VT *Fam* to clout, to cuff

Baffin [bafɛ̃] NM **la terre de B.** Baffin Island

baffle [bafl] NM *Électron (enceinte)* speaker; *(dans une enceinte)* baffle

bafouer [bafwe] VT *(personne)* to ridicule, to jeer at; *(règlement, autorité)* to flout; **mari bafoué** cuckold

bafouillage [bafujaʒ] NM *Fam (défaut de prononciation)* stammering, spluttering; *(propos incohérents)* gibberish, nonsense; *(de moteur)* misfiring, missing

bafouille [bafuj] NF *Arg* letter

bafouiller [bafuje] VI *Fam (mal prononcer)* to stammer, to splutter; *(être incohérent)* to talk gibberish *or* nonsense; *(d'un moteur)* to misfire, to miss ■ VT to stammer (out), to splutter (out); **je ne sais pas ce qu'il m'a bafouillé** I don't know what he was babbling about

bâfrer [bɑfre] *Arg* VI to stuff oneself, to guzzle, to pig out ■ VT *(nourriture)* to guzzle, to wolf

bâfreur, -euse [bɑfrœr, -øz] N *Arg* glutton, *Br* greedy-guts

bagage [bagaʒ] NM **1** *(équipement)* kit; **plier b.** to pack one's bags *or Mil* one's kit **2** **bagages** luggage, *surtout Am* baggage; **retrait des bagages** baggage (re)claim; **fourgon à bagages** luggage van, *Am* baggage car; **voyager avec peu de bagages** to travel light; **faire ses bagages** to pack one's bags **3** *Fig (connaissance)* knowledge (**en** of); **avoir un bon b. en sciences éco** to know a lot about economics; **son b. en physique est nul** he doesn't know any physics
▸▸ **bagages accompagnés** accompanied luggage *or* baggage; **bagages non accompagnés** unaccompanied luggage *or* baggage, luggage *or* baggage in advance; **bagages enregistrés** checked luggage *or* baggage; **bagages non-enregistrés** unchecked luggage *or* baggage; **bagages à main** hand luggage *or* baggage, cabin *or* carry-on baggage; **bagages de soute** hold luggage *or* baggage

bagagerie [bagaʒri] NF luggage room

bagagiste [bagaʒist] NM **1** *(dans une gare, un aéroport)* luggage *or* baggage handler **2** *(fabricant de bagages)* luggage manufacturer, travel goods manufacturer

bagarre [bagar] NF fight, brawl; **b. de rue** street fight; **il va y avoir de la b.** there's going to be a fight; **il cherche la b.** he's looking *or* spoiling for a fight; *Fig* **entre eux, c'est la b.** they've got it in for each other, they're at daggers drawn

bagarrer [bagare] *Fam* VI to fight, to battle (**pour** for); **aimer b.** to like a fight; *Fig* **il faudra b. pour l'avoir** you'll have to fight *or* battle to get it ■ VPR **se bagarrer** *(physiquement)* to fight, to scrap, to brawl; *(se quereller)* to quarrel, to argue

bagarreur, -euse [bagarœr, -øz] *Fam* ADJ *(personne, caractère)* aggressive; *Fig* **elle est bagarreuse** *(elle ne se laisse pas faire)* she's a fighter ■ N brawler; *Fig* **c'est une bagarreuse** she's a fighter

bagatelle [bagatɛl] NF **1** *(chose sans importance)* trifle, bagatelle; **se fâcher pour une b.** to take offence at a (mere) trifle; **elle perd son temps à des bagatelles** she's frittering away her time, she's wasting her time on trifles; **pour la b. de mille euros** for a mere thousand euros **2** *(plaisir sexuel)* lovemaking; **il ne pense qu'à la b.** he's got a one-track mind

bagnard [baɲar] NM convict

bagne [baɲ] NM *Hist (prison)* convict prison; **b. flottant** hulks; **condamné à cinq ans de b.** sentenced to five years' penal servitude; *Fig Fam* **c'est le b., la vie avec elle!** life with her is torment *or* a real nightmare!

bagnole [baɲɔl] NF *Fam* car; *Péj (vieille)* **b.** (old) jalopy, *Br* (old) banger; **ça, c'est de la b.!** that's some car!

bagou(t) [bagu] NM *Fam* glibness (of tongue); **avoir du b.** to have the gift of the gab

baguage [bagaʒ] NM *(des oiseaux, des arbres)* ringing

bague [bag] NF **1** *(bijou)* ring; **porter des bagues** to wear rings; **b. en argent/en or** silver/gold ring; **avoir la b. au doigt** to be married; **passer à qn la b. au doigt** to put a ring on sb's finger **2** *(d'une boîte de conserve)* ring-pull; *(de cigare)* band **3** *Tech* bush, ring **4** *(d'oiseau)* ring
▸▸ **b. d'appui** washer; **b. d'assemblage** collar, sleeve; **b. à bride** adapter; **b. d'espacement** sleeve; **b. de fiançailles** engagement ring; **b. (de garniture) de piston** piston ring, packing ring; **b. (d'une caméra)** extender lens; **b. de réglage** setting ring; **b. de roulement** ball race, bearing race; **b. de serrage** jubilee clip

baguenauder [bagnode] *Fam* VI to stroll *or* wander around ■ VPR **se baguenauder** to stroll *or* wander around

baguer¹ [bage] VT *(oiseau, arbre)* to ring; **cigare bagué d'or** cigar with a gold band

baguer² VT *Couture (plis etc)* to tack, to baste

baguette [bagɛt] NF **1** *(tige)* switch, stick; *(pain)* French stick; **baguettes** *(pour manger)* chopsticks; **tu ne crois pas que tout va changer, comme ça, d'un coup de b.?** surely you don't believe everything's going to change, just like that, as if by magic or as if by the wave of a magic wand?; *Fig* **avoir les cheveux raides comme des baguettes (de tambour)** to have hair that's as straight as a poker; *Fam* **commander** *ou* **mener** *ou* **faire marcher qn à la b.** to rule sb with a rod of iron *or* with an iron hand; **être sous la b. de qn** to be under someone's thumb; **passer par les baguettes** to run the gauntlet **2** *Menuis etc* moulding, beading **3** *(de bas, chaussette)* clock **4** *Aut* **b. de pavillon** roof bar; **b. de protection latérale** side-impact bar
▸▸ **b. de chef d'orchestre** conductor's baton; **b. magique** magic wand; **d'un coup de b. magique** with a wave of my/his/*etc* magic wand; **baguettes de tambour** drumsticks

baguier [bagje] NM ring case

bah [ba] INT bah!, pooh!

Bahamas [baamas] NFPL **les (îles) B., l'archipel des B.** the Bahamas VOIR GRAMMAIRE A11-12

Bahreïn [barɛ̃], **Bahrayn** [barɛ̃] NM Bahrain, Bahrein

bahut [bay] NM **1** *(coffre)* (round-topped) chest; *(buffet)* sideboard **2** *Arg (collège, lycée)* school **3** *Arg (taxi)* cab, taxi

bai [bɛ] ADJ *(cheval)* bay; **b. châtain** chestnut bay

baie¹ [bɛ] NF *Géog* bay; **une petite b. abritée** a sheltered cove; **la grande b. australienne** the Great Australian Bight; **la b. d'Hudson** Hudson Bay

baie² NF **1** *Archit* opening; **b. vitrée** picture window **2** *Ordinat* bay

baie³ NF *Bot* berry

baignade [bɛɲad] NF **1** *(activité)* swimming, *Br* bathing; **b. interdite** no swimming *or Br* bathing **2** *(endroit)* swimming *or Br* bathing place

baigner [beɲe] VT *(pieds, doigt etc)* to bathe; *(bébé, chien etc)* to bath *or Am* bathe; *(de la mer)* *(côte etc)* to wash; *(d'une rivière)* *(région)* to water; *Fig* **baigné de soleil** bathed in sunlight; **pièce baignée de lumière** room flooded with *or* bathed in light; **il était baigné de sueur** he was dripping with *or* bathed in sweat; **son visage est baigné de larmes** his face is bathed in tears ■ VI *(tremper)* to soak, to steep (**dans** in); **les légumes baignent dans une sauce à la tomate** the vegetables are swimming in a tomato sauce; *Fam* **ça baigne (dans l'huile)!**

everything's great or fine!; **OK, ça baigne!** OK, no problem!; **il baignait dans son sang** he was lying in a pool of his own blood; **la ville baigne dans la brume** the town is shrouded or swathed in mist; **maison qui baigne dans la lumière** house that is flooded with or bathed in light; **cette histoire/maison baigne dans le mystère** this story/house is shrouded in mystery

vpr se baigner 1 (se laver) to have or take a bath, Br to bath, Am to bathe **2** (nager) (dans la mer, un lac etc) to have a swim, Br to (have a) bathe; (dans une piscine) to have a swim, to swim; **on va se b.?** shall we go for a swim?, shall we go swimming?

baigneur, -euse [bɛɲœr, -øz] **N** Vieilli swimmer, Br bather

   NM (en porcelaine ou en plastique) doll

baignoire [bɛɲwar] **NF 1** (dans la salle de bains) bath, (bath)tub **2** Théâtre ground-floor box **3** Naut (de sous-marin) upper part of the conning tower

   ▸▸ **b. encastrée** sunken bath; **b. sabot** hip bath

bail, pl **baux** [baj, bo] **NM** lease; **b. commercial** commercial lease; **b. à ferme** farming lease; **b. emphytéotique** long lease; **b. à loyer** rental agreement, lease; **prendre une maison à b.** to take a lease on or to lease a house; **donner une maison à b.** to lease (out) a house; **renouveler un b.** to renew a lease; **résilier un b.** to cancel a lease; Fam **ça fait un b. que je ne l'ai pas vu** I haven't seen him for ages

baille [baj] **NF** Naut (baquet) bucket; (mauvais bateau) tub; Fam **la (grande) b.** the drink, the sea; **tomber à la b.** to fall into the drink

bâillement [bajmɑ̃] **NM 1** (de personne) yawn; **étouffer un b.** to stifle a yawn; **bâillements** yawning, yawns **2** (d'une couture etc) gaping; **b. des rideaux** gap between the curtains

bâiller [baje] **VI 1** (d'une personne) to yawn; **b. de sommeil/d'ennui/de fatigue** to yawn drowsily/with boredom/with tiredness; Fig **son histoire me fait b.** his/her story is one big yawn; Fam **b. à s'en** ou **se décrocher la mâchoire** to yawn one's head off **2** (des coutures, d'un col etc) to gape; (d'une porte) to be or stand ajar

bâilles [baj] **NFPL** Belg **faire des b.** to yawn

bailleur, -eresse [bajœr, bajrɛs] **N 1** Jur lessor **2** Com **b. de fonds** (investisseur) (financial) backer, sponsor; (associé passif) Br sleeping partner, Am silent partner; **b. de licence** licensor, licenser

bailli [baji] **NM** Hist bailiff

bailliage [bajaʒ] **NM** Hist (district) bailiwick; (tribunal) bailiff's court

bâillon [bajɔ̃] **NM** gag; **mettre un b. à qn** to gag sb; **mettre un b. à la presse/l'opposition** to gag or muzzle the press/the opposition

bâillonner [bajone] **VT** to gag; **b. la presse/l'opposition** to gag or muzzle the press/the opposition

bain [bɛ̃] **NM 1** (pour se laver) bath; (baignoire) bath(tub); **prendre un b.** to have or take a bath, Br to bath, Am to bathe; **donner un b. à qn** to give sb a bath, to bath or bathe sb; **salle de bain(s)** bathroom; **peignoir** ou **sortie de b.** bathrobe; **le b. est rempli/vidé** the bath is full/empty; **fais-moi couler un b.** run me a bath; Fig Fam **être dans le b.** (être compromis) to be implicated; (être habitué) to be in the swing of things; **elle n'a pas eu de mal à se mettre dans le b.** she had no trouble getting into the swing of things; Fig **ils sont dans le même b.** they're in the same boat; **on peut les mettre dans le même b.** you can lump them all together; **je dé-**

teste les bains de foule I hate crowds; **prendre un b. de foule** (d'une personne célèbre) to go on a walkabout; (d'un politicien) to press the flesh; **petit b.** (à la piscine) small or children's pool; **grand b.** (à la piscine) large pool **2** (à la mer etc) swim, Br bathe; **bains de mer** swimming in the sea, Br sea bathing; Vieilli (lieu) seaside resort; **b. en piscine** swimming or Br bathing in a pool

   3 Phot bath; **b. révélateur** ou **de développement** developing bath; **b. de fixage** ou **fixateur** fixing bath

   4 Tex dye; **ce n'est pas le même b.** it's not the same dye lot

   5 (pour moutons) (sheep) dip

   ▸▸ Phot **b. d'arrêt** stop bath; **b. de bouche** mouthwash; **faire un b. de bouche** to use a mouthwash; **b. de boue** mud bath; **b. bouillonnant** spa bath; Phot **b. de fixateur** fixing bath; Fig **b. de jouvence** rejuvenating experience; **ça m'a fait l'effet d'un b. de jouvence** it rejuvenated me, it made me feel years younger; **b. moussant** bubble bath; **b. de pieds** footbath; **prendre un b. de pieds** to soak or bathe one's feet; **b.-de-soleil** (corsage) halter top; **b. de soudure** solder bath; **b. turc** Turkish bath; **b. de vapeur** steam bath; **bains (publics)** (public) baths, Am bathhouse; **bains romains** Roman baths; **bains de soleil** sunbathing; **prendre un b. de soleil** ou **des bains de soleil** to sunbathe

bain-marie, pl **bains-marie** [bɛ̃mari] **NM** bain-marie, double saucepan or boiler; **faire cuire qch au b.** to cook sth in a bain-marie

baïonnette [bajɔnɛt] **NF** bayonet; **mettre/remettre la b.** to fix/unfix bayonets; **charge à la b.** bayonet charge; Tech **joint en b.** bayonet joint; Élec **douille à b.** bayonet socket; Élec **ampoule à b.** bulb with a bayonet fitting

baïram [bairam] **NM** Bairam

baisable [bɛzabl] **ADJ** Vulg fuckable, Br shaggable

baise [bɛz] **NF 1** Vulg (acte sexuel) screwing; **il ne pense qu'à la b.** all he ever thinks of is screwing **2** Belg (baiser) kiss

baise-en-ville **NM INV** Fam overnight bag; (pochette) (man's) handbag

baisemain [bɛzmɛ̃] **NM** hand kissing, kissing of hands; **faire le b. à qn** to kiss sb's hand

baiser¹ [beze] **VT 1** (embrasser) to kiss; **b. qn au front** to kiss sb on the forehead; **elle lui baisa les pieds** she kissed his feet **2** Vulg (coucher avec) to fuck, to screw **3** Arg (tromper) to screw; **il m'a bien baisé** he screwed me good and proper; **se faire b.** to be or get screwed **4** Arg (comprendre) **qu'est-ce qu'il dit? on n'y baise rien** what's he saying? you can't make head nor tail of it

   VI Vulg **elle baise bien** she's a good screw or fuck

baiser² **NM** kiss; **gros baisers** (dans une lettre) love and kisses; **b. de paix** kiss of peace; **b. d'adieu** parting or goodbye or farewell kiss; **b. de Judas** Judas kiss; **faire un b. à qn** to give sb a kiss

baiseur, -euse [bezœr, -øz] **N** Vulg **c'est un sacré b./une sacrée baiseuse** he's/she's a great screw

baisse [bɛs] **NF** fall, drop, downturn; (de la marée) ebb; **la b. de la natalité** the fall or drop in the birthrate; **la b. du niveau scolaire** the fall in educational standards; **b. des prix** fall or drop in prices, price cut; (action) price cutting; Bourse **b. sensible (des cours)** sharp fall (in prices); **être en b.** (de la température, du nombre des adhésions etc) to be falling or dropping; (de la popularité de qn) to be on the decline or the wane; (d'une rivière) to subside; **le moral du malade est en b.** the patient's morale is sinking; Bourse **spéculations à la b.** bear speculations; **jouer à la b.**

to bear; **revoir à la baisse** to revise downwards; **actions en b.** falling shares

BAISSER [bese] **VT** (rideau) to lower; (store) to lower, to pull down; (vitre de voiture) to open, to lower; **une étagère d'un cran** to lower a shelf by one notch; Aut **b. ses phares** to dip or Am dim one's headlights; **le store est baissé** the blind is down or lowered; **b. la lumière** to turn down or dim the light; **b. la radio/le chauffage** to turn down the radio/the heating; **b. pavillon** Naut to strike one's flag, to surrender; Fig (céder) to admit defeat, to give in; **b. la tête** ou **le front** to bend or lower one's head; (de honte, découragement etc) to hang one's head; **b. brusquement la tête** to duck; **donner tête baissée dans un piège** to fall headlong into a trap; **b. les yeux** to look down, to lower one's eyes; **les yeux baissés** with downcast eyes; **b. le nez** to hang one's head in shame; Fig **il ne faut pas b. les bras, battez-vous!** don't give in, fight!; **b. la voix** to lower one's voice; **b. le ton** (après une dispute) to climb down; **je vous prie de b. le ton!** please keep your voice down!; **b. le prix de qch** to lower or reduce or cut the price of sth

   VI 1 (de la température) to fall, to go or come down; (de la marée) to ebb; (du feu) to burn low, to burn down; (de la vue, de la mémoire) to fail; Théâtre **les lumières baissent** the lights are going down; **le baromètre baisse** the barometer is falling; **le jour baisse** night is falling, it's getting dark

   2 (s'affaiblir) (d'un malade) to get weaker, to deteriorate; (de l'enthousiasme) to fall off, to decline, to weaken; **il a beaucoup baissé dernièrement** (physiquement) he has got a lot weaker lately, he has deteriorated a lot lately; (intellectuellement) his mind has been going or deteriorating a lot lately; **le moral baisse** morale is sinking; **elle a baissé dans mon estime** she's gone down in my estimation

   3 (des prix) to fall, to come or go down; **la valeur de ces maisons a baissé** these houses have gone down in value; **faire b. les prix** to bring down prices; **le dollar a baissé** the dollar has weakened; **le niveau scolaire a beaucoup baissé** educational standards have fallen a lot

   VPR se baisser to bend down, to stoop; (pour éviter un coup etc) to duck; **c'est en se baissant qu'il s'est cogné** he banged himself as he bent down; Fig **il n'y a qu'à se b. pour les ramasser** there are loads of them around

baissier [besje] Bourse **NM** bear

   ADJ bearish

bajoues [baʒu] **NFPL** (d'animal) chops; Péj (d'une personne) flabby cheeks

bakchich [bakʃiʃ] **NM** Fam Br backhander, bung, Am payoff

Bakélite® [bakelit] **NF** Bakelite®; **téléphone en B.** Bakelite® telephone

baklava [baklava] **NM** Culin baklava, baclava

bal, pl **bals** [bal] **NM 1** (fête) (populaire) dance; (chic) ball, dance; **b. costumé** ou **masqué** ou **travesti** fancy dress ball; **donner un b.** to give a dance; **aller au b.** to go dancing; **robe de b.** ball gown, evening dress; **ouvrir le b.** to open the ball; Fig to set the ball rolling **2** (endroit) dance hall

   ▸▸ **b. populaire** = free, open-air dance to popular music; **b. public** public dance

balade [balad] **NF** Fam (à pied) walk, stroll; (en voiture) drive, run; **faire une b.** (à pied) to go for a walk or stroll; (en voiture) to go for a drive or run (in the car); **être/partir en b.** (à pied) to be out for/go off for a walk; (en voiture) to be out for/go off for a drive

balader [balade] Fam **VT** (personne, chien) to take (out) for a walk; (avoir avec soi) (objet) to carry or drag around; **il balade toujours cette vieille valise avec lui** he always carries or drags that old suitcase around with him **VPR se balader** (à pied) to go for a walk; (en voiture) to go for a drive; **se b. en montagne** to walk in the mountains; **tu ne vas pas te b. en ville avec cette casquette?** surely you're not going to walk around town in that cap?; **ses affaires se baladent dans la maison** his things are lying around all over the house

baladeur, -euse [baladœr, -øz] **ADJ** (instinct) wandering, roving; **j'ai l'âme baladeuse** I'm a wanderer at heart; (en ce moment) I want to be up and away; Fam **avoir les mains baladeuses** to have wandering hands; Tech **train b.** sliding gear
  NF baladeuse (lampe) portable lamp, inspection lamp
  NM personal stereo, Walkman®

baladin [baladɛ̃] **NM** strolling player, wandering actor

baladisque [baladisk] **NM** portable compact disc player, Discman®

balafre [balafr] **NF 1** (coupure) gash, slash, cut; (au sabre) sabre cut **2** (cicatrice) scar

balafré [balafre] **NM** scarface

balafrer [balafre] **VT** to slash, to gash, to cut; **les agresseurs lui ont balafré le visage** the attackers slashed his face; **visage balafré** scarred face

balai [balɛ] **NM 1** (de ménage) broom; **passer le b.** to sweep the floor, to give the floor a sweep; **donner un coup de b. dans** ou **à la cuisine** to give the kitchen a sweep, to sweep the kitchen; Fig **donner un coup de b.** (dans une entreprise) to have a shake-out; Fig **il y a eu un coup de b.** there's been a shake-out; **(allez,) du b.!** clear off!, scram!; Arg **con comme un b.** as stupid as they come, bloody stupid, Br as daft as a brush **2** Fam **(voiture-) b.** (autobus) last bus; (métro) last underground or Am subway **3** Élec brush **4** Aut (d'essuie-glace) blade **5** Fam (an) year; **il a cinquante balais** he's fifty
  ▸▸ **b. mécanique** carpet sweeper

balai-brosse, pl **balais-brosses NM** (long-handled) scrubbing brush

balaise [balɛz] **ADJ, N** Fam = **balèze**

balalaïka [balalaika] **NF** Mus balalaika

balan [balɑ̃] **NM** Suisse **être sur le b.** (être sur le point de tomber) to be tottering; (hésiter) to be indecisive; (être inquiet quant à son sort) to wait nervously

balance [balɑ̃s] **NF 1** (appareil) (pair of) scales; (publique) weighing machine; **monter sur la b.** to stand on the scales VOIR GRAMMAIRE A10
  2 Astron, Astrol **la B.** Libra, the Scales; **être (du signe de la) B.** to be Libra or a Libran **3** Fig **candidat mis en b.** candidate who is still being considered; **la victoire/la décision restait en b.** victory/the decision hung in the balance; **mettre qch en b.** to weigh up the pros and cons of sth; **il faut mettre ces deux arguments en b.** you have to weigh each argument against the other; **ce facteur pèse dans la b.** this is an important factor; **cet argument est un poids dans la b.** this argument has great weight; **il y a divers facteurs à mettre dans la b.** there are various factors to take into account; **faire pencher** ou **incliner** ou **emporter la b.** to tip the scales or balance; **votre qualification fera pencher la b. en votre faveur** your qualification will tip the balance in your favour
  4 Compta, Com **b. d'un compte** balance or balancing of an account; **faire la b.** to make up the balance (sheet); **la b. de l'actif et du passif** the balance of assets and liabilities, credit and debit balance; **compte en b.** account that balances; **la b. est en excédent** there is a surplus
  5 Pêche shrimp net
  6 Fam (mouchard) squealer, Br grass
  ▸▸ **b. automatique** shop scales; **b. avant inventaire** pre-inventory balance; **b. à bascule** weighbridge; Cin, TV **b. des blancs** white balance; **b. du commerce** ou **commerciale** trade balance, balance of trade; **b. créditrice** credit balance; **b. de cuisine** ou **de ménage** kitchen scales; **b. déficitaire** trade deficit; Pol **b. des forces** ou **des pouvoirs** balance of power; **b. d'inventaire** inventory balance; **b. du main courantier de nuit** (dans un hôtel) night auditor's report; **b. des paiements** balance of payments; **b. de Roberval** Roberval's balance; **b. romaine** steelyard; **b. de salle de bains** bathroom scales; **b. de vérification** trial balance

  > Il faut noter que le nom anglais **balance** est un faux ami. Il signifie le plus souvent **équilibre** et ne s'emploie jamais pour désigner un instrument de mesure.

balancé [balɑ̃se] **ADJ (bien) b.** (phrase, tournure) well-balanced; Fam **elle est bien balancée** she's got a great figure

balancelle [balɑ̃sɛl] **NF** (de jardin) Br swing chair, Am glider

balancement [balɑ̃smɑ̃] **NM 1** (de bateau, de train, des arbres etc) swaying, rocking; (des hanches) swaying; **balancements** (en politique) wavering, shilly-shallying **2** Beaux-Arts, Littér (équilibre) balance

balancer [balɑ̃se] (je **balançai(s)**; n. **balançons**) **VT 1** (bras, jambes, trompe) to swing; (personne dans un hamac) to rock; (hanches) to sway; **tu pourrais me b.?** (sur la balançoire) can you push me or give me a push?; **b. un enfant sur ses genoux** to rock a child on one's knees
  2 Fam (lancer) (pierres, stylo etc) to chuck, to throw; **tu pourrais me b. le journal** can you chuck or throw me the paper?; **b. des pierres à qn** to chuck or throw stones at sb; **il est toujours en train de b. des vannes** he's always making snide remarks
  3 Com **b. un compte** to balance an account; Fig **b. le pour et le contre** to weigh up the pros and cons; **tout bien balancé, c'est d'accord** all things considered, I agree
  4 Fam (se débarrasser de) (objet) to chuck or throw out or away; **b. qn** to give sb the push or Br the elbow; **elle a tout balancé** (tout abandonné) she's given it all up
  5 Fam (moucharder) to squeal on, Br to grass on, Br to shop
  VI Litt (hésiter) to waver, to hesitate
  VPR se balancer 1 (d'arbres, de blés etc) to sway; **se b. sur ses ancres** (d'un navire) to ride at anchor; **se b. sur sa chaise** to rock (backwards and forwards) on one's chair; **se b. d'un pied sur l'autre** to rock from one foot to the other
  2 (sur une balançoire) to swing; (sur une bascule) to see saw
  3 Arg **je m'en balance!** I don't give a damn!, I couldn't care less!; **je me balance complètement de ce qu'ils pensent** I really don't give a damn or I really couldn't care less what they think
  4 Fam **il s'est balancé du haut de la tour Eiffel** he chucked or threw himself off the top of the Eiffel Tower

balancier [balɑ̃sje] **NM 1** (d'un funambule) balancing pole **2** (dans une horloge) pendulum; (d'une montre) balance wheel **3** (d'une pompe) handle

balançoire [balɑ̃swar] **NF** (bascule) seesaw; (suspendue) swing; (dans une foire) swingboat; **faire de la b.** to have a go on the seesaw/the swing

balayage [balɛjaʒ] **NM 1** (d'une pièce etc) sweeping; (de la saleté etc) sweeping up; **b. intermittent** (d'essuie-glace) intermittent wipe; **b. unique** (d'essuie-glace) flick wipe **2** Radio, Électron, TV scan(ning), sweep; **fréquence de b.** sweep frequency; TV **b. de télévision** raster scan; TV **b. de trame** raster scan **3** (de cheveux) streaks; **se faire faire un b.** to have streaks put in one's hair, to have one's hair streaked

balayer [balɛje] **VT** (je **balaie**, je **balaye**; je **balaierai**, je **balayerai**) **1** (pièce etc) to sweep (out); (saleté etc) to sweep up; **le vent a balayé les nuages** the wind has swept the clouds away; **b. l'ennemi** to drive away the enemy; **b. les critiques/objections/obstacles** to brush aside criticism/objections/obstacles; **les communistes ont été balayés aux dernières élections** the Communists were swept from power or were swept out at the last elections; Fig **b. devant sa porte** to put one's (own) house in order; **cette nouvelle a balayé tous mes soucis** this news has swept away all my worries
  2 Radio, Électron, TV to scan, to sweep; (caméra) to pan across; **le radar balaie jusqu'à 100 km** the radar has a sweep of 100 kilometres; **les projecteurs de la prison balaient les champs tout autour** the prison searchlights sweep the fields all around
  3 Aut to scavenge

balayette [balɛjɛt] **NF** (small) brush

balayeur, -euse [balɛjœr, -øz] **N** (personne) (road) sweeper
  NF balayeuse 1 (machine) road sweeper **2** Can (aspirateur) vacuum cleaner

balayures [balɛjyr] **NFPL** sweepings

balbutiant [balbysjɑ̃] **ADJ** (voix) stuttering, stammering; **il répondit, tout b.** he stammered an answer; Fig **la psychanalyse, encore toute balbutiante** psychoanalysis, still in its infancy or still in its early stages

balbutiement [balbysimɑ̃] **NM** stuttering, stammering; (dans sa barbe) mumbling, muttering; **les balbutiements d'un jeune enfant** the babbling of a young child; Fig **l'informatique n'était alors qu'à ses balbutiements** data processing was then only in its infancy or in its early stages

balbutier [balbysje] (pr subj, impf n. **balbutiions**, v. **balbutiiez**) **VI** to stutter, to stammer; (parler dans sa barbe) to mumble, to mutter **VT** (des excuses) to stammer (out); (en parlant dans sa barbe) to mumble, to mutter

balcon [balkɔ̃] **NM 1** Archit balcony; Fam **il y a du monde au b.** she's well endowed, she's a big girl **2** Théâtre circle; **premier b.** dress circle; **nous étions placés au deuxième b.** we were in the upper circle

balconnet [balkɔnɛ] **NM** half-cup bra

baldaquin [baldakɛ̃] **NM** (de lit) tester, canopy; (de trône) canopy, baldachin; **lit à b.** tester bed

Bâle [bɑl] **N** Basle, Basel

Baléares [balear] **NFPL les B.** the Balearic Islands, the Balearics

baleine [balɛn] **NF 1** Zool whale; **b. à bosse** humpbacked whale; **b. blanche** white whale; **blanc de b.** spermaceti; Fig **rire comme une b.** to laugh like a drain **2** (d'un corset etc) (whale)bone; (d'un parapluie) rib

baleiné [balene] **ADJ** (soutien-gorge) boned; (col) stiffened

baleineau, -eaux [baleno] **NM** whale calf

baleinier, -ière [balenje, -jer] **ADJ** (bateau, industrie) whaling
  NF baleinière whaleboat, whaler; **baleinière de sauvetage** lifeboat

balèze [balɛz] Fam **ADJ** (grand et fort) hefty, brawny; Fig **elle est vraiment b.!** (intelli-

gente) she's so brainy!; **b. en maths** brilliant at maths

N *(personne grande et forte)* hefty or brawny sort; *(personne intelligente)* brainy sort

balier [balje] *Can Fam* **VT** *(nettoyer) (plancher, pièce)* to sweep (up or out); *(tapis)* to brush, to sweep

VI to sweep up

balisage [balizaʒ] **NM 1** *(signaux), Naut* beacons, buoys; *Aviat* lights; *Radio* beacons; **projecteur de b.** direction beacon **2** *(action), Naut* beaconing, buoying; *Aviat* lighting; *Radio* marking out with beacons

balise [baliz] **NF 1** *Naut* beacon, buoy; *Aviat* light; *Radio* beacon; *(de piste de ski, d'épave)* marker; *Naut* **b. flottante** buoy; *Radio* **b. radar** radar beacon **2** *Ordinat (d'un texte)* tag; **traitement de texte à balises** word processing with embedded visible commands

baliser [balize] **VT** *Naut (chenal)* to beacon, to buoy, to mark out; *Aviat (aéroport)* to equip with lights; *(route)* to mark out with beacons; **b. une piste de ski** to mark out a ski run

VI *Fam (avoir peur)* to have the jitters (**pour qch** about sth); **ne m'en parle pas, ça me fait b.** don't talk to me about it, it gives me the jitters

baliseur [balizœr] **NM 1** *(bateau)* **b.** buoy-laying boat **2** *(personne)* person who lays buoys

balistique [balistik] **ADJ** ballistic; **engin b.** ballistic missile

NF ballistics

baliverne [balivern] **NF** stupid remark; **balivernes** twaddle, nonsense; **débiter des balivernes** to talk twaddle or nonsense

balkanique [balkanik] **ADJ** Balkan

balkanisation [balkanizasjɔ̃] **NF** *Pol, Fig* Balkanization

Balkans [balkɑ̃] **NMPL** **les B.** the Balkans

ballade [balad] **NF** *(poème court)* ballade; *(poème long), Mus* ballad

ballant [balɑ̃] **ADJ** *(bras, jambes)* swinging, dangling; **assis les pieds ballants** sitting with one's feet dangling

NM 1 *(mouvement) (d'un véhicule)* sway, roll **2** *Naut (d'un cordage)* slack

ballast [balast] **NM 1** *Constr (d'une route, d'une voie ferrée)* ballast **2** *Naut* ballast tank

ballaster [balaste] **VT 1** *Constr (voie ferrée etc)* to ballast **2** *Naut (remplir)* to ballast; *(vider)* to unballast

balle¹ [bal] **NF 1** *(pour jouer)* ball; **b. de golf/de tennis/de ping-pong** golf/tennis/table-tennis ball; **jouer à la b.** to play ball; **b. au mur** ≃ fives; *Am* handball; *Can* **b. de neige** snowball; *Sport* **renvoyer/lancer la b.** to return the ball/to serve; *Sport Fam* **c'est une belle b.!** good shot or ball!; *Tennis* **faire des ou quelques balles** to have a knock-up; *Fig* **prendre** ou **saisir la b. au bond** to seize the opportunity or chance; *Fig* **se renvoyer la b.** to pass the buck; *Fig* **renvoyer la b. à qn** *(dans un débat)* to answer sb back; *Fig* **la b. est dans votre camp** the ball's in your court **2** *(d'arme)* bullet; **b. de fusil** rifle bullet; *Fam* **recevoir douze balles dans la peau** to go before the firing squad; **à l'épreuve des balles** bullet-proof

▸▸**b. de filet** net (ball); **b. de match** match point; **b. morte** spent bullet; **b. perdue** stray bullet; **b. plastique** plastic bullet, baton round; **b. de set** set point; **b. traçante** tracer bullet

balle² **NF 1** *Com (de coton, laine etc)* bale **2** *Arg (visage)* mug, *Br* dial; **il a une drôle de b.** he's an odd-looking guy; **quelle b.!** what an ugly mug!

balle³ **NF** *(de blé)* husk, chaff; *Bot (de fleur)* glume

baller [bale] **VI** *(de bras, jambes)* to dangle; *(de tête)* to hang

ballerine [balrin] **NF 1** *Théâtre* ballerina, ballet dancer **2** *(chaussure)* pump

balles [bal] **NFPL** *Anciennement Fam* francs; **je te le vends pour deux cents b.** I'll sell it to you for two hundred francs; **t'as pas cent b.?** *(dit dans la rue etc)* ≃ have you got any (spare) change?

ballet [balɛ] **NM** *Théâtre* ballet; **maître de b.** ballet master; **les ballets du Bolshoï** the Bolshoï Ballet; *Pol Fig* **le b. de ministres** the ministerial merry-go-round; **le b. diplomatique** diplomatic to-ings and fro-ings

ballon [balɔ̃] **NM 1** *(aéronef, vessie)* balloon; **faire un voyage en b.** to make a balloon journey; **monter en b.** to go up in a balloon; **envoyer** ou **lancer un b. d'essai** to send up a pilot balloon; *Fig* to put out feelers, to fly a kite; **marchand de ballons** balloon-seller

2 *Sport etc (pour jouer)* ball; *(au base-ball) (chandelle)* highball; **b. de football/de rugby/de volley** football/rugby ball/volleyball; **jouer au b.** to play with a ball; **b. d'entraînement (pour boxeurs)** punchball

3 *(de bande dessinée)* balloon

4 *(pour boire)* **(verre) b.** round wine glass; **un b. de vin blanc** a glass of white wine; *Suisse* **un b. (de vin)** = decilitre of wine

5 *Chimie* balloon flask; *Ind* carboy

6 **b. (d'Alcootest®)** (breathalyser) bag; **souffler dans le b.** to blow into the bag

7 *Suisse (petit pain)* (bread) roll

▸▸**b. de barrage** barrage balloon; **b. dirigeable** airship, dirigible; **b. gonflable** balloon; *(de football etc)* inflatable ball; **b. d'observation** observation balloon; **b. ovale** rugby ball; *(sport)* rugby; *Méd* **b. d'oxygène** oxygen bottle; **b. de protection** barrage balloon; **b. rond** football; *(sport)* football

ballonné [balone] **ADJ** *(bombé, arrondi) (joues)* chubby, round; *(nuages)* puffy; *(ventre)* bloated, distended

ballonnement [balonmɑ̃] **NM** *(du ventre, de l'estomac)* distending; **avoir des ballonnements** to feel bloated

ballonner [balone] **VT** *(gonfler) (cape, jupe, joues)* to puff out; *(ventre, estomac)* to distend; **manger ce genre de choses me ballonne** eating that kind of thing makes me feel bloated or gives me wind; **cette herbe risque de b. les bêtes** this grass is liable to bloat the livestock

ballon-panier **NM INV** *Can Sport* basketball

ballon-sonde, *pl* **ballons-sondes NM** *Météo* sounding balloon

ballot [balo] **NM 1** *(paquet)* bundle, package **2** *Fam (imbécile)* twit, wally

ADJ *Fam* **t'es pas b.?** are you mad?; **c'est vraiment b. de l'avoir prévenu** it's really crazy to have warned him

ballotin [balotɛ̃] **NM** sweet or *Am* candy box; **b. de chocolats** small box of chocolates

ballottage [balotaʒ] **NM** *Pol etc* **scrutin de b.** second ballot, run-off; **il y a b.** there will be a second ballot or a run-off; **M. Martin est en b.** Mr Martin has to stand again or *Am* run again in a second ballot

ballottement [balotmɑ̃] **NM** *(de train)* rocking, swaying; *(des passagers)* shaking, jolting; *(de porte)* swinging to and fro; *(de navire)* tossing

ballotter [balote] **VT** *(bateau)* to toss (about); *(passagers)* to shake or jolt (about); **être ballotté par des sentiments opposés** to be pulled this way and that by contradictory feelings; **un enfant ballotté entre ses parents** a tug-of-love child; **un enfant ballotté entre des écoles/villes** a child that has been

moved around from school to school/from town to town

VI *(de bagages)* to be tossed about; *(de porte)* to swing to and fro; *(de bateau)* to toss (about); *(de poitrine)* to bounce (up and down)

ballottine [balotin] **NF** *Culin* meat roll

balloune [balun] **NF** *Can Fam* **être en b.** *(enceinte)* to be in the (pudding) club

ball-trap, *pl* **ball-traps** [baltrap] **NM** *(sport)* clay-pigeon shooting, skeet shooting; *(appareil)* trap

balluchon [balyʃɔ̃] **NM** *Fam (de vêtements)* bundle; **faire son b.** to pack one's bags

balnéaire [balneɛr] **ADJ** **station b.** seaside resort

balnéothérapie [balneoterapi] **NF** *Méd* balneotherapy

baloche [balɔʃ] **NM** *Fam* local dance

balourd, -ourde [balur, -urd] **ADJ** *(personne)* awkward, clumsy; *(peu délicat)* loutish, uncouth

N *(maladroit)* clumsy oaf; **un grand b.** *(grand gars)* a great hulking fellow; **c'est le roi des balourds** he's a great oaf

NM *Tech* unbalance

balourdise [balurdiz] **NF 1** *(manque de finesse)* awkwardness, clumsiness **2** *(gaffe)* stupid blunder, *Fam* clanger

balsa [balza] **NM** balsa (wood)

balsamier [balzamje] **NM** balsam tree

balsamine [balzamin] **NF** *(plante)* balsam

balte [balt] **ADJ** Baltic; **les pays baltes** the Baltic States

balthazar [baltazar] **NM** *(de champagne)* Balthazar

Baltique [baltik] **NF** **la (mer) B.** the Baltic (Sea)

baluchon [balyʃɔ̃] **NM** *Fam* = **balluchon**

balustrade [balystrad] **NF 1** *Archit* balustrade **2** *(clôture)* railing

balustre [balystr] **NM** *Archit* baluster

balzacien, -ienne [balzasjɛ̃, -jɛn] **ADJ** *Littér* typical of Balzac; **une description très balzacienne** a description very typical of Balzac; **dans le plus pur style b.** in a style that is pure Balzac

balzan [balzɑ̃] **ADJ** **cheval b.** horse with white stockings

balzane [balzan] **NF** *(de cheval)* white stocking

bambin, -ine [bɑ̄bɛ̃, -in] **N** *Fam* toddler

bamboche [bɑ̄bɔʃ] **NF** *Fam* spree, lark; **faire b.** to live it up

bambocher [bɑ̄bɔʃe] **VI** *Fam* to live it up

bambocheur, -euse [bɑ̄bɔʃœr, -øz] **N** *Fam* reveller; **c'est un b.** he likes living it up

bambou [bɑ̄bu] **NM** *(plante)* bamboo; *Culin* **pousses de b.** bamboo shoots; *Fig Fam* **coup de b.** *(insolation)* sunstroke; *Fam* **il a le coup de b.** *(fou)* he's nuts or crazy; *(épuisé)* he's shattered or whacked; *Fam* **c'est le coup de b.** *(très cher)* it's a rip-off

bamboula [bɑ̄bula] **NF** *Fam* spree, lark; **faire la b.** to live it up

ban [bɑ̄] **NM 1** *(bannissement)* banishment; **mettre qn au b.** to banish sb; **pratique mise au b.** outlawed practice; **être au b. de la société** to be outlawed by society; **être en rupture de b.** to have illegally returned from banishment; *Fig* **être en rupture de b. avec** to have broken with **2 bans** *(de mariage)* banns; **publier les bans** to publish the banns **3 le b. et l'arrière-b.** *Hist* the ban and the arrière-ban; *Fig (tout le monde)* the world and his wife **4** *(applaudissements)* round of applause; **faire un b. pour qn** to give sb a round of applause, to applaud sb; **un b. pour Monsieur le maire!** a round of applause for the mayor!, ≃ three cheers for the mayor! **5** *(avant une annonce officielle)* drum roll; *Arch (d'un événement)* (public) proclamation

banal [banal] **ADJ 1** (*pl* **banals**) *(objet)* ordinary, commonplace; *(gens, occupation)* ordinary, run-of-the-mill; *(idée, remarque, style)* trite, banal; *(accident, exemple, excuse)* common; **parler de choses banales** to engage in small talk; **ça, c'est peu b.!** that's unusual, that's a bit out of the ordinary!; **c'est d'un b.!** it's dead ordinary!; *(idée)* it's so trite! **2** (*pl* **banaux**) *Hist (moulin, fournil)* communal

banalement [banalmɑ̃] **ADV** in an ordinary manner; **notre rencontre s'est passée très b.** our meeting took place in very ordinary circumstances

banalisation [banalizasjɔ̃] **NF 1** *(de la violence, du sexe dans les médias)* trivialization; **la b. des transports aériens** the fact that air travel has become commonplace *or* has become an everyday phenomenon; **la b. des voitures de police** the use of unmarked police cars **2** *Rail (pour une voie à deux sens)* signalling for two-way working; **la b. d'une locomotive** the manning of an engine by several crews

banaliser [banalize] **VT 1** *(sexe, violence etc)* to trivialize; **voiture** *ou* **véhicule banalisé(e)** unmarked police car **2** *Rail (voie ferrée)* to signal for two-way working; **b. une locomotive** to have an engine manned by several crews
VPR se banaliser to become commonplace

banalité [banalite] **NF 1** *(caractère) (d'objet, de gens, d'occupation)* ordinariness; *(d'idée, de remarque, de style)* triteness, banality; *(d'accident, d'exemple)* commonness **2 banalités** small talk, *Péj* platitudes; **un tissu** *ou* **ramassis de banalités** a collection of platitudes

banane [banan] **NF 1** *(fruit)* banana **2** *Mil Fam (médaille)* medal, *Br* gong **3** *Aviat Fam (hélicoptère)* chopper **4** *(coiffure)* quiff; **porter la b.** to have a quiff **5** *(petit sac)* bum-bag, *Am* fanny pack

bananier, -ière [bananje, -jɛr] **NM 1** *(arbre)* banana tree **2** *Naut* banana boat
ADJ *(plantation, production)* banana; **république bananière** banana republic

banc [bɑ̃] **NM 1** *(siège)* bench, seat **2** *(de rocher etc)* layer, bed; *Min (de charbon)* seam; *Naut* **toucher au b.** to run aground **3** *(colonie) (de poissons)* shoal, school; **b. d'huîtres** oyster bed **4** *(de brume)* bank; **b. de brouillard** fog bank **5** *Tech* (work)bench; *(d'un tour)* bed
▸▸ *Jur* **b. des accusés** dock; *Géog* **b. continental** continental shelf; **b. à coulisses** *(à l'aviron)* sliding seat; **b. d'école** school bench; **ils se sont connus sur les bancs de l'école** they got to know each other at school; **b. d'église** pew; **b. d'essai** *Ind* test bed; *Mktg* benchtest; *Ordinat* benchmark; *Fig* testing ground; **faire passer au b. d'essai** to benchtest; **mettre qch au b. d'essai** to test sth (out); **b. de glace** ice floe, ice field; **b. de jardin** garden bench *or* seat; *Jur* **b. des magistrats** magistrates' bench; *Ordinat* **b. de mémoire** memory bank; *Pol* **le b. des ministres** *Br* ≃ the (government) front bench; *TV, Cin* **b. de montage** editing desk, edit controller; *Can* **b. de neige** snowbank; **b. d'œuvre** churchwardens' pew; *Jur* **b. des prévenus** dock; **b. de roches** reef; **b. de sable** sandbank; **b. des témoins** witness box *or Am* witness stand; **le B. de Terre-Neuve** the Banks (of Newfoundland); **b. de vase** mudbank

bancable [bɑ̃kabl] **ADJ** *Fin* bankable, negotiable

bancaire [bɑ̃kɛr] **ADJ** bank(ing); **opérations bancaires** bank(ing) transactions; **chèque**

b. bank cheque; **compte b.** bank account; **informatique b.** computerized banking

bancal, -ale, -als, -ales [bɑ̃kal] **ADJ** *(personne)* lame; *(meuble etc)* wobbly, rickety; *Fig (raisonnement, idée)* shaky, unsound; *(projet)* unsound

bancarisation [bɑ̃karizasjɔ̃] **NF la b. de l'économie** the growing role of banks in the economy; **la b. de la population française** the spread of the use of banking services amongst the French population

bancarisé [bɑ̃karize] **ADJ être b.** to have an account with a bank, to use the banking system; **presque toutes les PME sont bancarisées** almost all small businesses have accounts with a bank *or* use the banking system

bancassurance [bɑ̃kasyrɑ̃s] **NF** *Banque* bancassurance

bancassureur [bɑ̃kasyrœr] **NM** insurance banker

bancatique [bɑ̃katik] **NF** electronic *or* computerized banking

banco [bɑ̃ko] **NM** *Cartes* banco; **faire b.** to go banco

bancomat [bɑ̃komat] **NM** *Suisse* ATM, cash dispenser

banc-titre, *pl* **bancs-titres** **NM** *Cin, TV* rostrum camera

bandage [bɑ̃daʒ] **NM 1** *(pansement)* bandage; *(action) (d'une blessure)* bandaging, binding up; **b. herniaire** truss **2** *(d'une roue) (en caoutchouc)* tyre, *Am* tire; *(en métal)* hoop, band **3** *(d'un ressort)* tightening; *(d'un arc)* bending

bandagiste [bɑ̃daʒist] **N** *Méd* truss manufacturer *or* supplier

bandana [bɑ̃dana] **NM** bandan(n)a

bandant [bɑ̃dɑ̃] **ADJ** *Vulg* sexy; *Fig* orgasmic; *Fig* **une proposition bandante** a turn-on; **ce n'est pas très b., comme idée de vacances** it doesn't really turn me on, as holiday ideas go

BANDE¹ [bɑ̃d] **NF 1** *(de tissu, de papier, de métal etc)* strip, band; *(de terre)* strip, stretch, belt; *(motif)* stripe; *Fig* **par la b.** in a roundabout way, indirectly; **mettre un journal sous b.** to put a wrapper round a newspaper; **b. de téléimprimeur** ticker tape; *Agr* **culture en bandes de niveau** strip contour farming **2** *Méd* bandage; **mettre une b. à qn** to put a bandage on sb, to bandage sb **3** *(magnétique)* tape; *(pellicule)* film; **tourner une b. d'essai** to have a screen test; **faire tourner une b. d'essai à qn** to give sb a screen test **4** *(de roue)* hoop, band **5** *Tél, Ordinat* **à large b.** broadband **6** *Billard* cushion **7** *Opt (du spectre)* band **8** *(d'une mitrailleuse)* (feeding) belt **9** *Hér* bend **10** *Naut (de navire)* side; *(inclinaison)* list; **donner de la b.** to list, to have a list
▸▸ *Cin* **b. amorce** (film) leader; **b. d'arrêt d'urgence** hard shoulder; *Cin* **b. audionumérique** digital audio tape, DAT; **b. en bobine** open-reel tape, reel-to-reel tape; *Ordinat* **b. en cassettes** cassette tape; **b. cyclable** cycle lane; *Ordinat* **b. de défilement** scroll bar; *Cin* **b. démo** demo tape; **b. dessinée** comic strip, strip cartoon; *Ordinat* **b. de données** data tape; **b. enregistrée** recorded tape; *Aviat* **b. d'envol** airstrip, landing strip; **b. ferrique** ferric tape; *Fin* **b. de fluctuation** *(d'une monnaie)* fluctuation band; *Ordinat* **b. sans fin** endless tape; *Radio* **b. de fréquences** frequency band; **b. illustrée** comic strip, strip cartoon; *TV, Cin* **b. internationale** music and effects track, M&E track; *Radio* **b. latérale** sideband; **b. magnétique** magnetic tape; **b. magnétique au-**

dio audio tape; **b. maîtresse** *ou* **mère** master tape; *Aut* **b. médiane** *(sur la route)* central (white) line; *Mil* **b. molletière** puttee; **b. noire** terrorist gang; **b. originale (d'un film)** original (film) soundtrack; *Ordinat* **b. de papier** paper tape; *Aut* **b. pare-soleil** shadeband; *Cin* **b. parole** dialogue track; *Électron, Ordinat* **b. passante** bandwidth; *Ordinat* **b. perforée** perforated tape, *Br* punched paper tape; **b. de présentation** *(d'une chanson etc)* demo tape; *Aut* **b. de protection latérale** side-impact bar; **b. de roulement** *(de pneu)* tread; **b. son** *ou* **sonore** sound reel *or* track; *Aut* **b. de stationnement** layby, *Am* rest stop; **b. Velpeau®** crepe bandage; **b. vidéo** videotape; **b. vidéo promotionnelle** promotional video; **b. vierge** blank tape; **bandes vierges** (film) stock

bande² **NF 1** *(de personnes)* band, group; **b. d'amis** group of friends; **b. de voleurs** gang *or* band of thieves; **b. armée** armed gang; **elle fait b. à part** she keeps (herself) to herself; **viens avec nous, ne fais pas b. à part** come with us, don't stay all on your own *or* all by yourself; **cet artiste fait un peu b. à part dans le mouvement minimaliste français** this artist is rather a special case *or* is something of an exception in the French minimalist movement; **faire qch en b.** to do sth in a group; **être de la b. de qn** to belong to sb's gang; **toute la b.** the whole gang, the whole lot of them; **une b. de fous/d'incapables** a bunch of madmen/incompetents; **b. d'imbéciles!** you bunch of idiots! **2** *(d'oiseaux)* flock, flight; *(de loups)* pack; *(de buffles)* herd; *(de marsouins)* school; *(de lions)* pride

bandé [bɑ̃de] **ADJ 1** *(main, cheville etc)* bandaged; **les yeux bandés** blindfold(ed) **2** *Hér* bendy

bande-annonce, *pl* **bandes-annonces** **NF** *Cin* trailer, *Am* preview (**de** for)

bandeau, -eaux [bɑ̃do] **NM 1** *(pour les cheveux)* headband; **cheveux en bandeaux** hair parted in the middle and swept back round the sides **2** *(sur les yeux)* blindfold; **mettre un b. à qn** to blindfold sb, to put a blindfold on sb; *Fig* **avoir un b. sur les yeux** to be blind **3** *Archit* string course **4** *Journ (titre)* streamer **5** *Ordinat (dans un site web)* banner

bandelette [bɑ̃dlɛt] **NF** *(de tissu)* strip, band; **bandelettes** *(de momies)* bandages, wrappings; **b. réactive** *Méd* testing strip; *(pour analyse d'urine)* dipstick; *Aut* **b. talon** chafer strip

bander [bɑ̃de] **VT 1** *(blessure, main etc)* to bandage (up), to put a bandage on; **b. les yeux à** *ou* **de qn** to blindfold sb, to put a blindfold on sb **2** *(ressort)* to tighten; **b. un arc** to bend a bow; **b. ses muscles** to tense one's muscles
VI *Vulg* to have a hard-on *or* an erection; *Fig* **faire b. qn** to excite sb; **le théâtre, ça la fait b.** she gets a real buzz from the theatre

banderille [bɑ̃drij] **NF** *(en tauromachie)* banderilla

banderole [bɑ̃drɔl] **NF** banderole; *(publicitaire)* streamer; *(de manifestant)* banner

bandit [bɑ̃di] **NM** *(escroc)* crook, swindler, rogue; *Vieilli (brigand)* bandit, brigand; **b. de grand chemin** highwayman

banditisme [bɑ̃ditism] **NM** crime; **recrudescence du b.** crime wave; **le grand b.** organized crime

bandonéon [bɑ̃dɔneɔ̃] **NM** bandoneon

bandouiller [bɑ̃duje] **VI** *Vulg* to have a semi

bandoulière [bɑ̃duljɛr] **NF 1** *(d'un sac etc)* shoulder strap; **porter/mettre qch en b.** to carry/sling sth over *or* across one's shoulder; **le sac en b.** with one's bag slung over *or* across one's shoulder **2** *Mil* bandolier

bang [bãg] NM INV *Aviat* (super)sonic boom

Bangladesh [bãgladɛʃ, bɛ̃gladɛʃ] NM Bangladesh

banian [banjã] NM banyan (tree)

banjo [bã(d)ʒo] NM *Mus* banjo VOIR GRAMMAIRE A12

banlieue [bãljø] NF suburbs *pl*; **la grande/petite b.** the outer/inner suburbs; **vivre en b.** to live in the suburbs *or* in suburbia; **maisons de b.** suburban houses; *Rail* **ligne/gare de b.** suburban line/station; **b. rouge** communist-voting suburb
NM *Belg* stopping train

> **Banlieue**
> In France the word "banlieue" often refers not to the upmarket areas of a city – as the word "suburbia" can suggest in English-speaking countries – but to the impoverished suburban areas on the outskirts of some cities. These neighbourhoods are culturally and ethnically diverse and are frequently associated with social problems such as delinquency, unemployment and unrest.

banlieusard, -arde [bãljøzar, -ard] N *Fam* suburbanite

banne [ban] NF **1** *(pour le charbon etc)* cart **2** *(panier)* (wicker) basket **3** *(de magasin etc)* awning, canopy

banneret [banrɛ] NM *Hist* banneret; **chevalier b.** knight banneret

banneton [bantɔ̃] NM **1** *(pour le pain)* basket **2** *(pour la pêche)* corf

banni, -ie [bani] ADJ *(personne)* banished, exiled
N exile

bannière [banjɛr] NF *(étendard)* banner; **il s'est rangé sous la b. des écologistes** he's joined the ranks of the ecologists; **la b. étoilée** the Star-Spangled Banner; *Fig* **c'est la croix et la b. pour le faire manger** it's a devil of a job *or* a heck of a job getting him to eat; **c'est la croix et la b., ce job!** this job is a real devil!

bannir [banir] VT *(personne)* to banish, to exile; **bannissez les pensées négatives de votre esprit** banish negative thoughts from your mind; **il a complètement banni la cigarette** he has completely given up smoking; **vous devez b. le sucre de votre alimentation** you must exclude sugar from your diet, you must cut sugar out of your diet

bannissement [banismã] NM banishment

banquable [bãkabl] ADJ *Fin* bankable, negotiable

banque [bãk] NF **1** *(commerce)* banking; *(établissement)* bank; **avoir de l'argent à la b.** to have money in the bank; **porter un chèque à la b.** to bank a cheque; **opération de b.** bank(ing) transaction; **billet de b.** banknote, *Am* bank bill; **chèque de b.** *Br* bank cheque; **carnet** *ou* **livret de b.** bankbook; **travailler dans la b.** to be in banking; **avoir un compte en b. chez ...** to have an account *or* to bank with ...; **employé/directeur de b.** bank clerk/manager; **b. privée/de l'État** privately owned/State bank **2** *Cartes* bank; **tenir la b.** to be (the) banker; **faire sauter la b.** to break the bank
▸▸ **b. d'acceptation** *Br* accepting *or* *Am* acceptance house; **b. d'affaires** investment bank, *Br* merchant bank; **b. centrale** central bank; **B. centrale européenne** European Central Bank; **b. commerciale** commercial bank; **b. compensatrice** clearing bank; **b. confirmatrice** confirming bank; **b. de crédit** credit bank; **b. de dépôt** clearing bank; **b. de détail** retail bank; *(activité)* retail banking; **b. à distance** direct banking; **b. à domicile** tele-

banking, home banking; *Ordinat* **b. de données** data bank; **b. d'émission** bank of issue; **b. d'entreprise** corporate banking; **b. d'épargne** savings bank; **b. d'escompte** discount house *or* bank; **B. européenne d'investissement** European Investment Bank; **B. européenne pour la reconstruction et le développement** European Bank for Reconstruction and Development; **B. de France** Bank of France; **b. de gestion de patrimoine** trust bank; **b. de gros** wholesale bank; **b. d'images** *Ordinat* image bank; *TV* television archives, image bank; **B. internationale pour la reconstruction et le développement** International Bank for Reconstruction and Development; **la B. mondiale** the World Bank; **b. notificatrice** advising bank; **b. de placement** issuing bank *or* house; *Radio, TV* **b. de programmes** programme library, programme archives; **b. de recouvrement** collecting agency *or* bank; *Méd* **b. de** *ou* **du sang** blood bank; **b. du sperme** sperm bank; **b. statistique** statistics bank; **b. des yeux** eye bank

banquer [bãke] VI *Fam* to cough up, *Br* to stump up; **c'est toujours moi qui banque** it's always me that has to cough up

banqueroute [bãkrut] NF *Jur* bankruptcy; **faire b.** to go bankrupt

banqueroutier, -ière [bãkrutje, -jɛr] N bankrupt; *(frauduleux)* fraudulent bankrupt

banquet [bãkɛ] NM banquet, feast; **salle de b.** banqueting hall

banquette [bãkɛt] NF **1** *(siège)* seat; **b. de piano** piano stool; *Aut* **la b. arrière** the back seat **2** *Constr (de terre)* bank; *(de pont, de tunnel)* (foot)path; *Archit* **b. de fenêtre** window seat **3** *(d'un couloir d'autobus)* = kerb separating a bus lane from the rest of the roadway

banquier, -ière [bãkje, -jɛr] N *Fin, Cartes* banker; *Fig* **crois-tu que je vais être ton b.?** do you think I'm going to finance *or* *Am* bankroll you?; **je ne suis pas b.** I'm not made of money
▸▸ **b. d'affaires** merchant banker; **b. prêteur** lending bank

banquise [bãkiz] NF ice floe, pack ice, ice pack

bantou, -oue [bãtu] ADJ Bantu
N B. Bantu

bantoustan [bãtustã] NM Bantustan, Bantu Homeland

baobab [baɔbab] NM baobab (tree)

baptême [batɛm] NM **1** *Rel* baptism, christening; **conférer** *ou* **donner le b. à qn** to baptize *or* christen sb; **recevoir le b.** to be baptized *or* christened; **nom de b.** Christian name, first *or* *Am* given name **2** *(d'une cloche)* blessing; *(d'un navire)* naming, christening
▸▸ **b. de l'air** first flight; *Mil* **b. du feu** baptism of fire; *Naut* **b. de la ligne** crossing of the line

baptiser [batize] VT **1** *Rel (personne)* to baptize, to christen; *(surnommer)* to christen, to nickname; **ses parents l'ont baptisée Léa** her parents christened her Léa; **on l'avait baptisé 'le Balafré'** they had christened *or* nicknamed him 'Scarface'; **b. son vin/son lait** to water down one's wine/milk **2** *Rel (cloche)* to bless; *(navire)* to name

baptismal, -ale, -aux, -ales [batismal, -o] ADJ baptismal

baptisme [batism] NM baptism

baptistaire [batistɛr] ADJ **registre b.** register of baptisms; **extrait b.** certificate of baptism

baptiste [batist] ADJ, N *Rel* Baptist

baptistère [batistɛr] NM *Rel* baptist(e)ry

baquer (se) [səbake] VPR *Fam* to go for a dip

baquet [bakɛ] NM **1** *(cuve)* tub **2** *Aut (siège en)* **b.** bucket seat

bar¹ [bar] NM *(poisson)* bass; **b. commun** sea perch

bar² NM *(café, comptoir)* bar; **le b. du coin** the bar on the corner, the local; **prendre une consommation au b.** to have a drink at the bar; **b. américain** *(dans une cuisine)* bar; **b.-tabac** = bar where tobacco, stamps and lottery tickets are also sold over the counter; **b. à vin** wine bar

bar³ NM *Météo* bar

barachois [baraʃwa] NM *Can (dans une rivière)* sandbar

baragouin [baragwɛ̃] NM *Fam* gibberish, gobbledegook

baragouinage [baragwinaʒ] NM *Fam* jabbering

baragouiner [baragwine] *Fam* VT *(langue étrangère)* to speak badly; **b. l'anglais** to talk broken English; **qu'est-ce qu'il baragouine?** what's he jabbering (on) about?
VI to jabber (on)

baragouineur, -euse [baragwinœr, -øz] N *Fam* jabberer

baraka [baraka] NF *Fam* (good) luck; **avoir la b.** to be lucky

baraque [barak] NF **1** *(logement provisoire)* hut, shack, shed **2** *Fam (foyer)* place; *Péj (lieu)* hole, dump; **casser la b.** to bring the house down; **il n'y a rien à manger dans cette b.!** there's nothing to eat in this joint! **3** *(de foire etc)* stall, stand

> Il faut noter que le nom anglais **barracks** est un faux ami. Il signifie **caserne**.

baraqué [barake] ADJ *Fam* hefty

baraquement [barakmã] NM shacks; *Mil* camp

baraquer [barake] VI *(d'un chameau)* to kneel down

baratin [baratɛ̃] NM *Fam (bavardage)* chatter; *(d'un vendeur)* sales talk, patter, spiel; *(pour draguer)* sweet *or* smooth talk; **b. publicitaire** *(écrit)* blurb; *(parlé)* sales pitch; **quel b.!** *(je n'y comprends rien)* what gibberish!; **faire du b. (à qn)** to spin (sb) a yarn, to shoot (sb) a line; **ce type me fait du b.** *(pour draguer)* this guy's chatting me up *or* *Am* hitting on me; **faire son b. à un client** to give a customer the patter *or* sales talk *or* spiel; **avoir du b.** to be a smooth talker

baratiner [baratine] *Fam* VI *(parler beaucoup)* to chatter; *(parler sans sincérité)* to shoot a line, to spin a yarn; *(d'un vendeur)* to give one's patter *or* sales talk *or* spiel
VT to sweet-talk; **b. un client** to give a client the patter *or* sales talk *or* spiel; **b. une fille** to chat up *or* *Am* hit on a girl

baratineur, -euse [baratinœr, -øz] N *Fam* smooth talker, smoothie

baratte [barat] NF churn

baratter [barate] VT *(lait)* to churn

barbacane [barbakan] NF **1** *(ouvrage)* barbican, outwork; *(meurtrière)* loop(hole) **2** *(canalisation)* drainage channel

Barbade [barbad] NF Barbados

barbant [barbã] ADJ *Fam* boring

barbaque [barbak] NF *Fam* meat; *(de mauvaise qualité)* lousy meat

barbare [barbar] ADJ *(cruel, sauvage)* barbaric, barbarous; *Fam* **il écoute de la musique b.** he's listening to that awful racket he calls music
N barbarian

barbaresque [barbarɛsk] *Vieilli* ADJ Berber; **les États barbaresques** the Barbary States
N B. Berber

Barbarie [barbari] NF *Vieilli* **la B.** the Barbary States

barbarie [barbari] NF **1** *(cruauté, action cruelle)* barbarity **2** *(manque de civilisation)* barbarism

barbarisme [barbarism] NM *Gram* barbarism

barbe¹ [barb] NF **1** *(d'homme)* beard; **sans b.** *(adulte)* clean-shaven; *(jeune adolescent)* beardless; **avoir de la b.** *(d'un homme)* to need a shave; *(d'un adolescent)* to have some hairs on one's chin; **se faire pousser la b.** to grow a beard, to let one's beard grow; **faire la b. à qn** to shave sb; **il avait une b. de huit jours** he had a week's beard *or* growth; **tu n'as pas encore de b. au menton et tu crois tout savoir** you're still in short pants and you think you know everything; **brosse/savon à b.** shaving brush/soap; **parler dans sa b.** to mutter, to mumble; **femme à b.** bearded lady; *Fig* **faire qch à la b. de qn** to do sth right under sb's nose; **rire dans sa b.** to laugh up one's sleeve; *Fam* **quelle b.!** what a drag!, what a bore!; *Fam* **la b.!** shut it!, shut up!; *Fam* **vieille b.** old fogey
2 *(de chèvre, d'oiseau etc)* beard; *(de chat)* whiskers; *(de poisson)* barbel, wattle; *(de plume, d'hameçon)* barb; *(du blé)* beard
3 *Tech (sur moulage etc)* bur(r); **barbes** *(sur papier)* deckle edge
▶▶ **b. à papa** candy floss, *Am* cotton candy

barbe² NM *(cheval)* **b.** barb, Barbary horse

barbeau [barbo] NM **1** *(poisson)* **b. commun** barbel; **b. de mer** red mullet **2** *Bot* cornflower **3** *Arg (souteneur)* pimp
ADJ INV **(bleu) b.** cornflower blue

Barbe-Bleue N Bluebeard

barbecue [barbəkju] NM barbecue; **faire un b.** to have a barbecue

barbelé [barbəle] ADJ *(flèche)* barbed; **fil de fer b.** barbed wire
NMPL **barbelés** barbed wire; *Mil* barbed wire entanglement; **être derrière les barbelés** to be in a prison camp

barber [barbe] *Fam* VT *(personne)* to bore stiff, to bore to death
VPR **se barber** to be bored stiff *or* bored to death

barbeux, -euse [barbø, -øz] *Can Fam* ADJ **être b.** to be a pain (in the neck)
NM pain (in the neck)

barbiche [barbiʃ] NF goatee (beard)

barbichette [barbiʃɛt] NF *Fam* small goatee (beard)

barbichu [barbiʃy] ADJ with a goatee (beard)
NM man with a goatee (beard)

barbier [barbje] NM **1** *Vieilli (qui rase le visage)* barber **2** *Can (coiffeur pour hommes)* (men's) hairdresser, barber; **salon de b.** (men's) hairdresser's, barber's, barbershop

barbillon [barbijɔ̃] NM **1** *(d'un poisson)* barbel; **barbillons** *(de cheval, bœuf)* barbs **2** *(poisson)* barbel; **b. de mer** red mullet

barbital, *pl* **barbitals** [barbital] NM *Pharm* barbitone, *Am* barbital

barbiturique [barbityrik] *Pharm* ADJ barbituric
NM barbiturate

barbiturisme [barbityrism] NM *Méd* barbiturate poisoning; *(dépendance)* barbiturism, addiction to barbiturates

barbon [barbɔ̃] NM *Litt* **vieux b.** greybeard

barbotage [barbɔtaʒ] NM *(dans l'eau)* paddling, splashing (about); *Chimie (d'un gaz dans un liquide)* bubbling

barboter [barbɔte] VI *(dans l'eau)* to paddle, to splash (about); *(du gaz)* to bubble *(through liquid)*; **les enfants barbotent dans la piscine** the children are splashing about in the swimming pool
VT *Arg (voler)* to pinch, *Br* to nick; **quelqu'un m'a barboté mon stylo** someone's pinched my pen

barboteur, -euse [barbɔtœr, -øz] N **1** *(dans l'eau)* paddler **2** *Arg (voleur)* thief
NM *Chimie* bubbler, blower
NF **barboteuse** playsuit, rompers

barbotin [barbɔtɛ̃] NM *Tech* sprocket wheel

barbouillage [barbujaʒ] NM **1** *(action de peindre)* daubing, smearing; *(action d'écrire)* scrawling, scribbling **2** *(mauvaise peinture)* daub; *(griffonnage)* scrawl, scribble

barbouiller [barbuje] VT **1** *(avec de la peinture)* to daub, to smear; *(salir) (visage)* to smear; *(papier avec de l'encre)* to blot; **visage barbouillé de larmes/de chocolat** tear-stained face/face smeared with chocolate; **b. des toiles** to do a bit of painting **2** *(griffonner)* to scribble, to scrawl; **b. un article** to dash off an article **3** *Fam* **ça me barbouille l'estomac** *ou* **le cœur** it makes me feel sick, it turns my stomach; **avoir l'estomac barbouillé** to feel queasy

barbouilleur, -euse [barbujœr, -øz] N **1** *(de peinture)* dauber, so-called artist **2 b. (de papier)** scribbler, hack

barbouze [barbuz] NF *Fam* **1** *(barbe)* beard **2** *(agent secret)* secret agent

barbu, -ue [barby] ADJ bearded
NM **1** bearded man **2** *Fam (fondamentaliste islamique)* Islamic fundamentalist **3** *Vulg (poils pubiens de la femme)* bush
NF **barbue** *(poisson)* brill

barcarolle [barkarɔl] NF *Mus* barcarol(l)e

barcasse [barkas] NF *Naut* launch, boat

Barcelone [barsəlɔn] N Barcelona

barda [barda] NM *Arg* gear, kit, stuff; *Mil* kit

bardage [bardaʒ] NM **1** *(de matériaux lourds)* hand transport **2** *(pour protéger un tableau etc)* boarding; *(d'un bâtiment)* weatherboarding, *Am* siding

bardane [bardan] NF *(plante)* burdock

bardas [barda] NM *Can (pagaille)* shambles; **être de b.** *(déranger)* to be a nuisance

barde¹ [bard] NF **1** *Culin (sur un rôti)* bard **2** *Hist (protégeant les chevaux de bataille)* bard

barde² NM bard, poet

bardeau, -eaux [bardo] NM **1** *Constr* shingle; **toit de bardeaux** shingle roof **2** *Zool* hinny **3** *Can Fam* **manquer un b.** to be not quite right in the head, to have a slate loose

barder¹ [barde] V IMPERS *Fam* **ça va b.!** there's going to be trouble!; **c'est là que ça a commencé à b.!** and then the fun began!, and then the sparks flew!

barder² VT **1** *Culin (volaille etc)* to bard **2** *Hist (cheval)* to bard; **chevalier bardé de fer** steel-clad knight; *Fig* **malle bardée d'étiquettes** trunk stuck all over with labels; **il est bardé de diplômes/décorations** he's got a whole string of qualifications/decorations

bardot [bardo] NM *Zool* hinny

barème [barɛm] NM **1** *(de notes, de salaires)* scale; **b. fiscal** *ou* **d'imposition** tax schedule, tax scale; **b. des prix** price list, schedule of prices **2** *(pour calcul rapide)* ready reckoner

barge¹ [barʒ] NF *Naut* barge, lighter

barge² ADJ *voir* **barjo**

baril [baril] NM *(de vin)* cask, barrel; *(de poudre)* keg; *(d'anchois)* barrel; *Pétr* barrel *(42 gallons)*; **b. de lessive** drum of washing powder

barillet [barijɛ] NM **1** *(petit baril)* small barrel *or* cask **2** *(d'une pompe)* barrel piston chamber; *(d'un revolver, d'une serrure)* cylinder, barrel; **il n'y avait rien dans le b.** the gun was empty; **b. (de ressort)** *(dans une horloge)* spring box, spring drum; **serrure à b.** cylinder lock, Yale® lock

bariolage [barjɔlaʒ] NM *(de peinture)* painting *or* daubing with bright colours; *Fig (de couleurs)* medley, riot; *Péj (motif)* gaudy colour scheme

bariolé [barjɔle] ADJ *(tissu)* multicoloured, *Péj* gaudy; **audience bariolée** colourfully dressed audience

barioler [barjɔle] VT to paint *or* daub in bright *or* *Péj* gaudy colours

bariolure [barjɔlyr] NF bright *or* *Péj* gaudy colours

barjo(t) [barʒo] *Fam* N nut, *Br* nutter
ADJ crazy

barmaid [barmɛd] NF barmaid

barman, *pl* **barmen, barmans** [barman, -mɛn] NM barman

barn [barn] NM *Phys* barn

barographe [barɔgraf] NM *Météo* barograph

baromètre [barɔmɛtr] NM *Météo, Fig* barometer; **b. anéroïde** aneroid barometer; **b. enregistreur** recording barometer

barométrique [barɔmetrik] ADJ barometric

baron [barɔ̃] NM **1** *(seigneur)* baron; *Fig* **les barons de la finance/de l'industrie** financial/industrial tycoons **2** *Arg (protecteur)* protector; *(compère)* plant **3** *Culin* **b. d'agneau** baron of lamb

baronnage [barɔnaʒ] NM *(titre)* barony, baronage

baronne [barɔn] NF baroness

baronnet [barɔnɛ] NM baronet

baronnie [barɔni] NF *Hist* barony

baroque [barɔk] ADJ *(idées etc)* bizarre, odd, strange; *Archit, Beaux-Arts, Mus* baroque; *(perle)* tear-shaped
NM Baroque

baroud [barud] NM *Mil Fam* fighting; **b. d'honneur** last-ditch battle, last stand

barouder [barude] VI *Fam (voyager)* to knock about

baroudeur [barudœr] NM *Mil Fam (qui aime le combat)* (keen) fighter; **c'est un b.** *(voyageur)* he's knocked about a bit

barouf(le) [baruf(l)] NM *Fam* din, row, racket; **faire du b.** to make a din *or* row *or* racket

barque [bark] NF *Naut* **1** *(embarcation)* boat; **b. de pêcheur** fishing boat; **patron de b.** skipper; *Fig* **bien mener** *ou* **bien conduire sa b.** to manage one's affairs well; *Fig* **c'est elle qui mène la b.** she's the boss, she's in charge; **charger la b.** to overdo it **2 trois-mâts b.** barque

barquette [barkɛt] NF **1** *(récipient) (pour plat à emporter etc)* container; *(de fraises, framboises etc)* punnet **2** *(gâteau)* pastry boat

barracuda [barakyda] NM barracuda

barrage [baraʒ] NM **1** *(fait de bloquer) (d'une route, rue)* blocking (off), closing; *(d'un port)* blocking; *(d'une vallée)* damming; **faire b. à qn/qch** to block sb/sth **2** *(fermeture)* barrier, obstruction; *(d'un port)* boom; **b. routier** *ou* **de route** roadblock; **b. de police** police roadblock, police cordon; **b. (de retenue)** dam, barrage; *(de petite taille)* weir; *Mil* **b. aérien** anti-aircraft barrage; **(tir de) b.** barrage (fire)

BARRE [bar] NF **1** *(de métal)* bar, rod; *(de bois etc)* rod; *Sport* bar; *(de danse)* barre; *Fam* **c'est le coup de b.** it's a rip-off; *Fig Fam* **avoir un coup de b.** to be shattered *or* whacked; **s'exercer à la b.,** **faire des exercices à la b.** to do exercises at the barre; **avoir barre(s) sur qn** to have an advantage over sb; **passer la b./sous la b. de 1000 euros** to rise above/drop below the 1,000 euro mark; *Archit* **b. (de) HLM** ≃ large block of council flats
2 *Naut (de bateau)* tiller; *(de navire)* helm; **homme de b.** helmsman; **être à** *ou* **tenir la b.**

to be at the helm; **prendre la b.** to take the helm; *Fig* **à partir d'aujourd'hui, je prends la b.** as from today, I'm in charge

3 *Jur (d'un tribunal)* bar; **b. des témoins** witness box *or Am* stand; **paraître à la b. to appear before the court** *or* at the bar; **être appelé à la b.** to be called to the witness box *or* stand

4 *(d'une rivière, d'un port)* (sand) bar; *(artificielle)* boom; **b. d'eau** (tidal) bore; **b. de flot** tidal wave; **b. de plage** surf

5 *(trait)* line, dash, stroke; **b. d'un t** cross(-bar) of a t; **mettre une b. à un t** to cross a t; *Mus* **b. de mesure** bar (line); **double b.** double bar

6 *(de cheval)* bar

7 *Hér* bend sinister

8 **jeu de barres** = prisoners' base

▸▸ **b. d'accouplement** tie rod, coupling bar; *(de direction)* steering rod; *Aut* **b. antidévers** *ou* **anti-roulis** anti-roll bar; *Aut* **b. antivol** locking bar; **b. d'appui** *(d'une fenêtre)* rail; **barres asymétriques** asymmetric bars; *Aut* **b. de calandre** nudge bar; **b. de chocolat** bar of chocolate; **b. chocolatée** chocolate bar; *Aut* **b. de connexion** *(de la boîte de direction)* crossbar, tie rod; *Typ, Ordinat* **b. d'espacement** space bar; *Ordinat* **b. de défilement** scroll bar; *Gym* **b. fixe** horizontal bar; *Ordinat* **b. d'icônes** icon bar; *Ordinat* **b. de menu** menu bar; *Ordinat* **b. de navigation** navigation bar; *Typ* **b. oblique** oblique, slash; *Typ* **b. oblique inversée** backslash; *Ordinat* **b. d'outils** tool bar; **barres parallèles** parallel bars; *Aut* **b. de remorquage** towing rod, towbar; *Aut* **b. de renfort latéral** side-impact bar; **b. de savon** bar of soap, cake of soap; *Ordinat* **b. de sélection** menu bar; *Aut* **b. stabilisatrice** stabilizer bar; *Ordinat* **b. de style** style bar; *Ordinat* **b. de titre** title bar; *Aut* **b. de toit** roof bar; *Aut* **b. de torsion** torsion bar, torque strut

barré [bare] ADJ **1** *(chemin, passage, route)* closed; **'route barrée'** 'road closed' **2** **chèque b.** crossed cheque *or Am* check; **chèque non b.** open cheque **3** **dent barrée** impacted tooth **4** *(à l'aviron)* **un deux b.** a coxed pair **5** *Fam* **on est mal b.** things don't look good

barreau, -eaux [baro] NM **1** *(d'une fenêtre, cage)* bar; *(d'une échelle)* rung; *(d'une chaise)* rung, crosspiece; *Fig* **b. de chaise** fat cigar; **fenêtre garnie de barreaux** barred window, window with bars; **être derrière les barreaux** to be behind bars **2** *Jur* **le b.** the bar; **être reçu** *ou* **admis au b.** to be called to the bar; **radier qn du b.** to disbar sb

barrement [barmã] NM *(d'un chèque)* crossing

barrer [bare] VT **1** *(porte, fenêtre)* to bar; *Can (fermer à clef)* to lock; *(route, passage, chemin)* to block (off), to close; **b. le passage** *ou* **la route à qn** to block *or* bar sb's way; *Fig* **to stand in sb's way, to thwart sb 2** *(chèque)* to cross; **b. un t** to cross a t **3** *(mot etc)* to cross out, to strike out; **je vais pouvoir b. ça de ma liste** I can cross that off my list **4** *Naut (bateau)* to steer; *(à l'aviron)* to cox

VPR **se barrer** *Fam* to clear off, to beat it, to scram

barrette¹ [baret] NF *Rel* biretta

barrette² NF **1** *(pour les cheveux)* (hair) slide, *Am* barrette **2** *(broche)* brooch; *(de médaille)* bar **3** *Fam (de haschich)* thin strip

▸▸ *Ordinat* **b. de mémoire vive** RAM module; *Aut* **b. verticale** overrider

barreur [barœr] NM **1** *Naut* helmsman **2** *(à l'aviron)* cox; **un deux sans b.** a coxless pair

barricade [barikad] NF **b. (de rue)** (street) barricade; *Fig* **de l'autre côté de la b.** on the opposing side, on the other side of the fence

barricader [barikade] VT *(route, porte etc)* to barricade

VPR **se barricader** to barricade oneself in; **se b. dans une chambre** to barricade oneself in a room *(contre against)*; *(pour ne pas être dérangé)* to shut *or* lock oneself up in a room

barrière [barjɛr] NF **1** *(obstacle)* barrier; *(clôture)* fence; *(dans le métro)* gate, barrier; *(d'un passage à niveau)* gate; **barrières culturelles/sociales** cultural/social barriers; *Géog* **b. naturelle** natural barrier; **la Grande B.** the Great Barrier Reef **2** *Hist (d'une ville, d'un château etc)* gate; *(péage)* toll gate, turnpike

▸▸ *Com* **b. d'accès** access barrier; *Aviat* **b. antisouffle** blast wall; **b. à bascule** drop-arm barrier; **b. commerciale** trade barrier; *Aut* **b. de dégel** = ban on the use of a road by heavy traffic during a thaw; *Com* **barrières douanières** trade barriers; *Com* **b. à l'entrée** entry barrier; *Phys* **b. de potentiel** potential barrier; *Com* **b. à la sortie** exit barrier; *Phys* **b. thermique** thermal barrier, heat barrier; **b. Vauban** security barrier

barrique [barik] NF barrel, cask *(containing approx 200 litres)*; *Fam* **il est gros comme une b.** he's as round as a barrel; *Fig Fam* **plein** *ou* **rond comme une b.** blind drunk, (as) drunk as a lord

barrir [barir] VI *(d'un éléphant)* to trumpet

barrissement [barismã], **barrit** [bari] NM *(d'un éléphant)* trumpeting

bartavelle [bartavɛl] NF **(perdrix) b.** rock partridge

barycentre [barisãtr] NM *Math* barycentre

baryte [barit] NF *Chimie, Minér* baryta, barium oxide

baryté [barite] ADJ *Méd* **bouillie barytée** barium meal

baryton [baritɔ̃] *Mus* ADJ *(voix)* baritone
NM baritone

baryum [barjɔm] NM *Chimie, Minér* barium

barzoï [barzɔj] NM *(chien)* borzoi

BAS [beas] NM *Admin (abrév* **Bureau d'aide sociale)** welfare office

BAS¹, BASSE [ba, bas]

ADJ	low **1, 2, 4** ▪ late **3** ▪ mean **4** ▪ petty **4**
ADV	low **1, 4** ▪ down **5, 6**
NM	bottom **1**

ADJ **1** *(de peu de hauteur, d'altitude)* low; *(station de ski etc)* low(-lying); *(baromètre, température, prix)* low; **maison basse de toit** *ou* **à toit b.** low-roofed house, house with a low roof; **b. de plafond** low-ceilinged, with a low ceiling; **b. sur pattes** short-legged; *Boxe, Fig* **coup b.** blow below the belt; **enfant en b. âge** infant; **avoir la vue basse** to be short-sighted *or* near-sighted; **basse saison** low season; **à b. prix** cheaply, for a low price; **maintenir les prix b.** to keep prices down *or* low; **prix les plus b.** rock-bottom prices, lowest possible prices; **en ce b. monde** here on earth; **au b. mot** at the very least, at the lowest estimate; **le soleil est b.** the sun is low; *Météo* **plafond b.** low ceiling (of cloud); **mer basse** low water *or* tide; **quand la mer est basse** when it's low tide, when the tide is low *or* out; **la marée est basse** the tide is out *or* low; **à marée basse** at low tide; *Fig* **la tête basse** with a hang-dog look; **le moral est très b.** morale is very low; **elle est au plus b.** she's really low, she's at a very low ebb; **terres** *ou* **régions basses** lowlands; **le b. Rhin** the lower Rhine; **la basse Normandie** Lower Normandy; **les Bas Bretons** the inhabitants of Lower Britanny

2 *(dans hiérarchie)* lower; **les basses classes**

(de la société) the lower classes; *Pol* **la Chambre basse** the Lower House; **la partie basse d'une ville, la basse ville** the lower (part of a) town

3 *(dans le temps)* late; **le b. Moyen Âge** the late Middle Ages; **le B.-Empire** the Late Empire **4** *Péj (acte)* mean, base, low; *(besognes)* menial; **b. motif** base *or* contemptible motive; **terme/style b.** vulgar expression/style; **c'est une basse vengeance** that was a petty revenge; **c'est vraiment b. de sa part** it's really mean of him; **de basse naissance** of low(ly) birth; **de basse condition** from a poor family **5** *(son, note)* low; *(voix)* low, deep; *(dans le réglage de la tonalité)* bass; **parler à voix basse** to speak in a low voice *or* in a whisper *or* under one's breath; **clarinette basse** bass clarinet

ADV **1** *(dans l'espace)* low (down); **être assis trop b.** to be sitting too low (down); **mettre une étagère plus b.** to put a shelf lower (down); **quelques marches plus b.** a few steps lower down *or* farther down; **plus b. dans la rue** farther down the street; **dix lignes plus b.** ten lines (further) down; **les hirondelles volent b.** the swallows are flying low; **voir plus b.** see below; *Fig* **mettre qn plus b. que terre** to treat sb like dirt; *Bourse* **les cours sont tombés très b.** shares are well down; **la température est tombée b. pendant la nuit** the temperature plummeted during the night; **comment a-t-elle pu tomber si b.?** how could she sink so low?; **le malade est bien b.** the patient is very low

2 **chapeau b.!** *(bravo)* bravo!; *Fam* **b. les mains** *ou* **les pattes!** hands off!, keep your paws off!; **b. les pattes!** *(à un chien)* paws (down)!; *Naut* **mettre b. une voile** to haul down a sail; **mettre pavillon b.** *Naut* to lower *or* strike the colours; *Fig Fam* to climb down

3 *(des animaux)* **mettre b.** to give birth, *Spéc* to drop (its young); *(d'une jument)* to foal; *(d'une brebis)* to lamb; *(d'une chèvre)* to kid; *(d'une chienne)* to pup, to whelp; *(d'une truie)* to farrow; **mettre b. avant terme** to cast *or* slip its young

4 *(en intensité)* low; **vous chantez trop b.** *(dans le registre)* you are singing too low; *(doucement)* you are singing too softly; **parler (tout) b.** to (speak in a) whisper; **parlez plus b., je vous prie** please speak more quietly, please lower your voice; **rire tout b.** to chuckle *or* laugh to oneself; **tu pourrais mettre la télévision/le chauffage plus b.?** could you turn down the television/the heating?

5 **en b.** *(à l'étage inférieur)* downstairs; **aller en b.** to go downstairs *or* down; **les gens d'en b.** the people below *or* downstairs; **ça a l'air de venir d'en b.** it seems to come from below *or* from downstairs; **agiter les bras de haut en b.** to move one's arms up and down; **de haut en b.** from top to bottom, downwards; **regarder qn de haut en b.** to look sb up and down, to look at sb from head to foot *or* toe; **il est vêtu de neuf de haut en b.** he's dressed from head to toe in new clothes; **de b. en haut** upwards; **la tête en b.** upside down; **ce vase est plus large en b.** this vase is wider at the bottom; **la jupe tombe mal en b.** the skirt hangs wrong at the bottom; **en** *ou* **au b. de** at the bottom of; *(escalier, page)* at the foot *or* bottom of; **en b. du village** at the lower end of the village

6 **à b. la dictature/la police!** down with dictatorship/the police!; **à b. Martin!** down with Martin!; **mettre** *ou* **jeter à b.** *(maison)* to pull down, to demolish; *(personne, gouvernement)* to bring down, to overthrow; **mettre b. les armes** *Mil* to lay down one's arms; *Fig (dans une dispute)* to give in

NM **1** *(partie inférieure)* foot, bottom; **les gens du b.** the people below *or* downstairs; **l'étagère**

qu'il est parti he left a long time ago or ages ago; **une belle tranche de tarte** a nice slice of tart; **une belle paie** a good salary, good wages; **c'est une belle sole** that's a lovely piece of sole; **belle fortune** large or tidy fortune; **b. poulet** good-sized or sizeable chicken; **un b. kilo** a good kilo

7 (mauvais) **une belle congestion pulmonaire** a bad attack of pneumonia; **belle correction** good thrashing; **b. tapage** terrific din or racket; **il a fait un b. désordre** he made a terrible mess; **un b. gâchis** a fine mess; **son bras est dans un bel état** his arm is in an awful or a terrible state; **j'ai eu une belle peur** I had an awful or a terrible fright; **Arg un b. salaud** a real or right bastard

8 bel et bien well and truly; **il est bel et bien venu** he really did come; **tu l'avais bel et bien dit** you definitely said so; **vous voilà bel et bien grand-père!** so you've actually become a grandfather!

9 tout b.! steady (on)!, gently!

10 de plus belle with a vengeance; **il reprit l'entraînement de plus belle** he resumed training with a vengeance, more enthusiastically than ever; **les discussions/batailles ont recommencé de plus belle** the arguing/fighting has started again with a vengeance, worse than ever

11 je l'ai échappé belle I had a narrow escape or a close shave

12 il ferait b. voir cela that would be a fine thing to see

13 j'ai b. le lui dire, il ne veut rien entendre it's no good my trying or however much I try to tell him, he just won't listen; **j'avais b. chercher, je ne trouvais rien** however hard I looked or no matter how hard I looked or look as I might, I found nothing; **vous avez b. parler ...** you can talk until you're blue in the face ...

NM 1 un vieux b. an old roué; **faire le b.** (d'un chien) to sit up and beg; Can (d'un homme) to strut about; Arch **un b.** a dandy, a beau, a buck

2 (beauté) **le b.** the beautiful, beauty; **l'amour du b.** the love of beauty; **le b., le bien et le vrai** beauty, goodness and truth

3 le b. de l'histoire, c'est que ... the best bit or part of the story is that ...; **mais le plus b., c'est que ...** but the best bit or part is that ...; Fam Iron **c'est du b.!** that's great!

4 Météo **le temps est au b. (fixe)** the weather is set fair; Fig **avoir l'humeur au b. fixe** to be permanently in a good mood

5 (beaux objets) **le b.** beautiful things; **ne vouloir/vendre que du b.** to want/sell only or nothing but the best

NF belle 1 (jolie femme) beauty, belle; (amie, amante) lady friend; **la Belle et la Bête** the Beauty and the Beast; **la Belle au bois dormant** Sleeping Beauty; **allez ma belle, ça suffit** now that's quite enough, my dear

2 Sport decider, deciding game; Cartes rubber game; **jouer** ou **faire la b.** Sport to play the decider or the deciding game; Cartes to play the rubber game

3 Naut (d'un navire) waist; **en b.** abeam

4 Fam **se faire la b.** (de prison) to break out, to escape

5 Fam **il en dit de belles!** he comes out with some good ones!, he really comes out with them!; **j'en ai entendu de belles sur votre compte!** I've heard some nice things about you!; **vous en avez fait une b.!** you've put your foot in it!

▶▶ **un bel âge** a ripe old age; **le b. monde** fashionable society; Iron **pour satisfaire tout ce b. monde** in order to satisfy all these fine people; **beaux quartiers** fashionable or smart districts; **le b. sexe** the fair sex

La Belle Époque

This term refers to the period of apparent stability and prosperity from the closing years of the 19th century to the beginning of the First World War, which found its expression in café and theatre society, fashion, art and architecture. Its chief surviving monument is the area on the south side of the Champs-Élysées containing the "Petit Palais" and the "Grand Palais", erected at the time of the Universal Exhibition of 1900.

BEAUCOUP [boku] ADV VOIR GRAMMAIRE A22–3
(une grande quantité) a lot, a great deal; **il reste encore b. à faire** there's still a lot or a great deal or much to do; **b. de** (nombre) a lot of, (a great) many; (quantité) a lot of, a great deal of, much; **b. de monde** a lot of people; **b. de vin/chance** a lot or a great deal of wine/luck; **avoir b. d'argent** to have plenty of or a lot of money; **ils n'ont pas b. d'argent** they don't have much or a lot of or a great deal of money; **je n'ai pas eu b. d'occasions** ou l'occasion de le faire I haven't had much (of an) opportunity to do it; **avec b. de soin** very carefully; **avoir besoin de b. d'attention/d'eau** to need a lot of attention/water; **j'en veux b., 20!** I want a lot, 20!; **il n'en reste pas b.** (de la tarte etc) there's not much left; (des bonbons etc) there aren't many left; **y a-t-il b. de champignons cette année? – oui, b./non, pas b.** are there many or a lot of mushrooms this year? – yes, there are/no, there aren't; **b. plus/moins de temps/de sel** a lot or much more/less time/salt; **b. plus/moins d'enfants/de livres** a lot or many more/fewer children/books; **elle veut b.** she wants a lot out of life; **c'est déjà b. s'il veut bien** ou qu'il veuille bien vous parler it's (quite) something that he condescended to speak to you; **b. pensent que ...** a lot of or many people think that ...; **il y est pour b.** he has had a great deal to do with it; **b. d'entre nous/d'entre vous** many or a lot of us/you; **de b.** by far; **c'est de b. le meilleur** it's by far or it's far and away the best, it's the best by a long chalk; **il s'en faut de b. que je sois riche** I'm far from being rich; **elle vous aime b.** she is very fond of you, she likes you a lot or a great deal; **il parle b.** he talks a lot or a great deal; **il a b. voyagé/lu** he has travelled/read a lot or a great deal; **elle ne lit pas b.** she doesn't read much or a lot or a great deal; **il parle b. trop** he talks far too much; **je me sens b. mieux** I feel a lot better; **ambitieuse, elle l'est, et b.** she's ambitious, very ambitious; **b. moins/plus vite** a lot or much slower/faster; **il est b. plus âgé que sa femme** he is much or a lot older than his wife; **ça te plaît? – pas b.** do you like it? – not much or not a lot; **j'y tiens b.** it means a lot to me

beauf [bof] Fam NM 1 (beau-frère) brother-in-law 2 Fig Péj narrow-minded middle-class type
ADJ Fig Péj **il est un peu b.** he's a bit of a narrow-minded middle-class type

beau-fils, pl **beaux-fils** NM 1 (gendre) son-in-law 2 (après remariage) stepson

beau-frère, pl **beaux-frères** NM brother-in-law

beaujolais [boʒɔlɛ] NM Beaujolais

beaujolpif [boʒɔlpif] NM Fam Beaujolais

beau-père, pl **beaux-pères** NM 1 (père du conjoint) father-in-law 2 (après remariage) stepfather

beaupré [bopre] NM Naut bowsprit

beauté [bote] NF 1 (de femme, paysage etc) beauty; **apparaître dans toute sa b.** to appear in all one's beauty; **être en b.** to be look-

ing one's best; **une femme/une vue de toute b.** a magnificent woman/view; Fam **finir en b.** to end with a flourish or on a high note; **faire qch pour la b. du geste** to do sth for its own sake; **grain de b.** beauty spot, mole; **institut de b.** beauty parlour; **produits de b.** beauty products, cosmetics; **la b. du diable** youthful beauty; Fam **se (re)faire une b.** to do one's face, to put one's face on 2 (femme) beauty 3 **les beautés artistiques de l'Italie** the art treasures of Italy; **les beautés touristiques** the sights

beaux-arts [bozar] NMPL fine arts; Univ **l'École des b.,** Fam **les B.** the Art School

beaux-parents NMPL parents-in-law, Fam in-laws

bébé [bebe] NM 1 (nourrisson) baby; **avoir/vouloir un b.** to have/want a baby; **attendre un b.** to be expecting (a baby); Fig **c'est un vrai b., il ne sait rien faire seul** he's a real baby or he's just like a child, he can't do anything for himself; **faire le b.** to behave childishly or like a baby; **il/elle est très b.** he/she is very childish or babyish 2 Com (poupée) (baby) doll 3 Zool **b. gazelle/lapin** baby gazelle/rabbit

bébé-éprouvette, pl **bébés-éprouvette** NM test-tube baby

bébelle [bebɛl] NF Can (gadget) gadget; (bibelot) ornament

bébelleux, -euse [bebɛløs, -øz] ADJ Can gadget mad; (bibelots) ornament mad

bébête [bebɛt] Fam ADJ silly; **rire b.** giggle, titter
NF little insect, Br creepy-crawly

bec [bɛk] NM 1 (d'oiseau) beak, bill; (de tortue, pieuvre etc) beak; **au b. long/court/jaune** long-/short-/yellow-billed; **coup de b.** peck; **donner un coup de b. à qn** to peck sb; Fig Fam **avoir un dig at sb; l'oiseau se fait le b.** the bird is sharpening its beak; Fig **se défendre b. et ongles** to fight tooth and nail

2 Fam (bouche) mouth, Br Fam gob; **claquer du b.** to be starving; **fin b.** gourmet; **être** ou **rester le b. dans l'eau** to be left high and dry; **il n'a pas ouvert le b. de la journée** he hasn't said a single word all day, there hasn't been a peep out of him all day; **il n'ouvre pas beaucoup le b., ton copain** your friend hasn't got much to say for himself, not the world's greatest talker, your friend, is he?; **avoir la cigarette/pipe au b.** to have a cigarette/one's pipe in one's mouth; **ferme ton b.!** shut up!, shut your mouth or gob!; **clouer** ou **clore le b. à qn** to shut sb up; **avoir bon b.** to have the gift of the gab; **prise de b.** quarrel, slanging match

3 (d'outil) nose; (de tube) nozzle; (de pot) lip; (de cafetière) spout; (de selle de bicyclette) peak; (de clarinette, flûte etc) mouthpiece; Arg **tomber sur un b.** to come a cropper; Aviat **b. d'attaque** (d'une aile) leading edge; **b. de plume** pen nib

4 Géog (nom de localité) bill; **le B. de Portland** Portland Bill

5 Belg, Can, Suisse Fam (baiser) kiss, peck; **donner un b. à qn** to give sb a kiss or peck; Can **b. pincé** snob

▶▶ **b. Bunsen** Bunsen burner; **b. à gaz** gas jet or burner; **b. de gaz** gas lamp; **b. verseur** lip

bécane [bekan] NF Fam (vélo) bike; (machine, ordinateur) machine

bécarre [bekar] Mus ADJ (signe) natural; **mi b.** E natural
NM natural

bécasse [bekas] NF 1 (oiseau) **b. (des bois)** woodcock; **b. de mer** oystercatcher 2 Fam (idiote) silly woman/girl, silly goose

bécasseau, -eaux [bekaso] NM (échassier)

sandpiper; *(petit de la bécasse)* young woodcock

bécassine [bekasin] NF **1** *(oiseau)* snipe **2** *Fam (fille niaise)* silly naive girl

bec-croisé, *pl* **becs-croisés** NM *(oiseau)* crossbill

bec-de-cane, *pl* **becs-de-cane** NM **1** *(serrure)* catch **2** *(poignée)* (door) handle

bec-de-lièvre, *pl* **becs-de-lièvre** NM *Méd* harelip

becfigue [bɛkfig] NM *(oiseau)* (garden) warbler; *(fauvette)* blackcap; *(jaseur)* waxwing; *(pipi)* pipit

bêchage [bɛʃaʒ] NM *(de la terre)* digging (over), turning over

béchamel [beʃamɛl] ADJ, NF *Culin* **(sauce) b.** béchamel sauce, white sauce

bêche [bɛʃ] NF spade

bêcher [beʃe] VT **1** *(terre)* to dig (over), to turn over; *(plate-bande)* to dig (over) **2** *Fam (personne)* to run down, to pull to pieces ▸ VI *Fam* to put on airs

bêcheur, -euse [beʃœr, -øz] N *Fam* **1** *(critiqueur)* knocker **2** *(snob)* stuck-up person

bécot [beko] NM *Fam* kiss, peck; **gros b.** smacker

bécoter [bekɔte] *Fam* VT to kiss ▸ VPR **se bécoter** to smooch, to kiss (and cuddle)

becquée [beke] NF beakful; *Fam* **encore une b.!** *(à un enfant)* another little mouthful!; **donner la b. à son bébé** to feed one's baby

becquerel [bɛk(ə)rɛl] NM *Nucl* becquerel

becquet [bekɛ] NM **1** *Aut* spoiler **2** *Typ* pasteon

becquetance [bɛktɑ̃s] NF *Arg* grub, *Br* nosh

becqueter [bekte] VT *(je becquette, n. becquetons; je becquetterai) (d'un oiseau)* to peck at; *Arg (d'une personne)* to eat; **il n'y a rien à b.** there's no grub *or Br* nosh; **on a bien becqueté** we had a good feed

bectance [bɛktɑ̃s] NF *Arg* grub, *Br* nosh

becter [bɛkte] VT = **becqueter**

bedaine [bədɛn] NF *Fam* pot(belly), paunch; **avoir de la b.** to be pot-bellied *or* paunchy; **prendre de la b.** to get a paunch

bédane [bedan] NM mortise, (cold) chisel

bédé [bede] NF *Fam* comic strip

bedeau, -eaux [bədo] NM *Rel* verger

bédéphile [bedefil] N *Fam* comic-strip freak

bedon [bədɔ̃] NM *Fam* pot(belly), paunch

bedonnant [bədɔnɑ̃] ADJ *Fam* potbellied, paunchy

bedonner [bədɔne] VI *Fam* to get a paunch

bédouin, -ouine [bedwɛ̃, -win] ADJ Bedouin ▸ N **B.** Bedouin

bée [be] ADJ **bouche b.** gaping, open-mouthed; **rester bouche b. devant qch** to stand gaping *or* open-mouthed in front of sth; **j'en suis resté bouche b.** I was flabbergasted (by it) *or* gobsmacked, it staggered me; **son culot me laisse bouche b.** I am staggered *or* flabbergasted by his cheek; **regarder qch bouche b.** to gape at sth

béer [bee] VI *Litt* **1 b. d'étonnement/d'admiration** to gape in astonishment/admiration **2** *(être grand ouvert)* to be wide open

beffroi [befrwa] NM **1** *(tour)* belfry **2** *(cloche)* **entendre sonner le b.** to hear the bell sound

bégaiement [begɛmɑ̃] NM **1** *(pathologique)* stuttering, stammering **2** *(des petits enfants)* lispings **3** *Fig* **bégaiements** hesitant *or* tentative beginnings

bégayant [begɛjɑ̃] ADJ *(involontairement)* stuttering, stammering; *Fig Litt* hesitant, faltering

bégayer [begeje] *(je bégaye, je bégaie, n. bégayons; je bégayerai, je bégaierai)* VI **1** *(pathologiquement)* to stutter, to stammer **2** *(des petits enfants)* to lisp ▸ VT to stammer (out); **b. une excuse** to stammer out an excuse

bégayeur, -euse [begejœr, -øz] ADJ stuttering, stammering

bégonia [begɔnja] NM *(plante)* begonia

bègue [bɛg] ADJ stuttering, stammering ▸ N stutterer, stammerer

bégueule [begœl] ADJ prudish; **ne sois pas b.** don't be prudish, don't be a prude ▸ NF prude

béguin [begɛ̃] NM **1** *Fam* **avoir le b. pour qn/qch** to have a crush on sb/to have taken a fancy to sth; **voilà son nouveau b.** that's his/her latest crush **2** *(pour un petit enfant)* bonnet; *Rel* hood

béguinage [beginaʒ] NM *Rel* Beguine convent

béguine [begin] NF *Rel* Beguine (nun)

bégum [begɔm] NF begum

behaviorisme [biavjɔrism, biev-] NM *Psy* behaviorism, *Am* behaviorism

behavioriste [biavjɔrist, biev-] *Psy* ADJ behaviourist(ic), *Am* behaviorist(ic) ▸ N behaviourist, *Am* behaviorist, behavioural *or Am* behavioral scientist

BEI [beɔi] NF *(abrév* **Banque européenne d'investissement)** EIB

beige [bɛʒ] ADJ, NM beige

beigne[1] [bɛɲ] NF *Arg* slap, clout; **filer** *ou* **flanquer une b. à qn** to give sb a clout, to clout sb one

beigne[2] NM *Can, Région* doughnut, *Am* donut

beignet [bɛɲɛ] NM fritter; *(au sucre, à la confiture)* doughnut, *Am* donut; **b. de** *ou* **aux pommes** apple fritter; **b. de crevettes** prawn cracker; *(avec de la pâte)* prawn fritter

beïram [biram] NM = **baïram**

béké [beke] N white Creole *(in the French Indies)*

bel[1] [bɛl] NM *Phys* bel

bel[2] ADJ *voir* **beau**

bélandre [belɑ̃dr] NF canal barge

bêlant [belɑ̃] ADJ *aussi Fig* bleating

bel canto [bɛlkɑ̃to] NM *Mus* bel canto

bêlement [bɛlmɑ̃] NM *Zool, Fig* bleating

bélemnite [belɛmnit] NF *(fossile)* belemnite

bêler [bele] VI *Zool, Fig* to bleat; *Fig* **qu'est-ce que vous avez à b. comme ça?** what on earth are you bleating about?

bel-étage, *pl* **beaux-étages** [bɛletaʒ, bozetaʒ] NM *Belg (rez-de-chaussée surélevé)* mezzanine ground floor, *Am* mezzanine first floor

belette [bəlɛt] NF **1** *Zool* weasel **2** *Fam (jeune femme)* Br bird, *Am* chick

Belga [bɛlga] NF *Journ* = Belgian press agency

belge [bɛlʒ] ADJ Belgian; **histoire b.** = joke told at the expense of the Belgians, *Br* ≃ Irish joke, *Am* ≃ Polish joke, *Can* ≃ Newfie joke ▸ N **B.** Belgian

belgicain, -aine [bɛlʒikɛ̃, -ɛn] *Belg Péj* ADJ **être b.** *(partisan de l'unité belge)* to be in favour of a united Belgium; *(attaché aux traditions nationales)* to be attached to conservative (Belgian) tradition ▸ N *(partisan de l'unité belge)* Belgian nationalist *(in favour of national unity)*; *(personne attachée aux traditions nationales)* conservative (Belgian)

belgicisme [bɛlʒisism] NM *(mot)* Belgian-

French word; *(tournure)* Belgian-French expression

Belgique [bɛlʒik] NF Belgium

Belgrade [bɛlgrad] N Belgrade

bélier [belje] NM **1** *(animal)* ram **2** *Mil* battering ram **3** *Constr* **b. (à pilotage)** pile driver, ram(mer); **b. mécanique** bulldozer **4 b. hydraulique** hydraulic ram; **coup de b.** water hammer **5** *Astron, Astrol* **le B.** Aries, the Ram; **être (du signe du) B.** to be (an) Aries

bélière [beljɛr] NF **1** *(d'une cloche)* clapper ring; *(d'une montre etc)* ring **2** *(du bélier qui conduit le troupeau)* (sheep) bell

Belize [beliz] NM Belize

belladone [beladɔn] NF *(plante)* belladonna, deadly nightshade

bellâtre [belɑtr] NM *Péj* smoothie

belle [bɛl] ADJ, NF *voir* **beau**

belle-dame, *pl* **belles-dames** NF **1** *(plante)* deadly nightshade **2** *(papillon)* painted lady

belle-de-jour, *pl* **belles-de-jour** NF *(plante)* convolvulus, bindweed

belle-de-nuit, *pl* **belles-de-nuit** NF **1** *(plante)* marvel of Peru, four o'clock **2** *Fam (prostituée)* lady of the night

belle-doche, *pl* **belles-doches** [bɛldɔʃ] NF *Fam* mother-in-law

belle-famille, *pl* **belles-familles** NF *(de l'époux)* wife's family, *Fam* in-laws; *(de l'épouse)* husband's family, *Fam* in-laws

belle-fille, *pl* **belles-filles** NF **1** *(épouse du fils)* daughter-in-law **2** *(après remariage)* stepdaughter

bellement [bɛlmɑ̃] ADV *Arch* well and truly; **voilà la vérité, tout b.** that's the simple truth

belle-mère, *pl* **belles-mères** NF **1** *(mère du conjoint)* mother-in-law **2** *(après remariage)* stepmother

belle-sœur, *pl* **belles-sœurs** NF sister-in-law

bellicisme [belisism] NM bellicosity, warmongering

belligérance [beliʒerɑ̃s] NF belligerence

belligérant, -ante [beliʒerɑ̃, -ɑ̃t] ADJ belligerent ▸ N belligerent, combatant

belliqueux, -euse [bel(l)ikø, -øz] ADJ *(nation, pays, peuple)* warlike, bellicose; *(personne etc)* aggressive, quarrelsome; *(humeur, tempérament)* aggressive; **tenir des propos b.** to speak aggressively

belote [bəlɔt] NF *Cartes* belote *(card game)*; *Fam* **faire une b.** to have a game of belote

bélouga, **béluga** [beluga] NM **1** *(mammifère)* beluga, white whale **2** *(caviar)* beluga (caviar)

belvédère [bɛlvedɛr] NM **1** *(construction)* belvedere, gazebo **2** *(sur un site naturel)* viewpoint

Belzébuth [bɛlzebyt] N *Bible* Beelzebub

bémol [bemɔl] NM *Mus* flat; **clarinette en si b.** B-flat clarinet; *Fig* **mettre un b. à ses critiques** to tone down one's criticism; *Fig Fam* **mettre un b.** to tone it down

bémoliser [bemɔlize] VT *Mus (note)* to flatten, *Am* to flat

ben [bɛ̃] ADV *Arg* = **bien; b. oui!** well, yes!; **b. voilà, euh …** yeah, well, er …

bénarde [benard] NF pin key lock, double-sided lock

bène [bɛn] NM *Fam* trousers, keks, *Am* pants

bénédicité [benedisite] NM *(avant le repas)* grace; **dire le b.** to say grace

bénédictin, -ine [benediktɛ̃, -in] *Rel* ADJ *(moine, sœur)* Benedictine ▸ N Benedictine; *Fig* **un vrai b.** a painstaking scholar; **un travail de b.** a work of painstaking scholarship ▸ NF **Bénédictine**® *(liqueur)* Benedictine

bénédiction [benediksjɔ̃] NF *Rel* blessing, benediction; *Fig* blessing; *(d'une église, des couleurs)* consecration; **donner la b.** *(d'un prêtre)* to give *or* pronounce the blessing; *Fig* **vous avez ma b.** you have my blessing; **il a donné sa b. au projet** he gave the plan his blessing; **quelle b.!** what a blessing!, what a godsend!; **il a dit oui, c'est une b.!** it's a blessing he said yes!

bénef [benɛf] NM *Arg* profit; **petits bénefs** perks; **faire 50 euros de b.** to make 50 euros profit

bénéfice [benefis] NM **1** *(gain)* profit; **b. brut/net** gross/net profit; **bénéfices non commerciaux** non-trading profits; **réaliser de gros bénéfices** to make large *or* handsome profits; **rapporter des bénéfices** to yield a profit; **faites-vous du b.?** do you make *or* any profit?; **participation aux bénéfices** profit-sharing; **être intéressé aux bénéfices** to share in the profits; **petits bénéfices** perquisites, *Fam* perks; **avec b.** *(investir)* profitably; **vendre qch à b.** to sell sth at a profit
2 *(avantage)* benefit, advantage; **tirer un certain b. de qch** to derive some benefit *or* advantage from sth; **c'est tout à son b. de suivre cette formation** it's wholly to his benefit *or* advantage to do this training; **c'est tout b.** it's all to his/their/*etc* advantage; **quel b. aurais-je à te mentir?** what good would it do me to lie to you?, what advantage *or* benefit would I get from lying to you?; **avoir le b. de l'âge** to have the benefit of age; *Jur* **b. du doute** benefit of the doubt; **on peut lui accorder** *ou* **laisser le b. du doute** we can give him the benefit of the doubt; *Théâtre, Sport* **représentation/match à b.** benefit performance/match; **concert donné au b. de la Croix-Rouge** concert given in aid of the Red Cross; *Can* **concert/repas-b.** fund-raising concert/dinner
3 *Rel* living, benefice
▸▸ **b. par action** earnings per share; **b. brut avant impôt** pre-tax profit; **b. brut d'exploitation** gross operating profit; *Mktg* **b. consommateur** *(d'un produit)* consumer benefit; **b. cumulé** cumulative profit; **b. escompté** desired profit; **bénéfices exceptionnels** windfall profit; **b. d'exploitation** operating profit; **b. imposable** taxable profit; **b. transféré** profit transferred

bénéficiaire [benefisjɛr] ADJ *Com* **solde b.** profit balance; **compte b.** account in credit, account showing a credit balance; **marge b.** profit margin
N *(d'un chèque etc)* recipient, payee; *Rel, Jur etc* beneficiary; **b. conjoint** joint beneficiary

bénéficier [benefisje] VT *(impf, pr sub* n. **bénéficiions**, v. **bénéficiiez)** to benefit *(de* from); **faire b. qn de son expérience** to give sb the benefit of one's experience; **cette carte d'abonnement vous fait b. d'une remise de 20 pour cent** this season ticket entitles you to a 20 per cent reduction; **à qui vont b. ces mesures?** who are these measures going to benefit?, who is going to benefit from these measures?; **cet article bénéficie d'une remise de dix pour cent** this article carries a ten per cent discount, there is a discount of ten per cent on this article; *Jur* **il a bénéficié d'une ordonnance de non-lieu** he was discharged

bénéfique [benefik] ADJ beneficial *(à* to); *Astrol (planète)* beneficent; **ce séjour à la montagne vous sera b.** this stay in the mountains will do you good *or* will be beneficial to you

Benelux [benelyks] NM **le B.** Benelux

benêt [bənɛ] ADJ silly, stupid
NM simpleton

bénévolat [benevɔla] NM voluntary work; **faire du b.** to do voluntary work

bénévole [benevɔl] ADJ **1** *(service, travail, conseiller, infirmière)* voluntary, unpaid; **aide b.** voluntary help; **organisation b.** voluntary organization **2** *Litt (bienveillant) (personne)* benevolent, kindly
N volunteer, voluntary worker

bénévolement [benevɔlmã] ADV **1** *(sans être payé)* voluntarily, without pay, unpaid; **il travaille b.** he does voluntary work **2** *Litt (avec bienveillance)* benevolently, kindly

Bengale [bɛ̃gal] NM **1** Bengal **2** **feu de B.** Bengal light

bengali [bɛ̃gali] ADJ Bengali, Bengalese
NM *Ling* Bengali
N B. Bengali

bénignité [beniɲite] NF **1** *(du climat, d'une maladie)* mildness **2** *Litt (d'une personne)* benignity, kindness

Bénin [benɛ̃] NM Benin

bénin, -igne [benɛ̃, -iɲ] ADJ **1** *(accident)* slight, minor; *(opération)* minor; **tumeur bénigne** benign *or* non-malignant tumour; **forme bénigne de (la) rougeole** mild form of measles **2** *Litt (personne, tempérament, critique etc)* benign, kindly

béninois, -oise [beninwa, -waz] ADJ Beninese
N B. Beninese

béni-oui-oui [beniwiwi] NM INV *Fam* yes-man

bénir [benir] VT *aussi Fig* to bless; *(église, pain etc)* to consecrate; **(que) Dieu vous bénisse!** (may) God bless you!; **le ciel en soit béni!** thank heaven(s)!; **je bénis cette journée où …** I bless the day when …; **b. la mémoire de qn** to glorify sb's memory; **je bénis cette occasion de parler avec elle** I'm thankful *or* grateful for this opportunity of speaking to her

bénit [beni] ADJ consecrated; **pain b.** consecrated bread, holy bread; **eau bénite** holy water

bénitier [benitje] NM **1** *Rel* stoup, stoop, holy-water basin; *(pour le baptême)* font **2** *(mollusque)* giant clam

benjamin, -ine [bɛ̃ʒamɛ̃, -in] N youngest child; **le b. de la famille** the youngest of the family

benjoin [bɛ̃ʒwɛ̃] NM *(gum)* benzoin, benjamin

benne [bɛn] NF *Min etc* tub, truck; *(d'une grue)* scoop; *(d'une dragueuse)* bucket; *(de ski etc)* (cable) car; *(de camion)* tipping *or* dump body; **camion à b. (basculante)** tip(-)per truck, dump(er) truck

Benoist, **Benoît** [bənwa] NM *Fam* **j'te crois, B!** tell me about it!

benoît [bənwa] ADJ ingratiating

benthique [bɛ̃tik] ADJ *(faune etc)* benthic

benthos [bɛ̃tɔs] NM benthos

benzène [bɛ̃zɛn] NM *Chimie* benzene

benzine [bɛ̃zin] NF **1** *(mélange d'hydrocarbures)* benzine **2** *Suisse (essence)* petrol, *Am* gas

benzol [bɛ̃zɔl] NM *Chimie* benzol(e)

benzolisme [bɛ̃zɔlism] NM *Méd* benzole poisoning

béotien, -ienne [beɔsjɛ̃, -jɛn] ADJ *Péj* philistine

BEP [beape] NM *Scol abrév* **brevet d'études professionnelles**

BEPC [beapese] NM *Scol Ancienneté abrév* **brevet d'études du premier cycle**

béquet [bekɛ] NM *Typ* paste-on

béquille [bekij] NF **1** *Méd* crutch; *Fig* prop; **marcher avec des béquilles** to walk on crutches **2** *(d'une moto)* stand; *Aviat* tail skid;

Naut shore, prop; *(du gouvernail)* tiller **3** *(de serrure)* catch; *(poignée)* (door) handle

béquiller [bekije] VT *Naut (bateau)* to shore up, to prop up
VI *Fam Arch* to walk on crutches

berbère [bɛrbɛr] ADJ Berber
NM *Ling* Berber
N B. Berber

bercail [bɛrkaj] NM *(de l'Église etc)* fold; **ramener au b. la brebis égarée** to bring the lost sheep back to the fold; *Fam* **rentrer au b.** to go (back) home; *(d'un mari etc qui a abandonné le foyer)* to return to the fold

berçante [bɛrsɑ̃t] ADJ, NF *Can* **(chaise) b.** rocking chair

berce [bɛrs] NF **1** *(plante)* **b. commune** hogweed **2** *Belg (berceau)* cradle

berceau, -eaux [bɛrso] NM **1** *(de bébé)* cradle; **dès la b.** from the cradle, from birth; *Fig* **le b. d'un mouvement populaire** the birthplace *or* cradle of a popular movement; *Fam* **il les prend au b.** he's a cradle-snatcher **2** *Typ* cradle, bed, support; *Mil (d'un fusil)* cradle; *(treillage)* bower, arbour, *Am* arbor; *Aut, Aviat* **b. (du) moteur** engine cradle; *Archit* **voûte en b.** barrel vault; **b. de verdure** leafy bower

bercelonnette [bɛrsəlɔnɛt] NF rocking cradle

bercement [bɛrsəmɑ̃] NM rocking

bercer [bɛrse] *(je berçai(s), n. berçons)* VT **1** *(bébé, passager)* to rock; **bateau bercé par la houle** boat rocked by the waves **2** *Litt (calmer) (chagrin)* to soothe **3** **b. qn de promesses/de belles paroles** to delude sb with promises/fine words
VPR **se bercer 1 se b. d'illusions** to delude oneself, to give oneself false hopes; **se b. d'un espoir** to indulge in a hope **2** *Can (se balancer)* to rock (back and forth) *(in a rocking chair)*

berceur, -euse [bɛrsœr, -øz] ADJ soothing, lulling
NF **berceuse** *Can (fauteuil)* rocking chair; *(chanson)* lullaby, cradle song; *Mus* berceuse

BERD [bɛrd] NF *(abrév* **Banque européenne pour la reconstruction et le développement)** EBRD

béret [berɛ] NM **b. (basque)** beret

bergamasque [bɛrgamask] NF bergamask

bergamote [bɛrgamɔt] NF bergamot; **thé à la b.** Earl Grey tea, tea with bergamot

berge¹ [bɛrʒ] NF *(de rivière, de voie ferrée, de route)* bank; *(d'une vallée)* slope, side; **voie sur b.** embankment road

berge² NF *Fam* **il a quarante berges** he's forty; **un type de trente-cinq berges** a guy of thirty-five

berger, -ère [bɛrʒe, -ɛr] N shepherd, *f* shepherdess; *Rel* shepherd, pastor; **chien de b.** sheepdog; **l'étoile du b.** the evening star
NM **(chien) b. allemand** German shepherd, *Br* Alsatian
NF **bergère** *(fauteuil)* wing chair

bergerette [bɛrʒərɛt] NF *(oiseau)* wagtail

bergerie [bɛrʒəri] NF **1** *(pour moutons etc)* sheepfold, sheep pen; *Fig* **enfermer le loup dans la b.** to set the fox to mind the geese **2** *Beaux-Arts, Littér (tableau, poème etc)* pastoral

bergeronnette [bɛrʒərɔnɛt] NF *(oiseau)* wagtail

béribéri [beriberi] NM *Méd* beriberi; **avoir le b.** to have beriberi

Béring [beriŋ] N **le détroit de B.** the Bering Strait; **la mer de B.** the Bering Sea

berk [bɛrk] INT yuk!

berkélium [bɛrkeljɔm] NM *Chimie* berkelium

berlander [bɛrlɑ̃de] VI *Can* to dawdle, to waste time

Berlin [bɛrlɛ̃] N Berlin; *Anciennement* B.-Ouest/-Est West/East Berlin

berline [bɛrlin] NF *Min* truck, tub; *Aut* (four-door) saloon, *Am* (four-door) sedan; *Arch* (voiture à cheval) berlin(e); **b. familiale** family saloon; **b. trois/cinq portes** (three-/five-door) hatchback

berlingot [bɛrlɛ̃go] NM **1** (bonbon) boiled sweet, *Am* hard candy; (à la menthe) humbug **2** (de lait) (pyramid-shaped) carton; (de shampoing) sachet; (de liquide ménager) pack

berlinois, -oise [bɛrlinwa, -waz] ADJ of/from Berlin ▶ N B. Berliner

berlue [bɛrly] NF **avoir la b.** to be seeing things; (se faire des illusions) to delude or deceive oneself

berme [bɛrm] NF (ouvrage) berm; (le long d'un canal, d'un fossé etc) (foot)path, verge

bermuda [bɛrmyda] NM Bermuda shorts, Bermudas

Bermudes [bɛrmyd] NFPL **les (îles) B.** Bermuda

bernache [bɛrnaʃ], **bernacle** [bɛrnakl] NF **1** (crustacé) barnacle **2** (oiseau) barnacle goose

bernardin, -ine [bɛrnardɛ̃, -in] N *Rel* Bernardine, Cistercian

bernard-l'(h)ermite [bɛrnarlɛrmit] NM INV (crustacé) hermit crab

Berne [bɛrn] N Bern

berne [bɛrn] NF **1** *Naut* **pavillon en b.** flag at half mast or *Am* half staff **2** *Mil* **drapeau en b.** furled flag

berner [bɛrne] VT **1** (duper) to fool, to hoax; (ridiculiser) to ridicule **2** *Arch* (brimer) to toss in a blanket

bernicle [bɛrnikl], **bernique**[1] [bɛrnik] NF (mollusque) limpet

bernique[2] INT *Fam* nothing doing!

bernois, -oise [bɛrnwa, -waz] ADJ Bernese ▶ N B. Bernese

berrichon, -onne [beriʃɔ̃, -ɔn] ADJ from Berry

Berry [beri] NM **le B.** Berry (region in central France)

bertillonnage [bɛrtijɔnaʒ] NM (en anthropométrie) Bertillon system

béryl [beril] NM *Minér* beryl

béryllium [beriljɔm] NM *Chimie* beryllium

berzingue [bɛrzɛ̃g] NM *Fam* **à tout b.** at full speed, double quick

besace [bəzas] NF *Arch* (de mendiant) bag; (de pèlerin) scrip

bésef [bezef] ADV *Fam* = **bézef**

besicles [bəzikl], **bésicles** [bezikl] NFPL *Fam* specs; *Arch* spectacles

bésigue [bezig] NM *Cartes* bezique

besogne [bəzɔɲ] NF (piece of) work, task, job; **se mettre à la b.** to set to work; **rude b.** hard job; **aller vite en b.** to get things done quickly; *Fam Péj* to rush things; **il est allé vite en b.!** he didn't hang about or mess about!; **abattre de la b.** to get through a lot of work; **voilà de la belle b.!** here's a fine mess!; *Fig* **mâcher la b. à qn** to spoon-feed sb

besogner [bəzɔɲe] VI *Péj* to slave away, to toil away ▸ VT *Vulg* to hump, to screw, *Br* to shaft

besogneux, -euse [bəzɔɲø, -øz] ADJ **1** (travailleur lent) plodding; **faire son travail de façon besogneuse** to plod away (at one's work) **2** *Arch* (dans le besoin) poor ▸ N **1** (travailleur lent) plodder **2** *Arch* (dans le besoin) poor person

besoin [bəzwɛ̃] NM **1** (nécessité) need; **un b. de chaleur humaine** a need for human warmth; **éprouver le b. de faire qch** to feel the need to do sth; **b. d'appartenance** need to belong; **pourvoir** ou **subvenir aux besoins de qn** to provide for sb's needs; **si le b. s'en faisait sentir** if the need or necessity arose; **pour les besoins de la cause** for the sake of the cause; **cet enfant a de grands besoins** this child is very demanding; *Fam* **faire ses besoins** (d'une personne) to relieve oneself; (d'un animal) to do its business; **au b.** if necessary, if need(s) be; **en cas de b.** in an emergency; **avoir b. de qn/qch** to need sb/sth; **j'en ai b. pour lundi** I need it for Monday; **j'ai grand b. de son aide** I'm badly in need of or I really need his help; **avoir b. de faire qch** to need to do sth; **il n'a pas b. de venir lundi** he needn't come or there's no need for him to come on Monday; **cette maison a grand b. d'être nettoyée** this house really needs to be cleaned or is badly in need of a clean; (il n'y a ou je n'ai) **pas b. de dire qu'elle était là** needless to say (that) or it goes without saying (that) she was there; **j'ai b. que tu me laisses tranquille maintenant** I need to be left alone now; **elle a b. qu'on lui parle** she needs someone to talk to; **vous aviez bien b. d'aller lui parler de cela!** you would go and tell him about that!; **tu n'as pas b. de me parler sur ce ton!** there's no need to talk to me in that tone of voice!; *Litt* **il n'est pas b. d'insister** there is no need to insist; **s'il (en) est b., si b. (en) est** if necessary, if need(s) be; *Compta* **b. en fonds de roulement** working capital requirements; **besoins de trésorerie** cash requirements VOIR GRAMMAIRE A40–1 **2** (misère) need, poverty, indigence; **être dans le b.** to be in need; **vieillards dans le b.** needy or impoverished old people, old people in need

bessemer [besmɛr] NM *Tech* (convertisseur) **b.** Bessemer converter

bestiaire [bestjɛr] NM *Litt* bestiary

bestial, -iale, -iaux, -iales [bestjal, -jo] ADJ (personne, colère, air) brutish; **sensualité bestiale** animal sensuality

bestialement [bestjalmɑ̃] ADV brutishly

bestialité [bestjalite] NF brutishness; (perversion) bestiality

bestiaux [bestjo] NMPL livestock; **parqués comme des b.** herded together like cattle

bestiole [bestjɔl] NF (bête) small or tiny animal or creature; (insecte) insect, bug

best of [bestɔf] NM INV greatest hits compilation; **un b. des Rolling Stones** a compilation of the greatest hits of the Rolling Stones

best-seller, *pl* **best-sellers** [bestsɛlœr] NM bestseller

bêta[1] **, -asse** [beta, -as] *Fam* ADJ silly, stupid ▸ N twit, idiot; **oh le gros b.!** (à un enfant) you silly billy!

bêta[2] [beta] NM **1** (lettre de l'alphabet grec) beta **2** *Nucl* **particules/rayons b.** beta particles/rays

bêtabloquant [betablɔkɑ̃] NM *Pharm* beta-blocker

bétail [betaj] NM livestock; **gros b.** livestock (including cattle, horses, asses, mules); **menu** ou **petit b.** smaller livestock; *Fig* **on était traité comme du b.** we were treated like cattle VOIR GRAMMAIRE A11

bétaillère [betajɛr] NF cattle truck

bêta-test, *pl* **bêta-tests** NM *Ordinat* beta test; **bêta-tests** beta testing

bêtatron [betatrɔ̃] NM *Nucl* betatron

bête [bɛt] NF **1** (animal) animal, *Litt* beast; **b. à cornes** horned animal; **b. de trait** draught animal; **les bêtes** (à la ferme) the animals, the livestock; *Fam* **reprendre du poil de la b.** (reprendre le dessus) to perk up, to pick up; **les bêtes féroces** wild animals; **une b. sauvage** a wild animal; **nos amies les bêtes** our animal friends, our four-legged friends; **sale b.** nasty little animal; **elle m'a regardé comme une b. curieuse** she looked at me as if I was from another planet; *Fam* **c'est une b. en maths!** he/she's a genius or a wiz at maths!; **travailler comme une b.** to work all out or flat out; **c'est une bonne b.** he's/she's a good sort; **grosse b.!** you silly(billy)! **2** (insecte) insect, bug; **petites bêtes** insects; (nocives) vermin; *Fig* **chercher la petite b.** to be over-critical, *Fam* to nit-pick; **jouer à la b. qui monte, qui monte** = to play 'round and round the garden like a teddy bear' **3** (idiot) fool, idiot, twit; **faire la b.** to act stupid, to pretend to be stupid; (sans le vouloir) to act stupidly or foolishly ▸ ADJ stupid, silly, foolish; **que je suis b.!** how silly or stupid of me!; **ce que tu peux être b. parfois!** you can be really stupid sometimes!; **pas si b.!** I'm/she's/etc not such a fool (as all that)!; **c'est vraiment b., j'ai oublié mes clés** how stupid, I've forgotten my keys; **c'est trop b., tu aurais dû venir** that's a pity or a shame, you should have come; **c'est b., on a loupé le film!** what a pity or a shame, we've missed the film!; **il n'est pas si b. qu'il en a l'air** he's not as stupid or silly as he looks; **elle est loin d'être b.** she's no fool; *Fam* **elle est b. comme un âne** ou **comme ses pieds** ou **à manger du foin** she's as thick as a brick or *Br* as two short planks; **une histoire/une fille b. à pleurer** a pitifully stupid story/girl, a story/girl that is too stupid for words; **mon Dieu qu'il est b.!** God he's stupid!; **l'âge b.** the difficult age; **b. et méchant** stupid and nasty; **c'est b. comme chou, c'est tout b.** it's as easy as pie or as anything; **ce n'est pas b.** that's not a bad idea, *Br* that's not daft; *Can* **rester tout b.** (décontenancé) to be stupefied; **une mort b.** a stupid or senseless death

▸▸ **b. à bon Dieu** ladybird, *Am* ladybug; *Péj* **b. à concours** swot, *Am* grind; **b. noire:** *Fig* **c'est sa b. noire** (personne) he's/she's his/her bête noire; **les maths, c'est ma b. noire** maths are my pet aversion or hate or my bête noire; **b. de scène** complete performer; **b. de somme** beast of burden

bétel [betɛl] NM (plante) betel

bêtement [bɛtmɑ̃] ADV stupidly, foolishly, idiotically; **mourir b.** to die senselessly; **tout b.** quite simply, purely and simply

Bethléem [betleɛm] N *Bible* Bethlehem

bêtifiant [betifjɑ̃] ADJ idiotic

bêtifier [betifje] (pr sub, impf **n. bêtifiions, v. bêtifiiez**) VT to make stupid ▸ VPR **se bêtifier ils se bêtifient à trop regarder la télévision** too much television is bad for their minds ▸ VI to talk nonsense; (faire l'idiot) to act or play the fool; **quand il parle à un enfant, il bêtifie** he uses baby-talk to children

bêtise [betiz] NF **1** (imbécillité) stupidity, silliness; **être d'une rare b.** to be exceptionally stupid; **elle a eu la b. de dire oui** she was stupid enough to say yes; **tu ne crois pas que c'est de la b. de l'acheter?** don't you think it's a stupid idea or it's stupid to buy it? **2** (action idiote) stupid thing (to do); (parole idiote) stupid remark, stupid thing to say; **dire des bêtises** to talk nonsense or *Br* rubbish; **quelle b.!** what nonsense!, how ridiculous!; **faire des bêtises** to do silly things; **ne faites pas de bêtises, les petits** don't do anything silly, children; **faire une (grosse) b.** to do something (very) stupid or silly; **ça, c'est une grosse b.** that is/was very stupid; **il**

ne faudrait pas qu'elle fasse une b. we don't want her to do anything silly; **se disputer pour des bêtises** to argue over nothing; **perdre son temps à des bêtises** to waste one's time on trifles; **dépenser tout son argent en bêtises** to fritter away one's money; **elle achète énormément de bêtises** she buys lots of rubbish *or Am* trash
 3 *Can* **bêtises** *(injures)* insults
 4 bêtises de Cambrai ≃ mint humbugs, *Am* ≃ hard mint candies

bêtisier [betizje] NM *(sous forme écrite)* collection of howlers; *(émission de télévision)* compendium of out-takes

béton [betɔ̃] NM **1** *Constr* concrete; **b. armé** reinforced concrete; *Fig* **des muscles en b.** rock-hard muscles; *Fam* **un alibi en b.** a cast-iron alibi; **il est b., leur dossier** their dossier is watertight **2** *Ftbl* **faire le b.** to pack the defence **3** *Fam* **laisse b.!** let it drop!, drop it!

bétonnage [betɔnaʒ] NM **1** *Constr* concreting **2** *Ftbl* packing the defence

bétonner [betɔne] VT **1** *Constr* to concrete **2** *Fam (préparer avec soin)* to work hard on; **il a bétonné son discours/son dossier** he's worked really hard on his speech/his application
 VI *Ftbl* to pack the defence

bétonneuse [betɔnøz], **bétonnière** [betɔnjer] NF cement mixer, concrete mixer

bette [bet] NF (spinach) beet; **b. à carde (blanche), b. à côtes** seakale beet, Swiss chard

betterave [betrav] NF **b. (rouge)** beetroot, *Am* beet; **b. sucrière** sugar beet; **b. fourragère** mangel-wurzel

betteravier, -ière [betravje, -jer] ADJ **l'industrie betteravière** the beet industry
 NM sugar beet grower

beuglant [bøglɑ̃] NM *Fam Vieilli (café-concert)* dive, *Am* honky-tonk

beuglante [bøglɑ̃t] NF *Fam (cri)* yell; *(chanson)* song; **pousser une b.** *(crier)* to shout one's head off; *(chanter)* to bawl out a song

beuglement [bøgləmɑ̃] NM *(du bétail)* lowing; *(du taureau)* bellow(ing); *Fam (d'une personne)* bawling, bellowing; *(de la radio etc)* blaring; **pousser des beuglements** to bawl, to bellow

beugler [bøgle] VI *(du bétail)* to low; *(d'un taureau)* to bellow; *Fam (d'une personne)* to bawl, to bellow; *(de la radio etc)* to blare; **pas la peine de b., je t'entends!** no need to yell, I can hear you!; **les voisins font b. leur télévision** the neighbours have got their television blaring away
 VT *Fam* **b. une chanson** to bawl out *or* bellow out a song

beur [bœr] NM = young man born in France, of North African immigrant parents
 ADJ INV *(culture, mode, musique)* = of North Africans born in France, of immigrant parents

beurette [bœret] NF = young woman born in France, of North African immigrant parents

beurre [bœr] NM butter; **b. salé/demi-sel** salted/slightly salted butter; **b. fondu** melted butter; **une motte de b.** a lump of butter; *Culin* **au b.** *(pâtisserie)* made with butter; *(légumes)* with melted butter; **faire la cuisine au b.** to cook with butter; **crème au b.** butter cream; **au b. noir** with black butter; **avoir un œil au b. noir** to have a black eye; **c'est entré comme dans du b.** it went in very easily; *Fam* **cela compte pour du b.** that doesn't count; *Fam* **il a fait son b.** he's made a packet; **ça mettra du b. dans les épinards** that will improve matters *or* ease the situation; **elle veut le b. et l'argent du b.** she wants to have her cake and eat it

▸▸ **b. d'anchois** anchovy butter; **b. de cacahouètes** peanut butter; **b. de cacao** cocoa butter

beurrée [bœre] NF *Can (tartine)* slice of bread and butter

beurre-frais ADJ INV buttercup-yellow

beurrer [bœre] VT *(pain, plat etc)* to butter; *Arg* **être complètement beurré** to be plastered *or* smashed
 VPR **se beurrer** *Arg* to get plastered *or* smashed

beurrerie [bœrri] NF **1** *(laiterie)* dairy **2** *(industrie)* butter industry

beurrier, -ière [bœrje, -jer] ADJ **l'industrie beurrière** the butter industry; **région beurrière** butter-producing region
 NM butter dish

beuverie [bøvri] NF binge, drinking session, *Br Fam* booze-up

bévatron [bevatrɔ̃] NM *Nucl* bevatron

bévue [bevy] NF blunder, mistake, slip; **commettre une b.** to blunder, to make a blunder

bey [bɛ] NM bey

Beyrouth [berut] N Beirut

bézef [bezɛf] ADV *Fam* **il n'y en a pas b.** *(non comptable)* there's not much *or* a lot (of it); *(comptable)* there aren't many *or* a lot (of them)

BF [beɛf] NF *(abrév* **Banque de France***)* Bank of France

BFCE [beɛfseə] NF *(abrév* **Banque française du commerce extérieur***)* French foreign trade bank

Bhoutan [butɑ̃] NM Bhutan

bi [bi] NM *Can* **donner** *ou* **faire un bi** to lend a hand

bi- [bi-] PRÉF bi-; **bilatéral/bipartisan/etc** bilateral/bipartisan/etc

biacide [biasid] ADJ, NM *Chimie* diacid

biais [bjɛ] ADJ *Archit* oblique, slanting; **voûte biaise** skew(ed) arch
 NM **1** *(d'un outil, d'une arche)* skew; *(d'un mur)* slant; **en b.** at an angle, slantwise; *Couture* **tailler un tissu dans le b.** to cut material on the bias **2** *(moyen)* way; *(détour)* expedient; **par le b. de son voisin** through his neighbour; **aborder** *ou* **prendre de b. une personne/une question** to approach a person/a question indirectly *or* in a roundabout way; **regarder qn de b.** to look sideways *or* askance at sb **3** *(aspect)* angle; **par quel b. envisager la chose?** from what angle should we look at the issue? **4** *Couture* bias binding

biaiser [bjeze] VI **1** *(obliquer)* to be on the slant; *(vers qch)* to veer off **2** *Fig* to dodge the issue; **pour éviter cela, il va falloir b.** we'll have to manoeuvre to avoid that
 VT **l'échantillon a été biaisé** the sample has been distorted

biathlon [biatlɔ̃] NM *Sport* biathlon

bibande [bibɑ̃d] *Tél* ADJ dual-band
 NM *(téléphone portable)* dual-band mobile phone *or Am* cellphone

bibasique [bibazik] ADJ *Chimie* dibasic

bibelot [biblo] NM curio, knick-knack; **bibelots sans valeur** trinkets

biberon [bibrɔ̃] NM (baby's *or* feeding) bottle; **nourrir** *ou* **élever un enfant au b.** to bottle-feed a child; **il est encore au b.?** is he still being bottle-fed?; **il prend trois biberons par jour** he has three feeds a day; **l'heure du b.** feeding time

biberonner [bibrɔne] VI *Fam* to booze, to tipple

bibi [bibi] NM **1** *Arg (moi)* yours truly; **et ça, c'est pour b.** that's for yours truly **2** *Fam (chapeau)* (woman's) hat

bibine [bibin] NF *Fam (boisson)* dishwater; **c'est de la b., cette bière** this beer is (like) dishwater

bibite [bibit] NF *Can Arg* bug, insect

bible [bibl] NF bible; **la B.** the Bible; **la b. du bricoleur** the DIY bible; *Ordinat* **b. de paragraphes** library of standard paragraphs

bibliobus [biblijɔbys] NM mobile library, *Am* bookmobile

bibliographe [biblijɔgraf] N bibliographer

bibliographie [biblijɔgrafi] NF bibliography

bibliographique [biblijɔgrafik] ADJ bibliographical

bibliomane [biblijɔman] N book lover, *Fml* bibliomaniac

bibliomanie [biblijɔmani] NF love of books, *Fml* bibliomania

bibliophile [biblijɔfil] N bibliophile, book lover

bibliophilie [biblijɔfili] NF love of books, *Fml* bibliophily

bibliothécaire [biblijɔtekɛr] N librarian

bibliothéconomie [biblijɔtekɔnɔmi] NF library science

bibliothèque [biblijɔtɛk] NF **1** *(bâtiment, salle)* library; **b. de prêt** lending library; **b. municipale** municipal *or* public library; **b. universitaire** university library; **B. nationale** the former national library in Paris *(now part of the Bibliothèque nationale de France)*; **B. nationale de France** = the French national library in Paris **2** *(meuble)* bookcase **3** *(série)* series; *Ordinat* **la b. verte/rose** = series of books aimed at 7- to 15-year-olds/at 5- to 7-year-olds; *Fam* **c'est une b. ambulante** *ou* **vivante** he's a walking encyclopaedia; *Ordinat* **b. de programmes** program library

biblique [biblik] ADJ biblical

Bi-bop® [bibɔp] NM *Tél* = mobile telephone system run by France Télécom

Bic® [bik] NM **pointe B.** ballpoint pen, *Fam* Biro®

bic® ADJ **stylo b., pointe b.** ballpoint pen, *Br* Biro®
 NM ballpoint, *Br* Biro®

bicaméral, -ale, -aux, -ales [bikameral, -o] ADJ *Pol (système etc)* bicameral

bicaméralisme [bikameralism], **bicamérisme** [bikamerism] NM *Pol* bicameral system

bicarbonate [bikarbɔnat] NM *Chimie* bicarbonate; **b. de soude** bicarbonate of soda, sodium bicarbonate

bicentenaire [bisɑ̃tnɛr] NM bicentenary, *Am* bicentennial

bicéphale [bisefal] ADJ *(animal)* two-headed, *Spéc* bicephalous

biceps [bisɛps] *Anat* ADJ *(muscle)* biceps
 NM biceps; *Fam* **avoir des b.** to have muscles

biche [biʃ] NF **1** *(mammifère)* hind, doe; **ventre de b.** *(couleur)* reddish-white; **table à pieds de b.** table with cabriole legs; **aux yeux de b.** doe-eyed **2** *Fam* **ma b.** my darling, my dear

bicher [biʃe] VI *Fam* **1** *(aller bien)* **ça biche?** how's things? **2** *(se réjouir)* to be tickled pink, *Br* to be as pleased as Punch

bichette [biʃet] NF **1** *(mammifère)* young *or* small hind **2** *Fam* **ma b.** my darling, my dear

bichlorure [biklɔryr] NM *Chimie* bichloride, dichloride

bichon, -onne [biʃɔ̃, ɔn] N **1** *(chien)* lapdog, toy dog **2** *Fam* **mon b.** my darling, my love, my dear

bichonner [biʃɔne] VT **1** *(préparer) (personne)* to make spruce *or* smart **2** *(soigner) (personne)* to pamper, to mollycoddle
 VPR **se bichonner** to spruce oneself up

bichromate [bikrɔmat] NM *Chimie* bichromate, dichromate

bichromie [bikrɔmi] NF *Typ* two-colour *or Am* two-color *or* two-tone printing

biclic [biklik] NM *Ordinat* double click

bicliquer [biklike] VI *Ordinat* to double-click

biclo [biklo], **biclou** [biklu] NM *Fam* bike

bicolore [bikɔlɔr] ADJ two-colour(ed) *or Am* -color(ed), two-tone

biconcave [bikɔ̃kav] ADJ biconcave

biconvexe [bikɔ̃vɛks] ADJ biconvex

bicoque [bikɔk] NF *(maison)* shack

bicorne [bikɔrn] ADJ *Biol, Anat* two-horned; *Spéc* bicorn(u)ate
NM cocked hat

bicot [biko] NM 1 *(biquet)* kid 2 *Fam (terme injurieux) (Arabe)* Arab; *Br* ≃ wog

bicross [bikrɔs] NM *Sport* cyclo-cross bicycle; **faire du b.** to cyclo-cross, to go cyclo-crossing

biculturalisme [bikyltyralism] NM biculturalism

biculturel, -elle [bikyltyrɛl] ADJ bicultural

bicyclette [bisiklɛt] NF bicycle; **aller en ville à** *ou Fam* **en b.** to cycle to town, to go to town by bicycle; **faire de la b. tous les week-ends** to go cycling *or* to cycle every weekend; **il ne sait pas faire de la b.** he can't ride a bicycle

bidasse [bidas] NM *Mil Arg* squaddie, *Am* GI

bide [bid] NM *Arg* 1 *(ventre)* belly; **avoir/prendre du b.** to have/develop a belly; *Fig* **c'est du b.** it's a load of baloney *or Br* codswallop 2 **la pièce/le film a fait un b.** the play/film flopped *or* bombed; **un b. complet** a total flop

bidet [bidε] NM 1 *(de toilette)* bidet 2 *Vieilli Fam (cheval)* nag

bidimensionnel, -elle [bidimɑ̃sjɔnɛl] ADJ bidimensional

bidirectionnel, -elle [bidirɛksjɔnɛl] ADJ bidirectional; *Tél* **b. simultané** full duplex

bidoche [bidɔʃ] NF *Arg* meat

bidon [bidɔ̃] NM 1 *(d'huile, d'essence)* can; *Mil etc (gourde)* water bottle; **b. d'essence** petrol can, jerry can; **b. à lait** milk churn 2 *très Fam (ventre)* belly; **se remplir le b.** to stuff oneself; **c'est du b.** it's a load of baloney *or Br* codswallop; **c'est pas du b.** it's the honest truth
ADJ *Fam* phoney, fake; *(élections)* rigged
NMPL *Belg Fam* **bidons** *(frusques)* togs, gear, threads; *(affaires)* things, stuff

bidonnant [bidɔnɑ̃] ADJ *Arg* hilarious, screamingly funny; **c'est b.** it's a scream

bidonner [bidɔne] VI *Fam* to create false news
VT *Fam (truquer)* to fake
VPR **se bidonner** *Fam* to laugh one's head off, to split one's sides (laughing)

bidonville [bidɔ̃vil] NM shantytown

bidouillage [biduja3] NM *Fam* 1 *(bricolage)* **c'est du b.** it's just been thrown together 2 *Ordinat* patching

bidouiller [biduje] VT *Fam* to patch up; *Ordinat (programme)* to patch

bidouilleur, -euse [bidujœr, -øz] N *Ordinat* hacker, expert user

bidule [bidyl] NM *Arg* thingy, thingummy, whatsit; **j'ai vu B.** I saw whats-his-name, *f* whats-her-name

bief [bjεf] NM 1 *(portion du cours d'eau)* reach 2 *(d'un moulin)* millcourse, millrace

bielle [bjεl] NF *Aut* connecting rod, conrod; *Tech (sous tension)* (tie) rod; *(sous compression)* push rod, crank arm; *Aut* **b. d'accouplement** track link; **tête de b.** crank head; *(de*

moteur) big end; **pied de b.** crosshead; *(de moteur)* little end; *Aut* **b. de connexion** track rod; *Aut* **b. pendante** drop arm, drag link bar

biellette [bjεlεt] NF *Tech (petite bielle)* small rod; *Aut* **b. de direction** drag link, track rod

biélorusse [bjelorys] ADJ B(y)elorussian
N **B.** B(y)elorussian

Biélorussie [bjelorysi] NF B(y)elorussia

BIEN [bjɛ̃]

ADV well 1, 3, 11 ▪ right 2, 3 ▪ really 3 ▪ very 4 ▪ a lot 5 ▪ although *(bien que)* ▪ 8 ▪ otherwise *(ou bien)* ▪ 10	
INT well	
ADJ INV good 1, 4 ▪ comfortable 2 ▪ well 3 ▪ good-looking 4	
NM good 1 ▪ possession 2 ▪ property 2	

ADV 1 *(convenablement)* well; **livre b. écrit** well-written book; **c'est du travail b. fait** it's a fine *or* well-executed piece of work; **j'aime le travail b. fait** I like work that's done well; **il parle b.** he is a good speaker, he speaks well; **on y mange très b.** the food there is very good, you eat very well there; **cette couleur/ce rôle lui va b.** this colour/this role suits him well; **ça te va b. de critiquer le travail des autres sans rien faire** you're a fine one to criticize the work of others without doing anything yourself; **aller** *ou* **se porter b.** to be well *or* in good health; **tout va b.** all's well, everything's OK *or* fine; **s'y prendre b.** to go about it the right way; *Iron* **voilà qui commence b.!** that's a good *or* fine start!; **vous arrivez b.** you've come just at the right moment; **b.!** good!; *(ça suffit)* that's enough!, that will do!; *(entendu)* all right!; **très b.!, fort b.!** very good!, well done!; *(signalant son accord avec le locuteur)* hear, hear!; **écoutez b. ceci** now listen carefully to this; **il faut b. les soigner** they must be well looked after

2 *(moralement)* **vous avez b. fait** you did the right thing, you did right; **se conduire** *ou* **se tenir b.** to behave (well); **veux-tu te conduire b.!** will you behave!; **c'est b. fait (pour lui)** it serves him right; **voilà qui est b. dit!** well said!; **tu fais b. de me le dire** it's a good thing *or* job you've told me, you've done well to tell me; **tu ferais b. de te méfier** you would do well to beware

3 *(emphatique)* **est-ce b. raisonnable?** is that really reasonable?; **c'est b. cela** that's right; **il y a b. deux ans que je ne l'ai vue** it's at least *or* it must be two years since I (last) saw her; **j'ai b. dû lire dix de ses livres** I must have read at least ten of his books; **je l'ai regardé b. en face** I looked him full *or* right in the face; **j'irais b. avec vous, mais …** I'd love to go with you, but …; **j'y suis b. obligé** I just *or* really have to; **conduis b. à droite** drive well over on the right; **b. au milieu** right *or Fam* bang in the middle; **être b. d'accord** to be entirely *or* completely in agreement, to be in complete agreement; **c'est b. d'accord/compris?** is that agreed/understood?; **b. à vous** *(dans une lettre)* yours; **je veux b. le croire** I can quite believe it; **je sais b.** I know full well, I'm well aware of it; **qu'est-ce que ça peut b. être/vouloir dire?** whatever can it be/mean?, what on earth can it be/mean?; **je me demande b. ce qu'il pouvait en penser** I really wonder what he might think of it; **c'est b. lui** it *is* him; **ce sont b. mes lunettes** those *are* my glasses; **c'est b. une erreur** that's definitely a mistake; **c'est b. de lui** it's just like him, that's typical of him; *Fam* **c'est b. à moi, ça?** that's really mine?; **est-ce b. le train pour Paris?** is this the right train for Paris?, is this train OK for Paris?; **c'est b. Apollinaire qui a écrit ces poèmes?** am I right in thinking Apollinaire wrote these poems?, Apollinaire did write

these poems, didn't he?; **je l'avais b. dit!** didn't I say so?; **on vous avait b. dit que tous les magasins seraient fermés** you were told all the shops would be shut; **voulez-vous b. vous taire!** *do* shut up!, will you *please* be quiet!; **il est b. entendu que …** it is understood, of course, that …; **b. entendu, b. sûr, b. évidemment** of course; **je m'en doutais b.** I thought as much; **c'est b. ce que je pensais** that's just what I thought; **il faut b. qu'on mange quelque chose** we really must eat something; **il est b. venu, mais j'étais occupé** he did come, but I was busy; **je ne veux pas que tu fasses cela – mais vous le faites b., vous!** I don't want you to do that – but *you* do it, don't you?; *Iron* **c'est b. le moment de parler comme ça!** a fine time *or* what a time to talk like that!; **c'est b. ma chance!** (it's) just my luck!; **c'était b. la peine** it wasn't worth the trouble; **voilà b. les hommes!** just like men!, that's men all over!

4 *(très)* very; **b. malheureux** very unhappy; **vous venez b. tard** you're very late; **b. souvent** quite often; **c'est b. loin de Paris** it's a long way (away) from Paris; **b. loin de moi l'idée de vous accuser** far be it from me to accuse you; **c'est b. gentil, mais …** that's very kind, but …; **c'est b. simple** it's quite *or* very simple; **je voudrais que ce soit b. clair entre nous** I want us to be quite clear on this

5 *(beaucoup) (souffrir, réfléchir, changer etc)* a lot, a great deal; **b. plus** much *or* a lot more; **b. moins** much *or* a lot less; **tu t'es b. amusé?** did you have a good time?, did you enjoy yourself?; **b. de …** a lot of …, a great deal of …; **b. des …** a lot of …, a good many …; **j'ai eu b. de la peine** *ou* **du mal à la convaincre** I had a lot of *or* a great deal of trouble convincing her; **j'ai reçu b. des lettres** I received a lot of *or* a good many letters; **nous avons eu b. des inquiétudes à son sujet** he caused us a lot of *or* a great deal of worry; **je l'ai vu b. des fois** I have seen him many times; **b. d'autres** many others, lots more

6 **aussi b.** just as well, just as easily; **on fera aussi b. d'y aller par nous-mêmes** we can just as well *or* just as easily go there by ourselves

7 **tant b. que mal** somehow (or other), after a fashion; **je m'en suis acquitté tant b. que mal** I got through

8 **b. que** + *sub* although, though; **je le respecte, b. qu'il ne me soit pas sympathique** I respect him (even) though I don't like him
SEE GRAMMAR B33

9 **si b. que** + *ind* and so; **il ne reparut plus, si b. qu'on le crut mort** he failed to come back, and so he was thought dead

10 **ou b.** or else, otherwise; **il faut le lui dire ou b. il l'apprendra par quelqu'un d'autre** we'll have to tell him or else *or* otherwise he'll hear about it from someone else; **viens à la maison, ou b. on se retrouve dans un café** come to my place, or (else) we could meet in a café; **ou b. … ou b. …** either … or …

INT eh b.! well!; **eh b. donc!** well then!; **eh b. ça alors!** well, fancy that!

ADJ INV 1 *(satisfaisant)* good; *Scol (sur un devoir)* good; **c'est b.!** good!; **ce serait b. si …** it would be good if …; **comme c'est b. à vous d'être venu!** how good of you to come!; **ce n'est pas b. de vous moquer de lui** it's not nice *or* kind of you to make fun of him; **des gens b.** nice *or* decent people; **il est très b., le nouvel assistant** the new assistant is very good; **il est très b., ce petit gars** he's a nice fellow; **il me faut quelque chose de b.** I'm looking for something good

2 *(à l'aise)* **êtes-vous b. dans ce fauteuil/ces chaussures?** are you comfortable in that armchair/those shoes?; **qu'est-ce qu'on serait b., dans une maison comme la tienne!** I'd really feel at home in a house like yours!;

se sentir b. dans un pays to like it *or* to feel at home in a country; **je suis b. partout** I'm at home anywhere; **ne t'occupe pas de moi, je suis b. comme ça** don't worry about me, I'm fine *or* all right as I am; **nous voilà b.!** we're in a right mess!; **être b. avec qn** to be on good terms with sb, to be well in with sb; **se mettre b. avec qn** to get into sb's good books, to get well in with sb
3 *(en forme)* well; **je ne me sens pas très b.** I don't feel very well; **vous vous sentez b. maintenant?** do you feel better now?; **il est moins b.** he's not as well (as he was)
4 *(beau) (personne)* good-looking, attractive; **il est b. de sa personne** he's a fine figure of a man; **tu es très b. dans cette robe** you look very good in that dress, that dress suits you very well; **elle est b. sur cette photo** she looks good in this photo
NM 1 *Phil, Rel etc* good; **le b. et le mal** good and evil, right and wrong; **faire le b.** to do good; **homme de b.** good *or* upright man; **le b. public** the public good; **c'est pour votre b.** it's for your own good; **cela m'a fait beaucoup de b.** it did me a lot of good; **ça pourrait peut-être faire du b. à mes rhumatismes** that could perhaps do my rheumatism some good; **faire le plus grand b. à qn** to do sb a great deal of good; **grand b. vous fasse!** much good may it do you!; **vouloir du b. à qn, vouloir le b. de qn** to wish sb well; **je ne veux que votre b.** I only want the best for you; **un ami qui vous veut du b.** a well-wisher; **tout le monde dit du b.** *ou* **parle en b. de lui** everyone speaks well of him; **on m'a dit beaucoup de b. de vous/de ce produit** I've heard a lot of good things about you/about this product; **je trouve qu'il a changé en b.** I think he's changed for the better; **mener une affaire à b.** to bring a matter to a satisfactory conclusion
2 *(chose matérielle)* possession, property; *Jur* assets; *(argent)* wealth, fortune; **biens** possessions, property; **il a du b. (au soleil)** he's a man of property, he has property; **c'est mon b. le plus cher** it's my dearest possession; **biens et services** goods and services
3 *Fam* **en tout b. (et) tout honneur** with the best of intentions
▶▶ **biens capitaux** capital goods *or* items; **b. collectif** collective good; **b. commun** common good; **biens consommables** consumables; **biens de consommation** consumer goods *or* products; **biens de consommation durables** consumer durables; **biens de consommation finale** final consumer goods; **biens de consommation intermédiaire** intermediate consumer goods; **biens de consommation non durables** disposable goods, non-durable consumer goods; **biens corporels** tangible assets; **biens dotaux** dowry; **biens durables** (consumer) durables; **biens d'équipement** capital equipment *or* goods; **biens fonciers** landed property; **biens immeubles** *or* **immobiliers** real estate *or* property; **b. industriel** industrial good; **biens intermédiaires** semi-finished goods; **biens meubles** *ou* **mobiliers** personal property *or* estate; **biens de première nécessité** staples; **biens de production** capital goods; *Compta* **biens sociaux** corporate assets *or* funds; **biens successoraux** hereditaments; **biens tangibles** physical goods; **biens vacants** ownerless property

bien-aimé, -ée, *pl* **bien-aimés, -ées** [bjɛ̃neme] **ADJ** beloved; **mon ami b.** my very dear friend
N beloved; *Hist* **(Louis) le Bien-Aimé** Louis XV

bien-être [bjɛ̃nɛtr] **NM INV 1** well-being; *(d'une population etc)* welfare; **sentiment de b.** feeling of well-being; **b. du consommateur** consumer welfare **2** *Can* **b. social** *Br* social security, *Am* welfare

bienfaisance [bjɛ̃fəzɑ̃s] **NF** *(générosité)* benevolence; *(charité)* charity; **bureau de b.** welfare office; **organisation** *ou* **œuvre de b.** charitable organization, charity

bienfaisant [bjɛ̃fəzɑ̃] **ADJ 1** *(personne)* charitable, kindly **2** *(remède etc)* beneficial, salutary; *(vent, pluie)* refreshing

bienfait [bjɛ̃fɛ] **NM 1** *(avantage)* benefit; **les bienfaits de la technique/du traitement** the benefits of technology/of the treatment **2** **un b. du ciel** a godsend; *Prov* **un b. n'est jamais perdu** a good deed will have its reward

bienfaiteur, -trice [bjɛ̃fɛtœr, -tris] **N** benefactor, *f* benefactress; **b. du peuple** people's friend

bien-fondé, *pl* **bien-fondés NM** *(d'une opinion, d'un argument, d'une revendication)* validity, merits; *Jur* cogency

bien-fonds, *pl* **biens-fonds NM** real estate, landed property

bienheureux, -euse [bjɛ̃nørø, -øz] **ADJ 1** *(heureux)* blissful, happy **2** *Rel* blessed
N *Rel* blessed person; **dormir comme un b.** to sleep the sleep of the just; **les b.** the blessed, the blest

bien-jugé NM INV *Jur* just and lawful decision

biennal, -ale, -aux, -ales [bjenal, -o] **ADJ** biennial, two-yearly; **contrat b.** two-year contract; **fonction biennale** two-year post; **exposition biennale** biennial exhibition
NF biennale biennial

bien-pensant, -ante, *pl* **bien-pensants, -antes ADJ** *(personne)* right-thinking, right-minded, *Péj* self-righteous
N *Péj* self-righteous person, prig

bienséance [bjɛ̃seɑ̃s] **NF** propriety, decorum; **respecter les bienséances** to observe the proprieties

bienséant [bjɛ̃seɑ̃] **ADJ** decorous, proper; **il est b. aux jeunes gens de respecter la vieillesse** it is right and proper for young people to respect old age; **il n'est pas b. de manger avec ses doigts** it is not proper *or* it is not the done thing to eat with your fingers

bientôt [bjɛ̃to] **ADV** soon, before long; **on est b. arrivé?** are we nearly there?, will we soon be there?; **il est b. deux heures** it'll soon be two o'clock; **tu vas b. arrêter de répéter la même chose?** will you please stop repeating the same thing?; **à b.!** see you soon!, goodbye for now!; **on s'est dit à b.** we said we'd see each other soon; **on se dit adieu ou on se dit à b.?** is it goodbye or just au revoir?; **les beaux jours seront b. là** the fine days will soon be here; **c'est pour b., ce bébé?** is the baby due soon?; *Vieilli* **c'est b. dit!** that's easier said than done! VOIR GRAMMAIRE A21

bienveillance [bjɛ̃vɛjɑ̃s] **NF** benevolence, kindness (**envers, pour** to); **avec b.** kindly

bienveillant [bjɛ̃vɛjɑ̃] **ADJ** kind, kindly, benevolent (**envers, pour** to); **examinateur b.** lenient examiner

bienvenu, -ue [bjɛ̃vny] **ADJ** *(remarque)* opportune, apposite; *(repas, explication etc)* welcome
N soyez le b./la bienvenue! welcome!; **vous êtes toujours le b.** you're always welcome; **votre proposition est la bienvenue** your suggestion is welcome

bienvenue [bjɛ̃vny] **NF** welcome; **souhaiter la b. à qn** to welcome sb; **b. à nos amis de Russie!** welcome to our Russian friends!; **b. à Nice!** welcome to Nice!; **allocution de b.** welcoming speech
INT Can de rien) you're welcome!

bière¹ [bjɛr] **NF** *(boisson)* beer; **b. blonde** lager; **b. brune** brown ale, *Am* dark beer; **b. pression** draught *or* *Am* draft beer; *Fig* **ce n'est pas de la petite b.** it's no small matter; **c'est de la petite b.** it's small beer

bière² **NF** *(cercueil)* coffin, *Am* casket; **assister à la mise en b.** to be present when the body is placed in the coffin

biffe [bif] **NF** *Mil Arg* infantry

biffer [bife] **VT** *(mot etc)* to cross out, to strike out, to put a line through; **tu peux b. ce nom de ta liste** you can cross or strike this name off your list

biffeton [biftɔ̃] **NM** = **bifton**

biffin [bifɛ̃] **NM 1** *Arg (chiffonnier)* ragman, *Br* rag-and-bone man **2** *Mil Fam* infantryman

biffure [bifyr] **NF** crossing out, striking out

bifide [bifid] **ADJ** bifid

bifidus [bifidys] **NM** *Biol* live culture

bifocal, -ale, -aux, -ales [bifɔkal, -o] **ADJ** *(lentille etc)* bifocal; **lunettes bifocales** bifocals

bifteck [biftɛk] **NM** (beef)steak; **b. de cheval** horse(meat) steak; *Fam* **gagner son b.** to earn a living

bifton [biftɔ̃] **NM** *Fam (billet de banque)* note, *Am* greenback; *(de transport, de spectacle)* ticket

bifurcation [bifyrkasjɔ̃] **NF** *(d'une route)* junction, fork; *(d'un tronc d'arbre etc)* fork; *(professionnelle)* change of direction; **tournez à droite à la b.** take the right fork

bifurquer [bifyrke] **VI** *(d'une route, d'un chemin)* to fork, to divide, to branch off; **nous avons bifurqué vers** *ou* **sur la ville** we turned *or* forked off towards the town; **bifurquez à droite** take the right fork; **b. vers la politique/dans la recherche** to branch out into politics/research

bigame [bigam] **ADJ** bigamous
N bigamist

bigamie [bigami] **NF** bigamy

bigarade [bigarad] **NF** *(fruit)* bitter *or* Seville orange

bigarré [bigare] **ADJ** *(tissu, chemise etc)* multicoloured, *Am* multicolored; *(groupe, société etc)* mixed; *(foule)* motley, mixed

bigarreau, -eaux [bigaro] **NM** *(cerise)* bigarreau

bigarrer [bigare] **VT** to colour *or* *Am* to color in many shades

bigarrure [bigaryr] **NF** mixture *or* medley of colours *or* *Am* colors; *(d'un groupe, style etc)* variety, motley nature; **les bigarrures du costume d'Arlequin** Harlequin's multicoloured *or* *Am* multicolored costume; **une b. de gens** a motley collection of people

big band [bigbɑ̃d] **NM** *Mus* big band

big(-)bang [bigbɑ̃g] **NM** *Astron* big bang

bigle [bigl] *Vieilli, Hum* **ADJ** cross-eyed
N cross-eyed person

bigler [bigle] *Fam* **VI** *(loucher)* to squint, to have a squint; **b. sur qch** to squint at sth
VT *(quelque chose)* to squint at; *(fille)* to eye (up)

bigleux, -euse [biglø, -øz] *Fam* **ADJ** *(personne) (qui louche)* cross-eyed; *(myope)* short-sighted; **t'es b.?** are you blind?
N *(qui louche)* cross-eyed person; *(qui myope)* short-sighted person

bigophone [bigɔfɔn] **NM** *Fam (téléphone)* phone, *Br* blower; **passer un coup de b. à qn** to give sb a buzz *or* *Br* a ring

bigophoner [bigɔfɔne] **VI** *Fam* to make a phone call; **b. à qn** to give sb a buzz *or* *Br* a bell

bigorneau, -eaux [bigɔrno] **NM** *(mollusque)* winkle

bigorner [bigɔrne] **VT** *Métal* to work on an anvil; *Arg (abîmer)* to smash up
VPR se bigorner *Arg* to have a punch-up, to scrap

bigot, -ote [bigo, -ɔt] *Péj* **ADJ** excessively devout, zealously religious
N religious zealot

> Il faut noter que le terme anglais **bigot** est un faux ami. Il se rapporte au sectarisme religieux et non à une attitude excessivement dévote.

bigoterie [bigɔtri] **NF** *Péj* (religious) bigotry

bigoudi [bigudi] **NM** (hair) curler, (hair) roller; **se mettre des bigoudis** to put one's hair in curlers *or* rollers; **tu ne vas pas sortir en bigoudis!** you're not going out in (your) curlers!

bigre [bigr] **INT** *Fam Vieilli* gosh!, *Br* crikey!

bigrement [bigrəmɑ̃] **ADV** *Fam* **vous avez b. raison!** you're dead right!; **il fait b. froid** it's awfully cold; **il a b. changé/grandi** he's changed/grown a heck of a lot; **il était b. surpris** he was dead surprised; **tu étais content? – oui, et b.!** were you satisfied? – yes, and how!

biguine [bigin] **NF** *Mus* beguine

bihebdo [biɛbdo] **NM** biweekly

bihebdomadaire [biɛbdɔmadɛr] **ADJ** (*magazine etc*) twice-weekly, biweekly

bijection [biʒɛksjɔ̃] **NF** *Math* bijection

bijou, -oux [biʒu] **NM** jewel; **bijoux** jewellery, *Am* jewelry, jewels; **un b. fantaisie** a piece of costume jewellery; *Fig* **c'est un b.** it's a gem; **cette montre est un b. d'exactitude/de précision** this watch is a marvel of accuracy/precision; **bijoux de famille** family jewels; *Fig Arg (sexe masculin)* family jewels, *Br* wedding tackle; *Fam* **mon b.!** my precious!, my pet!

bijouterie [biʒutri] **NF 1** (*boutique*) jeweller's *or Am* jeweler's (shop); (*commerce, fabrication*) jeweller's trade *or* business **2** (*bijoux*) jewellery, *Am* jewelry, jewels **3** (*art*) jewellery-making, *Am* jewelry-making

bijoutier, -ière [biʒutje, -jɛr] **N** jeweller, *Am* jeweler

Bikini® [bikini] **NM** bikini

bilabial, -iale, -iaux, -iales [bilabjal, -jo] *Ling* **ADJ** bilabial
NF bilabiale bilabial

bilan [bilɑ̃] **NM 1** *Fin* (*état*) balance sheet; **faire** *ou* **dresser un b.** to draw up a balance sheet; **déposer son b.** to file one's petition (in bankruptcy); **déposer le b.** to file for bankruptcy; **un dépôt de b.** a petition in bankruptcy **2** (*appréciation*) (*d'une situation, de faits*) assessment, evaluation; (*résultats*) results; **faire le b. de la situation** to take stock of *or* assess *or* evaluate the situation; **arrivé à 40 ans, on fait souvent le b.** you often stop to take stock when you reach 40; **'accident sur l'autoroute, b. quatre morts'** 'motorway accident, four dead'; **le b. d'un tremblement de terre** the toll of an earthquake
▸▸ *Mktg* **b. annuel** annual accounts; **b. commercial** market report; **b. de compétences** = summary of one's skills; **b. comptable** balance sheet; *Compta* **b. condensé** summary balance sheet; **b. financier** financial statement; *Compta* **b. intérimaire** interim statement; **b. de liquidation** statement of affairs; *Compta* **b. d'ouverture** opening balance sheet; *Compta* **b. prévisionnel** forecast balance sheet; **b. de santé** complete (medical) check-up; **votre b. de santé est excellent** your state of health is excellent, you are in excellent health; **faire le b. de santé de qn** to give sb a (medical) check-up; **faire le b. de santé d'une entreprise** to assess *or* evaluate the state of a company; *Compta* **b. social** social report

bilantiel [bilɑ̃sjɛl] **ADJ** balance-sheet

bilatéral, -ale, -aux, -ales [bilateral, -o] **ADJ** (*paralysie, traité, discussions etc*) bilateral, two-sided; **stationnement b.** parking on both sides (of the road)

bilboquet [bilbɔkɛ] **NM 1** (*jouet*) = cup-and-ball; (*poussah*) tumbler **2** *Typ* small job

bile [bil] **NF 1** *Physiol* bile **2** (*colère*) **échauffer la b. de** *ou* **à qn** to rouse sb's anger; **décharger sa b. sur qn** to vent one's spleen on sb **3** (*inquiétude*) **se faire de la b.** to fret, to be worried sick (**pour** about); **elle ne se fait pas de b.** she doesn't let things get on top of her; **ne te fais pas de b.!** don't fret!; **ses humeurs de b. noire** his black moods

biler (se) [səbile] **VPR** *Fam* to get worked up, to get all hot and bothered; (*être inquiet*) to be worried sick, to fret; **ne te bile pas!** don't fret!; **elle ne se bile pas, elle!** she's not bothered!

bileux, -euse [bilø, -øz] **ADJ** *Fam* easily upset; **elle n'est pas bileuse** she doesn't let things worry her *or* get on top of her

biliaire [biljɛr] **ADJ** *Anat* (*vaisseaux etc*) biliary; *Méd* **calcul b.** gallstone, *Spéc* biliary calculus; **vésicule b.** gall bladder; **cirrhose b.** cirrhosis (of the liver)

bilieux, -ieuse [biljø, -jøz] **ADJ 1** (*tempérament, teint*) bilious **2** (*personne*) (*colérique*) irritable, irascible; (*inquiet*) sick with worry

bilingue [bilɛ̃g] **ADJ 1** (*personne, dictionnaire etc*) bilingual **2** *Can Fam* (*bisexuel*) bi

bilinguisme [bilɛ̃gɥism] **NM** bilingualism

billard [bijar] **NM 1** (*jeu*) billiards; **jouer au b.** to play billiards; **faire un b.** *ou* **une partie de b.** to play *or* have a game of billiards **VOIR GRAMMAIRE A10 2** (*table*) billiard table; *Fig Fam* **monter** *ou* **passer sur le b.** to have an operation, to be operated on **3** (*salle*) billiard saloon; (*dans une maison*) billiard room
▸▸ **b. américain** pool; **b. électrique** pinball; **b. russe** bar billiards

bille¹ [bij] **NF 1** (*pour le billard*) (billiard) ball **2** *Arg* (*visage*) mug, face; **il a une bonne b.** he looks pleasant enough; **une b. de clown** a funny face; **quelle b., il ne comprend rien!** what a mug, he just doesn't twig! **3** (*de verre*) marble; **jouer aux billes** to play marbles; *Fig* **reprendre ses billes** to pull out; *Fam* **elle touche sa b. en informatique** she knows a thing or two about computers; *Fam* **il ne touche pas une b. au flippeur** he's hopeless *or* lousy at pinball; *Fig* **savoir placer ses billes** to play one's cards right **4** *Tech* ball; **roulement à billes** ball bearing; **stylo (à) b.** ballpoint (pen), *Br* Biro®; **flacon (à) b.** roll-on (bottle); **déodorant à b.** roll-on deodorant

bille² **NF** (*pièce de bois*) billet

billet [bijɛ] **NM 1 b. (de banque)** (bank)note, *Am* bill; **un faux b.** a forged banknote; **un b. de cent euros** a hundred-euro note; *Fam* **je te fiche mon b. qu'il pleuvra!** I bet my bottom dollar it'll rain! **2** *Com, Fin* (*effet*) note, bill **3** (*pour voyager*) ticket; **prendre un b. pour Valence** to buy a ticket for Valence **4** *Théâtre etc* ticket; **b. de théâtre** theatre ticket **5** *Litt* (*lettre*) note, short letter **6** *Journ* diary column
▸▸ *Scol* **b. d'absence** absence slip; **b. d'aller** single *or Am* one-way ticket; **b. d'aller (et) retour** return *or Am* round-trip ticket; **b. d'avion** plane ticket; **b. bradé** discounted ticket; **b. circulaire** round-trip ticket; **b. de complaisance** accommodation bill; **billets complémentaires** conjunction tickets; **b. demi-tarif** half-fare ticket; **b. doux** love letter, billet doux; *Vieilli* **b. de faire-part** = card announcing a birth/wedding/death in the family; **b. 'famille nombreuse'** = special SNCF rates for families with 3 children or more; **b. de faveur** complimentary ticket;

Mil **b. de logement** billet; **b. de naissance** birth certificate; **b. neutre** blank ticket; **b. open** open(-date) ticket; *Fin* **b. à ordre** promissory note; **b. ouvert** open ticket; *Fin* **b. au porteur** bill payable to bearer; **b. de première** first class ticket; **b. de reconnaissance de dettes** IOU; *Scol* **b. de retard** = note given to pupil who is late, specifying the time of arrival; **b. de retour** return *or Am* round-trip ticket; **b. sans condition** flexible ticket; **b. de santé** certificate *or* bill of health; **b. de seconde** second class ticket; **b. simple** single *or Am* one-way ticket; *Scol* **b. de sortie** pass, *Br Fml* exeat; **b. souple** flexible ticket; **b. de train** train ticket; **b. de transport** ticket; **b. du Trésor** Treasury bill; *Fin* **b. de trésorerie** commercial paper; **b. vert** dollar, *Am Fam* greenback

billétique [biletik] **NF** *Banque, Ordinat* cash dispenser technology

billette [bijɛt] **NF 1** (*du bois de chauffage, du métal*) billet **2** *Archit* billet (moulding)

billetterie [bijɛtri] **NF 1** (*opérations*) ticketing; (*lieu*) ticket office **2** (*distributeur de billets de banque*) cash dispenser; **b. automatique** automatic ticket machine

billettiste [bijetist] **N** ticketing clerk; *Journ* diary column writer

billevesées [bilvəze] **NFPL** nonsense, *Fam* twaddle; **b. que tout cela!** that's absolute nonsense!

billion [biljɔ̃] VOIR GRAMMAIRE A76 **1** (*million de millions*) trillion, *Br Vieilli* billion **2** *Arch* (*milliard*) billion, *Br Vieilli* milliard

billot [bijo] **NM** (*de boucher, bourreau*) block; (*dans la cuisine*) butcher's block table; (*de cordonnier*) last; **b. d'enclume** anvil block *or* stock; **périr** *ou* **mourir sur le b.** to be beheaded, to die on the block; *Fam* **j'en mettrais ma tête sur le b.** I'd stake my life on it

bilobé [bilɔbe] **ADJ** *Archit, Biol* bilobate, bilobed

bimane [biman] *Zool* **ADJ** bimanous
N bimanous animal

bimbeloterie [bɛ̃blɔtri] **NF 1** (*fabrication, commerce*) fancy goods business *or* trade **2** (*objets*) fancy goods, knick-knacks, odds and ends

bimbelotier [bɛ̃blɔtje] **NM** (*fabricant*) maker of fancy goods; (*vendeur*) dealer in fancy goods

bi-média [bimedja] **ADJ** bi-media

bimensuel, -elle [bimɑ̃sɥɛl] **ADJ** bimonthly, *Br* fortnightly, *Am* semimonthly
NM bimonthly (magazine), *Br* fortnightly magazine

bimestriel, -ielle [bimɛstriɛl] **ADJ** bimonthly
NM bimonthly

bimétallique [bimetalik] **ADJ** bimetallic

bimétallisme [bimetalism] **NM** *Écon* bimetallism

bimillénaire [bimilenɛr] **ADJ** bimillenary

bimoteur [bimɔtœr] **ADJ, NM** (*avion*) **b.** twin-engine (aircraft)

binage [binaʒ] **NM** *Agr* harrowing, hoeing; (*de jardin*) hoeing

binaire [binɛr] **ADJ** *Math etc* binary; **langage b.** binary notation

biner [bine] **VT** *Agr* (*sol*) to harrow, to hoe; (*jardin*) to hoe
VI *Rel* to celebrate Mass twice in one day

binette [binɛt] **NF 1** *Agr* hoe **2** *Arg* (*visage*) mug, face **3** *Can, Suisse Ordinat* smiley, emoticon

bineuse [binøz] **NF** *Agr* cultivator

bing [biŋ] **INT** bam!, wham!

bingo [biŋgo] **NM** bingo; **jouer au b.** to play bingo

biniou [binju] NM **1** *Mus* Breton bagpipes **2** *Fam (téléphone)* phone, *Br* blower; **donner un coup de b. à qn** to give sb a buzz *or* a call *or Br* a ring

binoclard, -arde [binɔklar, -ard] N *Fam* specs wearer; **hé, b.!** hey, four-eyes!

binocle [binɔkl] NM pince-nez; *Fam* **binocles** *(lunettes)* specs

binoculaire [binɔkylɛr] ADJ *(vision, microscope etc)* binocular

binôme [binom] NM **1** *Math* binomial; **le b. de Newton** the binomial theorem **2** *travailler en b. (d'étudiants etc)* to work in twos

binomial, -iale, -iaux, -iales [binɔmjal, -jo] ADJ *Math* binomial

binot [bino] NM *Agr* = **bineuse**

binz [bins] NM *Fam* **1** *(chose compliquée)* **quel b. pour trouver sa maison!** it was a real hassle finding his/her house! **2** *(désordre)* shambles

bio [bjo] *Fam* ADJ *(abrév* **biologique)** *(produits, agriculture)* organic ▪ NF *(abrév* **biographie)** biog; **une b. d'Elvis** an Elvis biog

biocarburant [bjokarbyrã] NM biofuel

biochimie [bjoʃimi] NF biochemistry

biochimique [bjoʃimik] ADJ biochemical; **demande b. en oxygène** biochemical oxygen demand

biochimiste [bjoʃimist] N biochemist

bioclimat [bjoklima] NM bioclimate

bioclimatique [bjoklimatik] ADJ bioclimatic

bioclimatologie [bjoklimatɔlɔʒi] NF bioclimatology

biodégradable [bjodegradabl] ADJ biodegradable

biodiversité [bjodivɛrsite] NF biodiversity

bioénergétique [bjoenɛrʒetik] ADJ bioenergetic ▪ NF bioenergetics

bioéthique [bjoetik] NF *Méd* bioethics

biogenèse [bjoʒənɛz] NF *Biol* biogenesis

biographe [bjograf] N biographer

biographie [bjografi] NF biography

biographique [bjografik] ADJ biographical

bio-industrie [bjoɛ̃dystri] NF biotechnology industry

bio-informatique [bjoɛ̃fɔrmatik] NF bio-IT, bio-information technology

biologie [bjɔlɔʒi] NF biology

biologique [bjɔlɔʒik] ADJ biological; **horloge b.** biological clock; **parents biologiques** biological parents; **agriculture/jardinage b.** organic farming/gardening; **aliments biologiques** organic food

biologiste [bjɔlɔʒist] N biologist

biomasse [bjomas] NF biomass

biomatériau [bjomaterjo] NM biomaterial

biomédical, -ale, -aux, -ales [bjomedikal, -o] ADJ biomedical

biométrie [bjometri] NF biometrics

biomoléculaire [bjomɔlekylɛr] ADJ biomolecular

bionique [bjɔnik] NF bionics

biophysicien, -ienne [bjofizisjɛ̃, -jɛn] N biophysicist

biophysique [bjofizik] NF biophysics

biopsie [bjɔpsi] NF *Chir* biopsy

biopuce [bjopys] NF biochip

biorythme [bjoritm] NM biorhythm

BIOS [bjɔs] NM *Ordinat* BIOS

biosphère [bjosfɛr] NF biosphere

biosynthèse [bjosɛ̃tɛz] NF biosynthesis

biotechnique [bjotɛknik], **biotechnologie** [bjotɛknɔlɔʒi] NF *Pharm, Chimie* biotechnology

biotechnologique [bjotɛknɔlɔʒik] ADJ biotechnological

bioterrorisme [bjotɛrɔrism] NM bioterrorism

bioterroriste [bjotɛrɔrist] N bioterrorist

biothérapie [bjoterapi] NF biotherapy

biotope [bjɔtɔp] NM biotope

biovigilance [bjoviʒilãs] NF biovigilance

bioxyde [bjɔksid] NM *Chimie* dioxide

bip [bip] INT beep ▪ NM **1** *(son)* beep; **après le b. sonore** after the beep; **faire b.** to beep; *TV, Radio* **b. de censure** censor bleep **2** *(appareil)* beeper, pager, bleeper

bipale [bipal] ADJ *(hélice)* twin-bladed

biparti [biparti] ADJ bipartite

bipartisme [bipartism] NM *Pol* bipartite system

bipartite [bipartit] ADJ = **biparti**

bip-bip, *pl* **bips-bips** NM beep

bipède [bipɛd] ADJ, NM biped

biper [bipe] VT *(personne)* to page

biphasé [bifaze] *Élec* ADJ *(courant)* two-phase, diphase ▪ NM two-phase *or* diphase current

biplace [biplas] ADJ, NM *Aut, Aviat* two-seater

biplan [biplã] ADJ, NM *(avion)* **b.** biplane

bipolaire [bipɔlɛr] ADJ *Élec, Phys etc* bipolar, two-pole

bipolarisation [bipɔlarizasjɔ̃] NF *Pol* separation into two blocs

bipolarité [bipɔlarite] NF bipolarity

biquadratique [bikwadratik] *Math* ADJ *(équation)* biquadratic ▪ NF biquadratic

bique [bik] NF *Fam* **1** *(chèvre)* nanny goat; **peau de b.** goatskin **2** *Péj (femme)* **vieille b.** old bag *or* hag

biquet, -ette [bikɛ, -ɛt] N **1** *(petit de la chèvre)* kid **2** *Fam* **mon b.** my pet, my love

biquotidien, -ienne [bikɔtidjɛ̃, -jɛn] ADJ twice-daily

birbe [birb] NM *Fam* **vieux b.** old fogey, old fuddy-duddy

BIRD [bird] NF *(abrév* **Banque internationale pour la reconstruction et le développement)** IBRD

bircher [birʃer] NM *Suisse* muesli

biréacteur [bireaktœr] NM twin-jet (aircraft)

biréfringence [birefrɛ̃ʒãs] NF *Opt* double refraction, birefringence

biréfringent [birefrɛ̃ʒã] ADJ *Opt* doubly refractive, birefringent

birman, -ane [birmã, -an] ADJ Burmese ▪ NM *Ling* Burmese ▪ N **B.** Burmese

Birmanie [birmani] NF Burma

biroute [birut] NF **1** *Mil, Aviat Fam* (wind) sock, wind sleeve **2** *Arg (pénis)* dick, cock

bis¹ [bi] ADJ greyish-brown, brownish-grey; **teint b.** dark *or* swarthy complexion; **toile bise** unbleached linen; **pain b.** brown bread

bis² [bis] ADV **1** *Théâtre* encore; *Mus* repeat **2** *(dans une adresse)* **10 b.** 10A **3 itinéraire b.** alternative route

bisaïeul, -eule, *pl* **bisaïeuls, -eules** [bizajœl] N *Litt* great-grandfather, *f* great-grandmother

bisannuel, -elle [bizanɥɛl] ADJ biennial; **plante bisannuelle** biennial (plant)

bisbille [bisbij] NF *Fam* squabble, petty quarrel, tiff; **être en b. avec qn** not to see eye to eye with sb, to be at odds with sb

Biscaye [biskaj] N Biscay; **le golfe de B.** the Bay of Biscay

biscôme [biskom] NM *Suisse* = Swiss gingerbread

biscornu [biskɔrny] ADJ **1** *(de forme) (chapeau)* crooked; *(personne, nain)* crooked, misshapen; *(sac, maison, bâtiment, cactus)* oddly shaped **2** *Fam (idées)* bizarre, weird, cranky; *(raisonnement, esprit)* tortuous

biscoteaux [biskoto] NMPL *Fam* biceps; **avoir des b.** to have bulging biceps

biscotte [biskɔt] NF rusk

biscuit [biskɥi] NM **1** *Culin* biscuit, *Am* cookie; **b. au chocolat** chocolate biscuit; **b. au fromage** cheese biscuit **2** *Cér* bisque; **un b.** a piece of biscuitware ▸ **b. à la cuiller** sponge finger, *Am* lady finger; **b. de fourrage** *(d'avoine etc)* cake; **b. de mer** ship's biscuit; **b. pour chien** dog biscuit; **b. de Savoie** sponge cake; **b. salé** cracker

biscuiterie [biskɥitri] NF **1** *(usine)* biscuit *or Am* cookie factory **2** *(commerce)* biscuit *or Am* cookie trade **3** *(fabrication)* biscuit *or Am* cookie making

bise¹ [biz] NF *(vent)* north wind

bise² NF *Fam (baiser)* kiss; **donner** *ou* **faire une b. à qn** to give sb a kiss, to kiss sb; **on se fait la b.** we give each other a kiss, we kiss each other; **grosses bises** *(sur une lettre)* love and kisses

biseau, -eaux [bizo] NM **1** *Menuis etc (bord)* chamfer, bevel, chamfered *or* bevelled edge; **taillé en b.** bevel-edged, bevelled, chamfered **2** *(d'horloge etc)* bezel; *Mus (d'instrument à vent)* lip **3** *(outil)* bevel

biseautage [bizotaʒ] NM **1** *Menuis etc* bevelling, chamfering **2** *(de cartes à jouer)* marking

biseauter [bizote] VT **1** *Menuis etc* to bevel, to chamfer **2** *(cartes à jouer)* to mark

biser¹ [bize] VI *Agr (du grain)* to darken, to deteriorate

biser² VT *Fam* to kiss

biset [bizɛ] NM *(oiseau)* rock pigeon

bisexualité [bisɛksɥalite] NF bisexuality

bisexué [bisɛksɥe] ADJ bisexual; **animal b.** hermaphrodite

bisexuel, -elle [bisɛksɥɛl] ADJ bisexual

bismuth [bismyt] NM bismuth

bison [bizɔ̃] NM *Zool* bison, buffalo **VOIR GRAMMAIRE A12**

Bison Futé NM *Aut* = body which advises drivers of road conditions and congestion on French motorways

bisou [bizu] NM *Fam* kiss; **faire un b. à son papa** to give Daddy a kiss

bisque [bisk] NF *Culin* bisque; **b. de homard** lobster bisque

bisquer [biske] VI *Fam* to be riled; **ça va le faire b.** that'll rile him, *Br* that'll get right up his nose

bissecteur, -trice [bisɛktœr, -tris] ADJ *(ligne etc)* bisecting ▪ NF **bissectrice** bisector, bisecting line

bissection [bisɛksjɔ̃] NF *Math* bisection

bisser [bise] VT **1** *(d'un artiste) (chanson etc)* to give an encore of, to repeat **2** *(d'un spectateur) (chanson, artiste etc)* to call on to give an encore **3** *Belg Scol (redoubler)* to repeat

bissextile [bisɛkstil] ADJ **année b.** leap year

bistandard [bistãdar] ADJ *TV* dual-standard

bistouquette [bistukɛt] NF *Fam Br* willy, *Am* peter

bistouri [bisturi] NM *Chir* lancet, *Spéc* bistoury

bistre [bistr] ADJ bistre, blackish-brown; **teint b.** swarthy *or* dark complexion ▪ NM bistre

bistré [bistre] ADJ *(peau)* swarthy, dark
bister [bistre] VT *(teint)* to darken, to tan
bistro(t) [bistro] NM *Fam* ≃ café

Bistrot

This word can refer either to a small café or to a cosy restaurant, especially one frequented by regulars. These establishments are usually less classy than bistros in English-speaking countries. The "style bistrot" refers to a style of furnishing inspired by the chairs, tables and zinc countertops typical of the traditional "bistrot".

---

bisulfate [bisylfat] NM *Chimie* bisulphate
bisulfite [bisylfit] NM *Chimie* bisulphite
bisulfure [bisylfyr] NM *Chimie* disulphide, bisulphide
BIT [beite] NM *(abrév* **Bureau international du travail***)* ILO
bit [bit] NM *Ordinat* bit; **b. d'arrêt** stop bit; **b. de contrôle** control bit, check bit; **b. de départ** start bit; **b. de parité** parity bit; **bits par seconde** bits per second
bite [bit] NF *Vulg (pénis)* cock, prick, dick
biter [bite] VT *Vulg* **j'y bite rien** I don't understand a bloody *or Am* goddamn thing
biterrois, -oise [biterwa, -waz] **1** ADJ of/from Béziers
  N **B.** *(natif)* native of Béziers; *(habitant)* inhabitant of Béziers
bitmap [bitmap] *Ordinat* ADJ bitmap
  NM bitmap
bitonal, -ale, -aux, -ales [bitɔnal, -o] ADJ *Tél* **sonnerie bitonale** two-tone ring
bitoniau [bitɔnjo] NM *Fam* thingy, whatsit
bitte¹ [bit] NF *Vulg* = **bite**
bitte² NF *Naut (sur un bateau)* bitt; **b. d'amarrage** bollard
bitter [biter] NM bitters
bitture [bityr] NF **1** *Naut* range of cable **2** *Arg* **prendre une b.** to get plastered *or* canned; **il tient une sacrée b.** he's absolutely plastered, *Br* he's paralytic
bitturer (se) [səbityre] VPR *Arg* to get plastered *or* canned
bitumage [bitymaʒ] NM **1** *(de route)* asphalting **2** *(de papier etc)* tarring
bitume [bitym] NM *Minér* **1** *(asphalte)* bitumen, asphalt; *Fam* **arpenter le b.** to walk the streets **2** *(goudron)* bitumen, tar
bitumer [bityme] VT **1** *(route)* to asphalt **2** *(goudronner)* to tar; **carton bitumé** tarred felt
bitum(in)eux, -euse [bitym(in)ø, -øz] ADJ *Minér* bituminous
biture [bityr] NF = **bitture**
biturer (se) [səbityre] VPR *Arg* = **bitturer (se)**
biunivoque [biynivɔk] ADJ *Math* one-to-one
bivalent [bivalɑ̃] ADJ *Chimie etc* bivalent, divalent
bivalve [bivalv] ADJ, NM bivalve
bivouac [bivwak] NM bivouac; **faire un b.** to bivouac; **feu de b.** watchfire; **cet endroit sera un excellent b.** this will be an excellent place to bivouac
bivouaquer [bivwake] VI to bivouac
bizarre [bizar] ADJ odd, strange, peculiar, bizarre; **c'est b., ce n'est pas ce qu'elle m'avait dit** that's odd *or* strange, that's not what she told me; **le plus b., c'est que ...** the strangest *or* oddest *or* funniest thing of all is that ...
  NM **le b.** the bizarre; **le b. de l'affaire, c'est que ...** the strange *or* odd *or* funny thing is that ...

bizarrement [bizarmɑ̃] ADV strangely, oddly, peculiarly; **et b., elle est venue toute seule** and for some strange reason, she came all alone
bizarrerie [bizarri] NF *(de situation, d'idée, d'attitude etc)* strangeness, oddness, peculiarity; *(de personne)* eccentricity; **bizarreries** oddities; *(de personne)* eccentricities
bizarroïde [bizarɔid] ADJ *Fam* weird; **ce type est b.** that guy's a weirdo
bizut [bizy] NM *Univ Fam* fresher, *Am* freshman
bizutage [bizytaʒ] NM *Univ Fam (des nouveaux arrivés)* ragging, *Am* hazing

---

Bizutage

In some French schools and colleges, students in fancy-dress take to the streets and play practical jokes, sometimes of a very cruel nature, on each other and on passers-by at the beginning of the school year. This is part of the traditional initiation ceremony known as "bizutage". As a consequence of the excessive behaviour to which it has often led, a law was passed in 1998 to make it an offence.

---

bizuter [bizyte] VT *Univ Fam (nouvel arrivé)* to rag, *Am* to haze
bizuth [bizy] NM *Univ Fam* = **bizut**
blabla(bla) [blabla(bla)] NM *Fam* claptrap, baloney; *(dans un discours, texte etc)* padding, waffle
blablater [blablate] VI *Fam* to waffle on, *Br* to witter on
black [blak] *Fam* N *(personne de race noire)* Black
  NM **travailler au b.** *(clandestinement)* = to work without declaring one's earnings; *(en plus de son travail habituel)* to moonlight
blackboulage [blakbulaʒ] NM blackballing; *Fam (d'un candidat à un examen)* failing
blackbouler [blakbule] VT to blackball; *Fam (à un examen)* to fail; **se faire b. d'un bureau à l'autre** to get shunted from one office to another
black-out [blakawt] NM INV blackout; *Fig* **faire le b. sur un scandale** to hush up *or* cover up a scandal; **c'est le b. total, on ne sait rien** there's a complete blackout, we don't know a thing
blad [blad] NM *Typ* blad
blafard [blafar] ADJ *(lune, lumière, teint etc)* pallid, wan, pale
blague [blag] NF **1** *(plaisanterie)* joke; *(tour)* (practical) joke, trick, hoax; **faire une b. (à qn)** to play a joke *or* trick (on sb); **il m'a fait une sale b.** he played a dirty trick on me; **tout ça, c'est de la b.** it's all bunkum *or* nonsense; **ne racontez pas de blagues** you're kidding (me), you're having *or Am* putting me on; **b. à part** seriously, joking apart; **sans b.?** really?, no kidding? **2 b. (à tabac)** (tobacco) pouch **3** *Vieilli (erreur)* mistake, blunder
blaguer [blage] *Fam* VI to joke; **il aime bien b.** he likes a joke; **là, tu es en train de b.!** you're joking *or* kidding!, you're having *or Am* putting me on!
  VT *(personne)* to tease, to make fun of
blagueur, -euse [blagœr, -øz] *Fam* N *(qui dit des blagues)* joker, comedian; *(qui fait des blagues)* practical joker, prankster
  ADJ *(remarque)* teasing, bantering; **il est très b.** he really likes a joke
blair [blɛr] NM *Arg (nez)* conk, *Br* hooter
blaireau, -eaux [blɛro] NM **1** *(mammifère)* badger **2** *(pour se raser)* shaving brush **3** *Beaux-Arts* (badger-hair) brush **4** *Fam (imbécile)* nerd, prat

blairer [blere] VT *Arg* **je ne peux pas le b.** I can't stick *or* stand *or* stomach him
blâmable [blɑmabl] ADJ blameworthy; **vous n'êtes pas b.** you're not to blame
blâme [blɑm] NM **1** *(reproche)* blame; **rejeter le b. de qch sur qn** to lay the blame for sth on sb; **s'attirer le b. de ses parents** to incur one's parents' disapproval **2** *Admin (sanction)* reprimand; **donner un b. à qn** to reprimand sb, to give sb a reprimand; **recevoir un b.** to be reprimanded
blâmer [blɑme] VT **1** *(condamner) (personne, gouvernement, acte etc)* to blame; **b. qn de faire/d'avoir fait qch** to blame sb for doing/having done sth **2** *Admin (réprimander)* to reprimand
  VPR **se blâmer** to blame oneself; **je ne peux que me b. d'avoir dit oui** I can't forgive myself for having said yes
blanc, blanche [blɑ̃, blɑ̃ʃ] ADJ **1** *(drap, pain, vin, chocolat etc)* white; **b. comme (la) neige** *(tissu, drap etc)* white as snow, snow-white; *Fig* **il est sorti du procès b. comme neige** he came out of the trial whiter than white; **vieillard à cheveux blancs** white-haired old man, old man with white hair; **fromage b.** cream cheese; **verre b.** colourless *or Am* colorless glass; **bruit b.** white noise
  2 *(peau)* pale, light-coloured, *Am* light-colored; *(pas bronzé)* white; **la race blanche** the white race; **b. de peur** white with fear; **b. de colère** livid with anger; **b. comme un linge** as white as a sheet; **b. comme un cachet d'aspirine** completely white; **il a la peau blanche** *(fragile)* he has a pale skin
  3 *Litt (innocent)* innocent, pure; **j'ai les mains blanches** my hands are clean, I'm innocent
  4 *(vierge) (page etc)* blank; *(papier)* plain, unlined; **j'ai besoin d'une feuille blanche** I need a clean piece of paper; **nuit blanche** sleepless night; **examen b.** mock (examination); *Scol* **rendre copie blanche** to hand in a blank paper; **mariage b.** unconsummated marriage; **voix blanche** toneless voice; **vers blancs** blank verse; *Tennis* **jeu b.** love game
  NM **1** *(couleur)* white; **b. éclatant** brilliant white; **robe d'un b. sale** dingy white dress; **peint en b.** painted white; **être habillé de b., être en b.** to be dressed in white; **mariage en b.** white wedding; **le b. est très à la mode** white is very fashionable; **je vous l'écris noir sur b.** I'm putting it in black and white for you
  2 *(d'une cible)* bull's-eye; **donner** *ou* **mettre dans le b.** to hit the bull's-eye
  3 *(espace)* blank, space, gap; *Ordinat* blank; **laisser des blancs** to leave blanks *or* spaces *or* gaps; **chèque en b.** blank cheque *or Am* check
  4 *(aux dominos)* blank; **double b.** double blank
  5 **saigner qn à b.** to bleed sb white; **chauffer un métal à b.** to bring a metal to a white heat; **chauffé à b.** white-hot; **cartouche à b.** blank (cartridge); **tirer à b.** to fire a blank/blanks
  6 *Culin* **b. de poulet** breast of chicken, chicken breast; **tu veux le b. ou la cuisse?** would you like breast or leg *or Am* white meat or dark?
  7 *(colorant)* **b. de billard** billiard chalk; **b. de chaux** whitewash; **b. de zinc** zinc white, oxide of zinc; **b. de céruse** *ou* **d'argent** *ou* **de plomb** white lead; **b. d'Espagne** whiting, whitening
  8 *(linge)* **(articles de) b.** linen; **il est préférable de laver le b. séparément** it's preferable to wash whites separately; **magasin de b.** linen shop; **vente de b.** white *or* linen sale
  9 *(vin)* white wine; **du rouge ou du b.?** red or white?; **b. de b.** = white wine made from white grapes

10 b. du rosier/de la vigne rose/vine mildew **11** *TV, Radio* drop-out **12** *Can, Suisse (trou de mémoire)* blank; **avoir un b.** to have a blank **NF blanche 1** *Billard* white (ball) **2** *Mus* minim, *Am* half note ▪ **B.** White (man, *f* woman); **réservé aux Blancs** reserved for Whites ▸▸ **b. cassé** off-white; *Typ* **b. de grand fond** gutter, fore-edge; *Typ* **b. de petit fond** gutter, back margin; **b. d'œuf** egg white; **le b. des yeux** the white of the eye; **regarder qn dans le b. des yeux** to look sb straight in the eye

blanc-bec, *pl* **blancs-becs NM** *Péj* greenhorn; *(adolescent)* callow youth

blanchaille [blɑ̃ʃaj] **NF 1** *Pêche (poisson)* small fry, bait **2** *Culin* whitebait

blanchâtre [blɑ̃ʃatr] **ADJ** whitish, off-white

Blanche-Neige [blɑ̃ʃnɛʒ] **N** Snow White; **B. et les sept nains** Snow White and the Seven Dwarfs

blanchet [blɑ̃ʃɛ] **NM** *Typ* blanket

blancheur [blɑ̃ʃœr] **NF** whiteness; *Fig* purity, innocence; **d'une b. de perle** pearl-white; **sa peau est d'une telle b.!** his skin is so white!

blanchiment [blɑ̃ʃimɑ̃] **NM 1** *(d'un plafond, mur etc)* whitewashing **2** *Culin (de légumes)* blanching **3** *Tex* bleaching **4** *(de l'argent)* laundering

> Do not confuse with **blanchissement**.

blanchir [blɑ̃ʃir] **VT 1** *(dents etc)* to whiten, to make white; **b. (à la chaux)** *(plafond, mur etc)* to whitewash; **la neige qui blanchit les sommets** the snow that turns the peaks white; *Typ* **b. la composition** to space out the matter **2** *(linge)* to launder; *Tex* to bleach; **donner du linge à b.** to send clothes to the laundry; *Fig* **cette déclaration l'a blanchi complètement** this statement has completely exonerated him or completely cleared his name; **b. de l'argent** to launder money **3** *Culin (légumes)* to blanch; *Ind (sucre)* to refine **4** *Can Sport (équipe)* to shut out **5** *Typ (texte, page)* to space, to space out **6** *Phot* to bleach out **VI 1** *(devenir blanc)* to turn or go white **2** *(pâlir)* to turn pale **VPR se blanchir** to clear oneself or one's name, to exonerate oneself; **se b. d'une accusation** to clear oneself of or exonerate oneself from a charge

blanchissage [blɑ̃ʃisaʒ] **NM 1** *(du linge etc)* laundering; **liste de b.** laundry list **2** *Ind (du sucre)* refining **3** *Can Sport* shutout

blanchissant, -ante [blɑ̃ʃisɑ̃] **ADJ 1** *(chevelure)* whitening; *(peau etc)* paling; **l'aube blanchissante** the brightening dawn **2** **agent b.** whitener

blanchissement [blɑ̃ʃismɑ̃] **NM 1** *(des cheveux)* whitening **2** *(de la peau)* blanching, turning pale

> Do not confuse with **blanchiment**.

blanchisserie [blɑ̃ʃisri] **NF 1** *Com* laundry **2** *Tex* bleachery

blanchisseur, -euse [blɑ̃ʃisœr, -øz] **N** launderer, laundryman, *f* laundress, *Vieilli* washerwoman

blanchon [blɑ̃ʃɔ̃] **NM** *Can* whitecoat *(seal pup)*

blanc-manger, *pl* **blancs-mangers NM** *Culin* = almond milk jelly, *Arch* blancmange

blanc-seing, *pl* **blancs-seings NM** signature to a blank document; *Fig* **donner un b. à qn** to give sb a free hand

blanquette [blɑ̃kɛt] **NF** *Culin (de veau)* blanquette

blanquette [blɑ̃kɛt] **NF b. de Limoux** = sparkling white wine from Limoux

blasé, -ée [blaze] **ADJ** blasé ▪ **N** blasé person; **faire le b.** to act all blasé

blaser [blaze] **VT** *(personne)* to make blasé; **être blasé de qch** to be indifferent to sth **VPR se blaser** to become blasé; **se b. de qch** to become indifferent to sth

blason [blazɔ̃] **NM** *Hér* **1** *(armes)* coat of arms, armorial bearings, blazon **2** *(héraldique)* heraldry

blasonner [blazɔne] **VT** *Hér* **b. un écu** to blazon an escutcheon

blasphémateur, -trice [blasfematœr, -tris] **N** blasphemer ▪ **ADJ** blaspheming, blasphemous

blasphématoire [blasfematwar] **ADJ** blasphemous

blasphème [blasfɛm] **NM** blasphemy; **dire** *ou* **prononcer des blasphèmes** to blaspheme

blasphémer [blasfeme] *(je blasphème, n. blasphémons; je blasphémerai)* **VI** to blaspheme **(contre** against) ▪ **VT** *Vieilli* to blaspheme; **b. le nom de Dieu** to take the Lord's name in vain

blastoderme [blastɔdɛrm] **NM** *Biol* blastoderm

blatérer [blatere] **VI** *(il blatère; il blatérera)* *(d'un chameau)* to roar; *(d'un bélier)* to bleat

blatte [blat] **NF** *(insecte)* cockroach, black beetle

blaze [blaz] **NM** *Arg* **1** *(nez)* conk, *Br* hooter **2** *(nom)* name, handle

blazer [blazœr] **NM** blazer

bld *abrév* **boulevard**

blé [ble] **NM 1** *(céréale)* wheat, *Br* corn; **b. dur** hard or durum wheat; **b. tendre** soft wheat; **champ de b.** wheatfield; **grenier à b.** granary; **halle aux blés** corn exchange; **b. en herbe** wheat in the blade; *Fig* **manger son b. en herbe** to eat one's seed corn **2** *Fam Fig (argent)* bread, dough, *Br* lolly ▸▸ *Can* **b. d'Inde** maize, *Am* (Indian) corn; **b. noir** buckwheat

bled [blɛd] **NM** *(en Afrique du Nord)* inland country, interior; *Fam (région ou village reculé(e))* backwater, place in the middle of nowhere; *(petite ville)* one-horse town; *Fam* **dans mon b.** in my part of the country; *Fam Péj* **un sale b., un b. perdu** a godforsaken place, a dump, a hole

blême [blɛm] **ADJ 1** *(personne, visage, teint)* pallid, wan; **b. de peur** white with fear; **un visage b. de fatigue** a tired, wan face; **b. de rage/colère** white with rage/anger; **elle est devenue b. quand je le lui ai dit** she went white or she blanched when I told her **2** *Fig* **lueur b.** pale or wan light; **matin b.** pale morning

blêmir [blemir] **VI 1** *(de personne)* to turn or go pale; **b. de rage/colère** to turn or go livid or white with rage/anger **2** *Fig (de la lumière)* to grow dim or faint or wan

> Il faut noter que le verbe anglais **to blemish** est un faux ami. Il ne signifie jamais **devenir pâle**.

blêmissement [blemismɑ̃] **NM** paling, turning pale

blennorragie [blenɔraʒi] **NF** *Méd* gonorrhoea

blennorragique [blenɔraʒik] *Méd* **ADJ** gonorrhoeal ▪ **N** gonorrhoea sufferer

blépharite [blefarit] **NF** *Méd* blepharitis

blèsement [blɛzmɑ̃] **NM** lisping, lisp

bléser [bleze] **VI** *(je blèse, n. blésons; je bléserai)* to lisp

blésité [blezite] **NF** lisping

blessant [blesɑ̃] **ADJ** *(remarque etc)* hurtful, cutting; *(personne)* hurtful

blessé, -ée [blese] **ADJ** *(par arme)* wounded; *(dans un accident)* injured, hurt; *(moralement)* hurt, upset ▪ **N** *(victime d'une agression)* wounded person, casualty; *(victime d'un accident)* injured person, casualty; **les blessés** the wounded/injured, the casualties; **les blessés légers** the slightly wounded/injured; **les grands blessés** the severely wounded/injured; **un mort et trois blessés** one dead and three wounded/injured; **les blessés de guerre** the war wounded; **b. de la face** person with facial wounds/injuries

blesser [blese] **VT 1** *(par arme)* to wound; *(dans un accident)* to injure, to hurt; **la chute l'a grièvement blessée** she was severely injured or hurt in the fall; **vous êtes blessé?** are you hurt?; **ces souliers me blessent** these shoes hurt me; **il a été blessé au bras** *(par arme)* he was wounded in the arm; *(dans un accident)* his arm was injured; **être blessé à mort** *(par arme)* to be fatally wounded; *(dans un accident)* to be fatally injured **2** *(moralement) (personne)* to offend, to hurt, to upset; **b. la vue** *ou* **les yeux/l'oreille** to offend the eye/to grate on the ear; **b. qn au vif** to cut sb to the quick; **b. l'amour-propre de qn, b. qn dans son orgueil** *ou* **amour-propre** to hurt or injure sb's pride or self-esteem; **cette suspicion de ta part me blesse** I resent your suspiciousness; **cela blesse notre sens des convenances** that offends (against) our sense of propriety ▪ **VPR se blesser** *(physiquement) (avec une arme)* to wound oneself; *(dans un accident)* to hurt or injure oneself (**avec** with); **il s'est blessé à la tête** *(avec une arme)* he's wounded himself in the head; *(dans un accident)* he's hurt or injured his head

blessure [blesyr] **NF** *(par arme)* wound; *(dans un accident)* injury; **faire une b. à qn** to wound sb; **b. légère** *ou* **superficielle** slight or flesh wound; **b. profonde** deep wound; *Jur* **coups et blessures** assault and battery; **une b. d'amour-propre** a blow to one's pride or self-esteem; *Fig* **rouvrir une b.** to open an old wound

blet, blette [blɛ, blɛt] **ADJ** *(fruit)* overripe, soft

blette [blɛt] **NF** = **bette**

blettir [bletir] **VI** *(d'un fruit)* to become overripe, to go soft

blettissement [bletismɑ̃] **NM** *(d'un fruit)* overripeness

bleu [blø] **ADJ** blue; *(bifteck)* very rare; **avoir les yeux bleus** to have blue eyes, to be blue-eyed; **b. de froid** blue with cold; *Can* **un froid b.** extreme cold; **il fait un froid b.** it's freezing (cold); **colère bleue** towering rage; **j'en suis resté b.** I was flabbergasted; *Méd* **maladie bleue** blue disease, *Spéc* cyanosis; *Méd* **enfant b.** blue baby; *Aut* **zone bleue** restricted parking area ▪ **NM 1** *(couleur)* blue; *Fig* **n'y voir que du b.** not to catch on, *Br* not to twig; **le b. du ciel** the blue(ness) of the sky; *Mil* **tirer dans le b.** to fire at random; **b. (de lessive)** blue, blueing; **passer du linge au b.** to blue laundry; *Tex* **b. de teinturier** blue, blueing **2** *(ecchymose)* bruise; **j'ai le bras couvert de bleus** my arm's covered in bruises, my arm's black and blue; **se faire un b.** to bruise oneself **3** *Fam (novice)* novice, greenhorn, *Am* tenderfoot; *Mil* raw recruit, rookie **4** *(fromage)* blue cheese **5** *Culin* **truite au b.** trout au bleu *(boiled alive in vinegar bouillon)* **6** **bleu(s) (de chauffe** *ou* **de travail)** *(combi-*

naison) overalls, Br boiler suit; (salopette) dungarees; (à deux pièces) overalls
7 Tech blueprint
8 Can Pol Conservative
9 Vieilli **petit b.** telegram
▸▸**b. ciel** sky blue; **b. clair** light blue; **b. foncé** dark blue; **b. horizon** sky blue; **b. marine** navy (blue); **b. d'outremer** ultramarine; **b. de Prusse** Prussian blue; **b. roi** royal blue; **b.-noir** bluish-black; **encre b.-noir** blue-black ink; **b.-nuit** midnight blue

bleuâtre [bløɑtr] ADJ bluish

bleuet [bløɛ] NM **1** (plante) cornflower **2** Can (baie) blueberry

bleuetière [bløɛtjɛr] NF Can blueberry field

bleuir [bløir] VT to turn or make blue
VI to turn or go blue

bleuissement [bløismɑ̃] NM turning blue

bleuté [bløte] ADJ (lumière, couleur etc) bluish, blue-tinged; (verres de lunettes etc) blue-tinted

bleuter [bløte] VT (verre, acier etc) to give a blue tinge to

blindage [blɛ̃daʒ] NM **1** Constr, Min (d'une tranchée) timbering, sheeting **2** Mil etc armour(-plate or -plating), Am armor(-plate or -plating); **plaque de b.** armour-plate **3** Élec (d'une valve etc) screen(ing); (d'un transformateur etc) shrouding; Ordinat shield

blinde [blɛ̃d] NF Fam **à toute b.** at full speed, like lightning, Br like the clappers

blindé [blɛ̃de] ADJ **1** Mil etc armoured, armour-plated, Am armored, Am armor-plated; (division, train) armoured; **porte blindée** steel security door; **abri b.** bombproof shelter; **non b.** (véhicule) soft-skinned **2** Fam **je suis b.** (ce n'est pas la première fois que ça m'arrive) I'm hardened or immune to it; **b. contre qch** hardened or immune to sth **3** Arg (ivre) blind drunk, plastered **4** Élec (valve) screened; (transformateur) shrouded
NMPL Mil **les blindés** the armour, Am the armor

blinder [blɛ̃de] VT **1** Constr, Min (tranchée, puits de mine etc) to sheet, to timber **2** Mil etc to armour(-plate), Am to armor(-plate); (abri) to make bombproof; **b. sa porte** to reinforce one's door (with steel) **3** Élec to screen, to shroud **4** Fam (personne) to harden, to make immune (**contre qch** to sth)
VPR **se blinder 1** (s'endurcir) to harden oneself, to become thick-skinned **2** Fam (s'enivrer) to get plastered or wasted

blinis [blini(s)] NM Culin blini

blinquer [blɛ̃ke] Belg Fam VT to polish
VI to shine

blister [blistɛr] NM Com blister pack; **marchandise vendue sous b.** goods sold in blister packs

blizzard [blizar] NM blizzard

bloblote [blɔblɔt] NF Fam **avoir la b.** to have the shakes

bloc [blɔk] NM **1** (de bois, de pierre etc) block, lump; **taillé d'un seul b.** cut from a solid block; **elle s'est retournée tout d'un b. et l'a giflé** she turned round smartly and slapped him in the face; **coulé en b.** cast in one piece; **acquérir des droits en b.** to buy rights outright; **il a tout refusé/critiqué en b.** he rejected/criticized everything in its entirety; **visser ou serrer qch à b.** to screw sth (up) as tightly as possible; **serrer les freins à b.** to jam the brakes on hard; Fam **gonflé à b.** full of beans, raring to go
2 (de maisons) block; **il habite dans ce b.** lives in this block
3 Pol etc bloc, group, coalition; **faire b.** to join forces, to unite (**avec** with; **contre** against); **les deux partis font b.** the two parties have formed a bloc or group or coali-

tion; **former un b.** to make up or form a group; **le b. occidental** the Western bloc; **le b. des gauches** the left-wing bloc or group or coalition
4 (de papier) pad; **b. à dessin** sketch pad, drawing pad; **b. de papier à lettres** writing pad; **b. de bureau** office pad, desk pad
5 (ensemble d'éléments) unit; Cin **b. sonore** sound unit; **former un b.** to make up or form a unit
6 Fam (prison) clink, Br nick; **être au b.** to be in the clink or the nick
7 Ordinat block; **quelle commande faut-il utiliser pour déplacer un b.?** what's the command for moving a block?; **b. d'alimentation secteur** mains power unit; **b. de données** data block; **b. numérique** numeric keypad; **b. de texte** text block, block of text; **b. de touches** keypad
▸▸**b. adresse** address block; Fin **b. de contrôle** controlling shareholding; Sport **b. de départ** starting block; Aut **b. des feux arrière** rear light cluster; **b. logique** package; **b. monétaire** currency bloc; **b. opératoire** theatre block, operating theatre or Am room; Aut **b. optique** sealed beam unit; **b. sanitaire** toilet block; **b. technique** (d'une usine etc) technical services block; **b. de titres** block of securities

blocage [blɔkaʒ] NM **1** (de mécanismes etc) jamming, sticking; (des freins) locking, seizing; Écon, Fin freezing; Sport (du ballon) blocking; Psy block; **b. des prix et des salaires** wage and price freeze; Psy **il a** ou **fait un b.** he's got a (mental) block; Aut **b. des roues** wheel lock, wheel lock-up; Aut **b. du volant** steering wheel clamp; Aut **b. de maintien du corps** bodylock seat restraints; **vis de b.** locking screw **2** Constr rubble (stone); Typ (des lettres) turning; Ordinat **b. majuscule** caps lock **3** Ordinat (dans réseau) lockout

blocaille [blɔkaj] NF Constr rubble (stone)

bloc-appartement, pl **blocs-appartements** NM Can Br block of flats, Am apartment building

bloc-cuisine, pl **blocs-cuisines** NM kitchen unit

bloc-cylindres, pl **blocs-cylindres** NM Aut cylinder block

bloc-diagramme, pl **blocs-diagrammes** NM Géog block diagram

bloc-évier, pl **blocs-éviers** NM sink unit

blockbuster [blɔkbœstœr] NM Cin blockbuster

blockhaus [blɔkos] NM **1** Mil blockhouse, pillbox **2** Naut armoured or Am armored tower; **b. de commandement** conning tower

bloc-moteur, pl **blocs-moteurs** NM Aut engine block

bloc-notes, pl **blocs-notes** NM notepad, memo pad; Ordinat notepad, scratchpad; **mémoire b.** scratchpad memory; **b. électronique** electronic notepad

bloc-sièges NM INV block of seats

bloc-système, pl **blocs-systèmes** NM Rail block system

blocus [blɔkys] NM **1** blockade; **faire le b. d'un port** to blockade a port; **lever/forcer le b.** to raise/to run the blockade

blond, -onde [blɔ̃, -ɔ̃d] ADJ (cheveux) fair, blond; (personne) fair(-haired), blond; (sable, blés) golden; **être b. comme les blés** (des cheveux) to be golden(-blond), Litt to be corn-coloured; (d'une personne) to have golden(-blond) hair, to be golden-haired; **bière blonde** lager; **un demi de blonde** = a half of lager; **(cigarette) blonde** Virginia cigarette; **tabac b.** Virginia tobacco
N (personne) **un b.** a fair(-haired) man; **une blonde** a blonde, a fair(-haired) woman; **blonde décolorée** peroxide blonde; Can

Fam **il va voir sa blonde** he's off to see his girl(friend)
NM **cheveux (d'un) b. doré** golden(-blond) hair; **se teindre (les cheveux) en b.** to dye one's hair blond
▸▸**b. ardent** auburn; **b. cendré** ash blond; **b. platine** platinum blond; **b. vénitien** strawberry blond, Titian red

blondasse [blɔ̃das] ADJ (cheveux) washed-out blond

blondeur [blɔ̃dœr] NF (des cheveux) blondness, fairness; (du sable, des blés) goldenness, gold

blondin¹, -ine [blɔ̃dɛ̃, -in] N fair-haired child

blondin² NM Tech cableway

blondinet, -ette [blɔ̃dinɛ, -ɛt] N fair-haired child

blondir [blɔ̃dir] VI (des cheveux) to go or turn blond, to get fairer or lighter; (d'une personne) to go or turn blond; **il faut faire b. les oignons dans du beurre** cook the onions in butter until they turn pale yellow
VT (cheveux) to bleach; **l'eau de mer blondit les cheveux** sea water bleaches the hair
VPR **se blondir** **elle s'est blondi les cheveux** she's bleached her hair

bloquer [blɔke] VT **1** (mécanisme etc) to jam; (porte) to jam, to wedge; (port etc) to blockade; **b. les roues** to lock (up) the wheels; **b. les freins** to jam the brakes on; **bloqué par la neige/le brouillard** snowbound/fogbound; **il m'a bloqué contre un mur** he jammed me up against a wall; Fam **me voilà bloqué à l'hôpital** here I am stuck in hospital
2 (réunir) to group together; **les cours sont bloqués sur six jours** the classes are grouped together over six days; **b. ses jours de congés** to lump together one's days off
3 Constr (mur) to block up or fill up (with rubble); Typ **b. une lettre** to turn a letter
4 (chèque) to stop; (compte en banque) to block; (prix, salaires) to freeze; (négociations) to hold up, to block
5 (route etc) to block; Sport (ballon) to block; **b. le chemin** ou **le passage à qn** to block or be in sb's way
6 Belg Fam (sujet) to bone up on, Br to swot up
7 Can Fam (échouer à) (examen) to fail, to flunk
8 Psy **ça me bloque de me sentir observé** I get a (mental) block if I feel I'm being watched; **être bloqué** to have a (mental) block
VPR **se bloquer 1** (de machine, d'ascenseur etc) to get stuck; (d'une carte à puce) to be automatically invalidated; (de papier) to jam **2** Psy to have or get a (mental) block

blottir (se) [səblɔtir] VPR to snuggle up, to curl up; **se b. dans son lit** to curl up or snuggle up or snuggle down in bed; **se b. contre qn/dans les bras de qn** to snuggle up to sb/ in sb's arms; **blottis les uns contre les autres** huddled up or snuggled up together; **blotti dans un coin** huddled or huddling in a corner; **village blotti au fond de la vallée** village tucked away or nestling in the valley

blousant [bluzɑ̃] ADJ loose-fitting

blouse [bluz] NF **1** (d'écolier, de femme de ménage, de mécanicien etc) overall; (de médecin) (white) coat; (de paysan) smock; **b. (de laboratoire)** (lab) coat **2** (chemisier) blouse

blouser [bluze] VT Fam (personne) to con, to take in, to cheat
VI (d'un corsage etc) to be loose-fitting
VPR **se blouser** Fam to make a mistake or a blunder

blouson [bluzɔ̃] NM (lumber)jacket; (plus léger) blouson; **b. en** ou **de cuir** leather jacket; **b. d'aviateur** bomber jacket; *Fam* **b. noir** young hoodlum (*wearing a black leather jacket*), *Br* rocker

blue chip [blutʃip] NM *Bourse* blue chip

blue-jean(s), *pl* **blue-jeans** [blu(d)ʒin(z)] NM jeans

blues [bluz] NM *Mus* blues

Bluetooth [blutus] NM *Tél* Bluetooth

bluff [blœf] NM bluff; **faire du b.** to bluff; **c'est un coup de b.** it's all bluff, he's/they're/*etc* bluffing *or Br* trying it on; **il faut y aller au b.** you'll have to try and bluff

bluffer [blœfe] VT **1** (*tromper*) to take in, to trick; *Cartes* to bluff **2** *Fam* (*impressionner*) to blow away; **ils m'ont vraiment bluffé lors du concert qu'ils ont donné à Paris** they really blew me away when they played Paris ▸ VI to bluff; **il ne fait que b.** he's only bluffing, *Br* he's just trying it on

bluffeur, -euse [blœfœr, -øz] N bluffer

blush [blœʃ] NM (*fard*) blusher

blutage [blytaʒ] NM (*de la farine*) bolting

bluter [blyte] VT (*farine*) to bolt

BMTN [beemteen] NM *Fin* (*abrév* **bon à moyen terme négociable**) MNT

BN [been] NF *abrév* **Bibliothèque nationale**

BNF [beenɛf] NF *abrév* **Bibliothèque nationale de France**

BO [beo] NF *abrév* **bande originale** ▸ NM *abrév* **Bulletin officiel**

boa [bɔa] NM **1** (*serpent*) boa; **b. constricteur** boa constrictor **2** (*tour de cou*) boa

boat people [botpipœl] NMPL boat people

bob [bɔb] NM *Fam* **1** *Sport* bob(sleigh) **2** (*chapeau*) sun hat

bobard [bɔbar] NM *Fam* tall story

bobet [bɔbɛ] *Suisse Fam* ADJ stupid ▸ NM idiot

bobinage [bɔbinaʒ] NM **1** (*opération*) winding, reeling **2** *Élec* coil

bobinard [bɔbinar] NM *très Fam* whorehouse, *Br* knocking shop

bobine [bɔbin] NF **1** (*de ruban, fil etc*) reel; (*dans une machine à coudre*) bobbin; (*de machine à écrire, d'appareil photo etc*) spool; (*de papier*) roll; *Cin, Phot* reel; **une b. de pellicule** a roll of film; *Cin, Phot* **à bobines** reel-to-reel **2** *Élec* coil; **b. de dérivation** shunt coil; **b. d'allumage** ignition coil; **b. HT** ht coil; **b. d'induction** induction coil; **b. exploratrice** pick-up coil; **b. haute tension** high-tension coil; **b. magnétique** magnet coil; **b. réceptrice** pick-up coil; **b. à faible inductance** low-inductance coil **3** *Arg* (*visage*) mug, face; **elle a fait une drôle de b.** she pulled a (funny) face

bobiner [bɔbine] VT (*fil de coton etc*) to wind, to reel; (*fil de fer etc*) to coil

bobineur, -euse [bɔbinœr, -øz] N *Tex, Élec* winder ▸ NF **bobineuse** winding machine, winder

bobinoir [bɔbinwar] NM *Tex, Élec* winding machine, winder

bobinot [bɔbino] NM *Cin, TV* reel

bobo [bobo] NM *Enf* (*blessure légère*) cut; **ça fait b.?** does it hurt?, is it sore?; **j'ai un b. au doigt** my finger hurts; **se faire b.** to hurt oneself ▸ N *Fam* (*abrév* **bourgeois(e) bohème**) bobo

bobonne [bɔbɔn] NF **1** *Arg Péj* missus, old girl; **il est toujours accompagné de b.** he always has his missus *or* old girl with him **2** *Belg Fam* grand-mama, grandma

bobsleigh [bɔbslɛ(g)] NM *Sport* bobsleigh

bobtail [bɔbtɛjl] NM (*chien*) Old English sheepdog

boc [bɔk] NM *Suisse* goatee (beard)

bocage [bɔkaʒ] NM **1** *Litt* (*bois*) copse **2** *Géog* bocage (*countryside with many hedges, trees and small fields*)

bocager, -ère [bɔkaʒe, -ɛr] ADJ wooded

bocal, -aux [bɔkal, -o] NM jar; **mettre des fruits en bocaux** to bottle fruit; **b. à poissons rouges** goldfish bowl

bocard [bɔkar] NM *Métal* ore crusher, stamping mill

Boccace [bɔkas] N Boccaccio

BOCE [beoseø] NM (*abrév* **Bulletin officiel des communautés européennes**) = official listing of all new EC directives

boche [bɔʃ] *Fam Péj* ADJ Boche, Kraut ▸ N **B.** Boche, Kraut

bock [bɔk] NM **1** (*verre*) beer glass **2** (*contenu*) glass of beer (c) *Fam* **aller pisser un b.** to go for a pee

bocson [bɔksɔ̃] NM *Fam* **quel b.!** what a shambles!; **ils ont mis le b. dans la chambre** they make a real mess in the room

body [bɔdi] NM (*vêtement*) body

body-building NM *Sport* body building; **faire du b.** to do body building

boentje [buntjə] N *Belg Fam Hum* (*attirance*) **avoir un b. pour qn** to have a crush on sb

Boer [bur] ADJ, N Boer

boët(t)e [bwɛt] NF *Pêche* bait

bœuf, *pl* **bœufs** [bœf, bø] NM **1** (*mammifère*) bullock, steer; (*de trait*) ox; **bœufs à l'engrais** beeves; **b. gras** fatted ox, prize ox; **bœufs de boucherie** beef cattle; **fort comme un b.** as strong as an ox; *Fam* **on n'est pas des bœufs** I'm/we're not superhuman; **avoir un b. sur la langue** to keep mum VOIR GRAMMAIRE A13 **2** (*viande*) beef **3** *Mus* jam session; **faire un b.** to have a jam session, to jam ▸ ADJ INV *Fam* fantastic, tremendous, amazing; **il a eu un succès b.** he was incredibly successful; **ça a fait un effet b.** it made a really big impression

▸▸ *Zool* **b. à bosse** zebu; **b. bourguignon** bœuf bourguignon; **b. gros sel** boiled beef; *Culin* **b. (à la) mode** stewed beef; **b. musqué** musk ox

bof [bɔf] INT **ça te plaît? – b., pas tellement** do you like it? – not really, no; **ça te dirait de venir avec nous? – b.** would you like to come with us? – I don't know *or* I'm not bothered; **il est chouette, hein, mon nouveau pull? – b.** my new sweater's great, isn't it? – I suppose so

boggie [bɔgi], **bogie** [bɔʒi] NM *Rail* bogie, bogy

Bogota [bɔgɔta] N Bogota

bogue¹ [bɔg] NF *Bot* chestnut bur, *Am* shuck

bogue² NM *Ordinat* bug; **dépourvu/plein de bogues** bug-free/-ridden; **b. de logiciel** software bug; **le b. de l'an 2000** the millennium bug

bogué [bɔge] ADJ *Ordinat* bug-ridden

boguet [bɔgɛ] NM *Suisse* (*cyclomoteur*) moped

bohème [bɔɛm] ADJ bohemian; **un esprit b.** an unconventional thinker ▸ N bohemian; **mener une vie de b.** to lead a bohemian *or* an unconventional life ▸ NF **la b.** (*milieu*) bohemia

Bohême [bɔɛm] NF Bohemia

bohémien, -ienne [bɔemjɛ̃, -jɛn] ADJ Bohemian ▸ N gipsy

boire [bwar] (*prp* **buvant**; *pp* **bu, bue**; *pr ind* **je bois** [bwa], **il boit, nous buvons, ils boivent**; *pr sub* **je boive, n. buvions**; *impf* **je buvais**; *p hist* **je bus, n. bûmes**; *fu* **je boirai**) VT **1** (*avaler*) to drink; **b. qch à petits coups** to sip sth; **b. qch d'un (seul) trait** *ou* **d'un seul coup** to drink sth at one gulp, to swig sth down, *Br* to

knock sth back; **je ne bois pas d'alcool** I don't drink (alcohol); **b. une bouteille à quatre** to drink a bottle between four; **b. un verre jusqu'à la dernière goutte** to drain a glass; *Fam* **b. un coup** to have a drink; **il a bu un coup (de trop)** he's had one too many; **tu viens b. un verre?** are you coming for a drink?; *Fig* **b. les paroles de qn** to drink in sb's every word; *Fam Fig* **b. la** *ou* **une tasse** (*en nageant*) to get a mouthful; *Fig Fam* **ce n'est pas la mer à b.** it's not that bad, it's no big deal; **b. un bouillon** (*en nageant*) to get a mouthful; *Fin* to make a big loss, to come a cropper; *Fig* **il boit du petit lait** (*il est content*) he's as pleased as Punch; **quand on le flatte, il boit du petit lait** when people flatter him, he laps it up

2 (*des plantes, des matières poreuses etc*) (*eau*) to soak up, to absorb

▸ VI **1** (*d'une personne*) to drink; (*des plantes*) to soak up *or* absorb water; *Can* (*d'un bébé*) to feed; **b. à la bouteille** to drink from the bottle; **b. à sa soif, b. jusqu'à plus soif** to drink one's fill; **b. à la santé de qn** to drink (to) sb's health; **b. au succès de qch** to drink to the success of sth; **faire b. qn** to give sb a drink *or* something to drink; **faire b. les chevaux** to water the horses; *Fig* **il y a à b. et à manger là-dedans** it's got its good and its bad points, it's a bit of a mixed bag; *Prov* **qui a bu boira** old habits die hard; **il a commandé à b.** (*pour lui*) he ordered a drink; (*pour deux, trois etc*) he ordered the drinks; **vous avez commandé à b.?** have you ordered something to drink?

2 (*d'un alcoolique*) to drink; **tu bois trop** you drink too much; **elle boit comme un trou** she drinks like a fish; **je ne sais pas b.** I'm not much of a drinker

▸ NM **le b. et le manger** food and drink, eating and drinking; *Fig* **il était si triste qu'il en avait perdu le b. et le manger** he was so upset that he couldn't eat or drink; *Can* **c'est l'heure de son b.** (*tétée*) it's his feeding time

▸ VPR **se boire** (*de boisson*) to be drunk; **les vins sucrés se boivent au dessert** sweet wines are drunk with dessert; **ce vin se boit bien** *ou* **se laisse b.** this wine is very drinkable *or* goes down well

bois [bwa] NM **1** (*forêt*) wood; **petit b.** grove, *Br* spinney; **b. de chênes/sapins** oak/fir wood; **Robin des B.** Robin Hood; **je n'aimerais pas le rencontrer un soir au coin d'un b.** I wouldn't like to meet him in a dark alley

2 (*arbres*) timber (trees); **abattre** *ou* **couper le b.** to cut down *or* fell timber; *Fam* **casser du b.** (*d'un avion*) to crash-land

3 (*matériau*) wood; **petit b.** kindling; **chantier de b.** timber yard; **travail du b.** woodwork; **train de b.** float *or* raft of timber; **jambe de b.** wooden leg; **meubles en b.** wooden furniture; *Can* **maison en b. rond** log house; *Fig* **elle n'est pas de b.** she's only human; *Fig* **être du b. dont on fait les flûtes** to be easy-going; *Fig* **je leur ferai voir de quel b. je me chauffe** I'll show them (what I'm made of); *Fam* **touchez du b.!** touch wood!, *Am* knock on wood!; *Fam* **chèque en b.** rubber cheque, cheque that bounces; *Fam* **ça envoie le b.** (*c'est excellent*) it's the business

4 (*gravure*) woodcut

5 (*de chaise, raquette etc*) frame; *Tennis* **faire un b.** to hit the ball off the wood *or* the frame

6 *Mus* **les b.** the woodwind

7 **les b.** (*d'un cerf*) the antlers

▸▸ **b. blanc** deal, whitewood; **b. à brûler** firewood; **b. de charpente** timber, *Am* lumber; **b. de chauffage** firewood; *surtout Can* **b. debout** standing timber; **b. dur** hardwood; *Can* **b. franc** hardwood; **b. des îles** West Indian hardwood; **b. de lit** bedstead; **b. de mai** hawthorn; **b. mort** deadwood; **b. d'œuvre** timber, *Am* lumber; **b. de rose** rosewood; **b. de** sapin deal, whitewood; **b. tendre** softwood; **b. vert** unseasoned *or* green timber

boisage [bwazaʒ] NM *Min* **1** *(action)* *(d'un puits, d'une galerie etc)* timbering **2** *(ensemble des bois)* timbering, timber work

boisé [bwaze] ADJ *(région)* wooded; **pays b.** woodland(s), wooded country

boisement [bwazmã] NM *(d'une région)* afforestation

boiser [bwaze] VT **1** *(planter d'arbres)* to afforest, to plant with trees **2** *(mine, galerie)* to timber

boiserie [bwazri] NF *Constr* woodwork, wainscot(ing), panelling

boisseau, -eaux [bwaso] NM **1** *Can, Arch (mesure)* bushel; *Fig* **mettre la lumière sous le b.** to keep things hidden **2** *Tech (tuyau)* drain tile; *(de cheminée)* chimney (flue) tile; *(de moteur)* throttle chamber

boisson [bwasɔ̃] NF **1** *(liquide à boire)* drink, *Fml* beverage; **b. gazeuse** fizzy drink; **b. fraîche** cold drink; **boissons alcoolisées/non alcoolisées** alcoholic/soft drinks; **b. chaude** hot drink **2** *(alcool)* drink; **il s'est adonné à la b.** he's taken to drink; **pris de b.** inebriated, intoxicated; **débit de boissons** bar **3** *Can (spiritueux)* hard liquor, spirits; **être/se mettre en b.** to be/get drunk

boîte [bwat] NF **1** *(récipient)* box; *(de conserves)* can, *Br* tin; **b. à bijoux** jewel box; **b. à couture** *ou* **ouvrage** sewing box; **b. en fer** tin; **une b. de chocolats** a box of chocolates; **des haricots en b.** canned *or Br* tinned beans; *TV, Cin* **en b.** in the can; **mettre en b.** *(marchandises)* to box; *(sardines, légumes etc)* to can, *Br* to tin; *Fig Fam* **mettre qn en b.** to pull sb's leg; **b. à violon** violin case; *Fig Fam* **fermer sa b.** to shut one's trap *or* mouth **2** *Tech (de serrure)* case
3 *Fam (entreprise)* firm; *(école)* school; **je travaille dans une b. d'informatique** I work for a computer firm *or* company; **sale b.** rotten hole
4 b. (de nuit) nightclub; **aller** *ou* **sortir en b.** to go (out) to a nightclub
▸▸ **b. d'allumettes** *(pleine)* box of matches; *(vide)* matchbox; **b. à bachot** crammer; **b. de conserve** can, *Br* tin; **ils se nourrissent de boîtes de conserve** they live on canned *or Br* tinned food; *Anat* **b. crânienne** *ou* **du crâne** cranium; **b. de dérivation** junction box; *Ordinat* **b. de dialogue** dialog box; **b. de l'embrayage** clutch casing; *Rail* **b. de l'essieu** axle box; **b. à feu** firebox; *Élec* **b. à fusibles** fuse box; *Aut* **b. à gants** glove compartment; **b. à** *ou* **aux lettres** *(pour envoyer)* letterbox, postbox, pillarbox, *Am* mailbox; *(chez soi)* letterbox, *Am* mailbox; *Ordinat* **b. à lettres électronique** (electronic) mailbox, e-mail box; **b. à malice** secret toy box; **b. à musique** music box, *Br* musical box; *Aviat* **b. noire** flight recorder, black box; **b. à outils** *(sens informatique également)* toolbox; **b. à pain** bread bin; **b. postale** Post Office box; **b. à rythmes** drum machine; **b. de secours** first-aid box; **b. à vapeur** steam chest; *Aut* **b. de vitesses** gearbox; **b. vocale** voice mail

boîte-pont, *pl* **boîtes-ponts** NF *Aut* transaxle

boiter [bwate] VI *(en marchant)* to limp, to walk with a limp; **b. d'un pied** to be lame in one foot; **b. bas** to limp badly

boiterie [bwatri] NF lameness

boiteux, -euse [bwatø, -øz] ADJ *(personne, cheval)* lame; *Fig (meuble)* wobbly, rickety; *(explication)* lame; *(raisonnement, projet)* shaky; *(traduction, phrase)* iffy; *(paix)* fragile, uncertain; *(période)* uncertain; **le facteur est b.** the postman walks with *or* has a limp; **vers b.** limping verses; **cette phrase est**

un peu **boiteuse** this sentence doesn't hang together very well *or* doesn't work very well
N **lame man,** f **lame woman**

boîtier [bwatje] NM case, casing, housing; *Phot* (camera) body; **b. de montre** watch case; **b. de chirurgien** surgeon's instrument case
▸▸ *Ordinat* **b. de commande** command box; *Ordinat* **b. commutateur** data switch; *Ordinat* **b. compact** compact case; *Aut* **b. de direction** steering box; *Aut* **b. de direction à crémaillère** rack and pinion steering box; *Ordinat* **b. grande tour** large tower case; *Ordinat* **b. mini-tour** minitower case; *Ordinat* **b. moyenne tour** miditower case; *Ordinat* **b. de partage** *(pour imprimante)* data switch; *Aut* **b. de raccordement** junction box; **b. de télécommande** remote control; *Ordinat* **b. vertical** tower

boitillement [bwatijmã] NM slight limp

boitiller [bwatije] VI to limp slightly, to have a slight limp

boit-sans-soif [bwasãswəf] NM INV *Arg* boozer, tippler

bol[1] [bɔl] NM **1** *Physiol* **b. alimentaire** *(alimentary)* bolus **2** *Pharm, Vét* bolus, pellet

bol[2] NM **1** *(pièce de vaisselle)* bowl **2** *Arg (chance)* luck; **manque de b.** bad luck; **coup de b.** stroke of luck; **ne pas avoir de b.** to be unlucky, to be out of luck; **pas de b.!** what rotten luck! **3** *(contenu)* bowl(ful); **avaler son b. de café** to drink one's coffee; **on a pris un b. d'air frais** *ou* **pur** we got a good breath of fresh air

bolchevik, bolchevique [bɔlʃəvik] ADJ, N Bolshevik, Bolshevist

bolchevisme [bɔlʃəvism] NM Bolshevism

bolcheviste [bɔlʃəvist] ADJ, N Bolshevik, Bolshevist

bolduc [bɔldyk] NM gift-wrap ribbon

bolée [bɔle] NF *(de cidre etc)* bowl(ful)

boléro [bɔlero] NM *(vêtement), Mus* bolero

bolet [bɔlɛ] NM *(champignon)* boletus

bolide [bɔlid] NM *(voiture de course)* racing car; *Astron* meteor, fireball, *Spéc* bolide; **lancé comme un b. sur la route** hurtling along the road; **s'éloigner** *ou* **partir comme un b.** to shoot off like a rocket; **il est arrivé comme un b.** he arrived at top speed

bolivar [bɔlivar] NM *(monnaie)* bolivar

Bolivie [bɔlivi] NF Bolivia

bolivien, -ienne [bɔlivjɛ̃, -jɛn] ADJ Bolivian
N **B.** Bolivian

bolognais, -aise [bɔlɔɲɛ, -ɛz] ADJ Bolognese; *Culin* **spaghetti bolognaise** spaghetti bolognese; **sauce bolognaise** bolognese sauce
N **B.** Bolognese

Bologne [bɔlɔɲ] N Bologna

bombage [bɔ̃baʒ] NM *Fam* (aerosol) graffiti; **faire des bombages sur un mur** to spray-paint a wall with graffiti

bombance [bɔ̃bãs] NF *Fam* feast; **faire b.** to go on a spree *or* a binge; *(manger)* to have a feast

bombardement [bɔ̃bardəmã] NM **1** *(avec des obus)* bombardment, shelling; *(avec des bombes)* bombing, bombardment; *(avec des pierres etc)* pelting; **b. de questions** flood of questions; **b. aérien** air raid; **avion de b.** bomber; **le b. atomique d'Hiroshima** the dropping of the atomic bomb on Hiroshima **2** *Phys* bombardment

bombarder [bɔ̃barde] VT **1** *(avec des obus)* to bombard, to shell; *(avec des bombes)* to bomb, to bombard; **maison bombardée** shelled/bombed house; **b. qn de pierres** to pelt sb with stones; **b. qn de questions** to fire questions at sb, to bombard sb with ques-

tions; **être bombardé de lettres/coups de téléphone** to be bombarded *or* inundated with letters/phone calls **2** *Phys (de neutrons etc)* to bombard (**de** with) **3** *Fam* **on l'a bombardé ministre** he's been pitchforked into the post of minister *or* made a minister out of the blue
VI *Fam (fumer beaucoup)* to smoke like a chimney

bombardier [bɔ̃bardje] NM *Mil* **1** *Aviat (avion)* bomber; *(aviateur)* bombardier **2** *Arch* bombardier

bombe [bɔ̃b] NF **1** *Mil etc* bomb; **b. de fabrication artisanale** home-made bomb; **attaque** *ou* **attentat à la b.** bomb attack; **lâcher** *ou* **larguer une b.** to release *or* drop a bomb; *Fam* **entrer en** *ou* **comme une b.** to come bursting in; *Fig* **cela a fait l'effet d'une b.** it was a real bombshell **2** *(atomiseur)* spray, aerosol; **b. de peinture/d'insecticide** paint/fly spray; **déodorant en b.** deodorant spray **3** *Équitation* riding hat *or* cap **4** *Fam* **faire la b.** to live it up **5** *Can (bouilloire)* kettle
▸▸ **b. A** A bomb; **b. atomique** atom(ic) bomb; *Méd* **b. au cobalt** cobalt bomb; **b. à eau** water bomb; **b. à fragmentation** fragmentation *or* scatter bomb; **b. fumigène** smoke bomb; *Culin* **b. glacée** bombe glacée; **b. H** H bomb; **b. à hydrogène** hydrogen bomb; **b. incendiaire** fire bomb, incendiary bomb; **b. lacrymogène** tear-gas grenade; **b. au plastic** plastic bomb; **b. à retardement** time bomb, delayed-action bomb; **b. volante** flying bomb, *Fam* doodlebug

bombé [bɔ̃be] ADJ bulging; *(forme)* rounded, curved; **avoir le front b.** to have a bulging forehead; **se tenir droit, la poitrine bombée** to stand up straight with one's chest thrown out; **chaussée bombée** cambered road

bombement [bɔ̃bmã] NM bulge, bulging; *(d'une route)* camber

bomber [bɔ̃be] VT **1** *(gonfler)* to cause to bulge; *(route)* to camber; **b. la poitrine** *ou* **le torse** to throw out one's chest; *Fig* to swagger (around) **2** *(écrire à la bombe)* to spray; **b. des graffiti/des slogans** to spray graffiti/slogans
VI **1** *(d'un mur etc)* to bulge (out) **2** *Fam (aller très vite)* to bomb along, to belt along

bombinette [bɔ̃binɛt] NF *Fam* **1** *(petite bombe)* little bomb **2** *(petite voiture très nerveuse)* nippy little car

bombonne [bɔ̃bɔn] NF = **bonbonne**

bôme [bom] NF *Naut* boom

BON[1]**, BONNE** [bɔ̃, bɔn]

ADJ	good **1–7, 9–11, 13** ▪ nice **2** ▪ kind **5** ▪ right **4, 13** ▪ fit **7**
ADV	good

ADJ **1** *(moralement)* good; **le b. M. Seguin** good old Mr Seguin; **mon b. monsieur** my dear sir; **défendre la bonne cause** to fight the good fight; **bonne action** good deed; *Fam* **b. chic b. genre** ≃ Sloany, *Am* ≃ preppy; **la bonne société** polite society
2 *(agréable) (livre, histoire, odeur, ambiance, travail etc)* good; **bonne soirée** pleasant evening; **installé dans un b. fauteuil** settled in a nice *or* comfortable armchair; **j'ai trouvé b. le rôti** I enjoyed the roast, I thought the roast was good; **je ne trouve pas ça très b.** I don't think it's very good, I don't much like it; **qu'est-ce que c'est b.!** that's really good!; **l'eau est bonne** *(en se baignant)* the water's great; **elle est bonne?** *(en se baignant)* what's the water like?; **ils aiment les bonnes choses** they like the good things in life; **elle lui fait de bons petits plats** she makes him nice little meals; **être en bonne compagnie** to be in good company;

être de bonne **compagnie** to be good company

3 (*capable, apte*) good; **un b. médecin/père** a good doctor/father; **les bons élèves** the good or bright pupils; **b. en anglais** good at English; *Fin* **b. pour aval** guaranteed by

4 (*correct*) (*travail, qualité etc*) good; (*réponse, clé, côté, bus etc*) right; **si j'ai bonne mémoire** if my memory serves me (well); **c'est de la bonne qualité** it's good quality; **oui, c'est b.** yes, that's right; **maintenant, c'est b.** (*à qn qui fixe une étagère etc*) it's right or fine now; **pour le b. fonctionnement de l'appareil** to ensure the appliance functions correctly; **pour lui, tous les moyens sont bons pour réussir** he'll do anything to succeed, he'll stop at nothing to succeed; **prends le marteau par le b. bout** hold the hammer the right way round; **tourner dans le b. sens** to turn in the right direction; **un intellectuel, dans le b. sens du terme** an intellectual in the true sense of the term; **en b. état** in good condition; *Fig* **frapper/ne pas frapper à la bonne porte** to come to the right/wrong person; *Fig* **la bonne voie** ou **route** the right path or track; **il a encore de bonnes jambes** he still has a good pair of legs; **avoir une bonne vue** to have good eyesight; **sa vue n'est plus très bonne** he doesn't see too well any more; *Tennis* **la balle est bonne** the ball is in or good; **les yaourts sont-ils encore bons?** are the yoghurts still good or all right?; **le fusible n'est plus b., il faut le changer** the fuse has gone, we'll have to change it

5 (*généreux*) good, kind (**pour, envers, avec** to); **c'est un b. garçon** ou *Fam* **type** ou **gars** he's a good sort, he's all right; **tu es trop bonne pour moi** you're too good to me; **être b. avec** ou **envers les animaux** to be kind to animals; **c'est parti d'une bonne intention, l'intention était bonne** the intention was good; **être b. public** to be a good audience; **vous êtes bien b. de m'inviter** it's very good or kind of you to invite me; *Fam Iron* **tu es b.!** oh *very* funny!

6 (*profitable, utile*) (*investissement etc*) good; **bonne affaire** bargain; **c'est b. à savoir/à se rappeler** it's worth knowing/remembering; **c'est toujours b. à avoir** it's always worth having; **à quoi b.?** what's the point?, what's the good of it?; **à quoi b. se plaindre?** what's the use or the good or the point of complaining?; **c'est un b. conseil** it's a good piece of advice; **quelle bonne idée!** what a good idea!; **puis-je vous être b. à quelque chose?** can I do anything for you?, can I be of any help (to you)?; **cet exercice est b. pour le dos** this exercise is good for the back; **ce qui est b. pour les uns n'est pas toujours b. pour les autres** what is good for some is not necessarily good for others

7 b. à manger good to eat; (*comestible*) fit or safe to eat; **b. pour le service** *Mil* fit for duty; *Fig* serviceable; **c'est b. pour les nerfs** it's good for your nerves; **il n'est b. qu'à cela** that's all he's fit for; **elle n'est bonne à rien** she's useless, she's good for nothing, she's no good at anything; **c'est b. à jeter** you can throw that away, *Fam* chuck it out

8 (*souhaitable*) **si b. vous semble** if you think it advisable; **il est b. de s'en informer tout de suite** it's best to get information straightaway; **il est b. que vous le sachiez** it's just as well that you should know; **juger** ou **croire** ou **trouver b. de faire qch** to think it best or advisable to do sth

9 (*présage*) good, favourable, *Am* favorable; **souhaiter une** ou **la bonne année à qn** to wish sb a happy New Year; **b. Noël** Merry Christmas; **b. anniversaire!** happy birthday!; **avoir la bonne vie** to have it easy; **b. week-end!**, *Can* **bonne fin de semaine!** have a good weekend!; **bonne chasse!** good hunt-

ing!; **b. voyage!** have a good trip!, bon voyage!; **bonne journée!** have a good or nice day!; **b. appétit!** bon appetit!; (*surtout dans un restaurant*) enjoy your meal!, *Am Fam* enjoy!; **bonne nuit** good night; **bonnes vacances!** have a good or enjoy your holiday!

10 (*caution, crédit etc*) good; **billet b. pour trois mois** ticket valid or good for three months; **ta carte d'étudiant n'est plus bonne** your student card isn't valid any more or is out of date; *Com* **b. pour une entrée gratuite/cinq euros de réduction sur votre prochain achat** this entitles you to free admission/to five euros off your next purchase; **son affaire est bonne!, son compte est b.!** he's in for it!; **elle est bonne pour deux mois de prison** she's looking at or she's going to get two months in prison; **tu es b. pour la contravention** you're in for a fine; *Fam* **on est b.!** (*c'est raté*) we've had it!

11 (*intensif*) good; **j'ai attendu deux bonnes heures** I waited a full or a good two hours, I waited (for) two solid hours; **deux bons kilos** two good kilos; **il m'a fallu un b. moment pour comprendre** it took me a (good or little) while to understand; **arriver b. premier** to come in an easy first; **il était b. dernier** he was way behind all the others, he brought up the rear; **b. nombre de** a number of, a good many; **prendre une bonne moitié de qch** to take a good half of sth; **donner bonne mesure** to give good or full measure; **elle a reçu une bonne fessée** she got a good spanking; **b. gros rire** big resounding laugh; **un b. rhume** a bad cold; **il faudrait qu'on ait une bonne discussion** we must have a good or proper discussion or talk; **une bonne fois pour toutes** once and for all

12 *Litt* **tout de b.** in earnest, really; **est-ce pour de b.?** are you serious?; **on se quitte pour de b.** we're splitting up for good; **il pleut pour de b.** it's raining in real earnest; **cette fois, elle pleure pour de b.** this time she's really crying

13 b.! right!, good!, fine!; **b., je viendrai** right or good or fine, I'll come; **il est malade, allons b.?** he's ill, eh?; **ah b., je ne le savais pas** oh, I didn't know; **b., b., d'accord** all right, all right, OK, OK; **c'est b., j'ai compris** all right or OK, I understand

▸ **ADV tenir b.** (*résister*) to stand fast, to hold one's own; **tenez b.!** hold tight!, hold on (tight)!; (*ne lâchez pas*) don't give up or in; **sentir b.** to smell good; **il fait b. vivre** it's good to be alive; **un pays où il fait b. vivre** a country that's good to live in; **il ne fait pas b. se promener dans ce quartier** it's not safe to walk in this district

▸ **N les bons** the good, the righteous; *Fam* (*dans un film etc*) the goodies; **une histoire de bons et de méchants** a goodies and baddies story; **un b./une bonne à rien** a good-for-nothing

▸ **NM cela a du b.** it has its good points, it has some advantages, there's some good in it; **il y a du b. à ne pas travailler** there's something to be said for not working; **le b. de l'histoire** the best part of the story

▸ **NF bonne** *voir* **bonne**

bon² **NM 1** (*billet*) voucher, coupon, slip **2** *Fin* bond, bill; **b. d'exécution de contrôle** performance bond

▸▸**b. d'achat** gift voucher; **b. d'agence** (*d'une agence de voyages*) travel agent's voucher; **b. d'annulation** cancellation form; **b. de caisse** (*justifiant sortie de fonds*) cash voucher; *Compta* interest-bearing note; *Typ* **b. à clicher** machine proof; **b. de commande** order form; *Typ* **b. à copier** machine proof; **b. de débours** (*pour services aux clients d'un hôtel*) visitors paid out voucher, VPO voucher; **b. de décaissement** disbursement voucher, paid out voucher; **b. à délivrer**

freight release; **b. d'échange** (*d'une agence de voyages*) (travel agent's) voucher; *Com* **b. d'entrée** stock received docket/form; **b. d'épargne** savings certificate; **b. d'essence** petrol coupon; *Com* **b. d'expédition** dispatch note, consignment note; **b. de garantie** guarantee; *Com* guarantee slip; *Com* **b. de livraison** delivery note; **b. au porteur** bearer bond; **b. de réception des marchandises** receipt note; **b. de réduction** money-off coupon or voucher, discount voucher; *Com* **b. de remboursement** money-off voucher; **b. de réservation** reservation form; *Com* **b. de sortie** stock issued docket/form; *Fin* **b. de souscription d'actions** warrant; *Tex* **b. teint** colourfast, *Am* colorfast; (*couleur*) fast; *Fig* (*syndicaliste, socialiste etc*) dyed-in-the-wool, staunch; **b. à tirer** press proof, final corrected proof; **donner le b. à tirer** to pass the proofs for press; **b. du Trésor** treasury bond, exchequer bill; **b. vacances** = voucher supplied by holiday associations to less well-off families to help cover holiday expenses

bonace [bɔnas] **NF** lull, calm (*before or after a storm*)

bonapartisme [bɔnapartism] **NM** Bonapartism

bonapartiste [bɔnapartist] **ADJ, N** Bonapartist

bonard [bɔnar] **ADJ** *Fam* great

bonasse [bɔnas] **ADJ** *Péj* soft, mild; **il est b.** he's too easy-going or too soft; **répondre d'un ton b.** to answer mildly

bonbon [bɔ̃bɔ̃] **NM 1** sweet, *Am* candy, *Austr* lolly; **b. anglais** fruit drop; **b. acidulé** acid drop; **b. à la menthe** mint **2** *Belg* (*biscuit*) biscuit, *Am* cookie

▸ **ADV** *Fam* **coûter b.** to cost an arm and a leg or a bundle

bonbonne [bɔ̃bɔn] **NF 1** *Ind* carboy **2** (*récipient*) demijohn; **b. en verre** glass demijohn; **une b. de vin** a demijohn of wine

bonbonnière [bɔ̃bɔnjer] **NF 1** (*pour les bonbons*) sweet or *Am* candy box, bonbonnière **2** *Fig* bijou residence

bond [bɔ̃] **NM 1** (*saut*) leap, bound, spring, jump; **faire un b.** to leap up, to jump up; **franchir qch d'un b.** to clear sth at one bound or leap or jump; **se lever d'un b.** to spring or to leap or to jump to one's feet; **les loyers/prix ont fait un b.** rents/prices have shot up; **progresser par bonds** to advance by leaps and bounds; **b. en avant** (*technologique etc*) breakthrough **2** (*d'une balle etc*) bounce, rebound; **saisir** ou **prendre la balle au b.** to catch the ball on the bounce or the rebound; *Fig* to seize or grasp the opportunity; **faire faux b. à qn** to leave sb in the lurch, to let sb down

bonde [bɔ̃d] **NF 1** (*bouchon*) (*d'un évier, d'une baignoire*) plug; (*d'un tonneau*) bung; (*d'un bassin*) sluice gate; **lâcher** ou **lever la b.** to pull the plug out; *Fig* **lâcher la b. à sa colère** to give vent to one's anger **2** (*trou d'évacuation*) (*d'un évier, d'une baignoire*) plughole; (*d'un tonneau*) bunghole; (*d'un bassin*) drainage hole, outlet

bondé [bɔ̃de] **ADJ** (*bus, cinéma, ville etc*) packed, jam-packed; **des trains bondés de vacanciers** trains packed or crammed with holiday-makers; *Théâtre* **salle bondée** packed house

bondieuserie [bɔ̃djøzri] **NF** *Péj* **1** (*bigoterie*) religiosity, over-religious zeal **2** (*objet*) devotional object, religious knick-knack

bondir [bɔ̃dir] **VI 1** (*sauter*) to leap (up), to spring (up), to jump (up); **b. en avant/arrière** to leap or spring or jump forward/back; **b. sur qn/qch** to pounce on sb/sth; *Fig* **il a bondi de colère** he flew into a rage; *Fig* **cela me**

fait b. it makes me mad, it makes me see red **2** (courir) to rush (off), to dash (off); **j'ai bondi jusqu'à la poste la plus proche** I rushed (off) or dashed (off) to the nearest post-office; **b. au secours de qn** ou **pour aider qn** to spring or leap to sb's assistance **3** (gambader) to gambol, to leap (about), to skip (about) **4** (d'une balle etc) to bounce

bondissement [bɔ̃dismɑ̃] NM **1** (saut) bound, leap **2** (des agneaux etc) gambolling, frisking

bon enfant [bɔ̃nɑ̃fɑ̃] ADJ INV (personne, manières etc) easy-going, good-natured; (atmosphère) easy-going

bonheur [bɔnœr] NM **1** (chance) good fortune, (good) luck; **j'ai eu le b. de la connaître** I had the good fortune to know her; **porter b. à qn** to bring sb (good) luck; **il ne connaît pas son b.** he doesn't know how lucky he is, he doesn't know his luck; **quel b.!** how marvellous!; **par b.** luckily, fortunately, as luck would have it; **au petit b. (la chance)** at random **2** (bien-être) happiness; **la recherche du b.** the quest for happiness; **le b. de vivre** the joy of living; **faire le b. de qn** to make sb happy; **ces chocolats font mon b.** I adore these chocolates; **l'argent ne fait pas le b.** money can't buy you happiness; **il fait tout pour mon b.** he does everything he can to make me happy; **j'ai eu le b. de voir ma fille naître** I had the joy of seeing my daughter being born; **quel b. de voyager en avion** what a pleasure or delight it is to travel by air **3** Litt (réussite) **avec b.** felicitously; **texte écrit avec b.** felicitous text; **le salé et le sucré s'allient avec b.** savoury and sweet combine happily or are a happy combination

bonheur-du-jour, pl **bonheurs-du-jour** NM escritoire

bonhomie [bɔnɔmi] NF good-heartedness, good-naturedness, bonhomie; **avec b.** goodnaturedly

bonhomme, pl **bonshommes** [bɔnɔm, bɔ̃zɔm] NM Fam (homme, type) fellow, guy, Br chap, Br bloke; **un petit b.** a little fellow; **un vilain b.** a nasty piece of work; **c'est un sacré b.** he's a hell of a guy; **pourquoi pleures-tu, mon b.?** (à un petit garçon) what are you crying for, little fellow?; Fig **il va son petit b. de chemin** he's jogging along nicely; **dessiner des bonshommes** to draw little people
▸▸**b. de neige** snowman; **faire un b. de neige** to make or build a snowman; **b. de** ou **en pain d'épice** gingerbread man; Tech **b. de verrouillage** plunger

boni [bɔni] NM (bénéfice) profit; (excédent) surplus, balance in hand

boniche [bɔniʃ] NF Péj (maid)servant, Br skivvy; **je ne suis pas ta b., fais-le tout seul!** I'm not your servant, do it yourself!; **faire la b. pour qn** to do sb's menial jobs for them, Br to skivvy for sb

bonification [bɔnifikasjɔ̃] NF **1** (d'une terre, d'un vin) improvement **2** Com bonus; **b. pour non sinistre** no claims bonus **3** Sport advantage

bonifié [bɔnifje] ADJ (prêt) at a reduced rate of interest

bonifier [bɔnifje] (pr sub, impf n. bonifiions, v. bonifiiez) VT **1** (terre, caractère etc) to improve **2** Com (pénurie etc) to make up, to make good
VPR **se bonifier** (d'une personne, du vin etc) to improve; **ses humeurs vont se b. avec le temps** his/her nature will improve with time

boniment [bɔnimɑ̃] NM **1** Com sales talk or pitch, patter; **faire du b. à qn** (d'un vendeur) to give sb the sales talk or the patter; **faire du b. à une femme** to chat a woman up; **faire**

du b. à qn pour qu'il fasse qch to try to coax or talk sb into doing sth **2** Fam (blague) tall story; **tout ça, c'est du b.** that's all eyewash or claptrap

bonimenter [bɔnimɑ̃te] VI Fam to dish out the sales talk or the patter

bonite [bɔnit] NF (poisson) bonito

bonjour [bɔ̃ʒur] NM **1** hello, Fam hi, Fml good day; (le matin) good morning; (l'après-midi) good afternoon; (quand on est présenté à qn) hello, how do you do?; Can (au revoir) (pendant la journée) goodbye, bye, see you later; **dis b. à la dame** (à un enfant) say hello to the lady; **(dis) b. à ta mère (de ma part)** (give) my regards to your mother, say hello to your mother for me; **c'est facile** ou **simple comme b.** it's as easy as pie, it's child's play **2** Fam Iron **b. les dégâts!** what a mess!; (ça va aller mal) there'll be trouble!; **b. la soirée/l'odeur!** what an evening/a smell!; **b. la propreté ici!** I don't think much of the way things are cleaned round here!; **le périphérique le soir à six heures, b.!** the ring road at six o'clock at night, no way or forget it!

bon marché ADJ INV cheap; **acheter/vendre qch (à) b.** to buy/sell sth cheap(ly)

bonnard [bɔnar] ADJ Fam great; **c'est b.!** cool!

bonne [bɔn] NF **1** (domestique) maid, Vieilli maidservant; **b. à tout faire** general help, Vieilli maid of all work; **b. d'enfants** nurse, Br nanny **2 en voilà une (bien) b.!** that's a good one!; **il en a de bonnes!** he must be joking or kidding!; **tu en as de bonnes!** you're having a laugh, aren't you?; **il m'en a raconté de bonnes sur toi!** he told me some interesting things about you!; **avoir qn à la b.** (d'un employeur, d'un professeur) to have a soft spot for sb; Fam **il t'a à la b.** you're well in with him

Bonne-Espérance N cap **de B.** Cape of Good Hope

bonne-main, pl **bonnes-mains** NF Suisse tip

bonne-maman, pl **bonnes-mamans** NF Vieilli grandmama

bonnement [bɔnmɑ̃] ADV **tout b.** simply; **je lui ai dit tout b. que …** I simply or just told him that …

bonnet [bɔnɛ] NM **1** (coiffure) hat; (de bébé) bonnet; **b. de ski** ski cap; Fig **prendre qch sous son b.** (faire de sa propre initiative) to take it upon oneself to do sth, Fam to do sth off one's own bat; (prendre la responsabilité) to take on the responsibility for sth, to take sth on; **opiner du b.** to nod (one's) assent, to nod in agreement; Fig **avoir la tête près du b.** to have a short fuse; Fig **jeter son b. par-dessus les moulins** to kick over the traces, to throw caution to the winds; **c'est b. blanc et blanc b.** it's six of one and half a dozen of the other; Fig Fam **gros b.** big shot, big noise, bigwig; Fam **te casse pas le b.!** don't worry about it, don't let it bother you!
2 (d'un soutien-gorge) cup; **quelle profondeur de b.?** what size cup?
3 Zool (d'un ruminant) second stomach, reticulum, honeycomb
▸▸**b. de bain** bathing or swimming cap; **b. de douche** shower cap; **b. d'évêque** bishop's mitre; **b. de nuit** nightcap; **être triste comme un b. de nuit** to be as cheerful as the grave; **b. phrygien** ou **rouge** Phrygian cap (in French Revolution); Mil **b. de police** forage cap

bonneterie [bɔnɛtri] NF **1** (bas) hosiery **2** (commerce) hosiery trade; (magasin) hosier's (shop)

bonnetier, -ière [bɔntje, -jɛr] N hosier

bonnette [bɔnɛt] NF (objectif) supplementary lens; (de micro) windshield; **b. anti-vent** (d'un microphone) windscreen, windshield

bonniche [bɔniʃ] NF Péj = **boniche**

bonobo [bɔnɔbo] NM Zool bonobo

bon-papa, pl **bons-papas** NM Vieilli grandpapa

bonsaï [bɔnzaj, bɔ̃zaj] NM (arbre) bonsai

bonsoir [bɔ̃swar] NM (en partant le soir) good evening; (en partant le soir) goodbye; (quand on prend congé tard le soir) goodnight; **dire b.** ou **souhaiter le b. à qn** to say good evening/goodnight to sb

bonté [bɔ̃te] NF **1** (qualité) kindness, goodness, kindliness; **une femme d'une grande b.** a very kind or good woman; **sourire plein de b.** kind(ly) or benevolent smile; **ayez la b. de me dire qui …** be so good as to tell me who …, please tell me who …; **auriez-vous la b. de …?** would you be so good as to …?; **faire qch par b. d'âme** to do sth out of the goodness or kindness of one's heart; Fam **b. divine** ou **du ciel!** good heavens!
2 bontés kindnesses, acts of kindness, kind acts; **avoir des bontés pour qn** to show kindness towards sb; **remercier qn pour ses bontés** to thank sb for his/her kindness; **je ne m'attendais pas à tant de bontés** I didn't expect such kindness
3 Vieilli (de choses) goodness, excellence

bonus [bɔnys] NM (dans les assurances) no-claims bonus

bonus-malus [bɔnysmalys] NM INV (en assurances) no-claims bonus system

bon vivant ADJ **il est b.** he enjoys life
NM man who enjoys life; **des bons vivants** people who enjoy life

bonze [bɔ̃z] NM **1** Rel Buddhist priest or monk, bonze **2** Fig Fam (personnage important) big shot, bigwig **3** Fam **vieux b.** bigheaded old fool

bonzerie [bɔ̃zri] NF Buddhist monastery

bonzesse [bɔ̃zɛs] NF Buddhist nun, bonze

boogie-woogie, pl **boogie-woogies** [bugiwugi] NM Mus boogie-woogie

book[1] [buk] NM (d'un mannequin, d'un artiste etc) portfolio; **b. de contacts** contacts book

bookmaker [bukmɛkœr], Fam **book**[2] NM bookmaker, Fam bookie

bookmark [bukmark] NM Ordinat bookmark

booléen, -éenne [buleɛ̃, -ɛn] ADJ Math, Ordinat Boolean

boom [bum] NM Com, Fin boom

boomerang [bumrɑ̃g] NM boomerang; **avoir un effet b.** to have a boomerang effect; Fam **son projet a fait b.** his plan boomeranged or backfired

booster[1] [bustœr] NM (amplificateur), Astronaut booster

booster[2] [buste] VT Fam (stimuler) to boost

booter [bute] VI Ordinat **b. (sur le lecteur B)** to boot (off the B drive)

boots [buts] NMPL ankle boots

boquer [bɔke] VI Can (s'entêter) to dig one's heels in

borate [bɔrat] NM Chimie borate

borax [bɔraks] NM Chimie borax

borborygme [bɔrbɔrigm] NM (usu pl) (de l'estomac) rumbling(s), gurgling(s); Fig **je ne comprenais pas ses borborygmes** I didn't understand his mumblings or mutterings; **borborygmes de la plomberie** gurgling noises in the plumbing

bord [bɔr] NM **1** Naut (d'un navire) side; **jeter qch/tomber** ou **passer par-dessus b.** to throw sth/to fall overboard; **moteur hors b.** outboard motor; **les hommes du b.** the ship's company, the crew; Fig **être du même b.** to be on the same side or of the same opinion; Can **se trouver du bon/mauvais b.** to be on the right/wrong side; **à b. d'un navire/d'un avion** on board or aboard a ship/a plane; **monter à b. (d'un bateau/d'un avion)** to go/come on board or aboard (a boat/a plane), to board (a boat/a plane); **prendre qn à son b.** to take sb on board or aboard; Fig **vous êtes (le) seul maître à b.** you're the one in charge **2** Naut (bordée) tack; **courir ou tirer un b.** to tack, to make a tack **3** (d'une table, d'une assiette, d'un biscuit, des paupières) edge; (d'un vêtement) border, hem; (d'une falaise, d'un chemin) edge, verge; (d'un chapeau) brim; (d'un vase, d'une tasse) rim; (d'une blessure) lip; (de l'œil) rim; **b. du trottoir** kerb, Am curb; **remplir un verre jusqu'au** ou **à ras b.** to fill a glass to the brim; **sur le** ou **au b. de la route** at or on the roadside, at or on the side of the road; Can **de l'autre b. de la rue** on the other side of the street; **auberge au b.** ou **sur le b. de la route** wayside or roadside inn; **hôtel au b. du lac** lakeside hotel; **se promener au b. du lac** to walk along the edge of the lake; **je l'ai trouvé au b. de la rivière** I found it on the river bank; **aller au b. de la mer** to go to the seaside; **se promener au b. de la mer** to walk by the sea; **maison au b. de la mer** house by the sea, seaside house; **maison sur le** ou **en b. de mer** house on the sea front or the (sea)shore; **vivre au b. de la mer** to live at the seaside or by the sea; **le b. de mer est très construit** there is a lot of development along the sea front; **b. à b.** edge to edge; Can **de b. en b.** from end to end; **chapeau à larges bords** broad- or wide-brimmed hat; Fig **au b. de la tombe** at death's door; **au b. des larmes** on the verge of tears; **au b. de la crise de nerfs/du désespoir/de la catastrophe** on the verge or brink of hysteria/of despair/of disaster; **un peu voleur/bête sur les bords** a bit light-fingered/stupid; **il est un peu menteur/provocateur sur les bords** he's a bit of a liar/an agitator

▸▸ Aviat **b. d'attaque** (d'une aile) leading edge; **b. de fuite** (d'une aile) trailing edge; Ordinat **b. de reliure** inside margin

bordage [bɔʁdaʒ] NM **1** Couture edging; **b. de pierres** stone kerb or Am curb **2** Can bordages (glace) inshore ice **3** Naut (d'un navire) (en bois) planking; (en fer) plating

bordé [bɔʁde] ADJ edged, bordered (de with); **mouchoir b. de dentelle** lace-edged handkerchief; **boulevard b. d'arbres** tree-lined boulevard

▸ NM **1** Couture edging, border **2** Naut (d'un navire) planking, planks; (en fer) plating

bordeaux [bɔʁdo] NM Bordeaux (wine); **b. rouge** claret

▸ ADJ INV claret(-coloured), maroon

bordée [bɔʁde] NF **1** Naut (de coups de feu) broadside; **lâcher une b.** to let fly a broadside; Fig **b. de jurons** ou **d'injures** torrent or hail of abuse **2** Naut (distance) tack; **courir une b.** to tack, to make a tack; **tirer des bordées** to tack; Fam Fig **tirer** ou **courir une b.** to go on a binge; Fam **être en b.** to be on a binge **3** Naut (équipe) watch; **b. de tribord/de bâbord** starboard/port watch **4** Can **b. (de neige)** heavy snowfall

bordel [bɔʁdɛl] NM très Fam (hôtel de passe) brothel; Arg (désordre) mess; **quel b.!** what a mess!, what a shambles!; **tu as rangé ton b.?** have you cleared up your mess?; **mettre** ou **foutre le b. dans qch** to make a mess of sth, to mess sth up; (dans une pièce) to make a mess in sth; **tout le b.** the whole damn lot; **b.!** hell!; Arg **b. de merde!** shit!; Vulg **putain de b. de merde!** fucking hell!, fuck!; **mais qu'est-ce qu'il fout, bordel!** what the fuck is he doing?

bordelais, -aise [bɔʁdəlɛ, -ɛz] ADJ of/from Bordeaux

▸ NM **le B.** (région) the Bordeaux region

▸ NF **bordelaise** (futaille) = cask of about 225 litres; (bouteille) = type of bottle for Bordeaux wine

▸ N **B.** (natif) native of Bordeaux; (habitant) inhabitant of Bordeaux

bordélique [bɔʁdelik] ADJ Fam (pièce, bureau, organisation etc) shambolic; **tu es très b.** you're a real slob

border [bɔʁde] VT **1** (garnir) (robe, manches etc) to edge, to border (de with); **les peupliers qui bordent le chemin** the poplars lining the road; **les villes qui bordent la frontière** the towns that border the frontier; Naut **navire qui borde les côtes** ship skirting the coast; **b. le lit/les draps** to tuck in the bedclothes/the sheets; **b. qn (dans son lit)** to tuck sb in or up **2** Naut (navire) (de bois) to plank; (de fer) to plate **3** (avirons) to ship **4** (voile) to haul taut

bordereau, -eaux [bɔʁdəʁo] NM (formulaire) form; Com statement; (de marchandises) invoice, account; (dans un devis) list, schedule

▸▸ Com **b. d'achat** inventory of purchases; Compta **b. de caisse** cash statement; Com **b. de chargement** cargo list; Compta **b. de codification** accounts coding sheet/form; Compta **b. de compte** statement of account; **b. de crédit** credit note; **b. de débit** debit note; Banque **b. d'encaissement** pay-in slip; Com **b. d'escompte** list of bills for discount; Com **b. d'expédition** ou **d'envoi** dispatch note; Compta **b. d'imputation** accounting entry sheet/form; Com **b. de livraison** delivery note; **b. de paie** wage slip, salary advice; **b. de(s) prix** price list; Banque **b. de remboursement** withdrawal slip; Banque **b. de remise (d'espèces** ou **de chèques)** pay-in or paying-in slip; **b. de réservations** reservation sheet; Compta **b. de saisie** accounting input sheet/form, record form; **b. de salaire** wage slip, salary advice; (liste des salaires payés) wages sheet; Banque **b. de versement** paying-in slip

bordure [bɔʁdyʁ] NF **1** (bord) edge; (d'un vêtement) border, edge; (d'un chapeau) binding; (de gant) welt; Tricot band; **la b. du trottoir** the kerb, Am the curb; **papier à b. noire** black-edged paper; **la banlieue se développe en b. de la ville** suburbs grow up around the edge of the town; **la maison est en b. de route** the house is by or at the roadside; **hôtel en b. de mer** seaside hotel, hotel by the sea **2** (d'un miroir, d'un tableau etc) frame, surround **3** Typ, Ordinat (de paragraphe, de cellule) border

bordurette [bɔʁdyʁɛt] NF = kerb separating a bus lane from the rest of the roadway

bore [bɔʁ] NM Chimie boron

boréal, -ale, -aux, -ales [bɔʁeal, -o] ADJ boreal, north(ern)

borgne [bɔʁɲ] ADJ **1** (personne) one-eyed, blind in one eye; Tech **trou b.** recessed hole; **mur b.** blind wall; **fenêtre b.** obstructed window **2** Fig (maison, rue etc) disreputable, shady

▸ N **1** (personne) one-eyed man/woman **2** Vulg **étrangler le b.** (se masturber) to bang or Br bash the bishop

borique [bɔʁik] ADJ Chimie (acide) boric, boracic

boriqué [bɔʁike] ADJ Pharm pommade boriquée boracic ointment; **compresse en coton b.** boracic lint compress

bornage [bɔʁnaʒ] NM (des limites d'un terrain) demarcation, marking out; **pierre de b.** boundary stone

borne [bɔʁn] NF **1** (limite) boundary marker; (pierre) boundary stone; Fam (kilomètre) kilometre, Am kilometer; **b. kilométrique** kilometre marker, ≃ milestone; Fig **il était**

planté là comme une b. he stood there as if he had taken root; Fam **il y a 200 bornes entre les deux villes** the two towns are 200 kilometres apart; **bornes** (d'un royaume, du savoir etc) boundaries, limits, bounds; **dépasser toutes les bornes** to go too far; **sans bornes** boundless, limitless; **une joie sans bornes** boundless happiness; **il n'y a pas de bornes à la vanité humaine** human vanity knows no bounds **2** Élec terminal; **b. de mise à la terre** ou **de masse** earth or Am ground terminal

▸▸ Naut **b. d'amarrage** (d'un quai) bollard; **b. d'incendie** (fire) hydrant

borné [bɔʁne] ADJ (intelligence) limited, restricted; (esprit) narrow; (personne) narrow-minded

borne-fontaine, pl bornes-fontaines NF **1** (fontaine) (public) drinking fountain **2** Can (bouche d'incendie) (fire) hydrant

borner [bɔʁne] VT (terrain) to mark out, to mark the boundary of, to demarcate; Fig (vue, pouvoir, ambition, désirs, enquête etc) to limit, to restrict (à to); **b. une route** to set up kilometre markers along a road; **le chemin qui borne la forêt** the path bordering the forest; **les pays qui bornent la France à l'est** the countries that border France in the east or that form France's eastern border

▸ VPR **se borner 1** (d'une personne) to restrict or limit oneself (à to); **je me borne au strict nécessaire** I restrict or limit myself to the absolute essentials; **se b. à faire qch** to limit or restrict oneself to doing sth **2** (des choses) to be limited, to be restricted, to be confined (à qch to sth); **toute leur science se borne à cela** this is the (full) extent of their knowledge; **voici à quoi se borne son raisonnement** this is what his argument comes down to or boils down to; **ses visites se bornent à quelques jours** his visits are never any longer than a few days

borsalino [bɔʁsalino] NM fedora

bortch [bɔʁtʃ] NM Culin borsch(t), bortsch

bosco [bɔsko] NM Naut bosun, boatswain

bosniaque [bɔsnjak, bɔznjak] ADJ Bosnian
▸ N **B.** Bosnian

Bosnie [bɔsni] NF Bosnia; **B.-Herzégovine** Bosnia-Herzegovina

bosnien, -ienne [bɔsnjɛ̃, -jɛn] ADJ Bosnian
▸ N **B.** Bosnian

Bosphore [bɔsfɔʁ] NM **le B.** the Bosphorus

bosquet [bɔskɛ] NM copse, grove, thicket

boss [bɔs] NM Fam boss; Fig **c'est toi le b., après tout** you're the boss or you're in charge, after all

bossage [bɔsaʒ] NM Archit boss

bossa-nova, pl bossas-novas [bɔsanɔva] NF Mus bossa nova

bosse [bɔs] NF **1** (d'un bossu, d'un chameau etc) hump; Fam **il a roulé sa b. un peu partout** he's knocked about or been about a bit **2** (sur la tête etc) bump, lump, swelling; (sur la surface du sol) bump, unevenness; **se faire une b. en tombant** to fall and get a bump; **la route est pleine de bosses** the road is very bumpy or uneven; Ski **sauter dans les bosses** to jump moguls; Fig **avoir la b. du commerce/des maths** to have a good head for business/maths

bosselage [bɔslaʒ] NM embossing

bosseler [bɔsle] VT (je bosselle, n. bosselons; je bossellerai) **1** (travailler) to emboss **2** (par accident) to dent, to bash; **casserole toute bosselée** battered saucepan

bosselure [bɔslyʁ] NF **1** (sur l'argenterie) relief **2** (de terrain, mur etc) bumpiness, unevenness

bosser [bɔse] Fam VI to work
▸ VT Scol to bone up on, Br to swot up

bossette [bɔsɛt] NF *Aut* boss

bosseur, -euse [bɔsœr, -øz] N *Fam* hard worker, slogger

bossoir [bɔswar] NM *Naut* **1** (*pour l'ancre*) cathead; (*de navire*) bow **2** (*appareil de levage*) davit; **les bras de b.** the davit guys

bossu, -ue [bɔsy] ADJ (*personne*) hunchbacked; (*animal*) humped; **tiens-toi droit, tu es complètement b.** straighten up, you're all bent; **tu deviens b.** you're getting a stoop ▪ N hunchback; *Fam* **rire comme un b.** to laugh one's head off, to split one's sides (laughing)

bossué [bɔsɥe] ADJ (*bouilloire etc*) battered; (*front*) bony

bossuer [bɔsɥe] VT = **bosseler 2**

boston [bɔstɔ̃] NM **1** *Cartes* boston **2** (*danse*) boston

bostonien, -ienne [bɔstɔnjɛ̃, -jɛn] ADJ Bostonian ▪ N **B.** Bostonian

bot [bo] ADJ **pied b.** club foot; (*personne*) clubfooted person; **main bote** club hand

botanique [bɔtanik] ADJ botanical ▪ NF botany

botaniste [bɔtanist] N botanist

Botswana [bɔtswana] NM Botswana

botte[1] [bɔt] NF (*de fleurs*) bunch; (*de carottes, radis etc*) bunch, bundle; (*de foin, chanvre*) bale, bundle

botte[2] NF (*chaussure*) (high) boot; **une paire de bottes** a pair of boots; **des bottes en cuir** leather boots; *Fig* **sous la b. de l'envahisseur/l'ennemi** under the heel of the invader/the enemy; *Fig* **on entend le bruit des bottes** war is in the air; *Géog* **la b. de l'Italie** the boot of Italy; *Fam* **en avoir plein les bottes** to be fed up; *Fam* **cirer ou lécher les bottes de qn** to lick sb's boots; *Vulg* **il lui a proposé la b.** he asked her straight out to sleep with him
▸▸**bottes de ou en caoutchouc** rubber boots, *Br* wellingtons, wellington boots, *Fam* wellies; **bottes de cavalier ou de cheval** riding boots; **bottes cuissardes ou d'égoutier** waders; **bottes de sept lieues** seven-league boots

botte[3] NF *Escrime* thrust, lunge, pass; **porter une b.** to thrust, to lunge; *Fig* **b. secrète** secret weapon

botte[4] NF *Scol Fam* = students who leave the École Polytechnique with the highest marks; **sortir dans la b.** to be among the best students in one's year

botté [bɔte] NM *Can* (*au football américain*) punt

botter [bɔte] VT **1 b. qn** (*le chausser*) to put sb's boots on; (*le fournir*) to supply sb with boots; **être bien botté** to be well shod; **botté de cuir** wearing leather boots; **le Chat botté** Puss in Boots **2** (*donner un coup de pied dans*) to kick; **b. la balle en touche** (*au football*) to kick the ball into touch; *Fig* to dodge the issue; *Fam* **il lui a botté les fesses ou le derrière** he booted him up the backside *or* gave him a kick up the backside **3** *Fam* (*plaire à*) **ça me botte** I like that; **ça m'a vraiment botté de revoir ce film** I really enjoyed seeing that film again; **ça me botte de partir avec vous** I'm really glad *or Br Fam* chuffed I'm going with you
▪ VI *Ftbl Fam* to kick the ball
▪ VPR **se botter** to put one's boots on

bottier [bɔtje] NM shoemaker, bootmaker

bottillon [bɔtijɔ̃] NM (*de femme*) ankle boot

Bottin® [bɔtɛ̃] NM telephone directory, phone book; **être dans le B.** to be in the telephone directory *or* phone book; **B. mondain** ≃ Who's Who

bottine [bɔtin] NF (*de femme*) ankle boot; (*de bébé*) bootee

botulisme [bɔtylism] NM *Méd* botulism

boubou [bubu] NM bubu, boubou

bouc [buk] NM (*billy*) goat; (*barbe*) goatee (beard); **b. émissaire** scapegoat; *Fam* **puer comme un b., puer le b.** to stink (to high heaven), *Br* to pong

boucan [bukɑ̃] NM *Arg* row, din, racket; **un b. de tous les diables** the devil of a row; **faire un sacré ou du b.** to make *or* kick up a row *or* din

boucane [bukan] NF *Can* smoke

boucané [bukane] ADJ (*teint*) tanned, weatherbeaten

boucaner [bukane] VT (*viande, poisson etc*) to smoke, to cure; (*la peau de qn*) to tan

boucanier [bukanje] NM buccaneer

bouchage [buʃaʒ] NM (*d'une conduite etc*) blocking (up); (*d'une bouteille*) corking

bouche [buʃ] NF **1** (*de personne*) mouth; **avoir/parler la b. pleine** to have/to talk with one's mouth full; **une pipe à la b.** with a pipe in his mouth; **j'ai la b. sèche** my mouth is dry, I've got a dry mouth; **j'ai la b. pâteuse** my tongue is coated; **garder qch pour la bonne b.** to save sth until last; **cela fait venir l'eau à la b.** it makes your mouth water; *Fig* **faire la fine b.** to be fussy *or* choosy; **dire qch la b. en cœur** to say sth with a simper; **embrasser qn à pleine b.** to kiss sb passionately; **elle l'embrasse sur la b.** she kisses him on the mouth *or* lips; **manger à pleine b.** to eat greedily, to gobble one's food; **provisions de b.** food; **dépenses de b.** expenditure on food, money spent on food; **c'est une fine b.** he's a gourmet; **avoir une douzaine de bouches à nourrir** to have a dozen mouths to feed; **les bouches inutiles** unproductive people; **elle n'osait pas ouvrir la b.** she didn't dare open her mouth; **je l'ai appris de sa propre b.** I had it from his own lips; *Fig* **ôter ou enlever le pain de la b. de qn** to take the bread from sb's mouth; **son nom est dans toutes les bouches** everyone's talking about him, his name is on everyone's lips; **elle n'a que ce mot à la b.** that's all she ever says; **demeurer ou rester b. close** to remain silent, to hold one's tongue; **b. cousue!** not a word!, mum's the word!, don't breathe a word (of it)!; *Arg* **ta b.!** shut your mouth!, shut up!; *Fam* **il en avait la b. pleine ou plein la b.** he was full of it, he couldn't talk of anything else; **de b. à oreille** by word of mouth; (*officieusement*) off the record, unofficially; **la nouvelle est passée de b. en b.** the news went round *or* did the rounds, the news went round *or* circulated **2** (*de cheval, de poisson etc*) mouth; **cheval sans b. ou fort en b.** hard-mouthed horse; **cheval à la b. chatouilleuse** tender-mouthed horse **3** (*d'une rivière, d'un cratère, d'un puits, d'un four etc*) mouth; (*d'un fusil, d'un canon*) muzzle
▸▸*Constr etc* **b. d'accès** (*d'un égout*) manhole; **b. d'aération** air vent; **b. de chaleur** hot air vent; **b. d'eau** hydrant; **b. d'égout** manhole; **b. d'incendie** fire hydrant, *Am* fireplug; **b. de métro** underground *or Am* subway entrance

bouché [buʃe] ADJ **1** (*conduite etc*) blocked; **j'ai le nez b.** my nose is blocked, my nose is stuffed up; **j'ai les oreilles bouchées** my ears are blocked up; *Fig* **avoir l'esprit b., être b.** to be dense *or* thick; **être b. à l'émeri** to be a complete moron; **cette voie est bouchée** this is a dead-end job; **temps b.** cloudy *or* overcast weather **2 cidre b.** bottled cider

bouche-à-bouche NM INV mouth-to-mouth resuscitation, *Br* kiss of life; **pratiquer ou faire le b. à un blessé** to give an injured person mouth-to-mouth resuscitation *or* the kiss of life

bouchée [buʃe] NF **1** (*quantité*) mouthful; **juste une b. pour goûter** just a mouthful to taste; *Fig* **acheter qch pour une b. de pain** to buy sth for a song *or* for next to nothing; **ne faire qu'une b. d'un mets** to polish off a dish quickly; *Fig* **ne faire qu'une b. de qn/qch** to make short work of sb/sth; *Fig* **mettre les bouchées doubles** to really get a move on, to really get going **2** *Culin* titbit; **b. (au chocolat)** chocolate; **b. à la reine** chicken vol-au-vent

boucher[1] [buʃe] VT (*fente, trou*) to fill up *or* in, to stop (up); (*conduite, fenêtre etc*) to block (up); (*vue*) to block; (*bouteille*) to cork; *Fig* **cela servira à b. un trou** that will do as a stopgap, that will tide us/them/*etc* over; **j'ai l'impression d'être là uniquement pour b. un trou** I have the feeling I'm there just as a stopgap *or* a fill-in; **b. un creux** (*à l'estomac*) to fill a hole; **b. le passage à qn** to block sb's way, to stand in sb's way; **ta voiture bouche le passage** your car is in the way; **pousse-toi, tu me bouches la vue** move over, you're blocking my view; *Fam* **elle/ça m'en a bouché un coin** she/that shut me up, she/that took the wind out of my sails
▪ VPR **se boucher** (*d'une conduite*) to get blocked (up) *or* clogged (up); **se b. le nez** to hold one's nose; **se b. les oreilles** to put one's fingers in one's ears; *Fig* to refuse to listen; **se b. les yeux** to put one's hands over one's eyes

boucher[2] NM *aussi Fig* butcher

bouchère [buʃɛr] NF (*woman*) butcher; (*épouse du boucher*) butcher's wife

boucherie [buʃri] NF (*boutique*) butcher's (shop); (*activité*) butchery; *Fig* (*massacre*) butchery, slaughter; **b. chevaline** horse butcher's (shop); **animaux de b.** animals for slaughter; *Fig* **ce fut une vraie b.** it was a real slaughter *or* bloodbath

bouche-trou, pl **bouche-trous** NM *Fam* stopgap, fill-in, stand-in; *Journ, Radio, TV* filler; **servir de b.** to act as a stopgap *or* fill-in *or* stand-in

bouchon [buʃɔ̃] NM **1** (*d'une bouteille de limonade, d'un tube de colle etc*) cap, top; (*d'un tonneau*) stopper, plug, bung; **b. (de liège)** cork; **vin qui sent le b.** corked wine; **b. de verre** glass stopper; **b. à l'émeri** ground(-glass) stopper **2** (*embouteillage*) (traffic) hold-up, traffic jam; **il y a un b. sur la Nationale 7** there's a hold-up *or* traffic jam on the N7; **trois kilomètres de b.** a three-kilometre tailback **3** *Pêche* (*d'une ligne*) float, bob **4** (*de paille*) wisp **5** *Région* (*petit restaurant*) **b. (lyonnais)** = small restaurant serving specialities of Lyons **6 tu pousses le b. un peu loin** you're going a bit too far
▸▸**b. antivol** anti-theft cap; *Aut* **b. de pressurisation** pressure cap; *Aut* **b. de radiateur** radiator cap; *Aut* **b. de remplissage** filler plug *or* cap; *Aut* **b. de réservoir** fuel cap; *Tech* **b. de trop plein ou de vidange** drain(ing) plug

bouchonné [buʃɔne] ADJ corked

bouchonner [buʃɔne] VI *Aut Fam* **ça risque de b. sur l'autoroute** there's a risk of hold-ups *or* congestion on the motorway; **ça bouchonne à partir d'Évreux** traffic is at a standstill from Évreux onwards
▪ VT (*cheval*) to rub down

bouchot [buʃo] NM mussel bank *or* bed *or* farm

bouclage [buklaʒ] NM **1** *Fam* (*de prisonnier etc*) imprisonment, locking up **2** (*d'un quartier etc*) surrounding, sealing off, cordoning off **3** *Ordinat* looping; (*acoustique*) (audio) feedback, howl-round; **b. acoustique** acoustic feedback **4** *Typ* (*d'un journal*) putting to bed, edition time

boucle [bukl] NF **1** *(de ceinture, chaussure, harnais etc)* buckle
 2 *(de ruban, de ficelle, de cordage, d'une rivière, d'une route)*, *Aviat* loop; **faire une b. pour retourner à …** to loop back to …; **b. à nœud coulant** running loop; **décrire de nombreuses boucles** *(d'une rivière)* to meander; **la Seine fait des boucles avant d'arriver à Rouen** the Seine twists and turns before it gets to Rouen
 3 *(anneau)* ring; **b. de rideau** curtain ring
 4 *(de cheveux)* curl, ringlet, lock
 5 *Sport* lap; **la Grande boucle** the Tour de France
 6 *TV, Cin* dialogue loop, film loop
 7 *Ordinat* **b. d'attente** wait loop; **b. de bande** tape loop; **b. sans fin** endless loop
 ▸▸ *TV, Cin* **b. de dialogue** dialogue *or* tape loop; *Tél* **b. locale** local loop; **b. locale radio** wireless local loop; **Boucle d'or** Goldilocks; **b. d'oreille** earring

bouclé [bukle] ADJ *(cheveux)* curly; *(personne)* curly-haired; *Ordinat* **système b.** looped system

bouclement [bukləmɑ̃] NM **1** *(de taureau, porc)* ringing **2** *Suisse (des comptes, d'un budget)* closing

boucler [bukle] VT **1** *(ceinture etc)* to buckle, to fasten; *(chambre, maison etc)* to lock (up); **b. sa valise** to fasten one's suitcase; *(se préparer à partir)* to pack one's bags; *Aut* **b. sa ceinture** to put on *or* fasten one's belt, to belt up; *Fam* **b. une affaire** to finish off *or* settle a matter; *Bourse* **b. une position** to close (out) a position; **il a du mal à b. ses fins de mois** he finds it hard to make ends meet at the end of the month; *Fam* **boucle-la!** belt up!, shut up!; *Typ* **b. une édition** *ou* **un journal** to put a newspaper to bed; *Journ* **b. un sujet** to file a story; **b. les comptes** to close the books
 2 b. la boucle *Aviat* to loop the loop; *Fig* to come full circle; **et voilà, la boucle est bouclée** and so we/they/*etc* come full circle
 3 *Fam (prisonnier etc)* to lock up, *Fam* to bang up
 4 *(quartier etc)* to surround, to seal off, to cordon off
 5 *Sport (adversaire)* to lap
 VI **1** *(des cheveux)* to curl, to be curly; **ses cheveux bouclent quand il pleut** her hair goes curly when it rains **2** *Ordinat* to get stuck in a loop, to loop round and round
 VPR **se boucler 1 se b. chez soi** to shut oneself away **2** *Fam* **se la b.** to keep quiet **3** *Ordinat (lignes)* to wrap

bouclette [buklɛt] NF **1** *(de cheveux)* small curl, ringlet **2** *(de laine, moquette)* curl
 ADJ *Tex* **laine b.** bouclé wool

bouclier [buklije] NM **1** *(arme défensive)*, *Constr*, *Géol* shield; **il lui fit un b. de son corps** he shielded him with his body; *Fig* **on s'attend à une levée de boucliers** an outcry is expected **2** *Aut* bumper; **b. inférieur** undershield
 ▸▸ **b. atomique** *ou* **nucléaire** nuclear shield; **b. humain** human shield; *Astronaut* **b. thermique** heat shield

Bouddha [buda] N Buddha

bouddhique [budik] ADJ Buddhist

bouddhisme [budism] NM Buddhism

bouddhiste [budist] ADJ, N Buddhist

bouder [bude] VI to sulk; **laisse-le b. dans son coin** leave him to sulk
 VT **b. qn/qch** to refuse to have anything to do with sb/sth; **tu me boudes?** aren't you talking to me?; **b. son plaisir** to deny oneself; **il boude la peinture moderne** he's not interested in modern art, he doesn't like modern art; **en été les Parisiens boudent les salles de cinéma** Parisians stay away from *or* don't go to the cinema in summer; **le soleil boudera**

la plus grande partie du pays most of the country won't have *or* see any sun
 VPR **se bouder** not to talk to each other, to refuse to have anything to do with each other

bouderie [budri] NF *(état)* sulkiness; *(action)* sulk, fit of the sulks; **j'en ai marre de tes bouderies!** I'm fed up with your sulking!

boudeur, -euse [budœr, -øz] ADJ sulky, sullen
 N sulky person
 NF **boudeuse** *(siège)* courting couch

boudin [budɛ̃] NM **1** *Culin* **b. (noir)** black pudding, *Am* blood sausage; **b. blanc** white pudding; *Fam* **s'en aller en eau de b.** *(d'un projet, d'une démarche etc)* to go to pot *or* down the drain *or* down the tubes **2** *Fam* **boudins** *(doigts)* fat *or* podgy fingers **3** *Fam* **faire du b.** to sulk *Belg (traversin)* bolster **5** *Péj Fam (fille)* fat lump, lump of a girl **6** *Min etc (d'explosif)* sausage; *(de pâte à modeler, terre)* roll; *Naut* **b. gonflable** inflatable fender

boudiné [budine] ADJ **1 b. dans un pantalon trop étroit** bursting *or* bulging out of a tight pair of trousers; **je suis complètement b. dans cette jupe** I'm bursting out all over in this skirt **2** *(doigts)* podgy, fat

boudiner [budine] VT **1** *Tex* to rove, to slub **2** *Tech (fil de fer)* to coil **3** *Fam* **cette robe me boudine** this dress shows all my bulges, I'm bursting out of this dress
 VPR **se boudiner se b. dans ses vêtements** to squeeze into one's clothes

boudoir [budwar] NM **1** *(salon)* boudoir **2** *(biscuit)* sponge finger, *Am* ladyfinger

boue [bu] NF **1** *(terre détrempée)* mud; *Fig* **traîner qn dans la b.** to drag sb through the mud; *Fig* **couvrir qn de b.** to throw *or* sling mud at sb **2** *Constr (pisé)* (building) clay **3** *(vase)* sludge, sediment; *(dans une rivière etc)* silt; *(de l'océan)* ooze; **bain de b.** mud bath; **boues activées** radioactive mud; *(épuration des eaux)* activated sludge

bouée [bwe] NF *Naut* buoy; *(pour nager)* rubber ring; **b. sonore** sonobuoy; **b. à sifflet** whistling buoy; **b. à cloche** bell buoy; **b. d'amarrage** *ou* **de corps-mort** mooring buoy; **b. lumineuse** light buoy, floating light; **b. de sauvetage** lifebelt, lifebuoy; *Fig* lifeline; **elle se cramponne à cet espoir comme à une b.** she is clinging to this hope like a lifeline

boueux, -euse [buø, -øz] ADJ *(route, bottes etc)* muddy; *(écriture, impression etc)* smudged, blurred
 NM *Fam* dustman, *Am* garbage man *or* collector

bouffant [bufɑ̃] ADJ *(manche)* puff(ed); *(jupe)* full; *(pantalon)* baggy; **cheveux bouffants** bouffant hair
 NM *(d'une manche)* puff; *(des cheveux)* body

bouffarde [bufard] NF *Fam (pipe)* pipe

bouffe¹ [buf] ADJ *Mus* **opéra b.** opera bouffe, comic opera

bouffe² NF *très Fam (aliments)* grub, *Br* nosh; **faire** *ou* **préparer la b.** to make the grub *or* nosh; **c'est l'heure de la b.!** grub('s) up!; **on pourrait se faire une petite b.** we could have a bite together

bouffée [bufe] NF **1** *(de fumée)* puff; *(de parfum)* whiff; *(d'air)* breath; **le souffle du printemps entrait dans la pièce par bouffées** spring air wafted into the room; **tirer une b. de sa pipe** to take a puff at one's pipe; **avoir une b. délirante** to be/become delirious; **b. de chaleur** blast of hot air; *Méd* hot flush, *Am* hot flash **2** *(d'éloquence, de colère etc)* (out)burst, fit; *(d'orgueil)* fit

bouffer [bufe] VI **1** *(d'une manche, d'un corsage etc)* to puff out, to balloon out; *(des cheveux)* to have body; **faire b. ses cheveux** to

give body to one's hair **2** *Fam (manger)* to eat; **j'ai bien bouffé** I've had a really good meal; **quand est-ce qu'on bouffe?** when are we eating?
 VT *Fam* **1** *(manger)* to eat; **on n'a rien à b.** there's no grub, there's nothing to eat; *Fig* **il ne va pas te b.** he won't eat you; *Fig* **je l'aurais bouffé** I could have killed him; **ça me bouffe!** it really gets me!; **elle se laisse b. par ses enfants/son travail** she has no time for anything but her children/work, all her time is taken up by her children/work; **b. de l'essence** *(d'une voiture)* to be heavy on petrol, to be a gas guzzler; **b. des kilomètres** to drive around; **b. du curé** to be very anticlerical **2** *(argent, économies)* to blow, to run through
 VPR **se bouffer** *Fig Fam* **elles se bouffent le nez constamment** they're always bickering, they're always having a go at each other

bouffetance [buftɑ̃s] NF *Fam* grub, *Br* nosh

bouffeur, -euse [bufœr, -øz] N *Fam* guzzler; **un gros b. de viande** a great meat-eater; **c'est un b. de curé** he's very anti-clerical

bouffi [bufi] ADJ *(yeux, visage)* puffy, puffed up, swollen; **b. d'orgueil** puffed up *or* swollen with pride; *Com* **hareng b.** bloater
 NM bloater

bouffir [bufir] VT to swell, to puff up
 VI *(des yeux, du visage)* to become swollen, to puff up

bouffissure [bufisyr] NF **1** *(des yeux, du visage)* puffiness, swollenness **2** *(du style)* turgidity

bouffon, -onne [bufɔ̃, -ɔn] NM buffoon, clown, fool; *Hist* jester
 ADJ farcical, comical

bouffonner [bufɔne] VI *Vieilli* to play *or* act the buffoon

bouffonnerie [bufɔnri] NF *(caractère)* buffoonery; **faire des bouffonneries** to play *or* act the buffoon

bougainvillée [bugɛ̃vile] NF, **bougainvillier** [bugɛ̃vilje] NM bougainvillea

bouge [buʒ] NM *Péj (maison)* hovel, dump; *(bar)* low dive, sleazy bar

bougeoir [buʒwar] NM *(plat)* candleholder; *(haut)* candlestick

bougeotte [buʒɔt] NF *Fam* **avoir la b.** to be fidgety, to have the fidgets; *(voyager sans cesse)* to have itchy feet

bouger [buʒe] (**je bougeai(s)**, n. **bougeons**)
 VI *(remuer, se déplacer)* to move; **rester sans b.** to keep still; **ne bougez pas!** don't move!, keep still!; **ne bouge pas (de là)!** stay where you are!, don't move!; *Phot* **ne bougeons plus!** hold it!; **je ne bougerai pas de la terrasse** I won't move from the terrace, I'll stay on the terrace; **je n'ai pas bougé de chez moi pendant deux jours** I haven't been out *or* I've stayed in for two days; *Fig* **ce chemisier ne bouge pas au lavage** *(ne déteint pas)* this blouse doesn't run in the wash; *(ne rétrécit pas)* this blouse doesn't shrink in the wash; **les prix ne bougent pas** prices are (holding) steady; **les ouvriers/étudiants bougent** the workers/students are restless; *Fam* **ça bouge pas mal, dans cette ville** there's a lot going on *or* happening in this town; **tu la connais, c'est difficile de la faire b.** you know what she's like, it's hard to get her to do anything
 VT *Fam* to move, to shift; *Fig* **elle n'a pas bougé le petit doigt** she didn't lift a finger
 VPR **se bouger** *Fam* to move; **bouge-toi de là!** shift yourself!; **il ne veut pas se b.** he won't shift himself; **bouge-toi un peu, fais quelque chose!** get up off your backside and do something!; **il faut te b. si tu veux avoir le poste** you'll have to get a move on if you want the job

bougie [buʒi] NF **1** *(en cire)* candle; **à la b., aux bougies** by candlelight; *Fam* **tu as mis de la b. partout sur la nappe!** you've got candle wax all over the tablecloth!; *Arch* **ampoule de 100 bougies** 100 watt bulb **2** *Aut* **b. (d'allumage)** spark plug, *Br* sparking plug **3** *Arg (visage)* mug, *Br* dial

bougnat [buɲa] NM *Vieilli* coal-merchant

bougnoul(e) [buɲul] N *Arg (terme injurieux)* Arab, *Br* ≃ wog

bougon, -onne [bugɔ̃, -ɔn] *Fam* N grumbler, grouch
  ADJ grumpy, grouchy

bougonnement [bugɔnmɑ̃] NM *Fam* grumbling, grousing

bougonner [bugɔne] VI *Fam* to grumble, to grouse

bougre [bugr] NM *Fam* **1** *Vieilli (type)* fellow, *Br* chap, *Br* bloke; **le pauvre b.** the poor devil; **ce n'est pas un mauvais b.** he's not a bad sort **2 b. d'imbécile** damn(ed) fool, *Br* bloody idiot **3** *Arch* **b.!** blast!, damn it!; **b. que ça fait mal!** heck, that hurts! **4** *Vieilli (sodomite)* bugger

bougrement [bugrəmɑ̃] ADV damn(ed); **il fait b. chaud** it's damn(ed) hot

boui-boui, *pl* **bouis-bouis** [bwibwi] NM *Fam* café, *Péj* dingy café

bouillabaisse [bujabɛs] NF *Culin* bouillabaisse *(Provençal fish soup)*

bouillant [bujɑ̃] ADJ **1** *(qui bout)* boiling; *(très chaud)* boiling hot; **il est b.** *(il a de la fièvre)* he's boiling hot **2** *Fig (ardent)* fiery, hot-headed, impetuous; **b. de colère** seething with anger; **b. d'impatience** bursting with impatience

bouille [buj] NF **1** *Arg (visage)* mug, *Br* dial; **il a une bonne b.** he looks a good sort **2** *(pour la vendange)* grape tub

bouilleur [bujœr] NM **1** *(distillateur)* distiller; **b. de cru** home distiller **2** *(d'une chaudière)* water space

bouilli [buji] *Culin* ADJ boiled
  NM boiled meat, *Can* = beans, cabbage, potatoes, salt pork and ham cooked together for several hours; **b. de bœuf** boiled beef

bouillie [buji] NF **1** *(pour bébés)* baby food; *(à base de céréales)* baby cereal; **préparer la b. du bébé** to prepare the baby's food; **réduire en b.** *(légumes, fruits etc)* to mash, to pulp; **b. de légumes** mashed vegetables; **légumes en b.** mushy vegetables; *Fig* **les voitures ont été réduites en b.** the cars were completely smashed up; *Fam* **s'il me provoque, je vais le mettre** *ou* **réduire en b.!** if he provokes me, I'll beat him to a pulp *or* I'll smash his head in! **2** *(pour le papier)* pulp **3** *Agr* **b. bordelaise** Bordeaux mixture

bouillir [bujir] *(prp* **bouillant;** *pp* **bouilli;** *pr ind* **je bous** [bu]**, tu bous, il bout,** *n.* **bouillons,** *v.* **bouillez, ils bouillent;** *pr sub* **je bouille,** *n.* **bouillions;** *imp* **bous, bouillez;** *impf* **je bouillais;** *p hist* **je bouillis;** *p sub* **je bouillisse;** *fu* **je bouillirai)** VI to boil; **commencer à b.** to come to the boil; **cesser de b.** to go off the boil; **faire b. qch** to boil sth; **faire b. du linge** to boil laundry; *Fam* **cela fera b. la marmite** that will keep the pot boiling; *Fig* **b. de colère** to seethe with anger; **b. d'impatience** to burst with impatience; **cela me fait b.** that makes my blood boil
  VT *Fam (lait, linge etc)* to boil

bouilloire [bujwar] NF kettle

bouillon [bujɔ̃] NM **1** *(d'un liquide en ébullition)* bubble; *(dans le verre)* (air) bubble; *(dans du métal)* blowhole; *(d'une étoffe)* puff; **bouillir à gros bouillons** to boil fast *or* hard; **au premier b.** as soon as it comes to the boil; **le sang sortait à gros bouillons** the blood was gushing out **2** *Culin (liquide)* stock,

bouillon; **b. gras/maigre** meat/clear stock; **b. de légumes** vegetable stock; **b. cube** stock cube; **boire un b.** *(en nageant)* to get a mouthful; *Fam (professionnellement)* to come to grief, to suffer a heavy loss; **b. de culture** culture medium; *Fig* **b. d'onze heures** poisoned drink **3** *Com* **bouillons** *(de livres, de journaux)* returns, unsold copies

bouillonnant [bujɔnɑ̃] ADJ bubbling; *(torrent)* foaming, seething; *Fig* **b. de vie/d'idées** bubbling over with life/ideas

bouillonnement [bujɔnmɑ̃] NM bubbling; *(de torrent)* foaming, seething; *Fig* **b. de la jeunesse** effervescence *or* impetuousness of youth

bouillonner [bujɔne] VI **1** *(d'eau, de soupe, de bain)* to bubble; *(de torrent)* to foam, to seethe; *Fig* **toutes les idées qui bouillonnent dans sa tête** all the ideas seething in his head; **b. de colère** to seethe with anger; **b. d'impatience** to burst with impatience **2** *Com (d'un journal, d'un magazine)* to remain unsold
  VT *Couture* **b. une manche** to gather a sleeve into a puff

bouillotte [bujɔt] NF hot-water bottle

bouillotter [bujɔte] VI to boil gently, to simmer

boul *abrév* boulevard

boulaie [bulɛ] NF birch plantation

boulange [bulɑ̃ʒ] NF *Fam* bakery trade

boulanger [bulɑ̃ʒe] NM baker
  VT *(je* **boulangeai(s),** *n.* **boulangeons)** *(farine)* to work

boulangère [bulɑ̃ʒɛr] NF (woman) baker; *(épouse du boulanger)* baker's wife

boulangerie [bulɑ̃ʒri] NF **1** *(industrie)* bakery trade **2** *(lieu de fabrication)* bakery; *(magasin)* baker's (shop), bakery; **b.-pâtisserie** bread and cake shop

boule [bul] NF **1** *(sphère)* ball; *Fam (tête)* nut, head; **b. de poils** *(régurgité)* hairball; **quelle jolie petite b. de poils** *(chaton)* what a lovely fluffy little thing; **arbre en b.** bushy-topped tree; **se rouler** *ou* **se mettre en b.** *(d'un hérisson etc)* to roll *or* curl (itself) up into a ball; *Fam* **se mettre en b.** *(en colère)* to fly off the handle, to go up the wall; *Fam* **elle/ça me met en b.** she/it gets my back up *or* makes me see red; *Fam* **j'ai les nerfs en b.** I'm a bundle of nerves, my nerves are all on edge; **avoir une b. dans la gorge** to have a lump in one's throat; *Fam* **perdre la b.** to go off one's head, to go round the bend; *Fam* **tu perds la b. ou quoi?** are you off your head?; *Can* **sortir qch des boules à mites** to take sth out of mothballs, to dust sth off
  2 *(pour jouer)* *(aux boules)* bowl; *(au billard, croquet, hockey)* ball; **jouer aux boules** to play bowls; **lancer la b.** to bowl; **la b.** *(au casino)* boule; *Fam* **avoir les boules** to be pissed off; *(avoir peur)* to be wetting oneself; **ça m'a foutu les boules** it pissed me off VOIR GRAMMAIRE A10
  3 *(de machine à écrire)* golf ball; **imprimante à b.** golf-ball printer
  ▸▸ **b. de billard** billiard ball; *Ordinat* **b. de commande** trackball; **b. de feu** fireball; **b. de naphtaline** mothball; **b. de neige** snowball; *Fig* **faire b. de neige** to snowball; **histoire qui fait b. de neige** story that snowballs; **b. de nerfs** bundle of nerves; *Ordinat* **b. de pointage** pointer; **b. puante** stink bomb; **b. Quiès®** earplug; *Ordinat* **b. de la souris** mouse ball; **b. à thé** tea ball

bouleau, -eaux [bulo] NM (silver) birch (tree); *(bois)* birch (wood)

boule-de-neige, *pl* **boules-de-neige** NF *(fleur)* guelder rose, snowball tree

bouledogue [buldɔg] NM bulldog

bouler [bule] VI to roll; *Fam* **envoyer b. qn** to send sb packing

VT **b. les cornes d'un taureau** to pad a bull's horns

boulet [bulɛ] NM **1** *Mil* **b. (de canon)** cannonball; *Fig* **tirer à boulet(s) rouge(s) sur qn** to go for sb hammer and tongs; **passer comme un b. (de canon)** to hurtle past *or* by **2** *(de bagnard)* ball and chain; *Fig* **c'est un b. qu'il traînera toute sa vie** it will be a millstone round his neck all his life **3** *Com (de charbon)* (coal) nut **4** *(de cheval)* fetlock (joint)

boulette [bulɛt] NF **1** *(de papier etc)* pellet, small ball **2** *Culin* meatball **3** *Vét* poison ball **4** *Fam (gaffe)* **faire une b.** to put one's foot in it, *Br* to drop a brick *or* a clanger

boulevard [bulvar] NM boulevard; **les grands boulevards** *(à Paris)* the main boulevards; **les boulevards extérieurs** *(à Paris)* the outer boulevards; **b. périphérique** orbital road, ring road; **théâtre de b.** light comedies; *Théâtre* **c'est du bon b.** it's good light comedy; *Fig* **ouvrir un b. à qn/qch** to leave the way open for sb/sth

boulevardier, -ière [bulvardje, -jɛr] ADJ *(humour)* facile

bouleversant [bulvɛrsɑ̃] ADJ profoundly *or* deeply moving, shattering; *(pénible, effrayant)* deeply distressing; **c'était b. de vérité** it was a shattering experience; **elle est bouleversante dans le rôle de ...** she gives a profoundly *or* deeply moving performance as ...

bouleversé [bulvɛrse] ADJ shattered; **j'en suis encore tout b.** I still haven't got over it; **d'une voix bouleversée** in a voice full of emotion, in a very emotional voice; **le visage b. par l'émotion** his/her face twisted with emotion

bouleversement [bulvɛrsəmɑ̃] NM **1** *(de projets, de programmes, des habitudes etc)* disruption; **bouleversements politiques/économiques** political/economic upheavals **2** *(d'une personne)* emotion; **son b. était tel que ...** he was in such an emotional state that ..., he was so emotional that ...; **sa voix trahissait un b. bien plus profond que ...** his/her voice betrayed a far deeper emotion than ...

bouleverser [bulvɛrse] VT **1** *(projets, habitudes etc)* to disrupt; *(la vie de qn)* to turn upside down; *(paysage)* to change radically; **ce changement de majorité a bouleversé la vie du pays** this change of government threw the whole country into confusion **2** *(émouvoir)* to shatter; **la nouvelle l'a complètement bouleversé** he was totally shattered by the news; **son accident l'a profondément bouleversé** his accident was something he found it hard to get over; **voir sur l'écran l'enfant qu'elle portait l'a profondément bouleversée** seeing the child she was carrying on the screen was a deeply *or* profoundly moving experience; **la voix de Piaf me bouleverse** I find listening to Piaf's voice a deeply *or* profoundly moving experience

boulier [bulje] NM **1** **b. (compteur)** abacus, counting frame **2** *Billard* scoring board

boulimie [bulimi] NF *Méd* bulimia; **faire de la b.** to eat compulsively; *Fig* **avoir une b. de connaissance** to have an unquenchable thirst for knowledge

boulimique [bulimik] ADJ, N *Méd* bulimic

boulingrin [bulɛ̃grɛ̃] NM lawn *(bordered by hedges etc)*

bouliste [bulist] N bowls player
  ADJ **club b.** bowling club

boulle [bul] NM boul(l)e, buhl; **cabinet de b.** buhl *or* boul(l)e cabinet

boulocher [bulɔʃe] VI *(d'un pull etc)* to pill

boulodrome [bulɔdrom] NM bowling alley

boulon [bulɔ̃] NM bolt; **b. à écrou** screw bolt; **b. à œil** eyebolt; **b. à oreilles** wing bolt; *Aut* **b.**

de roue wheel bolt; **b. mécanique** machine bolt; *Rail* **b. d'attelage** coupling pin; *Fig* **le gouvernement doit à présent resserrer les boulons** the government must now tighten the screws

boulonnage [bulɔnaʒ] NM bolting

boulonner [bulɔne] VT *Tech etc* to bolt
VI *Fam* to slog *or* slave (away)

boulonnerie [bulɔnri] NF **1** *(fabrique)* nut-and-bolt works; *(industrie)* nut-and-bolt trade **2** *(objets)* nuts and bolts

boulot¹, -otte [bulo, -ɔt] ADJ *Fam* dumpy, plump, tubby
N dumpy *or* tubby person

boulot² [bulo] *Fam* NM *(travail)* work; *(emploi)* job; **allez, au b.!** come on, (get) to work!; **refaire les peintures dans une maison, c'est du b.** to repaint a whole house is a lot of work *or* is quite a job; **aller au b.** to go to work; **rentrer du b.** to come back from work; *Fig* **c'est toujours moi qui fais le sale b.** it's always me that does the dirty work
ADJ INV **être b. b.** to be a workaholic, to be work-mad

boulotter [bulɔte] *Fam* VT to eat; **il n'y a rien à b.** there's no grub, there's nothing to eat
VI to eat, *Br* to nosh

boum [bum] INT *(explosion)* bang!, boom!; *(chute)* bang!, crash!; *Enf* **bébé a fait b.** baby's had a tumble
NM **1** *(bruit)* bang; **on a entendu un grand b.** we heard a big bang **2 en plein b.** in full swing
NF *(fête)* party *(for young people)*

boumer [bume] VI *Arg* **ça boume!** things are great!; **ça boume?** how's things?

bouquet¹ [buke] NM **1** *(fleurs)* bunch of flowers, bouquet; *(petit)* posy; *(d'arbres)* clump; *(de plumes)* plume, tuft; **le b. de la mariée** the bride's bouquet **2** *(d'un vin)* bouquet, nose **3** *(d'un feu d'artifice)* final display; *Fam* **ça, c'est le b.!** that takes the biscuit *or Am* cake!, that's the last straw! **4** *TV* **b. (de programmes)** multichannel package; **b. numérique** digital package; **b. satellitaire, b. satellite** satellite package
▸▸ **b. final** final display; *Culin* **b. garni** bouquet garni, mixed herbs

bouquet² NM **1** *(lièvre)* hare; *(lapin mâle)* buck rabbit **2** *(crevette)* prawn

bouquetière [buktjɛr] NF flower seller

bouquetin [buktɛ̃] NM ibex

bouquin¹ [bukɛ̃] NM *Fam (livre)* book

bouquin² NM *(lièvre)* hare; *(lapin mâle)* buck rabbit

bouquiner [bukine] VI *Fam (lire)* to read

bouquiniste [bukinist] N second-hand bookseller

bourbe [burb] NF mud, mire

bourbeux, -euse [burbø, -øz] ADJ muddy, miry

bourbier [burbje] NM bog, quagmire; *Fig* mess; *Fig* **se tirer d'un b.** to get out of a mess

bourbillon [burbijɔ̃] NM *(d'un abcès, d'un furoncle etc)* core

bourbon [burbɔ̃] NM *(whisky)* bourbon

bourdaine [burdɛn] NF black alder

bourde [burd] NF *Fam* **1** *(balivernes)* tall story; **raconter des bourdes à qn** to have *or Am* to put sb on **2** *(faute)* blunder, *Br* boob, boo-boo; **faire une b.** to put one's foot in it, *Br* to drop a brick *or* a clanger

bourdon¹ [burdɔ̃] NM *(bâton)* pilgrim's staff

bourdon² NM **1** *Mus (de cornemuse)* drone; *(d'un orgue)* bourdon stop; *(note)* drone bass **2** *(cloche)* great bell **3** *(insecte)* bumblebee; **faux b.** drone; *Arg* **avoir le b.** to be down (in the dumps)

bourdon³ NM *Typ* omission

bourdonnement [burdɔnmɑ̃] NM *(d'insectes)* buzz(ing), hum(ming); *(d'un moteur)* hum(ming); *Méd* **b. d'oreilles** buzzing *or* ringing in the ears; **avoir des bourdonnements d'oreilles** to have a buzzing *or* ringing in one's ears

bourdonner [burdɔne] VI *(d'insectes)* to buzz, to hum; *(d'une machine, d'un moteur)* to hum; *(des oreilles)* to buzz, to ring

bourg [bur] NM *(gros village)* small market town

bourgade [burgad] NF village, township

bourge [burʒ] *Fam Péj (abrév* **bourgeois)** ADJ middle-class
N middle-class person

bourgeois, -oise [burʒwa, -waz] ADJ **1** *(personne)* middle-class; **la classe bourgeoise** the middle class, the bourgeoisie; **quartier b.** middle-class area; **cuisine bourgeoise** simple *or* family *or* home cooking; **une belle maison bourgeoise** a grand house **2** *Péj (conventionnel)* middle-class, bourgeois, conventional
N **1** middle-class person; **les grands b.** the upper middle class; **les petits b.** the lower middle class; **en b.** in plain *or* civilian clothes **2** *Péj (béotien)* philistine; **chercher à épater le b.** to try to shock the establishment **3** *(roturier)* commoner **4** *Hist (citoyen)* burgess, burgher, citizen **5** *Suisse (citoyen)* citizen; **les b.** the townspeople
NF *Arg* **bourgeoise** *(épouse)* wife; **la bourgeoise** the old lady, the wife, the missus

bourgeoisement [burʒwazmɑ̃] ADV conventionally; **vivre b.** to live comfortably *or* in a middle-class way; *Admin* **occuper b. un local** to occupy premises for residential purposes

bourgeoisie [burʒwazi] NF **1** middle class(es), bourgeoisie; **la haute/petite b.** the upper/lower middle class; **la moyenne b.** the middle class **2** *Hist (d'une ville)* burgesses, citizens, freemen

bourgeon [burʒɔ̃] NM **1** *Bot* bud; **en bourgeons** in bud **2** *Fam Vieilli (bouton)* spot, pimple **3** *Anat* **b. gustatif** taste bud, *Spéc* gustatory bud

bourgeonnement [burʒɔnmɑ̃] NM **1** *Bot* budding; *(saison)* budding time **2** *Méd* granulation

bourgeonner [burʒɔne] VI **1** *Bot* to bud **2** *Fam (avoir des boutons)* to come out in spots **3** *Méd (d'une blessure)* to granulate

bourgmestre [burgmɛstr] NM burgomaster

Bourgogne [burgɔɲ] NF Burgundy
NM **(vin de) b.** Burgundy (wine)

bourgot [burgo] NM *Can* moose caller

bourguignon, -onne [burgiɲɔ̃, -ɔn] ADJ Burgundian; *Culin* **bœuf b.** bœuf bourguignon *(beef and vegetables cooked in red wine)*
NM *Culin* bœuf bourguignon
N **B.** Burgundian

bourlingue [burlɛ̃g] NF *Fam (errance)* knocking about

bourlinguer [burlɛ̃ge] VI **1** *Naut (d'un navire)* to make heavy weather, to labour, *Am* to labor, to toil **2** *(beaucoup naviguer)* to sail the seven seas; **il a bourlingué dans les mers de Chine** he has sailed the China Seas **3** *Fam (beaucoup voyager)* **b. de par le monde** to knock about the world; **il a beaucoup bourlingué** he's knocked about a lot

bourlingueur, -euse [burlɛ̃gœr, -øz] *Fam* ADJ adventurous
N adventurer, rolling stone; **c'est un grand b.** he's knocked about a bit

bourrache [buraʃ] NF *(plante)* borage

bourrade [burad] NF push, shove; *(dans le dos etc)* thump, slap; *(dans les côtes)* dig, poke, prod

bourrage [buraʒ] NM **1** *(d'une chaise, d'un coussin etc)* stuffing, padding; *(d'un placard, d'un sac etc)* cramming, packing tight; *(d'une pipe avec du tabac)* filling; *(d'une mine, d'une arme à feu etc)* tamping; *(dans une imprimante)* jam; *(répété)* jamming; **b. papier** paper jam, paper blockage **2** *(matériau)* stuffing, filling
▸▸ **b. de crâne** *Fam* eyewash; *surtout Pol (propagande)* brainwashing

bourrasque [burask] NF squall, gust (of wind); **b. de neige** snow flurry; **le vent souffle en b.** the wind is gusting *or* squalling; *Fig* **une b. d'injures** a flurry of insults; *Fig* **elle est passée en b.** she paid a lightning visit; **arriver en b.** to arrive at top speed

bourrasser [burase] VT *Can* to push around, to bully

bourratif, -ive [buratif, -iv] ADJ *Fam (aliment)* stodgy, filling

bourre¹ [bur] NF **1** *(pour rembourrer les chaises etc)* stuffing, padding, filling; *(de coton etc)* waste, fluff; *Bot (des bourgeons)* down, floss; *Tex etc* **b. de soie** floss silk, silk waste **2** *(d'arme à feu)* wad **3** *Arg* **de première b.** first-class, first-rate **4** *Fam* **à la b.** in a rush

bourre² NM *Arg (policier)* cop

bourré [bure] ADJ **1** *(plein)* packed, crammed (**de** with); **b. à craquer** full to bursting; **le coffre est b.** the boot is crammed full; **la tête bourrée de rêves** with his/her head full of dreams; **être b. de complexes** to be one big bundle *or* a mass of complexes; **il est b. d'antibiotiques** he's pumped full of antibiotics; **les kiwis sont bourrés de vitamines** kiwi fruits are packed *or* crammed with vitamins **2** *Arg (ivre)* plastered, smashed; **être complètement b.** to be smashed out of one's mind, to be legless

bourreau, -eaux [buro] NM **1** *(exécuteur)* executioner; *(qui pend)* hangman; *(tortionnaire)* torturer **2** *Fig* tormentor, torturer; **être le b. de qn** to torment *or* torture sb
▸▸ **b. des cœurs** ladykiller; **b. d'enfants** child-beater; **b. de travail** workaholic

bourrée [bure] NF *(danse)* bourrée

bourrelé [burle] ADJ **b. de remords** stricken with remorse

bourrèlement [burɛlmɑ̃] NM *Litt* torment, anguish; *(de remords)* pangs

bourrelet [burlɛ] NM **1** *Fam* **b. (de graisse)** *(au ventre)* spare tyre *or Am* tire, roll of fat **2** *(contre les courants d'air)* weather strip, *Br* draught excluder **3** *(petit coussin)* pad, cushion

bourrelier [burəlje] NM saddler, harness maker

bourrellerie [burɛlri] NF saddlery

bourre-pif, *pl* **bourre-pifs** NM *Fam (coup de poing)* punch on the nose

bourrer [bure] VT **1** *(chaise, coussin etc)* to stuff, to pad; *(placard, sac etc)* to cram, to pack tight; *(pipe)* to fill; **b. une dissertation de références** to stuff *or* cram an essay with references; *Fam* **b. le crâne à qn** to stuff *or* fill sb's head with nonsense; *(d'un professeur)* to stuff *or* fill sb's head with facts; *Pol* to brainwash sb; **on nous bourre le crâne de publicités** we're brainwashed by advertising; *Fam* **b. le mou à qn** to pull the wool over sb's eyes; **b. qn de coups** to beat sb up **2** *(de nourriture)* to fill up; **ne le bourre pas de biscuits** don't fill him up with biscuits **3** *Mil, Min (chargement)* to ram home; *(trou d'explosion, mine)* to stem, to tamp
VI *aliment qui bourre* stodgy *or* filling food; **les bananes, ça bourre** bananas are filling
VPR **se bourrer 1** *(trop manger)* to stuff oneself, to fill oneself up (**de chocolat** with chocolate)
2 *Fam (se saouler)* to get plastered *or*

smashed; **se b. la gueule** to get smashed out of one's mind, to get legless

bourrette [burɛt] NF *Tex* floss (silk)

bourriche [buriʃ] NF *(d'huîtres, de gibier etc)* basket, hamper

bourrichon [buriʃɔ̃] NM *Fam* **se monter le b.** to get worked up *or* excited, to work oneself up into a state; **monter le b. à qn contre qn** to stir sb up against sb, to set sb against sb

bourricot [buriko] NM (small) donkey

bourrin [burɛ̃] NM *Fam* **1** *(cheval)* nag **2** *(policier)* cop

bourrique [burik] NF *(ânesse)* she ass; *Fam (personne têtue)* pigheaded individual; **faire tourner qn en b.** to drive sb crazy *or* round the bend; **têtu comme une b.** as stubborn as a mule

bourru [bury] ADJ surly, gruff, rough

bourse [burs] NF **1** *(porte-monnaie)* purse, *Am* coin-purse; **c'est trop cher pour sa b.** it's beyond his means, he can't afford it; **b. bien garnie** well-lined purse; **la b. ou la vie!** your money or your life!; **tenir les cordons de la b.** to hold the purse-strings; **sans b. délier** without spending a penny; **faire b. à part** to have separate finances; **faire b. commune** to pool one's money, to share expenses
2 *Anat* **bourses** scrotum; **b. séreuse** bursa
3 *Scol, Univ* **b. (d'études)** grant; **b. de recherche** research grant
4 *Fin* **la B. (des valeurs)** the Stock Exchange, the Stock Market; **la B. monte/est calme** the market is rising/is quiet; **en B.** on the Stock Exchange *or* Stock Market; **valeur cotée en B.** listed *or* quoted share; **jouer à la B.** *ou* **en B.** to play the market, to speculate
▸▸**b. de commerce** commodities exchange; *Fig* **b. coulisse** unlisted market; **b. de l'emploi** = employment exchange; *Com* **b. de fret** shipping exchange; **b. du travail** *(réunion)* = meeting of local trade unions for the purpose of reaching agreement on how best to defend their interests and provide community services; *(endroit)* = local trade union centre

boursicotage [bursikɔtaʒ] NM *Bourse* dabbling on the Stock Market

boursicoter [bursikɔte] VI *Bourse* to dabble on the Stock Market

boursicoteur, -euse [bursikɔtœr, -øz], **boursicotier, -ière** [bursikɔtje, -jɛr] N *Bourse* small-time speculator

boursier, -ière [bursje, -jɛr] ADJ **1** *Bourse* **opérations boursières** Stock Exchange *or* Stock Market transactions **2** *Scol, Univ* **étudiant b.** grant holder
N **1** *Scol, Univ* grant holder **2** *Bourse* (Stock Exchange) operator

boursouflage [bursuflaʒ] NM *(de la chair, du visage etc)* puffiness; *Fig (du style)* turgidity

boursouflé [bursufle] ADJ *(visage, yeux)* swollen, puffy; *(peinture)* blistered; *Fig (style, discours)* turgid

boursouflement [bursufləmɑ̃] NM = **boursouflage**

boursoufler [bursufle] VT *(visage)* to cause to swell, to puff up; *(peinture)* to blister
VPR **se boursoufler** *(de la peinture)* to blister; *(du visage)* to swell, to puff up

boursouflure [bursuflyr] NF *(du visage etc)* swelling, puffiness; *(de peinture)* blister, bubbling; *(de pneu)* blister; *Fig (du style, d'un discours)* turgidity

bousculade [buskylad] NF *(agitation)* jostling, pushing and shoving, hustle; *(hâte)* rush; **une b. vers la porte** a rush for the door; **être pris dans la b.** to be caught up in the rush

bousculer [buskyle] VT **1** *(faire tomber)* to knock over; *Fig (habitudes, journée)* to disrupt; **cela va b. vos idées** that'll liven up your ideas **2** *(pousser)* **b. qn** to jostle sb, to bump *or* knock into sb, to knock against sb **3** *(presser)* to rush; **je n'aime pas être bousculé** I don't like being rushed; **il est toujours bousculé** he's always in a rush
VPR **se bousculer** *(d'une foule etc)* to jostle, to push and shove; **les idées se bousculaient dans sa tête** his head was swimming *or* buzzing with ideas; **aux heures de pointe, les voyageurs se bousculent au portillon** in the rush hour, the passengers jostle to get on; **les candidats ne se bousculent pas au portillon** applicants aren't exactly queuing up for the job; *Fig* **ça se bouscule au portillon** he can't get his words out

bouse [buz] NF dung; **b. de vache** cow dung; **une b.** a cowpat

bouseux [buzø] NM *Fam Péj* yokel, bumpkin, *Am* hick

bousier [buzje] NM *(insecte)* dung beetle

bousillage [buzijaʒ] NM **1** *Fam (d'un travail)* botching, bungling; *(résultat)* botch(-up), bungle **2** *Constr* cob, daub

bousiller [buzije] *Fam* VT *(travail)* to botch (up), to bungle; *(voiture, vélo, appareil photo etc)* to wreck; **b. qn** to bump sb off, to do sb in; **b. sa santé** to ruin one's health
VPR **se bousiller se b. la santé** to ruin one's health

bousilleur, -euse [buzijœr, -øz] N *Fam* botcher, bungler

boussole [busɔl] NF compass; **b. de marine** mariner's compass; **b. de poche** pocket compass; *Fam* **perdre la b.** to go off one's head

boustifaille [bustifaj] NF *Arg* grub, *Br* nosh

BOUT [bu] NM **1** *(extrémité)* end; **assembler deux planches b. à b.** to join two planks end to end *or* end on; **l'autre b.** *(de la rue, de la ville etc)* the other *or* far end; **de b. en b.** *(reprendre un travail etc)* from start to finish; *Naut* from stem to stern; **d'un b. à l'autre** *(dans l'espace)* from one end to the other; *(dans le temps)* from beginning to end; **lire un livre d'un b. à l'autre** to read a book from cover to cover *or* from start to finish; **d'un b. à l'autre de son œuvre** throughout his works, all through his works; **d'un b. de la semaine/de l'année à l'autre** from one end of the week/year to the next; *Fam* **il n'y a personne à l'autre b.** *(au téléphone)* there's nobody on the other end; *Fig* **je n'en vois pas le b.** I'm nowhere near the end of it; *Fig* **je n'arrive pas à joindre les deux bouts** I can't make ends meet; **au b. du compte** after all, at the end of the day, when all's said and done; **au b. de la rue** at the end/bottom/top of the street; **aller au b. du monde** to go to the ends of the earth; *Fam* **c'est le b. du monde** *(d'un lieu)* it's a godforsaken hole *or* a dump; **Roubaix, ce n'est tout de même pas le b. du monde!** it's not as though Roubaix is miles from anywhere!; **au b. d'une heure/de quelques jours** after an hour/a few days; **au b. d'un moment** after a while; **c'est ce qu'elle répète à tout b. de champ** that's what she keeps saying all the time *or* at every opportunity; **nous ne sommes pas encore au b.** we're not through yet, we're not out of the wood(s) yet; **il n'est pas au b. de ses peines** his troubles aren't over yet; **jusqu'au b.** to the (very) end; **aller jusqu'au b.** to go the whole way *or Fam* hog; *(d'un projet etc)* to see it through; *(avoir des rapports sexuels)* to go the whole way; **aller jusqu'au b. de ses idées** to follow one's ideas through (to their logical conclusion); **il est au b. de sa carrière** he's reached *or* he's at the end of his career; **être à b.** to be exhausted; *Fam* to be all in; **pousser** *ou* **mettre qn à b.** to exasperate sb, *Fam*

to drive sb round the bend; **à b. de patience** at the end of one's patience *or* tether; **être à b. de ressources** *(n'avoir plus rien à dire)* to have run out of ideas *or* suggestions; *(n'avoir plus d'argent)* to have run out of money *or* resources; **être à b. d'arguments** to have run out of arguments; **il est à b. de forces** he has no strength left (in him); **être au b. du rouleau** *(n'en pouvoir plus)* to be at the end of one's tether; *(n'avoir plus d'argent)* to have run out of money; **venir à b. de qch** *(achever)* to get through sth; **venir à b. de la résistance/l'opposition de qn** to break down *or* overcome sb's resistance/opposition; **venir à b. d'une épidémie** to stamp out an epidemic
2 *(pointe)* tip, end; *(de tuyau de pipe)* mouthpiece; *(de fusil)* muzzle; *(d'une canne)* ferrule; **b. du doigt/du nez/de la langue** tip *or* end of the finger/nose/tongue; **avoir un mot sur le b. de la langue** to have a word on the tip of one's tongue; **b. du sein** *(de femme)* nipple; **à b. de bras** at arm's length; *Fig* **porter une entreprise à b. de bras** to carry a firm; **b. de pied, b. renforcé** toecap; **ciseaux à bouts ronds** round-ended scissors; **b. de l'archet** *(d'un violon)* point of the bow; **à b. portant** point-blank, at point-blank range; *Fig* **tenir le bon b.** to be well on the way to success; *Fam* **elle est diplomate jusqu'au b. des ongles** she's a diplomat to her fingertips; **on ne sait jamais par quel b. le prendre** you never know how to approach *or* tackle him; *Arg* **mettre les bouts** to skedaddle, *Br* to hop it
3 *(morceau)* *(de ficelle, fromage, pain etc)* bit, piece; **b. de papier/tissu** scrap *or* piece *or* bit of paper/material; **b. de cigarette** cigarette end *or* butt *or* stub; **un b. de jardin/terrasse** a bit of garden/terrace; **un b. de ciel bleu** a patch of blue sky; **elle en connaît un b. sur la question** she knows a thing or two about it; **un tout petit b. de femme** a tiny little (slip of a) woman; **un b. de temps** a little while, some while; **un bon b. de temps** quite a while; **nous avons fait un b. de chemin ensemble** we went part of the way together; *Fig (de deux amants)* we were together for a while; *(de deux étudiants)* we studied together for a while; **nous avons fait un bon b. de chemin** we've come/gone a long way; **pour aller à Paris, cela fait un b. de chemin** it's quite a (long) way to Paris
▸▸*Rel* **(messe du) b. de l'an** Mass, memorial service *(held on the anniversary of sb's death)*; **b. de chou** small child; **quel adorable b. de chou!** what an adorable child!; *Cin, TV* **b. d'essai** screen test; **b. ferré** *(d'une canne)* ferrule; **b. filtre** *(d'une cigarette)* filter tip; *Élec* **b. mort** *(d'une bobine)* dead end; *Cin, TV* **b. de rôle** walk-on *or* bit part

bout-à-bout, *pl* **bouts-à-bouts** [butabu] NM *Cin, TV* rough cut, rough edit

boutade [butad] NF **1** *(trait d'esprit)* joke, jest **2** *(caprice)* whim, caprice

bout-dehors, *pl* **bouts-dehors** NM *Naut* boom; **b. de foc** jib boom

boute-en-train [butɑ̃trɛ̃] NM INV live wire; **c'est le b. de la soirée** he's the life and soul of the party; **c'est le b. de la classe** he's the bright spark of the class

bouteille [butɛj] NF bottle; *(contenu)* bottle(ful); **panier à bouteilles** bottle carrier; **nous allons boire une b.** we'll have a bottle (of wine) together; **c'est une bonne b.** it's a good drop (of wine); **mettre du vin en bouteilles** to bottle wine; **mise en bouteilles** bottling; *Fam* **aimer la b.** to like one's drink, to be fond of the bottle; **avoir dix ans de b.** *(d'un vin)* to be ten years old; *Fam* **prendre de la b.** to be getting on a bit, to be getting long in the tooth; **la b. de gaz est vide** the gas cylinder is empty; **acheter une b. de**

gaz/butane to buy a cylinder of gas/butane ▸▸ **b. isolante** vacuum flask, Thermos® (flask); *Élec* **b. de Leyde** Leyden jar, electric jar; **b. d'oxygène** cylinder of oxygen; **b. Thermos®** vacuum flask, Thermos® (flask)

bouter [bute] vt **1** *Arch* **b. l'ennemi hors de France** to drive the enemy out of France **2** *Belg, Suisse* **b. le feu à qch** to set fire to sth, to set sth on fire

bouteur [butœr] NM *Constr* bulldozer

boutiquage [butikaʒ] NM = system of having a range of separate staffed counters within a single retail outlet

boutiquaire [butikɛr] NM shopping area

boutique [butik] NF shop, *surtout Am* store; *Fig Péj (lieu)* dump, hole; **b. de mode** clothes or fashion shop, boutique; **b. de vêtements/de produits diététiques** clothes/health food shop; **b. de cadeaux** gift shop; **b. de souvenirs** souvenir shop; **b. hors taxe** duty-free shop, tax-free shop; **tenir b.** to run a shop; **fermer b.** to shut up shop; **parler b.** to talk shop; *Fig* **être de la b.** to be in the same business; *Fam* **j'en ai assez de cette sale b.!** I'm sick of this rotten dump or hole!; *Fam* **il est temps que je change de b.** it's time I had a change of job; **robe b.** designer dress; **confection b.** boutique-styled

boutiquier, -ière [butikje, -jɛr] N shopkeeper, *Am* storekeeper

boutoir [butwar] NM *(d'un sanglier etc)* snout; *Fig* **coup de b.** attack (**contre** on)

bouton [butɔ̃] NM **1** *(de fleur)* bud; **b. de rose** rosebud; **en b.** in bud, budding **2** *(sur un vêtement)* button; **b. à queue** shank button; **b. de plastron de chemise** stud; **b. de col** collar stud **3** *(d'une porte, d'une radio etc)* knob; *Ordinat* push button; *(qu'on pousse)* (push) button; *(d'un fleuret)* button; **b. (électrique)** switch; **appuyer sur le b.** to press the button; **b. de sonnerie** ou **de sonnette** ou **d'appel** bellpush **4** *(sur le visage)* spot, pimple; *(à la suite d'une maladie)* spot; **b. d'acné** spot caused by acne; **avoir des boutons** to have spots, to be spotty; *Fig* **ça me donne des boutons** it brings me out in a rash ▸▸ **b. d'arrêt** *(d'alimentation électrique)* off switch; *Ordinat (pour interrompre le téléchargement)* stop button; **b. de contraste** contrast button; **b. de contrôle de luminosité** brightness control button; *Ordinat* **b. de défilement** scroll button; **boutons de manchette** cufflinks; **b. de marche** on switch; **b. marche-arrêt** on/off switch, power switch; *Ordinat* **b. de navigation** navigation button; *Ordinat* **b. d'option, b. radio** radio button; **b. de réglage du contraste** contrast control button; **b. de réglage (du volume)** volume control (knob); *Ordinat* **b. de réinitialisation** reset button; *Ordinat* **b. de souris** mouse button; *Ordinat* **b. de turbo** turbo button

bouton-d'or, *pl* **boutons-d'or** NM *(plante)* buttercup

boutonnage [butɔnaʒ] NM buttoning (up); **b. devant/dans le dos** front/back fastening; **b. à droite/gauche** right/left buttoning; **veste avec double b.** double-buttoning jacket

boutonner [butɔne] vt **1** *(manteau etc)* to button (up), to fasten (up), to do up **2** *Escrime (adversaire)* to button

vPR se boutonner *(d'un manteau etc)* to button (up); *Fam* **il a encore du mal à se b. tout seul** he still has difficulty doing up his buttons by himself; **la robe se boutonne par derrière** the dress buttons (up) at the back

boutonneux, -euse [butɔnø, -øz] ADJ *(adolescent, visage etc)* spotty, pimply

boutonnière [butɔnjɛr] NF **1** *(de vêtement)* buttonhole; **faire une b.** to make a buttonhole; **porter une fleur à la b.** to wear a buttonhole or *Am* boutonnière; **porter une médaille à la b.** to wear a medal on one's lapel **2** *Chir* buttonhole; **faire une b. à qn** to make a buttonhole in sb; *Fig (avec une épée etc)* to pink sb

bouton-poussoir, *pl* **boutons-poussoir** NM push button

bouton-pression, *pl* **boutons-pression** NM press stud, *Am* snap fastener, *Br Fam* popper

bouturage [butyraʒ] NM *(de plantes)* propagation by cuttings

bouture [butyr] NF cutting; **faire des boutures** to take cuttings

bouturer [butyre] vi *(des plantes)* to make suckers

vt to propagate by cuttings

bouvet [buvɛ] NM grooving plane

bouvier, -ière [buvje, -jɛr] N *(pour les bœufs)* cowherd, cowhand; *(pour les troupeaux)* drover

NM *(chien)* sheepdog

bouvillon [buvijɔ̃] NM steer, young bullock

bouvreuil [buvrœj] NM bullfinch

bovarysme [bɔvarism] NM = tendency to romanticize reality as a way of escaping from the limitations of one's own existence

bovidés [bɔvide] NMPL *Zool* bovids, *Spéc* Bovidae

bovin [bɔvɛ̃] ADJ *(race, regard etc)* bovine; **un air b.** a bovine look

NMPL **bovins** bovines, cattle

bovinés [bɔvine] NMPL *Zool* bovines, cattle

bowling [buliŋ] NM **1** *(jeu)* (tenpin) bowling **2** *(endroit)* (tenpin) bowling alley

box ¹, *pl* **boxes** [bɔks] NM **1** *(dans un dortoir)* cubicle; *Jur* **b. des accusés** dock **2** *Aut* lock-up (garage) **3** *(dans une étable)* stall, *Br* loose box

box ², box-calf [bɔks(kalf)] NM *(cuir)* box calf

boxe [bɔks] NF boxing; **faire de la b.** to box; **gants/match de b.** boxing gloves/match; **b. anglaise** boxing; **b. française** kick boxing

boxer ¹ [bɔkse] vi to box; **b. contre qn** to box against or fight sb

vt to box against, to fight; *Fam (frapper)* to punch up

boxer ² [bɔksœr] NM *(chien)* boxer (dog)

boxer ³ [bɔksœr] NM *(short)* shorts

boxer ⁴ [bɔksɛr] NM *(moteur)* boxer engine

boxeur [bɔksœr] NM boxer

box-office, *pl* **box-offices** [bɔksɔfis] NM box office; *(recettes)* box-office takings; **une pièce/un film/un chanteur en tête du b.** a box-office hit

boxon [bɔksɔ̃] NM *Fam* brothel; *Fig* **quel b.!** what a mess!; **mettre le b. dans qch** to make a mess of sth

boy [bɔj] NM *(domestique)* boy

boyau, -aux [bwajo] NM **1** *(d'animal)* gut, bowel; **(corde de) b.** (cat)gut; **boisson à tordre les boyaux** *(fort)* drink that burns the throat; *(de mauvaise qualité)* rotgut **2** *(tuyau)* hose(pipe); *(de vélo)* tubular tyre or *Am* tire **3** *(allée)* narrow alley(way); *Min* narrow gallery; *Mil* communication trench

boycott(age) [bɔjkɔt(aʒ)] NM boycott(ing)

boycotter [bɔjkɔte] vt to boycott

boycotteur, -euse [bɔjkɔtœr, -øz] N boycotter

boy-scout, *pl* **boy-scouts** [bɔjskut] NM *Vieilli* boy scout; *Fig* **mentalité de b.** boy-scout mentality

BP [bepe] NF *(abrév* **boîte postale)** PO Box; **BP 5000** = consumer information/protection body

NM *(abrév* **brevet professionnel)** vocational qualification; **BP de barman** vocational qualification in bar work; **BP de cuisinier** vocational qualification in catering

BPA [bepea] NM *Fin (abrév* **bénéfice par action)** EPS

BPF [bepeɛf] *Fin Anciennement (abrév* **bon pour francs)** *(sur chèque)* = abbreviation printed on cheques and invoices before the amount to be written in figures

bpp [bepepe] NMPL *Ordinat (abrév* **bits par pouce)** bpi

bps [bepeɛs] NMPL *Ordinat (abrév* **bits par seconde)** bps

brabançon, -onne [brabɑ̃sɔ̃, -ɔn] ADJ of/from Brabant

N **B.** *(natif)* native of Brabant; *(habitant)* inhabitant of Brabant

NF **la Brabançonne** the Belgian national anthem

Brabant [brabɑ̃] NM **1** *Géog* Brabant **2** *Agr* **b.** all-metal wheel plough; **charrue à double b.** two-furrow plough

bracelet [braslɛ] NM **1** bracelet; *(rigide)* bangle; *(de montre)* strap, bracelet, band; **b. de force** (leather) wrist-band; **b. électronique** ou **de cheville** ou **de détention** electronic tag **2** *Fam* **bracelets** *(menottes)* cuffs, bracelets **3** *(lien)* band

bracelet-montre, *pl* **bracelets-montres** NM wristwatch

brachial, -iale, -iaux, -iales [brakjal, -jo] ADJ *Anat (artère etc)* brachial

brachiopode [brakjɔpɔd] NM *(mollusque)* brachiopod

brachycéphale [brakisefal] ADJ, N brachycephalic

braconnage [brakɔnaʒ] NM poaching

braconner [brakɔne] vi to poach

braconnier [brakɔnje] NM poacher

bractée [brakte] NF *Bot* bract

bradé [brade] ADJ cut-price

brader [brade] vt *(marchandises)* to sell off; *(à prix réduits)* to sell dirt cheap or at knock-down prices

braderie [bradri] NF *(foire)* ≃ jumble sale, *Am* ≃ rummage sale; *(magasin)* cut-price or discount store; *(liquidation)* clearance sale

braguette [bragɛt] NF *(de pantalon)* flies, fly

brahmane [braman] NM Brahman, Brahmin

brahmanisme [bramanism] NM Brahmanism, Brahminism

brahmine [bramin] NF Brahmani

brai [brɛ] NM pitch, tar

braillard, -arde [brajar, -ard] ADJ *Fam (foule etc)* yelling, noisy; *(enfant)* howling, bawling

N bawler; **petit b.** noisy brat

braille [braj] NM Braille; **lire en b.** to read Braille

braillement [brajmɑ̃] NM yelling; *(d'enfant)* howling, bawling; **pourquoi ces braillements?** *(d'un nourrisson)* what's all the howling about?

brailler [braje] vi to yell; *(d'un enfant)* to howl, to bawl; **faire b. sa télévision** to have one's television blaring (out)

vt *(chanson)* to bawl (out); *(slogan)* to chant

brailleur, -euse [brajœr, -øz] ADJ, N *Fam* = braillard

braiment [brɛmɑ̃] NM *(d'un âne)* bray(ing)

brainstorming [brɛnstɔrmiŋ] NM brainstorming; **un b.** a brainstorming session

brain-trust, *pl* **brain-trusts** [brɛntrœst] NM brains trust

braire [brɛr] vi *(pr ind* **il brait, ils braient;** *fu* **il braira, ils brairont;** *cond* **il brairait, ils braraient)** **1** *(d'un âne)* to bray **2** *Fam* = **brailler**

braise [brɛz] NF **1** *(charbons)* (glowing) embers; *(charbon de bois)* (live) charcoal; **cuire qch sur/sous la b.** to cook sth over/in the embers (of a fire); **des yeux de b.** glowing *or* burning eyes; *Fig* **être sur la b.** to be on tenterhooks **2** *Arg Vieilli (argent)* bread, dough

braiser [brɛze] VT *Culin* to braise

braisière [brɛzjɛr] NF *Culin* braising pan

bramement [brammɑ̃] NM *(hurlement)* howl(ing), wail(ing); *(de cerf)* bell(ing)

bramer [brame] VI *(hurler)* to howl, to wail; *(de cerf)* to bell

bran [brɑ̃] NM *(de son)* bran; **b. de scie** sawdust

brancard [brɑ̃kar] NM **1** *(bras) (d'une civière, d'une charrette etc)* shaft, pole; **ruer dans les brancards** *(d'un cheval)* to kick when between the shafts; *Fig* to kick over the traces, to rebel **2** *(civière)* stretcher

brancardier, -ière [brɑ̃kardje, -jɛr] N stretcher bearer

branchage [brɑ̃ʃaʒ] NM *(des arbres)* branches, boughs; **branchages** cut *or* lopped-off branches

branche [brɑ̃ʃ] NF **1** *(d'un arbre)* branch, bough; *(d'un nerf, d'une rivière etc)* branch; *(de l'industrie etc)* branch, sector; *(d'activité)* line of business; **b. d'activité** area of operations; **la maîtresse b.** the main branch; **céleri en branches** celery; **une b. de céleri** a stick of celery; *Arg* **vieille b.** old mate; *Fig* **avoir de la b.** to look distinguished; **notre b. de la famille** our branch of the family; **la b. maternelle** the mother's side, *Fml* the maternal line; **les branches de la physique** the branches of physics; **c'est une b. très littéraire** it is a very literary discipline; **branches des bois d'un cerf** tines of a stag's antlers
2 *(d'un compas)* leg; *(d'une monture de lunettes)* side; *(d'une fourche)* prong; *(d'une hélice)* blade; *(d'une clé)* shank; *(d'un fer à cheval)* arm; **les branches d'un chandelier** the branches of a candelabra; **b. à coulisse** *(d'un trépied)* telescopic leg
3 *Suisse Scol, Univ* subject; **b. principale** main subject, *Am* major; **b. secondaire** secondary subject, *Am* minor
4 *Suisse (chocolat)* = cylindrical bar of chocolate

branché [brɑ̃ʃe] ADJ *Fam* trendy, hip; **être b. sur qch** to be really into sth; **il est b. tennis/techno** he's really into tennis/techno music; **c'est très b. d'avoir des lunettes** wearing glasses is very trendy *or* is the in thing

branchement [brɑ̃ʃmɑ̃] NM **1** *(d'un appareil électrique, d'un téléphone)* connecting (up), connection; *(à une prise)* plugging in; *(de canalisations, de fils électriques)* branch(ing), junction; **(tube de) b.** branch pipe **2** *Rail* branch line; **b. de voie** junction, points **3** *Ordinat* branch

brancher [brɑ̃ʃe] VT **1** *(appareil électrique, téléphone)* to connect (up); *(à une prise)* to plug in; *Tél* **b. qn** to put sb through, to connect sb; **b. une sonnerie sur le circuit de lumière** to connect a bell up to *or* run a bell off the light circuit; *Fig* **b. qn sur un sujet** to get sb onto *or* started on a subject; **il faut que je le branche sur cette affaire** I must get him interested in this business **2** *Fam (plaire à)* **b. qn** to give sb a buzz; **la peinture, ça te branche?** are you into painting?; **on se fait un resto ce soir, ça te branche?** fancy going to a restaurant tonight?; **ta sœur a l'air de le b.** he seems to be interested in your sister
VI *(des oiseaux)* to perch, to roost *(on a branch)*
VPR **se brancher 1** *(des oiseaux)* to perch, to roost; *(d'un appareil électrique)* to plug in;

(canalisation) to connect up to; **se b. sur les grandes ondes** to tune in to long waves **2** *Can Fam (se décider)* to decide, to make up one's mind

branchette [brɑ̃ʃɛt] NF small branch, twig

branchial, -iale, -iaux, -iales [brɑ̃ʃjal, -jo] ADJ *Zool* branchial

branchie [brɑ̃ʃi] NF *(d'un poisson)* branchia, gill

branchitude [brɑ̃ʃityd] NF *Fam* hipness, trendiness; **cette boîte est l'un des hauts lieux de la b. parisienne** this club is one of the trendiest *or* hippest in Paris

branchu [brɑ̃ʃy] ADJ branchy, branching

brandade [brɑ̃dad] NF *Culin* **b. (de morue)** = salt cod pounded with garlic, oil and cream

brande [brɑ̃d] NF **1** *(bruyère)* heather **2** *(terrain)* heath(land)

Brandebourg [brɑ̃dbur] NM **1** Brandenburg **2** *Couture* **b.** frog; **brandebourgs** frogging; **à brandebourgs** frogged

brandir [brɑ̃dir] VT *(arme)* to brandish, to flourish; *(pour attirer l'attention)* to brandish, to wave; *(la menace de qch)* to hold up

brandon [brɑ̃dɔ̃] NM firebrand; *(flambeau de paille)* torch; *Fig* **c'est un b. de discorde** *(personne)* he's a firebrand; *(sujet, affaire)* it's a bone of contention

brandy [brɑ̃di] NM brandy

branlant [brɑ̃lɑ̃] ADJ shaky; *(dent)* loose; *(chaise, escalier)* rickety; *(immeuble)* ramshackle; *Fig (raison, réputation, vérité)* shaky

branle [brɑ̃l] NM *(mouvement)* swing; *Fig* impulse, impetus; **mettre une cloche en b.** to set a bell swinging *or* ringing; *Fig* **donner le b. à qch** to get sth going, to give an impetus to sth; **mettre qch en b.** to set sth in motion; **se mettre en b.** to get going

branle-bas NM INV **1** *Naut* **faire le b. de combat** to clear the decks for action; **b.!** action stations! **2** *Fig* commotion; **c'était le b. (de combat) dans la ville entière** the whole town was in turmoil; **dans le b. du départ** in the commotion of setting off; **que signifie tout ce b.?** what's all the commotion about?; **il met toute la maison en b.** he's turning the whole house upside down

branlée [brɑ̃le] NF *Fam* thrashing; **prendre ou recevoir une b.** to get a thrashing, to get thrashed

branlement [brɑ̃lmɑ̃] NM *(de la tête)* wagging, shaking

branler [brɑ̃le] VT **1** *(tête)* to wag, to shake **2** *Vulg (masturber)* to jerk off, *Br* to wank off; *Fig* **mais qu'est-ce qu'il branle? il devrait être là!** what the hell's he up to? he should be here!
VI to be shaky; *(de dent)* to be loose; *(de chaise, d'escalier)* to be rickety; *(de maison)* to be ramshackle; **b. dans le manche** *(d'un outil)* to have a loose handle
VPR **se branler** *Vulg (masturber)* to jerk off, *Br* to wank (off); *Fig* **franchement, je m'en branle** to be honest, I don't *or* couldn't give a fuck *or* a shit

branlette [brɑ̃lɛt] NF *Vulg* hand-job, *Br* wank; **se faire une b.** to jerk off, *Br* to have a wank

branleur, -euse [brɑ̃lœr, -øz] N *Vulg (bon à rien etc)* nerd, *Br* wanker

branque [brɑ̃k] *Fam* ADJ *(fou)* bonkers, nuts
N *(imbécile)* dope, jerk; *(fou)* nutter, headcase, *Am* wacko

braquage [brakaʒ] NM **1** *Aut (des roues)* turning; **(angle de) b.** *(d'une voiture)* steering lock; **rayon ou cercle de b.** turning circle; **b. (au) maximum** full lock **2** *Arg (vol)* hold-up; **faire un b.** to do a hold-up

braque [brak] NM *(chien)* pointer
ADJ *Fam* nutty, crazy

braquemart [brakmar] NM **1** *(épée)* cutlass **2** *Vulg (pénis)* dick, prick, *Br* knob

braquer [brake] VT **1** *(diriger, tourner)* to point; **b. un fusil sur qn/qch** to aim *or* point a gun at sb/sth; **b. une lunette sur qn/qch** to fix *or* train a telescope on sb/sth; **il a toujours l'œil braqué sur nous** he's got his eye on us all the time; **b. son attention sur qch** to fix one's attention on sth **2** *Aut (voiture etc)* to turn **3** *(monter) (personne)* to antagonize; **b. qn contre qn/qch** to turn sb against sb/sth; **il est braqué contre le projet** he's dead set against the plan **4** *Arg* **b. une banque** to hold up a bank
VPR **se braquer** to dig one's heels in; **se b. contre qn** to set one's face against sb
VI *Aut* to turn the (steering) wheel; **b. (à fond)** to apply full lock; **b. à gauche** to turn the wheel hard over to the left; **b. au maximum** to apply full lock; **voiture qui braque mal** car that has a poor lock

braquet [brakɛ] NM gear ratio; **changer de b.** to change gear

braqueur, -euse [brakœr, -øz] N armed robber

bras [bra] NM **1** *Anat* arm; **b. droit/gauche** right/left arm; **allonger le b. vers qch** to reach (out) for sth, to stretch out one's arm for sth; **offrir/donner le b. à qn** to offer/give sb one's arm; **prendre le b. de qn** to take sb's arm; **avoir un panier au b.** to have a basket on one's arm; **au b. de qn** on sb's arm; **il est entré, un dossier sous le b.** he came in with a file under his arm; **b. dessus, b. dessous** arm in arm; **les b. m'en tombent** I'm astounded, I'm flabbergasted; **cela m'a coupé b. et jambes** it stunned me; **assis, les b. croisés** sitting with one's arms folded *or* with folded arms; **rester les b. croisés** *(ne pas travailler)* to twiddle one's thumbs; *(être passif)* to stand idly by; *Fig* **avoir le b. long** to have a lot of influence *or Fam* clout; **accueillir qn à b. ouverts** to welcome sb with open arms; **avoir qn/qch sur les b.** to have sb/sth on one's hands; *Fig* **elle a la responsabilité de l'affaire sur les b.** she carries all the responsibility for the matter; **elle s'est retrouvée avec une famille sur les b.** she found herself with a family to look after *or* to take care of; *Litt Hum* **être dans les b. de Morphée** to be in the arms of Morpheus; **voiture à b.** handcart; **tenir qch à b. tendus** *ou* **à bout de b.** to hold sth in one's outstretched arms; **en b. de chemise** in (one's) shirtsleeves; **il m'est tombé dessus à b. raccourcis** he pitched *or* laid into me; **une partie de b. de fer** an arm-wrestling match; *Fig* a trial of strength; **les syndicats sont engagés dans une partie de b. de fer avec le gouvernement** the unions are at loggerheads with the government; **lancer qch/ frapper à tour de b.** to throw sth/strike with all one's might; **faire un b. d'honneur (à qn)** ≃ to stick two fingers up (to sb), *Br* ≃ to give (sb) the V-sign
2 *(homme)* hand, worker; **manquer de b.** to be short handed; **elle c'est la tête, et moi les b.** she's the brains, I'm the brawn
3 *(d'un fauteuil)* arm(rest); *(d'un levier, d'une ancre)* arm; *(d'une grue)* jib; *(d'une croix)* limb; *(d'une pompe)* handle; *Naut (de la vergue)* brace
4 *(de fleuve)* arm
5 *(pouvoir)* arm; **le b. séculier** the secular arm; **le b. de la justice** the arm of the law; **b. armé d'une organisation** the armed wing of an organization; **le b. politique d'une organisation** the political arm *or* wing of an organization
6 *(de mollusque)* tentacle
▸ ▸ *Aut* **b. compensateur** compensator arm; *Aut* **b. de contrôle** control arm; *Aut* **b. de direction** steering arm; **b. droit: être le b. droit de qn** to be sb's right hand (man); **b. fisher**

(microphone) fisher boom; **b. de lecture** pick-up arm; **b. de manivelle** crank arm; *Aut* web; *Géog* **b. de mer** arm of the sea; **b. mort** backwater; *Aut* **b. oscillant** radius arm *or* rod; **b. pivotant** *(pour moniteur)* swivel arm; **b. porte-copies** *(pour claviste)* copy-holder; *Aut* **b. de suspension** suspension arm; *Can* **b. de vitesse** *Br* gear lever, *Am* stick shift

brasage [brazaʒ] **NM** *Métal* brazing

braser [braze] **VT** *Métal* to braze

brasero [brazero] **NM** brazier

brasier [brazje] **NM** *(incendie)* blaze, inferno; **la voiture n'était plus qu'un b.** the car was a ball of flames; *Litt* **le b. du couchant** the fiery glow of the setting sun; **l'ardent b. des passions mortelles** the burning fire of human passion

Brasilia [brazilja] **N** Brasilia

brasiller [brazije] **VI** *(de la mer)* to glitter, to sparkle

bras-le-corps (à) **ADV** saisir qn à b. to seize sb round the waist; **prendre un problème à b.** to get to grips with a problem, to tackle a problem head on

brassage [brasaʒ] **NM 1** *(de la bière)* brewing **2** *(mélange)* mixing; *Aut* **b. des gaz** mixing; *Fig* **le b. de peuples/cultures** the (inter)mingling *or* (inter)mixing of races/cultures **3** *Naut (de la vergue)* bracing; *Aviat (d'une hélice)* swinging

brassard [brasar] **NM** armband; **b. de deuil** black armband

brasse [bras] **NF 1** *Natation* b. (coulée) breaststroke; **nager la b.** to swim breaststroke; **b. papillon** butterfly (stroke); **en quelques brasses, tu es au bout de la piscine** in a few strokes, you'll be at the end of the pool **2** *(ancienne mesure)* fathom

brassée [brase] **NF** armful; **par brassées** by the armful

brasser [brase] **VT 1** *(bière etc)* to brew **2** *(mélanger)* to mix; **b. des affaires** to be doing good business; **b. les cartes** to shuffle the cards; **b. de l'argent** to handle large amounts of money; **b. de l'air ou du vent** to work without getting anything done **3** *Naut (vergue)* to brace; *Aviat (hélice)* to swing

brasserie [brasri] **NF 1** *(fabrique)* brewery; *(industrie)* brewing, beer-making (industry) **2** *(restaurant)* restaurant (with bar), brasserie

brasseur, -euse [brasœr, -øz] **N 1** *(fabricant de bière)* brewer **2** *Fig* **b. d'affaires** big businessman, tycoon **3** *Sport* breaststroke swimmer

brassière [brasjɛr] **NF 1** *(de bébé)* (baby's) *Br* vest *or Am* undershirt **2** *Can (soutien-gorge)* bra, *Am* brassière **3** **b. de sauvetage** life jacket, life vest

brasure [brazyr] **NF 1** *(résultat)* braze, (brazed) seam **2** *(opération)* brazing, hard-soldering **3** *(alliage)* hard solder

Bratislava [bratislava] **N** Bratislava

bravache [bravaʃ] **NM** swaggerer, blusterer **ADJ** swaggering, blustering; **d'un air b.** blusteringly

bravade [bravad] **NF** bravado; **par b.** out of bravado

brave [brav] **ADJ** SEE GRAMMAR B10 **1** *(courageux)* brave, courageous **2** *(preceding the noun) (bon)* good; **ce sont de braves gens** they are good *or* decent people; **c'est un b. homme** *ou Fam* **type** he's a good *or* decent man *or* sort; **eh oui, ma b. dame, c'est la vie** well, my dear lady, that's life I suppose **3** *Péj* **il est bien b.** *(pas futé)* he's nice enough, he's OK

NM 1 *(héros)* brave man **2** **mon b.** my good man **3** *Péj* **faire le b.** to bluster, to swagger

---

Il faut noter que l'adjectif anglais **brave** ne signifie jamais **gentil**.

---

bravement [bravmɑ̃] **ADV 1** *(courageusement)* bravely, courageously **2** *(avec résolution)* boldly

braver [brave] **VT 1** *(affronter) (la mort, le danger)* to brave, to face bravely; **toujours prêt à b. le danger** always ready to face danger **2** *(défier) (personne)* to defy, to stand up to; **b. les lois/le règlement** to defy *or* flout the law/the rules

bravo [bravo] **INT** bravo!; *(dans un débat)* hear, hear!; **un grand b. à toute l'équipe technique** a big hand *or* cheer for all the technical crew; **ah b.!** *(tu as encore fait une sottise!)* oh, well done!

NM bravo; **des bravos** applause, cheers

bravoure [bravur] **NF 1** *(courage)* bravery, courage **2** *Mus* **chanter son air de b.** to sing one's bravura passage; *Littér* **morceau de b.** purple passage

Brazzaville [brazavil] **N** Brazzaville

break¹ [brɛk] **NM** *Aut* estate (car), *Am* station wagon

break² **NM** *Mus, Tennis, Fig* break; *Boxe* **b.!** break!; **balle de b.** break point

brebis [brəbi] **NF 1** *Zool* ewe; **lait/fromage de b.** ewe's milk/ewe's-milk cheese **2** *Rel* sheep; **les b.** the flock

▸▸ **b. égarée** lost sheep; *Fig* **b. galeuse** black sheep

brèche [brɛʃ] **NF** *(dans un mur, une haie etc)* gap, opening; *(dans la coque d'un bateau)* hole; *(dans une lame)* notch; *Mil* breach; *Mil* **monter sur la b.** to stand in the breach; *Fig* **être toujours sur la b.** to be always on the go; **battre qch en b.** to demolish sth

bréchet [breʃɛ] **NM** *Orn* breastbone

bredouillage [brəduja3], **bredouillement** [brədujmɑ̃] **NM** mumbling, muttering

bredouillant [brədujɑ̃] **ADJ** mumbling

bredouille [brəduj] **ADJ** empty-handed; **rentrer ou revenir b.** to come back empty-handed

bredouiller [brəduje] **VT & VI** to mumble, to mutter

bredouilleur, -euse [brədujœr, -øz] **ADJ** mumbling, muttering **N** mumbler, mutterer

bref, brève [bref, brɛv] **ADJ** brief, short; **soyez b.!** be brief!, make it short!; **répondre d'un ton b.** to answer curtly; *Ling* **voyelle brève** short vowel; **dans les plus brefs délais** as soon as possible

ADV in short; **en b.** in brief; **raconter qch en b.** to relate sth in a few words *or* briefly; **b., il accepte** in short *or* in a word *or* to cut a long story short, he accepts; *Fam* **enfin b., elle n'est pas satisfaite** well, in short, she isn't satisfied; **une cousine ou une tante, enfin b., quelqu'un de sa famille** a cousin or an aunt, well anyway, one of his relatives **NM** *Rel* (papal) brief

bréhaigne [breɛɲ] **ADJ** *Vieilli (jument etc)* barren

brelan [brəlɑ̃] **NM** *Cartes* three of a kind, pair royal; **b. d'as** three aces

brêle [brɛl] **NF** *Fam* cretin, jerk, *Br* tosspot

breloque [brələk] **NF 1** *(sur un bracelet etc)* charm; **bracelet à breloques** charm bracelet **2** *Mil* break-off; **battre la b.** to sound the dismiss; *(d'une montre)* to be on the blink; *Fig (intellectuellement)* to wander; **mon cœur bat la b.** *(bat vite)* my heart is racing; *(fonctionne mal)* my heart is playing me up

brème [brɛm] **NF** *(poisson)* bream

Brême [brɛm] **N** Bremen

Brésil [brezil] **NM** Brazil

---

brésilien, -ienne [breziljɛ̃, -jɛn] **ADJ** Brazilian; **maillot/slip b.** high-cut swimsuit/briefs **N B.** Brazilian

brésiller [brezije] *Tech, Litt* **VT** to break into small pieces; *(broyer)* to crumble, to pulverize **VI** to crumble **VPR se brésiller** to crumble

Bretagne [brətaɲ] **NF** Brittany; **Basse-B.** Lower *or* Western Brittany

bretelle [brətɛl] **NF 1** *(de soutien-gorge, robe etc)* (shoulder) strap; **(paire de) bretelles** *(de pantalon)* (pair of) braces *or Am* suspenders; *Fam* **se faire remonter les bretelles** to get bawled out **2** *(lanière)* strap; **b. de fusil** rifle sling; **l'arme à la b.** with one's rifle slung over one's shoulder **3** *(route)* access road; *Rail* crossover; **b. d'autoroute** motorway link road, *Br* slip road, ramp; *Aut* **b. d'accès** spur, slip road; *(vers autoroute surélevée)* on-ramp; *Aut* **b. de sortie** exit; *(d'autoroute surélevée)* exit, off-ramp **4** *TV, Radio (magnétophone)* portable tape recorder

breton, -onne [brətɔ̃, -ɔn] **ADJ** Breton **NM** *Ling* Breton **N B.** Breton

bretonnant [brətɔnɑ̃] **ADJ** Breton **b.** = Breton-speaking Breton who preserves local traditions; **la Bretagne bretonnante** = Breton-speaking Brittany where local traditions are preserved

brett(el)er [brɛtle, brɛte] **VT** *(je brettelle [brɛtɛl], n. brettelons [brɛtlɔ̃]) (pierre etc)* to tool, to tooth; *(bijoux)* to hatch, to chase

bretzel [brɛtzɛl] **NM** pretzel

breuvage [brœvaʒ] **NM 1** *(boisson)* beverage, drink **2** *(potion particulière)* potion; **b. magique** magic potion

brève [brɛv] **ADJ** *voir* **bref** **NF 1** *Journ* short (news) item **2** *Ling (syllabe)* short syllable; *(voyelle)* short vowel

brevet [brəvɛ] **NM 1** *(titre)* diploma, certificate; *Naut* **passer son b. de capitaine** to obtain one's master's certificate, *Fam* to get one's ticket; *Jur (acte en)* **b.** contract delivered by a notary in the original **2** **b. (d'invention)** patent; **prendre un b.** to take out a patent **3** *Fig (d'honnêteté)* guarantee **4** *Hist (du roi)* (royal) warrant

▸▸ **b. d'apprentissage** indentures, articles; *Scol* **b. (des collèges)** = general exam taken at fifteen, *Br* ≃ GCSE; *Mil* **b. d'état-major** = staff college certificate; *Scol* **b. d'études du premier cycle** *Br* ≃ GCSE, *Am* ≃ high school graduation; **b. d'études professionnelles** = vocational diploma; **b. de pilote** *Aviat* pilot's licence; *Mil* wings; **b. professionnel** vocational qualification; **b. de technicien** = vocational training certificate (for 16-year-olds); **b. de technicien supérieur** = advanced vocational training certificate

brevetable [brəvtabl] **ADJ** patentable

breveté [brəvte] **ADJ 1** *(invention)* patented; **inventeur b.** inventor holding letters patent **2** *(diplômé)* qualified; **officier b. (d'état-major)** = officer who has passed staff college

breveter [brəvte] **VT** *(je brevette [brəvɛt], n. brevetons; je brevetterai) (invention)* to patent; **faire b. une invention** to take out a patent on an invention

bréviaire [brevjɛr] **NM** *Rel* breviary; *Fig* bible

brévité [brevite] **NF** *Ling (d'une voyelle etc)* shortness

briard [brijar] **NM** *(chien)* Briard

bribes [brib] **NFPL** **b. de conversation** snatches *or* scraps of conversation; **des b. de finlandais** scraps *or* bits of Finnish; **les b. de sa fortune/du repas** the remnants of his fortune/the leftovers of the meal; **apprendre qch par b.** to learn sth piecemeal *or* bit by bit

bric-à-brac [brikabrak] NM INV **1** *(vieux objets)* odds and ends, bric-à-brac, jumble; *Fig* jumble (de of); **marchand de b.** second-hand dealer **2 (boutique de) b.** second-hand shop, *Fam* junk shop

bric et de broc (de) [dǝbrikedǝbrɔk] ADV from one source and another, haphazardly; **maison meublée de b.** house furnished with bits and pieces

bricheton [briʃtɔ̃] NM *Fam (pain)* bread

brick [brik] NM **1** *Naut* brig **2** *Culin* **b. à l'œuf** brik, = egg enclosed in filo pastry and deep fried **3** *(carton)* carton; **b. de lait/de jus d'orange** carton of milk/orange juice; **lait vendu en b.** milk sold in cartons

bricolage [brikɔlaʒ] NM **1** *(travail)* do-it-yourself, *Br* DIY; **faire du b.** to do (some) do-it-yourself *or* DIY; **grande surface de b.** do-it-yourself centre, DIY superstore; **rayon b.** do-it-yourself department; **un mordu du b.** a do-it-yourself enthusiast, a do-it-yourselfer **2** *Péj (réparation)* botch-up; **c'est du b.!** it's a botch-up!

bricole [brikɔl] NF **1** *(babiole)* trifle, little thing; **bricoles** *(objets)* odds and ends; *(travaux)* odd jobs; **offrir une petite b. à qn** to give sb a little something; *Fam* **il va lui arriver des bricoles** he's going to get into a pickle; **s'occuper à des bricoles** to do odd jobs **2** *(pour tirer une charrette etc)* breast strap; *(de cheval)* breast harness

bricoler [brikɔle] VT **b. une affaire** to arrange a piece of business *(often shady)*; **elle a bricolé une table** she's knocked together *or* knocked up a table; **il a bricolé le moteur** he's tinkered with the engine
VI to do do-it-yourself *or Br* DIY; **j'ai passé la matinée à b. dans la maison** I spent the morning doing odd jobs about the house

bricoleur, -euse [brikɔlœr, -øz] N handyman, *f* handywoman
ADJ **être b.** to be good with one's hands

bride [brid] NF **1** *(du harnais)* bridle; **lâcher la b. à un cheval/à qn** to give free rein to a horse/to sb, to give a horse/sb his head; *Fig* **lâcher la b. à un élève** to allow a pupil more freedom, to give a pupil his head; **laisser à un cheval/à qn la b. sur le cou** to give a horse his head/to give sb a free rein; *Fig* **elle a la b. sur le cou** she has a free rein; **tenir un cheval en b., tenir la b. haute à un cheval** to curb *or* check a horse; *Fig* **tenir qn en b., tenir la b. haute à qn** to keep a tight rein on sb; **tenir ses passions en b.** to keep a tight rein on one's passions; **aller à b. abattue** *ou* **à toute b.** to ride at full speed, to ride full tilt, *Fam* to ride hell for leather; **partir à b. abattue** to set off at top speed; **fureur sans b.** unbridled fury **2** *Couture (de boutonnière)* bar; *(pour un bouton)* loop; *(de bonnet)* string **3** *Tech* strap, tie; *(d'un cylindre, d'un tuyau)* flange, collar; **b. de serrage** clamp, cramp; **tuyau à brides** flanged pipe

bridé, -e [bride] ADJ **1 yeux bridés** slant(ing) eyes, *Péj* slitty eyes **2** *Aut* **moteur b.** governed engine
N *très Fam* slant-eye, *Am* gook

brider [bride] VT **1** *(cheval)* to bridle; *(personne, colère, passions, déception etc)* to restrain, to curb, to keep in check; **cette contrainte le bride** it's a restraint on him **2** *Culin (volaille)* to truss; *Naut (câble etc)* to lash **3** *Couture (boutonnière)* to bind **4** *(tuyaux)* to flange, to clamp

bridge [bridʒ] NM **1** *Cartes* bridge; **b. aux enchères** auction bridge; **b. contrat** contract bridge; **tournoi/club de b.** bridge tournament/club; **faire un b.** to have *or* play a game of bridge **2** *(prothèse dentaire)* bridge

bridger [bridʒe] VI (je bridgeai(s); n. bridgeons) to play bridge

bridgeur, -euse [bridʒœr, -øz] N bridge player

bridon [bridɔ̃] NM snaffle (bridle)

brie [bri] NM Brie

briefer [brife] VT to brief; **b. ses collègues sur une affaire** to brief one's colleagues on a matter

briefing [brifiŋ] NM briefing; **faire un b.** to hold a briefing

brièvement [brievmɑ̃] ADV briefly

brièveté [brievte] NF brevity, briefness, shortness; *(de style, d'expression)* brevity

brigade [brigad] NF **1** *Mil* brigade **2** *(de policiers)* squad; *(d'ouvriers)* gang; **chef de b.** foreman
▸▸ *Aviat* **b. aérienne** group, *Am* wing; **b. anti-gang** organized crime squad; **b. de gendarmerie** squad of gendarmes; *Hist* **Brigades internationales** International Brigades; **b. de police** police squad; **b. des stupéfiants** *ou Fam* **des stups** drug squad

brigadier [brigadje] NM **1** *Mil* corporal; *(d'artillerie)* bombardier **2 b. (de police)** (police) sergeant **3** *(d'un groupe d'ouvriers)* foreman **4** *Naut* bowman, bow oar(sman)

brigadier-chef, *pl* **brigadiers-chefs** NM *Mil* rank between corporal and sergeant, lance sergeant

brigand [brigɑ̃] NM *(pillard)* brigand, bandit; *(personne malhonnête)* crook; **le petit b.** the little scoundrel *or* rascal

brigandage [brigɑ̃daʒ] NM (armed) robbery, banditry; **des actes de b.** (armed) robbery

brigantin [brigɑ̃tɛ̃] NM *Hist, Naut* brigantine

brigantine [brigɑ̃tin] NF *Naut* spanker

brigue [brig] NF *Litt* intrigue

briguer [brige] VT *(faveur, amitié, poste etc)* to solicit; **b. des voix** to canvass (for votes)

brillamment [brijamɑ̃] ADV brilliantly

brillance [brijɑ̃s] NF *(d'un bijou, du regard)* brilliance; *Opt* brilliancy; *TV (de l'image etc)* brightness; *Mus* brightness of tone

brillant [brijɑ̃] ADJ *(carrière, élève, orateur etc)* brilliant; *(lumière, couleur)* bright, brilliant; *(pierre précieuse)* sparkling, glittering; *(cheveux, chaussures, cuir)* shiny, glossy; *(conversation)* sparkling; **spectacle b.** splendid sight; **elle avait les yeux brillants de fièvre/joie** her eyes were bright with fever/sparkling with joy; **la situation n'est pas brillante** the situation isn't brilliant; **il est promis à un b. avenir** he has a brilliant future ahead of him
NM **1** *(d'un métal)* brilliance, brightness; *(d'une pierre précieuse)* sparkle, glitter; *(d'un papier, d'un tissu)* shininess, glossiness, sheen; *(de chaussures)* shine, polish; *(de conversation)* sparkle; *(d'esprit, d'intelligence)* brilliance; **et vos cheveux retrouveront leur b. naturel** and your hair will regain its natural shine **2** *(diamant)* brilliant; **monté/taillé en b.** mounted/cut as a brilliant
▸▸ **b. à lèvres** lip gloss

brillantine [brijɑ̃tin] NF brilliantine

briller [brije] VI **1** *(du soleil)* to shine; *(de l'acier)* to glint, to gleam; *(d'une bougie)* to glimmer; *(de l'eau)* to shimmer, to glisten; *(des étoiles)* to glitter, to twinkle; *(de la lune)* to gleam, to shine; *(du satin)* to shimmer, to shine; *(des phares)* to glare; *(des braises)* to glow; *(des yeux)* to shine, to gleam; *Prov* **tout ce qui brille n'est pas or** all that glitters is not gold; **faire b. ses chaussures** to shine *or* polish one's shoes; **des yeux qui brillent de colère/de joie** eyes shining *or* gleaming with anger/happiness; **la joie brillait sur son visage** his/her face shone with joy
2 *Fig (exceller)* to shine, to excel, to do well;

il brille en société he shines in company; **b. dans la conversation** to be a brilliant conversationalist; **b. par son savoir/son intelligence** to be extraordinarily knowledgeable/intelligent; **b. par ses dons d'orateur** to be an extraordinarily gifted speaker; **b. par son absence** to be conspicuous by one's absence; **elle ne brille pas par sa ponctualité** she's not noted for her punctuality

brimade [brimad] NF *(tour)* rag; *Scol, Mil* brimades ragging, *Am* hazing; *(plus grave)* bullying, victimization; **faire subir des brimades à qn** to rag *or Am* to haze sb; *(plus gravement)* to bully *or* victimize sb

brimbalement [brɛ̃balmɑ̃] NM *(de voiture, charrette etc)* shaking about; *(de bateau)* swaying, rocking

brimbaler [brɛ̃bale] VT & VI *Fam* = **bringuebaler**

brimborion [brɛ̃bɔrjɔ̃] NM bauble, knick-knack

brimer [brime] VT *(recrue etc)* to rag, *Am* to haze; *(plus gravement)* to bully, to victimize; **il se croyait brimé** he felt he was being picked on *or* got at

brin [brɛ̃] NM **1** *(d'herbe)* blade; *(de myrte, persil, romarin etc)* sprig; *(de mimosa, de muguet)* spray; *(de paille)* wisp; **un beau b. de fille** a fine-looking girl **2** *Fam (petite quantité)* bit (de of); **un b. d'air** a breath of air; **un b. d'ironie/de jalousie** a touch *or* hint of irony/jealousy; **sa voix laissait transparaître un b. d'inquiétude** one could detect a note of concern in his voice; **faire un b. de toilette** to have a quick wash (and brush up); **faire un b. de causette** to have a little chat; **il lui a fait un b. de cour** he had a bit of a flirt with her **3** *(de laine, corde, fil etc)* strand **4 brins d'une antenne** wires of an aerial
ADV **un b.** a bit; **il est un b. ennuyeux** he's a bit of a bore

brindezingue [brɛ̃dzɛ̃g] ADJ *Fam* crazy

brindille [brɛ̃dij] NF twig

bringue [brɛ̃g] *Arg* NF **1 grande b.** *(fille)* beanpole **2** *(fête)* party; **faire la b.** to party **3** *Suisse Fam (querelle)* row; *(rengaine)* refrain

bringuebaler [brɛ̃g(ǝ)bale], **brinquebaler** [brɛ̃kbale] VI *Fam (d'une voiture, charrette etc)* to shake about; *(d'un bateau)* to sway, to rock; *(d'une chaîne)* to rattle
VT *Litt* to shake about

bringuer [brɛ̃ge] *Fam* VI **1** *(faire la fête)* to party **2** *Suisse* **arrête de b.!** stop going on about it!
VT *Suisse (harceler)* to go on at
VPR **se bringuer** *Suisse (se disputer)* **ils se bringuaient** they were having a row

brio [brijo] NM **avec b.** with panache, brilliantly; *Mus* **con b.** con brio

brioche [brijɔʃ] NF *Culin* brioche; *Fam* **prendre de la b.** to develop a paunch *or* pot

brioché [brijɔʃe] ADJ **pain b.** = milk bread

brique [brik] NF **1** *(de construction)* brick; **maison de** *ou* **en briques** brick(-built) house; **mur de briques** brick wall; *Arg* **bouffer des briques,** *Fam* **manger des briques à la sauce caillou** to have nothing to eat; **ne t'attends pas à ce que je mange des briques à la sauce caillou** you can't expect me to live on air **2** *(de savon)* bar, cake; *(de béton etc)* block, slab **3** *(de lait, jus de fruit)* carton **4** *Ancienne ment Arg (dix mille francs)* ten thousand francs
ADJ INV brick-red
▸▸ **b. creuse** hollow brick; **b. pleine** solid brick; **b. tubulaire** hollow brick

briquer [brike] VT *(nettoyer)* to scrub down; *Naut (pont)* to holystone

briquet¹ [brikɛ] NM *(appareil)* (cigarette)

lighter; *Arch (à amadou)* tinder box; **b.-tempête** pipe lighter, windproof lighter; **battre le b.** to strike a light

briquet² NM *(chien)* beagle

briquetage [brik(ə)taʒ] NM *(maçonnerie)* brickwork; *(trompe-l'œil)* imitation brickwork

briqueter [brik(ə)te] VT (**je briquette, n. briquetons; je briquetterai**) *(construire)* to brick; *(en trompe-l'œil)* to face with imitation brickwork

briqueterie [brikɛtri] NF brickworks, brickyard

briqueteur [brik(ə)tœr] NM bricklayer

briquetier [brik(ə)tje] NM brick manufacter

briquette [brikɛt] NF briquette

bris [bri] NM **1** *(de verre, des scellés etc)* breaking **2** *Jur* **b. de prison** prison breakout; **b. de clôture** breaking and entering, *Spéc* breach of close

brisant [brizɑ̃] ADJ **explosif b.** high explosive; **obus b.** high-explosive shell
▪ NM **1** *(écueil)* reef, shoal; **brisants** *(vagues)* breakers **2** = **brise-lames**

brise [briz] NF breeze; *Naut* **forte b.** stiff breeze

brisé [brize] ADJ *(détruit)* broken; **ligne brisée** broken line; *Fig* **il est b.** he's a broken man; **b. de fatigue** exhausted, tired out; **b. de chagrin** crushed by grief, brokenhearted

brise-bise [briz] NM INV half curtain *(in lower half of window)*

brisées [brize] NFPL *(pour marquer la voie)* broken branches; *(d'un cerf etc)* track; *Fig* **suivre les b. de qn** to follow in sb's footsteps, to follow sb's lead *or* example; *Fig* **aller** *ou* **marcher sur les b. de qn** to poach on sb's territory

brise-fer NM INV clumsy person (who breaks everything)

brise-glace NM INV **1** *(navire)* ice breaker **2** *(d'une pile de pont)* ice breaker; *(d'un navire)* ice beam

brise-jet NM INV tap *or Am* faucet nozzle

brise-lames NM INV **1** *(digue)* breakwater, mole **2** *(le long d'une plage)* groyne

brisement [brizmɑ̃] NM *Fig* **b. de cœur** heartbreak

brise-mottes NM INV *Agr* brake harrow

briser [brize] VT *(casser)* to break, to smash; *(mottes de terre, navire)* to break up; *(minerai)* to pound (up), to crush; *(opposition)* to crush, to break down; *(enthousiasme, espérances)* to crush; *(carrière, vie)* to ruin, to wreck; *(grève)* to break; *Vieilli (conversation)* to break off; **b. qn** *(d'une marche etc)* to exhaust sb, to wear *or* tire sb out; *(de difficultés, paroles pessimistes etc)* to wear sb down; **b. une porte** to break open *or* burst open a door; **b. qch en mille morceaux** to smash sth to smithereens *or* into a thousand pieces; **b. qch en éclats** to smash sth to bits *or* to pieces; **porter cette caisse m'a brisé les reins** carrying that box has done my back in; **brisé par la douleur** crushed by grief, heartbroken; **la voix brisée par l'émotion** his voice choked with emotion; **cela me brise le cœur** it breaks my heart; **c'est à vous b. le cœur** it's heartbreaking; *Fig* **il/ça me les brise** he/it really bugs me *or Br* hacks me off
▪ VI **1 b. avec qn** to break with sb; *Litt Vieilli* **brisons là!** not another word!, enough! **2** *(des vagues)* to break
▪ VPR **se briser 1** *(des vagues, de la porcelaine, du verre etc)* to break; **se b. en mille morceaux** to break *or* smash into a thousand pieces; **cela se brise comme du verre** it's as fragile as glass **2** *Fig (des espoirs)* to be shattered, to be dashed; *(des efforts)* to fail, to come to nothing

brise-tout N INV clumsy person (who breaks everything); **c'est un b.** he's like a bull in a china shop

briseur, -euse [brizœr, -øz] N **b. de grève** strike breaker, *Fam Péj* scab

brise-vent NM INV windbreak

bristol [bristɔl] NM Bristol board, thin cardboard; *(carte de visite)* visiting card

brisure [brizyr] NF **1** *(cassure)* break, crack **2** *(d'un gond)* break; *(d'un volet)* folding joint **3** **brisures** *(petits morceaux)* tiny pieces **4** *Hér* brisure

britannique [britanik] VOIR GRAMMAIRE A18
ADJ British; **les îles Britanniques** the British Isles
▪ N **B.** Briton, *Am* Britisher; **les Britanniques** the British

broc [bro] NM pitcher, (large) jug

brocante [brɔkɑ̃t] NF *(commerce)* bric-à-brac trade; *(magasin)* second-hand shop; *(marché aux puces)* second-hand market

brocanter [brɔkɑ̃te] VI to deal in secondhand goods
▪ VT *(meubles anciens, objets d'occasion etc)* to deal in

brocanteur, -euse [brɔkɑ̃tœr, -øz] N second-hand dealer

brocarder [brɔkarde] VT *Vieilli Litt (personne)* to gibe at

brocart [brɔkar] NM *Tex* brocade; **rideaux de b.** brocade curtains

brochage [brɔʃaʒ] NM **1** *(de livre)* stitching, sewing **2** *Tex* brocading, figuring

broche [brɔʃ] NF **1** *Culin* spit; **faire cuire qch à la b.** to spit-roast sth; **poulet à la b.** chicken on the spit; **b. de boucher** meat skewer **2** *(bijou)* brooch **3** *Tech, Élec* pin; *(d'une serrure)* gudgeon; **b. de charnière** hinge pin; *Élec* **fiche à deux broches** two-pin plug; *Ordinat* **b. de sortie** pinout **4** *Tex* spindle **5** *(de dentiste)* broach; *Chir* pin

broché [brɔʃe] ADJ **1** *Tex* brocaded **2** **livre b.** paperback (book)
▪ NM *Tex (procédé)* brocading; *(tissu)* brocade

brocher [brɔʃe] VT **1** *(livre)* to stitch, to sew **2** *Tex (tissu)* to brocade, to figure; **tissu broché d'or** gold brocade

brochet [brɔʃɛ] NM *(poisson)* pike VOIR GRAMMAIRE A12

brochette [brɔʃɛt] NF **1** *Culin (broche)* skewer; *(plat)* kebab; **b. de fruits de mer** seafood kebab **2** *(de gens)* band, group; **b. de décorations** row of medals *or* decorations; *Iron* **vous faites une belle b.!** you're a fine lot!

brocheur, -euse [brɔʃœr, -øz] N *(de livre)* bookbinder
▪ NF *Typ* **brocheuse** stitching machine; **b. automatique sans couture** perfect binder
▪ NM *Tex* brocade loom

brochure [brɔʃyr] NF **1** *(prospectus etc)* brochure, pamphlet, booklet; **b. publicitaire/touristique** advertising/tourist brochure **2** *(de livres)* stitching, sewing **3** *Tex* brocaded pattern

brocoli [brɔkɔli] NM broccoli; **mange tes brocolis** eat your broccoli

brodequin [brɔdkɛ̃] NM laced boot; *Hist, Théâtre* buskin; *Hist* **appliquer les brodequins à un supplicié** to put the boots on a torture victim

broder [brɔde] VT *Couture* to embroider; *Fig* **b. une histoire** to embroider *or* embellish a story
▪ VI **tu brodes** *(c'est inexact)* you're embroidering; **b. sur des faits** to embroider *or* embellish the facts; **b. sur un sujet** to elaborate on a subject

broderie [brɔdri] NF **1** *(ouvrage)* (piece of) embroidery; **broderies** embroidery **2** *(activité)* embroidery; **faire de la b.** to do embroidery, to embroider; **b. anglaise** broderie anglaise

brodeur, -euse [brɔdœr, -øz] N embroiderer
▪ NF **brodeuse** *(machine)* embroidering machine

broiement [brwamɑ̃] NM = **broyage**

brol(l) [brɔl] NM *Belg (tas d'objets, bric-à-brac)* clutter, jumble, bric-à-brac

bromate [brɔmat] NM *Chimie* bromate

brome [brom] NM *Chimie* bromine

bromure [brɔmyr] NM *Chimie* bromide; *Typ* **b. de page** page bromide

bronca [brɔ̃ka] NF *(huées)* booing, jeering; *(protestation collective)* general outcry

bronche [brɔ̃ʃ] NF *Anat* bronchus, *pl* bronchi; **elle est fragile des bronches** she has weak lungs *or* a weak chest; **affection des bronches** bronchial disorder

broncher [brɔ̃ʃe] VI **1** *(de cheval)* to stumble **2** *(réagir)* to react; **sans b.** without batting an eyelid, without turning a hair; **il n'a pas bronché** he didn't bat an eyelid; **le premier qui bronche aura des ennuis!** *(qui bouge)* the first one to move will get it!; *(qui se plaint)* the first one to complain will be in trouble!

bronchiole [brɔ̃ʃjɔl] NF *Anat* bronchiole

bronchique [brɔ̃ʃik] ADJ *Anat* bronchial

bronchite [brɔ̃ʃit] NF *Méd* bronchitis; **faire** *ou* **avoir une b.** to have bronchitis

bronchitique [brɔ̃ʃitik] ADJ, N *Méd* bronchitic

broncho-pneumonie [brɔ̃kopnømɔni], *pl* **broncho-pneumonies** NF *Méd* bronchopneumonia

bronchoscopie [brɔ̃kɔskɔpi] NF *Méd* bronchoscopy

brontosaure [brɔ̃tɔzɔr] NM brontosaurus

bronzage [brɔ̃zaʒ] NM **1** *(de la peau)* tanning; *(hâle)* (sun)tan; **b. intégral** all-over tan **2** *(d'une statue etc)* bronzing; *(d'un canon, de canons de fusil etc)* blueing

bronze [brɔ̃z] NM *(métal, objet d'art)* bronze; **b. à canon** gunmetal; *Fig* **un cœur de b.** a heart of stone; **c'est un homme de b.** he has a heart of stone

bronzé [brɔ̃ze] ADJ **1** *(visage etc)* (sun)tanned, bronzed **2** *(statue etc)* bronze(d)

bronzer [brɔ̃ze] VT **1** *(peau etc)* to tan **2** *(statue etc)* to bronze; *(canon de fusil etc)* to blue
▪ VI to tan, to get a tan; *(de la peau)* to tan; **il bronze vite** he tans quickly
▪ VPR **se bronzer** to sunbathe

bronzette [brɔ̃zɛt] NF *Fam* sunbathing; **faire (de la) b.** to do a bit of sunbathing, to sunbathe

bronzier [brɔ̃zje] NM *Beaux-Arts* maker of bronzes

brook [bruk] NM *Sport* water jump

broquette [brɔkɛt] NF (tin)tack

brossage [brɔsaʒ] NM brushing

brosse [brɔs] NF **1** *(ustensile)* brush; **b. métallique** wire brush; **b. de chiendent** scrubbing brush; **laver le sol à la b.** to give the floor a scrub, to scrub the floor; **donner un coup de b. à qch** to give sth a brush; **donner un coup de b. à qn** to give sb's hair a brush; **enlever la boue d'un coup de b.** to brush off the mud; **cheveux en b.** crew cut; **se faire couper les cheveux en b.** to have a crew cut; **il porte la b.** he has a crew cut; *Fig* **passer** *ou* **manier la b. (à reluire)** to crawl, to bow and scrape; *Can Fam* **partir sur une b.** *(biture)* to go on a pub crawl, *Am* to go bar-hopping **2** *(pinceau large)* (paint)brush **3** *(d'un renard)* brush
▪ ▪ **b. à cheveux** hairbrush; **b. à dents** toothbrush; **b. à habits** clothes brush; **b. à ongles** nailbrush

brosser [brɔse] **VT 1** *(tapis, manteau, cheveux etc)* to brush; *(sol)* to scrub; *(cheval)* to brush down; *Belg* **b. un cours** to skip *or* cut a lecture **2** *(peindre)* to paint; **b. les décors d'une pièce** to paint the scenery for a play; **il nous a brossé un rapide tableau de la situation** he gave us a brief outline of the situation; **son article brosse un vaste tableau de la situation** his article paints a broad picture of the situation **3** *Sport (balle, ballon)* to cut, to put spin on
VPR se brosser *(se nettoyer)* to brush oneself down, to brush one's clothes; **se b. les dents** to brush *or* clean one's teeth; **se b. les cheveux** to brush one's hair; *Fam* **tu peux te b.!** you can whistle for it!

brou [bru] **NM 1** *(enveloppe des noix etc)* husk, hull, *Am* shuck **2** *(teinture)* **b. de noix** walnut stain

broue [bru] **NF** *Can Arg* froth; *Fig* **faire ou péter de la b.** to talk big, to show off

brouet [bruɛ] **NM** gruel, *Br* skilly, *Péj* slop

brouette [bruɛt] **NF 1** *(de jardin)* wheelbarrow **2** *Hist (chaise fermée)* sedan chair *(on two wheels)*

brouettée [bruete] **NF** (wheel)barrowful, barrowload

brouetter [bruete] **VT** to carry in a wheelbarrow, to wheelbarrow

brouhaha [bruaa] **NM** hubbub, brouhaha

brouillage [bruja3] **NM** *Radio, Électron (accidentel)* interference; *(intentionnel)* jamming; *Tél* scrambling; **b. sonore/visuel** sound/visual interference

brouillard [brujar] **NM 1** *Météo* fog; **il y a du b.** it's foggy; **arrêté par le b., pris dans le b.** fogbound; *Fig* **je suis dans le b.** I'm in a fog; **b. givrant** freezing fog; **voir à travers un b., avoir un b. devant les yeux** to see things through a haze; *Fig* **foncer dans le b.** to push on regardless **2** *Com* day book; *Compta* **b. de caisse** cash book **3** *Phys* aerosol **4** *Aut* **b. carburé** fuel spray

brouillasse [brujas] **NF** = **bruine**

brouillasser [brujase] **V IMPERS** = **bruiner**

brouille [bruj] **NF** quarrel, disagreement; **être en b. avec qn** to be on bad terms with sb, to have fallen out with sb; **c'est une petite b. qui ne durera pas** it's just a tiff, it won't last long

brouillé [bruje] **ADJ 1** *(mélangé)* jumbled (up), mixed (up); *(contours etc)* blurred, fuzzy; *Tél* scrambled; **œufs brouillés** scrambled eggs; **teint b.** blotchy complexion **2 être b. avec qn** to be on bad terms with sb, to have fallen out with sb; **ils sont brouillés** they're on bad terms *or* they've fallen out (with each other); **je suis b. avec les dates/la grammaire** I'm hopeless at dates/grammar

brouille-ménage **NM** *Fam (vin rouge)* red wine, *Br* plonk

brouiller [bruje] **VT 1** *(mélanger)* *(idées)* to mix up, to jumble (up); **b. des œufs** to scramble eggs; **b. les cartes** to shuffle the cards; *Fig* to confuse the issue, to confuse things; **b. la combinaison d'un coffre** to scramble the combination of a safe; **b. la vue à qn** to blur sb's vision; **l'alcool brouille le teint** alcohol ruins your complexion; **b. les pistes** to cover one's tracks; **cela risquerait de me b. les idées** it might get me into a muddle; **cela a brouillé mes souvenirs** it's confused my memories **2** *(amis etc)* to set against each other, to cause a disagreement between; **je ne voudrais pas vous b. avec elle** I wouldn't want to make you fall out with her **3** *Radio, Électron (émission) (accidentellement)* to cause interference to; *(intentionnellement)* to jam; *Tél* to scramble
VPR se brouiller 1 *(d'idées)* to get mixed up *or* jumbled (up); **tout s'est brouillé dans ma**

tête I got all muddled up *or* mixed up; **le temps se brouille** it's clouding over
2 *(de la vue, des yeux)* to get blurred; **yeux brouillés de larmes** eyes blurred with tears
3 *(se disputer)* to quarrel, to fall out *(avec qn* with sb*)*; *Fam* **elle s'est brouillée avec la physique** she's taken a dislike to physics

brouillerie [brujri] **NF** *Fam* tiff

brouilleur [brujœr] **ADJ** *Radio, Électron* **émetteur b.** jamming station; **signal b.** jamming signal
NM *Radio, Électron* jammer, jamming transmitter; *Tél* **(circuit) b.** scrambler

brouillon, -onne [brujɔ̃, -ɔn] **ADJ** muddleheaded; *(au travail)* disorganized, unmethodical; **esprit b.** muddled mind; **travail b.** unmethodical work
N muddler
NM *(ébauche)* (rough) draft; *Scol (notes etc)* rough work; **(papier) b.** scrap *or* *Am* scratch paper; *Ordinat* **version b.** draft version; **prendre des notes au b.** to take rough notes; **faire un exercice au b.** to do an exercise in rough; **je ne vais pas lire ce b.!** I'm not going to read this scribble!; **(cahier de) b.** rough (note)book; *Fig* **cette présentation n'est qu'un b.** this is only a rough presentation

broum [brum] **INT** brum, brum!

broussaille [brusaj] **NF** *(souvent pl)* scrub, brushwood; **cheveux en b.** tousled *or* unkempt hair; **sourcils en b.** shaggy *or* bushy eyebrows

broussailleux, -euse [brusajø, -øz] **ADJ** *(région)* scrubby, bushy; *(cheveux)* tousled, unkempt; *(sourcils)* bushy, shaggy; **terrain b.** scrubland

broussard [brusar] **NM** bushman

brousse¹ [brus] **NF** **la b.** the bush, *Austr* the outback; *Fam Fig* the back of beyond, the middle of nowhere; **feux de b.** bush *or* brush fires; *Fam* **son village est perdu en pleine b.** his village is at the back of beyond *or* in the middle of nowhere

brousse² **NF** *Région (fromage)* = cream cheese made from goats' or ewes' milk

broutage [bruta3], **broutement** [brutmɑ̃] **NM 1** *(par les bêtes)* grazing, browsing **2** *Tech (des freins, de l'embrayage, d'un outil)* juddering, grabbing

brouter [brute] **VT** *(herbe etc)* to graze, to feed on; *Fig Fam* **elle me les broute, celle-là!** she's a real pain!, she really gets on my nerves!
VI 1 *(des bêtes)* to graze **2** *(des freins, de l'embrayage, d'un outil)* to judder, to grab

broutille [brutij] **NF** trifle, trifling matter; **ils se sont disputés pour une b.** they argued over nothing

brownien [broniɛ̃] **ADJ** *Phys* **mouvement b.** Brownian movement

browning [broniŋ] **NM** Browning

broyage [brwaja3] **NM** *(d'une pierre, des aliments par les dents etc)* crushing, grinding; *(du charbon)* pulverizing; *Tex (du chanvre etc)* braking

broyer [brwaje] **VT** *(je broie, n. broyons; je broierai)* *(pierre, aliments etc)* to crush, to grind; *(documents)* to shred; *(charbon)* to pulverize; *Tex (chanvre etc)* to brake; **b. des couleurs** to grind colours; **la machine lui a broyé la main** the machine crushed his hand; *Fig* **quand il te serre la main, il te la broie!** he has a crushing handshake!; *Fig* **b. du noir** to be down in the dumps

broyeur, -euse [brwajœr, -øz] **ADJ** *(appareil etc)* crushing, grinding
N *(personne)* crusher, grinder; *Tex* hemp braker *or* dresser
NM *(machine)* crusher, grinder; *(de documents)* shredder; *(de charbon)* pulverizer

▸▸ **b. d'évier** sink disposal unit; **b. d'ordures** waste *or* *Am* garbage disposal unit

brrr [br] **INT** *Fam* brrr!

bru [bry] **NF** *Vieilli* daughter-in-law

bruant [bryɑ̃] **NM** *(oiseau)* bunting; **b. jaune** yellowhammer

brucelles [brysɛl] **NFPL** tweezers

brucellose [bryseloz] **NF** *Vét, Méd* brucellosis

bruche [bryʃ] **NF** *Entom* **b. des pois** pea beetle, weevil

brugnon [bryɲɔ̃] **NM** *(fruit)* nectarine

brugnonier [bryɲɔnje] **NM** nectarine (tree)

bruine [bryin] **NF** drizzle

bruiner [bryine] **V IMPERS** to drizzle; **il bruine** it's drizzling

bruineux, -euse [bryinø, -øz] **ADJ** drizzly

bruire [bryir] **VI** *(prp bruissant; pr ind il bruit, ils bruissent; impf il bruissait)* *(des feuilles, d'une étoffe)* to rustle; *(d'une machine)* to hum; *(d'un ruisseau, du vent)* to murmur; *(des abeilles)* to buzz

bruissement [bryismɑ̃] **NM** *(des feuilles, d'une étoffe)* rustle, rustling; *(d'une machine)* hum(ming); *(d'un ruisseau, du vent)* murmur(ing); *(des abeilles)* buzzing

bruit [bryi] **NM 1** *(son)* sound, noise; *(vacarme)* noise; *(tapage, scandale)* commotion, fuss; **on n'entend pas les bruits de la rue** you can't hear the noise from the street; **c'est très calme, il n'y a pas un b.** it's very quiet, there's not a sound; **quel b.!** what a row *or* din *or* racket!; **lutte contre le b.** noise abatement campaign; **b. métallique** clang; **b. de vaisselle** clatter of dishes; **b. de marteaux** (sound of) hammering; **b. de pas** (sound of) footsteps; **il y avait des bruits de voix** there was the sound of voices, voices could be heard; **b. sourd** thud; **c'est tombé avec un b. sourd** it fell with a thud; **faire du b.** *(d'un enfant, moteur etc)* to make a noise, to be noisy; **il fait du b. quand il mange** he's a noisy eater; **ça a fait un b. formidable** it made an incredible noise; **enlève tes chaussures, tu feras moins de b.** take off your shoes, you'll make less noise; **ne faites pas de b.!** *(soyez silencieux)* don't make a sound!; *(ne chahutez pas)* don't be noisy!; *Fig* **cette histoire a fait du b. à l'époque** the affair caused a sensation *or* scandal at the time; **beaucoup de b. pour rien** much ado about nothing; **faire grand b. de qch** to make a great to-do *or* a great fuss about sth; **sans b.** without a sound, silently; *Électron etc* **b. parasite** interference, noise
2 *Méd (cardiaque, respiratoire)* murmur
3 *(rumeur)* rumour, *Am* rumor; **répandre ou faire courir un b.** to spread a rumour; **le b. court que ...** rumour has it that ...; **des bruits courent sur la démission du Premier ministre** there are rumours that the Prime Minister is going to resign; **des bruits circulent** rumours are circulating *or* are going about *or* round; **faux b.** false rumour
▸▸ **b. d'ambiance** background noise; **b. blanc** white noise; **b. de fond** background noise; **b. du moteur** engine noise; **b. de piste** *(d'un enregistrement)* hiss; **b. de roulement** road noise

bruitage [bryita3] **NM** *Théâtre, Cin, TV* sound effects

bruiter [bryite] **VT** *Théâtre, Cin, TV* to add sound effects to

bruiteur, -euse [bryitœr, øz] **N** *Théâtre, Cin, TV* sound-effects man, *f* woman

brûlage [bryla3] **NM 1** *(des mauvaises herbes, de l'herbe etc)* burning; *(de la peinture)* burning off; *(des cheveux)* singeing; **se faire faire un b.** to have one's hair singed **2** *(du café)* roasting

brûlant [brylɑ̃] ADJ *(très chaud)* burning (hot); *(café)* boiling (hot), scalding (hot); *(soleil)* burning, scorching, blazing; *Fig (paroles etc)* fiery, passionate; **il a les mains brûlantes** his hands are burning (hot); **désir b.** burning desire; **question brûlante** burning question; **le sujet est d'une actualité brûlante** it's one of the burning issues of the day

brûlé, -ée [bryle] ADJ burnt; *Méd* **il est b. au premier/deuxième/troisième degré** he has first-/second-/third-degree burns; *Culin* **crème brûlée** crème brûlée; **vin b.** mulled wine; *Fam* **tête brûlée** hothead; *Fam* **être b.** *(être compromis)* to be finished

NM **1** odeur de b. smell of burning, burnt smell; **goût de b.** burnt taste; **avoir un goût de b.** to taste burnt; **sentir le b.** *(être louche)* to look fishy; *(d'opinions)* to smack of heresy **2** *Can* burnt-out woodland area

N *(accidenté)* burns victim; *Méd* **les grands brûlés** people with third-degree burns; **crier comme un b.** to scream like a madman

brûle-parfum(s), *pl* **brûle-parfums** [brylparfœ̃] NM perfume burner

brûle-pourpoint (à) [abrylpurpwɛ̃] ADV *(sans détour)* point-blank; *Arch* **tirer sur qn à b.** to fire at sb at point-blank range

brûler [bryle] VT **1** *(papier, bois, objet, les morts etc)* to burn; *(détruire entièrement) (maison etc)* to burn down; *(métal)* to burn away; *(résistance électrique etc)* to burn out; *(peinture)* to burn off; *(blessure)* to cauterize; *(d'un acide)* to corrode; *(d'un consommateur) (électricité, combustible)* to use, to burn; *(bougie)* to burn; **elle fut brûlée vive** *(par accident)* she was burnt to death *or* burnt alive; *(par supplice)* she was burnt at the stake; **b. la cervelle à qn** to blow sb's brains out; *Agr* **b. le terrain** *ou* **la brousse** to burn the ground; **la chaudière brûle beaucoup de charbon** the boiler burns *or* uses a lot of coal; *Fig* **ils ont brûlé leurs dernières cartouches** they've shot their bolt

2 *(pain, gâteau, rôti etc)* to burn; *(café)* to roast; *(cheveux)* to singe; *(linge)* to scorch; *(personne, peau, yeux etc)* to burn; **le lait est brûlé** the milk has caught; **l'argent lui brûle les doigts** money burns a hole in his pocket; **terre brûlée par le soleil** sun-scorched earth; **le soleil me brûle le dos** the sun is burning *or* scorching my back; *Fam* **b. la route** *ou* **le pavé** to scorch along *or* tear along the road; **la gelée a brûlé les bourgeons** the frost has nipped the buds; **la fumée me brûlait les yeux** the smoke made my eyes burn *or* sting *or* smart; *Fig* **b. les planches** to give an inspired performance

3 *Aut* **b. un feu rouge** to jump the lights, to go through a red light; **b. un stop** to go straight through a stop sign, not to stop at a stop sign; **b. la politesse à qn** to leave sb abruptly, to leave without saying goodbye to sb; *(passer devant qn dans une queue)* to push in front of sb; *Sport* **b. un concurrent** to race past a competitor, to leave a competitor standing; **b. un signal** to overrun a signal

VI **1** *(flamber) (de bois, charbon etc)* to burn; *(de maison etc)* to burn, to be on fire, to be alight; *(être très chaud)* to be burning (hot); *(de l'eau)* to be boiling (hot), to be scalding (hot); *Méd* to be feverish; *(d'une blessure)* to smart; **j'ai la gorge qui brûle** my throat is burning; **j'ai les yeux qui brûlent** my eyes are burning *or* stinging *or* smarting; **b. lentement** *ou* **sans flamme** to smoulder; **laisser b. la lumière/l'électricité** to leave the light/the lights on *or* burning; **aïe, ça brûle!** ow, that's hot!; *Fam* **tu brûles** *(dans un jeu)* you're getting very warm; **b. de fièvre** to be burning (with fever)

2 *Fig* **b. de curiosité** to be consumed with

curiosity; **b. d'impatience de faire qch** to be burning (with impatience) *or* bursting (with impatience) to do sth; **b. (du désir) de faire qch** to be burning *or* dying to do sth; *Fam* **les mains lui brûlent** he's dying to be doing things; *Fam* **les pieds lui brûlent** he's itching to be off

3 *(de la viande)* to burn; *(du lait)* to catch; **j'ai encore fait b. mon repas!** I've burnt my food again!

4 *Litt, Vieilli* **b. (d'amour) pour qn** to languish for sb

VPR **se brûler** *(par accident)* to burn oneself (**avec** on); *(exprès)* to set fire to oneself; **se b. les doigts** to burn one's fingers; **se b. la langue** to burn *or* scald one's tongue; **se b. la cervelle** to blow one's brains out

brûleur [brylœr] NM **1** *(d'une cuisinière à gaz etc)* burner **2 b. de café** coffee roaster

brûloir [brylwar] NM *(machine)* coffee roaster

brûlot [brylo] NM **1** *(écrit)* fierce attack **2** *Culin (au sucre)* burnt brandy **3** *Can (moustique)* gnat, midge **4** *Hist, Naut* fire ship

brûlure [brylyr] NF **1** *(blessure)* burn; *Méd* **b. au premier/deuxième/troisième degré** first-/second-/third-degree burn; **des traces de b. de cigarette sur un fauteuil** cigarette burns on an armchair **2** *(sensation de)* **b.** burning (sensation); **brûlures d'estomac** heartburn **3** *Agr* frost nip; *(par le soleil)* scorching; *(du maïs)* blight

brume [brym] NF mist, haze; **un banc de b.** a bank of mist; *Fig* **dans les brumes du sommeil** heavy with sleep; **englué dans les brumes de l'ivresse** in a drunken haze

▸▸ **b. de beau temps** heat haze; **b. de chaleur** heat haze

brumeux, -euse [brymø, -øz] ADJ misty, hazy; *Fig (idées, explication etc)* hazy, vague, woolly

brumisateur® [brymizatœr] NM atomizer, spray

brun, brune [brœ̃, bryn] ADJ *(tissu, cheveux etc)* brown; *(peau, personne)* dark, swarthy, dusky; *(teint) (bronzé)* brown, tanned; **tabac b.** dark tobacco; **une bière brune** a brown ale; **il est b. de peau** he's dark-skinned; **elle est naturellement brune** she is a natural brunette

N *(personne)* dark-haired man, *f* woman; **une belle brune** a lovely brunette

NM *(couleur)* brown; **b. foncé** dark brown

NF **brune 1 à la brune** at dusk, at twilight **2** *(bière)* dark beer, *Br* ≃ brown ale

brunante [brynɑ̃t] NF *Can* dusk, twilight

brunâtre [brynɑtr] ADJ brownish

brunch [brœ̃ʃ] NM brunch

brunette [brynɛt] NF brunette

brunir [brynir] VI *(de peau, personne)* to tan, to become tanned; *(de cheveux)* to darken, to go dark; *(de feuillages)* to turn brown; *Culin (de sucre)* to brown; **b. au soleil** to tan

VT *(peau)* to tan; *(cheveux)* to darken; *Tech (or, métal)* to burnish, to polish

brunissage [brynisaʒ] NM *Tech* burnishing, polishing

brunissement [brynismɑ̃] NM *(de la peau)* tanning; *(résultat)* tan

brunisseur, -euse [brynisœr, -øz] N *Tech* burnisher

brunissoir [bryniswar] NM *Tech* burnisher, polisher

brunissure [brynisyr] NF **1** *(des métaux)* burnish, polish **2** *Agr* (potato) blight *or* rot

Brushing® [brœʃiŋ] NM blow-dry; **se faire un B.** to blow-dry one's hair; **faire un B. à qn** to give sb a blow-dry, to blow-dry sb's hair; **coupe et B.** cut and blow-dry

brusque [brysk] ADJ **1** *(personne, manière,*

ton) abrupt, curt, brusque; *(geste)* abrupt, brusque **2** *(arrêt, changement, départ etc)* sudden, abrupt; *Aut* **tournant b.** sharp bend

brusquement [bryskəmɑ̃] ADV **1** *(soudainement)* suddenly, abruptly; **il a b. changé** he suddenly changed; **la route plonge b./ tourne b. à droite** the road dips sharply/turns sharply to the right **2** *(sans ménagements)* abruptly, brusquely, curtly

brusquer [bryske] VT **1 b. qn** *(être impoli envers)* to be abrupt *or* curt with sb; *(maltraiter)* to treat sb harshly **2** *(hâter) (décision)* to rush; **b. les choses** to rush things; **il ne faut rien b.** we mustn't rush things; **attaque brusquée** surprise attack; *Fam* **arrête de me b.** stop rushing me

brusquerie [bryskəri] NF abruptness, brusqueness; **avec b.** abruptly, brusquely

brut [bryt] ADJ **1** *(pétrole)* crude; *(sucre)* unrefined; *(diamant)* rough, uncut; *(champagne)* extra-dry, brut; *(cidre)* dry; *(marbre, albâtre)* unpolished; *(bois, peau)* undressed; **toile brute** unbleached cloth; **produit b.** primary product; *Ordinat* **données brutes** raw data; **matières brutes** raw materials; **fonte brute** pig iron; **or b.** gold in nuggets; **b. de décoffrage** *(béton)* unsurfaced exposed; *Fig (non encore peaufiné)* rough around the edges; *(personne)* unrefined; *Métal* **b. de fonte** *ou* **de coulée** rough cast; **à l'état b.** in its raw state; **il nous a exposé le projet à l'état b.** he gave us a general outline of the project; **faire de l'art b.** to produce primitive art; **faits bruts** bald *or* hard facts

2 *Com (bénéfice, valeur, poids etc)* gross; **salaire b.** gross salary; **marge brute** gross profit margin; **montant b.** gross amount, gross

NM **1** *(pétrole)* crude (oil) **2** *(champagne)* brut *or* extra-dry champagne

ADV **le colis pèse b. 20 kilos** *ou* **20 kilos b.** the parcel weighs 20 kilos gross; **elle gagne b. 5000 euros** *ou* **5000 euros b.** she earns 5,000 euros gross, she grosses 5,000 euros

brutal, -ale, -aux, -ales [brytal, -o] ADJ *(violent) (personne, mort)* brutal, violent; *(impoli, brusque) (personne, paroles, révélation, franchise etc)* brutal; **force brutale** brute force; **coup b.** brutal *or* savage blow; **les faits brutaux** the hard *or* brutal facts; **vérité brutale** plain *or* unvarnished truth; **cette vérité était trop brutale pour elle** the truth was too shocking for her; **être b. avec qn** to treat sb roughly *or* harshly; **avec sa manière brutale de dire les choses** with his harsh way of saying things; **arrêt b.** sudden *or* abrupt stop; **frein/embrayage b.** fierce brake/clutch

brutalement [brytalmɑ̃] ADV *(violemment)* brutally, violently; *(rudement)* harshly, roughly; *(sans ambages)* bluntly, plainly; *(soudainement)* abruptly, suddenly; **la route tourne b.** there is a sudden bend in the road, the road bends suddenly; **il a b. changé** he has suddenly changed

brutaliser [brytalize] VT *(femme, enfant, matériel etc)* to ill-treat, to maltreat; *Fam* **il ne faut pas me b.** *(laisse-moi réfléchir)* don't rush me

brutalité [brytalite] NF **1** *(de personne) (violence)* brutality, violence; *(grossièreté)* roughness; **il lui parle avec b.** he has such a rough tone when he speaks to him; **pas de b.!** no violence! **2** *(d'animal)* brutality, savagery **3** *(rapidité)* suddenness, abruptness **4** *(acte violent)* brutal act, brutality; **brutalités de la police** police brutality

brute [bryt] NF **1** *(personne violente)* brute, beast; *(personne grossière)* boor; **sale b.!** filthy beast!; **frapper qn comme une b.** to hit sb brutally *or* violently; **j'ai dû taper dessus comme une b. pour que ça entre** I had to bang at it like mad to get it to go in; **espèce**

de b. épaisse! you great oaf!; **le gangster m'envoya une de ses brutes épaisses** the gangster sent one of his heavies to visit me **2** *Litt (animal)* brute beast

Bruxelles [brysɛl] N Brussels

bruyamment [brɥijamɑ̃] ADV *(parler, rire)* loudly; *(manger)* noisily

bruyant [brɥijɑ̃] ADJ *(rue, voisin)* noisy; *(succès)* resounding; *(rire, applaudissement)* loud; **un quartier peu b.** a quiet neighbourhood

bruyère [brɥijɛr] NF **1** *(plante)* heather, heath; *(terre)* heath(land), moor(land) **2** **racine de b.** briar root; **pipe en** *ou* **de b.** briar pipe

bryone [brijɔn] NF *(plante)* bryony

BSPCE [beɛspeseə] NM *Bourse (abrév* **bon de souscription de parts de créateurs d'entreprise)** = stock option in a start-up company with tax privileges

BT [bete] NM *abrév* **brevet de technicien**

BTH [beteaʃ] NM *abrév* **brevet de technicien hôtelier**

B2B [bitubi] ADJ *(abrév* **business to business)** B2B

B2C [bitusi] ADJ *(abrév* **business to consumer)** B2C

BTP [betepe] NM *(abrév* **bâtiment et travaux publics)** = building and public works sector

BTS [beteɛs] NM *(abrév* **brevet de technicien supérieur)** = advanced vocational training certificate; **B. Action Commerciale** professional marketing qualification; **B. Force de Vente** professional sales qualification

buanderie [bɥɑ̃dri] NF laundry (room)

Buba [byba] NF *(abrév* **Bundesbank)** Bundesbank

bubon [bybɔ̃] NM *Méd* bubo

bubonique [bybɔnik] ADJ *Méd (peste)* bubonic

Bucarest [bykarɛst] N Bucharest

buccal, -ale, -aux, -ales [bykal, -o] ADJ *Anat (cavité etc)* buccal; *Méd* **vaccin b.** oral vaccine

buccodentaire [bykodɑ̃tɛr] ADJ *(hygiène)* oral

bucco-génital, -ale, -aux, -ales [byko-ʒenital, -o] ADJ **rapports bucco-génitaux** oral sex

bûche [byʃ] NF *(morceau de bois)* log; *Fam (personne stupide)* blockhead; *Fam* **ramasser une b.** to come a cropper; *Fam* **ne reste pas là comme une b.!** don't just stand/sit there like a dummy!
▸▸ *Culin* **b. de Noël** Yule log

bûcher¹ [byʃe] NM **1** *(pour le bois)* woodshed **2** *(de supplice)* stake; **monter** *ou* **mourir sur le b.** to be burnt at the stake; **condamné au b.** sentenced to be burnt at the stake **3** *(funéraire)* (funeral) pyre
VT *Can (arbre)* to fell, to cut down

bûcher² *Scol Fam* VT *(matière)* to bone up on, *Br* to swot up
VI to slog, to work hard; *(d'un élève, d'un étudiant)* to swot, *Am* to grind

bûcheron [byʃrɔ̃] NM woodcutter, woodman, lumberjack

bûchette [byʃɛt] NF *(de bois sec)* stick, twig; *(pour apprendre à compter)* stick

bûcheur, -euse [byʃœr, -øz] *Fam* N slogger, hard worker; *(élève, étudiant)* swot, *Am* grind
ADJ *(étudiant etc)* hard-working

bucolique [bykɔlik] *Littér* ADJ *(poème)* bucolic, pastoral
NF pastoral poem, bucolic

budget [bydʒɛ] NM budget; *(dans la publicité, dans le marketing)* account; **b. de l'éducation** education budget; **b. de la marine/de**

---

la guerre navy/army estimates; **inscrire** *ou* **porter qch au b.** to budget for sth; **boucler le b.** to balance the budget; **vacances/prix pour les petits budgets** budget holidays/prices; **de quel b. disposez-vous pour vos vacances?** what's your holiday budget?, what's the budget for your holiday?
▸▸ **b. des approvisionnements** purchase budget; **b. des charges** overhead budget, cost budget; **b. commercial** sales budget; *UE* **b. communautaire européen** European Community budget; **b. équilibré** balanced budget; **b. de l'État** state budget; **b. d'exploitation** operating budget; **b. de fonctionnement** operating budget; **b. glissant** rolling budget; **b. global** master *or* overall budget; *Compta* **b. des investissements** capital budget; **b. marketing** marketing budget; **b. mensuel** monthly budget; **b. prévisionnel** provisional budget; **b. de production** production budget; *Mktg* **b. de prospection** market exploration budget; **b. publicitaire** advertising budget; **b. des recettes** revenue budget; **b. renouvelable** continuous budget; *Compta* **b. de trésorerie** cashflow, cash budget; **b. des ventes** sales budget

budgétaire [bydʒetɛr] ADJ *(dépenses, contrôle)* budgetary; *(année)* financial; **comptabilité b.** budgeting; **contrainte b.** budget constraint; **déficit/excédent b.** budget deficit/surplus

budgétisation [bydʒetizasjɔ̃] NF inclusion in the budget; **b. base zéro** zero-base budgeting

budgétiser [bydʒetize] VT to include in the budget, to budget for

buée [bɥe] NF *(sur les vitres etc)* condensation, steam; *(sur un miroir)* mist; **les vitres sont couvertes de b.** the windows are steamed up *or* covered with condensation; **faire de la b.** *(d'une cuisinière etc)* to make *or* produce steam

buffet [byfɛ] NM **1** *(meuble)* sideboard; **b. de cuisine** (kitchen) dresser **2 b. (d'orgue)** organ chest **3** *(repas)* buffet (meal); **b. froid** cold buffet; **b. de salades** salad bar; **b. du petit déjeuner** breakfast buffet; **b. à volonté** unlimited buffet; **b. campagnard** = cold buffet made with country produce; **b. de gare** station buffet, refreshment room **4** *Fam (ventre)* belly; **je n'ai rien dans le b. depuis hier soir** I haven't had a bite to eat since last night; **se mettre quelque chose dans le b.** to get something inside one

buffetier, -ière [byftje, -jɛr] N *Vieilli (d'un buffet de gare etc)* buffet manager, f buffet manageress

buffle [byfl] NM buffalo; **cuir (de) b.** buffalo hide VOIR GRAMMAIRE A12

bufflesse [byflɛs], **bufflonne** [byflɔn] NF cow buffalo

bug [bœg] NM *Ordinat* bug

bugle¹ [bygl] NM *Mus* (key) bugle, flugelhorn

bugle² NF *(plante)* bugle

building [bildiŋ] NM *(d'appartements, de bureaux)* tower block

buire [bɥir] NF ewer, flagon

buis [bɥi] NM *(arbre)* box (tree); *(bois)* box(-wood); *Rel* **b. bénit** (blessed) palm

buisson [bɥisɔ̃] NM bush; *(plusieurs plantes)* thicket; **un b. de mûres** a bramble thicket
▸▸ *Bible* **b. ardent** burning bush; *Culin* **b. d'écrevisses** = crayfish served piled up on a dish

buissonneux, -euse [bɥisɔnø, -øz] ADJ *(terrain etc)* bushy; *(végétation)* scrubby

buissonnière [bɥisɔnjɛr] ADJ F **faire l'école buissonnière** to play truant *or Am* hook(e)y

bulbe [bylb] NM **1** *Bot* bulb, corm **2** *Anat*

---

bulb; **b. (rachidien)** medulla oblongata **3** *Archit* onion dome

bulbeux, -euse [bylbø, -øz] ADJ *Bot* bulbous

bulgare [bylgar] ADJ Bulgarian
NM *Ling* Bulgarian
N **B.** Bulgarian

Bulgarie [bylgari] NF Bulgaria

bulldozer [byldozœr] NM bulldozer; *Fig Fam* **c'est un b., sa sœur** his sister just bulldozes *or* steamrollers her way through things

bulle [byl] NF **1** *(d'air etc)* bubble; *Méd (vésicule)* blister; *(enceinte stérile)* bubble; *(de bandes dessinées)* balloon; *Ordinat* **b. d'aide** help pop-up; *Tech* **b. d'air** air-lock; **b. d'encre** *(d'une imprimante)* ink bubble; **b. de savon** soap bubble; **faire des bulles** to blow bubbles; *Méd* **enfant-/bébé-b.** = child/baby kept in sterile surroundings; *Fig Fam* **coincer la b.** to laze *or* lounge around
2 *Bourse* **b. boursière** stock market bubble; **b. Internet** Internet bubble; **b. spéculative** speculative bubble
3 *(lettre du pape)* (papal) bull; **b. d'excommunication** bull of excommunication
4 *Fam (à un devoir)* zero; **prendre une b.** to get a zero
ADJ INV **papier b.** Manila paper
NM *(papier)* Manila paper

buller [byle] VI *Fam* to laze about

bulletin [byltɛ̃] NM **1** *(communiqué)* bulletin; *Scol* **b. (scolaire)** (school) report; *TV* **b. d'actualités** *ou* **d'informations** news bulletin *or* report, news sheet; **b. d'entreprise** newsletter; **b. radiophonique** radio bulletin; *TV, Radio* **b. spécial** newsflash **2** *(papier, certificat)* **b. (d'enregistrement) de bagages** luggage ticket, *Am* baggage check; **b. de consigne** left-luggage *or Am* checkroom ticket
▸▸ **b. d'annulation** cancellation form; **b. blanc** blank ballot paper; *Com* **b. de commande** order form; *Bourse* **b. des cours** (Stock Exchange) price list; *Journ* **b. électronique** electronic news sheet; **b. d'expédition** dispatch note, consignment note; **b. de garantie** guarantee (certificate); **b. d'inscription** registration form; **b. météorologique** weather report; **B. officiel** = official listing of all new laws and decrees; **B. officiel des communautés européennes** = official listing of all new EC directives; **b. de paie** pay (advice) slip, salary advice (note); **b. de participation** entry form; **b. de salaire** pay (advice) slip, salary advice (note); *Méd* **b. de santé** medical bulletin; **b. de souscription d'actions** share subscription form; *Scol* **b. trimestriel** end-of-term report; *UE* **B. de l'Union européenne** Bulletin of the European Union; **b. de vente** sales note; *Suisse* **b. de versement** paying-in slip *or* form; **b. de vote** ballot paper; **b. (de vote) nul** spoiled ballot paper

bulletin-réponse, *pl* **bulletins-réponse** NM reply form *or* coupon; *(pour un concours)* entry form

bulleux, -euse [bylø, -øz] ADJ *Méd* covered with blisters; *Géol, Méd (pierre, fièvre)* vesicular

bull-terrier, *pl* **bull-terriers** [bulterje] NM bull terrier

bumping [bœmpiŋ] NM *Aviat* bumping

bungalow [bɛ̃galo] NM bungalow

bunker [bunkœr] NM *Mil* bunker; *Golf* bunker, *Am* sand trap

buraliste [byralist] N *(de bureau de poste)* clerk; *(d'impôts)* receiver of taxes; *(de bureau de tabac)* tobacconist

bure [byr] NF *Tex* frieze, rough homespun; *(habit religieux)* frock

bureau, -eaux [byro] NM **1** *(meuble)* desk;

ordinateur de b. desk-top computer; *Pol* déposer un projet de loi sur le b. to table a bill
2 *(lieu)* office; *(à la maison)* study; **ceci fera
d'excellents bureaux** this will be very good
office space; **je dois passer au b. à midi** I
have to drop by the office at midday; **il y a
une bonne ambiance au b.** there's a good atmosphere at *or* in the office; **fournitures de
b.** office supplies; **b. central** *(de poste)* main
post office; *Tél* exchange; **b. de police** police
station; **b. de douane** customs house; **b. informatisé** electronic office, paperless office
3 *(personnel)* office (staff)
4 *(assemblée)* committee; **élire le b.** to elect
the committee
5 *(service d'une administration etc)* department, division, bureau; **Deuxième B.** Intelligence Branch *or* Service
▶▶ *Com* **b. d'achat** buying *or* purchase office; *Ordinat* **b. actif** active desktop; **b. d'aide
sociale** welfare office; **b. de change** bureau
de change; **b. à cylindre** roll-top desk; *Com*
b. de départ port of departure; *Com* **b. de
destination** port of destination; **b. distributeur (des Postes)** main sorting post office;
b. de douane customs office; *Ordinat* **b. électronique** electronic desktop; *Com* **b. d'enregistrement** registration office; *Com* **b.
d'entrée** port of entry; **b. d'études** design *or*
planning department *or* office; *(de recherche)* R&D department; *Com* **b. d'expédition** shipping office; **b. d'exportation** export
office; **b. des illustrations** picture desk; **b.
d'information** information office; **b. d'inscriptions** registration desk; **Bureau international du travail** International Labour
Office; **b. de location** box office; **b. des méthodes** organization and methods department, O&M department; **b. ministre**
pedestal *or* kneehole desk; **b. d'ordonnancement** scheduling and planning department; *Com* **b. de passage** port of transit; **b.
paysager** open-plan office; **b. de perception**
tax office; **b. de placement** employment
agency *or* bureau; **b. de poste** post office;
b. de publicité advertising agency; *Journ* bureaux de rédaction newspaper office; **b. de
renseignements** enquiry *or* information
desk; *(pièce)* information office; **b.-satellite**
branch office; *Can* **b. spécial de scrutin** advance poll; **b. de tabac** tobacconist's (shop);
b. de traduction translation agency; **Bureau
de vérification de la publicité** = French advertising standards authority, *Br* ≃ ASA

Il faut noter que le nom anglais **bureau** est
un faux ami. Il ne s'emploie jamais pour
désigner une pièce mais pour faire référence à une institution.

bureaucrate [byrokrat] N *Péj* bureaucrat
bureaucratie [byrokrasi] NF *Péj (système)*
bureaucracy; *(ensemble des fonctionnaires)*
officialdom
bureaucratique [byrokratik] ADJ *Péj* bureaucratic
bureaucratisation [byrokratizasjɔ̃] NF *Péj*
bureaucratization
bureaucratiser [byrokratize] VT *Péj* to bur-
eaucratize
bureautique [byrotik] NF office automation
burette [byrɛt] NF *(pour l'huile)* oilcan, oiler;
Chimie burette; *Rel* cruet; *Vulg* **il me casse les
burettes** he gets on my tits
burin [byrɛ̃] NM **1** *(de graveur)* graver, burin;
(gravure) engraving, print **2** *(ciseau d'acier)*
(cold) chisel
burinage [byrinaʒ] NM *Tech* chiselling,
chipping
buriner [byrine] VT **1** *(avec un burin)* to engrave; **visage buriné** *(par le vent etc)* seamed
face **2** *Tech (metal)* to chisel, to chip

burineur [byrinœr] NM *Tech* chipper,
chiseller
Burkina [byrkina] NM Burkina-Faso
burkinabé, -ée [byrkinabe] ADJ of/from
Burkina-Faso
▶ N **B.** *(natif)* native of Burkina-Faso; *(habitant)* inhabitant of Burkina-Faso
burlesque [byrlɛsk] ADJ **1** *(air, situation,
projet etc)* ludicrous, ridiculous **2** *Littér
(poème, genre etc)* burlesque
▶ NM *Littér* **le b.** the burlesque
burlingue [byrlɛ̃g] NM *Fam* office
burnes [byrn] NFPL *Vulg* balls, nuts, *Br* bollocks; **casser les b. à qn** to piss sb off, *Br* to
get on sb's tits, *Am* to break sb's balls
burnous [byrnu(s)] NM *(d'Arabe)* bur-
nous(e); *(de bébé)* hooded coat; *Fam* **faire
suer le b.** to use sweated labour
bus [bys] NM **1** *(autobus)* bus **2** *Élec* bus (bar)
3 *Ordinat* bus; **b. d'adresses** address bus; **b.
de contrôle** control bus; **b. de données** data
bus; **b. entrée/sortie** input/output bus; **b.
d'interface** interface bus; **b. local** local bus;
b. multimédia multimedia bus; **b. rapide**
high-speed bus; **b. système** system bus
busard [byzar] NM *(oiseau)* harrier
buse¹ [byz] NF **1** *(oiseau)* buzzard **2** *Fam
(idiot)* fool
buse² NF *(tuyau)* pipe; *Métal* blast pipe; **b.
d'injection** injector nozzle; *Aut* **b. de carburateur** carburettor choke tube; *Min* **b. d'aérage** air channel *or* pipe *or* shaft; **b. de
ventilation** air vent
buse³ NF *Belg (échec)* failure
business [biznɛs] NM *Fam (affaire)* business;
mais qu'est-ce que c'est que ce b.? what's going on?, what's all this?
businessman [biznɛsman], *pl* **businessmen**
[biznɛsmɛn] *ou* **businessmans** NM businessman
businesswoman [biznɛswuman], *pl* **businesswomen** [biznɛswumɛn] *ou* **businesswo-
mans** NF businesswoman
busqué [byske] ADJ *(nez)* hook(ed), aquiline, Roman
buste [byst] NM *(haut du corps)* chest; *(seins)*
bust; *Beaux-Arts* **b. (en hermès)** bust; **peindre qn en b.** to paint a half-length portrait
of sb
bustier [bystje] NM *(soutien-gorge)* long-line
(strapless) bra; *(corsage)* bustier; **robe de
bal/maillot à b.** strapless evening gown/
swimming costume
but [by(t)] NM **1** *(objectif)* aim, purpose, object, goal; *(d'un voyage, d'une promenade
etc)* destination, goal; **il faut avoir un b. dans
la vie** you must have a goal *or* an aim *or* a
purpose in life; **il l'a fait avec ce b. en tête**
he did it with this aim *or* object in mind; **je
vous ai blessé, ce n'était pas mon b.** I've hurt
you, it wasn't my intention *or* I didn't mean
to; **mesure ayant pour b. d'assurer …** measure intended to ensure …; **remplir un b.** to
serve a purpose; **un b. personnel** a personal
goal; **dans le b. de vous aider** with the object
or aim *or* intention of helping you; **dans le b.
de frauder** with intent to defraud; **dans ce b.**
with this aim in view; **se fixer un b.** to set
oneself a goal *or* target; **je suis encore loin
du b.** I still have a long way to go; **nous sommes tout près du b.** we don't have far to go;
poursuivre son b. to pursue one's goal *or*
aim; **cette loi vise un double b.** this law has
a two-fold objective; **il touche au b.** he has
nearly reached his goal *or* achieved his
aim; **aller droit au b.** to go straight to the
point; **errer sans b.** to wander about aimlessly; **c'est le b. recherché** that's what we're
aiming for; **c'est le b. de l'opération** that's the
(whole) point of the operation; **un coup au b.**

a direct hit; **à b. lucratif** profit-making; **association à b. non lucratif** non-profit-making
association, *Am* not-for-profit association
2 *Ftbl etc* goal; **ligne de b.** goal line; **entrée
du b.** goal mouth; **marquer un b.** to score a
goal; **gagner/perdre (par) 3 buts à 1** to win/
lose by 3 goals to 1; **être dans les buts, garder les buts** to be in goal; **b. en** *or* golden
goal
3 tirer de b. en blanc to fire point-blank;
faire une offre/répondre de b. en blanc to
make an offer/answer on the spur of the
moment; **elle me l'a dit de b. en blanc** she
told me point-blank
butane [bytan] NM *Chimie* butane; **gaz b.**
butane (gas)
butanier [bytanje] NM *Naut* butane tanker
buté [byte] ADJ stubborn, obstinate; **visage
b.** fixed *or* set *or* determined expression
butée [byte] NF **1** *Tech* thrust; **palier de b.**
thrust block *or* bearing; **b. (d'arrêt)** stop **2**
Constr abutment, buttress **3** *Aut* stop; **en b.**
in full lock; **en b. à droite/gauche** in full
right/left lock **4** *Typ* **texte en b. gauche/
droite** left/right justified text
buter [byte] VI **1 b. contre qch** *(cogner)* to
bump *or* bang into *or* against sth, to knock
against sth; *(trébucher)* to stumble *or* trip
over sth; **b. contre** *ou* **sur un problème/une
difficulté** to come up against a problem/a
difficulty **2** *(de poutres etc)* to abut, to rest
(contre against)
▶ VT **1** *(braquer)* **b. qn** to put sb's back up **2**
(mur) to prop up, to buttress, to shore up **3**
Arg (tuer) to bump off
▶ VPR **se buter** *(s'entêter)* to dig one's heels in,
to get stubborn
buteur [bytœr] NM *Ftbl* goalscorer; *Rugby*
kicker; **le meilleur b.** the top goalscorer
butin [bytɛ̃] NM booty; *(de pilleur)* spoils,
plunder; *(de voleur)* loot; **le b. des recherches archéologiques** the finds from the archaeological dig
butiner [bytine] VI *(des abeilles)* to gather
pollen
▶ VT *(renseignements etc)* to gather, to collect
butineur, -euse [bytinœr, -øz] ADJ pollen-
gathering
▶ NM *Ordinat* browser
butoir [bytwar] NM *Tech* stop, check; *Rail*
buffer; **b. d'une porte** door stop(per); *Aut* **b.
de pare-chocs** bumper guard, overrider
butor [bytor] NM **1** *(oiseau)* bittern **2** *Fam
(lourdaud)* lout, *Br* yob
buttage [bytaʒ] NM *(de plantes)* earthing up
butte [byt] NF **1** *(colline)* hillock, knoll,
mound; *Géol* **b. témoin** outlier **2 b. (de tir)**
butts; *Fig* **être en b. à qch** to be exposed *or*
open to sth
butter [byte] VT **1** *Agr (sol)* to ridge; *(plantes,
un rosier)* to earth up **2** *Arg (tuer)* **b. qn** to
bump sb off
buvable [byvabl] ADJ **1** *(potable)* drinkable;
il est tout à fait b., ce petit vin! it's a very
drinkable little wine, this **2** *Méd* to be taken
orally
buvard [byvar] ADJ **papier b.** blotting paper
▶ NM *(matière)* blotting paper; *(feuille)* piece
or sheet of blotting paper; *(sous-main)*
blotter
buvette [byvɛt] NF **1** *(dans une gare etc)* refreshment bar **2** *(dans une station thermale)*
pump room
buveur, -euse [byvœr, -øz] N drinker; **c'est
un grand** *ou* **gros b.** he's a heavy drinker;
une buveuse de bière a beer-drinker
BVP [bevepe] NM *(abrév* **bureau de vérification de la publicité)** French advertising standards authority, *Br* ≃ ASA
bye(-bye) [baj(baj)] INT bye-bye

by-pass [bajpas] NM INV *Chir, Aut* bypass

byronien, -ienne [birɔnjɛ̃, -jɛn] ADJ Byronic

Byzance [bizɑ̃s] N Byzantium; *Fam* **c'est B.** it's the last word in luxury; **c'est pas B.** it's not exactly luxurious

byzantin, -ine [bizɑ̃tɛ̃, -in] ADJ Byzantine; *Fig Péj (querelles etc)* byzantine N **B.** Byzantine

C¹, c [se] NM (lettre) C, c; **c cédille** c cedilla

C² (abrév **Celsius**) C

C++ [seplysplys] NM Ordinat C++

c' voir **ce**

CA [sea] NM **1** Élec (abrév **courant alternatif**) AC **2** Com (abrév **chiffre d'affaires**) turnover

CA [sa] PRON DÉM SEE GRAMMAR B15 **1** (cela) it, that; (ceci) it, this; **donne-moi ça** give it to me, give me that; **c'est dégoûtant ça** that's disgusting; **une petite femme haute comme ça** a little woman no taller than that or only so high; **je suis comme ça** I'm like that; Fam **alors comme ça, vous déménagez?** so you're moving, are you?; **allons, pas de ça!** hey! none of that!; **pas de ça chez nous** we don't want any of that here; **ce n'est pas si facile que ça** it isn't as easy as (all) that; **ça oui!** oh yes!, definitely!; **ça non!** oh no!, not on your life!; **il ne manquait plus que ça** that's all we/I/etc needed; **ça dépend** it or that depends; **à part ça, tout va bien** apart from that, everything's fine; **il y a un peu de ça, effectivement** yes, there's an element of or a bit of that; **ça me fait de la peine de le voir malade** it upsets me to see him ill; **elle n'était pas comme ça avant** she wasn't like that before; **ça va? – comme ci comme ça** how are you? – so-so; **... tout ça quoi** ... et cetera, et cetera; **qui/quand/où ça?** who/when/where('s that)?; **comment ça?** how's that?; **comment ça, elle est partie?** what do you mean 'she's gone'?; **c'est qui/quoi ça?** who's/what's that?; **ça alors!** goodness (me)!; **ça alors, c'est incroyable!** well I never! or blow me! that's incredible!; **ça y est!** that's it!; **c'est ça!** that's it!, that's right!

2 Fam **ça bavarde là-bas dans le fond de la classe** there's talking going on at the back of the classroom; **regarde-moi ça!** just look at that!; **écoute-moi ça!** just listen to this!; **c'est ça les hommes!** that's men for you!; **ça va, ça vient** (les touristes etc) they come and go; **ça arrive en retard et ça veut qu'on l'attende** he/she/etc arrives late, and then expects me/us/etc to wait for him/her/etc

3 Fam (le sexe) it; **il ne pense qu'à ça** he's got a one-track mind, that's all he thinks about NM Psy **le ça** the id

çà [sa] ADV **çà et là** here and there

INT **ah çà!** now then!; **ah çà! par exemple!** well, I'm blowed or damned!

cabale [kabal] NF **1** Rel cab(b)ala **2** (complot) cabal, plot; **monter une c. contre qn** to plot against sb **3** (ligue) cabal, faction

cabaliste [kabalist] NM Rel cab(b)alist

cabalistique [kabalistik] ADJ cab(b)alistic; Fig **des formules cabalistiques** arcane formulae

caban [kabā] NM car coat; Naut peajacket, reefer

cabane [kaban] NF **1** (bicoque) hut, Péj shack; (en rondins) (log) cabin; (à outils etc) shed; Can **c. à sucre** saphouse **2** Arg (prison) **en c.** in (the) clink, Br in the nick; **trente ans de c.** thirty years in (the) clink or Br in the nick; **faire de la c.** to do time, to be inside

▸▸ **c. à lapins** (rabbit) hutch; Fig **ils vivent dans des cabanes à lapins** they live in rabbit hutches or shoeboxes

cabanon [kabanō] NM **1** (petite cabane) hut, shed **2** (en Provence) (maison de campagne) (country) cottage **3** (chalet de plage) (beach) hut, cabin, chalet **4** (cellule) padded cell; Fam **il est bon pour le c.** he ought to be locked up

cabaret [kabarɛ] NM **1** (boîte) night club, cabaret **2** Arch (auberge) tavern, inn

cabaretier, -ière [kabartje, -jɛr] N Arch innkeeper, tavern keeper

cabas [kaba] NM **1** (panier) shopping basket; (en tissu) shopping bag **2** (pour les fruits) basket

cabestan [kabɛstā] NM Naut capstan; **c. horizontal** windlass; **grand c.** main capstan; **virez au c.!** heave!

cabillaud [kabijo] NM (fresh) cod

cabine [kabin] NF **1** (de bateau, d'avion, vaisseau spatial etc) cabin; Naut **c. de luxe** stateroom, de luxe cabin **2** (de piscine) changing cubicle **3** (de grue) cab, house; (de locomotive, camion) cab; (d'ascenseur) cage, Am car; Aut **c. basculante** tilt cab **4** TV etc **c. du commentateur** commentary booth; **c. de montage** edit suite; **c. de présentation** announcer booth; **c. de projection** projection room; **c. de régie** control room, control cubicle; **c. speak** presentation booth

▸▸ Rail **c. d'aiguillage** signal box; **c. de bain(s)** (de plage) beach hut; (de piscine) changing cubicle; **c. de douche** shower cubicle; **c. d'essayage** fitting room; **c. Internet** Internet booth; Aviat **c. de pilotage** cockpit, flight deck; **c. téléphonique** (tele)phone or call box, telephone booth

cabinet [kabinɛ] NM **1** (petite pièce) small room; Fam **les cabinets** the toilet, Br the loo, Am the john

2 (lieu de consultation etc) office; (d'avocat) chambers; (de médecin) consulting room, Br surgery, Am office; (patients, clients etc) practice; **c. conseil** consultancy; **c. de conseil en gestion** management consultancy; **c. d'experts-conseils** consultancy (firm); **c. d'audit** firm of auditors; Mktg **c. d'études** market research firm; **c. d'expertise comptable** accounting firm; **c. immobilier** Br estate agent's or Am realtor's office; **c. juridique** law firm; **c. de recrutement** recruitment agency; **c. de traduction** translation company

3 Pol Vieilli cabinet; (d'un ministre) departmental staff; **question de c.** ministerial question; **homme de c.** adviser; **chef de c.** = principal private secretary

4 (meuble) cabinet

5 (au musée) **c. d'estampes** print room

▸▸ Hist **c. de lecture** library, reading room; **c. noir** cubbyhole; **c. particulier** (au restaurant) private dining room; **c. de toilette** (small) bathroom or Am washroom

câblage [kablaʒ] NM **1** Élec (d'une maison, fils) wiring, cabling; Tél **c. en paire torsadée** twisted pair cabling **2** Tex, Élec (de fils etc) twisting together **3** (de message) cabling **4** TV (pose du réseau) cable (TV) installation, cabling; **le c. d'une ville** installing cable (television) in a town

câble [kabl] NM **1** Élec cable, lead; Tél cable; **poser un c.** to lay a cable; **la télévision par c., le c.** cable television; TV **avoir le c.** to have cable; TV **transmettre par c.** to cablecast **2** (corde) cable; **c. métallique** wire cable; (à brins) stranded wire **3** (message) cable, cablegram; **envoyer un c. à qn** to send sb a cable, to cable sb

▸▸ **c. d'alimentation** supply or feed or power cable; Naut **c. d'amarrage** mooring cable; Électron **c. coaxial** coaxial cable; Aut **c. de démarrage** jump lead, Am jumper cable; **c. en fibres optiques** fibre-optic or Am fiber-optic cable; **c. en fibre(s) de verre** glass fibre cable; Tech **c. de frein** brake cable; **c. hertzien** radio link; **c. d'imprimante** printer cable; **c. de masse** earth cable, Am ground cable; **c. optique** fibre-optic cable; Tél **c. en paire torsadée** twisted pair cable; Ordinat **c. parallèle** parallel cable; **c. péritel** SCART cable; **c. de raccordement** connecting cable; **c. de remorque** towrope, towline; **c. de retour (à la masse)** return cable; Ordinat **c. série** serial cable; Ordinat **c. de souris** mouse cable; Ordinat **c. USB** USB cable

câblé [kable] ADJ **1** (ville, région) with cable television; TV cabled; Ordinat, Tél hardwired; **l'immeuble est c.** the building is wired for cableTV; **réseau c.** cable (TV) network **2** Fam (à la page) hip, trendy

câbler [kable] VT **1** (tordre ensemble) (fils) to twist together **2** (message) to cable **3** TV (ville, quartier) to install cable television in; (émission) to cable

câbleur, -euse [kablœr, -øz] N Tech cablelayer

câbliste [kablist] N (personne) cable man, cable operator

câblodiffuseur [kablodifyzœr] NM cable company

câblodistributeur [kablodistribytœr] NM cable company

câblodistribution [kablodistribysjō] NF cable television; Am Admin community antenna television

câblogramme [kablogram] NM Arch cablegram, cable

câblo-opérateur, pl **câblo-opérateurs** [kablooperatœr] NM cable company

cabochard, -arde [kabɔʃar, -ard] *Fam* **ADJ** pigheaded
N pigheaded person

caboche [kabɔʃ] **NF 1** *Fam (tête)* nut; **mets-le toi dans la c.!** get that into your thick skull!; **avoir la c. dure** *(être bête)* to be thick; *(être têtu)* to be pigheaded, to be as stubborn as a mule **2** *(clou)* heavy-headed nail; *(de cordonnerie)* hobnail; *(pour les meubles)* stud (nail)

cabochon, -onne [kabɔʃɔ̃, ɔn] **NM 1** *(pierre précieuse)* cabochon **2** *(de carafe à liqueur)* (glass) stopper **3** *(pour les meubles)* stud (nail)
N *Can (têtu)* stubborn person; *(incompétent)* bad worker

cabosser [kabɔse] **VT** *(métal, voiture etc)* to bash up; *(chapeau)* to bash in; **vieux chapeau cabossé** battered old hat; **voiture cabossée** bashed-up *or* beat-up car

cabot [kabo] *Fam* **ADJ** = **cabotin ADJ 1**
NM 1 *(acteur)* = **cabotin N 1 2** *Péj (chien)* pooch, mutt **3** *Mil* corporal, corp

cabotage [kabɔtaʒ] **NM** *Naut* coasting, coastal trade, cabotage; *Aviat* cabotage; **grand/petit c.** offshore/inshore coastal traffic

caboter [kabɔte] **VI** *Naut* to coast

caboteur [kabɔtœr] **NM** *Naut* coaster

cabotin, -ine [kabɔtɛ̃, -in] *Fam Péj* **ADJ 1** *(acteur)* ham **2** *(personne)* histrionic; **il est c.** he's a show-off
N 1 *(mauvais acteur)* ham (actor, *f* actress), third-rate actor, *f* actress **2** *(vantard)* show-off

cabotinage [kabɔtinaʒ] **NM** *Fam Péj* **1** *Théâtre* ham *or* third-rate acting **2** *(en politique etc)* histrionics; *(vantardise)* showing off

cabotiner [kabɔtine] **VI** *Fam Péj* to play to the gallery, to show off

caboulot [kabulo] **NM** *Arg* seedy pub, dive

cabrage [kabraʒ] **NM** *(de cheval)* rearing (up); *Aviat* pulling up

cabré [kabre] **ADJ** *(cheval)* rearing; *(avion)* tail down

cabrer [kabre] **VT 1** *(cheval)* to rear up; *(avion)* to nose up **2** *Fig* **c. qn contre qn** to turn *or* set sb against sb
VI *Aviat* to nose up
VPR se cabrer *(d'un cheval)* to rear (up); *Fig* **se c. contre qn/qch** to rebel against sb/sth

cabri [kabri] **NM** *Zool* kid; *Fig* **sauter comme un c.** to jump for joy

cabriole [kabrijɔl] **NF** *(saut, bond)* leap, caper; *(en danse)* cabriole; *Équitation* capriole, goat's leap; *(de gymnaste)* somersault; *Fig* clever manoeuvre *or* *Am* maneuver; **faire des cabrioles** to caper about, to cavort about; **elle s'en est tirée par une c.** she cleverly manoeuvred *or* *Am* maneuvered her way out of it

cabrioler [kabrijɔle] **VI** to caper *or* cavort about

cabriolet [kabrijɔlɛ] **NM 1** *Aut* convertible **2** *Hist (voiture à cheval)* cabriolet

CAC [kak] **NF** *(abrév* **Compagnie des agents de change)** **l'indice C. 40, le C. 40** the CAC 40 (index) *(Paris Stock Exchange Index)*

caca [kaka] **NM** *Enf, Fam (excrément)* poo, *Am* poop; **as-tu fait c.?** *(à un enfant)* have you done a poo *or* a number two *or* a big job?; **jette ça, c'est (du) c.** throw that away, it's nasty *or* dirty; **c. d'oie** yellowish green; *Fam* **il nous fait un caca nerveux, l'autre!** he's having kittens!, he's having a fit!

cacah(o)uète, cacahouette [kakawɛt] **NF** peanut; **beurre de c.** peanut butter

cacao [kakao] **NM** *(boisson, poudre)* cocoa; *Bot* cocoa bean, cacao bean

cacaoté [kakaɔte] **ADJ** cocoa-flavoured

cacaotier [kakaɔtje] **NM** *Bot* cacao (tree)

cacaoui [kakawi] **NM** *Can* long-tailed duck

cacaoyer [kakaɔje] **NM** *Bot* cacao (tree)

cacatoès [kakatɔɛs] **NM** cockatoo

cacatois [kakatwa] **NM** *Naut* royal (sail); **(mât de) c.** royal mast; **c. de perruche** mizzen royal

cachalot [kaʃalo] **NM** sperm whale, cachalot

cache [kaʃ] **NF** hiding place, cache; **c. d'armes** arms cache, cache of arms
NM cover; *Phot, Ordinat, Cin (pour tirage)* mask; *(de caméra)* hood; *(pour corriger les bromures)* patch; *(volet)* vignette; **c. d'avant-plan** foreground matte; *TV, Cin* **c. de caméra** camera matte; *TV, Cin* **c./contre c. (électronique)** (electronic) matte; **c. latéral** slide matte; *Ordinat* **c. disque physique** physical disk cache; *Ordinat* **c. du disque dur** hard disk cache; *Ordinat* **c. externe** external cache

caché [kaʃe] **ADJ** hidden; *(sentiment)* secret

cache-antivol **NM INV** *Aut etc* security cover

cache-cache **NM INV** hide-and-seek; **jouer à c.** to play hide-and-seek

cache-col **NM INV** scarf, muffler

cachectique [kaʃɛktik] **ADJ** *Méd* cachectic

cache-culbuteur **NM INV** *Aut* rocker cover

Cachemire [kaʃmir] **NM** Kashmir

cachemire [kaʃmir] **NM** *Tex (laine)* cashmere; *(motif)* paisley pattern; **chemise de c.** paisley(-pattern) shirt

cache-misère **NM INV 1** *(vêtement)* = coat or wrap hiding shabby appearance **2** *(destiné à cacher des défauts)* **cette mesure n'est qu'un c.** this is just a cosmetic measure designed to distract attention from the real problems

cache-moyeu **NM INV** *Aut* hub cover

cache-nez **NM INV** scarf, muffler

cache-pot **NM INV** flowerpot holder

cache-poussière **NM INV** dust coat, *Am* duster

cacher [kaʃe] **VT** *(personne, chose)* to hide, to conceal; *(ses sentiments)* to hide, to conceal, to mask; *Ordinat, Phot* to mask out; **où a-t-il pu c. la clé?** where could he have hidden the key?; **le mur nous cache la vue** the wall blocks *or* hides our view; **c. qch à qn** to hide *or* conceal sth from sb; **c. son jeu** to keep one's cards hidden *or* close to one's chest; *Fig* **il a bien caché son jeu** he kept his cards close to his chest; **il n'y a rien de caché dans cette affaire** everything is open and aboveboard in this transaction; **je ne vous cache pas que je suis déçu** I won't hide *or* conceal from you that I'm disappointed, I won't hide *or* conceal my disappointment from you; **c. son âge** to keep one's age a secret; **pour ne rien te c.** to be completely open with you; **il ne cache pas que ...** he makes no secret of the fact that ...
VPR se cacher *(d'une personne)* to hide; *(d'une chose)* to be hidden; **les voleurs se cachent** the thieves are (in) hiding; **le soleil se cache** the sun isn't shining, the sun is behind a cloud; **elle ne se cache pas pour dire qu'elle est communiste** she doesn't hide the fact she's a communist; **se c. de qn** to hide from sb; **sa timidité se cache derrière une certaine rudesse** his shyness is hidden behind a bluff exterior; **je ne m'en cache pas** I make no secret of it; **en se cachant** secretly, *Péj* on the sly; **sans se c.** openly

cache-radiateur **NM INV** radiator cover

cachère [kaʃɛr] **ADJ** *Rel* kosher

cache-sexe **NM INV** G-string; *(d'indigène)* apron

cachet [kaʃɛ] **NM 1** *(empreinte)* stamp;

(sceau) seal; *(de fabricant)* (trade)mark; *Hist* **lettre de c.** = order under the King's private seal; *Fig* **le c. du génie** the stamp *or* hallmark of genius; **il a beaucoup de c.** he has a lot of style *or* a certain cachet; **manteau qui a du c.** stylish coat **2** *(d'artiste, avocat, conseiller etc)* fee; **courir le c.** *(d'un acteur)* to do any job that's going **3** *Pharm* tablet, pill; **un c. d'aspirine** an aspirin (tablet)
▸▸ **c. de fabrique** maker's trademark; **c. d'oblitération** postmark; **c. de la poste** postmark

cachetage [kaʃtaʒ] **NM** *(de lettres etc)* sealing

cache-tampon **NM INV** hunt-the-thimble *or* -slipper

cacheter [kaʃte] **VT** (**je cachette, n. cachetons; je cachetterai**) *(lettre, bouteille etc)* to seal; **cire à c.** sealing wax; **vin cacheté** vintage wine

cacheton [kaʃtɔ̃] **NM** *Fam (cachet d'artiste)* fee; **courir le c.** = to try to get little jobs here and there

cachetonner [kaʃtɔne] **VI** *Fam (artiste)* = to try to get little jobs here and there

cachette [kaʃɛt] **NF** *(pour chose)* hiding place; *(pour personne)* hiding place, hideaway; **en c.** secretly, *Péj* on the sly; **vendre en c.** to sell under the counter; **boire en c.** *(habituellement)* to be a secret drinker; **il boit en c. de sa famille** he hides his drinking from his family; *Can* **jouer à la c.** to play hide-and-seek

cachexie [kaʃɛksi] **NF** *Méd* cachexia

cachot [kaʃo] **NM 1** *(cellule)* dungeon **2** *(isolement)* solitary confinement

cachotterie [kaʃɔtri] **NF** mystery; **faire des cachotteries** to be secretive

cachottier, -ière [kaʃɔtje, -jɛr] **ADJ** *(personne)* secretive
N secretive person; **petit c.!** you secretive little thing!

cachou [kaʃu] **NM 1** *(bonbon)* cachou **2** *(teinture)* catechu
ADJ INV reddish-brown

cacique [kasik] **NM** *(chef)* cacique; *Fam (personne importante)* bigwig, big shot; **les caciques du parti** the party bigwigs

cacochyme [kakɔʃim] **ADJ** *Hum* doddery

cacophonie [kakɔfɔni] **NF** cacophony

cacophonique [kakɔfɔnik] **ADJ** cacophonous

cacou [kaku] **NM** *Fam* **faire le c.** to act smart, to show off

cactus [kaktys] **NM** cactus VOIR GRAMMAIRE A14

CAD [seade] **NM** *(abrév* **Comité d'aide au développement)** DAC

c.-à-d. *(abrév* **c'est-à-dire)** i.e.

cadastrage [kadastraʒ] **NM** *Admin* land registration

cadastral, -ale, -aux, -ales [kadastral, -o] **ADJ** *(registre, relevé)* cadastral

cadastre [kadastr] **NM** *Admin (registre)* cadastre; **employés du c.** survey staff

cadastrer [kadastre] **VT** *Admin (propriété)* to register in the cadastre

cadavéreux, -euse [kadaverø, -øz] **ADJ** *(teint)* deathly pale, *Litt* cadaverous

cadavérique [kadaverik] **ADJ** *(teint)* deathly pale; *Méd* cadaveric; **rigidité c.** rigor mortis; **la rigidité c. s'était déjà installée** rigor mortis had already set in

cadavre [kadavr] **NM 1** *(de personne)* corpse, (dead) body, *Fml* cadaver; *(d'animal mort)* carcass, body; *Fam* **c'est un c. ambulant** he's a walking corpse **2** *Arg (bouteille)* empty (bottle), dead man

Caddie® [kadi] **NM** *(chariot)* trolley, *Am* cart

caddie [kadi] **NM** *Golf* caddie

cadeau, -eaux [kado] NM **1** present, gift; **en c.** as a present, as a gift; **faire un c. à qn** to give sb a present *or* gift; **acheter un c. à** *ou* **pour qn** to buy sb a present *or* gift; **je n'en voudrais pas comme c.** I wouldn't have it as a gift; **j'aimerais mieux en faire c.** I'd rather give it away; *Fam* **il ne lui a pas fait de c.** (*il ne l'a pas épargnée*) he didn't spare her; *Fam* **ton frère, ce n'est pas un c.** your brother's a real pain; **partir avec eux, ce n'était pas un c.** going away with them was no picnic **2** *Mktg* free gift, freebie; **c. publicitaire** freebie, giveaway, free gift

▸ ▸ **c. d'anniversaire** birthday present; **c. de Noël** Christmas present

cadenas [kadna] NM padlock; **fermer la porte au c.** to padlock the door

cadenasser [kadnase] VT (*porte etc*) to padlock

VPR se cadenasser 1 (*d'une personne*) to lock oneself away **2** (*d'une porte*) to padlock

cadence [kadɑ̃s] NF **1** (*d'un vers, mouvement*) cadence, rhythm; **en c.** rhythmically, in time; **taper dans ses mains en c.** to clap (one's hands) in time; **marcher en c.** to march, to walk in time; **forcer la c.** to force the pace; **à la c. de …** at the rate of …; **c. de production** rate of production; *Mil etc* **c. du tir** rate of fire; **prendre la c.** to get in(to) step; **garder la c.** to keep in step **2** *Mus* (*accords*) cadence; (*de concerto*) cadenza

cadencé [kadɑ̃se] ADJ **1** rhythmic(al); **pas c., marche!** quick march!; **marcher au pas c.** to march, to walk in time; (*rapidement*) to march *or* walk in quick time **2** *Ordinat* **c. à** running at

cadencer [kadɑ̃se] VT (**je cadençai(s), n. cadençons**) (*son style etc*) to give rhythm to; **c. son pas** to walk in time

cadet, -ette [kadɛ, -ɛt] ADJ **la sœur cadette** (*de deux*) the younger sister; (*de plus de deux*) the youngest sister; **avoir trois frères cadets** to have three younger brothers; **la branche cadette** the younger branch

N **1** (*de deux enfants*) younger (child *or* one); (*de plus de deux enfants*) youngest (child *or* one); **mon c.** my younger brother; **ma cadette** my younger sister; **il est mon c. de deux ans** he's two years younger than I am, he's two years my junior; **c'est le c. de mes soucis** that's the least of my worries **2** *Sport* junior; **épreuve des cadets** junior event **3** *Golf* caddie **4** *Hist, Mil* cadet

Cadix [kadis] NF Cadiz

cadmium [kadmjɔm] NM *Chimie* cadmium

cadogan [kadɔgɑ̃] NM = **catogan**

cador [kadɔr] NM *Fam* **1** (*chien*) mutt **2** (*personne influente*) big cheese, big shot

cadrage [kadraʒ] NM *Cin, Phot etc* (*de l'image*) centring, *Am* centering; (*plan*) frame; (*action*) framing; *Ordinat* positioning; *Typ, Ordinat* (*des dimensions*) cropping; *Typ, Ordinat* (*des couleurs*) masking

cadran [kadrɑ̃] NM **1** (*d'horloge, de baromètre etc*) face, dial; (*d'instrument, de téléphone etc*) dial; *Can* (*réveil*) alarm-clock; **c. solaire** sundial; **faire le tour du c.** (*d'une personne*) to sleep (right) round the clock **2** *Naut* **c. de transmission d'ordres** engine-room telegraph; *Aut* **cadrans (de bord)** display panels

cadrat [kadra] NM *Typ* quadrat, quad

cadratin [kadratɛ̃] NM *Typ* em space

CADRE [kadr] NM **1** (*de tableau, porte, miroir etc*) frame; (*de vélo etc*) frame(work); **une photo sous c.** a framed photo
2 (*domaine*) limits, bounds; (*structure*) framework; **sortir du c. de ses fonctions** to exceed (the scope of) one's duties; **ne pas sortir du c. de la légalité** to remain within the bounds of the law; **l'analyse régionale ne**

rentre pas dans le c. de cet article regional analysis is beyond the scope of this article; **s'inscrire dans le c. de** to come within the framework of; **dans le c. de ce programme/des réformes entreprises par le gouvernement** as part of this programme/the government's programme of reform
3 (*décor*) setting; (*milieu*) environment; **c'est un c. splendide!** it's a splendid setting!; **le manoir et son c. de verdure** the manor and its leafy surroundings; **vivre dans le c. familial** to live in a family environment
4 *Litt* (*de livre etc*) framework, outline
5 (*dans un formulaire*) space, box; *Ordinat* (*pour graphique*) box; (*section d'une page*) frame; **c. réservé à l'administration** for official use only
6 *Naut* berth
7 *Radio* frame aerial, loop aerial
8 (*caisse*) **c. d'emballage** packing case
9 (*dans une entreprise*) executive, manager; **les cadres** the managerial staff, the management; *Mil* the (commissioned and non-commissioned) officers; (*d'unité réduite etc*) cadre, staff; **passer c.** (*dans une entreprise*) to become an executive, to be promoted to management; **une femme c.** a female executive *or* manager; **elle est c.** she's an executive, she's in management; **jeune c. dynamique** dynamic young executive, *Fam* whizz kid; **hors c.** seconded, on secondment; **être mis hors c.** to be seconded *or* detached; **rayé des cadres** dismissed; **c. en marketing** marketing executive

▸ ▸ **c. moyen** middle manager; *Mil* **le C. Noir** = military riding school in Saumur; *Mil* **c. de réserve** reserve list; **c. supérieur** senior executive *or* manager; **c. de vie** environment; **cadres moyens** middle management; **cadres supérieurs** senior management

---

Cadre
In French companies, employees are divided into two categories, "employés" and "cadres". "Cadres", who are better qualified, tend to occupy more senior posts and consequently enjoy higher salaries, more benefits and more prestige. They are also expected to work longer hours.

---

cadré [kadre] ADJ *TV, Cin* in-frame, on-frame

cadre-adresse, *pl* **cadres-adresses** NM address space

cadre-châssis, *pl* **cadres-châssis** NM *Aut* chassis frame

cadrer [kadre] VI to tally (**avec** with)
VT *Cin, Phot* to centre, *Am* to center; (*plan etc*) to frame; *Ordinat* to position

cadreur, -euse [kadrœr, -øz] N *TV, Cin* cameraman, *f* woman, camera operator

caduc, -uque [kadyk] ADJ **1** *Bot* (*feuille etc*) deciduous **2** *Jur* (*legs*) null and void; (*accord*) lapsed; (*dette*) statute-barred

caducée [kadyse] NM (*symbole de la profession pharmaceutique*) caduceus

caducité [kadysite] NF (*d'un système etc*) outmoded nature

cæcum [sekɔm] NM *Anat* caecum

CAF [seaɛf] **1** *Com* (*abrév* **coût, assurance, fret**) cif; **vente C.** sale on cif basis **2** (*abrév* **Caisse d'allocations familiales**) ≃ child benefit office

cafard, -arde [kafar, -ard] NM **1** (*insecte*) cockroach, *Am* roach **2** *Fam* **avoir le c.** to feel down *or* low, to be down in the dumps; **avoir un coup de c.** to feel a bit down *or* low
N **1** *Fam* (*rapporteur*) sneak, telltale **2** *Arch* (*faux dévot*) hypocrite
ADJ **air c.** hypocritical *or* sanctimonious air

cafardage [kafardaʒ] NM *Fam* sneaking, telling tales

cafarder [kafarde] *Fam* VT to sneak on, to tell tales on, *Am* to snitch
VI **1** (*rapporter*) to sneak, to tell tales **2** (*avoir le cafard*) to feel down *or* low, to be down in the dumps

cafardeur, -euse [kafardœr, -øz] N *Fam* sneak, telltale, *Am* snitch

cafardeux, -euse [kafardø, -øz] ADJ *Fam* (*endroit, soir*) miserable, depressing; **se sentir** *ou* **être c.** to feel down *or* low, to be down in the dumps

caf'conc' [kafkɔ̃s] NM INV *Fam abrév* **café-concert**

café [kafe] NM **1** (*produit, boisson*) coffee; **c. vert/torréfié** unroasted/roasted coffee; **grain de c.** coffee bean; **c. en grains** whole coffee, coffee beans; **c. moulu** ground coffee; **c. en poudre** *ou* **instantané** instant coffee; **un c. (bien) serré** a (very) strong coffee; **un c. léger** a weak coffee; **deux cafés** two coffees; **glace au c.** coffee ice cream **2** (*lieu*) café (*also serving alcoholic drinks*); **c. tabac** = cafe cum tobacconist's; **quand on les entend parler, on se croirait au c. du commerce** all they come out with are platitudes **3** *Hist, Littér* coffee-house

ADJ INV **c. (au lait)** coffee-coloured

▸ ▸ **c. complet** = continental breakfast; **c. crème** white coffee, coffee with hot milk; **c. décaféiné** decaffeinated coffee; **c. au lait** white coffee, *Br* coffee with milk; **c. liégeois** = coffee ice cream topped with whipped cream; **c. noir** black coffee; **c. turc** Turkish coffee

---

Café
In French cafés, a small cup of strong black coffee is called "un (petit) café", "un express" or, colloquially, "un petit noir". This may be served "serré" (extra-strong), "léger" (weak) or "allongé" (diluted with hot water). An "express" with a tiny amount of milk added is called "un noisette". A large cup of black coffee is "un grand café", "un double express" or, colloquially, "un grand noir". Coffee with frothy, steam-heated milk is called "un (grand/petit) crème". The term "café au lait" is almost never used in cafés.

---

café-concert, *pl* **cafés-concerts** NM = cabaret (club)

caféier [kafeje] NM coffee tree

caféière [kafejɛr] NF coffee plantation

caféine [kafein] NF caffeine; **sans c.** decaffeinated, caffeine-free; **teneur en c.** caffeine content

cafet [kafɛt] NF *Fam abrév* **cafétéria**

cafetan [kaftɑ̃] NM kaftan, caftan

cafeter [kafte] VI = **cafter**

cafétéria [kafeterja] NF cafeteria

café-théâtre, *pl* **cafés-théâtres** NM = café where theatrical performances take place

cafetier, -ière [kaftje, -jɛr] N café owner
NF **cafetière 1** (*récipient*) coffee pot; (*électrique*) coffee machine *or* maker; **cafetière automatique** *ou* **à pression** percolator **2** *Fam* (*tête*) nut, *Br* bonce

cafetier-limonadier, *pl* **cafetiers-limonadiers** NM café owner

cafouillage [kafujaʒ] NM *Fam* muddle, shambles, mess; (*de moteur de voiture*) missing, misfiring

cafouiller [kafuje] VI *Fam* to get into a muddle; (*de projet*) to fall apart *or* to pieces; (*de moteur de voiture*) to miss, to misfire; (*de poste de télévision*) to be on the blink

cafouilleur, -euse [kafujœr, -øz] *Fam* **ADJ** *(personne)* muddle-headed
  N muddler

cafouillis [kafuji] **NM** *Fam* shambles, muddle; **c'est un énorme c.** it's a complete shambles; **il y a beaucoup de c. dans la gestion de cette entreprise** the management of this company is really shambolic

caftan [kaftã] **NM** kaftan, caftan

cafter [kafte] **VI** *Fam* to sneak, to tell tales, *Am* to snitch

cafteur, -euse [kaftœr, -øz] **N** *Fam (indicateur)* sneak, *Am* snitch
  NM *Ordinat* cookie

cage [kaʒ] **NF 1** *(pour animaux)* cage; *(pour poules)* coop; *(pour lapins)* hutch; *(de puits de mine)* cage; *(de maison)* shell, carcass; *Ftbl* goal; **mettre un oiseau en c.** to cage a bird, to put a bird in a cage; **c. à oiseau/aux lions** bird/lions'cage; *Fig Fam* **c. à lapins** rabbit hutch; *Fig* **être comme un lion en c.** to be like a caged animal; *Fig* **une c. dorée** a gilded cage; *Ftbl* **être dans les cages** to be in goal **2** *(de montre etc)* (protective) cover, case, casing
  ▸▸**c. d'ascenseur** lift *or Am* elevator shaft; *Ordinat* scroll box; *Tech* **c. à billes** ball race; **c. d'escalier** stairwell; *Élec* **c. de Faraday** Faraday cage, electrostatic screen; *Anat* **c. thoracique** rib cage

cageot [kaʒo] **NM 1** crate **2** *Fam Péj (fille très laide)* dog

cagette [kaʒɛt] **NF** crate

cagibi [kaʒibi] **NM** *Fam* **1** *(remise)* shed, hut **2** *(débarras etc)* storage room, *Br* boxroom, lumber room

cagna [kaɲa] **NF** *Fam* (small) house

cagnard [kaɲar] **NM** *Fam* blazing sunshine

cagne [kaɲ] **NF** *Scol Fam* = second-year arts class preparing to compete for entrance to the École normale supérieure

cagneux, -euse [kaɲø, -øz] **ADJ** *(personne)* knock-kneed; *(jambes)* crooked; **genoux c.** knock knees
  N 1 *Scol Fam* = student in the cagne **2** *(personne qui a les genoux cagneux)* knock-kneed person

cagnotte [kaɲɔt] **NF** *(caisse commune)* kitty; *(de jeux)* pool, kitty, *surtout Am* pot; *Fam (économies)* nest egg

cagot, -ote [kago, -ɔt] *Péj* **N** (sanctimonious) hypocrite
  ADJ hypocritical, sanctimonious

cagouille [kaguj] **NF** *(escargot)* snail

cagoule [kagul] **NF 1** *(de moine)* cowl **2** *(de pénitent, cambrioleur)* hood **3** *(passe-montagne)* balaclava (helmet)

cahier [kaje] **NM 1** notebook; *Scol* exercise book **2** *Typ* signature, gathering, section; *(en reliure)* quire **3** *(d'un journal)* section **4** *(revue)* review, journal
  ▸▸*Compta* **c. des achats** purchase ledger; **c. de bord** logbook; **c. de brouillon** rough (notebook); *Com, Ind* **c. des charges** *(d'un contrat)* specifications; *(d'une vente)* articles and conditions; *Hist, Fig* **c. de doléances** list of grievances; **c. d'enregistrement** *(de courrier)* mail book; *(d'appels reçus)* telephone log; **c. des prix** price manual; **c. de réclamations** complaints book; **c. de textes** homework book; **c. de travaux pratiques** special notebook for practical work

cahin-caha [kaɛ̃kaa] **ADV** *Fam* **aller c.** *(de la santé)* to be so-so; *(d'une personne)* to struggle *or* limp along; **les affaires vont c.** business is slow *or* slack; **la vie continue c.** life goes on (as it must)

cahot [kao] **NM** *(de véhicule)* jolt; *(de route)* bump

cahotage [kaotaʒ] **NM** = **cahotement**

cahotant [kaotã] **ADJ 1** *(voiture)* jolting, jolty **2** *(route)* bumpy, rough

cahotement [kaotmã] **NM** *(mouvement)* jolting, shaking, bumping; *(heurt)* jolt

cahoter [kaote] **VT** to jolt, to shake; **vie cahotée** life full of ups and downs; **des enfants cahotés par le divorce** children shaken up by divorce
  VI *(d'une voiture, d'une brouette etc)* to jolt along

cahoteux, -euse [kaotø, -øz] **ADJ** *(route)* bumpy, rough

CAHT [seaaʃte] **NM** *Com (abrév* **chiffre d'affaires hors taxes)** pre-tax turnover

cahute [kayt] **NF** shack, shanty, hut

caïd [kaid] **NM 1** *(en Afrique du Nord)* kaïd **2** *Arg (chef de bande)* gang leader; **un c. de la drogue** a drug(s) baron; **c'est le gros c. en maths** he's the maths expert; *Fam* **jouer les caïds** *ou* **au c. dans la cour de récréation** to be a playground bully; **il fait le c.** he's acting all high and mighty

caïdat [kaida] **NM 1** *(en Afrique du Nord)* kaidship **2** *Arg (d'un chef de bande)* gang leadership

caillage [kɑjaʒ] **NM** = **caillement**

caillant [kɑjã] **ADJ** *Belg Fam* freezing (cold); **il fait c.** it's freezing (cold)

caillassage [kajasaʒ] **NM** *Fam* throwing *Br* stones *or Am* rocks (de at); **il a été assez souvent question du c. des bus dans les banlieues chaudes** the fact that, in the rougher areas, buses often got pelted with *Br* stones *or Am* rocks was much talked about

caillasse [kajas] **NF 1** *Géol* (gravelly) marl **2** *Fam (cailloux etc)* loose stones, scree; **marcher dans la c.** to walk on loose stones *or* scree

caillasser [kajase] **VT** *Fam* to stone

caille [kɑj] **NF** quail; **gras comme une c.** (as) plump as a partridge; **elle est chaude comme une c.** she's as snug as a bug in a rug; *Fam* **ma c.** my little dove

caillé [kaje] **NM** curds

caillebotis [kajbɔti] **NM 1** *Naut etc* grating **2** *(treillis, plancher)* duckboard(s)

caillebotte [kajbɔt] **NF** curds

caillebotter [kajbɔte] **VT** *Arch (lait)* to curdle

caillement [kajmã] **NM** *(du lait)* curdling; *(du sang)* clotting, coagulating, coagulation

cailler [kaje] **VT** *(lait)* to curdle; *(sang)* to clot, to coagulate
  VI 1 *(du lait)* to curdle; *(du sang)* to clot, to coagulate; **faire c. du lait** to curdle milk **2** *Fam* **ça caille** it's freezing (cold), *Br* it's perishing
  VPR se cailler *Fam* **on se (les) caille** it's freezing (cold), *Br* it's perishing

caillera [kajra] **NF** *Fam* scum

caillette [kajɛt] **NF** *(des ruminants)* fourth stomach

caillot [kajo] **NM** *(de sang)* clot

caillou, -oux [kaju] **NM 1** *(petite pierre)* stone; **cailloux d'empierrement** (loose) chippings, road metal; **avoir un c. dans sa chaussure** to have a stone in one's shoe; *Fig* **avoir le cœur dur comme un c.** to have a heart of stone **2** *(grosse pierre)* boulder, rock **3** *Fam (pierre précieuse)* stone **4** *Arg (tête)* nut, *Br* bonce; **il n'a plus un poil sur le c.** he's as bald as a coot **5** *Fam* **le C.** *(la Nouvelle-Calédonie)* New Caledonia

cailloutage [kajutaʒ] **NM 1** *(action)* *(de route)* metalling; *(de voie ferrée)* ballasting **2** *(pierres)* *(de route)* road metal; *(de voie ferrée)* ballast

caillouter [kajute] **VT** *(route)* to metal; *(voie ferrée)* to ballast

caillouteux, -euse [kajutø, -øz] **ADJ** *(route etc)* stony; *(plage)* pebbly, shingly

cailloutis [kajuti] **NM** broken stones, chippings, gravel; *(de route)* road metal

caïman [kaimã] **NM** cayman, caiman

Caïn [kaɛ̃] **NM** Cain

Caire (le) [(lə)kɛr] **NM** Cairo

cairn [kɛrn] **NM** cairn

cairote [kɛrɔt] **ADJ** of/from Cairo
  N C. Cairene, person from Cairo

caisse [kɛs] **NF 1** *(pour marchandises)* (packing) case; *(à outils, de rangement)* box, chest; *(à thé etc)* chest; *(de champagne, vin)* case; *(pour plantes)* tub; **c. à savon** soapbox; **c. de melons** crate of melons; **mettre des marchandises en c.** to case goods **2** *(de piano, d'horloge)* case; *(de véhicule)* body(work), bodyshell; *(de poulie)* shell; *Aut* **c. de l'embrayage** clutch casing **3** *Arg (voiture)* car, *Br* motor **4** *Arg (poitrine)* chest; **il s'en va de la c.** his chest is giving out **5** *Mus* drum; **c. claire** side *or* snare drum; **grosse c.** bass drum **6** *Anat* **c. du tympan** middle ear **7** *Com, Fin (coffre)* cash box; *(d'une caisse enregistreuse)* till; *(dans un magasin, un garage etc)* cash desk; *(dans un grand magasin)* cashpoint; *(dans un supermarché)* checkout; **c. (enregistreuse)** cash register; **les caisses de l'État** the coffers of the State; **payez à la c.** pay at the (cash) desk *or* at the till; **tenir la c.** to be in charge of the cash; *(dans un restaurant, un magasin etc)* to be the cashier; **passer à la c.** to go to the cash desk; *(dans un supermarché)* to go through the checkout; *(payer)* to pay; *(se faire payer)* to be paid; *(se faire licencier)* to be paid off **8** *(argent)* cash (in hand); *(recette)* takings; **livre de c.** cashbook; **faire la** *ou* **sa c.** to balance (up) one's cash, to do the takings, *Br* to cash up; **avoir tant d'argent en c.** *(disponible)* to have so much money in hand; **elle est partie avec la c.** she made off with the cash *or* the takings; **'la c.!'** hurla le malfaiteur 'hand over the cash!' shouted the robber **9** *(organisme)* fund; **c. de défense** *(d'une association etc)* fighting fund **10** *Suisse Fam* **prendre une c.** to get plastered; **être (fin) c.** to be (completely) plastered
  ▸▸**c. d'allocations familiales** ≃ child benefit office; *Compta* **c. d'amortissement** sinking fund; **c. de chômage** unemployment fund; **c. à claire-voie** crate; **c. de compensation** = equalization fund for payments such as child benefit, sickness benefit, pensions; **c. comptable** cash register; **C. des dépôts et consignations** = administrative department of the French government, in charge of investing and lending public money; *Naut* **c. à eau douce** freshwater tank; **c. électronique** electronic billing machine; **c. enregistreuse** cash register; **c. d'épargne** savings bank; **c. d'épargne-logement** *Br* ≃ building society, *Am* ≃ savings and loan association; **c. de garantie** credit guarantee institution; **c. à laser** laser checkout; **C. nationale d'assurance vieillesse** = French government department dealing with benefit payments relating to old age pensions; *Pol* **c. noire** slush fund; *Can* **c. populaire** credit union; **c. de prévoyance** provident fund; **c. primaire d'assurance maladie** = French government department dealing with health insurance; **c. régionale** ≃ local (bank) branch; **c. de retraite** ≃ pension fund

caissette [kɛsɛt] **NF** small box

caissier, -ière [kesje, -jer] **N** *(dans un restaurant, un magasin etc)* cashier; *(dans un supermarché)* checkout operator; *Banque*

cashier, teller; **c. de nuit** *(dans un hôtel)* night auditor

caisson [kɛsɔ̃] NM **1** *(caisse)* box, case; *Mil (de munitions etc)* wagon, caisson; *Fam* **se faire sauter le c.** to blow one's brains out **2** *Archit* **plafond à caissons** panelled *or* coffered ceiling **3** *(pour travail sous-marin)* caisson; *Méd* **mal(adie) des caissons** caisson disease, decompression sickness, *Fam* the bends; **c. à air comprimé** decompression chamber **4** *Aut* bay **5** *Cin, TV* **c. de graves** subwoofer; **c. d'insonorisation** blimp

cajoler [kaʒɔle] VT **1** *(câliner)* to cuddle, to make a fuss of **2** *Vieilli (flatter)* to cajole, to coax, to wheedle

cajolerie [kaʒɔlri] NF *(câlin)* cuddle

cajoleur, -euse [kaʒɔlœr, -øz] ADJ **1** *(câlin)* affectionate **2** *Vieilli (flatteur)* cajoling, wheedling, coaxing
▪ N *Vieilli (flatteur)* cajoler, wheedler, coaxer

cajou [kaʒu] NM cashew (nut)

cake [kɛk] NM fruit cake; **mascara en c.** block mascara; *Fam* **être dans le c.** *(avoir la gueule de bois)* to be hung over, to have a hangover; *(être très fatigué)* to be all in

cal, pl cals [kal] NM *Bot, Méd* callus, callosity

calabrais, -aise [kalabrɛ, -ɛz] ADJ Calabrian
▪ NM *Ling* Calabrian dialect
▪ N **C.** Calabrian

Calabre [kalabr] NF Calabria

calage [kalaʒ] NM **1** *(de pied de chaise etc)* wedging; *(de roue)* chocking **2** *(fait d'appuyer)* propping (up) **3** *(de manivelle à un axe etc)* wedging, keying; *(de roue à un axe etc)* fixing; *(de valve etc)* jamming, locking **4** *Aut (de moteur)* stalling **5** *(réglage)* adjustment; *(de valve, moteur)* tuning; *Aut* **c. d'allumage** ignition timing **6** *Typ* setting

calamar [kalamar] NM = **calmar**

calamine [kalamin] NF **1** *Minér* calamine **2** *(dépôt)* carbon deposits

calaminer (se) [səkalamine] VPR to get covered with carbon deposits

calamistré [kalamistre] ADJ **cheveux calamistrés** brilliantined hair

calamité [kalamite] NF *(désastre)* calamity, disaster; *(malheur)* (great) misfortune; **quelle c.!** what a disaster! *Fam* **ce mec, c'est une vraie c.!** this guy is a real *or* a walking disaster!

calamiteux, -euse [kalamitø, -øz] ADJ disastrous, *Fml* calamitous

calancher [kalɑ̃ʃe] VI *très Fam* to croak, *Br* to snuff it, *Am* to check out

calandrage [kalɑ̃draʒ] NM *(dans la fabrication du papier), Tex & Typ* calendering; *(de pneu)* liner

calandre [kalɑ̃dr] NF **1** *(dans la fabrication du papier), Tex, Typ* calender **2** *Aut* radiator grille

calandrer [kalɑ̃dre] VT *Tex, Typ etc* to calender

calandreur, -euse [kalɑ̃drœr, -øz] N *(pour les papiers), Tex, Typ* calenderer

calanque [kalɑ̃k] NF *(en Méditerranée)* deep narrow creek

calao [kalao] NM hornbill

calbar [kalbar] NM *Fam (slip) Br* scants, *Am* shorts

calcaire [kalkɛr] ADJ *(sol, terrain)* chalky; *(roche)* calcareous; *Chimie* **sel c.** calcium salt; **eau c.** hard water
▪ NM **1** *Géol* limestone **2** *(dans les bouilloires)* fur

calcanéum [kalkaneɔm] NM *Anat* heel bone, *Spéc* calcaneum

calcédoine [kalsedwan] NF *Minér* chalcedony

calcif [kalsif] NM *Fam* = **calecif**

calcination [kalsinasjɔ̃] NF calcination

calciner [kalsine] VT *(brûler)* to char; *Chimie, Ind* to calcine; **rôti calciné** joint burnt to a cinder; **désert calciné par le soleil** sun-baked desert
▪ VPR **se calciner** to burn

calcium [kalsjɔm] NM *Chimie* calcium

calcul[1] [kalkyl] NM **1** *(compte)* calculation, reckoning, computation; **faire un c.** to make a calculation; **faux c., erreur de c.** miscalculation; *Ordinat* **calculs très rapides** number crunching **2** *Scol* **le c.** arithmetic; **sums; faible en c.** bad at sums *or* arithmetic; **enseigner le c.** to teach arithmetic; **apprendre le c.** to learn (how) to count; **règle à c.** slide rule; **problème de c.** arithmetic problem **3** *(prévision)* calculation; **agir par c.** to act from selfish *or* ulterior motives; **ça a été un bon c. de notre part** it was a good move on our part, we did the right thing; **un mauvais c.** a miscalculation; **faire un bon c.** to calculate correctly; **faire un mauvais c.** to miscalculate; **selon nos calculs** according to our calculations
▪ ▪ *Math* **c. différentiel** differential calculus; *Math* **c. intégral** integral calculus; **c. mental** mental arithmetic; **c. des probabilités** theory of probability

calcul[2] NM *Méd (dans la vésicule)* stone, *Spéc* calculus; **avoir des calculs** to have stones in the bladder; *(aux reins)* to have kidney stones; **c. biliaire** gall stone; **c. rénal** kidney stone

calculable [kalkylabl] ADJ calculable

calculateur, -trice [kalkylatœr, -tris] ADJ *(personne, politique)* calculating
▪ N *(personne)* **c'est un bon c.** he's good at *or* with figures
▪ NM **1** *Ordinat* (desktop) calculator; **c. (électronique)** (electronic) computer **2** *(de poche)* calculator
▪ NF **calculatrice** *(machine)* (desktop) calculator; **calculatrice de bureau** desktop calculator; **calculatrice imprimante** print-out calculator; **calculatrice de poche** pocket calculator

calculé [kalkyle] ADJ *(insulte, risque)* calculated; *(méchanceté)* premeditated, calculated; *(insolence)* deliberate; **une bonté calculée** an act of kindness motivated by self-interest

calculer [kalkyle] VT *(compter) (prix, surface d'un triangle etc)* to work out, to calculate; *(comportement, réflexions etc)* to plan, to calculate; *(conséquences)* to weigh (up); **c. qch de tête** to work sth out *or* calculate sth in one's head; **tout bien calculé** taking everything into account; **c. ses chances de réussite** to calculate *or* to weigh up one's chances of success; **c. ses dépenses au plus juste** to work out *or* calculate one's expenses to the nearest penny
▪ VI to calculate; *Péj (économiser)* to count every penny; **c. vite et bien** to be quick and accurate at *or* with figures; **machine à c.** adding machine, (desk) calculator

calculette [kalkylɛt] NF **1** *(appareil)* (pocket) calculator **2** *Fam Hum (personne qui souffre d'acné)* pizza face; **elle sort avec un mec, une vraie c.!** she's going out with this real pizza face guy

caldoche [kaldɔʃ] ADJ = pertaining to the European community of New Caledonia
▪ N **C.** = New Caledonian of European descent

cale[1] [kal] NF *Naut* **1** *(de navire)* hold; **eau de c.** bilge water; **fond de c.** bilge; **à fond de c.** down in the hold; *Fam Fig* **être à fond de c.** to be stony-broke *or* *Am* stone-broke **2** **mettre un navire sur c.** to lay down a ship
▪ ▪ **c. à charbon** bunker; **c. de construction/ de lancement** stocks/slip(way); **c. à eau wa-**

ter tank; c. de radoub dry dock, graving dock; **c. sèche** dry dock

cale[2] NF **1** *(pour mettre un meuble d'aplomb etc)* wedge; *(pour bloquer une roue etc)* chock, block; *Aut (pour augmenter le jeu entre deux pièces)* shim, spacer; **c. de réglage** adjusting shim; **mettre une voiture sur cales** to put a car on blocks; *Aviat* **enlevez les cales!** chocks away! **2** *(support)* prop, strut; *Tech (d'arbre etc)* key

calé [kale] ADJ **1** *Fam (problème, question, devoir etc)* difficult, tough; **être c. en qch** to be well up in sth, to know all about sth; **ça, c'est c.!** that's cunning!, that's clever! **2** *Belg (prêt)* ready

calebasse [kalbas] NF *(fruit, récipient)* calabash, gourd

calèche [kalɛʃ] NF *(voiture)* barouche

calecif [kalsif] NM *Fam* boxer shorts

caleçon [kalsɔ̃] NM boxer shorts; *(de femme)* leggings; *Vieilli* **c. long** long underpants, *Fam* long johns; *Vieilli* **c. de bain** (swimming *or* bathing) trunks

calédonien, -ienne [kaledɔnjɛ̃, -jɛn] ADJ Caledonian
▪ N **C.** Caledonian

calembour [kalɑ̃bur] NM pun, play on words; **faire** *ou* **dire des calembours** to make puns, to pun, to play on words

calembredaine [kalɑ̃brədɛn] NF joke
▪ NFPL **calembredaines** nonsense

calendes [kalɑ̃d] NFPL *Antiq* calends; **renvoyer qn/qch aux c. grecques** to put sb/sth off indefinitely

calendos [kalɑ̃dos] NM *Fam* Camembert (cheese)

calendrier [kalɑ̃drije] NM **1** *(système, tableau)* calendar; **bloc c.** block calendar; **c. à effeuiller** tear-off calendar; **c. perpétuel** perpetual calendar; **c. grégorien** gregorian calendar **2** *(de voyage, travail etc)* timetable, programme, schedule; **avoir un c. chargé** to have a busy schedule *or* timetable; **le c. de ses visites n'a pas encore été établi** her visits haven't been timetabled *or* scheduled yet; **c. de campagne** media schedule; *Bourse* **c. des émissions** calendar of issues; **c. des remboursements** repayment schedule

cale-pied, pl cale-pieds NM toe clip

calepin [kalpɛ̃] NM **1** notebook **2** *Belg (cartable)* briefcase

caler[1] [kale] VT **1** *(pied de chaise etc)* to wedge; *(roue)* to chock; **c. un chargement** to secure a load (firmly); **c. un malade avec des coussins** to prop up a patient on cushions **2** *(manivelle à un axe etc)* to wedge, to key; *(roue sur un axe etc)* to fix; *(valve etc)* to jam, to lock **3** *Aut (moteur)* to stall **4** *(régler) (valve, moteur etc)* to adjust, to tune **5** *Fam (remplir)* **ça vous cale (l'estomac)** it fills you up, it's really filling; **je suis calé** I'm full (up)
▪ VI *(moteur)* to stall
▪ VPR **se caler 1** *(dans un fauteuil etc)* to settle (oneself) comfortably **2** *Fam* **se c. les joues, se les c.** to stuff oneself, to have a good feed

caler[2] VT *Naut (mât)* to house; *(voile)* to strike
▪ VI **1** *Naut* **navire qui cale vingt pieds** ship that draws *or* whose draught is twenty feet (of water); **navire qui cale trop** ship that is too deep in the water **2** *Fam (abandonner)* to give up **3** *Can (se dégarnir)* to have a receding hairline

caleter (se) [səkalte] VPR *Arg* = **calter**

calfat [kalfa] NM *Naut* ca(u)lker

calfatage [kalfataʒ] NM *Naut* ca(u)lking

calfater [kalfate] VT *Naut* to ca(u)lk

calfeutrage [kalføtraʒ], **calfeutrement** [kalføtrəmɑ̃] NM **1** *(de brèches)* blocking up, stopping (up), filling (in) **2** *(d'une pièce etc)* draught-proofing

calfeutrer [kalføtre] **VT 1** *(brèches)* to block up, to stop (up), to fill (in) **2** *(pièce etc)* to draught-proof, to make draught-proof
VPR se calfeutrer *(pour avoir chaud)* to make oneself snug; *(pour être seul)* to shut oneself up *or* away

calibrage [kalibraʒ] **NM 1** *(de pièce)* gauging, measuring; *(de thermomètre etc)* calibration; *Com (d'œufs, de fruits etc)* grading **2** *Phot (d'épreuve)* trimming **3** *Typ (de copie)* cast-off

calibre [kalibr] **NM 1** *(d'arme à feu, tuyau etc)* calibre, *Am* caliber, bore; *(de balle etc)* calibre, size; *(d'œufs, de fruits etc)* grade; **fusil de c. 8 mm** *Mil* 8-mm calibre rifle; *Sport* 8-mm gauge gun; **canon de gros c.** heavy gun, large-bore gun; *Fig* **sa sœur est d'un autre c.** his sister is of quite a different calibre, *Fam* his sister is in a different league; **il n'est pas de ce c.-là** he's not a man of that calibre; **j'ai rarement vu une bêtise de ce c.!** I've rarely seen stupidity on such a scale!
2 *(outil)* gauge, *Am* gage; **c. d'épaisseur (à lames)** feeler gauge, set of feelers; **c. de profondeur** depth gauge
3 *(pour la reproduction)* template
4 *(de machine-outil)* jig, former
5 *Arg (revolver)* shooter, *Am* rod; **un gros c.** a heavy pistol

calibrer [kalibre] **VT 1** *(pièce)* to gauge, to measure; *(thermomètre etc)* to calibrate; *Com (œufs, fruits etc)* to grade; *Ordinat (couleurs)* to calibrate **2** *Phot (épreuve)* to trim **3** *Typ (copie)* to cast off

calibreur, -euse [kalibrœr, -øz] **N** calibrator; *Aut* **c. d'air** air bleed jet, air correction jet

calice[1] [kalis] **NM** *Rel* chalice; *Fig* **boire le c. jusqu'à la lie** to drain the cup to the dregs **INT** *Can* hell!

calice[2] **NM** *Bot, Anat* calyx

calicot [kaliko] **NM 1** *Tex Br* calico, *Am* unbleached muslin **2** *(portant une publicité etc)* banner **3** *Vieilli (personne)* draper's assistant

califat [kalifa] **NM** caliphate

calife [kalif] **NM** caliph; **vouloir être c. à la place du c.** to want to be top dog

Californie [kaliforni] **NF** California

californien, -ienne [kalifornjɛ̃, -jɛn] **ADJ** Californian
N C. Californian

californium [kalifornjɔm] **NM** *Chimie* californium

califourchon [kalifurʃɔ̃] **ADV à c.** astride; **se mettre à c. sur qch** to sit astride sth, to straddle sth; **monter à c. sur un cheval** to ride a horse astride
NM *Can* bottom, backside, behind

câlin, -ine [kɑlɛ̃, -in] **ADJ** *(enfant, regard, ton etc)* affectionate
N *(personne)* affectionate person
NM cuddle; **faire un c. à qn** to give sb a cuddle

câliner [kɑline] **VT** *(choyer) (enfant etc)* to make a fuss of; *(caresser)* to cuddle

câlinerie [kɑlinri] **NF 1** *(tendresse)* fondness, tenderness **2** *(caresses etc)* caress; *(dans les bras)* cuddle; **faire des câlineries à qn** to cuddle sb

calisson [kalisɔ̃] **NM** = lozenge-shaped sweet made of marzipan

calleux, -euse [kalø, -øz] **ADJ** callous, horny

call-girl, *pl* **call-girls** [kolgœrl] **NF** call girl

calligramme [kaligram] **NM** *Littér* calligramme

calligraphe [kaligraf] **N** calligrapher, calligraphist

calligraphie [kaligrafi] **NF** calligraphy

calligraphier [kaligrafje] **VT** *(impf, pr sub* **n. calligraphiions, v. calligraphiiez)** *(lettre etc)* to write beautifully (and ornamentally); **nom calligraphié** beautifully (hand)written name

calligraphique [kaligrafik] **ADJ** calligraphic

callosité [kalozite] **NF** callus, callosity

calmant [kalmɑ̃] **ADJ** *(mots etc)* calming, soothing; *Méd (pour les nerfs)* tranquillizing, sedative; *(pour la douleur)* painkilling
NM *Méd (pour les nerfs)* tranquillizer, sedative; *(pour la douleur)* painkiller

calmar [kalmar] **NM** squid

calme [kalm] **NM** *(absence d'agitation)* calm, calmness; *(dans une situation difficile)* coolness, composure; *(de l'air, de la nuit)* stillness; *(du paysage)* peace and quiet, quiet(ness), peacefulness; **je cherche un peu de c.** I'm looking for some peace and quiet; **j'ai besoin d'être au c. pour écrire** I need (to have) peace and quiet in order to write; **moment de c.** lull; **je n'ai pas eu un moment de c. de toute la journée!** I haven't had a minute's peace all day!; **dans le c. de la nuit** in the still of the night; **du c.!** keep cool *or* calm!; **perdre son c.** to lose one's composure *or Fam* cool; **retrouver son c.** to regain one's composure, to calm down; **garder son c.** to keep one's composure, to keep calm *or* cool, *Fam* to keep one's cool; **il est toujours d'un c. incroyable** he is always incredibly calm *or* cool *or* composed; *Naut* **c. plat** dead calm; **les commerçants se plaignent que c'est le c. plat** traders are complaining that business is in the doldrums; **c'est le c. plat dans ma vie sentimentale** my love life is in the doldrums, there's nothing happening in my love life; **calmes équatoriaux** doldrums
ADJ *(nuit etc)* calm, still, quiet; *(personne, air)* calm, cool, composed; *(mer)* calm, smooth; *(ciel)* clear; *Com (marché)* quiet, flat, dull; **elle a des enfants très calmes** she has very placid children; **les affaires sont calmes en août** business is quiet in August; **la Bourse a été c.** the Stock Market has been quiet *or* has had a quiet day

> Attention: ne pas confondre **calm** et **quiet** lorsqu'on traduit **calme**. Le terme **calm** se rapporte généralement à la maîtrise de soi, alors que **quiet** désigne un comportement ou une situation paisible.

calmement [kalmǝmɑ̃] **ADV** calmly

calmer [kalme] **VT** *(personne) (rendre serein)* to calm (down); *(faire taire)* to quieten (down), *Am* to quiet down; *(foule etc)* to calm, to pacify; *(craintes)* to calm, to allay; *(douleur)* to soothe, to ease; *(conscience)* to ease; *(soif)* to quench; *(faim)* to appease; *(ardeur, passion)* to damp, to cool; *(fièvre)* to reduce, to bring down; *Fam* **je vais te le c. en moins de deux!** I'll soon shut him up *or* sort him out!; **c. le jeu** *(dans un jeu de ballon)* to slow down the pace of play; *Fig* to calm things down
VPR se calmer *(de personne) (devenir serein)* to calm down; *(se taire)* to quieten down, *Am* to quiet down; *(de tempête)* to abate, to die down, to blow over; *(de vent)* to drop, to subside; *(de mer)* to become calm; *(de pluie)* to ease off; **la douleur se calme** the pain is easing *or* subsiding

calmos [kalmos] **INT** *Fam* chill (out)!, take it easy!

calomel [kalɔmɛl] **NM** *Pharm* calomel

calomniateur, -trice [kalɔmnjatœr, -tris] **N** *(qui parle)* slanderer; *(qui écrit)* libeller
ADJ *(paroles)* slanderous; *(écrits)* libellous

calomnie [kalɔmni] **NF** *(parlée)* slander, *Fml* calumny; *(écrite, publiée)* libel; **répandre** des calomnies sur qn to cast aspersions on sb; **elle a été en butte à la c.** she has been a victim of slander/libel, she has been slandered/libelled

calomnier [kalɔmnje] **VT** to slander, to malign, *Fml* to calumniate; *(par écrit)* to libel

calomnieusement [kalɔmnjøzmɑ̃] **ADV** slanderously; *(par écrit)* libellously

calomnieux, -ieuse [kalɔmnjø, -jøz] **ADJ** *(paroles)* slanderous; *(écrits)* libellous

caloporteur [kalɔpɔrtœr] **ADJ fluide** *ou* **liquide c.** coolant
NM coolant

calorie [kalɔri] **NF** calorie; **régime basses calories** low-calorie diet; **l'avocat est riche en calories** avocados are high in calories; **ration de calories** calorie intake; **attention aux calories!** watch the calories!

calorifère [kalɔrifɛr] **ADJ** heat-conveying
NM *(slow-combustion)* stove; *Can* radiator

calorifique [kalɔrifik] **ADJ** *Phys* calorific, thermal; **capacité c.** heat capacity

calorifuge [kalɔrifyʒ] **ADJ** (heat-)insulating; *(vernis etc)* heat-proof; **le bois est c.** wood is a poor conductor of heat
NM heat insulator *or* insulation; *(pour chaudière, tuyau)* lagging

calorifugeage [kalɔrifyʒaʒ] **NM** (heat) insulation; *(de chaudière, tuyau)* lagging

calorifuger [kalɔrifyʒe] **VT** *(je calorifugeai(s); n. calorifugeons)* to insulate; *(chaudière, tuyau)* to lag

calorimètre [kalɔrimɛtr] **NM** *Phys* calorimeter

calorimétrie [kalɔrimetri] **NF** *Phys* calorimetry

calorimétrique [kalɔrimetrik] **ADJ** *Phys (unité etc)* calorimetric(al)

caloriporteur [kalɔripɔrtœr] **ADJ, NM** = **caloporteur**

calorique [kalɔrik] **ADJ** calorific; **ration c.** calorie intake

calorisation [kalɔrizasjɔ̃] **NF** *Tech* calorization, aluminium plating

calorstat [kalɔrsta] **NM** *Aut* thermostat

calot[1] [kalo] **NM 1** *(grosse bille)* (large) marble **2** *Arg (œil)* peeper

calot[2] **NM** *Mil* forage cap, *Am* garrison cap

calotin [kalɔtɛ̃] **NM** *Fam Péj* **1** *(prêtre)* priest **2** *(bigot)* pious churchgoer

calotte [kalɔt] **NF 1** *(chapeau rond)* skullcap; *Rel* calotte; *(de chapeau)* crown; *Arg Péj* **la c.** *(le clergé)* the priests; *Pol* the clerical party **2** *Litt* **la c. des cieux** the vault *or* canopy of heaven **3** *Fam (gifle)* cuff, clout; **flanquer une c. à qn** to give sb a clout, to box sb's ears
▸▸ *Anat* **c. du crâne, c. crânienne** top part of the skull, skullcap; *Géol* **c. glaciaire** ice cap; *Math* **c. sphérique** portion of a sphere

calotter [kalɔte] **VT** *Fam (personne)* to cuff, to clout

calquage [kalkaʒ] **NM** tracing

calque [kalk] **NM 1** *(copie)* tracing; *(de poème, de portrait etc)* exact copy; **prendre un c. de qch** to make a tracing of sth, to trace sth; **(papier-)c.** tracing paper **2** *Ling* loan translation, calque

calquer [kalke] **VT** *(reproduire)* to trace, to make a tracing of; *Fig* to copy exactly, to imitate; **dessin calqué** tracing; **expression calquée sur l'anglais** expression copied from *or* modelled on the English; **c. sa conduite sur celle de qn que l'on admire** to model one's behaviour on that of sb one admires

calter [kalte] **VI** *Arg (s'enfuir)* to scram, *Br* to scarper

calumet [kalymɛ] **NM** peace pipe, calumet; *Fig* **fumer le c. de la paix avec qn** to smoke the pipe of peace with sb

calva [kalva] NM *Fam abrév* **calvados**

calvados [kalvados] NM calvados, apple brandy

calvaire [kalvɛr] NM *(épreuve pénible)* agony, ordeal; *Rel* calvary; *(croix)* calvary, wayside cross; *Rel* **Le C.** (Mount) Calvary; **c'est un c. de devoir la supporter** it's agony having to put up with her; **sa vie fut un long c.** his life was one long ordeal

calvinisme [kalvinism] NM Calvinism

calviniste [kalvinist] ADJ Calvinistic, Calvinist
N Calvinist

calvitie [kalvisi] NF baldness; **c. naissante** incipient baldness; **c. précoce** premature baldness

calypso [kalipso] NM *(danse), Mus* calypso

cama [kama] NM *Belg Fam (camarade)* pal, mate, friend

camaïeu, -eux [kamajø] NM *(peinture)* monochrome *(painting)*; *(gravure)* tint drawing

camail [kamaj] NM 1 *Cathol (porté par-dessus le surplis)* cape 2 *Orn (du coq)* neck feathers, hackles

camarade [kamarad] N friend, *Fam* mate, pal; *Pol (terme d'adresse)* comrade, brother; **le c.** Gorbatchev comrade Gorbachev; **c. d'école** *ou* **de collège** school friend; **c. de classe** *ou* **de promotion** classmate; **c. de jeu** playmate; **c. de régiment** old army friend

camaraderie [kamaradri] NF camaraderie, comradeship

camard, -arde [kamar, -ard] ADJ *(nez)* flat; *(personne)* flat-nosed, with a flat nose
NF **camarde** *Fam* **la camarde** the (Grim) Reaper

camarguais, -aise [kamargɛ, -ɛz] ADJ of/from the Camargue
N **C.** *(natif)* native of the Camargue; *(habitant)* inhabitant of the Camargue

cambiste [kɑ̃bist] *Fin* N foreign exchange dealer
ADJ **marché c.** exchange market

Cambodge [kɑ̃bɔdʒ] NM Cambodia

cambodgien, -ienne [kɑ̃bɔdʒjɛ̃, -jɛn] ADJ Cambodian
N **C.** Cambodian

cambouis [kɑ̃bwi] NM dirty oil, grease

cambrage [kɑ̃braʒ] NM bending; *(du pied, du dos)* arching; *(du bois etc)* cambering, curving

cambré [kɑ̃bre] ADJ bent; *(poutre)* cambered, arched; **pied très c.** foot with a high instep; **taille cambrée** arched *or* curved back; **jambes cambrées** bow legs

cambrement [kɑ̃brəmɑ̃] NM = **cambrage**

cambrer [kɑ̃bre] VT to bend; *(le dos, le pied)* to arch; *(bois etc)* to camber, to curve; **c. la taille** *ou* **les reins** to arch one's back
VPR **se cambrer** to arch one's back

cambrien, -ienne [kɑ̃brijɛ̃, -jɛn] ADJ, NM *Géol* Cambrian

cambriolage [kɑ̃brijɔlaʒ] NM *(métier)* burglary, housebreaking; *(événement)* burglary, break-in

cambriole [kɑ̃brijɔl] NF *Fam (métier)* burglary, housebreaking

cambrioler [kɑ̃brijɔle] VT *(maison)* to break into, to burgle, *Am* to burglarize; **nous avons été cambriolés pendant les vacances** we were burgled *or* we had a burglary *or* break-in while we were on holiday

cambrioleur, -euse [kɑ̃brijɔlœr, -øz] N burglar, housebreaker

cambrouse [kɑ̃bruz], **cambrousse** [kɑ̃brus] NF *Fam (campagne)* country; **maison à la c.** *ou* **en pleine c.** house in the middle of nowhere *or* (out) in the sticks *or* at the back of beyond

cambrure [kɑ̃bryr] NF *(du bois etc)* camber, curve; *(du pied, du dos)* arch; **chaussures à forte c.** shoes with a high instep; **c. des reins** small of the back

cambuse [kɑ̃byz] NF 1 *Naut* storeroom 2 *(de chantier naval)* canteen 3 *Arg (chambre)* hole, place, room

cambusier [kɑ̃byzje] NM 1 *(à la cantine)* canteen keeper 2 *(de stocks)* storekeeper

came¹ [kam] NF *Tech* cam; **arbre à cames** camshaft; **moteur avec arbre à cames en tête** overhead camshaft engine; **à c. unique** single-cam; **c. de frein** expander

came² *Arg* NF 1 *(drogue)* dope, junk 2 *(diminutif de camelote) (objet de mauvaise qualité)* junk

camé, -ée [kame] N *Arg* junkie, druggie

camée [kame] NM cameo

caméléon [kamele5] NM *(reptile), Fig* chameleon

camélia [kamelja] NM camellia

camelot [kamlo] NM 1 *Fam (marchand dans la rue)* street vendor *or* seller 2 *Arch (vendeur de journaux)* newsvendor 3 *Hist* **camelots du roi** royalists

camelote [kamlɔt] NF *Fam* 1 *(pacotille)* junk, trash, *Br* rubbish; **n'achète pas cette voiture, c'est de la c.!** don't buy that car, it's a pile of junk *or* an old junk heap! 2 *(toute marchandise)* stuff

camembert [kamɑ̃bɛr] NM 1 *(fromage)* Camembert *(cheese)* 2 *(diagramme)* pie-chart

camer (se) [səkame] VPR *Arg* to do drugs, to be on drugs; **il se came à l'héroïne** he's on heroin; **elle est complètement camée** she's as high as a kite

caméra [kamera] NF *Cin, TV* camera; **il s'est expliqué devant les caméras** he gave an explanation in front of the television cameras; **c. de télévision** television camera; **c. asservie** *ou* **esclave** slave camera; **c. banc-titre** rostrum camera; **c. cachée** hidden camera; **c. d'animation** rostrum camera; **c. fixe** fixed camera; **c. Internet** Web cam, live cam; **c. invisible** hidden camera; **c. de reportage** hand-held camera; **c. en studio** studio (broadcast) camera; **c. grande vitesse** high speed camera; **c. isolée** isolated camera, ISO; **c. légère** lightweight camera, portable single camera; **C. d'or** = important prize awarded at the Cannes Film Festival to a first full-length film; **c. oculaire** eye (movement) camera; **c. portable** portable camera; **c. portative** press camera; **c. sans film** filmless camera; **c. sonore** sound camera; **c. super-8** super 8 camera; **c. vidéo** video camera; **c. vidéo numérique** digital video camera

> Il faut noter que le mot anglais **camera** signifie également **appareil photo**.

caméra-film, *pl* **caméras-film** NF film camera, motion picture camera, *surtout Am* movie camera

cameraman [kameraman], *pl* **cameramen** [kameramɛn] NM *Cin, TV* cameraman

camérier [kamerje] NM *(du Pape, de cardinal)* chamberlain

camériste [kamerist] NF *Hist* lady-in-waiting

Cameroun [kamrun] NM **le C.** Cameroon; *Hist* the Cameroons

camerounais, -aise [kamrunɛ, -ɛz] ADJ Cameroonian
N **C.** Cameroonian

Caméscope® [kameskɔp] NM camcorder; **C. numérique** digital camcorder

camion [kamjɔ̃] NM 1 *Aut* truck, *Br* lorry; **c. de déménagement** removal van; **c. bâché** curtainsider; **c. de dépannage** breakdown truck, *Am* wrecker; **c. pour transport d'auto-**

mobiles (car) transporter; **c. réfrigéré** refrigerated lorry; **chauffeur de c.** lorry *or* truck driver; *TV* **c. d'enregistrement (du son)** sound van 2 *(chariot)* dray, wag(g)on

camion-benne, *pl* **camions-bennes** NM dump(er) truck

camion-citerne, *pl* **camions-citernes** NM tanker, *Am* tank truck *or* trailer

camion-magasin, *pl* **camions-magasins** NM mobile shop

camionnage [kamjɔnaʒ] NM *(prix, service)* haulage, *Am* truckage; **une entreprise de c.** a haulage firm, *Am* a trucking business

camionner [kamjɔne] VT *(marchandises)* to transport by *Br* lorry *or* truck, *Am* to truck

camionnette [kamjɔnɛt] NF van, panel van, *Am* delivery truck; **c. de livraison** delivery van

camionneur [kamjɔnœr] NM 1 *(conducteur)* *Br* lorry driver, truck driver, *Am* trucker, teamster; *(de camionnette)* van driver 2 *(transporteur)* haulier, *Am* hauler, *Am* trucker

camisole [kamizɔl] NF 1 *Can, Suisse (tricot de corps)* vest, *Am* undershirt 2 *Arch (chemise de nuit)* nightshirt 3 *(corsage)* camisole
▸▸ **c. de force** strait-jacket

camomille [kamɔmij] NF camomile; **tisane de c.** camomile tea; **prendre une c.** to have a cup of camomile tea

camouflage [kamuflaʒ] NM camouflage; *(de la vérité etc)* disguising, hiding; **le c. d'une rentrée d'argent** the concealment of a sum of money received; **le c. d'une faute** the covering up of a mistake

camoufler [kamufle] VT to camouflage; *(vérité, intentions etc)* to disguise, to hide; *(faute)* to cover up; *(rentrée d'argent)* to conceal; **c. un bouton** to cover up *or* camouflage a spot; *Compta* **c. un bilan** to window-dress the accounts; **c. un meurtre en suicide** to make a murder look like suicide
VPR **se camoufler** to camouflage oneself

camouflet [kamufle] NM affront, snub; **essuyer un c.** to be snubbed

camp [kɑ̃] NM 1 *(campement)* camp; **établir un c.** to pitch camp; **lever le c.** to strike camp; **lit de c.** camp bed; **feu de c.** campfire; **partir faire un c., partir en c.** to go camping; *Fam* **ficher le c.** to clear off, to scram; *Fam* **fous-moi le c.!** clear off!, beat it! 2 *(parti)* camp; **changer de c.** to change sides; **le c. adverse** the opposing camp, the other side; **ils ne sont pas dans le même c.** they're on different sides 3 *(de jeux)* side; **tirer les camps** to pick sides; **faire deux camps** to form two teams
▸▸ **c. (de vacances)** (children's) holiday camp, *Am* summer camp; **c. d'adolescents** holiday camp for teenagers, *Am* camp; **c. de concentration** concentration camp; **c. d'internement** internment camp; **c. de loisirs** holiday camp; **c. de la mort** death camp; **c. de prisonniers** prison camp; *Mil* **c. volant** temporary camp

campage-caravanage [kɑ̃paʒkaravanaʒ] NM INV camping-caravanning

campagnard, -arde [kɑ̃paɲar, -ard] ADJ *(allure, accent etc)* country; *(simplicité)* rustic
N countryman, *f* countrywoman, *Péj* rustic

campagne [kɑ̃paɲ] NF 1 *(par opposition à la ville)* country(side); **à la c.** in the country; **en pleine c.** deep in the countryside; **vie à la c.** country life; **battre la c.** to scour *or* comb the countryside; *Fig* **son esprit bat la c.** his mind is wandering; **en rase c.** in (the) open country; **maison de c.** country house, place in the country 2 *Mil* **en c.** in the field, on active service; **artillerie de c.** field artillery; **tenue de c.** field dress, combat dress; **entrer** *ou* **se mettre en c.** to begin operations, to take the field; *Fig* to set to work **3** *Mil, Pol etc* campaign; *Mil* **faire c.** to fight a campaign; *Fig* **faire c.** *ou* **se mettre en c. pour qn/contre qch** to campaign on sb's behalf/against sth; **faire c. pour** *ou* **en faveur d'un candidat** to canvass *or* campaign for *or* on behalf of a candidate; *Pol* **entrer en c.** to start to campaign; **partir en c. contre le tabac** to launch an anti-smoking campaign; **c. d'affichage** poster campaign; **c. publicitaire** *ou* **de publicité** advertising *or* publicity campaign, publicity drive; **c. commerciale/de vente** sales campaign; **c. de marketing/de promotion** marketing/promotional campaign; **c. télévisée** television campaign; **c. de presse** press campaign; **c. électorale** election campaign; *Mktg* **c. de dénigrement** countermarketing campaign; **c. de calomnies** *ou* **de diffamation** smear campaign; *Mil* **la c. d'Égypte** the Egyptian campaign

> Attention: ne pas confondre **country** et **countryside** lorsqu'on traduit **campagne**. On utilise **countryside** lorsqu'il risque d'y avoir confusion avec **country** dans le sens de **pays**, ou bien lorsqu'on parle de paysages campagnards.

campagnol [kãpaɲɔl] **NM** vole

campanile [kãpanil] **NM** *Archit* campanile, bell tower

campanule [kãpanyl] **NF** campanula

campé [kãpe] **ADJ** **bien c.** *(personne)* well-built; **bien c. sur ses jambes** standing firmly on his feet; **portrait bien c.** well-sketched portrait; **récit bien c.** well-constructed story

campement [kãpmã] **NM 1** *(action)* camping **2** *(installation)* camp, encampment; *(lieu)* camping ground *or* place; **établir un c.** to camp, to pitch camp; **replier le c.** to strike camp; **matériel de c.** camping equipment

camper [kãpe] **VI 1** *(faire du camping)* to camp; *(dans le jardin etc)* to camp out **2** *(établir un campement)* to camp, to pitch camp, *Mil* to encamp; *Fig (dans un hôtel etc)* to camp out; *Fig* **ils campent ici depuis quinze jours** they've been camping out here for two weeks

VT *(troupes)* to encamp; *(planter) (histoire etc)* to put *or* place in context; **il a campé son chapeau sur sa tête** he stuck *or* planted his hat on his head; **un écrivain qui campe bien ses personnages** an author whose characters are well-rounded; *Théâtre* **c. un personnage** to play a part effectively

VPR se camper se c. devant qn to plant oneself in front of sb

campeur, -euse [kãpœr, -øz] **N** camper

camphre [kãfr] **NM** camphor; **essence de c.** camphor oil

camphré [kãfre] **ADJ** *(huile etc)* camphorated

camphrier [kãfrije] **NM** camphor tree

camping [kãpiŋ] **NM 1** *(activité)* camping; **faire du c.** to go camping; **c. libre** = non-site camping in suitable spots with permission if required; **c. à la ferme** farm camping; **c. sauvage** unauthorized camping **2** *(lieu)* camp(-ing) site; **c. aménagé** camp site (with facilities)

camping-car, *pl* **camping-cars NM** camper, *Br* Dormobile®, *Am* motor-home, *Am* recreational vehicle

camping-caravaning **NM INV** camping-caravanning

Camping-Gaz® **NM INV** camping stove

campos [kãpo] **NM** *Fam* **donner c. à qn** to give sb a day/an afternoon/*etc* off

campus [kãpys] **NM** campus; **vivre sur le c.** to live on campus VOIR GRAMMAIRE A14

camus [kamy] **ADJ 1** *(personne)* flat-nosed **2** *(nez)* flat

CAN NM *(abrév* **convertisseur analogue-numérique)** ADC

Canada [kanada] **NM** Canada; **être/aller au C.** to be in/to go to Canada

Canadair® [kanadɛr] **NM** fire-fighting plane

canadianisme [kanadjanism] **NM** *Ling* Canadianism

canadien, -ienne [kanadjɛ̃, -jɛn] **ADJ** Canadian

N C. Canadian; **C. français(e)** French Canadian **NF canadienne** *(veste)* sheepskin jacket; *(canoë)* Canadian canoe; *(tente)* ridge tent

canaille [kanaj] **NF** *(crapule)* scoundrel, rogue; **petite c.!** *(à un enfant)* you little devil *or* rascal!; *Vieilli* **la c.** the rabble, the riff-raff **ADJ** *(action)* low, crooked; *(chanson, paroles)* vulgar, coarse; **il a un petit air c.** he has a roguish air about him

canaillerie [kanajri] **NF 1** *(acte)* low(-down) *or* mean *or* dirty trick **2** *(d'une action)* lowness, crookedness; *(d'une chanson, d'une histoire etc)* vulgarity, coarseness

canal, -aux [kanal, -o] **NM 1** *Constr* canal; **c. d'irrigation** irrigation canal; **c. maritime** *ou* **de navigation** ship canal; **c. de dérivation** diversion *or* bypass channel; **le c. de Mozambique** the Mozambique Channel; **le c. de Suez** the Suez Canal; **la zone du c. (de Panama)** the Canal Zone

2 *(de rivière)* channel

3 *(conduite)* conduit, duct, pipe; **c. à air** *ou* **d'aérage** air passage *or* duct; **c. d'amenée** feeder; **c. de fuite** waste pipe; **c. de graissage** oil groove; **c. encreur** *(d'une imprimante)* ink channel

4 *Anat, Bot* canal, duct; **c. alimentaire** alimentary canal; **c. biliaire** bile duct; **c. lymphatique** lymph vessel

5 *Radio, TV, Ordinat* channel; *Can TV (chaîne)* (TV) channel; **c. d'accès** access channel; *Radio* **c. de fréquence à large bande** wide-band frequency channel; **c. IRC** IRC channel; *TV* **c. mosaïque** multi-screen channel; *TV* **C. Plus** = French pay television channel; **c. de télévision** television channel; **c. vidéo** video channel

6 *Fig (moyen)* channel; **par le c. de la poste** through the post

7 *Écon, Mktg* channel; **c. de distribution** distribution channel; **c. de distribution court** one-level channel; **c. de distribution long** two-/three-level marketing channel; **c. de communication** promotional *or* communications channel; **c. de communication commerciale** marketing communications channel

> ### Canal+
> Canal+, France's first private television channel, was established in 1982 and started broadcasting in 1984. It broadcasts programmes that have to be unscrambled using a special decoding unit, although for part of the day its programmes can be seen without this device. Canal+ also plays a prominent role in funding international films.

canalisable [kanalizabl] **ADJ** **eau c.** water which can be channelled *or* canalized; *Fig* **une énergie difficilement c.** energy which is difficult to channel *or* direct

canalisation [kanalizasjɔ̃] **NF 1** *(de rivière etc)* canalization **2** *(conduite)* conduit, pipe; *(conduites)* (system of) pipes, piping; *Élec* wiring **3** *(pour pétrole etc)* pipeline **4** *Ordinat* **c. des commandes** command piping

canaliser [kanalize] **VT 1** *(région, rivière etc)*

to canalize **2** *(ressources)* to channel, to concentrate **3** *(trafic, foule etc)* to direct

cananéen, -enne [kananeɛ̃, -ɛn] *Bible* **ADJ** Canaanite

NM *Ling* Canaanite **N C.** Canaanite

canapé [kanape] **NM 1** *(meuble)* sofa, couch, settee; **c. deux places** two-seater sofa, *Am* loveseat; **c. trois places** three-seater sofa; **c. convertible** sofa bed, bed settee **2** *Culin* canapé

canapé-lit, *pl* **canapés-lits NM** sofa bed, bed settee

canaque [kanak] **ADJ** Kanak

N C. Kanak *(indigenous inhabitant of New Caledonia)*

canard [kanar] **NM 1** *(oiseau)* duck; *(mâle)* drake; **mare aux canards** duck pond; **chasse aux canards** duck shooting *or* hunting; *Fam* **mon petit c.** my pet, my darling; *Fam* **marcher comme un c.** to waddle; **marcher en c.** to walk with one's feet turned out VOIR GRAMMAIRE A12 **2** *Fam (fausse nouvelle)* false report, *Lit* canard **3** *Fam (journal)* rag **4** *(morceau de sucre)* = sugar lump dipped in coffee, brandy etc **5** *Mus* false note **6** *Can (bouilloire)* kettle

► **c. de Barbarie** Muscovy duck; *Culin* **c. laqué** Peking duck; *Culin* **c. à l'orange** duck à l'orange; **c. sauvage** wild duck; **c. siffleur** wi(d)geon

canardeau, -eaux [kanardo] **NM** duckling

canarder [kanarde] **VI 1** *(de navire)* to pitch **2** *Mus Fam* to play a false note; *(en chantant)* to sing a false note

VT *Fam* to snipe at, to take pot shots at; **se faire c. à coup de boules de neige** to be pelted with snowballs; *Fig* **il s'est fait c. de questions** he was bombarded with questions

canardière [kanardjɛr] **NF 1** *(mare)* duck pond **2** *(lieu) (pour la chasse aux canards)* screen **3** *(fusil)* duck gun, punt gun

canari [kanari] **NM** canary **ADJ INV (jaune) c.** canary yellow

Canaries [kanari] **NFPL les (îles) C.** the Canary Islands, the Canaries

canasson [kanasɔ̃] **NM** *Arg (cheval)* nag

canasta [kanasta] **NF** *Cartes* canasta; **jouer à la c.** to play canasta

cancale [kãkal] **NF** Cancale oyster

cancan [kãkã] **NM 1** *Fam (racontar)* (piece of) gossip; **cancans** tittle-tattle, gossip; **dire** *ou* **faire des cancans** to gossip, to tittle-tattle, to talk (**sur** about) **2** *(danse)* cancan; **danser le c.** to do *or* dance the cancan

cancaner [kãkane] **VI 1** *Fam (médire)* to gossip, to tittle-tattle, to talk (**sur** about) **2** *(d'un canard)* to quack

cancanier, -ière [kãkanje, -jɛr] *Fam* **ADJ** gossipy, fond of tittle-tattle

N gossip, scandalmonger

cancer [kãsɛr] **NM 1** *Méd* cancer; **c. du poumon/du sein** lung/breast cancer, cancer of the lung/breast; **c. de la peau** skin cancer; **avoir un c.** to have cancer; **avoir un c. à** *ou* **de l'estomac/au** *ou* **du poumon** to have stomach/lung cancer; **mourir d'un c.** to die of cancer; *Fig* **le chômage est le c. du monde moderne** unemployment is the cancer of the modern world **2** *Astron, Astrol* **le C.** Cancer, the Crab; **être (du signe du) C.** to be (a) Cancer *or* Cancerian **3** *Géog* **le tropique du C.** the tropic of Cancer

cancéreux, -euse [kãserø, -øz] **ADJ** *(tumeur etc)* cancerous

N cancer victim *or* sufferer; **les c. en phase terminale** people with terminal cancer, people who are terminally ill with cancer

cancériforme [kãseriform] **ADJ** *Méd* cancriform, cancroid wrong **2** *Fam (travailler)* **ça carbure ici** everyone here's working like mad; **qu'est-ce qu'on a carburé hier!** we worked like mad yesterday! **3** *(fonctionner à)* **il carbure au whisky** whisky keeps him going

carcajou [karkaʒu] NM wolverine, *Am* carcajou

carcan [karkɑ̃] NM *Hist* iron collar; *Fig (contrainte)* yoke, restraint; **le c. des horaires** scheduling constraints

carcasse [karkas] NF **1** *(pour la boucherie)* carcass; *Fam (de personne vivante)* body; *Fam* **promener sa c.** to walk **2** *(de parapluie, capote de voiture, abat-jour etc)* frame(-work); *(de maison, bateau)* shell, skeleton; *(de moteur électrique)* carcass; *(de pneu)* casing, carcass, frame; *(caisse)* bodyshell; **c. diagonale** *(d'un pneu)* diagonal-ply carcass; **c. radiale** *(d'un pneu)* radial-ply carcass; **à c. radiale** *(pneu)* radial-ply

carcéral, -ale, -aux, -ales [karseral, -o] ADJ prison life; **vie carcérale** prison life

carcinogène [karsinoʒɛn] ADJ *Méd* carcinogenic

carcinologie [karsinɔlɔʒi] NF *Méd* oncology, study of cancer

carcinome [karsinom] NM *Méd* carcinoma

cardage [kardaʒ] NM *Tex* **1** *(de la laine etc)* carding, combing **2** *(de tissu)* teaselling

cardan [kardɑ̃] NM *Aut* **c., joint de C.** universal joint, Cardan joint

carde [kard] NF **1** *Culin* chard **2** *Tex* card, carding brush; *(tambour)* teasel

carder [karde] VT *Tex* **1** *(laine etc)* to card **2** *(tissu)* to teasel

cardeur, -euse [kardœr, -øz] *Tex* N carder **NF cardeuse** *(machine)* carding machine, carder

cardiaque [kardjak] ADJ *(nerfs, murmure etc)* cardiac; **crise c.** heart attack; **être c.** to have heart trouble *or* a weak heart **N** person with heart disease

cardigan [kardigɑ̃] NM cardigan

cardinal, -ale, -aux, -ales [kardinal, -o] ADJ *(point, nombre, vertu)* cardinal SEE GRAMMAR A76; B58

NM **1** *Cathol* cardinal **2** *Orn* cardinal (bird)

cardinalat [kardinala] NM *Cathol* cardinalship

cardinalice [kardinalis] ADJ *Cathol* of a cardinal; **revêtir la pourpre c.** to don the scarlet; **élever qn à la dignité c.** to make sb a cardinal

cardiogramme [kardjogram] NM *Méd* cardiogram

cardiographe [kardjograf] NM *Méd* cardiograph

cardiographie [kardjografi] NF *Méd* cardiography

cardiologie [kardjolɔʒi] NF *Méd* cardiology

cardiologue [kardjolɔg] N *Méd* cardiologist, heart specialist; **chirurgien c.** heart surgeon

cardiorespiratoire [kardjorɛspiratwar] ADJ *Méd* cardiorespiratory

cardio-training, *pl* **cardio-trainings** [kardjotrɛniŋ] NM cardiovascular fitness training

cardio-vasculaire [kardjovaskyler] ADJ *Anat, Méd* cardiovascular; *Méd* **accident c.** cardiovascular accident, *Fam* heart stroke

cardite [kardit] NF *Méd* carditis

cardon [kardɔ̃] NM *Bot, Culin* cardoon

carême [karɛm] NM **1** *(période)* Lent **2** *(jeûne)* (Lenten) fast(ing); **faire (son) c.** to keep Lent, to fast; *Fig* **face de c.** dismal face **3** *Litt (sermons)* (course of) Lenten sermons

carême-prenant, *pl* **carêmes-prenants** NM *Arch* Shrovetide

carénage [karenaʒ] NM **1** *Naut (de bateau)* careening, careenage; *(lieu)* careenage **2** *Aviat, Aut* streamlining

carence [karɑ̃s] NF **1** *Méd* deficiency (**de** in, of); **c. en vitamine E** deficiency in vitamin E, vitamin E deficiency; **maladie de** *ou* **par c.** deficiency disease; **c. alimentaire** nutritional deficiency; **c. affective** emotional deprivation; *Fig* **c. en personnel** staff shortage, shortage of staff **2** *(insuffisance)* shirking of one's obligations; **la c. du père** *(dans l'éducation de son enfant)* the father's non-participation **3** *Jur* insolvency

carencé [karɑ̃se] ADJ *Psy* emotionally deprived

carène [karɛn] NF *(de navire)* bottom, (underwater) hull; **abattre un navire en c.** to careen a ship

caréner [karene] VT (**je carène; je carénerai**) **1** *Naut* to careen **2** *Aviat, Aut* to streamline

carentiel, -ielle [karɑ̃sjɛl] ADJ **maladie carentielle** deficiency disease

caressant [karɛsɑ̃] ADJ *(regard, voix)* tender; *(vent)* soft, gentle; *(enfant)* affectionate; **d'une voix caressante** tenderly, affectionately

caresse [karɛs] NF **1** *(d'affection)* caress; **faire des caresses à** *(personne)* to caress; *(animal)* to stroke; *Litt* **la c. du soleil** the sun's caress **2** *Vieilli (flatterie)* flattery

caresser [karese] VT **1** *(par affection) (personne)* to caress; *(animal)* to stroke; **c. qn du regard** to look affectionately *or* tenderly at sb **2** *(espoir, rêve)* to cherish; *(idée)* to toy with; **c. un projet** to nurture a project **3** *Vieilli (flatter)* to flatter; **cette idée caresse son amour-propre** the idea flatters his self-esteem

car-ferry, *pl* **car-ferrys** NM car ferry

cargaison [kargɛzɔ̃] NF **1** *(marchandises)* cargo, freight; **c. de charbon/de marchandises** cargo of coal/merchandise; **c. en vrac** bulk cargo; **c. flottante** cargo afloat; **c. mixte** mixed cargo VOIR GRAMMAIRE A12 **2** *Fam (de passagers, cadeaux etc)* load (**de** of); **toute une c. d'histoires belges** a whole load *or* repertoire of Belgian jokes; **j'avais préparé toute une c. d'excuses** I had all sorts of *or* a whole load of excuses prepared

cargo [kargo] NM *Naut* cargo boat, freighter; **c. mixte** cargo and passenger vessel

> Il faut noter que le nom anglais **cargo** est un faux ami. Il signifie **cargaison**.

cargue [karg] NF *Naut (de voile)* brail

carguer [karge] VT *Naut (voile)* to take in, to brail (up)

cariant [karjɑ̃] ADJ **substance cariante** substance that causes tooth decay

cariatide [karjatid] NF *Archit* caryatid

caribou [karibu] NM *Zool* caribou

caricatural, -ale, -aux, -ales [karikatyral, -o] ADJ *(récit, description etc)* caricatured

caricature [karikatyr] NF *(dessin, description etc)* caricature; **le film est une c. de la vie ouvrière** the film is a caricature of working-class life; *Fam* **quelle c. que cette femme!** what a fright that woman is!

caricaturer [karikatyre] VT to caricature

caricaturiste [karikatyrist] N caricaturist

carie [kari] NF **1** *Méd (d'os)* caries, decay; **c. dentaire** tooth decay, *Spéc* dental caries; **avoir une c.** to have a tooth that needs filling **2** *(d'arbres)* blight; *(de céréales)* smut, bunt

carié [karje] ADJ *Méd (dent)* decayed, bad

carier [karje] *Méd* VT to rot, to decay **VPR se carier** to rot, to decay

carillon [karijɔ̃] NM *(sonnerie)* chime(s), *Litt* carillon; *(ensemble de cloches)* peal of bells; *(de porte)* (door) chime(s); *Mus* tubular bells, chimes; **(horloge à) c.** chiming clock

carillonnement [karijɔnmɑ̃] NM *(de cloches)* chiming, ringing

carillonner [karijɔne] VI *(faire sonner les cloches)* to ring the bells; *(des cloches)* to chime, to ring; **c. à la porte** to ring the (door) bell loudly **VT** *(air)* to chime; *(fête religieuse)* to announce with a peal of bells; *Fig* **c. la nouvelle** to spread the news far and wide, to tell the news to all and sundry; **fête carillonnée** high festival

carillonneur, -euse [karijɔnœr, -øz] N bellringer

cariste [karist] N *Tech* fork-lift truck driver

caritatif, -ive [karitatif, -iv] ADJ charitable; **association caritative** charitable organization, charity

carlin [karlɛ̃] NM *(chien)* pug

carlingue [karlɛ̃g] NF **1** *Naut* ke(e)lson **2** *Aviat* cabin

carliste [karlist] N *Hist* Carlist

carmagnole [karmaɲɔl] NF *Hist* **1** *(veste)* jacket *(worn by Revolutionaries in 1793)* **2** *Mus (ronde)* carmagnole

carme [karm] NM *Rel* Carmelite (friar), White Friar

Carmel [karmɛl] NM **1** *Rel* **le C.** the Carmelite order **2** *(couvent) (de carmes)* Carmelite monastery; *(de carmélites)* Carmelite convent

carmélite [karmelit] NF *Rel* Carmelite (nun)

carmin [karmɛ̃] ADJ INV carmine, crimson **NM** carmine

carminé [karmine] ADJ carmine, crimson

carnage [karnaʒ] NM carnage, slaughter; *Fig* **s'il n'arrête pas, je vais faire un c.** if he doesn't stop, I'll kill him

carnassier, -ière [karnasje, -jer] ADJ *(animal)* carnivorous, flesh-eating; *Zool (dent)* carnassial; *Fig (cruel) (regard, sourire)* predatory **NM** carnivore; **les carnassiers** carnivores, *Spéc* the Carnivora **NF carnassière 1** *Zool* carnassial (tooth) **2** *(sac)* game bag

carnation [karnasjɔ̃] NF **1** *(teint)* complexion; **c. de blonde** fair skin *or* complexion **2** *Beaux-Arts* flesh tint, *Spéc* carnation

carnaval, -als [karnaval] NM *(fête)* carnival; **un masque de c.** a carnival mask; **Sa Majesté C.** King Carnival

carnavalesque [karnavalɛsk] ADJ **tenue c.** carnival costume; *Péj* **un accoutrement c.** a ridiculous get-up

carne [karn] NF **1** *Fam (viande)* tough meat; *(vieux cheval)* old nag **2** *Arg* **quelle c.!** *(cet homme)* what a bastard!; *(cette femme)* what a bitch *or* cow!

carné [karne] ADJ **1** *(rose)* flesh-coloured *or Am* -colored **2** **régime c.** meat diet

carneau, -eaux [karno] NM *Tech* flue

carnet [karnɛ] NM *(cahier)* notebook
▸▸*Scol* **c. (de notes)** = (school) report; **c. d'adresses** address book; *(de publipostage)* address list; *Com* **c. ATA** ATA carnet; *Vieilli* **c. de bal** dance card; **c. blanc** marriages column; *Aut* **c. de bord** logbook, memorandum; **c. de chèques** cheque *or Am* check book; *Com* **c. de commandes** order book; *Com* **c. communautaire** Community carnet; *Aut* **c. de constat amiable** = set of insurance documents to be completed at scene of accident; *Scol* **c. de correspondance** = school report book; *Aut* **c. d'entretien** *(d'une voiture)* servicing booklet; *Belg, Suisse (livret d'épargne)* **c. d'épargne** savings account; *Journ* **c. mondain** society column; *Com* **c. de passage en douanes** carnet; **c. rose** births

column; **c. de route** logbook; **c. de santé** health record; **c. à souche(s)** counterfoil book; **c. de tickets** book of tickets; **c. de timbres** book of stamps; *Aviat* **c. de vol** log(-book); **c. de voyage** travel documents

carnier [karnje] NM game bag

carnivore [karnivɔr] *Zool* ADJ *(animal)* carnivorous, flesh-eating
NM carnivore; **les carnivores** carnivores, *Spéc* the Carnivora

carnotzet [karnotsɛt] NM *Suisse* = room set aside for drinking with friends, usually in a cellar

carolingien, -ienne [karɔlɛ̃ʒjɛ̃, -jɛn] *Hist* ADJ Carolingian, Carlovingian
N **C.** Carolingian, Carlovingian

caroncule [karɔ̃kyl] NF *Anat, Bot, Zool* caruncle; *(de dindon)* wattle

carotène [karɔtɛn] NM carotene

carotide [karɔtid] ADJ *(artère)* carotid

carottage [karɔtaʒ] NM **1** *Fam (vol)* pinching, *Br* nicking; *(escroquerie)* swindling, diddling **2** *Min* taking of cores

carotte [karɔt] NF **1** *(plante)* carrot; *Fam* **Poil de c.** Ginger; *Fam* **les carottes sont cuites** you've/he's/*etc* cooked your/his/*etc* goose, you're/he's/*etc* done for; *Suisse* **c. rouge** beetroot **2** *(promesse)* carrot; **la c. et le bâton** the carrot and stick **3** *Min* core (sample) **4** *(de tabac)* plug; *(enseigne)* tobacconist's sign **5** *Fam* **tirer une c. à qn** to swindle *or* diddle sb **6** *Tennis Fam* drop shot
ADJ INV **cheveux (rouge) c.** ginger *or* red *or Fam* carroty hair

carotter [karɔte] VT **1** *Fam (voler) (chose)* to pinch, *Br* to nick; *(escroquer) (personne)* to swindle, to diddle, *Br* to do; **c. une permission/une signature** to wangle leave/a signature **2** *Min* to take a core (sample) of

carotteur, -euse[1] [karɔtœr, -øz], **carottier, -ière** [karɔtje, -jer] N *Fam (voleur)* thief; *(escroc)* swindler

carotteuse[2] NF *Min* core sampler

caroube [karub] NF *Bot* carob (bean)

caroubier [karubje] NM *Bot* carob (tree)

carpaccio [karpatʃjo] NM *Culin* carpaccio

Carpates [karpat] NFPL **les C.** the Carpathian Mountains, the Carpathians

carpe[1] [karp] NM *Anat* carpus

carpe[2] NF *(poisson)* carp; **faire des yeux de c.** to make sheep's eyes; **être muet comme une c.** *(discret)* to be as silent as the grave; **tu es resté muet comme une c. toute la soirée** you didn't open your mouth all evening; **bâiller comme une c.** to yawn one's head off

carpeau, -eaux [karpo] NM *(poisson)* young carp

carpette [karpɛt] NF *(tapis)* rug; *Fam Péj* **s'aplatir comme une c.** to behave like a doormat; *Fam Péj* **c'est une vraie c.** he's a complete doormat

Il faut noter que le nom anglais **carpet** est un faux ami. Il signifie **moquette**.

carpiculture [karpikyltyr] NF carp farming

carpien, -ienne [karpjɛ̃, -jɛn] ADJ *Anat (os etc)* carpal

carquois [karkwa] NM quiver; *Litt* **il a vidé son c.** he has shot his bolt

carrare [karar] NM Carrara marble

carre [kar] NF *(de patin, ski)* edge; *(de livre etc)* corner; *(de planche etc)* cross section; *Ski* **lâcher les carres** to flatten *or* take the edge off the skis

carré, -ée [kare] ADJ **1** *(figure, jardin etc)* square; *(épaules)* square, broad; *Math* **nombre c.** square number; **dix mètres carrés** ten square metres; **partie carrée** ≃ wife-swapping party **2** *(tranché) (réponse)* plain,

straightforward, blunt; *(personne)* straightforward; **être c. en affaires** to be straightforward in one's business dealings
NM **1** *(figure)* square; *Can (place)* (public) square; **c. de papier** slip of paper; **c. de soie** silk square; **c. de choux** cabbage patch; *Naut* **c. (des officiers)** wardroom; *Mil* **former le c.** to get into square formation; *Cartes* **c. de valets** four jacks; **avoir une coupe au c.** *ou* **un c.** to have one's hair in a bob; *Fam* **s'il continue, je vais lui faire une tête au c.!** if he goes on like that, I'm going to punch his face in! **2** *Math (d'un nombre)* square; **élever au c.** to square; *Math* **le c. de six, six au c.** six squared
SEE GRAMMAR B59
3 *Culin* **c. d'agneau** rack of lamb; **c. de l'Est** = type of soft cheese **4** *(élève)* = second-year student *(in certain Grandes Écoles)*
NF **carrée 1** *Hist, Mus* breve **2** *Fam (chambre)* room
▸▸ *Rail* **c. Jeunes** = reduced-rate rail travel card for young people within France

carreau, -eaux [karo] NM **1** *(motif)* square; *(sur du tissu)* check; *(tissu)* check(ed) material; *Beaux-Arts* **mettre un croquis au c.** to square up a sketch **2** *(de céramique etc)* tile; *(dalle)* flag(stone) **3** *(de fenêtre)* (window) pane; **laveur de carreaux** window cleaner *or Am* washer; **regarder aux carreaux** to look in at the window; **un c. cassé** a broken window **4** *Fam* **carreaux** *(lunettes)* specs, glasses **5** *(sol)* (tiled) floor; **laver le c.** to wash the floor; **coucher qn sur le c.** to lay sb out; **rester sur le c.** *(être tué)* to be killed on the spot; *(être blessé)* to be critically injured; *(être éliminé)* to be out of the running; *(d'un boxeur)* not to get up, to stay on the canvas or floor; *Anciennement* **le c. des Halles** *(à Paris)* the (floor of the) market **6** *Cartes* diamond; *Fig* **se tenir à c.** to keep a low profile
▸▸ *Min* **c. de mine** pit head

carreauté [karote] ADJ *Can (chemise)* check(ed)

carrefour [karfur] NM **1** *(de route)* crossroads; **tête de c.** T-junction; **c. décalé** staggered junction; **c. ferroviaire** railway junction; *Fig* **être à un c.** to be at a crossroads; **un c. de nouvelles idées/de tendances** a place for the exchange of new ideas/trends VOIR GRAMMAIRE A13 **2** *(réunion)* forum, symposium

carrelage [karlaʒ] NM **1** *(action)* tiling **2** *(carreaux)* tiling, tiles; *(sol)* (tiled) floor; *(mur)* tiled wall

carreler [karle] VT (**je carrelle, n. carrelons; je carrellerai**) **1** *(mettre des carreaux sur) (sol, murs)* to tile **2** *(tracer des carreaux sur) (feuille de papier etc)* to draw squares on, to square

carrelet [karlɛ] NM **1** *(règle)* square ruler **2** *(aiguille)* large needle **3** *Pêche* square dipping net **4** *(poisson)* plaice

carreleur [karlœr] NM tiler, tile layer; *(d'une cour)* paver

carrément [karemɑ̃] ADV **1** *Géom* square(-ly); **pièce coupée c.** square-cut piece **2** *Fam* **il y est allé c.** he got straight to the point, he didn't beat about the bush, he didn't mess about; **je lui ai dit c. ce que je pensais** I told him straight (out) *or* bluntly *or* in no uncertain terms what I thought; **tu as c. tort** you're simply wrong, you're wrong and that's that

carrer [kare] VT *(planche)*, *Math (nombre etc)* to square
VPR **se carrer** to settle (down) (**dans un fauteuil** in an armchair)

carrier [karje] NM *(ouvrier)* quarryman, quarrier; **(maître) c.** quarry master

carrière[1] [karjer] NF **1** *(professionnelle etc)*

career; **faire c.** to make a career for oneself; **suivre une c.** *ou* **faire c. dans le commerce** to make a career in business; **en début/fin de c.** at the start/end of one's career; **c. politique/des armes** political/military career; **militaire de c.** regular (soldier); **diplomate de c.** professional *or* career diplomat; **elle est de la c.** she is in the diplomatic service **2** **donner c. à un cheval** to give free rein to a horse; *Fig* **donner (libre) c. à son imagination** to give free rein *or* free play *or* full scope to one's imagination; **donner c. à ses sentiments, se donner c.** to let oneself go, to give free expression to one's feelings

carrière[2] NF *(lieu)* quarry; **c. à ciel ouvert** open quarry

carriérisme [karjerism] NM *Péj* careerism

carriériste [karjerist] ADJ, N *Péj* careerist

carriole [karjɔl] NF **1** *(petite charrette)* light cart **2** *Can* sleigh, sled

carrossable [karɔsabl] ADJ *(chemin, route)* suitable for motor vehicles

carrossage [karɔsaʒ] NM *Aut* rake, camber

carrosse [karɔs] NM (horse-drawn) coach; **c. d'apparat** state coach; *Fam* **rouler c.** to live in great style; *Can* **c. de bébé** pram, *Am* baby carriage

carrosser [karɔse] VT *Aut (voiture etc)* to fit the body to; *Arg* **elle est bien carrossée** she's got curves in all the right places

carrosserie [karɔsri] NF *Aut* **1** *(construction)* coachbuilding **2** *(caisse) (de voiture etc)* body, coachwork, bodywork

carrossier [karɔsje] NM *Aut* coachbuilder

carroté [karɔte] ADJ *Can (chemise etc)* check(ed), *Am* checkered

carrousel [karuzɛl] NM **1** *Hist (tournoi)* tournament; *(lieu)* tiltyard; *Équitation* carousel; *(manège de chevaux de bois)* roundabout, *Am* carousel **2** *Fig (succession rapide)* **le c. des ministres** the ministerial merry-go-round **3** *(d'une aérogare)* carousel; **c. de livraison des bagages** baggage carousel **4** *Belg, Can, Suisse (manège)* merry-go round, carousel

carrure [karyr] NF **1** *(de personne)* build; *(de manteau)* width across the shoulders; **homme d'une belle c.** well-built man **2** *(de mâchoire etc)* broadness, squareness **3** *Fig* **elle est d'une grande c.** she's a very impressive woman; **il est d'une autre c. que ses concurrents** he is much more impressive than his competitors; **avoir la c. d'un cadre supérieur** to be senior management material

carry [kari] NM = **curry**

cartable [kartabl] NM school bag; *(à bretelles)* satchel

CARTE [kart] NF **1** *(géographique)* map; *Naut* chart; **dresser la c. d'une région** to map (out) an area
2 *(feuille de carton)* card; *Com* business card; *Cartes* (playing) card; **jeu de (52) cartes** pack *or Am* deck of cards; **laisser sa c. chez qn** *or* to leave one's card with sb; **avoir sa c. au parti** to be a card-carrying member of the party; **jouer aux cartes** to play cards; **une partie de cartes** a game of cards; **donner** *ou* **faire les cartes** to deal (the cards); *Fig* **donner c. blanche à qn** to give sb carte blanche *or* a free hand; **château de cartes** house of cards; **être balayé/s'écrouler comme un château de cartes** to be swept away/collapse like a house of cards; *Fig* **jouer cartes sur table** to put one's cards on the table; *Fig* **jouer la c. des libéraux** to play the liberal card *or* hand; *Fig* **jouer sa dernière c.** to play one's last card; **abattre ses cartes** to lay one's cards on the table; *Fig* **nous avons encore quelques bonnes cartes en main** we still have several cards up our sleeves; **c. maî-**

tresse *Cartes* master card; *Fig* trump card; *Fig* c'était la c. forcée it was Hobson's choice; *Fig* connaître le dessous des cartes to know the inside story; *Fig* brouiller les cartes to complicate matters, to confuse the issue; femme en c. registered prostitute

3 c. (de restaurant) menu; c. du jour today's menu, menu for the day; c. des vins wine list; manger à la c. to eat à la carte; horaires à la c. flexitime; nous vous proposons un vaste choix d'activités à la c. choose from a vast range of activities

4 *Ordinat* card; *(de clavier etc)* map

5 *Com (de boutons etc)* card; c. d'échantillons sample card

▸▸ c. d'abonnement *(pour la bibliothèque etc)* membership card *or* ticket; *(pour les transports, le théâtre etc)* season ticket; *Ordinat* c. accélérateur graphique graphics accelerator card; *Ordinat* c. accélératrice accelerator card; *Aviat* c. d'accès à bord boarding pass, embarkation card; c. accréditive charge card; c. d'adhérent membership card; c. d'affaires business card; *Ordinat* c. d'affichage display card; c. d'alimentation ration book; c. American Express® American Express®(card); c. Amex Amex (card); c. d'animation d'images vidéo video image animation card; c. d'anniversaire birthday card; *Ordinat* c. audio audio card; c. bancaire cash card, cheque card, banker's card; c. bancaire à puce banker's card; c. Bleue® = bank card with which purchases are debited directly from the customer's bank account; *Ordinat* c. bus bus board; c. de chemin de fer season ticket; c. du ciel astronomical map *or* chart; *Ordinat* c. à circuit imprimé *ou* de circuits imprimés printed circuit board, PCB; *Ordinat* c. à circuit(s) intégré(s) integrated circuit card, IC card; c. de circulation (rail/bus) pass; *Admin* c. de commerce trading licence; *Ordinat* c. de communication communication card; *Ordinat* c. de connexion connection card; *Ordinat* c. de contrôle control card; *Ordinat* c. contrôleur de disque disk controller card; c. de crédit credit card; c. de débarquement landing card; c. d'électeur voting card; *Aviat* c. d'embarquement boarding pass, embarkation card; *Ordinat* c. enfichable slot-in card; c. d'entrée pass (card); *Ordinat* c. d'E/S I/O card; c. d'état-major ≃ Ordnance Survey map, *Am* ≃ Geological Survey map; c. d'étudiant student card; c. Eurocard Mastercard® Mastercard®, Access® card; *Ordinat* c. d'extension expansion card *or* board; *Ordinat* c. d'extension mémoire memory expansion card *or* board; *Rail* c. famille nombreuse reduced-rate card for families with three or more children; c. fax fax card; c. de fidélité frequent user card, valued customer card; *Ordinat* c. fille daughterboard; *Biol* c. du génome humain map of the human genome; *Ordinat* c. graphique numérique digital graphics card; *Aut* c. grise ≃ (vehicle) registration document; c. d'identité identity card; c. d'identité bancaire bank card; *Ordinat* c. d'interface interface card; *Ordinat* c. interface réseau network interface card; c. internationale d'étudiant International Student Identity Card; *Rail* c. Inter-rail Inter-Rail Card; c. d'invitation invitation (card); *Rail* c. Jeunes = reduced-rate rail travel card for young people within France; c. à jouer (playing) card; c. de journaliste press card; c. de lecteur library *or* reader's ticket; *Ordinat* c. logique logic card; c. magnétique magnetic card; c. mécanographique punch card; *Ordinat* c. mémoire memory card; c. à mémoire smart card; *Ordinat* c. mère motherboard; c. météorologique meteorological *or* weather map *or* chart; *Ordinat* c. à microcircuit microcircuit card; *Ordinat* c. modem mo-

dem card; c. orange *(à Paris)* = combined monthly pass for the underground, bus and suburban train; c. de paiement payment card; *Tél* c. Pastel phone card *(use of which is debited to one's own phone number)*; *Mktg* c. perceptuelle de marques brand mapping; *Mktg* c. perceptuelle de produits product mapping; c. perforée punch card; *Ordinat* c. à piste magnétique magnetic stripe card; *Ordinat* c. de polices de caractères font card; c. postale (post)card; *Tél* c. à prépaiement phonecard *(with prepaid units)*; c. prépayée prepaid card; c. de presse press card; *Ordinat* c. principale main board; *Ordinat* c. processeur processor card; c. professionnelle professional certificate; c. à puce smart card; c. de réduction discount card; c. de représentant sales representative's official identity card; *Ordinat* c. réseau network card; *Ordinat* c. de réseau sans fil wireless network card; *Ordinat* c. RNIS ISDN card; c. routière road map; *Ordinat* c. SCSI SCSI card; c. de Sécurité sociale National Insurance Card; c. de séjour residence permit; *Ordinat* c. son *ou* sonore sound card; *Ordinat* c. système systems board; c. T reply-paid card; c. de télécopie fax card; c. de téléphone phonecard; c. de train railcard; *(abonnement, forfait)* rail pass; *Ordinat* c. unité centrale CPU board; *Rail* c. Vermeil ≃ Senior Citizen's railcard; *Aut* c. verte green card; *Ordinat* c. vidéo video card; *Ordinat* c. vidéo accélératrice video accelerator card; c. Visa® Visa® card; c. de visite (visiting *or Am* calling) card; *Ordinat* c. vocale voice card; c. de vœux greetings card

carte-adaptateur, *pl* **cartes-adaptateurs** NF *Ordinat* c. réseau network adaptor card

carte-clé, *pl* **cartes-clés** NF key card; c. électronique electronic key card

carte-guide, *pl* **cartes-guides** NF *(pour séparer des fiches)* file separator *or* divider

cartel [kartɛl] NM **1** *Écon* cartel, trust, combine; c. de l'acier/de la drogue steel/drug cartel; c. de production production cartel **2** *Pol* cartel, coalition **3** *(horloge)* wall clock

carte-lettre, *pl* **cartes-lettres** NF letter-card

cartellisation [kartelizasjɔ̃] NF *Écon* cartelization

carter [kartɛr] NM *(d'engrenages)* casing, housing; *(de mécanisme)* cover; *Aut (de vilebrequin)* crankcase; *(d'huile)* engine sump, oil sump; fond de c. sump

carte-réponse, *pl* **cartes-réponses** NF reply card *or* coupon

carterie [kartəri] NF *Com* card shop

cartésianisme [kartezjanism] NM *Phil* Cartesianism

cartésien, -ienne [kartezjɛ̃, -jɛn] ADJ, N *Phil, Math* Cartesian

carte-vue, *pl* **cartes-vues** [kart(ə)vy] NF *Belg* picture postcard

carthaginois, -oise [kartaʒinwa, -waz] *Hist* ADJ Carthaginian

N C. Carthaginian

cartilage [kartilaʒ] NM *Anat* cartilage; *(dans la viande)* gristle

cartilagineux, -euse [kartilaʒinø, -øz] ADJ *Anat* cartilaginous; *(viande)* gristly

cartographe [kartɔgraf] N cartographer

cartographie [kartɔgrafi] NF cartography; c. des gènes gene *or* genetic mapping

cartographier [kartɔgrafje] VT to chart, to make a map of

cartographique [kartɔgrafik] ADJ cartographic(al)

cartomancie [kartɔmɑ̃si] NF fortune telling (by cards), cartomancy

cartomancien, -ienne [kartɔmɑ̃sjɛ̃, -jɛn] N fortune teller *(who uses cards)*

carton [kartɔ̃] NM **1** *(matière)* cardboard; *(feuille, support)* piece of cardboard, (piece of) card; poupée/masque de c. cardboard doll/mask; *Fam* maison de c. jerry-built house; envoyer un c. to send (out) an invitation

2 *(boîte)* (cardboard) box, carton; *(dossier)* (cardboard) file; des cartons de déménagement cardboard boxes for moving (house); faire ses cartons to pack (up) one's things in cardboard boxes; le projet est resté dans les cartons the project never got off the ground; ça dort dans les cartons depuis des mois it's been shelved for months

3 *Beaux-Arts* cartoon, sketch

4 faire un c. *(au tir)* to fill a target; faire un c. *(obtenir un bon résultat)* to make a good score; *Scol Fam* se payer un c. to get a bad *or Fam* rotten mark

5 *Géog* inset (map)

▸▸ *TV* c. aide-mémoire cue card; c. bristol Bristol board; c. à chapeau(x) hatbox; c. de classement file box; c. à dessin portfolio; c. épais millboard; *TV* c. de générique title card; c. d'invitation invitation (card); *Ftbl* c. jaune yellow card; c. ondulé corrugated cardboard; *TV* cartons de prompteur prompt cards; *Ftbl* c. rouge red card; se prendre un c. rouge to get a *or* the red card; *TV* c. volant flip card

cartonnage [kartɔnaʒ] NM **1** *(objets en carton)* cardboard articles; *(fabrication)* making of cardboard articles **2** *(reliure) (action)* board binding; *(couverture)* paper boards; c. pleine toile cloth boards; c. souple limp boards

cartonner [kartɔne] VT *(livre)* to bind in boards, to case; livre cartonné hardback (book)

VI *Fam* to do very well

cartonnerie [kartɔnri] NF **1** *(usine)* cardboard factory **2** *(commerce)* cardboard trade

cartonneux, -euse [kartɔnø, -øz] ADJ like cardboard; neige cartonneuse snow with a crust on top; fromage c. cheese that's gone hard

cartonnier [kartɔnje] NM **1** *(fabricant)* cardboard manufacturer **2** *(meuble)* filing cabinet

carton-paille, *pl* **cartons-pailles** NM strawboard

carton-pâte, *pl* **cartons-pâtes** NM pasteboard; décor de c. cardboard scenery

cartoon [kartun] NM cartoon

cartouche [kartuʃ] NM **1** *Archit etc* cartouche; *(pour titre)* title **2** *Ordinat (sur plan)* box; c. de titre masthead

NF *(de fusil, d'explosif, de stylo, de lecteur de cassettes)* cartridge; *(de machine à écrire)*, *Phot* cartridge, cassette; *Mil etc* cent cartouches a hundred rounds (of ammunition)

▸▸ c. à blanc blank cartridge; c. de chasse sporting cartridge; c. de cigarettes carton of cigarettes; c. d'encre *(d'une imprimante etc)* ink cartridge; c. d'encre en poudre *(d'une imprimante)* toner cartridge; *Ordinat* c. de polices font cartridge; c. de rechange *(de stylo)* refill; *Ordinat* c. de stockage amovible removable storage cartridge; c. de toner toner cartridge; c. vidéo video cartridge

cartoucherie [kartuʃri] NF *(fabrique)* cartridge *or* ammunition factory; *(dépôt)* cartridge *or* ammunition store

cartouchière [kartuʃjɛr] NF *(sac)* cartridge pouch; *(ceinture)* cartridge belt

carvi [karvi] NM *(plante)* caraway; (graines de) c. caraway seeds

caryatide [karjatid] NF *Archit* caryatid

caryotype [karjotip] NM *Biol* karyotype

CAS [kɑ] NM **1** *(situation)* case, situation; *(événement)* occurrence; *Jur, Méd* case; **c. imprévu** unforeseen event; **c. général/particulier** general/particular case; **c. urgent** emergency *or* urgent case; **c'était un c. de légitime défense** it was self-defence; **c. litigieux** dispute; **dans le premier c.** in the first instance; **c'est le c. de le dire** you can say that again; **en pareil c.** in a similar situation, in similar circumstances; **que faire dans un c. de ce genre?** what can one do in a case *or* situation like this?; **c. de rougeole** case of measles; **ce malade est un c. désespéré** this patient is a hopeless case; *Fig* **c'est un c.!** he is a case!; **avez-vous envisagé tous les c.?** have you considered all possibilities *or* eventualities?; **il parle plusieurs langues étrangères, mais ce n'est pas mon c.** he speaks several foreign languages, but I don't; **dans son c., on peut faire une exception** an exception can be made in his case; **dans le c. qui nous occupe** in the case that we are concerned with; **si tel est votre c.** if that's your case
2 faire (grand) c. de qn/qch to value sb/sth (highly), to have a high opinion of sb/sth, to set great store by sb/sth; **faire peu de c. de qch** to have a low opinion of sth, to set little store by sth; **je ne fais pas grand c. de votre ami** I don't think much of your friend; **ne faire aucun c. de qch** to take no notice of sth, to pay no attention to sth
3 *Gram* case; **au c. nominatif** in the nominative (case)
4 *(locutions)* **en** *ou* **dans ce c.** in that case, if that's the case, under those circumstances; **en aucun c.** under no circumstances, on no account, not on any account; **en tout c., dans tous les c.** in any case, anyway, in any event; **dans tous les c., il est trop tard** it's too late now anyway *or* anyhow; **dans ce c.-là, auquel c.** in that case; **le c. échéant** if necessary, if need be, should the need arise; **selon le c.** as the case may be; **en c. de nécessité** if need be, if necessary; **en c. de pluie/décès/d'absence** in the event of rain/death/absence; **en c. d'accident** in the event of an accident; **en c. d'urgence** in an emergency; **en c. de besoin, tu peux m'appeler à n'importe quelle heure** if need be, you can call me at any time; **j'ai pris un pull supplémentaire en c. de besoin** I took an extra sweater just in case; **au c. où** *ou* **dans le c. où il viendrait** in case he comes, if he should come; **au c. où ce serait exact** should it prove correct; *Fam* **je te le laisse au c. où** I'll leave it for you just in case
▸▸ **c. de conscience** matter of conscience; **c. de divorce** divorce case; *(raisons)* grounds for divorce; **c. d'école** textbook case; **c. d'espèce** special case; **c. de figure** scenario; **c. limite** borderline case; **c. social** person with social problems

casanier, -ière [kazanje, -jɛr] ADJ home-loving, *Péj* stay-at-home
N homebody, *Péj* stay-at-home

casaque [kazak] NF *(de jockey)* blouse, jacket; *Fig* **tourner c.** *(partir)* to turn tail, to flee; *(changer d'opinion)* to turn one's coat

casbah [kazba] NF **1** casbah, kasbah **2** *Fam (maison)* place, pad

cascade [kaskad] NF **1** *(chute d'eau)* cascade, waterfall; *Fig (de boucles)* cascade; **c. de glace** ice fall; *Fig* **cascades de rires** peals of laughter; **ils ont connu des catastrophes en c.** they experienced a whole string *or* chain of disasters; *Élec* **montage en c.** connection in series; *Ordinat* **menus en c.** pull-down menus **2** *Cin* stunt; **faire de la c.** to do stunts

cascader [kaskade] VI *Litt (tomber)* to cascade **2** *Fam Vieilli (faire la noce)* to lead a wild life

cascadeur, -euse [kaskadœr, -øz] ADJ *Fam*

Vieilli (vie etc) wild, loose
N **1** *Cin* stuntman, f stuntwoman; *(de cirque)* acrobat **2** *Fam Vieilli (noceur)* person of disorderly habits

cascher [kaʃɛr] ADJ INV = **kascher**

case [kaz] NF **1** *(hutte)* hut, cabin
2 *(de tiroir etc)* compartment, division; *(pour le courrier)* pigeonhole; *(de formulaire)* box; *(de grille de mots croisés, damier)* square; **cocher la bonne c.** tick the appropriate box; *Fam* **il lui manque une c., il a une c. vide** *ou* **une c. en moins** he's got a screw loose
3 *Radio, TV* slot
4 *Ordinat* button; *(en forme de boîte)* box; **c. d'aide** help button; **c. 'annuler'** cancel button; **c. à cocher** check box; **c. de commande** command button; **c. de contrôle de taille** *ou* **de dimensionnement** size box; **c. de fermeture** close box; **c. 'marche'** walk button; **c. d'option** check box, option button; **c. de pointage** check box; **c. de saisie** input box; **c. zoom** zoom box
5 *Suisse* **c. postale** postbox
▸▸ **c. départ** *(dans les jeux)* start; *Fig* **retour à la c. départ** back to square one

caséeux, -euse [kazeø, -øz] ADJ caseous

caséine [kazein] NF *Chimie* casein

casemate [kazmat] NF *Mil* blockhouse, pillbox

caser [kaze] VT **1** *(placer)* to put; **je ne sais pas où c. tous mes livres** I don't know where to put all my books; **j'ai réussi à tout c. dans ma chambre** I managed to find space for everything in *or* to get everything into my room; **c. des papiers** to file papers (away) **2** *Fam (établir dans une situation)* to fix up with a job, to find a job for; **elle est bien casée** she's got a good job **3** *Fam (marier)* **elle a trois filles à c.** she has three daughters to marry off *or* to find husbands for
VPR **se caser** *Fam (se marier)* to (get married and) settle down; *(trouver un emploi)* to get oneself a job, to find a job

caserne [kazɛrn] NF *Mil, Fig, Fam Péj* barracks; **quand j'étais à la c.** when I was in the army; **plaisanteries de c.** locker room jokes, coarse jokes; **c. de pompiers** fire station **VOIR GRAMMAIRE A13**

casernement [kazɛrnəmɑ̃] NM *Mil* **1** *(de troupes)* quartering in barracks, barracking **2** *(lieu)* barrack block

caserner [kazɛrne] VT *Mil (troupes)* to quarter in barracks, to barrack

cash [kaʃ] ADV *Fam* cash; **payer c.** to pay cash (down)

cash and carry [kaʃɛndkari] *Com* NM INV cash-and-carry (store)
ADJ INV cash-and-carry

cash-flow, *pl* **cash-flows** [kaʃflo] NM *Com* cash flow

casier [kazje] NM **1** *(pour le courrier)* *(meuble)* (set of) pigeonholes; *(compartiment)* pigeonhole; *(pour ses vêtements etc)* locker; *(à tiroirs)* filing cabinet, *Am* file cabinet; **c. à bagages** luggage locker; **c. à clés et à courrier** key and mail rack; **c. à skis** ski rack; **c. à bouteilles** bottle rack; **c. à disques** record rack; **c. à musique** music cabinet **2** *Jur* **avoir un c.** to have a record **3** *Pêche* pot; **relever ses casiers** to go and lift one's pots
▸▸ **c. judiciaire** police *or* criminal record; **avoir un c. judiciaire** to have a record; **avoir un c. judiciaire vierge** to have a clean record

casino [kazino] NM casino

casoar [kazɔar] NM **1** *(oiseau)* cassowary **2** *(plumet)* plume *(worn by cadets of Saint-Cyr)*

Caspienne [kaspjɛn] NF **la mer C.** the Caspian Sea

casque [kask] NM **1** *(de soldat, pompier etc)* helmet; *(de motocycliste)* (crash) helmet; **le**

port du c. est obligatoire helmets must be worn **2** *Radio etc* headphones, headset, earphones; **écouter un disque au c.** to listen to a record on (one's) headphones **3** *Orn* casque; *Bot* helmet **4** *(de salon de coiffure)* (hair) drier
▸▸ **c. colonial** pith helmet, topee; *Radio* **c. à écouteurs** headphones, headset, earphones; **c. intégral** crash helmet *(full-faced)*; *TV, Radio* **c. interphone** headphone talkback; **Casques blancs** United Nations military observers; **Casques bleus** Blue Berets, United Nations peacekeeping force

casqué [kaske] ADJ helmeted

casquer [kaske] VI *Arg (payer)* to fork out, to shell out

casquette [kaskɛt] NF *(chapeau)* cap; *Fig* **avoir plusieurs casquettes** *(responsabilités)* to wear several hats; *Fig Fam* **avoir la c. (de plomb)** to be hungover, to have a hangover

cassable [kasabl] ADJ breakable

Cassandre [kasɑ̃dr] NF Cassandra
N *Fig* prophet of doom, Cassandra; **jouer les C.** to be a Cassandra *or* a prophet of doom and gloom, to prophesy doom and gloom

cassant [kasɑ̃] ADJ **1** *(fragile)* fragile; *(cheveux)* brittle; **c. comme du verre** as fragile as glass **2** *Fig (brusque)* *(personne, ton etc)* abrupt, brusque **3** *Arg (fatigant)* **c'est pas trop c.** it's not (exactly) back-breaking work

cassate [kasat] NF *Culin (glace)* cassata

cassation [kasasjɔ̃] NF **1** *Jur (de jugement, testament etc)* annulment, *Spéc* cassation; **Cour de c.** Supreme Court of Appeal; **se pourvoir en c.** to take one's case to the Supreme Court of Appeal **2** *Mil* reduction to the ranks

casse[1] [kas] NF *Typ (boîte)* case; **bas/haut de c.** lower-/upper-case letter

casse[2] NF *(arbre)* cassia

casse[3] NF *(action)* breaking, breakage; *(ce qui est cassé)* damage, breakages; **il va y avoir de la c.** something will get broken; *Fam (des ennuis)* there'll be trouble; **est-ce qu'il y a eu de la c.?** was anything broken?, were there any breakages?; **payer la c.** to pay for the breakages *or* the damage; **vendre qch à la c.** to sell sth for scrap; **envoyer une voiture à la c.** to send a car to the scrapyard; **aller** *ou* **partir à la c.** *(d'une voiture etc)* to go for scrap
NM *Arg (cambriolage)* break-in, burglary

cassé [kase] ADJ **1** *(objet, jambe etc)* broken; *(vieillard)* bent, bowed; *(voix)* cracked; *Fam (ivre)* smashed, plastered; *(drogué)* stoned; **blanc c.** off-white **2** *Can (sans argent)* broke; **c. comme un clou** stony broke

casseau, -eaux [kaso] NM *Typ* half-case

casse-bonbons *Fam* ADJ INV **être c.** to be a pain (in the neck)
N INV pain (in the neck)

casse-cou NM INV **1** *(passage)* danger *or* dangerous spot **2 crier c. à qn** to warn sb *(of a danger)* **3** *(personne)* daredevil
ADJ INV *(endroit)* dangerous; *(personne)* reckless

casse-couilles *Vulg* ADJ INV **être c.** to be a pain in the arse *or Am* ass
N INV pain in the arse *or Am* ass

casse-croûte NM INV **1** *(repas)* snack, bite **2** *Can (snack)* snack bar

casse-cul *Fam* ADJ INV damned annoying
N INV *(personne)* pain (in the arse *or Am* ass)

casse-dalle NM INV *Fam* sandwich

casse-graine NM INV *Fam* snack

casse-gueule *Fam* NM INV *(endroit)* danger *or* dangerous spot; *(entreprise)* risky *or Br Fam* dodgy undertaking
ADJ INV *(endroit)* dangerous; *(entreprise)* risky, *Br* dodgy

cassement [kasmã] NM **1** *Vieilli* c. de tête (*souci*) headache, worry; (*migraine*) splitting headache **2** *Arg, Vieilli* (*cambriolage*) break-in, burglary

casse-noisettes NM INV (pair of) nutcrackers, *Am* nutcracker

casse-noix NM INV **1** (pair of) nutcrackers, *Am* nutcracker **2** (*oiseau*) nutcracker

casse-pieds *Fam* ADJ INV damned annoying; **ce qu'il est c.** what a pain in the neck (he is)
▸ N INV (*personne*) pain (in the neck)

casse-pierre(s) NM INV (*masse*) stonebreaker's hammer; *Constr* (*machine*) stonebreaker, stone-crusher

casse-pipes NM INV *Arg* **aller au c.** *Mil* to go (off) to war *or* to the front; *Fig* to be heading for failure

CASSER [kase] VT **1** (*briser*) (*assiette, jouet, jambe, bras etc*) to break; (*voiture*) to wreck; (*mur*) to break down, to pull down; (*brindille, ficelle*) to break, to snap; (*noix*) to crack; (*pierres*) to break, to crush; **j'ai dû c. le carreau** I had to smash the window; **c. du bois** to chop wood; *Aviat* to crash on landing
2 (*moral*) to break; (*voix*) to strain; *Fam* (*personne*) to humiliate; (*billet, pièce*) (*dépenser*) to break; (*chaussures*) (*pour assouplir*) to break in; (*atmosphère*) to ruin; (*syndicats etc*) to break; **c. une grève** to break a strike; **c. les prix** to slash prices; **c. le marché** to break the market; **cette nouvelle m'a cassé le moral** the news depressed me; *Fig* **c. du sucre sur le dos de qn** to talk about sb behind his/her back; *Théâtre Fam* **c. la baraque** to bring the house down; *Fam* **c. la baraque à qn** to ruin *or* spoil things for sb; *Fig* **c. la croûte** *ou* **la graine, c. une petite graine** to have a snack *or* a bite *or* something to eat; *Fam* **c. sa pipe** to kick the bucket, *Br* to snuff it; *Arg* **c. le morceau** (*avouer*) to spill the beans, to come clean; (*dénoncer*) to grass; *Fam* **ça ne casse rien, ça ne casse pas trois pattes à un canard, ça ne casse pas des briques** it's not up to much, it's nothing to write home about, it's no great shakes; **un spectacle à tout c.** a marvellous *or* fantastic *or* super show; **applaudir à tout c.** to bring the house down; **cela vaut 1000 euros à tout c.** it's worth 1,000 euros at the very most *or* at the outside; **un homme cassé par l'adversité/la douleur/les échecs** a man broken by adversity/pain/failure
3 (*locutions avec parties du corps*) *Fam* **c. les pieds à qn** to do sb's head in; *Fam* **elle me casse les pieds** (*m'ennuie*) she bores the pants off me; (*m'agace*) she gets on my nerves *or Br* wick; **ça fait deux mois qu'elle me casse les pieds pour que je t'en parle** she's been on at me for two months now to talk to you about it; *Vulg* **il nous casse les bonbons** *ou* **les couilles, il nous casse** he gets on our tits; *Fam* **c. le cou** *ou Arg* **la gueule à qn** to smash sb's face in; **c. la tête** *ou* **les oreilles à qn** to deafen sb; **c. les reins à qn** to ruin *or* break sb; **c. bras et jambes à qn** to knock sb for six
4 (*dégrader*) (*officier*) to break, to reduce to the ranks; (*employé*) to demote
5 *Jur* (*verdict*) to quash, to set aside; **c. un mariage** to annul *or* dissolve a marriage; **c. ses fiançailles** to break off one's engagement
6 *très Fam* **c. de l'arabe** ≃ to go Paki-bashing; **c. du pédé** to go gay-bashing
▸ VI to break; (*de brindille, ficelle*) to break, to snap; **attention, ça casse!** be careful, it's fragile!; **cela casse comme du verre** it's as fragile as glass; *Fig Fam* **ils ont cassé** (*se sont séparés*) they've broken up *or* split up
▸ VPR **se casser 1** (*se briser*) to break; (*de brindille, ficelle*) to break, to snap; **la poutre se**

cassa sous son poids the beam broke under his weight; **elle s'est cassé la jambe** she's broken her leg; *Fam* **il ne s'est pas cassé pour m'aider** he didn't overstrain himself helping me; **le jour où je l'ai rencontré, j'aurais mieux fait de me c. une jambe** I wish I'd never set eyes on him; *Fam* **se c. la figure** (*tomber*) to fall flat on one's face, to come a cropper; (*se blesser*) to smash oneself up; (*rater, faire faillite*) to come a cropper; **se c. la tête** to rack one's brains; *Fam* **ne te casse pas la tête!** don't worry about it!; *Iron* **dis donc, tu ne t'es pas cassé la tête!** well, you didn't exactly strain yourself, did you!; *Fig* **se c. le nez à la porte de qn** to find nobody in *or* at home; *Fig* **il s'est cassé le nez** he's failed, *Fam* he's come a cropper; **se c. les dents** to come a cropper; *Fig* **ne grimpe pas sur cet échafaudage, tu vas te c. le cou!** don't climb up on that scaffolding, you'll break your neck!; *très Fam* **je me suis cassé le cul à lui trouver cette adresse** I really went out of my way *or Arg* bust a gut to find him that address
2 *Arg* (*partir*) to split, to clear off; **tu viens? on se casse** we're out of here, are you coming?; **casse-toi!** get out of here!, get lost!, beat it!; **elle s'est cassée de chez ses parents** she cleared out of her parents' place

casserole [kasʀɔl] NF **1** (*de cuisine*) (sauce)pan; **veau à la** *ou* **en c.** braised veal; *Arg* **passer à la c.** (*subir des épreuves*) to go through it; (*sexuellement*) to get screwed *or* laid, *Br* to get a good seeing-to; (*être tué*) to get bumped off **2** *Arg* (*mauvais piano*) tinny piano; **chanter comme une c.** to screech, to sing appallingly **3** *Cin Arg* projector

> Il faut noter que le nom anglais **casserole** est un faux ami. Il signifie **ragoût** ou **cocotte**, selon le contexte.

casse-tête NM INV **1** (*massue*) club; (*matraque*) cosh **2** (*jeu*) puzzle, brainteaser; **c. chinois** Chinese puzzle; *Fig* **c'est un c. chinois** it's baffling **3** (*problème*) headache; **ça a été un c. pour placer tout le monde à table** it was a headache seating everyone at the table

cassetin [kastɛ̃] NM *Typ* box

cassette [kasɛt] NF **1** (*magnétique*) cassette, tape; **écouter/passer une c.** to listen to/to put on *or* play a cassette; **enregistrer qch sur c.** to record sth on (to) cassette, to tape sth; (*vidéo*) to make a video (recording) of sth **2** (*de bijoux*) casket; *Arch* **c. du roi** King's privy purse; **il ne veut jamais puiser dans sa c. personnelle** he never wants to pay for things out of his own pocket
▸ ▸ **c. d'alimentation** (*de copieuse*) paper tray; **c. audio** audio cassette; **c. audionumérique** digital audio tape; *Ordinat* **c. à bande magnétique** mag tape cassette; **c. compacte numérique** digital compact cassette, DCC; **c. de démonstration** demo (tape); *Typ, Ordinat* **c. de fontes** font cassette; **c. numérique** digital audio tape; **c. pirate** pirate tape; *TV etc* **c. prête à diffuser** *ou* **PAD** master tape; **c. de ruban** (*d'une imprimante*) ribbon cassette; **c. de toner** (*d'une imprimante*) toner cassette; **c. vidéo** video (cassette)

cassettothèque [kasetɔtɛk] NF cassette library

casseur, -euse [kasœʀ, -øz] N **1 c. de pierres** stonebreaker **2** (*manifestant*) rioter **3** (*ferrailleur*) scrap (metal) merchant, breaker; **dépôt de c.** breaker's yard; **c. de voitures** (car) breaker **4** *Arg* (*cambrioleur*) burglar
▸ ADJ **il est c.** he's always breaking things

Cassin [kasɛ̃] NM **le mont C.** Monte Cassino

cassine [kasin] NF *Arch* (*petite maison*) small house

Cassiopée [kasjɔpe] NF Cassiopeia

cassis [kasis] NM **1** (*baie*) blackcurrant **2** (*arbuste*) blackcurrant bush **3** (*liqueur*) cassis, blackcurrant liqueur; **blanc c.** kir

cassis [kasi(s)] NM (*creux en travers d'une route*) dip

cassis [kasi] NM *Arg* (*tête*) nut, block

cassolette [kasɔlɛt] NF **1** (*pour parfums*) incense burner **2** *Culin* dish (for one person)

cassonade [kasɔnad] NF brown sugar

cassoulet [kasulɛ] NM *Culin* cassoulet (*stew of beans, pork, goose etc, a speciality of Languedoc*)

cassure [kasyʀ] NF break; (*dans du plâtre etc*) crack; *Fig* (*dans une amitié etc*) break, rupture; *Géol* fault; (*de tissu*) fold mark, crease; (*d'un pantalon*) crease

castagne [kastaɲ] NF *Fam* (*coup*) clout, wallop; **va y avoir de la c.** there's going to be a punch-up *or Am* fist fight

castagner [kastaɲe] *Fam* VT to clout, to wallop
▸ VPR **se castagner** to have a *Br* punch-up *or Am* fist fight

castagnette [kastaɲɛt] NF castanet; **jouer des castagnettes** to play the castanets; *Fig Fam* **j'avais les dents qui jouaient des castagnettes** my teeth were chattering; **ses genoux jouaient des castagnettes** his knees were knocking

caste [kast] NF caste; **la c. des prêtres** the priest caste; **esprit de c.** class consciousness; **avoir l'esprit de c.** to be class conscious; **être hors c.** to be an outcast

castel [kastɛl] NM (*manoir*) manor (house), mansion; (*petit château*) small castle

castillan, -ane [kastijã, -an] ADJ Castilian
▸ NM *Ling* Castilian
▸ N **C.** Castilian

Castille [kastij] NF Castile

casting [kastiŋ] NM *Cin, Théâtre* casting; **passer un c.** to go to a casting

castor [kastɔʀ] NM **1** (*mammifère, fourrure*) beaver; **c. du Chili** (*mammifère*) coypu; (*fourrure*) nutria; **c. du Canada** (*mammifère*) muskrat; (*fourrure*) musquash (fur) **2** *Fig* (*association*) **(mouvement des) castors** = group of people building their own houses

castrat [kastʀa] NM eunuch; *Mus* castrato

castrateur, -trice [kastʀatœʀ, -tʀis] ADJ *Psy* castrating; *Fig* (*autoritaire*) repressive

castration [kastʀasjɔ̃] NF castration; (*d'un étalon*) gelding; (*d'un chat, d'un chien*) neutering; (*d'une chatte, d'une chienne*) spaying; *Psy* **complexe de c.** castration complex; **c. chimique** chemical castration

castrer [kastʀe] VT to castrate; (*étalon*) to geld; (*chat, chien*) to neuter; (*chatte, chienne*) to spay

castrisme [kastʀism] NM *Pol* Castroism

castriste [kastʀist] ADJ, N *Pol* Castroist

casuel, -elle [kazɥɛl] ADJ **1** (*accidentel*) fortuitous **2** *Gram* **flexions casuelles** case endings **3** *Belg* (*fragile*) fragile
▸ NM (*revenu variable*) perquisites

casuiste [kazɥist] NM *Rel, Fig Péj* casuist

casuistique [kazɥistik] NF *Rel, Fig Péj* casuistry

casus belli [kazysbɛlli] NM INV casus belli

cata [kata] NF *Fam* **c'est la c.** it's a disaster

cataboliser [katabɔlize] VT *Biol* to catabolize

catabolisme [katabɔlism] NM *Biol* catabolism

catachrèse [katakʀɛz] NF *Ling* catachresis

cataclysmal, -ale, -aux, -ales [kataklismal, -o] ADJ cataclysmal

cataclysme [kataklism] NM *Géol* cataclysm; *Fig* disaster, cataclysm

cataclysmique [kataklismik] ADJ cataclysmic, cataclysmal; *Fig* disastrous, cataclysmic

catacombes [katakɔ̃b] NFPL catacombs

catadioptre [katadiɔptr] NM *(de véhicule etc)* reflector; *(sur la route)* cat's-eye®

catafalque [katafalk] NM catafalque

cataire [katɛr] NF catmint, catnip

catalan, -ane [katalɑ̃, -an] ADJ Catalan
NM *Ling* Catalan
N **C.** Catalan

catalepsie [katalɛpsi] NF *Méd* catalepsy; **tomber en c.** to have a cataleptic fit

cataleptique [katalɛptik] ADJ, N *Méd* cataleptic

catalogage [katalɔgaʒ] NM *(de livres etc)* cataloguing, *Am* cataloging

Catalogne [katalɔɲ] NF **1** Catalonia **2** *Can Tex* rag rug

catalogue [katalɔg] NM catalogue, *Am* catalog; **c. de vente par correspondance** mail-order catalogue; **je n'achète jamais rien sur c.** I never buy anything from a catalogue; **faire le c. de** to catalogue; **c. de films** film library; **c. méthodique** subject catalogue; **c. de normes** standards catalogue

cataloguer [katalɔge] VT *(livres)* to catalogue, *Am* to catalog; *Fig Péj (étiqueter)* to label; **les médias l'ont cataloguée parmi les révolutionnaires** the media labelled her a revolutionary; **je l'ai catalogué tout de suite** I sized him up immediately

catalpa [katalpa] NM *Bot* catalpa

catalyse [kataliz] NF *Chimie* catalysis; **four à c.** self-cleaning oven

catalyser [katalize] VT *Chimie, Fig* to catalyse

catalyseur [katalizœr] NM *Chimie, Fig* catalyst

catalytique [katalitik] ADJ *Chimie* catalytic; *Aut* **pot c.** catalytic converter

catamaran [katamarɑ̃] NM *Naut* catamaran; *Aviat (d'un hydravion)* floats

Cataphote® [katafɔt] NM = **catadioptre**

cataplasme [kataplasm] NM *Méd* poultice; **c. sinapisé** mustard poultice *or* plaster; *Fig* **c'est comme un c. sur une jambe de bois** it's worse than useless

catapultage [katapyltaʒ] NM catapulting; *Aviat* catapult launch(ing); *Fig (dans un poste etc)* catapulting; *Aviat* **crochet de c.** catapulting hook

catapulte [katapylt] NF *Aviat, Mil etc* catapult

catapulter [katapylte] VT to catapult; *Fig (personne)* to catapult (**dans un poste** into a post)

cataracte [katarakt] NF **1** *(d'eau)* cataract, falls; **des cataractes (de pluie)** torrents of rain **2** *Méd* cataract; **se faire opérer de la c.** to have a cataract operation

catarrhal, -ale, -aux, -ales [kataral, -o] ADJ *Méd* catarrhal

catarrhe [katar] NM *Méd* catarrh

catarrheux, -euse [katarø, -øz] *Méd* ADJ *(personne)* catarrhal
N catarrhal person

catastrophe [katastrɔf] NF catastrophe, disaster; **c. ferroviaire/aérienne** rail/air disaster; **c. financière** crash; **c'est la c.!** it's a disaster!; **ce n'est tout de même pas une c.!** it's not the end of the world!; **cet enfant/votre devoir est une c.** this child/your homework is a disaster; **c'est déjà là!** panic stations! he's here already!; *Aviat* **atterrir en c.** to make a forced *or* emergency landing; **je suis passé au bureau en c.** I went to the office in a mad rush *or* a panic

catastrophé [katastrɔfe] ADJ *Fam* stunned;

il était c. de l'apprendre he was stunned to learn it

catastropher [katastrɔfe] VT *Fam (personne)* to stun, to be a (great) blow to

catastrophique [katastrɔfik] ADJ *(événement, conséquence etc)* catastrophic, disastrous; *Fig (très mauvais)* disastrous, appalling

catastrophisme [katastrɔfism] NM catastrophism; *Fam* **sans vouloir faire du c.** without wishing to be pessimistic

catatonie [katatɔni] NF *Méd* catatonia

catatonique [katatɔnik] ADJ, N *Méd* catatonic

catch [katʃ] NM *Sport* (all-in) wrestling; **faire du c.** to wrestle; **match** *ou* **rencontre de c.** wrestling match

catcher [katʃe] VI *Sport* to wrestle

catcheur, -euse [katʃœr, -øz] N *Sport* (all-in) wrestler

catéchèse [kateʃɛz] NF *Rel* catechism

catéchisation [kateʃizasjɔ̃] NF *Rel* catechization

catéchiser [kateʃize] VT *Rel* to catechize; *Fig (endoctriner)* to indoctrinate; *(sermonner)* to preach at, to lecture

catéchisme [kateʃism] NM *Rel (instruction, livre)* catechism; **aller au c.** to go to catechism class; *Fig* **ce livre est son c.** this book is his bible

catéchiste [kateʃist] N *Rel* catechist

catéchumène [katekymɛn] N *Rel* catechumen; *Fig* novice, tyro

catégorie [kategɔri] NF category; *(d'hôtel, de personnel)* grade; *(de légumes, fruits)* category, grade, class; *(de boxeur)* class; **légumes de première c.** grade one *or* class one *or* prime vegetables; **de dernière c.** of poor quality; **morceau de viande de première/deuxième c.** prime/second cut of meat; **il appartient à cette c. de gens qui …** he belongs to that category *or* group of people who …; **c. de produit** product category *or* class; **c. sociale** social category; **c. socioprofessionnelle** socio-professional group, social stratum

catégoriel, -ielle [kategɔrjɛl] ADJ **1** *Ind, Pol* **revendications catégorielles** differential claims **2** *Ling* **symbole c.** category symbol **3** *Phil* categorical

catégorique [kategɔrik] ADJ *(clair) (réponse etc)* categoric(al); *Phil (proposition etc)* categorical; **refus c.** categoric *or* flat refusal; **elle a été c. sur ce point** she was categorical *or* quite emphatic on this point; **il est c., il faut aller à l'hôpital** there's no question about it, you/etc will have to go to hospital; **je suis absolument c., c'est bien l'homme que j'ai vu** I'm absolutely positive that's the man I saw

catégoriquement [kategɔrikmɑ̃] ADV categorically

catégorisation [kategɔrizasjɔ̃] NF categorization; *(de personnel)* grading

catégoriser [kategɔrize] VT to categorize; *(personnel)* to grade

catelle [katɛl] NF *Suisse* ceramic tile

caténaire [katenɛr] ADJ **1** *Rail* **suspension c.** catenary **2** **réaction c.** chain reaction
NF *Rail* catenary

catgut [katgyt] NM *Chir* catgut

cathare [katar] *Hist, Rel* ADJ Cathar
N **C.** Cathar

catharsis [katarsis] NF *Psy, Littér* catharsis

cathartique [katartik] ADJ *Psy, Littér* cathartic

cathédrale [katedral] NF cathedral

cathèdre [katɛdr] NF cathedra

Catherine [katrin] NF **coiffer sainte C.** *(d'une femme)* to be 25 and still unmarried, to be left on the shelf

catherinette [katrinɛt] NF unmarried woman of 25 or over

cathéter [katetɛr] NM *Méd* catheter

cathétérisme [kateterism] NM *Méd* catheterization

catho [kato] ADJ *Fam* Catholic

cathode [katɔd] NF *Élec* cathode

cathodique [katɔdik] ADJ *Élec* cathodic; **l'univers c.** the world of television; **rayons cathodiques** cathode rays; **tube à rayons cathodiques, tube c.** cathode-ray tube

catholicisme [katɔlisism] NM (Roman) Catholicism

catholicité [katɔlisite] NF **1** **la c.** *(catholiques)* the (Roman) Catholic Church **2** *(orthodoxie)* Catholicity

catholique [katɔlik] ADJ **1** *Rel* (Roman) Catholic; *(universel)* catholic, universal **2** *Fam* **il/ce n'est pas (très) c.** he's/it's a bit fishy; *Hum* **cette façon de faire la soupe n'est pas très c.** this isn't a very orthodox way of making soup
N (Roman) Catholic

catilinaire [katilinɛr] NF lampoon

catimini (en) [ɑ̃katimini] ADV *Fam* stealthily, on the sly *or* quiet; **entrer/sortir en c.** to steal *or Fam* sneak in/out; **je suis allé l'acheter en c.** I went to buy it on the quiet

catin [katɛ̃] NF **1** *Arg, Vieilli (prostituée)* trollop, whore **2** *Can (poupée)* doll **3** *Can (pansement)* finger bandage

cation [katjɔ̃] NM *Élec* cation

catogan [katɔgɑ̃] NM hair ribbon *(for ponytail)*

Caton [katɔ̃] NM Cato

Caucase (le) [lǝkokaz] NM the Caucasus

caucasien, -ienne [kokazjɛ̃, -jɛn] ADJ Caucasian
N **C.** Caucasian

cauchemar [koʃmar] NM *aussi Fig* nightmare; **faire un c.** to have a nightmare; **vision de c.** nightmarish vision; **ça me donne des cauchemars rien que d'y penser** it gives me nightmares just thinking about it; **il me donne des cauchemars** I have nightmares about him; *Fig* **les réceptions officielles étaient son c.** official receptions were a nightmare to *or* for him

cauchemarder [koʃmarde] VI to have nightmares; *Fig* **cette idée me fait c.** the idea gives me nightmares

cauchemardesque [koʃmardɛsk], **cauchemardeux, -euse** [koʃmardø, -øz] ADJ *(vision etc)* nightmarish; **sommeil cauchemardeux** sleep disturbed by nightmares

caudal, -ale, -aux, -ales [kodal, -o] ADJ *Zool* caudal

cauri(s) [kori] NM cowrie (shell)

causal, -ale, -als *ou* **-aux, -ales** [kozal, -o] ADJ *Gram, Phil* causal

causalité [kozalite] NF *Phil* causality; **rapport/principe de c.** causal relation/principle

causant [kozɑ̃] ADJ *Fam (personne)* chatty, talkative

CAUSE [koz] NF **1** *(origine)* cause; **c. réelle/apparente** real/apparent cause; **c. de défiance** cause *or* reason for distrust; *Phil* **c. première/seconde** first/secondary cause; **quelle est la c. de son départ?** what caused him to leave?; **on ne connaît pas la c. de sa mort** the cause of death is unknown; **être (la) c. de qch** to be the cause of sth; **les enfants sont souvent c. de soucis** children are often a cause of worry; **c'est elle qui en est c.** it's her fault, she's to blame; **il s'est fâché, et non sans c.** he got angry, and with good reason; **il s'est mis en colère, et pour c.** he got angry, and for a very good reason; **absent pour c. de santé** absent for health reasons *or* on medical grounds; **fermé pour c. de décès/d'inventaire** closed owing to bereavement/for stocktaking; **à c. de** because of, on account of; **c'est à c. de moi qu'il a manqué le train** it was because of me (that) he missed the train, it was my fault he missed the train; **c'est à c. de toi!** it's all because of you!, it's all your fault!

2 *Jur* case, (law)suit, action; **c. civile/criminelle** civil/criminal action *or* case; **plaider/gagner une c.** to argue/to win a case; **avocat sans causes** briefless barrister; **confier une c. à un avocat** to brief a barrister; **affaire en c.** case before the court; **entendre une c.** to hear a case; *Fig* **la c. est entendue** there's nothing more to be said; **être en c.** *(d'une personne, d'intérêts etc)* to be involved; **votre probité n'est pas en c.** your honesty is not in question *or* in doubt; **mettre en c. la probité de qn** to question sb's honesty; **mettre qn en c.** *Jur* to summon *or* sue sb; *(impliquer)* to implicate sb; **mettre qn hors de c.** to clear *or* exonerate sb; **il est maintenant hors de c.** he has now been cleared; **en tout état de c.** at all events, in any case; **en connaissance de c.** with full knowledge of the facts

3 *(parti)* cause; **prendre fait et c. pour qn/qch** to take up sb's/sth's cause; **c'est une c. perdue (d'avance)** it's a lost cause; **faire c. commune avec qn** to side with sb, to join forces with sb

▸▸ **c. célèbre** famous trial, cause célèbre

causer¹ [koze] **VT** *(chose)* to cause, to be the cause of; **c. un changement** to bring about a change; **son départ nous a causé beaucoup de chagrin** his departure distressed us greatly *or* caused us great distress; **c. des ennuis à qn** to cause sb problems, to give sb trouble

causer² **VI 1** *(parler)* to chat, to talk *(de* about); **c. avec** *ou Fam* **à qn** to have a chat *or* a talk with sb; *Fam* **je ne lui cause plus!** *(je suis fâché avec elle)* I'm not talking to her!; **c. de** to talk about; **c. de la pluie et du beau temps, c. de choses et d'autres** to talk about this and that; **c. affaires/chiffons** to talk business/clothes; **cause toujours, tu m'intéresses!** how interesting!; **faire c. qn** to make sb talk, to get sb to talk **2** *(cancaner)* to talk, to gossip; **on commence à en c.** people are beginning to talk *or* gossip (about it)

causerie [kozri] **NF 1** *(discussion)* chat, talk **2** *(conférence)* (informal) talk

causette [kozɛt] **NF 1** *Fam* little chat; **faire la c.** *ou* **un brin de c. avec qn** to have a little chat *or Br* a bit of a natter with sb **2** *Ordinat* chat

causeur, -euse [kozœr, -øz] **N** *(personne)* chatterer
  NF causeuse *(siège)* loveseat
  ADJ chatty, talkative

causse [kos] **NM** *Géog* = limestone plateau in central and southern France

causticité [kostisite] **NF** *Chimie* causticity; *Fig (d'une personne)* causticity; *(d'une remarque etc)* biting *or* caustic nature

caustique [kostik] **ADJ** *Chimie* caustic; *Fig (personne, esprit, humour)* caustic; *(remarque etc)* biting, caustic, cutting
  NM *Chimie* caustic
  NF *Opt* caustic

caustiquement [kostikmã] **ADV** *Fig* caustically, bitingly, cuttingly

cautèle [kotɛl] **NF** *Litt* wiliness, cunning

cauteleux, -euse [kotlø, -øz] **ADJ** *Litt* wily, cunning

cautère [kotɛr] **NM** *Méd* cautery; *Fam* **c'est un c. sur une jambe de bois** it's worse than useless, it won't do any good whatsoever

cautérisation [koterizasjɔ̃] **NF** *Méd* cauterization

cautériser [koterize] **VT** *Méd (blessure etc)* to cauterize

caution [kosjɔ̃] **NF 1** *(gage)*, *Com, Fin* security, guarantee; *Jur* bail; *Fig (appui)* support, backing; **c. de banque** bank guarantee; *Fin* **c. de bonne fin** performance bond; *Fin* **c. de soumission** bid bond; **il faut verser 1000 euros de c.** you/*etc* must pay a deposit of 1,000 euros; *Jur* **donner** *ou* **fournir c. pour qn** to go *or* stand bail for sb, to bail sb out; *Jur* **mettre qn en liberté sous c.** to release sb on bail; *Fig* **sujet à c.** *(nouvelles etc)* to be treated with caution, unreliable, unconfirmed; *Fig* **le gouvernement a donné sa c. au rachat** the takeover has the government's support *or* backing; *Fin* **c. d'adjudication** bid bond
  2 *(personne)* surety, security, guaranty; **se porter c. pour qn** *Jur* to go *or* stand bail for sb; *Com, Fin* to stand surety *or* security for sb

> Il faut noter que le nom anglais **caution** est un faux ami. Il signifie **prudence**.

cautionnement [kosjɔnmã] **NM 1** *(contrat)* surety bond **2** *(somme d'argent)* security, guarantee, guaranty; **c. électoral** deposit

cautionner [kosjɔne] **VT 1** *(personne)* *Com, Fin* to stand surety for, to act as guarantor for; *Jur* to go *or* stand bail for, to bail out **2** *Fig (répondre de) (chose)* to answer for, to guarantee; **c. l'honnêteté de qn** to vouch for sb's honesty **3** *Fig (approuver) (idée, action, gouvernement etc)* to support, to back

> Il faut noter que le verbe anglais **to caution** est un faux ami. Il signifie **mettre en garde**.

cavalcade [kavalkad] **NF 1** *(défilé)* cavalcade, procession **2** *Fig (bousculade)* swarm, stampede

cavalcader [kavalkade] **VI 1** *(d'un groupe de gens etc)* to swarm (about) **2** *Arch* to ride *(in a cavalcade)*

cavale [kaval] **NF 1** *Arg (évasion)* escape; **être en c.** to be on the run **2** *Litt (jument)* mare

cavaler [kavale] *Arg* **VI** to rush around; *(fuir)* to take off, *Br* to scarper, *Br* to do a runner; **c. après qn** *(poursuivre de ses assiduités)* to chase after sb; **je n'ai pas envie de c. le jour de Noël** I don't want to be rushing around on Christmas Day
  VT c. qn to get on sb's nerves, to plague *or* pester sb

cavalerie [kavalri] **NF 1** *Mil* cavalry; **c. légère** light cavalry, light horse; **c. motorisée** motorized cavalry; **grosse c.** heavy *or* armoured cavalry; *Fig Fam* **Wagner et sa grosse c. de cuivres** Wagner and his heavy brass **2** *(ensemble de chevaux)* stable

cavaleur, -euse [kavalœr, -øz] *Arg* **ADJ** *(homme)* womanizing; *(femme)* man-chasing
  N *(homme)* skirt chaser, womanizer; *(femme)* man-chaser

cavalier, -ière [kavalje, -jɛr] **N 1** *(à cheval)* rider, horseman, *f* horsewoman; **habit de c.** riding costume; *Bible* **les (Quatre) Cavaliers de l'Apocalypse** the (four) Horsemen of the Apocalypse **2** *(qui danse)* partner; *Fig* **faire c. seul** to go it alone, to act alone
  NM 1 *Mil* trooper, cavalryman; *Échecs* knight; *Arch (gentilhomme)* gentleman; *Br Hist* **Cavaliers et Têtes rondes** Cavaliers and Roundheads **2** *(accompagnateur de dame)* escort **3** *Ordinat* jumper **4** *Tech (clou)* staple; *(languette de fichier)* tab
  ADJ 1 allée *ou* **piste cavalière** bridle path **2** *(manière, personne)* cavalier, offhand

cavalièrement [kavaljɛrmã] **ADV** in a cavalier manner, off-handedly

cave¹ [kav] **ADJ 1** *(joues, yeux)* hollow, sunken **2** *Anat* **veine c.** vena cava

cave² **NF 1** *(cellier, vins)* cellar; **c. à charbon** coal cellar; **c. à vin** wine cellar; **avoir une bonne c.** to have *or* keep a good cellar; *Fig* **de la c. au grenier** *(ranger, repeindre etc)* from top to bottom, thoroughly **2** *(cabaret)* nightclub **3** **c. à liqueurs** *(meuble)* drinks cabinet

> Il faut noter que le nom anglais **cave** est un faux ami. Il signifie **grotte**.

cave³ **NF** *Cartes* = stake

cave⁴ **NM** *Arg* **1** *(personne ne faisant pas partie du milieu)* outsider **2** *(dupe)* sucker, mug
  ADJ ce qu'il est c.! what a sucker *or* mug (he is)!

caveau, -eaux [kavo] **NM 1** *(petite cave)* small cellar **2** *(cabaret)* nightclub **3** *(funéraire)* burial vault

caver¹ [kave] **VT** *Arch, Litt* to hollow (out), to dig (out), to excavate
  VPR se caver *(des yeux etc)* to become hollow *or* sunken

caver² *Cartes* **VT** *Arch (miser)* to put up
  VI to put up a stake
  VPR se caver se c. de deux cents euros to put up two hundred euros *(as a stake)*

caverne [kavɛrn] **NF** cave, cavern; *Anat (dans les poumons etc)* cavity; **homme des cavernes** caveman; **la c. d'Ali Baba** Ali Baba's cave; *Fig* **c'est une véritable c. d'Ali Baba** it's a real Aladdin's cave

caverneux, -euse [kavɛrnø, -øz] **ADJ 1** *(rocher)*, *Anat (tissu)* cavernous **2** *(voix, grognement)* sepulchral

caviar [kavjar] **NM 1** *Culin* caviar; **c. rouge** salmon roe **2** *Fig* blue pencil; **passer au c.** *(article de presse etc)* to blue-pencil, to censor

caviardage [kavjardaʒ] **NM** *(censure)* blue-pencilling, censoring

caviarder [kavjarde] **VT** *(article de presse etc)* to blue-pencil, to censor

caviste [kavist] **NM** cellarman

cavité [kavite] **NF** cavity, hollow; *Anat, Méd* cavity; **c. articulaire** *(d'un os)* socket; **c. buccale** oral cavity

Cayenne [kajɛn] **N** *(ville)* Cayenne; **poivre de C.** cayenne (pepper)

CB [sibi] **NF** *(abrév* **citizens' band, canaux banalisés)** CB

CC [sese] **NM** *Banque (abrév* **compte courant)** CA

cc [sese] **NM** *Élec (abrév* **courant continu)** DC

C/C **NM** *(abrév* **compte (de) chèque)** C/A

CCB [sesebe] **NM** *(abrév* **compte de chèque bancaire)** C/A

CCI **NF 1** *(abrév* **Chambre de commerce et de l'industrie)** CCI **2** *(abrév* **Chambre de commerce internationale)** ICC

CCP [sesepe] **NM** *(abrév* **compte courant postal, compte chèque postal)** ≃ Giro account

CCR [seseɛr] **NM** *Fin (abrév* **coefficient de capitalisation des résultats)** p/e ratio

CD [sede] **NM 1** *(abrév* **corps diplomatique)** CD **2** *(abrév* **compact disc)** CD; **CD audio** audio CD; **CD réinscriptible** CD-RW; **CD vidéo** video CD

CDD [sedede] **NM** *(abrév* **contrat à durée déterminée)** fixed-term contract

CDI [sedei] **NM 1** *(abrév* **centre des impôts)** tax centre, tax office **2** *(abrév* **contrat à durée indéterminée)** permanent contract

CD-I *(abrév* **compact disc-interactif)** CDI

CD-interactif **NM** interactive CD

CD-Photo **NM** photo CD

CD-R **NM** *(abrév* **compact disc recordable)** CD-R

CD-Rom NM INV CD-ROM; **C. d'installation** setup CD-ROM; **C. interactif** interactive CD-ROM

CDV NM (*abrév* **compact disc video**) CDV

CE [seə] NM (*abrév* **Conseil de l'Europe**) Council of Europe
NF (*abrév* **Communauté européenne**) EC

CE¹ [s(ə)] PRON DÉM SEE GRAMMAR B15 (*c'* before parts of *être* beginning with a vowel) **1** (*with adj or adv complement*) **c'est exact!** that's right!; **c'est tout à fait possible/fort probable** it's quite possible/highly probable; **ce doit être faux** it's probably untrue; **c'est sur votre bureau** it's on your desk; **le voilà, ce n'est pas trop tôt!** there he is, and about time too!; **est-ce** [εs] **assez?** is that enough?; **c'est facile** it's easy; **demain c'est dimanche** tomorrow is Sunday, it's Sunday tomorrow; **c'était inutile de sonner** you needn't have rung; **c'est assez qu'il veuille bien pardonner** it is enough that he is willing to forgive; **c'est à vous de vous en occuper** it's up to you to see to it; **c'est à toi, ce livre? – non, c'est à Paul** is this book yours? – no, it's Paul's SEE GRAMMAR B66

2 (*with noun or pron as complement; with a third person pl complement, the verb should be in the plural but colloquial usage allows the singular*) **c'est moi/c'est nous/ce sont eux** *ou Fam* **c'est eux** it's me/us/them, *Fml* it is I/we/they; **c'est le médecin/c'est Monsieur Pierrot** (*à la porte, au téléphone etc*) it's the doctor/it's Mr Pierrot; **qui a dit ça? – c'est moi/lui/***etc* who said that? – me/him/*etc or* I/he/*etc* did; **est-ce vous, Jean?** is that you, Jean?; **qui est-ce?** who is it?, who's that?; **c'est un ami que j'avais quand j'étais étudiante** he was a friend of mine when I was a student; **c'est un bon soldat** he's a good soldier; **ce n'est pas un hôtel ici!** this is not a hotel!; **ce n'est pas là mon parapluie** that is not my umbrella; **est-ce que ce sont là vos enfants?** are those your children?; **ce ne sont pas mes chaussures** they *or* these *or* those aren't my shoes; *Fam* **c'est elles qui me l'ont dit** it was them who told me SEE GRAMMAR B66

3 si *ce* **n'est** except; **personne si ce n'est vos parents** no one except (possibly) your parents

4 (*representing a subject which has been isolated in order to stress it*) **Paris, c'est bien loin!, c'est bien loin, Paris!** it's a long way to Paris!, Paris is a long way away!; **le temps, c'est de l'argent** time is money; **c'est incroyable, ce vent** this wind is incredible

5 (*used with* que *or* qui *to bring a word into prominence*) **c'est toi qui le dis!** that's what you say!, says you!; **c'est moi qui lui ai écrit** it was I *or Fam* me who wrote to him; **est-ce à moi que vous parlez?** are you speaking to me?; *Litt* **c'est un bon petit garçon que Jean!** what a fine little chap Jean is!; *Litt* **ce serait imprudence que d'y aller** it would be unwise to go (there)

6 (*used with* que *to introduce a statement*) **c'est que maman est malade** mother's ill, you see, the point is mother's ill; **c'est qu'il fait froid!** it's cold and no mistake!; **s'il chante, c'est qu'il est de bonne humeur** when *or* if he sings, it means *or* it's because he's in a good mood; **ce n'est pas qu'il n'y tienne pas** it's not that he isn't keen on it, it isn't that he's not keen on it

7 (*used in* est-ce que [εskə] *to introduce a question*) **est-ce que je peux entrer?** may I come in?; **est-ce qu'il est là?** is he there? SEE GRAMMAR B64

8 (*locutions*) **pour ce faire** in order to do this; **ce faisant** in so doing, whilst doing so; **ce disant** saying which *or* this, so saying, with these words; **on l'a attaqué et ce** [sə] **en plein jour** he was attacked, and in broad daylight (too); **sur ce ...** thereupon ..., on that note ...; **sur ce, il sortit son album de photos** whereupon he brought out his photo album; *Arch* **depuis ce ...** since then ...; **tenez-vous beaucoup à ce qu'il vienne?** are you very anxious for him to come?; **je ne m'attendais pas à ce qu'il soit là** I wasn't expecting him to be there; **tu te plains de ce que personne ne te téléphone** you're complaining that no one telephones you; **pour ce qui est de la qualité et du prix** with regard to *or* as regards quality and price; **pour ce qui est de cela** for that matter; **c'est te dire s'il était content** that shows you how happy he was; **c'est tout dire** that says it all; *Litt* **voilà, ce me semble, un avis excellent** that, to my mind, is excellent advice

9 (*with a rel pron*) **ce qui, ce que** what; **je sais ce qui est arrivé** I know what has happened; **c'est ce qui est important** this is what's important; **voilà ce que j'ai répondu** this is what I answered; **je sais ce que c'est que la pauvreté** I know what poverty is; **si vous saviez ce que c'est que de vivre seul** if you knew what it meant *or* what it's like to live alone; **voilà ce que c'est que de mentir** that's what comes of telling lies; **c'est ce qu'il a dit** that's what he said, so he said; **voici ce dont il s'agit** this is the point, this is what it's all about; **ce qu'il y a de plus remarquable, c'est que ...** what is most remarkable is that ..., the most remarkable thing about it is ...; **à ce qu'on dit** according to *or* from what they say; **voici ce à quoi j'avais pensé** this is what I had thought of SEE GRAMMAR A32; A33; B17–18; B23

10 (*referring back to a clause*) **ce qui, ce que** which; **ce qui compte, c'est que tu sois satisfait** what counts is that you're happy; **il faut avoir de l'argent, ce qu'elle n'a pas** you need to have money, which she doesn't have; **il l'a quittée, ce qui est dommage** he has left her, which is a pity; **il est déjà parti, ce que je ne savais pas** he has already gone, which I didn't know SEE GRAMMAR A33; B17–18; B23

11 tout ce qui, tout ce que everything, all (that); **voici tout ce que j'ai d'argent** here's all the money I've got; **faites tout ce que vous voudrez** do whatever you like

12 *Fam* **ce que ...!** (*comme*) how ...!; **(qu'est-)ce qu'elle a changé!** how she has changed!; **ce que tu as grandi!** how you've grown!, well, you have grown!; **ce qu'il peut être pénible!** he can be really tiresome!; **ce que j'ai faim!** I'm really hungry!

13 (*with à* + *inf*) **c'est à mourir de rire** it's absolutely hilarious; **c'est à se demander s'il n'est pas fou** one may well wonder if he isn't mad; **c'est à voir** (*ça reste à prouver*) that remains to be seen, we'll have to (wait and) see; (*il faut le voir absolument*) you have to see it; **c'est à refaire** it will have to be done again

CE², CET, CETTE, CES [sə, sεt, se *or* sε] ADJ DÉM (*the form* cet *is used before a* n *or adj beginning with a vowel or* h *mute*) **1** (*désigne quelque chose de proche dans l'espace ou dans le temps*) this, that, *pl* these, those; **un de ces jours** one of these days; **tu dois connaître cette histoire, tout le monde la connaît!** you must know this story, everyone does!; **il fera de l'orage cette nuit** there will be a storm tonight; **j'ai mal dormi cette nuit** I slept badly last night; **je l'ai vu/je le verrai ce matin/cet été/cette semaine** I saw him/I'll see him this morning/this summer/this week; **c'est une de ces femmes qui se plaignent tout le temps** she's one of those women who complain *or* she's the sort of woman who complains all the time SEE GRAMMAR A30–1; B14

2 (*par référence à une chose connue*) the; **j'ai encore cette impression que ...** I still have the feeling that ...; **rien de ce genre** nothing of the kind; **je n'ai jamais rien entendu/vu de ce genre** I've never heard/seen anything of the kind *or* anything like it

3 ce dernier the latter

4 ces the; **que prendront ces messieurs?** what will you take *or* have, gentlemen?; **ces dames sont au salon** the ladies are in the drawing room

5 ce ...-ci this; **ce ...-là** that; **de ce côté-ci/de ce côté-là** on this/that side; **je ne connais pas ce livre-là** I don't know that book; **j'ai vu tous ces films, mais j'ai préféré ce film-ci à tous les autres** I've seen all these films, but I prefer this one to all the others; **prenez cette tasse-ci** take this cup; **je n'oublierai jamais ce jour-là** I'll never forget that day; **je la verrai ces jours-ci** I'll see her in a day or two; **il fait chaud ces jours-ci** it's been warm lately *or* the(se) last couple of days

6 *Fam* (*en intensif*) **eh bien, et cette jambe?** well, how's that leg of yours *or* how's the leg?; **alors, cette lettre, tu me la fais lire?** so, do I get to read that letter of yours?; **et ce café, il arrive?** is that coffee on its way or what?; **et ce vent, qui ne tombe pas!** will that wind ever die down?; **mais laissez-la donc, cette enfant!** do leave that child alone!; **mais c'est qu'elle a grandi, cette petite!** that little girl has really grown!; **cette question!** what an absurd question!; **cette foule!** what a crowd!; **je lui ai écrit une de ces lettres!** I wrote him such a letter!; **j'ai une de ces faims!** I'm ravenous!; **elle a une de ces têtes!** (*elle est fatiguée, malade*) she looks awful!; (*elle est laide*) she's as ugly as sin!; **elle a fait une de ces têtes quand je le lui ai montré** you should have seen his face when I showed it to him

CEA [seəa] NM (*abrév* **Commissariat à l'énergie atomique**) = French atomic energy commission

céans [seã] ADV *Arch* (here) within, in this house; *Hum* **le maître de c.** the master of the house

ceci [səsi] PRON DÉM INV this; **et tout c. pour rien, puisqu'il a fallu recommencer** and it was all for nothing, since we/*etc* had to start again; **c. étant dit, il faut quand même reconnaître qu'il a du talent** having said that, it must be admitted that he's talented; **écoutez bien c.** (now) listen to this; **le cas a c. de particulier que ...** the case is peculiar in that ...; **c. n'explique pas cela** one thing doesn't explain the other SEE GRAMMAR B15

cécité [sesite] NF blindness; **être frappé de c.** to be struck blind; **être atteint de c.** to be blind; **c. verbale** word blindness

cédant, -ante [sedã, -ãt] *Com, Jur* ADJ (*partie*) granting, assigning
N grantor, assignor

céder [sede] (**je cède; je céderai**) VT (*donner*) (*chose*) to give up, to part with (**à** to); (*droit*) to give up, to surrender; *Jur* to transfer, to make over, to assign (**à** to); (*bail*) to dispose of, to sell; **c. qch à bail** to lease sth; **c. sa place à qn** to give up one's seat to sb; **c. le pas à qn** to let sb go first, to give way to sb; **c. du terrain** to give *or* lose ground; *Fig* to back down; **'cédez le passage'** 'give way', *Am* 'yield'; **fonds de commerce à c.** business for sale; **'à c.'** 'for sale'; **je vous le cède pour cent euros** I'll let you have it for a hundred euros; *Vieilli* **ne le c. en rien à qn** to be in no way inferior to sb; **pour l'intelligence, elle ne (le) cède à personne** when it comes to intelligence, she's second to none; **ces artistes russes ne le cédaient en rien à leurs contemporains français** these Russian artists were every bit as good as their French contemporaries
VI (*se soumettre*) (*d'une personne*) to yield, to give in (**à** to); (*s'écrouler*) (*d'une construction, corde etc*) to give way; **le terrain a cédé sous mes pieds** the ground gave way beneath me;

cervidé [sɛrvide] NM cervid; **les cervidés** the deer family, *Spéc* Cervidae

Cervin [sɛrvɛ̃] NM **le (mont) C.** the Matterhorn

cervoise [sɛrvwaz] NF *Antiq* barley beer

CES [seəes] NM **1** *Scol* (*abrév* **collège d'enseignement secondaire**) ≃ secondary school, *Am* ≃ high school **2** *abrév* **contrat emploi-solidarité**

ces *voir* **ce²**

César [sezar] NM **1** *Hist* **Jules C.** Julius Caesar **2** *Cin* = French cinema award

césarien, -ienne [sezarjɛ̃, -jɛn] ADJ *Hist* Caesarean
  NF *Méd* **césarienne** Caesarean (section), *Fam* C section; **on lui a fait une césarienne** she had a Caesarean; **elle est née par césarienne** she was born by Caesarean, she was a Caesarean

césium [sezjɔm] NM *Chimie* caesium

cessant [sɛsɑ̃] ADJ **toute(s) affaire(s)** *ou* **chose(s) cessante(s)** immediately

cessation [sɛsasjɔ̃] NF cessation; **c. de paiements** suspension of payments; **cette entreprise est en c. de paiements** the company is unable to meet its financial obligations; **c. d'entreprise** ceasing of trading; **après la c. de l'entreprise** after the company ceased trading; **fermé pour cause de c. d'activité** business closed down; **c. des hostilités** ceasefire

cesse [sɛs] NF **1 sans c.** constantly, continually, incessantly; **il est sans c. en train de travailler** he's constantly *or* continually working, he works incessantly; **il a plu sans c. pendant les vacances** it rained non-stop during the holidays; **il parle sans c.** he never stops talking, he talks non-stop **2** *Litt* **il n'aura (pas) de c. qu'il ne réussisse** he won't stop *or* rest until he has succeeded

cesser [sese] VI to cease, to stop; **le vent a cessé** the wind has died down; **faire c. qch** to put a stop to sth; **la douleur devrait bientôt c.** the pain should go away *or* stop soon; **il faudra que ça cesse** this has to stop; **faire c. une rumeur** to scotch a rumour
  VT **c. le travail** (*pour grève*) to walk out, to down tools; **c. les affaires** to close down; **c. toutes relations avec qn** to break off all relations with sb; **c. les paiements** to suspend *or* discontinue payment(s); **cessez ces cris!** stop that shouting!; *Mil* **cessez le feu!** cease fire!; **c. de faire qch** to stop doing sth; **il n'a pas cessé de neiger pendant plusieurs jours** it didn't stop snowing for several days; **c. de fumer** to give up *or* stop smoking; **il n'a pas cessé de nous observer** he's been watching us all this time; **je n'ai jamais cessé de les voir** I've never stopped seeing them; *Litt* **ne c. de faire qch** to keep doing sth, to persist in doing sth; **il ne cesse de le dire et je pense qu'il a raison** he never stops saying so and I think he's right

cessez-le-feu [seselfø] NM INV ceasefire

cessible [sesibl] ADJ *Jur* transferable, assignable; (*pension etc*) negotiable

cession [sɛsjɔ̃] NF *Jur* transfer, assignment; **faire c. de qch à qn** to transfer *or* assign *or* surrender sth to sb; **acte de c.** certificate *or* deed of transfer; **c. de bail** leaseback; *Com* **c. de licence** licensing; **c. de licence de marque** corporate licensing; *Mktg* **c. de licence de nom** name licensing; **c. de parts** sale *or* disposal of securities; **c. d'actifs** sale of assets

cession-bail, *pl* **cessions-baux** NF *Fin* leaseback

cessionnaire [sɛsjɔnɛr] N **1** *Com* transferee, assignee; (*d'un effet de commerce, d'une créance*) holder; *Jur* assignee, cessionary **2** (*d'un chèque*) endorser

c'est-à-dire [sɛtadir] CONJ that is (to say),

i.e.; **un parent, c. son oncle** a relative, that is to say, his uncle; **vous l'avez prévenu? – c. que non** did you let him know? – well, actually, I'm afraid I didn't; **c. que je n'étais pas au courant** the thing is that no one told me; **j'ai raté mon train, c. que je serai en retard** I missed my train so I'll be late; **elle m'en veut – c. qu'elle t'a attendue deux heures** she's annoyed with me – well, you did keep her waiting for two hours; **il m'agace! – c.?** he gets on my nerves! – what do you mean by that?

césure [sezyr] NF caesura; *Ordinat* break, hyphenation; *Ordinat* **c. automatique** soft hyphen; *Ordinat* **c. imposée** hard hyphen; *Ordinat* **c. interactive** interactive *or* prompted hyphenation

CET [seəte] NM *Scol Anciennement* (*abrév* **collège d'enseignement technique**) ≃ technical college

cet *voir* **ce²**

cétacé [setase] ADJ, NM *Zool* cetacean

cétane [setan] NM cetane

C et F (*abrév* **coût et fret**) C&F

cette *voir* **ce²**

ceux *voir* **celui**

cévenol, -ole [sevnɔl] ADJ (*habitant, natif*) of the Cévennes
  N **C.** (*habitant*) inhabitant of the Cévennes; (*natif*) native of the Cévennes

Ceylan [selɑ̃] NM *Anciennement* Ceylon

cézigue [sezig] PRON *Fam* his lordship, *Br* his nibs

cf cf

CFA [seɛfa] (*abrév* **Communauté financière africaine**) franc **C.** CFA franc

CFAO [seɛfao] NF (*abrév* **conception et fabrication assistées par ordinateur**) CADCAM

CFC [seɛfse] NMPL *Chimie* (*abrév* **chlorofluorocarbures**) CFCs

CFDT [seɛfdete] NF (*abrév* **Confédération française démocratique du travail**) = French trade union

CFF [seɛfɛf] NMPL *Suisse Rail* (*abrév* **Chemins de fer fédéraux**) = Swiss railways

CFP [seɛfpe] NM (*abrév* **centre de formation professionnelle**) = training centre

CFTC [seɛftese] NF (*abrév* **Confédération française des travailleurs chrétiens**) = French trade union

CGC [seʒese] NF (*abrév* **Confédération générale des cadres**) = French trade union of managerial staff

CGI [seʒei] NM *Admin* (*abrév* **Code général des impôts**) general tax code
  NF *Ordinat* (*abrév* **common gateway interface**) CGI

CGT [seʒete] NF (*abrév* **Confédération générale du travail**) = French trade union

chablon [ʃablɔ̃] NM *Suisse* (*pochoir*) stencil

chabot [ʃabo] NM (*poisson*) (*de mer*) bullhead; (*d'eau douce*) chub

chabrot [ʃabro] NM **faire c.** = to finish one's soup by adding wine to it and drinking it straight from the bowl

chacal, -als [ʃakal] NM *aussi Fig* jackal

cha-cha-cha [tʃatʃatʃa] NM INV *Mus* cha-cha(-cha)

chacon(n)e [ʃakɔn] NF *Mus* chaconne

chacun, -une [ʃakœ̃, -yn] PRON INDÉF **1** (*chaque personne d'un groupe*) each (one), every one; **chacune d'elles a refusé** each (one) *or* every one of them refused; **trois euros c.** three euros each; **ils ont pris c. son** *ou* **leur chapeau** each of them took their *or Fml* his hat, they each took their hat; **nous avons pris c. notre chapeau** each of us took our *or Fml* his hat, we each took our hat; **ils ont c.**

leurs qualités et leurs défauts they each have their good and bad points; **ils sont partis c. de son** *ou* **de leur côté** they (each *or* all) went their separate ways **2** (*tout le monde*) everybody, everyone; **c. pour soi** every man for himself; **c. ses goûts** everyone to their own taste; **c. son tour** each in turn; **on est passé c. son tour** everyone went past in turn; **c. son tour!** wait your turn!; *Fam* **tout un c.** all and sundry, everyTom, Dick and Harry; **c'est à la portée de tout un c.** it's within everyone's reach

chaebol [kebɔl] NM *Écon* chaebol

chafouin [ʃafwɛ̃, -in] ADJ (*air*) foxy, sly; **personne à la mine chafouine** foxy- *or* sly-looking person

chagatte [ʃagat] NF *Vulg* pussy, snatch, *Br* fanny

chagrin¹ [ʃagrɛ̃] ADJ *Litt* chagrined; *Vieilli* sad, downcast; **esprits chagrins** malcontents
  NM (*peine*) grief, sorrow, *Fml* affliction; *Vieilli* vexation, chagrin; **avoir du c.** to be sorrowful, to grieve; **il a un gros c.** (*d'un enfant*) he's very upset; **faire du c. à qn** to grieve *or* distress sb; **usé par le c.** careworn; **mourir de c.** to die of grief *or* of a broken heart; **un c. d'amour** an unhappy love affair

chagrin² NM (*cuir*) shagreen

chagrinant [ʃagrinɑ̃] ADJ distressing; *Vieilli* annoying, vexing

chagriner¹ [ʃagrine] VT (*peiner*) to grieve, to distress; *Vieilli* to vex, to annoy; (*chiffonner*) to worry, to bother; **cela me chagrine lorsque je vois que …** it grieves *or* pains me when I see that …; **je ne voulais pas vous c. en vous le disant** I didn't want to upset you by telling you
  VPR **se chagriner** (*se désoler*) to grieve; (*s'inquiéter*) to fret; *Can* **le temps se chagrine** it's clouding over, it's getting cloudy

chagriner² VT (*cuir*) to shagreen, to grain

chah [ʃa] NM shah

chahut [ʃay] NM *Fam* racket, din; **faire du c.** to make a din, to kick up a din *or* a racket *or* a rumpus, to create an uproar; **les élèves ont fait un c. pour protester contre la décision** the pupils kicked up a racket to show their disapproval of the decision

chahuter [ʃayte] *Fam* VI to make a din, to kick up a din *or* a racket *or* a rumpus, to create an uproar
  VT (*orateur*) to heckle, to boo, to barrack; **se faire c.** (*d'orateur*) to be *or* get heckled; **les filles se sont fait c. par les garçons** the boys gave the girls a hard time; **elle se fait c. par ses élèves** she can't control her pupils

chahuteur, -euse [ʃaytœr, -øz] *Fam* ADJ (*étudiant etc*) rowdy, disorderly
  N rowdy (person); (*dans un meeting politique*) heckler

chai [ʃɛ] NM wine and spirits store(house)

chaînage [ʃɛnaʒ] NM **1** (*arpentage*) chaining, chain measuring **2** *Constr* (*des murs*) tying, clamping; (*armature*) tie irons, (series of) clamps, ties **3** *Ordinat* chaining; (*de commandes*) piping

chaîne [ʃɛn] NF **1** (*d'acier, d'or etc*) chain; *Naut* cable; **la c. saute facilement** (*sur ma bicyclette*) the chain keeps coming off; **mettre un chien à la c.** to chain up a dog; **briser ses chaînes** to break free from one's chains; *Fig* to throw off one's chains *or* shackles; **faire la c.** (*pour faire passer des seaux etc*) to form a chain; *Ind* **travail/travailleur à la c.** assembly line *or* production line work/worker; **travailler à la c.** to work on the assembly *or* production line; *Naut* **le navire a cassé sa c.** the ship has parted her cable
  2 (*série*) (*d'hôtels, de magasins, de petits lacs*) chain; **une grande c. de supermarchés**

a large supermarket chain; *Com* **c. intégrée** corporate-operated group; **c. volontaire** consortium; **c. volontaire de détaillants** voluntary retailer chain; **c. d'idées** train of thought; **réaction en c.** chain reaction **3** *(par correspondance)* chain letter **4** *Chimie, Électron etc* chain **5** *TV* channel; **c. de télévision** television channel; **je regarde la première c.** I'm watching channel one; **changeons de c.** let's change channel; **qu'est-ce qu'il y a sur les autres chaînes?** what's on the other channels?; **c. publique/à péage** *ou* **payante** public *or* state-owned/subscription *or* pay channel; **c. à la carte** pay-per-view channel; **c. commerciale** commercial channel; **c. d'information continue** news channel; **c. de cinéma** movie channel; **c. de jeux (interactifs)** (interactive) games channel; **c. musicale** music channel; **c. de télé-achat** shopping channel; **c. généraliste** general-interest channel; **c. numérique** digital channel; **c. ouverte** public access channel; **c. par satellite** satellite channel; **c. spécialisée** specialized *or* specialist channel; **c. thématique** thematic *or* theme *or* specialist channel **6** *Tex* warp **7** *Ordinat* string; **c. de caractères** character string; **c. de recherche** search string; **c. à rechercher** search string
▸▸ **c. alimentaire** food chain; **c. d'arpenteur** surveying chain, surveyor's chain; *Aviat* **c. de charters** back-to-back; *Aut* **c. de distribution** timing *or* camshaft chain; *Ind* **c. de fabrication** production line; *Ind* **c. du froid** cold chain; **c. (haute-fidélité)** hi-fi; **c. laser** CD system; *Ind* **c. de montage** assembly line; **c. de montagnes** range *or* chain of mountains; **c. de montre** watch chain; *Aut* **chaînes à neige** snow chains; *Ling* **c. parlée** speech chain; *Naut* **c. de port** harbour (chain) boom; **c. de solidarité** network of support; **c. de sûreté** door chain, safety chain; **c. de vélo** bicycle chain

chaîner [ʃene] VT **1** *Constr (murs etc)* to tie **2** *Aut* to put chains on **3** *Ordinat (fichiers)* to join; *(commandes)* to pipe

chaînette [ʃenet] NF **1** *(bijou, petite chaîne etc)* small chain; **c. antivol** chain lock **2** *Math* **(arc en) c.** catenary (curve) **3** *Couture* **point de c.** chain stitch

chaînon [ʃenɔ̃] NM **1** *(dans une chaîne)* link; *Fig* **le c. manquant** the missing link **2** *Géog (de montagnes)* secondary chain

chair [ʃɛr] NF **1** *(chez l'homme et les animaux)* flesh; *(de pêche, de melon etc)* flesh, pulp; **en c. et en os** in the flesh, in person; **être (bien) en c.** *(d'un poulet)* to be nice and plump; *(d'une personne)* to be plump *or Fam* tubby; *Fig* **n'être ni c. ni poisson** to be neither fish nor fowl (nor good red herring); **une odeur de c. fraîche** a smell of fresh meat; *Fig* **il aime la c. fraîche** *(d'un séducteur)* he likes them young
2 *Beaux-Arts* **chairs** flesh tints **3** *Rel* body, *Péj* flesh; **la résurrection de la c.** the resurrection of the body; *Bible* **le Verbe s'est fait c.** the Word was made flesh; **c. de sa c.** his own flesh and blood; **souffrir dans sa c.** to suffer in the flesh; **la c. est faible** the flesh is weak; **péché de c.** sin of the flesh; **œuvre de c.** carnal knowledge
ADJ INV **(couleur) c.** flesh-coloured, *Am* flesh-colored
▸▸ **c. à canon** cannon fodder; **c. à pâté** sausagemeat; **c. de poule** gooseflesh, goose pimples, *Am* goose bumps; **cela vous donne** *ou* **on en a la c. de poule** it gives you goose pimples, it makes your flesh creep, *Fam* it gives you the creeps; **c. à saucisses** sausagemeat; *Fig Fam* **je vais en faire de la c. à saucisses** I'll make mincemeat of him

chaire [ʃɛr] NF **1** *(dans une église)* pulpit; **monter en c.** to go up into the pulpit **2** *Univ (fonction)* chair, professorship; *(tribune)* chair; **elle a été nommée à la c. d'anglais** she has been appointed to the chair of English; **être titulaire d'une c.** to hold a chair **3** *(trône)* chair, throne; **la c. de saint Pierre, la c. pontificale** the Chair of St Peter, the Holy See; **c. d'un évêque** bishop's throne

chaise [ʃɛz] NF **1** *(siège)* chair, seat; **c. de paille/cannée** straw/cane chair; **prenez donc une c.** have *or* take a seat; *Fig* **être assis** *ou* **très Fam avoir le cul entre deux chaises** to be in an awkward position; **porter qn en c., faire la c. à qn** to give sb a chair; **(jeu des) chaises musicales** (game of) musical chairs **2** *Naut etc* rope sling; **nœud de c.** bowline hitch
▸▸ **c. à bascule** rocking chair; *Can* **c. berçante/berceuse** rocking chair; **c. de cuisine** kitchen chair; *Jur* **c. électrique** electric chair; **passer à la c. électrique** to go to the (electric) chair; **c. d'enfant** (baby's) high chair; **c. haute** (baby's) high chair; **c. de jardin** garden chair; **c. longue** chaise longue; *(transatlantique)* deckchair; **faire de la c. longue** to have a rest, to put one's feet up; **c. percée** (night) commode; **c. pivotante** swivel chair; **c. à porteurs** sedan chair; **c. de poste** post chaise; **c. roulante** wheelchair

chaisier, -ière [ʃezje, -jɛr] N chairmaker
NF *Vieilli* **chaisière** *(dans un jardin public etc)* chair attendant

chaland¹ [ʃalɑ̃] NM *Naut* barge, lighter; **transport par chalands** lighterage

chaland², -ande [-ɑ̃d] N *Vieilli* client; **attirer le c.** to attract customers *or* custom

chalandage [ʃalɑ̃daʒ] NM *Com* shopping

chalazion [ʃalazjɔ̃] NM *Méd* chalazion

chaldaïque [kaldaik] ADJ Chaldean
N **C.** Chaldean

Chaldée [kalde] NF *Hist, Géog* Chaldea

chaldéen, -enne [kaldeɛ̃, -ɛn] ADJ Chaldean
NM *Ling* Chaldean
N **C.** Chaldean

châle [ʃal] NM shawl

chalet [ʃalɛ] NM **1** *(de montagne etc)* chalet **2** *Can* cottage **3** *Arch* **c. de nécessité** public convenience

chaleur [ʃalœr] NF **1** *(température)* heat, warmth; *Fig* warmth; *(d'un plaidoyer etc)* passion; **c. sèche/humide** dry/humid heat; **il fait une c. terrible dans ces dortoirs** it's terribly hot in these dormitories; **tu ne vas pas sortir par cette c.?** you're not going out in this heat, are you?; **vague de c.** heatwave; **il fait une c. lourde/accablante** it's very muggy/it's oppressively hot; **craint la c.** *(sur une étiquette)* store in a cool place; **c. spécifique/latente** specific/latent heat; *Méd* **éprouver des chaleurs, avoir des bouffées de c.** *(d'une femme ménopausée)* to have hot flushes; **sensation de c.** *(après un bain froid etc)* glow; **on a une impression de c. dès qu'on enfile ces gants** you feel warm as soon as you put these gloves on; *Méd* **coup de c.** heatstroke; **les chaleurs** the hot weather; **pendant les grandes chaleurs** during the hot season; **c. de coloris** warmth of colour; **rechercher la c. humaine** to look for human warmth; **parler avec c.** to speak warmly *or* enthusiastically; **il sera accueilli avec c.** he will receive a warm welcome
2 *(des animaux)* heat, rut; **en c.** on heat, *surtout Am* in heat; *Fig Vulg* **il/elle est en c., celui-là/celle-là!** he's/she's randy *or* horny *or* on heat, that one!
▸▸ **c. animale** body heat; *Phys* **c. atomique d'un corps** atomic heat of a body

chaleureusement [ʃalœrøzmɑ̃] ADV warmly

chaleureux, -euse [ʃalørø, -øz] ADJ *(accueil etc)* warm, cordial, hearty; *(termes, paroles)* glowing; *(applaudissements etc)* enthusiastic; **remercier qn en termes c.** to thank sb warmly

châlit [ʃali] NM bedstead

challenge [ʃalɑ̃ʒ] NM **1** *Sport* challenge match, tournament **2** *Fig (défi)* challenge; **c'est un réel c. que de vouloir changer de travail à son âge** it's a real challenge to want to change jobs at his age

challenger [tʃalɑ̃dʒɛr] NM *Sport etc* challenger

chaloir [ʃalwar] V IMPERS *Arch, Litt (used only in)* **peu me chaut, peu m'en chaut** I don't give a fig, I care not

chaloupe [ʃalup] NF *Naut* launch, longboat, tender; *(à rames)* rowing boat, *Am* rowboat; **c. de sauvetage** lifeboat; **c. à moteur** motor launch; **c. de pêche** fishing boat

chaloupé [ʃalupe] ADJ *(danse, démarche)* swaying

chalumeau, -eaux [ʃalymo] NM **1** *Tech* blowlamp, blowtorch; **faire une soudure au c.** to weld with a blowlamp; **c. oxyacétylénique** oxyacetylene torch **2** *Mus* pipe **3** *Vieilli (paille)* (drinking) straw; **c. de roseau** reed **4** *Can* spout *(for collecting sap of maple tree)*

chalut [ʃaly] NM *Pêche* trawl; **pêcher au c.** to trawl

chalutage [ʃalytaʒ] NM *Pêche* trawling

chalutier [ʃalytje] NM *(bateau)* trawler; *(pêcheur)* trawlerman

chamade [ʃamad] NF **mon cœur battait la c.** my heart was thumping *or* beating wildly

chamailler (se) [səʃamaje] VPR *Fam* to bicker, to squabble

chamaillerie [ʃamajri] NF *Fam (dispute)* squabble, row

chamailleur, -euse [ʃamajœr, -øz] ADJ quarrelsome
N quarrelsome person, squabbler

chaman [ʃaman] NM *Rel* shaman

chamanisme [ʃamanism] NM *Rel* shamanism

chamarré [ʃamare] ADJ richly- *or* brightly-coloured *or Am* -colored; **c. d'or** with gold brocade

chamarrer [ʃamare] VT *Litt* to bedeck, to adorn

chambard [ʃabar] NM *Fam* **1** *(désordre)* disorder, shambles; *(bouleversement)* upset, upheaval **2** *(bruit)* din, racket; **faire du c.** to make *or* kick up a row; *Fig* **ça va faire du c. quand il l'apprendra!** there'll be an unholy row when he finds out *or* hell to pay when he finds out!

chambardement [ʃabardəmɑ̃] NM *Fam* upset, upheaval; **un grand c. d'idées** a great shake-up of ideas

chambarder [ʃabarde] VT *Fam (mettre en désordre) (maison etc)* to turn upside down, to ransack; *(révolutionner) (un ordre établi, la société)* to turn upside down; **tout c.** to turn everything upside down; **c. les plans de qn** to upset sb's applecart

chambellan [ʃabelɑ̃] NM chamberlain

chambouler [ʃabule] VT *Fam (projets, maison etc)* to turn upside down; **il a fallu tout chambouler** everything's all topsy-turvy *or* upside down

chambranle [ʃabrɑl] NM *(d'une porte, d'une fenêtre)* frame; *(d'une cheminée)* mantelpiece

chambre [ʃabr] NF **1** *(pièce)* bedroom; *(d'un hôtel etc)* room; **c. à coucher** *(pièce)* bedroom; *(mobilier)* bedroom furniture; **c.**

d'amis spare (bed)room, guest room; **c. d'enfants** children's room; *(pour bébé)* nursery; **c. meublée** furnished room, *Br* bedsit(ter); **c. de bonne** maid's room; *(petit appartement)* attic room; **c. pour deux personnes** *ou* **double** double room; **c. à deux lits** room with twin beds, twin-bedded room; **c. pour une personne** *ou* **à un lit, c. individuelle** single room; **c. à lits jumeaux** twin(-bedded) room; **chambres attenantes** adjoining rooms; **chambres communicantes** connecting rooms; **c. avec petit déjeuner** bed and breakfast; **vous auriez une c. (de) libre?** do you have any vacancies?; **faire c. à part** to sleep in separate rooms; **faire sa c.** to clean (out) *or* tidy (up) one's room; **garder la c.** to keep to one's room; **travailler en c.** to work at home; **ouvrier en c.** homeworker; **sportif/stratège en c.** armchair sportsman/strategist; **musique de c.** chamber music
  2 *Admin, Jur* chamber, house, division of a court of justice
  3 *Pol* **la C.** the House; **siéger à la C.** to sit in the House
  4 *Physiol (de l'œil)* chamber
  5 *Tech (d'un fusil, d'une serrure etc)* chamber; **pneu sans c.** tubeless tyre
  6 *Belg, Suisse (pièce quelconque)* room; **une maison de six c.** a six-roomed house
  ▶▶ *Jur* **c. d'accusation** court of criminal appeal; **c. d'agriculture** = farmers' association; **c. à air** *(d'un pneu)* inner tube; *Aut* **c. d'air** air *or* plenum chamber; *Aut* **c. d'alimentation** feed chamber; **c. ardente** ≃ Star Chamber; *Parl* **C. basse** Lower House, Lower Chamber; *Phys* **c. à bulles** bubble chamber; *Aut* **c. de carburation** mixing chamber; *Naut* **c. des cartes** charthouse, chart room; **c. de chauffe** boiler room; *Naut* stokehold; **c. claire** camera lucida; *Fin* **c. de clearing** clearing house; *Tech* **c. de combustion** *ou* **d'explosion** combustion chamber; **C. de commerce (internationale)** (International) Chamber of Commerce; *Fin* **c. de compensation** clearing house; *Fin* **c. de compensation automatisée** automated clearing house; *Jur* **c. correctionnelle** District Court; *Anciennement* **c. des députés** Chamber of Deputies; **c. d'écho** echo chamber; **c. forte** safety vault, strong room; **c. frigorifique** *ou* **froide** cold (storage) room, cold store; **c. à gaz** gas chamber; *Parl* **C. haute** Upper House, Upper Chamber; **c. d'hôte** bed and breakfast; *Nucl* **c. d'ionisation** ionization chamber; *Suisse* **c. à lessive** *(buanderie)* laundry room; **c. des machines** engine room; *Aut* **c. de mélange** mixing chamber; **c. des métiers** ≃ guild chamber; **c. noire** *Phot* darkroom; *TV, Cin* loading room; *Jur* **c. des requêtes** appeal court; *Aut* **c. de résonance** resonating chamber; *Aut* **c. de turbulence** swirl chamber, turbulence combustion chamber; **c. de vapeur** steam room

chambrée [ʃɑ̃bre] NF **1** *(occupants d'une chambre)* room(ful) **2** *Mil* barrackroom

chambrer [ʃɑ̃bre] VT **1 c. un vin** to bring wine to room temperature; **chambré** at room temperature **2** *Fam (se moquer de)* **c. qn** to pull sb's leg **3** *Vieilli* **c. qn** to confine sb, to lock sb up, to keep sb locked up

chambrette [ʃɑ̃brɛt] NF little (bed)room

chambrière [ʃɑ̃brijɛr] NF **1** *Arch* chambermaid **2** *(fouet)* long whip, lunging whip

chameau, -eaux [ʃamo] NM *Zool* camel; **en** *ou* **à dos de c.** on camel (back); **quel c.!** *(d'un homme)* what a bastard!; *(d'une femme)* what a cow *or* bitch!
  ADJ *Fam* **ce qu'il/qu'elle est c.!** what a bastard he is/bitch she is!; **ce qu'il peut être c. avec elle!** he can be such a bastard to her!

chamelier [ʃaməlje] NM camel-driver, cameleer

chamelle [ʃamɛl] NF she-camel

chamois [ʃamwa] NM **1** *Zool* chamois; **(peau de) c.** chamois leather, shammy (leather) **2** *Sport* **c. d'or/d'argent/de bronze** = gold/silver/bronze skiing proficiency medal
  ADJ INV buff

champ¹ [ʃɑ̃] NM **1** *Agr* field; **c. de blé** field of wheat, wheatfield; **fleur des champs** wild flower; **courir les champs** to wander about the country; **aux champs** in the fields; **prendre** *ou* **couper à travers champs** to go *or* cut across country; **prendre la clef des champs** to run off, to decamp; **en plein(s) champ(s)** in the open (fields); **à tout bout de c.** repeatedly, at every possible opportunity; *Fig* **laisser le c. libre à qn** to leave the field free for sb, to give sb a free hand; **son assistante a le c. libre** his assistant has a free hand *or* rein; **donner le c. libre à qch** to give free rein to sth; *Fig* **le c. est libre** the coast's clear
  2 *(espace)* **prendre du c.** to give oneself (plenty of) room **(pour sauter** to jump); **donnez-moi du c.** give me (some) elbow room
  3 *Fig (domaine)* field; **ses lectures embrassent un c. très étendu** his reading covers a very wide field *or* a very wide range of subjects; **élargir le c. de son activité** to extend the scope *or* range of one's activities; **le c. de la connaissance** the field of (human) knowledge
  4 *Cin etc* shot, picture; *Opt (d'un télescope etc)* field; **c. optique** *ou* **visuel** *ou* **de vision** field of view *or* of vision; *Phot* **profondeur de c.** depth of focus; **hors c.** off camera; **en dehors du c.** out of shot *or* vision; **être dans le c.** to be in shot; **sortir du c.** to go out of shot; **récit hors c.** voice over
  5 *Élec, Électron, Radio* field
  6 *Ordinat* field; **c. d'action** sensitivity; **c. alphanumérique** alphanumeric(al) field; **c. calculé** calculated field; **c. mémo** memo field; **c. numérique** numeric field; **c. de saisie** form field; **c. de texte** text field; **c. variable** variable field
  7 *Beaux-Arts (d'un tableau)* field, ground; *Hér (d'armoiries)* field
  8 *Chir* **c. opératoire** field of operation
  ▶▶ **c. d'aviation** airfield; *Mil* **c. de bataille** battlefield; *Hist* **c. clos** lists; **c. de courses** racecourse, *Am* racetrack; **c. de foire** fairground; **c. de glace** icefield; *Mil* **c. d'honneur** battlefield; **mort** *ou* **tombé au c. d'honneur** killed in action; *Phys* **c. magnétique** magnetic field; **c. de manœuvres** drill *or* exercise *or* parade ground; **c. de mines** minefield; **c. de neige** snowfield; *Ling* **c. sémantique** semantic field; **c. de tir** firing *or* shooting *or* rifle range; *Mil* practice ground; *(d'un fusil)* field of fire

champ² [ʃɑ̃p] NM *Fam (abrév* **champagne***)* bubbly, *Br* champers

Champagne [ʃɑ̃paɲ] NF **1** *(région)* Champagne; **C. humide** wet Champagne; **C. pouilleuse** dry Champagne **2** *(eau-de-vie)* **fine c.** liqueur brandy
  NM **(vin de) C.** champagne

champagnisation [ʃɑ̃paɲizasjɔ̃] NF champagnization

champagniser [ʃɑ̃paɲize] VT *(vin)* to champagnize

champenois, -oise [ʃɑ̃pənwa, -waz] ADJ **1** *(de la région)* of Champagne **2 méthode champenoise** (natural) champagnization method, champagne method
  N **C.** *(natif)* native of Champagne; *(habitant)* inhabitant of Champagne

champêtre [ʃɑ̃pɛtr] ADJ rustic, rural; **vie c.** country life; *Admin* **garde c.** country *or* village policeman

champignon [ʃɑ̃piɲɔ̃] NM **1** *Bot* **c. (comestible)** mushroom; **c. vénéneux** poisonous mushroom, toadstool; *Fig* **pousser comme**

un c. to (spring up like a) mushroom; *Fig* **ville c.** mushroom *or* boom town **2** *Méd* fungus, fungoid growth VOIR GRAMMAIRE A14 **3** *(de modiste)* hatstand **4** *Aut Fam* accelerator (pedal); **appuyer sur le c.** to put one's foot down, *Am* to step on the gas
  ▶▶ **c. atomique** mushroom cloud; **c. de couche** button mushroom; **c. hallucinogène** hallucinogenic mushroom, *Fam* magic mushroom; *Culin* **c. noir** dried mushroom; **c. de Paris** button mushroom

champignonnière [ʃɑ̃piɲɔnjɛr] NF mushroom bed

champignonniste [ʃɑ̃piɲɔnist] N mushroom grower

champion, -ionne [ʃɑ̃pjɔ̃, -jɔn] N **1** *Sport etc* champion; **le c. du monde d'escrime** the world fencing champion; **un c. de ski** a ski champion; **une championne de gym** a champion gymnast; *Fam* **c'est un c. du bricolage** he's a first-class handyman; **je suis vraiment le c. de la gaffe** I'm a great one for putting my foot in it **2** *(d'une cause etc)* champion, defender; **se poser en** *ou* **se faire le c. de la protection des animaux** to champion the protection of animals
  ADJ **1** *Sport* **l'équipe championne du monde** the world champions **2** *Fam* great, *Br Dial* champion; **c'est c.!** it's first-rate!; **elle est championne, ta copine!** your girlfriend is terrific!; **pour les gaffes, il est c.!** he's a great one for putting his foot in it!

championnat [ʃɑ̃pjɔna] NM championship; **c. du monde de course à pied** world running championship

chançard, -arde [ʃɑ̃sar, -ard] *Fam* ADJ *(personne)* lucky
  N lucky person; **quel c.!** (he's a) lucky devil!

chance [ʃɑ̃s] NF **1** *(possibilité)* chance, likelihood; **vous avez toutes les chances d'être accusé, il y a toutes les chances (pour) que vous soyez accusé** there is every chance *or* likelihood that you will be accused; **il a compris qu'il fallait mettre toutes les chances de son côté** he realized he had to leave nothing to chance; **il a des chances d'être choisi** he stands a good chance of being chosen; **il a peu de chances de réussir** *ou* **de succès** he has little chance of succeeding, he's very unlikely to succeed; **elles ont des chances égales d'être nommées** they have an even chance of being appointed; **donner une** *ou* **sa c. à qn/qch** to give sb/sth a chance; **elle a une c. sur deux de gagner** she has a fifty-fifty chance of winning; **il y a une c. sur cent (pour) qu'elle le voie** there's a chance in a hundred that she'll see him; **il n'a aucune c. (de réussir)** he doesn't stand a chance *or* he has no chance (of succeeding); **calculer** *ou* **évaluer ses chances de succès** to work out one's chances of success; *Fam* **il y a une c.** *ou* **des chances** it's just possible; **il y a très peu de chances qu'elle puisse le faire à temps** there's very little chance that she'll be able to do it on time; **il y a de grandes** *ou* **fortes chances pour qu'on le lui propose** there's every chance that he will be offered it
  2 *(sort)* (good) luck, fortune; **la c. lui sourit** fortune smiles on him; **tenter sa c.** to try one's luck, to chance it; **la c. peut tourner à tout moment** our/your/etc luck could change at any time; **souhaiter bonne c. à qn** to wish sb luck; **bonne c.!** good luck!; **quelle c.!** what a bit of stroke of luck!; **avec un peu de c., on pourra le faire** with a bit of luck, we'll be able to do it; **elle a eu la c. de le rencontrer de son vivant** she was lucky enough to meet him when he was still alive; **avoir de la c.** to be lucky *or* fortunate; **elle n'a pas eu de c.** she was unlucky; **il y a vraiment des gens qui n'ont pas de c.** some people really don't have any luck, *Fam* some people

really get all the bad breaks; **porter c. à qn** to bring sb luck; **jour de c.** lucky day; **c'est bien ma c.!** just my luck!; **pas de c.!** hard luck!; **par c.** luckily, fortunately, by a stroke of luck; **la c. est avec nous** our luck's in

> Il faut noter que le nom anglais **chance** ne signifie jamais **bonne fortune**.

chancelant [ʃɑ̃slɑ̃] ADJ unsteady, wavering, shaky; *(courage, détermination)* wavering; *(mémoire)* shaky; **pas chancelants** staggering *or* tottering *or* unsteady footsteps; **une autorité chancelante** shaky *or* wavering authority; **le pouvoir est c.** the government is tottering *or* is on the brink of collapse; **santé chancelante** *(d'un vieillard etc)* delicate *or* poor health

chanceler [ʃɑ̃sle] VI (**je chancelle, n. chancelons; je chancellerai**) *(action)* to stagger, to totter; *(état)* to be unsteady (on one's legs); *(d'une chose)* to wobble; **avancer/reculer/entrer/sortir en chancelant** to stagger *or* totter forward/back/in/out; **l'uppercut le fit c.** the uppercut sent him reeling; **le régime chancelle** the government is tottering; **c. dans sa résolution** to waver *or* falter in one's resolution

chancelier [ʃɑ̃səlje] NM chancellor; *Admin* **c. de l'université** chancellor of the university; **Grand C.** *(en Grande-Bretagne)* Lord Chancellor; **c. de l'Échiquier** Chancellor of the Exchequer

chancelière [ʃɑ̃səljɛr] NF *(pour les pieds)* footmuff

chancellerie [ʃɑ̃sɛlri] NF *Hist (d'une ambassade)* chancery

chanceux, -euse [ʃɑ̃sø, -øz] ADJ *(personne)* lucky, fortunate; **vous voilà bien c.!** you're lucky!, you're in luck!; **Can c.!** (you) lucky devil!

chanci [ʃɑ̃si] ADJ *Vieilli* mouldy, *Am* moldy

chancre [ʃɑ̃kr] NM *Bot, Méd, Vét, Fig* canker; *Méd* **c. syphilitique** chancre; **c. mou** soft chancre; *Arg* **manger comme un c.** to eat like a horse, to make a pig of oneself

chandail [ʃɑ̃daj] NM sweater, jumper

Chandeleur (la) [laʃɑ̃dlœr] NF *Rel* Candlemas

chandelier [ʃɑ̃dəlje] NM *(à une branche)* candlestick; *(à plusieurs branches)* candelabra

> Il faut noter que le nom anglais **chandelier** est un faux ami. Il signifie **lustre**.

chandelle [ʃɑ̃dɛl] NF **1** *(bougie en cire)* candle; *(de suif)* (tallow) candle; **s'éclairer à la c.** to use candlelight; **économies de bouts de c.** cheeseparing; **faire des économies de bouts de c.** to scrimp and save; **travailler/dîner à la c.** to work/dine by candlelight; **un dîner aux chandelles** a candlelit dinner; *Fig* **brûler la c. par les deux bouts** to burn the candle at both ends; *(dépenser trop d'argent)* to be extravagant (with money); *Fig* **le jeu n'en vaut pas la c.** the game is not worth the candle; *Fig* **tenir la c.** to play gooseberry, *Am* to feel like a fifth wheel; *Fig* **en voir trente-six chandelles** to see stars; *Fig* **je vous dois une fière c.** I owe you more than I can repay; **lancer qch en c.** to throw sth straight up in the air

2 *Fam (de morve) (au bout du nez)* snot

3 *Tennis* lob; *Ftbl* high ball; *Rugby* garryowen, up and under; *Gym* shoulder stand; **faire une c.** *Rugby* to do an up and under; *Tennis* to lob the ball; *Gym* **faire la c.** to do a shoulder stand

4 *Aviat* **(montée en) c.** vertical climb; **monter en c.** *(d'un avion)* to climb vertically

5 *Aut* chassis stand

6 *Typ, Journ* full column

chanfrein¹ [ʃɑ̃frɛ̃] NM *(de cheval)* nose, forehead

chanfrein² NM *Archit* chamfered edge, chamfer, bevelled edge

chanfreiner [ʃɑ̃frene] VT *Tech* to chamfer

change [ʃɑ̃ʒ] NM **1** *Fin* exchange; **le c. est avantageux** the exchange rate is good; **au c. du jour** at the current rate of exchange; **c. du dollar** dollar exchange; *Fig* **gagner** *ou* **ne pas perdre au c.** to gain on *or* by the exchange, to lose nothing on the deal; *Fig* **je n'y ai pas perdu au c.** I came out (of it) ahead, I didn't lose by it; **lettre de c.** bill of exchange; **bureau de c.** bureau de change; **opérations de c.** (foreign) exchange transactions; **cours du c.** exchange rate, rate of exchange; **marché des changes** foreign exchange; **agent de c.** stockbroker; **contrôle des changes** exchange control

2 *(chasse)* **donner le c. aux chiens** to put hounds on the wrong scent; *Fig* **donner le c. à qn** to put sb on a false scent *or* trail

3 *(couche-culotte)* **c. (complet)** disposable nappy *or Am* diaper

> Il faut noter que le nom anglais **change** signifie **petite monnaie** quand il se réfère à de l'argent.

changeable [ʃɑ̃ʒabl] ADJ changeable

changeant [ʃɑ̃ʒɑ̃] ADJ changeable, variable; **caractère c.** changeable *or* fickle disposition; **d'humeur changeante** moody; **temps c.** unsettled weather; **soie changeante** shot silk

changement [ʃɑ̃ʒmɑ̃] NM **1** *(d'air, de résidence, de condition etc)* change; *Scol* **c. (de section/de classe)** transfer; **il va y avoir du c.** there are going to be some changes, things are going to change; **ça va te faire un drôle de c. d'avoir un enfant** things will be very different for you when you've got a child; **il vous faudrait un c. d'air** *ou* **d'occupation** you need a change (of scenery); *Théâtre* **c. de décor** scene shift *or* change; *Fig* **un c. de décor peut lui faire du bien** a change of scene *or* scenery may do him good; **il n'y a pas de c.** *(dans son état)* there's (been) no change; **la situation est restée longtemps sans c.** the situation stayed the same *or* remained unchanged for a long time; **son c. est radical, ce n'est plus le même!** he's changed completely, he isn't the same person any more!; **c. de programme** *TV, Cin* change in the (advertised) schedule; *Fig (de projets)* change of plan; **c. de programme, on ne va plus chez Paul** there's been a change of plan, we're not going to Paul's any more; **c. de prix** price change; *Mktg* **c. de marque** brand switching; **'c. de propriétaire'** 'under new ownership'; **'c. de direction'** 'under new management'; **c. de régime** change of government; **c. climatique** *ou* **du climat** climate change, change in the climate; **c. de vent** shift of wind; *Rail* **il y a un c. à Valence** you have to change at Valence; **le voyage est sans c. jusqu'à Paris** the train *etc* goes straight through to Paris

2 *Typ* **c. de page** page break; **c. de page obligatoire** hard page break; **c. conditionnel de page** soft page break; **c. de ligne facultatif** soft return; *Ordinat* **c. de ligne** line feed

▶▶ **c. de focale** *(d'une caméra)* zooming; *Cin, TV* **c. de plan** cutaway shot, cutaway; *Aut* **c. de rapports** gear shifting; **c. de vitesse** *(action)* change of gear, (manual) gear change; *(levier)* gear lever; *Théâtre* **c. à vue** transformation scene

CHANGER [ʃɑ̃ʒe] (**je changeai(s), n. changeons**) VT **1** *(remplacer)*, *Fin* to change, to exchange; **c. qch contre qch** to change *or* exchange sth for sth; **elle changerait bien sa place contre** *ou* **pour la tienne** *(situation*

professionnelle, familiale etc) she'd happily swap places with you; **il doit c. sa voiture** he has to change his car, he has to get a new car; **c. les draps** to change the sheets; *Théâtre* **c. le décor** to shift *or* change the scenery; **c. (la couche d')un bébé** to change a baby('s nappy *or Am* diaper); **c. un malade** to put clean clothes on a sick person; **c. un billet de banque** to change a (bank)note; **c. des dollars contre des euros** to change dollars into euros; **c. de l'argent** to change money; **c. un métal en or** to turn *or* change a metal into gold; **la grenouille fut changée en prince** the frog was turned *or* changed into a prince

2 *(modifier)* to change, to alter; *(divertir)* to be a change for; **ils partent vivre en Écosse, ça va les c.!** they're going to live in Scotland, that will be a change for them!; **cela te changera agréablement** *ou* **en bien** that will make a nice change for you; **une promenade me changera les idées** a walk will take my mind off things; **ça nous change du cinéma du coin** that makes a change from the local cinema; **c. sa façon de vivre** to change one's way of life; **ça ne change rien à rien** that doesn't change *or* alter anything, it makes absolutely no difference; **tu n'y changeras rien** there's nothing you can do about it; **elle ne changera pas une virgule au texte** she won't change *or* alter as much as a comma of the text; **cela ne change pas grand-chose** *ou* **rien au fait que ...** that doesn't change *or* alter the fact that ...; **cela ne change rien** *ou* **pas grand-chose à l'affaire** that makes no difference; **cette robe vous change** that dress makes you look different *or* changes you; **cette expérience l'a beaucoup changée** the experience has changed her a lot; **tu ne le changeras pas!** he'll never change!; *Fam* **ça vous change un homme!** it changes a man!; **voilà qui change les choses du tout au tout** that makes all the difference; **mais cela change tout!** that changes everything!; **c. un livre de place** to move a book; **c. les meubles de place** to change *or* move the furniture around; **c. un fonctionnaire de poste** to transfer a civil servant; **c. l'ordre des mots** to change the word order

VI **1** *(se modifier)* to (undergo a) change, to alter; **cette région a beaucoup changé** this region has changed a lot; **ça n'a pas changé, rien n'a changé** nothing has changed; **le temps va c.** the weather's going to change; **il a changé en mal** *ou* **en pire/en bien** *ou* **en mieux** he's changed for the worse/the better; *Iron* **pour c.** (just) for a change; **et pour c., il était de mauvaise humeur** and just for a change, he was in a bad mood; **tu n'as pas changé** you haven't changed (a bit); *Rail etc* **où dois-je c.?** where do I change?; **je dois c. à Bordeaux** I have to change at Bordeaux; **ça ne pourra pas toujours durer comme ça, il faudra que ça change!** it can't go on like this, things will have to change!

2 **c. de** to change; **c. de position** to change position; **c. de secrétaire/de train/de travail** to change secretaries/trains/jobs; **c. de gouvernement** to have a change of government, to have a new government; **c. de main** to change hands, to use the other hand; *Fig* **c. de mains** to change hands; **c. de place avec qn** to change seats with sb; **c. d'amis** to change one's friends; **c. de vie** to change one's way of life; **c. de maison** to move (house); **la rue a changé de nom** the name of the street has been changed, the street has changed its name; **le magasin a changé de propriétaire** the shop is under new management; **c. de genre/de coiffure** to change one's style/hairstyle; **c. de vêtements** to change (one's clothes), to get changed; *Fam* **ton chapeau me va mieux, on**

turn; **descendre une piste en c.** to snow-plough down a ski slope

chasse-pierres NM INV cowcatcher

chasser [ʃase] VT **1** *(animaux)* to hunt; **c. le renard/la perdrix** to go foxhunting/partridge shooting

2 *(personne)* to drive away, to chase out *or* away; *(employé)* to dismiss, *Fam* to sack; *(brouillard etc)* to dispel; **c. qn du pays** to drive sb from the country; **il fut chassé de la classe** he was expelled from the class; **si tu ne paies pas ton loyer, les propriétaires vont te c.** if you don't pay your rent, the owners will evict you; **chasse le chat de la maison!** chase the cat out (of the house)!; **se faire c. de la maison par ses parents** to get thrown out by one's parents; **je ne veux pas vous c., mais il est tard** I'm not trying to get rid of you, but it's getting late; **nous avons été chassés par les moustiques** we were chased away *or* driven away by mosquitoes; **c. une mouche (du revers de la main)** to brush away a fly; **le vent chassait la pluie contre les vitres** the wind was driving the rain against the windowpanes; **le vent va c. les nuages** the wind will blow the clouds away; **c. une mauvaise odeur** to get rid of a bad smell; *Fig* **c. qn/qch de son esprit** to dismiss sb/sth from one's mind *or* thoughts

VI **1** to hunt, to go hunting; *(au fusil)* to shoot, to go shooting; **c. à courre** to hunt, to go hunting; **c. au furet** to ferret; *Fig* **c. sur les terres de qn** to poach on sb's preserve *or* territory

2 *(venir)* to drive; **nuages qui chassent du nord** clouds driving from the north

3 *Naut (d'une ancre)* to drag; **navire qui chasse sur ses ancres** ship dragging her anchors

4 *Aut* to skid

5 *Typ (d'un caractère)* to drive out; *(d'un texte)* to overrun

> Il faut noter que le verbe anglais **to chase** est un faux ami. Il signifie **poursuivre**.

chasseresse [ʃasrɛs] NF *Littér* huntress; **Diane c.** Diana the Huntress

chasseur, -euse [ʃasœr, -øz] N hunter, *f* huntress; *(surtout à courre)* huntsman; **c'est un bon c.** he's a good shot

NM **1** *(dans un hôtel etc)* pageboy, *Am* bellboy, bellhop **2** *Mil, Aviat* fighter; *Naut* **c. de sous-marins** submarine hunter **3** *Mil* rifleman, light infantryman, chasseur; **les chasseurs (à pied)** the light infantry; **les chasseurs alpins** the mountain light infantry ▸▸ **c. d'autographes** autograph hunter; **c. d'images** keen photographer; *(professionnel)* professional photographer; **c. de primes** bounty hunter; *aussi Fig* **c. de têtes** headhunter; *Fig* **elle a été recrutée par un c. de têtes** she was headhunted

chasseur-bagagiste, *pl* **chasseurs-bagagistes** NM luggage porter, porter

chasseur-bombardier, *pl* **chasseurs-bombardiers** NM fighter-bomber

chassie [ʃasi] NF *(dans les yeux)* matter, rheum

chassieux, -ieuse [ʃasjø, -jøz] ADJ *(yeux)* rheumy

châssis [ʃasi] NM **1** *(charpente)* frame; *Beaux-Arts* stretcher; **c. de porte/fenêtre** door/window frame; **c. mobile** sash; **c. dormant** sash (frame); **c. à guillotine** sash window **2** *(de jardin)* (cold) frame; **culture sous c.** forcing **3** *Aut* chassis; **c. treillis** box section chassis; **c. tubulaire** box section chassis, space frame chassis; *Fam* **quel beau c.!** *(d'une femme)* she's got a great figure!, *Vieilli* what a chassis! **4** *Typ* chase

chaste [ʃast] ADJ chaste, pure; **un baiser c.** a chaste kiss; *Iron* **oreilles chastes** delicate ears

chastement [ʃastəmɑ̃] ADV chastely, innocently

chasteté [ʃastəte] NF chastity, purity

chasuble [ʃazybl] NF **1** **robe c.** pinafore dress, *Am* jumper **2** *Rel* chasuble

chat¹, chatte [ʃa, ʃat] N cat, *m* tom(cat); **le C. botté** Puss in Boots; **petit c.** kitten; *Fam* **mon petit c., ma petite chatte** my dear, my pet, my darling; *Fig* **il n'y avait pas un c. dans la rue** there wasn't a soul in the street; **langues de c.** langues de chat, finger biscuits; *Fig* **appeler un c. un c.** to call a spade a spade; **acheter c. en poche** to buy a pig in a poke; **avoir un c. dans la gorge** to have a frog in one's throat; **faire une toilette de c.** to give oneself a cat('s) lick *or* a lick and a promise; *Prov* **il ne faut pas réveiller le c. qui dort** let sleeping dogs lie; **à bon c. bon rat** tit for tat; **c. échaudé craint l'eau froide** once bitten twice shy; **quand le c. n'est pas là, les souris dansent** when the cat's away the mice will play; **jouer au c. et à la souris avec qn** to play cat and mouse with sb; **la nuit tous les chats sont gris** all cats are grey in the dark

NM *(jeu)* tag, tig; *(celui qui cherche)* it; **jouer à c.** to play tag *or* tig; **c. perché** off-ground tag *or* tig; **c'est toi le c.!** you're it! ▸▸ **c. de gouttière** alley cat; **c. à neuf queues** cat-o'-nine-tails; **c. persan** Persian (cat); **c. sauvage** wildcat; **c. siamois** Siamese (cat)

chat² [tʃat] NM *Ordinat (sur Internet)* chat

châtaigne [ʃatɛɲ] NF **1** *(fruit)* (sweet) chestnut **2** *Fam (coup de poing)* smack, clout; **je vais lui flanquer une c.** I'm going to clobber him; **je me suis pris une c.** *(léger choc électrique)* I got a shock ▸▸ **c. d'eau** water chestnut

châtaigner [ʃatɛɲe] VT *Fam* to clout, to thump

châtaigneraie [ʃatɛɲrɛ] NF chestnut grove, chestnut plantation

châtaignier [ʃatɛɲe] NM *(arbre, bois)* chestnut

châtain [ʃatɛ̃] ADJ *(féminin rare)* (chestnut-)brown; **une femme c.** *ou* **aux cheveux châtains** a brunette; **cheveux c. clair** (light) brown hair

NM chestnut brown

château, -eaux [ʃato] NM **1** castle; *(manoir)* mansion, manor, hall; *(demeure de famille aristocratique)* stately home; *Hist* (royal) palace; **le c. de Versailles** the palace of Versailles; **les châteaux de la Loire** the Châteaux of the Loire; *Fig* **c'est la vie de c.** it's the life of Riley; *Fig* **elle mène la vie de c.** she leads a life of luxury; *Fig* **bâtir des châteaux en Espagne** to build castles in Spain *or* in the air **2** *(exploitation vinicole)* château; **vin mis en bouteille au c.** château-bottled wine; *Arg* **C.-la-Pompe** (drinking) water, Adam's ale ▸▸ *Naut* **c. d'arrière** afterdeck; *Naut* **c. d'avant** forecastle, fo'c'sle; **c. de cartes** house of cards; **c. d'eau** water tower; *Rail* **c. fort** (fortified) castle; *Naut* **c. de poupe** afterdeck; *Naut* **c. de proue** forecastle, fo'c'sle

chateaubriand, châteaubriant [ʃatobrijɑ̃] NM *Culin* chateaubriand, porterhouse steak

châtelain [ʃatlɛ̃] NM **1** *Hist* lord of the manor **2** *(propriétaire d'un château)* owner of a/the château

châtelaine [ʃatlɛn] NF **1** *Hist* lady (of the manor) **2** *(propriétaire)* (woman) owner of a/the château; *(épouse du propriétaire)* wife of an owner of a château/the owner of the chateau **3** *(pour clés etc)* chatelaine

châtelet [ʃatlɛ] NM *Hist* small castle

chat-huant, *pl* **chats-huants** [ʃayɑ̃] NM tawny owl, brown owl

châtié [ʃatje] ADJ *(style)* polished; **en langage c.** in refined language

châtier [ʃatje] VT *(impf, pr sub* n. **châtiions,** v. **châtiiez)* **1** *Litt (enfant etc)* to chastise; **c. son corps** to mortify the flesh; **c. l'audace de qn** to punish sb for his impudence; *Prov* **qui aime bien châtie bien** spare the rod and spoil the child **2** *(style)* to polish

chatière [ʃatjɛr] NF **1** *(pour chat)* cat flap **2** *(pour aération)* ventilation hole **3** *(passage étroit)* narrow underground passage

châtiment [ʃatimɑ̃] NM *Litt* punishment, chastisement, castigation; **c. corporel** corporal punishment; **il a reçu un c. sévère** he was severely punished

chatoiement [ʃatwamɑ̃] NM shimmer, iridescence, sheen

chaton¹ [ʃatɔ̃] NM **1** *(petit chat)* kitten **2** *Bot* catkin

chaton² NM **1** *(d'une bague)* bezel, setting **2** *(pierre)* stone

chatouille [ʃatuj] NF *Fam* **faire des chatouilles à qn** to tickle sb; **craindre la c.** *ou* **les chatouilles** to be ticklish

chatouillement [ʃatujmɑ̃] NM tickling; **éprouver** *ou* **avoir un c. dans la gorge** to have a tickle in one's throat

chatouiller [ʃatuje] VT to tickle; **arrête de c. ta sœur!** stop tickling your sister!; *Fam* **c. les côtes à qn** to give sb a thrashing; **vin qui chatouille le palais** wine that pleases *or* titillates the palate; **de bonnes odeurs de cuisine nous chatouillaient les narines** delicious cooking smells were making our mouths water; **c. la curiosité** to excite *or* arouse curiosity; **c. l'amour-propre de qn** to flatter sb's vanity; **l'envie me chatouille d'aller voir ce qu'ils font** I'm itching to go and see what they're doing; **il ne faut pas le c. sur cette question, il risque de se mettre en colère** don't needle him on the subject, he might get angry

VI to tickle; **ah! ça chatouille!** oh! that tickles!

chatouilleux, -euse [ʃatujø, -øz] ADJ ticklish; *Fig* sensitive, touchy; **elle est très chatouilleuse** she's very ticklish; *Fig* **c. sur le point d'honneur** touchy where honour is concerned, touchy on a point of honour

chatouillis [ʃatuji] NM *Fam* gentle tickling, light tickling; **faire des c. à qn** to tickle sb gently

chatoyant [ʃatwajɑ̃] ADJ shimmering, iridescent; *(pierre, imagination etc)* sparkling; **soie chatoyante** shot silk

chatoyer [ʃatwaje] VI *(il chatoie; il chatoiera)* to shimmer; *(d'une pierre)* to sparkle; *Fig* **style qui chatoie** sparkling style

châtré [ʃatre] ADJ *(homme)* castrated; **taureau c.** steer, castrated bull; **étalon c.** gelding, castrated stallion

NM eunuch; *Fam* **voix de c.** high-pitched *or* falsetto voice

châtrer [ʃatre] VT **1** to castrate, to emasculate; *(étalon)* to geld; *(chat)* to neuter **2** *(texte)* to censor, to expurgate

chatte [ʃat] NF **1** *voir* **chat 2** *Vulg (sexe féminin)* pussy

chattemite [ʃatmit] NF **faire la c.** to simper

ADJ *(manière)* smooth, ingratiating; *(air)* smooth

chatter [tʃate] VI *Ordinat (sur Internet)* to chat

chatteries [ʃatri] NFPL **1** *(gestes de tendresse etc)* caresses; **se faire des c.** to caress each other **2** *(friandises)* delicacies, dainties

chatterton [ʃatɛrtɔn] NM *Élec* (adhesive) insulating tape, *Am* friction tape

chat-tigre, *pl* **chats-tigres** NM tiger cat

CHAUD [ʃo] ADJ **1** *(modéré)* warm; *(intense)* hot; **un bon pull c.** a good warm jumper; **pendant la chaude saison** during the warm weather; **la soupe est toute chaude** the soup is steaming or piping hot; **repas c.** hot meal; **animal à sang c.** warm-blooded animal; *Culin* **à mettre dans un four c.** cook in a hot oven; **pleurer à chaudes larmes** to weep bitterly; **il est c., il a de la fièvre** he's very warm or hot, he's running a fever; **le soleil est déjà c.** the sun's already (quite) warm or hot; *Prov* **il faut battre le fer pendant qu'il est c.** strike while the iron is hot, make hay while the sun shines; *Fig* **avoir la tête chaude** to be hotheaded; **l'été va être c.** it'll be a hot summer; *Fig* there will be a lot of unrest this summer; **l'alerte fut chaude** it was a close or near thing; **les points chauds du Proche-Orient** the hot spots or flash points of the Middle East; **chaude discussion** heated discussion; *Fig* **elle n'est pas chaude pour le projet** she's not keen on or not over-enthusiastic about the project; **c'est un c. partisan/défenseur de …** he's a keen supporter/defender of …; **nouvelle toute chaude** hot news, hot gossip; **tout c. de …** straight from …, hotfoot from …; *Fig* **voix chaude** sultry voice; *Beaux-Arts* **tons chauds** warm tints

2 *Fig* **avoir un tempérament c.** to be hot-tempered; **avoir le sang c.** to be hot-blooded; *Fam* **être c.** to be hot stuff; *Fam* **c'est un c. lapin** he's a randy devil

ADV **j'aime manger c.** I like my food hot; **le malade doit manger c.** the patient must eat hot food; **il fait très c.** it's hot, it's very warm; **cela ne me fait ni c. ni froid** it makes no difference, it's all the same to me

NM *(intense)* heat; *(modéré)* warmth; **garder ou tenir qch au c.** to keep sth hot; **il doit rester au lit, gardez-le bien au c.** he must stay in bed, keep him warm; **je garde ton assiette au c.** I'll keep your plate warm; **chez soi, au c.** at home, in the warmth; **prendre un c. et froid** to catch a chill; **avoir c.** *(d'une personne)* to be or feel warm/hot; **tu as assez c.?** are you warm enough?; **tu n'as pas trop c.?** you're not too hot?; *Fam* **il a eu c.** he had a narrow escape; **je crève de c.!** I'm dying of heat!; **travailler un métal à c.** to hot-work a metal; **être opéré à c.** to have an emergency operation; **interroger les spectateurs à c.** to question the audience on the spot; *Fig* **souffler le c. et le froid** to blow hot and cold

chaudement [ʃodmã] **ADV** warmly; **être vêtu c.** to be warmly dressed; **approuver c.** to approve heartily; **il a été c. défendu par elle** he was hotly defended by her

chaude-pisse [ʃodpis] **NF** **INV** *Arg* VD, clap

chaud-froid, *pl* **chauds-froids** **NM** *Culin* **c. de poulet/gibier** chaudfroid of chicken/game

chaudière [ʃodjɛr] **NF 1** *(de chauffage)* boiler; **c. de chauffage central** central heating boiler; **c. à mazout/à gaz** oil-fired/gas boiler; **c. à vapeur** steam boiler or generator **2** *Arch (pour la lessive etc)* copper **3** *Can (seau)* bucket; **c. à sucre** = bucket for collecting maple sap

chaudron [ʃodrɔ̃] **NM** cauldron, *Am* caldron

chaudronnerie [ʃodrɔnri] **NF 1** *Ind* boiler-making **2** *(objets)* boilers **3** *(atelier)* boiler works

chaudronnier, -ière [ʃodrɔnje, -jɛr] **N** *(fabricant)* boiler maker

ADJ **industrie chaudronnière** boiler-making

chauffage [ʃofaʒ] **NM** *(d'une pièce etc)* heating; *(appareils etc)* heating system; *(dans une voiture)* (car) heater; **bois de c.** firewood; **appareil de c.** heater; **c. central** central heating; **c. urbain** district heating; **c. par le sol** underfloor heating; **c. à l'électricité/au gaz/au mazout** electric/gas/oil heating; **installer le c.** to put central heating in; **le c. est détraqué** the boiler or the heat-

ing is out of order; **mettre/arrêter le c.** to turn on/turn off the heating

chauffagiste [ʃofaʒist] **N** *Tech* heating engineer

chauffant [ʃofã] **ADJ** heating, warming; **couverture chauffante** electric blanket; **plaque chauffante** hotplate

chauffard [ʃofar] **NM** *Fam (mauvais conducteur)* roadhog, reckless driver

chauffe [ʃof] **NF** *Tech* firing, stoking; **surface de c.** heating surface; **chef de c.** head stoker; *Naut* **chambre de c.** stokehold; **bleu de c.** boiler suit

chauffe-assiettes **NM** **INV** plate warmer

chauffe-bain, *pl* **chauffe-bains** **NM** water heater

chauffe-biberon, *pl* **chauffe-biberons** **NM** bottle-warmer

chauffe-eau **NM** **INV** water heater; *(à réservoir)* immersion heater

chauffe-pieds **NM** **INV** footwarmer

chauffe-plat, *pl* **chauffe-plats** **NM** chafing dish, hotplate

chauffer [ʃofe] **VT 1** to heat (up), to warm (up); **c. une maison au gaz** to heat a house with gas, to have gas heating; **la chambre n'est pas chauffée** there's no heating in the bedroom, the bedroom's not heated; **c. le fer à blanc/au rouge** to make iron white-/red-hot; **chauffé à blanc/au rouge** white-/red-hot; *Aut* **c. le moteur** to warm up the engine; **c. une chaudière/une locomotive** to fire/stoke (up) a boiler/an engine

2 *Fam* **c. qn** to cram or coach sb for an examination; **c. son public** to warm up one's audience; **il faut c. l'affaire** we're going to have to get things moving or hurry things along; **c. qn à blanc** to whip sb into a frenzy

VI 1 *(devenir chaud)* to get or become hot or warm; **ce radiateur chauffe bien/mal** this radiator gives out/doesn't give out a lot of heat; **la soupe chauffe** the soup's heating or warming up, the soup's on; **mets la soupe à c.** put the soup on (to heat); *Fam* **faites c. la colle!** that didn't sound very healthy!

2 *Fam* **ça chauffe, ça va c.** things are beginning to heat up; **je te promets que ça va c. s'il est en retard!** I promise you there'll be trouble if he's late!; **ça chauffe, ce soir!** things are hotting up this evening!; **tu chauffes!** *(dans un jeu)* you're getting warmer!

3 *(d'un roulement à billes etc)* to overheat, to run hot; **le moteur a tendance à c.** the engine tends to overheat or to get overheated

VPR **se chauffer** to warm oneself (**au soleil** in the sun); **se c. (les muscles)** to warm up, to limber up; **se c. au mazout** to have oil-fired (central) heating; **nous ne nous chauffions toujours pas** we still hadn't turned the heating on; *Fig* **je vais lui montrer de quel bois je me chauffe!** I'll show him what I'm made of!

chaufferette [ʃofrɛt] **NF** *(pour les pieds)* footwarmer

chaufferie [ʃofri] **NF** boiler room

chauffeur, -euse[1] [ʃofœr, -øz] **N 1** *(de voiture, bus, camion)* driver; *(employé)* chauffeur, driver; **c. de camion** truck or *Br* lorry driver; **c. routier** long-distance truck or *Br* lorry driver; **elle est chauffeuse de taxi** she's a taxi driver; **les chauffeurs du dimanche** Sunday drivers; **je n'ai pas l'intention de faire le c. toute la journée** I've no intention of chauffeuring people around all day **2** *(d'une locomotive à vapeur)* stoker

chauffeuse[2] [ʃoføz] **NF** *(chaise)* low fireside chair

chaulage [ʃolaʒ] **NM** *(des murs etc)* whitewashing; *(du sol etc)* liming

chauler [ʃole] **VT** *(murs etc)* to whitewash; *(sol etc)* to treat with lime

chaume [ʃom] **NM 1** *(paille)* thatch; **couvrir un toit de ou en c.** to thatch a roof; **toit de c.** thatched roof **2** *(ce qui reste des céréales)* stubble; *(champ)* stubble field

chaumer [ʃome] **VT** *Agr* **c. les champs** to clear fields (of stubble)

chaumière [ʃomjɛr] **NF** thatched cottage; *Fig* **un roman à faire pleurer dans les chaumières** a tear-jerking novel; **on en parlera longtemps dans les chaumières** tongues will be wagging about this for a long time

chaussant [ʃosã] **ADJ** *(chaussure)* that fits well

chaussée [ʃose] **NF 1** *(route)* roadway, *Am* pavement; **'c. glissante'** 'slippery (road) surface'; **'c. déformée'** 'temporary road surface' **2** *(digue)* dyke, embankment; *(dans un endroit marécageux)* causeway; **la C. des Géants** the Giant's Causeway **3** *(écueil)* reef, line of rocks

chausse-pied, *pl* **chausse-pieds** [ʃospje] **NM** shoehorn

chausser [ʃose] **VT 1** *(chaussures, bottes etc)* to put on; **chaussé de pantoufles** wearing (his) slippers; **c. les étriers** to put one's feet into the stirrups; **c. ses lunettes** to put one's glasses on

2 *(personne)* *(mettre des chaussures à)* to put shoes on; *(fournir en chaussures)* to supply with footwear, to make footwear for; **se faire c. chez Adrian** to buy or get one's shoes at Adrian's

3 *(aller à)* to fit; **ce modèle te chausse mieux que l'autre** this style fits you better than the other one

4 *Aut (voiture)* to put tyres on

5 *(arbre)* to earth up

VI to fit; **souliers qui chaussent bien** shoes that fit well; **ce soulier chausse étroit** this shoe comes in a narrow fitting; **du combien chaussez-vous?** what size do you take (in shoes)?; **elle chausse du 37** she takes a (size) four

VPR **se chausser** to put one's shoes on; **se c. tout seul** *(d'un enfant)* to put one's shoes on all by oneself; **se c. chez Simone** to buy one's shoes at Simone's

chausses [ʃos] **NFPL** *Hist* breeches; **coller aux c. de qn** to dog sb's footsteps

chausse-trap(p)e, *pl* **chausse-trap(p)es** [ʃostrap] **NF** *Fig Litt* trap

chaussette [ʃosɛt] **NF** sock; **une paire de chaussettes** a pair of socks; **en chaussettes** in one's socks, in one's stockinged feet; **c. de ski/de sport/de tennis** ski/sports/tennis sock; *Arg* **un vrai jus de c.** watery coffee; **laisser tomber qn comme une vieille c.** to cast sb aside like an old rag

chausseur [ʃosœr] **NM** *(magasin)* shoe shop; *(fabricant)* shoe manufacturer

chausson [ʃosɔ̃] **1 NM** *(pantoufle)* slipper; *(de danse)* ballet shoe; *(de bébé)* (baby's) bootee; **se mettre en chaussons** to put one's slippers on **2** *Culin* turnover; **c. aux pommes** apple turnover

chaussure [ʃosyr] **NF 1** *(soulier)* shoe; **une paire de chaussures** a pair of shoes; **c. de ville/de sport/habillée** town/sports/dress shoe; **chaussures de marche** *ou* **de montagne** walking boots; **c. à talon** *ou* **haute** high-heeled shoe; **c. basse** flat shoe; **c. montante** ankle boot; **chaussures de ski** ski boots; *Fam* **trouver c. à son pied** to find the right woman/man **2** *Ind* (boot and) shoe industry or trade **3** *(sens large)* footwear

chauve [ʃov] **ADJ** bald; *Fig (colline etc)* bare; *Fam* **c. comme un genou** *ou* **comme un œuf** *ou* **comme une bille** as bald as a coot

N bald(-headed) person

chauve-souris, *pl* **chauves-souris** **NF** bat

chauvin, -ine [ʃovɛ̃, -in] *Péj* **N** jingoist, chauvinist
ADJ jingoistic, chauvinistic

> Il faut noter que le nom anglais **chauvinist** est un faux ami. Il est désormais employé le plus souvent dans le sens de **phallocrate**.

chauvinisme [ʃovinism] **NM** *Péj* jingoism, chauvinism

> Il faut noter que le nom anglais **chauvinism** est un faux ami. Il signifie le plus souvent **phallocratie**.

chauviniste [ʃovinist] **ADJ, N** *Péj* = **chauvin**

chaux [ʃo] **NF** lime; **c. vive** quicklime; **c. éteinte** slaked lime; **blanchir un mur à la c.** to whitewash a wall; **bâtir à c. et à sable** *ou* **à c. et à ciment** to build firmly *or* solidly; *Fig* **être bâti à c. et à sable** (*d'une personne*) to have an iron constitution

chavirer [ʃavire] **VI 1** (*d'un bateau etc*) to capsize, to overturn, *Fam* to turn turtle; *Fig* (*sombrer*) to collapse; **faire c.** to capsize; **les plus grands empires chavirent** even the greatest empires collapse *or* fall **2** (*tourner*) to reel, to spin (round); **tout chavire autour de moi** everything's spinning; **ses yeux chaviraient** he was showing the whites of his eyes
VT 1 (*bateau*) to capsize, to overturn **2** *Fam* (*retourner*) to overwhelm, to bowl over; **il en est tout chaviré** it's knocked him for six

chébran [ʃebrã] **ADJ INV** *Fam* (*branché*) trendy

chèche [ʃɛʃ] **NM** North African scarf

chéchia [ʃeʃja] **NF** fez

check-list, *pl* **check-lists** [tʃɛklist] **NF** *Aviat etc Fam* checklist

check-point [tʃɛkpɔint] **NM INV** *Mil* checkpoint

check-up [tʃɛkœp] **NM INV** *Méd* check-up; **faire un c. à qn** to give sb a check-up; **le médecin me conseille de faire un c.** the doctor is advising me to have a check-up

chef [ʃɛf] **NM 1** (*de famille etc*) head; (*d'une tribu etc*) chief, chieftain; (*d'un parti politique etc*) leader; (*d'une entreprise*) head, manager; *Fam* (*patron*) boss; (*de jurés*) foreman; (*d'une école de pensée etc*) founder; **c. (cuisinier** *ou* **de cuisine**) (head) chef, chef de cuisine; **le plat du c.** the chef's special; **ingénieur en c.** chief engineer; **rédacteur en c.** chief editor; *Mil* **commandant en c.** commander-in-chief; **jouer au petit c.** to throw one's weight around; **il se débrouille comme un c.** he's getting on *or* doing very well; **bravo, tu es un c.!** well done, you're a marvel! **2** *Arch, Hum* (*tête*) head; *Litt* **faire qch de son (propre) c.** to do sth on one's own authority *or Fam* off one's own bat; **au premier c.** first and foremost
  ▸▸ *Jur* **c. d'accusation** charge, count (of an/ the indictment); **c. d'antenne** programme supervisor; *Ind* **c. d'atelier** (shop) foreman; **c. de bande** ringleader; **c. de bataillon** major; *Admin* **c. de bureau** office manager, *Vieilli* (*senior clerk*; *Parl* **c. de cabinet** = (minister's) principal private secretary; **c. chasseur** head porter, *Am* bell captain; **c. comptable** chief accountant; *Cin, TV* **c. costumier** wardrobe supervisor, costume supervisor; **c. de cuisine** head chef, chef de cuisine; **c. de la diplomatie** foreign minister; *Cin, TV* **c. électricien** gaffer; **c. d'équipe** *Sport* captain; *Ind* foreman, charge hand; **c. d'État** head of state; **c. des exploitations** operations manager; **c. de fabrication** production manager, manufacturing manager; **c. de famille** head of the family; **c. de file** leader, lead manager; (*produit*) (market) leader;

Rail **c. de gare** station manager; **c. du gouvernement** head of government; **c. de groupe** group supervisor *or* manager *or* leader; **c. infirmier** charge nurse; **c. des informations** public relations *or* PR manager; **c. de magasin** store manager; **c. de marque** brand manager; *TV, Cin* **c. montage** editor; **c. de musique** bandmaster; **c. de nage** stroke (oar); *TV, Cin* **c. opérateur** cinematographer, head of cameras; **c. opérateur cadreur** lighting-cameraman; **c. d'orchestre** conductor; **c. de partie** chef de partie; **c. de partie boucher** larder chef; **c. de partie poissonnier** fish cook; **c. pâtissier** chef patissier, pastry chef; **c. de patrouille** patrol leader; **c. du personnel** personnel manager, head of personnel; **c. de petit déjeuner** breakfast chef; *TV* **c. de plateau** stage manager, floor boss; *TV etc* **c. de production** production head; *Com* **c. de produit** product manager; **c. de publicité** advertising manager *or* executive; *Naut* **c. de quart** officer of the watch; **c. de rang** head waiter, chef de rang, station waiter, *Am* captain; **c. de rayon** (*dans un magasin*) head of department, department(al) manager, department head; (*dans un hôpital*) consultant; **c. de réception** (*dans un hôtel*) reception manager, front office manager; *Journ* **c. de rubriques** features editor; **c. scout** scout leader; **c. serveur** waiting chef; **c. de service** head of department, departmental manager; *TV etc* **c. de studio** studio supervisor; **c. de train** guard, *Am* conductor; **c. des traitements** data processing *or* DP manager; **c. des ventes** sales manager; *Com* **c. de zone** area manager

chefaillon [ʃefajɔ̃] **NM** *Fam* little Hitler

chef-d'œuvre, *pl* **chefs-d'œuvre** [ʃɛdœvr] **NM** masterpiece; **c'est un c. de la littérature/de la peinture** it's a literary/artistic masterpiece

chef-garde, *pl* **chefs-gardes** **NM** *Belg Rail* ticket inspector

chef-lieu, *pl* **chefs-lieux** **NM** chief town (of department), ≃ county town, *Am* ≃ county seat

cheftaine [ʃɛftɛn] **NF** (*des Guides*) captain; (*des jeannettes*) Brown Owl; (*des louveteaux*) cubmistress

cheik(h) [ʃɛk] **NM** sheik(h)

chelem [ʃlɛm] **NM** *Cartes* slam; **grand c.** grand slam; **petit c.** little slam; **faire c. à qn** to make a slam against sb; **elle a fini par me faire c.** I ended up not winning a trick against her; *Tennis etc* **Grand c.** Grand Slam

CHEMIN [ʃ(ə)mɛ̃] **NM 1** (*route*) way, road; (*voie*) path, track; **le c. de la gare** the way to the station; **le c. de la gloire/réussite** the road to glory/success; **le plus court c. d'un point à un autre** the shortest distance between two points; *Fam* **prendre le c. des écoliers** to take a roundabout way *or* the long(est) way round; **demander son c.** to ask one's way; **c'est sur mon c.** it's on my way; *aussi Fig* **nous avons beaucoup de c. à faire** we've a long way to go; *Fig* **il a du c. à faire s'il veut vraiment devenir un concurrent important** he has a long way to go if he wants to become a serious contender; **il faut compter deux ou trois heures de c.** it will take two or three hours to get there; **nous avons fait la moitié du c. ensemble/à pied** we went half the way together/on foot; *Fig* **nous avons déjà fait la moitié du c.** we're already halfway there; **aller son c., aller son petit bonhomme de c.** to jog along; **s'arrêter en c.** to stop on the way; *Fig* **maintenant que tu as fait le plus gros du travail, ce serait bête de t'arrêter en (si bon) c.** now that you've done most of the work, it would be silly to stop; **être en bon c.** to be getting on well; **nous ne pouvons pas nous arrêter en si**

bon c. we can't give up now that we're doing so well; **leur affaire est en bon c.** their business is off to a good start; **elle n'en prend pas le c.** she's not going the right way about it; **c. faisant** on the way; **faire le c. à pied/en vélo/en voiture** to walk/cycle/drive all the way; **faire un bout de c. avec qn** to go part of the way with sb; *Fig* (*vivre*) to live with sb for a while; **ils ont fait un bout de c. ensemble** (*dans la vie professionnelle*) their careers followed similar paths for a while; **suivre le droit c.** to stay on the straight and narrow; *aussi Fig* **montrer le c.** to lead *or* show the way; *Fig* **il leur montre le c.** he's showing them the way; **à mi-c.** halfway; **pourquoi s'arrêter à mi-c.?** why stop halfway?; **se mettre en c.** to set out *or* off; **se mettre en c. pour** *ou* **prendre le c. de Paris** to set out *or* off for Paris; **être dans** *ou* **sur le c. de qn** to be *or* stand in sb's way; **ton vélo est sur le c., pousse-le** your bike is in the way, move it; **il a trouvé un certain nombre de difficultés sur son c.** he found a certain number of difficulties standing in his way; **se mettre dans le c. de qn** to stand in sb's way; **il n'a pas intérêt à se trouver sur mon c.** he'd better keep out of my way; *Fig* **trouver son c. de Damas** to see the light; **ne pas y aller par quatre chemins** *ou* **par trente-six chemins** to go straight to the point; *Fig* **elle fera son c.** she'll get on *or* make her way in life; **il est très ambitieux, il fera du c.** he's very ambitious, he'll go far *or* a long way *or* he'll go places; *Fig* **cette idée fait du c.** the idea is gaining ground; *Arch* **grand c.** highway, high road; **voleur de grand c.** highwayman; *Fam* **être toujours sur les chemins** to be always on the go
  2 *Ordinat* path
  ▸▸ *Ordinat* **c. d'accès** path; *Ordinat* **c. d'accès aux données** data path; *Ordinat* **c. du courrier électronique** mail path; **c. creux** sunken road; **c. critique** critical path; **c. de fer** railway, *Am* railroad; *Ordinat* (*affichage*) thumbnail; *Journ* page allocation; *Typ* page plan; **aller** *ou* **voyager en** *ou* **par c. de fer** to go *or* travel by rail *or* by train; **c. de fer omnibus/rapide** local/express service; **accident de c. de fer** rail(way) accident; **c. de fer français** French railways; **Chemins de fer nationaux du Canada** Canadian National Railways; **c. de halage** towpath; *Ordinat* **c. du papier** (*d'une imprimante*) paper path; **c. piéton(nier)** footpath; **c. de randonnée** hiking trail; **c. de ronde** covered way; *Tech* **c. de roulement pour billes** ball race; **c. de table** (table) runner; **c. de terre** dirt track; *Can Jur* **c. de tolérance** right of way; **c. de traverse** side road; **c. vicinal** byroad, minor road

chemineau, -eaux [ʃ(ə)mino] **NM** tramp, vagrant

cheminée [ʃ(ə)mine] **NF 1** (*dans une maison*) fireplace; (**manteau de**) **c.** mantelpiece, chimneypiece; **il y a une c. dans chaque pièce** there's a fireplace in every room; **un feu dans la c.** a fire in the grate; **c'est sur la c.** it's on the mantelpiece; **c. en marbre** marble mantelpiece **2** (*conduit*) chimney (stack); (*de bateau à vapeur*) funnel, smokestack; **c. d'usine** factory chimney; (**conduit de**) **c.** flue; **le Père Noël passe par la c.** Father Christmas comes down the chimney; **feu de c.** chimney fire; **c. d'aération** air shaft, ventilating shaft **3** (*de lampe à huile*) chimney; **col c.** (*de pull etc*) cowl neck(line) **4** *Géol* chimney; **faire une c.** (*d'un alpiniste*) to chimney
  ▸▸ *Géol* **c. de fée** fairy chimney; *Géol* **c. volcanique** vent

cheminement [ʃ(ə)minmã] **NM 1** (*progression*) progression, movement; **le c. des touristes devant les toiles célèbres** the filing past of the tourists in front of the famous paintings; **le c. des eaux** the advance of the water **2** *Mil (vers les positions ennemies)* advance **3 c. de la pensée** advance *or* progress *or* development of thought; *(processus)* thought processes

cheminer [ʃ(ə)mine] **VI 1** *(avancer)* to advance, to move along; **la caravane chemine dans le désert** the caravan makes its way through the desert; **les eaux cheminent dans des canaux souterrains** the water travels through the underground canals **2** *Mil (vers les positions ennemies)* to advance; *Fig* to gain ground; **laisser une idée c.** to let an idea gain ground

cheminot [ʃ(ə)mino] **NM** rail(way) worker, railwayman, *Am* railroader; *(employé)* rail(-way) employee

chemisage [ʃ(ə)mizaʒ] **NM** *(d'une chaudière, d'un cylindre etc)* jacketing, casing; *(d'un fusil, d'un cylindre etc)* lining

chemise [ʃ(ə)miz] **NF 1** *(vêtement)* shirt; **c. à manches longues/courtes** long-/short-sleeved shirt; **en (bras** *ou* **en manches de) c.** in one's shirtsleeves; *Fig* **il change d'avis comme de c.** he changes his mind as often as he changes his shirt; **se moquer de qch comme de sa première c.** not to give a damn *or* two hoots about sth; **il donnerait sa c. au premier venu** he'd give you the shirt off his back

  2 *(classeur)* folder; **mettre un livre sous c.** to cover a book

  3 *(de chaudière, de cylindre etc)* jacket(ing), casing, sheathing; *(de cylindre, de fourneau etc)* lining; *(de mur)* facing; *Aut* **c. flottante/ humide/sèche** slip/wet/dry liner

  ▸▸**c. américaine** (woman's) vest, *Am* undershirt; **c. de nuit** (woman's) nightdress; *(d'homme)* nightshirt; *Hist* **Chemises brunes** Brownshirts; *Hist* **Chemises noires** Blackshirts; *Hist* **Chemises rouges** Red Shirts

chemiser [ʃ(ə)mize] **VT** *(chaudière, cylindre etc)* to jacket, to case; *(fusil, cylindre etc)* to line

chemiserie [ʃ(ə)mizri] **NF** *Ind* shirt making; *(ensemble de vêtements)* shirts, underwear and ties; *(fabrique)* shirt factory; *(magasin)* gents' outfitters

chemisette [ʃ(ə)mizɛt] **NF** *(pour hommes)* short-sleeved shirt

chemisier [ʃ(ə)mizje] **NM 1** *(fabricant)* shirtmaker; *(marchand)* men's outfitter **2** *(corsage)* blouse; **robe c.** shirt-waister

chênaie [ʃɛnɛ] **NF** oak grove *or* plantation

chenal, -aux [ʃ(ə)nal, -o] **NM 1** *(d'une rivière, d'un port etc)* channel, fairway; **au milieu du c.** in mid channel **2** *(courant d'eau)* millrace

chenapan [ʃ(ə)napɑ̃] **NM** *Hum* rogue, scoundrel

chêne [ʃɛn] **NM** *(arbre)* oak; **c. vert** evergreen oak, holm oak, ilex; **table en c. (massif)** (solid) oak table; *Fig* **être fort comme un c.** to be as strong as an ox

chéneau, -eaux [ʃeno] **NM** *(d'un toit)* gutter

chêneau, -eaux [ʃeno] **NM** oak sapling

chêne-liège, *pl* **chênes-lièges NM** cork oak

chenet [ʃ(ə)nɛ] **NM** firedog, andiron

chènevière [ʃɛnvjɛr] **NF** hemp field

chènevis [ʃɛnvi] **NM** hempseed

cheni [ʃni] **NM** *Suisse Fam* **1** *(balayures)* sweepings; *(débris, déchets)* rubbish **2** *(désordre)* mess, shambles **3** *(objets sans valeur)* junk, stuff

chenil [ʃəni(l)] **NM** *(pour chiens)* kennels

chenille [ʃ(ə)nij] **NF 1** *(insecte)* caterpillar; *(d'une autochenille)* band; **c. processionnaire** processionary caterpillar; **véhicule à chenilles** tracked vehicle **2** *Tex* chenille

chenillé [ʃ(ə)nije] **ADJ** *(véhicule)* tracked

chenillette [ʃ(ə)nijɛt] **NF** small tracked vehicle; *Mil* carrier

chenu [ʃəny] **ADJ** *Litt (personne, tête)* hoary; **arbres chenus** old leafless trees

cheptel [ʃɛptɛl] **NM 1** *(troupeaux)* livestock; **c. ovin d'une région** sheep population of a region **2** *Jur* **bail à c.** lease of livestock; **c. (vif)** livestock leased; **c. mort** farm equipment leased

chèque [ʃɛk] **NM** cheque, *Am* check; **c. de 60 euros** cheque for 60 euros; **carnet de chèques** cheque book; **endosser un c.** to endorse a cheque; **faire** *ou* **remplir un c.** to write (out) *or* make out a cheque; **je peux vous faire un c.?** can I give you a cheque?; **à qui dois-je adresser le c.?** who should I make the cheque out to?; **payer qch par c.** to pay for sth by cheque; **toucher un c.** to cash a cheque; **encaisser un c. (en espèces)** to cash a cheque; *(le mettre sur son compte)* to pay in a cheque; **déposer** *ou* **mettre un c. à la banque** to pay a cheque into the bank

  ▸▸**c. bancaire** (bank) cheque; **c. de banque** banker's draft, *Am* cashier's check; **c. barré** crossed cheque; **c. en blanc** blank cheque; **c. bloqué** stopped cheque; **c. en bois** rubber cheque; **c. certifié** certified cheque; **c. compensé** cleared cheque; **c. emploi-service** = special cheque used to pay casual workers such as part-time cleaners, babysitters etc; **c. d'entreprise** company cheque; **c. nominatif** cheque made out to name; **c. non endossable** non-negotiable cheque; **c. à ordre** cheque to order; **c. ouvert** open cheque; **c. au porteur** bearer cheque; **c. postal** post office cheque; **c. retourné** returned cheque; **c. sans provision** bad cheque, rubber cheque, cheque that bounces; **j'ai fait un c. sans provision** my cheque bounced; **c. stimulation-voyage** = incentive travel cheque issued by companies; **c. de virement** transfer cheque; *Can* **c. visé** certified cheque; **c. de voyage** traveller's cheque

chèque-cadeau, *pl* **chèques-cadeaux NM** gift token *or* voucher; **un c. d'une valeur de 200 euros** a gift token to the value of 200 euros

chèque-dividende, *pl* **chèques-dividendes NM** *Fin* dividend warrant

chèque-livre, *pl* **chèques-livres NM** book token

chèque-repas, *pl* **chèques-repas NM, chèque-restaurant,** *pl* **chèques-restaurant NM** luncheon voucher

chéquier [ʃekje] **NM** cheque *or Am* check book

CHER, CHÈRE [ʃɛr] **ADJ** SEE GRAMMAR B10 **1** *(aimé)* dear, beloved; **être c. à qn** to be dear to sb; **tout ce qui m'est c.** all that I hold dear; **ses espérances les plus chères** his most cherished hopes; **c'est mon vœu le plus c.** it's my dearest wish; **il a retrouvé sa chère maison/son c. bureau** he's back in his beloved house/office; **bien chers frères** dearly beloved brethren; **C. Monsieur** *(dans une lettre)* Dear Mr Smith/*etc*; *(officiel)* Dear Sir; **chers amis de la nature** dear nature lovers; **bonjour, chère Madame** hello, my dear lady; *Iron* **écoutez, chère Madame, c'est tout ce que nous sommes en mesure de vous proposer** I'm sorry, Madam, but that's all we're able to offer you; **cette chère Marie!** dear old Marie!

  2 *(coûteux)* dear, expensive; **c'est trop c. pour moi** I can't afford it; **un petit restaurant pas c.** an inexpensive little restaurant; **la vie est chère en ville** it's expensive living in town, the cost of living is high in town(s); **ce n'est pas vendu assez c.** it's underpriced

  ADV **payer qch c./trop c.** to pay a high price/ too much for sth; **c'est c. payer (sa liberté)** it's a high price to pay (for one's freedom); **il**

me le payera c. I'll make him pay for it; **coûter c.** to cost a lot, to be expensive; **ça coûte trop c. pour moi** it's too expensive for me, I can't afford it; *Fig* **ça m'a coûté c. de dire ce que je pensais** speaking my mind cost me dearly; *Fig* **ça va vous coûter c.!** you'll pay dearly for this!; *Fam* **je donnerais c. pour savoir ce qu'il lui a dit** I'd give anything *or* a lot to know what he said to him; **je ne donne pas c. de son succès** I don't give much for his chances of success; **cela ne vaut pas c.** it's not worth much; *Fam* **je l'ai eu pour pas c.** I got it cheap

  N mon c. my dear (fellow); **ma chère** my dear (girl); **ah, ma chère! quel plaisir de vous voir!** *(avec préciosité)* how nice to see you, my dear!

chérant [ʃerɑ̃] **ADJ** *Can* pricey; **un plombier pas c.** a plumber who doesn't charge too much, an inexpensive plumber

CHERCHER [ʃɛrʃe]

VT to look for **1** ▪ to seek **1** ▪ to search for **1** ▪ to fetch **2** ▪ to try to *(chercher à)* **3** ▪ to get at **5**
VI to look
VPR to try to find oneself

VT 1 *(essayer de trouver) (chose, personne)* to look for, to search for, *Fml* to seek; **je l'ai cherché partout** I searched for *or* looked for it high and low, I hunted for it everywhere; **c. une maison à acheter** to look for a house to buy, to be house-hunting; **c. du regard** *ou* **des yeux** to look around for sb; **c. un mot dans un dictionnaire** to look up a word in a dictionary; **il cherchait des moyens de s'évader** he looked around for a means of escape; **c. un emploi** to look for a job; **c. son chemin** *ou* **sa voie/une solution** to try to find one's way/a solution; **c. ses mots** to search for words; **je cherche son nom** I'm trying to think of his name; *Fam* **où va-t-il donc c. tout cela?** where on earth does he get that from?; **mais qu'est-ce que tu vas c. là, pourquoi faut-il toujours que tu compliques les choses?** what on earth are you going on about, why do you always have to complicate matters?; **c. sa ruine** to court one's own ruin; **partir c. du secours** to go for help; *Fam* **il l'a bien cherché** he was asking for it

  2 aller c. qn/qch to (go and) fetch sb/sth; **envoyer c. qn/qch** to send for sb/sth; **je suis allé le c. à la gare** I went to meet him at the station; **viens me c. à 17 heures** come for me at 5 pm

  3 c. à faire qch to try to do sth; **c. à se faire connaître** to try to get oneself known, to try to make a name for oneself; **c. à se faire aimer** to try to make oneself popular; **c. à plaire** to aim to please; *Iron* **il ne faut pas c. à comprendre** don't even try to understand

  4 *Fam (atteindre)* **cela va c. dans les 10 000 euros** it will cost about 10,000 euros, you're talking about something like 10,000 euros; **ça va c. dans les deux ans de prison** that will get you about two years in prison; **injures à magistrat, ça peut aller c. loin!** insulting a magistrate can get you into serious trouble!

  5 *Fam (provoquer)* to get at, to pick on; **tu me cherches?** are you looking for a fight?; **si tu me cherches, tu vas me trouver** if you want a fight, you'll get one

  VI to look, to search; **qui cherche trouve** seek and ye shall find; **il faut c. plus** you'll have to look harder; **cherche! (à un chien)** fetch!

  VPR se chercher to try to find oneself

chercheur, -euse [ʃɛrʃœr, -øz] **ADJ 1** *(spéculateur)* **esprit c.** enquiring mind **2 tête chercheuse** *(d'un missile)* homing head

  N 1 researcher, research worker **2 c. d'or** gold digger unemployment affects a high proportion of the population; **le c. des femmes/des jeunes** female/youth unemployment, unemployment among women/young people; **être au c.** to be unemployed *or* out of work *or Fam* jobless; **allocation** *ou* **indemnité de c.** unemployment benefit, *Br Fam* dole; **toucher le c.** to claim unemployment benefit, to be on unemployment *or Br Fam* on the dole; **s'inscrire au c.** to sign on; **c. d'une usine** closure of a factory

▸▸ **c. chronique** chronic unemployment; **c. conjoncturel** cyclical unemployment; **c. déguisé** hidden unemployment; **c. frictionnel** frictional unemployment; **c. de longue durée** long-term unemployment; **c. partiel** short-term (working); **être en c. partiel** to be on short time; **c. récurrent** periodic *or* recurrent unemployment; **c. saisonnier** seasonal unemployment; **c. structurel** structural *or* long-term unemployment; **c. technique** lay-offs; **être en c. technique** to have been laid off

chôm'du, chômedu [ʃomdy] **NM** *Fam* (*chômage*) **être au c.** to be out of work; **pointer au c.** to be *Br* on the dole *or Am* on welfare

chômer [ʃome] **VT** (*jour férié*) to keep; **jour chômé** public holiday, *Br* bank holiday

VI 1 (*ne pas travailler*) (*d'une usine*) to be *or* lie idle; (*d'un employé*) to be unemployed *or* out of work; *Fig* to do nothing; **vous n'avez pas chômé!** you've not been idle *or* twiddling your thumbs!; **l'an dernier, je n'ai pas eu le temps de c.** I didn't have a spare moment all last year; **laisser c. une terre** to let land lie fallow; **laisser c. son argent** to let one's money lie idle **2** (*faire le pont*) **c. entre Noël et le jour de l'an** to take time off between Christmas and New Year

chômeur, -euse [ʃomœr, -øz] **N** unemployed person; **un million de chômeurs** a million unemployed; **les chômeurs** the unemployed; **les chômeurs de longue durée** the long-term unemployed

chope [ʃop] **NF** (*récipient*) beer mug, tankard; (*contenu*) mugful

choper [ʃope] **VT** *Arg* **1** (*voler*) to pinch, to nick; **on m'a chopé mon portefeuille** I've had my wallet pinched *or* nicked, somebody's lifted my wallet **2** (*arrêter, prendre*) to catch, to nab; **se faire c.** to get caught *or* nabbed; **je l'ai chopé en train de fouiller dans mes affaires** I caught him rummaging through my things **3** (*attraper*) (*rhume*) to catch

chopine [ʃopin] **NF 1** *Fam* (*contenant*) half-litre *or Am* -liter bottle; **tu viens boire une c.?** (are you) coming for a drink? **2** *Can* (*mesure*) pint (*0.568 litre*)

choquant [ʃokã] **ADJ** (*attitude etc*) shocking; **un abus c.** a gross *or* shocking abuse

choqué [ʃoke] **ADJ** shocked; **il les regardait d'un air profondément c.** he looked at them, visibly shocked; *Can* **être c.** (*contre qn*) to be angry (at sb); *Am* to be mad (at sb)

choquer [ʃoke] **VT 1** (*percuter*) to strike, to knock; **nous avons choqué nos verres** we clinked *or* chinked glasses

2 (*contrarier, être désagréable à*) to shock, to offend; **ce qui choque le plus dans ces images, c'est que ...** the most shocking thing about these pictures is ...; **être choqué de qch** to be scandalized *or* shocked at *or* by sth; **nous avons été choqués par son manque d'égard** we were shocked *or* appalled by his lack of consideration; **je suis tout à fait choqué par sa vulgarité** I am deeply shocked by his coarseness; **cela risque de c.** it might cause offence; **sons qui choquent l'oreille** sounds that grate on *or* offend the ear; **mot qui choque** offensive *or* rude word; **de telles paroles choquent**

dans la bouche d'une jeune fille such language is shocking in the mouth of *or* coming from a young girl

3 (*blesser moralement*) to shock; **j'ai été choqué de le voir tellement changé** I was shocked *or* it gave me a shock to see such a change in him; **la vue du sang l'a choqué** the sight of blood has shaken him

VPR se choquer 1 (*d'objets*) to knock against each other **2** (*être scandalisé*) to be shocked, to take offence (**de** at); **il n'y a pas de quoi se choquer** there's nothing to be shocked at

choral, -ale, -als, -ales [koral] **ADJ** choral; **chant c.** choral singing; **société chorale** choral society

NM choral(e)

NF chorale (*société*) choral society; (*chanteurs*) choir; **la chorale de l'église** the church choir VOIR GRAMMAIRE A11

chorée [kore] **NF** *Méd* chorea; *Fam* Saint Vitus's dance

chorégraphe [koregraf] **N** choreographer

chorégraphie [koregrafi] **NF** choreography; **faire la c. d'un spectacle** to choreograph *or* do the choreography for a show

chorégraphier [koregrafje] **VT** to choreograph

chorégraphique [koregrafik] **ADJ** choreographic

choria [ʃorja] **NF** *Rel* (*Islam*) sharia

choriste [korist] **N** *Mus* choir member; (*dans une église*) chorister; (*dans un opéra*) chorus singer; (*d'une comédie musicale*) chorus member; (*d'un chanteur*) backing singer

chorizo [tʃorizo] **NM** *Culin* chorizo

chorus [korys] **NM 1 faire c.** to voice one's agreement; **ils ont fait c. avec lui** they voiced their agreement with him **2** (*dans le jazz*) chorus; **reprendre un c.** to take up the chorus

CHOSE [ʃoz] **NF 1** (*objet inanimé*) thing; **il aime les belles choses** he likes nice things; **les êtres et les choses** living creatures and objects *or* things; *Scol Vieilli* **leçon de choses** nature lesson; *Fig* **être la c. de qn** to belong to sb; **il la considère comme sa c.** he thinks he owns her

2 (*abstrait*) thing; **j'ai appris une c. incroyable** I've heard something unbelievable; **une c. très grave vient de se passer** something very serious has just happened; **il se passe des choses au ministère** there's something going on in the department; **quelque c. se prépare** something's brewing; **j'ai un tas de choses à faire** I've loads *or* masses of things to do; **c'est de deux choses l'une, soit il parle, soit ...** either he talks, or ...; **chaque c. en son temps** everything in its own time; **on m'a dit des tas de choses à son sujet** I've been told heaps of things about him; **dites bien des choses de ma part à ...** remember me to ..., give my regards to ...; **il a dit des choses sur moi?** has he been saying things about me?; **elle dit de ces choses parfois!** the things she comes out with sometimes!; **j'ai bien des choses à vous raconter** I've a lot (of things) to tell you; **ce n'est pas c. aisée de ...** it's no easy matter to ...; **réaliser cela est une c., l'admettre en est une autre** being aware of it is one thing, admitting it is another; **la c. en question** the case in point; **je vais vous expliquer la c.** I'll explain it *or* the matter to you; **il a très bien pris la c.** he took it very well; **c'était vraiment la c. à éviter** that was the last thing to do; **cela n'est plus la même c.** that alters the case *or* things; **nous y sommes retournés, mais ce n'est plus la même c.** we went back (there), but it wasn't the same; *Fam* **être porté sur la c.** to be obsessed with sex, to have a one-track mind; **je vais te dire une (bonne) c.** I'm

going to *or* let me tell you something; **c. curieuse, personne n'en savait rien** curiously enough, nobody knew anything about it; **avant toute c.** first of all, above all; **et, c. rare** for once; *Jur* **c. jugée** res judicata; *Pol* **la c. publique** the state, *Fml* res publica

3 les choses things; **voici comment se sont passées les choses** here's how things happened; **il a bien/mal pris les choses** he took it well/badly; **prendre les choses à cœur** to take things to heart; **l'état des choses** the state of things; **dans l'état actuel des choses** as things are *or* stand at the moment; **les choses de ce monde** the things of this world; **par la force des choses** by *or* through force of circumstance; **il fait bien les choses** he does things in style; **il faut bien voir les choses en face** *ou* **telles qu'elles sont** you have to face up to things, you have to face facts; **les choses étant ce qu'elles sont** things being as *or* what they are; **ne pas faire les choses à demi** not to do things by halves; **ce documentaire sur l'alcoolisme va au fond des choses** this documentary on alcoholism gets to the heart of the matter *or* problem; **n'aie pas peur d'appeler les choses par leur nom** don't be afraid to call a spade a spade *or* to speak your mind

NM *Fam* (*truc*) whatsit, what's-its-name, thingummy; **passe-moi le c.** pass me the whatsit *or* the what-d'you-call-it; **Monsieur/Madame C.** Mr/Mrs what-d'you-call-him/her, what's-his-name/what's-her-name, Mr/Mrs thingummy; **le petit C.** little what's-his-name

ADJ INV *Fam* **être** *ou* **se sentir/avoir l'air tout c.** to feel/look funny *or* a bit peculiar

chosifier [ʃozifje] **VT** *Phil* to reify

chott [ʃɔt] **NM** *Géog* saline lake, shott

chou¹, -oux [ʃu] **NM 1** (*plante*) cabbage; *Fam* **aller planter ses choux** to go and live in the country, to retire to the country; **faire ses choux gras de qch** (*s'enrichir*) to get rich on sth; **l'opposition a fait ses choux gras de ce scandale** the opposition had a field day with the scandal; **faire c. blanc** to draw a blank; **mon petit c.** darling, dear; **être dans les choux** to be in a fix *or* a mess; **rentrer dans le c. à qn** to attack *or* go for sb; **c'est bête comme c.** it's as easy as pie; *Fig* **feuille de c.** (*journal*) rag **2** (*ruban*) bow, rosette **3** *Culin* **pâte à choux** choux pastry

▸▸ **c. de Bruxelles** Brussels sprout; *Culin* **c. à la crème** = cream bun; **c. frisé** kale; **c. de Milan** Savoy (cabbage); **c. pommé** round cabbage; **c. rouge** red cabbage

chou², choute [ʃu, ʃut] **ADJ** *Fam* **elle est c.** *ou* **choute!** she's cute!; **c'est d'un c.!** it's so cute!

chouan [ʃwã] **NM** *Hist* Chouan

Chouannerie [ʃwanri] **NF** *Hist* **la C.** the Chouan revolt

choucas [ʃuka] **NM** jackdaw

chouchou, -oute [ʃuʃu, -ut] **N** *Fam* (*préféré*) pet, *m* blue-eyed boy; **le c. du prof** the teacher's pet; **tu es sa chouchoute** you're his favourite *or* pet

NM (*pour mettre dans les cheveux*) scrunchy

chouchouter [ʃuʃute] **VT** *Fam* to pamper, to spoil; **il aime se faire c.** he enjoys being pampered

choucroute [ʃukrut] **NF** *Culin* sauerkraut; **c. garnie** sauerkraut with meat

chouette¹ [ʃwɛt] **NF 1** (*oiseau*) **c. des clochers, c. effraie** screech owl, barn owl; **c. des bois** wood *or* brown owl; **c. hulotte** tawny owl **2** *Fam Péj* (*femme désagréable*) old shrew

chouette² *Fam* **ADJ** terrific, marvellous, great; **c'est c.!** that's great *or* smashing!; **un type vraiment c.** a really great guy; **il a été**

très c. avec elle he's been really good to her; *Iron* tu as l'air c. avec ton chapeau! you look (like) something else in that hat! **INT c. (alors)!** great!, fantastic!

chou-fleur, *pl* **choux-fleurs NM** cauliflower; **oreille en c.** cauliflower ear

chouïa [ʃuja] **NM** *Fam* **un c. (de)** a tiny bit (of), a smidgen (of); **tu devrais te reposer un c.** you should have a bit of *or* a little rest

chou-navet, *pl* **choux-navets NM** swede, *Am* rutabaga

chou-palmiste, *pl* **choux-palmistes NM** *Bot* palm cabbage

chou-rave, *pl* **choux-raves NM** kohlrabi

chouraver [ʃurave], **chourer** [ʃure] **VT** *Fam* to pinch, to nick; **on m'a chouravé mon vélo** I've had my bike pinched *or* nicked

chow-chow, *pl* **chows-chows** [ʃoʃo, ʃawʃaw] **NM** chow (dog)

choyer [ʃwaje] **VT** (**je choie; je choierai**) to pamper, to coddle; **c. un espoir** to cherish a hope

chrême [krɛm] **NM** *Rel* chrism, holy oil

chrétien, -ienne [kretjɛ̃, -jɛn] **ADJ** Christian **N** Christian; **un bon c.** a good Christian

chrétiennement [kretjɛnmɑ̃] **ADV** in a Christian manner, like a Christian; **mourir c.** to die a Christian death

chrétienté [kretjɛ̃te] **NF** Christendom

Chris-Craft® [kriskraft] **NM INV** *Naut* Chris-Craft®

Christ [krist] **NM 1 le C.** Christ; **Jésus-C.** [ʒezykri] Jesus Christ **2 c.** crucifix; **un c. d'ivoire/d'ébène** an ivory/ebony crucifix

christiania [kristjanja] **NM** *Ski* christiania, christie (turn)

christianisation [kristjanizasjɔ̃] **NF** christianization

christianiser [kristjanize] **VT** to christianize

christianisme [kristjanism] **NM** Christianity

chromage [kromaʒ] **NM** chromium plating

chromate [kromat] **NM** *Chimie* chromate

chromatique [kromatik] **ADJ 1** *Mus, Opt etc* chromatic **2** *Biol* chromosomal

chromatiquement [kromatikmɑ̃] **ADV** *Mus* chromatically

chromatisme [kromatism] **NM** *Mus* chromaticism; *Beaux-Arts* range of colours

chrome [krom] **NM 1** *Chimie* chromium **2** (*matière*) chrome; (*sur auto etc*) chrome fitting; **jaune de c.** chrome yellow; *Fam* **faire (briller) les chromes** (*de voitures, de bicyclettes etc*) to polish the chrome

chromé [krome] **ADJ** (*métal*) chromium-plated; **acier c.** chrome steel

chromer [krome] **VT 1** (*métal*) to chromium-plate **2** (*acier*) to chrome

chrominance [krominɑ̃s] **NF** *TV* chrominance

chromo [kromo] **NM** *Fam* chromo(lithograph), colour print

chromosome [kromozom] **NM** *Biol* chromosome; **c. somatique** autosome, somatic chromosome

chromosomique [kromozomik] **ADJ** *Biol* chromosomal; **maladie c.** chromosomal *or* genetic illness

chronicité [kronisite] **NF** (*d'une maladie, du chômage etc*) chronic nature, *Fml* chronicity

chronique [kronik] **ADJ** (*maladie, chômage etc*) chronic; **mévente c.** slump in sales **NF 1** *Journ* (*financière etc*) news, report, column; **tenir la c. sportive** to write the sports column; *Fig* **défrayer la c.** to be the talk of the neighbourhood *or* town, to be the main topic of conversation; **c. boursière** markets column; **c. financière** financial news; **c. judiciaire** court column; **c. littéraire** book reviews; **c. mondaine** society column; **c. des**

spectacles (entertainments) listings **2** (*annale*) chronicle

chroniquement [kronikmɑ̃] **ADV** chronically

chroniqueur, -euse [kronikœr, -øz] **N 1** *Journ* columnist, editor; **c. boursier** market commentator; **c. judiciaire** court reporter; **c. littéraire** book editor, book reviewer; **c. mondain** gossip columnist **2** (*historien*) chronicler

chrono [krono] **NM** *Fam* stopwatch; **du 220 (km/h) (au) c.** recorded speed of 220 (km/h); **son temps était de 4 minutes 6 secondes, c.** his time by the clock was 4 minutes (and) 6 seconds

chronobiologie [kronobjɔlɔʒi] **NF** *Biol* chronobiology

chronogramme [kronogram] **NM** planner

chronographe [kronograf] **NM** *Tech* chronograph

chronologie [kronolɔʒi] **NF** chronology; *Cin, TV* chronology, time sequence

chronologique [kronolɔʒik] **ADJ** chronological

chronologiquement [kronolɔʒikmɑ̃] **ADV** chronologically

chronométrage [kronometraʒ] **NM** timekeeping; (*d'une course*) timing

chronomètre [kronometr] **NM 1** (*pour le sport etc*) stopwatch **2** (*montre de précision*) chronometer; *Ordinat* timer

chronométrer [kronometre] **VT** (**je chronomètre; je chronométrerai**) *Sport* to time

chronométreur [kronometrœr] **NM 1** *Sport* timekeeper **2** *Ind* time and motion (study) expert

chronométrique [kronometrik] **ADJ** chronometric(al)

Chronopost [kronopost] **NM** = express mail service in France

chrysalide [krizalid] **NF** *Entom* chrysalis, pupa; *Fig* **sortir de sa c.** to come out of one's shell

chrysanthème [krizɑ̃tɛm] **NM** chrysanthemum

Chrysanthèmes

Chrysanthemums are often associated with funerals in France, and so are never offered as gifts. They are traditionally used to decorate graves, especially on All Saints' Day.

---

chrysolithe [krizɔlit] **NF** *Minér* chrysolite, olivine

CHS [seaʃɛs] **NM** (*abrév* **centre hospitalier spécialisé**) psychiatric hospital

chtarbé [ʃtarbe] **ADJ** *Fam* crazy, nuts, off one's rocker

ch'timi [ʃtimi] *Fam* **ADJ** from Northern France **N** person from Northern France

chtouille [ʃtuj] **NF** *très Fam* **la c.** the clap

CHU [seaʃy] **NM INV** (*abrév* **centre hospitalier universitaire**) ≃ teaching hospital

chuchotement [ʃyʃɔtmɑ̃] **NM** whisper; **chuchotements** whisperings, whispers

chuchoter [ʃyʃɔte] **VI** to whisper; **parler en chuchotant** to speak in a whisper **VT c. qch à l'oreille de qn** to whisper sth in sb's ear

chuchoterie [ʃyʃɔtri] **NF** whispering, whispered conversation

chuchoteur, -euse [ʃyʃɔtœr, -øz] **ADJ** whispering **N** whisperer

chuintant, -ante [ʃɥɛ̃tɑ̃, -ɑ̃t] *Ling* **ADJ** **sons chuintants** hushing sounds (*eg* S, Z);

consonne chuintante palato-alveolar fricative

NF chuintante palato-alveolar fricative

chuintement [ʃɥɛ̃tmɑ̃] **NM 1** *Ling* pronunciation of s as sh **2** (*sifflement*) hissing

chuinter [ʃɥɛ̃te] **VI 1** (*de la chouette*) to hoot **2** *Ling* to pronounce s as sh **3** (*de la vapeur etc*) to hiss

chut [ʃyt] **INT** hush!, sh!

chute [ʃyt] **NF 1** (*fait de tomber*) fall; *Fig* (*d'un ministère etc*) fall, collapse; (*de pression, de température etc*) drop, fall; (*de ventes etc*) slump; **faire une c. (de cheval/moto)** to have a fall *or* a tumble *or* a spill (from one's horse/motorbike), to fall off (one's horse/motorbike); **une c. de 10 mètres** a 10-metre fall; **il a fait une c. de dix mètres** he fell ten metres; **'c. de pierres'** 'danger! falling rocks'; **c. de pluie/neige** rainfall/snowfall; **c. du jour** nightfall; *Litt* **c. des feuilles** autumn, *Am* fall; **la c. des feuilles** the Fall; **il m'a entraîné dans sa c.** he has dragged me down with him; *Théâtre* **c. d'une pièce** failure *or Fam* flop of a play; *Cartes* **avoir deux levées de c.** to be two tricks down; *Élec* **c. de potentiel** voltage drop **2 c. d'eau** waterfall; **les chutes Victoria** the Victoria Falls; **c. naturelle** natural waterfall; **hauteur de c.** (*d'eau*) fall, head **3** (*du toit*) pitch; (*d'une robe*) hang; (*de la voix etc*) cadence; (*d'un poème, roman, d'une pièce etc*) end; (*d'histoire drôle*) punchline **4** (*de bois*) off-cut; (*de tissu etc*) scraps, trimmings; (*de métal*) scrap **5** *Cin, TV* waste film; *Journ* last line (*of article*), tag line ▸ ▸ **c. libre** free fall; **descendre en c. libre** (*to be in*) free fall; *Fig* **ses résultats scolaires descendent en c. libre** his marks are plummeting *or* have taken a nose-dive; **c. des reins** small of the back; *Théâtre* **c. du rideau** fall of the curtain

chuter [ʃyte] **VI** *Fam* (*tomber*) to fall (down); *Fig* to come a cropper, to come to grief; *Théâtre* (*d'une pièce de théâtre*) to be a failure, to flop; *Cartes* **c. de deux levées** to be two tricks down

chyme [ʃim] **NM** *Méd* chyme

Chypre [ʃipr] **NF** (**l'île de**) **C.** Cyprus

chypriote [ʃiprijɔt] **ADJ** Cypriot **N C.** Cypriot

CI [sei] **NM** *Fin* (*abrév* **certificat d'investissement**) investment certificate

ci¹ [si] **ADV** here; **ce livre-ci** this book; **ces jours-ci** these days; **de-ci, de-là** here and there, on all sides; **par-ci, par-là** here and there; **ci-gît …/-gisent …** here lies …/lie …

ci² **PRON DÉM INV** *Fam* **faire ci et ça** to do this and that; **comme ci comme ça** so-so

CIA [seia] **NF** (*abrév* **Central Intelligence Agency**) CIA

ciao [tʃao] **INT** *Fam* ciao

ci-après **ADV** (*dans la suite du texte etc*) later, further on, below; *Jur* here(in)after

cibiche [sibiʃ] **NF** *Fam* fag, ciggie

cibiste [sibist] **N** user of Citizens' Band radio, CB user

ciblage [siblaʒ] **NM** *Mktg* targeting; **c. stratégique** strategic targeting

cible [sibl] **NF** target, mark; (*en publicité*) target; **servir de c. aux railleries de qn** to be the butt *or* the target for sb's jokes; **déterminer/atteindre la c.** to define/reach the target; **langue c.** target language; *Mktg* **marché c.** (*pour un produit*) target market; **c. commerciale/de communication** marketing/promotional target

ciblé [sible] ADJ *(campagne etc)* targeted (**sur** at)

cibler [sible] VT *Mktg* to target

ciboire [sibwar] NM *Rel* pyx, ciborium

ciboule [sibul] NF *Bot, Culin* spring onion, *Am* scallion

ciboulette [sibulɛt] NF *(plante), Culin* chive(s)

ciboulot [sibulo] NM *Arg (tête)* noddle, nut; **se creuser le c.** to rack one's brains; **en avoir dans le c.** to have a lot between one's ears; **elle en a dans le c., cette petite!** she's not just a pretty face, this girl!

cicatrice [sikatris] NF scar; *Fig* **cette séparation a laissé une c. profonde en lui** the separation scarred him deeply *or* left a deep scar on him

cicatriciel, -ielle [sikatrisjɛl] ADJ **tissu c.** scar tissue

cicatrisant [sikatrizɑ̃] ADJ *(pommade etc)* healing, *Spéc* cicatrizing
▪ NM healing lotion *or* cream

cicatrisation [sikatrizasjɔ̃] NF *(de blessure etc)* healing, closing (up), *Spéc* cicatrization

cicatriser [sikatrize] VT *(blessure etc)* to heal; **le temps cicatrise toutes les blessures** time heals all wounds
▪ VI *(d'une blessure etc)* to heal (up)
▪ VPR **se cicatriser** to heal up; *Fig* to heal

cicéro [sisero] NM *Typ* pica, twelve-point type

ciclée [sikle] NF *Suisse Fam (cri)* shriek

cicler [sikle] VI *Suisse Fam (crier)* to shriek

ciclosporine [siklɔspɔrin] NF *Chimie* cyclosporin A

ci-contre ADV **1** *(en regard)* opposite; *Compta* **porté c.** as per contra **2** *(document etc)* attached

CICR [seiseɛr] NM *(abrév* **Comité international de la Croix-Rouge**) IRCC

ci-dessous [sid(ə)su] ADV below

ci-dessus [sid(ə)sy] ADV above

ci-devant [sid(ə)vɑ̃] ADV previously, formerly
▪ N INV *Hist* aristocrat

CIDEX [sidɛks] NM *(abrév* **courrier individuel à distribution exceptionnelle**) = system grouping letter boxes in country areas

CIDJ [seidɛʒi] NM *(abrév* **centre d'information et de documentation de la jeunesse**) = library offering careers information and literature to young people

cidre [sidr] NM cider; **c. bouché** bottled cider; **c. doux/brut** sweet/dry cider

cidrerie [sidrəri] NF *(fabrique)* cider house

Cie *(abrév* **Compagnie**) Co

ciel [sjɛl] *pl* **ciels, cieux** [sjø] NM **1** *(espace)* sky; **il s'est suspendu entre c. et terre** to hang in mid-air; **(couleur) bleu (de) c.** sky-blue; **trouée de c. (bleu)** patch of (blue) sky; **les ciels de l'Italie** the skies of Italy; *Beaux-Arts* **les ciels de Turner** Turner's skies; **carte du c.** map of the heavens; **à c. ouvert** in the open air, out of doors; **sous d'autres cieux** beneath other skies, in other climes; **lever les bras au c.** to raise one's hands to the sky *or* heavenwards; **lever les yeux au c.** to raise one's eyes to heaven; *Fam* **tomber du c.** to be thunderstruck; *Fig* **ça ne va pas te tomber du c.** it won't fall into your lap, you won't get it handed to you on a plate; *Fig* **remuer c. et terre** to move heaven and earth (**pour faire qch** to do sth); **être au septième c.** to be in seventh heaven; *Fig* **élever qn aux cieux** *ou* **jusqu'au c.** to laud sb to the skies

2 *(paradis)* heaven; **il est monté au c.** he's gone to heaven; **notre Père qui es** *ou* **êtes aux cieux** our Father which *or* who art in Heaven; **le royaume des cieux** the Kingdom of Heaven; **le c. m'en est témoin** (as) Heaven is my witness; **(juste) c.!** (good) heavens!, heavens above!; **aide-toi, le c. t'aidera** God helps those who help themselves; **grâce au c.** thank heavens

3 *pl* **ciels** *Rel (baldaquin)* baldachin, canopy; *(de lit)* canopy; *Min (d'une carrière etc)* roof; **carrière/mine à c. ouvert** opencast quarry/mine

cierge [sjɛrʒ] NM *Rel* candle; **brûler un c. à un saint** to burn a candle to a saint

cigale [sigal] NF *(insecte)* cicada; *Fig Fam (dépensier)* spendthrift

cigare [sigar] NM **1** *(à fumer)* cigar **2** *Arg (tête)* nut, bonce; **avoir mal au c.** to have a headache; **mets-toi ça dans le c.** get that into your thick skull

cigarette [sigarɛt] NF cigarette; **c. (à) bout filtre** filter-tip cigarette; **la c. du condamné** the condemned man's last cigarette; **c. russe** = long roll-shaped biscuit

cigarettier [sigarɛtje] NM cigarette manufacturer

cigarillo [sigarijo] NM cigarillo

cigogne [sigɔɲ] NF **1** *(oiseau)* stork **2** *(levier)* crank lever

ciguë [sigy] NF *(plante), Méd* hemlock

ci-inclus [siɛ̃kly] ADJ *(inv when it precedes the noun)* **la copie ci-incluse** the enclosed copy
▪ ADV **(vous trouverez) c. copie de votre lettre** please find enclosed a copy of your letter

CIJ [seiʒi] NF *(abrév* **Cour internationale de justice**) ICJ

ci-joint ADJ *(inv when it precedes the noun)* attached, enclosed; **les pièces ci-jointes** the enclosed *or* attached documents
▪ ADV **vous trouverez c. quittance** please find receipt attached *or* enclosed

cil [sil] NM **1** (eye)lash; **battre des cils** to flutter one's eyelashes; **faux cils** false eyelashes **2** *Biol* cilium, hair, filament

cilice [silis] NM hair shirt

cillement [sijmɑ̃] NM blinking

ciller [sije] VI to blink; *Fig* **il n'a pas cillé** he didn't bat an eyelid

cimaise [simɛz] NF ogee moulding; *(à hauteur d'appui)* dado (rail)

cime [sim] NF *(d'une montagne etc)* summit; *(pic)* peak; *(d'un arbre, d'un mât etc)* top; *Fig* **être à la c. de la réussite** to be at the height *or* peak of one's success

ciment [simɑ̃] NM cement; **c. à prise rapide** quick-setting cement; **c. armé** reinforced concrete; **c. dentaire** amalgam

cimentation [simɑ̃tasjɔ̃] NF cementing

cimenter [simɑ̃te] VT to cement; *Fig* **c. une alliance/une amitié/une relation** to cement *or* consolidate an alliance/a friendship/a relationship

cimenterie [simɑ̃tri] NF *Ind* cement works

cimeterre [simtɛr] NM scimitar

cimetière [simtjɛr] NM cemetery, graveyard; *(d'église)* churchyard; **c. de voitures** scrapyard; **c. d'éléphants** elephants' graveyard

cimier [simje] NM **1** *(d'un casque)* crest **2** *(d'un cerf etc)* haunch; *(d'un bœuf)* rump

cinabre [sinabr] NM cinnabar

ciné [sine] NM *Br Fam (spectacle)* pictures, *Am* movies; *(édifice) Br* cinema, *Am* movie theater; **aller au c.** to go to the pictures

cinéaste [sineast] N film maker

ciné-club, *pl* **ciné-clubs** NM film club

cinéma [sinema] NM **1** *(art)* cinema, movies, *Am* motion pictures; **le c. de Pasolini** Pasolini's films; **l'invention du c.** the invention of cinema *or* motion pictures; **studio de c.** film studio; **faire du c.** *(d'un acteur)* to be a film *or* movie actor, to act in films; *(d'un metteur en scène, technicien etc)* to work in films; **acteur/actrice de c.** film *or* movie actor/actress; **critique de c.** cinema *or* film critic; **industrie du c.** film *or* movie industry, *Am* motion picture industry; *Fam* **c'est du c.** it's all an act, it's all put on; **elle a fait tout un c. pour ne pas y aller** she made a scene so that she didn't have to go; **arrête (un peu) ton c. et va te coucher!** stop making such a fuss and go to bed!

2 *(salle)* cinema, *Am* movie theater, *Br Fam* pictures; **aller au c.** to go to the cinema; **ouvreuse de c.** usherette
▪ ▪ **c. d'amateurs** amateur film-making, home movies; **c. d'animation** animation; **c. d'art et d'essai** *(genre, bâtiment)* art-house cinema; **c. d'auteur** auteur cinema; **c. direct** direct cinema; **c. à domicile** home cinema; **c. muet** silent films; **c. multi-salle** multi-screen cinema, multiplex; **c. parlant** talking films, *Fam* talkies; **c. permanent** continuous performance; **c. en relief** three-dimensional *or* 3-D films

CinémaScope® [sinemaskɔp] NM CinemaScope®

cinémathèque [sinematɛk] NF film library *or* archives; **la C. française** = the French film institute

cinématique [sinematik] ADJ kinematic(al)
▪ NF kinematics

cinématographe [sinematɔgraf] NM cinematograph

cinématographie [sinematɔgrafi] NF cinematography

cinématographier [sinematɔgrafje] VT to film

cinématophotographie [sinematɔfɔtɔgrafi] NF camerawork

cinématographique [sinematɔgrafik] ADJ cinematographic; *(production etc)* cinema, film; **les techniques cinématographiques** cinematic techniques; **une grande carrière c.** a great career in the cinema

cinéma-vérité NM cinéma vérité

cinémomètre [sinemɔmɛtr] NM *Tech* speedometer, speed gauge

ciné-parc, *pl* **ciné-parcs** NM *Can* drive-in cinema

cinéphile [sinefil] ADJ film- *or* movie-loving; **public c.** cinema-going public; **ils sont tous très cinéphiles dans cette famille** they're all great film-lovers *or* film buffs *or* movie buffs in that family
▪ N film *or* movie enthusiast *or* buff

cinéraire [sinerɛr] ADJ *(urne etc)* cinerary
▪ NF *(plante)* cineraria

Cinérama® [sinerama] NM Cinerama®

ciné-roman, *pl* **ciné-romans** NM = picture book of a film; *Arch (film)* (film) serial

cinétique [sinetik] ADJ *(énergie etc)* kinetic
▪ NF kinetics

cing(h)alais, -aise [sɛ̃galɛ, -ɛz] ADJ Sin(g)halese
▪ NM *Ling* Sin(g)halese
▪ N **C.** Sin(g)halese

cinglant [sɛ̃glɑ̃] ADJ *(pluie etc)* lashing; *(vent etc)* cutting, biting; *(froid)* bitter; *(remarque)* stinging, cutting, scathing

cinglé, -ée [sɛ̃gle] *Fam* ADJ cracked, crazy; **il est complètement c.** he's off his rocker, he's round the twist
▪ N loony, nutcase

cingler[1] [sɛ̃gle] VI *Naut* **un voilier qui cingle vers les Canaries** a yacht making for *or* bound for the Canary Islands

cingler[2] VT *(visage) (du vent)* to sting; *(cheval etc)* to lash, to whip; *(personne)* to lash out at; **une branche m'a cinglé la figure** a branch whipped (against) my face; **la grêle lui cinglait le visage** the hail was stinging his face

cinoche [sinɔʃ] NM *Fam* cinema, *Am* movie theater; **aller au c.** to go to the pictures *or* movies; **je me ferais bien un petit c. ce soir** I quite fancy going to the pictures tonight

cinoque [sinɔk] *Arg* ADJ batty, crazy ▸ N nutcase, headbanger

cinq [sɛ̃k] ADJ INV **1** five; **à c. heures** at five o' clock **c. (petits) garçons** [sɛ̃(pti)garsɔ̃] five (little) boys; **c. hommes** [sɛ̃kɔm] five men; **j'en ai c.** [sɛ̃k] I've got five; **c. par c.** five by five, in fives; *Euph* **les c. lettres** ≃ a four-letter word; **je lui ai répondu en c. lettres** I told him where to go; **il était moins c.** it was a near thing *or* a close shave; *Aut* **c. places** five-seater; *Aut* **c. portes** five-door model; *Fig* **faire qch en c. sec** to do sth in five seconds flat; *Radio* **recevoir qn c. sur c.** to receive sb loud and clear; *Journ* **c. colonnes à la une** a banner headline
2 *(dans des séries)* fifth; **page/numéro c.** page/number five; **Henri C.** Henry the Fifth
3 *(pour exprimer les minutes)* **trois heures c.** five past three; **trois heures moins c.** five to three; **attends c. minutes** just give me a minute, *Fam* hang on a sec
▸ NM INV five; **le c. mars** [sɛ̃(k)mars] (on) the fifth of March, (on) March the fifth, *Am* (on) March fifth; *Cartes* **un c. de pique** a five of spades; **j'habite au c.** I live at number five

cinquantaine [sɛ̃kɑ̃tɛn] NF *(about)* fifty; **une c. de personnes** about *or* some fifty people, fifty or so people; **approcher la c.** to be getting on for fifty; **passer la c.** to be in one's fifties

cinquante [sɛ̃kɑ̃t] ADJ & INV fifty; **billet de c. euros** fifty-euro note; **page c.** page fifty; **demeurer au numéro c.** to live at number fifty; **les années c.** the fifties
▸ NM INV fifty; **le numéro c.** the number fifty, 50; **c. pour cent ont refusé** fifty per cent refused

cinquantenaire [sɛ̃kɑ̃tnɛr] NM fiftieth anniversary
▸ ADJ fifty-year-old, fifty years old

cinquantième [sɛ̃kɑ̃tjɛm] ADJ fiftieth ▸ N fiftieth; **être le c. dans un classement** to be placed *or* come fiftieth in a classification *or* grading
▸ NM *(partie)* fiftieth (part)

cinquième [sɛ̃kjɛm] ADJ fifth; **loger au c. étage** to live on the fifth *or Am* sixth floor; **être la c. roue de la charrette** *ou* **du carrosse** to feel out of it, *Am* to feel like a fifth wheel
▸ N fifth; **elle est arrivée la c.** she came (in) fifth, she came in in fifth place
▸ NM *(partie)* fifth (part)
▸ NF **1** *Scol* **(classe de) c.** ≃ second form *or* year (of secondary school), *Am* ≃ seventh grade **2** *Aut* fifth gear

cinquièmement [sɛ̃kjɛmmɑ̃] ADV fifthly, in (the) fifth place

cintrage [sɛ̃traʒ] NM *(action)* bending; *(résultat)* bend

cintre [sɛ̃tr] NM **1** *(pour les vêtements)* coat-hanger, clothes hanger; **suspendre sa veste à un c.** to put one's jacket on a (clothes) hanger **2** *(courbure)* curve **3** *Archit (d'un tunnel etc)* arch; *(d'une voûte)* soffit; **arc en plein c.** semicircular arch **4** *Théâtre* **les cintres** the flies; **c. de lumière** lighting batten

cintré [sɛ̃tre] ADJ **1** *(fenêtre etc)* arched; *(poutre etc)* bent, curved; *(veste etc)* fitted; **taille cintrée** nipped-in waist **2** *Fam* crazy

cintrer [sɛ̃tre] VT **1** *(tuyau, rail etc)* to bend, to curve **2** *(fenêtre)* to arch **3** **c. une veste** to take in a jacket at the waist

CIO [seio] NM *(abrév* **Comité international olympique)** IOC

cipaye [sipaj] NM sepoy; *Hist* **la révolte des cipayes** the Indian Mutiny

cirage [siraʒ] NM **1** *(des sols etc)* waxing, polishing; *(des chaussures)* polishing **2** *(substance)* (shoe) polish; **c. de couleur/incolore** coloured/neutral polish; **c. pour cuir/parquet** leather/floor polish; *Fam* **être dans le c.** to be a bit fuzzy, to be confused; *Aviat* to be flying blind

circadien [sirkadjɛ̃] ADJ *Biol* **rythme c.** circadian rhythm

circlip [sirklip] NM *Tech* circlip

circoncire [sirkɔ̃sir] VT *(prp* **circoncisant;** *pp* **conconcis;** *pr ind* **je circoncis;** *pr sub* **je circoncise;** *p hist* **je circoncis;** *fu* **je circoncirai)** to circumcise

circoncis [sirkɔ̃si] ADJ circumcised
▸ NM circumcised boy/man

circoncision [sirkɔ̃sizjɔ̃] NF circumcision

circonférence [sirkɔ̃ferɑ̃s] NF **1** *Géom* circumference; *(d'un arbre)* circumference, girth; **avoir dix centimètres de c.** to have a circumference of ten centimetres, to be ten centimetres in circumference **2** *(d'une ville etc)* perimeter, boundaries

circonflexe [sirkɔ̃flɛks] ADJ *(accent)* circumflex

circonlocution [sirkɔ̃lɔkysjɔ̃] NF circumlocution; **parler par circonlocutions** to speak in a roundabout way, *Fam* to beat about the bush; **après de longues circonlocutions, il finit par nous déclarer que ...** after much beating about the bush, he eventually announced that ...

circonscription [sirkɔ̃skripsjɔ̃] NF *Admin etc* division, district, area; **c. électorale** *(au niveau municipal)* ward; *(au niveau national)* constituency, *Can* riding; **c. téléphonique** telephone code area

circonscrire [sirkɔ̃skrir] *(conj like* **écrire)** VT *Math* to circumscribe, to draw a line round; *(espace, bloc de maisons)* to surround, to encircle (**par** with, by); *(limiter)* to limit; **c. son sujet** to define the scope of one's subject; **c. un incendie** to bring a fire under control, to contain a fire
▸ VPR **se circonscrire** to be bounded, to be limited; **le débat se circonscrit autour d'une seule idée** the whole debate centres *or* is centred around one idea

circonspect [sirkɔ̃spɛ(kt)] ADJ circumspect, cautious, wary; **il était c. dans ses propos** he spoke cautiously; **il était c. dans le choix de ses fréquentations** he was careful in his choice of company

circonspection [sirkɔ̃spɛksjɔ̃] NF circumspection, caution, wariness; **avec c.** cautiously, warily

circonstance [sirkɔ̃stɑ̃s] NF **1** *(cas)* circumstance; **dans les circonstances actuelles, il faut se montrer prudent** given the circumstances *or* as things stand, we must tread carefully; **se retrouver dans des circonstances difficiles** to find oneself in difficult circumstances; **en pareille c.** under such circumstances, in such a case; **à la hauteur des circonstances** equal to the occasion; **eu égard aux** *ou* **étant donné les circonstances** all things considered, in *or* given the circumstances; **par un concours de circonstances** by a combination of circumstances; **profiter de la c.** to make the most of the opportunity; **vers de c.** occasional verse; **paroles de c.** words suited to the occasion, appropriate *or* suitable words; **ce ne serait pas de c.** it would not be appropriate
2 *Jur* **circonstances et dépendances** appurtenances; **circonstances atténuantes** extenuating circumstances; **circonstances aggravantes** aggravating circumstances

circonstancié [sirkɔ̃stɑ̃sje] ADJ *(rapport)* detailed

circonstanciel, -ielle [sirkɔ̃stɑ̃sjɛl] ADJ **1** *Litt* circumstantial; **des mesures rigoureusement circonstancielles** measures dictated by exceptional circumstances; **déclaration/mesure circonstancielle** declaration/measure dictated by the circumstances **2** *Gram* **complément c. (de temps/de lieu)** adverbial complement (of time/place)

circonvenir [sirkɔ̃vnir] VT *(conj like* **venir)** *(personne)* to take in

circonvolution [sirkɔ̃vɔlysjɔ̃] NF *Anat, Archit* convolution; *Archit (de volutes etc)* circumvolution

circuit [sirkчi] NM **1** *Sport* round, lap; *(d'une course de motos etc)* circuit; **c. automobile** racing circuit; **c. de petites voitures** racing track
2 *(itinéraire)* **c. (touristique)** (organized) trip, tour; **c. en car** coach tour; **faire le c. des châteaux de la Loire** to tour the Loire châteaux
3 *(chemin)* way; **refaire tout le c. à pied** to go all the way back on foot; **c. touristique** scenic *or* tourist route; **il faut faire un long c. pour passer d'un côté de l'île à l'autre** you have to make a long detour to get from one side of the island to the other
4 *Élec* circuit; **c. ouvert/fermé** open/closed circuit; **télévision en c. fermé** closed circuit television; **c. basse tension** low-tension circuit; **c. haute tension** high-tension circuit; **c. d'induction** inductive circuit; **c. intégré** integrated circuit; **c. de retour à la masse** earth return circuit; **mettre en c.** to connect, to switch on; **couper le c.** to switch off; **rétablir le c.** to switch on (again); **mettre une lampe hors c.** to disconnect a lamp; *Fig* **ils ont tendance à vivre en c. fermé** they tend to lead their own separate existence *or* to live in a closed world; *Fig* **ça fait longtemps que je ne suis plus dans le c.** I've been out of it for ages, I'm hopelessly out of touch; *Fig* **il est complètement hors c.** he's completely out of touch
5 *Tech, Aut* **c. d'allumage** ignition system; **c. d'allumage par bobine** coil-ignition system; **c. de carburant étanche** sealed fuel system; **c. de charge** *(de batterie)* charging system; **c. de démarrage** starting circuit; **c. d'eau** water circuit; **c. de freinage** braking system; **c. de graissage** lubrication circuit; **c. hydraulique** hydraulic circuit; **c. d'injection d'essence** petrol injection system; **c. de lubrification** lubrication system; **c. oléopneumatique** air/hydraulic system; **c. de préchauffage** pre-heating system; **c. de refroidissement** cooling system
6 *Ordinat* **c. de commande** command circuit; **c. ET** AND circuit; **c. de liaison** link circuit; **c. logique** logic circuit; **circuits de rafraîchissement** *ou* **de régénération** refresh circuitry
7 *Écon* **c. de commercialisation** marketing network, trade *or* marketing channel; **c. de distribution** distribution channels *or* network; **circuits de vente** commercial channels
▸▸ **c. aventure** adventure holiday; *Radio* **c. de cryptage** scrambling circuit; *Électron* **c. imprimé** printed circuit

circulaire [sirkylɛr] ADJ circular; **billet c.** excursion ticket; **scie c.** circular saw; *Tech* **mouvement c.** rotary motion
▸ NF circular

circulairement [sirkylɛrmɑ̃] ADV in a circle

circulant [sirkylɑ̃] ADJ *Fin (billets, devises)* in circulation; *(capitaux)* circulating

circulation [sirkylasjɔ̃] NF **1** *(d'autos, d'avions)* traffic; **c. routière** road traffic; **c. aérienne** air traffic; **c. des trains** running of trains; **c. à sens unique/à deux sens** one-/two-way traffic; **c. interdite** no thoroughfare; **les embarras de la c.** traffic congestion; **route à grande c.** trunk road; **accident de la c.** road accident; **la c. est très difficile** the traffic is very heavy; **il y a beaucoup de c. sur les routes** there's a lot of traffic on the roads; *Fig* **disparaître de la c.** to drop out of circulation

2 *(de l'air, du sang, de l'information, des marchandises etc)* circulation; *Méd* **problèmes de c.** circulation *or* circulatory problems; **mettre un livre en c.** to put a book into circulation; **mise en c. de qch** circulation of sth; **retirer un produit de la c.** to take a product off the market

3 *Fin (des billets etc)* circulation; **c. des capitaux/des devises** circulation of capital/currency; **c. monétaire** circulation of money

4 *Pol, Écon* **libre c. des travailleurs/des citoyens** free movement of workers/of citizens

> Il faut noter que le mot anglais **circulation** ne s'emploie jamais pour faire référence à la circulation routière.

circulatoire [siʀkylatwaʀ] ADJ *Anat* circulatory

circuler [siʀkyle] VI **1** *(du sang, de l'air etc)* to circulate, to flow; *(d'une rumeur)* to circulate; **faire c. l'air** to circulate the air; *Fin* **les capitaux qui circulent** capital in circulation, circulating capital; *Fin* **faire c. des effets** to keep bills afloat; **faire c. la bouteille** to pass *or* hand the bottle round; **faire c. une nouvelle** to spread a piece of news; **faire c. une pétition** to circulate a petition

2 *(en voiture)* to travel, to move about; **circulez, il n'y a rien à voir!** move along now, there's nothing to see!; **les autobus circulent jour et nuit** the buses run day and night; **on a du mal à c. en ville** it's not easy to drive in town; **on circule très mal à ce moment de la journée** it's very difficult to get anywhere at this time of day

circumnavigation [siʀkɔmnavigasjɔ̃] NF circumnavigation

cire [siʀ] NF wax; *(encaustique)* (wax) polish; **bouchon de c.** *(dans l'oreille)* plug of earwax; **c. d'abeille** beeswax; **c. à cacheter** sealing wax; **personnage en c.** waxwork; **c. anti-corrosion** anti-corrosion wax

ciré [siʀe] ADJ polished; **parquet c.** polished *or* waxed floor; **chaussures bien cirées** well-polished shoes; **toile cirée** oilcloth ▪ NM oilskin

cirer [siʀe] VT *(sols, meubles etc)* to polish, to wax; *(corde etc)* to wax; **c. ses chaussures** to polish one's shoes; *Fam* **c. les bottes à qn** to lick sb's boots; *Arg* **il n'en a rien à c. (de tes histoires)** he doesn't give a damn (about your stories)

cireur, -euse [siʀœʀ, -øz] N **1** *(de chaussures)* shoeblack, *Am* shoeshine boy; *Fam* **un c. de pompes** a bootlicker **2** *(de sols)* (floor) polisher ▪ NF **cireuse** *(machine)* (electric) (floor) polisher

cireux, -euse [siʀø, -øz] ADJ waxy

cirque [siʀk] NM **1** circus; **c. forain** *ou* **ambulant** travelling circus; **aller au c.** to go to the circus; **gens du c.** circus people; **le c. Zavatta** Zavatta's circus **2** *Fam (chambard)* **quel c., ici!** it's like a zoo in here!; **quel c. pour obtenir ces renseignements!** what a performance *or* carry-on just to get this information!; **faire le c.** to rampage around; **faire tout un c.** to make a scene, to kick up a fuss; **arrête de faire ton c.!** stop your silly nonsense! **3** *Géol* cirque, corrie

cirrhose [siʀoz] NF *Méd* cirrhosis; **c. du foie** cirrhosis of the liver; **avoir une c. du foie** to have cirrhosis (of the liver)

cirrocumulus [siʀokymylys] NM INV *Météo* cirrocumulus

cirrostratus [siʀostʀatys] NM INV *Météo* cirrostratus

cirrus [siʀys] NM INV *Météo* cirrus, *Fam* mare's tail

cisaille [sizaj] NF **1** *(rognures en métal)* parings, cuttings **2** *(massicot)* guillotine **3** **cisailles** shears; *(pour câble)* wirecutters; **c. à haies** hedge clipper(s); **c. à bordures** edging shears VOIR GRAMMAIRE A10

cisaillement [sizajmɑ̃] NM **1** *(du métal)* cutting, shearing; *(des branches)* pruning **2** *Tech (usure)* shearing, shear

cisailler [sizaje] VT **1** *(branches)* to prune **2** *(métal)* to cut, to shear **3** *(joue, main etc)* to slash
▪ VPR **se cisailler** *(d'un métal)* to shear (off)

cisalpin [sizalpɛ̃] ADJ *Antiq* on the Roman side of the Alps, Cisalpine; *Hist* **République cisalpine** Cisalpine Republic

ciseau, -eaux [sizo] NM **1 (paire de) ciseaux** (pair of) scissors; *(de jardin)* shears, clippers; **ciseaux à bouts ronds** blunt- *or* round-ended scissors; **ciseaux à ongles** nail scissors; **ciseaux de couturière** dressmaking scissors; *Couture* **ciseaux à denteler** pinking shears; **coup de ciseaux** snip (of the scissors); **donner des coups de ciseaux dans qch** to snip away at sth with a pair of scissors; *Fig* **donner des coups de ciseaux dans un texte** to cut down *or* prune a text VOIR GRAMMAIRE A10 **2** *Sport* **c.**, **saut en ciseaux** scissors (jump); *Gym* **faire des ciseaux** to do the scissors **3** *Tech* chisel

ciselage [sizlaʒ] NM = **ciselement**

ciseler [sizle] VT **(je cisèle; je cisèlerai)** *(or, argent)* to chase, to engrave; *(marbre)* to chisel; *Fig (poème etc)* to polish up, to work on; **c. un bijou** to engrave a design on a piece of jewellery; **visage délicatement ciselé** finely chiselled features

ciseleur [sizlœʀ] NM engraver

cisellement [sizɛlmɑ̃] NM *(de l'or, de l'argent)* chasing, engraving

ciselure [sizlyʀ] NF *(en or, en argent)* chasing, engraving; *(sur le bois)* chiselling, carving; *(sur un bijou, une pièce d'orfèvrerie)* (engraved) design

Cisjordanie [sisʒɔʀdani] NF **la C.** the West Bank

cisjordanien, -ienne [sisʒɔʀdanjɛ̃, -jɛn] ADJ from the West Bank
▪ N **C.** = native or inhabitant of the West Bank

cistercien, -ienne [sistɛʀsjɛ̃, -jɛn] *Rel* ADJ *(moine, architecture)* Cistercian
▪ NM Cistercian

citadelle [sitadɛl] NF citadel, stronghold; *Fig* **une c. du protestantisme** a Protestant stronghold, a stronghold of Protestantism

citadin, -ine [sitadɛ̃, -in] N town-dweller, city-dweller
▪ ADJ (belonging to a) town *or* city
▪ NF *Aut* **citadine** supermini

citation [sitasjɔ̃] NF **1** *(extrait)* quotation; **la référence de la c.** the reference for the quotation, the quotation reference; **fin de c.** end of quotation; *(dans une dictée)* close quotation marks **2** *Jur* (writ of) summons; **c. des témoins** subpoena of witnesses; **notifier une c. à** *(accusé)* to serve a summons on; *(témoin)* to subpoena
▪ ▸ *Mil* **c. (à l'ordre du jour)** ≃ mention in dispatches; *Jur* **c. à comparaître** *(accusé)* summons; *(témoin)* subpoena

cité [site] NF **1** *(ville)* city, (large) town; **droit de c.** freedom of the city; *Fig* **le c genre d'original n'a pas droit de c. dans notre entreprise** there is no room for eccentrics like him in our company, our company doesn't take kindly to eccentrics like him; *Fig* **ga-**

gner droit de c. to be accepted **2** *(groupe d'immeubles)* (housing) estate
▪ ▸ **c.-dortoir** dormitory town; **c.-ghetto** ghetto housing estate; **c.-jardin** garden city; **c. ouvrière** (company-built) housing estate; **c. de transit** temporary settlement; **c. universitaire** = students' hall(s) of residence

Cîteaux [sito] NM *Rel* **l'ordre de C.** the Cistercian Order

citer [site] VT **1** *(rapporter)* to quote, to cite; **c. un auteur** to cite *or* quote (from) an author; **c. qn en exemple** to quote sb as an example, to hold sb up as an example; **c. les paroles de qn** to quote sb's words; **il a dit, je cite: …** he said, and I quote, … **2** *(énumérer)* to name, to list **3** *Jur (qn en justice)* to summon; *(témoin)* to subpoena **4** *Mil* **c. qn (à l'ordre du jour)** ≃ to mention sb in dispatches

citerne [sitɛʀn] NF tank, cistern; **c. à mazout** oil tank

cithare [sitaʀ] NF *Mus* **1** *(instrument moderne)* zither **2** *Antiq* cithara

citizen band [sitizɛnbɑ̃d] NF Citizens' Band, CB

citoyen, -enne [sitwajɛ̃, -ɛn] N citizen; **droits du c.** civic rights; **accomplir son devoir de c.** *(voter)* to do one's civic duty, to vote; **c. d'honneur** = freeman of a city; **elle se déclare citoyenne du monde** she claims that she's a citizen of the world; *Fam* **c'est un drôle de c.!** he's a queer customer!
▪ ADJ *(relatif à la citoyenneté)* civic; **il s'est produit une sorte de rassemblement c. contre l'extrême-droite** there was a sort of citizens' movement against the far right; **il faut encourager l'engagement c. au niveau local pour renforcer le tissu social** civic engagement on a local level should be encouraged as a way of strengthening the fabric of society; **on attend de nos élus un véritable projet c, pas une simple gestion de l'économie** we expect those we elected to come up with a manifesto which truly benefits society, not one which simply manages the economy; **cette société rêve de troquer sa réputation de pollueuse contre celle d'entreprise citoyenne** this company wants to banish its reputation as a polluter and instead to be known for being socially responsible

citoyenneté [sitwajɑ̃te] NF citizenship; **la c. française** French citizenship; **c. d'honneur d'une ville** = freedom of a city

citrate [sitʀat] NM *Chimie* citrate

citrique [sitʀik] ADJ *Chimie (acide)* citric

citron [sitʀɔ̃] NM **1** *(fruit)* lemon; **jus de c.** lemon juice; **c. pressé** freshly squeezed lemon juice; **c. givré** = lemon sorbet served inside the skin of a whole lemon; **essence de c.** lemon oil; **écorce de c.** lemon peel; **c. vert** lime **2** *Fam (tête)* nut; **se presser** *ou* **se creuser le c.** to rack *or Am* to cudgel one's brains
▪ ADJ INV lemon-yellow, lemon; **jaune c.** lemon-yellow

citronnade [sitʀɔnad] NF still lemonade, lemon squash

citronné [sitʀɔne] ADJ *(par l'odeur)* lemon-scented; *(par le goût)* lemon-flavoured

citronnelle [sitʀɔnɛl] NF **1** *(plante)* citronella **2** *(liqueur)* lemon liqueur

citronnier [sitʀɔnje] NM *(arbre)* lemon tree

citrouille [sitʀuj] NF **1** *(plante)* pumpkin; **tarte à la c.** pumpkin pie; *Fam* **j'ai la tête comme une c.** my head is fit to burst **2** *Arg (tête)* nut

cive [siv] NF *Bot, Culin* chives

civelle [sivɛl] NF elver

civet [sivɛ] NM *Culin (de gibier etc)* stew; **c. de lièvre** = jugged hare; **un c. de lapin** (a) rabbit stew

civette¹ [sivɛt] NF **1** *Zool* civet (cat) **2** *(parfum)* civet (perfume)

civette[2] NF *Bot, Culin* chives

civière [sivjɛr] NF *(brancard)* stretcher

civil [sivil] ADJ **1** *(de l'État, du citoyen) (droits etc)* civil; **année civile** calendar year; **guerre civile** civil war; *Jur* **droit c.** civil law; *Jur* **se porter partie civile** = to sue for damages someone being tried in a criminal court; **tribunal c.** civil court **2** *(non ecclésiastique)* lay, secular; *(non militaire)* civilian; **mariage c.** civil marriage; **enterrement c.** non-religious burial; **dans la vie civile** in private *or* civilian life **3** *Arch, Litt (courtois)* polite, courteous
■ NM **1** *(personne)* **un c.** *(non ecclésiastique)* a layman; *(non militaire)* a civilian **2 dans le c.** in private *or* civilian life; **en c.** *(police)* in plain clothes; *Mil* in civilian clothes, in mufti, *Fam* in civvies **3** *Jur* **poursuivre qn au c.** to sue sb in the civil courts, to bring a civil action against sb

> Attention: ne pas confondre **civil** et **civilian** lorsque l'on traduit le terme français **civil**. Le terme **civilian** signifie uniquement **non militaire**.

civilement [sivilmã] ADV **1** *Jur* **se marier c.** to be married at a registry office; **enterré c.** buried without religious ceremony; *Jur* **poursuivre qn c.** to bring a civil action against sb; **c. responsable** liable for damages **2** *Arch, Litt (courtoisement)* politely, courteously, civilly

civilisable [sivilizabl] ADJ civilizable

civilisateur, -trice [sivilizatœr, -tris] ADJ civilizing
■ N civilizer

civilisation [sivilizasjɔ̃] NF civilization; **la c. pré-colombienne** the pre-Columbian civilization; **les bienfaits de la c.** the benefits of civilization

civilisé [sivilize] ADJ civilized

civiliser [sivilize] VT to civilize; *Fam* **c. qn** to make sb less uncouth *or* more refined
■ VPR **se civiliser** to become civilized; *Fam* **il commence à se c.** he's starting to become more civilized *or* refined

civilité [sivilite] NF **1 civilités** courtesies, respects; **présenter ses civilités à qn** to pay one's respects to sb **2** *Litt, Vieilli (politesse)* civility, politeness, courtesy

civique [sivik] ADJ *(devoirs etc)* civic; *(droits)* civil; **avoir/développer le sens c.** to have/ foster a sense of civic responsibility; *Scol Anciennement* **instruction c.** civics; *surtout Can* **bibliothèque c.** municipal *or* public library

civisme [sivism] NM good citizenship, public-spiritedness

clabaudage [klabodaʒ] NM *Litt (médisance)* (spiteful) gossip, backbiting

clabauder [klabode] VI *Litt* **1** *(d'un chien de chasse)* to bark (a lot) **2** *Fig* **c. sur** *ou* **contre qn** to say nasty things about sb

clabauderie [klabodri] NF = **clabaudage**

clabaudeur, -euse [klabodœr, -øz] ADJ **1** *(chien)* barking **2** *Fig* gossiping, backbiting
■ N *Fig* gossip, scandalmonger

clac [klak] INT click!; *(d'un fouet)* crack! *(d'un objet qui se casse)* snap!

clafoutis [klafuti] NM *Culin* **c. aux pommes/ limousin** apples/(black) cherries baked in batter

claie [klɛ] NF **1** *(clôture)* fence **2 c. à fruits** (wicker) fruit tray **3** *(crible)* screen, riddle

CLAIR [klɛr]

ADJ	clear **1, 4** ■ bright **2** ■ light **2, 3, 5** ■ obvious **4** ■ thin **5**
ADV	clearly
NM	light **1**

ADJ **1** *(limpide, transparent) (eau etc)* clear; **teint c.** clear complexion; **ciel c.** clear *or* cloudless sky; **par temps c.** in clear weather, on a clear day; **voix claire** clear voice; *Mus* **caisse claire** side *or* snare drum
2 *(pièce etc)* bright, light; **il fait c.** *(jour)* it's (day)light; *(lumière)* there's plenty of light; **dans cette pièce, il fait plus c.** this room is brighter, there's more light in this room; **il ne fait pas très c. ici** there isn't much light here
3 *(couleur)* light, pale; **robe bleu c.** pale blue dress
4 *(sens etc)* clear, obvious, plain; **explication claire** clear *or* lucid explanation; **ce n'est pas très c., précisez** it's not very clear, be more precise; **il a été très c. là-dessus** he was very clear about it; **je vais être très c.** I'm going to make myself very clear; **il est c. qu'elle a tort** she is obviously *or* clearly wrong; **voilà qui est c.!** that's clear (enough)!; **c. comme le jour** *ou* **comme de l'eau de roche** crystal clear, as clear as daylight *or* crystal; **sa conduite n'est pas claire** his behaviour is suspicious *or Fam* fishy; **avoir l'esprit c.** *ou* **les idées claires** to be clear in one's mind *or* in one's ideas; **je n'avais pas les idées très claires ce jour-là** I wasn't thinking very clearly that day; **c'est c. et net** there are no two ways about it; **ils n'ont aucune intention de prolonger notre contrat, c'est c. et net** it's quite obvious that they have absolutely no intention of extending our contract; **je veux une réponse claire et nette** I want a definite answer
5 *(soupe)* thin; *(tissu)* light, thin
■ ADV plainly, clearly; **voir c.** to see clearly; **il ne voit plus très c.** he can't see too clearly *or* well; **parler c.** to speak clearly; *Fig* **je commence à (y) voir c.** I'm beginning to see *or* understand; **son explication est très confuse, je n'y vois pas très c.** his explanation is very confused, I don't quite follow it
■ NM **1** *(lumière)* light; **c. de lune** moonlight; **au c. de (la) lune** in the moonlight; **les clairs d'une peinture** the (high)lights in a painting **2 en c.** in plain language; **message en c.** message in clear; *TV* **émission en c.** *(non crypté)* non-crypted broadcast
3 tirer du vin au c. to decant wine; **sabre au c.** with drawn sword; *Fig* **tirer une affaire au c.** to clear a matter up; **mettre ses idées au c.** to get one's ideas straight; **mettre qch au c. avec qn** to sort sth out with sb, to get sth straight with sb
4 il passe le plus c. de son temps à rêvasser he spends most *or* the better part of his time daydreaming

clairance [klɛrɑ̃s] NF *Méd (rénale)* clearance

claire [klɛr] NF oyster bed; **fines de c.** = particularly fine variety of fattened oysters, with a green tinge caused by algae

clairement [klɛrmɑ̃] ADV clearly, plainly; **on le voit c. sur le tableau** it's clearly visible on the board; **expliquer c. qch à qn** to explain sth clearly to sb; **je te le dis c.** I'm telling you quite plainly

clairet, -ette [klɛrɛ, -ɛt] ADJ **vin c.** light-red wine; **voix clairette** thin *or* high-pitched *or* reedy voice
■ NM light-red wine
■ NF **clairette** light sparkling wine

claire-voie, *pl* **claires-voies** NF **1** *(treillage)* openwork, lattice(work); **porte à c.** (wicket) gate; **clôture à c.** fence, paling; **cloison à c.** grating; **caisse à c.** crate **2** *Archit* clerestory; *Naut* skylight, deadlight

clairière [klɛrjɛr] NF **1** *(dans forêt)* clearing, glade **2** *Tex* thin place

clair-obscur, *pl* **clairs-obscurs** NM **1** *Beaux-Arts* chiaroscuro, light and shade **2** *(lumière)* twilight

clairon [klɛrɔ̃] NM **1** *(trompette)* bugle; **jouer du c.** to play the bugle; **sonner le c.** to sound the bugle **2** *(joueur)* bugler

claironnant [klɛrɔnɑ̃] ADJ *(son)* loud, brassy; *(voix)* piercing, loud

claironner [klɛrɔne] VI to sound the bugle; *Fig (crier)* to shout loudly
■ VT **c. une nouvelle** to broadcast *or* proclaim a piece of news; **il claironna que ...** he proclaimed that ...

clairsemé [klɛrsəme] ADJ *(population etc)* scattered, sparse; *(cheveux)* thin; *(maïs etc)* thinly sown; *(gazon)* sparse; *(arbres)* scattered

clairvoyance [klɛrvwajɑ̃s] NF perceptiveness, clearsightedness; *(pouvoir paranormal)* clairvoyance; **il l'avait analysé avec c.** he had analysed it perceptively

clairvoyant [klɛrvwajɑ̃] ADJ perceptive, clear-sighted; *(paranormal)* clairvoyant; **esprit c.** perceptive mind
■ NM clairvoyant

clam [klam] NM *(mollusque)* clam

clamecer [klamse] VI *Arg (mourir)* to snuff it, to kick the bucket

clamer [klame] VT to shout out, to proclaim; **c. son innocence** to proclaim *or* protest one's innocence; **c. son mécontentement** to proclaim one's displeasure

clameur [klamœr] NF clamour; *(du vent, de la tempête)* howling, roaring; **une c. de joie** a shout of joy; **on entendit une c. épouvantable lorsque le bateau coula** there were horrendous screams when the boat went down; **c. publique** hue and cry

clamser [klamse] VI *Arg (mourir)* to kick the bucket, to snuff it

clan [klɑ̃] NM **1** *(tribu)* clan; **c. irlandais/écossais** Irish/Scottish clan; **chef de c.** clan chief **2** *(groupe)* clan, clique

clandestin, -ine [klɑ̃dɛstɛ̃, -in] ADJ *(réunion, atelier)* clandestine, secret; *(travailleur, pari)* illegal; **armée clandestine** underground forces; **mouvement c.** underground movement; **passager c.** stowaway
■ N *(voyageur)* stowaway; *(immigré)* illegal immigrant; *(travailleur)* illegal worker

clandestinement [klɑ̃dɛstinmɑ̃] ADV *(se réunir)* clandestinely, secretly; *(travailler, transporter, entrer dans un pays)* illegally; **voyager c.** to stow away

clandestinité [klɑ̃dɛstinite] NF clandestineness; **dans la c.** in secret; **entrer dans/sortir de la c.** to go into/come out of hiding; **passer dans la c.** to go underground

clanique [klanik] ADJ clan

clanisme [klanism] NM clannishness

clap [klap] NM *Cin* clapperboard; **c. de fin** tail slate

clapet [klapɛ] NM **1** *Tech* valve; *(de moteur)* poppet valve, mushroom valve; **c. d'admission/d'échappement** inlet/exhaust valve; **c. de dérivation** by-pass valve; **c. de limitation de pression** pressure limiting valve **2** *Élec* rectifier **3** *Arg (bouche)* trap, *Br* gob; **ferme ton c.!** shut your trap!; **il a un de ces clapets!** he never stops (talking)!

clapier [klapje] NM **1** *(terriers)* rabbit warren **2** *(case)* **c. à lapins** rabbit hutch; **(lapin de) c.** tame rabbit; *Fig Fam* **vivre dans un c. à lapins** to live in a rabbit hutch **3** *Géol (dans les Alpes)* scree

clapir [klapir] VI *(d'un lapin)* to squeal
■ VPR **se clapir** *(d'un lapin)* to hide, to cower

clapotage [klapɔtaʒ] NM, **clapotement** [klapɔtmɑ̃] NM *(des vagues)* lapping

clapoter [klapɔte] VI *(des vagues)* to lap; **mer qui clapote** choppy sea

clapotis [klapɔti] NM *(des vagues)* lap(ping)

clappement [klapmɑ̃] NM *(de la langue)* click

clapper [klape] VI **c. de la langue** to click one's tongue

claquage [klakaʒ] NM **1** *(d'un muscle)* strain, pulling; **se faire un c.** to pull *or* strain a muscle **2** *Élec* (electric) breakdown; **c. thermique** thermal breakdown

claquant [klakɑ̃] ADJ *Arg (fatigant)* killing, knackering

claque[1] [klak] NF **1** *(gifle)* slap, smack; **donner** *ou* **mettre** *ou très Fam* **foutre une c. à qn** to give sb a slap *or* a smack; **recevoir** *ou* **prendre une c.** to get a slap *or* a smack; *Fig* **se prendre une c.** to get a slap in the face; *Fig* **les centristes se sont pris une c. aux dernières élections** the last elections were a slap in the face for the centre party; **il mérite une bonne paire de claques** he deserves a good slap; *Fam* **c'est vraiment une tête à claques!** he's got a face you just want to slap! **2** *Arg* **il (en) a sa c.** *(il est fatigué)* he's knackered *or* shattered; *(il en a assez)* he's fed up with it, he's had enough of it **3** *Théâtre* claque **4** *Can* **claques** *(chaussures)* galoshes, *Am* rubbers

claque[2] ADJ, NM **(chapeau) c.** opera hat, crush hat
    NM *Arg (maison close)* whorehouse, *Br* knocking shop; *(tripot)* gambling den

claqué [klake] ADJ *Fam* knackered, shattered

claquement [klakmɑ̃] NM *(de porte)* slam(ming), bang(ing); *(de dents)* chattering; *(d'un fouet)* crack(ing); *(d'un drapeau)* flap(ping); *(des doigts)* snap(ping); *(des talons, de la langue)* click(ing); *(des sabots)* clatter(ing); *(dans un moteur)* slapping of pistons; **entendre un c. de porte** to hear a door bang, to hear the sound of a door banging; **des claquements de fouets** the cracking of whips

claquemurer [klakmyre] VT **c. qn** to shut sb up
    VPR **se claquemurer** to shut oneself up; **se c. dans sa chambre** to shut oneself up in one's room, to stay cooped up in one's room

claquer [klake] VI **1** *(d'une porte)* to slam, to bang; *(d'un drapeau)* to flap; *(des talons)* to click; *(des sabots)* to clatter; *(d'un piston)* to slap; **c. des mains** to clap, to applaud; **elle claque des dents** her teeth are chattering; **c. des doigts** to snap one's fingers; **faire c. sa langue** to click one's tongue; **faire c. la porte en sortant** to slam the door on the way out; *Fam* **c. du bec** to be hungry *or* starving
    2 *Arg (d'une personne)* to kick the bucket, to snuff it; *(d'un appareil)* to conk out; *(d'une ampoule électrique)* to go, to blow; *Fam* **l'affaire lui a claqué dans les doigts** *ou* **mains** the deal fell through; **il nous a claqué dans les mains avant que l'ambulance arrive** he died on us before the ambulance arrived
    VT **1** *(porte)* to slam, to bang; *(ses doigts)* to snap; *(ses talons)* to click; **c. la langue** to click one's tongue
    2 *(gifler)* *(enfant etc)* to slap, to smack
    3 *Fam (fatiguer)* *(personne)* to tire *or* wear out
    4 *Fam (dépenser)* *(argent)* to squander, to blow; **il claque un fric monstre** he spends money like water; **il claque un fric monstre chez le coiffeur** he spends a fortune at the hairdresser's
    VPR **se claquer 1** *Fam (se fatiguer)* to tire *or* wear oneself out **2 se c. un muscle/un ligament** to pull a muscle/tear a ligament

claquette [klakɛt] NF **1** *Cin* clapperboard **2** *(type de danse)* **(danse à) claquettes** tap dancing, tap dance; **faire des claquettes** to do tap (dancing); **danseur de claquettes**

tap dancer **3 claquettes** *(tongs)* flip-flops, *Am* thongs

claquoir [klakwar] NM clapper; *Cin* clapperboard

clarification [klarifikasjɔ̃] NF *(d'un liquide)* clarifying; *Fig (d'informations)* clarification

clarifier [klarifje] VT to clarify; **c. la situation** to clarify the situation, to clear the matter up
    VPR **se clarifier** to (become) clear; **la situation se clarifie** the situation is becoming clear

clarine [klarin] NF cowbell

clarinette [klarinɛt] NF clarinet

clarinettiste [klarinɛtist] N clarinettist

clarisse [klaris] NF *Rel* **(sœur) c.** nun of the order of St Clare

clarté [klarte] NF **1** *(lumière etc)* light, brightness; **une douce/faible c.** a soft/dim light; **à la c. de la lune** by the light of the moon, by moonlight; **la c. de l'aurore** *ou* **de l'aube** the early morning light **2** *(transparence)* clearness, clarity; *(d'un verre etc)* transparency; *(du style etc)* clarity, lucidity; **la c. de son teint** the clearness of his complexion; **la c. de l'expression** clarity of expression; **parler avec c.** to speak clearly; **c. d'esprit** clear-headedness; **manquer de c.** *(d'une personne)* not to make oneself clear; *(d'un texte, un devoir, un argument)* to be unclear; *Litt* **avoir des clartés sur un sujet** to have some knowledge of a subject

clash [klaʃ] NM *Fam* clash, conflict; **je voudrais éviter tout c. avec elle** I want to avoid clashing with her

classable [klasabl] ADJ classifiable; **une personne difficilement c.** a person who is difficult to classify

CLASSE [klas] NF **1** *(catégorie)* class, division, category; *Admin etc* rank, grade; **c. d'âge** age group; *Aviat etc* **c. touriste/club** tourist/club class; **c. affaires** business class, club class, executive class; **c. économique** economy class; **voyager en c. affaires/club** to travel business/club class; *Rail* **billet de première/deuxième** *ou* **seconde c.** first-/second-class ticket; **différence de c. sociale** difference in *or* of social class; **les hautes classes (de la société)** the upper classes; **la c. moyenne/ouvrière** the middle/working class(es); **c. dirigeante/dominante** ruling/dominant class; **société sans c.** classless society; **conscience de c.** class consciousness
    2 *(qualité)* class; **elle n'est pas de la même c. que les autres** she's not in the same class as the others; **un biologiste/sportif de c. internationale** a biologist/sportsman of international rank, a world-class biologist/sportsman; **produits de première c.** top-quality *or* first-class goods; **avoir de la c.** to have class *or* style; **cette robe a beaucoup de c.** that's a very classy *or* stylish dress, that dress has got a lot of class *or* style; **c'est la c.!** what class!
    3 *Scol (niveau)* class, form, *Am* grade; *(ensemble des élèves)* class; **c'est un cadeau offert par toute la c.** it's a present from the whole class; **il y a plusieurs classes de sixième au collège** there are several first-year classes at high school; **grandes classes, classes supérieures** upper forms, senior school; **c. de sixième/première/terminale** ≃ first year/lower sixth/upper sixth; **les petites classes** the junior school, the juniors; **il est dans quelle c.?** which *or* what class is he in? VOIR GRAMMAIRE A11
    4 *(leçon)* class, lesson; **c. de français** French class; **aller en c.** to go to school; **être en c.** to be in *or* at school; **faire la c.** to teach; **livre de c.** schoolbook

5 (salle de) c. classroom, schoolroom; **en sortant de c.** on coming out of school
    6 *Mil (de conscrits)* annual contingent; **la c. 1965** the 1965 class, the 1965 levy; **faire ses classes** to undergo basic training; *Fig* to learn the ropes
    7 *Mil (rang)* **(soldat de) deuxième c.** private; *Mil, Aviat* aircraftman, *Am* airman (basic); **(soldat de) première c.** lance-corporal, *Am* private first class; *Mil, Aviat* leading *or* senior aircraftman, *Am* airman first class
    8 *Compta* group of accounts
    ADJ INV *Fam* classy, stylish; **il s'habille très c.** he is a classy *or* stylish dresser
    ▸▸ *Scol* **c. de mer** = school study trip to the seaside; **c. de nature** = nature study trip; **c. de neige** = school study and skiing trip to the mountains; **partir en c. de neige** = to go skiing with the school; **c. préparatoire** = preparatory class for the entrance examinations for the grandes écoles; **c. unique** = class where pupils of different levels are taught together by one teacher; **c. verte** = school study trip to the countryside; **partir en c. verte** = to spend time in the countryside with the school

Classes préparatoires
This term refers to the two years of intensive preparation required for students who have passed their baccalauréat and wish to enter the "grandes écoles". These two years of study are extremely competitive and highly demanding. Students are completely immersed in their subject, which can be in humanities, economics or the sciences, and do little other than study for the "grandes écoles" exams. For students who are not successful in these exams, two years of "prépas" are considered equivalent to a **DEUG** *(see box at this entry)*, and these students often go on to study at a university.

classé [klase] ADJ **1** *Sport* ranked, graded; *Tennis* seeded **2** *(information)* classified; **cette information est classée** that information is classified **3** *(monument etc)* listed

classement [klasmɑ̃] NM **1** *(hiérarchie)* *(dans une classe, une course etc)* position, place; *(des plantes etc)* classification; **c. alphabétique/chronologique** alphabetical/chronological order; *Scol* **c. trimestriel** end of term results; *Scol* **ce trimestre, je suis troisième au c.** I'm third in the class this term; **donner le c.** *(d'un concours)* to give the results; **avoir un bon/mauvais c.** to be well/badly placed; **c. hôtelier** hotel classification; **c. par étoiles** *(d'un hôtel etc)* star rating **2** *(rangement)* *(de documents)* filing; *(d'articles)* sorting out, arranging; **faire du c.** to do some filing; **c. géographique** filing by geographical area; **c. horizontal** horizontal filing; **c. par ordre alphabétique** alphabetical filing

classer [klase] VT **1** *(classifier)* to classify, to class; **les livres sont classés par ordre alphabétique d'auteurs** the books are arranged *or* classified in alphabetical order of author; **monument classé** listed monument; **classés par pays** classified according to country; **ce chanteur, que l'on classe parmi les meilleurs ténors …** this singer, who is ranked among the best tenors …; *Courses de chevaux* **non classés** also ran; *Fam* **je n'ai pas eu de mal à le c.** it didn't take me long to size him up *or* to work out what sort of a person he was **2** *(documents)* to file; *(articles)* to sort out, to arrange; **c. une affaire** to consider a matter closed; **c'est une affaire classée** the matter's closed

VPR se classer to be classified, to rank; **ces faits se classent dans une autre catégorie** these facts fall into another category; **elle se classe parmi les meilleurs de son année** she's among the best in her year; *Sport etc* **se c. troisième** to be placed third, to come in third; *Tennis etc* **il n'a pas réussi à se c.** he failed to get into the rankings

classeur [klasœr] **NM** *(meuble)* filing cabinet; *(d'écolier etc)* (looseleaf) binder, folder; *Ordinat* filer; **c. à anneaux** ring binder; **c. distributeur** index card box; **c. à levier** lever-arch file

classicisme [klasisism] **NM** classicism

classieux, -ieuse [klasjø, -jøz] **ADJ** *Fam* classy

classificateur, -trice [klasifikatœr, -tris] **N** classifier
ADJ classifying

classification [klasifikasjɔ̃] **NF** classification; **c. socioéconomique** socio-economic grouping

classifier [klasifje] **VT** *(impf, pr sub* n. **classifiions, v. classifiiez)* to classify

classique [klasik] **ADJ 1** *Scol* academic, for school use; **faire des études classiques** to study classics; **langues classiques** classical languages; **auteurs classiques** classical authors **2** *(période, musique etc)* classical; *(beauté etc)* classic **3** *(travail etc)* standard; *(exemple, plaisanterie, question etc)* classic; **vêtement/tenue c.** classic garment/outfit; **aimer le style c.** to like the classic style; **guerre c.** conventional warfare; *Fam* **c'est le coup c.!** *(une chose qui se reproduit fréquemment)* that's typical!; *(une ruse connue)* it's the usual trick!; **ça, c'est c.** that's just typical(, that is)
NM 1 *(auteur)* classical author **2** *(livre)* classic; **les classiques grecs/français** the Greek/French classics; **relire ses classiques** to re-read the classics; **c'est un grand c. du jazz/des années soixante** it's a great jazz standard *or* classic/a great sixties classic; **c'est un c. du genre** it's a classic of its kind *or* of the genre **3** *Mus* classical music

Attention: ne pas confondre **classic** et **classical** lorsque l'on traduit l'adjectif **classique**. Le terme **classic** signifie généralement **typique**, **habituel**, alors que **classical** signifie **traditionnel** et s'oppose à **modern**.

classiquement [klasikmɑ̃] **ADV** classically

claudication [klodikasjɔ̃] **NF** *Méd, Litt* limp(-ing), *Spéc* claudication

claudiquer [klodike] **VI** *Litt* to limp

clause [kloz] **NF** *Jur etc* clause; **c. additionnelle** additional clause, rider; **c. pénale** penalty clause; **c. de style** formal clause; *Fin* **c. au porteur** pay to bearer clause; **c. d'annulation** cancellation clause; **c. d'arbitrage** arbitration clause; **c. compromissoire** arbitration clause; **c. contractuelle** clause of a/the contract; *Com* **c. d'exclusivité** exclusivity clause, exclusive rights clause; **c. d'exonération** exemption clause; *Fin* **c. d'indexation** cost escalation clause, indexation clause; **c. de franchise** excess clause; **c. limitative** limiting clause; **c. de la nation la plus favorisée** most-favoured-nation status; **c. de non-concurrence** non-competition clause; **c. de remboursement** refunding clause; **c. de réserve de propriété** retention of title clause; **c. de résiliation** termination clause, cancellation clause; **c. résolutoire** resolutive clause; **c. de sauvegarde** safeguard clause; *Com* **c. ducroire** del credere clause; **c. dérogatoire** derogatory clause; *Fin* **c. à ordre** clause 'to the order of'; **c. de sortie** escape *or* get-out clause

clausé [kloze] **ADJ** *Com (connaissance)* dirty
claustra [klostra] **NM** stone railings
claustral, -ale, -aux, -ales [klostral, -o] **ADJ** monastic
claustration [klostrasjɔ̃] **NF** *(isolation)* confinement
claustrer [klostre] **VT** *(isoler)* to confine, to shut up
VPR se claustrer to shut oneself up; **se c. dans le silence** to retreat into silence
claustrophobe [klostrofɔb] **ADJ** *Méd* claustrophobic
claustrophobie [klostrofɔbi] **NF** *Méd* claustrophobia
clavardage [klavardaʒ] **NM** *Can Ordinat* chat
claveau, -eaux [klavo] **NM** *Constr, Archit* archstone; **c. droit** keystone
clavecin [klavsɛ̃] **NM** *Mus* harpsichord
claveciniste [klavsinist] **N** *Mus* harpsichord player, harpsichordist
claveter [klavte] **VT** *(je clavette; je clavetterai)* *Tech* to key, to wedge, to cotter
clavette [klavɛt] **NF** *Tech* key (bolt), pin, cotter (pin)
clavicorde [klavikɔrd] **NM** *Mus* clavichord
clavicule [klavikyl] **NF** *Anat* collarbone, clavicle
clavier [klavje] **NM 1** *(de piano, de machine à écrire etc)* keyboard; *(de téléphone)* keypad; *Ordinat* **c. numérique** numerical *or* numeric keypad; **c. AZERTY** AZERTY keyboard; **c. QWERTY** QWERTY keyboard; **c. multifonction(s)** multifunctional keyboard; **c. national** country keyboard; **c. par défaut** default keyboard (layout); **c. à infrarouge** infrared keyboard; **c. sans fil** cordless *or* wireless keyboard **2** *Fig* **le c. des émotions amoureuses** the range *or* gamut of love's emotions
claviste [klavist] **N** typesetter; *Ordinat* keyboarder
clayette [klɛjɛt] **NF 1** *(petite claie)* wire tray *or* rack; *(dans un réfrigérateur)* (wire) shelf **2** *(cageot)* crate
clayon [klɛjɔ̃] **NM** *(pour les fromages)* wicker tray; *(pour les gâteaux)* cake rack
clé [kle] **NF** = **clef**
clean [klin] **ADJ INV** *Fam* straight, clean-living; **elle a un look c.** she has a clean-living *or* straight image
clearing [kliriŋ] **NM** *Écon* clearing; **accord de c.** clearing agreement
clébard [klebar] **NM**, **clebs** [klɛps] **NM** *Arg (chien)* pooch, mutt
CLEF [kle] **NF 1** *(d'une porte, d'un code, d'un mystère)* key; **c. de maison** house key; **mes clefs de voiture** my car keys; **fausse c.** skeleton key; **trousseau de clefs** bunch of keys; **fermer une porte à c.** to lock a door; **donner un tour de c. à la porte** to lock the door; **tenir/mettre qch sous c.** to keep/put sth under lock and key; **on l'a mis sous c. depuis hier** he's been under lock and key since yesterday; **la c. est sur la porte** the key is in the lock; **louer une maison clefs en main** to rent a house with immediate *or* vacant possession; **usine clefs en main** turnkey factory *or Am* plant; **prix clefs en main** *(d'une voiture)* on-the-road price; *(d'une maison)* all-inclusive price; **les clefs de la ville** the keys to the city; **la philosophie, c. de la connaissance** philosophy, the key to (all) knowledge; **roman à c.** = novel introducing real characters under fictitious names; **mettre la c. sous la porte** to scarper, to do a runner; **prendre la c. des champs** *(d'un prisonnier etc)* to make a bid for freedom; **position-c.** key position; **industrie-c.** key industry; **un secteur(-)c. de la recherche** a key sector *or* area of research; *Fig* **enquête avec ré-**

compense à la c. an investigation, for the successful conclusion of which there is a reward; **il y a une forte somme d'argent à la c.** there is a large sum of money at stake *or* involved
2 *Mus* clef; *(armature)* key signature; *(d'un instrument à cordes)* peg; *(d'un instrument à vent)* key; **c. de sol/de fa** treble/bass clef; **jouer avec des dièses à la c.** to play in sharp keys
3 *Tech* wrench, spanner
4 *Élec* switch (key); *Tél* **c. Morse** Morse key
5 *(prise de lutte)* lock
6 *Ordinat* key; *(du DOS)* switch; **c. d'accès** enter key; **c. de chiffrement** encryption key; **c. de contrôle** control key; **c. électronique** electronic key; **c. gigogne** dongle; **c. d'index** index key; **c. de protection** data protection ▸▸ **c. allen** allen key; **c. anglaise** adjustable spanner, monkey wrench; **c. à bougie** (spark)plug spanner; **c. à cliquet** ratchet handle; *Aut* **c. de contact** ignition key; *Aut* **c. en croix** wheelbrace, spider; **c. cruciforme** cruciform key; **c. à douille** box spanner; **c. dynamométrique** torque wrench; **c. mixte** combination spanner, *surtout Am* monkey wrench; **c. à œil** ring spanner; **c. ouverte** open-ended spanner; **c. passe-partout** passkey, master key; **c. à pipe** box spanner; **c. plate** (open) end wrench; **c. à puce** computerized key; *Banque* **c. RIB** bank details; **c. des songes** *(livre)* = how to interpret your dreams; *Archit* **c. de voûte** *(d'une arche)* keystone, crown; *Fig* **c'est la c. de voûte de notre entreprise** he's the cornerstone of our firm

clématite [klematit] **NF** clematis
clémence [klemɑ̃s] **NF 1** *Fig (de la température)* mildness; **si la c. du temps le permet** if the weather's mild enough **2** *Litt (pardon)* clemency, mercy, leniency (**pour, envers** to(wards))
clément [klemɑ̃] **ADJ 1** *Fig (température etc)* mild **2** *Litt (indulgent)* clement, merciful, lenient (**pour, envers** to, towards)
clémentine [klemɑ̃tin] **NF** *(fruit)* clementine
clenche [klɑ̃ʃ] **NF**, **clenchette** [klɑ̃ʃɛt] **NF 1** *(d'un loquet)* latch **2** *Belg (poignée)* doorhandle
Cléopâtre [kleopatr] **NF** *Antiq* Cleopatra
cleptomane [klɛptɔman] **N** kleptomaniac
cleptomanie [klɛptɔmani] **NF** kleptomania
clerc [klɛr] **NM 1** *(dans un bureau)* clerk; **c. de notaire** = solicitor's clerk; **petit c.** junior clerk **2** *Rel* cleric **3** *Arch (savant)* learned man, scholar **4** **il n'est pas besoin d'être grand c. pour …** you don't have to be a genius in order to …
clergé [klɛrʒe] **NM** clergy VOIR GRAMMAIRE A11
clérical, -ale, -aux, -ales [klerikal, -o] **ADJ, NM** *Rel* clerical
cléricalisme [klerikalism] **NM** *Rel* clericalism
clic [klik] **NM 1** *(bruit)* click, clicking; **entendre un c.** to hear a click *or* a clicking sound **2** *Ordinat* click; **double c.** double click; **c. de souris** mouse click
INT click
clic-clac **NM INV** *(d'un appareil photo, d'une ceinture de sécurité)* click; *(des talons)* click-clack; *(des sabots)* clatter
cliché [kliʃe] **NM 1** *(lieu commun)* cliché **2** *Phot (pellicule)* negative; *(photo)* photograph, shot **3** *Typ* stereotype; *(de caractères)* plate; *(d'illustration)* block; **c. au trait** line block **4** *Ordinat* format, layout; **c. de disque** disk dump; **c. mémoire** dump
clicheton [kliʃtɔ̃] **NM** *Fam (cliché)* cliché; **l'histoire est d'une banalité affligeante; tous les clichetons sont au rendez-vous** the story is as banal as can be and completely cliché-ridden

clicheur [kliʃœr] **NM** *Ordinat* screen dump program

client, -ente [klijɑ̃, -ɑ̃t] **N** *Com* client, customer; *(d'un médecin)* patient; *(d'un chauffeur de taxi)* fare; *(d'un hôtel)* guest; *(dans la publicité)* account; **c'est un bon c.** he's a good customer; **ici, le c. est roi** the customer is always right; **la France est un gros c. du Japon pour la robotique** France is one of Japan's big customers for robotics; **c. actuel** existing customer; *Compta* **c. douteux** doubtful debt, possible bad debt; **c. de passage** passing customer; **clients de passage** passing trade; **c. imprévu** chance customer; *Ordinat* **c. de messagerie électronique** e-mail client, mail reader; **c. potentiel** suspect, potential client, potential customer; **clients potentiels** potential clients, suspect pool; **c. régulier** regular customer; **c. sans réservation** *(dans un hôtel)* chance guest, walk-in; *Fig* **désolé, je ne suis pas c.** sorry, I'm not interested; *Fam* **c'est un drôle de c.** he's a queer customer

clientèle [klijɑ̃tɛl] **NF 1** *(d'un magasin)* customers, clientèle; *(d'une entreprise)* customer base; *(d'un médecin, d'un avocat)* practice; **c. actuelle** existing customers; **c. de passage** passing trade **2** *(fait d'acheter)* custom; **obtenir la c. d'un consommateur/d'un pays** to obtain a consumer's/a country's custom *or* business; **accorder sa c. à** to give one's custom to, to patronize

clientélisme [klijɑ̃telism] **NM** *Péj* (political) patronage, *Spéc* clientelism

clignement [kliɲmɑ̃] **NM** blink; **faire un c. d'œil** to wink

cligner [kliɲe] **VT c. les yeux** to blink
VI c. des yeux to blink

clignotant [kliɲɔtɑ̃] **ADJ** *(yeux)* blinking; *(paupière)* twitching; *(étoile)* twinkling; *(lumière)* flickering, flashing; **feu** *ou* **signal c.** *Naut* intermittent signal; *Aut* flashing light
NM 1 *Aut* indicator, *Am* turn signal; **mettre son c. (à droite/gauche)** to indicate (right/left), *Am* to put on one's turn signal (to turn right/left) **2** *Écon* signal, indicator; **le c. de la hausse des prix/de la crise** the warning light *or* signal that prices are rising/that a recession is on the way

clignotement [kliɲɔtmɑ̃] **NM** *(des yeux)* blinking; *(des paupières)* twitching; *(d'une étoile)* twinkling; *(d'une lumière)* flickering, flashing

clignoter [kliɲɔte] **VI** *(des paupières)* to twitch; *(d'une étoile)* to twinkle; *(d'une lumière)* to flicker, to flash; *Ordinat (d'un marqueur etc)* to flash, to blink

clignoteur [kliɲɔtœr] **NM** *Belg* **1** *Aut (lampe)* indicator, *Am* turn signal; **mettre son c. (à droite/gauche)** to indicate (right/left), *Am* to put on one's turn signal (to turn right/left) **2** *(signal)* warning light

clim [klim] **NF** *Fam (abrév* **climatisation)** air-conditioning

climat [klima] **NM** *aussi Fig* climate; **sous des climats plus ensoleillés** in sunnier climes; **c. de détente** relaxed atmosphere *or* climate; **c. économique** economic climate; **travailler dans un c. d'hostilité** to work in a hostile atmosphere *or* in an atmosphere of hostility

climatique [klimatik] **ADJ** *(conditions etc)* climatic; **station c.** health resort

climatisation [klimatizasjɔ̃] **NF** air conditioning; **avoir la c. dans toutes les pièces** to have air conditioning in every room

climatiser [klimatize] **VT** to air-condition; **chambre climatisée** air-conditioned bedroom

climatiseur [klimatizœr] **NM** air conditioner; *Aut* climate control system

climatologie [klimatɔlɔʒi] **NF** climatology

climatologique [klimatɔlɔʒik] **ADJ** climatological

clin [klɛ̃] **NM** *Naut* **bordé à clin(s)** clinker built

clin d'œil [klɛ̃dœj] **NM** wink; **faire un c. à qn** to wink at sb; **en un c.** in the twinkling of an eye, in a flash; **dans ce film, le réalisateur fait un c. à Bergman** in this film, the director makes passing references to Bergman *or* passing nods to Bergman

clinicien [klinisjɛ̃] **ADJ, NM (médecin) c.** clinician

clinique [klinik] **ADJ** *(médecine, essais etc)* clinical; **les signes cliniques d'une maladie** the clinical symptoms of an illness
NF 1 *(hôpital privé)* clinic; **chef de c.** senior registrar **2** *(observation des étudiants de médecine)* clinic; *(médecine)* clinical medicine

cliniquement [klinikmɑ̃] **ADV** clinically

clinquant [klɛ̃kɑ̃] **NM** tinsel; *(bijoux)* flashy jewellery; **c. du style** flashiness of style; **un journaliste qui donne dans le c. et la vulgarité** a journalist who tends to be flashy and vulgar
ADJ flashy, showy

clip [klip] **NM 1** *(broche)* clip; *(boucle d'oreille)* clip-on earring **2** *(pince)* clip **3** *(film)* clip; *(musical)* (music) video; **c. vidéo** video (clip)

clipart [klipart] **NM** *Ordinat* clip art

clipper¹ [klipœr] **NM 1** *Aviat* transport aircraft **2** *Naut* clipper

clipper² [klipe] **VT** to clip

clique [klik] **NF 1** *(gang)* clique, gang; *Fam* **et toute la c.** and the rest of the gang, and all the rest of them **2** *Mil (tambours et clairons)* band

cliquer [klike] **VI** *Ordinat* to click (**sur** on); **c. deux fois** to double-click; **c. avec le bouton gauche/droit de la souris** to left-click/right-click; **c. et glisser** to click and drag

cliques [klik] **NFPL** *Fam* **prendre ses c. et ses claques** to pack up and leave, to pack one's bags and go

cliquet [klikɛ] **NM** *Tech etc* catch, pawl, ratchet

cliqueter [klikte] **VI** (**je cliquette; je cliquetterai**) *(de chaînettes etc)* to rattle; *(de fleurets, d'aiguilles à tricoter)* to click; *(de pièces de monnaie)* to clink, to chink; *(de clés etc)* to jingle, to jangle; *Aut* to knock, to pink

cliquetis [klikti] **NM** *(de chaînettes)* rattling; *(de pièces de monnaie, de breloques etc)* clink(ing), chinking; *(de clés etc)* jingling, jangling; *(de couverts)* clinking; *(de vaisselle)* clattering; *(de fleurets, d'aiguilles à tricoter)* clicking; *(d'une machine à écrire)* clack; *Aut* knocking, pinking; **j'entendis un léger c.: on essayait de crocheter la serrure** I heard a slight scratching noise: somebody was trying to pick the lock

clisse [klis] **NF** *(pour bouteilles)* wicker covering; *(pour faire sécher des fromages)* wicker tray

clitoridien, -ienne [klitɔridjɛ̃, -jɛn] **ADJ** clitoral

clitoris [klitɔris] **NM** *Anat* clitoris

clivage [klivaʒ] **NM 1** *(dans la société)* divide; *(dans un parti politique)* split; **c. social** social divide; **c. idéologique** ideological divide **2** *(de roches etc)* cleavage **3** *(de diamants etc)* cleaving

cliver [klive] **VT** *(diamants etc)* to cleave, to split
VPR se cliver *(de roches etc)* to cleave, to split

cloaque [klɔak] **NM 1** *aussi Fig* cesspool; **c. de vices** den of iniquity; **comment peut-il vivre dans ce c.?** how can he live in that pigsty *or* midden? **2** *Anat, Zool* cloaca **3** *Antiq* **le grand C.** the Cloaca Maxima

clochard, -arde [klɔʃar, -ard] **N** *Fam* tramp, *Am* hobo; **si tu continues comme ça, tu vas finir c.** if you carry on like that, you're going to end up destitute

clochardisation [klɔʃardizasjɔ̃] **NF** destitution

clochardiser [klɔʃardize] **VT** to reduce to destitution; *(sans domicile)* to make homeless, to reduce to a state of vagrancy
VPR se clochardiser to be reduced to destitution; *(sans domicile)* to be made homeless

cloche [klɔʃ] **NF 1** bell; **sonner les cloches** to ring the bells; *Fam* **sonner les cloches à qn** to give sb a good ticking off *or* a good rollicking; **se faire sonner les cloches** to get a good ticking off *or* a good rollicking; **fleurs en c.** bell-shaped flowers; *Fam* **déménager à la c. de bois** to do a moonlight flit; *Fig* **voilà un autre son de c.** that's quite a different version of events **2** *Chimie* bell jar; *(en horticulture)* cloche; *Culin* **c. (de métal)** metal dish cover **3** *(chapeau)* **c.** cloche (hat) **4** *Fam (vagabondage)* **la c.** vagrancy; **être de la c.** to be a vagrant, to be of no fixed abode **5** *Arg* **se taper la c.** to pig out, to stuff oneself **6** *Fam (idiot)* twit, idiot
ADJ *Fam* idiotic, stupid; **avoir l'air c.** to look stupid
▸ ▸ *Aut* **c. d'embrayage** clutch bell housing; **c. à fromage(s)** cheese dish cover; **c. à plongeur** diving bell

cloche-pied (à) [klɔʃpje] **ADV** **sauter à c.** to hop; **s'éloigner à c.** to hop away

clocher¹ [klɔʃe] **NM 1** *(d'une église etc)* bell tower, steeple; **course au c.** point-to-point (race) **2** *(paroisse)* home town, home patch; **querelles** *ou* **disputes de c.** petty local quarrels, parish-pump quarrels; **esprit** *ou* **mentalité de c.** small-town mentality, parochialism

clocher² [klɔʃe] **VI 1** *Fam* **il y a quelque chose qui cloche** there's something wrong somewhere; **il y a quelque chose qui cloche dans son histoire** there's something not right about his story; **je ne sais pas ce qu'il y a, mais ça cloche quelque part** I don't know what it is, but something's not right somewhere **2** *Arch (boiter)* to limp, to hobble

clocheton [klɔʃtɔ̃] **NM** *Archit (d'une église)* (small) steeple; *(ornement)* pinnacle (turret)

clochette [klɔʃɛt] **NF 1** *(petite cloche)* small bell, handbell **2** *Bot* bell-flower, bell-shaped flower

clodo [klodo] *Fam* **NM** tramp, down-and-out, *Am* hobo
ADJ down-and-out

cloison [klwazɔ̃] **NF 1** *(entre des pièces)* partition; **mur de c.** dividing wall; **percer une c.** to knock through a (dividing) wall; **coller l'oreille** *ou* **écouter à la c.** to listen through the wall **2** *Naut, Aviat* bulkhead; *Aut* partition, bulkhead; **c. étanche** *Naut* watertight bulkhead; *Aviat* pressure bulkhead; *Fig* watertight compartment; *Fig* **faire tomber les cloisons entre les classes** to bring down class barriers **3** *Biol* septum; *Anat* **c. nasale** nasal septum

cloisonnage [klwazɔnaʒ] **NM** partitioning

cloisonné [klwazɔne] **ADJ 1** *(pièce)* partitioned (off); *Fig* **ces services sont très cloisonnés** these departments are highly compartmentalized **2** *Beaux-Arts (émaux)* cloisonné **3** *Biol* septate(d)
NM cloisonné

cloisonnement [klwazɔnmɑ̃] **NM** *(d'une pièce etc)* partitioning (off); *Fig* compartmentalization

cloisonner [klwazɔne] **VT** *(pièce etc)* to partition (off); *Fig* **c. la société** to put up class barriers

cloître [klwatr] **NM 1** *(partie d'un monastère*

etc) cloister(s) **2** *(monastère)* monastery, convent; **vie de c.** cloistered life

cloîtrer [klwatre] VT *(personne)* to cloister; *Fig* to shut up *or* away; **nonne cloîtrée** enclosed nun

VPR **se cloîtrer** *(de religieux)* to enter a convent *or* a monastery; *Fig* to shut oneself up *or* away, to live the life of a recluse

clonage [klɔnaʒ] NM *Biol, Ordinat* cloning

clone [klon] NM *Biol, Ordinat* clone

cloner [klone] VT *Biol, Ordinat* to clone

cloneur [klɔnœr] NM *Mktg* cloner

clope [klɔp] *Arg* NF OU M *(cigarette)* fag, ciggie, smoke; **la c. jaunit les doigts** cigarettes make your fingers go yellow; **des clopes!** nothing doing!, no way!

NM *(mégot)* (cigarette-)end *or* butt

cloper [klɔpe] VI *Fam* to smoke

clopin-clopant [klɔpɛ̃klɔpɑ̃] ADV *Fam* **aller c.** to limp along, to hobble about; *Fig* **commerce qui va c.** business that struggles along

clopiner [klɔpine] VI to hobble

clopinettes [klɔpinɛt] NFPL *Fam* sweet FA, *surtout Am* zilch; **je ne vais pas travailler pour des c.** I'm not going to work for peanuts

cloporte [klɔpɔrt] NM *(insecte)* woodlouse, *Am* sow bug

cloque [klɔk] NF **1** *(sur la peau, sur la peinture etc)* blister; **faire des cloques** to blister **2** *Agr (des arbres)* blight **3** *Arg* **être en c.** *(enceinte)* to be up the spout, to be knocked up, to be in the club

cloqué [klɔke] ADJ *(peinture)* blistered; *Agr (feuille)* blighted, curled; *Tex* **tissu c.** seersucker

NM *Tex* seersucker

cloquer [klɔke] VI *(de la peinture)* to blister; *(de la peau)* to blister, to come up in a blister

clore [klɔr] *(pp* **clos;** *pr ind* **je clos, il clôt, ils closent;** *fu* **je clorai)** VT *(= fermer, which has taken its place in most uses)* **1** *(discussion etc)* to end; *(marché)* to conclude; *(compte)* to close; *Bourse (position)* to close out; **l'image qui clôt le livre** the image which ends the book, the image on which the book closes; **c. le débat** to close the meeting, to adjourn; *Ordinat* **c. une session** to log off, to log out **2** *Litt (passage, porte)* to close (off), to shut (up); *(terrain etc)* to enclose

VPR **se clore** *(d'une réunion etc)* to (come to an) end

clos [klo] ADJ **1** *(fermé)* closed, shut; **volets c.** closed shutters; **trouver porte close** to find nobody in, to find nobody (at) home; **à la nuit close** after dark; *Jur* **à huis c.** in camera; **réunion à huis c.** closed session; **en vase c.** in isolation; **vivre en vase c.** to live in isolation, to live without any contact with the outside world **2** *(achevé)* finished, concluded; **la discussion est close** the discussion is closed; **l'incident est c.** the matter is closed; **les inscriptions seront closes le 5 mars** the closing date for applications is 5 March; **exercice c. le 31 décembre 2004** year ended 31 Dec 2004 **3** *(entouré) (jardin, monde)* enclosed

NM enclosure; **c. (de vigne)** vineyard

close-combat [klozkɔ̃ba] NM *Sport* close combat

closerie [klozri] NF small park

clôture [klotyr] NF **1** *(enceinte)* enclosure, fence; *(en fer)* railing; *Can Sport (au hockey sur glace)* rink; *(au base-ball)* fence; **c. métallique** wire fence; **mur de c.** enclosing wall **2** *(fermeture) (d'une réunion etc)* conclusion, end; *(d'un débat)* close; **c. des inscriptions le 3 mars** closing date for applications: March 3rd; **discours de c.** closing speech; **prononcer la c. des débats** to pronounce

closure; *Bourse* **cours en c.** closing price; **valeur du mark en c.** closing value of the mark, value of the mark at the close; **c. de la chasse** close of season

3 *Ordinat* close; **c. de session** logging off **4** *Com (d'un compte)* closing; *Bourse (d'une position)* closing (out); *Bourse* **c. par rachat** closure by repurchase; *Compta* **c. annuelle des livres** year-end closing of accounts; *Compta* **c. de l'exercice** end of the financial year

5 *Rel* enclosure; **faire vœu de c.** to take a vow of enclosure

clôturer [klotyre] VT **1** *(champ etc)* to enclose; *(avec barrière)* to fence in **2** *(session)* to close, to end, to conclude; *Pol* **c. les débats** to close the debate **3** *Com (comptes etc)* to close

VI *Bourse* to close; **le CAC 40 a clôturé en baisse/hausse de 9 points** the CAC 40 closed 9 points down/up; **c. à perte** to close at a loss

clou [klu] NM **1** nail; **souliers à gros clous** hobnail(ed) boots; **enfoncer un c. avec un marteau** to hammer in a nail; **ceinture à clous** studded belt; *Fam* **ça ne vaut pas un c.** it's not worth a penny *or Am* a red cent; *Fam* **des clous!** nothing doing!, no chance!, *surtout Am* no way!; **pour des clous** for nothing; *Fam* **elle est maigre comme un c.** she's as thin as a rake; *Fam* **mettre qch au c.** to pawn sth

2 *(d'un passage piéton)* stud; **traverser dans les clous** to cross at a pedestrian crossing *or Am* at a crosswalk

3 *Fam (d'un spectacle etc)* star turn, chief attraction; **ça a été le c. de la soirée** it was the high point *or* highlight of the evening

4 *Mil Arg (prison)* cooler, slammer

5 *Méd* boil, carbuncle

6 **(vieux) c.** *(voiture)* old banger; *(vélo)* old boneshaker

▸▸ **c. cavalier** staple; **c. à crochet** hook; **c. doré** brass-headed nail, stud; **c. de girofle** clove; **c. sans tête** brad; **c. à souliers** shoe tack; **c. de tapissier** (upholstery *or* carpet) tack

clouer [klue] VT **1** to nail; **c. une caisse** to nail down a crate; *Fig Fam* **c. le bec à qn** to shut sb up **2** *Fig (chose, personne)* to pin down; **c. qn au sol** to pin sb down; **rester cloué sur place** to be rooted to the spot; **la neige a cloué tous les avions au sol** all planes were grounded due to snow; **être cloué au lit** to be confined to *or Fam* stuck in bed

clouté [klute] ADJ *(chaussures etc)* studded; **passage c.** pedestrian crossing, *Am* crosswalk

clouter [klute] VT *(chaussures etc)* to stud

clovisse [klɔvis] NF *(mollusque)* clam

clown [klun] NM clown; **numéro de clowns** clown act; *Fig* **ne fais pas le c.!** stop acting the fool *or* goat!, stop clowning around!; **c'est un vrai c.** he's a real comic *or* clown

clownerie [klunri] NF clowning; *Fig* clowning around, playing the fool

clownesque [klunɛsk] ADJ clownish

club [klœb] NM **1** *(association) (sportif, politique)* club; **c. de foot** football club; **c. sportif ou de sport** sports club; **c. de gymnastique** fitness centre, gym; **c. de vacances** holiday club, *Am* vacation center; **c. de compagnie aérienne** airline club; **c. d'investissement** investment club; *Bourse* **c. des amis** fan club **2** *(de golf)* (golf) club **3** **(fauteuil) c.** club chair

cluse [klyz] NF *Géog* cluse, transverse valley

clystère [klistɛr] NM *Méd Arch* clyster, enema

cm *(abrév* **centimètre)** cm

CMJN [seɛmʒiɛn] *Ordinat (abrév* **cyan, magenta, jaune, noir)** CMYK

CMP [seɛmpe] NM *Fin (abrév* **coût moyen pondéré)** weighted average cost

CMU [seɛmy] NF *(abrév* **couverture maladie universelle)** = law introduced in France to ensure free health care for people on low incomes who have no social security cover

CNA [seɛna] NM *(abrév* **convertisseur numérique analogique)** DAC

CNAM [knam] NF *(abrév* **Caisse nationale d'assurance maladie)** = French government department dealing with health insurance and sickness benefit

NM *(abrév* **Conservatoire national des arts et métiers)** = school of engineering in Paris

CNCE [seɛnseə] NM *(abrév* **Centre national du commerce extérieur)** = national export organization

CNIL [knil] NF *(abrév* **Commission nationale de l'informatique et des libertés)** = board which enforces data protection legislation

CNPF [seɛnpeɛf] NM *Anciennement (abrév* **Conseil national du patronat français)** = former name of the French employers' association, *Br* ≃ CBI

CNRS [seɛnɛrɛs] NM *(abrév* **Centre national de la recherche scientifique)** *Br* ≃ SRC (Science Research Council), *Can* ≃ Science Council of Canada

coaccusé, -ée [koakyze] N *Jur* co-defendant

coach [kotʃ] NM **1** *Aut* two-door car **2** *(entraîneur)* coach

coacquéreur [koakerœr] NM joint purchaser

coadjuteur, -trice [koadʒytœr, -tris] N *Rel* coadjutor

coadministrateur, -trice [koadministratœr, -tris] N co-director; *Jur* co-trustee

coagulable [kɔagylabl] ADJ capable of coagulating, coagulable

coagulant [kɔagylɑ̃] ADJ coagulating, coagulative

NM coagulant

coagulateur, -trice [kɔagylatœr, -tris] ADJ coagulative

coagulation [kɔagylasjɔ̃] NF coagulation, coagulating

coaguler [kɔagyle] VT *(sang)* to coagulate; *(lait)* to curdle

VI *(du sang)* to coagulate, to clot; *(du lait)* to curdle

VPR **se coaguler** *(du sang)* to coagulate, to clot; *(du lait)* to curdle

coalescence [kɔalɛsɑ̃s] NF coalescence

coalisé [kɔalize] ADJ allied

N **les coalisés** the allies

coaliser [kɔalize] VT *(partis)* to unite into a coalition

VPR **se coaliser** to unite; *Pol* to form a coalition; *Fig* **ils se sont tous coalisés contre moi** they all ganged up on me *or* joined forces against me

coalition [kɔalisjɔ̃] NF **1** *(alliance)* coalition; **gouvernement de c.** coalition government **2** *Fig Péj* conspiracy; **former une c. contre qn/qch** to join forces against sb/sth

coaltar [koltar] NM coal tar; *Fam* **être dans le c.** to be completely out of it, to be in a daze

coassement [kɔasmɑ̃] NM *(de la grenouille)* croak; **des coassements** croaking, croaks

coasser [kɔase] VI *(d'une grenouille)* to croak

coassocié, -ée [kɔasɔsje] N copartner, joint partner

coassurance [kɔasyrɑ̃s] NF mutual assurance

coassurer [kɔasyre] VT to co-insure

coauteur [kootœr] NM **1** *(d'un livre etc)* joint author, co-author **2** *(d'un crime)* accomplice

coaxial, -iale, -iaux, -iales [koaksjal, -jo] ADJ coaxial

COB [seobe] NF Bourse (abrév **Commission des opérations de Bourse**) = Stock Exchange watchdog, Am ≃ SEC

cobalt [kobalt] NM cobalt; **bleu de c.** cobalt blue; **bombe au c.** cobalt bomb

cobaye [kobaj] NM (mammifère), Fig guinea pig; Fig **servir de c.** to act as a guinea pig

cobelligérant [kobeliʒerɑ̃] ADJ, NM cobelligerent

Coblence [koblɑ̃s] NF Koblenz

cobol [kobɔl] NM Ordinat COBOL

cobra [kobra] NM cobra

coca [koka] NM 1 Fam (boisson) Coke®; **prendre un c.** to have a Coke® 2 Bot coca NF Pharm coca

cocagne [kokaɲ] NF **mât de c.** greasy pole; **pays de c.** land of milk and honey, land of plenty

cocaïne [kokain] NF Pharm cocaine

cocaïnomane [kokainoman] N cocaine addict

cocard [kokar] NM Fam black eye, shiner

cocarde [kokard] NF rosette; Hist (sur un chapeau) cockade; Aviat roundel, fuselage marking; (dans un avion) company crest; **la c. tricolore** = tricolour cockade, worn on 14 July; **course à la c.** = traditional sport in southern France in which rosettes are snatched from the horns of young cattle

cocardier, -ière [kokardje, -jɛr] ADJ (chauviniste) chauvinistic, jingoistic N chauvinist, jingoist

cocasse [kokas] ADJ Fam comical, laughable

cocasserie [kokasri] NF Fam comical nature, ridiculousness

coccinelle [koksinɛl] NF 1 (insecte) ladybird, Spéc coccinella 2 Fam (voiture) (Volkswagen®) beetle

coccyx [koksis] NM Anat coccyx

coche¹ [kɔʃ] NM Arch stagecoach; Fig **faire la mouche du c.** to buzz around self-importantly; Fam **rater ou louper ou manquer le c.** to miss the boat

coche² NF 1 Vieilli notch, nick; (d'une flèche) nock 2 Ordinat tick, Am checkmark

cochenille [kɔʃnij] NF cochineal

cocher¹ [kɔʃe] NM coachman, driver; Arch **c. de fiacre** cabman, Fam cabby

cocher² VT 1 (nom etc) to tick (off), Am to check; **c. la case appropriée** tick the appropriate box 2 Vieilli (faire une entaille dans) to nick, to notch

cochère [kɔʃɛr] ADJ **porte c.** carriage gateway or entrance

cochet [kɔʃɛ] NM cockerel

cocheur [kɔʃœr] NM Can (au golf) **c. d'allée** pitching wedge; **c. de sable** sand wedge

Cochinchine [kɔʃɛ̃ʃin] NF Hist Cochin-China

cochon, -onne [kɔʃɔ̃, -ɔn] NM 1 Zool pig; Fig **copains comme cochons** as thick as thieves; Fam **tu es sale comme un c.** you're filthy; **petite cochonne!** you dirty little thing!; **quel c.!** (qui ne nettoie pas après soi) he leaves such a mess behind him!; **gros ou gras comme un c.** as round as a barrel; **manger comme un c.** to eat like a pig; **tu écris comme un c.** your writing is appalling; **avoir des yeux de c.** to have piggy eyes; Fig **temps de c.** rotten or stinking weather; Fig Fam **eh ben mon c.!** you old rogue or devil!; **c'est une tête de c.** he's really pig-headed; Fam **un c. n'y retrouverait pas ses petits!** what a pigsty!

2 Fam Péj (vicieux) dirty old man; **tu es une petite cochonne!** you've got a filthy mind or a mind like a sewer!; **c'est un c.** (il raconte des histoires immondes) he's got a filthy mind or a mind like a sewer; **quel vieux c.!** what a dirty old man!

3 Arg Péj dirty pig, swine; **jouer un tour de c. à qn** to play a dirty or rotten trick on sb ADJ (histoire etc) dirty, smutty, filthy; **film c.** dirty or porn or blue film; **dix mille euros? c'est pas c.** ten thousand euros? that's not bad; **c. qui s'en dédit** it's a deal

▸▸ **c. d'Amérique** peccary; **c. d'Inde** guinea pig; **c. de lait** suck(l)ing pig; **c. de mer** porpoise

cochonceté [kɔʃɔ̃ste] NF Fam (propos) filthy talk, foul language; (vacherie) dirty trick; (action obscène) repulsive act; **allez faire vos cochoncetés ailleurs!** go and do that sort of thing somewhere else!; **dire des cochoncetés** to use dirty language, to talk dirty

cochonnaille [kɔʃɔnaj] NF Fam foodstuffs made from pork

cochonner [kɔʃɔne] VT Fam 1 (mal faire) (travail) to bungle, to botch, to muck up 2 (salir) to dirty, to make a mess of

cochonnerie [kɔʃɔnri] NF Arg 1 (saleté) mess; **faire des cochonneries** (des saletés) to make a mess; **dire des cochonneries** to say dirty or smutty things 2 (chose sans valeur) trash, rubbish; (plat) pigswill; **il ne mange que des cochonneries** he only eats junk food

cochonnet [kɔʃɔnɛ] NM 1 (petit cochon) piglet 2 (aux boules) jack

cocker [kɔkɛr] NM cocker spaniel

cockpit [kɔkpit] NM (de voitures de courses), Naut, Aviat cockpit

cocktail [kɔktɛl] NM (boisson) cocktail; (soirée) cocktail party; Fig (mélange) cocktail, mixture; **c. de fruits** fruit cocktail; **c. Molotov** Molotov cocktail

coco¹ [koko] NM 1 (plante) **noix de c.** coconut; **huile/beurre de c.** coconut oil/butter 2 Arg (tête) nut, bonce; (estomac) belly; **mets-toi ça dans le c.!** get that into your thick skull! 3 (boisson) = drink made from liquorice, lemon juice and water

coco² NM 1 Enf (œuf) egg 2 Fam (type) fellow, bloke; **drôle de c.** odd bloke, strange guy; **toi, mon c., je t'ai à l'œil** just watch it, mate or chum 3 **mon petit c.** my darling, my pet

coco³ NF Arg (cocaïne) coke, Charlie

coco⁴ NM Fam (communiste) commie, red

cocoler [kɔkɔle] VT Suisse (dorloter) to cosset

cocon [kɔkɔ̃] NM (du vers à soie etc) cocoon; Fig **le c. familial** the family nest; **s'enfermer dans son c.** to retire into one's shell; **il faut sortir de ton c.** you must come out of your shell

cocontractant, -ante [kokɔ̃traktɑ̃, -ɑ̃t] N Jur contracting partner

cocooning [kɔkuniŋ] NM cocooning; **faire du c.** to cocoon

cocorico [kɔkɔriko] INT (du coq) cock-a-doodle-doo!
NM 1 (cri du coq) cock-a-doodle-doo 2 (cri) = French victory cheer; **faire c.** to crow

cocoter [kɔkɔte] VI Fam to stink; **ça cocote ici** it stinks in here

cocotier [kɔkɔtje] NM (arbre) coconut palm; Fig Fam **secouer le c.** to get rid of the dead wood

cocotte [kɔkɔt] NF 1 Enf (poule) hen, chicken; (en papier) = bird made out of folded paper 2 Fam **ma c.** darling 3 Péj (prostituée) tart 4 Culin (large) stewpan, casserole (dish) 5 Fam **hue, c.!** gee up! 6 Can (pomme de pin) pine cone

Cocotte-Minute®, pl **Cocottes-Minute** NF pressure cooker

cocréancier, -ière [kokreɑ̃sje, -jɛr] N Fin joint creditor

cocu, -ue [kɔky] Fam N deceived husband, f deceived wife; (homme) Fml cuckold; **faire c. son mari** to cheat on one's husband; **avoir une chance ou une veine de c.** to have the luck of the devil; **va donc, eh c.!** get lost, you sucker!
ADJ deceived, Fml cuckold(ed); **je suis c.** my wife is cheating on me

cocuage [kɔkyaʒ] NM Arg cuckoldry

cocufier [kɔkyfje] VT Fam to be unfaithful to, to cheat on, Fml to cuckold

coda [koda] NF Mus coda

codage [kodaʒ] NM 1 (chiffrement) coding; **c. de données** data encryption 2 Ling encoding

code [kod] NM 1 (symbole) code; **ils communiquent par c.** they communicate in code; **écrire un message en c.** to write a message in code, to write a coded message; **déchiffrer un c.** to decipher or break or crack a code

2 Ordinat code; **les codes** the codes, the coding; **c. alphanumérique** alphanumeric(al) code; **c. d'erreur** error code; **c. hexadécimal** hexa(decimal) code; **c. abrégé** shortcode; **c. machine** machine code; **c. couleurs** colour coding; **c. d'accès** access code; **c. d'arrêt** stop code; **c. d'autorisation d'accès** access authorization code; **c. d'identification** identification code; **c. d'imprimante** printer code; **c. d'instruction** instruction code; **c. de caractère** character code; **c. de commande** command code; **c. de contrôle** control code; **c. de contrôle de l'imprimante** printer control code; **c. de départ** start code; **c. inhibiteur** inhibit code; **c. natif** source code; **c. objet** object code; **c. source** source code; **c. ASCII** ASCII code

3 (ensemble de règles) law; (livre) (copy of the) code; Jur statute book; Aut **passer le c.** to sit the written part of a driving test; **c. de la morale** moral code; **c. de l'honneur** code of honour

4 Aut **se mettre en code(s)** to dip or Am dim one's headlights; **rouler en code(s)** to drive with dipped headlights; **phares code(s)** dipped headlights

▸▸ **c. assujetti TVA** VAT registration number; **c. civil** civil code, ≃ common law; **c. client** customer code, customer reference number; **c. de commerce** commercial law; **c. confidentiel** security code; (d'une carte bancaire) PIN; **c. général des impôts** general tax code; Biol **c. génétique** genetic code; Banque **c. guichet** bank branch code; **c. de justice militaire** military law; **c. maritime** navigation laws; **c. pénal** penal code; Banque **c. personnel, c. porteur** PIN, personal identity number; **c. postal** postcode, postal code, Am zip code; **C. de la route** Highway Code; **c. secret** secret code; **c. du travail** employment code, employment law, Am labor code, labor laws

---

Code postal

In France, the first two numbers of a given post code correspond to the administrative code number of the relevant "département". Thus all postal codes for Paris begin with 75.

---

codé [kode] ADJ coded; (pour sécurité) security-coded; (image) scrambled

code-barres, pl **codes-barres** NM bar code

codébiteur, -trice [kodebitœr, -tris] N Jur joint debtor

codécision [kodesizjɔ̃] NF joint decision; UE codecision (procedure)

codéine [kodein] NF Chimie codeine

codemandeur, -deresse [kodəmɑ̃dœr, -drɛs] N Jur joint plaintiff

coder [kɔde] VT (*message*) to code

codétenteur, -trice [kɔdetɑ̃tœr, -tris] N *Jur* joint holder

codétenu, -ue [kɔdetny] N fellow prisoner *or* inmate

codeur [kɔdœr] NM *Tech* coder

codéveloppement [kɔdevlɔpmɑ̃] NM co-operative development

CODÉVI [kɔdevi] NM (*abrév* **compte pour le développement industriel**) = savings account, money from which is invested in industrial development

codex [kɔdeks] NM pharmacopoeia

codicillaire [kɔdisiler] ADJ *Jur* codicillary

codicille [kɔdisil] NM *Jur* codicil

codification [kɔdifikasjɔ̃] NF (*des lois etc*) codification, classification; *Ordinat* **c. binaire** binary code; **c. décimale** decimal coding; **c. significative** coding by means of symbols, symbol coding

codifier [kɔdifje] VT (*lois etc*) to codify; (*mettre en système*) to systematize

codirecteur, -trice [kɔdirɛktœr, -tris] N joint manager, f joint manageress; (*d'un PDG etc*) co-director

coédition [kɔedisjɔ̃] NF (*procédé*) joint publishing; (*livre*) joint publication

coefficient [kɔefisjɑ̃] NM **1** *Math* coefficient; (*dans un concours ou examen*) coefficient, weighting factor; **on peut s'attendre à un c. d'erreur** a certain margin of error is to be expected; **c. d'occupation des sols** (*en urbanisme*) plot ratio **2** *Fin* **c. d'activité** activity ratio; **c. de capital** output ratio; **c. de capitalisation des résultats** price-earnings ratio; *Compta* **c. d'exploitation** performance *or* operating ratio; **c. de liquidité** current ratio; **c. de rotation** stock turnover ratio; **c. de solvabilité** risk asset ratio; **c. de trésorerie** cash ratio **3** *Tech* **c. de dilatation** coefficient of expansion; **c. d'écrasement/d'élasticité** modulus of compression/of elasticity; **c. de sécurité** safety factor; **c. de température** the rate of increase; *Aut* **c. aérodynamique** *ou* **de pénétration dans l'air** drag coefficient; *Aut* **c. de traînée** drag coefficient, drag factor

cœlacanthe [selakɑ̃t] NM *Zool* coelacanth

cœliaque [seljak] ADJ, N *Méd* coeliac, *Am* celiac

cœliochirurgie [seljoʃiryrʒi] NF *Méd* laparotomy

cœlioscopie [seljoskopi] NF *Méd* laparoscopy

coentreprise [kɔɑ̃trəpriz] NF joint venture

coéquation [kɔekwasjɔ̃] NF *Admin* proportional assessment

coéquipier, -ière [kɔekipje, -jɛr] N *Sport etc* team-mate

coercible [kɔɛrsibl] ADJ **1** *Phys* (*gaz etc*) coercible **2 un bâillement difficilement c.** a yawn that is hard to suppress *or* stifle

coercitif, -ive [kɔɛrsitif, -iv] ADJ coercive; **le pouvoir c. de son discours** the persuasive power of his speech

coercition [kɔɛrsisjɔ̃] NF coercion

CŒUR [kœr] NM **1** *Anat* heart; **maladie de c.** heart disease; **greffe du c.** heart transplant; **c. droit/gauche** right/left side of the heart; **subir une opération à c. ouvert** to have open-heart surgery; **tué d'une balle en plein c.** killed by a bullet in the heart; (*en forme de*) **c.** heart-shaped; *Fig* **faire la bouche en c.** to simper; **il est arrivé la bouche en c. pour me demander si …** he came simpering up to me to ask if …; *Fig* **joli comme un c.** as pretty as a picture; **serrer** *ou* **presser qn contre** *ou* **sur son c.** to hold sb close; *Fam* **faire le joli c.** to put on airs (and graces)

2 (*ventre*) **avoir mal au c.** to feel sick *or Am* nauseous; **ça fait mal au c. de voir tout cet argent gaspillé** it makes you sick to see all that money wasted *or* go to waste; **cela soulève le c.** it's nauseating *or* sickening; *Fam* **avoir le c. solide** *ou* **bien accroché** to have a strong stomach

3 (*siège des sentiments*) heart; **il a l'air dur, mais il a le c. sensible** he looks tough, but he has a tender heart; **avoir** *ou* **garder qch sur le c.** to have sth on one's mind; **tu ne peux pas garder ça sur le c., il faut que tu en parles** you can't keep that to yourself, you'll have to talk about it; **dire ce qu'on a sur le c.** to get it off one's chest; *Fig* **en avoir le c. net** to get to the bottom of it; *Fig* **ouvrir son c. à qn** to open one's heart to sb; **parler à c. ouvert** to speak freely; **avoir la rage au c.** to be seething with anger; **au fond du c.** in one's heart of hearts; **remercier qn de tout (son) c.** *ou* **du fond de son c.** to thank sb wholeheartedly *or* from the bottom of one's heart; **je l'espère de tout mon c.** I sincerely hope so; *Euph* **je sais qu'elle ne me porte pas dans son c.** I know she doesn't like me much *or* isn't very fond of me; **partir le c. léger** to set off with a light heart; **avoir le c. triste** *ou* **lourd** to be heavy-hearted; **avoir le c. gros** *ou* **serré** to have a heavy heart, to be sad at heart; **à c. joie** to one's heart's content; **de gaieté de c.** with a light heart; **ce n'était pas de gaieté de c. que je l'ai fait** I wasn't happy about doing it, I didn't enjoy doing it; **prendre** *ou* **avoir à c. de faire qch** to have one's heart set on doing sth; **la chose qui lui tient** *ou* **qu'il a** *ou* **prend à c. est de donner une éducation à sa fille** he has his heart set on giving his daughter an education; **ce projet lui tient à c.** this project is close to his heart; **ne pas avoir le c. de faire qch** not to have the heart to do sth; **elle n'a plus le c. à rien** she hasn't the heart for anything any more; **avoir le c. à rire** to be in the mood for laughing; **avoir le c. sur la main** to be very generous; **à votre bon c., m'sieurs dames** can you spare a few coins?; **femme de c.** warm-hearted woman; **je serai de c. avec vous** I'll be with you in spirit; **à vous briser** *ou* **fendre le c.** heartbreaking; **histoire d'une tristesse à vous fendre** *ou* **briser le c.** heartbreakingly sad story; **j'en avais le c. brisé** I was broken-hearted; **si le c. vous en dit** if you feel like it; **des gens selon mon c.** people after my own heart; **le c. a ses raisons** the heart has its reasons; **ta proposition lui est allée droit au c.** your offer went straight to his heart

4 par c. by heart; **c'est du par c.** it's been learnt (off) by heart *or* learnt parrot-fashion; **apprendre/savoir qch par c.** to learn/know sth by heart; *Fam* **je la connais par c.** I know her inside out

5 (*courage*) courage, spirit; **avoir le c. de faire qch** to have the heart to do sth; **donner du c. à qn** to give sb courage; *Fam* **avoir du c. au ventre** to have plenty of guts; **faire contre mauvaise fortune bon c.** to make the best of a bad job, to put a good face on it

6 (*énergie*) heart, will; **avoir** *ou* **mettre du c. à l'ouvrage** to put one's heart into one's work; **je n'ai pas le c. à l'ouvrage aujourd'hui** I haven't the heart for work today; **il était clair qu'il n'avait pas le c. à l'ouvrage** it was obvious that his heart wasn't in it; **faire qch de bon c.** *ou* **de grand c.** to do sth willingly *or* gladly; **rire de bon c.** to laugh heartily; **y aller de bon c.** to get down to it; **le c. n'y est pas** his/my/*etc* heart isn't in it

7 (*amour*) **donner son c. à qn** to lose one's heart to sb; **aimer qn de tout son c.** to love sb with all one's heart; *Prov* **loin des yeux, loin du c.** out of sight, out of mind; **des histoires de c.** affairs of the heart; **une affaire de c.** an affair of the heart

8 (*bonté*) **c'est un** *ou* **il a bon c.** he's kind-hearted, he's a kind-hearted soul; **avoir un c.**

d'or/de pierre to have a heart of gold/of stone; **ne pas avoir de c.** to be heartless

9 (*centre*) middle, core; *Fig* **le c. du problème** the heart of the matter; **au c. de la ville** in the centre of the town, in the heart of the city; **c. de palmier** heart of palm; **c. d'un chou/d'un artichaut** heart of a cabbage/artichoke heart; *Fam* **avoir un c. d'artichaut** to fall in love with every girl/man one meets, to be always falling in love; **fromage fait à c.** ripe cheese; **au c. de l'hiver** in the depths of winter; **au c. de l'été** at the height of summer

10 *Cartes* hearts; **dame de c.** queen of hearts; **avez-vous du c.?** have you any hearts?

11 (*d'imprimante laser*) engine

coexistence [kɔɛgzistɑ̃s] NF coexistence (**avec** with); *Pol* **c. pacifique** peaceful coexistence

coexister [kɔɛgziste] VI to coexist (**avec** with)

COFACE [kɔfas] NF (*abrév* **Compagnie française d'assurances pour le commerce extérieur**) ≃ Export Credit Guarantee Department

coffrage [kɔfraʒ] NM **1** (*pour ouvrages en béton*) formwork, *Br* shuttering **2** *Min* (*pour galerie etc*) coffering, lining

coffre [kɔfr] NM **1** (*meuble*) chest; (*pour l'argent*) safe; (*à la banque*) safe(ty) deposit box; *Banque* **c. de nuit** night safe; **c. en bois** wooden chest; **c. à jouets** toy box; **c. à linge** linen chest; **percer** *ou* **ouvrir un c.** to break open *or* into a safe; **les coffres de l'État** coffers of State

2 *Anat Fam* chest; **avoir du c.** (*avoir du souffle*) to have a sound chest, to have a lot of puff; (*avoir de la voix*) to have a powerful voice

3 *Aut* (*d'une voiture*) boot, *Am* trunk; *Aut* **c. de toit** car roof box, luggage box; **c. porte-skis** ski box; *Aviat* **c. à bagages** baggage compartment

4 (*d'une serrure, d'un piano etc*) case

5 *Naut* **c. d'amarrage** mooring buoy

coffre-fort, *pl* **coffres-forts** NM safe

coffrer [kɔfre] VT **1** *Fam* **c. qn** to put sb behind bars *or* inside *or* away; **faire c. qn** to have *or* get sb put behind bars *or* inside **2** *Min* (*galerie etc*) to coffer, to line

coffret [kɔfre] NM **1** small box, casket; **c. à bijoux** jewellery box; **c. de disques** boxed set **2** *Ordinat* case; **modèle en c.** cased model **3** *Tél* **c. avec carte prépayée** prepay package

cogénération [kɔʒenerasjɔ̃] NF *Tech* co-generation

cogérance [kɔʒerɑ̃s] NF co-management, joint management

cogérant, -ante [kɔʒerɑ̃, -ɑ̃t] N joint manager

cogérer [kɔʒere] VT **c. qch** to manage sth jointly

cogestion [kɔʒestjɔ̃] NF joint management, co-management

cogitation [kɔʒitasjɔ̃] NF *Iron, Vieilli* cogitation, reflection

cogiter [kɔʒite] VI *Vieilli* to cogitate, to think; **c. sur un problème** to ponder over a problem

cogito [kɔʒito] NM *Phil* cogito; **le c. de Descartes** the Cartesian cogito, Descartes' cogito

cognac [kɔɲak] NM cognac

cognassier [kɔɲasje] NM quince (tree)

cogne [kɔɲ] NM *Arg* (*policier*) cop; (*bagarre*) punch-up; **il va y avoir de la c.!** there's going to be trouble *or* a punch-up!

cognée [kɔɲe] NF axe, *Am* ax, hatchet; **jeter le manche après la c.** to throw in one's hand

cognement [kɔɲmɑ̃] NM (*bruit*) thumping,

banging; *(d'un moteur etc)* knocking, combustion knock; **c. (du moteur) diesel** diesel knock

cogner [kɔɲe] **VT** *(heurter)* to knock, to bump; *Fam (épouse, enfants etc)* to knock about; **c. qn en passant** to bump into sb (in passing); *Fam* **se faire c.** to get beaten up *or* knocked about; **il l'a cogné dur** he hit him hard

VI 1 *(frapper, battre)* to bang (**sur** on); **il est tombé de la chaise et sa tête a cogné contre le bureau** he fell off his chair and bumped *or* banged his head on the desk; **c. du poing sur la table** to bang (one's fist) on the table, to thump the table; *Fam* **il cogne dur** he knows how to use his fists; *Fam* **son mari lui cogne dessus chaque fois qu'il est ivre** her husband knocks her about *or* gives her a thumping every time he gets drunk; **c. à une porte** to bang *or* hammer on a door; **j'entends un volet** **c.** I can hear a shutter banging

2 *(d'un moteur etc)* to knock **3** *Fam (chauffer)* to be scorching; **ça cogne dur dehors** it's absolutely scorching outside, *très Fam* it's bloody hot outside **4** *Fam (puer)* to stink (to high heaven), *Br* to pong

VPR se cogner 1 *(se heurter)* to bump oneself; **se c. à** *ou* **contre qch** to knock against sth; *Fam* **ils se cognent dessus chaque fois qu'ils boivent** they bash each other about whenever they get drunk; *Fig* **se c. la tête contre les murs** to bang one's head against a brick wall **2** *Fam* **se c. qn/qch** to get stuck *or Br* lumbered *or* landed with sb/sth

cogneur [kɔɲœr] **NM** *Boxe etc* hard hitter, bruiser

cogniticien, -ienne [kɔgnitisjɛ̃, -jɛn] **N** *Ordinat* knowledge engineer

cognitif, -ive [kɔgnitif, -iv] **ADJ** *Phil* cognitive; **thérapie cognitive** cognitive therapy

cognition [kɔgnisjɔ̃] **NF** *Phil* cognition

cohabitation [kɔabitasjɔ̃] **NF** cohabitation, living together; *Pol* **sous le régime de la c.** during the period of cohabitation

---

Cohabitation

Originally, this term referred to the period (1986–1988) during which the socialist President (François Mitterrand) had a right-wing Prime Minister (Jacques Chirac), following the victory of the RPR in the legislative elections and Mitterrand's decision not to resign as President. It has since been used to refer to the similar situation which arose following the 1993 elections (with Édouard Balladur as Prime Minister) and more recently the 1997 elections (with the left-wing government of Lionel Jospin co-ruling with the President Jacques Chirac).

---

cohabiter [kɔabite] **VI** to cohabit (**avec** with), to live together; **elle cohabite avec des amies** she lives with friends

cohérence [kɔerɑ̃s] **NF** *(d'un discours)* coherence; *(d'un comportement)* consistency; *(d'une argumentation)* coherence, consistency; **cette explication/ce raisonnement/il manque de c.** that explanation/that line of argument/he is inconsistent; **parler sans aucune c.** to be totally incoherent

cohérent [kɔerɑ̃] **ADJ** *(argumentation)* coherent, consistent; *(comportement)* consistent; *(dans un discours)* coherent

cohéritier, -ière [kɔeritje, -jɛr] **N** coheir, *f* coheiress, joint heir, *f* joint heiress

cohésif, -ive [kɔezif, -iv] **ADJ** cohesive

cohésion [kɔezjɔ̃] **NF** cohesion, cohesiveness

cohorte [kɔɔrt] **NF 1** *Fam (de gens)* horde, band **2** *Hist* cohort

cohue [kɔy] **NF** crowd, mob, throng

coi, coite [kwa, kwat] **ADJ** **se tenir c.** to keep quiet, to lie low; **en rester c.** to be (left) speechless

coiffage [kwafaʒ] **NM 1** *(de cheveux)* hairdressing, doing someone's hair; *(de ses cheveux)* doing one's hair **2** *(pour recouvrir)* covering

coiffe [kwaf] **NF 1** *(surtout de costume régional)* headdress **2** *(doublure de chapeau)* lining **3** *(pour recouvrir)* cover; *Mil* breech cover; **c. de fusée** fuse cap **4** *(du nouveau-né)* caul

coiffé [kwafe] **ADJ 1** **être c. d'un chapeau** to be wearing a hat; **il est né c.** he was born with a caul; *Fig* he was born with a silver spoon in his mouth **2** **elle est bien coiffée ce soir** her hair is lovely this evening; **je ne suis pas encore coiffée** I haven't done my hair yet; **il est mal c.** his hair's a mess; **c. en arrière** with one's hair combed back; **il est c. en brosse** he has a crew cut

coiffer [kwafe] **VT 1** *(tête)* to cover; *(bouteille etc)* to cap; **c. un enfant d'un bonnet** to put a bonnet on a child('s head); **ce chapeau vous coiffe bien** that hat suits you; **il était coiffé d'un sombrero** he was wearing a sombrero; **montagne coiffée de neige** snow-capped mountain; **des nuages coiffent presque en permanence le mont Blanc** Mont Blanc is almost permanently covered by clouds *or* has a near permanent cloud-cover; *Fig* **c. sainte Catherine** to be (left) on the shelf, to be 25 and still unmarried

2 *(d'un coiffeur etc)* **c. qn** to do sb's hair; **il coiffe bien** he's a good hairdresser; **se faire c. (les cheveux)** to have one's hair done; **qui vous coiffe?** who does your hair?, who's your hairdresser?; **sur ces photos, les mannequins sont coiffés par Maniatis** in these photos, the models' hair-styling is by Maniatis; **se faire c. chez qn/par qn** to get one's hair done at sb's/by sb **3** *Sport Fam* to overtake; *aussi Fig* **se faire c. (au poteau)** to be pipped at the post **4** *Fam (organisation, service etc)* to head

VPR se coiffer 1 *(mettre)* **se c. d'une casquette** to put on a cap **2** *(se peigner)* to do one's hair; **tu ne t'es pas coiffé aujourd'hui, tes cheveux sont emmêlés** you haven't done your hair today, it's all tangled

coiffeur, -euse [kwafœr, -øz] **N** hairdresser, hair stylist; **c. pour hommes** barber

NF coiffeuse *(meuble)* dressing table

coiffure [kwafyr] **NF 1** *(de cheveux)* hairstyle; **changer de c.** to change one's hairstyle *or* hairdo **2** *(métier)* hairdressing; **salon de c.** hairdresser's, hairdressing salon; *(pour hommes)* barbershop, barber's **3** *(chapeau etc)* headgear; *(de costume régional etc)* headdress

COIN [kwɛ̃] **NM 1** *(angle)* *(de la bouche, de l'œil etc)* corner; **maison du** *ou* **qui fait le c.** corner house; **à tous les coins de rue** on every street corner; **l'épicier du c.** the grocer on the corner; *(du village etc)* the local *or* corner grocer; *Fam* **je ne voudrais pas le rencontrer au c. d'un bois** I wouldn't like to meet him down a dark alley *or* on a dark night; **mettre un enfant au c.** *(pour le punir)* to make a child stand in the corner; **regard en c.** sidelong glance; **lancer un regard en c. à qn** to look at sb sideways, to give sb a sidelong glance; **sourire en c.** half smile; **regarder qn du c. de l'œil** to look at sb out of the corner of one's eye; *Journ* **le c. du jardinier/santé** the gardener's/health page; **ici, c'est le c. des enfants** this is the children's corner; **c. enfants** *(au restaurant)* children's area; *Rail* **c. fenêtre/couloir** window/aisle seat; **aux quatre coins du monde** in the four corners of the earth; **elle a visité les quatre coins du monde** she has travelled all over the world; **reliure avec coins** binding with leather corners

2 *(endroit)* spot, place; **un petit c. pas cher** a cheap *or* inexpensive little place; **il habite dans le c.** he lives around here; **je ne suis pas du c.** I'm not local, I'm not from round here, I don't live round here; **les gens du c.** the locals; *Fam* **le petit c.** the smallest room (in the house), *Br* the loo; **coins et recoins** nooks and crannies; **il est resté dans son c. toute la journée** he's been very quiet all day; **c'est quelqu'un qui reste tout le temps dans son c.** he doesn't mix much, he stays in the background; **dans un c. de ma mémoire** in a corner of my memory, in the back of my mind; **mon stylo est introuvable, il a dû tomber dans un c.** I can't find my pen anywhere, it must have got lost somewhere; **j'ai dû le mettre dans un c.** I must have put it somewhere; **chercher qch dans tous les coins** to look everywhere *or* high and low for sth; *Fam* **connaître qch dans les coins** to know sth inside out; **au c. du feu** by the fireside

3 *(parcelle)* patch; **c. des légumes** vegetable patch *or* plot; **c. de ciel bleu** patch of blue sky **4** *(cale)* wedge; **en c.** wedge-shaped; **tranchant du c.** thin end of the wedge **5** *(pour frapper les monnaies)* stamp, die; *Fig* **marqué au c. du génie** bearing the stamp *or* hallmark of genius

coinçage [kwɛ̃saʒ] **NM, coincement** [kwɛ̃smɑ̃] **NM** wedging, jamming

coincé, -ée [kwɛ̃se] **ADJ** *(bloqué)* *(fermeture, porte, mécanisme)* jammed, stuck; *Psy Fam* uptight (about sex)

N *Fam* **c'est qui, ces deux coincés?** who are those two uptight-looking characters?

coincer [kwɛ̃se] (**je coinçai(s), n. coinçons**) **VT 1** *(tiroir etc)* to jam; *(rails etc)* to wedge (up), to chock (up); **j'ai coincé mes cheveux dans ma fermeture Éclair®** I got my hair stuck *or* caught in my zip; **sa main était coincée derrière le radiateur** his hand was trapped *or* caught behind the radiator; **la voiture est coincée entre deux camions** *(en stationnement)* the car is boxed in by two lorries; **je ne peux pas doubler, je suis coincé entre deux camions** I can't overtake, I'm stuck between two lorries; **je suis resté coincé dans un embouteillage** I got snarled up in a traffic jam; **je suis coincé à Prague/dans l'ascenseur** I'm stuck in Prague/in the lift; *Fig* **il est coincé tout le week-end** he's tied up all weekend

2 *(acculer)* to corner; **il m'a coincé** *(je n'ai pas su répondre)* he had me cornered; *Fig* **il faut que je paie, je suis coincé** I'll have to pay, I'm stuck *or* I've no choice; **je vais me retrouver coincé avec deux mensualités à payer** I'll be stuck with two monthly instalments to pay

3 *Fam (arrêter)* to run in, to nick; **il va finir par se faire c.** he'll end up getting nicked

VI 1 *(être bloqué)* to jam, to stick; *Fig* **notre proposition n'a pas été acceptée, ça coince au niveau de la direction** our proposal hasn't been accepted, there's a problem as far as management is concerned

2 *très Fam (sentir mauvais)* to stink, to pong, *Br* to hum

VPR se coincer to jam, to stick; **se c. la tête dans des barreaux** to get one's head stuck in railings; **se c. le doigt dans la porte** to catch one's finger in the door; **évite de te c. le dos!** be careful not to hurt your back!; **il s'est coincé une vertèbre cervicale** he's got a trapped nerve

coïncidence [kɔɛ̃sidɑ̃s] **NF** coincidence; **par une étrange c.** by a strange coincidence

coïncident [kɔɛ̃sidɑ̃] ADJ coincident, coinciding

coïncider [kɔɛ̃side] VI to coincide (**avec** with); **leurs intérêts coïncident** they have similar interests; **tout coïncide! je connais le coupable** it all fits! I know who did it; **votre réponse ne coïncide pas avec la question posée** there is some discrepancy between your answer and the question that was asked; **tous les témoignages coïncident** the witnesses all bear each other out *or* tell the same story; **ces deux figures géométriques coïncident** the two shapes match each other perfectly

coin-coin NM INV *(des canards)* quacking; **des c.** quacks, quacking
  INT quack! quack!

coin-cuisine, *pl* **coins-cuisine(s)** NM kitchen area, kitchenette

coïnculpé, -ée [kɔɛ̃kylpe] N co-defendant, co-accused

coing [kwɛ̃] NM *(fruit)* quince

coin-repas, *pl* **coins-repas** NM dining area *or* recess

coït [kɔit] NM coitus, coition

coke [kɔk] NM *(combustible)* coke
  NF *Fam (cocaïne)* coke

cokéfaction [kɔkefaksjɔ̃] NF coking

cokéfier [kɔkefje] VT to coke

cokerie [kɔkri] NF coking plant

co-koter [kɔkɔte] VI *Belg Fam* to share a room

co-koteur, -euse [kɔkɔtœr, -øz] N *Belg Fam* (student) roommate

col [kɔl] NM **1** *(d'une robe, d'une chemise etc)* collar; **faux c.** *(sur une chemise)* detachable collar; *(sur un verre de bière)* head; **c. de fourrure/de dentelle** fur/lace collar **2** *(d'une bouteille etc)* neck **3** *Géog* col **4** *Arch, Litt (de personne)* neck; **se hausser** *ou* **se pousser du c.** to push oneself forward **5** *Anat (d'un os)* neck
  ▸▸**c. blanc** white-collar worker; **c. bleu** blue-collar worker; **c. cassé** wing collar; **c. châle** shawl collar; **c. cheminée** turtleneck; **c. Claudine** Peter Pan collar; *Anat* **c. du fémur** neck of the femur; **c. marin** sailor's collar; **c. rond** round neck; **c. roulé** polo-neck (jumper); *Anat* **c. de l'utérus** cervix; **cancer du c. de l'utérus** cervical cancer; **c. en V** V-neck

cola [kɔla] NM *(plante)* cola, kola

colback [kɔlbak] NM *Fam* **attraper/prendre qn par le c.** to catch/grab sb by the scruff of the neck

colbertisme [kɔlbɛrtism] NM = economic policy of state intervention and protectionism, from Jean-Baptiste Colbert (1619-1683), finance minister to Louis XIV

col-bleu, *pl* **cols-bleus** NM *Fam (marin)* sailor, bluejacket

colchique [kɔlʃik] NM *(plante)* meadow saffron, autumn crocus, *Spéc* colchicum

cold-cream [koldkrim] NM cold cream

col-de-cygne, *pl* **cols-de-cygne** NM *Tech* swan neck

colégataire [kɔlegatɛr] N *Jur* co-legatee, joint legatee

coléoptère [kɔleɔptɛr] NM beetle; **les coléoptères** the Coleoptera

colère [kɔlɛr] NF anger, *Litt* wrath; **il s'est mis** *ou* **il est entré dans une c. bleue** *ou* **noire** he flew into a towering rage; **piquer** *ou* **faire une c.** to fly into a rage, to throw a tantrum; **être blanc** *ou* **blême/rouge de c.** to be white/flushed with anger; **c. froide** cold fury; **être en c.** to be angry; **se mettre en c.** to get angry, to lose one's temper (**contre qn** with sb, *Am* at sb); **je suis en c. contre moi-même** I'm

angry with myself; **mettre qn en c.** to make sb angry, to anger sb; **avec c.** angrily; **il avait des colères terribles** he was subject to terrible fits of anger; **pas la peine de passer ta c. sur moi** there's no point (in) taking your anger out *or* working your anger off on me; *Litt* **la c. de Dieu** the wrath of God
  ADJ *(voix)* irate, angry; *(personne)* bad-tempered

coléreux, -euse [kɔlerø, -øz], **colérique** [kɔlerik] ADJ *(personne)* quick-tempered; *(disposition)* irritable

colibacille [kɔlibasil] NM colon bacillus

colibacillose [kɔlibasiloz] NF *Méd* colibacillosis

colibri [kɔlibri] NM hummingbird

colifichet [kɔlifiʃɛ] NM trinket, knick-knack

colimaçon [kɔlimasɔ̃] NM snail; **escalier en c.** spiral staircase

colin [kɔlɛ̃] NM *(poisson)* hake, *Br* coley VOIR GRAMMAIRE A12

colinéaire [kɔlineɛr] ADJ *Math* colinear

colin-maillard [kɔlɛ̃majar] NM *(jeu)* blind man's buff

colin-tampon NM *Fam Hum ou Vieilli* **se soucier de qch comme de c.** not to give two hoots about sth

colique [kɔlik] ADJ *Anat (artère etc)* colic
  NF severe stomach pains; *(surtout de bébé)* colic; *Méd* **c. néphrétique/hépatique** renal/biliary colic; **avoir la c.** *(douleur)* to have stomach ache; *(diarrhée)* to have diarrhoea *or Am* diarrhea; *Fig Fam* to have the wind up; *Fam* **cette idée suffit pour me donner la c.** the very idea puts the wind up me; *Fam* **quelle c.!** what a bore!, what a bind!

colis [kɔli] NM **1** *(paquet)* parcel, packet, package; **par c. postal** by parcel post; **c. chargé** registered and insured parcel; **c. exprès** special delivery parcel; **c. contre remboursement** cash on delivery parcel, *Am* collect on delivery parcel **2** *Fam* **un joli petit c.** a knockout, a babe, *Br* a cracker

Colisée (le) [kɔlize] NM the Coliseum

colis-épargne NM INV *Com* saving stamps scheme

colistier, -ière [kɔlistje, -jɛr] N *Pol* fellow candidate, *Am* running mate

colite [kɔlit] NF *Méd* colitis

collabo [kɔlabo] N *Fam* = **collaborateur 2**

collaborateur, -trice [kɔlabɔratœr, -tris] N **1** *(associé)* fellow worker, associate, *Am* co-worker; *Journ* contributor; **collaborateurs d'une revue** contributors to a magazine **2** *Pol, Hist* collaborator, collaborationist

collaboration [kɔlabɔrasjɔ̃] NF **1** *(aide, soutien)* collaboration, co-operation (**avec** with); **travailler en étroite c.** to work closely together, to co-operate **2** *Pol, Hist* collaboration

collaborationniste [kɔlabɔrasjɔnist] N *Pol, Hist* collaborationist

collaborer [kɔlabɔre] VI **1** *(participer)* to collaborate, to co-operate (**avec** with); **c. à un journal** to contribute to a newspaper; **c. à un projet** to take part in a project; **les deux services collaborent étroitement** the two departments work closely together **2** *Pol, Hist* to collaborate

collage [kɔlaʒ] NM **1** *(d'affiches)* sticking up, putting up; *(de boîtes etc)* gluing, sticking; *(de papier etc)* pasting; *Beaux-Arts* collage; *Tech* sizing; *(de produits manufacturés)* bonding; *Typ* **c. et endossage** forwarding **2** *(du vin)* fining, clarifying

collagène [kɔlaʒɛn] NM collagen; **crème de beauté au c.** collagen(-based) cream

collant [kɔlɑ̃] ADJ **1** *(adhésif)* sticky; *(pein-*

ture, vernis) tacky; **papier c.** gummed paper **2** *(qui moule) (vêtement)* tight- *or* close-fitting; **pantalon c.** skintight trousers **3** *Fam (personne)* **qu'est-ce qu'il est c.!** you just can't shake him off *or* get rid of him!; **je m'en méfie, il est très c.** I'm wary of him, he's very clingy
  NM (pair of) tights, *Am* pantihose; **c. uni/fantaisie** self-coloured/patterned tights
  VOIR GRAMMAIRE A10

collante [kɔlɑ̃t] NF *Scol Fam* = letter giving notice of the date and place of an examination

collapsus [kɔlapsys] NM *Méd (d'un malade)* collapse; **c. cardio-vasculaire** circulatory collapse

collatéral, -ale, -aux, -ales [kɔlateral, -o] ADJ collateral; *Archit* **nef collatérale** side aisle; *Jur* **parents collatéraux** collaterals, relatives; **succession collatérale** collateral succession
  NM **1** *Archit* side aisle **2** *Jur* **collatéraux** collaterals, relatives

collation [kɔlasjɔ̃] NF **1** *(repas)* light meal, snack **2** *(de documents etc)* collation **3** *(d'un titre etc)* granting, conferment

collationnement [kɔlasjɔnmɑ̃] NM *(de documents etc)* collating, collation

collationner [kɔlasjɔne] VT *(deux documents écrits)* to collate, to compare

colle [kɔl] NF **1** glue; *(pour papier peint)* (wallpaper) paste; **c. en pot/stick/tube** pot/stick/tube of glue; **papier sans c.** unsized paper; *Fam* **c'est un vrai pot de c.** you just can't get rid of him, he sticks like a leech *or* like glue **2** *Scol etc Fam (question difficile)* difficult *or* sticky question, poser; *(examen oral)* oral exam; *(punition)* detention; **là, me poses une c., je ne sais pas** you've got me there, I don't know **3** *Arg* **vivre** *ou* **être à la c.** to be shacked up together
  ▸▸**c. blanche** paste; **c. à bois** wood glue; **c. de bureau** (paper) glue; **c. au caoutchouc** rubber solution; **c. forte** glue; **c. de poisson** isinglass

collecte [kɔlɛkt] NF **1** *(ramassage)* collection; *(pour les pauvres etc)* collection; **la c. des ordures ménagères** the rubbish collection; **faire** *ou* **organiser une c.** to make *or* take a collection; **nous faisons une c. au profit des enfants malades** we're collecting for sick children *or* on behalf of sick children; **c. de données** data collection *or* gathering; **c. de fonds** fundraising **2** *Rel (prière)* collect

collecter [kɔlɛkte] VT to collect

collecteur, -trice [kɔlɛktœr, -tris] N collector; **c. d'impôts** tax collector
  NM *Élec (d'une dynamo etc)* ring, commutator; *Radio* **c. d'ondes** aerial; **c. d'échappement** exhaust manifold; *Aut* **c. d'admission** inlet manifold, throttle line; *Aut* **c. de sortie** *(turbine)* outlet manifold
  ADJ **égout c.** main sewer

collectif, -ive [kɔlɛktif, -iv] ADJ *(action, compte-rendu etc)* collective, joint; **billet (de train) c.** group (rail) ticket; **une vague de licenciements collectifs** a wave of mass redundancies; **ferme collective** collective (farm); **contrat c.** collective agreement; **l'inconscient c.** the collective subconscious; **radiographie collective** mass radiography; *Can Jur* **recours c.** class action suit
  NM **1** *Gram* collective noun SEE GRAMMAR A11, BB **2** *Fin* **c. budgétaire** bill of supply **3** *(association)* co-operative

collection [kɔlɛksjɔ̃] NF **1** *(action)* collecting, gathering; **depuis l'âge de dix ans, il fait la c. des timbres** he's been collecting stamps since he was ten; **tu n'as jamais fait de c.?** have you never collected anything? **2** *(de papillons etc)* collection; *(de livres)* series, collection; *Com (d'échantillons)* line; **sa c. de timbres** his stamp collection; **je possède la c. complète des Astérix** I own the complete set of Asterix stories; **pièce de c.** collector's item; **la c. d'hiver** the winter collection; **la nouvelle c. de chez Dior** Dior's new collection; *Beaux-Arts* **c. privée** private collection; *Fam* **j'en ai toute une c.** I've got a whole collection *or* set of them

collectionner [kɔlɛksjɔne] **vt** *(timbres etc)* to collect

collectionneur, -euse [kɔlɛksjɔnœr, -øz] **N** *(de timbres etc)* collector

collectivement [kɔlɛktivmɑ̃] **ADV** collectively; **protester/agir c.** to protest/act as a group

collectivisation [kɔlɛktivizasjɔ̃] **NF** *Écon* collectivization

collectiviser [kɔlɛktivize] **vt** *Écon* to collectivize

collectivisme [kɔlɛktivism] **NM** *Écon* collectivism

collectiviste [kɔlɛktivist] **ADJ, N** *Écon* collectivist

collectivité [kɔlɛktivite] **NF** **1** *(groupe)* community; **le sens de la c.** community spirit; **vie en c.** community life *or* living; *Admin* **collectivités locales** *(dans un État)* local authorities; *(dans une fédération)* federal authorities; **la c. nationale** the nation, the country; **collectivités professionnelles** professional organizations; **c. publique** government organization; **c. territoriale** = administrative division with a higher degree of autonomy than a *département* **2** *(propriété en commun)* common ownership

collector [kɔlɛktɔr] **NM** *(objet de collection)* collector's item *or* piece

collège [kɔlɛʒ] **NM 1** *Scol* school; **c. d'enseignement secondaire** ≃ secondary (modern) school, *Am* ≃ high school; *Anciennement* **c. d'enseignement technique** technical college; **c. privé** private school; **le brevet des collèges** ≃ school leaving certificate; *Univ* **le C. de France** the Collège de France *(prestigious higher education institution)* VOIR GRAMMAIRE A6 **2** *Pol* **c. électoral** electoral body *or* constituency, *surtout Am* electoral college **3** *Rel* college; **le Sacré C.** the College of Cardinals

collégial, -iale, -iaux, -iales [kɔleʒjal, -jo] **ADJ** collegial, collegiate   **NF collégiale** collegiate church

collégialité [kɔleʒjalite] **NF** *(d'une société etc)* collegial structure

collégien, -ienne [kɔleʒjɛ̃, -jɛn] **N 1** *Scol* schoolboy, schoolgirl **2** *Iron* innocent; **je n'aime pas être traité en c.** I don't like being treated like a child; **rougir comme un c.** to blush like a schoolboy; **je me suis fait avoir comme un c.** I fell for it like a fool, I should have known better

collègue [kɔlɛg] **N c. (de travail)** colleague, fellow worker, *surtout Am* co-worker

COLLER [kɔle]

VT to stick **1, 2** ▪ to glue **1** ▪ to paste **1, 6** ▪ to put **2** ▪ to keep in **3** ▪ to fail **3** ▪ to follow closely **4**
VI to stick **1** ▪ to be OK **2**
VPR to stick (together) **1** ▪ to shack up (with) **2**

---

vt 1 to stick; *(avec de la colle)* to stick, to glue, to paste **(à, sur** to, on); **c. le timbre sur l'enveloppe** to stick the stamp on the envelope; **la sueur avait collé ses cheveux** his hair was matted with sweat; **elle avait les paupières collées** her eyelids were stuck together; **c. son visage à** *ou* **contre la vitre** to press one's face to the window; **il est resté collé à la télé toute la soirée** he was glued to the TV all evening; **il est toujours le nez collé dans ses bouquins** he's always got his nose stuck in a book; **elle a toujours l'oreille collée aux portes** she's always listening at doors; *Fig* **c. qn au mur** to stick sb up against a wall (and shoot him/her)

2 *Fam (mettre)* to stick, to put; **elle a collé le paquet dans un coin** she stuck the parcel in a corner; **ils ont collé le bébé chez la grand-mère** they've dumped the baby on the grandmother; **si tu continues, je te colle en pension** carry on like that and I'll pack you off to boarding school; **on m'a collé ce boulot sans que j'aie dit oui** I got stuck *or* saddled *or Br* lumbered with this job without any say in the matter; **c. une gifle à qn** to slap sb in the face; **si tu continues, je t'en colle une!** if you don't stop, I'll give you one!; **c. une punition à qn** to punish sb; **c. une contravention à qn** to slap a fine on sb

3 c. un élève *(le retenir)* to keep a pupil in; *(lui poser une question difficile)* to catch a pupil out (with a difficult question); **c. un candidat** to fail a candidate

4 *Fam (suivre)* to follow closely; **il me colle!** he sticks to me like glue!; **arrête de me c. au derrière** *ou* **très** *Fam* **au cul!** stop following me everywhere!

5 *Ind (papier)* to size; *(produits manufacturés)* to bond; *(vin)* to clarify, to fine

6 *Ordinat* to paste; *TV etc (bande etc)* to splice; **c. et endosser** to forward

vi 1 *(adhérer)* to stick (à to); **les pâtes ont collé à la casserole** the pasta has stuck to the pan; **robe qui colle au corps** clinging dress; *Fig* **il faut essayer de c. au style de l'auteur** you must try to stick to the author's style; **la peur qui lui collait à la peau** the fear that was ingrained in him *or* that was part of him

2 *Fam (aller bien)* **ça ne colle pas entre eux** they don't hit it off; **ce qu'elle a dit ne colle pas** what she said doesn't make sense *or* doesn't add up; **leurs témoignages ne collent pas** their testimonies don't tally; **ça colle!** that's OK!; **ça ne va pas c. pour mercredi** it's no go for Wednesday

vpr se coller 1 *(adhérer)* to stick; **les feuilles se sont collées entre elles** the leaves were all stuck together; **elle se colla contre le mur** she flattened herself against the wall; **elle s'est collée contre lui** she clung to him; **c'est toi qui t'y colles** you're landed with it

2 *Arg* **se c. avec qn** to shack up with sb

collerette [kɔlrɛt] **NF 1** *(de vêtement)* collar; *Hist (fraise)* ruff **2** *Bot (de champignon)* annulus **3** *Tech (de tuyau)* flange

collet [kɔlɛ] **NM 1** *(de manteau, robe etc)* collar; **saisir qn au c.** to collar sb, to seize sb by the scruff of the neck; **la police lui mit la main au c.** the police arrested him; **elle est très c. monté** she is very prim (and proper) *or* strait-laced **2** *(cape)* short cape **3** *(de dent, vis, violon etc)* neck; *(de raquette etc)* shoulder; *Bot (de champignon etc)* neck, collar; *Culin* **c. de mouton** neck *or* scrag of mutton **4** *Tech etc (de tuyau etc)* flange, collar, fillet **5** *(pour attraper de petits animaux)* snare, noose; **prendre des lapins au c.** to snare rabbits

colleter [kɔlte] *(je collette, n. colletons; je colletterai)* **vt** to collar, to seize by the collar   **vpr se colleter** *Fam* to tussle; **se c. avec qn** to tussle *or* grapple with sb; **se c. avec les difficultés** to struggle *or* grapple with problems

colleur, -euse [kɔlœr, -øz] **N 1** *(personne qui colle)* gluer, paster; **c. d'affiches** billsticker, billposter **2** *Scol Fam* examiner   **NF** *Cin* **colleuse** (film) splicer, splicing unit

collier [kɔlje] **NM 1** *(bijou)* necklace, necklet; **c. de perles** pearl necklace, string of pearls; **c. de fleurs** garland of flowers **2** *(de chien, d'esclave etc)* collar; **cheval de c.** draught horse; **cheval franc du c.** a willing *or* hard-working horse; *Fig* **elle a toujours été franche du c.** she's always been very frank and open; *Fig* **donner un coup de c.** to put one's back into it, to make a special effort; *Fig* **reprendre le c.** to get back into harness; **c. de barbe** narrow beard, fringe of beard **3** *Tech* collar, ring; *Tech (de renfort)* clip; *Aut* clamp; **c. de serrage** clamping ring, clamp; **c. de fixation** bracket, clip; **c. de frein** brake band; **c. de palier** bearing collar **4** *Zool (d'oiseau etc)* collar, ring; **pigeon à** *ou* **au c.** ringed *or* ring-necked pigeon **5** *Culin (de bœuf, mouton)* neck

collimateur [kɔlimatœr] **NM** *Astron, Opt* collimator; *Fig* **attention, je vous ai dans mon** *ou* **le c.** careful, I've got my eye on you

colline [kɔlin] **NF** hill

collision [kɔlizjɔ̃] **NF** *(entre véhicules etc)* collision; **entrer en c. avec qch** to collide with *or* run into sth; **c. frontale** head-on collision, frontal collision; **c. latérale** side-on collision, side impact; **c. nucléaire** nuclear collision; *Fig* **c. des intérêts** clash of interests

collocation [kɔlɔkasjɔ̃] **NF 1** *Jur* establishing the order of priority of creditors *(in bankruptcy)* **2** *Ling* collocation

collodion [kɔlɔdjɔ̃] **NM** *Chimie etc* collodion

colloïdal, -ale, -aux, -ales [kɔlɔidal, -o] **ADJ** *Chimie etc* colloidal

colloïde [kɔlɔid] **NM** *Chimie* colloid

colloque [kɔlɔk] **NM 1** *(conférence)* seminar **2** *Fam (conversation)* confab; **avoir un c. avec qn** to have a confab with sb; **être en c.** to be having a confab

collusion [kɔlyzjɔ̃] **NF** *Jur etc* collusion; **c. d'intérêts** merging of interests

collusoire [kɔlyzwar] **ADJ** *Jur* collusive

collutoire [kɔlytwar] **NM** *Pharm* oral medication

collyre [kɔlir] **NM** *Pharm* eyewash, eye lotion

colmatage [kɔlmataʒ] **NM 1** *(de trous dans la route etc)* filling in; *(de trou etc)* plugging (up); *Mil (de position)* consolidation **2** *Agr (de terrain)* warping

colmater [kɔlmate] **vt** *(trous dans la route etc)* to fill in; *(trou etc)* to plug (up); *Mil (position)* to consolidate

colo [kɔlo] **NF** *abrév Fam* **colonie de vacances**

colocataire [kɔlɔkatɛr] **N** flatmate, *Am* roommate; *Jur* joint tenant, co-tenant

Colomb [kɔlɔ̃] **NM Christophe C.** Christopher Columbus

colombage [kɔlɔ̃baʒ] **NM** *Constr* half-timbering; **maison à colombages** half-timbered house

colombe [kɔlɔ̃b] **NF** *(oiseau), Pol Fig* dove; **c. biset** rock dove *or* pigeon; *Fam* **ma c.** my (little) dove

Colombie [kɔlɔ̃bi] **NF 1** Colombia **2** **la C.-Britannique** British Columbia

colombien, -ienne [kɔlɔ̃bjɛ̃, -jɛn] **ADJ** Colombian   **N C.** Colombian

colombier [kɔlɔ̃bje] **NM** *(pigeonnier)* dovecot(e), pigeon loft

colombin [kɔlɔ̃bɛ̃] **NM** *Fam (étron)* turd

Colombine [kɔlɔ̃bin] **NF** *Théâtre* Columbine

colombophile [kɔlɔ̃bɔfil] **ADJ** pigeon-fancying, pigeon-fanciers'   **N** pigeon fancier

colombophilie [kɔlɔ̃bɔfili] **NF** pigeon fancying

colon[1] [kɔlɔ̃] **NM 1** *(pionnier)* settler, colonist **2** *(enfant dans une colonie de vacances)* child (at camp) **3** *Agr* farmer, smallholder

colon² NM *Mil* Arg colonel; **ben, mon c.!** well, I'm damned!

côlon [kolɔ̃] NM *Anat* colon; **c. transverse** transverse colon

colonel [kɔlɔnɛl] NM *Mil* colonel; *Aviat* group captain, *Am* colonel; *Mil* **oui, mon c.** yes, Colonel

colonelle [kɔlɔnɛl] NF *Mil* colonel's wife; *Aviat* group captain's wife, *Am* colonel's wife

colonial, -iale, -iaux, -iales [kɔlɔnjal, -jo] ADJ colonial
NM *(habitant)* colonial; *(soldat)* soldier of the colonial troops
NF *Hist, Mil* **la coloniale** the Colonial Army

colonialisme [kɔlɔnjalism] NM *Pol* colonialism

colonialiste [kɔlɔnjalist] ADJ, N *Pol* colonialist

colonie [kɔlɔni] NF **1** *(lieu)* colony, settlement; **vivre aux colonies** to live in the colonies; **administrations des colonies** administration *or* government of the colonies, colonial administration; **c. de vacances** (children's) holiday camp, *Am* summer camp; **envoyer ses enfants en c.** to send one's children to camp; **la c. anglaise de Paris** the English colony in Paris; **c. pénitentiaire** penal settlement *or* colony **2** *(d'animaux)* colony

> ### Colonie de vacances
> The "colonie de vacances" or "colo" is an integral part of childhood for many French people. The children's parents do not stay with them at the "colonie", the group being supervised by "moniteurs" or "animateurs" (group leaders), who organize games and activities.

colonisateur, -trice [kɔlɔnizatœr, -tris] ADJ *(nation etc)* colonizing
N colonizer

colonisation [kɔlɔnizasjɔ̃] NF colonization, settlement; *Fig* invasion

coloniser [kɔlɔnize] VT *(région)* to colonize, to settle

colonnade [kɔlɔnad] NF *Archit* colonnade

colonnage [kɔlɔnaʒ] NM putting into columns

colonne [kɔlɔn] NF **1** *Archit* column, pillar; **lit à colonnes** four-poster bed **2** *(file de personnes, soldats, choses)* column; **c. par deux/trois/quatre** column of twos/threes/fours; **c. de secours** relief column; **c. de véhicules en marche** column of moving vehicles; *Pol* **cinquième c.** fifth column **3** *(d'un dictionnaire, journal)* column; **disposé en colonnes** tabular; *Journ* **écrire une c.** to write *or* have a column; **comme je l'écrivais hier dans ces colonnes** as I wrote yesterday in these pages; *Journ* **cinq colonnes à la une** a front-page five-column spread; *Math* **dans la c. des dizaines** in the tens column; **des colonnes de chiffres/de noms** columns of figures/names ▸▸ *Compta* **c. créditrice/débitrice** credit/debit column; *Aut* **c. de direction** steering column; **c. de fumée** column *or* plume of smoke; *Naut* **c. d'habitacle** binnacle; **c. de mercure** column of mercury; **c. montante** *Ind* rising main, riser (pipe); *Élec* service cable, service conductor, riser; **c. Morris** = pillar used to advertise forthcoming events; *Journ* **c. rédactionnelle** editorial column; *Anat* **c. vertébrale** spinal column, spine

colonnette [kɔlɔnɛt] NF *Archit* small column, colonnette

colopathie [kɔlɔpati] NF *Méd* colitis

colophane [kɔlɔfan] NF rosin, colophony

coloquinte [kɔlɔkɛ̃t] NF **1** *(plante)* colocynth, bitter apple **2** *Arg (tête)* nut, *Br* bonce

colorant [kɔlɔrɑ̃] ADJ *(matière etc)* colouring, *Am* coloring
NM **1** *(pour teindre)* colorant, dye **2** *(alimentaire)* colouring, *Am* coloring; **sirop garanti sans c.** syrup guaranteed free from (artificial) colour(s)

coloration [kɔlɔrasjɔ̃] NF **1** *(fait de colorer)* colouring, *Am* coloring; *(de daguerréotype etc)* tinting; **se faire faire une c.** to have one's hair tinted; *Fig Litt* **la tristesse donnait une c. inhabituelle à sa voix** sadness had altered his tone of voice; *Fig* **c. politique** politics, political colour **2** *(de la peau)* colour(ing), *Am* color(ing)

colorature [kɔlɔratyr] NF *Mus* coloratura

coloré [kɔlɔre] ADJ coloured, *Am* colored; **teint c.** florid *or* ruddy complexion; *Fig* **style c.** colourful *or Am* colorful style

colorer [kɔlɔre] VT to colour, *Am* to color; **c. qch en vert** to colour sth green; *Fig* **c. un récit** to lend colour to a tale
VPR **se colorer** *(de fruit)* to colour, *Am* to color; *(de visage)* to become flushed; **sa voix s'est colorée de tendresse** a note of tenderness crept into his voice

coloriage [kɔlɔrjaʒ] NM *(action)* colouring, *Am* coloring; *(dessin)* coloured *or Am* colored drawing; **album** *ou* **livre de c.** colouring(-in) book

colorier [kɔlɔrje] VT *(impf, pr sub n. coloriions, v. coloriiez)* *(carte, dessin)* to colour *or Am* color (in); **c. qch en rouge/en bleu** to colour sth red/blue

coloris [kɔlɔri] NM shade; *(de tableau, fruit etc)* colours, *Am* colors; *Com* **carte de c.** shade card; **disponible en quatre c.** available in four shades *or* colours; *(combinaison de couleurs)* available in four colourways

colorisation [kɔlɔrizasjɔ̃] NF *Cin* colourization, *Am* colorization

coloriser [kɔlɔrize] VT *Cin* to colourize, *Am* to colorize

coloriste [kɔlɔrist] N **1** *Beaux-Arts* colourist, *Am* colorist **2** *(de cartes postales, jouets etc)* colourer, *Am* colorer, painter **3** *(coiffeur)* colourist, *Am* colorist

colossal, -ale, -aux, -ales [kɔlɔsal, -o] ADJ *(somme)* colossal, huge, gigantic; *(énergie)* colossal, enormous

colossalement [kɔlɔsalmɑ̃] ADV colossally, hugely

colosse [kɔlɔs] NM *(statue)* colossus; *(homme, institution)* giant; **le C. de Rhodes** the Colossus of Rhodes; *Fig* **un c. aux pieds d'argile** a giant with feet of clay

colostomie [kɔlɔstɔmi] NF *Chir* colostomy; **subir une c.** to have a colostomy

colostrum [kɔlɔstrɔm] NM *Physiol* colostrum

colportage [kɔlpɔrtaʒ] NM *(de marchandises)* hawking, peddling; **c. de fausses nouvelles** spreading of rumours

colporter [kɔlpɔrte] VT *(marchandises)* to hawk, to peddle; *(nouvelle, rumeurs)* to spread

colporteur, -euse [kɔlpɔrtœr, -øz] N hawker, pedlar; *Péj* **c. de ragots** gossipmonger

colposcopie [kɔlpɔskɔpi] NF *Méd* colposcopy

colt [kɔlt] NM Colt®

coltinage [kɔltinaʒ] NM *(d'une charge sur le dos)* porterage, carrying

coltiner [kɔltine] VT *(charges)* to carry on one's back
VPR **se coltiner** *Fam* **se c. qn/qch** to get stuck *or* landed *or Br* lumbered with sb/sth

coltineur [kɔltinœr] NM porter *(who carries heavy loads)*; **c. de charbon** coal heaver

columbarium [kɔlɔ̃barjɔm] NM columbarium

colvert [kɔlvɛr] NM *(oiseau)* mallard

colza [kɔlza] NM *(plante)* rape, colza; **huile de c.** rapeseed oil, colza oil

coma [kɔma] NM *Méd* coma; **être dans le c.** to be in a coma; **tomber dans le c.** to go *or* lapse into a coma; **il est dans un c. dépassé** he's brain-dead

comarketing [komarketiŋ] NM comarketing

comateux, -euse [kɔmatø, -øz] *Méd* ADJ comatose
N patient in a coma

combat [kɔ̃ba] NM **1** *Mil (bataille)* fight, battle; *(activité)* combat; **c. corps à corps** hand-to-hand fight; *(activité)* hand-to-hand fighting; **c. aérien** dog fight; *(activité)* aerial combat; **c. naval** naval engagement *or* action; *(activité)* naval combat; **c. terrestre** land operation; *(activité)* land fighting; **tenue de c.** battledress; **gaz de c.** nerve gas; **c. de rue** street fight; **engager le c.** to go into action (**avec qn** against sb); **mettre hors de c.** to disable, to put out of action; **hors de c.** disabled, out of action; *(régiment)* out of action
2 *(dispute)* fight; **c. de boxe** boxing match; **c. de coqs** cockfight
3 *Fig (lutte)* fight; **c. contre la mort** fight against death; **le c. contre l'inflation** the battle *or* fight against inflation; **c'est un c. quotidien** it's a daily struggle; **même c.!** we're fighting for the same thing!; **continuons le c.!** the fight goes on!

combatif, -ive [kɔ̃batif, -iv] ADJ combative, pugnacious; **esprit c.** fighting spirit; **il n'a rien de c.** he's no fighter
N fighter, battler

combativité [kɔ̃bativite] NF combativeness, pugnacity

combattant [kɔ̃batɑ̃] ADJ fighting, combatant; *Mil* **unité combattante** combatant *or* fighting unit
NM **1** *(soldat)* combatant, fighter; **anciens combattants** ex-servicemen, *Am* veterans **2** *(dans une dispute)* fighter, brawler **3** *(oiseau)* ruff **4** *Mktg* **c. de front** front-line person

combattre [kɔ̃batr] *(conj like battre)* VT *(ennemi)* to fight (against); *(maladie, théorie)* to fight; *(inflation etc)* to combat, to fight
VI to fight; **c. pour/contre qn/qch** to fight for/against sb/sth

combe [kɔ̃b] NF *Géog* coomb, anticlinal valley

COMBIEN [kɔ̃bjɛ̃] ADV *(conj when introducing a clause)* **1** *(comme)* how (much); **si tu savais c. je t'aime!** if you knew how (much) I love you!; **j'ai pu constater c. tu avais changé** I could see how much you'd changed; **c. crédules sont tous ces hommes!** how gullible all these men are!
2 *(en nombre)* how many; **c. de** how many; **c. de fois?** how many times?, how often?; **c. sont-ils?** how many (of them) are there?; **je ne sais pas c. il y en a** I don't know how many (of them) there are; **c'est à c. de kilomètres d'ici?** how many kilometres away is it? how far (away) is it?; **et c. de gens furent tués dans cette guerre!** what a lot of people were killed in that war!
3 *(en quantité)* how much; **c. de** how much; **c. vous dois-je?** how much do I owe you?; **tu veux c.?** *(d'argent)* how much do you want?; *Fam* **ça fait c.?, c'est c.?** how much (is that)?, how much does that come to?; **depuis c. de temps est-il ici?** how long has he been here?; **il y en a pour c. de temps?** how long will it take?; **tu en as pour c. de temps?** how long will it take you?, how long will you be?; **c. de**

temps vous a-t-il fallu pour venir? how long did it take you to come?; **c'est arrivé il y a je ne sais c. de temps** it happened such a long time ago; **c. y a-t-il d'ici à Londres?** how far is it (from here) to London?; **à c. sommes-nous de Paris?** how far are we from Paris?; **c. pèse-t-elle?** how much does she weigh?; **c. mesure-t-il?** how tall is he?; **elle est enceinte – de c.?** she's pregnant – how far gone is she orhow many months?; **il a fait c. au saut à la perche?** how high did he jump in the pole vault?, what was his height in the pole vault?

NM INV *Fam* **le c. sommes-nous?, on est le c. aujourd'hui?** what's the date (today)?, what's today's date?; **il y a un c. pour les bus?** how often is there a bus?; **tu chausses du c.?** what's your shoe size?, what shoe size are you?, what shoe size do you take?

combientième [kɔ̃bjɛ̃tjɛm] *Fam*ADJ **tu as été reçu c. à l'examen?** where did you come in the exam?; **tu es c. dans la liste?** where are you on the list?, what position are you in the list?; **c'est la c. fois que tu viens?** how often have you been now?

N elle est arrivée la c.? where did she come in?; **tu veux le c.?** which of them do you want?

combinaison [kɔ̃binɛzɔ̃] NF **1** *(de lettres, d'idées etc)*, *Math, Chimie* combination; *(de coffre-fort, cadenas)* combination; **c. financière** combine; **la c. gagnante** *(au tiercé)* the winning combination (of numbers); **une heureuse c. de couleurs** a pleasing combination of colours orcolour scheme; *Ordinat* **c. de touches** key combination **2** *(solution)* scheme, plan **3** *(vêtement)* *(tenue de travail)* boiler suit; *Aviat* flying suit; *(de femme)* slip; **c. de plongée** *ou* **de planche à voile** wet suit

combinard, -arde [kɔ̃binar, -ard] *Fam* ADJ scheming, devious; **il est c.** he's a real schemer

N schemer

combinateur [kɔ̃binatœr] NM *Élec* controller, multiple-contact *ou*selector switch; *Rail* switchgroup

combinatoire [kɔ̃binatwar] ADJ combinative; *Math* combinatorial

combine [kɔ̃bin] NF *Fam* scheme, trick; **il a une c. pour entrer sans payer** he knows a way of getting in without paying; **il a trouvé la c. pour se faire embaucher** he's found a way of getting taken on; **il faut le mettre dans la c.** we'll have to let orbring him in on it

combiné [kɔ̃bine] ADJ *(action etc)* combined, joint

NM 1 *Chimie* compound **2 c. (téléphonique)** receiver, handset **3** *(hi-fi)* radiogram; *Radio etc* **c. micro-casque** headset **4** *Ski* combined downhill and slalom competition **5** *Vieilli* *(sous-vêtement)* corselet

combiner [kɔ̃bine] VT **1** *(forces, efforts etc)* to combine, to unite; *(nombres, idées etc)*, *Chimie* to combine **2** *Fam* *(plan)* to devise, to think out, to concoct; **qu'est-ce que tu as combiné?** what have you come up with?; **elle combine un sale coup** she's plotting something nasty, she's planning a dirty trick

VPR se combiner to combine, to go together **(à, avec** with)

comble [kɔ̃bl] NM **1** *(maximum)* *(du bonheur, de l'insolence)* height; *(du désespoir)* depth; *(de la gloire etc)* height, peak, summit; **le c. du ridicule serait de …** it would be the height of absurdity to …; **pour c. de malheur** to cap or crown it all; **ça, c'est le** *ou* **un c.!** that's the limit or the last straw!; **elle était au c. de la joie** she was overjoyed, she was beside herself with joy **2** *Archit* *(en bois)* roof timbers; *(en métal)* roof structure; **c. à deux pans** span roof; **c. brisé** curb roof; **loger sous les combles** to live in an/the attic; **combles aménageables** attic suitable for conversion;

Fig **de fond en c.** from top to bottom; **modifier une organisation de fond en c.** to effect a major shake-up of an organization, to make sweeping changes in an organization ADJ *(train, autobus, pièce etc)* (jam-)packed; *(mesure)* piled high; *Théâtre* **on a fait salle c.** we had a full *or*capacity house; *Fig* **la mesure est c.** enough is enough, that's the limit

comblé [kɔ̃ble] ADJ *(personne)* happy, contented, satisfied; **il est c.** he has everything he could wish for

combler [kɔ̃ble] VT **1** *(puits, fossé, trou etc)* to fill in, to fill (up); *(une perte)* to make up, to make good; *(découvert)* to pay off; **c. une lacune** to fill a gap; **c. un besoin** to satisfy a need; **c. un retard** to make up for lost time **2** *(satisfaire)* *(personne)* to satisfy; **c. les vœux de qn** to fulfil *or*satisfy sb's desires; **vous me comblez** you are too kind, I'm overwhelmed; **c. qn de cadeaux** to shower sb with gifts; **elle a été comblée par la nature** she has been blessed by nature

comburant [kɔ̃byrã] *Chimie etc* ADJ combustive

NM combustive agent; *Astronaut* oxidant

combustibilité [kɔ̃bystibilite] NF combustibility

combustible [kɔ̃bystibl] ADJ combustible; **assemblage d'éléments combustibles** fuel assembly

NM fuel; *(de fusée)* propellant, fuel; **c. nucléaire** nuclear fuel; **c. liquide** liquid fuel

combustion [kɔ̃bystjɔ̃] NF combustion; **poêle à c. lente** slow-combustion stove; **c. vive** external combustion; **moteur à c. interne** internal combustion engine; **c. détonante** detonation, combustion knock

Côme [kom] NF Como; **le lac de C.** Lake Como

come-back [kɔmbak] NM INV *(d'une vedette)* come-back; **faire un c.** to make a come-back

comédie [kɔmedi] NF **1** *Théâtre* *(pièce comique, genre)* comedy; **la c. et la tragédie** comedy and tragedy; **jouer la c.** to act; *Fig* to put on an act; **allons! pas de c.!** come on, stop acting!; **c'est une vraie c. quand il faut aller à l'école** it's a real fuss *or* palaver when it's time to go to school; **c'est toujours la même c.** it's the same old thing *or* story every time **2** *Arch* *(pièce de théâtre)* play

▸▸ **c. de caractères** character comedy; **c. dramatique** drama; **c. de mœurs** comedy of manners; **c. musicale** musical; **c. de situation** situation comedy

Comédie–Française

This state-subsidized company dates back to the seventeenth century; the theatre itself, officially called "le Théâtre-Français" or "le Français", is situated in the rue Richelieu in Paris. Its repertoire consists mainly of classical works, although modern plays are sometimes staged. Actors who perform in the Comédie-Française fall into two categories: the "sociétaires" who are fully-fledged members of the company, and the "pensionnaires" who work with the company on a fixed salary but are not shareholders in it.

comédien, -ienne [kɔmedjɛ̃, -jɛn] N *(acteur)* actor, f actress; *(acteur comique)* comic actor, f comedienne; *Fig* show-off; **comédiens ambulants** strolling players; *Fig* **c'est une comédienne** she is always putting on an act

ADJ **il est très c.** he's very theatrical *or*affected; **être plus c. que tragédien** to be more of a comic than a tragic actor

> Il faut noter que le nom anglais **comedian** est un faux ami. Il signifie **comique**.

comédon [kɔmedɔ̃] NM blackhead

comestible [kɔmɛstibl] ADJ edible; **denrées comestibles** food, foodstuffs, *Fml* comestibles

NMPL **comestibles** food, foodstuffs, *Fml* comestibles

comète [kɔmɛt] NF **1** *Astron* comet; *(feu d'artifice)* sky rocket; **l'année de la C.** the year of the comet *(1811, when Halley's Comet was seen for the first time)*; *Fig* **tirer** *ou* **faire des plans sur la c.** to build castles in Spain, to indulge in pipe-dreams **2** *(tranchefile)* headband

comice [kɔmis] NM **1 c. agricole** agricultural association; **comices agricoles** *(foire)* agricultural show **2** *Hist* **comices** electoral meeting

comics [kɔmiks] NMPL comic strips, cartoon strips, *surtout Am Fam* funnies

comique [kɔmik] ADJ **1** *Théâtre* *(acteur, auteur, rôle etc)* comic; **le genre c.** comedy **2** *(amusant)* *(histoire, visage etc)* comical, funny

NM 1 *(genre)* comedy; *(acteur)* comic actor; *(auteur)* comic author, writer of comedy; *(boute-en-train)* comic, comedian; **c. de répétition** comedy based on repetition; **c. de situation** situation comedy; **c. troupier** *(genre)* coarse *or* vulgar comedy **2 le c. de l'histoire, c'est que …** the funny part or the joke is that …

> Attention: ne pas confondre **comic** et **comical** lorsqu'on traduit l'adjectif **comique**. Le terme **comic** se rapporte au genre comique, alors que **comical** signifie **amusant**. En outre, l'adjectif **comic** ne s'utilise jamais comme attribut.

comiquement [kɔmikmã] ADV comically

comité [kɔmite] NM VOIR GRAMMAIRE A11 committee; **faire partie d'un c.** to sit on a committee; **cette décision sera prise en petit c.** the decision will be made by a select group; **ils se sont mariés en petit c.** they had a quiet wedding; **pour leur anniversaire, ils seront en petit c.** they'll celebrate their anniversary with just a few friends (and relations); **un dîner en petit c.** a small dinner party

▸▸ **c. consultatif** advisory committee *or* board; **c. de direction** executive *or*management committee; **c. d'enquête** board of enquiry; **c. d'entreprise** works council *or* committee; **C. européen de normalisation** European Standards Commission; **c. d'hygiène et de sécurité** health and safety committee; **C. international olympique** International Olympic Committee; **c. de lecture** reading *or* selection committee; **c. secret** secret session; *Mktg* **c. synectique** idea committee; **c. d'usagers** users' committee

Comité d'entreprise

The "Comité d'entreprise" or "CE" looks after the general welfare of company employees and organizes subsidised leisure activities, outings, holidays etc. It also deals with industrial problems.

commandant, -ante [kɔmãdã, -ãt] NM **1** *(officier)* *(d'unité etc)* commander, commanding officer; *(de camp, base etc)* commandant; *Naut* *(de bateau)* captain *(whatever his rank)*; **c. en chef** commander-in-chief; *Naut* executive officer, first lieutenant; *Aviat* **c. de bord** captain **2** *(rang)*, *Mil* major; *Mil, Aviat* squadron leader, *Am* major; **c. en chef des forces aériennes** ≃ Marshal of the Royal Air Force, *Am* ≃ General of the Air Force

NF commandante commanding officer's wife

commande [kɔmɑ̃d] **NF 1** *Com* order; **faire** *ou* **passer une c.** to put in *or* place an order; **livrer une c.** to deliver an order; **fait sur c.** made to order; **ouvrage écrit sur la c. de l'éditeur** work commissioned by the publisher; **payable à la c.** payment with order, cash with order; **c. export** export order; **c. ferme** firm order; **c. renouvelée** repeat order; **c. téléphonique, c. par téléphone** telephone order; *Fig* **sourire de c.** forced smile; **on ne peut pas rire sur c.** you can't laugh to order

2 *Tech (action)* control, operation; *(dispositif)* control; *(mécanisme)* drive, driving (gear); **c. à distance** remote control; **c. manuelle/à pied** hand *or* manual/foot control; **c'est à c. manuelle** it has hand *or* manual controls, it is manually controlled; **levier de c.** control lever; *Aviat* control column; **prendre les commandes** *(d'un avion etc)* to take over the controls; *(d'une société etc)* to take over, to take control; **avion à double c.** dual-control plane; *Élec* **machine à c. électrique** electrically driven machine; *Aut* **c. d'allumage** ignition trigger; *Aut* **c. de démarreur** starter switch; *Aut* **c. de starter** choke control; *Aut* **c. de vitesse de croisière** cruise control; **c. par poignée** *(d'une moto etc)* twist grip; **c. tactile** *(des vitres d'une voiture etc)* one-touch operation; *Aut* **c. électronique du moteur** engine management system; *Aut* **commandes de conduite** driving controls

3 *Ordinat* command; **c. d'annulation** undo command; **c. à bascule** toggle switch; **c. binaire** bit command; **c. de copie** copy command; **c. DOS** DOS command; **c. écran précédent** screen up command; **c. écran suivant** screen down command; **c. d'effacement** delete command; **c. erronée** bad command; **c. de formatage** formatting command; **c. imbriquée** embedded command; **c. d'insertion** insert command; **c. numérique** digital control; **à c. numérique** digitally controlled *or* operated; **c. de recherche** search *or* find command; **c. de recherche et remplacement** search and replace command, find and replace command; **c. de sauvegarde** save command; **c. de soulignage** underline command; **c. du système d'exploitation** operating system command; **à c. vocale** voice-activated

commandement [kɔmɑ̃dmɑ̃] **NM 1** *(ordre)* command, order; *Jur* summons to pay before execution; **dès que je vous en donnerai le c., à mon c.** when I give the command *or* order, on my command; *Rel* **les Dix Commandements** the Ten Commandments **2** *(pouvoir)* command; **avoir/prendre le c.** to be in/take command; **avoir le c. sur ...** to be in command of ..., to have command over ...; *Mil, Naut* **c. en chef** command-in-chief; **c. suprême, haut c.** high command

commander [kɔmɑ̃de] **VT 1** *(diriger)* to command, to be in command of; *(ordonner)* to command, to order; **il commande deux cents hommes** he has two hundred men under his command; **il n'aime pas qu'on le commande** he doesn't like being ordered about; *Fam* **sans vouloir vous c., est-ce que vous pourriez fermer la fenêtre?** I don't want to give orders, but could you close the window? **2** *(marchandises, dîner etc)* to order; *(peinture, ouvrage)* to commission; **c. qch à qn** to order/commission sth from sb; **c. qch par correspondance** to order sth by mail *or* Br

through the post, to mail-order sth; **c. qch par téléphone** to order sth by phone *or* over the phone **3** *(susciter)* to command; **c. le respect/l'attention** to command respect/attention **4** *(dominer)* *(vallée etc)* to dominate, to command **5** *(maîtriser)* *(sentiment, réaction etc)* to control **6** *Tech (mouvement, valve etc)* to control; *(machine, arbre etc)* to drive **7** *Ordinat* to drive; **commandé par menu** menu-driven; **commandé à la voix** voice-activated

VI je lui ai commandé de se taire I told *or* ordered him to be quiet; **qui est-ce qui commande ici?** who's in charge here?; **avez-vous déjà commandé?** *(au restaurant)* have you ordered yet?

VPR se commander 1 ces choses-là ne se commandent pas *(sont incontrôlables)* these things are beyond our control; **il faut apprendre à vous c.** you must learn to control yourself **2 les pièces de cet appartement se commandent** the rooms of this flat connect up *or* communicate with each other

commanderie [kɔmɑ̃dri] **NF** *(résidence)* commander's residence

commandeur [kɔmɑ̃dœr] **NM** commander

commanditaire [kɔmɑ̃diter] **ADJ, NM** *Com* **(associé) c.** sleeping *or Am* silent partner; **nous ne savons pas qui sont les commanditaires de l'attentat** we don't know who is behind the attack

commandite [kɔmɑ̃dit] **NF** *Com* **1 (société en)** mixed liability company, limited partnership **2** *(fonds)* interest *or* capital invested by sleeping partner(s)

commandité [kɔmɑ̃dite] **ADJ, NM** *Com* **(associé) c.** active partner, general partner

commanditer [kɔmɑ̃dite] **VT** to finance; *Mktg (tournoi, spectacle)* to sponsor; *(meurtre, attentat etc)* to be behind

commando [kɔmɑ̃do] **NM** *Mil* commando (unit) VOIR GRAMMAIRE A12

COMME [kɔm]

ADV as **1, 7, 8** ▪ like **1, 6** ▪ alike **1** ▪ as if *(comme si)* **2** ▪ like that *(comme ça)* **4** ▪ such as **6** ▪ in the way of **8** ▪ how *(interjection)* **9**
CONJ as **1, 2** ▪ since **1**

ADV 1 *(comparaison)* as; *(de la même manière)* like; **faites c. moi** do as I do; **se conduire c. un fou** to behave like a madman; **il n'est pas c. les autres** he isn't like the others; **tous furent appelés à participer à l'effort de guerre, les femmes c. les hommes** they were all called upon to join in the war effort, men and women alike; **sortir tous les jours, été c. hiver** to go out every day, summer and winter alike; **tout le monde fera la vaisselle, toi c. les autres** everyone will do the washing-up, and that includes *or* goes for you as well as the others; **tout c. un autre** (just) like anyone else; **nous étions c. un seul homme** we were as one man; **c. qui dirait** as one might say; **c. dit l'autre** as they say; **rusé c. un (vieux) renard** (as) sly *or* cunning as a fox; **doux c. un agneau** (as) gentle as a lamb; **haut c. trois pommes** knee-high to a grasshopper; **blanc c. neige** snow-white, white as snow; *Fam* **c. par hasard** as if by chance; **c. prévu** as planned; **il a été puni c. de juste** he's got his just deserts, he's been punished as he deserved; **quelque chose c. deux cents personnes** something like two hundred people; **A c. abricot** A as in apricot; *(en apprenant l'alphabet)* A is for apricot

2 c. (si) *(si is expressed only before a finite verb)* as if, as though; **il travaille c. s'il avait vingt ans** he works as if *or* as though he were twenty, he works like a twenty-year-old; **ils faisaient c. si rien ne s'était passé** they acted as if *or* as though nothing had happened; **c. si de rien n'était** as if *or* as though nothing had happened; **c. si je ne le savais pas!** as if I didn't know!; **tu n'es pas content, mais tu n'as qu'à faire c. si** you're not happy, but you can act as if *or* as though you are; **il leva la main c. pour me frapper** he lifted his hand as if *or* as though to strike me; *Fam* **c'est tout c.** it comes *or* amounts to the same thing

3 c. quoi je ne m'étais pas trompé! which only goes to show I was right!; *Fam* **voici un certificat c. quoi j'ai été malade** here's a certificate to say that I've been ill

4 c. ça like that; *Fam* **c'est c. ça et c'est pas autrement** that's the way it is; **alors c. ça, on fait le mur?** so we're making a run for it, are we?; **(alors) c. ça, vous venez de Paris?** so you come from Paris?; **elle est toujours c. ça?** is she always like that?; **puisque c'est c. ça, je m'en vais** if that's the way it is *or* things are, I'm going; **elle était grande comment, ta truite? – c. ça!** how big was your trout? – this big!; *Fam* **il me fait c. ça ...** he says to me just like that ...; **comment ça va? – c. ci c. ça** how are you? – so-so

5 drôle c. tout as funny as anything, incredibly funny; **c'est mignon c. tout!** it's as cute as anything! it's so cute!; **c'est facile c. tout!** it's as easy as pie!, it's dead easy!

6 *(tel que)* such as, like; **les bois durs c. le chêne et le noyer** hard woods such as *or* like oak and walnut

7 *(immediately before finite verbs)* as; **faites c. il vous plaira** *ou* **vous voulez** do as you please; **insolent c. il est** insolent as he is; **belle c. elle est, elle n'aura pas de mal à trouver un mari** being as beautiful as she is, she won't have any trouble finding a husband; **c'est arrivé à peu près c. je l'avais prédit** it happened more or less as I predicted; **des montres c. on n'en fait plus maintenant** the kind of watches they don't make any more

8 *(en tant que)* as, in the way of; **qu'est-ce que vous avez c. légumes?** what have you got in the way of vegetables?, what (kinds of) vegetables do you have?; **avoir qn c. ami** to have sb as a friend; **je l'ai eue c. professeur** I had her as my *or* a teacher; **il a été vendu c. esclave** he was sold as a slave; **ce n'est pas mal c. film** it's not bad as films go

9 *int* how; **c. vous avez grandi!** how you've grown!; **c. elle est bête!** how stupid she is!; **c. je suis content de vous voir!** how glad I am to see you!, am I glad to see you!; **c. tu as de grandes dents!** what big teeth you have!; **c. de bien entendu, il ne m'a pas appelé** as I might have known, he didn't call me; **c. c'est curieux! j'aurais juré l'avoir laissé là!** how odd! I could have sworn I left it there!; *Fam* **c. tu y vas!** that's a bit much!

10 *Fam (comment)* how; **il y est arrivé Dieu sait c.** he managed it, God (only) knows how; **voilà c. elle est** that's just like her; **elle a fait les carreaux, faut voir c.!** you should see the way she's done the windows!

11 *Fam* **elle a eu c. une hésitation avant de répondre** she seemed to hesitate before answering; **il était c. pantelant** he seemed to be gasping for breath; **à mon avis, on a c. un problème** I think we've got a bit of a problem (here); **j'ai c. l'impression qu'on s'est trompé de route** I have a feeling we're on the wrong road; **il y a là c. un hic!** there seems to be a bit of a catch!; **j'étais c. hypnotisé** it was as if *or* as though I was hypnotized

CONJ SEE GRAMMAR B58 **1** *(puisque)* as, since, seeing that; **c. vous êtes mon ami, je vous dirai tout** as *or* since *or* seeing that you're my friend, I'll tell you everything

2 *(alors que)* (just) as; **c. il allait frapper, on l'arrêta** (just) as he was about to strike, he was arrested

commémoratif, -ive [kɔmemɔratif, -iv] **ADJ** commemorative (**de** of); **service c.** memorial service; **monument c.** memorial

commémoration [kɔmemɔrasjɔ̃] **NF** commemoration; **en c. d'un événement/d'une personne** in commemoration of an event/a person

commémorer [kɔmemɔre] **VT** to commemorate

commençant, -ante [kɔmɑ̃sɑ̃, -ɑ̃t] **ADJ** **une fièvre commençante** the beginnings of a fever; **se lever au jour c.** to get up at daybreak ▪ **N** beginner; **manuel pour grands commençants** handbook for complete beginners

commencement [kɔmɑ̃smɑ̃] **NM** beginning, start; **commencements** beginnings, initial stage(s); **au c.** at the beginning or start or outset; *Bible* **au c. était le verbe** in the beginning was the word; **du c. jusqu'à la fin** from beginning to end, from start to finish; **il faut un c. à tout** you've got to start somewhere; *Fam* **c'est le c. de la fin** it's the beginning of the end

▌**COMMENCER** [kɔmɑ̃se] (**je commençai(s), n. commençons**) **VT 1** *(entreprendre)* to begin, to start (on), *Fml* to commence; **c. les hostilités** *ou* **la guerre** to commence hostilities, to start a war; **c. un traitement** to go on *or* start a course of treatment; **nous avons mal commencé l'année** we've made a bad start to the year; *Vieilli* **c. un élève en chimie** to give a pupil a grounding in chemistry
2 *(être au début de)* to begin, to start (**par** with); **le mot qui commence la phrase** the word which starts the sentence
3 *Typ* **c. en retrait** to indent
VI to begin, to start, *Fml* to commence; **c. à** *ou* **de faire qch** to begin *or* start to do sth, to begin *or* start doing sth; **l'année commence le 1er janvier** the year begins *or* starts on 1 January; **il commence à pleuvoir** it's beginning *or* starting to rain; **la pluie vient de c.** it's just started raining; **c. par faire qch** to begin *or* start by doing sth; **commençons par votre frère/le commencement** let's start *or* begin with your brother/at the beginning; **pour c., je dois vous dire …** to begin with *or* to start with *or* first of all, I must tell you …; **par où c.?** *(il y a tellement de choses à dire)* where should *or* shall I begin?; **nous allions c. sans vous** we were going to start *or* begin without you; **à c. par …** beginning *or* starting with …; **je commence à en avoir assez!** I've had just about enough!; *Fam* **ça commence à bien faire** it's getting a bit too much, it's getting beyond a joke; *Iron* **ça commence bien!** that's a great start!; *Fam* **tu ne vas pas c.!, ne commence pas!** don't start!; *Enf* **c'est lui qui a commencé!** he started it!

commensal, -ale, -aux, -ales [kɔmɑ̃sal, -o] **N 1** *(hôte)* table companion **2** *Biol* commensal

commensurable [kɔmɑ̃syrabl] **ADJ** commensurable (**avec** with, to)

comment [kɔmɑ̃] **ADV 1** *interr* how; **c. allez-vous?** how are you?; **c. (dites-vous)?** I beg your pardon?, what did you say?; **c. faire?** what can *or* should I/we/etc do?, what's to be done?; **c. s'appelle-t-il?** what's his name?, what's he called?; **c. dit-on 'soleil' en japonais?** how do you say 'sun' in Japanese?; **c. est-il, ce garçon?** what's this young man like?, what sort of young man is he?; **c. peut-il me dire des choses pareilles?** how can he talk to me like that *or* say such things to me?; **c. se fait-il que vous soyez toujours en retard?** how *or* why is it that you're always late?

2 *(affirmation)* how, the way; **elle me dira c. faire** she'll tell me how (to do it); **il faut voir c. elle lui parle** you should hear the way *or* how she speaks to him; **faire qch n'importe c.** to do sth in a slapdash manner *or Fam* anyhow *or* any old how
3 *int* what!; **c.! vous n'êtes pas encore parti!** what! haven't you gone yet!; **mais c. donc!** why of course!, by all means!; *Fam* **ça vous a plu? – et c.!** did you like it? – and how! *or* you bet!
NM INV les pourquoi et les c. the whys and wherefores

commentaire [kɔmɑ̃tɛr] **NM 1** *(remarque)* comment, remark; **faire des commentaires** to make comments *or* remarks; **je te dispense de tes commentaires** I don't need *or* I can do without your comments; **un c. pertinent** a pertinent observation; *Fam* **cela se passe de c.** it speaks for itself, it's obvious; *Fam* **sans c.!**, *pas de c.!* no comment!; *Fam* **je ne veux pas de c.!** that's final!, don't argue!; *Péj* **les commentaires vont bon train** comment is rife **2** *Radio, TV* commentary; *(lecture d'un texte préparé)* narration; **c. sportif** sports commentary; **c. en direct** live commentary; **c. sur image** voice-over, voice-over narration; **c. en voix off** off-screen narration
▸ ▸ *Scol* **c. de texte** textual commentary

commentateur, -trice [kɔmɑ̃tatœr, -tris] **N** *Radio, TV* commentator; **c. sportif** sports commentator
NM *Littér* commentator

commenter [kɔmɑ̃te] **VT 1** *(expliquer)* *(texte)* to comment on; *Radio, TV* **c. une course** to do the commentary for *or* to give the commentary on a race; **c. l'actualité** *ou* **les événements** to comment on current events **2** *(donner son avis sur)* to comment on

commérage [kɔmeraʒ] **NM** *Fam* (piece of) gossip; **commérages** gossip, tittle-tattle

commerçant, -ante [kɔmɛrsɑ̃, -ɑ̃t] **ADJ** commercial; **quartier c.** shopping area; **rue très commerçante** busy shopping street; **un sourire c.** a PR-type smile; **il n'est pas très c.** he doesn't look after his customers very well
▪ **N** trader, merchant; *(qui tient un magasin)* shopkeeper; **c. en gros** wholesaler; **c. en détail** retailer; **commerçants** traders, tradespeople; **petits commerçants** small traders *or* shopkeepers

commerce [kɔmɛrs] **NM 1** **le c.** *(activité)* trade; *(secteur)* trade, commerce; *(affaires)* business, trade; **c. de demi-gros** cash and carry; **c. en** *ou* **de gros/détail** wholesale/retail trade; **le petit c.** shopkeepers, small traders; **c. équitable** fair trade; **c. éthique** ethical trading, ethical trade; **c. intérieur/extérieur** home/foreign *or* overseas trade; **c. international** world trade, international trade; **il est dans le c.** he's in business; **ça se trouve dans le c.** you can buy it in the shops; **maison de c.** firm; **voyageur de c.** commercial traveller, sales rep(resentative); **école de c.** business school; **port de c.** commercial port; **faire du c.** to trade, to be in business; **faire du c. avec le Japon** to do business with Japan, to have business dealings with Japan; **faire le c. de qch** to trade in sth; **cela fait marcher le c.** it's good for business *or* trade; **hors c.** not for (general) sale; **c. des chevaux** horse dealing; **c. associé** voluntary group, association of distributors; **c. d'exportation/d'importation** export/import trade; **c. d'échange** countertrade; *Ordinat* **c. électronique** electronic commerce, e-commerce, e-business
2 *(magasin)* **(fonds de) c.** business; **commerces high-street shops**; **c. de proximité** local shop *or Am* store; **ouvrir un c.** to open a business

3 *Péj (trafic)* traffic, trade; **faire c. de son honneur/nom** to trade on one's honour/name; **faire c. de son corps** to sell one's body **4** *Arch, Litt (relations)* intercourse, dealings; **avoir** *ou* **être en c. avec qn** to have dealings with sb; **être d'un c. agréable** to be easy to get on with *or* pleasant to deal with; **fuir le c. des hommes** to flee the company of men **5** *Suisse Fam (ensemble d'objets disparates, affaires)* **range ton c.!** tidy up your stuff *or* things!

commercer [kɔmɛrse] **VI** (**je commerçai(s); n. commerçons**) to trade, to deal (**avec** with)

commercial, -iale, -iaux, -iales [kɔmɛrsjal, -jo] **ADJ** *(rapports, pratiques etc)* business, commercial; *(embargo, tribunal)* trade; *(droit)* commercial; *(délégué, direction, service)* sales; *Péj* **film c.** commercial film; **suivre une formation commerciale** to train in business studies
NF commerciale *(voiture)* estate car, *Am* station wagon; *(camionnette)* small van
▪ **N** salesman, representative; **c'est un c.** he's in sales

commercialement [kɔmɛrsjalmɑ̃] **ADV** commercially

commercialisable [kɔmɛrsjalizabl] **ADJ** marketable

commercialisation [kɔmɛrsjalizasjɔ̃] **NF** marketing

commercialiser [kɔmɛrsjalize] **VT** *(produit)* to market; *(art)* to commercialize; *Fin (effet)* to negotiate

commère [kɔmɛr] **NF** gossip

commettant [kɔmetɑ̃] **NM 1** *Com, Jur* principal **2** *Pol* **commettants** constituents

commettre [kɔmɛtr] (*conj like* **mettre**) **VT 1** *(accomplir)* *(crime, péché, injustice)* to commit; **c. une erreur** to make a mistake; *Hum* **il a déjà commis deux pièces de théâtre** he's already to blame for *or* he's already perpetrated two plays **2** *Jur* **c. qn à qch** to appoint sb to sth, to put sb in charge of sth; **c. un avocat d'office à qn** to assign a lawyer to sb **3** *Arch (compromettre)* to expose; **c. sa réputation** to risk one's reputation **4** *Arch (confier)* **c. qch à qn** to commit *or* entrust sth to sb *or* to sb's keeping, to entrust sb with sth
VPR se commettre *Litt* to compromise oneself; **se c. avec qn** to compromise oneself by associating with sb

comminatoire [kɔminatwar] **ADJ 1** *(lettre)* threatening **2** *Jur (décret etc)* comminatory

commis [kɔmi] **NM 1** *(employé)* clerk; *(dans un magasin)* (shop) assistant; *(à la Bourse)* floor trader; *Culin* **c. chef** commis waiter; **c. de banque** bank clerk; **c. aux comptes** government auditor; **c. de cuisine** commis chef; **c. de rang** trainee chef de rang; **c. de salle** waiter; **c. principal** senior clerk; **c. aux écritures** book-keeper; **les grands c.** the senior civil servants **2** *Arch* **c. voyageur** commercial traveller

commisération [kɔmizerasjɔ̃] **NF** commiseration; **éprouver/avoir de la c.** to feel/have sympathy; **témoigner de la c. à qn** to show sb sympathy

commis-greffier, *pl* **commis-greffiers NM** assistant to the clerk of court

commissaire [kɔmisɛr] **N 1** *Sport* steward; *Sport* **c. des courses** race steward; **c. (de police)** ≃ (police) superintendent, *Am* ≃ (police) captain; **c. principal** ≃ chief superintendent, *Am* ≃ chief of police; *Naut* **c. de la Marine** = supply officer; *Naut* **c. du bord** purser; *Fin* **c. aux comptes** government auditor; **c. d'avaries** average adjuster; *Can* **c. d'école** school commissioner **2** *(membre d'une commission)* commissioner, commission member; *UE* Commissioner, member of the Commission; **c. près du Conseil d'État**

government representative on the Council of State; **c. du gouvernement** government representative; **c. parlementaire** parliamentary commissioner

commissaire-priseur, *pl* **commissaires-priseurs** NM auctioneer

commissariat [kɔmisarja] NM **1** c. **(de police)** police station **2** *(fonction)* commissionership; **c. aux comptes** auditorship; *Naut* **c. du bord** pursership **3** c. **de la marine** *ou* **maritime** = supply branch **4** C. **à l'énergie atomique** = French atomic energy commission

commission [kɔmisjɔ̃] NF **1** *(course)* purchase; **il faut que j'aille faire les commissions** I have to go shopping
2 *(comité)* commission, committee; *Parl* **renvoi d'un texte en c.** referral of a bill to a committee
3 *(pourcentage), Com* commission; *Fin* brokerage; **c. de deux pour cent** commission of two per cent; **3% de c.** 3% commission; **être payé à la c.** to be paid on a commission basis; *Com* **maison de c.** firm of commission agents, commission agency; **vente à c.** sale on commission
4 *(charge)* commission; **avoir la c. de faire qch** to be commissioned *or* empowered to do sth
5 *(service)* errand; **faire une c.** to run an errand; **on ne m'a pas fait la c.** I wasn't given the message
6 *Enf* **la petite/grosse c.** a number one/two
▸▸ **c. d'acceptation** acceptance fee; **c. d'affacturage** factoring charges; **c. d'arbitrage** arbitration committee *or* board; **c. d'arrangement** over-riding commission; **c. bancaire** bank commission *or* charge *or* fee; **c. de change** exchange commission; *Banque* **c. de compte** account fee; **c. de confirmation** confirmation fee *or* commission; *(pour crédit)* facility fee; **c. consultative** advisory committee; **c. d'encaissement** collection charge *or* fee; **c. d'endos** endorsement fee; **c. d'engagement** commitment fee; **c. d'enquête** board *or* committee of inquiry; **C. européenne** European Commission; **c. de garantie** guarantee commission; **c. de normalisation** standards commission; **C. des opérations de Bourse** = Stock Exchange watchdog, *Am* ≃ Securities and Exchange Commission; **c. de paiement** collection charge, collection fee; **c. paritaire** joint commission *(with both sides equally represented)*; **c. parlementaire** parliamentary commission; **c. permanente** standing committee; **c. de rachat** redemption fee; **c. de souscription** front load; **c. de tenue de compte** account handling fee; **c. de vente** sales commission

commissionnaire [kɔmisjɔnɛr] NM **1** *(messager)* messenger; *(à l'hôtel, au théâtre)* commissionaire **2** *Com (commission)* agent, broker; **c. exportateur/importateur** export/import agent; **c. de transport** *ou* **de roulage** forwarding agent, carrier; **c. en banque** outside broker; **c. en douane** customs agent *or* broker; **c. agréé en douane** authorized customs broker; **c. en gros** factor; **c. de transport** shipping agent; **c. ducroire** del credere agent; **c. à l'export** export agent

commissionner [kɔmisjɔne] VT to commission

commissure [kɔmisyr] NF *(de la bouche)* corner; *Anat, Bot etc* commissure

commode [kɔmɔd] ADJ **1** *(pratique) (heure, lieu)* convenient, suitable; *(outil etc)* handy; *(maison etc)* convenient, comfortable; **c'est très c. pour ranger ses affaires** it's very handy for storing things in **2** *(facile)* easy; **ce que vous me demandez là n'est pas c.** what you

are asking me isn't very easy **3** *(caractère etc)* easy-going, *Fml* accommodating; *Fam* **il n'est pas c.** he's a tough *or* an awkward customer
NF chest of drawers, commode

commodément [kɔmɔdemɑ̃] ADV *(assis)* comfortably; *(situé)* conveniently

commodité [kɔmɔdite] NF **1** *(facilité)* convenience; **pour plus de c.** for greater convenience; **les commodités de la vie (moderne)** the comforts of (modern) life **2** **commodités** *(toilettes)* toilets, *Am* rest rooms

commodore [kɔmɔdɔr] NM *Mil* commodore

commotion [kɔmosjɔ̃] NF **1** c. **politique** political upheaval; *Méd* **c. cérébrale** concussion **2** *(émotion)* shock

commotionner [kɔmosjɔne] VT **1** *Méd* to concuss; **il a été fortement commotionné** he was severely concussed, he had severe concussion **2** *(choquer)* to shake (up), to shock; **cette nouvelle m'a commotionné** this news has given me a shock *or* has shaken me

commuable [kɔmɥabl] ADJ *Jur (peine)* commutable

commuer [kɔmɥe] VT *Jur (peine)* to commute (**en** to)

commun [kɔmɛ̃] ADJ **1** *(non exclusif)* common (**à** to); *(travail)* joint; *(ami)* mutual; *Math* **dénominateur c.** common denominator; **jardin c. à deux maisons** garden shared by two houses; **salle commune** common room; *(d'hôpital)* ward; **parties communes** communal areas; **maison commune** town hall; **avoir des intérêts communs** to have interests in common, to have common interests; **faire cause commune avec qn** to make common cause *or* join forces with sb; **il n'y a rien de c. entre eux** they've (got) nothing in common; **c'est sans commune mesure** there's no possible comparison; **vie commune** communal life; *(de couple)* conjugal life; **la vie commune n'est pas facile** living together isn't easy; **rechercher le bien c.** to seek the common good; **d'un c. accord** with one accord; **en c.** in common; **travailler en c.** to work together; **vivre en c.** to live communally; **mettre l'argent/les ressources en c.** to pool money/resources; **on s'est mis en c. pour lui acheter un cadeau** we all clubbed together to buy him a present **2** *(courant) (coutume, opinion etc)* common, universal, general; *(événement etc)* common, usual, ordinary, everyday; **sens c.** common sense; *Gram* **nom c.** common noun VOIR GRAMMAIRE A9; **lieu c.** commonplace; **il est d'une force peu commune** he's unusually strong **3** *(vulgaire)* common, vulgar
NM **1** *(de personnes etc)* common run, generality; **le c. des mortels** the ordinary *or* average man; **le c. des spectateurs n'a pas compris** the ordinary *or* average member of the audience didn't understand; **hors du c.** out of the ordinary **2** **communs** outhouses, outbuildings

communal, -ale, -aux, -ales [kɔmynal, -o] ADJ **1** *(conjoint) (terrain, propriété)* common, communal **2** *(de la commune) (propriété etc) Br* ≃ council; **école communale** ≃ local primary school
NMPL **communaux** common land
NF **communale** ≃ local primary school

communard, -arde [kɔmynar, -ard] ADJ *Hist* of the Commune
N **1** *Hist* Communard **2** *Péj (communiste)* commie, red

communautaire [kɔmynotɛr] ADJ communal; *Pol (aide, politique)* community; *(surtout UE)* Community; **centre c.** community centre

communautarisme [kɔmynotarism] NM =

emphasis on issues relating to minorities and ethnic communities within society

communauté [kɔmynote] NF **1** *(collectivité)* community; *Rel* community, order; **la c. internationale** the international community; **c. de travail** working community; **c. urbaine** urban community; **C. urbaine de Montréal** Montreal Urban Community; **c. de hippies** hippie commune; **vivre en c.** to live communally; **elle est partie vivre en c.** she's gone off to live in a commune **2** *(d'intérêts, d'idées etc)* similarity, *Fml* community; *Jur* **c. de biens** joint estate *(of husband and wife)*
▸▸ **C. économique européenne** European Economic Community

commune [kɔmyn] NF **1** *Admin* commune *(smallest territorial division in France)* **2** *Hist (ville autonome)* free town **3** *Pol* **la Chambre des communes, les Communes** the (House of) Commons **4** *Hist* **la C.** the Commune *(in 1789 and 1871)*

> ### Commune
> There are over 36,000 "communes" or administrative districts in France, some with fewer than 25 inhabitants. Each "commune" has an elected mayor and a town council.

communément [kɔmynemɑ̃] ADV commonly

communiant, -ante [kɔmynjɑ̃, -ɑ̃t] N *Rel* communicant; **premier c., première communiante** person taking his/her first communion

communicable [kɔmynikabl] ADJ *(impression, idée etc)* that can be communicated; *Jur (droit)* transferable; *(dossier etc)* that can be made available

communicant [kɔmynikɑ̃] ADJ *(chambres etc)* communicating, connecting

communicateur, -trice [kɔmynikatœr, -tris] ADJ *(fil etc)* connecting

communicatif, -ive [kɔmynikatif, -iv] ADJ **1** *(qui parle)* communicative, talkative; **peu c.** uncommunicative **2** *(rire etc)* infectious

communication [kɔmynikasjɔ̃] NF **1** communication; **avoir des problèmes de c.** to have problems *or* difficulties (in) communicating; **c. d'idées** interchange of ideas; **entrer** *ou* **se mettre en c. avec qn** to get in touch *or* in contact with sb; **mettre deux personnes en c.** to put two people in touch *or* in contact with each other; **je n'ai pas eu c. de ce message** the message wasn't passed on to me, I didn't get the message; **voies de c.** lines of communication, communication routes; **portes de c.** communicating doors; **toutes les communications sont coupées** all lines of communication are cut (off); **études de c.** media studies; **travailler dans la c.** to work in the media; *Ordinat* **progiciel de c.** communications *or Fam* comms package; *Mktg* **c. commerciale** marketing communications; **c. de données** data communications, datacomms; *Ordinat* **c. homme-machine** man-machine dialogue; **c. en ligne** on-line communication; **c. de masse** mass communication
2 *Tél* **c. téléphonique** (telephone) call; **mettez-moi en c. avec M. Martin** put me through to Mr Martin; **je vous passe la c.** I'll put you through; **vous avez la c.** you're through; **la c. est mauvaise** the line is bad; **c. en PCV** reverse charge *or* transferred charge call, *surtout Am* collect call; **c. interurbaine** long-distance call; **c. locale** local call; **c. longue distance** long-distance call; **c. télématique** datacommunications, datacomms
3 *Mktg (publicité)* promotion; **c. événementielle** event promotion; **c. institutionnelle** corporate promotion, corporate identity; **c.**

produit product promotion; **c. sur le lieu de vente** point-of-sale promotion **4** *(message)* communication, message; *(dans la presse)* statement; **transmettre une c. à qn** to pass on a message to sb; **le président a une importante c. à nous faire** the president has an important message for us *or* has something important to communicate to us; **faire une c. dans un colloque** to read a paper to a conference; *Jur* **donner c. des pièces** to communicate documents

communier [kɔmynje] VI *(impf, pr sub n. communiions, v. communiiez) Rel* to receive (Holy) Communion

communion [kɔmynjɔ̃] NF **1** *(communauté)* communion; **être en c. de sentiments avec qn** to be in sympathy with sb; **être en c. avec la nature** to commune with nature **2** *Rel* Communion; **première c., c. privée** first Communion; **faire sa première c.** to make one's first Communion; **c. solennelle** solemn Communion

communiqué [kɔmynike] NM communiqué, official statement; **c. de presse** press release, press hand-out; **c. de sécurité routière** traffic news

communiquer [kɔmynike] VT *(transmettre) (information, renseignements etc)* to communicate, to convey (**à qn** to sb); *(joie, peur etc)* to communicate (**à qn** to sb); *(maladie)* to pass on, to give (**à qn** to sb); **c. qch par écrit à qn** to communicate *or* convey sth in writing to sb; **c. ses impressions** to pass on *or* communicate one's impressions
  VI **1** *(être en relation)* to communicate (**avec** with); **avoir du mal à c. avec qn** to find it hard *or* difficult to communicate with sb; **refus total de c.** total unwillingness to communicate **2** *(d'une pièce)* to communicate (**avec** with); **toutes les chambres communiquent** all the bedrooms communicate with one another; **porte qui communique au** *ou* **avec le jardin** door that leads into the garden; **canal qui fait c. deux rivières** canal that connects two rivers
  VPR **se communiquer 1** *(se transmettre)* to spread; **l'incendie s'est communiqué aux maisons voisines** the fire has spread to the neighbouring houses **2** *Vieilli (être communicatif)* to be communicative

communisant, -ante [kɔmynizɑ̃, -ɑ̃t] ADJ *(personne, journal, parti etc)* with communist sympathies
  N communist sympathizer, fellow traveller

communisme [kɔmynism] NM communism

communiste [kɔmynist] ADJ, N communist

commutable [kɔmytabl] ADJ *Tél* switchable

commutateur [kɔmytatœr] NM *Élec* **1** *(de dynamo etc)* commutator **2** *(bouton)* switch; **c. sélecteur** selector switch; **c. téléphonique** exchange; *Ordinat* **c. de données** data switch

commutatif, -ive [kɔmytatif, -iv] ADJ *Jur, Math* commutative

commutation [kɔmytasjɔ̃] NF **1** *Jur (de sentence)* commutation **2** *(changement)* substitution, *Fml* commutation; *(entre documents)* switching; *Gram* replacement, substitution; **le patron a décidé de la c. de deux employés** the boss decided to swap the duties of two employees **3** *Élec* commutation, change-over; *TV etc* **c. de l'image** switching **4** *Ordinat, Tél* switch-over, switching; **c. de bande/ de circuits** tape/circuit switching; **c. de message/de paquets** message/packet switching

commutatrice [kɔmytatris] NF *Élec* rotary converter, transformer

commuté [kɔmyte] ADJ *(réseau)* switched

commuter¹ [kɔmyte] VT **1** *Jur (sentence)* to commute **2** *Élec (courant)* to commutate, to

switch over, to change over **3 c. les fonctions** to swap duties
  VI *(entre documents, écrans)* to switch; **deux employés qui vont c.** two employees who are going to swap duties
  VPR **se commuter** *Ordinat* to switch

commuter² [kɔmytœr] NM *Aviat* commuter plane

Comores [kɔmɔr] NF *Géog* **les îles C.** the Comoro Islands

comorien, -ienne [kɔmɔrjɛ̃, -jɛn] ADJ Comoran
  N **C.** Comoran

compacité [kɔ̃pasite] NF *(de la terre etc)* compactness; *(d'un métal)* density; *(de la foule)* denseness

compact [kɔ̃pakt] ADJ **1** *(de petit format)* compact; **voiture compacte** small car, *Am* compact; **disque c.** compact disc **2** *(masse, formation etc)* compact, dense; *(foule)* dense; *(terre)* compact; *(métal)* dense; **majorité compacte** large *or* solid majority; **poudre compacte** pressed (face-)powder
  NM compact disc; **disponible en c.** available on CD

Compact Disc® [kɔ̃paktdisk] NM compact disc

compacter [kɔ̃pakte] VT *(fichier, données)* to compress; *(base de données)* to pack

compacteur [kɔ̃paktœr] NM *Ordinat* **c. d'exécutables** execute file compressor; **c. de données** data compressor

compagne [kɔ̃paɲ] NF **1** *(camarade)* (female) companion; **mes compagnes de captivité** my fellow captives **2** *(concubine)* partner; *(épouse)* wife; *(d'un animal)* mate

compagnie [kɔ̃paɲi] NF **1** *(présence)* company, companionship; **n'avoir qu'un vieux chien pour toute c.** to have only an old dog for company; **tenir c. à qn** to keep sb company; **fausser c. à qn** to give sb the slip; **je vais vous fausser c.** this is where I leave you; **dame de c.** (lady's) companion; **être en c. d'amis proches** to be in the company of close friends, to be with close friends; **rechercher la c. de gens simples** to seek the company of simple people; **aller de c. avec …** to go hand in hand with …; **être de bonne/mauvaise c.** to be good/poor company; **être c. agréable** to be pleasant company; **je l'ai trouvé en joyeuse/galante c.** I found him in cheerful company/in the company of a lady; **ils ont voyagé de c.** they travelled together
  2 *(groupe)* company, party; **toute la c.** everybody, all of them/us
  3 *Com, Théâtre etc* company; *Com* **la maison Thomas et C.** (the firm of) Thomas and Company; *Fam* **ces mecs, c'est arnaqueurs et c.!** those guys are just a bunch of crooks!
  4 *Mil* company; **c. de débarquement** landing party
  5 *(de perdrix)* covey
  ▸▸ **c. aérienne** airline; **c. aérienne nationale** flag *or* national airline; **c. d'assurances** insurance company; **c. d'aviation civile** civil airline; *Rel* **la C. de Jésus** the Society of Jesus; **c. maritime** shipping line; **c. mère** parent company; **c. de navigation** shipping company; **c. pétrolière** oil company; **compagnies républicaines de sécurité** riot police; **c. de transports** carrier; **c. de transports nationale** flag carrier

compagnon [kɔ̃paɲɔ̃] NM **1** *(camarade)* companion; *(d'ouvrier)* mate; **c. d'études** fellow student; **c. de voyage** travelling companion; **c'était mon c. de jeu** I used to play with him; *Pol* **c. de route** fellow traveller; **c. d'infortune/de misère** companion in misfortune/in suffering **2** *(ouvrier)* journeyman **3** *Fam (plante)* **c. blanc/rouge** white/red campion **4** *(concubin)* partner; *(époux)* husband

comparable [kɔ̃parabl] ADJ comparable (**à** *ou* **avec qn/qch** to *or* with sb/sth); **ce n'est pas c.** there's no comparison

comparablement [kɔ̃parabləmɑ̃] ADV comparatively

comparaison [kɔ̃parɛzɔ̃] NF **1** comparison; **c. des prix** price comparison; **faire la c. entre deux choses** to compare two things, to make a comparison between two things; **tu peux faire la c. toi-même** you can judge *or* see *or* make the comparison for yourself; **soutenir la c.** to bear *or* stand comparison; **il n'y a pas de c. possible** there's no possible comparison; **c'est sans c. avec …** it can't be compared with …; **il est sans c. le plus grand** he is by far *or* he is far and away the tallest; *Prov* **c. n'est pas raison** comparisons are odious; *Gram* **adverbe de c.** adverb of comparison, comparative adverb; **les degrés de c.** the degrees of comparison; **c. par paire** paired comparison
  2 *(locutions)* **en c. de …** compared with, in comparison with …; **par c.** by comparison; **par c. avec** *ou* **à** compared with
  3 *Littér* simile

comparaître [kɔ̃parɛtr] VI *(conj like paraître) Jur* **c. (en justice)** to appear (before a court); **c. en personne** to appear in person; **c. par avoué** to be represented by counsel; **c. comme témoin** to appear as a witness; **être appelé à c.** to be summoned to appear

comparant, -ante [kɔ̃parɑ̃, -ɑ̃t] *Jur* ADJ appearing in court
  N person appearing in court

comparateur [kɔ̃paratœr] NM *Aut etc* dial gauge

comparatif, -ive [kɔ̃paratif, -iv] ADJ comparative; **publicité comparative** comparative advertising
  NM *Gram* comparative; **adjectif au c.** comparative adjective; **c. d'infériorité** comparative of lesser degree SEE GRAMMAR A24–7; B11; B13–14

comparatiste [kɔ̃paratist] N *Ling* specialist in comparative linguistics; *Littér* specialist in comparative literature

comparativement [kɔ̃parativmɑ̃] ADV comparatively; **il fait bien plus beau aujourd'hui, c. à hier** it's much nicer today compared with *or* to yesterday

comparé [kɔ̃pare] ADJ *(anatomie, histoire, littérature etc)* comparative; **c. à** compared with *or* to

comparer [kɔ̃pare] VT to compare (**à** to; **avec** with); **il compare les étoiles filantes à des cheveux** he compares *or* likens shooting stars to strands of hair; **c. deux objets/textes** to compare two objects/texts; **tu peux c., ma robe est plus large** you can see the difference, my dress is wider
  VPR **se comparer je ne peux pas me c. à toi** I can't compare myself with *or* to you; **Haendel ne peut pas se c. à Mozart** Handel can't be compared with *or* to Mozart; **ça ne se compare pas** there's no comparison

comparse [kɔ̃pars] N *Cin* extra; *Théâtre* walk-on, super, *Fml* supernumerary; *Fig Péj* associate; *Théâtre* **rôle de c.** walk-on part

compartiment [kɔ̃partimɑ̃] NM *(de wagon, boîte, tiroir etc)* compartment; *(d'échiquier, de damier)* square; *Rail* **c. de première classe** first-class compartment; **c. fumeurs** smoking compartment, smoker; **c. non-fumeurs** no-smoking compartment, non-smoker; **c. moteur** engine compartment; **c. à bagages** *(d'autocar)* luggage compartment

compartimentage [kɔ̃partimɑ̃taʒ] NM partitioning; *(d'une administration etc)* compartmentalization

compartimenter [kɔ̃partimɑ̃te] VT **1** *(diviser en espaces)* to partition, to divide into compartments **2** *(administration etc)* to compartmentalize

comparution [kɔparysjɔ̃] **NF** *Jur (au tribunal)* appearance; **défaut de c.** failure to appear

compas [kɔpa] **NM 1** *Géom* (pair of) compasses; **c. à pointes sèches** dividers; **c. quart de cercle** wing compasses; *Tech etc* **c. d'épaisseur** callipers; *Fig Fam* **tout faire au c.** to do everything with precision; *Fig* **avoir le c. dans l'œil** to have an accurate eye **2** *Naut* **c. (de mer)** (mariner's) compass; **c. de route** steering compass; **c. gyroscopique** gyrocompass

compassé [kɔpase] **ADJ** *(personne, manières, ton etc)* stiff, formal

compasser [kɔpase] **VT 1** *(distances sur la carte etc)* to measure with compasses; *Naut (carte)* to prick **2** *Litt (ses actes etc)* to control, to regulate

compassion [kɔpasjɔ̃] **NF** compassion; **avec c.** compassionately

compatibilité [kɔpatibilite] **NF** compatibility

compatible [kɔpatibl] **ADJ** compatible (**avec** with); *Ordinat* **c. abc** abc-compatible; **ces deux applications ne sont pas compatibles** these two applications are incompatible *or* not compatible; **compatible vers le haut/vers le bas** upward/downward compatible; **compatible avec les versions antérieures** backward compatible; **compatible IBM** IBM-compatible; **compatible Mac** Mac-compatible
NM *Ordinat* **c. (PC)** (PC) compatible

compatir [kɔpatir] **VI** to sympathize; **c. au chagrin de qn** to sympathize with *or* feel for sb in his/her grief

compatissant [kɔpatisɑ̃] **ADJ** compassionate, sympathetic

compatriote [kɔpatrijɔt] **N** compatriot, fellow countryman, *f* countrywoman

compensable [kɔpɑ̃sabl] **ADJ** that can be compensated for; *(chèque)* clearable; *Fin* **c. à Paris** to be cleared at Paris

compensateur, -trice [kɔpɑ̃satœr, -tris] **ADJ** *(ressort, aimant etc)* compensating; *Élec (courant)* equalizing; *(dynamo)* balancing; **indemnité compensatrice** compensatory payment, compensation; **pendule c.** compensation pendulum
NM *(de boussole etc)* compensator, balancer; *Aviat* trimming tab, trimmer; *Aut* **c. de frein** brake compensator

compensation [kɔpɑ̃sasjɔ̃] **NF 1** *(de perte)* compensation; **en c. de mes pertes** to compensate for *or* as compensation for my losses; **en c., vous avez droit à deux jours de vacances** to compensate (for it) *or* to make up for it, you can have two days off; **il y a des compensations** there are compensations; *Jur* **c. des dépens** sharing of the costs; *Fin* **chambre de c.** clearing house **2** *Élec etc (de forces etc)* equalization, balancing; *(de son)* equalization; *Math* **loi de c.** law of large numbers **3** *Naut (de boussole)* adjustment **4** *(de chèque)* clearing; **caisse de c.** = equalization fund for payments such as child benefit, sickness benefit, pensions etc **5** *Psy* compensation

compensatoire [kɔpɑ̃satwar] **ADJ** compensatory; **droits compensatoires** countervailing duties

compenser [kɔpɑ̃se] **VT 1** *(perte)* to compensate for, to make up for, to make good; *(défaut etc)* to compensate for, to make up for, to offset; *Jur etc (dettes)* to set off, to balance (out); *(chèque)* to clear; **talon *ou* semelle compensé(e)** built-up heel; **son efficacité compense son mauvais caractère** his efficiency compensates for *or* makes up

for *or* offsets his bad temper; *Jur* **c. les dépens** to divide the costs **2** *Naut (boussole)* to adjust
VPR se compenser to make up for each other, to offset each other

compère [kɔpɛr] **NM 1** *(de prestidigitateur etc)* accomplice, associate **2** *Fam Vieilli (camarade)* comrade, crony; **un bon c.** a pleasant companion

compère-loriot, *pl* **compères-loriots NM 1** *(oiseau)* golden oriole **2** *Méd (sur la paupière)* sty

compète [kɔpɛt] **NF** *Fam (abrév* **compétition)** competition *(in sport)*; **faire de la c.** to enter competitions

compétence [kɔpetɑ̃s] **NF 1** *(capacité)* competence, ability, skill (**pour faire qch** to do sth); **avoir toutes les compétences requises pour faire qch** to have all the necessary skills to do sth; **c'est en dehors de mes compétences** it's beyond my capabilities; **faire qch avec beaucoup de c.** to do sth very competently **2** *Jur (de cour de justice etc)* competence, jurisdiction, powers; **cela ne rentre pas dans *ou* cela n'est pas de sa c.** that does not come within his province, that is outside his scope; **sortir de sa c.** to exceed one's powers; **c. universelle** universal competence

compétent [kɔpetɑ̃] **ADJ** *Jur etc (tribunal, autorité etc)* competent; **c. en matière de finance** conversant with finance; **je ne suis pas c. en la matière** I am not well up in the subject; **il est très c.** he's very competent; *Com* **adressez-vous au service c.** apply to the appropriate *or* relevant department, apply to the department concerned

compétiteur, -trice [kɔpetitœr, -tris] **N** competitor

compétitif, -ive [kɔpetitif, -iv] **ADJ** *Com (prix etc)* competitive

compétition [kɔpetisjɔ̃] **NF 1** *(rivalité)* competition, rivalry; **être en c. avec qn** to be in competition with sb, to compete with sb; **c. entre partis politiques** rivalry between political parties; **esprit de c.** competitive spirit **2** *Sport (épreuve)* competition, event; **c. sportive** sports competition, sporting event; **faire de la c.** to go in for competitive sport; **du ski de c.** competitive *or* competition skiing

compétitivité [kɔpetitivite] **NF** competitiveness

compilateur, -trice [kɔpilatœr, -tris] **NM** *Ordinat* compiler; **c. croisé** cross-compiler
N 1 *(auteur)* compiler **2** *Péj (plagiaire)* plagiarist

compilation [kɔpilasjɔ̃] **NF 1** *Ordinat* compilation **2** *(enregistrement)* compilation **3** *(de documents)* compiling, compilation **4** *Péj (plagiat)* plagiarism

compiler [kɔpile] **VT 1** *Ordinat* to compile **2** *(réunir)* to compile **3** *Péj (plagier)* to plagiarize

complainte [kɔplɛ̃t] **NF 1** *Arch (plainte)* plaint **2** *Littér, Mus* lament

complaire [kɔplɛr] *(conj like* **plaire)** **VI** *Litt* **c. à qn** to please sb
VPR se complaire to delight, to revel (**dans qch** in sth; **à faire qch** in doing sth); **elle se complaît dans le malheur** she wallows in her misery

complaisamment [kɔplɛzamɑ̃] **ADV 1** *(avec obligeance)* obligingly, kindly **2** *(avec vanité)* complacently, smugly

complaisance [kɔplɛzɑ̃s] **NF 1** *(bienveillance)* obligingness, kindness; **faire qch par c.** to do sth out of kindness; **faire qch par c. pour qn** to do sth to oblige sb; **auriez-vous la c. de le faire?** would you be so good *or* so kind as to do it?, would you oblige me by do-

ing it?; **avoir des complaisances pour qn** to be indulgent towards sb; **sourire de c.** polite smile; **sourire d'un air de c.** to smile politely, to give a polite smile; *Com* **billet *ou* effet de c.** accommodation bill; **on a fini par lui délivrer un certificat de c.** he was finally issued with a medical certificate *(to which he was not entitled)* **2** *(auto-satisfaction)* complacency, smugness, self-satisfaction; **il s'écoute avec c.** he likes the sound of his own voice; **ton plein de c.** self-satisfied *or* smug tone

complaisant [kɔplɛzɑ̃] **ADJ 1** *(bienveillant)* obliging, accommodating, kind (**envers, pour** towards); **prêter une oreille complaisante à qn** to lend sb a sympathetic *or* willing ear **2** *(indulgent) (médecin)* indulgent; *(mari)* complaisant, indulgent **3** *(satisfait)* complacent, smug, self-satisfied

complément [kɔplemɑ̃] **NM** *(reste)* rest, remainder; *Gram, Biol, Chimie, Math* complement; **il faudra racheter cinq livres de lecture pour faire le c.** we'll have to buy five more readers to make up the numbers; **si on manque de dessert, on fera le c. avec des yaourts** if we're short of desserts, we'll use yoghurts instead; **demander un c. d'information** to ask for more *or* additional information; *Gram* **c. circonstanciel de temps** adverbial phrase of time; *Gram* **c. (d'objet)** object; *Gram* **c. d'objet direct/indirect** direct/indirect object [SEE GRAMMAR A78-9; B52-3] ; *Admin* **c. (de) retraite** supplementary pension

complémentaire [kɔplemɑ̃tɛr] **ADJ** *(angle, couleur etc)* complementary; **pour tout renseignement c., s'adresser à …** for further *or* additional information, apply to …

complémentarité [kɔplemɑ̃tarite] **NF** complementarity

COMPLET, -ÈTE [kɔplɛ, -ɛt] **ADJ 1** *(entier, intégral) (tenue, service etc)* complete, whole, entire; **rapport très c.** very full *or* comprehensive report; **se faire une idée complète de la situation** to get an overall picture *or* a complete picture *or* an overview of the situation; **deux jours complets** two full *or* whole days; **examen c.** full *or* thorough examination; **voyager dans le plus c. anonymat** to travel completely incognito; **votre devoir est loin d'être c.** your homework is a long way *or* far from being complete; **athlète c.** all-round athlete; **un c. abruti** a complete *or* a total *or* an absolute moron; **échec c.** complete *or* total *or* utter failure; **collection complète d'un auteur** complete works of an author, complete set of an author's works; **formation très complète** thorough training; *Fam* **c'est c.!** that's the last straw!, that's the limit!; **pain c.** wholemeal bread; **pâtes complètes** wholemeal pasta; **riz c.** brown rice **2** *(rempli) (bus)*, *Théâtre (salle etc)* full; **'c.'** 'full (up)'; *(signe devant pension, hôtel etc)* 'no vacancies'
NM 1 **c.(-veston)** suit
2 **nous étions au grand c.** we turned out in full force; **j'ai invité la famille au c. pour Noël** I've invited the whole family for Christmas; **j'attends que l'assistance soit au c. pour commencer** I'm waiting for everyone to arrive before I begin

complètement [kɔplɛtmɑ̃] **ADV** completely, totally, wholly; *(ruiné, perdu, idiot)* utterly, completely, totally; **c. nu** stark naked, completely naked; **finir c. un pot de crème** to finish off *or* polish off a pot of cream; **je n'ai pas pu le lire c.** I couldn't read all of it *or* the whole thing

compléter [kɔplete] (**je complète, n. complétons; je compléterai**) **VT** *(collection, garde-robe, formation etc)* to complete; *(formulaire)* to complete, to fill in *or* out; **c. une somme** to make up a sum (of money); **c. une**

gamme de produits to add to a range of products; *Fig* pour c. le tableau ... to cap it all ...

VPR se compléter to complement one another; **ils se complètent bien l'un l'autre** they're well-matched, they complement each other well

complétif, -ive [kɔ̃pletif, -iv] ADJ, NF *Gram* (proposition) complétive noun clause

complexe [kɔ̃plɛks] ADJ (caractère, question etc) complex, complicated; *Gram* sujet c. compound subject; *Math* nombre c. complex number

NM 1 *Constr, Écon* complex; **vivre dans un grand c.** to live in a complex; **le c. industriel de la vallée du Rhône** the Rhone valley industrial complex; **c. commercial/sportif** shopping/sports centre or complex; **c. de loisirs** leisure complex; **c. hôtelier** hotel complex; **c. touristique** holiday or tourism complex 2 *Psy* complex; **c. d'infériorité** inferiority complex; **c. d'Œdipe** Oedipus complex; *Fam* **ça me donne des complexes** it gives me a complex, it gives me hang-ups; *Fam* **avoir des complexes** to have a complex or a hang-up, to be hung up (à cause de about); *Fam* **être sans c.** to have no hang-ups; *Fam* **il est bourré de complexes** he's really hung up, he's full of complexes

complexé [kɔ̃plɛkse] ADJ *Fam* hung up, full of complexes (par about)

complexer [kɔ̃plɛkse] VT *Fam* **c. qn** to give sb a complex or a hang-up

complexifier [kɔ̃plɛksifje] VT to make (more) complex

VPR se complexifier to become (more) complex

complexion [kɔ̃plɛksjɔ̃] NF constitution; *Vieilli* (caractère) temperament, disposition; **je suis gros de c.** I'm naturally fat, I'm predisposed to be fat

complexité [kɔ̃plɛksite] NF complexity

complication [kɔ̃plikasjɔ̃] NF 1 (ennui) complication; **faire des complications** to complicate the issue, to create or cause complications or problems 2 (de situation etc) complexity, intricacy 3 *Méd* complications complications

complice [kɔ̃plis] ADJ **être c. de qch** to be party to sth; **des regards complices** knowing glances

N accomplice

complicité [kɔ̃plisite] NF complicity; *Jur* aiding and abetting; *Jur* **agir en c. avec qn** to act in collusion or complicity with sb; **accusé de c. de meurtre** accused of being an accessory to murder

complies [kɔ̃pli] NFPL *Rel* compline

compliment [kɔ̃plimɑ̃] NM 1 (félicitation) compliment; **avec les compliments de** with the compliments of; **avec les compliments de la maison** with the compliments of the house; **mes compliments au chef** my compliments to the chef; **faire des compliments à qn** to pay sb compliments, to compliment sb; **on lui a fait c. de sa jolie robe** she was complimented on her pretty dress; **(je vous fais) mes compliments** I congratulate you; *Iron* **mes compliments!** congratulations!; **faites-lui mes compliments** (please) give her my regards 2 (discours) speech of congratulation, congratulatory speech

complimenter [kɔ̃plimɑ̃te] VT **c. qn pour** (courage, présence d'esprit) to congratulate sb on; **c. qn sur** (toilette, coiffure) to compliment sb on; **il faut la c. pour son nouveau travail** we must congratulate her on her new job

complimenteur, -euse [kɔ̃plimɑ̃tœr, -øz]

Péj ADJ (personne) obsequious; **discours c.** flattering speech

N flatterer

compliqué, -ée [kɔ̃plike] ADJ (mécanisme, système etc) complicated, intricate; (style, texte, théorie etc) complicated, involved; (personne) complicated; **je n'y arrive pas, c'est trop c.** I can't do it, it's too complicated; *Fam* **ce n'est pas c.!** it's quite simple!

N *Fam* complicated individual

compliquer [kɔ̃plike] VT to complicate; **ça risque de c. les choses** that may or might well complicate matters

VPR se compliquer (d'une situation, de la vie, d'un problème) to get complicated; *Littér, Théâtre* (d'une intrigue) to thicken; **ça se complique!** things are getting a bit complicated!; **il se complique l'existence** he's making life complicated or difficult for himself

complot [kɔ̃plo] NM plot, conspiracy; **tramer un c.** to hatch a plot; **mettre qn dans le c.** to let sb in on the plot

comploter [kɔ̃plɔte] VI to plot, to conspire (contre against); **c. de faire qch** to plot or conspire to do sth

VT to plot; *Fam* **qu'est-ce que vous complotez là?** what are you cooking up or plotting now?

VPR se comploter **je me demande ce qui se complote par ici** I wonder what's being hatched or plotted here

comploteur [kɔ̃plɔtœr] NM plotter, conspirator

compo [kɔ̃po] NF *Scol Fam* test; (plus important) exam

componction [kɔ̃pɔ̃ksjɔ̃] NF 1 *Rel* (contrition) compunction 2 *Iron* **avec c.** gravely, solemnly

comportement [kɔ̃pɔrtəmɑ̃] NM 1 behaviour, *Am* behavior; **elle a un c. très bizarre avec les enfants** her behaviour towards children is very strange, she behaves very strangely towards children; **psychologie du c.** behaviourism, *Am* behaviorism; **type de c.** behaviour pattern 2 *Mktg* **c. d'achat** buying or purchase or purchasing behaviour or *Am* behavior; **c. de l'acheteur** buyer or purchaser behaviour; **c. du consommateur** consumer behaviour; **c. post-achat** post-purchase behaviour 3 *Bourse, Fin* (du marché, des cours, des actions) performance 4 *Aut* **c. en courbe** ou **en virage** cornering (ability); **c. routier** (road) handling; **c. sous-vireur** understeer; **c. survireur** oversteer

comportemental, -ale, -aux, -ales [kɔ̃pɔrtəmɑ̃tal, -o] ADJ behavioural, *Am* behavioral

comporter [kɔ̃pɔrte] VT 1 (admettre) to allow, *Fml* to allow of, *Fml* to admit of; **règle qui comporte des exceptions** rule that allows of or admits of exceptions 2 (comprendre) to comprise; **la fusée comporte quatre étages** the rocket comprises or is made up of four stages; **les difficultés que cela comporterait** the difficulties this would involve or entail

VPR se comporter to behave (vis-à-vis de, envers towards); **mal se c.** to misbehave, to behave badly; **se c. en** ou **comme un lâche** to act or behave like a coward; **la voiture se comporte aussi bien sur neige que sur terrain sec** the car handles equally well on snow or dry ground; **ses actions se sont bien comportées** his shares have performed well

composant, -ante [kɔ̃pozɑ̃, -ɑ̃t] ADJ (partie) component, constituent

NM composant, constituent

NF **composante** (de voltage, force, vitesse etc) component; **c'est une des composantes de la vie de couple** it's one of the components of married life, it's one of the things that make up married life

composé, -ée [kɔ̃poze] ADJ 1 (salade) mixed; (intérêt, mot etc) compound; *Chimie* **corps c.** compound; *Gram* **temps c.** compound tense **SEE GRAMMAR B26-8**; **nom c.** compound (noun) **VOIR GRAMMAIRE A14** 2 *Bot* (fleur) composite 3 (compassé) (attitude, comportement etc) studied

NM *Chimie, Gram etc* compound

NFPL *Bot* **composées** Compositae

composer [kɔ̃poze] VT 1 (créer) (poème, symphonie etc) to compose, to write; (bouquet), *Pharm* (ordonnance) to make up 2 *Typ* (fonte) to set, to compose, to typeset; **c. sur ordinateur** to computer-typeset; *Tél* **c. un numéro** to dial a number 3 (faire partie de) to make up; **quels sont les ingrédients qui composent ce plat?** which ingredients make up or go into this dish?; **les personnes qui composent notre famille** the people who make up our family, all the members of our family; **ce médicament est composé de nombreuses substances** this medicine is made up of or is composed of or consists of numerous substances 4 **c. son visage** to compose one's features

VI 1 (s'entendre) to compromise (avec with) 2 *Mus* to compose 3 *Scol* to take or sit a test; **les élèves composeront en anglais demain** the pupils will take or sit an English test tomorrow

VPR se composer 1 se c. de to be made up of, to be composed of, to consist of 2 **se c. un visage de circonstance** to put on a suitable expression

composeur [kɔ̃pozœr] NM *Tél* **c. de numéros** dialler

composeuse [kɔ̃pozøz] NF *Typ* photosetter, typesetting machine

composite [kɔ̃pozit] ADJ composite; **matériau c.** composite (material)

compositeur, -trice [kɔ̃pozitœr, -tris] N 1 *Mus* composer 2 *Typ* compositor, typesetter

composition [kɔ̃pozisjɔ̃] NF 1 (de sonate, roman, poème etc) composition, writing; (d'une ordonnance etc) making up; (d'un bouquet) arrangement; (d'un portefeuille d'actions) building up; **un poème de ma c.** a poem I wrote (myself)

2 (éléments), *Chimie, Phys* (de l'eau etc) composition; **la c. d'un repas** the composition of a meal; **la c. des équipes n'est pas encore connue** the teams haven't been announced yet

3 *Mus, Littér etc* (œuvre) composition

4 *Scol* (dissertation) essay; (examen) test

5 (arrangement) arrangement, compromise; **entrer en c. avec qn** to come to terms with sb

6 **être de bonne c.** to be good-natured

7 *Typ* typesetting, composition; **c. (des caractères)** body setting; **c. informatisée** computer typesetting; **c. programmée** automatic typesetting; *Tél* **c. automatique de numéros** automatic dialling

compost [kɔ̃pɔst] NM *Agr* compost

compostage [kɔ̃pɔstaʒ] NM (de billet) (date-)stamping; (poinçonnage) punching

composter[1] [kɔ̃pɔste] VT *Agr* (terre) to compost

composter[2] VT (billet) to (date-)stamp; (poinçonner) to punch

composteur [kɔ̃pɔstœr] NM 1 (machine) date stamp; (pour poinçonner) ticket-punching machine 2 *Typ* composing stick

compote [kɔ̃pɔt] NF *Culin* compote, stewed fruit; **c. de pommes** apple sauce, stewed apples; *Fam* **j'ai les jambes en c.** my legs feel like jelly; *Fam* **j'ai la tête en c.** my brain's gone to mush; *Fam* **il lui a mis le visage en c.** he smashed his face to a pulp

compotier [kɔ̃pɔtje] NM fruit dish

compréhensibilité [kɔ̃preãsibilite] NF comprehensibility

compréhensible [kɔ̃preãsibl] ADJ **1** *(clair)* comprehensible, understandable; **c. du** *ou* **par le grand public** understandable by *or* comprehensible to the general public **2** *(justifié)* understandable; **c'est tout à fait c. de sa part** it's altogether understandable on his part

> Attention: ne pas confondre **comprehensible** et **understandable** lorsqu'on traduit **compréhensible**. Le terme **comprehensible** signifie **intelligible**, alors que **understandable** signifie **concevable, qui se comprend**.

compréhensif, -ive [kɔ̃preãsif, -iv] ADJ **1** *(personne)* understanding; **elle s'est montrée très compréhensive là-dessus** she was very understanding about it **2** *(vaste)* comprehensive

> Il faut noter que l'adjectif anglais **comprehensive** est un faux ami. Il signifie le plus souvent **complet, exhaustif**.

compréhension [kɔ̃preãsjɔ̃] NF **1** *(fait de comprendre)* comprehension, understanding; **pour la bonne c. du texte** (in order) to fully understand the text; **cet élève a des problèmes de c.** this pupil has problems understanding *or* problems of comprehension **2** *(bienveillance)* understanding; **il est plein de c.** he is very understanding

COMPRENDRE [kɔ̃prãdr] *(conj like* **prendre***)*

> | **VT** to understand **1** ▪ to comprise **2** ▪ to include **3**
> | **VI** to understand ▪ to see
> | **VPR** to understand each other ▪ to be understandable

VT **1** *(par l'esprit)* to understand, *Fml* to comprehend; **je ne comprends pas ce que vous voulez dire** I don't understand what you mean, *Fam* I don't get you; **difficile à c.** difficult *or* hard to understand; **c. une langue étrangère** to understand a foreign language; **je n'arrive pas à c. cette phrase** I can't make sense of this sentence; **c. la portée d'un acte** to realize *or* understand the consequences of an action; **je ne comprends pas comment/pourquoi il a fait ça** I don't understand *or* see how/why he did it; **dois-je c. que ...?** am I to understand *or* do you mean to say that ...?; **vous m'avez mal compris** you've misunderstood me; **on ne te comprend pas** *(tu parles trop vite)* nobody can understand *or* make out what you say; **je ne le comprends pas** *(il est étrange)* I can't understand him *or* fathom him out, I can't make him out; **il ne comprend rien à rien** he hasn't a clue about anything; **tu peux lui expliquer, il comprend les choses** you can explain to him, he understands about these things; **elle ne comprend pas la plaisanterie** she can't take a joke; **elle n'a pas compris la plaisanterie** she didn't get the joke; **tu comprends ce que je te dis?** do you understand what I'm saying?; **je n'y comprends rien** I can't make head or tail of it, it makes no sense to me; **c'est à n'y rien c.** it's incomprehensible; **ne cherche pas, il n'y a rien à c.** don't even try to understand; **va y c. quelque chose!** you try to make head or tail of it!, *Am* go figure!; **je lui ai fait c. que ... +** *ind* I gave him to understand that ...; *(avec autorité)* I made it clear to him that ...; **se faire c.** to make oneself understood; **me suis-je bien fait c.?** have I made myself clear?; **comment c. ce tableau/ce poème/l'art?** what is one to make of this picture/this poem/art?; **il faut la c.** you have to see things from her point of

view, you have to put yourself in her shoes; **tu n'as pas encore compris qu'il n'en veut qu'à ton argent!** you still haven't realized *or* understood that he's only after your money!; **je n'ai toujours pas compris ce qui s'est passé** I still haven't quite realized *or* grasped *or* understood what has happened; *Fam* **j'ai compris ma douleur** I realized what I had let myself in for

2 *(être composé entièrement de)* to comprise, to be made up of, to consist of; **cet organe comprend trois parties distinctes** this organ is made up of *or* comprises three separate parts

3 *(inclure)* to include; **service non compris** service not included; **le prix comprend tous les frais d'hébergement** the price is fully inclusive of accommodation; **ils ont tous été punis, y compris le plus jeune** they were all punished, including the youngest *or* the youngest included

VI to understand; **ai-je bien compris?** have I understood correctly?; **ah! je comprends!** oh! I see!; **ça va, j'ai compris, ce n'est pas la peine de me faire un dessin!** OK, I understand, you don't need to spell it out to me!; **elle comprend vite** she's quick on the uptake, she catches on quickly; **tu comprends, on ne pouvait pas se le permettre** you see, we just couldn't afford it; **elle finira par c.** she'll understand eventually; **je comprends bien!** I understand!; *Fam* **elle est belle, n'est-ce pas? – je comprends!** she's lovely, isn't she? – you bet! *or* and how!

VPR **se comprendre** *(des gens)* to understand each other; *Fam* **ça se comprend!** it's understandable!, it's not surprising!; **je me comprends!** I know what I'm talking about!

comprenette [kɔ̃prənɛt] NF *Fam* **il a la c. un peu dure** he's a bit slow on the uptake

comprenure [kɔ̃prənyr] NF *Belg, Can Fam* **être dur de c.** to be slow (on the uptake)

compresse [kɔ̃prɛs] NF compress

compresser [kɔ̃prɛse] VT to compress; *Ordinat (fichier)* to compact, to compress, to zip

compresseur [kɔ̃prɛsœr] NM **1** *Tech (à air, de gaz, de fluide)* compressor; *(de moteur)* supercharger, impeller, compressor; *(d'air conditionné)* blower, fan; *Aut* **c. Roots** Roots blower; *Aut* **c. centrifuge** centrifugal compressor; *Aut* **c. sur vilebrequin** crankshaft compressor; *Aut* **c. à palettes** vane compressor **2** *Ordinat* **c. de données** data compressor

ADJ M compressing; *Constr* **rouleau c.** road roller, steamroller

compressibilité [kɔ̃prɛsibilite] NF *Phys* compressibility; *(de dépenses, peine de prison etc)* reducibility; **vous êtes assez optimiste quant à la c. des dépenses publiques** you're quite optimistic about the possibility of reducing *or* cutting government spending

compressible [kɔ̃prɛsibl] ADJ **1** *(comprimable)* compressible **2** *(dépenses, peine de prison etc)* reducible

compressif, -ive [kɔ̃prɛsif, -iv] ADJ *(bandage etc)* compressive

compression [kɔ̃prɛsjɔ̃] NF **1** *(de gaz, vapeur etc)* compression; **temps de c.** compression stroke **2** *(réduction)* reduction, cutback; *Ordinat (de données)* compression; **c. des dépenses** spending cuts; **c. des dépenses budgétaires** budget cuts; **c. de crédit** credit squeeze; **c. du personnel** reduction of staff, cutback in staff; **mesure de c.** cutback, reduction

comprimable [kɔ̃primabl] ADJ compressible

comprimé [kɔ̃prime] ADJ compressed; **air c.**

compressed air; **outil à air c.** pneumatic tool ▪ NM *Pharm* tablet; **un c. d'aspirine** an aspirin

comprimer [kɔ̃prime] VT **1** *(gaz, artère), Ordinat (fichier)* to compress; **c. la taille** to squeeze the waist in; **c. les dépenses** to cut down *or* reduce expenditure **2** *(sa colère, sa jalousie etc)* to curb, to repress, to restrain; *(larmes)* to repress, to hold back

compris [kɔ̃pri] ADJ **1** *(enregistré)* **bien c.** (fully) understood; **mal c.** misunderstood; **alors, c'est c.?** so, do you understand *or* have you understood?; **la leçon n'a pas été comprise** (the point of) the lesson wasn't understood; **tu fais tes devoirs immédiatement, c.!** you'll do your homework right now, (is that) understood *or* (do you) understand? **2** *(situé)* **la maison est comprise entre deux avancées de la mer** the house lies between *or* is bounded by two arms of the sea; **le passage c. entre les deux dialogues** the passage between the two dialogues

compromettant [kɔ̃prɔmetã] ADJ *(situation)* compromising; *(documents, photos)* incriminating, compromising

compromettre [kɔ̃prɔmɛtr] *(conj like* **mettre***)* VT **1** *(entacher) (personne, la réputation de qn etc)* to compromise; **être compromis dans un crime** to be implicated in a crime **2** *(mettre en péril) (vie, sécurité, vacances etc)* to jeopardize, to put in jeopardy

VPR **se compromettre** to compromise oneself; *(s'engager)* to commit oneself; **il s'est compromis dans une affaire de fausses factures** he became implicated in a matter of forged invoices

compromis [kɔ̃prɔmi] NM **1** *(arrangement)* compromise, arrangement; **parvenir à un c.** to reach a compromise, to come to an arrangement; **cette robe est un c. entre l'élégance et la décontraction** this dress is neither too elegant nor too casual **2** *Jur* **mettre une affaire en c.** to submit an affair for arbitration; **c. de vente** provisional *or* preliminary sales agreement **3** *(en assurances)* **c. d'avarie** average bond

compromission [kɔ̃prɔmisjɔ̃] NF *souvent Péj* **1** *(avec sa conscience)* compromising **2** *(résultat)* compromise

compta [kɔ̃ta] NF *Fam* accounting

comptabilisation [kɔ̃tabilizasjɔ̃] NF *Fin* posting, entering in *or* into the accounts; *(dénombrement)* counting; **la c. de l'actif d'une société** recording the assets of a company in the accounts; *Bourse* **c. au prix de marché** marking to market

comptabiliser [kɔ̃tabilize] VT **1** *(dénombrer)* to count **2** *Fin* to post, to enter in the accounts; *Bourse* **c. au prix de marché** to mark to market

comptabilité [kɔ̃tabilite] NF **1** *(livres)* accounts; *(technique)* book-keeping, accounting, accountancy; **c. en partie simple/double** single-/double-entry book-keeping; **livre de c.** account book; **méthode de c.** book-keeping *or* accounting method; **tenir la c. d'une maison** to keep the books *or* the accounts of a firm; *Fin* **c. matières** stock record, stores accounts; **c. analytique** cost accounting; **c. bancaire** bank accounting; **c. budgétaire** budgeting; **c. de caisse** cash basis accounting; **c. commerciale** business accounting; **c. des coûts variables** direct cost accounting; **c. d'exploitation** cost accounting; **c. financière** financial accounting; **c. générale** general accounts; *(système)* financial accounting; **c. de gestion** management accounting; **c.-gestion financière** financial management accounting; **c. informatisée** computerized accounts; **c. de prix de revient** cost accounting; **c. publique** public finance; **c. uniforme** uniform accounting **2** *(service)* accounts department

conductivité [kɔ̃dyktivite] NF *Élec* conductivity

CONDUIRE [kɔ̃dɥir] (*prp* **conduisant**; *pp* **conduit**; *pr ind* **je conduis**, n. **conduisons**, ils **conduisent**; *impf* **je conduisais**; *p hist* **je conduisis**; *fu* **je conduirai**) VT **1** (*emmener*) to take; (*en voiture*) to take, to drive; **j'ai dû le c. chez le dentiste de toute urgence** I had to rush him to the dentist; **c. qn à la gare** to take *or* drive sb to the station; **on la conduisit à sa chambre** she was shown *or* taken to her room

2 (*mener*) (*cheval, aveugle etc*) to lead; **c. qn à faire qch** to lead sb to do sth; **ses pas la conduisirent jusqu'à la chapelle** her footsteps led her to the chapel; **les traces de sang nous conduisirent jusqu'au lieu du crime** the bloodstains led us to the scene of the crime; **c. ses hommes au combat** to lead one's men into battle; **cela va nous c. à la catastrophe/ruine** it's going to lead us to disaster/ruin; **c. qn au désespoir/suicide** to drive sb to despair/suicide; **c'est l'appât du gain qui conduit tous ses actes** the thirst for wealth dictates his every action

3 (*piloter*) (*voiture etc*) to drive; (*bateau*) to steer

4 (*l'eau, le gaz etc*) to carry, to convey; **corps qui conduit bien l'électricité** good conductor of electricity

5 (*diriger*) (*entreprise, affaire*) to manage, to run; **c. un orchestre** to conduct an orchestra

VI **1** *Aut* to drive; **elle conduit bien** she is a good driver

2 (*mener*) to lead; **quel est le chemin qui conduit à la gare?** which is the way to the station?; **cette porte ne conduit nulle part** this door doesn't lead anywhere; **elle se laissa c. comme une enfant jusqu'à la cuisine** she let herself be led like a child into the kitchen

VPR **se conduire 1** (*se diriger*) (*d'un engin*) **ça se conduit comment?** how do you drive it?

2 (*se comporter*) to behave; **se c. mal** (*d'un enfant*) to behave badly, to misbehave; **se c. bien/mal avec qn** to behave well/badly towards sb

conduit [kɔ̃dɥi] NM **1** *Tech* conduit, pipe; *Constr, Tech* **c. d'aération** air duct; **c. de ventilation** ventilation shaft; *Naut* **c. de chaîne** hawse hole; *Aut* **c. d'aspiration** suction pipe; *Aut* **c. de carburant** fuel pipe; *Aut* **conduits d'échappement** exhaust manifold **2** *Anat* **c. auditif** auditory canal, *Spéc* meatus; **c. lacrymal** tear *or* *Spec* lachrymal duct; **c. urinaire** urinary canal

conduite [kɔ̃dɥit] NF **1** (*action d'accompagner*) **les chiens qui assurent la c. du troupeau** the dogs which drive the herd; *Fam* **faire un bout de c. à qn** to go part of the way with sb

2 (*de voiture, charrette etc*) driving; (*de bateau, ballon*) steering; **c. à gauche/droite** (*d'une voiture*) left-/right-hand drive; (*d'un pays*) driving on the left/right; **ma voiture a la c. à gauche** my car is left-hand drive; **leçons de c.** driving lessons; **c. dangereuse** dangerous driving

3 (*d'une entreprise, des affaires, opérations*) management, running; (*d'une armée, flotte etc*) command; (*d'une guerre*) conduct; **être sous la c. de qn** (*suivre des ordres*) to be under sb's leadership; (*suivre des conseils*) to be under sb's guidance; **c. des travaux** supervision of works

4 (*comportement*) behaviour, *Am* behavior, conduct; **je ne sais vraiment plus quelle c. adopter avec elle** I really don't know any more what line to take with her; **c'est ma seule ligne de c.** it's my guiding principle; **mauvaise c.** bad behaviour, misbehaviour, misconduct; **il a été relâché pour bonne c.** he was released for good behaviour; **adop-**

ter une c. différente to start to behave differently; **un écart de c.** a misdemeanour; *Vieilli* **il manque de c.** he has no manners, he doesn't know how to behave; *Hum* **s'acheter une c.** to turn over a new leaf; *Scol* **zéro de c.** no marks for conduct

5 *Tech* pipe, conduit, duct; **c. à air** *ou* **d'air** air duct; **c. d'eau** water pipe *or* main(s); **c. de gaz** gas pipe *or* main(s); **c. souple** hose, flexible pipe; **tuyau de c.** conduit pipe; *Aut* **c. d'arrivée du combustible** supply pipe

▶▶ **c. accompagnée** = learning to drive accompanied by someone holding a full driving licence; *Psy* **c. d'échec** defeatist behaviour; **c. en état d'ivresse** drunk driving; *Tech etc* **c. forcée** (*pressure*) pipeline; *Aut* **c. fractionnée** stop-go driving; *Aut* **c. de frein** brake line; **c. intérieure** saloon (car), *Am* sedan; **c. montante** flow pipe, rising main; **c. normale** (*de boîte auto*) drive

condyle [kɔ̃dil] NM *Anat* condyle

cône [kon] NM (*objet, forme*) cone; **en forme de c.** cone-shaped; **c. de pin** pine cone; *Géol* **c. de déjection** alluvial cone; *Astron* **c. d'ombre** (*d'une planète etc*) umbra; *Naut* **c. de tempête** storm cone; **c. de signalisation** signal cone; **c. de chantier** traffic cone; *Aut* **c. d'embrayage** clutch cone; *Aut* **c. de friction** friction cone; *Aut* **c. de synchronisation** synchromesh cone, baulking cone

confection [kɔ̃feksjɔ̃] NF **1** (*d'un vêtement etc*) making; (*d'un repas*) preparation, making; **elle nous a offert des gâteaux de sa c.** she offered us some of her home-made cakes **2** (*industrie*) (ready-to-wear) clothing industry; **robe/vêtements de c.** ready-made *or* off-the-peg dress/clothes; **maison de c.** (ready-to-wear) clothes company; **travailler dans la c.** to work in the clothing industry *or* *Fam* rag trade

confectionner [kɔ̃feksjɔne] VT (*robe*) to make; (*plat*) to prepare, to make

confectionneur, -euse [kɔ̃feksjɔnœr, -øz] N clothes manufacturer

confédéral, -ale, -aux, -ales [kɔ̃federal, -o] ADJ confederal; **débat c.** debate within the confederation

confédération [kɔ̃federasjɔ̃] NF confederation, confederacy

confédéré [kɔ̃federe] ADJ (*nations*) confederate; *Ind, Pol* **syndicat non c.** non-affiliated union

NMPL *Hist* **les Confédérés** the Confederates

confédérer [kɔ̃federe] VT (**je confédère**, n. **confédérons**; **je confédérerai**) to confederate

confer [kɔ̃fɛr] VT (*impératif*) cf, compare

conférence [kɔ̃ferɑ̃s] NF **1** (*congrès, colloque*) conference, meeting; **tenir c.** to hold a conference; **être en c.** to be in a meeting **2** *Univ etc* (*exposé*) lecture; **maître de conférences** lecturer; **salle de conférences** lecture room; **faire une c. sur l'alcoolisme** to lecture *or* to give a lecture on alcoholism

▶▶ **c. au sommet** summit (conference); *Com, Naut* **c. maritime** shipping conference; *Journ* **c. de rédaction** (editors') conference

conférencier, -ière [kɔ̃ferɑ̃sje, -jɛr] N lecturer, speaker; *Univ* lecturer; **c. invité** guest speaker

conférer [kɔ̃fere] (**je confère**, n. **conférons**; **je conférerai**) VT **1** (*privilèges etc*) to confer, to bestow (**à** on); **c. le grade de docteur à qn** to confer a doctor's degree on sb; **ils lui ont conféré tous les pouvoirs** they invested him with *or* granted him full authority; **en vertu des pouvoirs qui me sont conférés** by the authority vested in me **2** (*textes*) to compare, to collate

VI to confer (**avec** with); **nous avons conféré**

de l'affaire we talked the matter over, we conferred on the matter

confesse [kɔ̃fɛs] NF **aller/être à c.** to go to/be at confession

confesser [kɔ̃fese] VT **1** (*reconnaître*) to confess, to admit; **je confesse mon ignorance** I confess *or* admit my ignorance; **j'ai menti, je vous le confesse, mais …** I admit *or* confess I lied, but …, I lied, I admit it, but …; **il confesse qu'il s'est trompé** he admits he was mistaken **2** *Rel* (*ses péchés, sa foi*) to confess **3** (*du prêtre*) (*pénitent*) to confess; *Fig Fam* **on trouvera les moyens de le c.** we'll find a way to make him talk

VI **ce prêtre ne confesse pas** this priest doesn't hear confessions

VPR **se confesser** to confess; *Rel* to confess (one's sins); *Rel* **se c. toutes les semaines** to go to confession every week

confesseur [kɔ̃fesœr] NM **1** *Rel, Fig* (father) confessor **2** *Hist* (*de sa religion, foi*) confessor

confession [kɔ̃fesjɔ̃] NF **1** (*aveu*) confession, admission; **faire la c. de qch** to confess to sth, to own up to sth; **je vais vous faire une c.** I've got a confession to make to you **2** *Rel* (*aveu*) confession; *Fam* **on te donnerait le bon Dieu sans c.** you look as though butter wouldn't melt in your mouth **3** *Rel* (*par un prêtre*) hearing of confession; **entendre qn en c.** to hear sb's confession **4** (*croyance*) denomination, faith, religion; **des élèves de toutes confessions** pupils of all denominations; **une école avec des élèves de toutes confessions** a multi-denominational school

confessionnal, -aux [kɔ̃fesjɔnal, -o] NM *Rel* confessional

confessionnel, -elle [kɔ̃fesjɔnɛl] ADJ (*querelles, affaires*) denominational

confetti [kɔ̃feti] NM (piece of) confetti; **confettis** confetti; *Fam* **tu peux en faire des confettis!** you can chuck it out!, you can throw it in the bin! **VOIR GRAMMAIRE A14**

confiance [kɔ̃fjɑ̃s] NF **1** (*foi*) trust, confidence, faith; **avoir c. en** *ou* **faire c. à qn/qch** to trust sb/sth, to have confidence *or* faith in sb/sth; **il n'a pas c. dans les médecins** he doesn't trust doctors, he has no confidence *or* faith in doctors; **elle a une c. aveugle en toi** she trusts you blindly *or* implicitly; **acheter qch en toute c.** to buy sth with complete confidence; **il me faut un homme de c.** I need a man I can trust *or* rely on; **c'est l'homme de c. du président** he's the one who has the president's confidence; **comment regagner sa c.?** how can I/we/*etc* win back *or* regain his confidence *or* trust?; **abuser de la c. de qn** to abuse sb's trust; **digne de c.** trustworthy, reliable; **maison de c.** reliable firm; **c'est un poste** *ou* **emploi de c.** it's a position of trust; **avec c.** (*avec espoir*) confidently; **je vous parle en toute c.** I know I can trust you (with what I have to say); **tu sais que tu peux me faire c.** you know you can trust me; **faites-moi c.** trust me; *Fam* (*croyez-moi*) believe me; *Pol* **vote de c.** vote of confidence; **un climat de c. économique** a climate of economic confidence

2 (*assurance*) confidence; **manquer de c. en soi** to lack (self-)assurance *or* (self-)confidence

confiant [kɔ̃fjɑ̃] ADJ **1** (*qui fait confiance*) trusting, trustful **2** (*optimiste*) (*nature*) confident (**dans** in) **3** (*qui a confiance en soi*) (*manières etc*) (self-)confident, (self-)assured

confidence [kɔ̃fidɑ̃s] NF confidence; **faire une c. à qn** to confide something to sb, to tell sb a secret; **il ne me fait jamais de c.** he never confides in me; **faire c. de qch à qn** to confide sth to sb; **mettre qn dans la c.** to let sb into the secret; **dire qch en c.** to say sth in confidence *or* confidentially; **confidences sur l'oreiller** pillow talk

> Il faut noter que le nom anglais **confidence** signifie également **confiance**.

confident, -ente [kɔ̃fidɑ̃, -ɑ̃t] N confidant, *f* confidante

confidentialité [kɔ̃fidɑ̃sjalite] NF confidentiality; *Ordinat* **c. des données** data privacy

confidentiel, -ielle [kɔ̃fidɑ̃sjɛl] ADJ confidential; *(mention sur document)* private and confidential; **à titre c.** confidentially, in confidence; *(non officiel)* off-the-record; **succès c.** modest *or* limited success

confidentiellement [kɔ̃fidɑ̃sjɛlmɑ̃] ADV confidentially, in confidence

confier [kɔ̃fje] *(impf, pr sub* n. **confiions**, v. **confiiez)** VT **1** *(laisser)* to entrust; **c. qch à qn** to entrust sb with sth, to entrust sth to sb; **c. qch à la garde de qn** to entrust sth to sb's care; **je leur ai confié les enfants** I left the children with them; **je n'oserais pas c. mes économies à cette banque** I wouldn't dare entrust my savings to this bank *or* entrust this bank with my savings **2** *(dire)* to confide; **c. qch à qn** to confide sth to sb, to tell sb sth in confidence; **est-ce que je peux te c. un secret?** can I tell you a secret?, can I share a secret (with you)?
▶ VPR **se confier 1** *Fml (s'en remettre)* **se c. à qn/qch** to put one's trust in sb/sth **2** *(s'épancher)* **se c. à qn** to confide in sb; **il ne se confie jamais** he never confides in anyone

configurable [kɔ̃figyrabl] ADJ *Ordinat* configurable

configuration [kɔ̃figyrasjɔ̃] NF **1** configuration; *(de bâtiment)* form, shape; *(du terrain)* lie **2** *Ordinat* configuration; **c. matérielle** hardware configuration

configurer [kɔ̃figyre] VT *Ordinat etc* to configure

confiné [kɔ̃fine] ADJ **1** *(atmosphère etc)* enclosed; *(air)* stale **2** *(enfermé)* shut away *or* up; **vivre c. chez soi** to live shut away *or* up indoors

confinement [kɔ̃finmɑ̃] NM confinement

confiner [kɔ̃fine] VI **c. à** *ou* **avec un pays** *(d'un pays etc)* to border on *or* adjoin a country; *Fig* **courage qui confine à la témérité** courage verging *or* bordering on foolhardiness
▶ VT to confine, to shut away *or* up
▶ VPR **se confiner** to confine oneself; **se c. chez soi** to shut oneself away *or* up indoors

confins [kɔ̃fɛ̃] NMPL *(de pays, d'État)* confines, borders; **aux c. de la science et de la métaphysique** on the border between science and metaphysics

confiote [kɔ̃fjɔt] NF *Fam (confiture)* jam

confire [kɔ̃fir] VT *(prp* **confisant;** *pp* **confit;** *pr ind* **je confis,** n. **confisons, ils confisent;** *impf* **je confisais;** *p hist* **je confis;** *fu* **je confirai)** *(fruits etc)* to preserve; *(écorce, zeste etc)* to candy; **c. qch au sel/au vinaigre** to salt sth down/pickle sth

confirmatif, -ive [kɔ̃firmatif, -iv] ADJ *(déclaration)* corroborative; *(jugement)* confirmative

confirmation [kɔ̃firmasjɔ̃] NF **1** *(de nouvelle etc)* confirmation, corroboration; **c. écrite** written confirmation; **c. de commande** confirmation of an/the order; **c. de réservation** confirmation of a/the reservation; **c. d'un jugement** confirmation of a sentence; **il m'en a donné c.** he gave me confirmation of it; **c'est la c. de ce que je pensais** that (just) confirms what I thought; **en c. de** in confirmation of **2** *Rel* confirmation; **donner la c. à qn** to confirm sb

confirmer [kɔ̃firme] VT **1** *(nouvelle, juge-*

ment etc) to confirm; **c. un traité** to ratify a treaty; **cela me confirme dans mon opinion** that confirms *or* strengthens me in my opinion; **elle n'a pas été confirmée dans ses fonctions** she was not given the job (which she had been doing temporarily); **l'exception confirme la règle** the exception proves the rule **2** *Rel (personne)* to confirm
▶ VPR **se confirmer** *(d'un rapport, de doutes etc)* to be confirmed; **le bruit ne s'est pas confirmé** the rumour proved false; **je pensais qu'il était bête et là, ça se confirme** I thought he was stupid and there's the proof of it *or* and I've been proved right

confiscation [kɔ̃fiskasjɔ̃] NF *(de propriété etc)* confiscation, seizure

confiserie [kɔ̃fizri] NF **1** *(de fruits etc)* preserving in sugar **2** *(magasin)* confectioner's (shop), *Br* sweetshop, *Am* candy store **3** *(bonbon)* sweet, *Am* candy; **des confiseries** confectionery, *Br* sweets, *Am* candy

confiseur, -euse [kɔ̃fizœr, -øz] N confectioner

confisquer [kɔ̃fiske] VT *(marchandises, propriété etc)* to confiscate, to seize; **le prof m'a confisqué ma balle** the teacher confiscated my ball; **le président veut c. le pouvoir** the president wants to seize power

confit [kɔ̃fi] ADJ **fruits confits** crystallized *or* candied fruit; *Fig* **être c. en dévotion** to be steeped in piety
▶ NM *Culin* **c. d'oie/de canard** conserve of goose/of duck

confiture [kɔ̃fityr] NF *Culin* jam; **c. de fraises** strawberry jam; **c. d'oranges** (orange) marmalade; *Fig* **ce serait donner de la c. aux cochons** that would be throwing *or* casting pearls before swine

confiturerie [kɔ̃fityrri] NF **1** *(commerce)* jam manufacture **2** *(fabrique)* jam factory

confiturier [kɔ̃fityrje] NM jam maker *or* manufacturer

conflagration [kɔ̃flagrasjɔ̃] NF cataclysm

conflictuel, -elle [kɔ̃fliktɥɛl] ADJ *(témoignages, intérêts etc)* conflicting; **situation conflictuelle** situation of conflict; **ils ont des rapports très conflictuels** they have a very adversarial relationship

conflit [kɔ̃fli] NM **1** *(divergence)* conflict; *(d'intérêts)* conflict, clash; **être en c.** to be at variance *or* *Fam* loggerheads (**avec** with); *(d'intérêts)* to conflict, to clash (**avec** with); **entrer en c. avec qn** to come into conflict with sb, to clash with sb; **le c. des générations** the generation gap; **arbitrage des conflits internationaux** arbitration of international disputes; **conflits sociaux** industrial disputes; **c. du travail** industrial dispute; **c. salarial** pay dispute; *Jur* **tribunal des conflits** = jurisdictional court which decides whether a matter should be dealt with by a civil or other court **2** *(lutte armée)* **c. (armé)** (armed) conflict, war

confluence [kɔ̃flɥɑ̃s] NF confluence

confluent [kɔ̃flɥɑ̃] NM *(de fleuves, veines etc)* confluence

confluer [kɔ̃flɥe] VI to meet, to join, to unite; **l'Oise conflue avec la Seine** the Oise flows into the Seine

confondant [kɔ̃fɔ̃dɑ̃] ADJ *(qui met en confusion)* confusing; *(qui trouble)* astounding

confondre [kɔ̃fɔ̃dr] VT **1** *(réunir)* to merge, to mingle, to intermingle; **toutes tendances confondues, les électeurs ont voté en masse pour lui** voters of all political tendencies voted massively for him
2 *(mélanger) (noms)* to confuse, to mix up; **je les confonds toujours** I always confuse them *or* mix them up, I always get them confused *or* mixed up
3 *(sidérer) (personne)* to astound, to stag-

ger; **son insolence me confond** I'm astounded by his insolence, his insolence astounds me
4 *(démasquer) (criminel etc)* to find, to track down; **c. un menteur** to show up a liar
▶ VI to be mistaken; **tu dois c., ce n'est pas ça** you must be mistaken, that's not it at all
▶ VPR **se confondre 1** *(de couleurs etc)* to merge, to blend (**en** into)
2 *(de ruisseaux etc)* to merge, to flow into each other; *(d'intérêts etc)* to merge, to be identical; **se c. en excuses/remerciements** to apologize profusely/be profuse in one's thanks; **se c. en excuses/remerciements devant qn** to apologize profusely to sb/thank sb profusely; **leurs voix se confondent au loin** their voices merge *or* mingle in the distance

confondu [kɔ̃fɔ̃dy] ADJ **1** *(décontenancé)* disconcerted; **je suis tout c. de votre bonté** I am overwhelmed by your kindness **2** *(sidéré)* astounded, dumbfounded (**de** at); **en rester c.** to be (left) dumbfounded

conformation [kɔ̃fɔrmasjɔ̃] NF *(de collines, parties du corps etc)* conformation, structure

conforme [kɔ̃fɔrm] ADJ **1** *(identique)* **copie c. à l'original** exact copy; *Admin* **pour copie c.** certified true copy; *Fig* **elle est la copie c. de sa mère** she is the exact *or* very image of her mother **2** *(qui correspond à)* **il mène une vie c. à ses moyens** he lives according to his means; **la réalisation n'est pas c. à ce qui avait été prévu** it is not being carried out in keeping with *or* in accordance with what was agreed; **les sanitaires ne sont pas conformes** the sanitary installations are not standard; **non c.** *(pensée, idée)* unorthodox

conformé [kɔ̃fɔrme] ADJ **bien c.** *(enfant etc)* well-formed; **mal c.** *(membre etc)* misshapen

conformément [kɔ̃fɔrmemɑ̃] ADV **c. à** in accordance with; **c. à la loi** according to *or* in accordance with the law; **c. à vos ordres** in accordance with your orders; **c. à ce qui a été prévu** according to *or* in accordance with what was planned; **tout se passe c. aux plans** everything's going according to plan

conformer [kɔ̃fɔrme] VT to model (**à** on); **c. sa vie à certains principes** to shape one's life according to certain principles
▶ VPR **se conformer** **se c. à qch** to conform to sth, to comply with *or* abide by sth; **se c. à la règle** to conform to the rule; *Com* **se c. au modèle** to keep (to) the pattern

conformisme [kɔ̃fɔrmism] NM *(traditionalisme)* conformism, conventionalism; *Rel* conformism, conformity

conformiste [kɔ̃fɔrmist] N *(traditionaliste)* conformist, conventionalist; *Rel (de l'Église anglicane)* conformist
▶ ADJ conformist

conformité [kɔ̃fɔrmite] NF *(ressemblance)* similarity; *Rel* conformity; *(d'un produit aux normes)* compliance; **en c. avec** in accordance with; **être en c. de goûts avec qn** to have similar tastes to sb

confort [kɔ̃fɔr] NM comfort; **hôtel avec tout le c. moderne** hotel with every modern convenience *or Fam* with all mod cons; **manquer de c.** to be lacking in comfort, to be uncomfortable; **une maison sans c.** an uncomfortable house; **elle aime bien son petit c.** she likes her creature comforts *or* her little comforts; **c. d'écoute** *(d'une station de radio)* quality of reception; **c. d'emploi** *(d'un ordinateur etc)* user-friendliness, ease of use; **c. visuel** *(d'un écran)* easiness on the eye; **médicament de c.** = medicine not considered essential and not reimbursed by Social Security

confortable [kɔ̃fɔrtabl] ADJ *(fauteuil,*

maison, chaussures etc), *Fig* comfortable; (*financièrement*) comfortable, well-off, comfortably off; **des appointements confortables** a comfortable *or* good salary; **une vie c.** a comfortable life(style); *Fig* **il est plus c. de penser que tout va bien** it's easier *or* more comfortable to think that everything is going well

NM *Can (édredon)* quilt, *Am* comforter

confortablement [kɔ̃fɔrtabləmɑ̃] ADV comfortably; **installe-toi c.** make yourself comfortable; **être c. rémunéré** to be on a good salary, to be well paid

conforter [kɔ̃fɔrte] VT to reinforce, to strengthen, to confirm; *(position, avance)* to consolidate; **cela me conforte dans mon opinion** that reinforces *or* strengthens *or* confirms my opinion

confraternel, -elle [kɔ̃fratɛrnɛl] ADJ fraternal, brotherly

confraternité [kɔ̃fratɛrnite] NF brotherliness

confrère [kɔ̃frɛr] NM *(de profession)* colleague; *(de société)* fellow member

confrérie [kɔ̃freri] NF *Rel* brotherhood, confraternity

confrontation [kɔ̃frɔ̃tasjɔ̃] NF **1** *Jur (d'un accusé avec un témoin)* confrontation, confronting; *Fig (d'opinions, d'idéaux etc)* clash, conflict **2** *(comparaison)* comparison (**à, avec** with); *(de textes)* comparison, collation

confronter [kɔ̃frɔ̃te] VT **1** to confront; *(prisonnier)* to confront, to bring face to face (**avec, à** with); **être confronté à un problème** to be confronted with a problem **2** *(comparer)* to compare (**avec, à** with); *(textes)* to collate

VPR se confronter se c. à un adversaire to confront an opponent; **nous nous sommes confrontés** we confronted each other (**au sujet de** about)

confucéen, -éenne [kɔ̃fyseɛ̃, -eɛn] ADJ Confucian

confucianisme [kɔ̃fysjanism] NM Confucianism

confus [kɔ̃fy] ADJ **1** *(mélangé) (masse etc)* confused, jumbled, chaotic; *(explication)* confused, muddled; *(bruit)* indistinct; *(vision)* dim, blurred; *(style, texte)* obscure, unclear; **une affaire pour le moins confuse** a confused *or* muddled business to say the least **2** *(embarrassé)* embarrassed, abashed; **je suis c.** *(après un faux pas)* I'm so embarrassed, I don't know where to put myself; *(devant votre bonté)* I don't know what to say; **je suis c. de vous déranger** I'm so sorry to disturb you

Il faut noter que l'adjectif anglais **confused** est un faux ami. Il signifie le plus souvent **désorienté, embrouillé**.

confusément [kɔ̃fyzemɑ̃] ADV confusedly, vaguely, indistinctly; **j'entrevoyais c. la solution du problème** I was slowly beginning to see a solution to the problem

confusion [kɔ̃fyzjɔ̃] NF **1** *(désordre)* confusion, disorder, disarray; **il a réussi à s'échapper, profitant de la c. générale** he managed to escape in the general confusion; **mettre la c. dans l'assemblée** to throw the audience into confusion; **jeter la c. dans les esprits** to confuse people; *Méd* **c. mentale** mental aberration; **un moment de c.** a moment of confusion, a moment's confusion **2** *(erreur) (de noms, dates etc)* mix-up, confusion; **il y a eu c. entre deux personnes** they got two people mixed up *or* confused; **c'est une grossière c.** it's a stupid mix-up **3** *(gêne)* embarrassment, confusion; **être rouge de c.** to be red with embarrassment, *Fml* to be covered in confusion **4** *Jur* **avec c. des peines** the sentences to run concurrently

congé [kɔ̃ʒe] NM **1** *(vacances)* holiday, *Am* vacation; *Mil* leave; **il ne me reste plus de c. à prendre** I've used up all my holiday (entitlement); **en c.** on holiday, *Am* on vacation; *Mil* on leave; **un après-midi de c.** an afternoon off; **on a c. lundi** we've got Monday off, Monday's a holiday; **prendre c. de qn** to take (one's) leave of sb; **donner c. à qn** to dismiss sb **2** *(avis de renvoi)* notice; **donner son c. à qn** to give sb his notice; **demander son c.** to hand in *or* give in one's notice, to give notice; **donner c. à un locataire** to give a tenant notice (to quit) **3** *(autorisation)* authorization, permit; *(de vin en douane)* release; *Naut* **c. de navigation** clearance certificate

▸▸ *Admin* **c. annuel** annual leave, annual holiday, *Am* vacation leave; **c. de longue durée** extended leave; **c. de maladie** sick leave; **c. de maternité** maternity leave; **c. parental d'éducation** = maternity/paternity leave; **c. de paternité** paternity leave; **congés payés** paid holidays *or* leave, *Am* paid vacation; **c. pour convenance personnelle** leave for personal reasons, compassionate leave; **c. sabbatique** sabbatical; **c. sans solde** unpaid leave *or* holidays, *Am* unpaid vacation

congédiable [kɔ̃ʒedjabl] ADJ liable to be dismissed at any time; *Mil* due for discharge

congédier [kɔ̃ʒedje] VT *(impf, pr sub n. congédiions, v. congédiiez)* **1** *(employé)* to dismiss **2** *(visiteur)* to dismiss; *Mil, Naut (hommes)* to discharge

congelable [kɔ̃ʒlabl] ADJ suitable for freezing, freezable; **aliment non c.** foodstuff unsuitable for freezing

congélateur [kɔ̃ʒelatœr] NM freezer, deep-freeze

congélation [kɔ̃ʒelasjɔ̃] NF *(d'aliments)* (deep-)freezing; *(de l'eau etc)* freezing; *(de l'huile)* congealing; **point de c. de l'eau** freezing point of water; **sac (de) c.** freezer bag

congeler [kɔ̃ʒle] *(il congèle; il congèlera)* VT *(aliments)* to (deep-)freeze; *(eau etc)* to freeze; **viande congelée** frozen meat; **ne pas c.** do not freeze

VPR se congeler to freeze

congélo [kɔ̃ʒelo] NM *(abrév* **congélateur***)* freezer

congénère [kɔ̃ʒenɛr] ADJ *Biol* congeneric; *Anat (muscle)* congenerous

N *Biol* congener; *Fam* **lui et ses congénères** him and his sort *or* his like

congénital, -ale, -aux, -ales [kɔ̃ʒenital, -o] ADJ congenital; *Méd* **malformation congénitale** congenital malformation; *Fam* **inconscience congénitale** innate *or* congenital thoughtlessness

congère [kɔ̃ʒɛr] NF snowdrift

congestif, -ive [kɔ̃ʒɛstif, -iv] ADJ *Méd* congestive

congestion [kɔ̃ʒɛstjɔ̃] NF *Méd* congestion; **c. cérébrale** stroke; **c. pulmonaire** congestion of the lungs

congestionné [kɔ̃ʒɛstjɔne] ADJ *(visage)* flushed, red; *(routes)* congested; **les routes sont très congestionnées** the roads are very congested, there's a lot of congestion on the roads

congestionner [kɔ̃ʒɛstjɔne] VT **1** *Méd* to congest; *(visage)* to flush **2** *(boucher)* to block, to congest; **les voitures congestionnent la rue** the cars are blocking the street

VPR se congestionner to become congested

conglomérat [kɔ̃glɔmera] NM *Écon, Géol* conglomerate

conglomération [kɔ̃glɔmerasjɔ̃] NF conglomeration

conglomérer [kɔ̃glɔmere] *(* **je conglomère, n. conglomérons; je conglomérerai** *)* VT to conglomerate

VPR se conglomérer to conglomerate

Congo [kɔ̃go] NM **le C.** the Congo

congolais, -aise [kɔ̃gɔlɛ, -ɛz] ADJ Congolese

N C. Congolese

NM *Culin* coconut cake

congratulations [kɔ̃gratylasjɔ̃] NFPL congratulations; **mes c. pour ta réussite** congratulations on your success

congratuler [kɔ̃gratyle] VT *(personne)* to congratulate (**pour** on)

VPR se congratuler to congratulate oneself, *Fam* to pat oneself on the back

congre [kɔ̃gr] NM conger (eel)

congrégation [kɔ̃gregasjɔ̃] NF **1** *Rel (communauté)* community *(group of monasteries)*; *(de cardinaux)* congregation **2** *Fig* assembly

congrès [kɔ̃grɛ] NM conference, convention; **C. des États-Unis** United States Congress; **membre du C.** congressman, *f* congresswoman; **palais des c.** conference centre; **c. annuel** *(d'un parti politique)* annual conference

congressiste [kɔ̃gresist] N conference participant, *Am* conventioneer; *Pol* conference delegate

congru [kɔ̃gry] ADJ **1** portion congrue *(income providing a)* bare living; *Rel (de prêtre)* emolument; **réduire qn à la portion congrue** to put sb on short allowance **2** *Math* congruent **3** *Arch (adéquat)* sufficient, adequate

congruence [kɔ̃gryɑ̃s] NF *Math* congruence

congruent [kɔ̃gryɑ̃] ADJ *Math* congruent

conifère [kɔnifɛr] NM *Bot* conifer

conique [kɔnik, ko-] ADJ **1** *Géom* conical, cone-shaped; *Math* **section c.** conic section **2** *Tech etc (tige, goupille etc)* coned, tapering; **engrenage c.** bevel gearing

conjectural, -ale, -aux, -ales [kɔ̃ʒɛktyral, -o] ADJ conjectural

conjecture [kɔ̃ʒɛktyr] NF conjecture, surmise; **se perdre en conjectures** to get lost *or* lose oneself in conjecture(s); **ce n'est que pure c.** it's sheer conjecture

conjecturer [kɔ̃ʒɛktyre] VT to conjecture about, to guess at

VI to conjecture, to hypothesize; **il conjecture sur ce qu'il ignore** he conjectures *or* makes guesses about things he knows nothing about

conjoint, -ointe [kɔ̃ʒwɛ̃] ADJ **1** joint, united; *Fin* **compte c.** joint account; *Jur* **legs c.** joint legacy; **légataires conjoints** co-legatees **2** *Jur (marié)* married

N spouse; **les conjoints** the husband and wife; **féliciter les conjoints** to congratulate the couple; **les conjoints n'ont pas été invités** partners weren't invited

conjointement [kɔ̃ʒwɛ̃tmɑ̃] ADV jointly; *Jur* **c. et solidairement** jointly and severally

conjoncteur [kɔ̃ʒɔ̃ktœr] NM *Élec* circuit closer

conjoncteur-disjoncteur, *pl* **conjoncteurs-disjoncteurs** NM *Aut* cut-out (valve), *Élec* make-and-break (switch)

conjonctif, -ive [kɔ̃ʒɔ̃ktif, -iv] ADJ *(tissu etc)* connective, *Gram* **locution/proposition conjonctive** conjunctive phrase/clause

conjonction [kɔ̃ʒɔ̃ksjɔ̃] NF **1** *(réunion)* union; **la c. de nos efforts** our combined efforts **2** *Gram* conjunction; **c. de subordination/coordination** subordinating/coordinating conjunction SEE GRAMMAR A73–6; B57–8

conjonctive [kɔ̃ʒɔ̃ktiv] NF *(de l'œil)* conjunctiva

conjonctivite [kɔ̃ʒɔ̃ktivit] NF *Méd* conjunctivitis; **faire** *ou* **avoir de la c.** to have conjunctivitis

conjoncture [kɔ̃ʒɔ̃ktyr] NF *(situation)* circumstances, situation; **dans la c. actuelle** at this (present) juncture, under the present circumstances, in the present situation; *Pol, Écon* **c. économique** overall economic situation; **on assiste à une dégradation de la c. économique** the economic situation is deteriorating; **étude de c.** study of the state of the economy

conjoncturel, -elle [kɔ̃ʒɔ̃ktyrɛl] ADJ relating to the current economic climate, economic; *(chômage)* cyclical; **crise conjoncturelle** economic crisis

conjoncturiste [kɔ̃ʒɔ̃ktyrist] NM *Écon* economic analyst

conjugable [kɔ̃ʒygabl] ADJ *Gram* conjugable

conjugaison [kɔ̃ʒygɛzɔ̃] NF *Gram, Biol etc (de verbe, de cellules etc)* conjugation; *Fig Litt* **grâce à la c. de leurs efforts** thanks to their joint efforts SEE GRAMMAR B24

conjugal, -ale, -aux, -ales [kɔ̃ʒygal, -o] ADJ *(devoir)* marital, conjugal; **vie conjugale** married life; **le domicile c.** the marital *or* matrimonial home; **bonheur c.** wedded *or* married bliss; **le lit c.** the marriage bed

conjugalement [kɔ̃ʒygalmã] ADV conjugally; **vivre c.** to live together as a married couple *or* as man and wife

conjugué [kɔ̃ʒyge] ADJ *(efforts etc)* joint, combined; *Tech* paired, twin; *Math, Opt* conjugate; *Bot* **feuilles conjuguées** conjugate leaves; **machines conjuguées** paired engines

conjuguer [kɔ̃ʒyge] VT **1** *Gram* to conjugate **2** *(unir) (efforts)* to combine
   VPR **se conjuguer** *Gram* to be conjugated

conjuration [kɔ̃ʒyrasjɔ̃] NF **1** *(complot)* conspiracy, plot **2** *(charme)* exorcism, conjuration

conjuré, -ée [kɔ̃ʒyre] N conspirator

conjurer [kɔ̃ʒyre] VT **1** *(implorer)* **c. qn de faire qch** to entreat *or* beg *or* beseech *or* implore sb to do sth; **je t'en conjure** I beg *or* beseech *or* implore you **2** *(écarter) (danger, mauvais sort etc)* to avert, to ward off **3** *(démon)* to cast out, to exorcise **4** *Arch (conspirer)* to plot
   VPR **se conjurer** to conspire (together) **(contre** against)

connaissable [kɔnɛsabl] ADJ knowable

connaissance [kɔnɛsɑ̃s] NF **1** *(savoir)* knowledge; **prendre c. de qch** to make oneself acquainted with sth, to study *or* examine sth; **avoir c. de qch** to know sth; **donner c. de qch à qn, porter qch à la c. de qn** to inform sb of sth, to make sth known to sb; **il n'a jamais, à ma c., été malade** he has never, to my knowledge *or* as far as I know, had a day's illness; **en (toute) c. de cause** with full knowledge of the facts, advisedly; **je souhaite que vous preniez la décision en toute c. de cause** I hope you're making an informed decision; *Mktg* **c. de la marque** brand familiarity, brand awareness; **connaissances en informatique** computing skills
   2 *(contact)* **faire c. avec qn, faire la c. de qn** to make sb's acquaintance, to meet sb; **quand je fis sa c.** when I first knew him; **lier c. avec qn** to strike up an acquaintance with sb; **une figure de c.** a familiar face; **en pays de c.** *(parmi des gens)* among familiar faces; *Fig* on familiar ground; **une personne de ma c.** someone I know, an acquaintance of mine; **je ne la connais pas, c'est une vague**
   3 *(personne)* acquaintance; **c'est une de mes connaissances** he is an acquaintance of mine; **je ne la connais pas, c'est une vague**

---

c. I don't (really) know her, she's just an acquaintance; *Fam* **c'est une vieille c.** I've known him for ages, he's an old acquaintance; *Fam Vieilli* **je l'ai rencontré avec sa c.** I met him with his girlfriend
   4 *(maîtrise)* knowledge; *Jur* cognizance; *Phil* cognition; **la c. de soi** self-knowledge; **avoir la c. de plusieurs langues** to know several languages; **ma c. du russe/du droit** my knowledge of Russian/the law; **connaissances** knowledge; **connaissances informatiques** computer literacy; **avoir des connaissances en informatique** to be computer-literate; **avoir de grandes connaissances en mathématiques** to be very knowledgeable about *or* very well versed in mathematics; **elle a des connaissances en maths** she has some knowledge of maths; **avoir des connaissances sommaires sur qch** to have a basic *or* rudimentary knowledge of sth, to know the basics *or* rudiments of sth; **l'acquisition des connaissances** the acquisition of knowledge, the learning process
   5 *(conscience)* consciousness; **perdre c.** to lose consciousness; **avoir des pertes de c.** to have blackouts *or* fainting fits; **reprendre c.** to regain consciousness, to come round, to come to; **sans c.** unconscious; **il a toute sa c.** he's fully conscious

connaissement [kɔnɛsmã] NM *Naut, Com* bill of lading, waybill; **c. aérien** air waybill; **c. clausé** dirty bill; **c. de groupage** groupage bill; **c. de transbordement** transshipment bill of lading; **c. de transport combiné** combined transport bill of lading; **c. direct** through bill; **c. embarqué** shipped bill; **c. fluvial** inland waterway bill of lading; **c. maritime** marine bill of lading; **c. net** clean bill of lading; **c. périmé** stale bill

connaisseur, -euse [kɔnɛsœr, -øz] N connoisseur, expert; **être bon c. en qch** to be an expert judge of sth
   ADJ expert, knowledgeable; **je ne suis pas du tout c.** I'm by no means an expert; **regarder qch d'un œil c.** to look at sth with an expert eye

CONNAÎTRE [kɔnɛtr] *(prp* **connaissant;** *pp* **connu;** *pr ind* **je connais, il connaît, n. connaissons;** *impf* **je connaissais;** *p hist* **je connus;** *fu* **je connaîtrai)**

VT to know **1–5** ▪ to be acquainted with **1, 2** ▪ to be familiar with **1, 3** ▪ to meet **2** ▪ to recognize **4**	
VPR to know oneself **1** ▪ to know all about **2** ▪ to meet **3**	

VT 1 *(détails)* to know, to be aware of, to be acquainted with; *(paroles d'une chanson)* to know; **c. les chemins** to be familiar with the roads; **tu connais la route?** do you know the way?; **je lui connaissais du talent** I knew he had talent; **faire c. qch** to bring sth to light, to make sth known; **faire c. ses intentions** to make one's intentions known; **je vous ferai c. mes intentions** I'll let you know what I intend to do; **il n'a jamais connu l'amour** he has never known *or* experienced love; **il a connu un destin tragique** his was a tragic fate; **elle n'a jamais connu la faim** she's never known hunger *or* what hunger means; **cette région connaît actuellement une famine** this region is now experiencing a famine; **je ne connais pas Milan** I don't know Milan, I'm not familiar with *or* acquainted with Milan; *Fam* **mais bien sûr, je ne connais que ça** it's something I'm totally familiar with, it's a subject I'm quite at home with; **connaissez-vous la nouvelle?** have you heard the news?; **sa bonté ne connaît pas de limites** his goodness knows no bounds; **il est sorti, ni vu ni connu** he went out without anyone noticing; **elle ne connaît que son travail** she's only in-

---

terested in her work, she lives for her work; *Fam* **elle en connaît un rayon sur la question** she knows a thing or two *or* quite a bit about the matter; **tu ne connais pas ta chance** you don't know how lucky you are, you don't know your luck; *Fam* **je connais la musique** *ou* **la chanson** I've heard it all before, it's the same old story
   2 *(personne)* to know, to be acquainted with; *(rencontrer)* to meet, to make the acquaintance of; **c. qn de nom/vue** to know sb by name/sight; **c. qn de réputation** to know sb by reputation, to have heard of sb; **c. son monde** to know the people one has to deal with; **méfie-toi, il connaît du monde** watch out, he knows people; **il est connu comme le loup blanc** everybody knows him *or* has heard of him; **il est connu ici** he's well known around here; **se faire c.** to introduce oneself; *(par le public etc)* to make a name for oneself, to become well known; **je vous le ferai c.** I'll introduce him to you; *Fam* **j'en connais un qui ne va pas être content!** somebody's not going to be happy!; *Fam* **je le connais par cœur/comme ma poche** I know him through and through/can read him like a(n open) book; **ça, c'est un diamant bleu ou je ne m'y connais pas!** that's a blue diamond or I'm a Dutchman *or* I'm very much mistaken!; *Fam* **le foot, ça me connaît** I know all there is to know about football; *Fam* **si tu fais ça, je ne te connais plus** if you do that, I'll have nothing more to do with you *or* I'll disown you
   3 *(langue)* to know; *(science, art)* to know about, to be familiar with; **c. à fond** to have a thorough knowledge of, to be thoroughly conversant with; *(une langue)* to have a thorough command of; **elle connaît très bien le russe** she knows Russian very well, she has a very good command of Russian; **je ne connais pas cette théorie** I don't know *or* I'm not familiar with that theory; **il n'y connaît rien** he doesn't know anything about it
   4 *(reconnaître)* to know, to recognize; **c. le bien du mal** to know good from evil
   5 *Bible (femme)* to know
   VI *Jur* **c. de qch** to take cognizance of sth
   VPR se connaître 1 se c. (soi-même) to know oneself
   2 elle s'y connaît en hommes/en œnologie she knows all about men/wine; *Fam* **il s'y connaît** he's an expert
   3 *(se rencontrer)* to meet; **ils se sont connus en 1990** they met in 1990
   4 il ne se connaît plus he has lost control of himself; **il ne se connaît plus de joie** he's beside himself with joy, he's walking on air

connard, -arde [kɔnar, -ard] ADJ, N = **conard**

connecter [kɔnɛkte] VT *Élec, Électron* to connect; *Ordinat* **connecté** on line; **ne pas être connecté** not to be on line, to be off line; **connecté en anneau/bus/étoile** in a ring/bus/star configuration; **connecté en série** series-connected; **c. en boucle** to daisy-chain
   VPR **se connecter** *Élec, Électron* to be connected; *Ordinat* **se c. à un système** to log on to a system

connecteur [kɔnɛktœr] NM *Élec, Électron* connector; *Ordinat* **c. d'extension** expansion slot

connectivité [kɔnɛktivite] NF *Ordinat* connectivity

connement [kɔnmã] ADV *très Fam* stupidly; **il s'est fait c. piquer sa caisse** the stupid idiot got his car pinched; **et c. j'ai accepté** and like the idiot that I am, I said yes

connerie [kɔnri] NF *très Fam* damned *or Br* bloody stupidity; *(remarque, acte)* damned *or Br* bloody stupid thing; **c'est de la c., ne le crois pas!** it's bullshit *or* crap, don't believe it!; **tu as fait là une c. magistrale** that was bloody stupid of you; **dire** *ou* **raconter des conneries** to talk bullshit *or* crap; **ce sont des conneries** it's a load of crap *or Br* bollocks; **c'est bientôt fini, vos conneries?** will you stop pissing about!; **il a fait quelques conneries dans sa jeunesse** he did some pretty stupid things when he was young

connétable [kɔnetabl] **NM** *Hist* constable

connexe [kɔnɛks] **ADJ** connected, related

connexion [kɔnɛksjɔ̃] **NF 1** *(d'éléments, d'idées etc)* connection **2** *Élec* connection; *Ordinat* **c. directe au réseau** direct network connection; **c. à un autre réseau** *(d'un téléphone portable)* roaming

connivence [kɔnivɑ̃s] **NF** connivance, complicity; **agir/être de c. avec qn** to act/be in connivance *or* in collusion with sb, to connive with sb; **des regards de c.** conniving looks

connotation [kɔnɔtasjɔ̃] **NF** connotation

connoter [kɔnɔte] **VT** to imply, to connote; *Ling* to connote

connu [kɔny] **ADJ** *(écrivain, chanteur etc)* well-known, famous; **c'est (un fait) bien c.!** that's a well-known fact!; everyone knows that!; **elle est bien connue, celle-là!** that's an old one!, that's an old joke!

NM passer *ou* **aller du c. à l'inconnu** to go from the known to the unknown

conque [kɔ̃k] **NF 1** *(coquille)* conch **2** *Anat* external ear, *Spéc* concha

conquérant, -ante [kɔ̃kerɑ̃, -ɑ̃t] **ADJ** *(nation etc)* conquering; *Fam* **air c.** swaggering air, swagger

N conqueror; **Guillaume le C.** William the Conqueror

conquérir [kɔ̃kerir] *(prp* **conquérant;** *pp* **conquis;** *pr ind* **je conquiers, n. conquérons, ils conquièrent;** *impf* **je conquérais;** *p hist* **je conquis;** *fu* **je conquerrai) VT** *(pays, peuple)* to conquer; *(personne, animal)* to win over; **ils ont tout de suite été conquis par son charme** they were immediately won over by his charm; **se battre pour c. un marché** to fight (in order) to conquer *or* capture *or* win a market; **c. l'estime de qn** to win *or* gain sb's esteem

VPR se conquérir to be (hard) won *or* earned

conquête [kɔ̃kɛt] **NF 1** *(action de conquérir)* conquest; **faire la c. d'un pays** to conquer a country; **faire la c. de qn** to make a conquest of sb; **vous avez fait sa c.!** you've made a conquest!; **se lancer à la c. du pouvoir** to make a bid for power; **la c. de nouveaux marchés en Asie est une des priorités de l'entreprise** conquering new Asian markets is one of the company's priorities **2** *(territoire)* conquered territory **3** *Fam (personne)* conquest; **il nous a présenté sa dernière c.** he introduced us to his latest conquest

conquistador [kɔ̃kistadɔr] **NM** conquistador

consacré [kɔ̃sakre] **ADJ 1** *Rel (vaisseau etc)* consecrated, sacred; *(terrain)* hallowed **2** *(coutume etc)* established; **selon l'expression consacrée** as the saying goes; **c. par l'usage** sanctioned by usage

consacrer [kɔ̃sakre] **VT 1** *Rel (autel, le pain et le vin etc)* to consecrate; **c. un évêque/un prêtre** to consecrate a bishop/ordain a priest **2** *(sa vie à Dieu)* to dedicate (à to); *(son temps, énergie à qch)* to devote (à to); **c. sa vie à la lecture et à l'étude** to devote one's life to reading and study; **combien de temps pouvez-vous me c.?** how much time can you spare *or* give me? **3** *(souvenir, endroit etc)* to sanctify, to hallow **4** *(entériner)* to establish

VPR se consacrer se c. à son travail/foyer to devote oneself to one's work/family; **se c. à Dieu** to dedicate oneself to God

consanguin [kɔ̃sɑ̃gɛ̃] **ADJ 1 frère c./sœur consanguine** half-brother/-sister (on the father's side); **mariage c.** marriage between blood relations, intermarriage **2** *(cheval etc)* inbred

consanguinité [kɔ̃sɑ̃g(ɥ)inite] **NF 1** consanguinity *(through the father)* **2** *(de cheval etc)* inbreeding

consciemment [kɔ̃sjamɑ̃] **ADV** consciously, knowingly, wittingly

conscience [kɔ̃sjɑ̃s] **NF 1** *Physiol, Psy* consciousness; *Phil* (self-)consciousness; **perdre c.** to lose consciousness; **reprendre doucement c.** to slowly regain consciousness *or* come round; **à 80 ans, elle a encore toute sa c.** at the age of 80, she is still very alert; **avoir c. de qch/d'avoir fait qch** to be aware *or* conscious of sth/of having done sth; **avoir c. de ses capacités** to be aware of one's abilities; **prendre c. de qch** to become aware of sth; **il finira par prendre c. de la gravité de la situation** he'll eventually wake up to the seriousness of the situation; **c'est la première fois que j'en ai pris c.** it's the first time that I have been aware of it; **prise de c.** sudden awareness

2 *(morale)* conscience; **mauvaise c.** guilty *or* bad conscience; **j'ai bonne c.** my conscience is clear; **c'est un moyen pour se donner bonne c.** it's a way of easing one's conscience; **c. large** accommodating conscience; **écouter la voix de sa c.** to listen to (the voice of) one's conscience; *Fam* **il a la c. élastique** he is not over-scrupulous; **pour avoir la c. tranquille, je vais vérifier que tout est bien fermé** to set my mind at rest, I'll just make sure everything's locked up; **faire qch par acquit de c.** to do sth for the sake of one's conscience; **dire qch en c.** to say sth in all conscience; **manque de c.** unscrupulousness; **avoir qch sur la c.** to have sth on one's conscience; **ça m'est longtemps resté sur la c.** it was on my conscience *or* preyed on my mind for a long time; **liberté de c.** freedom of conscience; **fais selon ta c.** do as you think right

3 *(dans son travail)* conscientiousness; **faire qch avec c.** to do sth conscientiously

▶ ▶ **c. de classe** class-consciousness; **c. collective** collective consciousness; **c. professionnelle** professional integrity; **c. de soi** self-awareness

> Attention: ne pas confondre **conscience** et **consciousness** lorsque l'on traduit le terme français **conscience**. Le terme anglais **conscience** se rapporte à la conscience morale, alors que **consciousness** se rapporte à la conscience psychologique et s'oppose à l'inconscience.

consciencieusement [kɔ̃sjɑ̃sjøzmɑ̃] **ADV** conscientiously

consciencieux, -ieuse [kɔ̃sjɑ̃sjø, -jøz] **ADJ** *(personne, travail)* conscientious

conscient [kɔ̃sjɑ̃] **ADJ 1** *(lucide etc)* conscious; *Phil* (self-)conscious; **un être c.** a conscious being; **c'est un choix tout à fait c.** it's an entirely conscious choice; **être c. de qch** to be aware *or* conscious of sth; **être c. de ses devoirs** to be aware of one's duties, to know where one's duty lies; **es-tu c. que tu as failli tous nous tuer?** are you aware *or* do you realize that you nearly killed us all? **2** *Méd* conscious; **le malade n'est plus c.** the patient is no longer conscious *or* has lost consciousness

conscription [kɔ̃skripsjɔ̃] **NF** *Mil* conscription, *Am* draft

conscrit [kɔ̃skri] **NM 1** *Mil (qui a l'âge d'être inscrit)* person liable to conscription; *(qui fait son service)* conscript, recruit, *Am* draftee **2** *Vieilli Fig* novice, greenhorn

consécration [kɔ̃sekrasjɔ̃] **NF 1** *(d'église, d'évêque etc)* consecration; *(de prêtre)* ordination **2** *(du pain et du vin)* consecration **3** *(établissement) (de coutume, réputation)* establishing; **exposer dans cette galerie sera pour lui la c.** exhibiting in that gallery will establish his reputation

consécutif, -ive [kɔ̃sekytif, -iv] **ADJ 1** *(qui se suivent)* consecutive; **pendant trois jours consécutifs** for three days running *or* in a row, for three consecutive days; *Gram* **proposition consécutive** consecutive clause **2 c. à** following on from; **fatigue consécutive à une longue marche** fatigue resulting from a long walk

consécutivement [kɔ̃sekytivmɑ̃] **ADV** consecutively, in succession; **c. à** following

conseil [kɔ̃sɛj] **NM 1** *(recommandation)* (piece of) advice, *Fml* counsel; *(en marketing, promotion, finance etc)* consultancy; **c'est un homme de bon c.** he gives good *or* sound advice; **c'est un bon c.** that's a good piece of advice, that's good advice; **donner un c. à qn** to advise sb; **demander c. à qn** to ask sb's advice, to ask sb for advice; **j'ai besoin de tes conseils** *ou* **ton c.** I need your advice; **suivre les conseils de qn** to follow *or* heed sb's advice; **j'écoutais les conseils de son expérience** I learned from his experience; **pouvez-vous me donner quelques conseils?** can you give me some hints *or* tips?; *Prov* **la nuit porte c.** sleep on it

2 *(assemblée)* council, committee; *(d'une entreprise)* board; *(réunion)* meeting; **les membres du c.** the members of the board, the board members; **tenir c.** to hold a meeting; *Fig* **tenir un c. de guerre** to hold a council of war; *Mil* **passer en c. de guerre** to be court-martialled

3 *(conseiller)* *Arch* counsellor, counsel, adviser; *(en marketing, finance etc)* consultant; **avocat-c.** legal consultant; **ingénieur-c.** consulting engineer

4 *Arch, Litt (résolution)* (firm) resolution; **ne savoir quel c. prendre** not to know what decision to make

▶ ▶ *Com* **c. d'administration** board of directors; **c. d'arbitrage** conciliation *or* arbitration board; **C. des Bourses de Valeurs** regulatory body of the Paris Stock Exchange; *Scol* **c. de classe** = staff meeting, with possible participation of class representatives, to discuss individual pupils and their work, disciplinary matters etc; **c. en communication** media consultant, PR consultant; **C. constitutionnel** = independent body which may be appealed to, to pronounce on the constitutionality of government decisions; *Scol etc* **c. de discipline** disciplinary committee; **passer en c. de discipline** to appear before the disciplinary committee; **c. Ecofin** ECOFIN; **c. économique** economic council; **c. d'entreprise** works committee; **C. d'État** Council of State; **C. de l'Europe** Council of Europe; *Can* **c. exécutif** council of ministers, Cabinet; **c. de famille** *Jur* family council; *Hum* family conference; **c. financier** financial consultant *or* adviser; **c. fiscal** tax consultant; **C. général** regional council; **c. en gestion** management consultant; **c. interministériel** interministerial council; *Jur* **c. judiciaire** guardian, administrator, trustee *(of estate of mentally deficient young person)*; **c. juridique** legal adviser; **c. en mercatique** marketing consultancy; **le c. des ministres** the Cabinet; **c. monétaire** Currency Board; **c. municipal** local council; **C. de la politique monétaire** Monetary Policy Committee; **c. en promotion** advertising consultancy; **c.**

des prud'hommes industrial tribunal, industrial court of arbitration; **c. en publicité** advertising consultant; **c. en recrutement** recruitment consultant; **c. régional** regional council; **C. de sécurité** *(de l'ONU)* Security Council; **c. de surveillance** supervisory board; **c. syndical** trade union council; **C. de l'Union Européenne** Council of the European Union

> ## Conseil de classe
> The French school year is divided into three terms. In secondary schools, a "conseil de classe", or staff meeting, is held at the end of each term to discuss the progress made by pupils in a given class. A report containing the marks obtained during the term with teachers' comments is filled in for each pupil. The "conseil de classe" is initially held behind closed doors, attended by the teachers of a given class and the head teacher, and then with two elected class representatives present. During the last "conseil de classe" of the year, decisions are taken such as which pupils repeat a year and which should change courses.

conseiller [kɔseje] **vt c. qn** to advise sb, to give advice to sb; *(d'un psychiatre etc)* to counsel sb; **c. qch à qn** to recommend sth to sb; **c. un jeune dans ses sorties/lectures/fréquentations** to advise a youngster as to where he should go/what he should read/the company he should keep; **je ne vous le conseille pas** I wouldn't if I were you, I wouldn't recommend it; **c. à qn de faire qch** to advise *or* recommend sb to do sth; **l'expérience me conseille d'attendre** experience tells me to wait; **nous avons été très mal conseillés** we were very badly advised, we were given very bad advice; **il est conseillé de ne pas fumer** it is advisable not to smoke

conseiller ², -ère [kɔseje, -ɛr] **n** *(qui donne son avis)* counsellor, adviser; *(spécialiste)* adviser, consultant; **la jalousie est mauvaise conseillère** do not be guided by jealousy; **c'est un très bon c.** he gives very good advice

▸▸**c. artistique** artistic adviser; **c. de clientèle** customer consultant; **c. commercial** marketing *or* sales consultant; *Jur* **c. à la cour (d'appel)** appeal court judge; **c. économique** economic adviser; **c. financier** financial adviser *or* consultant; **c. financier indépendant** independent financial adviser; **c. fiscal** tax consultant; **c. général** regional councillor; **c. en gestion (d'entreprise)** management consultant; **c. juridique** legal adviser; **c. en mercatique** marketing consultant; *Admin* **c. municipal** local councillor; *Scol* **c. d'orientation** careers adviser; **c. en placements** investment adviser; **c. technique** technical adviser; **c. du travail** personnel consultant

conseilleur, -euse [kɔsejœr, -øz] **n** *Péj* giver *or* dispenser of (unwanted) advice; *Prov* **les conseilleurs ne sont pas les payeurs** it's easy to give advice when you don't have to pay the price

consensuel, -elle [kɔsɑ̃sɥɛl] **adj** *(accord, décision)* reached by consensus

consensus [kɔsɛ̃sys] **nm** consensus (of opinion)

consentant [kɔsɑ̃tɑ̃] **adj 1** *Jur* in agreement; *(partie)* consenting **2 elle est consentante** she's willing

consentement [kɔsɑ̃tmɑ̃] **nm** consent; **il lui faut le c. de ses parents** he needs his parents' consent; **donner son c. à qch** to give one's consent to sth, to consent to sth; **divorce par c. mutuel** divorce by mutual consent

consentir [kɔsɑ̃tir] *(conj like* **sentir***)* **vi** to consent, to agree; **c. à qch/à faire qch** to consent *or* agree to sth/to do sth; **je consens (à ce) qu'il vienne** I consent *or* agree to his coming; **il a fini par c.** he finally agreed, *Fam* he came round in the end; *Prov* **qui ne dit mot consent** silence means consent
vt c. un prêt to grant a loan; **c. une remise à qn** to allow sb a discount

conséquemment [kɔsekamɑ̃] **adv 1 c.** as a result of, *Fml* in consequence of **2** *Arch, Litt* consequentially

conséquence [kɔsekɑ̃s] **nf 1** *(résultat)* consequence, result; **il faut en subir les conséquences** we/you/etc must take the consequences; **tu traînes, tu traînes, c. on est encore en retard** you keep dawdling and as a result we're late again; **quelles en seront les conséquences?** what will be the consequences *or* outcome?; **cela ne tire pas à c.** it's of no consequence; **cet événement eut plus d'une heureuse c.** this event had several happy results; **cette erreur n'a pas eu de conséquences graves** this mistake didn't have any serious consequences *or* repercussions; **ton acte sera sans c. sur ton avenir** your action will have no effect on your future; **en c.** *(par conséquent)* consequently, as a result; **agir en c.** to take appropriate action; **en c. de** as a result of, *Fml* in consequence of; *(selon)* according to
2 *(conclusion)* inference, conclusion
3 *(importance)* importance, consequence; **personne sans c.** person of no importance *or Fml* consequence

conséquent [kɔsekɑ̃] **adj 1** *(cohérent)* consistent; *(esprit)* rational; **il n'est pas c. dans ses actions** he's not consistent in his actions; **être c. avec soi-même** to be consistent **2** *Mus* **partie conséquente d'une fugue** answer of a fugue **3** *Fam* *(important)* *(somme)* tidy; *(affaire)* important **4 par c.** consequently, accordingly, therefore
nm *Gram, Math* consequent

conservateur, -trice [kɔsɛrvatœr, -tris] **n 1** *(gardien)* *(de musée)* curator, keeper; **c. de bibliothèque** librarian; **c. des hypothèques** registrar of mortgages; **c. des eaux et forêts** ≃ forestry commissioner **2** *Pol* conservative
nm *(alimentaire)* preservative; **sans c.** preservative-free, free of preservatives
adj 1 *Pol* conservative **2** *(procédé etc)* preserving, preservative

conservation [kɔsɛrvasjɔ̃] **nf 1** *(de fruits, viande etc)* preserving; **c. par le froid** refrigeration; *(congélation)* freezing **2** *(de bâtiments, santé etc)* preservation; *Biol* **instinct de c.** instinct of self-preservation; **des bâtiments en bon état de c.** well-preserved buildings; **c. des eaux et forêts** ≃ Forestry Commission **3** *(de droits, situation etc)* retention **4** *(d'archives)* keeping **5** *(d'hypothèques)* registration **6** *(état)* (state of) preservation; **des ossements en parfait état de c.** perfectly preserved bones, bones in a perfect state of preservation

conservatisme [kɔsɛrvatism] **nm** *Pol etc* conservatism

conservatoire [kɔsɛrvatwar] **adj** *Jur* *(acte etc)* conservatory; **mesures conservatoires** measures of conservation
nm 1 *(musée)* repository, museum; **C. national des arts et métiers** = school of engineering in Paris **2** *(de musique, d'art dramatique)* school, academy, conservatoire, *Am* conservatory; **le C. (de Paris)** the (Paris) Conservatoire

conserve [kɔsɛrv] **nf 1** *(alimentaire)* canned *or Br* tinned food; *(en bocal)* preserve; **boîte**

de c. can, *Br* tin; **conserves au vinaigre** pickles; **petits pois en c.** canned *or Br* tinned peas; **mettre en c.** to can, *Br* to tin; **évitez de manger trop de conserves** try not to eat too much canned *or Br* tinned food, *Fam* try not to live out of cans *or Br* tins; *Fam* **tu ne vas en faire pas des conserves!** they're not museum pieces! **2** *Naut* **naviguer de c.** to sail together (**avec** with); *Fig* **de c.** together

conservé [kɔserve] **adj** **femme bien conservée** well-preserved woman

conserver [kɔserve] **vt 1** *(fruits, viande etc)* to preserve; **aliments conservés** *(dans des boîtes)* canned *or Br* tinned food; **c. des tomates en bocaux** to bottle tomatoes; **à c. à l'abri de la lumière** keep away from direct sunlight; **à c. à 6°C** store at 6°C
2 *(bâtiments, meubles, vêtements etc)* to preserve; **cette vie de plein air l'a bien conservé** this outdoor life has kept him well preserved **3** *(droits etc)* to retain, to keep, to maintain; *(emploi)* to keep; **il a conservé précieusement toutes ses lettres d'amour** he carefully kept *or* preserved all her love letters; **je n'en ai pas conservé un bon souvenir** I don't have good memories of it; **c. son sang-froid** *ou* **sa tête** to remain cool, to keep one's head; **elle a réussi à c. ses cheveux malgré le traitement** she has managed to keep *or* not to lose her hair in spite of the treatment; **c. l'allure** to keep up *or* maintain the speed; *Mil* **c. une position** to hold a position
vpr se conserver *(d'un aliment)* to keep; **articles qui ne se conservent pas** perishable goods

conserverie [kɔservəri] **nf 1** *(industrie)* canning industry **2** *(fabrique)* cannery, canning factory

considérable [kɔsiderabl] **adj** *(nombre, population)* considerable, substantial; *(propriété etc)* considerable, substantial, extensive; *(changement etc)* considerable, significant; **il lui reste un travail c. à faire** he has still got a considerable *or* substantial amount of work to do; **un changement d'une importance c.** a substantial change; **j'ai fait des dépenses considérables** I have been *or* have gone to considerable expense; **l'émotion fut c.** there was quite a stir

considérablement [kɔsiderabləmɑ̃] **adv** considerably, significantly

considérant [kɔsiderɑ̃] **nm** *Jur* preamble

considération [kɔsiderasjɔ̃] **nf 1** *(examen attentif)* consideration, attention, thought; **sans c. de prix** without considering the price *or* thinking about the price; **cette offre mérite toute notre c.** this offer deserves our full attention *or* consideration; **après c. de votre demande** having considered *or* studied your application; **prendre en c.** to take into consideration *or* account; *(offre, demande d'emploi etc)* to consider; **en c. de** in consideration of
2 *(constatation)* consideration, factor; **je ne peux pas entrer dans ces considérations** I can't go into that; **poussé par de nombreuses considérations** motivated by a variety of factors *or* considerations
3 *(estime)* regard, esteem, respect; **agir avec/sans c.** to act considerately/inconsiderately; **n'avoir de c. pour personne** to have no consideration for anyone; **tu as agi sans aucune c.** that was most inconsiderate of you; **jouir d'une grande c.** to be highly respected; **veuillez agréer, Monsieur, l'assurance de ma parfaite** *ou* **haute c.** *(dans une lettre)* yours truly; **agréez l'assurance de ma c. distinguée** yours faithfully, *Am* yours truly; **par c. pour** out of consideration *or* regard for
4 considérations *(observations)* observations, reflections, thoughts (**sur** on)

considéré [kɔ̃sidere] ADJ *(personne)* highly regarded or respected

considérer [kɔ̃sidere] (**je considère**, n. **considérons; je considérerai**) VT **1** *(étudier) (problème etc)* to consider, to weigh up; **tout bien considéré** taking everything into consideration or account, all things considered, on the whole; **c'est à c.** it's worth bearing in mind; *(à étudier)* it's worth considering; **considérant que …** considering that … **2** *(regarder)* to consider, to gaze at, to contemplate **3** *(respecter) (personne)* to respect; **on la considère beaucoup** she is highly thought of or respected, she is held in high regard **4** *(juger)* **je considère votre lettre comme frivole** I think your letter is flippant, I regard your letter as flippant; **je le considère comme mon meilleur ami** I regard him or consider him or look on him as my best friend; **je considère ce livre comme le meilleur de l'année** I consider this book (to be) the best of the year; **je considère que tu aurais pu te renseigner auparavant** I really think you could have found out beforehand ▸ VPR **se considérer** to consider or regard oneself; **se c. comme responsable** to consider or hold oneself responsible

consignataire [kɔ̃siɲatɛr] NM **1** *Jur* depositary **2** *Com, Naut* consignee

consignation [kɔ̃siɲasjɔ̃] NF **1** *(d'argent)* deposit **2** *Com (de marchandises)* consignment; **marchandises en c.** goods on consignment **3 un système pour la c. des bouteilles** a money-back system for bottles

consigne [kɔ̃siɲ] NF **1** *(donnée à la sentinelle etc)* orders, instructions; **il a pour c. de ne laisser passer personne** his orders are to let nobody pass; **observer la c.** to obey orders; **c'est la c.** those are the orders; **consignes en cas d'incendie** fire notice, fire regulations **2** *(punition) Mil* confinement to barracks; *Scol* detention; **deux heures de c.** two hours' detention **3** *Rail* **c. (à bagages)** left-luggage office, *Am* checkroom; **c. automatique** lockers, *Br* left-luggage lockers **4** *(de bouteille etc)* deposit

consigner [kɔ̃siɲe] VT **1** *(argent etc)* to deposit; **bouteille consignée** returnable bottle; **c. l'emballage** to charge a refundable deposit on the packaging; **emballage non consigné** non-returnable packing **2** *Com (marchandises etc)* to consign (**à** to) **3** *(fait etc)* to record, to write down; **c. des impressions par écrit** to commit one's impressions to paper **4** *Mil (soldat)* to confine to barracks; *Scol (élève)* to keep in; **c. sa porte à qn** to bar one's door to sb **5** *Rail* **c. ses bagages** to put or deposit one's luggage in the left-luggage office or *Am* checkroom

consistance [kɔ̃sistɑ̃s] NF **1** *(d'un sirop, d'une crème etc)* consistency, consistence; **prendre c.** to thicken; *Fig* **ses projets semblent prendre (de la) c.** his plans seem to be taking shape; **tout cela n'était que rêve sans c.** it was all just a vague dream or *Fml* a dream without substance; **bruit sans c.** unfounded or groundless rumour; **donner de la c. à qch** to thicken sth; *Fig* **donner de la c. à un personnage** to flesh out or give substance to a character **2** *(de l'esprit, du caractère)* firmness, strength; **sans c.** spineless

consistant [kɔ̃sistɑ̃] ADJ *(substance)* firm, solid; *(sauce etc)* thick; *(repas)* substantial; *(argument)* well-founded, sound

> Il faut noter que l'adjectif anglais **consistent** est un faux ami. Il signifie le plus souvent **cohérent**.

consister [kɔ̃siste] VI **c. en qch** to consist of sth; **le repas consiste en un sandwich et en une pomme** the meal consists of or comprises a sandwich and an apple; **en quoi consiste cette tâche?** what does the task consist of or involve or entail?; **c. dans qch** to consist in sth; **c. à faire qch** to consist in doing sth

consistoire [kɔ̃sistwar] NM *Rel* consistory

conso [kɔ̃so] NF *Fam (abrév* **consommation)** drink

consœur [kɔ̃sœr] NF *(female)* colleague

consolable [kɔ̃sɔlabl] ADJ consolable

consolant [kɔ̃sɔlɑ̃] ADJ consoling, comforting; **ce qui est c., c'est que …** the comforting thing (about it) is that …

consolateur, -trice [kɔ̃sɔlatœr, -tris] N *Litt* comforter, consoler
▸ ADJ consoling, consolatory

consolation [kɔ̃sɔlasjɔ̃] NF *(soulagement)* consolation, solace, comfort; **chercher une c. dans qch** to seek consolation or solace or comfort in sth; **paroles de c.** words of comfort, comforting or consoling words; **lot** ou **prix de c.** consolation prize; **c'est ma seule c.** it's my only consolation

console [kɔ̃sɔl] NF **1** *Ordinat* console; *Ordinat* **c. opérateur** operator console; *Aut* **c. centrale** central console; **c. de jeux** games console; **c. de visualisation** visual display unit, VDU; *TV etc* **c. de mixage** sound mixer, mixing desk; *TV* **c. vidéo** video console, switcher **2** *(meuble)* console (table) **3** *Archit* console, corbel, bracket **4** *Mus (d'un orgue)* console; *(d'une harpe)* neck

consoler [kɔ̃sɔle] VT to console, to comfort; **c. qn de sa peine** to comfort or console sb in his/her grief; **le temps console** time is a great healer; **si ça peut te c.** if that's any consolation or comfort to you; **ça me console de voir que ça t'est déjà arrivé** it consoles me or is a consolation that it's happened to you too
▸ VPR **se consoler** to console oneself, to find comfort or consolation; **se c. en pensant que …** to console oneself with the thought that …; **se c. avec qn** to console oneself with sb; **se c. d'une perte/d'un échec/de la mort de qn** to get over a loss/a failure/sb's death; **elle s'en est vite consolée** she soon got over it; **je ne pourrai jamais m'en c.** I'll never get over it; **elles se sont consolées mutuellement** they consoled or comforted each other

consolidation [kɔ̃sɔlidasjɔ̃] NF **1** *(d'un édifice, d'un mur)* strengthening, reinforcement; *(d'une position, du pouvoir, d'une amitié etc)* consolidation, strengthening **2** *Méd (d'une blessure)* healing; *(d'une fracture)* knitting, setting **3** *Fin (d'une dette flottante)* funding; *(d'un bilan)* consolidation; *Mktg* **c. de ligne** line filling

consolidé [kɔ̃sɔlide] *Fin* ADJ **dette consolidée** funded debt; **fonds consolidés** consols; **bilan c.** consolidated balance sheet
▸ NMPL **consolidés** consols

consolider [kɔ̃sɔlide] VT **1** *(édifice, mur, coutures)* to strengthen, to reinforce; *(position, régime, amitié etc)* to consolidate, to strengthen **2** *Méd (blessure)* to heal; *(fracture)* to knit, to set **3** *Fin (dette)* to fund; *(bilan)* to consolidate
▸ VPR **se consolider 1** *(se renforcer) (d'un régime)* to consolidate its position; *(d'une amitié, de liens)* to become stronger **2** *Méd (d'une blessure)* to heal; *(d'une fracture)* to knit, to set

consommable [kɔ̃sɔmabl] ADJ *(solide)* edible; *(liquide)* drinkable; **ce produit n'est c. que cru/cuit** this product must be eaten raw/cooked before eating

consommateur, -trice [kɔ̃sɔmatœr, -tris] N *(en général)* consumer; *(dans un restaurant, un café)* customer; **ce pays est un des premiers consommateurs de pétrole** this country is one of the biggest oil consumers; **mes grands-parents sont de grands consommateurs de café** my grandparents are great coffee drinkers; **défense des consommateurs** consumer protection; *Mktg* **c. cible** target consumer; *Mktg* **c. final** end-user; **c. moyen** average user
▸ ADJ **pays c.** consuming country

consommation [kɔ̃sɔmasjɔ̃] NF **1** *(d'électricité, de pétrole)* consumption, use; *(de nourriture)* consumption, eating; *(de boisson)* consumption, drinking; *(d'une voiture)* (petrol or *Am* gas) consumption; **cette viande est impropre à la c.** this meat is unfit for (human) consumption; **faire une grande c. de papier** to get through or go through or use (up) a lot of paper; **ils font une grande c. de viandes fumées** they get through or consume a lot of smoked meat; **c. quotidienne de vitamines** daily intake of vitamins; **c. intérieure** home consumption; **c. des ménages** household consumption; **c. mondiale** world consumption; **biens de c.** consumer goods; **produits de grande c.** mass market products; **société de c.** consumer society; **crédit à la c.** consumer credit; *Aut* **c. d'huile** oil consumption; *Aut* **c. de carburant** fuel consumption; **c. de masse** mass consumption; *Aut* **c. en ville** urban fuel consumption; *Aut* **c. en vitesse de croisière** touring consumption; *Aut* **c. spécifique** specific fuel consumption, sfc; *Compta* **consommations de l'exercice** total annual expenses **2** *(dans un café)* drink **3** *Litt (d'un travail etc)* accomplishment; *(d'un crime)* perpetration; *(du mariage)* consummation; **jusqu'à la c. des siècles** until the end of time

consommatique [kɔ̃sɔmatik] NF consumer research

consommé [kɔ̃sɔme] ADJ *(habileté etc)* consummate; *(écrivain, diplomate etc)* consummate, accomplished
▸ NM *Culin* consommé; **c. de poulet** chicken consommé

consommer [kɔ̃sɔme] VT **1** *(électricité, pétrole etc)* to consume, to use; *(nourriture)* to consume, to eat; *(boisson)* to consume, to drink; **'à c. avant fin novembre'** 'best before end November'; **cette voiture consomme trop (d'essence)** this car is heavy on petrol or *Am* gas **2** *(crime)* to perpetrate; *(mariage)* to consummate; *Litt (œuvre)* to accomplish, to achieve; **la rupture est consommée** they have broken up for good
▸ VI to consume; *(dans un café)* to drink, to have a drink; **c. au bar** to (have a) drink at the bar; **c. sur place** to eat in
▸ VPR **se consommer** *(de la nourriture, de boissons etc)* to be consumed; **ce plat se consomme froid** this dish is eaten cold

consomption [kɔ̃sɔpsjɔ̃] NF **1** *Méd* wasting, decline; *Arch (tuberculose)* consumption **2** *Arch, Litt (par le feu)* consuming

consonance [kɔ̃sɔnɑ̃s] NF *Mus, Ling* consonance; **mots aux consonances harmonieuses/bizarres** harmonious/odd-sounding words; **langue à c. germanique** German-sounding language

consonant [kɔ̃sɔnɑ̃] ADJ *Mus, Ling* consonant

consonantique [kɔ̃sɔnɑ̃tik] ADJ *Ling* consonant(al)

consonne [kɔ̃sɔn] NF *Ling* consonant; **c. occlusive/labiale/dentale** plosive/labial/dental (consonant)

consort [kɔ̃sɔr] ADJ **prince c.** prince consort
▸ NMPL *Péj* **et consorts** and company

consortial, -iale, -iaux, -iales [kɔ̃sɔrsjal, -jo] ADJ *Com, Fin* consortium, *Fml* consortial

consortium [kɔ̃sɔrsjɔm] NM *Com, Fin*

consortium, syndicate; **c. de banques** banking consortium

conspirateur, -trice [kɔ̃spiratœr, -tris] N conspirator; **ils se donnaient des airs de conspirateurs** they had a conspiratorial air about them
ADJ conspiratorial

conspiration [kɔ̃spirasjɔ̃] NF conspiracy, plot; **Fam mais c'est une c.** it's a conspiracy

conspirer [kɔ̃spire] VI **1** (comploter) to conspire, to plot (**contre** against) **2** (contribuer) to conspire; **tout conspire à me mettre en retard** everything's conspiring to make me late; **tout semble c. à son bonheur/la réussite du projet** everything seems to be conspiring to make him happy/to make the project a success

conspuer [kɔ̃spɥe] VT (pièce de théâtre, orateur etc) to boo, to shout down

constamment [kɔ̃stamɑ̃] ADV constantly, continually, continuously

constance [kɔ̃stɑ̃s] NF **1** (dans une tâche) persistence, perseverance; (en amour) constancy; **manquer de c. en amour** to be fickle; **il a de la c. à t'attendre depuis cinq ans** he's patient to have waited for you for five years; **faire preuve d'une grande c. en amitié** to be unswerving in one's friendships; **travailler avec c.** to work steadily **2** (de la température, d'un phénomène etc) constancy, invariability

constant, -ante [kɔ̃stɑ̃, -ɑ̃t] ADJ **1** (cœur, préoccupation, souci) constant; (effort) persistent; (amitié, intérêt) steady, unwavering; **être c. dans la recherche de qch** to be persistent in one's search for sth **2** Rare (fait) established **3** (température) constant; (circulation) continuous, uninterrupted; **à niveau c.** at a constant level **4** Com **en euros constants** in real terms
NF Math, Phys etc **constante** constant

constat [kɔ̃sta] NM **1** Jur certified or official statement or report; **dresser un c. d'accident** to write out an accident report; **c. amiable** (formulaire) = insurance form to be completed at the scene of an accident; **c. d'huissier** process server's affidavit; **c. de dommages** damages report **2** (fait) observation; **c. d'échec** acknowledgement or admission of failure; **faire un c. d'échec** to acknowledge or admit failure

constatation [kɔ̃statasjɔ̃] NF **1** (d'un fait etc) noting, noticing; **procéder aux constatations d'usage** to make the usual or routine investigations or inquiries **2** (fait) observation; **constatations d'une enquête** findings of an enquiry; **la première c. est la suivante** the first point to note is the following; **c'est une simple c.** it's a simple statement of fact **3** Compta **c. de stock** stock take **4** (en assurances) **c. des dommages** assessment of damages

constaté [kɔ̃state] ADJ Fin (valeur) registered; **c. d'avance** (charge) prepaid

constater [kɔ̃state] VT **1** (remarquer) (fait, amélioration etc) to note, to notice, to observe; **c. une erreur** to discover or find a mistake; **je constate que ce que je propose n'est jamais retenu** I notice that what I suggest is never accepted; **vous pouvez c. vous-même qu'elle est partie** you can see for yourself that she's gone; **constate par toi-même!** see for yourself!; **je suis obligé de c. que je me suis trompé** I'm forced to the conclusion or to conclude that I've made a mistake **2** (enregistrer) to record; **c. un décès** to certify a death; **les experts sont venus c. les dégâts** the experts came to assess the damage

constellation [kɔ̃stelasjɔ̃] NF constellation; **la c. de la Croix du Sud** the Southern Cross;

Fig **une c. de personnes célèbres** a constellation or galaxy of famous people

consteller [kɔ̃stele] VT to spangle, to stud; **ciel constellé d'étoiles** star-spangled or star-studded sky; **robe constellée de pierreries** dress studded with jewels; **des taches de sang constellent sa chemise** his shirt is spattered with blood
VPR **se consteller le ciel se constella d'étoiles** the stars came out in the sky; **la neige se mit à tomber et le sol se constella de taches blanches** the snow began to fall and the ground was spotted with white

consternant [kɔ̃stɛrnɑ̃] ADJ (nouvelles) alarming, dismaying; **d'une bêtise consternante** alarmingly stupid

consternation [kɔ̃stɛrnasjɔ̃] NF consternation, dismay; **jeter la c. dans un groupe** to fill a group with consternation or dismay; **à la c. générale** to everyone's consternation or dismay

consterner [kɔ̃stɛrne] VT (personne) to dismay, to fill with consternation or dismay; **prendre un air consterné** to look dismayed

constipation [kɔ̃stipasjɔ̃] NF Méd constipation

constipé, -ée [kɔ̃stipe] ADJ Méd constipated; Fam (air, manière etc) ill at ease, stiff, Fam constipated; **arrête de prendre cet air c.!** loosen up or relax a bit!
N Méd constipated person, sufferer from constipation; Fig Fam **quel c.!** what a stuffed shirt!

constiper [kɔ̃stipe] Méd VT to constipate
VI **nourriture qui constipe** constipating food

constituant, -ante [kɔ̃stitɥɑ̃, -ɑ̃t] ADJ **1** (partie, élément) constituent, component **2** Hist **l'Assemblée constituante** the Constituent Assembly (of 1789)
NM constituent part; Hist **les constituants** the members of the Constituent Assembly
NF Hist **la Constituante** the Constituent Assembly (of 1789)

constitué [kɔ̃stitɥe] ADJ **1** (autorité etc) constituted, organized; **corps constitués** official bodies **2** Anat constituted, formed; **enfant bien c.** fine, healthy child; **enfant mal c.** child of poor constitution

constituer [kɔ̃stitɥe] VT **1** (faire partie de) to form, to constitute, to make up; **parties qui constituent le tout** parts that form or constitute or (go to) make up the whole; **ce mobilier constitue tout mon bien** this furniture represents all my worldly goods, this furniture is all I own; **cet acte constitue un outrage aux bonnes mœurs** this action constitutes or represents an affront to public decency; **cela devrait c. un délit** that ought to constitute an offence; **être constitué de ...** to be made up of or consist of ...; **appartement constitué de six pièces** six-roomed flat
2 (créer) (comité, société commerciale, ministère, équipe etc) to form, to set up; (bibliothèque, fortune) to build up
3 Jur etc (nommer) to appoint; **c. qn président** to appoint sb president; **c. qn son héritier** to make sb one's heir; **c. une rente/une dot à qn** to settle an annuity/a dowry on sb
VPR **se constituer 1** (devenir) **se c. prisonnier** to give oneself up; **se c. partie civile** to bring a civil suit for damages **2** (se réunir) **ils se constituèrent en commission/en association** they formed a committee/an association

constitutif, -ive [kɔ̃stitytif, -iv] ADJ **1** (composant) constituent, component; **les éléments constitutifs de l'air** the constituent elements of air **2** Jur constitutive; **titre c.** (d'une propriété) title deed

constitution [kɔ̃stitysjɔ̃] NF **1** (physique) constitution; **avoir une bonne c.** to have a sound constitution, to be fit **2** (création) (de comité) formation, setting up, constitution; (de société commerciale) formation, setting up; (de ministère) formation; (de stocks) constitution; (de bibliothèque) building up **3** Jur (de rente, dot) settlement; **c. de partie civile** institution of civil action; **c. d'avoué** briefing or instructing of a lawyer **4** (de l'air, de l'eau) composition **5** Pol constitution; **loi conforme à la c.** law complying with the constitution

constitutionnaliser [kɔ̃stitysjɔnalize] VT Jur to constitutionalize

constitutionnalité [kɔ̃stitysjɔnalite] NF constitutionality

constitutionnel, -elle [kɔ̃stitysjɔnel] ADJ constitutional

constitutionnellement [kɔ̃stitysjɔnelmɑ̃] ADV constitutionally

constricteur [kɔ̃striktœr] ADJ **1** Anat **muscle c.** constrictor muscle **2 boa c.** boa constrictor
NM Anat constrictor (muscle)

constriction [kɔ̃striksjɔ̃] NF (des vaisseaux sanguins) constriction

constrictor [kɔ̃striktɔr] ADJ, NM **(boa) c.** boa constrictor

constructeur, -trice [kɔ̃stryktœr, -tris] NM Constr builder, constructor; **c. automobile ou d'automobiles** car or motor manufacturer; **c. naval** shipbuilder
ADJ (esprit, démarche) constructive; Zool **animaux constructeurs** home-building animals

constructible [kɔ̃stryktibl] ADJ **terrain c.** building land, land approved for development

constructif, -ive [kɔ̃stryktif, -iv] ADJ constructive

construction [kɔ̃stryksjɔ̃] NF **1** (d'une maison, d'une route, d'un voilier etc) construction, building, constructing; (d'un roman, poème etc) construction; (d'une phrase) structure, construction; **matériaux de c.** building or construction materials; **c. aéronautique** aircraft manufacturing; **c. mécanique** (mechanical) engineering; **c. navale** shipbuilding; **maison en c.** house under construction; **il y a plusieurs maisons en c. de l'autre côté de la rue** several houses are being built on the other side of the street; **appareil de c. japonaise** Japanese-built appliance, appliance of Japanese manufacture; **jeu de c.** construction set; Fig **c'est une c. de l'esprit** it's purely hypothetical
2 (bâtiment) building, construction, structure; **un grand nombre de nouvelles constructions** a large number of new buildings
3 Géom figure, construction

constructivisme [kɔ̃stryktivism] NM constructivism

constructiviste [kɔ̃stryktivist] N constructivist

construire [kɔ̃strɥir] (prp **construisant**; pp **construit**; pr ind **je construis, il construit, n. construisons**; impf **je construisais**; p hist **je construisis**; fu **je construirai**) VT **1** (maison, route, etc) to build, to construct; **pendant qu'on construit la maison** while the house is being built; **région très construite** heavily built-up area; **c. l'Europe** to build a new Europe
2 (machine, bateau, avion etc) to build, to construct; (roman, poème etc) to construct; (théorie) to construct, to put together; Gram **c. une phrase** to construct a sentence
VPR **se construire** (d'une résidence etc) to be built, to be constructed; **la région s'est beaucoup construite** there has been a lot of

particular about one's appearance; *Vieilli (sourire)* coquettish, flirtatious **2** *(ville, jardin, intérieur etc)* charming; *(vêtements)* smart, stylish; *Fam* **coquette somme** tidy sum, nice little sum
NF *Vieilli* **coquette** coquette, flirt

coquetel [kɔktɛl] NM *Can* cocktail

coquetier [kɔktje] NM egg-cup; *Fam* **gagner le c.** to hit the jackpot; *Iron* **ça y est, j'ai gagné le c.!** that's it, I've really done it now!

coquettement [kɔkɛtmɑ̃] ADV *(habillé)* smartly, stylishly; *(meublé)* stylishly, elegantly; *(sourire)* flirtatiously, coquettishly; *Fam (dédommager qn)* handsomely

coquetterie [kɔkɛtri] NF **1** *(vestimentaire)* consciousness of one's appearance; *Vieilli (désir de plaire)* coquetry, flirtatiousness; **faire des coquetteries** to put on an affected manner; **avec c.** *(habiller, meubler)* stylishly, elegantly **2** *Fam* **avoir une c. dans l'œil** to have a cast in one's eye

coquillage [kɔkijaʒ] NM **1** *(mollusque)* shellfish; **manger des coquillages** to eat shellfish **2** *(coque vide)* shell

coquillard [kɔkijar] NM **1** *Hist* ruffian, rogue **2** *Arg* **je m'en tamponne le c.** I don't give a damn *or* a monkey's

coquille [kɔkij] NF **1** *(d'escargot, d'huître, d'œuf, de noix etc)* shell; *Fig* **sortir de sa c.** to come out of one's shell; *Fig* **rentrer dans sa c.** to go back *or* withdraw into one's shell **2** *(plat)* (scallop-shaped) dish **3** *(d'épée)* hand guard *or* shell **4** *Constr (d'un escalier en colimaçon)* soffit, underpart **5** *Métal* chill, chill mould; *Sport* box, shield; *Méd* **c. (plâtrée)** spinal plaster **6** *Typ* misprint, typo, literal
▸▸ **c. de beurre** (shell-shaped) pat of butter; **c. de noix** walnut shell; *(bateau)* cockleshell; **c. d'œuf** eggshell; **peinture c. d'œuf** eggshell paint; **c. Saint-Jacques** scallop; *(coquillage)* scallop shell

coquillettes [kɔkijɛt] NFPL *Culin* pasta shells

coquin, -ine [kɔkɛ̃, -in] N **1** *(garnement)* rascal, scamp, rogue; **c. de sort!** *(en Provence)* hang it!, damn it!; **petit c.!/petite coquine!** you little rascal! **2** *(canaille)* rogue, scoundrel
ADJ *(sourire)* mischievous; *(sous-vêtement)* naughty; **un air c.** a flirtatious *or* coquettish look; **des histoires coquines** risqué stories
NF *Arch* **coquine** loose woman, hussy

coquinement [kɔkinmɑ̃] ADV *(d'une manière espiègle)* mischievously; *(coquettement)* coquettishly, flirtatiously; **avec un petit bibi c. posé sur l'oreille** with a little hat worn coquettishly over one ear

coquinerie [kɔkinri] NF mischievousness, roguishness; *(tour)* mischievous *or* roguish trick

cor [kɔr] NM **1** *Mus* horn; **c. (de chasse)** (hunting) horn; **sonner du c.** to sound *or* blow the horn; **les cors** *(dans un orchestre)* the horns; *Fig* **réclamer qch à c. et à cri** to clamour *or* *Am* clamor for sth **2** *(sur l'orteil, le pied)* corn; **avoir un c. au pied** to have a corn on one's foot **3** *(d'un andouiller)* tine; **un cerf (de) dix cors** a ten-pointer
▸▸ **c. anglais** cor anglais, English horn; **c. d'harmonie** French horn; **c. à piston** valve horn

corail¹, -aux [kɔraj, -o] NM *Zool* coral; **récif de c.** coral reef; *Litt* **lèvres de c.** coral lips
ADJ INV *(couleur)* coral; **des lèvres rouge c.** coral-red lips

corail² NM *Rail* express (train)
ADJ INV *Rail* **train c.** express (train)

corailleur, -euse [kɔrajœr, -øz] N *(pêcheur)* coral gatherer; *(artisan)* coral worker

corallien, -ienne [kɔraljɛ̃, -jɛn] ADJ coral-line; **récif c.** coral reef

Coran (le) [lǝkɔrɑ̃] NM the Koran

coranique [kɔranik] ADJ Koranic

corbeau, -eaux [kɔrbo] NM **1** *(oiseau)* crow; **grand c.** raven; **c. freux** rook; **noir comme un c.** raven- *or* crow-black **2** *(auteur de lettres anonymes)* writer of poison-pen letters **3** *Fig Péj (prêtre)* priest; *Vieilli (homme avide)* shark **4** *Archit* corbel, bracket

corbeille [kɔrbɛj] NF **1** *(panier)* basket **2** *(massif)* (round *or* oval) flower-bed **3** *Archit (d'un chapiteau corinthien)* bell, corbeil **4** *Bourse* ring, pit **5** *Théâtre* dress circle **6** *Ordinat* wastebasket, *Am* trash; *(dans Windows)* recycle bin; **c. d'arrivée** *(pour courrier électronique)* inbox; **c. de départ** *(pour courrier électronique)* outbox
▸▸ *Bot* **c. d'argent** sweet alyssum; **c. à courrier** desk tray; **c. de fruits** fruit basket; **c. de mariage** wedding presents; **c. des obligations** bond-trading ring; *Bot* **c. d'or** rock alyssum; **c. à ouvrage** work basket; **c. à pain** bread basket; **c. à papier** wastepaper basket

corbillard [kɔrbijar] NM hearse

cordage [kɔrdaʒ] NM **1** *(action) (d'une raquette)* stringing **2** *(corde)* rope; **c. en chanvre** hemp rope; *Naut* **cordages** rigging; **le c.** *(d'une raquette)* the strings

corde [kɔrd] NF **1** *(lien)* rope; **danseur de c.** tightrope walker; **semelle/échelle de c.** rope sole/ladder; **sauter à la c.** to skip, *Am* to jump rope; *Gym* **grimper à la c.** to climb the rope; *Fig* **tirer sur la c.** to go too far, to push one's luck; *Fig Fam* **il pleut des cordes** it's raining cats and dogs, *Br* it's bucketing down **2** *(d'instrument)* string; **c. (de boyau)** catgut; **c. de violon** violin string; **instrument à cordes** stringed instrument; **les cordes** *(dans un orchestre)* the strings; **orchestre à cordes** string orchestra; **double c.** double stopping; *Fig* **tu as touché** *ou* **fait vibrer la c. sensible** you've touched on a subject close to his/her heart; *Fig* **avoir plus d'une c. à son arc** to have more than one string to one's bow **3** *(de pendu)* (hangman's) rope; *Fig Fam* **se mettre la c. au cou** to put one's head in the noose, to put a rope round one's own neck; *Arg (se marier)* to get spliced *or* hitched; **dire cela, c'était comme parler de c. dans la maison d'un pendu** that was a very tactless thing to say, you/he/etc really put your/his/etc foot in it; *Fig* **il ne mérite pas la c. pour le pendre** hanging's too good for him **4** *Courses de chevaux* **la c.** the rails; **tenir c.** *(de coureur)* to be on the inside; *Courses de chevaux* **à la c.** to hug the rails, to be on the inside; *Fig Vieilli* to have the advantage; *Aut* **prendre un virage à la c.** to hug the bend; *Boxe* **les cordes** the ropes; *Boxe, Fig* **être dans les cordes** to be on the ropes; **être renvoyé dans les cordes** to be thrown onto the ropes **5** *Tex* thread; **drap/manteau usé jusqu'à la c.** *ou* **qui laisse voir la c.** threadbare cloth/coat; *Fig* **plaisanterie/histoire usée jusqu'à la c.** well-worn joke/story, old joke/story **6** *Math (d'un arc)* chord **7** *Fig* **ce n'est pas dans mes cordes** it's not in my line, it's not up my street, it's not my province
▸▸ **c. cervicale** cervical nerve; **c. dorsale** spinal cord; **c. à linge** clothes *or* washing line; *Gym* **c. lisse** climbing rope; **c. à nœuds** knotted climbing rope; **c. raide** tightrope; *Fig* **être sur la c. raide** to be walking a tightrope; **c. à sauter** skipping rope, *Am* jump-rope; *Anat* **cordes vocales** vocal cords

cordé [kɔrde] ADJ *Bot etc* cordate, heart-shaped

cordeau, -eaux [kɔrdo] NM **1** *(petite corde)* string, line; **un c. de jardinier** garden string *or* line; *Fig* **tiré au c.** perfectly straight, as straight as a die; *Fig* **lettres tracées au c.** per-

fectly regular letters **2** *Min, Mil (mèche)* fuse, match; **c. Bickford** Bickford *or* safety fuse **3** *Pêche* paternoster (line)

cordée [kɔrde] NF **1** *Com* **c. de bois** cord of wood **2** *(d'alpinistes)* rope, roped party; **premier de c.** leader, first on the rope **3** *Pêche* hook length

cordelette [kɔrdǝlɛt] NF cord, string

cordelier, -ière [kɔrdǝlje, -jɛr] N **1** *Rel (religieux)* Franciscan friar, Cordelier; *(religieuse)* Franciscan nun **2** *Hist* **le Club des Cordeliers** = a left-wing club of the Revolutionary period
NF **cordelière** *(de robe de chambre etc)* cord; *Archit* cable moulding

corder [kɔrde] VT **1** *(chanvre etc)* to twist into rope **2** *(malle etc)* to rope up **3** *(raquette)* to string **4** *Com (mesurer)* **c. du bois** to cord wood

cordial, -iale, -iaux, -iales [kɔrdjal, -jo] ADJ **1** *(accueil, atmosphère)* cordial, hearty, warm; *(paroles)* warm **2** *(haine, ennui, mépris etc)* deep(-seated) **3** *Pharm (médicament)* stimulating
NM *Pharm* tonic

cordialement [kɔrdjalmɑ̃] ADV cordially, heartily, warmly; **c. vôtre** *(dans une lettre)* yours sincerely; **bien c.** best wishes; *Iron* **elle le déteste c.** she heartily detests him

cordialité [kɔrdjalite] NF cordiality, heartiness, warmth; **parler avec c.** to speak warmly

cordier [kɔrdje] NM **1** *Ind* ropemaker **2** *Mus (d'un violon etc)* tailpiece

cordillère [kɔrdijɛr] NF *Géog* cordillera

cordon [kɔrdɔ̃] NM **1** *(lien)* cord, string; *(d'un câble, d'une corde)* strand, twist; *(d'un ordre)* ribbon; *Électron, Élec* lead; **corde à trois cordons** three-stranded rope; *Arch* **demander le c.** to ask the concierge to open the door; *Fig* **tenir les cordons de la bourse** to hold the purse-strings; *Fig Fam* **il faut couper le c.** you must get away from your mother's apron strings, you must branch out on your own **2** *(d'arbres etc)* row, line; *(de police, de troupes)* cordon; *Archit (dans un mur)* string course, cordon; *(d'une pièce de monnaie)* milled edge
▸▸ *Géog* **c. littoral** offshore bar; *Anat* **c. médullaire** spinal cord; *Anat* **c. ombilical** umbilical cord; *Élec* **c. prolongateur** extension cable *or* lead; **c. sanitaire** cordon sanitaire; **c. de soie** silk cord; **c. de sonnette** bellpull

cordon-bleu, *pl* **cordons-bleus** NM *Fam* cordon bleu (cook)

cordonnerie [kɔrdɔnri] NF **1** *(métier)* shoe-repairing, shoemending; *(fabrication)* shoemaking **2** *(boutique)* shoe repairer's (shop), shoemender's (shop), cobbler's (shop)

cordonnet [kɔrdɔnɛ] NM braid, cord, twist

cordonnier, -ière [kɔrdɔnje, -jɛr] N **1** *(réparateur)* shoe repairer, shoe-mender, cobbler **2** *(fabricant)* shoemaker; *Prov* **les cordonniers sont les plus mal chaussés** the shoemaker's wife is always the worst shod

Cordoue [kɔrdu] NF Cordoba

co-rédiger [korediʒe] VT to co-author

Corée [kɔre] NF Korea; **C. du Nord/du Sud** North/South Korea

coréen, -enne [kɔreɛ̃, -ɛn] ADJ Korean
N **C.** Korean

coreligionnaire [kɔrǝliʒjɔnɛr] N co-religionist

Corfou [kɔrfu] NF Corfu

coriace [kɔrjas] ADJ **1** *(viande)* tough, leathery **2** *(personne, adversaire)* tough; **être c. en affaires** to be hard-headed in business
N *Fam* hard-headed *or* tough customer

coriandre [kɔrjɑ̃dr] NF *Bot, Culin* coriander

coricide [kɔrisid] NM *Pharm* corn remover

corindon [kɔrɛ̃dɔ̃] NM *Minér* corundum

Corinthe [kɔrɛ̃t] NF Corinth; *Culin* raisins de C. currants

corinthien, -ienne [kɔrɛ̃tjɛ̃, -jɛn] ADJ Corinthian

N **C.** Corinthian

cormoran [kɔrmɔrɑ̃] NM *(oiseau)* cormorant

cornac [kɔrnak] NM elephant keeper, mahout

cornaline [kɔrnalin] NF cornelian

cornaquer [kɔrnake] VT *Fam* to show around

cornard [kɔrnar] NM *Arg* cuckold

corne [kɔrn] NF 1 *(d'animal, d'escargot)* horn; *(d'un insecte)* horn, antenna; **les cornes du diable** the devil's horns; **bêtes à cornes** horned animals; **vipère à cornes** horned viper; **donner un coup de c. à qn** *(d'un taureau)* to gore sb; *(d'un bélier, d'une chèvre)* to butt sb; *Fig Fam* **montrer** *ou* **faire les cornes à qn** to jeer at sb, to mock sb; *Fam* **ouh les cornes!** shame on you/him/*etc*!; *Fig Fam* **avoir** *ou* **porter des cornes** to be a cuckold; *Fig Fam* **faire (porter) des cornes à qn** to cuckold sb; *Fig* **prendre le taureau par les cornes** to take the bull by the horns
2 *(matériau)* horn; **peigne de c.** horn comb
3 *(cor)* horn
4 *Naut (d'une voile aurique)* gaff
5 *(d'un objet pointu)* tip; *(de la lune)* horn, cusp; *(d'une page)* dog-ear; *(d'un croissant)* end, tip; **chapeau à cornes** cocked hat; **faire une c. à une page** to turn down the corner of a page
6 *(sur les pieds etc)* hard skin; **avoir de la c. au pied** to have hard skin *or* calluses on one's foot
▸▸ **c. d'abondance** horn of plenty, cornucopia; **la c. de l'Afrique** the Horn of Africa; *Naut* **c. de brume** foghorn; **c. à chaussure** shoehorn; *Culin* **c. de gazelle** = horn-shaped cake

corné [kɔrne] ADJ 1 *(pied, main etc)* horny 2 **page cornée** dog-eared page

corned-beef [kɔrnbif] NM corned beef

cornée [kɔrne] NF *Anat* cornea

cornéen, -enne [kɔrneɛ̃, -ɛn] ADJ *Anat* corneal

corneille [kɔrnɛj] NF crow; **c. noire** carrion crow; **c. mantelée** *ou* **grise** *ou* **cendrée** hooded crow

cornélien, -ienne [kɔrneljɛ̃, -jɛn] ADJ *Littér (tragédie etc)* Cornelian; **situation cornélienne** = situation where there is a conflict between love and duty

cornemuse [kɔrnəmyz] NF *Mus* bagpipes; **joueur de c.** (bag)piper; **c. écossaise/bretonne** Scottish/Breton bagpipes

cornemuseur [kɔrnəmyzœr] NM (bag)piper

corner[1] [kɔrne] VT 1 *(clamer)* to blare out; **c. les ordres à qn** to bawl out *or* yell out orders to sb; **c. qch aux oreilles de qn** to shout sth into sb's ear 2 *(page)* to turn down the corner of
VI 1 *(souffler dans une corne)* to sound a horn; *Aut Vieilli* to sound one's horn, to hoot, to honk 2 *Fam* **la télé nous cornait aux** *ou* **dans les oreilles** the telly was blaring; **les radios leur cornaient dans les oreilles que …** radios were blaring out that … 3 *(des oreilles)* to ring; **les oreilles lui cornent** his ears are ringing

corner[2] [kɔrnɛr] NM *Ftbl* corner; **tirer un c.** to take a corner

cornet [kɔrnɛ] NM 1 *(de papier)* cone; *(de bonbons, de dragées, de frites)* cornet; **c. de papier** paper cone; **il cria, les deux mains en c. pour mieux se faire entendre** he shouted, cupping his hands to his mouth to make

himself heard better; *très Fam* **se mettre quelque chose dans le c.** *(manger)* to get something inside one; **qu'est-ce qu'on s'est mis dans le c.!** we really stuffed ourselves *or* our faces!
2 *Mus (instrument)* cornet; *(d'un orgue)* cornet stop
3 *Arch (petit cor)* small horn
4 *Anat* scroll *or* turbinate bone
5 *Suisse (sac en papier)* paper bag; *(sac en plastique)* plastic bag
▸▸ **c. acoustique** ear trumpet; **c. à dés** dice cup; **c. de glace** ice cream cone *or Br* cornet; *Mus* **c. à pistons** cornet

cornette [kɔrnɛt] NF 1 *(salade)* endive 2 *(coiffe religieuse)* cornet 3 *Mil Arch (de la cavalerie)* pennant, standard
NM *Mil Arch (officier)* cornet, ensign
NFPL *Suisse* **cornettes** *(sorte de pâtes alimentaires)* (elbow) macaroni

cornettiste [kɔrnetist] N *Mus* cornetist, cornet player

corn flakes [kɔrnflɛks] NMPL cornflakes

corniaud [kɔrnjo] NM 1 *(chien)* mongrel 2 *Fam (personne)* idiot, twit

corniche [kɔrniʃ] NF 1 *Archit* cornice 2 *(de rochers)* ledge; *(de glace, de neige)* cornice; *(route en)* **c.** corniche (road)

cornichon [kɔrniʃɔ̃] NM 1 gherkin 2 *Fam (personne)* idiot, nitwit

cornier, -ière [kɔrnje, -jɛr] ADJ (at the) corner, angle; *Constr* **poteau c.** corner *or* angle post
NF **cornière** 1 *Constr (sous les combles)* valley 2 *(pièce en équerre)* angle (iron *or* bar)

cornique [kɔrnik] ADJ Cornish
NM *Ling* Cornish

corniste [kɔrnist] N *Mus* horn player

cornouaillais, -aise [kɔrnwajɛ, -ɛz] ADJ of *or* from Cornouaille
NM *Ling* Cornouaillais (dialect)
N **C.** *(natif)* native of Cornouaille; *(habitant)* inhabitant of Cornouaille

Cornouaille [kɔrnwaj] NF Cornouaille *(in Britanny)*

Cornouailles [kɔrnwaj] NF Cornwall

cornouille [kɔrnuj] NF *Bot* dogberry, cornel berry

cornouiller [kɔrnuje] NM 1 *Bot* corneltree 2 *(bois)* dogwood

cornu [kɔrny] ADJ *(animal, diable)* horned

cornue [kɔrny] NF 1 *Chimie* retort; **charbon de c.** retort carbon 2 *Métal* steel converter

corollaire [kɔrɔlɛr] NM *(suite)* consequence, corollary; *Math* corollary

corolle [kɔrɔl] NF *Bot* corolla

coron [kɔrɔ̃] NM *(maison)* miner's cottage; *(quartier)* mining village

coronaire [kɔrɔnɛr] ADJ *Anat* coronary

coronarien, -ienne [kɔrɔnarjɛ̃, -jɛn] ADJ *Méd* coronary

corporatif, -ive [kɔrpɔratif, -iv] ADJ corporate, corporative

corporation [kɔrpɔrasjɔ̃] NF *(ordre)* corporate body; *Hist (trade)* guild; **la c. des pharmaciens** the guild of pharmacists, the pharmacists' guild; **c. de droit public** public corporation *or* body

corporatisme [kɔrpɔratism] NM corporatism

corporatiste [kɔrpɔratist] ADJ corporatist

corporel, -elle [kɔrpɔrɛl] ADJ *(être, nature)* corporeal; *(punition)* corporal; *(besoins, exercice)* bodily; *(hygiène)* personal; **expression corporelle** self-expression through movement; **odeur corporelle** body odour, *Fam* BO; *Psy* **schéma c.** body image

corporellement [kɔrpɔrɛlmɑ̃] ADV corporeally, corporally, bodily

CORPS [kɔr] NM 1 *Anat* body; **un c. robuste/lourd** a strong *or* robust/heavy frame *or* body; **soigner son c.** to look after one's body, to take care of oneself; **elle a conservé un c. jeune** she still has a youthful body, she's well-preserved; **entrer dans l'eau à mi-c.** to go into the water up to one's waist; **un petit c. et de grandes jambes** a short body and long legs; **pleurer toutes les larmes de son c.** to cry one's heart out; **frémir/trembler de tout son c.** to quiver/tremble all over; **passer sur le c. de** *ou* **à qn** to run over sb; *Fig* to trample sb underfoot; *Fig* **il te passerait sur le c. pour obtenir ce qu'il veut** he'd sell his grandmother to get what he wants; *Fig* **il faudra d'abord qu'il me passe sur le c.!** he'll have to do it over my dead body!; *Fig* **je me demande ce qu'il a dans le c.** I wonder what makes him tick; **il n'a rien dans le c.** *(il n'a rien mangé)* he hasn't eaten anything; *Fig* he has no strength *or* energy; **ça va te tenir au c.** *(tu n'auras plus faim)* that'll fill you up, that'll stick to your ribs; **c'est une nourriture qui tient au c.** it's filling food; *Fam Vieilli* **c'est un drôle de c.** he's a strange character *or Br* bod; *Fig* **faire qch à son c. défendant** to do something reluctantly; *Fig* **se jeter à c. perdu dans un projet/son travail** to throw oneself heart and soul into a project/one's work; **se donner c. et âme à qn/à un travail** to give *or* devote oneself body and soul to sb/to a task; *Jur* **séparation de c.** legal *or* judicial separation; *Jur* **ils ont fait une séparation de c.** they are legally separated; **lutter c. à c.** to fight hand to hand; *Fig* **affronter la réalité à c.** to get to grips with reality
2 *(cadavre)* body, corpse; **deux c. ont été retrouvés** two bodies have been recovered; **la levée du c. aura lieu à onze heures** the coffin will leave the house at eleven o'clock
3 *Chimie, Phys* body; **c. simple** simple body; **c. composé** compound (body)
4 *(consistance) (de vin)* body; **avoir du c.** to have body; **vin qui a du c.** full-bodied wine, wine that has body; *Fig* **son projet manque de c.** his plan lacks substance; *Fig* **donner du c. à qch** to give substance to sth; *Fig* **prendre c.** *(d'un projet, d'une idée)* to take shape
5 *(partie principale)* main part; *(d'un texte, d'un article etc)* body; *(d'une robe)* body, bodice; *(d'un cylindre, d'une pompe etc)* barrel; *Typ (de lettre)* body; **faire c. avec qch** to be an integral part of sth; *Naut* **perdu c. et biens** lost with all hands; *Typ* **force de c.** size of type body
6 *(d'ancrage)* dolphin, moorings; **(bouée de) c. mort** (anchor) buoy
7 *(groupe)* **le c. médical/enseignant** the medical/teaching profession; **les grands c. de l'État** = the highest sections of the French administration *(Conseil d'État, Cour des comptes etc)*; **avoir l'esprit de c.** to have esprit de corps
8 *(écrits)* corpus; **c. de lois** body of law(s)
▸▸ *Mil* **c. d'armée** army corps; **c. de ballet** corps de ballet; *Constr* **c. de bâtiment** main (part of a/the) building; *Astron* **c. céleste** celestial *or* heavenly body; *Jur* **c. du délit** corpus delicti; **le c. diplomatique** the diplomatic corps; **c. électoral** electorate; *Méd, Chimie* **c. étranger** foreign body; **c. de garde** guardroom; **plaisanterie de c. de garde** barrackroom joke; *Physiol* **c. jaune** yellow body; *Constr* **c. de logis** main (part of a/the) building; **c. de la magistrature** magistrature; **c. de métier** trade; *Hist* corporation, g(u)ild; *Nucl* **c. noir** black body

corps-à-corps NM INV hand-to-hand fight, tussle; *Boxe* clinch

corpulence [kɔrpylɑ̃s] NF stoutness, corpulence; **être d'une forte c.** to be stoutly built *or* of stout build; **un homme d'une faible c.** a slightly built man; **ils n'ont pas la même c.** they are not of the same build

corpulent [kɔrpylɑ̃] ADJ stout, corpulent

corpus [kɔrpys] NM *Jur, Ling* corpus

corpusculaire [kɔrpyskyler] ADJ corpuscular

corpuscule [kɔrpyskyl] NM corpuscle

corral, -als [kɔral] NM corral, enclosure

correct [kɔrɛkt] ADJ **1** *(sans fautes) (langage, emploi etc)* correct; *(copie, plan etc)* accurate; **il serait plus c. d'employer le subjonctif** it would be more correct to use the subjunctive; *Can Fam* **il a dit oui? – c.!** did he agree? – correct! *or* right! **2** *(courtois) (personne)* correct, proper; **cela n'est pas c. de sa part** that's not right of him; **elle a été correcte avec moi** she behaved correctly towards me; **être c. en affaires** to behave correctly *or* honestly in one's business dealings **3** *Fam (acceptable) (repas, traduction etc)* acceptable, decent, reasonable; **son travail est c., sans plus** his work is all right, but nothing special

correctement [kɔrɛktəmɑ̃] ADV **1** *(parler, employer)* correctly; **vous n'avez pas répondu c. à la question posée** you didn't answer the question correctly; *(sans faire d'erreur)* you didn't answer the question accurately **2** *(agir, être habillé)* correctly, properly; **veux-tu bien répondre c. quand on te parle!** will you talk properly when you're spoken to! **3** *(de façon acceptable)* reasonably; **elle gagne c. sa vie** she makes a decent *or* reasonable living

correcteur, -trice [kɔrɛktœr, -tris] N *(personne)* corrector; *Scol (de copies d'examen)* examiner, marker; *Typ* proofreader; *Journ* copy reader; *Journ* **c. de mise en page** stone sub(-editor)

■ NM *Ordinat* checker; *Tech* corrector; **c. liquide** correcting fluid; *Ordinat* **c. grammatical** grammar checker; *Ordinat* **c. d'orthographe** *ou* **orthographique** spell-checker; *Ordinat* **c. de style** stylechecker; **c. de tonalité** tone control; *TV etc* **c. colorimétrique** colour corrector

■ ADJ *(verres etc)* correcting, corrective

correctif, -ive [kɔrɛktif, -iv] ADJ corrective; *Méd* **gymnastique corrective** remedial exercises

■ NM **1** *(mise au point)* qualifying statement; **apporter des correctifs à une déclaration** to qualify a statement; *Com* **c. d'ajustement monétaire** currency adjustment factor **2** *Méd* corrective

correction [kɔrɛksjɔ̃] NF **1** *(d'une faute etc)* correction, correcting; *Scol (d'un exercice)* correcting, marking; *Typ (d'épreuves)* proofreading, correction, proofing; **faire des corrections dans un texte, apporter des corrections à un texte** to make corrections to a text; **les corrections sont en rouge** the corrections are in red; **maison de c.** reformatory; **je crois, sauf c., qu'il vient demain** unless I'm mistaken, he's coming tomorrow; *Ordinat* **c. d'orthographe** spellcheck; *Aviat, Naut etc* **c. de compas** compass adjustment; *Aut* **c. d'avance** *(à l'allumage)* ignition advance adjustment **2** *(pour punir)* beating, thrashing; **tu vas recevoir une bonne c.!** you'll get a good hiding! **3** *(d'une robe, d'un discours, d'un style etc)* correctness; *(d'un comportement)* correctness, propriety; **il a été d'une parfaite c. avec moi** he behaved very correctly towards me; **c'est la plus élémentaire des corrections** it's basic good manners; **j'apprécie la c. en affaires** I appreciate honesty in business

correctionnel, -elle [kɔrɛksjɔnɛl] ADJ *Jur* **peine correctionnelle** = penalty of more than five days' (but less than five years') im-

prisonment; **tribunal de police correctionnelle** court of summary jurisdiction

■ NF *Fam* **correctionnelle** criminal court; **passer en correctionnelle** to go before the criminal court

corrélatif, -ive [kɔrelatif, -iv] ADJ, NM correlative

corrélation [kɔrelasjɔ̃] NF correlation; **être en c. étroite** to be closely connected *or* related

corrélativement [kɔrelativmɑ̃] ADV correlatively

correspondance [kɔrɛspɔ̃dɑ̃s] NF **1** *(échange de lettres)* correspondence; *(lettres)* letters, correspondence; **être en** *ou* **entretenir une c. avec qn** to correspond with sb, to be in correspondence with sb; **enseignement par c.** correspondence courses; **prendre des cours d'anglais par c.** to take a correspondence course in English; **c. commerciale** commercial *or* business correspondence; **publier la c. d'un auteur** to publish an author's correspondence *or* (collected) letters

2 *(entre les trains)* connection; *Aviat* connecting flight; *Can (ticket)* transfer; **assurer la c. avec ...** *(d'un train, d'un bateau etc)* to connect with ...; **j'attends la c.** I'm waiting for my connection

3 *(de goûts, entre deux choses etc)* correspondence; *(d'idées, de principes etc)* conformity

correspondant, -ante [kɔrɛspɔ̃dɑ̃, -ɑ̃t] ADJ **1** *(page, illustration)*, *Géom (angle)* corresponding (**à** to) **2 membre c.** *(d'un institut etc)* corresponding member

■ N **1** *Journ* correspondent; **c. de guerre** war correspondent *or* reporter; **c. permanent** permanent *or* resident correspondent; **c. sur place** local correspondent; **c. à l'étranger** foreign correspondent

2 *(au téléphone)* caller; *(ami à qui l'on écrit)* pen friend; *Tél* **le numéro de votre c. a changé** the number you have dialled has been changed; **votre c. est en ligne** your party is on the line

3 *(agent de voyages)* **c. d'agréments** = travel agent (for rail and sea) who has not yet obtained qualifications; **c. de licence** travel agent (for airlines) who has not yet obtained qualifications; **c. local** *(pour les voyagistes)* resort representative

correspondre [kɔrɛspɔ̃dr] VI **1 c. à qch** to correspond to sth; **ce qu'il dit ne correspond pas à ses déclarations antérieures** what he is saying doesn't tally with *or* square with his previous statements; **cela ne correspond pas à votre promesse** that wasn't what you promised; **la théorie ne correspond pas aux faits** the theory does not square with the facts; **son attitude correspond à ce qu'on m'en avait dit** his attitude fits in with *or* corresponds to what I was told; **j'ai les vis, mais pas les écrous qui correspondent** I have the screws, but I don't have the nuts that go with them *or* the corresponding nuts

2 *(communiquer) (de chambres etc)* to communicate; **ces deux pièces correspondent** these two rooms communicate with one another

3 *(par lettres)* **c. avec qn** to correspond with *or* write to sb; **ils ont cessé de c.** they have stopped writing *or* are no longer writing (to each other)

■ VPR **se correspondre** *(être en relation)* to correspond; **leurs goûts se correspondent** they have similar *or* the same tastes; **ils se correspondent parfaitement** they are perfectly matched *or* suited

corrida [kɔrida] NF **1** *(de taureaux)* bullfight, corrida; **c. pédestre** road race **2** *Fam (à l'aéroport, dans les magasins etc)* hassle, *Br*

carry-on; *(dispute)* ding-dong argument; **quelle c.!** all hell broke loose!; **faire la c. dans sa chambre** to kick up a shindig *or* racket in one's bedroom

corridor [kɔridɔr] NM corridor, passage

corrigé [kɔriʒe] ADJ corrected; *(press)* subbed; **données corrigées des variations saisonnières** seasonally adjusted figures; **en données corrigées des variations saisonnières** seasonally adjusted, adjusted for seasonal variations

■ NM *Scol (d'un exercice)* fair copy, correct version; *(ouvrage donnant les solutions)* key, *Fam* crib; **le professeur a donné un c. de l'exercice** the teacher gave a model answer to the exercise

corriger [kɔriʒe] *(je corrigeai(s), n. corrigeons)* VT **1** *(erreur etc)* to correct, to put right, to rectify; *(mot mal orthographié, les défauts de qn, myopie)* to correct; *Scol (exercice etc)* to correct, to mark; *Typ (épreuves)* to (proof)read, to correct; *Journ (article)* to sub-edit, to sub; *Naut (compas)* to adjust; **je voudrais c. ce que vous avez dit** I'd like to correct what you've said; **c. le tir** *Mil* to adjust the fire; *Fig* to adjust one's position; **c. son jugement** to alter one's judgment; **c. qn d'une mauvaise habitude** to cure *or* break sb of a bad habit **2** *(pour punir)* **c. qn** to give sb a beating *or* a thrashing; **se faire c.** to get a beating *or* a thrashing

■ VPR **se corriger** *(d'une personne)* to mend one's ways, to turn over a new leaf; **se c. de sa gourmandise** to cure oneself of one's greed; **elle ne s'est donc pas corrigée!** she hasn't mended her ways, then!

corrigible [kɔriʒibl] ADJ corrigible, rectifiable

corroboration [kɔrɔbɔrasjɔ̃] NF corroboration

corroborer [kɔrɔbɔre] VT to corroborate

corrodant [kɔrɔdɑ̃] ADJ, NM corrosive

corroder [kɔrɔde] VT *(métal, pierre)* to corrode, to eat away

corrompre [kɔrɔ̃pr] VT **1** *(pervertir) (personne, jeunesse, mœurs, goût etc)* to corrupt; *(air)* to pollute; *(langage)* to debase **2** *(soudoyer)* to bribe

■ VPR **se corrompre** *(de vin)* to go off; *(de goût)* to become corrupt(ed)

corrompu [kɔrɔ̃py] ADJ *(personne, mœurs, goût, texte, disquette)* corrupt; *(viande)* tainted, putrid; *(chairs)* putrid

corrosif, -ive [kɔrozif, -iv] ADJ corrosive; *Fig (propos, humour, style)* caustic, scathing

■ NM corrosive

corrosion [kɔrozjɔ̃] NF *(d'un métal)* corrosion

corroyage [kɔrwajaʒ] NM *(du cuir)* currying; *(du métal)* welding

corroyer [kɔrwaje] VT *(pr ind* **je corroie,** *n.* **corroyons;** *fu* **je corroierai)** *(cuir)* to curry; *(métal)* to weld; *(bois)* to trim, to roughplane

corroyeur [kɔrwajœr] NM currier

corrupteur, -trice [kɔryptœr, -tris] N *(des mœurs)* corrupter; *(de témoins etc)* briber

■ ADJ *(influence, pouvoir etc)* corrupting

corruptible [kɔryptibl] ADJ *(juge, conscience)* corruptible; *(matériau)* corruptible, perishable

corruption [kɔrypsjɔ̃] NF corruption; *(de nourriture etc)* decomposition; *(fait de soudoyer)* bribery

corsage [kɔrsaʒ] NM **1** *(chemisier)* blouse **2** *(d'une robe)* bodice, body

corsaire [kɔrsɛr] NM **1** *Hist (navire, homme)* corsair, privateer **2** *(pantalon)* breeches

■ ADJ **pantalon c.** breeches

Corse [kɔrs] NF *Géog* Corsica

La Corse

Since the 1970s, the Corsican independence movement has become more radical, with the FLNC (the Corsican Liberation Movement) engaged in a bloody conflict against the French government. In 1982, as part of the law on decentralization, Corsica was attributed a "statut spécial" (special status) allowing for the election of its own assembly, and became a "collectivité locale" in 1991. In 2001 a devolution bill was passed granting Corsica partial control of its own affairs and making the teaching of the Corsican language mandatory in schools.

corse [kɔrs] ADJ Corsican NM Ling Corsican N **C.** (personne) Corsican

corsé [kɔrse] ADJ (vin) full-bodied; (sauce, plat etc) spicy; (fromage) strong, full-flavoured; **café (au goût) c.** full-flavoured coffee; Fig **histoire corsée** risqué or spicy story; **affaire corsée** tricky business

corselet [kɔrsəlɛ] NM Entom, Mil etc corselet

corser [kɔrse] VT (vin) to strengthen, to fortify (by adding spirits); (plat) to spice up; (café) to strengthen; (récit) to liven up, to enliven; **c. l'action d'un drame** to intensify the action of a drama
VPR **se corser** to intensify; **l'affaire se corse** (d'une enquête etc) the plot thickens; (dans la vie) things are getting serious; **ça se corse** things are getting difficult

corset [kɔrsɛ] NM corset; **c. orthopédique** ou **médical** (surgical) corset

corseter [kɔrsəte] VT (pr ind **je corsète, n. corsetons;** fu **je corsèterai**) to corset; Fig to restrict, to constrain

corsetier, -ière [kɔrsətje, -jɛr] N corset maker

corso [kɔrso] NM **c. (fleuri)** procession of floral floats

cortège [kɔrtɛʒ] NM **1** (d'un souverain etc) retinue, suite, train **2** (défilé) procession; **c. funèbre** funeral cortège; **c. nuptial** bridal procession; **défiler en c.** to go past in a procession, to process past; Fig **la vie de famille et son c. de problèmes** family life and its accompanying problems

cortex [kɔrtɛks] NM Anat, Bot cortex; **c. cérébral** cerebral cortex

cortical, -ale, -aux, -ales [kɔrtikal, -o] ADJ Anat, Bot cortical

corticoïde [kɔrtikɔid] NM Méd corticoid

corticosurrénal, -ale, -aux, -ales [kɔrtikɔsyrenal, -o] ADJ Méd adrenocortical

corticothérapie [kɔrtikɔterapi] NF Méd corticotherapy

cortisol [kɔrtisɔl] NM Méd hydrocortisone, cortisol

cortisone [kɔrtizɔn] NF Méd cortisone

corvée [kɔrve] NF **1** (obligation pénible) chore; **les corvées ménagères** the household chores; **je suis de c. de vaisselle ce soir** I'm on washing-up duty tonight; **quelle c.!** what a drag or bind!; **c'est une c. que d'aller chez eux** going to see them is a real chore; Can **faire une c.** to pitch or muck in together (to get a job done) **2** Mil fatigue (duty); **(détachement de) c.** fatigue party; **être de c.** to be on fatigue (duty); **c. de cuisine(s)** cookhouse fatigue, Am kitchen police; **c. de ravitaillement** supply duty **3** Hist corvée

corvette [kɔrvɛt] NF Naut corvette

coryphée [kɔrife] NM **1** (dans un corps de ballet) ballerina **2** (d'une secte, d'un parti) leader, chief

coryza [kɔriza] NM Méd head cold, Spéc coryza

cosaque [kɔzak] NM cossack

cosécante [kosekɑ̃t] NF Math cosecant

cosignataire [kosiɲater] ADJ, N cosignatory

cosinus [kɔsinys] NM Math cosine

cosmétique [kɔsmetik] ADJ cosmetic NM **1** Vieilli hair cream **2** **les cosmétiques** cosmetics

cosmétologue [kɔsmetɔlɔg] N cosmetics expert, beautician

cosmique [kɔsmik] ADJ (rayons etc) cosmic

cosmogonie [kɔsmɔgɔni] NF cosmogony

cosmographie [kɔsmɔgrafi] NF cosmography

cosmologie [kɔsmɔlɔʒi] NF cosmology

cosmonaute [kɔsmɔnot] N cosmonaut

cosmopolite [kɔsmɔpɔlit] ADJ cosmopolitan

cosmopolitisme [kɔsmɔpɔlitism] NM cosmopolitanism

cosmos [kɔsmos] NM Phil cosmos; Astronaut outer space

cossard, -arde [kɔsar, -ard] Arg N lazybones ADJ lazy

cosse [kɔs] NF **1** (de petits pois, fèves etc) pod, husk, hull **2** Naut (d'un cordage) thimble, eyelet **3** Élec (d'un câble) terminal **4** Arg **avoir la c.** to feel lazy

cossin [kɔsɛ̃] NM Can Fam (truc) whatsit, thingumabob, thingumajig, thingummy

cossu [kɔsy] ADJ (personne) well-to-do, well-off, wealthy; (maison, intérieur etc) opulent

costal, -ale, -aux, -ales [kɔstal, -o] ADJ Anat costal

costard [kɔstar] NM Arg suit

costard-cravate, pl **costards-cravates** NM Fam suit (person)

Costa Rica [kɔstarika] NM Costa Rica

costaud [kɔsto] ADJ (personne, valise etc) sturdy; Fam (alcool, épice) strong NM strong or sturdy man; Fam **tu peux avoir confiance, c'est du c.** trust me, it's sturdy stuff or it's sturdily made

costume [kɔstym] NM (habit) costume; (complet) suit; **c. trois-pièces** three-piece suit; **c. national** national costume or dress; **c. ecclésiastique** clerical dress; **c. de cérémonie** ou **d'apparat** ceremonial or formal dress; Fam **c. d'Adam** birthday suit; Fam **en c. d'Adam** in one's birthday suit, in the altogether; Théâtre **répéter en c.** to have a dress rehearsal; Can, Suisse **c. de bain** (de femme) swimsuit, Br swimming costume; (d'homme) swimming trunks, Am swimming shorts

costumé [kɔstyme] ADJ **bal c.** fancy-dress ball

costumer [kɔstyme] VT **c. qn** to dress sb up; **il était costumé en Turc** he was dressed (up) as a Turk
VPR **se costumer** to put on fancy dress, to dress up; **se c. en Turc** to dress up as a Turk

costumier, -ière [kɔstymje, -jɛr] N **1** Com costum(i)er, dealer in (fancy) costumes **2** Théâtre wardrobe master, f mistress; Cin costume supervisor

cosy [kɔzi] NM corner divan (with shelves) ADJ Fam cosy, Am cozy, comfy

cotangente [kɔtɑ̃ʒɑ̃t] NF Math cotangent

cotation [kɔtasjɔ̃] NF Bourse quotation; **c. à la criée** open-outcry trading; **c. à vue** spot quotation

cote [kɔt] NF **1** Bourse, Com quotation; (liste) list; **actions inscrites à la c.** listed shares; **retirer de la c.** (société, action) to delist; **hors c.** (actions) unlisted; (marché) unofficial, Am over-the-counter; Courses de chevaux **c.**
d'un cheval odds on a horse; **c. d'une voiture à l'argus** listed price of a car in the car buyer's guide; Pol **pour faire monter sa c. de popularité** ou **d'amour** to increase his popularity (rating); Fam **avoir la c.** to be popular (**avec, auprès de** with); **alors, tu as la c.?** oh, you're popular!
2 Com, Jur (d'un document etc) (classification) mark; (d'un livre de bibliothèque) classification or shelf mark, pressmark; Jur (d'un navire) character, classification
3 (de dépenses, d'impôts etc) quota, share
4 (taille) (indication of) dimensions; **c. d'origine** standard size
5 Géog height; (au-dessus de la mer) elevation; (d'un point dans un diagramme) altitude; **la c. 304** hill 304; **c. moins/plus 500** 500 below/above sea level
▸▸ **c. d'alerte** Tech critical or flood level; Fig danger point; Fin **c. de clôture** closing price; **c. mal taillée** rough and ready settlement; Admin **c. mobilière** assessment on income; Bourse **c. officielle** official list; **c. des prix** Bourse sharelist; Com list of prices

côte [kot] NF **1** Anat rib; **c. à c.** side by side; Fam **se tenir les côtes** to split one's sides laughing; **on lui compterait les côtes, on lui voit les côtes** he's nothing but skin and bone; Fig Fam **avoir les côtes en long** to be bone-idle, to be lazy; Culin **plat de côtes** dish of spare ribs **2** (de melon, salade, feuille) rib; **tissu à côtes** ribbed or corded material **3** (de colline) slope; (à monter, à descendre) hill; Constr gradient; **vitesse en c.** speed uphill; Aut **démarrage en c.** hill start; **ma voiture a du mal à monter les côtes** my car has problems getting up hills; **à mi-c.** halfway up/down the hill **4** (rivage) coast, coastline; **les côtes de (la) France** the coast of France, the French coast; **la C. (d'Azur)** the (French) Riviera; **faire c.** to beach, to run aground; Naut **jeter à la c.** to drive ashore, to strand; Fig Fam **être à la c.** to be on one's beam ends, to be hard up
▸▸ **c. d'agneau** lamb chop or cutlet; **c. de bœuf** rib of beef; Culin **côtes découvertes** middle neck; Anat **côtes flottantes** floating ribs; Géog **la C. d'Ivoire** the Ivory Coast; **c. de porc** pork chop; Culin **c. première** loin chop

CÔTÉ [kote]

| side **1–4** ▪ aspect **3** ▪ direction **4** ▪ way **4** ▪ aside (de côté) **6** ▪ nearby (à côté) **7** ▪ next to (à côté de) **7** |

NM **1** (du corps humain) side; **il a le c. gauche entièrement paralysé** his left side is completely paralysed; **couché sur le c.** lying on one's side; **assis à mes côtés** sitting by my side; **aux côtés de qn** at sb's side; **avoir un point de c.** to have a stitch (in one's side)
2 (d'une montagne, d'une route, d'une table, d'une feuille etc) side; **les côtés d'un rectangle** the sides of a rectangle; **les côtés de la médaille** the (two) sides of the medal; **une feuille de papier écrite des deux côtés** a sheet of paper written on on both sides; **de l'autre c. de** on the other side of; **passer de l'autre c. de la rue** to cross the street; Théâtre **c. jardin** stage right; **appartement c. jardin** flat overlooking the garden; **la tour penche d'un c.** the tower leans to one side or leans sideways; **ta jupe est plus longue d'un c. que de l'autre** your skirt is longer on one side than (on) the other; Naut **présenter le c. à qch** to be broadside on to sth; **navire sur le c.** ship on her beam ends
3 (aspect) side, aspect; **le bon/le mauvais c. d'une affaire** the good/bad side or aspect of a matter; **le c. recherche m'intéresse plus que le c. enseignement** the research side interests me more than the teaching side; **il a un c. méchant** he has or there's a mean

health cover; **c. sociale** social security cover; **c. à terme** term insurance cover

couveuse [kuvøz] NF **1** (*poule*) brooder, sitter; **c. artificielle** (*pour œufs*) incubator **2** (*pour nouveau-nés*) incubator; **il a dû être mis en c. à sa naissance** he had to be put in an incubator when he was born

couvrant [kuvrã] ADJ **1** (*qui protège*) covering **2** (*peinture etc*) that covers well

couvrante [kuvrãt] NF *Fam* blanket, cover

couvre-chef, *pl* **couvre-chefs** [kuvrəʃɛf] NM *Fam Hum* headdress, headgear, hat

couvre-feu, *pl* **couvre-feux** [kuvrəfø] NM *Mil* curfew

couvre-lit, *pl* **couvre-lits** [kuvrəli] NM bedspread, coverlet, counterpane; **c. piqué** quilt, *Am* comforter

couvre-livre, *pl* **couvre-livres** [kuvrəlivr] NM (dust) jacket, dust cover

couvre-nuque, *pl* **couvre-nuques** [kuvrənyk] NM (*de casquette*) flap (*to protect back of neck from sun*)

couvre-pied(s), *pl* **couvre-pieds** [kuvrəpje] NM quilt

couvre-plat, *pl* **couvre-plats** [kuvrəpla] NM dish cover

couvreur [kuvrœr] NM roofer; **c. en tuiles/ardoises** tiler/slater; **c. en chaume** thatcher

COUVRIR [kuvrir] (*prp* **couvrant;** *pp* **couvert;** *pr ind* **je couvre, il couvre, n. couvrons;** *pr sub* **je couvre;** *impf* **je couvrais;** *p hist* **je couvris;** *fu* **je couvrirai**) VT **1** (*casserole, meuble, livre, Fin (frais etc)* to cover (**de** with); (*emprunt*) to secure; **il faut c. cet enfant** that child needs to be covered up or wrapped up; **être couvert de poussière** to be covered with or in dust; **mur couvert de lierre** wall covered orovergrown with ivy, ivy-clad wall; **c. qn de cadeaux** to shower sb with gifts; **c. qn de son corps** to shield sb with one's body; **c. qn** (*contre les risques, avec une arme*) to cover sb; **lorsqu'il a agi, il était couvert par ses supérieurs** when he acted, it was with the authority of his superiors; **c. la retraite de l'armée** to cover the army's retreat; **c. les risques** to insure against risks; **le bruit de la cascade couvre les voix** the noise of the waterfall drowns the sound of voices; *Cartes* **c. une carte** to cover a card; **c. cinquante kilomètres en une heure** to cover fifty kilometres in an hour; **c. un défaut/une faiblesse** to hide a fault/a weakness; **prière de nous c. par chèque** kindly remit by cheque; **c. une enchère** to make a higher bid **2** *Journ* **c. un événement** to cover an event **3** *Constr* **c. un toit d'ardoises/de tuiles/de chaume** to slate/tile/thatch a roof **4** *Zool* (*de mâle*) (*femelle*) to cover **5** *Bourse* (*position*) to hedge

VPR **se couvrir 1** (*pour sortir*) to wrap up, to put on warm clothes, to dress warmly; (*pour cacher sa nudité*) to cover oneself up; (*mettre son chapeau*) to put on one's hat; **se c. de gloire** to cover oneself with or in glory **2** *Sport* to cover or protect oneself; *Escrime* to guard one's body; *Fig (se protéger)* to cover oneself; **se c. d'un alibi** to provide oneself with an alibi **3** **le temps** *ou* **ça se couvre** it's clouding over, it's becoming overcast **4** **les arbres se couvrent de feuilles** the trees are coming into leaf

covalent [kɔvalã] ADJ *Chimie* covalent

cover-girl, *pl* **cover-girls** [kɔvœrgœrl] NF *Fam* cover girl

covoiturage [kɔvwatyraʒ] NM car-pooling (*for commuting to the workplace*)

cow-boy, *pl* **cow-boys** [kobɔj] NM cowboy

coxal, -ale, -aux, -ales [kɔksal, -o] ADJ *Anat* coxal; **os c.** hip bone

coxalgie [kɔksalʒi] NF *Méd* coxalgia

coxarthrose [kɔksartroz] NF *Méd* arthritis of the hip

coyote [kɔjɔt] NM coyote, prairie wolf

CP [sepe] NM (*abrév* **cours préparatoire**) = first year of primary school

CPAM [sepeaɛm] NF *Admin* (*abrév* **caisse primaire d'assurance maladie**) = French government department dealing with health insurance

CPI [sepei] NF *Jur* (*abrév* **Cour pénale internationale**) ICC

CPM [sepeɛm] NM *Com* (*abrév* **coût par mille**) cost per thousand

cpp *Ordinat* (*abrév* **caractères par pouce**) cpi

cps *Ordinat* (*abrév* **caractères par seconde**) cps

CQFD [sekyɛfde] (*abrév* **ce qu'il fallait démontrer**) QED

crabe [krab] NM **1** (*crustacé*) crab; **marcher en c.** to walk sideways or crabwise **2** (*véhicule*) caterpillar-tracked vehicle

crabot [krabo] NM *Aut* dog clutch

crac [krak] INT (*de bois*) crack!, snap!; (*de tissu*) rip!; *Fam* **et c.!** **il est tombé par terre** and bang! there he was on the floor
  NM (*de bois*) crack, snap; (*de tissu*) rip

crac-crac NM *Fam* **faire c.** to do it

crachat [kraʃa] NM **1** (*salive*) spit, spittle; *Méd* sputum; **un c.** a gob of spit **2** *Fam* (*décoration*) gong

craché [kraʃe] ADJ *Fam* **c'est sa mère tout c.,** **c'est le portrait c. de sa mère** he's the spitting image of his mother; **c'est lui tout c.!** that's just like him!, that's him all over!

crachement [kraʃmã] NM spitting; (*de haut-parleur*) crackling; **c. de sang** spitting of blood; **c. d'étincelles** shower of sparks; **c. de flammes** burst of flames

cracher [kraʃe] VI (*de personne*) to spit; (*de stylo*) to splutter; (*de haut-parleur*) to crackle; *Fam* **il ne crache pas sur le champagne** he doesn't turn up his nose at champagne, he never says no to champagne; *Fig Péj* **c. sur qn** to spit at or on sb
  VT (*salive etc*) to spit (out); (*d'une cheminée, d'un volcan etc*) (*fumée etc*) to belch out; **c. du sang** to spit blood; **il va finir par c. ses poumons** he's going to end up coughing his lungs up; **c. des injures** to hurl abuse; *Fam* **j'ai dû c. mille euros** I had to fork out or cough up a thousand euros

cracheur, -euse [kraʃœr, -øz] N **c. de feu** fire-eater

crachin [kraʃɛ̃] NM (*fine*) drizzle; **il tombe un petit c.** there's a light drizzle

crachiner [kraʃine] V IMPERS to drizzle

crachoir [kraʃwar] NM spittoon, *Am* cuspidor; *Fig Fam* **tenir le c.** to monopolize the conversation; *Fig Fam* **tenir le c. à qn** to listen to sb rambling on and on

crachotement [kraʃɔtmã] NM (*de personne, feu, moteur*) spluttering, sputtering; *Radio* crackling

crachoter [kraʃɔte] VI (*d'une personne, d'un feu, d'un moteur*) to splutter, to sputter; *Radio* to crackle

crack [krak] NM **1** (*poulain*) crack or star horse; (*personne*) genius, ace; **c'est un c. en math** he's a genius at maths **2** (*drogue*) crack

cracker [krakœr] NM **1** *Culin* cracker **2** (*pirate informatique*) cracker

cracking [krakiŋ] NM *Pétr* (*de pétrole brut*) cracking

Cracovie [krakɔvi] NF Cracow

cracra [krakra] ADJ INV *Fam* dirty

cradingue [kradɛ̃g], **crado** [krado], **crade**

[krad] ADJ *Fam* filthy, *Br* grotty; **la cuisine était vraiment crado** the kitchen was really filthy

craie [krɛ] NF chalk; **falaise de c.** chalk cliff; **c. de tailleur** tailor's or French chalk; **bâton de c.** stick of chalk; **inscrire qch à la c.** to chalk sth up

craignos [krɛɲos] ADJ INV **1** (*louche*) shady, *Br* dodgy **2** (*laid*) hideous **3** (*mauvais*) crap, lousy, the pits

CRAINDRE [krɛ̃dr] (*prp* **craignant;** *pp* **craint;** *pr ind* **je crains, il craint, n. craignons, ils craignent;** *pr sub* **je craigne;** *impf* **je craignais;** *p hist* **je craignis;** *fu* **je craindrai**) VT **1** (*redouter*) to fear, to be afraid of; **c. la mort** to fear or be afraid of death; **ne craignez rien!** (*n'ayez pas peur*) don't be frightened!; (*ne vous inquiétez pas*) don't worry!; **je crains de le laisser entrer** I am afraid to let him in; **je crains qu'il (ne) soit parti** I'm afraid he's left; **il est à c.** *ou* **il y a lieu de c. que ... (ne) ...** it is to be feared that ...; **il n'y a pas à c. qu'il revienne** there is no fear of his coming back; **elle craint de le revoir** she's frightened or afraid of seeing him again; **c. pour qn** to fear for sb, to be anxious about sb
2 (*ne pas supporter*) **ces plantes craignent le gel** these plants don't like or can't stand the frost; **je crains le froid** I can't stand or bear the cold; **craint l'humidité/le froid** keep in a dry/warm place, keep dry/warm
VI *Fam* **j'ai raté mon exam/mon train, ça craint** I've failed my exam/missed my train, what a pain; **du rose et du jaune, ça craint** pink and yellow together, that looks terrible; **pour mon voyage, ça craint** things don't look too good for my trip; **ça craint dans ce pays-là** things are in a real mess over there; **elle craint** she's really awful; **il commence à c., ton copain** that mate of yours is getting beyond a joke

crainte [krɛ̃t] NF fear; **de c. de tomber** for fear of falling; **de c. de se faire mal** for fear of hurting oneself, lest one should hurt oneself; **de c. que ... (ne)** + *sub* lest; **il a parlé plus bas de c. qu'on (ne) l'entende** he spoke more quietly lest he (should) be overheard or for fear of being overheard; **il n'a rien dit par c. de ses parents** he said nothing for fear of his parents' reaction; **sans c.** (*employé comme adjectif*) fearless; (*employé comme adverbe*) fearlessly; **soyez sans c., n'ayez c.** have no fear; **la c. du gendarme** the fear of being caught; **un sujet de c.** a matter for concern, a worrying business; **avoir des craintes au sujet de qch** to have some fears or worries about sth; **je n'ai aucune c. quant à l'issue de ce projet** I've no fears or worries about how this project will turn out

craintif, -ive [krɛ̃tif, -iv] ADJ timid, timorous

craintivement [krɛ̃tivmã] ADV timidly, timorously

cramé [krame] NM *Fam* **ça sent le c.** I can smell burning

cramer [krame] *Fam* VI to burn; **tout a cramé** everything went up in flames or in smoke
VT to burn
VPR **se cramer** to burn oneself; **se c. les doigts** to burn one's fingers

cramoisi [kramwazi] ADJ crimson; **devenir c.** (*de honte, de timidité etc*) to flush crimson; (*de colère*) to go purple in the face

crampe [krãp] NF *Méd* cramp; **avoir une c.** to have cramp; **j'ai une c. au pied** I've got (a) cramp in my foot; **c. de l'écrivain** writer's cramp; **crampes d'estomac** stomach cramps; *Vulg* **tirer sa c.** to get one's leg over

crampon [krãpɔ̃] NM **1** *Constr etc* cramp (iron), staple, clamp, holdfast **2 c. (à glace)** crampon **3** (*pour semelle de botte*) stud; (*de chaussure de course*) spike; (*de fer à cheval*) calk, cog **4** *Bot* tendril **5** *Fam (personne)* **quel c.!** what a leech!

ADJ INV *Fam (personne)* clinging

cramponnement [krɑ̃pɔnmɑ̃] **NM** clinging

cramponner [krɑ̃pɔne] **VT 1** *Constr (pierres etc)* to clamp, to cramp together **2** *Fam* **c. qn** *(s'accrocher à)* to cling to sb; *(importuner)* to pester sb

VPR se cramponner to hold on, to hang on; **cramponne-toi!** hold on!; **se c. à qn/qch** to hold on *or* to to hang on *or* to cling (on) to sb/sth; *Fig* **se c. à qn** to cling to sb; *Fig* **se c. à la vie/au pouvoir** to cling to *or* hang on to life/power; *Fig* **se c. à un espoir** to clutch at a hope; *Fig* **il se cramponne à cette idée** he clings to this idea

cran [krɑ̃] **NM 1** *(entaille)* notch; *(de roue à rochet)* tooth; *(de ceinture, lanière etc)* hole; *Fig (degré)* rung, step; **c. de l'armé** full cock notch; **c. de sûreté** *ou* **d'arrêt** safety catch; **le c. de sûreté est mis** the safety catch is on; **lâcher une courroie d'un c.** to let a strap out a hole; **resserrer sa ceinture d'un c.** to take one's belt in a notch; **avancer d'un c. dans la hiérarchie** to go up a rung *or* step in the hierarchy; *Fam* **être à c.** to be wound up; *Fam* **avoir du c.** to have guts **2** *(coiffure)* wave; **se faire faire des crans** to have one's hair crimped

crâne [krɑn] **NM** *Anat* skull, *Spéc* cranium; **fracture du c.** fracture of the skull; **défoncer le c. à qn** to smash sb's skull *or* head in, to bash sb's brains in; *Fam* **avoir mal au c.** to have a headache; *Fam* **mets-toi ça dans le c.** get that into your head *or* thick skull

ADJ *Vieilli (air)* gallant

crânement [krɑnmɑ̃] **ADV** *Vieilli* gallantly, bravely

crâner [krɑne] **VI** *Fam* to swagger, to show off

crâneur, -euse [krɑnœr, -øz] *Fam* **N** show-off

ADJ swaggering, showy

crânien, -ienne [krɑnjɛ̃, -jɛn] **ADJ** *Anat* cranial; **la boîte crânienne** the cranium, the skull

craniologie [kranjɔlɔʒi] **NF** craniology

cranter [krɑ̃te] **VT 1** *(roue etc)* to notch **2** *(cheveux)* to crimp

crapahuter [krapayte] **VI** *Fam* **1** *(d'un enfant etc)* to crawl about (all over the place) **2** *Mil (sur un terrain difficile)* to trudge along

crapaud [krapo] **NM 1** *Zool* toad; *Fam (gamin)* kid, child; *Fam* **c'est un vilain c.** he's an ugly little squirt *or* toad **2 c. de mer** angler-fish **3** *(défaut)* flaw, blemish **4** *(fauteuil)* tub chair **5** *(piano)* baby grand (piano)

ADJ 1 fauteuil c. tub chair **2 piano c.** baby grand (piano)

crapaudine [krapodin] **NF 1** *Minér* toadstone **2** *Culin* **poulet à la c.** spatchcock (chicken) **3** *Tech (de tuyau d'arrivée d'eau)* grating, strainer **4** *Tech* pivot bearing *or* box *or* hole; *(de gond etc)* socket, gudgeon

crapette [krapet] **NF** *Cartes* Russian bank

crapoteux, -euse [krapotø, -øz] **ADJ** *Fam (personne)* grubby, dirty; *(endroit)* scuzzy, grimy

crapule [krapyl] **NF** *Fam (canaille)* scoundrel, villain

crapuleusement [krapyløzmɑ̃] **ADV** crookedly, dishonestly

crapuleux, -euse [krapylø, -øz] **ADJ 1** sordid **2** *Arch (débauché)* debauched, dissolute

> Il faut noter que l'adjectif anglais **crapulous** est un faux ami. Il signifie **intempérant**.

craquage [krakaʒ] **NM** *Tech (de pétrole brut)* cracking

craquant [krakɑ̃] **ADJ** *Fam (personne)* irresistible

craque [krak] **NF** *Fam (mensonge)* lie, fib, *Br* porky (pie)

craquelé [krakle] **ADJ** cracked; *Cér* crackled

NM *Cér (faïence, porcelaine, verre)* crackle

craqueler [krakle] *(je craquelle, n. craquelons; je craquellerai)* **VT** to crack; *Cér* to crackle

VPR se craqueler to crack, to become cracked

craquelure [kraklyr] **NF** crack; *Cér* crackle; *Beaux-Arts* craquelure

craquement [krakmɑ̃] **NM** *(de bois qui casse)* crack, snap; *(d'escalier, de plancher etc)* creak(ing); *(de feuilles mortes)* crackling, crackle; *(de neige)* crunching; *(de chaussures)* squeak(ing), creak(ing); **des craquements effrayants** terrifying cracking/creaking noises

craquer [krake] **VI 1** *(faire un bruit sec)* *(de bois qui casse)* to crack, to snap; *(d'escalier, de plancher etc)* to creak; *(de feuilles mortes)* to crackle; *(de neige dure)* to crunch; *(de chaussures)* to squeak, to creak; **faire c. ses doigts** to crack one's fingers

2 *(se déchirer)* to rip, to tear; **les coutures ont craqué** the seams have split; **plein à c.** full to bursting

3 *Fam (échouer)* *(d'une amitié, d'une entente)* to be breaking down

4 *(perdre le contrôle de soi)* to crack up; **elle craque nerveusement** she's cracking up; **j'étais sur le point de c.** I was at breaking point, I was about to crack up; **au bout d'une heure, j'ai craqué et je …** after an hour I just couldn't take any more and I …

5 *Fam (être attiré)* **je craque** I can't resist it/them/etc; **elle craque toujours devant un éclair en chocolat** she can never say no to *or* resist a chocolate éclair; **ce mec me fait c.** that guy drives me wild; **j'ai fini par c.** I finally cracked *or* gave in *or* succumbed

6 *Can Fam* **riche à c.** really rich; **fou à c.** totally mad

VT 1 c. une allumette to strike a match **2** *Tech (pétrole)* to crack **3** *(déchirer)* to split, to rip

craqueter [krakte] **VI** *(il craquette; il craquettera)* to crackle; *(de grillon)* to chirp; *(de cigogne)* to call, to cry

crash [kraʃ] **NM** *Aviat* crash

crasher (se) [səkraʃe] **VPR** *Fam* **1** *Aviat (s'écraser)* to crash; *(atterrir accidentellement)* to crash-land **2** *(conducteur, véhicule)* to crash; **il s'est crashé contre un arbre** he smashed *or* crashed into a tree; **il s'est crashé en voiture** he crashed his car

crasse [kras] **ADJ** *(ignorance etc)* crass, gross; **être d'une humeur c.** to be in a foul mood

NF 1 *(saleté)* filth, dirt; **vivre dans la c.** to live in squalor **2** *Métal* dross, scum, slag; *(résidus)* scale **3** *Fam (mauvais tour)* dirty trick; **faire une c. à qn** to play a dirty trick on sb, *Br* to do the dirty on sb **4** *Can (personne malhonnête)* crook

crasseux, -euse [krasø, -øz] **ADJ** *(mains, draps etc)* filthy, dirty; *(logement etc)* squalid

crassier [krasje] **NM** slag heap, *Scot* bing

cratère [kratεr] **NM 1** *Géog (de volcan)* crater **2** *Antiq* crater, (wine) bowl

cravache [kravaʃ] **NF** *(riding)* crop; *Fig* **à la c.** brutally

cravacher [kravaʃe] **VT** *(cheval)* to use the crop on; *(personne)* to horsewhip

VI *Fam (pour finir qch)* to work like mad, *Br* to slog away

cravate [kravat] **NF 1** *(d'homme)* tie, *Am* necktie; **c. blanche** *(sur carton d'invitation)* white tie, tails; **c. noire** *(sur carton d'invitation)* black tie, dinner jacket, *Am* tuxedo; **épingle de c.** tiepin; *Mil* **c. d'un drapeau** bow and tassels of a colour stave; *Fig Fam* **c.**

de chanvre hangman's rope; *Fam* **s'en jeter un derrière la c.** to knock back a drink **2** *(décoration)* insignia, ribbon **3** *(prise de lutte)* headlock **4** *Naut* sling

cravater [kravate] **VT 1** *(mettre une cravate à)* to put a tie on **2** *(attraper par le cou)* to grab round *or* by the neck; *Sport* to get in a headlock **3** *Arg (duper)* to take in, to take for a ride; *(arrêter)* to nick; **je me suis fait c.** *(dupé)* I got taken in *or* taken for a ride; *(arrêté)* I got nicked

VPR se cravater to put a *or* one's tie on

crawl [krol] **NM** *Natation* crawl; **nager le c., faire du c.** to do the crawl

crawler [krole] **VI** *Natation* to do the crawl; **dos crawlé** backstroke, back crawl

crayeux, -euse [krɛjø, -øz] **ADJ** chalky; **d'un blanc c.** chalky-white; **teint c.** chalky *or* chalk-white complexion

crayon [krɛjɔ̃] **NM 1** *(pour écrire)* pencil; **c. de plombagine** *ou* **à mine de plomb** lead pencil; **c. gras** soft lead pencil; *Spéc, TV etc* Chinagraph®; **c. de couleur** coloured pencil, crayon; **c. feutre** felt(-tip) pen; **c. à bille** ballpoint pen; **c. lithographique** litho crayon, *Am* grease pencil; *Ordinat* **c. lumineux** *ou* **optique** light pen; **écrit au c.** written in pencil; **dessin au c.** pencil drawing

2 *(dessin)* pencil drawing *or* sketch

3 *(bâton)* stick; *Méd* pencil; **c. à lèvres** lip pencil; **c. noir** eye pencil, eyeliner; **c. à sourcils** eyebrow pencil

crayonnage [krɛjɔnaʒ] **NM 1** *(action) (gribouillage)* doodling; *(dessin)* sketching; *(traits)* pencil marks **2** *(dessin)* pencil sketch

crayonner [krɛjɔne] **VT 1** *(dessiner)* to draw *or* sketch in pencil, to make a pencil drawing *or* sketch of; *(gribouiller)* to doodle; *Typ* **crayonné** rough **2** *(noter)* to note down *or* write down (in pencil)

CRDS [seerdees] **NF** *(abrév* **contribution au remboursement de la dette sociale)** = income-based tax deducted at source as a contribution to paying off the French social security budget deficit

créance [kreɑ̃s] **NF 1** *(foi)* credence, belief; **hors de c.** unbelievable, incredible; **trouver c.** to be believed; **ajouter c. à qch** to give credence to sth

2 *(dette)* debt; *Jur* claim; **mauvaises créances** bad debts; **c. chirographaire** unsecured debt; **c. contestée** contested debt; **c. douteuse** doubtful debt, possible bad debt; **c. exigible** debt due; **c. garantie** secured debt; **c. hypothécaire** debt secured by a mortgage; **c. impayée** unpaid debt *or* unrecovered debt; **c. litigieuse** contested debt; **c. principale** principal debt; **c. privilégiée** preferred debt; **c. recouvrable** recoverable debt; **créances receivables**, accounts receivable; **créances clients** accounts receivable, trade debtors; **créances gelées** frozen credits

3 *Arch (confiance)* trust; **lettres de c.** credentials

créancier, -ière [kreɑ̃sje, -jɛr] **N, ADJ** creditor; **c. d'exploitation** trade creditor; **c. hypothécaire** mortgagee; **c. nanti** secured creditor; **c. ordinaire** ordinary *or* unsecured creditor; **c. privilégié** preferred creditor

créateur, -trice [kreatœr, -tris] **ADJ** *(pouvoir, génie)* creative; **une impulsion créatrice** creative impulse *or* urge; **industrie créatrice d'emplois** job-creating industry

N creator; *Com* creator, designer; *Rel* **le C.** the Creator; **le c. exclusif d'un modèle** the sole *or* exclusive creator *or* designer of a model; **c. d'entreprise(s)** entrepreneur

créatif, -ive [kreatif, -iv] **ADJ** creative

N designer

création [kreasjɔ̃] **NF 1** *(fait de créer)* creation, creating; *(d'institution etc)* creation, founding, establishment; *Com (d'un nouveau produit)* creation, designing; *Théâtre (d'une pièce)* first production; *(d'un rôle)* creation; **les merveilles de la c.** the wonders of creation *or* of the universe; **c. d'emplois** job creation; **il y a eu 3 000 créations d'emplois en mai** 3,000 new jobs were created in May; **la c. (du monde)** the creation (of the world); **je connais cette société depuis sa c.** I have known this firm since it was founded; *Ordinat* **c. de pages Web** web authoring; **c. télévisuelle** television production

2 *(chose créée)* creation; *Com* new product; **une des plus belles créations humaines** one of the finest works of man; **sa robe était une c. de chez Jacques Fath** her dress was a creation by Jacques Fath; **la dernière c. d'un constructeur automobile** a car manufacturer's latest model; **la dernière c. d'un metteur en scène** a director's latest production

créativité [kreativite] NF creativity

créature [kreatyr] NF **1** *(être vivant)* creature; **c. humaine** human being **2** *(personne)* creature; *Fam* **une belle c.** a beautiful creature; **une pauvre c.** a poor *or* wretched creature **3** *Péj (protégé)* creature; *(prostituée)* trollop

crécelle [krɛsɛl] NF rattle; **quelle c.!** *(bavard)* what a chatterbox!; **voix de c.** rasping voice

crèche [krɛʃ] NF **1** *(garderie)* crèche, day nursery; **mettre ses enfants à la c.** to put one's children in the crèche **2** *Arg (chambre)* pad **3** *(de Noël)* crib, crèche; **c. vivante** ≃ nativity play

---

Crèche

State-subsidized care for children under three years of age of working families is well established in France, although this is subject to the availability of places.

---

crécher [kreʃe] VI *Arg (habiter)* to live; *(passer la nuit)* to crash

crédence [kredãs] NF credence (table), credenza

crédibilité [kredibilite] NF credibility

crédible [kredibl] ADJ credible

crédit [kredi] NM **1** *Fin, Com* credit; **lettre de c.** letter of credit; **carte de c.** credit card; **vendre/acheter qch à c.** to sell/buy sth on credit *or Fam* on tick; **faire c. à qn** to give sb credit; *Fig* to trust sb; **ouvrir un c. chez qn** to open a credit account with sb; **'la maison ne fait pas c.'** 'we do not give credit', 'no credit given', 'please do not ask for credit', as a refusal often offends)'; **établissement** *ou* **société de c.** loan society, credit establishment; *Journ* **c. photographique** photographer's credit

2 *Litt (influence)* credit, influence, repute; **être en c. auprès de qn** to have credit *or* influence with sb; **avoir du c. auprès de qn** to enjoy sb's confidence *or* trust; **il faut dire à son c. que …** it must be said to his credit that …

3 *(du grand livre, bilan)* credit(or) side; **porter une somme au c. de qn** to credit sb with a sum, to place *or* carry a sum to sb's credit

4 *(subvention)* **crédits** funds, allocation; **voter des crédits** to vote supplies

5 *Can Scol* credit

▶▶ *Fin* **c. back to back** back to back credit; **c. bancaire** bank credit *or* loan; **c. en blanc** blank *or* open credit; **c. bloqué** frozen credit; **c. de campagne** stock financing loan; **c. commercial** trade credit; **c. à la consommation** *ou* **au consommateur** consumer credit; **c. (à) court terme** short-term credit; *Bourse* **c. croisé** cross-currency swap; **c. à découvert** open credit; **crédits de développement**

---

development loans; **c. documentaire** documentary credit, letter of credit; **c. documentaire révocable/irrévocable/renouvelable** revocable/irrevocable/revolving letter of credit; **c. dos à dos** back to back credit; **c. de droits** delay in payment of indirect taxes; **c. épargne-logement** home purchase loan; **crédits d'équipements** equipment financing; **c. à l'exportation** export credit; **c. foncier** ≃ (government-controlled) building society; **c. gratuit** interest-free credit; **c. immobilier** home loan, mortgage; **c. d'impôt** *(abattement)* tax rebate; *(report)* tax credit; **c. irrévocable** irrevocable letter of credit; **c. (à) long terme** long-term credit; **c. (à) moyen terme** medium-term credit; **c. permanent** revolving credit; **c. personnalisé** individual personal credit arrangement; **c. 'red clause'** red clause credit; **c. renouvelable** revolving *or* revolver credit; **c. à reporter** credit to be carried forward; **c. revolving** revolving credit; **c. de sécurité** swing line; **c. à taux réduit** low-interest loan; **c. à terme** term loan; **c. transférable** transferable letter of credit; **crédits de trésorerie** (short term) credit facilities; **c. de TVA** VAT credit; **c. utilisable à vue** sight letter of credit

crédit-acheteur, *pl* **crédits-acheteurs** NM buyer credit

crédit-bail NM leasing

créditer [kredite] VT **1** *Fin* **c. qn d'une somme** to credit sb *or* sb's account with a sum, to place *or* carry a sum to sb's credit; **c. un compte** to credit an account **2** *Fig* **c. qn de qch** to give sb credit for sth, to credit sb with sth

créditeur, -trice [kreditœr, -tris] N customer in credit

ADJ *(solde etc)* credit; *(qui concerne les créditeurs)* creditor; **être c.** to be in credit; **compte c.** account in credit; **solde c.** credit balance; **nation créditrice** creditor nation

crédit-fournisseur, *pl* **crédits-fournisseurs** NM supplier credit

crédit-relais, *pl* **crédits-relais** NM bridging loan

credo [kredo] NM INV credo, creed; *Rel* **le C.** the (Apostles') Creed; **c. politique** political credo *or* creed

Credoc [kredɔk] NM *(abrév* **crédit documentaire)** = large state-funded market research company in Paris

crédule [kredyl] ADJ credulous

crédulité [kredylite] NF credulity, credulousness

créer [kree] VT to create; **c. des emplois** to create jobs; **c. une chaire** to found *or* establish a chair; **c. une armée** to form an army; **c. l'événement** to be big news; **c. qch de toutes pièces** to create sth out of nothing; **c. une entreprise** to set up a business; **agence récemment créée** recently established agency; **c. une hypothèque** to create a mortgage; **le pouvoir de c.** the power of creation; **cette attitude va lui c. des problèmes** that attitude is going to cause him problems *or* create problems for him; **c. des difficultés à qn** to create *or* cause difficulties for sb; *Théâtre* **c. un rôle** to create a part; **c. un spectacle/une pièce** to produce a show/a play (for the first time); **chemises créées par Dumaine** shirts created *or* designed *or* styled by Dumaine

VPR **se créer 1** *(se former)* to be created **2** *(se faire)* **se c. une clientèle** to build up a clientele; **se c. des problèmes** to create problems for oneself

crémaillère [kremajɛr] NF **1** *(dans la cheminée)* trammel (hook); **pendre la c.** to have a housewarming (party) **2** *Tech etc* (toothed) rack; *Rail* rack rail; **c. (et pignon)** rack and

---

pinion; **engrenage à c.** rack(-and-pinion) gearing; **chemin de fer à c.** rack *or* cog railway; *Aut* **c. de direction** steering rack

crémant [kremã] ADJ, NM **(champagne) c.** slightly sparkling champagne

crémation [kremasjɔ̃] NF cremation

crématoire [krematwar] ADJ crematory; **four c.** cremator, *Am* cinerator
NM cremator, *Am* cinerator

crématorium [krematɔrjɔm] NM crematorium

crème [krɛm] NF **1** *Culin* cream; *(sur le lait bouilli)* skin; **fromage à la c.** cream cheese; **fraises à la c.** strawberries and cream; **café c.** white coffee, coffee with milk; *Fig* **c'est la c. des hommes** he's the best of men, he's one of the best; *Fig Fam* **la c.** *(personnes)* the cream **2** **c. pour chaussures** shoe cream *or* polish **3** *(liqueur)* **c. de menthe** crème de menthe, peppermint liqueur; **c. de cassis** (crème de) cassis, blackcurrant liqueur
NM *Fam* **un grand c.** a large (cup of) white coffee
ADJ INV cream(-coloured), *Am* cream(-colored)

▶▶ **c. anglaise** (egg) custard; **c. anti-rides** anti-wrinkle cream; **c. de beauté** skin cream; **c. au beurre** butter cream; **c. brûlée** crème brûlée; **c. (au) caramel** caramel custard, crème caramel; **c. Chantilly** whipped cream; **c. écran** barrier cream; **c. fouettée** whipped cream; **c. fraîche** crème fraîche; **c. fraîche épaisse** double cream; **c. glacée,** *Can* **c. à la glace** ice cream; **c. hydratante** moisturizing cream; **c. de marrons** chestnut purée; **c. pâtissière** confectioner's custard; **c. à raser** shaving cream; **c. renversée** crème caramel *(turned out of its mould)*; *Chimie* **c. de tartre** cream of tartar

crémer[1] [kreme] VT (**je crème, n. crémons; je crémerai**) *(incinérer)* to cremate

crémer[2] VI *(du lait)* to cream

crémerie [kremri] NF *(magasin)* dairy, creamery; *Fam* **changer de c.** to go elsewhere

crémeux, -euse [kremø, -øz] ADJ creamy

crémier, -ière [kremje, -jɛr] N dairyman, *f* dairywoman

Crémone [kremɔn] NF Cremona

crémone [kremɔn] NF **1** *(de porte, de fenêtre)* espagnolette **2** *Can (cache-nez)* scarf

crénage [krenaʒ] NM *Typ* kerning

créneau, -eaux [kreno] NM **1** *(de rempart)* crenel, crenelle; *(meurtrière)* loophole, slit; **à créneaux** crenellated; *Fig* **monter au c.** to take a stand **2** *Aut* gap, space; **faire un c.** to reverse into a (parking) space; **stationnement en c.** parallel parking; **elle a raté son c.** she's parked badly *or* made a mess of parking **3** *Com (market)* niche, gap in the market, opening; **c. porteur** potentially lucrative market; **exploiter un nouveau c.** to fill a new gap *or* niche in the market **4** *Radio, TV* slot; **c. horaire** time slot; **c. publicitaire** advertising slot

crénelage [krenlaʒ] NM **1** *(de rempart)* crenellation **2** *(de pièce de monnaie)* milling **3** *Ordinat (en PAO)* aliasing

crénelé [krenle] ADJ **1** *(rempart)* crenellated; *(muni de meurtrières)* loopholed **2** *Bot (feuille etc)* crenate(d) **3** *(pièce de monnaie)* milled; *(écrou)* castellated

créneler [krenle] VT (**je crénelle, n. crénelons; je crénellerai**) **1** *(mur etc) (munir de créneaux)* to crenellate; *(munir de meurtrières)* to cut loopholes in, to loophole **2** *(roue etc)* to notch, to tooth; *(pièce de monnaie)* to mill

crénelure [krenlyr] NF crenellation; *Bot (de feuille)* crenelling

créner [krene] VT *Typ* to kern

crénom [krenɔ̃] INT **c. d'un pétard!, c. de nom!** for Pete's sake!

créole [kreɔl] ADJ Creole; **boucles d'oreille créoles** hoop earrings
  NM *Ling* Creole
  N **C.** Creole
  NFPL **créoles** *(boucles d'oreille)* hoop earrings

créosote [kreɔzɔt] NF creosote

créosoter [kreɔzɔte] VT to creosote

crêpage [krɛpaʒ] NM *(de cheveux)* back-combing; *Fam* **c. de chignon** dust-up, bust-up

crêpe [krɛp] NF *Culin* pancake; **pâte à c.** pancake batter; **faire sauter des crêpes** to toss pancakes
  NM **1** *Tex* crêpe, crape; *(pour le deuil)* black mourning crêpe; **c. de Chine** crêpe de Chine; **c. satin** satin crêpe; **voile de c.** mourning veil **2** *(caoutchouc)* crêpe (rubber); **semelles (de) c.** crêpe(-rubber) soles

crêpelé [krɛple] ADJ *(cheveux)* frizzy

crêper [krɛpe] VT *(cheveux)* to backcomb; *(tissu)* to crimp
  VPR **se crêper** *Fig Fam* **se c. (le chignon)** to have a dust-up *or* bust-up

crêperie [krɛpri] NF creperie, pancake house

crépi [krepi] ADJ, NM *Constr* roughcast

crêpier, -ière [krɛpje, -jɛr] N *(personne)* pancake seller *or* maker
  NF **crêpière** pancake griddle

crépine [krepin] NF **1** *(de meubles capitonnés)* fringe **2** *Culin* caul **3** *(de pompe etc)* strainer, filter

crépir [krepir] VT *Constr (mur etc)* to roughcast

crépissage [krepisaʒ] NM *Constr* roughcasting

crépitation [krepitasjɔ̃] NF **1** *(du feu, d'étincelles etc)* crackling **2** *Méd* **c. osseuse** crepitation, crepitus; **c. pulmonaire** crepitations, crepitant rale

crépitement [krepitmɑ̃] NM *(de feu)* crackling; *(de la pluie)* pattering; *(de flamme de bougie)* sputtering, spluttering

crépiter [krepite] VI *(du feu)* to crackle; *(de la pluie)* to patter; *(d'une flamme de bougie, de beurre fondu etc)* to sputter, to splutter; **les applaudissements crépitèrent** there was a ripple of applause

crépon [krepɔ̃] NM *Tex* crepon; **papier c.** crêpe paper

crépu [krepy] ADJ *(cheveux)* frizzy, fuzzy, woolly

crépusculaire [krepyskyler] ADJ twilight; *Zool* crepuscular; **lumière c.** twilight, half light; **papillon c.** moth; **oiseau c.** night-bird

crépuscule [krepyskyl] NM twilight, dusk; *Fig* twilight; *Fig* **quand on arrive au c. de la vie** when one is in one's twilight years *or* in the twilight of one's life

crescendo [kreʃɛndo] *Mus* ADV crescendo; **aller c.** to grow louder and louder; *Fig (de besoin, plaintes etc)* to get more and more urgent
  NM INV crescendo

cresson [kresɔ̃] NM *Bot* cress; **c. de fontaine** watercress

cressonnière [kresɔnjɛr] NF watercress bed *or* pond

Crésus [krezys] NM *Antiq* Croesus; **il est riche comme C.** he's fabulously wealthy

crésyl [krezil] NM *Chimie* cresol, methyl phenol

crétacé [kretase] ADJ, NM *Géol* Cretaceous

Crète [krɛt] NF Crete

crête [krɛt] NF **1** *(d'oiseau)* crest; *(de coq)* comb; *(de crapaud)* horn; **c. de coq** cockscomb; *Fam* **baisser la c.** to look crestfallen **2** *(de montagne)* crest, ridge; *(de vague)* crest;

Constr (de toit) crest, ridge; *(de parapet, mur)* crest, top; *Anat (d'os)* crest; *(de casque)* crest; *Géog* **(ligne de) c.** watershed **3** *Élec* peak

crête-de-coq, *pl* **crêtes-de-coq** NF *Bot* cockscomb

crétin, -ine [kretɛ̃, -in] N *Méd* cretin; *Fam (idiot etc)* cretin, moron, idiot
  ADJ *Fam* cretinous, moronic, idiotic; **vous êtes encore plus c. que lui** you're even more of a cretin *or* a moron *or* an idiot than he is

crétinerie [kretinri] NF *(caractère)* imbecility, stupidity, idiocy; **des crétineries** stupid *or* idiotic things

crétinisant [kretinizɑ̃] ADJ mind-numbing

crétiniser [kretinize] VT to turn into a moron *or* an idiot

crétinisme [kretinism] NM *Fam* stupidity, idiocy; *Méd* cretinism

crétois, -oise [kretwa, -waz] ADJ Cretan
  N **C.** Cretan

cretonne [krətɔn] NF *Tex* cretonne

cretons [krətɔ̃] NMPL *Can* potted meat *(made from pork)*

creusage [krøzaʒ], **creusement** [krøzmɑ̃] NM *(d'un trou etc)* digging; *(d'un puits)* sinking, digging; *(d'un canal)* cutting, digging

creuser [krøze] VT **1** *(trou, tranchée etc)* to dig; *(puits)* to sink, to dig; *(canal)* to cut, to dig; *Fig (un problème, une question etc)* to examine (closely), to look into (closely); **c. un chemin sous terre** to burrow one's way underground; *Fig* **c. un écart** to widen a gap; *Fig* **c. sa fosse** *ou* **sa tombe** to dig one's own grave; *Fig* **cela a creusé un abîme entre eux** it has created a gulf between them **2** *(faire un trou dans)* to hollow (out); *Agr (sillon)* to plough; **c. la terre** to dig; **front creusé de rides** brow furrowed with wrinkles, deeply lined forehead; **la maladie lui avait creusé les joues** illness had hollowed his cheeks; *Fig* **travail qui creuse l'estomac** work that gives you an appetite
  VI to dig; **c. dans le sable** to dig *or* burrow in the sand; **c. très profond** to dig down deep; *Fig* **plus on creuse, plus c'est intéressant** the more (deeply) you go into it, the deeper you go, the more interesting it gets
  VPR **se creuser 1** *(de visage)* to grow hollow; **ses joues se creusent** his cheeks are falling in; **l'écart entre eux s'est creusé** the gap between them has widened *or* has got wider **2** *Fig* **se c. (la tête)** to rack *or* cudgel one's brains (**pour faire** to do)

creuset [krøzɛ] NM **1** *Chimie, Ind* crucible, melting pot; *Fig* melting pot **2** *Métal (de haut-fourneau)* crucible **3** *Litt (épreuve de purification)* crucible; **au c. du malheur/de la souffrance** in the crucible of misfortune/ suffering

creux, -euse [krø, -øz] ADJ *(arbre, mur, dent)* hollow; *(voix)* hollow, deep; *(chemin)* sunken; **assiette creuse** soup plate; **yeux c.** sunken *or* deep-set eyes; **joues creuses** gaunt *or* hollow cheeks; *Fig* **avoir l'estomac** *ou* **le ventre c.** to be ravenous; **travailler le ventre c.** to work on an empty stomach; *Fig* **avoir la tête creuse** to be empty-headed; *Fig Fam* **avoir le nez c.** to be shrewd *or* far-sighted; **heures creuses** off-peak hours; **période creuse** *(dans l'industrie touristique)* slack season; **l'électricité coûte moins cher en période creuse** electricity costs less offpeak; *Péj* **paroles creuses** empty *or* meaningless words; **spéculations creuses** pointless speculation; *Couture* **pli c.** inverted *or* box pleat; *Fin* **marché c.** sagging market; *Naut* **mer creuse** rough sea
  ADV **sonner c.** to sound hollow; *Fig* to sound empty *or* false
  NM *(de la main, de l'épaule etc)* hollow; *(d'ar-*

bre, dans un mur) hole, cavity; *(dans le sol, une route)* hollow, dip; *(dans un rocher)* crevice, cavity; *(de l'estomac)* pit; *(d'une vague, d'une courbe)* trough; *(d'une voile)* belly; **tenir qch dans le c. de la main** to hold sth cupped in one's hand; **c'est si petit que ça tient dans le c. de la main** it's so small you can hold it in the palm of your hand; **succession de c. et de bosses** succession *or* series of bumps and hollows; **le c. des reins** the small of the back; **c. de l'aisselle** armpit; *Fig* **être au c. de la vague** *(d'une personne)* to be in the depths of despair, to have hit rock bottom; *(d'une entreprise)* to have hit rock bottom; *Litt* **dans le c. de, du c. de** in the depths of; *Fam* **avoir un c. dans l'estomac** to be ravenous; **j'ai un petit c.** I'm a bit peckish; **ce chanteur a du c.** *ou* **un bon c.** this singer has a fine bass voice; **une période de c.** a slack period

crevaison [krəvɛzɔ̃] NF *(d'un pneu)* puncture, flat

crevant [krəvɑ̃] ADJ *Fam* **1** *(travail, chaleur)* killing, exhausting, murderous; *(enfant)* exhausting, fagged out **2** *(histoire etc)* hilarious, priceless, killing

crevard, -arde [krəvar, -ard] *Fam* ADJ **1** *(malingre)* pitifully thin **2** *(affamée)* hungry, starving
  N **1** *(personne malingre)* pitifully thin person **2** *(personne affamée)* **c'est un c.**, **celui-là** he's always hungry, he's a bottomless pit

crevasse [krəvas] NF *(dans la peau)* crack; *(dans un mur, le sol)* crack, crevice, fissure; *(dans un glacier)* crevasse; **avoir des crevasses aux mains** to have chapped hands

crevasser [krəvase] VT *(mains)* to chap; *(terre, mur)* to crack, to make cracks *or* fissures in
  VPR **se crevasser** *(des mains)* to chap, to get chapped; *(de la terre)* to crack, to fissure

crevé [krəve] ADJ burst; *(pneu)* punctured, flat; *Fam (mort)* dead; *Fam (fatigué)* worn out, fagged out, dead beat; **ça sent le rat c., ici** it smells as if something has died in here
  NM *(dans une manche)* slash; **manches à crevés** slashed sleeves

crève [krɛv] NF *Arg (gros rhume)* stinker of a cold, stinking cold; **attraper la c.** to catch one's death of cold

crève-cœur NM INV *(peine profonde)* heartbreak, bitter disappointment; **c'est un vrai c. de devoir te quitter** it's heartbreaking *or* heartrending having to leave you

crève-la-faim NM INV *Fam (miséreux)* down-and-out

crever [krəve] (**je crève, n. crevons; je crèverai**) VI *(éclater)* to burst, to split; *(d'une bête, une plante)* to die; *Arg (d'une personne)* to snuff it, to kick the bucket; **mon pneu a** *ou* *Fam* **j'ai crevé** I've got a puncture *or* a flat; **c. de jalousie/d'orgueil** to be bursting with jealousy/pride; **il va en c. de jalousie** he's going to be madly jealous; **c. d'envie de faire qch** to be dying to do sth; **j'en crève d'envie** I'm dying to; **c. de rire** to split one's sides laughing; *Fam* **c. de faim** *(mourir)* to starve to death; *(avoir faim)* to be starving *or* famished; **très** *Fam* **je crève la dalle** I'm dying of hunger, I'm absolutely starving; **c. d'ennui** to be bored to death; *Fam* **je crève de froid/de chaleur** I'm freezing/boiling *or* roasting; **il fait une chaleur à c.** it's stifling *or* boiling; *Fam* **qu'il crève!** he can go to hell!; *Fam* **plutôt c.!** I'd rather die!, I'll die first!
  VT *(ballon, sac etc)* to burst; *(pneu)* to puncture; *Fig* **c. le cœur à qn** to break sb's heart; *Fig* **ça me crève le cœur de devoir abandonner cette maison** I'm heartbroken about *or* it's heartrending having to leave this house; **c. un œil à qn** to put out *or* gouge out sb's eye; *(accidentellement)* to blind sb in one eye; *Fig Fam* **ça crève les yeux** it stands out

cruellement [kryɛlmã] ADV cruelly; **c. déçu** bitterly disappointed; **c. éprouvé** sorely tried; **faire c. défaut** to be sorely lacking

cruiser [kruzœr] NM (petit yacht) cruiser

crûment [krymã] ADV **1** (durement) (parler) (sans détours) bluntly; (ouvertement) openly, unabashedly **2** éclairé **c.** garishly lit

crustacé [krystase] NM **crustacés** shellfish, crustaceans, Spéc Crustacea; **la crevette est un c.** the prawn is a shellfish, prawns are shellfish; Culin **assiette de crustacés** seafood platter

cruzado [kruzado] NM crusado, cruzado

cryobiologie [krijobjɔlɔʒi] NF cryobiology

cryochirurgie [krijoʃiryrʒi] NF cryosurgery

cryoconservation [krijokɔ̃sɛrvasjɔ̃] NF cryoconservation

cryogène [krijoʒɛn] ADJ cryogenic; **mélange c.** freezing mixture

cryogénie [krijoʒeni] NF cryogenics

cryothérapie [krijoterapi] NF Méd cryotherapy

cryptage [kriptaʒ] NM encryption, encoding; TV scrambling, encrypting

crypte [kript] NF Archit, Anat crypt

crypté [kripte] ADJ **1** TV (chaîne, film) scrambled **2** (message) coded, in code

crypter [kripte] VT to encode; Tél, TV to encrypt, to scramble

cryptocommuniste [kriptokɔmynist] ADJ, N crypto-communist

cryptogénétique [kriptoʒenetik] ADJ Méd idiopathic

cryptogramme [kriptogram] NM cipher (message)

cryptographie [kriptografi] NF writing in cipher

cryptographique [kriptografik] ADJ cryptographic

cryptologie [kriptɔlɔʒi] NF cryptology, cryptography

CSA [seɛsa] NM (abrév Conseil supérieur de l'audiovisuel) = French broadcasting supervisory body

CSCE [seɛseə] NF (abrév Conférence sur la sécurité et la coopération en Europe) CSCE

CSG [seɛsʒe] NF (abrév contribution sociale généralisée) = income-based tax deducted at source as a contribution to paying off the French social security budget deficit

cubage [kybaʒ] NM **1** (action) (d'un tas de bois etc) calculating the cubic content **2** (volume) (d'un réservoir etc) cubic capacity, volume

cubain, -aine [kybɛ̃, -ɛn] ADJ Cuban
▪ N **C.** Cuban

cube [kyb] NM **1** Géom, Math cube; **élever un nombre au c.** to cube a number; **jeu de cubes** building blocks, (wooden) bricks **2** Scol Arg = student repeating a class for the second time **3** Arg **gros c.** (moto) large motorbike (over 500 cc); **les gros cubes** heavy metal
▪ ADJ (mètre, centimètre etc) cubic

cuber [kybe] VT Math (nombre etc) to cube; (évaluer) to calculate the cubic capacity of
▪ VI **1** (contenir) to have a cubic capacity of; **réservoir qui cube vingt litres** tank with a cubic capacity of twenty litres **2** Fam (revenir cher) to be expensive, to work out expensive; **ça cube, ça finit par c.** it mounts up

cubique [kybik] ADJ cubic; Math **racine c.** cube root
▪ NF cubic (curve)

cubisme [kybism] NM Beaux-Arts Cubism

cubiste [kybist] ADJ, N Beaux-Arts Cubist

cubitainer [kybitenɛr] NM = large cubic plastic container (for bulk purchase of wine etc)

cubital, -ale, -aux, -ales [kybital, -o] ADJ Anat ulnar

cubitus [kybitys] NM Anat ulna

cuchaule [kyʃol] NF Suisse (brioche) brioche

cucu(l) [kyky] ADJ INV Fam **c. (la praline)** (personne, décoration) twee; (film, livre) corny; **elle est gentille, mais un peu c.** she is nice, but she's not really clued up

cueillette [kœjɛt] NF (action) gathering, picking; (fruits, noisettes, baies) crop, harvest; **aller faire la c. de mûres** to go blackberry picking or blackberrying; **une tribu qui vit de la chasse et de la c.** a tribe of hunters and gatherers

cueilleur, -euse [kœjœr, -øz] N (de fruit etc) picker, gatherer

cueillir [kœjir] VT (prp **cueillant**; pp **cueilli**; pr ind **je cueille, il cueille, n. cueillons**; impf **je cueillais**; p hist **je cueillis**; fu **je cueillerai**) (fleurs, fruits etc) to gather, to pick; **c. un baiser** to steal or snatch a kiss; Fig **c. des lauriers** to win laurels; Fig Litt **c. le jour, c. les roses de la vie** to make the most of life; Fig Litt **cueillez le jour** seize the day; Fig Litt **il faut c. les roses de la vie** gather ye rosebuds while ye may; Fig **le crochet du gauche l'a cueilli en plein estomac** the left hook got him right in the stomach; Fig **la mort l'a cueilli en pleine jeunesse** he was cut down in his prime; Fam **c. qn** (passer le chercher) to collect sb, to pick sb up; (l'arrêter) to pick sb up, to nab sb

cuesta [kwɛsta] NF Géog cuesta

cui-cui [kɥikɥi] NM INV cheeping, chirping, chirruping
▪ INT cheep

cuiller, cuillère [kɥijɛr] NF **1** spoon; (contenu) spoon(ful); **c. à dessert** ou **à entremets** dessertspoon; **c. à soupe** soup spoon; (pour mesurer) tablespoon; **c. à café** teaspoon; (plus petite) coffee spoon; **petite c.** teaspoon; **c. à pot** ladle; **avaler une c. de sirop** to swallow a spoonful of medicine; **une c. pour papa, une c. pour maman** (à un enfant) one (spoonful) for Daddy, one (spoonful) for Mummy; **deux cuillers de sucre** two spoons or spoonfuls or spoonsful of sugar; Fig Fam **il n'y a pas avec le dos de la c.** he goes the whole hog, he doesn't go in for half measures, there are no half measures with him; (il est franc) he doesn't pull his punches or mince his words; Fig Fam **en deux** ou **trois** ou **cinq coups de c. à pot** in no time at all, in two shakes (of a lamb's tail); Fig Fam **être à ramasser à la petite c.** (blessé) to be badly hurt or smashed up; (épuisé) to be completely exhausted or all in; (déprimé) to be thoroughly depressed or down in the dumps; Fig Fam **on l'a ramassé à la petite c.** he was scraped off the pavement
   2 Pêche spoon (bait), trolling spoon; **pêcher la truite/etc à la c.** to troll or spin for trout/etc
   3 (d'une grenade) safety catch
   4 Constr (d'une drague) scoop, bucket
   5 Arg (main) paw, mitt

cuillerée [kɥijere] NF spoonful; **une c. à soupe de sucre** a tablespoonful of sugar; **deux cuillerées à café de sel** two teaspoons or teaspoonfuls or teaspoonsful of salt; **une c. pour maman** (à un enfant) one (spoonful) for Mummy

cuilleron [kɥijrɔ̃] NM (d'une cuillère) bowl

cuir [kɥir] NM **1** (tanné) leather; (veste) leather jacket; **c. vert** ou **brut** rawhide; **c. en croûte** undressed leather; **c. verni** patent leather; **pantalon en** ou **de c.** leather trousers; **chaussures en c.** leather shoes; **c. à rasoir** razor strop; **cuirs de motocycliste**

motorcycle leathers **2** (d'un éléphant), Fam (d'une personne) hide; **c. chevelu** scalp; **tanner le c. à qn** to tan sb's hide, to give sb a good hiding **3** Fam (mauvaise prononciation) incorrect liaison (intrusive t or z); **faire un c.** to make an incorrect or a false liaison (par exemple **cent idées** [sãzide]; **moi aussi** [mwazosi])

cuirasse [kɥiras] NF **1** (protection) cuirass, breastplate; Fig **trouver le défaut dans la c. de qn** to find sb's weak or vulnerable spot, to find a chink in sb's armour; Fig **une c. de froideur** an air of aloofness **2** (d'un navire de guerre, blindé) armour (plating); **plaque de c.** armour plate

cuirassé [kɥirase] ADJ (armé) armour-plated, Am armor-plated, armoured, Am armored; Naut **croiseur c.** armour-plated cruiser; Fig **être c. contre les attaques** to be hardened to attack
▪ NM Mil, Naut armoured or Am armored ship; **c. (de ligne)** battleship

cuirassement [kɥirasmã] NM **1** (d'un navire) armouring, Am armoring **2** (cuirasse) armour-plating, Am armor-plating

cuirasser [kɥirase] VT **1** (navire) to armour(-plate), Am to armor(-plate); (machine) to enclose, to protect **2** Arch (soldat) to put a cuirass or breastplate on
▪ VPR **se cuirasser** Arch to put on one's cuirass or breastplate; Fig **se c. contre qch** to arm or steel oneself against or harden oneself to sth

cuirassier [kɥirasje] NM Mil cuirassier

cuire [kɥir] (prp **cuisant**; pp **cuit**; pr ind **je cuis, il cuit, n. cuisons, ils cuisent**; impf **je cuisais**; p hist **je cuisis**; fu **je cuirai**) VT **1** Culin to cook; **c. à l'eau** to boil; **c. des légumes à la vapeur** to steam vegetables; **c. la viande sur le gril** to grill or Am broil the meat; **c. au four** to bake; **un four en terre cuit bien le pain** bread bakes well in a clay oven
   2 (briques, poterie etc) to fire, to bake
   3 (détruire) (du soleil) to bake; (du gel) to kill (off); **le gel a cuit les géraniums** the frost has nipped the geraniums
   4 Suisse (eau, lait) to boil; (vêtements, linge) to boil-wash
▪ VI **1** (des aliments) to cook; **le poulet a cuit trop longtemps** the chicken is overcooked; **pommes à c.** cooking apples; **chocolat à c.** cooking or baking chocolate; **c. à petit feu** ou **à feu doux** to cook slowly, to simmer; Fig Fam **au lieu de me laisser c. à petit feu** instead of keeping me on tenterhooks; Fig Fam **c. (dans son jus)** (avoir très chaud) to be boiling; Fig **laisser c. qn dans son jus** to let sb stew (in their own juice); Fig Fam **on cuit dans cette salle** this room's like an oven; Fam **va te faire c. un œuf!** go to hell!
   2 (brûler) (des mains, joues) to burn; (des yeux) to smart
▪ VPR **se cuire se c. au soleil/sur la plage** to bake or roast in the sun/on the beach
▪ V IMPERS **il vous en cuira** you'll be sorry (for it), you'll regret it

cuisant [kɥizã] ADJ (douleur) smarting, burning; (froid) biting; (remarques) caustic, biting, bitter; **déception cuisante** bitter disappointment; **un échec c.** a stinging defeat

cuiseur [kɥizœr] NM large cooking pot

cuisine [kɥizin] NF **1** (pièce) kitchen; Naut (cook's) galley; **éléments de c.** kitchen units; **ustensiles de c.** cooking utensils; **batterie de c.** (set of) pots and pans; Mil **c. roulante** field kitchen; Ling **latin de c.** dog Latin
   2 (préparation) (art of) cooking, cookery, cuisine; **faire la c.** to cook; **c'est lui qui fait la c.** he does the cooking; **il fait de la bonne c., il fait bien la c.** he's a good cook; **c. au beurre/à l'huile** cooking with butter/oil; **c.**

bourgeoise plain or home cooking; **livre de c.** cookery or recipe book, cookbook **3** (plats) food; **restaurant renommé pour sa c.** restaurant famed for its food or cuisine; **la nouvelle c.** nouvelle cuisine **4** Fam (intrigue) (dirty) tricks; **la c. parlementaire** parliamentary intrigue

cuisiner [kɥizine] VI to cook; **elle cuisine bien** she's a good cook **VT 1** (dîner) to make, to cook; **plats cuisinés** ready-cooked dishes, takeaway meals **2** Fig Fam **c. qn** to interrogate or grill sb

cuisinette [kɥizinɛt] NF kitchenette

cuisinier, -ière [kɥizinje, -jɛr] N chef, cook; **c. en chef** executive chef
▪ NF **cuisinière** cooker, stove; **cuisinière électrique** electric cooker or stove

cuisinier-pâtissier, pl **cuisiniers-pâtissiers** NM pastry cook

cuissage [kɥisaʒ] NM **droit de c.** Fig sexual harassment (by a superior); Hist droit du seigneur

cuissard [kɥisar] NM **1** (pour cycliste) racing shorts **2** Arch (partie de l'armure) cuisse, thigh piece

cuissardes [kɥisard] NFPL (bottes de femme) thigh boots; (de pêche) waders

cuisse [kɥis] NF Anat thigh; Culin **c. de poulet** chicken leg, Fam drumstick; **cuisses de grenouilles** frogs' legs; Fig **avoir la c. légère** to sleep around; Fam **se croire sorti de la c. de Jupiter** to think a lot of oneself, to think one is the cat's whiskers

cuisseau, -eaux [kɥiso] NM Culin (de veau) leg

cuissettes [kɥisɛt] NFPL (pour sportifs) = short shorts

cuisson [kɥisɔ̃] NF **1** (d'aliments) cooking; **temps de c.** cooking time; **le porc demande une longue c.** pork has to be cooked for a long time; **plaque de c.** hob; **c. au gril** grilling; **c. en bain de friture** deep-fat frying; **c. à la vapeur** steaming **2** (des briques, de la porcelaine) burning, firing **3** (sensation) **une impression de c.** a burning sensation or feeling; **la c. de la fessée qu'elle avait reçue l'empêchait de s'asseoir** she was smarting so much after the spanking that she couldn't sit down

cuissot [kɥiso] NM Culin (de venaison) haunch

cuistance [kɥistɑ̃s] NF Arg cooking; (nourriture) grub, nosh; **qui est-ce qui fait la c. ce soir?** who's cooking tonight?

cuistot [kɥisto] NM Fam cook

cuistre [kɥistr] Péj Litt NM **1** (vaniteux) pedant **2** (grossier personnage) scoundrel ▪ ADJ pedantic

cuistrerie [kɥistrəri] NF Péj **1** Litt pedantry **2** (grossièreté) scoundrelly behaviour

cuit [kɥi] ADJ **1** Culin cooked; **bien c.** well done; **c. à point** done to a turn; **trop c.** overdone, overcooked; **pas assez c.** underdone, undercooked; **c. au four** baked; **terre cuite** terracotta; **vin c.** = aperitif wine **2** Fig Fam **être c.** to be done for, to have had it; **c'est c.!** that's it!, we've had it!; **le cinéma, c'est c. pour ce soir** the cinema's out tonight; **c'est c. pour nos vacances** we've had it as far as a holiday is concerned; **c'est du tout c.** it's a cinch or a walkover or a doddle **3** Fam (ivre) plastered, smashed

cuite [kɥit] NF **1** (de briques, poterie) baking, firing **2** Fam **(se) prendre une (bonne) c.** to get plastered or tight, Am to tie one on

cuiter (se) [səkɥite] VPR Fam to get tight or plastered, Am to tie one on

cuivre [kɥivr] NM **1** (métal) **c. (rouge)** copper; **casserole en c.** copper saucepan; **doublé en c.** (plaqué) copper-plated; (par le fond) copper-bottomed; Minér **minerai de c.** copper ore; **c. jaune** brass; **les cuivres** copper(ware); (jaunes) brasses; **faire (briller) les cuivres** to polish the brassware, to do the brasses **2** Mus **les cuivres** the brass (section) **3** (planche) copperplate

cuivré [kɥivre] ADJ **1** (hâlé) (peau, teint) (naturellement) copper-coloured; (par le soleil) bronzed; **cheveux aux reflets cuivrés** auburn hair; **d'un rouge c.** coppery red **2** (voix) resonant, ringing; Mus **sons cuivrés** brassy tones

cuivrer [kɥivre] VT **1** (couvrir de cuivre) to copper, to coat with copper **2** (la peau, le teint) to bronze
▪ VPR **se cuivrer** to turn the colour of copper, to turn coppery

cuivreux, -euse [kɥivrø, -øz] ADJ Chimie (oxyde) cuprous

cul [ky] NM **1** Arg (d'une personne) arse, Fam bum, Am ass, Fam fanny; **un beau c.** a great bum, a lovely arse; Am (d'homme) nice buns; Vulg **trou du c.** arsehole, Am asshole; **faux c.** bustle; Fig **c'est un faux c.** he's two-faced; **renverser qn c. par-dessus tête** to send sb flying or head over heels or Vulg arse over elbow; Fig **il en est tombé ou resté sur le c.** he was flabbergasted; **se taper le c. par terre** to roar with laughter, to split one's sides laughing; **des vacances? mon c.!** holidays? my arse!; Vulg **parle à mon c., ma tête est malade!** (personne ne m'écoute) I might as well talk to the fucking wall!; (laisse-moi tranquille) fuck off!; **avoir le feu au c.** to be in a hell of a rush; (sexuellement) to be randy as hell; **être porté sur le c.** to be sex-mad; **revue** ou **bouquin de c.** porn magazine; **film de c.** blue or porn movie; **être comme c. et chemise** to be as thick as thieves; **ça vaut mieux qu'un coup de pied au c.** it's better than a kick in the pants; **avoir qn dans le c.** to hate sb's guts; **en avoir plein le c.** to be pissed off (**de qch** with sth), to have had a bellyful (**de qch** of sth); **ils l'ont dans le c.** they've had it, that's really screwed them up, that's them buggered; **on a les flics au c.** we've got the cops on our tail; Mil Arg **tirer au c.** to swing the lead, to shirk; **c'est un tire-au-c.** he's a shirker or skiver; Can Fam **n'avoir rien que le c. et les dents** to be at rock-bottom; Arg **quel c.!** what a bloody fool or prat or arsehole or Am asshole! **2** Arg (chance) luck; **avoir du c.** to be lucky or jammy; **avoir le c. bordé de nouilles** to be a lucky bastard; **j'ai/elle a gagné le gros lot – quel c.!** I/she won the jackpot – you/the jammy devil! **3** (d'un animal) haunches, rump **4** (d'un sac, tonneau) bottom; (d'une bouteille) bottom, base; **boire c. sec** to down one's drink in one go; **c. sec!** bottoms up! **5** Naut (d'un navire) stern ▪ ADJ INV silly; **elle est un peu c.** she's a bit of a twerp or twit or nerd

culasse [kylas] NF **1** Mil (de fusil, pistolet) breech; **c. mobile** (de carabine) bolt; **fusil se chargeant par la c.** breech loader; **bloc de c.** breech block **2** (de moteur) cylinder head; **joint de c.** cylinder head gasket; Aut **c. à flux opposés** cross-flow or hemispherical head; Aut **c. à flux transversal** cross-flow head

cul-blanc, pl **culs-blancs** NM (oiseau) wheatear

culbute [kylbyt] NF **1** (cabriole) somersault; **faire la c.** to turn a somersault **2** (chute) tumble, heavy fall; **faire une** ou **la c.** to fall; **le gamin chuta de son vélo et fit une c.** the kid came off his bike head over heels; Fig Fam **faire la c.** (d'un gouvernement) to fall; (d'une entreprise) to go bust; Com **les revendeurs font la c.** the dealers are making a killing or a huge profit

culbuter [kylbyte] VI **1** (se renverser) (d'un vase, d'un arbre, d'une statue etc) to topple over; (de qn) to take a tumble; **la voiture a culbuté dans le fossé** the car overturned and landed in the ditch **2** Fam (d'une entreprise) to go bust or Arg belly up; (d'un banquier, homme d'affaires etc) to come a cropper
▪ VT **1** (renverser) to knock down or over; (gouvernement) to bring down **2** très Fam (femme) to lay

culbuterie [kylbytri] NF Aut rocker arms

culbuteur [kylbytœr] NM **1** (jouet) tumbler **2** (de moteur) rocker (arm) **3** Tech tripper device; (de camion) tipper

cul-de-basse-fosse, pl **culs-de-basse-fosse** [kydbɑsfos] NM dungeon

cul-de-jatte, pl **culs-de-jatte** [kydʒat] NM legless cripple

cul-de-lampe, pl **culs-de-lampe** [kydlɑ̃p] NM **1** Archit (ornement) bracket, corbel **2** Typ tailpiece

cul-de-poule [kydpul] NM Arg **faire la bouche en c.** to purse one's lips

cul-de-sac, pl **culs-de-sac** [kydsak] NM blind alley, cul-de-sac; Fig dead end; **la rue se termine en c.** the street ends in a cul-de-sac or is a dead end; Fig **être dans un c.** to have reached a dead end

culée [kyle] NF Archit (d'un contrefort) pier; Constr (d'un pont) abutment (pier)

culinaire [kylinɛr] ADJ culinary; **l'art c.** the art of cooking, the culinary art; **les talents culinaires de son mari** her husband's talents as a cook; **recettes culinaires** recipes

culminant [kylminɑ̃] ADJ **point c.** (d'une chaîne de montagnes) highest point; (du pouvoir) zenith; (de la renommée, gloire, d'une carrière) height, peak

culminer [kylmine] VI **1 le mont Blanc culmine à 4807 mètres** Mont Blanc is 4,807 metres at its highest point **2** Fig Bourse (de cours) to reach its highest level, to peak; **sa carrière culmine** it's the crowning point or pinnacle of his career; **alors que sa carrière culminait** when his career was reaching its height or peak

culot [kylo] NM **1** Fam (audace) cheek, nerve; **tu ne manques pas de c.!, tu as du c.!** you've got a nerve or a cheek!; **il a un sacré c.!** he's got a helluva nerve!; **il a tous les culots** he's got a lot of nerve, cheek is his middle name; **y aller au c.** to put a brave face on it, to brazen it out; **vas-y au c. et demande-lui son autographe** just breeze up and ask him for his autograph **2** (de lampe, bouteille etc) bottom, base; Mil (de douille de cartouche, d'obus) base; (de cartouche) head; Élec (d'ampoule) base; Aut (d'une bougie) body **3** (dans une pipe) dottle **4** Tech (résidu) residue

culottage [kylotaʒ] NM (d'une pipe) colouring, seasoning

culotte [kylot] NF **1** (pantalon) **c. courte** short trousers; **c. de cheval** jodhpurs, riding breeches; Fig Fam **jodhpur thighs**; **c. de golf** plus fours; **c. de peau** lederhosen; Fig Fam **c'est la femme qui porte la c.** it's the wife who wears the trousers; Can **avoir des culottes** to have guts; Fam **user ses fonds de c. sur les bancs de l'école** to idle away one's time at school; Fam **faire dans sa c.** to be scared stiff, to have the jitters, Arg to wet or pee oneself **2** (sous-vêtement) (de femme) panties, knickers; (d'enfant) pants VOIR GRAMMAIRE A10 **3** Fam **prendre une c.** to lose heavily, Am to take a bath **4** Culin (de bœuf) rump

culotté [kylote] ADJ **1** (pipe) seasoned; **un plafond c. par la fumée du tabac** a ceiling black with tobacco smoke **2** Fam (audacieux) full of cheek or nerve, cheeky; **il est**

c. he's got one hell of a nerve (**de faire qch** doing sth)

culotter [kylɔte] VT *(pipe)* to colour, to season

culpabilisation [kylpabilizasjɔ̃] NF *Psy* **1** *(action)* **la c. de qn** making sb feel guilty **2** *(résultat)* (feeling of) guilt

culpabiliser [kylpabilize] *Psy* VT **c. qn** to make sb feel guilty
▸ VI to feel guilty

culpabilité [kylpabilite] NF guilt; **nier sa c.** to deny that one is guilty; *Jur* **verdict de c.** guilty verdict; **sa c. dans cette affaire a été établie** his guilt in the matter has been established; **sentiment de c.** feeling of guilt, guilty feeling

culte [kylt] ADJ *(livre, film, émission, auteur)* cult
▸ NM **1** *(vénération)* worship; *Fig* cult; *Fig* **c. de la personnalité** personality cult, cult of the personality; **avoir le c. de l'argent** to worship money; *Fig* **avoir un c. pour qn, rendre** *ou* **vouer un c. à qn** to (hero-)worship sb **2** *(religion)* form of worship, creed, religion; **liberté du c.** freedom of worship; **changer de c.** to change one's religion **3** *(service protestant)* (church) service

cul-terreux, *pl* **culs-terreux** NM *Fam Péj* country bumpkin, yokel, *Am* rube, redneck

cultivable [kyltivabl] ADJ suitable for cultivation

cultivateur, -trice [kyltivatœr, -tris] N farmer; **petits cultivateurs** small farmers, smallholders
▸ NM *(machine)* cultivator
▸ ADJ agricultural, farming; **les peuples cultivateurs** agricultural people, farming communities

cultivé [kyltive] ADJ **1** *Agr (terre, champs)*, *Biol (virus)* cultivated **2** *(personne)* cultivated, cultured; **gens cultivés** cultivated *or* educated people

cultiver [kyltive] VT **1** *(sol)* to cultivate, to farm **2** *Agr (céréales, artichauts)* to raise, to grow, to cultivate; *(roses)* to raise, to grow; *Biol (virus)*, *Fig (l'amitié de qn etc)* to cultivate; **c. son esprit** to cultivate *or* improve one's mind; **c. un goût** to cultivate *or* develop a taste; **il cultive la goujaterie** he makes a point of being boorish, he works hard at being boorish; *Fig* **il faut c. son jardin** = concentrate on things close to home and don't try to change the world
▸ VPR **se cultiver** to improve one's mind

cultuel, -elle [kyltɥɛl] ADJ of *or* pertaining to worship; **édifice c.** place of worship

culture [kyltyr] NF **1** *(du sol)* cultivation; **c. fruitière** fruit farming; **c. sèche** dry farming; **cultures** land under cultivation **2** *(de céréales, artichauts etc)* growing, raising; *Biol* **c. (microbienne/de tissus)** culture (of bacteria/of tissue); **bouillon de c.** culture medium **3** *(espèce cultivée)* crop **4** *(intellectuelle)* culture, education; **c. scientifique** scientific knowledge *or* background; **question de c. générale** question of general knowledge; **avoir une solide c.** to have a sound education; **maison de la c.** ≃ arts centre **5** *(civilisation)* culture; **la c. gréco-romaine** Graeco-Roman culture *or* civilization; **c'est une autre c.** it's a different culture *or* way of life
▸▸**c. d'entreprise** corporate culture; **c. physique** physical training, *Fam* PT

culturel, -elle [kyltyrɛl] ADJ *(relations, milieu, attaché)* cultural; *(voyage)* educational; **centre c.** community arts centre; **choc c.** culture shock; **subir un choc c.** to suffer (from) culture shock

culturisme [kyltyrism] NM body building, *Fam* pumping iron

culturiste [kyltyrist] N body builder

cumin [kymɛ̃] NM cumin; **c. des prés** caraway; **munster au c.** Munster (cheese) with caraway seeds

cumul [kymyl] NM **c. des fonctions, c. des mandats** plurality of offices, pluralism; **c. des traitements** drawing of more than one salary

cumulable [kymylabl] ADJ **des fonctions cumulables** offices which can be held simultaneously *or* concurrently; **des traitements cumulables** salaries which can be drawn concurrently *or* simultaneously; **ces deux réductions d'impôts ne sont pas cumulables** these two tax reductions may not be claimed at the same time

cumulard, -arde [kymylar, -ard] N *Fam Péj* holder of several official positions *(for each of which a salary is drawn)*

cumulatif, -ive [kymylatif, -iv] ADJ cumulative

cumuler [kymyle] VT **c. des fonctions** to hold more than one office; **c. deux traitements** to draw two (separate) salaries; **il cumule plusieurs emplois** he has several jobs

cumulo-nimbus [kymylonɛ̃bys] NM INV *Météo* cumulo-nimbus

cumulo-stratus [kymylostratys] NM INV *Météo* strato-cumulus, cumulo-stratus

cumulus [kymylys] NM INV *Météo* cumulus

cunéiforme [kyneifɔrm] ADJ cuneiform

cupide [kypid] ADJ greedy, grasping, moneygrubbing

cupidement [kypidmɑ̃] ADV greedily

cupidité [kypidite] NF cupidity, greed

Cupidon [kypidɔ̃] NM *Myth* Cupid

cuprifère [kyprifɛr] ADJ copper-bearing, *Spéc* cupriferous

cuprique [kyprik] ADJ cupric

curable [kyrabl] ADJ *(maladie etc)* curable; **la lèpre est c.** leprosy can be cured, leprosy is curable

curaçao [kyraso] NM curaçao (liqueur)

curage [kyraʒ] NM *(de canalisation, port)* clearing *or* cleaning out; *(de tuyau)* flushing

curare [kyrar] NM curare

curatelle [kyratɛl] NF *Jur (d'une succession)* trusteeship; *(d'un mineur, aliéné)* guardianship

curateur, -trice [kyratœr, -tris] N *Jur (d'une succession etc)* trustee; *(d'un mineur, aliéné)* guardian

curatif, -ive [kyratif, -iv] ADJ curative

cure [kyr] NF **1** *Méd (course of)* treatment; **c. thermale** hydrotherapy, course of treatment at a spa; **c. d'amaigrissement** diet; **faire une c. de lait/de repos** to go on a milk diet/rest cure; **elle a fait une c. à Vichy** she took the waters at Vichy; **c. de sommeil** sleep cure; **c. de sevrage** detoxification programme **2** *(fonction de curé)* office of a parish priest; *(paroisse)* parish; *(presbytère)* presbytery; **obtenir une c.** to be appointed parish priest **3** **n'avoir c. de qch** not to care about sth; **je n'ai c. de toutes ses médailles** I don't care about all his medals; **tu peux toujours essayer de l'impressionner, elle n'en a c.** she won't take any notice of your attempts to impress her

curé [kyre] NM *Cathol* parish priest; *Fam (sans aucune distinction de rang)* priest; **monsieur le c.** Father; **il veut se faire c.** he wants to become a priest *or* to enter the priesthood; *Fig Fam* **bouffer** *ou* **manger du c.** to be (violently) anti-clerical

cure-dent(s), *pl* **cure-dents** NM toothpick

curée [kyre] NF = parts of the stag given to the hounds; *(mise à mort)* kill; *Fig* **pays livré à la c. des mercenaires étrangers** country handed over to the tender mercies of foreign mercenaries; *Fig* **ce fut la c. entre les héritiers** the heirs started to fight over the spoils; *Fig* **les journalistes s'emparèrent de l'affaire et ce fut une véritable c.** the press acted like jackals once they got wind of the story

cure-ongles NM INV nail cleaner

cure-pipe, *pl* **cure-pipes** NM pipe-cleaner

curer [kyre] VT *(ses dents)* to pick; *(une canalisation, un port)* to clear *or* clean out; *(une rivière, un canal, un étang)* to dredge; *(pipe)* to scrape, to clean out; **se c. les ongles/les oreilles** to clean one's nails/clean (out) one's ears

curetage [kyrtaʒ] NM *Chir* curetting, curettage

cureter [kyrte] VT *Chir* to curette

cureton [kyrtɔ̃] NM *Fam Péj* priest

curette [kyrɛt] NF *Tech* scraper; *Chir* curette

curie¹ [kyri] NF *Antiq, Cathol* curia

curie² NM *Phys* curie

curieusement [kyrjøzmɑ̃] ADV *(étrangement)* curiously, oddly; **les gens le regardaient c.** people looked at him curiously *or* gave him curious *or* funny looks

curieux, -ieuse [kyrjø, -jøz] ADJ **1** *(intéressé)* curious, interested; *(esprit)* inquiring, curious; **être c. de tout/de la vie** to be curious about *or* interested in everything/life; **elle est curieuse d'archéologie** she's interested in archaeology; **je serais c. de voir cela** I'd be interested in seeing that **2** *(indiscret)* curious, inquisitive, *Fam* nos(e)y **3** *(étrange)* curious, odd, funny, peculiar; **par une curieuse coïncidence** by a strange coincidence; **chose assez curieuse** curiously *or* funnily enough; **ne me regarde pas comme une bête curieuse** don't look at me as if I had two heads
▸ N inquisitive person, *Fam* nos(e)y parker, busybody; **méfie-toi, c'est un c.** watch out, he's nos(e)y; **un attroupement de c.** a crowd of onlookers *or* bystanders; **il était venu en c.** he came just to have a look
▸ NM **le plus c. de l'affaire est que ...** the strangest *or* oddest part *or* thing about it is that ...

curiosité [kyrjozite] NF **1** *(intellectuelle)* curiosity, interest; **c. intellectuelle** intellectual curiosity; **pour développer la c. de votre enfant** to arouse your child's sense of curiosity; **satisfaire sa c.** to satisfy one's curiosity; **regarder qn avec c.** to look at sb curiously *or* enquiringly **2** *(indiscrétion)* curiosity, inquisitiveness, *Fam* nosiness; **par c.** out of curiosity; **par simple c., dites-moi ...** just out of curiosity, tell me ...; **la c. est un vilain défaut** curiosity killed the cat **3** *(monument)* interesting feature *or* sight; *(objet)* curio; **curiosités d'une ville** sights of a town

curiste [kyrist] N patient taking the waters *(at a spa)*

curling [kœrliŋ] NM *Sport* curling

curriculum vitae [kyrikylɔmvite] NM INV curriculum vitae, CV, *Am* résumé; **envoyer/établir son c.** to send (off)/draw up one's CV

curry [kyri] NM *Culin* curry; **poulet au c., c. de poulet** curried chicken, chicken curry

curseur [kyrsœr] NM *Ordinat* cursor; *Tech (de règle à calcul, compas)* cursor, slide, runner; *Ordinat* **position/déplacement du c.** cursor position/movement

cursif, -ive [kyrsif, -iv] ADJ **1** *(écriture)* cursive **2** *(rapide)* cursory

cursus [kyrsys] NM *Univ* programme, *Am* program, course of study, curriculum; **établir son c.** to arrange one's course of study; **le c. médical** the medical degree course

curviligne [kyrvilliŋ] ADJ curvilinear

cuspide [kyspid] NF *Anat, Bot* cusp

custode [kystɔd] NF **1** Rel (pour hostie) custodial **2** (de voiture) rear quarter panel; (glace) quarterlight

cutané [kytane] ADJ skin, Spéc cutaneous; **maladie cutanée** skin disease

cuti [kyti] NF Méd skin test; Fam **virer sa c.** to have a positive reaction to a skin test; Fig to have changed radically

cuticule [kytikyl] NF Anat epidermis, cuticle

cutiréaction [kytireaksjɔ̃] NF Méd = cuti

cutter [kœtœr, kytɛr] NM Stanley® knife

cuvage [kyvaʒ] NM, **cuvaison** [kyvɛzɔ̃] NF (de vin, bière) fermenting or fermentation in vats

cuve [kyv] NF (storage) tank, cistern; (de machine à laver) tub; (pour la fermentation des alcools, du vin) vat, tun; Vieilli **c. à lessive** laundry tub; Phot **c. à laver/à développement** washing/developing tank

cuvée [kyve] NF **1** (quantité) vatful, tunful **2** (produit) vintage; Fig batch; **vin de première c.** wine of the first growth or vintage; **c. de la maison** ou **du patron** house wine; Fig **être de la même c.** (d'étudiants) to be classmates, to be in the same year; Fig **la dernière c. du festival de Cannes** the latest batch of films from the Cannes festival

cuver [kyve] VI **1** (de vin, bière) to ferment (in the vats) **2** Fam (d'une personne) to sleep it off VT Fam **c. son vin** to sleep it off; **c. sa colère** to simmer down

cuvette [kyvɛt] NF **1** (wash)basin, (wash)bowl; **c. (de lavabo)** washbasin **2** (de W.-C.) bowl, pan; (de thermomètre) bulb; Phot (developing) dish **3** (dépression), Géog basin, depression, Br punchbowl

CV [seve] NM **1** Aut (abrév **cheval-vapeur**) = French administrative unit for car tax purposes **2** (abrév **curriculum vitae**) CV, Am résumé

CVG [seveʒe] NM Bourse (abrév **certificat de valeur garantie**) CVR

cyan [sjɑ̃] ADJ INV, NM cyan

cyanhydrique [sjanidrik] ADJ **acide c.** prussic acid

cyanose [sjanoz] NF Méd cyanosis

cyanure [sjanyr] NM Chimie cyanide; **empoisonnement au c.** cyanide poisoning

cyber [sibɛr] NM cyber

cybercafé [sibɛrkafe] NM cybercafé

cybercommerce [sibɛrkɔmɛrs] NM e-commerce

cybercrime [sibɛrkrim] NM cybercrime

cyberculture [sibɛrkyltyr] NF cyberculture

cyberespace [sibɛrɛspas] NM cyberspace; **dans le c.** in cyberspace

cybermonde [sibɛrmɔ̃d] NM cyberspace; **dans le c.** in cyberspace

cybernaute [sibɛrnot] NM cybernaut

cybernéticien, -ienne [sibɛrnetisjɛ̃, -jɛn] N cybernetics expert, cyberneticist

cybernétique [sibɛrnetik] ADJ cybernetic NF cybernetics

cyberpunk [sibɛrpœnk] NM cyberpunk

cybersexe [sibɛrsɛks] NM cybersex

cyclable [siklabl] ADJ **piste c.** cycle track

cyclamen [siklamɛn] NM cyclamen

cycle [sikl] NM **1** (d'événements, de poèmes etc), Biol, Chimie cycle; (de conférences) series; Mktg **c. commande-livraison-facturation** order-to-remittance cycle; Mktg **c. de commercialisation** trade cycle; Mktg **c. de la distribution** wheel of retailing; **c. économique** economic cycle; Com **c. d'exploitation** operating cycle; Ordinat **c. d'exécution** execute cycle; **c. menstruel** menstrual cycle; **c. solaire** solar cycle; Mktg **c. de vie** life cycle; Mktg **c. de vie du produit** product life cycle, PLC

2 Scol **premier/second c.** junior/senior classes (in secondary school); **elle est prof dans le premier c.** she's a junior school teacher, Am she teaches junior school; **élèves du premier c.** junior pupils; **c. primaire/supérieur** primary/higher education

3 Aut **c. d'allumage** ignition cycle; **c. à deux temps** two-stroke cycle; **c. à quatre temps** four-stroke cycle; **c. urbain** urban cycle

4 (véhicule) cycle; **magasin/fabricant de cycles** cycle shop/manufacturer

cyclique [siklik] ADJ cyclical

cyclisme [siklism] NM Sport cycling

cycliste [siklist] Sport N cyclist ADJ (course) cycle; **coureur c.** racing cyclist

cyclo-cross [siklokrɔs] NM Sport cyclo-cross

cycloïdal, -ale, -aux, -ales [siklɔidal, -o] ADJ Math (courbe etc) cycloidal

cycloïde [s.iklɔid] NF Math cycloid

cyclomoteur [siklomɔtœr] NM moped

cyclomotoriste [siklomɔtɔrist] N moped rider

cyclonal, -ale, -aux, -ales [siklɔnal, -o] ADJ Météo cyclonic

cyclone [siklon] NM Météo (tempête) cyclone; (zone de basse pression) area of low pressure, depression, cyclone; **œil du c.** eye of the storm; Fig **elle est entrée comme un c.** she came in like a whirlwind

cyclonique [siklɔnik] ADJ Météo cyclonic

cyclope [siklɔp] NM Myth Cyclops; Fig **travail de c.** colossal undertaking, Herculean task

cyclopéen, -enne [siklɔpeɛ̃, -ɛn] ADJ Fig gigantic, colossal; **travail c.** Herculean task

cyclopousse [siklopus] NM trishaw, rickshaw (drawn by a bicycle)

cyclorama [siklorama] NM TV, Cin cyclorama, cyc

cyclothymie [siklotimi] NF Psy manic-depression

cyclothymique [siklotimik] ADJ Psy manic-depressive

cyclotourisme [sikloturism] NM bicycle touring, cycling holidays

cyclotron [siklotrɔ̃] NM Nucl cyclotron

cygne [siɲ] NM swan; **jeune c.** cygnet; **c. mâle** cob; **c. femelle** pen; **duvet de c.** swans-down; **une robe d'une blancheur de c.** a pure or snowy white dress; Fig **c'est son chant du c.** it's his swansong; Tech **col de c.** swan neck

cylindrage [silɛ̃draʒ] NM (de route, d'acier etc) rolling; Métal **c. à froid** cold rolling

cylindre [silɛ̃dr] NM **1** Géom cylinder **2** (de moteur) cylinder; (de laminoir, essoreuse à rouleaux, calandre etc) roller; Aut **c. de roue** wheel cylinder; **moteur à quatre cylindres** four-cylinder engine; Aut **une quatre cylindres** a four-cylinder (car); Typ **c. d'impression** printing cylinder, drum; **c. compresseur** road roller; **c. de friction** (dans une imprimante) friction cylinder

cylindrée [silɛ̃dre] NF (de cylindre, moteur) (cubic) capacity; **petite c.** (voiture) small car, Am compact; **grosse c.** large car, Fam tank

cylindrer [silɛ̃dre] VT (route, pelouse, métal etc) to roll

cylindrique [silɛ̃drik] ADJ cylindrical

cymbale [sɛ̃bal] NF Mus cymbal

cymbalier, -ière [sɛ̃balje, -jɛr] NM cymbal player, cymbalist

cynégétique [sineʒetik] NF hunting ADJ hunting; **les plaisirs cynégétiques** the pleasures of hunting

cynique [sinik] ADJ **1** (personne, attitude etc) cynical **2** Phil Cynic NM **1** cynic **2** Phil Cynic

cyniquement [sinikmɑ̃] ADV cynically

cynisme [sinism] NM **1** cynicism **2** Phil Cynicism

cynocéphale [sinosefal] NM dog-faced baboon

cynodrome [sinodrom] NM greyhound (racing) track, Fam dog track

cynophile [sinofil] ADJ **équipe c.** (police) dog-handlers, dog-handling team N dog lover

cynor(r)hodon [sinɔrɔdɔ̃] NM (fruit) rosehip; **confiture/tisane de c.** rosehip jam/tea

cyprès [siprɛ] NM cypress (tree)

cypriote [siprijɔt] ADJ Cypriot N C. Cypriot

cyrillique [sirilik] ADJ (alphabet etc) Cyrillic

cystique [sistik] ADJ Anat, Méd (conduit, bile, calcul etc) cystic

cystite [sistit] NF Méd cystitis

cytise [sitiz] NM laburnum

cytologie [sitolɔʒi] NF Biol cytology

cytologique [sitolɔʒik] ADJ Biol cytological

cytomégalovirus [sitomegalovirys] NM Méd cytomegalovirus, CMV

cytoplasme [sitoplasm] NM Biol cytoplasm

cytoplasmique [sitoplasmik] ADJ Biol cytoplasmic

czar [tsar] NM tsar, czar

(d'un orateur) delivery; **il a un de ces débits!** he really has the gift of the gab!

débit² NM *Fin* debit; **porter 1 000 euros au d. de qn** to debit sb with 1,000 euros; **d. cumulé** cumulative debit; **d. de caisse** cash debit; **d. immédiat** immediate debit

débitable¹ [debitabl] ADJ *(bois etc)* that can be cut up

débitable² ADJ *(compte)* that can be drawn on

débitant, -ante [debitã, -ãt] N **d. de tabac** tobacconist; **d. de boissons** pub owner, *Am* bar owner

débiter¹ [debite] VT **1** *Com (vendre)* to sell retail **2** *(bois)* to cut up, to convert; *(viande)* to cut up **3** *Tech (tant de litres par heure etc)* to discharge; *Ind* to produce; *Ordinat* to output; **les ascenseurs de la tour débitent 500 personnes par heure** the lifts in the tower handle 500 people per hour; **cette usine débite 250 voitures par jour** the output from the factory is 250 cars a day, the factory produces 250 cars a day **4** *(texte, harangue)* to deliver; **l'acteur débite son texte de plus en plus vite** the actor's speaking his lines faster and faster; **ce n'est pas un acteur, il ne fait que d. le texte** he's no actor, he's merely reciting the text; *Péj* **d. des sottises** to talk rubbish; **il m'a débité toutes ces sottises sans s'arrêter** he trotted out all that nonsense to me non-stop; **d. des mensonges** to trot out one lie after another

débiter² VT *Com (inscrire au débit)* to debit; **d. une somme à qn, d. qn d'une somme** to debit sb with an amount; **d. un compte** to debit an account; **d. une somme d'un compte** to debit an account with an amount, to debit an amount to an account

débiteur¹, -euse [debitœr, -øz] N **1** *Péj Vieilli (diseur)* person who holds forth *or* talks rubbish; **d. de calomnies** scandalmonger **2** *Tech* feeding device **3** *(dans un magasin)* shop assistant

débiteur², -trice [debitœr, -tris] N *(qui doit de l'argent)* debtor; *Fig* **je suis votre d.** I am indebted to you, I am in your debt ▪ ADJ **1** *Com* **compte d.** debit account; **votre compte est d. de trois mille euros** your account is three thousand euros overdrawn **2** *Cin* **bobine débitrice** top *or* delivery spool ▸▸ **d. concordataire** = bankrupt who has reached a settlement with his debtors; **d. hypothécaire** mortgagor; **d. insolvable** insolvent debtor; **d. principal** primary *or* principal debtor; **d. solidaire** joint and several debtor

débitmètre [debitmɛtr] NM *Tech* flowmeter

déblai [deblɛ] NM *Constr, Rail etc* **1** excavation, cut(ting); **route en d.** sunken road **2 déblais** spoil earth

déblaiement [deblɛmã] NM *(de terrain etc)* clearing

déblatérer [deblatere] (**je déblatère; je déblatérerai**) VT **d. des sottises** to talk nonsense; **d. des injures** to fling abuse (**contre** at); **il ne cesse de d. les pires insultes à ton égard** he's always extremely abusive about you ▪ VI **d. contre** *ou* **sur qn/qch** to rail against sb/sth

déblayage [deblɛjaʒ] NM clearing; *(d'une chambre)* clearing out

déblayer [deblɛje] VT (**je déblaye, je déblaie**) **1** *(déblais etc)* to clear away, to remove; **d. la neige** to shovel away the snow **2** *(chambre)* to clear out; **d. un terrain** to clear a piece of ground; *Fig* **d. le terrain** *(pour des négociations etc)* to prepare *or* clear the ground *or* the way

déblocage [deblɔkaʒ] NM freeing, releasing; *(de machine)* unjamming; *Fin (des prix etc)* unfreezing; *Psy* **le d. d'inhibitions/de complexes** getting rid of inhibitions/complexes

débloquer [deblɔke] VT **1** *(libérer, mettre en marche)* to free, to release; *(machine)* to unjam; *Tél (téléphone portable)* to unlock; *Fin (prix etc)* to unfreeze; *(compte)* to free, to unfreeze; **d. des fonds** to release funds, to make funds available **2** *Psy* **d. qn** *(ôter les complexes de)* to rid sb of his/her complexes; *(rendre moins timide)* to make sb less inhibited ▪ VI *Fam* **1** *(être fou)* to be off one's rocker; *(raconter n'importe quoi)* to talk nonsense; **son grand-père est vieux, il commence à d.** his grandfather is old and going gaga **2** *(ne pas fonctionner correctement)* to be on the blink, *Am* to be on the fritz

débobiner [debɔbine] VT *(rouleau, fil etc)* to unwind

débogage [debɔgaʒ] NM *Ordinat* debugging

déboguer [debɔge] VT *Ordinat* to debug

débogueur [debɔgœr] NM *Ordinat* debugger

déboires [debwar] NMPL *(déceptions)* disappointments; *(ennuis)* problems, trouble; **essuyer bien des d.** to suffer many disappointments *or* setbacks

déboisement [debwazmã] NM deforestation

déboiser [debwaze] VT *(région)* to deforest, to clear; *Fam* **se faire d. la colline** to have one's hair cropped

déboîtement [debwatmã] NM **1** *(d'un membre, d'une articulation)* dislocation **2** *Aut* pulling out

déboîter [debwate] VT **1** *Tech (tuyau etc)* to disconnect, to uncouple **2** *(articulation, membre)* to dislocate **3** *(montre etc)* to remove from its case ▪ VI *Aut* to pull out ▪ VPR **se déboîter** *(d'une cheville etc)* to become dislocated; **se d. l'épaule/le genou** to dislocate one's shoulder/knee, to put one's shoulder/knee out

débonder [debɔde] VT *(lavabo)* to unblock; *(fût)* to unbung; *Fig Vieilli* **d. son cœur** to pour out one's heart ▪ VPR **se débonder** *(d'un lavabo etc)* to unblock; *(d'un fût)* to become unbunged; *Fig Vieilli (d'une personne)* to pour out one's heart

débonnaire [debɔnɛr] ADJ goodnatured, easy-going; **répondre d'un ton d.** to answer goodnaturedly

débordant [debɔrdã] ADJ **1** *(expansif)* overflowing, brimming over (**de** with); **d. de santé** bursting with health; **avoir une imagination débordante** to be brimful of imagination; **faire preuve d'un enthousiasme/ d'une activité débordant(e)** to be brimming *or* bubbling over with enthusiasm/brimful of energy **2** *(qui dépasse)* projecting, protruding; *(en se chevauchant)* overlapping

débordé [debɔrde] ADJ **1** *(de travail etc)* snowed under **2 drap d.** *(pour préparer le lit)* turned-back sheet; *(défait)* untucked sheet; **mon lit est d.** my sheets have come untucked

débordement [debɔrdəmã] NM **1** *(d'une rivière etc)* overflowing; *Fig (d'enthousiasme, injures etc)* outburst, outpouring **2 débordements** excesses, dissipation, dissolute living **3** *Mil (de l'ennemi)* outflanking

déborder [debɔrde] VI **1** *(du contenu d'un verre etc)* to overflow, to brim over, to run over; **verre plein à d.** glass full to overflowing *or* to the brim; **la rivière a débordé** the river has overflowed its banks; **le lait a dé-**

bordé de la casserole the milk has boiled over; **les papiers débordent de la corbeille** the papers are spilling out of the wastepaper basket; **essaie de colorier la maison sans d.** try to colour in the house without going over the edges; **c'est la goutte d'eau qui fait d. le vase** it's the last straw; *TV, Radio etc* **d. sur le temps prévu** to overrun **2** *Fig* **elle déborde de vie** she is bubbling over with *or* brimful of vitality; **d. d'imagination** to be brimful of imagination; **son cœur déborde de reconnaissance** his heart is brimming over with gratitude ▪ VT **1** *(dépasser)* to project *or* extend beyond; *Mil (l'ennemi)* to outflank; **d. son adversaire** *(dans une course)* to overtake one's competitor; **cela déborde le cadre de mes responsabilités/de notre débat** that exceeds my responsibilities/the limits of our discussion **2 d. (les couvertures d')un lit** to untuck a bed; *Naut* **d. une embarcation** to shove off, to sheer off; **d. les avirons** to unship the oars **3** *(enlever les bords de)* to remove the edging from; *Tech* **d. une tôle** to trim the edges of an iron plate

débotté [debɔte] NM **au d.** immediately, *Am* off the bat

débotter [debɔte] VT **d. qn** to take off sb's boots ▪ VPR **se débotter** to take off one's boots

débouchage [debuʃaʒ] NM **1** *(d'un tuyau)* unblocking **2** *(d'une bouteille)* uncorking

débouché [debuʃe] NM **1** *(d'un passage etc)* opening; *(d'une vallée)* entrance **2** *(possibilité)* opening, opportunity; *Com, Mktg* outlet, market; **cette formation n'offre aucun d.** the training does not lead to any career openings; **créer de nouveaux débouchés pour un produit** to create new outlets for a product

déboucher [debuʃe] VT **1** *(tuyau bouché etc)* to clear, to unblock **2** *(bouteille)* to uncork, to remove the cork from ▪ VI to emerge (**de** from), to come out (**de** of); **cet escalier débouche dans le grenier** the staircase leads to the attic; **cette rue débouche sur la place** this street runs into the square; **voilà sur quoi débouche la guerre** that's what war leads to; **ces études débouchent sur un métier intéressant** this course of study leads to a worthwhile career; **vos expériences ne débouchent sur aucun résultat** your experiments aren't leading anywhere, you're not getting any results with your experiments ▪ VPR **se déboucher** *(de tuyau)* to clear, to become unblocked; **la bouteille se débouche facilement** the bottle opens easily, the cork is easily removed from the bottle

déboucheur [debuʃœr] NM drain clearer

débouchoir [debuʃwar] NM *(pour les sanitaires)* (rubber) plunger

déboucler [debukle] VT **1** *(ceinture etc)* to unbuckle **2** *(cheveux)* to take the curl out of

déboulé [debule] NM **tirer un lapin au d.** to shoot a rabbit as it bolts from cover

débouler [debule] VI **1** *(tomber)* to fall head over heels **2** *Fam (arriver)* to turn up, to show up; **ils ont déboulé chez moi sans prévenir** they showed up at my place without any warning **3** *(du gibier)* to start, to bolt (from cover) ▪ VT *Fam* **d. l'escalier** to run down the stairs

déboulonnage [debulɔnaʒ] NM, **déboulonnement** [debulɔnmã] NM **1** *Tech* unriveting, unbolting **2** *Fig (renvoi)* dismissal; **il procéda ensuite au d. systématique de ses anciens collègues** he then proceeded to systematically debunk his former colleagues

déboulonner [debulɔne] VT **1** *Tech* to unrivet, to unbolt **2** *Fig (discréditer)* to debunk; *(de son poste)* to get rid of, to kick out

débourber [deburbe] **VT 1** *(étang, canal)* to clean out; **d. le vin** to draw off *or* decant wine **2** *(voiture etc)* to haul out of the mud

débourrer [debure] **VT 1 d. un cheval** to break in a horse **2 d. sa pipe** to scrape out one's pipe

VI *Fam (ne plus être saoul)* to sober up; **il n'a pas débourré depuis huit jours** he's been drunk for a week; **il ne débourre plus** he's never sober

débours [debur] **NM** expenses; *(pour services aux clients)* visitors paid out, VPO; **faire des d.** to lay out money

déboursement [debursəmɑ̃] **NM** paying out, *Fml* disbursement

débourser [deburse] **VT** *(argent)* to spend, to lay out, to pay, *Fml* to disburse; **sans rien d.** without spending a penny; **je suis toujours en train de d.** I'm always putting my hand in my pocket

déboussoler [debusɔle] **VT** *Fam* to disorientate, *surtout Am* to disorient; **je suis un peu déboussolée dans ce nouveau pays/dans mon nouvel appartement** I'm a bit disorientated *or* lost in this new country/in my new apartment; **cette nouvelle l'a complètement déboussolé** the news completely threw him

debout [dəbu] **ADV 1** *(chose)* upright, on end; *(personne)* standing; **mettre qch d.** to stand sth up *or* on end; **mettre les bouteilles d.** to stand the bottles up(right); **cent ans plus tard, la maison est encore d.** the house is still standing a hundred years later; **elle est d. toute la journée** she's on her feet all day; **rester d.** to stand; **places d. seulement** standing room only; **tenir d.** to be (standing) upright; **c'est si bas qu'on ne peut tenir d.** it's so low that you can't stand up straight; *Fig* **argument qui ne tient pas d.** argument that won't hold water *or* won't stand up; *Fig* **cette institution est** *ou* **tient encore d.** the institution is still in existence; **se tenir d.** to stand; **se tenir d. (sur ses pattes arrières)** *(d'un chien)* to stand on its hind legs; **se (re)mettre d.** to stand up; **conte** *ou* **histoire à dormir d.** silly *or* extravagant *or Fam* cock-and-bull story; **tous les matins je suis d. à six heures** I'm up *or* I get up at six o'clock every morning; **allons, d.!** *(hors du lit)* come on, get up!; **il va mieux, il est déjà d.** he's better, he's up *or* out of bed already

2 *Naut* **d. à la mer** *ou* **à la lame/au vent** head on to the sea/to the wind

ADJ INV 1 *Jur* **magistrature d.** = public prosecutors **2** *Naut* **vent d.** head wind

débouté [debute] **NM**, **déboutement** [debutmɑ̃] **NM** *Jur* nonsuit

débouter [debute] **VT** *Jur* to dismiss; **d. qn (de sa demande/de sa plainte)** to nonsuit sb

déboutonner [debutɔne] **VT** to unbutton; *Vieilli* **rire à ventre déboutonné** to split one's sides laughing

VPR se déboutonner 1 *(d'une personne)* to undo one's buttons; *(d'une robe, d'une chemise etc)* to unbutton; *Fig (se confier)* to get it off one's chest **2** *Can (se montrer généreux)* to splash out

débraillé [debraje] **ADJ** *(personne)* untidy, slovenly; *(tenue)* untidy, sloppy; **manières débraillées** bad manners

NM untidiness, slovenliness; **même au bureau, il est en d.** he's a sloppy dresser even at work

débrailler (se) [sədebraje] **VPR** *Fam* to loosen one's clothing; *Fig* **la conversation se débraille** the conversation is getting a bit out of hand

débranchement [debrɑ̃ʃmɑ̃] **NM** *Élec* disconnection, unplugging

débrancher [debrɑ̃ʃe] **VT** *Élec* to disconnect, to unplug; *Fam* **débranchez-le!** shut him up, will you!

débrayage [debrɛjaʒ] **NM 1** *Aut, Tech* declutching **2** *Fam (grève)* stoppage

débrayer [debrɛje] **(je débraye, je débraie) VT** *Tech* to throw out of gear

VI 1 *Aut* to disengage the clutch, to declutch **2** *Fam (se mettre en grève)* to down tools; *(à la fin de la journée)* to down tools, to knock off

débridé [debride] **ADJ** *(passion)* unbridled; *(imagination)* vivid

débridement [debridmɑ̃] **NM 1** *(d'un cheval)* unbridling **2** *Chir (d'une adhérence etc)* incision, slitting up; *(d'un furoncle)* lancing **3** *(déchaînement)* **le d. de son comportement/imagination** his unbridled behaviour/extremely vivid imagination

débrider [debride] **VT 1** *(cheval)* to unbridle **2** *Chir (adhérence etc)* to incise, to slit up; *(furoncle, plaie)* to lance **3** *Culin (volaille)* to untruss

VI *Fig* **travailler dix heures sans d.** to work ten hours at a stretch

débriefer [debrife] **VT** to debrief

débris [debri] **NMPL** *(d'un avion, une voiture)* remains, debris, wreckage; *(de verre, de bois)* splinters, fragments; **d. de métal** scrap (metal); **les d. d'une armée** the remnants of an army; **les d. de sa fortune** the remnants *or* remains of his fortune

NM *Fam* **ce n'est plus qu'un vieux d.** he's just an old wreck

débronzer [debrɔ̃ze] **VI** to lose one's tan

débrouillard, -arde [debrujar, -ard] **ADJ** resourceful, smart

N resourceful person; **c'est vraiment un d.** he's really resourceful

débrouillardise [debrujardiz] **NF** resourcefulness; **faire preuve de d.** to be resourceful

débrouiller [debruje] **VT 1** *(fil etc)* to unravel, to disentangle; **d. une affaire** to clear up *or* straighten out a situation; **d. une signature** to make out *or* decipher a signature **2** *Fam* **d. qn** to wise sb up; **il faut le d. en anglais/en cuisine** he'll need to be taught some basic English/cooking

VPR se débrouiller to cope, to manage; *Fam* **qu'il se débrouille!** he'll have to manage!, he'll have to sort it out for himself!; **débrouillez-vous!** you'll just have to manage!, you'll just have to sort it out for yourself!; **il a un peu de mal à se d. avec son ordinateur** he's having some trouble coping with his computer; **je me débrouille en russe** I can get by in Russian; **elle s'est débrouillée pour rencontrer le directeur** she worked it so that she got to meet the director

débroussailler [debrusaje] **VT** to clear of undergrowth; *Fig* **d. une question** to clarify a matter

débudgétisation [debydʒetizasjɔ̃] **NF** = transfer from one budget to another

débudgétiser [debydʒetize] **VT** = to transfer from one budget to another; **il faut d. l'État des dépenses de la sécurité sociale** the burden of social security should no longer be borne by the State

débusquer [debyske] **VT** to flush out (of cover)

début [deby] **NM 1** *(commencement)* beginning, start; **au d.** at the start *or* beginning *or* outset; **au d. des hostilités** at the outbreak of hostilities; **au tout d., tout au d.** at the very start *or* beginning; **dès le d.** right at the start, from the outset (**de** of); **je l'ai su dès le d.** I knew from the outset *or* (right) from the beginning; **je le savais depuis le d.** I knew all along *or* from the start; **du d. à la fin** from start to finish; **appointements de**

d. starting salary; **être en d. de carrière** to be at the start of one's career; *Hum* **il faut** *ou* **il y a un d. à tout** there's a first time for everything **2** *(d'un acteur etc)* **débuts** first appearance, début; **faire ses débuts** to make one's first appearance *or* one's début, *Am* to début; **faire ses débuts dans le monde** *(d'une jeune fille)* to come out; **société/entreprise à ses débuts** association/enterprise in its infancy **3** *Ordinat* home; **aller au d.** *(commande)* go top

débutant, -ante [debytɑ̃, -ɑ̃t] **ADJ** novice; **cours pour les skieurs débutants** skiing classes for beginners; **si vous êtes skieur d.** if you're learning (how) to ski; **conducteur d.** newly qualified driver

N 1 *(dans une matière, une discipline etc)* beginner; **cours pour grands débutants** classes for complete beginners **2** *Théâtre* actor/actress making his/her début

NF débutante *(dans la haute société)* debutante, *Fam* deb

débuter [debyte] **VI 1** *(commencer)* to begin, to start, to commence; **vous travaillerez ici pour d.** you'll work here to begin with *or* start with; **le film débute par une séquence de meurtre** the film opens with a murder; **le concert a bien/mal débuté** the concert started well/badly, the concert got off to a good/bad start **2** *Cin, Théâtre etc (de personne)* to make one's first appearance *or* one's début, *Am* to début; **mal/bien d. dans la vie** to get off to a bad/good start in life; **je débute dans le métier** I'm new to the business; **d. dans le monde** *(d'une jeune fille)* to come out; **faire d. une jeune fille dans le monde** to bring a girl out; **d. comme professeur** to start off as a teacher

déc [dɛk] **VI** *Fam* **sans d.!** *(je t'assure)* no kidding!, *Br* straight up!; **sans d.?** *(est-ce vrai?)* no kidding?, yeah?

déca [deka] **NM** *Fam (café)* decaf

deçà [dəsa] **PRÉP en d. de qch** (on) this side of sth; **rester (très) en d. de la vérité** to be (very) short of the truth

ADV *Arch* on this side; **d. delà** here and there, on all sides

décachetage [dekaʃtaʒ] **NM** *(d'une lettre)* unsealing, opening

décacheter [dekaʃte] **VT** *(conj like* **cacheter***)* *(lettre)* to unseal, to open

décade [dekad] **NF** *(période de dix jours)* period of ten days; *(période de dix ans)* decade

Il faut noter que le nom anglais **decade** est un faux ami. Il signifie uniquement **décennie**.

décadenasser [dekadnase] **VT** to unlock, to take the padlock off

décadence [dekadɑ̃s] **NF** decadence; **la d. d'une civilisation** *(processus)* the decline of a civilization; *(résultat)* the decadence of a civilization; **tomber en d.** to fall into decay; *(d'une personne)* to start to decline

décadent, -ente [dekadɑ̃, -ɑ̃t] **ADJ** decadent

N *Littér, Beaux-Arts* Decadent

décadrage [dekadraʒ] **NM** *Cin* off-centring

décadré [dekadre] **ADJ** *Cin* off-centre

décaèdre [dekaɛdr] *Math* **ADJ** decahedral

NM decahedron

décaféiné [dekafeine] **NM** decaffeinated (coffee); **j'achète toujours du d.** I always buy decaffeinated

décaféiner [dekafeine] **VT** to decaffeinate; **un café décaféiné** a (cup of) decaffeinated coffee

décagonal, -ale, -aux, -ales [dekagɔnal, -o] **ADJ** *Math* decagonal

décagone [dekagon] **NM** *Math* decagon

décaissable [dekɛsabl] ADJ (charge) payable

décaissement [dekɛsmã] NM Com (d'une somme) cash withdrawal or disbursement; **faire un d.** to make an outlay; Compta **décaissements** outgoings

décaisser [dekese] VT **1** (marchandises etc) to unpack **2** (plante, arbuste) to plant out **3** Com (somme) to pay (out); (TVA) to pay

décalage [dekalaʒ] NM **1** (écart) gap; **le d. entre la réalité et les espoirs** the gap between reality and hopes; **d. d'opinions** difference of opinion **2** (d'un instrument) shifting the zero; (quantité) (amount of) shift; **d. vers le haut** upward movement; **d. à droite/gauche** movement to the right/left **3** (retard) time lag; **un d. est prévu pour la date de la réunion** the meeting has been postponed
▸▸ **d. horaire** time difference; **souffrir du d. horaire** to have jet lag

décalaminage [dekalaminaʒ] NM (de moteur) decarbonizing, Fam decoking, decoke

décalaminer [dekalamine] VT (moteur) to decarbonize, Fam to decoke

décalcifiant [dekalsifjã] ADJ Méd decalcifying

décalcification [dekalsifikasjɔ̃] NF Méd decalcification

décalcifier [dekalsifje] Méd VT to decalcify
VPR **se décalcifier** to become decalcified

décalcomanie [dekalkɔmani] NF Cér etc (procédé) decal(comania); (résultat) decal(-comania), transfer; **faire de la d.** to decal

décalé [dekale] ADJ Fam (personne) out of it, out of touch with reality; (discours, approche) unrealistic

décaler [dekale] VT **1** (meuble) to move, to shift; (instrument) to shift the zero of; **d. l'heure** to alter the time, to change the time or the clock; **d. ses rendez-vous d'une heure** (les avancer) to bring one's meetings forward by an hour; (les reculer) to put one's meetings back by an hour **2** Tech (rivets) to stagger
VPR **se décaler** to move, to shift; **vous pourriez vous d. d'un rang/vers la gauche** you could move up a row/move to the left

décalitre [dekalitr] NM decalitre, Am decaliter

décalogue [dekalɔg] NM Rel Decalogue

décalotter [dekalɔte] VT **1** Fam **d. une bouteille** to open or crack a bottle **2** Méd to pull back the foreskin of

décalquage [dekalkaʒ] NM (de dessin) tracing; (par la chaleur etc) transferring

décalque [dekalk] NM **1** (de dessin) tracing; (par la chaleur etc) transferring; **papier (à) d.** tracing paper **2** (dessin) tracing; (image) transfer; (imitation) copy

décalquer [dekalke] VT (dessin) to trace; (par la chaleur) (plan, image en couleur) to transfer

décamètre [dekamɛtr] NM decametre, Am decameter

décamper [dekãpe] VI Fam to clear out or off; **décampez d'ici!** clear out or off!, get lost!; **tu vas d. et plus vite que ça!** clear off or clear out or get out, on the double!

décan [dekã] NM Astrol decan

décanat [dekana] NM deanship

décanewton [dekanjutɔn] NM decanewton

décaniller [dekanije] VI Fam = **décamper**

décantation [dekãtasjɔ̃] NF decantation, decanting

décanter [dekãte] VT (vin) to decant; Fig **d. ses projets** to mull over one's plans
VPR **se décanter** (de vin) to settle; Fig (de projets) to become clearer; (d'une situation) to settle down, to become clearer; **laisser aux choses le temps de se d.** to give things time to settle down

décapage [dekapaʒ] NM (d'un meuble etc) stripping; (au papier de verre) sanding (down)

décapant [dekapã] ADJ **1 produit d.** stripper **2** Fig (humour) caustic, vitriolic
NM (pour vernis, peinture) remover, stripper

décaper [dekape] VT (peinture, vernis) to strip, to remove; Tech (métal etc) to scour, to clean; Tech (objets métalliques) to pickle, to dip; **d. un meuble au papier de verre** to sand down a piece of furniture; **d. une surface à peindre** to strip a surface for painting; **d. à la sableuse** to sand-blast
VI Fig Fam **des plaisanteries qui décapent** caustic or vitriolic jokes

décapeuse [dekapøz] NF Tech scraper

décapitation [dekapitasjɔ̃] NF decapitation, beheading

décapiter [dekapite] VT (personne) to decapitate, to behead; (arbre) to pollard; Fig **d. un complot/une association** to root out the ringleaders of a plot/the leaders of a society

décapode [dekapɔd] NM decapod

décapotable [dekapɔtabl] Aut ADJ convertible, open-top; (coupé) drop-head
NF convertible, open-top

décapotage [dekapɔtaʒ] NM lowering the hood

décapoté [dekapɔte] ADJ open

décapoter [dekapɔte] VT Aut to lower the hood of

décapsulage [dekapsylaʒ] NM (de bouteille) opening

décapsuler [dekapsyle] VT (bouteille) to open, to take the top off

décapsuleur [dekapsylœr] NM bottle opener

décapuchonner [dekapyʃɔne] VT to take the top off

décarcasser (se) [sədekarkase] VPR Fam to bust a gut

décarreler [dekarle] VT (surface, pièce) to remove the tiles from

décarrer [dekare] VI Fam to get going, to hit the road

décartellisation [dekartɛlizasjɔ̃] NF Écon, Hist break-up of a cartel

décasyllabe [dekasilab] ADJ decasyllabic
NM decasyllabic verse

décasyllabique [dekasilabik] ADJ decasyllabic

décathlon [dekatlɔ̃] NM Sport decathlon

décathlonien, -ienne [dekatlɔnjɛ̃, -jɛn] N Sport decathlete

décati [dekati] ADJ (visage) wrinkled, that has lost its freshness; (immeuble) shabby, rundown; **vieillard d.** decrepit old man

décatir [dekatir] VT Tex (étoffe) to take the gloss or finish off
VPR **se décatir** to lose one's freshness or one's beauty, to age

décauser [dekoze] VT Belg to malign

décavé [dekave] ADJ **1** Fam (personne riche) ruined; (aux cartes) cleaned out **2** (visage) drawn, pinched

décédé, -ée [desede] ADJ, N surtout Admin deceased

décéder [desede] VI (conj like **céder**, aux **être**) surtout Admin to die

décelable [deslabl] ADJ detectable

déceler [desle] VT (je décèle; je décèlerai) **1** (découvrir) to detect; **on a décélé des traces de pneus dans le jardin** tyre marks were found in the garden; **on décèle l'importance qu'a eue sa mère dans tous ses écrits** the importance of his mother can be detected in all his writings **2** (indiquer) to point to, to indicate; **sa voix décelait la peur** there was (a note of) fear in his voice

décélération [deselerasjɔ̃] NF deceleration, slowing down

décélérer [deselere] VI to decelerate, to slow down

décembre [desãbr] NM December; **en d., au mois de d.** in (the month of) December; **le 25 d.** the 25th of December, December the 25th
SEE GRAMMAR A81–2; B60–2

décemment [desamã] ADV **1** (convenablement) properly, Fml with decorum **2** (correctement) **elle parle anglais d.** her English is reasonable or quite good, she speaks quite decent English **3** (raisonnablement) reasonably; **d., je ne pouvais pas refuser** I couldn't reasonably refuse

décence [desãs] NF **1** (bienséance) (de comportement) propriety, decorum; (d'habillement) decency; **se tenir avec d.** to behave properly or Fml with decorum; **choquer la d.** to offend against decency; **des mots/un comportement qui choque(nt) la d.** offensive words/behaviour **2** (tact) decency; **il aurait dû avoir la d. de s'excuser** he ought to have had the decency to apologize **3** (réserve) decency; **parler avec d.** to speak in restrained terms

décennal, -ale, -aux, -ales [desenal, -o] ADJ decennial

décennie [deseni] NF decade

décent [desã] ADJ **1** decent; (vêtements etc) modest; (comportement, attitude etc) proper; **peu d.** indecent, unseemly **2** (correct) reasonable; **lire d'une manière décente** to read reasonably well

décentrage [desãtraʒ] NM moving off centre or Am center

décentralisateur, -trice [desãtralizatœr, -tris] ADJ decentralizing
N Pol advocate of decentralization, decentralizer

décentralisation [desãtralizasjɔ̃] NF decentralization; **la d. des grandes écoles est devenue nécessaire** it has become necessary to move the grandes écoles out of Paris

décentraliser [desãtralize] VT (administration) to decentralize; (entreprise) to move away from the capital

décentration [desãtrasjɔ̃] NF Opt, Phot decentring, throwing off centre or Am center

décentré [desãtre] ADJ off centre or Am off center

décentrement [desãtrəmã] NM = **décentration**

décentrer [desãtre] VT (table, tableau) to move off centre or Am center; Opt, Tech etc to put out of or off centre, to decentre or Am decenter
VPR **se décentrer** to come or move off centre or Am center

déception [desɛpsjɔ̃] NF disappointment, Fam let-down; **éprouver une d.** to be disappointed; **d. sentimentale** unhappy love affair, disappointment in love

> Il faut noter que le nom anglais **deception** est un faux ami. Il signifie **tromperie**.

décérébrer [deserebre] VT to lobotomize

décernement [desɛrnəmã] NM (d'un prix etc) award

décerner [desɛrne] VT **1** (prix etc) to award; **d. un honneur à qn** to confer an honour on sb **2** Jur **d. un mandat d'arrêt contre qn** to issue a warrant for the arrest of sb

décès [desɛ] NM surtout Admin decease, (natural) death, demise; **acte de d.** death certificate; **fermé pour cause de d.** closed on account of bereavement

décevant [des(ə)vɑ̃] ADJ **1** *(résultat, livre, attitude etc)* disappointing **2** Arch *(mensonger)* *(apparence etc)* deceptive

décevoir [des(ə)vwar] VT *(conj like* **recevoir***)* **1** to disappoint; **il m'a beaucoup déçu** I was very disappointed in him; **ce voyage m'a profondément déçu** I was very disappointed with the trip; **d. l'attente de qn** to disappoint sb, not to live up to sb's expectations; *Suisse* **d. qn en bien** *(le surprendre agréablement)* to give sb a pleasant surprise **2** Arch *(tromper)* to deceive, to delude

> Il faut noter que le verbe anglais **to deceive** est un faux ami. Il signifie **tromper**, **abuser**.

déchaîné [deʃene] ADJ *(passion)* unrestrained, unbridled; *(spéculation)* wild; **craindre les éléments déchaînés** to fear the fury of the elements; **elle a dû faire face à une presse déchaînée** she had to face a press in full cry; **il est complètement d. à l'idée de la fête** he's hyper *or* pretty worked up at the thought of the party; **être d. contre qn** to be furious with sb

déchaînement [deʃɛnmɑ̃] NM *(des éléments)* fury; *(des passions)* outburst; **d. de rage** outburst of fury, fit of rage; **pourquoi a-t-il fait preuve d'un tel d. contre moi?** why did he fly into a rage with me like that?; **le d. de la tempête** the breaking of the storm; **un d. de l'opinion** a great wave of public opinion

déchaîner [deʃene] VT *(d'une personne)* *(passions, colère etc)* to arouse, to provoke; **d. l'hilarité** to provoke laughter
VPR **se déchaîner** to break out; **la tempête s'est déchaînée** the storm broke; **se d. contre qn** to fly into a rage with sb

déchanter [deʃɑ̃te] VI *Fam* to become disillusioned

décharge [deʃarʒ] NF **1** *(tirs)* discharge, volley; **on lui a envoyé une d. de plombs pour le faire fuir** they fired a few rounds at him to scare him off; **de nombreuses décharges ont été entendues cette nuit** a lot of firing was heard last night; **d. (électrique)** electric shock; **d. d'adrénaline** rush of adrenalin **2** *Jur (d'un accusé)* release, acquittal; *(d'une obligation)* discharge; **témoin à d.** witness for the defence; **dire qch à la d. de qn** to say sth in sb's defence **3** *Fin* (tax) rebate; **porter une somme en d.** to mark a sum as paid; **d. de 50 pour cent** composition of 50p in the pound **4** *Tech (sortie etc)* discharge, outlet; **tuyau de d.** waste pipe **5** *Typ* set-off sheet, offset sheet **6** *(d'ordures)* dumping, tipping; **d. (publique)** rubbish dump, tip; **d. interdite** no dumping, tipping prohibited; **décharges sauvages** fly tipping, *Am* illegal dumping

déchargement [deʃarʒəmɑ̃] NM *(de bateau, cargaison etc)* unloading; *(de marchandises)* offloading, unloading

décharger [deʃarʒe] *(je* **déchargeai(s)***;* **nous déchargeons)** VT **1** *(vider) (camion, bateau, cargaison etc)* to unload; *(marchandises)* to offload, to unload; *(d'un camion) (gravier)* to tip, to dump; *(réservoir etc)* to discharge, to empty; *(arme à feu)* to fire, to discharge; *(accumulateur)* to discharge; **d. son fusil sur** *ou* **contre qn** to fire one's gun at sb; *Fig* **d. sa conscience** to ease one's conscience *(de* of); **d. sa conscience auprès de qn** to unburden oneself to sb; **d. son cœur** to unburden one's heart; **d. sa colère sur qn** to vent one's anger on sb

2 *(soulager) (cheval)* to relieve, to ease of part of its load; *(bateau)* to lighten; *(poutre)* to take the strain off; **d. qn d'une tâche/ d'une responsabilité** to relieve sb of a task/

a responsibility; *Jur* **d. qn d'une accusation** to acquit sb of a charge; **d. qn d'une dette** to discharge sb from a debt; **failli déchargé/non déchargé** discharged/undischarged bankrupt
VI **1** *Typ* **encre qui décharge** ink that rubs off **2** *Vulg (éjaculer)* to shoot one's load
VPR **se décharger 1** *(d'une personne)* **se d. de qn/qch** to get rid of sb/sth; **se d. d'un fardeau** to put down *or* lay down a load; **se d. de qch sur qn** to shift the responsibility for sth onto sb; **se d. d'une tâche sur qn** to unload a task onto sb **2** *(se vider) (d'une arme)* to go off; *(d'une pile)* to run down, to discharge; *(d'une colère)* to vent itself *(sur* on); **le fleuve se décharge dans un lac** the river flows into a lake

décharné [deʃarne] ADJ *(corps, membres etc)* emaciated; *(visage)* emaciated, gaunt; *(os)* stripped of flesh; *Fig (arbre)* bare; *(style)* bald

décharner [deʃarne] VT *(personne)* to emaciate; *(os)* to strip the flesh off

déchaussé [deʃose] ADJ **1** *(sans chaussures)* barefoot(ed) **2** **avoir les dents déchaussées** to have receding gums; **bâtisse aux murs déchaussés** building with unsound foundations

déchaussement [deʃosmɑ̃] NM *(de murs)* laying bare of foundations; **d. de dents** receding gums

déchausser [deʃose] VT **1** *(enlever ses chaussures à)* **d. qn** to take off sb's shoes; **d. ses skis** to take off one's skis **2** *(arbre)* to expose *or* (lay) bare the roots of; *(dent, fondations)* to expose
VPR **se déchausser 1** *(enlever ses chaussures)* to take off one's shoes **2** **ses dents se déchaussent** he has receding gums, his gums are receding

dèche [deʃ] NF *Fam* **être dans la d.** to be stony broke; **c'est la d.** I'm/we're/*etc* stony broke

déchéance [deʃeɑ̃s] NF **1** *(dégradation, chute) (physique)* deterioration, decline; *(morale)* downfall, ruin; **sa d. a été causée par l'alcool** drink was his downfall; **c'est la mort de son fils qui est à l'origine de sa d.** it was the death of his son which started him on the downward path

2 *Jur, Fin (de droits etc)* forfeiture; **action en d. de brevet** action for forfeiture of patent; **d. parentale** loss of parental authority; **d. d'une police** expiry of a policy

3 *Pol (d'un monarque)* deposition, deposing; *(d'un président)* removal *(after impeachment)*

4 *Compta* **tomber en d.** to lapse

déchet [deʃɛ] NM **1** **déchets** waste; **des déchets de tissu** scraps of fabric; **déchets radioactifs/industriels** radioactive/industrial waste; **déchets domestiques** household waste *or* rubbish; **déchets de métal** scrap (metal); **déchets de viande** scraps of meat **2** *Com (de poids, valeur)* loss, decrease; **il y a du d.** there is some wastage; **d. de route** loss in transit **3** *Péj (personne)* down-and-out; **un d. de la société** a social outcast

déchetterie [deʃɛtri] NF dump, *Br* rubbish dump, tip

déchiffonner [deʃifɔne] VT to smooth out the creases in

déchiffrable [deʃifrabl] ADJ *(inscription)* decipherable; *(écriture)* decipherable, legible; **code facilement d.** code that is easy to crack *or* break

déchiffrage [deʃifraʒ] NM *Mus* sight-reading

déchiffrement [deʃifrəmɑ̃] NM deciphering; *Ordinat* decryption; *Ordinat* **d. de données** data decryption

déchiffrer [deʃifre] VT **1** *(inscription, écriture etc)* to decipher, to make out; *(message)*

to decode; *(signaux)* to read, to interpret; *Ordinat* to decrypt; **d. les sentiments d'une personne** to fathom *or* make out sb's feelings; **d. un mystère** to unravel a mystery **2** *(musique)* to read, to play at sight, to sight-read; **d. un morceau** to sight-read a piece; **je suis juste en train de d. ce morceau** I'm just learning this piece
VI *Mus* to sight-read

déchiffreur, -euse [deʃifrœr, -øz] N *(d'inscription)* decipherer; *(de message)* decoder; *(de message secret)* code-breaker

déchiqueté [deʃikte] ADJ **1** *(bord)* jagged; *(littoral)* jagged, ragged; **papier à bords déchiquetés** deckle-edge paper **2** *(objet)* cut to bits *or* shreds; **une couverture déchiquetée** a tattered blanket

déchiqueter [deʃikte] VT *(je* **déchiquette;** **je déchiquetterai)** *(papier)* to rip to shreds; *(de machine)* to shred; *(chair)* to cut *or* tear to shreds; *(corps, poulet)* to hack to pieces

déchiqueteuse [deʃiktøz] NF shredder

déchiqueture [deʃiktyr] NF slash, long tear

déchirant [deʃirɑ̃] ADJ *(spectacle)* heartrending, harrowing; *(douleur)* agonizing; **des adieux déchirants** heartrending farewells

déchiré [deʃire] ADJ **1** *(vêtement, couverture, Méd muscle, Fig nation etc)* torn; **être d. entre deux personnes** to be torn between two people **2** *Fam (ivre)* wasted, trashed, *Am* fried; *(drogué)* stoned

déchirement [deʃirmɑ̃] NM *(de tissu, vêtement etc)* tearing, *Fml* rending; *Méd (de muscle)* tearing; *Fig (peine)* heartbreak; **cette famille/ce parti connaît des déchirements terribles** the family/party is tearing itself apart

déchirer [deʃire] VT **1** *(tissu, vêtement etc)* to tear, *Fml* to rend; *(papier)* to tear up; *(enveloppe)* to tear open; **d. qch en morceaux** to tear sth to pieces *or* bits *or* shreds **2** *Fig (famille, pays)* to tear apart; **d. le cœur à qn** to break sb's heart; **des cris qui déchiraient le cœur** heartrending cries; **un cri aigu déchira le silence** a shrill scream pierced the silence; **des sons qui déchirent le tympan** ear-splitting sounds; **une toux qui déchire la poitrine** a hacking cough; **être déchiré de douleur/ remords** to be racked with pain/remorse
VPR **se déchirer 1** *(d'un tissu)* to tear; **il s'est déchiré un muscle** he's torn a muscle **2** *Fig* **un couple qui se déchire** a couple who are tearing each other apart; **mon cœur s'est déchiré** I was heartbroken

déchirure [deʃiryr] NF *(dans un tissu)* tear, rip, *Fml* rent; *(blessure)* laceration; *Fig (peine, chagrin)* heartbreak; **le fait de quitter ses parents a été pour lui une véritable d.** it was heartbreaking *or* heartrending leaving his parents; **une d. musculaire** a torn muscle

déchoir [deʃwar] VI *(pp* **déchu;** *pr ind* **je déchois, n. déchoyons, ils déchoient;** *p hist* **je déchus;** *fu* **je déchoirai;** *aux* **être** *or* **avoir)** **ce quartier a déchu** the area has gone down; **sa popularité déchoit** his popularity is declining; **la maison déchoit de son prestige** the firm is losing its prestige; **par ce mariage/à cause de cet emploi, il déchoit de son rang** he is marrying/the job is beneath him; **ce serait d. (que de s'abaisser à ces tâches vulgaires)** it would be demeaning (to stoop to such common tasks)

déchristianisation [dekristjanizasjɔ̃] NF dechristianization

déchristianiser [dekristjanize] VT to dechristianize, to turn from Christianity
VPR **se déchristianiser** to turn (away) from Christianity

déchu [deʃy] ADJ **ange d.** fallen angel; **roi d.**

to order; *(loi)* to enact; **il a décrété qu'il n'irait plus jamais sur la Côte d'Azur** he has vowed that he will never go to the French Riviera again; **quand elle décrète quelque chose** when she vows to do something; *Jur* **d. un moratoire** to declare a moratorium

décret-loi, *pl* **décrets-lois** NM *Br* ≃ Order in Council, *Am* ≃ executive order

décrier [dekrije] VT to disparage, to run down; **il a été beaucoup décrié** a lot of people have disparaged him *or* run him down; **ce genre de pratique est assez décrié** a lot of people deplore this kind of thing

décrire [dekrir] VT *(conj like* **écrire)** **1** *(représenter)* to describe, to depict **2** *Math (courbe, cercle)* to describe, to draw; **la route décrit une courbe** the road bends; **les oiseaux décrivaient de grands cercles** the birds were circling

décrispation [dekrispasjɔ̃] NF *Pol* détente; **climat de d.** atmosphere of détente

décrisper [dekrispe] VT *(personne)* to relax, to make less tense; **d. l'atmosphère** to lighten the atmosphere, to make the atmosphere less tense; **d. la situation** to ease the situation, to make the situation less tense; **la plaisanterie l'a décrispé** the joke made him relax *or* calmed him down
  VPR **se décrisper** to relax, *Fam* to lighten up

décrochage [dekrɔʃaʒ] NM *(de wagon)* uncoupling, disconnection; *(d'un tableau)* removal, taking down; *Radio, TV* **diffuser en d.** to broadcast on own programmes; *Radio, TV* **le d. a lieu à 19 h** regional programming begins at 7 pm

décrochement [dekrɔʃmɑ̃] NM *Géol* thrust

décrocher [dekrɔʃe] VT **1** *(détacher) (manteau d'une patère, rideaux, tableau etc)* to take down; *(wagons etc)* to uncouple, to disconnect; *(fermoir)* to undo; *Tél (combiné)* to pick *or* lift up; **d. le téléphone** *(pour ne pas être dérangé)* to take the phone off the hook; *(pour répondre)* to pick up the phone; **décrochez** lift the receiver; **le téléphone est décroché** the phone's off the hook
  2 *(recevoir) (poste, prix, contrat etc)* to land; **d. la timbale** to hit the jackpot; **d. la croix** to receive a military decoration
  VI **1** *Tél* to pick up the phone; *(pour ne pas être dérangé)* to take the phone off the hook
  2 *Mil* to beat a retreat, to withdraw
  3 *Fig Fam (ne plus se concentrer)* to switch off; **au bout de trois heures de réunion, je décroche** I just switch off after three hours in a meeting; **si cet élève décroche, il est perdu** if this pupil fails to keep up, he won't have a chance; **il commence souvent de nouvelles activités, mais il décroche très vite** he often starts new activities, but loses interest very quickly
  4 *Fam (arrêter de se droguer)* to kick the habit; **ça fait trois mois qu'il a décroché** he's been clean for three months
  5 *Can Fam (abandonner l'école)* to drop out (of school)
  VPR **se décrocher** to come unhooked; **la médaille s'est décrochée** the medal has come unpinned; **se d. la mâchoire** to dislocate one's jaw; *Fam* **bâiller à se d. la mâchoire** to yawn one's head off

décrocheur, -euse [dekrɔʃœr, -øz] N *Can* dropout

décroisement [dekrwazmɑ̃] NM uncrossing

décroiser [dekrwaze] VT *(ses jambes etc)* to uncross

décroissance [dekrwasɑ̃s] NF *(de population)* decrease, decline

décroissant [dekrwasɑ̃] ADJ decreasing; **par ordre d.** in descending order

décroissement [dekrwasmɑ̃] NM *(de la lune)* waning; *(des jours)* shortening

décroît [dekrwa] NM **la lune est sur** *ou* **dans son d.** the moon is in its last quarter

décroître [dekrwatr] VI *(prp* **décroissant;** *pp* **décru;** *pr ind* **il décroît, ils décroissent;** *p hist* **il décrut;** *fu* **il décroîtra)** *(de force, population, nombre etc)* to decrease, to decline, to diminish; **les jours commencent à d.** the days are beginning to draw in *or* get shorter; **la lune décroît** the moon is on the wane; **l'intensité de son amour/de la lumière décroît** her love/the light is becoming less intense; **les eaux décroissent** the water level is dropping; **aller (en) décroissant** to be decreasing, to grow gradually less

décrottage [dekrɔtaʒ] NM *(de bottes etc)* cleaning

décrotter [dekrɔte] VT *(bottes etc)* to clean, to remove the mud from; *(semelles)* to scrape; *Fig Fam* **d. qn** to knock the rough edges off sb, to knock sb into shape; **il a vraiment fallu le d.** he had to have the rough edges knocked off him, he had to be knocked into shape

décrottoir [dekrɔtwar] NM shoe scraper; **tapis d.** (wire) doormat

décrue [dekry] NF **1** *(de rivière etc)* fall, drop in level; **la d. des eaux** the drop in the water level **2** *(en nombre etc)* decrease, decline, fall

décryptage [dekriptaʒ] NM deciphering; *(de signaux)* decoding; *Ordinat* decrypting; *Tél, TV* descrambling

décrypter [dekripte] VT to decipher; *(signaux)* to decode; *Ordinat* to decrypt; *Tél, TV* to descramble

DECS [deɔsees] NM *(abrév* **diplôme d'études comptables supérieures)** = postgraduate qualification in accounting

déçu [desy] ADJ disappointed; *Fig Iron* **elle ne va pas être déçue (du voyage)** she's got another think coming; *Fig Iron* **je ne suis pas d. du voyage!** a fine state of affairs!

décuiter [dekɥite] VI *Fam* to sober up

déculottée [dekylɔte] NF *Fam* hammering

déculotter [dekylɔte] VT **d. qn** *(enlever son slip)* to take sb's panties/underpants off; *(enlever son pantalon)* to take sb's trousers off, *Fam Vieilli* to debag sb
  VPR **se déculotter** *(enlever son slip)* to take one's panties/underpants off; *(enlever son pantalon)* to let down *or* to drop one's trousers; *Fig Fam* to grovel **(devant, pour** to)

déculpabilisation [dekylpabilizasjɔ̃] NF **la d. de l'avortement** removing the guilt surrounding abortion; **la d. des malades atteints du sida** removing the guilt feelings of AIDS victims

déculpabiliser [dekylpabilize] VT **d. qn** to stop sb feeling guilty **(de qch** about sth); **d. la contraception** to take the guilt out of (using) contraception, to remove the guilt surrounding contraception
  VPR **se déculpabiliser** to get rid of one's guilt feelings, to stop feeling guilty

déculturation [dekyltyrasjɔ̃] NF loss of culture

décuple [dekypl] ADJ tenfold; **le prix de leur maison est d. de la nôtre** their house cost ten times as much as ours
  NM tenfold increase

décuplement [dekyplmɑ̃] NM multiplication by ten; *Fig* quantum leap

décupler [dekyple] VT to increase *or* multiply tenfold; *Fig* **la peur décuplait mon allure** fear quickened my pace (until I was almost running); **la douleur décupla ses forces** the pain gave him a surge of strength; **sa joie a été décuplée quand il a su que tu venais aussi** he was ecstatic when he found out you were coming too
  VI to increase tenfold

dédaignable [dedɛɲabl] ADJ worthy of disdain; **cette somme n'est pas d.** this is a not inconsiderable sum; **cette offre n'est pas d.** it is not an offer to be sniffed at

dédaigner [dedɛɲe] VT *(offre, proposition etc)* to turn up one's nose at, to sniff at, *Fml* to disdain, to scorn; *(injure, conseil)* to disregard; **d. qn** to treat sb with disdain *or* contempt, *Fml* to scorn sb; *Litt* **elle dédaigna de répondre** she disdained to reply; **cette proposition n'est pas à d.** it is not a proposal to be sniffed at; **il ne dédaigne pas un cigare de temps en temps** he is not averse to the occasional cigar, *Fam* he doesn't say no to the odd cigar

dédaigneusement [dedɛɲøzmɑ̃] ADV disdainfully, contemptuously, scornfully

dédaigneux, -euse [dedɛɲø, -øz] ADJ disdainful, contemptuous, scornful **(de** of)

dédain [dedɛ̃] NM disdain, contempt, scorn **(de, pour** for); **avec d.** disdainfully, contemptuously, scornfully, with disdain *or* contempt; **témoigner du d. à qn** to show contempt for sb; **avoir du d. pour qch** to despise sth; **elle n'a que du d. pour lui** she has nothing but contempt for him; **considérer qn avec d.** to look down on sb

Dédale [dedal] NM *Myth* Daedalus

dédale [dedal] NM *(de rues)* labyrinth, maze; **perdu dans le d. de ses réflexions** lost in the maze of one's thoughts

DEDANS [dədɑ̃] ADV inside; **la lettre est d.** the letter is inside; **une voiture nous est rentrée d., nous nous sommes fait rentrer d.** a car smashed into us; *Fam* **je vais lui rentrer d.** I'll smash his face in; *Fig Fam* **mettre** *ou* **ficher qn d.** *(le tromper)* to take sb for a ride; *Fig Fam* **donner d.** to fall into the trap; **marcher les pieds en d.** to be pigeon-toed; **en d.** (on the) inside, within; **il n'était pas si calme en d.** inwardly, he was not so calm; **en d. de** within; **de d.** from within; **il y a vraiment quelqu'un qui vit là-d.?** is somebody actually living there?; *Fam* **c'est un bon film, mais il y a trop de violence à.** it's a good film, but there's too much violence in it
  NM *(d'une maison, d'une boîte)* inside, interior; *(d'une personne)* innermost heart; **agir du d.** to act on the *or* from inside; **au-d. et au-dehors** inside and out; **au-d.** (on the) inside, within; **au-d. de** inside, within; **elle le savait au-d. d'elle** inwardly, she knew it

dédicace [dedikas] NF **1** *(de livre etc)* dedication **2** *Rel (d'un édifice etc)* dedication, consecration

dédicacer [dedikase] VT *(je* **dédicaçai(s); n. dédicaçons)** *(livre)* to write a dedication in; **d. son dernier livre** to sign copies of one's latest book; **livre dédicacé par l'auteur** signed copy of a book

dédicatoire [dedikatwar] ADJ dedicatory

dédié [dedje] ADJ *Ordinat* dedicated

dédier [dedje] VT **1** *(livre, film etc)* to dedicate **2** *Rel (édifice etc)* to dedicate, to consecrate

dédire (se) [sədedir] VPR *(conj like* **dire** *except pr ind* **v. v. dédisez)** **se d. de** *(déclaration)* to retract, to withdraw; *(accusation)* to withdraw; **se d. d'une promesse** to go back on one's word

dédit [dedi] NM *(de déclaration)* retraction, withdrawal; *(d'accusation)* withdrawal; *(de promesse)* breaking; *(pour rupture de contrat etc)* forfeit, penalty; **en cas de d., vous devrez payer 10% de la somme initiale** in the event of cancellation, you will be required to pay 10% of the initial sum

dédommagement [dedɔmaʒmɑ̃] NM compensation; **50 000 euros de d.** 50,000 euros (in) compensation; **recevoir une**

somme en d. de qch to receive a sum as or in compensation for sth; **en d. de la peine que je vous ai causée** to make up for the pain I caused you; **c'est un d. à** ou **pour votre patience** it's in recognition of your patience; **d. de non accès à bord** denied boarding compensation

dédommager [dedɔmaʒe] (**je dédommageai(s); n. dédommageons**) **VT** to compensate, *Fml* to indemnify; **d. qn de qch** to compensate sb for sth; **comment pourrai-je te d.?** how can I ever repay you?; **d. qn d'une perte** to compensate sb for a loss, to make good sb's loss; **pour me d., il m'a invité au restaurant** he took me out to dinner to make up for it; **tiens, dédommage-toi avec ce billet** here, take it out of this

dédoré [dedɔre] **ADJ** tarnished, with the gilt rubbed off

dédorer [dedɔre] **VT** to remove the gilt from

dédouanage [dedwanaʒ] **NM** clearance (through customs)

dédouanement [dedwanmɑ̃] **NM** clearance through customs; *Fig* **le d. de la conscience** salving one's conscience

dédouaner [dedwane] **VT** to clear (through customs), to take out of bond; **d. ses bagages** to clear one's luggage through customs; *Fig* **d. qn** to clear sb
VPR se dédouaner *Fig* to clear one's name

dédoublage [dedublaʒ] **NM 1** (*d'alcool*) diluting **2** (*de manteau etc*) removing the lining

dédoublement [dedubləmɑ̃] **NM 1** (*d'une étoffe pliée etc*) opening out **2** *Psy* dividing or splitting into two; **d. de la personnalité** split personality **3** *Rail* **d. d'un train** running an extra train

dédoubler [deduble] **VT 1** (*étoffe pliée etc*) to open out; **d. les rangs** to form single file **2** (*partager*) to divide or split into two **3** *Rail* **d. un train** to run an extra train **4** (*vêtement*) to remove the lining of
VPR se dédoubler 1 (*d'une couverture*) to unfold **2** (*se diviser*) to divide, to split; (*cheveux, ongle*) to split; *Psy* to have a split personality; *Fam* **je ne peux pas me d.** I can't be in two places at once

dédramatisation [dedramatizasjɔ̃] **NF gouvernement travaille à la d. de l'événement** the government is trying hard to play down the significance of the event; **cela a contribué à la d. de la situation** this helped make the situation less tense

dédramatiser [dedramatize] **VT** (*situation*) to take the tension out of; (*événement*) to play down the significance of

déductibilité [dedyktibilite] **NF** deductibility

déductible [dedyktibl] **ADJ** deductible; **d. des impôts** tax deductible

déductif, -ive [dedyktif, -iv] **ADJ** *Phil* deductive

déduction [dedyksjɔ̃] **NF 1** *Com etc* deduction, allowance; **faire d. des sommes payées d'avance** to deduct sums or allow for sums paid in advance; **d. fiscale** tax allowance; **d. forfaitaire** (*d'impôts*) standard allowance; **sous d. de 10%** less 10%; **sans d. terms** net cash; **d. faite des frais d'essence** after deduction of petrol costs **2** (*raisonnement*) deduction, inference

déduire [dedɥir] (*conj like* **conduire**) **VT 1** (*enlever*) to deduct; **d. 5%** to take off or deduct 5%, to allow a deduction of 5%; **tous frais déduits** after deduction of expenses **2** (*conclure*) to deduce, to infer; **de là, on peut d. que ...** from this, it may be deduced that ...

déesse [deɛs] **NF** goddess

défaillance [defajɑ̃s] **NF 1** (*faiblesse*) (*morale*) failing, lapse; (*physique*) deficiency; **cet enfant a de sérieuses défaillances en lecture** the child has serious reading difficulties; **les défaillances des dirigeants de l'entreprise** management's failings; **sans d.** without flinching; **courage sans d.** unflagging or unfailing courage; **travailler sans d.** to work tirelessly; **d. de mémoire** memory lapse; **d. cardiaque** heart failure; **d. mécanique** mechanical failure; **la machine a eu une d.** the machine developed a fault; **d. d'entreprise** business failure

2 (*évanouissement*) fainting fit; **avoir une d.** (*s'évanouir*) to faint; (*faiblir*) to flag; **soudain, ce fut la d.** (*il faiblit*) all of a sudden, he flagged

3 *Jur* default(ing)

défaillant, -ante [defajɑ̃, -ɑ̃t] **ADJ 1** (*force, mémoire*) failing; (*santé*) declining; (*cœur*) weak; **d. de fatigue** exhausted **2** (*qui s'évanouit*) (*voix, personne*) faint; **il avançait d'un pas d.** he walked with a faltering step; **elle était défaillante de bonheur** she was giddy with delight **3** *Jur* defaulting
N *Jur* defaulter, absconder

défaillir [defajir] **VI** (*prp* **défaillant**; *pp* **défailli**; *pr ind* **il défaille, n. défaillons**; *impf* **défaillais**; *p hist* **je défaillis**; *fu* **je défaillirai** ou *parfois* **je défaillerai**) **1** (*faiblir*) to become feeble; **sa mémoire/sa force commence à d.** his/her memory/strength is beginning to fail; **à cette nouvelle, son cœur défaillit** his heart sank at the news; **j'accomplirai le travail sans d.** I'll do the job without flinching **2** (*s'évanouir*) to faint; **d. de faim** to feel faint with hunger

défaire [defɛr] (*conj like* **faire**) **VT 1** (*nœud*) to undo, to untie; (*paquet*) to undo, to unwrap; (*valise*) to unpack; (*ourlet*) to unpick; (*robe etc*) to undo; (*fermeture Éclair®*) to unzip; **d. le lit** (*enlever les draps*) to strip the bed; (*pour se coucher*) to turn down the bed; (*le mettre en désordre*) to rumple the bedclothes; **d. ses cheveux** to let one's hair down

2 (*détruire*) (*puzzle*) to take apart, to take to pieces; (*traité*) to cancel, to annul; (*alliance, mariage*) to break up; *Fam* **d. un marché** to cancel a deal

3 *Ordinat* (*opération*) to undo

4 *Litt* (*battre*) (*armée etc*) to defeat; (*personne*) to get the better of

5 *Litt* **d. qn de qn/qch** to rid sb of sb/sth

6 (*miner*) to devastate; **cette nouvelle l'a complètement défait** he was completely devastated by the news
VPR se défaire 1 (*de vêtements, d'un nœud*) to come undone; (*de cheveux*) to come down; (*de choses jointes les unes aux autres*) to come apart; (*de mariage*) to break up, to fall apart; (*de viande à la cuisson*) to fall apart **2 se d. de qn/qch** to get rid of sb/sth; **se d. de ses marchandises** to get rid of or sell off one's stock; **je ne veux pas m'en d.** I don't want to part with it; **se d. d'une mauvaise habitude** to get out of or break oneself of a bad habit **3** (*s'altérer*) (*de personne, visage*) to become haggard or drawn

défait [defɛ] **ADJ 1** (*traits, visage*) drawn, haggard; **la mine défaite** with a haggard expression; **il est arrivé à l'hôpital, complètement d.** he arrived at the hospital in a state of collapse; **elle était quelque peu défaite après l'échec de son livre** she was somewhat depressed after her book's lack of success **2** (*cheveux, apparence*) dishevelled **3** (*armée etc*) defeated

défaite [defɛt] **NF** defeat; **connaître une d.** to suffer a defeat

défaitisme [defɛtism] **NM** defeatism

défaitiste [defɛtist] **ADJ, N** defeatist

défalcation [defalkasjɔ̃] **NF** deduction; **d. faite des frais** after deduction of expenses

défalquer [defalke] **VT** (*une somme d'un total*) to deduct

défatigant [defatigɑ̃] **ADJ** relaxing
NM muscle relaxant

défatiguer [defatige] **VT** to relax; **un bon bain chaud va vous d.** a hot bath will relax you or help you (to) unwind
VPR se défatiguer to unwind; **se d. les yeux** to rest one's eyes; **j'ai besoin de me d. la tête** I need to clear my mind

défaufiler [defofile] **VT** *Couture* to remove the tacks from

défausser [defose] **VT** (*clé, tournevis etc*) to straighten (out)
VPR se défausser *Cartes* to discard; **se d. à cœur** to discard one's hearts

défaut [defo] **NM 1** (*imperfection*) (*d'une personne*) fault, shortcoming; (*de pierre précieuse, métal, verre, tissu*) flaw; (*d'une machine*) defect; **chacun a ses défauts** everyone has their faults; **la curiosité est un vilain d.** curiosity killed the cat; **c'est là son moindre d.** that's the least of his faults; **les défauts d'une explication/d'une théorie** the flaws in or shortcomings of an explanation/a theory; **avoir un d.** (*d'une machine*) to be defective; **il y a un d. de fonctionnement** it isn't working properly; **cette école n'a qu'un d.** the school has only one drawback; **sans d.** faultless, flawless; **mettre les chiens en d.** to throw the hounds off the scent; *Fig* **mettre qn en d.** to put sb on the spot; **prendre qn en d.** to catch sb napping; **être en d.** to be wrong; **d. de prononciation** speech impediment; **d. de fabrication** manufacturing fault or defect; *Com* **défauts apparents** visible defects; *Com* **défauts cachés** hidden defects

2 (*manque*) lack; *Jur* default; **il y a, chez cet enfant, un d. de concentration** the child lacks concentration; **le temps me fait d.** I haven't got the time; **le courage lui a fait d.** his courage failed him; **les provisions font d.** there is a shortage of supplies, supplies are short; **les bonnes places font d.** there is a shortage of good jobs, good jobs are hard to come by; **la place fait d. chez moi** there is a shortage of space or space is in short supply at my place; **l'argent fait d. en ce moment** money is tight at the moment; **l'argent lui fait cruellement d.** he is very short of money; **le bon sens lui fait cruellement d.** he is sadly lacking in common sense; **sa** ou **la mémoire lui fait d.** he can't remember; **si ma mémoire ne me fait pas d.** if I'm not mistaken, if my memory serves me right; **pécher par d.** to sin by omission, to commit a sin of omission; **ou, à d., ...** or, failing that, ...; **à d. de qch** for lack of sth; **à d. de salaire intéressant, elle a au moins l'avantage de travailler près de chez elle** she might not have a very good salary, but at least she works close to home; **le d. de l'épaule** the hollow of the shoulder; *Fig* **j'ai trouvé le d. de la cuirasse** ou **de l'armure** I've found the chink in his/etc armour; **frapper au d. de la cuirasse** ou **de l'armure** to aim for the chink in his/etc armour; *Jur* **faire d.** to fail to appear, to default; *Jur* **jugement par d.** judgment by default; **d. de comparution** failure to appear; **d. de paiement** failure to pay, non-payment, default on payment; **d. de livraison** default on delivery; *Banque* **chèque refusé pour cause de d. de provision** cheque refused by the bank because of insufficient funds; **'d. de provision'** (*tampon sur chèque*) ≃ 'refer to drawer'

3 *Math* **total approché par d.** total rounded down; *Ordinat* **lecteur/clavier par d.** default drive/keyboard

défaveur [defavœr] NF disfavour, Am disfavor, discredit; **être en d.** to be in disfavour (**auprès de** with); **il faut vraiment être très désagréable pour s'attirer la d. de mon grand-père** you have to be really unpleasant for my grandfather to take against you

défavorable [defavɔrabl] ADJ unfavourable, Am unfavorable (**à** to); **être d. à qn/qch** to be against sb/sth; **les conditions (nous) sont défavorables** conditions are against us

défavorablement [defavɔrabləmɑ̃] ADV unfavourably, Am unfavorably

défavorisé [defavɔrize] ADJ (enfant, pays) underprivileged; **candidat d.** candidate at a disadvantage; **les milieux les plus défavorisés** the underprivileged classes

défavoriser [defavɔrize] VT to put at a disadvantage, to disadvantage; **cette nouvelle loi défavorisera les couples non mariés** this new law will put unmarried couples at a disadvantage or will be unfair to unmarried couples; **d. les candidates** to favour male candidates over female ones; **le climat du désert défavorise les soldats occidentaux** Western soldiers are at a disadvantage in desert climates; **il est défavorisé par sa timidité** his shyness puts him at a disadvantage; **dans son testament, il a défavorisé sa femme par rapport à ses enfants** he favoured his children over his wife in his will

défécation [defekasjɔ̃] NF Physiol defecation

défectif, -ive [defɛktif, -iv] ADJ (verbe etc) defective

défection [defɛksjɔ̃] NF Pol defection; (de partisan, soldat, allié) defection, desertion; **je ne m'attendais pas à sa d.** I did not expect him to defect; **au moment de son divorce, il a assisté à la d. de tous ses amis** all his friends deserted him when he got divorced; **elle a été très déçue par les défections qui se sont produites la veille de la réception** she was very disappointed by the number of people who cancelled the day before the party; **à mon mariage, il n'y a eu qu'une seule d.** only one person didn't attend my wedding; **en cas de d.** in the event of cancellation; **faire d.** to desert, to defect, Fam to rat

défectueusement [defɛktɥøzmɑ̃] ADV defectively

défectueux, -euse [defɛktɥø, -øz] ADJ defective, faulty

défectuosité [defɛktɥozite] NF 1 (défaut) defect, flaw 2 (mauvaise qualité) defectiveness

défendable [defɑ̃dabl] ADJ (position, point de vue, théorie etc) defensible; **ses théories ne sont absolument pas défendables** his theories are totally indefensible

défendeur, -deresse [defɑ̃dœr, -drɛs] N Jur defendant

DÉFENDRE [defɑ̃dr] VT 1 (lutter pour ou contre, soutenir) (théorie, politique, la mémoire de qn), Jur (accusé) to defend; (cause) to defend, to champion; (droit, opinion) to defend, to uphold; (ses amis, ses idées) to defend, to stand up for (**contre** against); **il sait d. ses opinions** he can hold his own; **cette organisation défend les droits de l'homme** this organization defends or champions human rights; Sport **d. son titre de champion du monde/les couleurs de ...** to defend one's world championship title/the colours of ...

2 (protéger) to defend, to guard (**contre** against, from); Tennis (service) to defend; **d. son pays contre l'envahisseur** to defend one's country against the invader; **la propriété est défendue par deux chiens** the estate is guarded by two dogs; **d. ses intérêts** to protect one's interests; **il a fait cela pour d.**

mes intérêts he did it to defend or in defence of my interests; Fig **d. son bifteck** to look after number one; **de lourdes tentures défendaient la pièce contre les regards indiscrets** heavy curtains shielded the room from prying eyes; **l'isolation défend la pièce du froid** the insulation shields the room from cold; **les fourrures défendent les Esquimaux du froid** fur clothing protects the Eskimos from the cold; Ftbl **Durant défendra les buts de l'équipe d'Aix** Durant will play in goal for Aix

3 (interdire) to forbid, to prohibit; **fruit(s) défendu(s)** forbidden fruit; **d. qch à qn** to forbid sb sth; **son père lui a défendu l'entrée de sa maison** his father has forbidden him to set foot over the doorstep; **d. sa porte à qn** to close one's door to sb; **ce médicament est défendu aux enfants** this medicine must not be given to children; **il défend qu'on passe par là** he forbids anyone to go that way; **une herse de fer défendait l'entrée de la crypte** an iron portcullis barred the entrance to the crypt

4 d. à qn de faire qch to forbid sb to do sth; **je te défends d'y aller** I forbid you to go; **son père lui défend de sortir le soir** his father does not allow him to go out at night; **il est défendu de fumer dans les classes** smoking is prohibited in the classrooms; **il m'est défendu de fumer** I'm not allowed or I'm forbidden to smoke; **il est défendu de parler au chauffeur** please do not speak to the driver

VPR **se défendre 1** (se protéger) to defend oneself; **se d. de** ou **contre qch** to defend oneself against sth, to protect or shield oneself from or against sth; **se d. des agressions** to defend oneself against attack; **se d. avec un couteau** to defend oneself with a knife; **se d. de la pluie** to shelter from the rain; **se d. du froid** to protect oneself from the cold; **se d. contre la critique** to defend oneself against criticism; **se d. des tentations** to steer clear of temptation

2 Fam (se débrouiller) **je me défends** I'm holding my own, I'm getting by or along; **je me défends en anglais/en tennis** I can hold my own or I can get by in English/at tennis; **il se défend bien en affaires** he's a good businessman; **il ne se défend pas mal avec son ordinateur** he's getting on quite well with his computer

3 (nier) **se d. de faire/d'avoir fait qch** to deny doing sth

4 (se justifier) **cette attitude peut se d.** this attitude is justifiable; **c'est une idée qui se défend** there is something to be said for the idea

5 (s'empêcher) (the pron is the indirect object) **se d. de faire qch** to refrain from doing sth; **on ne peut se d. de l'aimer** you can't help liking him; **elle ne peut se d. d'un certain sentiment de culpabilité** she can't help feeling guilty; **se d. tout plaisir/toute gourmandise** to deny oneself all pleasure/sweet things

défenestration [defənɛstrasjɔ̃] NF defenestration

défenestrer [defənɛstre] VT to defenestrate

défense¹ [defɑ̃s] NF 1 (soutien) (d'une politique, d'une théorie, d'une opinion etc), Jur defence, Am defense; **prendre la d. de qn** to defend sb; **sans d.** defenceless; **la meilleure d., c'est l'attaque** attack is the best form of defence; Jur **la parole est à la d.** the defence may now speak; Jur **assurer la d. de qn** to defend sb; **qu'avez-vous à dire pour votre d.?** what do you have to say in your defence?

2 (protection), Mil, Sp defence, Am defense; **combattre pour la d. de son pays** to fight in defence of one's country; **ligne de d.** line of defence; **moyen de d.** means of defence; **d. nationale** national defence; **d. côtière/aé-**

rienne coastal/air defence; **d. contre avions** anti-aircraft defence; **d. passive** civil defence; Physiol **la d. de l'organisme** the organism's defence mechanisms; Physiol **défenses immunitaires** immune defences; **d. des consommateurs** consumer protection; Mktg **d. contre-offensive** counteroffensive defence; Mktg **d. mobile** mobile defence; Mktg **d. préventive** pre-emptive defence; Jur **légitime d.** self-defence

3 (interdiction) **d. d'entrer/de fumer/de stationner** no entry or admittance/smoking/parking; **d. d'afficher** stick no bills; **c'est un secret, d. d'en parler à ton père!** it's a secret so don't go telling your father about it!; Vieilli **faire d. à qn de faire qch** to forbid sb to do sth

défense² NF (d'éléphant, de sanglier etc) tusk

défenseur [defɑ̃sœr] NM 1 (d'un enfant, d'une ville etc) protector, defender; (d'une cause) supporter, upholder; Sport defender **2** Jur counsel for the defence; **qui est son d.?** who's defending him?; **c'est le d. de la veuve et de l'orphelin** he's a champion of the underdog

défensif, -ive [defɑ̃sif, -iv] ADJ defensive NF **défensive** defensive; **être** ou **se tenir sur la défensive** to be on the defensive

défensivement [defɑ̃sivmɑ̃] ADV defensively

déféquer [defeke] VI (je défèque, n. déféquons; je déféquerai) Physiol to defecate

déférence [deferɑ̃s] NF deference (**pour** for); **par d. pour ...** in or out of deference to ...

déférent [deferɑ̃] ADJ (manière etc) deferential

déférer [defere] (je défère; je déférerai) VT **1** Jur (une affaire devant un tribunal) to submit, to refer; **d. qn à la justice** to hand sb over or give sb up to the police **2** Arch (honneur) to confer, to bestow (**à** on) VI **d. à qn** to defer to sb; **d. aux ordres de qn** to comply with sb's orders; **d. à une demande** to accede to a request

déferlant, -ante [defɛrlɑ̃, -ɑ̃t] ADJ, NF (vague) **déferlante** breaker, beachcomber; Fig surge; **une d. de lettres de protestation** a deluge of letters of complaint; **la d. des jeux électroniques** the sudden influx of video games

déferlement [defɛrləmɑ̃] NM (de vagues) breaking; Fig (d'enthousiasme, de violence, de racisme) wave; **d. de colère** fit of anger; **d. de touristes/journalistes** invasion of tourists/reporters; **le d. des touristes sur la Côte d'Azur en juillet** the July invasion of the French Riviera by tourists, the descent of tourists on the French Riviera in July

déferler [defɛrle] VT (drapeau), Naut (voile) to unfurl
VI (de vagues) to break; **la foule déferle dans la rue** the crowd is surging down the street; **la joie/la colère/une rumeur déferlait dans toute la ville** joy/anger/a rumour spread through the entire city; **les vacanciers déferlent sur les routes** holiday-makers are taking to the roads in droves

défet [defɛ] NM Typ waste sheet

défi [defi] NM 1 challenge; **lancer** ou **jeter un d. à qn** to challenge sb; **relever un d.** to take up a challenge; **la jeunesse a besoin de d.** young people need a challenge 2 (provocation) defiance; **mettre qn au d. de faire qch** to defy or dare sb to do sth; **avec un sourire de d.** with a smile of defiance, with a defiant smile; **d'un air de d.** defiantly, with a defiant air or an air of defiance; **son attitude est un d. à votre autorité** his attitude is a challenge to your authority; **son numéro est un d. aux**

lois de la pesanteur his act defies the laws of gravity

défiance [defjɑ̃s] NF mistrust, distrust, suspicion, wariness; **inspirer** *ou* **éveiller la d.** to arouse suspicion; **mettre qn en d.** to make sb wary; *Pol* **motion de d.** motion of no confidence; **d. de soi-même** diffidence, lack of self-confidence

défiant [defjɑ̃] ADJ mistrustful, distrustful, cautious, wary

défibrillateur [defibrijatœr] NM *Méd* defibrillator

défibrillation [defibrijasjɔ̃] NF *Méd* defibrillation

déficeler [defisle] (*conj like* **ficeler**) VT (*paquet etc*) to untie, to undo
VPR se déficeler to come untied *or* undone

déficience [defisjɑ̃s] NF deficiency; **d. intellectuelle** mental deficiency; **d. (alimentaire)** malnutrition; **d. musculaire** muscle deficiency; **d. immunologique** immune deficiency; **d. en vitamine B** vitamin B deficiency

déficient, -iente [defisjɑ̃, -jɑ̃t] ADJ deficient; (*muscle*) wasted, atrophied, deficient; (*raisonnement, théorie*) weak; **intelligence déficiente** (*insuffisance*) mental deficiency; **enfant d.** (*mentalement*) mentally deficient child; (*physiquement*) physically handicapped *or surtout Am* challenged child
N **d. moteur** person with motor deficiency; **d. mental** mentally deficient person; **les déficients visuels** the visually impaired *or surtout Am* challenged

déficit [defisit] NM *Fin* deficit; **d. de la balance commerciale** trade deficit; **d. budgétaire/commercial** budget/trade deficit; *Pol* **d. démocratique** democratic deficit; **d. extérieur** external deficit, balance of payments deficit; **d. fiscal remboursable** negative income tax; *Compta* **d. reportable** loss carry forward; **d. du secteur public** public sector deficit; **d. social** public spending deficit; **d. de trésorerie** cash deficit; **d. psychologique/mental** psychological/mental deficiency; **être en d.** to be in deficit; **combler un d.** to make good a deficit; **accuser un d.** to show a deficit

déficitaire [defisiter] ADJ (*entreprise*) loss-making, unprofitable; (*compte*) showing a debit balance; (*budget etc*) showing a deficit; (*bilan*) showing a loss; **être d.** (*d'un compte*) to be in debit; (*d'un budget, d'une entreprise*) to be in deficit; *Agr* **récolte d.** short crop

défier [defje] VT 1 (*provoquer*) (*dans une lutte etc*) to challenge; **d. qn au combat/aux échecs** to challenge sb to a fight/to a game of chess 2 (*inciter*) to defy; **je vous défie de faire mieux** I defy you to do better 3 (*braver*) (*danger, mort, balles*) to brave, to face; (*la police*) to taunt; (*la presse*) to confront; **il ne craint pas de d. l'autorité paternelle** he's not afraid to stand up to his father 4 (*résister à*) **d. l'imagination** to defy the imagination; **le spectacle défie toute description** the sight defies *or* is beyond description; **des prix qui défient toute concurrence** unbeatable prices
VPR se défier *Fml* **se d. de qn/qch** to mistrust *or* distrust sb/sth; **se d. de soi-même** to be diffident

défigurement [defigyrmɑ̃] NM (*d'une personne*) disfigurement; (*d'une statue*) defacement; (*de la vérité, du sens*) distortion

défigurer [defigyre] VT (*personne, paysage*) to disfigure; (*statue*) to deface; (*la vérité, sens*) to twist, to distort; (*la pensée, les intentions de qn*) to misrepresent; **l'acné la défigure** her acne disfigures her face; **d. un texte** (*d'un acteur*) to ruin a script

défilé [defile] NM 1 *Géog* defile, (mountain) pass 2 (*file*) parade, procession; *Mil* march past; *Aviat* flypast; (*de souvenirs, d'idées*) series; **un d. ininterrompu de touristes** an endless stream of tourists
▸▸ *Aviat* **d. aérien** flypast; **d. de mode** fashion show

défilement [defil(ə)mɑ̃] NM 1 (*de bande magnétique, de pellicule*) running 2 *Ordinat* scrolling

> Il faut noter que le nom anglais **defilement** est un faux ami. Il signifie **souillure** ou **profanation**, selon le contexte.

défiler¹ [defile] VT (*perles, collier*) to unstring, to unthread
VPR se défiler 1 (*de perles etc*) to come unstrung **2** *Mil* **se d. du feu de l'adversaire** to take cover from enemy fire **3** *Fam* (*se dérober*) to slope off

défiler² VI (*passer en colonne*) to walk in procession; *Mil* to march past, to parade; **les manifestants défilent depuis ce matin** the demonstrators have been marching *or* trooping past since this morning; **des centaines de voitures défilent vers la côte** hundreds of cars are streaming towards the coast; **les images défilaient devant nos yeux** the pictures passed before our eyes; **les souvenirs défilaient dans sa mémoire** the memories came thick and fast; **le paysage défilait à toute vitesse** the countryside sped past *or* flashed past; *Mil* **d. en colonne par deux** to file off in twos; **faire d. une bande/une bobine de film** to run a tape/reel of film; *Ordinat* **faire d. un document** to scroll a document; *Ordinat* **d. vers le bas** to scroll down; *Ordinat* **d. vers le haut** to scroll up

défini [defini] ADJ 1 (*précis*) clearly defined; **mot bien/mal d.** well-defined/badly defined word; **un travail bien d.** a clearly defined piece of work; *Ordinat* **d. par l'utilisateur** user-defined; *Ordinat* **pouvant être d. par l'utilisateur** user-definable **2** *Gram* definite; **passé d.** past definite, preterite, past historic SEE GRAMMAR A6–8; B3–4

définir [definir] VT (*conditions, mot etc*) to define; **c'est difficile à d.** it's difficult to define; **il faut d. le poste** we'll have to define what the job entails, we'll have to draw up a job description
VPR se définir to describe oneself; **comment vous définissez-vous?** how would you describe yourself?

définissable [definisabl] ADJ definable; *Ordinat* **d. par l'utilisateur** user-definable

définitif, -ive [definitif, -iv] ADJ 1 (*résolution, jugement, version etc*) final, definitive; (*argument*) definitive; **la biographie définitive de Proust** the definitive biography of Proust; **une séparation définitive** a permanent separation; **nommé à titre d.** permanently appointed; **ma décision est définitive** my decision is final; **veuillez noter la fermeture définitive du magasin** please note that the shop has closed down **2 en définitive** when all is said and done

définition [definisjɔ̃] NF 1 (*d'un mot, de conditions etc*) definition; (*de mots croisés*) clue; **par d.** by definition; **d. de poste** job description **2** *Cin, TV, Phot* definition; **télévision à haute d.** high-definition television

définitivement [definitivmɑ̃] ADV (*décider qch*) definitely; (*partir, s'installer*) for good; (*nommé*) permanently

défiscalisation [defiskalizasjɔ̃] NF removal *or* lifting of taxes

défiscalisé [defiskalize] ADJ tax-free

défiscaliser [defiskalize] VT to remove *or* lift the tax on

déflagration [deflagrasjɔ̃] NF (*explosion*) explosion

déflagrer [deflagre] VI to combust

déflation [deflasjɔ̃] NF *Écon* deflation

déflationniste [deflasjɔnist] *Écon* ADJ deflationary
N deflationist

déflecteur [deflɛktœr] NM *Aut etc* (*sur vitre*) deflector, quarterlight; **d. de faisceau** beam deflector; **d. de ventilateur** cowl, cowling

défleuraison [deflœrɛzɔ̃] NF falling of blossom

défleurir [deflœrir] VI (*d'arbre etc*) to lose its blossom
VT (*plante*) to take the flowers off

déflexion [deflɛksjɔ̃] NF deflection

déflocage [deflɔkaʒ] NM **le d. d'un bâtiment** the removal of asbestos insulation from a building

défloraison [deflɔrɛzɔ̃] NF = **défleuraison**

défloration [deflɔrasjɔ̃] NF (*d'une vierge*) deflowering

déflorer [deflɔre] VT 1 (*vierge*) to deflower **2** *Fig* (*révéler*) (*nouvelle*) to announce; (*secret*) to give away

défoliant [defɔljɑ̃] NM *Agr* defoliant

défoliation [defɔljasjɔ̃] NF defoliation

défonçage [defɔ̃saʒ] NM (*d'une boîte, d'une porte etc*) smashing in; (*d'un mur*) knocking down

défonce [defɔ̃s] NF *Fam* (*par la drogue*) trip; **être en pleine d.** to be on a trip

défoncé [defɔ̃se] ADJ 1 (*détérioré*) (*porte*) bashed in; (*fauteuil*) battered; **un matelas d.** a mattress with all the stuffing hanging out; **chemin d.** rough *or* bumpy road **2** *Fam* (*qui a pris de la drogue*) high, stoned

défoncement [defɔ̃smɑ̃] NM = **défonçage**

défoncer [defɔ̃se] (**je défonçai(s); n. défonçons**) VT (*boîte, porte etc*) to smash in, to bash in; (*mur etc*) to knock down; (*tonneau, bateau*) to stave in; (*route*) to break up, to cut up; **il a eu le crâne défoncé dans l'accident** his head was smashed in in the accident; *très Fam* **d. la gueule à qn** to smash sb's face in, to punch sb's lights out, *Am* to punch sb out
VPR se défoncer *Fam* **1** (*avec de la drogue*) to get high **2** (*faire un grand effort*) to sweat blood; **il s'est défoncé pour que tu aies ta voiture à temps** he sweated blood *or* bust a gut so you would get your car back in time

déforestation [defɔrɛstasjɔ̃] NF deforestation

déformant [defɔrmɑ̃] ADJ distorting

déformation [defɔrmasjɔ̃] NF (*d'un membre*) deformation; (*d'un visage, de la vérité*), *Phot* (*d'une image*) distortion; (*des faits, de la réalité*) distortion, misrepresentation; (*de la pensée*) misrepresentation; (*de vêtement, chaussure*) stretching out of shape; (*de métal*) buckling; (*de bois*), *Fig* (*de l'esprit*) warping; **avoir une d. du pied** to have a deformed foot; **à cause de la d. de vos chaussures** because your shoes are all stretched out of shape; **il fume tellement qu'il souffre d'une d. du goût** he smokes so much that he's ruined his palate; **c'est son métier de psychanalyste qui conduit à cette d. de l'esprit chez lui** it's being a psychoanalyst that has warped his mind
▸▸ **d. professionnelle** = habits acquired through doing the type of work one does; **elle est professeur, c'est donc par d. professionnelle qu'elle répète tout tout le temps** it must be because she's a teacher that she repeats things all the time; **il fait de la d. professionnelle** he's like that because of his job

déformer [defɔrme] VT (*membre*) to deform; (*vêtement, chaussure*) to stretch out of

Delco® [dɛlko] NM *Aut* distributor

déléatur [deleatyr] NM INV *Typ* delete (mark), dele

délectable [delɛktabl] ADJ delicious, delightful

délectation [delɛktasjɔ̃] NF delight; *Fml, Hum* delectation

délecter [delɛkte] VT *Litt* to delight
VPR se délecter to enjoy oneself; **se d. à (faire) qch** to take delight in (doing) sth

délégant, -ante [delegɑ̃, -ɑ̃t] N *Jur* delegant

délégataire [delegater] N *Jur* delegatee

délégateur, -trice [delegatœr, -tris] N *Jur* delegator

délégation [delegasjɔ̃] NF 1 *(action de déléguer) (de représentants)* delegation, deputing; *(de dette)* assignment, transfer; **agir en vertu d'une** *ou* **par d.** to act on the authority invested in one; **d. de pouvoir** delegation of authority; **d. de signature** power of attorney; *Scol* **d. rectorale** (one-year) transfer; **d. de vote** proxy voting 2 *(groupe)* delegation, body of delegates; **envoyer une d. auprès d'un ministre** to send a delegation to a minister; **venir en d.** to come in a delegation

délégué, -ée [delege] ADJ **membre d.** delegate; **ministre d. à l'environnement** Minister for the Environment, Environment Minister
N *(à une réunion)* delegate; *Scol* representative *(at class meetings)*
▸▸ *Scol* **d. de classe** class representative *(at class meetings)*; **d. commercial** sales rep(resentative); **d. des parents** parent representative *(at class meetings)*; **d. du personnel** staff representative; *(syndiqué)* union representative; *Scol* **d. rectoral** = teacher on a one-year placement *(in a job other than the one to which he or she was originally assigned)*; **d. syndical** union representative; *(d'usine)* shop steward

déléguer [delege] (je délègue; je déléguerai) VT 1 *(désigner)* **d. qn pour faire qch** to delegate sb to do sth 2 *(transmettre) (pouvoirs)* to delegate; **c'est un patron qui sait d. ses fonctions** he's a boss who knows how to delegate; **d. une créance** to assign a debt
VI to delegate

délestage [delɛstaʒ] NM *(d'un navire, d'un ballon)* unballasting; *Élec* power cut; **pour assurer le d. des grandes artères** to relieve congestion on the main roads; **itinéraire de d.** alternative route

délester [delɛste] VT *(navire, ballon)* to unballast; *Élec* to cut off the power to; *(voie de communication)* to relieve congestion on; **d. qn d'un fardeau** to relieve sb of a burden; *Fam* **d. qn de son argent** to relieve sb of his/her money
VPR se délester *(d'un navire, d'un ballon)* to jettison ballast; **se d. de ses paquets** to set down *or* relieve oneself of one's parcels

délétère [deletɛr] ADJ harmful, *Fml* deleterious; *(gaz)* noxious, poisonous; *(influence etc)* pernicious

délibérant [deliberɑ̃] ADJ *(assemblée)* deliberative

délibératif, -ive [deliberatif, -iv] ADJ *(fonction)* deliberative; **avoir voix délibérative** to be entitled to speak and vote

délibération [deliberasjɔ̃] NF 1 *(examen)* deliberation, debate, discussion; **pendant la d. du jury** during the jury's deliberations, *Fam* the jury was out; **la question est en d.** the matter is under discussion *or* being deliberated 2 *(réflexion)* consideration, reflection, cogitation; **après mûre d.** after careful consideration 3 *(décision) (d'une assemblée)* resolution, decision, vote

délibéré [delibere] ADJ 1 *(intentionnel)* deliberate, intentional; **agir de propos d.** to act

deliberately *or* intentionally 2 *(résolu) (ton, manière)* deliberate, determined, resolute
NM *Jur (de juges)* consultation, private sitting; **mettre une affaire en d.** = to submit a matter for decision by the Bench, *Am* ≃ to take a matter under advisement

délibérément [deliberemɑ̃] ADV deliberately

délibérer [delibere] VI 1 *(discuter)* to deliberate, to confer; **d. (avec qn) sur qch** to discuss a matter (with sb); **le jury s'est retiré pour d.** the jury retired to consider its verdict 2 *(réfléchir)* to deliberate, to reflect 3 *(décider)* **d. de qch** to decide sth; **le tribunal populaire délibérait de le condamner à mort** the people's tribunal was deciding whether to condemn him to death

délicat, -ate [delika] ADJ 1 *(fragile) (peau)* sensitive, tender; *(fleur etc)* delicate; *(santé)* delicate, frail, weak
2 *(fin) (dentelle, ouvrage)* delicate; *(travail)* fine; *(plat)* fine, refined; **d'une facture très délicate** very delicately made
3 *(raffiné) (goût, personne)* fine, refined, discerning; *(geste)* graceful; *(comportement)* considerate; *(toucher)* delicate, gentle; **avoir les oreilles délicates** to dislike bad language; **avoir le palais d.** to have a discerning palate; **avoir des gestes délicats** to move gracefully; **il est toujours très d. avec les vieilles dames** he's always very considerate towards old ladies; **il a eu une attention délicate pour nous à l'occasion de notre mariage** he was very thoughtful *or* considerate when we got married; **quelle attention délicate!** how thoughtful!, how considerate!
4 *(difficile) (situation, question, opération)* delicate, difficult, tricky; *(problème, travail)* difficult, tricky
5 *(souvent avec négation) (scrupuleux) (personne)* scrupulous; *(conscience)* tender; **peu d.** not very scrupulous, rather unscrupulous
6 *(exigeant)* **d. sur la nourriture** fussy about food; **qu'est-ce qu'il est d.!** isn't he fussy!
N **faire le d.** *(devant un mets)* to be fussy; *(devant le sang)* to be squeamish

délicatement [delikatmɑ̃] ADV delicately; *(s'exprimer)* with delicacy; *(se comporter)* considerately, thoughtfully; *(poser des verres sur un plateau)* to put glasses down gently on a tray; **annoncer d. un décès à qn** to gently break the news of a death to sb; **d. brodé** finely embroidered; **plat d. préparé** dish prepared with great care

délicatesse [delikates] NF 1 *(fragilité) (de la peau)* tenderness; *(d'une fleur, d'un tissu)* delicacy; *(d'un objet)* fragility; *(de la santé)* frailty
2 *(finesse) (d'une dentelle, d'un ouvrage)* delicacy, fineness; *(d'un tableau)* fineness; *(d'une texture, d'un coloris)* fineness, softness; *(d'un plat)* refinement
3 *(raffinement) (de goût)* refinement; *(d'un geste)* gracefulness; *(de toucher)* delicacy, gentleness; **d'un geste plein de d.** with an extremely graceful movement; **elle posa les verres sur la table avec d.** she gently put the glasses down on the table
4 *(difficulté) (d'une situation)* delicacy, difficulty, awkwardness; *(d'une opération, d'une question, d'un problème, d'un travail)* difficulty; **ce que vous me demandez de lui dire est vraiment d'une d. incroyable** what you're asking me to tell him is extremely difficult *or* awkward; **il est en d. avec la police/le gouvernement** he has to watch his step with the police/the government; **nous sommes en d.** we've had words
5 *(gentillesse)* considerateness, consideration; *(sensibilité)* tact; **agir avec d.** to behave considerately/tactfully; **elle avait des délicatesses pour moi** she treated me very considerately; **c'est une personne pleine de**

d. he's/she's extremely thoughtful *or* considerate

délice [delis] NM delight, extreme pleasure; **cette tarte est un vrai d.** this tart is delicious; **quel d. de se plonger dans un bon bain chaud** what a delight it is to sink into a warm bath

délices [delis] NFPL delight(s), pleasure(s); **faire les d. de qn** to delight sb, to be the delight of sb; **faire ses d. de qch** to delight in sth; **c'est un lieu de d.** this place is heavenly

délicieusement [delisjøzmɑ̃] ADV delightfully; *(en rapport avec le goût)* deliciously; **elle nous a reçus d.** she entertained us delightfully, she was a delightful hostess; **elle réussit d. la paella** she makes a delicious paella; **elle se laissa glisser d. dans l'eau** she slid into the water with delight

délicieux, -ieuse [delisjø, -jøz] ADJ *(nourriture)* delicious; *(personne, robe etc)* delightful, charming

délictuel, -elle [deliktɥɛl] ADJ *Jur* = délictueux

délictueux, -euse [deliktɥø, -øz] ADJ *Jur* punishable; **acte d.** misdemeanour, offence, *Am* offense

délié [delje] ADJ slender, fine; *(doigts)* nimble, agile; **taille déliée** slim figure; **avoir la langue déliée** to be talkative; **un esprit d.** a sharp *or* astute mind
NM *Typ etc* thin stroke

délier [delje] VT 1 *(défaire) (corde, rubans etc)* to untie, to undo; *(chaînes)* to undo, to loose; *Fig* **le vin lui a délié la langue** the wine loosened his tongue 2 *(libérer) (prisonnier)* to untie; **d. les mains à qn** to untie sb's hands; **d. qn d'une promesse/d'une responsabilité** to release sb from a promise/a responsibility
VPR se délier 1 *(se défaire)* to come undone *or* untied, to come loose; *Fig* **sa langue s'est déliée** he began to talk, he found his tongue 2 **se d. d'un serment/d'une promesse** to free oneself from an oath/a promise

délimitation [delimitasjɔ̃] NF *(d'un territoire)* delimitation, demarcation; *(d'une responsabilité, d'un sujet etc)* definition; **poteau de d.** boundary post

délimiter [delimite] VT *(territoire)* to delimit, to demarcate; *(responsabilité, sujet etc)* to define, to set the limits of

délimiteur [delimitœr] NM *Ordinat* delimiter; **d. de bloc** block delimiter, block marker; **d. de champ** field delimiter

délinquance [delɛ̃kɑ̃s] NF delinquency; **d. juvénile** juvenile delinquency; **la petite d. des banlieues** petty crime in the suburbs

délinquant, -ante [delɛ̃kɑ̃, -ɑ̃t] *Jur* ADJ delinquent; **la jeunesse délinquante** juvenile delinquents
N offender; **d. juvénile** juvenile delinquent; **d. primaire** first offender; **d. sexuel** sex offender

déliquescence [delikesɑ̃s] NF 1 *Chimie* deliquescence 2 *Fig Péj (de civilisation, mœurs)* decay, decline; *(de relation, mariage etc)* deterioration; *(d'une personne)* decline; **tomber en d.** *(d'une civilisation)* to fall into decay *or* decline; *(d'un mariage)* to fall apart; *(d'une personne)* to decline

déliquescent [delikesɑ̃] ADJ 1 *Chimie* deliquescent 2 *Fig Péj (civilisation)* in decay, decaying; *(personne)* declining; *(relation, mariage)* deteriorating; **mœurs** *ou* **habitudes déliquescentes** decadent ways

délirant [delirɑ̃] ADJ *Méd (malade, fièvre etc)* delirious; *Fam* **c'est d. de lui demander de tout payer!** it's madness to ask him to pay for everything!; **joie délirante** frenzied joy; **avoir une imagination délirante** to have a wild imagination; **une atmosphère complètement délirante** an atmosphere of total delirium

délire [delir] NM **1** *Méd* delirium; **d. alcoolique** alcoholic dementia; **d. de persécution** persecution mania; **d. de grandeur** delusions of grandeur; **d. hallucinatoire** hallucination; **être victime de délires hallucinatoires** to hallucinate; **d. collectif** mass hysteria; **avoir le d.** to be delirious; **crise** *ou* **accès de d.** attack of delirium; *Fig* **c'est du d.!** it's madness!; **c'est du d. de croire qu'il va divorcer pour toi** you must be off your head if you think that he's going to get a divorce for your sake **2** *(frénésie)* frenzy; **foule en d.** delirious *or* ecstatic crowd; **son amour pour elle va jusqu'au d.** he is madly in love with her; **sa jalousie va jusqu'au d.** he is insanely jealous; *Fam* **cette soirée, c'est le d.!** this is a wild party!; **quand il arrive sur scène, c'est un vrai** *ou* **du d.** the audience goes wild when he appears on stage; *Fam* **on s'est tapé un super d.!** we had a wicked *or* awesome *or Br* mental time!

délirer [delire] VI **1** *(de malade)* to be delirious; *(dire n'importe quoi)* to rave; **d. de joie** to be delirious, to be mad with joy; **tu délires!** you're raving! **2** *Fam (s'amuser)* to have a great time, *Am* to have a blast

delirium tremens [delirjɔmtremɛ̃s] NM delirium tremens, *Fam* DTs; **avoir le d.** to have delirium tremens *or Fam* the DTs

délit [deli] NM *Jur* offence, misdemeanour, *Am* misdemeanor; **en flagrant d.** red-handed; *Jur* in flagrante delicto; **prendre qn en flagrant d.** to catch sb red-handed *or* in the act; **pris en flagrant d. d'adultère** caught in flagrante delicto; *Fig* **pris en flagrant d. de gourmandise/de mensonge/d'ignorance** caught being greedy/lying/showing one's ignorance; **d. politique** political offence; *Fam* **ils l'ont arrêté pour d. de sale gueule** they arrested him because they didn't like the look of him

▸▸**d. d'abus de biens sociaux** misappropriation of corporate funds; **d. civil** tort; **d. de fuite** failure to report an accident; **d. d'initié** insider dealing *or* trading; **d. d'opinion** failure to toe the party line; **d. de presse** violation of the press laws

déliter (se) [sədelite] VPR *(se désintégrer)*, *Fig* to fall apart

délivrance [delivrɑ̃s] NF **1** *(libération)* rescue, release **2** *(soulagement)* relief; **c'est fini! quelle d.!** it's over! what a relief!; **son départ fut une vraie d.** it was a real relief when he left, his departure came as a real relief; **ses aveux lui furent une d.** it was a relief for him to confess; **il attendait la mort comme une d.** he was waiting for death as a release **3** *(de marchandises)* delivery, handing over; *(de certificat, tickets)* issue **4** *(accouchement)* delivery; *(expulsion du placenta)* delivery of the afterbirth; **la d. a été difficile** it was a difficult delivery

délivrer [delivre] VT **1** *(libérer) (captif, otage etc)* to rescue; *(détenu)* to release, to set free; *Fig* to set free (**de** from); **d. qn de ses liens** to free sb from his/her bonds **2** *(soulager)* **d. qn d'un secret trop lourd** to share the burden of a secret with sb; **tu me délivres d'un grand poids** you've taken a weight off my shoulders **3** *(remettre) (marchandises etc)* to deliver, to hand over; *(certificat, ticket)* to issue; *(licence)* to grant **4** *Obst* **d. une femme** *(du placenta)* to deliver a woman of the afterbirth; *(l'accoucher)* to deliver a woman (of a child)

VPR **se délivrer** *(se libérer)* to free oneself; *Fig* **se d. de qn/qch** to get rid of sb/sth; **se d. de ses soucis** to shed one's worries

délocalisation [delɔkalizasjɔ̃] NF *Admin*

(d'entreprise, de production) relocation; *(de capitaux)* expatriation

délocaliser [delɔkalize] VT *Admin* to relocate, to shift; *(capitaux)* to expatriate

VPR **se délocaliser** *(d'une entreprise, d'une usine)* to relocate

délogement [delɔʒmɑ̃] NM *(de locataire)* eviction; *(dans un hôtel)* room change

déloger [delɔʒe] *(conj like* **loger***)* VI **1** to leave (home); **délogez de là!** get out of here! **2** *Belg (découcher)* to sleep out; **il a délogé hier** he didn't come home last night

VT to drive out; *(locataire)* to evict; *(l'ennemi, objet coincé)* to dislodge; **quand il est devant la télé, c'est vraiment difficile de le d.** you just can't shift him when he's in front of the telly

déloquer (se) [sədelɔke] VPR *Fam* to strip off, to get undressed

déloyal, -ale, -aux, -ales [delwajal, -o] ADJ *(ami etc)* disloyal, unfaithful; *(pratique)* unfair; **concurrence déloyale** unfair competition; *Sport* **jeu d.** foul play; *Sport* **coup d.** foul

déloyalement [delwajalmɑ̃] ADV *(agir) (d'un ami)* disloyally; *(d'un concurrent)* unfairly; *(jouer aux cartes)* dishonestly

déloyauté [delwajote] NF *(d'un ami)* disloyalty, treachery; *(d'un concurrent, d'une pratique)* unfairness

Delphes [delf] NFPL Delphi

delta [dɛlta] NM *(lettre grecque)*, *Géog* delta; *Aviat* **aile (en) d.** delta wing

deltaïque [dɛltaik] ADJ *Géog* delta, of a/the delta

deltaplane [dɛltaplan] NM *Sport* hang-glider; **faire du d.** to go hang-gliding

deltoïde [dɛltɔid] ADJ, NM *Anat* deltoid

déluge [delyʒ] NM deluge, flood; *(de pluie)* downpour; *(d'injures)* torrent; *(de larmes)* flood; **elle l'a noyé sous un d. de compliments** she showered *or* overwhelmed him with compliments; *Rel* **le D.** the Flood; **après moi, le d.!** when I'm gone, I don't care what happens!; **cela remonte au d.** it's as old as the hills

déluré [delyre] ADJ *(vif)* sharp, smart; *Péj (provocant)* forward

délurer [delyre] VT *(dégourdir)* **d. qn** to teach sb a thing or two; *Péj* **ses années d'étudiante l'ont un peu trop délurée** she went a bit off the rails when she was a student

VPR **se délurer** *(se dégourdir)* to learn a thing or two; *Péj* to run wild

délustrer [delystre] VT *Tex (étoffe)* to take the shine off

DEM *Anciennement (abrév* **Deutsche Mark***)* DM

démagnétisation [demaɲetizasjɔ̃] NF *Phys* demagnetization

démagnétiser [demaɲetize] VT *Phys* to demagnetize

démago [demago] *Fam* ADJ *(abrév* **démagogique***)* demagogic

N *(abrév* **démagogue***)* demagogue

démagogie [demagɔʒi] NF demagogy, demagoguery

démagogique [demagɔʒik] ADJ demagogic

démagogue [demagɔg] N demagogue

ADJ demagogic, rabble-rousing

démaillage [demɑjaʒ] NM laddering

démailler [demɑje] VT *(tricot)* to unravel; **tes bas sont démaillés** your stockings are laddered, *Am* you have a run in your stockings

VPR **se démailler** *(d'un collant)* to ladder, *Am* to run; **le filet se démaille** the net is torn

démailloter [demɑjɔte] VT **d. un bébé** to take the swaddling clothes off a baby

demain [dəmɛ̃] ADV tomorrow; **d. soir** to-

morrow evening; **d. en huit** a week tomorrow, *Br* tomorrow week; **à d.!** see you tomorrow!; **remettre un travail à d.** to postpone *or* put off a job till tomorrow; **d'ici d.** between now and tomorrow; **réponds-moi d'ici d.** give me an answer by tomorrow; **le journal de d.** tomorrow's paper; *Fam* **ce n'est pas pour d., ce n'est pas d. la veille** that won't happen for a long time yet; **d. il fera jour** tomorrow is another day; *Fam* **et d. on rase gratis!** pigs might fly!; *Fig* **les parents de d.** tomorrow's parents

NM tomorrow; **tu as d. pour réfléchir** you've got tomorrow to think about it; *Fig* **des demains peu heureux** a not-too-rosy future

démanché [demɑ̃ʃe] ADJ *(outil etc)* without a handle; *(épaule etc)* dislocated

NM *Mus* shift

démanchement [demɑ̃ʃmɑ̃] NM *(d'un outil etc)* removal of the handle; *(de l'épaule etc)* dislocation

démancher [demɑ̃ʃe] VT *(outil etc)* to remove the handle of

VI *Mus* to shift

VPR **se démancher 1** *(d'un outil etc)* to lose its handle **2** *(se déboîter)* **se d. l'épaule/le bras** to put one's shoulder/arm out, to dislocate one's shoulder/arm; *Fam* **se d. pour obtenir qch** to move heaven and earth to get sth

demande [dəmɑ̃d] NF **1** *(requête)* request, application, query (**de** for); *Cartes* bid; **faire la d. de qch** to ask for sth; **faire qch à** *ou* **sur la d. de qn** to do sth at sb's request; **faire qch à la** *ou* **sur d.** to do sth on request; **d. (en mariage)** proposal (of marriage); *Vieilli* offer of marriage; **faire sa d. (en mariage)** to propose; **à la d. générale** by popular request; **il faut remplir une d.** you must fill in an application form; **adresser une d.** to apply in writing; **d. d'intervention** request for action; **d. de renseignements** enquiry, request for information

2 *Écon* demand; **l'offre et la d.** supply and demand; **répondre à la d.** to meet demand; **répondre à la d. en qch** to meet the demand for sth; **la d. est en hausse/en baisse** demand is up/down; **d. des consommateurs** consumer demand; **d. déclinante** declining *or* falling demand; **d. dérivée** derived demand; **d. effective** effective demand; **d. élastique** elastic demand; **d. excédentaire** overdemand; **d. globale** global demand, aggregate demand; **d. indésirable** unwholesome demand; **d. du marché** market demand; **d. prévisionnelle** projected demand; **d. soutenue** full demand; **d. surabondante** overfull demand

3 *Jur* **d. en divorce** divorce petition; **d. de dommages-intérêts** claim for damages; **d. principale** main claim; **d. accessoire** related claim; **d. subsidiaire** subsidiary claim; **d. en renvoi** request for referral to another court

4 *(besoin) (de soins, d'affection)* need; **il est perpétuellement dans un état de d. affective** he's always looking for affection

5 *(question)* question, inquiry, enquiry

▸▸**'demandes d'emploi'** *(rubrique)* 'situations wanted'; **d. d'emploi** job application; *(petite annonce)* 'job wanted' advertisement; **faire une d. d'emploi** to apply for a job; **d. de rançon** ransom demand

> Il faut noter que le nom anglais **demand** est un faux ami. Il signifie **exigence**.

DEMANDER [dəmɑ̃de]

VT to ask **4** ▪ to ask for **1, 5** ▪ to claim **1** ▪ to apply for **1** ▪ to need **2** ▪ to demand **2, 3** ▪ to want **5**		
VI to ask		
VPR to wonder		

VT **1** *(réclamer, vouloir) (une augmentation,*

l'addition, de l'argent, du travail, des preuves etc) to ask for; **d. qch à qn** to ask sb for sth; **d. un renseignement à qn** to ask sb something, to ask sb for information; **d. à qn de faire qch** to ask sb to do sth; **on nous a demandé nos passeports** we were asked for our passports; **d. à qn son aide/sa protection/un conseil** to ask sb for help/protection/advice; **d. à qn son avis** to ask sb's opinion; **d. la permission/l'autorisation** to ask (for) permission (**de faire qch** to do sth); *Mil* **d. une permission** to ask for *or* apply for leave; **d. des dommages et intérêts** to claim damages; **d. le divorce** to apply for a divorce; **puis-je vous d. une faveur ou un service?** can I ask you a favour?; **d. l'ouverture d'une enquête** to call for an inquiry; **d. un rendez-vous** to request a meeting; *(chez le médecin)* to ask for an appointment; **d. audience** to request an audience; **d. la main de qn** to ask for sb's hand (in marriage); **il a fini par la d. en mariage** he eventually proposed (to her); **combien demandez-vous de l'heure?** how much do you charge an hour?; **combien en demande-t-elle?** how much is she asking for it?; **il ne demande que ça** he'd be only too pleased; *Hum* **que demande le peuple?** what more could I/he/*etc* ask (for)?; **je ne demande qu'une seule chose: qu'on me laisse tranquille** all I ask is to be left alone; **je ne demande qu'une seule chose: qu'il fasse beau** all I ask for is good weather; **je ne demande pas mieux que de vous aider** I'll be only too pleased to help you; **il demande qu'on lui rende justice** he wants justice; **d. la parole** to ask to speak; **je demande la parole!** may I speak!

2 *(nécessiter)* to need, to require; **la situation demande le plus grand tact** the situation needs *or* requires *or* calls for tactful handling; **ça demande de gros sacrifices** great sacrifices are called for; **cela demande mûre réflexion** that calls for careful consideration; **le voyage demande trois heures/une semaine** the journey takes three hours/a week; **ce travail demande toute votre attention** the work demands all your attention; **on demande un maçon** builder wanted; **article très demandé** article in great demand

3 *(exiger)* to demand; **d. à qn plus qu'il n'en peut faire** to demand *or* expect from sb more than he can do; **c'est trop me d.** it's too much to ask of me, it's asking too much; **il ne faut pas lui en d. trop** you mustn't expect too much from him; **d. la lune** to ask for the moon; **d. l'impossible** to ask (for) the impossible

4 *(s'enquérir de)* *(prix, cause, raison)* to ask, to enquire; **d. l'heure, d. l'heure qu'il est** to ask the time; **d. son nom à qn** to ask sb his/her name; **je n'ai pas compris ce qu'il m'a demandé** I didn't understand what he asked me; **d. son chemin à qn** to ask sb the way; **il m'a demandé de tes nouvelles** he asked me how you were; *Fam* **je ne t'ai rien demandé!** I didn't ask for your advice *or* opinion!; *Fam Hum* **je ne t'ai pas demandé l'heure qu'il est!** mind your own business!; **je vous (le) demande!, je vous demande un peu!** I ask you!

5 *(appeler)* **on vous demande** you're wanted, somebody wants to see you; **on vous demande au téléphone** there is a call for you; **M. Dubois est demandé au téléphone** Mr Dubois is wanted on the telephone; *(annonce)* telephone for Mr Dubois; **un conseiller en peinture est demandé à la caisse no 3** paint consultant to checkout 3, please; **qui demandez-vous?** who do you want to speak to?; **d. un médecin/un prêtre** to ask for a doctor/priest

vi d. à faire qch to ask (permission) to do sth; **il a demandé à sortir** he asked to leave the room; **je demande à parler** may I speak?,

please let me speak; **d. à manger/boire** to ask for something to eat/drink; **je ne demande qu'à rester ici** I would dearly love to stay here; **les suspects ne demandaient qu'à parler** the suspects were only too willing to speak; **il demande à ce qu'on lui rende son argent** he's asking for *or* he wants his money back; **demande à ce qu'on vienne te chercher** ask someone to come and collect you; **ce vin demande à être bu frais** this wine requires to be drunk chilled; **tu vois, ce n'était pas difficile, il suffisait de d.!** see, it wasn't difficult, you only had to ask!; **il n'y a qu'à d.** you/he/*etc* only have/has to ask; **d. après qn** to ask after *or* for sb

VPR se demander to wonder, to ask oneself; **c'est ce que je me demande** that's what I'd like to know; **c'est à se d. ou on se demande ou on peut se d. s'il ne l'a pas fait exprès** it makes you wonder whether he didn't do it on purpose; **je me demande bien pourquoi/ce que/où …** I really can't think why/what/where …; **des choses comme ça, cela ne se demande pas!** you don't ask that sort of question!

> Il faut noter que le verbe anglais **to demand** est un faux ami. Il signifie **exiger**.

demandeur¹, -deresse [dəmɑ̃dœr, -drɛs] N *Jur* plaintiff; **d. en divorce** petitioner; **d. en appel** appellant

demandeur², -euse [dəmɑ̃dœr, -øz] N **1 d. d'asile** asylum-seeker; **d. d'emploi** job seeker **2** *Com* customer, buyer; **si tu trouves la même robe en solde, je suis demandeuse** if you find the same dress in the sales, I'll take it **3** *Tél* **d. (de la communication)** caller

démangeaison [demɑ̃ʒɛzɔ̃] NF itching; **j'ai une d.** I've got an itch, I'm itching; **j'ai des démangeaisons dans les jambes** my legs itch; *Fig Fam* **une d. de faire qch** a longing *or* an itching to do sth

démanger [demɑ̃ʒe] VI *(il démangea(it))* to itch; **l'épaule me démange** my shoulder's itching; *Fig* **la main lui ou le démangeait** he was itching *or* dying for a fight; **ça me démange de lui dire ce que je pense** I'm dying *or* itching to tell him what I think

démantèlement [demɑ̃tɛlmɑ̃] NM *(de fortifications)* demolition, demolishing; *(d'organisation, d'empire)* dismantling, breaking up

démanteler [demɑ̃tle] VT *(je démantèle; je démantèlerai)* *(fortifications etc)* to demolish, to destroy; *(organisation, empire etc)* to dismantle, to break up

démantibuler [demɑ̃tibyle] *Fam* VT *(objet)* to break *or* smash up; **d. une machine** to smash a machine to pieces
VPR se démantibuler to come to pieces

démaquillage [demakijaʒ] NM removal of make-up; **crème pour le d.** cleansing cream, make-up remover

démaquillant [demakijɑ̃] ADJ **lotion/crème démaquillante** cleansing lotion/cream **NM** cleanser

démaquiller [demakije] VT **d. qn** to remove sb's make-up
VPR se démaquiller to remove one's make-up; **se d. les yeux** to remove one's eye make-up

démarcage [demarkaʒ] NM = **démarquage**

démarcatif, -ive [demarkatif, -iv] ADJ **ligne démarcative** line of demarcation

démarcation [demarkasjɔ̃] NF demarcation; **ligne de d.** dividing line, boundary line, demarcation line; *Hist* demarcation line; **c'est sur ce problème que la d. entre les deux partis s'affirme** it is on this problem that the dividing line between the two parties is most evident; **on voit la d. de son fond**

de teint you can see where her foundation stops, *Fam* she's got a tide mark

démarchage [demarʃaʒ] NM *Com (porte-à-porte)* door-to-door selling; *(prospection)* canvassing; **d. à distance** telephone prospecting and selling

démarche [demarʃ] NF **1** *(allure)* gait, step, walk; **d. majestueuse** majestic bearing; **reconnaître qn à sa d.** to recognize sb by his/her walk; **elle avait une d. digne** she moved with dignity **2** *(requête)* step; **faire une d. auprès de qn** to approach sb; **faire les démarches nécessaires pour s'inscrire** to take the necessary steps to enrol; **faire les premières démarches** to take the first steps **3** *Fig (cheminement)* process; **d. intellectuelle** thought process

démarcher [demarʃe] *Com* VI *(faire du porte-à-porte)* to sell door-to-door; **d. pour des calendriers** to sell calendars door-to-door
VT *(prospecter)* *(clients)* to canvass for

démarcheur, -euse [demarʃœr, -øz] N *Com* **1** *(représentant)* door-to-door salesman/saleswoman **2** *(prospecteur)* canvasser; **d. en publicité** advertisement canvasser

démariage [demarjaʒ] NM *(en horticulture)* thinning out

démarketing [demarketiŋ] NM demarketing

démarquage [demarkaʒ] NM **1** *(de linge, de plat)* removal of the (identification) mark(s) **2** *(plagiat)* copying, plagiarizing **3** *Sport* breaking free from one's opponent

démarque [demark] NF *Com* marking down, markdown; **la d. inconnue** shrinkage

démarqué [demarke] ADJ **1** *Com* marked down **2** *Sport* unmarked

démarquer [demarke] VT **1** *(linge, plat etc)* to remove the identification mark(s) from **2** *Com (marchandises)* to mark down **3** *(livre)* to plagiarize **4** *Sport (partenaire)* to free from a marker
VPR se démarquer *Sport* to break free from one's opponent; *Fig* **un élève qui se démarque des autres** a pupil who stands out *or* apart from the others

démarrage [demaraʒ] NM **1** *(de moteur etc)* start, starting; *(de voiture etc)* moving off; *Sport (soudain)* spurt; *(d'entreprise)* start-up; *Sport* **faire un d.** to put on a spurt; *Ordinat* **d. automatique** autostart; *Ordinat* **d. à chaud/froid** warm/cold start; **faire un d. en trombe** to shoot off; *Fig* **d. d'une affaire/d'une campagne publicitaire** start of a business/publicity campaign **2** *(d'un navire)* casting off ▸▸ *Aut* **d. à l'aide de câbles** jump start; **d. en côte** hill start; **d. à l'embrayage** clutch start; **d. poussé** bump start

démarrer [demare] VI **1** *(d'un train, d'une voiture etc)* to start, to move off; *(d'un conducteur)* to drive away or off; *(d'un coureur)* to put on a spurt; **d. en trombe** *(en voiture)* to shoot off; **d. à froid** to start from cold; *Fig* **son affaire commence à d.** his business is beginning to take off; **j'ai toujours du mal à d. le matin** *(en voiture)* I always have trouble starting in the morning; *Fam Fig* I always have trouble getting started *or* getting going in the morning **2** *(commencer)* to start; **bien/mal d.** to get off to a good/bad start **3** *(de navire)* to cast off
VT 1 *(voiture, travaux etc)* to start; *Fig (affaire, campagne)* to start (up); *(caméras)* to roll; *Ordinat* to boot (up), to start up; **d. le moteur** *(sens mécanique)* to crank the engine; **d. en remorque** to tow-start; **d. à l'aide des câbles** to jump start **2** *(navire)* to unmoor, to cast off

démarreur [demarœr] NM *Aut* starter (motor); *Ordinat* boot program

démasquer [demaske] VT *(enlever le masque de)* to unmask; *(imposteur, espion)* to unmask, to expose; *(complot, mensonge)* to expose; *Fig* **d. ses batteries** to show one's hand
VPR **se démasquer** to take off one's mask; *Fig* to drop the mask

démâtage [demataʒ] NM dismasting

démâter [demate] VI **le voilier a démâté** the yacht lost its mast
VT to dismast

démêlage [demelaʒ] NM untangling

démêlant [demelɑ̃] ADJ **produit d., crème démêlante** conditioner
NM conditioner

démêlé [demele] NM argument; **avoir un d. avec un collègue** to have an argument or *Fml* altercation with a colleague; **démêlés** *(unpleasant)* dealings; **avoir des démêlés avec la justice** to be in trouble with the law; **il a eu des démêlés avec la police** he's had a few run-ins with the police

démêler [demele] VT *(fil, soie etc)* to disentangle, to unravel; *(cheveux)* to untangle, to comb out; *Fig* **d. un problème/un malentendu** to sort out a problem/clear up a misunderstanding; *Fig* **avoir qch à d. avec qn** to have sth to clear up or sort out with sb; *Fig* **on va d. ça ensemble** we'll sort it out together
VPR **se démêler se d. de** to extricate oneself from

démêloir [demelwar] NM large-toothed comb

démembrement [demɑ̃brəmɑ̃] NM **1** *(d'un empire etc)* breaking up, dismemberment; *(d'un poulet etc)* jointing; *(d'une propriété, d'un domaine)* dividing up, division **2** *Bourse* stripping

démembrer [demɑ̃bre] VT *(empire)* to break up, to dismember; *(poulet etc)* to cut up, to joint; *(royaume, domaine)* to divide (up)

déménagement [demenaʒmɑ̃] NM *(action)* moving (house); *(meubles)* furniture, things; **c'est pour quand le d.?** when are you/we/*etc* moving?; **entreprise de d.** removal firm; **camion de d.** furniture or removal van; **frais de d.** moving expenses or costs; **votre d. est arrivé** your furniture has arrived; **le d. de ta chambre dans la pièce du fond va prendre du temps** it's going to take some time to move you or your things into the back room; **le d. de l'entreprise ne s'est pas fait sans mal** the company's move did not go smoothly; **cette entreprise fait une moyenne de six déménagements par semaine** the company does an average of six removals a week; **en sept ans, j'ai fait sept déménagements** I've moved seven times in seven years; **tu veux bien m'aider à faire mon d.?** will you help me move (house)?

déménager [demenaʒe] (je déménageai(s); n. déménageons) VT to move; **qui est-ce qui vous déménage?** who's moving you?, which removal company are you using?; **d. ses meubles** to move house
VI **1** to move; *(d'une entreprise)* to move, to relocate; **où déménage-t-il?** where's he moving to?; *Fam* **d. à la cloche de bois** to do a moonlight flit; *Fig Fam* **il déménage!** he's off his head!, he's round the bend! *Fam* **allez! déménagez!** scram! get out of here! **2** *Fig Fam* **moutarde qui déménage** mustard that takes the top of your head off; **musique qui déménage** powerful music

déménageur [demenaʒœr] NM removal man, furniture remover or *Am* mover

démence [demɑ̃s] NF *(folie)* insanity, madness, lunacy; *Méd* dementia; *Méd* **d. précoce** dementia praecox, *Fam* premature senility; *Fam* **c'est de la pure d.!** it's sheer madness!, it's insane!

démener (se) [sədemne] VPR *(conj like* **mener***)* **1** *(s'agiter)* to thrash about, to throw oneself about, to struggle; **se d. comme un beau diable** *(pour échapper)* to struggle or fight like a madman; *(en dansant)* to thrash around; **se d. comme un beau diable pour faire qch** to break one's back to do or doing sth **2** *(se dépenser)* to exert oneself, to make a great effort; **ils se sont tellement démenés que ...** they exerted themselves to such an extent that ...; **ils avaient beau se d., l'incendie ne s'éteignait pas** despite their tremendous efforts, the fire continued to burn

dément, -ente [demɑ̃, -ɑ̃t] ADJ *(fou)* mad, insane; *Méd* demented; *Fam* **quel monde! c'est d.!** what a crowd! it's unbelievable!; *Fam* **ce concert était d.** it was a great or terrific concert
N mad or insane person, lunatic; *Méd* demented person

démenti [demɑ̃ti] NM *(flat)* denial, contradiction; *Journ* disclaimer; **donner ou opposer un d. formel à une accusation** to deny an accusation; **publier ou faire paraître un d.** to issue a denial; *Journ* to publish a disclaimer; **ses actions donnent un d. à ses paroles** his actions belie his words; **ces rumeurs restent sans d.** the rumours have not been denied

démentiel, -ielle [demɑ̃sjɛl] ADJ mad, insane; *Fam (idée)* mad, insane, crazy; *Fam (tenue, prix)* wild, wicked

démentir [demɑ̃tir] *(conj like* **mentir***)* VT to deny; **je démens absolument avoir passé la nuit là-bas** I flatly deny spending the night there; **leur attitude dément complètement leur réputation** their attitude totally belies their reputation; *Litt* **il a démenti nos espérances** he has not come up to our expectations, he has disappointed us
VPR **se démentir** *(cesser)* **politesse qui ne se dément jamais** unfailing courtesy; **il a fait preuve d'une attention qui ne s'est jamais démentie** he showed unfailing attention

démerdard, -arde [demɛrdar, -ard] *Arg* ADJ resourceful; **il n'est vraiment pas d.** he's absolutely hopeless or useless
N resourceful person; **c'est un d.** he's pretty sharp, he's a smart cookie

démerde [demɛrd] NF *Fam* **dans ce pays, tout marche à la d.** you have to use your wits to get anything done in this country

démerder (se) [sədemɛrde] VPR *très Fam* **1** *(s'en sortir)* to get out of the shit; **tu peux te d.?** can you cope or manage?
2 *(se débrouiller)* to cope, to manage, to get by; **elle est assez grande pour se d. seule** she's old enough to take care of or look after herself; **tu ne voulais pas que je t'aide, maintenant démerde-toi!** you didn't want me to help you, so you can manage on your own now!; **elle se démerde pas mal en cuisine/tennis** she's not a bad cook/tennis player; **elle se démerde pas mal en anglais** she gets by quite well in English; **la prochaine fois, tu te démerderas mieux et tu auras un billet à meilleur prix** if you manage things better next time, you'll get a cheaper ticket; **se d. pour obtenir qch** to wangle sth; **je sais pas comment il se démerde, il casse tout ce qu'il touche** I don't know how he does it, he breaks everything he lays his hands on
3 *(se dépêcher)* to get a move on, *Am* to get it in gear

démerdeur, -euse [demɛrdœr, -øz] ADJ, N *Arg* = **démerdard**

démérite [demerit] NM *Litt* **je ne vois pas où est mon d.** I don't see how I'm at fault; **son d. vient du fait qu'elle n'a pas fait ce qu'elle avait promis** she's at fault because she didn't do what she promised; **faire à qn un d. de qch** to reproach sb for sth

démériter [demerite] VI to be at fault; **je vois pas en quoi il a démérité** I don't see how he is at fault; **d. auprès de qn** to come down in sb's estimation

démesure [deməzyr] NF disproportion, excessiveness

démesuré [deməzyre] ADJ *(mains, jardin)* huge, enormous; *(orgueil)* excessive, *Fml* inordinate; *(ambition)* excessive, *Fml* inordinate, unbounded; **il est d'une taille démesurée** he's enormously tall; **il a des mains démesurées par rapport à ses bras** his hands are out of proportion to his arms

démesurément [deməzyremɑ̃] ADV *(haut)* enormously, *Fml* inordinately; *(augmenter ses prix)* excessively

démettre¹ [demɛtr] *(conj like* **mettre***)* VT *(articulation)* to dislocate
VPR **se démettre se d. l'épaule/le genou** to dislocate one's shoulder/knee, to put one's shoulder/knee out

démettre² VT **1** *(renvoyer)* **d. qn de ses fonctions** to deprive sb of (his/her) office, to remove sb from office or from his/her post **2** *Jur (débouter)* **d. qn de son appel** to dismiss sb's appeal
VPR **se démettre** *(démissionner)* to resign; **se d. de ses fonctions** to resign office, to resign from one's job

demeurant (au) [odəmœrɑ̃] ADV **il n'est pas très vif, mais bien gentil au d.** he's not very bright, but he's very nice all the same or for all that; **je ne vous donne pas mon avis, au d., je ne suis pas concerné** I'm not telling you what I think, after all, it's none of my business

demeure [dəmœr] NF **1** *(résidence)* (place of) residence; **une belle d.** a beautiful home, *Fml, Litt* a fine residence; **dernière d.** last resting place **2** **il est ici à d.** he's here for good or to stay or permanently; *Jur* **meuble à d.** fixture **3** *Jur* **mettre qn en d. de payer** to give sb notice to pay; **mise en d.** formal notice, summons; *Fig* **je vous mets en d. de le faire immédiatement** I'm warning you that I want it done immediately **4** **il y a péril en la d.** you/I/he/*etc* must act immediately; **il n'y a pas péril en la d.** there's no great rush

demeuré, -ée [dəmœre] ADJ mentally retarded, *Péj* halfwitted; *Fam* **il est complètement d., ce mec** the guy's a complete halfwit
N mentally retarded person, *Péj* halfwit

demeurer [dəmœre] VI **1** *(conj with* **être***)* *(rester)* to remain; **je demeure convaincu que ...** I remain convinced that ...; **d. fidèle à qn** to stay faithful to sb; **l'affaire n'en demeurera pas là** the matter won't rest there; **demeurons-en là** let's leave it at that; **elle ne pouvait pas d. en place** she couldn't keep still; **elle demeurait assise à nous écouter** she sat listening to us; *Litt* **je suis demeuré des heures à t'attendre** I waited hours for you; *Litt* **il est demeuré des mois sans nouvelles** he had no news for months; *Fml* **l'affaire lui est demeurée de sa famille** he inherited the business from his family **2** *(conj with* **avoir***)* *(habiter)* to live, *Fml* to reside; **d. à la campagne** to live in the country; **il demeure rue de Rivoli** he lives in or *Am* on the rue de Rivoli

demi, -ie [dəmi] ADJ **1** *(après un nom)* half; **deux heures et demie** *(durée)* two and a half hours; *(moment)* half past two; **un litre/kilo/centimètre et d.** a litre/kilo/centimetre and a half; **il gagne trois fois et demie ce que je gagne** he earns three and a half times as much as I do **2** *(avant un nom ou un adjectif)* half; **un d.-congé** a half-holiday; **une d.-cuillère de sucre** half a teaspoon of sugar, a half-teaspoon of sugar; **d.-cuit** half cooked
NM **1** *(moitié)* half; **deux plus un d.** two plus a half **2** *(bière)* **un d.** ≃ half a pint, a half **3** *Ftbl*

les demis the halfbacks; *Rugby* **d. de mêlée** scrum half; **d. d'ouverture** stand-off (half), fly half **4** *Suisse (vin)* = half a litre of wine
  NF demie half hour; **il est la demie** it's half past; **à la demie** at half past
  ADV half; **d. plein** full full; **à d.** half; **à d. mort** half dead; **à d. transparent** semi-transparent; **faire les choses à d.** to do things by halves; **croire qn à d.** to half believe sb; **ouvre la fenêtre à d.** open the window half way
  NOTE *in the following compounds, unless otherwise stated, demi is inv and the second component takes the plural*

demi-arbre NM half-shaft

demiard [dəmjar] NM *Can* half pint

demi-arrière NM *Ftbl* halfback

demi-bas NM knee-length sock; *(pour femmes)* popsock

demi-botte NF half boot

demi-bouteille NF half bottle

demi-canton [dəmikɑ̃tɔ̃] NM *Suisse* = state of the Swiss confederation which is one half of a divided canton

demi-centre NM *Ftbl* centre half

demi-cercle NM semicircle, half-circle; **en d.** in a semicircle

demi-circulaire ADJ semicircular

demi-clef NF half hitch

demi-deuil NM half mourning

demi-dieu NM demigod

demi-douzaine NF half dozen; **une d. d'œufs** half a dozen eggs, a half-dozen eggs; **une d. de fois** half a dozen times

demi-droite NF *Géom* semi-infinite line, half-line

demi-écrémé ADJ semi-skimmed

demi-fin ADJ **1** *(petits pois, haricots etc)* medium **2** *(or)* twelve-carat
  NM twelve-carat gold; **bracelet en d.** twelve-carat bracelet

demi-finale NF *Sport* semifinal

demi-finaliste N *Sport* semifinalist

demi-fond NM INV *Sport* **(course de) d.** middle distance race

demi-frère NM half-brother

demi-gros NM retail wholesale; **(commerce de) d.** cash and carry

demi-grossiste N cash-and-carry merchant

demi-heure [dəmijœr] NF **une d.** half an hour; **deux demi-heures** two half-hours; **de d. en d., toutes les demi-heures** every half-hour

demi-jour NM half-light; *(crépuscule)* twi-light, dusk

demi-journée NF half a day; *(de travail, de congé)* half day; **faire des demi-journées** to work half days; **j'ai pris ma d.** I took a half day

démilitarisation [demilitarizasjɔ̃] NF de-militarization

démilitariser [demilitarize] VT to de-militarize

demi-litre NM half litre *or Am* liter; **un d. de vin** half a litre *or* a half litre of wine

demi-longueur NF *Sport* **une d.** half a length, a half-length

demi-lune NF half-moon; *(fortification)* demi-lune
  ADJ INV semicircular

demi-mal, *pl* **demi-maux** NM **il n'y a que** *ou* **ce n'est que d.** it could have been worse

demi-mesure NF **1** *(compromis)* half measure; **avec elle, il n'y a jamais de d.** there are never any half measures with her **2** *(pour chaussures etc)* half-size

demi-mondain, -aine ADJ belonging to the demi-monde *or* fringes of society
  NF **demi-mondaine** demi-mondaine

demi-monde NM demi-monde, fringes of society

demi-mort ADJ half dead

demi-mot (à) [ad(ə)mimo] ADV **comprendre à d.** to (know how to) take a hint; **il a compris à d.** he took the hint; **nous nous comprenons à d.** we don't have to spell everything out (to each other)

déminage [deminaʒ] NM mine clearance; *Naut* minesweeping

déminer [demine] VT to clear of mines

déminéralisation [demineralizasjɔ̃] NF demineralization

déminéraliser [demineralize] VT to demineralize
  VPR **se déminéraliser** to become demineralized

démineur [deminœr] NM *(personne)* bomb disposal expert; *(navire)* minesweeper

demi-pause NF *Mus* minim rest, *Am* half-note rest

demi-pension NF *(à l'hôtel)* half board, *Am* American plan; **sept jours en d.** seven days' half board; *Scol* **mon fils est en d.** my son is a day boarder

demi-pensionnaire N *Scol* day boarder

demi-place NF *(en voyage)* half-fare; *(au théâtre etc)* half-price ticket

demi-pointe NF *(position)* demi-point; **(chausson de) d.** demi-point shoe

demi-portion NF *Fam Péj* weed; **eh toi, la d., viens ici!** come here, titch!

demi-produit NM *Écon* semi-finished product

demi-quart NM **1** *(de compas)* half point **2** *(mesure)* ≃ two ounces

demi-queue ADJ, NM **(piano) d.** baby grand (piano)

demi-reliure NF quarter-binding; **d. à (petits) coins** half-binding

démis [demi] ADJ *(épaule)* dislocated

demi-saison NF between season, mid season; **vêtements (de) d.** spring/autumn clothes

demi-salaire NM half-pay

demi-sang NM INV halfbred (horse)

demi-sel ADJ INV *(beurre etc)* slightly salted
  NM INV **1** *(fromage)* (slightly salted) cream cheese **2** *Fam (souteneur)* small-time pimp; *(voyou)* small time gangster

demi-sœur NF half-sister

demi-solde NF *Mil* half-pay; **en d.** on half-pay
  NM INV half-pay officer

demi-sommeil NM drowsiness, somnolence

demi-soupir NM *Mus* quaver rest, *Am* eighth-note rest

démission [demisjɔ̃] NF **1** *(au travail)* resignation; **donner sa d.** to hand in *or Fml* tender one's resignation, to resign; *Fig* to give up **2** *Fig (abandon)* renunciation; **la d. du père** the father's abdication of his responsibilities

démissionnaire [demisjɔnɛr] ADJ who has resigned; *Fig* **père/mère d.** father/mother who has abdicated his/her responsibilities

démissionner [demisjɔne] VI to resign (**de** from); *Fig* **je démissionne!** I give up!
  VT *Fam* to sack

demi-tarif NM half price; **billet d.** *(transports)* half-fare (ticket); *Théâtre, Cin* half-price ticket

demi-teinte NF *Beaux-Arts, Phot* half-tone; **en d.** half-tone; *Fig* **il ne fait pas dans la d.** there are no half measures with him

demi-ton NM *Mus* semitone

demi-tonneau NM *Aviat* half roll

demi-tour NM half-turn; *Mil* about-turn; *Aut* U-turn; *Aut* **en trois temps** three-point turn; **un d. de clé** a half-turn of the key; **faire d.** to turn and go back

démiurge [demjyrʒ] NM demiurge

demi-voix (à) [ad(ə)mivwa] ADV in an undertone, under one's breath

demi-volée NF *Tennis* half volley

démo [demo] NF *(abrév* **démonstration**) demo

démobilisateur, -trice [demɔbilizatœr, -tris] ADJ *(paroles, actions)* demotivating, discouraging

démobilisation [demɔbilizasjɔ̃] NF **1** *(de troupes)* demobilization, *Fam* demob **2** *(désintérêt)* apathy, lack of interest

démobiliser [demɔbilize] VT **1** *(troupes)* to demobilize, *Fam* to demob **2** *(décourager)* to demotivate, to discourage; **cette campagne de presse a beaucoup contribué à d. les militants** the press campaign had a very demotivating effect on the militants
  VPR **se démobiliser** to become apathetic *or* discouraged

démocrate [demɔkrat] ADJ democratic
  N democrat

démocrate-chrétien, -ienne, *pl* **démocrates-chrétiens, -iennes** ADJ, N *Pol* Christian Democrat

démocratie [demɔkrasi] NF democracy; *Fam* **on est en d., après tout!** it's a free country!; **d. directe** direct democracy; **d. participative** participatory democracy; **d. populaire** people's democracy; **d. représentative** representative democracy

démocratique [demɔkratik] ADJ democratic

démocratiquement [demɔkratikmɑ̃] ADV democratically

démocratisation [demɔkratizasjɔ̃] NF democratization

démocratiser [demɔkratize] VT to democratize
  VPR **se démocratiser** to become (more) democratic

démodé [demɔde] ADJ *(personne, manières)* old-fashioned; *(vêtement)* old-fashioned, out-of-date, out-of-fashion; *(équipement)* old-fashioned, out-of-date; *(idée, théorie)* old-fashioned, out-of-date, outmoded

démoder (se) [sədemɔde] VPR *(de vêtements etc)* to go out of fashion, to become old-fashioned

demodex [demɔdɛks] NM demodex, follicle mite

démodulation [demɔdylasjɔ̃] NF demodulation

démographe [demɔɡraf] N demographer

démographie [demɔɡrafi] NF demography

démographique [demɔɡrafik] ADJ demographic; **statistiques démographiques** demographics; **poussée d.** population growth

demoiselle [dəmwazɛl] NF **1** *(femme célibataire)* single *or* unmarried woman; *Vieilli, Admin* spinster; **les demoiselles Dupin** the Misses Dupin; **c'est une vieille d.** she never married **2** *(jeune fille, employée)* young lady; **les demoiselles du téléphone** the young ladies on the switchboard **3** *(insecte)* dragonfly; **d. (de Numidie)** demoiselle (crane), Numidian crane **4** *Tech* paving beetle
  ▸▸**d. de compagnie** lady's companion; **d. d'honneur** *(d'une souveraine)* lady-in-waiting, *Vieilli* maid of honour; *(d'une mariée)* bridesmaid

démolir [demɔlir] VT **1** *(maison, immeuble, quartier etc)* to demolish, to pull down; *(navire)* to break up; *(voiture, jouet etc)* to demolish, to wreck, to smash up; **d. une porte à coups de pied** to kick a door down

2 *Fig (argument, théorie, adversaire, concurrent etc)* to demolish; *(réputation)* to ruin; *(gouvernement, autorité etc)* to undermine; *(auteur, cinéaste, roman, film)* to criticize severely, *Fam* to slate

3 *Fam (battre)* to beat up, to bash about; *(fatiguer)* to tire; **je vais lui d. le portrait!** I'll smash his face in!; **il s'est fait d.** he got beaten up; **cette mauvaise grippe m'a démoli** that bad bout of flu laid me low *or* put me flat on my back; **tout ce travail l'a démolie** she's exhausted *or* shattered after all that work; **d. le foie de qn** *(de l'alcool)* to play havoc with *or* ruin sb's liver; **les piments m'ont démoli l'estomac** those chillis are playing havoc *or Fam* merry hell with my stomach

démolissage [demɔlisaʒ] NM *(d'un auteur etc)* severe criticism, *Fam* slating; *(d'une théorie, d'un argument)* demolition

démolisseur, -euse [demɔlisœr, -øz] N **1** *(de bâtiments)* demolition contractor; *(de bateaux)* shipbreaker **2** *Fig (d'un argument etc)* demolisher, destroyer

démolition [demɔlisjɔ̃] NF **1** *(d'une structure)* demolition, pulling down; **chantier de d.** demolition yard **2** *Fig (d'une théorie)* demolition **3 démolitions** *(matériaux)* debris, rubble

démon [demɔ̃] NM **1** demon, devil, fiend; **le d.** *(Satan)* the Devil; **cette femme est un d.** that woman's a (she-)devil; **cet enfant est un petit d.** that child is a little devil; **le d. de la jalousie** the demon of jealousy, the greeneyed monster; **d. de midi** *(d'un homme)* male menopause, midlife crisis; *(d'une femme)* midlife crisis **2** *(génie, esprit etc)* (good/evil) genius; *Myth* daemon **3** *Can* **être en d.** to be furious, to be mad

démonétisation [demɔnetizasjɔ̃] NF *Fin (d'argent)* demonetization, withdrawal from circulation **2** *Fig (d'une personne)* discrediting; **sa d. au sein de l'entreprise a été rapide** he quickly became discredited throughout the company; **pour accélérer sa d.** to speed up the process of discrediting him

démonétiser [demɔnetize] VT **1** *Fin* to demonetize, to withdraw from circulation **2** *Fig (personne)* to discredit

démoniaque [demɔnjak] ADJ demonic, possessed by the devil; *Fig (personne, rire)* fiendish

   N person possessed by the devil

démonstrateur, -trice [demɔ̃stratœr, -tris] N demonstrator

démonstratif, -ive [demɔ̃stratif, -iv] ADJ **1** *(convaincant)* (logically) conclusive **2** *(personne)* demonstrative; **peu d.** undemonstrative **3** *Gram* demonstrative

   NM *Gram* demonstrative SEE GRAMMAR A30–1; B14–15

démonstration [demɔ̃strasjɔ̃] NF **1** *(preuve)* *(de théorème etc)* demonstration, proof; **d. par l'absurde** reductio ad absurdum; **faire la d. de qch** to demonstrate *or* prove sth

   2 *Com (d'article)* demonstration; **je ne peux pas vous vendre cet appareil, il est en d.** I can't sell you this appliance, it's a demonstration model; **d. sur le lieu de vente** in-store demonstration; *Boxe* **assaut de d.** sparring match; *Mus* **cassette de d.** demo (tape); **appareil de d.** demonstration model; **est-ce que vous pouvez me faire la d. de cette machine à laver?** could you give me a demonstration of this washing machine?

   3 *(manifestation)* *(de tendresse, joie etc)* demonstration; **faire de grandes démonstrations d'amitié** to make a great show of friendship; *Mil* **d. de force** display *or* show of force; **d. navale** naval display

démontable [demɔ̃tabl] ADJ *(machine, armoire etc)* that can be dismantled

démontage [demɔ̃taʒ] NM dismantling, taking to pieces, taking apart

démonté [demɔ̃te] ADJ **1** *(cavalier)* thrown; *Fig (déconcerté)* disconcerted, *Fam* thrown; *(troublé)* upset **2** *(mécanisme etc)* dismantled, taken to pieces, taken apart **3** *(mer)* stormy, raging

démonte-pneu, pl **démonte-pneus** [demɔ̃tpnø] NM tyre *or Am* tire lever

démonter [demɔ̃te] VT **1** *(appareil, moteur, armoire etc)* to dismantle, to take to pieces, to take apart; *(tente)* to dismantle, to take down; *(porte)* to remove from its hinges; *(pneu)* to remove; *(décor)* to strike

   2 *(cavalier)* to throw (off), to unseat

   3 *(déconcerter)* to disconcert, *Fam* to throw; *(troubler)* to upset; **la nouvelle m'a démonté** I was greatly upset *or* put out by the news; **ça me démonte de le voir dans un tel état** it upsets me to see him in such a state; **elle est complètement démontée depuis qu'elle sait qu'il va partir** she's been in a dreadful state since she found out that he was leaving; **se laisser d.** to get upset *or* flustered, to be thrown

   4 *Can (décourager)* to discourage

   VPR **se démonter 1** *(d'un mécanisme)* to come apart, to dismantle

   2 *Fam* **elle ne se démonte pas pour si peu** she's not so easily put out *or* thrown

démontrable [demɔ̃trabl] ADJ demonstrable, provable

démontrer [demɔ̃tre] VT *(théorème, vérité)* to demonstrate; **d. qu'il est nécessaire de faire qch** to show *or* demonstrate *or* prove that it is necessary to do sth; *Fam* **d. qch par A + B** to prove sth conclusively

démoralisant [demɔralizɑ̃] ADJ demoralizing, disheartening

démoralisateur, -trice [demɔralizatœr, -tris] ADJ demoralizing, disheartening

démoralisation [demɔralizasjɔ̃] NF demoralization

démoralisé [demɔralize] ADJ **il était complètement d.** he was completely demoralized *or* downcast

démoraliser [demɔralize] VT to demoralize, to dishearten

   VPR **se démoraliser** to become demoralized, to lose heart

démordre [demɔrdr] VI **ne pas d. de ses opinions** to stand by *or* stick to one's opinions; **elle ne veut pas en d.** she won't give up, she's sticking to her guns; **quand il a une idée, il n'en démord jamais** once he gets an idea in his head, you can't shift him; **ça va être difficile de le faire d. de sa décision** it's going to be difficult to get him to change his mind

démotivation [demɔtivasjɔ̃] NF demotivation; **il ne faut pas laisser s'installer la d. au sein de l'équipe** we mustn't let the team become demotivated

démotiver [demɔtive] VT to demotivate; **ne te laisse pas d. par ses arguments stupides** don't let his stupid arguments put you off

démoulage [demulaʒ] NM *(d'un moulage)* removal from the mould *or Am* mold; *Culin* turning out

démouler [demule] VT *(moulage)* to remove from the mould *or Am* mold; *Culin* to turn out

démoustication [demustikasjɔ̃] NF clearing of mosquitoes; **il faut procéder à la d. de la région** the region must be cleared of mosquitoes

démoustiquer [demustike] VT to clear mosquitoes from

démultiplicateur, -trice [demyltiplikatœr, -tris] *Tech* ADJ *(dispositif)* reducing, reduction

   NM reduction system; **d. de vitesse** motor reduction unit

démultiplication [demyltiplikasjɔ̃] NF *Tech* **1** *(de voiture, machine)* gearing down, (gear) reduction **2** *(de vitesses)* reduction ratio

démultiplier [demyltiplije] VT *Tech (voiture, machine)* to gear down; *(de boîte de vitesses)* to reduce the gear ratio of

démuni [demyni] ADJ penniless; **d. de vêtements/papiers d'identité** without any clothes/identification; **d. d'argent** without any money, penniless; **d. de tout** destitute; **d. d'intérêt/d'intelligence/de talent** devoid of interest/intelligence/talent; *Com* **être d. de qch** to be out of sth, to be sold out of sth

démunir [demynir] VT to deprive

   VPR **se démunir** to leave oneself short; **se d. de qch** to part with sth

démuseler [demyzle] VT **(je démuselle; je démusellerai)** *(chien)* to unmuzzle; *Fig* **d. la presse** to ungag the press

démystifiant [demistifjɑ̃] ADJ *(histoire, étude etc)* which demystifies; **son film sur Mozart est tout à fait d.** his film gives us an insight into the real Mozart

démystificateur, -trice [demistifikatœr, -tris] ADJ *(histoire, étude etc)* which demystifies

   N demystifier

démystification [demistifikasjɔ̃] NF demystification

démystifier [demistifje] VT *(impf, pr subj* n. **démystifiions,** v. **démystifiiez)** to demystify

démythification [demitifikasjɔ̃] NF demythologization; **on assiste à la d. de l'ordinateur** computers are no longer regarded with awe *or* are losing their mystique

démythifier [demitifje] VT to demythologize; *(ordinateur)* to remove the mystique surrounding

dénatalité [denatalite] NF fall in the birth rate

dénationalisation [denasjɔnalizasjɔ̃] NF denationalization

dénationaliser [denasjɔnalize] VT to denationalize

dénatter [denate] VT *(cheveux)* to unplait

dénaturalisation [denatyralizasjɔ̃] NF denaturalization

dénaturaliser [denatyralize] VT to denaturalize

dénaturant [denatyrɑ̃] *Chimie* ADJ denaturing

   NM denaturant, denaturing agent

dénaturation [denatyrasjɔ̃] NF *Chimie* denaturing

dénaturé [denatyre] ADJ **1** *(dépravé)* *(parents)* unnatural; *(goût)* unnatural, perverted **2** *Chimie (transformé)* denatured

dénaturer [denatyre] VT *(mots)* to misrepresent, to distort; *(actions)* to misrepresent; *Chimie (alcool etc)* to denature; **d. les faits** to distort the facts; **d. les paroles de qn** to misrepresent what sb has said

dénazification [denazifikasjɔ̃] NF denazification

dénazifier [denazifje] VT to denazify

dénégateur, -trice [denegatœr, -tris] N denier

dénégation [denegasjɔ̃] NF denial

déneigement [denɛʒmɑ̃] NM snow clearance *or* removal

déneiger [denɛʒe] VT to clear (away) *or* remove snow from

déneigeuse [denɛʒøz] NF *Can* snowblower

dengue [dɛ̃g] NF *Méd* dengue fever

déni [deni] NM *Jur* denial, refusal; **d. de justice** denial of justice

déniaiser [denjeze] **vт 1** (dégourdir) **d. qn** to teach sb a thing or two, to smarten or Fam wise sb up **2** Fam (faire perdre sa virginité à) c'est lui qui l'a déniaisée he was her first **vpr se déniaiser** (se dégourdir) to smarten up, to get smart

dénicher [denife] **vт 1** Fam (trouver) (objet) to find, to unearth; (personne) to find, to track down; **nous avons déniché une maison superbe** we've found a beautiful house; **on a déniché un restaurant très chouette** we've found or Fam sussed out a great restaurant; **elle est allée d. l'homme de sa vie au Canada** she went to Canada to find the man of her dreams **2** (oiseau, œufs) to take out of the nest **3** (animal) to drive out of hiding **vi** (d'un oiseau) to leave the nest

dénicheur, -euse [denifœr, -øz] **n 1** Fig (d'objets) searcher; **d. de curiosités/d'antiquités** curio/antique hunter; **c'est un d. de talents** he's good at spotting talent **2** (d'oiseaux) bird nester

dénicotinisation [denikɔtinizasjɔ̃] **nf** reduction of nicotine

dénicotiniser [denikɔtinize] **vt** to reduce the amount of nicotine in; **du tabac dénicotinisé** low nicotine tobacco

denier [dənje] **nm 1** Antiq denarius; Hist denier; **je l'ai payé de mes deniers** I paid for it with my own money; **payer jusqu'au dernier d.** to pay to the last farthing; **les deniers publics** public money or funds; Cathol **d. du culte** church offering (given privately to parish priest) **2** (de bas) denier; **bas de 30 deniers** 30-denier stockings

dénier [denje] **vт 1** (crime etc) to deny; (responsabilité) to deny, to disclaim **2 d. qch à qn** to refuse or deny sb sth; **d. à qn le droit de faire qch** to deny sb the right to do sth

dénigrant [denigrɑ̃] **adj** disparaging, denigrating

dénigrement [denigrəmɑ̃] **nm** disparagement, denigration

dénigrer [denigre] **vt** to disparage, to denigrate

dénivelé [denivle] **adj** (surface) uneven **nm** difference or variation in level or height

dénivelée [denivle] **nf** difference or variation in level or height

déniveler [denivle] **vt** (conj like **niveler**) to make uneven

dénivellation [denivelasjɔ̃] **nf**, **dénivellement** [denivelmɑ̃] **nm 1** (écart) difference in level or height; **d. d'une route** gradients or ups and downs of a road **2** (action) making uneven

dénombrable [denɔ̃brabl] **adj** countable
VOIR GRAMMAIRE A9–12

dénombrement [denɔ̃brəmɑ̃] **nm** counting, Fml enumeration; (de la population) census; Méd **d. des hématies** blood count

dénombrer [denɔ̃bre] **vt** to count, Fml to enumerate; (population) to take a census of

dénominateur [denɔminatœr] **nm** Math denominator; **d. commun** common denominator; **plus petit d. commun** lowest common denominator

dénominatif, -ive [denɔminatif, -iv] **adj**, **nm** Ling denominative

dénomination [denɔminasjɔ̃] **nf** name, denomination, designation; **comment a été décidée la nouvelle d. de certaines régions?** how were the new names for certain regions decided on?; Pharm **d. commune** generic name; **d. commerciale** (de produit) trade name; **d. sociale** company name

dénommer [denɔme] **vt** to name; parfois Péj **un dénommé Charles** someone by the name of Charles; **est-ce que le dénommé Laurent va …?** is that man/boy Laurent going to …?; **le dénommé Jacques Duval est prié de se rendre à la caisse no. 3** would Jacques Duval go to checkout 3; **ci-après dénommé …** hereinafter referred to as …

dénoncer [denɔ̃se] (**je dénonçai(s); n. dénonçons**) **vt 1** (à la police) (personne) to denounce, to inform against; (crime etc) to expose; **d. qn à la police** to denounce sb to the police; **c'est elle qui a dénoncé son frère à ses parents** it was she who gave her brother away or told on her brother to her parents **2** (protester contre) (traité, abus de pouvoir, la pollution etc) to denounce; **d. un contrat** to terminate a contract, to cancel a contract **3** (révéler) to indicate, to reveal; **son attitude dénonce sa méfiance des autres** his attitude betrays his mistrust of others
vpr se dénoncer to give oneself up

dénonciateur, -trice [denɔ̃sjatœr, -tris] **n** (d'une personne) informer; **il est le d. de ces crimes** he exposed the crimes
adj (lettre) of denunciation, accusing

dénonciation [denɔ̃sjasjɔ̃] **nf** denunciation

dénotation [denɔtasjɔ̃] **nf** denotation

dénoter [denɔte] **vt** to denote, to show, to indicate

dénouement [denumɑ̃] **nm** (d'un événement) result, outcome; (d'une difficulté) solution; (d'une intrigue, d'une histoire) ending; Théâtre dénouement

dénouer [denwe] **vt** (nœud) to untie, to undo, to loosen; **d. ses cheveux** to undo or let down one's hair; **d. une intrigue** to unravel a plot
vpr se dénouer (d'un nœud) to come undone; (de cheveux) to come down; (d'un mystère) to be solved; (d'une histoire, d'une enquête) to end; **sa langue se dénoue** he's finding his tongue

dénoyautage [denwajotaʒ] **nm** (d'un fruit) stoning, Am pitting; Fig Écon removal of political appointees from the board

dénoyauter [denwajote] **vt** (fruit) to stone, Am to pit; Fig Écon **d. une entreprise** to remove political appointees from the board of a company

dénoyauteur [denwajotœr] **nm** (machine) stoner

denrée [dɑ̃re] **nf** (pour l'homme) foodstuff; (pour le bétail) feed; **denrées alimentaires** food products, foodstuffs; **denrées périssables** perishable goods; **denrées de consommation courante** staple foods, staples; Fig **la patience est une d. rare** patience is a rare commodity

dense [dɑ̃s] **adj 1** Phys dense **2** (foule) dense; (brouillard, forêt) dense, thick; (style) concise, condensed, dense

densité [dɑ̃site] **nf 1** Phys density; **d. moyenne** mean specific weight; **flacon à d. moyenne** specific gravity flask **2** (de population etc) density; Ordinat **à double d.** double-density; Ordinat **d. quadruple** quad density; **haute d.** high density **3** Phot (de négatif) density

dent [dɑ̃] **nf 1** Anat tooth; **d. du fond/de devant/du haut/du bas** back/front/top/bottom tooth; **sans dents** toothless; **percer** ou **faire ses dents** (d'un enfant) to cut one's teeth, to be teething; **se faire les dents sur qch** (d'un chat, d'un enfant) to cut one's teeth on sth; Fig **se faire les dents sur qn** to take it out on sb; **mal** ou **rage de dents** toothache; **coup de d.** bite; Fig Fam **avoir la d.** to be hungry; **manger/rire à belles dents** to eat hungrily or with relish/laugh heartily; **manger du bout des dents** to pick at one's food; **rire du bout des dents** to force a laugh; **avoir les dents longues** (être ambitieux) to be ambitious, Fam to be hungry; **avoir la d. dure** to

have a sharp tongue; **montrer les dents** to show one's teeth; aussi Fig **serrer les dents** to grit one's teeth; **ne pas desserrer les dents** not to open one's mouth; **avoir** ou **conserver** ou **garder une d. contre qn** to have a grudge against sb; **ils n'ont rien à se mettre sous la d.** they don't have a bite to eat; **parler entre ses dents** to mumble, to mutter; **être sur les dents** (épuisé) to be worn out; (surmené) to be overworked
2 (de peigne, scie) tooth; (de roue) cog; (de fourchette) prong; (de montagne) (jagged) peak; (de timbre) perforation; **en dents de scie** serrated, jagged; Fig (évolution, progrès) uneven; **roue à dents** cogged wheel
▸▸ **d. d'éléphant** elephant's tusk; **d. de lait** milk tooth, first tooth; **d. de sagesse** wisdom tooth

dentaire [dɑ̃ter] **adj** Anat (hygiène, plaque, pulpe etc) dental; **l'art d.** dentistry

dental, -ale, -aux, -ales [dɑ̃tal, -o] Ling **adj** (consonne) dental
nf dentale dental consonant

dent-de-lion, pl **dents-de-lion** [dɑ̃d(ə)ljɔ̃] **nf** dandelion

dent-de-loup, pl **dents-de-loup** [dɑ̃dlu] **nf** Aut ratchet tooth, catch

denté [dɑ̃te] **adj** Tech (couronne, anneau) cogged, toothed; (feuille) jagged, Spéc dentate; **roue dentée** cogwheel

dentelé [dɑ̃tle] **adj** (rivage) jagged, indented; (bord) jagged; (feuille) serrated; (timbre) perforated

denteler [dɑ̃tle] **vt** (je dentelle; je dentellerai) to notch, to jag, to indent; (timbre) to perforate

dentelle [dɑ̃tel] **nf 1** (tissu) lace; **d. aux fuseaux** pillow lace; **d. à l'aiguille** ou **au point** point lace; **robe de** ou **en d.** lace dress; **des dentelles de papier** paper doilies; Culin **crêpe d.** very thin pancake, crêpe; Fig **ne pas faire dans la d.** (y aller carrément) not to mince one's words; (manquer de finesse) to be clumsy; **ça n'est pas de la d.** it's nothing fancy **2** Archit = wrought ironwork that has the appearance of lace, Am ≃ gingerbread

dentellerie [dɑ̃telri] **nf** lacemaking

dentellier, -ière [dɑ̃təlje, -jer] **adj** (industrie etc) lace(making)
n lacemaker
nf dentellière (machine) lacemaking machine

dentelure [dɑ̃tlyr] **nf** (d'un rivage) indentation; (d'une montagne) jagged summit; (d'une feuille) serration; (d'un timbre) perforation

dentier [dɑ̃tje] **nm** set of false teeth, dentures

dentifrice [dɑ̃tifris] **nm** toothpaste, Vieilli toothpowder
adj **pâte d.** toothpaste; **eau d.** mouthwash; **poudre d.** toothpowder

dentine [dɑ̃tin] **nf** Anat dentine

dentiste [dɑ̃tist] **n** dentist

dentition [dɑ̃tisjɔ̃] **nf 1** (croissance) cutting of teeth, teething; **d. définitive** ou **permanente** permanent teeth **2** (arrangement) arrangement of the teeth, Spéc dentition

denture [dɑ̃tyr] **nf 1** (dents) set of teeth **2** Tech teeth, cogs, gearing; (du rotor) rotor gear; **à d. hélicoïdale** spiral

> Il faut noter que le nom anglais **dentures** est un faux ami. Il signifie **dentier**.

dénucléarisation [denyklearizasjɔ̃] **nf** denuclearization

dénucléariser [denyklearize] **vt** to denuclearize

dénudation [denydasjɔ̃] **nf** Fml stripping, laying bare

dénudé [denyde] ADJ *(campagne, arbre)* bare; *(crâne)* bald; *Élec (fil)* bare

dénuder [denyde] VT *(colline)* to strip, to lay bare; *(arbre)* to strip; *(d'une robe)* to leave bare; **d. un arbre de son écorce** to strip a tree of its bark, to strip the bark off a tree
• VPR **se dénuder 1** *(d'une colline)* to grow bare; *(d'un arbre)* to lose its leaves **2** *(se mettre à nu)* to strip (naked); **crâne qui se dénude** balding head

dénué [denye] ADJ **d. de** *(raison, intelligence, intérêt etc)* devoid of; **une famille dénuée de tout** a family with absolutely nothing, a destitute family; **d. de tout fondement** totally without foundation

dénuement [denymã] NM destitution, penury; **être dans le d.** to be destitute *or* poverty-stricken

dénuer (se) [sədenye] VPR *Littr* to deprive oneself (**de** of); **se d. de ses biens** to part with all one's possessions

dénutrition [denytrisjõ] NF *Méd* malnutrition

déodorant [deɔdɔrã] ADJ, NM deodorant

déodoriser [deɔdɔrize] VT to deodorize

déontologie [deɔ̃tɔlɔʒi] NF professional ethics; **code de d.** professional code of ethics; *(écrit)* code of practice

déontologique [deɔ̃tɔlɔʒik] ADJ ethical; **règles déontologiques** rules of ethics

dépannage [depanaʒ] NM **1** *(d'un moteur, d'une voiture en panne etc)* (emergency) repairs; *(remorquage)* recovery; *Ordinat* trouble-shooting; **service de d.** breakdown service **2** *(pour rendre service)* helping out; **elle a eu besoin d'un petit d.** she needed a hand *or* a bit of help

dépanner [depane] VT **1** *(moteur, voiture en panne etc)* to repair, to fix; **il m'a dépanné** he got my car/TV/*etc* going again **2** *Fam (aider)* to help out; *(financièrement)* to tide over, to bail out; **peux-tu me d. de 50 euros?** could you give me 50 euros to bail me out?

dépanneur [depanœr] NM **1** *(de voiture)* breakdown mechanic; *(de téléviseur)* (television) repairman **2** *Can (magasin)* corner shop, *Am* convenience store

dépanneuse [depanøz] NF *Aut* breakdown van *or* lorry, recovery vehicle, *Am* wrecker

dépaquetage [depaktaʒ] NM unpacking

dépaqueter [depakte] VT *(conj like* **paqueter***)* to unpack

déparasiter [deparazite] VT *(poste de radio)* to eliminate the interference in

dépareillé [depareje] ADJ **1** *(gant)* odd; *(service de table)* incomplete; *Com* **articles dépareillés** oddments, job lot **2** *Can (sans pareil)* **c'est un mari d.** he's a husband in a million

dépareiller [depareje] VT *(paire d'objets)* to break up; *(paire de gants, chaussettes)* to lose one of; *(service, collection)* to make incomplete; **en cassant cette assiette, tu as dépareillé mon service de table** my dinner service is incomplete now that you've broken that plate

déparer [depare] VT to spoil, to mar; **d. le paysage** to be a blot on the landscape; **ce tableau ne dépare pas dans le salon** the painting looks very good in the living room

déparier [deparje] VT *(impf, pr sub n.* **dépariions, v. dépariiez***)* to split up, to separate

départ [depar] NM **1** *(d'une personne, d'un véhicule etc)* departure; *(de bateau)* departure, sailing; **quel est le jour de ton d.?** when do you leave?; **dès son d., j'ai rangé sa chambre** I tidied his room as soon as he left; **mon d. de la maison a été douloureux** my leaving home was a painful experience; **le décès de sa mère l'a obligé à un d. précipité** his mother's death forced him to leave hurriedly;

les grands départs (en vacances) the great holiday exodus; **c'était le grand d.** it was the final departure; **le d. de la navette spatiale** the launch of the space shuttle; **le d. du courrier a été retardé** the post has been delayed; **être sur le d.** to be on the point of leaving *or* of departure; **produit de d.** original material; **excursions au d. de Nice** trips (leaving) from Nice; **le train au d. de la voie 9** the train standing at platform 9; **le train à destination de Lille est au d. de la voie 9** the train to Lille will leave from platform 9; **d. anticipé** early departure; **d. différé** delayed departure; **d. matinal** early morning departure; *Com* **d. entrepôt** ex warehouse; *Com* **d. usine** ex works; *Com* **prix d. usine** price ex works; **d. volontaire** *(d'employé)* voluntary redundancy

2 *(du travail)* departure; **exiger le d. d'un employé** to insist on the dismissal of an employee; **il accepte mal son d. en retraite/en préretraite** he's finding it difficult to come to terms with the prospect of retirement/early retirement

3 *(début)* *(d'un projet, d'une entreprise etc)* start, beginning; **le d. d'une association** the foundation of an association; **point de d.** starting point, point of departure; **prendre qch comme point de d.** to take sth as one's starting point; **langue de d.** *(d'une traduction)* source language; **qui a eu l'idée de d.?** who had the original idea?; **prix de d.** *(à une vente aux enchères)* upset price; **salaire de d.** starting salary; **ça ne ressemble plus du tout au modèle de d.** it doesn't look anything like the original model now; **au d.** at first, to start *or* begin with; **si tu me l'avais dit au d.** if you had told me that at the start *or* the outset; *Banque* **d. d'un compte** opening date of an account

4 *Sport (d'une course etc)* start; **ligne de d.** starting line; *Golf* **(tertre de) d.** tee; **d. arrêté** standing start; **d. lancé** flying start; **faux d.** false start; **donner le d.** to start the race, *Fam* to give the off; *Sp, Fig* **prendre un bon/mauvais d.** to get off to a good/bad start

départager [departaʒe] VT *(conj like* **partager***)* *(candidats, chansons etc)* to decide between; **d. les gagnants** to decide the winners; **d. les votes** to give the casting vote

département [departamã] NM *Admin* **1** *(dans un ministère)* **d. (ministériel)** department; **le d. de la peinture moderne** *(dans un musée)* the modern art section **2** *(de la France)* = subdivision administered by a prefect

Département

A "département" is the chief administrative division of France. There are 95 "départements" in metropolitan France and 4 overseas and each is administered by a "conseil général" and a "préfet". The number of the "département" corresponds to the first two figures in a postcode and the last two figures in a car registration number.

départemental, -ale, -aux, -ales [departamãtal, -o] ADJ departmental
• NM *Journ* regional (paper)
• NF **départementale** secondary *or Br* B road

départir [departir] *(conj like* **partir***, occ like* **finir***)* VT *Littr (faveurs)* to distribute, to dispense, to deal out; *(tâches)* to distribute, to allocate
• VPR **se départir il ne se départ jamais de son calme** he never gets excited; **elle ne se départ jamais de sa bonne humeur** her good humour *or Am* humor never deserts her, she is unfailingly good-humoured *or Am* good-humored; **il est connu pour sa bonne**

humeur, dont effectivement il ne se départ jamais he is famous for his good humour, which never fails *or* deserts him

dépassé [depase] ADJ **1** *(démodé)* *(mode, technique, langage)* old-fashioned, out of date; **c'est d.** *(de faire ça)* it's medieval; **se marier à 20 ans, c'est complètement d.** nobody gets married at 20 nowadays **2** *(perdu)* overwhelmed; **je suis d. (par les événements)** things are getting too much for me

dépassement [depasmã] NM **1** *Aut* overtaking, *Am* passing; **d. interdit** no overtaking, *Am* no passing **2** *Fin* **nous avons un d. de crédit à déplorer** we have failed to keep within our spending limit; **il y a un d. de crédit de plusieurs millions** the budget has been exceeded by several million; **pratiquer le d. d'honoraires** to charge more than will be reimbursed by Social Security; **d. budgétaire** failure to keep within the budget; *Ordinat* **d. de capacité** overflow; *Compta* **d. de coût** cost overrun **3** **d. (de soi-même)** surpassing oneself

DÉPASSER [depase] VT **1** *(aller plus loin que)* *(personne, chose)* to pass, to go past *or* beyond; *(signal)* to overrun; **nous avons dépassé la boulangerie** we have passed *or* gone past the baker's; **cette maison dépasse l'alignement** the house projects beyond the building line; **d. le but** to overshoot the mark

2 *(excéder)* to exceed; **d. la limite de vitesse** to exceed the speed limit; **d. la date limite** to miss the deadline; **ce produit a dépassé la date limite de vente** this product is past its sell-by date; **l'entretien ne dépassera pas un quart d'heure** the interview won't take *or* last more than a quarter of an hour; **d. la durée autorisée de 20 minutes** to take more than the 20 minutes allowed; *Fin* **d. un crédit** to exceed a credit limit; **toutes ces voitures dépassent nos moyens** all these cars are beyond our means; **ne pas d. la dose prescrite** do not exceed the stated dose; **il a dépassé la trentaine** he has turned thirty, he is over thirty

3 *(à la course, en voiture)* to overtake, *Am* to pass

4 *(surpasser)* **d. qch en hauteur** to top sth, to be higher than sth; **d. qn de la tête** to stand a head taller than sb; **d. qn en intelligence/en beauté** to be more intelligent/beautiful than sb; **la beauté des lieux dépasse l'imagination** the scene is beautiful beyond all imagination; **les résultats ont largement dépassé nos espérances** the results far exceeded our expectations *or* were much better than we hoped for

5 *(outrepasser)* **cela dépasse ma compétence** it lies beyond *or* outside my area of responsibility; **les mots ont dépassé ma pensée** I said it in the heat of the moment; **d. les bornes** to overstep the bounds *or* the mark, *Am* to be out of line; **cela dépasse mon entendement, cela me dépasse** *(d'un comportement)* it's beyond me; *(d'une discussion savante)* it's beyond me, it's over my head; **être dépassé par les événements** to be overtaken by events

• VI **1** *Aut* to overtake, *Am* to pass; **il est interdit de d. sur ce pont** no overtaking *or Am* passing on this bridge

2 *(être trop long)* **votre jupon dépasse** your underskirt is showing; **son mouchoir dépasse de sa poche** his handkerchief is sticking out of his pocket
• VPR **se dépasser** to surpass oneself

dépassionner [depasjone] VT *(débat, conversation)* to take the heat out of; **il faisait tout ce qu'il pouvait pour d. la conversation** he was doing everything he could to cool *or* calm things down

dépatouiller (se) [sədepatuje] VPR *Fam* to cope, to manage

dépaver [depave] VT *(cour, rue)* to take up the paving from

dépaysé [depeize] ADJ out of one's element; **je me sens d.** I feel like a fish out of water, I don't feel at home; **depuis qu'on l'a changé d'école, il se sent d.** he feels totally lost since changing schools; *Iron* **il pleut autant que chez moi! – eh bien, comme ça tu ne seras pas d.!** it rains as much here as it does at home! – well at least you won't feel homesick!

dépaysement [depeizmɑ̃] NM *(négatif)* disorientation; *(positif)* change of scene; **c'est un grand d. pour lui d'être dans cette ville** he feels really lost in this town; **elle a besoin de d.** she needs a change of scene; **cela te ferait un d.** it would be a change of scene for you

dépayser [depeize] VT *(positivement)* to be a change of scene for; *(négativement)* to disorientate; **mes vacances m'ont beaucoup dépaysé** my holiday provided a great change of scene

dépeçage [depəsaʒ] NM, **dépècement** [depɛsmɑ̃] NM cutting up; *Fig* **le d. du pays fut achevé par les barbares** the barbarians completed the dismemberment of the country

dépecer [depəse] VT (**je dépèce, n. dépeçons; je dépècerai**) **1** *(carcasse, volaille)* to cut up; *(baleine)* to flense; **le lion dépèce sa proie** the lion tears into its prey; **un corps dépecé** a dismembered body **2** *Fig (territoire)* to dismember

dépeceur, -euse [depəsœr, -øz] N cutter-up; **d. (de baleines)** flenser; **d. d'entreprises** asset-stripper

dépêche [depɛʃ] NF **1** *(lettre officielle)* (official) dispatch, message **2** *(nouvelle)* news item *(sent through an agency)*; **d. (télégraphique)** telegram, *Fam* wire; *Journ* **d. d'agence** agency copy; **nous avons appris par d. la démission du président** we have just heard over the wire that the president has resigned

dépêcher [depeʃe] VT *(un courrier, un messager)* to dispatch
VPR **se dépêcher** to hurry, to be quick; **dépêchez-vous!** hurry up!; **se d. de faire qch** to hurry to do sth; **dépêche-toi de finir ton travail** hurry up and finish your work; **se d. de rentrer** to hurry home

dépeigner [depeɲe] VT **d. qn** to ruffle sb's hair, to make sb's hair untidy; **elle est toute dépeignée** her hair's all dishevelled

dépeindre [depɛ̃dr] VT *(conj like* **peindre***)* to depict, to picture, to describe

dépenaillé [dep(ə)naje] ADJ *(veste, pantalon etc)* ragged, tattered, in rags, in tatters; *(personne)* in rags, in tatters

dépénalisation [depenalizasjɔ̃] NF decriminalization

dépénaliser [depenalize] VT to decriminalize

dépendance [depɑ̃dɑ̃s] NF **1** *(solidarité)* dependence **2** *(d'un pays)* dependency; *Archit* **dépendances** outbuildings **3** *(asservissement)* dependence, *surtout Am* dependancy; **l'abus de somnifères peut créer une d.** excessive use of sleeping tablets can lead to dependence; **vivre dans la d. complète de qn** to be completely dependent on sb; **être sous la d. de qn** to be under sb's domination or control

dépendant [depɑ̃dɑ̃] ADJ dependent; **fonctions dépendantes l'une de l'autre** functions dependent on each other, interdependent functions; **être d. de qn** to be dependent on sb; **être d. de la drogue** to be dependent on drugs

dépendre¹ [depɑ̃dr] VT *(linge etc)* to take down

dépendre² VI to depend; **d. de qn/qch** to depend on sb/sth; **un pays qui dépend d'un autre** a country which is dependent on another; **tout dépend des circonstances** everything depends on the circumstances; **ces événements ne dépendent pas de nous** such events are beyond our control; **cela ne dépend que de toi** that depends on you alone; **il dépend de vous de le faire** it lies or rests with you to do it; **cela dépend,** *Fam* **cela dépend des fois** it depends; *Fam* **ça dépend s'il est marié** it depends whether he's married; **il dépend financièrement de ses parents** he is financially dependent on his parents; **je ne dépends pas de lui** I don't take orders from him; **ne d. que de soi(-même)** to be one's own boss; **l'étang dépend aussi de leur domaine** the pond is also part of their estate

dépens [depɑ̃] NMPL **1 aux d. de** at the expense of; **faire qch aux d. d'autrui** to do sth at other people's expense; **vivre aux d. de qn** to live at sb's expense; **s'amuser aux d. de ses études** to enjoy oneself at the expense of one's studies; **il apprit à ses d. que ...** he learnt to his cost that ... **2** *Jur* costs; *Com* cost, expenses; *Jur* **être condamné aux d.** to be ordered to pay costs

dépense [depɑ̃s] NF **1** expenditure, expense, outlay; **dépenses** spending; **dépenses du ménage** household expenses; **dépenses courantes** current expenditure or expenses; **faire des dépenses** to spend money; **engager une d.** ou **des dépenses** to incur expenditure; **nous avons décidé d'engager les dépenses pour les travaux** we decided to go ahead and incur the expenditure of having the work done; **j'ai acheté une voiture, mais je n'arriverai pas à couvrir la d.** I bought a car, but I'll never be able to pay for it; **je n'arriverai pas à couvrir tes dépenses** I won't be able to pay for your extravagance; **je n'aurais pas dû faire cette d.** I shouldn't have spent that money; **pousser à la d.** to encourage people to spend; **c'est une grosse d.** it's a lot of money; **faire trop de dépenses** to spend too much (money); **on ne regardait pas à la d.** there was no stinting, they didn't mind the cost, they spared no expense; **faire de folles dépenses** to spend money extravagantly; **recettes et dépenses** income or receipts and expenditure

2 *Tech* **d. à vide** wasted energy; *Fig* **d. de temps/d'énergie** expenditure of time/energy; **d. physique** physical exertion

3 *(d'une communauté religieuse)* bursary
▸▸ *Compta* **dépenses de caisse** cash expenditure; **dépenses en capital** capital expenditure; *Écon* **dépenses des consommateurs** consumer expenditure; *Compta* **dépenses de création** above-the-line costs; *Compta* **dépenses diverses** sundry expenses; **dépenses d'équipement** capital expenditure; *Compta* **dépenses d'exploitation** operating costs; *Compta* **dépenses de fonctionnement** operating costs; *Écon* **dépenses des ménages** household expenditure; *Écon* **d. nationale** national expenditure, government spending; **dépenses publiques** public spending, government spending; **dépenses de santé** *(de l'État)* health spending, health expenditure; **dépenses sociales** spending on social services

dépenser [depɑ̃se] VT **1** *(de l'argent)* to spend; **il dépense peu en livres** he doesn't spend much on books **2** *(temps)* to spend; *(énergie)* to use, to consume; **la voiture dépense très peu d'essence** the car uses or consumes very little petrol; **d. toute son énergie/ses forces (à faire qch)** to use up all one's energy/one's strength (in doing sth); **d. sa salive pour rien** ou **inutilement** to waste one's breath

VI to spend (money); **d. sans compter** to spend lavishly, to be free with one's money; **qu'est-ce que tu peux d. en un mois!** the amount you spend in a month!

VPR **se dépenser** to use up or consume energy; **j'ai besoin de me d.** I need some physical exercise; **se d. pour qn** to spare no trouble on sb's behalf; **il s'est dépensé sans compter pour obtenir ton passeport plus vite** he went to a great deal of trouble to get your passport faster; **se d. en démarches inutiles** to waste one's energies in useless activities

dépensier, -ière [depɑ̃sje, -jɛr] ADJ extravagant
N **1** *(personne prodigue)* spendthrift **2** *(d'une communauté religieuse)* bursar

déperdition [deperdisjɔ̃] NF *(de tissu etc)* waste, wastage; *(de chaleur, d'énergie)* loss

dépérir [deperir] VI *(d'une personne)* to waste away; *(de la santé)* to decline; *(d'une fleur)* to wither; *(d'un arbre)* to decay; *(d'une affaire)* to go downhill

dépérissement [deperismɑ̃] NM *(d'une personne)* wasting away; *(d'une fleur)* withering; *(d'un arbre)* decay; *(d'une affaire, de la santé)* decline

dépersonnalisation [depersɔnalizasjɔ̃] NF depersonalization

dépersonnaliser [depersɔnalize] VT to depersonalize
VPR **se dépersonnaliser** to lose one's personality or character

dépêtrer [depetre] *Fam* VT *(de la boue)*, *Fig (d'une situation difficile etc)* to extricate, to free; **d. qn d'une mauvaise affaire** to get sb out of a scrape
VPR **se dépêtrer** *(de la boue, de racines etc)* to extricate or free oneself; *Fig* **se d. de qn** to get rid of sb, to shake sb off

dépeuplé [depœple] ADJ *(pays, région)* depopulated; *(étang)* empty; *(forêt)* cleared, thinned

dépeuplement [depœpləmɑ̃] NM *(d'un pays, d'une région)* depopulation; *(d'un étang)* unstocking; *(d'une forêt)* thinning, clearing

dépeupler [depœple] VT *(pays, région)* to depopulate; *(étang)* to unstock; *(forêt)* to thin, to clear
VPR **se dépeupler** *(d'un pays, d'une région)* to become depopulated; *(d'une salle)* to empty; *(d'un étang)* to become unstocked; *(d'une forêt)* to thin

déphasage [defazaʒ] NM **1** *Élec* phase displacement; **d. en avant** (phase) lead; **d. en arrière** lag **2** *Fig Fam* **il y a vraiment un d. entre les connaissances qu'on demande à un professeur et la réalité de l'enseignement** there's a big difference between the knowledge demanded of a teacher and the realities of teaching; **le d. est de plus en plus important entre le PDG et le conseil d'administration** the chairman is increasingly out of step with the board

déphasé [defaze] ADJ **1** *Élec, Cin, TV* out-of-phase; **d. en arrière** lagging; **d. en avant** leading **2** *Fig Fam (personne) (désorienté)* disoriented, *surtout Am* disoriented

déphaser [defaze] VT **1** *Élec* to dephase **2** *Fig Fam (personne)* to disorientate, *surtout Am* to disorient

dépiauter [depjote] VT *Fam (lapin etc)* to skin, to flay; *Fig* **d. un texte/un article** to pull a text/an article to pieces

dépigmentation [depigmɑ̃tasjɔ̃] NF *Méd* loss of pigmentation

dépilation [depilasjɔ̃] NF loss of hair

dépilatoire [depilatwar] ADJ depilatory; **crème d.** hair removing cream, depilatory

dépiler [depile] **vt** *Méd* to cause loss of hair from

dépiquer¹ [depike] **vt** *(pousses)* to transplant, to prick out

dépiquer² **vt** *Couture* to unstitch, to unpick

dépistage [depistaʒ] **nm** *(d'un criminel etc)* tracking down, detection; *(d'une maladie, d'un virus etc)* (early) detection; **d. obligatoire du sida** compulsory AIDS screening

dépister [depiste] **vt 1** *(gibier, criminel)* to track down; *(maladie)* to detect; **d. un traquenard** to spot a trap; **il a été dépisté séropositif** he tested HIV-positive **2** *(chiens de chasse)* to put off the scent; *(poursuivant)* to throw off the scent; **il a dépisté la police** he threw the police off the scent, he gave the police the slip

dépit [depi] **nm 1** *(ressentiment)* spite, resentment; **un accès de d.** a fit of pique; **par d.** out of spite; **elle s'est mariée avec lui par d. amoureux** she married him on the rebound; **il a agi par d. amoureux** he did it because he was disappointed in love; **pleurer de d.** to cry with vexation; **concevoir du d. de qch** to resent sth **2 en d. de** in spite of, despite; **en d. du bon sens** *(illogiquement)* contrary to common sense

dépité [depite] **adj** annoyed; **être tout d.** to be thoroughly annoyed

dépiter [depite] **vt** to spite, to offend

déplacé [deplase] **adj 1** *(pas à sa place)* out of (its) place; **avoir une vertèbre déplacée** to have a slipped disc; *Fig* **se sentir d.** to feel out of place **2** *(inconvenant) (observation, attitude etc)* unwarranted, uncalled-for **3** *Pol* **personne déplacée** displaced person

déplacement [deplasmã] **nm 1** *(de meubles etc)* moving, shifting; *(de fonctionnaire, service)* transfer; *Méd* **d. de vertèbre** slipped disc; *Ordinat* **d. du curseur** cursor movement; *Ordinat* **d. entre fichiers** movement between files; *TV, Cin* **d. latéral** *(d'une caméra)* crabbing **2** *(voyage)* trip, journey; **déplacements** travel; **ces déplacements continuels** this constant travel or travelling; **les déplacements des cadres** executive travel; **être en d.** to be on a (business) trip; **frais de d.** travelling expenses **3** *Naut (d'un navire)* displacement; **d. en charge** displacement loaded, load displacement; **d. d'air** air displacement

déplacer [deplase] *(je déplaçai(s); n. déplaçons)* **vt 1** *(changer de place) (objet)* to move, to shift; *(fonctionnaire, service)* to transfer; *(fonds)* to move; **il ne peut rien d., il a mal au dos** he can't carry anything, he has a bad back; *Fig* **d. la question** *ou* **le problème** to shift the focus of a problem; **vous déplacez le problème** you're dodging the issue; *Hum* **tout ce qu'il sait faire, c'est d. de l'air** he just runs around in circles **2 ce navire déplace dix mille tonnes** this ship has a displacement of ten thousand tons

vpr se déplacer 1 *(changer de place)* to change one's place, to move (around); **il est interdit de se d.** please remain seated; **avoir du mal à se d.** to have difficulty in moving or getting around; **se d. une vertèbre** to slip a disc **2** *(voyager)* to move about, to travel; **son métier l'oblige à se d. souvent** he does a lot of travelling in his job **3** *(bouger) (d'un bateau, d'un poisson etc)* to move

déplafonnement [deplafɔnmã] **nm** removal of the upper limit or ceiling

déplafonner [deplafɔne] **vt** *(prix)* to remove the upper limit or the ceiling on; *Fin* **d. un crédit** to raise the ceiling on a credit, to raise a credit limit

déplaire [depleʁ] *(conj like plaire)* **vi d. à qn** *(irriter)* to displease or offend sb; *(ne pas plaire à)* to fail to please sb, to be displeasing to sb; **odeur qui déplaît** offensive or disagreeable smell; **tu lui déplais** he dislikes you; **il me déplaît de le faire** I dislike or don't like doing it; **il me déplaît d'avoir à vous le dire, mais ...** I hate or I don't like having to tell you this, but ...; **il me déplairait vraiment d'avoir à vous faire d'autres remarques** I would be extremely displeased if I had to make any further comment; **cela ne me déplairait pas** I wouldn't mind (it); **il a tout fait pour nous d.** he has been utterly disagreeable; **cela m'a profondément déplu** I was greatly or most displeased by that; *Iron* **n'en déplaise à la compagnie** with all due respect to those present; **n'en déplaise à votre Altesse!** may it please Your Highness!; **ne vous/leur en déplaise** whether you/they like it or not; **n'en déplaise à mes parents** whether my parents like it or not

vpr se déplaire to be displeased or dissatisfied; **il se déplaît à Paris** he doesn't like Paris; **il ne se déplaît pas à Paris** he quite likes Paris

déplaisant [depleza̰] **adj** unpleasant, disagreeable

déplaisir [deplezir] **nm** displeasure, annoyance; **à son grand d.** to his great annoyance

déplantage [deplɑ̃taʒ] **nm** digging up, lifting

déplanter [deplɑ̃te] **vt** to take or dig up, to lift

déplantoir [deplɑ̃twar] **nm** hand fork

déplâtrage [deplɑtraʒ] **nm 1 le d. d'un mur** taking or stripping the plaster off a wall **2 le d. d'un bras/d'une jambe** taking an arm/a leg out of plaster

déplâtrer [deplɑtre] **vt 1** *(mur etc)* to strip the plaster from **2** *(membre)* to take the plaster off; **on la déplâtre demain** she's having the plaster off tomorrow

dépliage [deplijaʒ] **nm** unfolding, opening out

dépliant [deplijã] **adj** *(qui se déplie)* folding **nm** leaflet; *(plus luxueux)* brochure; *(feuille pliée)* fold-out page; **d. promotionnel** promotional leaflet

dépliement [deplimã] **nm** = **dépliage**

déplier [deplije] *(impf, pr sub* **n. dépliions, v. dépliiez**) **vt** *(journal, carte)* to unfold, to open out, to spread out; *(mouchoir)* to unfold; *(canapé)* to open out; **d. les jambes** to stretch one's legs

vpr se déplier to unfold, to open out

déplissage [deplisaʒ] **nm** *(d'un tissu etc)* taking the creases out, smoothing out

déplisser [deplise] **vt** *(tissu etc)* to take the creases out of, to smooth out

vpr se déplisser *(d'un tissu etc)* to lose its creases

déploiement [deplwamã] **nm 1** *(d'ailes etc)* spreading out, unfolding; *(du drapeau)* unfurling; *(des troupes, navires etc)* deployment **2** *(de force, courage)* display; **un d. d'attentions** a display or show of attention

déplombage [deplɔ̃baʒ] **nm 1** *(d'un compteur d'électricité, d'un paquet etc)* removal of the seal **2** *(d'une dent)* removal of the filling **3** *Ordinat* decoding, decrypting

déplomber [deplɔ̃be] **vt 1** *(compteur d'électricité, paquet etc)* to remove the seal from **2** *(dent)* to remove the filling from **3** *Ordinat (logiciel)* to decode, to decrypt

déplorable [deplɔrabl] **adj** *(incident etc)* deplorable, regrettable; *(comportement, résultats etc)* deplorable, disgraceful

déplorablement [deplɔrabləmã] **adv** deplorably

déplorer [deplɔre] **vt** to deplore; **vous avez très mal agi et je le déplore** I think it is deplorable that you behaved so badly; **il est à d. que vous ayez eu cette conduite** it is deplorable that you behaved in such a way; **d. la mort de qn** to grieve over or mourn sb's death

déployer [deplwaje] (**je déploie, n. déployons; je déploierai**) **vt 1** *(journal, carte)* to unfold, to open out; *(drapeau)* to unfurl; *(voiles, ailes)* to spread; *(troupes, police)* to deploy; **rire à gorge déployée** to roar with laughter **2** *(marchandises, patience etc)* to display, to show; **il a déployé un énorme effort** he made a tremendous effort; **il va falloir d. des trésors d'ingéniosité** we're/they're/etc going to have to be extremely ingenious

vpr se déployer *(d'une voile, d'un drapeau)* to unfurl; *(de troupes, de police)* to deploy; *Mil* **se d. en éventail** to fan out

déplumé [deplyme] **adj** featherless; *Fam (chauve)* bald

déplumer (se) [sədeplyme] **vpr** *(d'un oiseau)* to moult; *Fam (d'une personne)* to go bald

dépoitraillé [depwatraje] **adj** *Fam Péj* with one's shirt/etc all undone (at the front)

dépolarisant [depɔlariza̰] *Phys* **adj** depolarizing **nm** depolarizer

dépolarisation [depɔlarizasjɔ̃] **nf** *Phys* depolarization

dépolariser [depɔlarize] **vt** *Phys* to depolarize

dépoli [depɔli] **adj** *(verre)* frosted

dépolir [depɔlir] **vt** *(surface)* to dull, to tarnish; *(verre)* to frost

vpr se dépolir to become dull, to tarnish

dépolissage [depɔlisaʒ] **nm**, **dépolissement** [depɔlismã] **nm** *(de surface)* dulling, tarnishing; *(de verre)* frosting

dépolitisation [depɔlitizasjɔ̃] **nf** depoliticization

dépolitiser [depɔlitize] **vt** to depoliticize

dépolluer [depɔlɥe] **vt** to clean up

dépollution [depɔlysjɔ̃] **nf** cleaning up

déponent [depɔnã] **adj, nm** *Gram* deponent

dépopulation [depɔpylasjɔ̃] **nf** depopulation

déportation [depɔrtasjɔ̃] **nf 1** *(d'un prisonnier)* transportation **2** *(en camp de concentration)* internment

déporté, -ée [depɔrte] **n 1** *(exilé)* transported criminal **2** *(de camp de concentration)* internee, prisoner

déportement [depɔrtəmã] **nm 1** *Aut* skidding, swerving **2** *Vieilli* **déportements** excesses, dissolute life

déporter [depɔrte] **vt 1** *(prisonnier)* to transport **2** *(en camp de concentration)* to send to a concentration camp **3** *(navire, avion)* to carry off course; **voiture déportée par la violence du vent** car blown off the road by the force of the wind

déposant, -ante [depoza̰, -ãt] **n 1** *Fin* depositor **2** *Jur* deponent, witness

dépose [depoz] **nf** *(de tapis, moquette)* lifting, taking up; *(de moteur, radiateur)* removal

déposer¹ [depoze] **vt** *(enlever) (tapis, moquette)* to lift, to take up; *(rideaux)* to take down; *(moteur, radiateur)* to remove

déposer² **vt 1** *(valise, sac etc)* to put or set down; **d. une gerbe sur un tombeau** to lay a wreath on a grave; **ma voiture vous déposera à l'hôtel** my car will drop you at the hotel; **puis-je vous d. quelque part?** can I drop you somewhere?; **d. une lettre/un paquet chez qn** to drop off a letter/a parcel at sb's house; **d. la clé à la réception** to leave the key at reception; **défense de d. des ordures** no dumping, *Br* no tipping; **d. les armes** to lay down one's arms, to surrender; *Fml* **d. un baiser sur la joue/le front de qn** to kiss sb on the cheek/forehead; *Fml* **d. ses hommages aux pieds de qn** to pay homage to sb **2** *(confier)* to deposit, to lodge in a safe place; *Com (marque, brevet)* to register; **d. une caution** to leave a deposit; **d. son argent à la banque** to deposit one's money at the bank; *Com* **marque déposée** registered trademark; *Jur* **d. une plainte contre qn** to prefer a charge *or* lodge a complaint against sb; *Com* **d. son bilan** to file one's petition (in bankruptcy); **d. un projet de loi** to table a bill, to bring in a bill **3** *(monarque etc)* to depose **4** *(d'un liquide) (dépôt)* to deposit **VI 1** **il faut laisser au liquide le temps de d.** the liquid must be given time to settle **2** *Jur* **d. (en justice)** to give evidence (**contre** against) **VPR se déposer** *(d'une substance)* to settle, to form a deposit

dépositaire [depozitɛr] **N 1** *(de papiers confidentiels)* depositary; *Com* consignee; **d. de valeurs** holder of securities on trust; *Admin* **d. de l'autorité publique** = officer of the State; *Admin* **d. public** = government official with responsibility for the management of public funds **2** *Com (de produits)* agent; **d. agréé/exclusif** authorized/sole agent; **d. de journaux** newsagent

déposition [depozisjɔ̃] **NF 1** *Jur* statement, deposition *(made by witness)*; **faire/recueillir une d.** to make/take a statement **2** *(d'un monarque)* deposing **3** *Beaux-Arts* **D. de Croix** Deposition

dépositionner [depozisjɔne] **VT** *Mktg* to deposition

déposséder [depɔsede] **VT** (**je dépossède, n. dépossédons; je déposséderai**) to dispossess, to deprive (**de** of); **d. qn de sa place** to deprive sb of *or* oust sb from his seat; **d. qn de sa charge** to remove sb from office, to deprive sb of his/her office; **se sentir dépossédé** to feel dispossessed

dépossession [depɔsɛsjɔ̃] **NF** dispossession

dépôt [depo] **NM 1** *(action)* deposit, depositing; *(chose confiée)* deposit; **d. d'une gerbe** laying of a wreath; **le d. des manteaux au vestiaire est conseillé** customers are advised to leave their coats in the cloakroom; **faire un d.** *(d'argent)* to make a deposit; **banque de d.** deposit bank; **compte de d.** deposit account; *Com* **d. d'une marque de fabrique** registration of a trademark; *Pol* **d. d'un projet de loi** bringing in *or* tabling of a bill; **avoir** *ou* **détenir qch en d.** to hold sth in trust; **marchandises en d.** *(à la douane)* goods in bond; *Com* **goods on sale or return 2** *(entrepôt)* depot, depository, repository; *Rail* engine shed; *(prison)* prison, jail; **il a passé la nuit au d.** he spent the night in the cells; *Jur* **mandat de d.** warrant of committal *or* commitment *(of prisoner)* **3** *(de précipité, boue etc) (action)* deposition, settling; *(résultat)* deposit, sediment; *(limon)* silt; *(dans une bouilloire)* fur; *(dans un chauffe-eau)* scale; **le d. d'un vin** the sediment in a wine; **il y a du d.** there is a sediment; *Géol* **d. calcaire/sédimentaire** calcareous/sedimentary deposit

▸▸ **d. bancaire** bank deposit; *Com* **d. de bilan** (filing of a petition in) bankruptcy; **d. de bois** timber yard; **d. de bouteilles** bottle bank; **d. de distributeur** distribution depot; **d. à échéance fixe** fixed deposit; **d. d'espèces** cash deposit; **d. d'essence** petrol storage depot; **d. d'expédition** sending depot; **d. de fret** freight depot; **d. de garantie** security deposit; **d. interbancaire** interbank deposit;

Jur **d. légal** copyright deposit *(in France, copies of published or recorded documents have to be deposited at the Bibliothèque nationale)*; **d. de(s) marchandises** goods depot; *(entrepôt)* warehouse; *Mil* **d. de munitions** munitions depot; **d. d'ordures** rubbish dump *or Br* tip; **d. de pain** ≃ bread shop *(which does not make its own bread)*; **d. pour conteneurs** container depot; **d. de réception** receiving depot; **d. sacré** sacred trust; *Fin* **d. à terme** term deposit; **d. à terme fixe** fixed deposit; **d. de verre** bottle bank; *Fin* **d. à vue** demand deposit, sight deposit

dépotage [depɔtaʒ], **dépotement** [depɔtmã] **NM 1** *(de liquide)* decanting **2** *(de plantes)* repotting; *(de semis)* planting out

dépoter [depɔte] **VT 1** *(liquide)* to decant **2** *(plantes)* to repot; *(semis)* to plant out

dépotoir [depɔtwar] **NM 1** *(dépôt d'ordures)* dump, *Br* rubbish tip; *Fig* **cette chambre est un vrai d.** this room is a real tip *or* dump **2** *Ind* sewage works

dépôt-vente, *pl* **dépôts-ventes NM** sales room

dépouille [depuj] **NF 1** *(d'animal)* skin, hide; *(de serpent)* slough; **d. (mortelle)** (mortal) remains **2 dépouilles** *(trésor de guerre)* spoils, booty

dépouillé [depuje] **ADJ** *(style)* bald; *(arbre)* bare; **vin d.** = wine that has lost its alcohol content; **d. de** lacking in; **ils vivent dans un décor très d.** they live in very spartan surroundings

dépouillement [depujmã] **NM 1** **d. volontaire de ses biens** relinquishment *or* renouncement of one's property; **ils vivent dans le d.** they live in utter poverty **2** *(examen)* **d. d'un rapport** examination *or* analysis of a report; **d. des votes** *ou* **du scrutin** counting of the votes; **d. du courrier** going *or* sorting through the mail **3** *TV etc (avant enregistrement)* breakdown

dépouiller [depuje] **VT 1** *(priver)* to deprive, to strip (**de** of); **d. qn de ses vêtements** to strip sb; **d. qn de ses droits** to strip sb of his/her rights; **se faire d.** *(dans une affaire)* to lose all one's money; **se faire d. par des voleurs** to be robbed of all one's money; **d. un pays** to plunder a country; **d. un héritier** to rob an heir of his inheritance; **le décor est dépouillé de tout** ornement the surroundings are bare of all ornament; *Fig* **dans le film, le personnage est dépouillé de tout son charme** all the character's charm is lost in the film; *Litt* **la bise a dépouillé les bois** the wind has stripped all the trees bare **2** *(examiner) (le courrier, numéros d'une revue)* to sort, to go through; *(appels d'offres)* to check; **d. un inventaire** to examine *or* analyse an inventory; **d. le scrutin** to count the votes; **pour faire son mémoire, il a dépouillé tout Balzac** he analysed all of Balzac line by line for his thesis **3** *(lapin etc)* to skin **VPR se dépouiller 1** *(d'un insecte, serpent)* to cast (off) its skin; *(d'un arbre)* to shed its leaves; *(du vin)* to lose its strength **2** **se d. de qch** to deprive *or* divest *or* rid oneself of sth; **se d. de ses vêtements** to strip off one's clothes, *Fam* to strip; **les arbres se dépouillaient de leurs feuilles** the trees were dropping *or* shedding their leaves

dépourvu [depurvy] **ADJ** **d. d'intelligence/d'intérêt** devoid of intelligence/interest; **pays d. d'arbres** treeless country; **être d. (d'argent)** to be penniless **NM être pris au d.** to be caught off (one's) guard, to be taken by surprise

dépoussiérage [depusjeraʒ] **NM** *Ind* vacuum cleaning, dust removal

dépoussiérant [depusjerã] **NM** furniture polish

dépoussiérer [depusjere] **VT** *Ind* to vacuum-clean, to remove the dust from; *Fig (institution, traduction etc)* to modernize, to bring up to date; *(connaissances)* to brush up

dépravation [depravasjɔ̃] **NF** (moral) depravity

dépravé, -ée [deprave] **ADJ** depraved **N** degenerate, depraved person

dépraver [deprave] **VT** to deprave **VPR se dépraver** to become depraved

dépréciateur, -trice [depresjatœr, -tris] **N** disparager, belittler

dépréciatif, -ive [depresjatif, -iv] **ADJ** *(expression, mot etc)* derogatory; **en termes dépréciatifs** in derogatory *or* disparaging terms

dépréciation [depresjasjɔ̃] **NF 1** *(dévaluation)* depreciation, fall in value **2** *(mauvaise évaluation)* underrating, undervaluing; *(dénigrement)* disparagement; *Compta* **d. de créances** write-down of accounts receivable

déprécier [depresje] *(impf, pr sub* **n. déprécions, v. dépréciiez***)* **VT 1** *(biens)* to undervalue; *(mérites, personne, livre)* to underrate **2** *(mal évaluer)* to undervalue **VPR se déprécier 1** *(de valeurs)* to depreciate, to fall; *(de marchandises)* to depreciate, to fall in value **2** *(de personne)* to belittle oneself

déprédateur, -trice [depredatœr, -tris] **N 1** pillager **2** *Fin* embezzler **ADJ** pillaging, *Fml* depredatory

déprédation [depredasjɔ̃] **NF 1** *(pillage)* pillaging, *Fml* depredation **2** *Fin (de fonds etc)* misappropriation, embezzlement

déprendre (se) [sədeprɑ̃dr] **VPR** *(conj like* **prendre***)* to detach oneself, to get free; **se d. d'une habitude/d'une personne** to get out of a habit/get clear *or* free of a person

dépressif, -ive [depresif, -iv] **ADJ** depressive

dépression [depresjɔ̃] **NF 1** *(affaissement)* depression; *(dans le sol)* hollow, dip; *(dans l'océan)* trough; *Astron (de l'horizon)* dip; *Mil* **angle de d.** *(d'une arme)* angle of depression **2** *(chute) (de valeur)* fall; **d. économique** economic depression, slump; *Météo* **d. (barométrique)** (barometric) depression, low, trough **3** *Psy (mental)* depression; **faire de la d.** to be in a state of depression; *Méd* **d. nerveuse** nervous breakdown; **d. hivernale** seasonal affective disorder, SAD

dépressionnaire [depresjɔnɛr] **ADJ 1** *Météo* **zone** *ou* **centre d.** trough, area of low pressure; **système d.** low-pressure system **2** *Écon* slump; **le marché a des tendances dépressionnaires** the market is sliding towards a slump

dépressurisation [depresyrizasjɔ̃] **NF** depressurization

dépressuriser [depresyrize] **VT** *(avion, véhicule spatial)* to depressurize

déprimant [deprimã] **ADJ** depressing

déprime [deprim] **NF** *Fam* depression; **la d.** the blues; **c'est la d. dans tous les secteurs de l'économie** all sectors of the economy are depressed; **faire de la d.** to be in a state of depression; **avoir un (petit) coup de d.** to be (a bit) depressed

déprimé [deprime] **ADJ 1** *(personne)* depressed **2** *(surface etc)* depressed, low, flat, flattened; **front d.** low forehead **3** *Bourse (marché)* depressed

déprimer [deprime] **VT 1** *(personne)* to depress **2** *(surface etc)* to depress, to lower **VI** *Fam* to be depressed

de profundis [deprɔfɔ̃dis] **NM** *Rel* de profundis

déprogrammation [deprɔgramasjɔ̃] **NF** *(de rendez-vous, d'émission TV ou radio)* cancellation

déprogrammer [deprɔgrame] VT *(rendez-vous, émission TV ou radio)* to cancel; *Ordinat* to remove from a program

déprotection [deprɔteksjɔ̃] NF *Ordinat* unprotecting

DEPS [deapees] Com *(abrév* **dernier entré, premier sorti)** LIFO

dépucelage [depyslaʒ] NM *Fam* loss of one's virginity; **son d. a eu lieu l'été de ses 15 ans** she had sex for the first time the summer she was 15, the first time for her was the summer she was 15

dépuceler [depysle] VT *Fam* to take the virginity of, to deflower; **se faire d.** to lose one's virginity, to have sex for the first time; **il faudrait qu'il se fasse d.** he needs to lose his virginity; **elle a été dépucelée très jeune** she first had sex at a very young age; **c'est lui qui l'a dépucelée** he was her first

DEPUIS [dəpɥi]

> PRÉP ▪ since **1** ▪ for **2** ▪ from **2–4**
> ADV ▪ since (then) ▪ later
> CONJ ▪ since *(depuis que)*

PRÉP SEE GRAMMAR A72; B31; B55 **1** *(temps)* since; **je ne suis pas sorti d. hier** I haven't been out since yesterday; **en vigueur d. le 1er avril** in force since 1 April; **elle est handicapée d. l'âge de cinq ans** she has been disabled since she was five *or* from the age of five; **ils ne se sont plus quittés d. leur rencontre** they haven't been apart since they first met; **d. ce temps-là, d. lors** since then, since that time; **d. ce jour, tout a changé** everything changed after that, since that day everything has changed; **je suis là d. le déjeuner** I've been here (ever) since lunch; **d. quand êtes-vous ici?** how long have you been here?; **d. quand est-il permis d'entrer sans frapper?** since when can you come in without knocking? **2** *(durée)* for; **je suis ici d. trois jours** I've been here for three days; **d. combien de temps êtes-vous mariés?** how long have you been married (for)?; **il l'aime/vit ici d. toujours** he has always loved her/lived here; **d. le matin jusqu'au soir** from morning till night; **d. le temps que je te le dis** considering how often I've told you; *Fam* **comment vas-tu, d. le temps?** how have you been all this time?; **ça devait casser, d. le temps!** it had to break sometime!, it was bound to break sometime!; **arrivé d. peu** arrived a short while ago; **d. la nuit des temps** since the dawn of time; **d. des siècles** for centuries **3** *(lieu etc)* from; **d. ma chambre, j'entends tout** I can hear everything from my room; **il ne m'a pas parlé d. Rouen** he hasn't spoken to me since (we left) Rouen; *Radio* **concert transmis d. Londres** concert broadcast from London; **un embouteillage d. La Rochelle** a traffic jam all the way from La Rochelle; **téléphoner d. chez soi** to ring from home **4** *(ordre, quantité)* **chemises d. 30 euros** (jusqu'à 150 euros) shirts from 30 (to 150) euros; **des robes d. la taille 34** dresses from size 34 upwards

ADV since (then), since that time; *(par la suite)* afterwards, later; **d., je comprends mieux son attitude** I've understood his attitude better since then *or* since that time; **je l'ai connu d.** I made his acquaintance later

CONJ **d. que** + *ind* since; **nous ne l'avons pas vu d. qu'il est marié** we haven't seen him since he got married; **d. qu'il sait qu'il va la voir, il ne tient plus en place** he hasn't been able to keep still since he found out he was going to see her; **d. qu'elle couche avec le patron, elle ne nous dit plus bonjour** she hasn't acknowledged us since she's been sleeping

with the boss, now that she's sleeping with the boss she doesn't acknowledge us any more; **d. que le monde est monde** since the world began

dépuratif, -ive [depyratif, -iv] ADJ, NM *Méd* purgative

dépuration [depyrasjɔ̃] NF *(du sang)* cleansing

dépurer [depyre] VT *(sang)* to cleanse

députation [depytasjɔ̃] NF **1** *(action)* delegation, deputing, delegating; *(groupe)* deputation, delegation **2** *Pol (fonction de député)* membership of Parliament; **la d. n'est pas une chose facile** it is not easy being a Member of Parliament; **candidat à la d.** parliamentary candidate; **se présenter à la d.** to stand for Parliament

député [depyte] NM **1** *(représentant)* deputy, delegate **2** *Pol Br* ≃ Member of Parliament *(de* for), *Am* ≃ Congressman, *f* Congresswoman; **d. du Parlement européen** Member of the European Parliament, MEP; **la Chambre des députés** *Br* ≃ the House of Commons, *Am* ≃ the House of Representatives; **elle a été élue d. ou députée** she was elected a Member of Parliament *or* to Parliament; **d.-maire** = MP and mayor

députer [depyte] VT to appoint as deputy *or* delegate, to depute; **on l'a député comme ambassadeur au Vatican** he has been appointed ambassador to the Vatican; **c'est lui qui a été député pour les négociations** he's been appointed *or* delegated to take charge of the negotiations

déqualification [dekalifikasjɔ̃] NF **la d. (professionnelle) est de plus en plus fréquente** more and more people are overqualified for their jobs *or* for the work they do; **les jeunes souffrent de la d.** young people are overqualified

déqualifier [dekalifje] VT *(de l'automatisation)* *(ouvrier)* to deskill; **on est souvent obligé de d. les gens qu'on embauche** it is frequently necessary to recruit people for jobs they are overqualified for

der [dɛr] NM OU NF INV *Fam (abrév* **dernier)** **la d. des d.** the war to end all wars

déracinable [derasinabl] ADJ which can be uprooted; **le racisme n'est guère plus d. aujourd'hui qu'il y a un siècle** it is no easier to uproot *or* eradicate racism now than it was a century ago

déraciné, -ée [derasine] ADJ uprooted
▪ N person who has been uprooted

déracinement [derasinmɑ̃] NM *(d'une souche)*, *Fig (d'une personne)* uprooting; *(d'un défaut, d'un abus, d'une idée reçue etc)* eradication

déraciner [derasine] VT *(souche, arbre)* to uproot, to tear up by the roots; *Fig (personne)* to uproot; *(défaut, abus, idée reçue)* to eradicate; *(racisme, sexisme)* to uproot, to eradicate

déraidir [derɛdir] VT *(membre, tissu etc)* to take the stiffness out of; *Fig (caractère de qn)* to soften
▪ VPR **se déraidir** *(d'un membre, tissu etc)* to lose its stiffness; *(d'une personne)* to unbend, to thaw

déraillement [derajmɑ̃] NM *Rail* derailment

dérailler [deraje] VI **1** *(d'un train, d'un tram)* to become derailed, to leave the rails; *(d'une pointe de lecture)* to jump *or* leave the sound groove; **faire d. un train** to derail a train **2** *Fam (d'une machine etc)* to be on the blink; *(d'une personne)* (dire une bêtise, se tromper) to talk nonsense; *(divaguer)* to rave; *(devenir gâteux)* to go gaga

dérailleur [derajœr] NM *(de bicyclette)* derailleur (gears)

déraison [derɛzɔ̃] NF *Litt* unreasonableness, folly

déraisonnable [derɛzɔnabl] ADJ foolish

déraisonnablement [derɛzɔnabləmɑ̃] ADV foolishly

déraisonner [derɛzɔne] VI *Litt* to talk nonsense

dérangé [derɑ̃ʒe] ADJ *(esprit)* deranged, unbalanced; *(estomac)* upset; *Fam* **tu es complètement d.!** you're off your rocker!

dérangeant [derɑ̃ʒɑ̃] ADJ *(film, personnage)* disturbing

dérangement [derɑ̃ʒmɑ̃] NM **1** *(gêne)* disturbance, trouble; *(perturbation)* disturbed *or* unsettled state; **causer du d. à qn** to put sb to trouble *or* bother; **je ne veux pas te causer de d.** I don't want to put you to any trouble *or* bother; **excusez-moi pour le d.** I'm sorry to disturb *or* trouble you; **il faudrait le dédommager de son d.** we'll have to give him something for his trouble **2** *(désordre)* *(de livres, meubles etc)* disarrangement, disorder; *Élec (dans la ligne etc)* fault; *Tél* **la ligne est en d.** the line is out of order, there's a fault on the line; **d. d'esprit** mental derangement; **d. de l'intestin** upset stomach

déranger [derɑ̃ʒe] (je **dérangeai(s); n. dérangeons**) VT **1** *(papiers, livres etc)* to disturb, to put out of order, to disarrange; *(chignon, mise)* to rumple; **il a dérangé ma chambre** he's made my room untidy
2 *(gêner) (personne)* to disturb; **ne pas d.** *(sur panneau)* do not disturb; **je ne peux pas travailler, je suis sans arrêt dérangé** I can't work with all these interruptions; **cela vous dérange si j'ouvre la fenêtre?** would you mind if I opened the window?; **je vous dérange?** am I disturbing you?; *Iron* **je ne te dérange pas trop?** am I in your way?; **excusez-moi de vous d.** I'm sorry to disturb *or* trouble you; **si cela ne vous dérange pas** if it's no trouble to you, if that's all right by you, if you don't mind; **je ne voudrais pas vous d. pour rien** I wouldn't want to bring you out for nothing; *Fam Iron* **ça te dérangerait de me laisser tranquille?** would you mind very much leaving me alone?; *Fam* **et alors, ça te dérange?** what business is it of yours?, what's it to you?
3 *(perturber) (personne, projets)* to upset; **d. l'esprit de qn** to affect the balance of sb's mind; **avoir le cerveau dérangé** to be deranged; **quelque chose lui a dérangé l'estomac** something has upset his stomach; *Tél* **la ligne est dérangée** the line is out of order; **le temps est complètement dérangé** the weather is all back to front
▪ VPR **se déranger merci de vous être dérangé** thank you for putting yourself out *or* for the trouble you've gone to; **ne vous dérangez pas pour moi** please don't put yourself out *or* go to any trouble on my account; **nous pouvons nous d. à toute heure de la nuit** we can come out at any time of the night; **il ne se dérange jamais, c'est toujours nous qui devons y aller** he never comes to us, we always have to go to him

dérapage [derapaʒ] NM **1** *Aut* skid; *Aviat, Ski* sideslip; *Pol, Fig (erreur)* bad mistake; *Fig (d'un budget, d'un horaire)* slippage; *(d'une conversation)* deterioration; *Aut* **d. contrôlé** controlled skid; *Fig* **le d. des prix** spiralling prices; **le d. inflationniste** the inflationary spiral; **il y a déjà eu plusieurs dérapages dans cette émission** there have already been several inappropriate outbursts in the programme; **il faudrait éviter tout d. dans les négociations de paix** there must be no hitches in the peace talks, the peace talks must not come unstuck *or* become derailed **2** *Naut (d'ancre)* dragging

déraper [derape] VI **1** *Aut* to skid; *Aviat, Ski* to sideslip; *Fig (des prix)* to be rising uncontrollably, to soar, to rise sharply; *(d'une conversation)* to deteriorate; *Fig* **le budget dérape** there's some slippage in the budget; **il faut éviter que les négociations ne dérapent** the talks must not go wrong or come unstuck or become derailed; **le débat a rapidement dérapé vers le duel** the discussion rapidly deteriorated into or turned into a fight; **les commentaires ont dérapé vers une critique sévère** comment has turned into severe criticism **2** *Naut (d'une ancre)* to drag

dératé [derate] NM *Fam* **courir comme un d.** to run flat out

dératisation [deratizasjɔ̃] NF extermination of rats

dératiser [deratize] VT to clear of rats

dérayage [derɛjaʒ] NM *Cin, TV* polishing out

dérayer [derɛje] VT *Cin, TV* to polish out

derby [dɛrbi] NM **1** *Courses de chevaux* derby; **le D. d'Epsom** the Derby **2** *Ftbl* local derby

derche [dɛrʃ] NM *très Fam* butt, *Br* bum, *Am* fanny; **se magner le d.** to move one's butt or *Br* bum; **un faux d.** a two-faced swine or *Am* stinker

derechef [dərəʃɛf] ADV *Arch, Litt* a second time, yet again, once more

déréférencement [dereferɑ̃smɑ̃] NM *Mktg (d'un produit)* delisting

déréférencer [dereferɑ̃se] VT *(produit)* to delist; **certains produits ont été déréférencés par le distributeur** some products have been delisted by the distributor

déréglé [deregle] ADJ **1** *(machine, horloge etc)* not working properly **2** *(estomac)* upset; *(esprit)* disordered; *(pouls)* irregular; *(temps)* unsettled **3** *(vie)* wild, dissolute; **il a des mœurs complètement déréglées** he is quite dissolute or debauched

dérèglement [deregləmɑ̃] NM **1** *(d'une machine, d'une horloge)* malfunctioning **2** *(du temps)* unsettled state; *(du pouls)* irregularity; **d. de l'esprit** mental derangement; **j'ai un d. de l'appétit** there is something wrong with my appetite; **d. hormonal** hormone disorder **3** *(de l'imagination)* disordered state; *(de la moralité)* dissoluteness; **il fait montre d'un d. de l'imagination** his imagination is getting out of control; *Vieilli, Hum* **dérèglements** dissolute behaviour

déréglementation [dereglmɑ̃tasjɔ̃] NF deregulation

déréglementer [dereglomɑ̃te] VT to deregulate

dérégler [deregle] (**je dérègle, n. déréglons; je déréglerai**) VT **1** *(horloge, machine etc)* to cause to malfunction; *Radio, TV* to detune; **tu as déréglé la pendule/le moteur à force de la/le démonter** you've dismantled the clock/the engine so many times that it's gone haywire **2** *(estomac)* to upset; *(personne, esprit, habitudes, temps)* to unsettle; **d. son sommeil** to disrupt one's sleeping pattern; **elle a complètement déréglé son appétit avec tous ses régimes** all these diets have completely disrupted her eating patterns
► VPR **se dérégler 1** *(d'horloge, de machine etc)* to go wrong **2** *(de pouls)* to be irregular; *(d'estomac)* to be upset; **son esprit se dérègle** his mind is going; **elle s'est déréglé le système digestif** she's ruined her digestive system **3** *(de moralité)* to become dissolute; *(d'imagination)* to run wild, to get out of control

dérider [deride] VT to cheer up, to brighten up; **c'est impossible de le d.** it's impossible to get a smile out of him
► VPR **se dérider** to cheer up, to brighten up

Il faut noter que le verbe anglais **to deride** est un faux ami. Il signifie **ridiculiser**.

---

dérision [derizjɔ̃] NF derision, mockery; **dire qch par d.** to say sth derisively or mockingly; **geste de d.** derisive gesture; **tourner qch en d.** to deride sth; **c'est une d.!** *(chose insignifiante)* it's ridiculous or laughable!

dérisoire [derizwar] ADJ *(offre, salaire)* derisory, laughable; *(prix)* very low, rock-bottom; **vendre qch à un prix d.** to sell sth at a ridiculously or an absurdly low price; **cette objection me paraît d.** that seems an absurd objection to me

dérisoirement [derizwarmɑ̃] ADV laughably, pathetically; **il est payé d.** he's paid a derisory or laughable or pathetic amount

dérivatif, -ive [derivatif, -iv] ADJ *Ling* derivative
▪ NM distraction (**à, de** from); **c'est un d. à sa douleur** it takes his mind off his grief; **le sport est un excellent d.** sport is an excellent way of taking your mind off things

dérivation [derivasjɔ̃] NF **1** *Aut* diversion; *Tech (d'un cours d'eau)* diversion, tapping; *Élec (du courant)* shunt(ing), branching, tapping; *Tech* by-pass; **canal de d.** headrace, penstock; *Élec* **monté en d.** shunt connected **2** *Ling, Math* derivation **3** *Naut, Aviat* drift

dérive [deriv] NF **1** *Naut* drift, leeway; *Aviat* drift; **(quille de) d.** *Naut* drop keel, centreboard; *Aviat* fin; **angle de d.** angle of drift, drift angle; **à la d., en d.** adrift; **navire en d.** drifting vessel; *Géog* **d. des continents** continental drift **2** *(évolution incontrôlée et dangereuse)* **tout va à la d.** everything has been left to drift; **un mariage/une entreprise qui part à la d.** a failing marriage/business; **des jeunes à la d. dans la grande ville** young people adrift in the big city; **une d. totalitaire est à craindre dans ce pays** this country is in danger of drifting into totalitarianism, there's a danger that this country might be overtaken by totalitarianism

dérivé, -ée [derive] ADJ **1** *(signification etc)* derived, secondary; *Math (fonction, courbe)* derived; **produit d.** *Chimie* by-product; *Bourse* derivative **2** *Élec* **courant d.** shunt current
▪ NM *Ling* derivative; *Chimie, Ind* derivative, by-product; **d. du sang** blood product
▪ NF *Math* **dérivée** derivative

dériver¹ [derive] VT **1** *Tech (cours d'eau)* to divert or tap the course of; *Élec (courant)* to shunt, to branch **2** *Ling, Math* to derive
▪ VI *Ling* to be derived (**de** from)

dériver² VT *Tech* to unrivet

dériver³ VI **1** *Naut, Aviat* to drift; **d. à vau-l'eau** to drift downstream **2** *Fig (du sujet etc)* to drift away (**de** from)

dériveur [derivœr] NM *Naut* **1** *(bateau)* sailing dinghy *(with centreboard)* **2** *(voile)* storm sail

dérivomètre [derivɔmɛtr] NM *Aviat* drift meter

dermatite [dɛrmatit] NF dermatitis

dermato [dɛrmato] N *Fam (abrév* **dermatologue)** dermatologist

dermatologie [dɛrmatɔlɔʒi] NF dermatology

dermatologique [dɛrmatɔlɔʒik] ADJ dermatological

dermatologiste [dɛrmatɔlɔʒist], **dermatologue** [dɛrmatɔlɔg] N dermatologist

dermatose [dɛrmatoz] NF *Méd* dermatosis

derme [dɛrm] NM *Anat* derm

dermique [dɛrmik] ADJ *Anat* dermic, dermal

---

dermite [dɛrmit] NF *Méd* = **dermatite**

DERNIER, -IÈRE [dɛrnje, -jɛr]

ADJ last **1–6** ▪ final **1** ▪ latest **2** ▪ utmost **4** ▪ bottom **3, 5** ▪ worst **5**
N last **1, 2** ▪ latest **2** ▪ latter **2**
NF final performance **1** ▪ last edition **2** ▪ latest **3**
ADV last *(en dernier)*

ADJ SEE GRAMMAR B10 **1** *(ultime)* last; *(marquant la fin)* final; **au d. moment** at the last (moment); **à la dernière minute** at the last minute; **des préparatifs de dernière minute** last minute preparations; **les derniers préparatifs** the final preparations; **faire un d. effort** to make a final or one last effort; **mettre la dernière main à qch** to give or put the finishing or final touches to sth; **j'ai dépensé jusqu'à mon d. sou** I've spent my last penny; **la dernière moitié du XVIᵉ siècle** the second half of the 16th century; **les derniers mètres de l'ascension** the final metres of the climb; **d. rappel** *(de facture)* final reminder; **d. paiement** final payment; **c'est mon d. prix** that's my final offer; *Bourse* **d. cours** closing price; *Journ* **dernière heure** copy deadline; *Journ* **dernière page** back page; *Journ* **dernière édition** final edition, late edition; **dernière épreuve** *(dans l'édition)* press proof; **dernière proposition** final offer; **d. délai pour l'inscription** deadline for registration; **il faut libérer la chambre à 9 h, d. délai** *ou Fam* **carat** the room has to be vacated by 9 o'clock at the very latest; **en d. recours** *ou* **ressort** as a last resort; **en dernière analyse** in the final analysis; **en d. lieu** lastly, last; **c'est la dernière personne à qui je demanderais un service** he's the last person I would ask a favour of; **pour la dernière fois** for the last time; **il veut toujours avoir le d. mot** he always has to have the last word; **je n'ai pas dit mon d. mot** I'm not done for yet, there's still fight left in me, you/they/etc haven't heard the last of me; **la peste n'a pas dit son d. mot** the plague is still with us, the plague has not been beaten; **c'est ma dernière chance** this is my last chance VOIR GRAMMAIRE A26
2 *(le ou la plus récent(e))* last; **mardi d.** last Tuesday; **le mois d.** last month; **au cours des dernières années** over the past or last few years; **la dernière fois, il allait bien** he was well (the) last time I saw him; **je l'ai déjà fait la dernière fois** I did that the last time; **ces derniers temps, ces temps derniers** lately; **dernières nouvelles** latest news; **aux dernières nouvelles, il s'est marié** the last I heard, he had got married; **ce sont les dernières nouvelles que j'ai eues de lui** that's the last I've heard of him; **dernière édition** latest edition; **les derniers développements d'une affaire** the latest developments of an affair; **le d. roman de cet auteur** this author's latest novel; **la dernière mode, le d. cri** the latest fashion, the latest thing; **le d. modèle** the latest model; **mon d. patron était anglais** my last boss was English VOIR GRAMMAIRE A7; A26
3 *(dans l'espace)* last; **la dernière maison du village** the last house in the village; **le d. rang** the back or last row; **la dernière marche de l'escalier** *(en haut)* the top step; *(en bas)* the bottom step; **au d. étage** on the top floor; **le d. tiroir de la commode** the bottom drawer of the chest of drawers
4 *Litt (extrême)* utmost; **vérité dernière** ultimate truth; **de la dernière importance** of the utmost or greatest importance; **au d. degré** to the utmost or highest degree; **le d. degré de la bêtise** the height of stupidity; **atteindre le d. degré de la bêtise** to be the height of or the last word in stupidity; **le d. degré de la misère** the depths of poverty; **dans la dernière misère** in utmost poverty; **être du d. bien avec qn** to be extremely friendly with

sb, to be great friends with sb; **ils sont du d. bien** they're the best of friends *or* on the best of terms; **être de la dernière insolence avec qn** to be most insolent to *or* with sb; **se débattre avec la dernière énergie** to put up a fierce struggle; **jeter dans le d. désespoir** to cast into the depths of despair; **c'est du d. chic/ridicule** it's the height of elegance/ridiculousness

5 *(le pire)* lowest, worst; **de d. ordre** very inferior; **être le d. élève de la classe** to be last in *or* bottom of the class; **il a été reçu d. au concours** he came in last in the competition; **un hôtel de dernière catégorie** a fourth-rate hotel; **une étoffe de la dernière qualité** *ou* **du d. choix** material of the poorest quality; **c'était la dernière chose à dire/faire** that's the last thing you/he/*etc* should have said/done; *Fml* **ils lui ont fait subir les derniers outrages** they subjected her to the worst outrages

6 *(avec idée de mort)* last; **ils ont bien cru que leur dernière heure était venue** they really thought that their last hour had come; **je m'en souviendrai jusqu'à mon d. jour** *ou* **jusqu'à ma dernière heure** I shall remember it to my dying day; **nous sommes restés avec lui jusqu'à son d. souffle** we stayed with him until the last *or* the end; **rendre le d. soupir** to breathe one's last; **rendre les derniers devoirs à qn** to lay sb out; **recevoir les derniers sacrements** to receive the last rites; **ce sont ses dernières volontés** that was his dying wish; **les dernières dispositions du défunt** the dead man's last will and testament; **accompagner qn à sa dernière demeure** to accompany sb to his/her final resting place

N 1 *(dans classement)* last; *Sport* **il est arrivé le d.** *ou* **bon d.** he came in last; **le d. arrivé** the last to arrive; **il est le d. de sa promotion** he is bottom of his year; **dans les derniers** among the last; **les six derniers** the last six; **c'est le d. de mes soucis** that's the least of my worries; **elle est la dernière à qui je demanderais de l'aide** she's the last person I'd ask for help; **je les arrêterai tous jusqu'au d.** I'll stop each and every last one of them

2 *(dans chronologie)* last, latest; **c'est notre petit d.** he's our youngest (child); **comment va la petite dernière?** how's the little one?; **ce d. répondit …** the latter answered …; **le d. en date** the most recent; **c'est toujours le d. à sortir** he's always last out

3 *Péj* **on la traite comme la dernière des dernières** they treat her like dirt *or* the lowest of the low; **ton frère est vraiment le d. des crétins/des menteurs** your brother is the world's biggest fool/liar; *très Fam* **c'est vraiment la dernière des connes** she really is an utter prat

NF dernière 1 *Théâtre* last night, final performance

2 *Journ (édition)* last edition; *(page)* back page

3 *(nouveauté)* **tu as entendu la dernière de ton frère?** have you heard your brother's latest?

ADV en d. last (of all); **cela vient en d.** that comes last; **il sort toujours en d.** he's always last out; **je mange toujours le meilleur en d.** I always keep the best till last

dernièrement [dɛrnjɛrmɑ̃] **ADV** lately, of late, recently

dernier-né, *pl* **-née,** *pl* **derniers-nés, dernières-nées N** youngest child

dérobade [derɔbad] **NF 1** *(de qn, qch)* evasion, avoidance; **c'est le spécialiste de la d.** he's a past master at avoiding the issue; **il pratique beaucoup la d. pour ne pas payer ce qu'il lui doit** he gets out of paying what he owes her as much as he can **2** *(d'un cheval)* swerve, jib

dérobé [derɔbe] **ADJ** *(escalier, porte etc)* hidden, concealed, secret

dérobée (à la) [aladerɔbe] **ADV** stealthily, secretly, on the sly; **regarder qn à la d.** to steal a glance at sb; **sortir à la d.** to steal out

dérober [derɔbe] **VT 1** *(voler)* to steal, to make away with; **d. qch à qn** to steal sth from sb; **d. un baiser** to steal a kiss **2** *(cacher)* to hide, to conceal; **d. qch à qn** to hide sth from sb; **ce mur dérobe la vue** this wall hides the view; **d. qn au danger** to snatch sb from danger

VPR se dérober 1 *(s'échapper)* to escape, to steal away, to slip away (**à** from); **se d. aux regards** to escape observation, to avoid notice; **se d. à la curiosité de qn** to avoid sb's prying eyes; **se d. à son devoir** to evade *or* shirk one's duty; **je le lui ai demandé, mais il s'est dérobé** I asked him, but he avoided the issue **2** *(manquer)* *(du sol, des genoux, des jambes)* to give way (**sous** beneath) **3** *(de cheval)* to swerve, to jib

dérogation [derɔgasjɔ̃] **NF** *(pour passer un examen)* waiver, exemption; *Jur* waiver; *(à une loi)* derogation, impairment (**à** of); **d. à qch** departure from sth, exception to sth; **par** *ou* **en d. à cette règle** this rule notwithstanding, as an exception to this rule; **je n'admettrai aucune d.** I will allow no exceptions

dérogatoire [derɔgatwar] **ADJ** *Jur* **clause d.** waiver, *Spéc* derogatory clause

déroger [derɔʒe] **VI** *(je dérogeai(s); n. dérogeons)* **d. à l'usage/à la loi** to depart from custom/the law; **d. à un principe** to waive a principle; *Hist* **d. (à noblesse)** to lose rank; **d. à son rang** to lower *or* demean oneself

dérougir [deruʒir] **VI 1** *Vieilli (perdre de sa rougeur)* to stop blushing **2** *Can Fam* **ne pas d.** *(du travail)* not to let up; *(être bondé)* to be jam packed; *(être en colère)* to be always raging; *(être soûl)* to be permanently pissed

dérouillée [deruje] **NF** *très Fam* beating, belting

dérouiller [deruje] **VT 1** *(enlever la rouille de)* to take *or* get the rust off **2** *très Fam (battre)* to beat up

VI *très Fam* **1** *(être battu)* to get beaten up, to catch it; **qu'est-ce qu'il a dérouillé!** he really took a beating! **2** *(souffrir)* to suffer, to have a hard time; **depuis qu'il a cette otite, qu'est-ce qu'il dérouille** he's suffered agonies with that earache

VPR se dérouiller **se d. les jambes** to stretch one's legs; **se d. la mémoire** to refresh one's memory

déroulement [derulmɑ̃] **NM 1** *(d'une intrigue, des événements)* unfolding, development, progress; **nous avons besoin de connaître le d. de votre journée** we need to know how you spent the day; **le d. des travaux s'est passé normalement** the work went smoothly; **pendant tout le d. de la cérémonie** throughout the ceremony; **il a surveillé tout le d. des opérations** he monitored operations from start to finish **2** *(d'une bobine etc)* unwinding

dérouler [derule] **VT** *(rouleau)* to unroll; *(store)* to let down; *(câble etc)* to unwind, to uncoil; **le serpent a déroulé ses anneaux** the snake uncoiled itself; *Ordinat* **d. un menu** to pull down a menu; *Fig Litt* **il a déroulé le fil de sa vie** he recounted *or* unfolded the story of his life

VPR se dérouler 1 *(d'un rouleau)* to come unrolled, to unroll; *(d'un store)* to come down; *(d'un câble etc)* to come unwound; *(d'un serpent)* to uncoil **2** *Fig* to unfold; **le paysage se déroule devant nous** the landscape unfolds *or* stretches out before us; **les événements qui se déroulent à Paris** the events (that are) unfolding *or* taking place in Paris; **la manifestation s'est déroulée dans le calme** the demonstration went off peacefully *or*

was peaceful; **son existence se déroule dans la plus grande monotonie** he leads the most monotonous of existences

dérouleur [derulœr] **NM** *Ordinat* tape drive, streamer; **d. de bandes** tape streamer

déroutage [derutaʒ] **NM d. de marchandises** rerouting of goods

déroutant [derutɑ̃] **ADJ** disconcerting

déroute [derut] **NF** *(débandade)* rout, disorderly retreat; **l'ennemi fut mis en d.** the enemy was put to flight *or* was routed

déroutement [derutmɑ̃] **NM** *Naut, Aviat* rerouting, diversion

dérouter [derute] **VT 1** *(confondre)* to nonplus, *Fam* to throw **2** *(tromper)* to lead astray; **d. la police** to throw the police off the scent; **d. les soupçons** to divert suspicion **3** *(navire, avion etc)* to divert, to reroute

derrick [derik] **NM** *Pétr* derrick

DERRIÈRE [dɛrjɛr] **PRÉP 1** *(au dos de)* behind, *Am* in back of; **il s'est caché d. le rideau** he hid behind the curtain; **les uns d. les autres** one behind the other; *aussi Fig* **les autres sont loin d. moi** the others are way behind me; **il faut toujours être d. elle** *ou* **son dos** you always have to be at her back; **il a laissé une femme et deux enfants d. lui** he left a wife and two children; **d. des abords chaleureux** behind a cordial façade; **faire qch d. (le dos de) qn** to do sth behind sb's back; **dire du mal d. (le dos de) qn** to say nasty things about sb behind his/her back; **c'est lui qui est d. tout ça** he's the one behind all this

2 de d. from behind; **sortir de d. un buisson** to come out from behind a bush

ADV 1 *(en arrière)* behind, at the back, in the rear; **laisser qn d.** to leave sb behind; **regarder d.** to look back; **ton parapluie est d.** your umbrella is at the back; **enfiler un pull sens devant d.** to put on a pullover back to front; **ça se ferme d.** it fastens (up) at the back; *Aut* **aller** *ou* **monter d.** to sit in the back *or Am* in back; **taisez-vous, d.!** *(en voiture)* quiet back there!; *(dans une pièce)* be quiet at the back!

2 par d. from behind; **attaquer qn par d.** to attack sb from behind *or* from the rear; **cette robe s'attache par d.** the dress does up at the back; **il a dû passer par d.** he had to go round the back; *Fig* **elle le critique par d.** she criticizes him behind his back

NM 1 *(d'édifice etc)* back, rear; **le d. de la tête** the back of the head; **porte de d.** back door; **pattes de d.** hind legs

2 *(postérieur)* behind, backside, bottom, *Am* butt; *(d'un animal)* hindquarters; *Fig Fam* **il en est tombé sur le d.** it knocked him for six, he nearly fainted (with surprise); **recevoir des coups de pied dans le** *ou* **au d.** to get kicked in the behind *or* up the backside

déruralisation [deryralizasjɔ̃] **NF** rural depopulation

dérushage [derœʃaʒ] **NM** *TV, Cin* first view

dérusher [deryʃe] **VT** *Cin, TV* to edit

derviche [dɛrviʃ] **NM** dervish; **d. tourneur** dancing *or* whirling dervish

des [de] *voir* **de**

dès [dɛ] **PRÉP** since, from, as early as, as long ago as; **d. sa jeunesse** from childhood; **d. l'abord** from the outset, from the (very) first; **d. maintenant,** *Fml* **d. à présent** from now on, *Fml* henceforth; **j'ai décidé de commencer le projet d. maintenant** I've decided to start on the project now *or* immediately; **d. 1840** as far back as 1840; **d. le matin** first thing in the morning; **d. son arrivée** the minute *or* the moment he arrives/arrived; as soon as he arrives/arrived; **d. mon retour** immediately on my return; **je te téléphonerai d. mon retour** I'll call you as soon as *or* immediately *or* the minute I get back; **d. sa première remarque, j'ai senti que …** as soon as he spoke *or* from the moment he spoke, I felt that …; **d. les premiers froids** as soon as it starts to get cold; **elle est ivre d. le premier verre** she's tipsy after one drink, one drink and she's tipsy; **d. la porte, il commença à crier** he had no sooner reached the door than he began to shout; **d. l'autoroute, on sentait la différence de température** as soon as we reached the motorway, we could feel the difference in temperature; **d. Paris, la pluie tombait** it rained all the way from Paris; **d. que** + *ind* as soon as, the moment that; **d. lors** *(dans le temps)* then; *(par conséquent)* consequently, therefore; **ils vendirent leur maison et d. lors, partirent habiter à Paris** as soon as they sold their house, they went off to live in Paris; **d. lors que vous refusez** seeing that *or* since you refuse SEE GRAMMAR B31–2

désabonnement [dezabɔnmɑ̃] NM cancellation (of subscription)

désabonner [dezabɔne] VT **d. qn à une revue** to cancel sb's subscription to a magazine
▸ VPR **se désabonner** to stop subscribing, to cancel one's subscription (**à** to)

désabusé [dezabyze] ADJ disillusioned, disenchanted

désabusement [dezabyzmɑ̃] NM disillusionment, disenchantment

désabuser [dezabyze] VT *Littr* **d. qn** to disillusion sb, to open sb's eyes; **c'est un esprit désabusé** he's disillusioned

désacclimater [dezaklimate] VT **d. qn/qch** to remove sb/sth from their/its natural habitat

désaccord [dezakɔr] NM *(mésentente)* disagreement; *(d'intérêts etc)* clash; **les désaccords entre les États-Unis et Cuba** the disagreements *or* the dissension between the United States and Cuba; **c'est un de leurs désaccords** it's one of the things they disagree about; **être** *ou* **se trouver en d. avec qn sur qch** to disagree *or* be at odds with sb about sth; **sujet de d.** bone of contention; **d. entre la théorie et la pratique** discrepancy between theory and practice; **il y a d. entre ses paroles et sa conduite** his words are inconsistent *or* not in keeping with his conduct; **vivre en d. avec son époque** to be out of step with one's time

désaccordé [dezakɔrde] ADJ *Mus* out of tune

désaccorder [dezakɔrde] *Mus* VT *(instrument)* to put out of tune
▸ VPR **se désaccorder** to go out of tune

désaccoupler [dezakuple] VT **1** *Tech (wagons)* to uncouple; *Élec* to disconnect **2** *(chiens de meute)* to slip, to uncouple

désaccoutumance [dezakutymɑ̃s] NF **d. de** *ou* **à la drogue** breaking the habit of taking drugs; **la d. à la drogue est quelque chose de pénible** overcoming drug addiction is a painful process; *Fig* **j'étais tellement bien avec toi que la d. va être longue et douloureuse** being with you was so good that learning to live without you will be a long and painful process

désaccoutumer [dezakutyme] VT **d. qn à (faire) qch** to get sb out of the habit of (doing) sth
▸ VPR **se désaccoutumer** to lose the habit; **se d. de (faire) qch** to get out of the habit of (doing) sth

désacralisation [dezakralizasjɔ̃] NF *(de la famille etc)* desanctification

désacraliser [dezakralize] VT *(famille etc)* to desanctify

désactivation [dezaktivasjɔ̃] NF *Nucl (d'un site)* cleaning up; *Ordinat* deactivation

désactiver [dezaktive] VT *Nucl (site)* to clean up; *Ordinat* to deactivate, to disable

désadaptation [dezadaptasjɔ̃] NF unsuitability; **il montre une d. au milieu scolaire** he shows signs of not being suited to school life

désadapter [dezadapte] VT **d. qn de qch** to wean sb away from sth; **le risque de les d. à** *ou* **de leur vie quotidienne** the danger of creating a gulf between them and their everyday life

désaffectation [dezafɛktasjɔ̃] NF *(fermeture)* *(d'un bâtiment)* closing down; *(d'une église)* deconsecration

désaffecté [dezafɛkte] ADJ disused; **église désaffectée** deconsecrated church

désaffecter [dezafɛkte] VT *(bâtiment public etc)* to put to another purpose; *(fermer)* *(bâtiment)* to close down

désaffection [dezafɛksjɔ̃] NF disaffection (**pour** with)

désagrafer [dezagrafe] VT *(vêtement)* to unfasten, to undo
▸ VPR **se désagrafer** to unfasten *or* undo one's dress/etc

désagréable [dezagreabl] ADJ *(personne, remarque)* unpleasant, disagreeable (**à** to); *(odeur)* unpleasant, nasty; *Euph* **ce n'est pas d.** that's (a bit of) all right

désagréablement [dezagreabləmɑ̃] ADV unpleasantly, disagreeably

désagrégation [dezagregasjɔ̃] NF disintegration, breaking up

désagréger [dezagreʒe] (**je désagrège, n. désagrégeons; je désagrégeai(s); je désagrégerai**) VT to cause to disintegrate; **la bombe a complètement désagrégé l'immeuble** the bomb completely destroyed the building, *Fam* the bomb smashed the building to smithereens; **la météorite a désagrégé la navette spatiale** the space shuttle disintegrated when the meteorite hit it
▸ VPR **se désagréger** to disintegrate, to break up

désagrément [dezagremɑ̃] NM trouble; **causer du d.** *ou* **des désagréments à qn** *(d'une personne)* to cause unpleasantness for sb; **sa voiture lui cause beaucoup de désagréments** his car gives him lots of problems; **il a beaucoup de désagréments avec sa voiture** he's got a lot of problems with his car; **les désagréments de la situation** the unpleasantness of the situation; **l'éloignement et la solitude font partie des désagréments de la situation** distance and loneliness are two of the things that make this a difficult situation

désaimantation [dezɛmɑ̃tasjɔ̃] NF demagnetization

désaimanter [dezɛmɑ̃te] VT to demagnetize

désaisonnalisé [desezɔnalize] ADJ seasonally adjusted

désaligné [dezaliɲe] ADJ out of alignment, out of line

désaltérant [dezalterɑ̃] ADJ thirst-quenching

désaltérer [dezaltere] (**je désaltère, n. désaltérons; je désaltérerai**) VT **d. qn** to quench sb's thirst
▸ VI **le thé désaltère mieux qu'une boisson glacée** tea is more thirst-quenching than an ice-cold drink
▸ VPR **se désaltérer** to quench one's thirst

désambiguïsation [dezɑ̃biguizasjɔ̃] NF clarification

désambiguïser [dezɑ̃biguize] VT *(situation)* to clarify, to clear up; **il faut absolument d. ta relation avec lui vis-à-vis de ta famille** you really must make your relationship with

him crystal-clear to your family; **un mot est souvent désambiguïsé par un contexte** a word in context is rarely ambiguous

désâmer (se) [sədezɑme] VPR *Can* to work oneself to death

désamiantage [dezamjɑ̃taʒ] NM removal of asbestos fireproofing

désamorçage [dezamɔrsaʒ] NM *(d'une bombe, d'un obus etc)*, *Fig (d'un conflit)* defusing

désamorcer [dezamɔrse] (**je désamorçai(s); n. désamorçons**) VT *(bombe, obus etc)*, *Fig (conflit, querelle)* to defuse; *Fig (neutraliser) (complot)* to render harmless

désamour [dezamur] NM **1** *(cessation de l'amour)* falling out of love **2** *(désillusion)* disenchantment, disillusionment

désanamorphoser [dezanamɔrfoze] VT *(image)* to unsqueeze

désannoncer [dezanɔ̃se] VT *Radio (morceau de musique, émission)* to back-announce

désaper (se) [sədezape] VPR *Fam* to strip off

désapparier [dezaparje] VT *(objets)* to remove one of a pair of, to spoil a pair of; *(couple d'oiseaux, d'animaux)* to separate; **j'ai un tas de gants désappariés** I've got piles of odd gloves

désappointement [dezapwɛ̃tmɑ̃] NM *Litt* disappointment

désappointer [dezapwɛ̃te] VT *Litt* to disappoint

désapprendre [dezaprɑ̃dr] VT *Fml* to forget; *(exprès)* to unlearn

désapprobateur, -trice [dezaprɔbatœr, -tris] ADJ disapproving; **regard d.** disapproving look, look of disapproval

désapprobation [dezaprɔbasjɔ̃] NF disapproval (**de** of); **regard de d.** disapproving look, look of disapproval; **murmure de d.** murmur of disapproval

désapprouver [dezapruve] VT to disapprove of; **elle désapprouve mon projet** she disapproves *or* doesn't approve of my plan; **il désapprouve que je vienne** he disapproves of my coming; **je le désapprouve de ne pas avoir travaillé** I disapprove of the fact that he didn't work

désapprovisionné [dezaprɔvizjɔne] ADJ *(compte)* overdrawn

désarçonner [dezarsɔne] VT *(de cheval)* to unseat, to throw; *Fig (d'un adversaire, d'une question, d'une situation)* to floor, to throw

désargenté [dezarʒɑ̃te] ADJ **1** *(fourchette, cuillère etc)* tarnished **2** *Fam (personne)* broke

désarmant [dezarmɑ̃] ADJ *(sourire etc)* disarming

désarmé [dezarme] ADJ **1** *(personne) (qui n'a plus d'arme)* disarmed; *(qui n'a jamais eu d'arme)* unarmed, defenceless **2** *(arme)* unloaded **3** *(navire)* laid up, out of commission

désarmement [dezarməmɑ̃] NM **1** *(d'une personne)* disarming; *Mil, Pol* disarmament; *Mil, Pol* **d. nucléaire** nuclear disarmament; **d. progressif/multilatéral/unilatéral** progressive/multilateral/unilateral disarmament **2** *Naut (de navire)* laying up

désarmer [dezarme] VT **1** *(une personne, un pays)* to disarm; *Fig* **il montrait une franchise qui vous désarmait** he was disarmingly frank **2** *(arme) (enlever les balles de)* to unload; *(placer le cran de sûreté de)* to uncock **3** *Naut (navire)* to lay up
▸ VI *(cesser) (always neg)* **haine/désir de vengeance qui ne désarme pas** unrelenting *or* relentless hatred/desire for vengeance; **sa colère ne désarme pas** he is still angry

désarrimage [dezarimaʒ] NM *Naut etc (d'une cargaison)* shifting

désarrimer [dezarime] VT *Naut etc (cargaison)* to shift

désarroi [dezarwa] NM disarray, confusion; **jeter qn dans le d.** to throw sb into disarray; **il est en plein** *ou* **dans un grand d.** he's in a state of utter disarray *or* confusion

désarticulation [dezartikylasjɔ̃] NF *Méd* dislocation

désarticuler [dezartikyle] VT *Méd* to dislocate; *Fig* **d. un échafaudage** to dismantle scaffolding

▶ **se désarticuler** to be double-jointed

désassemblage [dezasɑ̃blaʒ] NM dismantling

désassembler [dezasɑ̃ble] VT to dismantle, to take apart

désassembleur [dezasɑ̃blœr] NM *Ordinat* disassembler

désassortir [dezasɔrtir] VT *(conj like assortir)* **1** *(série, collection etc)* to spoil, to break up; **service de table désassorti** dinner service made up of odd pieces **2** *(magasin)* to clear (of stock)

désastre [dezastr] NM disaster, calamity; **d. financier** financial disaster, crash; **la soirée fut un vrai d.** the party was a disaster; **courir au d.** to court disaster

désastreusement [dezastrøzmɑ̃] ADV disastrously

désastreux, -euse [dezastrø, -øz] ADJ disastrous; **un travail d.** a dreadful *or* an appalling piece of work

désatellisation [dezatelizasjɔ̃] NF **la d. d'un pays** making a country more autonomous

désatomisation [dezatɔmizasjɔ̃] NF nuclear disarmament

désatomiser [dezatɔmize] VT to undertake the nuclear disarmament of

désavantage [dezavɑ̃taʒ] NM disadvantage, drawback; **avoir un d. par rapport à qn** to be at a disadvantage compared with sb; **tourner au d. de qn** to go against sb; **cette solution a le d. d'être trop coûteuse** the drawback to *or* disadvantage of this solution is its expense; **c'est un d. de taille** it's a sizeable drawback; **il vous a été présenté à son d.** you saw him in a disadvantageous *or* an unfavourable light

désavantagé [dezavɑ̃taʒe] ADJ at a disadvantage, disadvantaged (**par** by); **être désavantagé par rapport à qn** to be at a disadvantage compared with sb; **être très désavantagé par sa taille** to be greatly handicapped by one's size, to be at a great disadvantage because of one's size

désavantager [dezavɑ̃taʒe] VT (**je désavantageai(s); n. désavantageons**) to put at a disadvantage, to disadvantage; **il désavantage toujours son fils par rapport à sa fille** he always favours his daughter over his son

désavantageusement [dezavɑ̃taʒøzmɑ̃] ADV disadvantageously, unfavourably, *Am* unfavorably

désavantageux, -euse [dezavɑ̃taʒø, -øz] ADJ disadvantageous, unfavourable, *Am* unfavorable

désaveu [dezavø] NM **1** *(reniement) (d'une action, d'une œuvre, d'une opinion)* disowning; *(d'une promesse, d'une parole)* retraction; *Jur* **d. de paternité** repudiation of paternity; **faire un d. public** to make a public retraction **2** *(condamnation)* disapproval; **encourir le d. de ses supérieurs** to incur the disapproval of one's superiors; **il a été l'objet du d. de toute la population** he was universally condemned

désavouer [dezavwe] VT **1** *(renier) (action, œuvre, enfant, opinion etc)* to disown; *(promesse, parole)* to go back on, to retract; *(paternité)* to disclaim, to deny; **d. un man-**

dataire to withdraw recognition from an agent **2** *(condamner) (le comportement, les propos, l'attitude etc de qn)* to deplore

▶ **se désavouer** to go back on one's word

désaxé, -ée [dezakse] ADJ **1** *Tech (came etc)* eccentric; **roue désaxée** wheel out of true **2** *(esprit)* unbalanced

▶ N unbalanced person

désaxer [dezakse] VT **1** *Tech (cylindre etc)* to set over; *(roue)* to put out of true **2** *(esprit)* to unbalance

descellement [desɛlmɑ̃] NM *(d'un cachet)* breaking; *(d'un document)* breaking the seal; *(d'une pierre)* loosening

desceller [desele] VT *(cachet)* to break; *(document)* to unseal, to break the seal of; *(pierre)* to loosen

descendance [desɑ̃dɑ̃s] NF **1** *(origine)* descent, *Fml* lineage **2** *(postérité)* descendants

descendant, -ante [desɑ̃dɑ̃, -ɑ̃t] ADJ *(mouvement)* downward; **marée descendante** ebbing tide; *Mil* **garde descendante** old guard; **ligne descendante** (genealogical) line of descent; *Mus* **gamme descendante** descending scale

▶ N descendant

descendeur, -euse [desɑ̃dœr, -øz] N *Ski* downhill specialist *or* skier; *Cyclisme* downhill racer

---

DESCENDRE [desɑ̃dr]

| **VI** to come down **1, 2, 4–6** ▪ to go down **1, 2, 8, 9** ▪ to get off **3** ▪ to fall **4, 5, 9** ▪ to stay **7** ▪ to raid **10** |
| **VT** to go down **1** ▪ to take down **2** ▪ to bring down **2, 5** ▪ to lower **3** ▪ to put away **4** ▪ to shoot down **5** |

VI *(aux* **être**, *occ* **avoir**) **1** *(allant vers le point de référence fixé)* to come down, *Fml* to descend; *(s'éloignant du point de référence fixé)* to go down, *Fml* to descend; **tu descends par l'escalier ou par l'ascenseur?** are you going to walk down or take the lift?; **d. d'un arbre/ d'une échelle** to come down *or* get down from a tree/a ladder; **d. d'une colline** to come down a hill; **peux-tu faire d. les enfants de cet arbre?** can you get the children down out of *or* down from that tree?; **peux-tu m'aider à d.?** can you help me down?; **d. en glissant/en courant/en boitant** to slide/run/limp down; *Aviat* **d. en vol plané** to glide down; **d. en parachute** to parachute down; **d. en rappel** to abseil down; **d. (de Paris) en province** to go to the provinces (from Paris); **d. (du nord) en voiture/en train** to travel down (from the north) by car/train; **d. dans le midi en voiture/en train** to travel to the south by car/train; **d. en ville** to go into town; **il faut d. par ce chemin** you have to go down by this path *or* take this path down; **on peut d. en une nuit?** can we do the journey down in one night?; *Fig* **d. dans la rue** to take to the streets; *Fig* **d. dans l'arène** to enter the fray; **d. du trône** to leave the throne; *Fig* **descends de ton nuage!** come down to earth!; **les scaphandriers sont descendus à 150 m de profondeur** the divers reached a depth of 150 m; **le premier nageur à d. en dessous des 23 secondes au 50 m nage libre** the first swimmer to break 23 seconds in the 50 m freestyle; *Sport* **d. en seconde division** to move down to the second division; *Fig* **d. plus avant** *ou* **plus à fond dans une question** to consider a question at a deeper level; *Fig* **d. en soi-même** to take a close look at oneself

2 *(par l'escalier etc) (allant vers le point de référence fixé)* to come downstairs; *(s'éloignant du point de référence fixé)* to go downstairs; **tu peux d.?** **j'ai besoin de toi à la cuisine** can you come down(stairs)? I need

you in the kitchen; **il est descendu à la cave** he's gone down(stairs) to the cellar; **il n'est pas encore descendu** he isn't down yet; **faites-le d.** *(en l'envoyant chercher)* send him down; *(en l'appelant)* call him down

3 *(d'un véhicule)* to get off, *Fml* to alight; **je descends à Lille/à la prochaine** I'm getting off at Lille/at the next stop; **'aucun voyageur ne descend dans cette gare'** 'the train does not stop here'; **c'est ici que je descends** this is where I get off; **tout le monde descend!** *(au terminus)* all change!; **d. du train** to get off the train; **d. de cheval/de vélo/de moto** to dismount; **d. à terre** *(d'un bateau)* to go ashore, to land

4 *(baisser) (de prix)* to come down, to fall; *(de température)* to drop, to fall; *(de marée)* to fall, to go out; **le baromètre descend** the glass is falling; **il faut faire d. la fièvre** we must bring his temperature down; **sa voix ne descend pas plus bas** his voice won't go any lower

5 *(tomber) (de brouillard)* to come down; *(des ombres)* to fall; **le fleuve descend vers la mer** the river flows down to the sea; **le soleil descend sur l'horizon** the sun is sinking below the horizon; **la nuit** *ou* **le soir va d.** it will soon be nightfall *or* dark; **le précipité descend au fond de l'éprouvette** the precipitate drops to the bottom of the test-tube; **une grande paix était descendue en lui** a great sense of peace came over him

6 *(s'étendre)* to extend downwards; *(de route, rue)* to go downhill; **les cheveux lui descendent jusqu'à la taille** her hair comes down to her waist; **une robe qui descend jusqu'aux chevilles/genoux** an ankle-/ knee-length dress, a dress that comes down to the ankles/knees; **ce chemin descend au village** this path goes down to the village; **la colline descend (en pente douce) jusqu'à la mer** the hill slopes (gently) down to the sea; **la route descend en lacets** the road winds down

7 *(loger)* **d. chez des amis** to stay with friends; **d. à l'hôtel** to put up *or* stay at a hotel

8 *Fam* **mon dîner ne descend pas** my dinner won't go down; **un petit verre pour faire d. mon repas** a drop of something to wash down my meal; **qu'est-ce qu'il descend dans les soirées!** he can really put it away at parties!

9 *Fig (s'abaisser)* to lower oneself; **il est descendu bien bas** he has fallen very low; *Péj* **d. jusqu'au mensonge** to stoop to lying; **d. dans l'estime de qn** to go down in sb's estimation

10 *(faire irruption)* **la police est descendue dans la boîte de nuit** the police raided the nightclub

11 *Fig (venir de)* to be descended (**de** from); **ces gens-là descendent d'une ancienne famille** these people are descended from an ancient family

12 *TV (image)* to slip

VT *(aux* **avoir**) **1** *(dévaler)* **d. les marches/la rue** to go down the steps/the street; **d. la rivière** to go downriver; **d. la rivière en nageant/en canoë/en radeau** to swim/canoe/ raft downriver; **d. un escalier quatre à quatre** to race downstairs; *Mus* **d. la gamme** to run down the scale

2 *(porter vers le bas) (allant vers le point de référence fixé)* to bring down; *(s'éloignant du point de référence fixé)* to take down; *Fam (déposer)* to drop, to put down; **d. la poubelle** to take the rubbish down; **peux-tu me d. mon pull?** will you bring me down my sweater?; **je vous descendrai à votre porte** I'll drop you at your door

3 *(abaisser) (store, étagère)* to lower; **descends le tableau un peu plus vers la droite** move the picture down a bit on the right

4 *Fam (repas, boisson)* to put away, to knock

back, to sink; **il a descendu toutes les bières** he's guzzled all the beer

5 *Fam (animal, homme, avion)* to bring down, to shoot down; **la police l'a descendu, il s'est fait d. par la police** he was shot down *or* shot dead by the police; *Fig* **d. qn en flammes** to shoot sb down in flames; *Fig* **ils l'ont descendu en beauté** they crucified him

descente [desɑ̃t] **NF 1** *(action de descendre)* descent; *Ski (course)* downhill (race); *Ski* **faire de la d.** to do downhill (skiing); **j'ai fait une d. en rappel** I abseiled down; **la d. en rappel est dangereuse** abseiling is dangerous; *Cyclisme* **être bon en d.** to be good downhill *or* on the downhill sections; **c'était une d. difficile** *(en alpinisme)* it was a difficult descent; **d. de cheval** dismounting; *Aviat* **d. en vol plané** glide; **d. en parachute** parachute jump; **accueillir qn à la d. du train** to meet sb off the train; **d. interdite** *(sur panneau)* up only

2 *(incursion)* raid; **d. de police** police raid; *Jur* **d. sur les lieux** visit to the scene *(of a crime etc)*; *Fig* **faire une d. en boîte (de nuit)** to go to a nightclub; *Ftbl* **d. des avants** attack by the forwards

3 *Méd (d'un organe)* prolapse

4 *(pente)* slope, incline; **une d. rapide** a steep slope; **d. dangereuse** dangerous hill; **ralentir dans la d.** to slow down when going downhill

5 *(tuyau)* downpipe, rainwater pipe

6 *Fam* **il a une bonne d.** he can really put it away

▸▸ *Beaux-Arts* **D. de Croix** Deposition; **d. de lit** bedside rug

déscolarisation [deskɔlarizasjɔ̃] **NF** *(action)* removal from school; *(résultat)* lack of schooling *or* education; **les impératifs des travaux agricoles conduisent à la d. des enfants en milieu rural** children in rural areas are taken out of school because of the demands of farm work; **on assiste à une d. massive des jeunes gitans** the level of school attendance among young gipsies is falling drastically

déscolariser [deskɔlarize] **VT** to remove from *or* take out of school

descripteur [dɛskriptœr] **NM** *Ordinat* descriptor

descriptible [dɛskriptibl] **ADJ** describable

descriptif, -ive [dɛskriptif, -iv] **ADJ** descriptive

NM *(d'une maison)* description; *(d'une machine, d'un appareil)* instructions, explanatory leaflet; *Constr* specification; **un d. de vos souhaits** a list of what you would like, your wish list

description [dɛskripsjɔ̃] **NF** description; **d. orale/écrite** verbal/written description; **faire la d. de qn/qch** to give a description of sb/sth, to describe sb/sth; *Tech* **conforme à la d.** as described *or* represented; **d. de brevet** patent specification; **d. commerciale** trade description; **d. de poste** job description

désectorisation [desɛktɔrizasjɔ̃] **NF** freedom of choice *(by virtue of the fact that parents no longer need to send their children to the school designated for their area)*; **la d. de l'école primaire se fera plus vite que celle de l'école secondaire** freedom of choice will come about in primary schools sooner than in secondary schools

désectoriser [desɛktɔrize] **VT d. le primaire/ secondaire** = to allow parents to choose which primary/secondary school they send their children to, regardless of where they live

désembourber [dezɑ̃burbe] **VT** *(véhicule etc)* to extricate from the mud

désembourgeoiser [dezɑ̃burʒwaze] **VT** *(personne)* to make less conventional *or* less middle-class; *(profession, activité etc)* to make less middle-class, to remove the middle-class aura surrounding

VPR se désembourgeoiser to become less conventional *or* less middle-class; **les facs de droit ont beaucoup de mal à se d.** law faculties are finding it very difficult to attract students from outside the middle classes

désembouteiller [dezɑ̃buteje] **VT** *(route)* to unblock; *(ligne téléphonique)* to unjam

désembrouiller [dezɑ̃bruje] **VT** *(signaux, données)* to unscramble

désembrouilleur [dezɑ̃brujœr] **NM** *(de signaux etc)* descrambler

désembuage [dezɑ̃bɥaʒ] **NM** demisting; **d. arrière** rear demister

désembuer [dezɑ̃bɥe] **VT** to demist

désembueur [dezɑ̃bɥœr] **NM** demister

désemparé [dezɑ̃pare] **ADJ 1** *(personne)* at a loss; **il reste d.** he's quite at a loss; **très d.** very much at a loss **2** *(navire, avion)* disabled

désemparer [dezɑ̃pare] **VT** *Naut (navire)* to disable

VI sans d. without stopping; **ils travaillent des heures sans d.** they work for hours on end

désemplir [dezɑ̃plir] **VT** *(bouteille etc)* to partially empty

VI son magasin ne désemplit pas his shop is always full (of customers)

VPR se désemplir to empty

désencadrement [dezɑ̃kadrəmɑ̃] **NM** *Écon (des crédits)* unblocking

désenchaîner [dezɑ̃ʃene] **VT d. qn** to unchain sb, to remove sb's chains

désenchanté [dezɑ̃ʃɑ̃te] **ADJ** *(personne)* disillusioned; *(sourire)* wistful

désenchantement [dezɑ̃ʃɑ̃tmɑ̃] **NM 1** *(déception)* disillusion **2** *Vieilli (désensorcellement)* removal of a/the spell

désenchanter [dezɑ̃ʃɑ̃te] **VT 1** *(décevoir)* to disillusion **2** *Vieilli (désensorceler)* to remove a/the spell from

désenclavement [dezɑ̃klavmɑ̃] **NM** opening up

désenclaver [dezɑ̃klave] **VT** to open up

désencombrement [dezɑ̃kɔ̃brəmɑ̃] **NM** *(d'un passage etc)* clearing, freeing

désencombrer [dezɑ̃kɔ̃bre] **VT** *(passage etc)* to clear, to free (**de** of)

désencrasser [dezɑ̃krase] **VT** to clean

désencroûter [dezɑ̃krute] **VT d. qn** to get sb out of his/her rut

VPR se désencroûter to get out of the *or* one's rut; **j'ai besoin de me d.** I need to get out of this rut I'm in *or* out of my rut

désendettement [dezɑ̃dɛtmɑ̃] **NM** debt reduction, reduction in borrowings; **il faut aboutir au d. des ménages** household debt must be reduced; **le d. des pays de l'Est se fera progressivement** Eastern countries will gradually be relieved of their debt burden

désendetter (se) [sədezɑ̃dete] **VPR** to get out of debt, to clear one's debts

désenfiler [dezɑ̃file] **VT** *(aiguille)* to unthread; *(perles etc)* to unstring

VPR se désenfiler *(d'une aiguille)* to come unthreaded; *(de perles)* to come unstrung

désenflammer [dezɑ̃flame] **VT** *Méd (plaie etc)* to reduce the inflammation in

désenfler [dezɑ̃fle] **VI** to become less swollen; **ma joue/cheville désenfle** the swelling in my cheek/ankle is going down, my cheek/ankle is less swollen

VPR se désenfler = **VI**

désenfumer [dezɑ̃fyme] **VT** to get rid of the smoke in

désengagement [dezɑ̃gaʒmɑ̃] **NM** disengagement

désengager [dezɑ̃gaʒe] (**je désengageai(s); n. désengageons**) **VT d. qn** to release sb from an obligation; **d. sa parole** to go back on one's word

VPR se désengager to free oneself of an obligation; **je ne peux pas me d.** I can't get out of it

désengorgement [dezɑ̃gɔrʒəmɑ̃] **NM** *(d'un tuyau etc)* unblocking

désengorger [dezɑ̃gɔrʒe] **VT** (**je désengorgeai(s); n. désengorgeons**) *(tuyau etc)* to unblock

désenivrer [dezɑ̃nivre] **VT d. qn** to sober sb up

VI to sober up, to become sober; **il ne désenivre pas** he's never sober

désennuyer [dezɑ̃nɥije] (**je désennuie, n. désennuyons; je désennuierai**) **VT d. qn** to keep sb amused

VPR se désennuyer to amuse oneself, to keep oneself amused

désensabler [dezɑ̃sable] **VT 1** *(bateau)* to get off the sand; *(voiture etc)* to dig out of the sand **2** *(chenal etc)* to dredge of sand

désensevelir [dezɑ̃səvlir] **VT** *(objet)* to dig up; *(cadavre)* to disinter, to exhume

désensibilisateur [dezɑ̃sibilizatœr] **NM** *Phot* desensitizer

désensibilisation [dezɑ̃sibilizasjɔ̃] **NF** *Méd, Phot* desensitization

désensibiliser [dezɑ̃sibilize] **VT** *Méd, Phot* to desensitize; *Fig* **de telles images ont désensibilisé l'opinion** people have become hardened as a result of pictures such as these

désensorceler [dezɑ̃sɔrsəle] **VT** (**je désensorcelle, n. désensorcelons; je désensorcellerai**) to free from a/the spell

désensorcellement [dezɑ̃sɔrsɛlmɑ̃] **NM** removal of a/the spell

désentortiller [dezɑ̃tɔrtije] **VT** *(fil etc)* to untwist; *(laine etc)* to disentangle

désentraver [dezɑ̃trave] **VT** *(personne)* to unshackle; *(animal)* to unhobble

désenvaser [dezɑ̃vaze] **VT 1** *(égout)* to clear out, to remove the sludge from; *(port)* to remove the silt from **2** *(voiture)* to get out of the mud, to extract from the mud

désenvoûtement [dezɑ̃vutmɑ̃] **NM** removal of a/the spell; **procéder au d. de qn** to remove a/the spell from sb

désenvoûter [dezɑ̃vute] **VT** to remove a/the spell from

désépaissir [dezepesir] **VT** *(sauce, cheveux)* to thin

déséquilibrant [dezekilibrɑ̃] **ADJ** *(effet)* unbalancing; **être d.** to have an unbalancing effect (**pour** on)

déséquilibre [dezekilibr] **NM** imbalance; **la chaise était en d.** the chair wasn't balanced properly; *Psy* **d. émotif** emotional maladjustment; *Méd* **d. nutritionnel** nutritional imbalance; **d. financier** financial imbalance; **d. de la balance commerciale** unfavourable trade balance

déséquilibré, -ée [dezekilibre] **ADJ** unbalanced

N unbalanced person

déséquilibrer [dezekilibre] **VT** *(personne) (mentalement, physiquement)* to unbalance; *(déconcerter)* to throw off balance; *(objet)* to unbalance, to throw out of balance

désert [dezɛr] **ADJ** *(lieu)* deserted; *(pays, région)* uninhabited; **une île déserte** a desert island

NM desert; **d. de sable** sandy desert; **un d. de glace** an icy waste; *Fig* **prêcher dans le d.** to be a voice crying in the wilderness; *Fig* **en-**

tamer sa traversée du d. to go into the wilderness; **après cinq années de traversée du d.** after five years in the wilderness

> Do not confuse with the adjective **désertique**.

déserter [dezɛrte] **vt** to desert; *Fig (cause)* to desert, to abandon; *(idéal)* to abandon; *Mil* **d. son poste** to desert one's post; **d. l'armée** to desert (from the army); **nos amis désertent notre maison depuis quelque temps** we've been deserted by our friends recently, our friends have been staying away recently **vi** to desert

déserteur [dezɛrtœr] **NM** deserter

désertification [dezɛrtifikasjɔ̃] **NF** *Géog* desertification; *Fig* **la d. du Massif central** the desertion of the Massif Central

désertion [dezɛrsjɔ̃] **NF** *(de l'armée, d'un parti)* desertion

désertique [dezɛrtik] **ADJ** *Géog* desert, of the desert; **région d.** desert region

> Do not confuse with the adjective **désert**.

désertisation [dezɛrtizasjɔ̃] **NF** = **désertification**

désescalade [dezɛskalad] **NF** *Pol, Mil* de-escalation

désespérance [dezɛsperɑ̃s] **NF** *Litt* loss of hope, despair

désespérant [dezɛsperɑ̃] **ADJ 1** **c'est d.** it's enough to drive you to despair; **cet enfant est d.** that child will drive me to despair; **il fait un temps vraiment d.** the weather's really appalling; **tu es vraiment d'une stupidité désespérante** you really are incredibly stupid, you're so stupid you'll drive me to despair; **tu es vraiment d'une nullité désespérante** you really are absolutely hopeless **2** *Litt (image, vision)* heartbreaking

désespéré, -ée [dezɛspere] **ADJ** *(sans espoir) (regard, discours)* desperate, of despair, despairing; *(situation)* desperate; *(extrême) (mesure, solution)* desperate; *(après décès, accident)* in despair, distressed; **être dans un état d.** to be in a hopeless *or* desperate state; **il est d. depuis la mort de sa femme** he's been in despair since his wife died; **sa voix était désespérée** he sounded desperate

N 1 desperate person; **agir en d.** to act out of desperation, to commit an act of despair **2** *(suicidé)* suicide (victim)

désespérément [dezɛsperemɑ̃] **ADV** *(avec désespoir)* despairingly, hopelessly; *(avec acharnement)* desperately

désespérer [dezɛspere] (**je désespère, n. désespérons; je désespérerai**) **vi** to despair, to lose hope; **je ne désespère pas d'y arriver un jour** I still hope to get *or* I haven't given up hope of getting there one day; **d. de qn** to despair of sb; **il désespère de pouvoir rentrer chez lui** he despairs of ever getting home; **il désespère de sa situation** he's in despair about the situation he's in; **il désespère sa femme par son attitude** he drives his wife to despair with his attitude

vpr se désespérer to be in despair, to give way to despair

désespoir [dezɛspwar] **NM 1** despair; **être au d.** to be in despair; **elle était au d. de ne pouvoir vous aider** she was distressed *or* extremely upset that she wasn't able to help you; **enfant qui fait** *ou* **est le d. de sa famille** child who is the despair of his family; **cette cuisine fait mon d.** this kitchen will drive me to despair; **réduire qn au d.** to drive sb to desperation *or* to despair; **en d. de cause** in desperation, as a last resort **2** *(plante)* **d. des peintres** London pride

désétatisation [dezetatizasjɔ̃] **NF** denationalization

désétatiser [dezetatize] **vt** *Écon, Pol (industrie)* to denationalize

désexualiser [desɛksɥalize] **vt** to desexualize, to desex

déshabillage [dezabijaʒ] **NM** undressing

déshabillé [dezabije] **NM** négligé

déshabiller [dezabije] **vt** to undress; **d. qn du regard** to undress sb with one's eyes, to mentally undress sb

vpr se déshabiller to undress (oneself), to take off one's clothes; *(enlever son manteau etc)* to take off one's coat/*etc*

déshabituer [dezabitɥe] **vt d. qn de (faire) qch** to get sb out of *or* break sb of the habit of (doing) sth

vpr se déshabituer to get out of *or* lose the habit (**de** of)

désherbage [dezɛrbaʒ] **NM** weeding

désherbant [dezɛrbɑ̃] **NM** weedkiller

désherber [dezɛrbe] **vt** *(jardin, champ)* to weed

déshérence [dezerɑ̃s] **NF** *Jur* default of heirs, escheat; **tomber en d.** to escheat

déshérité [dezerite] **ADJ** *(sans héritage)* disinherited; *(démuni)* deprived

NMPL les déshérités the underprivileged

déshéritement [dezeritmɑ̃] **NM** disinheritance

déshériter [dezerite] **vt** to disinherit; *Fig Hum* **être déshérité par la nature** *(d'une personne inintelligente)* to be not very bright; *(d'une personne laide)* to be no oil painting

déshonnête [dezɔnɛt] **ADJ** *Arch* improper, immodest, unseemly

déshonnêtement [dezɔnɛtmɑ̃] **ADV** *Arch* improperly, immodestly

déshonnêteté [dezɔnɛt(ə)te] **NF** *Arch, Litt* impropriety, immodesty, unseemliness

déshonneur [dezɔnœr] **NM** dishonour, *Am* dishonor

déshonorant [dezɔnɔrɑ̃] **ADJ** *(comportement, métier)* dishonourable, *Am* dishonorable; **des paroles déshonorantes pour notre famille/la profession** remarks that bring dishonour on *or* discredit the family/the profession

déshonorer [dezɔnɔre] **vt 1** *(discréditer)* to disgrace, to bring disgrace *or* dishonour *or* *Am* dishonor on, to dishonour; **il se croirait déshonoré de serrer la main à des étrangers** he would feel it reflected on his honour *or* he would think it beneath him to shake hands with a foreigner; **être déshonoré par un jeune blanc-bec** to be put to shame by a complete beginner; *Vieilli* **d. une jeune fille/une femme** to seduce a girl/a woman **2** *Fig (abîmer) (paysage, édifice etc)* to disfigure, to spoil

vpr se déshonorer to disgrace oneself

déshuiler [dezɥile] **vt** to extract *or* separate *or* remove oil from

déshumaniser [dezymanize] **vt** to dehumanize

déshumidification [dezymidifikasjɔ̃] **NF** dehumidification

déshydratation [dezidratasjɔ̃] **NF** dehydration

déshydrater [dezidrate] **vt** to dehydrate; **je suis déshydraté** I'm dehydrated; **noix de coco déshydratée** desiccated coconut

vpr se déshydrater to become dehydrated; **on se déshydrate beaucoup en avion** you get very dehydrated when you fly

déshydrateur [dezidratœr] **NM** dehydrator

déshydrogénation [dezidrɔʒenasjɔ̃] **NF** *Chimie* dehydrogenation

déshydrogéner [dezidrɔʒene] **vt** (**je dés-**

hydrogène, n. déshydrogénons; je déshydrogénerai) *Chimie* to dehydrogenate

déshypothéquer [dezipɔteke] **vt** *(conj like* **hypothéquer** *) (domaine)* to free from mortgage

desiderata [deziderata] **NMPL** desiderata; **quels sont vos d.?** what can I do for you?

design [dizajn] **NM** design; **ils sont entièrement meublés en d.** they have nothing but designer furniture; **société de d.** design company; **il fait du d. (industriel)** he's a(n industrial) designer, he's in (industrial) design

ADJ INV designer; **un intérieur très d.** a designer interior

désignation [deziɲasjɔ̃] **NF 1** *(appellation)* designation; *(de marchandises etc)* description **2** *(choix)* appointment; **d. de qn pour un poste** appointment of sb to a position

designer [dizajnœr] **NM** designer; **d. graphiste** graphics designer; **d. presse** newspaper designer

désigner [deziɲe] **vt 1** *(signaler)* to point out, to indicate; **est-ce que tu peux le d.?** can you point him out?; **d. qch du doigt** to point sth out, to point at sth; **il a pris le siège qu'on lui avait désigné** he took the seat they pointed to *or* indicated; **d. qch à l'attention de qn** to call *or* draw sb's attention to sth; **je désigne à votre attention que ...** I would call *or* draw your attention to the fact that ...

2 *(choisir)* to appoint; **d. qn à un jour** to appoint *or* set *or* fix a day; **d. qn à** *ou* **pour un poste** to appoint sb to a position; **il est tout désigné pour le faire** he's just the man to do it, he's cut out for it; **sa compétence la désigne à cet emploi** her ability makes her the right person for the job; **il a été désigné pour nous représenter** he was chosen to represent us **3** *(nommer)* to refer to; **d. qn par son nom** to refer to sb by name; **d. qn par un surnom** to call sb by a nickname; **on désigne, sous ce nom, tous les gaz de cette famille** this name is applied to all the gases in the family

vpr se désigner se d. volontaire to volunteer

désillusion [dezilyzjɔ̃] **NF** disillusion

désillusionnement [dezilyzjɔnmɑ̃] **NM** disillusionment

désillusionner [dezilyzjɔne] **vt** to disillusion

désincarcération [dezɛ̃karserasjɔ̃] **NF** *(des débris d'une voiture etc)* release, freeing

désincarcérer [dezɛ̃karsere] **vt** *(des débris d'une voiture etc)* to free

désincarné [dezɛ̃karne] **ADJ** disembodied; *souvent Iron* **il paraît totalement d.** he seems above it all

désincarner (se) [sədezɛ̃karne] **vpr** to become disembodied

désincrustant [dezɛ̃krystɑ̃] **ADJ** *Tech (substance)* scaling; **masque d.** *(cosmétique)* face pack

NM *Tech* scale preventive

désincrustation [dezɛ̃krystasjɔ̃] **NF** *Tech (d'une chaudière etc)* scaling

désincruster [dezɛ̃kryste] **vt** *Tech (chaudière etc)* to scale; **un masque pour d. la peau** a mask for removing impurities from the skin

désindexation [dezɛ̃dɛksasjɔ̃] **NF** de-indexing

désindexer [dezɛ̃dɛkse] **vt** to de-index

désindustrialisation [dezɛ̃dystrijalizasjɔ̃] **NF** de-industrialization

désindustrialiser [dezɛ̃dystrijalize] **vt** to de-industrialize

désinence [dezinɑ̃s] **NF** *Gram* (flexional) ending

désinfectant [dezɛ̃fɛktɑ̃] **ADJ, NM** disinfectant

désinfecter [dezɛ̃fɛkte] **VT** to disinfect

désinfection [dezɛ̃fɛksjɔ̃] **NF** disinfection

désinflation [dezɛ̃flasjɔ̃] **NF** *Écon* disinflation

désinformation [dezɛ̃fɔrmasjɔ̃] **NF** disinformation

désinformer [dezɛ̃fɔrme] **VT** to disinform

désinscrire (se) [sədezɛ̃skrir] **VPR** *Ordinat* to unsubscribe

désinsectisation [dezɛ̃sɛktizasjɔ̃] **NF** pest control

désinsectiser [dezɛ̃sɛktize] **VT** to clear of insects, to remove the insects from

désinstallateur [dezɛ̃stalatœr] **NM** *Ordinat* deinstaller

désinstallation [dezɛ̃stalasjɔ̃] **NF** *Ordinat* deinstallation

désinstaller [dezɛ̃stale] **VT** *Ordinat* to deinstall

désintégration [dezɛ̃tegrasjɔ̃] **NF** *(des roches)* weathering; *Nucl* (nuclear) disintegration; *(de l'atome)* splitting; *Fig (d'un groupe)* break-up; *(de la famille, de la société)* disintegration

désintégrer [dezɛ̃tegre] **(je désintègre, n. désintégrons; je désintégrerai) VT** *(roches)* to weather; *Nucl (matière)* to disintegrate; *(atome)* to split; *Fig (groupe, famille etc)* to break up
VPR se désintégrer *(de roches)* to weather; *Nucl (de matière)* to disintegrate; *(d'atome)* to split; *Fig (d'un groupe, d'une famille)* to break up; *(d'un mariage)* to break up, to fall apart; *(de la société, de la famille)* to disintegrate

désintéressé [dezɛ̃terese] **ADJ** *(opinion, avis etc)* disinterested, impartial; *(motif)* disinterested, unselfish; *(personne)* disinterested, selfless; **il agit de manière tout à fait désintéressée** he is being quite impartial

désintéressement [dezɛ̃teresmɑ̃] **NM 1** *(d'opinion, d'avis)* disinterestedness, impartiality; *(de motif)* disinterestedness, unselfishness; *(de personne)* disinterestedness, selflessness **2** *Com (de partenaire)* buying out; *(de créditeur)* paying off

> Do not confuse with **désintérêt**.

désintéresser [dezɛ̃terese] **VT** *Com (partenaire)* to buy out; *(créditeur)* to pay off
VPR se désintéresser se d. de qn/qch to take no further interest in sb/sth

désintérêt [dezɛ̃terɛ] **NM** disinterest

> Do not confuse with **désintéressement**.

désintermédiation [dezɛ̃tɛrmedjasjɔ̃] **NF** disintermediation

désintoxication [dezɛ̃tɔksikasjɔ̃] **NF** *Méd* detoxification; **faire une cure de d.** to undergo treatment for alcoholism/drug addiction, *Am Fam* to be in detox

désintoxiquer [dezɛ̃tɔksike] *Méd* **VT** to treat for alcoholism/drug addiction; *Fig* **il ne fait que regarder la télévision, il faut le d.!** all he does is watch television, we'll have to break him of the habit!
VPR se désintoxiquer to come off alcohol/drugs; *Fig* **je cours tous les jours pour me d.** I run every day to clean out my system; *Fig* **aller à la campagne pour se d.** to go to the countryside to clean out one's system *or* to get the city air out of one's lungs

désinvestir [dezɛ̃vɛstir] **VI** *Fin* to disinvest *(dans* in)
VPR se désinvestir depuis qu'il sait qu'il va être licencié, il s'est désinvesti de son travail since finding out that he's going to be made

redundant, he has ceased to take an interest in his job *or* he no longer makes any effort at work

désinvestissement [dezɛ̃vɛstismɑ̃] **NM** *Fin* divestment

désinvolte [dezɛ̃vɔlt] **ADJ** *(manière)* casual, airy, unselfconscious; *(mouvements)* easy, free; **d. à l'égard de qn** casual *or* offhand with sb; **il a quand même été très d. en ne venant pas à mon anniversaire** it was very offhand of him not to come to my birthday party

désinvolture [dezɛ̃vɔltyr] **NF** *(naturel) (de manières)* unselfconsciousness; *(de mouvement)* ease; *(sans-gêne)* casualness; **avec d.** casually; **sa d. devient insupportable** his casualness *or* his offhand *or* airy manner is becoming unbearable; **il travaille avec une d. qui commence à agacer au bureau** his casual approach to work is beginning to irritate people in the office

désir [dezir] **NM 1** *(souhait)* desire; **avoir un d. de qch** to have a desire for something; **d. de plaire** desire to please; **d. ardent** craving, longing; **ardent d. de réussir** ardent desire to succeed; **selon le d. de son père** in accordance with his father's wishes; **éprouver le d. de faire qch** to want to do sth; **prendre ses désirs pour des réalités** to indulge in wishful thinking; **tes désirs sont des ordres** your wish is my command **2 d. (sexuel)** *(sexual)* desire

désirabilité [dezirabilite] **NF** desirability

désirable [dezirabl] **ADJ** desirable; **peu d.** undesirable

désirer [dezire] **VT 1** *(souhaiter)* to want, to desire; **d. ardemment qch** to crave sth, to yearn *or* long for sth; **d. qch de qn** to want sth of *or* from sb; **je désire le voir** I want *or* wish to see him; **je désire qu'il vienne** I want him to come; **cela laisse à d.** it leaves a lot to be desired; **elle se fait d.** *(elle n'arrive pas)* she's keeping us waiting; **elle aime se faire d.** *(ce n'est pas une femme facile)* she plays hard to get; **je n'avais plus rien à d.** I had nothing left to wish for; **que désirez-vous?,** *Fam* **vous désirez?** *(dans un magasin)* can I help you?; *(qu'est-ce que je vous sers?)* what would you like? **2** *(sexuellement)* to desire; **je te désire** I want you

désireux, -euse [dezirø, -øz] **ADJ** desirous *(* **de** of); **d. de plaire** anxious to please; **je serais très d. de la connaître** I would very much like to meet her

désistement [dezistəmɑ̃] **NM 1** cancellation; *Jur (de réclamation)* waiver; *(de procès)* withdrawal **2** *Pol* withdrawal of one's candidature, standing down

désister (se) [sədeziste] **VPR 1** *Jur* se d. d'une poursuite to withdraw an action; **se d. d'une demande** to waive a claim **2** *Pol* to withdraw (one's candidature), to stand down

desk [dɛsk] **NM** *Journ* desk

deskman, *pl* **deskmen, deskmans** [dɛskman, men] **NM** *Journ* deskman

désobéir [dezɔbeir] **VI** to be disobedient; **d. à qn/un ordre** to disobey sb/an order; **d. à une règle** to break a rule

désobéissance [dezɔbeisɑ̃s] **NF** disobedience *(* **à** of); **d. à une règle** disregard for *or* breaking of a rule; **d. civile** civil disobedience

désobéissant [dezɔbeisɑ̃] **ADJ** disobedient

désobligeance [dezɔbliʒɑ̃s] **NF** disagreeableness *(* **envers** to)

désobligeant [dezɔbliʒɑ̃] **ADJ** *(personne, manière, mots etc)* disagreeable, ungracious *(* **envers** to)

désobliger [dezɔbliʒe] **VT (je désobligeai(s); n. désobligeons)** to offend

désobstruer [dezɔpstrye] **VT** *(tuyau, passage, tunnel etc)* to clear (of an obstruction)

désodé [desɔde] **ADJ** salt-free

désodorisant [dezɔdɔrizɑ̃] **ADJ** deodorant
NM *(pour le corps)* deodorant; *(pour la maison)* air freshener

désodoriser [dezɔdɔrize] **VT** to deodorize

désœuvré [dezœvre] **ADJ** unoccupied, idle; **me trouvant d.** finding myself with nothing to do, *Fam* being *or* finding myself at a loose end; **je ne supporte pas de rester d. plus de cinq minutes** I can't bear to be idle for more than five minutes
NMPL les désœuvrés people with nothing to do

désœuvrement [dezœvrəmɑ̃] **NM** idleness; **par d.** to kill time, for want of something to do

désolant [dezɔlɑ̃] **ADJ** *(nouvelle etc)* distressing; **tu es vraiment d.** you drive me to despair; **ce temps est d.** this weather is very depressing

désolation [dezɔlasjɔ̃] **NF 1** *(dévastation)* desolation, devastation, laying waste **2** *(affliction)* grief, sorrow; **être plongé dans la d.** to be grief-stricken; **sa fille ne fait plus de danse et c'est sa grande d.** she is heartbroken that her daughter has given up dancing

désolé [dezɔle] **ADJ 1** *(région etc)* desolate, dreary **2** *(navré)* sorry; **je suis (terriblement) d. de vous avoir fait attendre** I'm (so *or* very) sorry to have kept you waiting; **d., je n'ai pas le temps** sorry, I haven't got the time; **je suis d. mais ce n'est pas la meilleure candidate** I'm sorry but she isn't the best candidate **3** *(affligé)* upset

désoler [dezɔle] **VT 1** *(affliger)* to distress, to grieve; **son échec à l'examen le désole** he's very upset about failing the exam **2** *Vieilli, Litt (pays etc)* to devastate, to ravage, to lay waste
VPR se désoler to be distressed, to be upset

désolidariser (se) [sədesɔlidarize] **VPR** *(d'une personne)* to break away, to break ranks; **se d. de** *ou* **d'avec ses collègues** to break with one's colleagues; **se d. d'une cause** to withdraw one's support from a cause; **se d. d'un projet** to withdraw from a project

désopilant [dezɔpilɑ̃] **ADJ** screamingly funny, hilarious

désordonné [dezɔrdɔne] **ADJ 1** *(chambre, bureau etc)* untidy; *(personne) (qui n'est pas organisé)* disorganized; *(qui ne range pas)* untidy; *(mouvements)* uncoordinated; **une fuite désordonnée** a disorderly flight; **il a un esprit trop d.** he's too scatterbrained **2** *Litt (vie etc)* disorderly; *(dépenses)* reckless

désordre [dezɔrdr] **NM 1** *(manque d'organisation)* disorder, confusion; *(manque d'ordre)* untidiness; **quel d.!** what a mess!; **il règne dans leur maison un d. incroyable** their house is incredibly untidy; **tu as mis du d. dans toute la maison, tu as mis toute la maison en d.** you've made the entire house untidy; **c'est un peu le d. dans ses papiers** his papers are not altogether in order; **c'est le d. dans sa dissertation** his thesis lacks organization *or* is not clearly thought out; **être en d.** *(d'une pièce etc)* to be untidy; **cheveux en d.** tangled *or* untidy hair; *Fig* **ça fait d.!** *(ça ne se fait pas)* it's just not done!; *(ce n'est pas sérieux)* that's a laugh!
2 *(agitation)* **mettre le d. dans les rangs** to cause confusion in the ranks; **il arrive toujours à mettre un d. infernal dans la classe** he always manages to cause an uproar in the classroom; *Fam* **il a fait du d. dans la rue** he caused a disturbance in the street; **le d. qui règne à l'Assemblée nationale ces jours-ci** the present commotion in the Natio-

nal Assembly; **d. de la pensée** confused thinking

3 désordres (émeutes) disturbances, riots; **de graves désordres ont éclaté** serious disturbances have broken out

4 Litt (licence) licentiousness; **vivre dans le d.** to lead a life of licentiousness

5 Méd disorder; **d. nerveux/fonctionnel/ hormonal** nervous/functional/hormone disorder; **d. affectif saisonnier** seasonal affective disorder, SAD

désorganisation [dezɔrganizasjɔ̃] NF disorganization

désorganisé [dezɔrganize] ADJ disorganized

désorganiser [dezɔrganize] VT (système etc) to disrupt; (plans etc) to upset
VPR **se désorganiser** to become disorganized

désorientation [dezɔrjɑ̃tasjɔ̃] NF disorientation; (déconcertation) confusion, bewilderment

désorienté [dezɔrjɑ̃te] ADJ (perdu) disorientated, surtout Am disoriented; (déconcerté) confused, bewildered; **après l'anesthésie, il était complètement d.** he was completely disorientated or totally confused after the anaesthetic

désorienter [dezɔrjɑ̃te] VT **1** (égarer) (personne) to disorientate, surtout Am to disorient; (compas, instrument) to throw out (of adjustment) **2** (déconcerter) to confuse, to bewilder; **l'anesthésie l'a désorienté** he is disorientated or confused because of the anaesthetic

désormais [dezɔrmɛ] ADV from now on(wards), in future, Litt henceforth

désorption [dezɔrpsjɔ̃] NF Chimie desorption

désossé [dezose] ADJ (viande, poisson) boned; (gigot, jambon) off the bone; Fig (personne) supple; Péj (style etc) flabby, flaccid

désossement [dezosmɑ̃] NM (de viande, poisson) boning

désosser [dezose] VT (viande, poisson) to bone; Fig (phrase, livre) to dissect
VPR **se désosser** to contort oneself

désoxydant [dezɔksidɑ̃] Chimie ADJ deoxidizing
NM deoxidizer

désoxyder [dezɔkside] VT Chimie, Métal to deoxidize

desperado [dɛsperado] NM desperado

despote [dɛspɔt] NM despot; Fam **sa fille est un d.!** her daughter is a regular tyrant!
ADJ **mari/femme d.** despotic husband/wife

despotique [dɛspɔtik] ADJ (pouvoir etc) despotic

despotiquement [dɛspɔtikmɑ̃] ADV despotically

despotisme [dɛspɔtism] NM despotism

desquamation [dɛskwamasjɔ̃] NF peeling, Spéc exfoliation; Méd (pathologique) desquamation

desquamer [dɛskwame] VT to exfoliate
VI to peel (off); Méd to desquamate
VPR **se desquamer** to peel

desquels, desquelles [dekɛl] voir lequel

DESS [deɛsɛs] NM (abrév **diplôme d'études supérieures spécialisées**) = postgraduate diploma

dessaisir [desezir] VT Jur **d. un tribunal d'une affaire** to remove a case from a court
VPR **se dessaisir se d. de qch** to relinquish sth, to part with sth, to give sth up

dessaisissement [desezismɑ̃] NM **1** Jur **d. d'un tribunal d'une affaire** removal of a case from a court **2** (abandon) **d. de qch** relinquishment of sth

dessalage [desalaʒ] NM (du poisson, de la viande etc) soaking (to remove salt)

dessalaison [desalɛzɔ̃] NF **1** (du poisson, de la viande etc) soaking (to remove salt) **2** (de l'eau de mer) desalination

dessalé [desale] ADJ **1** (viande, poisson etc) soaked (to remove salt) **2** Fam (personne) wide awake, sharp

dessalement [desalmɑ̃] NM (de l'eau de mer) desalination

dessaler [desale] VT **1** (viande, poisson) to remove the salt from (by soaking); (eau de mer) to desalinate **2** Fam **d. qn** to sharpen sb's wits
VI Naut to capsize
VPR **se dessaler 1** (devenir moins salé) to become less salty **2** Fam (d'une personne) to learn a thing or two

dessangler [desɑ̃gle] VT (horse) to ungirth, to take the girths off

dessaouler [desule] VT & VI Fam = **dessoûler**

desséchant [deseʃɑ̃] ADJ (vent) drying

desséché [deseʃe] ADJ (étang, rivière) dry, dried-up; (sol, bouche) dry, parched; (peau) dry; (bois) seasoned, dried; (plante) dry, withered; Fig (personne) (maigre) shrunken; (insensible) without feelings, without emotions, dried-up; **il est d.** (insensible) he's dead inside, he's got no feelings left

dessèchement [deseʃmɑ̃] NM (d'un étang, d'une rivière) drying up; (d'un sol) drying; (du bois) seasoning, drying; (d'une plante) withering; Vieilli Fig (du corps) shrunkenness; Fig (dureté) (d'une personne) lack of feeling

dessécher [deseʃe] (je **dessèche**, n. **desséchons**; je **dessécherai**) VT (sol, étang, rivière) to dry up; (bois) to season; (denrées alimentaires) to dry; (noix de coco) to desiccate; (du vent, de la chaleur etc) (plante) to wither; (peau) to dry; (bouche) to dry, to parch; (de maladie, l'âge etc) (corps) to shrink; Fig **d. le cœur de qn** to harden sb's heart
VPR **se dessécher** (du sol) to dry up, to become dry; (d'un étang, d'une rivière etc) to dry up, to go dry; (d'une plante) to wither; (d'une personne) (maigrir) to waste away; Fig (devenir insensible) to become insensitive

dessein [desɛ̃] NM intention, purpose, Litt design; **avoir le d. de faire qch** to intend to do sth; **former le d. de faire qch** to plan to do sth; **dans ce d.** with this intention, with this in mind; **à d.** on purpose, purposely, intentionally; **c'est à d. que je n'ai pas répondu** I deliberately didn't answer; **à d. ou dans le d. de vous revoir** in order to see you again

desseller [desele] VT (cheval) to unsaddle

desserrage [desɛraʒ] NM (d'une vis) loosening; (d'une ceinture, d'un nœud) slackening, loosening

desserrement [desɛrmɑ̃] NM loosening

desserrer [desere] VT (vis) to loosen; (ceinture, nœud) to loosen, to slacken; (poing, dents) to unclench; (frein à main) to release, to take off; **d. son étreinte** to relax one's hold; **je n'ai pas desserré les dents** I didn't open my mouth, I didn't utter a word; **peux-tu d. les livres sur l'étagère?** can you move the books on the shelf so they're a bit less tightly packed?
VPR **se desserrer** (d'une vis) to work loose; (d'une ceinture, d'un nœud) to come loose; (d'étreinte) to relax

dessert [desɛr] NM dessert, Br pudding, Br sweet; **venez pour le d.** come for dessert; **être privé de d.** to go without dessert; **qu'est-ce qu'il y a comme ou au d.?** what's for dessert?; **carte des desserts** dessert menu

desserte [desɛrt] NF **1** (service) service; **d.**

d'un port par voie ferrée rail service to a port; **chemin de d.** service road **2** Rel ministry

desserte [2] NF (meuble) sideboard; **d. (roulante)** trolley

dessertir [desɛrtir] VT (pierre précieuse) to remove from its setting

desservant [desɛrvɑ̃] NM Rel incumbent

desservir [1] [desɛrvir] VT (conj like **servir**) **1** (de chemins de fer etc) to serve; (de porte) to lead into; **ce train ne dessert pas toutes les gares** this train does not stop at every station; **ville bien desservie** town with efficient public transport **2** Rel (paroisse etc) to minister to

desservir [2] (conj like **servir**) VT **1** (table) to clear **2** (nuire à) to do harm to; **d. qn** to do sb a disservice; **cela risque de vous d.** that may be to your disadvantage; **cela desservirait mes intérêts** it would be detrimental to my interests; **son perfectionnisme la dessert** her perfectionism isn't doing her any good
VI to clear away
VPR **se desservir** to do oneself a disservice; **il se dessert par sa malhonnêteté** he's not doing himself any good by being dishonest

dessiccatif, -ive [desikatif, -iv] Méd ADJ (produit) drying
NM drying agent

dessiccation [desikasjɔ̃] NF desiccation

dessiller [desije] VT (yeux) to open; Fig **d. les yeux à ou de qn** to open sb's eyes (to the facts)
VPR **se dessiller** (des yeux) to open; Fig **ses yeux se dessillèrent** his eyes were opened

dessin [desɛ̃] NM **1** (art) (art of) drawing, sketching; (croquis etc) drawing; **être bon en d.** to be good at drawing, to be a good drawer; **d. à la plume** pen-and-ink sketch; **d. au trait** line drawing; **d. à main levée** free-hand drawing; **un d. d'enfant** a child's drawing; **les dessins de Degas** Degas' drawings; **faire du d. publicitaire** to be a commercial artist; Fam **faut-il que je te fasse un d.?** do I have to draw a picture or spell it out for you?; Tech **planche à d.** drawing board; **d. d'ensemble** general assembly drawing; **d. de profil** profile drawing
2 (motif) design, pattern; **tissu à dessins** patterned fabric; **une robe avec de jolis dessins** a pretty patterned dress
3 (contour) (d'un visage etc) outline
▸▸ Cin **dessin(s) animé(s)** cartoon(s); **d. assisté par ordinateur** computer-assisted design; **d. humoristique** cartoon; **d. industriel** industrial drawing; **d. de mode** fashion design

dessinateur, -trice [desinatœr, -tris] N **1** (artiste) sketcher, drawer; **d. humoristique** cartoonist **2** (de papier peint etc) designer; (de mode) fashion artist **3** Tech draughtsman, f draughtswoman, Am draftsman, f draftswoman; **d. industriel** draughtsman; **d. cartographe** cartographer; **d. concepteur** (de mobilier etc) designer

dessiner [desine] VT **1** to draw, to sketch; **d. qch d'après nature** to draw sth from nature; **d. à l'encre/à la craie** to draw in ink/chalk **2** (papier peint, tissu, plan etc) to design **3** Fig (tracer) to show, to outline; **les montagnes dessinent leur courbe sur le ciel** the line of the mountains stands out against the sky; **vêtement qui dessine bien la taille** garment that shows off the waist; **visage bien dessiné** finely chiselled face
VPR **se dessiner 1** (se voir) to stand out, to be outlined; **les arbres se dessinent à l'horizon** the trees stand out or are outlined on the horizon; **parfois, un sourire se dessinait sur ses lèvres** a smile occasionally played or hovered on her lips **2** (se préciser) to take

shape; **nos projets de vacances se dessinent vaguement** our holiday plans are beginning to take shape; **on voit se d. un virage à gauche de l'opinion** we can see the beginnings of a shift to the left in public opinion

dessouder [desude] **VT 1** *Tech* to unsolder **2** *Arg (tuer)* to waste, *Br* to do in
VPR se dessouder le tuyau s'est dessoudé the pipe has come unsoldered

dessoûler [desule] *Fam* **VT** to sober up, to make sober
VI to become sober, to sober up; **il ne dessoûle pas depuis son mariage** he hasn't been sober since he got married

dessous [dəsu] **ADV** underneath; **passez (par-)d.** go underneath (it); **prendre/porter qch par (en) d.** to take hold of/carry sth from underneath; *Fig* **il fait des choses par (en) d.** he does things in an underhand way; **en d.** underneath; **l'appartement d'en d.** the downstairs flat, the flat downstairs; **regarder qn (par) en d.** to look at sb furtively *or* stealthily; **rire en d.** to laugh up one's sleeve; **agir en d.** to act in an underhand way; **ci-d.** below; **dans la note ci-d.** in the note below; **là-d.** under there; *Fig* **il y a quelque chose de bizarre là-d.** there's something funny about it; **au-d.** below; **son bureau est au-d.** his office is on the next floor down; **une maison avec un garage au-d.** a house with a garage underneath (it); *Fig* **pour vingt euros et au-d., vous ne trouverez rien de bien** you won't find anything decent for less than twenty euros
PRÉP 1 de d. from under(neath) *or* beneath **2 par-d.** underneath **3 au-d. de** under; **au-d. de 100 euros, on ne trouve rien** you won't find anything under 100 euros; **un peu au-d. de Paris** slightly to the south of Paris; *Fig* **elle est bien au-d. de toi** she's not nearly as good as you; **il est au-d. de sa tâche** he's not up to the job; **être au-d. de tout** to be beneath contempt **4 en d.** under(neath); **tu es très en d. de la vérité** you're not even close
NM les gens du d. the people on the floor below, the downstairs neighbours; **d. d'une assiette** underside of a plate; **d. de robe** slip, *Vieilli* petticoat; *Fig* **avoir le d.** to get the worst of it, to be defeated; **être dans le troisième** *ou* **trente-sixième d.** to be in the depths of despair; **les d. de la politique** the shady side of politics; **je voudrais bien connaître le d. de toute cette histoire** I'd really like to know what they're not telling us (in this whole affair); *Fig* **connaître le d. des cartes** to be in the know, to know what's going on
NMPL *(sous-vêtements)* (ladies') underwear, *Fam* undies; *(raffiné)* lingerie

dessous-de-bouteille [d(ə)sudbutɛj] **NM INV** coaster

dessous-de-bras [d(ə)sudbra] **NM INV** dress shield

dessous-de-plat [d(ə)sudpla] **NM INV** table mat

dessous-de-table [d(ə)sudtabl] **NM INV** backhander; *Fig* **verser un d. à qn** to pay sb a bribe, to give *or* slip sb a backhander

dessous-de-tasse [d(ə)sud(ə)tas] **NM INV** saucer

dessous-de-verre [d(ə)sudvɛr] **NM INV** coaster

dessus [dəsy] **ADV** (up)on (it/them); **il a marché d.** he trod on it; **mais il n'y a pas l'adresse d.** but the address isn't on it, but it doesn't have the address on (it); **avec du chocolat d.** with chocolate on top; **j'ai failli lui tirer d.** I nearly shot him; **vous avez mis le doigt d.** you've put your finger on it, you've hit the nail on the head; *Fig Fam* **il m'est tombé d. dans le métro** he buttonholed me *or*

grabbed hold of me in the underground; **la police finira bien par lui mettre la main d.** the police will track him down eventually; **impossible de mettre la main d.!** *(d'une chose)* I just can't/couldn't lay my hands on it!; **marcher bras d. bras dessous** to walk arm in arm; **au-d.** at the top, on top, above; **mettre les meilleures pommes (au-)d.** to put the best apples on top *or* at the top; **l'appartement au-d.** the flat upstairs, the upstairs flat; **avec de la crème au-d.** with cream on top; **vous ne trouverez rien au-d.** you'll find nothing better; **voir ci-d.** see above; **là-d.** up there; **il y a beaucoup à dire là-d.** a lot could be said on that score; *Fam* **ne compte pas là-d.!** don't count on it!; **là-d., elle partit** and with that, she left
PRÉP 1 de d. from, off; **elle ne leva pas les yeux de d. son ouvrage** she didn't lift her eyes from *or* look up from *or* take her eyes off her work
2 au-d. de above; **au-d. de 15 ans** over 15, more than 15 (years old); **au-d. de Lyon** *(au nord de)* north of Lyons; **nous volons au-d. de l'Alsace** we are flying over Alsace; *Fig* **il est bien au-d. de toi** he's much better than you are; **je suis au-d. de tout cela** I'm above all that; **au-d. de tout soupçon** above suspicion; **c'est au-d. de mes forces** I'm not strong enough (to do it); **c'est au-d. de mes capacités/moyens** I can't do/afford it; **rien n'est au-d. de sa foi** his faith can move mountains
3 par-d. above, over; *Fam* **j'en ai par-d. la tête** I've had it up to here
NM *(de table etc)* top; **l'étage du d.** the top floor; *Théâtre* **les d.** the flies; **avoir le d.** to have the upper hand, to be on top; **(re)prendre le d.** to get over it

dessus-de-cheminée [d(ə)sydʃəmine] **NM INV** mantelshelf runner

dessus-de-lit [d(ə)sydli] **NM INV** coverlet, bedspread

déstabilisant [destabilizɑ̃], **déstabilisateur, -trice** [destabilizatœr, -tris] **ADJ** unsettling; *Pol, Fin* destabilizing; **cet incident a été très d. pour les élèves** the incident was very unsettling for *or* had a very unsettling effect on the pupils; **cela a été très d. pour le gouvernement** it has had an extremely destabilizing effect on the government

déstabilisation [destabilizasjɔ̃] **NF** unsettling; *Pol, Fin* destabilization

déstabiliser [destabilize] **VT** to unsettle; *Pol, Fin* to destabilize

déstalinisation [destalinizasjɔ̃] **NF** *Pol* de-stalinization

déstaliniser [destalinize] **VT** *Pol* to de-stalinize

destin [dɛstɛ̃] **NM** fate, destiny; **avoir un d. tragique** to be ill-fated; **qui aurait pu prévoir son d.?** who could have predicted his fate *or* what would become of him?; **le d. a voulu que ...** fate decreed that ...; **le d. nous a réunis** fate brought us together; **accepter son d.** to accept one's fate *or* destiny; **se mettre dans les mains du d.** to trust to fate; **nous nous souviendrons du d. tragique qui fut le sien** we shall remember his tragic fate

destinataire [dɛstinatɛr] **N** *(de lettre etc)* addressee, recipient; *(de marchandises)* consignee; *(de mandat postal)* payee

destination [dɛstinasjɔ̃] **NF 1** *(direction)* destination; **quelle est votre d.?** where are you going (to) *or* heading (for) *or* bound (for)?; **d. touristique** tourist destination; **trains/vols à d. de Paris** trains/flights to Paris; **articles à d. de la province et de l'étranger** goods for the provinces and for export; **arriver à d.** to arrive at one's destination **2** *(d'un édifice, d'une somme d'argent etc)* purpose

destinée [dɛstine] **NF 1** *(vie)* destiny; **unir sa**

d. à celle de qn to marry sb; *Litt* **il était promis à de si grandes destinées** he was destined for such great things **2 = destin**

destiner [dɛstine] **VT 1 d. qch à qn** to mean *or* intend sth for sb; **le sort qui nous est destiné** what fate holds in store for us; **cette remarque t'était personnellement destinée** that remark was meant for *or* aimed at you; **ce paquet vous est destiné** this parcel is meant for *or* addressed to you; **d. une somme d'argent à un achat** to allot *or* assign a sum of money to a purchase; **la recette du concert est destinée à la recherche contre le sida** the money from the concert will go to *or* towards AIDS research; **des marchandises destinées à l'exportation** goods intended for export; **il avait destiné son fils au barreau** he had intended his son for the bar; **on la destinait au fils du maire** they intended that she should marry the mayor's son; **cette salle est destinée aux répétitions** this room is used for rehearsals
2 *Vieilli (prédestiner)* to destine; **nous étions destinés à nous rencontrer** we were destined *or* fated to meet
VPR se destiner se d. à qch to intend to take up sth (as a profession); **il se destine à la médecine** he intends to be a doctor

destituable [dɛstituabl] **ADJ** *(fonctionnaire)* dismissible; *(souverain)* deposable; **il n'est pas destituable** *(fonctionnaire)* he cannot be dismissed (from his post); *(officier)* he cannot be stripped of his rank

destituer [dɛstitɥe] **VT** *(renvoyer)* to dismiss, to discharge; *Mil* to discharge; *(fonctionnaire)* to remove from office; *(souverain)* to depose; **d. un général de son commandement** to relieve a general of his command

destitution [dɛstitysjɔ̃] **NF** dismissal; *Mil* discharge; *(d'un souverain)* deposition

déstockage [destɔkaʒ] **NM** *Com* destocking, reduction in stocks; *Compta* **d. de production** *(poste de bilan)* decrease in stocks

déstocker [destɔke] **VT** *Com* to destock, to reduce stocks of

destrier [dɛstrije] **NM** *Arch* charger, war horse

destroy [dɛstrɔj] **ADJ INV** *Fam (musique)* = loud, fast and aggressive; *(personne)* self-destructive; *(jean)* ripped; *(voiture)* beat up, wrecked, *Br* knackered; **avoir une allure complètement d.** to look wasted

destroyer [dɛstrɔjœr, dɛstrwaje] **NM** *Naut, Mil* destroyer

destructeur, -trice [dɛstryktœr, -tris] **ADJ** *(enfant, guerre etc)* destructive
N destroyer
NM *(appareil)* **d. de documents** shredder

destructible [dɛstryktibl] **ADJ** destructible

destructif, -ive [dɛstryktif, -iv] **ADJ** destructive

destruction [dɛstryksjɔ̃] **NF** *(de preuves, papiers, ville etc)* destruction; *(de rats etc)*, *Fig (d'une race)* extermination

déstructuration [destryktyrasjɔ̃] **NF** *(de la société)* breakdown, disintegration

déstructuré [destryktyre] **ADJ 1** *(vêtement)* unstructured, deconstructed **2 une société déstructurée** a society in which traditional structures have broken down

déstructurer [destryktyre] **VT 1** *(vêtement)* to deconstruct **2** *(société)* **le chômage a déstructuré la société** society has been undermined by unemployment; **des populations déstructurées par le chômage/la guerre** people whose lives have been destroyed *or* shattered by unemployment/war

désuet, -uète [desɥɛ, -ɥɛt] **ADJ** *(mot)* obsolete; *(théorie)* obsolete, antiquated, out-of-date; *(vêtement)* out-of-date, old-fashioned; *(charme)* old-fashioned

désuétude [desɥetyd] **NF** disuse; **tomber en d.** to fall into disuse; *(d'un mot)* to become obsolete; *Jur (d'un droit etc)* to lapse; *(d'une loi)* to fall into abeyance; **d. calculée** planned *or* built-in obsolescence

désuni [dezyni] **ADJ** *(personnes)* divided, disunited; *(manœuvre)* uncoordinated; **des amis désunis par la guerre** friends divided by war

désunion [dezynjɔ̃] **NF** *(de personnes)* lack of unity; *(dans la famille etc)* dissension

désunir [dezynir] **VT** *(personnes, famille etc)* to divide; **questions qu'on ne peut pas d.** questions that cannot be treated separately (from each other), indissolubly linked questions; **des amants que le temps a désunis** lovers who grew apart with the passage of time
▪ **VPR se désunir** *(d'un athlète)* to lose one's stride

désynchronisé [desɛ̃krɔnize] **ADJ** out of synch

désyndicalisation [desɛ̃dikalizasjɔ̃] **NF** *(de la classe ouvrière)* decline in union membership (**de** among)

désyndicaliser [desɛ̃dikalize] **VT** *(entreprise)* to de-unionize

détachable [detaʃabl] **ADJ** detachable

détachage [detaʃaʒ] **NM** *(de vêtements etc)* stain *or* spot removal

détachant [detaʃɑ̃] **ADJ** stain- *or* spot-removing
▪ **NM** stain *or* spot remover

détaché [detaʃe] **ADJ 1** loose, detached; *(animal)* untethered; **pièces détachées** spare parts **2** *(délégué)* seconded *(to another department)*; *Mil* detached **3** *Fig (manière etc)* detached; **d. des biens de ce monde** detached from the world, unworldly

détachement [detaʃmɑ̃] **NM 1** *(d'un employé)* secondment; **il est en d. à l'université de Cambridge** he has been seconded *or* is on secondment to the University of Cambridge **2** *Mil (de troupes)* detachment, draft, *Am* detail; **d. de corvée** fatigue party **3** *(indifférence)* detachment (**de** from); **d. des biens de ce monde** detachment from the world, unworldliness

détacher[1] [detaʃe] **VT 1** *(défaire)* to detach; *(rideau)* to take down; *(chaîne)* to undo; *(animal)* to untether; *Rail (wagon à plate-forme)* to uncouple; **je ne peux pas en d. mes yeux** I can't take my eyes off it; **d. un chèque du carnet** to tear out a cheque; **d. les pétales d'une fleur** to pick *or* pluck the petals off a flower
2 *Fig* **d. qn de qch** to turn sb away from sth; **son indiscrétion a détaché de lui tous ses amis** his lack of discretion cost him all his friends *or* caused all his friends to turn away from him; **ses parents ont réussi à le d. de ce chien** his parents managed to free him *or* get him away from the dog
3 *(déléguer)* to attach, to second; *Mil* to detach; *Mil* **d. un officier auprès de qn** to detach an officer to serve with sb; **fonctionnaire détaché à un autre service** official temporarily attached *or* seconded to another department; **se faire d.** to be seconded; *Mil* to be detached
4 *(découper)* **d. une figure dans un tableau** to make a figure stand out in a picture; **d. les syllabes d'un mot** to pronounce each syllable of a word separately; *Mus* **d. les notes** to detach the notes
▪ **VPR se détacher 1** *(de nœud etc)* to come undone; *(d'animal)* to break loose; *(de poignée)* to break *or* come off, to become detached; *(de bouton)* to come off; *(de pièces)* to come apart; *(de peinture)* to flake *or* come away *or* off; **l'écorce se détache** the bark is peeling off *or* coming away

2 *Fig* **se d. de sa famille/qn** to separate *or* break away from one's family/sb; *(se désintéresser)* to grow apart from one's family/sb; **il s'est complètement détaché de toutes ces choses qui autrefois l'intéressaient** he has completely cut himself off from everything that used to interest him; **ils se sont beaucoup détachés l'un de l'autre** they've grown wide apart; **il s'est détaché peu à peu de la maison où il avait passé son enfance** he has gradually detached himself from his childhood home

3 *(se séparer)* **un petit groupe de coureurs se détacha en avant** a small group of runners broke away (from the field) *or* pulled ahead (of the field)

4 *(ressortir)* **se d. sur un fond/l'horizon** to stand out against a background/the horizon

détacher[2] **VT** *(nettoyer)* *(vêtements etc)* to remove stains *or* spots from

détacheur, -euse [detaʃœr, -øz] **ADJ** **flacon d.** (bottle of) stain remover
▪ **NM** stain remover

détail [detaj] **NM 1** *(élément)* detail; **donner tous les détails** to enter into *or* go into all the details, to give full details; **elle n'a pas donné de détails** she didn't go into detail, she didn't give any details; **raconter qch en d.** *ou* **dans les détails** to give a detailed account of sth; **décrire qch en d.** to describe sth in detail, to give a detailed description of sth; **elle va encore me faire le d. de ses vacances** she's going to give me yet another detailed account of her holiday; *Fig Fam* **ne pas faire de détails** not to make any exceptions; **sans faire de détails** without exception; **demander plus de détails** to ask for more details (**sur, à propos de** about, of); **nous n'avons pas encore de détails** there are no details as yet; **pour plus de détails** for more details; **c'est un d.** it's not important, it's a detail; **se perdre dans les détails** to get bogged down in detail; *Com* **le d. d'un compte** the items of an account; **le d. d'une facture** the breakdown of an invoice; **faire le d. de ses dépenses** to itemize one's expenses
2 *Com* retail; **vendre au d.** to sell (goods) retail; **magasin de vente au d.** retail store; **marchand au d.** retailer; **prix de d.** retail price; **commerce de d.** retailing; **être dans le commerce de d.** to be in retailing
3 *Admin, Mil* **service de d.** executive duties; **officier de d.** ≃ quartermaster officer

détaillant, -ante [detajɑ̃, -ɑ̃t] **N** *Com* retailer; **d. indépendant** independent retailer; **d. spécialisé** specialist retailer

détaillé [detaje] **ADJ 1** *(récit, description etc)* detailed **2** *Com* **état d. de compte** detailed *or* itemized statement of account

détailler [detaje] **VT 1** *Com (marchandises)* to retail, to sell retail **2** *(énumérer) (raisons)* to list; *Com (facture)* to itemize **3** **d. qn (de la tête aux pieds)** to scrutinize sb, to look sb up and down

détaler [detale] **VI** *Fam (d'une personne)* to bolt, to take off; *(d'un cheval etc)* to bolt; **la souris détala vers son trou** the mouse bolted for *or* scuttled off to *or* scurried off to its hole

détartrage [detartraʒ] **NM** *(de chaudière)* descaling; *(de dents)* tartar removal, scaling

détartrant [detartrɑ̃] **NM** *(pour chaudière)* scaler
▪ **ADJ** **dentifrice d.** toothpaste for tartar removal

détartrer [detartre] **VT** *(chaudière)* to (de)scale; *(dents) (d'un dentiste)* to scale, to remove the tartar from; *(d'un dentifrice)* to remove the tartar from

détartreur [detartrœr] **NM** *(pour chaudière)* scaler

détaxation [detaksasjɔ̃] **NF** removal of tax

détaxe [detaks] **NF 1** *(levée)* **la d. des tabacs** *(réduction)* the reduction of duty *or* tax on tobacco; *(suppression)* the lifting of tax or duty on tobacco; **vendu en d.** duty-free; **la d. des marchandises à l'exportation** the lifting of duty on exports **2** *(remboursement)* refund; **cela m'a fait cent euros de d.** I got a hundred euros in duty refunded

détaxé [detakse] **ADJ** *(produits, articles)* duty-free

détaxer [detakse] **VT** to take the tax off, to remove the tax on; **marchandises détaxées** duty-free goods

détectable [detɛktabl] **ADJ** detectable

détecter [detɛkte] **VT** to detect

détecteur, -trice [detɛktœr, -tris] **ADJ** *Tech* detecting, sensing; *Électron* **lampe détectrice** detector valve
▪ **NM** *Tech* detector; *Électron* detector, sensor
▸▸ *Aut* **d. d'anomalie** fault warning sensor; *Aut* **d. anti-pincement** anti-pinch sensor; *Aut* **d. de choc** crash sensor; *Aut* **d. de cognement** knock sensor; *Aut* **d. de collision** crash sensor; *Com* **d. de faux billets** forged banknote detector; **d. de fumée** smoke detector *or* alarm; **d. de mensonges** lie detector, *Spéc* polygraph; **d. de mines** mine detector; *Électron* **d. d'ondes** wave detector; *Électron* **d. de particules** particle detector; **d. de radar** radar detector; *TV etc* **d. transistorisé** solid-state sensor; *Ordinat* **d. de virus** virus detector

détection [detɛksjɔ̃] **NF** detection, location; **d. électromagnétique** radio location; **d. sous-marine** underwater detection; *Mil, Naut* **d. des mines** mine detection; **d. à ultrasons** ultrasound detection; *Ordinat* **d. d'erreurs** error detection; *Ordinat* **d. virale** virus detection

détective [detɛktiv] **NM** detective; **d. privé** private detective; **d. d'hôtel** house detective, hotel detective

déteindre [detɛ̃dr] *(conj like* **teindre)** **VT** to take the colour out of
▪ **VI** *(d'un tissu)* to fade, to lose colour; **d. au lavage** to run in the wash; **le ruban a déteint sur ma robe** the colour of the ribbon has come off on my dress; *Fig* **cela déteint sur eux** it rubs off on them; *Fig* **j'espère que leur politesse déteindra sur elle** I hope some of their politeness rubs off on her

dételage [detlaʒ] **NM 1** *(de chevaux)* unharnessing, unhitching **2** *Rail (de wagons)* uncoupling

dételer [detle] (**je dételle, n. dételons; je detellerai)** **VT 1** *(chevaux)* to unharness, to unhitch; *(bœufs)* to unyoke **2** *Rail (wagons)* to uncouple
▪ **VI** *Fam* to ease off, to stop working; **travailler dix heures sans d.** to work for ten hours without letting up, to work non-stop for ten hours; **on dételle à six heures** we stop (work) at six o'clock

détendeur [detɑ̃dœr] **NM** *Tech* pressure reducer, relief valve

détendre [detɑ̃dr] **VT** *(cordage de raquette, cordes de guitare)* to slacken, to loosen; *(arc)* to unbend; **d. un ressort** to release a spring; **d. des relations/l'atmosphère** to make relations/the atmosphere less strained; **d. les nerfs** to steady the nerves
▪ **VPR se détendre** *(de tissu)* to stretch; *(de ressort)* to uncoil; *(de vapeur)* to be reduced in pressure; *(d'un gaz, de l'air chaud)* to expand; *(se relaxer)* to relax; **se d. pendant une heure** to relax for an hour; **son visage se détendit dans un sourire** his face relaxed into a smile; **la situation se détend** the situation is easing *or* is becoming less tense

détendu [detɑ̃dy] **ADJ** *(lâche)* slack; *(conversation etc)* relaxed

détenir [detnir] **VT** (*conj like* **tenir**) **1** (*passeport, titres etc*) to hold, to be in possession of; (*le pouvoir, Sport coupe, record du monde*) to hold; **d. un objet volé** to be in possession of a stolen object; **d. un secret** to have a secret; **ils détiennent 30% des parts de la société/des parts de marché** they have a 30% shareholding in the company/a 30% market share **2** (*personne*) to detain, to keep *or* hold prisoner

détente [detãt] **NF 1** (*relaxation*) recreation; **dans ses rares moments de d.** in the little time he has to relax; **j'ai besoin de quelques instants de d.** I need to relax for a few moments, I need a few moments' relaxation

2 (*de qch de tendu*) loosening, slackening; (*de relations etc*) easing; *Pol* détente; (*d'un athlète*) spring; **avoir une belle d.** to jump well, to be a good jumper; **d'une d. de la jambe droite, il envoya le ballon dans le but anglais** stretching out his right leg, he sent the ball into the England goal; **travaillant tout en d.**, il parvint à sauter les 2 mètres with a powerful spring, he managed to clear the 2-metre mark

3 (*d'une arme*) trigger; *Fam* **il est dur à la d.** (*pingre*) he's tight-fisted *or* stingy; (*il ne comprend pas vite*) he's slow on the uptake

4 *Tech* (*de la vapeur, des gaz*) expansion; (*dans un moteur*) explosion *or* power stroke; **soupape de d.** expansion valve

5 *Écon* (*des taux d'intérêt*) lowering, easing

détenteur, -trice [detãtœr, -tris] **N** (*de droits d'auteur, titres, coupe etc*) holder; **d. de titres** stockholder, shareholder; **d. d'obligations** bondholder; **d. du record du monde** world record holder

détention [detãsjã] **NF 1** (*de titres etc*) holding; (*d'armes à feu etc*) possession **2** (*captivité*) detention, imprisonment; **d. provisoire** detention pending trial

détenu, -ue [detny] **N** prisoner, inmate

détergence [deterʒãs] **NF** detergency

détergent [deterʒã] **ADJ, NM** detergent

déterger [deterʒe] **VT** *Tech* (*taches d'huile etc*) to clean, to remove

détérioration [deterjɔrasjã] **NF** deterioration

détériorer [deterjɔre] **VT** (*matériel, santé*) to damage; (*marchandises*) to spoil; **la radio m'est revenue complètement détériorée** the radio came back absolutely ruined; **détérioré en cours de transport** damaged in transit
VPR se détériorer to deteriorate

déterminable [determinabl] **ADJ** determinable, which can be determined

déterminant [determinã] **ADJ** (*facteur, cause etc*) deciding, decisive; **sa présence a été déterminante pour la signature du contrat** his presence was the determining factor in the decision to sign the contract
NM *Ling* determiner; *Math* determinant

déterminatif, -ive [determinatif, -iv] **VOIR GRAMMAIRE A32** *Ling, Gram* **ADJ** (*mot etc*) determinative, defining; **phrase déterminative** defining clause
NM determiner, determinative

détermination [determinasjã] **NF 1** (*fermeté*) determination, resolution; **avec d.** with determination, determinedly, resolutely **2** (*résolution*) resolve, determination; **rien ne pourra faire flancher ma d.** nothing will make me any less determined, nothing will shake my resolve **3** (*d'une espèce, d'une date, d'une zone etc*) determination; (*du sang, d'une bactérie*) typing; **d. des prix** price setting

déterminé [determine] **ADJ 1** (*domaine, objectif etc*) specific, particular; (*durée*) specific, set, definite; **dans un sens d.** in a given

direction; **il faut arriver au but/à l'objectif d.** we have to achieve the goal/the objective that was set; **il l'a fait dans un but d.** he did it for a specific reason **2** (*personne, manière etc*) determined, resolute; **être d. à faire qch** to be determined to do sth

déterminer [determine] **VT 1** (*définir*) (*date, fait, nom, valeur etc*) to determine, to establish; (*espèce*) to determine; (*sang, bactérie*) to type; **d. un lieu de rendez-vous** to fix *or* decide on a meeting place **2** (*causer*) (*changement*) to cause, to give rise to; (*action, décision*) to determine, to dictate **3** (*décider*) **d. qn à faire qch** to induce *or* move *or* impel sb to do sth; **qu'est-ce qui vous a déterminé à partir?** what made you (decide to) leave? **4** *Gram* to determine
VPR se déterminer to make up one's mind (**à faire qch** to do sth)

déterminisme [determinism] **NM** *Phil* determinism

déterministe [determinist] *Phil* **N** determinist
ADJ determinist(ic)

déterré, -ée [detere] **N** *Fam* **il a un air** *ou* **une mine** *ou* **une tête de d.** he looks like death warmed up

déterrer [detere] **VT** (*trésor enfoui etc*) to dig up, to unearth; (*arbre*) to uproot; (*cadavre*) to exhume; *Fig* (*vieux livre etc*) to dig up

détersif, -ive [detersif, -iv] **ADJ, NM** detergent

détersion [detersjã] **NF** (*nettoyage*) cleaning with a detergent; *Méd* (*d'une plaie etc*) cleansing

détestable [detestabl] **ADJ** (*personne*) detestable, hateful; (*travail etc*) (*de mauvaise qualité*) awful, dreadful, very bad; (*inintéressant*) awful, ghastly; (*temps, humeur*) foul, ghastly

détestablement [detestabləmã] **ADV** (*se conduire, chanter, parler*) extremely badly, appallingly; **faire la cuisine d.** to be an extremely bad *or* an appalling cook; **il parle anglais/travaille d.** his English/work is extremely bad *or* is appalling

détester [deteste] **VT** to detest, to hate; **je déteste être dérangé** I hate to be *or* I hate *or* detest being disturbed; **elle ne déteste pas (de) courir** she's quite fond of running; **il ne déteste pas les bonbons** he rather likes sweets

déthéiné [deteine] **ADJ** (*thé*) decaffeinated

détonant [detonã] **ADJ** (*substance*) explosive; **explosif d.** high explosive; *Tech, Fig* **mélange d.** explosive mixture
NM explosive

détonateur [detonatœr] **NM** detonator; *Fig* **être le d. de qch** to spark sth off

détonation [detonasjã] **NF** (*explosion*) detonation; (*bruit*) explosion; (*bruit d'arme à feu*) report, bang; *Aut* knocking, detonation

détoner [detone] **VI** (*de dynamite etc*) to detonate, to explode; (*de carburant*) to knock; **faire d. qch** to detonate sth

Do not confuse with **détonner**.

détonner [detone] **VI** (*d'un instrument*) to be out of tune; (*d'un chanteur*) to sing out of tune *or* off-key; (*d'un pianiste etc*) to play out of tune; (*de couleurs*) to clash; **ses bijoux détonnent dans ce milieu** her jewels are out of place *or* out of keeping in these circles; **il détonne dans cet entourage** he looks out of place in that circle; **la remarque détonne dans ce texte** the remark jumps out in this text *or* looks really out of place in this text

Do not confuse with **détoner**.

détordre [detɔrdr] **VT** (*fil etc*) to untwist

VPR se détordre (*de fil etc*) to come untwisted, to untwist

détortiller [detɔrtije] **VT** (*fil etc*) to untwist; (*cheveux etc*) to disentangle

détour [detur] **NM 1** (*tracé*) (*d'une route, d'une rivière*) turn, curve, bend; **la route fait un brusque d.** the road makes a sharp turn *or* bends sharply; **je l'ai aperçue au d. du chemin** I spotted her at the bend in the path; *Fig* **au d. de la conversation** in the course of the conversation

2 (*dans un parcours*) detour; **faire un long d.** to make a long detour; **d. obligatoire de 5 km** (mandatory) 5 kilometre diversion; **ça vaut le d.** it's worth the trip; *Fig* **tu verras son nouveau copain, il vaut le d.** her new boyfriend is really something

3 *Fig* (*biais*) **user de détours pour arriver à un but** to achieve one's end in a roundabout way; **répondre sans d.** to give a plain *or* straightforward answer; **vous pouvez me parler sans d.** you can speak frankly to me

détourage [deturaʒ] **NM** *Cin* cropping

détourné [deturne] **ADJ** (*route, itinéraire*) indirect, roundabout; **chemin d.** by-road; *Fig* **par des voies détournées, de façon détournée** indirectly, in a roundabout way; **ce n'est pas la peine de prendre des chemins détournés pour me le dire** you might as well tell me straight out, why go all around the houses to tell me

détournement [deturnəmã] **NM** (*d'une rivière etc*) diversion, diverting; (*du trafic*) diversion, rerouting

▸▸ *Fin* **d. d'actif** embezzlement of assets; **d. d'avion** hijacking; *Fin* **d. de fonds** misappropriation of funds, embezzlement; *Jur* **d. de mineur** corruption of a minor; **d. de pouvoir** takeover (of power)

détourner [deturne] **VT 1** (*trafic, rivière etc*) to divert; **d. un avion** to hijack a plane; **d. l'attention de qn** to divert *or* distract sb's attention; **d. qn de** (*son travail, mauvaises fréquentations*) to get sb away from; **d. qn de sa route** to take sb out of his/her way; **comment as-tu pu te laisser d. de ton devoir?** how could you have let yourself be distracted from your duty?; **d. qn du droit chemin** to lead sb astray; **il faut absolument le d. de ce projet** we really must get him to drop the idea; **d. la conversation** to change the subject; **d. les soupçons** to avert suspicion **2** (*fonds*) to misappropriate, to embezzle **3 d. la tête pour éviter de voir qn** to look the other way *or* to turn one's head away so as not to see sb; **d. les yeux** to avert one's gaze, to look away, to turn one's eyes away
VPR se détourner to turn away *or* aside (**de** from); *Fig* **se d. de ses études/amis** to neglect one's studies/friends

détoxication [detɔksikasjã] **NF** detoxication

détoxiquer [detɔksike] **VT** to detoxicate

détracter [detrakte] **VT** *Litt* to denigrate, to disparage

détracteur, -trice [detraktœr, -tris] **N** detractor, disparager

détraqué, -ée [detrake] **ADJ** (*appareil*) out of order; (*digestion, estomac*) upset; (*santé*) ruined; *Fam* (*personne*) (*psychologiquement*) unhinged; **ma radio est toute détraquée** there is something very wrong with my radio; **il a le cerveau d.** his mind is unhinged; **avoir les nerfs détraqués** to be a nervous wreck; **le temps est d.** the weather is unsettled
N *Fam* psycho

détraquement [detrakmã] **NM** (*d'un appareil, de la santé etc*) breakdown

détraquer [detrake] **VT** (*appareil*) to put out

of order; *(mécanisme)* to throw out of gear; *Fam* **cette déception lui a détraqué le cerveau** the disappointment has unhinged his mind; **ça va te d. l'estomac** that'll upset your stomach

VPR se détraquer *(d'un appareil, de la santé etc)* to break down; *(de l'estomac)* to be upset; *(du temps)* to become unsettled; **se d. l'estomac/les nerfs** to upset one's stomach/ruin one's nerves

détrempe¹ [detrɑ̃p] **NF** *(de mur)* distemper; *Beaux-Arts* tempera

détrempe² **NF** *(d'acier)* annealing

détremper¹ [detrɑ̃pe] **VT** *(gorger d'eau)* to soak; **champ/terre détrempé(e)** sodden *or* waterlogged field/earth

détremper² **VT** *(acier)* to anneal

détresse [detrɛs] **NF 1** *(angoisse)* distress, grief, anguish; **elle est dans une grande d.** she is extremely distressed *or* heartbroken **2** *(dénuement)* financial straits *or* difficulties; **être en d.** to be in financial difficulties, to have money problems **3** *(perdition)* **en d.** *(navire)* in distress; *(voiture, avion)* in difficulties; **signal de d.** distress signal, SOS; *Aut* **feux de d.** hazard warning lights, *Fam* hazards; *Méd* **d. respiratoire** respiratory distress syndrome

détriment [detrimɑ̃] **NM au d. de qn/qch** to the detriment of sb/sth; **je l'ai appris à mon d.** I found it out to my cost

détritus [detritys] **NM** rubbish, refuse

détroit [detrwa] **NM** *Géog* strait(s), sound

détromper [detrɔ̃pe] **VT d. qn** to put sb right **VPR se détromper** to realize that one was wrong; **il a fini par se d.** he finally realized his mistake *or* that he was wrong *or* mistaken; **je ne demande pas mieux que de me d.** I'll be quite happy to admit that I was mistaken; **détrompez-vous!** open your eyes!

détrôner [detrone] **VT 1** *(monarque)*, *Sport* *(champion)* to dethrone **2** *(supplanter)* *(ancienne méthode etc)* to supersede

détrousser [detruse] **VT d. qn** *Hum* to relieve sb of his/her valuables; *Arch* to rob sb

détrousseur [detrusœr] **NM** *Arch* highwayman, footpad

détruire [detrɥir] *(prp* **détruisant;** *pp* **détruit;** *pr ind* **je détruis,** n. **détruisons;** *impf* **je détruisais;** *p hist* **je détruisis;** *fu* **je détruirai)** **VT 1** *(démolir)* *(édifice, ville etc)* to destroy; *(empire etc)* to destroy, to overthrow; *(bateau etc)* to break up, to scrap; *(voiture, avion etc)* to destroy, *Fam* to demolish, to write off **2** *(anéantir)* *(maison, village)* to destroy; *(mariage)* to destroy, to wreck; *(moisson, alibi)* to ruin, to destroy; *(santé)* to ruin; **d. les espérances de qn** to destroy *or* dash sb's hopes; **il a détruit sa fortune au jeu** he spent all his money gambling **3** *(tuer)* to kill; **l'épidémie va d. 200 000 personnes** the epidemic is likely to kill 200,000 people **VPR se détruire** *(se suicider)* to kill oneself

dette [dɛt] **NF** *Fin*, *Fig* debt; **faire des dettes** to run into debt; **avoir des dettes** to be in debt, to have debts; **avoir 10 000 euros de dettes** to be 10,000 euros in debt; **être criblé de dettes** to be crippled with debt; **avoir une d. de reconnaissance envers qn** to owe sb a debt of gratitude, to be under an obligation to sb; **être en d. envers qn** to be indebted to sb, to be under an obligation to sb; **payer sa d. à la justice** *ou* **à la société** to pay one's debt to society

▸▸ *Compta* **dettes actives** accounts receivable, assets; **dettes bancaires** bank debts; **d. caduque** debt barred by the Statute of Limitations; **dettes compte** book debts; **d. consolidée** consolidated debt; **d. à court terme** short-term debt; *Compta* **dettes à court terme** current liabilities; **la d. de l'État**

the national debt; **d. exigible** debt due for (re)payment; **d. d'exploitation** trade debt; **d. extérieure** foreign debt; **d. flottante** floating debt; **d. foncière** property charge; *Compta* **dettes fournisseurs** accounts payable; **d. d'honneur** debt of honour; *(hypothécaire)* mortgage debt; **d. inexigible** unrecoverable debt; **d. inscrite** consolidated debt; **d. de jeu** gambling debt; **d. liquide** liquid debt; *Compta* **dettes à long terme** long-term liabilities; *Compta* **dettes à moyen terme** medium-term liabilities; *Compta* **dettes passives** accounts payable, liabilities; **d. privilégiée** preferred debt; **la d. publique** the national debt; **d. sociale** social debt; **d. véreuse** bad debt

deuche [dœʃ], **deudeuche** [dœdœʃ] **NF** *Fam* Citroën 2CV

DEUG [dœg] **NM** *(abrév* **diplôme d'études universitaires générales)** = university degree awarded after a two-year course of study

> **DEUG**
> In French universities, students take the "DEUG" or the "DEUST" ("diplôme d'études universitaires scientifiques et techniques") after two years of courses. They may then take further courses leading to the "licence" (the equivalent of a bachelor's degree). Most students who obtain the "DEUG" choose to do this, while the majority of students who obtain the "DEUST" leave university and go straight into employment.

deuil [dœj] **NM 1** *(perte)* bereavement; **fermé pour cause de d.** *(annonce)* closed owing to bereavement; **il y a eu plusieurs deuils dans leur famille** there have been several deaths in their family

2 *(manifestation)* mourning; **porter le d.,** **être en d.** to be in mourning; **porter le d. de qn** to be in mourning for sb; *Fig* **elle porte le d. de sa jeunesse/de sa fortune** she is mourning the loss of her youth/her fortune; **se mettre en d., prendre le d.** to go into mourning; **quitter le d.** to come out of mourning; *Fig* **la montagne est en d.** the mountain looks desolate; *Fig Fam* **il avait toujours les ongles en d.** his fingernails were always dirty; **grand d.** deep mourning; **semaine de d.** week of mourning; **décréter une journée de d. national** to order a day of national mourning, ≃ to order the flags to be flown at half mast *or Am* half-staff; *Vieilli* **conduire le d.** to be chief mourner; *Fam* **faire son d. de qch** to give sth up as *or* for lost

DEUST [dœst] **NM** *(abrév* **diplôme d'études universitaires scientifiques et techniques)** = university degree awarded after a two-year course of study in science and/or technical subjects

deutérium [døterjɔm] **NM** *Chimie* deuterium

Deutéronome [døterɔnɔm] **NM** *Bible* Deuteronomy

deutsche Mark [dɔjtʃmark, døtʃmark] **NM** *Anciennement* Deutschmark

deux [dø, *before a vowel sound in the same word group* døz] **ADJ INV 1** two; **d. enfants** [døzɑ̃fɑ̃] two children; **j'en ai d.** [dø] I have two (of them); **d. ou trois** [døzutrwa] two or three; **d. fois** twice; **on a dû lui enlever les d. yeux** they had to remove both his eyes; **des d. côtés du fleuve** on either side *or* on both sides of the river; **tous (les) d.** both; **tous les d. jours** every other day, every two days, every second day; **nous/vous/eux d.** *(sujet)* we/you/those two, the two of *or* both of us/you/them; *(complément)* us/you/

those two, the two of *or* both of us/you/them; **entre d. âges** middle-aged; **être pris entre d. feux** to be caught in the middle; **être assis** *ou* **avoir le derrière** *ou très Fam* **le cul entre d. chaises** to be in an awkward position; **vivre à d.** to live together; **à d. tranchants** *(lame)* double-edged; *Fig* two-edged; *Fig* **une économie/une Europe à d. vitesses** a two-speed economy/Europe; **faire d. poids d. mesures** to apply double standards; **de d. choses l'une, il viendra seul ou il ne viendra pas** he'll either come on his own or he won't come at all; **de d. choses l'une, soit tu pars en vacances avec nous, soit tu restes à la maison** either you come on holiday with us or you stay at home – take your pick *or* it's up to you; **en d. temps, trois mouvements** in no time at all, in next to no time; **les mathématiques/les ordinateurs et moi, ça fait d.** I just don't get on with mathematics/computers; **ma sœur et moi, ça fait d.** *(ne nous confondez pas)* my sister and I are two different people; *(nous sommes fâchés)* my sister and I just don't get along; *Vulg* **cette voiture de mes d.** that fucking car

2 *(peu de)* **j'ai d. mots à lui dire** I've a bone to pick with him; **c'est à d. pas** *ou* **d. minutes d'ici** it's only a short distance away, it's two minutes away; **je reviens dans d. minutes** I'll be back in a minute *or Fam* a tick; **tu peux venir? – d. secondes!** can you come here? – just a minute!; **ça va te prendre d. secondes** it will only take you a minute; *Fam* **être à d. doigts de faire qch** to be on the verge of *or* within an inch of doing sth; **je suis à d. doigts de terminer** *ou* **d'avoir terminé** I've very nearly finished

3 *(deuxième)* **Charles D.** Charles the Second; **chapitre d.** chapter two; *Fam* **il est arrivé d. ou troisième** he came in second or third; **il est numéro d. dans mes pensées** he takes second place *or* comes second in my thoughts; **c'est le numéro d. des fabricants de produits textiles** it's the second largest textile manufacturer

NM INV two; *Cartes* two, deuce; *Cartes* **le d. de cœur** the two of hearts; **la table de d.** the two times table; **d. fois d. font quatre** two times two *or* twice two is four; *Fig* **c'est clair comme d. et d. font quatre** it's as clear as day; **aujourd'hui nous sommes le d.** today is the second, it's the second today; **casser qch en d.** to break sth in two; **diviser** *ou* **couper une ligne en d.** to bisect a line; **marcher par d.** to walk in pairs *or* twos; *(dans une procession)* to march two abreast; **entrer d. par d.** to come in two by two *or* in twos; **à nous d.** *(entre amis)* let's get on with it (together); *(à un adversaire)* let's fight it out; *Fam* **il fera ça en moins de d.** he'll do it in two ticks *or* in no time at all *or* in next to no time; *Fam* **comme pas d.** as anything; **pas de d.** *(danse)* pas de deux; *Fig* **entre les d.** average, OK; **tu as froid ou chaud? – entre les d.** are you hot or cold? – I'm just right; **tu as réussi ton examen? – entre les d.** how did your exam go? – so-so; **alors, tu l'aimes ou tu ne l'aimes pas? – entre les d.** well, do you like it or not? – I'm not sure one way or the other; **tu as envie de venir? – je ne sais pas, entre les d.** do you want to come? – I don't know, I do and I don't; **jamais d. sans trois** it never rains but it pours; *Fam* **je n'ai fait ni une ni d.** I didn't think twice

deux-chevaux [døʃ(ə)vo] **NF INV** *Aut* deux-chevaux, 2CV

deux-deux (à) **ADJ** *Mus* in two-two time

deux-huit (à) **ADJ** *Mus* in two-eight time

deuxième [døzjɛm] **ADJ** second; **appartement au d. étage** second-floor flat, *Am* third-floor apartment; **le d. exportateur/annonceur du monde** the world's second largest exporter/advertiser; *Math* **équation du d. degré** quadratic equation; **d. classe** second class, standard class; **d. épreuve** *(dans l'édition)* revise; *Rugby* **d. temps** second phase

N second; **elle est née la d.** she is the second child

NM *(étage)* **habiter au d.** to live on the second *or Am* third floor

NF *Journ* **d. de couverture** inside front cover, IFC

deuxièmement [døzjɛmmɑ̃] **ADV** secondly, in the second place

deux-mâts [døma] **NM INV** *Naut* two-master

deux-pattes [døpat] **NF INV** *Fam* Citroën 2CV

deux-pièces [døpjɛs] **NM INV 1** *(maillot de bain)* two-piece (swimsuit); *(ensemble, tailleur)* two-piece **2** *(appartement)* two-roomed flat *or Am* apartment

deux-points [døpwɛ̃] **NM INV** *Typ* colon

deux-ponts [døpɔ̃] **NM INV** *Naut* two-decked ship; *Aviat* double-decker (aircraft)

deux-quatre **NM INV** *Mus* two-four time

deux-roues [døru] **NM INV** two-wheeled vehicle, two-wheeler; **je circule en d.** I get around on two wheels

deux-temps **NM INV 1** *Mus* two-two time **2** *(moteur)* two-stroke (engine); **(mélange) d.** two-stroke mixture

deuzio [døzjo] **ADV** *Fam* second(ly)

dévaler [devale] **VI** to go down, to descend; *(de cours d'eau)* to rush down; **le jardin dévale jusqu'à la rivière** the garden slopes down *or* extends down to the river

VT d. l'escalier to rush down the stairs; **d. la rue à toute vitesse** to race down the street

dévaliser [devalize] **VT** *(banque)* to rob; *(maison)* to burgle; *Fam (frigo, placard etc)* to raid; *Fig* **j'ai dévalisé la boutique** I bought up the shop; **on a été dévalisé en manteaux rouges** all the red coats have been snatched up

dévalorisation [devalɔrizasjɔ̃] **NF 1** *(action)* *(de la monnaie)* devaluation; *Com (de marchandises)* marking down; *(résultat)* *(de la monnaie)* fall in value, depreciation; *Com (de marchandises)* mark-down **2** *Fig (d'une personne, d'une politique)* discrediting

dévaloriser [devalɔrize] **VT** *(monnaie)* to devalue; *Com (marchandises)* to mark down

VPR se dévaloriser *(de monnaie)* to depreciate; *Com (de marchandises)* to lose value; *(d'une personne)* to put oneself down; **se d. dans l'esprit du public** to discredit oneself in the eyes of the public

dévaluation [devalɥasjɔ̃] **NF** *Écon (de la monnaie)* devaluation

dévaluer [devalɥe] **VT** *(monnaie)* to devalue **VPR se dévaluer** to lose value

devancement [dəvɑ̃smɑ̃] **NM** *Mil* **d. d'appel** enlistment before call-up; *Fin* **d. d'une échéance** payment before the due date, pre-payment

devancer [dəvɑ̃se] **VT** (**je devançai(s); n. devançons**) **1** *(dans un classement)* to come ahead of; **d. ses concurrents** to be ahead of the competition **2** *(distancer)* to leave behind, to out-distance, to outstrip; **je vous ai devancé** I got here before you **3** *(prévenir)* *(personne, critiques)* to forestall; *(demande, désirs de qn)* to anticipate; **d. son époque** to be ahead of one's time; *Mil* **d. l'appel** to enlist before call-up; *Fin* **d. une échéance** to settle an account early, to pay a bill before the due date

devancier, -ière [dəvɑ̃sje, -jɛr] **N** predecessor

DEVANT [dəvɑ̃] SEE GRAMMAR B55

> **PRÉP** in front of **1**, **2** ▪ ahead of **1** ▪ in the face of **3**
> **ADV** in front **1**, **2** ▪ past **1** ▪ ahead **2**
> **NM** front **1**

PRÉP 1 *(en face de, en avant de)* in front of; **assis d. moi** sitting in front of me; **il est loin d. nous** he is a long way in front of *or* ahead of us; **marchez tout droit d. vous** carry straight on; **regardez d. vous** look where you're going; **je passe d. elle tous les jours** I pass her every day; **elle est passée d. moi dans la queue** she went in front of *or* ahead of me in the queue; **avoir du temps/de l'argent d. soi** to have time/money to spare; **tu as la vie d. toi** you've got your whole life ahead of you; **assis d. un verre de vin** sitting over a glass of wine; **navire d. Calais** ship off Calais

2 *(en présence de)* in front of; **il l'a frappée d. les enfants** he hit her in front of the children; **éprouver de la gêne d. qn** to feel ill at ease with sb *or* in sb's presence; **je n'ai su que faire d. cette petite fille en pleurs** I didn't know what to do when faced *or* confronted with this little girl in tears; **s'incliner d. qn** to bow to sb; **paraître d. ses pairs** to appear before one's peers

3 *(face à)* **être courageux d. le danger** to show courage in the face of danger; **égaux d. la loi** equal in the eyes of the law; **sa position d. ce problème** his position on the problem; **il ne sait quelle attitude adopter d. de tels problèmes/mon malheur** he doesn't know what attitude to adopt when faced with *or* in the face of such problems/my unhappiness; **d. cet état de choses/votre silence** in view of *or* given this state of affairs/your silence

ADV 1 *(en face)* in front; **tu cherches la bibliothèque? tu es (juste) d.** you're looking for the library? you're right in front of it; **son magasin? je passe d. tous les jours** his shop? I pass *or* go past it every day; **il est passé d. et il ne l'a même pas vu** he went right past it and didn't even see it; **passer (par) d.** to come in the front way; **porter qch sens d. derrière** to wear sth back to front; **sa robe se ferme d.** her dress closes at the front *or Am* in front

2 *(en avant)* **aller d.** to go in front, to lead the way; **marcher/courir d.** to walk on/run on ahead; **partir d. pour arriver le premier** to go on ahead so as to get there first; **envoyer qn d.** to send sb on (in front); **passe d.** go ahead of *or* in front of me/us/*etc*; **s'asseoir d.** *(en voiture)* to sit in the front *or Am* in front; **ils sont d. sur la photo** they're at the front in the photograph; **tu n'as pas vu Martin? – je crois qu'il est d.** have you seen Martin? – he's up ahead, I think; **les voleurs sont loin d. maintenant** the thieves are far ahead of us by now; **avoir des places d.** to have seats at the front; **vous pouvez passer des verres d.?** will you pass some glasses to the front?

3 *Arch, Litt* **d.** as before

NM 1 front (part); **d. (de chemise)** (shirt) front; *Tricot* **d. gauche/droit** left/right front; **chambre sur le d.** front room; **dents de d.** front teeth; **pattes de d.** forelegs; *Com* **d. de caisse** checkout display; **prendre les devants** to go on ahead; *Fig* to make the first move; **gagner les devants** to take the lead

2 **aller au-d. de qn** to meet sb on the way; **aller au-d. des vœux de qn** to anticipate sb's wishes; **courir au-d. du danger** to court danger, to go to meet danger; **tu vas au-d. de gros ennuis** you're looking for trouble

---

devanture [dəvɑ̃tyr] **NF** *(d'un édifice)* façade, front; **d. de magasin** *(façade)* shopfront; *(vitrine)* shop window

dévastateur, -trice [devastatœr, -tris] **ADJ** devastating

dévastation [devastasjɔ̃] **NF** devastation, destruction, havoc

dévaster [devaste] **VT** *(pays)* to devastate, to lay waste, *Fml* to ravage; *(cultures)* to devastate, to destroy, to ruin

déveine [devɛn] **NF** *Fam* (run of) bad luck; **être dans la d.** to be down on one's luck; **quelle d.!** (what) hard luck!

développé [devlɔpe] **NM 1** *Sport (en haltérophilie)* press **2** *(en danse)* développé

développement [devlɔpmɑ̃] **NM 1** *(du corps)* development, growth; *(des muscles, des fleurs, des facultés etc)* development; **d. d'une entreprise** growth of a business; **d. durable** sustained development; **mon entreprise est en plein d.** my business is growing fast; **d. de produit** product development; **d. régional** regional development; *Écon* **un pays en voie de d.** a developing country; **personne n'aurait pu s'attendre à de tels développements** no one could have expected such developments; **suivre les développements d'une affaire** to follow the developments of an affair; **un des développements possibles de l'affaire** one of the possible consequences of the scandal

2 *Phot (traitement complet)* processing, developing; *(étape du traitement)* developing

3 *(des ailes)* spreading out, opening out; *(des branches d'un arbre etc)* spread; *Math (d'une expression contractée etc)* expansion, development

4 *Cyclisme* roll out, development, = distance covered by a bicycle in one revolution of the pedals; **bicyclette avec un d. de six mètres** ≃ bicycle with a six-metre gear *or* geared to six metres

5 *Mus, Beaux-Arts (d'un thème, d'une dissertation)* development; *Fig* **se lancer dans de grands développements** to go into detailed explanations *or* great detail

développer [devlɔpe] **VT 1** *(muscles, facultés, commerce etc)* to develop **2** *(ailes)* to spread out, to open out; *Math (expression contractée etc)* to expand, to develop **3** *Phot (traiter)* to process; *(révéler)* to develop; **faire d. une pellicule** to have a film developed *or* processed; **faire d. des photos** to have photos developed **4** *(élargir) (sujet, idée, sa pensée)* to develop **5** *Aut (chevaux)* to deliver; *Cyclisme* **bicyclette qui développe six mètres** bicycle that has a gear of six metres *or* that is geared to six metres

VPR se développer 1 *(d'un enfant, d'un pays, de fleurs, de l'intelligence etc)* to develop; **l'affaire ne va pas tarder à se d. et se transformer en un véritable scandale** the affair will soon develop into a real scandal **2** *(s'étendre)* to spread out, to expand, to extend; **la plaine se développe à perte de vue** the plain extends *or* stretches out as far as the eye can see

développeur [devlɔpœr] **NM** *(société de logiciels)* developer

développeuse [devlɔpøz] **NF** *(pour imprimante laser)* developer

devenir [dəvnir] **NM** gradual change, development; **la langue est dans un perpétuel d.** the language is in a constant state of flux

VI *(conj like* **venir***, the aux is* **être***)* to become; **il devint général** he became a general; **il était devenu (un) homme** he had grown into a man; **il devient vraiment indiscret** he's becoming *or* getting really indiscreet; **que devenez-vous ces temps-ci?** what are you up to these days?; **que devient votre cousin?** how is your cousin getting on?; **qu'est-il devenu?** what has become of him?; **que vais-je d. sans toi?** what will become of me without you?, what will I do without you?, where will I be without you?; **qu'est devenu mon livre?** what's happened to my book?; **d. grand** *(en taille)* to grow tall; *(en âge)* to grow up; **d. vieux** to grow old, to get old; **c'est à d. fou!** it's enough to drive you mad!; **d. tout rouge** to go all red, to blush; **quand je lui ai dit ça, il est devenu tout heureux/tout dépité** he was delighted/extremely annoyed when I told him

dévergondage [devɛrgɔ̃daʒ] **NM 1** *(d'attitude, de personne)* shamelessness **2** *(de style, d'imagination)* extravagance

dévergondé, -ée [devɛrgɔ̃de] **ADJ 1** *(attitude, personne)* shameless **2** *(style, imagination)* extravagant
▪ **N** shameless person; **cette petite dévergondée** the little hussy

dévergonder (se) [sədevɛrgɔ̃de] **VPR** to become (quite) shameless

dévernir [devɛrnir] **VT** *(meubles etc)* to take the varnish *or* the polish off

déverrouillage [devɛrujaʒ] **NM** *(de porte etc)* unbolting, unlocking; *Ordinat* unlocking; *Aut* **d. du capot par l'intérieur** internal bonnet release; *Aut* **d. du hayon par l'intérieur** internal hatchback release

déverrouiller [devɛruje] **VT** *(porte etc)* to unbolt, to unlock; *(arme)* to release the bolt of; *Ordinat* to unlock; *(majuscules)* to lock off; *Ordinat* **d. en écriture** *(fichier)* to unlock, to remove the read-only lock on

dévers [devɛr] **NM 1** *(d'un mur etc)* inclination, slope; *(d'une route dans un virage)* banking; *Rail* vertical slant, cant *(of outer rail at curve)* **2** *(dans le bois etc)* warp, twist

déversement [devɛrsəmɑ̃] **NM** *(liquide)* discharge, overflow; *(action)* pouring out

déverser¹ [devɛrse] **VT** *(eau)* to pour; *(trop-plein d'un canal etc)* to discharge; *(détritus etc)* to tip, to dump; *(déchets)* to dump; **le train déversa des centaines de vacanciers sur le quai** the train deposited hundreds of holiday-makers on the platform; *Fig* **il a déversé des torrents d'injures sur sa femme** he showered his wife with abuse, he heaped abuse on his wife; **d. sa colère sur qn** to take one's anger out on sb
▪ **VPR se déverser** *(d'une rivière etc)* to empty, to flow *(dans* into)

déverser² **VT 1** *(mur etc)* to slope; *(route)* to bank; *(voie ferrée)* to raise the outer rail of **2** *(planche de bois)* to warp
▪ **VI 1** *(d'un mur etc)* to incline, to lean **2** *(du bois)* to warp

déversoir [devɛrswar] **NM 1** *(de citerne, bassin etc)* overflow; *Tech (de barrage)* spillway **2** *Fig (exutoire)* outlet, safety valve

dévêtir [devetir] *(conj like* **vêtir***)* **VT** to undress, to strip
▪ **VPR se dévêtir** *(complètement)* to undress, to strip, to take off one's clothes; *(partiellement)* to take off some of one's clothing

déviance [devjɑ̃s] **NF** *Psy* deviance

déviant [devjɑ̃] **ADJ** *Psy* deviant

déviation [devjasjɔ̃] **NF** deviation; *Aut* detour, *Br* diversion; *(d'un compas)* variation; *(de la colonne vertébrale)* curvature; *(de l'utérus)* displacement

> Il faut noter que le nom anglais **deviation** ne s'utilise jamais dans un contexte routier.

déviationnisme [devjasjɔnism] **NM** *Pol* deviationism

déviationniste [devjasjɔnist] **ADJ, N** *Pol* deviationist

dévidage [devidaʒ] **NM** *Tex etc (de bobine)* unwinding; *(pour faire une bobine)* reeling, spooling

dévider [devide] **VT** *Tex etc (dérouler)* to unwind; *(pour faire une bobine)* to reel, to spool; **d. son rosaire** to reel off the rosary;

Fam **il m'a dévidé son chapelet** he reeled off his whole story to me

dévideur [devidœr] **NM** *Ordinat* streamer

dévidoir [devidwar] **NM** *Tex* reeling machine, reel; *(pour tuyaux)* hose reel; *(pour câbles)* drum

dévier [devje] *(impf, pr sub* **n. déviions, v. déviiez***)* **VI 1** to deviate, to swerve; *Tech* to run out of true; *(de la colonne vertébrale)* to be out of alignment, not to be straight; **faire d. une balle** to deflect a bullet; *Naut, Aviat* **d. de sa route** *(par accident)* to go *or* stray off course; *(volontairement)* to turn off *or* deviate from course **2** *Fig* to deviate *(de* from); **elle ne dévie jamais de ses principes** she never deviates *or* departs from her principles; **cette conversation dévie** this conversation is getting out of hand
▪ **VT** *(coup, balle)* to turn aside, to deflect; *Phys (rayon)* to deflect; *(circulation)* to divert

devin, devineresse [dəvɛ̃, dəvinrɛs] **N** diviner; *(prophète)* soothsayer, *f* fortune teller; *Fam* **je ne suis pas d.** I can't tell *or* predict the future

devinable [dəvinabl] **ADJ** foreseeable

deviner [dəvine] **VT** *(énigme, secret etc)* to guess; *(futur)* to predict; *(la pensée de qn)* to read; **vous ne devinez pas?** can't you guess?; **devine qui j'ai vu/pourquoi il est là/comment il est venu** guess who I saw/why he's here/how he came; *Fam* **je ne pouvais pas d.!** how was I supposed to know!

devineresse *voir* **devin**

devinette [dəvinɛt] **NF** riddle, conundrum; *(jeu)* guessing game; **poser une d. à qn** to ask sb a riddle

devis [dəvi] **NM** *(descriptif)* estimate; *Tech* specification; **d. estimatif** estimate, quote, quotation; **ils m'ont fait un d. de 5 000 euros** they quoted me *or* they gave me a quote of 5,000 euros; **je voudrais qu'on me fasse un d.** I'd like an estimate *or* quote *(* **pour** for)

dévisager [deviʒaʒe] **VT** *(je* **dévisageai(s)***; n.* **dévisageons***)* to stare *or* look hard at

devise [dəviz] **NF 1** *Fin* currency; **devises étrangères** foreign currency; **d. internationale** international currency; **d. forte** strong *or* hard currency; **d. faible** soft *or* weak currency; **d. contrôlée** managed currency; **d. convertible** convertible currency; **d. non convertible** non-convertible currency; **marché des devises** currency market **2** *Hér* device; *(d'une personne)* motto; *Fig* **telle est ma d.** that's my motto **VOIR GRAMMAIRE A12**

deviser [dəvize] **VI** to converse

devise-titre, *pl* **devises-titres** **NF** *Fin* foreign security, exchange currency

dévissage [devisaʒ] **NM 1** *(d'un écrou)* unscrewing **2** *(en montagne)* fall

dévisser [devise] **VT** *(boulon, écrou etc)* to unscrew
▪ **VI** *(d'alpiniste)* to fall
▪ **VPR se dévisser** to unscrew; *(par accident)* to come unscrewed; *Fig* **se d. la tête** *ou* **le cou** to screw one's head round

de visu [dəvizy] **ADV** with my/his/*etc* own eyes; **je préférerais me rendre compte d.** I'd rather see it with my own eyes, I'd rather see for myself; **je veux m'assurer d. que tu as fait le travail** I want to see for myself that you've done the work

dévitalisation [devitalizasjɔ̃] **NF** *(d'une dent)* root canal treatment, *Spéc* devitalization; **subir plusieurs dévitalisations** to have root canal treatment on several teeth

dévitaliser [devitalize] **VT** *(dent)* to carry out root canal treatment on, *Spéc* to devitalize

dévitaminé [devitamine] **ADJ** lacking in vitamins

dévoiement [devwamɑ̃] **NM** *(d'un conduit etc)* canting, tilting

dévoilement [devwalmɑ̃] **NM** *(de visage, statue, plaque etc)* unveiling; *Fig (d'un nom, un secret etc)* disclosure, revelation; *(d'une conspiration)* unmasking; *(d'une fraude)* uncovering

dévoiler [devwale] **VT** *(visage, statue, plaque etc)* to unveil; *Fig (nom, secret etc)* to reveal, to disclose; *(conspiration)* to unmask; *(fraude etc)* to uncover; **d. ses charmes** to show *or* reveal all
▪ **VPR se dévoiler** *(de secret etc)* to come to light

DEVOIR¹ [dəvwar] **NM 1** *(obligation morale ou sociale)* duty; **je l'ai fait par d.** I did it from a sense of duty; **avoir le sens** *ou* **le sentiment du d.** to have a sense of duty; **un homme/une femme de d.** a man/woman with a sense of duty; **manquer à son d.** to fail in one's duty; **faire** *ou* **remplir son d. (envers qn/la patrie)** to do one's duty (by sb/one's country); **se faire un d. de faire qch** to make a point of doing sth; **se mettre en d. de faire qch** to make it one's duty *or* responsibility to do sth; **il est de mon d. de vous le dire** it is my duty *or* my responsibility to tell you; **je sais ce qui est de mon d.** I know my duty, I know where my duty lies; **mes devoirs de citoyen/de père** my duties *or* obligations as a citizen/as a father; **avoir un d. de réserve** to be bound by professional secrecy; *Pol* **d. d'ingérence** duty to intervene
2 *Scol (en classe)* test; *(à la maison)* homework; **un d. de latin** a Latin test; **faire ses devoirs** to do one's homework; **d. sur table** class test; **d. à rendre** take-home (exam); **devoirs de vacances** holiday homework
3 *Vieilli (hommage)* **devoirs** respects; **rendre ses devoirs à qn** to pay one's respects to sb; **rendre à qn les derniers devoirs** to pay one's last respects to sb

DEVOIR² *(prp* devant*; pp* dû*, f* due*; pr ind* je dois, n. devons, ils doivent; *pr sub* je doive, n. devions, ils doivent; *impf* je devais; *p hist* je dus; *fu* je devrai*)*

> **VT** to owe
> **V AUX** must **1, 2, 4** ▪ to be obliged to **2** ▪ to be bound to **2** ▪ to have to **1–3** ▪ to be supposed to **3** ▪ to be due to **3**

VT *(être redevable de)* **d. qch à qn** to owe sb sth, to owe sth to sb; **il me doit mille euros** he owes me a thousand euros; **il ne veut rien d. à personne** he doesn't want to owe anyone anything, he doesn't want to be indebted to anyone for anything; **d. du respect à son père** to owe respect to one's father; **je lui dois d'être en vie, je lui dois la vie** I owe my life to him, I owe him my life; **je lui dois bien cela** it's the least I can do for him, I owe him that at least; **il doit sa réussite à ses parents, sa réussite est due à ses parents** he owes his success to his parents; **je te dois une fière chandelle** I'm forever in your debt

V AUX **SEE GRAMMAR A60~1; B39 1** *(obligation)* **vous devez** *ou* **devrez vous trouver à votre poste à trois heures** you must *or* you have to be at your post at three o'clock; **elle a cru d. refuser** she thought it advisable to refuse; **tu dois honorer tes parents** you must honour your parents; **fais ce que dois, advienne que pourra** do your duty, come what may; **les commandes doivent être adressées à …** orders should be sent to …; **je ne savais pas ce que je devais faire** I didn't know what (I ought) to do; **il aurait dû m'avertir** he should have warned me, he ought to have warned me
2 *(nécessité)* **tous les hommes doivent mourir** all men must die; **finalement, j'ai dû céder**

I had to or I was obliged to give way in the end; **tu dois absolument lui en parler** you really must talk to him about it; **il ne devait plus les revoir** he was (destined) never to see them again; **cela devait arriver!** it was bound to or it had to happen!; **dût-il m'en coûter la vie** were I to die for it

3 *(intention)* **je dois partir demain** I am (supposed) to or I have to leave tomorrow; **je devais la rencontrer à Paris** I was (supposed) to meet her in Paris; **je ne devais pas être là, mais j'ai changé d'avis** I hadn't planned on being there, but I changed my mind; **le train doit arriver à midi** the train is due (to arrive) at twelve o'clock

4 *(supposition)* **vous devez avoir faim** you must be hungry; **il doit être trois heures** it must be three o'clock; **il ne doit pas avoir plus de 40 ans** he can't be more than 40; **il a** *ou* **avait dû me prendre pour un autre** he must have taken me for someone else; **elle devait avoir cinq ans quand elle a eu son accident** she must have been five when she had the accident; **la pollution devrait s'accroître d'ici à la fin du siècle** pollution is expected to increase by the end of the century **VPR se devoir 1** *(être obligé de se consacrer à)* **je me dois à ma famille/mon travail** I must devote myself to my family/my work; **je me dois de le faire** it's my duty to do it **2 comme il se doit** as is (only) right and proper

dévoisé [devwaze] **ADJ** *Ling* devoiced

dévoisement [devwazmɑ̃] **NM** *Ling* devoicing

dévoltage [devɔltaʒ] **NM** reduction of voltage

dévolter [devɔlte] **VT** *Élec (courant)* to reduce the voltage of

dévolu [devɔly] **ADJ** *Jur (héritage etc)* devolving (**à** to, upon); **part dévolue à la ligne paternelle** share that falls to the heirs on the father's side; **c'est le terrain qui lui a été d.** the land went to him; **être d. à qn de faire qch** to fall to sb's lot to do sth; **voilà la tâche qui vous a été dévolue** that is the task which has been assigned to you

NM jeter son d. sur qn/qch to set one's heart on sb/sth, to be determined to have sb/sth, *Hum Péj* to have designs on sb/sth

dévolution [devɔlysjɔ̃] **NF** *Jur* devolution; **d. d'un héritage à l'État** escheat

dévorant [devɔrɑ̃] **ADJ 1** *(envie, besoin)* overwhelming; **avoir une faim dévorante** to be ravenous; **j'ai une envie dévorante de le voir** I've got a burning desire to see him **2** *(maladie)* wasting; *(passion)* devouring

dévorer [devɔre] **VT 1** *(manger) (proie)* to devour; *(nourriture)* to devour, *Fam* to gobble up, to wolf down; **pour ne pas être dévoré par les moustiques** so as not to be eaten alive by mosquitoes; **d. qn des yeux** *ou* **du regard/de baisers** to devour sb with one's eyes/with kisses; *Fig* **d. un livre** to devour or gobble up a book; *Fig* **d. la route** to tear along, to eat up the miles; **d. sa fortune** to squander one's fortune **2** *(consumer) (de flammes)* to devour; *Fig* **l'ambition/la jalousie la dévore** she is consumed by or devoured by or eaten up with ambition/jealousy; **il ne faut pas que cela dévore tout votre temps** don't let it take up all your time; **l'angoisse le dévore** he's sick with worry; **dévoré de remords** eaten up or stricken with remorse

dévoreur, -euse [devɔrœr, -øz] **N** devourer; *Fig* **d. de livres** avid reader, bookworm; **d. de films** avid cinemagoer; **d. de pellicule** *Cin* avid or keen cinemagoer; *Phot* avid or keen photographer

dévot, -ote [devo, -ɔt] **ADJ** *(fervent)* devout,

religious, pious, *Péj* sanctimonious; *Rel* **être d. à un saint** to be a votary of a saint

N devout person, *Péj* bigot; *Arch* **faux d.** hypocrite

dévotement [devɔtmɑ̃] **ADV** devoutly

dévotion [devɔsjɔ̃] **NF 1** *(ferveur)* devoutness, piety; **faire ses dévotions** to make one's devotions, to say one's prayers; *Péj* **être confit en d.** to be sanctimonious; **fausse d.** hypocrisy **2** *(adoration)* devotion; **avoir une grande d. pour qn/qch** to be devoted or extremely attached to sb/sth; **avoir une grande d. pour un acteur/écrivain** to be a great admirer or a devotee of an actor/a writer; **être à la d. de qn** to be fanatically attached to sb

> Do not confuse with **dévouement**.

dévoué [devwe] **ADJ** *(ami etc)* devoted, staunch, loyal; **votre (tout) d.** *(dans une lettre)* yours sincerely; **être très/entièrement d. à qn** to be very attached/utterly devoted to sb

dévouement [devumɑ̃] **NM 1** *(devoir)* self-sacrifice, dedication to duty; *(d'un scientifique etc)* dedication **2** *(amour)* devotion, devotedness; **soigner qn avec d.** to nurse or look after sb devotedly or with devotion

> Do not confuse with **dévotion**.

dévouer (se) [sədevwe] **VPR 1** *(se consacrer)* to sacrifice oneself (**pour qn** for sb); **il faut que quelqu'un se dévoue** somebody has to do it **2** *Vieilli* **se d. à** to devote oneself to, to dedicate oneself to

dévoyé, -ée [devwaje] **ADJ** astray

N delinquent

dévoyer [devwaje] (**je dévoie, n. dévoyons; je dévoierai**) **VT** *Litt* to lead astray

VPR se dévoyer to go astray, to leave the straight and narrow

dextérité [dɛksterite] **NF** dexterity, skill; **conduire ses affaires avec d.** to manage one's business cleverly or skilfully

dextre [dɛkstr] **NF** *Vieilli, Hum* right hand; **veux-tu t'asseoir à ma d.?** will you sit on my right?

dextrine [dɛkstrin] **NF** *Chimie, Ind* dextrin

dézinguer [dezɛ̃ge] **VT** *Fam* **1** *(détruire)* to wreck **2** *(critiquer)* to pull to pieces, to slam **3** *(tuer)* to bump off

dézipper [dezipe] **VT** *Ordinat (fichier)* to unzip

DG [deʒe] **NM** *(abrév directeur général)* GM, *Am* CEO

NF *(abrév direction générale)* general management, senior management

DGA [deʒea] **NM** *(abrév directeur général adjoint)* assistant general manager

NF *(abrév Délégation générale pour l'armement)* = section of the French armed forces responsible for building and testing armaments

DGSE [deʒeɛsə] **NF** *(abrév Direction générale de la sécurité extérieure)* = French military intelligence service, *Br* ≃ MI6

DHEA [deaʃəa] **NF** *(abrév déhydroépiandrostérone)* DHEA

DI [dei] **NF** *(abrév déclaration d'importation)* import declaration

diabète [djabɛt] **NM** *Méd* diabetes; **d. sucré** (sugar) diabetes, *Spéc* diabetes mellitus; **avoir du d.** to have diabetes

diabétique [djabetik] *Méd* **ADJ** diabetic; **être d.** to be (a) diabetic, to have diabetes

N diabetic; **chocolat/confiture pour diabétiques** diabetic chocolate/jam

diable [djabl] **NM 1** devil; **le d.** *(Satan)* the Devil, Satan, *Fam* Old Nick; *Fam* **s'agiter** *ou*

se démener comme un beau d. *ou* **comme un d. dans un bénitier** to struggle or fight like mad; *Fam* **il s'est défendu comme un beau d.** he put up quite a fight; **faire le d. (à quatre)** to kick up a row; **avoir le d. au corps** to be possessed; **tirer le d. par la queue** to be hard up; *Can* **parler au d.** to be psychic; **que le d. l'emporte!** the devil take him!; **(que) le d. m'emporte si j'y comprends quelque chose!** I'll be hanged or damned if I understand (it)!; **c'est le d. pour lui faire entendre raison** it's damned hard to make or it's the devil of a job making him see reason; **c'est bien le d. si ...** it would be surprising if ...; **ce n'est pas le d.** *(c'est facile)* it's not that difficult; **d. de mer** devil fish, (manta) ray

2 d.! (good) heavens!, goodness!; **où d. est-il allé?** where the devil has he gone?; **que d. cherche-t-il?** what the devil is he looking for?; **pourquoi d. m'a-t-il demandé cela?** why the devil did he ask me that?; **du d. si je peux te répondre!** I'm damned if I can tell you!; **que d.!** for heaven's or goodness' sake!

3 en d. extremely, *Fml* in the extreme; **têtu en d.** extremely obstinate, obstinate in the extreme; **il demeure au d.** he lives miles away; **au d. vauvert** a long way (away); **allez au d.!** go to hell!, *Vieilli* go to the devil!; **tu peux aller au d. avec tes belles promesses** you and your promises can go to hell; **envoyer qn au d.** to tell sb to go to hell; **au d. l'avarice/le régime!** to hell with the expense/the diet!; **à la d.** anyhow; *Culin* in a spicy sauce; **c'est fait à la d.** it's been done any old how; *Culin* **steak à la d.** devilled steak; **ce d. de parapluie** that wretched umbrella; **un d. de temps, un temps du d.** wretched or dreadful weather; **j'ai une faim du d.** *ou* **de tous les diables** I'm ravenous; **il fait un froid/une chaleur du d.** it's dreadfully cold/hot; **un bruit de tous les diables** a hell of a din

4 un petit d. *(enfant)* a little devil; **pauvre d.!** poor devil or beggar!; **un drôle de petit d.** a funny little chap or beggar; **un grand d.** a big fellow; **c'est un bon d.** he's not a bad sort

5 *(chariot)* (two-wheeled) trolley; *Rail* (railway porter's) barrow, luggage truck

6 *(jouet)* jack-in-the-box

diablement [djabləmɑ̃] **ADV** *Fam (fort, bon, amusant etc)* damn, damned, *Vieilli* devilish(ly); **il y a d. longtemps que je ne l'ai pas vu** I haven't seen him for a hell of a long time; **il faisait d. froid** it was hellish(ly) cold

diablerie [djabləri] **NF 1** *Fam (espièglerie)* devilry, devilment **2** *Arch (sorcellerie)* devilry, sorcery **3** *(intrigue)* machination, intrigue

diablesse [djablɛs] **NF** *(diable femelle, méchante femme)* she-devil; *(jeune fille)* devil

diablotin [djablɔtɛ̃] **NM 1** *(petit diable, enfant coquin)* little devil, imp **2** *(pétard)* (Christmas) cracker

diabolique [djabɔlik] **ADJ** diabolic(al), fiendish

diaboliquement [djabɔlikmɑ̃] **ADV** diabolically, fiendishly

diabolisation [djabɔlizasjɔ̃] **NF** demonization

diaboliser [djabɔlize] **VT** to demonize

diabolo [djabɔlo] **NM 1** *(jouet)* diabolo **2** *(boisson)* lemonade (drink) with syrup; **d. menthe** mint and lemonade syrup

diachromie [djakrɔmi] **NF** *Phot* screenplate colour photography

diachronie [djakrɔni] **NF** *Ling* diachrony

diachronique [djakrɔnik] **ADJ** *Ling* diachronic

diaconesse [djakɔnɛs] **NF** *Rel* deaconess

diacre [djakr] **NM** *Rel* deacon

diacritique [djakritik] ADJ *Ling* diacritic(al); **signe d.** diacritic(al)

diadème [djadɛm] NM tiara

diagnostic [djagnɔstik] NM *Méd (de maladie)* diagnosis; **porter** *ou* **faire un d.** to make a diagnosis; **le d. de la maladie doit être porté le plus tôt possible** the disease must be diagnosed as soon as possible; **ce médecin a un d. très sûr** this doctor makes very reliable diagnoses; **quel est votre d.?** what's your diagnosis?; *Ordinat* **d. d'autotest** self-test diagnosis; **d. financier** financial health-check, diagnostic audit

diagnostique [djagnɔstik] ADJ *Méd (aptitude, signe etc)* diagnostic

diagnostiquer [djagnɔstike] VT *Méd, Fig* to diagnose; **on a diagnostiqué un diabète** the illness has been diagnosed as diabetes

diagnostiqueur [djagnɔstikœr] NM *Méd* diagnostician; **elle n'est pas bon d.** she's not a good diagnostician, diagnosis is not her strong point

diagonal, -ale, -aux, -ales [djagɔnal, -o] ADJ *Math etc* diagonal
NF diagonale diagonal (line); **en diagonale** diagonally; *Fig* **lire qch en diagonale** to skim sth

diagonalement [djagɔnalmɑ̃] ADV diagonally

diagramme [djagram] NM diagram; **d. circulaire** *ou* **à secteurs** pie chart; **d. en bâtons** *ou* **à barres** bar chart; **d. de circulation** flow chart; **d. de relations fonctionnelles** functional relations diagram; **d. des flux** flowchart

dialectal, -ale, -aux, -ales [djalɛktal, -o] ADJ *Ling* dialectal

dialecte [djalɛkt] NM dialect; **en d.** in dialect

dialecticien, -ienne [djalɛktisjɛ̃, -jɛn] N dialectician

dialectique [djalɛktik] ADJ *(argument)* dialectic(al)
NF dialectics

dialectiquement [djalɛktikmɑ̃] ADV dialectically

dialogue [djalɔg] NM dialogue, *Am* dialog; *Pol* dialogue, talks; **d. Nord-Sud** dialogue *or* talks between North and South; **écrire les dialogues d'un film** to write the dialogue for a movie *or Br* film; **le d. est de Valérie Devaux** dialogue by Valérie Devaux; *Ordinat* **mode de d.** interactive mode; *Ordinat* **d. d'établissement de liaison** handshake, handshaking; *Ordinat* **d. en direct** Internet Relay Chat, IRC; **c'est un d. de sourds** it's a dialogue of the deaf

dialoguer [djalɔge] VI to hold a dialogue *or Am* dialog, to converse; *Ordinat* to communicate; **d. avec son ordinateur** to interact with one's computer
VT *Littér* to write in dialogue *or Am* dialog form

dialoguiste [djalɔgist] N *Cin* dialogue *or Am* dialog writer

dialyse [djaliz] NF *Méd, Chimie* dialysis; *Méd* **il faut qu'on lui fasse une d. tous les mois** he has to have dialysis once a month

dialyser [djalize] VT *Chimie* to dialyse

dialyseur [djalizœr] NM *Méd* dialysis machine

diam [djam] NM *Fam (abrév* **diamant)** sparkler, rock

diamant [djamɑ̃] NM diamond; *Typ* gem; **d. de première eau** diamond of the first water; **d. brut** rough diamond; **d. de vitrier** glass cutter, *Spéc* glazier's diamond, diamond point

diamantaire [djamɑ̃tɛr] ADJ *Tech (pierre)* diamond-like, sparkling
NM *(tailleur)* diamond cutter; *(vendeur)* diamond merchant

diamantifère [djamɑ̃tifɛr] ADJ *Géol etc (région)* diamantiferous; *(gravier etc)* diamond-yielding *or* -bearing

diamétral, -ale, -aux, -ales [djametral, -o] ADJ diametric(al), diametral

diamétralement [djametralmɑ̃] ADV diametrically; **opinions d. opposées** diametrically opposed views

diamètre [djamɛtr] NM diameter; **la roue a 60 cm de d.** the wheel is 60 cm in diameter *or* 60 cm across; *Aut* **d. de braquage hors tout** overall turning circle

diane [djan] NF *Mil Arch, Litt* reveille; **battre** *ou* **sonner la d.** to sound reveille

diantre [djɑ̃tr] INT *Arch, Litt* **que d. désirez-vous?** what the devil do you want?; **d., c'est cher!** it's devilishly expensive!; **d., comme vous y allez!** good heavens! that's going a bit far!

diapason [djapazɔ̃] NM *Mus* **1** *(ton)* pitch, diapason; *Fig* **se mettre au d. de la compagnie** to adapt oneself to the company, to fall in with the mood of the company **2** *(appareil)* tuning fork; *(à vent)* pitch pipe **3** *(registre)* compass, range

diaphane [djafan] ADJ diaphanous

diaphonie [djafɔni] NF *Radio etc* crosstalk

diaphragme [djafragm] NM **1** *Anat* diaphragm **2** *Tech (d'un télescope, d'une cellule électrique etc), Cin, TV* diaphragm; *Phot (d'un objectif)* diaphragm, T-stop, iris; *Mus (d'une enceinte)* soundbox; *Méd (contraceptif)* diaphragm, *Fam* (Dutch) cap; *Phot* **d. iris** iris diaphragm

diaphragmer [djafragme] VT, VI *Phot* to stop down; **diaphragmez à 11** stop down to 11, use stop number 11

diaphyse [djafiz] NF shaft, diaphysis

diapo [djapo] NF *Fam (abrév* **diapositive)** slide, transparency

diaporama [djapɔrama] NM slide show

diapositive [djapozitiv] NF *Phot* slide, transparency; **d. en couleurs** colour slide

diapré [djapre] ADJ variegated, mottled, speckled

diaprer [djapre] VT to variegate, to mottle, to speckle

diaprure [djapryr] NF *Litt* iridescence; **elle portait une robe dont le satin faisait des diaprures** she wore a gown of iridescent *or* shimmering satin

diariste [djarist] N diarist

diarrhée [djare] NF *Méd* diarrhoea, *Am* diarrhea; **avoir la d.** to have diarrhoea; **d. du voyageur** holiday tummy; *Fig Péj* **ce type fait de la d. verbale** that guy suffers from verbal diarrhoea

diarrhéique [djareik] ADJ *Méd* diarrhoeic, *Am* diarrheic; diarrhoeal, *Am* diarrheal
N person subject to diarrhoea *or Am* diarrhea

diaspora [djaspɔra] NF *Rel, Pol* diaspora

diastole [djastɔl] NF *Physiol* diastole

diatomée [djatɔme] NF *(algue)* diatom

diatomique [djatɔmik] ADJ *Chimie* diatomic

diatonique [djatɔnik] ADJ *Mus (échelle, intervalle)* diatonic

diatoniquement [djatɔnikmɑ̃] ADV *Mus* diatonically

diatribe [djatrib] NF diatribe (**contre** against)

dichotomie [dikɔtɔmi] NF dichotomy

dichotomique [dikɔtɔmik] ADJ dichotomous; *Psy* **test d.** yes/no test, true/false test

dichromatique [dikrɔmatik] ADJ dichromatic

dico [diko] NM *Fam (abrév* **dictionnaire)** dictionary

dicotylédone [dikɔtiledɔn] *Bot* ADJ dicotyledonous
NF dicotyledon

Dictaphone® [diktafɔn] NM Dictaphone®

dictateur [diktatœr] NM dictator; **ton de d.** dictatorial tone

dictatorial, -iale, -iaux, -iales [diktatɔrjal, -jo] ADJ dictatorial

dictatorialement [diktatɔrjalmɑ̃] ADV dictatorially

dictature [diktatyr] NF *Pol, Fig* dictatorship; **d. militaire** military dictatorship; **d. du prolétariat** dictatorship of the proletariat; *Fig* **il fait de la d. intellectuelle** he tells people what to think

dictée [dikte] NF dictation; *Scol* dictation (exercise); **d. musicale** musical dictation; **prendre qch sous la d.** *(d'une secrétaire)* to take sth down in shorthand; **écrire qch sous la d. de qn** to write sth at sb's dictation; **agir sous la d. de son cœur/de sa conscience** to follow the dictates of one's heart/one's conscience

dicter [dikte] VT *(lettre etc)* to dictate; **d. ses conditions** to dictate *or* lay down one's conditions; **votre conscience vous dictera votre devoir** you must follow the dictates of your conscience; **d. sa volonté à qn** to impose one's will on sb; **je ne veux pas qu'on me dicte ma conduite!** I won't be dictated to!; **ces mesures ont été dictées par la conjoncture économique** these measures were dictated by the economic situation

diction [diksjɔ̃] NF diction; **professeur de d.** elocution teacher

dictionnaire [diksjɔnɛr] NM dictionary; **d. de langue** dictionary; **d. anglais-français** English-French dictionary; **le d. d'un enfant de 10 ans** the vocabulary of a 10-year-old child; **c'est un d. ambulant** he's a walking encyclopaedia; **elle parle comme un d.** she talks as if she's swallowed a dictionary
▸▸ **d. analogique** thesaurus; **d. de césure** hyphenation dictionary; **d. électronique** electronic dictionary; **d. encyclopédique** encyclopaedic dictionary; **d. géographique** gazetteer; **d. de poche** pocket dictionary; **d. de synonymes** thesaurus

dicton [diktɔ̃] NM *(common)* saying

didacthèque [didaktɛk] NF *Ordinat* set of educational software, *Am* set of teachware

didacticiel [didaktisjɛl] NM *Ordinat* tutorial (program); *(à l'école)* courseware, educational software, *Am* teachware

didactique [didaktik] ADJ **1** *(ouvrage, voyage)* educational **2** *(mot, langage)* technical
NF didactics

didactiquement [didaktikmɑ̃] ADV educationally

didactyle [didaktil] ADJ *Zool* didactyl(e)

dièdre [djɛdr] *Math* ADJ *(angle)* dihedral
NM dihedron

diélectrique [dielɛktrik] *Élec* ADJ dielectric; *(milieu)* insulating, non-conducting
NM dielectric

diérèse [djerɛz] NF *Ling, Chir* diaeresis

dies academicus [djesakademikys] NM INV *Suisse* = annual public ceremony in universities marking the start of the new academic year and the conferment of honorary doctorates

dièse [djɛz] *Mus* NM sharp; **double d.** double sharp
ADJ sharp; **fa d.** F sharp

diesel [djezɛl] NM *(carburant)* diesel; **moteur d.** diesel engine
NF *(voiture)* diesel

diéséliste [djezelist] N *Tech* diesel fitter

diéser [djeze] **VT** (**je dièse**, n. **diésons**; je **diéserai**) *Mus (note)* to sharpen, *Am* to sharp

diète¹ [djɛt] **NF** diet; *(jeûne)* fast; **d. lactée** milk diet; **être à la d.** *(régime)* to be on a diet; *(jeûne)* to be fasting; **mettre qn à la d.** to put sb on a diet

diète² **NF** *Hist, Pol* diet

diététicien, -ienne [djetetisjɛ̃, -jɛn] **N** dietitian, dietician

diététique [djetetik] *Méd* **ADJ** *(menu, repas)* diet; *(supplément)* dietary; **magasin/restaurant d.** health food shop/restaurant **NF** dietetics

DIEU, *pl* **dieux** [djø] **NM 1** god; **les dieux de l'Égypte ancienne** the gods of ancient Egypt; **beau comme un d. (grec)** like a Greek god; **il danse comme un d.** he's a wonderful dancer, *Vieilli* he dances divinely; **être aimé** *ou* **béni des dieux** to be blessed with good fortune, to be a favourite of the gods; **jurer ses grands dieux** to swear (by all that's holy) **2** D. God; **D. le père** God the Father; *Fig* **ce n'est pas D. le père** he's not God Almighty; **la voix de D.** the voice of God; **croire en D.** to believe in God; **un homme de D.** a holy man; **s'il plaît à D., si D. (le) veut** please God, God willing; **D. merci!**, **D. soit loué!** thank God!; **le bon D.** God; **recevoir le bon D.** to receive the Holy Sacrament; **on lui donnerait le bon D. sans confession** he looks as though butter wouldn't melt in his mouth; **mais qu'est-ce que j'ai fait au bon D. pour mériter ça/avoir un mari aussi stupide!** what in heaven's *or* God's name have I ever done to deserve this/ to deserve such a stupid husband!; *Fam* **y a pas de bon D.** there's no justice in the world!; **pour l'amour de D.** for goodness' *or* God's sake; **devant D. et devant les hommes** by Almighty God; **D. vous bénisse** God bless you; **D. vous garde** God keep you; **D. m'en garde, à D. ne plaise** God forbid; **D. vous entende** may your prayers be answered; **D. sait si j'ai travaillé** goodness *or* heaven *or* God knows I've worked hard enough; **D. sait quoi** God knows what; **D. seul le sait** God only knows; *Fam* **il va y aller D. sait comment** he's going, God knows how (he's going); **D. m'est témoin que je n'ai pas dit cela** as God is my witness, I never said that; **chaque jour** *ou* **tous les jours que D. fait** every day that God sends; *Vieilli* **à D. vat!** it's in God's hands now! **INT 1** *(admis)* **mon D.!**, **grand D.!** God!, my God!, good God!; **grands dieux!** heavens!; **mon D. oui!** God, yes!; **mon D. je veux bien!** well, I don't mind!; **D. qu'elle est petite!** goodness *or* God she's small!; *Fam* **c'est pas D. possible!** it's just not possible!, I refuse to believe it!; **c'est pas D. possible d'être aussi bête!** it's just not heavenly possible to be that stupid! **2** *(profane)* **bon D.!**, **D. de D.!**, **bon D. de bon D.!**, *(sacré)* **nom de D.!** for Christ's sake!, God almighty!, hell!

diffamant [difamɑ̃] **ADJ** *(paroles)* slanderous, defamatory; *(écrits)* libellous, defamatory

diffamateur, -trice [difamatœr, -tris] **N** *(en paroles)* slanderer; *(par écrit)* libeller

diffamation [difamasjɔ̃] **NF** defamation (of character); *(paroles)* slander; *(écrits)* libel; **campagne de d.** smear campaign; **poursuivre qn en d.** to sue sb for defamation of character; **procès en d.** slander/libel trial

diffamatoire [difamatwar] **ADJ** defamatory; *(paroles)* slanderous; *(écrits)* libellous

diffamer [difame] **VT** to defame; *(en paroles)* to slander; *(par écrit)* to libel

différé [difere] **ADJ 1** *(paiement, rente)* deferred **2** *Radio, TV* prerecorded; *Élec* **coupe-circuit à action différée** time-lag cut-out;

Phot **obturateur à action différée** delayed action shutter; *Ordinat* **traitement d.** off-line processing **NM** *Radio, TV (émission)* prerecording, prerecorded programme; **émission en d.** (pre-)recorded broadcast

différemment [diferamɑ̃] **ADV** differently (**de** from)

différence [diferɑ̃s] **NF** difference; **d. de goûts** difference of taste; **la d. de A à B** *ou* **entre A et B** the difference between A and B; **d. d'âges** age difference; **d. d'opinions** difference of opinions; *Élec* **d. de potentiel** potential difference, pd; **d. de prix** price difference; **quelle d. avec ...!** what a difference from ...!; **il n'y a pas de d. entre eux** there's nothing to choose between them; **cela ne fait pas de d.** it makes no difference *or* Br Fam no odds; **il ne faut pas faire de d. entre ses enfants** you shouldn't treat your children differently, you should not discriminate between your children; **il y a trop de d. d'âge entre eux** there's too much of *or* too big an age gap *or* age difference between them; **faire la d. d'une chose avec une autre** *ou* **entre une chose et une autre** to distinguish *or* discriminate between one thing and another; **c'est ça qui a fait la d.** that's what made the difference; **je vous dois la d.** I'll owe you the difference; **à la d. de ...** unlike ...; **à la d. que ...** except that ...

différenciateur, -trice [diferɑ̃sjatœr, -tris] **ADJ** differentiating **NM d. sémantique** semantic differential

différenciation [diferɑ̃sjasjɔ̃] **NF** differentiation; *Mktg* **d. de ligne** line featuring

différencier [diferɑ̃sje] *(impf, pr sub n.* **différenciions**) **VT** to differentiate (**de, d'avec** from); *Math (équation etc)* to obtain the differential (coefficient) of; **rien ne les différencie** there's nothing to differentiate them **VPR se différencier 1** *(de deux personnes)* to be different (from each other), to differ; **ils se différencient par leurs écharpes de couleurs différentes** you can tell them apart by their different-coloured scarves **2** *(d'une personne)* **se d. de** to differentiate oneself from

différend [diferɑ̃] **NM** dispute, difference of opinion, disagreement (**entre** between); *Jur* dispute; **avoir un d. avec qn** to disagree *or* have a disagreement with sb (**sur** about); **ils ont un d. sur l'éducation des enfants** they disagree *or* differ on how the children should be educated; **il a un d. avec son voisin à propos de la clôture du jardin** he is at odds with his neighbour over the garden fence; **il a un d. avec son père qui empoisonne leurs relations depuis de nombreuses années** a long-standing difference of opinion between him and his father has poisoned their relationship

différent [diferɑ̃] **ADJ 1** *(distinct)* different (**de** from, *Am* than); **un avis d. du premier** a different opinion from the first, an opinion that differs from the first; **elle utilise une recette différente de la tienne** her recipe is different from yours **VOIR GRAMMAIRE A70 2** *(divers)* *(toujours au pl)* **différents** various; **différentes personnes l'ont vu** different people *or* various people *or* a number of people saw him; **à différentes reprises** at various times, off and on

différentiation [diferɑ̃sjasjɔ̃] **NF** *Math* differentiation

différentiel, -ielle [diferɑ̃sjɛl] **ADJ** differential **NM** *Aut etc* differential; *Com* **d. de prix** price differential; *Ling* **d. sémantique** semantic differential; **d. de taux d'intérêt** interest rate differential **NF** *Math* **différentielle** differential

différer [difere] (**je diffère**, n. **différons**; je **différerai**) **VT** *(retarder)* *(jugement)* to defer, to postpone; *(paiement)* to defer; *(décision, départ)* to postpone, to put off; *Fml* **d. de faire qch** to defer doing sth **VI** *(être différent)* to differ; **nos origines diffèrent complètement** our backgrounds are completely different; **ils diffèrent de race et de langue** they differ in race and speech; **nous différons d'opinion** our opinions differ; **nous différons en tout** we differ on everything; **ils diffèrent par la taille** they differ in height, they are of different heights; **nous différons sur le choix de l'école des enfants** we differ *or* do not agree on which school the children should go to

difficile [difisil] **ADJ 1** *(ardu)* *(travail, situation etc)* difficult, hard; **d'accès d.** difficult to get to; **le plus d. est fait** the hardest *or* most difficult part is over; **il est très d. de le joindre** it is very difficult to contact him, he is very difficult to contact **2** *(délicat)* difficult; **circonstances difficiles** difficult *or* trying circumstances; **les temps sont difficiles** times are hard; **il m'est d. d'accepter** it is difficult for me to accept, I can't very well accept; **les fins de mois sont difficiles** things are difficult at the end of the month **3** *(personne)* difficult to get on with, hard to please; **enfant d.** difficult *or* problem child; **elle est d. à vivre** she is difficult to get on with; **il est d. sur la nourriture** he's difficult *or* fussy about his food; **elle est très d. sur la ponctualité/l'orthographe** she is very fussy about punctuality/spelling; **si la maison ne te plaît pas, c'est que tu es vraiment d.** you must be really hard to please *or* fussy if you don't like the house **N faire le/la d.** to be hard to please; **ne faites pas le d.** don't be difficult, stop fussing **ADV** *Belg* **avoir d. à** *ou* **de faire qch** to have problems *or* difficulty doing sth

difficilement [difisilmɑ̃] **ADV** with difficulty, not easily; **il apprend d.** he is a slow learner; **on peut d. lui dire une chose pareille** you can hardly *or* you can't possibly tell him something like that; **c'est d. faisable** it's virtually impossible

difficulté [difikylte] **NF** difficulty; **être en d.** to be in difficulties *or* trouble; **cela ne présente aucune d.** that doesn't present any difficulty; **c'est sans d.** it's easy, it's not difficult; **aimer la d.** to like to make things difficult for oneself; **tourner la d.** to get round a difficulty; **faire** *ou* **soulever des difficultés** to create obstacles, to raise objections, to make difficulties; **cela ne fera pas de d., que je sache** there won't be any difficulty as far as I know; **se heurter à de graves difficultés** to come up against serious difficulties; **avoir de la d. à faire qch** to have difficulty doing sth, to find it hard *or* difficult to do sth; **avoir des difficultés matérielles** to be in financial difficulties; **créer des difficultés à qn** to put difficulties in sb's way, to make difficulties for sb; **difficultés de trésorerie** cashflow problems

difforme [difɔrm] **ADJ** *(personne)* deformed; *(membre)* malformed, misshapen, twisted; **troncs d'arbres difformes** gnarled treetrunks

difformité [difɔrmite] **NF** *(d'une personne)* deformity; *(d'un membre)* malformation; **la d. de son bras n'est pas irrémédiable** his malformed arm *or* the malformation in his arm is not incurable

diffracter [difrakte] **VT** *Opt* to diffract

diffraction [difraksjɔ̃] **NF** *Opt* diffraction

diffus [dify] **ADJ** *(lumière)* diffused; *(matière)* diffuse; *(pensée, idées)* vague; **éclairs d.** sheet lightning; **style d.** diffuse *or* Fml prolix style; **écrivain d.** verbose *or Fml* prolix writer

diffusément [difyzemã] **ADV** *(penser)* vaguely; *(écrire)* in a diffuse style; **la musique/la conversation nous parvenait d.** we couldn't hear the music/the conversation very clearly

diffuser [difyze] **VT** *(lumière, chaleur)* to diffuse, to spread; *Radio, TV (émission etc)* to broadcast, to air; *(idées, nouvelles)* to spread; *(livres, journaux)* to distribute; *(rapport)* to circulate; **une émission diffusée en direct/différé** a live/prerecorded broadcast; **d. qch sur Internet** to webcast sth; **leurs produits sont diffusés sur une grande échelle** they are widely-available products
VPR se diffuser *(d'idées, de nouvelles, de lumière), Phys (des ondes)* to spread

diffuseur [difyzœr] **NM 1** *(de lumière, de sèche-cheveux)* diffuser; *(dans un moteur)* mixer, diffuser; *TV, Radio* broadcaster; *(écran diffuseur)* diffuser, scrim; *(compresseur)* diffuser; *(d'un chauffage)* air vent; **d. de parfum** room scenter; *Aut* **à d. fixe** fixed-choke **2** *(de livres, journaux)* distributor **3** *Ordinat* **d. en ligne** webcaster

diffusion [difyzjɔ̃] **NF 1** *(de lumière, chaleur)* diffusion **2** *(de nouvelles, d'idées)* spread, spreading; *Radio, TV (d'émission)* broadcasting, airing; *Cin* screening; *(de livres)* distribution; *(de journal)* circulation; **en deuxième d., en seconde d.** repeated, repeat; *TV etc* **d. audionumérique** digital audio broadcasting; *TV etc* **d. de données par satellite** satellite data broadcasting; **d. de masse** *(d'un journal etc)* mass circulation; **d. directe par satellite** direct satellite broadcasting, DSB; **d. hertzienne** terrestrial broadcasting; **d. numérique** *Com* stock holding distribution; *TV etc* digital broadcasting; *TV, Radio* **d. terrestre** terrestrial broadcasting

digérer [diʒere] (**je digère, n. digérons; je digérerai**) **VT 1** *(nourriture)* to digest; **je ne digère pas le porc** pork does not agree with me, I find pork difficult to digest **2** *Fig (ce qu'on lit, ce qu'on apprend)* to digest, to take in, to assimilate; *Fam (accepter) (insultes etc)* to swallow; **je n'ai toujours pas digéré le coup qu'il m'a fait à Noël** I still haven't got over what he did to me at Christmas; **des vérités dures à d.** unpalatable truths
VI je digère mal my digestion is bad, I have bad digestion

digest [daʒɛst, diʒɛst] **NM** *Journ* digest

digeste [diʒɛst] **ADJ** *Fam (aliment)* easily digestible; **ce livre est vraiment peu d.** the book is indigestible

digestibilité [diʒɛstibilite] **NF** digestibility

digestible [diʒɛstibl] **ADJ** digestible

digestif, -ive [diʒɛstif, -iv] **ADJ** *(de la digestion)* digestive; *(substance)* which aids digestion; **le tube d.** the digestive tract; **avoir des troubles digestifs** to have digestive problems, to have problems with one's digestion
NM liqueur, after-dinner drink

digestion [diʒɛstjɔ̃] **NF** digestion; **elle a une d. difficile** she has problems with her digestion *or* digestive problems

Digicode® [diʒikɔd] **NM** door code *(for entrance to a building)*

digit [diʒit] **NM** *Ordinat* **1** *(chiffre)* digit **2** *(caractère)* character

digital¹, -ale, -aux, -ales [diʒital, -o] **ADJ** *Ordinat* digital; **code d.** digital code; **affichage d.** digital display; **horloge/montre à affichage d.** digital watch/clock

digital², -ale, -aux, -ales **ADJ** *(nerf etc)* digital; **empreinte digitale** fingerprint; **prendre les empreintes digitales de qn** to take sb's fingerprints, to fingerprint sb

NF *Bot, Méd* **digitale** digitalis; *Bot* **digitale pourprée** foxglove

digitaline [diʒitalin] **NF** *Chimie, Pharm* digitalin

digitaliser [diʒitalize] **VT** *Ordinat* to digitize

digitaliseur [diʒitalizœr] **NM** *Ordinat* digitizer

digne [diɲ] **ADJ 1** *(méritant)* deserving, worthy (**de** of); **cela est d. de récompense** that deserves a reward; **d. d'éloges** praiseworthy; **d. de foi** reliable; **d. d'être remarqué** noteworthy; **il est d. d'être remercié** he deserves thanks *or* to be thanked; **il n'est pas d. d'être notre représentant** he does not deserve *or* he is not fit to be our representative; **il n'est pas d. de vivre** he is not fit to live; **ce film est d. d'être vu** it's a film worth seeing; **je ne suis pas d. de toi** I am not worthy of you, you're too good for me; **une mère d.** a fit mother
2 *(à la hauteur)* **d. de** worthy of; **une attitude peu d. d'un chef d'État** an attitude that is hardly worthy of a head of state; **d. d'une mère** of a mother, motherly; **son attitude n'est pas d. d'une mère** her attitude is not motherly *or* not that of a mother; **il est d'une gentillesse avec toi d. d'une mère** he is almost motherly towards you; **d. de ce nom** worthy of the name; **prouver qu'on est une mère d. de ce nom** to prove that one is a fit mother; *Hum* **tu es bien le d. fils de ton père** you're your father's son all right; **un adversaire d. de soi** a worthy opponent; **un roman d. de la grande tradition française** a novel in the great French tradition; **tâchez de vous montrer d. de (représenter) la France** try to show that you're worthy to represent France **3** *(honorable, décent) (air, personne etc)* dignified; **il est incapable de rester d. après trois verres de vin** after three glasses of wine, he is incapable of acting in a dignified fashion, he loses all dignity after three glasses of wine

dignement [diɲ(ə)mã] **ADV 1** *(avec dignité)* with dignity, in a dignified fashion; **il a réagi très d.** he reacted with great dignity **2** *(légitimement)* **être d. récompensé** to be justly rewarded

dignitaire [diɲitɛr] **NM** *(de l'Église)* dignitary

dignité [diɲite] **NF 1** *(grandeur)* dignity; **elle manque de d.** she's undignified; **elle fit une entrée pleine de d.** she came in with great dignity; **toute personne a droit à la d.** everyone is entitled to their dignity **2** *(haute fonction)* high office *or* position, *Fml* dignity; **installer qn dans une d.** to install sb in an office

digramme [digram] **NM** *Ling* digraph

digraphie [digrafi] **NF** *Com* double-entry bookkeeping

digression [digrɛsjɔ̃] **NF** digression; **faire une d.** to digress, to stray *or* wander from the point

digue [dig] **NF** *Tech* dyke; *(d'une voie navigable etc)* embankment; *(en pierre)* breakwater; *(contre l'érosion)* sea wall; *Fig (aux passions etc)* barrier

diktat [diktat] **NM** diktat, dictate

dilapidateur, -trice [dilapidatœr, -tris] **ADJ** spendthrift
N *(de fortune)* spendthrift, wastrel; *(de fonds publics, de biens)* embezzler

dilapidation [dilapidasjɔ̃] **NF** *(de fortune)* wasting, squandering; *(de fonds publics, de biens)* embezzlement, misappropriation

dilapider [dilapide] **VT** *(fortune)* to waste, to squander; *(fonds publics)* to misappropriate, to embezzle

dilatation [dilatasjɔ̃] **NF** *(des pupilles)* dilation; *(de l'estomac)* distension; *(des gaz)* expansion; *Constr* **joint de d.** expansion joint

dilater [dilate] **VT** *(agrandir) (pupilles)* to dilate; *(estomac)* to distend; *(gaz)* to expand; **il a les pupilles dilatées** his pupils are dilated; *Fig* **d. le cœur** to cheer *or* gladden the heart
VPR se dilater *(de pupilles)* to dilate; *(de l'estomac)* to become distended; *(d'un gaz)* to expand

dilatoire [dilatwar] **ADJ** *(tactique etc)* delaying; *Jur* dilatory; **faire des réponses dilatoires** to stall for time

dilemme [dilɛm] **NM** dilemma; **être devant un d.** to be in a dilemma; *Mktg (produit)* wildcat

dilettante [diletãt] **N** dilettante, amateur; **faire des sciences en d.** to dabble in science

dilettantisme [diletãtism] **NM** dilettantism, amateurism

diligemment [diliʒamã] **ADV** *Litt* **1** *(avec soin)* diligently **2** *(avec rapidité)* promptly, quickly

diligence [diliʒãs] **NF 1** *Litt (soin)* diligence, industry, application **2** *Litt (rapidité)* haste, dispatch; **faire d.** to hurry, to make haste **3** *(véhicule)* (stage)coach **4** *Jur* proceedings

diligent [diliʒã] **ADJ** *Litt* **1** *(appliqué)* diligent, industrious; **soins diligents** assiduous care **2** *(rapide)* speedy, prompt

diluant [dilɥã] **NM** thinner

diluer [dilɥe] **VT** *(boisson)* to dilute, to water down (**de** with); *(peinture)* to thin down (**de** with); *(pouvoir)* to weaken; *(discours, dissertation)* to pad

dilution [dilysjɔ̃] **NF** *(de peinture)* thinning down; *(de boisson)* dilution, watering down; *(de pouvoir)* weakening; *(de discours, dissertation)* padding; **d. de capital** dilution of capital

diluvien, -ienne [dilyvjɛ̃, -jɛn] **ADJ 1** *(fossiles etc)* diluvian; *(dépôt, argile etc)* diluvial **2** *Fig* **pluie diluvienne** torrential rain

dimanche [dimãʃ] **NM** Sunday; **d. des Rameaux/de Pâques** Palm/Easter Sunday; **ses habits du d.** one's Sunday clothes *or* best; *Fam* **un chauffeur du d.** a weekend *or* Sunday driver; **un peintre du d.** a weekend painter; **la promenade du d.** the (usual) Sunday stroll; **on passe tous les dimanches en famille** we spend every Sunday with the family; **je hais les dimanches** I hate Sundays *(voir aussi* **samedi** *)* SEE GRAMMAR A81–2; B61–2

dîme [dim] **NF** *Hist* tithe; *Fig* **l'État prélève sa d. sur le tabac** the government takes its cut on tobacco

dimension [dimãsjɔ̃] **NF 1** *(grandeur)* dimension, size; **à deux/trois dimensions** two-/three-dimensional; **quelles sont les dimensions de la pièce?** how large is the room?, what is the size of the room?; **prendre les dimensions de qch** to take the measurements of sth, to measure sth; **taillé à la d.** cut to size; **coupé dans sa plus grande/petite d.** cut lengthways/crossways SEE GRAMMAR B59
2 *(importance) (d'une faute)* magnitude, enormity; **te rends-tu compte de la d. de ta gaffe?** do you realize what an enormous blunder you made?; *Fig* **prendre les dimensions d'une expédition/d'une révolution** to take on the dimensions of an expedition/a revolution; **le suspens est une d. prépondérante de son œuvre** suspense is a significant feature of his work; **ce travail n'est pas à la d. de son talent** the work is not equal to his talent; **il n'a pas la d. d'un homme d'État** he is not the stuff that statesmen are made of; **cette découverte prend enfin ses vraies dimensions** people are finally realizing the true importance of this discovery

dimensionner [dimãsjɔne] **VT** *Ordinat (figure)* to size

diminué [diminye] ADJ **1** *Tex (tricot)* fully-fashioned; *Mus (intervalle)* diminished; *Archit* **colonne diminuée** tapering column **2** *(affaibli)* weakened, diminished; **c'est un homme d.** he is not the man he was; **il est très d. physiquement/mentalement** he is physically/mentally a lot weaker

diminuer [diminye] VT *(prix)* to reduce, to lower; *(dépenses)* to reduce, to decrease, to cut down; *(salaire)* to reduce, to decrease, to cut; *(autorité, pouvoir, crédibilité etc)* to lessen, to diminish; *(son capital, l'importance de qch)* to diminish; **d. les chances de succès** to diminish *or* lessen *or* reduce the chances of success; **d. sa consommation d'alcool** to reduce *or* cut down one's alcohol consumption; **d. l'ardeur des foules** to decrease the fervour *or Am* fervor of the crowds; **la maladie l'a considérablement diminuée** the illness has weakened her considerably; *Fig* **cela vous diminuerait aux yeux du public** it would lower *or* diminish you in the eyes of the public; **d. le son** to turn down the volume; **d. la semaine de travail** to reduce *or* cut the working week; **d. la longueur de qch** to make sth shorter, to shorten sth; **d. la hauteur de qch** to lower the height of sth; **d. la largeur de qch** to make sth narrower; *Tricot* **d. l'encolure de quatre mailles** to decrease four stitches at the neck

VI to diminish, to decrease, to lessen; *(de profits)* to decrease, to fall off, to decline; *(de prix)* to decrease, to fall; *(de fièvre)* to abate; *(de douleur)* to decrease, to diminish; **d. de vitesse** to slow down, to reduce speed; **les jours diminuent** the days are drawing in *or* are growing shorter; **ses forces ont diminué** his strength has declined; **sa toux a diminué** he is not coughing as much; *Naut* **d. de toile** to shorten sail

VPR **se diminuer** to lower *or* demean oneself

diminutif, -ive [diminytif, -iv] ADJ diminutive

NM *(d'un nom commun)* diminutive; *(d'un nom propre)* pet name, nickname; **'jupette' est le d. de 'jupe'** 'jupette' is the diminutive (form) of 'jupe'

diminution [diminysjɔ̃] NF *(de nombre)* decrease, decline; *(de prix)* reduction, decrease, lowering; *(de dépenses)* cutting down; *(de salaire)* decrease; *(de vitesse)* slackening; *(du son)* fading; *(de fièvre)* abatement; *(de douleur)* decrease, lessening; *Tricot* **commencer les diminutions** to begin decreasing; *Tricot* **faire trois diminutions** decrease three stitches

dimorphe [dimɔrf] ADJ *Biol* dimorphic, dimorphous

dimorphisme [dimɔrfism] NM *Biol* dimorphism

dinanderie [dinɑ̃dri] NF brassware; *(de cuisine)* brass kitchen utensils

dinar [dinar] NM dinar

dînatoire [dinatwar] ADJ *Fml, Hum (apéritif, goûter)* copious, *Hum* mammoth

dinde [dɛ̃d] NF **1** *(volaille)* turkey hen; *Culin* turkey **2** *Fam (femme sotte)* stupid woman

dindon [dɛ̃dɔ̃] NM turkey (cock); *Fig* **être le d. de la farce** to be fooled *or* duped, to be made a fool of; **c'est le fisc qui est le d. de la farce** it's the tax man who's been conned

dindonneau, -eaux [dɛ̃dɔno] NM young turkey, turkey poult

dîner¹ [dine] NM VOIR GRAMMAIRE A7 **1** *(repas du soir)* dinner; **prendre son d.** to have one's dinner; **je donne un d. ce soir** I'm having a dinner party tonight; **je ne peux pas venir ce soir, j'ai un d.** I can't come this evening, I'm already booked for dinner; **il y a des pâtes pour le ou au ou à d.** it's pasta for dinner; **d. dansant** dinner-dance; **d.-débat/-con-**

cert/-spectacle dinner-debate/-concert/-show; **d. de gala** gala dinner; **d. de famille** family dinner **2** *Belg, Can, Suisse (déjeuner)* lunch

dîner² VI **1** *(prendre le repas du soir)* to dine, to have dinner; **d. en ville** *ou* **à l'extérieur** to dine out; **d. dehors** to eat out; **d. chez des amis** to dine *or* have dinner with friends; **à quelle heure dînez-vous?** what time do you have dinner?; **il est resté à d.** he stayed for dinner; **avoir/inviter qn à d.** to have/invite sb for *or* to dinner; **nous avons les Dupont à d.** the Duponts are coming for dinner; **elle dîne de peu** she doesn't eat very much at dinner; **elle a dîné de peu** she didn't have much dinner, she didn't eat very much at dinner; **il dîna d'une tranche de jambon** he had a slice of ham for dinner; *Prov* **qui dort dîne** he who sleeps forgets his hunger **2** *Belg, Can, Suisse (déjeuner)* to (have) lunch; **elle est partie d.** she's gone to lunch

dînette [dinɛt] NF *Fam (service)* doll's teaset; *(repas)* dolls' tea party; **jouer à la d.** to have a dolls' tea party

dîneur, -euse [dinœr, -øz] N diner

ding [diŋ] INT ting-a-ling

dingo¹ [dɛ̃go] NM *(animal)* dingo

dingo² ADJ, N *Fam* = **dingue**

dingue [dɛ̃g] *Fam* ADJ **1** *(fou)* crazy, nuts (**de qn/qch** about sb/sth; **de faire qch** to do sth); **c'est complètement d. de croire qu'on va s'en sortir** it's absolutely crazy to think we're going to get out of this **2** *(incroyable) (fête, fringues, bouquin)* great, terrific; **c'est d. ce que la ville a changé** it's incredible how much the town has changed; **c'est d. ce que la vie est chère** the cost of living is terrible; **c'est d., la pluie qui tombe ici** it's terrible how much it rains here, it rains a terrific lot here; **il a fait un orage d.** there was a terrific storm N nutcase, crackpot, loony; **ce d. est arrivé chez moi sans prévenir** the nutcase turned up on my doorstep without warning; **envoyer qn chez les dingues** to send sb to the loony bin *or* funny farm; **c'est un d. de la moto** he's crazy *or* nuts about motorbikes; **d. d'informatique** computer freak

dinguer [dɛ̃ge] VI *Fam* **s'en aller d.** *(d'une personne)* to go flying; **sa voiture est allée d. contre un mur** his car went flying *or* headlong into a wall; **envoyer qn** *(le pousser)* to send sb flying (**contre** into); *(l'éconduire)* to send sb packing; **envoyer d. qch** to send sth flying; **je vais tout envoyer d.** I'm going to pack it all in

dinguerie [dɛ̃gri] NF *Fam* stupidity; **ce film est d'une d.!** it's an incredibly stupid film!; **voilà sa dernière d.: s'acheter une moto!** you know what his latest mad *or* crazy idea is? to buy a motorbike!; **ils ne savent faire que les dingueries** they get up to all sorts of nonsense; **il est capable des pires dingueries** he's capable of doing the most idiotic things

dinosaure [dinozɔr] NM *(animal)*, *Fig* dinosaur; *Fig* **dinosaures de la politique** political dinosaurs

diocésain, -aine [djɔsezɛ̃, -ɛn] ADJ, N *Rel* diocesan

diocèse [djɔsɛz] NM *Rel* diocese

diode [djɔd] NF *Radio* diode; *Ordinat* **d. électroluminescente** light-emitting diode

dionysiaque [djɔnizjak] ADJ Dionysiac NFPL **les dionysiaques** the Dionysia

diorama [djɔrama] NM diorama

dioxine [djɔksin] NF dioxin

dioxyde [djɔksid] NM *Chimie* dioxide

diphasé [difaze] ADJ *Élec (système etc)* two-phase

diphtérie [difteri] NF *Méd* diphtheria; **avoir la d.** to have diphtheria

diphtérique [difterik] ADJ *Méd* diphther(i-t)ic, diphtherial

diphtongue [diftɔ̃g] NF *Ling* diphthong

diphtonguer [diftɔ̃ge] VT *Ling* to diphthongize

diplodocus [diplɔdɔkys] NM diplodocus

diplomate [diplɔmat] N *(fonctionnaire, négociateur)* diplomat NM *Culin* ≃ trifle ADJ diplomatic

diplomatie [diplɔmasi] NF *(tact)*, *Pol* diplomacy; **entrer dans la d.** to enter the diplomatic service; **user de d.** to be diplomatic

diplomatique [diplɔmatik] ADJ **1** *(service, corps, immunité etc)* diplomatic; **valise d.** diplomatic bag, *Fam* bag, *Am* (diplomatic) pouch **2** *(habile)* diplomatic, tactful; **ce n'était pas très d. de sa part** that wasn't very diplomatic *or* tactful of him; **maladie d.** diplomatic flu

diplomatiquement [diplɔmatikmɑ̃] ADV diplomatically

diplôme [diplom] NM *(d'enseignant, de docteur etc)* diploma; *Univ* degree; **elle a des diplômes** she has qualifications

▸▸ **d. d'études approfondies** = postgraduate qualification which is a prerequisite for PhD candidates; **d. d'études supérieures spécialisées** = postgraduate diploma; **d. d'études universitaires générales** = university degree awarded after a two-year course of study; **d. d'études universitaires scientifiques et techniques** = university degree awarded after a two-year course of study in science and/or technical subjects; **d. universitaire de technologie** = post-baccalauréat technical qualification awarded after two-years

diplômé, -ée [diplome] ADJ *Univ* graduate; *(architecte, infirmière)* qualified, certified; **un ingénieur d. de l'École polytechnique** an engineering graduate of the École polytechnique N holder of a diploma; *Univ* graduate

diplômer [diplome] VT to confer a diploma on; *Univ* to confer a degree on, *Am* to graduate

diplopie [diplɔpi] NF *Méd* double vision, diplopia

dipode [dipɔd] ADJ, NM *Zool* biped

dipsomane [dipsɔman], **dipsomaniaque** [dipsɔmanjak] ADJ, N dipsomaniac

dipsomanie [dipsɔmani] NF dipsomania

diptère [diptɛr] *Entom* ADJ two-winged, *Spéc* dipterous NM dipter(an); **les diptères** the Diptera

diptyque [diptik] NM diptych; *Littér* two-part literary work

dirco [dirko] NM *(abrév directeur commercial)* marketing manager; *(en chef)* marketing director

dircom [dirkɔm] NM *(abrév directeur de la communication)* communications manager; *(en chef)* communications director

dire¹ [dir] NM statement, assertion; *Jur* allegation; **on ne peut pas se fier à leurs dires** you can't trust what they say; **au d. de l'expert** according to expert opinion *or* the experts; **selon son d., à son d., à ses dires** according to him, by his own account; **maintenir son d.** to stand by one's statement *or* what one said

DIRE² *(prp disant; pp dit; pr ind je dis, n. disons, v. dites, ils disent; impf je disais; p hist je dis; fu je dirai)*

VT to say **1–5, 7, 8, 11** ▪ to tell **1–4, 7, 9, 11** ▪ to think **6** ▪ to look/sound/*etc* like *(on dirait...)* **6** ▪ to show **9** ▪ to suit *(dire à)* **10** ▪ to recite **11** ▪ to mean *(vouloir dire)* **13**		
VPR to say **1, 3, 5, 6** ▪ to think **2, 4**		

VT 1 (*exprimer*) to say; **il ne savait plus quoi d.** he didn't know what to say; **dites 33** (*chez le médecin*) say 'Ah'; **elle a dit 'rénumération' au lieu de rémunération'** she said 'rénumération' instead of 'rémunération'; **c'est justement ce que j'allais d.!** that's just what I was about to say!; **alors, qu'est-ce qu'il t'a dit?** well, what did he say to you?; **vous ne m'en avez jamais rien dit** you never mentioned it or said a thing about it; **mettez que je n'ai rien dit** forget I said that; **il n'y a pas à d., c'est vraiment le meilleur** there are no two ways about it, it's really the best; **je ne sais que d. pour vous remercier** I don't know how to thank you; **je ne sais que d. pour vous consoler** I don't know what to say to comfort you; **elle n'a plus dit un mot** she didn't say another word; **ce ne sont pas des choses à d.** you don't say that kind of thing; **tu ne sais plus ce que tu dis!** (*tes mots dépassent ta pensée*) you don't know what you're saying!; **arrête de d. n'importe quoi** stop talking nonsense; **j'ai un mot à te d.** (*pour mettre au courant*) I've got something to tell you; (*d'un ton menaçant*) I've something to say to you; **d. ce qu'on pense** to say what one thinks, to speak one's mind; **j'ai dit ce que j'avais à d.** I've said what I had to say; **ce disant …, ceci dit …** with these words …, having said that …; **un ami, que dis-je! un frère** a friend, no, a brother!; **c'est facile à d., c'est plus facile à d. qu'à faire** (it's) easier said than done; **d. bonjour à qn** to say hello to sb; **d. bonjour de la main** to wave hello; **d. bonsoir à qn** to say goodnight to sb, to wish sb goodnight; **comme on dit** as the saying goes, as they say; **comment dites-vous cela en français?** how do you say that in French?, what is the French for that?; **d. du mal de qn** to speak ill of sb; **je vous dis que non** no, I said; **je t'ai déjà dit que oui!** I've already said yes!; **là je ne dis pas non** I wouldn't say no; **sans mot d.** without (saying) a word; *Prov* **qui ne dit mot consent** silence is tantamount to consent; **pour ainsi d.** so to speak, as it were; *Fam* **on a comme qui dirait des ennuis** we have what you might call a few problems; **faire des stocks de sucre lorsqu'on habite à Moscou, je ne dis pas, mais à Paris!** stocking up on sugar when you live in Moscow, that's fair enough or that's one thing, but in Paris!; **ou, pour mieux d. …** or, to be more specific …; **il est un peu lent, pour ne pas d. complètement idiot** he's a little slow or, to put it bluntly, he's a complete idiot; **autrement dit** in other words; **cela va sans d.** that goes without saying, of course, naturally; **il va sans d. que vous venez avec votre épouse** needless to say or naturally, your wife is invited as well, your wife is invited as well, of course; **comment dirais-je?** how shall I put it?; **je ne sais comment d.** I don't know how to put it; **qui dit mieux?** (*à une vente aux enchères*) any advance?; **dites toujours!** go on, say it!; *Fam* **fire away!**; **il faut le d. vite!** it's easy to say!; **c'est vite dit** it's easier said than done; *Enf* **c'est celui qui dit, qui l'est!** it takes one to know one!

2 (*informer*) to tell; **qui te l'a dit?** (*comment le sais-tu?*) who told you?; **elle m'a dit que tu étais à Paris** she told me (that) you were in Paris; **qui t'a dit ça?** (*ce n'est pas vrai*) who told you that?; **c'est Sophie qui me l'a dit** it was Sophie who told me; **elle a dit qu'elle arriverait en retard** she said she'd be late; **envoyer d. à qn que …** to send word to sb that …; **d. un secret** to tell a secret; **il faudra bien que tu le lui dises un jour** you'll have to tell him some day; **ne me dis rien, tu as gagné!** don't tell me or let me guess, you've won!; **ne me dis pas que tu as gagné!** don't tell me or don't say you've won!; **il dit dans sa lettre que …, sa lettre dit que …** he says in his let-ter that …; **faire d. qch à qn** (*en le forçant*) to make sb say sth; (*pour prévenir*) to send word of sth to sb; **je lui ai fait d. de venir** I sent for him; **elle ne se le fit pas d. deux fois** she didn't wait to be told twice; *Fam* **je ne te le fais pas d.!** tell me something I don't know!; **faire d. qch par qn** to send word of sth through sb; **il a fait d. à son patron qu'il ne viendrait pas** he sent word to his boss that he wouldn't be coming in

3 (*affirmer*) to tell; **moi, je vous dis qu'il ne viendra pas** I say he won't come; **je le dis et je le répète** let me make myself perfectly clear; **qui vous dit qu'elle est vraiment aveugle?** who says she's really blind?; **quand je vous le disais!, je vous l'avais bien dit!** I told you so!, didn't I say so?; (*puisque*) **je vous le dis!** take my word for it!; **il est vraiment parti avec elle?** – (*puisque*) **je vous le dis** has he really gone off with her? – you can take it from me (he has) or take my word for it; **je peux reprendre du gâteau?** – (*puisque*) **je vous le dis!** of course you can!; *Fam* **c'est lui, je te dis** it's him, I tell you; **c'est moi qui vous le dis** let me tell you, believe me; **c'est toi qui le dis!**, *Fam* **que tu dis!** if you say so!; **je sais ce que je dis!** I know what I'm talking about!; *Fam* **à qui le dites-vous?** you're telling me!; **tu ne crois pas si bien d.!** you're telling me!, how right you are!, *Am* you've said a mouthful!; **on peut d. qu'il a eu de la chance** he was lucky, you might say; *Fam* **tu l'as dit (bouffi)!** you('ve) said it!; **c'est beaucoup d.** that's say-ing (quite) a lot, that's going rather far; **c'est peu d.** that's putting it mildly; **c'est pas de d. qu'il est petit!** he's small, and that's putt-ing it mildly!, he's small, to put it mildly!, *Br* he isn't half small!; *Fam* **je ne te dis pas la fête démente que c'était!** the party was so wild, it was unreal!; *Fam* **je ne te dis que ça** say no more, enough said; **vous m'en direz tant!** you don't say!; *Enf Fam* **on dit qu'on est des astronautes** let's be astronauts; **vous m'avez dit adorer la musique** you told me you loved music; **on le dit mort** they say he is dead, he is said or reported to be dead; **enfin, ça c'est ce qu'elle dit!** well, that's what she says!

4 to say; *Enf* **je vais le d. à ma mère** I'm going to tell mum on you; **je vais le d.!** I'm going to tell!; *Fam* **je vais te d.** let me tell you; *Fam* **je te dis pas la surprise quand ils sont arrivés!** I can't tell you what a surprise it was when they arrived!; **il a fait une tête quand il m'a vue, je te dis pas!** I can't describe the ex-pression on his face when he saw me!; **à vrai d., à d. vrai** to tell the truth, to be truthful; **pour tout (vous) d.** to be honest (with you), to be truthful, to tell (you) the truth; **c'est (tout) d.** need I say more?; **c'est d. s'il t'aime** that shows how much he loves you; **à ce qu'elle dit** according to her; **entre nous soit dit, soit dit entre nous** between ourselves, between you and me, *Fam* between you, me and the gatepost; **soit dit en passant ou entre parenthèses** by the by, by the way, in-cidentally

5 (*décider*) **aussitôt dit, aussitôt fait** no soo-ner said than done; **alors c'est dit, voilà qui est dit** (well then,) that's settled or that's de-cided; **disons à quatre heures** let's say four o'clock, four o'clock, say; **ce qui est dit est dit** a promise is a promise; **tenez-vous cela pour dit** don't let me have to tell you again, that's my last word; **mais tout n'est pas dit** but that's not the last of it; **tant que tout n'est pas dit** while things are still up in the air, un-til things are definite one way or the other; **tant que tout n'est pas dit pour le mariage** until the wedding is definitely going to take place; **il est dit que je resterai célibataire** I'm destined to stay single

6 (*penser*) to think (**de** of); **alors, qu'est-ce que tu en dis?** well, what do you think?; **qu'en dira-t-on?, qu'est-ce que les gens vont d.?** what will people say or think?; **qu'est-ce que tu dirais d'aller au cinéma?** how about going to see a film?; **on aurait dit qu'elle était hypnotisée/que c'était la fin du monde** you would have thought she was hypnot-ized/it was the end of the world; **avec sa canne, on aurait dit Charlot** he looked like Charlie Chaplin with his cane; **qui eût dit qu'elle se marierait?** who would have thought she'd get married?; **et d. qu'elle n'a que vingt ans!** and to think that she's only twenty!; **on dirait qu'il va pleuvoir** it looks like rain; **on dirait qu'il pleut** it looks as if it is raining; **on dirait du Mozart** it sounds like Mozart; **on dirait du gin** it tastes like gin

7 (*ordonner*) **d. à qn de faire qch** to tell sb to do sth; **faites ce qu'on vous dit** do as you're told; **dites-lui d'entrer** tell or ask him to come in; **dites qu'on le fasse entrer** tell or ask them to show him in; **le prof a dit de lire le premier chapitre** the teacher said to read the first chapter; **taisez-vous, j'ai dit!** be quiet, I said!; **je ne le dirai pas deux fois!** I won't tell you twice or again!

8 (*protester*) to say; **il est trop tard, je ne peux plus rien d.** it's too late, I can't say anything now; **j'ai eu une augmentation conséquente, je n'ai rien à d.** I got a decent rise, I can't complain; **tu as quelque chose à d. à ça?** have you got any objection?; **très bon travail, rien à d.** this is very good work, I have no complaints; **il y a beaucoup à d. sur ton travail** there's quite a lot I'd like to say about your work; **tu n'as rien à d.!** I don't want to hear a word out of you!; **je n'ai rien à d. contre lui** I have no objection to him; **il n'y a pas à d.** there's no denying it, there's no doubt about it; **il n'y a pas à d. ou on a beau d., c'est utile d'avoir un homme chez soi** there's no denying that it's useful to have a man about the house; **vous avez beau d. (le contraire)** you can say what you like; **tu as beau d. qu'elle ne ment pas** you can say she doesn't lie until you're blue in the face; **j'ai beau d. (tout ce que je veux), il ne m'écoute jamais** I can talk until I'm blue in the face, he never listens to me; **ce n'est pas pour d., mais …** I hate to tell you this, but …; **ne pas avoir son mot à d.** not to have any say; **tu n'as pas ton mot à d. sur cette question** you don't have any say in the matter

9 (*indiquer*) to show, to express; **horloge qui dit l'heure exacte** clock that tells the right time; **cela en dit long sur son courage** it speaks volumes for his courage; *Litt* **sa dé-marche/son visage disait son désespoir** his despair was evident in his gait/face; **qu'est-ce qui vous dit qu'il viendra?** how do you know he will come?; **ce nom/cette musique ne me dit rien** the name/the music means or conveys nothing to me; **quelque chose me dit que …** something tells me that …

10 (*plaire*) **d. à** to suit, to appeal to; **ça te dit?** what about it?, how about it?; **ça te dit de partir en vacances avec nous?** how about coming on holiday with us?; **si cela te dit, si le cœur t'en dit** if you feel like it; **cela me dit (trop) rien, cela ne me dit pas** I don't feel like it; **cela ne me dit trop rien de manger chinois ce soir** I don't feel like eating Chinese this evening; **en hiver, rien ne me dit** I don't feel like doing anything in winter; *Fam* **alors, ton tricot, qu'est-ce que ça dit?** how did your sweater turn out?; **pour l'instant, il ne dit pas grand-chose** it doesn't look like much at the moment; **cela ne me disait rien de bon ou rien qui vaille** I didn't like the look of it; **le fait qu'il soit si hésitant ne me dit rien de bon ou rien qui vaille** I don't like the fact or I'm a bit concerned that he's hesitating so much

11 (*réciter*) (*ses prières, la messe*) to say; **d.**

des vers *ou* de la poésie to recite poetry; **d. son chapelet** to tell one's beads

12 *(nommer)* **Jacques, dit Jacko** Jacques, also known as *or* alias *or Fam* aka Jacko; *(en le présentant)* Jacques, or Jacko to us

13 *(signifier)* **vouloir d.** to mean; **je veux d. ...** that is to say ..., I mean ...; **que voulez-vous d. par là?** what do you mean by that?; **que veut d. ce mot?** what does this word mean?; *Fam* **ça fait bien ce que ça veut d.** it means what it says; **qu'est-ce à d.?** what does this mean?; **est-ce à d. qu'il ne viendra pas?** does this mean he won't come?; **qui dit bordeaux dit bon vin** Bordeaux is synonymous with good wine

14 laisse-les d., ils sont stupides! let them talk, they're stupid!; **je me suis laissé d. que ...** I hear that ...

15 dis donc, je viens de penser qu'on pourrait se voir ce week-end by the way *or Fam* hey, I've just had a thought, we could see each other this weekend; **tu as grandi, dis donc!** goodness *or* my word, you've grown!; **non mais dis donc, tu ne vas pas recommencer!** you're not going to start up again!; **dis donc, tu te fiches de moi!** you don't give a damn about me, do you?; **ben dis donc!** well I'm damned!; **tu m'emmènes, dis, sur ta moto?** take me for a ride on your motorbike, eh?, go on, give me a ride on your motorbike; **non mais, dis donc!** do you mind!

VPR se dire 1 *(réciproque)* **on se dit bonjour de temps en temps** we say hello from time to time

2 *(penser)* **je me disais que tout était fini** I thought it was all over; **dis-toi bien que ça aurait pu être plus grave** tell yourself it could have been worse; **je me disais bien que j'avais déjà vu quelque part** I knew I'd seen him before

3 *(être correct)* **ça se dit en français?** can you say that in French?; **cela ne se dit pas** that isn't said; **des choses pareilles ne se disent pas** you don't say things like that; **cela se dit d'une personne mais certainement pas d'un objet** you can say that about *or* of a person but definitely not about *or* of a thing

4 *(se croire)* **on se dirait en Suisse** you would think you were in Switzerland; **on se dirait en été** you would think it was summer

5 *(se prétendre)* **elle se dit écossaise/à Londres** she says she is Scottish/in London

6 comment ça se dit en français? how do you say that in French?

Attention: ne pas confondre **to say** et **to tell** lorsqu'on traduit **dire**. Le verbe **to tell** est toujours suivi d'un complément d'objet désignant la personne à qui l'on s'adresse.

---

direct [dirɛkt] **ADJ 1** *(sans détour) (question, chemin)* direct, straight; *(personne)* direct, straightforward; **quel est le chemin le plus d. pour aller à la mairie?** what's the most direct way to get to the town hall?; **d'ici, la route est directe** it's a straight road from here; **tu ne peux pas te tromper, c'est d.** you can't go wrong, it's a straight road; **il y a fait une allusion directe** he made a direct reference to it, he referred to it directly

2 *(sans intermédiaire) (impôts)*, *Tél (ligne)* direct; **descendre de qn en ligne directe** to be a direct descendant of sb; *Gram* **complément d'objet d.** direct object; **SEE GRAMMAR B18–19; B52–3 mon supérieur d.** my immediate superior; **il y a des ventes directes au grand public dans leur entrepôt** they sell direct to the public from their warehouse; **être en rapport** *ou* **contact d.** *ou* **en relations directes avec qn** to be in direct contact with sb; **d. sur cassette** live on tape

3 *(sans arrêt)* **train d.** through train, fast train; *Aviat* **vol d.** direct flight

NM 1 *Radio, TV* live broadcasting; **ce n'est jamais du d.** it's never broadcast live; **il préfère le d. au playback** he prefers performing live to miming; **émission en d.** live broadcast; **vous allez entendre ce concert en d. de l'Opéra de Paris** you will hear this concert live from the Paris Opera House

2 *Boxe* straight; **d. du droit/du gauche** straight right/left; **s'il continue de m'énerver, je lui mets un d. au menton** if he keeps on annoying me, I'll punch him on the jaw

3 *Rail* through *or* fast train (**pour** to)

4 *Ordinat* **en d.** in direct mode

ADV *Fam* directly; **je pars d. vers Grenoble** I'm going to Grenoble direct; **s'il recommence, je vais d. chez le proviseur** if he starts again, I'm going straight to the headmaster

directement [dirɛktəmã] **ADV 1** *(sans détour)* straight, directly; **en arrivant, je vais d. au lit** I'm going straight to bed when I arrive; **si tu prends ce chemin, tu arrives d. à la rivière** this road will take you straight to the river; **se précipiter d. sur un endroit/qch** to head straight for a place/sth; **elle est venue d. vers nous** she came straight towards us; **se diriger d. au nord** to go due north; **répondre d. à la question** to give a direct *or* straight answer to the question; **dis-moi d. combien tu veux** tell me straight out how much you want **2** *(sans intermédiaire)* directly; **expédier des marchandises d. à qn** to send goods direct to sb; **d. du producteur au consommateur** direct *or* straight from the producer to the consumer

directeur, -trice [dirɛktœr, -tris] **N** *Com (qui fait partie du conseil d'administration)* director; *(d'un magasin, d'un service)* manager; *Scol* head(teacher), *Am* principal; *Univ (d'une UER)* head; *(de prison)* governor; *(de journal)* editor; *(d'expédition etc)* leader; *Cin, Radio, TV* director

ADJ *(équipe, instances)* management, executive; *(force)* directing, managing, controlling; *(principe)* guiding; **comité d.** steering committee; **roue directrice** front wheel; **lignes directrices** guidelines; **l'idée directrice d'un livre** the central theme of a book

▸▸ **d. des achats** purchasing director/manager; **d. adjoint** deputy director/manager; **d. administratif** executive director; **d. administratif et financier** administrative and financial manager; **d. d'agence** branch manager; *Radio* **d. d'antenne** station director; **d. artistique** artistic director, production designer; *Journ* art editor, art director; **d. de banque** bank manager; *Pol* **d. de cabinet** *(d'un ministre)* ≃ principal private secretary; *TV, Cin etc* **d. de casting** casting director; *TV, Radio* **d. de chaîne** network controller; **d. de la clientèle** customer relations manager; **d. commercial** sales director/manager; **d. de la communication** communications director/manager; **d. des comptes-clients** accounts director/manager; *Rel* **d. de conscience** spiritual adviser; **d. de la création** creative director; **d. du crédit** credit manager; **d. de division** *(au siège)* divisional director; **d. d'exploitation** operations director/manager; **d. export** export director/manager; *Journ* **d. de la fabrication** production director/manager; **d. financier** financial manager; *(en chef)* financial *or* finance director; **d. général** *(d'un ministère)* ≃ permanent under-secretary; *Com* chief executive officer, managing director; *(d'organisation internationale, EDF etc)* director general; **d. gérant** executive director; **d. (de l')informatique** computer manager; **d. intérimaire** temporary director/manager, interim manager, acting manager; **d. de marché**

market manager; **d. du marketing** marketing director/manager; **d. de marque** brand manager; **d. mercatique-vente** sales and marketing director/manager; **d. du personnel** personnel director/manager; **d. de la photographie** *Cin* director of photography, cinematographer; *Journ* picture editor; **d. de production** production manager; **d. de produit** product manager, brand manager; **d. des programmes** director of programming, programme controller; **d. de projet** project director/manager; **d. de la publicité** advertising director/manager; **d. de recherche et développement** director of research and development, R&D director; **d. de recherche marketing** marketing research director/manager; **d. de (la) rédaction** managing editor; **d. régional** regional director/manager, area director/manager, district manager; **d. régional des ventes** regional sales manager; **d. des relations publiques** public relations director/manager; **d. des ressources humaines** human resources manager; **d. de service** head of department, unit manager; **d. des services techniques** technical director; *Rel* **d. spirituel** spiritual adviser; *TV, Radio* **d. de station** station manager; *TV, Radio* **d. de studio** studio manager; **d. de succursale** branch manager; **d. technique** technical manager; **d. de télévision** television director; *Univ* **d. de thèse** thesis director; **d. des ventes** sales director/manager; **d. des ventes et du marketing** sales and marketing director/manager

directif, -ive [dirɛktif, -iv] **ADJ** *Psy (entretien, questionnaire)* directive; *(question)* leading, directive; *Péj (personne, attitude)* managing; **ces instructions sont purement directives** these instructions are for guidance only; **c'est un chef très d.** he's the kind of manager who takes all the decisions himself; **il a des méthodes très directives** he's very managerial *or Fam* bossy

direction [dirɛksjɔ̃] **NF 1** *(d'une affaire, d'une usine, d'un théâtre, d'une école)* management, running; *(d'un parti, d'un pays)* leadership; *(d'un procès, d'une enquête)* conduct; *(d'une équipe, de travaux, d'opérations)* management, supervision; **elle a été promue à la d. du journal/du lycée** she's been promoted to editor/headmistress; **orchestre (placé) sous la d. de Karajan** orchestra conducted by Karajan *or Am* under the baton of Karajan; **projet mené sous la d. du Pr. Lacroix** *(qui y a travaillé activement)* project carried out under the leadership of Prof. Lacroix; *(qui l'a supervisé)* project carried out under the supervision of Prof. Lacroix; **c'est lui qui a pris la d. des opérations** he was in charge of operations; **on lui a confié la d. d'une nouvelle équipe de recherches** he was put in charge of a new research team

2 *(personnes) (d'une administration)* management; **une décision prise au niveau de la d.** a management decision; **j'irai me plaindre à la d.** I'll complain to the management

3 *(lieux) (d'un conseil)* offices; *(d'une firme etc)* head office

4 *Aut, Naut (mécanisme)* steering; *Aut* **la d. est un peu raide** the steering's a bit stiff

5 *(orientation)* direction; *Naut* bearing, course; **changer de d.** to change direction; *Naut* to alter course; **toutes/autres directions** *(sur panneau)* all/all other directions; **ton devoir part dans toutes les directions** your homework goes off in all directions; **quelle d. ont-ils prise?** which way did they go?; **ce train va en d. de Paris** this train is going to Paris; **ses recherches prennent une nouvelle d.** his research is taking a new direction; **chercher la solution dans une autre d.** to look elsewhere for the solution

6 *Cin, TV* directing, direction

▸▸*Aut* d. assistée power steering; d. collégiale collegiate management; d. commerciale sales management; d. du contentieux legal department; *Aut* d. à crémaillère rack and pinion steering; D. départementale de l'action sanitaire et sociale = office administering health and social services at regional level; d. des entreprises business management; d. de l'exploitation operations management; *(service)* operations department; d. financière financial management; *(service)* finance department; d. générale general management, senior management; D. générale des Impôts ≃ Inland Revenue, *Am* ≃ IRS; *Admin* D. générale de la santé = central administrative body for health and social services; *Admin* D. des hôpitaux = central government office for hospital administration; *Aut* d. mécanique manual steering; d. mercatique marketing department; d. par objectifs management by objectives; d. du personnel personnel management; *(service)* personnel department; d. de la production production control; d. de la rédaction editorial department; D. de la surveillance du territoire = French secret service; d. du trésor finance department; d. des ventes sales management; *Ordinat* d. systématisée systems management

directionnel, -elle [dirɛksjɔnɛl] ADJ *(antenne etc)* directional

directive [dirɛktiv] NF directive, order, instruction; *Pol* guideline

directoire [dirɛktwar] NM 1 *Hist* le D. the Directoire *(1795);* chaise D. Directoire chair 2 *Admin, Com* executive board

directorial¹, -iale, -iaux, -iales [dirɛktɔrjal, -jo] ADJ *Com etc* directorial, managerial

directorial², -iale, -iaux, -iales ADJ *Hist (constitution, gouvernement)* of the Directoire

directrice [dirɛktris] NF, ADJ *voir* directeur

dirham [diram] NM dirham

dirigé [diriʒe] ADJ controlled, managed; économie dirigée planned economy; *Scol* activités dirigées extra-curricular activities; *Univ* travaux dirigés classwork; *(en laboratoire)* lab work, practicals

dirigeable [diriʒabl] ADJ dirigible
NM *Aviat* dirigible (balloon), airship

dirigeant, -ante [diriʒɑ̃, -ɑ̃t] ADJ *(principe, philosophie etc)* guiding; classes dirigeantes ruling classes; *Pol* le rôle d. du parti Communiste the leading role of the Communist Party
N *(d'un parti etc)* leader; *(d'un pays)* leader, ruler; d. d'entreprise company manager; d. syndical union leader

DIRIGER [diriʒe] (je dirigeai(s); n. dirigeons) VT 1 *(être à la tête de) (entreprise, affaire, usine, théâtre, école etc)* to manage, to run; *(pays)* to lead, to run; *(orchestre)* to conduct; *(journal)* to edit; *(expédition, débat)* to lead; *(procès, enquête, séance etc)* to conduct; *(travaux, équipe)* to manage, to supervise; *(circulation, Cin, TV)* to direct; d. la production to control production
2 *(orienter) (fusil, arme, télescope)* to aim, to level, to point (sur at); *(personne)* to direct; *(navire)* to steer, to navigate; d. un colis sur Paris to send a parcel off to Paris; d. ses pas vers ... to go *or* move towards ..., to direct one's steps towards ...; peux-tu d. ta lampe vers le plafond? can you move your lamp so it's pointing towards the ceiling?; d. son regard vers *ou* sur qn/qch to look at sb/sth; d. son attention sur qch to turn one's attention to sth; d. ses accusations contre qn to level

or aim accusations at sb; vers qui sont dirigées tes critiques? who is your criticism aimed at?; les filles sont souvent dirigées vers des études littéraires girls are often steered towards arts subjects
VPR se diriger 1 *(aller)* se d. vers un endroit to make for *or* head for a place, to make one's way towards a place; le navire se dirigea vers le port the ship steered *or* headed for the harbour; se d. vers qn to go up to sb; nous nous dirigeons vers une crise encore plus profonde we are heading for an even greater crisis; de plus en plus de femmes se dirigent vers l'informatique more and more women are going into computers
2 *(s'orienter)* se d. à l'aide d'une boussole/du soleil to use a compass/the sun to guide oneself; je n'arrive jamais à me d. dans le noir I can never find my way around in the dark

dirigisme [diriʒism] NM *Écon* state control, dirigisme

dirigiste [diriʒist] *Écon* ADJ système d. state-controlled economy
N advocate of a state-controlled economy

dirlo [dirlo] N *Fam (abrév* directeur) head (teacher), *Am* principal

discal, -ale, -aux, -ales [diskal, -o] ADJ *Méd* hernie discale slipped disc

discernable [disɛrnabl] ADJ discernible, visible

discernement [disɛrnəmɑ̃] NM 1 *(distinction)* discrimination (de ... et de ... between ... and ...) 2 *(jugement)* judgment, discernment; agir sans d. to act rashly

discerner [disɛrne] VT 1 *(distinguer)* to discern, to distinguish; on discernait une maison dans le lointain we could (just) see *or* make out a house in the distance 2 *(différencier)* d. qch de qch to distinguish sth from sth, to discriminate between sth and sth; d. le bien du mal to tell right from wrong 3 *(sentir)* to detect, to discern; d. de la tristesse dans la voix de qn to detect a note of sadness in sb's voice

disciple [disipl] N disciple, follower

disciplinable [disiplinabl] ADJ that can be disciplined

disciplinaire [disiplinɛr] ADJ *(mesure, sanction etc)* disciplinary

discipline [disiplin] NF 1 *(règlement)* discipline; maintenir la d. to maintain discipline *or* order; un prof qui ne sait pas maintenir la d. a teacher who cannot keep discipline 2 *Scol (matière)* subject, discipline, branch of learning; quelles sont les disciplines enseignées ici? what subjects are taught here? 3 *(fouet)* scourge

discipliné [disipline] ADJ disciplined

discipliner [disipline] VT *(élèves)* to control, to maintain discipline over; d. ses cheveux avec de la laque to control one's hair with lacquer; *Fig* d. ses instincts to curb one's instincts
VPR se discipliner to discipline oneself, to exercise self-control

disc-jockey, *pl* disc-jockeys [diskʒɔkɛ] NM disc jockey

disco [disko] NF *Fam (abrév* discothèque) disco
ADJ, NM (musique) d. disco (music)

discobole [diskɔbɔl] NM *Sport* discus thrower

discographie [diskɔgrafi] NF discography

discographique [diskɔgrafik] ADJ *(rubrique, production)* record

discoïde [diskɔid], discoïdal, -ale, -aux, -ales [diskɔidal, -o] ADJ disc-shaped, *Spéc* discoid(al)

discompte [diskɔ̃t] NM discount

discontinu [diskɔ̃tiny] ADJ discontinuous; *(ligne)* broken
NM discontinuity

discontinuer [diskɔ̃tinɥe] VI to stop, to discontinue; parler pendant des heures sans d. to talk for hours on end without stopping *or* without a break
VT *Litt* to stop, to discontinue

discontinuité [diskɔ̃tinɥite] NF discontinuity

disconvenir [diskɔ̃vnir] VI *(conj like* venir, the aux is avoir) je n'en disconviens pas I admit it, I don't deny it

discophile [diskɔfil] N record enthusiast

discordance [diskɔrdɑ̃s] NF *(de sons)* discordance, dissonance; *(d'opinions)* difference; *(de personnalités, couleurs)* clash

discordant [diskɔrdɑ̃] ADJ *(son)* discordant, dissonant; *(bruit)* grating, jarring; *(couleurs, personnalités)* clashing; *(preuves, opinions etc)* conflicting

discorde [diskɔrd] NF discord, dissension, strife; semer la d. to make trouble, to sow discord

discorder [diskɔrde] VI *(de couleurs, témoignages)* to clash (avec with); sa voix discorde dans l'orchestre her voice clashes with the orchestra

discothèque [diskɔtɛk] NF 1 *(organisme)* record library; *(collection)* record collection *or* library; *(meuble)* record cabinet 2 *(boîte de nuit)* discothèque, *Fam* disco

discount [diskunt] NM 1 *(rabais)* discount 2 *(magasin)* discount shop *or* store

discounter¹ [diskunte] VT to reduce the price of; tout est discounté there's a discount on everything, everything's reduced

discounter², discounteur [diskuntœr] NM discount shop *or* store; *(personne)* discount trader

discoureur, -euse [diskurœr, -øz] N *Péj* speechifier

discourir [diskurir] VI *(conj like* courir) to discourse, *Péj* to air one's opinions (sur on)

discours [diskur] NM 1 *(allocution)* speech; prononcer *ou* faire un d. to make a speech; d. de clôture closing speech; *Pol* d. sur l'état de l'Union *(du président des États-Unis)* State of the Union Speech; d. d'ouverture opening speech; *Pol* d.-programme policy statement; d. de réception acceptance speech; d. du trône Speech from the Throne
2 *(exposé)* discourse, dissertation, treatise; *Littér* le D. de la méthode the Discourse on Method
3 *(langage)* speech; *Gram* parties du d. parts of speech; d. indirect/direct indirect *or* reported/direct speech; d. rapporté reported speech VOIR GRAMMAIRE A63; A78
4 *(paroles)* talk; tenir un d. à qn to address sb at length; se perdre en longs d. to talk endlessly; elle a *ou* tient un d. très clair she speaks very clearly; tous ces beaux d. ne nous avancent à rien all this talk isn't getting us anywhere

discourtois [diskurtwa] ADJ discourteous

discourtoisement [diskurtwazmɑ̃] ADV discourteously

discourtoisie [diskurtwazi] NF *Arch* discourtesy

discrédit [diskredi] NM discredit, loss of credit; être en d. auprès de qn to be in disfavour with sb; jeter le d. sur qn to bring discredit on sb

discréditer [diskredite] VT *(théorie etc)* to discredit
VPR se discréditer *(d'une idée, d'une théorie)* to become discredited (auprès *ou* aux yeux de qn in sb's eyes); *(d'une personne)* to discredit oneself (auprès *ou* aux yeux de qn with sb)

discret, -ète [diskrɛ, -ɛt] ADJ 1 *(plein de re-*

tenue) (*personne, comportement etc*) discreet; **sous pli d.** under plain cover; **tu sauras rester d.?** you'll keep it to yourself, won't you?; *Iron* **il m'énerve avec ses allusions discrètes** those subtle hints of his are getting on my nerves; **sois d., il ne faut pas qu'elle l'apprenne** don't go repeating this, she mustn't find out **2** (*modeste*) (*personne*) quiet, unobtrusive, unassuming; (*vêtements*) sober, simple, plain; (*apparence*) inconspicuous; (*endroit*) quiet, secluded; **une discrète touche de bleu** a discreet touch of blue **3** *Math* (*quantité*) discrete; *Phys* (*fonction*) discontinuous

discrètement [diskrɛtmã] ADV **1** (*avec retenue*) discreetly, with discretion; **il lui a parlé d.** he had a quiet word with him **2** (*modestement*) quietly, modestly, simply; **maquillé d.** discreetly made up

discrétion [diskresjɔ̃] NF **1** (*retenue*) discretion; **avoir de la d.** to be discreet; **d. assurée** discretion guaranteed; **la d. d'une intervention** the discreetness of an intervention; **user de qch avec d.** to use sth in moderation **2** (*sobriété*) **la d. avec laquelle elle se conduit** her unassuming behaviour; **s'habiller avec d.** to dress simply *or* plainly; **elle se maquille avec d.** she is always discreetly made up **3** she is always discreetly made up **3** **être à la d. de qn** to be in sb's hands; **pain à d.** unlimited bread, as much bread as one wants

discrétionnaire [diskresjɔnɛr] ADJ (*pouvoirs etc*) discretionary

discrètos [diskretɔs] ADV *Fam* on the quiet

discriminant [diskriminã] ADJ discriminating
     NM *Math* discriminant

discrimination [diskriminasjɔ̃] NF discrimination; **ils étaient victimes de d.** they were victims of discrimination, they were discriminated against; **d. raciale/sexuelle** racial/sexual discrimination; **sans d. de race ni de sexe** regardless of race or sex, without discrimination on the grounds of race or sex; **d. positive** positive discrimination, *Am* affirmative action

discriminatoire [diskriminatwar] ADJ discriminatory, discriminating

discriminer [diskrimine] VT *Littt* to discriminate, to distinguish

disculpation [diskylpasjɔ̃] NF exoneration; **sa d. n'a pas été facile à obtenir** it was not easy to clear him *or* to prove him innocent

disculper [diskylpe] VT **d. qn** to clear sb, to prove sb innocent, to exonerate sb (**de** of)
     VPR **se disculper** to clear oneself, to prove oneself innocent (**de** of)

discursif, -ive [diskyrsif, -iv] ADJ discursive

discussion [diskysjɔ̃] NF discussion; (*plus passionnée*) argument; (*émission*) discussion programme; **avoir une d.** to have a discussion/an argument (**sur, à propos de** about); **la question est en d.** the question is under discussion; **sans d. possible** indisputably; **il s'exécuta sans d.** he complied without arguing (the point); **pas de d., au travail!** don't argue, get to work!

discutable [diskytabl] ADJ debatable, questionable; **tu as agi d'une manière qui est tout à fait d.** your behaviour was altogether questionable

discutailler [diskytaje] VI *Fam Péj* (*chicaner*) to quibble

discuté [diskyte] ADJ (*question*) disputed; (*livre, sujet*) much discussed; **être très d.** to be hotly disputed *or* the subject of much discussion

discuter [diskyte] VT (*examiner*) to discuss, to debate; (*contester*) to question, to dispute; **d. un droit** to dispute a right; **d. un problème** to discuss a problem; **discutons la chose** let's

discuss it, let's talk it over; *Fam* **le coup** *ou* **le bout de gras** to have a natter *or* a chat; **prix à d.** negotiable
     VI **1** (*parler*) to discuss; (*débattre*) to debate; **d. avec qn sur qch** to debate sth with sb; **d. de politique** to discuss *or* talk politics, to argue about politics; **il faut qu'on en discute** we must discuss it; **d. du prix de qch** to haggle over the price of sth; **on ne peut pas d. avec toi** it's impossible to have a discussion with you; **on pourrait peut-être d. avant de se battre?** could we discuss it first before we start fighting? **2** (*protester*) to argue (**avec** with); **ne discutez pas** no arguing, don't argue; **il n'y a pas à d.** I don't want any arguments *or* arguing; **suis-moi sans d.** follow me without any arguments, follow me and don't argue; **on ne discute pas avec la loi** the law's the law
     VPR **se discuter** to be discussed *or* debated; **ça se discute** that's debatable

disert [dizɛr] ADJ *Littt* eloquent, fluent

disette [dizɛt] NF scarcity, *Fml* dearth; **d. d'eau** drought; **vivre dans la d.** to live in poverty

diseur, -euse [dizœr, -øz] N **1 d./diseuse de bonne aventure** fortune teller **2** (*qui déclame*) orator

disgrâce [disgrɑs] NF disfavour, disgrace; **encourir la d. de qn** to incur sb's displeasure; **tomber en d. (auprès de qn)** to fall into disfavour (with sb)

disgracié [disgrasje] ADJ out of favour, in disgrace

disgracier [disgrasje] VT (*impf, pr sub n. disgraciions, v. disgraciiez*) (*ministre*) to dismiss

disgracieux, -ieuse [disgrasjø, -jøz] ADJ (*personne, mouvement, geste*) awkward, ungraceful; (*visage etc*) ugly

> Il faut noter que l'adjectif anglais **disgraceful** est un faux ami. Il signifie **honteux, scandaleux**.

disjoindre [disʒwɛdr] (*conj like* **joindre**) VT to separate, to take apart; *Jur* **d. deux causes** to treat two cases separately
     VPR **se disjoindre** to come apart, to separate

disjoint [disʒwɛ̃] ADJ (*pièces*) separated; (*problèmes*) unconnected, separate

disjoncter [disʒɔ̃kte] *Élec* VT (*circuit*) to break
     VI to fuse; *Aut* to cut out; *Fig Fam* to crack up

disjoncteur [disʒɔ̃ktœr] NM *Élec* circuit breaker, cut-out

disjonctif, -ive [disʒɔ̃ktif, -iv] ADJ disjunctive SEE GRAMMAR B20

disjonction [disʒɔ̃ksjɔ̃] NF (*de tuyaux, lames de parquet*) separation

dislocation [dislɔkasjɔ̃] NF (*d'une articulation*) dislocation; (*d'une machine etc*) taking to pieces, dismantling; (*d'un empire, d'un État etc*) dismemberment; *Géol* fault; *Mil etc* (*des troupes etc*) dispersal, breaking up

disloqué [dislɔke] ADJ (*épaule, genou*) dislocated; (*machine*) dismantled; (*empire, État etc*) dismembered, broken up

disloquer [dislɔke] VT (*épaule, genou*) to dislocate; (*machine*) to take to pieces, to dismantle; (*troupes*) to break up, to disperse; (*empire, État*) to break up, to dismember
     VPR **se disloquer** (*d'un empire*) to break up, to fall to pieces; **son bras s'est disloqué** he's dislocated his arm

disparaître [disparɛtr] VI (*conj like* **paraître**) **1** (*s'en aller*) to disappear, to vanish; **elle a disparu sans laisser de traces** she has disappeared *or* vanished without trace; **la petite fille a disparu il y a une semaine** the little girl disappeared *or* went missing a week ago; *Fam* **disparais, je t'ai assez vu** clear off, I've had enough of you

2 (*devenir invisible*) to disappear, to vanish; **d. dans la foule** to disappear *or* vanish into the crowd; *Fam* **d. de la circulation** to vanish from *or* drop out of circulation; **d. aux regards** to vanish from sight, to disappear from view; *Cin, TV* **d. en fondu** to fade out
     3 (*mourir*) to die; **tous ses amis ont disparu** all his friends have died *or* are dead; *Naut* **disparu en mer** lost at sea; **faire d. qn** to get rid of sb
     4 (*finir*) (*d'un bouton*) to disappear, to vanish, to go away; (*d'une mode, d'une tradition*) to die out; **faire d. une tache/une difficulté** to get rid of *or* remove a stain/a difficulty; **faire d. la douleur** to make the pain disappear *or* go; **j'ai pris un cachet pour faire d. la douleur** I took a pill to relieve *or* get rid of the pain; **sa timidité disparaît peu à peu** his shyness is wearing off

disparate [disparat] ADJ (*différent*) dissimilar, *Fml* disparate; (*qui ne s'accorde pas*) ill-matched, ill-assorted; **couleurs disparates** clashing colours; **ils ont un mobilier très d.** no two pieces of their furniture are alike *or* the same

disparité [disparite] NF disparity

disparition [disparisjɔ̃] NF **1** (*départ, absence*) disappearance; **remarquer la d. de qch** to notice that sth has disappeared; **j'ai remarqué la d. de ma carte de crédit deux jours plus tard** I first missed my credit card two days later; **sa d. date de six mois** he disappeared *or* vanished six months ago, he has been missing for six months; *Cin, TV* **d. en fondu** fade **2** (*mort*) death; **depuis la d. de son mari** since the death of her husband, since her husband died; **la d. des dinosaures ne s'est pas faite en un jour** dinosaurs did not disappear *or* vanish *or* die out overnight

disparu, -ue [dispary] ADJ **1** *Mil* missing (in action); **être porté d.** to be reported missing; **marin d. en mer** sailor lost at sea **2** (*race, espèce etc*) extinct; (*monde, époque etc*) vanished, bygone **3** (*invisible*) **la cicatrice une fois disparue** once the scar has/had disappeared; **aussitôt le soleil d., elle rentra** she went home as soon as the sun had disappeared
     N **1** (*défunt*) deceased; **nos chers disparus** our dear departed **2** *Mil* missing soldier (*believed dead*), *Am* MIA (= *missing in action*)

dispatcher¹ [dispatʃœr] NM dispatcher

dispatcher² [dispatʃe] VT to dispatch

dispatching [dispatʃiŋ] NM dispatching; *Journ* assignment list

dispendieusement [dispɑ̃djøzmɑ̃] ADV *Littt* expensively

dispendieux, -ieuse [dispɑ̃djø, -jøz] ADJ *Littt* (*goûts, procédure etc*) expensive

dispensaire [dispɑ̃sɛr] NM free clinic, free health centre

dispensateur, -trice [dispɑ̃satœr, -tris] N (*de charité, justice etc*) dispenser

dispense [dispɑ̃s] NF **1** (*du service militaire etc*) exemption; *Rel* dispensation; **d. d'âge** age dispensation; **une d. d'âge peut être accordée dans les cas où ...** the age limit may be waived in cases where ... **2** (*certificat*) (certificate of) exemption

dispenser [dispɑ̃se] VT **1 d. qn de (faire) qch** to excuse *or* exempt sb from (doing) sth; **d. qn du service militaire** to exempt sb from military service; **dispensez-moi de ce voyage** spare me this journey; **se faire d. de sport** to be excused *or* let off sport, to get off sport; *Rel* **d. qn d'un vœu** to release sb from a vow; **je vous dispense de vos commentaires** you can keep your remarks to yourself **2** (*charité, faveurs etc*) to dispense, to distribute; *Méd* **d. des soins** to dispense care

VPR se dispenser se d. de (faire) qch to get out of (doing) sth; **on peut s'en d.** we can do without it; *Hum* **il se dispense toujours de dire bonjour** he never says hello; **c'est un élève qui peut se d. de travailler en français** he can afford not to work at his French

dispersal [dispɛʁsəl] NM *Aviat* apron

dispersant [dispɛʁsɑ̃] NM *Chimie* dispersant, dispersal agent

dispersé [dispɛʁse] ADJ *(feuilles, famille etc)* scattered, dispersed; *(travail etc)* lacking in order, disorganized

disperser [dispɛʁse] VT *(foule, famille)* to disperse, to scatter, to break up; *(feuilles)* to disperse, to scatter, to spread (far and wide); **d. une armée** to rout an army; *Fig* **d. son attention sur plusieurs choses** to divide one's attention among several things
VPR **se disperser** *(de nuages)* to disperse, to break up; *(de foule, de famille)* to disperse, to scatter, to break up; *Fig* **tu as tendance à trop te d.** you tend to spread yourself too thin(ly)

dispersion [dispɛʁsjɔ̃] NF **1** *(des gens, des feuilles)* scattering, dispersal; *(de la foule, des nuages)* dispersal, breaking up; *(de l'armée)* rout; *Fig* **la d. d'un esprit** an unfocused mind **2** *Opt (de la lumière)* dispersion, decomposition **3** *Suisse (peinture)* emulsion (paint)

disponibilité [dispɔnibilite] NF *(de personne, de sièges, de capital etc)* availability; **il a une grande d. d'esprit** he has a very receptive mind; *Mil* **la d.** the reserve; **mettre qn en d.** *Ind (en chômage)* to lay sb off; *Mil* to release sb temporarily from duty; **prendre une d.** to take a sabbatical, to take leave of absence; **demander une mise en d.** to ask for (a) leave of absence; *Com* **d. numérique** stock holding distribution; *Fin* **disponibilités** available funds, liquid assets; **disponibilités monétaires** money supply; **disponibilités du stock** items available in stock

disponible [dispɔnibl] ADJ available; *(actif)* liquid; **places disponibles** vacant *or* unoccupied seats; **il n'y avait plus un siège d.** there weren't any seats left, no seats were available; **êtes-vous d. ce soir?** are you free tonight?; *Mil* **officier d.** unattached officer, half-pay officer
NM **1** *Com* **marché du d.** spot market **2** *Fin* **le d.** liquid assets **3** *Mil* reservist

dispos [dispo] ADJ fit and well, in good form; **frais et d.** raring to go, bright-eyed and bushy-tailed; **esprit d.** alert mind; **je n'ai pas l'esprit d. aujourd'hui** I don't feel very alert today

disposé [dispoze] ADJ **1** *(personne)* **être bien/mal d.** to be in a good/bad mood; **être bien d. pour** *ou* **envers qn** to be well disposed towards sb; **être** *ou* **se sentir d. à faire qch** to feel disposed *or* willing *or* in the mood to do sth; **je suis tout d. à pardonner** I am quite willing *or* fully prepared to forgive **2** *(arrangé)* arranged, set out; **fleurs disposées avec goût** tastefully arranged flowers

disposer [dispoze] VT **1** *(objets)* to set out, to arrange; *(table)* to lay, to set; **il faudra d. le salon autrement** the living room will have to be rearranged; **comment vas-tu d. les invités?** what are the seating arrangements for the guests? **2 d. qn à (faire) qch** to dispose *or* incline sb to (do) sth
VI **1 d. de qn/qch** to have sb/sth at one's disposal; **disposez de moi** I am at your service; **de combien de temps disposons-nous?** how much time do we have?; **les renseignements dont je dispose** the information at my disposal; **vous pouvez en d.** you may use it; **d. de ses biens en faveur de qn** to dispose of *or* make over one's property to sb; **le droit des peuples à d. d'eux-mêmes** the right of peo-

ple to self-determination **2** *Fml (partir)* **vous pouvez d.** that will be all, you may go **3** *(décider) Prov* **l'homme propose, Dieu dispose** man proposes, God disposes
VPR **se disposer se d. à faire qch** to get ready to do sth; **se d. à partir** to get ready to leave

---

Il faut noter que le verbe anglais **to dispose of** est un faux ami. Il signifie **se débarrasser de**.

---

dispositif [dispozitif] NM **1** *Tech* device; **d. de commande/de manœuvre** driving/controlling gear *or* mechanism; **d. de sûreté** safety device **2** *(ensemble de moyens)* system, machinery; *Mil* plan of action; *(des troupes dans une bataille etc)* disposition, deployment; **d. d'attaque** attack force; **d. de défense** defence system; **un important d. policier sera mis en place** there will be a large police presence; **il s'agit d'un d. gouvernemental pour favoriser l'emploi des jeunes** it's a government plan to stimulate youth employment
▸▸*Ordinat* **d. d'alimentation** power unit; *(pour papier)* sheet feed; **d. d'alimentation feuille à feuille** *(d'une imprimante)* cut sheet feed, stacker; **d. d'alimentation papier** *(d'une imprimante)* sheet feed, paper feed; *Aut* **d. antidémarrage** engine immobilizer; *Aut* **d. d'avance centrifuge** centrifugal advance mechanism; *TV etc* **d. de balayage** scanner; *TV etc* **d. de colorisation** colourizer; **d. de coupure** cut-out (device); **d. d'entraînement à traction** *(d'une imprimante)* tractor feed; *Ordinat* **d. externe** external device; *Ordinat* **d. de pointage à boule** trackball; *Aut* **d. de préchauffage** pre-heater; *Tél* **d. de redirection d'appel** call-forwarding device; *Ordinat* **d. de sortie** output device; *Ordinat* **d. de stockage** storage device; *Aut* **d. de verrouillage 'sécurité enfant'** child lock; *Ordinat* **d. de visualisation** display unit

disposition [dispozisjɔ̃] NF **1** *(arrangement) (d'une maison, d'un jardin etc)* layout; **réfléchir à la d. des sièges** to think about the seating plan; **d. du terrain** lie of the land; **comment est la d. des lieux?** what's the layout of the place?; *Ordinat* **d. de texte/de clavier** text/keyboard layout
2 *(disponibilité)* disposal; **avoir la libre d. de son bien** to be free to dispose of one's property; **libre d. de soi-même** self-determination; **d. fiscale** tax provision; *Fin* **d. à vue** sight clause; **avoir qch à sa d.** to have sth at one's disposal; **mettre qch à la d. de qn** to put *or* place sth at sb's disposal, to make sth available to sb; **je suis à votre (entière) d.** I am at your disposal *or* (entirely) at your service
3 *(humeur)* **être dans de bonnes/mauvaises dispositions** to be in a good/bad mood; **être dans de bonnes dispositions à l'égard de qn** to be favourably disposed towards sb; **choisis un jour où il sera dans les meilleures dispositions pour t'écouter/te voir** choose a day when he'll be most likely to give you a favourable hearing/see you; **dans quelles dispositions est-il?** what kind of mood is he in?; **être en bonne d. pour faire qch** to be disposed *or* inclined *or* in the mood to do sth
4 *(dons)* **avoir des dispositions pour qch** to have a natural ability *or* an aptitude for sth; **dispositions naturelles pour la musique** aptitude *or* natural bent for music; **cet enfant a des dispositions** he is a (naturally) gifted child
5 *(tendance)* tendency, predisposition; **avoir une d. au rhumatisme** to have a tendency *or* to be predisposed to rheumatism; **d. à pleurer souvent** tendency to cry a lot
6 dispositions *(préparatifs)* arrangements; **prendre des dispositions pour faire qch** to

make the necessary arrangements to do sth; **prends tes dispositions pour être libre ce jour-là** make arrangements *or* arrange to be free that day; **vous n'avez qu'à prendre vos dispositions** you'll just have to make arrangements
7 *Jur* **dispositions** *(d'un testament)* provisions, conditions; *(d'une loi)* clauses, provisions, conditions; **les dispositions contenues dans l'article 34** the provisions of article 34

disproportion [dispʁɔpɔʁsjɔ̃] NF lack of proportion, disproportion (**entre** between)

disproportionné [dispʁɔpɔʁsjɔne] ADJ out of proportion, disproportionate (**par rapport à, avec** to)

dispute [dispyt] NF **1** *(querelle)* dispute, quarrel, *Fml* altercation; **c'est un sujet de d. entre eux** it is a subject of dispute *or* bone of contention between them **2** *Arch (débat)* debate; **sujet en d.** subject under discussion

disputé [dispyte] ADJ **une question très disputée** a very controversial *or* hotly disputed matter; **un match très d.** a very hard-fought match; **ce poste sera très d.** there will be a lot of competition for the position; **c'est un héritage d. par tous les membres de la famille** the entire family is quarrelling over the inheritance

disputer [dispyte] VT **1** *(contester)* **d. qch à qn** to contend with sb for sth; *Fml* **je ne peux imaginer palais qui puisse le d. en splendeur à celui-ci** I cannot imagine a palace to rival this one in splendour **2** *Sport* **d. un match** to play a match; **d. une course** *(sur mille mètres)* to run a (thousand-metre) race; *Fig* **d. le terrain** to fight every inch of the way **3** *Fam* **d. qn** to tick *or* tell sb off; **il s'est fait d. par son père** he got ticked off *or* told off by his father, he got a ticking off *or* telling off from his father
VI **1** *(discuter)* to quarrel, to argue (**avec** with); **d. d'un sujet avec qn** to quarrel *or* argue with sb about *or* over a subject **2** *Fml (rivaliser)* **d. de zèle/d'élégance avec qn** to vie with sb in zeal/elegance
VPR **se disputer 1** *(se quereller)* to quarrel, to argue, to wrangle (**pour** over, about; **avec** with) **2** *(se battre pour)* to fight for; **deux chiens qui se disputent un os** two dogs fighting over a bone; **ils se disputent à qui aura le plus gros morceau** they are arguing about who should get the biggest piece **3** *(se jouer)* **le match se disputera à Wimbledon** the match will be played *or* will take place at Wimbledon; **la finale devrait se d. entre les USA et l'Australie** the final is expected to be between the USA and Australia

disquaire [diskɛʁ] N record dealer; **en vente chez tous les disquaires** on sale in all record shops

disqualification [diskalifikasjɔ̃] NF *Sport* disqualification

disqualifier [diskalifje] *(impf, pr sub n.* **disqualifiions, v. disqualifiiez)** VT **1** *Sport* to disqualify **2** *Litt (discréditer)* to discredit
VPR **se disqualifier** *Litt* to disgrace oneself

disque [disk] NM **1** disc, *Am* disk; *Rail* disc signal; *Aut* **frein à d.** disc brake; **appareil photo à disques** disc camera **2** *Mus* record, disc; **mettre un d.** to play a record; *Fig Fam* **changer de d.** to change the record *or* subject **3** *Ordinat* disk; **station de travail sans d.** diskless workstation **4** *Sport* discus; **lanceur de d.** discus thrower; **arriver deuxième au lancer de d.** to come second in the discus
▸▸*Ordinat* **d. amovible** removable disk; **d. audionumérique** compact disc; *Ordinat* **d. cible** target disk; **d. compact** compact disc, CD; **d. compact interactif** interactive CD, CD-I; **d. compact vidéo** video compact disc; *Ordinat* **d. de démarrage** boot disk; **d. de dé-**

monstration demo (record); *Ordinat* **d. de destination** destination disk; *Ordinat* **d. dur** hard disk; *Ordinat* **d. dur externe** external hard disk; *Aut* **d. d'embrayage** clutch plate *or* disc; *Ordinat* **d. fixe** fixed disk; *Anat* **d. intervertébral** (intervertebral) disc; **d. laser** laser disc; **d. magnétique** magnetic disk; *Ordinat* **d. magnéto-optique** optical disk, optomagnetic disk; **d. maître** master disk; **d. microsillon** long-playing record, LP; *Ordinat* **d. optique** optical disk; *Ordinat* **d. optique compact** CD-ROM; *Ordinat* **d. souple** floppy disk; *Ordinat* **d. source** source disk; *Admin*, *Aut* **d. de stationnement** parking disc; *Ordinat* **d. système** system disk; **d. vidéo** video-disc; **d. vidéo numérique** digital versatile disk, digital video disk; **d. en vinyle** vinyl disc

disquette [disket] NF *Ordinat* diskette, disk, *Fam* floppy disk; **sur d.** on diskette, *Fam* on floppy; **d. de copie** copy disk; **d. de démarrage** boot disk, start-up disk; **d. de démonstration,** *Fam* **d. démo** demo disk; **d. de destination** destination disk; **d. de diagnostic** diagnostic disk; **d. de distribution** master disk; **d. (à) double densité** double density disk; **d. haute densité** high-density disk; **d. d'installation** installation disk, installer; **d. magnétique** magnetic disk; **d. optique** optical disk, floptical disk; **d. d'origine** source disk; **d. programme** program disk; **d. (à) simple densité** single density disk; **d. source** source disk; **d. système** system disk, systems disk; **d. de travail** working disk, work disk; **d. vierge** blank unformatted disk

disruptif, -ive [disryptif, -iv] ADJ *(force, décharge électrique etc)* disruptive

dissection [disɛksjɔ̃] NF *(d'un corps, d'une œuvre littéraire etc)* dissection

dissemblable [disɑ̃blabl] ADJ dissimilar, unlike, **d. à qch** unlike sth, different from *or Am* than sth

dissemblance [disɑ̃blɑ̃s] NF dissimilarity, difference (**entre** between)

dissémination [diseminasjɔ̃] NF *(de graines, de peuple, d'amis etc)* scattering; *(de germes)* spreading; *Mil (de troupes)* deployment; *(d'idées)* spread, dissemination; *(de nouvelles)* spread; **la d. de notre famille date de deux siècles** our family has been scattered for two centuries; **depuis la d. de mon groupe d'amis** since my group of friends scattered *or* broke up; **le territoire est si étendu que cela favorise la d. des entreprises** the vastness of the area means that companies tend to be spread rather thinly

disséminer [disemine] VT *(graines, groupe d'amis, peuple etc)* to scatter; *(germes)* to spread; *Mil (troupes)* to deploy; *(idées)* to spread, to disseminate; *(nouvelles)* to spread; **les écoles sont très disséminées** the schools are very thin on the ground

VPR **se disséminer** *(de personnes)* to scatter; *(de germes, idées)* to spread

dissension [disɑ̃sjɔ̃] NF dissension, discord

dissentiment [disɑ̃timɑ̃] NM disagreement

disséquer [diseke] VT (je **dissèque;** je **disséquerai**) *(cadavre, œuvre littéraire etc)* to dissect

dissert [disert] NF *Fam (abrév* **dissertation)** essay

dissertation [disertasjɔ̃] NF **1** *Scol* essay **2** *Vieilli (étude)* dissertation (**sur** (up)on)

disserter [diserte] VI **1 d. sur un sujet** to discourse on a subject **2** *Péj (parler beaucoup)* to talk at length, *Fam* to hold forth; **d. pendant des heures** to hold forth for hours

dissidence [disidɑ̃s] NF *Rel, Pol* dissidence, dissent; **la d.** *(dissidents)* the dissidents, the dissident movement

dissident, -ente [disidɑ̃, -ɑ̃t] ADJ *Pol* dissident; *Rel* dissenting

N *Pol* dissident; *Rel* dissenter, nonconformist

dissimilation [disimilasjɔ̃] NF *Ling* dissimilation

dissimilitude [disimilityd] NF dissimilarity

dissimulateur, -trice [disimylatœr, -tris] ADJ dissembling

N dissembler, deceiver

dissimulation [disimylasjɔ̃] NF **1** *(hypocrisie)* dissembling, deceit; **agir avec d.** to act in an underhand way **2** *(de la vérité, de ses sentiments)* concealment; *(d'une faute)* covering up; *Jur* **d. d'actif** (fraudulent) concealment of assets

dissimulé [disimyle] ADJ **1** *(caché) (sentiments, défauts, rides etc)* hidden, unconcealed; **avec un plaisir non d.** with unconcealed delight **2** *(secret) (homme, caractère)* secretive

dissimuler [disimyle] VT *(sentiments, vérité)* to hide, to conceal; *(faute)* to cover up; **d. qch à qn** to hide sth *or* keep sth (back) from sb; **il se dissimule la vérité** he's deceiving himself; **le rideau dissimule le siège des W.-C.** the curtain screens off the lavatory; **d. ses revenus** to conceal one's income; **je ne (vous) dissimule pas que je souhaite partir** I cannot hide the fact that I want to leave

VPR **se dissimuler** to be hidden, to hide; **sa jalousie ne peut se d.** he cannot hide his jealousy; **parmi tant de qualités se dissimule un défaut** a weakness lies hidden *or* lurks among so many qualities

dissipateur, -trice [disipatœr, -tris] N spendthrift, squanderer, waster

ADJ *(personne)* spendthrift; *(gestion)* wasteful

dissipation [disipasjɔ̃] NF **1** *(d'argent)* squandering, wasting; *(de temps, d'énergie)* wasting; *(de nuages)* dispersal; *(de craintes, soupçons)* dispelling; *(de malentendu)* clearing up; **après d. des brouillards matinaux** after the morning mist lifts/lifted *or* clears/cleared; **d. calorique** heat dissipation **2** *(débauche)* dissipation, dissolute living; **une vie de d.** a dissolute life, a life of dissipation **3** *(à l'école)* inattentiveness, lack of attention

dissipé [disipe] ADJ **1** *(débauché)* dissipated, dissolute; **mener une vie dissipée** to lead a riotous life **2** *Scol (élève)* inattentive

dissiper [disipe] VT **1** *(argent)* to squander, to waste; *(temps, énergie)* to waste; *(nuages)* to disperse, to scatter, to dispel; *(brouillard)* to disperse, to clear away, to dispel; *(malentendu)* to clear up; *(craintes, soupçons)* to dispel **2** *(distraire)* to distract; **il se laisse facilement d.** he is easily distracted

VPR **se dissiper 1** *(de soupçons, malentendu)* to vanish, to disappear; **le brouillard se dissipe** the fog is lifting *or* clearing (away); **ses doutes se sont dissipés** his doubts faded **2** *(se laisser distraire) (à l'école etc)* to be inattentive; **il dissipe vite** his attention soon wanders

dissociable [disɔsjabl] ADJ separable

dissociation [disɔsjasjɔ̃] NF separation; *Chimie* decomposition, dissociation; **la d. nécessaire entre la vie privée et la vie professionnelle** the need to keep one's private life separate from one's work

dissocier [disɔsje] VT *(idées etc)* to separate; *Chimie (composé)* to dissociate

VPR **se dissocier se d. d'un groupe** to dissociate oneself from a group

dissolu [disɔly] ADJ *(personne, vie)* dissolute

dissolubilité [disɔlybilite] NF dissolubility

dissoluble [disɔlybl] ADJ **1** *Pol (assemblée etc)* which can be dissolved, dissoluble **2** *Arch (substance)* soluble

dissolution [disɔlysjɔ̃] NF **1** *(d'un parlement, d'un mariage)* dissolution; *(d'un contrat)* dissolution, termination **2** *Chimie (d'une substance dans un liquide)* dissolving; *(colle)* rubber solution **3** *(d'un corps)* decomposition; *(d'une matière)* decomposition, breakdown **4** *Litt (débauche)* dissoluteness, licentiousness, profligacy

dissolvant [disɔlvɑ̃] ADJ **1** *(qui dissout)* solvent **2** *Vieilli (climat)* debilitating; *(doctrine)* corrupt

NM solvent; *(pour ongles)* nail varnish remover

dissonance [disɔnɑ̃s] NF *Mus* discord; *Fig* clash

dissonant [disɔnɑ̃] ADJ *Mus* dissonant, discordant; *Fig* clashing

dissoudre [disudr] *(prp* **dissolvant;** *pp* **dissous,** *f* **dissoute;** *pr ind* **je dissous, il dissout,** *n.* **dissolvons;** *impf* **je dissolvais;** *p hist & p sub are lacking; fu* **je dissoudrai)** VT **1** *(substance)* to dissolve **2** *(parlement, mariage)* to dissolve; *(association)* to dissolve, to break (up); *(entreprise)* to wind up

VPR **se dissoudre** to dissolve; **se d. dans l'eau** to dissolve in water; *Fig* **colère qui se dissout en larmes** anger that dissolves into tears

dissuader [disɥade] VT **d. qn de faire qch** to dissuade sb from doing sth, to talk sb out of doing sth; **d. qn de partir** to persuade sb not to leave, to dissuade sb from leaving, to talk sb out of leaving

dissuasif, -ive [disɥazif, -iv] ADJ dissuasive; **ils pratiquent vraiment des prix dissuasifs** their prices are enough to put you off

dissuasion [disɥazjɔ̃] NF dissuasion (**de** from); *Mktg* demarketing; **d. nucléaire** nuclear deterrence; *Mil, Pol* **force de d.** deterrent

dissyllabe [disilab] ADJ di(s)syllabic

NM di(s)syllable

dissyllabique [disilabik] ADJ di(s)syllabic

dissymétrie [disimetri] NF asymmetry

dissymétrique [disimetrik] ADJ asymmetric(al)

distance [distɑ̃s] NF SEE GRAMMAR 859 distance; **une faible d.** a short way *or* distance; **il y a une d. de cinq km entre ces deux points** there is a distance of five km between these two points, these two points are five km apart; **on ne voyait rien à cette d.** you couldn't see anything at that distance; **suivre qn à d./à peu de d.** to follow sb at a distance/at a short distance; **à quelle d. sommes-nous de la ville?** how far are we from the town?; **à une courte d.** a short distance away (**de** from), within easy reach (**de** of); **c'est à une grande d.** it's a long way away *or* off (**de** from); *Mil etc* **à petite** *ou* **faible d.** at short range; *Ordinat etc* **à d.** remote; *Tech* **commande à d.** remote control; **à d.** *(juger, influencer qn)* at *or* from a distance; **tenir qn à d.** to keep sb at a distance; **il me tient à d. de tous les projets intéressants** he keeps me away from all the interesting projects; **conserver** *ou* **garder ses distances, se tenir à d.** to keep at a distance, to remain aloof; *Fig* **il conserve** *ou* **garde ses distances par rapport à la gauche/aux intellectuels/à sa famille** he keeps at a distance *or* holds himself aloof from the left/intellectuals/his family; **se tenir à une d. respectueuse** to remain at a respectful distance; **je vous prie de vous tenir à une d. respectueuse de ma fille** please keep away from my daughter; **de d. en d.** at intervals; **prendre ses distances** *Mil* to dress; *Gym* to space out; *Fig* **prendre de la d.** to stand back (**par rapport à** from); *Sp, Fig* **tenir la d.** to go the distance, to stay *or* last the course

▶▶ *Aut* **d. d'arrêt** stopping distance; *Opt* **d.**

focale focal distance, focal length; **d. de freinage** braking distance; *Phot* **d. hyperfocale** hyperfocal distance; *Phot* **d. de mise au point minimale** minimum focusing distance, MFD; *Aut* **d. de sécurité** thinking distance; **d. tarifaire** *(dans un taxi)* chargeable distance

distancement [distãsmã] NM *(de cheval)* disqualification

distancer [distãse] VT (**je distançai(s)**; **n. distançons**) **1** *Sp, Fig (devancer)* to outdistance, to outrun, to outstrip; **se laisser d.** to drop away, to fall or lag behind; **il se laisse d. par les autres** he is letting the others outdistance him or pull ahead; **le parti socialiste distance la droite de deux points** the socialists are two points ahead of the conservatives; **ce périodique distance tous les autres par sa qualité** this periodical surpasses all the others in quality **2** *(disqualifier) (cheval)* to disqualify

distanciation [distãsjasjõ] NF detachment; *Théâtre* **l'effet de d.** the alienation effect

distancier (se) [sədistãsje] VPR **se d. de qn/qch** to distance oneself from sb/sth

distant [distã] ADJ **1** *(éloigné)* distant; *(PC, modem)* remote; **nos deux maisons sont distantes d'un kilomètre** l'une de l'autre our two houses are a kilometre apart **2** *Fig (froid)* distant, standoffish, aloof; **elle est très distante avec moi** she's being very distant towards me

distendre [distãdr] VT *(estomac)* to distend; *(muscle)* to strain, to pull; *(corde, fil etc)* to stretch to breaking point; *Fig* **le temps a distendu notre amitié** we've drifted apart with time
▪ VPR **se distendre** *(se relâcher) (d'une corde, d'un élastique, d'un vêtement, de la peau)* to stretch; *(de l'estomac)* to become distended, to swell; **il s'est distendu un muscle** he has pulled or strained a muscle; *Fig* **notre relation se distend** we're drifting apart

distension [distãsjõ] NF *(de l'estomac)* distension; *(d'un muscle)* straining, pulling; *(d'une corde, d'un fil etc)* slackening, loosening; *(de la peau, d'un élastique)* stretching

distillat [distila] NM *Chimie* distillate

distillateur [distilatœr] NM distiller

distillation [distilasjõ] NF *(du whisky)*, *Pétr* distillation, distilling; *Pétr* **d. fractionnée** fractional distillation

distiller [distile] VT **1** *(alcool, pétrole etc)* to distil, *Am* to distill; *Litt (ses pensées)* to refine; **eau distillée** distilled water **2** *(poison)* to distil, to exude; *Fig (colère, ennui etc)* to exude
▪ VI *Chimie* to distil, to exude (**de** from)

distillerie [distilri] NF *(lieu)* distillery; *(procédé)* distilling

distinct [distẽ(kt)] ADJ **1** *(séparé)* distinct, separate; **une organisation distincte de la nôtre** an organization that is distinct from ours, a different organization from ours; **mon poste est d. du sien en cela que je ...** my job differs from his in that I ... **2** *(clair) (silhouette, voix etc)* distinct, clear

distinctement [distẽktəmã] ADV distinctly, clearly

distinctif, -ive [distẽktif, -iv] ADJ *(signe, trait etc)* distinctive, characteristic, distinguishing

distinction [distẽksjõ] NF **1** *(différence)* distinction; **faire une d. entre deux choses** to make a distinction or differentiate or distinguish between two things; **sans d.** without distinction, indiscriminately; **sans d. de race ou de couleur** irrespective or regardless of race or colour; **d. sociale** social or class distinction **2** *(dignité)* distinction, honour, *Am* honor; *(décoration)* decoration **3** *(éminence)*

distinction, eminence; **un personnage de haute d.** a highly distinguished person **4** *(élégance)* air of distinction, elegance; **avoir de la d.** to be distinguished

distinguable [distẽgabl] ADJ distinguishable

distingué [distẽge] ADJ **1** *(remarqué) (écrivain, politicien etc)* distinguished, eminent, noted **2** *(élégant) (personne, maintien)* distinguished; *(goût)* refined; *(vêtement)* smart; **avoir un air d.** to look distinguished **3** **je vous prie d'agréer l'expression de mes sentiments distingués** *(dans une lettre)* Yours sincerely

distinguer [distẽge] VT **1** *(particulariser)* to distinguish, to mark, to characterize; **sa mise soignée le distinguait de la foule** his impeccable appearance made him stand out from or set him apart from the crowd **2** *(pour honorer)* to honour, *Am* to honor; **il a été distingué pour son premier roman** he received an award for his first novel **3** *(différencier)* to distinguish; **il a appris à d. les champignons** he has learnt how to tell the various kinds of mushroom apart or to distinguish between the various kinds of mushroom; **d. qch de qch** *ou* **d'avec qch** to distinguish or tell sth from sth; **on peut à peine les d. l'un de l'autre** you can hardly tell them apart; **à quoi les distingues-tu?** how do you tell them apart? **4** *(discerner)* to discern, to perceive; **je ne peux pas d. ses traits** I cannot make out his features; **je l'ai distinguée dans la foule** I spotted her in the crowd; **d. une nuance d'amertume dans la voix de qn** to detect a trace of bitterness in sb's voice
▪ VPR **se distinguer 1** *(s'illustrer)* to distinguish oneself (**par** by); **il s'est surtout distingué par ses articles en neurobiologie** he was particularly noted for his articles on neurobiology; **on ne peut vraiment pas dire qu'il se distingue par son intelligence** he hardly stands out as being very intelligent; **il ne se distingue ni par son physique ni par ses qualités intellectuelles** neither his physical nor his intellectual qualities are anything out of the ordinary **2** *(se différencier) (dans une foule etc)* to be noticeable or conspicuous, to stand out; **se d. des autres** to be distinguishable from others (**par** by); **il se distingue de son frère par son grand nez** you can tell him from his brother by his big nose; **leur maison se distingue des autres à cause de ses volets bleus** their house stands out from the others because of its blue shutters; **comment la reine se distingue-t-elle des autres abeilles?** in what way does the queen differ from the other bees? **3** *(être perçu)* **au loin se distinguait la côte** the coastline could be seen in the distance

distinguo [distẽgo] NM difference; **il y a un d. à faire entre l'élégance et le raffinement** elegance and refinement are not quite the same thing or are not one and the same; **faire des distinguos entre les mots** to bring out the shades of meaning between words

distique [distik] NM **1** *(vers français)* couplet **2** *Antiq* distich

distordre [distordr] VT *(traits, bouche)* to distort

distorsion [distorsjõ] NF *(d'un visage, d'une image optique, d'une impulsion électrique etc)* distortion; *(entre deux facteurs, deux salaires)* imbalance; *Radio* **d. de phase** phase distortion; *Radio etc* **d. de crête** peak distortion; *Radio etc* **d. de fréquence** frequency distortion; *Radio etc* **d. harmonique** harmonic distortion; *TV etc* **d. de l'image** image distortion; *TV* **d. géométrique** geometric distortion

distraction [distraksjõ] NF **1** *(inattention)*

absentmindedness, lack of attention, abstraction; **par d.** inadvertently, absentmindedly; **avoir des moments de d.** to have moments of absentmindedness; **c'est une d. que nous ne pouvons te pardonner** we cannot forgive such absentmindedness on your part **2** *(loisir)* amusement, recreation; **distractions** entertainment; **ce bled manque de d.** there's nothing to do around here; **la lecture et le cinéma sont mes distractions préférées** reading and going to the cinema are my favourite forms of recreation or what I like doing best in my spare time; **depuis que ses enfants sont partis, elle n'a plus aucune d.** she's got nothing to occupy her mind now that her children have left home; **distractions en vol** in-flight entertainment

distraire [distrer] *(conj like traire)* VT **1** *(l'attention de qn)* to distract, to divert; **d. qn de ses travaux** to distract sb from his/her work **2** *(divertir)* to divert, to entertain, to amuse; **j'aime bien que tu viennes me voir, ça me distrait** I like you to visit me, it gives me something else to think about
▪ VPR **se distraire** to amuse oneself; **elle a besoin de se d.** she needs to relax a bit or to enjoy herself

distrait [distre] ADJ absentminded; **air d.** absentminded or abstracted or distracted look; **d'une oreille distraite** with only half an ear; **vous êtes d.** you're not paying attention; **élève d.** inattentive pupil

> Il faut noter que l'adjectif anglais **distracted** est un faux ami. Il signifie **préoccupé**.

distraitement [distretmã] ADV absentmindedly, abstractedly

distrayant [distrejã] ADJ *(livre, spectacle)* diverting, entertaining

distribanque [distribãk] NF cash dispenser

distribuer [distribµe] VT **1** *(donner) (prix, bonbons etc)* to distribute, to hand out; *(provisions, vivres etc)* to distribute, to issue; *(ordres)* to hand out, to give out; *(cartes)* to deal; *(du facteur)* to deliver; **il a commencé à d. des coups** he started to lash out with his fists; **d. des sourires à tout le monde** to bestow smiles on everybody **2** *(répartir)* **d. les fleurs en plusieurs classes** to classify flowers; *Cin, Théâtre* **d. les rôles** to cast the parts (in a/the play), to cast a/the play; **d. un dividende** to pay a dividend; **appartement bien/mal distribué** well/badly laid out flat; **d. son temps de la façon la plus logique** to allocate or apportion one's time in the most logical fashion possible; **conduites qui distribuent l'eau dans la ville** pipes that supply water to the city; **expliquez de quelle manière le sang est distribué dans notre corps** explain how blood circulates through our body **3** *(commercialiser) (produit, film, livres etc)* to distribute

distributaire [distribµter] N *Jur* distributee

distributeur, -trice [distribµtœr, -tris] N *Com* distributor, dealer
▪ NM **1** *Cin* (film) distributor **2** *Tech, Aut* distributor
▸ ▪ **d. agréé** authorized dealer, authorized distributor; **d. automatique** automatic vending machine, slot machine; **d. (automatique) de billets** cashpoint, *Am* ATM; *Rail etc* ticket machine; **d. (automatique) de boissons** drinks machine, drinks dispenser, drinks vending machine; **d. automatique de titres de transport** automatic ticket dispenser; **d. de cigarettes** cigarette machine; *Élec* **d. de courant** distributor; **d. d'engrais** fertilizer spreader; **d. de presse** press distributor; *Tech* **d. de vapeur** steam distributor or regulator, steam valve

distributif, -ive [distribytif, -iv] ADJ *Gram (terme, pronom etc)* distributive

distribution [distribysjɔ̃] NF **1** *(don)* distribution; *(de fonctions, de tâches etc)* allocation, allotment; *(de rations, vivres)* issue; *(de lettres, marchandises)* delivery; *Scol* **d. des prix** prizegiving, speech day; **il va y avoir une d. gratuite de saucissons au rayon charcuterie** sausages will be given away at the meat counter **2** *(répartition) (d'une maison, d'un appartement)* layout; *Aut* distribution; *Bot* **d. des plantes** classification of plants; *Écon* **d. des richesses** distribution of wealth; *Théâtre* **d. des rôles** *(choix)* casting; *(liste)* cast; **une brillante d.** an all-star cast; *Théâtre, Cin* **d. par ordre d'entrée en scène** characters *or* cast in order of appearance; **d. des eaux** water supply; **d. d'une maladie selon les classes d'âge** incidence of a disease by age group; **d. d'un bénéfice** distribution of profits; **d. de dividende** payment of a/the dividend; **d. par câble** cable distribution **3** *Com* distribution; **réseau de d.** distribution network; **droits de d.** distribution rights; **grande d.** large-scale distribution; **d. à flux tendus** just-in-time distribution; **d. de masse** mass distribution; **d. exclusive** exclusive distribution; **d. numérique** stock holding distribution

distributionnel, -elle [distribysjɔnɛl] ADJ *Ling (analyse, linguistique)* distributive

distributivement [distribytivmã] ADV distributively

distributivité [distribytivite] NF *Math* distributive law

district [distrikt] NM district, region

dit [di] ADJ **1** *(décidé)* settled, fixed; **à l'heure dite** *(à l'heure convenue)* at the appointed *or* agreed time; *(à l'heure fixée)* at the time indicated; **au jour d.** on the appointed *or* agreed day **2** *(appelé)* called; **la zone dite tempérée** the temperate zone as it is called ▪ NM *Littér* traditional story *(usually in verse)*; **le d. des trois larrons** the story of the three thieves

dithyrambe [ditirãb] NM *(panégyrique)* eulogy; *Littér* dithyramb; **se lancer dans un d. sur qch** to go into raptures about sth

dithyrambique [ditirãbik] ADJ *(mots etc)* eulogistic; *Littér* dithyrambic

dito [dito] ADV ditto

diurèse [djyrez] NF *Méd* diuresis

diurétique [djyretik] ADJ, NM *Méd* diuretic

diurne [djyrn] ADJ *Bot, Zool* diurnal

diva [diva] NF **1** *Mus* diva **2** *(célébrité)* star

divagation [divagasjɔ̃] NF **1** *(propos)* divagations **d'un fou** ravings *or* ramblings of a madman **2** *(de rivière)* shifting from its course; *Jur (du bétail etc)* straying

divaguer [divage] VI **1** *(dans un discours)* to digress, to stray from the point; **malade qui divague** patient whose mind is wandering *or* who is rambling; **vous divaguez!** you're raving! **2** *(de rivière)* to shift its course; *Jur (de bétail etc)* to stray

divan [divã] NM **1** *(meuble)* divan, couch; **d.-lit** divan (bed) **2** *Hist* divan

divergence [divɛrʒãs] NF *(de lignes, de rayons etc)* divergence; *(d'opinions)* difference

divergent [divɛrʒã] ADJ *(lignes)* divergent; *(opinions)* differing, different

diverger [divɛrʒe] VI *(il divergea(it)*; n. **divergeons)** *(de lignes, de rayons)* to diverge *(de* from); *(d'opinion)* to differ, to diverge *(de* from); **nos opinions divergent sur certains points** our opinions differ on certain points

divers [divɛr] ADJ **1** *(différent)* different, varied; *(rubrique)* miscellaneous; **le dessert consistait en fruits d.** there was a variety of fruit for dessert, there were various kinds of

---

fruit for dessert; **à des heures diverses** at different times; **ils ont eu des fortunes diverses** they had varying fortunes; **des opinions très diverses** very varied opinions, a wide range of opinions; **une clientèle très diverse** a wide clientele, a wide range of customers; **frais d.** sundry expenses, sundries; *Journ* **faits d.** news items; **un fait d.** a minor incident **2** *(always preceding the noun)* *(plusieurs)* various, a number of **3** *Arch (nature etc)* changing, varying

diversement [divɛrsəmã] ADV in various *or* different ways; **les participants ont d. compris la question** the contestants understood the question in different ways; **mes élèves ont d. réussi l'examen** my pupils had varying degrees of success in the exam

diversification [divɛrsifikasjɔ̃] NF diversification; *Bourse* **d. de portefeuille** portfolio diversification

diversifier [divɛrsifje] *(impf, pr sub n. diversifiions, v. diversifiiez)* VT *(économie, cultures, produits, placements)* to diversify; *(activités, intérêts, couleurs etc)* to vary ▪ VPR **se diversifier** *(de compagnie)* to diversify

diversion [divɛrsjɔ̃] NF diversion; *(changement)* change, distraction; **faire d.** to create a diversion; **faire d. à la tristesse de qn** to cheer sb up; **cela fera une d. à tes ennuis** it will take your mind off your troubles

diversité [divɛrsite] NF *(variété)* variety, diversity; *(différence)* difference; **une grande d. de races/de milieux sociaux** a wide variety of races/classes; **étant donné la d. de leurs intérêts** given that they have such different *or* varying interests; **j'admire la d. de ses talents** I admire the variety of talents that he has; **d. biologique** biological diversity, biodiversity

divertir [divɛrtir] VT **1** *(amuser)* to entertain, to amuse **2** *Vieilli (coup etc)* to divert, to ward off; *(personne) (d'un projet, d'une intention etc)* to turn (away); *(attention)* to divert; *(somme d'argent)* to misappropriate ▪ VPR **se divertir** to enjoy oneself; **se d. de la stupidité/de la balourdise de qn** to laugh at sb's stupidity/clumsiness; **se d. l'esprit** to amuse *or* entertain oneself

divertissant [divɛrtisã] ADJ amusing, entertaining

divertissement [divɛrtismã] NM **1** *(amusement)* entertainment, amusement, diversion; **on manque de d. dans ce bled** there's nothing to do in this place; **il faut trouver des divertissements pour les enfants** we have to find something to amuse the children *or* for the children to do **2** *Mus* divertimento **3** *Jur* **d. de fonds** misappropriation of funds

dividende [dividãd] NM *Math, Fin* dividend; **d. anticipé** advance dividend; **d. brut** gross dividend; **d. cumulatif** cumulative dividend; **d. d'action** share dividend; **d. définitif** final dividend; **d. en espèces** cash dividend; **d. final** final dividend; **d. majoré** grossed-up dividend; **d. net** net dividend; **dividendes accrus** accrued dividends; **sans d.** ex dividend, *Am* dividend off

divin [divɛ̃] ADJ *(volonté etc)* divine; *Fam (musique, climat etc)* heavenly; **le d. Enfant** [divinãfã] the Holy Child ▪ NM **le d.** the divine

divinateur, -trice [divinatœr, -tris] N *Arch* diviner, soothsayer ▪ ADJ *(don, pouvoir etc)* of prophecy

divination [divinasjɔ̃] NF **1** *(occultisme)* divination, soothsaying; **l'astrologie et autres méthodes de d.** astrology and other methods of telling the future **2** *(intuition)* intuition; **faire preuve d'un peu de d.** to do a bit of guesswork

---

divinatoire [divinatwar] ADJ *(science, art, don)* of divination; **baguette d.** divining rod, dowsing rod

divinement [divinmã] ADV divinely

divinisation [divinizasjɔ̃] NF deification

diviniser [divinize] VT to deify

divinité [divinite] NF **1** *(nature de Dieu)* divinity, divine nature; *(du Christ)* godhead **2** *(dieu)* deity, god, divinity, f goddess

diviser [divize] VT **1** *(partager)* to divide; *(travail, gains, héritage)* to divide, to share out *(entre* among); **divise le gâteau en trois** divide the cake in *or* into three; **ce pays est divisé en plusieurs provinces** the country is divided into several provinces; **la semaine est divisée en jours** the week is divided *or* split up into days; **d. une question en plusieurs points** to break down a question into several points; *Math* **d. un nombre par un autre** to divide one number by another **2** *(opposer)* to divide; **les questions déontologiques divisent les scientifiques** scientists are divided on questions of ethics; **l'opinion est divisée au sujet de cette affaire** opinion on the matter is divided; **d. pour (mieux) régner** divide and rule **3** *Arch (délimiter)* les Pyrénées divisent la France d'avec l'Espagne the Pyrenees divide *or* separate France from Spain ▪ VPR **se diviser** to divide *(en* into); **l'examen se divise en trois parties** the examination is divided into three parts; **l'équipe s'est divisée en deux** the team divided itself *or* split up into two groups; **le chemin se divise en deux** the road divides *or* forks

diviseur [divizœr] NM **1** *Math* divisor; **plus grand commun d.** highest common factor; **nombre/fraction d.** divisor number/fraction **2** *Tech* divider; *Élec* **d. de courant** current divider

divisibilité [divizibilite] NF divisibility

divisible [divizibl] ADJ divisible

division [divizjɔ̃] NF **1** *(d'un tout en parties)*, *Math* division *(en* into); **j'ai des divisions à faire** I've got some division to do; **je déteste les divisions** *ou* **faire des divisions** I hate division; **d. du marché** market division SEE GRAMMAR A77; B59 **2** *(partie) (d'un tout)* part, portion, section; *Admin* division, department, branch; *Scol* group, section; *Mil, Naut* division; **les divisions d'un livre** the sections of a book; **d. de formation professionnelle** training division; **d. des exportations** export division; **d. internationale** international division **3** *(désaccord)* discord, dissension, disagreement; **semer la d. au sein d'une famille** to cause dissent in a family; **depuis le dernier congrès, c'est la d. qui règne dans le parti** division has reigned in the party since the last congress **4** *Typ* hyphen ▸▸ *Mil* **d. blindée** armoured division; *Biol* **d. cellulaire** cell division; **d. du travail** division of labour

divisionnaire [divizjɔnɛr] ADJ *Mil* divisional; *Admin* **commissaire d.** ≃ (police) superintendent ▪ NM ≃ (police) superintendent; *Mil* major general

divorce [divɔrs] NM *Jur* divorce; **les enfants sont ceux qui pâtissent le plus du d.** divorce is hardest on the children; **demander le d.** to ask for a divorce; *Jur* to sue for divorce, to file a petition for divorce; **obtenir le d.** to get a divorce; **être en instance de d.** to be getting a divorce, to have started divorce proceedings; **se solder par un d.** to end in divorce; *Fig* **le d. de la langue écrite (d')avec la langue parlée** the gulf between the written and the spoken language

▸▸ **d. à l'amiable** no-fault divorce; **d. par consentement mutuel** divorce by mutual consent

divorcé, -ée [divɔrse] ADJ divorced N divorced man, f woman, divorcee

divorcer [divɔrse] VI (**je divorçai(s)**; **n. divorçons**) **d. (d')avec qn** to divorce sb; **il veut d.** he wants a divorce; **ils ont divorcé l'année dernière** they got divorced *or* they got a divorce last year; **pourquoi est-ce que tu ne lui demandes pas de d.?** why don't you ask him for a divorce?; **un couple sur trois divorce** one marriage in three ends in divorce

divulgateur, -trice [divylgatœr, -tris] N (*police*) informer; (*de secrets*) betrayer

divulgation [divylgasjɔ̃] NF disclosure (**de** of)

divulguer [divylge] VT (*secret*) to divulge, to reveal, to disclose; (*nouvelle*) to reveal; **il a divulgué qu'il y aurait des licenciements** he revealed *or* disclosed that there would be layoffs

dix [dis] ADJ INV (*at the end of the word group* [dis]; *before n or adj beginning with a vowel sound* [diz]; *before n or adj beginning with a consonant* [di]) **1 il est d. heures** [dizœr] it's ten o'clock; **j'en ai d.** [dis] I have ten; **les d. commandements** the Ten Commandments; *Scol* **devoir noté sur d.** homework marked out of ten; **avoir d. sur d. à sa dictée** to get ten out of ten for dictation; **avoir d. sur d. à chaque œil** to have twenty-twenty vision **2** (*ordinal uses etc*) **le d. mai** [ladime] the tenth of May; **Charles D.** Charles the Tenth; **le numéro d.** number ten

NM INV (*souvent* [dis]) **d. et demi** [disedmi] ten and a half; **j'habite au d.** I live at number 10; *Cartes* **le d. de trèfle** the ten of clubs; **le X est le signe du d. romain** X is ten in Roman numerals

dix-huit [dizɥi(t)] ADJ INV eighteen; **le d. mai** the eighteenth of May

NM INV eighteen; **j'ai eu un d. en maths** I got 90% in maths

dix-huitième [dizɥitjɛm] ADJ, N eighteenth

dixième [dizjɛm] ADJ, N tenth

dixièmement [dizjɛmmɑ̃] ADV tenthly, in tenth place

dixit [diksit] **il faut couper tous les arbres, Papa d.** all the trees have to be cut down, Dad says *or* so Dad says

dix-neuf [diznœf] ADJ INV nineteen; **le d. mai** the nineteenth of May

NM INV nineteen

dix-neuvième [diznœvjɛm] ADJ, N nineteenth

dix-sept [dis(s)ɛt] ADJ INV seventeen; **le d. mai** the seventeenth of May

NM INV seventeen

dix-septième [dis(s)ɛtjɛm] ADJ, N seventeenth

dizain [dizɛ̃] NM *Littér* ten-line stanza

dizaine [dizɛn] NF *Math* ten; **une d.** (*environ dix*) about ten, ten or so; *Math* **compter par dizaines** to count in tens; **une d. de personnes** ten or so people, about ten people; **il y a une d. d'années** about ten years ago, ten or so years ago

dizygote [dizigɔt] *Biol* ADJ fraternal N fraternal twin

DJ [didʒe] NM DJ

djebel [dʒebɛl] NM jebel, mountain

djellaba [dʒelaba] NF djellaba

djembé [dʒembe] NM djembe (drum)

Djibouti [dʒibuti] N Djibouti

djihad [dʒiad] NM jihad

djinn [dʒin] NM djin(n), jinn

DLC [deɛlse] NF (*abrév* date limite de consommation) best-before date

DNS [deɛnɛs] NM *Ordinat* (*abrév* **Domain Name System**) DNS

do [do] NM *Mus* (*note*) C; (*solfège*) doh

doberman [dɔbɛrman] NM Doberman

doc [dɔk] NF *Fam abrév* documentation

docile [dɔsil] ADJ (*enfant, animal*) docile; (*cheveux*) manageable

docilement [dɔsilmɑ̃] ADV docilely

docilité [dɔsilite] NF docility

dock [dɔk] NM *Naut* **1** (*bassin*) dock; **les docks** the dock(s), the dockyard; **d. de carénage/flottant** dry/floating dock **2** *Com* warehouse; **d. entrepôt** dock-warehouse; **d. frigorifique** cold storage dock

docker [dɔkɛr] NM docker, dock worker, *Am* longshoreman

docte [dɔkt] ADJ *Litt, Iron* (*when it precedes noun*) learned

doctement [dɔktəmɑ̃] ADV *Litt, Iron* in a learned manner, learnedly

docteur [dɔktœr] NM **1 d. (en médecine)** doctor (of medicine); **leur fille est d.** their daughter is a doctor; **le d. Thomas** Dr Thomas; **bonjour, d.** good morning, doctor **2** *Univ* **d. ès lettres** ≃ PhD; **Mlle Laurent est d. ès sciences** Miss Laurent is a doctor of science; **d. en droit** doctor of law **3** *Rel* **les docteurs de l'Église** the Doctors of the Church

doctoral, -ale, -aux, -ales [dɔktɔral, -o] ADJ *Péj* (*air, ton*) pompous

doctoralement [dɔktɔralmɑ̃] ADV *Péj* pompously

doctorat [dɔktɔra] NM *Univ* doctorate; **d. d'État** ≃ D Litt/DSc/*etc*; **d. de 3ᵉ cycle** ≃ PhD

doctoresse [dɔktɔrɛs] NF *Vieilli* woman doctor

doctrinaire [dɔktrinɛr] ADJ doctrinaire

doctrinal, -ale, -aux, -ales [dɔktrinal, -o] ADJ doctrinal

doctrine [dɔktrin] NF doctrine, tenet

docudrame [dɔkydram] NM *TV* docudrama

document [dɔkymɑ̃] NM document
▸▸ *Com* **documents contre acceptation** documents against acceptance; *Com* **d. administratif unique** unique data folder; *TV, Cin* **d. d'archives** library document; *Aut* **documents de bord** vehicle documents; **d.-canevas** (*de publipostage*) form document; *Com* **documents d'embarquement** shipping documents; *Typ* **d. d'exécution** artwork; *Com* **d. d'expédition** shipping document; **d. interne à l'entreprise** internal company document; **d. maître** master document; *Com* **documents maritimes** shipping documents; *Com* **d. d'offre** tender document; *Com* **documents contre paiement** documents against payment; **d. source** source document; *Compta* **d. de synthèse** financial statements; **d. transmissible** transferable document; *Com* **d. de transport combiné** combined transport document; **d. de travail** working document; **d.-type** (*de publipostage*) form document; **documents de voyage** travel documents

documentaire [dɔkymɑ̃tɛr] ADJ (*intérêt, valeur etc*) documentary; **à titre d.** for (your) information; *Cin* **film d.** documentary
NM **1** *Cin* documentary **2 d. touristique** travelogue

documentaliste [dɔkymɑ̃talist] N **1** (*d'archives*) documentalist, archivist; *Admin* information officer **2** *TV etc* researcher

documentariste [dɔkymɑ̃tarist] N *Cin, TV* documentarist

documentation [dɔkymɑ̃tasjɔ̃] NF **1** (*informations, documents*) documentation; **la bibliothèque n'a aucune d. sur le sujet** the library has no documentation on the subject; **ils ont réuni une d. très riche pour leur film** they gathered a wide range of documentary evidence for their film; **d. iconographique** pictorial *or* iconographic documentation; **service de la d.** research department **2** (*publicités*) literature, information, documentation; **voulez-vous recevoir notre d.?** would you like us to send you our brochure? **3** (*technique*) documentation (technique)

▸▸ **d. automatique** automated information service; **système d. automatique** automated information service; **d. de presse** press kit; **d. touristique** travel literature, tourist literature **3** (*technique*) documentation (technique)

documenter [dɔkymɑ̃te] VT (*sujet*) to document; (*déclaration etc*) to support with documentary evidence; **d. qn sur une question** to brief sb on a question; **elle est bien documentée** she is well informed on the subject; **son étude n'était pas solidement documentée** his study was not well documented
VPR **se documenter** to gather documentation *or* information *or* material

dodécaèdre [dɔdekaɛdr] NM *Math* dodecahedron

dodécagonal, -ale, -aux, -ales [dɔdekagɔnal, -o] ADJ *Math* twelve-sided, dodecagonal

dodécagone [dɔdekagɔn] NM *Math* dodecagon

dodécaphonique [dɔdekafɔnik] ADJ *Mus* twelve-tone, dodecaphonic

dodécaphonisme [dɔdekafɔnism] NM *Mus* twelve-tone system, dodecaphony

dodelinement [dɔdlinmɑ̃] NM (*de la tête*) nodding

dodeliner [dɔdline] VI **il dodelinait de la tête** his head kept falling forward *or* nodding

dodo¹ [dodo] NM *Enf* (*sommeil*) sleep, bye-byes; (*lit*) bed; **faire d.** to sleep; **aller au d.** to go to bed *or* to bye-byes; **qui c'est qui va faire un gros d.?** who's a sleepy boy/girl then?; **d.!** go to sleep!; **allez, au d.!** bed!

dodo² NM (*oiseau*) dodo

dodu [dɔdy] ADJ *Fam* plump, chubby

doge [dɔʒ] NM *Hist* doge

dogmatique [dɔgmatik] ADJ dogmatic

dogmatiquement [dɔgmatikmɑ̃] ADV dogmatically

dogmatiser [dɔgmatize] VI to be dogmatic

dogmatisme [dɔgmatism] NM dogmatism

dogme [dɔgm] NM dogma

dogue [dɔg] NM mastiff; *Fig* **être d'une humeur de d.** to be like a bear with a sore head

doigt [dwa] NM **1** finger; *Anat, Zool* digit; **d. de pied** toe; *Fig* **mettre les doigts de pied en éventail** to relax thoroughly, to do absolutely nothing; **le petit d.** the little finger; *Fam* **mon petit d. me l'a dit** a little bird told me; **lever le d.** (*en classe etc*) to put one's hand up; *Fig* **ne pas lever ou remuer le petit d.** not to lift a finger; **compter sur ses doigts** to count on one's fingers; **je peux compter mes amis sur les doigts de la main** I can count my friends on the fingers of one hand; **je ne sais rien faire de mes dix doigts** I'm not good with my hands; **porter une bague au d.** to wear a ring on one's finger; **promener ses doigts sur qch** to run one's fingers over sth; **elle a des doigts de fée** she's good with her hands; **il a les doigts verts** he has green fingers *or Am* a green thumb; **se faire taper sur les doigts** to be rapped over the knuckles, to get a rap over the knuckles; *Mus* **avoir un morceau dans les doigts** to have mastered a piece; **savoir qch sur le bout des doigts** to know sth inside out, to have sth at one's fingertips; **elle est élégante/spirituelle/méchante jusqu'au bout des doigts** she is elegant/witty/nasty through and through;

elle est française jusqu'au bout des doigts she is French to her fingertips; **menacer qn du d.** to shake *or* wag one's finger at sb; **elle lui fit signe du d. (de venir)** she beckoned to him (to come over); **désigner** *ou* **montrer qn/qch du d.** to point at sb/sth; *Fam* **faire un d. d'honneur à qn** to give sb the finger, *Am* to flip sb the bird; *Fig* **mettre le d. dans l'engrenage** to get involved; **il a mis le d. dans l'engrenage de la drogue** he got involved *or* mixed up in drugs; **vous avez mis le d. dessus** you've put your finger on it, you've hit the nail on the head; **je crois que je touche le problème du d.** I think I see what the problem is; **nous touchons le but/la vérité du d.** we're very close to *or* within an inch of our goal/the truth; *Fam* **se mettre** *ou* **se fourrer le d. dans l'œil (jusqu'au coude)** to be completely wrong; **fourrer ses doigts partout** to be into everything; **croiser les doigts** to cross one's fingers; **je croise les doigts** I've got my fingers crossed; **croisons les doigts pour que ça marche** let's cross our fingers that it works; *Fam* **mener qn au d. et à l'œil** to keep a tight rein on sb; **elle se laisse mener au d. et à l'œil par son mari** her husband only has to raise a finger and she jumps; **obéir au d. et à l'œil** to obey immediately; **filer** *ou* **glisser entre les doigts de qn** to slip through sb's fingers; **s'en mordre les doigts** to regret it; **j'ai voulu lui tenir tête et je m'en mords les doigts** I tried standing up to her and I regret it *or* I'm sorry I did; **ils sont ensemble comme les (deux) doigts de la main** they are very close; *Fam* **gagner les doigts dans le nez** to win hands down; **faire qch les doigts dans le nez** to do sth as easy as winking; **être le petit d. sur la couture du pantalon** to be a lackey

2 *(mesure)* finger's breadth; **la robe est trop courte d'un d.** the dress is a fraction too short; **un d. de cognac** a nip *or* drop *or* spot of brandy; **être à deux doigts de la mort** to be within an inch of death; **il était à un d.** *ou* **à deux doigts de refuser** he was within an ace of refusing

3 *(objet)* **doigts d'un gant** fingers of a glove; *Aut* **d. de distribution** rotor arm

doigté [dwate] NM **1** *Mus (d'un morceau de musique)* fingering; **exercices de d.** five-finger exercises **2** *(de dactylo)* touch; *(d'un chirurgien)* skill **3** *Fig* tact, diplomacy; **manquer de d.** to be tactless

doigter [dwate] VT **1** *(d'un musicien)* to finger **2** *(d'un compositeur)* to mark with the proper fingering

VI to finger; **elle doigte bien/mal** her fingering is good/bad

doigtier [dwatje] NM fingerstall

doit [dwa] NM *Com* debit, liability; **d. et avoir** debits and credits; *(personnes)* debtors and creditors

dol [dɔl] NM *Jur* fraud, wilful misrepresentation

Dolby® [dɔlbi] NM Dolby®; **en D. stéréo** in Dolby stereo

dôle [dol] NF *Suisse* = red wine from the canton of Valais

doléances [dɔleãs] NFPL complaints; **faire ses d.** to air one's grievances

dolent [dɔlã] ADJ *(voix, personne etc)* doleful, plaintive

doline [dɔlin] NF *Géol* sink-hole, *Spéc* doline

dollar [dɔlar] NM dollar; **la zone d.** the dollar area; **d.-titre** dollar security; **d. américain** US dollar; **dollars constants** dollars in real terms; **dollars courants** actual dollars

dollarisation [dɔlarizasjõ] NF *Écon* dollarization

dolman [dɔlmã] NM dolman; *(de hussard)* short-skirted jacket

dolmen [dɔlmɛn] NM dolmen

dolomie [dɔlɔmi], **dolomite** [dɔlɔmit] NF *Minér* dolomite; *Géog* **les Dolomites** the Dolomites

dolomitique [dɔlɔmitik] ADJ *Géol* dolomitic

dolosif, -ive [dɔlɔzif, -iv] ADJ *Jur* fraudulent

domaine [dɔmɛn] NM **1** *(propriété)* estate, property; *Jur* demesne; **il est interdit de chasser sur leur d.** hunting is forbidden on their land; **ils ont plusieurs domaines dans le vignoble bordelais** they own several pieces of land in the Bordeaux wine-growing area; **domaines de la Couronne** Crown lands; **D. (de l'État)** State(-administered) property; **d. public** public property; **cet ouvrage est tombé dans le d. public** this work is out of copyright *or* has come into the public domain, the copyright on this work has run out *or* lapsed; **le d. forestier** the national forests; **d. skiable** skiing area; **cette pièce est mon d.** this room is my domain

2 *(rayon)* field; **d. d'une science** field *or* scope of a science; **d. des affaires** business domain; **d. de compétence** area of expertise, area of competence; **cela n'entre pas dans le d. de mes connaissances** that's not my field *or* domain; **ce n'est pas de mon d.** that's not my field *or* my line; **une intervention aussi délicate est du d. de la microchirurgie** such a delicate operation calls for microsurgery; **c'est du d. du possible** it is within the realm of possibility, it is not beyond the bounds of possibility; **il est bon dans tous les domaines** he is good in all fields *or* areas; **c'est son d. réservé** it's his private domain; *Mktg* **d. concurrentiel** competitive scope; *Mktg* **d. d'activité stratégique** strategic business area

3 *Ordinat (partie d'une adresse Internet)*

domanial, -iale, -iaux, -iales [dɔmanjal, -jo] ADJ *(domaines, forêts etc)* national, (belonging to the) State

dôme [dom] NM **1** *Archit* dome, cupola **2** *Litt (du ciel, des arbres)* vault, canopy; *Géog* dome

domestication [dɔmɛstikasjõ] NF domestication

domesticité [dɔmɛstisite] NF **1** *(service)* domestic service **2** *(personnel)* domestic staff, household **3** *(d'un animal)* domesticity; **la d. est impossible chez certaines races** some breeds are impossible to tame *or* domesticate

domestique [dɔmɛstik] ADJ **1** *(vie, soucis)* domestic; *(occupations, tâches, déchets)* household; *(querelle)* family, domestic; **économie d.** home economics; **accidents domestiques** accidents in the home **2** *animal* **d.** domestic animal; *(qu'on a chez soi)* pet; **éléphant d.** tame *or* domesticated elephant

N servant, *Fml, Am* domestic

domestiquer [dɔmɛstike] VT *(animal)* to domesticate; *(personne)* to subjugate, to bring to a state of subjection; *(énergie atomique etc)* to harness

domicile [dɔmisil] NM (place of) residence, home, *Jur* domicile; **sans d. fixe** of no fixed abode *or* address; **élire d. au 3, rue Hoche** to take up residence at no 3, rue Hoche; **dernier d. connu** last known address; **à d.** in one's home, at home; **travailler à d.** to work from home; **notre épicier livre à d.** our grocer has a (home) delivery service; **vous préférez être livré à d. ou au bureau?** do you want it delivered to your home or your office?; **franco à d.** carriage paid; *Jur* **d. conjugal** marital *or* matrimonial home; *Jur* **abandon du d. conjugal** desertion; **d. fiscal** tax domicile; *Sport* **match à d.** home game *or* match; **jouer à d.** to play *or* be at home;

le PSG joue à d. contre Lille PSG is at home to Lille

domiciliaire [dɔmisiljer] ADJ *(visite etc)* home

domiciliataire [dɔmisiljater] N *(de chèque)* paying bank; *(d'effet)* paying agent

domiciliation [dɔmisiljasjõ] NF *Com* domiciliation; **d. bancaire** payment by banker's order

domicilié [dɔmisilje] ADJ resident, domiciled *(à* at); *Com* domiciled

domicilier [dɔmisilje] VT *(impf, pr sub* n. **domiciliions, v. domiciliiez)** *Com* to domicile

domien, -ienne [dɔmjɛ̃, -jɛn] ADJ of/from the French overseas departments

N **D.** *(natif)* native of the French overseas departments; *(habitant)* inhabitant of the French overseas departments

dominance [dɔminãs] NF *Biol* dominance

dominant, -ante [dɔminã, -ãt] ADJ *(couleur, opinion etc)* predominating, prevailing; *(trait, idée etc)* dominant, outstanding; *Biol* **caractère d.** dominant (characteristic)

NF **dominante 1** *(ce qui domine)* chief characteristic; **un ameublement avec une dominante moderne** furniture which is predominantly *or* primarily modern; **la dominante de son programme politique est la protection de l'environnement** environmental protection is the main plank of his platform; **elle avait une tenue très pâle, avec une dominante rose** she was wearing a very pale outfit, in which pink predominated *or* was the main colour; **une classe à dominante scientifique** a class where the emphasis is on scientific subjects **2** *Mus* dominant (note)

dominateur, -trice [dɔminatœr, -tris] N *Litt* ruler

ADJ *(pays, caractère)* dominating; *Péj (personne, ton, attitude etc)* domineering, overbearing

domination [dɔminasjõ] NF domination; **la d. de l'URSS sur les autres pays de l'Est** the USSR's domination of the other Eastern bloc countries; **d. morale** dominance, domination; **il exerce sur elle une telle d. morale que ...** he dominates her so completely that ..., he has such sway over her that ...; **d. de soi-même** self-control; **être sous la d. de qn** to be under sb's thumb

dominer [dɔmine] VT **1** *(assujettir)* *(personne)* to dominate; *(empire)* to rule over; **l'ambition le domine** he is dominated by ambition; **se laisser d. par un collègue autoritaire** to let oneself be dominated by an authoritarian colleague; **d. une classe** *(d'un professeur)* to control a class

2 *(surpasser)* *(adversaire, concurrent)* to surpass, *Fam* to be streets ahead of; **sa voix dominait toutes les autres** his voice rose *or* was heard above all the others; **dans son domaine, il domine absolument tous les savants** he stands head and shoulders above all the other scientists in his field

3 *(prédominer dans)* *(travail, caractère, humeur)* to be the dominant feature of; **c'est la question du chômage qui domine les préoccupations du gouvernement** unemployment is predominant among the government's concerns; **le rouge domine toute sa garde-robe** red is the dominant colour in her wardrobe; **le sapin domine dans les forêts allemandes** fir is the predominant species of tree in German forests

4 *(maîtriser)* *(timidité, passions)* to master, to overcome; *(larmes)* *Fig (son sujet)* to master; *(paresse, envie de faire qch)* to overcome; **d. la situation** to be master of the situation, to have the situation under control; *Sport* **d. la partie** to dominate the game

5 *(surplomber)* to dominate; **le château do-**

mine la vallée the castle dominates the valley; **il domine les enfants de son âge d'une tête au moins** he stands at least a head above other children of his age; **de sa terrasse, on domine la mer** you overlook the sea from his balcony

VI 1 *(l'emporter)* to dominate; **notre équipe a dominé tout le long du match** our team dominated the entire match *or* was in control throughout the match; **ce sont ses arguments qui dominent** his arguments carry the day; **leur entreprise domine dans le secteur du prêt-à-porter féminin** their company dominates the women's ready-to-wear sector; **notre entreprise domine largement dans ce secteur** our company is by far the largest in the sector; **elle domine de très loin sur ses collègues** she is *or* stands head and shoulders above her colleagues, she is far better than *or* Fam streets ahead of her colleagues; **il domine en taille sur les autres enfants de son âge** he is taller than the other children in his age group

2 *(prédominer)* to be predominant; **c'est la couleur bleue qui domine** blue is the predominant *or* predominating colour; **les jeunes de moins de 15 ans dominent dans le club** young people under 15 are in the majority in the club; **chez lui, c'est l'égoïsme/la gentillesse qui domine** selfishness/kindness is his dominant characteristic; **parmi mes préoccupations, c'est l'avenir de mes enfants qui domine** my children's future is my main concern

VPR se dominer to be self-controlled, to control one's feelings; **il ne pouvait plus se d.** he couldn't control himself any longer; **dès qu'il boit deux verres, il n'arrive plus à se d.** two drinks and he loses all self-control

dominicain, -aine [dominikɛ̃, -ɛn] **ADJ 1** *Rel (moine, religieuse)* Dominican **2** *Géog (natif, habitant)* of Santo Domingo; **la République Dominicaine** the Dominican Republic, Santo Domingo
N 1 *Rel* Dominican **2** *Géog* **D.** Dominican

dominical, -ale, -aux, -ales [dominikal, -o] **ADJ l'oraison dominicale** the Lord's prayer; **repos d.** day of rest; **dans la religion chrétienne, le repos d. est une coutume** in Christianity, it is traditional for Sunday to be a day of rest; **ouverture dominicale des magasins** Sunday opening *or* shopping

dominion [dominjɔn] **NM** *Pol* dominion

Dominique [dominik] **NF** *Géog* **la D.** Dominica

domino [domino] **NM** domino; **jouer aux dominos** to play dominoes **VOIR GRAMMAIRE A12**

dommage [domaʒ] **NM 1** *(préjudice)* damage, injury; **causer un d. à qn** to do sb harm *or* an injury; **il s'en est tiré sans d.** he came out of it unscathed **2** *(dégâts matériels)* **dommages** damage; **aucun d. n'est à déplorer** no damage is reported; **les dommages causés par l'explosion sont énormes** the explosion caused tremendous damage; **dommages collatéraux** collateral damage **3** **(quel) d.!** what a pity!, what a shame!; **c'est (bien) d. qu'elle ne soit pas venue** it's a (great) pity that she didn't come; **le plus d. c'est que tu ne l'aies jamais rencontré** it's a great pity that you never met him; **d. que tu n'aies pas le temps** it's a pity you haven't the time
ADJ INV *Suisse (que l'on ne veut pas endommager)* **il ne faut pas mettre des habits d. pour faire le ménage** you shouldn't wear your good clothes to do the housework
▸▸ *Jur* **d. causé avec intention de nuire** malicious damage; **d. corporel** personal *or* physical injury; **dommages de guerre** war damages; **dommages et intérêts, dommages-intérêts** damages; **poursuivre qn en**

dommages-intérêts to sue sb for damages, to bring an action for damages against sb; **verser/obtenir des dommages-intérêts** to pay/to be awarded damages; **dommages-intérêts compensatoires** compensation; **d. matériel** damage to property; **d. moral** psychological damage; **dommages punitifs** punitive damages

dommageable [domaʒabl] **ADJ** detrimental, injurious; *Jur* prejudicial; *Jur* **acte d.** tort

domotique [domotik] **NF** home automation

domptable [dɔ̃(p)tabl] **ADJ** capable of being tamed *or* subdued, tamable

domptage [dɔ̃(p)taʒ] **NM** *(d'animal) (apprivoisement)* taming; *(dressage)* training; *(de cheval)* breaking in; *(de fleuve, de la nature)* taming; **le d. du criminel n'a pas été facile** it was not easy to subdue the criminal

dompter [dɔ̃(p)te] **VT** *(animal) (apprivoiser)* to tame; *(dresser)* to train; *(cheval)* to break in; *(ses sentiments, passions etc)* to subdue, to overcome; *(fleuve, la nature)* to tame; *(personne)* to subdue

dompteur, -euse [dɔ̃(p)tœr, -øz] **N** *(d'animaux)* tamer, trainer; **d. de chevaux** horsebreaker

DOM-TOM [domtom] **NMPL** *(abrév départements et territoires d'outre-mer)* = French overseas departments and territories

DON [deoɛn] **NM** *Ordinat (abrév disque optique numérique)* CD-ROM

don [dɔ̃] **NM 1** *(cadeau)* gift, present; *(à un musée, une œuvre)* donation; **d. de M. Roland** *(dans un musée)* gift of Mr Roland, donated by Mr Roland; **un d. en nature/espèces** a donation in kind/cash; **faire d. à qn de qch** to make a present *or* a donation of sth to sb; *Fig* **les dons de la terre** the fruits of the earth; **cet enfant est un d. du ciel** that child is a gift from heaven; **le d. de soi** self-sacrifice; **faire d. de sa vie à Dieu** to give one's life to God **2** *(aptitude)* gift, talent; **le d. des langues** a gift *or* talent for languages; *aussi Iron* **avoir le d. de faire qch** to have a gift *or* talent *or* genius for doing sth
▸▸ **d. d'organes** organ donation; **d. du sang** blood donation; **d. de sperme** sperm donation

donataire [donatɛr] **N** *Jur* donee

donateur, -trice [donatœr, -tris] **N** donor

donation [donasjɔ̃] **NF** donation, gift; *Jur* **d. entre vifs** gift *(made to avoid inheritance tax)*; **donations parents-enfants** donations from parents to children

donation-partage, *pl* **donations-partages NF** *Jur* = distribution of estate during one's lifetime to avoid inheritance tax

donc [dɔ̃k] **CONJ** *(marque la conséquence)* so; **il répond exactement à mes besoins, j'en suis d. très satisfait** it's exactly what I need, so I'm very satisfied with it; **je pense, d. je suis** I think, therefore I am
ADV 1 *(emphatique)* **vous voilà d. de retour** so you're back (again); **tu le savais d. depuis le début?** so you knew from the start?, you knew from the start then?; **que voulez-vous d.?** what(ever) do you want?; **mais taisez-vous d.!** do be quiet!, *Fam* do shut up!; **allons d.!** nonsense!, come on!, come now!; **comment d.?** how do you mean?; **pensez d.!** that's what you think!, that'll be the day!; **tu as d. oublié?** have you forgotten?; **où vas-tu d.?** [dɔ̃] where are you going?; **cela vous plaît d.?** you like it, then?, so you like it? **2** *(après interruption ou digression)* **d. pour en revenir à notre sujet** so *or* well, to come back to our subject; **je disais d. que ...** I was saying, then, that ..., as I was saying, ...

dondon [dɔ̃dɔ̃] **NF** *Fam* fat woman/girl; **grosse d.** great lump of a woman/girl

donjon [dɔ̃ʒɔ̃] **NM** *(d'un château)* keep, donjon

don Juan [dɔ̃ʒɥɑ̃] **NM** Don Juan

donjuanesque [dɔ̃ʒɥanɛsk] **ADJ** Don Juan

donjuanisme [dɔ̃ʒɥanism] **NM** Don Juanism

donnant-donnant [donɑ̃donɑ̃] **ADJ c'est d., je te prête ma voiture et tu me prêtes ton aspirateur** it's only fair, I lend you my car and you lend me your vacuum cleaner; **avec elle, c'est toujours d.** she always expects something in return; **désormais, ce sera d.** from now on, things are going to be a bit fairer around here, from now on, it's going to be a two-way street around here

donne [dɔn] **NF** *Cartes* deal; **à vous la d.!** your deal!; **faire la d.** to deal; **fausse d.** misdeal; *Fig* **il y a fausse d.** there's been a mistake; *Fig* **nouvelle d.** new state of affairs; **il y a une nouvelle d. des pays de l'Est** the situation in the Eastern bloc has changed; **le partage du travail sera une nouvelle d. dans la situation économique** job-sharing will be a new factor in the economic situation

donné [done] **ADJ 1** given; **propriété donnée en dot** property given as a dowry; *Fam* **c'est d.** it's dirt cheap, it's a gift, I'm/he's/*etc* giving it away **2** *(défini)* given; **à un point d./une distance donnée** at a given *or* certain point/distance; **des quantités données** given quantities; **à un moment d.** then; **à un moment d., tu seras bien obligé de le lui dire** you'll have to tell him sometime *or* sooner *or* later **3** **étant d. deux triangles** given two triangles; **étant d. l'heure tardive** since it's so late; **étant d. qu'il était mineur** since *or* as he was a minor

donnée [done] **NF** *(d'un problème etc)* given information; *(d'un roman etc)* fundamental idea *or* subject; **données** data; **VOIR GRAMMAIRE A11** **si je n'ai pas toutes les données du problème** if I don't have all the data *or* information on the problem; **données brutes** raw data; *Écon* **en données corrigées des variations saisonnières** with adjustments for seasonal variations, seasonally adjusted; **traitement des données** data processing; *Ordinat* **support de données** data carrier; *Ordinat* **commutateur de données** data switch; **données nominatives** personal data; *Ordinat* **données numériques** digital data; *Ordinat* **données à sept bits** seven-bit data; *Ordinat* **banque de données** data bank; *Ordinat* **base de données** database

DONNER [done]

VT to give **1–13** ▪ to donate **1, 2** ▪ to hand in **4** ▪ to leave **4** ▪ to cause **7** ▪ to yield **8** ▪ to produce **8**		
VI to give **1** ▪ to stretch **7** ▪ to deal **8**		
VPR to devote oneself **1** ▪ to give oneself **2, 3, 6** ▪ to choose **7** ▪ to be on **9**		

VT 1 *(offrir) (quelque chose de concret, siège, livre, travail etc)* to give; **d. son sang** to give blood; **d. un cadeau à qn** to give a present to sb, to give sb a present; **il m'a donné 100 euros** he gave me 100 euros; **d. son corps à la science** to donate one's body to science; **d. sa place à une vieille dame** to give (up) one's seat to an old lady; **d. à boire à qn** to give sb something to drink; **c'est toi qui nous donnes à manger?** are you giving us lunch/*etc*?; **d. c'est d.** a gift is a gift

2 *(faire don de) (temps, amour, hospitalité etc)* to give; **d. sa vie pour qn** to give one's life for sb; **d. son temps pour une cause** to give *or* donate one's time to a cause; **d. le jour** *ou* **la vie à un enfant** to give birth to a child; **d. la mort à qn** to kill sb

3 *(céder, vendre)* to give; **je vous en donne dix euros** I'll give you ten euros for it; **je lui**

donne 20 euros de l'heure I pay him 20 euros an hour; **je te donne mon pull contre ta jupe** I'll give you my sweater (in exchange) for your skirt, I'll swap my sweater for your skirt; **en d. à qn pour son argent** to give sb their money's worth; *Fig* **ah, il veut avoir plus de responsabilités, et bien, on va lui en d. pour son argent** if he wants more responsibility, we'll give him it and then some more *or* we'll give him as much as he wants and more; **elle donnerait n'importe quoi** *ou* **tout ce qu'elle a au monde pour que cela se réalise** she'd give anything for that to happen; **je donnerais beaucoup pour le savoir** I'd give a lot to know

4 *(confier)* to give; **d. à qn qch à garder** to give sb sth to look after, *Fml* to entrust sb with sth; **d. ses chaussures à ressemeler** to leave one's shoes to be resoled; **d. un vêtement à nettoyer** *ou* **au teinturier** to hand in a piece of clothing to be dry-cleaned; **d. ses enfants à garder** to leave one's children to be looked after

5 *(dire, communiquer)* *(avis, détails, description, ordres, conseils etc)* to give; **d. l'heure** to tell the time; **vous pourriez me d. l'heure?** could you give me the time?; **le journal donne des nouvelles alarmantes sur la crise** the newspaper gives alarming news of the crisis; **tu lui donneras le bonjour de ma part** say hello to him for me; **tu pourrais d. des nouvelles de temps en temps!** you could let me/us/*etc* hear from you occasionally!; **je vous le donne en cent** *ou* **en mille** you'll never guess; **donnez-moi le jour et l'heure de votre arrivée** give me your date and time of arrival; *Péj* **il faudrait qu'on lui donne du 'Maître' pour qu'il soit satisfait** he won't be happy unless he's addressed as 'Maître'; **il lui a donné du 'Madame la Comtesse' toute la soirée** he 'Countess'd her this and 'Countess'd her that all evening

6 *(octroyer)* *(sa parole, son accord, du temps, une chance, délai, occasion, pourboire etc)* to give; **j'y reviendrai plus tard, si l'occasion m'en est donnée** I'll go there again later if I get the chance; **d. sa fille en mariage à qn** to give one's daughter to sb in marriage; **d. sa confiance à qn** to put one's trust in sb

7 *(causer)* *(de l'énergie, de l'appétit, des coliques etc)* to give; **cette odeur me donne mal à la tête** this smell is giving me a headache; **d. du souci à qn** to cause sb worry; **d. sujet** *ou* **matière à discussion** to be a subject for discussion *or* debate; **cela m'a donné l'idée de …** that gave me the idea to …; **son histoire donne plus à rire qu'à pleurer** his story is funny rather than sad, his story makes you want to laugh rather than cry; **toute cette histoire m'a donné à réfléchir/à rire** the entire business made me think/laugh; **d. envie de rire** to be laughable *or* comical; **ça me donne envie de rire** that makes me want to laugh; **d. faim/soif/sommeil/ chaud/le vertige à qn** to make sb hungry/ thirsty/sleepy/hot/dizzy; **cette fenêtre donne de la lumière dans la pièce** that window makes the room brighter; **je lui ai donné à entendre que …** I gave him to understand that …; **cela me donne à croire que …** it leads me to believe that …

8 *(produire)* to give; *(récoltes)* to yield; **arbre qui donne de beaux fruits** tree that gives *or* yields *or* bears fine fruit; **les arbres donnent de l'ombre** the trees give shade; **elle a donné trois beaux enfants à son mari** she gave *or* bore her husband three beautiful children; **d. le la avec un diapason** to give an A with a tuning fork; **d. de l'électricité** to produce electricity; **essai qui ne donne rien** fruitless *or* unsuccessful attempt; **une méthode qui ne donne rien** a method that doesn't work; *Fam* **ça n'a rien donné** nothing came of it, it didn't work out; **je me demande ce que cela**

va d. I wonder what will come of it *or* what the result of it will be; *Fam* **qu'est-ce que ça donne?** how does it look?

9 *(mettre)* to give; **d. un baiser/une caresse/ une gifle/une fessée à qn** to give sb a kiss/a caress/a slap in the face/a spanking; **d. un coup de peigne à ses cheveux** to give one's hair a quick comb; **il faudrait d. une couche de peinture supplémentaire** we'll have to put on an extra coat of paint; **tu peux d. un coup de balai dans la cuisine?** can you give the kitchen a sweep?; *Fig* **tu donnes ta langue au chat?** do you give up *or* in?

10 *(organiser)* *(bal, dîner, conférence etc)* to give; **d. une pièce de théâtre** to put on *or* perform a play; **qu'est-ce qu'on donne au cinéma aujourd'hui?** what's on at the cinema today?

11 *(attribuer)* **on donne ses théories pour révolutionnaires** they say his theories are revolutionary, his theories are said to be revolutionary; **je lui donne vingt ans** I reckon he's about twenty; **les médecins lui donnent deux jours (à vivre)** the doctors give him two days (to live); **d. tort/raison à qn** to disagree/agree with sb

12 *(conférer)* *(impression)* to give; *(poids, valeur)* to give, to lend; **d. un sens à sa vie** to give (a) meaning to one's life; **ta nouvelle coiffure te donne un air jeune** your new hairdo makes you look younger

13 *(passer)* **tu peux me d. le livre qui est dans le tiroir/sur la table?** can you give me the book out of the drawer/off the table?; **il m'a donné son rhume** he gave me his cold, I caught his cold

14 *(accorder)* **il n'est pas donné à tout le monde d'être (un) écrivain** not everybody can be a writer

15 *Arg* *(vendre)* to grass on (à to)

VI 1 *(faire un don)* to give; **aimer d.** to like to give, to like giving

2 *(cogner)* **le navire a donné sur les rochers** the ship ran onto *or* struck the rocks; **d. de la tête contre qch** to knock *or* strike *or* bump one's head against sth; *Fig Fam* **ne pas savoir où d. de la tête** not to know which way to turn; **sa tête alla d. dans le ventre de son adversaire** his head went straight into his opponent's stomach; **le soleil donne dans la pièce** the sun is streaming into the room

3 *(tomber)* **d. dans le piège** *ou Fam* **le panneau** to fall into the trap; **d. dans** *(avoir un penchant pour)* to be given to; **il donne dans la bigoterie** he is rather bigoted; **il donne dans les petites minettes en ce moment** he really goes for young babes at the moment; **d. dans le genre théâtral** to lapse into the melodramatic

4 *(produire)* **si les blés donnent cette année** if there is a good crop of wheat this year; *Fam* **ça donne!** it's something else!, it's wicked *or Br* mental!; *Fam* **s'ils se disputent, ça va d.** if they argue, there'll be trouble; **leur chaîne/la musique a donné à fond toute la soirée** their stereo/the music was blaring all evening

5 *(charger)* **faire d. un bataillon** to send a battalion into action

6 *(déboucher)* **la fenêtre donne sur la cour** the window looks onto the yard; **cette porte donne sur** *ou* **dans le jardin** this door leads (out) into the garden

7 *(s'allonger)* *(d'une corde, d'une jupe)* to stretch

8 *Cartes* to deal; **mal d.** to misdeal; **c'est à qui de d.?** whose deal is it?

VPR se donner 1 *(se consacrer)* to devote oneself (à to); **elle s'est donnée entièrement** she gave fully of herself

2 *(s'offrir)* **se d. en spectacle** to make an exhibition of oneself; **se d. des airs** to put on airs, to give oneself airs; **se d. un genre** to make out one is something one is not; **c'est**

un genre qu'elle se donne it's just a front; *Fam* **se la d.** to show off, to pose

3 *(s'accorder)* **se d. toutes les chances de réussir** to give oneself every chance of succeeding; **se d. le temps de réfléchir** to give oneself *or* take time to think; **s'en d. (à cœur joie)** to enjoy oneself (to the full), to have a good time, to have a field day; **se d. du bon temps** to have a good time, to enjoy oneself; **se d. bonne conscience** to salve one's conscience; **se d. pour tâche de …** to set oneself the task of …; **se d. pour mission de …** to make it one's mission to …

4 se d. un coup de peigne/brosse to give one's hair a quick comb/brush; **se d. un coup de marteau sur le pouce** to hit one's thumb with a hammer; **se d. du tourment** to torment oneself

5 *(se prétendre)* **il se donne pour un grand musicien** he says he is *or* claims he is *or* claims to be a great musician

6 *(sexuellement)* to give oneself

7 *(choisir)* *(chef, président etc)* to choose, to select

8 *(échanger)* **se d. des coups** to exchange blows, to hit each other; **se d. des baisers** to kiss each other; **se d. l'accolade** to embrace each other; **se d. une poignée de main** to shake hands

9 *Cin* to be on, to be showing; **hier soir se donnait chez Maxim's la soirée d'adieu du Comte Orloff** Count Orloff's farewell party took place at Maxim's last night

V IMPERS c'est le spectacle le plus épouvantable qu'il m'a (jamais) été donné de voir it was the most horrifying sight I'd ever been unfortunate enough to witness

donneur, -euse [dɔnœr, -øz] **N 1** *Méd* donor; **d. de sang/sperme** blood/sperm donor; *Méd* **d. universel** universal donor; *Com* **d. d'ordre** principal; *Péj* **d. d'avis** *ou* **de conseils** know-all; **d. de caution** guarantor **2** *Cartes* dealer **3** *Arg* *(délateur)* grass

don-quichottisme [dɔ̃kiʃɔtism] **NM** quixotism

DONT [dɔ̃] **PRON REL** SEE GRAMMAR A33; B23; B62

1 *(exprimant le complément du verbe et indiquant la provenance)* **la pièce d. elle sort** the room she is coming out of; **la ville d. je viens** the town I come from; **la famille d. je descends** the family I am descended from *or* from which I am descended

2 *(exprimant le complément du verbe et indiquant le moyen, la manière etc)* **la façon d. il me regardait/était habillé** the way (in which) he looked at me/is dressed

3 *(au sujet de qui, de quoi)* **une fille d. on ne sait rien** a girl we know nothing about, *Fml* a girl about whom we know nothing; **un film d. on parle beaucoup** a film that is being talked about a lot; **un incident d. on se souviendra** an incident that will be remembered

4 *(exprimant l'objet du verbe)* **le livre d. j'ai besoin** the book (that) I need; **voici ce d. il s'agit** this is what it's all about; **l'homme d. il s'agit** the man in question; **l'homme d. elle se moque** the man she's making fun of, *Fml* the man of whom she is making fun

5 *(exprimant l'objet de l'adjectif)* **la femme d. il est amoureux** the woman he is in love with; **le groupe d'enfants d. vous êtes responsable** the group of children you are responsible for; **le souvenir d. elle est si honteuse** the memory she is so ashamed of

6 *(exprimant le complément de nom et indiquant la possession, la qualité, la matière)* **la dame d. je connais le fils** the lady whose son I know; **la dame d. le fils vous connaît** the lady whose son knows you; **la chambre d. la porte est fermée** the room with the closed door; **cet objet d. le nom m'échappe**

this object, the name of which escapes me **7** *(exprimant le complément de nom et indiquant une partie d'un tout)* **quelques-uns étaient là, d. votre frère** there were a few people there, including your brother; **un rêve d. il ne me reste que cette image** a dream of which I remember nothing but this image, a dream I remember nothing about except this image; **un film d. voici le résumé** a film of which the following is a summary; **la maison d. on voit le toit** the house whose roof can be seen; **le parti d. le chef vient de mourir** the party whose leader has just died

donzelle [dõzɛl] NF *Fam Péj* woman who puts on airs

dopage [dɔpaʒ] NM doping; *(en athlétisme, cyclisme etc)* drug-taking; *Fig (de l'économie)* boosting

dopant [dɔpɑ̃] ADJ **produit d.** drug
  NM drug

dope [dɔp] NF *Fam (drogue)* dope

doper [dɔpe] VT *Sport etc* to dope; *Fig (économie, monnaie etc)* to boost, to give a boost or fillip to
  VPR **se doper** to take stimulants, to dope oneself

dope sheet [dɔpʃit] NM *TV* dope sheet

doping [dɔpiŋ] NM doping

Doppler [dɔplɛr] ADJ *Phys* **effet D.** Doppler effect
  NM *Méd* = use of Doppler's method to determine speed at which the blood is circulating

dorade [dɔrad] NF *(poisson)* gilthead bream, sea bream

doré [dɔre] ADJ **1** *(recouvert d'or)* gilded, gilt; **d. sur tranche** gilt-edged; **papier d.** gold-coloured paper **2** *(couleur d'or)* *(blé, lumière)* golden, honey-coloured; *Am* honey-colored; *(yeux)* golden (brown); *(peau)* golden (brown), honey-coloured; *Culin (gâteau passé au jaune d'œuf)* glazed; *(viande, pommes de terre, gâteau cuit)* browned, golden; **cheveux blond d.** golden hair
  NM *Can (poisson)* wall-eyed pike, yellow pike

dorée [dɔre] NF *(poisson)* (John) Dory

dorénavant [dɔrenavɑ̃] ADV from now on, *Fml* henceforth

dorer [dɔre] VT **1** *(recouvrir d'or)* to gild; *Fig* **d. la pilule à qn** to sugar the pill for sb **2** *(donner une couleur dorée à)* *(peau)* to turn golden; *Culin (gâteau)* to glaze; *(viande, pommes de terre)* to brown; **le soleil dorait les cimes** the sun shed a golden light on the hilltops or turned the hilltops golden
  VI *Culin* to brown
  VPR **se dorer** to turn a golden colour or *Am* color; **elle se dore** ou *Fam* **se dore la pilule au soleil** she's sunbathing, she's getting a suntan

doreur, -euse [dɔrœr, -øz] N gilder

dorique [dɔrik] ADJ *Archit* Doric

dorlotement [dɔrlɔtmɑ̃] NM coddling, pampering

dorloter [dɔrlɔte] VT to coddle, to pamper; **se laisser/se faire d.** to let oneself be/to be coddled or pampered
  VPR **se dorloter** to coddle or pamper oneself

dormance [dɔrmɑ̃s] NF *Biol* dormancy

dormant [dɔrmɑ̃] ADJ **1** *(eau)* still, stagnant **2** *Tech* **serrure dormante** dead lock **3** *Fig Fml (passions, instincts, sensualité)* dormant **4** *Fin (capitaux, compte)* dormant
  NM *(d'une porte, d'une fenêtre)* frame, casing

dormeur, -euse [dɔrmœr, -øz] ADJ **poupée dormeuse** doll with eyes that close
  N *(personne endormie)* sleeper; **ne réveille pas les dormeurs** don't wake the people who're sleeping; **c'est un grand** ou **gros d.**

he sleeps a lot; **en vacances, je redeviens un gros d.** I sleep a lot when I'm on holiday; **je ne partirai plus en week-end avec ces dormeurs** I'm not going away with them for the weekend again, all they do is sleep
  NM *(crustacé)* edible crab

dormeuse NF *(boucle d'oreille)* sleeper

DORMIR [dɔrmir] VI *(prp* **dormant**; *pp* **dormi**; *pr ind* **je dors**, *n.* **dormons**; *impf* **je dormais**; *p hist* **je dormis)** **1** to sleep; **il dort** he's sleeping, he's asleep; **d. profondément** ou **d'un profond sommeil** to be fast asleep, to be in a deep sleep; **bien/mal d.** to sleep well/badly; **elle dort d'un sommeil léger** she's a light sleeper; **d. du sommeil du juste** to sleep the sleep of the just; **je n'ai pas dormi de la nuit** I haven't slept a wink, I didn't sleep a wink or get a wink's sleep (all night), I didn't sleep all night; **il n'en dort pas** he can't (get to) sleep for thinking of it; **parler/pleurer/crier en dormant** to talk/cry/shout in one's sleep; **le café m'empêche de d.** coffee keeps me awake; *Fam* **ce n'est pas ça qui va m'empêcher de d.** I won't lose any sleep over it; **d. trop longtemps** to oversleep; **d. à poings fermés** ou **comme une souche** ou **comme un loir** ou **comme une marmotte** ou **comme une brute** ou **comme un sonneur** to sleep soundly or like a log; **ne d. que d'un œil** to sleep with one eye open; **vous pouvez d. tranquille** ou **sur les** ou **vos deux oreilles** you can rest easy; **avoir envie de d.** to be or feel sleepy or drowsy; **il dort debout** he's asleep on his feet, he can't keep his eyes open; **une histoire** ou **un conte à d. debout** a tall or cock-and-bull story; **il dort sur son travail** he's falling asleep over his work; *Fam* **ce n'est vraiment pas le moment de d.** there's no time for sleeping now

2 *Fig (d'une ville, d'une forêt)* to be sleeping, to be asleep; **une espèce de génie dort en lui** he has a kind of latent genius; **elle a laissé ses projets d. trop longtemps** she waited too long to carry out her plans; **ce serait dommage de laisser d. tes talents de couturier** it would be a pity not to make use of your dressmaking talents or a pity to let your dressmaking talents go to waste; **un roman qui dort dans un tiroir** a novel languishing in a drawer; **c'est idiot d'avoir des capitaux qui dorment** it's stupid to have capital lying idle, it's stupid not to make your capital work for you; **eau qui dort** stagnant or still water; *Prov* **il n'est pire eau que l'eau qui dort** still waters run deep

dormitif, -ive [dɔrmitif, -iv] ADJ *Méd* soporific

dorsal, -ale, -aux, -ales [dɔrsal, -o] ADJ dorsal; **région dorsale de la main** back of the hand; *Aviat* **parachute d.** back-type parachute
  NF **dorsale 1** *Ling* dorsal consonant **2** *Géog* ridge; *Météo* **dorsale barométrique** ridge of high pressure

dort-en-chiant, *pl* **dorts-en-chiant** [dɔrɑ̃ʃjɑ̃] N *Fam* slowcoach, *Am* slowpoke

dortoir [dɔrtwar] NM dormitory; **ville-d., cité-d.** dormitory town

dorure [dɔryr] NF **1** *(couche d'or)* gilding **2** *Culin (d'un gâteau)* glazing (with egg yolk) **3** *(ornement doré)* gilt, gilding; **uniforme couvert de dorures** gold-braided uniform

doryphore [dɔrifɔr] NM Colorado beetle

DOS [dɔs] NM *Ordinat* DOS; **depuis le D., à partir du D.** through (the) DOS

DOS [do] NM **1** *Anat* back; **avoir le d. voûté** to be round-shouldered; *Fig* **il a bon d.** he's got a broad back or shoulders; **elle a bon d. la grève des postes, dis plutôt que tu n'as pas écrit** why don't you admit that you haven't written instead of blaming it on the postal

strike?; *Fam* **j'en ai plein le d.** I'm sick of it, I'm fed up with it; **faire le gros d.** *(d'un chat)* to arch its back; *Fig (faire des difficultés)* to dig one's heels in, *Br Fam* to turn bolshie; **mon fils fait toujours le gros d. pour aller se coucher** my son always kicks up a fuss at bedtime; **tourner le d. à qn** to turn one's back on sb; *(quand on est debout/assis)* to stand/sit with one's back to sb; *Fig* **tous mes amis m'ont tourné le d.** all my friends have turned their back on me; **avoir le d. tourné à qn/qch** to have one's back to sb/sth; **dès qu'il a le d. tourné** the moment or as soon as his back is turned; **en d. d'âne** ridged, razor-backed; **pont en d. d'âne** humpbacked bridge; **attention, d. d'âne** beware uneven road surface; **voyager à d. d'âne** to ride or travel on a donkey; *Fig* **d. à d.** back to back; *Fig* **leur mère les a renvoyés d. à d.** their mother couldn't decide which of them was the guilty party; **je les renvoie d. à d.** I think they're equally guilty or as bad as each other; **on peut les renvoyer d. à d.** they're equally guilty; *Fam* **se mettre tout le monde à d.** to set everybody against you; **partir sac au d.** to set off with one's pack on one's back; **faire qch derrière** ou **dans le d. de qn** to do sth behind sb's back; **robe décolletée dans le d.** low-backed dress; **elle porte ses cheveux dans le d.** she wears her hair loose or down; **ça fait froid dans le d.** it's scary or creepy, it gives you the shivers; **j'en ai un frisson dans le d.** it sends a shiver down my spine; *Fig Fam* **la maison, on l'a dans le d.** we can kiss the house goodbye; *Fig Fam* **faire un enfant dans le d. à qn** to stab sb in the back; **je ne l'ai vu que de d.** I only saw him from the back, I only got a back view of him; **dormir sur le d.** to sleep on one's back; *Fig Fam* **depuis un mois, j'ai mon patron/le fisc sur le d.** I've had my boss/the tax man on my back for a month; *Fam* **il me tombe toujours sur le d.** *(il m'attaque)* he's always on my back; *(il arrive à l'improviste)* he's always just turning up; **le fisc va te tomber sur le d.** you're going to have the tax man on your back, you're going to bring the tax man down on you; **le repassage, c'est toujours sur son d. que ça tombe** he always gets landed with the ironing; **quand mes frères font des bêtises, c'est toujours sur mon d. que ça tombe** I always get the blame when my brothers do something stupid; **mettre qch sur le d. de qn** to saddle sb with sth; **quand il a été interrogé, il a tout mis sur mon d.** when he was questioned, he put all the blame on me; **il a tout mis sur le d. des petits copains et est parti tranquillement en vacances** he offloaded everything onto his friends and blithely went off on holiday; **il s'est mis une sale histoire sur le d.** he's landed himself in real trouble; **gagner de l'argent** ou **s'enrichir sur le d. de qn** to get rich off sb, to make money on sb's back; **je n'ai rien à me mettre sur le d.** I haven't a thing to wear; *Fam Vieilli* **faire la bête à deux d.** to have it off; *Fam Vieilli* **faire la bête à deux d. avec qn** to sleep with or have it off with sb

2 *(d'une chaise, d'une page, d'un couteau etc)* back; *(du nez)* bridge; *(d'un livre)* spine; **signer au d. d'un chèque** to endorse a cheque; **voir au d.** see over or overleaf; *Fin* **d. d'un effet** back of a bill

3 *(nage)* **d. (crawlé)** backstroke; **nager le** ou **faire du d. (crawlé)** to do the backstroke

dosage [dozaʒ] NM *Chimie etc (d'ingrédients)* proportioning; *Méd (de médicaments)* dosage; *Méd* **d. hormonal** test to determine hormone levels

dos-d'âne [dodɑn] NM INV bump; **pont en d.** humpbacked bridge

dose [doz] NF *Chimie etc (d'un élément dans un mélange)* proportion, amount; *(de médi-*

cament) dose; **d. mortelle** lethal dose; **ne pas dépasser la d. prescrite** do not exceed the stated dose; _Fig_ **par** _ou_ **à petites doses, à d. homéopathique** in small doses; **une légère d. d'ironie** a tinge of irony; _Fam_ **il faut une sacrée d. de culot/d'humour pour faire cela** it takes a helluva nerve/a great sense of humour to do that; **forcer la d.** to overdo it; _Fam_ **avoir sa d.** to have had more than enough; **avoir sa d. de lecture/de ménage/de cinéma américain** to have had one's fill of reading/housework/American films; _Fam_ **en avoir sa d.** to have had one's fill, to have had more than enough; **la pluie, je t'assure que j'en ai ma d.** I've had my fill of rain _or_ more than enough rain, let me tell you

doser [doze] **VT** _Chimie etc_ (_pour évaluer_) to determine the quantity of; (_pour constituer_) to proportion; (_médicament_) to measure out; **je n'arrive jamais à d. la farine dans mes gâteaux** I never manage to get the right amount of flour in my cakes; _Fig_ **il faut savoir d. l'ironie** you have to get the amount of irony just right

doseur [dozœr] **NM** measure; **verre d.** _Culin_ measuring jug; (_pour l'alcool_) measure

doseur-distributeur, _pl_ **doseurs-distributeurs NM** (_de carburant_) fuel distributor

dossard [dosar] **NM** _Sport_ number

dossier [dosje] **NM 1** (_d'un siège_) back, backrest; **chaise à d. droit** straight-backed chair; **d. réglable** adjustable back; **d. rabattable** folding seatback; **d. repliable** folding seatback

2 (_pièces, documents_) file, dossier; (_d'un prisonnier, d'un malade etc_) record; (_chemise_) folder, file; _Ordinat_ file; **verser une pièce au d.** to file a document; **constituer un d. sur qn/qch** to build up a file on sb/sth; **d. d'appel d'offres** tender documents; **d. client** client file; **d. crédit** credit file; **d. de demande d'introduction en Bourse** listing agreement; **d. de demande de prêt** loan application form; **d. 'divers'** miscellaneous file; **d. de domiciliation** domiciliation papers, domiciliation file; **d. de douane** customs papers _or_ file; **d. d'information** information pack; **d. de lancement** (_d'un produit_) product launch file; **d. médical** medical record; _Fam_ **d. offre** tender documents; **d. de presse** book of press cuttings, scrap book; **d. scolaire** school records; **d. suspendu** suspension file; _Ordinat_ **d. système** system folder; **d. de voyage** travel documents

3 (_sujet_) question, matter; **le d. de la couche d'ozone est assez important** the ozone layer is a fairly important question _or_ matter; **le d. du GATT** the GATT question, GATT matters; **s'occuper du d. de l'environnement** to be responsible for environmental matters; **avoir un d. brûlant à traiter** to have a controversial issue to deal with; **je pense qu'il est temps de fermer le d. Staline** I think it's time to draw a line under the Stalin question

dot [dɔt] **NF 1** (_pour un mariage_) dowry, marriage settlement; **il l'a épousée pour sa d.** he married her for her dowry; **coureur de d.** fortune hunter **2** (_pour une religieuse_) dowry

dotal, -ale, -aux, -ales [dɔtal, -o] **ADJ** (_propriété_) dotal; _Jur_ **régime d.** (_marriage_) settlement in trust

dotation [dɔtasjɔ̃] **NF 1** (_fonds_) (_d'hôpital, de collège etc_) endowment, foundation; (_à la famille royale, à un chef d'État_) allowance **2** _Can Admin_ staffing; **agent de d.** staffing officer; **d. en effectifs** staff increase **3** _Compta_ provision; **d. aux amortissements** depreciation provision, allowance for depreciation, charge to depreciation; **d. aux provisions** charge to provisions; **d. en capital** capital contribution

doter [dɔte] **VT** (_hôpital, collège etc_) to en-

dow; _Vieilli_ (_mariée_) to dower; **être doté de toutes les vertus** to be endowed with every virtue; **d. une usine d'un matériel neuf** to equip a factory with new plant; **la nature l'a dotée d'une intelligence remarquable** nature has bestowed exceptional intelligence on her _or_ has endowed her with exceptional intelligence; **d. une provision** to make a provision

douaire [dwɛr] **NM** dower

douairière [dwɛrjɛr] **ADJ, NF** dowager

douane [dwan] **NF** _Admin_ customs; **(droits de) d.** (customs) duty; **passer à la d.** _ou_ **au bureau de d.** to go through customs; **passer qch (en fraude) à la d.** to smuggle sth through customs; **formalités de d.** customs formalities; **à l'aéroport, les formalités de d. sont vraiment simplifiées** it's really easy to go through customs at the airport; **agent des douanes** customs officer; **marchandises en d.** bonded goods; **franc de d.** duty paid; **d. volante** mobile customs and excise unit

douanier, -ière [dwanje, -jɛr] **ADJ** customs; **tarif d.** customs tariff; **union douanière** customs union; **barrières douanières** tariff barriers

N customs officer

doublage [dublaʒ] **NM 1** (_d'une feuille de papier, d'une couverture, d'un fil etc_) doubling, folding in half **2** (_d'une quantité, d'un salaire etc_) doubling **3** (_d'un manteau_) lining **4** _Cin_ (_de voix_) dubbing; (_dans une scène_) doubling (**de** for); **d. du film en anglais** English dubbing of the film; **d. du dialogue (en boucle)** dialogue looping **5** _Aut_ **d. d'aile** wing valance

DOUBLE [dubl] **ADJ 1** (_mesure, quantité, consonne, lit, chambre etc_) double; _Scol_ **copie d.** double sheet of paper; **valise à d. fond** suitcase with a false bottom; **faire qch en d. exemplaire** to do sth in duplicate; **coup d.** (_au tir_) right and left; **mot qui fait d. emploi (avec un autre)** redundant word; **'vends micro-ondes, cause d. emploi'** (_de petite annonce_) 'microwave for sale, duplicate item'; **sa canne à pêche a une longueur d. de la mienne** his fishing rod is twice the length of _or_ twice as long as mine; **fermer une porte à d. tour** to double-lock a door; **enfermer qn à d. tour** to lock sb in; **d. effet** dual- _or_ double-action; **outil à d. usage** dual-purpose tool; **à d. tranchant** (_couteau_) double-edged; _Fig_ two-edged; **comptabilité en partie d.** double-entry bookkeeping; **d. allumage** (_de moteur_) dual ignition; **avoir une d. nationalité** to have dual nationality; **foyer à d. revenu** two-income household; **d. whisky** double _or_ large whisky; _Mus_ **d. croche** semiquaver, _Am_ sixteenth note; **d. mètre** rule (_which measures two metres_); **d. nœud** double knot; **doubles rideaux** curtains, _Am_ drapes; _Fig_ **faire coup d.** to kill two birds with one stone; **test en d. aveugle** double blind test; _Fig_ **mettre les bouchées doubles** to work twice as hard; **d. vitrage** double glazing; **d. arbre à cames** twin cam, twin camshaft; _Tél_ **(à) d. bande** dual-band; **d. carburateur** twin carburettor; _UE_ **d. circulation** (_de monnaies_) dual circulation; _Journ_ **d. colonne** double column; _Ordinat_ **d. densité** double density; _Aut_ **d. ligne blanche** double white line; _Journ_ **d. page** (double-page) spread; **l'article prend une d. page** it's a two-page spread; _Jur_ **d. peine** double punishment (_consisting of a prison sentence followed by expulsion from the country_); _Typ, TV, Cin_ **d. prise** double-take; **d. interligne** double spacing; **en d. interligne** double-spaced; _Typ_ **d. soulignement** double underlining; _Typ_ **d. souligné** double underline

2 (_ambigu_) **d. personnalité** dual personality; **mener une d. vie** to lead a double

life; **mot à d. sens** ambiguous word; **agent d.** double agent; **jouer un d. jeu avec qn** to play a double game with sb; **je n'ai pas le don de d. vue** I'm not endowed with ESP, I'm not psychic, I don't have second sight

ADV voir d. to see double

NM 1 (_quantité_) double; **j'ai le d. de votre âge** I'm twice your age; **ça m'a coûté le d.** it cost me twice as much _or_ double; **mettre qch en d.** to double sth, to fold sth in two _or_ half; _Tennis_ **d. messieurs/dames/mixte** men's/ladies'/mixed doubles; **faire un d.** (_dans un jeu_) to throw a double

2 (_exemplaire_) duplicate, copy; _Ordinat_ backup; **faire qch en d.** (_lettre, devoir, clé_) to make two copies of sth; **je dois tricoter le pull en d.** I'll have to make two pullovers of the same pattern; **avoir un d. des clefs** to have duplicate keys _or_ a spare set of keys; **avoir un d. de tous les papiers importants** to have duplicates of all the important papers; **prends-le, je l'ai en d.** take it, I have two of them; **j'ai un timbre en d. dans ma collection** I have two copies of a stamp in my collection; **j'ai tous mes papiers en d. au cas où** I have duplicates _or_ copies of all my papers just in case

3 (_personne_) double

doublé [duble] **ADJ 1** doubled **2** (_veste, gants_) lined (**de** with) **3** _Cin_ dubbed, re-voiced

NM 1 d. (or) gold plate, rolled gold; (_bijouterie_) gold-plated jewellery _or Am_ jewelry; **d. argent** silver plate; (_bijouterie_) silver-plated jewellery **2** (_à la chasse_), _Sport_ double

double-bande, _pl_ **doubles-bandes** [dubləbãd] **NF** _TV_ double head

double-blanc, _pl_ **doubles-blancs** [dubləblã] **NM** (_aux dominos_) double blank

double-clic, _pl_ **doubles-clics** [dubləklik] **NM** _Ordinat_ double-click; **faire un d.** to double-click

double-cliquer [dubləklike] **VI** _Ordinat_ to double-click

double-commande, _pl_ **doubles-commandes** [dubləkɔmãd] **NF** _Aviat, Aut_ dual controls

double-corde, _pl_ **doubles-cordes** [dubləkɔrd] **NF** _Mus_ (_sur un violon etc_) double-stopping

double-crème, _pl_ **doubles-crèmes** [dubləkrɛm] **NM** (_type of_) cream cheese

double-débrayage [dublədebrɛjaʒ] **NM** _Aut_ double-declutching; **faire un d.** to double-declutch

double-décimètre, _pl_ **doubles-décimètres** [dublədesimɛtr] **NM** ruler

double-fenêtre, _pl_ **doubles-fenêtres** [dubləf(ə)nɛtr] **NF** sash window, double-hung window

doublement¹ [dubləmã] **ADV** doubly

doublement² **NM 1** (_d'un nombre, d'une somme, d'une lettre etc_) doubling; (_d'une feuille de papier_) folding in two _or_ in half; (_d'une couverture, d'un fil_) folding in two _or_ in half, doubling; _Ordinat_ **d. de vitesse d'horloge** clock speed doubling **2** _Aut_ overtaking, _Am_ passing; **tenter un d.** to try to overtake; **d. interdit** no overtaking

doubler [duble] **VT 1** (_montant, taille etc_) to double; **d. le pas** to quicken one's pace

2 (_feuille de papier_) to fold in two _or_ in half; (_couverture, fil_) to fold in two _or_ in half, to double; _Mus_ **d. une partie** to double a part

3 (_manteau, gant etc_) to line

4 _Belg, Can, Suisse Scol_ (_redoubler_) to repeat (_a school year_)

5 _Cin_ (_voix_) to dub; _Cin_ (_acteur_) to stand in for; _Théâtre_ (_rôle, acteur_) to understudy; **il se fait d. pour les cascades** he's got a stand-in for his stunts; _Cin_ **d. une prise** to do a double-take

6 *(passer)* **d. les gens dans une queue** to jump a queue, to sneak past the people in a queue; **d. une voiture** to overtake *or Am* pass a car; *Naut* **d. un cap** to double *or* make *or* weather a cape **7** *Fam (trahir)* to double-cross; **on s'est fait d.** we've been double-crossed

VI 1 *(de population etc)* to double, to increase twofold **2** *Aut* to overtake, *Am* to pass; **défense de d.** no overtaking, *Am* no passing **3** *Belg,Can, Suisse Scol (redoubler)* to repeat a year

VPR se doubler une haine qui se double de mépris hatred coupled with contempt

doublet [dublɛ] NM *(pierre précieuse)*, *Ling* doublet

doubleur [dublœr] NM *Ordinat* **d. de fréquence** clock speed doubler

doublon¹ [dublɔ̃] NM *Typ* double, word keyed twice

doublon² NM *Hist (monnaie)* doubloon

doublonner [dublɔne] VI **notre nouvelle imprimante doublonne avec l'ancienne** our new printer makes the old one redundant, our new printer means that we no longer need the old one

doublure [dublyr] NF **1** *(d'un vêtement, d'un sac de couchage etc)* lining **2** *Théâtre* understudy; *Cin* stand-in, body double; *(cascadeur)* stunt man/woman

douce [dus] *voir* **doux**

douce-amère, *pl* **douces-amères** [dusamɛr] NF woody nightshade, bittersweet

douceâtre [dusɑtr] ADJ sweetish, *Péj* sickly sweet

doucement [dusmɑ̃] ADV *(délicatement)* gently; *(bas)* softly; *(en faisant attention)* gently, carefully, slowly; **allez-y d.!** gently does it!, easy does it!; **les affaires vont d.** business is so-so; *Fam* **(allez-y) d. avec le vin** go easy on the wine, *Arg* **ça m'a fait d. rigoler** I had a good laugh over it; *Fam* **d. les basses!** take it easy!

doucereux, -euse [dusrø, -øz] ADJ **1** *(goût etc)* sweetish, *Péj* sickly (sweet) **2** *(personne)* smooth, smooth-tongued; *(voix, ton)* smooth, sugary

doucet, -ette [dusɛ, -ɛt] ADJ *Arch (personne)* meek, mild
  NF **doucette** *(plante)* corn salad, lamb's lettuce

douceur [dusœr] NF **1** *(d'un son, d'une matière)* softness; *(d'un climat)* mildness; *(d'une atmosphère)* pleasantness; **d. de vivre** easy *or* relaxed way of life; **les douceurs de l'amitié** the comforts *or* pleasures of friendship **2** *(de caractère)* gentleness; *(d'un sourire)* sweetness; **traiter qn avec d.** to treat sb gently *or* with kindness; **employer la d. avec un enfant/un animal** to be gentle with a child/an animal; **en d.** gently; **la voiture a démarré en d.** the car started smoothly; **allez-y en d.!** gently does it!, easy does it!; **poser un avion en d.** to land an aircraft smoothly, to make a smooth landing **3** *(sucreries)* **douceurs** sweets, sweet things; **aimer les douceurs** to have a sweet tooth; *Fig* **dire des douceurs à une femme** to whisper sweet nothings to a woman **4** *(du miel, d'un parfum etc)* sweetness

douche [duʃ] NF **1** shower; *(installation)* shower (unit); **prendre une d.** to take a shower; **être sous la d.** to be in the shower; **préférer la d. au bain** to prefer a shower to a bath; **passer à la d.** to take a shower; **les douches** the shower room(s), the showers **2** *Fam (de pluie)* **on s'est pris une de ces douches!** we got soaked! **3** *Fig* disappointment; **plus jamais je ne voudrais me prendre une d. pareille** I don't want another disappointment like that ever again

▸ ▸ **d. écossaise** (alternately) hot and cold shower; *Fig* **il a un caractère tellement changeant qu'avec lui, c'est toujours la d. écossaise** he's so unpredictable that you never know where you are with him; *Fig* **ça m'a fait l'effet d'une d. écossaise** it came as a bit of a shock; *Fig* **d. froide** terrible disappointment, let-down

doucher [duʃe] VT **1** *(pour laver)* **d. qn** to give sb a shower **2** *Fam (d'une averse)* to soak; **se faire d. par l'orage** to get soaked in the storm **3** *Fam (fustiger)* to tell off; *(décevoir)* to shock; **il s'est fait d. par le patron** he got a telling-off from the boss; **ça m'a vraiment douché** it came as a real shock
  VPR se doucher to take a shower, to shower

douchette [duʃɛt] NF **1** *(pomme)* shower head **2** *(pour codes-barres)* bar code reader

doudou [dudu] NF *(aux Antilles)* girlfriend

doudoune¹ [dudun] NF *(anorak)* down jacket

doudounes² NFPL *Fam (seins)* boobs

doué [dwe] ADJ *(acteur, musicien etc)* gifted, talented; **il n'est guère d. pour les langues** he has no gift for languages, he's no linguist; *Hum* **tu es vraiment d.!** that was really intelligent *or* clever!

douer [dwe] VT to endow *(de* with); **il est doué d'une bonne mémoire** he has a good memory

douille [duj] NF *(d'un outil etc)* socket; *(d'une ampoule électrique)* lamp socket; *(d'une cartouche etc)* case; *Culin* piping nozzle; **d. à (pas de) vis** screw lamp holder

douiller [duje] VI *Fam (coûter cher)* to cost an arm and a leg; **la prochaine facture de téléphone, ça va d.** the next phone bill is going to be sky-high; **c'est un restau qui douille** the prices are sky-high in that restaurant, it costs an arm and a leg to eat in that restaurant

douillet, -ette [dujɛ, -ɛt] ADJ **1** *(coussin)* soft, downy; *(lit)* cosy **2** *(trop délicat)* **ne sois pas si d.!** don't be such a baby *or Fam* wimp!
  NF **douillette 1** *(robe de chambre)* quilted housecoat *or Am* robe; *(de curé)* overcoat **2** *Can (couvre-lit)* quilted bedspread

douillettement [dujɛtmɑ̃] ADV *(confortablement)* cosily; **quand il fait froid, je m'installe d. sous la couette** when it's cold, I snuggle down under the quilt; **j'étais d. enroulée dans mon châle** I was all snug and cosy *or* I was wrapped up warmly in my shawl; **élever un enfant d.** to coddle a child; **il a été élevé trop d.** he was coddled too much as a child; **sa mère le traite toujours d.** his mother still coddles him

douleur [dulœr] NF **1** *(physique)* pain; *(diffuse)* ache; **d. aiguë** sharp pain; **pousser un cri/des cris de d.** to cry out with *or* in pain; **j'ai une d. persistante dans le genou** I have a persistent ache in my knee; **se sentir des douleurs par** *ou* **dans tout le corps** to ache all over; **j'ai des douleurs dans le ventre** I've got pains in my stomach; **sans d.** *(accouchement)* painless **2** *(morale)* sorrow, grief; **il a eu la d. de perdre sa mère** he had the painful experience of losing his mother; **partager la d. de qn** to share sb's sorrow *or* grief, to feel for sb; **nous avons la d. de vous faire part du décès de …** we regret to inform you of the death of …; *Fam* **si je le chope, il va comprendre sa d.!** if I catch him, he'll get what's coming to him *or* his worst nightmares will come true!

douloureusement [dulurøzmɑ̃] ADV painfully; *(regarder qn)* sorrowfully; **il s'est cogné le genou d.** he gave himself a painful knock on the knee; **c'est une perte qu'elle ressent d.** she feels the loss deeply; **il a été d. atteint par la mort de sa grand-mère** his grandmo-

ther's death upset him very much *or* affected him deeply

douloureux, -euse [dulurø, -øz] ADJ **1** *(coup, maladie, opération etc)* painful; *(au contact)* sore, tender; **mon dos est d. aujourd'hui** my back hurts *or* aches today, my back is hurting today **2** *(perte, événement etc)* sad, distressing; *(séparation)* painful; *(circonstances)* painful, distressing; *(regard)* pained, sorrowful; **des cris d.** heart-rending *or* mournful cries
  NF *Fam* **la douloureuse** the bill; **apportez-moi la douloureuse** let's see what the damage is

DOUTE [dut] NM **1** *(incertitude)* doubt, uncertainty; **être dans le d.** to be in doubt, to be doubtful *(au sujet de qch* about sth); **mettre qch en d.** to question sth, to cast doubt on sth; **mettre en d. la parole de qn** to doubt sb's word; **il n'y a pas de** *ou* **aucun d.** there's no doubt about it, it is beyond doubt *or* beyond (all) question; **laisser qn dans le d. est cruel** it's cruel to leave sb in doubt *or* in a state of uncertainty; **je ne lui ai laissé aucun d. quant à mes sentiments pour lui** I left him in no doubt about my feelings for him; **cela ne fait plus aucun d.** there is no longer any doubt about it; **nul d. qu'il (ne) soit mort** there is no doubt that he is dead; **sans d.** no doubt, probably; **sans aucun d.** without (any) doubt; **vous ne me reconnaissez pas, sans d.** I don't suppose you recognize me; **sans d. viendra-t-il, sans d. qu'il viendra** I expect he'll come, he'll probably come; *Prov* **dans le d., abstiens-toi** when in doubt, don't **2** *(soupçon)* doubt, misgiving, suspicion; **avoir des doutes sur** *ou* **au sujet de qn/qch** to have doubts *or* misgivings *or* suspicions about sb/sth; **avoir un d. (sur qch)** to have misgivings *or* doubts (about sth); **j'ai un d. sur la vérité de ce qu'il dit** I have doubts about whether he's telling the truth; **il y a quand même un d. sur son passé** there is still some doubt about his past

DOUTER [dute] VI to doubt; **il était à n'en point d. courageux** his courage was beyond all question; **d. de qn/qch** to doubt sb/sth; **je n'ai jamais douté de vos compétences** I have never doubted your ability; **je n'ai jamais douté de ta venue** I never doubted that you would come; **je n'ai jamais douté de te voir** I never doubted that I would see you; **d. du zèle de qn** to doubt *or* question sb's enthusiasm, to have doubts about sb's enthusiasm; **elle doute de vous avoir rencontré** she's not sure whether she's met you; **il ne doute de rien** he is full of self-confidence; **j'en doute** I doubt it, I have my doubts (about it); **j'en doute fort** I doubt it very much, I have very strong doubts

VT **je doute qu'il soit assez fort** I doubt whether he is strong enough; **je n'ai jamais douté que tu viennes** I never doubted that you would come; **je ne doute pas qu'il (ne) vous vienne en aide** I am confident that he will help you

VPR se douter se d. de qch to suspect sth; **il ne se doute de rien** he doesn't suspect anything; **je m'en doutais (bien)** I guessed *or* thought as much; **elle est surprise, je m'en doute** she is surprised, I'm sure *or* I dare say; **je ne me doutais pas qu'il fût là** I had no idea that he was there; **je me doute bien que c'est un peu difficile** I rather suspect *or* think it's going to be difficult; **j'étais loin de me d. que cela arriverait** I never thought for a moment that that would happen; *Fam* **on s'en serait douté!** I might have known *or* guessed!

douteux, -euse [dutø, -øz] ADJ **1** *(incertain)* doubtful; *(origine, authenticité)* doubtful, questionable; **il est d. qu'il vienne** it is doubtful whether he will come; **il n'est pas**

d. que ... (ne) + *sub ou plus souvent que* + *ind* there is no doubt that ...; **créance douteuse** bad debt **2** *(honneur, compagnie, fraîcheur, mœurs etc)* dubious; **jour d.** dubious *or* uncertain light; **des vêtements d.** *ou* **d'une propreté douteuse** dubious clothes; **d'un blanc d.** of a dubious white; **d'un goût d.** *(plaisanteries, vêtements, pièce)* in dubious taste; **il a des petites copines d'un goût d.** he has some rather dubious girlfriends

douve [duv] NF **1** *Agr* trench, ditch; *Courses de chevaux* water jump; **douves** *(d'un château)* moat **2** *(planche)* stave

Douvres [duvr] N Dover

doux, douce [du, dus] ADJ **1** *(au toucher)* smooth, soft; *(au goût)* mild; **eau douce** fresh water; *(non calcaire)* soft water; **poisson d'eau douce** freshwater fish; *Fam* **marin d'eau douce** landlubber; **peau douce** smooth *or* soft skin

2 *(air, ton etc)* pleasant, agreeable; **d. souvenir** pleasant memory; **mener une vie douce** to lead a calm *or* peaceful life; *Fam* **se la couler douce** to take it easy; **faire les yeux d. à qn** to make sheep's eyes at sb; *Iron* **douce perspective!** charming prospect!

3 *(mouvement, voix, pente)* gentle; *(couleur, son)* soft, subdued; *(lumière)* mellow, soft, subdued; *(climat, hiver)* mild; *(moteur, suspension)* sweet; **chaleur douce** moderate heat; *Culin* **faire cuire à feu d.** to cook on a low heat *or* in a low oven; **lime douce** smooth file; **drogue douce** soft drug; **des médecines douces** alternative forms of medicine; **consonne douce** soft consonant

4 *(nature, regard)* mild, gentle; **être d. avec les enfants** to be kind to children; *(d'un animal)* to be good *or* gentle with children; **être d. avec les animaux** to be kind to animals; **il est très d. avec son petit garçon** he's very gentle with his little boy; **d. comme un agneau** as gentle as a lamb

5 *Fam* **c'est de la folie douce!** it's sheer madness!

▸ ADV *Fam* **filer d.** to tread warily, to watch one's step; **là, tout d.!** steady, steady!

▸ NM **préférer le sec au d.** to prefer dry (wine) to sweet

▸ NF **douce 1** *Fam (petite amie)* girlfriend; **allez, viens, ma d.** come on, sweetheart **2 en d.** discreetly, quietly, *Fam* on the QT

▸ N *Fam* **c'est un d./une douce** he's/she's a gentle creature

douzain [duzɛ̃] NM *Littér* twelve-line poem

douzaine [duzɛn] NF dozen; **trois douzaines d'œufs** three dozen eggs; **une d. de personnes** about a dozen people, a dozen or so people; **il y a une d. d'années** about twelve years ago, a dozen or so years ago; **quand nous avions une d. d'années** when we were about twelve; **à la d.** by the dozen; *Fig* **il y en a à la d.** there are dozens *or* lots of them SEE GRAMMAR A12–13; B60

douze [duz] ADJ INV twelve; **le d. mai** the twelfth of May; **Louis D.** Louis the Twelfth; **d. heures** twelve o'clock (noon)
NM INV twelve

douzième [duzjɛm] ADJ, N twelfth

douzièmement [duzjɛmmɑ̃] ADV twelfthly, in the twelfth place

doyen, -enne [dwajɛ̃, -ɛn] N **1** *(d'un chapitre, d'une faculté)* dean; *(d'un corps, d'une association etc)* doyen **2** *(personne la plus âgée)* senior; **elle est la doyenne de notre groupe** she's the oldest in *or* the oldest member of our group; **d. d'âge** oldest member

doyenné [dwajɛne] NM *Rel (dignité, résidence)* deanery
NF **d. (du comice)** comice (pear)

dpi [depei] *(abrév* **dots per inch***)* dpi

drache [draʃ] NF *Région* downpour; **on s'est pris une de ces draches!** we got soaked *or* drenched!

dracher [draʃe] V IMPERS *Région* to pour

drachme [drakm] NF *Anciennement* drachma

draconien, -ienne [drakɔnjɛ̃, -jɛn] ADJ *(règlement)* draconian; **régime d.** very strict diet

dragage [dragaʒ] NM **1** *(nettoyage) (d'une rivière, d'un port etc)* dredging **2** *(d'une rivière pour retrouver un corps etc)* dragging; **d. des mines** mine-sweeping

dragée [draʒe] NF **1** *(confiserie)* sugar(ed) almond; *Pharm* sugar-coated pill; **tenir la d. haute à qn** to make sb dance to one's tune **2** *(petit plomb)* small shot; *Arg (balle)* bullet

dragéifier [draʒeifje] VT *Pharm (pilule)* to coat with sugar, to sugar; **comprimé dragéifié** sugar-coated tablet

drageon [draʒɔ̃] NM *Bot* sucker

dragon [dragɔ̃] NM **1** *Myth, Fig* dragon; *Fig* **c'est un d. de vertu** she pretends to be such a paragon of virtue; **d. volant** *(reptile)* flying lizard **2** *Mil* dragoon; **dragons portés** ≃ motorized cavalry

dragonne [dragɔn] NF *(d'une épée, d'un sabre)* sword knot; *(d'un parapluie)* strap

drague [drag] NF **1** *Tech* dredger; *(grappin)* drag, grappling hook; *Pêche* dredge, dragnet; **d. suceuse** pump dredger; **d. à godets** bucket dredger **2** *Fam (pour séduire)* chatting up men/women, *Am* hitting on men/women; **il y a de la d. dans l'air** someone's getting the come-on; **un champion** *ou* **professionnel de la d.** an expert at chatting up women; **c'est un lieu de d. idéal** it's an ideal place for chatting people up

draguer [drage] VT **1** *(nettoyer) (rivière, port etc)* to dredge **2** *(pour retrouver qch) (étang etc)* to drag; *(bras de mer)* to sweep; *Pêche (huîtres etc)* to dredge for **3** *Fam (hommes, femmes)* to chat up, to try to pick up, *Am* to hit on; **il m'a draguée** he tried to pick me up
▸ VI *Fam* to chat up men/women, *Am* to hit on men/women; **ça drague sec** *ou* **dur ici** there's a lot of chatting up going on here

dragueur, -euse [dragœr, -øz] NM **1** *(bateau)* dredger; **d. de mines** minesweeper **2** *(ouvrier), Tech* dredgerman; *(avec grappin)* dragman
▸ N *Fam* **c'est un d.** he's always on the pull *or Am* on the make; **c'est une sacrée dragueuse** she's always chatting up the men

drain [drɛ̃] NM **1** *(conduit)* drain(pipe) **2** *Chir* drainage tube

drainage [drenaʒ] NM **1** *(d'un champ, d'une plaie etc)* drainage, draining **2** *(d'argent, de capital)* drain

drainer [drene] VT **1** *(sol, abcès)* to drain **2** *(commerce, capital, talent, ouvriers etc)* to draw, to attract

Dralon® [dralɔ̃] NM Dralon®

DRAM [dram] NF *Ordinat (abrév* **dynamic random access memory***)* DRAM

dramatique [dramatik] ADJ *Théâtre* dramatic; **l'art d.** drama; **école d'art d.** drama school; **auteur d.** playwright; *Fig* **il est arrivé quelque chose de d.** something dreadful *or* terrible has happened; **mais c'est d.!** that's dreadful *or* terrible!; **je ne considère pas son départ comme d.** I don't think his leaving is a tragedy; *Fam* **c'est pas d.** it's not a tragedy, it's not the end of the world
▸ NF *TV* television play *or* drama; *Radio* radio play *or* drama

Il faut noter que l'adjectif anglais **dramatic** ne signifie jamais **terrible** ni **tragique**.

dramatiquement [dramatikmɑ̃] ADV tragically

Il faut noter que l'adverbe anglais **dramatically** est un faux ami. Il signifie le plus souvent **radicalement**.

dramatisation [dramatizasjɔ̃] NF dramatization

dramatiser [dramatize] VT **1** *(événement etc)* to dramatize **2** *(roman)* to dramatize, to adapt for the stage

dramaturge [dramatyrʒ] NM dramatist, playwright

dramaturgie [dramatyrʒi] NF dramatic art

drame [dram] NM **1** *(genre littéraire)* drama; *Arch (pièce)* play; **d. lyrique** *(opéra)* opera; *(oratorio)* oratorio; **d. psychologique** psychological drama **2** *Fig* drama, tragedy; **la scène a tourné au d.** the scene took a tragic turn; **il ne faut pas en faire un d.** there's no need to make a drama out of it *or* to dramatize it; **ce n'est pas un d.** it's not the end of the world, it's nothing to get upset about; **il nous a fait tout un d. parce que son stylo avait disparu** he made quite a scene because his pen had disappeared **3** *Cin, Radio, TV* drama; **d. judiciaire** courtroom drama; **d. reconstitué** drama documentary, dramadoc; **d. télévisé** television drama

drap [dra] NM **1** *Tex* cloth; **d. fin** broadcloth; **d. d'or/de soie** gold/silk brocade; *Hist* **le camp du D. d'or** the Field of the Cloth of Gold **2 d. (de lit)** sheet; **d. de dessous/dessus** bottom/top sheet; **se mettre dans** *ou* **entre les draps** to go to bed; *Fig* **être dans de beaux** *ou* **mauvais** *ou* **vilains draps** to be in a fine mess *or* in a pickle *or* in a predicament **3** *Belg (serviette)* towel; **d. de maison** table cloth
▸ ▸ **d. de bain** bath sheet; **d. mortuaire** pall; **d. de plage** beach towel

drapé [drape] ADJ **1** *(couvert d'un drap)* covered with a sheet *or* a cloth **2** *(à plis)* draped; **robe drapée sur les épaules** dress draped at the shoulders
▸ NM *(d'un vêtement)* drape

drapeau, -eaux [drapo] NM flag; *Mil (regimental)* colour; *Cin, TV (sur lumière)* flag, gobo; **arborer** *ou* **hisser un d.** to hoist a flag; *Mil* **présentation du d.** ≃ trooping the colour; *Fig* **être sous les drapeaux** to serve in the (armed) forces; **mourir pour le d.** to die for the flag *or* one's country; *Fig* **se ranger sous les drapeaux de la Serbie/des verts** to join the Serbian/greens' camp; *Arg* **planter un d.** to leave without paying (the bill); *Aviat* **mettre une hélice en d.** to feather a propeller; *Sport* **abaisser le d. à l'arrivée du premier concurrent** to flag in the winner
▸ ▸ **d. blanc** white flag; **d. noir** black flag; **d. rouge** red flag

drapement [drapmɑ̃] NM *(de tissu)* draping

draper [drape] VT **1** *Tex (laine)* to process **2** *(étoffe)* to drape
▸ VPR **se draper** to wrap oneself up, to drape oneself *(dans, de* in); *Fig* **se d. dans sa dignité** to stand on one's dignity

draperie [drapri] NF **1** *(usine)* cloth factory; *(commerce)* drapery (trade) **2** *Beaux-Arts* drapery **3** *(tenture)* curtains, *Am* drapes

drap-housse, *pl* **draps-housses** NM fitted sheet

drapier, -ière [drapje, -jɛr] N *(marchand)* draper; *(fabricant)* cloth manufacturer
▸ ADJ *(industrie)* cloth(-making); *(ouvrier, marchand)* cloth

DRASS [dras] NF *Admin (abrév* **Direction régionale des affaires sanitaires et sociales***)* = office administering health and social services at regional level

drastique [drastik] ADJ drastic

NM *Méd* drastic purgative

drave [drav] **NF** *Can (de rondins)* drive

draver [drave] **VT** *Can (rondins)* to float, to drive

draveur [dravœr] **NM** *Can* driver, raftsman

draw-back, *pl* **draw-backs** [drobak] **NM** *Com* drawback

dreadlocks [drɛdlɔks] **NFPL** dreadlocks

drelin [drəlɛ̃] **INT** *Vieilli* ting-a-ling, tinkle

Dresde [drɛzd] **N** Dresden

dressage [drɛsaʒ] **NM 1** *(d'un mât, d'un monument, d'un échafaudage etc)* erection, raising; *(d'une tente)* pitching **2** *Tech (d'un morceau de bois etc)* trimming, dressing; *(d'une tige, d'une barre)* straightening **3** *(d'un animal)* training; *Fam (d'un enfant)* strict upbringing; *Équitation* **d.** *(élémentaire)* breaking in; *Équitation* **d.** *(supérieur)* dressage; **ce n'est pas une éducation qu'ils donnent à cet enfant, c'est un d.** that child isn't being brought up, he's being trained

dresser [drese] **VT 1** *(ériger) (mât, monument, échafaudage etc)* to erect, to put up, to raise; *(échelle, lit)* to put up; *(tente)* to pitch, to put up; *(bûcher)* to erect; **d. la tête** to hold up *or* lift one's head; *(pour regarder)* to look up; **d. les oreilles** *(d'un animal)* to prick up *or* cock its ears; *Fig* **d. l'oreille** to prick up one's ears; **une histoire à faire d. les poils** *ou* **les cheveux (sur la tête)** a hair-raising story, a story to make your hair stand on end **2** *Tech (morceau de bois)* to trim, to dress; *(fil)* to straighten out **3** *(établir) (plan, rapport, estimation etc)* to prepare, to draw up; *(liste, inventaire)* to prepare, to draw up, to make out; **d. un contrat** to draw up a contract; **d. une carte** to make a map; **pourriez-vous me d. la liste de ce dont vous avez besoin?** could you make a list for me of what you need? **4** *(préparer) (piège)* to set; *Fig* **d. ses batteries** to draw up a battle plan *or* a plan of action *or* *Litt* one's batteries; **d. la table** *ou* **le couvert** to lay *or* set the table; **d. un plat** to put food on a plate, to arrange a dish **5** *(animal, Fam (enfant)* to train (**à faire qch** to do sth); *(cheval)* to break in; *Arch, Péj (recrue)* to train, to drill; *Fam* **ça le dressera!** that'll teach him!, that'll put him in his place!; *Fig* **d. une personne contre une autre** to set one person against another

VPR se dresser 1 *(se lever)* to stand up, to rise; *(sur une chaise, dans un lit)* to sit up; *(se tenir droit)* to hold oneself erect *or* straight; *(d'un cheval)* to rear (up); *(d'un chien)* to stand up; **se d. sur la pointe des pieds** to stand on tiptoe; **ses cheveux se dressaient (sur sa tête)** his hair stood on end; *Fig* **quand je le vois, j'ai les poils qui se dressent** my hackles rise whenever I see him; **les obstacles qui se dressent sur notre chemin** the obstacles that stand *or* lie in our way; *Fig* **se d. contre qch** to rise up (in protest) against sth, to revolt against sth **2** *(s'apprivoiser)* to be tamed; **les hérissons ne se dressent pas** hedgehogs can't be tamed

dresseur, -euse [drɛsœr, -øz] **N** *(d'animaux)* trainer; **d. de chevaux** horse-breaker; **d. de fauves** wild animal tamer

dressing(-room), *pl* **dressings** *ou* **dressing-rooms** [drɛsiŋ(rum)] **NM** dressing room

dressoir [drɛswar] **NM** dresser, sideboard

dreyfusard, -arde [drɛfyzar, -ard] **N** *Hist* supporter *or* defender of Dreyfus

DRH [deɛraʃ] **NM** *(abrév* **directeur des ressources humaines)** HRD, human resources manager

NF *(abrév* **direction des ressources humaines)** HRM, human resources management

dribble [dribl] **NM** *Ftbl etc* dribble

dribbler [drible] **Ftbl etc** **VI** to dribble

VT *(ballon)* to dribble; **d. un joueur** to dribble round a player

dribbleur [driblœr] **NM** *Ftbl etc* dribbler

dribbling [dribliŋ] **NM** *Rugby* forward ruck

drill¹ [drij] **NM** *(singe)* drill

drill² [dril] **NM** *Mil etc* drill

drille¹ [drij] **NM** *Fam Vieilli* **c'est un bon** *ou* **joyeux d.** he's always good for a laugh

drille² [drij] **NF** *Tech* hand drill

driller [drije] **VT** *Tech* to drill, to bore

dring [driŋ] **INT** ting-a-ling

drink [drink] **NM** *Fam* drink

drisse [dris] **NF** *Naut* halyard

drive [drajv] **NM** *Tennis, Golf* drive

drive-in [drajvin] **NM INV** drive-in

driver¹ [drajvœr] **NM 1** *Sport (dans les courses de trot)* driver **2** *Golf (club)* driver

driver² [drajve] **VI** *Tennis, Golf* to drive

VT 1 *Tennis, Golf (balle)* to drive **2** *(dans les courses de trot)* to drive

drogman [drɔgmã] **NM** *Vieilli* dragoman

drogue [drɔg] **NF 1** *(stupéfiant)* drug, narcotic; **d. dure/douce** hard/soft drug; **prendre de la d.** to take *or* be on drugs; **trafic de d.** drug trafficking; **l'argent de la d.** drug money; **il faut lutter contre la d. dans les lycées** we have to fight against drugs in high schools; *Hum* **moi, ma d., c'est le chocolat** chocolate is what I'm hooked on, I'm a chocaholic; *Fig* **la télévision est une d. pour beaucoup de gens** lots of people are television addicts *or* are hooked on television **2** *Vieilli (médicament)* remedy, medicine; *Péj* nostrum, quack remedy

drogué, -ée [drɔge] **N** drug addict; *Fig* **les drogués de l'information** information addicts; **les drogués de la cigarette** people hooked on cigarettes

droguer [drɔge] **VT 1** *(malade)* to dose (with medicine); **je déteste les médecins qui vous droguent** I hate doctors who force medicine on you **2** *(victime)* to drug; *(cheval de course etc)* to dope, *Arg* to nobble

VPR se droguer 1 *(prendre des stupéfiants)* to take drugs; **il se drogue** he's taking drugs, he's on drugs; **il se drogue à l'héro** he's on heroin **2** *Pharm* to be always taking drugs; **elle est obligée de se d. pour dormir** she has to take drugs in order to be able to sleep

droguerie [drɔgri] **NF** *(magasin)* ≃ hardware store, *Br* ironmonger's *(selling paint, cleaning materials etc)*; *(commerce)* ≃ hardware trade

droguet [drɔgɛ] **NM** *Tex Vieilli* drugget

droguiste [drɔgist] **NM** ≃ hardware dealer, *Br* ironmonger *(dealing in paints, cleaning materials etc)*; **épicier d.** grocer and general storekeeper

droit¹, droite [drwa, drwat] **ADJ 1** *(vertical)* straight; **se tenir d.** to hold oneself erect, to stand up straight; **d. comme un i** *ou* **un piquet** as straight *or* stiff as a poker; **col d.** stand-up collar; **jupe droite** straight skirt; **veste droite** boxy jacket; *(non croisée)* single-breasted jacket; *Math* **angle d.** right angle; **section droite** cross section

2 *(non courbe) (route, ligne)* straight; **coup d.** *Escrime* straight thrust; *Tennis* forehand drive; **en ligne droite** in a straight line, as the crow flies; *Fig* **ces boucles d'oreille me viennent en droite ligne de ma grand-mère** I inherited these earrings from my grandmother; **ses idées viennent en droite ligne de celles de son père** he gets his ideas from his father; *Fig* **ne pas s'écarter du d. chemin** not to leave the straight and narrow; **ramener qn dans le d. chemin** to bring sb back to the straight and narrow; *Couture* **dans le d. fil** on the straight; *Fig* **son étude est dans le d. fil des conceptions freudiennes** his study

is in line with Freudian concepts; *Naut* **mettre la barre droite** to right the helm; *Naut* **d. la barre!** helm amidships!

3 *(honnête) (personne, conduite)* upright, honest

ADV 1 c'est d. devant vous *ou* **tout d.** it's straight ahead of you; **marcher d.** to walk straight *or* in a straight line; *Fig* to toe the line; **aller d. au fait** to get straight to the point; **aller** *ou* **courir d. à qch** to be heading straight for sth; **votre cadeau/proposition m'est allé(e) d. au cœur** I am deeply touched *or* moved by your gift/suggestion; **écrire d.** to write straight *or* in a straight line; *Naut* **d. devant, d. droite** right ahead

2 *Suisse (tout à fait, exactement)* **c'est d. son père** he's the spitting image of his father; **elle est d. arrivée** *(tout juste)* she's just arrived

NF droite straight line; **tracer une droite reliant A à B** to draw a line connecting A and B

droit², droite ADJ *(main, jambe, gant etc)* right; **être le bras d. de qn** to be sb's right-hand man; **du côté d.** on the right-hand side

NF droite 1 *(côté droit)* right (hand), right-hand side; **tourner à droite** to turn (to the) right; **rouler à droite** to drive on the right; **tenir** *ou* **garder sa droite** to keep to the right; **à ma droite, le château** to *or* on my right is the castle; **sur la droite, il y a un feu** on the right there is a traffic light; **reconnaître sa droite de sa gauche** to know one's left from one's right; **le placard de droite** the right-hand cupboard, the cupboard on the right; **à droite du placard** to *or* on the right of the cupboard; **regarder de droite à gauche** to look from right to left; **courir à droite et à gauche** to run about all over the place; **j'entends dire à droite et à gauche** *ou* **de droite et de gauche que ...** I hear from all quarters *or* on all sides that ...; *Naut* **(la barre) à droite!** starboard!

2 *Pol* **la droite** the right (wing); **candidat/idées/journal de droite** right-wing candidate/ideas/newspaper; **voter à droite** to vote for the right; **droite dure** hard right; **droite modérée** soft right

NM *Boxe* right; **crochet du d.** right hook; **direct du d.** straight right

DROIT³

right **1** ▪ fee **2** ▪ tax **2** ▪ duty **2** ▪ law **3**		

NM 1 *(prérogative)* right; **d. de chasse/pêche** hunting/fishing rights; **le d. du plus fort** the law of the jungle; **avoir d. de vie et de mort sur qn** to have the power of life and death over sb; **avoir d. de regard sur qch** to have the right to approve sth, *Fam* to have a say on sth; **avoir le d. de savoir** to have the right to know; **tous droits réservés** all rights reserved; **faire valoir ses droits** to assert one's rights; **avoir d. à qch** to have a right to sth, to be entitled to sth; **il a d. à mes excuses** I owe him an apology; *Fam Iron* **il a eu d. aux inévitables recommandations** he was treated to the inevitable good advice; *Fam* **ce soir, on va encore y avoir d.** the same treat is in store for us again this evening; *Fam* **ils parlent de licencier 300 personnes, je sens que je vais y avoir d.** they're talking about laying off 300 people and I think that's going to include me; *Fam* **s'il pleut dans tout le pays, il n'y a pas de raison qu'on n'y ait pas d.** if it's raining all over the country, there's no reason why here should be any exception *or* why we should escape; **ce coupon (vous) donne d. à ...** this coupon entitles you to ...; **avoir le** *ou* **être en d. de faire qch** to have a right to do sth, to be justified in doing sth, to be entitled to do sth; **je n'ai pas le d. de le faire** I'm not allowed to do it; **tu n'as pas le d. de me reprocher cela** you've no right to hold that

against me; **avoir des droits sur qn/qch** to have rights over sb/sth; **tu n'as aucun d. sur les décisions de tes enfants** you have no say in your children's decisions; **à bon d.** *(d'une façon justifiée)* with good reason; *(selon la loi)* legitimately; **de d. et de fait** de facto and de jure; **à qui de d.** to whom it may concern; **s'adresser à qui de d.** to apply to the proper quarter *or* to an authorized person; **être dans son (bon) d.** to be within one's rights; **tu serais dans ton d. si tu lui demandais une compensation** you'd be within your rights asking him for compensation; **de quel d. me critiques-tu?** by what right do you criticize me?, what gives you the right to criticize me?, what right have you to criticize me?; **de quel d. êtes-vous entré?** what right had you *or* what gave you the right to come in?; **faire d. à une demande** to comply with *or* accede to a request; **les droits de l'amitié** the claims of friendship; **Commission européenne des droits de l'homme** European Commission of Human Rights; **Convention relative aux droits de l'enfant** Convention on the Rights of the Child

2 *(en argent)* fee, due; *(imposition)* duty; *(taxe)* tax; *Compta* **d. fixe** fixed rate of duty; **exempt de droits** duty-free; **allocation de fin de droits** = reduced amount of unemployment benefit (paid to people whose benefit period has almost expired); **(chômeur en) fin de droits** = unemployed person whose benefit period is running out

3 *Jur* law; **le d.** the law; **d. administratif** administrative law; **d. aérien** aviation law; **d. bancaire** banking law; **d. de brevet** patent law; **d. civil** civil law; **d. commercial** commercial law; **d. communautaire** Community law; **d. de la consommation** consumer law; **d. constitutionnel** constitutional law; **d. coutumier** common law; **d. commun** common law; **d. des contrats** contract law; **d. criminel** criminal law; **d. douanier** customs legislation; **d. écrit** statute law; **d. fiscal** tax law; **d. hôtelier** hotel law; **d. international** international law; **d. de marque** trademark law; **d. des obligations** ≃ law of contract; **d. pénal** criminal law; **d. public** public law; **d. privé** private law; **d. romain** Roman law; **d. des sociétés** corporate law; **d. du travail** labour laws; **faire son d.** to study *or* read law; **étudiant en d.** law student

▸▸ **d. d'accès** right of access; **droits acquis** vested rights; *Com* **droits acquittés** duty paid; **d. d'admission** *(prérogative)* right of entry; *(imposition)* import duty; *Fin, Com* **droits ad valorem** ad valorem duty; **d. d'aînesse** birthright; *TV* **droits d'antenne** broadcasting rights; **d. d'asile** right of asylum; **droits d'auteur** royalties; **d. au bail** *(bien incorporel)* leasehold; *(comme bien incorporel)* right to a lease; *Aviat, Naut* **droits de cabotage** cabotage rights; **d. canon** canon law; **d. de cité** freedom of a/the city; *Fig* **il n'a pas d. de cité dans cette maison** he is not welcome in this house; **droits civils** civil rights; **droits du consommateur** consumer rights; *Com* **d. de courtage** brokerage (fee); **droits de diffusion** broadcasting rights; **monarchie de d. divin** kingship by divine right; **droits de douane** (customs) duty; **d. d'entrée** *(coût)* admission fee; *(prérogative)* right of entry; *(imposition)* import duty; *Com* **droits exclusifs** sole rights; **droits d'exclusivité** exclusive rights; **droits d'exécution en public** performing rights; **droits d'exploitation d'un feuilleton** serial rights; **droits d'exploitation pour le monde entier** (wide) rights; **droits d'exploitation à la télévision** TV rights; **droits d'exploitation vidéo** video rights; **d. d'exportation** export duty; **d. de grève** right to strike; **d. d'importation** import duty; **droits d'inscription** registration fee; **droits internationaux** international

rights; **droits d'interprète** performing rights; **d. de licenciement** right to dismiss (employees); **d. de passage** right of way; **droits de port** harbour dues; *Jur* **d. de rachat** repurchase right, buyback right; *Journ* **d. de rectification** right of reply; *Journ* **d. de réponse** right of reply; **d. de reproduction** reproduction rights; **avoir le d. du sang** to have the nationality of one's parents; **avoir le d. du sol** to have the nationality of the country where one was born; *Fin, Com* **droits de sortie** export duty; **d. de souscription (d'actions)** subscription right; **droits statutaires** statutory rights; **droits de succession** death duties; *Admin* **d. de timbre** stamp duty; *Fin* **droits de tirage** drawing rights; **droits de tirage spéciaux** special drawing rights; **droits de trafic** *(des compagnies aériennes)* traffic rights; **d. d'usage** right of use; **d. aux vacances** holiday entitlement; **droits de vote** voting rights

droitement [drwatmɑ̃] ADV **faire son travail d.** to do an honest day's work; **il juge les gens d.** he judges people fairly

droitier, -ière [drwatje, -jɛr] ADJ **1** right-handed **2** *Pol Fam* right-wing N right-handed person

droiture [drwatyr] NF rectitude, honesty

drolatique [drɔlatik] ADJ *Litt* comic, humorous, droll

drôle [drol] ADJ **1** *(amusant)* funny, amusing; **je ne trouve pas ça très d.** I don't think that's very funny; **ça ne va pas être d.** it's not going to be much fun; *Fam* **vous êtes d.! qu'auriez-vous fait à ma place?** come on! what would you have done in my place?

2 *(étrange)* funny, odd, strange; **je l'ai trouvé d. hier** he was behaving rather oddly *or* strangely yesterday; **c'est d. que je ne t'aie pas reconnu tout de suite** it's funny *or* odd that I didn't recognize you immediately; **une d. d'odeur** a funny *or* a strange *or* an odd smell; **quelle d. d'idée!** what a funny *or* a strange *or* an odd idea!; **j'ai dû faire une d. de tête** I must have looked a bit taken aback; *Fam* **un d. de type** a queer fish, an odd sort; *Fam* **la d. de guerre** the phoney war

3 *Fam (sacré)* **il faut une d. de patience** it needs an awful lot *or* surtout *Am* a heck of a lot of patience; **il a une d. de force** he's awfully strong; **en voir de drôles** *(avoir des ennuis)* to have an awful time (of it); **ils en ont vu de drôles pendant leur voyage au Maroc** they had an incredible time on their trip to Morocco; **en faire voir de drôles à qn** to give sb an awful time (of it)

ADV *Fam* **ça m'a fait tout d. de te voir là** it gave me a funny *or* a strange *or* an odd feeling to see you there

NM **1** *Arch (mauvais sujet)* rascal, knave, scamp **2** *Région (jeune garçon)* lad

drôlement [drolmɑ̃] ADV **1** funnily, strangely, oddly **2** *Fam (sacrément)* awfully, awful; **les prix ont d. augmenté** prices have gone up an awful lot; **je me suis d. amusé** I had a great time, I had an awful(ly) good time *or* an awful lot of fun; **elle est d. bien** *(remarquable)* she's a terrific person; *(belle)* she's gorgeous, she's great-looking

drôlerie [drolri] NF *(caractère amusant)* funniness; *(action)* joke; *(parole)* joke, funny remark

drôlesse [droles] NF **1** *Vieilli (femme effrontée)* bitch **2** *Région (jeune fille)* lass

dromadaire [drɔmadɛr] NM dromedary

drop (goal) [drɔp(gol)] NM *Rugby* drop goal

droppage [drɔpaʒ] NM *Aviat* (parachute) drop; **zone de d.** drop zone

drosophile [drɔzɔfil] NF fruit fly

drosser [drɔse] VT *Naut (du vent, courant)* to drive

dru [dry] ADJ *(herbe, blé etc)* thick, dense; *(cheveux, barbe)* thick; *(pluie)* heavy
ADV **tomber d.** to fall thick and fast; **pousser d.** *(de l'herbe etc)* to grow thickly

drugstore [drœgstɔr] NM drugstore

druide, druidesse [drɥid, drɥidɛs] N druid, f druidess

druidique [drɥidik] ADJ druidic(al)

druidisme [drɥidism] NM druidism

drummer [drœmœr] NM *Mus* drummer

drupe [dryp] NF *Bot* drupe

dry [draj] ADJ INV dry; **champagne d.** dry champagne; **whisky d.** neat *or* straight whisky
NM INV dry Martini®

dryade [drijad] NF *(nymphe)* dryad, wood nymph

DST [deɛste] NF *(abrév* **Direction de la surveillance du territoire)** = French Secret Service

DTP [detepe] NM *(abrév* **diphtérie, tétanos, polio)** diphtheria, tetanus and polio vaccination

DTS [detees] NMPL *(abrév* **droits de tirage spéciaux)** special drawing rights

du [dy] *voir* de

dû, due [dy] ADJ **1** *(que l'on doit)* due, owing, owed; *Com* **en port dû** carriage forward **2** *(causé)* **ce retard est dû à ...** this delay is due to ...; **son licenciement est dû aux difficultés économiques de l'entreprise** he was made redundant because of *or* due to the company's economic difficulties; **sa maladresse est due à sa timidité** his clumsiness is caused by *or* is due to his shyness **3** *(approprié)* **en temps dû** in due course; **contrat rédigé en bonne et due forme** contract drawn up in due form, formal contract
NM due; **chacun sera rétribué selon son dû** everyone will be paid according to his due

dualisme [dɥalism] NM dualism

dualiste [dɥalist] ADJ dualistic
N dualist

dualité [dɥalite] NF duality

dubitatif, -ive [dybitatif, -iv] ADJ doubtful, dubious

dubitativement [dybitativmɑ̃] ADV doubtfully, dubiously

Dublin [dyblɛ̃] N Dublin

dublinois, -oise [dyblinwa, -waz] ADJ of/from Dublin
N D. Dubliner

duc [dyk] NM **1** duke **2** *(oiseau)* horned owl; **grand d.** eagle owl

ducal, -ale, -aux, -ales [dykal, -o] ADJ ducal

duché [dyʃe] NM duchy, dukedom

duchesse [dyʃɛs] NF **1** duchess; *Péj* **elle fait la d.** she puts on airs **2** *(fruit)* (poire) **d.** duchess pear **3** *Culin* **pommes (de terre) d.** duchesse potatoes

Duchnoque [dyʃnɔk] NM *Fam* pal, matey, *Am* bud, buddy

Ducon [dykɔ̃], **Ducon-la-joie** [dykɔ̃laʒwa] NM *très Fam* shit-for-brains, *Br* dick features

ducroire [dykrwar] NM *Com* del credere; *(agent)* del credere agent

ductile [dyktil] ADJ ductile, tensile

ductilité [dyktilite] NF ductility

duègne [dɥɛɲ] NF *Arch* duenna, chaperon

duel¹ [dɥɛl] NM duel; **se battre en d.** to fight a duel; **provoquer qn en d.** to challenge sb to a duel; **d. oratoire** battle of words

duel² NM *Gram* dual (number)

duelliste [dɥelist] NM duellist

duettiste [dɥetist] N *Mus* duettist

duffel-coat, duffle-coat, *pl* **duffel-coats, duffle-coats** [dœfølkot] NM duffel coat, duffle coat

dulcinée [dylsine] NF *Hum* love of one's life

dum-dum, *pl* **dum-dums** [dumdum] NF dumdum bullet

dûment [dymã] ADV duly, in due form

dumping [dœmpiŋ] NM *Com* dumping; **faire du d.** to dump; **être accusé de faire du d.** to be accused of dumping; **d. social** social dumping

dune [dyn] NF dune, sandhill

dunette [dynɛt] NF *Naut* poop (deck)

Dunkerque [dœ̃kɛrk] NF Dunkirk

duo [dɥo] NM *Mus* duet; *Théâtre* duo; *Fam* **d. d'injures** slanging match

duodécimal, -ale, -aux, -ales [dɥodesimal, -o] ADJ duodecimal

duodénal, -ale, -aux, -ales [dɥodenal, -o] ADJ *Anat* duodenal

duodénite [dɥodenit] NF *Méd* duodenitis

duodénum [dɥodenɔm] NM *Anat* duodenum

duopole [dɥopɔl] NM *Com* duopoly

dupe [dyp] NF dupe, *Fam* sucker; **prendre qn pour d.** to fool sb, to take sb in; **c'est un marché de dupes** I've/he's/*etc* been had *or* taken in *or* swindled
ADJ naive, gullible, easily deceived; **je ne suis pas d.** I'm not fooled *or* taken in; **il me ment, mais je ne suis pas d.** I'm well aware that he's lying to me

duper [dype] VT to dupe, to deceive, to fool, to take in
VPR **se duper** to deceive oneself

duperie [dypri] NF *(tromperie)* deception; **victime d'une d.** victim of deception; **une vaste d.** one vast deception

dupeur, -euse [dypœr, -øz] N *Litt* trickster, deceiver

duplex [dyplɛks] ADJ INV *Tél* duplex; *TV, Radio* link-up
NM INV **1** *Tél, TV* duplex, diplex; **(émission en) d.** link-up **2** *(appartement)* maison(-n)ette, *Am* duplex

duplexer [dyplɛkse] VT *Tél* to duplex

duplicata [dyplikata] NM INV duplicate (copy)

duplicateur [dyplikatœr] NM duplicator, duplicating machine

duplication [dyplikasjɔ̃] NF **1** *Math* duplication; *Biol* doubling **2** *Tél* duplexing; *Ordinat* **d. de logiciel** software copying

duplicité [dyplisite] NF duplicity, double dealing

dupliquer [dyplike] VT *Tél* to duplex

DUR, DURE [dyr]

ADJ	hard **1–5** ▪ tough **1** ▪ difficult **2–4** ▪ severe **4**
ADV	hard
N	tough guy ▪ hard liner

ADJ **1** *(rigide) (substance)* hard; *(viande)* tough; **œuf d.** hard-boiled egg; **pain d.** stale bread; **être d. à cuire** *(de viande)* to take a lot of cooking; *Fam (de personne)* to be a tough nut; **eau dure** hard water
2 *(qui résiste à l'effort)* hard, difficult; **cette porte est dure (à ouvrir)** this door is stiff, this door is hard *or* difficult to open; *Aut etc* **commande dure** stiff control; **être d. à la peine** to be a tireless worker; **avoir l'oreille dure, être d. d'oreille** *ou Fam* **de la feuille** to be hard of hearing; **avoir la tête dure** to be obstinate *or* pig-headed; **avoir la vie dure** *(d'une personne, d'un animal)* to be hard to kill; *Fig* **les idées reçues ont la vie dure** preconceived ideas die hard; *Fam* **être d. à la détente** *(lent à comprendre)* to be slow on the uptake
3 *(difficile) (travail etc)* hard, difficult; **c'est**

d. à croire it's hard *or* difficult to believe; **enfant d.** difficult *or* problem child
4 *(pénible)* hard, difficult; **hiver d.** hard *or* severe winter; **des scènes très dures** distressing *or* painful sights; **rendre la vie dure à qn** to make sb's life a misery; **la vie est dure** it's a hard life; **les temps sont durs** times are hard; **avoir un coup d.** to be dealt a severe blow; **une dure épreuve** a severe trial, a sore test; **être à dure école** to have a hard time of it
5 *(sévère, cruel)* hard; **avoir le cœur d.** to be hard-hearted *or* callous; **être d. envers** *ou* **pour** *ou* **avec qn** to be hard *or* rough on sb; **c'est un tendre sous ses dehors très durs** he's quite soft-hearted under that tough exterior of his
ADV *Fam (travailler, cogner)* hard; **le soleil tape d. ce matin** the sun is really beating down this morning; **croire qch d. comme fer** to be quite convinced of sth; **il croit d. comme fer que ...** he is quite convinced *or* really believes that ...; **d. d.!** (what a) bummer!; **d. d. la rentrée dans mon nouveau bahut!** what a bummer having to go to a new school next term!
NM **1** *Constr* **bâtiment en d.** permanent building
2 *Arg (train)* train
N *Fam (personne)* **un d.** a tough guy, a hard nut; *Pol* a hardliner; **un d./une dure à cuire** a hard-boiled man/woman; **il aime bien jouer les durs** he likes to act tough
NF **coucher sur la dure** *(sur le sol)* to sleep on the floor; *(dehors)* to sleep rough; **vivre à la dure** to rough it; **il a été élevé à la dure** he's had a hard upbringing, he was brought up in the school of hard knocks; *Fam* **en dire de dures à qn** to tell sb where to get off; *Fam* **elle en a vu de dures** she's had a hard *or* tough time (of it)

durabilité [dyrabilite] NF durability

durable [dyrabl] ADJ durable, lasting, long-lasting

durablement [dyrabləmã] ADV durably

duraille [dyraj] ADJ *Fam* hard; **il était d., le problème de maths** the maths question was a real pig; **se faire piquer son mec par sa meilleure copine, c'est plutôt d.** it's a bit of a bummer *or* downer when your best friend steals your man

Duralumin® [dyralymɛ̃] NM Duralumin®

durant [dyrã] PRÉP during; **d. toute sa vie, sa vie d.** during his whole life, throughout his life; **parler des heures d.** to talk for hours on end *or* for hours at a time; **d. quelques instants** for a few moments

durcir [dyrsir] VT to harden, to make hard; *Fig* **d. la ligne du parti** to harden *or* stiffen the party line; **il a durci son opinion** his opinion has stiffened; **la France a décidé de d. ses positions au sujet de GATT** France has decided to take a tougher position *or* a harder line on GATT
VI *(de pain, sol)* to harden, to become hard; *(du ciment etc)* to set, to harden
VPR **se durcir** to harden; *Fig (d'opposition)* to stiffen; **ses traits se sont durcis** his features have hardened

durcissement [dyrsismã] NM *(de pain, du sol)* hardening; *(du ciment etc)* setting, hardening; *Fig (d'opposition, d'opinion)* stiffening; *(d'une attitude)* hardening

durée [dyre] NF *(d'un règne, de la guerre etc)* duration; *(d'un tissu, d'édifice etc)* lasting quality, wear; *(d'une ampoule)* life; *Mus (d'une note)* length, value; *(d'un film, d'une émission)* running time, screen time; **bonheur de courte/longue d.** short-lived/lasting happiness; **d. d'un bail** duration *or* term of a lease; **contrat à d. illimitée** *ou* **indéterminée** permanent contract; **quelle est la d.**

de votre congé? how long is your leave?, how long does your leave last?; **disque longue d.** long-playing record, LP; *Cin* **d. de projection** running time; **d. de crédit** term of loan; **d. de séjour** length of stay; **d. de validité** period of validity; **d. de vie** lifespan; *(d'une pile etc)* life; *(d'une machine etc)* useful life; *(d'un produit)* shelf-life, life expectancy; **d. de vol** flight time; **d. de voyage** journey time; **d. du travail** working hours; *Compta* **d. d'amortissement** depreciation period; *Radio* **d. d'écoute** listening time; *Ordinat* **d. de connexion** on-line time

durement [dyrmã] ADV **1** *(avec vigueur) (se battre)* hard **2** *(péniblement)* **d. éprouvé** sorely tried **3** *(sévèrement, cruellement) (répondre, parler)* harshly, roughly; *(touché)* severely; **on l'a élevée d.** she had a harsh *or* hard upbringing; **très d. touché par qch** very hard hit by sth; **d. secoué dans un accident/par une nouvelle** severely *or* badly shaken up in an accident/by a piece of news

durer [dyre] VI **1** *(avoir une durée) (d'un congé, d'une opération etc)* to last; **voilà trois ans que cela dure** it's been going on for three years; **votre congé dure combien de temps?** how long does your leave last *or* is your leave?
2 *(continuer, perdurer)* to last; **cela ne durera pas** it can't *or* won't last; **pourvu que ça dure!** long may it last *or* continue!; **ça va d. longtemps, cette plaisanterie?** hasn't this gone on long enough?; **ça ne peut pas d.** this can't go on; *Fam* **ça durera ce que ça durera** it'll last as long as it's meant to last; **cette réparation n'est pas très solide, mais ça durera ce que ça durera** it's not a brilliant repair job, but it'll do for the moment *or* for the time being; **faire d. qch** *(une réunion, une conversation téléphonique, un repas)* to drag sth out; *(un manteau, un livre etc)* to make sth last; *Hum* **faire d. le plaisir** to prolong the agony; **tissu qui durera** material which will wear well; *Péj* **elle dure la mémé** the old woman is hanging on
3 *Fam Région* **il ne peut pas d. en place** he can't stay put *or* keep still

dureté [dyrte] NF **1** *(d'une substance, de l'eau)* hardness; *(de la viande)* toughness **2** *(d'une personne, d'une voix)* harshness; *(d'un hiver, d'un climat)* severity; *(de traits)* hardness; **d. de cœur** hard-heartedness; **parler avec d.** to speak harshly

durillon [dyrijɔ̃] NM *(sur la main)* callus; *(sur le pied)* corn, callus

Durit® [dyrit] NF *Aut, Aviat etc* hose (connection), flexible pipe; *Fam* **péter une D.** *(se mettre en colère)* to hit the roof *or Am* ceiling

DUT [deyte] NM *(abrév* **diplôme universitaire de technologie***)* = post-baccalauréat technical qualification awarded after two years

duvet [dyve] NM **1** *(sur le menton, un oisillon, une pêche etc)* down; **d. de l'eider** eiderdown; **d. du cygne** swan's down **2** *(sac de couchage)* sleeping bag **3** *Belg, Suisse (couette)* duvet, continental quilt

duveté [dyvte] ADJ downy

duveter (se) [sədyvte] VPR to become downy

duveteux, -euse [dyvtø, -øz] ADJ downy

DVD [devede] NM *(abrév* **Digital Video Disc** *ou* **Digital Versatile Disc***)* DVD

DVD-R [devedeɛr] NM *Ordinat (abrév* **Digital Video Disc-Recordable***)* DVD-R

DVD-ROM [devederɔm] NM *Ordinat (abrév* **Digital Video Disc-Read Only Memory***)* DVD-ROM

DVD-RW [devedeɛrdubləve] NM *Ordinat (abrév* **Digital Video Disc-Rewritable***)* DVD-RW

dwell [dwɛl] NM *Aut* dwell

dynamique [dinamik] ADJ dynamic; *Fam* c'est un type d. he's lively *or* dynamic *or* go-ahead

▮ NF dynamics; **d. de groupe** group dynamics; **d. du marché** market dynamics

dynamiquement [dinamikmã] ADV dynamically

dynamisant [dinamizã] ADJ motivating, stimulating

dynamisation [dinamizasjɔ̃] NF motivation, stimulation

dynamiser [dinamize] VT to motivate, to stimulate

dynamisme [dinamism] NM dynamism; *Fam (vitalité)* dynamism, vitality, drive

dynamiste [dinamist] N *Phil* dynamist

dynamitage [dinamitaʒ] NM dynamiting

dynamite [dinamit] NF dynamite

dynamiter [dinamite] VT *(édifice etc)* to dynamite, to blow up; *Fig (idée, certitude, conception)* to explode

dynamiteur, -euse [dinamitœr, -øz] N dynamiter

dynamo [dinamo] NF *Élec* dynamo

dynamoélectrique [dinamoelɛktrik] ADJ *Élec* dynamoelectric(al)

dynamogène [dinamoʒɛn] ADJ *Physiol* energy-giving

dynastie [dinasti] NF dynasty

dynastique [dinastik] ADJ dynastic

dyne [din] NF *Phys* dyne

dysenterie [disɑ̃tri] NF *Méd* dysentery

dysentérique [disɑ̃terik] ADJ *Méd* dysenteric

dysfonctionnement [disfɔ̃ksjɔnmã] NM *(d'un organe)* dysfunction, malfunction; *(d'une institution, d'un service)* failure

dyslexie [dislɛksi] NF *Méd* dyslexia

dyslexique [dislɛksik] ADJ dyslexic ▮ N dyslexic

dysménorrhée [dismenɔre] NF *Méd* dysmenorrhoea, *Am* dysmenorrhea

dyspepsie [dispɛpsi] NF *Méd* dyspepsia

dyspepsique [dispɛpsik], **dyspeptique** [dispɛptik] ADJ, N *Méd* dyspeptic

E¹, e [ə] NM *(lettre)* E, e

E² *(abrév* **Est**) E

EAO [ɜao] NM *Ordinat (abrév* **enseignement assisté par ordinateur**) CAL

EARL [ɜaɛrɛl] NF *abrév* **Exploitation agricole à responsabilité limitée**

eau, *pl* **eaux** [o] NF **1** *(liquide naturel)* water; **e. potable** drinking water; **e. non potable** water unfit for drinking; *(sur panneau)* not drinking water; **e. du robinet** tap water; **e. courante** running water; **faire installer l'e. courante** to have water laid on; **e. en bouteille** bottled water; **laver le plancher à grande e.** to swab down the floor; **passer à l'e.** to rinse; **cuire à l'e.** to boil; **pommes de terre à l'e.** boiled potatoes; **whisky sans e.** neat whisky; **se mettre à l'e.** to go on the wagon; **service des eaux** water supply; **e. de la ville** main(s) water; **château d'e.** water tower; **conduite d'e.** water main(s); **il est tombé beaucoup d'e.** a lot of rain fell; **chaussures qui prennent l'e.** shoes that let in water; **faire de l'e.** *(d'une locomotive, d'un bateau)* to water, to take on water; *Vieilli* **être comme l'e. et le feu** to be as different as or to be like chalk and cheese; *Fam* **compte là-dessus et bois de l'e.!** don't count on it!; *Fig* **mettre de l'e. dans son vin** to tone it down a bit; *Fam* **s'en aller en e. de boudin** to go down the tubes *or* up the spout; *Fam* **il y a de l'e. dans le gaz** there's trouble brewing

2 ville d'eau(x) spa; **prendre les eaux** to take *or* drink the waters

3 *(étendue, masse)* water; **au bord de l'e.** by the water's side *or* edge; **restaurant au bord de l'e.** waterside restaurant; **sur l'e.** afloat; **tomber à l'e.** to fall into the water; *Fig (d'un plan)* to fall through; *Fig Fam* **mes vacances sont à l'e.** my holiday is up the spout *or* down the tubes; **mettre un navire à l'e.** to launch a ship; **se mettre à l'e.** to go in (for a swim); *Fig* **se lancer** *ou* **se jeter à l'e.** to take the plunge; *Fig* **apporter de l'e. au moulin de qn** to strengthen sb's case, to provide sb with ammunition; *Fig* **porter de l'e. à la rivière** *ou* à la **mer** to take coals to Newcastle; *Fig* **de l'e. sous les ponts avant que** *ou* **d'ici à ce que … it will be a long time before …; mais depuis, bien de l'e. est passée sous les ponts** a lot of water has flowed under the bridge since then, that was a long time ago; *Fig* **pêcher en e. trouble** to fish in troubled waters; *Fig* **nager** *ou* **naviguer en e. trouble** to sail close to the wind; **faire e.** *(d'un bateau)* to leak, to spring a leak; **cours d'e.** *(rivière, fleuve)* river; *(ruisseau)* stream; **jet d'e.** fountain; **pièce d'e.** (ornamental) lake; *(petite)* pond, pool, water feature; **eaux internationales/françaises** international/French waters; **dimanche: grandes eaux à Versailles** the fountains will play at Versailles on Sunday; *Fig Fam* **c'était les grandes eaux** the waterworks started, he/she turned on the waterworks; *Fig Fam* **on va avoir droit aux grandes eaux** we'll be in for waterworks *or* floods of tears; *Fig* **dans ces eaux-là** or thereabouts; **mortes-eaux** neap tides; **vives-eaux** spring tides; **hautes/basses eaux** high/low water; *Fig* **nager entre deux eaux** *(ne pas s'engager)* to sit on the fence; **être dans les eaux d'un navire** to be in the wake of a ship; *Fig* **être** *ou* **naviguer dans les eaux de qn** *(rallier ses opinions)* to take the same line as sb; **il navigue dans les eaux de plusieurs peintres en vue** he hangs around several well known painters

4 *(sécrétions du corps humain)* **être tout en e.** to be dripping with perspiration; **cela me fait venir** *ou* **me met l'e. à la bouche** it makes my mouth water; **j'ai l'e. à la bouche rien que d'y penser** my mouth is watering just thinking about it; **j'en ai l'e. à la bouche!** my mouth is watering (already)!; **cloque pleine d'e.** water blister; **poche des eaux** amniotic sac, bag of waters; **elle a perdu les eaux** her waters have broken

5 *(d'un melon)* juice; **les concombres rendent beaucoup d'e.** cucumbers give off *or* out a lot of water

6 *(pureté)* **de la plus belle e.** *(diamant)*, *Fig (charlatan etc)* of the first water; **ces deux-là sont de la même e.** they're two of a kind, they're tarred with the same brush

▸▸ **e. bénite** holy water; **e. de Cologne** eau de Cologne; **e. déminéralisée** deionized water; **e. dentifrice** mouthwash; **e. distillée** distilled water; **e. douce** *(non salée)* fresh water; *(sans calcaire)* soft water; *Fam* **marin d'e. douce** landlubber; **e. dure** hard water; **e. de fleurs d'oranger** orange flower water; **e. gazeuse** carbonated *or* sparkling water; **e. grasse** washing-up water; **e. de Javel** bleach; **e. de lavande** lavender water; *Nucl* **e. lourde** heavy water; **e. de mélisse** = liqueur made from lemon balm; **e. minérale** (natural) mineral water; **e. oxygénée** hydrogen peroxide; **e. de parfum** eau de parfum; **e. plate** still water; **e. de pluie** rainwater; **e. de refroidissement** cooling water; **e. régale** aqua regia; **e. de roche** spring water; **e. de rose** rose water; *Fig* **roman/film à l'e. de rose** soppy *or* slushy novel/film; **e. rougie** = water with a drop of wine in it; **eaux de ruissellement** runoff; **e. de Seltz** soda water, Seltzer (water); **e. de source** spring water; **eaux territoriales** territorial waters; **eaux thermales** thermal *or* hot springs; **e. de toilette** toilet water, eau de toilette; **eaux usées** waste water; **traitement des eaux usées** waste water treatment; **e. de vaisselle** washing-up water

eau-de-vie, *pl* **eaux-de-vie** [odvi] NF *(de prune etc)* brandy

eau-forte, *pl* **eaux-fortes** NF **1** *Chimie* aqua fortis, nitric acid **2** *Beaux-Arts* etching, etched engraving

eaux-vannes [ovan] NFPL sewage (water)

ébahi [ebai] ADJ astounded, *Fam* flabbergasted, staggered; **un regard é.** a look of blank astonishment

ébahir [ebair] VT to astound, *Fam* to flabbergast, to stagger
   VPR **s'ébahir** to be dumbfounded (**de** by)

ébahissement [ebaismɑ̃] NM astonishment

ébarbage [ebarbaʒ] NM *(d'un livre)* trimming the pages; *(d'une feuille de papier)* trimming the edges; *(d'une haie, pelouse)* clipping; *(d'une surface métallique)* removal of the burrs

ébarber [ebarbe] VT *(feuille de papier)* to trim (the edges of); *(livre)* to trim the pages of; *(haie, pelouse)* to clip; *(surface métallique)* to remove the burrs from

ébarbure [ebarbyr] NF *(de métal etc)* burr, paring; *(de papier)* trimming

ébats [eba] NMPL playing (about); **é. (amoureux)** lovemaking; **au milieu de leurs é. (amoureux)** in the middle of their lovemaking, while they were making love

ébattre (s') [sebatr] VPR *(conj like* **battre**) to frolic, to play (about); *(des animaux)* to gambol

ébaubi [ebobi] ADJ *Fam* flabbergasted

ébauchage [eboʃaʒ] NM *(d'un tableau etc)* roughing out, sketching out; *(d'un roman etc)* roughing out, outlining

ébauche [eboʃ] NF *(d'un tableau)* rough sketch; *(d'un roman, poème etc)* outline, rough draft; *(d'une lettre, traduction)* draft; *(d'un projet)* outline; **faire l'é. de** *(roman, lettre, traduction)* to draft; *(tableau)* to make a rough sketch of, to sketch out; *(projet)* to outline; **ce projet n'est qu'à l'état d'é.** the plan is still sketchy; **l'architecte n'en est qu'à l'é. du plan** the architect is still only at the planning stage; **il semble qu'il y ait une é. de réconciliation entre l'OLP et Israël** there seem to be the first tentative signs of a reconciliation between the PLO and Israel; **il n'y a qu'une é. de relations entre eux** relations between them are very tentative; **je n'ai réussi à avoir avec lui qu'une é. de conversation** I managed only a rather stilted conversation with him; **il a marmonné l'é. d'un remerciement** he grudgingly muttered a few words of thanks; **é. d'un sourire** suspicion *or* ghost of a smile; **é. d'un espoir** glimmer of hope

ébaucher [eboʃe] VT *(tableau, roman)* to rough out; *(projet, mise en scène)* to sketch out, to outline; *(lettre)* to draft, to make a draft of; *(réconciliation, amitié)* to take the first tentative steps towards; *(statue)* to rough-hew; **é. une traduction** to make a draft *or* rough translation, to draft a translation; **é. un sourire** to give a faint smile, to smile faintly; **é. un geste** to make a vague gesture; **les négociations étaient à peine ébauchées et déjà …** talks had barely been mooted before …; **é. des hypothèses** to put forward tentative hypotheses; **é. une con-versation avec qn** to have a stilted conversation with sb

ébène [ebɛn] NF ebony; **(d'un noir) d'é., (noir) é.** jet black; *Hist* **(bois d')é.** slaves; **marchand d'é.** slave-trader

ébénier [ebenje] NM *(arbre)* ebony tree; **faux é.** laburnum

ébéniste [ebenist] NM cabinetmaker

ébénisterie [ebenistəri] NF *(métier)* cabinetmaking

éberlué [ebɛrlɥe] ADJ *Fam* flabbergasted

éblouir [ebluir] VT *aussi Fig* to dazzle; *Fig* **il a préparé ce plat pour vous é.** he prepared this dish to impress you

éblouissant [ebluisɑ̃] ADJ dazzling, blinding; *Fig* dazzling; **d'une beauté éblouissante** dazzlingly beautiful

éblouissement [ebluismɑ̃] NM dazzle, glare; *Fig (émerveillement)* amazement; *Fig* **quand on arrive chez eux, c'est un véritable é.** their place is dazzling; *Fig* **l'é. qu'il ressentit lorsqu'il la vit** his sense of dazzlement when he saw her; *Méd* **avoir des éblouissements** to have fits of dizziness

ébonite [ebɔnit] NF vulcanite, ebonite

éborgner [ebɔrɲe] VT **1 é. qn** to blind sb in one eye, to put sb's eye out; **j'ai failli m'é.** I nearly put my eye out **2** *(arbre fruitier)* to disbud

éboueur [ebwœr] NM dustman, *Am* garbage man

ébouillanter [ebujɑ̃te] VT to scald
VPR **s'ébouillanter** to scald oneself

éboulement [ebulmɑ̃] NM **1** *(écroulement) (de falaise, côte, remblai)* collapse; **l'é. de la falaise/carrière a fait deux morts** two people were killed when the cliff collapsed/the quarry fell in; **il y a eu un é. dans la mine** there has been a cave-in at the mine; **si vous allez vers la carrière, méfiez-vous des éboulements** if you're going in the direction of the quarry, watch out for falling rocks **2** *(tas)* landslide, landslip

> Do not confuse with **éboulis**.

ébouler (s') [sebule] VPR *(d'une falaise, une côte)* to collapse, to slip; *(d'une mine)* to cave in; *(d'un remblai)* to collapse

éboulis [ebuli] NM mass of fallen earth; *(en montagne)* scree

> Do not confuse with **éboulement**.

ébourgeonnage [eburʒɔnaʒ] NM, **ébourgeonnement** [eburʒɔnmɑ̃] NM disbudding

ébourgeonner [eburʒɔne] VT *(arbre fruitier)* to disbud

ébouriffant [eburifɑ̃] ADJ *Fam* breathtaking, hair-raising

ébouriffé [eburife] ADJ **1** *(cheveux, personne)* dishevelled **2** *Fam* amazed

ébouriffer [eburife] VT **1** *(les cheveux de qn)* to ruffle, to tousle; **é. qn** to ruffle *or* tousle sb's hair **2** *Fam* **e. qn** *(époustoufler)* to take sb's breath away

ébranchage [ebrɑ̃ʃaʒ] NM, **ébranchement** [ebrɑ̃ʃmɑ̃] NM *(d'un arbre)* stripping *or* lopping the branches

ébrancher [ebrɑ̃ʃe] VT *(arbre)* to lop off *or* strip the branches from

ébranchoir [ebrɑ̃ʃwar] NM billhook

ébranlement [ebrɑ̃lmɑ̃] NM **1** *(tremblement) (de vitres, mur, édifice)* shaking; **l'é. des murs a été si violent qu'ils se sont lézardés** the walls shook so violently that they cracked; *Fig* **ce scandale a provoqué l'é. du gouvernement** the scandal caused the government to totter, the scandal rocked the government **2** *(choc nerveux)* shock; **la mort**

de son ami a provoqué un véritable é. chez elle she went to pieces after her friend's death **3** *(départ, mise en route) (d'un train, une procession, un convoi)* departure

ébranler [ebrɑ̃le] VT **1** *(édifice, mur)* to shake, to rock; *(vitres)* to shake **2** *Fig (personne)* to shake (up), to upset; *(confiance, nerfs, régime, dictature, économie)* to shake; **il ne faut pas te laisser é. par ses critiques** don't let his criticism get to you; **il a été très é. par l'annonce de cet accident** he was very shaken *or* upset by the news of the accident; **la nouvelle a ébranlé le pays tout entier** the entire country was rocked by the news
VPR **s'ébranler** *(d'un train)* to start, to move off; *(d'une procession, un convoi, une cara-vane)* to move *or* set off

Èbre [ebr] NM **l'È.** the Ebro

ébréché [ebreʃe] ADJ chipped

ébrécher [ebreʃe] VT **(j'ébrèche; j'ébrécherai)** *(assiette, tasse, verre, lame etc)* to chip; *Fig Fam (réputation)* to damage; *Fig Fam (son capital)* to make a hole in

ébréchure [ebreʃyr] NF chip

ébriété [ebrijete] NF (state of) drunkenness *or* intoxication *or* inebriation; **en état d'é.** in a state of inebriation

ébrouement [ebrumɑ̃] NM **1** *(d'un cheval)* snorting, snort **2** *(d'ailes)* flap(ping); *(dans l'eau)* splashing about

ébrouer (s') [sebrue] VPR **1** *(d'un cheval)* to snort **2** *(d'ailes)* to flap; *(dans l'eau)* to splash about

ébruitement [ebrɥitmɑ̃] NM spreading

ébruiter [ebrɥite] VT *(secret)* to give away; *(accord, pourparlers)* to leak; *(nouvelle)* to spread
VPR **s'ébruiter** *(d'une nouvelle)* to spread, *Fam* to get (a)round

EBS [əbeɛs] NF *(abrév* **encéphalite bovine spongiforme**) BSE

ébullition [ebylisjɔ̃] NF boiling point; **l'é. de l'eau se fait à 100°C** the boiling point of water is 100°C, water boils at 100°C; **arriver à é.** to come to the boil; **amener à é.** to bring to the boil; **maintenir en é. pendant cinq minutes** boil for five minutes; *Fig* **en é.** *(village, maison)* in turmoil; *(personne)* very excited, worked up

écaillage [ekajaʒ] NM **1** *(d'un poisson)* scaling; *(des huîtres)* opening **2** *(de peinture)* flaking off, peeling off; *(d'émail)* scaling off, chipping

écaille [ekaj] NF *(d'un poisson)* scale; *(d'une tortue)* shell; *(de peinture)* flake; *(d'émail)* chip; *Litt Fig* **les écailles lui tombèrent des yeux** the scales fell from his eyes; **lunettes à monture d'é.** tortoiseshell-rimmed spectacles; **peigne en é.** tortoiseshell comb

écailler [ekaje] VT **1** *(poisson)* to scale; *(huître)* to open **2** *(chaudière)* to scale
VPR **s'écailler** *(de l'émail)* to chip (off); *(de la peinture)* to peel (off), to flake (off)

écailler, **-ère** [ekaje, -ɛr] N *(marchand)* oyster seller; *(dans un bar, un restaurant)* oyster opener
NF **écaillère** oyster knife

écailleux, -euse [ekajø, -øz] ADJ *(poisson)* scaly; *(ardoise)* flaky

écale [ekal] NF *(d'une noix)* hull, husk; *(d'une châtaigne)* shuck

écaler [ekale] VT *(noix)* to hull, to husk; *(châtaignes)* to shuck

écarlate [ekarlat] ADJ scarlet; **devenir é.** to blush, to go *or* turn scarlet
NF scarlet

écarquiller [ekarkije] VT **é. les yeux** to open one's eyes wide, to stare, *Fam* to goggle

écart¹ [ekar] NM **1** *(entre deux chiffres, deux températures)* difference (**de** in); *Compta*

spread, variance; *Bourse* spread; *Mktg* gap; *(stratégie d'attaque)* bypass attack; **é. d'opinions/de points de vue** difference of opinions/points of view; **on constate de grands écarts dans ses résultats** his results are very uneven; **il y a des écarts de niveau trop importants dans cette classe** ability differs *or* varies too much in the class; **il y a un é. important entre ma sœur et moi** there's a big (age) gap *or* a big difference in age between my sister and me; **il y a un é. de trois ans entre eux** there's a three-year gap *or* three years between them, they're three years apart; **l'é. entre les deux équipes s'est beaucoup réduit** the gap between the two teams has narrowed considerably; **é. de prix/de salaires** price/wage differential; **réduire l'é. entre deux salaires** to narrow the gap between two wages; *Com* **é. entre le prix de vente et le coût** margin between cost and selling price; *Bourse* **é. vertical** vertical spread; *Bourse* **écarts de cours** price spreads; *Tech* **é. admissible** tolerance **2** *(distance) (entre étagères, tableaux etc)* distance, space; **l'é. entre chaque soldat doit être de ...** there must be (a distance of) ... between each soldier, soldiers must be ... apart; **faire le grand é.** to do the splits **3** *(déviation) Tech (de l'aiguille d'une boussole)* deflection; **faire un é.** *(d'un piéton)* to step aside, to swerve; *(d'un cheval)* to shy; *(d'une voiture, un vélo)* to swerve; **il ne fait jamais d'écarts de régime** he never breaks his diet, he always keeps to *or Fam* sticks to his diet **4** **à l'é.:** **j'ai mis mes verres en cristal à l'é.** I've put my crystal glasses out of the way; **je mets sa suggestion à l'é. pour l'instant** I'm putting *or* setting his suggestion aside for the moment; **se sentir à l'é.** to feel isolated *or* out of things; **se tenir à l'é.** to keep *or* stay in the background; *(du monde, de la foule etc)* to keep oneself apart, to hold oneself aloof; **se tenir à l'é. de la politique** to keep out of *or* away from politics; **mettre** *ou* **tenir qn à l'é.** to keep sb at a distance; **les autres enfants le mettent** *ou* **tiennent à l'é.** the other children don't let him join in; **tenir qn à l'é.** to keep sb away (**de qch** from sth); **il tient sa femme à l'é. de ses affaires** he keeps his wife out of his business, he doesn't involve his wife in his business; **un terrain à l'é. de la ville** a piece of land outside the town; **habiter à l'é.** to live in a remote *or* lonely spot

▸▸ *Bourse* **é. d'acquisition** goodwill; **é. budgétaire** budgetary variance; **écarts de conduite** transgressions, misbehaviour; **ses écarts de conduite ont fini par lasser sa femme** his wife finally got tired of his behaviour *or Fam* carryings-on; **elle a cessé ses écarts de conduite** she's stopped misbehaving, she's settled down; *Fin* **écarts de conversion** exchange adjustments; **é. des coûts** cost variance; **écarts de jeunesse** youthful indiscretions; **écarts de langage** bad language; **faire des écarts de langage** to use bad language; *Compta* **é. net** net variance; **é. de prime** option spread; *Tech* **é. type** standard deviation

écart² NM *Cartes* **1** *(action)* discarding **2** *(carte)* discard

écartant [ekartɑ̃] ADJ *Can* disorienting

écarté¹ [ekarte] ADJ **1** *(maison, endroit)* isolated, lonely, remote **2** *(distant) (bras, pieds)* apart; *(yeux)* widely spaced; **avoir les dents écartées** to have gaps between one's teeth **3** *Can (personne)* lost

écarté² NM *Cartes* (game of) écarté

écartelé [ekartəle] ADJ *Hér* quartered, quarterly

écarteler [ekartəle] VT **(j'écartèle; j'écartèle-**

rai) **1** *(criminel)*, *Hér (écu)* to quarter **2** *Fig* **se sentir écartelé** to be torn (**entre** between)

écartement [ekartəmɑ̃] **NM 1** *(séparation)* separation; **l'é. des volets** the opening of the shutters; *Tech* **pièce d'é.** spacer **2** *(d'un obstacle)* setting aside; **depuis l'é. des gêneurs, la société va beaucoup mieux** things have been much better in the company since it got rid of the trouble-makers **3** *(distance) (entre des barres etc)* space, gap, clearance; *Rail (de la voie)* gauge; *Aut* **é. des essieux** wheelbase; *Aut* **é. des roues** track; *Aut* **é. des électrodes** spark or plug or electrode gap

écarter[1] [ekarte] **VT 1** *(séparer) (doigts)* to spread out; *(branches)* to part; *(rideaux)* to draw back, to open; *(ses bras)* to open; *(ses jambes)* to spread, to open; *(ses coudes)* to square; *(personnes, objets)* to move or push aside; **le service d'ordre devait é. les fans sur son passage** the marshals had to push a way for him through the crowd of fans; *Fig* **le temps nous écarte l'un de l'autre** we are drifting apart with time **2** *(éliminer, exclure) (candidat, réclamation, solution, proposition)* to turn down; *(soupçon)* to divert; *(coup, danger)* to ward off, to avert; **é. les obstacles de son chemin** to brush aside the obstacles in one's path; **é. qn de son chemin** to push sb out of one's way; **ses interventions nous ont écartés de notre sujet** his interruptions caused us to stray or wander from the subject or to digress; **être écarté du but** to be deflected from one's goal

VPR s'écarter 1 *(se séparer) (de personnes)* to move apart; *(de routes)* to diverge; **plus on avance vers le nord, plus les maisons s'écartent les unes des autres** the further north you go, the further apart the houses become; **la foule s'est écartée sur le passage des pompiers** the crowd parted or drew aside to let the firemen through; *Fig* **nos chemins s'écartent de plus en plus** we are drifting further and further apart; *Fig* **nos aspirations/nos vies s'écartent de plus en plus** our aims in life/our lives are increasingly different **2** *(s'éloigner) (de piéton)* to move or step aside; *(de voiture, de vélo)* to swerve; *(dévier)* to deviate, to stray (**de** from); **s'é. du sujet** to digress, to deviate or wander from the subject; **s'é. des règles** to depart from the rules; **ne vous écartez pas de la route** keep to the road; **s'é. du droit chemin** to stray from the straight and narrow **3** *Can (s'égarer)* to get lost, to go astray

écarter[2] **VT** *Cartes* to discard

écarteur [ekartœr] **NM** *Aut* **é. de mâchoire** shoe expander

ecchymose [ekimoz] **NF** bruise, *Spéc* ecchymosis

Ecclésiaste (l') [leklezjast] **NM** *Bible* (the book of) Ecclesiastes

ecclésiastique [eklezjastik] **ADJ** ecclesiastical
NM ecclesiastic, cleric, clergyman

écervelé, -ée [eservəle] **ADJ** harebrained, scatterbrained
N scatterbrain

ECG [əseʒe] **NM** *Méd (abrév* **électrocardiogramme)** ECG

échafaud [eʃafo] **NM 1** scaffold; **monter sur** *ou* **à l'é.** to go to the scaffold, to mount the scaffold; **finir sur l'é.** to die on the scaffold, *Hum* **tu vas finir sur l'é.** you'll end up hanged **2** *Vieilli (estrade)* stand, platform

échafaudage [eʃafodaʒ] **NM 1** *(passerelles etc)* scaffolding; *(d'objets)* pile; *Fig (d'une argumentation, théorie)* structure, fabric; **é. pour caméra** (camera) tower **2** *(procédé)* erection of scaffolding; *Fig (d'une fortune)*

building up; *(d'une argumentation, théorie)* construction; *(de projets)* devising, putting together

échafauder [eʃafode] **VI** to erect (a) scaffolding
VT *Fig (projet, système)* to put together, to devise; *(argumentation)* to put together, to construct

échalas [eʃala] **NM** *(pour soutenir une plante)* cane, stake; *Fig* **grand é.** beanpole; **il est comme un é.** he's a real beanpole

échalier [eʃalje] **NM 1** *(clôture)* barrier, hurdle *(closing gap)* **2** *(échelle)* stile

échalote [eʃalɔt] **NF** *(plante)* shallot, *Can* scallion; *Can* **é. française** shallot

échancré [eʃɑ̃kre] **ADJ** low-cut; **robe échancrée dans le dos** dress cut low in the back, dress with a low back

échancrer [eʃɑ̃kre] **VT** *(robe etc)* to cut out the neckline of; *(planche)* to notch; **littoral échancré** indented coastline

échancrure [eʃɑ̃kryr] **NF** *(décolleté)* low neckline; *(découpe de veste)* vent, slit; *(d'une planche)* notch; *(d'un littoral)* indentation

échange [eʃɑ̃ʒ] **NM 1** *(de prisonniers, d'idées, de coups etc)* exchange; **faire l'é. de qch pour** *ou* **contre qch** to exchange sth for sth; **recevoir/donner qch en é.** to receive/give sth in exchange or in return (**de qch** for sth); **est-il possible de faire l'é.?** is it possible to exchange it?, can it be exchanged?; *Fam* **on fait é.?** want to swap?; **é. d'appartement** flat swap; **de violents échanges entre la police et les manifestants** *(physique)* violent clashes between the police and demonstrators; *(verbal)* violent exchanges between the police and demonstrators; **échanges culturels** cultural exchanges; **c'est un é. de bons procédés** one good turn deserves another, I'm/he's/*etc* returning a favour or *Am* favor; **nous faisons des échanges de bons procédés** we do favours for each other, we help each other out
2 *Fin* exchange; *(commerce)* trade; **échanges commerciaux** trade; **échanges internationaux** international trade; **échanges intracommunautaires** intra-Community trade; **le volume des échanges** the volume of trade; **les échanges entre la France et l'Allemagne** trade between France and Germany
3 *Bourse* **é. d'actions** share swap; **é. cambiste** treasury swap; **é. de créances** debt swap; **é. de créances contre actifs** debt equity swap; **é. de devises** currency swap; **é. financier** swap; **é. de taux d'intérêt** interest rate swap
4 *Tennis* rally; **on va faire quelques échanges?** shall we knock a few balls about?
► ► *Ordinat* **é. de données** data exchange or swap; *Ordinat* **é. de données dynamique** dynamic data exchange; *Ordinat* **é. de données informatisé** electronic data interchange; **é. linguistique** language exchange holiday; *Tech* **é. standard** standard replacement; **é. à terme** forward swap; *Pol* **é. de voix** vote-trading

échangeable [eʃɑ̃ʒabl] **ADJ** exchangeable

échanger [eʃɑ̃ʒe] **VT** (**j'échangeai(s); n. échangeons**) *(coups, idées, injures, lettres)* to exchange; *(objets, articles)* to exchange, to trade, *Fam* to swap, *Vieilli* to barter (**contre** for); **les articles soldés ne sont ni repris ni échangés** sales goods may not be returned or exchanged; **il m'a échangé un timbre espagnol contre un anglais** he traded or *Fam* swapped me a Spanish stamp for an English one; **é. des impressions** to exchange or compare impressions

échangeur [eʃɑ̃ʒœr] **NM 1** *(sur une autoroute)* interchange; *(sur une route)* (clover leaf) intersection **2** *Phys* (heat) exchanger; *Aut* **é. air/air** air-to-air exchanger

échangisme [eʃɑ̃ʒism] **NM** partner swapping

échangiste [eʃɑ̃ʒist] **N** partner swapper
ADJ partner-swapping

échanson [eʃɑ̃sɔ̃] **NM** *Hist* cup-bearer

échantillon [eʃɑ̃tijɔ̃] **NM 1** *(de tissu)* sample; *(d'un travail)* sample, specimen; *(pour un sondage)* population sample; *Méd* specimen; **prendre** *ou* **prélever des échantillons de qch** to take samples of sth, to sample sth; **catalogue d'échantillons** sample or pattern book; *Mktg* **non conforme à l'é.** not up to sample **2** *Vieilli* **brique/tuile d'é.** standard brick/tile
► ► *Mktg* **é. aléatoire** random sample; **é. aréolaire** cluster (area) sample; **é. gratuit** free sample; **é. gratuit, ne peut être vendu** free sample, not for resale; **é. par quotas** quota sample; **é. probabiliste** probability sample; **é. publicitaire** free sample; **é représentatif** representative sample

échantillonnage [eʃɑ̃tijɔnaʒ] **NM 1** *(vérification)* sampling, testing; *(groupe de personnes)* sample; **l'é. se fait sur un produit sur cent** one product in a hundred is sampled or tested; **un é. est effectué systématiquement** sampling is done systematically **2** *Com* making up of samples; *(d'un tissu etc)* making up of patterns; **un é. de ce que je sais faire/de mes capacités** a sample of what I can do/of my ability; **voici un é. de sa bêtise** here's an example of how stupid he is
► ► *Mktg* **é. aléatoire** random sampling; **é. empirique** purposive or non-random sampling; **é. non probabiliste** non-random or non-probability sampling; **é. par zone** area sampling

échantillonner [eʃɑ̃tijɔne] **VT 1** *(vin)* to sample, to taste; *(population)* to sample **2** *Com (préparer des échantillons de)* to prepare samples of; *(tissues etc)* to prepare patterns of **3** *(étalonner) (articles)* to make according to sample

échantillonneur, -euse [eʃɑ̃tijɔnœr, -øz] **N** *Com (personne)* tester, sampler

échappatoire [eʃapatwar] **NF** way out; **le sommeil est mon é.** sleep is my escape mechanism; **é. fiscale** tax loophole
ADJ **clause é.** escape clause

échappé [eʃape] **NM** *Sport* breakaway; **les trois échappés** the three breakaway riders

échappée [eʃape] **NF 1** *Sport (dans une course)* breakaway; **être dans l'é.** to be part of the breakaway group **2** *(espace libre)* space, gap, interval; **é. (de vue)** vista (**sur** over); **é. de lumière** shaft of light; **é. de ciel** patch of sky; **é. de soleil** burst of sunshine; **é. de beau temps** short spell of fine weather; *Fig* **faire qch par échappées** to do sth in fits and starts **3** *(pour véhicules)* turning space **4** *(d'un escalier)* headroom

échappement [eʃapmɑ̃] **NM 1** *(de vapeur)* exhaust, release; *Aut (mouvement)* exhaust stroke; **(tuyau d')é.** waste-steam pipe; *Aut* exhaust (pipe); *Aut* **pot d'é.** silencer, *Am* muffler; *Aut* **(soupape d')é. libre** cut-out; **gaz d'é.** exhaust fumes; **clapet d'é.** exhaust cut-out **2** *(d'une montre)* escapement; **montre à é.** lever watch **3** *Ordinat* escape

échapper [eʃape] **VI 1 é. à** *(quelqu'un)* to escape from; *(grippe, punition)* to escape or *Fam* dodge; *(corvées)* to get out of, to dodge; **é. à la mort** to escape death; **é. à un coup** to dodge a blow; **é. aux recherches** *(d'un criminel, un animal)* to evade capture; **cette édition a échappé à mes recherches** I missed this edition in my research; **é. à l'impôt** to avoid tax; **le prisonnier nous a échappé** the prisoner got away from us or escaped; **le vase m'a échappé des mains** the vase slipped out of my hands; **é. à tout contrôle** to be out of control; **cet enfant/ce chien**

échappe à notre contrôle this child/dog has got out of hand *or* is beyond our control; **il n'y a pas moyen d'y é.** there is no escaping it *or* getting away from it; **je n'échapperai pas à une leçon de morale** I'm in for a sermon; **peux-tu é. quelques heures à ton patron?** can you get away from work for a few hours?; **on ne m'échappe pas comme ça** you don't get away *or* escape that easily; **é. à toute définition** to defy definition; **à la règle** to be an exception to the rule; **tu n'échappes pas à la règle** you're no exception to the rule; **leurs baisers n'ont pas échappé à mes regards** it did not escape my notice that they were kissing; **l'enfant a échappé à la vue de sa mère cinq minutes seulement** the child was out of his mother's sight for only five minutes; **ce fait a échappé à mon attention, ce fait m'a échappé** this fact escaped *or* slipped my attention, this fact escaped me; **rien ne lui échappe** he doesn't miss a thing; **son nom m'échappe** his name escapes *or* eludes me, his name has slipped my mind; *Fam* **vous l'avez échappé belle** you've had a narrow escape

2 laisser é. *(personne, animal)* to let escape; *(de l'air d'un ballon)* to let out; *(vapeur)* to let off; *(larme)* to let fall; *(secret, soupir, cri, grossièreté)* to let out; *(faute d'orthographe, détail)* to overlook; **laisser é. son stylo** to let one's pen slip from one's fingers; **laisser é. l'occasion** to let the opportunity slip

3 *(parole, cri etc)* **pas un mot ne lui a échappé** he didn't let anything slip, he didn't say a word; **je n'aurais pas dû le dire mais ça m'a échappé** I shouldn't have said it but it just slipped out; **un sanglot/une injure lui échappa** he let out a sob/an oath

VPR s'échapper *(s'évader)* to escape (**de** from); **s'é. de prison** to escape from prison, to break out of prison; **je n'arriverai jamais à m'é. de cette réunion de famille** I'll never manage to get out of this family reunion; *Fam* **il faut que je m'échappe pendant quelques minutes** I've got to go somewhere (else) for a few minutes, I must be off; **le gaz s'échappe** the gas is leaking; **un cri s'échappa de ses lèvres** a cry burst from his lips; **de hautes flammes s'échappaient de tous côtés** great flames were shooting from every side

vt *Can (laisser échapper)* to drop

écharde [eʃaʀd] NF splinter

écharpe [eʃaʀp] NF scarf VOIR GRAMMAIRE A12; *(de cérémonie)* sash; *(au bras)* sling; **porter le bras en é.** to have one's arm in a sling; **en é.** diagonally, crosswise; **prendre une voiture en é.** to hit a car sideways on; **se prendre en é.** *(de voitures)* to collide at an angle; *(de trains)* to collide at the points

écharper [eʃaʀpe] VT *(membre, personne)* to slash; *(viande)* to hack (up); *(troupes)* to cut to pieces; **vous allez vous faire é.!** you'll get torn to pieces!

échasse [eʃas] NF **1** stilt; **être monté sur des échasses** to be on stilts; *Fam (avoir de longues jambes)* to have long legs, to be long in the leg **2** *Orn* stilt

échassier [eʃasje] NM *Orn* wader

échauder [eʃode] VT *(théière)* to warm; *Fig* **se faire é., être échaudé** to get one's fingers burnt, to burn one's fingers; **elle hésite à se remarier car son premier mariage l'a échaudée** she's reluctant to get married again because she got her fingers burnt the first time

échauffant [eʃofɑ̃] ADJ *Arch (aliment)* that causes constipation

échauffement [eʃofmɑ̃] NM **1** *(d'une pièce, d'un moteur)*, *Fig Fin (de l'économie)* overheating; *(d'une céréale, du foin)* fermenting; *(d'une corde)* chafing **2** *(excitation)* overexcitement; **le débat a provoqué l'é. des esprits**

the discussion got people worked up, people got rather worked up *or* tempers got rather heated during the discussion; **dans l'é. de la discussion** in the heat of the argument; **l'é. de l'économie** the overheating of the economy **3** *(d'un athlète)* warm(ing)-up; **exercices d'é.** warm-up *or* limbering-up exercises **4** *Arch (constipation)* constipation

échauffer [eʃofe] VT **1** *(chauffer) (pièce, moteur)* to overheat; *(céréales, foin)* to cause fermentation in; **frottement qui échauffe les roues** friction that overheats the wheels **2** *(exciter)* **discussion qui échauffe les esprits** discussion that gets people worked up; *Fam* **é. la bile** *ou* **les oreilles** *ou* **les sangs à qn** to get up sb's nose, to get on sb's nerves **3** *(athlète)* to warm up

VPR s'échauffer to become *or* get overheated; *(d'un athlète etc)* to warm *or* limber up; *Tech* to run hot, to heat; *(de céréales, du foin)* to ferment; **ne vous échauffez pas** don't get excited

échauffourée [eʃofure] NF scuffle, skirmish; *(entre bandes)* clash; *Mil* skirmish

échéance [eʃeɑ̃s] NF date of payment; *(terme d'un effet)* falling due, maturity; *(de contrat)* expiry date; **venir à é.** to fall due; **payable à l'é.** payable at maturity; **à trois mois d'é.** at three months' date; **billet à longue/courte é.** long-/short-dated bill; **politique à longue/courte é.** long-/short-term policy; **emprunter/prêter à courte é.** to borrow/lend short; **faire face à une é.** to meet a bill; **avoir de lourdes échéances** to have a lot of bills to pay each month, to have a lot of monthly payments to make

▸▸ *Fin* **é. commune** equation of payment; *Fin* **é. à court terme** short-term maturity; **l'é. électorale** election day, the elections; *Fin* **é. emprunt** loan maturity; *Fin* **é. fixe** fixed maturity; *Compta* **échéances de fin de mois** end of month payments; *Fin* **é. à long terme** long-term maturity; *Fin* **é. proche** short maturity, near month; *Fin* **é. à vue** sight bill *or* maturity

échéancier [eʃeɑ̃sje] NM **1** *Fin* bill book; *Compta* due date file, aged debtor schedule; *Com* **é. de paiement** payment schedule **2** *(calendrier pour les travaux etc)* timetable, schedule

échéant [eʃeɑ̃] ADJ **1** *Fin* falling due **2** **le cas é.** if necessary, if need be

échec [eʃɛk] NM **1** *(défaite)* failure; *(revers)* check, setback; **l'é. des discussions** the failure *or* breakdown of the negotiations; **l'é. scolaire** doing badly at school, poor performance at school; **les problèmes familiaux sont très souvent à l'origine de l'é. scolaire** family problems are often the reason why children do badly at school; **voué à l'é.** bound to fail, doomed to failure; **reconnaître son é.** to admit defeat *or* failure; **cela va se solder par un é.** it will end in failure; **subir un é.** to suffer a setback; *Can* **mettre en é.** *(au hockey)* to check; *Fig* **tenir l'ennemi en é.** to hold the enemy in check; **faire é. à** *(activités, agissements etc)* to put a stop to; **faire é. à qn/aux projets de qn** to foil *or* frustrate sb/sb's plans

2 *(jeu)* **é.!** check!; **é. et mat** checkmate; **faire é. au roi** to check the king; **échecs** chess; **une partie d'échecs** a game of chess; **joueur d'échecs** chess player

échelle [eʃɛl] NF **1** ladder; **é. d'incendie** *ou* **de pompiers** fireman's ladder; **é. double** stepladder; **é. de corde** rope ladder; **é. coulissante** extension *or* extending ladder; **faire la courte é. à qn** to give sb a leg up *or Am* a boost; *Fam* **vous voulez me faire monter à l'é.** you're having *or Am* putting me on, you're pulling my leg

2 *Fig* **l'é. sociale** the social ladder; **être en**

haut *ou* **au sommet de l'é.** to be at the top of the tree *or* the ladder

3 *(d'une carte, maquette etc)* scale; **l'é. est de 1/10 000** the scale is 1/10,000; **ton train électrique est à quelle é.?** what scale is your electric train?; **carte à petite/grande é.** small-/large-scale map; *Fig* **faire les choses sur une grande é.** to do things on a large scale; **à l'é. mondiale/nationale** on a world/national scale; **à l'é. de l'homme** on a human scale; **à l'é. de temps humain** on a human time scale; *Ordinat* **intégration à grande/petite é.** large-/small-scale integration

4 *Hist* **les échelles du Levant** the (commercial) ports of the Levant; **les échelles de Barbarie** the Barbary ports

5 *(dans un collant)* ladder, *Am* run; **j'ai fait une é. à mon collant** I've laddered my tights, *Am* I have a run in my tights

6 *(dans les cheveux)* **elle me fait des échelles** she cuts my hair in steps; **dommage qu'il y ait toutes ces échelles** it's a pity that it's all so uneven *or* all so up and down

▸▸ *Mktg* **é. d'attitudes** attitude scale; **é. de Beaufort** Beaufort scale; *Mus* **é. chromatique/diatonique/harmonique** chromatic/diatonic/harmonic scale; *Mktg* **é. de classement** rating scale; *Naut* **é. de commandement** *ou* **d'honneur** companion ladder; **é. des êtres** evolutionary ladder; **dans l'é. des êtres** on the evolutionary ladder; *Typ, Ordinat* **é. des gris** levels of grey; *Mktg* **é. d'importance** importance scale; *Rel* **é. de Jacob** Jacob's ladder; **é. de marée** tide gauge; **é. de meunier** open staircase; **é. mobile** *(des prix etc)* sliding scale; *Naut* **é. de revers** Jacob's ladder; **é. de Richter** Richter scale; **sur l'é. de Richter** on the Richter scale; **é. à saumons** salmon ladder; *Mus* **é. des sons** scale; *Naut* **é. de tirant d'eau** water *or* draught marks, *Am* immersion scale; **é. des traitements** *ou* **des salaires** salary scale; **é. des valeurs** scale of values

échelon [eʃlɔ̃] NM **1** *(d'une échelle)* rung **2** *(degré d'une hiérarchie, organisation)* step, grade, *Fml* echelon; **monter par échelons** to rise by degrees *or* by successive stages; **les échelons de l'administration** the grades of the civil service; **le dernier/premier é.** the bottom/top grade *or* step; **il a gravi rapidement tous les échelons** he climbed the ladder rapidly; **j'en suis au dernier é.** I'm at *or* I've reached the top of my grade **3** *(niveau)* level; **à l'é. ministériel/directoriel** at ministerial/managerial level; **à l'é. régional/national** on a regional/national level; **à tous les échelons** at all levels, at every level; *Bourse* **é. de cotation** tick size

échelonnement [eʃ(ə)lɔnmɑ̃] NM **1** *(des paiements)* spreading out; *(des vacances)* staggering; **l'é. des travaux se fera sur plusieurs mois** the work will be spread out over several months; **le cours suit un é. bien précis** the course timetable is laid out very precisely **2** *(de poteaux, maisons)* row

échelonner [eʃ(ə)lɔne] VT **1** *(objets)* to space out, to place at intervals; *(paiements)* to spread (out), to stagger; **congés échelonnés** staggered holidays **2** *Mil (troupes)* to dispose in echelon *or* in depth

VPR s'échelonner *(d'objets)* to be spaced out; **les paiements s'échelonnent sur deux ans** the payments are spread (out) over two years; **les arbres s'échelonnent sur plusieurs kilomètres** the trees stretch for several kilometres; **le cours s'échelonne sur dix niveaux** there are ten levels of difficulty in the course; **le remboursement de la dette s'échelonnera sur dix ans** the repayment of the debt will be spread out *or* staggered over a ten year period

écheniller [eʃ(ə)nije] VT *(arbres fruitiers)* to clear of caterpillars

écheveau, -eaux [eʃ(ə)vo] NM *(de fil etc)* hank, skein; *Fig* **é. de rues** maze of streets; **l'é. d'une intrigue** the intricacies *or* complexities of a plot; **un é. de mensonges/problèmes** a tissue of lies/a host of problems

échevelé [eʃəvle] ADJ **1** *(personne)* dishevelled **2** *Fig (danse, fête)* wild; *(course)* mad

échevin [eʃ(ə)vɛ̃] NM **1** *Arch* municipal magistrate **2** *Belg* deputy mayor

échine [eʃin] NF **1** *Anat* spine, backbone; *Fig* **courber** *ou* **plier l'é.** to submit, to kowtow (**devant qn** to sb); *Fig* **avoir l'é. souple** *ou* **flexible** to bow and scrape **2** *Culin* loin (of pork); **une côte de porc dans l'é.** a pork loin chop

échiné [eʃine] ADJ *Can* tired out, exhausted

échiner (s') [seʃine] VPR *(se fatiguer)* to exhaust oneself, to tire oneself out (**à faire qch** doing sth); *(se donner du mal)* to go to great lengths, to make a great effort (**à faire qch** to do sth)

échiquier [eʃikje] NM **1** *(damier)* chessboard; **en é.** in a chequered *or Am* checkered pattern; *Pol Fig* **l'é. mondial/européen** the world/European stage *or* arena **2** *Br Pol* **l'É.** the Exchequer

écho [eko] NM **1** echo; **faire é.** to echo (back); **il y a de l'é.** there's an echo; *Fig* **se faire l'é. des opinions de qn** to echo *or* repeat sb's opinions; *Fig* **je n'ai eu aucun é. de leur discussion** I've heard nothing about their discussion; *Fig* **ma proposition/mon offre est restée sans é.** I got no feedback on my suggestion/offer, I never heard any more about my suggestion/offer; *Fig* **trouver un é.** to get a response VOIR GRAMMAIRE A12 **2** *Ordinat* echo; *Électron* **éliminateur** *ou* **suppresseur d'é.** echo suppressor; **échos parasites** clutter; **é. local** local echo **3** *TV* ghost(ing); *Radio* echo **4** *Journ* **échos** news in brief; **échos mondains** gossip column

échocardiographie [ekokardjografi] NF echocardiography

échographie [ekografi] NF *(ultrasound)* scan; **passer une é.** to have a scan

échoir [eʃwar] VI *(prp* **échéant***; pp* **échu***; pr ind* **il échoit, ils échoient***; impf* **il échoyait***; p hist* **il échut***; fu* **il échoira***; aux souvent* **être**) **1** *Litt* **é. à qn** to fall to sb; **le devoir m'échut de lui apprendre la nouvelle** it fell to me to break the news to him **2** *Fin (d'une dette etc)* to fall due; *(d'un investissement etc)* to mature; **abonnement échu** expired subscription; **billets échus** bills (over)due; **intérêts échus** outstanding interest, interest due; **intérêts à é.** accruing interest; **le terme échoit le 20 de ce mois** the date for payment is the 20th of this month; **le délai est échu** the deadline has expired

échoppe [eʃɔp] NF *Com* booth, stall; *(de cordonnier)* (cobbler's) small (work)shop

écho-sondeur, *pl* **écho-sondeurs** NM *Naut* echo sounder, sonic depth finder

échotier, -ière [ekɔtje, -jɛr] N *Journ* gossip columnist

échouage [eʃwaʒ] **échouement** [eʃumɑ̃] NM running aground; *(sur la plage)* beaching

échouer [eʃwe] VI **1** *Naut* to run aground, to be stranded, to ground; *(d'une baleine)* to beach; **navire échoué** ship aground, stranded vessel *or* ship; **échoué à sec** high and dry; *Fig* **é. dans** *(pays hostile, bar mal famé etc)* to end *or* land up in **2** *(ne pas réussir) (d'un plan etc)* to fail, to come to nothing; *(d'une personne)* to fail; **é. à un examen** to fail an examination; **faire é.** *(projet)* to wreck, *(complot)* to foil

▸ VT *Naut (bateau)* to beach, to run aground

▸ VPR **s'échouer** *Naut* to run aground, to be driven ashore; *(d'une baleine)* to beach

écimage [esimaʒ] NM *(d'un arbre)* topping, pollarding

écimer [esime] VT *(arbre)* to top, to pollard

éclaboussement [eklabusmɑ̃] NM splashing, spattering

éclabousser [eklabuse] VT *(avec un liquide)* to splash, to spatter (**de** with); *Fig* **é. qn** *(salir)* to damage sb's reputation, to sully sb's (good) name

éclaboussure [eklabusyr] NF *(de boue etc)* splash, spatter; *Fig (à la réputation)* blemish, blot, smirch; **le président n'a reçu aucune é. dans cette histoire** the president came out of the business with his reputation intact, none of the mud stuck to the president

éclair [eklɛr] NM **1** *Météo* flash of lightning; **éclairs** lightning; **éclairs de chaleur** heat lightning; **il y a des éclairs** there's lightning; **rapide comme l'é.** quick as lightning *or* as a flash; *Fig* **en un é.** in a flash, quick as a flash; **la voiture passa comme un é.** the car flashed by; **cette pensée traversa mon esprit comme un é.** the thought flashed through my mind **2** *(d'une arme etc)*, *Fig (de lucidité, génie)* flash; **lancer des éclairs** *(d'un diamant, des yeux etc)* to flash **3** *Culin* éclair

▸ ADJ INV *(visite, attaque)* lightning; **guerre é.** blitzkrieg; **il a fait un passage é. au sein de la rédaction** he had a very brief spell on the editorial team

éclairage [eklɛraʒ] NM **1** *(fait d'éclairer)* lighting, illumination; *Cin, Théâtre* lighting; *(par projecteurs)* floodlighting; *Phot* light; **é. doux** soft lighting **2** *Fig* light; **sous cet é.** (seen) in this light; **montrer qch sous un autre é.** to show sth in a different light **3** *Mil, Naut* scouting

▸▸ **é. d'ambiance** background light; **é. d'appoint** fill light; **é. sur batterie** sungun; **é. clair-obscur** Rembrandt *or* chiaroscuro lighting; **é. en contre-jour** backlighting; **é. de cyclorama** cyclorama light; **é. direct/indirect** direct/indirect lighting; **é. à l'électricité/au gaz** electric/gas lighting; **é. de faible intensité** low-key lighting; **é. frisant** rimming; *Aut* **é. intérieur automatique** courtesy light; **é. de plateau** stage lighting; **é. aux projecteurs** floodlighting; **é. public** street lighting; **é. rasant** rim light; **é. à la Rembrandt** Rembrandt lighting; *Aut* **é. de route** full-beam headlights; **é. de sécurité** emergency lighting; **é. en trois points** three-point lighting; *Aut* **é. de ville** dipped headlights

éclairagiste [eklɛraʒist] N *Cin, Théâtre* lighting technician *or* engineer

éclairant [eklɛrɑ̃] ADJ *(pouvoir etc)* lighting, illuminating; **fusée éclairante** flare; *Fig* **une explication éclairante** an enlightening *or* illuminating explanation

éclaircie [eklɛrsi] NF **1** *(dans les nuages etc)* break, opening, rift; *Météo* bright interval; *Fig* improvement **2** *(dans une forêt)* clearing, glade

éclaircir [eklɛrsir] VT **1** *(rendre plus clair)* *(couleur, teinte, les cheveux etc)* to lighten; **é. le teint** to clear the complexion **2** *Fig (élucider) (mystère)* to throw light on, to clear up; *(situation)* to clarify **3** *(rendre moins épais)* *(forêt, sauce)* to thin; *(jeunes plants etc)* to thin out

▸ VPR **s'éclaircir 1** *(du temps)* to clear (up), to become bright(er); *(du ciel)* to clear, to brighten; *(du teint, de la voix)* to clear, to become clear(er); **s'é. la voix** to clear one's throat; *Fig* **l'avenir semble s'é.** the future seems to be getting brighter; **son visage s'éclaircit** his/her face brightened up *or* lit up; **mes idées se sont peu à peu éclaircies** my ideas gradually became clearer **2** *(se dissiper) (d'un mystère, de doutes)* to be cleared up; *(de brouillard)* to clear (up) **3** *(des cheveux)* to grow thin, to be thinning; **enfin**

les arbres s'éclaircirent at length the trees thinned out

éclaircissage [eklɛrsisaʒ] NM **1** *(du verre)* polishing **2** *(de plantes)* thinning out

éclaircissant [eklɛrsisɑ̃] ADJ lightening, highlighting

éclaircissement [eklɛrsismɑ̃] NM **1** *(élucidation)* clarification, *Fml* elucidation; *(explication)* explanation; **l'é. de ce mystère a pris des mois** it was months before the mystery was cleared up; **demander des éclaircissements sur qch** to ask for an explanation of sth; **s'ils me demandent des éclaircissements sur mon rapport** if they ask me for clarification on my report **2** *(de cheveux)* lightening; **je me suis fait faire un é.** I had my hair lightened

éclairé [eklere] ADJ lit; *Fig (personne, esprit, public)* enlightened

éclairement [eklɛrmɑ̃] NM illumination, lighting

éclairer [eklere] VT **1** *(pièce, vitrine)* to light, to illuminate; *(personne)* to light the way for; *Cin, Phot, TV* to light; **é. un angle sombre** to light up a dark corner; **cafés éclairés au néon** cafés with neon lights, neon-lit cafés; **une pièce bien/mal éclairée** a well-lit/badly lit room; **éclaire-moi, que j'ouvre la serrure** give me some light so that I can open the lock; *Fig* **un sourire éclaira son visage** a smile lit up his/her face **2** *(expliquer)* *(sujet)* to shed *or* throw light on; **é. qch d'un jour nouveau** to shed *or* throw new light on sth **3** *(informer)* to enlighten; **éclairez-moi sur ce sujet** tell me what it's all about; *Fam* **si tu pouvais é. ma lanterne sur cette affaire** if you could put me in the picture about this matter **4** *Mil* **é. le terrain** *ou* **la marche** to reconnoitre the ground, to scout

▸ VI *(donner de la lumière)* **cette lampe éclaire mal** this lamp doesn't give a very good light

▸ VPR **s'éclairer 1** *(pour avoir de la lumière)* **il s'éclaire toujours au pétrole/gaz** he still has *or* uses oil lamps/gaslight; **s'é. à la bougie/avec une lampe de poche** *(pour voir le chemin)* to light one's way with a candle/torch, to use a candle/torch to see by **2** *(devenir lumineux) (d'un bâtiment etc)* to light up; **son visage s'est éclairé** his/her face lit up *or* brightened **3** *Fig (devenir compréhensible) (d'une situation etc)* to become clear(er); **tout s'éclaire!** things are *or* everything is becoming clear(er)!

éclaireur, -euse [eklɛrœr, -øz] NM **1** *Mil* scout; *Naut* scouting vessel, scout; *Aviat* **avion é.** reconnaissance aircraft; *Mil, Fig* **partir en é.** to go off for a scout around; *Fig* **il est parti en é. pour voir s'il y avait de la place au restaurant** he's gone to check the seat situation in the restaurant; **il part un mois avant, en é.** he's leaving a month in advance to check things out **2** *Aut* **é. de coffre** boot *or Am* trunk light

▸ N (boy) scout, f (girl) guide; **chef é.** scoutmaster, f guide captain

éclampsie [eklɑ̃psi] NF *Méd* eclampsia

éclat [ekla] NM **1** *(fragment) (de bois)* splinter; *(de pierre)* chip; *(de mica)* flake; **é. d'obus** piece of shrapnel; **éclats d'obus** shrapnel; **voler en éclats** to fly *or* burst into pieces; **un é. de verre** a fragment *or* splinter of glass; **éclats de verre** *(bris)* broken glass; *(projeté)* flying glass

2 *(son) (de rire)* burst; **é. de colère** outburst of anger; **de grands éclats de voix** loud voices; **partir d'un grand é. de rire** to burst out laughing; **rire aux éclats** to roar with laughter

3 *Fig (scandale)* scandal, stir, fuss; **elle fait**

des éclats à chaque fois qu'elle sort she causes commotion wherever she goes; **j'espère qu'il n'y aura pas d'é. pendant la réunion** I hope the meeting passes off quietly, I hope nobody makes a fuss at the meeting; **il adore provoquer des éclats dans les soirées mondaines** he loves creating a commotion at parties; **sans é.** quietly, without any fuss **4** *(du soleil)* glare; *(d'un diamant)* glitter, lustre; *(du regard)* sparkle; *(de couleurs)* brilliance, vividness; **l'é. de ses yeux** the sparkle in his/her eyes; **l'é. de la jeunesse** the bloom *or* freshness of youth; **le soleil brille de son plus vif é.** the sun is (shining) at its brightest *or* most brilliant **5** *(de style etc)* brilliance; *(d'une cérémonie, période, de la gloire etc)* splendour, *Am* splendor; **action** *ou* **coup d'é.** brilliant feat; **il aime faire les choses avec é.** he likes to do things with style

éclatant [eklatɑ̃] ADJ **1** *(son, rire)* loud, ringing **2** *(lumière, couleur, succès)* dazzling, brilliant; *(bijoux)* sparkling, glittering; **teint é.** glowing *or* blooming complexion; **être dans une forme éclatante** to be on brilliant *or* dazzling form; **é. de santé** glowing *or* blooming with health

éclate [eklat] NF *Fam* **c'est l'é.** it's a laugh *or* a hoot; **c'est pas l'é.** it's not exactly a barrel of laughs

éclaté [eklate] ADJ *(groupe)* scattered, dispersed; *(programme, mesures)* fragmented, fragmentary; **paysage politique é.** fragmented political landscape; **avoir une vision éclatée des choses** to have a fragmented view of things ▪ NM *Tech* exploded view

éclatement [eklatmɑ̃] NM *(d'un obus)* bursting, explosion; *(d'une arme)* explosion; *(d'un pneu)* bursting, blow-out; *(d'un tuyau)* bursting; *(d'un verre)* shattering; *(du foie, de la rate)* rupture; *(d'un convoi, un groupe)* dispersal; *Pol (d'un parti)* splitting (up), fragmentation; *Aut* **é. de l'étincelle** spark

éclater [eklate] VI **1** *(d'un obus)* to burst, to explode; *(d'une arme)* to explode; *(d'une mine)* to blow up; *(d'un pneu, un ballon)* to burst; *(d'un verre)* to shatter; **faire é. qch** to burst/explode/shatter sth; **faire é. un pétard** to set off a firework; *Fig* **le groupe a fini par é.** the group finally split up **2** *(de la guerre, un incendie, une épidémie, un conflit)* to break out; *(d'un orage, un scandale)* to break; *(de la colère)* to burst out; **quand la guerre éclata** at the outbreak of the war, when war broke out; **le tonnerre éclata** there was a clap of thunder; **l'hymne national éclata dans la salle** the people in the room broke into the national anthem **3** *Fig (de personne)* **é. de rire** to burst out laughing; **é. en applaudissements** to burst into applause; **é. en sanglots** to burst into tears; **é. de colère** to fly into a rage **4** *(se manifester)* to be obvious *or* evident, to stand out; **les préjugés de l'auteur éclatent à chaque page** the author's prejudices stand out on every page; **l'indignation éclatait dans ses yeux** his eyes were blazing with indignation
▪ VPR **s'éclater** *Fam* to have a wild *or* a really good time; **s'é. comme une bête** to freak out ▪ VT *Fam (pneu)* to burst; *Fig Fam* **je vais l'é., je vais lui é. la tête** *ou* **la gueule** I'll smash his head in

éclateur [eklatœr] NM *Aut* spark gap

éclectique [eklɛktik] ADJ, N eclectic

éclectisme [eklɛktism] NM eclecticism

éclipse [eklips] NF *(de soleil, lune)* eclipse; *Fig* **é. totale de la raison/mémoire** total loss of reason/memory; *Fig* **après une longue é.** after a long absence

éclipser [eklipse] VT **1** *Astron (soleil, lune)* to

eclipse **2** *Fig (surpasser) (personne)* to eclipse, to outshine, to overshadow, *Fam* to put in the shade; *(événement, exploit etc)* to eclipse, to overshadow
▪ VPR **s'éclipser 1** *Fam (s'esquiver)* to make off, to make oneself scarce **2** *Astron* to be eclipsed; *(être voilé)* to be obscured

écliptique [ekliptik] ADJ, NM *Astron* ecliptic

éclisse [eklis] NF **1** *(plaque de bois)* (wooden) wedge **2** *(éclat)* piece of split wood **3** *Méd* splint **4** *Rail* fishplate

éclisser [eklise] VT *Méd (membre)* to put in splints, to splint

éclopé, -ée [eklɔpe] ADJ lame, limping
▪ NM *Mil* temporarily disabled soldier
▪ N *Hum* person with a limp

éclore [eklɔr] VI *(pp* **éclos**; *pr ind* **il éclôt, ils éclosent;** *impf* **il éclosait;** *no p hist; fu* **il éclora;** *aux souvent* **être,** *parfois* **avoir) 1** *(d'œufs, de poussins)* to hatch (out), to be hatched; **faire é. un œuf** to hatch (out) an egg **2** *(de fleurs, bourgeons)* to open; *Fig (d'un talent)* to be born, to appear; **roses fraîches écloses** roses that have just opened; *Litt* **le jour est près d'é.** dawn is near; *Fig* **faire é. un talent** to nurture *or* develop a talent

éclosion [eklozjɔ̃] NF **1** *(d'œufs, de poussins)* hatching **2** *(de fleurs)* opening, blooming; *Fig (d'un talent)* birth

écluse [eklyz] NF **1** *(de canal)* lock; **droit d'é.** lock fee, lockage; **(porte d')é.** lock gate, sluice (gate); **é. de moulin** mill dam; *Fam Fig* **lâcher** *ou* **ouvrir les écluses** to turn on the waterworks **2** *(d'un dock)* tide gate **3** *Ordinat* firewall

éclusée [eklyze] NF *Tech* lock water

écluser [eklyze] VT **1** *(canal)* to equip with locks **2** *(péniche)* to pass through a lock **3** *Fam (boire)* to knock back
▪ VI *Fam* **qu'est-ce qu'elle écluse!** she doesn't half knock it back!

éclusier, -ière [eklyzje, -jɛr] N lock keeper

éco- [eko, eko] PRÉF eco-

écobilan [ekobilɑ̃] NM life-cycle analysis

écœurant [ekœrɑ̃] ADJ **1** *(dégoûtant) (nourriture)* nauseating, sickening; *(personne)* disgusting, sickening; **c'est un peu é. si on en mange trop** it's a bit sickly if you eat too much of it; **il a une manière de manger vraiment écœurante** it's quite sickening *or* disgusting *or Fam* sick-making watching him eat, it really turns the stomach watching him eat **2** *(décourageant)* disheartening, discouraging, demoralizing; **c'est é., elle a encore eu une augmentation!** it's sickening, she's got another rise!; **tu as une chance écœurante!** what disgusting luck!; **c'est é. ce que tu peux avoir de la chance** you're so lucky it makes me sick; *Can* **Steven est é. dans le rôle de Jake** Steven is unreal in the role of Jake
▪ NM *Can* disgusting *or* loathsome man

écœuranterie [ekœrɑ̃tri] NF *Can Fam* **1** *(saleté)* filth **2** *(coup bas)* dirty trick; **elle m'a fait une é.** she played a dirty trick on me

écœurement [ekœrmɑ̃] NM **1** *(physique)* nausea; *(dégoût)* disgust, loathing; **manger du chocolat jusqu'à é.** to eat chocolate until you feel sick *or* to the point of nausea; *Fig* **j'ai jardiné jusqu'à é.** I've done so much gardening I'm sick (and tired) of it *or* I'm fed up; **sa cruauté a provoqué l'é. de tout le monde** everyone was disgusted *or* nauseated by his/her cruelty, his/her cruelty turned everyone's stomach; **on ne peut le regarder agir sans é.** it's impossible to watch him at work without feeling disgust **2** *(découragement)* discouragement, dejection; **maintenant c'est l'é.** now I've/he's/*etc* become discouraged *or* lost heart; **ça a été l'é. dans toute la classe** the entire class lost heart

écœurer [ekœre] VT **1** *(physiquement)* **e. qn** to nauseate sb, to make sb feel sick *or Am* nauseous; *(dégoûter)* to disgust sb, to make sb feel sick; *(révolter)* to disgust sb **2** *(décourager)* to dishearten, to discourage; **son attitude l'écœure tellement que ...** he finds his/her attitude so disheartening *or* discouraging that ...; *Fam* **elle est écœurée de son job** she is sick of *or* fed up with her job; **ça m'écœure que ...** it sickens me *or* makes me sick that ... **3** *Can Fam (donner envie)* **e. qn** to make sb green with envy

écoinçon [ekwɛ̃sɔ̃] NM *Constr* corner piece *or* stone

écolabel [ekolabɛl] NM ecolabel

écolage [ekolaʒ] NM **1** *Suisse (frais de scolarité)* school fees **2** *Belg (formation)* training

école [ekɔl] NF VOIR GRAMMAIRE A6–7 **1** *(établissement)* school; **maîtresse/maître d'é.** (primary) school teacher; **les grandes écoles** = prestigious university-level colleges which prepare students for senior posts in public administration, engineering and business **2** *(enseignement)* school; **aller à l'é. jusqu'à 16 ans** to go to school until the age of 16; **faire l'é.** to teach; **faire l'é. buissonnière** to play truant *or Am Fam* hooky; **reprendre l'é.** to go back to school; **Fam je n'ai pas é. aujourd'hui** there's no school today; *Fig Hum* **tu peux retourner à l'é.** what did they teach you at school?; *Fig* **vous êtes à bonne é.** you're in good hands; *Fig* **à l'é. de la vie** in the university of life **3** *(mouvement) (de pensée, d'art, de littérature)* school; **faire é.** *(d'une théorie, d'un penseur)* to win a following **4** *Mil (exercice)* drill, training; **é. du soldat** drill; **é. de tir** rifle drill, knotting and splicing; *Aviat* **appareil d'é.** training aircraft
▸ ▸ **é. de l'air** flying school; **École des Arts et Métiers** = engineering college *(of university level)*; **é. des Beaux-Arts** art school; **é. de cinéma** film school; **é. de commerce** business school; **é. de conduite** driving school; **é. confessionnelle** ≃ independent *or* private school; **é. de danse** dance *or* dancing school; **é. de dessin** art school; *Suisse* **é. enfantine** nursery school; **é. d'équitation** riding school; **é. hôtelière** hotel school; **é. de journalisme** school of journalism; **é. libre** ≃ independent *or* private school; **é. maternelle** nursery school, kindergarten; **é. militaire** military academy; **é. de musique** music school; **É. nationale d'administration** = prestigious university-level college preparing students for senior posts in the civil service and public management; **É. nationale supérieure d'ingénieurs** = university-level college for the continuing education of qualified engineers; *Anciennement* **é. normale** ≃ teacher training college; **É. normale supérieure** = university-level college that prepares students for senior posts in teaching and other professions; **é. de police** police college *or Am* academy; **é. primaire** primary school; **é. privée** ≃ independent *or* private school; **é. publique** state *or Am* public school; *Suisse* **é. de recrues** *(instruction militaire obligatoire)* compulsory military training; **é. secondaire** secondary school, *Am* high school; **é. de secrétariat** secretarial college; **É. supérieure des sciences économiques et commerciales** = grande école for management and business studies

écolier, -ière [ekɔlje, -jɛr] N *(du primaire)* (primary) schoolboy, *f* (primary) schoolgirl; **écoliers** schoolchildren; *Fig* **le chemin des écoliers** the longest way round; **papier é.** exercise paper

écolo [ekɔlo] ADJ, N *Fam (abrév* **écologiste)** green

écologie [ekɔlɔʒi] NF ecology

écologique [ekɔlɔʒik] ADJ ecological, environmental

écologisme [ekɔlɔʒism] NM concern for the environment, environmental awareness

écologiste [ekɔlɔʒist] N ecologist; *Pol* ecologist, environmentalist
ADJ *(parti)* green, ecology; *(politique)* green, environmentalist

e-commerce [ikɔmɛrs] NM e-commerce

écomusée [ekomyze] NM ecomuseum

éconduire [ekɔ̃dɥir] VT *(conj like* **conduire***)* **1** *(congédier)* **é. qn** to get rid of sb, to show sb the door; **j'ai eu beaucoup de mal à les é.** I had a lot of trouble getting rid of them **2** *(refuser)* *(prétendant)* to reject, to turn down; *(suppliant, requérant)* *(en personne)* to turn away; *(par lettre)* to turn down

éconocroques [ekɔnɔkrɔk] NFPL *Arg* savings

économat [ekɔnɔma] NM **1** *(fonction)* stewardship, bursarship **2** *(bureau)* steward's or bursar's office **3** *(magasin)* staff (discount) store; *Com (coopérative)* multiple or chain store

économe [ekɔnɔm] N *(d'un collège, d'une institution etc)* steward, bursar
ADJ economical, thrifty; **é. de paroles/de son temps** sparing with words/of one's time
NM potato peeler

> Note that **économe** means **thrifty** and cannot be used to translate **economic**, for which the correct translation is always **économique**.

économètre [ekɔnɔmɛtr] N econometrician, econometrist

économétrie [ekɔnɔmetri] NF econometrics

économétrique [ekɔnɔmetrik] ADJ econometric

économie [ekɔnɔmi] NF **1** *(système)* economy; **é. de troc** barter economy; **nouvelle é.** new economy; **la fermeture de l'usine a eu des conséquences désastreuses sur l'é. de la région** the closure of the factory has had disastrous consequences for the region's economy
2 *(gain)* economy, saving; *(vertu)* economy, thrift; **avoir le sens de l'é.** to be thrifty, to be good with money; **elle n'a aucun sens de l'é.** she's no good at managing money, she's got no idea about money; **é. de temps** time saving; **faire une é. de temps/d'énergie/de vingt pour cent** to save time/energy/twenty per cent; **ça représentera une énorme é. de temps** it will be an enormous saving of time or an enormous time saver, it will save an enormous amount of time; **je vais faire l'é. d'un coup de fil** I'll save myself a phone call; **je pense qu'on ne pourra pas faire l'é. d'une réunion** I don't think we can do without a meeting, I think a meeting is essential; **le mariage a vraiment été fait à l'é.** the wedding was really done on the cheap
3 *(discipline)* economics
4 **économies** savings; **j'ai quelques économies** I have a few or some savings; **faire des économies** to save money; **je n'arrive pas à faire d'économies** I can't manage to save; **réaliser d'importantes économies** to save a lot of money, to make major savings; **faire des économies de chauffage** to save money or economize on heating; **prendre sur ses économies** to break into or draw on one's savings; **il n'y a pas de petites économies** every little helps
5 *(organisation)* *(d'une œuvre littéraire, loi etc)* arrangement, structure
▸ ▸ **é. du bien-être** welfare economy; *Fam* **économies de bouts de chandelles** cheeseparing (economy); **é. capitaliste** capitalist

economy; **é. classique** classical economics; **é. de la demande** demand-side economics; **é. à deux vitesses** two-speed economy; **é. dirigée** planned economy; **économies d'échelle** economies of scale; **é. d'entreprise** business management or studies; **é. de l'environnement** environmental economics; **é. éthique** caring economy; **é. immergée** underground economy; **é. industrielle** industrial economics; **é. informelle** informal economy; **é. libérale** open market economy; **é. de libre entreprise** free-enterprise economy; **é. de marché** market economy; **é. mixte** mixed economy; **é. mondiale** world economy; **é. noire** black economy; **é. de l'offre** supply-side economics; **é. ouverte** open economy; **é. parallèle** black economy; **é. planifiée** planned economy; **é. politique** political economy, economics; **é. sociale** social economy; **é. solidaire** economy of solidarity, socially responsible economy; **é. souterraine** black economy, underground economy; **é. de subsistance** subsistence economy; **é. de transition** transition economy; **é. de troc** barter economy

économique [ekɔnɔmik] ADJ **1** *(problème, doctrine)* economic; **science é.** economics **2** *(bon marché, avantageux)* economical; **vitesse é.** *(d'une voiture etc)* economical speed; **cycle é.** *(d'un lave-vaisselle etc)* economy cycle; *Aviat* **classe é.** economy class; **bouteille/voiture é.** economy (size) bottle/economy car

> Attention: ne pas confondre **economic** et **economical** lorsque l'on traduit **économique**. Economic signifie **qui se rapporte à l'économie** alors que **economical** signifie **qui permet d'économiser**.

économiquement [ekɔnɔmikmɑ̃] ADV *(à peu de frais)*, *Écon* economically, inexpensively; **les é. faibles** people on low incomes

économiser [ekɔnɔmize] VT *(argent)* to economize, to save; *(temps, énergie)* to save; *(électricité, gaz)* to economize on, to save on; *(ressources etc)* to conserve; **économisez 100 euros** 100 euros off, save 100 euros; **é. ses paroles** to be sparing of one's words; **é. ses forces** to conserve one's strength; **é. sa salive** to save one's breath
VI to economize, to save (**sur** on)

économiseur [ekɔnɔmizœr] NM *Aut* fuel-saving device, economizer; *Ordinat* **é. d'écran** screen saver

économiste [ekɔnɔmist] N economist

écope [ekɔp] NF *Naut* bailer, scoop

écoper [ekɔpe] VT **1** *(barque)* to bail (out); **é. l'eau d'une embarcation** to bail out a boat or the water out of a boat **2** *Fam (recevoir comme punition)* **c'est encore moi qui ai écopé de la punition** it was me that caught it again; **é. (de) cinq ans de prison** to cop or get five years' prison
VI to get the blame, to catch or cop it; **j'en ai marre d'é. pour les autres** I'm sick of getting the blame for what other people do

écoproduit [ekoprɔdɥi] NM eco-friendly product, environmentally-friendly product

écorçage [ekɔrsaʒ] NM *(d'arbres)* barking; *(d'oranges)* peeling; *(de riz)* husking

écorce [ekɔrs] NF **1** *(d'un arbre)* bark; *(d'une orange)* rind, peel; *(de riz)* husk; *(de châtaigne)* skin **2** *Géog* **l'é. terrestre** the earth's crust **3** *Bot* cortex **4** *Fig (apparence)* outward appearance

écorcer [ekɔrse] VT (j'écorçai(s); n. écorçons) *(arbre)* to bark; *(orange)* to peel; *(riz)* to husk

écorché, -ée [ekɔrʃe] NM **1** *Beaux-Arts* anatomical model, écorché **2** *Tech* sectional or cutaway view
N *Fig* **é. vif** tortured soul

écorchement [ekɔrʃəmɑ̃] NM *(d'un animal)*, skinning

écorcher [ekɔrʃe] VT **1** *(animal)* to skin; *(criminel)* to flay; *Fig Fam* **é. les clients** to fleece the customers **2** *(érafler)* *(jambe, peau etc)* to graze, to scrape; *(la gorge)* *(de l'alcool)* to burn, to rasp; *(d'un plat pimenté)* to burn; *(d'un bonbon)* to scratch; *Fig Fam* **é. une langue/un nom** to murder a language/name; **son qui écorche l'oreille** sound that grates on the ear
VPR **s'écorcher** to graze oneself; **s'é. le genou** to graze or scrape one's knee; **s'é. le tibia** to graze or bark one's shin

écorcheur, -euse [ekɔrʃœr, -øz] N **1** *(d'animal)* skinner **2** *Fig Fam (voleur)* extortionist; **ce sont de véritables écorcheurs** they rob you blind

écorchure [ekɔrʃyr] NF graze, scratch

éco-recharge, *pl* **éco-recharges** NF eco-refill

écorner [ekɔrne] VT **1** *(meuble, statue etc)* to chip or damage the corner(s) of; **é. (les pages d')un livre** to dog-ear (the pages of) a book **2** *Fig* **é. son capital/ses économies** to break into one's capital/savings **3** *Can (animal)* to dehorn; *Fig* **un vent à é. les bœufs** a fierce gale

écornifler [ekɔrnifle] VT *Fam Vieilli (repas, argent)* to cadge, to scrounge (**à qn** off sb)
VI *Can (être indiscret)* to snoop (around), to pry

écornifleur, -euse [ekɔrniflœr, -øz] N **1** *Fam Vieilli* sponger, cadger, scrounger **2** *Can Fam (personne indiscrète)* snooper
ADJ *Can Fam* snooping, prying

écossais, -aise [ekɔsɛ, -ɛz] VOIR GRAMMAIRE A19 ADJ *(paysage, personne etc)* Scottish; *(whisky)* Scotch; **tissu é.** tartan, plaid
N **É.** Scot, Scotsman, f Scotswoman
NM **1** *(tissu)* tartan, plaid **2** *Ling (dialecte de l'anglais)* Scots; *(langue celtique)* (Scots) Gaelic

Écosse [ekɔs] NF Scotland

écosser [ekɔse] VT *(pois)* to shell, to pod; *(haricots)* to shell

écosystème [ekosistɛm] NM *Biol* ecosystem

écot [eko] NM **payer son é.** to pay one's share

écotaxe [ekotaks] NF ecotax

écotourisme [ekoturism] NM ecotourism

écoulement [ekulmɑ̃] NM **1** *(d'un liquide)* flow, discharge; *Constr (du toit etc)* run-off; **fossé d'é.** drain; *(tube d')é.* *(d'une baignoire)* waste pipe; **l'é. se fait mal** it's not flowing very well; *Aviat* **é. (des filets) d'air** air flow **2** *Méd* discharge **3** *(de la circulation)* flow; **l'é. de la foule dans le métro** the streams of people moving through the metro **4** *Com (de marchandises)* sale; **marchandises d'é. facile** goods that sell easily or fast, goods with a ready sale; **l'é. de ces vieux parapluies sera plus facile** it will be easier to sell or dispose of these old umbrellas **5** *(du temps)* passage, passing; **vous n'avez pas le droit de répondre après é. du temps** you must answer before the time is up

écouler [ekule] VT *(marchandises)* to sell (off), to dispose of, to move; **é. des faux billets** to put forged notes into circulation; *Com* **é. à perte** to sell at a loss
VPR **s'écouler 1** *(d'un liquide)* to flow out, to run out (**de** of); *(de la circulation)* to flow; **le public s'écoulait sagement du théâtre** the audience was leaving the theatre quietly; **faire s'é. l'eau** to run off or drain off the water; **mon argent s'écoule à une vitesse!** I just don't know where my money goes to! **2** *(de marchandises)* to sell, to move **3** *(du temps)* to pass, to elapse

écourter [ekurte] VT *(robe, texte, citation)* to

shorten; *(visite, discours)* to curtail, to cut short; *(barbe, moustache)* to trim; *(queue de chien)* to dock

écoute [ekut] NF **1** *Vieilli* être *ou* se tenir aux écoutes to listen, to eavesdrop; *Fig* to keep one's ears open; être aux écoutes derrière la porte to be listening at the door; *Mil* poste d'é. listening post

2 *Radio (fait d'écouter)* listening; *(audience)* listeners; é. de contrôle monitoring; se mettre *ou* se porter à l'é., prendre l'é. to listen in, to tune in; *Mil, Radio* être à l'é. to be listening (de to); *Radio* ne quittez pas l'é.!, restez à l'é.! stay tuned (in)!, keep listening!; heure de grande é. *Radio* peak listening time; *TV* peak viewing time; aux heures de grande é. during prime time; émission programmée à une heure de grande é. prime-time programme; cette émission bénéficie d'une grande é. the programme has a large audience *or* stands high in the ratings; dès la première é. ... *(d'un disque, d'un morceau)* the first time you hear it ...; indice d'é. ratings; *Tél* table d'é. tapping equipment; elle est sur l'é. (table d')é. her phone is being tapped; écoutes téléphoniques telephone tapping

3 être à l'é. de *(électeurs, opinion publique)* to be in touch with; *(enfants)* to be attentive to the needs of; être toujours à l'é. des autres to be always willing to lend a sympathetic ear to others

4 *(d'un sanglier)* écoutes ears

écoute² NF *Naut (d'une voile)* sheet; nœud d'é. sheet bend; point d'é. clew

écouter [ekute] VT **1** to listen to; *Radio* vous écoutez France Inter you are listening *or* tuned to France Inter; savoir é. to be a good listener; je vais te faire é. un morceau I'll play you some music; é. qn jusqu'au bout to hear sb out; é. aux portes to listen at doors, to eavesdrop; écoutez! listen!, look (here)! **2** *(suivre) (personne, avis)* to listen to, to pay attention to; ne les écoutez pas! don't listen to them, don't pay them any attention!; é. sa conscience to listen to *or* be guided by one's conscience; savoir se faire é. to know how to command respect; il faudrait quand même que tu te fasses é. par tes enfants/élèves even so, your children/pupils ought to listen to you *or* obey you *or* be obedient; il est très écouté au sein du gouvernement the government listens closely to him *or* to what he has to say, he has the ear of the government

VPR s'écouter il s'écoute trop he coddles himself; elle a tendance à s'é. parler she likes the sound of her own voice; si je m'écoutais if I did what I wanted

écouteur [ekutœr] NM *Tél* receiver; prendre l'é. to listen in; *Radio* écouteurs earphones, headphones; *TV, Radio* é. auriculaire earpiece

écoutille [ekutij] NF *Naut* hatchway

écouvillon [ekuvijɔ̃] NM *(pour bouteille, biberon)* (bottle) brush; *Méd* swab

écouvillonner [ekuvijɔne] VT *(bouteille)* to clean out; *Méd (cavité)* to swab

écrabouillage [ekrabujaʒ] NM, **écrabouillement** [ekrabujmɑ̃] NM *Fam* squashing, crushing

écrabouiller [ekrabuje] VT *Fam* to squash, to crush; se faire é. par une voiture to get flattened by a car

écran [ekrɑ̃] NM **1** *(pour protéger)* screen; elle fit un é. de sa main she shielded *or* shaded her eyes with her hand; on ne peut pas voir le lac car les arbres font é. you can't see the lake because it's screened by the trees; elle se cachait derrière l'é. de ses cheveux she was using her hair as a screen to hide behind; il m'a fait é. de son corps pour me

protéger he shielded me with his body **2** *TV, Cin, Phot* screen; porter une pièce à l'é. to adapt a play for the screen; la technique de l'é. film technique; Delon crève l'é. dans ce film Delon gives a riveting performance in this film; vedette de l'é. film star; sur les écrans, cette semaine what's on this week (at the movies *or* Br cinema); prochainement sur vos écrans coming to a cinema *or* Am movie theater near you; le petit é. the small screen, television; le grand é. the big screen, cinema; téléviseur à é. plat flat-screen television **3** *Ordinat* screen, display; à l'é. on screen; plein é. full screen

▸▸ *Ordinat* é. d'accueil logo screen; *TV, Radio* é. acoustique acoustic screen; *Ordinat* é. à affichage accéléré accelerated display screen; *Ordinat* é. d'aide help screen; é. antibruit noise barrier; é. antireflets antiglare screen; é. basse radiation low radiation screen; é. cathodique cathode ray tube screen; é. de cheminée fire screen; é. de cinéma cinema *or* movie screen, motion picture screen; *TV* é. de contrôle control monitor; *TV* é. de contrôle de l'image picture monitor (screen); *TV* é. de contrôle studio studio monitor; *Ordinat* é. couleur colour screen *or* display; *Ordinat* é. à cristaux liquides liquid crystal screen; *Ordinat* é. de dialogue dialog(ue) screen; *Ordinat* é. divisé split screen; *Ordinat* é. à fenêtres split screen; é. de fumée smoke screen; é. haute résolution high resolution screen; é. à matrice active/passive active/passive matrix screen; é. monochrome monochrome screen; *TV* é.-mosaïque, *pl* écrans-mosaïques multi-screen, multi-split screen; *Cin* é. panoramique wide screen; *Ordinat* é. (à) plasma (gas) plasma screen; *Ordinat, TV* é. plat flat screen; *Ordinat* é. pleine page A4 screen; é. de prévisualisation preview monitor; *Cin* é. de projection projection screen; *Ordinat* é. protecteur *ou* de protection shield; é. publicitaire commercial break; *Ordinat* é. rétro-éclairé back-lit screen; *Ordinat* é. de saisie input screen; é. solaire sun block; *Cin* é. de sûreté *(de projecteur)* cut-off; *Ordinat* é. tactile touch *or* touch-sensitive screen; é. de télévision TV screen; *TV* é.-témoin, *pl* écrans-témoins monitor; é. TFT TFT screen; é. total sun block; *Ordinat* é. de travail working *or* work screen; *TV* é. de vision review screen; *TV* é. de visualisation display screen

écrasant [ekrazɑ̃] ADJ *(poids, défaite, impôts, responsabilité etc)* crushing; *(preuve, majorité, victoire)* overwhelming; *(travail)* back-breaking; *(chaleur)* overpowering

écrasé [ekraze] ADJ nez é. flat nose

écrasement [ekrazmɑ̃] NM *(d'un fruit)* crushing; *(accidentellement)* squashing; *(d'une personne, un animal) (par une voiture)* running over; *Fig (d'un peuple)* oppression; *(d'une armée, une équipe)* crushing defeat; *Ordinat (de données, d'un fichier)* zapping; *Aviat* é. (au sol) crash

écrase-merde [ekrazmɛrd] NMPL *Fam* clodhoppers

écraser [ekraze] VT **1** *(fruit)* to crush; *(accidentellement)* to squash; *(boîte, membre, ail)* to crush; *(carton)* to flatten; *(cafard)* to squash; *(mouche)* to swat; *(cigarette)* to stub out; *(piéton, chien, hérisson)* to run over *or* down; é. des œufs durs pour un plat to mash up hard boiled eggs for a dish; il s'est fait é. par une voiture he was *or* got run down *or* over by a car; *Fam* é. l'accélérateur *ou* le champignon to step on the gas; é. le frein to slam on the brakes; *Fig Fam* je compte sur toi pour é. le coup I'm relying on you to keep quiet *or* not to say anything

2 *Fig (assommer)* é. d'impôts to overburden with taxes; écrasé d'impôts crushed by

taxation, staggering under the burden of taxation; écrasé de travail overwhelmed with *or* Fam snowed under with work; Fam é. le marché to glut *or* flood the market; être écrasé de chaleur to be dropping with the heat; il écrase les gens de sa richesse he uses his wealth to put other people down

3 *(vaincre) (adversaire, troupes etc)* to crush; il écrase tout le monde en latin he is much better than everyone else at Latin

4 *Ordinat (fichier)* to zap

5 *Arg* en é. to sleep like a log

VI *Arg* écrase! shut up!, drop dead!, put a sock in it!

VPR s'écraser s'é. au sol *(d'une personne)* to crash to the ground; *(d'un avion)* to crash; la neige s'écrasait sous nos pieds the snow crunched under our feet; *Fig* on s'écrase devant le cinéma there's a tremendous crush outside the cinema; *Fig Fam* à sa place, je m'écraserais if I were him I'd keep my head down *or* keep a low profile; *Arg* écrase-toi! shut it!, button it!

écraseur, -euse [ekrazœr, -øz] N *Fam* road hog

écrémage [ekremaʒ] NM **1** *(du lait)* creaming, skimming **2** *Fig* ce lycée n'aurait pas de si bons résultats sans un sévère é. des élèves the school wouldn't get such good results if it didn't choose only the very best pupils *or* if it didn't pick and choose its pupils; le recrutement de leurs élèves passe par un sacré é. they only take the crème de la crème; *Mktg* é. du marché market skimming

écrémer [ekreme] VT *(j'écrème; j'écrémerai)* *(lait)* to cream, to skim; *Mktg (marché)* to skim; *Fig* to take the best *or* the cream of, to cream off; lait écrémé skim(med) milk

écrémeuse [ekremøz] NF (cream) separator, creamer

écrêter [ekrete] VT **1** *(coq)* to remove the comb of **2** *Fig (revenus, prix etc)* to even out

écrevisse [ekrəvis] NF *(crustacé)* (freshwater) crayfish; *Fam* rouge comme une é. as red as a lobster; *Fam* marcher comme une é. to walk backwards

écrier (s') [sekrije] VPR to cry (out), to exclaim

écrin [ekrɛ̃] NM *(jewel)* case

écrire [ekrir] *(prp écrivant; pp écrit; pr ind j'écris, n. écrivons, ils écrivent; p hist j'écrivis; fu j'écrirai)* VT *(lettre, livre, chanson, mémoires)* to write; *(noter)* to write down; é. qch à *ou* avec de l'encre to write with ink; machine à é. typewriter; écrit à la main longhand, handwritten; é. une lettre à la machine to type a letter; é. un mot à la hâte to scribble a note; é. un mot à qn to drop sb a line; é. à qn to write to sb; je lui ai écrit de venir I've written asking him to come; *Ordinat* é. qch sur un disque to write sth to disk; il est écrit que je n'irai jamais I'm fated not to get there; c'est écrit it is bound to happen; c'est écrit sur sa figure you can tell from his/her face, it's written all over his/her face; é. qch noir sur blanc *ou* en toutes lettres to put sth in black and white; tant que je ne verrai pas mon nom écrit noir sur blanc until I see my name in black and white

VI to write; il écrit bien his (hand)writing is good, he has good handwriting; *(d'un écrivain)* he's a good writer, he writes well; ce stylo écrit très bien this pen writes very well; é. dans les journaux to write for the papers; é. à l'encre to use ink

VPR s'écrire **1** *(s'orthographier)* to be spelled; comment ça s'écrit? how do you spell it? **2** *(correspondre)* ils s'écrivent they write to each other

écrit [ekri] NM **1** consigner *ou* coucher qch par é. to put *or* set sth down in writing; convention par é. written agreement

2 *(texte)* (written) document; **faire/signer un é.** to draw up/to sign a document; **les écrits de Bossuet** the writings *or* works of Bossuet; *Journ* **é. diffamatoire** libel **3** *Scol* **échouer à l'é.** to fail in the written examination

écriteau, -eaux [ekrito] NM notice

écritoire [ekritwar] NF *(coffret)* writing case

écriture [ekrityr] NF **1** *(système, caractères)* writing, script; *Typ* script; *Ordinat* write **2** *(main)* (hand)writing; **elle a une belle é.** her handwriting is good, she has good handwriting; **elle a une vilaine é.** her handwriting is dreadful **3** *Compta* entry, item **4** *Com* **écritures** accounts; **tenir les écritures** to keep the accounts; **employé aux écritures** accounts *or* ledger clerk **5** *Rel* **l'É. sainte, les saintes Écritures** Holy Scripture, Holy Writ **6** *Littér* writing; *TV, Cin* **é. de scénarios** scriptwriting, screenwriting ▸▸ **é. abrégée** speedwriting; **é. d'ajustement** corrected entry; **é. automatique** automatic writing; *Compta* **é. de clôture** closing entry; *Compta* **écritures comptables** accounting entries; *Compta* **é. conforme** corresponding entry; *Typ* **é. cursive** cursive; *Typ* **é. droite** upright script; *Typ* **é. grasse** bold typeface, boldface; *Compta* **é. d'inventaire** closing entries; *Typ* **é. en italique** italic script; *Compta* **écritures en partie double** double entry bookkeeping; *Compta* **écritures en partie simple** single-entry bookkeeping; **é. phonétique** phonetic script; *Compta* **é. regroupement** consolidated entry; *Compta* **é. de régularisation** adjusting entry; *Cin, TV* **é. de scénarios** scriptwriting, screenwriting; *Compta* **é. de virement** transfer entry

écrivailler [ekrivaje] VI *Péj* to be a hack (writer), to scribble

écrivailleur, -euse [ekrivajœr, -øz] N, **écrivaillon** [ekrivajɔ̃] NM *Péj* hack (writer), scribbler

écrivain [ekrivɛ̃] NM **1** *(auteur)* author, writer; **femme é.** woman writer **2** *Arch* **é. public** (public) letter writer

écrivasser [ekrivase] VI *Péj* = **écrivailler**

écrivassier, -ière [ekrivasje, -jɛr] N *Péj* hack (writer), scribbler

écrou[1] [ekru] NM *Jur* committal (to prison); **sous é.** detained, in detention; **levée d'é.** release, discharge (from prison)

écrou[2] NM *Tech* nut; **é. à ailettes** *ou* **à oreilles** thumb *or* wing *or* butterfly nut; **é. crénelé** *ou* **à créneaux** *ou* **à encoches** castellated nut; **é. de réglage** adjusting *or* adjuster nut

écrouelles [ekruɛl] NFPL *Arch* scrofula, king's evil

écrouer [ekrue] VT *Jur* to imprison, to commit to prison

écroulement [ekrulmɑ̃] NM *(d'un édifice, un pont, une personne, de prix etc)* collapse; *(de terre, roche)* fall; *(d'un empire)* fall, collapse

écrouler (s') [sekrule] VPR **1** *(d'un édifice, un pont, une personne, de prix)* to collapse; *(d'espoirs)* to crumble away; **empire près de s'é.** empire on the verge of collapse **2** **s'é. sur une chaise** to drop *or* flop onto a chair; **s'é. de fatigue** to collapse *or* drop with exhaustion; **écroulé dans un fauteuil** slumped in an armchair; *Fam* **écroulé (de rire)** doubled up with laughter

écru [ekry] ADJ *(tissu)* unbleached, ecru, natural-coloured; **soie écrue** raw silk; **toile écrue** holland

ecsta [ɛksta] NF *Fam (abrév* **ecstasy)** E

ecstasy [ɛkstasi] NF ecstasy

ectoplasme [ɛktɔplasm] NM *Biol* ectoplasm

ECU [eky] NM INV *Anciennement (abrév* **European Currency Unit)** ECU

écu [eky] NM **1** *(monnaie)* ECU; *Arch Fin* crown **2** *(bouclier)* shield; *Hér* escutcheon, coat of arms

écubier [ekybje] NM *Naut* hawsehole

écueil [ekœj] NM *Naut* reef, shelf; *Fig (danger)* pitfall; **donner sur les écueils** *(d'un bateau)* to strike the rocks; *Fig* **se heurter à un é.** to hit a snag

écuelle [ekɥɛl] NF *(assiette large)* bowl; **une é. de soupe** a bowl(ful) of soup; **é. du chien/chat** dog's/cat's bowl *or* dish

éculé [ekyle] ADJ *(chaussure)* down-at-heel; *Fig (tour, plaisanterie, argument)* well-worn, hackneyed

écumage [ekymaʒ] NM *(de la soupe, la confiture, du métal fondu)* skimming

écume [ekym] NF *(dans la bouche, sur la bière)* froth, foam; *(sur la mer)* foam; *(sur la soupe, la confiture, le métal fondu)* scum; **il avait l'é. à la bouche** he was foaming at the mouth; **cheval couvert d'é.** foam-covered horse; *Minér* **é. (de mer)** *(magnésite)* meerschaum

écumer [ekyme] VT **1** *(soupe, confiture, métal fondu etc)* to skim **2** *(piller)* to scour, to pillage; **é. les mers** *(des pirates)* to scour the seas, to buccaneer; *Fig* **j'ai écumé tous les magasins pour le trouver** I scoured the shops looking for it ◊ VI *(du vin, de la bouche etc)* to foam, to froth; *(de la mer)* to foam; *(de la soupe, la confiture, du métal fondu etc)* to form a scum; **cheval qui écume** foaming horse; **é. (de rage)** to foam (with rage)

écumeur [ekymœr] NM **é. (de mer)** buccaneer, pirate

écumeux, -euse [ekymø, -øz] ADJ *(mer, vagues)* foaming; *(bière)* foamy, frothy; *(confiture etc)* scummy

écumoire [ekymwar] NF skimmer, perforated spoon; **é. à friture** slotted spoon; *Fig* **troué comme une é.** riddled with holes

écureuil [ekyrœj] NM squirrel; **é. volant** flying squirrel

écurie [ekyri] NF stable; **é. (de courses)** *(de chevaux, voitures)* (racing) stable; **mettre les chevaux à** *ou* **dans l'é.** to stable the horses; *Fam* **quelle é.!** what a pigsty!; *Myth* **les écuries d'Augias** the Augean stables

écusson [ekysɔ̃] NM **1** *(de serrure)* key-plate, keyhole scutcheon **2** *Hér* escutcheon, shield, coat of arms **3** *(emblème d'étoffe)* badge; *Mil* tab, badge, (collar) patch

écuyer, -ère [ekɥije, -ɛr] NM **1** *(instructeur)* riding master **2** *Arch (gentilhomme)* squire, armour-bearer; *(servant la famille royale)* equerry; *Hist* **grand é.** Master of the Horse ◊ N rider, horseman, f horsewoman; **é. de cirque** circus rider, equestrian, f equestrienne; **bottes à l'écuyère** riding boots

eczéma [ɛgzema] NM *Méd* eczema; **avoir** *ou* **faire de l'é.** to have eczema

eczémateux, -euse [ɛgzematø, -øz] ADJ *Méd* eczematous

édam [edam] NM Edam

edelweiss [edɛlvɛs, -vajs] NF *(plante)* edelweiss

Éden [edɛn] NM *Bible* **l'É., le jardin d'É.** Eden, the Garden of Eden; *Fig* **un é.** a paradise, a Garden of Eden

édénique [edenik] ADJ *Litt* idyllic

édenté [edɑ̃te] ADJ *(personne, peigne)* toothless; *(animal)* toothless, *Spéc* edentate

édenter [edɑ̃te] VT *(peigne, scie, lame)* to break the teeth of

EDF [ədeɛf, edeɛf] NF *(abrév* **Électricité de France)** (French) Electricity Board

EDI [ədei] NM *Ordinat (abrév* **échange de données informatisé)** EDI

édicter [edikte] VT *(loi)* to enact, to decree; *(peine)* to decree, to prescribe

édicule [edikyl] NM *(urinoir)* public convenience

édifiant [edifjɑ̃] ADJ edifying

édification [edifikasjɔ̃] NF **1** *(d'un monument, d'un bâtiment)* erecting, erection, building; *Fig (d'un empire, d'une fortune)* building up **2** *(instruction morale)* edification, moral improvement; **pour votre é.** for your edification

édifice [edifis] NM building, *Fml* edifice; **édifices publics** public buildings; *Fig* **apporter sa pierre à l'é.** to make a contribution, to do one's bit; *Fig* **tout l'é. social** the whole fabric *or* structure of society

édifier [edifje] VT **1** *(bâtiment)* to build; *Fig (empire, fortune etc)* to build up; *(système)* to develop, to put together **2** *(d'un sermon)* to edify; *Iron* **ces dernières révélations nous ont tous édifiés** these latest revelations were an education for us all; **c'est sans doute pour nous é. qu'il a tenu ce discours** he probably made the speech for our edification

édile [edil] NM **1** *Antiq* aedile, *Am* edile **2** *(magistrat officiel)* municipal official, town councillor

Édimbourg [edɛ̃bur] N Edinburgh

édimbourgeois, -e [edɛ̃burʒwa, -az] ADJ of Edinburgh ◊ N **É.** person from Edinburgh

édit [edi] NM *Hist* edict

éditer [edite] VT **1** *(publier)* *(livre etc)* to publish; *(disque)* to produce **2** *(commenter)* *(texte)* to edit **3** *Ordinat* to edit; **pouvant être édité** editable

> Il faut noter que le verbe anglais **to edit** ne s'emploie jamais pour dire **publier**.

éditeur, -trice [editœr, -tris] N **1** *(d'une maison d'édition)* publisher **2** *(commentateur)* editor ◊ NM *Ordinat (de programme)* editor ▸▸ **é. de disques** record producer; *Cin* **é. de film** film releasing company; *Ordinat* **é. d'icônes** icon editor; *Ordinat* **é. HTML** HTML editor; *Ordinat* **é. d'images** image editing program, image editor; *Ordinat* **é. de liens** linker, link editor; *Ordinat* **é. de logiciels** software company; *Ordinat* **é. orienté en lignes** line editor; **é. de presse** newspaper publisher; **é. de texte** text editor; **é. de vidéo** video publisher

édition [edisjɔ̃] NF **1** *(activité, métier)* publishing; **maison d'é.** publishing house *or* firm; **é. de disques** record production; **é. électronique** e-publishing; **é. musicale** music publishing; **travailler dans l'é.** to work in publishing; **le monde de l'é.** the publishing world; **é. sur le Web** Web publishing **2** *(texte commenté)* edition; *(exemplaire)* edition, issue, impression; **é. de luxe** library edition; **é. scolaire** school edition; **é. originale** first edition; **é. (entièrement) revue et corrigée** major new edition; *Hum* **où est le sucre? – dans le placard, troisième é.!** where's the sugar? – for the third time, it's in the cupboard! **3** *Journ (de journaux)* edition; **dernière é.** final edition; **l'é. du matin/soir** the morning/evening edition; *TV* **l'é. du journal télévisé** the (television) news bulletin; **é. spéciale** *(de journal)* special edition; *(de revue)* special issue; **é. exceptionelle** extra; **é. locale** local edition **4** *(action de commenter)* editing **5** *Ordinat* editing; **é. de liens** linking; **é. pleine page** full page editing; **é. électronique** electronic publishing

> Il faut noter que le terme anglais **edition** est un faux ami. Il ne désigne jamais **l'industrie du livre**.

éditique [editik] NF *Ordinat* desktop publishing

édito [edito] NM *Journ* (*abrév* **éditorial**) leading article, leader, editorial

éditorial, -iale, -iaux, -iales [editɔrjal, -jo] *Journ* ADJ editorial
NM leading article, leader, editorial

éditorialiste [editɔrjalist] N *Journ* leader writer, editorialist, editorial writer

édouardien, -ienne [edwardjɛ̃, -jɛn] ADJ *Hist* Edwardian

édredon [edrədɔ̃] NM eiderdown, quilt

éducable [edykabl] ADJ teachable, *Fml* educable

éducateur, -trice [edykatœr, -tris] N (*enseignant*) educator, instructor; (*spécialiste*) educationalist; **é. spécialisé** special education teacher
ADJ educational

éducatif, -ive [edykatif, -iv] ADJ educational

éducation [edykasjɔ̃] NF **1** (*enseignement*) education; **faire l'é. de qn** to educate sb; *Hum* **toute ton é. est à (re)faire!** your education has been sadly neglected!; **en rock, toute mon é. est à faire** I know absolutely nothing *or* I'm totally ignorant about rock music; **l'é. politique de la jeunesse** the political education of young people **2** (*par les parents*) upbringing; **sans é.** ill-bred, uncouth; **avoir de l'é.** to be well-bred, to have good manners; **il manque d'é.** he has no manners, he is ill-mannered *or* ill-bred; **quel manque d'é.!** what manners! **3** *Fig* (*de la volonté, de l'esprit*) training
▸▸**é. manuelle et technique** handicraft classes; **l'É. nationale** *Br* ≃ Department for Education and Employment, *Am* ≃ Department of Education; **é. permanente** continuing education; **é. physique** physical training *or* education; **é. professionnelle** vocational training; **é. religieuse** religious instruction; **é. sexuelle** sex education

> Il faut noter que le nom anglais **education** ne fait référence qu'à l'instruction scolaire et à l'enseignement et non à la façon dont on est élevé.

édulcorant [edylkɔrɑ̃] ADJ sweetening
NM sweetener; **é. de synthèse** artificial sweetener

édulcorer [edylkɔre] VT **1** (*médicament, boisson etc*) to sweeten **2** *Fig* (*théorie, compte rendu*) to water down; (*roman pornographique*) to tone down

éduquer [edyke] VT **1** (*donner un enseignement à*) (*enfant, peuple etc*) to educate **2** (*élever*) to bring up; **mal éduqué** ill-bred, ill-mannered **3** *Fig* (*volonté, esprit etc*) to train; **le goût est quelque chose qui s'éduque** taste has to be learnt

EED [əəde] NM *Pol* (*abrév* **échange électronique de données**) EDI

EEE [əəə] NM (*abrév* **Espace économique européen**) EEA

EEG NM (*abrév* **électroencéphalogramme**) EEG

effaçable [efasabl] ADJ **1** (*encre, crayon, inscription*) erasable **2** *Ordinat* (*mémoire*) erasable

effaçage [efasaʒ] NM erasing

efface [efas] NF *Can Fam Br* rubber, *Am* eraser

effacé [efase] ADJ (*personne, manières*) self-effacing, retiring; (*rôle*) small, insignificant; (*menton*) receding; **mener une vie très effacée** to live very quietly

effacement [efasmɑ̃] NM **1** (*d'un mot*) (*en gommant*) erasure; (*de message*) erasing; (*d'une bande magnétique*) blanking, erasing;

Ordinat deletion; (*d'une tache*) removal; (*par le temps, les éléments*) (*d'une inscription*) wearing away; (*des souvenirs*) fading **2** (*d'une personne*) self-effacement

effacer [efase] (**j'effaçai(s); n. effaçons**) VT **1** (*enlever*) (*mot*) to erase, to rub out; (*enregistrement, bande*) to wipe, to erase; *Ordinat* to erase, to delete; **e. le tableau** to clean the blackboard; *Ordinat* **e. l'écran** to clear the screen; **e. une tache** to remove a stain; (*en lavant*) to wash out a stain; (*avec un chiffon*) to wipe off a stain; **e. des imperfections** to smooth out imperfections; **sculptures effacées par le temps** carvings worn away by time; **e. toutes traces de son passage** to remove *or* eliminate all traces of one's presence
2 *Fig* (*faire oublier*) **e. un mauvais souvenir** to erase *or* wipe out *or* blot out an unhappy memory; **e. qch de sa mémoire** to blot sth out of *or* erase sth from one's memory; **il a réussi à e. toutes mes craintes** he made my fears vanish; **on efface tout et on recommence** we'll wipe the slate clean and make a fresh start
3 (*éclipser*) *Fig* to put in the shade
4 e. le corps to stand sideways; **e. les épaules** to throw back one's shoulders
VPR **s'effacer 1** (*disparaître*) (*d'une inscription*) to wear away; *Fig* (*d'un sentiment, un souvenir*) to fade (away); **cela s'effacera à l'eau** it will wash off; **la tache ne s'est pas effacée au lavage** the stain didn't come out in the wash; **cette encre ne s'efface pas bien** anything written in this ink doesn't rub out very well; *Fig* **avec le temps, tout s'efface** everything fades with time; **ton chagrin s'effacera** you'll get over it
2 (*s'écarter*) to stand *or* move aside, to move to one side; *Fig* **depuis quelque temps il s'était effacé** for some time he had kept in the background; **il s'est effacé devant moi pour me laisser passer** he stood aside to let me pass; **il a tendance à s'e. derrière elle** he tends to hide behind her

effaceur [efasœr] NM **e. (d'encre)** ink eraser *or Br* rubber

effarant [efarɑ̃] ADJ frightening, alarming; **ils pratiquent des prix effarants** their prices are frightening *or* shocking; **il y avait un monde e. sur les plages** there was an awful lot of people on the beach; **d'une naïveté effarante** alarmingly *or* shockingly naive

effaré [efare] ADJ alarmed

effarement [efarmɑ̃] NM alarm

effarer [efare] VT to alarm, to scare; **son hypocrisie m'effare!** his/her hypocrisy astounds me!; **je suis effaré par les prix!** the prices are frightening *or* shocking!, I'm astounded at the prices!

effarouchement [efaruʃmɑ̃] NM startling, frightening (away)

effaroucher [efaruʃe] VT **1** (*effrayer*) to scare, to alarm; (*faire reculer*) to scare away, to frighten away **2** (*choquer*) to shock
VPR **s'effaroucher 1** (*s'effrayer*) to be scared *or* alarmed (**de** by); **elle s'effarouche pour un rien** she gets frightened at the least little thing, the least little thing frightens her; **il ne risque pas de s'e. pour si peu** he's unlikely to let a little thing like that frighten him **2** (*s'offusquer*) to be shocked (**de** by, at)

effectif, -ive [efɛktif, -iv] ADJ **1** (*efficace*) (*traitement etc*) effective, efficacious **2** (*réel*) (*travail, rendement etc*) effective, actual; *Fin* (*circulation*) active; (*valeur*) real
NM (*employés*) manpower, (number of) employees, staff; (*d'un club, bataillon*) strength, numbers; *Naut* complement; **à e. réduit** under *or* below strength; *Scol* **réduire l'e. des classes à 25** to reduce the size of classes *or* reduce class numbers to 25; **l'e. est au**

complet we are at full strength *or* up to strength; *Mil* **les effectifs** the total strength; **crise d'effectifs** manpower crisis; **e. budgétaire** budgetary strength, *Am* authorized strength

effectivement [efɛktivmɑ̃] ADV **1** (*réellement, de manière effective*) actually, in reality, really; **contribuer e. au processus de paix** to make a real contribution to the peace process **2** (*en effet*) actually, in (actual) fact; **c'est pratique, hein? – e.!** it's practical, isn't it? – (yes) indeed! *or* indeed it is!; **e., on aurait pu prévoir un parapluie** we should have thought about bringing an umbrella, *Fam* we should have brought an umbrella right enough; **il a e. travaillé sur ce projet** he did actually work on the project

> Il faut noter que l'adverbe anglais **effectively** est un faux ami. Il signifie **efficacement**.

effectuer [efɛktɥe] VT (*réforme, mesure etc*) to carry out, to bring into effect; (*mouvement, opération*) to execute; (*paiement*) to make, *Fml* to effect; (*voyage, calcul*), *Mil* (*retraite*) to make; (*réconciliation*) to bring about; **e. des démarches** to take steps; *Com* **e. une commande** to place an order; **e. une réservation** to make a reservation
VPR **s'effectuer** (*d'une réforme etc*) to be carried out, to be brought into effect; (*d'un mouvement, d'une opération*) to be executed; (*d'un paiement, voyage*) to be made; (*d'une réconciliation*) to be brought about

efféminé [efemine] ADJ effeminate

efféminer [efemine] VT to make effeminate; (*pensée*) to emasculate

effervescence [efɛrvesɑ̃s] NF (*bouillonnement*) effervescence; *Fig* (*agitation*) agitation, turmoil; (*excitation*) excitement; **ville en e.** town seething with excitement *or* in (a) turmoil; **il avait l'esprit en e.** his mind was in a ferment

effervescent [efɛrvesɑ̃] ADJ (*comprimé, aspirine*) effervescent; *Fig* (*tempérament*) excitable, exuberant; (*foule*) excited

effet [efɛ] NM **1** (*résultat, conséquence*) effect (**sur** on); **les mesures du gouvernement n'ont eu aucun e.** the government's measures have had no effect; **cela a eu pour e. de le mettre en colère** it had the effect of making him angry; **sa fréquentation a un e. désastreux sur ma fille** going out with him has had a disastrous effect on my daughter; **ce poison a pour e. de paralyser le système nerveux** this poison results in the paralysis of the nervous system; **faire de l'e.** to have an effect, to be effective; **son départ précipité a fait de l'e.** his hurried departure caused a stir; **faire de l'e. sur** to have an effect on; **ma remarque a fait son petit e.** my remark caused a stir; **faire e.** to take effect; **produire l'e. voulu** to produce the desired effect; **une relation de cause à e.** a cause and effect relationship; **à cet e.** with that in mind, *Fml* to that end, with this end in view; **cet appareil n'a pas été conçu à cet e.** the machine was not designed for that purpose; **sans e.** ineffective, ineffectual; **mes conseils sont restés** *ou* **demeurés sans e.** my advice had no effect *or* was ineffective; **sous l'e. de l'alcool/la drogue** under the influence of alcohol/drugs; **il t'a injurié sous l'e. de la colère** he insulted you because he was angry; **je suis encore sous l'e. de la colère** I'm still angry, I still haven't calmed down; **les feuilles sont tombées sous l'e. de la chaleur** the leaves dropped off with the heat; **ce n'est qu'un e. de sa timidité** it's only because he is shy; **à quel e.?** to what end?; **e. secondaire** side effect; **ce n'était que l'e. du hasard** it was only by pure *or* sheer chance; **créer un**

e. de surprise to cause a stir; **nous ne gagnerons cette bataille qu'en créant un e. de surprise** we won't win this battle unless we can take the enemy by surprise

2 *(impression)* impression; **c'est l'e. que cela m'a fait** that's how it impressed *or* struck me; **quel e. ça te fait qu'elle revienne?** how do you feel about her coming back?; **les pleurs de sa femme ne lui firent aucun e.** his wife's tears had no effect on him; **elle me fait l'e. d'une fille plutôt équilibrée** she strikes me as being a fairly well-balanced girl; **sa réponse a fait l'e. d'une bombe** his answer came as *or* was a bombshell; *Fam* **et c'est tout l'e. que ça te fait?** is that all it means to you?; **à chaque fois qu'il me parle, ça me fait un drôle d'e.** I feel all funny inside whenever he talks to me; **ça m'a fait un drôle d'e.** it gave me a funny *or* strange feeling, it made me feel all funny *or* strange; **ça fait un drôle d'e. de penser que …** it's funny *or* strange to think that …; **il fit une pause pour mieux juger de l'e. de ses paroles** he paused to see what effect his words were having; **cela fait mauvais e. de le faire attendre** it looks bad to keep him waiting; **ça a fait bon e. que tu aies mis une jupe** your wearing a skirt made a good impression; **faire bon/mauvais e. à qn** to make a good/bad impression on sb; **faire de l'e.** to make a show, to attract attention; **dès que je l'ai vu, il m'a fait de l'e.** I fancied him the minute I saw him; **eh bien! elle te fait de l'e.!** she's got quite an effect on you, I see!; *Fam* **ça m'a fait de l'e. de la voir si pâle** it gave me quite a turn to see her so pale

3 *(but recherché, force artistique)* **manquer son e.** *(d'un discours)* not to have the desired effect; *(d'une plaisanterie)* to misfire, to fall flat; **il voulait faire une entrée triomphale mais il a manqué son e.** he wanted to make a triumphant entry but it fell flat; **soigner ses effets** to work hard to make the right impression; **rechercher les effets** to try to make an impression; **ménager ses effets** to have a sense of the dramatic; **un e. de contraste** contrasting effect; **e. de style** stylistic effect; *Litt* **phrases à e.** words used for effect; **un orateur qui fait des effets de voix** a speaker who makes striking use of his voice; **faire des effets de jambes** to show off one's legs, to draw attention to one's legs; **faire des effets de manches** *(d'un avocat)* to have a dramatic courtroom style; *Beaux-Arts* **e. de lune** moonlight effect

4 *(application)* effect; **mettre un projet à e.** to put a plan into action *or* into effect; **prendre e.** *(d'une loi etc)* to take effect, to come into effect *or* force; **e. rétroactif d'une loi/d'un accord** retroactive effect of a law/an argument; **augmentation avec e. rétroactif au 1er avril** rise retroactive *or* backdated to April 1st

5 *Tennis* spin; **balle qui a de l'e.** ball that has spin; **donner de l'e. à sa balle** to put spin on one's ball; *Billard* **e. de côté** side (screw); **mettre trop d'e.** to put on too much spin

6 *Tech* **e. utile** efficiency; **à simple e.** single-action, single-acting; **à double e.** double-action, double-acting; **e. Edison** Edison effect; **e. photoélectrique** photoelectric effect

7 *Fin* bill; **e. accepté** accepted bill; **e. bancable** eligible list; **e. bancaire** bill, draft; **e. de commerce** bill, draft; **e. de complaisance** accommodation bill; **e. à courte échéance** short, short-dated bill; **e. à date fixe** fixed-term bill; **e. domicilié** domiciled bill; **e. à l'encaissement** bill for collection; **effets à encaisser** accounts receivable; **e. endossé** endorsed bill; **e. escompté** discounted bill; **e. libre** clean bill; **e. à longue échéance** long, long-dated bill; *Bourse* **effets nominatifs** registered stock; **e. à ordre** promissory note; **effets à payer** bills payable; **e. au porteur**

bearer bill, bill made out to bearer; **effets publics** government stock *or* securities; **effets à recevoir** bills receivable; **e. en souffrance** overdue bill; **e. à taux flottant** floating rate note, FRN; **e. à terme** period *or* term bill; **e. à usance** usance bill; **e. à vue** sight bill *or* draft

8 effets *(affaires)* possessions, belongings; **effets personnels** personal effects; *Jur* goods and chattels

9 en e. *(réellement)* actually, in (actual) fact; **oui, je m'en souviens, en e.** yes, I do remember; **en e., c'est ce que je me suis dit** that's just what I thought; **mais c'est monstrueux! – en e.!** it's abominable! – isn't it just!

▸▸ *Fin* **e. balançoire** see-saw effect; **e. boomerang** boomerang effect; **avoir un e. boomerang** to boomerang; **e. boule de neige** snowball effect; *Aut* **e. de chasse** caster action; **e. Doppler** Doppler effect; *Cin, TV* **effets d'éclairage** lighting effects; *Typ* **e. d'escalier** jagged appearance, jaggy; *TV, Radio* **e. Larsen** audio *or* acoustic feedback, howl-round; **e. d'optique** visual effect; *Cin, TV* **effets optiques** camera effects; **e. pervers** undesired effect; *Méd* side effect; **e. de serre** greenhouse effect; **des gaz à e. de serre** greenhouse gases; *Cin etc* **effets sonores** sound effects; *Cin etc* **effets spéciaux** special effects; *Ordinat, TV* **e. de transition** melt; *Phys* **e. tunnel** tunnel effect; **effets vidéo** video effects; *Cin, TV* **effets visuels** visual effects

effeuillage [efœjaʒ] NM **1** *(d'arbres fruitiers etc)* thinning out of leaves **2** *Fam* striptease, strip

effeuillaison [efœjezɔ̃] NF, **effeuillement** [efœjmã] NM leaf fall

effeuiller [efœje] VT *(d'une personne) (arbre fruitier)* to thin out the leaves of; *(fleur)* to pluck the petals of; *(du vent) (arbre)* to blow off the leaves of; **e. la marguerite** to play 'he/she loves me, he/she loves me not'

effeuilleuse [efœjøz] NF *Fam* stripper, striptease artist

efficace [efikas] ADJ *(action, remède)* effective, *Fml* efficacious; *(machine)* efficient; *(personne)* efficient, capable; **prêter à qn un appui e.** to give sb useful *or* helpful support

> Attention: ne pas confondre **effective** et **efficient** lorsqu'on traduit **efficace**. **Effective** signifie **qui fait de l'effet** alors que **efficient** signifie **compétent**.

efficacement [efikasmã] ADV effectively; *(avec le minimum d'effort)* efficiently

efficacité [efikasite] NF *(d'un remède, d'une prière etc)* effectiveness, *Fml* efficacy; *(d'une machine etc)* efficiency; *Écon* **e. économique** economic efficiency

efficience [efisjãs] NF efficiency

efficient [efisjã] ADJ efficient

effigie [efiʒi] NF **1** *(portrait)* effigy; **pendre qn en e.** to hang sb in effigy **2** *(sur une pièce etc)* effigy, head

effilage [efilaʒ] NM *(d'un tissu)* fraying, ravelling out

effilé [efile] ADJ **1** *(tissu)* frayed; **une frange effilée** a ragged fringe **2** *(allongé) (outil)* tapered, pointed; *(doigts)* tapering; *(silhouette)* rangy; **amandes effilées** slivered almonds **3** *(poulet)* dressed, drawn
▪ NM *Tex* fringe

effilement [efilmã] NM **1** *(des doigts)* tapering **2** *(de tissu)* fraying

effiler [efile] VT **1** *Tex* to fray **2 e. les cheveux** to taper hair
▪ VPR **s'effiler 1** *(d'un tissu)* to fray **2** *(d'un visage)* to taper, to come to a point

effilochage [efilɔʃaʒ] NM *Tex (en peignant)* teasing out

effiloche [efilɔʃ] NF *(de fils laissés libres)* fringe

effilocher [efilɔʃe] VT *Tex (avec un peigne)* to tease out
▪ VPR **s'effilocher** *(d'un tissu)* to fray

efflanqué [eflãke] ADJ *(animal)* lean, rawboned; *(personne)* skinny, lanky

effleurement [eflœrmã] NM *(frôlement)* (light gentle) touch; *(de l'eau)* skimming; **touche à e.** touch-sensitive key

effleurer [eflœre] VT **1** *(frôler)* to touch lightly; *(accidentellement)* to brush (against); *(surface de l'eau)* to skim; *Fig* **e. un sujet** to touch on a topic; *Fig* **quelques soupçons l'avaient effleuré** some misgivings had crossed his mind; *Fig* **cette idée ne m'a jamais effleuré** the idea never crossed *or* entered my mind **2** *(égratigner) (peau)* to graze

efflorescence [eflɔresãs] NF **1** *Chimie* efflorescence **2** *(sur les fruits)* bloom **3** *Litt* **être en pleine e.** to be flourishing

efflorescent [eflɔresã] ADJ *Chimie* efflorescent

effluent [eflyã] ADJ effluent
▪ NM effluent; *(sewage)* effluent; **effluents radioactifs** radioactive waste

effluve [eflyv] NM *(émanation)* emanation; **de riches effluves** rich fragrance; *Fig Litt* **les effluves du passé** the ghosts of the past

effondré [efɔ̃dre] ADJ *(personne)* grief-stricken

effondrement [efɔ̃drəmã] NM *(d'un pont, un mur, un bâtiment etc)* collapse; *(d'un toit)* collapse, falling in; *(d'une mine)* caving in; *Géol* subsidence; *Fig (d'un plan)* falling through; *(d'une personne, une fortune, une monnaie)* collapse; *(d'un gouvernement, empire)* collapse, downfall; *Com (des prix, marchés)* slump (**de** in), collapse; **il est dans un état d'e. complet** he is in a state of total collapse

effondrer [efɔ̃dre] VT *(briser) (toit)* to bring down; *(mur)* to break down
▪ VPR **s'effondrer** *(d'un pont, un mur, un bâtiment)* to collapse; *(d'un toit)* to collapse, to fall in, to cave in; *(d'une mine)* to cave in; *Fig (d'un projet)* to fall through; *(des prix)* to slump; *(d'une monnaie, de cours)* to collapse; *(d'une personne, d'un gouvernement, d'un empire)* to collapse; **toute son histoire s'effondre** his whole story is collapsing *or* falling to pieces; **s'e. en larmes** to break down and cry, to dissolve into tears; **s'e. dans un fauteuil** to collapse *or* sink *or* flop into an armchair; **le marché s'est effondré** the bottom has fallen out of the market

efforcer (s') [sefɔrse] VPR **(je m'efforçai(s); n. n. efforçons)** to strive, to endeavour, *Am* to endeavor; **s'e. de faire qch** to do one's utmost *or* one's best to do sth, to make every effort to do sth; **je m'y efforce** I'm doing my best *or* utmost

effort [efɔr] NM **1** effort; **allons, encore un (petit) e.** come on, try again *or* a bit more effort; **son médecin lui a interdit tout e.** his doctor has forbidden any exertion; **cela va te demander un certain e.** you'll need to exert yourself a bit; **après bien des efforts** after a great deal of effort; *Fam* **après l'e., le réconfort** I/you/etc deserve this; *Fam* **appliquer la loi du moindre e.** to take the line of least resistance; *Fam* **il est partisan du moindre e.** he doesn't believe in exerting himself; *Péj* **son travail sent l'e.** his work reeks of effort; **il a progressé mais doit encore faire des efforts** he's made progress but still needs to make an effort; **sans e.** effortlessly, without effort; **elle parle anglais sans e.** she speaks English effortlessly; **je suis prêt à faire un e. pour ton projet** I'm willing to help with your project; **faire un e.**

pour faire qch to make an effort to do sth; **faire un violent e. pour se lever** to make a great effort to get up; **faire un e. d'adaptation** to make an effort to adapt; **faire un e. d'imagination** to use one's imagination; **fais un petit e. d'imagination!** use a bit of imagination!; **cela demande un sacré e. d'imagination** it takes an awful lot of imagination, it puts quite a strain on the imagination; **faire un e. de mémoire** to rack one's brains; **faire un e. sur soi-même** to exercise self-control; **faire tous ses efforts pour réussir** to make every effort *or* do one's utmost to succeed; **faire l'e. de faire qch** to make the effort to do sth; **e. de volonté** effort of (the) will; **ce travail demande un e. intellectuel immense** this is a very demanding job intellectually

2 *Méd* Vieilli strain, rick; **se donner** *ou* **attraper un e.** to rick one's back

3 *Tech* strain, stress

▸▸ *Tech* **e. de cisaillement** shearing stress; *Mktg* **e. de commercialisation** *ou* **de marketing** marketing effort; **e. financier** financial outlay; **e. de guerre** war effort; *Tech* **e. de rupture** breaking strain; *Tech* **e. de tension** tensile stress; *Tech* **e. de torsion** torque; *Aut* **e. de traction** tractive effort, pull; *Aut* **efforts en virage** cornering force

effraction [efraksjɔ̃] **NF** *Jur* breaking and entering; **entrer par e.** to break in; **vol avec e.** burglary; **il n'y a pas eu e.** there was no sign of a burglary

effraie [efrɛ] **NF** *(oiseau)* barn owl, screech owl

effranger [efrɑ̃ʒe] *(j'effrangeai(s); n. effrangeons)* **VT** *(bords d'un tissu)* to fray
VPR s'**effranger** to fray, to become frayed

effrayant [efrɛjɑ̃] **ADJ** frightening; *Fig (chaleur, appétit, charme)* tremendous; *(prix, bêtise, laideur)* frightening

effrayer [efrɛje] *(j'effraie, j'effraye, n. effrayons; j'effraierai, j'effrayerai)* **VT** *(faire peur à)* to frighten, to scare; *(inquiéter)* to alarm; **l'énormité de la besogne nous effraie** the magnitude of the task appals *or* alarms us
VPR s'**effrayer** to be frightened *(de* at); **elle s'effraie pour un rien** the least little thing frightens her, she takes fright at the least little thing; **je m'effraie de la lenteur avec laquelle elle travaille** I'm alarmed by how slowly she works; **d'après lui, il n'y a aucune raison de s'e.** according to him there's no need to be frightened *or* alarmed *or* there's no need for alarm

effréné [efrene] **ADJ** *(passion, curiosité)* unbridled, unrestrained; *(efforts)* frantic; *(galop)* frantic, mad

effritement [efritmɑ̃] **NM** *(du plâtre, d'un revêtement)* crumbling (into dust); *(de la roche)* weathering; *Fig (d'une autorité, une majorité, de fonds)* erosion

effriter [efrite] **VT** to cause to crumble *or* disintegrate; *(du vent) (roche)* to weather
VPR s'**effriter** *(de plâtre, d'un revêtement)* to crumble, to disintegrate; *(de la roche)* to weather, *Fig (d'une autorité, une majorité, de fonds)* to be eroded

effroi [efrwa] **NM** *Litt* terror, fear, dread; **je fus saisi d'e.** I was seized by terror, I was terror-stricken

effronté [efrɔ̃te] **ADJ** *(personne, manières)* impudent, insolent; *(mensonge, menteur)* barefaced, brazen

effrontément [efrɔ̃temɑ̃] **ADV** impudently, insolently; *(mentir)* brazenly

effronterie [efrɔ̃tri] **NF** *(d'une personne, de manières)* effrontery, insolence, impudence; *(d'un mensonge)* brazenness

effroyable [efrwajabl] **ADJ** *(qui fait peur)* dreadful, appalling, horrifying; *Fam (énorme) (dépense, foule, erreur)* dreadful, terrible

effroyablement [efrwajabləmɑ̃] **ADV** *Fam* dreadfully, terribly

effusion [efyzjɔ̃] **NF 1 e. de sang** bloodshed **2** *(exubérance)* effusiveness; **avec e.** effusively, gushingly; **une e. de tendresse** an outpouring of affection

égaiement [egɛmɑ̃] **NM** cheering up

égailler (s') [segaje] **VPR** to disperse, to scatter

égal, -ale, -aux, -ales [egal, -o] **ADJ 1** *(équivalent) (part, poids etc)* equal; **être e. à** to be equal to, to equal; **toutes choses égales (d'ailleurs)** all (other) things being equal; **à travail é., salaire é.** equal pay for equal work; **la partie n'est pas égale** they/we/you are not evenly matched; **ils sont de force/d'intelligence égale** they are equally strong/intelligent; **à surface égale, je préfère mon appartement au sien** square foot for square foot, I prefer my flat to his/hers; **à expérience égale, ils préfèrent recruter un homme qu'une femme** if they have two candidates with identical experience, they prefer to hire a man rather than a woman

2 *(constant) (respiration, son)* even, regular; *(allure, pouls)* steady; *(sol)* level, even; *(climat)* equable; **homme d'humeur égale** even-tempered man; **fournir un effort é.** to work steadily; **il reste é. à lui-même** he's still his same old self

3 cela m'est (bien) é. it's all the same *or* all one to me; *(cela ne m'intéresse pas)* I don't care; **c'est é., elle aurait pu venir!** all the same, she could have come!

N equal; **s'associer avec ses égaux** to associate with one's equals; **elle est mon égale** she is my equal; **traiter qn d'é. à é., traiter qn en é.** to treat sb as an equal; **nous avons eu une discussion d'é. à é.** we had a discussion as equals *or* on equal terms *or* on an equal footing; **sans é.** unequalled, matchless; **elle est d'une malhonnêteté sans é.** she is incredibly dishonest; **il me chérit à l'é. d'un fils** he loves me like a son; **sa beauté n'a d'é. que sa bêtise** her beauty is only equalled by her stupidity

égalable [egalabl] **ADJ** which can be equalled *or* matched; **c'est un exploit difficilement é.** it's a achievement that will be difficult to match, it'll be a hard act to follow

également [egalmɑ̃] **ADV 1** *(de la même manière)* equally; **é. bon** equally good; **servir tout le monde é.** to give everyone an equal serving; **j'aime é. sa mère et son père** I like his/her mother as much as I do his/her father **2** *(aussi)* also, as well, too; **j'en veux é.** I want some too *or* as well

égaler [egale] **VT 1** *(être égal à) (personne, score)* to equal, to match (up to) *(en* for); **deux et deux égalent quatre** two and two equal *or* make four; **é. un record** to equal a record; **rien n'égale sa beauté** her beauty is unequalled **2** *Arch (rendre égal)* to make equal; **la douleur égale les hommes** grief makes all men equal; **peut-on é. Mozart à Bach?** can Mozart be considered the equal of Bach?

égalisateur, -trice [egalizatœr, -tris] **ADJ** *(système, effet etc)* equalizing, levelling; *Sport* **but/point é.** equalizer

égalisation [egalizasjɔ̃] **NF 1** *(équilibrage)* equalization, equalizing; *Math* **é. à zéro** equating to zero; *Sport* **(but/point d')é.** equalizer; **réussir l'é.** to score the equalizer **2** *(nivellement) (du sol)* levelling, evening out

égaliser [egalize] **VT 1** *(salaires, pression etc)* to equalize, to make equal; **é. les cheveux de qn** to trim sb's hair; *Math* **é. une expression à**

zéro to equate an expression to zero; *Sport* **é. la marque** to equalize, to draw level **2** *(sol)* to level, to even out
VI *Sport* to equalize

égaliseur [egalizœr] **NM** *Électron* equalizer; **é. graphique** graphic equalizer

égalitaire [egaliter] **ADJ, N** egalitarian

égalitarisme [egalitarism] **NM** egalitarianism

égalitariste [egalitarist] **ADJ, N** egalitarian

égalité [egalite] **NF 1** *(équivalence)*, *Pol* equality; *Tennis* deuce; **être sur un pied d'é. avec qn** to be on an equal footing *or* on equal terms with sb; **é. des chances** equal opportunities; **é. des salaires** equal pay; *Sport* **à é.** *(équipes)* level; *(résultat)* drawn, tied; *Golf* all square; *Fig* **maintenant, nous sommes à é.** now we're even; *Sport* **course à é.** dead heat, tie; *Courses de chevaux* **parier à é. sur un cheval** to lay evens on a horse **2** *(constance) (de la respiration, d'un son etc)* evenness, regularity; *(d'une allure, du pouls)* steadiness; *(du sol)* evenness; *(de l'esprit)* equanimity; **é. d'humeur** even-temperedness

égard [egar] **NM 1** *(attention)* consideration; **avoir é. à qch** to take sth into consideration *or* into account, to make allowance(s) *or* to allow for sth; **eu é. aux circonstances** in view of *or* considering the circumstances; **eu é. à son âge** in view of *or* given his age; **sans é. à** regardless of, irrespective of

2 à tous (les) égards in all respects, in every respect; **à certains égards** in some respects; **n'ayez aucune crainte à cet é.** don't worry about that, don't have any worries on that score; **être injuste à l'é. de qn** to be unjust to(wards) sb; **il a été très gentil à mon é.** he has been very kind to me

3 *(respect)* consideration, respect, regard; **faire qch par é. pour qn** to do sth out of respect *or* consideration for sb; **être sans é.** *ou* **n'avoir aucun é. pour qn** to have no consideration for sb; **avoir des égards pour qn** to be considerate towards sb, to show sb consideration; **elle est toujours accueillie avec les égards dus à son rang** she is always greeted with the respect due to her rank; **il nous a reçus avec beaucoup d'égards** he received us very warmly

égaré [egare] **ADJ 1** *(personne)* lost; *(animal)* stray, lost **2** *(hagard) (regard)* distraught; *(yeux)* wild

égarement [egarmɑ̃] **NM 1** *(délire, distraction)* é. **(d'esprit)** (mental) aberration; **il a parfois des moments d'é.** sometimes what he says/does doesn't make much sense, *Fam* there are times when he's not all there **2 égarements** *(dérèglements de conduite)* wild behaviour, wildness; **il est revenu de ses égarements** he has seen the error of his ways

égarer [egare] **VT** *(perdre) (personne)* to lose; *(en donnant de mauvaises indications)* to mislead; *(objet)* to mislay, to lose; **il jouait à é. les nouveaux arrivants** it amused him to get the newcomers lost; *Fig* **égaré par tant de malheurs** distraught by so many misfortunes; **la douleur/colère vous égare** you don't know what you're saying because of the pain/because you're so angry; **il faut à tout prix é. ses soupçons** we have to avert his/her suspicions at all costs
VPR s'**égarer 1** *(se perdre) (personne)* to lose one's way, to get lost; **colis qui s'est égaré** parcel that has got lost *or* gone astray **2** *(dévier)* s'é. **du droit chemin** to wander from the straight and narrow **3** *(sortir du sujet)* to stray *or* wander from the point; **son esprit s'égare** his mind is wandering

égayer [egeje] *(j'égaie, j'égaye, n. égayons; j'égaierai, j'égayerai)* **VT** *(malade, personne* *déprimée*) to cheer up; *(invités)* to amuse; *(conversation)* to liven up; *(pièce, robe, la vie de quelqu'un)* to brighten (up)

VPR s'égayer *(s'amuser)* to have fun, to enjoy oneself; *(s'animer)* to cheer up; **s'é. aux dépens de qn** to have fun at sb's expense, to make fun of sb

Égée [eʒe] **ADJ la mer É.** the Aegean (Sea)

égéen, -éenne [eʒeɛ̃, -ɛɛn] **ADJ** Aegean

égérie [eʒeri] **NF** muse

égide [eʒid] **NF** aegis, shield; *Fig* **sous l'é. de** under the aegis *or* care of; *Fig* **se mettre sous l'é. des lois** to take refuge in the law

églantier [eglɑ̃tje] **NM** wild rose *or* dog rose (bush)

églantine [eglɑ̃tin] **NF** *(fleur)* wild *or* dog rose

églefin [egləfɛ̃] **NM** haddock

église [egliz] **NF** VOIR GRAMMAIRE A6-7 **1 l'É. (catholique romaine)** the (Roman) Catholic Church; **l'É. anglicane** the Church of England, the Anglican Church; **l'É. et l'État** Church and State; **gens d'É.** churchmen **2** *(bâtiment)* church; **l'é. Saint-Pierre** St. Peter's (church); **aller à l'é.** to go to church; **se marier à l'é.** to get married in (a) church, to have a church wedding

églogue [eglɔg] **NF** *Littér* eclogue

ego [ego] **NM INV** ego

égocentrique [egosɑ̃trik] **ADJ** self-centred, egocentric

N self-centred *or* egocentric person

égocentrisme [egosɑ̃trism] **NM** egocentricity, self-centredness; *Psy* egocentrism

égoïne [egɔin] **NF (scie) é.** handsaw

égoïsme [egɔism] **NM** selfishness, egoism

égoïste [egɔist] **N** egoist, selfish person
ADJ selfish, self-centred, egoistic

égoïstement [egɔistəmɑ̃] **ADV** selfishly, egoistically

égorgement [egɔrʒəmɑ̃] **NM** *(d'un cochon, d'une personne)* cutting the throat

égorger [egɔrʒe] (**j'égorgeai(s); n. égorgeons**) **VT 1** *(animal, personne)* to cut the throat of **2** *Vieilli (ruiner)* to bleed white *or* dry

VPR s'égorger *Fig* to kill each other

égorgeur, -euse [egɔrʒœr, -øz] **N** *(assassin)* cut-throat

égosiller (s') [segozije] **VPR** *(en parlant)* to bawl, to shout (oneself hoarse); *(en chantant)* to sing at the top of one's voice, *Fam* to sing one's head off; **mais je m'égosille à vous le dire!** I've told you till I'm blue in the face *or* I'm hoarse!

égotisme [egotism] **NM** egotism

égotiste [egotist] **N** egotist
ADJ egotistic(al)

égout [egu] **NM** *(canalisation souterraine)* sewer; **eaux d'é.** sewage; **é. collecteur** main sewer; **bouche d'é.** manhole; **rat d'é.** sewer rat

égoutier [egutje] **NM** sewerman

égouttage [eguta3] **NM** *(de la vaisselle, d'un fromage frais etc)* draining

égouttement [egutmɑ̃] **NM 1** *(de l'eau)* dripping **2** *(égouttage)* draining

égoutter [egute] **VT** *(fromage frais, pâtes etc)* to drain
VPR s'égoutter *(d'un fromage frais, de vaisselle etc)* to drain
VI to drain; **laisser é. la vaisselle** to leave the dishes to drain

égouttoir [egutwar] **NM 1** *(dans l'évier)* draining board; *(mobile)* drainer, draining rack **2** *(passoire)* colander; **panier é.** *(d'une friteuse)* basket

égrappage [egrapa3] **NM** *(de raisins)* picking off

égrapper [egrape] **VT** *(raisins, baies)* to pick off from the bunch

égratigner [egratiɲe] **VT** *(écorcher)* to scratch; *Fig* to have *or* take a dig at
VPR s'égratigner to scratch oneself

égratignure [egratiɲyr] **NF** *(écorchure)* scratch; *Fig* dig, gibe; **je m'en suis sorti sans une é.** I escaped without a scratch

égrenage [egrəna3] **NM**, **égrènement** [egrɛnmɑ̃] **NM** *(de pois, maïs etc)* shelling; *(de raisins, baies)* picking off

égrener [egrəne] (**j'égrène, n. égrenons; j'égrènerai**) **VT 1** *(maïs, pois etc)* to shell; *(raisins, baies)* to pick off **2** *Fig* **é. son chapelet** to tell one's beads; **la pendule égrenne les heures** the clock ticks away; **é. ses souvenirs** to call up one's memories one by one
VPR s'égrener 1 *(de raisins, baies)* to fall *or* drop from the bunch; *(du blé)* to seed **2** *Fig* *(d'un cortège)* to become strung out; **des lumières s'égrenaient le long du quai** a string of lights stretched along the quay

égrillard [egrijar] **ADJ** *(personne, chanson, histoire etc)* bawdy, ribald; **en société, il a des manières égrillardes** he tends to be bawdy in company

Égypte [eʒipt] **NF** Egypt

égyptien, -ienne [eʒipsjɛ̃, -jɛn] **ADJ** Egyptian
N É. Egyptian
NM *Hist, Ling* Egyptian

égyptologie [eʒiptɔlɔʒi] **NF** Egyptology

égyptologue [eʒiptɔlɔg] **N** Egyptologist

eh [e] **INT** hey!; **eh bien!** well!, now then!; **eh bien, comment ça va aujourd'hui?** so how are you today?; **eh bien, je ne sais pas** well I don't know; **eh bien, je vais m'en occuper** oh well, I'll deal with it; **eh oui!** that's right!; **eh! que voulez-vous que j'y fasse?** well what do you want me to do about it?

éhonté [eɔ̃te] **ADJ** *(mensonge, menteur)* shameless, barefaced, brazen

eider [ɛdɛr] **NM** *(oiseau)* eider (duck)

einsteinien, -ienne [ajnʃtajnjɛ̃, -jɛn] **ADJ** of/typical of Einstein

éjaculateur [eʒakylatœr] **NM** *Physiol* **é. précoce** premature ejaculator

éjaculation [eʒakylasjɔ̃] **NF** *Physiol* ejaculation; **é. précoce** premature ejaculation

éjaculer [eʒakyle] **VI** *Physiol* to ejaculate

éjectable [eʒɛktabl] **ADJ** *Aviat* **siège é.** ejector seat

éjecter [eʒɛkte] **VT** *(cartouche, pilote etc)* to eject; *Fam (expulser)* to throw *or* kick out (**de** of); **elle s'est fait é.** she was *or* got thrown *or* kicked out

éjection [eʒɛksjɔ̃] **NF** *(d'une cartouche, d'un pilote etc)* ejection; *Fam (expulsion)* throwing out, kicking out; **éjections volcaniques** ejecta

élaboration [elabɔrasjɔ̃] **NF** *(d'un plan, d'une idée)* working out, development; *(d'une constitution, une loi etc)* drawing up; **é. de concept** concept development; *Mktg* **é. de produit** product development

élaboré [elabɔre] **ADJ** *(technique, machine)* sophisticated; *(plan)* elaborate

élaborer [elabɔre] **VT** *(plan, idée)* to work out, to develop; *(constitution, loi etc)* to draw up; **é. le profil de qn** to profile sb

élagage [elaga3] **NM** *(d'un arbre)*, *Fig (d'un film, un roman etc)* pruning; *Mktg* **é. de la ligne** line pruning

élaguer [elage] **VT** *(arbre)*, *Fig (film, roman etc)* to prune

élagueur, -euse [elagœr, -øz] **N** pruner

élan¹ [elɑ̃] **NM 1** *Sport etc (action de s'élancer)* *(avec les jambes)* run-up; *(avec les bras)* swing; *Sport* **prendre de l'é.** *ou* **son é.** to take

a run (-up); **saut sans/avec é.** standing/running jump; **mal calculer son é.** to misjudge one's run-up; **d'un seul é.** *(en sautant)* at one bound; *(en courant)* in one burst; *Fig* **elle courut chez sa mère d'un seul é.** she ran all the way to her mother's without stopping

2 *Fig (impulsion)* **donner de l'é. à l'industrie** to give a boost to industry

3 *(vitesse)* momentum, impetus; **emporté par son é., il trébucha** carried away by his own momentum, he tripped; **emportée par son é., la voiture alla au fossé** gathering momentum, the car went into the ditch; **perdre de l'é.** to lose momentum; *Fig* **le général Dupont brisa l'é. des forces ennemies** General Dupont broke the momentum of the enemy forces; **impossible de les arrêter dans leur é.** it's impossible to stop them once they've got going *or* started

4 *(transport)* *(d'enthousiasme)* burst, outburst; *(de tendresse, passion)* surge; **un é. créatif** a creative outburst; **dans un é. amoureux** in a surge of love; **il ne connaissait plus aucun des élans de sa jeunesse** he no longer felt the impulses of his youth; **éprouver un é. (naturel) vers qn** to feel (naturally) drawn to sb; **rien n'a jamais pu briser l'é. qui me portait vers elle** nothing could ever break the force which drew me towards her; **contenir** *ou* **maîtriser ses élans** to keep one's impulses in check

5 *(ferveur)* fervour, *Am* fervor; **parler avec é.** to speak with fervour *or* fervently

6 *(accent)* **sa voix avait des élans lyriques** her voice had a lyrical ring; **le violon avait des élans plaintifs** the violin had plaintive tones

7 *Phil* **é. vital** life force

élan² **NM** *(animal)* (Scandinavian) elk; **é. du Canada** moose

élancé [elɑ̃se] **ADJ** *(silhouette, personne, arbre)* slim, slender; **aux formes élancées** *(bateau, voiture)* streamlined

élancement [elɑ̃smɑ̃] **NM** *(douleur)* shooting pain

élancer [elɑ̃se] (**j'élançai(s); n. élançons**) **VI** **ma jambe m'élance, ça m'élance dans la jambe** I've got shooting pains in my leg
VPR s'élancer *(en courant)* to rush, to dash; *Sport (prendre son élan)* to take a run-up; **s'é. dans une course effrénée** to break into a mad dash; **s'é. sur qn** to rush *or* make a rush at sb; **le chat s'élança sur moi** the cat flew at me; **s'é. à l'assaut des vagues** *(d'un navire, un surfeur)* to take to the water, *Litt* to brave the seas; **s'é. à l'assaut d'un sommet** to attack *or* tackle a peak; **s'é. vers le ciel** to soar skywards
VT la cathédrale élance ses flèches vers le ciel the cathedral's spires soar skywards

élargir [elarʒir] **VT 1** *(route, rue)* to widen, to broaden; *(robe)* to let out; *(chaussures)* to stretch; *(tube)* to expand; *(trou)* to enlarge; *(propriété)* to enlarge, to extend, to add to; **robe qui élargit les épaules** dress which makes the shoulders look broader

2 *Fig (groupe, gamme de produits)* to expand; *(connaissance, débat)* to broaden, to widen, to expand; *(horizon)* to broaden; **é. un marché** to broaden a market

3 *Jur (prisonnier)* to release, to set free
VPR s'élargir 1 *(d'une route, une rue)* to widen (out), to broaden (out); *(de hanches, d'épaules)* to broaden (out); *(de chaussures, d'un jean etc)* to stretch

2 *Fig (d'un groupe)* to expand; *(de son horizon)* to broaden; *(de débat)* to broaden, to widen; **ses idées se sont élargies au contact des jeunes** he became more broadminded through being in contact with young people

élargissement [elarʒismɑ̃] **NM 1** *(d'une route, d'une rue etc)* widening, broadening;

(d'une robe) letting out; *(de chaussures)* stretching; *(d'une propriété)* extension, enlargement **2** *Fig (d'un groupe, des connaissances)* expansion; *(de son horizon)* broadening; *(d'un débat)* broadening, widening, expansion; **l'é. de l'Union européenne** the enlargement of the EU; *Mktg* **é. du marché** market rollout **3** *Jur (d'un prisonnier)* release

élasticité [elastisite] NF *(d'un corps, de la peau, d'une matière)* elasticity; *(d'un pas)* springiness (**de** of), spring (**de** in); *Fig (de principes etc)* flexibility; *Com* **é. de l'offre/ de la demande** elasticity of supply/demand; *Com* **é. des prix** price elasticity

élastine [elastin] NF elastin

élastique [elastik] ADJ **1** *(corps, matière etc)* elastic; **gomme é.** india rubber; **balle é.** rubber ball; **d'un pas é.** with a springy or buoyant step **2** *Fig (règlement, principes)* flexible; **conscience é.** accommodating conscience
NM **1** *Couture etc* elastic; **en é.** elastic **2** *(de bureau)* elastic or *Br* rubber band; *Fig Fam* **les lâcher avec un é.** to have moths in one's wallet **3** *(jeu)* **jouer à l'é.** to play at elastics; **saut à l'é.** bungee jumping

élastiqué [elastike] ADJ elasticated

élastomère [elastɔmɛr] NM *Chimie, Ind* elastomer

Elbe [ɛlb] NF **(l'île d')E.** (the island of) Elba
NM (river) Elbe

eldorado [ɛldɔrado] NM eldorado; **il veut faire de son pays un véritable e. pour les investisseurs étrangers** he wants to turn his country into a land of opportunity for foreign investors

électeur, -trice [elɛktœr, -tris] N **1** *Pol* elector, voter; **mes électeurs** the people who voted for me; **carte d'é.** voting or polling card **2** *Hist* **É.** Elector; **Électrice** Electress

électif, -ive [elɛktif, -iv] ADJ elective

élection [elɛksjɔ̃] NF **1** *(d'un député, un pape, une reine de beauté etc)* election; **é. partielle** by-election; **jour des élections** polling or election day; **annuler l'é. de qn** to unseat sb; **se présenter aux élections** to stand as a candidate (in the elections), to stand for election; **remporter les élections** to win the election **2** *(choix)* election, choice; **mon pays d'é.** the country of my choice; *Jur* **faire é. de domicile** to elect domicile; *Rel* **le peuple d'é.** the chosen people
▸▸ **élections européennes** European elections; **élections législatives** (parliamentary) election(s), general election; **élections municipales** = local (council) elections; **é. présidentielle** presidential election

---

Élections
All French citizens of eighteen or over are entitled to vote in elections, which take place on a Sunday. Polling stations are often set up in local schools. Voters collect leaflets (each corresponding to the different political parties or candidates), go to a booth and put their chosen leaflet into the envelope provided. It is then placed in the ballot box ("l'urne") supervised by an "assesseur", who utters the words "a voté!". Unlike Britain with its first-past-the-post system, the French electoral system is based on a type of proportional representation. As from 2002 presidential elections take place every five years. General elections are also held every five years.

électoral, -ale, -aux, -ales [elɛktɔral, -o] ADJ *(campagne, comité, promesses)* election;

circonscription électorale constituency, *Can* riding; **liste électorale** electoral register or roll; **corps é.** electorate

électoralisme [elɛktɔralism] NM *Péj* electioneering

électoraliste [elɛktɔralist] ADJ electioneering, vote-catching

électorat [elɛktɔra] NM **1** *Pol* voters, electorate; **consulter l'é.** to go to the country; **l'é. communiste/féminin** the communist/female vote, communist/female voters **2** *(droit de vote)* franchise **3** *Hist* **É.** electorate

Électre [elɛktr] N Electra

électricien, -ienne [elɛktrisjɛ̃, -jɛn] N electrician; **ingénieur é.** electrical engineer

électricité [elɛktrisite] NF electricity; **panne d'é.** power cut or failure; **faire poser** ou **installer l'é.** to have electricity put in or installed; **il faut refaire l'é. de la cuisine** we're going to have to rewire the kitchen; *Fig Fam* **il y a de l'é. dans l'air** the atmosphere is electric
▸▸ **é. atmosphérique** atmospherics; **é. statique** static (electricity)

électrification [elɛktrifikasjɔ̃] NF electrification

électrifier [elɛktrifje] VT *(chemin de fer)* to electrify; *(village)* to bring electricity to, to electrify

électrique [elɛktrik] ADJ **1** *(courant, train etc)*, *Fig (atmosphère)* electric **2** *(ingénierie)* electrical

électriquement [elɛktrikmɑ̃] ADV electrically

électrisant [elɛktrizɑ̃] ADJ *Fig* electrifying

électrisation [elɛktrizasjɔ̃] NF *Élec* electrification; **à é. positive** positively charged, charged with positive electricity

électriser [elɛktrize] VT *Élec, Fig (audience)* to electrify; *Élec* **fil électrisé** live wire

électro- [elɛktro] PRÉF electro-

électro-acousticien, -ienne N electroacoustics expert
ADJ electroacoustics

électro-aimant, pl **électro-aimants** NM electromagnet

électrocardiogramme [elɛktrokardjɔgram] NM *Méd* electrocardiogram

électrocardiographe [elɛktrokardjɔgraf] NM *Méd* electrocardiograph

électrocardiographie [elɛktrokardjɔgrafi] NF *Méd* electrocardiography

électrochimie [elɛktroʃimi] NF electrochemistry

électrochimique [elɛktroʃimik] ADJ electrochemical

électrochoc [elɛktroʃɔk] NM *Méd, Fig* electric shock; **traitement par électrochocs** electric shock treatment; **on lui a fait des électrochocs** he was given electric shock treatment

électrocopie [elɛktrokɔpi] NF xerography

électrocuter [elɛktrokyte] VT to electrocute; **se faire é.** to be electrocuted

électrocution [elɛktrokysjɔ̃] NF electrocution

électrode [elɛktrɔd] NF electrode; **é. de masse** earth electrode

électrodomestique [elɛktrodɔmestik] ADJ **appareils électrodomestiques** household electrical appliances or *Am* electricals
NM **l'é.** electrical goods or *Am* electricals

électrodynamique [elɛktrodinamik] ADJ electrodynamic
NF electrodynamics

électro-encéphalogramme, pl **électro-encéphalogrammes** NM *Méd* electroencephalogram

électro-encéphalographie NF *Méd* electroencephalography

électrogène [elɛktrɔʒɛn] ADJ **groupe é.** generator; **appareil é.** *(d'un poisson)* electric organ

électroluminescent [elɛktrolyminesɑ̃] ADJ light-emitting

électrolyse [elɛktrɔliz] NF electrolysis

électrolyser [elɛktrɔlize] VT to electrolyse

électrolyte [elɛktrɔlit] NM electrolyte

électrolytique [elɛktrɔlitik] ADJ electrolytic

électromagnétique [elɛktromaɲetik] ADJ electromagnetic

électromagnétisme [elɛktromaɲetism] NM electromagnetism

électromécanicien, -ienne [elɛktromekanisjɛ̃, -jɛn] N electrical engineer

électromécanique [elɛktromekanik] ADJ electromechanical
NF electromechanics

électroménager [elɛktromenaʒe] ADJ **appareils électroménagers** household appliances or *Am* electricals
NM household appliances or *Am* electricals

électrométallurgie [elɛktrometalyrʒi] NF electrometallurgy

électrométallurgique [eletrometalyrʒik] ADJ electrometallurgical

électromètre [elɛktrɔmɛtr] NM electrometer

électromoteur, -trice [elɛktromɔtœr, -tris] ADJ electromotive
NM electromotor

électron [elɛktrɔ̃] NM *Phys* electron

électronégatif, -ive [elɛktronegatif, -iv] ADJ electronegative

électronicien, -ienne [elɛktrɔnisjɛ̃, -jɛn] N electronics specialist; **ingénieur é.** electronics engineer

électronique [elɛktronik] ADJ *(équipement, musique, point de vente, argent, réservation)* electronic; *(faisceau, flux, microscope, télescope)* electron; **l'industrie é.** the electronics industry
NF electronics; **é. aérospatiale** avionics

électroniquement [elɛktrɔnikmɑ̃] ADV electronically

électronucléaire [elɛktronykleɛr] ADJ *(industrie, centrale)* nuclear power; **énergie é.** nuclear power
NM nuclear power

électronvolt [elɛktrɔ̃vɔlt] NM electronvolt

électrophone [elɛktrɔfɔn] NM record player

électropositif, -ive [elɛktropozitif, -iv] ADJ electropositive

électroscope [elɛktrɔskɔp] NM electroscope

électrosensible [elɛktrosɑ̃sibl] ADJ electrosensitive

électrostatique [elɛktrostatik] ADJ electrostatic
NF electrostatics

électrotechnique [elɛktroteknik] ADJ electrotechnical
NF electrical engineering

électrothérapie [elɛktroterapi] NF *Méd (pratique)* electrotherapy; *(étude)* electrotherapeutics

électrovalve [elɛktrovalv] NF *Aut* solenoid; **é. de starter** starter solenoid

électrovanne [elɛktrovan] NF solenoid valve

élégamment [elegamɑ̃] ADV *(vêtu)* elegantly, smartly; *(maquillée)* smartly; *(agir)* courteously; **coiffée é.** with an elegant or smart hairstyle

élégance [elegɑ̃s] NF elegance; *(d'un geste, d'un comportement)* courtesy; *(d'une méthode, d'une solution)* neatness; **l'é. du chat siamois** the elegance *or* grace of a Siamese cat; **habillé avec é.** elegantly *or* smartly dressed; **savoir perdre avec é.** to be a good loser; **elle a eu l'é. de ne pas protester** she had the courtesy not to protest

élégant, -ante [elegɑ̃, -ɑ̃t] ADJ *(vêtements, restaurant, style etc)* elegant; *(méthode, solution)* neat; *(geste, comportement)* courteous; **c'était une façon élégante de me dire que ...** it was a polite *or* diplomatic way of telling me that ...; **il use de procédés peu élégants** he uses rather callous measures
▪ NM *Arch* dandy
▪ NF **élégante** well- *or* smartly *or* fashionably dressed woman

élégiaque [eleʒjak] ADJ elegiac

élégie [eleʒi] NF elegy

élément [elemɑ̃] NM **1** *(naturel)* element; **les quatre éléments** the four elements; *Fig* **être dans son é.** to be in one's element; *Fig* **je ne me sens pas dans mon é. ici** I'm not in my element here, I'm like a fish out of water here
2 *Chimie* element; *Phys* **é. radioactif** radioactive element
3 *(partie)* *(d'une structure, un problème etc)* element, component, constituent; *(d'un médicament)* ingredient; *(d'un compte)* item; **les éléments d'un ensemble** the elements *or* parts of a whole; *Tech* **é. chauffant** heating unit *or* element; *Aut* **é. filtrant en papier** paper filtering element; *Ordinat* **é. de menu** menu item; *Tech* **é. mobile** working part; *Électron* **é. de calculateur** *ou* **de calculatrice** *ou* **électronique** computer unit; **éléments préfabriqués** prefabricated *or* ready-made units; **mobilier formé d'éléments** modular furniture
4 *(personne)* element; **les éléments indésirables de la population** the undesirable elements of the population; **l'é. féminin** the female element *or* contingent; **l'é. féminin est faiblement représenté dans cette société** there are few women in the company; **j'ai de bons éléments dans ma classe** I've got some good material in my class; **avec lui, nous avons perdu un très bon é.** we've lost a good man in him
5 *Élec (d'une batterie, d'un accumulateur)* cell; **batterie de cinq éléments** five-cell battery
6 *(rudiment)* *(de science etc)* **éléments** elements, rudiments; **avoir quelques éléments en espagnol** to have elementary *or* rudimentary Spanish; **Éléments de chimie** *(livre)* Elementary Chemistry
7 *(donnée)* **éléments** data, information; **l'é. décisif** the deciding factor; **aucun é. nouveau à signaler** nothing new to report
8 *Mil* **éléments blindés/motorisés** armoured/motorized units

élémentaire [elemɑ̃tɛr] ADJ **1** *Chimie, Phys (analyse chimique, particule d'atome etc)* elementary **2** *(de base)* *(connaissance)* elementary, rudimentary; *(cours, problème etc)* elementary; *(minimal)* *(habitation)* basic, rudimentary; *Scol* **cours é.** = second and third years of primary school; **cours é. de ski/danse** skiing/dance classes for beginners; **c'est é.!** *(évident)* it's elementary!, it's simple!; *(le minimum)* it's the least I/you/*etc* could do!; **c'est la politesse la plus é.** it's only common courtesy

éléphant [elefɑ̃] NM elephant; **é. mâle/femelle** bull/cow elephant; **é. d'Afrique/d'Asie** African/Indian elephant; **é. marin** *ou* **de mer** elephant seal, sea elephant; **comme un é. dans un magasin de porcelaine** like a bull in a china shop

éléphanteau, -eaux [elefɑ̃to] NM elephant calf; *(très jeune)* baby elephant

éléphantesque [elefɑ̃tɛsk] ADJ *Fam* elephantine, gigantic, colossal; **elle est d'une bêtise é.** she is colossally stupid

éléphantiasis [elefɑ̃tjazis] NM *Méd* elephantiasis

élevage [elvaʒ] NM **1** *(de bovins, chevaux, moutons etc)* breeding, rearing; **l'é.** stock breeding; **é. intensif/en batterie** intensive/battery farming; **é. des animaux à fourrure** fur farming; **faire de l'é.** to breed *or* rear cattle, to be a stock breeder; **région d'é.** breeding area; **poulet d'é.** battery-reared chicken **2** *(ferme)* (stock) farm, *Am* ranch, *Austr* station

élévateur, -trice [elevatœr, -tris] ADJ **chariot é. à fourche** fork-lift truck
▪ NM **1** *(appareil)* elevator, lift, hoist; **é. à bascule** tip; **é. à augets** *ou* **à godets** bucket elevator; **é. (à fourche)** fork-lift truck **2** *Élec* **é. de tension** step-up transformer

élévation [elevasjɔ̃] NF **1** *(action d'élever)* *(d'un mur, de la voix etc)* raising; *(de la température, des prix etc)* raising, increasing; *(d'une statue etc)* erection, setting up; *Rel (de l'hostie)* elevation; *Math* **é. d'un nombre au carré/à la puissance 10** raising a number to the square root/to the power of 10
2 *(action de s'élever)* *(de température, prix etc)* rise, increase; **é. du niveau des eaux** rise in water level; **é. du pouls** quickening of the pulse
3 *Fig* **lire Platon contribue à l'é. de l'esprit** reading Plato improves the mind; **é. des sentiments/du caractère** nobility of sentiments/character
4 *Archit (projection)* elevation
5 *(tertre)* rise (in the ground), mound

élévatoire [elevatwar] ADJ *(appareil)* lifting, hoisting

élevé [elve] ADJ **1** *(montagne, prix)* high; *Fig (style, esprit)* noble, elevated; *(rang, position)* high, exalted; **l'officier ayant le grade le plus é.** the senior *or* highest-ranking officer; **il occupe un rang é. dans ce parti** he ranks high in the party; **de rang é.** high-ranking; **pouls é.** rapid pulse **2** *(éduqué)* **bien é.** well brought up, well-bred; **mal é.** badly brought up, ill-bred, ill-mannered; *Fam* **c'est très mal é. de parler la bouche pleine** it's very rude *or* very bad manners to speak with your mouth full; **c'est un mal é., ce garçon** he has bad manners, that boy

élève [elɛv] N *Scol* pupil, student; *(d'un peintre, un musicien etc)* pupil
▪ NF **1** *(animal)* young stock animal **2** *(plante)* seedling
▸▸ **é. infirmière** student nurse; *Mil* **é. officier** cadet; **é. pilote** trainee *or* student pilot

élever [elve] (j'élève, n. élevons; j'élèverai) VT **1** *(faire monter)* *(niveau d'eau, voix etc)* to raise; *(prix, température etc)* to increase, to raise; *(charge)* to lift up, to raise; **é. un nombre au carré/au cube** to square/cube a number; **é. un nombre à la puissance 4** to raise a number to the power 4; **é. une perpendiculaire** to raise a perpendicular
2 *(dresser)* *(monument, statue, mur etc)* to erect, to put up; *(les bras, le poing, les yeux)* to raise; *Fig (objection, difficultés)* to raise; *Fig* **quelqu'un a-t-il une critique à é.?** does anyone have any criticism to make?; *Fig* **é. des autels à qn** to praise sb to the skies
3 *(rehausser)* *(immeuble, mur etc)* to raise, to make higher; *(plafond, plancher)* to raise; **é. un mur de 20 cm** to raise a wall by 20 cm, to make a wall 20 cm higher
4 *(porter à un rang supérieur)* to promote (**au rang de** to)
5 *(édifier)* *(esprit)* to improve; **é. le débat** to raise the tone of the proceedings
6 *(éduquer)* *(enfant)* to bring up, to raise; **bébé élevé au sein/au biberon** breast-/bottle-fed baby; *Fam* **é. qn dans du coton** to raise sb in cotton wool, to coddle sb
7 *(faire l'élevage de)* *(bovins, chevaux etc)* to rear, to breed; *(lapins)* to breed; *(abeilles, volaille)* to keep
▪ VPR **s'élever 1** *(avec mouvement)* to rise (up); **l'hélicoptère s'élevait doucement dans les airs** the helicopter rose smoothly into the air; **un cri s'éleva** a shout went up
2 *(sans mouvement)* to stand; **le château s'élève sur la colline** the castle stands on the hill; **la maison s'élevait dans le soleil couchant** the house stood silhouetted against the setting sun
3 *(monter)* *(de la température, des prix etc)* to rise, to increase, to go up
4 *(paraître)* *(de doutes, difficultés)* to arise
5 *(protester)* **s'é. contre qch/qn** to rise up against sth/sb; **je m'élève contre la validité de ce testament** I contest the validity of this will
6 *Fig* **s'é. à force de travail** to work one's way up; **s'é. socialement** to climb up the social ladder; **s'é. au-dessus des préjugés** to rise above prejudice; **ses pensées ne s'élèvent jamais au-delà de sa petite personne** his thoughts never rise above himself; **des lectures qui permettent à l'âme de s'é.** spiritually uplifting reading matter
7 *(atteindre)* **s'é. à** to come to, to amount to; **la note s'élève à 1000 euros** the bill comes to *or* adds up to *or* totals 1,000 euros

éleveur, -euse [elvœr, -øz] N *(de bovins)* stock breeder, cattle farmer; **é. de chevaux/chiens** horse/dog breeder; **é. de moutons/poulets** sheep/poultry farmer
▪ NF **éleveuse** *(pour poussins)* brooder

elfe [ɛlf] NM elf VOIR GRAMMAIRE A12

élider [elide] *Ling* VT *(voyelle)* to elide
▪ VPR **s'élider** to be elided, to elide

éligibilité [eliʒibilite] NF *Pol* eligibility

éligible [eliʒibl] ADJ *Pol* eligible

élimé [elime] ADJ *(tissu, vêtement)* worn, threadbare

élimer [elime] VT *(tissu, vêtement)* to wear thin
▪ VPR **s'élimer** to wear thin

élimination [eliminasjɔ̃] NF *aussi Physiol* elimination; **procéder par é.** to use a process of elimination; **en procédant par é.** by a process of elimination; *Ind etc* **é. des déchets** waste disposal; *Radio* **é. des parasites** suppression of noise *or* interference

éliminatoire [eliminatwar] ADJ *(examen)* qualifying; **5 est une note é.** five counts as a fail; **il a eu une note é.** he didn't get a pass mark; **épreuve é.** qualifying heat *or* round, qualifier
▪ NF qualifying *or* eliminating heat *or* round, qualifier

éliminer [elimine] VT **1** *(candidat, suspect)* to eliminate; *(possibilité, théorie)* to rule out, to exclude; *Physiol (déchets)* to get rid of, to eliminate; **être éliminé** *(d'un candidat)* to be knocked out *or* eliminated; **ils ont tous été éliminés pour dopage** they were all disqualified for drug-taking **2** *(tuer)* to liquidate
▪ VI *Physiol* to get rid of *or* eliminate body wastes

élire [elir] VT *(conj like lire)* **1** *(candidat, représentant etc)* to elect; **é. un député** ≃ to elect *or* return a Member of Parliament; **é. qn président** to elect sb president, to vote sb in as president **2 é. domicile** to take up residence (**à** in); *Jur* to elect domicile (**à** in); **une souris a élu domicile dans notre grenier** a mouse has moved into *or* taken up residence in our attic

élisabéthain, -aine [elizabetɛ̃, -ɛn] ADJ Elizabethan

N É. Elizabethan

élision [elizjɔ̃] NF Ling elision SEE GRAMMAR B2

élite [elit] NF élite, elite; **les élites** the élite; **l'é. de ...** the cream or élite of ...; **personnel d'é.** select or hand-picked personnel; **régiment/tireur d'é.** crack regiment/shot

élitisme [elitism] NM elitism

élitiste [elitist] ADJ, N elitist

élixir [eliksir] NM elixir; **l'é. de longue vie** the elixir of life; **é. parégorique** = medicine for treating diarrhoea, Spéc paregoric (elixir)

elle, pl **elles** [ɛl] PRON PERS F SEE GRAMMAR A27; B18; B66 **1** (sujet) (personne) she; (chose) it; (bébé, animal, nation, navire) it, she; **elles** they; **e. chante** she sings; **elles dansent** they dance; **e. arrivée, la fête a pu commencer** once she had arrived the party was able to start; **e., dégoûtée, a fait la grimace** she grimaced in disgust; **e., e. n'aurait même pas levé le petit doigt** she wouldn't have raised a finger; **e., se marier? tu ne la connais pas!** her get married? you don't know her!; **qui a fait ça? – c'est e.** who did that? – she did or her; **ah!, e. est bien bonne, celle-là!** that's a good one!

2 (objet) (personne) her; (chose) it; (bébé, animal etc) it, her; **elles** them; **et e., tu l'oublies?** and are you forgetting her?; **tu la connais, e.?** do you know her?; **tu les imagines, e. et lui, sur des skis!** imagine the pair of them on skis!

3 (avec qui, que) **c'est e. qui est partie la première** she left first; **c'est e. que j'ai rencontrée dans la rue** it was her I met in the street; **son père est déjà là et e. qui n'arrive pas** her father's here already and she hasn't arrived yet; **c'est à e. qu'il veut avoir affaire** it's her he wants to talk to

4 (avec préposition) **je suis content d'e./d'elles** I am pleased with her/them; **e. ne pense qu'à e.** she thinks only of herself; **dis-le-lui, à e.** tell her, **ce n'est pas à moi, c'est à e.** it's not mine, it's hers; **c'est à e. de dire si e. veut venir** it's up to her to say if she wants to come or not; **e. possède une entreprise à e.** she has her own company; **je l'ai entendu dire par une relation à e.** I heard it from a relation of hers; **un portrait d'e.** (qu'elle a fait) a portrait by her; (où elle est représentée) a portrait of her; **il aimait sa patrie et mourut pour e.** he loved his country and died for it

5 (dans comparaisons) **il est mieux qu'e.** he is better than she is or than her; **il boit plus qu'e.** he drinks more than she does or than her; **je fais mon travail aussi bien qu'e.** I work as well as she does, my work is as good as hers; **je fais comme e.** I do what she does

6 (interrogatif, emphatique) **viendra-t-e.?** will she come?; **ta directrice est-e. toujours en activité?** is your boss still working?; **la télévision est-e. toujours en panne?** is the television still not working?; **qu'e. est jolie, cette broche!** how pretty that brooch is!; **eh bien, ta cousine, e. n'est pas près de me revoir** well, your cousin isn't likely to see me again in a hurry

ellébore [elebɔr] NM (plante) helebore

elle-même [elmɛm] PRON PERS (d'une personne) herself; (d'une chose) itself; (d'un bébé, d'un animal, d'une nation) itself, herself; **elles-mêmes** themselves; **mais e. n'est pas sans défauts** but she's no paragon herself; **c'est e. qui me l'a dit** she told me so herself, she herself told me so

ellipse [elips] NF **1** Gram ellipsis **2** Géom ellipse

ellipsoïdal, -ale, -aux, -ales [elipsɔidal, -o] ADJ Géom ellipsoidal

ellipsoïde [elipsɔid] Géom ADJ ellipsoidal NM ellipsoid

elliptique [eliptik] ADJ Gram, Géom elliptical; **style e.** elliptical style

elliptiquement [eliptikmɑ̃] ADV Gram elliptically

élocution [elɔkysjɔ̃] NF **1** (diction) elocution; (débit) delivery; **avoir une é. trop rapide** to speak too quickly; **avoir une é. claire** to speak or enunciate clearly; **défaut d'é.** speech impediment or defect **2** Belg Scol (exposé) talk, presentation

éloge [elɔʒ] NM **1** (discours) eulogy; **é. funèbre** eulogy, funeral oration **2** (louange) praise; **faire l'é. de qn/qch** to speak very highly of or in praise of sb/sth; **faire son propre é.** to sing one's own praises, Br to blow one's own trumpet; **digne d'éloges** praiseworthy; **c'est tout à votre é. d'avoir accepté** it's to your credit that you accepted; **il fait du bénévolat et c'est tout à son é.** to his credit, he does volunteer work

élogieusement [elɔʒjøzmɑ̃] ADV **parler é. de** to speak very highly of

élogieux, -ieuse [elɔʒjø, -jøz] ADJ (discours, article) of praise, Fml eulogistic, laudatory; **parler de qn/qch en termes é.** to speak very highly of sb/sth; **les critiques ont été é. avec son dernier film** the critics praised his last film

éloigné [elwaɲe] ADJ (endroit, passé, futur etc) distant, remote; (parent) distant; **la ville est très éloignée** the town is a long way away or off, the town is very far off; **la ville est éloignée de cinq kilomètres** the town is five kilometres away; **ils sont éloignés d'un kilomètre** they are one kilometre apart, there is a kilometre between them; **maison éloignée de la gare** house a long way from the station; **notre mariage est encore à une date éloignée** our wedding is still a long way off; **la date en est trop éloignée pour que je puisse savoir si je serai libre** it's too far away for me to say whether I'll be free or not; **dans un avenir peu é.** in the near or not-too-distant future; **rien n'est plus é. de ma pensée** nothing is further from my thoughts; **se tenir é. de qch** to keep away from sth, to steer clear of sth; Fig **je ne suis plus é. de croire que ...** I'm coming round to believe that or to the belief that ...

éloignement [elwaɲ(ə)mɑ̃] NM **1** (action) (d'une personne indésirable) removal; **l'é. de sa famille est nécessaire à sa guérison** his family must be kept away if he is to recover **2** (fait d'être éloigné) absence; **je ne supporte plus notre é.** I can't bear us to be apart any longer; **plus l'é. dure, plus il renforce notre amour** the longer we are apart or the longer the separation lasts, the stronger our love grows; **l'é. est difficile à vivre** it is difficult to be apart or separated **3** (distance) (dans l'espace) distance, remoteness; (dans le temps) remoteness; **l'é. de nos deux bureaux ne favorise pas la communication** the distance between our two offices does not help communication; **avec l'é. on arrive mieux à comprendre ce qui s'est passé** with the benefit of hindsight or the passage of time it is easier to understand what happened

éloigner [elwaɲe] VT **1** (écarter dans l'espace) (personne, objet) to move away, to take away, to remove; **é. qch de qch** to move sth away from sth; **é. qn du feu/de la voiture** to move sb away from the fire/car; **ce trajet nous éloigne du centre ville** this route takes us away from the centre of town; **é. les loups/les moustiques** to keep the wolves/mosquitoes away or at bay; **tes parents cherchent à m'é. de toi** your parents are trying to keep me away from you; **mon travail m'éloigne de toute vie sociale** my work makes it impossible to socialize

2 (dans le temps) **chaque jour m'éloigne un**

peu plus de cette époque that time recedes with each day that passes

3 (distraire, détourner) **é. une crainte/une pensée/des soupçons** to banish a fear/dismiss a thought/avert suspicion; **é. qn de son travail** to keep sb away from his work

VPR **s'éloigner 1** (s'écarter dans l'espace) (d'une personne) to move away (**de** from); (d'un objet) to move away or off; **voudriez-vous vous é. un peu?** would you please stand further away or back, would you please move back or away a little; **ne vous éloignez pas!** don't go too far away!; **l'orage s'éloigne** the storm is passing; Fig **avec le temps, ce souvenir s'éloignera** the memory will fade with time

2 (se distraire, se détourner) **s'é. de la vérité** to stray or wander from the truth; **s'é. de son devoir** to neglect one's duty; **s'é. du sujet** to wander from the subject; **s'é. de tout le monde** to distance oneself from everybody; **je sens bien que tu t'éloignes (de moi)** I feel you're growing away from me; **le temps a fait qu'ils se sont éloignés l'un de l'autre** they drifted apart with time

élongation [elɔ̃gasjɔ̃] NF Méd pulled muscle; **se faire une é.** to pull a muscle

éloquemment [elɔkamɑ̃] ADV eloquently

éloquence [elɔkɑ̃s] NF **1** (loquacité) (d'une personne), Fig (d'un tableau, de l'expression du visage) eloquence **2** (rhétorique) oratory

éloquent [elɔkɑ̃] ADJ (personne, discours) eloquent; Fig (silence, geste etc) eloquent, expressive; **ces chiffres sont éloquents** the figures speak volumes or speak for themselves; **52 à 0, le score est é.** 52-nil: the score speaks for itself; **son expression dégoûtée était éloquente** his expression of disgust said it all

élu, -ue [ely] ADJ Pol elected; **président é.** president elect; Bible **le peuple é.** the chosen people

N **1** Rel **les élus** the elect **2** Pol (député, conseiller) elected representative; **les élus du peuple** the people's representatives; **les élus locaux** local or town councillors **3** Hum **qui est l'heureuse élue?** who's the lucky girl or lady?; **l'é. de son cœur** the man of her choice

élucidation [elysidasjɔ̃] NF elucidation

élucider [elyside] VT (mystère) to clear up; (question, problème) to clarify

élucubrations [elykybrasjɔ̃] NFPL Péj flights of fancy, wild imaginings

élucubrer [elykybre] VT Péj to dream up

éluder [elyde] VT to evade, to elude; **é. le paiement de l'impôt** to evade payment of tax

élusif, -ive [elyzif, -iv] ADJ (réponse, attitude) evasive

Élysée [elize] NM **1** Myth **L'É.** Elysium **2** Pol (le palais de) **l'É.** the Élysée palace (the residence of the President of the French Republic) ADJ **les champs Élysées** Myth the Elysian Fields; **les Champs-Élysées** (à Paris) the Champs Élysées

---

Élysée

This eighteenth-century palace near the Champs-Élysées in Paris is the official residence of the French President. The name is often used to refer to the presidency itself.

élyséen, -enne [elizeɛ̃, -ɛn] ADJ **1** Myth Elysian **2** Pol of the Élysée palace

em [ɛm] NM Typ em

émaciation [emasjasjɔ̃] NF emaciation

émacié [emasje] ADJ (silhouette, visage etc) emaciated

émacier (s') [semasje] VPR to become emaciated

émail, -aux [emaj, -o] NM enamel; *Cér* glaze; **en é.** *(casserole etc)* enamel(led)

e-mail, email [imɛl] NM e-mail

émaillage [emaja3] NM **1** *(des métaux précieux etc)* enamelling **2** *Cér* glazing

émailler [emaje] VT **1** *(métal etc)* to enamel; **émaillé au four** stove-enamelled **2** *Cér (porcelaine)* to glaze **3** *Fig (des fleurs, étoiles etc) (champs, ciel etc)* to stud, to spangle; **texte émaillé de métaphores** text littered with or full of metaphors

émailleur, -euse [emajœr, -øz] N enameller

émaillure [emajyr] NF enamelling, enamel work

émanation [emanasjɔ̃] NF emanation; **é. fétide** foul odour; *Fig* **cet ordre, é. de sa volonté …** this order, an expression or a product of his will …; **être l'é. de qch** to emanate from sth

émancipateur, -trice [emɑ̃sipatœr, -tris] ADJ liberating, emancipating N emancipator

émancipation [emɑ̃sipasjɔ̃] NF emancipation; *Fig (de l'esprit, de la pensée etc)* liberation, freeing

émancipé [emɑ̃sipe] ADJ *(femme, populations)* emancipated

émanciper [emɑ̃sipe] VT *(peuple, esclave)* to emancipate; *(femme)* to emancipate, to liberate; *Jur (mineur)* to emancipate ▪ VPR **s'émanciper** to become emancipated; *Fig* to become liberated; *Fig* **elle n'a jamais réussi à s'é. de l'éducation stricte qu'elle a reçue** she never managed to break free from her strict upbringing; **elle s'est drôlement émancipée** she's become very liberated

émaner [emane] VI **é. de qch** *(de fumée etc)*, *Fig (d'un ordre, du pouvoir, du charme)* to emanate from sth

émargement [emar3əmɑ̃] NM **1** *(initiales)* initialling (in the margin); *(signature)* signature; **feuille d'é.** *(de présence)* attendance sheet; *(de paie)* pay sheet; **é. du courrier** signing for the mail **2** *(annotation)* marginal note **3** *Typ (de pages)* trimming

émarger [emar3e] (j'**émargeai(s)**; n. émargeons) VT **1** *Admin (document, compte etc)* to initial (in the margin); *(signer)* to sign; *(courrier)* to sign for **2** *(annoter) (livre etc)* to make marginal notes in **3** *Typ (pages etc)* to cut down or trim the margins of ▪ VI to draw one's salary; **il émarge aux fonds secrets** he's paid out of the secret funds

émasculation [emaskylasjɔ̃] NF emasculation

émasculer [emaskyle] VT to emasculate

embâcle [ɑ̃bɑkl] NM *(obstruction dans un cours d'eau)* blockage; *(par un bloc de glace)* ice block or jam

emballage [ɑ̃bala3] NM **1** *(action)* packing; *(dans du papier)* wrapping; **papier d'e.** wrapping paper **2** *(boîte etc)* packaging, packing (material); *(papier)* wrapping; **emballages vides** (returned) empties **3** *Cyclisme* (final) spurt ▸▸ **e. bulle** blister pack; **e. consigné** returnable or refundable packaging; **e. gratuit** packaging free of charge; **e. perdu** non-returnable or throwaway or disposable packaging; *Com* **e. récupérable** recoverable packaging; **e. sous vide** vacuum-packed

emballé [ɑ̃bale] ADJ *Fam* (mad) keen, enthusiastic

emballement [ɑ̃balmɑ̃] NM **1** *(de moteur)* racing; *(de cheval)* bolting; **l'e. du cheval a provoqué la mort du cavalier** the rider was killed when the horse bolted **2** *(enthousiasme soudain)* burst of enthusiasm; *(colère)* surge of anger; **prompt aux emballements** easily carried away; **pas d'e.** *(par en-*

thousiasme) let's not get carried away!; *(par colère)* let's not get worked up! **3** *Bourse* boom (**de** in); **cela aboutirait certainement à l'e. de l'économie** that would definitely lead to the economy spiralling out of control

emballer [ɑ̃bale] VT **1** *(empaqueter)* to pack; *(dans du papier)* to wrap; *(marchandises)* to package; **emballé sous vide** vacuum-packed; *Arg* **e. qn** *(arrêter)* to nick sb; *Arg* **e. une fille** *(draguer)* to pull a girl **2** *(moteur)* to race, to rev **3** *Fam (enthousiasmer)* to excite, to thrill; **ça ne m'emballe pas vraiment de les voir** I'm not exactly thrilled about seeing them or mad keen to see them; **être emballé par qn/qch** to be (mad) keen on sb/sth ▪ VPR **s'emballer 1** *(d'un moteur)* to race; *(d'un cheval)* to bolt, to run away **2** *Fam (se laisser emporter)* *(par enthousiasme)* to get carried away, to get excited; *(par colère)* to get worked up **3** *Bourse (des cours, d'une monnaie)* to spiral out of control

emballeur, -euse [ɑ̃balœr, -øz] N packer

embarbouiller [ɑ̃barbuje] VT *(personne)* to muddle, to confuse ▪ VPR **s'embarbouiller** to get muddled up

embarcadère [ɑ̃barkadɛr] NM landing stage, jetty

embarcation [ɑ̃barkasjɔ̃] NF (small) boat, small craft

embardée [ɑ̃barde] NF *Aut* swerve; *Naut* yaw; **faire une e.** *(d'une voiture)* to swerve; *(d'un bateau)* to yaw

embargo [ɑ̃bargo] NM embargo; **mettre l'e. sur** to put an embargo on, to embargo; **lever l'e. sur** to raise or lift the embargo on; **e. économique** economic embargo

embarqué [ɑ̃barke] ADJ **1** *Aut, Aviat etc* onboard **2** *(journaliste)* embedded

embarquement [ɑ̃barkəmɑ̃] NM **1** *(action d'embarquer) Naut (de passagers)* embarkation; *(de marchandises)* shipping; *(dans un train, avion, car) (de passagers)* boarding; *(de marchandises)* loading; *Rail, Mil (de troupes)* entrainment; *Rail* **quai d'e.** departure platform; *(de chargement)* loading platform **2** *(action de s'embarquer) Naut* embarkation, boarding; *Rail, Aviat, Aut* boarding; **le vol 123 est prêt pour l'e.** flight 123 is ready for boarding or is now boarding; **e. immédiat porte 5** now boarding at gate 5; **carte d'e.** boarding card

embarquer [ɑ̃barke] VT **1** *Naut (passagers)* to embark; *(marchandises)* to ship; *(dans un train, avion, car) (passagers)* to take on board; *(marchandises)* to load; *Rail, Mil (troupes)* to entrain **2** *Naut* **e. de l'eau** to take in or ship water **3** *Fam (emmener)* to take (with one); *(voler)* to pinch, to nick; *(arrêter)* to nick **4** *Fam (entraîner)* *(en week-end, au cinéma)* to take or carry off; **son divorce l'a embarqué dans un procès sans fin** his divorce got him involved or embroiled in an endless lawsuit; **elle embarque toujours sa copine dans ses escapades** she always involves her friend in her escapades; **une entreprise mal embarquée** an undertaking that has got off to a bad start ▪ VI **1** *Naut (partir)* to embark (**pour** for); **e. (sur un navire)** to go on board, to board (a ship); **e. (dans un train/un autobus)** to board or get on (a train/bus); **une personne supplémentaire peut e. dans ma voiture** there's room for one more in my car; **on embarque à 7h demain matin** we're leaving at 7 o'clock tomorrow morning **2** *Naut* **le bateau embarque** the boat is taking in water ▪ VPR **s'embarquer 1** *(partir)* to embark (**pour** for); **s'e. sur un navire** to go on board or to board a ship

2 *Fig* **s'e. dans** to get mixed up or involved in; *(une entreprise, une discussion)* to embark on; **dans quoi est-ce que je me suis embarqué?** what have I got myself into?

embarras [ɑ̃bara] NM **1** *(situation difficile)* difficulty, trouble, *Fam* fix; **tirer qn d'e.** to help sb out of trouble or a difficulty or *Fam* a fix; **n'avoir que l'e. du choix** to be spoiled for choice; **je suis dans l'e.** I'm in trouble or *Fam* in a fix or a bind

2 *(difficulté financière)* **se trouver** ou **être dans l'e.** to be in (financial) difficulties

3 *(gêne)* embarrassment; **répondre avec e.** to reply with embarrassment, to reply embarrassedly or in confusion; **plonger qn dans l'e.** to embarrass sb

4 *(obstacle)* **je vous donne beaucoup d'e.** I'm putting you to a lot of bother or trouble; **faire des** ou **de l'e.** to make a fuss, to make a song and dance (**au sujet de** about); **être un e. pour les autres** to be a bother to other people

5 *Aut* **e. de voitures, e. de la circulation** traffic hold-up

6 *Méd* **e. gastrique** upset stomach

embarrassant [ɑ̃barasɑ̃] ADJ **1** *(qui encombre)* *(colis, valise etc)* cumbersome **2** *(qui gêne)* *(question, situation)* embarrassing, awkward

embarrassé [ɑ̃barase] ADJ **1** *(encombré)* *(table, pièce etc)* cluttered; **avoir les mains embarrassées** to have one's hands full

2 *(confus)* *(gestes)* hampered; *(style)* awkward; **prononciation embarrassée** unclear or garbled pronunciation; **explications embarrassées** involved or confused explanations; **dès qu'il met un costume, ses gestes sont embarrassés** he feels hampered in a suit

3 *(gêné)* *(personne, sourire, manière etc)* embarrassed; **je suis très e. de devoir lui dire** I am very embarrassed about having to tell him; **me voilà bien e.** I'm in a really awkward situation, I'm really embarrassed

4 *Méd* **avoir l'estomac e.** to have an upset stomach; **avoir la langue embarrassée** to have a coated or furred tongue

embarrasser [ɑ̃barase] VT **1** *(encombrer)* *(personne)* to hamper; *(table, pièce etc)* to clutter up (**de** with); **cette valise t'embarrasse, laisse-moi la porter** that suitcase is cumbersome for you, let me carry it; **je peux poser mon manteau?** **il m'embarrasse** can I put my coat down? it's a bit of a nuisance **2** *(gêner)* to embarrass; **tu m'embarrasses beaucoup en me demandant ce service** you're really embarrassing me or putting me in a very awkward situation by asking me this favour ▪ VPR **s'embarrasser 1** *(s'encombrer)* to burden oneself (**de** with) **2** *(s'inquiéter) (toujours négativement)* to trouble or bother oneself (**de** with), to be concerned (**de** about); **elle ne s'embarrasse pas de scrupules** she doesn't let scruples get in her way, she's not over-scrupulous **3** *(s'embrouiller)* **s'e. dans** *(vêtements)*, *Fig (mensonges etc)* to get tangled up in

embastiller [ɑ̃bastije] VT *Hist, Hum* to put in jail

embauchage [ɑ̃boʃa3] NM *(de travailleurs etc)* taking on, hiring, engaging

embauche [ɑ̃boʃ] NF **1** *(action)* taking on, hiring, engaging **2** *(emploi)* employment; **chercher de l'e.** to look for a job or for employment; **il n'y a pas d'e.** there are no jobs or vacancies, *Am* we're/they're/etc not hiring at the moment

embaucher [ɑ̃boʃe] VT *(travailleur)* to take on, to hire, to engage; **e. qn pour le poste de** ou **comme** to engage or recruit sb as; *Fam* **je**

me suis encore fait e. pour faire la vaisselle I got hired again to do the washing-up **VI** to recruit, to take on *or* hire *or* engage people

embaucheur, -euse [ɑ̃boʃœr, -øz] **N** employer; **les embaucheurs ne sont pas légion de nos jours** not many companies are recruiting people *or* taking people on these days

embauchoir [ɑ̃boʃwar] **NM** shoe tree; *(pour bottes)* boot tree

embaumement [ɑ̃bommɑ̃] **NM** *(de corps)* embalming

embaumer [ɑ̃bome] **VT 1** *(corps)* to embalm **2** *(parfumer)* to perfume, to scent; *(répandre une odeur de)* to be fragrant with; **air embaumé** fragrant *or* balmy air; **l'église embaume l'encens** the church is heavy with (the scent of) incense; **l'encens embaume l'église** the scent of incense fills the church **VI** to be fragrant

embaumeur [ɑ̃bomœr] **NM** *(de corps)* embalmer

embéguiner (s') [sɑ̃begine] **VPR** *Vieilli* **s'e. de qn** to become infatuated with sb

embellie [ɑ̃beli] **NF** *(éclaircie)* bright spell; *Naut* calm spell, lull; *Fig (de l'économie, d'une situation etc)* improvement; **courte e.** bright interval

embellir [ɑ̃belir] **VT** *(pièce, parc etc)* to make (more) attractive; *(personne)* to make look (more) beautiful, to improve the looks of; *Fig (histoire, vérité etc)* to improve on, to embellish; **le mariage/la maternité l'embellit** married life/motherhood suits her **VI** to grow (more) beautiful

embellissement [ɑ̃belismɑ̃] **NM 1** *(fait de rendre plus beau) (d'une pièce, d'un parc)* improvement; *Fig (d'une histoire, de la vérité etc)* embellishment; **e. de qn** improving sb's looks **2** *(décoration)* embellishment, embellishing touch; **il faudra apporter des embellissements à l'appartement** the flat needs improving *or* needs a few embellishing touches

emberlificoter [ɑ̃berlifikɔte] *Fam* **VT 1** *(empêtrer)* to tangle up, to entangle **2** *(duper)* to take in **VPR s'emberlificoter s'e. dans** *(vêtements)*, *Fig (mensonges etc)* to get tangled up in

embêtant [ɑ̃betɑ̃] **ADJ** *Fam (personne, problème etc)* annoying; *(situation)* awkward; **c'est drôlement e.!** it's really annoying!

embêtement [ɑ̃betmɑ̃] **NM** *Fam (agacement)* annoyance; *(souci)* worry, trouble; **faire des embêtements à qn** to cause *or* make trouble for sb

embêter [ɑ̃bete] *Fam* **VT** *(agacer)* to annoy; *(ennuyer)* to bore; **ça m'embête d'y aller** *(ça m'ennuie)* I can't be bothered going *or* to go; *(ça me gêne)* I wish I didn't have to go; **ça m'embête d'arriver en retard** I don't like being late; **je suis drôlement embêté avec ma fille** I'm having a lot of trouble with my daughter **VPR s'embêter** to be/get bored (stiff); *Iron* **je vois que tu ne t'embêtes pas!** I see you don't do badly for yourself!; **s'e. avec** *(des histoires d'argent, des scrupules, sa belle-mère etc)* to bother oneself about *or* with

emblée (d') [dɑ̃ble] **ADV** directly, right away, straight off; *(réussir)* at the first attempt

emblématique [ɑ̃blematik] **ADJ** emblematic(al); *Fig* symbolic

emblème [ɑ̃blɛm] **NM** *(insigne)* emblem, device; *Fig (symbole)* symbol; *Mktg* **e. de marque** brand mark

embobiner [ɑ̃bɔbine] **VT** *Fam (duper)* to take in; *(enjôler)* to get round; **ne vous laissez pas e.** don't let yourself be had *or* taken in

emboîtable [ɑ̃bwatabl] **ADJ** *(chaise)* stacking, stackable; *(boîte, table etc)* that fits into a nest

emboîtage [ɑ̃bwataʒ] **NM 1** *(action d'emboîter) (de chaises)* stacking; *Constr (de tuyaux, poutres etc)* jointing **2** *(d'un livre)* casing; *(étui d'un livre)* slipcase

emboîtement [ɑ̃bwatmɑ̃] **NM** *(de chaises)* stacking; *Constr (de tuyaux, poutres etc)* jointing

emboîter [ɑ̃bwate] **VT 1** *(assembler) (morceaux, pièces etc)* to fit together *or* into each other; *(boîtes, tables etc)* to nest; *(chaises)* to stack; *Constr (tuyaux, poutres etc)* to joint; **e. le pas à qn** to follow close on sb's heels; *Fig* to follow suit, to follow sb's lead **2** *(envelopper)* **e. un livre** to case a book **VPR s'emboîter** *(de pièces, morceaux etc)* to fit together *or* into each other; *(de boîtes, tables etc)* to nest; *(de chaises)* to stack

embolie [ɑ̃bɔli] **NF** *Méd* embolism; **e. gazeuse/pulmonaire** air/pulmonary embolism; **e. cérébrale** clot on the brain, *Spéc* cerebral embolism

embonpoint [ɑ̃bɔ̃pwɛ̃] **NM** stoutness, corpulence; **avoir de l'e.** to be stout *or* corpulent

embouché [ɑ̃buʃe] **ADJ** *Fam* **mal e.** *(grossier)* foul-mouthed; *(de mauvaise humeur)* in a foul mood

emboucher [ɑ̃buʃe] **VT 1** *(trompette etc)* to put to one's mouth; *Fig Vieilli* **e. la trompette** to trumpet the news **2** **un cheval** to put the bit in a horse's mouth

embouchure [ɑ̃buʃyr] **NF 1** *(d'une trompette, sarbacane etc)* mouthpiece **2** *(d'un sac, vase)* opening, mouth **3** *(d'un fleuve)* mouth

embourber (s') [sɑ̃burbe] **VPR 1** *(d'une voiture)* to get stuck (in the mud) **2** *Fig Péj* to flounder, to get bogged down; **il s'est embourbé dans des explications compliquées** he got bogged down in complicated explanations

embourgeoisement [ɑ̃burʒwazmɑ̃] **NM** attainment of middle-class respectability; *(d'un quartier)* gentrification

embourgeoiser (s') [sɑ̃burʒwaze] **VPR** to become bourgeois *or* middle-class; *(d'un quartier)* to become gentrified

embout [ɑ̃bu] **NM** *(d'un parapluie, d'une canne etc)* ferrule, tip; *(d'un câble)* terminal; *(d'un tuyau)* nozzle; *(d'un tirant, fil etc)* connector

embouteillage [ɑ̃buteja ʒ] **NM 1** *(encombrement)* (traffic) hold-up, traffic jam, *Fam* snarl-up; **tomber dans les embouteillages** to get caught in traffic **2** *(de navires)* bottling up

embouteiller [ɑ̃buteje] **VT 1** *(rue, autoroute etc)* to block (up), to jam (up); *(circulation)* to tie up, to hold up, *Fam* to snarl up; **circulation embouteillée** congested traffic; **route embouteillée** road blocked with traffic **2** *(navires)* to bottle up

emboutir [ɑ̃butir] **VT 1** *(véhicule)* to bash in; **tout l'arrière de ma voiture est embouti** the entire rear end of my car is bashed in; **je me suis fait e. par mon voisin** my neighbour crashed into me **2** *(métal)* to stamp, to press; **châssis en tôle emboutie** pressed steel frame **3** *(arrondir)* to emboss

emboutissage [ɑ̃butisaʒ] **NM 1** *(de voitures)* collision; **l'e. d'une voiture par un autobus** the collision between a bus and a car **2** *(de métaux)* stamping, pressing **3** *(fait d'arrondir)* embossing

embranchement [ɑ̃brɑ̃ʃmɑ̃] **NM 1** *(croisement) (d'une route, d'un rail, d'une conduite etc)* junction; *(bifurcation) (sur une route)* fork **2** *Rail* branch line **3** *Biol* sub-kingdom, *Spéc* phylum

embrancher [ɑ̃brɑ̃ʃe] **VT** *(route, conduite etc)* to connect up, to join up (**à** to) **VPR s'embrancher** to join (up) (**sur** with)

embrasement [ɑ̃brazmɑ̃] **NM 1** *Arch (incendie)* conflagration **2** *Litt* **l'e. des cieux au soleil couchant** the blazing sunset **3** *Litt (agitation)* agitation, turmoil; **il ne pouvait pas lutter contre l'e. de son cœur** he could not fight against the love that flared up in his heart

embraser [ɑ̃braze] **VT** *Litt* **1** *(maison, champs etc)* to set ablaze **2** *(d'un coucher de soleil)* to set aglow **3** *Fig (imagination)* to fire; *(foule)* to fire, to set alight, *Péj* to inflame **VPR s'embraser 1** *(prendre feu)* to blaze up **2** *(rougeoyer)* to glow **3** *Fig Litt* **dès que je l'ai vu, mon cœur s'est embrasé** the mere sight of him kindled a flame; **l'imagination des jeunes romantiques s'embrase trop vite** young romantics have an imagination that is too readily inflamed; **quand j'entendais des histoires sur l'Afrique, mon imagination s'embrasait** hearing stories about Africa fired my imagination; **les esprits s'embrasaient dans ces réunions** the meetings had an inflammatory effect on those present

embrassade [ɑ̃brasad] **NF** embrace, hug; **ce furent des embrassades à n'en plus finir lorsqu'ils se retrouvèrent** they hugged and kissed for ages when they met again

embrasse [ɑ̃bras] **NF** *(d'un rideau)* tieback

embrasser [ɑ̃brase] **VT 1** *(donner un baiser à)* to kiss; **je t'embrasse de tout mon cœur** *(dans une lettre)* with fondest love; **e. qn sur la bouche/la joue** to kiss sb on the mouth/cheek **2** *Vieilli (étreindre)* to embrace **3** *(adopter) (croyance, religion, doctrine, théorie)* to embrace; *(carrière)* to take up; *(cause)* to embrace, to take up; **e. la carrière diplomatique** to enter the diplomatic service **4** *(contenir) (sujet, période, cas de figure)* to embrace, to cover, to take in; **il faut e. tous les problèmes** we have to look at all the problems; **le cours embrassera l'ensemble du moyen âge** the course will cover the whole of the Middle Ages; **e. qch du regard** to take sth in at a glance; **il embrassa toute sa famille d'un regard satisfait** he cast a satisfied eye over his family **VPR s'embrasser** to kiss (each other)

Il faut noter que le verbe anglais **to embrace** ne signifie jamais **donner un baiser**.

---

embrasure [ɑ̃brazyr] **NF 1** *Constr* embrasure; **l'e. de la porte/fenêtre** the door/window recess **2** *Mil (dans un mur)* embrasure; *Naut* gun port

embrayage [ɑ̃brejaʒ] **NM 1** *(action) Aut* letting in *or* engaging the clutch; *Tech (de pièces de moteur)* coupling, engaging **2** *(pièce) Aut* clutch; *Tech* coupling (gear); **pédale d'e.** clutch pedal
► ► **e. à cônes** cone clutch; **e. à crabot** dog clutch; **e. à diaphragme** diaphragm spring *or* DS clutch; **e. électromagnétique** magnetic clutch; **e. à friction** friction clutch; **e. hydrodynamique** fluid clutch; **e. monodisque** single-plate *or* disc clutch; **e. multidisque** multi-disc clutch pack; **e. de prise directe** lock-up clutch

embrayer [ɑ̃breje] (**j'embraie, j'embraye, n. embrayons; j'embraierai, j'embrayerai**) **VT** *Tech (pièces de moteur)* to couple, to engage **VI 1** *Aut* to let in *or* engage the clutch **2** *Fam (commencer à parler de)* **e. sur** to get going *or* started on; **on pourrait peut-être e. sur un autre sujet** maybe we could change the subject **3** *Can Fam (se dépêcher)* **embraye!** get a move on!, hurry up!

embrigadement [ɑ̃brigadmɑ̃] **NM** *(de supporters etc)* recruitment (**dans** to, into)

embrigader [ɑ̃brigade] **VT** *(supporter etc)* to recruit (**dans** to, into)

embringuer [ɑ̃brɛ̃ge] *Fam* **VT e. qn dans qch** to get sb mixed up in sth; **il ne veut pas se laisser e. dans cette histoire** he doesn't want to get mixed up in it
▶ **VPR s'embringuer** to get mixed up (**dans** in)

embrocation [ɑ̃brɔkasjɔ̃] **NF** *Méd* embrocation

embrocher [ɑ̃brɔʃe] **VT 1** *Culin (viande etc)* to put on a/the spit **2** *Fam* **e. qn** *(d'un coup d'épée)* to skewer sb

embrouillage [ɑ̃brujaʒ] **NM** = embrouillement

embrouillamini [ɑ̃brujamini] **NM** *Fam* confusion, muddle; **sa vie sentimentale est un tel e. que …** his love life is so complicated *or* involved that …; **comment veux-tu que je m'y retrouve dans cet e. de papiers?** how can I be expected to know what I'm doing when these papers are in such a muddle?

embrouillé [ɑ̃bruje] **ADJ 1** *(fils)* tangled **2** *Fig (papiers, lettres etc)* mixed up, in a mess; *(situation, idées, arguments etc)* confused, muddled; *(style, affaire)* complicated, involved

embrouillement [ɑ̃brujmɑ̃] **NM 1** *(de fils) (action)* tangling; *(état)* tangle **2** *Fig (d'une situation, d'idées etc) (action)* muddling, confusing; *(état)* muddle, confusion; **l'e. de la situation est tel que …** the situation is so confused that …; **cela a provoqué un tel e. dans son esprit que …** this confused him so much that …

embrouiller [ɑ̃bruje] **VT 1** *(fils)* to tangle (up) **2** *Fig (personne, situation, idées etc)* to confuse, to muddle (up); **il a embrouillé la situation encore plus** he confused the situation even further, he made the situation even more confused; **il a réussi à m'e.** *ou* à **e. mes idées** he managed to confuse me; *Fam* **ni vu ni connu je t'embrouille** hey presto; *Fam* **… alors qu'il était avec une autre: ni vu ni connu je t'embrouille …** while all the time he was with another woman – talk about a con artist *or* about being conned!
▶ **VPR s'embrouiller** *(d'une personne, d'une situation, d'idées etc)* to get muddled (up) *or* confused; **je me suis embrouillé dans mes rendez-vous** I got my appointments muddled, I got into a muddle with my appointments

embroussaillé [ɑ̃brusaje] **ADJ** *(sentier, jardin, dunes etc)* covered with *or* in bushes; **cheveux embroussaillés** tousled hair; **le jardin est complètement e.** the garden is completely overgrown

embrumé [ɑ̃bryme] **ADJ** *(temps)* misty; *(horizon)* hazy; *Fig (esprit) (par l'alcool)* fuddled, fogged; **il avait l'esprit e. par toutes ces paroles** all that talking had left him feeling less than clear-headed

embrumer [ɑ̃bryme] **VT** *(paysage, ville etc)* to cover with mist *or* haze; *Fig (de l'alcool) (esprit)* to fuddle, to fog; **tous ces discours lui ont embrumé l'esprit** his/her mind is less than clear after all those speeches
▶ **VPR s'embrumer** *(du ciel)* to become misty *or* hazy; *(du paysage, d'une ville, une île)* to become covered with mist *or* haze; *Fig (des idées)* to become foggy *or* cloudy; **avec chaque verre, mon esprit s'embrumait un peu plus** with each glass, my brain became a little more fogged

embruns [ɑ̃brœ̃] **NMPL** spray, spindrift

embryologie [ɑ̃brijɔlɔʒi] **NF** *Biol* embryology

embryologique [ɑ̃brijɔlɔʒik] **ADJ** *Biol* embryologic(al)

embryologiste [ɑ̃brijɔlɔʒist] **N** *Biol* embryologist

embryon [ɑ̃brijɔ̃] **NM** embryo; *Fig* **un e. de roman/dissertation** an embryonic novel/dissertation; **ne nous emballons pas, ce n'est encore qu'un e. de projet** don't let's get carried away, it's still just a vague plan

embryonnaire [ɑ̃brijɔnɛr] **ADJ** *Biol* embryonic; **sac e.** embryo sac; *Fig* **à l'état e.** in an embryonic state, in embryo; **le projet en est encore à un stade e.** the project is still at a very early stage *or* in its very early stages

embryotomie [ɑ̃brijɔtɔmi] **NF** *Obst* embryotomy

embu [ɑ̃by] *Beaux-Arts* **ADJ** *(couleur, tableau)* flat, dull
▶ **NM** *(d'une couleur)* flatness, dullness

embûches [ɑ̃byʃ] **NFPL** traps; **tendre** *ou* **dresser des e. à qn** to set traps for sb; **sujet plein d'e.** tricky subject; **la vie est semée d'e.** life is full of pitfalls

embuer [ɑ̃bɥe] **VT** *(de la vapeur etc) (verre etc)* to mist up, to cloud; **yeux embués de larmes** eyes dimmed *or* clouded with tears; **pare-brise embué** misted(-up) windscreen

embuscade [ɑ̃byskad] **NF** ambush; **dresser** *ou* **tendre une e. à qn** to lay *or* set an ambush for sb; **attirer qn dans une e.** to ambush *or* waylay sb; **se tenir en e.** to lie in ambush *or* in wait; **tomber dans une e.** to be ambushed *or* waylaid

embusqué [ɑ̃byske] **NM 1** *Mil* shirker, dodger **2** *Rugby* **les embusqués** the back row of forwards

embusquer [ɑ̃byske] *Mil* **VT 1** *(placer en embuscade)* to place in ambush **2** *(affecter loin du front)* to find a cushy posting for
▶ **VPR s'embusquer 1** *(se mettre en embuscade)* to lie in ambush **2** *(se faire affecter loin du front)* to get a cushy posting

éméché [emeʃe] **ADJ** *Fam* slightly the worse for wear *or* drink, tipsy

émeraude [emrod] **NF** *Minér* emerald
▶ **NM** *(couleur)* emerald green
▶ **ADJ INV** emerald green

émergence [emɛrʒɑ̃s] **NF** emergence; **c'est là que se trouve le point d'é. de la source** the spring emerges here; **on assistait à l'é. de nouvelles théories politiques** new political theories were emerging *or* were coming to the fore

émergent [emɛrʒɑ̃] **ADJ** emergent, emerging

émerger [emɛrʒe] **VI** (j'émergeai(s); n. émergeons) **1** to emerge (**de** from) **2** *Fig (de la vérité, d'un fait etc)* to emerge, to come to light; *(d'un nouvel écrivain etc)* to emerge; *(d'une personne)* to come to; *Fam* **le dimanche, il n'émerge jamais avant midi** he never surfaces before noon on Sundays

émeri [emri] **NM** emery; **papier** *ou* **toile (d')é.** emery paper; **bouchon à l'é.** (ground glass) stopper; **bouché à l'é.** *(flasque)* stoppered; *Fam (personne)* bone-headed

émerillon [emrijɔ̃] **NM** *(oiseau)* merlin

émeriser [emrize] **VT** to coat with emery

émérite [emerit] **ADJ 1** *(expérimenté) (artisan, ouvrier, médecin etc)* skilled, experienced **2** *(professeur)* emeritus

émerveillement [emɛrvɛjmɑ̃] **NM 1** *(enchantement)* wonder, amazement **2** *(chose)* amazing *or* wonderful thing; **c'était un é.** it was amazing *or* wonderful; **un é. perpétuel** a constant source of amazement

émerveiller [emɛrvɛje] **VT** *(enchanter)* to fill with wonder, to amaze; **être émerveillé par** to marvel at, to be filled with wonder by
▶ **VPR s'émerveiller s'é. de** *ou* **devant** *(s'étonner de)* to be amazed by; *(s'enchanter de)* to marvel at; **la jeunesse s'émerveille de pas grand-**

chose it doesn't take much to amaze young people

émétique [emetik] **ADJ**, **NM** emetic

émetteur, -trice [emetœr, -tris] **ADJ 1** *Fin (banque, organisme)* issuing; **é. de cartes** card issuer **2** *Radio* transmitting; **poste é.** transmitter; **station émettrice** transmitting *or* broadcasting station
▶ **N** *(de billets, d'actions etc)* issuer; *(d'un chèque)* drawer
▶ **NM 1** *TV, Radio* transmitter; **é. monophonique/stéréo** monoaural/stereo transmitter; **é. terrestre** ground transmitter **2** *Phys (de radiation, son etc)* emitter

émetteur-récepteur, *pl* **émetteurs-récepteurs** **NM** *Radio* transmitter-receiver, transceiver; **é. (portatif)** walkie-talkie; **é. additionnel** transverter

émettre [emetr] *(conj like* **mettre***)* **VT 1** *(cri)* to give, to utter, to emit; *(rot, soupir)* to give; *(son)* to make, to emit; *(fumée)* to give off, to emit; *(chaleur)* to give out *or* off; *(lumière)* to give (out); **la seiche émet de l'encre** the cuttlefish ejects ink; **mon ordinateur émet un bruit bizarre** my computer is making a funny noise
2 *Fig (opinion, avis)* to voice, to express; *(objection)* to voice, to raise, to put forward; *(idée)* to voice, to put forward
3 *Radio, TV (programme)* to transmit, to broadcast; *(onde, signal)* to send out
4 *Fin (chèque, nouveau billet etc)* to issue; *(prêt)* to float; *Jur (fausse monnaie)* to utter; *Fin* **é. un emprunt** to issue loan stock, to make a bond issue; *Fin* **é. une lettre de crédit** to open a letter of credit
▶ **VI** *Radio, TV* to transmit, to broadcast

émeu, *pl* **émeus** [emø] **NM** *(oiseau)* emu

émeute [emøt] **NF** riot, outbreak, disturbance; **tourner à l'é.** to turn into a riot; **de terribles émeutes ont éclaté dans tout le pays** dreadful riots *or* rioting broke out throughout the country

émeutier, -ière [emøtje, -jɛr] **N** rioter

émietter [emjete] **VT 1** *(pain, fromage, roche etc)* to crumble (up) **2** *Fig (domaine, empire etc)* to break up; *(pouvoir)* to erode, to eat away at; *(fortune)* to fritter away, to squander; *(énergie, forces)* to waste
▶ **VPR s'émietter 1** *(du pain, fromage, d'une roche etc)* to crumble **2** *Fig (d'un domaine, un empire, un pouvoir etc)* to crumble away; **sa fortune s'émiettait au fil des années** his fortune disappeared little by little over the years

émigrant, -ante [emigrɑ̃, -ɑ̃t] **ADJ** migrant
▶ **N** emigrant

émigration [emigrasjɔ̃] **NF 1** emigration; **pays à forte/faible é.** country with high/low emigration **2** *Zool* migration

émigré, -ée [emigre] **N** *Pol, Écon* migrant; *Hist* (political) exile, émigré; **travailleurs émigrés** migrant workers

émigrer [emigre] **VI 1** to emigrate **2** *Zool* to migrate

émincé [emɛ̃se] **NM** *Culin (plat)* = thinly sliced meat or poultry in sauce; *(tranche)* thin slice *(of meat)*

émincer [emɛ̃se] **VT** (j'éminçai(s); n. éminçons) *(de la viande, des légumes etc)* to slice thinly

éminemment [eminamɑ̃] **ADV** eminently

éminence [eminɑ̃s] **NF 1** *(géographique)* hill, *Litt* eminence **2** *Anat* eminence; **l'é. du pouce** the ball of the thumb **3** *Rel* **son É.** le cardinal his Eminence the Cardinal; *Fig* **l'É. grise** the power behind the throne, the éminence grise **4** *Arch (excellence)* eminence

éminent [eminɑ̃] **ADJ** *(personne)* eminent, distinguished; **il nous a rendu d'éminents services** he rendered us outstanding service

émir [emir] NM emir

émirat [emira] NM emirate; **les Émirats arabes unis** the United Arab Emirates

émissaire [emisɛr] ADJ **bouc é.** scapegoat
NM **1** (envoyé) emissary **2** (d'un lac) outlet, drainage channel

émission [emisjɔ̃] NF **1** (de son, fluide etc) emission; (de sons, cris etc) utterance; (de chaleur, lumière) emission, giving out; **tuyau d'é.** discharge pipe
2 Radio, TV (action) transmission, broadcasting; (programme) programme, Am program, broadcast, show; **poste d'é.** transmitter; **station d'é.** transmitting or broadcasting station; **une é. pour les enfants** a children's programme or broadcast
3 Électron é. **électronique** electron emission; Nucl é. **de particules** particle emission
4 Fin (de billets de banque, timbres-poste etc) issue; Bourse é. **boursière** ou **d'actions** share issue; Bourse é. **de conversion** conversion issue; Bourse é. **d'actions gratuites** scrip issue; Banque é. **fiduciaire** fiduciary or note issue; Bourse é. **obligataire** ou **d'obligations** bond issue; é. **par séries** block issues
5 Jur uttering
▸▸ Radio, TV é. **en différé** recorded broadcast; é. **diffusée simultanément** simultaneous broadcast; é. **en direct** live broadcast; é. **éducative** educational programme; é. **pour enfants** children's television; é. **pour enfants d'âge pré-scolaire** pre-school programme; é. **d'expression directe** live debate programme; é. **d'expression directe (de formation politique)** party political broadcast; é. **en extérieur** outside broadcast, Spéc OB; é. **d'informations** news programme; é. **de jeux (télévisés)** (TV) game(s) show; é. **magazine** magazine programme; é. **payante** premium programme; é. **pilote** pilot; é. **en public** audience show; é. **de radio** radio programme; é. **radiotélévisée** simulcast; é. **relayée** relay; é. **de reportage** feature programme; **émissions scolaires** schools broadcasting; **émissions de service public** public-service broadcasting; é. **sportive** sports programme; é. **de télévision** television programme; é. **tout public** family programme; é. **de variétés** variety programme or show

emmagasinage [ɑ̃magazinaʒ] NM (de marchandises) storage, warehousing; (d'électricité, de chaleur) storing up, accumulation

emmagasiner [ɑ̃magazine] VT (marchandises) to store, to warehouse; (électricité, chaleur) to store up, to accumulate; Fig (souvenirs, connaissances) to store up

emmailloter [ɑ̃majɔte] VT **1** (membre etc) to wrap (up), to swathe; **l'infirmière m'a emmailloté la cheville dans un bandage** the nurse wrapped a bandage round my ankle; **bien emmailloté dans des couvertures** well wrapped up in blankets **2** (langer) (nourisson) to swaddle

emmanchement [ɑ̃mɑ̃ʃmɑ̃] NM **1** fitting or fixing of a handle (**d'un outil** (on) to a tool) **2** (d'une pièce à une autre) fitting; **cela rendait l'e. des deux pièces impossible** it made it impossible to fit the two parts together

emmancher [ɑ̃mɑ̃ʃe] VT **1** (outil) to fit or fix a handle to **2** (tuyaux) to fit together, to joint; (pièce dans une autre) to fit (**dans** to) **3** Fig Fam (travail, affaire etc) to get started on
VPR **s'emmancher** (de deux pièces) to fit together; Fig Fam **bien/mal s'e.** to get off to a good/bad start

emmanchure [ɑ̃mɑ̃ʃyr] NF **1** armhole; **la veste me serre aux emmanchures** the jacket's too tight at the armpits **2** Belg (combine) scheme, trick

emmêlement [ɑ̃mɛlmɑ̃] NM (de fils, laine etc) tangling; (état) tangle; Fig (de faits, d'une histoire) mixing up, muddling; (état) mix-up, muddle

emmêler [ɑ̃mɛle] VT (fil, cheveux etc) to tangle; Fig (faits, histoire) to mix up, to muddle
VPR **s'emmêler** (de fils, cheveux etc) to become tangled, to get in a tangle; Fig (de faits, d'une histoire) to become mixed up or muddled, to get into a muddle; Fam **s'e. les pédales** to get all mixed up or confused

emménagement [ɑ̃menaʒmɑ̃] NM moving in; **nous avons dû remettre notre e. à plus tard** we had to put off moving in or we had to put our move off to later; **comment s'est passé ton e.?** how did the move go?

emménager [ɑ̃menaʒe] (**j'emménageai(s)**) VI to move in; **e. dans** to move into
VT (meubles, personne) to move in; **e. qn/qch dans** to move sb/sth into

emmener [ɑ̃mne] VT (**j'emmène; j'emmènerai**) **1** (prendre avec soi) (enfant etc) to take (with one); (prisonnier etc) to lead or take away; Fam (objet) to bring; **je vous emmène avec moi** I'm taking you with me; **je t'emmène passer le week-end à Florence** I'm taking you (off) to Florence for the weekend; **cette année nous emmenons les enfants** we're taking the children away this year; **il m'a emmené à l'aéroport en voiture** he drove me to the airport; **e. promener qn** to take sb for a walk
2 (entraîner) (soldats, équipe de sport, peloton etc) to lead; (sprint) to lead (in); **les coéquipiers se sont relayés pour e. leur leader** the other members of the team took turns acting as pacemaker for their leader
3 (transporter) (d'un bateau, d'un avion etc) (passagers) to take, to carry

emment(h)al [emɛtal] NM (fromage) Emment(h)al (cheese)

emmerdant [ɑ̃mɛrdɑ̃] ADJ Arg (qui contrarie) damned or Br bloody annoying; (qui ennuie) damned or Br bloody boring; **ce que tu peux être e.!** you can be a real pain (in the bum or neck or Am butt)!

emmerde [ɑ̃mɛrd] NF Arg = **emmerdement**

emmerdement [ɑ̃mɛrd(ə)mɑ̃] NM Arg emmerdes (damned) bother, trouble; **depuis le début de l'année, il ne lui arrive que des emmerdements** he's had a helluva time of it since the beginning of the year; **pour les emmerdements, j'ai été servi aujourd'hui!** I've had a bloody awful day!; **un e.** a damned or Br bloody nuisance; **j'ai encore eu un e. avec la bagnole/les flics** I had trouble with the car/the police again; **tu parles d'un e.!** what an absolute pain (in the neck or bum or Am butt)!

emmerder [ɑ̃mɛrde] Arg VT **1 e. qn** (contrarier) to get up sb's nose or on sb's nerves; (ennuyer) to bore sb stiff or silly or rigid; **ça m'emmerde mais il va vraiment falloir que j'y aille** it's a real pain (in the neck or bum or Am butt), but I'm going to have to go; **arrête d'e. ta sœur!** stop annoying your sister! **2** (comme défi) dis-lui que je l'emmerde! tell him from me he can (go and) get stuffed!; **toi je t'emmerde!** get stuffed!, Vulg fuck you!; **moi, les gens, je les emmerde!** I don't give a shit or Vulg a fuck what people think!
VPR **s'emmerder 1** (s'ennuyer) to be bored stiff or silly or rigid; **qu'est-ce qu'on s'emmerde en colonie de vacances/avec eux** holiday camp is/they're bloody boring!; Iron **tu ne t'emmerdes pas!** you're not doing badly for yourself!; (tu as du culot) you've got some or a helluva nerve! **2** (se donner du mal) **je me suis vraiment emmerdé à monter ces étagères** it was a real pain putting up those shelves; **je ne me suis pas emmerdée à faire le ménage pour que …** I didn't go to all the

bother or trouble of doing the housework just so that …; **tu t'emmerdes beaucoup pour pas grand-chose** you're putting yourself to a lot of trouble for nothing

emmerdeur, -euse [ɑ̃mɛrdœr, -øz] N Arg (qui contrarie) damned or Br bloody nuisance, pain (in the neck or bum or Am butt); (qui ennuie) helluva or Br bloody bore

emmitoufler [ɑ̃mitufle] VT to wrap or muffle up (**dans, de** in)
VPR **s'emmitoufler** to get muffled up (**dans, de** in); **tâche de bien t'e.** try to wrap up well

emmurer [ɑ̃myre] VT (victime) to immure, to wall in or up; (d'une chute de pierres) (mineurs) to trap

émoi [emwa] NM (trouble) emotion, agitation; (plaisir) excitement; (anxiété) anxiety; **être (tout) en é.** (troublé) to be all excited or all in a flutter; **toute la ville était en é.** the whole town was in a commotion; **non sans é.** in some agitation

émollient [emɔljɑ̃] ADJ, NM emollient

émoluments [emɔlymɑ̃] NMPL emoluments, remuneration; **percevoir des é.** to receive payment

émondage [emɔ̃daʒ] NM **1** (d'un arbre) pruning, trimming **2** (de graines) cleaning

émonder [emɔ̃de] VT (arbre), Fig (livre, texte) to prune, to trim

émondeur, -euse [emɔ̃dœr, -øz] N pruner

émondoir [emɔ̃dwar] NM pruning hook

émoticon [emɔtikɔ̃] NM Ordinat smiley, emoticon

émotif, -ive [emɔtif, -iv] ADJ (personne, réaction etc) emotional
N emotional person

émotion [emosjɔ̃] NF emotion; Fam (inquiétude) fright, shock; **vive é.** strong emotion; (exaltation) excitement, thrill; **le meurtre de l'enfant a provoqué une vive é.** people were shocked by the child's murder; **l'atterrissage mouvementé a provoqué une vive é. parmi les passagers** the bumpy landing frightened the passengers; **ressentir une vive é.** (attendrissement) to be greatly moved; (exaltation) to be thrilled; (peur) to be very frightened; **parler avec é.** to speak emotionally; Fam **j'ai eu une é.** I've had a fright or shock; Fam **tu nous as vraiment donné des émotions** you gave us a real fright, you really frightened us

émotionnel, -elle [emosjɔnɛl] ADJ Psy (réaction etc) emotional

émotionner [emosjɔne] VT Fam to affect

émotivité [emotivite] NF emotionalism; **être d'une trop grande é.** to be too emotional

émoulu [emuly] ADJ Fam **jeune homme frais é. du collège/de son université** young man fresh from school/university

émoussé [emuse] ADJ (pointe, lame) blunt; Fig (sentiment, qualité etc) blunted, diminished; **une patience émoussée par le temps** patience diminished or worn thin by time; **il a l'appétit é. par la maladie** illness has blunted or taken the edge off his appetite

émousser [emuse] VT (lame, pointe, crayon, angle) to blunt; Fig (sens, passions etc) to dull, to blunt; (appétit) to take the edge off; **le temps a émoussé sa résistance** time has lessened or worn away his resistance
VPR **s'émousser** (d'une lame, pointe) to get blunt; Fig (des sens, passions) to become blunted or dulled; **mon appétit s'est émoussé depuis que je suis malade** I've not had much appetite or I haven't felt much like eating since I fell ill

émoustillant [emustijɑ̃] ADJ arousing, titillating

émoustiller [emustije] VT to arouse, to titillate

émouvant [emuvã] **ADJ** *(attendrissant)* moving, touching; *(bouleversant)* stirring, thrilling

émouvoir [emuvwar] *(pp* **ému;** *otherwise conj like* **mouvoir) VT** *(toucher)* to move, to touch; *(inquiéter)* to upset; **é. qn (jusqu')aux larmes** to move sb to tears; **cela ne m'émeut pas le moins du monde** that doesn't upset me in the least; **encore tout ému de la rencontre** still very upset by the meeting; **facile à é.** emotional, easily moved *or* upset; **ça n'a pas eu l'air de l'é.** he seemed quite unsympathetic
▪ **VPR s'émouvoir** *(se troubler)* to be touched *or* moved; **rester sans s'é. à la vue de leur malheur** to remain unmoved by their plight; **ce qu'il me déclara sans s'é.** le moins du monde which he announced to me with perfect composure; *Fam* **pas de quoi s'é.** it's nothing to get worked up about

empaffé [ãpafe] **NM** *Vulg* dickhead, prick, *Br* wanker

empaillage [ãpajaʒ] **NM 1** *(d'animaux morts)* stuffing **2** *(de plantes)* mulching with straw **3** *(de chaises)* bottoming with straw

empaillé, -ée [ãpaje] **ADJ** *(oiseau, renard etc)* stuffed; *Fam* **avoir l'air e.** to be self-conscious *or* awkward

empailler [ãpaje] **VT 1** *(animal mort)* to stuff **2** *(plantes)* to mulch with straw **3** *(chaise)* to bottom with straw
▪ **VPR s'empailler** *Fam (se quereller violemment)* to lay into each other

empailleur, -euse [ãpajœr, -øz] **N** *(d'animaux)* taxidermist

empalement [ãpalmã] **NM** impalement

empaler [ãpale] **VT** to impale
▪ **VPR s'empaler** to impale oneself

empanaché [ãpanaʃe] **ADJ** plumed, decorated with plumes; *Fig* **style e.** pompous *or* flowery style

empannage [ãpanaʒ] **NM** *Naut* gybe

empanner [ãpane] **VI** *Naut* to gybe

empapaouter [ãpapaute] **VT** *Vulg* to bugger; **va te faire e.!** go to hell!, *Br* bugger off!, sod off!

empaquetage [ãpaktaʒ] **NM** packing (up)

empaqueter [ãpakte] **VT** *(* **j'empaquette,** **j'empaquetterai)** to pack up, to package

empaqueteur, -euse [ãpaktœr, -øz] **N** packer

emparer (s') [sãpare] **VPR s'emparer de** *(ville, otage, butin, pouvoir)* to seize; *(téléphone, porte-monnaie etc)* to grab (hold of), to seize; *Sport (ballon)* to take possession of, to get hold of; *(d'un doute, une obsession, de la jalousie etc) (personne)* to take hold of; **depuis que cette idée s'est emparée de mon esprit** since the idea took hold of me; **la presse s'est emparée de cette histoire** the press got hold of the story; **il s'est emparé de ce prétexte pour partir** he used it as a pretext to leave

empâté [ãpate] **ADJ** *(visage)* fleshy, bloated

empâtement [ãpatmã] **NM 1** *(de la volaille)* fattening (up) **2** *(d'une personne, d'un visage)* bloating; *(d'un corps)* bloating, thickening **3** *Beaux-Arts* impasto

empâter [ãpate] **VT 1** *(engraisser) (volaille)* to fatten (up) **2** *(épaissir) (corps)* to bloat, to thicken; *(visage)* to bloat, to coarsen; **la vie à la campagne l'a empâtée** she has put on weight in the country **3** *(couvrir d'une pâte) (langue)* to coat, to fur up; *Beaux-Arts* to impaste
▪ **VPR s'empâter 1** *(d'une personne, d'un corps)* to become bloated; *(d'un visage)* to coarsen; **elle s'est empâtée depuis quelque temps** she has put on weight recently **2** *(de la langue)* to become coated, to fur up

empattement [ãpatmã] **NM 1** *(d'une voiture)* wheelbase **2** *Typ* serif; **sans e.** sans serif **3** *(d'un mur)* footing

empatter [ãpate] **VT** *(mur)* to give footing to

empaumer [ãpome] **VT 1** *(au jeu de paume) (attraper)* to catch in the palm of the hand; *(frapper)* to strike with the palm of the hand **2** *Fam Vieilli* **se laisser** *ou* **se faire e.** to be tricked *or* taken in **3** *(d'un magicien etc) (carte, pièce etc)* to palm

empêché [ãpeʃe] **ADJ** *(retenu)* held up, detained

empêchement [ãpeʃmã] **NM 1** *(contretemps)* **j'ai eu un e.** I got held up *or* detained, something came up at the last minute; **en cas d'e., veuillez prévenir 24 heures à l'avance** please give us 24 hours notice if you cannot keep the appointment; **en cas d'e., nous remettrons la réunion à la semaine suivante** if anybody can't make the meeting, we'll postpone it to the following week **2** *Jur* **e. de mariage** impediment to marriage

empêcher [ãpeʃe] **VT 1** *(action, événement etc)* to prevent; *(mouvement, progrès etc)* to obstruct, to impede; **ce vent empêchera la pluie** this wind will keep the rain off
2 e. qn de faire qch to stop *or* prevent *or* keep sb from doing sth; **rien ne m'empêchera de te rejoindre** nothing will stop me (from) joining you; **il sera difficile de l'en e.** it will be difficult to stop *or* prevent him/her; **tu ne m'empêcheras pas de penser que j'ai raison** I still think I'm right, you won't convince me that I'm wrong; *Fam* **ce n'est pas ça qui m'empêchera de dormir** I won't lose any sleep over it; **la pluie empêche que nous (ne) sortions** the rain is preventing *or* stopping us from going out; **il n'y a rien qui t'empêche de lui téléphoner** there's nothing to stop you telephoning him/her; **je ne vous empêche pas de partir/dîner, au moins?** I hope I'm not keeping you from going/your dinner?
3 il n'empêche que cela nous a coûté cher all the same *or* nevertheless it has cost us dear; **cela n'empêche pas qu'il aurait pu s'excuser** all the same *or* nevertheless, he could have apologized; *Fam* **n'empêche** all the same; *Fam* **qu'est-ce que ça empêche?** what does that matter?, what odds *or* difference does that make?; *Fam* **ça n'empêche rien!** that doesn't matter!, it makes no odds *or* difference!
▪ **VPR s'empêcher** *(souvent nég)* **s'e. de faire qch** to stop oneself *or* prevent oneself *or* refrain from doing sth; **je ne pouvais m'e. de rire** I couldn't help laughing, I had to laugh; **je ne peux pas m'e. de la taquiner** I can't help teasing her; **elle ne peut jamais s'e. de dire ce qu'il ne faut pas** she can never stop herself from saying what she shouldn't; **je ne peux pas m'en e.** I can't help it, I can't stop myself

empêcheur, -euse [ãpeʃœr, -øz] **N** *Fam* **e. de danser** *ou* **de tourner en rond** spoilsport, wet blanket

empeigne [ãpεɲ] **NF** *(de chaussure)* upper, vamp; *Arg* **gueule d'e.** ugly mug

empennage [ãpenaʒ] **NM** *(d'une flèche)* feathering, feathers; *(d'une bombe)* fins, vanes; *(d'une torpille)* fins; *(d'un avion)* empennage, tail

empenner [ãpene] **VT** *(flèche)* to feather

empereur [ãprœr] **NM** emperor

emperlousé [ãpεrluze] **ADJ** *Fam* dripping with pearls

empesage [ãpəzaʒ] **NM** *(d'un col, d'une chemise etc)* starching

empesé [ãpəze] **ADJ 1** *(col, chemise etc)* starched **2** *Fig (manière)* stiff, starchy, unbending; *(style)* stiff

empeser [ãpəze] **VT** *(* **j'empèse;** **j'empèserai)** *(col, chemise etc)* to starch

empester [ãpεste] **VT** **e. l'alcool/le parfum** to reek *or* stink of alcohol/perfume; **le frigo empeste le fromage** the fridge stinks of cheese; **le fromage empeste le frigo** the cheese is stinking out the fridge; **e. qn (avec sa fumée)** to stink sb out (with one's smoke) ▪ **VI** to stink, to smell to high heaven

empêtrer (s') [sãpetre] **VPR** to become entangled; **s'e. les pieds dans les broussailles** to get one's feet caught in the undergrowth; *Fig* **s'e. dans** *(explications, discours, mensonges)* to get tangled up in; *Fig* **s'e. dans une sale affaire** to get involved *or* mixed up in a bad business

emphase [ãfaz] **NF** pompousness, pomposity; **avec e.** pompously; **solennel mais sans e.** solemn but not pompous; **parler sans e.** to speak simply

emphatique [ãfatik] **ADJ** pompous

> Il faut noter que l'adjectif anglais **emphatic** est un faux ami. Il signifie **énergique** ou **catégorique**.

emphatiquement [ãfatikmã] **ADV** pompously

> Il faut noter que l'adverbe anglais **emphatically** est un faux ami. Il signifie **énergiquement** ou **catégoriquement**.

emphysémateux, -euse [ãfizematø, -øz] **N** *Méd* emphysema sufferer

emphysème [ãfizεm] **NM** *Méd* emphysema

empiècement [ãpjεsmã] **NM** *(d'un vêtement)* yoke

empierrement [ãpjεrmã] **NM 1** *(action) (d'une route)* metalling, macadamization; *Rail* ballasting **2** *(couche de pierres) (d'une route)* macadam, (road) metal; *Rail* ballast

empierrer [ãpjere] **VT** *(route)* to metal, to macadamize; *Rail* to ballast

empiétement [ãpjetmã] **NM** encroachment (**sur** on); **c'est un e. sur ma vie privée** it's an encroachment on my private life; **cette barrière est un e. sur mon terrain** that fence encroaches on my land; **e. sur les droits de qn** infringement of sb's rights

empiéter [ãpjete] **VI** *(* **j'empiète;** **j'empiéterai) e. sur** *(le terrain, le temps, la vie privée de quelqu'un)* to encroach on; **cette affiche empiète sur l'autre** this poster overlaps the other; **son collègue essaie d'e. sur ses attributions** his colleague is trying to trespass on his/her territory; **e. sur les droits de qn** to infringe sb's rights

empiffrer (s') [sãpifre] **VPR** *Fam* to stuff *or* gorge oneself (**de** with)

empilable [ãpilabl] **ADJ** *(chaise, boîte etc)* stacking

empilage [ãpilaʒ] **NM, empilement** [ãpilmã] **NM 1** *(action) (de livres, bois etc)* stacking, piling (up) **2** *(pile)* pile, stack

empiler [ãpile] **VT 1** *(livres, bois)* to stack, to pile (up) **2** *(passagers dans un véhicule)* to cram **3** *Fam (duper)* to do; **se faire e.** to be done *or* had; **se faire e. par qn** to be done by sb
▪ **VPR s'empiler 1** *(de livres, dossiers etc)* to pile up; *(former une pile)* to be piled up **2** *(de passagers)* **s'e. dans** to cram into

empire [ãpir] **NM 1** *(domination)* authority, dominion; *(contrôle)* influence, control; **sous l'e. d'un tyran** ruled by a tyrant, under the rule *or Litt* sway of a tyrant; **avoir de l'e. sur qn** to have influence over sb; **user de** *ou* **exercer son e. sur qn** to use one's power over sb; **la religion exerce un véritable e. sur lui** religion has a real hold on him; **avoir de l'e. sur soi-même** to be self-controlled; **avoir**

peu d'e. sur soi-même to have little self-control; **avoir beaucoup d'e. sur soi-même** to be very self-controlled, to have a lot of self-control; **quand j'ai bu, je n'ai plus aucun e. sur moi-même** I lose all self-control when I drink; **faire qch sous l'e. de la boisson/de la colère** to do sth under the influence of drink/in a fit of anger; **elle s'est enfuie sous l'e. de la peur** she fled in fear **2** *Hist, Pol* **impero; le Saint E. romain germanique** the Holy Roman Empire; **le premier E., l'E.** the First Empire; **le second E.** the Second Empire; **style/meubles E.** Empire style/furniture; **je ne changerais pas de travail pour un e.** I wouldn't change my job for all the tea in China *or* if you paid me **3** *(groupe commercial)* empire

▸▸ **le Céleste E.** the Middle Kingdom, the Celestial Empire; **l'E. du Milieu** the Middle Kingdom, the Celestial Empire; **l'E. du Soleil-Levant** the Land of the Rising Sun

empirer [ɑ̃piʀe] **VI** to worsen, to get *or* to grow worse, to deteriorate; **est-ce que les choses s'arrangent avec ton mari? – non, elles empirent** are things any better with your husband? – no, they're (getting) worse **VT** to worsen, to make worse, to aggravate

empirique [ɑ̃piʀik] **ADJ** empiric(al)

empirisme [ɑ̃piʀism] **NM** empiricism

empiriste [ɑ̃piʀist] **ADJ, N** *Phil* empiricist

emplacement [ɑ̃plasmɑ̃] **NM 1** *(d'une tente, d'un édifice etc)* site, location; *(sur un marché, dans un parking)* space; **à l'e. d'un ancien tombeau** on the site of an old tomb; **e. publicitaire** *(sur un mur, dans un journal)* advertising space; *Naut* **e. de chargement** loading berth **2** *Ordinat* slot; **e. pour carte d'extension** expansion slot; **e. (pour) périphériques** extension slot; **e. d'évolutivité** upgrade slot; **e. pour carte** card slot

emplafonner [ɑ̃plafɔne] **VT** *Fam* to crash into; **elle s'est fait e. par mon voisin** my neighbour crashed into her

emplâtre [ɑ̃plɑtʀ] **NM 1** *Pharm (pansement)* (sticking *or* adhesive) plaster; **e. contre** *ou* **pour les cors** corn plaster; *Fig* **c'est un e. sur une jambe de bois** it's (of) no earthly use; *Fam* **cette purée, quel e.!** this mashed potato is really stodgy **2** *Fam (personne)* wimp

emplette [ɑ̃plɛt] **NF 1** *(achat)* purchase; **aller faire ses emplettes** to go shopping; **faire l'e. de qch** to buy *or* purchase sth **2** *(choses achetées)* emplettes shopping, purchases; **mes dernières emplettes** my latest purchases, the latest things I've bought

emplir [ɑ̃pliʀ] **VT** to fill (**de** with); **la foule emplissait les rues** the crowd filled the streets; **cette nouvelle m'emplit de joie** the news fills me with delight; **les enfants emplissaient la cour de rires** the playground was full of children's laughter

VPR s'emplir to fill (up) (**de** with)

emploi [ɑ̃plwa] **NM 1** *(utilisation)* use; **l'e. du béton est de plus en plus courant** concrete is being used increasingly; **ce mot est d'un e. rare** the word is rarely used; **je n'en aurais pas l'e.** I wouldn't have any use for it *or* get any use out of it; **quel e. vas-tu faire de tout cet argent/ce temps?** what are you going to do with all that money/time?; **je me demande quel e. il peut bien faire de ce vieux meuble?** I wonder what use he has for that old piece of furniture; **faire bon/mauvais e. de qch** to make good/bad use of sth, to put sth to good/bad use; **mode d'e.** directions *or* instructions for use; **prêt à l'e.** ready to use **2** *(situation)* job; *(travail)* employment, work; **être sans e.** to be out of work *or* out of a job, to be unemployed; **chercher un e.** to be looking for work *or* a job; **avoir un e.** to have a job, to be in work; **la crise/situation de l'e.** the employment crisis/situation; **il**

faut faire quelque chose pour l'e. something has to be done about employment; **agence nationale pour l'e.** = (French state) employment agency, *Br* ≃ Jobcentre®; *Journ* **demandes d'e.** situations wanted; **j'ai adressé plusieurs demandes d'e.** I sent off several job applications; *Journ* **offres d'e.** situations vacant; **création d'emplois** job creation; **sécurité de l'e.** job security; **partage de l'e.** job-sharing; *Écon, Pol* **plein e.** full employment; **les sans e.** the jobless; **e. à plein temps** full-time job; **e. à temps partiel** part-time job

3 *Théâtre* **c'est elle qui tient l'e. de la fille de la star** she is cast as the star's daughter, she plays (the part of) the star's daughter; **on le cantonne dans des emplois de grand amoureux** he is typecast as the great lover; *Fig* **il a le physique** *ou* **la tête** *ou Fam* **la gueule de l'e.** he looks the part

▸▸ **emplois-jeunes** = jobs created for young people, particularly in the public sector and in education, as part of a programme to combat unemployment; **emplois de proximité** = employment in the community *(as a way of reducing unemployment)*; **e. saisonnier** seasonal employment; **e. du temps** timetable, schedule; **elle a un e. du temps très chargé** she has a very busy *or* full timetable *or* schedule; **e. vacant** vacancy

employabilité **NF** employability

employé, -ée [ɑ̃plwaje] **N** employee; **e. (de bureau)** office worker; **e. de banque** bank clerk; **e. d'une administration** government employee, civil servant; **l'e. du gaz vient demain** the gas man's coming tomorrow; **e. aux écritures** accounts *or* ledger clerk; **e. des postes** post office clerk; **e. de mairie** town hall employee; **e. occasionnel** casual worker; **e. à plein temps/à temps partiel** full-time/part-time employee; **être e. des postes/de mairie** to work for the Post Office/at the town hall; **e. de chemin de fer** railway employee; **e. à l'enregistrement des bagages** check-in clerk; **être e. de maison** to do domestic work

employer [ɑ̃plwaje] (**j'emploie; j'emploierai**) **VT 1** *(utiliser)* (outil, mot, technique, force etc) to use; **e. toute son énergie à faire qch** to devote all one's energies to doing sth; **j'emploierai tous les moyens** I'll use whatever means I have; **e. les grands moyens** to go to great lengths; **e. son temps à nettoyer/étudier** to spend one's time cleaning/studying; **il ne sait à quoi e. son temps** he doesn't know what to do with his time; **bien e. son temps** to use one's time well, to make good use of one's time, to put one's time to good use; **elle ne sait pas e. son argent** she doesn't know how to use her money; **à quoi vas-tu e. cette somme?** what are you going to spend the money on?; **cet ordinateur n'emploie que des disquettes de double densité** the computer only takes double-density disks

2 *Com* **e. une somme en recette** to put *or* enter an amount in the receipts

3 *(faire travailler) (ouvrier, personnel etc)* to employ; **e. qn comme secrétaire** to employ sb as secretary; **e. qn à des corvées/des petits travaux** to employ sb to do the chores/odd jobs; **je suis employé par plusieurs sociétés** I am employed by *or* I work for several companies

VPR s'employer 1 *(d'une personne)* **s'e. à faire qch** to work on doing sth; **je m'y emploie** I'm working on it **2** *(être utilisé)* to be used **3** *Vieilli* **s'e. pour qn** to exert oneself on sb's behalf

employeur, -euse [ɑ̃plwajœʀ, -øz] **N** employer

emplumé [ɑ̃plyme] **ADJ** feathered

empocher [ɑ̃pɔʃe] **VT 1** *(toucher) (argent,*

chèque etc) to pocket, to receive **2** *(mettre dans sa poche)* to pocket

empoignade [ɑ̃pwaɲad] **NF** *Fam* brawl, punch-up

empoigne [ɑ̃pwaɲ] **NF** *Fam* **c'était la foire d'e. dans les magasins** it was bedlam in the shops, the shops were full of people pushing and shoving; **c'est la foire d'e. pour se faire servir** it's a real scrum getting served; **quelle foire d'e. ici!** what a scrum!; **la vie n'est qu'une foire d'e.** life's just a rat race *or* a free-for-all

empoigner [ɑ̃pwaɲe] **VT** *(attraper) (objet)* to grab (hold of), to grasp, to seize; *(personne)* to seize, to grab (hold of), *Fam* to collar

VPR s'empoigner to brawl, to have a punch-up

empois [ɑ̃pwa] **NM** (laundry) starch; *Tex* dressing

empoisonnant [ɑ̃pwazɔnɑ̃] **ADJ** *Fam (irritant)* annoying, irritating; *(ennuyeux)* boring; **c'est vraiment e., ces retards continuels** these constant delays are an absolute pain

empoisonné **ADJ** *Fig (trait, paroles)* poisonous, vicious; *Fig* **cadeau empoisonné** poisoned chalice; **il m'a fait un cadeau empoisonné en me nommant à ce poste** he wasn't exactly doing me a favour by appointing me to that job

empoisonnement [ɑ̃pwazɔnmɑ̃] **NM 1** *(intoxication) (d'une personne, de la nourriture)* poisoning **2** *Fam (souci, ennui)* problem; **je n'ai que des empoisonnements** I've got nothing but problems; **la vie avec lui est un e. continuel** life with him is just one thing after another; **quel e.!** what a pain (in the neck)!

empoisonner [ɑ̃pwazɔne] **VT 1** *(intoxiquer) (personne, nourriture, animal, flèche, étang)* to poison

2 *(empester)* **du poisson pourri empoisonnait la pièce** there was a smell of rotten fish in the room, the room smelled of rotten fish; **des odeurs de cuisine empoisonnaient la pièce** the room was full of cooking smells; **odeur qui empoisonne l'air** smell that taints the air

3 *Fig (altérer) (existence, mariage)* to poison; *Fam (irriter)* to annoy, to irritate; *(ennuyer)* to bore; **e. la vie de qn** to make sb's life a misery; **vraiment, ça m'empoisonne de devoir y aller** I'm really fed up about having to go; **il m'empoisonne à toujours me téléphoner** I'm fed up with his constant telephoning

VPR s'empoisonner 1 *(se tuer)* to poison oneself

2 *Fig (s'ennuyer)* to be bored; **qu'est-ce qu'on s'empoisonne dans cette soirée!** this is a really boring party!; **s'e. l'existence** to make one's life a misery; **essaie de trouver ce livre mais ne t'empoisonne pas l'existence avec ça** try to find the book but don't go to too much trouble over it

empoisonneur, -euse [ɑ̃pwazɔnœʀ, -øz] **N 1** *(criminel)* poisoner **2** *Fam (personne qui ennuie)* bore; *(personne qui irrite)* nuisance, pest

empoissonner [ɑ̃pwasɔne] **VT** to stock with fish

emporté, -ée [ɑ̃pɔʀte] **ADJ** *(personne)* irascible, quick-tempered; **avoir un caractère e.** to be irascible *or* quick-tempered, to be quick to lose one's temper; **d'un ton e.** irascibly

N irascible *or* quick-tempered person

emportement [ɑ̃pɔʀtəmɑ̃] **NM 1** *(colère)* (fit of) anger; **répondre avec e.** to reply angrily **2** *Litt, Vieilli (élan) (d'enthousiasme, d'excitation etc)* burst, surge; **dans l'e. de la discussion** in the heat of the debate

emporte-pièce [ɑ̃pɔʀtəpjɛs] **NM INV** *Tech*

punch; *Culin* pastry cutter; **découper qch à l'e.** to stamp *or* punch sth out; *Culin* to cut out (with a pastry cutter); *Fig* **style à l'e.** incisive style; *Fig* **mots à l'e.** biting *or* cutting words; *Fig* **répondre à l'e.** to reply incisively *or* trenchantly

emporter [ɑ̃pɔrte] **vt 1** *(partir et prendre avec soi)* to take (with one); *(enlever d'un lieu)* to take away; *(emmener)* to carry *or* take away; **e. un blessé sur un brancard** to carry off *or* take away a wounded man on a stretcher; **ils ont emporté de quoi manger** they took some food with them; **plats à e.** take-away food; *Fam* **il ne l'emportera pas au paradis** he'll live to regret it; **(que) le diable l'emporte!** to hell with him!; **le train qui m'emporte vers le nord** the train which is carrying *or* taking me northwards; **il a emporté son secret dans la tombe** he took his secret to the grave (with him)
2 *(entraîner, arracher) (du courant, de la lave)* to sweep *or* carry away; **le choléra l'emporta** cholera carried him off; **il a eu une jambe emportée par un obus** a shell took *or* blew one of his legs off; **le vent emporta son chapeau** the wind blew his/her hat off *or* away; **la tempête a emporté le toit** the roof came off in the storm; *Fig* **autant en emporte le vent** promises are cheap, talk is easy; **cette moutarde vous emporte la bouche** *ou Arg* **la gueule** this mustard takes the roof off your mouth; *Fig* **se laisser e. par** *(la colère, l'enthousiasme, l'imagination, les sentiments)* to get *or* let oneself be carried away by
3 *(conquérir) (fort, ville etc)* to take (by assault); **e. la victoire** to be victorious, to be the victor (**contre** over); **e. la décision** to win out, to carry the day; *Fam* **e. le morceau** to win one's case; **l'équipe nantaise l'a emporté par deux buts à zéro** the Nantes team won (by) two goals to nil; **le coureur hollandais l'emporte haut la main** the Dutch runner is winning hands down; **avec lui, c'est toujours l'amitié qui l'emporte** friendship is always the most important consideration *or* outweighs everything else as far as he's concerned; **considérations qui l'emportent sur toutes les autres** considerations that override *or* outweigh all others; **ce dossier/ ce candidat/ce prototype l'emporte sur tous les autres** this file/candidate/prototype stands head and shoulders above the others *or* is streets ahead of the others; **en ce qui concerne le culot, elle l'emporte vraiment sur tout le monde** she's streets ahead of everybody when it comes to cheek; **ici, la pluie l'emporte sur le soleil** there's much more rain than sunshine here; **ici, le rugby l'emporte sur le foot** rugby is more important *or* popular than football here
vpr s'emporter 1 to lose one's temper, to fly into a rage (**contre qn** with sb)
2 *(d'un cheval)* to bolt

empoté, -ée [ɑ̃pɔte] *Fam* **adj** cack-handed **n** cack-handed idiot

empoter [ɑ̃pɔte] **vt** *(plantes)* to pot

empourprer [ɑ̃purpre] **vt** to tinge with crimson
vpr s'empourprer *(d'un visage)* to flush, to go crimson; *(du ciel)* to turn crimson

empoussiéré [ɑ̃pusjere] **adj** covered with dust, dusty

empreindre [ɑ̃prɛ̃dr] *(prp* **empreignant;** *pp* **empreint;** *pr ind* **j'empreins, il empreint,** n. **empreignons, ils empreignent;** *impf* **j'empreignais;** *p hist* **j'empreignis;** *fu* **j'empreindrai)** **vt** *(dans la cire)* to impress, to imprint, to stamp; *Fig* **visage empreint de mélancolie/de terreur** face marked *or* stamped with sadness/full of terror; *Fig* **article empreint d'un certain sérieux** article with serious overtones; *Fig* **des histoires empreintes**

---

d'onirisme stories with a dreamlike quality
vpr s'empreindre *(d'un visage, d'une expression etc)* to be marked *or* stamped (**de** with)

empreinte [ɑ̃prɛ̃t] **nf 1** *(trace, impression)* impression, (im)print; *Typ* mould, *Am* mold; *(de satellite)* footprint; **prendre l'e. de qch** to take an impression of sth; **les loups ont laissé des empreintes dans la neige** the wolves left tracks *or* footprints in the snow; **e. des roues** tyre tracks; **e. de pas** footprint; **e. de doigt** fingermark; **prendre** *ou* **relever les empreintes de qn** to take sb's fingerprints, to fingerprint sb; **relever les empreintes sur un revolver** to fingerprint a revolver **2** *Fig (du génie, du passé, de l'éducation etc)* stamp, (hall)mark; **mettre son e. sur qch** to put one's stamp *or* mark on sth; **marquer qn/ qch de son e.** to put one's stamp *or* mark on sb/sth; **être marqué de l'e. de qn** to bear sb's stamp *or* mark
▸▸**e. digitale** fingerprint; **e. génétique** genetic fingerprint; **e. en plâtre** plaster cast; **e. vocale** voice print

empressé, -ée [ɑ̃prese] **adj 1** *(prévenant) (vendeur)* eager, willing; *(serviteur, docteur, admirateur etc)* attentive; **des soins empressés** assiduous attentions; **ils m'ont entouré de soins empressés** they gave me every care and consideration; **il lui fait une cour empressée** he is courting her assiduously **2** *Litt (pressé)* **il est e. à vous revoir** he is eager to see you again
n *Péj* **faire le. auprès de qn** to dance attendance on sb

empressement [ɑ̃presmɑ̃] **nm 1** *(prévenance) (d'un vendeur)* eagerness, willingness (**à faire qch** to do sth); *(d'un serviteur, docteur, admirateur etc)* attentiveness; **témoigner de l'e. auprès de qn** to pay marked attention(s) to sb; **son e. auprès des femmes est presque gênant** he is almost embarrassingly attentive to women **2** *(hâte)* eagerness; **il montre peu d'e. à faire les travaux** he doesn't seem to be very eager *or* keen to do the work; **avec e.** eagerly; **tous les soirs il rentre chez lui avec e.** he hurries home every evening, he is eager to get home every evening; **mettre beaucoup d'e. à faire qch** to hasten to do sth

empresser (s') [ɑ̃prese] **vpr 1** *(se dépêcher)* **s'e. de faire qch** to hurry to do sth; **il s'empressa de répondre à ma lettre** he lost no time in answering my letter **2** *(être prévenant)* **s'e. à faire qch** to do sth eagerly, to hasten to do sth; **s'e. auprès de qn** to pay marked attention(s) to sb; **s'e. autour d'un accidenté de la route** to be busy attending to the victim of a road accident; **tout le monde s'empresse autour d'elle** everyone crowds *or* flocks round her

emprise [ɑ̃priz] **nf 1** *(domination)* hold; **avoir de l'e. sur qn** to have a hold over sb; **sous l'e. de l'alcool** under the influence of alcohol; **sous l'e. de son amour pour elle** swayed by his love for her; **c'est sous l'e. de la colère qu'il l'a mise à la porte** he fired her in a fit of anger **2** *Jur (de terres etc à des fins publiques)* expropriation, acquisition

emprisonnement [ɑ̃prizɔnmɑ̃] **nm** imprisonment; **e. à perpétuité** life imprisonment; **peine d'e.** prison sentence; **il a été condamné à une peine d'e. de cinq ans** he was sentenced to five years in prison *or Fml* to a five-year term of imprisonment, he was given a five-year prison sentence

emprisonner [ɑ̃prizɔne] **vt 1** *(mettre en prison)* to imprison, to put in prison **2** *Fig (serrer) (esprit)* to imprison; **e. le buste dans un corset** to squeeze into a corset; **col qui emprisonne le cou** collar that is too tight

emprunt [ɑ̃prœ̃] **nm 1** *(action)* borrowing; **ce n'est pas à moi, c'est un e.** it's not mine, it's

---

borrowed; **nom d'e.** assumed name; **son nom de scène est un nom d'e.** he acts under an assumed name
2 *(somme)* loan; **faire un e. à qn** to borrow (money) from sb; **faire un e.** *(auprès d'une banque etc)* to take out a loan; **contracter un e.** to raise a loan; **couvrir un e.** to cover a loan; **e. public** public loan; **e. d'État** government loan; *Bourse* state bond; **e. à court/ long terme** short-/long-term loan; **procéder à un nouvel e.** to make a new loan issue; **faire un e. de plusieurs millions à la banque** to borrow several million from the bank, to take out a bank loan of several million; **e. de conversion** conversion loan; **e. à découvert** unsecured loan; **e. en devises** currency loan; **e. garanti** secured loan; **e. indexé** indexed loan; **e. obligataire** bond issue, loan stock; *(titre)* debenture bond; **e. obligataire convertible** convertible loan stock; **e. perpétuel** perpetual loan; **e. remboursable sur demande** call loan, loan repayable on demand; **e. de remboursement** refunding loan; **emprunts à taux fixe** fixed-rate borrowing; **e. à terme** term loan; **e. sur titres** loan on securities *or* stock
3 *Ling* borrowing (**à l'anglais** from English)

emprunté [ɑ̃prœ̃te] **adj** *(manière, personne)* self-conscious, stiff, awkward; **il était tellement impressionné par elle qu'il en devenait e.** he was so impressed by her that it made him self-conscious; **dit-elle d'un ton e.** she said self-consciously *or* awkwardly

emprunter [ɑ̃prœ̃te] **vt 1** *(objet, argent)* to borrow (**à** from); **est-ce que je peux t'e. ton fiancé pour cette danse?** can I borrow your fiancé for this dance?; **elle a emprunté ses manières à sa mère** she copies her mother's ways **2** *(route, chemin)* to take; **le cortège emprunta la rue de Rivoli** the procession took *or* went down the Rue de Rivoli
vi to take out a loan, to borrow; **e. à long/ court terme** to borrow long/short; **e. à intérêt** to borrow at interest

emprunteur, -euse [ɑ̃prœ̃tœr, -øz] **n** borrower

empuantir [ɑ̃pɥɑ̃tir] **vt** to make stink; *(pièce)* to stink out, to make stink

EMS [ɛmɛs] **nm** *Ordinat (abrév* **enhanced messaging service)** EMS

ému [emy] **adj** *(touché)* moved, touched; *(passionné)* roused; **voix émue** voice filled with emotion; **garder un souvenir é. de qch** to retain a touching memory of sth; **j'en suis encore tout é.** I still haven't got over it; **être é. (jusqu')aux larmes par qch** to be moved to tears by sth; **il était trop é. pour s'asseoir/lui parler** he was too nervous to sit down/talk to her

émulateur [emylatœr] **nm** *Ordinat* emulator; **é. de terminal** terminal emulator; **é. graphique** graphics emulator

émulation [emylasjɔ̃] **nf 1** *(concurrence)* competitiveness **2** *Ordinat* emulation; **é. de terminal** terminal emulation

émule [emyl] **n** *(imitateur)* emulator; *(concurrent)* competitor; **j'ai fait des émules** people followed my lead *or* example

émuler [emyle] **vt** *Ordinat* to emulate

émulseur [emylsœr] **nm** *(appareil)* emulsifier

émulsif, -ive [emylsif, -iv] **adj** *Pharm* emulsive; *Chimie* emulsifying

émulsifiable [emylsifjabl] **adj** *Chimie* emulsifiable

émulsifiant [emylsifjɑ̃] **adj** emulsifying **nm** emulsifier

émulsifier [emylsifje] **vt** to emulsify

émulsion [emylsjɔ̃] **nf** emulsion

émulsionner [emylsjɔne] **vt** to emulsify

EN [əɛn] NF *Anciennement abrév* École normale

EN¹ [ɑ̃]

> in **1–4, 6, 8, 9** ▪ to **1, 7, 8** ▪ at **1, 4, 6** ▪ on **1, 4, 11** ▪ about **2** ▪ within **2** ▪ made of **5** ▪ into **7** ▪ by **9** ▪ as **10, 11** ▪ like **10** ▪ + ing **11**

PRÉP SEE GRAMMAR B55–6 **1** *(lieu)* in; *(avec mouvement)* to; **être/aller en ville/montagne** to be in/to go (in)to town/the mountains; **en province** in the country, in the provinces; **il est parti en mer** he's gone to sea; **une promenade en mer** a boat trip; **en tête/queue** at the head/in the rear; **la suite en page quatre** continued on page four; **aller en France/Amérique** to go to France/America; **être en Avignon/Arles** to be in Avignon/Arles; **être en Saône-et-Loire** to be in Saône-et-Loire; **regarder en l'air** to look up at the sky; **le mariage aura lieu en l'église Saint-Jean** the marriage will be celebrated *or* held at St. John's (Church); **c'était comment en classe aujourd'hui?** how was school today?; **le Christ en croix** Jesus on the cross; **garde ça en mémoire** keep that in mind; **de branche en branche** from branch to branch

2 *(avec pron pers)* **il y a quelque chose en lui que j'admire** there is something I admire about him; **un homme en qui** *ou* **en lequel j'ai confiance** a man whom I trust; **c'est en nous-mêmes que nous devons chercher la réponse** we must look for the answer within ourselves; **en chaque être** in every being

3 *(temps)* in; **en été/automne/hiver** in (the) summer/autumn/winter; **né en 1967** born in 1967; **en avril** in April; **aujourd'hui en huit** a week today; **on peut y aller en cinq heures** you can get there in five hours; **en l'an 1800** in (the year) 1800; **en ce temps-là** in those days, at that time; **d'année en année** from year to year, year by year; **son état s'aggravait de jour en jour** he was getting worse by the day; **fermé en semaine** closed weekdays; **il a été guéri en deux semaines** he was cured (with)in two weeks

4 *(état)* in; **être en deuil/en loques/en tenue de sport** to be in mourning/in rags/in sports clothes; **lait en poudre** powdered milk; **en vers/prose** in verse/prose; **en direct** live; **laisser les choses en l'état** to leave everything as it is; **en l'absence du chef** in the absence of the boss; **en présence de mon avocat** in the presence of my lawyer; **arbres en fleur** trees in blossom *or* flower; **être en guerre** to be at war; **en vacances** on holiday

5 *(composition)* made of; **montre en or** gold watch; **c'est en or** it's made of gold; **table en marbre** marble table; **évier en inox®** stainless-steel sink; **pull en laine** woollen sweater

6 *(description)* **escalier en spirale** spiral staircase; **chemin en pente** sloping road; **docteur en médecine** doctor of medicine; **peintre en bâtiment** house painter; **fort/faible en mathématiques** good/bad at mathematics; **parler en français/anglais** to speak in French/English; **marcher en silence** to walk in silence; **en votre honneur** in your honour

7 *(annonce un changement)* into; **changé en serpent** changed into a serpent; **traduire une lettre en français** to translate a letter into French; **peindre qch en bleu** to paint sth blue; **de mal en pis** from bad to worse; **tomber en admiration devant qn/qch** to be filled with admiration for sb/sth

8 *(indique une division)* **briser qch en morceaux** to break sth (in)to bits; **casser qch en deux** to break sth in two; **pièce en trois actes** play in three acts; **vendre en paquets/feuilles** to sell in packets/sheets

9 *(manière)* **s'épuiser en d'inutiles efforts** to exhaust oneself in useless efforts; **venir en taxi/avion** to come by taxi/by plane *or* air; **en trois bonds** in three jumps

10 *(comme)* **envoyer qch en cadeau** to send sth as a present; **donner qch à qn en compensation** to give sb sth by way of *or* as compensation; **il mourut en brave** he died like the brave man that he was; **agir en honnête homme** to act like an honest man; **prendre la chose en philosophe** to take it philosophically

11 *(avec gérondif)* **il marchait en lisant son journal** he walked along reading his paper; **il répondit en riant** he answered with a laugh; **elle entra/sortit en dansant** she danced in/out; **on apprend en vieillissant** we learn as we grow older; **il s'est aigri en vieillissant** he has become embittered with age; **en faisant cela vous l'offenserez** you'll offend him by doing that; **en arrivant à Paris** on arriving in Paris; **en vous écrivant hier j'ai oublié de vous le dire** I forgot to mention it when writing to you yesterday; **en attendant** while waiting, in the meantime; **tout en tricotant, elle nous racontait des histoires** as she knitted she told us stories; **s'enrhumer en marchant sous la pluie** to catch a cold (through *or* from) walking in the rain; **tout en étant riche, il vit très simplement** whilst (he is) rich, he leads a very simple life SEE GRAMMAR B38

EN²

> from there **1** ▪ it **2–7** ▪ some/any **6–8**

PRON SEE GRAMMAR B19–20 **1** *(de cet endroit)* from there; **il en revient** he's just come back from there; **où en étions-nous?** *(dans un livre, travail etc)* where were we?; **j'en sors à l'instant** I'm just leaving

2 *(de ce fait)* **si vous étiez riche, en seriez-vous plus heureux?** if you were rich, would you be happier for it *or* any the happier?; **je n'en dors plus la nuit** it keeps me awake at night, I can't sleep at night for it; **j'en ris encore** I still laugh about it; **en tirer une conclusion** to draw a conclusion from it; **j'en suis encore toute retournée** I'm still all of a flutter

3 *(remplaçant un nom régi par* de*)* **j'aime mieux ne pas en parler** I would rather not speak about it; **combien en demande-t-il** *ou* **en veut-il?** how much does he want for it?; **qu'en pensez-vous?** what do you think of *or* about it?; **les rues en sont pleines** the streets are full of it/them; **il reçut une blessure et en mourut** he received a wound and died of *or* from it; **il en devint amoureux** he fell in love with her; **il faut en faire un film!** they should make a film of it *or* turn it into a film!; **que vais-je en faire, de cette table?** what am I going to do with this table?; *Fam* **en être** *(être homosexuel)* to be one of them

4 *(de choses, remplaçant le possessif)* **j'ai la valise mais je n'en ai pas la clef** I have the suitcase but I haven't (got) the key (for it); **prends la boîte mais n'en perds pas le couvercle** take the box, but don't lose the lid (of it); **je ne savais rien de cet endroit, je n'en connaissais que le nom** I didn't know anything about the place, I only knew the name

5 *(remplaçant une proposition)* **il ne l'a pas fait, mais il en est capable** he didn't do it but he's (quite) capable of it

6 *(nombre, quantité)* **j'en ai un/trois/plusieurs** I have one/three/several (of them); **combien en voulez-vous?** *(quantité)* how much do you want?; *(nombre)* how many do you want?; **elle en a déjà vu beaucoup pour son âge** she has already seen a lot for her age; **j'en ai** I have some; **je n'en ai pas** I don't have any, I have none; **en avez-vous?** do you

have any, have you (got) any?; **parmi ses livres il y en a d'excellents** some of his books are excellent; **il en a mangé deux cuillerées** he ate two spoonfuls (of it)

7 *(locutions)* **je n'en ai pas encore fini avec lui** I haven't done *or* finished with him yet; **si le cœur vous en dit** if you feel so inclined, if you feel like it; **en venir aux mains** to come to blows; **est-ce à ça que tu en es réduit?** have you been reduced to that?; **ne t'en fais pas!** don't worry!; **il en va de même pour toi** it's the same for you; **il en est ainsi** that's the way it is; **je n'en puis plus** I can't bear it any longer; **elle en aime un autre** she loves someone else; **à en croire les racontars** if we are able to believe the tales; **il y en a qui … some people …**

8 *(après un impératif)* **prenez-en** take some; **prenez-en dix** take ten (of them); **va-t'en, allez-vous-en** go away; **va en chercher** go and get some; **donne-m'en!, ** *Fam* **donne-moi-z-en!** give me some!; **souvenez-vous-en!** remember!

9 *(après la forme pronominale de certains verbes)* **s'en aller** to go away; **il s'en est allé** he went away; **s'en retourner** to go back, to return

en³ [ɛn] NM *Typ* en

ENA [ena] NF *abrév* École nationale d'administration

enamouré [ɑ̃namure], **énamouré** [enamure] ADJ *(regard, sourire etc)* amorous; **être e.** *ou* **é. de qn** to be enamoured *or Am* enamored of sb

enamourer (s') [sɑ̃namure], **énamourer (s')** [senamure] VPR to become enamoured *or Am* enamored **(de** of)

énarchie [enarʃi] NF *Fam* = elite system dominated by the graduates of the École nationale d'administration

énarque [enark] N = graduate of the École nationale d'administration

en-arrière [ɑ̃narjɛr] NM INV *(au patinage)* backward glide

énarthrose [enartroz] NF *Anat* ball-and-socket joint, *Spéc* enarthrosis

en-avant [ɑ̃navɑ̃] NM INV **1** *Rugby* forward pass; *(dans les mains)* knock-on **2** *(au patinage)* forward glide

en-but [ɑ̃by(t)] NM INV *Rugby* in-goal

encabaner (s') [sɑ̃kabane] VPR *Can* to shut oneself up in a hut

encablure [ɑ̃kablyr] NF *Arch (mesure)* cable (length) *(approx 200 m)*; *Hum* **je n'habite qu'à quelques encablures du bureau** I live a stone's throw from the office

encadré [ɑ̃kadre] NM *Journ, Typ (dans un texte)* boxed; *(presse écrite)* boxed article; *(petites annonces)* display advertisement; *Ordinat* **e. graphique** graphics box; *Ordinat* **e. texte** text box
ADJ panelled-in, boxed

encadrement [ɑ̃kadrəmɑ̃] NM **1** *(d'un tableau, d'une fenêtre etc)* *(action)* framing; *(cadre)* frame; **dans l'e. de la porte** in the doorway; *Tech* **e. en caoutchouc** rubber seal
2 *Admin, Ind, Sport etc (action d'encadrer)* *(du personnel, d'une équipe sportive)* management; *(d'un groupe d'enfants, de handicapés, d'étudiants)* supervision; *Mil (d'une unité)* officering; *(personnes qui encadrent)* *(du personnel, d'une équipe sportive)* management, managers; *Mil* officers; *(cadres)* executives; **fonctions d'e.** executive functions; **personnel d'e.** management, managerial staff; **e. d'une colonie de vacances** supervisory staff of a holiday camp
3 *Écon* **e. du crédit** restriction on credit, credit restriction(s) *or* squeeze; **diminuer l'e. du crédit** to reduce credit restrictions, to loosen the credit squeeze; **e. des loyers** rent control; **e. des prix** price control(s)

encadrer [ãkadre] VT **1** *(tableau, photo, porte etc)* to frame

2 *(entourer) (des mots, une phrase)* to circle; *(le visage)* to frame; **jardin encadré de haies** garden enclosed by hedges; **il était encadré par deux gendarmes** flanked by two policemen; **encadré de ses gardes du corps/de jolies filles** surrounded by his bodyguards/by pretty girls

3 *Admin, Ind, Sport etc (personnel, équipe)* to manage; *(groupe d'enfants, de handicapés, d'étudiants)* to supervise; *Mil (unité)* to officer; **nous sommes bien encadrés** our management is good

4 *Écon (prix, loyers, crédits)* to control

5 *Fam (supporter)* **je ne peux pas l'e.** I can't stand *or* abide him

6 *Fam (entrer dans)* **il a encadré un arbre** he wrapped his vehicle round a tree

encadreur, -euse [ãkadrœr, -øz] N picture framer

encager [ãkaʒe] VT (j'encageai(s); n. encageons) *(oiseau, animal)* to cage; **tenir qn encagé** to keep sb caged up; **tenir un oiseau/un animal encagé** to keep a bird/an animal in a cage *or* caged up

encagoulé [ãkagule] ADJ hooded

encaissable [ãkesabl] ADJ cashable, *Br* encashable

encaisse [ãkes] NF *Com* cash (in hand); **e. de 1000 euros** cash balance of 1,000 euros; **e. or et argent** *ou* **e. métallique d'un pays** gold and silver holding of a country; *Banque* **pas d'e.** no funds

encaissé [ãkese] ADJ *(vallée)* deep; *(rivière)* deeply embanked; *(route)* sunken

encaissement [ãkesmã] NM **1** *(d'un chèque)* cashing, paying in, *Br* encashment; *(d'argent)* receipt, collection; *(d'une traite)* collection; **donner un chèque à l'e.** to cash a cheque; **encaissements et décaissements** cash inflows and outflows **2** *(d'une vallée)* depth; *(d'une rivière)* deep embankment; **dans l'e. de la route** in the deep cutting made by the road

encaisser [ãkese] VT **1** *(chèque)* to cash, *Br* to encash; *(argent)* to receive, to collect; *(traite)* to collect; **e. de l'argent** *(sur son compte)* to pay in cash; *Bourse* **e. un premium** to receive a premium **2** *Fam (supporter) (des coups, des remarques, des critiques)* to take; **je ne sais comment il fait pour e. les coups aussi bien** I don't know how he stands up to being hit; **je n'arrive plus à e. ma belle-mère** I can't take my mother-in-law any more; **je ne peux pas l'e.** I can't stand him/her **3** *(resserrer) (de collines)* to hem in; *Tech (rivière etc)* to embank **4** *Com* **e. des marchandises** to pack goods

VPR **s'encaisser** *(d'une rivière, route etc)* to be hemmed in; **la route s'encaisse profondément entre les montagnes** mountains tower above the road on both sides

VI *Fam* **il sait e.** he can take it; **qu'est-ce qu'il a encaissé!** he took a lot of punishment; **elle a plutôt bien encaissé** she took it rather well; **e. sans broncher** to grin and bear it

encaisseur [ãkesœr] NM *(de loyer, dettes etc)* collector

encan [ãkã] NM **vendre qch à l'e.** to sell sth by *or* at auction; *aussi Fig* **mettre qch à l'e.** to put sth up for auction; *Fig* **la loi semble mettre la justice à l'e.** the law seems to put a low price on justice

encanaillement [ãkanajmã] NM slumming it

encanailler (s') [sãkanaje] VPR to like slumming it, to hang around with doubtful characters; **il faudrait qu'elle s'encanaille un peu** she ought to break out *or* loosen up a bit and live

encapuchonner [ãkapyʃɔne] VT *(personne, la tête de quelqu'un)* to put a hood on; *(machine)* to put a hood on, to cover (with a hood); *(stylo)* to put the top on; **encapuchonné** hooded

VPR **s'encapuchonner** to put on a *or* one's hood

encart [ãkar] NM *Journ* slip sheet; *(attaché)* inset; *(mobile)* (loose) insert; **e. dépliant** gatefold; **e. publicitaire** *Journ* advertising supplement; *TV, Radio* commercial break

encartage [ãkartaʒ] NM *Typ* inserting, insetting

encarté [ãkarte] ADJ *(membre)* card-carrying; **il est e. au PC** he's a card-carrying *or* paid-up member of the communist party

encarter [ãkarte] VT **1** *Typ (pages)* to inset; *(notice dans un livre)* to insert **2** *(épingles, boutons etc)* to card

en-cas [ãka] NM INV snack (meal)

encaserner [ãkazɛrne] VT *Mil* to put in barracks; **être encaserné à** to be barracked at

encastrable [ãkastrabl] ADJ *(machine à laver, cuisinière etc)* that can be built in *or* fitted

encastré [ãkastre] ADJ *(machine à laver, cuisinière)* built-in, fitted; *(four, baignoire)* built-in; *(interrupteur)* flush-fitting, set-in

encastrement [ãkastrəmã] NM **1** *(action) (d'une machine à laver, cuisinière)* fitting, building in; *(d'un interrupteur)* flush-fitting, setting in **2** *(espace prévu)* recess

encastrer [ãkastre] VT *(machine à laver, cuisinière)* to build in, to fit; *(four, baignoire)* to build in; *(interrupteur)* to flush fit, to set in

VPR **s'encastrer** *(de deux éléments)* to fit together; **s'e. dans** *(d'une machine à laver, une cuisinière)* to fit into; **la voiture s'est encastrée sous un camion** the car embedded itself under a lorry

encaustiquage [ãkɔstikaʒ, ãko-] NM *(d'un parquet, de meubles)* waxing, wax-polishing

encaustique [ãkɔstik, ãko-] NF *(pour les meubles)* wax, polish

encaustiquer [ãkɔstike, ãko-] VT *(parquet, meubles)* to wax, to polish

encavage [ãkavaʒ] NM *Suisse (de vin)* cellarage, cellaring; *(de fromage, légumes, fruits)* storage in a cellar

encavement [ãkavmã] NM *(du vin)* cellaring

encaver [ãkave] VT *(vin etc)* to cellar

encaveur [ãkavœr] NM **1** *(ouvrier)* cellarman **2** *Suisse (négociant)* wine-maker, wine producer

enceindre [ãsɛdr] VT *(conj like* **ceindre***)* to surround (**de** with)

enceinte¹ [ãsɛ̃t] NF **1** *(mur)* (surrounding) wall; *(palissade)* fence **2** *(espace)* enclosure; *(d'église, de couvent)* precinct(s); *Courses de chevaux* ring; **dans l'e. du parc** within *or* inside (the confines of) the park; **il est interdit de pénétrer en voiture dans l'e. du parc** cars may not enter the park, cars are not allowed into the park; **dans l'e. de l'école** on school premises; **en dehors de l'e. de l'école** outside school **3** *(sonore)* **e. (acoustique)** speaker

enceinte² ADJ F pregnant, *Fam* expecting, *Litt* with child; **femme e.** pregnant woman, expectant mother; **e. de cinq mois** five months pregnant; **être e. d'un petit garçon/de jumeaux** to be expecting a little boy/twins; **elle est e. de Paul** she's pregnant by Paul, she's expecting Paul's child; **mettre qn e.** to make *or* get sb pregnant

encens [ãsã] NM incense

encensement [ãsãsmã] NM **1** *Rel* censing **2** *Fig* flattery, toadying

encenser [ãsãse] VT **1** *Rel* to cense **2** *Fig* **e. qn** to flatter sb outrageously

VI *(d'un cheval)* to toss its head up and down

> Attention: le verbe anglais **to incense** est un faux ami. Il signifie **rendre furieux**.

encenseur, -euse [ãsãsœr, -øz] N **1** *Rel* thurifer, censer bearer **2** *Fig Vieilli* sycophant

encensoir [ãsãswar] NM *Rel* censer; *Fig Péj* **donner des coups d'e.** to butter people up; **donner des coups d'e. à qui il faut** to butter up the right people

encéphale [ãsefal] NM brain, encephalon

encéphalite [ãsefalit] NF *Méd* encephalitis; **e. léthargique** sleeping sickness; *Vét* **e. bovine spongiforme** bovine spongiform encephalopathy, BSE

encéphalogramme [ãsefalɔgram] NM *Méd* (electro)encephalogram

encéphalographie [ãsefalɔgrafi] NF *Méd* (electro)encephalography

encéphalomyélite [ãsefalɔmjelit] NF *Méd* encephalomyelitis

encerclement [ãsɛrkləmã] NM encircling, surrounding; **après l'e. de l'ennemi** after the enemy was surrounded *or* encircled

encercler [ãsɛrkle] VT **1** *(ennemi, manifestants etc)* to encircle, to surround **2** *(mot)* to circle, to ring

enchaîné [ãʃene] NM *TV, Cin* dissolve, mix

enchaînement [ãʃɛnmã] NM **1** *(série) (d'événements)* series, chain, train; *(d'idées, de mesures)* series **2** *(liaison) (d'idées, de séquences etc)* linking, connection; *TV, Cin (entre deux vues)* melt; **l'e. des paragraphes est très important** the way in which the paragraphs follow on from each other *or* the paragraphs are linked is very important **3** *(en danse)* sequence (of steps); *(en ballet)* enchaînement **4** *(dans un spectacle)* filler **5** *Ordinat* concatenation

enchaîner [ãʃene] VT **1** *(animal)* to chain up; *(prisonnier)* to chain up, to put in chains; *Fig (la presse, les passions)* to curb; **e. à un poteau** to chain (up) to a post **2** *(lier) (idées, faits, mots etc)* to link (up), to connect; **il est incapable d'e. deux phrases** he can't string *or* put two sentences together; **ils enchaînaient les sujets très vite** they moved very quickly from one subject to another; **e. le tournage de plusieurs épisodes** to shoot several episodes one after the other; **pour la répétition de ce soir, on enchaîne toutes les scènes/chansons** at this evening's rehearsal we'll run through all the scenes/songs one after the other without a break **3** *Cin, TV* to dissolve

VI **1** *(continuer)* to move on, to go on, to carry on; **e. sur un sujet** to move on to a subject; **on enchaîne avec les nouvelles internationales** we'll move on to the international news **2** *Cin* to dissolve, to fade *(into next scene)*; *Théâtre* to carry straight on

VPR **s'enchaîner** *(de faits, d'épisodes etc)* to be linked together; **on voit comme les choses s'enchaînent** you can see how things hang together *or* are linked together; **les événements se sont enchaînés très vite** things moved *or* happened very quickly

enchanté [ãʃãte] ADJ **1** *(magique etc) (personne, objet, endroit)* enchanted; **la Flûte enchantée** the Magic Flute **2** *(ravi)* enchanted, delighted; **être e. de qch** to be enchanted by *or* delighted with sth; **e. (de faire votre connaissance)** pleased to meet you, how do you do?

enchantement [ãʃãtmã] NM **1** *(magie)* enchantment, magic; *(effet)* (magic) spell; **rompre un e.** to break a spell; **comme par e.** as if by magic; **c'est par e. qu'elle s'est transformée en princesse** she was magically turned into a princess **2** *(ravissement)* enchantment, delight; *(merveille)* delight; **être dans l'e.** to be enchanted *(* **de** *by)*

enchanter [ɑ̃ʃɑ̃te] **VT 1** *(ensorceler)* to enchant, to bewitch, to cast a spell on **2** *(ravir, plaire à)* to enchant, to delight; **cette idée ne l'enchante pas** he's not taken with the idea *or* keen on the idea

enchanteur, -eresse [ɑ̃ʃɑ̃tœr, -res] **NM 1** *(sorcier)* enchanter **2** *Fig (charmeur)* charmer

  NF enchanteresse enchantress

  ADJ *(sourire)* bewitching, captivating; *(discours, endroit etc)* enchanting, delightful, charming

enchâssement [ɑ̃ʃɑsmɑ̃] **NM** *(d'un bijou)* setting, mounting

enchâsser [ɑ̃ʃase] **VT 1** *Rel (relique)* to enshrine **2** *(bijou)* to set, to mount **3** *Fig (dans un texte)* to insert, to slot in

  VPR s'enchâsser to fit perfectly *(* **dans** *into)*

enchâssure [ɑ̃ʃasyr] **NF** *(support) (d'un bijou)* setting, mount

enchère [ɑ̃ʃɛr] **NF** bid; **les enchères, l'e.** the bidding; **commencer les enchères à 2000 euros** to start the bidding at 2,000 euros; **faire** *ou* **porter une e.** to make a bid; **vente aux enchères** (sale by) auction; **enchères publiques** public auction; **couvrir une e.** to make a higher bid, to bid higher; **couvrir l'e. de qn** to bid higher than sb, to outbid sb; **pousser** *ou* **faire monter les enchères** to raise *or* push up the bidding; *Fig* to increase the stakes; **vendre/acheter qch aux enchères** to sell/buy sth at auction; **mettre qch aux enchères** to put sth up for auction, to auction sth (off); *Fig* **il l'a pour ainsi dire mise aux enchères** he auctioned her off *or* sold her to the highest bidder, so to speak; *Cartes* **manille aux enchères** auction bridge; **système des enchères** *(au bridge)* bidding system

enchérir [ɑ̃ʃerir] **VI 1** *(dépasser)* to make a higher bid; **e. de dix euros** to bid another ten euros; **e. sur qn** to outbid sb, to make a higher bid than sb; *Fig* to go one better than sb; **e. sur le prix des marchandises** to make a higher bid for the goods **2** *Vieilli (devenir plus cher)* to rise *or* go up in price

enchérissement [ɑ̃ʃerismɑ̃] **NM** *Vieilli (de prix)* rise, increase

enchérisseur, -euse [ɑ̃ʃerisœr, -øz] **N** bidder; **au plus offrant et dernier e.** to the highest bidder

enchevaucher [ɑ̃ʃ(ə)voʃe] **VT** *(tuiles etc)* to fix *or* lay with an overlap

enchevêtré [ɑ̃ʃ(ə)vetre] **ADJ** *(écheveau, fils)* tangled, in a tangle; *(style, idées)* confused; *(affaires, revues)* in a mess; **un amas de branches enchevêtrées** a tangle of branches

enchevêtrement [ɑ̃ʃ(ə)vetrəmɑ̃] **NM** *(de fils, branches)* tangle; *(d'objets, d'idées)* confusion, muddle; **l'e. de ses idées est tel que ...** he is so confused that ...; **comment s'y retrouver dans cet e. d'événements?** how on earth are you supposed to make sense of these events when they're all so confused?

enchevêtrer [ɑ̃ʃ(ə)vetre] **VT** *(fils, branches etc)* to tangle (up); *(situation)* to confuse, to muddle

  VPR s'enchevêtrer *(de fils, branches etc)* to get tangled *or* in a tangle; *(d'objets)* to get muddled (up) *or* mixed up; *(d'une situation)* to get confused *or* muddled

enchifrené [ɑ̃ʃifrəne] **ADJ** *Vieilli* **il est e.** his nose is blocked

enclave [ɑ̃klav] **NF** *(terrain)*, *Fig* enclave; **l'escalier fait e. dans la pièce** the staircase leads directly from *or* into the room

enclaver [ɑ̃klave] **VT 1** *(poutres etc)* to wedge in, to fit in **2** *(territoire)* to enclose, to make

an enclave of; **domaine qui enclave deux petites terres** estate which encloses two small properties **3** *(une pièce dans une autre)* to fit *(* **dans** *into)*; **e. deux anneaux l'un dans l'autre** to interlock two rings, to fit two rings together

enclenchement [ɑ̃klɑ̃ʃmɑ̃] **NM** *Tech (d'une vitesse, d'un mécanisme etc)* engaging; *(de pièces)* interlocking

enclencher [ɑ̃klɑ̃ʃe] **VT** *(vitesse, mécanisme etc)* to engage; *(pièces)* to interlock; *Fig (entreprise, projet etc)* to set in motion, to get under way; *Fig* **maintenant que le processus est enclenché, ça va être difficile de faire marche arrière** now that things have been set in motion *or* are under way, there's no going back

  VPR s'enclencher *(d'une vitesse, d'un mécanisme etc)* to engage; *(de pièces)* to interlock; *Fig* **bien/mal s'e.** to get off to a good/bad start

enclin [ɑ̃klɛ̃] **ADJ** inclined, disposed (**à faire qch** to do sth); **elle est encline à la paresse/à la panique** she is inclined *or* tends to be lazy/to panic; **il est e. à l'alcoolisme** he is inclined to drink, he has alcoholic tendencies

enclitique [ɑ̃klitik] **NM** *Ling* enclitic

enclore [ɑ̃klɔr] **VT** *(conj like* **clore***)* to enclose; *(d'une palissade)* to fence in; *(d'un mur)* to wall in

enclos [ɑ̃klo] **NM 1** *(espace)* enclosure; *(pour chevaux)* paddock **2** *(clôture)* enclosure; *(mur)* (enclosing) wall

enclume [ɑ̃klym] **NF 1** anvil; **e. de cordonnier** (shoemender's) last; *Fig* **être entre le marteau et l'e.** to be between the devil and the deep (blue) sea **2** *Anat (de l'oreille interne)* anvil

encoche [ɑ̃kɔʃ] **NF** *(dans un morceau de bois)* notch (**à, sur** in); *(d'une flèche)* nock; *(pour répertoire à onglets)* notch; *Ordinat* **e. de protection contre l'écriture** write-protect notch; *Élec* **armature à encoches** slotted armature

encochement [ɑ̃kɔʃmɑ̃] **NM** notching

encocher [ɑ̃kɔʃe] **VT** *(morceau de bois)* to notch; *(livre)* to thumb-index

encodage [ɑ̃kɔdaʒ] **NM** *Ling, Ordinat* encoding

encoder [ɑ̃kɔde] **VT** *Ling, Ordinat* to encode

encodeur [ɑ̃kɔdœr] **NM** *Ordinat* encoder

encoignure [ɑ̃kwaɲyr] **NF 1** *(d'une pièce)* corner, angle **2** *(petit meuble)* corner cupboard

encollage [ɑ̃kɔlaʒ] **NM** *(à l'aide de colle) (de papier)* pasting; *(de bois)* glueing; *(à l'aide d'apprêt) (de papier, tissu, plâtre etc)* sizing; *Typ* perfect binding

encoller [ɑ̃kɔle] **VT** *(à l'aide de colle) (papier)* to paste; *(bois etc)* to glue, to apply glue to; *(à l'aide d'apprêt) (papier, tissu, plâtre etc)* to size

encolure [ɑ̃kɔlyr] **NF 1** *(de chameau, d'autruche etc)* neck; *Courses de chevaux* **gagner d'une e.** to win by a neck **2** *(tour de cou)* neck size; **homme de forte e.** thickset *or* stocky man **3** *(échancrure) (d'un vêtement)* neck (opening); **e. carrée** square neck

encombrant [ɑ̃kɔ̃brɑ̃] **ADJ** *(meuble, valise etc)* cumbersome, bulky; *(colis)* bulky; **ce canapé est e.** the sofa is too big, the sofa takes up too much space *or* is in the way; **ils l'ont liquidé** *car* **il devenait trop e.** they bumped him off because he was becoming too much of a liability; **un témoin e.** an unwanted witness

  NMPL *Région* **les encombrants passent demain** the bulk refuse disposal people are coming tomorrow; **mettre qch aux encombrants** to put sth out for collection; **j'ai**

trouvé cette table aux encombrants I found this table in among rubbish put out for collection

encombre [ɑ̃kɔ̃br] **NM** **sans e.** without mishap, safely; **il a obtenu son diplôme sans e.** he got his degree without any problem

encombrement [ɑ̃kɔ̃brəmɑ̃] **NM 1** *(état) (de la circulation)* congestion; *(des rues, de l'espace aérien)* overcrowding; *(de lignes téléphoniques)* jamming, blocking; *(de texte)* clutter, litter; **il y a un tel e. de livres dans son bureau** his/her office is so cluttered up with books **3** *(espace, volume) (d'une voiture, d'un meuble etc)* (overall) dimensions **4** *Ordinat* footprint; **faible e. sur le disque dur** low use of hard disk space

encombrer [ɑ̃kɔ̃bre] **VT** *(pièce)* to clutter (up); *(passage, route etc)* to obstruct, to block; *(lignes téléphoniques)* to jam, to block; **e. les rues** to congest the streets; **table encombrée de papiers** table littered with papers; **sentier encombré de ronces** path overgrown with brambles; **les lignes téléphoniques sont vraiment encombrées** the telephone lines are really busy; **e. le marché** to glut *or* saturate the market; **j'ai les mains encombrées** my hands are full; **je ne veux pas de ce divan, il m'encombrerait** I don't want this sofa, it would just clutter my place up; **tu m'encombres, sors d'ici!** you're getting under my feet, get out!

  VPR s'encombrer s'e. de *(colis, équipement etc)* to load oneself down with; *Fig (obligations, enfants etc)* to burden oneself *or* saddle oneself with; **je ne vais pas m'e. de scrupules** I'm not going to be over-scrupulous

encontre (à l') [alɑ̃kɔ̃tr] **ADV** in opposition; **cela va à l'e. de la loi** that's against the law; **tu n'as pas le droit d'aller à l'e. du projet** you have no right to try to stop *or* go against the project; **cela va à l'e. de ce qu'il proposait la semaine dernière** that's the opposite of *or* contradicts what he was saying last week; **ces nouvelles méthodes vont à l'e. de tout ce qu'on m'a toujours appris** these new methods go against *or* are contrary to *or* run counter to everything I've been taught; **cela va à l'e. du bon sens** it goes against common sense

encorbellement [ɑ̃kɔrbɛlmɑ̃] **NM** *Archit (d'un mur etc)* corbelling; *(d'un étage supérieur)* overhang; **fenêtre en e.** oriel window

encorder (s') [sɑ̃kɔrde] **VPR** *(en alpinisme)* to rope up

ENCORE [ɑ̃kɔr]

still **1–3** ▪ not yet *(pas encore)* **2** ▪ more **3** ▪ another **3, 4** ▪ again **4** ▪ even more/less *(encore plus/moins)* **3** ▪ moreover **5** ▪ if that *(et encore)* **6** ▪ although *(encore que)* **7** ▪ only **9**

ADV 1 *(toujours)* still; **je cherche e. une explication** I am still looking for an explanation; **je ne suis e. qu'étudiant** I'm still only a student, I'm only a student as yet

  2 pas e. not yet; **elle n'est pas e. mariée** she isn't married yet, she's still not married; **elle n'est e. jamais** *ou* **e. pas venue me voir** she hasn't come to see me yet, she still hasn't come to see me; **un homme que je n'avais e. jamais vu** a man I'd never seen before

  3 *(davantage)* more; **e. un mot** (just) one word more; **en voulez-vous e.?** would you like some more?; **e. du vin, s'il vous plaît!** some more wine please!; **e. une tasse de café** another cup of coffee; **pendant trois mois e., pendant e. trois mois** for three months longer, for another three months; **il est e. plus beau que je ne le pensais** he's even better looking than I thought; **il y a e.**

moins de relief que dans mon pays it's even flatter than where I come from; **réduire e. le prix** to reduce the price still or even further or more; **c'est e. pire** it's even worse, it's worse still

4 (de nouveau) again; **voilà e. la pluie!** here's the rain again!; **nous l'avons e. vu hier** we saw him again yesterday; **qu'est-ce qu'il a e. fait?** now what's he done?, what's he done now or this time?; **il y a e. eu un meurtre d'enfant** another child has been murdered; **quoi e.?** now what?; **e. une fois** once more, once again; **e. autant** as much again; **e. vous!** (what) you again?

5 (en plus) moreover, furthermore; **non seulement stupide, mais e. têtu** not only stupid, but also pigheaded or Fam but pigheaded to boot; **que faut-il que je prenne e.?** what else do I need to take?

6 (restrictif) **e. s'il était reconnaissant!** if only he was at least grateful!; **si e. je savais où il se cache** if I only knew or if only I knew where he was hiding; **il aura peut-être une chance là-bas, et e.!** perhaps he'll have a chance over there, but only just or but not much of one!; **il vous en donnera dix euros et e.!** he'll give you ten euros for it, if that!; Fam **il faudrait e. que je trouve une voiture!** for a start or first I would have to find a car!; **(mais) e. faudrait-il qu'elle accepte!** she has to agree first!

7 e. que + sub (al)though, even though; **e. qu'il ne me soit rien** (al)though he is nothing to me; **temps agréable e. qu'un peu froid** pleasant if or though rather cold weather

8 il a dit qu'il avait bien aimé – mais e.? he said he liked it – but what exactly did he say?; **elle est sympa – mais e.?** she's nice – yes, go on!

9 (pas plus tard que) **hier e. je lui ai parlé** I spoke to him only yesterday, I just spoke to him yesterday; **c'est ce que nous nous disions e. hier soir** ou **hier soir e.** that's what we were saying only or just last night

encorné [ãkɔrne] ADJ (animal) horned

encorner [ãkɔrne] VT (d'un taureau) to gore

encornet [ãkɔrnɛ] NM (mollusque) squid

encoubler (s') [sãkuble] VPR Suisse to trip over

encourageant [ãkuraʒã] ADJ (personne) encouraging; (nouvelles, résultat, événement etc) encouraging, heartening

encouragement [ãkuraʒmã] NM encouragement; **prime d'e.** incentive; **e. à la vertu/au crime** incentive to virtue/to crime; **recevoir peu d'encouragements à faire qch** to receive little encouragement or little inducement to do sth

encourager [ãkuraʒe] (j'encourageai(s)) **1** (personne) to encourage; (athlète, équipe) to encourage, to cheer on; **ils m'ont beaucoup encouragé** they gave me a lot of encouragement; **être encouragé par qn** to be encouraged by sb, to receive or get encouragement from sb; **encouragé par les premiers résultats** encouraged or heartened by the first results; **elle l'a encouragé d'un sourire** she gave him an encouraging smile, she smiled at him encouragingly; **e. qn à faire qch** to encourage sb to do sth **2** (arts) to encourage, to foster, to promote; (plan) to promote; **la presse encourage l'utilisation de certaines drogues** the press encourages the use of certain drugs; **l'oisiveté encourage le vice** idleness encourages or promotes vice

encourir [ãkurir] VT (conj like courir) (dépense) to incur; (punition, reproches, sanctions) to incur, to bring (up)on oneself; **e. des risques** to run risks; **il sait qu'il encourt une lourde punition** he knows he risks being severely punished

en(-)cours [ãkur] NM INV **1** Banque loans outstanding, exposure; **e. de crédit** exposure; **e. débiteur autorisé** authorized overdraft facility **2** Compta **e. de production de biens** work-in-progress

encrage [ãkraʒ] NM Typ inking (up)

encrassé [ãkrase] ADJ (tuyau) clogged-up; (bougie) sooted-up; (chaudière) scaled-up

encrassement [ãkrasmã] NM (des vêtements, mains etc) dirtying; Aut (d'une bougie) fouling, sooting (up); (d'une machine etc) clogging, choking

encrasser [ãkrase] VT (ses vêtements, mains etc) to dirty; Aut (bougie) to soot up; (machine etc) to clog, to choke

▸ **s'encrasser** VPR to get dirty; Aut (d'une bougie) to soot up; (d'une machine) to get clogged or choked

encre [ãkr] NF **1** ink; **écrit à l'e.** written in ink; **cela a fait couler beaucoup d'e.** a lot has been written about it; **doigts couverts d'e.** inky fingers, fingers covered in ink; **noir comme de l'e.** inky black, black as ink; Fig **nuit d'e.** inky black night; Fam **c'est la bouteille à l'e.** it's got everyone scratching their head or stumped; Psy **test de la tache d'e.** inkblot or Rorschach test **2** Zool (de seiche) ink

▸ ▸ **e. de Chine** Indian ink; **e. d'impression** printing ink; **e. d'imprimerie** printing ink, printer's ink; **e. en poudre** toner; **e. sympathique** invisible ink

encrer [ãkre] VT Typ to ink (up)

encreur [ãkrœr] ADJ **ruban e.** (typewriter) ribbon; Typ **rouleau e.** inker

encrier [ãkrije] NM inkwell, inkpot, inkstand

encroûté [ãkrute] ADJ Fam (personne) (stuck) in a rut, set in one's ways; **qu'est-ce que tu peux être e.!** what a stick-in-the-mud you are!; **vieux bonhomme e.** old fogey or stick-in-the-mud; **il mène une vie très encroûtée** he is very set in his ways

encroûtement [ãkrutmã] NM **1** (d'une tuyauterie) encrustation **2** Fam (d'une personne) sinking into a rut; **sortir** ou **tirer qn de son e.** to get sb out of his/her rut

encroûter [ãkrute] VT **1** (tuyauterie) to encrust **2** Fam (personne) **la retraite l'a encroûté** retirement has made him set in his ways or got him into a rut

▸ **s'encroûter** VPR **1** (d'une tuyauterie) to become encrusted (**de** with) **2** Fam (d'une personne) to get into a or stuck in a rut, to become set in one's way

enculé, -ée [ãkyle] N Vulg bugger, arsehole, Am asshole

enculer [ãkyle] VT Vulg to bugger; **va te faire e.!** bugger off!, sod off!; Fig **e. les mouches** to nit-pick

encuver [ãkyve] VT (peaux, raisins) to vat

encyclique [ãsiklik] NF Rel encyclical

encyclopédie [ãsiklɔpedi] NF encyclop(a)edia; Fam **une e. vivante** a walking encyclop(a)edia

encyclopédique [ãsiklɔpedik] ADJ encyclop(a)edic

encyclopédiste [ãsiklɔpedist] N encyclop(a)edist

endéans [ãdeã] PRÉP Belg within

endémie [ãdemi] NF endemic (disease)

endémique [ãdemik] ADJ Méd, Fig endemic (à to)

endenter [ãdãte] VT **1** (roue etc) to tooth, to cog, to ratchet **2** (assembler) (roues) to mesh

endetté [ãdɛte] ADJ in debt; Fig in debt, indebted (envers to); **très e.** deep(ly) or heavily in debt

endettement [ãdɛtmã] NM (action) running or getting into debt; (état) debt; Compta indebtedness, gearing; **e. des consommateurs** consumer debt; **e. extérieur** foreign debt; **e. intérieur** internal debt; **e. public** public debt; **l'e. des pays du Tiers Monde** the debt burden of Third World countries; **cela a provoqué l'e. du pays** this caused the country to get into debt; **ratio d'e.** debt ratio; **facilité d'e.** borrowing capacity

endetter [ãdɛte] VT to get into debt; **l'acquisition de nouvelles machines a endetté la société** the purchase of new machinery has got the company into debt

▸ **s'endetter** VPR to run or get into debt; **s'e. trop lourdement** to take on too many debts

endeuiller [ãdœje] VT (famille, nation etc) to plunge into mourning; (événement) to cast gloom over; **maison endeuillée** house in mourning

endêver [ãdeve] VT & VI Can Fam **il m'endêve, il me fait e.** he infuriates me

endiablé [ãdjable] ADJ (personne) lively, full of life; (musique, rythme etc) wild, frenzied

endiguement [ãdigmã] NM **1** (action) (d'un cours d'eau) embanking, dyking (up) **2** (digue) embankment, dyke **3** Fig (de l'inflation) containment, holding in check; (de la violence, la pauvreté, du chômage) containment; **tenter l'e. de la violence/de la hausse des prix** to attempt to contain violence/price increases

endiguer [ãdige] VT **1** (cours d'eau) to embank, to dyke (up) **2** Fig (foule, colère, hausse des prix) to hold back, to contain; (inflation, pauvreté, chômage, violence) to contain

endimanché [ãdimãʃe] ADJ all dressed up, in one's Sunday best

endimancher (s') [sãdimãʃe] VPR to put on one's best clothes or one's Sunday best, to get all dressed up

endive [ãdiv] NF endive; (chicorée) chicory; Fam **pâle comme une e.** as white or pale as a sheet

endocarde [ãdɔkard] NM Anat endocardium

endocardite [ãdɔkardit] NF Méd endocarditis

endocarpe [ãdɔkarp] NM Bot endocarp

endocrine [ãdɔkrin] ADJ F Physiol (glande) endocrine

endocrinien, -ienne [ãdɔkrinjɛ̃, -jɛn] ADJ Physiol (glande etc) endocrine, endocrinal

endocrinologie [ãdɔkrinɔlɔʒi] NF endocrinology

endoctrinement [ãdɔktrinmã] NM indoctrination

endoctriner [ãdɔktrine] VT to indoctrinate, Fam to brainwash

endogame [ãdɔgam] ADJ endogamous

endogamie [ãdɔgami] NF endogamy

endogène [ãdɔʒɛn] ADJ endogenous

endolori [ãdɔlɔri] ADJ (bras etc) sore, painful

endolorir [ãdɔlɔrir] VT (bras etc) to make sore or painful

▸ **s'endolorir** VPR to become sore or painful

endolorissement [ãdɔlɔrismã] NM Litt pain, soreness

endommagement [ãdɔmaʒmã] NM (action) damaging (**de** of); (résultat) damage (**de** to)

endommager [ãdɔmaʒe] (j'endommageai(s)) VT **1** to damage, to do damage to **2** Ordinat to corrupt; **fichier endommagé** damaged or corrupt file

endomorphine [ãdɔmɔrfin] NF Physiol endorphin

endormant [ãdɔrmã] ADJ (ennuyeux) (discours, réunion etc) boring, wearisome; (tâche) boring, humdrum

endormi, -ie [ãdɔrmi] **ADJ 1** (personne) asleep, sleeping; (voix, village) sleepy; **avoir l'air e.** to look sleepy; **j'ai la jambe endormie** my leg has gone to sleep or is numb **2** Fam (inerte, lent) (personne) inattentive, half-asleep **3** Fig (passion, intérêt etc) dormant ▪ **N** (personne inerte, lente) slowcoach

> Attention: le terme **asleep** n'est jamais utilisé comme épithète.

endormir [ãdɔrmir] (conj like **dormir**) **VT 1** (d'une drogue, un hypnotiseur etc) to put or send to sleep; (d'une mère) (enfant) to send or lull to sleep **2** (ennuyer) to send or put to sleep **3** (apaiser) (douleur) to deaden; **e. les soupçons** to allay suspicion ▪ **VPR s'endormir 1** to fall asleep, to go to sleep, Fam to drop off (to sleep) **2** Fig (d'une douleur) to die away; (de soupçons) to be allayed

endormissement [ãdɔrmismã] **NM 1** falling asleep, Fam dropping off (to sleep) **2** Ordinat hibernation, sleep mode

endorphine [ãdɔrfin] **NF** Physiol endorphin

endos [ãdo] **NM** (sur chèque) endorsement

endoscope [ãdɔskɔp] **NM** Méd endoscope

endoscopie [ãdɔskɔpi] **NF** Méd endoscopy

endossable [ãdosabl] **ADJ** (chèque) endorsable

endossataire [ãdosatɛr] **N** endorsee

endossement [ãdosmã] **NM** (d'un chèque) endorsement; **e. en blanc** blank endorsement

endosser [ãdose] **VT 1** (veste etc) to put on **2** (responsabilité) to assume, to shoulder; **je ne vais pas encore e. tes erreurs** I'm not going to take the responsibility or shoulder the blame for your mistakes again **3** (chèque) to endorse; **e. en blanc** to blank endorse **4** (en reliure) (livre) to back

endosseur, -euse [ãdosœr, -øz] **N** (d'un chèque) endorser

endroit [ãdrwa] **NM 1** (lieu) place, spot; **c'est l'e. idéal pour un magasin** it's the ideal place or spot for a shop; **je ne sais plus à quel e. j'ai rangé mes lunettes** I don't know where I put my glasses; **je me suis arrêté à cet e. du livre, j'ai arrêté ma lecture à cet e.** this is where I stopped reading, I stopped reading here; **ça me fait mal à cet e.** it hurts me (just) here; **c'est à cet e. que ça vous fait mal?** is this where it hurts?; **par endroits** here and there, in places; **en plusieurs/certains endroits** in several/certain places; **rire au bon e.** to laugh in the right place; Fam **le petit e.** Br the loo, Am the john
2 (bon sens) right side; **ton pull n'est pas à l'e.** your sweater's on the wrong way round; (les coutures ne sont pas à l'intérieur) your sweater's on inside out; **remets la bouteille à l'e.** turn the bottle the right way up; Tricot **maille à l'e.** plain stitch; **deux à l'e., deux à l'envers** knit two, purl two

enduire [ãdɥir] (prp **enduisant**; pp **enduit**; pr ind **j'enduis, il enduit**; impf **j'enduisais**; p hist **j'enduisis**; fu **j'enduirai**) **VT e. de** (peinture, ciment, colle etc) to coat or cover with; (crème, boue etc) to smear with ▪ **VPR s'enduire s'e. de crème à bronzer** to smear or rub or cover oneself with suntan cream

enduit [ãdɥi] **NM 1** (de goudron, peinture etc) coat, application **2** Constr (plâtre) plastering, coat of plaster; **e. de ciment** cement rendering; **e. imperméable** proofing **3** Cér glaze, glazing

endurable [ãdyrabl] **ADJ** endurable

endurance [ãdyrãs] **NF 1** (physique) stamina, staying power, endurance **2** (morale) endurance, powers of resistance; **il n'a pas eu l'e. nécessaire pour résister à la pression** he wasn't tough enough to stand up to the pressure **3** Aut etc **épreuve/course d'e.** endurance trial/run

endurant [ãdyrã] **ADJ 1** (résistant) tough; **elle n'était pas assez endurante** she wasn't tough enough or didn't have enough stamina **2** Vieilli (patient) enduring, long-suffering

endurci [ãdyrsi] **ADJ 1** (dur) (personne) hard, callous; (cœur) hard **2** (invétéré) (criminel) hardened; (célibataire) confirmed; (haine) inveterate

endurcir [ãdyrsir] **VT 1** (cuirasser) (quelqu'un, le cœur de qn) to harden; **son séjour dans l'armée l'a endurci** his time in the army toughened him up **2** (rendre résistant) to harden, to toughen (up); **être endurci à la fatigue** to be inured or hardened to fatigue ▪ **VPR s'endurcir 1** (moralement) to become hard; **il s'est beaucoup endurci** he has become very hard **2** (physiquement) to toughen up, to become hardened

endurcissement [ãdyrsismã] **NM 1** (action) (moral) hardening; (physique) hardening, toughening (up) **2** (état) (moral) hardness, callousness; (physique) hardness, toughness

endurer [ãdyre] **VT** (épreuve, mauvais traitements) to endure, to bear; **je ne vois pas pourquoi je devrais e. cela** I can't see why I should put up with that

enduro [ãdyro] **NM** Sport enduro

Énée [ene] **N** Aeneas

Énéide (l') [leneid] **NF** Littér the Aeneid

énergétique [enɛrʒetik] **ADJ 1** (médicament, nourriture etc) energizing, energy-giving; **dépense é.** expenditure of energy **2** Écon (ressources, besoins etc) energy ▪ **NF** energetics

> Note that **énergétique** means **energy-giving**: it should not be confused with **énergique** which means **energetic**.

énergie [enɛrʒi] **NF 1** (force) energy; **apporter ou appliquer ou mettre toute son é. à une tâche/à faire qch** to devote or direct all one's energies to a task/to doing sth; **je n'ai pas assez d'é. pour sortir ce soir** I haven't got the energy to go out this evening; **je ne me sens pas beaucoup d'é.** I'm not feeling very energetic; **avec é.** energetically; (refuser, répondre) forcefully, vigorously; **elle conduit avec é.** she's an aggressive driver; **il a fait face à la situation avec é.** he faced up to the situation with spirit; **l'é. d'un passage/d'un style** the vigour of a passage/style; **sans é.** (adjectivement) listless; (adverbialement) listlessly; **faire qch avec l'é. du désespoir** to do sth with the strength born of desperation **2** Ind energy, power; **faire des économies d'é.** to save energy; **la crise de l'é.** the energy crisis
▸▸ **é. atomique** atomic energy, nuclear power; **é. cinétique** kinetic energy; **é. électrique** electrical power; **é. éolienne** wind power; **é. hydraulique** hydraulic power; **é. nucléaire** nuclear power; **é. potentielle** potential energy; **é. solaire** solar power or energy; **é. thermique** thermal power

énergique [enɛrʒik] **ADJ 1** (personne) energetic, dynamic; (vendeur) aggressive; (personnalité) forceful; **une jeune femme é.** a young woman with plenty of spirit or drive; **un visage é.** a strong face **2** (mesures) strong, drastic; (langage) strong, forceful; (geste) emphatic, forceful; (coup de pied, coup) forceful; (médicament, remède) powerful

> Note that **énergique** means **energetic**: it should not be confused with **énergétique** which means **energy-giving**.

énergiquement [enɛrʒikmã] **ADV** (nier) energetically, forcefully; (agir, parler) forcefully; (refuser, répondre) forcefully, vigorously; (conduire) aggressively; **s'y mettre é.** to put one's back into it

énergisant [enɛrʒizã] **ADJ** (médicament, nourriture etc) energizing, energy-giving ▪ **NM** Méd antidepressant

énergumène [enɛrgymɛn] **N** Fam maniac; **c'est un drôle d'é.** he's a queer fish

énervant [enɛrvã] **ADJ 1** (personne, habitude etc) irritating; (bruit) nerve-racking **2** Vieilli (climat) enervating

énervé [enɛrve] **ADJ** (agacé) irritated; (excité) (personne) on edge, edgy, agitated; (rire) nervous

énervement [enɛrvəmã] **NM** (agacement) irritation; (excitation) edginess

énerver [enɛrve] **VT 1 é. qn** (agacer) to get on sb's nerves, to irritate sb; (exciter) to get sb worked up, to agitate sb **2** Vieilli (débiliter) to enervate, to weaken ▪ **VPR s'énerver** to get excited or agitated or (all) worked up

> Il faut noter que le verbe anglais **to unnerve** est un faux ami. Il signifie **troubler**.

enfaîteau, -eaux [ãfɛto] **NM** Constr ridge tile

enfaîtement [ãfɛtmã] **NM** Constr ridge tiling, ridging

enfaîter [ãfɛte] **VT** Constr (toit) to ridge

enfance [ãfãs] **NF 1** (jeunesse) childhood; (de garçon) boyhood; (de fille) girlhood; **elle a eu une e. heureuse/difficile** she had a happy/difficult childhood; **dans mon e.** in my childhood, when I was a child; **depuis mon e.** ever since I was a child; **souvenir/camarade d'e.** childhood memory/friend; **petite e.** infancy, early childhood; **des souvenirs datant de la petite e.** memories of when one was very small, early childhood memories; **l'e. d'une civilisation** the dawn or beginning of a civilization; Fam **c'est l'e. de l'art** it's (mere) child's play; **industrie encore dans son e.** industry still in its infancy; **retomber en e.** to sink into one's second childhood or one's dotage **2** (enfants) l'e. children

enfant [ãfã] **N 1** (jeune) child, pl children; Jur (mineur) infant; **c'est une belle e.** she's a beautiful child; **e. en bas âge** infant; **éducation des enfants** children's education; **babil d'e.** childish prattle; **elle me parle comme à un e.** she talks to me as if I was a child; **les droits de l'e.** children's rights; **menu e.** children's menu; **l'e. qui est en chacun de nous** the child in all of us; **je l'ai connu e.** I have known him since he was a child; Fam **c'est un jeu d'e.** it's child's play; Fam **il n'y a plus d'enfants** honestly, kids nowadays!; **se conduire en e., faire l'e.** to act or behave childishly or like a child, to be childish; **e. surdoué** exceptionally gifted child
2 (fils, fille) child; **elle attend un e.** she's expecting a child or baby; Fam **il lui a fait un e.** she had a child by him; **être en mal d'e.** (d'une femme) to be broody; Fam **c'est son e.** (création) it's his baby or his brainchild; **couple sans e.** childless couple; **mourir sans enfants** to die childless or Jur without issue
3 (descendant) **un e. du peuple** a child of the people; **un e. de Paris** a native of Paris
4 (terme d'affection) Fam **salut, les enfants!** (à des adultes) hello people!, hi guys or gang!
▸▸ **e. de l'amour** love child; **e. de la balle** child who follows in his father's footsteps; **c'est un e. de la balle** he was born in a trunk;

Méd **e. bleu** blue baby; **e. bulle** = child who has to be kept in a sterile environment because of an immune deficiency; **e. de chœur** *Rel* altar boy; *Fig* naive person; *Fig* **je ne suis pas un e. de chœur** I'm no saint *or* no angel; **e. gâté** spoilt child; **les enfants d'Israël** the children of Israel; *Rel* **l'E. Jésus** the Christ Child, *Enf* Baby Jesus; *Rel* **les enfants de Marie** the Legion of Mary; *Fig* **c'est une e. de Marie** she's an innocent; **cela fait bien longtemps que ce n'est plus une e. de Marie** it's a long time since she was as pure as the driven snow; **e. martyr** battered baby/child; **e. naturel** illegitimate child; *Jur* natural child; **e. prodige** child prodigy; *Rel, Fig* **e. prodigue** prodigal son; **e. terrible** enfant terrible; **e. de troupe** army child *or Fam* brat; **e. trouvé** foundling; **e. unique** only child

enfantement [ãfãtmã] NM childbirth; *Fig (d'une œuvre littéraire)* production

enfanter [ãfãte] VT *(enfant)* to bear, to give birth to; *Fig (œuvre littéraire)* to produce, to give birth to; **la discorde enfante le crime** discord begets crime

enfantillage [ãfãtijaʒ] NM **enfantillage(s)** childishness, infantile behaviour; **de l'e. pur et simple** sheer childishness; **ne fais pas d'enfantillages!** don't be childish *or* infantile!

enfantin [ãfãtɛ̃] ADJ 1 *(voix)* child's; *(jeu, littérature)* children's; *Péj (remarque, action etc)* childish, infantile; **des voix enfantines** children's voices; **babil e.** childish prattle 2 *(élémentaire)* elementary; **c'est e.** it's child's play; **c'est d'une simplicité enfantine** it's childishly simple

enfarger [ãfarʒe] *Can* VI to trip
  VPR **s'enfarger** to trip over

enfariné [ãfarine] ADJ *(visage, cheveux etc)* *(de farine)* covered with flour; *(de poudre)* smothered in powder; *Fam* **je suis arrivée, la gueule enfarinée, demander mon augmentation** I arrived in all innocence *or* quite unsuspecting to ask for my rise; **à chaque fois qu'il casse quelque chose, il vient la gueule enfarinée** whenever he breaks something he turns up looking all innocent *or* as if butter wouldn't melt in his mouth

enfer [ãfɛr] NM 1 *Rel etc* **l'e.** hell; **les enfers** the underworld; *Myth* Hades; **l'E. de Dante** Dante's Inferno; *Fig* **aller en e.** to go to hell; **il fait de ma vie un e.** he's making my life hell; **elle a vécu un véritable e.** she's been through sheer *or* a living hell; **c'est vraiment l'e. à la maison** it's sheer hell at home; **quelquefois c'est l'e. pour se garer ici** it can be hell trying to park here; **l'e. de la drogue/de la prostitution/du chômage** the living hell of drug addiction/of prostitution/of unemployment; **descente aux enfers** *ou* **en e.** descent into hell; **une vision d'e.** a vision of hell; **aller un train d'e.** to go at top speed *or Fam* hell for leather; **bruit d'e.** hellish noise; *Fam* **une soirée d'e.** *(excellent)* a great *or* terrific party; **cette fille est d'e.!** she's a great *or* terrific girl
  2 *(dans une bibliothèque)* = library department containing books not available to the public

enfermement [ãfɛrməmã] NM imprisonment

enfermer [ãfɛrme] VT 1 *(personne, objet)* to shut up; **e. qch/qn (à clef)** to lock sth/sb up; **tenir qn enfermé** to keep sb shut up *or* locked up; **e. qn dehors** to shut *or* lock sb out; **j'ai été enfermé dans une pièce toute la journée** I've been shut up *or* cooped up in a room all day; **vivre trop enfermé** to stay at home too much; *Fam* **il est bon à e.** he ought to be locked up; *Fig* **e. un mot dans une définition trop étroite/qn dans un rôle inadéquat** to confine a word in an excessively

narrow definition/sb in an inadequate role; **e. qn dans ses contradictions** to trap sb in his own contradictions; **e. le savoir dans les bibliothèques** to lock away *or* shut away knowledge in libraries; **être enfermé dans ses pensées** to be wrapped up in one's thoughts
  2 *(entourer)* *(jardin, terrain, bâtiment)* to enclose, to surround; *Sport (concurrent)* to hem *or* box in
  VPR **s'enfermer** to shut oneself up; *(à clef)* to lock oneself in; **s'e. dehors** to lock oneself out; *Fig* **s'e. dans le silence/un rôle** to retreat into silence/to confine oneself to a role; **depuis qu'il est prof, il s'est enfermé dans le rôle de M. je sais tout** he's turned into a real know-it-all since he became a teacher; **Johnny Weissmuller s'est enfermé dans le rôle de Tarzan** Johnny Weissmuller never tried to be anybody but Tarzan

enferrer (s') [sãfere] VPR to impale oneself **(sur** on); *Fig (dans une explication, ses mensonges etc)* to get tangled up *or* bogged down

enfichable [ãfiʃabl] ADJ *Élec* that can be plugged in; *Ordinat* slot-in

enficher [ãfiʃe] VT *Élec* to plug in

enfiévré [ãfjevre] ADJ *(front)*, *Fig (imagination)* fevered; *Fig (atmosphère)* feverish; *(foule)* in a fever *(of excitement)*, at fever pitch

enfièvrement [ãfjevrəmã] NM fever *(of excitement)*

enfiévrer [ãfjevre] **(j'enfièvre; j'enfiéverai)** VT 1 *(énerver)* *(personne, imagination)* to excite, to fire, to stir 2 *Méd Vieilli* to make feverish
  VPR **s'enfiévrer** 1 *(se passionner)* to get excited *or* all worked up; **s'e. pour une cause** to become passionate about a cause 2 *Méd Vieilli* to grow feverish

enfilade [ãfilad] NF 1 *(de portes, maisons, colonnes, couloirs etc)* succession, series; *(de pièces etc)* series, suite; **nos deux chambres sont en e.** we have adjoining rooms; **la cuisine et la buanderie sont en e.** the kitchen and the laundry room are next to *or* adjoin each other; **maisons en e.** row of houses; **je me suis perdue dans l'e. des couloirs** I got lost in the maze of corridors *or* the endless corridors 2 *Mil* enfilade; **tir d'e.** raking *or* enfilading fire

enfiler [ãfile] VT 1 *(aiguille)* to thread; *(perles)* to string 2 *(rue, couloir etc)* to take, to go along 3 *(vêtements)* to slip on, to pull on; *(pantalon, bas)* to pull on 4 *Vulg (sexuellement)* to screw, to lay; **ce que je cherche, moi, le samedi soir, c'est une fille à e.** I'm out to get laid on a Saturday night 5 *(troupes etc)* to enfilade, to rake
  VPR **s'enfiler** 1 *(s'engager)* **s'e. dans un couloir/une rue** to go along a corridor/street 2 *Fam (consommer)* *(boisson)* to down, to knock back; *(nourriture)* to put away, to guzzle; **s'e. un bon dîner** to have a slap-up meal; **je me suis enfilé un sandwich en vitesse** I grabbed a sandwich, I had a quick sandwich 3 *Fam (avoir à supporter)* *(tâche)* to get stuck *or* landed with 4 *(de gants, bottes)* to pull on; *(d'un étui)* to slide on

enfin [ãfɛ̃] ADV 1 *(en dernier lieu)* last, finally, lastly; **e. et surtout** last but not least
  2 *(plutôt)* **blonde, e. châtain clair** blond, well, light brown; **elle n'est pas mal, e. pour son âge** she's not bad – for her age, that is; **c'était une soirée géniale, e. je veux dire qu'on ne s'est pas ennuyé** it was a good party – we weren't bored, I mean
  3 *(finalement)* at last, finally, at length; **e. vous voilà!, vous voilà e.!** here you are at last!; **j'y suis e. arrivée** I finally managed, I managed it at last

4 *(résignation)* that's that!; **e. c'est la vie** well, that's life!; **mais e., si elle est heureuse!** but as long as she's happy!; **mais e. bon, c'est son problème** oh well, that's <u>his</u> problem!; **e., n'en parlons plus!** let's forget it!; **e.! ce qui est fait est fait** what's done is done
  5 *(exaspération)* **e. quoi, tu n'as plus 10 ans!** after all, you're not 10 any more!; **on est en République e., quoi!** it's a free country after all!; **mais e. je te l'avais déjà dit!** I'd already <u>told</u> you!; **mais e., c'est pas vrai!** I don't believe it!; **e., lâche-moi un peu!** give me some peace!, give it a rest!
  6 *(hésitation, pour résumer)* well; **e. je ne dis pas non, mais …** well, I'm not saying no, but …; **mais e., s'il acceptait!** but still, if he did accept!; **e. (bref) c'était la panique!** in short *or* in a word *or* to cut a long story short, it was panic!; **c'est un homme, e.! il a sa dignité!** he's a man after all! he has his dignity!

enfirouâper [ãfirwape] *Can* VT 1 *Fam (tromper)* to fool, to hoodwink; **se faire e.** *(se faire avoir)* to get taken for a ride, to be had; *(être enjôlé)* to be taken in; *(se faire mettre enceinte)* to get knocked up 2 *Fam (nourriture)* to gulp down, to wolf down

enflammé [ãflame] ADJ 1 *(bois, brindille, torche)* burning, blazing; *(allumette)* burning; *(soleil, coucher de soleil)* fiery 2 *(joues)* *(de froid)* glowing; *(de fièvre, gêne, chaleur)* burning 3 *Méd (plaie, gorge etc)* inflamed 4 *Fig (discours, caractère etc)* fiery, passionate; **faire une déclaration enflammée à une femme** to make a passionate declaration to a woman

enflammer [ãflame] VT 1 *(mettre en flammes)* to set light to, to set ablaze; **e. une allumette** to strike a match 2 *Méd (plaie, gorge etc)* to inflame 3 *Fig (personne, imagination de qn)* to excite, to fire, to stir up; **la colère enflamme son regard** his/her eyes are blazing with anger; **l'urgence de la situation enflamme ses talents d'orateur** the urgency of the situation is arousing his talents as a speaker
  VPR **s'enflammer** 1 *(prendre feu)* to catch fire, to burst into flames, to blaze up 2 *(d'une plaie, de la gorge)* to become inflamed 3 *(d'une personne, de l'imagination)* to be stirred; **chaque jour, il s'enflamme pour une cause nouvelle/un auteur nouveau** he develops a passion for a new cause/a different author every day; **s'e. de colère** *(d'une personne)* to flare up

enfle [ãfl] ADJ *Suisse (cheville, joue)* swollen

enflé [ãfle] ADJ *(rivière, membre etc)* swollen; *(prix)* inflated, turgid, bombastic
  NM *Fam* idiot

enfléchure [ãfleʃyr] NF *Naut* ratline

enfler [ãfle] VT 1 *(membre, rivière, paupières etc)* to swell, to cause to swell; *(prix)* to inflate; **e. les joues** to puff out *or* blow out one's cheeks; **e. les voiles** *(du vent)* to fill the sails; **e. la voix** to raise one's voice; **des paupières enflées** swollen eyelids; *Vieilli* **e. le nombre/ la dépense** to swell *or* add to the number/ the expense 2 *Fig (exagérer)* *(histoire, son succès etc)* to exaggerate; **e. son style** to inflate one's style
  VI *(d'un membre, des paupières, des joues etc)* to swell (up)
  VPR **s'enfler** 1 *(d'un membre, des paupières, des joues etc)* to swell (up); *(d'une voix)* to rise 2 *(d'une rivière etc)* to swell, to rise 3 *(d'un style)* to become inflated *or* turgid

enflure [ãflyr] NF 1 *(d'un membre etc)* swelling 2 *(d'un style)* turgidity 3 *Fam (imbécile)* jerk

enfoiré, -ée [ãfware] N *Vulg* bugger, bastard

enfoncé [ãfɔ̃se] ADJ *(yeux)* deep-set; *(ca-*

vité, ravin etc) sunken, deep; *(sol, village)* low-lying

enfoncement [ɑ̃fɔ̃smɑ̃] NM **1** *(action d'enfoncer) (d'un pieu, clou etc)* driving in; *(d'une aiguille etc)* sticking in, pushing in; *(d'une porte etc)* forcing, breaking open **2** *(action de s'enfoncer) (du sol)* giving way **3** *(creux) (dans le sol)* hollow, depression; *(dans le mur)* alcove, recess; *Naut* bay, bight; **dans l'e. de la porte** in the doorway

enfoncer [ɑ̃fɔ̃se] (**j'enfonçai(s)**) VT **1** *(pieu, clou)* to drive in; *(aiguille, épingle)* to stick in, to push in; **e. un clou dans une planche** to drive a nail into a plank; **e. un couteau dans** to thrust *or* plunge *or* stick a knife into; **e. au marteau** to hammer in; **e. la main dans sa poche** to thrust one's hand into one's pocket; **e. son chapeau sur sa tête** to jam *or* cram one's hat on one's head; **e. la clef dans la serrure** to insert the key in the lock; *Fig* **e. qn dans la misère** to plunge sb into poverty; *Fig Fam* **je ne peux pas lui e. cela dans la tête** I can't get it into his head; *Fig Fam* **tu n'étais pas obligé de l'e. comme ça!** you didn't have to be so hard on him/her!

2 *(défoncer) (porte)* to break down *or* open; *(fût)* to stave in; *(voiture)* to smash into; **e. une porte à coups de pied** to kick a door in *or* down; *Fig* **e. une porte ouverte** *ou* **des portes ouvertes** to state the obvious

3 *Fam (battre) (personne, équipe)* to hammer, to wipe the floor with

VI *(dans la boue, mer)* to sink; **nous enfoncions jusqu'aux genoux** we sank into it up to our knees

VPR **s'enfoncer** *(d'un clou, couteau etc)* to sink *or* go in; *(d'un bateau)* to sink; *(du sol)* to subside, to give way; **la balle s'enfonça dans le mur** the bullet embedded itself in the wall; **s'e. dans son fauteuil** to sink into one's armchair; **s'e. dans l'ombre** to disappear in *or* be swallowed up by the darkness; **s'e. dans une rue/dans un bois** to go down a street/to plunge into a wood; **il s'est enfoncé trop loin dans la rue** he went too far along the street; **s'e. dans l'étude/dans la rêverie** to bury oneself in study/to sink into reverie; **s'e. dans le crime** to sink deep(er) into crime; **s'e. dans son opinion** to become entrenched in one's opinion

enfonceur, -euse [ɑ̃fɔ̃sœr, -øz] N **c'est un e. de portes ouvertes** he's got a gift for stating the obvious

enfonçure [ɑ̃fɔ̃syr] NF depression, hollow

enfouir [ɑ̃fwir] VT to bury (**dans** in; **sous** beneath, under); *Agr (fumier)* to plough in; **les mains enfouies dans ses poches** with his hands buried in his pockets

VPR **s'enfouir** to bury oneself

enfouissement [ɑ̃fwismɑ̃] NM burying; *Agr (de fumier)* ploughing in

enfourcher [ɑ̃furʃe] VT *(cheval, vélo)* to get on, to mount; *Fig* **e. son dada** to get on one's hobbyhorse

enfourchure [ɑ̃furʃyr] NF *Vieilli (d'arbre, de jambes)* fork

enfournage [ɑ̃furnaʒ], **enfournement** [ɑ̃furnəmɑ̃] NM *(de pain etc)* putting in the oven; *(de poteries, briques etc)* putting in the kiln

enfourner [ɑ̃furne] VT *(pain etc)* to put in the oven; *(poteries, briques etc)* to put in the kiln; *Fam (avaler)* to put away; **e. les passagers dans un autobus** to pack *or* cram passengers into a bus

VPR **s'enfourner** *Fam* to pile, to pack (**dans** into)

enfourneur [ɑ̃furnœr] NM oven man; *Cér* kiln man

enfreindre [ɑ̃frɛ̃dr] VT *(prp* **enfreignant***; pp* **enfreint***; pr ind* **j'enfreins, il enfreint, ils en-**

freignent*; impf* **j'enfreignais***; p hist* **j'enfreignis***; fu* **j'enfreindrai***) (loi)* to infringe, to break; *(règlements)* to contravene, to act contrary to; *(ordres)* to disobey; *(vœu)* to break; **e. les dispositions d'un traité** to violate a treaty; **e. un contrat** to violate a contract

enfuir (s') [sɑ̃fɥir] VPR *(conj like* **fuir***)* to run away, *Litt* to flee, to fly; *(d'un escroc)* to abscond; *(d'amoureux)* to elope; **s'e. de prison** to escape from prison; **à mesure que les jours s'enfuyaient** as the days flew by; *Litt* **mon bonheur menace de s'e.** my happiness is in danger of evaporating

enfumé [ɑ̃fyme] ADJ **1** *(pièce, atmosphère)* smoky **2** *(murs etc)* smoke-blackened

enfumer [ɑ̃fyme] VT **1** *(pièce)* to fill with smoke **2** *(murs etc)* to blacken with smoke **3** *(personne, abeilles etc)* to smoke out

enfûtage [ɑ̃fytaʒ] NM *(d'un vin)* putting in barrels *or* casks

enfutailler [ɑ̃fytaje], **enfûter** [ɑ̃fyte] VT *(vin)* to put in barrels *or* casks

engagé [ɑ̃gaʒe] ADJ **1** *Littér, Pol etc (littérature, artiste etc)* committed **2** *Archit (colonne etc)* engaged **3** **navire e.** ship on her beam-ends **4** *Mil* **soldat e.** volunteer

NM *Mil* **e. (volontaire)** volunteer; *Courses de chevaux, Cyclisme* **la liste des engagés** the list of starters

> Il faut noter que l'adjectif anglais **engaged** est un faux ami. Il ne s'utilise jamais dans un contexte politique.

engageant [ɑ̃gaʒɑ̃] ADJ *(manière etc)* engaging, prepossessing; *(sourire)* winning, engaging; **il a écouté ma proposition d'un air e.** he listened to my suggestion sympathetically

engagement [ɑ̃gaʒmɑ̃] NM **1** *(promesse etc)* promise, undertaking, commitment; **faire honneur à** *ou* **tenir** *ou* **respecter ses engagements** to honour *or Am* honor *or* fulfil *or Am* fulfill one's commitments; **e. écrit** written undertaking; *Fin* **e. à court terme** short-term undertaking; **contracter** *ou* **prendre un e.** to enter into an undertaking; **elle a pris l'e. de le faire** she undertook to do it; **sans e. (de votre part)** without obligation (on your part), without any commitment (on your part)

2 *Fin (d'un capital)* tying up, locking up; *(de dépenses)* incurring; **e. à court terme** short-term undertaking

3 *(mise en gage) (de bijoux)* pawning, pledging; *(d'un domaine)* mortgaging

4 *(embauche) (d'un employé)* engagement, appointment, hiring; *(d'un pianiste etc)* booking; *Mil (voluntary)* enlistment; **se trouver sans e.** to be out of work; *Théâtre* to be resting

5 *Sport (pour un événement sportif)* entering, entry

6 *(commencement) (de conversation, négociations)* beginning, start, opening; *(d'entreprise, de projet etc)* setting in motion; *Jur (de poursuites)* institution; *Mil, Naut (bataille)* engagement, action; *(coup d'envoi) Ftbl* kick-off; *(au hockey)* bully-off; *Escrime* engagement; **l'e. des négociations ne pourra se faire avant le mois prochain** negotiations cannot begin *or* start before next month; **pour que l'e. du projet soit possible** in order to get the project under way *or* to set the project in motion

7 *(à une cause etc)* commitment (**à** to)

8 *(encouragement)* encouragement; **c'est un e. à poursuivre votre effort** it's an encouragement to continue your effort

9 *(introduction) (du pied)* putting; *(d'une clé)* fitting, inserting; *(d'un véhicule)* driving (**dans** into)

10 *Physiol* **e. du fœtus** engagement of the foetus

ENGAGER [ɑ̃gaʒe] (**j'engageai(s)**)

VT to commit **1** ▪ to tie up **2** ▪ to pawn **3** ▪ to hire **4** ▪ to begin **5** ▪ to involve **6** ▪ to urge **7** ▪ to engage **11**
VPR to commit oneself **1, 2** ▪ to promise **1, 2** ▪ to get involved in *(s'engager dans)* **3** ▪ to enlist **5** ▪ to fit into *(s'engager dans)* **6** ▪ to enter **7** ▪ to begin **8**

VT **1** *(lier par une obligation ou une promesse)* to commit, to bind; **e. sa parole** to pledge *or* give one's word; *(dans une affaire)* to commit oneself; **cette lettre ne vous engage pas** this letter does not bind *or* commit you; **cela vous engage à vie** it's a lifetime commitment; **cela ne vous engage à rien** it doesn't commit you to anything; **votre responsabilité est engagée dans cette affaire** you have certain responsibilities in this matter; **c'est ce que je crois, mais ça n'engage que moi** it's what I think, but it's just my way of looking at things

2 *Fin (argent)* to lock up, to tie up; *(dépenses)* to incur; **e. sa fortune/des capitaux dans une affaire** to lock up *or* tie up one's fortune/capital in a deal

3 *(mettre en gage) (au mont-de-piété)* to pawn; *(auprès de créanciers)* to pledge; *(propriété)* to mortgage

4 *(embaucher) (employé)* to hire, to take on; *(pianiste)* to book; *Mil (recrue)* to enlist; *(mercenaire)* to hire

5 *(commencer) (conversation, négociations)* to begin, to start, to open; *(entreprise, projet etc)* to get under way, to set in motion; *Jur (poursuites)* to institute, to start; **e. la partie** to begin the match *or* game; **la partie est maintenant bien engagée** the match is now well under way; **e. le jeu** *Ftbl* to kick off; *(au hockey)* to bully off; **e. le combat** to join battle, to engage; **e. les hostilités** to open hostilities; **e. des troupes** to bring troops into action, to engage troops

6 *(entraîner)* to involve (**dans** in); **le pays tout entier se voit engagé dans ce conflit** the whole country finds itself involved *or* caught up in this conflict; **e. qn dans une querelle** to involve sb in *or* draw sb into a quarrel

7 *(inciter)* **e. qn à faire qch** *(d'une personne)* to urge *or* encourage sb to do sth; *(d'une situation, d'un événement)* to encourage sb to do sth

8 *(introduire)* **e. le pied dans l'étrier** to put one's foot in the stirrup; **e. la clef dans la serrure** to fit *or* insert the key in the lock; **e. un véhicule dans une allée** to drive a vehicle into a lane

9 *Sport (inscrire sur liste des concurrents)* to enter; **cet entraîneur a deux chevaux engagés dans cette course** this trainer has two horses entered in the race

10 *(entraver) (corde etc)* to catch, to foul, to entangle; *(machinerie)* to jam; **e. une ancre** to foul an anchor; **e. un aviron** to catch a crab; **e. un vaisseau** to run a ship aground

11 *Tech (engrenage)* to engage, to put into gear; *Aut* **e. la première** to change into first (gear)

VPR **s'engager 1** *(promettre)* **s'e. à faire qch** to promise to do sth, to commit oneself to do sth, *Fml* to undertake to do sth; **s'e. par traité à faire qch** to contract to do sth; **je m'engage à vous payer dans les 30 jours** I promise to pay you within 30 days; **je me suis trop engagé pour reculer** I have gone too far *or* I'm too far in to pull out now; **s'e. vis-à-vis de qn** to commit oneself to sb; **je ne veux pas m'e.** *(sentimentalement)* I don't want to get involved

2 *(prendre position) (écrivain, intellectuel)* to commit oneself

3 *(se lancer)* **s'e. dans une aventure/un combat/une affaire** to get involved in an adventure/a fight/a deal

4 *(se faire embaucher)* **s'e. chez qn** to be *or* get taken on by sb; **s'e. comme cuisinier** to get (oneself) a job as *or* get taken on as a cook

5 *Mil* to enlist, to join up

6 *(se loger)* to fit; **un tube s'engage dans l'ouverture** a pipe fits into the opening

7 *(pénétrer)* **s'e. dans une rue/forêt** to turn into a street/to enter a forest; **il s'engagea dans le passage pour piétons sans regarder à droite ni à gauche** he stepped out onto the pedestrian crossing without looking left or right; **la voiture s'engagea dans le rond-point** the car pulled out onto the roundabout; **nous nous engageâmes dans un étroit boyau** we moved into a narrow passageway

8 *(commencer)* *(d'une bataille, conversation etc)* to begin

9 *Sport* **s'e. pour une course** to enter for a race

10 *(d'une corde, hélice etc)* to foul, to become fouled; *(d'une machine)* to jam

engazonnement [ɑ̃gazɔnmɑ̃] **NM** *(fait de semer)* sowing with grass seed

engazonner [ɑ̃gazɔne] **VT** *(semer)* to sow with grass seed

engeance [ɑ̃ʒɑ̃s] **NF** *Fam* **quelle e.!** what a crew!

engelure [ɑ̃ʒlyr] **NF** chilblain

engendrement [ɑ̃ʒɑ̃drəmɑ̃] **NM 1** *(d'enfant)* fathering, *Bible* begetting **2** *(de chaleur etc)* generation; *(de maladie, pauvreté)* breeding

engendrer [ɑ̃ʒɑ̃dre] **VT 1** *(enfant)* to father, *Bible* to beget; *(d'un étalon etc)* to sire **2** *Fig (conflit)* to engender, to give rise to; *(maladie, pauvreté)* to breed; *(chaleur etc)* to generate, to develop

engin [ɑ̃ʒɛ̃] **NM** *(machine)* machine; *(outil)* device, contrivance; *Mil (missile)* missile; *Fam (objet)* thing; **engins de pêche** fishing tackle; **passage d'engins** heavy plant crossing; **engins de guerre** engines of war; **e. amphibie** amphibious craft *or* vehicle; **e. blindé** armoured vehicle; **e. blindé de reconnaissance** armoured car; **e. de mort** deadly weapon; **e. prohibé** illegal hunting/fishing device; **e. spatial** spacecraft; **e. de terrassement** earthmoving machine; **e. de manutention** machine for handling goods

---
Il faut noter que le nom anglais **engine** est un faux ami. Il signifie **moteur**.
---

engineering [ɛndʒiniriŋ] **NM** engineering

englober [ɑ̃glɔbe] **VT 1** *(inclure)* to include (**dans** in); **e. les innocents parmi les coupables** to include the innocent with the guilty **2** *(annexer)* to merge (**dans** into); **ces états furent englobés dans l'Empire** these states were merged into the Empire

engloutir [ɑ̃glutir] **VT 1** *(avaler) (boisson)* to gulp down; *(nourriture)* to wolf down **2** *(submerger) (bateau, village etc)* to engulf, to swallow up **3** *(son capital etc) (d'une entreprise, projet etc)* to swallow up; *(d'une personne)* to sink (**dans** in)
VPR s'engloutir *(d'un bateau)* to sink

engloutissement [ɑ̃glutismɑ̃] **NM 1** *(d'une boisson)* gulping down; *(de la nourriture)* wolfing down **2** *(d'un village etc)* engulfing, swallowing up; *(d'un bateau)* sinking **3** *(d'une fortune etc)* swallowing up

engluage [ɑ̃glyaʒ], **engluement** [ɑ̃glymɑ̃] **NM 1** *(de brindilles, d'un oiseau)* liming **2** *(enduit)* (bird)lime

engluer [ɑ̃glye] **VT** *(brindilles, oiseau)* to lime
VPR s'engluer *(d'un oiseau)* to get caught in

lime; **s'e. les doigts** to get sticky fingers; *Fig* **s'e. dans une situation difficile/des problèmes/des dettes** to get bogged down in a difficult situation/problems/debts

engoncer [ɑ̃gɔ̃se] **VT** *(d'un vêtement)* **e. qn** to make sb look hunched up; **être engoncé dans sa veste** to be hunched up in one's jacket

engorgement [ɑ̃gɔrʒəmɑ̃] **NM 1** *(action)* *(d'un passage, tuyau etc)* choking, blocking, clogging; **e. des marchés** glutting of the markets **2** *(bouchon)* obstruction, stoppage; *Méd* engorgement, congestion

engorger [ɑ̃gɔrʒe] (**j'engorgeai(s)**) **VT 1** *(passage, tuyau etc)* to choke (up), to block, to clog **2** *(marché)* to glut **3** *Méd (organe)* to engorge, congest
VPR s'engorger 1 *(d'un tuyau etc)* to become choked (up) *or* blocked (up) *or* clogged **2** *Méd (d'un organe)* to become engorged *or* congested **3** *(d'une route, d'un carrefour)* to become blocked up *or* congested

engouement [ɑ̃gumɑ̃] **NM 1** *(admiration)* infatuation, craze (**pour qn/qch** for sb/sth) **2** *Méd (d'une hernie)* obstruction

engouer (s') [ɑ̃gwe] **VPR 1** *Méd (d'une hernie)* to become obstructed **2** **s'e. de qn/qch** to become infatuated with *or* go crazy over sb/sth

engouffrement [ɑ̃gufrəmɑ̃] **NM** *(d'un vaisseau par la mer etc)* engulfment, engulfing, swallowing up

engouffrer [ɑ̃gufre] **VT** *(bateau etc)* to engulf, to swallow up; **e. une fortune** to swallow up a fortune; *Fam* **e. sa nourriture** to devour *or* gulp down *or* wolf down one's food; *Fam* **qu'est-ce que j'ai engouffré!** I really wolfed *or* gulped it down!
VPR s'engouffrer *(d'un bateau etc)* to be engulfed *or* swallowed up; **il s'engouffra dans la gare** he plunged *or* dived into the station; **le vent s'engouffra par la porte** the wind swept in through the door

engoulevent [ɑ̃gulvɑ̃] **NM** *(oiseau)* nightjar

engourdi [ɑ̃gurdi] **ADJ 1** *(membre, corps etc)* numb; **j'ai le pied e.** my foot has gone to sleep *or* is numb **2** *Fig (esprit)* dull, sluggish

engourdir [ɑ̃gurdir] **VT 1** *(membre, corps etc)* to numb **2** *(endormir) (esprit, douleur)* to dull
VPR s'engourdir 1 *(d'un membre etc)* to grow numb, to go to sleep **2** *Fig (de l'esprit)* to become dull *or* sluggish **3** *(d'un animal qui hiberne)* to become dormant

engourdissement [ɑ̃gurdismɑ̃] **NM 1** *(état)* *(d'un membre etc)* numbness; *(de l'esprit)* dullness, sluggishness; *(d'un animal qui hiberne)* torpor **2** *(action)* *(d'un membre etc)* numbing; *(de l'esprit, d'une douleur)* dulling

engrais [ɑ̃grɛ] **NM 1** *(pour l'élevage)* **mettre des bœufs à l'e.** to put cattle to fatten **2** *(fertilisant)* fertilizer; **e. (animal)** manure; **e. chimiques** chemical fertilizers; **e. verts** green fertilizers

engraissage [ɑ̃grɛsaʒ], **engraissement** [ɑ̃grɛsmɑ̃] **NM** *(des animaux)* fattening

engraisser [ɑ̃grɛse] **VT 1** *(animaux)* to fatten **2** *(personne)* to make fat **3** *(terre)* to fertilize
VI *(d'une personne, d'un animal)* to get fat
VPR s'engraisser *(s'enrichir)* to grow fat; **l'État s'engraisse sur le dos des travailleurs** the State grows fat at the workers' expense

engrangement [ɑ̃grɑ̃ʒmɑ̃] **NM** *(des céréales)* getting in, *Litt* garnering

engranger [ɑ̃grɑ̃ʒe] (**j'engrangeai(s)**; **n. engrangeons**) *(céréales)* to get in, *Litt* to garner

engrenage [ɑ̃grənaʒ] **NM 1** *Tech (roues dentées)* gears; *(disposition du système)* gearing; **e. hélicoïdal** helical *or* screw gear; **système ou jeu d'engrenages** train *or* set of gears;

Aut **e. de démarrage** starter gear; **e. à train planétaire** planetary gearing; **engrenage(s) de transmission** driving gear; **e. en prise constante** constant-mesh gear; **e. à variations progressives** gradually variable gear; **e. à vis sans fin** worm gears **2** *Fig (des événements)* chain, mesh, web; **être pris dans l'e.** to be *or* get caught (up) in the system; **l'e. de la violence/de l'agressivité** the spiral of violence/aggression; **mettre le doigt dans l'e.** to get caught up in it

engrènement [ɑ̃grɛnmɑ̃] **NM 1** *Agr (d'un moulin etc)* feeding with grain **2** *Tech* engaging, meshing

engrener [ɑ̃grəne] (**j'engrène**; **j'engrènerai**) **VT 1** *Agr (moulin, batteuse)* to feed grain into **2** *Tech (pignons)* to engage, to mesh; **e. dans** to engage into, to mesh with; *Fam* **e. une affaire** to set a thing going
VPR s'engrener *Tech* to engage (**dans** into), to mesh (**dans** with)

engrenure [ɑ̃grənyr] **NF** *Tech (disposition de roues)* gearing

engrosser [ɑ̃grose] **VT** *Arg (femme)* to make pregnant, to knock up; **se faire e.** to get knocked up (**par** by)

engueulade [ɑ̃gœlad] **NF** *Fam (réprimande)* bawling out; *(querelle)* row, *Br* slanging match; **passer une e. à qn** to give sb a bawling out, to bawl sb out; **recevoir une e.** to get a bawling out

engueuler [ɑ̃gœle] *Fam* **VT e. qn** *(réprimander)* to give sb hell, to give sb a roasting; **se faire e.** to be given a roasting; **e. qn comme du poisson pourri** to call sb every name under the sun
VPR s'engueuler to have a row *or Br* slanging match

enguirlander [ɑ̃girlɑ̃de] **VT 1** *(décorer)* to garland (**de** with) **2** *Fam* = **engueuler**

enhardir [ɑ̃ardir] **VT** to embolden, to put courage into, to give courage to
VPR s'enhardir to become bold(er); **s'e. à faire qch** to pluck up the courage to do sth

enharmonie [ɑ̃narmɔni] **NF** *Mus* enharmonic change

enharmonique [ɑ̃narmɔnik] **ADJ** *Mus* enharmonic

enharnacher [ɑ̃arnaʃe] **VT** *(cheval)* to harness

énième [enjɛm] **ADJ** nth; **pour la é. fois** for the nth *or* umpteenth time
N nth

énigmatique [enigmatik] **ADJ** enigmatic

énigmatiquement [enigmatikmɑ̃] **ADV** enigmatically

énigme [enigm] **NF** *(problème, mystère)* enigma, riddle; *(devinette)* riddle; **proposer une é. à qn** to ask sb a riddle; **trouver le mot** *ou* **la clé de l'é.** to find the answer to the riddle, to guess *or* solve the riddle; **parler par énigmes** to speak in riddles; **ce garçon est une é. pour moi** I can't make the boy out; **ça, c'est une é. pour moi** it's a mystery to me

enivrant [ɑ̃nivrɑ̃] **ADJ** *(parfum)* intoxicating, heady; *(vitesse)* exhilarating, dizzying; **vivre dans un luxe e.** to live in fabulous luxury

enivrement [ɑ̃nivrəmɑ̃] **NM 1** *(par l'alcool)* intoxication, inebriation **2** *Fig* exhilaration; **dans l'e. de** intoxicated *or* exhilarated by

enivrer [ɑ̃nivre] **VT 1** *(avec de l'alcool)* to intoxicate, to inebriate, to make drunk **2** *Fig (exalter)* to intoxicate, to exhilarate; **enivré par le succès** intoxicated *or* exhilarated by success
VPR s'enivrer 1 *(devenir ivre)* to become intoxicated *or* inebriated (**de** with), to get drunk (**de** on) **2** *Fig* **s'e. de mots** to get drunk on words

enjambée [ãʒãbe] NF stride; **marcher à grandes enjambées** to stride along

enjambement [ãʒãbmã] NM *Littér* enjamb(e)ment

enjamber [ãʒãbe] VT *(obstacle, fossé etc)* to step over *or* across; *(d'un pont) (rivière etc)* to span

enjeu [ãʒø] NM **1** *(au jeu)* stake **2** *Mil, Pol etc* stakes; **quel est l'e.?** what is at stake?, what are the stakes?

enjoindre [ãʒwɛ̃dr] VT *(conj like* **joindre***) Littér* **e. à qn de faire qch** to enjoin *or* call upon *or* charge sb to do sth

enjôlement [ãʒolmã] NM **1** *(action)* cajoling, wheedling, coaxing **2** *(paroles etc)* cajolery, blandishment

enjôler [ãʒole] VT to cajole, to wheedle, to coax

enjôleur, -euse [ãʒolœr, -øz] N coaxer, cajoler, wheedler

ADJ coaxing, cajoling, wheedling

enjolivement [ãʒolivmã] NM *(ornement)* embellishment, ornament; *(dans un récit)* embellishment

enjoliver [ãʒolive] VT *(pièce, robe etc)* to embellish, to ornament; *(faits, histoire etc)* to embellish, to embroider

enjoliveur, -euse [ãʒolivœr, -øz] N **c'est un e.** he likes to embellish *or* embroider his stories

NM *Aut* hubcap, wheel trim; **e. de phare** headlamp rim

enjolivure [ãʒolivyr] NF *(ornement), Fig* embellishment

enjoué [ãʒwe] ADJ vivacious, lively, playful

enjouement [ãʒumã] NM vivaciousness, liveliness, playfulness

enkystement [ãkistəmã] NM *Méd* encystation, encystment

enkyster (s') [sãkiste] VPR *Méd (d'une tumeur)* to become encysted, to encyst

enlacement [ãlasmã] NM **1** *(de rubans, branches)* intertwining, interlacing **2** *(en entourant)* enlacing, entwining

enlacer [ãlase] *(j'enlaçais)* VT **1** *(rubans, branches)* to intertwine, to interlace; *(entourer)* to entwine, to enlace, to twine round; *(papiers)* to tie up **2** *(étreindre)* to clasp in one's arms, to hug, to embrace

VPR **s'enlacer 1** *(s'étreindre)* to hug, to embrace (each other); **amants enlacés** lovers (clasped) in an embrace **2** *(s'entrelacer)* to intertwine, to interlace

enlaidir [ãlɛdir] VT *(personne)* to make ugly, to disfigure; *(paysage, ville etc)* to disfigure; **cette robe l'enlaidit** that dress makes her look ugly

VI to grow ugly *or* plain

VPR **s'enlaidir** to make oneself look ugly *or* plain

enlaidissement [ãlɛdismã] NM *(de personne) (par accident)* disfigurement; *(naturel)* growing ugly *or* plain, loss of good looks; *(de paysage, ville etc)* disfigurement

enlevage [ãlvaʒ] NM *(dans une course d'aviron)* spurt

enlevé [ãlve] ADJ *(représentation, style etc)* lively, spirited; *(danse, sonate etc)* performed in a lively *or* spirited fashion

enlèvement [ãlɛvmã] NM **1** *(de meubles, d'une étiquette, d'une tache, de peinture)* removal, removing; *(des bagages, ordures)* collection; **e. des ordures** garbage disposal; *Com* **e. et livraison** collection and delivery **2** *(kidnapping)* kidnapping, abduction; *Jur* **e. de mineur** abduction of a minor; **e. d'enfant** baby-snatching **3** *Mil (d'une position)* taking, storming, carrying

▸▸ *Hist* **l'e. des Sabines** the rape of the Sabine women

enlever [ãlve] *(j'enlève; j'enlèverai)* VT **1** *(vêtements, étiquette, bouton, couvercle etc)* to remove, to take off; *(meubles etc)* to remove, to take away; *(tapis)* to take up; *(rideaux)* to take down; *(pelure, peinture etc)* to peel off, to remove; *(tache)* to remove, to take out; **e. le couvert** to clear away, to clear the table; *Fam* **il a fallu lui e. les végétations** he had to have his adenoids removed *or* taken out; *Litt* **enlevé par la mer** carried away *or* washed away by the sea; **la mort l'enleva à vingt ans** death carried him off at twenty; **e. qch à qn** to take sth away from sb; **enlève-lui ces allumettes des mains** take those matches off him; **enlève-toi de là!** get off there!; **il m'a enlevé mes cors** he removed my corns; **cette erreur n'enlève rien à votre valeur** this mistake takes nothing away from *or* in no way detracts from your merit; **cela m'a enlevé tout mon courage/toute ma bonne humeur** it has drained me of all courage/of my good humour; **e. à qn la garde d'un enfant** to remove *or* take a child from sb's care *or* custody; **e. à qn le goût de qch** to take away sb's taste for sth

2 *(kidnapper)* to kidnap, to abduct; **se faire e. par son amant** to elope (with one's lover)

3 *(remporter) Mil (position)* to take, to carry, to storm; *Sport etc (course, victoire, prix)* to win; *(commande, contrat)* to win, to secure; **e. la décision** to win *or* carry the day, to win through; **e. les suffrages** *Pol* to win *or* capture votes; *Fig* to be liked by everyone, to be universally liked

4 *(soulever) (poids, couvercle)* to raise, to lift (up); *(ballon)* to send up; **le vent enlève la poussière** the wind raises the dust; **e. son cheval** *(le faire bondir)* to lift one's horse; *(le faire partir)* to set one's horse at full gallop; *Fig* **la foule fut enlevée par ces paroles** the crowd was carried away by these words

5 e. un morceau (de musique) to play a piece (of music) in a lively *or* spirited fashion

VPR **s'enlever 1** *(d'un couvercle)* to come off; *(de la peinture, peau etc)* to come *or* peel off; *(d'une tache)* to come out **2** *(de marchandises)* to sell quickly, to be snapped up **3** *(d'un ballon etc)* to rise **4** *(d'un cheval)* to take off

enlisement [ãlizmã] NM *(dans les sables mouvants etc)* sinking

enliser [ãlize] VT *(voiture, roue etc) (dans la boue, le sable etc)* to get stuck

VPR **s'enliser** *(d'une personne) (dans un marécage etc)* to sink, to be sucked down; *(d'une voiture etc) (dans la boue, le sable etc)* to sink, to get stuck; *Fig* **s'e. dans ses explications/habitudes** to get bogged down in one's explanations/habits

enluminer [ãlymine] VT **1** *(illustrer) (manuscrit, livre etc)* to illuminate **2** *(colorer) (gravure, carte etc)* to colour, *Am* to color **3** *Fig* **visage enluminé** flushed *or* glowing face

enlumineur, -euse [ãlyminœr, -øz] N *(artiste)* illuminator

enluminure [ãlyminyr] NF **1** *(action d'illustrer) (d'un manuscrit etc)* illumination, illuminating **2** *(action de colorer) (de gravures etc)* colouring, *Am* coloring **3** *Fig (d'un visage)* colour, *Am* color **4** *(lettre, dessin)* illumination

enneigé [ãneʒe] ADJ *(montagne, champ etc)* snow-covered; *(route, village etc)* snowbound, snowed-up

enneigement [ãneʒmã] NM *(action)* snowing up; *(état)* snow cover; **bulletin d'e.** snow report

ennemi, -ie [ɛnmi] N enemy; **se faire un e. de qn** to make an enemy of sb, to turn sb against one; **passer à l'e.** to go over to the enemy; **e. public numéro un** public enemy

number one; **les ennemis de la liberté** the enemies of freedom; *Prov* **le mieux est l'e. du bien** leave well alone VOIR GRAMMAIRE A11

ADJ enemy; **le camp e.** the enemy('s) camp; **en pays e.** in enemy country

ennoblir [ãnoblir] VT **1** *(esprit etc)* to ennoble, to elevate **2** *Tex (tissu etc)* to improve (the quality of)

> Do not confuse with **anoblir**, which means **to raise to the peerage**.

ennui [ãnɥi] NM **1** *(souci)* worry, anxiety; *(problème)* problem; **avoir des ennuis** *(soucis)* to be worried *or* anxious; *(problèmes)* to have problems; **avoir des ennuis de santé/d'argent/de voiture** to have health/money/car problems; **avoir des ennuis avec la police** to be in trouble with the police; **avoir des ennuis avec ses voisins** to have trouble *or* problems with one's neighbours; **si tu continues, tu vas avoir des ennuis** if you carry on, you'll be in trouble; **petits ennuis** minor worries, *Péj* petty worries; **créer** *ou* **susciter** *ou* **faire des ennuis à qn** to make trouble for sb, to create problems for sb; **je ne voudrais pas vous attirer d'ennuis** I wouldn't want to get you into trouble; **quel e.!** what a nuisance *or* bother *or Fam* bind!; **l'e., c'est que je ne lui ai rien expliqué** the trouble is that I haven't explained anything to him

2 *(lassitude)* boredom, *Litt* ennui; **ils me font mourir d'e.** they bore me to death *or* stiff; **sa conversation est d'un e.!** his/her conversation is so boring!

ennuyant [ãnɥijã] ADJ *Belg, Can* **1** *(lassant) (travail, conférencier, collègue)* boring, dull; **e. à mourir** *ou* **à périr** *ou* **comme la pluie** *ou* **comme la mort** (as) dull as ditchwater *or Am* dishwater, deadly boring **2** *(fâcheux)* annoying, tiresome; **c'est e. qu'il ne puisse pas venir** *(regrettable)* it's a pity (that) he can't come; *(contrariant)* it's annoying *or* a nuisance that he can't come

ennuyé [ãnɥije] ADJ **1** *(contrarié)* annoyed, bothered (**de** about) **2** *(las)* bored (**de** with)

ennuyer [ãnɥije] *(j'ennuie; j'ennuierai)* VT **1** *(contrarier)* to annoy, to bother; **cela vous ennuierait-il d'attendre?** would you mind waiting?; **je ne voudrais pas vous e.** I don't want to bother you; **cela m'ennuie de ne pouvoir le lui expliquer** it annoys me that I can't explain it to him; **je suis très ennuyé de la savoir fâchée** it bothers *or* upsets me a lot to know that she is angry

2 *(agacer)* to annoy, to irritate; **qu'est-ce qu'elle m'ennuie avec ses chichis!** I'm really getting tired of the fuss she makes!

3 *(lasser)* to bore; **il m'ennuie à mourir** he bores me to death

VPR **s'ennuyer** to be/get bored; **je m'ennuie à ne rien faire** *(maintenant)* I'm bored *or Fam* fed up with doing nothing; *(en général)* I get bored if I have nothing to do; **s'e. de faire qch** to get tired of doing sth

> Il faut noter que le verbe anglais **to annoy** signifie **importuner** ou **irriter** et non **lasser**.

ennuyeux, -euse [ãnɥijø, -øz] ADJ **1** *(contrariant)* annoying, irritating; **comme c'est e.!** what a nuisance! **2** *(lassant)* boring, tedious, dull; **mortellement e.** deadly boring *or* dull

énoncé [enõse] NM **1** *(des faits)* statement; *(d'un problème), Jur (d'une sentence)* terms; *(d'un contrat, d'une loi etc)* text, wording; *(d'une question)* wording **2** *Ling* utterance

énoncer [enõse] *(j'énonçai(s))* VT *(opinion, fait, conditions etc)* to state

VPR **s'énoncer** *(d'une opinion)* to be stated

énonciation [enɔ̃sjasjɔ̃] NF *(d'un fait etc)* stating, statement

enorgueillir [ɑ̃nɔrɡœjir] VT to make proud
VPR **s'enorgueillir s'e. de qch/d'avoir fait qch** to be proud of *or* pride oneself on sth/ having done sth

énorme [enɔrm] ADJ *(personne, édifice, succès, quantité, perte etc)* enormous, huge; **il a été élu à une é. majorité** he was elected by a huge *or* overwhelming majority; **mensonge é.** whopping lie, whopper; **raconter des choses énormes** to say outrageous things; **il n'est pas mort, c'est déjà é.** he's still alive, which is incredible

énormément [enɔrmemɑ̃] ADV enormously, hugely, tremendously; **je le regrette é.** I'm extremely *or Fam* awfully sorry; **elle a é. changé** she has changed enormously *or* a great deal; **é. de bien/d'argent** an enormous amount *or* a great deal of good/money; **é. de gens** a great many *or Fam* lots of people

énormité [enɔrmite] NF **1** *(d'une demande, d'un péché, d'un crime etc)* enormity, outrageousness **2** *(taille démesurée)* *(d'une personne, d'un édifice)* enormousness, hugeness; **l'é. du gaspillage** the huge *or* enormous amount wasted **3** *(bévue)* (dreadful) blunder; **commettre une é.** to put one's foot right in it, to make a (dreadful) blunder; **ce traité est plein d'énormités** this treaty is full of (written) mistakes *or Fam* howlers **4 dire des énormités** to say the most outrageous things

enquérir (s') [sɑ̃kerir] VPR *(conj like* **acquérir***)* to inquire, to make inquiries *(de* about); **s'e. du prix** to ask the price; **il s'est enquis de vous/de votre santé** he inquired *or* asked after *or* about you/your health

enquête [ɑ̃ket] NF *Jur, Parl etc* inquiry; *(policière)* investigation(s), inquiries; *(sondage)* survey, opinion poll; *Journ* (investigative) report, exposé; *Mktg* market probe; **l'inspecteur mène l'e.** the inspector is leading the investigation(s) *or* inquiries; **ouvrir une e.** to set up *or* open an inquiry; **faire** *ou* **procéder à une e. sur qch** *Jur etc* to hold *or* conduct an inquiry into sth; *(de la police)* to carry out *or* conduct an investigation into sth; **commission d'e.** court of inquiry; *Br Parl* select committee; **elle a décidé de faire sa petite e.** she decided to investigate; *Com* **e. sur les prix** price survey; **e. auprès des consommateurs** consumer survey
►► *Jur* **e. administrative** public inquiry; **e. omnibus** omnibus survey; **e. postale** postal survey; **e. par questionnaire** questionnaire survey; **e. scientifique** scientific investigation; **e. sociologique** sociological survey; **e. par sondage** sample survey; **e. téléphonique** telephone interview *or* survey

enquête-pilote, *pl* **enquêtes-pilotes** NF *Mktg* pilot survey

enquêter [ɑ̃kete] VI *Jur* to hold an inquiry; *(de la police)* to make investigations; *(faire un sondage)* to conduct a survey (**sur** into); **e. sur une affaire** to inquire into a matter, to investigate a matter

enquêteur, -euse [ɑ̃ketœr, -øz] ADJ *Jur* **commissaire e.** investigating commissioner
N investigator; *(qui fait un sondage)* researcher; *Journ* interviewer; *Mktg* pollster

enquêtrice [ɑ̃ketris] NF investigator; *(qui fait un sondage)* researcher; *Journ* interviewer; *Mktg* pollster

enquiquinant [ɑ̃kikinɑ̃] ADJ *Fam (agaçant)* irritating, annoying; *(lassant)* boring

enquiquinement [ɑ̃kikinmɑ̃] NM *Fam (souci, problème)* nuisance; **enquiquinements** trouble; **mon patron me fait des enquiquinements** my boss is giving me trouble; **je n'ai que des enquiquinements**

avec ma voiture I have nothing but trouble with my car, my car gives me nothing but trouble

enquiquiner [ɑ̃kikine] VT *Fam (agacer)* to irritate, to annoy; *(lasser)* to bore (stiff)

enquiquineur, -euse [ɑ̃kikinœr, -øz] N *Fam* nuisance, pest; *(raseur)* (crashing) bore

enraciné [ɑ̃rasine] ADJ *(habitude, haine etc)* deep-rooted, deep-seated; **elle est enracinée dans cette région/ses habitudes** she is firmly rooted in this region/her habits

enracinement [ɑ̃rasinmɑ̃] NM **1** *(action d'enraciner)* *(d'un jeune arbre)* digging in **2** *(action de s'enraciner)* *(d'un arbre)*, *Fig (d'une idée etc)* taking root; *(d'une personne)* putting down of roots

enraciner [ɑ̃rasine] VT **1** *(arbre etc)* to dig in, to root **2** *Fig (principes etc)* to establish, to implant
VPR **s'enraciner** *(d'un arbre)* to take root; *Fig (d'une personne)* to put down roots; *Fig (de sentiments, d'habitudes, d'une coutume etc)* to take root, to become established *or* deeply rooted

enrageant, -e [ɑ̃raʒɑ̃] ADJ infuriating, maddening

enragé, -ée [ɑ̃raʒe] ADJ **1** *(chien etc)* rabid **2** *Fam (partisan etc)* rabid, out-and-out; *(sportif etc)* keen
N *Fam* fanatic; **un e. de golf** a golf fanatic *or* enthusiast, a keen golfer

enrager [ɑ̃raʒe] VI *(* **j'enrageai(s);** *n.* **enrageons***)* to be furious; **elle enrage de ne pas pouvoir le faire** she's furious at not being able to do it; **faire e. qn** to infuriate *or* madden sb; *(taquiner)* to tease sb

enrayage [ɑ̃rɛjaʒ] NM **1** *(blocage)* *(d'une roue)* locking; *(d'un mécanisme, d'une arme etc)* jamming **2** *(montage des rayons)* *(d'une roue)* spoking

enrayer [ɑ̃reje] VT **1** *(bloquer)* *(arme à feu, machine etc)* to jam; *(roue)* to lock; *Fig* **e. une maladie/un fléau** to arrest *or* check a disease/scourge **2** *(équiper de rayons)* *(roue)* to spoke
VPR **s'enrayer 1** *(d'une arme à feu, machine etc)* to jam **2** *(d'une épidémie)* to abate

enrayure [ɑ̃rɛjyr] NF *(rayons)* *(d'une roue)* spokes

enrégimenter [ɑ̃reʒimɑ̃te] VT **1** *(dans un parti, une organisation etc)* to enrol **2** *Mil* to form into regiments

enregistrable [ɑ̃r(ə)ʒistrabl] ADJ *(musique, émission etc)* recordable

enregistrement [ɑ̃r(ə)ʒistrəmɑ̃] NM **1** *(action d'inscrire)* *(de faits etc)* recording; *Jur (de la naissance, d'un acte etc)* registration; *(d'une commande)* booking, entering (up); *(de bagages)* check-in; **guichet d'e.** *(à l'aéroport etc)* check-in (desk); **e. anticipé** advanced check-in; **e. d'une compagnie** incorporation of a company; *Admin* **droit d'e.** stamp duty; *Admin* **l'E.** the Registration department
2 *Tech (action, disque etc)* recording; *Ordinat (de données)* logging, recording; **e. comptable** accounting entry; *Ordinat* **e. de transactions** transaction logging; **e. haute fidélité** hi-fi recording; **e. laser** *(procédé)* laser recording; *(disque)* laser disc; **e. magnétoscope** video recording; **e. numérique** digital recording; **e. vidéo** video recording; **e. sur bande/cassette** tape/cassette recording; **studio d'e.** recording studio; *TV, Radio* **e. son** *ou* **sonore** audio *or* sound recording; **e. vocal** voice recording; *TV* **camion d'e. (du son)** sound van; **passer un e.** to play a recording
3 *Ordinat (article de base de données)* record

enregistrer [ɑ̃r(ə)ʒistre] VT **1** *(inscrire)* *(faits* *etc)* to record; *Jur (naissance, acte etc)* to register; *(commande)* to book, to enter (up); *(bagages)* to check in; **société enregistrée** incorporated company; **les meilleures ventes enregistrées depuis des mois** the best recorded sales for months; **e. le courrier** to log the mail **2** *Fam (mémoriser)* to note, to memorize **3** *Tech (musique, émission)* to record, to tape; *(cassette vidéo)* to record; *(CD-ROM)* to write; *(données)* to store; **e. un disque** to make a record; **e. sur bande** to tape, to record on tape; **e. au magnétoscope** to video, to record on video; **musique enregistrée** recorded music; *Ordinat* **programme enregistré** stored programme
VPR **s'enregistrer** *(d'une cassette etc)* to record

enregistreur, -euse [ɑ̃r(ə)ʒistrœr, -øz] ADJ *(appareil, mécanisme)* recording; **caisse enregistreuse** cash register
NM *(appareil)* recorder
►► **e. à bande** (strip) chart recorder; **e. de pression** pressure recorder; **e. de son** *ou* **sonore** sound recorder; **e. à tambour** drum recorder; *Ind* **e. de temps** time clock *or* recorder; *Aviat* **e. de vol** flight recorder, black box

enrhumer [ɑ̃ryme] VT **e. qn** to give sb a cold; **être enrhumé** to have a cold
VPR **s'enrhumer** to catch a cold

enrichi [ɑ̃riʃi] ADJ **1** *(personne)* wealthy, *Péj* nouveau riche; *Fig* **il est sorti e. de ses voyages** his travelling has enriched his mind; **céréales enrichies en vitamines** cereals with added vitamins, vitamin-enriched cereals; **liquide vaisselle e. en lanoline** washing-up liquid with added lanolin *or* enriched with lanolin **2** *Typ (texte)* enhanced **3** *Phys (uranium)* enriched

enrichir [ɑ̃riʃir] VT **1** *(personne, pays)* to enrich, to make rich(er) **2** *Fig (art, collection, esprit etc)* to enrich; **e. la langue française** to enrich the French language **3** *Phys (uranium etc)* to enrich; **e. la terre** to enrich the soil **4** *Typ (texte)* to enhance
VPR **s'enrichir 1** *(d'une personne, d'un pays)* to grow rich(er) **2** *Fig (d'une langue etc)* to grow *or* become richer (**de** with; **en** in); **s'e. à force de lectures/de voyages** to enrich one's mind through reading/travel

enrichissant [ɑ̃riʃisɑ̃] ADJ *(expérience etc)* enriching

enrichissement [ɑ̃riʃismɑ̃] NM **1** *(de l'esprit, d'une collection etc)* enriching, enrichment; *(d'entreprise)* increase in capital; **e. personnel** personal enrichment **2** *Phys (de l'uranium etc)* enrichment **3** *Typ (attribut)* enhancement, special typographical feature **4** *TV, Radio* **e. audio** audio sweetening

enrobage [ɑ̃rɔbaʒ], **enrobement** [ɑ̃rɔbmɑ̃] NM *(action, enveloppe)* coating; **e. de sucre/ chocolat** sugar/chocolate coating

enrobé [ɑ̃rɔbe] ADJ *Fam* chubby, plump

enrober [ɑ̃rɔbe] VT *(bonbon, pilule etc)* to coat (**de** with); *Fig* **e. une nouvelle peu agréable dans un flot de paroles** to wrap up a piece of unpleasant news in a mass of words

enrôlé [ɑ̃role] NM *Mil* enlisted man

enrôlement [ɑ̃rolmɑ̃] NM enrolment; *Mil* enlistment

enrôler [ɑ̃role] VT *(membres, travailleurs)* to enrol, to recruit; *Mil* to enlist; *Hist* **e. de force** to press-gang, to impress
VPR **s'enrôler** to enrol; *Mil* to enlist

enroué, -e [ɑ̃rwe] ADJ *(personne, voix)* hoarse, husky

enrouement [ɑ̃rumɑ̃] NM hoarseness, huskiness

enrouer [ɑ̃rwe] VT *(voix, personne)* to make hoarse *or* husky

VPR s'enrouer to get hoarse; **s'e. à force de crier** to shout oneself hoarse

enroulable [ɑ̃rulabl] ADJ winding; *Aut* **cein-ture de sécurité e.** inertia-reel seat belt

enroulement [ɑ̃rulmɑ̃] NM 1 *(de tissu, tapis etc)* rolling up; *(de câble, ruban etc)* winding up 2 *Élec (fil)* coil, winding; **e. du champ d'excitation** field winding; **e. en série** series winding 3 *(ornement)* scroll, volute

enrouler [ɑ̃rule] VT 1 *(rouler)* (carte, tapis etc) to roll up; *(câble, ruban etc)* to wind up 2 *(envelopper)* to wrap up **(dans** in)
VPR s'enrouler *(d'un serpent etc)* to coil (up); *(d'un film, fil etc)* to wind; **s'e. dans une cou-verture** to wrap oneself up in a blanket

enrouleur [ɑ̃rulœr] NM *Aut* **e. (de ceinture de sécurité)** inertia reel, seat-belt retractor; **ceinture de sécurité à e.** inertia-reel seat belt

enrubanner [ɑ̃rybane] VT to decorate with a ribbon/ribbons

ENS [øɛnɛs] NF *(abrév* **École normale supé-rieure)** = university-level college that pre-pares students for senior posts in teaching and other professions

ENSA [ɛnsa] NF *(abrév* **École nationale supé-rieure agronomique)** = one of five competi-tive-entry agricultural engineering schools

ensablement [ɑ̃sabləmɑ̃] NM 1 *(d'un ba-teau)* running aground, stranding 2 *(d'un port)* silting up; *(de tuyaux)* choking up (with sand) 3 *(dépôt) (amené par l'eau)* sandbank, sand bar; *(amené par le vent)* sand dune

ensabler [ɑ̃sable] VT 1 *(sur le sable) (bateau)* to strand, to run aground; *(véhicule)* to get stuck in the sand 2 *(d'une inondation) (terre)* to cover with sand; *(port, rivière)* to silt up, to sand up
VPR s'ensabler 1 *(d'un bateau, véhicule, pois-son)* to get stuck in the sand 2 *(d'un port, d'une rivière)* to silt up; *(de tuyaux)* to get choked up (with sand)

ensachage [ɑ̃saʃaʒ] NM *(de bonbons etc)* bagging; *(de céréales etc)* sacking

ensacher [ɑ̃saʃe] VT *(bonbons etc)* to put in-to bags, to bag; *(céréales etc)* to put into sacks, to sack

ensanglanter [ɑ̃sɑ̃glɑ̃te] VT *(chemise, corps etc)* to stain with blood; **e. une nation** to plunge a nation into a bloodbath; **mains en-sanglantées** bloodstained *or* bloody hands; **événement ensanglanté par un attentat** event marred by the bloody violence of an assassination attempt

ENSBA NF *(abrév* **École nationale supérieure des Beaux-Arts)** = leading art school in Paris

enseignant, -ante [ɑ̃sɛɲɑ̃, -ɑ̃t] ADJ teach-ing; **corps e.** teaching profession
N teacher

enseigne [ɑ̃sɛɲ] NF 1 *(panonceau) (d'un ma-gasin, cinéma etc)* sign; **e. au néon** neon sign; **à l'e. du Lion d'or** at the (sign of the) Golden Lion; **e. bancaire** big bank; *Fig Fam* **nous sommes tous logés à la même e.** we are all in the same boat; *Prov* **à bon vin point d'e.** good wine needs no bush 2 *Mktg* brand name 3 *Litt* **à telle e. que ...** so much so that ... 4 *Hist, Mil (drapeau etc)* ensign
NM 1 *Hist, Mil (soldat)* standard-bearer, en-sign 2 *Naut* **e. (de vaisseau)** sub-lieutenant, *Am* ensign

enseignement [ɑ̃sɛɲmɑ̃] NM 1 *(instruc-tion)* teaching; **l'e. de l'anglais** the teaching of English; **méthode d'e.** teaching method; **il est dans l'e.** he is a teacher, he teaches 2 *(éducation, formation)* education; **e. des** *ou* **pour adultes** adult education; **e. du pre-mier/second degré, e. primaire/secondaire** primary/secondary education; **e. supérieur** higher education 3 *(leçon tirée de l'expé-rience)* lesson; **tirer un e. de qch** to learn a lesson from sth

▶▶**e. assisté par ordinateur** computer-aided *or* -assisted learning; **e. par corres-pondance** teaching by correspondence courses; **e. à distance** distance learning; **e. en groupe** group teaching; **e. libre** private education; **e. mixte** coeducation; **e. tech-nique** technical education

enseigner [ɑ̃sɛɲe] VT 1 *(apprendre)* to teach; **e. la grammaire à qn** to teach sb grammar; **e. à qn à faire qch** to teach sb (how) to do sth; **e. l'anglais** to teach English; **l'expérience nous enseigne que ...** expe-rience teaches *or* shows us that ... 2 *Vieilli (indiquer)* to show, to point out; **e. à qn son devoir** to point out his/her duty to sb
VI to be a teacher, to teach

ensemble [ɑ̃sɑ̃bl] ADV together; **vivre e.** to live together; **ils se marièrent e.** they mar-ried (each other); **aller (bien) e.** *(de per-sonnes)* to be well-matched; *(de choses)* to go together; **ils vont mal e.** *(de personnes)* they're ill-matched; **on pourrait partir tous e.** we could all go together *or* in a group; **ne répondez pas tous e.** don't all answer at once *or* at the same time; **vendre tous ses meubles e.** to sell all one's furniture at once
NM 1 *(totalité)* whole, entirety; **l'e. du travail est bon** the work as a whole is good; **l'e. d'un tableau** the general effect of a picture; **vue d'e.** comprehensive *or* general view, overall picture; **idée d'e.** *(d'un sujet)* broad *or* gene-ral idea; **dans l'e.** on the whole, taken all round, by and large; **la classe, prise dans son e., a un bon niveau** the class, (taken) as a whole, is of a good standard
2 *(unité)* cohesion, unity; **mouvement d'e.** combined movement; **l'exécution manque d'e.** the execution lacks cohesion *or* is rag-ged; **avec e.** all together, in unison, as one
3 *(groupe) (de gens)* group; *(d'objets, de faits, de conditions)* set; *(de meubles)* suite; *(de services etc)* package; **e. vocal** (small) choir; **e. de couleurs** harmonious (group of) colours; **e. de données** set of data; *Mktg* **e. de besoins** need set; *Mktg* **e. de considéra-tions** consideration *or* product (choice) set
4 *(vêtements)* ensemble, outfit; **e. pantalon** trouser suit, *Am* pant suit
5 *(d'habitations)* block; **grand e.** residential estate
6 *Math* set; **e. vide** empty set
7 *Aut* **e. moteur-boîte** power unit

ensemblier [ɑ̃sɑ̃blije] NM interior decora-tor; *Cin, TV* assistant set designer

ensemencement [ɑ̃s(ə)mɑ̃smɑ̃] NM 1 *Agr* sowing 2 *Biol* seeding

ensemencer [ɑ̃s(ə)mɑ̃se] VT *(j'ensemen-çai(s))* 1 *Agr (champ)* to sow 2 *Biol (milieu de culture)* to seed

enserrer [ɑ̃sere] VT *(objet, partie du corps)* to encircle tightly; **e. qn dans ses bras** to clasp sb in one's arms, to embrace *or* hug sb

ensevelir [ɑ̃səvlir] VT 1 *Litt (enterrer) (corps)* to bury, to entomb; *Fig (secret)* to hide away; **l'avalanche a enseveli le village sous la neige** the avalanche buried the village in snow; *Fig* **il a été enseveli sous des tonnes de lettres** he was snowed under with letters 2 *(mettre dans un linceul) (corps)* to shroud
VPR s'ensevelir *(dans un livre, à la campagne etc)* to bury oneself

ensevelissement [ɑ̃səvlismɑ̃] NM *(de mort)* burial; *(dans un linceul)* shrouding; *(sous la neige, des décombres etc)* burying; *Fig (de se-cret)* hiding away

ENSI [ɛnsi] NF *(abrév* **École nationale supé-rieure d'ingénieurs)** = competitive-entry engineering institute

ensilage [ɑ̃silaʒ] NM *(de récoltes)* ensilage

ensiler [ɑ̃sile] VT *(récoltes)* to ensile

ensoleillé [ɑ̃sɔleje] ADJ *(lieu, jour etc)* sunny

ensoleillement [ɑ̃sɔlɛjmɑ̃] NM 1 *(état)* sun-niness 2 *(période)* sunny period; **cinq jour-nées d'e.** five days of sun(shine)

ensoleiller [ɑ̃sɔleje] VT 1 *(pièce, mur etc)* to bathe in sunlight 2 *Fig (la vie de qn etc)* to brighten (up), to light up

ensommeillé [ɑ̃sɔmeje] ADJ *(personne)* sleepy, drowsy; *(yeux, visage)* sleepy

ensorcelant [ɑ̃sɔrsəlɑ̃] ADJ *(sourire etc)* bewitching

ensorcelé [ɑ̃sɔrsəle] ADJ bewitched, under a spell

ensorceler [ɑ̃sɔrsəle] VT *(j'ensorcelle; j'en-sorcellerai)* 1 *(envoûter)* to bewitch, to cast *or* put a spell (up) on 2 *Fig (personne)* to be-witch, to captivate

ensorceleur, -euse [ɑ̃sɔrsəlœr, -øz] ADJ bewitching
NM sorcerer; *Fig* charmer
NF **ensorceleuse** sorceress; *Fig* enchan-tress

ensorcellement [ɑ̃sɔrsɛlmɑ̃] NM 1 *(action)* bewitching; *(état)* bewitchment; *(sorcel-lerie)* sorcery 2 *Fig (charme)* charm, spell

ensuite [ɑ̃sɥit] ADV *(plus tard)* after(wards), later; *(puis)* then, next, after that; **et e.?** what then?, what next?; *Fam* **e. de quoi/de cela, il s'est mis en colère** after which/after that he lost his temper; **les pompiers marchaient en tête, e. venait la musique** the firemen led the procession, next came the band; **d'abord, c'est très cher, et e. ça ne te va pas du tout** for one thing it's very expensive and for another it doesn't at all suit you

ensuivre (s') [sɑ̃sɥivr] **VPR** *(conj like* **suivre***)* to follow, to ensue, to result; **jusqu'à ce que mort s'ensuive** *(battre qn etc)* to death; **les ré-sultats qui s'ensuivent** the results which en-sue *or* follow; **il s'ensuit qu'il est sans emploi** the consequence is he's out of a job; *Fam* **et tout ce qui s'ensuit** and all the rest of it, and all that goes with it; *Litt* **vos erreurs s'en-suivront de graves sanctions** your errors will result in grave punishment

ensuqué [ɑ̃syke] ADJ *Région, Fam* dazed, in a daze

entablement [ɑ̃tabləmɑ̃] NM *Archit (au-dessus d'une colonnade)* entablature; *Constr (support de toit)* coping

entacher [ɑ̃taʃe] VT 1 *(l'honneur de qn)* to sully, to besmirch, to cast a slur on 2 *Jur (contrat etc)* to vitiate; **entaché de nullité** voidable

entaille [ɑ̃taj] NF 1 *(dans un morceau de bois etc)* notch; *(longue)* groove; **à entailles** notched; *(longues)* grooved 2 *(blessure)* gash, cut; *(superficielle)* nick, cut; **se faire une e. au menton** to cut one's chin

entailler [ɑ̃taje] VT 1 *(morceau de bois etc)* to notch; *(d'une longue encoche)* to groove 2 *(blesser)* to gash, to cut; *(superficiellement)* to nick, to cut
VPR s'entailler **s'e. le doigt** to cut one's finger

entame [ɑ̃tam] NF 1 *(de pain, jambon etc)* first slice 2 *Cartes (d'une couleur)* opening (card)

entamer [ɑ̃tame] VT 1 *(pain, jambon etc)* to start on, to cut into; *(fût)* to broach; *(bou-teille, pot de confiture etc)* to start on, to open; *(défense)* to penetrate, to breach; *(chair)* to cut into; **e. la peau** to break the skin; **doutes qui entament la foi/les convic-tions de qn** doubts that undermine *or* shake sb's faith/convictions; **e. l'honneur de qn** to damage sb's honour; **e. son capital** to break into one's capital
2 *(commencer à entreprendre) (travail, re-cherche etc)* to begin, to commence, to start (on); *(négociations)* to start, to open; **e. une conversation** to strike up a conversation; **e. des démarches** to begin to take steps, to ini-

tiate steps; **e. des relations avec qn** to enter into relations with sb; *Jur* **e. des poursuites contre qn** to initiate *or* institute proceedings against sb; **e. un sujet** to broach a subject; *Com* **e. une vente** to open a sale **3** *Cartes* **e. trèfle** to open clubs

entartrage [ɑ̃tartraʒ] **NM** *(d'une chaudière etc)* furring (up), scaling

entartrer [ɑ̃tartre] **VT** *(chaudière etc)* to fur (up), to scale
VPR s'entartrer *(d'une chaudière)* to fur (up), to become furred; *(des dents)* to scale up

entassement [ɑ̃tasmɑ̃] **NM 1** *(de pierres etc)* piling (up), heaping (up); *(de caisses etc)* stacking **2** *(de passagers, bétail etc)* crowding *or* packing together

entasser [ɑ̃tase] **VT 1** *(pierres, livres, vêtements etc)* to pile (up), to heap (up); *(caisses etc)* to stack (up); *(argent)* to amass, to pile up **2** *(serrer) (passagers, bétail etc)* to pack *or* crowd *or* cram together
VPR s'entasser 1 *(d'objets)* to pile up **2** *(de personnes)* to crowd *or* huddle together

ente [ɑ̃t] **NF 1** *Agr etc (greffe)* scion, graft; *(porte-greffe)* stock **2** *(de pinceau)* handle

entendement [ɑ̃tɑ̃dmɑ̃] **NM** understanding; **dépasser l'e.** to be beyond all understanding

entendeur [ɑ̃tɑ̃dœr] **NM à bon e. salut!** a word to the wise (is enough)

ENTENDRE [ɑ̃tɑ̃dr]

VT to hear **1, 2** ▪ to listen to **2** ▪ to understand **3** ▪ to insinuate *(laisser entendre)* **3** ▪ to mean **4** ▪ to intend **5**
VI to hear
VPR to get on **1** ▪ to agree **2** ▪ to be heard **3** ▪ to be understood **4** ▪ to know about *(s'y entendre à)* **5**

VT 1 *(ouïr)* to hear; **j'entendis un cri** I heard a cry; **je n'entends rien (de ce que tu dis)** I can't hear a thing (you're saying); **on l'entend à peine** you can hardly hear him/it, he/it is scarcely audible; **je pouvais à peine me faire e.** I could hardly make myself heard; **parlez plus fort, je ne vous entends pas bien** speak up, I can't hear you very well; **je l'entendis rire** I heard him laugh *or* laughing; **tu n'as pas entendu quelque chose?** didn't you hear anything?; **on n'entend que toi, ici! c'est lassant à la fin!** yours is the only voice we can hear, it's so annoying!; **e. qch de ses propres oreilles** to hear sth with one's own ears; **je ne veux plus e. parler de lui** I don't want to hear him mentioned again *or* to hear another word about him; **e. dire que ...** to hear (it said) that ...; **on a entendu dire que sa femme l'a quitté** it is rumoured *or* said that his wife has left him; **je le sais parce que je l'ai entendu dire** I know it by *or* from hearsay; **e. qn dire qch** to hear sb say sth; **e. parler de** *(connaître l'existence de)* to hear of; *(être au courant de)* to hear about; **je ne veux pas en e. parler!** I don't want to hear (a word) about it!; **celui-là, il va e. parler de moi** *ou* **du pays!** he'll get a piece of my mind *or* a good ear-bashing!; **celui-là, il va m'e.!** he'll hear *me*!; **je ne veux pas en e. plus!** I don't want to hear any more *or* another word about it!; **il répétait, à qui voulait l'e., que ...** he'd tell anyone who would listen that ...; **je l'entends d'avance** *ou* **d'ici!** I can hear it already!; **e. des voix** to hear voices; *Fam* **ce qu'il ne faut pas e.!** I've heard it all now!; *Fam* **qu'entends-je, qu'ouïs-je, qu'acoustiqué-je?** *ou* **qu'entends-je, qu'ouïs-je, rêvé-je ou dors-je?** ≃ I can't believe my ears! SEE GRAMMAR A39; B35
2 *(écouter) (suppliant etc)* to hear, to listen to; **on le congédia sans l'e.** he was dismissed without a hearing *or* without being heard; **e.**

la messe to hear a mass; **e. qn en confession** to hear sb's confession; **aller e. un concert** to go to a concert; **à vous e., il a eu tort** judging from *or* going by what you say, he was in the wrong; **refuser d'e. une requête** to turn a deaf ear to a request; **e. raison** to listen to reason; **il n'a rien voulu e.** he would not listen; *Jur* **l'affaire sera entendue demain** the case will be heard *or* comes up (for hearing) tomorrow; **le juge a entendu les témoins** the judge heard the witnesses; **que Dieu entende nos prières** may our prayers be answered
3 *(comprendre) (langue, passage d'un texte etc)* to understand; **ce n'est pas ainsi qu'il l'entend** he doesn't see it that way *or* like that; **donner à e. à qn que ...** *(faire croire)* to lead sb to believe that ...; *(faire comprendre)* to give sb to understand that ...; **laisser e. qch** to insinuate *or* imply sth; **il n'entend pas la plaisanterie** he can't take a joke; **je n'y entends rien** I don't know the first thing about it
4 *(vouloir dire)* to mean; **qu'entendez-vous par là?** what do you mean by that?
5 *(vouloir)* **e. faire qch** to intend *or* mean to do sth; **il n'y entend pas malice** he means *or* intends no harm; **faites comme vous l'entendez** do as you think best, do as you please; **j'entends que vous veniez** I expect you to come; **je n'entends pas qu'on le vende** I won't have it being sold; **elle voulait trouver du travail, mais lui ne l'entendait pas ainsi** she wanted to get a job, but he wouldn't hear of it
VI *(par l'ouïe)* to hear; **il entend mal** he is hard of hearing; **il est impossible de se faire e. ici!** it's impossible to make youself heard here!; **un bruit se fit e.** a noise was heard; **attends, j'ai mal entendu!** hold on, I don't think I heard you right!; **tu entends!** *(menace)* do you hear (me)!
VPR s'entendre 1 *(sympathiser)* to get on; **ils s'entendent bien** they get on (well); **je ne m'entends pas du tout avec elle** I don't get on at all with her; **je crois que nous sommes faits pour nous e.** I think we were made to get on well together; **nous n'étions pas faits pour nous e.** we weren't suited to each other; **ils s'entendent comme larrons en foire** they are as thick as thieves
2 *(se mettre d'accord)* to agree; **s'e. directement avec qn** to come to a direct understanding with sb; **s'e. pour commettre un crime** to conspire to commit a crime; **il faudrait vous e., il est venu ou il n'est pas venu?** get your story straight, did he come or not?; **entendons-nous bien!** *(mettons les choses au clair)* let's get things straight!
3 *(être perçu par l'ouïe)* to be heard; **sa voix ne s'entend guère** his/her voice is hardly audible *or* can hardly be heard; **on ne s'entend plus ici** you can't hear yourself speak *or* think here
4 *(être compris)* to be understood; **cela s'entend** of course, that goes without saying
5 s'e. à, s'y e. à *(être habile à) (chevaux, voitures etc)* to know (all) about, to understand; **s'e. aux affaires** to have a good head for business; **elle s'y entend à mettre de l'huile sur le feu** she has a knack for adding fuel to the fire

entendu, -ue [ɑ̃tɑ̃dy] **ADJ 1** *(complice, informé) (regard, sourire)* knowing; **d'un air e.** knowingly; **intérêt bien e.** enlightened self-interest **2** *(décidé)* très bien, **(c'est)** e. fine, agreed *or* all right!; **c'est une affaire entendue** that's agreed *or* settled; **et bien e., vous toucherez la moitié du bénéfice** and of course, you'll get half the profit
N *Vieilli* **faire l'e.** to pretend to know all about it

enténébrer [ɑ̃tenebre] **VT** (**il enténèbre; il**

enténébrera) *Litt* to envelop *or* plunge in darkness *or* gloom

entente [ɑ̃tɑ̃t] **NF 1** *(entre personnes) (accord)* agreement, understanding (**entre** *bet-* ween); *(relation)* harmony; **arriver à une e.** to reach an agreement *or* understanding; **terrain d'e.** common ground; **après e. avec les autorités** after consultation with the authorities; **il faut vivre en bonne e. avec ses voisins** one must live in harmony with one's neighbours; **la bonne/mauvaise e. qui règne dans la famille** the good/bad feeling that prevails in the family **2** *(compréhension)* **mot à double e.** word with a double meaning ▸▸ *Hist* **E. cordiale** Entente Cordiale; **e. industrielle** *(cartel)* combine

enter [ɑ̃te] **VT** *(arbre)* to graft

entérinement [ɑ̃terinmɑ̃] **NM** *Jur* ratification, confirmation; *Fig* endorsement

entériner [ɑ̃terine] **VT** *Jur* to ratify, to confirm; *Fig (approuver) (action, nouveau mot etc)* to endorse

entérique [ɑ̃terik] **ADJ** *Méd* enteric, intestinal

entérite [ɑ̃terit] **NF** *Méd* enteritis

enterrement [ɑ̃tɛrmɑ̃] **NM 1** *(sous la terre)* burial, *Fml* interment; *Fig* **c'est l'e. de tous mes projets/espoirs** that has killed off all my plans/hopes; *Hum* **c'était vraiment un e. de première classe** it really got the thumbs down; *Hum* **faire un e. de première classe à un projet** to give a plan the thumbs down, to shelve a plan for good **2** *(cérémonie)* funeral; *Fam* **figure** *ou* **tête d'e.** long face; **faire une tête d'e.** to look sombre **3** *(cortège)* funeral procession

enterrer [ɑ̃tere] **VT 1** *(enfouir) (chose)* to bury, to put in the earth; *(bulbes)* to plant **2** *(inhumer) (corps)* to bury, *Fml* to inter; *Fam* **il nous enterrera tous** he will outlive us all; *Fig* **e. un projet** to scrap a plan; *Fig* **e. un désaccord/une querelle** to bury a disagreement/a quarrel; *Fig* **elle désire e. toute cette affaire** she wants the whole thing buried and forgotten; *Fig* **e. sa vie de garçon** to have a stag party *or* Am bachelor party
VPR s'enterrer *Fig* **il s'est enterré au fin fond de la campagne normande** he buried himself in the depths of the Normandy countryside

entêtant [ɑ̃tɛtɑ̃] **ADJ** *(vin, parfum, musique etc)* heady

en-tête, *pl* **en-têtes** [ɑ̃tɛt] **NM** *(d'une lettre, d'un document)* heading; *Com* letterhead; *Typ (d'une page etc)* headline; *Ordinat* header; **e. de facture** billhead; *Journ* **e. de colonne** column header; **papier à e.** headed paper

entêté, -ée [ɑ̃tete] **ADJ** obstinate, stubborn
N obstinate *or* stubborn person

entêtement [ɑ̃tetmɑ̃] **NM** obstinacy, stubbornness; **e. à faire qch** persistence in doing sth

entêter [ɑ̃tete] **VT e. qn** *(d'un vin, d'une odeur, de la musique etc)* to go to sb's head, to make sb giddy
VPR s'entêter to persist, to be persistent; **s'e. dans une opinion** to persist in an opinion; **s'e. à faire qch** to persist in doing sth

enthousiasmant [ɑ̃tuzjasmɑ̃] **ADJ** *(plan, idée etc)* exciting

enthousiasme [ɑ̃tuzjasm] **NM** enthusiasm (**pour** for); **avec e.** enthusiastically, with enthusiasm; **faire qch sans e.** to do sth half-heartedly *or* without enthusiasm

enthousiasmer [ɑ̃tuzjasme] **VT** *(personne)* to fire *or* fill with enthusiasm; **il est revenu enthousiasmé** he came back full of *or* fired with enthusiasm
VPR s'enthousiasmer to be/become enthusiastic, to enthuse (**pour** about)

enthousiaste [ātuzjast] N enthusiast ADJ enthusiastic

entiché [ātiʃe] ADJ infatuated (**de** with), *Fam* crazy (**de** about)

enticher (s') [sātiʃe] VPR **s'e. de qn/qch** to become infatuated with *or Fam* crazy about sb/sth

entier, -ière [ātje, -jɛr] ADJ **1** (*sans division, sans diminution*) (*ville, boîte, quantité etc*) whole, entire; (*pas cassé, pas entamé*) (*assiette, gâteau etc*) intact, whole; (*boîte, bouteille etc*) full; **lait e.** whole milk, *Br* full-cream milk; **la France entière** the whole of France; **il a mangé le gâteau tout e.** he ate the whole (of the) cake; **pendant des heures entières** for hours on end; **conserver sa réputation entière** to keep one's reputation intact; **le problème reste e.** the problem is no nearer solution *or* remains unsolved; *Math* **nombre e.** integer, whole number; **cheval e.** stallion; **payer place entière** *Rail* to pay full fare; *Théâtre* to pay full price **2** (*absolu*) (*autorité, confiance etc*) complete, full; **l'entière direction de qch** the entire *or* sole management of sth; **se donner tout e. à son travail** to devote oneself entirely to one's work; **elle est tout(e) entière à ce qu'elle fait** she is engrossed in *or* intent on what she is doing; **jouir d'une entière liberté** to enjoy complete *or* total freedom; **donner entière satisfaction** to give complete *or* total satisfaction **3** (*sans compromis*) (*personne*) unyielding, uncompromising NM **1** (*totalité*) entirety; **raconter une histoire dans son e.** to relate a story in its entirety; **en e.** wholly, entirely, totally; **il a lu le livre en e.** he read the whole (of the) book *or* the entire book; **il a fait ses devoirs en e.** he has done all (of) his homework; **nom en e.** name in full, full name **2** *Math* (*nombre*) integer, whole number

entièrement [ātjɛrmā] ADV entirely, wholly, completely; **il n'est pas e. mauvais** he's not all bad

entièreté [ātjɛrte] NF entirety

entité [ātite] NF entity; *Compta* item

entoilage [ātwalaʒ] NM **1** (*action*) (*de carte etc*) mounting on canvas; *Couture* stiffening with canvas **2** (*toile*) canvas mount

entoiler [ātwale] VT (*carte etc*) to mount on canvas; *Couture* to stiffen with canvas; **carte entoilée** canvas-mounted map

entôler [ātole] VT *Arg* (*en particulier d'une prostituée*) (*client etc*) to fleece, to rob

entomologie [ātɔmɔlɔʒi] NF entomology

entomologique [ātɔmɔlɔʒik] ADJ entomological

entomologiste [ātɔmɔlɔʒist] N entomologist

entonner¹ [ātɔne] VT (*vin etc*) to barrel, to cask

entonner² VT (*commencer à chanter*) (*chanson*) to strike up, to start; *Vieilli* **e. les louanges de qn** to sing sb's praises

entonnoir [ātɔnwar] NM **1** (*ustensile*) funnel; **en (forme d')e.** funnel-shaped **2** (*cavité*) funnel; (*produit par une bombe etc*) crater

entorse [ātɔrs] NF **1** *Méd* sprain, wrench; **se faire une e. à la cheville/au poignet** to sprain *or* twist *or* wrench one's ankle/wrist **2** *Fig* **faire une e. à la loi/au règlement** to bend *or* stretch the law/the rules; **faire une e. à la vérité** to twist *or* distort the truth; **faire une e. à son régime** to break one's diet; **tu peux bien faire une petite e. à tes habitudes** you can surely make an exception

entortillement [ātɔrtijmā] NM **1** (*action*) (*d'un fil, papier etc*) twisting, wrapping; (*d'un serpent, du lierre etc*) twisting, twining, coiling **2** (*état*) entwinement

entortiller [ātɔrtije] VT **1** (*envelopper*) (*bonbon etc*) to wrap (up) (**dans** in); (*enrouler*) (*fil, papier etc*) to twist, to wrap (**autour de** round) **2** (*circonvenir*) (*personne*) to get round **3** (*embrouiller*) (*phrases, réponses etc*) to make convoluted; **e. une demande dans des explications fumeuses** to wrap up a request in woolly explanations

VPR **s'entortiller 1** (*d'un serpent, du lierre etc*) to twist, to twine, to coil (**autour de** round) **2** (*s'empêtrer*) to get entangled, to get tangled (up) (**dans** in); **il s'est entortillé les pieds dans le tapis** he got his feet entangled *or* tangled up in the carpet; *Fig* **elle s'entortillait dans des explications compliquées** she tied herself in knots with complicated explanations **3** (*s'enrouler*) (*dans une couette etc*) to wrap oneself up (**dans** in)

entour [ātur] NM **à l'e. de** (*ville etc*) round (about); *Litt* **les entours de** the environs *or* surroundings of

entourage [āturaʒ] NM **1** (*bordure*) (*d'une ouverture, d'un parterre de fleurs etc*) border; (*d'un bijou*) setting; **miniature avec un e. de perles** miniature set in pearls **2** (*amis, relations*) circle (of friends/acquaintances); (*collègues*) associates; (*de ministre etc*) attendants; (*de souverain*) entourage, suite; **dans son e. proche** in his/her close circle

entourer [āture] VT **1** (*border, enceindre*) to surround (**de** with); **e. un champ d'une clôture** to fence in a field; **veuillez e. la bonne réponse en rouge** please circle *or* ring the correct answer in red; **e. qn de ses bras** to put one's arms round sb, to hold *or* take sb in one's arms; **cheminée entourée de marbre** fireplace enclosed in marble **2** (*être autour de*) to surround; (*armée*) to encircle, to surround; **les gens qui vous entourent** the people around *or* about you; **le monde qui nous entoure** the world around us; **entouré d'amis** surrounded by friends; **un rang de perles entourait son cou** a string of pearls encircled her neck, she had a string of pearls round her neck; **entouré de mystère** wrapped *or* shrouded in mystery **3** (*s'occuper de*) (*personne*) to rally round; **il est très entouré (d'amis)** he is surrounded by friends; **e. qn de soins/respect** to lavish attention on sb/to show respect to sb; **au moment de son divorce, sa famille l'a beaucoup entouré** his family rallied round *or* supported him at the time of his divorce

VPR **s'entourer s'e. d'amis/de belles choses** to surround oneself with friends/fine things

entourloupe [āturlup], **entourloupette** [āturlupɛt] NF *Fam* dirty trick; **faire une e. à qn** to play a dirty trick on sb

entourlouper [āturlupe] VT *Fam* **e. qn** to play a dirty trick on sb, *Br* to do the dirty on sb, *Am* to do sb dirt

entourloupette [āturlupɛt] NF nasty *or* dirty trick; **faire une e. à qn** to play a dirty trick on sb

entournure [āturnyr] NF (*de vêtement*) armhole; *Fam* **être gêné aux entournures** (*mal à l'aise*) to feel awkward *or* ill at ease; (*financièrement*) to feel the pinch

entracte [ātrakt] NM **1** *Théâtre, Cin* (*intervalle*) intermission, *Br* interval; **à l'e.** in the intermission *or Br* interval **2** *Théâtre* (*pièce*) entr'acte, interlude

entraide [ātrɛd] NF mutual aid

entraider (s') [sātrede] VPR to help one another *or* each other

entrailles [ātraj] NFPL (*du corps*) entrails, intestines, bowels; *Litt* (*de la mère*) womb; *Fig* **les e. de la terre** the bowels of the earth; *Fig* **ce reportage m'a remué les e.** this report made a deep and painful impression on me; *Fig* **ne pas avoir d'e.** to be heartless

entrain [ātrɛ̃] NM (*d'une fête, musique, conversation etc*) liveliness, spirit; (*d'une personne*) high spirits, spirit, liveliness; **être plein d'e., avoir de l'e.** (*d'une personne*) to be full of life *or* of go; **musique pleine d'e.** lively music; **manger avec e.** to eat with gusto; **travailler avec e.** to work with a will; **donner plus d'e. à la conversation** to liven up the conversation; **ça manque d'e., tout ça** that's all a bit half-hearted; **faire qch sans e.** to do sth half-heartedly

entraînant [ātrɛnā] ADJ (*air, rythme, style*) lively; (*éloquence*) stirring

entraînement [ātrɛnmā] NM **1** (*d'un élève etc*), *Sport, Courses de chevaux* training; **un e.** a training session, a work-out; **suivre un e.** to follow a training programme; **à l'e.** in training; **il s'est blessé à l'e.** he hurt himself training; **il a marqué un but comme à l'e.** he scored a text-book goal; **match d'e.** practice game; **terrain d'e.** training *or* practice ground; **avoir de l'e.** to be well trained; *Fig Fam* **toi qui as de l'e., fais-le** you've had a lot of practice at this type of thing, you do it; **manquer d'e.** to be out of training **2** *Tech* drive; **arbre d'e.** drive shaft; *Aut* **e. par chaîne** chain drive; **e. à friction** (*d'une imprimante*) friction feed; *Ordinat* **e. du papier** (*d'une imprimante*) paper advance; **e. à picots** *ou* **à traction** (*d'une imprimante*) tractor drive *or* feed **3** *Litt* (*des passions*) force

entraîner [ātrene] VT **1** (*d'une rivière etc*) to sweep along, to carry away; (*d'une locomotive etc*) to pull, to draw (along); **e. qn quelque part** to drag *or* take sb off somewhere; **il m'a entraîné chez lui** he took me along to his house; **il vous entraînera dans sa chute** he will drag you down with him **2** *Tech* (*partie de machine etc*) to drive; *Tech* **entraîné par courroie** belt-driven **3** (*exercer une influence sur*) **e. qn à faire qch** to lead *or* induce sb to do sth; **être entraîné dans un piège** to be lured *or* led into a trap; **cela nous entraînera dans des problèmes** that will lead *or* get us into problems; **entraîné par l'éloquence de l'orateur** carried away by the speaker's eloquence; **se faire e.** to be *or* get led astray; **se laisser e.** to allow oneself to be led astray; **se laisser e. à faire qch** to be drawn into doing sth **4** (*causer*) (*accident, malheur etc*) to result in, to bring about; (*problème, dépense etc*) to entail, to involve; **cela entraînera un retard** it will involve *or* lead to delay; **décision qui peut e. des inconvénients** decision that may give rise to difficulties **5** (*former*) (*élève etc*) to train; *Sport* (*athlète, équipe*) to coach, to train; (*cheval de course etc*) to train; (*cycliste*) to pace; **e. qn à faire qch** to train sb to do sth

VPR **s'entraîner** (*d'un élève etc*) to train oneself; *Sport* to train; **s'e. à faire qch** to train oneself to do sth

entraîneur [ātrɛnœr] NM **1** *Sport* (*d'un athlète, d'une équipe*) coach, trainer; (*d'un cheval etc*) trainer; (*d'un cycliste*) pacemaker, pacer **2** (*chef*) **e. d'hommes** leader of men

entraîneuse [ātrɛnøz] NF **1** (*dans une boîte de nuit etc*) hostess **2** *Sport* (*d'une athlète, d'une équipe*) coach, trainer; (*d'un cheval etc*) trainer

entrant [ātrā] ADJ (*fonctionnaire*) newly appointed; (*représentant parlementaire*) newly elected; **les élèves entrants** the new pupils NLES **entrants et les sortants** those entering and those leaving

entrapercevoir [ātraparsəvwar] VT (*conj like* **apercevoir**) to catch a fleeting glimpse of

entrave [ātrav] NF **1** (*d'un cheval etc*) hobble; **entraves** (*d'un forçat etc*) fetters, shackles **2** *Fig* hindrance, impediment (**à** to); **e. à la cir-**

culation hindrance to traffic; **e. à la liberté/à la bonne marche de la justice** interference with freedom/with the due process of the law

entravé [ãtrave] ADJ **jupe entravée** hobble skirt

entraver [ãtrave] VT **1** *(cheval etc)* to hobble; *(forçat etc)* to put in fetters or shackles **2** *Fig (action, carrière etc)* to hinder, to hamper, to impede; **e. la circulation** to hold up or block the traffic **3** *Fam (comprendre)* to get; **je n'y entrave rien** *ou* **que dalle** I don't get it (at all)

ENTRE [ãtr]

between **1, 4, 5** ▪ among **2, 4, 5** ▪ in **2, 3** ▪ of **2** ▪ through **5**

PRÉP *SEE GRAMMAR A69; B56* **1** *(deux choses, personnes, dates etc)* between; **choisir e. deux choses** to choose between two things; **distance de 10 kilomètres e. deux villes** distance of 10 kilometres between two towns; **e. deux et trois (heures)** between two and three (o'clock); *Fig* **e. les deux** *(ni l'un ni l'autre)* between the two; *(comme ci comme ça)* so-so; **être e. la vie et la mort** to be between life and death; **être e. deux âges** to be middle-aged; *Fig* **voir qn/faire qch e. deux portes** to see sb/to do sth for a brief moment **2** *(parmi)* among(st); **un homme dangereux e. tous** a most dangerous man; **un homme qu'il admirait e. tous** a man he admired above all others; **un jour e. mille** a day in a thousand; **il y avait e. autres, un Dürer et un Rembrandt** there were, among(st) other things or others, a Dürer and a Rembrandt; **ce jour e. tous** this day of all days; **d'e.** (from) among; **plusieurs d'e. nous** several of us; **l'und'e. vous** one of you; **hésiter e. plusieurs solutions/routes/robes** to hesitate between several solutions/roads/dresses; **elle l'a choisi e. tous les hommes présents** she chose him from among all the men present **3** *(dans)* **tomber e. les mains de l'ennemi** to fall into the enemy's hands; **tenir qch e. les mains** to hold sth in one's hands; **serrer qn e. ses bras** to clasp sb in one's arms, to hug sb; **parler e. ses dents** to mumble, to mutter; **e. ces murs** within these walls **4** *(rapport réciproque) (deux personnes)* between; *(plus de deux personnes)* among(st); **ils se sont mis d'accord e. eux** they agreed among(st) themselves; **qu'est-ce qu'il y a de semblable e. lui et moi?** what similarities are there between him and me?; **mais qu'y a-t-il e. eux, exactement?** but what's (going on) between them exactly?; **soit dit e. nous** between ourselves; **nous dînerons e. nous** we'll have dinner alone or by ourselves; **nous sommes e. amis** we are among(st) friends; **se marier e. cousins** to intermarry with cousins; **discuter e. connaisseurs** to talk as one expert to another; *Fam* **il faut que je te parle e. quat'z'yeux** I've got to talk to you in private **5** *(à travers)* through; **se faufiler e. les arbres** to thread one's way through or between or among(st) the trees; **passer e. les mailles** to slip through the net; **lire e. les lignes** to read between the lines

entrebâillement [ãtrabajmã] NM **l'e. de la porte/fenêtre** the half-open door/window

entrebâiller [ãtrabaje] VT *(porte, fenêtre)* to half-open; **la porte était entrebâillée** the door was ajar or half open

entrebâilleur [ãtrabajœr] NM door chain

entrechat [ãtraʃa] NM **1** *(saut de danse)* entrechat **2** *(gambade)* leap; **faire des entrechats** to prance (about), to cavort

entrechoquer [ãtraʃoke] VT to knock or bang together; **e. des verres** to chink glasses ▪ VPR **s'entrechoquer** to knock or bang

against one another; *(de verres)* to chink; *Fig (de personnalités, d'idées etc)* to clash; **elle parle tellement vite que les mots s'entrechoquent** the words come tumbling out when she speaks

entrecôte [ãtrakot] NF *Culin* rib steak, entrecôte

entrecoupé [ãtrakupe] ADJ *(discours, sommeil, voyage etc)* interrupted, broken; *(représentation, lecture etc)* interrupted; **d'une voix entrecoupée** with a catch in one's voice

entrecouper [ãtrakupe] VT *(discours, voyage, représentation etc)* to interrupt (**de** with)

entrecroisement [ãtrakrwazmã] NM *(de lignes etc)* intersection, crisscross; *(de fils etc)* interlacing

entrecroiser [ãtrakrwaze] VT *(lignes etc)* to intersect, to (criss)cross; *(fils etc)* to interlace

▪ VPR **s'entrecroiser** *(de lignes, routes etc)* to intersect, to (criss)cross; *(de fils etc)* to interlace

entre-déchirer (s') [sãtradeʃire] VPR to tear each other to pieces

entre-deux [ãtradø] NM INV **1 il est arrivé dans l'e.** he arrived in the intervening period **2** *Couture (bande)* insertion

entre-deux-guerres [ãtradøgɛr] NM INV inter-war years *(1918-1939)*

entre-dévorer (s') [sãtradevɔre] VPR to devour one another or each other

ENTRÉE [ãtre] NF **1** *(action d'entrer)* entry, entrance; **e. (en scène) d'un acteur** an actor's entrance (on to the stage); **à leur e., tous se levèrent** as they entered, everybody stood up; **faire son e.** to make one's entrance; **faire une e. triomphale/discrète** to make a triumphal/discreet entrance; **faire son e. dans le monde** *(d'une fille)* to come out (into society); **l'e. en gare du train** the entry of the train into the station; **l'e. du Japon dans la seconde guerre mondiale** the entry of Japan into the Second World War; **depuis l'e. en guerre du pays** since the country entered the war; **mon e. dans cette société date de six mois** I joined this company six months ago; **e. en fonction** assumption or taking up of one's duties; **l'e. en fonction du nouveau directeur est prévue pour le ...** the new director is scheduled to take up his post on ...; **e. en fusion** beginning to melt; **e. en ébullition** coming to the boil; *Fig* **à l'e. de l'hiver** at the beginning of winter; *Fig* **d'e. (de jeu)** from the outset, from the very beginning **2** *(accès)* admission, admittance **(dans un** *ou* **d'un lieu** to a place); **se voir refuser l'e. d'un lieu** to find oneself refused admission or entry to a place; **avoir ses entrées dans un lieu** to have the run of a place; **avoir ses entrées chez** *ou* **auprès de qn** to have free access to sb; **e. interdite** no admittance, no entry; **e. interdite au public/aux moins de 12 ans** public/under 12s not admitted, no admittance to the public/to under 12s; **e. interdite à tout véhicule** vehicles prohibited; **payer son e.** to pay one's admission fee or entrance fee; **prendre une e. au musée/ théâtre** to buy a museum/theatre ticket; **film qui fait des records d'e.** film that breaks box-office records; **on a fait mille entrées le premier soir** a thousand people came on the first night; **e. à l'hôpital** admission into hospital **3** *(action de devenir membre)* **e. dans l'armée/le club/le parti** joining the army/club/ party; **e. dans l'enseignement/la finance** going into or taking up teaching/finance; **e. à l'université** going into university; **e. au couvent** going into a convent, taking the veil; **l'e. de la Norvège dans la CEE** Norway's en-

try into the EEC; **mon e. dans cette famille ne s'est pas vraiment bien passée** I didn't fit into the family very well

4 *Com* entry; *(de marchandises importées)* importation; **droit d'e.** import duty; **e. en douane** inward customs clearance

5 *(voie d'accès)* way in, entrance, entry (**de** to); *(d'un tunnel, port etc)* entrance, mouth; *(vestibule)* entrance hall; **e. réservée au personnel** staff entrance; **e. des fournisseurs** tradesmen's entrance; **e. principale** main entrance

6 *(ouverture)* **e. de clef** keyhole; **e. d'air** air intake; *Radio* **e. de poste** lead-in

7 *Ordinat (processus)* input, entry; *(information)* entry; *(touche)* enter (key); *(de caractère etc)* entering; **données d'e.** input (data); **e. (par le) clavier** keyboard input; **e. (à partir du) scanneur** scanned input; **e. de données** data input or entry; **e. de données à distance** remote data input or entry; **e. de gamme** entry level; **e. de papier** paper input; **e. opérateur** operator input; **e./sortie** input/ output; **e./sortie parallèles** parallel input/ output

8 *Culin* starter

9 *(de dictionnaire, livre de comptes etc)* entry

10 *Compta (dans un livre de comptes)* entry; **e. d'argent** cash received

▸ ▸ **e. des artistes** stage door; **e. libre** *(dans un musée)* admission free, free admission; *(dans une boutique)* no obligation to buy; **e. en matière: après cette e. en matière** after this introduction; *Radio* **e. de poste** lead-in; **e. de service** service entrance; **e. en vigueur** coming into force or effect or operation

entre-égorger (s') [sãtregɔrʒe] VPR to cut one another's or each other's throats

entrefaites [ãtrafɛt] NFPL **sur ces e.** at that moment

entrefilet [ãtrafilɛ] NM *Journ* paragraph, short item; **l'affaire a eu droit à un e.** there was a paragraph or there were a few lines in the newspaper about it

entregent [ãtraʒã] NM social sense, savoir-faire; **elle a de l'e.** she knows how to get on with people

entrejambe [ãtraʒãb] NM *Couture* crotch, crutch; **hauteur de l'e.** inside leg measurement

entrelacement [ãtralasmã] NM *(de rubans, fils, branches)* intertwining, interlacing, interweaving

entrelacer [ãtralase] *(conj like* **lacer***)* VT *(rubans, fils, branches)* to intertwine, to interlace, to interweave; **les mains entrelacées** with one's/their/*etc* fingers entwined; *Ordinat* **écran entrelacé** interlaced screen

▪ VPR **s'entrelacer** to intertwine, to interlace, to interweave

entrelacs [ãtrala] NM interlaced design, tracery

entrelarder [ãtralarde] VT *Culin (viande)* to lard; *Fig* **e. un discours de citations** to interlard a speech with quotations

entremêlement [ãtramɛlmã] NM **1** *(action)* (inter)mingling **2** *(résultat)* (inter)mixture

entremêler [ãtramele] VT to (inter)mix, to (inter)mingle; **e. des couleurs** to mix or blend colours; **ordres entremêlés de jurons** orders interspersed with oaths

▪ VPR **s'entremêler** to (inter)mix, to (inter)mingle

entremets [ãtramɛ] NM *Culin* dessert, *Br* sweet

entremetteur, -euse [ãtramɛtœr, -øz] N *(dans une querelle)* intermediary, mediator; *(dans une liaison amoureuse)* go-between

entremettre (s') [sãtramɛtr] VPR *(conj like* **mettre***)* *(dans une querelle)* to intervene, to mediate; *(dans une liaison amoureuse)* to act as go-between

entremise [ātrəmiz] NF intervention, mediation; **par l'e. de qn** through sb

entrepont [ātrəpɔ̃] NM *Naut* 'tween decks; **passager d'e.** steerage passenger

entreposage [ātrəpozaʒ] NM storing; *(en douane)* bonding

entreposer [ātrəpoze] VT to store; *(en douane)* to bond, to put in bond; **e. des marchandises** to warehouse goods, to put goods in a warehouse

entrepositaire [ātrəpozitɛr] NM *(employé)* warehouseman

entrepôt [ātrəpo] NM warehouse, store; **e. (de la douane)** bonded warehouse; **e. frigorifique** cold store; **e. de stockage** warehouse; **marchandises en e.** goods in store; *(en douane)* goods in bond; **e. privé/public** private/public bonded warehouse

entreprenant [ātrəprənā] ADJ enterprising, go-ahead; *(auprès des femmes)* forward

entreprenariat [ātrəprənarja] NM entrepreneurship

entreprendre [ātrəprādr] VT *(conj like* **prendre**) **1** *(commencer)* *(tâche, étude, voyage etc)* to undertake; **e. des démarches** to take steps; **e. de faire qch** to undertake to do sth **2 e. une femme** to make advances to(wards) a woman **3** *(entretenir)* **elle m'a entrepris sur son sujet favori** she engaged me in conversation about *or* started talking to me about her favourite subject

entrepreneur, -euse [ātrəprənœr, -øz] N **1** *Constr* contractor; **e. (en bâtiment)** building contractor; **e. de transports** carrier, *Br* haulier, *Am* hauler; **e. de pompes funèbres** undertaker, funeral director, *Am* mortician **2** *(patron)* businessman

entreprise [ātrəpriz] NF **1** *(action, initiative)* enterprise, undertaking, venture; *Écon* **libre e.** free enterprise; **l'e. privée** private enterprise

2 *(firme)* company, firm; **chef d'e.** company head; **e. commerciale** business enterprise *or* operation; *Mktg* **e. dauphine** runner-up company; *Mktg* **e. dominante/défendable/à la traîne** dominant/tenable/trailing firm; **e. exportatrice** export company; **e. familiale** family business; **e. industrielle** manufacturing concern *or* company; *Mktg* **e. innovatrice** innovator, market pioneer company; **e. d'investissement** investment company; **e. de messageries** parcel delivery company; **e. multinationale** multinational (company); **e. en participation** joint venture; **e. de pompes funèbres** undertaker's, funeral director's; **e. prestataire de services** service company; **e. privée** private company; **e. publique** public corporation; **e. de transports** haulage *or* carrying company; **e. de travail intérimaire** temp agency; **e. unipersonnelle** one-man business, sole trader; **e. unipersonnelle à responsabilité limitée** sole trader with limited liability

3 *Jur (louage)* contracting; **travail à l'e.** contract work, work by *or* on contract; **mettre qch à l'e.** to put sth out to contract

4 *Vieilli* **entreprises** *(tentatives de séduction)* advances

ENTRER [ātre]

VI to come in **1, 4** ▪ to go in **1, 4** ▪ to enter **1, 2, 4, 7** ▪ to go to **3** ▪ to fit **5** ▪ to log in **6** ▪ to go into *(entrer dans)* **9–11** ▪ to join *(entrer dans)* **2, 10**
VT to bring in **1** ▪ to take in **1** ▪ to enter **3** ▪ to input **3**

VI *(aux* **être**) **1** *(aller)* to go in, to enter; *(venir)* to come in, to enter; *(réussir à pénétrer)* to get in; **e. dans une salle** to enter *or* go into/

come into a room; **entrez!** come/go in!; **entre dans la voiture/l'ascenseur** get into the car/lift; **défense d'e.** no admittance, private; **il a réussi à e. sans payer** he managed to get in without paying; **je n'aime pas les gens qui entrent sans frapper** I don't like people who come in *or* enter without knocking; **faire e. qn** *(en l'appelant)* to call sb in; **faites e.** send *or* show him/her/them in, have him/her/them come in; **fais-le e.!** *(chez soi)* let him in; *(au bureau)* send *or* show him in; **laisser e. qn/qch** to let sb/sth in; **e. en passant** to drop in, to look in (**chez qn** on sb); **je n'ai fait qu'e. et sortir** I just dropped in for a moment; **empêcher qn d'e.** to keep sb out, to stop sb entering *or* getting in; **le voleur est entré par la fenêtre** the thief got in through the window; **il n'a pas pu e.** he couldn't get in; **le train entre en gare** the train is pulling into the station; **le navire entre au port** the ship is coming into harbour; **e. en courant/en dansant** to run/dance in; **e. furtivement** to sneak in, to steal in; **e. dans un pays** to enter a country; *Théâtre* **Hamlet entre (en scène)** enter Hamlet; **vous qui entrez ici, abandonnez toute espérance** abandon hope, all ye who enter here

2 *(devenir membre)* **e. dans l'armée/la police** to join the army/the police; *Mil* **e. dans la carrière** to become an officer; **e. en religion** to take (holy) orders; **il est entré à l'hôpital comme infirmier** he joined *or* started working at the hospital as a nurse; **e. aux PTT** to start working for the Post Office; **e. au service de qn** to enter sb's service; **e. dans la Communauté européenne** to join the European Community

3 *(être admis)* **e. à l'université** to go to university; **j'entre à l'hôpital demain** I'm going into hospital *or Am* the hospital tomorrow; **e. en maternelle** to start nursery school

4 *(pénétrer, s'infiltrer)* *(de l'eau, de l'air etc)* to go/come in; **le clou est entré dans le mur** the nail went into the wall; **nous constatons que la balle est entrée dans le crâne et l'a traversé de part en part** we can see that the bullet entered the skull and came through the other side; **la clef n'entre pas dans la serrure** the key won't *or* doesn't go *or* fit in the lock; **les liens étaient tellement serrés qu'ils lui sont entrés dans les chairs** the straps were so tight that they cut into his flesh; **une pareille idée ne lui serait jamais entrée dans la tête** such an idea never entered his head; **faire e. une idée dans la tête de qn** to put an idea in sb's head; *Fig* **le doute/la peur entra dans son esprit** his mind was filled with doubts/fear

5 *(tenir)* **on n'entrera jamais à vingt dans cette petite pièce** we'll never get twenty people into that small room; **la télévision n'entre pas dans le carton** the television won't *or* doesn't go *or* fit in the box; *Fam* **ça ne veut pas e.** it won't go in; **faire e. qch dans qch** to insert *or* put sth in sth; **je ne peux pas faire e. toutes mes affaires dans une seule valise** I can't get *or* fit all my things in one suitcase

6 *Ordinat* to log in *or* on

7 *Com (de marchandises importées)* to enter, to be imported; **ces marchandises sont entrées en fraude sur le territoire** these goods were smuggled into the country

8 *(marque le début de)* **e. dans une colère terrible** to get extremely angry; **la Roumanie entre en démocratie** Romania is embracing democracy; **elle entre tout juste en convalescence** she's just beginning to convalesce; **e. en ébullition** to begin to boil, to come to the boil; **e. en effervescence** to begin to effervesce; **e. en fonction** to take up one's duties; **e. dans la vie active** to start one's working life; **e. en vigueur** to come into force *or* effect *or* operation; **e. dans sa ving-**

tième **année** to turn nineteen; **e. dans une ère nouvelle** to enter a new era; *Mil* **e. en campagne** to take the field; *Mil* **e. en guerre** to enter the war; **e. en méditation** to begin to meditate; **on entre en hiver** winter is just beginning; *Com* **e. en liquidation** to go into liquidation

9 *(faire partie de)* **e. dans une catégorie** to fall into a category; **cela ne peut pas e. en ligne de compte** that cannot be taken into account *or* consideration; **cela entre dans ses projets** that is part of his plans; **il est entré dans ma vie tout d'un coup** he came into my life all of a sudden; **dans tout ceci l'imagination entre pour beaucoup** in all this imagination plays a large part; **e. dans la légende** to become a legend; **e. dans l'histoire** to go down in history; **aucun produit chimique n'entre dans la composition de ce dessert** no chemical product goes into the making of this dessert; *Com* **e. dans un marché** to enter a market

10 e. dans *(danse, débat etc)* to join in; *(les idées, les vues, les sentiments de qn etc)* to share, to go along with sb; **e. dans les détails/de longues explications** to go into the details *or* into detail/long explanations; *TV, Cin* **e. dans le champ** to come into shot

11 e. dans *(heurter)* *(arbre, mur etc)* to go into, to run into; *Fam* **on est entrés dans le décor** we went off the road

VT *(aux* **avoir**) **1** *(introduire)* to bring in; *(vu de l'extérieur)* to take in; **e. des marchandises en fraude** to smuggle in goods

2 *(enfoncer)* **elle a failli m'e. son parapluie dans l'œil** she nearly poked me in the eye with her umbrella; **il m'a entré ses dents/ongles dans le cou** he sank his teeth/nails into my neck

3 *Ordinat (données)* to enter, to input; *(au clavier aussi)* to key up *or* in

V IMPERS **il entre beaucoup de calculs dans sa générosité** there's a lot of calculation behind his/her generosity; **il n'entre pas dans mes projets de me marier tout de suite** getting married right away is not part of my plans

entre-rail, *pl* **entre-rails** [ātrəraj] NM *Rail (d'une voie)* gauge

entresol [ātrəsɔl] NM entresol, mezzanine (floor)

entre-temps [ātrətā] ADV meanwhile, in the meantime

NM INV *Arch* **dans l'e.** in the meantime

entretenir [ātrət(ə)nir] *(conj like* **tenir**) VT **1** *(soigner)* *(maison, jardin, routes etc)* to maintain, to keep up; *(machine)* to maintain; *(d'un fournisseur)* *(appareil)* to service; **e. qch en bon état** to keep sth in good condition *or* repair; **une moquette facile à e.** a carpet which is easily looked after; **j'entretiens la voiture moi-même** I look after the car myself; **e. sa santé/sa beauté** to look after *or* take care of one's health/beauty; **e. sa forme** to keep fit; **e. son français** to keep up one's French; **e. le feu** to keep the fire going

2 *(pourvoir à la subsistance de)* *(famille, maîtresse, flotte etc)* to maintain, to support, to keep; **je ne veux pas me faire e.** I don't want to be a kept man/woman

3 *(nourrir)* **e. des soupçons/des craintes** to entertain *or* harbour suspicions/fears; **e. une correspondance avec qn** to keep up a correspondence with sb; **e. l'espoir de qn** to keep sb's hopes alive; **e. qn dans l'ignorance** to keep sb in ignorance; **e. qn dans l'erreur** to allow sb to continue to labour under a misapprehension; **il faut e. l'idée que la paix va revenir** we must keep alive the idea that peace will return; **e. de bonnes relations avec** *(personne)* to remain on good terms with; *(pays)* to maintain good relations with

4 (parler à) **e. qn** to converse or talk with sb about sth, to discuss sth with sb **5** Compta (comptes) to keep in order **VPR s'entretenir 1 s'e. avec qn (de qch)** to converse or talk with sb (about sth) **2** (se maintenir en forme) to keep fit

> Il faut noter que le verbe anglais **to entertain** est un faux ami. Il signifie le plus souvent **divertir**.

entretenu [ɑ̃trətny] ADJ **1 femme entretenue** kept woman **2 bien/mal e.** (maison, jardin etc) well-kept/badly kept **3** Radio (oscillations) sustained; (ondes) undamped, continuous

entretien [ɑ̃trətjɛ̃] NM **1** (soins) (d'une maison, d'un jardin, des routes etc) upkeep, maintenance; (par le fournisseur) (d'un appareil) servicing, service; **facile/difficile d'e., d'e. facile/difficile** easy/difficult to maintain; **cher à l'e.** expensive to maintain; **e. des chambres** (d'hôtel) room servicing; **personnel d'e.** maintenance staff; **manuel d'e.** service manual; **produits d'e.** (household) cleaning materials
2 (subsistance) (d'une famille, armée etc) support, maintenance
3 (conversation) conversation, talk; (audience) interview; **j'ai eu un e. avec lui** I had a talk or conversation with him; **j'ai réussi à décrocher un e.** (pour une embauche) I managed to get myself an interview; **e. téléphonique** telephone conversation; **avoir des entretiens avec le patronat** to hold talks or discussions with the employers
4 Mktg **e. assisté par ordinateur** computer-assisted interviewing; **e. centré** structured interview; **e. de groupe** group interview; (activité) group interviewing; **e. libre** ou **non structuré** unstructured interview; **e. organisé** arranged interview; **e. spontané** intercept interview; **e. structuré** structured interview; **e. par téléphone** telephone interview; (activité) telephone interviewing

entretoile [ɑ̃trətwal] NF Couture (lace) insertion

entretoise [ɑ̃trətwaz] NF Aut spacer; (étai) strut; **e. de réglage** distance piece

entre-tuer (s') [sɑ̃trətɥe] VPR to kill one another or each other

entre-voie, pl **entre-voies** [ɑ̃trəvwa] NF Rail space between tracks

entrevoir [ɑ̃trəvwar] VT (conj like voir) to catch sight or a glimpse of; (indistinctement) to make out; **je n'ai fait que le v.** I caught only a glimpse of him; **il entrevoyait la vérité** he had an inkling of the truth; **j'entrevois des difficultés** I foresee difficulties

entrevue [ɑ̃trəvy] NF interview; (entre hommes politiques, hommes d'affaires etc) meeting; **avoir/fixer une e. avec qn** to have/arrange an interview or a meeting with sb

entrisme [ɑ̃trism] NM Pol entryism

entriste [ɑ̃trist] N, ADJ Pol entryist

entropie [ɑ̃trɔpi] NF Phys entropy

entrouvert [ɑ̃truvɛr] ADJ (fenêtre, fleur etc) half-open; (gouffre) gaping, yawning; **laissez la porte entrouverte** leave the door ajar; **la bouche entrouverte** with one's mouth half-open

entrouvrir [ɑ̃truvrir] VT (porte, yeux, bouche etc) to half-open **VPR s'entrouvrir** to half-open; (d'un gouffre) to open up, to gape, to yawn

entuber [ɑ̃tybe] VT très Fam (duper) to con, to have; **il s'est fait e.** he was conned or had

enturbanné [ɑ̃tyrbane] ADJ turbaned, wearing a turban

énucléation [enykleasjɔ̃] NF Chir enucleation

énucléer [enyklee] VT Chir (tumeur, œil) to enucleate

énumératif, -ive [enymeratif, -iv] ADJ enumerative

énumération [enymerasjɔ̃] NF enumeration, listing

énumérer [enymere] VT (j'énumère, n. énumérons; j'énumérerai) to enumerate, to list

énuquer (s') [senyke] VPR Suisse to break one's neck

énurésie [enyrezi] NF Méd enuresis

énurétique [enyretik] N, ADJ Méd enuretic

envahir [ɑ̃vair] VT (pays etc) to invade, to overrun; Com **e. le marché** to flood the market; **envahi par les mauvaises herbes** overgrown with weeds; **envahi par l'eau** flooded; **quand le doute/le sommeil nous envahit** when we are overcome with doubt/sleep; **la politique envahit tout** politics gets into everything; Fig Fam **je ne voulais pas les e.** (déranger) I didn't want to intrude (upon them)

envahissant [ɑ̃vaisɑ̃] ADJ (voisins) intrusive; (plantes) invasive; Fig (désir, soupçon, odeur etc) overwhelming

envahissement [ɑ̃vaismɑ̃] NM invasion

envahisseur [ɑ̃vaisœr] NM invader

envapé [ɑ̃vape] ADJ Fam out of it, ripped, Br off one's face

envasement [ɑ̃vazmɑ̃] NM (d'un port etc) silting up

envaser [ɑ̃vaze] VT (port etc) to silt up; (bateau) to run on the mud
VPR s'envaser (d'un port etc) to silt up; (d'un bateau, d'une personne) to get stuck in the mud

enveloppant [ɑ̃vlɔpɑ̃] ADJ **1** (couvrant) **ce manteau est bien e.** this coat covers well; **regard e.** look that takes everything in; Aut **pare-chocs e.** wraparound bumper **2** Fig (séduisant) (personne, mots, manières etc) captivating

enveloppe [ɑ̃vlɔp] NF **1** (d'un colis etc) wrapper, wrapping **2** (pour lettre) envelope; **envoyer qch sous e.** to send sth under cover; **e. timbrée** stamped envelope; **e. timbrée avec nom et adresse** stamped addressed envelope, SAE **3** (apparence) **un bon cœur sous une rude e.** a rough diamond; Litt **l'e. mortelle** ou **charnelle** this mortal coil **4** (somme d'argent) **l'e. de la recherche** the research budget; **de combien est l'e. du service/du projet?** how high is the departmental budget/the budget for the project?; **e. budgétaire** (allotted) budget, budget allocation; **e. fiscale** savings scheme with tax advantages; **e. salariale** wages bill; Fam **recevoir une e.** (pot-de-vin) to receive a bribe **5** (revêtement) (d'une chaudière) sheathing, casing, jacket; Aut (d'un pneu) outer cover, casing **6** (des graines etc) husk, hull
▸ ▸ **e. autocollante** self-seal envelope; **e. calorifuge** lagging; **e. à fenêtre** window envelope; **e. matelassée** padded envelope, Jiffy bag®; Philat **e. premier jour** first-day cover; **e.T** ≃ business reply or reply-paid envelope

enveloppé [ɑ̃vlɔpe] ADJ Fam **bien e.** (personne) well-padded, plump

enveloppement [ɑ̃vlɔpmɑ̃] NM **1** (action) (d'un colis etc) wrapping (up); Mil **manœuvre d'e.** pincer movement, envelopment **2** Méd (linges) pack; **e. froid** cold pack

envelopper [ɑ̃vlɔpe] VT **1** (marchandises, bébé etc) to wrap (up); **e. un paquet** to wrap up or do up a parcel; **enveloppé de bandages** swathed in bandages; **e. des remarques désagréables dans des phrases gentilles** to wrap up unpleasant remarks in kind words

2 (entourer) (personne) to surround, to encircle, to close in on; **la nuit nous enveloppa** darkness closed in on us; **enveloppé de mystère/brume** shrouded in mystery/in mist; **e. qch du regard** to take sth in with one's gaze
VPR s'envelopper s'e. dans une couverture to wrap oneself up in a blanket; Fig **s'e. dans son silence** to immure oneself in silence

enveloppe-réponse, pl **enveloppes-réponses** NF reply-paid envelope

envenimé [ɑ̃v(ə)nime] ADJ (plaie) poisoned, septic; Fig **discussion envenimée** acrimonious discussion

envenimement [ɑ̃v(ə)nimmɑ̃] NM (d'une plaie) poisoning; Fig (d'une querelle, discussion) embittering; (d'une situation) aggravation

envenimer [ɑ̃v(ə)nime] VT (plaie) to poison, to make septic; Fig (querelle, discussion) to envenom, to embitter; (situation) to aggravate
VPR s'envenimer (d'une plaie) to fester, to turn septic; Fig (d'une querelle, discussion) to grow acrimonious; (d'une situation) to become aggravated

envergure [ɑ̃vɛrgyr] NF **1** (d'un oiseau, avion) wingspread, wingspan **2** Fig (ampleur) scope; **de grande e., d'e.** (réforme, rapport, question) far-reaching, wide-ranging; (opération, firme) large-scale; **esprit de grande e.** wide-ranging mind; **leur affaire commence à prendre de l'e.** their business is beginning to expand or grow **3** (de personne) calibre, Am caliber; **homme d'e./de cette e.** man of calibre/of this calibre; **cet homme manque d'e.** this man is of a low calibre

envers¹ [ɑ̃vɛr] NM (d'un document, d'une assiette etc) reverse, back; (d'une médaille, pièce) reverse; **l'endroit et l'e. d'un tissu** the right and the wrong side of a material; **l'e. de la vie** the seamy side of life; Fig **l'e. du décor** the other side of the picture; **à l'e.** (du mauvais côté) inside out; (avec le haut en bas) the wrong way up, upside down; (dans le mauvais sens) the wrong way round, back to front; (en désordre) upside down; **le monde à l'e.** the world turned upside down; Hum **il travaille? c'est le monde à l'e!.** he's working? wonders will never cease!; **j'ai la tête à l'e.** my brain is in a whirl; Tricot **une maille à l'endroit, une maille à l'e.** knit one, purl one

envers² PRÉP toward(s); **juste e. tous** just to(wards) or with everyone; **leur devoir e. leur patrie** their duty to(wards) their country; **avoir une dette e. qn** to be indebted to sb; **e. et contre tous** in spite of everyone, in the face of all opposition

enviable [ɑ̃vjabl] ADJ enviable

envi (à l') [alɑ̃vi] ADV **faire qch à l'e.** to vie with one another in doing sth, to try to outdo each other doing sth

envie [ɑ̃vi] NF **1** (désir) desire (**de qch** for sth; **de faire** to do); **avoir e. de qch/de faire qch** to want sth/to do sth; **j'ai des envies de fraises** I have cravings for strawberries; Fam **j'ai une de ces envies de champagne!** I've got a real craving for champagne!, I could really do with some champagne!; **ce gâteau plein de crème me fait e.** I like the look of or Br I fancy that cake filled with cream; **j'avais e. de dormir/boire/manger** I felt sleepy/thirsty/hungry; **avoir e. de rire/de vomir** to feel like laughing/being sick, to want to laugh/be sick; **être pris d'une terrible e. de rire** to have a terrible urge to laugh; Fam **ça m'a pris comme une e. de pisser** it was a sudden urge; **avoir bien** ou **très e. de faire qch** to really want to do sth; **brûler d'e. de faire qch** to be burning or dying to do sth; **donner**

à qn l'e. de faire qch to make sb want to do sth; **il a e. que je fasse cela** he wants me to do that; **je n'ai pas e. que ça se sache** I don't want it to be known; **c'est une e. qui te passera** you'll get over your craving; *Fam* **ça va lui passer son e.** it'll be just what he wants; **je vais lui ôter l'e. de s'amuser** I'll stop his messing around; **avoir e. de qn** *(sexuellement)* to want sb; *Fam* **avoir e.** *(avoir besoin d'uriner)* to want *or* have to go; *(de sexe)* to want it

2 *(jalousie)* envy; **être dévoré d'e.** to be consumed *or* green with envy; **faire e. à qn** to make sb envious; **regarder qch avec e.** to look enviously at sth; **cette situation confortable, ça fait e.** a good job like that makes people envious; **porter e. à qn** to envy sb

3 *(au doigt)* hangnail; *(sur la peau)* birthmark

envier [ãvje] VT *(impf, pr sub n. enviions)* to envy, to be envious of; **e. qch à qn** to envy sb sth; **je t'envie de ne jamais avoir faim!** I envy your never being hungry!; **elle n'a rien à e. à personne** she has no cause to be envious of anyone

envieux, -ieuse [ãvjø, -jøz] ADJ envious *(de* of)

N envious person; **faire des e.** to make people envious

environ [ãvirɔ̃] ADV *(à peu près)* about, around; **il a e. quarante ans** he's about *or* around forty VOIR GRAMMAIRE A67

NMPL **environs** *(d'une ville etc)* surroundings, surrounding area; **habiter aux** *ou* **dans les environs de Paris** to live in the vicinity of *or* near Paris; **aux environs de Pâques/cinq heures** around Easter/five o'clock; **aux environs de cent euros** in the region *or* vicinity of a hundred euros, about *or* around a hundred euros

environnant [ãvironã] ADJ *(campagne etc)* surrounding

environnement [ãvironmã] NM **1** *(naturel, personnel)* environment; **protection de l'e.** environmental protection, protection of the environment; **qui ne nuit pas à l'e.** environment-friendly; **e. commercial** business environment; **e. du marché** market environment; *Com* **e. institutionnel/marketing** corporate/marketing environment **2** *Ordinat* environment; **e. partagé** shared environment

environnemental, -ale, -aux, -ales [ãvironmãtal, -o] ADJ environmental

environnementaliste [ãvironmãtalist] N environmentalist

environner [ãvirone] VT to surround; **environné de** surrounded by
VPR **s'environner s'e. d'intellectuels** to surround oneself with intellectuals

envisageable [ãvizaʒabl] ADJ conceivable, imaginable; **ce n'est pas e.** it's inconceivable *or* unimaginable

envisager [ãvizaʒe] VT *(j'envisageai(s))* *(considérer) (question, situation, remède etc)* to consider; *(imaginer comme possible, projeter) (conséquence, événement etc)* to envisage; **e. l'avenir** to look to the future; **le cas que nous envisageons** the case under consideration; **cas non envisagé** unforeseen case; **comment envisagez-vous la question?** what are your views on *or* how do you see the matter?; **il n'envisageait pas de partir** he wasn't thinking of leaving, he wasn't considering leaving; **e. un chiffre d'affaires** to forecast turnover

envoi [ãvwa] NM **1** *(action)* *(d'un représentant, de troupes etc)* sending; *(d'une lettre, d'un colis etc)* sending, dispatch(ing); *(d'argent, de fonds)* sending, remittance; *(de marchandises)* sending, dispatch(ing), for-

warding; **e. par mer** shipment; **faire un e. tous les mois** to send *or* dispatch goods every month; **e. exprès** express delivery; **e. groupé** grouped consignment; **e. postal** postal delivery; **e. recommandé** recorded delivery; **faire un e. de fonds à qn** to send *or* remit funds to sb; **e. contre paiement** cash with order

2 coup d'e. *Ftbl* kickoff; *(d'un événement, festival, projet etc)* start, *Fam* kickoff

3 *(ce qui est envoyé)* *(colis)* parcel; *(lettre)* letter; *(marchandises)* consignment *(de* of); **e. de l'auteur** presentation copy; **j'ai bien reçu votre e. du 10 octobre** I acknowledge receipt of your consignment of 10 October

4 *Ordinat* **e. multiple** crossposting; **faire un e. multiple de qch** to cross-post sth

5 *Littér (d'un poème)* envoi

envol [ãvɔl] NM *(d'oiseaux)* taking flight *or* wing; *(d'un avion)* takeoff; **piste d'e.** (takeoff) runway; *Naut* **pont d'e.** flight deck

envolée [ãvɔle] NF **1** *(action)* *(d'oiseaux)* flight **2** *Fig* **e. lyrique/oratoire** flight of lyricism/oratory **3** *Fin* *(hausse rapide)* **l'e. du dollar** the rapid rise in the dollar

envoler (s') [sãvɔle] VPR **1** *(d'un oiseau)* to fly away, to fly off; *(d'un avion)* to take off; **faire s'e. des oiseaux** to put birds to flight; **mon avion s'envole** *ou* **je m'envole dans une heure** my plane takes off *or* my flight leaves in an hour **2** *Fig* **l'euro s'envole** the euro is rising rapidly; **s'e. dans les sondages** to rise rapidly in the opinion polls **3** *(emporté par le vent)* *(d'un chapeau etc)* to blow off; *(de papiers etc)* to blow away; **le temps s'envole** time flies **4** *Fam (disparaître soudainement)* *(d'une personne, d'un sac à main etc)* to vanish, to disappear

envoûtant [ãvutã] ADJ *(fascinant)* bewitching, captivating

envoûtement [ãvutmã] NM **1** *(maléfice)* bewitchment **2** *Fig (fascination)* bewitchment, captivation; **cette région me fait l'effet d'un e.** this region has a bewitching *or* captivating effect on me

envoûter [ãvute] VT *(en employant la magie)* to bewitch; *Fig (fasciner)* to bewitch, to captivate

envoûteur, -euse [ãvutœr, -øz] N sorcerer, f sorceress

envoyé, -ée [ãvwaje] ADJ **bien e.** *Sport (balle)*, *Fig Fam (remarque)* well-aimed; *Fam* **c'est e.!** *(bien dit)* well said!; *(bien exécuté)* well done!

N *(messager)* messenger; *(d'un parti etc)* representative; *(d'un gouvernement)* envoy; *Journ* **e. spécial** special correspondent; *Journ* **e. de la rédaction** staff correspondent

envoyer [ãvwaje] *(j'envoie, n. envoyons; j'enverrai)* VT *(personne)* to send; *(lettre, colis etc)* to send, to dispatch; *(argent)* to send, to remit; *(marchandises)* to send, to dispatch, to ship; *(ses excuses, condoléances etc)* to send; **e. par courrier** to mail, *Br* to post; **e. qn à Paris** to send sb to Paris; **e. une lettre à qn** to send sb a letter, to send a letter to sb; **e. un publipostage à** to mailshot; **je lui ai envoyé mes félicitations** I sent him my congratulations; **envoyez-moi un petit mot** drop me a line; **sa démission** to send in *or Fml* to tender one's resignation; **elle lui a envoyé un regard noir/une gifle** she gave him a black look/slap (in the face); **e. un baiser à qn** to blow sb a kiss; **e. chercher qn** to send for sb; **j'ai envoyé Paul prendre de ses nouvelles** I sent Paul to ask after him; *Fam* **je ne le lui ai pas envoyé dire** I told him straight *or* to his face; *Fam* **e. promener** *ou* **balader** *ou* **paître qn** *ou* **sur les roses** to send sb packing; *Fam* **j'en ai assez, je vais tout e. promener** *ou* **valser** *ou* **dinguer** I've had enough,

I'm going to chuck it all in *or* throw in the towel; *Naut* **e. les couleurs/une vergue** to hoist the colours/send up a yard
VI *Naut* **envoyez!** about ship!
VPR **s'envoyer 1** *(par courrier etc)* **ils s'envoient des cartes postales régulièrement** they regularly send postcards to each other **2** *Fam* **s'e. un verre de vin** to knock back a glass of wine; *Fam* **s'e. une corvée** to get landed *or* stuck with a tedious job; *Arg* **il ne pense qu'à s'e. en l'air** all he thinks about is having sex *or Br* having it off *or* away; *Arg* **s'e. une fille/un mec** to have sex *or Br* have it off *or* away with a girl/guy

envoyeur, -euse [ãvwajœr, -øz] N sender; **retour à l'e.** return to sender

enzyme [ãzim] N enzyme; **produit de lavage aux enzymes** cleaning product with biological action

éocène [eɔsɛn] *Géol* ADJ *(période)* Eocene
NM Eocene

éolien, -ienne [eɔljɛ̃, -jɛn] ADJ **harpe éolienne** aeolian harp; **érosion éolienne** wind erosion; **énergie éolienne** wind energy; **moteur é.** wind-powered engine
NF **éolienne** wind turbine

épagneul [epaɲœl] NM spaniel

épais, -aisse [epɛ, -ɛs] ADJ *(cheveux, doigt, mur, tranche, sauce etc)* thick; *(feuillage, brouillard)* dense, thick; *(foule, buisson)* dense; *(livre)* thick, fat; *(ombre, nuit)* deep, dark; *(silence)* deep; **é. de deux mètres** two metres thick; **avoir la taille épaisse** to be thickset; *Fam* **avoir l'esprit é.** to be dense *or* thick; **peu é.** thin
ADV **1** *(pousser, semer)* thick(ly) **2** *Fam (beaucoup)* **il n'y en a pas é.** there's not much of it
NM **couper dans l'é.** to cut into the thick part; **au plus é. de la foule/forêt** in the heart of the crowd/forest

épaisseur [epɛsœr] NF **1** *(de cheveux, d'un mur, d'une sauce etc)* thickness; *(d'un feuillage, du brouillard)* density, thickness; *(d'une foule)* density; *(d'une ombre, de la nuit)* darkness; **le mur a deux pieds d'é.** the wall is two feet thick; **courroie en trois épaisseurs** three-ply belt; **une é. de tissu** a layer of material; **le peu d'é. d'une planche** the thinness of a board **2** *(d'un esprit)* dullness **3** *(profondeur) (d'une personne, d'un personnage de roman etc)* depth

épaissir [epesir] VT *(sauce, peinture etc)* to thicken; *(ombre, mystère)* to deepen
VI *(d'une sauce etc)* to thicken, to get thick(er); *(d'une personne)* to fill out
VPR **s'épaissir** *(de cheveux, du brouillard, d'une sauce etc)* to thicken, to get thick(er); *(d'une personne)* to fill out; *(d'une ombre, d'un mystère)* to deepen

épaississant [epesisã] NM *(substance)* thickener

épaississement [epesismã] NM *(du brouillard, d'une sauce etc)* thickening; *(d'une personne)* filling out

épanchement [epãʃmã] NM **1** *Arch, Litt (d'un liquide)* pouring out, discharge; *Méd* **é. de synovie** synovial extravasation **2** *Fig (de sentiments)* outpouring, *Litt* effusion; *(de pensées)* outpouring

épancher [epãʃe] VT **1** *Arch, Litt (liquide)* to pour out, to discharge; *Fig* **é. sa bile** to vent one's spleen **2** *Fig (son amour, ses soucis etc)* to pour out; **é. son cœur** to pour out one's heart, to unbosom oneself
VPR **s'épancher 1** *Arch, Litt (d'un liquide)* to pour out; *Méd (du sang etc)* to extravasate **2** *Fig (d'une personne)* to pour out one's heart, to unbosom oneself

épandage [epãdaʒ] NM *(de fumier etc)* spreading; **champs d'é.** sewage farm

épandeur, -euse [epɑ̃dœr, -øz] N *(machine) (de fumier, d'asphalte etc)* spreader

épandre [epɑ̃dr] VT *(fumier etc)* to spread
VPR **s'épandre** *Litt* to spread (**sur** over)

épanoui [epanwi] ADJ *(fleur)* in full bloom, full-blown; *(visage, sourire)* beaming; **une jeune femme épanouie** a young woman in full bloom

épanouir [epanwir] VT *(fleur, pétales)* to open out; *(voiles, plumes)* to spread; **un large sourire lui épanouit le visage** his face broadened into a grin
VPR **s'épanouir 1** *(d'une fleur)* to open out, to bloom **2** *(d'un visage)* to beam, to light up; *(d'une personne heureuse)* to beam **3** *(d'une jeune fille, personnalité, civilisation etc)* to blossom

épanouissant [epanwisɑ̃] ADJ *(travail, vie etc)* fulfilling

épanouissement [epanwismɑ̃] NM **1** *(action) (d'une fleur)* opening out, blooming; *(d'un visage)* lighting up; *(d'une jeune fille, personnalité, civilisation etc)* blossoming **2** *(plénitude)* (full) bloom; **elle a trouvé l'é. physique et moral** she is at her physical and mental peak

épargnant, -ante [eparɲɑ̃, -ɑ̃t] N saver, investor; **les petits épargnants** small savers *or* investors

épargne [eparɲ] NF **1** *(action, vertu)* saving, economy; *Fig (de temps, forces)* saving; **caisse d'é.** savings bank; **plan d'é.-logement** *Br* ≃ building society (savings) account, *Am* ≃ savings and loan association account; **é. des entreprises** company reserves; **é. liquide** on-hand savings; **é. mobilière** fixed savings; **é. privée** private investors; **é. productive** re-invested savings; **é. salariale** save as you earn, SAYE **2** *(sommes)* savings **3** *(épargnants)* **la petite é.** small savers *or* investors; **l'é. privée** private investors

épargne-retraite NF retirement savings scheme; **plan d'é.-retraite** personal pension scheme *or* plan

épargner [eparɲe] VT **1** *(argent, provisions)* to save (up), to put by; *(beurre, sel etc)* to be sparing with **2** *(énergie, temps)* to save; **é. ses forces** to save one's strength; **épargne-moi tes explications/tes jérémiades/les détails!** spare me your explanations/your complaining/the details!; **é. à qn la peine de faire qch** to save sb the trouble of doing sth **3** *(prisonnier etc)* to spare, to have mercy on; **elle a toujours tenté d'é. ses enfants** she has always tried to shield her children; **l'incendie a épargné notre village** the fire spared our village
VI to save (**sur qch** on sth)

éparpillement [eparpijmɑ̃] NM **1** *(action) (d'objets, de foin etc)* scattering; *(d'une foule, de troupes etc)* scattering, dispersal; *Fig (des efforts, de l'attention etc)* dissipation **2** *(état)* scattered state

éparpiller [eparpije] VT *(objets, foin etc)* to scatter, to strew about; *(foule, troupes etc)* to scatter, to disperse; *Fig (efforts, attention etc)* to dissipate
VPR **s'éparpiller** *(d'objets etc)* to scatter; *(d'une foule, de troupes etc)* to scatter, to disperse; *Fig (d'une personne)* to dissipate one's energies

épars [epar] ADJ *(maisons, moutons etc)* scattered; *(végétation, population, informations)* sparse; *(cheveux)* thin

éparvin [eparvɛ̃] NM *Vét (d'un cheval)* spavin

épatant [epatɑ̃] ADJ *Fam* splendid, wonderful

épate [epat] NF *Fam* swank, swagger; **faire de l'é.** to show off, to swank; **on l'a fait à l'é.** it was done to show off

épaté [epate] ADJ **1** *(table etc)* splay-footed;

(nez) flat **2** *Fam (étonné)* dumbfounded, flabbergasted

épatement [epatmɑ̃] NM **1** *(d'un nez)* flatness **2** *Fam (étonnement)* astonishment, amazement

épater [epate] VT **1** *(rendre plat)* to flatten out the base of **2** *Fam (étonner)* to astound, to amaze; **rien ne l'épate, il ne se laisse pas é.** nothing surprises him, he isn't easily impressed

épaulard [epolar] NM killer whale, grampus, orc

épaule [epol] NF shoulder; **large d'épaules** broad-shouldered; **hausser les épaules** to shrug (one's shoulders); *Culin* **é. d'agneau** shoulder of lamb; **donner un coup d'é. à qn** to shoulder sb; *Fig* to give sb a push in the right direction; **charger un fardeau sur son é.** to shoulder a burden; *Mil* **l'arme sur l'é.** with rifle at the slope; **rouler les épaules** *(en marchant)* to swagger

épaulé-jeté, *pl* **épaulés-jetés** [epoleʒ(ə)te] NM *(en haltérophilie)* clean-and-jerk

épaulement [epolmɑ̃] NM **1** *(mur)* revetment, retaining wall **2** *(rempart)* breastwork **3** *(d'une colline)* shoulder

épauler [epole] VT **1** *(fusil)* to bring to one's shoulder **2 é. qn** *(aider)* to back sb up **3** *(mur)* to retain, to support **4** *Couture* to attach shoulder pads to
VI to take aim

épaulette [epolɛt] NF **1** *(bretelle) (d'une combinaison)* shoulder-strap **2** *Mil* epaulette **3** *(rembourrage)* shoulder pad

épave [epav] NF *(navire, voiture)* wreck; *Fig (loque humaine)* (human) wreck; *Fig* **les épaves de la société** the flotsam of society; **épaves flottantes** flotsam; **épaves rejetées** jetsam

épeautre [epotr] NM spelt

épée [epe] NF sword; *Escrime* épée; **coup d'é.** swordthrust; *Fig* **coup d'é. dans l'eau** wasted effort; **Marc est une bonne é.** Marc is a good swordsman; *Fig* **é. de Damoclès** Sword of Damocles

épeiche [epɛʃ] NF *Orn* great spotted woodpecker

épeichette [epɛʃɛt] NF *Orn* lesser spotted woodpecker

épéiste [epeist] N *Escrime* épéeist

épeler [eple] VT *(j'épelle; j'épellerai)* VT **1** *(mot, nom etc)* to spell; **mot mal épelé** misspelt word **2** *(lire avec difficulté) (texte)* to spell out
VI to spell

épépiner [epepine] VT *(raisins, tomates etc)* to remove the seeds *or* pips from, to deseed; *(pommes)* to core

éperdu [eperdy] ADJ *(regard)* distraught, frantic; *(amour, besoin etc)* violent; *(résistance)* desperate; **é. de joie/douleur** frantic with joy/grief

éperdument [eperdymɑ̃] ADV *(aimer)* madly, to distraction; *(travailler)* desperately, frantically; **é. amoureux** head over heels in love, madly in love; *Fam* **je m'en fiche é.** I couldn't care less, I don't give a damn

éperlan [eperlɑ̃] NM *(poisson)* smelt, sparling

éperon [eprɔ̃] NM **1** *(d'un cavalier)* spur; **donner de l'é. à son cheval, piquer de l'é.** to spur (on) one's horse; **gagner ses éperons** to win one's spurs **2** *(d'une violette, d'une montagne, d'un coq)* spur **3** *Hist (d'un vaisseau de guerre)* ram **4** *(d'un pont)* cutwater

éperonner [eprɔne] VT **1** *(cheval)* to spur (on), to put spurs to; *Fig* **é. qn** to spur *or* urge sb on **2** *Hist (vaisseau ennemi)* to ram **3** *(bottes etc)* to spur, to put spurs on

épervier [epervje] NM **1** *(oiseau)* sparrowhawk; *Pol Fig* hawk **2** *Pêche* castnet

éphèbe [efɛb] NM *Iron (beau jeune homme)* Adonis

éphélide [efelid] NF freckle

éphémère [efemer] ADJ *(bonheur etc)* ephemeral, short-lived, fleeting; **ce chanteur n'a connu qu'un succès é.** this singer enjoyed only a short-lived *or* brief success
NM *Entom* mayfly, ephemera

éphéméride [efemerid] NF **1** *(calendrier)* tear-off *or* block calendar **2** *Astron (publication annuelle)* ephemeris; **éphémérides** *(tables)* ephemerides

Éphèse [efɛz] N Ephesus

épi [epi] NM **1** *(de grain)* ear; *(de fleur)* spike; **blés en é.** wheat in the ear; **monter en é.** *(de céréales)* to ear; **é. de maïs** *Agr* corncob; *Culin* corn on the cob **2** *(mèche de cheveux)* tuft of hair; **ses cheveux font des épis** his/her hair sticks up in tufts **3** *(jetée)* spur, groyne; *Rail (de voie)* spur; *Aut* **stationnement en é.** angle parking; *Constr* **appareil en é.** herringbone bond
▸▸ *Archit* **é. de faîtage** finial

épicarpe [epikarp] NM *Bot* epicarp

épice [epis] NF spice; **pain d'é.** ≃ gingerbread; **quatre épices** allspice

épicé [epise] ADJ *(nourriture, plat etc)* highly spiced, spicy, hot; *(assaisonnement)* spicy, hot; *Fam* **conte é.** spicy story

épicéa [episea] NM *(arbre)* spruce

épicentre [episɑ̃tr] NM *(d'un tremblement de terre)* epicentre

épicer [epise] VT *(j'épiçai(s))* *(nourriture, plat etc)* to spice; *Fam (histoire etc)* to spice up, to add a bit of spice to

épicerie [episri] NF **1** *(produits)* groceries; **é. fine** delicatessen; **être dans l'é.** to be in the grocery business **2** *(magasin)* grocer's (shop) **3** *Can Fig* **liste d'é.** *(de griefs etc)* shopping list

épicier, -ière [episje, -jɛr] N grocer; *Fig Péj* **d'é.** *(idées, littérature etc)* common-or-garden; *(encre, savon etc)* cheap, ordinary; *Fig Péj* **mentalité d'é.** small-town mentality

épicurien, -ienne [epikyrjɛ̃, -jɛn] ADJ epicurean; *Phil* Epicurean
N epicure; *Phil* Epicurean

épicurisme [epikyrism] NM **1** *Phil* Epicureanism **2** *(recherche du plaisir)* epicur(ean)ism

épicycloïdal, -ale, -aux, -ales [episiklɔidal] ADJ *Tech (engrenage)* epicyclic

épidémie [epidemi] NF *Méd, Fig* epidemic

épidémiologie [epidemjɔlɔʒi] NF epidemiology

épidémiologique [epidemjɔlɔʒik] ADJ epidemiological

épidémiologiste [epidemjɔlɔʒist] N epidemiologist

épidémique [epidemik] ADJ *Méd* epidemic; *Fig* contagious

épiderme [epiderm] NM *Anat, Bot* epidermis, skin; *Fig* **avoir l'é. sensible** *ou* **délicat** to be thin-skinned *or* touchy

épidermique [epidermik] ADJ *(tissu etc)* epidermal, epidermic; *Fig* **une réaction é.** a kneejerk reaction

épier [epje] VT *(impf, pr sub* **n. épiions, v. épiiez**) *(espionner) (personne, les activités de qn etc)* to spy on, to keep a watch on; *(observer pour découvrir) (signe, occasion etc)* to watch out for; *(la réaction de qn)* to watch for

épigastre [epigastr] NM *Anat* epigastrium

épigastrique [epigastrik] ADJ *Anat* epigastric

épiglotte [epiglɔt] NF *Anat* epiglottis

épigone [epigɔn] NM *Litt (successeur)* epigone

épigramme [epigram] NF epigram

épigraphe [epigraf] NF epigraph

épigraphie [epigrafi] NF epigraphy

épilation [epilasjɔ̃] NF removal of unwanted hair (*de* from); (*des sourcils*) plucking

épilatoire [epilatwar] ADJ (*crème etc*) hair-removing, depilatory

épilepsie [epilɛpsi] NF *Méd* epilepsy; **crise d'é.** epileptic fit

épileptique [epilɛptik] ADJ, N *Méd* epileptic

épiler [epile] VT to remove unwanted hair from; (*sourcils*) to pluck
VPR **s'épiler s'é. les jambes à la cire** to wax one's legs

épilogue [epilɔg] NM epilogue; *Fig* **j'attends l'é. de cette histoire** I'm waiting for the rest of the story

épiloguer [epilɔge] VT *Arch* to pass censure on
VI to go on (and on), to hold forth (*sur* about)

épinard [epinar] NM (*plante*) spinach; *Culin* **épinards** spinach; **épinards en branches** leaf spinach

épine [epin] NF **1** (*arbre*) thornbush **2** (*piquant*) *Bot* thorn, prickle; *Zool* spine, prickle; **tirer une é. du pied à qn** (*tirer d'embarras*) to get sb out of a mess; (*soulager*) to relieve sb's mind
▸▸ **é. blanche** hawthorn; *Anat, Ordinat* **é. dorsale** backbone; **é. noire** blackthorn; **é. de rat** butcher's broom

épinette [epinɛt] NF **1** *Can Bot* spruce **2** *Mus* spinet **3** (*cage*) hen coop

épinettière [epinɛtjer] NF *Can* spruce grove

épineux, -euse [epinø, -øz] ADJ **1** (*arbuste, tige*) thorny, prickly, spiky; (*poisson*) spiny; *Fig* (*question, problème*) thorny, tricky; *Fig* **être dans une situation épineuse** to be in a tricky *or* ticklish situation **2** *Anat* (*excroissance*) spinous
NM thornbush

épinglage [epɛ̃glaʒ] NM pinning

épingle [epɛ̃gl] NF pin; **attacher avec des épingles** (*cheveux, poster*) to pin up; (*morceau de tissu, feuilles*) to pin together; *Fig* **tiré à quatre épingles** dressed up to the nines; *Fig* **tirer son é. du jeu** to extricate oneself; *Fig* **chercher une é. dans une botte de foin** to look for a needle in a haystack; *Fig* **monter qch en é.** (*exagérer*) to make too much of sth
▸▸ **é. à chapeau** hatpin; **é. à cheveux** hairpin; **virage en é. à cheveux** hairpin bend *or* *Am* turn; **é. de cravate** tiepin; **é. à linge** clothes peg *or* *Am* pin; **é. de ou à nourrice** safety pin; **é. de signalisation** (*d'une fiche*) marker tag; **é. de sûreté** safety pin

épingler [epɛ̃gle] VT **1** (*attacher*) to pin, to fasten with a pin/pins (*à* to; **sur** on); **é. ses cheveux** to pin up one's hair **2** *Fam* (*arrêter*) to nab, to collar

épinière [epinjer] ADJ *Anat* **moelle é.** spinal cord

épinoche [epinɔʃ] NF stickleback

Épiphanie [epifani] NF *Rel* Epiphany

épiphénomène [epifenɔmɛn] NM epiphenomenon

épiphyse [epifiz] NF *Anat* epiphysis

épique [epik] ADJ epic; **poème é.** epic (poem)

épiscopal, -ale, -aux, -ales [episkɔpal, -o] ADJ *Rel* episcopal

épiscopat [episkɔpa] NM (*fonction, ensemble des évêques*) episcopate

épiscope [episkɔp] NM episcope

épisiotomie [epizjɔtɔmi] NF *Chir* episiotomy

épisode [epizɔd] NM episode; **feuilleton** *ou* **film à épisodes** serial; **feuilleton en six épi-** sodes six-part serial; **la suite au prochain é.** tune in again to find out what happens next; *Fig* watch this space; *Fig* **ce n'est qu'un é. malheureux** it's just an unfortunate episode

épisodique [epizɔdik] ADJ (*intermittent*) episodic; (*accessoire*) minor

épisodiquement [epizɔdikmɑ̃] ADV occasionally, now and again

épisser [epise] VT (*corde, câble*) to splice

épissure [episyr] NF splice

épistémologie [epistemɔlɔʒi] NF epistemology

épistémologique [epistemɔlɔʒik] ADJ epistemological

épistolaire [epistɔler] ADJ epistolary; **être en relation é. avec qn** to correspond with sb; **nous n'avons que des relations épistolaires** our only contact is by letter

épistolier, -ière [epistɔlje, -jer] N letter writer

épitaphe [epitaf] NF epitaph

épithélium [epiteljɔm] NM *Biol* epithelium

épithète [epitɛt] NF epithet; *Gram* attribute
VOIR GRAMMAIRE A17

épitoge [epitɔʒ] NF **1** *Univ* (*bande d'étoffe*) ≃ (graduate's) hood **2** *Antiq* (*vêtement*) cloak

épitomé [epitɔme] NM (*abrégé d'un ouvrage*) epitome

épître [epitr] NF epistle; (*partie de la messe*) Epistle; **côté de l'é.** (*de l'autel*) Epistle side

éploré [eplɔre] ADJ (*personne*) tearful, weeping; (*expression, voix*) tearful

épluchage [eplyʃaʒ] NM (*de fruits, pommes de terre etc*) peeling; (*d'une salade*) cleaning; (*de crevettes*) peeling, shelling; (*de noisettes, pois*) shelling; *Fig* (*d'un texte, journal etc*) detailed examination

épluche-légumes [eplyʃlegym] NM INV vegetable *or* potato peeler

éplucher [eplyʃe] VT (*fruits, pommes de terre etc*) to peel; (*salade*) to clean; (*crevettes*) to peel, to shell; (*noisettes, pois*) to shell; *Fig* (*texte, journal, publicités etc*) to go through *or* examine in detail; *Fig* **ma mère épluche mon emploi du temps** my mother checks up on how I spend my time

épluchette [eplyʃɛt] NF *Can* **é. de blé d'Inde** corn-husking party

éplucheur, -euse [eplyʃœr, -øz] N (*instrument, personne*) peeler; **é. de pommes de terre** potato peeler

épluchure [eplyʃyr] NF (*pelure*) peeling

EPO [epeo] NF (*abrév* **érythropoïétine**) EPO

épointage [epwɛ̃taʒ] NM (*en cassant*) (*d'un crayon*) breaking the point; (*en usant*) (*d'une aiguille, d'un crayon, d'un outil etc*) blunting

épointé [epwɛ̃te] ADJ (*aiguille, crayon, outil etc*) blunt

épointer [epwɛ̃te] VT (*en cassant*) (*crayon*) to break the point of; (*en usant*) (*aiguille, crayon, outil etc*) to blunt

éponge [epɔ̃ʒ] NF **1** (*naturelle*) sponge **2** *Com* **donner un coup d'é. à qch** to wipe sth with a sponge; **effacer une tache d'un coup d'é.** to sponge out a stain; *Fig* **passons l'é.** let's forget it; *Boxe* **jeter l'é.** to throw in the sponge *or* towel; *Fig* **l'industrie française jette l'é. dans le domaine de la construction automobile** French industry is throwing in the sponge *or* towel as regards the building of cars; *Tex* **tissu é.** (terry) towelling; **serviette é.** terry towel; *Fam* **il boit comme une é., c'est une véritable é.** he drinks like a fish
▸▸ **é. métallique** (pan) scourer, scouring pad; **é. végétale** vegetable sponge, loofah

épongeage [epɔ̃ʒaʒ] NM (*d'un liquide*) sponging up, mopping up; (*d'une surface*) sponging (down)

éponger [epɔ̃ʒe] (**j'épongeai(s)**; *n.* **épongeons**) VT **1** (*liquide*) to sponge up, to mop up **2** (*surface*) to sponge (down), to mop; (*cheval, voiture etc*) to sponge down; (*le front de qn*) to mop **3** *Fin* (*déficit etc*) to mop up, to absorb
VPR **s'éponger s'é. le front** to mop one's brow

épontille [epɔ̃tij] NF *Naut* shore, prop

épontiller [epɔ̃tije] VT *Naut* to prop, to shore (up)

éponyme [epɔnim] ADJ eponymous

épopée [epɔpe] NF *Littér, Fig* epic

époque [epɔk] NF **1** (*historique*) epoch, era, age; *Géol* age, period; **l'é. glaciaire** the ice age; **la Belle É.** the Belle Epoque; **quelle é. (nous vivons)!** what times we live in!; **il n'est plus de son é.** he's out of step *or* tune with the times; **meubles d'é.** period furniture, (genuine) antique furniture; **à l'é., elle était très reconnue** at the time she was highly regarded; **faire é.** (*d'une invention, déclaration etc*) to leave its mark on history; **découverte qui fait é.** epoch-making discovery
2 (*moment précis*) time; **à l'é. de sa naissance** at the time of his birth; **à cette é. de l'année** at this time of year; **à l'é., je faisais le grand écart** I was doing the splits at the time

épouillage [epujaʒ] NM delousing

épouiller [epuje] VT to delouse

époumoner (s') [sepumɔne] VPR (*en criant*) to shout oneself hoarse; (*en chantant*) to sing oneself hoarse; **c'est ce que je m'époumone à te dire!** I've told you so until I'm hoarse

épousailles [epuzaj] NFPL *Arch* nuptials, wedding

épouse [epuz] NF wife; *Admin* spouse VOIR GRAMMAIRE A12

épousée [epuze] NF *Vieilli* bride

épouser [epuze] VT **1** to marry, *Vieilli* to wed; **é. une grosse dot** to marry (into) money **2** *Fig* (*cause, doctrine etc*) to espouse, to take up, to adopt; **les Français ont épousé le golf** the French have taken up golf; **é. la forme de qch** to take on the exact shape of sth; **sa robe épousait les courbes de son corps** her dress hugged the curves of her body; **la route épouse la colline** the road follows the hill round

époussetage [epustaʒ] NM (*de meubles etc*) dusting

épousseter [epuste] VT (*conj like* **jeter**) (*meubles etc*) to dust; (*vêtements etc*) to brush (the dust from); (*cheval*) to rub down

époustouflant [epustuflɑ̃] ADJ *Fam* amazing, astounding

époustoufler [epustufle] VT *Fam* to amaze, to astound

épouvantable [epuvɑ̃tabl] ADJ dreadful, appalling

épouvantablement [epuvɑ̃tabləmɑ̃] ADV dreadfully, appallingly

épouvantail [epuvɑ̃taj] NM (*dans un jardin*) scarecrow; *Péj* (*personne laide ou bizarrement habillée*) fright; (*personne terrifiante*) bogey; (*chose terrifiante*) bugbear, bogey

épouvante [epuvɑ̃t] NF terror, fright; **jeter** *ou* **porter l'é. dans un pays** to spread terror in a country; **saisi d'é.** terror-stricken, frightened to death; **film d'é.** horror film; **elle pense à cette rencontre avec é.** she is dreading the meeting

épouvanté [epuvɑ̃te] ADJ terror-stricken

épouvanter [epuvɑ̃te] VT to terrify, to scare
VPR **s'épouvanter** to take fright (*de* at)

époux [epu] NM husband; *Admin* spouse; **les é.** the married couple, the husband and wife; **les é. Thomas** Mr and Mrs Thomas

éprendre (s') [seprɑ̃dr] VPR (*conj like pren-dre*) **s'é. de** (*personne*) to fall in love with; (*son travail, une idée etc*) to become passionate about

épreuve [eprœv] NF 1 (*essai*) test, trial; **faire l'é. de qch** to test sth; **mettre qch/qn à l'é.** to put sth/sb to the test; **à l'é. du feu/de l'eau** fireproof/waterproof; **à l'é. des balles** bulletproof; **l'é. de vérité pour …** the critical test for …; **mécanisme à toute é.** foolproof mechanism; **bonté/courage à toute é.** unfailing kindness/courage; **être mis à rude é.** (*d'une personne, de la patience, de l'honneur etc*) to be severely tested; (*de jouets etc*) to be roughly treated *or* handled; **les bateaux/arbres ont été mis à rude é. par la tempête** the boats/trees took a battering from the storm **2** *Scol, Univ* (*écrite*) (examination) paper; (*orale*) test **3** *Sport* (*d'une rencontre d'athlétisme*) event **4** (*adversité*) trial, ordeal; **dans l'é.** in adversity; **passer par de rudes épreuves** to go through a bad *or* hard time **5** *Typ* proof; **corriger les épreuves d'un livre** to proofread a book; **première é.** first proof; **dernière é.** final proof **6** *Phot* print; *Cin* **épreuves (de tournage)** rushes
▸▸ *Typ* **é. bonne à filmer** camera-ready copy, CRC; *Typ* **é. de calage** machine proof; *Sport* **é. contre la montre** time trial; *Sport* **é. éliminatoire** (preliminary) heat; *Sport* **é. d'endurance** endurance test; *Hist* **é. du feu** ordeal by fire; *Sport* **é. finale** final; **é. de force** trial of strength, showdown; *Typ* **épreuves d'imprimerie** printer's proofs; **épreuves d'initiation** initiation rites; **é. d'outrance** resistance test; *Typ* **é. ozalide** ozalid; *Typ* **é. de page** page proof; *Sport* **é.-phare** major event; *Typ* **é. en placard** galley (proof); *Sport* **épreuves sur piste** track events; **é. de résistance** resistance test

épris [epri] ADJ 1 **é. de qn** in love with sb 2 **é. de qch** passionate about sth

éprouvant [epruvɑ̃] ADJ (*pénible*) trying, tiring

éprouvé [epruve] ADJ 1 (*testé*) (*remède*) proven, well-tried; (*spécialiste, loyauté etc*) proven; (*allié*) trusty, staunch; (*matériaux*) tested 2 (*famille*) stricken; (*région*) hard-hit; **troupes très éprouvées** troops that have suffered a great deal

éprouver [epruve] VT 1 (*tester*) (*machine, matériaux, méthode etc*) to test; (*personne, courage etc*) to put to the test, to test 2 (*ressentir*) (*sensation, douleur etc*) to feel, to experience; **les sentiments qu'il éprouve pour moi** the feelings that he has for me 3 (*subir*) (*perte*) to sustain, to suffer; (*difficultés*) to meet with

éprouvette [epruvɛt] NF test tube
ADJ **bébé é.** test-tube baby

EPS [əpees] NF (*abrév* **éducation physique et sportive**) PE

epsilon [ɛpsilɔn] NM (*lettre grecque*) epsilon

épucer [epyse] VT (**j'épuçai(s)**; *n.* **épuçons**) (*chien etc*) to rid of fleas

épuisant [epɥizɑ̃] ADJ exhausting

épuisé [epɥize] ADJ 1 (*très fatigué*) exhausted, tired out, worn out 2 (*sol, mine*) exhausted, worked out; *Élec* **pile épuisée** dead battery; *Nucl* **uranium é.** depleted *or* impoverished uranium 3 *Com* (*livre, édition*) out of print; (*marchandises*) sold out, out of stock; **tous nos stocks sont épuisés** all our stocks are exhausted

épuisement [epɥizmɑ̃] NM 1 (*fatigue*) exhaustion; **danser/marcher jusqu'à é.** to dance/walk till one drops; **rouler/nager jusqu'à é.** to drive/swim until one is exhausted; **mort d'é.** dead with exhaustion 2 (*de provisions, de munitions, d'une mine, d'un sol, d'un*

stock etc) exhaustion; (*de ressources*) depletion; (*d'une citerne*) draining, emptying; *Nucl* (*de l'uranium*) depletion, impoverishment; *Com* **jusqu'à. é. des stocks** while stocks last

épuiser [epɥize] VT 1 (*fatiguer*) to exhaust, to wear *or* tire out 2 (*provisions, munitions etc*) to use up, to exhaust; (*mine, sol*) to exhaust, to work out; (*ressources*) to deplete; (*citerne*) to drain, to empty; (*stock*) to exhaust, to run low on; (*marchandises*) to sell out; **é. un sujet** to exhaust a subject; **cette marche a épuisé toute mon énergie** that walking has used up all my energy 3 (*lettre de crédit*) to use up
VPR **s'épuiser 1** (*se fatiguer*) to exhaust oneself, to tire *or* wear oneself out; **je m'épuise à vous le dire** I've told you so until I'm blue in the face 2 (*d'une source etc*) to dry up, to run dry; (*d'un stock, de l'argent, de provisions etc*) to run out, to give out

épuisette [epɥizɛt] NF 1 *Pêche* landing net 2 *Naut* (*pelle*) scoop, bailer

épurateur [epyratœr] NM *Tech* purifier; **é. de gaz** gas purifier, (gas) scrubber

épuration [epyrasjɔ̃] NF (*de l'eau*) purification; (*du gaz*) purification, scrubbing; (*du pétrole, d'un minerai*) refining; *Fig* (*d'une langue, d'un style*) refining; *Pol* purge, purging

épure [epyr] NF working drawing; (*dessin fini*) (*d'un édifice, moteur etc*) finished plan

épurer [epyre] VT (*eau*) to purify; (*gaz*) to purify, to scrub; (*pétrole, minerai*) to refine; *Fig* (*langue, style*) to refine; *Pol* (*parti, personnel etc*) to purge

équarrir [ekarir] VT 1 (*bois, pierre*) to square 2 (*animal*) to quarter, to cut up

équarrissage [ekarisaʒ] NM 1 (*du bois, de la pierre*) squaring 2 (*de carcasses d'animaux*) quartering, cutting up; **chantier d'é.** knacker's yard

équarrisseur [ekarisœr] NM knacker

équarrissoir [ekariswar] NM 1 (*couteau*) knacker's knife 2 (*abattoir*) knacker's yard

Équateur [ekwatœr] NM Ecuador

équateur [ekwatœr] NM equator; **sous l'é.** at *or* on the equator; **é. magnétique** magnetic equator; *Astron* **é. céleste** celestial equator

équation [ekwasjɔ̃] NF (*calcul*) *Math* **é. du premier/du deuxième degré** simple/quadratic equation; *Compta* **é. de bénéfice** profit equation; *Compta* **é. de coût** cost equation; *Mktg* **é. de la demande** demand equation; *Mktg* **é. de réponse de marché** sales-response function; *Mktg* **é. de vente** sales equation

équatorial, -iale, -iaux, -iales [ekwatɔrjal, -jo] ADJ equatorial
NM *Astron* equatorial (telescope)

équatorien, -ienne [ekwatɔrjɛ̃, -jɛn] ADJ Ecuadorian
N **É.** Ecuadorian

équerre [ekɛr] NF 1 (*instrument*) **é. (à dessin)** set square; **é. à coulisse** (sliding) calliper gauge; **fausse é.** bevel square; **é. à onglet** mitre square; **é. d'arpenteur** cross-staff 2 **en é., à l'é.** at right angles; **d'é.** square, straight; **mettre qch d'é.** to square sth 3 (*pièce métallique*) corner plate

équestre [ekɛstr] ADJ (*statue, sports etc*) equestrian; (*exercices etc*) (horse)riding

équeuter [ekøte] VT (*fruit*) to remove the stalk(s) from

équiangle [ekɥiɑ̃gl] ADJ *Géom* equiangular

équidés [ek(ɥ)ide] NMPL *Zool* Equidae

équidistance [ekɥidistɑ̃s] NF equidistance

équidistant [ekɥidistɑ̃] ADJ equidistant (**de** from)

équilatéral, -ale, -aux, -ales [ekɥilateral, -o] ADJ *Géom* equilateral

équilibrage [ekilibraʒ] NM balancing

équilibrant [ekilibrɑ̃] ADJ (*élément*) balancing; **poids é.** counterweight; *Psy* **c'est un facteur é. dans la vie d'un enfant** it's a stabilizing factor in a child's life

équilibre [ekilibr] NM 1 (*d'un corps, objet*) balance, equilibrium; (*d'un avion*) stability; **avoir le sens de l'é.** to have a sense of balance; **mettre qch en é.** to balance sth; **tenir qch en é. sur son nez** to balance sth on one's nose; **perdre l'é.** to lose one's balance; **faire perdre l'é. à qn** to throw sb off (his/her) balance; **cet acrobate fait de l'é. ou des tours d'é.** this acrobat does balancing tricks; **la chaise est en é. instable** the chair is precariously balanced **2** (*mental*) (mental) balance *or* equilibrium; **elle manque d'é.** she is unbalanced **3** *Pol* **budget en é.** balanced budget; **é. budgétaire** balanced budget; **é. européen** balance of power in Europe; **l'é. des rapports/des forces** (*entre deux pays*) the balance of relations/power; **l'é. de la terreur** the balance of terror **4** (*des éléments d'un ensemble*) balance, harmony; *TV, Cin* **é. des couleurs** colour balance

équilibré [ekilibre] ADJ (*chargement, repas etc*) balanced; (*personne*) well-balanced, stable; (*vie*) regular, stable; **mal é., non é.** unbalanced; **vie peu équilibrée** irregular *or* unstable life

équilibrer [ekilibre] VT (*charge, éléments d'une composition etc*) to balance; (*bateau, avion*) to trim; **é. qch par un contrepoids** to counterbalance sth; **é. un budget** to balance a budget, to break even; *Aut* **é. les roues** to balance the wheels; **cette expérience dans le monde du travail l'a équilibré** this work experience has stabilized him
VPR **s'équilibrer** to balance each other (out); (*budget*) to balance

équilibreur [ekilibrœr] NM *Aviat* stabilizer

équilibriste [ekilibrist] N (*acrobate*) equilibrist; (*funambule*) tightrope walker

équille [ekij] NF (*poisson*) launce, sand eel

équin [ekɛ̃] ADJ equine; **pied é.** club foot

équinisme [ekinism] NM *Méd* (*difformité*) club foot

équinoxe [ekinɔks] NM equinox; **é. de printemps/d'automne** spring/autumn(al) equinox; **vent d'é.** equinoctial gale

équinoxial, -iale, -iaux, -iales [ekinɔksjal, -jo] ADJ equinoctial

équipage [ekipaʒ] NM 1 (*d'un navire, avion*) crew; *Naut* **maître d'é.** boatswain; *Naut* **les hommes de l'é.** the crew; **les membres de l'é.** the crew VOIR GRAMMAIRE A11 2 (*suite*) équipage, retinue; **arriver en grand é.** to arrive in state 3 *Hist* (*voiture, chevaux etc*) équipage 4 *Vieilli* (*tenue*) attire 5 (*équipement*) *Mil* train, equipment; *Tech* equipment, gear; **é. de construction** builder's *or* building equipment *or* gear

équipe [ekip] NF VOIR GRAMMAIRE A11 1 *Sport* team; (*d'un canot à rames*) crew; **sport d'é.** team sport 2 (*personnes qui travaillent ensemble*) (*de chercheurs, médecins etc*) team; (*d'ouvriers*) gang; *Mil* working party; **travailler par équipes** to work in shifts; **chef d'é.** (gang) foreman; **encourager le travail d'é.** to encourage teamwork; **esprit d'é.** team spirit; **faire é. avec qn** to team up with sb; *Fam* **nous étions une é. de joyeux lurons** we were a cheerful crew *or* lot; *Fam* **en voilà une fine é.!** what a crew! 3 *Mktg* **é. commando** venture team; **é. commerciale** marketing team
▸▸ *TV, Cin* **é. caméra** camera crew; *Cin* **é. de cinéma** film crew; *Sport* **é. de cricket** cricket team *or* eleven; *Rail* **é. de conduite** *ou* de lo-

comotive engine crew; **é. de création** creative team; **é. de dactylos** typing pool; *Com* **é. dirigeante** management team; *Journ* **é. d'investigation** investigative team; **é. de jour** day shift; **é. de nuit** night shift; *Journ* back-bench; *TV, Cin* **é. de prise de vue** camera crew; *TV, Cin* **é. de production** production team; **é. de secours** rescue team; **é. du son** sound crew; *Journ* **é. de soutien** back-bench; **é. de télévision** television crew; *TV, Cin* **é. de tournage** camera crew, film crew; *Com* **é. de vente** sales team *or* force

équipée [ekipe] NF *(frasque)* escapade, lark; *(promenade, voyage)* jaunt

équipement [ekipmɑ̃] NM **1** *(action) (d'un atelier, d'une cuisine)* equipping, equipment, fitting out (**de** with); **é. en hommes** manning; **plan d'é. national** national development plan **2** *(matériel)* equipment; *(d'un soldat)* kit; *(de camping, ski etc)* gear, equipment **3** *(installations)* facilities
▸▸ **é. acoustique** audio equipment; **é. audiovisuel** audiovisual equipment; **é. automobile** car accessories; **équipements collectifs** public facilities *or* amenities; **é. électrique** electrical fittings; **é. industriel** industrial plant; *Ordinat* **é. informatique** computer equipment; *Aut* **é. intérieur** internal fittings; **é. routier** road signs; *Aut* **équipements spéciaux** *(chaînes)* chains; *(pneus cloutés)* studded tyres; **e. de survie** survival kit

équipementier [ekipmɑ̃tje] NM *Aut* parts manufacturer

équiper [ekipe] VT *(atelier, cuisine etc)* to equip, to fit out (**de** with); *(sportif, armée etc)* to equip, *Br* to kit out (**de** with); **é. un navire** *(d'appareils etc)* to equip *or* fit out a ship; *(en hommes)* to man a ship; **é. une voiture pour la neige** to equip a car for the snow; **é. une ville en terrains de sport** to provide a town with sports grounds; **appartement avec cuisine équipée** flat with cooking facilities; *Fam* **comme vous voilà équipé!** what a get-up!
VPR **s'équiper** to equip oneself

équipier, -ière [ekipje, -jɛr] N *Sport* team member; *Naut* crew member; *Naut* **mené par 14 équipiers** manned by a crew of 14, with a 14-man crew

équitable [ekitabl] ADJ **1** *(marché, partage etc)* equitable, fair, just **2** *(personne)* impartial, fair-minded, fair

équitablement [ekitabləmɑ̃] ADV equitably, fairly

équitation [ekitasjɔ̃] NF (horse)riding, *Fml* equitation; **faire de l'é.** to go riding; **école d'é.** riding school

équité [ekite] NF equity, equitableness, fairness

équivalence [ekivalɑ̃s] NF equivalence; *Univ* **avoir/obtenir une é.** to have/get an equivalent diploma; **ce diplôme est une é. du bac** this diploma is the equivalent of the baccalauréat

équivalent [ekivalɑ̃] ADJ equivalent (**à** to)
NM equivalent; **sans é.** without equal, unequalled

équivaloir [ekivalwar] VI *(conj like* **valoir***)* to be equivalent *or* equal (**à** to); **cela équivaut à un refus** that amounts to a refusal

équivoque [ekivɔk] ADJ **1** *(ambigu) (mots, faits, attitude etc)* equivocal, ambiguous **2** *(douteux) (conduite, honnêteté, passé etc)* questionable, doubtful, dubious
NF **1** *(ambiguïté)* ambiguity; **sans é.** *(adj)* unequivocal; *(adv)* unequivocally **2** *(malentendu)* misunderstanding (**sur** about)

érable [erabl] NM *(arbre, bois)* maple; **é. à sucre** sugar maple; **sirop/sucre d'é.** maple syrup/sugar

érablière [erablijɛr] NF *Can* maple grove

éradication [eradikasjɔ̃] NF eradication

éradiquer [eradike] VT to eradicate

érafler [erafle] VT *(genou etc)* to scratch, to graze; *(cuir etc)* to scuff; *(bois, meuble)* to scratch
VPR **s'érafler s'é. le coude** to graze *or* scrape one's elbow

éraflure [eraflyr] NF *(au genou etc)* scratch, graze; *(sur cuir etc)* scuff (mark); *(sur bois, meuble)* scratch (mark)

éraillé [eraje] ADJ **1** *(tissu)* frayed; *(surface)* scratched; *(corde)* fretted **2** **yeux éraillés** bloodshot eyes **3** *(voix)* hoarse

éraillement [erajmɑ̃] NM **1** *(d'un tissu)* fraying; *(d'une corde)* fretting; *(d'une surface)* scratching **2** *(éraflure)* scratch **3** *(de voix)* hoarseness

érailler [eraje] VT **1** *(tissu)* to fray; *(ourlet etc)* to unravel; *(corde)* to fret **2** *(peau, surface etc)* to scratch **3** *(voix)* to make hoarse
VPR **s'érailler 1** *(d'un ourlet etc)* to unravel, to come unravelled; *(d'un tissu)* to fray; *(d'une corde)* to fret **2** *(d'une voix)* to become hoarse

éraillure [erajyr] NF *(marque)* scratch

erbium [ɛrbjɔm] NM *Chimie* erbium

ère [ɛr] NF era; **en l'an 1150 de notre è.** in (the year) 1150 AD; **avant notre è.** BC; **è. de prospérité** period of prosperity

érecteur, -trice [erɛktœr, -tris] ADJ *Physiol* erector

érectile [erɛktil] ADJ erectile

érection [erɛksjɔ̃] NF **1** *(d'une statue, d'un mât etc)* erection, setting up, raising **2** *Physiol* erection; **être en é.** to have an erection

éreintage [erɛ̃taʒ] NM = **éreintement 2**

éreintant [erɛ̃tɑ̃] ADJ *Fam (travail etc)* backbreaking, exhausting

éreinté [erɛ̃te] ADJ *Fam* exhausted, worn out

éreintement [erɛ̃tmɑ̃] NM **1** *(fatigue)* exhaustion **2** *(critique sévère)* savage criticism, *Br* slating

éreinter [erɛ̃te] VT **1** *(fatiguer) (personne, animal)* to exhaust, to wear *or* tire out **2** *Fam (critiquer) (livre, représentation, auteur etc)* to criticize savagely, *Br* to slate
VPR **s'éreinter** to exhaust oneself, to wear *or* tire oneself out (**à faire** doing)

éreinteur, -euse [erɛ̃tœr, øz] N savage critic

érémiste [eremist] N *Fam* = person receiving the RMI benefit

Erevan [erevan] N Yerevan

erg¹ [ɛrg] NM *Phys (unité)* erg

erg² NM *Géog* erg

ergol [ɛrgɔl] NM *Astronaut* propellant

ergonome [ɛrgɔnɔm] N ergonomist

ergonomie [ɛrgɔnɔmi] NF ergonomics

ergonomique [ɛrgɔnɔmik] ADJ ergonomic

ergot [ɛrgo] NM **1** *(d'un coq etc)* spur; *Fam* **monter** *ou* **se dresser sur ses ergots** *(se montrer menaçant)* to show one's teeth **2** *(d'un chien etc)* dewclaw **3** *Agr, Pharm* ergot **4** *Tech* lug; **e. d'arrêt** stop lug; **e. de tracteur** *(d'imprimante)* tractor pin

ergotage [ɛrgɔtaʒ] NM quibbling, cavilling

ergoté [ɛrgɔte] ADJ **1** *(oiseau)* spurred; *(chien)* dewclawed **2** *Agr (seigle, blé)* affected with ergot

ergoter [ɛrgɔte] VI to quibble, to cavil (**sur** about)

ergoteur, -euse [ɛrgɔtœr, -øz] ADJ cavilling, quibbling
N quibbler, caviller

ergothérapeute [ɛrgoterapøt] N occupational therapist

ergothérapie [ɛrgoterapi] NF occupational therapy

Érié [erje] NM **le Lac É.** Lake Erie

ériger [eriʒe] **(j'érigeai(s))** VT **1** *(dresser) (statue, temple, mât etc)* to erect, to set up, to raise **2** *(créer) (bureau, tribunal etc)* to establish, to set up **3** *Fig* **é. qn en** to set sb up as, to elevate sb to the status of; **é. qch en** to elevate sth to the status of, to present sth as; **é. une église en cathédrale** to raise a church to (the dignity of) a cathedral
VPR **s'ériger s'é. en spécialiste** to set oneself up as a specialist

ermitage [ɛrmitaʒ] NM hermitage

ermite [ɛrmit] NM hermit; **vivre en e.** to live the life of a recluse

éroder [erɔde] VT *(côte, rochers etc)* to erode, to wear away; *(métaux etc)* to corrode, to eat away

érogène [erɔʒɛn] ADJ erogenous

éros [eros] NM **1** *Psy* **l'é.** Eros **2** *Myth* **É.** Eros

érosif, -ive [erozif, -iv] ADJ erosive

érosion [erozjɔ̃] NF erosion, wearing away; *Fig* erosion; **é. dentaire** dental erosion; *Fig* **é. monétaire** depreciation of money

érotique [erɔtik] ADJ erotic

érotiquement [erɔtikmɑ̃] ADV erotically

érotisation [erɔtizasjɔ̃] NF eroticization

érotiser [erɔtize] VT to eroticize

érotisme [erɔtism] NM *(caractère érotique)* eroticism; *(goût pour le plaisir sexuel)* erotism

érotologue [erɔtɔlɔg] N sexologist

érotomane [erɔtɔman] N erotomaniac

errance [ɛrɑ̃s] NF *Litt* roving, wandering; **vie d'e.** roving *or* wandering life

errant [ɛrɑ̃] ADJ *(personne, vie etc)* roving, wandering; **chevalier e.** knight errant; **le Juif e.** the Wandering Jew; **chien e.** stray dog; **pensées errantes** wandering thoughts

errata [erata] NM INV *Typ* errata; **feuille d'e.** errata slip

erratique [eratik] ADJ erratic

erratum, *pl* **errata** [eratɔm, -ta] NM *Typ* erratum, *pl* errata

erre [ɛr] NF **1** *Naut (lancée)* way; **e. pour gouverner** steerage way; **avoir de l'e.** to have way on; **perdre de l'e.** *ou* **son e.** to lose way **2** **erres** *(d'un cerf etc)* track, spoor, slot; *Fig* **suivre les erres de qn** to follow in sb's footsteps

errement [ɛrmɑ̃] NM *Fin* **é. du marché** market fluctuation
NMPL **errements** erring *or* bad ways; **retomber dans** *ou* **revenir à ses anciens errements** to fall back into one's bad old ways

errer [ɛre] VI **1** *(d'un marcheur etc)* to wander (about), to roam, to rove; **e. par les rues** to wander about *or* roam the streets; **e. comme une âme en peine** to wander about like a lost soul; **laisser e. ses pensées** to let one's thoughts wander *or* stray **2** *Litt (se tromper)* to err, to be mistaken

erreur [ɛrœr] NF **1** *(faute, inexactitude)* error, mistake; **e. de plume** slip of the pen; **e. de date** mistake in the date; **e. de jugement** error of judgment; **e. de sens** wrong meaning; **faire** *ou* **commettre une e.** to make a mistake; **faire e.** to be mistaken; **par e.** by mistake; **sauf e.** if I am not mistaken; **sauf e. ou omission** errors and omissions excepted; **il y a e. sur la personne** you've/they've/etc got the wrong person; **il n'y a pas d'e. (possible)** there's no doubt about it; *Fam* **c'est un malin, pas d'e.** he's a smart one and no mistake; **e.!** wrong!, not so!
2 *(opinion fausse)* error; **être dans l'e.** to be under a misapprehension, to be mistaken; **induire qn en e.** to mislead sb
3 *(action regrettable ou blâmable)* error; **revenir de ses erreurs** to turn over a new leaf

4 *Ordinat* error; **message d'e.** error message; **correction des erreurs** error correction

▸▸ *Ordinat* **e. aléatoire** random error; *Ordinat* **e. d'analyse (syntaxique)** parse error; *Ordinat* **e. d'arrondi** rounding error; **e. de calcul** miscalculation; *Ordinat* **e. de codage** coding error; **e. d'échantillonnage** sampling error; *Ordinat* **e. d'écriture** write error; *Ordinat* **e. d'entrée** input error; *Ordinat* **e. disque** disk error; **e. de jeunesse** youthful error; **e. judiciaire** miscarriage of justice; *Ordinat* **e. de lecture** read error; *Ordinat* **e. de logiciel** software *or* system error; *Ordinat* **e. de parité** parity error; *Ordinat* **e. de programmation** program *or* programming error; *Ordinat* **e. de saisie** keyboarding error; *Ordinat* **e. de syntaxe** syntax error; **e. système** system error; **e. typographique** printing error; *(coquille)* misprint

erroné [ɛrɔne] **ADJ** *(déclaration etc)* erroneous

erronément [ɛrɔnemɑ̃] **ADV** erroneously

ersatz [ɛrzats] **NM INV** ersatz, substitute; **e. de café/littérature** ersatz coffee/literature

erse[1] [ɛrs] **ADJ, NM** *Ling* Erse

erse[2] **NF** *Naut* grummet, grommet

éructation [eryktasjɔ̃] **NF** belch

éructer [erykte] **VI** to belch
VT *Fig* **é. des injures** to hurl abuse

érudit, -ite [erydi, -it] **ADJ** erudite, scholarly, learned
N scholar

érudition [erydisjɔ̃] **NF** erudition, learning, scholarship; **discourir avec é.** to talk learnedly

éruptif, -ive [eryptif, -iv] **ADJ** *(maladie, roche etc)* eruptive

éruption [erypsjɔ̃] **NF 1** *(d'un volcan)* eruption; **faire é., entrer en é.** to erupt **2 é. dentaire** *ou* **des dents** cutting of teeth **3** *Méd* rash, eruption **4** *Fig (de colère, joie etc)* eruption, outburst

> Do not confuse with **irruption**.

érysipèle [erizipɛl] **NM** *Méd* erysipelas

érythème [eritɛm] **NM** *Méd* rash, *Spéc* erythema; **é. fessier** nappy *or Am* diaper rash; **é. solaire** sunburn

Érythrée [eritre] **NF** Eritrea

érythréen, -enne [eritreɛ̃, -ɛn] **ADJ** Eritrean
N É. Eritrean

E/S *Ordinat (abrév* **entrée/sortie**) I/O

ès [ɛs] **PRÉP docteur ès lettres/sciences** ≃ PhD, DPhil; **licencié(e) ès lettres/sciences** ≃ Bachelor of Arts/Science, BA/BSc; *Admin, Jur* **ès qualités** ex officio

ESB [æɛsbe] **NF** *Vét (abrév* **encéphalite spongiforme bovine**) BSE

esbigner (s') [sɛsbiɲe] **VPR** *Fam* to clear off, to take off, *Am* to book it, to fade

esbroufe [ɛzbruf] **NF** *Fam* bluff(ing); **faire de l'e.** to show off, to overdo it; **avoir qn à l'e.** to bluff sb

esbroufeur, -euse [ɛzbrufœr, -øz] **N** *Fam* swaggerer

escabeau, -eaux [ɛskabo] **NM 1** *(tabouret)* (wooden) stool **2** *(marchepied)* stepladder, *Br* (pair of) steps; **e. de bibliothèque** library steps

escadre [ɛskadr] **NF** *Naut* squadron; *Aviat* **e. aérienne** wing; **chef d'e.** *Naut* squadron commander; *Aviat* wing commander

escadrille [ɛskadrij] **NF 1** *Naut* flotilla **2** *Aviat (unité)* flight

escadron [ɛskadrɔ̃] **NM 1** *Mil* squadron; **e. de chars** armoured squadron; **chef d'escadron(s)** major **2** *Aviat* squadron; **e. de**

chasse/bombardement fighter/bomber squadron **3** *Fig (groupe) (de touristes, journalistes etc)* troop, band

escagasser [ɛskagase] *Région* **VT 1** *(rouer de coups)* to beat up **2** *(irriter)* to annoy, to irritate
VPR s'escagasser *(s'épuiser)* to wear oneself out *(à faire qch* doing sth); *(se donner du mal)* to go to a lot of trouble *(à faire qch* to do sth)

escalade [ɛskalad] **NF 1** *(action) (d'un mur, d'une falaise etc)* climbing, scaling; *Sport* (rock)climbing; **faire de l'e.** to go (rock)climbing **2** *(parcours)* climb **3** *(d'une guerre, des prix, de la violence etc)* escalation; **les charges locatives n'ont pas cessé leur e.** service charges are still escalating; **on a remarqué son e. verbale** it was noted that he got more and more carried away as he spoke

▸▸ *Sport* **e. libre** free climbing

escalader [ɛskalade] **VT** to climb, to scale; *Hist, Mil (forteresse)* to escalade

escalator [ɛskalatɔr] **NM** escalator

escale [ɛskal] **NF 1** *(temps d'arrêt) Naut* call; *Aviat* stop(over), layover; **faire e.** *Naut* to put into port; *Aviat* to touch down; **faire e. à Londres** *Naut* to put in *or* call at London; *Aviat* to stop over at London; *Aviat* **escales prévues** scheduled stops; **vol sans e.** nonstop flight; **une e. de quatre heures** *Naut* a four-hour call; *Aviat* a four-hour stop(over) **2** *(lieu) Naut* port *or* place of call; *Aviat* stop(over)

escalier [ɛskalje] **NM 1** *(marches)* (flight of) stairs; *(cage)* staircase; **rencontrer qn dans l'e.** *ou* **dans les escaliers** to meet sb on the stairs; *Fig* **j'ai l'esprit de l'e.** I always think of an answer when it's too late; *Ski* **monter en e.** to sidestep; *Fig Fam* **avoir des escaliers dans les cheveux** to have unevenly cut hair **2** *Tech* step; **en e.** stepped **3** *Typ (de titres)* step effect; **courbe en e.** jaggy

▸▸ *Naut* **e. des cabines** companionway; **e. en colimaçon** spiral staircase; **e. d'honneur** main *or* grand staircase; **e. mécanique** escalator, *Can* **e. mobile** escalator; **e. roulant** escalator; **e. de secours** fire escape; **e. de service** backstairs; **e. à vis** spiral staircase

escalope [ɛskalɔp] **NF** *Culin* escalope

escamotable [ɛskamɔtabl] **ADJ** *(antenne)*, *Aviat (train d'atterrissage)* retractable; *(meuble)* foldaway, collapsible; *Aut (phares)* retractable

escamotage [ɛskamɔtaʒ] **NM 1** *(par un illusionniste)* conjuring away, vanishing; **tour d'é.** vanishing trick **2** *Fig (d'une tâche)* skipping; *(d'un problème, d'une question)* dodging **3** *Aviat (d'un train d'atterrissage)* retraction **4** *(vol)* stealing

escamoter [ɛskamɔte] **VT 1** *(d'un illusionniste)* to conjure away, to make vanish **2** *Fig (éviter) (tâche)* to skip; *(problème, question)* to dodge **3** *Aviat (train d'atterrissage)* to retract **4** *(voler)* to sneak off with, to steal; **on m'a escamoté ma montre** someone's sneaked off with *or* stolen my watch

escamoteur, -euse [ɛskamɔtœr, -øz] **N 1** *(illusionniste)* conjuror **2** *(voleur)* sneak thief

escampette [ɛskɑ̃pɛt] **NF** *Fam* **prendre la poudre d'e.** *(s'enfuir)* to make off, *Br* to do a bunk

escapade [ɛskapad] **NF** *(excursion)* jaunt; *(fugue)* running off *or* away; **faire une e.** to run off *or* away

escarbille [ɛskarbij] **NF** cinder

escarboucle [ɛskarbukl] **NF** *(pierre précieuse)* carbuncle

escarcelle [ɛskarsɛl] **NF tomber dans l'e. de qn** *(de l'argent, d'une collection de tableaux*

etc) to come sb's way; *(de la direction d'une entreprise etc)* to end up *or* wind up in sb's hands; **tout le département est tombé dans l'e. des socialistes** the whole department ended up *or* wound up in the hands of the socialists

escargot [ɛskargo] **NM** snail; **allure d'e.** snail's pace; *Fam* **il marche comme un e.** he's walking at a snail's pace; **nous avancions à la vitesse d'un e.** we were moving at a snail's pace; *Fig* **opération e.** slowing down of the traffic *(by protesting truck drivers)*

escargotière [ɛskargɔtjer] **NF 1** *(parc)* snailery **2** *(plat)* snail dish

escarmouche [ɛskarmuʃ] **NF** skirmish

escarpé [ɛskarpe] **ADJ** *(route, montagne, pente)* steep; *(falaise)* sheer

escarpement [ɛskarpəmɑ̃] **NM** *(versant)* steep slope; *Géog* escarpment; *Géog* **e. de faille** fault scarp

escarpin [ɛskarpɛ̃] **NM** pump, *Br* court shoe; *(pour danser)* pump

escarpolette [ɛskarpɔlɛt] **NF** *Vieilli (balançoire)* swing

escarre, eschare [ɛskar] **NF** *Méd* scab; *(dû aux draps etc)* bedsore

Escaut (l') [lɛsko] **NM** the Scheldt

eschatologie [ɛskatɔlɔʒi] **NF** eschatology

Éschyle [eʃil] **N** Aeschylus

escient [ɛsjɑ̃] **NM à bon e.** wisely, judiciously; **à mauvais e.** unwisely

esclaffer (s') [sɛsklafe] **VPR** to burst out laughing, to roar with laughter, to guffaw

esclandre [ɛsklɑ̃dr] **NM** *(scandale, tapage)* (noisy) scene; **faire** *ou* **causer un e., faire de l'e.** to make a scene

esclavage [ɛsklavaʒ] **NM** *(état)* slavery; *(action)* enslavement; **réduire qn en e.** to enslave sb, to reduce sb to slavery; *Fig* **l'e. du bureau** the drudgery of the office; *Fam* **mais c'est de l'e.!** *(exploitation)* but it's slave labour!

esclavagisme [ɛsklavaʒism] **NM** slavery; *(doctrine)* pro-slavery

esclavagiste [ɛsklavaʒist] **N** pro-slaver
ADJ état e. slave state

esclave [ɛsklav] **N** slave; **marchand d'esclaves** slave trader; **il fut vendu comme e.** he was sold into slavery; *Fig* **elle est l'e. de sa famille** she is a slave to her family; *Fig* **être l'e. de la mode/de son travail** to be a slave to fashion/one's work
ADJ être e. de ses habitudes to be a slave to *or* the slave of one's habits

escogriffe [ɛskɔgrif] **NM (grand) e.** *(homme grand)* beanpole

escomptable [ɛskɔ̃tabl] **ADJ** *Compta* discountable

escompte [ɛskɔ̃t] **NM 1** *Com* discount; **accorder** *ou* **faire un e. sur les prix** to allow *or* give a discount on the prices; **maison d'e.** cutprice *or* discount store; **à e.** at a discount; *Can* **50% d'e. sur toute la marchandise** 50% discount on all goods; **e. professionnel** *(au détaillant)* trade discount; **e. sur les achats en gros** *ou* **en quantité** volume purchase discount, quantity *or* bulk discount; **e. à forfait** forfaiting

2 *Fin* **e. (de banque)** discount; **e. officiel, taux d'e.** (bank) discount rate; **e. de caisse** *ou* **au comptant** cash discount; **e. commercial** trade discount; **e. de règlement** discount for early payment, settlement discount; **prendre à l'e. un effet de commerce** to discount a bill of exchange

3 *Can (remise)* discount; **50% d'e. sur toute la marchandise** 50% discount on all goods

escompter [ɛskɔ̃te] **VT 1** *Fin (traite)* to discount **2** *(s'attendre à)* to expect, to anticipate *(que* that); **e. une hausse** to anticipate an increase; **e. faire** to expect to do, to anticipate doing; **le succès escompté** the expected or anticipated success

escorte [ɛskɔrt] NF *Mil, Naut etc* escort; **faire e. à qn** to escort sb; **sous (bonne) e.** under escort; **conduire un prisonnier sous (bonne) e.** to escort a prisoner; *Naut* **sous l'e. d'une corvette** convoyed or escorted by a corvette

escorter [ɛskɔrte] VT to escort; *Naut* to convoy, to escort

escorteur [ɛskɔrtœr] NM *Naut* escort (vessel)

escouade [ɛskwad] NF **1** *(d'ouvriers)* squad, gang; *(de touristes, jeunes gens etc)* group **2** *Hist, Mil* squad

ESCP [ɛɛsɛspe] NF *(abrév* **École supérieure de commerce de Paris)** = prestigious business and management school

escrime [ɛskrim] NF *Sport* fencing; **faire de l'e.** to fence

escrimer (s') [sɛskrime] VPR to fight; **s'e. à faire qch** to do all one can to do sth, to try very hard to do sth

escrimeur, -euse [ɛskrimœr, -øz] N *Sport* fencer

escroc [ɛskro] NM swindler, crook

escroquer [ɛskrɔke] VT *(personne)* to swindle, to cheat, to trick; **e. qch à qn, e. qn de qch** to swindle or to cheat or to trick sb out of sth

escroquerie [ɛskrɔkri] NF *(action)* swindling; *(résultat)* swindle; *Jur (délit)* fraud; **mais c'est de l'e.!** it's a swindle, *Br* it's daylight robbery!

escudo [ɛskydo] NM *Anciennement* escudo

esgourde [ɛsgurd] NF *Arg* ear, *Br* lughole

eskimo [ɛskimo] ADJ INV Eskimo, Inuit; **les coutumes e.** Eskimo or Inuit customs

NM *Ling* Eskimo, Inuit

N **E.** Eskimo, Inuit

Ésope [ezɔp] N Aesop

ésotérique [ezɔterik] ADJ esoteric

ésotérisme [ezɔterism] NM esotericism

espace [ɛspas] NM **1** *(étendue, distance)* space; **laisser de l'e.** to leave space or room; **un e. de dix mètres entre deux choses** a distance or space or gap of ten metres between two things; **laisser un e. entre deux mots** to leave a space between two words; **l'e. parcouru** the distance covered

2 *(durée)* **pendant le même e. de temps** in the same space of time; **en l'e. d'une semaine** within a week

3 *(vide), Astron* space; **regarder dans l'e.** to stare into space; **e. extra-atmosphérique** outer space; **vol** *ou* **voyage dans l'e.** space flight

4 *Géom* space; **e. à trois/quatre dimensions** three-/four-dimensional space

5 *Ordinat* **e. disque** disk space; **e. insécable** hard space; **e. mémoire** memory space; **e. ressort** soft space; **e. de stockage** storage space; **e. Web** Web space

6 *Mktg* **e. d'exposition** display area; **e. de PLV** in-store advertising space

NF *Typ* space; **e. fine/moyenne/forte** hair/medium-sized/thick space

▸▸ **e. aérien** airspace; *Typ* **e. blanc** space; *Com* **e. cargo** cargo space; *TV, Cin* **e. filmique** filmic space; *Admin* **e. judiciaire européen** common European legal framework; **e. mort** dead space; *Aut* clearance volume; **e. publicitaire** advertising space; **e. de rangement** storage space; **e. de rayonnage** shelf space; **e. social européen** common European social legislation; **e. vital** living space; **espaces verts** green spaces

espacement [ɛspasmɑ̃] NM **1** *(action)* spacing out; *(résultat)* spacing; *(distance)* space, distance; *Ordinat* **e. arrière** backspace; *Aut*

e. des sièges seat pitch; **barre d'e.** *(d'une machine à écrire etc)* space bar **2** *Typ (entre deux lettres)* space; *(interligne)* space (between the lines), spacing; **e. des caractères/lignes** character/line spacing; **e. fixe/proportionnel** fixed/proportional spacing

espacer [ɛspase] **(j'espaçai(s))** VT *(objets, lignes, paiements, visites etc)* to space out; *Ordinat, Typ* to interspace; **e. des choses d'un mètre** to space things out a metre apart; **il faut e. nos rencontres** we must meet less often

VPR **s'espacer 1** *(de visites, lettres, cris etc)* to become less frequent **2** *(de personnes)* **espacez-vous** space yourselves out

espace-temps NM INV *Math, Phys* space-time (continuum)

espadon [ɛspadɔ̃] NM swordfish

espadrille [ɛspadrij] NF espadrille, rope-soled sandal

Espagne [ɛspaɲ] NF Spain

espagnol, -ole [ɛspaɲɔl] VOIR GRAMMAIRE A19 ADJ Spanish

NM *Ling* Spanish

N **E.** Spaniard; **les E.** the Spanish, the Spaniards

espagnolette [ɛspaɲɔlɛt] NF (window) fastener *(long vertical bar with pivoting central catch)*

espalier [ɛspalje] NM **1** *(mur)* wall *(for espaliers)*; **(arbre en) e.** espalier **2** *Gym* wall bars

espar [ɛspar] NM *Naut* spar

espèce [ɛspɛs] NF **1** *(sorte)* kind, sort; **gens/ livres de toute e.** people/books of all kinds or of every description; **il portait une e. de chemise à fleurs** he wore a kind or a sort of flowery shirt; **cela n'a aucune e. d'importance** that's of no importance whatsoever, that's not at all important; *Fam* **cette e. d'idiot** that stupid idiot, that silly fool; *Fam* **e. d'idiot!** you idiot!; *Fam* **une e. de mec bizarre** a strange sort of guy; *Péj* **l'e. de blonde qui lui sert de femme** that blonde he calls his wife; **des gens de son e.** people like him, people of his kind or sort; **un escroc/menteur/avare de la pire e.** a crook/liar/miser of the worst sort or kind, the worst sort or kind of crook/liar/miser

2 *Jur* **cas d'e.** specific case; **loi applicable en l'e.** law applicable to the case in point; *Fig Fam* **je suis un cas d'e.** I'm a special case

3 espèces *(argent)* cash; *Hist (monnaie métallique)* coin; **payer en espèces** to pay in cash; **espèces sonnantes et trébuchantes** hard cash; *Compta* **espèces en caisse** cash in hand

4 *Bot, Zool* species; **l'e. humaine** the human race, mankind; **e. en voie de disparition** endangered species VOIR GRAMMAIRE A13

5 *Rel* (Eucharistic) species

espérance [ɛsperɑ̃s] NF hope; **vivre dans l'e.** to live in hope; **dans l'e. de faire** in the hope of doing; **dans l'e. que** in the hope that; **contre toute e.** against or contrary to all expectation; **au-delà de nos espérances** beyond our expectations, beyond expectation; **fonder son e. sur qn/qch** to found one's hopes on sb/sth; **mettre ses espérances en qch** to pin one's hopes on sth; **l'affaire n'a pas répondu à nos espérances** the business did not come up or live up to our expectations; **cet enfant donne de grandes espérances** this child shows great promise or is very promising; *Hum* **avoir des espérances** to have expectations *(of an inheritance)*; **tu es toute mon e.** you are my only hope

▸▸ **e. de vie** *(d'une personne)* life expectancy; *(d'un produit)* life expectancy, shelf life

espérantiste [ɛsperɑ̃tist] *Ling* N Esperantist

ADJ *(société etc)* Esperanto

espéranto [ɛsperɑ̃to] NM *Ling* Esperanto

espérer [ɛspere] **(j'espère; j'espérerai)** VT *(quelque chose)* to hope for; *(s'attendre à) (personne, chose)* to expect; **j'espère vous revoir** I hope to see or I'll see you again; **j'espère qu'il viendra** I hope that he comes or will come; **je n'espère pas qu'il vienne** I don't expect him to come; **je ne vous espérais plus** I had given you up, I wasn't expecting you to come any more

VI **1 e. en Dieu** to trust in God **2 j'espère bien** I hope so; **espérons!** let's hope so!

esperluète, esperluette [ɛspɛrlɥɛt] NF ampersand

espiègle [ɛspjɛgl] ADJ *(enfant, réponse etc)* mischievous

N *(enfant)* imp; **petit(e) e.** little monkey

espièglerie [ɛspjɛgləri] NF **1** *(caractère)* mischievousness; **par pure e.** out of pure mischief **2** *(tour)* prank

espingouin [ɛspɛ̃gwɛ̃] *Arg* ADJ Dago

NM **E.** Dago

espion, -ionne [ɛspjɔ̃, -jɔn] N *(d'une puissance étrangère)* spy, secret agent; *(de police), Fig* spy; **avion-/satellite-e.** spy plane/satellite

espionnage [ɛspjɔnaʒ] NM espionage, spying; **faire de l'e.** to spy; **réseau/roman d'e.** spy network/novel; **l'e. industriel** industrial espionage

espionner [ɛspjɔne] VT *(quelqu'un, les mouvements de qn etc)* to spy on

VI to spy

espionnite [ɛspjɔnit] NF *Fam Hum* spy fever

esplanade [ɛsplanad] NF esplanade

espoir [ɛspwar] NM **1** *(espérance)* hope; **avoir l'e. de faire qch** to have hopes of or to be hopeful of doing sth; **avoir de l'e.** to have hope(s); **dans l'e. de vous revoir** in the hope of seeing you again; **avoir bon e.** to be full of hope; **reprendre e.** to be or become hopeful again; **mettre son e. en qch/qn** to put one's hopes in or to pin one's hopes on sth/sb; **nourrir l'e. de faire qch** to live in hope of doing sth; **c'est sans e.** it's hopeless; **il n'y a plus d'e.** there's no hope any more, all hope is gone or lost; **tous les espoirs sont permis** things look hopeful; *Prov Iron* **l'e. fait vivre** hope springs eternal

2 *(personne, chose)* hope; **vous êtes/ce plan est leur seul e.** you are/this plan is their only hope; **un e. du tennis français/de la chanson française** one of the most promising French tennis players/French singers; **ce sont les espoirs du patinage artistique** they are the most promising figure skaters around

ESPRIT [ɛspri]

| mind **1** ▪ spirit **2, 5–7** ▪ wit **1, 3** |
| ▪ person **4** |

NM **1** *(intellectuel)* mind; **d'e. lent** slow-witted; **d'e. vif** quick-witted; **avoir l'e. large/ étroit** to be broad-/narrow-minded; **avoir l'e. tranquille** to be easy in one's mind; **avoir l'e. libre** to have a clear mind; **avoir l'e. mal tourné** to have a dirty mind; **perdre l'e.** to go out of one's mind; **elle avait l'e. ailleurs** her thoughts were or her mind was elsewhere; **où aviez-vous l'e.?** what were you thinking of?; **c'est une vue de l'e.** that's theoretical or all theory; **présence d'e.** presence of mind; **ça m'est sorti de l'e.** it slipped my mind, it went clean out of my head; **qu'avez-vous à l'e.?** what are you thinking of?; **elle n'avait pas l'e. à ce qu'elle faisait** her mind wasn't on or she didn't have her mind on what she was doing; **je n'ai pas l'e. à plaisanter ce matin** I'm not in the mood for joking or in a joking mood this morning; *Hum* **l'e. est fort mais la chair est faible** the spirit is willing but the flesh is weak; **une pareille idée ne me serait jamais venue à l'e.**

such an idea would never have occurred to me *or* crossed my mind *or* entered my head; **dans mon e., ça ne veut pas dire la même chose** to my mind that doesn't mean the same thing; **dans mon e., ils arrivaient demain** I thought they were coming tomorrow; **avoir l'e. de se taire** to have the (good) sense to be silent; **perdre/reprendre ses esprits** to lose/regain consciousness

2 (*attitude, qualité*) spirit; **e. de compétition** competitive spirit; **e. d'entreprise** enterprise spirit, spirit of enterprise; **avoir bon e.** to be good-natured; **faire du mauvais e.** to be negative; **je n'ai pas l'e. de sacrifice** I'm not the sort to make sacrifices; **avoir l'e. d'analyse/scientifique** to have an analytical/a scientific (turn of) mind

3 (*humour*) wit; **avoir de l'e.** to be witty; **mots** *ou* **traits d'e.** witticisms, witty remarks; **faire de l'e.** to display one's wit

4 (*personne*) person; **un e. dangereux** a dangerous person *or* man/woman; **un e. fort** a freethinker; **les grands esprits de notre siècle** the great minds of our century; *Prov* **les grands esprits se rencontrent** great minds think alike

5 (*sens*) spirit; **s'attacher à l'e. de la loi plutôt qu'à la lettre** to go by the spirit of the law rather than the letter; **c'est dans cet e. qu'a été conçue cette organisation** it is in this spirit that the organization was conceived

6 (*désincarné*) spirit; (*fantôme*) spirit (of the dead), ghost; **le Saint-E., l'E. saint** the Holy Ghost, the Holy Spirit; *Hum* **je ne suis pas un pur e., il faut bien que je mange** I'm flesh and blood, I do have to eat; **l'e. malin** the Evil One; **e., es-tu là?** (*dans une séance de spiritisme*) is there anybody there?

7 *Chimie etc* (volatile) spirit

8 *Méd Arch* **esprits animaux** animal spirits ▸ ▸ **e.-de-bois** wood alcohol; **e. brut** raw spirits; **e. de caste** class consciousness; **e. de chapelle** cliquishness; **e. de clan** clannishness; **e. de clocher** parochialism; **e. de corps** esprit de corps; **e. d'équipe** team spirit; **e. de famille** family feeling; **e. frappeur** spirit-rapper; **e.-de-sel** spirits of salt; **e.-de-vin** spirits of wine

esquif [ɛskif] NM *Litt* (*embarcation*) skiff; **frêle e.** frail barque *or* vessel

esquille [ɛskij] NF splinter (of bone)

esquimau, -aude, -aux [ɛskimo, -od, -o] ADJ (*occ inv in feminine*) Eskimo, Inuit; **chien e.** husky

  N **E.** Eskimo, Inuit

  NM **1** (*glace*) **e.®** ≃ choc-ice (*on a stick*), *Am* ≃ ice-cream bar, Eskimo Pie® **2** *Ling* Eskimo, Inuit

esquimautage [ɛskimotaʒ] NM *Sport* Eskimo roll

esquintant [ɛskɛ̃tɑ̃] ADJ *Fam* (*travail, voyage etc*) exhausting, tiring; (*personne*) tiresome

esquinter [ɛskɛ̃te] *Fam* VT **1** (*fatiguer*) to do in, to wear out **2** (*abîmer*) (*montre, outil etc*) to do in, to ruin; (*voiture etc*) to bash up, *Br* to prang; (*blesser*) to do in; **il a eu le bras esquinté dans sa chute** he did his arm in when he fell **3** (*critiquer*) (*auteur, film etc*) to slam, *Br* to slate

  VPR **s'esquinter 1** (*se fatiguer*) to do oneself in, to wear oneself out (**à faire** doing) **2** (*s'abîmer*) **s'e. la santé/les yeux** to ruin one's health/eyes (**à faire** doing); **je me suis esquinté la jambe en tombant** I did my leg in when I fell

esquisse [ɛskis] NF *Beaux-Arts* (rough) sketch; *Typ* (*de page*) rough layout; *Fig* (*d'un projet, d'un roman etc*) sketch, outline; *Fig* **l'e. d'un sourire** the ghost *or* suggestion of a smile; *Fig* **l'e. d'une aide de la part du gouvernement** the tiniest amount of aid from the government

esquisser [ɛskise] VT (*portrait etc*) to sketch; *Fig* (*plan, roman, personnage etc*) to sketch, to outline; *Fig* **e. un sourire** to give a slight smile; *Fig* **e. un geste** to make a slight gesture; *Fig* **e. un geste de la main** to give a slight wave, to sketch a wave

  VPR **s'esquisser un sourire s'esquissa sur son visage** he gave a slight smile; *Fig* **un plan commençait à s'e. dans mon esprit** a plan started to take shape in my mind

esquive [ɛskiv] NF *Sport etc* (*mouvement*) dodge; *Fig* (*d'une question, d'un problème etc*) dodging, evasion; *Boxe etc* **e. de la tête** dodge

esquiver [ɛskive] VT (*coup*), *Fig* (*question, problème, devoir, créancier etc*) to avoid, to dodge, to evade

  VI **e. (de la tête)** to dodge

  VPR **s'esquiver** to slip away *or* off, to make oneself scarce

essai [ɛsɛ] NM **1** (*test, épreuve*) (*d'un produit, d'une machine, d'une voiture etc*) test, trial; *TV, Cin* audition; *Com* **à l'e.** on a trial basis; **faire l'e. de qch** to test sth, to try sth out; **faites un e. avant de vous décider** try it out before you decide; *TV, Cin* **faire faire un e. à qn** to audition sb; **mettre qn/qch à l'e.** to put sb/sth to the test; **essais comparatifs** comparative tests; **prendre qch/qn à l'e.** to take sth/sb on trial, to take sth on approval/sb on probation; **pilote d'e.** test pilot; *Cin* **bout d'e.** screen test

2 (*tentative*) attempt, try; **faire un e.** to have a try, to make an attempt; **elle fait des essais de jardinage plutôt infructueux** she makes rather fruitless attempts at gardening; **au premier e.** at the first attempt *or* try; **coup d'e.** trial go *or* attempt; **à titre d'e.** subject to approval

3 *Littér* essay

4 *Métal* (*de l'or, de l'argent*) assay(ing); **fourneau d'e.** assay furnace

5 *Rugby* try; **marquer un e.** to score a try; **transformer un e. (en but)** to convert a try ▸ ▸ *Ordinat* **e. approfondi** beta test; **e. à banc** bench test; *TV, Cin* **e. de caméra** screen test; *Aut* **e. de chute** drop test; *Aut* **e. de collision frontale** frontal impact test; *Tech* **e. en endurance** endurance test; *Mktg* **e. gratuit** free trial; *TV, Cin* **e. image** test shot; **e. nucléaire** nuclear test; *Ordinat* **e. de performance** benchmark; *Ordinat* **e. préliminaire** alphatest; **essais de produit** product testing; *Aut* **e. routier** *ou* **sur route** road test; *TV, Radio* **e. de voix** voice test; *Aviat* **essais en vol** test flights

essaim [ɛsɛ̃] NM (*d'abeilles, d'étudiants etc*) swarm; (*de filles*) bevy

essaimage [ɛsemaʒ] NM **1** (*d'abeilles*) swarming; *Fig* (*de la population, d'une famille*) spreading; *Fig* **l'e. de notre entreprise** the expansion of our firm's branch network **2** (*époque*) swarming time

essaimer [ɛseme] VI (*des abeilles*) to swarm; *Fig* (*d'une population, d'une famille*) to spread; (*d'une firme*) to expand

  VT (*d'une firme*) (*usines, filiales etc*) spread

essayage [ɛsɛjaʒ] NM (*de vêtements, chaussures etc*) trying on, fitting; **on fera les rectifications après le deuxième e.** adjustments will be made after the second fitting; **cabine** *ou* **salon d'e.** fitting room

essayer [ɛseje] (**j'essaie, j'essaye,** n. **essayons; j'essaierai, j'essayerai**) VT **1** (*tester*) (*machine, produit etc*) to test, to try out; (*pour la première fois, avant d'acheter etc*) (*nouveau gadget, restaurant, coiffeur etc*) to try (out); (*voiture*) to test-drive, to try out; (*vin, plat etc*) to try, to taste; (*vêtements, chaussures etc*) to try on; (*utiliser*) (*remède, politesse, sa force etc*) to try

2 (*tenter*) **e. de faire qch** to try *or* attempt to do sth; **n'essaie pas de me mentir** don't try

lying *or* to lie to me; **essayez de l'attraper** try to *or* and catch it; **laissez-moi e.** let me (have a) try; **sois courageux! – on va e.!** be brave! – I'll try!; **e. les maths/les agences matrimoniales** to try maths/the marriage bureaux VOIR GRAMMAIRE A43–4

3 *Métal* (*minerai*) to assay

  VPR **s'essayer s'e. à qch/à faire qch** to try one's hand *or* one's skill at sth/at doing sth

essayeur, -euse [ɛsɛjœr, -øz] N **1** (*de vêtements*) fitter **2** (*d'une machine, d'un produit etc*) tester **3** (*d'or, d'argent*) assayer

essayiste [ɛsɛjist] N essayist

esse [ɛs] NF **1** (*crochet*) S-hook **2** (*cheville d'essieu*) linchpin **3** (*de violon etc*) f-hole, sound hole

ESSEC [ɛsɛk] NF (*abrév* École supérieure des sciences économiques et commerciales) = university-level business school

essence [ɛsɑ̃s] NF **1** *Aut* petrol, *Am* gas, gasoline; **à e.** petrol-powered; **poste d'e.** filling station, petrol *or Am* gas station; *Fam* **faire de l'e.** to fill up **2** (*extrait*) (*de plante, café, viande etc*) essence; **e. de citron** lemon oil; **e. de roses** rose oil, attar of roses **3** (*caractère fondamental*), *Phil* essence; **par e.** essentially **4** (*espèce*) (*d'arbre*) species; **essences résineuses** resinous trees, conifers ▸ ▸ **e. à faible indice d'octane** low-octane petrol; **e. à indice d'octane élevé** high-octane petrol; **e. ordinaire** two-star petrol, *Am* regular gas; **e. sans plomb** unleaded (petrol *or Am* gas), lead-free petrol *or Am* gas; **e. de térébenthine** oil *or* spirits of turpentine

essentiel, -ielle [ɛsɑ̃sjɛl] ADJ **1** (*fondamental*) (*vérité, caractère etc*) essential; (*raison*) basic, main **2** (*nécessaire*) essential, necessary (**à, pour** for); **il est e. d'avoir compris ce point** it is essential *or* necessary to have understood this point **3** (*très important*) essential; **il est e. d'avoir lu ce livre** it is essential to have read this book

  NM **l'e.** (*le point central*) the main point; (*les points centraux*) the main points; (*la majeure partie*) the main *or* greater part (**de** of); **l'e. des effectifs est resté à la base** the greater part *or* most of the men stayed at base; **n'apportez que l'e.** bring only the (bare) essentials *or* the basics; **l'e. est d'agir/que tu lui parles** the main *or* important thing is to act/that you talk to him; **vous avez la santé, c'est l'e.** you're healthy, that's the main *or* important thing

essentiellement [ɛsɑ̃sjɛlmɑ̃] ADV **1** (*par nature*) essentially, fundamentally **2** (*principalement*) essentially, mainly; (*avant tout*) above all

esseulé [ɛsœle] ADJ (*abandonné*) alone; (*solitaire*) lonely

essieu, -ieux [ɛsjø] NM axle; (*de chariot*) axle tree; **e. avant/arrière** front/rear axle; **e. fixe** dead axle

essor [ɛsɔr] NM **1** (*d'un oiseau*) flight; **prendre son e.** to fly off *or* away **2** *Fig* (*d'une industrie, d'une économie, d'un pays etc*) (rapid) growth, expansion; **e. économique** economic expansion; **prendre son e.** to take off; **prendre un grand e.** to grow *or* expand very rapidly; **industrie en plein e.** booming *or* fast-growing industry; **donner un nouvel e. à qch** to give a lift *or* boost to sth; **l'économie connaît un nouvel e.** the economy is experiencing a new boom *or* is expanding rapidly again

essorage [ɛsɔraʒ] NM (*de linge*) spin-drying; (*à la main, avec une essoreuse à rouleaux*) wringing

essorer [ɛsɔre] VT (*vêtements*) to spin(-dry); (*à la main, avec une essoreuse à rouleaux*) to wring; (*salade*) to spin

essoreuse [esɔrøz] NF spin-dryer; **e. à rouleau** wringer, mangle; **e. à salade** salad spinner

essoufflé [esufle] ADJ out of breath, short of breath, winded

essoufflement [esufləmɑ̃] NM shortness of breath, breathlessness; *Fig* **en raison de l'e. de l'économie** because the economy is running out of steam

essouffler [esufle] VT *(personne, cheval)* to wind, to make out of breath
VPR s'essouffler to get out of breath *or Fam* puff; *Fig (d'un roman, d'une personne créative, de l'économie etc)* to run out of steam; *Fig* **s'e. à faire qch** to struggle to do sth

essuie [esɥi] NM *Belg (essuie-mains)* hand towel; *(torchon)* cloth, tea towel; *(serviette de bain)* bath towel

essuie-glace, *pl* **essuie-glaces** [esɥiglas] NM *Aut* windscreen *or Am* windshield wiper; **e. arrière** rear wiper; **e. deux vitesses** two-speed wiper

essuie-mains [esɥimɛ̃] NM INV hand towel

essuie-meubles [esɥimœbl] NM INV duster

essuie-phare, *pl* **essuie-phares** [esɥifar] NM headlamp wiper

essuie-pieds [esɥipje] NM INV doormat

essuie-tout [esɥitu] NM INV kitchen paper

essuie-verres [esɥiver] NM INV glass cloth

essuyage [esɥija3] NM *(de vaisselle)* wiping, drying; *(d'une surface mouillée)* wiping (down); *(d'eau etc)* wiping up, mopping up; *(nettoyage)* wiping (clean); *(époussetage)* dusting

essuyer [esɥije] **(j'essuie; j'essuierai)** VT **1** *(sécher) (assiettes etc)* to wipe, to dry; *(surface)* to wipe (down); *(nettoyer)* to wipe (clean); *(épousseter)* to dust; *(éponger) (liquide)* to wipe up, to mop up; *(larmes)* to wipe away; **e. la vaisselle** to dry the dishes, to dry up; **e. ses pieds avant d'entrer** to wipe one's feet before going/coming in **2** *(subir) (défaite, perte)* to suffer; *(insultes, reproches etc)* to suffer, to endure, to be subjected to; **e. un refus** to meet with a refusal; **e. le feu de l'ennemi** to come under enemy fire; **e. une tempête** to weather a storm
VPR s'essuyer to wipe oneself, to dry oneself; **s'e. les pieds/la bouche/les yeux** to wipe one's feet/mouth/eyes

est¹ [ɛ] *voir* **être²**

est² [ɛst] NM INV **1** *(point cardinal)* east; **à l'e., dans l'e.** in the east; **où est l'e.?** which way is east?; **la partie la plus à l'e. de l'île** the easternmost part of the island; **le vent vient de l'e.** it's an east *or* easterly wind, the wind is coming from the east; **un vent d'e.** an easterly wind; **le vent d'e.** the east wind; **aller au** *ou* **vers l'e.** to go east *or* eastwards; **les trains qui vont vers l'e.** trains going east, eastbound trains; **rouler vers l'e.** to drive east *or* eastwards; **aller droit vers l'e.** to head due east; **la cuisine est plein e.** *ou* **exposée à l'e.** the kitchen faces due east; **le soleil se lève à l'e.** the sun rises in the east **2** *(partie d'un pays, d'un continent)* east, eastern area *or* regions; *(partie d'une ville)* east; **l'e. de l'Italie** eastern Italy, the east of Italy; **dans l'e. de l'Espagne** in eastern Spain, in the east of Spain; **elle habite dans l'e.** she lives in the East; **il habite dans l'e. de Paris** he lives in the east of Paris; **elle est de l'e.** she's from the east; **les gens de l'e.** people who live in the east
ADJ INV *(côte, face)* east; *(banlieue, partie, région)* eastern; **la façade e. d'un immeuble** the east-facing wall of a building; **la chambre est côté e.** the bedroom faces east; **dans la partie e. de la France** in the East of France, in eastern France; **la côte e. des États-Unis** the East coast *or* Eastern seaboard of the

United States; **suivre la direction e.** to head *or* to go eastwards; *Pol, Hist* **l'E.** Eastern Europe, Eastern European countries; **les pays de l'E.** the countries of Eastern Europe, Eastern European countries; *Hist* **le bloc de l'E.** the Eastern bloc

establishment [ɛstabliʃmɛnt] NM *Pol* establishment

estacade [ɛstakad] NF *Naut (pieux)* stockade; *(jetée)* pier (on piles)

estafette [ɛstafɛt] NF **1** *Hist (courrier)* courier **2** *Mil (agent de liaison)* liaison officer **3** *(camionnette)* van

estafilade [ɛstafilad] NF *(d'un rasoir, d'une épée)* gash

est-allemand, -ande [ɛstalmɑ̃, -ɑ̃d] *Anciennement* ADJ East German
N **E.-A.** East German

estaminet [ɛstaminɛ] NM *(small)* café, bar *(esp in N France and Belgium)*

estampage [ɛstɑ̃pa3] NM **1** *Tech (d'un métal, d'une pièce, du cuir etc)* stamping **2** *Fam (action d'escroquer)* swindling, fleecing; *(résultat)* swindle

estampe [ɛstɑ̃p] NF **1** *(image)* print; **cabinet des estampes** *(d'une bibliothèque)* print room; *Hum* **tu es allée voir ses estampes japonaises?** did he show you his etchings? **2** *(outil)* stamp

estamper [ɛstɑ̃pe] VT **1** *Tech (métal, pièce, cuir etc)* to stamp **2** *Fam (escroquer)* to swindle, to fleece

estampeur, -euse [ɛstɑ̃pœr, -øz] N **1** *Tech (personne, outil)* stamper **2** *Fam (escroc)* swindler

estampillage [ɛstɑ̃pija3] NM *(d'un document etc)* stamping; *(de marchandises)* marking

estampille [ɛstɑ̃pij] NF *(sur un document etc)* stamp; *(sur un produit)* mark

estampiller [ɛstɑ̃pije] VT *(document etc)* to stamp; *(marchandises)* to mark

este [ɛst] ADJ Estonian
NM *Ling* Estonian
N **E.** Estonian

ester [ɛstɛr] NM *Chimie* ester

esthète [ɛstɛt] N aesthete, *Am* esthete

esthéticien, -ienne [ɛstetisjɛ̃, -jɛn] N **1** *(spécialiste des soins de beauté)* beautician, beauty therapist **2** *(artiste, poète etc)* aesthetician, *Am* esthetician

esthétique [ɛstetik] ADJ aesthetic, *Am* esthetic; *(beau)* aesthetically *or Am* esthetically pleasing; **chirurgie e.** plastic surgery
NF *(science)* aesthetics, *Am* esthetics; *(beauté)* aesthetic *or Am* esthetic quality; **ça manque d'e.** it's not very aesthetically *or Am* esthetically pleasing

esthétiquement [ɛstetikmɑ̃] ADV aesthetically, *Am* esthetically

esthétisme [ɛstetism] NM aestheticism, *Am* estheticism

estimable [ɛstimabl] ADJ **1** *(honorable) (personne, qualité)* estimable **2** *(assez bon) (travail, artiste etc)* fairly good **3** *(calculable) (frais, perte)* assessable

estimatif, -ive [ɛstimatif, -iv] ADJ *(coût etc)* estimated; **devis e.** estimate, quotation

estimation [ɛstimasjɔ̃] NF **1** *(détermination de la valeur) (d'un prix, d'une distance, d'un poids etc)* estimation; *(de marchandises)* valuation, appraising; *(de dommages, besoins)* assessment, estimation; **faire une e.** to give an estimation/a valuation/an assessment; **e. approximative** rough estimate; *Mktg* **e. des besoins** needs assessment; *Compta* **e. des frais** estimate of costs **2** *(valeur, quantité estimée)* estimate

estime [ɛstim] NF **1** *(respect)* esteem, regard;

avoir de l'e. pour qn/qch to esteem sb/sth; **avoir beaucoup d'e. pour qn/qch** to have great regard for sb/sth, to hold sb/sth in high regard; **tu as baissé dans mon e.** you have gone down in my estimation; **tenir qn en grande/en médiocre e.** to think highly/little of sb, to hold sb in high/low regard; **avoir un succès d'e.** to be a critical (though not a popular) success **2** *Naut* reckoning; **à l'e.** by dead reckoning; *Fig* by guesswork; **navigation à l'e.** dead reckoning

estimer [ɛstime] VT **1** *(déterminer la valeur de) (prix, distance, poids etc)* to estimate; *(marchandises)* to value, to appraise; *(dommages)* to assess; *Naut* to reckon; **faire e. une maison** to have a house valued; **les experts estiment que les pertes s'élèvent à plusieurs milliards** the experts estimate the losses at *or* that the losses total several hundred million; *Naut* **longitude estimée** longitude by dead reckoning
2 *(considérer)* to consider, to think **(que** that**)**; **j'estime qu'il est de mon devoir de parler** I consider *or* think it (is) my duty *or* that it is my duty to speak; **je n'estime pas que vous ayez besoin d'y aller** I don't consider *or* think it (is) necessary for you to go, I don't think you need to go; **il n'a pas estimé nécessaire de me prévenir** he didn't consider *or* think it (was) necessary to warn me
3 *(respecter) (personne)* to have a high opinion of, to think highly of, to esteem; *(les qualités de qn, la musique etc)* to value, to have a high opinion of; **elle est estimée de tous** she is highly thought of *or* is esteemed by everyone; **j'estime son dévouement à sa juste valeur** I value his dedication at its true worth
VPR s'estimer **s'e. satisfait/heureux** to consider oneself satisfied/lucky

estivage [ɛstiva3] NM *Agr (du bétail etc)* summering on mountain pastures

estival, -ale, -aux, -ales [ɛstival, -o] ADJ *(résidence, vêtements, travail etc)* summer; **station estivale** summer resort

estivant, -ante [ɛstivɑ̃, -ɑ̃t] N (summer) holiday-maker *or Am* vacationer

estiver [ɛstive] VT *Agr (bétail etc)* to summer on mountain pastures

estoc [ɛstɔk] NM **frapper d'e. et de taille** to cut and thrust

estocade [ɛstɔkad] NF *(en tauromachie)* deathblow; **donner l'e. à** *(taureau)*, *Fig (adversaire)* to deal the deathblow to

estomac [ɛstɔma] NM stomach; **avoir l'e. vide** *ou* **creux/plein** to have an empty stomach/be full (up); **creux de l'e.** pit of the stomach; **mal à l'e.** stomach ache; **avoir un e. d'autruche** to have a cast-iron stomach; **avoir l'e. dans les talons** to be ravenous *or* starving; *Fig Fam* **avoir de l'e.** *(courage)* to have plenty of guts; *(culot)* to have plenty of cheek; *Fig Fam* **la faire à l'e.** to try it on **(à qn** with sb**)**

estomaqué [ɛstɔmake] ADJ *Fam* staggered, astounded, flabbergasted

estomaquer [ɛstɔmake] VT *Fam* to stagger, to astound, to flabbergast

estompage [ɛstɔ̃pa3] NM *Beaux-Arts* stumping, shading off (with a stump)

estompe [ɛstɔ̃p] NF *Beaux-Arts* stump; **dessin à l'e.** stump drawing

estompé [ɛstɔ̃pe] ADJ *(contour, image, couleurs etc)* indistinct, blurred; *(souvenirs)* blurred, dim; *Ordinat* dimmed

estomper [ɛstɔ̃pe] VT *Beaux-Arts (dessin)* to stump, to shade off (with a stump); *Fig (paysage, contour, souvenir etc)* to blur, to dim; *(contraste)* to tone down; *(rides)* to smooth out; **le temps estompera la douleur** time will ease the pain

VPR s'estomper *(d'un souvenir)* to become blurred; *(de la douleur)* to ease; *(des rides)* to be smoothed out; *(des couleurs)* to fade; *(des contours)* to fade, to blur

Estonie [ɛstɔni] **NF** Estonia

estonien, -ienne [ɛstɔnjɛ̃, jɛn] **ADJ** Estonian
NM *Ling* Estonian
N E. Estonian

estoquer [ɛstɔke] **VT** *(d'un matador) (taureau)* to kill

estouffade [ɛstufad] **NF** *Culin* **e. de bœuf** beef stew

estourbir [ɛsturbir] **VT** *Fam* **1** *(tuer)* to do in **2** *(étonner)* to astound, to knock sideways; **je suis encore tout estourbi de la chance que j'ai eue** I'm still quite astounded how lucky I was

estrade [ɛstrad] **NF** dais, rostrum, platform; **e. réservée à la presse** press box

estragon [ɛstragɔ̃] **NM** *Bot, Culin* tarragon

estran [ɛstrɑ̃] **NM** strand, foreshore

estrapade [ɛstrapad] **NF** *Hist (supplice)* strappado; *Naut* dipping from the yard arm

estrogène [ɛstrɔʒɛn] **NM** *Physiol* oestrogen, *Am* estrogen

estropié, -ée [ɛstrɔpje] **ADJ** crippled, maimed
N cripple

estropier [ɛstrɔpje] **VT** *(impf, pr sub* **n. estropiions)** **1** *(personne)* to cripple, to maim **2** *Fig (valse, langue étrangère etc)* to murder; *(mot, nom)* to mispronounce; *(texte)* to mutilate

estuaire [ɛstɥɛr] **NM** estuary

estudiantin [ɛstydjɑ̃tɛ̃] **ADJ** *(vie, univers etc)* student

esturgeon [ɛstyrʒɔ̃] **NM** sturgeon

et [e] **CONJ** *(note there is no liaison with* **et**: j'ai écrit et écrit [ʒeekrieekri]) **1** and; **toi et moi partirons demain** you and I will leave tomorrow; **c'est un homme d'une grande énergie, et qui arrivera** he is a man of great energy, who will succeed; **et son frère et sa sœur** both his brother and his sister; **je ne peux pas et répondre au téléphone et ouvrir la porte** I can't answer the phone *and* open the door; **et d'un, il pleut et de deux, je n'ai pas envie d'y aller** first(ly) it's raining, and second(ly) I don't want to go; **j'aime le café, et vous?** I like coffee, do you?; **et les dix euros que je vous ai prêtés?** and (what about) the ten euros I lent you?; **et le garçon de se sauver** at this the boy ran off; **et elle de rire!** and she burst out laughing!
2 *(dans les nombres etc)* **vingt/trente/**etc **et un** twenty/thirty/*etc*-one; **soixante et onze** seventy-one; **il est quatre heures et demie** it's half past four
NM 1 et commercial ampersand **2** *Ordinat* **ET** AND; **circuit ET** AND gate

ETA [ɛta] **NF** *(abrév* **Euskadi ta Askatasuna)** ETA

étable [etabl] **NF** cowshed

Il faut noter que le nom anglais **stable** est un faux ami. Il signifie **écurie.**

établi¹ [etabli] **NM** (work)bench

établi² **ADJ** *(gouvernement, réputation etc)* established; **l'Église établie** the Established Church; **considérer qch comme chose établie** to take sth for granted; **l'ordre é.** the established order

établir [etablir] **VT 1** *(créer) (forme de gouvernement, affaire, paix, relations, contact etc)* to establish; *(agence)* to set up; *(édifice)* to put up, to erect; *(barrage, voie ferrée)* to construct; *(lieu de résidence)* to settle, to fix; *(machinerie)* to install, *Am* to instal; *(voile)* to set; *(camp)* to pitch; *(prix)* to fix, to set; *(taxe, tribunal etc)* to institute, to create;

(plan, proposition etc) to draw up; *(règlement)* to prescribe, to lay down; *(principe)* to lay down; *(devis, facture, bilan, budget)* to draw up; **é. un chèque** to make out *or* write a cheque; **é. un chèque à l'ordre de** to make a cheque payable to; **é. une balance** to strike a balance; **é. une moyenne** to work out an average; **é. un record** to set a record
2 *(démontrer) (fait, l'innocence de qn)* to establish, to prove; **é. une accusation** to establish *or* substantiate a charge; **é. un parallèle entre** to establish *or* draw a parallel between
3 *(asseoir) (autorité, droits, réputation etc)* to establish; *(fortune)* to establish, to build up *(*sur on*)*; **é. le silence** to establish silence; **é. une démonstration sur des arguments solides** to base a proof on sound arguments **4** *(pourvoir d'une situation)* to set up *(*dans in; comme as*)*; **il a établi tous ses enfants** he has settled all his children, he has set all his children up in life; *Vieilli* **il lui reste une fille à é.** *(à marier)* he still has a daughter at home
VPR s'établir 1 *(dans une ville, un pays etc)* to settle *(*à, dans, en in*)* **2** *(pour exercer un métier)* s'é. épicier to set (oneself) up as a grocer; **elle s'est établie à son compte** she set up (in) business on her own **3** *(se poser en)* s'é. chef/juge to set oneself up as a leader/judge **4** *(d'une coutume, d'une idée, de rapports etc)* to become established; **le silence s'est enfin établi** silence was established at last

établissement [etablismɑ̃] **NM 1** *(création) (de forme de gouvernement, affaire, paix etc)* establishment; *(d'agence)* setting up; *(d'édifice)* putting up, erection; *(d'un lieu de résidence)* settling, fixing; *(de machinerie)* installation; *(de voile)* setting; *(de camp)* pitching; *(de prix)* fixing; *(de taxe, tribunal)* institution, creation; *(de plan, proposition etc)* drawing up; *(de règlement)* prescribing, laying down; *(de principe)* laying down; *Tél* **é. d'appel** call connection; *Fin* **é. d'un compte** opening an account, setting up an account; **é. des menus** *(dans un restaurant)* menu planning; *Com* **é. des prix** pricing
2 *(démonstration) (de fait, innocence de qn)* establishment, proving
3 *(d'autorité, de droits, réputation etc)* establishment
4 *(de ses enfants)* settling
5 *(institution)* establishment, institution; **é. thermal** hydropathic establishment, spa; **é. hospitalier** hospital; **é. scolaire** educational establishment; **é. pénitentiaire** prison, penal establishment; **é. bancaire** bank; **é. de crédit** credit institution; *Compta* **é. déclarant** company making the return; **é. dépositaire** = financial institution holding securities on trust; **é. financier** financial institution; *Fin* **é. payeur** paying bank
6 *Hist* **établissements** *(colonies)* settlements, colonies
7 *Com* business, firm; **les établissements Martin** Martin & Co; **é. principal** main branch *or* office; **é. industriel** factory

étage [etaʒ] **NM 1** *(d'un bâtiment)* floor, storey, *Am* story; **à deux étages** two-storeyed, *Am* two-storied; **au troisième é.** on the third floor, *Am* on the fourth floor; **monter à l'é.** to go upstairs; **dévaler les étages** to race down the stairs; **elle est dans les étages** she's somewhere upstairs
2 *(d'une construction, d'un terrain)* level; *(d'un jardin)* terrace; *(d'un gâteau)* tier; **gâteau à quatre étages** four-tiered cake
3 *Géol* stage, formation
4 *Tech* stage; **compression par étages** compression by stages; **fusée à trois étages** three-stage rocket
5 *Péj* **de bas é.** *(esprit, histoire etc)* mediocre,

second-rate; **individu de bas é.** worthless individual
6 *Can Sport* **le deuxième é.** the (club) management

étagement [etaʒmɑ̃] **NM** *(de plantations, vignes)* terracing

étager [etaʒe] *(j'étageai(s))* **VT 1** *(sièges, livres, groupe de personnes etc)* to arrange in tiers; **jardin étagé** terraced garden; **vignes étagées** vines arranged in terraces; **poulie étagée** cone pulley **2** *Tech* **compression étagée** compression by stages, staged compression
VPR s'étager *(des maisons, vignes etc)* to rise in tiers

étagère [etaʒɛr] **NF** *(meuble)* (set of) shelves; *(planche)* shelf **VOIR GRAMMAIRE A12**

étai¹ [etɛ] **NM** *Naut (cordage)* stay; **voile d'é.** staysail

étai² **NM** *Constr etc* stay, prop, strut; **é. de mine** pit prop

étaiement [etɛmɑ̃] **NM** *Constr etc* shoring (up), propping (up)

étain [etɛ̃] **NM 1** *(métal)* tin; **é. battu, é. en feuilles** thin sheet tin; **papier d'é.** tinfoil, silver paper **2** *(pour la vaisselle, les bijoux)* pewter; **vaisselle d'é.** pewter (plate); **une très belle collection d'étains** a very fine collection of pewter (pieces)

étal, -als [etal] **NM 1** *(de boucher)* (butcher's) stall, meat stall **2** *(au marché)* (market) stall

étalage [etalaʒ] **NM 1** *Com (des marchandises)* display, show; *(vitrine)* (display) window; *(impôt)* = tax paid by street trader; **faire l'é.** to set out one's goods; *(vitrine)* to dress the window(s); **mettre qch à l'é.** to display sth for sale; **article qui a fait l'é.** shopsoiled *or Am* shopworn article; *Journ* **é. publicitaire** display advertising **2** *Fig (de richesse, des connaissances etc)* display, show, parading; **faire é. de ses bijoux/son savoir/sa richesse** to show off *or* parade one's jewels/knowledge/wealth; **faire é. de sa force** to show one's strength; **elle fait é. de sa vie privée** she flaunts her private life

étalager [etalaʒe] **VT** *(j'étalageai(s))* *Com (marchandises)* to display for sale

étalagiste [etalaʒist] **N** window dresser

étale [etal] *Naut* **ADJ** *(mer, marée)* slack; *(brise)* steady
NM OU NF é. du flot slack water

étalement [etalmɑ̃] **NM 1** *(du linge à sécher, de papiers sur la table etc)* spreading out; *(d'une nappe, du beurre etc)* spreading; *(de la peinture etc)* application; *(des marchandises)* displaying **2** *(des vacances)* staggering *(*sur over*)*; *(des travaux, d'un cours etc)* spreading (out) *(*sur over*)*; *(de paiements)* spreading, staggering *(*sur over*)*

étaler [etale] **VT 1** *(étendre) (linge à sécher, papiers etc)* to spread out, to lay out; *(nappe, beurre etc)* to spread; *(peinture, onguent)* to apply *(*sur to*)*; *(marchandises)* to display (for sale); *(ses cartes)* to lay down
2 *Fig (montrer) (sa richesse, ses connaissances)* to display, to show off, to parade; *(ses malheurs)* to parade, to draw attention to; **é. sa vie** to tell one's life story; **é. une affaire au grand jour** to make a matter public; **l'affaire était étalée à la une des journaux** the story was splashed across the front page; *Hum* **la culture, c'est comme la confiture: moins on en a, plus on l'étale** = people who don't have much culture have to make the most of it
3 *(échelonner) (vacances, paiements, envoi du courrier etc)* to stagger *(*sur over*)*; *(travaux, cours, opération etc)* to spread *(*sur over*)*; **é. les remboursements sur plusieurs exercices** to spread (out) the repayments over several financial years

4 *Naut (courant, vent)* to stem
5 *Fam (faire tomber) (personne)* to lay out, to floor
VPR s'étaler 1 *(d'un village, parc etc)* to spread out; **arbre à cime étalée** large-crowned tree; **cette peinture s'étale mal** this paint goes on badly
2 *(parader) (des gens riches etc)* to flaunt oneself; **son succès s'étale à la une des journaux** his success is splashed across the front pages
3 *(se vautrer)* to sprawl
4 *Fam (tomber)* **s'é. par terre** to fall flat on the ground; **s'é. de tout son long** to go *or* measure one's length
5 *(des vacances, paiements etc)* to be spread (**sur** over)

étalon¹ [etalɔ̃] **NM** *(cheval)* stallion

étalon² **NM** *(modèle de mesure)* standard; *Fig (modèle)* standard, yardstick; **mètre é.** standard metre; *Écon* **l'é.-or** the gold standard; **é.-or lingot** gold bullion standard; **é. monétaire** monetary standard

étalonnage [etalɔnaʒ] **NM**, **étalonnement** [etalɔnmɑ̃] **NM 1** *(action de vérifier) (d'un poids, d'une mesure)* standardization; *(d'un instrument)* gauging, testing **2** *(action de graduer) (d'un thermomètre etc)* calibration; *Cin, TV* calibration, grading **3** *Psy (d'un test)* standardization

étalonner [etalɔne] **VT 1** *(vérifier) (poids, mesure)* to standardize; *(instrument)* to gauge, to test **2** *(graduer) (thermomètre, baromètre etc)* to calibrate; *Cin, TV* to calibrate, to grade **3** *Psy (test)* to standardize

étamage [etamaʒ] **NM 1** *(de cuivre etc)* tinning; *(d'une tôle de fer)* tinplating **2** *(d'un miroir)* silvering

étambot [etɑ̃bo] **NM** *Naut* sternpost

étamer [etame] **VT 1** *(cuivre etc)* to tin; *(tôle de fer)* to tinplate **2** *(miroir)* to silver

étameur [etamœr] **NM** tinner, tinsmith

étamine¹ [etamin] **NF** *Tex* muslin; *(pour filtrer, cribler)* butter muslin, cheesecloth; **passer à l'é.** *(liquide)* to filter; *(farine etc)* to sift

étamine² **NF** *Bot* stamen

étanche [etɑ̃ʃ] **ADJ** *(bateau, toit etc)* watertight; *(montre, bottes etc)* waterproof; **é. à l'eau/à l'air/à la poussière** watertight/air-tight/dustproof; **cloison é.** *Naut* watertight bulkhead; *Fig (entre services, disciplines etc)* impenetrable barrier, *esp Am Fam* Great Wall of China

étanchéité [etɑ̃ʃeite] **NF** *(d'un bateau, toit etc)* watertightness; *(d'une montre, de bottes etc)* waterproofness; **é. à l'eau/à l'air** water-tightness/airtightness; **vérifier l'é.** to check for leaks (**de** in)

étancher [etɑ̃ʃe] **VT 1** *(liquide)* to check the flow of; *(sang)* to staunch; *(les larmes de qn)* to dry; *Naut* **é. une voie d'eau** to stop a leak **2** *(sa soif)* to quench, to slake **3** *(rendre étanche)* to make watertight

étançon [etɑ̃sɔ̃] **NM** *Constr, Naut (étai)* shore, stanchion

étançonnement [etɑ̃sɔnmɑ̃] **NM** shoring up

étançonner [etɑ̃sɔne] **VT** to shore up

étang [etɑ̃] **NM** pond, pool

étant [etɑ̃] *voir* **être²**

étape [etap] **NF 1** *(lieu)* stop(over), stopping place; **faire é.** to stop; **nous avons fait é. à Bordeaux** we stopped over(night) at Bordeaux; **brûler une é.** *(d'un train, un autobus)* to go past *or* miss a stop, to fail to stop (at a scheduled stop); **comme nous étions pressés, nous avons brûlé l'é. de Strasbourg** since we were in a hurry, we missed out Strasbourg *or* we didn't stop in Strasbourg;

brûlons la prochaine é. et continuons jusqu'à Lyon let's press on to Lyons without stopping; *Fig* **brûler les étapes** *(dans une entreprise, un métier)* to move up the ladder very quickly; *(dans une tâche)* to cut corners
2 *(distance à parcourir) (d'un voyage, d'une course etc)* stage, leg; **à ou par petites étapes** by *or* in easy stages; **nous avons fait hier une é. de 500 kilomètres** we covered *or* did 500 kilometres yesterday
3 *Fig (phase) (d'une vie, d'un processus etc)* stage; **une procédure en deux étapes** a two-stage *or* -step procedure; **l'é. suivante consiste à …** the next step is to …; **é. par é.** stage by stage, step by step, one stage *or* step at a time; **par étapes** by *or* in stages *or* steps

ÉTAT [eta]

state **1, 5, 6, 8** ▪ condition **1** ▪ position **1** ▪ profession **3** ▪ form **7** ▪ list **7**	

NM 1 *(façon d'être)* state, condition; *Phys* state; **à l'é. solide/liquide/naturel** in its solid/liquid/natural state; **é. du ciel** weather conditions; **é. de la mer** conditions at sea; **l'é. des routes** road conditions; **é. du marché** state of the market; **à l'é. neuf** *(dans une petite annonce)* as new; **à l'é. pur** *(métal)* unalloyed; *Fig* **c'est de la bêtise/de l'incompétence à l'é. pur** it is sheer *or* downright stupidity/incompetence; **retourner à l'é. sauvage** to revert to the wild; **une plante qui pousse à l'é. sauvage** a plant which grows in the wild; **dans l'é. actuel des choses** given the current state of affairs; **dans l'é. actuel de nos connaissances** given what we know at the moment; **être dans un triste/piteux é.** to be in a sorry/pitiful state; *Hum* **elle est dans un é. intéressant** *(enceinte)* she's in the family way; **tu ne devrais pas porter cette valise dans ton é.** you shouldn't be carrying that case in your condition; *Fam* **être dans tous ses états** to be in a real *or* terrible *or* dreadful state; **il n'y a pas de quoi se mettre dans un é. pareil!** there's no point getting into such a state (about it)!; **te voilà dans un bel é.!** that's some state you're in!; **tu as vu dans quel é. tu t'es mis?** have you seen the state you've got yourself into?; **on a retrouvé des ossements en parfait é. de conservation** we found some perfectly preserved bones; **en (bon) é.** *(machine, voiture, maison etc)* in good condition *or* repair; **navire en bon é. (de navigabilité)** seaworthy ship; **en mauvais é.** in bad condition; **en é. de rouler** *(voiture)* roadworthy; **en é. de voler** *(avion)* airworthy; **être en é. de marche** to be in working order; *Aut* **to be roadworthy, to be in a roadworthy condition**; *Méd* **être en é. de manque** to have withdrawal symptoms; *Psy* **en é. de veille** in a waking state; **remettre en é.** *(maison etc)* to renovate, to repair; *(moteur)* to overhaul, to recondition; **tenir qch en é.** to look after sth, to keep sth in good repair; **laisser les choses en l'é.** to leave things as they are *or* stand; **vendre qch en l'é.** to sell sth as it is; **être/se sentir en é. de faire qch** to be/feel up to doing sth; **elle n'est plus en é. de travailler** she's not up to working any more; **tu n'es pas en é. de conduire** you're in no condition *or* in no fit state to drive; **le blessé n'est pas encore en é. de parler** the injured man is still not in a condition to talk; **je ne suis pas en é. de vous répondre** I am not in a position to give you an answer; **êtes-vous en é. de le recevoir?** *(décemment habillé)* are you presentable?, are you fit to be seen?; *(assez bien portant)* do you feel up to seeing him?, are you up to seeing him?; **nous sommes maintenant en é. d'affirmer que les otages ont tous été libérés** we are now in a position to confirm that the hostages have all been released; **être hors**

d'é. to have broken down; **il faut mettre ces terroristes hors d'é. de nuire** these terrorists must be prevented from doing harm
2 faire é. de to refer to, to mention
3 *(profession)* **militaire/épicier de son é.** soldier by profession/grocer by trade
4 *Hist (groupe social)* **le Tiers É.** the Third Estate
5 *(nation, autorité centrale)* **l'É.** the state *or* State; **coup d'É.** coup (d'état); **le budget de l'É.** the state budget; **homme d'É.** statesman; **femme d'É.** stateswoman; **pour des raisons d'É.** for reasons of state; **un É. dans l'É.** a state within a state; **É. croupion** rump state; **É. de droit** legitimate state; **É. fédéral** federal state; **É. membre** member state; **É. neutre** neutral state; **É. paria** rogue state; **É. paternaliste** nanny state; **É. providence** welfare state; **servir d'É. tampon** to serve as a buffer state; **É. voyou** rogue state
6 *(territoire aux États-Unis)* state
7 *(rapport) (imprimé)* form; *(des dépenses, ventes)* statement, list; *(des paiements, marchandises)* schedule, list; **rayer qn des états** to strike sb off the rolls
8 *Ordinat* **en é. de veille** in standby mode; **é. d'attente** wait state; **sans é. d'attente** with zero wait states
▶▶ **é. d'alerte** state of alert; **être en é. d'alerte** to be on the alert; *Mil* to be in a state of alert; **états d'âmes: avoir des états d'âme** to engage in soul-searching; **je n'ai pas eu d'états d'âme avant de le virer** I didn't engage in too much soul-searching before I fired him; **tu nous embêtes avec tes états d'âme** you're getting on our nerves with your constant soul-searching; *Compta* **é. de caisse** cash statement; **é. de choc: en é. de choc** in a state of shock; **é. de choses** state of affairs, situation; *Admin* **é. civil** *(d'une personne)* (civil) status; *(à la mairie)* register *or Br* registry office; **actes de l'é. civil** = birth, marriage and death certificates; **informer l'é. civil d'un décès** to register a death; *Compta* **états comptables** accounting records; *Compta* **états comptables et commerciaux** internal company records; **é. de compte** *Can* bank statement, statement of account; *Compta* **position on an account**; *Pol* **é. d'ébriété: en é. d'ébriété** in a state of intoxication; **é. d'esprit** state *or* frame of mind; *Pol* **é. d'exception** state of emergency; **é. de fait: c'est un é. de fait** it's an undeniable *or* established fact; *Jur* **é. de frais** bill of costs; **les États généraux** the States General; **é. de grâce** *Rel* state of grace; *Pol* honeymoon period; **é. de guerre** state of war; **l'é. de guerre a été déclaré** a state of war has been declared; **é. d'impression** report form; *Fin* **é. imprimé** printed statement *or* form; **é. d'ivresse: en é. d'ivresse** in a state of intoxication; **é. des lieux** inventory of fixtures *(in rented premises)*; **le propriétaire est tenu de faire l'é. des lieux avec son locataire** the landlord is obliged to agree an inventory of fixtures with the tenant; **é. néant** nil return; **é. nominatif** list of names, (nominal) roll; *Compta* **é. de rapprochement** reconciliation statement; *Compta* **é. récapitulatif** final assessment, adjustment account; **é. de santé** state of health; **é. second** (state of) trance; *Admin, Mil* **états de service** service record; **é. de siège** state of siege; **é. de situation** status *or* state-of-play report; *Compta* **é. TVA** VAT statement *or* return; **é. d'urgence** state of emergency

étatique [etatik] **ADJ** *Pol* (of the) state; **l'appareil é.** the machinery of state

étatisation [etatizasjɔ̃] **NF** *(action)* establishment of state control (**de** over); *(doctrine)* state control

étatisé [etatize] **ADJ** state-controlled, state-run

étatiser [etatize] VT *(firme etc)* to bring under state control

étatisme [etatism] NM state control

étatiste [etatist] ADJ **système é.** system of state control
  N partisan of state control

état-major, *pl* **états-majors** NM **1** *Mil (officiers)* (general) staff; *(lieu)* headquarters; **officier d'é.** staff officer; **carte d'é.** *Br* ≃ Ordnance Survey map, *Am* ≃ Geological Survey map **2** *(d'une firme)* senior staff, management; *(d'un parti politique)* leadership

États-Unis [etazyni] NMPL **les É. (d'Amérique)** the United States (of America), *Fam* the States VOIR GRAMMAIRE A12

étau, -aux [eto] NM **1** *Tech* vice, *Am* vise; **é. d'établi** bench vice **2** *Fig (restrictions)* stranglehold; **les kidnappeurs sentaient l'é. se resserrer autour d'eux** the kidnappers could feel the net closing around them; **je suis prise là-dedans comme dans un é.** I can't get out of it, they've/he's/*etc* got me in a stranglehold

étayage [eteja ʒ] NM *Constr etc* shoring, propping (up)

étayer [eteje] (**j'étaie, j'étaye; j'étaierai, j'étayerai**) VT **1** *Constr etc (mur etc)* to prop (up), to shore (up) **2** *Fig (argumentation)* to buttress; *(déclaration, théorie etc)* to support, to back up; **pour é. ses allégations** in support of his/her allegations
  VPR **s'étayer s'é. sur** *(d'une théorie, de la défense etc)* to be based *or* founded on

etc [ɛtsetera] ADV etc

et c(a)etera [ɛtsetera] ADV etcetera

été¹ [ete] NM VOIR GRAMMAIRE A7 summer; **é. comme hiver il se rend à son travail à vélo** he cycles to work winter and summer alike; **en é.** in (the) summer *or* summertime; **pendant l'é. 2004** in the summer of 2004; **l'é. prochain** next summer; **un jour d'é.** a summer('s) day; **heure d'é.** summer time, *Am* daylight (saving) time; **temps/vêtements d'é.** summer weather/clothes
  ▸▸ **é. indien** Indian summer; **é. de la Saint-Martin** Indian summer

été² *voir* **être²**

éteignoir [eteɲwar] NM (candle) snuffer; **en é.** conical

éteindre [etɛ̃dr] (*conj like* **teindre**) VT **1** *(incendie, bougie, cigarette etc)* to extinguish, to put out; *(gaz)* to turn off; *(lumière, radio, radiateur etc)* to switch off, to turn off; *Fam (pièce)* to switch off (the lights) in **2** *Tech (chaux)* to slake, to slack; *(fer chauffé au rouge etc)* to quench **3** *Fig (mettre fin à) (dette)* to pay off; *(querelle)* to put an end to; **é. le feu de l'ennemi** to silence the enemy's guns **4** *Fig (affaiblir) (couleur)* to fade, to soften; **les couleurs ont été éteintes par le temps** the colours have faded with time; **le temps éteint les passions** passions fade with time
  VPR **s'éteindre 1** *(d'un incendie, d'une cigarette, d'une lampe etc)* to go out **2** *Fig (s'affaiblir) (d'une couleur, une passion)* to fade; *(d'un son, de rires)* to die away, to subside; *(d'une voix)* to die away; **le jour s'éteint** daylight is failing *or* fading **3** *Fig (disparaître) (d'une personne)* to pass away, to die; *(d'une race, famille)* to become extinct, to die out
  VI **1** to switch off (the lights) (**dans** in) **2** **laisser é. le feu** to let the fire go out

éteint [etɛ̃] ADJ **1** **être é.** *(d'un incendie, d'une cigarette, d'une lampe etc)* to be out; *(de l'électricité, d'une radio etc)* to be off; *Aut* **rouler tous feux éteints** to drive without (any) lights **2** *(race, famille, volcan)* extinct **3** *Fig (couleur)* dull; *(yeux)* dull, lacklustre, *Am* lackluster; *(voix)* faint, lifeless; **depuis qu'elle l'a quitté, il a l'air tout é.** all the life

seems to have gone out of him *or* all of the stuffing seems to have been knocked out of him since she left him; **je l'ai trouvée éteinte hier soir** I found her rather subdued last night

étendard [etɑ̃dar] NM **1** *Mil (drapeau)* standard **2** *Fig (symbole)* banner; **lever l'é. de la révolte** to raise the standard of revolt; **se ranger sous l'é. de qn** to join sb's camp

étendoir [etɑ̃dwar] NM **1** *(cordes)* clotheslines **2** *(cour)* drying yard; *(salle)* drying room

étendre [etɑ̃dr] VT **1** *(déployer) (carte, nappe etc)* to spread (out); *(linge)* to hang up; *(beurre, onguent, fumier etc)* to spread; *(peinture)* to apply (**sur** to), to spread (**sur** on, over); **é. qn** to stretch sb out; **é. le bras** to stretch out *or* reach out (one's arm); **é. les bras** to open one's arms wide, to spread out one's arms; **é. ses ailes** to spread its wings; **é. qn (par terre) d'un coup de poing** to knock sb down *or Fam* flat, *Fam* to deck sb; *Boxe etc* **se faire é.** to go down, *Fam* to get decked; *Fam* **se faire é. à un examen** to fail an exam
  2 *(développer) (influence, pouvoir, connaissances etc)* to extend, to widen, to expand; *(limites, propriété)* to extend; **é. une peau** to stretch a skin; **é. la pâte** to roll out the dough; **é. les termes d'une loi** to widen *or* broaden the terms of a law; **é. sa connaissance des langues étrangères au chinois** to expand *or* extend one's knowledge of foreign languages to include Chinese
  3 *(diluer) (vin, lait etc)* to dilute; **é. d'eau une boisson** to water down a drink
  4 *Ordinat (mémoire)* to upgrade
  VPR **s'étendre 1** *(s'allonger)* to lie down, to stretch out; *Fig* **s'é. sur un sujet** to dwell on a subject; *Fig* **il ne s'est pas étendu sur les raisons de son absence** he didn't enlarge *or* expand on the reasons for his/her absence **2** *(aller)* to stretch, to extend; **la ligne s'étend depuis Ivry jusqu'à Charenton** the line extends *or* runs from Ivry to Charenton; **aussi loin que le regard peut s'é.** as far as the eye can see; **notre parc s'étend sur plusieurs hectares** our grounds spread over several acres **3** *(se développer) (d'un incendie, d'une épidémie, d'une grève etc)* to spread; *(d'une fortune, d'une affaire, d'un empire etc)* to expand, to grow larger; *(d'un pouvoir)* to widen, to increase; *(d'une influence)* to spread, to widen, to increase; *(des connaissances, du vocabulaire)* to widen, to broaden

étendu, -ue [etɑ̃dy] ADJ **1** *(plaine, forêt), Fig (connaissances, vocabulaire)* wide, extensive; *Fig (influence)* far-reaching, widespread **2** *(bras, jambes)* outstretched; **é. sur un divan** stretched out *or* lying on a couch **3** *(dilué)* diluted (**de** with)
  NF **étendue** *(d'un champ, d'une région etc)* area, extent; *(d'une calamité, grève, épidémie)* scale, extent; *(d'eau, de sable etc)* expanse, stretch; *(de terre etc)* expanse, tract; *(d'une voix, d'un instrument)* range, compass; *(des connaissances, du vocabulaire, du pouvoir de qn etc)* extent, scope; **sur une grande étendue** over a wide area; **sur toute l'étendue du champ** over the entire field; **te rends-tu compte de l'étendue de ton erreur?** do you realize the extent *or* the magnitude of your error?

éternel, -elle [etɛrnɛl] ADJ **1** *(être, Dieu etc)* eternal; **le père é.** the everlasting Father **2** *(vie, joie etc)* eternal, everlasting; **neiges éternelles** eternal snow **3** *Fig (regrets)* eternal, endless; *(amour)* eternal, undying; *(discussion, recommandations, bavardages)* endless, never-ending; **vous aurez droit à ma reconnaissance éternelle** I shall be eternally grateful to you; **un é. causeur** an inve-

terate chatterer; **tu es un é. mécontent** you're never satisfied; **fumant son éternelle cigarette** smoking the inevitable cigarette
  NM **1 l'É.** *(Dieu)* the Eternal; *Hum* **c'est un grand fumeur/grand paresseux devant l'É.** he's an incurable smoker/incurably lazy **2 l'é. féminin** the archetypal female

éternellement [etɛrnɛlmɑ̃] ADV **1** *(durer, attendre, rester etc)* for ever; **é. reconnaissant** eternally grateful **2** *(continuellement)* constantly, for ever; **il est é. mécontent** he's never satisfied; **elle a é. raison** she's always right; **il est é. en retard** he's constantly *or* always late

éterniser [etɛrnize] VT **1** *Litt* **é. le nom/la mémoire de qn** to immortalize sb's name/memory; **si nous pouvions é. cette heure** if only we could make this hour last for ever **2** *(prolonger) (discussion, crise, procès etc)* to drag out (for ever)
  VPR **s'éterniser** *(d'une discussion, d'une crise, d'un procès etc)* to drag on (for ever); **j'ai horreur que les adieux s'éternisent** I hate long drawn-out goodbyes; **s'é. chez qn** to outstay one's welcome

éternité [etɛrnite] NF eternity; **de toute é.** from time immemorial; **il y a une é.** *ou* **des éternités que je ne vous ai vu** it's ages since I saw you, I haven't seen you for ages; **j'aimerais autant que notre visite ne dure pas une é.** I really don't want to stay longer than necessary; **j'ai attendu pendant une é.** I waited an eternity, I waited for ages

éternuement [etɛrnymɑ̃] NM sneeze

éternuer [etɛrnɥe] VI to sneeze

êtes [ɛt] *voir* **être²**

étêtage [eteta ʒ], **étêtement** [etɛtmɑ̃] NM *(d'un arbre)* pollarding, topping

étêter [etete] VT *(poisson, clou etc)* to remove the head from; *(arbre)* to pollard, to top

éthane [etan] NM *Chimie* ethane

éthanol [etanɔl] NM ethanol

éther [etɛr] NM ether; *Litt (air, ciel)* ether

éthéré [etere] ADJ ethereal

Ethernet® [etɛrnɛt] NM *Ordinat* Ethernet®

éthéromane [eterɔman] N ether addict

Éthiopie [etjɔpi] NF Ethiopia

éthiopien, -ienne [etjɔpjɛ̃, -jɛn] ADJ Ethiopian
  N **É.** Ethiopian

éthique [etik] ADJ **1** *(problème etc)* ethical **2** *Gram* **datif é.** ethical dative
  NF *(science, règles de conduite)* ethics; **l'é. puritaine** the Puritan ethic

ethnie [etni] NF ethnic group

ethnique [etnik] ADJ *(groupe etc)* ethnic

ethnocentrisme [etnosɑ̃trism] NM ethnocentrism

ethnographe [etnɔgraf] N ethnographer

ethnographie [etnɔgrafi] NF ethnography

ethnographique [etnɔgrafik] ADJ ethnographic(al)

ethnolinguistique [etnolɛ̃gɥistik] NF ethnolinguistics

ethnologie [etnɔlɔʒi] NF ethnology

ethnologique [etnɔlɔʒik] ADJ ethnological

ethnologue [etnɔlɔg] N ethnologist

éthologie [etɔlɔʒi] NF ethology

éthologique [etɔlɔʒik] ADJ ethological

éthologiste [etɔlɔʒist] N ethologist

éthyle [etil] NM *Chimie* ethyl

éthylène [etilɛn] NM *Chimie* ethylene

éthylène-glycol NM INV ethylene glycol

éthylique [etilik] ADJ *Chimie* ethylic; **alcool é.** ethyl alcohol
  N *Méd* alcoholic

éthylisme [etilism] NM *Méd* alcoholism

éthylomètre [etilɔmɛtr], **éthylotest** [etilotɛst] NM Breathalyzer®

étiage [etjaʒ] NM (baisse d'eaux) low water; (niveau le plus bas) lowest water level; **échelle d'é.** water gauge

étincelage [etɛ̃slaʒ] NM **1** Tech **soudure par é.** flash welding **2** Méd electrotherapy

étincelant [etɛ̃slɑ̃] ADJ (diamant, métal, lac etc) sparkling, glittering; (étoile) twinkling, glittering; (yeux) Fig esprit, conversation, livre etc) sparkling; **un diamant plus é. que celui-là** a diamond that sparkles more than that one; **le lac était é. sous le soleil** the lake sparkled in the sunlight; **elle avait les yeux étincelants de colère/de convoitise/de joie** her eyes glinted or flashed with anger/gleamed with envy/sparkled with joy

étinceler [etɛ̃sle] VI (il étincelle; il étincelait; il étincellera) (d'un diamant, métal, lac etc) to sparkle, to glitter; (d'une étoile) to twinkle, to glitter; (des yeux) Fig (de l'esprit, la conversation, un livre etc) to sparkle; **ses yeux étincelaient de joie/de colère/de convoitise** his eyes sparkled with joy/glinted or flashed with anger/gleamed with envy; **é. de propreté** to be sparkling clean

étincelle [etɛ̃sɛl] NF **1** (du feu, d'allumage etc) spark; **lancer des étincelles** to throw out sparks; (d'un diamant, des yeux) to sparkle, to flash; Fig **elle a fait des étincelles à ses derniers examens** she was brilliant or she shone in her last exams; Fig Fam **ça va faire des étincelles, il va y avoir des étincelles** sparks will fly **2** Fig (de vie, génie) spark; (de bon sens) spark, glimmer; **il a eu une é. de génie** he had a stroke of genius, he had a brilliant idea; **une é. de courage** a fleeting moment of courage

étincellement [etɛ̃sɛlmɑ̃] NM (d'un diamant, métal, lac etc) sparkle, glitter; (d'une étoile) twinkle, glitter; (des yeux) sparkle

étiolement [etjɔlmɑ̃] NM **1** (d'une plante) legginess, straggliness; Agr (intentionnel) blanching; **pour empêcher l'é. de vos plantes** to stop your plants going leggy or straggly **2** Méd etiolation **3** Fig (de l'esprit, la mémoire etc) deterioration

étioler [etjɔle] VT **1** (plante) to make leggy; Agr (intentionnellement) to blanch; **une plante étiolée** a leggy or straggly plant **2** é. qn (du manque d'air) to weaken sb, to make sb sickly; (de la maladie) to leave sb in a weakened condition or sickly; **une intelligence étiolée** an intellect in decline
VPR s'étioler 1 (d'une plante) to go leggy **2** (d'une personne) to grow sickly, to go into a decline **3** (de l'esprit, de la mémoire etc) to deteriorate

étiologie [etjɔlɔʒi] NF Méd (étude, causes) aetiology, Am etiology

étique [etik] ADJ emaciated

étiquetage [etiktaʒ] NM (de bagages, colis etc) labelling; (de marchandises) labelling, ticketing; **é. de l'apport nutritionnel** nutritional labelling; **é. de la composition** ingredient labelling; **é. des pourcentages** (des principaux ingrédients) percentage labelling; **é. du prix** price marking

étiqueter [etikte] VT (j'étiquète; j'étiquèterai) **1** (bagage, colis etc) to label; (marchandises) to label, to ticket **2** Fig (personne) to label (**comme** as)

étiqueteur, -euse [etiktœr, -øz] N (personne) labeller
NF **étiqueteuse** (machine) labelling machine, labeller

étiquette [etikɛt] NF **1** (d'une valise, d'un colis etc) label; (indiquant le prix) (price) label, ticket; **coller une é. sur un paquet** to label a parcel, to stick a label on a parcel **2** Fig (désignation) (d'une personne) label; **coller une é.**

à qn to stick a label on sb, to label sb; **é. politique** political affiliation; **quelle est son é. politique?** what are his/her politics? **3** (protocole) etiquette; **l'é. de la cour** Court etiquette or ceremonial

▸▸ **é. d'adresse** address label; **é. autocollante** self-adhesive or sticky label; Com **é. de calibrage** (d'un produit) grade label; Com **é. descriptive** descriptive label; **é. 'fabriqué en'** 'made-in' label; **é. gommée** sticky label; **é. d'identification** (d'un produit) identification label; Com **é. magnétique** security tag; Com **é. porte-prix** price label; Com **é. promotionnelle** promotional label

étirable [etirabl] ADJ **film é.** cling film

étirage [etiraʒ] NM (d'un métal, du verre etc) drawing (out); **é. à chaud/froid** hot/cold drawing; **é. du fil** wire drawing

étirement [etirmɑ̃] NM (des membres, du corps) stretching; **faire des étirements** to do stretching exercises

étirer [etire] VT (métal, verre etc) to draw (out); (fil, textiles) to draw
VPR **s'étirer 1** (se détendre) (d'une personne) to stretch **2** (s'allonger) (d'un tissu, vêtement) to stretch **3** (se prolonger) (d'une journée, d'une réunion etc) to drag on (for ever)

étoffe [etɔf] NF **1** Tex material, fabric; **étoffes de soie** silk fabrics **2** Fig **avoir l'é. d'un chef d'état/d'un écrivain/d'un héros** to have the makings of a statesman/writer/hero; **elle a de l'é.** she's got character, there's a lot to her; **manquer d'é.** (d'un film, un roman) to lack substance, to be thin or insubstantial

étoffé [etɔfe] ADJ (voix) rich, full; **homme é.** stout or thickset man; **discours é.** pithy speech

étoffer [etɔfe] VT Fig (discours, livre, personnage) to flesh out; (effectifs, équipe) to beef up
VPR **s'étoffer** (d'une personne) to fill out

étoile [etwal] NF **1** Astron star; **à la clarté des étoiles** in the starlight; **un ciel sans étoiles** a starless sky; **un ciel (par)semé d'étoiles** a starry or star-studded sky; **coucher ou dormir à la belle é.** to sleep in the open or out of doors; **né sous une bonne/mauvaise é.** born under a lucky/an unlucky star; **croire ou avoir foi en son é.** to believe in or trust to luck; Fam **voir des étoiles (en plein midi)** to see stars
2 (ornement, objet etc) star; Typ asterisk, star; **é. à cinq branches** five-pointed star; **les graviers ont fait des étoiles sur le pare-brise** the gravel starred the windscreen; **hôtel cinq étoiles** five-star hotel; **c'est un deux étoiles** it has a two-star rating
3 Aut roundabout, Am traffic circle
4 Cin, Théâtre (vedette) star; **une grande é. de la chanson** a big singing star; **é. montante** rising star
5 Ordinat **connecté en é.** in a star configuration
▸▸ Astron **é. du berger** evening star; **é. de David** Star of David; Astron **é. filante** shooting star; Zool **é. de mer** starfish; Astron **é. polaire** Pole Star; Astron **é. triple** triple star

étoilé [etwale] ADJ **1** (ciel) starry, star-studded; (nuit) starry, starlit **2** (fêlé) (pare-brise) starred

étoiler [etwale] VT **1** (parsemer d'étoiles) to stud with stars; Fig (parsemer) to stud (**de** with); **la nuit étoile le ciel** the night sky is studded with stars **2** (pare-brise, verre etc) to star, to make a star-shaped crack in
VPR **s'étoiler** (du ciel) to fill with stars

étole [etɔl] NF (fourrure), Rel stole

étonnamment [etɔnamɑ̃] ADV astonishingly, amazingly, surprisingly

étonnant [etɔnɑ̃] ADJ astonishing, amazing; **rien d'é. à cela** that's not surprising,

no wonder; **ce n'est pas é. qu'il soit malade** it's not surprising or it's no wonder that he's ill; **comme c'est é., il m'avait dit le contraire** how strange or odd, he had told me the opposite; **c'est é. mais personne n'a été blessé** it's amazing or astonishing that no one was hurt; **chose étonnante, il est arrivé** astonishingly or amazingly or surprisingly (enough), he arrived; **vous êtes é.!** you amaze me sometimes!
NM **l'é. est qu'il soit venu** the astonishing or amazing or surprising thing is that he came

étonné [etɔne] ADJ surprised; (plus fort) astonished, amazed (**de qch** at sth; **de voir** to see); **un regard é.** a surprised look; (plus fort) a look of astonishment or amazement, an astonished look; **je suis très é. qu'on ne m'ait rien dit** I'm amazed or astonished or extremely surprised that nobody said anything to me

étonnement [etɔnmɑ̃] NM astonishment, amazement, surprise; **frappé ou saisi d'é.** taken aback; **à mon grand é.** to my great surprise, much to my surprise, to my amazement; **imaginez (quel a été) mon é. quand …** imagine my surprise or astonishment when …; **faire l'é. de tout le monde** to astonish or surprise everybody

étonner [etɔne] VT to astonish, to amaze, to surprise; **cela ne m'étonnerait pas** it wouldn't surprise me, I wouldn't be the least bit surprised; **ça ne m'étonne pas du tout** it doesn't surprise me in the least, I'm not the least bit surprised; **ce qui m'étonne, c'est qu'il a menti** what surprises or astonishes me is that he lied; **cela m'étonne qu'elle soit venue** I'm surprised or astonished or amazed that she came; **il n'est pas venu? ça m'étonne ou voilà qui m'étonne** he didn't come? that's surprising; Fam **alors ça, ça m'étonnerait** that'll be the day; **ça m'étonne de toi, tu m'étonnes** I'm surprised at you; Fam **tu m'étonnes!** you don't say!, tell me something I don't know!; **tu m'étonneras toujours!** you never cease to astonish me!
VPR **s'étonner** to be astonished, to be surprised, to wonder (**de** at); **je m'étonne de vous voir** I'm astonished or surprised to see you; **je m'étonne qu'il ne voie pas le danger** it amazes me or I am astonished that he does not see the danger; **comment s'é. qu'il ait refusé?** can you wonder or is it any wonder that he refused?; **je ne m'étonne plus de rien** nothing surprises me any more; **essaie, tu pourrais t'é. toi-même** try, you might surprise yourself

étouffant [etufɑ̃] ADJ (air, chaleur), Fig (atmosphère) stifling, suffocating; (temps) oppressive, sultry; **une journée étouffante** a stifling hot day

étouffe-chrétien [etufkretjɛ̃] NM INV Fam **sa tarte est un é., c'est de l'é., sa tarte** his/her tart is pure stodge; **c'est un peu é.** it's a bit stodgy

étouffée [etufe] NF Culin **cuire à l'é.** to braise

étouffement [etufmɑ̃] NM **1** (asphyxie) suffocation; **sensation d'é.** feeling of breathlessness, stifling feeling; **la victime a été tuée par é.** the victim was suffocated (to death); **mourir d'é.** to die of or from suffocation **2** Fig (d'un scandale) hushing up; (de rumeurs, d'un complot, d'une révolte) suppression

étouffer [etufe] VT **1** (personne) (avec un oreiller etc) to suffocate, to smother; (en serrant) to suffocate, to choke; (de plantes) to choke; **la chaleur m'étouffe** the heat is stifling (me); Iron **ce ne sont pas les scrupules qui l'étouffent** he's/she's not overscrupulous; **ça t'étoufferait de dire merci?** would it choke you to say thank you?; **ça t'étouffe-**

rait d'être poli? it wouldn't kill you to be polite!

2 *Fig (cri, passion, créativité)* to stifle; *(bâillement, rire)* to stifle, to smother, to suppress; *(feu)* to smother; *(révolte)* to quell, to suppress; *(scandale, affaire)* to hush up; *(son)* to muffle; *Mus* to damp; *Élec (étincelle)* to quench; **é. un sanglot** to stifle a sob, to choke back a sob; **é. un scandale dans l'œuf** to nip a scandal in the bud

VI to suffocate; **é. de rire/colère** to choke with laughter/anger; *Fig* **dans cette ville, j'étouffais** I was suffocating in that town; **on étouffe ici** it's stifling here

VPR s'étouffer to suffocate; *(en mangeant)* to choke; **je me suis étouffé avec une bouchée de pain** I choked on a piece of bread; **plantes qui s'étouffent** plants that choke one another

étouffoir [etufwar] NM *(d'un piano)* damper

étourderie [eturdəri] NF **1** *(caractère)* carelessness, thoughtlessness, *Fam* scattiness; **faute d'é.** careless mistake; **par é.** inadvertently, in an unthinking moment; **il est d'une é. incroyable** he is incredibly scatterbrained *or Fam* scatty **2** *(action)* foolish mistake

étourdi, -ie [eturdi] ADJ *(irréfléchi)* thoughtless, careless; *(écervelé) (personne)* scatterbrained, featherbrained, *Fam* scatty

N *(écervelé)* scatterbrain, featherbrain

NF *Arch* **à l'étourdie** thoughtlessly, heedlessly

étourdiment [eturdimã] ADV without thinking

étourdir [eturdir] VT *(personne) (d'un coup, choc etc)* to stun, to daze; *Fig (d'un vin, d'éloges etc)* to make dizzy *or* giddy; *Fig* **je suis tout étourdie** my head's spinning

VPR s'étourdir to let one's hair down, to live it up; **s'é. dans la boisson** to drown one's sorrows (in drink)

étourdissant [eturdisã] ADJ **1** *(bruit)* deafening, ear-splitting **2** *(nouvelles, succès etc)* staggering, stunning, astounding; **e. de beauté** astoundingly *or* staggeringly *or* stunningly beautiful, stunning; **e. de bêtise** astoundingly *or* staggeringly stupid

étourdissement [eturdismã] NM **1** *(vertige)* giddiness, dizziness; **avoir un é.** to feel giddy *or* dizzy; **cela me donne des étourdissements** it makes me feel giddy *or* dizzy, it makes my head spin *or* swim **2** *Litt (griserie)* (feeling of) euphoria

étourneau, -eaux [eturno] NM **1** *(oiseau)* starling **2** *Fam (personne)* scatterbrain

étrange [etrãʒ] ADJ strange, peculiar, odd; **chose é., il est revenu** strange to say *or* strangely enough *or* oddly enough, he came back

étrangement [etrãʒmã] ADV strangely, oddly, peculiarly; **cela ressemble é. à la rougeole** it looks suspiciously like measles

étranger, -ère [etrãʒe, -er] ADJ **1** *(d'un autre pays)* foreign **2** *(inconnu)* strange, unfamiliar (à to); **sa voix ne m'est pas étrangère** his voice is not unfamiliar; **la haine lui est étrangère** he doesn't know what hatred is; **la musique lui est étrangère** he has no knowledge of music, *Fam* music is a closed book to him **3** *(extérieur)* foreign (à to); *Méd, Fig* **corps é.** foreign body; **entrée interdite à toute personne étrangère** no entry to unauthorized personnel; **des éléments étrangers se sont introduits dans l'enceinte de l'école** outsiders entered the school premises; **elle est étrangère à cette firme/au projet** she isn't a member of this firm/involved in the plan; **il est é. à tout ce qui s'est passé ici** he doesn't have anything to do with what happened here

N 1 *(d'un autre pays)* foreigner; *Admin* alien **2** *(d'un autre groupe)* stranger, outsider; **ce**

club est fermé aux étrangers the club is for members only; **je suis un é. ici** I'm a stranger here, *Fam* I'm a foreigner in these parts

NM l'é. *(pays étrangers)* foreign countries *or* parts; **aller/vivre à l'é.** to go/live abroad; **correspondant à l'é.** foreign correspondent; **voyages à l'é.** foreign travel; **investissement à l'é.** foreign *or* outward investment

> Attention: ne pas confondre **foreigner** et **stranger** lorsqu'on traduit le nom **étranger**. **Foreigner** s'applique uniquement à quelqu'un venant d'un autre pays, alors que **stranger** désigne quelqu'un d'extérieur à un groupe donné.

étrangeté [etrãʒte] NF *(d'une conduite, d'une robe etc)* strangeness, oddness, peculiarity

étranglé [etrãgle] ADJ *(passage, vallée etc)* narrow; *(taille)* nipped-in; *(voix)* strangled, choked, choking; *Méd (hernie)* strangulated

étranglement [etrãgləmã] NM **1** *(d'une personne)* strangling, strangulation; *(en lutte)* stranglehold; *Fig (de la liberté, la presse)* stifling; **il est mort par é.** he died of strangulation, he was strangled; **ce n'est pas l'é. qui a provoqué la mort** strangulation was not the cause of death **2** *(action de resserrer) (de la taille)* narrowing; *(d'un tube etc)* constriction, narrowing; *Aut, Tech* throttling; **soupape d'é.** throttle valve; *Méd* **é. herniaire** strangulated hernia **3** *(partie resserrée) (d'une rivière)* narrow part, narrows; *(d'une route)* bottleneck; **la route présente un é.** the road bottlenecks *or* forms a bottleneck

étrangler [etrãgle] VT **1** *(personne)* to strangle, to throttle; *Fig (liberté, la presse)* to stifle; **sa cravate l'étrangle** his tie is choking *or* strangling him; **la colère l'étrangle** he/she is choking with rage; *Fig* **les impôts m'étranglent** taxes are killing me **2** *(resserrer) (taille, tube etc)* to constrict; *Tech (vapeur etc)* to throttle; *Méd (vaisseau sanguin)* to strangulate; *Aut* **é. le moteur** to throttle (down) the engine

VPR s'étrangler 1 *(en mangeant)* to choke (**avec** on); **s'é. (de colère/d'indignation/de rire)** to choke (with anger/indignation/laughter) **2** *(de voix)* to choke; *(de paroles)* to stick in one's throat; **j'entendis un sanglot s'é.** I heard a choked sob; **mais les mots se sont étranglés** but the words died on his lips, but he couldn't get the words out **3** *(se resserrer) (d'une rivière)* to narrow; *(d'une rue)* to narrow, to (form a) bottleneck

étrangleur, -euse [etrãglœr, -øz] N *(personne)* strangler

NM *Aut, Tech* throttle

étrave [etrav] NF *Naut* stem; **de l'é. à l'étambot** from stem to stern; **lame d'é.** bow wave

être¹ [etr] NM **1** *Phil (existence)* being; **l'ê. et le néant** being and nothingness

2 *(âme)* being; **tout mon ê. se révolte à cette idée** my entire being rebels at the idea; **du fond de son ê.** from the depths of her/his being

3 *(personne)* being; *Biol, Litt* being, creature; **je ne veux partager ce secret qu'avec un ê. cher** I want to share this secret only with someone close to me; **elle pensait aux êtres chers qui étaient si loin** she thought of her loved ones so far away; **l'ê. aimé** the beloved; **pauvres petits êtres!** poor little things!; **c'est un ê. hors du commun** he/she is someone out of the ordinary *or* is no common mortal; **c'est un ê. méprisable** he's a despicable creature; **un ê. supérieur** a higher *or* superior being; **nul ê. au monde ne t'a aimé plus que moi** no one in the world loved you more than I; **ê. fantastique/mythique/surnaturel** fantastic/mythical/supernatural creature; *Litt* **un ê. de feu/lumière/ténèbres** a creature of fire/light/darkness

▶▶ ê. humain human being; **l'Ê. suprême** the Supreme Being; **ê. vivant** living creature; **on n'a trouvé aucun ê. vivant sur cette planète** we found no living creature on the planet

ÊTRE²

to be **1–8, 10, 11**	impersonal verb **9**
to belong to **12**	auxiliary verb **13, 14**
passive form **15**	to go **16**

VI *(prp* étant; *pp* été; *pr ind* je suis, tu es, il est, n. sommes, v. êtes, ils sont; *pr sub* je sois, tu sois, il soit, n. soyons, v. soyez, ils soient; *imp* sois, soyons, soyez; *impf* j'étais; *p hist* je fus, tu fus, il fut, n. fûmes, v. fûtes, ils furent; *p sub* je fusse; *fu* je serai) **1** *(exister)* to be; **je pense, donc je suis** I think, therefore I am; *Rel* **je suis celui qui est** I am that I am; **ce temps n'est plus où …** the days are gone when …; **l'ancien projet n'est plus** the old plan is a thing of the past; *Fml* **elle n'est plus** she is no longer with us; **quand on pense que tout cela aurait pu ne pas ê.** to think that all that may never have happened; **si cela était** if that were the case; **(et) quand cela serait** even if it were the case; **cela étant** that being so *or* the case; **la plus belle voiture qui soit** the finest car there is; **eh bien, soit!** very well then!; **ainsi soit-il** so be it, amen; *Rel* **amen!; maudit soit-il!** damn him to hell!; *Prov* **on ne peut pas ê. et avoir été** you can't stay young for ever; **nous sommes le dix** it's the tenth (today); **la vérité est entre ces extrêmes** the truth lies between these extremes

2 *(copule)* to be; **c'est ma mère** this is my mother; *(au téléphone)* it's my mother; **c'est le chef de gare** he's the stationmaster; **c'est un ou il est chef de gare** he's a stationmaster; **soit AB la base d'un triangle** let AB be the base of a triangle; **soit un triangle ABC** given a triangle ABC; **l'homme est mortel** man is mortal; **nous étions deux/plusieurs** there were two/several of us; **vous êtes tout pour moi** you mean everything to me; **c'est quelqu'un!** he/she's somebody!; *Fam* **est-il drôle!** he's *so* funny!

3 *(+ adv)* to be; **vous êtes ici chez vous** treat this place like your own; **elle est très mal/beaucoup mieux** she is very ill/much better; **ê. bien avec qn** to be on good terms with sb **4** *(locutions avec 'à' + nom)* **ê. au travail/à son bureau** to be at work/at one's desk; **ê. à l'agonie** to be dying; **vous n'êtes pas à ce que je dis** you're not paying attention to what I'm saying; **il est tout à son travail** he is entirely engrossed in his work; **il est à Paris** he is in Paris; **le temps est au beau** the weather's set fair; **le temps est à l'orage** there's a storm brewing; **les prix sont à la baisse** prices are on the decrease, prices are coming down

5 *(locutions avec 'de' + nom)* **ce tableau est de Gauguin** this picture is by Gauguin; **il est de Londres** he is from London; **il était de la CIA** he was a member of the CIA; **il n'est pas des nôtres** he isn't one of us, he isn't with us; **serez-vous des nôtres, ce soir?** will you be joining us this evening?; **il est de mes amis** he's a friend of mine, he's one of my friends; **ê. de service** to be on duty; **ils sont de la même promotion** they're in the same year *or Am* class; **cet enfant est d'un caractère étrange** this child has a strange character *or* nature; **l'enfant est-il de lui?** is the child his?; **c'était d'un simple!** it was *so* simple!; **je suis de noce samedi prochain** I've got a wedding next Saturday

6 *(+ à + inf)* **j'étais là à l'attendre** I was there waiting for him; **la maison est à louer** the house is to let; **elle est tout le temps à se plaindre** she's always *or* forever complaining; **elles étaient encore à médire** they were running people down again; **c'était à pré-**

voir it was to be expected; **c'est à craindre** I fear so

7 (+ à + inf avec idée d'obligation) **cette idée est à creuser** this idea will have to be thoroughly looked into; **c'est à prendre ou à laisser** take it or leave it; **lui seul est à blâmer** he alone is to blame

8 (avec 'ce') **je sais ce qui est arrivé** I know what happened; **savez-vous ce que c'est?** do you know what it is?; **est-ce vrai?** is it true?; **serait-ce vrai?** can it be or could it (possibly) be true?; **ce n'est pas qu'il soit ingrat, mais ...** it's not that he's ungrateful, but ...; **ne fût-ce que, ne serait-ce que** if only; **vous venez, n'est-ce pas?** you're coming, aren't you?; **vous ne venez pas, n'est-ce pas?** you're not coming, are you?; **n'est-ce pas qu'il a de la chance?** isn't he lucky?; Litt **je le ferais (si ce) n'était que je dois partir** I would do it if I didn't have to leave; **n'était mon rhumatisme** if it weren't or wasn't for my rheumatism; **il l'aurait bien épousée, n'eût été qu'il la trouvait trop orgueilleuse** he would gladly have married her, were it not for the fact that he found her too proud SEE GRAMMAR B64

9 (impers) **il est midi** it is twelve o'clock; **il est temps de partir** it is time to go; **il est de mon devoir de rester** it is my duty to stay; Litt **il n'est que de comparer les deux pour se rendre compte de leur différence** one need only compare the two to become aware of the difference between them; **il n'est point d'amours sans larmes** there is no love without tears; **comme si de rien n'était** as if nothing had happened; **soit dit sans offense** if you don't mind my saying so; **il était une fois une fée** once upon a time there was a fairy; **un héros, s'il en fut (jamais)** a hero, if ever there was one; **il est à craindre/prévoir que ...** it's feared/expected that ...; **il est à croire/espérer que ...** it's to be believed/hoped that ...; **il fut un temps où ...** there was a time when ...; **il m'est très douloureux de vous annoncer ...** it is with great sorrow that I inform you ...; **il m'est impossible de vous répondre** it's impossible for me to give you an answer; **il est probable qu'ils sont déjà mariés** they're probably already married SEE GRAMMAR B29

10 (avec 'en' indéterminé) **où en sommes-nous?** how far have we got?, where are we?; **où en êtes-vous de vos travaux?** how far have you got with your work?; **l'affaire en est là** that is how things stand; **j'en étais là de mes suppositions quand ...** I'd reached that point or I'd got that far in my assumptions when ...; **si vous m'aviez écouté, on n'en serait pas là** if you had listened to me, we wouldn't be where we are now; **vous n'en êtes pas encore là!** you haven't come to that (point or stage) yet!; **il n'en est pas à son coup d'essai** this is not his first attempt; **je ne sais plus où j'en suis** I don't know where I am or what I'm doing; **j'en suis à me demander si ...** I'm beginning to wonder whether ...; **nous n'en sommes pas à le renvoyer** we haven't reached the point of sacking him yet; **on n'en est pas à un euro près** we're not going to quibble over a euro; **j'en suis pour mon argent** I've spent my money to no purpose, I've thrown my money away; **j'en suis pour mille euros** I'm a thousand euros the poorer; **c'en est trop!** it's too much!, this is past bearing!; **c'en est assez!** enough!; **il en est de l'homme comme de la nature** it's the same with man as with nature; **puisqu'il en est ainsi** since that's how things are; **il n'en est rien!** nothing of the kind!; **comment pourrait-il en ê. autrement?** how could it be any other way?, how could things be any different?; **il en est** (d'un complot, d'une société secrète etc) he's one of them; (est homosexuel) he's one of them, he's the other way in-

clined; **nous allons faire une partie de golf, vous en êtes?** we're going to have a round of golf, can we count you in? or are you game? or are you up for it?

11 (avec 'y' indéterminé) **il y est pour quelque chose** he's got something to do with it; **j'y suis pour un tiers** I'm in for a third share; **ça y est!** that's it!; **ça y est? tu as fini?** is that it? have you finished?; **vous y êtes?** (vous comprenez?) are you with me?, have you got it?; (vous avez trouvé?) have you got it?

12 (appartenir) **ê. à qn** to belong to sb; **à qui sont ces livres?** whose books are these?, who do these books belong to?; **la victoire est à nous** victory is ours; **je suis à vous dans un moment** I'll be with you in a moment; **sois à moi!** be mine!; **c'est à vous de jouer** it's your turn to play; **c'est à vous de veiller sur l'enfant** it's your job or it's up to you to look after the child

13 (avec aller, rester, tomber etc aux temps composés) **il est déjà arrivé** he has already arrived; **il est arrivé hier** he arrived yesterday; **elle est née en 1974** she was born in 1974 SEE GRAMMAR B27–8; B38–9

14 (avec vpr aux temps composés) **nous nous sommes trompés** we (have) made a mistake; **ils se sont aimés** they loved each other; **elle s'est fait mal** she (has) hurt herself SEE GRAMMAR B38–9

15 (pour indiquer le passif) to be; **il fut puni par son père** he was punished by his father; **il est aimé de tout le monde** he is loved by everyone; **j'entends ê. obéi** I mean to be obeyed SEE GRAMMAR A54–5; B38–9

16 Fam (= aller, aux temps composés et au passé simple) **j'avais été à Paris** I had been to Paris; **j'ai été voir Martin** I've been or I went to see Martin; **vous avez été trop loin** you went too far, you've gone too far; **ça a été (ça a marché)** it went OK

17 (= s'en aller, au passé simple) **il s'en fut ouvrir la porte** he went off to open the door

18 **quand il fut pour partir** just as he was about to leave

étreindre [etrɛ̃dr] VT (prp **étreignant**; pp **étreint**; pr ind **j'étreins, il étreint**, n. **étreignons**; impf **j'étreignais**; p hist **j'étreignis**; fu **j'étreindrai**) (personne) to embrace, to clasp in one's arms; **spectacle qui vous étreint le cœur** sight that wrings one's heart, heart-rending sight; **la peur/la douleur l'étreignait** fear/pain gripped him; **la douleur l'étreignait trop fort** the pain had too strong a grip or hold (on him); Prov **qui trop embrasse mal étreint** = that's what comes of trying to do too much at once

étreinte [etrɛ̃t] NF **1** (entre personnes) embrace; **ils ne pouvaient cesser leurs étreintes** they couldn't stop embracing or hugging **2** (en lutte) lock **3** Fig (pression) grip; **tu ne peux imaginer ce qu'est l'é. de la misère** you cannot imagine what it's like to be in the grip of poverty; **l'é. de la douleur se faisait sentir de plus en plus** the pain was strengthening its grip or hold

étrenne [etrɛn] NF **1** (cadeau) **étrennes** New Year's gift; **les étrennes du facteur/de l'éboueur** ≃ the postman's/dustman's Christmas box **2** (premier usage) **avoir l'é. de qch** to have the first use of sth, to be the first person to use sth, Fam to christen sth; **pour une fois, tu auras l'é. d'un manteau** you'll have a new coat for once

étrenner [etrene] VT (objet) to use for the first time, Fam to christen; (vêtement) to wear for the first time; **c'est moi qui vais é. les nouveaux bureaux** I'll be the first person to use the new offices

VI Arg **tu vas é.!** (être puni) you're going to catch or get it!

êtres [ɛtr] NMPL Arch **connaître les ê. d'une maison** to know one's way about a house

étrette [etrɛt] Can Fam ADJ narrow; (personne) narrow-minded

NF (personne d'esprit étroit) narrow-minded person

étrier [etrije] NM **1** Équitation stirrup; **vider les étriers** to be thrown; Fig to be thrown or disconcerted; Fig **avoir le pied à l'é.** to be on the point of leaving; (être en bonne voie pour réussir) to be off to a good start; Fig **il a eu du mal à mettre le pied à l'é.** he had trouble getting started or getting off the ground; Fig **mettre le pied à l'é. à qn** to give sb a helping hand; **boire** ou **prendre le coup de l'é.** to have one for the road **2** Méd **é.** (de soutien) stirrup, leg rest; **é.** (de traction ou de réduction) calliper **3** Anat (de l'oreille) stirrup bone **4** Aut stirrup, shackle; (de frein) caliper

étrille [etrij] NF **1** (brosse) currycomb **2** Zool small edible crab

étriller [etrije] VT **1** (cheval) to curry **2** Fam (réprimander) **é. qn** to give sb a dressing-down or a telling-off **3** Fam (faire payer trop cher) to fleece, to sting

étripage [etripaʒ] NM (d'un poisson, d'un lièvre) gutting; (d'un poulet etc) drawing; Fam (tuerie) bloodbath, slaughter

étriper [etripe] VT (poisson, lièvre) to gut; (poulet etc) to draw; Fig Fam **je vais l'é.** I'll murder or slaughter him, I'll have his guts for garters

VPR **s'étriper** Fam (se battre) to make mincemeat of each other

étriqué [etrike] ADJ **1** (vêtement) skimpy, tight **2** Fig (perspective, vie) narrow; (avenir) limited

étriquer [etrike] VT Couture (vêtement) to make too tight; **cette robe vous étrique** that dress is too tight on you

étriver [etrive] Can VT to irritate, to annoy

VI **faire é.** to drive mad

étrivière [etrivjɛr] NF stirrup leather

étroit [etrwa] ADJ **1** (peu large) (ruban, sentier, épaules), Fig (esprit, vue) narrow; (espace, pièce etc) narrow, confined, cramped; Fig (idées) hidebound; Fig **la voie étroite** the straight and narrow; Fig **avoir l'esprit é.** to be narrow-minded

2 (serré) (nœud) tight; (manteau etc) tight(-fitting); Fig (amitié, lien etc) close; **je suis en rapport é. avec sa sœur** I am in close contact or touch with his sister; **être en étroite collaboration avec** to work closely or in close co-operation with; **règlements étroits** strict rules; **sous étroite surveillance** under close surveillance; **le sens é. d'un mot** the strict meaning of a word

3 **être à l'é.** (dans son logement etc) to be cramped for room; (financièrement) to be in straitened circumstances

étroitement [etrwatmɑ̃] ADV **1** (nouer, tenir) tightly; Fig (lier, collaborer) closely **2** (observer une règle) strictly; **surveiller qn é.** to watch sb closely, to keep a close watch on sb

étroitesse [etrwatɛs] NF (d'un ruban, d'un sentier, des épaules etc) narrowness; Fig **é. d'esprit** narrow-mindedness; **l'é. de ce bureau** the lack of space in this office

étron [etrɔ̃] NM piece of excrement, Vulg turd

étrusque [etrysk] ADJ Etruscan

N **É.** Etruscan

Ets Com (abrév **établissements**) **E. Legrand** Legrand

étude [etyd] NF **1** Scol, Univ etc (action) (d'un sujet, texte, auteur etc) study, survey; **voyage d'études** educational or study tour; **aimer l'é.** to like studying; **faire des études de français/de droit** to study or Br read French/law; **il a fait ses études à Eton/Oxford** he was educated at Eton/he went to or studied at

Oxford; **payer les études de qn** to pay for sb's education; **faire de brillantes études** to do extremely well at university; **j'ai arrêté mes études à 16 ans** I left school when I was 16; **négliger ses études** to neglect one's studies; **achever ses études** to finish one's studies *or* education; *Péj* **cela sent l'é.** it reeks of effort **2** *Scol (heure)* (private) study period, *Br* prep; **(salle d')é.** (private) study room, *Br* prep room; **je laisse mes enfants à l'é. jusqu'à 5 heures** = I leave them in home-work class until 5 o'clock

3 *(action de considérer) (d'une question, d'un plan etc)* study, investigation, survey; *Constr* survey; **bureau d'études** research department; **ingénieur d'études** design engineer; **voyage d'études** study *or* field trip; **procéder à l'é. d'une question, mettre une question à l'é.** to study *or* investigate *or* go into a question

4 *(texte, musique, peinture etc)* study; *Mus* **é. pour violon** violin study; *Beaux-Arts* **é. de tête** study of a head

5 *(bureau)* office; *(d'un avocat)* office, *Br* chambers; *(charge) (d'un juriste)* practice
► ► *Mktg, Com* **é. AIO** AIO research; *Mktg, Com* **é. d'audience** audience research; *Mktg, Com* **é. des besoins** needs study *or* analysis; **é. de cas** case study; **é. client** customer survey; *Mktg, Com* **é. commerciale** marketing study; **études commerciales** *Mktg* marketing research; *(dans école de commerce etc)* business studies; **é. de communication** communications study; **études de communication** media studies; **é. comparative** comparative study; **é. du comportement** behavioural study *or* analysis; *Mktg, Com* **é. du comportement du consommateur** consumer behaviour study; *Mktg, Com* **é. auprès des consommateurs** consumer *or* customer survey; *Mktg, Com* **é. auprès des consommateurs finaux** end-user survey; **é. documentaire** desk research; **é. de faisabilité** feasibility study; **é. du lectorat** readership survey; *Mktg, Com* **é. de marché** market research; *Mktg, Com* **une é. de marché** a market study; **faire une é. de marché** to do market research; **ce cabinet est spécialisé dans les études de marché** the company specializes in market research; *Mktg, Com* **é. de marché standard** omnibus survey; **é. marketing** marketing study; **é. des performances** *(d'un employé)* performance appraisal; **é. préliminaire** preliminary study; *Mktg, Com* **é. de produit** product analysis; **études qualitatives** qualitative research; **études quantitatives** quantitative research; *Mktg, Com* **é. de satisfaction de la clientèle** customer satisfaction survey; **é. sur le terrain** field study; **études sur le terrain** field research; *Mktg, Com* **études sur les ventes** sales research

étudiant, -ante [etydjɑ̃, -ɑ̃t] N student; **é. en médecine/en droit/en lettres** medical/law/arts student; **é. de première/seconde année** first/second-year student, *Am* freshman/sophomore
ADJ *(vie, mouvement etc)* student

étudié [etydje] **ADJ 1** *(soigneusement préparé) (effet, discours etc)* carefully prepared; **prix très étudiés** very fair prices **2** *Péj (affecté) (politesse, geste)* affected, studied; *(manières, sourires)* affected

étudier [etydje] *(impf, pr sub n.* **étudiions)** **VT 1** *Scol, Univ etc (sujet, texte, auteur etc)* to study; *Scol (leçon)* to prepare; *Mus, Théâtre (instrument, rôle etc)* to study; **é. une matière en vue d'un examen** to read up a subject for an examination **2** *Péj (son apparence etc)* to study; **elle étudie ses poses** she strikes poses **3** *(considérer) (question, plan, théorie etc)* to study, to examine; **sa demande mérite d'être étudiée** his application merits examination

4 *(observer) (société, personne, visage etc)* to study
VI to study
VPR **s'étudier 1** *(se regarder, s'analyser)* to study *or* examine oneself, to take stock of oneself; *Péj (manquer de naturel)* to be affected **2** *(s'observer l'un l'autre)* to study each other, to take stock of each other; **ils se sont longuement étudiés** they took careful stock of each other **3** *Arch* **s'é. à faire qch** to take pains to do sth, to make a point of doing sth; **il s'étudiait à m'éviter** he studiously avoided me

étui [etɥi] **NM** case; **é. (de revolver)** holster; **é. de cartouche** cartridge case; **é. de cassette** cassette case; **é. à lunettes** glasses case; *Naut* **é. de voile** sail cover

étuvage [etyvaʒ] **NM** *Chimie, Ind (séchage)* drying; *(stérilisation)* sterilization

étuve [etyv] **NF 1** *(aux thermes)* steam room; **é. sèche** hot-air steam cabinet; **é. humide** steam *or* vapour bath **2** *Chimie, Ind etc (pour sécher)* drying oven; *(pour stériliser)* sterilizer; **é. à incubation** *ou* **à cultures** incubator **3** *Fam (lieu où il fait trop chaud)* oven

étuvée [etyve] **NF** *Culin* **à l'é.** braised

étuver [etyve] **VT 1** *(sécher) (fruit etc)* to dry; *(stériliser) (vêtements contaminés etc)* to sterilize **2** *Culin* to braise

étymologie [etimɔlɔʒi] **NF** etymology

étymologique [etimɔlɔʒik] **ADJ** etymological

étymologiquement [etimɔlɔʒikmɑ̃] **ADV** etymologically

étymologiste [etimɔlɔʒist] **N** etymologist

étymon [etimɔ̃] **NM** etymon

eu [y] *voir* **avoir¹**

eucalyptus [økaliptys] **NM** eucalyptus; **essence d'e.** eucalyptus oil

Eucharistie (l') [løkaristi] **NF** *Rel* the Eucharist

eucharistique [økaristik] **ADJ** *Rel* Eucharistic(al)

Euclide [øklid] **N** Euclid

euclidien, -ienne [øklidjɛ̃, -jɛn] **ADJ** *Math* Euclidean

eugénique [øʒenik] **NF**, **eugénisme** [øʒenism] **NM** eugenics

euh [ø] **INT** er

eunuque [ønyk] **NM** eunuch

euphémique [øfemik] **ADJ** euphemistic

euphémiquement [øfemikmɑ̃] **ADV** euphemistically

euphémisme [øfemism] **NM** euphemism

euphonie [øfɔni] **NF** euphony

euphonique [øfɔnik] **ADJ** euphonious, euphonic

euphorbe [øfɔrb] **NF** *Bot* euphorbia

euphorie [øfɔri] **NF** euphoria

euphorique [øfɔrik] **ADJ** euphoric

euphorisant [øfɔrizɑ̃] **ADJ** *(effet, atmosphère etc)* exhilarating; *Méd (drogue)* antidepressant, *Spéc* euphoriant
NM anti-depressant drug, *Spéc* euphoriant

Euphrate (l') [løfrat] **NM** the Euphrates

eurafricain, -aine [ørafrikɛ̃, -ɛn] **ADJ** Eurafrican
N **E.** Eurafrican

Eurasie [ørazi] **NF** Eurasia

eurasien, -ienne [ørazjɛ̃, -jɛn] **ADJ** Eurasian
N **E.** Eurasian

eurêka [øreka] **INT** eureka

eurent [yr] *voir* **avoir¹**

Euripide [øripid] **N** Euripides

EURL [əyɛrɛl] **NF** *Com (abrév* **entreprise unipersonnelle à responsabilité limitée)** trader with limited liability

euro [øro] **NM** *(monnaie)* euro

euro- **PRÉF** Euro-

eurobanque [ørobɑ̃k] **NF** Eurobank

eurobudget [ørobydʒe] **NM** Eurobudget

euro-certificat **NM** *Bourse* euro-certificate

eurochèque [ørofɛk] **NM** Eurocheque

eurocommunisme [ørokɔmynism] **NM** Eurocommunism

Eurocorps [ørokɔr] **NM** *Mil* Eurocorps

eurocrate [ørokrat] **N** Eurocrat

eurocrédit [ørokredi] **NM** Euroloan

eurodéputé [ørodepyte] **NM** *Pol* Euro MP

eurodevise [ørodəviz] **NF** *Fin* Eurocurrency

eurodollar [ørodɔlar] **NM** *Fin* Eurodollar

eurofranc [ørofrɑ̃] **NM** eurofranc

Euroland(e) [ørolɑ̃d] **NF** Euroland

euromarché [øromarʃe] **NM** *Fin* Euromarket

euromissile [øromisil] **NM** Euromissile

euromonnaie [øromɔnɛ] **NF** *Fin* Eurocurrency

euro-obligation **NF** *Fin* Eurobond

Europe [ørɔp] **NF** Europe; **l'E. verte** (European) Community agriculture *or* farming; **l'E. des quinze** the European Union *(comprising fifteen member states)*; **l'E. sociale** social Europe *(a united Europe committed to a progressive social and welfare policy)*

européanisation [øropeanizasjɔ̃] **NF** Europeanization

européaniser [øropeanize] **VT** to Europeanize
VPR **s'européaniser** to become Europeanized

européen, -enne [øropeɛ̃, -ɛn] **ADJ** European
N **E.** European

euroscepticisme [ørosɛptisism] **N** *Pol* Euroscepticism

eurosceptique [ørosɛptik] **N** *Pol* Eurosceptic

Euro Stoxx [ørostɔks] **NM** Euro Stoxx; **l'E. 50** the Euro Stoxx 50 index

eurostratégique [ørostrateʒik] **ADJ** *Mil* Eurostrategic

Eurotunnel [ørotynɛl] **NM** Channel tunnel

Eurovision [ørovizjɔ̃] **NF** Eurovision

eut [y] *voir* **avoir¹**

euthanasie [øtanazi] **NF** euthanasia

eutrophe [øtrɔf], **eutrophique** [øtrɔfik] **ADJ** eutrophic

eutrophisation [øtrɔfizasjɔ̃] **NF** eutrophication

eux [ø] *voir* **lui²**

eux-mêmes [ømɛm] **PRON PERS** themselves

évacuateur, -trice [evakɥatør, -tris] **ADJ** *(tuyau etc)* drainage

évacuation [evakɥasjɔ̃] **NF 1** *(de matières du corps)* evacuation, voiding, discharge; *(d'eau, de pus etc)* draining (off); **course d'é.** *(d'un moteur)* exhaust stroke **2** *(de population, troupes, blessés etc)* evacuation; *(d'une salle etc)* evacuation, clearing; *Naut (d'un bateau)* abandoning; *Mil* **hôpital d'é.** clearing hospital

évacué, -ée [evakɥe] **N** evacuee

évacuer [evakɥe] **VT 1** *(matières du corps)* to evacuate, to discharge, to void; *(vapeur)* to vent; *(eau, pus etc)* to drain (off) **2** *(faire partir)* to evacuate; **faire é. tous les habitants** to evacuate all the inhabitants **3** *(quitter) (forteresse, ville etc)* to evacuate, to vacate; **faire é. une salle** to evacuate *or* clear a hall; *Naut* **é. le bâtiment** to abandon ship **4** *Fig (problème)* to get rid of, to solve; **c'est une question que je préfèrerais é. le plus vite**

possible it's a matter I'd like to dispose of as soon as possible

évadé, -ée [evade] **N** escaped prisoner, fugitive

évader (s') [sevade] **VPR** *(de prison, de la réalité etc)* to escape (**de** from)

> Il faut noter que le verbe anglais **to evade** est un faux ami. Il signifie **éviter**.

évaluateur, -trice [evalɥatœr, -tris] **N** *Can* valuer, appraiser

évaluation [evalɥasjɔ̃] **NF 1** *(action) (d'une propriété, d'un bien etc)* valuation, appraisal; *(des dommages)* assessment; *(d'un poids, d'un nombre etc)* estimation; *Com* **é. du coût** cost assessment; **é. des coûts** cost analysis; **é. financière** financial appraisal; **é. des risques** risk assessment **2** *(quantité, valeur) (d'une propriété, d'un bien etc)* valuation; *(des dommages)* assessment; *(d'un poids, d'un nombre etc)* estimate

évaluer [evalɥe] **VT** to evaluate; *(propriété, bien etc)* to value, to appraise; *(dommages)* to assess (**à** at); *(poids, nombre, risques etc)* to estimate; *Fin* **é. le(s) coût(s) de** to cost

évanescent [evanesɑ̃] **ADJ** evanescent

évangélique [evɑ̃ʒelik] **ADJ** *Rel* evangelical

évangélisateur, -trice [evɑ̃ʒelizatœr, -tris] *Rel* **ADJ** evangelistic **N** evangelist

évangélisation [evɑ̃ʒelizasjɔ̃] **NF** *Rel* evangelization

évangéliser [evɑ̃ʒelize] **VT** *Rel* to evangelize

évangélisme [evɑ̃ʒelism] **NM** *Rel* evangelism

évangéliste [evɑ̃ʒelist] **NM** *Rel* evangelist; *(auteur de l'un des Évangiles)* Evangelist

évangile [evɑ̃ʒil] **NM 1** *Rel* **l'É.** the Gospel; **l'É. selon saint Jean** the Gospel according to St. John; **l'é. du jour** the gospel for the day; *Fig* **prendre qch pour parole d'é.** to take sth for gospel (truth); *Fig* **ce n'est pas l'é.** it's not Holy Writ **2** *Fig (livre important)* bible

évanoui [evanwi] **ADJ** unconscious; **tomber é.** to fall down in a faint; **on l'a trouvé é.** he was found unconscious *or* in a (dead) faint

évanouir (s') [sevanwir] **VPR 1** *(disparaître) (d'une silhouette, apparition, ombre)* to vanish, to disappear; *(d'un souvenir, rêve)* to fade (**away**); *(d'un son)* to die away, to fade away **2** *(perdre conscience)* to faint

évanouissement [evanwismɑ̃] **NM 1** *(disparition) (d'un fantôme, d'une personne etc)* vanishing, disappearance; *(d'un souvenir, rêve)* fading; *Radio* fade-away **2** *(syncope)* faint(ing fit); **avoir un é.** to faint **3** *Aut (de freins)* fade

évaporation [evapɔrasjɔ̃] **NF** evaporation

évaporé, -ée [evapɔre] *Péj* **ADJ** featherbrained, scatterbrained **N** featherbrain, scatterbrain

évaporer [evapɔre] **VI faire é. un liquide** to evaporate a liquid **VT** *Arch* **é. un liquide** to evaporate a liquid **VPR s'évaporer 1** *(d'un liquide, parfum etc)* to evaporate **2** *Fam (disparaître)* to vanish (into thin air)

évasé [evaze] **ADJ** *(vase, tuyau etc)* widemouthed; *(vêtement)* flared

évasement [evazmɑ̃] **NM** *(d'un vase, tuyau etc)* wide mouth; *(d'un vêtement)* flare

évaser [evaze] **VT** *(vase, verre etc)* to widen (out) the opening of; *(tuyau, conduite etc)* to open out; *(ouverture)* to widen; *Couture (vêtement)* to flare **VPR s'évaser** to widen, to open out; *Couture* to flare

évasif, -ive [evazif, -iv] **ADJ** evasive

évasion [evazjɔ̃] **NF 1** *(de prison etc)* escape

(**de** from); **réussir son é.** to succeed in escaping; **le roi de l'é.** the master escaper **2** *Fig (distraction)* escape; *(hors de la réalité)* escapism; **avoir besoin d'é.** to need to escape; **littérature d'é.** escapist literature ▸▸ **é. de capitaux** flight *or* exodus of capital; **é. fiscale** tax evasion

> Il faut noter que le nom anglais **evasion** est un faux ami. Il signifie le plus souvent **dérobade**.

évasivement [evazivmɑ̃] **ADV** evasively

Ève [ɛv] **N** Eve; *Fam* **je ne le connais ni d'È. ni d'Adam** I don't know him from Adam

évêché [eveʃe] **NM** *(diocèse)* bishopric, see; *(palais)* bishop's palace; *(dignité)* bishopric

éveil [evɛj] **NM 1** *(action) (de la nature, la curiosité, la nation etc)* awakening; **être en é.** *(d'une personne)* to be on the alert; *(de l'esprit)* to be alert **2** *(alerte)* **donner l'é.** to raise the alarm; **donner l'é. à qn** to alert sb, to put sb on his/her guard

éveillé [eveje] **ADJ 1** *(non endormi)* awake; **rêve é.** waking dream; **tenir qn é.** to keep sb awake; **é. ou endormi** waking or sleeping **2** *(vif) (personne)* wide-awake, alert, bright; **garçon (à l'esprit) é.** bright boy

éveiller [eveje] **VT** *Litt (personne)* to awake(n); *Fig (curiosité, soupçons, jalousie etc)* to arouse, to awaken; *(intelligence, imagination etc)* to bring out, to develop **VPR s'éveiller** *(d'une personne)* to awake(n); *Fig (de la curiosité, des soupçons etc)* to be aroused; *(de l'imagination, de l'imagination etc)* to show itself, to develop; *Litt* **elle s'éveille à l'amour** she is awakening to love

événement [evɛnmɑ̃] **NM** event, occurrence; *Fig (livre, spectacle etc important)* event; **attendre la suite des événements** to await the course of events; **créer l'é.** to make big news; **semaine fertile en événements** eventful week; **é. médiatique** media event; **les événements (de mai 68)** the events of May 1968; *Hum* **quand il fait la vaisselle, c'est (tout) un é.** it's a real event when he does the dishes

événementiel, -elle [evɛnmɑ̃sjɛl] **ADJ** *(information, histoire, programme télévisé etc)* factual

évent [evɑ̃] **NM 1** *(de la nourriture, d'un vin, d'un parfum)* mustiness; *(de la bière)* flatness, staleness **2** *(d'une baleine)* blowhole, spout **3** *Tech* vent(hole)

éventail [evɑ̃taj] **NM 1** *(instrument)* fan; **en é.** fan-shaped; *Fam* **elle est restée les doigts de pied en é. toute la matinée** she lazed around all morning; **voûte en é.** fan vaulting **2** *(choix) (de marchandises, salaires, possibilités etc)* range, mix, set; **é. de produits** product *or* sales mix; **é. des prix** price range

éventaire [evɑ̃tɛr] **NM 1** *(d'un marchand ambulant etc)* tray **2** *(étal)* (street) stall

éventé [evɑ̃te] **ADJ** *(nourriture, vin, parfum etc)* musty; *(bière)* flat, stale; *Fig (secret)* well-known

éventer [evɑ̃te] **VT 1** *(vêtements)* to air; *(grain)* to expose to the air; *(mine, mèche)* to ventilate **2** *(avec un éventail etc)* to fan **3** *Fig (découvrir) (secret, complot)* to find out, to discover; **é. la mèche** to discover *or* find out the secret; **le secret est éventé** the secret is out **VPR s'éventer 1** *(de la nourriture, d'un vin, d'un parfum)* to go musty; *(de la bière)* to go flat *or* stale **2** *(avec un éventail etc)* to fan oneself

éventration [evɑ̃trasjɔ̃] **NF** *Méd* rupture, hernia

éventrer [evɑ̃tre] **VT** *(personne, animal)* to disembowel, to eviscerate; *(poisson)* to gut;

(volaille) to draw; *(colis)* to rip *or* tear open; *(fût, boîte)* to break *or* smash open; *(porte)* to burst open; *(sac, matelas)* to slit open

éventreur [evɑ̃trœr] **NM** disemboweller; **Jack l'É.** Jack the Ripper

éventualité [evɑ̃tɥalite] **NF 1** *(circonstance)* eventuality, contingency, possibility; **parer à toute é.** to provide for all eventualities *or* contingencies; **dans l'é. d'un changement de date** in the event of a change of date; **dans cette é.** if that happens *or* should happen **2** *(possibilité) (de guerre etc)* possibility

éventuel, -elle [evɑ̃tɥɛl] **ADJ** *(successeur, profits, guerre etc)* possible, potential; **client é.** potential *or* prospective customer

> Il faut noter que l'adjectif anglais **eventual** est un faux ami. Il signifie **final**.

éventuellement [evɑ̃tɥɛlmɑ̃] **ADV** possibly; **il viendra avec sa cousine et é. avec sa tante** he'll come with his cousin and possibly with his aunt; **faites cet exercice en vous servant é. d'un dictionnaire** do this exercise using a dictionary if necessary; **j'aurais é. besoin de votre concours** I may need your help (later); **tu veux venir avec nous? – é.!** do you want to come with us? – possibly!

> Il faut noter que l'adverbe anglais **eventually** est un faux ami. Il signifie **finalement**.

évêque [evɛk] **NM** *Rel* bishop; *Prov* **un chien regarde bien un é.** a cat may look at a king; **bonnet d'é.** bishop's mitre; *Fam (d'une volaille)* parson's nose

évertuer (s') [severtɥe] **VPR s'é. à faire qch** to do one's utmost *or* make every effort to do sth; **je m'évertue à lui répéter que c'est impossible** I'm tired of telling him that it's impossible; **s'é. sur qch** to struggle with sth

éviction [eviksjɔ̃] **NF** *(d'un rival, d'une tête de parti etc)* ousting, supplanting; *(d'un locataire)* eviction; **depuis son é. du parti** since his/her ousting *or* since being ousted from the party

évidage [evidaʒ] **NM** *(d'une pierre, du bois etc)* hollowing out, scooping out

évidement [evidmɑ̃] **NM** *(action) (d'une pierre, du bois etc)* hollowing out, scooping out; *Chir* scraping out

évidemment [evidamɑ̃] **ADV 1** *(bien sûr)* of course **2** *Arch (manifestement)* obviously, clearly

> Il faut noter que l'adverbe anglais **evidently** est un faux ami. Il signifie **manifestement, à l'évidence**.

évidence [evidɑ̃s] **NF 1** *(d'un fait, de la vérité etc)* obviousness, clearness; **se rendre à l'é.** to yield to *or* face the facts; **nier** *ou* **refuser l'é.** to deny the obvious *or* what is obvious; **de toute é., à l'é.** clearly, obviously; **mais c'est une é.!, mais c'est l'é.** même but it's obvious *or* self-evident! **2 être en é.** *(d'un objet)* to be in a prominent position, to be conspicuous; **mettre en é.** *(marchandises)* to display prominently; *(idée)* to give prominence to, to underline; **je vais les laisser bien en é. sur la table** I'll leave them in a prominent position on the table; **se mettre en é.** to try to get oneself noticed

> Il faut noter que le nom anglais **evidence** est un faux ami. Il signifie le plus souvent **preuve**.

évident [evidɑ̃] **ADJ** *(erreur, vérité, preuve, raisonnement)* obvious, clear, plain; **il est é. qu'elle se trompe** it is obvious *or* clear that she is mistaken; **il était d'une évidente mauvaise foi** he was obviously *or* clearly insincere; **tu crois qu'on va réussir? – c'est é.!** do you think we'll succeed? – of course (we will)!; *Fam* **c'est pas é.!** *(pas facile)* it's not easy

évider [evide] **VT** *(pierre, bois etc)* to hollow out, to scoop out; *Culin (tomate, pomme etc)* to scoop out

évier [evje] **NM** sink

évincer [evɛ̃se] **VT** **(j'évinçai(s))** *(rival, tête de parti etc)* to oust (**de** from), to supplant; *(locataire)* to evict

---

Il faut noter que le verbe anglais **to evince** est un faux ami. Il signifie **faire preuve de, manifester**.

éviscération [eviserasjɔ̃] **NF** *Chir* evisceration

éviscérer [evisere] **VT** **(j'éviscère, n. éviscérons)** to eviscerate

évitable [evitabl] **ADJ** avoidable

évitage [evitaʒ] **NM** *Naut* **1** *(mouvement) (d'un bateau)* swinging; **bassin d'é.** turning basin **2** *(espace)* room to swing, sea room

évitement [evitmɑ̃] **NM** **1** *(action d'éviter)* avoidance; **faire une manœuvre d'é.** to take evasive action; *Biol* **réaction d'é.** avoiding reaction **2** *Rail* **voie** *ou* **gare d'é.** siding; **ligne d'é.** loop line

éviter [evite] **VT 1** *(ne pas heurter)* to avoid, to miss; *(ne pas subir)* to avoid, to steer clear of; *(ne pas rencontrer) (personne)* to avoid, to keep clear of; *(regard)* to avoid; **é. l'alcool/ le sucre** to avoid *or* keep off alcohol/sugar; **é. un coup** to avoid *or* dodge a blow; **é. la question** to avoid *or* dodge the issue; **é. de faire qch** to avoid doing sth; **j'essaie d'é. qu'il ne le découvre** I'm trying to avoid his discovering it; **é. que le vent n'entre dans la maison** to prevent the wind getting into the house, to keep the wind out of the house; **évite que ça se sache** don't let it get out, prevent it getting out **2** *(épargner)* **é. des ennuis/une corvée à qn** to save *or* spare sb trouble/a chore; **ça m'évitera d'avoir à le faire** it will save me having to do it **VI** *Naut* **é. sur l'ancre** to swing at anchor; **évité au vent** riding the wind **VPR s'éviter 1 s'é. qch** to avoid sth **2** *(se fuir)* to avoid each other

évocable [evɔkabl] **ADJ** *Jur* **cause é.** = case that may be transferred to a higher court

évocateur, -trice [evɔkatœr, -tris] **ADJ** evocative, suggestive (**de** of)

évocation [evɔkasjɔ̃] **NF 1** *(par la magie) (d'un esprit etc)* evocation, calling forth, conjuring up **2** *(d'un souvenir, du passé etc)* evocation, conjuring up, recalling; **à l'é. de son premier amour** when she recalled her first love; *(mentionné par un tiers)* when reference was made to her first love; **le pouvoir d'é. d'un lieu/mot** the evocative power of a place/word

évolué [evɔlɥe] **ADJ** *(race, pays, société)* (highly) developed, advanced; *(personne)* mature, broadminded; *Ordinat (langage)* high-level

évoluer [evɔlɥe] **VI 1** *(se déplacer) (d'un bateau, de troupes etc)* to manœuvre, *Am* to maneuver; *(d'un danseur, d'un cerf-volant, d'un poisson etc)* to move around; *Fig* **é. dans la haute société** to move in high society; **j'ignore dans quel milieu elle évolue maintenant** I don't know what circles she moves in now **2** *(se développer) (d'une théorie, d'une science, d'une ville, d'une entreprise etc)* to evolve, to develop; *(d'une personne, d'une maladie)* to develop **3** *Ordinat* **faire é.** to upgrade

évolutif, -ive [evɔlytif, -iv] **ADJ** evolutionary; *Méd (maladie)* progressive; *Ordinat* up-

gradeable; **méthode évolutive, ski é.** short-ski method; **poste é.** position with promotion prospects

évolution [evɔlysjɔ̃] **NF 1** *(déplacement) (d'un bateau, de troupes etc);* **évolutions** manœuvres, *Am* maneuvers; *(d'un patineur etc)* movements **2** *(développement) (d'une théorie, d'une science, d'un peuple, d'un conflit etc)* evolution, development; *(d'une personne, d'une maladie)* development; *Biol* evolution; **être contre toute é.** to be against any development; **suivre une lente é.** to evolve *or* develop slowly

évolutionnisme [evɔlysjɔnism] **NM** *Biol* evolutionism

évolutionniste [evɔlysjɔnist] *Biol* **ADJ** evolutionist(ic)
N evolutionist

évolutivité [evɔlytivite] **NF** *Ordinat* upgradeability

évoquer [evɔke] **VT 1** *(se remémorer) (souvenir, passé etc)* to recall, to conjure up, to evoke **2** *(faire penser à)* to be reminiscent of; **qu'est-ce que cela vous évoque?** what does that remind you of *or* conjure up for you?; **son nom/ce visage ne m'évoque rien** his name/this face means nothing to me *or* doesn't ring a bell with me **3** *(aborder)* to touch on, to mention; **nous n'avons fait qu'é. le sujet** we've only touched on the subject **4** *(par la magie) (esprit, démon, mort etc)* to evoke, to call forth, to conjure up

ex [eks] **N** *Fam* ex; **un de mes ex** one of my exes

ex- [ɛks] **PRÉF** ex-; **ex-femme/-champion** ex-wife/-champion

ex abrupto [eksabrypto] **ADV** straight off

exacerbation [ɛgzasɛrbasjɔ̃] **NF** exacerbation

exacerber [ɛgzasɛrbe] **VT** *(douleur, irritation etc)* to exacerbate, to aggravate; **susceptibilité exacerbée** exaggerated sensitivity; **nationalisme exacerbé** extreme nationalism
VPR s'exacerber to become acute

exact [ɛgza(kt)] **ADJ 1** *(précis) (quantité, poids, nombre, calcul etc)* exact, precise; *(fidèle) (rapport, description, copie etc)* exact, accurate; *(juste) (solution, mot, réponse etc)* right, correct; **l'heure/la date exacte** the right *or* correct *or* exact time/date; **une montre exacte** a precise *or* accurate watch; **e. à un millimètre près** correct *or* accurate to within a millimetre; **c'est e.** *(vrai)* it's quite true, it's a fact; **il est e. que j'ai dit cela** it's quite true that I said that; **vous vous appelez bien Martin? – e.!** your name is Martin? – correct! **2** *(ponctuel)* punctual, on time; **il est e. à payer son loyer** he is punctual in paying his rent, he pays his rent on time; **je n'ai pu être e. au rendez-vous** I couldn't be on time for the appointment **3** *Litt (strict) (discipline, obéissance etc)* strict, rigorous

exactement [ɛgzaktəmɑ̃] **ADV** *(précisément) (calculer, placer etc)* exactly, precisely; *(fidèlement) (rapporter, reproduire etc)* exactly, accurately; *(avec justesse) (répondre, raisonner etc)* correctly; **il est e. deux heures** it is exactly *or* precisely two o'clock; **c'est très e. ce que je veux dire** that's exactly *or* precisely what I mean; **je sais e. combien** I know exactly *or* precisely how much; **un effet e. contraire** a directly opposite effect

exaction [ɛgzaksjɔ̃] **NF 1** *(d'impôt etc)* exaction; *(vol)* extortion **2 exactions** *(actes cruels)* atrocities

exactitude [ɛgzaktityd] **NF 1** *(précision) (d'une quantité, d'un calcul etc)* exactness, precision; *(fidélité) (d'un rapport, d'une copie etc)* exactness, accuracy; *(justesse) (d'une solution, réponse etc)* correctness; **calculer/**

mesurer avec e. to calculate/measure exactly *or* precisely **2** *(ponctualité)* punctuality; **avec e.** punctually; *Prov* **l'e. est la politesse des rois** punctuality is the politeness of kings

ex æquo [ɛgzeko] **ADV** *Scol, Sport etc* **être (classés) e.** to tie, to be equally placed; **être troisième e.** to tie for third place, to be placed equal third; **être e. avec qn** to tie with sb, to be placed equal with sb
N INV il y avait trois e. pour la première place three people tied for first place; **départager les e.** to break the tie

exagération [ɛgzaʒerasjɔ̃] **NF** exaggeration; **sans e.** *(faire un récit)* without exaggerating; *(boire, aimer le chocolat etc)* in moderation; **on peut dire sans e. que ...** it is no exaggeration to say *or* one can say without exaggeration that ...; **se montrer ferme sans e.** to be firm without overdoing it *or* going to extremes

exagéré [ɛgzaʒere] **ADJ** *(commentaire, récit, geste)* exaggerated; *(prix, salaire)* exorbitant, excessive; *(pessimisme, nationalisme)* excessive; **confiance exagérée** overconfidence; **il n'est pas e. de dire que ...** it is no exaggeration to say that ...; **dire qu'il est bête, c'est un peu e.** it's a bit much *or* a bit excessive to say that he's stupid

exagérément [ɛgzaʒeremɑ̃] **ADV** excessively; **il lui fait e. confiance** he trusts him/her far too much; **elle a e. tardé avant de répondre** she delayed for far too long before replying

exagérer [ɛgzaʒere] **VT** *(faits, vérité, danger, qualités de qn etc)* to exaggerate, to overstate; *(forme, proportions etc)* to exaggerate; **il ne faut rien e., n'exagérons rien** things should be kept in proportion, let's not exaggerate
VI *(en parlant)* to exaggerate; *(abuser)* to go too far, to overstep the mark; **il faut toujours que tu exagères!** you always exaggerate!; **il ne faut pas e.!** that's a bit excessive *or* much!; *Fam* **tu exagères e., mon vieux** don't exaggerate!; **sans e., il y en avait bien soixante** without exaggeration there were sixty of them
VPR s'exagérer s'e. qch to overestimate sth

exaltant [ɛgzaltɑ̃] **ADJ** *(discours, musique, expérience etc)* exciting

exaltation [ɛgzaltasjɔ̃] **NF 1** *(excitation)* (great) excitement; *Méd* overexcitement; **e. mystique** exaltation; **il a préparé son départ dans l'e.** he got ready to leave in (a state of) great excitement **2** *(action de louer) (de la vertu, d'une personne etc)* exalting, extolling **3** *Rel* **E. de la Sainte Croix** Exaltation of the Cross

exalté, -ée [ɛgzalte] **ADJ** *Péj (discours, sentiment)* wild, impassioned; *(imagination, esprit)* wild; *(personne)* fanatical, hot-headed
N *Péj* fanatic, hothead

exalter [ɛgzalte] **VT 1** *(exciter) (imagination, esprit)* to stir, to fire; *(ressentiment, orgueil etc)* to intensify; **ses voyages/lectures/expériences l'ont exalté** his travels/reading/experiences fired his imagination **2** *(louer) (personne, les qualités de qn)* to exalt, to extol, to glorify
VPR s'exalter to get excited

exam [ɛgzam] **NM** *Fam* exam

examen [ɛgzamɛ̃] **NM 1** *(observation, analyse) (d'un document, d'un spécimen, de faits etc)* examination; *(des comptes)* inspection; **après un e. attentif de la situation/du problème** after a careful examination of the situation/problem; **cette assertion ne supporte pas l'e.** this assertion will not bear examination; **mettre une question à l'e.** to examine *or* look into *or* go into a matter;

après e., e. fait (up)on examination 2 *Méd* e. (médical) (medical) examination, medical, checkup; e. de la vue sight *or* eye test; e. médical complet complete checkup 3 *Scol, Univ etc* exam, examination; passer un e. to sit *or* take an exam; faire passer un e. à qn to examine sb; être reçu/refusé à un e. to pass/fail an exam; jury d'e. examining body, examiners

▸▸e. blanc mock exam; e. de conscience soul-searching; *Jur* e. contradictoire examination made in the presence of both parties to a contract; e. d'entrée entrance exam; e. financier financial review; e. partiel (d'année) half-year exam; (de semestre, trimestre) half-term exam; e. de passage end-of-year exam, *Am* final exam; e. prénuptial premarital checkup

examinateur, -trice [ɛgzaminatœr, -tris] N examiner

examiner [ɛgzamine] VT 1 (étudier, analyser) (document, spécimen, faits etc) to examine; (comptes) to inspect, to go through; (machinerie) to check; e. une question to examine *or* look into *or* go into a matter; e. une demande to consider a request; e. les lieux to inspect the premises
2 (regarder, observer) e. l'horizon to scan *or* survey the horizon; *Fig* elle m'a examiné de la tête aux pieds she eyed me from head to toe *or* up and down
3 *Méd* (patient) to examine; se faire e. par un médecin to have oneself *or* be examined by a doctor
4 *Scol, Univ etc* *Arch* to examine; e. qn en algèbre to examine sb in algebra
VPR s'examiner 1 (dans une glace etc) to examine oneself 2 (de plusieurs personnes) (s'observer) to examine each other

exanthème [ɛgzɑ̃tɛm] NM *Méd* exanthema

exaspérant [ɛgzasperɑ̃] ADJ exasperating, irritating, aggravating

exaspération [ɛgzasperasjɔ̃] NF 1 (énervement) exasperation, irritation, aggravation 2 *Vieilli* (d'une douleur, d'un sentiment) aggravation

exaspérer [ɛgzaspere] (j'exaspère; j'exaspérerai) VT 1 (énerver) (personne) to exasperate, to irritate, to aggravate 2 (douleur, sentiment) to aggravate
VPR s'exaspérer (d'une douleur, d'un sentiment) to become acute

exaucement [ɛgzosmɑ̃] NM (d'un souhait, désir) granting, fulfilment

exaucer [ɛgzose] VT (j'exauçai(s), n. exauçons) 1 (souhait, désir) to grant, to fulfil, *Am* to fulfill; exauce ma prière! hear my prayer! 2 e. qn to grant sb's wish, to hear *or* answer sb's prayer; te voilà exaucé your prayer is answered

ex cathedra [ɛkskatedra] ADV *Rel, Fig* ex cathedra

excavateur, -trice [ɛkskavatœr, -tris] N *Constr* excavator, (mechanical) digger

excavation [ɛkskavasjɔ̃] NF 1 (trou) excavation; (creusée par une bombe) crater 2 (action) excavation, excavating

excaver [ɛkskave] VT to excavate

excédant [ɛksedɑ̃] ADJ exasperating, tiresome

excédent [ɛksedɑ̃] NM (de nourriture, de sucre dans le sang etc) surplus, excess; (d'un budget, d'une balance) surplus; somme en e. sum in excess; dégager un e. to show a surplus; budget en e. surplus budget; e. budgétaire budget(ary) surplus; vous garderez l'e. you will keep what is left over; e. de poids excess weight; e. de dépenses deficit; e. de bagages excess luggage *or* baggage; e. de blé wheat surplus; la balance commerciale est en e. the trade balance shows a surplus,

there is a trade surplus; *Compta* e. de caisse cash overs; e. commercial trade surplus; e. d'exploitation operating profit; excédents et déficits overs and shorts

excédentaire [ɛksedɑ̃tɛr] ADJ (production) excess, surplus; (poids) excess; (budget) surplus; balance commerciale e. trade surplus

excéder [ɛksede] VT (j'excède, n. excédons; j'excéderai) 1 (dépasser) (quantité, somme, période), *Fig* (limite etc) to exceed; e. les moyens de qn to be beyond sb's means; nos pertes excèdent nos bénéfices our losses are greater than our profits 2 (outrepasser) (forces, compétences) to be beyond; e. ses pouvoirs to exceed *or* overstep one's powers 3 (irriter) to exasperate; j'étais excédé I was exasperated, I had lost all patience 4 *Vieilli* (épuiser) to tire *or* wear out; excédé de fatigue worn out, tired out

excellemment [ɛksɛlamɑ̃] ADV *Litt* excellently

excellence [ɛksɛlɑ̃s] NF 1 excellence; *Scol* prix d'e. class prize (for all-round standard); c'est le chercheur/l'homme à femmes par e. he's the researcher/ladies' man par excellence; c'est un têtu/paresseux par e. he's stubbornness/laziness itself 2 (titre) Son/Votre E. His/Her/Your Excellency

excellent [ɛksɛlɑ̃] ADJ excellent, first-rate (en at, in); en excellente santé in the best of health, in excellent health

exceller [ɛksele] VI to excel (en at, in; à faire qch in doing sth)

excentré [ɛksɑ̃tre] ADJ 1 (quartier, maison etc) far from the centre, remote 2 *Tech* off centre

excentricité [ɛksɑ̃trisite] NF 1 (caractère, acte bizarre) eccentricity 2 (d'un quartier, d'une maison etc) remoteness 3 *Math etc* (d'un cercle, d'une orbite etc) eccentricity

excentrique [ɛksɑ̃trik] ADJ 1 (bizarre) (personne, comportement, idée etc) eccentric, odd 2 (loin du centre) (faubourg, quartier etc) remote, far from the centre 3 *Math etc* (cercle, orbite etc) eccentric
N (personne) eccentric
NM (mécanisme) eccentric

excentriquement [ɛksɑ̃trikmɑ̃] ADV centrically

excepté [ɛksɛpte] PRÉP except, apart from, with the exception of; tous les jours e. quand il pleut every day except *or* apart from *or* with the exception of when it rains; la maison nous convient e. qu'il n'y a pas de garage the house suits us except (for the fact) that there's no garage
ADJ les femmes exceptées except for *or* apart from the women; j'aime tous leurs meubles, le bahut e. I like all their furniture except for *or* apart from the sideboard

excepter [ɛksɛpte] VT to exclude, to except (de from), to make an exception of; si l'on excepte une seule rue with the exception of *or* apart from one street; sans e. les enfants without excluding the children, including the children

exception [ɛksɛpsjɔ̃] NF 1 exception (à to); faire une e. to make an exception (pour for); faire une e. à une règle to make an exception to a rule; faire e. à une règle to be an exception to a rule; c'est l'e. qui confirme la règle it's the exception that proves the rule; à quelques exceptions près with a few exceptions; à quelques rares exceptions près with very few exceptions; à une e. près with one exception; sans e. without exception; tous, à l'e. du docteur *ou* e. faite du docteur all, except (for) *or* with the exception of the doctor; c'est un être d'e. he's an exceptional person; l'e. culturelle the cultural exception 2 *Jur* objection, plea (by the defence)

Exception française

The term "l'exception française" is used to describe France's individual status in terms of economic development. It is characterized by a very large public sector, by a larger degree of state intervention in the economy than in Britain or the US and by the persistence of a relatively generous welfare State coupled with greater investment in public services, all of which goes against the principles of market-driven economics. France is also keen to safeguard its film industry and has been campaigning in favour of "l'exception culturelle" – the notion that cultural products should not be treated in the same way as commercial products and that consequently governments should be authorized to subsidize their film industries.

exceptionnel, -elle [ɛksɛpsjɔnɛl] ADJ 1 (qui fait exception) (circonstances, situation etc) exceptional; congé e. special leave 2 (remarquable) exceptional, outstanding; sa femme/sa voiture/son livre n'a rien d'e. his wife/his car/his book is nothing special

exceptionnellement [ɛksɛpsjɔnɛlmɑ̃] ADV exceptionally; e. tu peux partir maintenant just this once you can leave now; nous ouvrirons e. le soir de Noël we will open specially on Christmas Eve

excès [ɛksɛ] NM 1 (excédent, démesure) excess; e. de l'offre sur la demande excess of supply over demand; pécher par e. de zèle, faire de l'e. de zèle to be overzealous; l'e. de ses prétentions his/her excessive claims, the excessive nature of his/her claims; c'est un peu un e. de précautions these are rather excessive precautions; avec e. (boire, fumer, travailler etc) excessively, to excess; manger avec e. to overeat, to eat excessively *or* to excess; dépenser avec e. to overspend; réagir avec e. to overreact (à qch to sth); sans e. (manger, utiliser etc) in moderation; (jusqu')à l'e. to excess, excessively; se dépenser à l'e. to overexert oneself; gentil/scrupuleux à l'e. kind/scrupulous to a fault, overkind/overscrupulous; tomber dans l'e. to overdo it, *Fam* to go over the top; tomber dans l'e. inverse to go to the other extreme
2 (abus) excess; commettre *ou* se laisser aller à des e. to overdo things, to go too far; des e. (de table) overeating, overindulgence; faire des e. (de table) to overeat, to overindulge; évitez tout e. avoid overdoing things; (alimentaire) avoid overeating
▸▸des e. de conduite loose living; des e. de langage immoderate language; *Jur* e. de pouvoir action ultra vires; *Aut* e. de vitesse speeding, exceeding the speed limit; faire un e. de vitesse to speed, to exceed the speed limit

excessif, -ive [ɛksɛsif, -iv] ADJ (longueur, chaleur, quantité etc) excessive; (opinion, idée) extreme; (optimisme, idéalisme) excessive, unwarranted; (prix) exorbitant, excessive; (langage) immoderate; (orgueil) inordinate; des mois de travail e. l'a rendu malade he has become ill through months of overwork; il est e. he goes to extremes; il fait un vent e. pour sortir le bébé it's far too windy to take the baby out

excessivement [ɛksɛsivmɑ̃] ADV 1 (trop) excessively; manger e. to overeat, to eat excessively *or* to excess; il avait bu e. he had been drinking to excess 2 (extrêmement) extremely

exciper [ɛksipe] VI *Jur* to put in a plea; *Litt* e. de son ignorance/sa bonne foi to plead ignorance/one's good faith

excipient [ɛksipjã] NM *Pharm* excipient

exciser [ɛksize] VT *Chir* to excise, to cut out

exciseur, -euse [ɛksizœr, -øz] N *Chir* excisor, excisionist

excision [ɛksizjɔ̃] NF *Chir* excision

excitabilité [ɛksitabilite] NF excitability

excitable [ɛksitabl] ADJ excitable

excitant [ɛksitã] ADJ *(nouvelles, débat, film, perspective, sexuelles etc)* exciting; *(effet)* stimulating
▸ NM stimulant

excitation [ɛksitasjɔ̃] NF **1** *(action)* *(à la violence, au racisme etc)* incitement (**à** to); **e. à la révolte** incitement to rebellion **2** *(résultat)* excitement; **e. (sexuelle)** *(sexual)* arousal *or* excitement; **dans l'e. du moment** in the excitement of the moment **3** *Élec, Physiol* excitation
▸▸ *Jur* **e. des mineurs à la débauche** incitement of minors to commit immoral acts

excité, -ée [ɛksite] ADJ **1** *(énervé)* worked-up; *(plein d'anticipation)* excited **2** *(sexuellement)* excited
▸ N *(personne)* hothead

exciter [ɛksite] VT **1** *(attiser)* *(curiosité, jalousie etc)* to excite, to arouse; *(pitié)* to arouse; *(appétit)* to whet; *(rire)* to provoke; **e. l'envie de tout le monde** to make everybody envious; **e. la pitié de qn** to move sb to pity, to arouse sb's pity
2 *(encourager)* to urge on; **e. qn à la révolte** *ou* **à se révolter** to incite sb to revolt; **e. qn contre qn** to set sb against sb; **e. la meute contre le gibier** to urge on the pack to hunt their quarry
3 *(énerver)* *(intellectuellement)* to excite, to thrill; *(physiquement)* to excite; *(sexuellement)* to arouse, to excite; **excité à l'idée de partir en vacances** excited *or* thrilled at the idea of going on holiday; **trop e. qn** to overexcite sb; **le café/le tabac excite** coffee/tobacco acts as a stimulant
4 *Fam (irriter)* to irritate, to annoy
5 *Physiol (nerf, muscle)* to excite, to stimulate; *Élec (dynamo)* to excite
▸ VPR **s'exciter** *Fam* to get excited, to get worked up; *(sexuellement)* to get aroused *or* excited; **t'excite pas, je vais te le rendre, ton fric!** calm down *or* don't get worked up, I'll give you your money back!

exclamatif, -ive [ɛksklamatif, -iv] ADJ exclamatory; *Gram* **proposition exclamative** exclamation, interjection

exclamation [ɛksklamasjɔ̃] NF exclamation; **pousser des exclamations** to exclaim

exclamer (s') [sɛksklame] VPR *(de joie, de surprise, d'admiration)* to exclaim, to shout out; *(de douleur, colère)* to cry out, to shout out *(de* in, with); **'toi ici!' s'exclama-t-il** 'you here!' he exclaimed; **s'e. sur la montée du chômage/de la violence** to make a lot of noise about rising unemployment/violence

exclu, -ue [ɛkskly] ADJ **1** *(non compris)* **le prix des travaux, TVA exclue** the cost of the work, excluding VAT; **le mois d'août jusqu'au 31 e.** the month of August excluding the 31st **2** *(impensable)* out of the question, impossible; **il est e. que** + *sub* it's out of the question *or* impossible that; **il est e. qu'il vienne avec nous** it's out of the question for him to come with us, *Fam* there's no way he's coming with us; **il n'est pas e. que ...** it's not out of the question that ...
▸ N outcast; **les exclus de la société** social outcasts, the outcasts of society; **les exclus du progrès** those whom progress has ignored *or* passed by

exclure [ɛksklyr] *(prp* excluant; *pp* exclu; *pr ind* j'exclus, n. excluons; *impf* j'excluais; *p hist* j'exclus; *fu* j'exclurai) VT **1** *(expulser)* *(d'un parti, d'une école etc)* to expel; *(d'une fonc-*

tion publique) to remove; *(d'une salle, réunion)* to eject (**de** from)
2 *(ne pas permettre ou admettre)* to exclude (**de** from); **e. le pain de son régime** to exclude *or* cut out bread from one's diet; **e. l'alcool de sa table** not to allow alcohol in the house; **elle a exclu le rouge dans ses vêtements** she doesn't wear anything with red in it; **e. la TVA de la somme** to exclude the VAT from *or* leave the VAT out of the sum; **l'alcool est exclu de la vente le dimanche** alcohol is not allowed to be sold on Sundays
3 *(ne pas considérer)* to rule out; **e. la possibilité d'un accord** to rule out the possibility of an agreement; **cette hypothèse est à e.** this possibility is out of the question; **cela n'exclut pas que vous puissiez enseigner** that doesn't rule out the possibility of your teaching
▸ VPR **s'exclure** *(de théories etc)* to be mutually exclusive

exclusif, -ive [ɛksklyzif, -iv] ADJ **1** *(non partagé)* *(occupation, intérêt etc)* exclusive; *(but, mission)* sole; *Com (droit, agent etc)* exclusive, sole; *(article, modèle, reportage, interview etc)* exclusive; **une interview exclusive** an exclusive (interview); **il a un intérêt e. pour les papillons** he is solely interested in butterflies; **pendant les vacances, son occupation exclusive a été de courir** during the holidays, running was his sole activity **2** *(sélectif)* *(dans ses opinions)* self-opinionated; *(dans ses goûts)* selective; **elle est très exclusive dans ses amitiés** she is very selective in her choice of friends; **il est e. en amour** he's a one-woman man
▸ NF **exclusive** *(mesure d'exclusion)* bar; **prononcer l'exclusive contre, frapper d'exclusive** to bar, to debar; **sans exclusive** without exception

exclusion [ɛksklyzjɔ̃] NF **1** *(expulsion)* *(d'un parti, d'une école etc)* expulsion; *(d'une fonction publique)* removal; *(d'une salle, réunion)* ejection (**de** from); **e. temporaire** suspension **2 e. (sociale)** social exclusion **3 à l'e. de** to the exclusion of; *(à l'exception de)* with the exception of

exclusivement [ɛksklyzivmã] ADV exclusively, solely; **parking e. réservé aux clients de l'hôtel** customer parking only; **il aime e. les opéras de Verdi** he likes Verdi's operas to the exclusion of all others; **de lundi jusqu'à vendredi e.** from Monday to Friday exclusive

exclusivisme [ɛksklyzivism] NM exclusivism

exclusiviste [ɛksklyzivist] N exclusivist

exclusivité [ɛksklyzivite] NF **1** *Com (droit)* sole *or* exclusive rights (**de** in); *TV, Cin (de film)* first run; **en e.** exclusively; **avoir un contrat d'e.** to have an exclusive contract *(chez* with); **ce modèle se trouve en e. chez ...** this model is exclusive to *or* can only be found at ...; **nous avons l'e. de la vente de ce produit** we have the (sole) rights for this product; **c'est notre journal qui a eu l'e. de son interview** our paper had an exclusive with him; **en e. dans le Figaro** a Figaro exclusive; **film en e.** exclusive film; **film en première** movie *or Br* film receiving its first showing; *Fig* **ne pas avoir l'e. de l'intelligence/de la beauté** not to have a monopoly on intelligence/beauty **2** *Com (article)* exclusive article; *(film)* movie *or Br* film on general release; *Journ (article)* exclusive, scoop; **c'est une e. Mercedes** it's exclusive to Mercedes **3** *(des sentiments)* selectiveness

excommunication [ɛkskɔmynikasjɔ̃] NF excommunication

excommunier [ɛkskɔmynje] VT *(impf, pr sub* n. **excommuniions**) to excommunicate

excoriation [ɛkskɔrjasjɔ̃] NF *(éraflure)* graze, *Spéc* excoriation

excorier [ɛkskɔrje] VT *(peau)* to graze, *Spéc* to excoriate

ex-coupon [ɛkskupɔ̃] ADV *Bourse* ex coupon

excrément [ɛkskremã] NM **excrément(s)** excrement

excrémentiel, -elle [ɛkskremãsjɛl] ADJ excremental

excréter [ɛkskrete] VT *(j'excrète; j'excréterai)* to excrete

excréteur, -trice [ɛkskretœr, -tris] ADJ excretory

excrétion [ɛkskresjɔ̃] NF **1** *(action)* excretion, excreting **2** *(déchet)* **excrétions** excreta

excrétoire [ɛkskretwar] ADJ excretory

excroissance [ɛkskrwasãs] NF excrescence

excursion [ɛkskyrsjɔ̃] NF *(en car, voiture etc)* excursion, trip; *(d'une journée)* day trip, day tour; *(de plusieurs jours)* tour; *(lors d'une escale)* shore excursion, trip ashore; *(à pied)* hike, long walk; **faire une e., partir en e.** to go on an excursion *or* a trip *or* a tour/a hike or a walk; **e. en car** coach trip

excursionner [ɛkskyrsjɔne] VI *Vieilli (en car, voiture etc)* to go on excursions *or* trips; *(pendant plusieurs jours)* to go touring; *(à pied)* to go hiking *or* walking

excursionniste [ɛkskyrsjɔnist] N *(en car, voiture etc)* tourist, excursionist, *Br* tripper; *(à pied)* hiker, walker

excusable [ɛkskyzabl] ADJ excusable, forgivable; **ce n'est absolument pas e.** it's absolutely inexcusable *or* unforgivable

excuse [ɛkskyz] NF **1** *(raison)* excuse; **bonne e.** a good excuse; **ce n'est pas une e.!** that's no excuse!; **trouver une e. à qch/pour faire qch** to find an excuse for sth/for doing sth; **je prends mon travail comme e. pour ne pas partir** I'm making my work the excuse for not going; **tu lui trouves toujours des excuses** you're always finding excuses for him; **tu n'as aucune e. de ne pas avoir prévenu** you have no excuse for not letting us know; **c'est sans e.** it's inexcusable *or* unforgivable
2 **excuses** *(regrets)* apology; **faire** *ou* **présenter ses excuses à qn** to make one's apologies *or* to apologize to sb; **je vous fais mes plus plates excuses** *ou* **mes excuses les plus plates** you have my humble apologies; **il exige des excuses** he is demanding an apology; **je vous dois des excuses** I owe you an apology; **lettre d'excuses** letter of apology
3 *Fam* **faites e.!** sorry!
4 *(au tarot)* excuse

excuser [ɛkskyze] VT **1** *(justifier)* *(personne, action)* to excuse, to make excuses for, to apologize for; **e. qn auprès de qn** to apologize for sb to sb; **l'ignorance n'excuse rien** ignorance is no excuse
2 *(pardonner)* *(personne, erreur, colère etc)* to excuse; **excusez-moi, veuillez m'e.** excuse me, pardon me, I'm sorry; **excuse-moi de te déranger** I'm sorry to disturb you, excuse me for disturbing you; **excuse-moi de ne pas t'avoir téléphoné** I'm sorry I didn't phone you; **excusez-moi de vous le faire remarquer** excuse me for saying so, I hope you don't mind my mentioning it; *Fml* **je vous prie de m'e.** I do beg your pardon; **excusez ma curiosité mais ...** excuse *or* forgive my curiosity but ...; **tu es tout excusé** there's no need to apologize, that's quite all right; *Hum* **excusez du peu!** would you believe!, if you please!
3 *(dispenser)* to excuse; **se faire e.** to ask to be excused; **peux-tu m'e. auprès de lui?** can you ask him to excuse me?; **liste des présents, absents, excusés** list of those present, those absent and those from whom apologies have been received; **e. un juré** to excuse a juror (from attendance)

VPR s'excuser to apologize; *Iron* surtout ne t'excuse pas! an apology wouldn't go amiss!; s'e. auprès de qn to apologize to sb; s'e. de qch/de faire qch to apologize for sth/doing sth; *Fam* je m'excuse! sorry!, excuse me!; *Prov* qui s'excuse s'accuse he who excuses himself accuses himself

ex-dividende [ɛksdividɑ̃d] **ADV** *Fin* ex dividend

ex-droit [ɛksdrwa] **ADV** *Bourse* ex rights

exécrable [ɛgzekrabl] **ADJ** atrocious, abominable, execrable

exécrablement [ɛgzekrabləmɑ̃] **ADV** atrociously, abominably, execrably

exécration [ɛgzekrasjɔ̃] **NF** *Litt* (*du crime etc*) execration, detestation; avoir qn/qch en e. to loathe sb/sth

exécrer [ɛgzekre] **VT** (*j'exècre; j'exécrerai*) *Litt* to execrate, to loathe, to detest

exécutable [ɛgzekytabl] **ADJ** feasible; *Ordinat* (*programme*) executable

exécutant, -ante [ɛgzekytɑ̃, -ɑ̃t] **N** *Mus* performer, executant; il n'a été qu'un simple e. he was just doing what he was told *or* carrying out orders

exécuter [ɛgzekyte] **VT 1** (*effectuer*) (*travail, plan*) to execute, to carry out; (*ordres, décision*) to carry out, to act upon; (*promesse*) to carry out, to fulfil; (*danse, morceau de musique, contrat*) to perform, to execute **2** (*confectionner*) (*peinture, décor etc*) to produce, to execute **3** *Ordinat* (*programme*) to execute, to run; (*commande*) to execute, to carry out **4** *Jur* (*débiteur*) to distrain upon; (*décret, loi etc*) to enforce, to give effect to **5** (*mettre à mort*) (*criminel etc*) to execute, to put to death; *Sport Fam* (*battre*) (*adversaire*) to slaughter; *Fam* (*critiquer*) (*travail, auteur etc*) to savage **6** *Bourse* (*spéculateur*) to hammer; (*client*) to sell out against
VPR s'exécuter to comply; il faudra bien vous e. you'll have to bring yourself to do it

exécuteur, -trice [ɛgzekytœr, -tris] **N 1** *Jur* e. testamentaire executor; exécutrice testamentaire executrix **2** *Arch* (*d'un plan, d'une tâche*) executant
NM (*bourreau*) e. (des hautes œuvres) executioner

exécutif, -ive [ɛgzekytif, -iv] *Pol* **ADJ** (*pouvoir etc*) executive
NM l'e. the executive

exécution [ɛgzekysjɔ̃] **NF 1** (*d'un plan, travail*) execution, carrying out; (*d'ordres, d'une décision*) carrying out; (*d'une promesse*) fulfilment; (*d'une danse, d'un morceau de musique*) performance, execution; (*d'une peinture, d'un roman etc*) execution; *Mil, Hum* e.! jump to it! at the double!; droit d'e. performing rights; difficultés d'e. d'un morceau de musique difficulties in the execution of a piece of music; mettre un projet à e. to put a plan into execution *or* operation, to carry out a plan; travaux en voie d'e. work in progress **2** *Ordinat* running, execution **3** *Jur* (*d'un débiteur*) distraint (de upon); (*d'une loi, d'un décret etc*) enforcement **4** (*mise à mort*) e. (capitale) execution; ordre d'e. death warrant; *Mil* peloton d'e. firing squad *or* party **5** *Bourse* e. au prix du marché execution at market

exécutoire [ɛgzekytwar] **ADJ** *Jur* **1** jugement (de force) e. enforceable decision (*of the court*) **2** (*formule*) executory

exégèse [ɛgzeʒez] **NF** exegesis

exégète [ɛgzeʒet] **N** exegete

exemplaire¹ [ɛgzɑ̃plɛr] **ADJ 1** (*comportement, courage*) exemplary **2** c'était une puni-

tion e. the punishment was intended as an example

exemplaire² **NM 1** (*livre, gravure etc*) copy; en deux/trois exemplaires in duplicate/triplicate; photocopier un texte en 20 exemplaires to make 20 photocopies of a text; le livre a été tiré à 10 000 exemplaires 10,000 copies of the book were published; le journal tire à 150 000 exemplaires the newspaper has a circulation of 150,000; e. gratuit presentation copy; e. de lancement advance copy; exemplaires de passe overs; e. de service de presse press copy **2** (*spécimen*) (*de plante, d'animal etc*) example

exemplairement [ɛgzɑ̃plɛrmɑ̃] **ADV** exemplarily; elle a vécu e. she led an exemplary life; il a été puni e. he was punished as an example to others

exemple [ɛgzɑ̃pl] **NM 1** (*modèle*) example, model (pour to); donner l'e. to set an example (à to); suivre l'e. de qn, prendre e. sur qn to follow sb's example; suivre le mauvais e. de qn to follow sb's bad example; prendre qn pour *ou* comme e. to take sb as one's model, to model oneself on sb; citer qn/qch en e. to quote sb/sth as an example; prêcher d'e. to practise what one preaches; faire un e. (*en punissant qn*) to set an example; servir d'e. à qn (*d'une réussite etc*) to be an example to sb; (*d'une punition etc*) to be a lesson *or* a warning to sb; infliger une punition à qn pour l'e. to punish sb as an example *or* a warning to others **2** (*cas*) example, instance; (*mot, phrase*) example; il est l'e. même du type qui ne sait pas ce qu'il veut he's the perfect example of someone who doesn't know what he wants; sans e. without parallel, unparalleled; être d'une gentillesse/d'un égoïsme sans e. to be of unparalleled kindness/egoism; j'en connais plein: e., ma mère I know lots: my mother, for example *or* for instance **3** par e. for example, for instance; un de ces jours, par e. dimanche one of these days, say *or* for example *or* for instance on Sunday; *Fam* par e.! (*étonnement*) well really!; *Fam* ah ça par e.! (*stupeur*) oh no!; ah non, par e.! I should think not!

exemplification [ɛgzɑ̃plifikasjɔ̃] **NF** exemplification

exemplifier [ɛgzɑ̃plifje] **VT** to exemplify

exempt, -te [ɛgzɑ̃, -ɑ̃t] **ADJ** e. de (*service militaire etc*) exempt from; (*anxiété, danger, maladie etc*) free from; e. de soucis free from care, carefree; e. de droits (de douane) free of duty, duty-free, non-dutiable; e. d'impôts tax exempt, exempt from tax; e. de TVA zero-rated; e. de port carriage free; elle a eu une vie dont tout souci était e. she has had a life free from all care; sa remarque n'était pas exempte d'une certaine amertume his remark was not without a trace of bitterness
N (*personne*) exempt (de from)

exempter [ɛgzɑ̃te] **VT** (*d'impôt, de service militaire etc*) to exempt (de from); (*d'anxiété, de risques etc*) to safeguard (de against); e. qn de faire qch to exempt *or* excuse sb from doing sth
VPR s'exempter s'e. de qch/de faire qch to get out of sth/doing sth

exemption [ɛgzɑ̃psjɔ̃] **NF** exemption (de from); liste d'exemptions (*de la douane*) free list; e. d'impôts tax exemption

exerçable [ɛgzɛrsabl] **ADJ** *Bourse* exerciseable

exercé [ɛgzɛrse] **ADJ** (*œil, oreille*) trained; (*main*) practised; avoir l'œil/l'oreille exercé(e) pour *ou* à faire qch to have a trained eye/ear for doing sth

exercer [ɛgzɛrse] (*j'exerçai(s)*) **VT 1** (*former*) (*son corps, esprit*) to exercise; (*mémoire*) to train; *Mil* (*soldats*) to drill; e. qn à qch/à faire

qch to train sb in sth/to do sth; e. son esprit à l'art de la rhétorique to train one's mind in the art of rhetoric **2** (*user de*) (*autorité, talent etc*) to exercise; e. son influence sur qn to exert *or* exercise one's influence on sb, to bring one's influence to bear on sb; e. une pression sur qch/qn to exert pressure on sth/sb; e. ses droits to exercise one's rights; e. un contrôle sur to exercise control over **3** (*profession*) to practise; e. des fonctions to carry out duties; j'exerce le métier de journaliste I'm a journalist by profession **4** *Bourse* (*option*) to exercise; e. par anticipation to exercise in advance
VI (*d'un médecin, juriste etc*) to practise, to be in practice
VPR s'exercer **1** (*d'un chanteur, sportif etc*) to practise; s'e. à qch/à faire qch to practise sth/doing sth; s'e. au piano to practise the piano **2** (*se manifester*) (*autorité, pouvoir*) to make itself felt; sa mauvaise foi s'exerce aussi contre ses proches his/her close relations also feel the effects of his/her dishonesty

exercice [ɛgzɛrsis] **NM 1** (*physique*) exercise; faire des exercices to do (some) exercises; prendre *ou* faire de l'e. to (take) exercise; manquer d'e. to lack exercise; e. physique physical exercise **2** *Mil* drill(ing); être à l'e. to be on parade; faire l'e. to drill **3** *Sport, Mus, Scol etc* (*mouvement, tâche*) exercise; exercices de grammaire grammar exercises; faire ses exercices to do one's exercises; faire des exercices au piano to do (some) piano exercises; e. d'évacuation en cas d'incendie fire drill **4** (*du pouvoir, d'un droit*) exercise; (*d'une profession*) practice; dans l'e. de ses fonctions in the exercise *or* discharge of one's duties; être en e. (*d'un avocat etc*) to be in practice, to be practising; avocat en e. practising lawyer; le président en e. the president in office; être condamné pour e. illégal de la médecine to be sentenced for the illegal practice of medicine *or* for practising medicine illegally **5** *Rel* l'e. du culte public worship **6** (*en comptabilité*) financial year, *Am* fiscal year; bilan en fin d'e. end-of-year balance sheet; e. bénéficiaire profitable year
▸▸ *Compta* e. budgétaire financial *or Am* fiscal year; e. comptable financial *or* accounting *or Am* fiscal year; e. en cours current financial year, *Am* current fiscal year; e. écoulé last financial *or Am* fiscal year; e. financier financial *or Am* fiscal year; e. fiscal tax year

exerciseur [ɛgzɛrsizœr] **NM** (*appareil de gymnastique*) exerciser; (*pour poitrine*) chest expander

exergue [ɛgzɛrg] **NM** (*d'une médaille*) inscription, *Spéc* exergue; (*d'une illustration*) inscription; (*d'un texte*) epigraph; *Fig* mettre une idée en e. to highlight an idea, to point up an idea

exfoliant [ɛksfɔljɑ̃] **ADJ** exfoliating
NM face/body scrub, *Spéc* exfoliant

exfoliation [ɛksfɔljasjɔ̃] **NF** exfoliation

exfolier (s') [sɛksfɔlje] **VPR** to exfoliate, to scale off

exhalaison [ɛgzalɛzɔ̃] **NF** (*odeur, vapeur*) exhalation

exhalation [ɛgzalasjɔ̃] **NF** (*action*) exhalation, exhaling

exhaler [ɛgzale] **VT** (*odeur, vapeur etc*) to give off; (*soupir*) to breathe; *Fig* (*joie, colère etc*) to give vent to, to vent; *Fig* cette maison exhale la tristesse sadness pervades this house
VPR s'exhaler (*d'une odeur, de la vapeur etc*) to be given off

exhaussement [εgzosmɑ̃] NM *(d'un mur, édifice etc)* increase in the height

exhausser [εgzose] VT *(mur, édifice etc)* to heighten, to increase the height of; **e. une maison d'un étage** to add a storey to a house

exhaustif, -ive [εgzostif, -iv] ADJ exhaustive

exhaustivement [εgzostivmɑ̃] ADV exhaustively

exhaustivité [εgzostivite] NF exhaustiveness

exhiber [εgzibe] VT **1** *(documents etc)* to produce; *(passeport, carte d'identité etc)* to present, to show **2** *(animaux)* to exhibit, to show **3** *Péj (ses connaissances, richesses, vêtements)* to show off, to flaunt; *(photos etc)* to show off; **e. ses muscles** to show off or display one's muscles
▸ **VPR s'exhiber** to flaunt oneself

exhibition [εgzibisjɔ̃] NF **1** *Jur (de documents)* production **2** *(présentation) (d'animaux)* show **3** *Péj (étalage) (de connaissances, richesses)* flaunting, showing off; *(de muscles)* display

Il faut noter que le nom anglais **exhibition** est un faux ami. Il signifie le plus souvent **exposition**.

exhibitionnisme [εgzibisjɔnism] NM exhibitionism

exhibitionniste [εgzibisjɔnist] N exhibitionist

exhibo [εgzibo] N *Fam (abrév* **exhibitionniste***)* exhibitionist

exhortation [εgzɔrtasjɔ̃] NF exhortation (**à qch** to sth; **à faire qch** to do sth)

exhorter [εgzɔrte] VT to exhort (**à qch** to sth; **à faire qch** to do sth), to urge (**à faire qch** to do sth)

exhumation [εgzymasjɔ̃] NF *(d'un corps)* exhumation; *(d'un trésor, des vestiges d'une ville etc)* digging up, excavation; *Fig (de vieux documents etc)* unearthing; *(de vieilles rancunes, souvenirs etc)* digging up; *(d'une ancienne loi, coutume etc)* exhumation

exhumer [εgzyme] VT *(corps)* to exhume; *(trésor, vestiges d'une ville etc)* to dig up, to excavate; *Fig (vieux documents etc)* to unearth; *(vieilles rancunes, souvenirs etc)* to dig up; *(ancienne loi, coutume etc)* to exhume

exigeant [εgziʒɑ̃] ADJ *(personne, travail etc)* demanding, exacting; **être trop e.** *(d'une personne)* to expect too much, to be too demanding; *Iron* **je ne suis pas e., je demande juste la fortune et la célébrité!** I don't want much, just fame and fortune!

exigence [εgziʒɑ̃s] NF **1** *(caractère)* **elle est d'une e. insupportable** she's intolerably demanding **2** *(condition) (d'un client etc)* demand, requirement; *(d'un métier, milieu)* demand; **l'e.** *ou* **les exigences de l'étiquette** the demands or requirements of etiquette

exiger [εgziʒe] VT *(* **j'exigeai(s)** *)* **1** *(demander en insistant) (action, paiement, silence etc)* to demand, to require, to insist on (**de** from); *(rançon)* to demand; **trop e. des forces de qn** to overtax sb's strength; **e. qu'une chose soit faite** to insist on a thing being done, to demand that a thing be done; **j'exige des excuses/que vous vous excusiez** I demand an apology/that you apologize; **j'exige réparation** I demand redress; **j'exige d'être payé immédiatement** I demand to be paid or I insist on being paid immediately, I demand or insist on immediate payment; **le port de la cravate est exigé** ties must be worn
2 *(nécessiter) (soin, action etc)* to require, to necessitate, to call for; **prendre les mesures qu'exigent les circonstances** to take the ne-

cessary measures; **ces plantes exigent des engrais particuliers** these plants require or need special fertilizer; **aucune qualification particulière n'est exigée pour ce poste** no special qualification is required or needed for this post

exigibilité [εgziʒibilite] NF *Fin* **date d'e.** due date; **e. de taxe** tax liability; **e. immédiate** immediately due

exigible [εgziʒibl] ADJ *(dette, impôt)* payable, due (for payment); **le paiement est e. dès réception de la facture** payment is due upon receipt of the invoice; **e. à vue** payable at sight

exigu, -uë [εgzigy] ADJ *(lieu)* cramped, tiny; *Vieilli (somme)* meagre, slender

exiguïté [εgziguite] NF *(d'un lieu)* crampedness, tininess; *Vieilli (d'une somme)* meagreness

exil [εgzil] NM *(expulsion)* exile; **envoyer qn en e.** to send sb into exile, to exile sb; **vivre en e.** to live in exile; **se sentir en e.** to feel like an exile

exilé, -ée [εgzile] N *(personne)* exile

exiler [εgzile] VT *(d'un pays)* to exile (**de** from); *(d'une ville, de la cour etc)* to banish (**de** from); *Fig* **on l'a exilé à l'autre bout de la classe** he was banished or exiled to the other end of the classroom
▸ **VPR s'exiler** *Pol* to go into (voluntary) exile; *Fig* to cut oneself off or withdraw (from the world); **il s'est exilé à la campagne pour terminer son livre** he withdrew to the country to finish his book; **s'e. à l'autre bout du monde** to go into self-imposed exile on the other side of the world; **s'e. de la ville** to cut oneself off from the town

existant [εgzistɑ̃] ADJ existing; **lois existantes** existing laws, laws in force
NM *Com* **e. en caisse/en magasin** cash/stock in hand

existence [εgzistɑ̃s] NF **1** *Phil (être)* existence, (state of) being **2** *(vie)* existence, life; **changer d'e.** to change one's (way of) life; **mener une e. tranquille** to lead a quiet existence or life; **dans l'e.** in life **3** *(présence, réalité)* existence (**de** of) **4** *(durée) (d'une institution etc)* life; **il est improbable que ce gouvernement puisse dépasser un an d'e.** it's unlikely that this government can stay in existence for longer than a year **5** *Compta* **existences en caisse** cash on hand

existentialisme [εgzistɑ̃sjalism] NM *Phil* existentialism

existentialiste [εgzistɑ̃sjalist] ADJ, N *Phil* existentialist

existentiel, -elle [εgzistɑ̃sjεl] ADJ existential

exister [εgziste] VI *(vivre, être réel, se trouver)* to exist; *Com* to be available; **il existe** *(il y a)* there is, *pl* there are; **existe-t-il une vie sur Mars?** does life exist on Mars?, is there life on Mars?; **la maison existe toujours** the house still exists or is still standing; *Com* the firm still exists or is still in existence; **je n'arrive pas à croire qu'un autre monde puisse e.** I just can't believe that there is another world or that another world exists; **les roses noires, ça n'existe pas** there is no such thing as a black rose, black roses don't exist; **rien n'existe pour lui que l'art** nothing but art matters to him; **pour elle, l'amour/le bonheur/le danger n'existe pas** love/happiness/danger doesn't exist for her; **et l'amitié, cela existe, non?** there is such a thing as friendship, isn't there?; **je ne veux pas vous déranger, faites comme si je n'existais pas** I don't want to disturb you, pretend I'm not here or I don't exist; *Hum* **si ta sœur/le vélo n'existait pas, il faudrait l'inventer** if your sister/the bicycle didn't exist, we would have to invent her/it

exit [εgzit] ADV *Théâtre* exit, *Fml* exeunt; **e. les gardes** exit or esp *Fml* exeunt the guards; *Fig Fam* **e. le ministre des affaires étrangères** out goes or exit the foreign minister

ex-libris [εkslibris] NM *(vignette)* bookplate, ex-libris

ex navire [εksnavir] ADJ, ADV *Com* ex ship

ex nihilo [εksniilo] ADV, ADJ INV out of or from nothing, ex nihilo

exo [εgzo] NM *(abrév* **exercice***) Fam* exercise

exocet [εgzɔsε(t)] NM **1** *(poisson)* flying fish **2** **Exocet®** *(missile)* Exocet

exocrine [εgzɔkrin] ADJ *Physiol* exocrine

exode [εgzɔd] NM **1** *(émigration)* exodus; *Hist* **l'e.** = the flight of the French civilian population during the 1940 German invasion **2** *Bible* **l'E.** *(livre)* Exodus; *(émigration des Hébreux)* the Exodus
▸ ▸ **e. des capitaux** flight of capital; **l'e. des cerveaux** the brain drain; **e. rural** rural depopulation

exogame [εgzogam] ADJ *(tribu etc)* exogamous

exogamie [εgzogami] NF exogamy

exogène [εgzɔʒεn] ADJ exogenous

exonération [εgzonerasjɔ̃] NF exemption; **e. d'impôts** *or* **fiscale** tax exemption; **e. de TVA** exemption from VAT; **e. de responsabilité** exemption from liability

exonérer [εgzonere] VT *(* **j'exonère; j'exonérerai** *)* *(personne)* to exempt; *(marchandises)* to exempt from import duty; **être exonéré d'impôts** to be exempt from tax; **exonéré de TVA** VAT-exempt, zero-rated

exophtalmie [εgzɔftalmi] NF *Méd* exophthalmus, exophthalmos

exophtalmique [εgzɔftalmik] ADJ *Méd (goitre)* exophthalmic

exoplanète [εgzoplanεt] NF *Astron* exoplanet

exorbitant [εgzɔrbitɑ̃] ADJ *(prix, demande etc)* exorbitant

exorbité [εgzɔrbite] ADJ *(yeux)* protruding; *Fig* **ils regardaient, les yeux exorbités** they were watching with their eyes bulging (out of their heads)

exorciser [εgzɔrsize] VT *(démon, possédé)* to exorcize; *(démon)* to cast out; *(fantôme)* to lay; *Fig (ses peurs, les démons de sa jeunesse etc)* to exorcize

exorcisme [εgzɔrsism] NM exorcism

exorciste [εgzɔrsist] N exorcist

exorde [εgzɔrd] NM exordium

exosmose [εgzɔsmoz] NF *Phys* exosmosis

exotique [εgzɔtik] ADJ exotic; **une collection d'objets exotiques** a collection of exotica; **poisson e.** tropical fish

exotisme [εgzɔtism] NM exoticism

expansé [εkspɑ̃se] ADJ *(polystyrène)* expanded

expansibilité [εkspɑ̃sibilite] NF *(d'un gaz, de l'eau)* expansibility

expansible [εkspɑ̃sibl] ADJ *(gaz, eau)* expansible

expansif, -ive [εkspɑ̃sif, -iv] ADJ **1** *(exubérant) (personne)* expansive, outgoing **2** *Phys (force etc)* expansive

expansion [εkspɑ̃sjɔ̃] NF **1** *Phys (des gaz, de l'univers etc)* expansion; **l'univers en e.** the expanding universe **2** *(développement) (d'une ville, industrie etc)* expansion; *(d'idées, d'une culture etc)* spread(ing); **e. coloniale** colonial expansion; **taux d'e. économique** economic growth rate; **être en pleine e.** *(d'une économie, entreprise)* to be booming **3** *(exubérance)* expansiveness; **avec e.** expansively **4** *Ordinat* **carte d'e.** expansion card

expansionnisme [ɛkspɑ̃sjɔnism] **NM** expansionism

expansionniste [ɛkspɑ̃sjɔnist] **ADJ, N** expansionist

expansivité [ɛkspɑ̃sivite] **NF** expansiveness

expatriation [ɛkspatrijasjɔ̃] **NF** expatriation; *Fin* **e. de capitaux** movement of capital abroad

expatrié, -ée [ɛkspatrije] **ADJ** expatriate, *Fam* expat; *(réseau de vente etc)* overseas **N** expatriate, *Fam* expat

expatrier [ɛkspatrije] **(impf, pr sub n. expatriions) VT** *(personne)* to expatriate; *(capitaux)* to move abroad **VPR** s'**expatrier** to settle abroad

expectative [ɛkspɛktativ] **NF** *(attente)* expectation (**de** of); **nous vivons dans l'e.** we are living in hope; **rester dans l'e.** to wait and see

expectorant [ɛkspɛktɔrɑ̃] **ADJ, NM** *Méd* expectorant

expectoration [ɛkspɛktɔrasjɔ̃] **NF** *(action, crachat)* expectoration

expectorer [ɛkspɛktɔre] **VT** to expectorate

expédient [ɛkspedjɑ̃] **ADJ** *Fml* expedient **NM** expedient, makeshift; **vivre d'expédients** to live by one's wits; **user d'expédients** to resort to evasion

expédier [ɛkspedje] **VT** *(impf, pr sub n. expédiions)* **1** *(envoyer)* to dispatch, to send off; *Com* to dispatch, to ship; **e. des marchandises par navire** to send goods by sea, to ship goods; **e. un colis par chemin de fer** to dispatch *or* send *or* ship a parcel by rail; **e. par fret aérien** to airfreight; *Fam* **expédiez-le-moi!** *(personne)* send him along (to me)!; *Fam* **e. qn dans l'autre monde** *ou* **au cimetière** to dispatch sb to the next world **2** *(se débarrasser de)* to get rid of, to dispose of; **elle a expédié ses enfants chez sa belle-mère/en colonie de vacances/au lit** she sent *or* packed her children off to her mother-in-law's/to camp/to bed; **il a tendance à e. ses patients un peu vite** *(d'un médecin)* he tends to pack his patients out of the surgery rather quickly **3** *(faire rapidement) (tâche etc)* to deal promptly with; *(ses devoirs, sa dissertation)* to dash off; **e. son déjeuner** to make short work of one's lunch; **e. les affaires courantes** to deal with *or* get rid of the day-to-day matters **4** *Jur (contrat, acte etc)* to draw up

expéditeur, -trice [ɛkspeditœr, -tris] **N 1** *(d'une lettre, d'un colis etc)* sender; **e./expéditrice J. Martin** from *or* sender J. Martin **2** *Com (de marchandises)* shipper, consigner; *(par bateau)* shipper **ADJ** *(bureau, compagnie, gare etc)* shipping, dispatching

expéditif, -ive [ɛkspeditif, -iv] **ADJ** speedy, expeditious; **il est toujours très e. avec ses patients** he spends very little time with his patients; **je n'aime pas beaucoup ces méthodes expéditives** I don't appreciate this hasty way of doing things

expédition [ɛkspedisjɔ̃] **NF 1** *(envoi)* dispatch, sending; *Com* shipping, shipment; **e. par mer** shipping, shipment; *Com* **bulletin d'e.** waybill; *Com* **e. de détail** retail shipment; **e. exclusive** exclusive shipment; **e. maritime** maritime shipment; **e. par avion** airfreighting; **e. par bateau** shipping; **e. par chemin de fer** sending by rail, railfreighting; **e. par courrier** mailing; **e. par la poste** mailing; *Com* **e. partielle** part shipment *or* consignment; *Com* **e. port à port** port-to-port shipment; *Com* **expéditions** *(service)* dispatch (department), shipping (department) **2** *(marchandises)* consignment, shipment **3** *(voyage, opération militaire)*, *Fig* expedi-

tion; **partir en e.** to go (off) on an expedition; *Fig* **dis donc, pour venir chez toi, quelle e.!** it's quite an expedition *or* a trek getting to your place! **4** *Admin* **il est chargé de l'e. des affaires courantes** he is in charge of day-to-day matters; **je préfère m'occuper d'abord de l'e. des affaires courantes** I prefer to deal with *or* get rid of the day-to-day matters first **5** *Jur (d'un contrat etc)* (authentic) copy

expéditionnaire [ɛkspedisjɔnɛr] **ADJ** *Mil* expeditionary **N** *Com* shipping clerk

expérience [ɛksperjɑ̃s] **NF 1** *(pratique)* experience; **avec l'e., tu sauras que ...** you'll find out with experience that ...; **il a de l'e.** he's got experience, he's experienced; **elle a deux ans d'e.** she has two years' experience; **il nous faut quelqu'un qui a de l'e.** we need someone with experience; **avoir l'e. de qch** to have experience of sth, to be experienced in sth; **il a l'e. des enfants/de ce genre de voitures** he is used to children/this kind of car; **savoir qch par e.** to know sth from experience; **sans e.** inexperienced (**de** in), with no experience (**de** of); **il est sans e. de la vie** he has no experience of life **2** *(essai)* experiment; **faire l'e. de** *(mauvaise humeur, douleur)* to experience; *(la vie à deux)* to experience, to try; *(machine)* to try out; **j'ai fait l'e. de la douleur** I've experienced pain, I've had experience of pain; **j'en ai malheureusement fait l'e.** that has been my experience unfortunately *or* as I've discovered to my cost; **nous avons décidé de tenter l'e.** we've decided to give it a try *or* a go; **tu pourrais tenter l'e. des clubs de rencontre** you could give dating agencies a try **3** *(test scientifique)* experiment; **e. en laboratoire** laboratory experiment; **e. sur le terrain** field experiment; **faire une e.** to carry out *or* do an experiment (**sur** on)

> Attention: ne pas confondre **experience** et **experiment** lorsque l'on traduit **expérience**. **Experience** s'applique à la pratique que l'on a d'une chose, alors que **experiment** ne s'utilise que pour l'essai d'une chose nouvelle.

expérimental, -ale, -aux, -ales [ɛksperimɑ̃tal, -o] **ADJ** experimental

expérimentalement [ɛksperimɑ̃talmɑ̃] **ADV** experimentally

expérimentateur, -trice [ɛksperimɑ̃tatœr, -tris] **N** experimenter; *(scientifique)* (scientific) research worker

expérimentation [ɛksperimɑ̃tasjɔ̃] **NF** experimentation; **l'e. de ce produit n'a pas encore été faite** the product has not yet been tested; **e. sur l'homme** *(d'un vaccin etc)* human experiments, tests on humans

expérimenté [ɛksperimɑ̃te] **ADJ** experienced; **elle a un œil e. pour repérer les bonnes affaires** she's got a good eye for a bargain

expérimenter [ɛksperimɑ̃te] **VT** *(tester) (remède, modèle, vaccin etc)* to test, to try out (**sur** on); **cette machine a été longuement expérimentée** the machine has been thoroughly tested **VI** to experiment, to carry out experiments

expert [ɛkspɛr] **ADJ** expert, skilled (**en, dans** in; **à faire qch** in doing sth); **elle est experte à vous faire douter de vous-même** she is an expert at making you doubt yourself; **être e. en la matière** to be an expert in the matter **NM** expert; *(d'assurance, d'objets d'art)* valuer, appraiser; *Naut* surveyor; **e. financier/fiscal** financial/tax expert

expert-comptable, *pl* **experts-comptables NM** *Br* ≃ chartered accountant, *Am* ≃ certified public accountant

expert-conseil, *pl* **experts-conseils NM** consultant

expertise [ɛkspɛrtiz] **NF 1** *(évaluation) (d'une œuvre d'art etc)* (expert) valuation, appraisal; *(dans les assurances) (de dommages)* (expert) assessment; *Jur* expert opinion *or* testimony; *(dans les assurances)* **rapport d'e.** assessor's report, claims adjuster's report; *Naut* **e. d'avarie** damage survey; **e. médico-légale** forensic examination; *Jur* **e. contradictoire** valuation made in the presence of both parties to a contract **2** *(rapport)* expert's report **3** *(compétence)* expertise

expertiser [ɛkspɛrtize] **VT** *(œuvre d'art etc)* to value, to appraise; *(dommages)* to assess

expert-répétiteur, *pl* **experts-répétiteurs NM** *Fin* loss *or* average adjuster

expiable [ɛkspjabl] **ADJ** which can be atoned for; **tu as commis une faute, certes, mais elle est e.** yes, you made a mistake but you can make up for it

expiation [ɛkspjasjɔ̃] **NF** atonement (**de** for), expiation (**de** of)

expiatoire [ɛkspjatwar] **ADJ** expiatory

expier [ɛkspje] **VT** *(impf, pr sub n. expiions)* *(péché, crime)* to atone for, to pay the penalty for, *Fml* to expiate; *(erreur)* to atone for, to make up for

expirant [ɛkspirɑ̃] **ADJ** *Litt (personne)* dying; *(flamme)* dying, guttering; **voix expirante** faint *or* barely audible voice

expiration [ɛkspirasjɔ̃] **NF 1** *(respiration)* breathing out, exhalation, *Spéc* expiration; **pendant** *ou* **sur l'e.** on exhalation, as you/he/etc exhale(s) *or* breathes out **2** *(d'un contrat, un bail etc)* expiry, *Am* expiration; **venir** *ou* **arriver à e.** to expire, to run out

expirer [ɛkspire] **VI 1** *Litt (mourir)* to die, *Fml* to expire; *Fig (d'une flamme, d'une vague)* to die; *(d'un feu)* to go out; *(d'un son)* to die *or* fade away **2** *(d'un contrat, un bail etc)* to expire, to run out; **mon congé est expiré** my leave is up *or* has expired **3** *(respirer)* to breathe out, to exhale, *Spéc* to expire **VT** *(air)* to breathe out, to exhale, *Spéc* to expire

explétif, -ive [ɛkspletif, -iv] **ADJ, NM** *Gram* expletive

explicable [ɛksplikabl] **ADJ** explicable, explainable; **ces phénomènes ne sont explicables que par le paranormal** such phenomena can only be explained *or* accounted for in terms of the paranormal; **sa conduite est difficilement e.** his behaviour is difficult to explain, it is difficult to account for his behaviour

explicatif, -ive [ɛksplikatif, -iv] **ADJ** explanatory; *Com* **notice explicative** directions for use; *Gram* **proposition relative explicative** non-defining relative clause

explication [ɛksplikasjɔ̃] **NF** explanation (**à** for); **je ne comprends pas les explications de la machine** I don't understand the instructions for the machine; **il a quitté la réunion sans aucune e.** he left the meeting without (giving) any explanation; **donner l'e. de qch** to account for *or* explain sth; **j'exige des explications!** I demand an explanation!; **avoir une e. avec qn** *(discuter)* to talk things over with sb; *(se disputer)* to have it out with sb; **je crois qu'il va falloir que nous ayons une petite e. tous les deux** I think we're going to have to have a little talk, you and I; **il y a eu une violente e. entre les deux équipes** there was a violent altercation between the two teams

▸▸*Scol, Univ* **e. de textes** critical analysis

explicite [ɛksplisit] **ADJ** explicit (**sur** about)

explicitement [ɛksplisitmɑ̃] **ADV** explicitly;

formuler e. une demande to make an explicit request

expliciter [ɛksplisite] **VT** *(texte, pensées, clause d'un contrat etc)* to clarify; **il n'a pas voulu e. ses intentions** he did not want to be explicit about what he meant to do

expliquer [ɛksplike] **VT 1** *(communiquer) (ses idées, plans etc)* to explain *(à qn* to sb); **ce serait trop long à e.** it would take too long to explain; *Fam* **on s'est pris un de ces savons, je t'explique pas...** you wouldn't have believed the telling-off we got...
2 *(élucider) (doctrine, théorème etc)* to explain, to expound, to elucidate; *(mystère, signification)* to explain
3 *(indiquer la raison de) (action, fait, attitude etc)* to explain, to account for
VPR s'expliquer 1 *(communiquer ses idées)* to explain oneself; *(se justifier)* to justify one's behaviour, to explain oneself; **me serais-je mal expliqué?** perhaps I didn't make myself clear *or* wasn't plain enough; **je m'explique** this is what I mean, let me explain; **elle s'est expliquée sur différents reproches qu'on lui faisait** she justified herself with regard to the things they reproached her with
2 *(comprendre)* **je ne m'explique pas pourquoi** I can't understand why
3 *(être explicable)* **cela s'explique facilement** that's easily understandable *or* explainable; **il y a des choses qui ne s'expliquent pas** some things can't be explained; **c'est bizarre mais ça s'explique** it's strange but it can be explained *or* there's an explanation for it; **sa mort ne s'explique que par un suicide** his death can only be put down to suicide, suicide is the only explanation for his death; **le mauvais temps s'explique par la présence d'une dépression** the presence of a depression explains the bad weather; **et bien voilà, tout s'explique!** so you see, there's a reason for everything!
4 *(de plusieurs personnes)* to talk things over; **s'e. avec qn** *(discuter)* to talk things over with sb; *(se disputer)* to have it out with sb; **expliquez-vous une bonne fois pour toutes** get it sorted out once and for all; **viens un peu, on va s'e. dehors** come on, we'll settle this outside; **ils se sont expliqués au couteau** they settled it with knives

exploit [ɛksplwa] **NM 1** *(sportif, oratoire etc)* feat, achievement; *(militaire, amoureux)* exploit; **il est arrivé à l'heure, tu te rends compte d'un e.!** he arrived on time, which was quite an achievement for him! **2** *Jur* **e. (d'huissier)** writ

exploitable [ɛksplwatabl] **ADJ** *(terre)* farmable; *(mine, forêt)* workable; *(ressources naturelles)*, *Fig*, *Péj* exploitable; **tes documents ne sont pas exploitables dans l'optique de mes recherches** I can't make use of your documentation for my research; **e. par ordinateur** machine readable; **corpus e. par ordinateur** computerized corpus; *Fig Péj* **elles sont facilement exploitables** they are easily exploited *or* easy to exploit

exploitant [ɛksplwatɑ̃] **N 1** *Com, Ind (de mine)* operator; **les exploitants de l'entreprise** the people running the company; **e. (agricole)** farmer; **petits exploitants** small farmers **2** *Cin (propriétaire)* owner; *(directeur)* manager, *Am* exhibitor

exploitation [ɛksplwatasjɔ̃] **NF 1** *(action) (d'une mine, forêt etc)* working; *(d'une ligne de chemin de fer, ligne aérienne, ferme etc)* running, operation; *(d'une terre)* farming; *(des ressources naturelles)*, *Fig*, *Péj* exploitation; *Com (d'un brevet)* commercialization; *Ordinat* **système d'e.** operating system; **société d'e.** development company; **mettre une terre en e.** to bring a piece of land into cultivation; **faire l'e. industrielle de qch** to produce sth on an industrial scale; **e. capita-** **liste** capitalist exploitation; **l'e. de l'homme par l'homme** the exploitation of man by man; *Fig Péj* **c'est de l'e.!** it's exploitation! **2** *(entreprise)* concern; **e. agricole** farm; **petite e. agricole** small farm, smallholding; **e. forestière** forestry concern *or* operation; **e. minière** mine; **e. à ciel ouvert** open cast mine; **e. industrielle** industrial concern; **e. commerciale** business (concern); **e. familiale** family business

exploiter [ɛksplwate] **VT 1** *(mine)* to work; *(forêt)* to work, to exploit; *(ressources naturelles, brevet)* to exploit; *(invention)* to use; *(chemin de fer, ferme, journal etc)* to run, to operate; *(terre)* to farm; *Fig (situation, talent, idée etc)* to exploit, to make the most of, to capitalize on **2** *Péj (abuser de) (personne, l'ignorance de qn etc)* to exploit, to take (unfair) advantage of

exploiteur, -euse [ɛksplwatœr, -øz] **N** *(de main-d'œuvre, de l'ignorance de qn etc)* exploiter

explorateur, -trice [ɛksplɔratœr, -tris] **N** *(personne)* explorer

exploration [ɛksplɔrasjɔ̃] **NF 1** *(d'un pays, d'une maison)*, *Fig (d'un sujet etc)* exploration; **voyage d'e.** voyage of discovery; **partir en e.** to go off exploring *or* on an exploration **2** *Méd* exploration

exploratoire [ɛksplɔratwar] **ADJ** exploratory

explorer [ɛksplɔre] **VT 1** *(pays, maison)*, *Fig (sujet, possibilité etc)* to explore **2** *Méd (blessure, cavité)* to explore, to probe

exploser [ɛksploze] **VI 1** *(d'une bombe)* to explode, to go off; *(d'un avion, d'une chaudière etc)* to explode, to blow up; *(d'un gaz)* to explode; **faire e. une bombe** to explode a bomb **2** *Fig (se mettre en colère)* **e. (de colère)** to explode, *Fam* to blow one's top **3** *Fam (apparaître)* **ils ont explosé sur la scène rock il y a vingt ans** they burst onto the rock scene twenty years ago **4** *Fam (augmenter de façon spectaculaire)* to soar, to (sky) rocket
VT *Fam* **1** *(battre)* **e. qn** to kick sb's head in, to smash sb's face in **2** **être explosé (de rire)** to be killing oneself (laughing), to be cracking up, to be in stitches

explosible [ɛksplozibl] **ADJ** *(gaz etc)* explosive

explosif, -ive [ɛksplozif, -iv] **ADJ** *(obus, force etc)*, *Fig (situation, question, tempérament etc)* explosive; *Ling (consonne)* plosive; **il est d'un tempérament e.** he tends to explode *or* erupt *or Fam* blow his top
NM explosive

explosion [ɛksplozjɔ̃] **NF** *aussi Fig* explosion; **e. atomique** atomic explosion; **e. volcanique** volcanic explosion *or* eruption; **faire e.** to explode; **e. de fureur/rires** explosion *or* (out)burst of fury/laughter; **e. démographique** population explosion; **e. des naissances** baby boom

expo [ɛkspo] **NF** *Fam (abrév* **exposition)** exhibition

exponentiel, -ielle [ɛkspɔnɑ̃sjɛl] **ADJ, N** *Math* exponential

export [ɛkspɔr] **NM** export; **l'e., le service e.** the export branch; *Ordinat* **e. de données** data export

exportable [ɛkspɔrtabl] **ADJ** exportable

exportateur, -trice [ɛkspɔrtatœr, -tris] **N** exporter
ADJ exporting; **pays e. de vin** wine-exporting country

exportation [ɛkspɔrtasjɔ̃] **NF** *(action)* export(ation), exporting; *(produit)* export; *Ordinat (d'un fichier)* exporting; *Ordinat (données exportées)* exported data; **le montant des exportations a augmenté de 10%** cette année exports have risen by 10% this year; **ce produit marche très fort à l'e.** this product is doing very well on the export market, we export a lot of this product; **l'e. de nos produits a rencontré un vif succès** our products have been very successful on the export market; **réservé à l'e.** reserved for export, for export only; **articles d'e.** exports; **faire de l'e.** to export; **exportations visibles/invisibles** visible/invisible exports; **e. de capitaux** export of capital; **commerce d'e.** export trade; **e. kangourou** piggybacking

exporter [ɛkspɔrte] **VT** *Com, Ordinat* to export *(vers* to); **ces articles s'exportent mal** these items are difficult to export; *Fig* **ce genre de coutume s'exporte mal** this type of custom does not export *or* travel well; **cette mode a été** *ou* **s'est exportée dans le monde entier** the fashion has spread throughout the world

exposant, -ante [ɛkspozɑ̃, -ɑ̃t] **N** *(artiste, firme etc)* exhibitor
NM 1 *Math* exponent, (power) index **2** *Typ (chiffre, lettre)* superscript, superior **3 en exposant** superscript 3

exposé [ɛkspoze] **NM 1** *(de faits, d'une situation etc)* statement, account, report; *Scol, Univ* presentation; **faire un e. des faits** to give an account of the facts; **après avoir fait un bref e. de la situation** after outlining the situation; **faire l'e. d'un projet** to sketch out a plan; **e. verbal (de mission)** briefing; *Compta* **e. de la situation de l'entreprise** statement of the company's position **2** *(discours)* (short) talk; **faire un e.** to give a (short) talk **3** *Jur* **e. des motifs** *(d'un projet de loi)* preamble

exposer [ɛkspoze] **VT 1** *(montrer) (marchandises, œuvres d'art etc)* to exhibit, to show, to display; **objet exposé** exhibit; **ça fait très longtemps qu'il n'a pas exposé** he hasn't exhibited anything for a very long time; **être exposé (sur un lit de parade)** to lie in state; **e. des marchandises en vitrine** to display goods for sale
2 *(expliquer) (plans, raisons, problème etc)* to set out, to unfold, to expound; *(ses griefs, problèmes, son point de vue)* to air; **je leur ai exposé ma situation** I explained my situation to them
3 *(présenter) (à la chaleur, lumière etc)* to expose *(à* to); *(à la critique, un danger etc)* to expose, to lay open *(à* to); *Hist (nouveau-né)* to expose; **il faut e. cette plante à la lumière le plus possible** the plant must receive *or* get as much light as possible; **parce que la plante n'était pas du tout exposée** because the plant wasn't getting any light at all; **exposé à tous les vents** exposed *or* open to the four winds; **maison exposée au nord** house facing north *or* with a northern outlook; *Phot* **e. un film à la lumière** to expose a film
4 *(risquer) (sa vie, son honneur etc)* to risk, to take chances with; **e. qn** to put sb in danger
5 *Mus* to introduce; *Littér* to set out
VPR s'exposer to put oneself in danger; **s'e. à des critiques** to lay oneself open *or* expose oneself to criticism; **il s'expose à des poursuites** he is laying himself open to prosecution; **s'e. au soleil** to expose oneself to the sun; **si tu t'exposes trop longtemps** if you stay in the sun too long

exposition [ɛkspozisjɔ̃] **NF 1** *(action de montrer) (de marchandises, d'œuvres d'art, de fleurs etc)* display; *(d'un corps)* lying in state **2** *(dans un musée, une galerie)* exhibition **3** *(salon, foire)* exhibition, show; **salle d'e.** exhibition room, *Can* showroom; **e. interprofessionnelle** trade exhibition *or* show; **e. commerciale** trade exhibition; **E. universelle** world fair; *Mktg* **e. sur le lieu de vente** point of sale display; *Mktg* **e. sur le marché** market exposure

4 *(de faits, raisons etc)* exposition

5 *(au froid, danger etc)* exposure (**à** to); *(d'une maison)* aspect, exposure; *Phot* exposure; **e. solaire** exposure to the sun; **il lui faut au minimum une heure d'e. (à la lumière) par jour** it needs at least an hour of light a day; *Fin* **e. aux risques** exposure

6 *Littér, Mus* exposition, introduction; *Mus* **d'e.** introductory, expository; *Littér* **scène d'e.** prologue, *Am* prolog

7 *Typ* **e. directe des plaques** computer to plate, CTP

exposition-vente, *pl* **expositions-ventes** NF *Com* show, exhibition *(where the items are for sale)*

exprès¹, -esse [ɛksprɛs] ADJ *(explicite)* *(ordre, mise en garde etc)* express, distinct, explicit; **vous avez l'interdiction expresse de jouer dans la rue** you are expressly forbidden to play in the street; **défense expresse de fumer** smoking strictly prohibited ADJ INV, NM *Arch* **(lettre/paquet) e.** special delivery *or Br* express letter/parcel; **par ou en e.** (by) special *or Br* express delivery

exprès² [ɛksprɛ] ADV *(à dessein)* on purpose, intentionally, deliberately; *(spécialement)* specially, especially; **elle est sortie e. pour l'acheter** she went out specially *or* expressly to buy it; **je ne l'ai pas fait e.** I didn't mean to do it, I didn't do it on purpose *or* intentionally *or* deliberately; **je n'ai pas fait e. d'être méchante avec elle** I didn't mean to *or* set out to be nasty to her, I wasn't nasty to her on purpose; **j'ai déclenché l'alarme sans le faire e.** I set off the alarm without meaning to; **il fait e. de vous contredire** he makes a point of contradicting you; **j'aurais voulu le faire e., je n'y serais pas arrivé** I couldn't have done it if I'd tried *or* if I'd wanted to; **c'est fait e.** it's (quite) intentional *or* deliberate; **c'est fait e. pour ranger des crayons** it's designed *or* meant for holding pencils; **elle est trop grande, ta robe – c'est fait e.** your dress is too big for you – it's meant to be (that way *or* like that); **on dirait un fait e.** you'd think it was done on purpose *or* was intentional; *Iron* **comme (par) un fait e., il pleuvait** and of course *or* wouldn't you know it, it was raining

express [ɛksprɛs] ADJ **1** *(train)* fast, express **2** *(coffee)* espresso

NM **1** *(train)* fast train **2** *(café)* espresso *(coffee)*

expressément [ɛkspresemā] ADV **1** *(catégoriquement)* expressly **2** *(spécialement)* expressly, specially

expressif, -ive [ɛkspresif, -iv] ADJ *(langage, musique, regard, visage etc)* expressive

expression [ɛkspresjɔ̃] NF **1** *(d'un sentiment, d'une pensée, d'une opinion, d'une douleur etc)* expression; *(du visage)* expression, look; **il faudrait que tu soignes l'e.** you'll have to express yourself better; **l'e. de nos idées doit se faire par le biais d'un journal** we must express our ideas in a newspaper; **au-delà de toute e.** *(employé comme adjectif)* inexpressible; *(employé comme adverbe)* inexpressibly; **veuillez recevoir l'e. de mes sentiments distingués** *(en fin de lettre)* *(quand le destinataire n'est pas nommé dans l'introduction)* yours faithfully; *(quand le destinataire est nommé)* yours sincerely; **l'e. de son visage ne changea pas** his expression didn't change; **un visage plein d'e.** a very expressive face, a face full of expression; **auteur d'e. anglaise** author writing in English; **sans e.** expressionless; *Mus* **jouer avec e.** to play with expression *or* feeling

2 *(locution)* expression, phrase; **e. familière** colloquialism, colloquial expression;

e. figée, e. toute faite set *or* fixed expression

3 *Math* expression; *Fig* **la famille, réduite à sa plus simple e.** the family, reduced to its simplest expression; *Hum* **une jupe réduite à sa plus simple e.** a skirt that leaves little to the imagination; *Fig* **un meublé dont le mobilier était réduit à sa plus simple e.** a furnished room that hardly merited the term

▸ ▶ **e. algébrique** algebraic expression; **e. corporelle** self-expression, music and movement; *Ordinat* **e. logique** logical expression; *Ordinat* **e. de sélection** selection command; *Ordinat* **e. de tri** sort command

expressionnisme [ɛkspresjɔnism] NM *Beaux-Arts* expressionism

expressionniste [ɛkspresjɔnist] ADJ, N *Beaux-Arts* expressionist

expressivement [ɛkspresivmā] ADV expressively

expressivité [ɛkspresivite] NF expressiveness

exprimable [ɛksprimabl] ADJ which can be expressed, expressible; **sa douleur/joie n'était pas e.** his pain/happiness was inexpressible

exprimer [ɛksprime] VT **1** *(par des mots)* *(sentiment, pensée, opinion, douleur etc)* to express (**à qn** to sb); *(d'un regard, geste etc)* *(douleur, plaisir etc)* to express, to show **2** *Math (quantité, valeur etc)* to express **3** *(extraire en pressant) (jus)* to squeeze out (**de** from)

VPR **s'exprimer** *(en parlant, en agissant etc)* to express oneself; **si l'on peut s'e. ainsi** if one may put it this way *or* like this; **le président n'est pas encore exprimé sur ce sujet** the president has yet to voice an opinion on the matter; **s'e. par gestes** to use sign language

expropriation [ɛksproprijasjɔ̃] NF *Jur (de propriété, propriétaire)* expropriation

exproprier [ɛksproprije] VT *(impf, pr sub n.* **expropriions)** *Jur* to expropriate

expulser [ɛkspylse] VT **1** *(étranger)* to deport, to expel; *(locataire)* to evict; *(perturbateur etc)* to eject; *(élève, étudiant, membre de parti etc)* to expel (**de** from); *Sport (joueur)* to send off **2** *Physiol* to expel

expulsif, -ive [ɛkspylsif, -iv] ADJ *Méd* expulsive

expulsion [ɛkspylsjɔ̃] NF **1** *(d'un étranger)* deportation; *(d'un locataire)* eviction; *(d'un perturbateur etc)* ejection; *(d'un élève, d'un membre de parti etc)* expulsion; *Sport (joueur)* sending off **2** *Physiol* expulsion

expurgation [ɛkspyrgasjɔ̃] NF *(d'un livre etc)* expurgation

expurger [ɛkspyrʒe] VT *(j'expurgeai(s))* *(livre etc)* to expurgate; **un récit très expurgé de cette histoire** an expurgated *or* sanitized version of the matter

exquis [ɛkski] ADJ **1** *(manières, goût, nourriture etc)* exquisite; *(personne, sourire, temps)* delightful **2** *(douleur)* exquisite

exsangue [ɛksɑ̃g, ɛgzɑ̃g] ADJ *(patient, organe, visage etc)* anaemic, *Am* anemic; *Fig (œuvre d'art etc)* anaemic, bloodless; *(pays)* bled white; *(entreprise, région)* on its knees; *Fig* **elle est devenue e.** she turned deathly pale, the blood drained from her face; *Fig* **il est sorti e. de cette épreuve** he was drained by the ordeal

exsanguino-transfusion, *pl* **exsanguino-transfusions** [ɛksɑ̃g(ɥ)inotrɑ̃sfyzjɔ̃] NF *Méd* exchange transfusion

exsudation [ɛksydasjɔ̃] NF exudation

exsuder [ɛksyde] VT & VI to exude

exta [ɛksta] NF *Fam (abrév* **ecstasy)** E

extase [ɛkstaz] NF **1** *Rel, Psy* ecstasy, trance

2 *(admiration)* rapture, ecstasy; **être en e. devant qch/qn** to be in raptures *or* ecstasies over sth/sb, to be rapturous about sth/sb; **tomber en e. devant qn/qch** to go into raptures over sb/sth

extasié [ɛkstazje] ADJ *(personne, regard)* ecstatic, enraptured

extasier (s') [sɛkstazje] VPR *(impf, pr sub n.* **n. extasiions)** to be in *or* go into ecstasies *or* raptures (**sur** about; **devant** over); **elle s'est longuement extasiée sur ses enfants/devant mes géraniums** she went into great raptures about her children/my geraniums

extatique [ɛkstatik] ADJ *(personne, regard)* ecstatic, enraptured; *(état, vision)* ecstatic

extenseur [ɛkstɑ̃sœr] ADJ *Anat (muscle)* extensor

NM **1** *Gym* (chest) expander **2** *Anat* extensor

extensibilité [ɛkstɑ̃sibilite] NF *(de fibres)* ability to stretch, stretchability; *(d'un métal)* tensile nature

extensible [ɛkstɑ̃sibl] ADJ **1** *(métal)* tensile; *(vêtement, tissu)* stretch; *Fig (idée, définition etc)* flexible; *Fig* **ma fortune n'est malheureusement pas e.** unfortunately my funds are not limitless *or Fam* I'm not made of money **2** *Ordinat* upgradeable; *(mémoire)* expandable, upgradeable

extensif, -ive [ɛkstɑ̃sif, -iv] ADJ **1** *Agr* **culture extensive** extensive farming **2** *sens* **e.** *(d'un mot)* extended meaning

extension [ɛkstɑ̃sjɔ̃] NF **1** *(d'un muscle, bras, ressort etc)* stretching, extension; **être en e.** *(d'un ressort)* to be released; *(d'un gymnaste etc)* to be stretched out

2 *Fig (d'un territoire, d'une firme etc)* enlargement, expansion; *(d'un contrat)* extension; *(d'une maladie, d'une langue, d'un incendie etc)* spread; **leur but est l'e. du territoire** territorial expansion is their aim; **il veut l'e. de ses pouvoirs** he wants to extend his powers; **il faut éviter l'e. de l'épidémie/de l'incendie** the epidemic/fire must be prevented from spreading; **cette langue a forcément une e. restreinte** the language is necessarily restricted to a fairly small area; **donner de l'e. à une loi** to extend a law; **e. du commerce** business expansion; **prendre de l'e.** *(d'une entreprise etc)* to expand, to grow; *(d'une maladie, d'un incendie)* to spread

3 *(d'un mot)* extended meaning; **par e.** by extension

4 *Ordinat* expansion; **e. du nom de fichier** filename extension; **e. mémoire** memory expansion *or* upgrade; **carte d'e.** expansion board

5 *Mktg* **e. de la gamme** range stretching; **e. de la marque** brand extension; **e. de ligne** line extension; **e. de marché** market expansion

exténuant [ɛkstenɥɑ̃] ADJ exhausting

exténuation [ɛkstenɥasjɔ̃] NF *(du corps, de l'esprit)* exhaustion

exténuer [ɛkstenɥe] VT to exhaust; **être exténué (de fatigue)** to be exhausted *or* worn out

VPR **s'exténuer** to exhaust oneself, to tire oneself out (**à faire** doing); **je m'exténue à lui dire de ne pas y aller** I'm tired of telling him not to go

Il faut noter que le verbe anglais **to extenuate** est un faux ami. Il signifie **atténuer**.

extérieur [ɛksterjœr] ADJ **1** *(surface, partie etc)* exterior, outer, external; *(escalier, éclairage, poche, intérêts etc)* outside; *(port, boulevards)* outer; *(signe, apparence etc)* outward, external; *(facteur, cause)* external; *Péj (gentillesse, pitié etc)* superficial; *(fragilité, assurance)* outward; **il habite dans un quartier e. à la ville** he lives outside the city;

pour des raisons qui te sont complètement extérieures for reasons that have absolutely nothing to do with you; **elle est extérieure à cette entreprise/ce service** she doesn't work for this company/this department; **avoir des activités extérieures** to have outside interests; *Péj* **sa fragilité est toute extérieure** her fragility is all on the surface; **le côté e. de qch** the outer side *or* outside of sth; **le monde e.** the outside world; **fonds extérieurs** external financing; **sans aide extérieure** without outside help, *Fam* under one's own steam

2 (*étranger*) (*commerce, politique etc*) external, foreign

NM 1 (*d'un bâtiment, d'une boîte etc*) exterior, outside; **vu de l'e.** seen from the outside; **vue de l'e., cette entreprise a l'air de bien marcher** judging by appearances, the company seems to be doing well; **à l'e.** (*d'un bâtiment*) outside; (*d'une boîte etc*) on the outside; **à l'intérieur et à l'e.** inside and out; **juger de l'e.** to judge by appearances; *Sport* **match à l'e.** away match; **à l'e. de la gare/ville** outside the station/town; **cette peinture est prévue pour l'e.** the paint is intended for outside use

2 l'e. (*pays étrangers*) foreign countries; **à l'e.** abroad; **de l'e.** from abroad; **les relations avec l'e.** foreign relations

3 *Cin* location shot; **il tourne en e.** he's on location; **extérieurs tournés à Rueil** shot on location in Rueil; **émission en e.** outside broadcast, OB

extérieurement [εksterjœrmɑ̃] ADV **1** (*dehors*) externally, on the outside **2** (*en apparence*) on the surface

extériorisation [εksterjɔrizasjɔ̃] NF (*d'un sentiment*) manifestation, display; *Psy* exteriorization, externalization

extérioriser [εksterjɔrize] VT (*sentiment*) to show, to express; *Psy* to exteriorize, to externalize

VPR s'extérioriser (*d'un sentiment*) to show *or* manifest itself; (*d'une personne*) to express oneself, to externalize; **il s'extériorise très peu** he shows little of what he's feeling

extériorité [εksterjɔrite] NF exteriority

exterminateur, -trice [εkstεrminatœr, -tris] ADJ (*rage*) destructive N exterminator, destroyer

extermination [εkstεrminasjɔ̃] NF (*d'une race, d'une armée etc*) extermination, destruction

exterminer [εkstεrmine] VT (*race, armée etc*) to exterminate, to destroy, to wipe out

externalisation [εkstεrnalizasjɔ̃] NF outsourcing

externaliser [εkstεrnalize] VT to outsource

externat [εkstεrna] NM **1** (*école*) day school **2** (*élèves*) day pupils **3** *Méd* non-resident (medical) studentship

externe [εkstεrn] ADJ **1** (*surface, partie etc*) external, outside, outer; (*cause*) external; **côté e.** outside; **angle e.** exterior angle; *Ordinat* **dispositif e.** external device; *Pharm* **à usage e.** for external use only **2 élève e.** day pupil

N **1** (*élève*) day pupil **2** *Méd* **e. (des hôpitaux)** non-resident (medical) student, *Am* extern

exterritorialité [εkstεritɔrjalite] NF ex(tra)territoriality

extincteur, -trice [εkstε̃ktœr, -tris] ADJ (*matériel etc*) extinguishing NM fire extinguisher

extinction [εkstε̃ksjɔ̃] NF **1** (*d'un incendie etc*) extinguishing, putting out; *Mil* **e. des feux** lights out; **l'e. des feux ou des lumières se fait à 22h** lights out at 10 pm; *Aut* **e. retardée** (*d'une lumière*) delayed cut-off **2** *Jur* (*d'un droit etc*) extinguishment; (*d'un con-*

trat) termination; (*d'une hypothèque*) redemption; *Compta* **e. d'une dette** discharge of a debt **3** (*d'une race, espèce*) extinction; **espèce menacée** *ou* **en voie d'e.** endangered species; **depuis l'e. des dinosaures** since dinosaurs became extinct **4 e. de voix** loss of one's voice; **avoir une e. de voix** to have lost one's voice

extirpateur [εkstirpatœr] NM *Agr* (*instrument*) weeder

extirpation [εkstirpasjɔ̃] NF (*d'une plante, de mauvaises herbes*) uprooting; *Chir* (*d'une tumeur etc*) extirpation

extirper [εkstirpe] VT (*plante*) to root out *or* up; *Fig* (*vices*) to eradicate, to root out; *Fam* **e. qn de son lit** to drag sb out of bed; **e. qn d'une situation impossible/un piège** to extricate sb from an impossible situation/a trap; **je n'ai pas réussi à lui e. un mot** I couldn't drag *or* get a word out of him

VPR s'extirper s'e. de son lit/de dessous la couette to drag oneself out of bed/from beneath the quilt; **s'e. de son pull/d'un enchevêtrement de racines** to extricate oneself from one's pullover/a tangle of roots

extorquer [εkstɔrke] VT (*argent, promesse etc*) to extort, to wring (**à qn** from sb)

extorqueur, -euse [εkstɔrkœr, -øz] N extortioner

extorsion [εkstɔrsjɔ̃] NF extortion; **e. de fonds** extortion of funds

extra [εkstra] NM INV **1** *aussi Culin* (special) treat; **faire/s'offrir un e.** to do/treat oneself to something special; **on s'est fait un petit e. en achetant du homard** we treated ourselves a little and bought lobster **2** (*serviteur*) extra help *or* hand; **faire des e. chez qn** to do occasional work for sb; **pour la soirée, on prendra deux e.** we'll take on two extra people for the party

ADJ INV **1** (*de qualité supérieure*) (*vin, repas, vêtement etc*) first-class, first-rate; *Fam* (*remarquable*) (*personne, roman, vacances etc*) terrific, fantastic, fabulous; **tu viens passer le week-end avec nous? c'est e.!** you're spending the weekend with us? (that's) fantastic *or* terrific! **2** *Can Fam* (*en supplément*) extra; **la taxe est e.** the tax is extra *or* on top

extra- [εkstra] PRÉF extra-

extra-comptable ADJ *Compta* (*ajustement*) off-balance sheet

extraconjugal, -ale, -aux, -ales [εkstrakɔ̃ʒygal, -o] ADJ extramarital

extracteur [εkstraktœr] NM (*appareil, instrument*) extractor

extractible [εkstraktibl] ADJ (*autoradio*) removable

extractif, -ive [εkstraktif, -iv] ADJ extractive

extraction [εkstraksjɔ̃] NF **1** (*de dents*) extraction, *Fam* pulling; (*de charbon, minerai*) extraction, mining; (*de pierres*) quarrying; (*de pétrole, de gaz etc*) extraction; *Chir* (*d'une balle etc*) removal **2** *Math* (*d'une racine carrée ou cubique*) extraction **3** *Fig* **de haute/basse e.** of noble/humble extraction *or* birth

extrader [εkstrade] VT to extradite

extradition [εkstradisjɔ̃] NF extradition

extra-dry ADJ INV (*boisson alcoolisée*) extra dry

extra-fin ADJ **1** (*petit, fin*) (*pois, aiguille etc*) extra-fine **2** *Com* (*de qualité supérieure*) (*chocolat*) superfine, top-quality; (*beurre*) top quality

extra-fort ADJ extra-strong NM *Couture* bias binding

extra(-)galactique ADJ *Astron* extra-galactic

extraire [εkstrεr] (*conj like* **traire**) VT (*épingle, clou etc*) to pull out, to draw out; (*dent*)

to extract, to take out, to pull (out); (*charbon, minerai*) to extract, to mine; (*pierre*) to quarry; (*pétrole, gaz, jus etc*) to extract; (*citation, passage etc*) to extract, to excerpt; (*balle, chose de son portefeuille etc*) to take out, to remove; (*blessés, corps*) (*d'une voiture, des décombres*) to free; **cette citation est extraite du Roman de la rose** this quotation is taken from the Roman de la rose; **e. des plants** to lift seedlings; *Math* **e. une racine** to extract a root

VPR s'extraire s'e. de sa voiture to free oneself from *or* wriggle out of *or* squeeze out of one's car

extrait [εkstrε] NM **1** (*produit*) extract, essence; **e. de viande** meat extract; **e. de lavande** lavender essence; **e. de café** coffee extract **2** (*d'un livre, discours, auteur etc*) extract, excerpt; (*de film*) extract, clip; *Jur, Fin* (*d'un acte, compte rendu*) abstract; **e. de presse** press cutting; *TV* **extraits pré-enregistrés** recorded highlights

▸▸ **extraits d'archives** archive footage; **e. de baptême** certificate of baptism, baptismal certificate; **e. de casier judiciaire** = documentary evidence that one does not have a criminal record; **e. de compte** *Compta* statement of account; *Banque* bank statement; **e. de film** film clip; **e. de naissance** birth certificate

extrajudiciaire [εkstraʒydisjεr] ADJ extrajudicial

extra-légal, -ale, -aux, -ales ADJ bordering on the illegal; **ils ont employé des méthodes extra-légales** they used methods that bordered on the illegal *or Fam* that were legally a bit iffy; **les procédés extra-légaux ne lui font pas peur** he's not bothered about sailing a bit close to the wind *or* doing things that are not altogether above board

extralinguistique [εkstralε̃gɥistik] ADJ extralinguistic

extralucide [εkstralysid] ADJ, N (**voyante**) **e.** clairvoyant

extra-muros [εkstramyros] ADJ INV (*quartier*) suburban, outside town

ADV (*habiter*) outside town, in the suburbs; **se promener e.** to go for a stroll in the suburbs

extranet [εkstranεt] NM *Ordinat* extranet

extraordinaire [εkstraɔrdinεr] ADJ **1** (*spécial*) (*réunion, mesures etc*) extraordinary, special; (*messager, mission*) special; **assemblée générale e.** extraordinary general meeting; **frais** *ou* **dépenses extraordinaires** (*non prévues*) extras; (*uniques*) non-recurring expenditure

2 (*étonnant*) (*nouvelles, événement etc*) extraordinary, astonishing; **cela n'a rien d'e.** that's nothing out of the ordinary; **cela n'a rien d'e. après ce que tu lui as dit** that's not surprising given what you said to him

3 (*remarquable*) (*personne, beauté, succès*) extraordinary, outstanding; (*chaleur, prix*) extraordinary; *Fam* (*très bon*) (*livre, vin etc*) really good; **elle est vraiment e. dans cette robe** she looks quite extraordinary in that dress; **elle a fait un travail e.** she did outstanding work; **par e.** by *or* some remote chance; **si par e. tu la voyais** if by some remote chance you should see her; **quand par e. nous nous rencontrons** when we meet, which we rarely do

extraordinairement [εkstraɔrdinεrmɑ̃] ADV extraordinarily

extra-parlementaire ADJ extra-parliamentary

extraplat [εkstrapla] ADJ (*montre, calculette etc*) slimline

extrapolation [εkstrapɔlasjɔ̃] NF extrapolation

extrapoler [ɛkstrapɔle] **vi** to extrapolate (à partir de from)

extrascolaire [ɛkstraskɔlɛr] **ADJ** (activités etc) extra-curricular

extrasensible [ɛkstrasɑ̃sibl] **ADJ** (phénomène) extrasensory

extra(-)sensoriel, extra(-)sensorielle ADJ Psy (perception etc) extrasensory

extrasystole [ɛkstrasistɔl] **NF** Physiol extrasystole

extra(-)terrestre, pl **extra(-)terrestres ADJ, N** extraterrestrial

extraterritorial, -ale, -aux, -ales [ɛkstratɛritɔrjal, -o] **ADJ** extraterritorial

extraterritorialité [ɛkstratɛritɔrjalite] **NF** extraterritoriality

extra-utérin ADJ Méd grossesse extra-utérine ectopic pregnancy

extravagance [ɛkstravagɑ̃s] **NF 1** (d'une idée, d'un comportement, de vêtements etc) extravagance; (d'une personne) eccentricity; (de dépenses) exorbitance; (d'un désir) immoderateness; **des idées d'une telle e.** such extravagant ideas **2** (action, remarque) piece of nonsense; **il a dit un tas d'extravagances** he talked a lot of nonsense

> Il faut noter que le nom anglais **extravagance** signifie également **gaspillage, dépense inconsidérée.**

extravagant, -ante [ɛkstravagɑ̃, -ɑ̃t] **ADJ** (idée, comportement, vêtements etc) extravagant; (personne) eccentric; (prix, demande) exorbitant; (désir) immoderate **N** eccentric (person)

> Il faut noter que l'adjectif anglais **extravagant** signifie également **dépensier.**

extraversion [ɛkstravɛrsjɔ̃] **NF** Psy extroversion

extraverti, -ie [ɛkstravɛrti] **ADJ, N** Psy extrovert

extrême [ɛkstrɛm] **ADJ 1** (point, limite etc) far, extreme, farthest; (jeunesse, vieillesse) extreme; (froid, plaisir etc) extreme, intense; **à l'e. limite, j'accepterai d'attendre une semaine de plus** I'll agree to wait another week at the most or at the outside; **il pousse la pingrerie jusqu'à son point e.** he takes meanness to extremes; **tu ne m'appelles qu'en cas d'e. urgence** only call me in cases of extreme urgency or if it's extremely urgent; **d'une maigreur e.** extremely thin; **j'ai l'e. regret de vous annoncer que ...** I am extremely sorry to tell you that ...; Pol **e. droite/gauche** far or extreme right/left **2** (excessif) (mesure, solution) extreme, drastic, severe; (cas, situation, opinion) extreme; **elle est e. en tout** she is extreme in everything; **être e. dans ses opinions** to hold extreme opinions

NM extreme; **les extrêmes** (de chaleur et froid), Math (d'une proportion) the extremes; **il passe d'un e. à l'autre** he goes from one extreme to the other; **prudent à l'e.** cautious in the extreme or to a fault; **pousser les choses à l'e.** to take or carry matters to extremes; **elle a réagi à l'e.** her reaction was rather extreme; **il la déteste à l'e.** he cordially detests her; **les extrêmes se touchent** extremes meet

extrêmement [ɛkstrɛmmɑ̃] **ADV** extremely, exceedingly

extrême-onction NF Rel extreme unction

Extrême-Orient (l') NM the Far East

extrême-oriental, -ale, -aux, -ales ADJ Far East, Far Eastern **N** E. Oriental

extrémisme [ɛkstremism] **NM** extremism

extrémiste [ɛkstremist] **ADJ, N** extremist

extrémité [ɛkstremite] **NF 1** (bout) (d'un lac, d'une route, d'une jambe, d'une corde etc) end; (d'un doigt, d'une aile etc) tip; (d'une aiguille, une épée etc) point; **les extrémités** (pieds et mains) the extremities, the hands and feet; **j'ai les extrémités glacées** my hands and feet are frozen

2 (excès) **extrémité(s)** extremes; **pousser qch à l'e.** to carry or take sth to extremes; **pousser qn à une e.** ou **à des extrémités** to drive sb to extremes; **en venir à des extrémités** to resort to extreme measures; (à la violence) to resort to violence

3 (situation désespérée) extremity; **dans cette e.** in this extremity; **réduit à l'e.** in dire distress or straits, reduced to extremity; **être à la dernière** ou **à toute e.** to be at the point of death, to be close to death

extrinsèque [ɛkstrɛ̃sɛk] **ADJ** extrinsic; **valeur e.** (de monnaie) face value

extroversion [ɛkstrovɛrsjɔ̃] **NF** Psy extroversion, extraversion

extroverti, -ie [ɛkstrovɛrti] **ADJ, N** Psy extrovert, extravert

extrusion [ɛkstryzjɔ̃] **NF** Tech extrusion

exubérance [ɛgzyberɑ̃s] **NF** (d'une personne, de la végétation, d'un style etc) exuberance; **avec e.** with exuberance, exuberantly

exubérant [ɛgzyberɑ̃] **ADJ** (personne, végétation, joie, style etc) exuberant

exultation [ɛgzyltasjɔ̃] **NF** exultation

exulter [ɛgzylte] **vi** to exult, to rejoice (**de faire** in doing)

exutoire [ɛgzytwar] **NM** outlet (à sa colère for one's anger)

ex-voto [ɛksvɔto] **NM INV** Rel ex-voto, votive offering

eye-liner, pl **eye-liners** [ajlajnœr] **NM** eyeliner

ezine, e-zine [izin] **NM** e-zine, ezine

F¹ 1 (*abrév* **franc(s)**) F, fr **2** (*abrév* **Fahren-heit**) F

F², f¹ [ɛf] NM INV (*lettre*) F f; **un F2/3/etc** (*appartement*) a two-/three-/etc roomed flat or *Am* apartment

f² (*abrév* **féminin**) f

fa [fa] NM INV *Mus (note)* F; (*quand on chante la gamme*) fa; **clef de fa** bass clef, F clef

FAB [ɛfabe] *Com (abrév* **franco à bord**) FOB

fable [fabl] NF **1** (*légende*) fable; **célèbre dans la f.** famous in fable **2** (*invention*) story, tale; **c'est pure f.** it's pure invention; **être la f. de la ville** to be the laughing stock of the whole town

fabliau, -aux [fablijo] NM *Littér* fabliau

fablier [fablije] NM book of fables

fabricant, -ante [fabrikɑ̃, -ɑ̃t] N maker, manufacturer; **f. de chapeaux** hat maker or manufacturer; **f. d'automobiles** car maker or manufacturer; **gros/petit f.** large/small manufacturer

fabricateur, -trice [fabrikatœr, -tris] N **f. de fausse monnaie** counterfeiter, forger; **f. de faux papiers** forger of documents; **f. de fausses nouvelles** scandalmonger

fabrication [fabrikasjɔ̃] NF **1** (*à la main*) making; *Ind* manufacture, manufacturing; **f. artisanale** production by craftsmen; **produits de f. artisanale** handmade products; **f. industrielle** industrial manufacture; **f. par lots** batch production; **f. assistée par ordinateur** computer-aided manufacture; **f. intégrée par ordinateur** computer-integrated manufacturing; **f. sous contrat** contract manufacturing; **défaut de f.** manufacturing defect; **secret de f.** trade secret; **f. en série** mass production; **elle a amené une tarte de sa f.** she brought along a tart she had made herself; **n'employer que la meilleure f.** to employ only the best workmanship; **article de f. française** article made in France **2** (*de fausses nouvelles*) fabrication; (*de document, fausse monnaie*) forging **3** *Typ* production

fabrique [fabrik] NF **1** (*fabrication*) manufacture; **prix de f.** manufacturer's or factory price; **marque de f.** trademark **2** (*établissement*) factory; **f. de papier** paper mill **3** *Rel* (**conseil de**) **f.** = (parochial) church council, vestry

> Il faut noter que le nom anglais **fabric** est un faux ami. Il signifie le plus souvent **tis-su**.

fabriquer [fabrike] VT **1** *Ind* (*étoffes, bicyclettes etc*) to manufacture; **f. des véhicules en série** to mass-produce vehicles; **fabriqué en série** mass-produced

2 (*artisanalement*) to make; **nous fabriquons nos produits à la main** we make our products by hand; **fabriqué sur mesure** made to measure; *Fig* **l'entraîneur qui a fa-**briqué le champion de ski the coach who created or made the ski champion; **cela a contribué à f. son personnage médiatique** that helped to turn him/her into a media figure or to make a media figure out of him/her **3** (*pour tromper*) (*mensonge, histoire*) to make up, to fabricate; (*faux papiers*) to forge; **f. de la fausse monnaie** to counterfeit or forge money; **histoire fabriquée de toutes pièces** completely made-up or fabricated story

4 *Fam* (*faire*) to do; **qu'est-ce qu'il fabrique?** what's he up to?, what's he doing?; **qu'est-ce que j'ai pu f. avec mon briquet?** what can I have done with my lighter?; **je me suis tout à coup demandé ce que je fabriquais là** I suddenly wondered what I was doing there

fabulateur, -trice [fabylatœr, -tris] ADJ *aussi Psy* fantasizing

N compulsive liar

fabulation [fabylasjɔ̃] NF fantasizing; (*pathologique*) compulsive lying

fabuler [fabyle] VI to fantasize; (*pathologique*) to make things up, to fabricate

fabuleusement [fabyløzmɑ̃] ADV fabulously

fabuleux, -euse [fabylø, -øz] ADJ **1** (*qui appartient à la légende*) (*bête*) fabulous, mythical; (*caractère, exploits*) mythical, legendary **2** *Fig* (*incroyable*) (*aventure, temps, somme d'argent, film etc*) fabulous, fantastic

fabuliste [fabylist] NM fabulist

FAC [ɛfase] NM *Admin abrév* **fonds d'aide et de coopération**

fac [fak] NF *Fam* university; **f. de droit/de lettres** faculty of law/arts; **à la f., en f.** at university, *Fam* at uni

façade [fasad] NF **1** (*de bâtiment*) façade; **hôtel en f. sur la place** hotel facing the square **2** (*apparence*) pretence, façade, show (**de** of); **elle a l'air méprisant – non, ce n'est qu'une f.** she looks scornful – no, it's just a pretence or a front; **ne faire qch que pour la f.** to do sth just for show; **générosité/patriotisme de f.** sham generosity/patriotism **3** *Fam* (*visage*) **se ravaler la f.** (*se maquiller*) to put one's face on; **démolir la f. à qn** to smash sb's face in **4** (*d'un modem etc*) front panel **5** (*en assurances*) fronting

face [fas] NF **1** (*visage*) face; **jeter des accusations à la f. de qn** to throw accusations in sb's face; **elle n'a pas hésité à lui jeter à la f. qu'il était hypocrite** she told him straight to his face that he was a hypocrite; **les blessés de la f.** those with facial injuries; **sauver la f.** to save (one's) face; **perdre la f.** to lose face; **tomber f. contre terre** to fall flat on one's face; **f. de carême** long face; *Péj* **f. de rat** rat-face; *Fig* **la f. du monde** the face of the world; **crier à la f. du monde** to shout to the whole world

2 *Litt* (*surface*) **la f. des eaux/de la terre** the face of the waters/of the earth

3 (*côté*) (*d'une lame d'épée*) flat; (*d'une lentille, d'un disque*) side; (*d'une médaille*) ob-verse; (*d'une pièce*) head (side); **f.!** (*en jouant à pile ou face*) heads!; **f. avant** front; **f. arrière** back; **polyèdre à douze faces** twelve-sided polyhedron; **à deux faces** (*disquette*) double-sided; **tissu (à) double f.** reversible fabric; **ruban adhésif à double f.** double-sided adhesive tape; **la f. cachée de la lune** the hidden side of the moon; **considérer qch sous toutes ses faces** to consider sth from all sides or from every angle; **c'est une des nombreuses faces du problème** it's one of the many aspects of the problem; **change le disque de f.!** turn the record over!; **dans son nouveau disque, je préfère la f. A à la f. B** on his new record I prefer the A side to the B side or I prefer side A to side B

4 faire f. à to face, to be facing or opposite; *Fig* (*responsabilités, dépenses, besoins*) to meet; (*situation, difficultés*) to face up to; **faire f. à ses créanciers** to face up to one's creditors; **les deux maisons se font f.** the two houses face or are facing or are opposite each other

5 portrait de f. full-face portrait; **vue de f.** front view; *Théâtre* **place de f.** front-facing seat; **se présenter de f.** to be face on; **il l'a attaquée de f.** he attacked her from the front; *Fig* he attacked her openly; **la maison (d')en f.** the house opposite; **regarder qn (bien) en f.** to look sb (full or straight) in the face; **si elle l'apprend, je n'oserais plus la regarder en f.** if she found out, I wouldn't be able to look her in the face again; **il n'ose pas le lui dire en f.** he daren't tell him/her to his/her face; **regarder les choses/la mort en f.** to face facts/death; **en f. de** opposite, facing; **les maisons en f. de l'école** the houses opposite or facing the school; **en f. l'un de l'autre, l'un en f. de l'autre** opposite each other, facing each other; **si tu les mets l'un en f. de l'autre** if you put them face to face or opposite each other; **en f. du professeur, il change d'attitude** in front of the teacher his attitude changes; **on est en f. d'un problème difficile** we are faced with a difficult problem

6 f. à facing; **la chambre f. à la mienne** the room facing mine; **f. à cette situation, on n'avait pas le choix** faced with that situation we had no choice; **f. à f.** face to face (**avec** with); **mettre deux témoins f. à f.** to bring two witnesses face to face; **on s'est retrouvé f. à f.** we found ourselves face to face

face-à-face NM INV face-to-face encounter/debate

face-à-main, *pl* **faces-à-main** NM lorgnette

face-texte, *pl* **faces-textes** NM *Journ* facing matter

facétie [fasesi] NF joke; **dire des facéties** to crack jokes; **faire des facéties** to play jokes or pranks

facétieux, -ieuse [fasesjø, -jøz] ADJ (*petit garçon, regard*) mischievous

facette [fasɛt] NF (d'un diamant, de l'œil d'un insecte, Fig d'une personnalité, d'un problème etc) facet; **(taillé) à facettes** (cut) in facets, facetted; **une personnalité/une histoire/une réalité à facettes** a multi- or many-facetted personality/story/reality; **examiner un problème sous toutes ses facettes** to examine a problem from every angle

facetter [fasete] VT to facet

fâché [faʃe] ADJ **1** (mécontent) angry, annoyed; **être f. contre qn** to be angry or annoyed with sb; **être f. avec qn** to have fallen out with sb; **ils sont fâchés** they've fallen out or they're on bad terms (with each other); **tu n'es pas f., au moins?** you're not angry, are you?; **elle est fâchée avec les maths** she can't get on with maths, she has problems or trouble with maths; Hum **tu es f. avec l'ordre/ton rasoir?** being tidy/shaving doesn't come naturally to you, does it? **2** (désolé) sorry; **être f. de qch/pour qn** to be sorry about sth/for sb; Iron **je ne suis pas f. que ça soit terminé** I'm not exactly sorry or sad that it has finished; **je ne suis pas f. de m'asseoir** I'm glad to get the weight off my feet

fâcher [faʃe] VT **1** (rendre mécontent) to annoy, to make angry, to anger; **ton attitude me fâche beaucoup** your attitude annoys me a lot or makes me very angry **2** (affliger) to grieve

VPR **se fâcher 1** (se mettre en colère) to get angry or annoyed, to lose one's temper; **attention! je vais me f.!** be careful or I'll get angry!; **se f. contre qn** to get annoyed or angry with sb; Fam **se f. tout rouge** to blow one's top, to go up the wall **2** (se brouiller) to fall out, to quarrel (**avec qn** with sb)

fâcherie [faʃri] NF quarrel, disagreement

fâcheusement [faʃøzmɑ̃] ADV **1** (malheureusement) unfortunately **2** (surpris) unpleasantly; (impressionné) unfavourably, Am unfavorably

fâcheux, -euse [faʃø, -øz] ADJ (événement, question, complication, changement etc) unfortunate, annoying; (position, situation) awkward, unfortunate; (nouvelles) annoying; (exemple) unfortunate; **j'ai eu la fâcheuse idée de lui en parler** I had the unfortunate idea of talking to him/her about it; **il serait f. que tu arrives en retard** it would be a pity if you arrived late; **c'est f.!** what a nuisance!, how annoying!

N (importun) nuisance

facho [faʃo] ADJ, N Fam Péj fascist

facial, -ale, -iaux, -ales [fasjal, -jo] ADJ (muscle, angle etc) facial; **massage f.** facial or face massage

faciès [fasjɛs] NM **1** (aspect du visage) features; Méd facies **2** Bot, Géol facies

facile [fasil] ADJ **1** (travail, problème, vie etc) easy; **c'est f. à faire** it's easy to do or easily done; **c'est f. à dire** that's easily said; **c'est plus f. à dire qu'à faire** it's easier said than done; **avoir la vie f.** to have an easy life; **c'est f. comme bonjour** it's as easy as pie, it's child's play; **il lui est f. de le faire** it's easy for him (to do it); **f. d'emploi** easy to use; **d'une mise en place f., f. à installer** easily installed; **besognes faciles** light or easy tasks **2** (caractère) easy-going; **homme f. à vivre** man easy to get along with or to get on with; **il n'a pas l'air f. en affaires** he doesn't seem an easy man to do business with; **f. à émouvoir** easily moved; **cet enfant est f.** this child is no problem; Péj **femme f.** woman of easy virtue, loose woman **3** (superficiel) (plaisanterie, littérature, style etc) facile **4** (qui vient facilement) **il n'a pas la parole f.** words don't come easily to him; **il n'a pas l'argent f.** he's a bit tight-fisted; **un milieu où**

l'argent est f. an environment where there's plenty of money around; **elle a les larmes faciles** she is easily moved to tears; **avoir la gâchette f.** to be trigger-happy; **elle a la plume f.** she is a fluent writer, writing comes easily to her

ADV **1** (au moins) easily, at least; **on met trois jours f. pour traverser l'île** it takes easily or at least three days to cross the island; **en trois jours, j'aurai lu f. deux livres** I'll easily read two books in three days

2 Belg **avoir f. à** ou **de faire qch** to find it easy to do sth, to have no problem doing sth

facilement [fasilmɑ̃] ADV easily; **il rit f.** it's easy to make him laugh; **je mettrai f. deux jours pour le faire** it'll take me easily or at least two days to do it

facilité [fasilite] NF **1** (d'une tâche, d'un problème etc) easiness; (à faire qch) ease; **avec f.** easily, with ease; **les enfants comprennent l'informatique avec une f. déconcertante** children understand computers with disconcerting ease; Péj **elle choisit toujours la f.** she always chooses the easy option or the easy way out; **c'est une solution de f.** it's the easy solution or way out **2** (moyen, occasion) **avoir toutes facilités pour faire qch** to have every opportunity of doing sth **3** (aptitude) aptitude, talent (**pour qch** for sth); **écrire avec f.** to write fluently or with ease; **f. à faire qch** aptitude for doing sth; **f. de parole** fluency; **elle a beaucoup de facilités pour les/en maths** she has great aptitude for maths

▸▸ **f. d'accès pour fauteuils roulants** wheelchair access; **f. d'accès pour personnes handicapées** disabled access; Banque **f. de caisse** overdraft or cash facility; Banque **facilités de crédit** credit facilities; **f. d'écoulement** (d'un produit) saleability; **f. d'emploi** (d'un ordinateur etc) user-friendliness; Fin **facilités d'endettement** borrowing capacity; Fin **facilités de paiement** credit or payment facilities; Com **f. de reprise** trade-in facility; **facilités de transport** transport facilities

faciliter [fasilite] VT to make easier; **f. qch à qn** to make sth easier for sb; **cela ne va pas f. les choses** it won't make things (any) easier

facob [fakɔb] NM (abrév **traité facultatif obligatoire**) open cover

FAÇON [fasɔ̃]

way **1**	▪ manner **1**	▪ so as to (de façon à) **3**	▪ so that (de façon que) **4**
▪ behaviour (façons) **5**	▪ making **7**

NF **1** (manière de faire qch) way, manner; **ils vivent encore à la f. de leurs ancêtres** they still live in the manner of their ancestors or as their ancestors did; **il n'y a pour toi qu'une seule f. de t'en sortir** there's only one way for you to come through all right; **il n'y a pas trente-six façons de le faire** there are no two ways of doing it; **avoir une f. à soi de faire qch** to have one's own way of doing sth; **je le ferai à ma f.** I shall do it (in) my own way; **ce n'est qu'une f. de parler** it's just a manner of speaking; **ce n'est pas une f. de parler à son père** that's no way to speak to one's father; **ce n'est pas une f. de parler pour un petit garçon** that's no way for a little boy to speak; **je ne tolérerai pas ces façons de parler** I won't tolerate that sort of language; **tu pars en vacances? – oui, f. de parler, je vais garder mes neveux** are you going on holiday? – yes, I suppose you could say that or in a manner of speaking or sort of, I'm looking after my nephews; **ce n'est pas ma f. de faire** it's not my way of doing things; **ils agissent tous de la même f.** they all act alike or in the same way; **elle a une curieuse f. de voir les choses** she has a strange way of

looking at things; **de la bonne f.** properly, in the right way; **la f. dont l'anglais est enseigné** the way (in which) English is taught; Suisse **avoir bonne/mauvaise f.** to look good/bad, to create a good/bad impression

2 de cette f. (in) this way, Fml thus; **venez avec nous, de cette f. cela ne vous coûtera rien** come with us, that way it won't cost you anything; **d'une** ou **de f. générale, on peut dire que …** generally speaking, one can say that …; **d'une f. ou d'une autre** one way or another, somehow or other; **de toute f. j'irai** anyhow or anyway or in any case I shall go; **en aucune f.!** not at all!, by no means!; **cela ne me dérange en aucune f.** it doesn't disturb me in any way

3 de f. à so as to; **parlez de f. à vous faire comprendre** speak so that you can be understood; **elle parle de f. à ce que tout le monde l'entende** she speaks so that or in such a way that everyone can hear her SEE GRAMMAR B33

4 de (telle) f. que so that; **parlez de f. qu'on vous comprenne** speak so that you can be understood; **il pleuvait de telle f. que je fus obligé de rentrer** it was raining so hard that I had to go home; Vieilli **il pleuvait, de f. que je fus obligé de rentrer** it was raining, (and) so I had to go home SEE GRAMMAR B33

5 façons (comportement) manners, behaviour; **en voilà des façons!** what a way to behave!; **ce ne sont pas des façons!** that's no way to behave!

6 sans façon(s) (personne) unaffected, straightforward; **traiter qn sans f.** to treat sb in an offhand manner; **un repas sans f.** an unpretentious or a simple meal; **non merci, sans f.** no thanks, really (not); **sans plus de façons** without further or any more ado; **faire des façons** to make a fuss; **on est entre nous, on ne va pas faire de façons** we're all friends here, we won't stand on ceremony

7 (exécution) making, fashioning; (style) style; **f. d'un manteau** making (up) of a coat; (coupe) cut of a coat; **matière et f.** material and labour; **compter 50 euros de f.** to charge 50 euros for labour; **on travaille f.** (dans une annonce) customers' own materials made up; **un poème de sa f.** a poem of his own composition; **robe qui a bonne f.** well-cut dress; Agr **donner une f. à la terre** to cultivate the soil; **cuir f. porc** imitation pigskin; **sac f. cuir** imitation leather bag

faconde [fakɔ̃d] NF (de l'élocution) fluency, volubility, Péj garrulousness; **avoir de la f.** to be fluent or voluble, Péj to be garrulous; **quelle f.!** he/she talks so much!, Fam what a bletherer!

façonnage [fasɔnaʒ] NM **1** (action de travailler) (du bois) working, shaping; (sur un tour) turning; (de l'argile) fashioning **2** (fabrication) (à la main) making, fashioning; Couture making (up); Ind manufacturing **3** (dans l'édition) forwarding **4** Fig (d'une personne) shaping

façonné [fasɔne] ADJ Tex (tissu) figured

façonnement [fasɔnmɑ̃] NM = façonnage

façonner [fasɔne] VT **1** (travailler) (bois, métal, pierre etc) to work, to shape; (sur un tour) to turn; (argile) to fashion; Agr **f. la terre** to work the soil **2** (fabriquer) (à la main) to make, to fashion; Couture to make (up); Ind to manufacture **3** (dans l'édition) to forward **4** Fig (personne, caractère) to mould, Am to mold, to shape; **f. qn à son image** to mould sb in one's own image

façonnier, -ière [fasɔnje, -jɛr] ADJ (personne) affected, mannered

NM Ordinat computer bureau

fac-similé, pl **fac-similés** [faksimile] NM facsimile

factage [faktaʒ] NM **1** (de marchandises) carriage (and delivery); **payer le f.** to pay the carriage **2** *(de lettres etc)* delivery

facteur [faktœr] NM **1** *(de la poste)* postman, *Am* mailman **2** *(élément)* factor; **le f. chance/ humain/temps** the chance/human/time factor; **f. coût** cost factor; **f. économique** economic factor; *Méd* **f. de risque** risk factor; *Mktg* **f. de situation** situational factor; **f. déterminant** determining factor, determinant; *Méd* **f. rhésus** rhesus factor **3** *Math* factor; **f. premier/commun** prime/common factor; **mettre un nombre en facteurs** to factorize a number **4** *Mus (fabricant)* maker; **f. d'orgues** organ builder; **f. de pianos** piano maker

factice [faktis] ADJ **1** *(objet)* false, artificial; *(articles en vitrine)* dummy; *(moustache, barbe)* false; **cuir/diamant f.** imitation leather/diamond; **les bouteilles de parfum en vitrine sont factices** the bottles of perfume in the window are dummies **2** *Fig (joie, pitié etc)* false, feigned; *(sourire)* forced; *(beauté)* artificial

factieux, -ieuse [faksjø, -jøz] ADJ factious, seditious

■ N agitator, troublemaker

faction [faksjɔ̃] NF **1** *Mil* sentry duty, guard; **être de** *ou* **en f.** to be on guard *or* on sentry duty; **mettre qn en f.** to put sb on guard; *Fig* **j'ai dû me mettre en f. devant sa porte** I had to wait around outside his/her door **2** *(groupe)* faction

factionnaire [faksjɔner] NM *(sentinelle)* sentry, guard; **poser/relever un f.** to post/relieve a sentry *or* guard

factitif, -ive [faktitif, -iv] ADJ *Gram* causative, factitive

factoriel, -ielle [faktɔrjɛl] ADJ, NF *Math* factorial

factoring [faktɔriŋ] NM *Com* factoring

factorisation [faktɔrizasjɔ̃] NF *Math* factorization

factotum [faktɔtɔm] NM factotum

factrice [faktris] NF postwoman, *Am* mailwoman

factuel, -elle [faktɥɛl] ADJ factual

facturation [faktyrasjɔ̃] NF invoicing, billing; **(service de) f.** invoice department; *Ordinat* **f. à la durée** pay-as-you-go

facture[1] [faktyr] NF **1** *(style) (d'un morceau de musique, d'un poème, d'un tableau etc)* construction; *(d'un artiste etc)* style, technique **2** *Mus (fabrication)* making; *(d'orgues)* building

facture[2] NF *Com* invoice, bill (of sale); **faire** *ou* **dresser** *ou* **établir une f.** to make out an invoice; **f. d'électricité/de gaz** electricity/ gas bill; **selon** *ou* **suivant f.** as per invoice; *Écon* **la f. pétrolière de la France** France's oil bill

▸▸ **f. d'achat** purchase invoice; **f. d'avoir** credit note; **f. certifiée** certified invoice; **f. client** guest bill; **f. commerciale** commercial invoice; **f. de confirmation** confirmation invoice; **f. consulaire** consular invoice; **f. de débit** debit note; **f. détaillée** itemized invoice; **f. de doit** debit note; **f. douanière** customs invoice; **f. à l'exportation** export invoice; **f. originale** invoice of origin; **f. pro forma** pro forma invoice; **f. provisoire** pro forma invoice; **f. rectificative** amended invoice; **f. de transitaire** forwarding agent's invoice; **f. de vente** sales invoice

facturer [faktyre] VT *(marchandises)* to invoice; **le papier nous a été facturé 50 euros** we were invoiced 50 euros for the paper

facturette [faktyrɛt] NF credit card sales slip

facturier, -ière [faktyrje, -jer] NM *(livre)* sales book; **f. d'entrée** purchase ledger; **f. de sortie** sales ledger

■ N *(employé)* invoice clerk; **f. d'entrée** purchase ledger clerk; **f. de sortie** sales ledger clerk

facultatif, -ive [fakyltatif, -iv] ADJ optional; **arrêt f.** request stop

facultativement [fakyltativmɑ̃] ADV optionally

faculté [fakylte] NF **1** *(don, capacité)* faculty, ability, power; **facultés de l'esprit** *ou* **intellectuelles** intellectual faculties; **ne pas avoir la f. de marcher** to be unable to walk; **jouir de toutes ses facultés** to be in possession of all one's faculties; **elle n'a plus toutes ses facultés** she no longer has all her faculties; **homme doué de grandes facultés** man of great abilities

2 *(droit)* right; *(possibilité)* option; **avoir la f. de faire qch** *(droit)* to have the right to do sth; *(possibilité)* to have the option of doing sth; **f. de rachat** buy-back option

3 *Vieilli (ressources)* resources, means; **elle dépense au-dessus de ses facultés** she spends beyond her means

4 *Univ* faculty; **professeur de f.** = (university) professor; *Vieilli* **la F.** the Faculty of Medicine; *(les médecins)* the medical profession; *Hum* **la F. m'interdit de boire** I'm forbidden to drink, doctor's orders; **à la f., en f.** at university; **entrer en f.** to go to university

▸▸ *Com* **facultés assurées** insured cargo

fada [fada] *Fam* ADJ *(fou)* crazy

■ N crackpot

fadaise [fadɛz] NF silly remark; *(chose insignifiante)* trifle; **débiter des fadaises** to talk nonsense

fadasse [fadas] ADJ *Fam (goût, boisson, nourriture etc)* insipid, bland; *(couleur)* pale, washed-out; *(livre, style etc)* dreary, dull

fade [fad] ADJ *(plat, boisson, goût etc)* insipid, bland; *(plaisanterie)* tame; *(compliments)* banal, bland; *(couleur)* drab, washed-out; *(odeur)* stale; *(livre, conversation, style etc)* dull, dreary; *(beauté)* insipid

fadé [fade] ADJ *Fam* **être f.** *(remarquable)* to beat them all, to take the biscuit *or Am* the cake

fader (se) [səfade] VPR *Fam* **se f. qn/qch** to get landed with sb/sth

fadeur [fadœr] NF **1** *(d'un plat, d'une boisson, de goût etc)* insipidness, blandness; *(d'une plaisanterie)* tameness; *(de compliments)* banality; *(d'une couleur)* drabness; *(d'une odeur)* staleness; *(d'un livre, style etc)* dullness, dreariness; *(d'une beauté)* insipidness **2** **fadeurs** *(compliments)* banal *or* bland compliments; **dire des fadeurs à qn** to pay sb banal *or* bland compliments

fading [fadiŋ] NM *Radio* fading; *Aut* (brake) fade

faf [faf] N *Fam* fascist

fafiot [fafjo] NM *Arg* banknote, *Am* bill

fafouin, -ouine [fafwɛ̃, -win] *Can Fam* ADJ scatter-brained, *Br* scatty

■ N scatterbrain; **arrête de faire le f., tu vas avoir un accident!** stop acting the fool *or* clowning around, you'll have an accident!

fagot [fago] NM bundle of firewood; *Fig* **sentir le f.** to smack of heresy; *Fam* **bouteille de vin de derrière les fagots** bottle of wine from the hidden store *or* kept for special occasions; **un repas de derrière les fagots** an extra-special meal; **une idée de derrière les fagots** a remarkable idea

fagotage [fagɔtaʒ] NM **1** *(du bois)* tying up in bundles **2** *Péj (accoutrement)* ridiculous get-up *or* rig-out

fagoter [fagɔte] VT **1** *(bois)* to tie up in bundles **2** *Péj (accoutrer)* to rig *or* deck out; **mal/ bizarrement fagoté** badly/oddly dressed

■ VPR **se fagoter** *Péj* to rig *or* deck oneself out

FAI [ɛfai] NM *Ordinat (abrév* **fournisseur d'accès à l'Internet)** IAP

faiblard [fɛblar] ADJ *Fam* (a bit) weak, weakish

faible [fɛbl] ADJ **1** *(physiquement) (personne, membres etc)* weak, feeble; *(cœur, yeux, constitution)* weak; *(arche, branche etc)* weak, unstable; *(pays, armée etc)* weak; **avoir la vue f.** to have weak *or* poor eyesight; **le sexe f.** the weaker sex; **une f. femme** a helpless woman

2 *(intellectuellement) (personne, idée, style, film etc)* weak, poor; *(intelligence)* low; **élève f. en chimie** pupil weak *or* poor in *or* at chemistry; **f. d'esprit** feeble-minded; **côté/point f.** weak side/point; **et le terme est f.!** and that's putting it mildly!

3 *(moralement) (personne)* weak, soft; *(caractère)* weak; **être f. avec qn** to be weak *or* soft with sb; **f. de caractère** weak-willed

4 *(léger) (café, vin etc)* weak; *(son, voix)* faint, quiet; *(odeur)* faint, slight; *(lumière)* faint, dim; *(vent)* light; *Mus* **temps f.** weak *or* unaccented beat; **boisson f. en alcool** low-alcohol drink; **f. en calories** low-calorie

5 *(petit) (quantité, majorité etc)* small; *(avantage, différence, réaction, chance, espoir)* slight; *(prix, revenu, loyer etc)* low; *(récolte, rendement)* poor; *(vitesse)* low, slow; **à une f. hauteur/profondeur** not very high up/deep down; **cela ne vous en donne qu'une f. idée** that gives you only a vague idea of it; *Naut* **f. tirant d'eau** shallow draught; **à f. émission** low-emission

6 *Gram (verbe, conjugaison)* weak

■ N *(personne sans force morale)* weakling, weak person; **les faibles** the weak; **les faibles d'esprit** the feeble-minded; **défendre le f. et l'opprimé** to defend the weak and oppressed

■ NM **1** *(défaut)* weak point, weakness; **le f. chez moi, c'est …** my weak point *or* weakness is …

2 *(penchant)* weakness; **avoir un f. pour qch/qn** to have a weakness for sth/a soft spot for sb; **prendre qn par son f.** to take advantage of sb's weakness

faiblement [fɛbləmɑ̃] ADV *(résister, insister, protester)* weakly, feebly; *(éclairer)* faintly, dimly; *(parler, crier)* quietly, faintly; *(entendre)* faintly; **f. attiré/parfumé** slightly attracted/flavoured

faiblesse [fɛblɛs] NF **1** *(physique) (d'une personne, des membres etc)* weakness, feebleness; *(du cœur, de la vue, d'une constitution etc)* weakness; *(d'une arche, d'une branche, d'un gouvernement, d'une armée etc)* weakness; *(syncope)* (sudden) faintness; **elle eut une f.** she (suddenly) felt faint; **je tombais de f.** I was ready to drop (with exhaustion); **donner des signes de f.** *(d'une machine)* to be showing signs of wear and tear; *Vieilli* **tomber en f.** to swoon, to faint

2 *(intellectuelle) (d'un élève, argument, style etc)* weakness, poorness; **f. d'esprit** feeble-mindedness

3 *(morale)* weakness (**envers qn** towards sb); **f. de caractère** weakness of character; **la f. humaine** human weakness *or* frailty; **la f. d'une mère** a mother's indulgence; **avoir la f. de faire qch** to be weak enough to do sth; **dans un moment de f. je lui ai dit oui** in a moment of weakness I said yes to him; **avoir des faiblesses pour qn** to have a soft spot for sb

4 *(manque d'intensité) (d'un son, d'une odeur, d'une lumière)* faintness; *(du vent)* lightness

5 *(petitesse) (d'une quantité, majorité etc)* smallness; *(d'une différence, réaction etc)* slightness; **la f. de leurs revenus** their low income

6 *(défaut) (d'une personne)* weakness, fail-

fantasmagorique [fɑ̃tasmagɔrik] ADJ phantasmagoric(al)

fantasme [fɑ̃tasm] NM *(situation imaginée)* fantasy; **tu vis dans tes fantasmes** you're living in a fantasy world

fantasmer [fɑ̃tasme] VI to fantasize (**sur** about)

fantasque [fɑ̃task] ADJ *(personne, manières etc)* whimsical; *(histoire, forme etc)* odd, weird

fantassin [fɑ̃tasɛ̃] NM foot soldier, infantryman

fantastique [fɑ̃tastik] ADJ **1** *(imaginaire)* *(être, animal etc)* imaginary **2** *(surnaturel)* *(lumière, atmosphère etc)* weird, eerie **3** *(incroyable)* *(idée, histoire etc)* fantastic **4** *(formidable)* *(succès, plan, somme etc)* fantastic; **paysage d'une beauté f.** fantastically beautiful scenery **5** *Beaux-Arts, Cin, Littér* fantastic
NM **le f.** the fantastic; *(art)* fantasy art; *(littérature)* fantasy literature

fantastiquement [fɑ̃tastikmɑ̃] ADV fantastically; *(d'une manière surnaturelle)* weirdly, eerily

fantoche [fɑ̃tɔʃ] NM *(marionnette)*, *Fig (personne)* puppet
ADJ **gouvernement f.** puppet government

fantomatique [fɑ̃tɔmatik] ADJ ghostly

fantôme [fɑ̃tom] NM ghost, phantom; *Cin, TV* ghost, ghosting; **train f.** ghost train; *Mus* **le Vaisseau F.** the Flying Dutchman; **ville f.** ghost town; **membre(-) f.** phantom limb; *Fig* **ce n'est plus qu'un f.** *(très maigre)* he's just a skeleton, he's nothing but skin and bone; *Pol* **gouvernement/cabinet f.** shadow government/cabinet

fanzine [fɑ̃zin] NM fanzine

FAO NF *Ordinat (abrév* **fabrication assistée par ordinateur)** CAM

faon [fɑ̃] NM fawn, calf

FAQ [ɛfaky] *Ordinat (abrév* **frequently asked questions, foire aux questions)** FAQ

faquin [fakɛ̃] NM *Arch, Péj* varlet

FAR [far] NF *Mil (abrév* **force d'action rapide)** = (French) strike force, *Am* ≃ RDF

far [far] NM **f. breton** custard flan (with prunes)

farad [farad] NM *Élec (unité)* farad

faramineux, -euse [faraminø, -øz] ADJ *Fam* phenomenal, staggering; **il lui a fait des compliments pour le moins f.** his compliments were slightly over the top

farandole [farɑ̃dɔl] NF farandole

faraud, -aude [faro, -od] *Fam Vieilli* ADJ swanky, swaggering
N swaggerer; **faire le f.** to swagger

farce [fars] NF **1** *Culin* stuffing **2** *(tour)* *(practical)* joke, prank, trick; **faire des farces à qn** to play tricks *or* (practical) jokes on sb; *Com* **farces et attrapes** tricks and jokes; **magasin de farces et attrapes** joke shop; *Can Fam* **f. plate** sick *or* tasteless joke **3** *Théâtre, Fig* farce; **la situation va tourner à la f.** the situation is becoming farcical *or* is turning into a farce
ADJ *Fam Vieilli* funny, comical

farceur, -euse [farsœr, -øz] ADJ *(rire, œil)* roguish, mischievous
N **1** *(qui fait des tours)* (practical) joker, prankster; **je me demande qui est le petit f. qui m'a fait ça** I wonder who the joker is that I have to blame for this **2** *(blagueur)* joker, wag; **c'est un f. qui vous aura dit cela** somebody's been pulling your leg

farcir [farsir] VT **1** *Culin (volaille, légume etc)* to stuff **2** *Fig (bourrer)* to cram, to stuff (**de** with); **arrête de lui f. le crâne avec tes histoires** stop filling his/her head with your non-

sense; *Fam* **j'ai la tête farcie** my head's fit to burst
VPR **se farcir 1 se f. la tête d'idées romantiques** to fill one's head with romantic ideas **2** *Fam (travail, lessive etc)* to get landed *or* stuck *or Br* lumbered with; **on va encore devoir se f. ta mère tout le week-end** we're going to have to put up with your mother again all weekend; **il faut se le f.** he's impossible *or* really hard to get on with; **tu as lu son livre? il faut se le f.** have you read his book? it's really hard going **3** *Vulg (posséder sexuellement)* to screw, *Br* to have it off with, *Am* to ball

fard [far] NM make-up; **f. à joues** blusher; **f. à paupières** eye shadow; **la vérité sans f.** the plain unvarnished truth; **parler sans f.** to speak candidly *or* openly; *Fam* **piquer un f.** to go red, to blush

fardage [fardaʒ] NM *Com (de marchandises inférieures)* camouflaging

farde [fard] NF *Belg* **1** *(cahier)* exercise book **2** *(chemise)* folder **3** *(cartouche de cigarettes)* carton *(of cigarettes)*

fardeau, -eaux [fardo] NM burden, load; *Fig* burden; **le f. des impôts** the burden of taxation; *Fig* **c'est un lourd f. qu'il traîne** it's a millstone round his neck

farder [farde] VT **1** *(maquiller)* *(personne, son visage)* to make up; **trop fardé** over made-up; **f. la vérité/les faits** to gloss over *or* disguise the truth/facts; **le film présente une version fardée de cet événement** the film presents a dressed-up *or* cosmetic version of the event **2** *Com (marchandises inférieures)* to camouflage
VPR **se farder** to make up one's face, to put on one's make-up; **se f. les yeux** to put eye shadow on

farfadet [farfadɛ] NM (hob)goblin, sprite

farfelu, -ue [farfəly] *Fam* ADJ *(personne, idée etc)* weird, strange
N weirdo

farfouiller [farfuje] VI *Fam* to rummage (about)

faribole [faribɔl] NF *(propos)* piece of nonsense; **dire des fariboles** to talk nonsense

farinacé [farinase] ADJ farinaceous

farine [farin] NF **1** flour; **folle f.** flour dust, mill dust; **f. d'avoine** oatmeal; **f. de maïs** cornflour, *Am* cornstarch; **f. de moutarde** mustard powder; **f. de poisson** fish meal; **farines animales** bone meal; *Fam* **de la même f.** of the same kind; **ce sont gens de (la) même f.** they are birds of a feather; *Fam* **rouler qn dans la f.** to take sb for a ride **2** *Tech* **f. de forage** bore dust

fariner [farine] VT *Culin* to coat with flour, to flour

farineux, -euse [farinø, -øz] ADJ **1** *(qui est recouvert de farine)* floury, covered with flour; *Péj (au goût)* floury **2** *(contenant de la fécule)* *(nourriture)* starchy, *Spéc* farinaceous
NMPL starchy food, *Spéc* farinaceous food

farlouse [farluz] NF *Orn* meadow pipit

farniente [farnjɛnte] NM *(pleasurable)* idleness, dolce farniente

farouche [faruʃ] ADJ **1** *(pas apprivoisé)* *(animal, oiseau)* timid, shy; **leurs chats ne sont pas farouches** their cats are quite tame **2** *(timide)* *(personne)* shy **3** *(acharné, violent)* *(ennemi, résistance, regard etc)* fierce; **volonté f.** iron *or* unshakeable will **4** *(peu civilisé)* *(gens, pays etc)* wild, uncivilized

farouchement [faruʃmɑ̃] ADV fiercely

fart [far(t)] NM (ski) wax

fartage [fartaʒ] NM *(de skis)* waxing

farter [farte] VT *(skis)* to wax

fascicule [fasikyl] NM **1** *(d'une publication)* instalment, part, section; *(brochure)* bro-

chure, leaflet; **publier un livre par fascicules** to publish a book in parts *or* instalments **2** *Mil* **f. de mobilisation** call-up instructions

fasciculé [fasikyle] ADJ *Bot* fascicular, fasciculate

fascinant [fasinɑ̃] ADJ *(personne)* fascinating; *(beauté, yeux, sourire etc)* captivating, bewitching

fascinateur, -trice [fasinatœr, -tris] ADJ *Litt* captivating, bewitching

fascination [fasinasjɔ̃] NF fascination

fascine [fasin] NF *(de brindilles)* faggot; *Constr* fascine

fasciner [1](fasine) VT **1** *(d'un serpent)* *(proie)* to fascinate, to hypnotize **2** *(attirer l'attention de)* to fascinate; *(charmer)* to captivate, to bewitch; **elle est fascinée par l'argent** she is very impressed by money

fasciner [2] VT *Constr (rive etc)* to line with fascines; **route fascinée** corduroy road

fascisant [faʃizɑ̃] ADJ *Pol* fascistic

fasciser [faʃize] VT *Pol* to make fascist

fascisme [faʃism] NM *Pol* fascism

fasciste [faʃist] ADJ, N *Pol* fascist

faste [1](fast) NM INV *(d'une cérémonie)* pomp, splendour, *Am* splendor; *(d'une demeure)* sumptuousness, splendour; **mariage sans f.** quiet wedding; **la cérémonie aura lieu sans f.** the ceremony will be a simple affair

faste [2] ADJ **jour f.** *Antiq* lawful day; *(jour favorable)* lucky day; **période f.** good period; **je paie la note, je suis dans une période f.!** I'll pay the bill, I'm in the money, I'm flush

fast-food, pl fast-foods [fastfud] NM **1** *(restauration)* fast food **2** *(lieu)* fast-food restaurant, fast-food bar

fastidieusement [fastidjøzmɑ̃] ADV tiresomely, tediously

fastidieux, -ieuse [fastidjø, -jøz] ADJ dull, tiresome, tedious; **besognes fastidieuses** drudgery

> Il faut noter que l'adjectif anglais **fastidious** est un faux ami. Il signifie **pointilleux, difficile.**

fastoche [fastɔʃ] ADJ *Fam* dead easy

fastueusement [fastɥøzmɑ̃] ADV sumptuously, lavishly

fastueux, -euse [fastɥø, -øz] ADJ *(personne, vie)* lavish; *(ameublement, dîner etc)* sumptuous

FAT [fat] NF *Ordinat (abrév* **File Allocation Table)** FAT

fat [fa(t)] ADJ *(personne)* conceited, self-satisfied
NM conceited *or* self-satisfied person

fatal, -als [fatal] ADJ **1** *(mortel)* *(accident, résultat etc)* fatal; **heure fatale** fatal hour, hour of death; **coup f.** deadly *or* fatal blow; **le choc lui a été f.** the shock killed him **2** *(nuisible)* *(beauté, oubli)* fatal; **f. à qn** fatal *or* disastrous for sb; **erreur fatale** fatal mistake; *Ordinat* fatal error; **femme fatale** femme fatale **3** *(inévitable)* inevitable; **c'est f.** it's bound *or* sure to happen, it's inevitable; **on ne peut pas échapper au cours f. des choses** you can't avoid the inevitable

fatalement [fatalmɑ̃] ADV inevitably; **ils devaient f. se fâcher** they were bound to fall out

> Il faut noter que l'adverbe anglais **fatally** est un faux ami. Il signifie **mortellement** ou **irrémédiablement.**

fatalisme [fatalism] NM fatalism

fataliste [fatalist] N fatalist
ADJ fatalistic

fatalité [fatalite] NF **1** *(destin)* fate; **poursuivi**

par la f. pursued by fate; **c'est la f.!** it's just bad luck!; **c'est (comme) une f.** it's an awful coincidence **2** *(malédiction)* misfortune **3** *(inévitabilité)* inevitability

> Il faut noter que le nom anglais **fatality** signifie également **victime**.

fatidique [fatidik] **ADJ** fateful

fatigabilité [fatigabilite] **NF** tendency to get tired; **il est d'une grande f.** he gets tired very easily

fatigable [fatigabl] **ADJ** easily tired

fatigant [fatigã] **ADJ 1** *(épuisant)* tiring, exhausting; **c'est f. pour le cœur** it strains the heart; **c'est f. pour les yeux** it's tiring on the eyes, it's a strain on the eyes **2** *(lassant)* annoying, tiresome, wearisome; **c'est f. de ne jamais réussir** it's annoying or tiresome or wearisome never to be successful

> Attention: ne pas confondre **tiring** et **tiresome** lorsqu'on traduit **fatigant**. Tiring s'applique à la fatigue physique alors que **tiresome** exprime la lassitude.

fatigue [fatig] **NF 1** *(d'une personne, des membres etc)* tiredness, weariness, fatigue; **tomber** ou **être mort de f.** to be dead tired, to be ready to drop; **ressentir une grande/légère f.** to feel very/a bit tired or weary; **f. nerveuse** nervous exhaustion; **f. intellectuelle** mental strain; **f. oculaire** eyestrain; **état de f. générale** general fatigue **2** *Tech (d'un métal, d'une pièce etc)* fatigue **3** *(effort pénible)* strain, effort; **épargner** ou **éviter à qn la f. de qch/de faire qch** to save sb the strain or effort of sth/of doing sth

fatigué [fatige] **ADJ 1** *(épuisé)* *(personne, membres etc)* tired (out), weary; *(traits, regard, voix etc)* tired; *(yeux, cœur)* strained; *(cerveau)* tired, overworked; **f. par le voyage** travel-worn, travel-weary **2** *Fig* **f. de qch/qn** tired or weary of sth/sb; **f. de faire qch** tired or weary of doing sth **3** *Méd (dérangé)* *(estomac, foie etc)* upset **4** *(usé)* *(vêtements, chaussures etc)* worn (out), shabby; *(moteur)* worn out

fatiguer [fatige] **VT 1** *(épuiser)* *(personne)* to tire (out), to make tired or weary; *(cheval)* to tire; *(surmener)* to overwork; **f. le cœur/les yeux** to strain the heart/the eyes; *Iron* **si ça ne te fatigue pas trop évidemment** not if it's too tiring for you or it's not too much of an effort of course
2 *(soumettre à un long usage etc)* *(machine, moteur, solive etc)* to strain; *(vêtements, chaussures etc)* to wear out; *(champ, sol)* to exhaust, to impoverish; **f. un livre** to give a book a lot of hard wear
3 *(remuer)* *(salade)* to mix, to toss
4 *(importuner)* to annoy, to irritate; *(lasser)* to weary, to wear down
VI *(d'une personne)* to tire, to get tired (out); *(d'un bateau, moteur)* to labour, *Am* to labor; *(d'une solive etc)* to show strain; **je commence à f. sérieusement** I'm beginning to get really tired
VPR se fatiguer *(d'une personne)* to get tired (out), to tire; *(en travaillant beaucoup)* to tire oneself out (**à faire qch** doing sth); **se f. les yeux/le cœur** to strain one's eyes/heart; *Iron* **il ne s'est pas (trop) fatigué** he didn't exactly exert himself; **ne te fatigue pas, je m'en occupe** don't bother, I'll see to it; **c'était bien la peine que je me fatigue à préparer le repas** a fat lot of use it was me wearing myself out getting the meal ready; **ne vous fatiguez pas, je suis au courant** don't waste your breath, I know all about it; **se f. de qch/qn** to get tired or to tire of sth/sb; **se f. de faire qch** to get tired or to tire of doing sth

fatras [fatra] **NM** *(d'idées, de papiers etc)* jumble, muddle, hotchpotch

fatuité [fatɥite] **NF** (self-)conceit, self-satisfaction

fatwa [fatwa] **NF** *Rel* fatwa; **prononcer une f. contre qn** to declare or issue a fatwa against sb

fauber(t) [fobɛr] **NM** *Naut* (deck) swab, mop

faubourg [fobur] **NM 1** *(quartier périphérique)* suburb; **accent des faubourgs** (Parisian) working-class accent **2** *(quartier de grande ville)* district

faubourien, -ienne [foburjɛ̃, -jɛn] **ADJ** *(accent etc)* (Parisian) working-class
N working-class Parisian

fauchage [foʃaʒ] **NM 1** *(du blé, d'un champ de blé etc)* reaping; *(de l'herbe, d'une prairie etc)* mowing, cutting **2** *Mil (de troupes)* mowing down; *(procédé de tir)* sweeping of the ground (with machine-gun fire)

fauchaison [foʃɛzɔ̃] **NF 1** *(saison)* reaping time; *(où l'on fauche l'herbe)* mowing time **2** *(action)* = **fauchage 1**

fauchard [foʃar] **NM** *Agr* double-edged slasher

fauche [foʃ] **NF** *Fam* **1** *(vol)* pinching, thieving; **méfie-toi, il y a de la f. au lycée** watch out, there's a lot of thieving going on at school **2** *(manque d'argent)* pennilessness; **c'est vraiment la f. en ce moment** I'm really broke just now

fauché [foʃe] **ADJ** **fam f. (comme les blés)** (flat) broke, stony-broke, *Am* stone-broke

faucher [foʃe] **VT 1** *(blé, champ de blé etc)* to reap; *(herbe, prairie etc)* to mow, to cut; *Fam* **f. l'herbe sous le pied de qn** to cut the ground from under sb's feet **2** *(abattre)* *(d'une voiture, une mitraillette)* *(piétons, troupes etc)* to mow down; *(d'une guerre, une maladie)* to wipe out; *Rugby, Ftbl etc* **f. son homme** to bring down one's man **3** *Fam (voler)* to swipe, to pinch; **elle m'a fauché ma montre/mon mari** she has swiped or pinched my watch/husband
VI 1 *Fam* **ça fauche par ici** things get swiped or nicked round here **2** *Mil* to sweep the ground (with machine-gun fire)

faucheur, -euse [foʃœr, -øz] **N** *(personne)* reaper; *(qui fauche les herbes)* mower
NM *(insecte)* harvestman, *Am* daddy-long-legs
NF faucheuse *(machine)* reaper; *(pour herbes)* mower; **la Faucheuse** *(la Mort)* the Grim Reaper

faucheux [foʃø] **NM** *(insecte)* harvestman, *Am* daddy-long-legs

faucille [fosij] **NF** sickle, (reaping) hook; **la f. et le marteau** the hammer and sickle

faucon [fokɔ̃] **NM 1** *(oiseau)* falcon, hawk; **f. mâle** tercel, tiercel; **f. pèlerin** peregrine falcon; **chasser au f.** to hawk; **chasse au f.** hawking, falconry **2** *Pol* hawk

fauconneau, -eaux [fokono] **NM** *Orn* young falcon

fauconnerie [fokɔnri] **NF 1** *(lieu)* hawk house, falcon house **2** *(chasse)* falconry, hawking

fauconnier [fokɔ̃je] **NM** falconer

faufil [fofil] **NM** *Couture* basting or *Br* tacking thread

faufilage [fofilaʒ] **NM** *Couture* basting, *Br* tacking

faufiler [fofile] **VT** *Couture* to baste, *Br* to tack
VPR se faufiler *(se glisser)* to thread one's way (**dans, entre, parmi** through); *(entrer)* to slip in, to sneak in; **il s'est faufilé jusqu'au premier rang** he worked his way to the front; **il s'était faufilé parmi les invités** he had slipped in or sneaked in with the guests; **se f. entre les voitures** to nip in and out of the traffic, to thread one's way through the traffic

faufilure [fofilyr] **NF** *Couture* **1** *(résultat)* basted or *Br* tacked seam **2** *(action)* basting, *Br* tacking

faune [fon] **NM** *Myth* faun

faune [fon] **NF** *(animaux)* fauna, animal life; *Fig Péj* **la f. des boîtes de nuit** the nightclub set; **il fréquente une f. bizarre** he associates with a funny crowd

faunesque [fonɛsk] **ADJ** faun-like

faussaire [fosɛr] **N** forger

fausse [fos] **ADJ** *voir* **faux**

faussement [fosmã] **ADV** wrongly, falsely; **un sourire f. aimable** a deceptively pleasant smile

fausser [fose] **VT 1** *(sens, réalité, résultat, faits etc)* to distort; *(informations, chiffres)* to distort, to skew; *(l'esprit, le jugement de qn)* to warp **2** *(clé, serrure, axe etc)* to buckle, to bend, to twist **3** **f. compagnie à qn** to give sb the slip
VPR se fausser 1 *(d'une voix)* to become forced or strained **2** *(d'une clé, d'une serrure, d'un axe etc)* to buckle, to bend

fausset [fosɛ] **NM** *Mus* falsetto; **chanter f.** to sing falsetto; *Fig* **voix de f.** falsetto or high-pitched voice

fausset [fosɛ] **NM** *(d'un tonneau)* spigot, vent peg; **trou de f.** vent hole

fausseté [foste] **NF 1** *(d'une déclaration, idée etc)* falseness, falsity **2** *(de caractère)* duplicity

faustien [fostjɛ̃] **ADJ** Faustian

faut [fo] *voir* **falloir**

faute [fot] **NF 1** *(erreur)* mistake, error; **f. d'étourderie** ou **d'inattention** careless mistake or error; *Ordinat* **f. de frappe** miskey, keying error, typo; **f. d'impression** misprint; **f. de jugement** error of judgment; **f. d'orthographe** spelling mistake; **faire une f.** to make a mistake or an error
2 *(responsabilité)* fault; **être en f.** to be at fault; **trouver** ou **prendre qn en f.** to catch sb out; **c'est la f. de** ou *Fam* **à Pierre** it's Pierre's fault, Pierre's to blame; *Fam* **ce n'est quand même pas ma f. s'il pleut!** it's hardly my fault if it rains!, you can hardly blame me if it rains!; *Fam* **ce n'est pas (de) ma f.** it's not my fault, I'm not to blame; **à qui la f.?** whose fault is it?, who's to blame?; **c'est un peu (de) ma f.** I'm partly to blame; **il a été puni par ma f.** it's my fault he was punished; *Fam* **c'est la f. de personne** it's nobody's fault, nobody's to blame; **c'est la f. à pas de chance** it's just bad luck
3 *(manque)* **le courage lui a fait f.** his courage failed him; **la main-d'œuvre nous fait f.** we're short of labour; **votre jovialité nous a fait f.** we missed your joviality; **et pourtant ce n'est pas l'envie qui lui faisait f.** and yet it's not because he didn't want to; **ne se faire f. de rien** to deny oneself nothing; **nous ne nous faisons jamais f. de lui écrire** we never fail to write to him; **il ne s'est pas fait f. de le lui dire devant tout le monde** he made sure he told him in front of everybody; **sans f.** without fail; **f. d'argent/de temps** for lack or want of money/time; **f. d'essayer** for want of trying; **f. de preuves** for lack of evidence; **f. d'ordres précis** in the absence of definite instructions; **f. de paiement** for non-payment; *Compta* **f. de provision** for lack of funds; **f. de quoi** failing which, otherwise; **f. de réponse satisfaisante** failing a satisfactory reply; **f. de paiement sous quinzaine, nous serons dans l'obligation de majorer notre facture de 10%** should payment not be made within fourteen days, we shall be obliged to add a 10% surcharge to your bill
4 *(délit)* offence, *Am* offense; *(mauvaise action)* misdemeanour, *Am* misdemeanor;

(péché) sin, transgression; *(mauvaise conduite)* misconduct; **f. professionnelle** professional misconduct

5 *Ftbl* foul; *Tennis* fault; *Ftbl* **commettre une f. sur qn** to foul sb; *Tennis* **double f.** double fault; *Tennis* **f. de pied** foot fault; *Tennis* **faire une double f./une f. de pied** to double-fault/foot-fault; *Ftbl* **f. de main** hand ball; **faire une f. de main** to handle the ball

> Il faut noter que le nom anglais **faute** signifie également **défaut**.

fauter [fote] VI *Fam Vieilli (d'une femme)* to go astray

fauteuil [fotœj] NM **1** armchair, easy chair; **f. à oreillettes** wing chair; **f. à bascule** rocking chair; **f. pliant** folding chair; **f. de dentiste** dentist's chair; **f. roulant** wheelchair; *Théâtre* **f. d'orchestre** seat in the stalls *or Am* orchestra; *Théâtre* **f. de (premier) balcon** dress-circle seat, *Am* balcony seat; *Fig* **arriver dans un f.** *(sans peine)* to win hands down, *Br* to walk it; **il a remporté la course/les élections dans un f.** he won the race/election hands down **2** *(d'une assemblée)* chair; **occuper le f.** to be in the chair; **le f. de président** the chairmanship **3** **f. (d'académicien)** seat (in the Académie française)

fauteur [fotœr] NM **f. de troubles** *ou* **de désordre** agitator, troublemaker; **f. de guerre** warmonger

fautif, -ive [fotif, -iv] ADJ **1** *(incorrect)* faulty, incorrect; **calcul f.** miscalculation; **mémoire fautive** defective memory **2** *(coupable)* at fault, in the wrong

N person at fault *or* in the wrong; **va savoir qui est le f. dans cette histoire!** who knows who's at fault *or* to blame in this business!

fautivement [fotivmɑ̃] ADV incorrectly; **j'avais f. éteint mes phares** I had switched off my headlights by mistake

fauve [fov] ADJ **1** *(couleur)* fawn, tawny **2** **bête f.** *(grand félin)* big cat; *Arch (cerf, daim)* deer **3** **odeur f.** musky smell **4** *Beaux-Arts* Fauve, Fauvist

NM **1** *(grand félin)* big cat; **chasse aux (grands) fauves** big-game hunting; **cette chambre sent le f.** it smells sweaty *or* of sweat in this room; **tu sens le f.** you smell sweaty *or* of sweat **2** *(couleur)* fawn **3** *Beaux-Arts* Fauve, Fauvist

fauverie [fovri] NF *(dans un zoo)* big-cat house

fauvette [fovɛt] NF *Orn* warbler; **f. d'hiver** *ou* **des haies** hedge sparrow, dunnock; **f. des roseaux** reed warbler

fauvisme [fovism] NM *Beaux-Arts* Fauvism

FAUX¹, FAUSSE [fo, fos]

ADJ false **1–4** ▪ untrue **1** ▪ fake **2**	▪ bogus **2** ▪ deceitful **3** ▪ wrong **4**
ADV out of tune **1** ▪ wrong **1**	
NM false **1** ▪ imitation **2** ▪ forgery **3**	

ADJ **1** *(qui n'est pas vrai)* false, untrue; **il est f. qu'il soit …** it's false *or* untrue that he is …; **fausse nouvelle** false report; **f. témoin** perjurer; **f. témoignage** false evidence; *(délit)* perjury; **faire un f. témoignage** to give false evidence, to commit perjury; **donner de f. espoirs à qn** to give sb false hope

2 *(qui n'est pas d'origine) (cheveux, dents, cils etc)* false; *(bijoux etc)* imitation, fake; *(docteur)* bogus; **f. bilan** fraudulent balance sheet; **fausse écriture** false entry; **fausse facture** fake invoice; **fausse monnaie** fake *or* counterfeit money; **fabriquer de la fausse monnaie** to counterfeit money; **f. seins** false breasts, *Fam* falsies; **j'ai eu une fausse joie** I got excited about nothing; **elle m'a fait une fausse joie en me le faisant croire** she built up my hopes by making me believe it;

fausse clef skeleton key; **fausse cartouche** dummy cartridge; **f. plafond** false ceiling; **fausse fenêtre** blind window; *Ling* **f. ami** false friend; **faire un f. sens** to give an inaccurate translation/definition; **un f. Monet** a forged *or* fake Monet; *Anat* **fausses côtes** floating ribs; *TV, Cin* **f. raccord** jump cut; *Typ* **f. titre** half title; **fausse sortie** *Mil* feint sortie; *Théâtre* fake *or* sham exit; *Fig* **il a fait une fausse sortie** he pretended to leave

3 *Péj (hypocrite) (personne)* false, deceitful; *(honte, pudeur, modestie)* false; **c'est un f.** *Fam* **jeton** *ou* **très** *Fam* **cul** he's a hypocrite *or Fam* a phoney; **un f. frère** a false friend

4 *(incorrect)* wrong; **fausse date** wrong date; **vous avez fait un f. numéro** you've got *or* dialled *or Am* dialed the wrong number; **raisonnement f.** unsound *or* faulty reasoning; **présenter qch sous un f. jour** to present sth in a false light, to misrepresent sth; **situation fausse** awkward situation; **balance fausse** inaccurate scales; *Aut* **f. alignement** misalignment; **f. poids** false weight; **faire un f. mouvement** to make an awkward movement; **f. pas** slip, stumble; *Fig* faux pas, (social) blunder; **faire un f. pas** *(en marchant)* to stumble, to trip; *Fig* to put one's foot in it, to make a faux pas; *(faire un écart de conduite)* to make a faux pas; **un f. pas en montagne peut vous coûter la vie** one false step in the mountains can cost you your life; *Méd* **fausse couche** miscarriage; **faire fausse route** to take the wrong road; *Fig* to be on the wrong track; **f. calcul** miscalculation; **faire un f. calcul** to miscalculate; *Mus* **fausse note** wrong note; *Fig* false note; *Fig* **il n'y a eu aucune fausse note** there were no hitches, everything went smoothly

ADV **1** **chanter f.** to sing out of tune, to sing off key; **cela sonne f.** that doesn't sound right; **ses paroles sonnent f.** his words have a hollow ring (to them); **rire qui sonne f.** hollow laugh(ter); *Fam* **avoir tout f.** to have it all wrong

2 **poser le pied à f.** to miss one's footing; **accuser qn à f.** to wrongly *or* falsely accuse sb; **porter à f.** to be out of true

NM **1** *(ce qui n'est pas vrai)* **le f.** the false; **distinguer le vrai du f.** to distinguish truth from falsehood

2 *(imitation) (œuvre d'art)* forgery, fake; **(bijouterie en) f.** costume *or* imitation jewellery

3 *(contrefaçon)* forgery; *Jur* **usage de f.** use of forgeries; **inculpé pour f. et usage de f.** charged with forgery and use of forgeries; **s'inscrire en f. contre qch** to dispute the validity of sth; *Compta* **f. en écritures** forgery

faux² NF *Agr* scythe **2** *Anat* falx

faux-bourdon, *pl* **faux-bourdons** NM **1** *Mus* fauxbourdon **2** *Entom* drone

faux-cul, *pl* **faux-culs, faux-derche,** *pl* **faux-derches** NM *Fam* two-faced *Br* swine *or Am* stinker

faux-facturier, *pl* **faux-facturiers** NM = person using fake invoices to commit fraud

faux-filet, *pl* **faux-filets** NM *Culin* sirloin, tenderloin

faux-fuyant, *pl* **faux-fuyants** NM **1** *(prétexte)* subterfuge, evasion, dodge; **chercher des faux-fuyants** to hedge, to prevaricate; **une réponse claire et nette, sans f.** a straight answer with no hedging *or* without any ifs and buts **2** *Arch (sentier)* bypath

faux-monnayeur, *pl* **faux-monnayeurs** NM forger, counterfeiter

faux-rond, *pl* **faux-ronds** NM *Aut* run-out

faux-semblant, *pl* **faux-semblants** NM pretence, sham

faux-titre, *pl* **faux-titres** NM *Typ* half-title

faveur [favœr] NF **1** *(aide, considération)* favour, *Am* favor; **gagner** *ou* **obtenir la f. de qn** to gain sb's favour; **recevoir des marques de f. de qn** to receive signs of favour from sb; **avoir la f. de qn** to be in favour with sb; **être en (grande) f. auprès de qn** to be in (high) favour with sb; **perdre la f. de qn** to fall out of favour with sb; **prix/traitement de f.** preferential *or* special price/treatment; **billet de f.** complimentary ticket; *Jur, Fin* **en f. de** in favour of

2 *(bienfait)* favour, *Am* favor; **faire une f. à qn** to do sb a favour; **nous feriez-nous la f. de venir dîner chez nous** would you do us the favour of coming to have dinner with us; **par f. spéciale** as a special favour; **elle lui accorde ses faveurs** she bestows her favours on him

3 **plaider en f. de qn** to plead in sb's favour *or Am* favor; *Vieilli* **on lui fit grâce en f. de sa jeunesse** he was let off in consideration of his youth; **quête en f. de qn/qch** collection in aid of sb/sth

4 **à la f. de qch** with the help of sth; **à la f. de la nuit** under cover of darkness

5 *(ruban)* ribbon

favorable [favɔrabl] ADJ **1** *(bienveillant) (opinion)* favourable, *Am* favorable (à to); **il est f. à cette idée** he is in favour *or Am* favor of this idea; **elle vous est f.** she is favourably *or Am* favorably disposed towards you; **elle a présenté les choses sous un jour f.** she presented things in a favourable light *or* favourably **2** *(convenable)* favourable, *Am* favorable; *(situation, occasion, circonstances)* auspicious; *(vent)* favourable, fair; **le moment était f. pour lui parler** it was a good moment to speak to him; **recevoir un accueil f.** to be given a favourable reception; **peu f.** unfavourable, *Am* unfavorable

favorablement [favɔrabləmɑ̃] ADV favourably, *Am* favorably

favori, -ite [favɔri, -it] ADJ *(personne, objet, cheval de course etc)* favourite, *Am* favorite

N *(personne)* favourite, *Am* favorite

NF **favorite** *(maîtresse du roi)* favourite *or Am* favorite (mistress)

NM **1** *Courses de chevaux* favourite, *Am* favorite; **le grand f.** the odds-on *or* clear favourite **2** *Ordinat* **favoris** favourites

favoris [favɔri] NMPL sideburns, (side) whiskers

favorisé [favɔrize] ADJ *(milieu, famille)* privileged

favoriser [favɔrize] VT **1** *(avantager) (personne)* to favour, *Am* to favor; **le fait qu'elle soit une femme peut la f.** the fact that she's a woman may work in her favour; **les événements l'ont/ne l'ont pas favorisé** events turned out in her favour *or* on his side/not in his favour *or* against him; **favorisé par le destin** blessed by fate **2** *(encourager) (commerce, arts, crime, maladie, croissance etc)* to encourage, to promote **3** *(faciliter) (entreprise, fuite etc)* to assist, to further

favorite [favɔrit] ADJ, NF *voir* **favori**

favoritisme [favɔritism] NM favouritism, *Am* favoritism; **essayez de ne pas faire de f.** try not to show favouritism

fax [faks] NM *(appareil)* fax (machine); *(message)* fax; **envoyer qch par f.** to send sth by fax, to fax sth; **numéro de f.** fax number; *Ordinat* **f. modem** fax modem; **f. sur papier ordinaire** plain paper fax

faxer [fakse] VT to fax; **je vous faxe les chiffres** I'll fax the figures to you

fayot, -ote [fajo] *Arg* NM *(haricot sec)* bean N *Péj* crawler, creep

fayotage [fajotaʒ] NM *Arg Péj* crawling

fayoter [fajɔte] VI *Arg Péj* to crawl, to creep

FB NM *Anciennement abrév* franc belge

fco ADV *Com abrév* franco

FCP [εfsepe] NM *Fin* (*abrév* **fonds commun de placement**) investment trust, mutual fund

FCPE [εfsepeə] NM *Fin* (*abrév* **fonds commun de placement d'entreprise**) company investment fund

FCPR [εfsepeεr] NM *Fin* (*abrév* **fonds commun de placements à risques**) VCT

f. c(t). (*abrév* **fin courant**) at the end of this month

FDM (*abrév* **fin de mois**) end of month

FDR [εfdeεr] NM (*abrév* **fonds de roulement**) working capital

féal, -ale, -aux, -ales [feal, -o] ADJ *Arch* (*vassal etc*) feal, faithful, trusty

fébrifuge [febrifyʒ] ADJ, NM *Méd* febrifuge; *Pharm* antifebrile, antipyretic

fébrile [febril] ADJ (*pouls, patient etc*) feverish, febrile; *Fig* (*activité, conversation etc*) feverish; **tout le village était f.** the entire village was in a state of excitement

fébrilement [febrilmã] ADV feverishly; (*parler, préparer qch*) excitedly, hurriedly

fébrilité [febrilite] NF feverishness

fécal, -ale, -aux, -ales [fekal, -o] ADJ faecal, *Am* fecal; **matières fécales** faeces, *Am* feces

fèces [fεs] NFPL **1** faeces, *Am* feces **2** *Chimie* sediment, precipitate

FECOM [fekom] NM (*abrév* **Fonds européen de coopération monétaire**) EMCF

fécond [fekɔ̃] ADJ (*femme, animal, œuf, esprit*) fertile; (*terre*) fruitful; (*travail, idée*) fruitful, productive; (*sol, imagination*) fertile, rich; (*auteur, peintre, sculpteur etc*) prolific, productive; **ses films sont féconds en** … his/her films are full of …

fécondabilité [fekɔ̃dabilite] NF *Physiol* fertilizability; **taux de f.** fertility rate

fécondable [fekɔ̃dabl] ADJ fertilizable

fécondateur, -trice [fekɔ̃datœr, -tris] ADJ fertilizing

fécondation [fekɔ̃dasjɔ̃] NF *Biol* (*d'un œuf, ovule*) fertilization; (*d'une femme, d'un animal femelle*) impregnation; (*d'une fleur, plante*) pollination; **f. in vitro** in vitro fertilization; **f. artificielle** (*d'une femme*) artificial insemination; (*d'une fleur, plante*) artificial pollination

féconder [fekɔ̃de] VT *Biol* (*œuf, ovule*) to fertilize; (*femme, animal femelle*) to impregnate; (*fleur, plante*) to pollinate

fécondité [fekɔ̃dite] NF **1** *Physiol* fertility, *Fml* fecundity; **taux de f.** reproduction rate **2** *Fig* (*d'un sol, de l'imagination etc*) fertility; (*d'une idée*) fruitfulness, productiveness; (*d'un écrivain*) productiveness

fécule [fekyl] NF starch; *Culin* **f. de pommes de terre** potato starch or flour

féculent [fekylã] ADJ (*aliment*) starchy
NM starchy food; **tu manges trop de féculents** you eat too much starchy food or starch

FED [εfəde] NM (*abrév* **Fonds européen de développement**) EDF

FEDER [fedεr] NM (*abrév* **Fonds européen de développement régional**) ERDF

fédéral, -ale, -aux, -ales [federal, -o] ADJ **1** federal **2** *Suisse* federal (*relative to the Swiss Confederation*)
NM *Hist Am* Federal; **les fédéraux** (*le FBI*) the Feds

fédéraliser [federalize] VT to federalize

fédéralisme [federalism] NM federalism

fédéraliste [federalist] ADJ, N federalist

fédérateur, -trice [federatœr, -tris] ADJ (*politique*) federative; **élément/principe f.** unifying element/principle
N unifier

fédératif, -ive [federatif, -iv] ADJ federative

fédération [federasjɔ̃] NF (*d'états*) federation; **f. de syndicats (ouvriers)** amalgamated (trade) unions; **f. sportive** sports federation

fédéré [federe] ADJ (*états*) federate
NM *Hist* federate

fédérer [federe] (**je fédère; je fédérai**) VT (*états*) to federate, to federalize
VPR **se fédérer** to federate

fée [fe] NF fairy; **pays des fées** fairyland; *Fig* **doigts de f.** nimble fingers; **une f. du logis** an ideal homemaker; *Suisse* **f. verte** absinthe

feed-back [fidbak] NM INV *Électron, Physiol etc* feedback

feeder [fidœr] NM **1** *Élec* feeder (cable) **2** (*de gaz*) (gas) pipeline

feeling [filiŋ] NM (*sensibilité*) feeling; **avoir un bon f. pour qch** to have a good feeling about sth; **faire qch au f.** to do sth by feel

féerie [fe(e)ri] NF **1** *Théâtre, Cin* fantasy, extravaganza **2** (*spectacle merveilleux*) enchantment; **une f. de lumières** an enchanting display of lights **3** *Vieilli* (*pouvoir des fées*) (power of) enchantment; (*monde des fées*) fairyland

féerique [fe(e)rik] ADJ **1** (*château, monde etc*) fairy, magic **2** *Fig* (*d'une beauté irréelle*) (*vue, paysage etc*) magical, enchanting

feignant, -ante [feɲã, -ãt] ADJ, N *Fam* = **fainéant**

feignasse [fεɲas] NF *Arg* lazy so-and-so

feignasser [fεɲase] VI *Arg* to lounge or laze around

feindre [fɛ̃dr] (*prp* **feignant**; *pp* **feint**; *pr ind* **je feins, n. feignons**; *pr sub* **je feigne**; *impf* **je feignais**; *p hist* **je feignis**; *fu* **je feindrai**) VT (*maladie, surprise etc*) to feign, to simulate, to sham; **f. de faire qch** to pretend to do sth, to make a pretence of doing sth
VI *Litt* to dissemble; **inutile de f.** it's no use pretending

feint [fɛ̃] ADJ **1** (*simulé*) (*maladie, joie etc*) feigned, assumed, sham **2** *Archit* (*porte, fenêtre*) blind, dummy

feinte [fɛ̃t] NF **1** *Boxe, Escrime, Mil* feint; *Ftbl, Rugby etc* **faire une f. (de passe)** to (sell a) dummy **2** (*ruse*) ruse, trick, dodge; *Vieilli* (*dissimulation*) sham, pretence, *Am* pretense; **sans f.** frankly, without pretence

feinter [fɛ̃te] VI *Boxe, Escrime* to feint, to make a feint; *Ftbl, Rugby etc* to (sell a) dummy
VT *Fam* (*duper*) to take in

feldspath [fεldspat] NM *Minér* fel(d)spar

fêlé, -ée [fele] ADJ **1** (*verre, voix etc*) cracked **2** *Fig Fam* **il a le cerveau f.** ou **la tête fêlée, il est f.** he's a bit cracked or crazy; **tu es complètement f. de le lui avoir dit!** you're absolutely crazy to have told him!
N *Fam* maniac; **f. du jazz/des chocolats** jazz/chocolate freak

fêler [fele] VT (*verre, porcelaine etc*) to crack
VPR **se fêler** (*du verre, de la porcelaine, de la voix etc*) to crack

félicitations [felisitasjɔ̃] NFPL congratulations; **adresser des f. à qn** to congratulate sb (**pour qch** on sth); **(toutes mes) f.!** (many) congratulations!; **il a eu les f. du jury** he was congratulated by the jury, he received the jury's congratulations

félicité [felisite] NF bliss, felicity, happiness

féliciter [felisite] VT to congratulate; **f. qn pour** ou **sur qch/d'avoir fait qch** to congratulate sb on sth/on having done sth; **je ne vous félicite pas!** you'll get no praise from me!
VPR **se féliciter** (*être content*) to be pleased or satisfied (**de qch** with sth); (*se louer*) to congratulate oneself (**de qch** on sth; **d'avoir**

fait qch on having done sth); **félicitons-nous de ce que nous avons la vie sauve** let us be thankful we came out alive

félidé [felide] NM *Zool* feline; **les f.** the cat family, *Spéc* the Felidae

félin, -ine [felɛ̃, -in] ADJ (*race*) feline; *Fig* (*grâce, souplesse etc*) feline, cat-like
NM **1** feline; **les grands félins** the big cats; *Spéc* the great felines **2** *Bourse* stripped bond

fellah [fella] NM fellah, Arab peasant

fellation [felasjɔ̃] NF fellatio

félon, -onne [felɔ̃, -ɔn] *Hist, Litt* ADJ treacherous, disloyal
N traitor

félonie [feloni] NF *Hist, Litt* (*déloyauté*) treachery, disloyalty; (*acte*) act of treachery

felouque [fəluk] NF (*bateau*) felucca

fêlure [felyr] NF crack; **f. du crâne** fracture of the skull; *Fig* **une f. dans notre amitié/leur couple** a rift between us/them

femelle [fəmεl] ADJ **1** (*sexe*) female; (*animal*) she-, female; (*éléphant, baleine*) cow; (*oiseau*) hen **2** *Tech* (*vis*) female; *Élec* **prise f.** socket **3** *Bot* female, *Spéc* pistillate
NF (*animal*) female; *très Fam Péj* (*femme*) female

féminin, -ine [feminɛ̃, -in] ADJ (*personne, charme etc*) feminine; (*hormone, population*) female; (*équipe, groupe, magazine, mode etc*) women's; **le sexe f.** the female sex; **vêtements féminins** women's clothes, clothes for women; **les conquêtes féminines d'un homme** a man's female conquests
NM *Gram* feminine; **ce mot est du f.** this word is feminine; **au f.** in the feminine SEE GRAMMAR A16-17; B5-8

> Attention: ne pas confondre **female** et **feminine** lorsque l'on traduit **féminin**. On utilise **feminine** pour décrire les qualités que la société associe traditionnellement aux femmes, alors que **female** s'utilise pour qualifier ce qui est propre au sexe féminin.

féminisant [feminizã] ADJ (*gène*) feminizing

féminiser [feminize] VT **1** (*donner le caractère féminin à*) to make feminine; (*rendre efféminé*) to make effeminate; **f. une profession** to bring or introduce more women into a profession; **profession très féminisée** largely female profession, female-dominated profession **2** *Biol* (*animal mâle*) to feminize **3** *Gram* (*mot*) to make feminine
VPR **se féminiser 1** (*d'une femme*) to become more feminine; (*devenir efféminé*) to become effeminate; **la profession se féminise** the profession is attracting more and more women **2** *Biol* (*d'un animal mâle*) to feminize

féminisme [feminism] NM feminism

féministe [feminist] ADJ, N feminist

féminité [feminite] NF femininity

femme [fam] NF **1** (*personne*) woman, *pl* women; **les femmes, la f.** (*le sexe féminin*) women, womankind; **l'émancipation de la f.** the emancipation of women; **cherchez la f.** there's got to be a woman behind it; **elle est très f.** she's very feminine; **la f. de ma vie** the woman of my dreams, the only woman for me; **être très f. du monde** to be a wonderful hostess; **f. auteur** woman author, authoress; **f. ministre** female minister; **metteur en scène** woman or female director; **f. de tête** woman with a good head on her shoulders; **f. médecin** woman or lady doctor; **parapluie de f.** lady's umbrella; **elle n'est pas f. à se plaindre** she's not the sort (of woman) to complain; **une bonne f.** a simple or good-natured woman; *Fam* (*femme*) a wo-

ficelé [fis(ə)le] ADJ **1** *(lié) (colis, prisonnier etc)* tied up **2** *Fam (habillé)* got up; **être f. comme l'as de pique** to be dressed like a scarecrow **3** *Fam* **c'est bien/mal f.** *(d'un texte, d'une histoire, d'un film)* it hangs/ doesn't hang together well; **un scénario bien f.** a well-crafted screenplay

ficeler [fis(ə)le] VT (**je ficelle; je ficellerai**) *(colis, prisonnier)* to tie up

ficelle [fisɛl] NF **1** *(mince corde)* string; **les ficelles de la marionnette** the puppet's strings **2** *Fig* **c'est lui qui tire les ficelles** he's the one who pulls the strings; **les ficelles du métier** the tricks of the trade; **connaître les ficelles (du métier)** to know the ropes, to know the tricks of the trade; **la f. est un peu grosse** that won't fool anybody **3** *(pain)* small French stick
ADJ *Vieilli* crafty, wily

fiche¹ [fiʃ] NF **1** *Élec (prise)* plug; *(broche)* pin; *Tél (patch)* plug; *(électrique)* jack plug **2** *(morceau de papier)* slip (of paper); *(formulaire)* form; *(dépliant)* leaflet; **remplir une f.** to fill in *or* fill out a form; **faire des fiches de lecture** to write a book report; **fiches-cuisine/-tricot/-santé** *(dans un magazine)* cookery/knitting/health cards **3** *(carte)* (index) card; **jeu de fiches** card index; **mettre des informations en** *ou* **sur fiche(s)** to card-index data **4** *(cheville) (en fer, bois etc)* peg, pin
▸▸ **f. d'accueil** registration form; *Admin* **f. anthropométrique** = (criminal) dossier; **f. d'appréciation** customer satisfaction questionnaire; **f. d'arrivée** registration form; **f. de blocage** *(d'un hôtel etc)* block card, reservation rack card, room rack card; **f. cartonnée** index card; **f. client** customer record; *(d'un hôtel etc)* room rack card; *(sur ordinateur)* guest folio, guest file; **f. de compte** accounts card; **f.-contact** contacts file; *Ind* **f. de contrôle** checking form, *Br* docket; **f. courrier** mail checklist *or* file; **f. dentaire** dental chart; **f. d'entretien** service record; *Ordinat* **f. d'état** report form; **f. d'état civil** = record of civil status *(birth details and marital status)*; **f. explicative** information sheet; **f. de facture** account card; **f. fournisseur** supplier file; *Ordinat* **f. gigogne** dongle; **f. d'hôtel** *(clé)* key card; *Compta* **f. d'imputation** data entry form; **f. d'inscription** registration form; **f. Kardex** *(d'un hôtel etc)* guest history card; **f. médicale** medical record (card); **f.-message** message form; **f. d'observations** *(questionnaire d'évaluation)* comment card; **f. d'occupation** *(d'un hôtel etc)* room rack card; **f. de paie** payslip; **f. à perforations marginales** edge punched card; **f. perforée** perforated card; *Com* **f. de pointage** clocking-in card; **f. de police** = registration card to be filled in by hotel guests from non-EU countries; *(au débarquement)* landing card; **f. de poste** *(descriptif des tâches à accomplir)* task sheet; **f. de présence** *(de salarié)* attendance sheet; **f.-prospect** potential-customer file; **f. signalétique** personal details card; **f. de stock** stock sheet; **f. en T** T-card; **f. technique** specifications sheet; **f. téléphonique** telephone jack plug; *(broche)* telephone jack; *(pour message)* telephone memo; **f. verticale suspendue** vertical suspension file; **f. à visibilité** visible card record; **f. voyageur** *(d'un hôtel etc)* = registration card for foreign guests; **f. Whitney** *(d'un hôtel etc)* Whitney card

fiche² VT, VPR *Fam*= **ficher²**

ficher¹ [fiʃe] VT **1** *(enfoncer) (clou, pieu etc)* to drive in; *(lame)* to plunge; *(épingle)* to stick in; **f. une épingle dans qch** to stick a pin into sth **2** *(mettre sur fiche) (informations)* to file (away), to put on file; *(personne)* to put on file; **il est fiché aux stups** the drugs squad have got him on their files
VPR **se ficher** to stick (**dans** in); **la flèche se**

ficha en plein milieu de la cible the arrow hit the middle of the target; **la balle se ficha dans le mur** the bullet became embedded in the wall

ficher² *(inf souvent* **fiche;** *pp* **fichu)** *Fam* VT **1** *(mettre)* to stick, to shove, *Br* to bung; **f. par terre** *(chapeau etc)* to chuck on the ground; *Fig (gouvernement)* to bring down, to overthrow; *(projet)* to mess up, to put paid to; **t'as tout fichu par terre** you've messed everything up; *Fig* **f. qn à la porte** to chuck sb out; **f. qn dedans** to land *or* drop sb in it **2** *(faire)* to do; **il n'a rien fichu de la journée** he's done damn all all day, he hasn't done a thing all day **3** *(donner)* **f. une gifle à qn** to give sb a slap in the face; **fiche-moi la paix!** leave me alone!, clear off!; **je t'en fiche!** no way!, you must be joking!; **je t'en ficherai, tiens, moi, des petits copains à ton âge!** boyfriends at your age – what are you thinking of!; **ça la fiche mal** *(fait mauvais effet)* it looks really bad (**de faire** to do) **4** **f. le camp** to shove off, to clear off; **fiche-moi le camp!** shove off!, clear off!; **va te faire fiche!** get lost!, go to hell!
VPR **se ficher 1** *(se mettre)* **se f. par terre** *(tomber)* to fall flat; **se f. dedans** *(se tromper)* to make a boo-boo *or* a blunder; **soyons attentifs pour ne pas nous f. dedans cette fois** let's take care we don't land ourselves in it this time **2** **se f. de qn/qch** *(tourner en ridicule)* to make fun of sb/sth; *(mépriser)* not to give a damn about sb/sth; **vous vous fichez de moi!** what do you take me for?; **ça, c'est se f. du monde!** well, what a damned cheek!, that's just not taking things seriously!; **je m'en fiche (pas mal)** I don't give a damn, I couldn't care less; **elle s'en fiche que son père ne soit pas d'accord** she doesn't give a damn *or* couldn't care less if her father doesn't agree

fichet [fiʃɛ] NM *(utilisé au trictrac)* peg

fichette [fiʃɛt] NF **f. client** *(d'un hôtel etc)* reservation card; **f. d'arrivée** arrival form

fichier [fiʃje] NM **1** *(ensemble de fiches)* card index, card-index system; **2** *(boîte)* card-index box; *(meuble)* card-index cabinet; *(à tiroirs)* card-index filing cabinet **3** *Ordinat* file; **volume du f.** file size
▸▸ **f. à accès aléatoire** random access file; **f. à accès limité** restricted file; **f. actif** active file; **f. d'adresses** address file; **f. d'application** application file; **f. ASCII** ASCII file; **f. de base de données** database file; **f. BAT** batch file; **f. binaire** binary file; **f. (des) clients** client *or* customer file; **f. de commande** command file; **f. compte-rendu** log file; *Journ* **f. de coupures** cuttings file; **f. en cours** current file; **f. de destination** target file; **disque** disk file; **f. document** document file; **f. d'entrée** input file; **f. exécutable** executable *or* execute file; **f. FAQ** FAQ file; **f. historique** history file; **f. à imprimer** print(er) file; **f. indexé** indexed file; **f. d'intendance** control file; **f. journal** logging file; **f. Kardex** *(d'un hôtel etc)* guest history file; **f. en lecture seule** read-only file; **f. lisez-moi** read-me file; **f. maître** master file; **f. MP3** MP3 file; **f. non structuré** flat file; **f. par points** bitmap file; **f. principal** master file; **f. rotatif** rotating card index, rotary (card) file; **f. des salariés** personnel files; **f. de sauvegarde** backup file; **f. de secours** backup file; **f. séquentiel** batch *or* sequential file; **f. signature** signature file; **f. de sortie** output file; **f. source** source file; **f. système** system file; **f. (de) texte** text file; **f. de travail** working *or* work file; **f. de tri temporaire** temporary sort file

fichtre [fiʃtr] INT *Vieilli, Fam* **1** *(étonnement)* golly!, good gracious! **2** *(admiration)* my!, *Br* I say! **3** *(contrariété)* blow!, blast! **4** *(intensif)*

f. oui! I should say so!, rather!; **f. non!** not likely!, no fear!

fichtrement [fiʃtrəmɑ̃] ADV *Vieilli (extrêmement)* awfully, frightfully; **je n'en sais f. rien!** how the heck should I know?

fichu¹ [fiʃy] ADJ *Fam* **1** *(maudit)* rotten, awful; **quel f. pays!** what a godforsaken country!; **quel f. temps!** what filthy *or* awful weather!; **tu as vraiment un f. caractère!** nobody can say a word to you; **cette fichue machine** this damn *or* bloody machine **2** *(en mauvais état, perdu)* **il est f.** he's done for, it's all up with him, he's had it; **c'est f.!** *(sans espoir)* (we can) forget it!; **c'est f. pour dimanche** Sunday's out, we can forget Sunday; **ma robe/voiture est fichue** my dress/ car has had it **3** *(habillé)* **être bien/mal f.** to be well/badly turned out *or* dressed **4** *(bâti, conçu)* **elle est vraiment bien fichue, cette fille** that girl's got a great body on her; **c'est bien/mal f.** it's well/badly designed **5** **être mal f.** *(un peu malade)* to be out of sorts, *Br* to be off colour **6** *(capable)* **elle serait fichue d'oublier le rendez-vous** she'd be quite capable of forgetting the appointment, I wouldn't put it past her to forget the appointment; **il n'est pas f. de faire cuire des pâtes** he's not even capable of cooking pasta, even cooking pasta is beyond him

fichu² NM headscarf; *(couvrant les épaules)* fichu, (small) shawl

fictif, -ive [fiktif, -iv] ADJ **1** *(imaginaire)* fictitious, imaginary **2** *(faux) (promesse)* false; *(nom, adresse etc)* false, fictitious; *(lutte)* sham **3** *Fin* **valeur fictive** *(de billets)* face value

fiction [fiksjɔ̃] NF *(fait imaginé)*, *Littér* fiction; **film de f.** fictional film; **livre de f.** work of fiction; **la réalité dépasse la f.** truth is stranger than fiction; **la politique-f.** political pie in the sky; **roman de politique-f.** political novel

fictivement [fiktivmɑ̃] ADV **1** *(par la pensée)* in one's imagination *or* mind **2** *Littér* fictitiously

ficus [fikys] NM *Bot* ficus

fidéicommis [fideikɔmi] NM *Jur* trust

fidéicommissaire [fideikɔmisɛr] NM *Jur* trustee

fidèle [fidɛl] ADJ **1** *(loyal) (ami, supporter, serviteur etc)* faithful, loyal; *(époux, chien)* faithful; **lecteur/client f.** regular *or* loyal reader/customer; **rester f. à une promesse** to stand by *or* keep a promise; **rester f. à la mémoire de qn** to remain true *or* faithful to sb's memory; **être f. à ses engagements** to stand by one's commitments; **rester f. à ses idées** to remain true to one's ideas; **peu f.** unfaithful; *Iron* **f. à lui-même, il a oublié mon anniversaire** true to character *or* true to form, he forgot my birthday; **comment l'as-tu trouvé? – f. à lui-même** how did you find him? – his usual self; **elle est toujours f. au poste** she never misses a day; *Mktg* **f. à la marque** brand-loyal
2 *(exact) (copie, traduction, récit etc)* faithful, accurate; *(traducteur, historien, témoin)* accurate; *(mémoire, souvenir)* reliable; **la traduction n'est pas f. au texte** the translation is not faithful to the original; **le document est peu f. aux événements** the document is not a faithful *or* an accurate account of what happened
N *(partisan)* (loyal) supporter; *Com* regular *or* loyal customer; *(lecteur de journal)* regular *or* loyal reader; *TV* regular *or* loyal viewer; **je suis un f. de votre émission** I always watch *or* I never miss your programme; *Rel* **les fidèles** the faithful; *(à l'église)* the congregation

fidèlement [fidɛlmã] ADV **1** *(servir)* faithfully, loyally; *Com* loyally **2** *(traduire, reproduire etc)* accurately, faithfully

fidélisation [fidelizasjɔ̃] NF f. de la clientèle building of customer loyalty; **f. à la marque** creation of brand loyalty

fidéliser [fidelize] VT *(clients, lecteurs, spectateurs etc)* to win the loyalty of; **f. la clientèle** to create customer loyalty; **f. une équipe** to keep a team together

fidélité [fidelite] NF **1** *(loyauté) (d'un ami, chien etc)* faithfulness; *(d'un époux)* faithfulness, fidelity; *Com (d'un client, lecteur, spectateur etc)* loyalty; **serment de f.** oath of allegiance; **f. conjugale** marital fidelity; **f. à ses engagements** standing by one's commitments; *Mktg* **f. du consommateur** consumer loyalty; *Mktg* **f. à la marque** brand loyalty; **f. à** *ou* **de la couleur** colour fidelity **2** *(exactitude) (d'une traduction, copie etc)* faithfulness, accuracy; *(de la mémoire)* reliability; **haute f.** high fidelity, hi-fi

Fidji [fidʒi] NFPL **les îles F.** Fiji, the Fiji Islands

fidjien, -ienne [fidʒjɛ̃, -jɛn] ADJ Fijian
▪ NM *Ling* Fijian
▪ N F. Fijian

fiduciaire [fidysjɛr] ADJ *(prêt, devise etc)* fiduciary; **monnaie f.** paper money; **avoirs en monnaie f.** *(d'une banque)* cash holdings; **société f.** trust company; *Jur* **en dépôt f.** in trust
▪ NM *Jur* fiduciary, trustee

fiduciairement [fidysjɛrmã] ADV *Jur* in trust

fief [fjɛf] NM **1** *Hist* fief **2** *Fig (spécialité)* domain **3** **f. électoral** loyal constituency; **un f. socialiste** a socialist stronghold

fieffé [fjefe] ADJ *(menteur, ivrogne)* inveterate

fiel [fjɛl] NM **1** *(de bœuf, volaille etc)* gall **2** *Fig (venin)* bitterness, venom, malice; **plein de f.** venomous; **épancher son f.** to vent one's spleen

fielleux, -euse [fjelø, -øz] ADJ bitter

fiente [fjãt] NF *(d'oiseaux)* droppings

fienter [fjãte] VI *(d'un oiseau)* to leave droppings

fier[1], **-ère** [fjɛr] ADJ **1** *(digne)* proud; **courage f.** noble courage; **être trop f. pour mendier** to be too proud to beg; **être f. de ses enfants** to be proud of one's children; **je n'étais pas f. de moi** I wasn't proud of myself; **être f. de qch/d'avoir fait qch** to be proud of sth/of having done sth; **il n'y a pas de quoi être f.** that's nothing to boast about *or* to be proud of; **f. comme Artaban** as proud as a peacock
2 *(hautain)* proud, haughty; **alors, on est moins f., n'est-ce pas?** not quite so high and mighty now, are we?; *Fam* **c'est une fille pas fière** she's not a stuck-up girl; *Fam* **il n'est pas f. pour deux sous** he's not at all stuck-up
3 *(extrême)* **f. imbécile** first-rate *or* real idiot; **tu m'as fait une fière peur** you gave me a fine *or* real fright; **vous avez eu une fière idée** you've had a great idea
▪ N **faire le f.** to show off; **il fait le f. avec sa nouvelle voiture** he's showing off with his new car; **inutile de faire le f., ça sera pareil pour toi** it's no good giving yourself airs (and graces), it'll be the same for you

fier[2] **(se)** [səfje] VPR *(impf & pr sub n. n. fiions)* **se f. à qn/qch** *(avoir confiance en)* to trust sb/sth; *(compter sur)* to rely on *or* count on sb/sth; **fiez-vous à moi** *(action)* leave it to me; *(renseignement)* take my word for it; **ne te fie pas aux apparences** don't trust *or* go by *or* go on appearances; **se f. à la parole de qn** to take sb's word for it, to believe sb; **ne vous y fiez pas** beware!; *(n'y croyez pas)* don't count on it

fier-à-bras, *pl* **fiers-à-bras** NM swaggerer, braggart

fièrement [fjɛrmã] ADV **1** *(dignement)* proudly **2** *Arch (d'une manière hautaine)* haughtily **3** *Vieilli (extrêmement)* famously

fiérot, -ote [fjero, -ɔt] *Fam* ADJ *(personne)* cocky
▪ N **faire le f.** to swagger (around)

fierté [fjɛrte] NF **1** *(satisfaction)* pride; **tirer f. de qch** to take pride in sth; **ma fille/maison est ma f.** my daughter/house is my pride and joy; **la réussite de l'entreprise est notre f.** we pride ourselves on the success of the venture; **c'est avec f. que je vous présente …** I take pride in presenting to you …, I proudly present to you … **2** *(arrogance)* pride, haughtiness **3** *(amour-propre)* pride, self-respect

fiesta [fjɛsta] NF *Fam (fête)* binge, fling; **faire une** *ou* **la f.** to live it up, to have a wild time; **c'est la f.!** it's party time!

fièvre [fjɛvr] NF **1** *Méd (maladie)* fever; *(température)* temperature; **elle a 40 de f.** her temperature's at 40, she has a temperature of 40 degrees; **avoir beaucoup de f.** to have a high temperature; **avoir (de) la f.** to be feverish, to have a (high) temperature; *Fam* **avoir une f. de cheval** to have a raging fever **2** *(excitation)* excitement, frenzy; **sans f.** calmly; **dans la f. de la campagne électorale** in the heat *or* excitement of the electoral campaign; **dans la f. de l'action/des débats** in the heat of the action/debates; **travailler avec f.** to work feverishly; **elle en parle avec f.** she speaks of it excitedly **3** *(désir)* passion *(de qch* for sth); *(rage)* urge *(de faire qch* to do sth)
▸▸ **f. amarile** *ou* **jaune** yellow fever; **f. de Malte** Malta fever; **f. paludéenne** malaria; **f. quarte** quartan fever; **f. typhoïde** typhoid (fever)

fiévreusement [fjevrøzmã] ADV feverishly, frantically

fiévreux, -euse [fjevrø, -øz] ADJ **1** *Méd (pouls, personne etc)* feverish **2** *Fig (activité, préparations etc)* feverish, frantic; *(imagination)* feverish; *(attente)* anxious

fifille [fifij] NF *Fam* little girl, daughter; **f. à son papa** daddy's little girl

fifre [fifr] NM **1** *(instrument)* fife **2** *(joueur)* fife (player)

fifrelin [fifrəlɛ̃] NM *Vieilli* **ce ne vaut pas un f.** it's not worth a penny

fifty-fifty [fiftififti] ADV **faire f., partager f.** to go halves *or* fifty-fifty; **partager qch f.** to share sth fifty-fifty *or* half and half

figé [fiʒe] ADJ *(sauce, huile)* congealed; *(sourire)* fixed; *(style)* stilted; *(société)* fossilized; **locution figée** set phrase; **elle est figée dans cette situation** she is stuck in this situation

figer [fiʒe] **(figeant; il figeait)** VT *(sang)* to coagulate, to congeal; *(huile, sauce)* to congeal; **des cris à vous f. le sang** blood-curdling cries; **ce spectacle lui a figé le sang** the sight made his blood run cold; **figé sur place** rooted to the spot
▪ VPR **se figer** *(du sang)* to coagulate, to congeal; *(de l'huile, d'une sauce)* to congeal; *Fig (du regard, de traits)* to freeze; **elle se fige si on lui en parle** she justs stares past you if you talk to her about it; **se f. dans une attitude/un point de vue** to persist in an attitude/a point of view; **son sang se figea (dans ses veines)** his/her blood ran cold; **son sourire se figea quand il entendit la nouvelle** his smile froze when he heard the news

fignolage [fiɲɔlaʒ] NM *Fam (d'un travail, dessin etc)* touching up

fignoler [fiɲɔle] *Fam* VT *(travail, dessin etc)* to put the finishing touches to, to touch up
▪ VI to be meticulous

fignoleur, -euse [fiɲɔlœr, -øz] ADJ meticulous
▪ N perfectionist, meticulous worker

figue [fig] NF *(fruit)* fig; **f. de Barbarie** prickly pear

figuier [figje] NM fig (tree); **f. de Barbarie** prickly pear

figurant, -ante [figyrã, -ãt] N *Théâtre* walk-on, extra; *Cin* extra; **rôle de f.** *Théâtre* walk-on (part), bit part; *Cin* bit part; *Fig* **avoir un rôle de f. dans qch, n'être qu'un f. dans qch** to take no active part *or* be just an onlooker in sth

figuratif, -ive [figyratif, -iv] ADJ *(plan)* figurative; *(art, artiste)* figurative, representational
▪ N figurative *or* representational artist

figuration [figyrasjɔ̃] NF **1** *(représentation)* figuration, representation **2** *Théâtre (acteurs)* walk-on actors, *Fam* supers; *(rôle)* walk-on (part), bit part; **faire de la f.** to do walk-on parts, to play bit parts **3** *Cin (acteurs)* extras; *(rôle)* bit part; **faire de la f.** to play bit parts

figurativement [figyrativmã] ADV figuratively

figure [figyr] NF **1** *(visage)* face; **jeter qch à la f. de qn** to throw sth in sb's face; *Fam* **casser la f. à qn** to smash sb's face in; *Fam* **se casser la f.** to fall flat on one's face; *Fig (échouer)* to come a cropper; **je me suis cassé la f. en vélo/dans les escaliers** I fell off my bike/down the stairs
2 *(mine)* face, *Fml* countenance; **faire bonne f. à qn** to act pleasantly towards sb; **faire bonne f.** to make a good impression; **faire une drôle de f.** to pull a face, to give a funny look; **faire triste f.** to pull a long face; **ne plus avoir f. humaine** to be totally disfigured; *Hum* **mes vieilles chaussures n'ont plus f. humaine** my old shoes are falling to pieces **3** *(représentation, image)* figure; **figures de cire** waxworks, waxwork figures; *Cartes* **les figures** *Br* the court cards, the face cards; **figures géométriques** geometrical figures; **figure de proue** *(d'un bateau)*, *Fig (d'un parti politique etc)* figurehead; **livre avec figures dans le texte** book with figures *or* diagrams in the text; **prendre f.** to take shape; **faire f. de riche** to give an impression of wealth; **elle fait f. d'intellectuelle dans ce milieu** she gives the impression of *or* has the appearance of an intellectual amongst these people; **faire pauvre** *ou* **piètre f.** to cut a sorry figure **4** *(personnage)* figure; **les grandes figures de la Guerre** the great figures of the War **5** *(de danseur, patineur etc)* figure; **figures libres** freestyle; **figures imposées** compulsory figures **6** *Ling* figure; **f. de mots** *ou* **de rhétorique** figure of speech; **f. de style** stylistic device

> Il faut remarquer que lorsqu'il s'applique à une personne, le nom anglais **figure** signifie **silhouette**.

figuré [figyre] ADJ **1** *(plan)* diagrammatic **2** *Ling* **sens f.** figurative meaning
▪ NM *Ling* **au f.** in the figurative sense, figuratively; **au propre comme au f.** literally and figuratively

figurément [figyremã] ADV figuratively

figurer [figyre] VT to represent; **une croix figure une église sur le plan** a cross stands for *or* represents *or* indicates a church on the map; **la scène figure le camp des brigands** the scene shows *or* represents the brigands' camp
▪ VI **1** *(se trouver)* to appear, to figure; **je ne**

veux pas que mon nom **figure dans l'af-faire/le livre** I don't want my name to appear *or* figure in the matter/the book; **f. dans un catalogue/une bibliographie** to be listed *or* appear in a catalogue/a bibliography; **voici les chevaux qui figurent à l'arrivée** here are the names of the winning horses **2** *Théâtre* to have a walk-on (part); *Cin* to have a bit part

VPR se figurer to imagine (**que** that); **se f. qch** to imagine sth; **figurez-vous la situation** imagine the situation, picture the situation (to yourself); **ne vous figurez pas que je sois satisfait** don't get the idea that I'm satisfied; **si tu te figures que je vais te pardonner, tu te trompes** if you imagine I'm going to forgive you, you're mistaken; **je suis à sec, figure-toi** believe it or not, I'm broke; **figure-toi que, nous aussi, on a loué une maison dans ce village** would you believe it, we've rented a house in that village as well

figurine [figyrin] NF figurine, statuette

fil [fil] NM **1** *Tex (brin)* thread, yarn; *(de toile d'araignée)* thread; *(tissu)* linen; **f. de coton/nylon** cotton/nylon thread *or* yarn; **f. de lin** linen yarn *or* thread; **des draps pur f.** (pure) linen sheets; **gants de f.** cotton gloves; **laine trois/quatre fils** three-/four-ply wool; *Fig* **astuce cousue de f. blanc** obvious *or* blatant trick; *Fig* **c'est cousu de f. blanc** you can see right through it, it won't fool anybody; *Fig* **de f. en aiguille** little by little, bit by bit, gradually; **démêler les fils d'une intrigue** to unravel the threads of a plot; *Fig* **trouver le f. d'Ariane** *ou* **le f. conducteur** to find the clue (to the mystery); **le f. rouge** recurrent theme; **il n'y a pas de f. conducteur dans ce roman** there's no unifying thread in this novel; **mince comme un f.** as thin as a rake **2** *(de câble, corde etc)* strand; *(de marionnette)* string; *Fig* **c'est lui qui tient les fils** he's the one who holds (all) the strings; *Fig* **être dans le droit f. de qch** to be in line with sth; **le droit f. du parti n'a pas changé depuis dix ans** the party line hasn't changed in ten years; *Fig* **sa vie ne tenait qu'à un f.** his life hung by a thread; **il ne tenait qu'à un f. qu'il soit renvoyé** it was touch and go whether he would be dismissed; *Fam* **avoir un f. à la patte** *(être tenu par un engagement)* to be tied down; *Fam* **se mettre un f. à la patte** to tie oneself down; *Sport* **être coiffé sur le f.** to be pipped at the post, to be beaten at the wire **3** *(métallique)* wire; *Fam* **donner du f. à retordre à qn** to give sb trouble **4** *Élec* **f. (électrique)** (electric) wire; **f. (souple)** lead, cord, *Br* flex; **f. téléphonique** telephone wire; *Tél* **donner** *ou* **passer un coup de f. à qn** to give sb a call, to call sb (up), *Br* to give sb a ring, *Br* to ring sb (up); **recevoir** *ou* **avoir un coup de f. de qn** to get a (phone) call from sb; **être au bout du f.** to be on the line *or* phone; **je viens d'avoir Martin au bout du f.** I've just had Martin on the line *or* phone; **télégraphie/téléphonie sans f.** wireless telegraphy/telephony; **téléphone sans f.** cordless telephone **5** *(de bois, viande)* grain; **les haricots verts ont des fils** *ou* **sont pleins de fils** the green beans are stringy; **haricots sans fils** stringless beans; **contre le f., à contre-f.** against *or* across the grain; **dans le sens du f.** with the grain; **couper dans le droit f.** *(bois)* to cut along the grain; *(tissu)* to cut on the straight **6** *Fig (cours)* **au f. de l'eau** with the current, downstream; **se laisser aller au f. de l'eau** to let oneself drift (with the current); **au f. des jours/semaines/heures** as the days/weeks/hours go by, with the passing days/weeks/hours; **le f. des événements** the chain of events; **perdre/reprendre le f. de la conver-**

sation to lose/pick up the thread of the conversation; **j'ai perdu le f., je ne sais plus où j'en suis** I've lost the thread, I don't know where I am any more; **suivre le f. des idées de qn** to follow the thread of sb's ideas **7** *(d'un couteau, d'une épée etc)* edge; **donner le f. à un rasoir** to put an edge on a razor; *Fig* **le président est sur le f. du rasoir** the president is on a knife edge; *Litt* **passer des prisonniers au f. de l'épée** to put prisoners to the sword

▸ ▸ **f. à bâtir** basting thread; **f. de bougie** (spark) plug lead; **f. à coudre** (sewing) thread, cotton; **f. à couper le beurre** cheesewire; *Fig* **il n'a pas inventé le f. à couper le beurre** he'll never set the Thames on fire; **f. dentaire** dental floss; **f. d'Écosse** lisle thread; **chaussettes en f. d'Écosse** lisle socks; **f. de fer** wire; **fil(s) de fer barbelé(s)** barbed wire; **f. de masse** *ou* **de terre** earth (wire), *Am* ground (wire); **f. de la vierge** gossamer

filage [filaʒ] NM *Tex* spinning

filaire [filɛr] *Tél* ADJ corded, plug-in ▪ NM corded *or* plug-in phone

filament [filamã] NM **1** *(de viande)* fibre, *Am* fiber; *(de lampe électrique)* filament; **ça a trop de filaments pour être mangé** it's too stringy to eat **2** *Biol* filament

filamenteux, -euse [filamãtø, -øz] ADJ filamentous

filandière [filãdjɛr] NF *Tex Arch* (hand-)spinner

filandreux, -euse [filãdrø, -øz] ADJ **1** *(viande, légumes)* stringy **2** *Fig Péj (explication, phrase etc)* involved, confused

filant [filã] ADJ **1** *(qui coule)* fluid **2 étoile filante** shooting star, falling star

filasse [filas] NF *(matière)* tow; **f. de chanvre** hemp ▪ ADJ INV **cheveux (blond) f.** tow-coloured hair; **aux cheveux (blond) f.** tow-headed, tow-haired

filateur [filatœr] NM (spinning) mill owner

filature [filatyr] NF **1** *Tex (action)* spinning **2** *(fabrique)* (spinning) mill; **f. de coton** cotton mill **3** *(par un détective etc)* shadowing, tailing; **il a été pris en f.** he was shadowed *or* tailed

fil-de-fériste, *pl* **fil-de-féristes** [fildəferist] N high-wire artist

file [fil] NF **1** *(de gens, voitures etc)* line; **f. (d'attente)** queue, *Am* line; *Aviat* stacking; **se mettre** *ou* **se ranger en f.** to line up; **prendre la f., se mettre à la f.** to join the queue *or Am* line; *Ordinat* **f. d'attente** print queue *or* list; **mettre en f. d'attente** to spool, to queue; **marcher à la f.** *ou* **en f.** to walk in single file *or* one behind another; **à la** *ou* **en f. indienne** in single *or* Indian file; **entrer/sortir en f.** *ou* **à la f.** to file in/out; **cinq bières à la f.** five beers in a row *or* in succession *or* one after another; **trois jours à la f.** *ou* **de f.** three days in a row *or* in succession; *Aut* **stationner en double f.** to double-park **2** *Aut (couloir)* lane; **ne changez pas de f.** keep in lane; **rouler dans** *ou* **sur la f. de droite** to drive in the right-hand lane

filé [file] ADJ **1** *(bas, collant)* with a run, *Br* laddered **2 verre f.** spun glass ▪ NM *Tex, Tech* thread; **f. d'or** gold thread

filer [file] VT **1** *(coton, verre etc)* to spin; *Fig* **f. des jours heureux** to live very happily; *Fam* **ils filent le parfait amour** they are living love's dream **2** *Naut (câble)* to pay out, to run out; *(amarres)* to slip **3** *(métaphore)* to spin out, to draw out; *Mus (note)* to draw out, to sustain; *(huile)* to pour out in a trickle; *Cartes* **f. les cartes** to lay the cards down slowly; **il m'a filé entre les doigts** he slipped between my fingers

4 *(d'un détective etc) (suspect)* to shadow, to tail

5 *Fam (donner)* **f. qch à qn** to give sb sth; **je lui ai filé ma voiture/un conseil** I gave him my car/a piece of advice; **f. un coup de pied/une gifle à qn** to give sb a kick/a slap; **f. de l'aide** *ou* **un coup de main à qn** to give sb a hand

6 *(démailler) (bas, collant)* to put a run in, *Br* to ladder

▪ VI **1** *(passer très vite)* **le temps file** time flies; **laisser f. un câble** to pay out a cable; **l'argent lui file entre les mains** *ou* **les doigts** money runs through his hands *or* fingers like water; **train qui file à toute vitesse** train rushing along at full speed; **les voitures filaient sur la route** cars were speeding along the road; *Naut* **f. (à) vingt nœuds** to proceed at twenty knots

2 *Fam (partir en vitesse)* to dash *or* rush off; **f. (en douce)** to slip away *or* off; **allez, filez!** clear off!, scram!; *(dépêchez-vous)* off you go!; **f. à l'anglaise** to sneak off, to take French leave

3 *Fam* **f. doux** to toe the line, to behave oneself

4 *(de bas, collant)* to run, *Br* to ladder; **j'ai un bas qui file** I've got a run *or Br* ladder

5 la lampe file the lamp is smoking

6 *(de l'huile etc)* to run

filet¹ [file] NM **1** *(de lumière)* thin streak; *(d'air)* thin stream; *(d'eau, de bave)* trickle, dribble; *(de sang)* trickle; *(de fumée etc)* thread, wisp; *(de voix)* thin *or* weak voice; *Culin* **ajoutez-y un f. de citron/vinaigre** add a dash of lemon/vinegar; **f. d'une vis** thread *or Spéc* worm of a screw **2** *Anat (de la langue)* frenum, string **3** *Bot (d'étamine)* filament **4** *(de reliure), Archit* filet **5** *Typ* rule; **f. maigre** hairline (rule)

filet² NM *Culin* fillet; **f. mignon** filet mignon *(small fillet steak)*

filet³ NM **1** *(ouvrage à mailles)* net; *(au cirque)* (safety) net; **f. de pêche** fishing net; **f. à papillons** butterfly net; **être pris au f.** to be caught with a net; *Fig* **faire tomber** *ou* **attirer qn dans ses filets** to ensnare sb; **un beau coup de f. pour la police** a good haul for the police; **travailler sans f.** *(d'un trapéziste)* to work without a net; *Fig* to go out on a limb, to take risks; **f. à provisions** string *or* net bag; **f. pour cheveux** hairnet; *Rail* **f. à bagages** luggage rack **2** *Tennis, Ftbl etc* net; *Tennis* **monter au f.** to go up to the net; **balle de f.** let (ball); **juge de f.** net-cord judge

filetage [filtaʒ] NM *Tech* **1** *(action)* threading, screw cutting **2** *(filets) (de vis)* thread, *Spéc* worm; *Tech* **f. Acmé** Acme thread; **f. Whitworth** Whitworth thread

fileter [filte] VT *(je filète; je filèterai)* *Tech* **1** *(métal)* to wiredraw; *(fil)* to draw **2** *(boulon, tige etc)* to thread, to screw

fileur, -euse [filœr, -øz] N *Tex (de métier à tisser)* spinner

filial, -ale, -aux, -ales [filjal] ADJ filial ▪ NF *Com* **filiale** subsidiary (company); **filiale consolidée** consolidated subsidiary; **filiale de distribution** marketing subsidiary; **filiale de vente** sales subsidiary

filialement [filjalmã] ADV filially

filiation [filjasjɔ̃] NF **1** *(lien de parenté)* filiation; **en f. directe** in direct line; **un descendant en f. directe** a direct descendant **2** *Litt (famille)* descendants **3** *Fig (de mots, d'événements etc)* relationship (**de** between); **des théories en f. directe avec ce texte** theories directly related to this text

filière [filjɛr] NF **1** *Admin* channels; **la f. administrative** the (usual) official channels; **passer par** *ou* **suivre la f.** *(pour obtenir qch)* to go through official channels; *(comme employé)* to work one's way up; **choisir la f. nu-**

cléaire to go down the nuclear road, to choose the nuclear path; *Scol* **suivre une f. scientifique/commerciale** to study scientific/business subjects **2** *(de trafiquants, terroristes etc)* network; **remonter la f.** to go back along the network (to the person at the top); **démanteler une f.** to break up a ring **3** *Tech (pour fileter une vis)* screw plate; *(pour étirer)* draw(ing) plate; **travailler un métal à la f.** to draw a metal **4** *Zool (d'une araignée, d'un ver à soie)* spinneret **5** *Fin* **f. électronique** electronic transfer

filiforme [filiform] ADJ **1** *Zool* filiform, threadlike **2** *Fam (très mince) (personne, jambes etc)* spindly

filigrane [filigran] NM **1** *(ouvrage d'orfèvrerie)* filigree; **broche en f.** filigree brooch **2** *(de papier, billet de banque etc)* watermark; **à f.** watermarked; *Fig* **lire en f.** to read between the lines; **apparaître en f. dans qch** to be implicit in sth

filigrané [filigrane] ADJ **1** *(broche)* filigreed **2** *(papier)* watermarked

filin [filɛ̃] NM rope

fille [fij] NF **1** *(descendante directe)* daughter; *Fig* **la superstition est (la) f. de l'ignorance** superstition is born of ignorance **2** *(enfant)* girl; **petite f.** little girl; **jeune f.** girl, young woman; **faire la jeune f. de la maison** *(à un cocktail)* to pass *or* hand round the snacks; **ma pauvre f.!** my poor child *or* dear!; **nom de jeune f.** maiden name; **école de filles** girls' school; *Fig* **jouer la f. de l'air** to escape, to get out **3** *(femme)* woman; **vieille f.** old maid, spinster; **habitudes de vieille f.** old-maidish habits; *Vieilli* **rester f.** to remain single *or* unmarried **4** *Rel* **les filles de Port-Royal** the sisters *or* nuns of Port-Royal ▸▸ **f. de cuisine** kitchenmaid; **f. de ferme** farm girl; **f. d'honneur** maid of honour; *surtout Vieilli* **f. de joie** fille de joie, prostitute; **f. à matelots** prostitute *(whose customers are primarily sailors)*; **f. publique** prostitute; **f. des rues** streetwalker; **f. de salle** *(dans un hôtel)* waitress; *(dans un hôpital)* nursing auxiliary; **f. de service** maidservant; *Vieilli* **f. à soldats** prostitute *(whose customers are primarily soldiers)*

fille-mère, *pl* **filles-mères** NF *Péj, Vieilli* unmarried mother

fillette [fijɛt] NF **1** *(petite fille)* little girl **2** *(bouteille) (de vin)* half-bottle

filleul, -eule [fijœl] N godson, *f* goddaughter; **f. de guerre** = soldier in action 'adopted' by a woman, who sends letters, parcels etc

film [film] NM **1** *Phot* film **2** *Cin (pellicule)* film; *(œuvre)* film, picture, movie, *Am* motion picture; **le f.** *(art)* film, cinema; **tourner un f.** to make a film; *Fam* **il n'a rien compris au f.** he hasn't taken anything in; *Fam* **se faire un f.** to be living in a dream world; **f. en noir et blanc/en couleur** black and white/colour film **3** *Fig (déroulement) (d'événements)* sequence; **revoir le f. de sa vie** to look back over one's life **4** *(couche)* film; **f. alimentaire** cling film; **f. dentaire** (dental) plaque; **sous f. plastique** shrink-wrapped; **f. transparent** transparency; **recouvert d'un f. protecteur** covered with a protective film ▸▸ **f. d'action** action film, action movie; **f. d'actualité** newsreel, news film; **f. d'animation** animated film, cartoon; **f. d'archives** library film; **f. d'art et d'essai** arthouse film; **f. d'auteur** film d'auteur; **f. d'aventures** adventure film; **f. catastrophe** disaster film; **f. documentaire** documentary film; **f. dramatique** drama; **f. d'entreprise** corporate film, corporate video; **f. d'épouvante** horror film *or* movie, thriller; **f. d'espionnage** spy film; **f. à faible budget** low-budget movie; **f.**

fantastique science fiction film; **f. de genre** genre film; **f. à gros succès** blockbuster movie; **f. de guerre** war film; **f. d'horreur** horror film *or* movie; **f. institutionnel** corporate video; **f. long métrage** feature film; **f. muet** silent film, silent movie; **f. noir** film noir; **f. parlant** talkie; **f. plat** two-dimensional film; **f. policier** detective film; **f. pornographique** pornographic film, blue movie; **f. publicitaire** *(à la télévision)* commercial; *(au cinéma)* cinema advertisement; **f. en relief** 3D film; **f. de science-fiction** science fiction film; **f. semi-documentaire** semi-documentary; **f. de série B** B-movie, B-feature; **f. sonore** sound film; **f. à succès** box-office hit; **f. de suspense** thriller; **f. télévisé** television film; **f. en 3D** 3D film; **f. vidéo** video film; **f. classé X** adults-only movie *or Br* film, *Br* X-rated movie *or* film

filmage [filmaʒ] NM *Cin* filming

filmer [filme] VT **1** *Tech (enduire)* to cover with a film **2** *Cin* to film; *(scène)* to film, to shoot
VI *Cin* to film

filmique [filmik] ADJ cinematic, filmic

filmographie [filmɔgrafi] NF *Cin* filmography

filmologie [filmɔlɔʒi] NF film studies

filmothèque [filmɔtɛk] NF microfilm library

filoche [filɔʃ] NF *Fam* shadowing, tailing

filoguidé [filogide] ADJ wire-guided

filon [filɔ̃] NM **1** *Min* vein, seam, lode **2** *Fam (situation lucrative)* cushy job; **il tient le f., il a déniché** *ou* **trouvé le (bon) f.** he's struck it rich; *Fig* **trouver un f.** to find a goldmine; **j'ai un bon f. pour avoir des vidéos gratuites** I know where I can get free videos easily

filou [filu] NM **1** *(escroc)* rogue, swindler, crook **2** *(enfant)* rascal, rogue

filoutage [filutaʒ] NM swindling, cheating

filouter [filute] VT **1** *Vieilli* **f. qch à qn** to steal sth from sb **2 f. qn** to swindle *or* cheat sb

filouterie [filutri] NF **1** *(action)* swindling, cheating **2** *(manœuvre)* swindle, fraud

fils [fis] NM son; **elle et ses deux f.** she and her two boys *or* sons; **c'est bien le f. de son père** he's a chip off the old block; **être le f. de ses œuvres** to be a self-made man; **c'est le f. spirituel de René Char** he's the spiritual son of René Char; **M. Duval f.** Mr Duval junior; **le f. Duval** young Duval; *Rel* **le F. de Dieu/de l'homme** the Son of God/of Man ▸▸ **f. de famille** young man of good social standing; *Péj* **f. à papa** daddy's boy; *Vulg* **f. de pute** son of a bitch

filtrage [filtraʒ] NM **1** *(d'un liquide, gaz, son etc)* filtering **2** *Fig (contrôle) (des informations, visiteurs etc)* screening

filtrant [filtrɑ̃] ADJ filtering; **verre f.** filter glass; **lunettes à verres filtrants** glasses with filter lenses

filtration [filtrasjɔ̃] NF filtration, filtering

filtre [filtr] NM *Tech, Phot, Élec, Ordinat etc* filter; **(bout) f.** filter *(tip)*; **je fume des (cigarettes) f.** I smoke filter-tipped cigarettes *or* filter tips; **(café) f.** filter coffee; **papier f.** filter paper ▸▸ **f. à air** air filter; *Radio, TV* **f. anti-parasites** interference filter *or* suppressor; *Ordinat* **f. anti-reflet** glare screen; **f. audio** audio filter; **f. à brouillard** *(pour une caméra)* fog filter; **f. à café** coffee filter; **f. à carburant** fuel filter; **f. au charbon** carbon filter; **f. à combustible** fuel filter; **f. correcteur** corrective filter; **f. couleur** colour medium; *Phot* **f. de couleur** *ou* **coloré** colour filter; *Ordinat* **f. écran** screen filter; **f. à essence** petrol filter; **f. à huile** oil filter; *Ordinat* **f. d'importation/ exportation** import/export filter; **f. à parti-**

cules dust filter; **f. à pollen** pollen filter; *TV, Cin* **f. pour objectif de caméra** camera lens filter

filtrer [filtre] VT **1** *(eau, café, gaz, son, lumière etc)* to filter **2** *Fig (contrôler) (informations, visiteurs etc)* to screen
VI *(d'un liquide)* to filter, to percolate, to seep *(à travers* through); *(d'une nouvelle)* to leak out, to filter out; **la lumière filtrait à travers** *ou* **par les branches** the light filtered through the branches; **ils n'ont rien laissé f. de ses déclarations** they have said nothing about his statement, *Fam* they're keeping a very tight lid on what he said

end **1, 2**	= expiry **1**	= death **1**	= back
1 = purpose **2**	= aim **2**		

NF **1** *(dernier moment) (de film, réunion, travail etc)* end, conclusion; *(de contrat, de bail etc)* expiry, expiration; *(d'empire, de régime etc)* end, fall; *(d'un espoir, de malheurs etc)* end; *(mort)* end, death; *Cin* **'f.'** 'The End'; **le cinquième en partant de la f.** the fifth from the end, the last but four; **f. du jour** close of day; **f. du mois** end of the month; *Com* **f. de mois** monthly statement; **de f. de mois** end-of-month; **assurer ses fins de mois** to make sure one has enough money at the end of the month; **avoir des fins de mois difficiles** to be always short of money at the end of the month; **f. de l'exercice** end of the financial year; **de f. d'exercice** year-end; **en f. d'exercice** at the end of the financial year; **payable f. courant/prochain** payable at the end of this/next month; **on se reverra f. mars** *ou* **à la f. de mars** we'll meet again at the end of March; **en f. de soirée** towards the end of the evening; **il a faibli en f. de trimestre** his work fell off towards the end of the term; **il est venu vers la f. de l'après-midi** he came late in *or* towards the end of the afternoon; **en f. d'année** at the end of the year; **jusqu'à la f. des temps** *ou* **des siècles** till the end of time; **le vocabulaire est à la f. du livre** the vocabulary is at the back of the book; **à la f. de la liste, en f. de liste** at the bottom *or* end of the list; **sans f.** *(emploi adjectival)* endless; *(plaintes, interrogatoire)* endless, never-ending; *(emploi adverbial)* endlessly; **vis sans f.** endless screw; **il parle sans f.** he never stops talking, he talks endlessly; **f. prématurée** untimely death *or* end; **il a eu une belle f./une f. affreuse** he had a good/terrible end *or* death; **on sent bien que la f. n'est pas loin** we've a feeling the end is not far away *or* it can't be long now; **vers la f., il n'était plus le même** he wasn't the same towards the end; **le lave-vaisselle est sur sa f.** the dishwasher is on its last legs; **toucher** *ou* **tirer à sa f.** *(d'un projet, d'une union)* to come *or* draw to an end *or* a close; **l'année touche** *ou* **tire à sa f.** the year is drawing to an end *or* a close; **votre participation touche à sa f.** your participation will soon be over *or* at an end; **le contrat touche à sa f.** the contract will expire soon; **être en f. de course** *(d'une vis)* to be screwed fully home; *(d'un piston)* to have reached the end of its stroke; *Fig (d'une personne)* to have come to the end of the road; **chômeur en f. de droits** unemployed person who is coming to the end of his benefit; **mettre f. à qch** to put an end *or* a stop to sth; **mettre f. à sa vie** *ou* **ses jours** to put an end to one's life; **elle se marie pour faire une f.** she's getting married in order to settle down; **prendre f., avoir une f.** to come to an end; **mener une affaire à bonne f.** to bring a matter to a successful conclusion, to deal successfully with a matter; **c'est la f.** this is the end; **la f. du monde** the end of the world; **ce n'est pas la f. du monde** it's not the end of the world; *Fam* **c'est la f. de tout** that's the (absolute) end; **c'est Patrick qui a dit** *ou* **eu le mot de la f.** it was Patrick who had the last *or* final word; **à la f. il répondit** in the end *or* finally *or* at last he answered; *Fam* **tu es stupide à la f.** you really are very stupid; **tu m'ennuies à la f.!** you're really annoying me!; **en f. de compte** *(après tout)* in the end, after all; *(tout bien considéré)* all things considered, taking everything into account; *(pour conclure)* finally, to conclude; *Fam* **à la f. des fins** when all's said and done, at the end of the day

2 *(but)* end, aim, purpose; **la f. justifie les moyens** the end justifies the means; **arriver** *ou* **parvenir** *ou* **en venir à ses fins** to achieve one's ends *or* aims *or* purpose, to get what one wants; **une f. en soi** an end in itself; **à cette f. il faut avoir beaucoup de patience** to this end *or* in order to achieve this one must have a lot of patience; **à quelle f.?** for what purpose?, to what end?; **with what end in view?**; **je vous le fais parvenir à toutes fins utiles** I'm sending it to you should you need it; **aux fins de faire qch** with a view to doing sth; **à seule(s) fin(s) de l'aider** for the sole purpose of helping him; *Jur* **aux fins de débauche** for immoral purposes

3 *Jur* **renvoyé des fins de la plainte** discharged, acquitted

▶▶ *Ordinat* **f. de ligne** line end; *Ordinat* **f. de page** pagebreak; *Ordinat* **f. de page obligatoire** hard page break; *Ordinat* **f. de paragraphe** paragraph break; **f. de race: comportement f. de race** degenerate behaviour; *Com* **f. de série** discontinued line; *Ordinat* **f. de session** logoff; **f. de siècle: style/mœurs f. de siècle** f. de siècle *or* decadent style/morals

---

FIN², -INE [fɛ̃, fin]

ADJ	thin **1** ▪ fine **1–3** ▪ first-class **2** ▪ subtle **4**
NM	the ultimate *(le fin du fin)*
ADV	absolutely **1** ▪ finely **2**

ADJ 1 *(mince) (papier, tranche)* thin; *(étoffe)* fine, thin; *(cheveux, pluie, grains, sable, aiguille, pointe)* fine; *(traits)* fine, delicate; *(silhouette)* slender; *(cheville)* neat

2 *(de première qualité)* fine, first-class; **vins fins** choice *or* fine wines; **or f.** pure *or* fine gold; **lingerie fine** fine lingerie; **des souliers fins** elegant shoes; **un repas f.** a choice *or* exquisite meal; **fines herbes** mixed herbs, fines herbes; **épicerie fine** delicatessen

3 *(expert)* fine; **f. connaisseur de vins** fine judge of wine; **f. tireur** crack shot; **fine lame** fine swordsman; **f. stratège** fine *or* expert strategist; **fine cuisinière** gourmet cook; **avoir l'ouïe fine** to have sharp ears *or* an acute ear *or* a keen ear; **avoir le nez f.** to have a keen sense of smell; *Fig* **elle a le nez f.** she's sharp

4 *(subtil)* subtle; **une fine mouche** a sharp customer; **fine ironie** subtle irony; **il est trop f. pour vous** he's too clever for you; **elle n'est pas très fine, cette jeune femme** that young woman isn't very bright; **bien f. qui le prendra** it would take a smart man to catch him; *Iron* **qu'est-ce que c'est f.!** oh, very funny!

5 **dans le f. fond du hangar/du panier** right at the back of the shed/the bottom of the basket; **au f. fond de la Sibérie** in deepest Siberia; **au f. fond de moi** in my heart of hearts; **le f. mot de l'histoire** the truth of the matter

NM 1 le f. du f. the ultimate **2 jouer au (plus) f.** to have a battle of wits

ADV 1 tout était f. prêt everything was absolutely ready; **être f. soûl** to be blind drunk **2** *(finement)* finely; **café moulu f.** finely ground coffee; **des crayons taillés f.** sharp-pointed pencils

---

final, -ale, -als, -ales [final] **ADJ 1** final; **point f.** full stop, *Am* period; *Fig* **mettre un point f. à une affaire** to put a stop *or* an end to a matter; **va te coucher, point f.!** bed time! and that's final! **2** *Phil, Gram (cause, proposition)* final

NM 1 *Mus (d'opéra etc)* finale **2 au f.** in the end

finale [final] **NF 1** *Sport* final; **f. de coupe** cup final; **aller/être en f.** to go *or* get through to/to be in the finals **2** *Ling (de mot)* final *or* end syllable

NM *Mus (d'opéra etc)* finale

finalement [finalmɑ̃] **ADV** in the end, finally

finaliser [finalize] **VT** to finalize

finaliste [finalist] **ADJ, N** finalist

finalité [finalite] **NF** *(objectif)* aim, objective; *Phil* finality; *Biol* adaptation

finance [finɑ̃s] **NF 1** finance; **monde de la f.** financial world, world of finance; **la haute f.** high finance; *(le milieu)* the financiers, the bankers; **être dans la f.** to be in finance; **f. d'entreprise** corporate finance; *Fam* **faire qch moyennant f.** to do sth for a consideration *or* for a fee **2 finances** finances; **nos finances sont mal en point** our finances are in bad shape; **lois de finances** financial laws; **ministre des Finances** minister of Finance, *Br* ≃ Chancellor of the Exchequer, *Am* ≃ Secretary of the Treasury; **le Ministère des Finances** the Treasury

financement [finɑ̃smɑ̃] **NM** financing, funding; *(surtout d'un mécène)* (financial) backing; **f. à court terme** short-term financing; **f. par endettement** debt financing; **f. initial** start-up capital; **f. à long terme** long-term financing; **f. à moyen terme** medium-term financing

financement-relais, *pl* **financements-relais NM** *Fin* bridge financing

financer [finɑ̃se] **VT** (**je finançai(s), n. finançons**) to finance, to fund; *(surtout d'un mécène)* to back, to put up the money for; **BP financera le projet à 50%** BP will put up half of the funding for the project; **l'opération a été entièrement financée par emprunt** the transaction was 100% financed through borrowing

financier, -ière [finɑ̃sje, -jɛr] **ADJ** financial; **avoir des problèmes financiers** to be in financial *or Fml* pecuniary difficulties; **crise financière** financial crisis; **le marché f.** the money market; *Culin* **sauce financière** = white sauce containing small pieces of sweetbread, dumplings and mushrooms

NM financier; **f. d'entreprise** corporate finance manager

financièrement [finɑ̃sjɛrmɑ̃] **ADV** financially

finasser [finase] **VI** to resort to trickery

finasserie [finasri] **NF** trick

finasseur, -euse [finasœr, -øz], **finassier, -ière** [finasje, -jɛr] **N** *Vieilli* trickster

finaud, -aude [fino, -od] **ADJ** wily, cunning **N** crafty devil

finauderie [finodri] **NF** trickery

fine [fin] **NF** liqueur brandy; **une f. à l'eau** = a brandy and soda

finement [finmɑ̃] **ADV 1** *(délicatement)* finely, delicately **2** *(subtilement)* *(analyser, apprécier)* subtly; **elle avait f. prévu ce coup-là** she had shrewdly *or* cleverly foreseen that that would happen

finesse [fines] **NF 1** *(d'un tissu)* fineness; *(d'exécution)* delicacy; *(du sable)* fineness; *(de taille)* slenderness, slimness **2** *(subtilité)* subtlety; **f. d'ouïe/de l'odorat** keenness *or* acuteness of hearing/of smell; **f. de goût** good taste; **f. d'esprit** shrewdness; **discours plein de f.** speech full of subtlety *or* finesse;

---

elle a beaucoup de f. she's very shrewd; **parodie pleine de f.** clever *or* subtle parody; **finesses d'un métier** niceties *or* subtleties *or* fine points of a craft; **il connaît toutes les finesses du métier** he knows all the tricks of the trade **3** *(d'une pointe, d'une image optique etc)* sharpness; *(d'une lame)* keenness

finette [finɛt] **NF** *Tex* brushed cotton

fini [fini] **ADJ 1** *(terminé)* finished, over; **c'est f. (tout cela), tout est f.** that's all over (and done with); **c'est f. entre nous** we're finished, it's all over between us; **(c'est) f. de rire** the fun's over; **c'est un homme f.** he's finished, he's done for **2** *(ouvrage)* well finished; **cette robe est mal finie** this dress is badly finished; *Péj* **un idiot f.** a complete idiot; **un alcoolo/voleur f.** an out-and-out drunkard/thief **3** *(espace, temps, nombre)* finite

NM 1 *(d'un produit manufacturé)* finish **2 le f. et l'infini** the finite and the infinite

finir [finir] **VT** *(tâche, études, conversation etc)* to finish; *(vie)* to end; **f. un tableau/une sculpture** to finish (off) a picture/sculpture; **tu as fini ton assiette?** have you finished what's on your plate?; **ils ont fini la soirée au poste** the evening ended with them in the police station; **je vais f. ces chaussures** I'll wear these shoes out

VI to end, to finish; **quand est-ce que ça finit?** when does it end *or* finish?; **comment est-ce que ça a fini?** how did it end?; **à quelle heure tu finis?** what time do you finish?; **f. en pointe** to end *or* terminate in a point; **une histoire qui finit bien/mal** a story with a happy/sad ending; **tout est bien qui finit bien** all's well that ends well; **il finira mal** he'll come to a bad end; **ça va mal f. tout ça!** no good will come of all that!, it will all end in disaster!; **l'histoire ne finit pas là** that's not the end of the story; **f. à l'hôpital/dans un fossé** to end up *or* finish up in hospital/a ditch; **en f. avec qn/qch** to be *or* have done with sb/sth; **il faut en f. avec ces idées reçues** we must break with *or* shake off these preconceived ideas; **je voudrais en f.** I want to get it over (with); **il voulait en f. (avec la vie)** he wanted to put an end to it all *or* to end it all; **vous n'avez pas encore fini tous les deux!** are you two still at it!; *Fam* **c'est pas bientôt fini, ce bordel?** is this racket going to stop soon?; **cela n'en finit pas** there's no end to it; **il n'en finit pas de se préparer dans la salle de bain** he takes ages in the bathroom getting ready; **pour f.** to cut a long story short; **histoires/ennuis à n'en plus f.** endless *or* interminable stories/problems; **et pour f., voici le dessert** and to finish (with), here's dessert; **cette route n'en finit pas** this road seems to go on (and on) for ever; **elle a des jambes à n'en plus f.** she has incredibly long legs; **f. de faire qch** to finish doing sth; **f. par faire qch** to end up (by) doing sth; **tu vas f. par le faire pleurer** you'll end up (by) making him cry; **elle finira par t'oublier/s'y habituer** she'll forget you/get used to it in the end *or* eventually; **la justice finit par triompher** justice triumphs in the end *or* in the long run *or* eventually; **tout finit toujours par arriver** everything comes to those who wait

finish [finiʃ] **NM** *Sport (fin)* finish; *(impulsion finale)* finish, final burst; **il a un bon f.** he has a strong finish; *Fig* **on l'a eu au f.** we got him in the end

finissage [finisaʒ] **NM** *Ind* finishing (off)

finissant [finisɑ̃] **ADJ** finishing; *(société)* in decline; **le jour f.** dusk, twilight

finisseur, -euse [finisœr, -øz] **N** *Ind, Sport* finisher

finition [finisjɔ̃] **NF** finishing; *(résultat)* finish; **les finitions** the finishing touches; *Cou-*

ture **les finitions sont très soignées** it's very well finished; *Tricot* **je déteste faire les finitions** I hate the sewing up

finlandais, -aise [fɛ̃lɑ̃dɛ, -ɛz] VOIR GRAMMAIRE A19 ADJ Finnish
N F. Finn

Finlande [fɛ̃lɑ̃d] NF Finland

finnois [finwa] VOIR GRAMMAIRE A19 ADJ Finnish
NM *Ling* Finnish

finno-ougrien, -ienne [finougriɛ̃, -jɛn] *Ling* ADJ Finno-Ugric
NM Finno-Ugric

fiole [fjɔl] NF **1** *(flacon)* phial, flask **2** *Arg (tête)* nut, *Br* bonce; *(visage)* mug; **se payer la f. de qn** to make a fool of sb

fion [fjɔ̃] NM **1** *Arg Vulg* arse, *Am* ass **2** *Can, Suisse* **lancer des fions à qn** to taunt sb

fiord [fjɔr] NM *Géog* fjord, fiord

fioriture [fjɔrityr] NF *(d'une écriture)* flourish; *(du style)* embellishment; *Mus* fioritura, ornament, embellishment; **une lettre pleine de fioritures** a flowery letter

fiotte [fjɔt] NF *Vulg* queer, *Br* poof, *Am* fag

fioul [fjul] NM fuel oil

FIP [fip] *(abrév* **France Inter Paris)** = French radio station broadcasting mainly light music

firmament [firmamɑ̃] NM *Litt* firmament

firme [firm] NF firm VOIR GRAMMAIRE A11

firmware [fœrmwɛr] NM *Ordinat* firmware

FIS [fis] NM *(abrév* **Front islamique du salut)** **le F.** the FIS, the Islamique Salvation Front

fisc [fisc] NM *Admin* tax department ≃ Inland Revenue, *Am* ≃ Internal Revenue; **avoir des ennuis avec le f.** to have problems with the taxman

fiscal, -ale, -aux, -ales [fiskal, -o] ADJ fiscal; **l'administration fiscale** the tax(ation) authorities; **timbre f.** revenue stamp; **fraude/évasion fiscale** tax evasion/avoidance; **paradis f.** tax haven; **abri f.** tax shelter

fiscalement [fiskalmɑ̃] ADV from a tax point of view, fiscally

fiscalisation [fiskalizasjɔ̃] NF taxing, taxation

fiscaliser [fiskalize] VT to tax

fiscaliste [fiskalist] N tax specialist

fiscalité [fiskalite] NF tax system; **f. directe** direct taxation; **f. écologique** green taxation; **f. indirecte** indirect taxation; **f. locale** local taxation; **f. des entreprises** corporate taxation; **optimiser la f. de qch** to improve the tax efficiency of sth, to make sth more tax efficient

fissa [fisa] ADV *Fam* **faire f.** to get a move on, to get one's skates on

fissible [fisibl] ADJ *Phys* fissionable, fissile

fissile [fisil] ADJ **1** = fissible **2** *(roche)* fissile, tending to split

fission [fisjɔ̃] NF *Nucl* fission; **f. de l'atome** atomic fission, splitting of the atom

fissuration [fisyrasjɔ̃] NF cracking, fissuring

fissure [fisyr] NF crack, fissure; *Fig (entre amis)* split; **les fissures du mur** the cracks in the wall; **cette dispute provoqua une f. dans notre amitié** this quarrel caused a rift in our friendship

fissurer [fisyre] VT to crack, to fissure; *Fig* to split (up)
VPR **se fissurer** to crack, to fissure; *Fig* to split (up)

fiston [fistɔ̃] NM *Fam* son, lad; **allons (mon) f.!** now then, young fellow *or* my lad *or* sonny!

fistule [fistyl] NF *Méd* fistula

fistuleux, -euse [fistylø, -øz] ADJ *Méd* fistulous

FIV [ɛfive] NF *Biol (abrév* **fécondation in vitro)** IVF

fivète [fivɛt] NF *Biol* in vitro fertilization

fixage [fiksaʒ] NM **1** *Phot* fixing; **bain de f.** fixing bath **2** *Bourse* fixing

fixateur, -trice [fiksatœr, -tris] NM *(de teintures)* fixer; *Phot* fixer, fixing solution *or* bath; *Biol* fixative; *(pour cheveux)* hair spray, lacquer
ADJ **bactéries fixatrices d'azote** nitrogen-fixing bacteria

fixatif [fiksatif] NM *(pour dessins)* fixative

fixation [fiksasjɔ̃] NF **1** *(de date)* fixing; **f. de prix** price setting *ou* fixing, pricing; **f. d'un prix d'appel** loss-leader pricing; **f. d'un prix de soumission** sealed-bid pricing; **f. de l'impôt** tax assessment; **f. du prix en fonction du coût** cost-plus pricing; **f. du prix en fonction du taux de rentabilité souhaité** target-return pricing; **f. du prix optimal** optimal pricing; **f. du prix unitaire** unit pricing **2** *(d'étagère etc)* fixing; *(de sables mouvants)*, *Chimie (d'azote)* fixation; **f. par bride** *ou* **par collier** clamping; **vis de f.** fixing screw, set screw; **patte de f.** anchor(ing) clip **3** *Tech* attachment, anchor; *Ski* (ski) binding **4** *Psy* fixation *(à qn* on sb*)*; **faire une f. sur qch/qn** to become obsessed with *or* fixated on sth/sb

fixe [fiks] ADJ **1** *(immobile)* fixed; **idée f.** obsession, idée fixe; **regard f.** fixed *or* steady gaze; **grue f.** fixed *or* stationary crane; **essieu f.** dead axle; *Mil* **f.!** attention! **2** *(arrêté)* fixed; **prix f.** fixed *or* set price; **à prix f.** at fixed prices; **frais fixes** fixed costs; **traitement f.** fixed salary; **adresse f.** permanent address; **sans domicile f.** of no fixed abode; **prendre ses repas à heure f.** to eat at fixed *or* set times; *Ordinat* **disque f.** fixed disk; **beau (temps) f.** set fair (weather); **arrêt f.** compulsory stop
NM **1** *(salaire)* fixed salary; **toucher un f.** to be on a fixed salary **2** *Fam (de drogue)* fix

fixé [fikse] ADJ **1** *(date, heure, jour)* agreed, appointed; **à la date fixée** on the agreed *or* appointed day **2** **être f. sur qch** to have made up one's mind about sth; **je ne suis pas f.** I haven't made my mind up yet; **eh bien, maintenant, tu es f.** well, now you know

fixe-chaussettes [fiks(ə)ʃosɛt] NM INV suspender, *Am* garter

fixement [fiksəmɑ̃] ADV fixedly; **regarder f. qch** to stare at sth

fixer [fikse] VT **1** *(immobiliser)* to fix; **les vis qui fixent la serrure** the screws that hold the lock; *Fig* **f. qch dans sa mémoire** to implant sth in one's memory; **f. l'attention de qn** to hold *or* engage sb's attention; **f. son attention sur qch** to fix *or* focus one's attention on sth; **f. les yeux sur qch/qn** to fix one's eyes on sth/sb, to gaze *or* stare at sth/sb; *(scruter)* to look hard *or* intently at sth/sb; **f. qn (du regard)** to stare at sb; **ça va le f.** that will make him settle down
2 *Chimie, Phot* to fix
3 *(déterminer) (date, heure, jour)* to fix, to set, to arrange; *(rendez-vous)* to fix, to arrange; *(dommages, taxes)* to fix, to set; *(conditions, règlements)* to fix, to lay down; **f. un salaire** to fix a salary; **f. le prix de** to price; **f. un prix** to set a price, to fix a price; *Bourse* **f. un cours** to make a price
4 f. qn sur qch to put sb in the picture about sth
VPR **se fixer 1** *(s'installer)* to settle down
2 *(s'arrêter)* to become fixed; **l'orthographe du mot se fixa au XVIIIᵉ siècle** the spelling of the word became fixed in the 18th century; **se f. un objectif** to set oneself a target; **elle s'est fixée sur cette idée** she's got the idea

in her head (and nothing will shift it); **il s'est fixé sur ce type d'écran** he has gone for *or* decided on this type of screen

fixette [fiksɛt] NF *Fam* **faire une f. sur qn/ qch** to be obsessed with sb/sth, *Br* to have sb/sth on the brain

fixeur [fiksœr] NM *Bourse* **f. de prix** price maker

fixisme [fiksism] NM *Biol* creationism

fixité [fiksite] NF *(du regard)* fixity, steadiness

fjord [fjɔr(d)] NM *Géog* fjord, fiord

flac [flak] NM, INT plop; **faire f.** to plop

flaccidité [flaksidite] NF flabbiness, flaccidity

flacon [flakɔ̃] NM small (stoppered) bottle; *(de laboratoire)* flask; **f. à parfum** perfume bottle; **f. à liqueur** liqueur decanter

fla-fla [flafla] NM *Fam* show, ostentation; **faire du f.** to show off

flagada [flagada] ADJ INV *Fam* washed out, all in, dead beat

flagellation [flaʒɛlasjɔ̃] NF flogging, whipping; *(sur soi-même)* flagellation

flagelle [flaʒɛl] NM *Biol* flagellum

flagellé [flaʒele] ADJ, NM *Biol* flagellate

flageller [flaʒele] VT to flog, to whip
VPR **se flageller** to scourge oneself

flageolant [flaʒɔlɑ̃] ADJ shaking, trembling; **j'ai les jambes flageolantes** my legs are shaking *or* trembling

flageoler [flaʒɔle] VI *(des jambes)* to shake, to tremble; **elle flageole sur ses jambes** *(de peur)* she is shaking at the knees; *(de fatigue)* she's dead on her feet

flageolet¹ [flaʒɔle] NM *Mus* flageolet

flageolet² NM *Bot, Culin* flageolet (bean)

flagorner [flagɔrne] VT *Péj* to fawn on, to toady to

flagornerie [flagɔrnəri] NF *Péj* fawning, toadying

flagorneur, -euse [flagɔrnœr, -øz] N *Péj* toady, sycophant

flagrant [flagrɑ̃] ADJ *(injustice, mensonge etc)* flagrant, blatant; **pris en f. délit** caught in the act, caught red-handed; **pris en f. délit de mensonge** caught (out) lying; *Fam* **c'est f.!** it's (glaringly) obvious!

flair [flɛr] NM **1** *(des chiens)* scent, (sense of) smell, nose **2** *(d'une personne)* intuition; **avoir du f.** to have good intuition

flairer [flere] VT **1** *(d'un chien) (gibier)* to scent, to smell (out), to nose out; *Fig* **f. le danger** to scent *or* smell *or* sense danger; **f. le mensonge** to detect a lie; **f. que** to sense that **2** *(sentir)* to smell **3** *Belg Fam Péj (empester)* to stink *or* to reek of

flamand, -ande [flamɑ̃, -ɑ̃d] ADJ Flemish
NM *Ling* Flemish
N F. Fleming

flamant [flamɑ̃] NM flamingo; **f. rose** pink flamingo VOIR GRAMMAIRE A12

flambage [flɑ̃baʒ] NM **1** *(des cheveux, d'un poulet etc)* singeing; *(d'une aiguille)* sterilization; *(d'un bûcher)* charring **2** *(d'une plaque de métal)* buckling, collapse

flambant [flɑ̃bɑ̃] ADV **1 f. neuf** brand new **2** *Can Fam (complètement)* completely, totally; **f. nu** stark naked, starkers
ADJ **1** *(bûche, soleil)* blazing, flaming **2** **houille flambante** bituminous *or* soft coal
NM bituminous *or* soft coal

flambard [flɑ̃bar] NM *Fam* **faire le f.** to show off

flambé [flɑ̃be] ADJ **1** *Culin* flambé(ed) **2** *Fam* **il est f.** he's done for, his goose is cooked

flambeau, -eaux [flɑ̃bo] NM **1** *(torche)* torch; **descente/retraite aux flambeaux**

torch-lit descent/procession; **à la lueur des flambeaux, aux flambeaux** by torchlight; *Fig* **reprendre le f.** to take up the torch; *Fig* **passer le f. aux futures générations** to hand on the torch to future generations **2** *(chandelier)* candlestick

flambée [flɑ̃be] NF **1** *(feu)* blaze, blazing fire; **faire une f. dans la cheminée** to light a fire in the hearth **2** *Fig (de violence)* flare-up, outbreak; *(des prix)* upsurge, escalation; *(de colère)* outburst

flambement [flɑ̃bmɑ̃] NM *(d'une plaque de métal)* buckling, collapse

flamber [flɑ̃be] VI **1** *(brûler)* to blaze; **f. comme une allumette** to burn like matchwood **2** *(prix)* to escalate **3** *(d'une barre de métal etc)* to buckle, to collapse
▪ VT *(cheveux, volaille etc)* to singe; *Culin* to flambé; **f. une aiguille** to sterilize a needle (in a flame); *Fig* **elle a flambé l'argent du ménage au jeu** she gambled away *or* blew the housekeeping money; **c'est fou ce qu'elle flambe comme argent** it's crazy the amount of money she throws away!

flambeur [flɑ̃bœr] NM *Arg* big-time gambler

flamboiement [flɑ̃bwamɑ̃] NM blazing, blaze

flamboyant [flɑ̃bwajɑ̃] ADJ **1** *(feu)* blazing; *(yeux)* blazing, flashing **2** *Archit* flamboyant

flamboyer [flɑ̃bwaje] VI (**il flamboie**) *(du feu)* to blaze; **f. de colère** *(des yeux)* to blaze *or* flash with anger

flamingant, -ante [flamɛ̃gɑ̃, -ɑ̃t] ADJ *(ville, personne)* Flemish-speaking
▪ N *Pol* Flemish nationalist

flamme [flam] NF **1** *(de feu)* flame; **en flammes** on fire, ablaze; **dévoré par les flammes** consumed by flames; **retour de f.** *(d'une arme)* back flash; *Tech* backfire, backfiring; *Fig* backlash; **passer à la f.** to singe **2** *Litt (amour)* passion, love; **déclarer sa f. à une femme** to declare one's love for a woman **3** *(enthousiasme)* fire, enthusiasm; **discours plein de f.** fiery speech **4** *(drapeau)* pennant, streamer **5** *(sur lettre) (marque postale)* slogan

flammèche [flamɛʃ] NF spark

flan [flɑ̃] NM **1** *Culin* (baked) custard; *(tarte)* custard pie; **f. chimique** *ou* **en poudre** custard powder **2** *(d'une pièce, d'un disque etc)* blank **3** *Typ* flong, mould, *Am* mold **4** *Fig* **en rester** *ou* **en être comme deux ronds de f.** to be flabbergasted; *Fam* **c'est du f.** it's rubbish!; *Fam* **j'ai dit ça au f.** I said it just for the sake of it *or* just for something to say; *Fam* **y aller au f.** to try it on, to bluff

flanc [flɑ̃] NM *(d'un animal)* side, flank; *(d'une personne)* side; *(d'un pneu)* wall, profile, side wall; **route à f. de coteau** road following the hillside; **être sur le f.** *(malade)* to be laid up; *(épuisé)* to be quite worn out; **ces difficultés l'ont mise sur le f.** these problems really took it out of her; **battre des flancs** *(d'un cheval)* to heave, to pant; *Mil* **par le f. droit!** by the right!; **attaquer de f.** to attack on the flank; **le navire se présentait de f.** the ship was broadside on; **prêter le f. à la critique** to lay oneself open to criticism; *Fam* **tirer au f.** to shirk, *Br* to skive

flancher [flɑ̃ʃe] VI *Fam (faiblir)* to give in, to weaken; **ce n'est pas le moment de f.!** don't give in now!; **son cœur a flanché** his heart gave out; **sans f.** without flinching

flanchet [flɑ̃ʃɛ] NM *Culin* flank

Flandre [flɑ̃dr] NF Flanders

flandrin [flɑ̃drɛ̃] NM *Arch Fam* **grand f.** gangling *or* gangly fellow

flanelle [flanɛl] NF *Tex* flannel; **f. (de) coton** flannelette; **pantalon de f. grise** grey flannels; *Fam* **il devrait mettre sa f.** he ought to wear his jacket

flâner [flɑne, flane] VI **1** *(se promener)* to stroll, to saunter **2** *(perdre son temps)* to hang about; **perdre son temps à f.** to idle away one's time

flânerie [flɑnri, flanri] NF *(balade)* strolling; *(oisiveté)* idling

flâneur, -euse [flɑnœr, flanœr, -øz] ADJ idle
▪ N **1** *(promeneur)* stroller **2** *(oisif)* idler, loafer

flanquer¹ [flɑ̃ke] VT *(bâtiment), Mil (colonne, ennemi)* to flank; **flanqué de deux agents** flanked by two policemen

flanquer² *Fam* VT *(jeter)* to chuck, to fling, to throw; **f. une gifle/un coup de pied à qn** to give sb a slap/kick; **f. qn à la porte** *ou* **dehors** to throw sb out; *(licencier)* to fire sb, *Br* to sack sb; **f. la trouille** *ou* **les jetons à qn** to give sb the jitters, to put the wind up sb
▪ VPR **se flanquer se f. par terre** to come a cropper, to take a tumble; **elle s'est flanquée dans le ravin** she plunged into the ravine

flapi [flapi] ADJ *Fam* dead beat, fagged out

flaque [flak] NF puddle; **f. de sang** pool of blood

flash, *pl* **flashes** [flaʃ] NM **1** *Phot* flash(light); **prendre une photo au f.** to take a picture using a flash **2** *Cin* flash; **f. publicitaire** commercial **3** *TV, Radio* newsflash; **f. d'informations** newsflash; *TV, Radio* **f. spécial** (special) newsflash

flashant [flaʃɑ̃] ADJ *Fam* flashy

flash-back [flaʃbak] NM INV flashback; **faire un f.** to flash back

flasher [flaʃe] VI *Fam* **f. sur qch/qn** to really fall for sth/sb

flasque¹ [flask] ADJ *(chair)* flabby, flaccid; *(style)* limp; *(chapeau)* floppy

flasque² NF flask

flasque³ NM *Mil (d'un affût de canon)* cheek; *Aut* hubcap, wheel disc; *(d'une roue)* flange

flatter [flate] VT **1** *(complimenter)* to flatter; **f. qn sur son bel esprit** to flatter sb on his wit; **je suis flatté de votre proposition** I am flattered by your proposal
2 *(avantager)* **cette coupe ne la flatte pas** that style doesn't flatter her; **peintre qui flatte ses modèles** painter who flatters his sitters
3 *(plaire) (l'oreille)* to delight, to be pleasing to, to please; **spectacle qui flatte les yeux** sight that is pleasing to the eye; **plat/vin qui flatte le palais** dish/wine that delights the taste buds *or* the palate; **f. les caprices de qn** to pander to *or* humour *or* indulge sb's whims
4 *(tromper)* to delude; **f. qn de l'espoir de qch** to hold out false hopes of sth to sb
5 *(animal)* to stroke, to caress; **f. un cheval** to pat a horse
▪ VPR **se flatter** to flatter oneself, to delude oneself; **elle se flattait de réussir** she flattered herself sure that she would succeed; **il se flatte qu'on a** *ou* **ait besoin de lui** he flatters himself that he is indispensable; **se f. de son habileté** to congratulate oneself on one's cleverness; **se f. d'avoir fait qch** to pride oneself on having done sth; **à ta place, je ne m'en flatterais pas** if I was in your place it's not something I'd be proud of

flatterie [flatri] NF flattery; **ce ne sont que de viles flatteries** it's just base flattery

flatteur, -euse [flatœr, -øz] ADJ *(remarque, portrait, couleur)* flattering; *(personne)* full of flattery; **peu f.** unflattering; **il a fait un tableau f. de la situation** he painted a rosy picture of the situation
▪ N flatterer

flatulence [flatylɑ̃s] NF *Méd* flatulence; **avoir des flatulences** to suffer from flatulence

flatulent [flatylɑ̃] ADJ *Méd* flatulent

flatuosité [flatɥozite] NF wind; *Méd* flatus

FLE [fla] NM *(abrév* **français langue étrangère)** French as a foreign language

fléau, -aux [fleo] NM **1** *(calamité)* scourge, curse; *Fig* plague, pest, bane; *Fam* **c'est un vrai f.!** he's/it's a real pain! **2** *(à céréales)* flail **3** *(d'une balance)* beam, arm

fléchage [fleʃaʒ] NM *(de direction)* signposting

flèche¹ [flɛʃ] NF **1** *(projectile)* arrow; **pistolet à flèches** dart gun; **fer de f.** arrowhead; **faire f. de tout bois** to use all available means, to use all means at one's disposal; **partir en** *ou* **comme une f.** *(d'une personne)* to shoot off; **monter en f.** *(d'un avion)* to shoot (straight) up; *(des prix)* to shoot up, to rocket; *Fig* **elle lui a décoché des flèches méchantes** she let fly a few barbed remarks in his direction; **je ne supporte plus ses petites flèches** I can't stand his digs at me any longer
2 *(direction)* arrow; **suivre les flèches** to follow the arrows; **f. lumineuse** pointer; *(de sortie de secours etc)* luminous arrow; *Aut* **f. de direction** trafficator
3 **chevaux attelés en f.** horses driven tandem; **cheval de f.** leader, leading horse
4 *(d'une église)* spire
5 *(d'une grue)* jib, boom
6 *Naut (d'un mât)* pole; *(d'un cutter)* topsail
7 *Archit (d'une arche)* rise; *Aviat (d'un plan à profil d'aile)* camber
8 *(d'un câble)* sag, dip
9 *Ordinat* **f. de défilement** scroll arrow; **f. vers la droite** right arrow; **f. vers la gauche** left arrow; **f. vers le bas** down arrow; **f. vers le haut** up arrow; **flèches verticales** up and down arrow keys

flèche² NF *(de lard)* flitch

flèche³ NM *Fam* **j'ai pas un f.** I'm totally broke

flécher [fleʃe] VT *(route, direction)* to arrow; **itinéraire fléché** arrowed *or* signposted route

fléchette [fleʃɛt] NF dart; **jouer aux fléchettes** to play darts VOIR GRAMMAIRE A10

fléchi [fleʃi] ADJ *Ling* **forme fléchie** inflected form

fléchir [fleʃir] VT **1** *(bras, jambe)* to bend, to flex; **f. le genou devant qn** to bend *or* bow the knee to sb **2** *(émouvoir)* to sway; **se laisser f.** to let oneself be swayed
▪ VI **1** *(se ployer)* to bend; *(des jambes, troupes etc)* to give way; *(d'un câble, d'une poutre)* to sag **2** *(diminuer) (de prix)* to fall; **les prix fléchissent** prices are falling, prices are coming down; **le dollar fléchit** the dollar is weakening *or* falling; **son autorité fléchit** his authority is weakening; **elle n'a pas fléchi** she didn't give in *or* yield

fléchissement [fleʃismɑ̃] NM **1** *(du genou etc)* bending; *(d'une poutre etc)* yielding, bending; *(d'un câble etc)* sagging **2** *(des prix)* falling, drop; *(des devises)* weakening; *Bourse* **f. des cours** fall *or* drop in share prices

fléchisseur [fleʃisœr] ADJ, NM *Anat* (muscle) **f.** flexor

flegmatique [flɛgmatik] ADJ phlegmatic, imperturbable

flegmatiquement [flɛgmatikmɑ̃] ADV phlegmatically, imperturbably

flegme [flɛgm] NM **1** *(imperturbabilité)* phlegm, imperturbability; **faire perdre son f. à qn** to make sb lose their composure *or Fam* cool; **le f. britannique** British phlegm **2** *Méd* phlegm

flémingite [flemɛ̃ʒit] NF *Fam* total laziness; **il fait de la f. aiguë** he's being bone idle

flemmard, -arde [flemar, -rd] N *Fam* lazy sod *or* so-and-so

flemmarder [flemarde] VI *Fam* to lounge about; **f. au lit** to laze in bed

flemmardise [flemardiz] NF *Fam* laziness, idleness

flemme [flεm] NF *Fam* laziness, idleness, slacking; **j'ai la f. de le faire** I can't be bothered to do it; **tirer sa f.** to lounge about

flet [flε] NM flounder

flétan [fletɑ̃] NM halibut

flétri [fletri] ADJ withered

flétrir[1] [fletrir] VT *(peau)* to wither; *(couleurs etc)* to fade; *(plantes)* to wither (up), to wilt VPR **se flétrir** *(des plantes)* to wither, to wilt; *(de la peau)* to wither

flétrir[2] VT **1** *(crime)* to stigmatize; *Hist (criminel)* to brand **2** *(la réputation de qn)* to blacken, to sully, to stain

flétrissure[1] [fletrisyr] NF withering

flétrissure[2] NF *(déshonneur)* stain, blemish

fleur [flœr] NF **1** *Bot* flower; *(d'arbre)* blossom, bloom; **arbre en fleur(s)** tree in blossom *or* in flower *or* in bloom; **fleurs des champs** wild flowers; **fleurs en pot** flowering pot plant; **ni fleurs, ni couronnes** ≃ no flowers by request; **envoyer des fleurs à qn** to send sb flowers; *Fig* to pat sb on the back; **f. artificielle/en papier** artificial/paper flower; **tissu à fleurs** flowered *or* flowery material; *Fig* **faire une f. à qn** to do sb a favour; *Fig* **elle le couvre de fleurs** she heaps praise (up)on him; **être f. bleue** to be (naively) romantic; *Fam* **elle y est arrivée comme une f.** she managed it without a hitch *or* a problem **2** *Fig Litt* **dans** *ou* **à la f. de l'âge** in the prime of life; **dans la première f. de la jeunesse** in the first flush *or* flower of youth; **la fine f. de la société** the cream of society **3** *(d'antimoine, de vin etc)* **fleurs** flowers **4** **à f. de** on the surface of; **à f. d'eau** just above (the surface of) the water; **voler à f. d'eau** to skim the water; **émotions à f. de peau** skin-deep emotions; **avoir les nerfs à f. de peau** to be all on edge **5** *(d'une peau)* hair side, grain side **6** **f. de farine** top-quality flour

fleurage [flœraʒ] NM *(sur un tissu, tapis)* floral pattern

fleurdelisé [flœrdəlize] ADJ decorated with fleurs-de-lis; *Hér* fleury NM *Can (drapeau du Québec)* flag of Quebec

fleurer [flœre] VT *Litt* to smell of; **f. la violette** to smell of violets; *Fig* **ça fleure l'intrigue/les pots-de-vin** it smacks of a plot/of bribery, I/he/*etc* can smell a plot/bribery

fleuret [flœrε] NM *(épée)* foil; *Min* borer

fleurette [flœrεt] NF **1 conter f. à qn** to whisper sweet nothings to sb **2 crème f.** ≃ single cream

fleuri [flœri] ADJ **1** *(en fleurs)* in bloom, in flower, in blossom; *(orné de fleurs) (tissu, robe)* flowered, flowery; *(vaisselle)* flower-patterned; **village f.** ≃ village taking part in a flower competition; **avoir la boutonnière fleurie** to have a flower in one's buttonhole; *(décoré)* to wear a decoration **2** *(sentier etc)* flowery; *(teint)* florid; *(style)* flowery, florid

fleurir [flœrir] *(prp* fleurissant, *Litt* florissant; *impf* il fleurissait, *Litt* il florissait) VI **1** *(des plantes)* to flower, to bloom, to blossom **2** *(de l'art, du commerce etc) (usu* florissant, florissait) to blossom, to flourish, to prosper VT *(table)* to decorate with flowers; *(boutonnière)* to put a flower in; *(tombe)* to lay flowers on

fleuriste [flœrist] N **1** *(commerçant)* florist, flower seller **2** *(horticulteur)* flower grower **3** *(de fleurs artificielles)* artificial flower maker

fleuron [flœrɔ̃] NM **1** *(ornement)* flower, fleuron; *Archit* finial; **c'est le plus beau f. de no-**tre collection it's the jewel in our collection **2** *Bot* floret

fleuve [flœv] NM river *(as opposed to tributary)*; **f. (côtier)** short coastal river; *Fig* **un f. de sang/de larmes** a river of blood/a flood of tears; **des fleuves de boue** rivers of mud ADJ INV **roman-f.** saga; **discours-f.** lengthy speech

flexibilité [flεksibilite] NF flexibility; *(de matériaux)* pliability; *(du corps)* flexibility, suppleness, litheness; *Fin (d'une entreprise, de la main-d'œuvre)* flexibility

flexible [flεksibl] ADJ **1** *(souple)* flexible, supple; *(matériaux)* pliable; **tuyau f.** hose(-pipe) **2** *(adaptable) (personne)* flexible; *(disposition)* accommodating; *(malléable)* pliable, pliant; **avoir des horaires flexibles** to work flexible hours, to be on flexitime NM *(tuyau)* hose(pipe); *Élec* flexible lead; *Br* flex; *Aut* **f. de frein** brake hose

flexion [flεksjɔ̃] NF **1** *(fléchissement)* flexion, bending; *Gym* **f. du corps** trunk exercise; *Tech* **effort de f.** bending stress **2** *(d'une tige)* buckling, collapse **3** *Ling (de mot)* inflexion; **langue à flexions** inflected language

flexionnel, -elle [flεksjɔnεl] ADJ *Ling* inflected; **langue flexionnelle** inflected language

flibuste [flibyst] NF *Hist (piraterie)* buccaneering, freebooting; *(pirates)* buccaneers, freebooters

flibustier [flibystje] NM **1** *Hist* buccaneer, freebooter **2** *Arch Fam (escroc)* cheat, crook

flic [flik] NM *Fam (policier)* cop, copper; **voilà les flics!** it's the cops!

flicage [flikaʒ] NM *Fam (par la police)* heavy policing; *Fig* heavy-handed supervision

flicaille [flikɑj] NF *Fam* **la f.** the pigs

flic flac NM splish splash; *(d'un fouet)* crack

flingue [flɛ̃g] NM *Fam (arme)* shooter, piece

flinguer [flɛ̃ge] *Fam* VT **1** *(tuer avec une arme à feu)* to gun down **2** *(abîmer)* to wreck, to bust; *Br* to knacker **3** *(critiquer sévèrement)* to shoot down, to savage VPR **se flinguer** to blow one's brains out; **il n'y a pas de quoi se f.** it's not the end of the world; **c'est à se f.!** it's enough to make you chuck yourself under a train!

flip [flip] NM *Fam* **1** *(déprime)* **être en plein f.** to be on a real downer; **c'est le f.!** what a downer! **2** *(après l'absorption de drogue)* depression, downer *(as the after-effect of taking cocaine or amphetamines)*

flip-flap, *pl* **flips-flaps** [flipflap] NM *Gym* back(ward) flip

flippant [flipɑ̃] ADJ *Fam (déprimant)* grim; *(effrayant)* creepy

flipper[1] [flipœr] NM *(appareil)* pinball (machine); *(jeu)* pinball; **jouer au f.** to play pinball

flipper[2] [flipe] VI *Fam* **1** *(d'un drogué)* to be spaced out **2** *(s'angoisser)* to freak out; **ça me fait f.** that freaks me out; **elle flippe à cause de son travail** her work is freaking her out

fliquer [flike] VT *Fam* to police heavily; **fliqué** overrun with cops; *Fig* **au bureau, on a vraiment l'impression d'être fliqués** in the office we really feel we're being watched like criminals; **il flique complètement sa femme** he watches his wife like a hawk

flirt [flœrt] NM **1** *(amourette)* flirtation, flirting; **ce n'est qu'un f.** I/he/*etc* was only flirting **2** *Vieilli* **mon f.** my boyfriend/girlfriend; **un de mes anciens flirts** an old flame of mine

flirter [flœrte] VI to flirt; *Fam* **f. avec le danger** to flirt with danger; *Fig* **il flirte avec la police/l'opposition** he's flirting with the police/the opposition

FLN [εfεlεn] NM *Hist (abrév* **Front de libération nationale**) = national liberation front in Algeria

FLNC [εfεlεnse] NM *(abrév* **Front de libération national de la Corse**) = Corsican liberation front

FLNKS [εfεlɛnkɑεs] NM *Can (abrév* **Front de libération nationale kanak et socialiste**) = Kanak national liberation front in New Caledonia

flo [flo] N *Can Fam* teenager, *Am* teen

floc [flɔk] INT, NM splash

flocage [flɔkaʒ] NM *Tex* flocking

floche [flɔʃ] ADJ flossy; **soie f.** floss silk

flocon [flɔkɔ̃] NM **1** *(de neige, céréale)* flake; **flocons d'avoine** oat flakes; *Can* **flocons de maïs** cornflakes; **purée en flocons** instant mashed potato **2** *(de laine, coton)* tuft, flock

floconneux, -euse [flɔkɔnø, -øz] ADJ fleecy, fluffy

floculation [flɔkylasjɔ̃] NF *Chimie* flocculation

flonflons [flɔ̃flɔ̃] NMPL tiddly-om-pom-pom

flop [flɔp] NM *Fam* flop; **faire un f.** to be a flop

flopée [flɔpe] NF *Fam* **une f., des flopées** *(d'enfants, de gens)* loads, masses

floquer [flɔke] VT *Tex* to flock

floraison [flɔrεzɔ̃] NF **1** *(d'arbre)* flowering, blossoming; **l'arbre est en pleine f.** the tree is in full flower *or* blossom **2** *Fig* upsurge *(*de in)

floral, -ale, -aux, -ales [flɔral, -o] ADJ floral; **exposition florale** flower show

floralies [flɔrali] NFPL flower show

flore [flɔr] NF *Bot* flora; *Physiol* **f. intestinale** intestinal flora

floréal [flɔreal] NM *Hist* = eighth month of the French Republican calendar *(April-May)*

florès [flɔrεs] NM *Litt Vieilli* **faire f.** to prosper

Floride [flɔrid] NF Florida

florifère [flɔrifεr] ADJ flower-bearing, *Spéc* floriferous; **plante très f.** prolific flowerer

florilège [flɔrilεʒ] NM anthology

florin [flɔrɛ̃] NM *Anciennement* florin

florissant [flɔrisɑ̃] ADJ *(affaire, pays, peuple)* flourishing, prosperous; *(santé, mine)* blooming; **d'une santé florissante** in the best of health

flot [flo] NM **1** *(marée)* flood (tide); *Litt* **les flots bleus** the ocean blue; **elle s'endormit, bercée par le bruit des flots** she fell asleep, lulled by the sound of the waves **2** *(de larmes)* flood; *(de sang, d'injures)* torrent, stream; *(de gens, voitures)* stream; **un f. de paroles** a torrent *or* flood of words; **entrer à flots** *(de gens, du soleil)* to flood in, to stream in; **f. de dentelle/rubans** cascade of lace/ribbons; **couler à flots** to pour out **3** **être à f.** *(d'un bateau)* to be afloat; *Fig (d'une personne)* to have one's head above water; **mettre un navire à f.** to launch a ship; **remettre un navire à f.** to refloat a ship; **mon compte en banque est à f.** my bank account is in the black *or* in credit; **remettre qn à f.** to put sb back in the black; **ce cours vous permettra de vous remettre à f. en russe** this course will get you going in Russian again *or* will bring your Russian back up to scratch again

flottabilité [flɔtabilite] NF buoyancy; **caisson** *ou* **réservoir de f.** buoyancy tank

flottable [flɔtabl] ADJ **1** *(d'un cours d'eau)* floatable *(for rafts of wood)* **2** *(du bois)* floatable, buoyant

flottage [flɔtaʒ] NM *(de bois)* floating; **bois de f.** raft wood; **train de f.** timber raft

flottaison [flɔtεzɔ̃] NF floating; *Naut* **(ligne de) f.** waterline; **f. en charge** load line; **f. lège** light waterline

flottant [flɔtɑ̃] ADJ **1** (dette, moteur etc) floating; (chiffre) fluctuating; Ordinat **virgule flottante** floating point **2** (toge, cheveux) flowing, loose; **filet f.** drift net **3** (électorat, opinion) undecided, wavering; **électeur f.** floating voter
▪ NM Bourse float

flotte [flɔt] NF **1** (bateaux) fleet; **f. de ligne** ou **de combat** battle fleet; **f. de commerce** merchant fleet; **être dans la f.** to be in the navy; **f. aérienne** air fleet; **f. marchande** merchant marine **2** Fam (pluie) rain; (eau) water; **il tombe de la f.** it's pouring with rain; **c'est de la f., ce café!** this coffee's like water!

flottement [flɔtmɑ̃] NM **1** (d'une ligne de troupes etc) wavering, swaying; (d'un drapeau) flapping, fluttering; (d'une chaîne, roue) wobble; (d'une devise) fluctuation **2** (hésitation) wavering, hesitation; **il y eut un moment de f.** there was a moment's hesitation; **il y a toujours des flottements dans ses exposés** there are always some uneven patches in his talks

flotter [flɔte] VI **1** (sur l'eau) to float **2** (au vent) to float, to stream; (des cheveux) to stream **3** (hésiter) to waver, to hesitate; (des pensées) to wander; **un sourire flottait sur ses lèvres** a smile played or hovered on his/her lips **4** (des devises) to fluctuate; **faire f.** to float **5** (des vêtements) to hang loosely; **il flotte dans ses vêtements** his clothes are far too big for him, Fam his clothes drown him
▪ VT **f. du bois** to float timber (down a stream); **bois flotté** driftwood
▪ V IMPERS Fam **il flotte** it's raining

flotteur [flɔtœr] NM **1** (ouvrier) raftsman (in charge of timber raft) **2** (d'une canne à pêche, d'un hydravion, carburateur etc) float **3** (d'un robinet) ball; **robinet à f.** ballcock

flottille [flɔtij] NF (de bateaux) flotilla; (d'avions) squadron; **f. de pêche** fishing fleet

flou [flu] ADJ (contour, peinture) blurred; (image) blurred, fuzzy, out of focus; (son) muffled, indistinct; (horizon) hazy; (idée) hazy, vague; (cheveux) soft, fluffy; (robe) loose (-fitting)
▪ NM (d'un contour, d'une image) blur, fuzziness; (d'un son) indistinctness; (de l'horizon) haziness; (d'une idée) haziness, vagueness; (des cheveux) softness, fluffiness; (d'une robe) looseness; **le f. revient à la mode** loose-fitting clothes are back in fashion; **f. artistique** Phot soft-focus effect; Fig deliberate vagueness; **elle a préféré rester dans un f. artistique** she preferred to remain deliberately vague

flouche [fluʃ] N Can Fam teenager

flouer [flue] VT Fam to swindle; **se faire f.** to be swindled, to be done

flouse, flouze [fluz] NM Arg (argent) bread, dough, cash

FLQ [ɛfɛlky] (abrév franco long du quai) FAS

fluctuant [flyktɥɑ̃] ADJ fluctuating; **un esprit f.** a weathercock; **elle est fluctuante dans ses projets** her plans are liable to change

fluctuation [flyktɥasjɔ̃] NF **1** (changement) fluctuation; **f. des prix** price fluctuation; **f. saisonnière** seasonal fluctuation; Écon **bande** ou **marge de f.** fluctuation band or margin **2** Élec **fluctuations de tension** voltage fluctuations

fluctuer [flyktɥe] VI to fluctuate

fluent [flɥɑ̃] ADJ (sol) flowing, loose; Méd **hémorroïdes fluentes** bleeding piles

fluet, -ette [flɥɛ, -ɛt] ADJ (personne) thin, slender; (voix) thin, reedy

fluide [flɥid] ADJ (huile, situation) fluid; (style, pensée) fluid, flowing; **la circulation était f.** the traffic was flowing steadily; **les**

accords fluides de la sonate the fluid chords of the sonata
▪ NM **1** fluid; **f. de nettoyage** cleaning fluid; Aut **f. de frein** brake fluid; **f. aéré** aerated fluid; **f. d'embrayage** clutch fluid; **f. glacial** = ice-cold liquid used by children for pranks; **f. de refroidissement** coolant; **f. moteur** engine fluid; Phys **la mécanique des fluides** fluid mechanics **2** avoir du f. (d'un médium) to have strange powers

fluidifier [flɥidifje] VT to thin, to fluidify

fluidité [flɥidite] NF fluidity; **f. de la circulation** steady flow of traffic

fluo [flyo] ADJ INV Fam fluorescent

fluor [flyɔr] NM Chimie fluorine; **dentifrice au f.** fluoride toothpaste; Minér **spath f.** fluorspar

fluoration [flyɔrasjɔ̃] NF (de l'eau) fluoridation

fluoré [flyɔre] ADJ **dentifrice f.** fluoride toothpaste

fluorescence [flyɔrɛsɑ̃s] NF fluorescence

fluorescent [flyɔrɛsɑ̃] ADJ fluorescent; **rose/vert f.** fluorescent pink/green

fluorine [flyɔrin] NF Minér fluorspar

fluorure [flyɔryr] NM Chimie fluoride

flûte [flyt] NF **1** (instrument) flute; **f. à bec** recorder; **f. de Pan** panpipes; **f. traversière, grande f.** concert flute; **petite f.** piccolo **2** (musicien) flautist, flute (player), Am flutist **3** (pain) small French stick; Suisse (biscuit) breadstick **4** (verre) flute; **f. à champagne** champagne flute **5** Fam **flûtes** (jambes) pins; **jouer** ou **se tirer des flûtes** to show a clean pair of heels
▪ INT Fam blow!, drat!; **f. alors, il est déjà parti!** blow it or drat it, he's gone already!

flûté [flyte] ADJ **voix flûtée** flute-like or piping voice

flûtiau, -aux [flytjo] NM penny whistle

flûtiste [flytist] N flautist, flute player, Am flutist

fluvial, -iale, -iaux, -iales [flyvjal, -jo] ADJ river attrib fluvial; **police fluviale** river police; **pêche fluviale** river fishing, angling; **alluvions fluviales** fluvial deposits; **port f.** river port

fluviatile [flyvjatil] ADJ **mollusques fluviatiles** river or freshwater molluscs

flux [fly] NM **1** (de mots) flow, stream **2** (marée montante) flow, flood; **le f. et le reflux** the ebb and flow; Pol Fam the swing of the pendulum; Fig **le f. et le reflux des visiteurs** the coming and going of visitors; **f. de fonds** flow of funds; **f. de trésorerie** cashflow; **f. monétaire** cashflow **3** Méd flow, flux; **f. menstruel** menstrual flow **4** Chimie, Métal flux **5** Phys, Élec **f. magnétique** magnetic flux; **f. lumineux** luminous or light flux; **f. électronique** electron flow or stream

fluxion [flyksjɔ̃] NF Méd inflammation; **f. à la joue** swollen cheek; **f. de la gencive** gumboil; **f. de poitrine** pneumonia

FM [ɛfɛm] NF (abrév modulation de fréquence) FM

FME [ɛfɛmə] NM (abrév Fonds monétaire européen) EMF

FMI [ɛfɛmi] NM (abrév Fonds monétaire international) IMF

FN [ɛfɛn] NM (abrév Front national) = French extreme right-wing party

FNAC [fnak] NF (abrév Fédération nationale d'achat des cadres) = chain of stores selling books, hi-fis, photographic equipment etc

FNE [ɛfɛnə] NM (abrév Fonds national de l'emploi) = state fund providing aid to job-seekers and workers who accept lower-paid work to avoid redundancy

FNGS [ɛfɛnʒeɛs] NM (abrév Fonds national de garantie des salaires) = national guarantee fund for the payment of salaries

FNI [ɛfɛni] NFPL Mil (abrév forces nucléaires intermédiaires) INF

FNSEA [ɛfɛnsəa] NF (abrév Fédération nationale des syndicats d'exploitants agricoles) farmers' union, Br ≃ NFU

FO [ɛfo] NF (abrév Force ouvrière) = French trade union

FOB, fob [ɛfɔbe] ADJ INV, ADV FOB; **vente f.** FOB sale

foc [fɔk] NM Naut jib; **grand f.** main or outer jib; **petit f.** fore staysail; **f. d'artimon** mizzen-topmast staysail

focal, -ale, -aux, -ales [fɔkal, -o] ADJ Math, Opt focal

focalisation [fɔkalizasjɔ̃] NF Opt, Électron focusing; Mktg targeting; Mktg **f. stratégique** strategic targeting

focaliser [fɔkalize] VT Opt, Électron to focus; Mktg to target Fig **f. son attention/l'attention de qn sur qch** to focus one's/sb's attention on sth
▪ VPR **se focaliser** to focus (**sur** on)

fœhn [føn] NM **1** (vent) foehn **2** Suisse (sèche-cheveux) hair-dryer

fœhner [føne] VT Suisse (sécher au sèche-cheveux électrique) to dry with a/the hair-dryer

fœtal, -ale, -aux, -ales [fetal, -o] ADJ f(o)etal

fœtus [fetys] NM f(o)etus

fofolle [fɔfɔl] Fam ADJ F nutty, daft
▪ NF nutty or daft woman

foi [fwa] NF **1** bonne **f.** sincerity, honesty; mauvaise **f.** insincerity, dishonesty; Phil bad faith; **il est de bonne/mauvaise f.** he is sincere/insincere; **je le lui ai dit en toute bonne f.** I told him that in good faith; **témoin de bonne/mauvaise f.** truthful/untruthful witness; **témoin digne de f.** trustworthy or reliable or credible witness; **ma f., oui!** yes indeed!; **c'est ma f. vrai** that is certainly or definitely true; Arch **f. d'honnête homme** on my word as a gentleman; **sur la f. de sa lettre** on the strength of his letter
2 (confiance) belief, trust, confidence; **avoir f. en qn/qch** to have faith in or to believe in sb/sth; **avoir f. en l'avenir** to have confidence in the future; **ajouter** ou **attacher f. à une nouvelle** to give credence to or to credit or to believe (in) a piece of news; **texte qui fait f.** authentic text; **la lettre doit partir avant le 29, le cachet de la poste faisant f.** the letter must be postmarked no later than the 28th; Jur **en f. de quoi** in witness whereof; **ligne de f.** Opt zero alignment; Naut, Aviat lubber line
3 Rel faith, belief; **avoir la f.** to have faith; Fig **il faut vraiment avoir la f.** you have to be really dedicated; Iron **il n'y a que la f. qui sauve** faith is a wonderful thing; **acte/article de f.** act/article of faith; **profession de f.** profession of faith; Cathol confirmation; Pol (d'un candidat) mission statement; **répandre la f.** to spread the Word; **la f. démocratique** faith or belief in democracy; **il n'a ni f. ni loi, il est sans f. ni loi** he fears neither God nor man

foie [fwa] NM Culin liver; **f. de veau/volaille** calf's/chicken liver; **huile de f. de morue** cod-liver oil; Fig Fam **se ronger** ou **se manger les foies** to be climbing the walls, to go berserk; très Fam **avoir les foies** to be scared out of one's wits; **ça m'a foutu les foies** it scared me out of my wits
▸ ▸ **f. gras** foie gras

foie-de-bœuf, pl **foies-de-bœuf** NM beefsteak fungus

foin [fwɛ̃] NM **1** (fourrage) hay; **faire les foins**

to make hay; **tas de f.** haycock; **meule de f.** haystack; **rhume des foins** hay fever; *Fam* **faire du f.** *(scandale)* to kick up *or* make a fuss; *(bruit)* to kick up *or* make a din; **ce scandale a fait du f. dans le milieu politique local** this scandal made waves in local political circles **2** *(d'artichaut)* choke **3** *Arch* **f. de ...** the devil take ...

foire [fwar] NF fair; **f. commerciale** trade show; **f. internationale** international (trade) fair; **f. professionnelle** trade fair; **f. commerciale de Marseille** Marseilles trade fair; *Ordinat* **f. aux questions** frequently asked questions, FAQ; **champ de f.** fairground; *Fam* **c'est la f. ici** *(désordre)* it's chaos in here; *(bruit)* it's bedlam in here; **faire la f.** to have a good time, to have fun

foire-exposition, *Fam* **foire-expo,** *pl* **foires-expositions, foires-expos** NF trade fair *or* exhibition

foirer [fware] *très Fam* VI *(rater)* **la mission/le plan/la soirée a complètement foiré** the mission/the plan/the evening was a complete balls-up *or Am* ballup *or* cockup; **ses prévisions ont complètement foiré** his predictions were a mile out; **il a tout fait f.** he cocked everything up; *Mil* **fusée qui foire** shell that doesn't go off
▶ VT to cock up, to mess up

foireux, -euse [fwarø, -øz] ADJ **1** *très Fam* *(qui échoue)* hopeless; **c'est un plan f.** that plan is going to be a cock up **2** *Fam (lâche)* chicken, yellow **3** *Vulg (qui a la diarrhée)* suffering from the runs *or* the trots

fois [fwa] NF **1** *(occasion)* time; **une f.** once; *Belg* **venez une f. voir** *(donc)* just come and see; **une f. et une seule** just the once, once and once only; **il était une f. un roi** once upon a time there was a king; **deux f.** twice; **par deux f.** not once but twice; **combien de f.?** how many times?, how often?; **trois f. quatre font douze** three times four is twelve; **trois f. plus grand** three times as big; **je l'ai acheté pour trois f. rien** I bought it for next to nothing; **il faut du beurre? – oui, mais trois f. rien** do you need some butter? – yes, just the smallest amount *or* but hardly any; **tu t'es fait mal? – non, c'est trois f. rien** have you hurt yourself? – no, it's nothing at all; **encore une f.** once more, once again; **y regarder à deux f. (pour faire qch)** to think twice (before doing sth); **une (bonne) f. pour toutes** once and for all; **la première/deuxième f.** the first/second time; **c'est la première f. que j'en fais** it's my first time, it's the first time I've done it; **une dernière f., arrête!** for the last time, stop it!; **cette f.** this time; **pour cette f.** this once; **une autre f.** another time, on another occasion; **d'autres f.** at other times; **bien des f.** many times, often; **deux f. par jour** twice daily *or* a day; **il faut le boire en une f.** you must drink it at *or* in one go *or Fam* in a oner; **toutes les f.** *ou* **chaque f. que j'y pense** every time that *or* whenever I think about it; **pour une f. tu as raison** you're right for once; **pour une f. que je peux y aller, il faut qu'il vienne aussi!** it's the one time I can go *or* for once I can go and he has to come as well!; **c'est la seule f. où j'ai regretté** that's the only time when *or* that I had regrets; **il y a des f. où je me demande à quoi tu penses** there are times when I wonder what you're thinking about; **une f. que vous aurez des informations** once you have *or* as soon as you have some information; **à la f.** at the same time, at once; **à la f. utile et pas cher** both useful and inexpensive; **pas trop vite, une chose à la f.** slow down, one thing at a time; **pas tous à la f.!** one at a time!, not all at once!, not all at the same time!; **je n'arrive pas à écouter de la musique et lire à la f.** I can't listen to music and read at the same time; *Fig* **tu ne peux** pas courir deux lièvres à la f. you can't do two things at once *or* at the same time **2** *Fam* **des f.** *(parfois)* sometimes; **vous n'auriez pas un câble de remorque, des f.?** you haven't by any chance got a towrope?; **des f. qu'il viendrait** in case he should come; **non, mais des f.!** really now!

foison [fwazɔ̃] NF **1** *Arch* abundance, plenty **2** **à f.** in abundance; **il y en a à f.** there are plenty of them, they are abundant; **des pommes à f.** apples in abundance, apples galore

foisonnant [fwazɔnɑ̃] ADJ abundant, plentiful

foisonnement [fwazɔnmɑ̃] NM **1** *(abondance)* abundance; **un f. de détails** an abundance of details; **le f. des idées** the proliferation of ideas **2** *(multiplication)* multiplying **3** *(augmentation de volume)* swelling, expansion

foisonner [fwazɔne] VI **1** to abound *(de, en* in, with); **le gibier foisonne ici** game is plentiful here; **il foisonne de bonnes idées** he's bursting with good ideas; **une école d'art où les jeunes talents foisonnent** an art school bursting with young talent **2** *(d'animaux)* to multiply **3** *(augmenter de volume)* to swell, to expand

fol [fɔl] ADJ *voir* **fou**

folâtre [fɔlɑtr] ADJ *(personne)* playful, lively; *(agneau, poulain)* frisky

folâtrer [fɔlɑtre] VI *(d'une personne)* to romp, to frolic; *(d'un agneau etc)* to gambol, to frisk about

folâtrerie [fɔlɑtrəri] NF *Arch* **1** *(d'un agneau)* friskiness; *(d'un chaton)* playfulness **2** *(blague)* frolic, romp

foldingue [fɔldɛ̃g] *Fam* ADJ crazy, nutty
▶ N nutter

folerie [fɔləri] NF *Can Fam* **elle a fait une f. en épousant cet homme** she was crazy *or* mad to marry that man; **faire des f.** *(faire le clown)* to clown about; *(dépenser beaucoup)* to be extravagant

foliacé [fɔljase] ADJ *Bot* foliaceous

foliaire [fɔljɛr] ADJ *Bot* foliar

foliation [fɔljasjɔ̃] NF *Bot* foliation

folichon, -onne [fɔliʃɔ̃, -ɔn] ADJ playful, lighthearted; *Fam* **ce n'est pas f.** it's not much fun

folichonner [fɔliʃɔne] VI *Arch* to play *or* romp about

folie [fɔli] NF **1** *Méd* madness, lunacy; **accès de f.** fit of madness; **être pris de f.** to go mad; **avoir un grain de f.** to be a bit touched; **aimer qn à la f.** to be madly in love with sb, to love sb to distraction; **aimer qch à la f.** to be mad on sth, to be crazy about sth; *Fam* **c'est de la f., tout ce monde!** all these people, it's crazy *or* madness! **2** *(inconscience)* folly; **c'est de la f.!** it's madness!, it's crazy!; **c'est de la f. douce** it's sheer madness!, it's absolutely crazy!; **il a eu la f. de céder** he was mad enough to give in; **dire des folies** to talk wildly, to say crazy things; **faire des folies** to do crazy things; *(faire des achats extravagants)* to go mad; *Hum* **faire des folies de son corps** to put oneself about **3** *Archit* folly
▶ ▶ **f. furieuse** raving madness; **f. des grandeurs** delusions of grandeur, megalomania

folio [fɔljo] NM folio

foliole [fɔljɔl] NF *Bot* leaflet

folioter [fɔljɔte] VT to folio; *(par page)* to paginate

folk [fɔlk] ADJ, NM *Mus* folk

folkeux, -euse [fɔlkø, -øz] N *Fam (amateur de musique folklorique)* folkie

folklo [fɔlklo] ADJ *Fam (bizarre)* weird; **il est f.** he's a weirdo *or* an oddball

folklore [fɔlklɔr] NM folklore; *Fam* **c'est du**

f., ce n'est pas sérieux it's a load of nonsense, you can't take it seriously

folklorique [fɔlklɔrik] ADJ *(costume)* traditional; **danses folkloriques** folk *or* country dances; *Fam* **c'était f.** it was bizarre

folkloriste [fɔlklɔrist] N folklorist, specialist in folklore

folle [fɔl] ADJ *voir* **fou**

follement [fɔlmɑ̃] ADV **1** *(avec excès)* madly, foolishly, rashly; **être f. amoureux** to be madly in love **2** *(au plus haut point)* madly, wildly; **s'amuser f.** to have a wonderful time

follet, -ette [fɔlɛ, -ɛt] ADJ **1** *Arch* **esprit f.** elfish spirit, sprite, (hob)goblin; **feu f.** will-o'-the-wisp, Jack-o'-lantern; *Fig* **c'est un vrai feu f.** he's here today and gone tomorrow **2** **poil f.** *(d'un oiseau, visage)* down; **cheveux follets** stray lock(s)

folliculaire [fɔlikylɛr] ADJ follicular

follicule [fɔlikyl] NM *Bot, Anat* follicle

folliculine [fɔlikylin] NF *Anat* folliculin

fomentateur, -trice [fɔmɑ̃tatœr, -tris] N agitator, troublemaker

fomentation [fɔmɑ̃tasjɔ̃] NF fomentation

fomenter [fɔmɑ̃te] VT to stir up, *Fml* to foment

fonçage [fɔ̃saʒ] NM **1** *(de tonneau)* bottoming, heading **2** *(de puits)* boring, sinking

foncé [fɔ̃se] ADJ *(couleur)* dark; **bleu f.** dark blue

foncer [fɔ̃se] (**je fonçai(s), n. fonçons**) VT **1** *(teinte)* to darken **2** *Culin (moule)* to line **3** *(tonneau)* to bottom, to head **4** *(pieu)* to sink, to drive (in); *(puits)* to sink, to bore
▶ VI **1** **f. sur qn** to rush at *or* swoop (down) on sb; *(d'un taureau, joueur de football)* to charge (at) sb **2** *Fam (se déplacer très vite)* to speed along; *(se hâter)* to get a move on; **la voiture a foncé dans la foule** the car ploughed into the crowd; *Fam* **f. dans le tas** to charge in with fists flying; *Fig Fam* **ne te pose pas de questions, fonce!** don't ask any questions, just do it! **3** *(s'assombrir)* to darken

fonceur, -euse [fɔ̃sœr, -øz] *Fam* N dynamic *or* go-ahead type
▶ ADJ dynamic, go-ahead

foncier, -ière [fɔ̃sje, -jɛr] ADJ **1** of land; **propriété foncière** landed property; **le propriétaire f.** the landowner; **rente foncière** ground rent; **impôt f.** land tax; **crédit f.** land bank **2** *Fig (fondamental) (honnêteté)* fundamental, basic
▶ NM land tax; **f. bâti** landed property; **f. non bâti** land for development

foncièrement [fɔ̃sjɛrmɑ̃] ADV fundamentally, basically

fonction [fɔ̃ksjɔ̃] NF **1** *(poste)* office; **la f. publique** the public *or* civil service; **entrer en fonction(s), prendre ses fonctions** to take up one's duties; **être en f.** to be in office; **cela ne fait pas partie de mes fonctions** that's not part of my duties, that doesn't come within my remit; **voiture/appartement de f.** company car/flat; *(de fonctionnaire)* car/flat that goes with the job
2 *(rôle)* function; **faire f. de gérant** to act as manager; **cette table fait f. de table à café** this table acts *or* serves as a coffee table; **adjectif qui fait f. d'adverbe** adjective that is used *or* functions as an adverb; *Anat* **fonctions de l'estomac/du cœur** functions of the stomach/heart; **c'est la f. qui crée l'organe** necessity is the mother of invention
3 *Math* function; **f. inverse** inverse function; **être f. de** to be a function of; *Mktg* **f. de la demande** demand function, market demand function
4 **en f. de** *(résultats etc)* according to; **exprimer une quantité en f. d'une autre** to ex-

press one quantity in terms of or as a function of another; **les prix varient en f. de la demande** prices vary in accordance with or according to demand

5 Ordinat **f. booléenne** Boolean function; **f. de comptage de mots** word count facility; **f. de contrôle** control function; **f. 'couper-coller'** cut-and-paste facility; **f. d'éditeur de texte** text editing feature; **f. multimédia** multimedia facility; **f. multitâche** multitasking facility; **f. recherche et remplacement** search and replace function; **f. de recopie** copy function; **f. de répétition** repeat function; **f. de réponse automatique** autoresponder, mailbox; **f. de sauvegarde** save function; **f. de vérité** truth function

fonctionnaire [fɔ̃ksjɔnɛr] N state employee; (dans l'administration) civil servant; **haut/petit f.** high-/low-ranking official or civil servant; Péj **mentalité de f.** bureaucratic mentality

---

Fonctionnaire

This term covers a broader range of public service employees than the term "civil servant", from high-ranking members of the state administration to public-sector teachers and post office workers. "Fonctionnaires", of whom there are more than four and a half million in France, are normally recruited through competitive state examination and enjoy greater job security and other privileges to which private sector employees are not automatically entitled.

---

fonctionnalisme [fɔ̃ksjɔnalism] NM functionalism

fonctionnaliste [fɔ̃ksjɔnalist] ADJ functionalist

fonctionnalité [fɔ̃ksjɔnalite] NF functionality

fonctionnariat [fɔ̃ksjɔnarja] NM employment by the state

fonctionnariser [fɔ̃ksjɔnarize] VT (employés, profession) to make part of the public or civil service

fonctionnarisme [fɔ̃ksjɔnarism] NM Péj officialdom, bureaucracy, Fam red tape

fonctionnel, -elle [fɔ̃ksjɔnɛl] ADJ functional

fonctionnellement [fɔ̃ksjɔnɛlmɑ̃] ADV functionally

fonctionnement [fɔ̃ksjɔnmɑ̃] NM **1** (du gouvernement, d'un plan etc) functioning, working; **pour le bon f. du service, il est préférable que tous les employés aient les mêmes horaires** if the department is to run efficiently it is preferable that all staff have the same working hours **2** (d'une machine etc) functioning, operation, running, working; **en (bon) état de f.** in (good) working order; **mauvais f.** malfunction, fault; **panne due à un mauvais f. du carburateur** breakdown due to a malfunction in the or a malfunctioning carburettor; **cycle de f.** operating cycle; Ordinat **f. en réseau** networking

fonctionner [fɔ̃ksjɔne] VI (d'une machine, d'un mécanisme) to function, to work; (d'une personne) to function, to operate; Ordinat to run; **les trains ne fonctionnent plus** the trains are no longer running; **les freins n'ont pas fonctionné** the brakes failed, the brakes didn't work; **faire f. une machine** to operate or work a machine; Élec **f. sur courant continu** to operate or run on direct current; **f. sur piles** to run on batteries, to be battery-operated; **dans cette atmosphère mon cerveau ne peut pas f.** my brain can't function in this atmosphere

FOND [fɔ̃]

bottom **1, 2** ▪ back **1** ▪ content **3** ▪ basically (au fond) **1** ▪ thoroughly (à fond) **1** ▪ background **4** ▪ long-distance running **5** ▪ cross-country skiing **5**

NM **1** (partie la plus profonde) bottom; (de chapeau) crown; (de chaise, de pantalon) seat; (de tonneau) bottom, head; (de la gorge) back; **abîme sans f.** bottomless chasm; **boîte à double f.** box with a false bottom; **bateau à f. plat** flat-bottomed boat; **f. de cylindre/chaudière** cylinder/boiler head; **f. de bouteille** dregs; **il n'en reste qu'un f.** there's only a drop left; **râcler ses fonds de tiroir** to scrape around (for money); **du f. du cœur** from the bottom of one's heart; **tu connais le f. de ma pensée** you know what my thoughts or feelings really are; Fig **au f., dans le f.** basically; **dans le f. elle n'est pas méchante** she's not a bad sort at heart or deep down or she's basically not a bad sort; **au f., c'est ce qu'il voulait** (deep down) that's what he really wanted; **au f. il était très flatté** in his heart of hearts he was extremely flattered; **aller au f. d'une affaire/d'un problème** to get to the bottom or root of a matter/problem; **à f.** (étudier) thoroughly; **enfoncer un clou à f.** to hammer a nail home, to drive a nail all the way in; **respire à f.** breathe deeply; **on a fait le ménage à f. dans la cuisine** we cleaned the kitchen thoroughly; **se consacrer** ou **se donner à f. à qch** to devote oneself totally to sth; **il s'est engagé à f. dans le combat écologique** he committed himself wholeheartedly or body and soul to the struggle for the environment; **connaître un sujet à f.** to have a thorough knowledge of a subject; **à f. (de train)** (at) full tilt; Fig **elle a touché le f.** she's hit rock bottom

2 (de l'océan) bottom, bed; **il n'y a pas assez de f. pour plonger/jeter l'ancre** the water isn't deep enough for diving/for dropping anchor; **f. de sable** sandy bottom; **prendre f.** (d'une ancre) to bite, to grip; **envoyer un navire par le f.** to send a ship to the bottom; **grands fonds** ocean depths or deeps; **courant de f.** undertow; **lame de f.** groundswell

3 (fondement) **rebâtir une maison de f. en comble** to rebuild a house from top to bottom; Fig **il a un bon f.** he's good at heart or basically good; **faire f. sur qn/qch** to rely or depend on sb/sth; **le f. et la forme** the form and the content or substance; **le f. de cette politique** the essential features of this policy; **question de f.** fundamental question; Journ **article de f.** feature (article); Mus **jeu de f.** (d'un orgue) pipe stop; **f. sonore** ou **musical** background music or sound

4 (partie la plus éloignée) (d'une peinture) background; (d'un espace clos) far end; **la salle du f.** the room at the end, the far room; Fam **fonds de boutique** oddments, old stock; **au (fin) f. du désert/de l'Australie** in the heart of the desert/Australia; **au fin f. de la campagne** in the depths of the country; Théâtre **toile de f.** backdrop, backcloth; Fig **avec la guerre en toile de f.** against a backdrop of war; Tennis **ligne de f.** baseline; **bruit de f.** background noise; **sur un f. de musique tzigane** with gipsy music in the background

5 Sport **le f.** long-distance running; **course de (grand) f.** long-distance race; Ski cross-country race; **coureur de f.** long-distance runner; **ski de f.** cross-country skiing, langlauf; **cheval qui a du f.** horse with staying power

6 Typ **f. perdu** bleed; **à f. perdu** bleeding; **(blanc de) petit f.** back margin, gutter; **(blanc de) grand f.** fore-edge, gutter

▸ ▸ **f. d'artichaut** artichoke heart; **f. de cale** bilge; **tous les mutins furent enfermés à f. de cale** the mutineers were all locked away in the bottom of the hold; **f. musical** background music; Méd **f. d'œil** examination of the retina; **f. de robe** (full-length) slip; **f. scénique** scenic background; **f. sonore** background music; **f. de teint** foundation (cream)

fondamental, -ale, -aux, -ales [fɔ̃damɑ̃tal, -o] ADJ (principe, postulat, différence, erreur, contradiction) basic, fundamental; **il est f. que tout soit prêt à temps** it is (absolutely) essential that everything is ready in time; **le vocabulaire f. d'une langue** the basic or base vocabulary of a language; **pierre fondamentale** foundation stone; **couleurs fondamentales** primary colours; Mus **son f.** (d'une corde) root, generator; Univ **recherche fondamentale** basic research

NMPL **fondamentaux les fondamentaux de qch** the basics or fundamentals of sth

fondamentalement [fɔ̃damɑ̃talmɑ̃] ADV fundamentally, basically

fondamentalisme [fɔ̃damɑ̃talism] NM Rel fundamentalism

fondamentaliste [fɔ̃damɑ̃talist] ADJ fundamentalist

N **1** (scientifique) scientist engaged in basic research **2** Rel fundamentalist

fondant [fɔ̃dɑ̃] ADJ melting; **poire fondante** pear that melts in the mouth; **un chocolat f.** a fondant chocolate; **viande fondante** very tender meat; **tons fondants** blended shades (of colour)

NM **1** (bonbon) fondant; **un f. au chocolat** a chocolate fondant **2** Tech flux

fondateur, -trice [fɔ̃datœr, -tris] ADJ **membre f.** founder or founding member; **les mythes fondateurs d'une culture** the underlying myths of a culture

N (d'une ville, société etc) founder

fondation [fɔ̃dasjɔ̃] NF **1** (d'une ville, d'un hôpital etc) founding, foundation; **f. d'une entreprise** setting up of a business **2** (fonds) endowment (fund), foundation **3** (établissement) foundation **4** Constr **fondations** foundations

fondé [fɔ̃de] ADJ (doutes, peurs) well-founded, justified; **vos craintes ne sont pas fondées** your fears are groundless or unfounded or unjustified; **mal f.** (soupçons) groundless, ill-founded; **établissement f. en 1850** established 1850; **être f. à croire** to have good reason(s) to believe; **qu'est-ce qu'il y a de f. dans ces bruits?** is there any justification for anything in these reports?, is anything in these reports justified?

NM Jur **f. de pouvoir** agent (holding power of attorney); (mandant) proxy; (directeur de banque) manager with signing authority

fondement [fɔ̃dmɑ̃] NM **1** (base) foundation, base; **soupçons sans f.** groundless or unfounded suspicions **2** Fam (derrière) behind, backside; (anus) back passage

fonder [fɔ̃de] VT (ville) to found; (société, journal) to start, to set up; **f. une famille** to start a family; **f. un hôpital** (en donnant un legs) to found a hospital; **f. ses espérances sur qch** to base or build one's hopes on sth; **document fondé sur des témoignages réels** document based on authentic accounts; **théorie fondée sur des textes scientifiques** theory based on scientific texts

VPR **se fonder se f. sur qch** (d'une personne) to go by sth, to base oneself on sth; (d'une remarque, théorie) to be based on sth; **sur quoi se fonde-t-il pour le nier?** what are his grounds for denying it?; **un espoir qui se fondait sur une information fausse** a hope that was based on misinformation

fonderie [fɔ̃dri] NF **1** *(extraction) (de minerai)* smelting; *(fusion) (de métaux)* founding, casting **2** *(usine) (d'extraction)* smelting works; *(de fusion)* foundry

fondeur¹ [fɔ̃dœr] NM *(maître de forges)* ironmaster; *(ouvrier) (d'extraction)* smelter; *(de fusion)* (metal) founder; **f. en cuivre** brass founder; **f. en caractères, f. typographe** type founder

fondeur², **-euse** [fɔ̃dœr, -øz] N *Ski* cross-country skier

fondre [fɔ̃dr] VT **1** *(liquéfier) (minerai)* to smelt; *(métal)* (metal) to melt down; *(sucre)* to dissolve; *(neige, cire etc)* to melt; **f. deux fils ensemble** to fuse two wires together **2** *(fabriquer) (cloche, arme etc)* to cast, to found **3** *TV etc* to fade; **f. des teintes** to blend colours **4** *Com (compagnies)* to amalgamate, to merge
▪ VI **1** *(se liquéfier)* to melt; *(de la neige)* to melt, to thaw; *(du sucre)* to dissolve; **le beurre fond au soleil** butter melts in the sun; **faire f. le beurre dans une casserole** melt the butter in a saucepan; *Élec* **faire f. un fusible** to blow a fuse; *Fig* **mon cœur fondit (de pitié)** my heart melted (with pity); **je fonds** my heart melts; **f. en larmes** to dissolve in(to) tears; **l'argent lui fond entre les doigts** money runs through his fingers; **il fond à vue d'œil** he's visibly wasting away **2 f. sur sa proie** to pounce upon *or* to swoop (down) upon one's prey
▪ VPR **se fondre** to merge; *(de compagnies)* to amalgamate, to merge; **se f. dans la brume** to disappear into the mist; **se f. dans la foule** to merge *or* blend into the crowd; **leur maison se fond dans le paysage** their house merges into the landscape; **se f. dans l'anonymat** to hide under the cloak of anonymity

fondrière [fɔ̃drijɛr] NF pothole *(full of water)*; **une f. marécageuse** a bog; *Can* **f. de mousse** muskeg

fonds [fɔ̃] NM VOIR GRAMMAIRE A10 **1** *(organisme)* fund; **F. européen de coopération monétaire** European Monetary Cooperation Fund; **F. monétaire européen** European Monetary Fund; **F. monétaire international** International Monetary Fund; **F. national de garantie des salaires** national guarantee fund for the payment of salaries; **F. européen de développement** European Development Fund; **F. européen de développement régional** European Regional Development Fund; **F. national de l'emploi** = French national employment fund; **F. social européen** European Social Fund; **F. de stabilisation des changes** exchange equalization account
2 *(dans un musée)* collection; *Fig* **c'est un f. inestimable pour les chercheurs** it is an invaluable resource for researchers; **le f. commun de toutes les langues indo-européennes** the common stock of all Indo-European languages
▪ NMPL **1** *(argent)* fund
2 *(ressources)* funds; **réunir des f.** to raise funds; **je n'ai pas les f. suffisants pour ouvrir un magasin** I don't have the (necessary) funds *or* capital to open a shop; **mise de f.** paid-in capital; **mouvement de f.** flow of capital; **rentrer dans ses f.** to recoup one's losses; **être en f.** to be in funds; **appel de f.** call upon shareholders; **ne pas toucher à ses f.** not to touch one's capital; **placer son argent à f. perdu** to purchase an annuity; **je l'ai aidé, mais je savais que c'était à f. perdu** I helped him, but I knew I wouldn't get my money back; **prêt à f. perdu** loan without security
3 *Bourse* **des fonds** stocks, securities; **f. d'État, f. publics** Government stock(s)
▸▸ **f. de caisse** float; **f. de chômage** unemployment fund; **f. de clientèle** customer

base; **f. de commerce** business; **f. de commerce à vendre** business for sale (as a going concern); **f. commercial** goodwill; **f. commun** common fund, pool; **f. commun de placement** investment trust, mutual fund; **f. de dotation** endowment fund; **f. d'épargne-retraite** retirement savings fund; **f. disponibles** liquid assets, available funds; **f. de garantie** guarantee fund; **f. de grève** strike fund; **f. d'investissement** investment fund; **f. liquides** available funds; **f. de pension** pension fund; **f. de prévoyance** contingency fund; **f. propres** equity; **f. publics** government funds; *(valeurs)* government stocks; **f. de réserve** reserve funds; **f. de roulement** working capital; **f. de secours** emergency fund; **f. social** company funds; **f. de terre** (piece of) land

fondu, -ue [fɔ̃dy] ADJ *(beurre)* melted; *(plomb, lave)* molten; **neige fondue** *(qui tombe)* sleet; *(par terre)* slush
▪ NM **1** *(de couleurs)* blending **2** *Cin* dissolve, fade; **faire un f.** to fade; **faire un f. au noir** to fade to black; **s'ouvrir en f.** to fade in; **ouverture en f.** fade-in; **fermeture en f.** fade-out; **f. enchaîné** mix, lap dissolve, dissolve; **faire un f. enchaîné** to fade in-fade out; **f. par ondulation** ripple dissolve; **f. par passage au flou** defocus dissolve
▪ NF *Culin* **fondue** *(savoyarde)* (cheese) fondue; **fondue bourguignonne** fondue bourguignonne, beef fondue
▪ N *Fam* **1** *(fou)* round the bend, out to lunch, off one's rocker **2** *(enthousiaste)* fanatic, freak; **un f. d'informatique/de skateboard** he's a computer/skateboard freak

fongible [fɔ̃ʒibl] ADJ fungible

fongicide [fɔ̃ʒisid] ADJ fungicidal
▪ NM fungicide

fongueux, -euse [fɔ̃gø, -øz] ADJ *Méd* fungous

fontaine [fɔ̃tɛn] NF **1** *(source)* spring; **F. de Jouvence** Fountain of Youth; *Prov* **il ne faut pas dire 'f., je ne boirai pas de ton eau'** never say never **2** *(construite)* fountain **3** *(petit réservoir)* cistern; **f. filtrante** *ou* **de ménage** (household) filter

fontainier [fɔ̃tenje] NM **1** water engineer **2** *(qui cherche de l'eau)* well borer *or* sinker

fontanelle [fɔ̃tanɛl] NF *Anat* fontanel(le)

fonte¹ [fɔ̃t] NF **1** *(de neige)* melting, thawing; *(d'or, d'argent etc)* melting down; *(de minerai)* smelting; *Métal* casting, founding; **pièces de f.** castings; **(fer de) f., f. de fer** cast iron; **f. d'acier** cast steel; **poêle en f.** cast-iron stove; *Méd* **f. musculaire** wasting of muscle **2** *Typ* font; **f. bitmap** bitmap font; **f. de caractère** character font; **f. écran** screen font; **f. imprimante** printer font; **f. reconnue optiquement** OCR-font; **f. vectorielle** outline font

fonte² NF *(d'une selle)* holster

fonts [fɔ̃] NMPL **f. baptismaux** (baptismal) font; **tenir un enfant sur les f. baptismaux** to be godfather/godmother to a child

foot [fut] NM *Fam* soccer, *Br* football; **jouer au f.** to play soccer *or Br* football

football [futbol] NM soccer, *Br* football

footballeur, -euse [futbolœr, -øz] N soccer player *or Br* football player

footballistique [futbolistik] ADJ *Hum (qui a trait au football)* soccer, *Br* football; **à la veille de la coupe du monde, la frénésie f. s'est à nouveau emparée du pays** on the eve of the World Cup, football fever has taken over the country again

footeux, -euse [futø] NM *Fam (joueur)* soccer player, *Br* football player; *(supporter)* soccer fan, *Br* football fan

footing [futiŋ] NM jogging; **faire son f.** to go jogging, to jog

for [fɔr] NM **le f. intérieur** the conscience;

dans *ou* en son f. intérieur in one's heart of hearts, deep (down) inside

forage [fɔraʒ] NM **1** *(action) (de puits)* drilling, boring, sinking; **f. pétrolier** drilling oil-wells **2** *(trou)* borehole, drill hole

forain, -aine [fɔrɛ̃, -ɛn] ADJ **1** *(itinérant)* itinerant; **spectacle f.** travelling show; **hercule f.** strongman *(at a fair)*; **baraque foraine** fairground stall; **fête foraine** funfair; **marchand f.** stallholder **2** *Naut* **mouillage f.** open berth
▪ N fair stallholder

forban [fɔrbɑ̃] NM pirate, buccaneer; *Fig* rogue, crook

forçage [fɔrsaʒ] NM **1** *(de plantes)* forcing **2** = **forcement 3** *Tech* **introduction d'air par f.** ram air induction

forçat [fɔrsa] NM *(prisonnier)* convict; *(galérien)* galley slave; *Fig* **mener une vie de f.** to slave away, to work like a slave; **la maçonnerie est un métier de f.** building work is really backbreaking; **je ne supporte plus cette vie de f.** I can't stand this slavery any more

FORCE [fɔrs]

| NF strength **1** ▪ force **4, 5** ▪ by (dint of) *(à force de)* **6** |
| ADJ INV many |

NF **1** *(vigueur)* strength; **être à bout de force(s)** to have no strength left; **je n'ai pas beaucoup de f.** I've not got much strength, I'm not very strong; **donner des forces** to give strength; **(re)prendre des forces** to (re)gain strength; **ménager ses forces** to save *or* conserve *or Fml* husband one's strength; **la maladie le laissa sans f.** the illness left him (feeling) weak, the illness sapped his strength; **ne pas sentir sa f.** not to know one's own strength; **cette épreuve est au-dessus de ses forces** this test is beyond him *or* is too much for him; **lui parler fut au-dessus de mes forces** it was too much for me to speak to him; **il le frappa avec f.** he hit him hard *or* forcefully; **mon doute revint avec f.** my doubts returned with renewed force; **de toutes ses forces** *(pousser, frapper etc)* with all one's strength *or* might; **j'essaie de toutes mes forces de le convaincre** I'm trying as hard as I can to convince him; **elle le veut de toutes ses forces** she wants it with all her heart; **vouloir à toute f. faire qch** to be determined to do sth, to want to do sth at all costs; **il veut à toute f. qu'on soit rentré à minuit** he wants us to be back at midnight at all costs; **elle n'avait plus la f. de répondre** she didn't have the strength (left) to answer, she had no strength left to answer; **je ne me sens pas/ne suis pas de f. à faire cela** I don't feel/I'm not up to *or* equal to doing it; **elle ne se sentait pas la f. de lui en parler** she didn't feel up to talking to him about it; **de f. égale, de même f.** equally matched, well matched; **ce qui fait votre f., c'est …** your strength is …; **être bâti en f.** to be stocky, to be strongly built; **dans la f. de l'âge** in the prime of life **2** *(courage)* **f. d'âme** moral strength, fortitude; **elle a une sacrée f. de caractère** she has incredible strength of character **3 tour de f.** tour de force; *Constr* **(jambe de) f.** force piece, strut; **f. de résistance à la tension** tensile strength **4** *(violence)* force; **faire appel à** *ou* **avoir recours à la f.** to resort to force; **céder à la f.** to give in *or* yield to force; **faire qch de vive f.** to do sth by sheer force; **entrer** *ou* **pénétrer de f. dans une maison** to force one's way into a house; **faire entrer qch de f. dans qch** to force sth into sth; **f. lui fut d'obéir** he was obliged to obey, he had no option but to obey; *Jur* **un cas de f. majeure** *(en assurance)* an act of God; **c'était un cas de f. majeur** there was no other option, circumstances were beyond my/our/your/*etc* control; *Naut* **faire f. de voiles** to crowd on (all) sail; **faire f. de rames** to row *or* pull hard; *Prov* **la f. prime le droit, f. passe droit** might is right; **il devra le faire, de gré ou de f.** he'll have to do it whether he wants to or not, he'll have to do it willy-nilly

5 *(d'un coup, du vent, d'un argument)* force; **vent de f. 8** force 8 gale; **les forces de la nature** the forces of nature; **c'est une f. de la nature** he's a mighty force; **par la f. des choses** through force of circumstance; **la f. de l'habitude** force of habit; **dans toute la f. du mot** in the strongest sense of the word, in every sense of the word

6 à f. de by (dint of); **à f. d'y penser** by (dint of) thinking about it; **à f. de travailler** by (dint of) hard work; **à f. d'explications** by (dint of) explanation; **à f. de volonté** by sheer force of will; **à f. de répéter** by constant repetition; **il s'est enroué à f. de crier** he shouted himself hoarse; **à f. de jouer dehors le soir, tu vas t'enrhumer** by playing outside in the evening you'll end up with a cold; **il va se lasser, à f.** he'll get tired of it in the long run

7 *Phys* **f. motrice** motive power; *Fig* driving force; **f. d'inertie** inertia; **f. vive** kinetic energy, momentum; *Élec* **f. (électrique)** (electric) power; **prise de f.** power point; **f. centrifuge** centrifugal force; **f. centripète** centripetal force; **f. de traction** traction *or* tractive force; **forces d'inertie** inertia forces; **forces de cisaillement** shear forces; *Aut* **forces en virage** cornering force

8 les forces armées the armed forces, the services; **f. de dissuasion** deterrence; **f. de frappe** strike force; **f. d'interposition** interposition force; **f. de paix** peacekeeping force; **f. tactique** *ou* **d'intervention** task force; **la f. publique, les forces de police** *ou* **de l'ordre** the police (force), the forces of law and order; **les forces vives du pays** the country's resources; **nous étions là en force(s)** we were there in (full) force; **ils sont arrivés en f.** they arrived in force; *Écon* **les forces du marché** market forces; *Mktg* **forces, faiblesses, opportunités et menaces** strengths, weaknesses, opportunities and threats, SWOT; **f. de travail** workforce; **f. de vente** sales force; **forces nucléaires intermédiaires** intermediate-range nuclear forces

ADJ INV *Arch, Litt* **f. gens/anecdotes** a great number of *or* (very) many people/anecdotes; **f. bière** copious amounts of beer

forcé [fɔrse] **ADJ 1** *(obligé)* forced; *Aviat* **atterrissage f.** forced *or* emergency landing; *Jur* **travaux forcés** hard labour; *Fam* **mariage f.** shotgun wedding, forced marriage; **la comparaison est un peu forcée** the comparison is a bit forced; **exemple f.** far-fetched example **2** *(affecté)* **rire/sourire f.** forced laugh/smile **3** *(involontaire)* **prendre un bain f.** to fall in (the water) **4** *Fam* **c'est f.!** it's inevitable!

forcement [fɔrsəmɑ̃] **NM** forcing (open); **f. de blocus** blockade running

forcément [fɔrsemɑ̃] **ADV** inevitably; **nous étions f. en retard** inevitably *or* of course, we were late; **elle le sait f. déjà** she's bound to *or* she must know already; **elle sera f. déçue** she's bound to be disappointed; **f.!** of course; **pas f.** not necessarily; **l'herbe est verte, f., il a plu tous les jours** the grass is green but it's not surprising, it has been raining every day

forcené, -ée [fɔrsəne] **ADJ 1** *Arch (personne)* lunatic, mad **2** *(extrême)* (marche, imagination) frenzied; *(amateur de bons vins etc)* passionate; *(individualisme)* fanatical, rabid; **un goût f. du travail** a fanatical liking for work

N maniac, madman, *f* madwoman; **crier comme un f.** to scream like a madman/madwoman

forceps [fɔrsɛps] **NM** *Obst* forceps; **accouchement au f.** forceps delivery

forcer [fɔrse] **(je forçai(s))** **VT 1** *(obliger)* to force, to compel; **f. qn à faire qch** to force *or* compel sb to do sth, to make sb do sth; **sans vouloir te f. il faudrait faire la vaisselle** I don't want to force you, but the washing-up has to be done; **personne ne t'y force** no one is forcing you; **f. la main à qn** to force sb's hand; **f. le respect/l'admiration (de qn)** to command sb's respect/admiration; **être forcé de faire qch** to be forced to do sth; **f. une femme** to violate *or* rape a woman; *Mil* **f. un poste** to take a post by storm *or* by force; **f. une serrure/un coffre** to force (open) a lock/a safe; **f. la caisse** to force open the till, to break into the till; **f. une porte** to force *or* break open a door; **f. la porte de qn** to force one's way into sb's place; **f. le destin** to force the hand of destiny

2 *(voix)* to force; *(mât)* to strain; *(plaque)* to buckle; *Fam* **f. la note** to overdo it; **f. l'allure** *ou* **le pas** to force the pace; **f. le sens** to strain *or* distort the meaning; **f. un cheval** to override a horse; **f. des fleurs** to force flowers; **f. un cerf** to run down a stag, to bring a stag to bay; **f. la dose d'un médicament** to take/give too large a dose of a medicine

3 *Ordinat (justification, coupure de page)* to force

VI *Naut* **f. de voiles** to crowd on sail; **f. sur les avirons** to strain at the oars; **le vent force** the wind is rising; *Cartes* **f. sur l'annonce de qn** to overcall *or* overbid sb; **tu y arriveras sans f.** you'll get there without straining yourself *or* without too much effort; **essayez de garder les jambes raides, mais ne forcez pas** try to keep your legs straight, but don't strain yourself; **ne force pas, ça doit se fermer tout seul!** don't force it, it has to close by itself!; *Fam* **f. sur la bouteille** to overdo the drinking; **je crains d'avoir forcé sur le poivre** I'm afraid I've overdone (it with) the pepper

VPR se forcer *(s'obliger)* to force oneself; **se f. à faire qch** to force oneself to do sth

forcing [fɔrsiŋ] **NM** *Sport* sustained pressure; *Fig Fam* **il a fallu faire le f. pour qu'il accepte** we had to put on a lot of pressure to get him to accept; **avoir qn au f.** to pressurize sb, to put pressure on sb

forcir [fɔrsir] **VI 1** *(d'une personne)* to fill out, to get bigger **2** *(des éléments)* **le vent/la tempête forcit** the wind is picking up/the storm is getting stronger

forclore [fɔrklɔr] **VT** *Jur* to debar

forclusion [fɔrklyzjɔ̃] **NF** *Jur* debarment; *Fin* foreclosure

forer [fɔre] **VT** *(roche)* to drill, to bore; *(puits)* to drill, to bore, to sink

forestier, -ière [fɔrɛstje, -jɛr] **ADJ** *(zone)* forest(ed); **chemin f.** forest road; **essences forestières** forest trees; **une exploitation forestière** a forestry development; **garde f.** forester, forest warden, *Am* ranger

NM forester

foret [fɔrɛ] **NM 1** *(vrille)* drill **2 f. à bois** gimlet; **f. de charpentier** auger **3** *(vilebrequin)* (brace) bit

forêt [fɔrɛ] **NF** forest; **f. vierge** virgin forest; **région couverte de forêts** forest(ed) region; *Admin* **le service des Eaux et Forêts** *Br* ≃ the Forestry Commission, *Am* ≃ the Forest Service; *Fig* **une f. de mâts** a forest of masts; *Prov* **les arbres vous cachent la f.** you can't see the wood *or Am* forest for the trees; **F.-Noire** Black Forest; *Culin* Black forest gateau

foreur [fɔrœr] **NM** borer, driller; *Pétr* **f. d'ex-**

ploration oil prospector, *Am Fam* wildcatter

foreuse [fɔrøz] **NF** *(outil)* drill; *Min etc* rock drill; **f. à main** hand drill

forfaire [fɔrfɛr] **VI** *(conj like* **faire***)* *Arch, Litt* **f. à son devoir** to fail in one's duty; **f. à l'honneur** to forfeit one's honour; **f. à sa parole** to break one's word

forfait [fɔrfɛ] **NM** *(crime)* heinous crime

forfait [fɔrfɛ] **NM** *(contrat)* fixed-price contract; *Fin* lump sum; **le f. comprend les frais de location et d'entretien du matériel** the set *or* fixed price includes the cost of hire and maintenance of the equipment; **f. (-voyage)** package (deal); **travail à f.** fixed-price work; **travailler au f.** to do fixed-price work; **prix à f.** all-in price; **et pour un f. de 500 euros, and for 500 euros** for an all-in price of 500 euros, and for 500 euros all in; **vente à f.** outright sale; **f. avion + location de voiture** fly drive; **f. de remontées mécaniques** ski *or* lift pass; **f. de ski** ski pass; **forfait-vacances** holiday package; *Com* **f. de port** carriage forward

forfait [fɔrfɛ] **NM** *Courses de chevaux* fine, forfeit *(paid for scratching a horse)*; **déclarer f. pour un cheval** to scratch a horse; **déclarer f.** *(d'un athlète, concurrent)* to scratch; *Fig* to throw in the towel; **l'équipe a déclaré f.** the team withdrew

forfaitage [fɔrfɛtaʒ] **NM** forfaiting

forfaitaire [fɔrfɛtɛr] **ADJ** **marché f.** fixed-price contract; **paiement f.** lump sum; **indemnités forfaitaires** basic allocation; **prix f.** all-in price; **voyage à prix f.** package tour

forfaitairement [fɔrfɛtɛrmɑ̃] **ADV** *Fin* in a lump sum; *(facturer)* in a lump sum, in one amount

forfaiture [fɔrfɛtyr] **NF** *(abus de pouvoir)* abuse of authority; **f. au devoir/à l'honneur** breach of duty/honour

forfanterie [fɔrfɑ̃tri] **NF** bragging, boasting

forge [fɔrʒ] **NF** forge; **f. (de maréchal-ferrant)** smithy; **mener un cheval à la f.** to take a horse to the blacksmith's; **f. de serrurier** locksmith's workshop; **maître de forges** ironmaster; **pièce de f.** forging

forgeable [fɔrʒabl] **ADJ** *(métal)* forgeable

forgeage [fɔrʒaʒ] **NM** forging

forger [fɔrʒe] **(je forgeai(s))** **VT 1** *(métal)* to forge; **fer forgé** wrought iron; **cela forge le caractère** it forms *or* moulds the character, it is character-forming; **f. un homme** to form a man's character; *Prov* **c'est en forgeant qu'on devient forgeron** practice makes perfect **2** *(inventer)* (histoire, excuse) to fabricate, to make up; *(mot)* to coin; *(accusation)* to trump up; *(vision)* to conjure up; **histoire forgée de toutes pièces** completely fabricated *or* made-up story

VPR se forger **se f. une réputation** to carve out a reputation for oneself; **se f. un idéal de vie** to create an ideal lifestyle for oneself

> Il faut noter que le verbe anglais **to forge** signifie également **contrefaire**.

forgeron [fɔrʒərɔ̃] **NM** (black)smith

forgeur, -euse [fɔrʒœr, -øz] **N** *(de nouvelles, mensonges)* inventor, fabricator; *(de mots)* coiner

NM *Litt (forgeron)* metal worker

formage [fɔrmaʒ] **NM** *Tech* forming

formaldéhyde [fɔrmaldeid] **NM** *Chimie* formaldehyde

formalisation [fɔrmalizasjɔ̃] **NF** formalization

formaliser [fɔrmalize] **VT** to formalize; **logique formalisée** formal logic

VPR se formaliser to take offence (**de** at), to take exception (**de** to)

formalisme [fɔrmalism] NM **1** formality; **f. administratif** bureaucracy, *Fam* red tape; **f. intransigeant** rigid obsession with formalities **2** *Beaux-Arts* formalism

formaliste [fɔrmalist] ADJ **1** formalistic **2** *Beaux-Arts* formalist
N formalist

formalité [fɔrmalite] NF **1** *(procédure)* formality; **c'est une pure f., ce n'est qu'une f.** it's just a formality; **formalités douanières** customs formalities; **formalités d'entrée** entry requirements; **sans autre f.** without further ado **2** *(cérémonie)* formality; **sans formalité(s)** informal

format [fɔrma] NM *(de livre)*, *Ordinat* format; *(de papier)*, *Phot* size, format; **f. de poche** pocket size; **papier f. A4/A3** A4/A3 paper format; *Typ* **f. paysage** landscape format; *Typ* **f. portrait** portrait format; **f. tabloïd** tabloid format; **f. de page** page format *or* layout; *Ordinat* **f. ASCII** ASCII format; **f. carte de crédit** credit card format; **f. d'impression** print format; **f. d'écran** screen format; **f. de fichier** file format; **f. de papier** paper format; **f. de paragraphe** paragraph format; *TV etc* **f. de présentation** show format

formatage [fɔrmataʒ] NM *Ordinat* formatting; **f. de bas niveau** low-level format(ting); **f. de haut niveau** high-level format(ting); **f. logiciel** soft sectoring

formater [fɔrmate] VT *Ordinat* to format

formateur, -trice [fɔrmatœr, -tris] ADJ formative; **expérience formatrice** formative experience
N trainer

formation [fɔrmasjɔ̃] NF **1** *(constitution)* formation; *(de caractère)* forming, development; **la f. du goût/de la personnalité** the development of taste/the personality; **volcan en voie** *ou* **en cours de f.** volcano in the process of formation; **mot de f. savante** word of learned origin; **la f. du pluriel en anglais** the formation of the plural in English **2** *(éducation)* training; **avoir une excellente f.** to have an excellent training; **elle a reçu une f. littéraire/scientifique** she received a literary education/a scientific training; **suivre une f.** to do *or* take a training course; **il lui faut une f.** he needs (some) training; **il est technicien de f.** he trained as a technician; **f. en alternance** *ou* **alternée** = training given partly in an educational institution and partly in the workplace; **f. continue** *ou* **permanente** continuing education, continuous training; **f. professionnelle** vocational training; **f. courte** *ou* **accélérée** intensive training; **être en f.** to be undergoing training; **stage de f.** training course; **f. sur le tas** *ou* **par la pratique** on-the-job training; **f. dans l'entreprise** in-house training **3** *(de roche)* formation; *Mil* **f. serrée** close formation **4** *(groupe)*, *Mil* unit; *Mus* group; **une petite f. de jazz** a small jazz band; **f. aérienne** aerial unit; **f. politique** political group

forme [fɔrm] NF **1** *(configuration)* form, shape; **formes** *(d'un bateau)* lines; *(d'une personne)* figure; *(d'une femme)* curves; **les formes d'un tableau/paysage** the lines of a picture/shapes of a landscape; **vêtement qui épouse les formes** close-fitting *or* figure-hugging garment; **en f. d'œuf** egg-shaped; **gomme en f. de voiture** eraser in the shape *or* form of a car, car-shaped eraser; **yeux en f. de billes** eyes like marbles; **sous la f. d'une nymphe** in the form *or* shape of a nymph; **c'est une différente f. d'esprit** it is a different way of thinking; **l'histoire racontée sous une nouvelle f.** history told in a new way; **présenter les choses sous une autre f.** to present things in a different *or* in

another way; **statistiques sous f. de tableau** statistics in tabular form; **le produit existe aussi sous f. de bombe aérosol** the product also comes as an aerosol spray; **sous toutes ses formes** in all its forms *or* guises; **sans f.** shapeless; **prendre f.** to take shape; **mettre en f.** *(texte)* to format **2** *(procédure)* form; **arrêt cassé pour vice de f.** judgment quashed on a technical point; **renvoyer qn sans autre f. de procès** to dismiss sb without further ado; **avertir qn dans les formes** to give sb formal *or* due warning; **il faut y mettre les formes** it must be done tactfully; **faire qch dans les formes** to do sth in the accepted way; **en bonne et due f.** in due form, according to the proper form; **faire une réclamation en bonne et due f.** to use the correct procedure in making a complaint; **de pure f.** purely formal; **vérification de pure f.** routine check; **pour la f.** as a matter of form **3** **être en f.** to be on form *or* in good form; **être très en f.** *ou* **en pleine f.** *ou* **en grande f.** to be in great form; *Fam* **tenir** *ou* **péter la f.** to be in cracking form; **ne pas être en f., être en mauvaise f.**, *Fam* **ne pas avoir la f.** not to be on form, to be in poor form; **c'est bon pour la f.** it's good for you, it'll do you good; *Fam* **alors, c'est la f.?** how are you doing? **4** *Ind* former, forming block; *(pour fromage etc)* mould, *Am* mold; *(de cordonnier)* last; *(pour élargir)* shoe tree; *(de chapelier)* block; **chapeau haut de f.** top hat **5** *Naut* dock **6** *Typ* forme, *Am* form **7** *Com* **f. sociale** type of company

formé [fɔrme] ADJ fully formed, fully developed; **jeune fille formée** fully-developed girl; **un personnel bien f.** well-trained staff

formel, -elle [fɔrmɛl] ADJ **1** *(ordre)* express; *(démenti)* flat, categorical; *(veto)* absolute; **défense formelle** strict prohibition; **il a été tout à fait f. sur ce point** he was quite adamant *or* definite on this point; **je suis f.** I'm (absolutely) positive **2** *(de principe)* *(distinction, attitude)* formal **3** *Phil (cause)* formal

formellement [fɔrmɛlmɑ̃] ADV **1** *(interdit)* strictly; **promettre f.** to promise faithfully; **s'engager f. à régler ses dettes** to vow to pay off one's debts; **accuser f. qn** to specifically accuse sb; **l'homme a été f. reconnu** the man was positively identified **2** *(en considérant la forme)* formally; **une argumentation f. inattaquable** an argument that cannot be attacked on formal grounds

Il faut noter que l'adverbe anglais **formally** signifie le plus souvent **officiellement** ou **de façon cérémonieuse**, selon le contexte.

former [fɔrme] VT **1** *(créer) (gouvernement, collection etc)* to form; *Rail (train)* to make up; **f. un projet/des idées** to form a plan/ideas; **les murs forment un carré** the walls form a square; **ils forment une famille unie** they are a united family; **ils forment une bonne équipe/un beau couple** they make a good team/a lovely couple **2** *(pilote, cheval etc)* to train; *(caractère)* to form, to mould, *Am* to mold; **f. son esprit/son goût** to develop one's mind/taste; **f. l'oreille/l'œil** to train the ear/eye; **cela forme le caractère** it forms *or* moulds the character, it is character-forming; **cette université a formé des hommes remarquables** this university has turned out *or* produced some remarkable men; *Tech* **f. par roulage** to roll **3** **nous avons formé des vœux pour sa réussite** we wished him every success
VPR **se former 1** *(se développer)* to form, to develop; *(apparaître) (d'un fruit)* to form; *(d'un plan)* to take shape; **des cristaux se forment dans la roche** crystals form in rock;

une jeune fille qui se forme a girl who is developing; **se f. en cortège/en carré** to form (into) a procession/(into) a square **2** *(apprendre son métier)* to train oneself; *(s'instruire)* to educate oneself; **se f. aux affaires** to acquire a business training; **se f. sur le tas** to learn on the job

formica® [fɔrmika] NM formica®; **en f.** formica

formidable [fɔrmidabl] ADJ **1** *(extraordinaire)* tremendous **2** *(bon)* great, fantastic; *Iron Fam* **tu es/c'est f.!** you're/it's incredible! **3** *Vieilli (effrayant)* fearsome, formidable

Il faut noter que l'adjectif anglais **formidable** est un faux ami. Il signifie le plus souvent **redoutable**.

formidablement [fɔrmidabləmɑ̃] ADV **1** *(énormément)* tremendously, fantastically; **nous avons été f. accueillis** we were given a tremendous *or* fantastic welcome **2** *Arch (de manière effrayante)* formidably, fearsomely

formique [fɔrmik] ADJ *Chimie (acide)* formic

formol [fɔrmɔl] NM *Chimie* formalin, formol

formulable [fɔrmylabl] ADJ **une opinion difficilement f.** an opinion that is difficult to formulate; **une théorie f. en termes clairs** a theory that can be clearly formulated

formulaire [fɔrmylɛr] NM **1** *(imprimé)* form; **remplir un f.** to fill in *or* out a form; **f. E111** form E111; **f. d'appréciation** customer satisfaction questionnaire; **f. d'assurance** insurance form; **f. de candidature** (job) application form; **f. de détaxe** tax free shopping form; *Ordinat* **f. de saisie** input form **2** *(recueil)* formulary; *(de pharmaciens)* formulary, pharmacopoeia

formulation [fɔrmylasjɔ̃] NF formulation, wording

formule [fɔrmyl] NF **1** *Math, Chimie etc* formula VOIR GRAMMAIRE A14 **2** *(paroles)* expression, phrase; **f. magique** magic formula; *Suisse Pol* = name given to the coalition that forms the executive body of the Swiss government; **f. de début** *(d'une lettre)* opening; **f. de politesse** *(au début d'une lettre)* standard opening; *(à la fin)* standard closure, letter ending; **f. finale** standard closure, letter ending; **selon la f. consacrée** as the expression goes; **trouver la f. juste** to find the right phrase **3** *(méthode)* formula; **c'est la f. idéale pour les vacances en famille** it's the ideal formula for a family holiday; **nous vous proposons différentes formules de crédit/de remboursement** we offer you various credit/repayment options *or* methods *or* formulae; **nous avons aussi une f. à 1000 euros** we also have a 1000-euro option **4** *Aut* **f. un/deux** Formula One/Two **5** *Admin (formulaire)* form; **f. de chèque** *Br* cheque form, *Am* blank cheque; **f. de demande de crédit** credit application form; **f. de réponse** reply form; *Com* **f. de soumission** tender form; **f. de télégramme** telegram form

formule-hôtel, *pl* **formules-hôtel** NF hotel package

formuler [fɔrmyle] VT *(doctrine)* to formulate; *(document)* to draw up; *(souhait)* to express; *(proposition)* to formulate, to put into words; *(plainte)* to lodge; *(règlement)* to formulate, to lay down

fornication [fɔrnikasjɔ̃] NF fornication

forniquer [fɔrnike] VI to fornicate

FORPRONU [fɔrprɔny] NF *(abrév* **Forces de protection des Nations unies**) UNPROFOR

fors [fɔr] PRÉP *Litt* except, save; **tout est perdu f. l'honneur** all is lost save honour

forsythia [fɔrsisja] NM *Bot* forsythia

FORT [fɔr]

ADJ strong **1, 2** ▪ intense **2** ▪ loud **2** ▪ large **5** ▪ big **5**	
ADV loud **1** ▪ hard **1** ▪ very **2**	
NM forte **1** ▪ fort **2**	

ADJ 1 *(vigoureux)* strong; **f. comme un Turc** *ou* **un bœuf** as strong as an ox; **utiliser la manière forte** to use strong-arm tactics, to use force; **trouver plus f. que soi** to meet one's match; **s'attaquer à plus f. que soi** to take on more than one can handle; **courage, il faut être f.** cheer up! you/we/*etc* must be strong; **f. de son expérience** with a wealth of experience behind one; **f. de son récent succès** bolstered by one's recent success; **f. de ses certitudes** secure in the strength of one's convictions; **f. de son bon droit** in the knowledge that right is on one's side; **c'est une forte tête** he's/she's very strong-minded; **un esprit f.** a freethinker; **avoir affaire à forte partie** to be up against a strong opponent; **être f. en mathématiques/en ski/aux échecs** to be good at mathematics/skiing/chess; **elle est forte sur la question** she is well up in *or* knowledgeable about the matter; **il est f. pour critiquer, mais quand il faut travailler …** he's good at criticizing, but when it comes to working …
2 *(corde, boisson, sauce, haleine etc)* strong; *(fièvre, vent)* high; *(chaleur)* intense, great; *(lumière)* strong, bright, intense; *(pluie, mer)* heavy; *(voix)* loud; **moutarde forte** strong mustard; *Fig* **elle a fait (une) forte impression** she made a strong impression; **avoir une forte odeur** to have a strong smell; **c'est plus f. que moi!** I can't help it!; **j'avais une forte envie de rire/de lui casser la figure** I was very tempted to laugh/to smash his face in; *Fam* **c'est trop f.!, c'est un peu f. (de café)!** that's a bit much!; **ce qu'il y a de plus f., c'est qu'on n'y peut rien** the worst of it is that nothing can be done about it; **à plus forte raison** all the more so (**que** since)
3 place/ville forte fortress/fortified town
4 se faire f. de faire qch to be sure *or* convinced one can do sth; **elles se font f. de le retrouver** they are sure *or* convinced they can find it
5 *(gros) (personne)* large, stout; *(lèvres)* thick, full; *(poitrine)* large; **homme à la forte charpente** solidly built man; **elle est forte des hanches** she's big round the hips, she has large hips; **forte somme** large sum of money; **forte différence** big *or* great difference; **forte baisse** *(de prix)* slump; **forte hausse des prix** sharp *or* big rise in prices; **forte pente** steep slope; **armée forte de cinq mille hommes** five-thousand-strong army, army five thousand strong; *Com* **prix f.** full price; **acheter qch au prix f.** to buy sth at *or* for the full price, to pay (the) full price for sth
ADV 1 *(parler, crier, chanter)* loudly, loud; *(tirer)* hard; **frapper f.** to strike *or* hit hard; *Fam* **y aller f.** to overdo it, to go over the top; **sentir f.** to smell strong; *Fam* **faire (très) f.** to do brilliantly, to do really well
2 *(très)* very, extremely; **il a été f. mécontent** he was very *or* extremely annoyed; **j'en suis f. aise** I'm very pleased; **c'est f. dommage** it's a great *or* real pity; **f. bien** very well; **f. heureusement, il était là** he was there, which was very fortunate
3 *(beaucoup)* **j'ai f. à faire** I have a great deal *or* a lot to do; **nous avons eu f. à faire avec cette jeune fille/ce radiateur électrique** we had our work cut out with that girl/that electric heater; **j'en doute f.** I very much doubt it
NM 1 *(spécialité)* strong point, forte; **la politesse n'est pas son f.** politeness is not his

strong point *or* his forte; **le f. et le faible de l'affaire** the strong and weak points of the matter; **le f. d'un bois** the heart of a wood; **au plus f. de l'hiver** in the depths of winter; **au f. de l'été/de l'épidémie** at the height of summer/of the epidemic; **au (plus) f. du combat** in the thick of the fight; **le plus f., c'est que je lui avais déjà dit** the best of it is, I'd always told him; *Prov* **la raison du plus f. est toujours la meilleure** might is right
2 *(citadelle)* fort, stronghold
▸▸ *Fam* **f. en gueule** loud-mouthed; **c'est un f. en gueule** he's a loudmouth; *Péj* **f. en thème** swot, *Am* grind; **forts des Halles** market porters

fortement [fɔrtəmɑ̃] ADV *(désirer, souhaiter, influencé)* strongly, greatly; *(tirer, pousser)* hard; *(impressionner)* greatly; **insister f. sur qch** to insist firmly *or* strongly on sth; **j'espère f. qu'il viendra** I very much *or* I sincerely hope he'll come; **f. épicé** highly spiced; **f. critiqué** strongly *or* highly criticized; **f. irrité** greatly *or* extremely irritated; **c'est f. conseillé** it's strongly advised; **f. charpenté** solidly built

forteresse [fɔrtəres] NF fortress, stronghold; **f. volante** flying fortress

fortiche [fɔrtiʃ] *Fam* ADJ clever, smart
N **1** clever *or* smart cookie; **c'est un f. en chimie** he's really good at chemistry **2** *Vieilli (personne robuste)* brawny person

fortifiant [fɔrtifjɑ̃] ADJ *(nourriture, boisson)* fortifying; *(air)* bracing, invigorating
NM *Méd* tonic

fortification [fɔrtifikasjɔ̃] NF *(action, ouvrages)* fortification

fortifier [fɔrtifje] *(impf & pr sub n. fortifiions)* VT **1** *(ville)* to fortify; *(mur, corps)* to fortify, to strengthen; *(muscles)* to tone up, to strengthen **2** *(sentiment, impression)* to strengthen; **cela m'a fortifié dans ma décision** that strengthened me in my decision
VPR **se fortifier 1** *(devenir plus fort)* to get *or* become stronger; **il faut qu'il se fortifie le dos** he has to strengthen his back **2** *Mil* to raise a line of defences; *(en creusant des tranchées)* to dig oneself in

Fortifs [fɔrtif] NFPL *Arg* **les F.** = the old defence works around Paris, once a favourite area for criminals

fortin [fɔrtɛ̃] NM small fort

Fortran [fɔrtrɑ̃] NM *Ordinat* FORTRAN

fortuit [fɔrtɥi] ADJ *(rencontre, événement)* chance, fortuitous; **dans cette affaire, rien n'est f.** nothing is fortuitous *or* nothing can be put down to chance in this matter; **toute ressemblance avec des personnes existantes ou ayant existé serait purement fortuite** any resemblance to persons living or dead is entirely coincidental; *Jur* **cas f.** act of God

fortuitement [fɔrtɥitmɑ̃] ADV by chance, fortuitously

fortune [fɔrtyn] NF **1** *(chance)* fortune, chance, luck; **chercher f.** to try one's luck; **revers de f.** reversal of fortune, setback in one's fortunes; **mauvaise f.** misfortune; **avoir la bonne/la mauvaise f. de rencontrer qn** to have the good fortune/misfortune to meet sb, to be fortunate/unfortunate enough to meet sb; **faire contre mauvaise f. bon cœur** to make the best of a bad job; **connaître des fortunes diverses** to have varying (degrees of) success; **la f. d'une théorie/d'une œuvre d'art** the fortunes of a theory/a work of art; **dîner à la f. du pot** to take pot luck; **inviter qn à la f. du pot** to invite sb to come and take pot luck; *Prov* **la f. sourit aux audacieux** fortune favours the brave; **installation de f.** temporary *or* makeshift installation; **lit de f.** makeshift bed; **réparations de f.** makeshift *or* emergency

repairs; **moyens de f.** makeshift means; *Naut* **mât de f.** jury mast; **(voile de) f.** cross-jack (foresail); **f. de mer** perils of the sea
2 *(richesse)* fortune, wealth; **faire f.** to make one's fortune *or* a fortune; **avoir de la f.** to be well off; **sa f. est importante** he has a considerable fortune *or* considerable wealth; **c'est une grosse f.** he's a very wealthy man; **être l'artisan de sa f.** to be a self-made man; **valoir une f.** to be worth a fortune; **voilà toute ma f.** that's all I've got

fortuné [fɔrtyne] ADJ **1** *(riche)* rich, wealthy, well-off **2** *Arch, Litt (chanceux)* fortunate, happy

Il faut noter que l'adjectif anglais **fortunate** signifie uniquement **qui a de la chance.**

forum [fɔrɔm] NM forum; *Ordinat* **f. de discussion** discussion group, forum; **f. Internet** Web forum; **f. en ligne** online forum; **f. sur l'éducation** forum *or* symposium on education; *Radio etc* **f. populaire** vox pop; **F. social mondial** World Social Forum

fosse [fos] NF **1** *(creux)* pit, hole; *(abyssale)* trough; *Sport* (sand) pit; *Anat* fossa; *Min* pit; **les animaux des grandes fosses** animals living on the ocean bed **2** *(tombe)* grave; **f. commune** common grave; *Fam* **avoir un pied dans la f.** to have one foot in the grave; **creuser sa f. avec ses dents** to eat oneself into an early grave
▸▸ **f. d'aisances** cesspool; **f. aux lions** lions' den; *Théâtre* **f. d'orchestre** orchestra pit; **f. à purin** liquid manure pit; *Aut* **f. (de réparation)** inspection pit; **f. septique** septic tank

Do not confuse with **fossé**.

fossé [fose] NM **1** *(tranchée, au bord de la route)* ditch; *(douve)* moat; *Géol* trough **2** *Fig (entre personnes)* gulf; **le f. ne cesse de se creuser entre eux** there is an ever-widening gulf between them; **le f. des générations** the generation gap
▸▸ *Géol* **f. d'effondrement** rift valley; *Aut* **f. d'inspection** inspection pit

Do not confuse with **fosse**.

fossette [fosɛt] NF dimple

fossile [fosil] NM fossil; *Fam* **un vieux f.** an old fossil
ADJ fossil

fossilifère [fosilifɛr] ADJ fossiliferous

fossilisation [fosilizasjɔ̃] NF fossilization

fossiliser [fosilize] VT to fossilize
VPR **se fossiliser** to fossilize, to become fossilized; *Fig* **les mentalités se sont fossilisées** attitudes have become fossilized

fossoyeur [foswajœr] NM gravedigger; *Fig* destroyer

fou [fu], **fol, folle** [fɔl] *(the form* **fol** *is used in the masculine before a vowel or h mute)* ADJ **1** *(dément)* mad, insane; **devenir f.** to go mad *or* insane; **f. à lier** raving mad, out of one's mind; **cette musique/situation me rend f.** the music/situation is driving me mad; **il y a de quoi devenir f.** it's enough to drive you mad; **f. de joie/de terreur/de rage/d'inquiétude** beside oneself with joy/fear/rage/worry; **être f. de qn** to be mad *or* crazy about sb; **être f. d'amour pour qn** *ou* **f. amoureux de qn** to be madly in love with sb; **entre eux, c'est l'amour f.** they're madly in love, they're crazy about each other; **vivre l'amour f.** to be madly in love; **f. de peinture/ski** mad *or* crazy about painting/skiing, dead keen on painting/skiing; **des diamants? mais tu es f.!** diamonds? you're mad *or* crazy!; **tu serais f. de ne pas accepter** you'd be mad *or* crazy not to accept; *Fam* **pas folle, la guêpe!** there are no flies on her!, she's not stupid!; **il n'est pas f.** he's no fool

2 folles illusions wild delusions; *Bible* **les vierges folles** the foolish virgins; **les années folles** the Roaring Twenties; **un fol espoir** a foolish *or* mad hope

3 *(énorme)* tremendous; **succès f.** tremendous *or* wild success; **mettre un temps f. à faire qch** to take absolutely ages to do sth; **il gagne un argent f.** he makes pots of money, he rakes it in; **à une allure folle** at breakneck speed; **il y avait un monde f.** there was an enormous *or* a tremendous crowd; **un prix f.** an exorbitant price; *Fam* **c'est f. ce que c'est grand!** it's incredible how big it is!; **d'une gaieté folle** wildly happy

4 *(incontrôlé) (mèche de cheveux)* stray, loose; *(camion)* runaway; *(boussole, aiguille)* crazy; *(roue)* idle, free; *(poulie)* loose; **f. rire** (uncontrollable) giggling; **avoir un f. rire** to have (a fit of) the giggles; *Fam* **avoir une patte folle** to have a gammy *or Am* gimpy leg; **herbes folles** rank weeds; *Bot* **folle avoine** wild oats

N lunatic, madman, *f* madwoman; **f. furieux** raving lunatic, maniac; **espèce de vieille folle!** crazy old woman!; *Fam* **il travaille comme un f.** he works like mad; **c'est une histoire de fous** I can't make head (n)or tail of it; *Fam* **maison de fous** madhouse; **f. du volant** reckless driver; *Litt* **la folle du logis** (wild *or* fevered) imagination; **faire le f.** to play *or* act the fool; **plus on est de fous plus on rit** the more the merrier

NM **1** *Échecs* bishop **2** *Hist (bouffon)* jester, fool **3** *Orn* **f. de Bassan** gannet

NF *Péj Fam* **folle** *(homosexuel)* queen; **grande folle** raving queen

fouace [fwas] NF *Culin* = **fougasse**

foucade [fukad] NF *Litt* caprice, passing whim

foudre[1] [fudr] NF lightning, *surtout Bible* thunderbolt; **la f. est tombée sur la maison** the house was struck by lightning; **maison frappée par la f.** house struck by lightning; *Fig* **coup de f.** love at first sight; **avoir le coup de f. pour qn** to fall in love at first sight; **j'ai eu le coup de f. pour cette maison** I fell in love with this house at first sight

NFPL **foudres** *(colère)* wrath

NM **un f. de guerre** a great warrior; *Fig* **ce n'est pas un f. de guerre** he wouldn't say boo to a goose; **f. d'éloquence** powerful orator

foudre[2] NM *(tonneau)* tun, large cask

foudroyant [fudrwajɑ̃] ADJ *(attaque, nouvelles)* devastating; *(regard)* withering; *(succès)* stunning, staggering; **progrès foudroyants** lightning progress; **une mort foudroyante** a sudden death; **poison f.** devastatingly lethal poison

foudroyer [fudrwaje] VT (je **foudroie**; je **foudroierai**) to strike; **être foudroyé** to be struck by lightning; **arbre foudroyé** tree struck by lightning; *Fig* **l'apoplexie l'a foudroyé** he was struck down by apoplexy; **la mort l'a foudroyé alors qu'il n'avait que 30 ans** he was struck down when he was only 30; **elle le foudroya du regard** she gave him a withering look; **cette nouvelle m'a foudroyé** I was thunderstruck *or* devastated by the news; **la division fut foudroyée par la puissance de feu de l'ennemi** the division was decimated by enemy fire power

fouet [fwɛ] NM **1** whip; **donner le f. à qn** to whip *or* flog sb; **faire claquer son f.** to crack one's whip; **coup de f.** lash, stroke; *Fig* fillip, stimulus; **l'air de la mer lui a donné un coup de f.** the sea air has perked him up *or* given him a lift; **donner un coup de f. à l'économie** to give a fillip to the economy, to stimulate *or* boost the economy; **être frappé de plein f.** *(d'une cible)* to receive a direct hit; **frapper la balle de plein f.** to connect well with the

ball; **il a reçu le ballon de plein f.** the ball came straight at him; **collision de plein f.** head-on collision **2** *(de cuisine)* whisk **3** *(de l'aile d'un oiseau, de la queue d'un chien)* tip; *Naut (d'une poulie)* tail

fouettard [fwɛtar] ADJ **le Père F.** the Bogeyman

fouettement [fwɛtmɑ̃] NM *(d'une voile)* flapping; *(d'une corde, de la pluie etc)* lashing

fouetter [fwete] VT **1** *(personne)* to whip, to flog; *(cheval)* to whip; *(œufs)* to beat, to whisk; *(crème)* to whip; **ils l'ont fouetté jusqu'au sang** they whipped *or* flogged him until he bled; **la pluie fouette les vitres** the rain is lashing (against) the panes; *Fam* **il n'y a pas de quoi f. un chat** there's nothing to make a fuss about; *Fam* **avoir d'autres chats à f.** to have other fish to fry **2** *Fig (exciter)* to excite, to stimulate; **vent qui fouette le sang** wind that makes the blood tingle; **le sang fouetté par le désir** spurred on *or* stimulated by desire

VI **1** *(d'un câble)* to lash, to whip; *(d'une voile)* to flap; **la pluie fouette contre les vitres** the rain is lashing (against) the panes **2** *Fam (sentir mauvais)* to stink, to pong **3** *Arg (avoir peur)* to be scared stiff

foufou [fufu] *Fam* ADJ M nutty, daft
NM nutter

foufoune [fufun], **foufounette** [fufunɛt] NF *Vulg (sexe de femme)* pussy, *Br* fanny

fougasse [fugas] NF *Culin* flat bread *(sometimes stuffed with anchovies, olives etc)*

fougeraie [fuʒrɛ] NF patch of ferns

fougère [fuʒer] NF fern; **f. aigle** bracken; **f. arborescente** tree fern

fougue [fug] NF fire, spirit, passion; **la f. de la jeunesse** youthful high spirits; **cheval plein de f.** spirited horse

fougueusement [fugøzmɑ̃] ADV fierily; *(embrasser)* passionately

fougueux, -euse [fugø, -øz] ADJ *(personne)* fiery, ardent, spirited; *(cheval)* spirited; **tempérament f.** fiery temperament

fouille [fuj] NF **1** *(fosse)* excavation, pit; **f. à ciel ouvert** open pit **2** *Archéol* **fouilles** dig, excavations; **faire des fouilles** to carry out excavations *or* a dig **3** *(d'un suspect, voyageur)* search(ing), frisking; *(d'un lieu)* search(ing); **passer à la f.** to be searched *or* frisked; **la police a fait une f. complète de ses bureaux** the police made a thorough search of his offices **4** *très Fam (poche)* pocket; *Fig* **se remplir les fouilles, s'en mettre plein les fouilles** to line one's pockets **5** *Can (chute)* fall; **prendre une f.** to fall, to tumble

fouillé [fuje] ADJ detailed

fouille-merde, *pl* **fouille-merdes** N *très Fam* muckraker

fouiller [fuje] VT *(maison)* to search; *(personne)* to search, to frisk; *(tiroir)* to search (through), to go through; *(valise)* to go through; *(bois)* to scour, to comb; *(terre)* to dig; *Archéol (emplacement d'un ancien site)* to excavate; **f. toutes ses poches** to go through *or* look in all one's pockets; **ses yeux fouillaient la salle** his eyes *or* he scanned the room; **f. un problème** to go thoroughly into a problem, to explore a problem thoroughly

VI **1** *(d'un lapin)* to burrow; *(d'un cochon)* to root **2 f. dans une armoire/sa poche** to search *or* rummage in a cupboard/in one's pocket; **j'ai fouillé dans toutes les poches sans rien trouver** I've gone through *or* searched all the pockets without finding anything; **f. dans les papiers de qn** to search through *or* go through sb's papers; **f. dans les librairies pour trouver un livre** to search around in bookshops for a book; **quand je**

n'ai rien à faire, je vais f. dans les librairies when I've nothing to do, I go and rummage around *or* poke around in bookshops; **f. dans le passé** to delve into the past; **f. dans sa mémoire** to search one's memory

VPR **se fouiller** to go through one's pockets; *Arg* **tu peux te f.!** nothing doing!; **il peut se f. s'il croit qu'on lui en donnera!** if he thinks we're going to give him some, he's got another think coming!

fouilleur, -euse [fujœr, -øz] N **1** *Archéol* excavator, digger **2** *(à la douane)* officer who carries out body-searches **3** *(fouineur)* rummager, searcher; **f. de brocantes/de bibliothèques** an avid frequenter of second-hand shops/libraries
NF *Agr* **fouilleuse** subsoil plough *or Am* plow

fouillis [fuji] NM *(de papiers, jouets etc)* jumble, muddle; *(de lianes)* tangle; **range ton f.** put away your mess; **c'est le f. ici** it's a mess in here

fouinard, -arde [fwinar, -ard] *Fam* ADJ nosy, prying, inquisitive
N nosy parker, pryer

fouine [fwin] NF *Zool* stone marten; *Fam* **à tête de f.** weasel-faced, ferret-faced

fouiner [fwine] VI *Fam* to ferret about, to nose about; **f. dans les affaires d'autrui** to poke one's nose into other people's business

fouineur, -euse [fwinœr, -øz] ADJ, N *Fam* = **fouinard**

fouir [fwir] VT to dig; *(d'animaux)* to burrow, to dig

fouisseur, -euse [fwisœr, -øz] ADJ *(animal)* burrowing
N burrower

foulage [fulaʒ] NM **1** *(de raisins)* pressing, crushing **2** *(du cuir)* tanning; *(de tissu)* fulling **3** *Typ* impression

foulant [fulɑ̃] ADJ pressing, crushing; **pompe foulante** force pump; *Fam* **ce n'est pas bien f.** it won't kill you/her/*etc*

foulard [fular] NM **1** scarf **2** *Tex* foulard

foule [ful] NF **1** *(de gens)* crowd, *Litt* throng; *(d'idées, de souvenirs)* host; **j'ai une f. de choses à te raconter/à faire** I've got lots of things to tell you/to do; **il y a une f. de choses à te raconter/à faire** there are crowds of people (there); **il n'y a pas f.** there's hardly anyone around; **psychologie des foules** crowd psychology; **mouvement de foule(s)** movement in the crowd; **entrer en f.** to crowd in; **les réfugiés arrivent en f. à la frontière** the refugees are flocking to the border; **faire f. autour de qn** to crowd round sb, to mob sb; **fuir la f.** to flee the crowds; **quelle f. dans les rues!** how crowded the streets are!; *Vieilli* **on en trouve en f.** there are loads of them **2** *Can (du caribou)* migration

foulée [fule] NF **1** *Sport, Équitation* stride; **parcourir les champs à longues foulées** to stride over the fields; **courir à petites foulées** to trot along; *Sport* **courir *ou* rester dans la f. d'un concurrent** to follow close behind a competitor, to slip-stream; *Fig* **dans la f., j'ai aussi vérifié les comptes** while I was at it, I also checked the accounts **2** **foulées** *(d'animaux sauvages)* track(s), spoor

fouler [fule] VT **1** *(herbe)* to trample (down), to tread down; *(raisins)* to press, to crush; **f. qch aux pieds** to trample sth underfoot; *Fig* **les droits de l'homme sont foulés aux pieds!** human rights have been trampled underfoot!; **nous foulions pour la première fois le sol de Grèce** we were setting foot for the first time on Greek soil **2** *Tex (tissu)* to full; *(cuir)* to tan

VPR **se fouler 1 se f. la cheville** to sprain *or* twist one's ankle **2** *Fam* **se f. (la rate)** to strain oneself, to overexert oneself; **tu ne t'es pas foulé!** you didn't (exactly) strain or overexert yourself!

fouleur, -euse [fulœr, -øz] **N 1** (de raisins) (personne) winepresser **2** Tex (personne) (de tissu) fuller; (de cuir) tanner

fouloir [fulwar] **NM** (pour le raisin) wine press

foulon [fulɔ̃] **NM** Tex (de tissu) fuller; **chardon à f.** fuller's teasel; **terre à f.** fuller's earth; **(moulin à) f.** fulling mill

foulonnier [fulɔnje] **NM** = **fouleur 2**

foulque [fulk] **NF** Orn coot

foultitude [fultityd] **NF** Fam **une f.** loads, masses (**de** of)

foulure [fulyr] **NF** sprain; **f. du poignet/de la cheville** sprained wrist/ankle

four [fur] **NM 1** (de cuisine) oven; **f. à gaz** gas oven; **f. électrique** electric oven; **f. de boulanger** baker's oven; **f. à micro-ondes** microwave (oven); **faire cuire au f.** (pain) to bake; (viande) to roast; **il fait noir comme dans un f.** it's pitch black; **vaisselle allant au f.** ovenware; **plat allant au f.** ovenproof dish; Fam **ouvrir une bouche (grande) comme un f.** to open one's mouth really wide; **on ne peut être à la fois au f. et au moulin** you can't be in two places at the same time; Culin **petits fours** petits fours
2 Ind kiln; (avec combustion du contenu) furnace; **f. à chaux** lime kiln; **f. à briques** brick kiln; **f. à émaux** enamelling kiln; **f. solaire** solar furnace
3 Fam (fiasco) flop; **la pièce/l'exposition a fait un f.** the play/exhibition was a flop; **il a fait un f. avec son discours** his speech was a flop

fourbe [furb] **ADJ** cheating, double-dealing, two-faced
N cheat, rogue, double-dealer

fourberie [furbəri] **NF 1** (hypocrisie) deceit, cheating, double-dealing **2** (action) underhand trick

fourbi [furbi] **NM** Fam **1** (attirail) gear, tackle, Br clobber; (de soldat) kit; **tout le f.** the whole (kit and) caboodle; **Fig quel f., je ne retrouve rien!** what a muddle or mess, I can't find anything! **2** (truc) thingummy, thingy

fourbir [furbir] **VT** (métal) to polish up, to shine up, to furbish; Fig **f. ses armes** to prepare for battle

fourbissage [furbisaʒ] **NM** (du métal) polishing, furbishing

fourbu [furby] **ADJ** exhausted, tired out

fourche [furʃ] **NF 1** Agr fork; **f. à foin** hayfork, pitchfork; **remuer le sol à la f.** to fork the ground; **chariot (élévateur) à f.** forklift (truck); Aut **f. d'attelage** trailer hitch **2** (de bicyclette, d'arbre, de route, de rivière) fork; (de pantalon) crotch, Br crutch; Aut **Y** junction; **mes cheveux ont des fourches** my hair has split ends; **en forme de f.** forked; **la route fait une f.** the road forks **3** Hist **les Fourches Caudines** the Caudine Forks; Fig **passer sous les fourches caudines** to suffer torments

fourchée [furʃe] **NF** (de foin) pitchforkful

fourcher [furʃe] **VI 1 sa langue a fourché** he made a slip of the tongue **2** Arch to fork, to divide
VT (sol) to fork

fourchet [furʃɛ] **NM** Vét foot rot

fourchette [furʃɛt] **NF 1** (ustensile) fork; **f. à poisson/à dessert** fish/dessert fork; Fam **il a un joli ou bon coup de f.**, **c'est une bonne f.** he's a hearty eater, he has a healthy or hearty appetite; **manger avec la f. du père Adam** to eat with one's fingers
2 Mil, Fin bracket; **prendre une cible en f.** ou

à la f. to bracket a target; **f. de salaire** wage bracket; **f. de prix** price bracket or range; Bourse **f. de cotation** trading range; **f. de cours de clôture** closing range; **f. de cours d'ouverture** opening range; **f. d'imposition** tax bracket; **f. de taux** rate band
3 Cartes tenace
4 (d'un volatile) wishbone; (d'un sabot de cheval) frog
5 (de balance) beam support
6 Tech belt guide, shifter; **f. de débrayage** clutch throw-out fork; **f. d'embrayage** clutch fork

fourchu [furʃy] **ADJ** forked; (bâton, menton) cleft; **pied f.** cloven hoof; **avoir les cheveux fourchus** to have split ends; **avoir la langue fourchue** to speak with a forked tongue

fourgon¹ [furgɔ̃] **NM** (de cheminée) poker; (de four) (fire) rake

fourgon² **NM 1** Aut van; **f. automobile** (motor) van; **f. blindé** armoured van **2** Rail **f. de queue** rear (brake) van, guard's van, Am caboose
▸ ▸ **f. à bagages** luggage van, Am baggage car; **f. à bétail** cattle truck; **f. cellulaire** police van or Am wagon; **f. funèbre, f. funéraire, f. mortuaire** hearse

fourgonner [furgɔne] **VT** (feu) to poke, to rake
VI to poke the fire; Fam **f. dans un tiroir** to poke about or rummage about in a drawer

fourgonnette [furgɔnɛt] **NF** (small or light) van

fourguer [furge] **VT** Fam (vendre) to flog; (donner) to unload; **f. qch à qn** (vendre) to flog sb sth; (donner) to unload sth onto sb

fourmi [furmi] **NF** ant; Fig **c'est une vraie f.** he's/she's a busy bee, he's/she's always beavering away (at something); **avoir des fourmis dans les jambes** to have pins and needles in one's legs

fourmilier [furmilje] **NM** anteater

fourmilière [furmiljer] **NF** anthill, ants' nest; Fig **cette banlieue est une véritable f. (humaine)** this suburb is swarming or teeming with people; **donner des coups de pied dans la f.** to stir things up

fourmi-lion, pl **fourmis-lions NM** Entom ant-lion

fourmillement [furmijmɑ̃] **NM 1** (d'insectes) swarming; **un f. de détails/d'idées** a welter of details/ideas **2** (dans les membres) pins and needles

fourmiller [furmije] **VI** to swarm, to teem; **les vers fourmillaient dans ce fromage** the cheese was alive with maggots; Fig **la ville fourmille d'ingénieurs** the town is swarming or teeming with engineers; **ouvrage qui fourmille de fautes** work teeming or riddled with mistakes; **f. d'idées** to be bursting with ideas; **f. d'impressions** to be full of impressions

fournaise [furnez] **NF** cette chambre est une (vraie) f. this room's like an oven

fourneau, -eaux [furno] **NM 1** (de chaudière) furnace; **f. d'une pipe** bowl of a pipe **2 f. de cuisine** (kitchen) range; **f. à gaz** gas stove or Br cooker; **c'est David qui est aux fourneaux ce soir** David is the chef this evening **3** Métal furnace; **haut f.** blast furnace **4** Min **f. de mine** mine chamber, blast hole

fournée [furne] **NF** (de pains) batch; Fig Fam batch, contingent

fourni [furni] **ADJ 1** (magasin, bibliothèque etc) (bien) **f.** well-stocked **2** (cheveux) thick; (barbe) bushy, thick; **barbe peu fournie** sparse or thin beard

fournil [furni] **NM** bakehouse

fourniment [furnimɑ̃] **NM** Fam gear, Br clobber

fournir [furnir] **VT 1** (approvisionner) to supply; **f. qch à qn, f. qn en qch** to supply sb with sth; **qui fournit la famille royale?** who is the Royal Family's supplier?, who supplies the Royal Family?
2 (produire) to supply, to provide; (documents) to produce, to furnish; (idées) to provide; **f. une caution** to give a guarantee, to provide security; **vignoble qui fournit un bon vin** vineyard that yields or produces a good wine; **l'ENA fournit de futurs hauts fonctionnaires** the ENA produces or turns out the senior civil servants of the future; **f. un effort considérable** to make a considerable effort; **f. des renseignements à qn** to supply or provide or furnish sb with information; **vous devez f. votre carte d'identité** you must present or show your identity card; **il pourra peut-être te f. du travail** he might be able to give you some work; **f. le gîte et le couvert** to provide board and lodging; **cela te fournira l'occasion de le rencontrer** it will provide you with or give you the opportunity of meeting him; **f. une bonne raison à qn** to provide sb with or give sb a good reason; **pièces à f.** required documents; Cartes **f. du trèfle** to follow a club lead; Sport **f. un jeu remarquable** to play an outstanding game
VI Vieilli **f. aux dépenses** to defray the expenses; **f. aux besoins de qn** to supply sb's wants
VPR se fournir 1 se f. en qch to get in supplies of sth; **ils se fournissent (en vin) chez ce négociant** they get their supplies (of wine) from this merchant
2 (d'une barbe etc) to grow thick

fournissement [furnismɑ̃] **NM** Fin contribution (in shares)

fournisseur, -euse [furnisœr, -øz] **N 1** Com supplier; **l'entrée des fournisseurs** the tradesman's entrance; **f. de navires** ou **de la marine** ships'chandler; **le plus grand f. français en meubles** the biggest French supplier of furniture; **f. attitré** approved or official supplier; (habituel) regular supplier; **f. exclusif** sole supplier; **f. principal** prime supplier; **f. secondaire** secondary supplier **2** Ordinat **f. d'accès** (Internet) access provider; **f. de contenu** content provider
ADJ les pays fournisseurs de la France the countries that supply France (with goods), France's suppliers

fourniture [furnityr] **NF 1** (approvisionnement) supplying, provision **2 fournitures** supplies; **façon et fournitures** making-up and materials; **fournitures et services** supplies and services
▸ ▸ **fournitures de bureau** office supplies; **fournitures de navires** ships' chandlery; **fournitures scolaires** educational stationery

---

Il faut noter que le mot anglais **furniture** est un faux ami. Il signifie **meubles**.

---

fourrage [furaʒ] **NM** fodder, forage; **f. sec/vert** hay/silage; **rentrer du f.** to harvest forage

fourrager¹ [furaʒe] (n. **fourrageons**; je **fourrageai(s)**) **VI** (pour s'alimenter) to forage; Fam (fouiller) to rummage, to forage
VT 1 Fam (papiers) to rummage through **2** Arch (pays) to pillage, to ravage

fourrager², -ère [furaʒe, -ɛr] **ADJ plantes fourragères** fodder crops; **betterave fourragère** mangel-wurzel
NF fourragère 1 (champ) field sown with fodder crop **2** Mil fourragère, shoulder braid

fourre [fur] **NF** Suisse (d'un oreiller) pillowcase; (d'un édredon) quilt cover; (d'un livre) jacket; (d'un disque) sleeve; (dossier, chemise) file, folder

fourré [fuʀe] ADJ **1** *(manteau, gants etc)* (fur-) lined; *(bois)* thick, dense; **chocolats fourrés à la crème** chocolate creams; **bonbon f.** sweet with a soft centre, *Am* candy with a soft center **2** *Escrime* **coup f.** exchanged hit, double hit; *Fig* **méfie-toi, c'est un coup f.** look out, it's a trap; **faire un coup f. à qn** to trick sb; *Vieilli* **paix fourrée** hollow *or* mock peace

NM thicket; *(à la chasse)* cover

fourreau, -eaux [fuʀo] NM *(d'épée)* sheath, scabbard; *(de parapluie)* cover; *(robe)* sheath dress; **remettre l'épée au f.** to sheathe one's sword; *Tech* **soupapes à fourreaux** sleeve valves

ADJ **jupe/robe f.** pencil skirt/sheath dress

fourrer [fuʀe] VT **1** *Fam (mettre)* to stick; **je les avais fourrés dans le coin** I'd stuck them in the corner; **f. ses mains dans ses poches** to stick *or* stuff *or* shove one's hands in one's pockets; **mais où ai-je bien pu f. ça?** where on earth have I stuck it?; **f. son nez partout** to poke *or* stick one's nose into everything; **f. qn au trou** to stick *or* chuck sb in jail; **il est toujours fourré dans mes pattes** he's always under my feet; **il est toujours fourré au bistrot** he's always stuck in the pub

2 *(avec de la fourrure)* to line (with fur)

3 *Tech (jointure)* to pack

4 f. un chocolat/une crêpe de liqueur to fill a chocolate/a pancake with liqueur; **f. une dinde de marrons** to stuff a turkey with chestnuts

VPR **se fourrer** *Fam* **il s'est fourré dans le coin/sous le lit** he got into the corner/under the bed; **où est-il allé se f.?** wherever has he got to? wherever has he hidden himself?; **je ne savais plus où me f.** I didn't know where to put myself; **se f. dans une sale affaire** to get involved in a nasty business; *Fam* **il se fourre les doigts dans le nez** he picks his nose; *Fig Fam* **si tu crois que je vais l'attendre, tu te fourres le doigt dans l'œil** if you think I'm going to wait for him, you've got another think coming

fourre-tout [fuʀtu] NM INV **1** *(pièce)* junk room; *(placard)* junk cupboard **2** *(sac)* hold-all, *Am* carryall; *Aut* storage pocket

ADJ INV **sac f.** holdall, *Am* carryall; **placard f.** junk cupboard; *Péj* **une loi f.** a mishmash *or* ragbag of a law

fourreur [fuʀœʀ] NM furrier

fourrier [fuʀje] NM *Mil* quartermaster sergeant

fourrière [fuʀjɛʀ] NF *(pour animaux, voitures)* pound; **mettre un chien/une voiture en f. ou à la f.** to impound a dog/a car

fourrure [fuʀyʀ] NF **1** *(peau préparée, vêtement)* fur; **manteau de f.** fur coat **2** *(pelage)* fur, coat **3** *(de jointure)* packing; *Aut* **f. de frein** brake lining

fourvoiement [fuʀvwamã] NM *Litt* going astray

fourvoyer [fuʀvwaje] *(je fourvoie; je fourvoierai)* *Litt* VT to mislead, to lead astray

VPR **se fourvoyer** to lose one's way; *Fig* to make a mistake, to go astray

foutage [futaʒ] NM *Fam* **c'est du f. de gueule** you/they/*etc* gotta be kidding!, *Br* that's just taking the piss!

foutaise [futɛz] NF *très Fam* bullshit, crap; **c'est de la f.!** that's (a load of) bullshit *or* crap!

fouteur, -euse [futœʀ, -øz] N *Fam* **f. de merde** shit-stirrer

foutimasser [futimase] VI *Suisse Fam (perdre son temps)* to mess about

foutoir [futwaʀ] NM *très Fam* dump, tip

foutraque [futʀak] ADJ *Fam* nuts, *Br* crackers

foutre¹ [futʀ] *(pp* **foutu;** *pr ind* **je fous,** n.

foutons) ADV *Fam Vieilli* damned; **je n'en sais f. rien** I know damn all about it

VT *très Fam* **1** *(mettre)* **je me demande où elle a pu le f.** where the hell has she put it?; **f. qch par terre** to chuck *or* fling sth on the ground; **f. qn à la porte** to chuck sb out; **f. le bordel** to create havoc *or* chaos; **f. qn en rogne** *ou* **en pétard** to make sb hopping mad; **ça la fout mal** that won't look too good; **ça a tout foutu en l'air** that screwed *or* *Vulg* fucked everything up

2 *(faire)* to do; **il ne fout rien** he does damn all *or Br* bugger all; **il n'a pas l'air de f. grand-chose** he doesn't seem to do much at all; **qu'est-ce que tu fous dans mon bureau?** what the hell are you doing in my office?; **ça fait deux heures que je t'attends, qu'est-ce que tu fous?** I've been waiting for you for two hours, what (the hell) are you playing at?; **je n'en sais pas quoi f. de lui/de cette vieille table** I don't know what the hell to do with him/this old table; **je n'en ai rien à f.** I couldn't give a damn, I couldn't care less; **qu'est-ce que ça peut f.?** so what?, what the hell does it matter?; **qu'est-ce que ça peut f. qu'on soit en retard?** so what if we're late, what the hell does it matter if we're late?; **qu'est-ce que ça peut te/lui f.?** what the hell is it to you/him?, what the hell does it matter to you/him?; **f. le camp** to piss off, *Br* to bugger off; **qu'il aille se faire f.** he can piss off *or* *Vulg* fuck off; **va te faire f.!** piss off!, *Vulg* fuck off!

3 *(donner)* **je vais lui f. une bonne raclée** I'll give him a good hiding; **elle m'a foutu la honte** *(d'elle)* I was ashamed of her; *(de moi)* she made me ashamed of myself; **f. la trouille à qn** to put the wind up sb, to scare sb stiff; **ça nous a foutu un coup** it gave us a nasty shock; **qu'est-ce qui m'a foutu un empoté pareil!** what an absolute oaf you are!; **je t'en fous!** some chance!, you'll be lucky!; **je t'en foutrais, du champagne!** champagne, you'll be lucky! *or* I should coco!

4 *Vieilli Vulg (posséder sexuellement)* to fuck

5 *Suisse* **f. qch bas** *(démolir)* to knock sth down; **f. qn bas** *(tuer)* to kill sb *or Br* to do sb in

VPR **se foutre** *très Fam* **1** *(se mettre)* **il s'est encore foutu dans une affaire louche** he's got (himself) mixed up in some shady business again; **se f. par terre** to fall flat on one's face; **se f. sur la gueule** to beat the living daylights out of each other; **se f. en l'air** to top oneself; **il s'est foutu dedans!** he got it wrong!

2 se f. de qn/qch *(se moquer de)* to make fun of sb/sth, to take the piss *or Br* the mickey out of sb/sth; *(être indifférent à)* not to give a damn about sb/sth; **se f. de la gueule de qn** to take the piss *or Br* the mickey out of sb; **tu te fous du monde ou quoi?** who the hell do you think you are?; **c'est vraiment se f. (de la gueule) du monde!** he/they/*etc* must think we're absolute idiots!; **elle se fout complètement de ce que j'en pense** she doesn't give a damn (about) what I think of it; **je m'en fous** I don't give a damn

3 *Suisse* **se f. bas** *(se suicider)* to commit suicide *or Br* to top oneself; **se f. en bas** *(tomber)* to fall

foutre² NM *Vulg (sperme)* come, *Br* spunk

foutrement [futʀəmã] ADV *Fam* damn, *Br* bloody; **f. bien** damn well, *Br* bloody well; **je n'en sais f. rien** I know damn all *or Br* bugger all about it

foutriquet [futʀikɛ] NM *Péj Vieilli* little runt *or* squirt

foutu [futy] ADJ *Vulg* **1** *(maudit)* damn (awful), *Br* bloody (awful) **2** *(en mauvais état, perdu)* ruined; **il est f.** he's had it, he's done for; **ma bagnole/robe est foutue** my car/dress has had it; **c'est f.!** forget it!; **pour la**

fête de demain, c'est f. you can forget the party tomorrow; **c'est f. pour mon augmentation** I can forget *or* it's goodbye to my pay rise **3** *(bâti, conçu)* **elle est plutôt bien foutue** she's got a great body; **c'est bien/mal f.** it's well/badly designed **4** *(malade)* **je suis mal f.** I feel really *or Br* bloody awful **5** *(capable)* **elle n'est même pas foutue de le faire** she's not up to doing it; **elle serait foutue de le lui dire** she's quite likely to tell him

fox(-terrier), *pl* **fox(-terriers)** [fɔks(teʀje)] NM fox terrier

fox-trot [fɔkstʀɔt] NM INV foxtrot

foyer [fwaje] NM **1** *(domicile)* home, household; *surtout Mktg* household unit; **le f. familial** the (family) home; **le f. conjugal** the marital home; **rentrer dans ses foyers** to return home; **mère** *ou* **femme au f.** housewife; **homme au f.** househusband; **fonder un f.** to start a family; *Fin* **f. fiscal** household *(as a tax unit)*

2 f. d'étudiants student residence; **f. de jeunes travailleurs** young workers' hostel; **f. d'accueil et d'hébergement** *(pour les gens à la rue)* hostel for the homeless

3 *Scol* common room; *Théâtre* foyer; **f. des artistes** green room

4 *(de chaleur, d'infection)* source; *(d'incendie, d'érudition, de conflits)* seat, centre, *Am* center; **f. d'intrigue** hotbed of intrigue

5 *(âtre)* fireplace, hearth; *(de locomotive)* firebox; **f. de chaudière** boiler furnace

6 *(de lentille, courbe etc)* focus; **verres à double f.** bifocal lenses, bifocals

frac [fʀak] NM tail coat, tails

fracas [fʀaka] NM *(de verre cassé, du tonnerre)* crash; *(de l'orage)* din; *(des armes)* clash; *(vacarme)* racket, din; **faire du f.** *(d'un événement)* to create a sensation; **à grand f.** with a lot of fuss, with a great to-do; **elle sortit avec f.** she stormed out

fracassant [fʀakasã] ADJ *(bruit)* deafening; *Fig* **c'est une nouvelle/révélation fracassante** it's a shattering *or* staggering piece of news/revelation; **succès f.** resounding success

fracasser [fʀakase] VT to smash (to pieces), to shatter; **il aurait eu la tête fracassée** he would have smashed his head in

VPR **se fracasser** to crash, to smash; **tu vas te f. la tête!** you'll smash your head in!

fractal, -ale, -aux, -ales [fʀaktal] ADJ fractal

NF **fractale** fractal

fraction [fʀaksjɔ̃] NF **1** *Math* fraction; **f. ordinaire** vulgar fraction; **f. décimale** decimal fraction; **f. périodique** recurring decimal SEE GRAMMAR A76; B59 **2** *(partie)* part, portion; *Pol* splinter group; **ça a duré une f. de seconde** it lasted a fraction of a second *or* a split second; *Compta* **f. imposable** part subject to tax; **f. d'intérêt** interest accrued **3** *Rel (du pain)* breaking

fractionnaire [fʀaksjɔnɛʀ] ADJ fractional; **nombre f.** improper fraction

fractionnel, -elle [fʀaksjɔnɛl] ADJ *(tactique)* divisive

fractionnement [fʀaksjɔnmã] NM **1** *(d'une propriété, d'un groupe)* dividing up, splitting up; *(de paiements)* spreading (out); *(d'actions)* splitting **2** *Chimie* fractional distillation; *(d'huiles minérales)* cracking **3** *Com* breaking bulk

fractionner [fʀaksjɔne] VT **1** *(diviser)* to divide up, to split up; *Math* to fractionize; **f. le paiement** to pay in instalments; **nous allons devoir f. l'opération en plusieurs phases** we'll have to break down *or* split the operation into several stages **2** *Chimie (distillation)* to fractionate; *(huiles minérales)* to crack

VPR se fractionner *(de gens, d'objets)* to split up, to divide up; **le groupe se fractionne en deux** the group splits *or* divides in two

fractionnisme [fraksjɔnism] NM *Pol (tactique)* divisive tactics; *(caractère)* factionalism

fractionniste [fraksjɔnist] N *Pol* factionalist

fracture [fraktyr] NF **1** *(d'une serrure, porte)* breaking open, forcing **2** *Méd, Géol* fracture; **f. du crâne** fractured skull; **f. simple** simple *or* closed fracture; **f. multiple** multiple fracture; **f. ouverte** open fracture **3** *Pol* **f. Nord-Sud** North-South divide; **la f. sociale** the gap between the haves and have-nots in society

fracturer [fraktyre] VT **1** *(serrure, porte, coffre-fort)* to break open, to force **2** *(os)* to fracture

VPR se fracturer to fracture, to break; **se f. le tibia** to fracture one's tibia

fragile [fraʒil] ADJ *(construction)* fragile, flimsy; *(verre)* brittle; *(personne, santé)* fragile, frail, delicate; *(estomac)* weak, delicate; *(autorité)* weak, unstable; *(bonheur)* precarious, fragile; *(équilibre)* delicate; *(hypothèse)* shaky; **elle est f. des poumons/de la gorge** she has delicate lungs/a delicate throat; **ne la brutalise pas, elle est encore f.** *(psychologiquement)* don't treat her roughly, she's still (feeling) fragile

fragilisation [fraʒilizasjɔ̃] NF weakening

fragiliser [fraʒilize] VT to weaken

fragilité [fraʒilite] NF *(d'une construction)* fragility; *(du verre)* brittleness; *(d'une personne)* frailty, weakness, fragility; *(d'une hypothèse)* shakiness; *(d'un équilibre)* delicacy

fragment [fragmɑ̃] NM *(de pierre)* fragment, piece; *(d'os)* fragment, splinter; *(de chanson, conversation)* fragment, snatch; *(d'un livre)* extract

fragmentaire [fragmɑ̃tɛr] ADJ fragmentary; *(connaissances)* sketchy, patchy, fragmentary

fragmentation [fragmɑ̃tasjɔ̃] NF fragmentation

fragmenter [fragmɑ̃te] VT to fragment, to split up; *(travail)* to divide up, to split up; **f. la publication d'un ouvrage** to publish a work in parts

frai [frɛ] NM **1** *(action, période)* spawning *(of fish)* **2** *(œufs)* spawn; *(poissons)* fry **3** *(de pièces de monnaie)* abrasion, wear

fraîche [frɛʃ] ADJ *voir* **frais¹**

fraîchement [frɛʃmɑ̃] ADV **1** *(recevoir)* coolly; **accueillir qn f.** to give sb a cool reception; *Fam* **ça va f. ce matin** it's a bit chilly this morning **2** *(récemment)* **f. marié/divorcé/arrivé** newly *or* recently married/divorced/arrived; **fleurs f. cueillies** freshly picked flowers

fraîcheur [frɛʃœr] NF **1** *(température)* freshness, coolness; **dans la f. du soir** in the cool of the evening; **une sensation de f.** a feeling of freshness; **rechercher un peu de f.** to seek out a cool spot **2** *(de fleurs, nourriture, couleurs, d'idées, de film etc)* freshness; *(de la jeunesse)* freshness, bloom; **elle a perdu sa f. d'esprit** she has lost her freshness of mind

fraîchir [frɛʃir] VI *Météo* **1** *(devenir frais)* to freshen, to grow colder *or* cooler **2** *(du vent)* to freshen

frais¹, fraîche [frɛ, frɛʃ] ADJ **1** *(froid) (vent)* fresh, cool; *Fig (réception)* cool; *(rafraîchi)* chilled; **un accueil plutôt f.** a rather cool welcome

2 *(récent) (pain, fruits, fleurs, traces)* fresh; *(souvenir)* recent, fresh; **air f.** fresh air; **œufs f.** fresh *or* new-laid eggs; **les croissants sont tout f. de ce matin** the croissants are fresh this morning; **de fraîche date** not long ago,

recently; **amis de fraîche date** recent friends; **l'encre est encore fraîche** the ink is still wet; **peinture fraîche** wet paint

3 teint f. fresh complexion; **avoir l'haleine fraîche** to have fresh breath; **cette robe n'est plus très fraîche, mais elle fera l'affaire** this dress isn't very fresh any more, but it will do; **f. et dispos** hale and hearty; **être f. comme un gardon** to be bright-eyed and bushy-tailed; **être fraîche comme une rose** to be as fresh as a daisy; *Fam* **me voilà f.!** I'm in a nice mess *or* a pretty fix!

4 avoir de l'argent f. to have new money

ADV il fait f. it's cool *or* fresh; **servir/boire f.** serve/drink chilled *or* cool; **roses toutes fraîches** *ou* **f. cueillies** freshly picked roses; **herbe f.** *ou* **fraîche coupée** freshly *or* newly cut grass; **il est f. débarqué de sa province** he is fresh from the country; **f. émoulu de l'université** fresh out of *or* from university; **rasé de f.** freshly shaven; **peint de f.** freshly painted

NM prendre le f. to take some *or* a breath of (fresh) air; **à mettre** *ou* **à conserver au f.** to be kept cool *or* in a cool place; **mettre le vin au f.** to put the wine to cool; *Fig Fam* **ils l'ont mis au f.** they've put him in the cooler, they've locked him up *or* put him inside; *Météo, Naut* **avis de grand f.** gale warning

NF fraîche 1 *Arg (argent)* cash, dough **2 à la fraîche** in the cool part of the day

frais² NMPL expenses, costs; **f. d'un procès** costs of a lawsuit; **j'ai eu beaucoup de f. ce mois-ci** I've had a lot of expense(s) this month; **faire de gros f.** to go to great expense; **faux f.** incidental expenses; **note de f.** expense account; **tous f. payés** all expenses paid; *Jur* **être condamné aux f.** to be ordered to pay costs; **rentrer dans ses f.** to cover one's expenses; *Fig* **j'ai fait les f. de la plaisanterie** the joke was at my expense; *Fig* **faire les f. de la conversation** to keep the conversation going; **(à ses dépens)** to be the subject of the conversation; **faire les f. d'une politique** to pay the price for a policy; **faire qch à ses f.** to do sth at one's own expense; **à grands/à peu de f.** at great/little cost; **se mettre en f.** to go to great expense, *Fam* to put oneself out of pocket; **se mettre en f. de politesse** to go out of one's way to be polite; **j'en suis pour mes f.** it's been a lot of trouble for nothing, I've been wasting my time; **exempt de f., sans f.** free of charge; *(sur une lettre de change)* no expenses; *Fam* **aux f. de la princesse** at the expense of the government/the firm/*etc*; **f. accessoires** incidental costs *or* expenses; **f. d'achat** purchase costs; **f. d'adhésion** membership charge; **f. administratifs** administrative costs; **f. d'administration** administrative costs; *(en échange d'un service)* handling charge; **f. d'administration générale** general overheads, general administration costs, *Am* general overhead; **f. d'agence** agency fee; **f. d'amortissement** amortization *or* depreciation charges; **f. d'annulation** cancellation charge; **f. de banque** bank charges; **f. de Bourse** transaction costs; **f. de camionnage** haulage; **f. de commercialisation** marketing costs; **f. de constitution** *(de société)* startup costs; *(de compte)* set-up fee; **f. consulaires** consular fees; *Bourse* **f. de courtage** brokerage, commission; **f. de déplacement** travelling *or* travel expenses; **f. différés** deferred charges; **f. de distribution** distribution costs; **f. de douane** customs duties; **f. d'encaissement** collection charges *or* fees; **f. d'entrée** *(d'une sicav)* front-end *or* front-load fees; **f. d'envoi** carriage costs; **f. d'établissement** startup costs; **f. d'exploitation** operating costs, operational costs; **f. extraordinaires** extraordinary expenses; **f. financiers** interest charges, financial costs;

f. fixes fixed charges; **f. de fonctionnement** operating costs; *Com* **f. généraux** overheads, *Am* overhead; **f. de gestion** administration costs; **f. inclus** inclusive of costs; **f. d'inscription** membership fee; **f. d'installation** initial expenses; **f. de lancement** set-up *or* start-up costs; **f. de liquidation** closing-down costs; **f. de livraison** delivery charges; **f. de main-d'œuvre** labour costs; **f. de manutention** handling charges; **f. de pilotage** pilotage; **f. de port** carriage; **f. de port et d'emballage** postage and packing; **f. portuaires** port charges; **f. de publicité** advertising costs; **f. de représentation** expense account, entertainment allowance *or* expenses; **f. de réservation** booking fee, reservation charge; **f. de scolarité** school fees; **f. de sortie** exit charges, back-end load; **f. de tenue de compte** account charges; *(de compte bancaire)* bank charges; **f. de transport** carriage; **f. de trésorerie** finance costs; **f. variables** variable costs

fraisage [frɛzaʒ] NM **1** *Métal (de surface)* milling; *(de trou)* reaming; *(de trou de vis)* countersinking **2** *(par le dentiste)* drilling

fraise¹ [frɛz] NF **1** *(fruit)* strawberry; **f. des bois** wild *or Am* field strawberry; **tarte aux fraises** strawberry tart; **confiture de fraises** strawberry jam; **sirop de f.** strawberry cordial; *Fig* **sucrer les fraises** to have the shakes; *Arg* **un coup en pleine f.** a punch in the kisser; *Arg* **amène ta f.!** get yourself over here!; *Arg* **il est tout le temps à ramener sa f.** he's always sticking his oar in **2** *Méd* strawberry (mark)

ADJ INV *(couleur)* strawberry-pink; **f. écrasée** crushed strawberry; **écharpe f.** strawberry-pink scarf

fraise² NF **1** *Culin (de veau, d'agneau)* caul **2** *Hist (col)* ruff **3** *(de dinde)* wattle **4** *Tech* milling cutter, mill; **f. (conique)** countersink **5** *(de dentiste)* drill

fraiser [frɛze] VT **1** *(dent)* to drill **2** *Tech (surface)* to mill; *(trou)* to ream; *(trou de vis)* to countersink

fraiseraie [frɛzrɛ] NF strawberry field

fraiseuse [frɛzøz] NF *Tech* milling machine

fraisier [frɛzje] NM **1** *Bot* strawberry plant **2** *Culin* strawberry cream cake

fraisil [frɛzi(l)] NM coal cinders

fraisure [frɛzyr] NF countersink, countersunk hole

framboise [frɑ̃bwaz] NF *(fruit)* raspberry; *(liqueur)* raspberry liqueur; **tarte aux framboises** raspberry tart

ADJ INV raspberry

framboisé [frɑ̃bwaze] ADJ raspberry-flavoured, *Am* raspberry-flavored

framboisier [frɑ̃bwazje] NM **1** *Bot* raspberry bush *or* cane **2** *Culin* raspberry cream cake

franc¹ [frɑ̃] NM *(monnaie)* franc; **f. suisse** Swiss franc; **f. or** gold value of the franc; **ancien/nouveau f.** old/new franc; **f. constant** inflation-adjusted franc, franc in real terms; **francs courants** actual francs; **je l'ai eu pour trois francs six sous** I got it for next to nothing; **f. symbolique** nominal sum; **un f. symbolique de dommages et intérêts** token damages

franc², franche [frɑ̃, frɑ̃ʃ] ADJ **1** *(sincère) (personne)* frank, open, candid; *(réponse, conversation)* frank, candid; **je serai f. (avec vous)** I'll be frank *or* candid *or* honest (with you); **pour être f.** to be frank *or* candid; **sa réponse a au moins le mérite d'être franche** at least he answered frankly *or* candidly; **un regard f.** an open look; **un oui f. et massif** a clear and overwhelming yes; **être f. comme l'or** to be totally frank; **être f. du collier** to be

completely open; *(serviable)* to be compliant
2 *(libre)* free; **f. de tout droit** duty-free; **f. d'avarie particulière** free of particular average; **f. d'impôts** tax free, free of tax; **f. de casse** free of breakage; **f. de toute avarie** free of average; **f. de port** carriage paid, carriage free; **zone/ville franche** free zone/city; **port f.** free port; *Ftbl* **coup f.** free kick; *Mil* **corps f.** commando (unit)
3 *(net) (couleur, vin)* pure; *(rupture)* clean; *(escroc)* downright, out-and-out; **situation franche** clear *or* unequivocal position; **c'est un f. Breton** he's a true Breton; **vin f. de goût** wine clean to the taste; **terre franche** loam; **ça a été une franche rigolade** it was an absolute scream; **huit jours francs** eight clear days
ADV **pour parler f.** frankly *or* candidly speaking; **parlons f.** let's be frank (with each other)

franc³, franque [frã, frãk] *Hist* ADJ Frankish
N F. Frank

français, -aise [frãsɛ, -ɛz] ADJ French; **impossible n'est pas f.** impossible? there's no such word (in the language); **c'est bien f. cette attitude** that's a typically French attitude
ADV **acheter f.** to buy French; **rouler/boire/manger f.** to drive French cars/drink French wine/eat French food
NM *Ling* French; **parler f.** to speak French; *(correctement)* to speak properly; *Fam* **tu ne comprends pas le f.?** ≃ don't you understand (plain) English?
N F. Frenchman, *f* Frenchwoman
NF *Ordinat* **imprimer à la française** to print portrait

franc-bord, *pl* **francs-bords** NM *Naut* freeboard; **bordé à f.** carvel built

franc-bourgeois, *pl* **francs-bourgeois** NM *Hist* freeman

France [frãs] NF France; **vivre/aller en F.** to live in/go to France; **les vins de F.** French wines; **être** *ou* **faire (très) vieille F.** to be rather old-fashioned; **F. 2** = French state-owned TV channel; **F.3** = French state-owned TV channel; **F. Info** = French state-owned news radio station; **F. Inter** = French state-owned radio station; **F. Télécom** = state-owned company which runs all telecommunications services, until 1991 part of the PTT

Francfort [frãkfɔr] N Frankfurt; **saucisse de F.** frankfurter

franchement [frãʃmã] ADV **1** *(ouvertement)* frankly, candidly, openly; **(très) f., je ne sais pas quoi dire à ça** (quite) frankly, I don't know what to say to that; **je vais te parler f.** I'll be frank with you; **il me l'a dit f.** he told me openly; **y aller f.** to go right ahead with it; **vas-y f., appuie sur la manette** go on, push the joystick hard **2** *(tout à fait, vraiment)* really; **c'était f. stupide/mauvais** it was really *or* downright stupid/bad; **j'en suis f. dégoûté** I'm absolutely sick of it; **f., tu comprends ça, toi?** honestly (now), do you understand that?; **non, mais f.!** no, honestly *or* really!; **tu as de ces idées, f.!** the ideas you have, honestly *or* really!

franchir [frãʃir] VT *(obstacle, difficulté)* to get over, to clear; *(fossé)* to jump (over), to clear; *(rapides)* to shoot; *(limite)* to exceed; *(porte)* to pass or walk through; *(rivière, frontière)* to cross; **la panthère franchit le mur d'un seul bond** the panther cleared *or* jumped over the wall in one bound; **f. la ligne d'arrivée** to cross the finishing line; **f. le Rubicon** to cross the Rubicon; **f. le pas** to take the plunge; **f. le seuil** to step over *or* to cross the threshold; **f. le mur du son** to break

(through) the sound barrier; **si l'on franchit un certain cap** if a certain point is passed; **f. la barre des 3 millions** to pass the 3 million mark

franchisage [frãʃizaʒ] NM *Com* franchising

franchise [frãʃiz] NF **1** *(sincérité)* frankness, openness, candour, *Am* candor; *(franc-parler)* plain speaking, outspokenness; **en toute f.** quite frankly; **parler avec f.** to speak frankly *or* candidly **2** *(exonération)* exemption; **faire entrer qch en f.** to import sth duty-free; **entrée en f.** free import; **bagages en f.** baggage allowance **3** *(d'assurance)* excess, *Am* deductible **4** *Hist* **charte de f.** charter (of freedom) *(of city)* **5** *Com* franchise
▸▸ **f. (de) bagages** baggage allowance; **f. douanière** exemption from customs duties; **f. fiscale** tax exemption; **f. postale** = official paid; **f. de TVA** VAT exemption, zero-rating; **en f. de TVA** VAT-exempt, zero-rated

Il faut noter que le nom anglais **franchise** ne signifie jamais **sincérité**.

franchisé, -ée [frãʃize] N *Com* franchisee
ADJ **magasin f.** franchise

franchiser [frãʃize] VT to franchise

franchiseur, -euse [frãʃizœr, -øz] N *Com* franchisor

franchissable [frãʃisabl] ADJ *(route)* passable; *(col de montagne)* negotiable; *(obstacle)* surmountable

franchissement [frãʃismã] NM *(d'obstacle)* clearing; *(de fossé)* jumping; *(de rivière)* crossing

franchouillard, -arde [frãʃujar, -ard] *Fam Péj* ADJ archetypally French
N archetypal Frenchman, *f* Frenchwoman

francilien, -ienne [frãsiljɛ̃, -jɛn] ADJ of *or* from the Île-de-France *(the greater Paris region)*
N F. inhabitant of the Île-de-France *(the greater Paris region)*

francisant, -ante [frãsizã, -ãt] N French specialist

francisation [frãsizasjɔ̃] NF **1** *(d'un mot étranger)* gallicizing, *Fam* Frenchifying **2** *Naut* registry as a French ship

franciscain, -aine [frãsiskɛ̃, -ɛn] ADJ, N *Rel* Franciscan

franciser [frãsize] VT **1** *(mot étranger)* to gallicize, *Fam* to Frenchify **2** *Naut (bateau)* to register as French

francisque [frãsisk] NF = emblem of the Vichy government

francité [frãsite] NF Frenchness

franc-maçon, *pl* **francs-maçons** NM freemason

franc-maçonnerie NF freemasonry

franc-maçonnique ADJ masonic

franco [frãko] ADV **1** *Com* **f. (de port)** post(age) paid, carriage free, carriage paid; **f. allège** free over side; **f. de port et d'emballage** post(age) and packing paid; **f. d'emballage** free of packing charges; **livré f.** delivered free *or* post(age) paid; **f. (à) bord** free on board, FOB; **f. de douane** free of customs duty; **f. frontière** free at frontier; **f. gare de réception** free on rail; **f. de tous frais** free of all charges; **f. le long du navire** free alongside ship; **f. long du bord** free alongside ship; **f. long du quai** free alongside ship; **f. rendu** free at; **f. transporteur** free carrier; **f. wagon** free on rail **2** *Fam* **vas-y f.!** go right ahead!

franco-allemand ADJ Franco-German

franco-américain ADJ Franco-American

franco-britannique ADJ Anglo-French

franco-canadien, -ienne ADJ French Canadian
NM *Ling* Canadian French

franco-français ADJ pure French; **une entreprise franco-française** a 100% French-owned company

francophile [frãkɔfil] ADJ, N francophile

francophilie [frãkɔfili] NF love of all things French

francophobe [frãkɔfɔb] N francophobe
ADJ francophobe, francophobic

francophobie [frãkɔfɔbi] NF francophobia

francophone [frãkɔfɔn] ADJ French-speaking
N French speaker

francophonie [frãkɔfɔni] NF French-speaking world

franc-parler NM plain speaking, outspokenness; **avoir son f.** to speak one's mind, to be outspoken, not to mince one's words

franc-tireur, *pl* **francs-tireurs** NM *Mil* franc-tireur, irregular (soldier); *Fig* maverick

frange [frãʒ] NF *(de carpette, cheveux etc)*, *Fig* fringe

franger [frãʒe] VT *(je frangeai(s))* to fringe, to border

frangin [frãʒɛ̃] NM *Fam* brother

frangine [frãʒin] NF *Fam* sister

frangipane [frãʒipan] NF *Culin* almond paste, frangipane

frangipanier [frãʒipanje] NM *Bot* frangipani (tree)

franglais [frãglɛ] NM Franglais

franquette [frãkɛt] NF **à la bonne f.** simply, without ceremony; **on mangera à la bonne f.** we will eat simply; **un repas à la bonne f.** a simple meal; **c'est à la bonne f. chez eux** they don't stand on ceremony at home

franquisme [frãkism] NM Francoism

franquiste [frãkist] ADJ pro-Franco
N supporter of Franco

frappadingue [frapadɛ̃g] ADJ *Fam* crazy, bonkers, *Br* mental

frappant [frapã] ADJ *(image, ressemblance etc)* striking

frappe [frap] NF **1** *(dactylographie)* typing; *Ordinat* keying; **elle a une f. rapide** she can type/key fast; **la lettre est à la f.** the letter is being typed/keyed; **faute de f.** typing/keying error; **vitesse de f.** typing/keying speed; *Ordinat* **f. au kilomètre** continuous input; *Ordinat* **f. en continu** type-ahead **2** *(de pièces de monnaie)* striking, minting **3** *(au base-ball)* hit; *Boxe* punch; *Ftbl* strike, kick **4** *Mil* **force de f.** strike force; **des frappes aériennes** airstrikes **5** *Arg* **petite f.** hoodlum

frappé [frape] ADJ **1** iced, well chilled; **café f.** iced coffee; **champagne f.** chilled champagne, champagne frappé **2** *Fam (fou)* crazy

frappement [frapmã] NM striking; *(bruit)* knocking

frapper [frape] VT **1** to hit, to strike; **f. légèrement** to tap; **être frappé à mort** to be fatally *or* mortally wounded; **la balle l'a frappé en plein cœur** the bullet hit him right in the heart; **f. des marchandises d'une taxe** to impose a duty on goods; **être frappé par une maladie** to be struck down by a disease; **être frappé par un deuil** to be suffering from bereavement; **être frappé de mutisme** to be struck dumb; **f. qn d'étonnement** to strike sb with amazement; **cela a frappé son imagination** that caught his/her imagination; **ce qui m'a frappé le plus, c'était son sang-froid** what struck *or* impressed me most was his coolness; **je fus frappé par leur ressemblance** I was struck by their resemblance; **je suis frappé de le retrouver dans cette situation** I'm surprised to find him in this situation; *Théâtre* **f. les trois coups** to give the three knocks *(at the start of a play)*; *Fig* **f. un**

grand coup to strike a decisive blow; *Fig* **f. à la tête** to strike at the top **2** *(médaille)* to strike; *(pièces de monnaie)* to strike, to mint; *(papier peint)* to emboss; *(motif)* to punch (out), to cut out; *(cuir)* to block **3** *(lettre)* to type; *Ordinat* to key; *Ordinat* **f. au kilomètre** to input continuously **4** *(refroidir)* to ice; *(boisson)* to chill; **f. le champagne** to put the champagne on ice **vi 1** to strike, to hit; **f. du poing sur la table** to bang (on) the table; **f. à la porte** to knock on *or* at the door; **f. doucement à la porte** to tap on *or* at the door; **la prochaine fois vous pourrez entrer sans f.** next time you can come in without knocking; **entrez sans f.** *(notice)* come *or* go straight in; **on frappe** there's someone (knocking) at the door; *Fig* **vous frappez à la bonne/mauvaise porte** you've come to the right/wrong place; **il va falloir f. à toutes les portes** we will have to ask for help from all quarters **2 f. des mains** *ou* **dans ses mains** to clap (one's hands); **f. du pied** to stamp (one's foot) **3** *Fam (agir)* to strike; **le gang a encore frappé** the gang has struck again; **la grippe va f. durement** the flu will hit everyone hard **vpr se frapper 1 se f. les cuisses** to slap one's thighs; **se f. le front** to slap one's forehead; **se f. la poitrine** to beat one's chest **2** *Fam* to get oneself worked up, to get oneself into a flap *or* panic; **ne vous frappez pas** don't panic, don't flap

frappeur, -euse [frapœr, -øz] **N** *Métal* striker; *(de papier peint)* embosser **ADJ esprit f.** spirit-rapper

frasque [frask] **NF** escapade, prank; **frasques** carryings-on, misbehaviour; **faire des frasques** to get up to mischief *or* to no good; **ses frasques de jeunesse** his youthful indiscretions

fraternel, -elle [fratɛrnɛl] **ADJ** fraternal, brotherly; **geste f.** friendly gesture

fraternellement [fratɛrnɛlmɑ̃] **ADV** fraternally, in a fraternal manner; **nous nous embrassâmes f.** we kissed like brothers

fraternisation [fratɛrnizasjɔ̃] **NF** fraternization

fraterniser [fratɛrnize] **VI** to fraternize

fraternité [fratɛrnite] **NF** fraternity, brotherhood; **on trouve une certaine f. d'esprit entre eux** you can see a certain kinship of spirit between them

fratricide [fratrisid] **ADJ** fratricidal **NM** *(crime)* fratricide **N** *(personne)* fratricide

fraude [frod] **NF** fraud; *(à un examen)* cheating; **f. électorale** electoral fraud, vote rigging; **f. fiscale** tax evasion; **en f.** fraudulently, unlawfully; **passer qch en f.** to smuggle sth in/out; **il entra en f. dans le pays** he entered the country illegally *or* unlawfully

frauder [frode] **VT** to defraud, to cheat, to swindle; **f. le fisc** to evade tax; **f. la douane** to defraud customs, to smuggle; **vin fraudé** adulterated wine **VI** to cheat (**sur** on); **f. sur la marchandise** to cheat the customer; **il a l'habitude de f. dans le métro** he always avoids buying a ticket for the underground, he's a fare-dodger

fraudeur, -euse [frodœr, -øz] **N** defrauder, cheat; *(trafiquant)* smuggler; **le nombre de fraudeurs dans les transports en commun a diminué** the number of fare-dodgers on public transport has decreased

frauduleusement [frodyløzmɑ̃] **ADV** fraudulently; **je le vis se glisser f. dans le cinéma** I saw him slipping into the cinema without paying

frauduleux, -euse [frodylø, -øz] **ADJ** frau-

dulent; **édition frauduleuse** pirated edition

frayer [freje] *(je fraye ou fraie, n. frayons; je frayerai ou fraierai)* **VT 1 f. un chemin** to clear a path; *Fig* to blaze a trail; **f. la voie à qn** to pave the way for sb **2** *(d'un cerf)* to scrape, to rub; *Vét (d'un cheval)* to gall **VI 1** *(d'un poisson)* to spawn **2** *Fig* **f. avec qn** to mix *or* associate with sb; **je ne fraye pas avec des gens de cette espèce** I don't mix with that sort of people; **elle fraye peu** she doesn't mix much, she's not much of a mixer **VPR se frayer se f. un passage** to clear a way (for oneself); **se f. un chemin à travers la foule** to force *or* push *or* elbow one's way through the crowd; *Fig* **se f. un chemin dans …** to make one's way in …

frayère [frɛjɛr] **NF** spawning ground *(of fish)*

frayeur [frɛjœr] **NF** fright *(de* of); **tu m'as fait une de ces frayeurs!** you really frightened me!, you gave me such a fright!; **j'ai eu une f., j'ai cru que j'avais oublié mes clés** I had *or* got a fright, I thought I had forgotten my keys; **vous me donnez des frayeurs** you're getting me worried; **se remettre de ses frayeurs** to recover from one's fright

FRBG [ɛfɛrbeʒe] **NM** *(abrév* **fonds pour risques bancaires généraux)** FGBR

fredaine [frɔdɛn] **NF** prank, escapade; **faire des fredaines** to get into *or* up to mischief; *(amoureuses)* to carry on

fredonnement [frɔdɔnmɑ̃] **NM** *(d'un air)* humming

fredonner [frɔdɔne] **VT, VI** to hum

free-jazz [fridʒaz] **NM** *Mus* free jazz, freeform jazz

free-lance [frilɑ̃s] **ADJ INV** freelance **NM INV travailler en f., faire du f.** to work freelance, to do freelance work, to freelance **N INV** freelance, freelancer

freesia [frezja] **NM** *Bot* freesia

freeware [friwɛr] **NM** *Ordinat* freeware; **freewares** freeware programs

freezer [frizœr] **NM** freezer compartment

frégate [fregat] **NF 1** *Naut* frigate; **capitaine de f.** commander **2** *Orn* frigate bird

frein [frɛ̃] **NM 1** *Aut* brake; **il a fallu donner un coup de f. très rapide** we had to brake very suddenly; *Fig* **donner un coup de f. à une entreprise** to put a brake on an undertaking; **un coup de f. à la création d'entreprises** a check to reduce the number of new firms; **mettre un f. à qch** to curb *or* check sth; **mettre un f. aux désirs de qn** to curb *or* bridle sb's desires; **mettre un f. à la montée de la colère** to stem *or* curb *or* check the rising tide of anger; **curiosité/imagination sans f.** unbridled curiosity/imagination; **f. à l'expansion** brake on growth **2** *(mors)* bit; **ronger son f.** *(d'un cheval)*, *Fig (d'une personne)* to champ at the bit **3** *Anat (de la langue)* fr(a)enum **▸▸ f. à air (comprimé)** airbrake; **freins arrière** rear brakes; **freins assistés** power brakes; **freins avant** front brakes; **freins à bande** band brakes; *Can* **f. à bras** handbrake, *Am* parking brake; **f. à disque** disc brake; **f. sur échappement** exhaust brake; **f. d'embrayage** clutch stop; **f. à main** handbrake, *Am* parking brake; **f. moteur** engine brake; **utilisez votre f. moteur** *(sur panneau)* engage low gear; **f. à pédale** foot brake; **f. au pied** foot brake; **f. secondaire** emergency brake; **f. de stationnement** handbrake, *Am* parking brake; **f. à tambour** drum brake; **f. sur transmission** transmission brake; **f. à vide** vacuum brake

freinage [frɛnaʒ] **NM 1** *(action)* braking; *Fig (de l'inflation)* curbing; *(de la production)* cutting back; *(des importations, des salaires)* reduction; **distance de f.** braking distance; **traces de f.** skid marks; *Aviat* **parachute de**

f. brake parachute 2 *(système)* brake system, brakes

freiner [frene, frɛne] **VT 1** *(véhicule)* to brake **2** *(ralentir)* to slow down; **des arbres ont freiné sa chute** trees broke his fall **3** *(inflation, production etc)* to curb, to check; **f. qn** to keep sb in check, to restrain sb **VI** to brake; **f. à bloc** to jam on *or* slam on the brakes; *Fig* **ce sont les patrons qui freinent** it's the bosses who are back-pedalling; **il voudrait moderniser l'usine mais son père freine des quatre fers** he'd like to modernize the factory, but his father is putting a brake on that idea **VPR se freiner** *Fig* to keep oneself in check, to restrain oneself

freinte [frɛ̃t] **NF** *Com* wastage, loss in volume/weight *(during transit or manufacture)*

frelatage [frɔlataʒ] **NM** *(du vin, de la nourriture etc)* adulteration

frelater [frɔlate] **VT** *(alcool, nourriture)* to adulterate

frêle [frɛl] **ADJ** *(personne, enfant, voix)* frail, weak; *(silhouette)* frail; *(embarcation, cabane)* flimsy, frail

frelon [frɔlɔ̃] **NM** hornet

freluquet [frɔlykɛ] **NM** *Fam* (young) whippersnapper

frémir [fremir] **VI 1** *(vibrer)* to quiver; *(des vitres)* to shake, to rattle; *(des feuilles)* to rustle; *(du vent)* to sigh; *(de l'eau chaude)* to simmer; **l'air frémissait encore des échos d'une flûte lointaine** the air was still vibrating to the echoes of a distant flute **2** *(d'une personne) (de peur)* to shake, to tremble, to shudder, to quake; *(de froid)* to shiver, to shudder; *(de plaisir, joie, d'impatience)* to tremble, to quiver; *(de colère, d'inquiétude)* to shake, to tremble, to quiver *(de* with); **il m'a fait si peur, j'en frémis encore** he scared me so much I'm still shaking *or* trembling

frémissant [fremisɑ̃] **ADJ** *(eau)* simmering; *(voix)* trembling, shaky; *(feuillage, chair)* quivering, trembling; **sensibilité frémissante** quivering sensitivity

frémissement [fremismɑ̃] **NM 1** *(des feuilles)* rustle; *(de l'eau chaude)* simmering; *(du vent)* sighing; **le f. des champs de blé sous la brise** the wheatfields quivering in the breeze **2** *(frisson) (de peur)* shudder; **f. de plaisir/joie** thrill of pleasure/joy; **un f. de colère/d'impatience/d'inquiétude** a quiver of anger/impatience/anxiety; **avec un f. de crainte** shaking *or* quaking with fear; **avec un f. dans la voix** with a trembling *or* shaky voice; **des frémissements parcouraient son corps** he was shaking *or* trembling all over; **un léger f. parcourut tous les auditeurs** a slight shudder went through the audience

frênaie [frɛnɛ] **NF** ash plantation

french-cancan [frɛnʃkɑ̃kɑ̃] **NM** cancan

frêne [frɛn] **NM** *(arbre)* ash (tree); *(bois)* ash

frénésie [frenezi] **NF** frenzy; **applaudir avec f.** to applaud frantically; **travailler/parler avec f.** to work/talk frenziedly; **f. d'achat** buying spree

frénétique [frenetik] **ADJ** *(activité)* frenzied, frantic; *(rythme)* frenetic, frenzied; *(passion)* wild

frénétiquement [frenetikmɑ̃] **ADV** frenziedly, frenetically

Fréon® [freɔ̃] **NM** Freon®

fréquemment [frekamɑ̃] **ADV** frequently

fréquence [frekɑ̃s] **NF 1** *(occurrence)* frequency; **la f. d'un mot dans un texte** the frequency of a word in a text; **f. du pouls** pulse rate; **f. d'achat** purchase frequency **2** *Phys, Radio etc* frequency; *(de son)* tone; **basse/haute f.** low/high frequency; **très haute f.** very high frequency; **bande de fréquences**

frequency band; **modulation de f.** frequency modulation; **f. absolue** absolute frequency; **f. cumulée** cumulative frequency; *Ordinat* **f. d'horloge** clock speed *or* frequency; **f. d'horloge du microprocesseur** microprocessor clock frequency; **f. porteuse** carrier; **f. radio** radio frequency; **f. de rafraîchissement** refresh rate; **f. réglée** adjusted frequency; **f. relative** relative frequency; **f. sonore** audio frequency

fréquent [frekɑ̃] **ADJ** frequent; **il est f. de voir des jeunes couples divorcer** you frequently *or* often see young couples getting divorced; **il est peu f. que …** it is not very often that …

fréquentable [frekɑ̃tabl] **ADJ** **des gens peu fréquentables** people you wouldn't want to associate with; **il redeviendra peut-être f. s'il paye des dettes** people will perhaps want to know him again if he pays his debts; *Hum* **tôt le matin, il n'est pas f.** he's not in the best of moods *or* he's not nice to know early in the morning

fréquentatif, -ive [frekɑ̃tatif, -iv] **ADJ** *Gram* frequentative

fréquentation [frekɑ̃tasjɔ̃] **NF 1** *(fait d'aller à)* frequenting (**de** of); **f. des théâtres** theatre-going; **la f. des cinémas a baissé** cinema-going has decreased; **cela demande une f. assidue** it requires regular attendance; **f. des grands auteurs** acquaintance with the great writers **2 fréquentations** company; **mauvaises fréquentations** bad company; **elle a de mauvaises fréquentations** she keeps bad company; **surveillez ses fréquentations** keep a watch on the company he keeps; **ce ne sont pas des fréquentations pour une jeune fille** these are not the sort of people a young girl should be associating with

fréquenté [frekɑ̃te] **ADJ** *(endroit, route)* busy; **bar f. par les étudiants** bar frequented by students, student bar; **hôtel bien f.** hotel with a good clientele; **endroit mal f.** place with a bad reputation

fréquenter [frekɑ̃te] **VT 1** *(endroit)* to frequent **2 f. qn** to see sb regularly; *(comme petite amie, petit ami)* to go out with sb; **nous ne nous fréquentons plus beaucoup** we don't see much of each other any more; **je fréquente peu ce genre de personnes** I don't associate much with that type of person; **quels gens fréquente-t-il?** who does he go around with?, what company does he keep?; **je t'interdis de f. les voisins** I forbid you to speak to the neighbours; **parmi tous ceux que je fréquente** amongst all my acquaintances ■ **VPR se fréquenter** to see each other regularly; *(d'un couple)* to go out with each other

frère [frɛr] **NM 1** brother; **ils s'aiment comme des frères** they love each other like brothers; **on va partager en frères** we'll share it amicably; *Fam* **tu es un f. (pour moi)** you're a real friend; **faux f.** false friend; **alors, vieux f., quoi de neuf?** well, old chum *or* pal, what's new?; **les hommes sont tous frères** all men are brothers; **pays/peuples frères** sister countries/nations **2** *Rel* friar; **mes bien chers frères** dearly beloved brethren VOIR GRAMMAIRE A13 ■; **j'ai fait mes études chez les frères** I studied with the brothers
▸▸ **f. lai** lay brother; **f. de lait** foster brother; *Fam* **f. trois-points** freemason; **frères d'armes** brothers-in-arms

frérot [frero] **NM** *Fam* kid *or* little brother

fresque [frɛsk] **NF** fresco; **peinture à f.** painting in fresco; **ce roman est une f. historique** this novel is a historical epic; **le film est une f. sociale sur l'Italie des années 50** the film is a social portrait of Italy in the 50s

fresquiste [frɛskist] **ADJ, N** **(peintre) f.** fresco painter

fressure [fresyr] **NF** *(d'un veau, mouton etc)* pluck; *Culin* fry

fret [frɛ(t)] **NM 1** *(prix) (de navire etc)* freight, freightage; **payer le f.** to pay the freight **2** *(louage)* chartering; **prendre un navire à f.** to charter a ship; **donner un navire à f.** to freight (out) a ship; **avion de f.** charter aircraft **3** *(cargaison) (d'un bateau, avion)* cargo, freight; *(d'un camion)* load, freight; **f. aérien** air freight; **expédier par f. aérien** to airfreight; **f. express** express freight; **f. intérieur** inland freight; **f. maritime** sea *or* ocean freight; **f. par conteneur** containerized freight; **f. à forfait** through freight

fréter [frete] **VT** (**je frète; je fréterai**) *(donner en location) (bateau)* to freight (out), to charter; *(avion)* to charter; *(prendre en location) (voiture)* to hire

fréteur [fretœr] **NM** ship charterer, freight forwarder; *(armateur)* shipowner; **f. et affréteur** owner and charterer

frétillant [fretijɑ̃] **ADJ** *(poisson)* wriggling, wriggly; *Fig (personne)* lively; **elle était toute frétillante à l'idée de le revoir** she couldn't keep still at the thought of seeing him again

frétillement [fretijmɑ̃] **NM** *(d'un poisson)* wriggling; *(d'une queue)* wagging; *Fig* fidgeting

frétiller [fretije] **VI** *(d'un poisson)* to wriggle; **le chien frétille de la queue** the dog is wagging its tail; **l'enfant frétille d'impatience** the child is fidgeting with impatience; **f. de joie** to quiver with joy

fretin [frətɛ̃] **NM** *Pêche, Fig* **(menu) f.** small fry

frette¹ [frɛt] **NF** *Tech* (binding) hoop, collar, ferrule; *(d'axe)* band; **f. de moyeu** *(de roue)* nave ring

frette² **NF** *Archit, Hér* fret

freudien, -ienne [frødjɛ̃, -jɛn] **ADJ** *Psy* Freudian

freudisme [frødism] **NM** *Psy* Freudianism

freux [frø] **NM** rook; **colonie de f.** rookery

friabilité [frijabilite] **NF** crumbliness, *Spéc* friability

friable [frijabl] **ADJ** crumbly, *Spéc* friable

friand [frijɑ̃] **ADJ** fond of delicacies; **être f. de qch** to be fond of sth; **être f. de sucreries** to have a sweet tooth; *Fig* **f. de louanges** fond of praise ■ **NM** *Culin (feuilleté)* small savoury pastry; *(gâteau)* small almond cake

friandise [frijɑ̃diz] **NF** titbit, delicacy

Fribourg [fribur] **N** *(en Allemagne)* Freiburg; *(en Suisse)* Fribourg

fric [frik] **NM** *Fam (argent)* dough, *Br* dosh; **j'ai plus de f.!** I'm out of dough!, I'm skint!

fricassée [frikase] **NF** *Culin* fricassee; *Belg* bacon omelette; *Fam* **f. de museaux** hugging and kissing

fricasser [frikase] **VT** *Culin* to fricassee

fricatif, -ive [frikatif, -iv] **ADJ, NF** *Ling* fricative

fric-frac, *pl* **fric-frac(s)** **NM** *Arg* burglary, break-in

friche [friʃ] **NF** fallow land; **f. industrielle** industrial wasteland; **rester** *ou* **être en f.** to lie fallow, to remain uncultivated; *Fig* **une idée/un projet qui est** *ou* **reste en f.** an idea/a plan which has not yet been taken up; **elle laisse son talent/son génie en f.** she's letting her talent/genius go to waste

frichti [friʃti] **NM** *Fam* grub, *Br* nosh

fricot [friko] **NM** *Fam* grub, *Br* nosh; **faire le f.** to do the cooking

fricotage [frikotaʒ] **NM** *Fam* fiddling

fricoter [frikote] *Fam* **VT** *Culin* to cook; *Fig (manigancer)* to scheme, to plot; **je me demande ce qu'il fricote** I wonder what he's up to *or* what he's cooking up
■ **VI 1** *(trafiquer)* to be on the fiddle **2** *(avoir des relations sexuelles)* **ils fricotent ensemble** they're sleeping together

fricoteur, -euse [frikotœr, -øz] **N** *Fam (trafiquant)* wide boy

friction [friksjɔ̃] **NF 1** *(massage)* rubdown; *(du cuir chevelu)* scalp massage **2** *Phys, Tech* friction; **embrayage à f.** friction clutch; **réduire les frictions** to reduce friction; **entraînement par f.** *(d'une imprimante)* friction feed **3** *Fig (heurt)* friction; **cause de f.** cause of friction; **cela reste un point de f.** that remains a bone of contention

frictionnel, -elle [friksjɔnɛl] **ADJ** *(chômage)* temporary

frictionner [friksjɔne] **VT** *(membre)* to rub; **f. qn** to rub sb down, to give sb a rubdown; **f. la tête de qn** to massage sb's scalp, to give sb a scalp massage ■ **VPR se frictionner** to rub oneself down

fridolin [fridɔlɛ̃] **NM** *Fam (terme injurieux)* Kraut, Fritz; **les fridolins** Jerry, the Jerries

frigidaire® [friʒidɛr] **NM** refrigerator, fridge; *Fam* **mettre un projet au f.** to put a plan into cold storage *or* on ice

frigide [friʒid] **ADJ** *(femme)* frigid; *Litt (cœur, caractère)* cold, icy

frigidité [friʒidite] **NF** frigidity, frigidness

frigo [frigo] **NM** *Fam* fridge, refrigerator; *Fam* **mettre un projet au f.** to put a plan into cold storage *or* on ice

frigorification [frigɔrifikasjɔ̃] **NF** *(de viande)* refrigerating, refrigeration

frigorifié [frigɔrifje] **ADJ** frozen; *Fam* **être f.** *(d'une personne)* to be frozen stiff

frigorifier [frigɔrifje] **VT** *(viande)* to refrigerate

frigorifique [frigɔrifik] **ADJ** refrigerating, *Am* frigorific; **appareil f.** refrigerator; **mélange f.** freezing mixture; **wagon f.** refrigerator van; **entrepôt f.** cold store

frigoriste [frigɔrist] **NM** refrigerating engineer

frileusement [friløzmɑ̃] **ADV** with a shiver

frileux, -euse [frilø, -øz] **ADJ** *(personne)* sensitive to the cold; **je suis très f.** I really feel the cold, I'm very sensitive to cold, I'm a chilly sort of person; **une attitude/réponse frileuse** a timid attitude/answer

frilosité [frilozite] **NF** *Litt* sensitivity to the cold; *Fig* nervousness, hesitancy

frimaire [frimɛr] **NM** *Hist* = third month of the French Republican calendar *(Nov-Dec)*

frimas [frima] **NM** *Litt* (hoar)frost, rime

frime [frim] **NF** *Fam* show, pretence; **tout ça, c'est de la f.** that's all show *or* all put on; **il le fait pour la f.** he does it for show

frimer [frime] **VI** *Fam* to show off

frimeur, -euse [frimœr, -øz] **N** *Fam* show-off

frimousse [frimus] **NF 1** *Fam* sweet *or* pretty little face **2** *Ordinat (smiley)* smiley

fringale [frɛ̃gal] **NF** *Fam* hunger; **avoir la f.** to be ravenous *or* starving *or* famished; *Fig* **une f. de qch** a craving for sth; **avoir une f. de voyage** to have itchy feet, to have an urge to travel

fringant [frɛ̃gɑ̃] **ADJ** *(cheval)* spirited, lively, frisky; *(personne)* dashing

fringuer [frɛ̃ge] **VT** *Fam* to dress; **bien fringué** well turned out, well dressed
■ **VI** *Arch ou Can Fam* to prance about, to skip about
■ **VPR se fringuer** to get dressed; **il ne sait pas se f.** *(il n'a aucun goût)* he's got no dress sense

fringues [frɛ̃g] NFPL *Fam (vêtements)* gear, togs, clothes; **elle est folle de f.** she's clothes-mad, she's mad about clothes

fripé [fripe] ADJ *Can Fam* exhausted, beat, *Br* knackered

friper [fripe] VT *(vêtement)* to crumple, to crush; **visage fripé** crumpled face
▸ **VPR se friper** *(d'un vêtement)* to get crushed *or* crumpled

friperie [fripri] NF *(magasin)* second-hand clothes shop; *(vêtements)* second-hand clothes

fripes [frip] NFPL second-hand clothes

fripier, -ière [fripje, -jɛr] N second-hand clothes dealer

fripon, -onne [fripɔ̃, -ɔn] N *Vieilli* rogue, knave; *Fig* **petit f./petite friponne!** you little rascal *or* devil!
▸ ADJ *(sourire, regard, air)* mischievous, roguish

friponnerie [fripɔnri] NF *Vieilli (caractère)* roguery, knavery; *(action)* mischievous prank

fripouille [fripuj] NF **1** *Fam* rogue, scoundrel **2** *Arch (racaille)* rabble, riff-raff

friqué [frike] ADJ *Fam* loaded, rolling in it

friquet [frikɛ] NM tree sparrow

frire [frir] *(pp* frit; *pr ind* je fris, tu fris, il frit; *no pl; fu* je frirai*)* VT to fry; **je fris du poisson** I'm frying fish
▸ VI to fry; **faire f. qch** to fry sth; **le poisson frit** the fish is frying

frisant [frizɑ̃] ADJ **lumière frisante** oblique light

frisbee® [frizbi] NM Frisbee®

Frise [friz] NF Friesland

frise [friz] NF *Archit* frieze; *Théâtre* **frises** border

frisé, -ée [frize] ADJ *(cheveux)* curly; *(personne)* curly-haired; **salade frisée** curly lettuce; **velours f.** uncut velvet, terry; **elle est frisée comme un mouton** she's got frizzy hair
▸ NF **frisée** *(chicorée)* curly endive
▸ N *Fam* **1** *(enfant)* curly-haired child **2** *Fam (terme injurieux)* Kraut, Fritz, *Br* Jerry

friselis [frizli] NM *Litt (des feuilles)* rustling

friser [frize] VT **1** *(cheveux)* to curl; **f. (les cheveux de) qn** to curl sb's hair; **fer à f.** curling tongs **2** *(approcher)* **f. l'accident** to have a narrow escape; **on a frisé la catastrophe** we came within a hair's-breadth *or* an inch of disaster; **on frise la dispute** we're close to arguing *or* to an argument; **cela frise l'impertinence** it's verging on the impertinent; **il frisait la soixantaine** he was close on sixty
▸ VI *(d'une personne)* to have curly hair

frisette [frizɛt] NF *(de cheveux)* ringlet, small curl

frison¹ [frizɔ̃] NM *(cheveux)* curl; *(de bois, papier etc)* shaving

frison², -onne [frizɔ̃, -ɔn] ADJ Friesian; **vache frisonne** Friesian cow
▸ NM *Ling* Friesian
▸ N **F.** Friesian

frisotter [frizɔte] VT **f. (les cheveux de) qn** to crimp sb's hair
▸ VI to curl, to be frizzy

frisquet, -ette [friskɛ, -ɛt] ADJ *Fam (vent)* chill(y); **il fait f.** it's a bit chilly *or Br Fam* parky

frisson [frisɔ̃] NM *(de froid, peur)* shiver, shudder; *(de plaisir)* thrill; **avoir des frissons** to shiver, *Fam* to have the shivers; **j'en ai des frissons** it makes me shudder; **ça me donne des frissons rien que d'y penser** it makes me shudder just thinking of it; *Fig* **le f. de l'eau/ des arbres** the rippling of the water/quivering of the trees

frissonnement [frisɔnmɑ̃] NM *(action)* shivering, shuddering; *(tremblement)* shudder, shiver; **un f. de plaisir** a thrill of pleasure

frissonner [frisɔne] VI **1** *(de froid, de peur)* to shiver, to shudder; **f. de joie** to be thrilled **2** *(du feuillage)* to quiver; *(de l'eau)* to ripple

frisure [frizyr] NF *(des cheveux)* curliness; **frisures** curls, curly hair; **se faire faire des frisures** to have one's hair curled

frit, -ite [fri, frit] ADJ **1** *Culin* fried; **pommes de terre frites** French fried potatoes, (French) fries, *Br* chips **2** *Arg* **il est f.** he's had it
▸ NF **1** *Culin* **frites** (French) fries, *Br* chips; **un steak frites, s'il vous plaît!** steak and chips, please **2** *Fam* **avoir la frite** to be on form; **ça va te donner la frite** that'll perk you up **3** *Fam (tape sur les fesses)* **faire une frite à qn** to flick sb on the bottom

friter [frite] *Fam* VT *(battre)* **f. qn** to beat sb up, to kick sb's head in
▸ VPR **se friter** to have a punch-up *or Am* fist fight

friterie [fritri] NF chip stall

friteuse [fritøz] NF deep fryer, *Br* chip pan; **f. électrique** electric fryer

fritillaire [fritilɛr] NF *Bot* fritillary

fritter [frite] VT *(métal)* to sinter

friture [frityr] NF **1** *(action) (de la nourriture)* frying; *(huile)* (deep) fat, oil *(for frying)*; *(aliments)* fried food; **f. (de poissons)** fried fish **2** *Radio, Tél* **(bruits de) f.** crackling (noise), interference **3** *Belg (friterie)* chip stall

Fritz [frits] NM INV *Fam (terme injurieux)* Fritz, *Br* Jerry

frivole [frivɔl] ADJ frivolous

frivolement [frivɔlmɑ̃] ADV frivolously

frivolité [frivɔlite] NF **1** *(caractère)* frivolity, frivolousness; *(vétille)* trifle **2** *Couture* **frivolités** (fancy) trimmings

froc [frɔk] NM **1** *(de moine)* habit, frock, gown; **prendre le f.** to become a monk; **jeter le f. aux orties** to leave the priesthood **2** *Fam (pantalon)* trousers, *Am* pants; *très Fam* **faire dans son f.** to shit oneself

froid [frwa] ADJ **1** *(vent, temps, bain, radiateur etc)* cold; **à table!, ça va être f.!** come and eat, it's getting cold!; **repas f.** cold meal; **buffet f.** cold buffet; **viandes froides** cold meat(s)
2 *Fig (personne)* cold; *(manière, accueil)* cold, chilly; *(style)* cold, unemotional; **se montrer ou être f. avec ou envers qn** to be cold towards sb, to treat sb coldly *or* coolly; **garder la tête froide** to remain cool (and collected), to keep one's composure; **cela me laisse f.** it leaves me cold; **colère froide** controlled *or* suppressed anger; **la guerre froide** the cold war
▸ ADV **soluble à f.** soluble when cold; *Aut* **démarrer à f.** to start from cold; **parler à f. d'une catastrophe** to speak calmly *or* unemotionally about a catastrophe; *Méd* **opérer à f.** to perform non-emergency surgery; **prendre ou cueillir un adversaire à f.** to catch an opponent unawares *or* off guard *or Br* on the hop
▸ NM **1** cold; **il fait f.** it's cold; *Fam* **il fait un f. de canard ou de loup** it's freezing (cold); *Météo* **coup de f.** cold snap; **prendre (un coup de) f.** to catch a chill *or* a cold; **les grands froids** the coldest part of the winter; **une vague de f.** a cold spell; **avoir f.** to be *or* feel cold; **j'ai f. aux mains** my hands are cold, I've got cold hands; *Fig* **cela m'a fait ou donné f. (dans le dos)** it sent (cold) shivers down my spine; *Fig* **elle n'a pas f. aux yeux** she's very determined, she's got plenty of nerve; **battre f. à qn** to cold-shoulder sb
2 *Fig* coolness; **ils sont en f.** there's a coolness between them; **je suis f. avec lui**

there's a coolness between me and him; **jeter un f.** to cast a chill
3 **l'industrie du f.** the refrigerating industry; **le f. industriel** refrigeration; **la chaîne du f.** the refrigeration chain

froidement [frwadmɑ̃] ADV **1** *(avec réserve)* coldly, coolly; **être f. accueilli** to be given a cold welcome *or* cool reception; **il les a abattus f.** he shot them in cold blood *or* cold-bloodedly **2** *(calmement)* calmly; **il faut étudier f. le problème** we must consider the problem calmly

froideur [frwadœr] NF **1** *(de manière)* coldness, chilliness; **sa f. me met mal à l'aise** his coldness makes me ill at ease; **il est toujours d'une très grande f. avec moi** he is always very cold towards me; **avec f.** coldly **2** *(indifférence)* coldness, indifference; **contempler le spectacle avec f.** to look coldly on; **analysons le problème avec f.** let us analyse the problem calmly **3** *(manque de sensualité)* coldness, iciness

froidure [frwadyr] NF *Litt* cold; **par ces temps de f.** in this cold weather

froissant [frwasɑ̃] ADJ hurtful, wounding

froissement [frwasmɑ̃] NM **1** *(action) (de muscle)* bruising; *(de papier, tissu etc)* crumpling, creasing **2** *(bruit) (du papier, de la soie etc)* rustle, rustling **3** *Fig Vieilli (d'intérêts)* conflict, clash **4** *(vexation)* **un f. d'amour-propre** a blow to one's pride; **éviter tous froissements** to avoid ruffling any feathers *or* hurting anyone's feelings; **il risque d'y avoir des froissements entre elles** there's a chance of some hurt feelings between them

froisser [frwase] VT **1** *(muscle)* to bruise; *(tissu, papier)* to crumple, to crease **2** **f. qn** to offend sb, to give offence to sb, to hurt *or* wound sb's feelings
▸ VPR **se froisser 1** *(d'un tissu)* to crease, to crumple **2** *(d'une personne)* to take offence *or* umbrage *(de* at), to take exception *(de* to)

frôlement [frolmɑ̃] NM *(contact)* brushing *(contre* against); *(son)* rustle

frôler [frole] VT *(effleurer)* to brush, to touch lightly; **l'avion a frôlé la cime des arbres** the plane skimmed the treetops; **f. les murs** to hug the walls; **il a frôlé la mort** he came close to death *or* had a brush with death; **on a frôlé la catastrophe/la dispute** we came close to disaster/to arguing; **ton attitude frôle le ridicule** your attitude verges on *or* borders on the ridiculous
▸ VPR **se frôler** to touch one another lightly, to brush each other; **les deux voitures se sont frôlées** the two cars brushed past each other

fromage [frɔmaʒ] NM cheese; **f. bien fait** ripe cheese; **omelette/soufflé au f.** cheese omelette/soufflé; *Fig Fam* **pas la peine d'en faire un f.** it's not worth making a fuss about; *Fam* **un gentil petit f.** a nice little earner
▸ ▸ **f. blanc** fromage frais; **f. fermenté** fermented cheese; **f. fondu** cheese spread; **f. frais** fromage frais; **f. à pâte molle/dure** soft/hard cheese; **f. à pâte persillée** blue(-veined) cheese; *Culin* **f. de tête** brawn, *Am* headcheese

fromager, -ère [frɔmaʒe, -ɛr] ADJ cheese; **industrie fromagère** cheese industry
▸ N *(commerçant)* cheese merchant, *Br* cheesemonger; *(fabricant)* cheesemaker

fromagerie [frɔmaʒri] NF *(lieu de fabrication)* cheese dairy; *(magasin)* cheese shop

froment [frɔmɑ̃] NM wheat; **pain de f.** wheaten bread; **farine de f.** wheat flour

fronce [frɔ̃s] NF *Couture* gather; **jupe à fronces** gathered skirt

froncement [frɔ̃smɑ̃] NM wrinkling, puckering; **f. de(s) sourcils** frown

froncer [frɔ̃se] VT (**je françai(s)**) **1** (*plisser*) to wrinkle, to pucker; **f. les sourcils** to frown, *Litt* to knit one's brows **2** *Couture* to gather

frondaison [frɔ̃dɛzɔ̃] NF (*apparition des feuilles*) foliation; (*feuillage*) foliage

fronde¹ [frɔ̃d] NF *Bot* frond

fronde² NF **1** (*arme*) sling; (*jouet*) catapult, *Am* slingshot **2** *Hist* **la F.** the Fronde; *Fig* **esprit de f.** spirit of revolt *or* rebellion

fronder [frɔ̃de] VT *Vieilli* (*critiquer*) to lampoon
▸ VI **1** *Hist* to belong to the Fronde; *Fig* to rebel **2** *Arch* to use one's sling

frondeur, -euse [frɔ̃dœr, -øz] N **1** *Hist* member of the Fronde **2** (*rebelle*) rebel
▸ ADJ rebellious, anti-authority

front [frɔ̃] NM **1** (*de personne*) forehead, *surtout Litt* brow; **marcher le f. haut** to walk with one's head (held) high; **relever le f.** to hold one's head high; **courber** *ou* **baisser le f.** to submit; **faire f. à qn/qch** to face up to *or* stand up to sb/sth; **faire f.** to face up to things; **et vous avez le f. de me dire cela!** you have the nerve to tell me that!
2 (*de bâtiment*) front, face; (*de colline*) brow; *Pol* front; **f. de bataille** battle front; *Mil* **le f.** the front (line); **partir sur le** *ou* **au f.** to go (up) to the front; **nouvelles du f.** news from the front; *Météo* **f. chaud/froid** warm/cold front; *Pol* **f. commun** united *or* common front; **faire f. commun contre qn/qch** to join forces against sb/sth
3 de f. (*côte à côte*) side by side, one next to the other; **marcher à trois de f.** to walk three abreast; **mener plusieurs choses de f.** to have several things on the go at once; *Mil* **marche de f.** march in line; *Naut* **en ligne de f.** line abreast
4 vue de f. front view; **attaque de f.** frontal attack; **attaquer qn de f.** to attack sb from the front; *Fig* to attack sb head-on; **aborder un problème de f.** to tackle a problem head-on; **heurter qn/qch de f.** to run head-on into sb/sth
▸▸ **f. de mer** (sea)front; **le F. populaire** = French left-wing coalition in power 1936-38; *Min* **f. de taille** working face, coal face

frontal, -ale, -aux, -ales [frɔ̃tal] ADJ frontal; (*collision*) head-on; *Ordinat* front-end; **ordinateur f.** front end; **os f.** frontal bone; **chargement f.** front loading; *Min* **lampe frontale** cap lamp
▸ NM *Anat* frontal bone; *Com* facing; **f. de rayonnage** shelf facing
▸ NF *Com* **frontale** shelf facing

frontalier, -ière [frɔ̃talje, -jɛr] ADJ **régions frontalières** frontier *or* border regions
▸ N inhabitant of the frontier zone; (*travailleur*) cross-border commuter

fronteau, -eaux [frɔ̃to] NM **1** *Archit* small pediment **2** *Rel* (*de nonne*) frontlet

frontière [frɔ̃tjɛr] NF *Pol* border; *Fig* boundary; **f. naturelle** natural border; **f. linguistique** linguistic boundary; **incident de f.** border incident; *Fig* **ma liberté ne connaît pas de f.** my freedom knows no bounds; **faire reculer les frontières du savoir** to roll back the frontiers of knowledge; **aux frontières de la vie et de la mort** between life and death; **se situer à la f. du possible** to stretch the bounds of what is possible; **dépasser les frontières du possible** to go beyond the bounds of what is possible
▸ ADJ (*ville*) frontier, border; **poste f.** border *or* frontier post

Attention: ne pas confondre **frontier** et **border** lorsque l'on traduit **frontière**. On ne peut utiliser que **border** pour décrire la limite qui sépare deux États.

frontispice [frɔ̃tispis] NM frontispiece

frontiste [frɔ̃tist] ADJ of the (French) National Front
▸ N member of the (French) National Front

front-office, *pl* **front-offices** [frɔ̃tɔfis] NM *Banque* front office

fronton [frɔ̃tɔ̃] NM *Archit* pediment; (*à la pelote basque*) fronton

frottage [frɔtaʒ] NM (*d'un membre etc*) rubbing, chafing; (*des sols etc*) polishing

frottée [frɔte] NF *Vieilli* **1** (*volée*) beating, thrashing **2 f. (d'ail)** = bread which has been toasted then rubbed with a clove of garlic

frotte-manche, *pl* **frotte-manches** [frɔtmɑ̃ʃ] N *Belg Fam* bootlicker

frottement [frɔtmɑ̃] NM **1** (*friction*) rubbing; *Méd* **f. pleural** pleural rub; *Phot* **marques de f.** stress marks; *Fig* **il y a quelques frottements entre eux** there is some friction between them **2** *Tech* friction; (*de freins*) binding; **f. de glissement** sliding friction; **usure par f.** abrasion

frotter [frɔte] VT (*membre*) to rub; (*sol*) to rub; (*avec une brosse*) to brush; (*cuivre*) to polish; **je vais te f. le dos pour te réchauffer** I'll rub your back to warm you up; **si je t'y reprends, je te frotterai les oreilles!** if I catch you at it again, I'll give you what for!; **f. une allumette** to strike a match; *Vieilli* **être frotté de latin** to have a smattering of Latin
▸ VI to rub; **la roue frotte (contre le frein)** the wheel is rubbing (against the brake)
▸ VPR **se frotter 1 se f. les mains** to rub one's hands (together); *Fig* to rub one's hands; **se f. les yeux** to rub one's eyes; **se f. contre qch/qn** to rub (up) against sth/sb **2** *Fig* **se f. aux artistes** to rub shoulders with artists; **se f. au monde professionnel** to be in contact with the professional world; **des gens auxquels il vaut mieux ne pas se f.** people it's best to keep away from *or* not to get involved with; **ne vous y frottez pas!** don't get involved!, don't meddle!; *Fig* **qui s'y frotte s'y pique** if you meddle, you'll get your fingers burnt

frotteur, -euse [frɔtœr, -øz] N (*personne*) floor polisher
▸ NM (*de train électrique*) sliding contact, (collecting) shoe; *Aut* slipper

frotti-frotta [frɔtifrɔta] NM *Fam* **faire du f.** to rub up against each other

frottis [frɔti] NM **1** *Beaux-Arts* scumble **2** *Biol* (*pour examen au microscope*) smear; **f. vaginal** cervical smear

frottoir [frɔtwar] NM (*ustensile*) rubber; (*brosse*) scrubbing brush; (*de boîte d'allumettes*) friction strip; (*de dynamo*) brush

frou(-)frou, *pl* **frou(-)frous** [frufru] NM (*bruit*) (*d'une robe en soie, de feuilles*) rustle, rustling; (*vêtement féminin*) frill

froufroutant [frufrutɑ̃] ADJ frilly

froufrouter [frufrute] VI to rustle

froussard, -arde [frusar, -ard] *Fam* ADJ yellow, chicken
▸ N chicken, coward

frousse [frus] NF *Fam* fear, fright; **avoir la f.** to be scared, to have the wind up; **avoir la f. de faire qch** to be scared to do *or* of doing sth; **ça m'a donné** *ou* **foutu la f.** that scared me to death *or* put the wind up me

fructidor [fryktidɔr] NM *Hist* = twelfth month of the French Republican calendar (*August-September*)

fructifère [fryktifɛr] ADJ fruitbearing

fructification [fryktifikasjɔ̃] NF (*d'un arbre*) fruition, fructification; (*d'un investissement*) yield; *Fig* (*d'une idée, d'un projet*) fruition

fructifier [fryktifje] VI (*d'arbres*) to bear fruit, *Spéc* to fructify; *Fig* **ses placements commencent à f.** his investments are beginning to show *or* yield a profit; **il sait faire**

f. son argent he knows how to get a return on his money

fructose [fryktoz] NM fructose

fructueusement [fryktɥøzmɑ̃] ADV fruitfully, profitably

fructueux, -euse [fryktɥø, -øz] ADJ fruitful, profitable

frugal, -ale, -aux, -ales [frygal, -o] ADJ (*personne, repas*) frugal

frugalement [frygalmɑ̃] ADV frugally

frugalité [frygalite] NF frugality

frugivore [fryʒivɔr] ADJ (*animal*) fruit-eating
▸ N fruit-eater

fruit¹ [frɥi] NM fruit; **manger des fruits** to eat (some) fruit; **manger un f.** to eat some fruit *or* a piece of fruit; **producteur de fruits** fruit grower; **f. vert** unripe fruit; **le f. d'un mariage** the offspring of a marriage; **le f. de plusieurs années de travail** the fruit of several years' work; **porter des fruits** (*d'un arbre*) to bear fruit; *Fig* **porter ses fruits** (*d'une action, d'un investissement etc*) to bear fruit; **avec f.** to good purpose
▸▸ **fruits des bois,** *Suisse* petits fruits fruits of the forest; **fruits confits** crystallized fruit; *Culin, Rel* **f. défendu** forbidden fruit; **fruits déguisés** = dates, prunes etc stuffed with almond paste; **fruits de mer** seafood; **f. de la passion** passion fruit; **fruits rafraîchis** fruit salad soaked in alcohol; **fruits rouges** red berries and currants; *Fig* **f. sec** failure; **fruits secs** dried fruit

fruit² NM *Constr* (*d'un mur, contrefort etc*) batter

fruité [frɥite] ADJ fruity

fruiterie [frɥitri] NF (*magasin*) fruiterer's *or* greengrocer's shop, *Am* fruit store; (*local*) fruit storeroom

fruiticulteur, -trice [frɥitikyltœr, -tris] N fruit grower

fruitier, -ière [frɥitje, -jɛr] ADJ **arbre f.** fruit tree
▸ N fruit dealer, *Br* fruiterer, greengrocer
▸ NM **1** (*local*) fruit storeroom; (*étagère*) stand of fruit trays **2** (*verger*) orchard

frusques [frysk] NFPL *Fam* (*vêtements*) gear, togs, *Br* clobber

fruste [fryst] ADJ (*style, personne*) rough, unpolished; (*pièce, statue*) worn

frustrant [frystrɑ̃] ADJ frustrating

frustration [frystrasjɔ̃] N **1** *Psy* frustration **2** (*d'un légataire*) cheating, defrauding

frustré, -ée [frystre] ADJ frustrated
▸ N frustrated person; **c'est un f.** he's so frustrated

frustrer [frystre] VT **1** *Psy* to frustrate **2** (*priver*) **f. qn de qch** to deprive sb of sth; **vous l'avez frustré de sa victoire/réussite** you robbed *or* deprived him of his victory/success; **on m'a frustré de mes biens** I have been cheated out of *or* defrauded of my property

FS [ɛfɛs] *abrév* franc suisse

FSE [ɛfɛsə] NM (*abrév* Fonds social européen) ESF

FSM [ɛfɛsɛm] NM (*abrév* Forum social mondial) WSF

FTP [ɛftepe] NMPL (*abrév* Francs-tireurs et partisans) = French Communist resistance group in the Second World War

fuchsia [fyʃja] NM *Bot* fuchsia
▸ ADJ INV fuchsia

fucus [fykys] NM fucus, sea wrack

fuel [fjul] NM fuel oil

fufute [fyfyt] ADJ *Fam* **il n'est pas très f.** he's a bit thick

fugace [fygas] ADJ fleeting, transient; **impression f.** fleeting impression

fugacité [fygasite] NF *Litt* fleetingness, transience

fugitif, -ive [fyʒitif, -iv] ADJ **1** *(personne)* fugitive, runaway **2** *(fugace) (désir, émotion)* transitory, fleeting, ephemeral, short-lived; **ombre fugitive** fleeting shadow
  N fugitive, runaway

fugitivement [fyʒitivmɑ̃] ADV fleetingly

fugue [fyg] NF **1** *Mus* fugue **2 faire une f.** to run away

fuguer [fyge] VI *Fam* to run away

fugueur, -euse [fygœr, -øz] ADJ who runs away a lot
  N runaway

fuir [fɥir] *(prp* **fuyant;** *pp* **fui;** *pr ind* **je fuis, n. fuyons, ils fuient)** VI **1** *(s'enfuir)* to run away, to flee **(devant** from); **f. de son pays** to flee one's country; **faire f.** to put to flight; **bête à faire f.** as stupid as can be; **le temps fuit** time flies, time is slipping by; **f. devant les responsabilités** to shirk one's responsibilities; *Naut* **f. devant le vent** to scud *or* run before the wind; **il a le regard qui fuit** he has shifty eyes; **f. à toutes jambes** to run off at top speed *or* as fast as one can **2** *(de l'horizon)* to recede **3** *(d'un robinet, tonneau etc)* to leak; *(de gaz, d'eau)* to leak, to escape
  VT **1** *(éviter) (responsabilité, amis, journalistes)* to shun, to avoid; *(question)* to evade, to avoid; **f. sa famille** to shun one's family; *Litt* **f. le monde** to flee society; **le sommeil me fuit** I cannot sleep **2** *(abandonner)* to flee, to run away from; **f. son pays** to flee one's country
  VPR **se fuir** *(s'éviter)* to avoid each other

fuite [fɥit] NF **1** flight **(devant** from); **prendre la f.** to take flight; **être en f.** to be on the run; **mettre l'ennemi en f.** to put the enemy to flight; *Fam* **la f. des cerveaux** the brain drain; **la f. des capitaux** the flight of capital; **renversé par une voiture qui a pris la f.** run over by a hit-and-run driver; *Fig* **la f. en avant de la consommation** the headlong rush of consumerism; **la course aux armements est une f. en avant** the arms race is being blindly pursued by all governments; **à partir de là, c'était la f. en avant** from then on there was no turning back; **la seule solution possible était la f. en avant** the only possible solution was to keep on going, the only way out was forward
  2 *(de liquide, gaz, d'information)* leak; **f. de gaz** gas leak; **il y a eu des fuites en histoire** some of the history questions leaked out
  3 *(devant des difficultés, des problèmes)* evasion, avoidance
  4 la f. du temps the passage *or* passing of time
  5 *Beaux-Arts* **point de f.** vanishing point

fulgurant [fylgyrɑ̃] ADJ *(lumière)* flashing; *(attaque, changement)* lightning; *Méd (douleurs)* stabbing, searing; **une découverte fulgurante** a dazzling discovery; **une idée fulgurante** a sudden and brilliant idea; **lancer un regard f. à qn** to look daggers at sb; **elle a connu un succès f.** she was brilliantly successful; **une explication d'une clarté fulgurante** a brilliantly clear explanation

fulguration [fylgyrasjɔ̃] NF lightning; *Méd* fulguration

fulgurer [fylgyre] VI to flash

fuligineux, -euse [fyliʒinø, -øz] ADJ *(couleur)* smoky, sooty; *(ciel)* murky

fulmicoton [fylmikɔtɔ̃] NM guncotton

fulminant [fylminɑ̃] ADJ *(ton)* exceedingly angry, furious; *(poudre)* fulminating; *Spéc (douleur)* fulminant

fulminer [fylmine] VT *(accusations)* to thunder, to roar
  VI **f. contre qn/qch** to fulminate *or* inveigh against sb/sth

fumage¹ [fymaʒ] NM, **fumaison** [fymɛzɔ̃] NF *(d'une terre)* manuring, dressing, dunging

fumage² NM, **fumaison** NF *(de poisson, viande)* smoking, smoke-curing

fumant [fymɑ̃] ADJ **1** *(âtre, cendres)* smoking **2** *(soupe, cheval etc)* steaming; *Fam* **de colère** fuming **3** *Fam (remarquable)* terrific, sensational; **faire un coup f.** to pull off a masterstroke

fumasse [fymas] ADJ *Fam* fuming

fumé [fyme] ADJ **1** *(poisson, viande etc)* smoked, smoke-cured **2 verre f.** smoked glass; **verres fumés** dark lenses; *(lunettes)* dark glasses, sunglasses

fume-cigare [fymsigar] NM INV cigar holder

fume-cigarette [fymsigarɛt] NM INV cigarette holder

fumée [fyme] NF **1** *(de feu, cigarette etc)* smoke; **rideau de f.** smokescreen; **noir de f.** lampblack; **la f. (du tabac) vous gêne-t-elle?** do you mind my smoking?; *Fig* **partir** *ou* **s'en aller en f.** to go up in smoke; *Prov* **il n'y a pas de f. sans feu** there's no smoke without fire **2** *(de la soupe etc)* steam; *(du charbon de bois)* fumes; *(d'alcool)* vapours, *Am* vapors

fumer¹ [fyme] VT *(terre)* to manure, to dress, to dung

fumer² VI **1** *(d'un âtre, d'une lampe, d'un moteur)* to smoke **2** *(d'un fumeur)* to smoke; **défense de f.** no smoking; **f. comme un pompier** *ou* **un sapeur** to smoke like a chimney; **f. tranquillement** to have a quiet smoke; **il est allé en f. une dans la cour** he went for a smoke *or* to have a smoke in the yard **3** *(de la soupe etc)* to steam **4** *Fam (de colère)* to fume
  VT **1** *(poisson, viande)* to smoke(-cure) **2** *(pipe, tabac etc)* to smoke; **il fumait cigarette sur cigarette** he was chainsmoking **3** *Arg (battre)* to clobber, to thump; *(tuer)* to kill, *Br* to do in

> Il faut noter que le verbe anglais **to fume** est un faux ami. Il signifie **fulminer**.

fumerie [fymri] NF **f. d'opium** opium den

fumerolle [fymrɔl] NF *(de volcan)* smoke and gas

fumet [fymɛ] NM **1** *(de la nourriture qui cuit)* aroma, (pleasant) smell; *(du vin)* bouquet **2** *(à la chasse)* scent

fumeterre [fymtɛr] NF *Bot* fumitory

fumette [fymɛt] NF *Fam* getting stoned; **c'est un habitué de la f.** he gets stoned regularly; **il y a que la f. qui l'intéresse** all he's interested in is getting stoned

fumeur, -euse [fymœr, -øz] N smoker; **f. de pipe/cigares** pipe/cigar smoker; **f. d'opium** opium smoker; *Rail* **compartiment fumeurs/non fumeurs** smoking/non-smoking compartment, *Fam* smoker/non-smoker

fumeux, -euse [fymø, -øz] ADJ *(lampe)* smoky, smoking; *(ciel, idées, explications, projets)* hazy; **quel esprit f.!** what a woolly mind!

fumier [fymje] NM **1** *(engrais)* manure, dung; **fosse à f.** slurry pit **2** *(tas)* dunghill, manure heap **3** *Vulg (salaud)* bastard; **espèce de f.!** you bastard!; **le f.!, il m'a menti!** he lied to me, the bastard!

fumigation [fymigasjɔ̃] NF fumigation; *Méd* inhalation

fumigène [fymiʒɛn] NM *(en horticulture)*, *Mil* smoke-producing device
  ADJ *Mil* **grenade f.** smoke grenade

fumiger [fymiʒe] VT (**je fumigeai(s)**) to fumigate

fumiste [fymist] NM **1** *Fam (sur qui on ne peut compter)* shirker, *Br* layabout; **c'est un f.** he doesn't exactly kill himself working **2** *(installateur)* heating engineer **3** *Vieilli (farceur)* practical joker
  ADJ *Fam* unreliable, irresponsible

fumisterie [fymistəri] NF **1** *(métier)* heating engineering **2** *Fam (farce)* con, farce; **c'est une vaste f.** it's a huge con, it's an absolute farce

fumivore [fymivɔr] ADJ smoke-absorbing

fumoir [fymwar] NM smoking room; *(pour la viande, le poisson etc)* smokehouse

fumure [fymyr] NF *(de champ)* manuring, dressing, dunging

fun [fœn] *Fam* ADJ *(amusant, divertissant)* fun; **c'est pas très f.** it's not much fun
  NM fun; **faire qch pour le f.** to do sth for fun

funambule [fynɑ̃byl] N tightrope walker, *Spéc* funambulist

funambulesque [fynɑ̃bylɛsk] ADJ **1 l'art f.** the art of tightrope walking; **acrobatie f.** high-wire acrobatics **2** *Fig (idées, projet etc)* *(original)* fantastic, bizarre; *(casse-cou)* reckless

funboard [fœnbɔrd] NM funboard

funèbre [fynɛbr] ADJ **1** *(cérémonie)* funeral; **hymne** *ou* **chant f.** dirge; **marche f.** funeral *or* dead march **2** *(lugubre)* funereal, gloomy

funérailles [fyneraj] NFPL funeral; **f. nationales** state funeral

funéraire [fynerɛr] ADJ *(dépenses)* funeral; *(urne)* funeral, funerary; **pierre f.** tombstone, gravestone; **drap f.** pall

funérarium [fynerarjɔm] NM funeral home, *Br* funeral parlour, *Am* funeral parlor

funeste [fynɛst] ADJ **1** *Litt (accident)* deadly, fatal **2** *(erreur, conséquences)* fatal, disastrous, catastrophic; **influence f.** disastrous influence; **être f. à qch** to be fatal to sth **3** *Arch (triste)* funereal, gloomy

funiculaire [fynikylɛr] ADJ funicular
  NM funicular (railway)

funk [fœnk] ADJ INV, NM INV *Mus* funk

funky [fœnki] *Mus* ADJ INV funky
  NM INV funky music

fur [fyr] NM **au f. et à mesure** as one goes along, bit by bit; **au f. et à mesure, j'ai compris comment ça fonctionnait** I understood how it worked as I went along *or* bit by bit; **au f. et à mesure des besoins** as and when required, as needed; **au f. et à mesure de la progression des travaux** as work progresses; **au f. et à mesure de ses recherches** as he progressed with his research; **au f. et à mesure que tu en as besoin** as and when you need it; **je repasse mon linge au f. et à mesure que je le lave** I iron my clothes as soon as I've washed them

furax [fyraks] ADJ *Fam* livid, *Am* fit to be tied

furet [fyrɛ] NM **1** *(animal)* ferret; **chasse au f.** ferreting; **chasser au f.** to go ferreting; **jeu du f.** ≃ hunt-the-slipper **2** *Fig Arch* nosy parker

furetage [fyrtaʒ] NM **1** *(pour lapins)* ferreting **2** *Fig* prying, nosing around; *(dans l'armoire)* rummaging (about), ferreting (about)

fureter [fyrte] VI (**je furette; je furetterai**) **1** *(chasser)* to ferret, to go ferreting **2** *(chercher)* to pry, to nose around; **f. dans les armoires** to ferret (about) *or* rummage (about) in the cupboards

fureteur, -euse [fyrtœr, -øz] N **1** *(chasseur)* ferreter **2** *Fam Péj* nosy parker
  NM *Can Ordinat* browser
  ADJ prying, *Fam* nosy; **regard f.** inquisitive look

fureur [fyrœr] NF **1** *(colère)* fury, rage; **être en f.** to be in a rage *or* fury, to be furious; **tu vas le mettre en f.** you'll infuriate *or* enrage him, you'll make him furious; **se mettre dans une f. (noire)** to fly into a (towering) rage; **la f. des combats dans le Golfe** the battle raging in the Gulf; **la f. des flots** the fury of the waves **2** *(passion)* passion; **aimer qn/qch avec f.** to be passionately fond of sb/sth; **avoir la f. de bâtir** to be mad on building; **la f. du jeu** a passion for gambling; **faire f.** to be all the rage

furia [fyrja] NF *Fam (d'une foule)* frenzy; **ils n'ont pas pu résister à la f. bordelaise** they had no answer to the Bordeaux team's furious onslaught

furibard [fyribar] ADJ *Fam* livid, *Am* fit to be tied

furibond [fyribɔ̃] ADJ furious; **elle lui a lancé un regard f.** she glared at him

furie [fyri] NF **1** *(passion)* fury; **critiquer qn/se battre avec f.** to criticize sb/fight furiously; **applaudir/crier avec f.** to applaud/shout frantically; **la f. du jeu** a passion for gambling; **en f.** infuriated, enraged; **se mettre en f.** to fly into a rage **2** *Myth* **les Furies** the Furies; *Fig* **c'est une f.** she's a shrew; **comme une f.** like a wild thing

furieusement [fyrjøzmɑ̃] ADV **1** furiously **2** *Vieilli, Hum (très)* extremely, really; **on s'est f. amusé** we had a great time

furieux, -ieuse [fyrjø, -jøz] ADJ **1** *(en colère)* furious; **être f. contre qn** to be furious with sb; **elle est furieuse qu'on ne l'ait pas prévenue** she's furious that nobody told her; **il est f. contre lui-même** he's furious with himself; **être f. de qch** to be furious with *or* at sth; **je suis f. de constater que vous n'avez fait aucun effort** I'm furious to see that you've made no effort at all; **rendre qn f.** to enrage *or* infuriate sb; **taureau f.** mad *or* raging bull; **tempête furieuse** raging *or* howling storm; **il a un f. appétit** he has a tremendous appetite; **un f. désir de vivre** a tremendous desire to live; **pousser des cris f.** to shout furiously **2** *(forcené)* mad; **c'est un fou f.** he's a raving lunatic
▸ N **c'est un f.** he's a raving lunatic

furoncle [fyrɔ̃kl] NM *Méd* boil, *Spéc* furuncle

furonculose [fyrɔ̃kyloz] NF *Méd* furunculosis

furtif, -ive [fyrtif, -iv] ADJ furtive, stealthy

furtivement [fyrtivmɑ̃] ADV furtively, stealthily; **entrer/sortir f.** to steal in/out, to enter/leave furtively

fusain [fyzɛ̃] NM **1** *(arbre)* spindle tree **2** *Beaux-Arts (crayon)* charcoal (pencil); *(dessin)* charcoal (drawing)

fusant [fyzɑ̃] ADJ fusing; **obus f.** time shell

fuseau, -eaux [fyzo] NM **1** *Tex* spindle; *(pour dentelle)* bobbin; **f. de quenouille** distaff; **en f.** tapered, tapering; **jambes en f.** slender legs **2 f. horaire** time zone **3 fuseaux** *(pantalon)* ski pants; **la mode du f.** *ou* **des fuseaux revient** ski pants are coming back into fashion

fusée [fyze] NF **1** *(projectile)* rocket; **lancer une f.** to launch a rocket; **avion-f.** rocket-propelled aircraft; **il est parti comme une f.** he shot off like a rocket **2** *(de bombe etc)* fuse, *Am* fuze **3** *(d'arbre, d'axe)* spindle; *Aut* stub axle, hub carrier
▸▸ **f. air-air** air-to-air missile; **f. d'appoint** booster; **f. de détresse** distress rocket; **f. de direction** stub axle; **f. éclairante** flare; **f.-engin** missile; **f. à étages** multistage rocket; **f. à un étage** one-stage rocket; *Astronaut* **f. interplanétaire** space rocket; **f. percutante** percussion fuse; **f. à pétard** maroon; *Naut* **f. porte-amarre** life(-saving) rocket; **f. porteuse** carrier rocket; **f. de signalisation** signal rocket; **f. sonde** probe; **f. à temps** time fuse; **f. volante** sky rocket

fuselage [fyzlaʒ] NM *Aviat* fuselage

fuselé [fyzle] ADJ *(colonne, doigts)* tapering; *Aut* streamlined

fuseler [fyzle] VT (**je fuselle; je fusellerai**) to taper; *Aut* to streamline

fuser [fyze] VI **1** *(de cire chaude)* to run, to melt; *Fig* **des rires fusèrent de toutes parts** there were bursts of laughter from all sides, laughter erupted from all sides; **des cris/des remarques fusèrent de toutes parts** cries/comments were suddenly heard from all sides **2** *Chimie (de sel)* to crackle **3** *(de fusible)* to burn slowly

fusibilité [fyzibilite] NF fusibility

fusible [fyzibl] ADJ fusible
▸ NM *Élec* fuse, *Am* fuze; *(fil métallique)* fuse wire; **f. de sûreté** safety fuse, cut-out

fusiforme [fyzifɔrm] ADJ spindle-shaped

fusil [fyzi] NM **1** *(arme)* gun, rifle; *Fig* **changer son f. d'épaule** to change (one's) tack; **entendre un coup de f.** to hear a shot; **c'est un de nos meilleurs fusils** he's one of our best shots; **coup de f.** gunshot, rifle shot; *Fam (dans un hôtel)* overcharging, fleecing; *Fam* **c'est le coup de f., dans ce restaurant** the prices in this restaurant are extortionate; *Fam* **quel coup de f.!** what a rip-off! **2** *(d'un briquet à amadou)* steel; *(pour aiguiser)* (sharpening) steel
▸▸ **f. à air comprimé** air gun; **f. automatique** automatic gun *or* rifle; **f. à chargeur** magazine rifle; **f. de chasse** shotgun, sporting gun; **f. à deux coups** double-barrelled gun; **f. harpon** harpoon gun; **f. rayé** rifle

fusilier [fyzilje] N fusilier; **f. marin** marine

fusillade [fyzijad] NF *(tir)* fusillade, rifle fire

fusiller [fyzije] VT **1** *(par un peloton d'exécution)* to shoot; *Fig* **f. qn du regard** to look daggers at sb **2** *Fam Vieilli (abîmer)* to wreck, to ruin

fusil-mitrailleur, *pl* **fusils-mitrailleurs** NM light machinegun

fusion [fyzjɔ̃] NF **1** *(par la chaleur)* melting; *Spéc* fusion; *Métal* smelting; **point de f.** melting point; **fer en f.** molten iron **2** *Nucl* fusion **3** *Fig (d'idées, de philosophies etc)* merging, combining **4** *(de compagnies, partis politiques etc)* merger; **fusions-rachats** mergers and acquisitions; *Ordinat* **f. de fichiers** file merge

fusion-acquisition, *pl* **fusions-acquisitions** NF merger acquisition

fusionnement [fyzjɔnmɑ̃] NM *Com (de compagnies)* merger, amalgamation

fusionner [fyzjɔne] VI *(de sociétés, communes, partis politiques)* to merge, to amalgamate
▸ VT *(sociétés, communes, partis politiques)* to merge, to amalgamate; *Ordinat* to merge

fustigation [fystigasjɔ̃] NF *Litt* castigation

fustiger [fystiʒe] VT (**je fustigeai(s)**) *Arch (battre)* to thrash, to beat; *Fig Litt (critiquer)* to castigate

fût [fy] NM **1** *(de fusil)* stock; *(de scie, de raquette etc)* handle **2** *(de colonne, cheminée)* shaft; *(de candélabre)* stem; *(de rivet)* shank; *(d'arbre)* bole **3** *(baril)* cask, barrel; *(pour l'huile)* drum; **tirer de la bière du f.** to draw beer from the wood *or* cask *or* barrel

futaie [fyte] NF forest *(producing timber from full-grown trees)*; **arbre de haute f.** full-grown tree

futaille [fytaj] NF *(baril)* cask, barrel

futaine [fytɛn] NF *Tex* fustian

futal [fytal], **fute** [fyt] NM *Fam* trousers, *Am* pants

futé, -ée [fyte] ADJ cunning, wily, crafty
▸ N **c'est un petit f.** he's a cunning *or* crafty devil

futile [fytil] ADJ *(argument, occupation)* trivial, trifling; *(prétexte)* idle; *(personne)* frivolous

futilement [fytilmɑ̃] ADV frivolously

futilité [fytilite] NF triviality; **s'occuper à des futilités** to fritter away one's time; **une conversation pleine de futilités** a conversation full of trivialities

futon [fytɔ̃] NM futon

futur, -ure [fytyr] ADJ future; **la vie future** the life to come; **les générations futures** future *or* coming generations; **f. acheteur** prospective buyer; **un f. artiste** a budding artist; **f. client** prospective client; **mon f. emploi/appartement** my next job/flat; **mon f. mari** my future husband, my husband-to-be
▸ N *Hum* **mon f./ma future** my fiancé/fiancée, my intended
▸ NM **1** *(avenir)* future; **le f. m'inquiète** I am worried about the future; **quel f. pour l'Europe?** what will Europe's future be? **2** *Gram* future (tense); **au f.** in the future (tense) SEE GRAMMAR A50–2; B24; B31

futurisme [fytyrism] NM *Beaux-Arts, Archit* futurism

futuriste [fytyrist] *Beaux-Arts, Archit* ADJ futuristic
▸ N futurist

fuyant [fɥijɑ̃] ADJ **1** *(ligne, menton)* receding; *Beaux-Arts* **lignes fuyantes** perspective lines **2** *(personne, attitude)* evasive; *(yeux)* shifty

fuyard, -arde [fɥijar, -ard] ADJ *Arch* shy, timid
▸ N fugitive, runaway

FV NF *(abrév* **fréquence vocale)** VF

G, g [ʒe] NM **1** *(lettre)* G, g; **une force égale à plusieurs G** a force of several G **2** *Belg Fam (abbr GSM) (téléphone portable)* mobile, *Am* cell(phone)

g. 1 *abrév* **gauche 2** *abrév* **gramme(s)**

G7 [ʒeset] NM *(abrév* **Groupe des Sept)** G7

G8 [ʒeɥit] NM *(abrév* **Groupe des Huit)** G8

gabardine [gabardin] NF **1** *Tex* gabardine **2** *(imperméable)* gabardine (raincoat)

gabare [gabar] NF **1** *Naut* sailing barge; *(pour charger, décharger un navire)* lighter; *(chaland)* transport vessel, store ship, scow **2** *Pêche* dragnet

gabarit [gabari] NM **1** *Naut (d'un bateau)* model; *(d'une pièce de bateau)* mould, *Am* mold; *Constr (d'un bâtiment)* outline **2** *Tech* template, templet; *Ordinat* template; **g. d'assemblage** assembly jig, assembling gauge; **g. de mise en page** master page; **tour à g.** copying lathe **3** *Rail (sous un pont)* clearance; **g. de chargement** loading gauge; **g. d'écartement (des voies)** rail *or* track gauge **4** *Fam* **un grand/petit g.** a huge/tiny man, *f* woman; **des gens de son g.** people of his calibre

gabegie [gabʒi] NF *(mauvaise gestion)* mismanagement; *(désordre)* muddle, chaos

gabelle [gabɛl] NF *Hist* salt tax

gabelou [gablu] NM *Péj* customs officer

gabier [gabje] NM *Naut* topman; **g. breveté** able(-bodied) seaman

gable [gabl], **gâble** [gɑbl] NM *Archit* gable; *(charpente)* (triangular) window canopy

Gabon [gabɔ̃] NM Gabon

gabonais, -aise [gabɔnɛ, -ɛz] ADJ Gabonese

N **G.** Gabonese

gâchage [gɑʃaʒ] NM **1** *(du mortier, du plâtre)* mixing **2** *(gaspillage)* waste, wasting **3** **g. des prix** price undercutting

gâche¹ [gɑʃ] NF **1** *(pour le plâtre)* trowel **2** *(de pâtissier)* spatula

gâche² NF **1** *(d'une serrure)* (box) staple, keeper; *(d'une fenêtre)* (latch) catch; *(d'un pêne)* striking box *or* plate, strike box; *Aut* **g. de porte** striker plate **2** *Tech (pour cliquet)* notch

gâchée [gɑʃe] NF *Constr (de ciment etc)* batch

gâcher [gɑʃe] VT **1** *(gâter)* to spoil; *(bâcler) (travail)* to bungle, to botch, to mess up; *(gaspiller) (nourriture, pellicule etc)* to waste; *(fortune)* to waste, to squander; **il a gâché notre plaisir/la soirée** he spoiled our pleasure/the evening; **tu as tout gâché en lui racontant ça** you've spoilt *or* ruined everything by telling him that; **g. ses chances de succès** to spoil one's chances; **g. sa vie** to waste one's life; **g. le métier** to spoil it for others *(by undercutting them)*; **g. le marché** to spoil the trade **2** *(mélanger) (mortier, plâtre)* to mix; **g. la chaux** to slack lime

gâchette [gɑʃɛt, gaʃɛt] NF **1** *(d'une arme)* trigger; *Fam* **avoir la g. facile** to be trigger-happy **2** *(d'une serrure)* spring catch **3** *Tech* pawl **4** *Électron* gate

gâcheur, -euse [gɑʃœr, -øz] ADJ wasteful
N waster
NM *Constr* plasterer's mate

gâchis [gɑʃi] NM **1** *(mortier)* wet mortar **2** *(désordre)* mess; *(gaspillage)* waste; **vous avez fait un beau g. dans la cuisine!** you've made a right mess in the kitchen!; **je ne supporte pas le g.** I can't stand waste *or* wastefulness; **quel g.!** what a waste!

gadelle [gadɛl] NF *Can Bot* redcurrant

gadget [gadʒɛt] NM gadget, *Fam* gizmo; **des mesures-gadgets** gimmicky measures

gadgétisation [gadʒetizasjɔ̃] NF **la g. des voitures/ordinateurs** the adding of gadgets to cars/computers; **la g. de la société** the increasing use of gadgets in society

gadgétiser [gadʒetize] VT to add gadgets to; **g. la société** to increase the use of gadgets in society; **g. une voiture** to customize a car (with gadgets)

gadgétomanie [gadʒetɔmani] NF *Fam* mania for gadgets

gadin [gadɛ̃] NM *Fam* **prendre** *ou* **ramasser un g.** to fall flat on one's face, *Br* to come a cropper

gaditan, -ane [gaditɑ̃, -an] ADJ of *or* from Cadiz
N **G.** *(natif)* native of Cadiz; *(habitant)* inhabitant of Cadiz

gadoue [gadu] NF *(boue)* mud, slush; *(engrais)* sewage sludge

Gaël [gaɛl] NM Gael

gaélique [gaelik] ADJ, NM *Ling* Gaelic

gaffe [gaf] NF **1** *Fam (maladresse)* blunder, booboo; **faire une g.** to put one's foot in it, to make a blunder **2** *(perche)* boathook; *Pêche* gaff; *Arg* **avaler sa g.** to croak, *Br* to kick the bucket **3** *Fam* **faire g.** to pay attention; **fais g.!** look out!, watch it! **4** *Arg* prison warder, screw

gaffer¹ [gafe] VT **1** *(objet flottant etc)* to hook; *Pêche (saumon etc)* to gaff **2** *Fam* **gaffe un peu la nana!** get a look at that chick!
VI *Fam* **1** *(commettre une bévue)* to put one's foot in it, to make a blunder **2** *Fam (regarder)* to look; **gaffe un peu!** have a look!
VPR **se gaffer** *Suisse Fam* to watch out

gaffer² [gafœr] NM *TV, Cin* gaffer

gaffeur¹, **-euse** [gafœr, -øz] N *Fam* blunderer, blundering fool; **c'est un g.** he's always putting his foot in it

gaffeur² NM *Cin, TV* **g. grip** alligator clip

gag [gag] NM *Théâtre, Cin etc* gag; **tu es renvoyé – c'est un g.?** you're fired – you're kidding *or* joking?; **son pantalon a craqué au milieu de la réunion, le g.!** his trousers split during the meeting, what a scream!

gaga [gaga] *Fam* N old dodderer
ADJ gaga

gage [gaʒ] NM **1** *Com, Jur* security; *(chez le prêteur sur gages)* pledge; *Fig (garantie)* guarantee; **laisser qch en g.** to leave sth as security; **mettre qch en g.** to pawn sth; **mise en g.** pawning; **prêteur sur gages** pawnbroker; **ma montre est en g.** my watch is in pawn; **lettre de g.** debenture bond; *(pour hypothèque)* mortgage bond; *Jur* **g. mobilier** mortgage over assets, mortgage over property; **rester en g.** to remain as surety; **votre parole sera le meilleur des gages** your word will be the best guarantee
2 *(preuve)* token; **les ambassadeurs nous ont apporté des gages de bonne volonté** the ambassadors brought us tokens of goodwill *or* goodwill tokens; **g. d'amour** token of love, love token; **je t'offre ce livre en g. de notre amitié** I offer you this book as a token of our friendship
3 *(aux jeux)* forfeit
4 *(salaire)* **gages** wages, pay; *Péj* **être aux gages de qn** to be in the pay of sb; **tueur à gages** hired assassin *or* killer

gagé [gaʒe] ADJ *(montre, bijoux etc)* pawned; *Jur* pledged; *(emprunt)* secured; **meubles gagés** furniture under distraint; **recettes non gagées** unassigned *or* unpledged revenue

gager [gaʒe] VT *(je gageai(s); n. gageons)* **1** *Litt* **je gagerais que …** I would wager *or* bet that … **2** *(emprunt)* to guarantee, to secure; **g. qch** to deposit sth as security, to pledge sth as security

gageur [gaʒœr] NM *Jur* pledgor

gageure [gaʒyr] NF **1** *(action difficile)* difficult undertaking, challenge; **réussir la g. de faire qch** to succeed in the difficult task of doing sth **2** *(pari)* *Litt* wager, bet

gagiste [gaʒist] NM *Jur* pledgee

gagnant, -ante [gaɲɑ̃, -ɑ̃t] ADJ *(billet, numéro, combinaison etc)* winning; **jouer un cheval g.** to back a winner *or* a winning horse
N winner; **partir g.** *(à une course)* to start favourite *or* *Am* favorite; *Fig* to be bound to succeed; **il joue g.** he can't lose

gagne-pain [gaɲpɛ̃] NM INV livelihood; **trouver un g.** to find a job; **il n'aime pas ce qu'il fait, c'est juste un g.** he doesn't like what he does, it's just a way of earning a living *or* of making his bread and butter

gagne-petit [gaɲpəti] NM INV low wage earner; *Péj (personne qui n'a aucune ambition)* small-timer

GAGNER [gaɲe]

VT	
▪ to earn **1**	▪ to gain **2, 3** ▪ to win **3, 4** ▪ to win over **2** ▪ to get to **5** ▪ to spread to **6**
VI to win **1**	▪ to increase **3**

VT **1** *(comme rémunération)* to earn; **g. cinq**

mille euros par mois to earn five thousand euros a month; **g. gros** to earn *or* make big money; *(d'une société)* to make large profits; **g. sa vie** to earn one's living; **g. bien/mal sa vie** to earn *or* make/not to earn *or* make a good living; **g. de quoi vivre** to earn a living, to earn enough to live on; *Fam* **g. sa croûte** *ou* **son bifteck** to earn one's crust; *Fam* **g. des mille et des cents** to earn *or* make a fortune *or* a packet; **ce que je gagne suffit à nos besoins** I earn enough to keep us; *Fam* **il l'a bien gagné** he's earned it; *Fam* **j'ai gagné ma journée!** it's just not my day!

2 *(obtenir)* *(réputation, fortune, avantages)* to gain; *(se concilier)* *(partisan, mari)* to win over; *(profiter)* to gain (**à** by); **g. du temps** to save time; *(sur un délai serré)* to gain time; **g. des parts de marché** to gain share; **chercher à g. du temps** to play for time; **g. de l'espace** to save space; **j'ai gagné trois places dans la queue** I've moved up three places in the queue; **c'est autant de gagné, c'est toujours ça de gagné** that's something, anyway; **nous ne gagnerons rien à attendre** there is nothing to be gained *or* we'll gain nothing by waiting; **nous n'y avons gagné que des problèmes** all it brought us was problems; **et moi, qu'est-ce que j'y gagne?** and what do I get out of it?, what's in this for me?, and where do I come in?; **tu as tout à g.** you've everything to gain; **il n'y a rien à y g.** there's nothing to be gained by it, it won't get you anywhere

3 *(victoire)* to win, to gain; *(bataille, guerre)* to win; *Fig* **la partie n'est pas gagnée** we haven't won yet; **je vais essayer de faire le travail que vous me demandez mais ce n'est pas gagné!** I'll try to do the work you want me to do, but I can't promise anything!; **si elle dit oui, c'est gagné** if she says yes, then everything's OK *or* all right

4 *(jeu, course, prix, somme)* to win; **g. qn à une cause** to win sb over to a cause; **g. qn à une idée** to sell sb an idea; **g. la confiance/l'estime/l'amitié de qn** to win *or* gain sb's confidence/respect/friendship

5 *(atteindre)* *(ville, sortie, porte)* to reach, to get to; **g. le haut** to reach *or* get to the top; *Naut* **g. le port** to reach port, *Spéc* to fetch into port

6 *(de maladie, d'infection)* to spread to; **l'enflure a gagné la gorge** the swelling has spread to the throat; **le rire gagna l'assemblée tout entière** the laughter spread through the whole audience

7 *(rattraper)* **g. un navire** to gain on *or* overhaul a ship; **g. le devant** to forge ahead, to take the lead; **la nuit nous gagna** darkness overtook us; **le feu/l'épidémie gagne** the fire/the epidemic is spreading; **g. du terrain** to gain ground; *(sur la mer etc)* to reclaim land; **la mer gagne du terrain** the sea is encroaching on the land; **la faim nous gagnait** we were getting hungry; **le doute/la peur/la joie les gagne** doubt/fear/joy overcomes them *or* sweeps over them; **gagné par le sommeil/la peur/les larmes** overcome by sleep/by fear/with tears; *Naut* **g. le vent** to make *or* fetch to windward; **g. le vent d'une pointe** to weather a headland; **g. de l'avant** to forge ahead

VI 1 *(être vainqueur)* to win; **g. dans un fauteuil** to walk it, to win by a walkover; **g. haut la main** to win hands down

2 *(profiter)* **g. à qch/à faire qch** to benefit from sth/from doing sth; **tu gagnerais à partir** it would be in your (best) interest *or* to your advantage to leave; **il ne gagne pas à se montrer trop empressé envers elle** it isn't to his advantage to be too attentive to her, he won't get anything out of being too attentive to her; **g. à être connu** to improve with acquaintance; **j'ai gagné au change** I got the best of the bargain *or* deal

3 *(croître)* to increase; **g. en intensité** to increase or gain in intensity; **g. en profondeur/beauté** to increase in depth/beauty, to become deeper/more beautiful; **g. en vigueur** to become stronger; **le mécontentement gagne en force** there is increasing discontent

4 *Naut* **g. au vent** to make *or* fetch to windward

---

gagneur, -euse [gaɲœr, -øz] **N** winner; **avoir un tempérament** *ou* **un caractère de g.** to be a winner

NF *Arg* **gagneuse** *(prostituée)* pro

gai [gɛ, ge] **ADJ** *(chanson)* cheerful, merry, lively; *(personne)* cheerful, merry, lively, in good spirits; *(voix)* cheerful, cheery; *(chambre, couleur etc)* bright, cheerful; **g. comme un pinson** happy as a lark *or* a sandboy; **avoir un naturel g.** to be of a cheerful disposition; *Fam* **être un peu g.** *(ivre)* to be tipsy *or* tight; **avoir le vin g.** to get merry when one drinks; *Iron* **ça va être g.!** that will be nice!; *Iron* **il vérifie en permanence ce que je fais, c'est g.** he's continually checking what I'm doing, it's charming *or* really nice; **tout cela n'est pas très g.** it's all a bit depressing

gaiement [gɛmɑ̃, gemɑ̃] **ADV** cheerfully, merrily, gaily; *Iron* **allons-y g.!** let's get on with it!

gaieté [gete] **NF** cheerfulness, gaiety; **vous n'êtes pas/cela n'est pas d'une g. folle!** you're/it's hardly a bundle of fun *or* laughs!; **déborder de g.** to be bubbling over with high spirits; **retrouver sa g.** to recover one's spirits, to perk up, to buck up; **je ne le fais pas de g. de cœur** I don't enjoy doing it, it's not something I do willingly

gaillard, -arde [gajar, -ard] **ADJ 1** *(vigoureux)* *(personne)* strong, vigorous; **un petit vent g.** a good stiff breeze, a lively breeze; **frais et g.** hale and hearty; **il se sentait g.** he felt in good form; **mon grand-père est encore très g. pour son âge** my grandfather is still very sprightly for his age **2** *Vieilli (jovial)* *(humeur)* merry, lively, cheerful; *(grivois)* *(histoire, commentaire)* bawdy, *Am* off-color

N *(homme)* hearty *or* vigorous type; **un grand et solide g.** a great strapping man; **tu ne vas pas pleurer, un grand g. comme toi!** you're not going to cry, a big guy like you!; **toi mon g., tu ne perds rien pour attendre!** just you wait, chum *or* Br mate *or* Am fella; **c'est un sacré g.!** *(vigueur sexuelle)* he's quite a lad *or* stud!; **une grande gaillarde** a strapping woman; *(légère)* a bit of a girl; *Arch* **un vert g.** a rip

NM *Naut* **g. d'avant** forecastle; **g. d'arrière** poop; **haut de g.** deep-waisted

NF **gaillarde** *(danse)* galliard

gaillardement [gajardəmɑ̃] **ADV 1** *(gaiement)* cheerfully, good-humouredly **2** *(sans faiblir)* boldly, bravely, gallantly

gaillardise [gajardiz] **NF** **conter des gaillardises** to tell risqué *or* off-colour stories *or* jokes

gaillette [gajɛt] **NF** *(de charbon)* lump

gaîment [gɛmɑ̃, gemɑ̃] **ADV** = **gaiement**

gain [gɛ̃] **NM 1** *(d'une compétition, d'une guerre etc)* winning; *Jur* **avoir** *ou* **obtenir g. de cause** to win one's case; **donner g. de cause à qn** to decide in favour of sb; **il y a chances égales de g. et de perte** it's an even chance, there's a fifty-fifty chance

2 *(profit)* gain, profit; *(salaire)* earnings; *(au jeu)* winnings; **g. d'argent** financial gain; **avoir l'amour du g.** to love making money; **un g. de temps/place** a saving of time/space; **ça nous fait un sacré g. de temps/de place** that saves us an awful lot of time/space; **g. retiré d'une lecture/d'une expérience** benefit *or* profit acquired from reading/from an experience; **gains de productivité** productivity gains

3 *Élec etc* gain; **g. en courant** current gain; **g. en tension** voltage magnification; *Électron* **g. d'étage** stage gain; *Nucl* **g. de régénération** breeding gain

▸▸ *Compta* **g. latent** unrealized gain; *TV etc* **g. vidéo** video gain

gainage [gɛnaʒ] **NM** *Tech, Constr etc* casing, sheathing, sleeving; *Nucl (du combustible etc)* canning, casing, cladding

gaine [gɛn] **NF 1** *(cache)* case, casing; **g. en cuir** leather case; **g. métallique** metallic sheath *or* sleeve; **câble sous g.** sheathed cable; **g. souple** flexible sheath; *Nucl* **g. d'électrons/d'ions** electron/ion sheath **2** *Anat, Bot* sheath **3** *(sous-vêtement)* girdle, corset, foundation (garment) **4** *Géol* gangue, matrix **5** *Constr, Min etc* shaft, duct

▸▸ **g. d'aération** ventilation shaft

gaine-combinaison, *pl* **gaines-combinaisons** **NF** corselet

gaine-culotte, *pl* **gaines-culottes** **NF** panty girdle

gainer [gene] **VT** *(de cuir, de soie, de nylon etc)* to sheath, to cover (**de** in)

Gal *Mil (abrév* **Général***)* Gen

gal [gal] **NM** *Phys* gal

gala [gala] **NM** gala; **en habit** *ou* **tenue de g.** in gala dress, in full dress; *Fig* in one's best clothes, in one's Sunday best; **inutile de mettre ton habit de g.** don't bother putting on your best clothes *or* getting dressed up; **dîner en grand g.** to dine in state, to dine with great ceremony; **g. de bienfaisance** *ou* **de charité** charity gala

Galaad [galaad] **NM** *Littér* Galahad

galactique [galaktik] **ADJ** galactic

galactogène [galaktɔʒɛn] **ADJ, NM** *Physiol* galactagogue

galamment [galamɑ̃] **ADV** *(avec politesse)* politely, courteously; *(d'un homme)* gallantly, like a gentleman; *Litt (noblement)* honourably, *Am* honorably; **se tirer g. d'une affaire** to come out of an affair with honour *or Am* honor

galandage [galɑ̃daʒ] **NM** *Constr* brick partition

galant [galɑ̃] **ADJ** *(homme)* gallant, chivalrous, gentlemanly; *Arch (élégant)* gay, elegant; **homme g.** ladies' man; **vers galants** love poems; **femme galante** woman of loose morals; *Hum* **être en galante compagnie** to be in the company of the opposite sex; **rendez-vous g.** romantic rendezvous; **g. homme** gentleman, man of honour; **se conduire en g. homme** to behave like a gentleman

NM *Vieilli, Litt* gallant; *(coureur de jupons)* philanderer; **faire le g. auprès d'une dame** to court *or* pay court to a lady; *(flirter)* to flirt with a lady

galanterie [galɑ̃tri] **NF 1** *(envers les femmes)* gallantry, chivalry, courteousness; **dire des galanteries à qn** to pay sb compliments **2** *(intrigue)* love affair, intrigue

galantine [galɑ̃tin] **NF** *Culin* galantine

Galapagos [galapagos] **NFPL** **les (îles) G.** the Galapagos (Islands)

Galatée [galate] **N** *Myth* Galatea

Galatie [galasi] **NF** Galatia

galaxie [galaksi] **NF** *Astron* galaxy

galbe [galb] **NM** *(d'un meuble, d'un balustre etc)* curve; *(des jambes, hanches etc)* curve(s), contour; *(d'une voiture)* sweep, lines

galbé [galbe] **ADJ** *(jambe etc)* shapely

galber [galbe] **VT** *(vase, commode etc)* to give curves to; *Tech (feuille de métal)* to curve, to bend (lightly)

gale [gal] NF **1** *Méd* scabies; *Méd* **g. bédouine** prickly heat; *Fig* **je n'ai pas la g.!** I haven't got the plague! **2** *Fam (personne)* nasty person; *Fam* **être mauvais comme la g.** to be a nasty character *or Br* nasty piece of work **3** *Vét (de mouton)* scab; *(de chien, chat)* mange **4** *Bot* scab

galée [gale] NF *Typ* composing galley

galéjade [galeʒad] NF *Région* tall story; **débiter** *ou* **dire des galéjades à qn** to pull sb's leg

galéjer [galeʒe] VI *Région* to tell tall stories

galène [galɛn] NF *Minér* galena, sulphide of lead

galéopithèque [galeɔpitɛk] NM *Zool* flying lemur

galère [galɛr] NF **1** *Hist (navire)* galley; *Naut* **avirons en g.!** rest on your oars!; **être condamné aux galères** to be sentenced to the galleys **2** *(locutions) Fam* **après plusieurs mois de g.** after several months of hassle; **je me suis mis dans une g. pas possible** I got myself into an incredible mess *or* pickle; **c'est une vraie g.** it's a real pain *or* drag; **il lui arrive g. sur g.** it's just one disaster after another for him; **c'est la g. pour se garer le samedi** it's a (real) hassle *or* pain to find a parking place on Saturdays; **et vogue la g.!** let's see what happens!; *Hum* **mais que diable allait-il faire dans cette g.?** but what the hell was he doing mixed up in that?; **dans quelle galère est-ce que je me suis embarqué?** what have I let myself in for?
▸ ADJ *Fam (plans)* crazy, madcap; *(vacances)* hassle-filled; **c'est g. de trouver une cabine téléphonique dans cette ville** it's a (real) hassle to find a phone box in this town

galérer [galere] VI *Fam* to have a hard time (of it)

galerie [galri] NF **1** *(passage, salle)* gallery; *Can (véranda)* porch **2** *Théâtre* balcony, gallery; **première g.** dress circle; **seconde g.** upper circle; **la troisième g.** the gallery, *Fam* the gods; **tout ce qu'il fait, c'est pour épater la g.** everything he does is just showing off *or* playing to the gallery **3** *Min* gallery, level, drift; **g. d'avancement** heading **4** *Aut (sur toit)* roof rack, roof rail **5** *(sur meuble)* cornice **6** *(d'une digue)* run
▸▸ **g. d'art** art gallery; *Élec* **g. des câbles** cable tunnel; **g. marchande** shopping arcade; **g. de portraits** portrait gallery

galérien [galerjɛ̃] NM galley slave; **travailler comme un g.** to work like a (galley) slave; *Fam* **mener une vie de g.** to lead a dog's life

galeriste [galrist] N gallery owner

galet [galɛ] NM **1** *(caillou)* pebble; **galets** shingle, pebbles; **plage de galets** shingly *or* shingle beach **2** *Tech* roller, runner, wheel; **g. de roulement** travelling *or* running wheel; *Aut* **g. de direction** roller **3** *Pêche (d'un filet)* float **4** *Ordinat (dans souris)* roller

galetas [galta] NM *(sous les toits)* garret, attic; *Péj (taudis)* hovel

galetouse [galtuz] NF *Arg* mess tin, dixie

galette [galɛt] NF **1** *(crêpe de blé noir)* buckwheat pancake **2** *(biscuit rond sablé)* butter biscuit; *Naut* (ship's) biscuit; *Fam* **plat comme une g.** flat as a pancake **3** *Fam (argent)* dough, bread; **il a de la g.** he's loaded, he's rolling in it **4** *Fam (disque, CD)* disc
▸▸ **galette:g. des Rois** Twelfth Night cake; **g. de fioul** *ou* **de mazout** *ou* **de pétrole** patch of oil

galetteux, -euse [galɛtø, -øz] ADJ *Vieilli* loaded, rolling in it

galeux, -euse [galø, -øz] ADJ *(chien)* mangy; *(arbre)* scabby; *(pelouse)* patchy; *Méd* **plaie galeuse** sore caused by scabies; **murs g.** peeling *or* flaking walls; *Fig* **des mauvais garçons g.** some evil-looking types

galgal, -als [galgal] NM *Archéol* cairn, barrow

galibot [galibo] NM *Min* pit boy

Galice [galis] NF *(en Espagne)* Galicia

Galicie [galisi] NF *(en Pologne)* Galicia

galicien, -ienne [galisjɛ̃, -jɛn] ADJ Galician *(in Spain or Poland)*
▸ N **G.** Galician *(in Spain or in Poland)*

Galien [galjɛ̃] NM Galen

Galilée [galile] NF *Bible* Galilee

Galilée [2] N *Hist* Galileo

galiléen, -enne [galileɛ̃, -ɛn] ADJ Galilean
▸ N **G.** Galilean

galimatias [galimatjɑ] NM gibberish

galion [galjɔ̃] NM *Naut* galleon

galipette [galipɛt] NF *Fam* somersault; **faire des galipettes** to do somersaults; *(ébats amoureux)* to have it off, to bonk

galipot [galipo] NM **1** *Com (résine)* galipot, white resin **2** *Can* **courir le g.** to chase women

galle [gal] NF *Bot* gall; **g. de chêne** oak apple

Galles [gal] NF **le pays de G.** Wales; **Prince de G.** Prince of Wales; *Tex* Prince of Wales check

gallican, -ane [galikɑ̃, -an] ADJ, N *Rel* Gallican

gallicanisme [galikanism] NM *Rel* Gallicanism

gallicisme [galisism] NM Gallicism

gallinacé [galinase] *Orn* ADJ gallinaceous
▸ NMPL **gallinacés** Gallinaceae

gallique [1] [galik] ADJ *Hist* Gallic

gallique [2] ADJ *Chimie (acide)* gallic

gallium [galjɔm] NM *Chimie* gallium

gallois, -oise [galwa, -waz] ADJ Welsh
▸ NM *Ling* Welsh
▸ N **G.** Welshman; *f* Welshwoman; **les G.** the Welsh

gallomanie [galɔmani] NF Gallomania

gallon [galɔ̃] NM gallon

gallo-romain, *pl* gallo-romains [galorɔmɛ̃] ADJ Gallo-Roman

gallup [galœp] N **sondage g.** Gallup poll

galoche [galɔʃ] NF **1** *(chaussure)* clog *(with leather upper)*; *Fam* **menton en g.** jutting chin **2** *très Fam* **rouler une g. à qn** to French-kiss sb, *Br* to snog sb

galon [galɔ̃] NM **1** *Couture* braid; **g. de finition** upholstery binding **2** *Mil* **galons** *(de sous-officier)* stripes; *(d'officier)* bands, gold braid; *Naut (d'officier)* stripes; *(dans la marine marchande)* bands; **priver qn de ses galons** to reduce sb to the ranks; **gagner ses galons** to win *or* get *or* earn one's stripes; *Fam* **prendre du g.** to be promoted; *Fam* **arroser ses galons** to celebrate one's promotion

galonné [galɔne] NM *Arg (officier)* officer; *(sous-officier)* NCO

galonner [galɔne] VT *Couture* to (trim with) braid; **habit galonné d'or** gold-trimmed coat

galop [galo] NM *Équitation* gallop; **prendre le g.** to break into a gallop; **au g.** at a gallop; **grand g., triple g.** full gallop; **g. de manège** hand gallop; **petit g.** canter; **partir au (grand** *ou* **triple) g.** to gallop away; *Fig* **arriver au (grand** *ou* **triple) g.** to come like a shot; *Fig* **faire qch au g.** to do sth double-quick *or* at top speed; **allez, au travail! et au g.!** come on, to work!, and be quick about it! *or* and make it snappy!; *Scol* **g. d'essai** mock exam; *Fig* **ce séminaire ne constitue qu'un g. d'essai** this seminar is just a trial run

galopade [galɔpad] NF **1** *Équitation* gallop; **le bruit d'une g.** the sound of galloping **2** *(bruit)* stampede

galopant [galɔpɑ̃] ADJ *(chevaux etc)* galloping; *(inflation etc)* galloping, runaway; **démographie galopante** rapid population growth; **phtisie galopante** galloping con-

sumption; **le flot g. des vagues** the rushing waves

galoper [galɔpe] VI **1** *Équitation* to gallop; **se mettre à g.** to break into a gallop **2** *Fig (courir)* to charge along; *(çà et là)* to gallop *or* rush around; **g. après qn/qch** to run after sb/sth; **il galopa jusqu'au bourg** he charged off to the village; **les enfants galopaient dans le salon** the children were charging around in the living room
▸ VT *Rare (cheval)* to gallop

galopeur, -euse [galɔpœr, -øz] N *(cheval)* galloper

galopin [galɔpɛ̃] NM *Fam* urchin, ragamuffin; **espèce de petit g.!** you little rascal *or* devil!

galure [galyr], **galurin** [galyrɛ̃] NM *Fam* hat, *Br* titfer

galvanique [galvanik] ADJ *(cellule etc)* galvanic; **plaqué g.** electroplate; **dorure g.** electrogilding

galvanisation [galvanizasjɔ̃] NF *(métallisation)* galvanization, galvanizing; *Élec* galvanism

galvaniser [galvanize] VT **1** *(entreprise)* to give new life to, to inject new life into; *(foule, corps, organe)* to galvanize **2** *Métal* to galvanize; *(de zinc)* to zinc; *Élec* to (electro)plate; **tôle galvanisée** galvanized (sheet) iron

galvanisme [galvanism] NM *Méd* galvanism

galvano [galvano] NM *Typ Fam* electro

galvanomètre [galvanɔmɛtr] NM *Élec* galvanometer

galvanoplastie [galvanɔplasti] NF galvanoplasty, electrodeposition; *Ind* electroplating; *Typ* electrotyping

galvanoplastique [galvanɔplastik] ADJ galvanoplastic

galvanoscope [galvanɔskɔp] NM galvanoscope; *Tél* (linesman's) detector

galvanotype [galvanɔtip] NM *Typ* electrotype

galvanotypie [galvanɔtipi] NF *Typ* electrotyping

galvaudage [galvodaʒ] NM *(de talent, capacités)* prostituting

galvauder [galvode] VT *(nom, réputation)* to bring into disrepute; *(talents, dons)* to prostitute; **g. un mot** to overuse a word
▸ VPR **se galvauder** to damage one's reputation

gambade [gɑ̃bad] NF leap, gambol, caper; *Équitation* gambade; **gambades** capers; **faire des gambades** to leap about, to gambol, to caper

gambader [gɑ̃bade] VI to leap *or* frisk about, to gambol, to caper

gambas [gɑ̃bas] NFPL large prawns

gamberge [gɑ̃bɛrʒ] NF *Arg* **ton plan manque de g.** your plan shows a lack of thought; **il va falloir une bonne g. pour s'en sortir** we'll need to have a good think to get out of this one; **être en pleine g.** to be deep in thought; *(rêver)* to be daydreaming

gamberger [gɑ̃bɛrʒe] *Fam* VI to think deeply; **tu gamberges trop pour être heureux** you spend too much time thinking to be happy; **tu ne vas pas te mettre à g. pour si peu** you're not going to start brooding over such a small thing
▸ VT to work out, to figure out; *Fam* **c'est lui qui a gambergé le coup de la banque** he's the one who masterminded the bank job

gambette [1] [gɑ̃bɛt] NM *(oiseau)* redshank

gambette [2] NF *Arg (jambe)* pin, leg; **jouer** *ou* **tricoter des gambettes** to beat it, to leg it

Gambie [gɑ̃bi] NF **la G.** the Gambia

gambiller [gɑ̃bije] VI *Arg Vieilli (danser)* to jig about

gambit [gãbi] NM Échecs gambit; **(pion de) g.** gambit pawn

gamelle [gamɛl] NF **1** *(de soldat)* dixie, mess tin; *(d'ouvrier)* billy(can); *Hum (assiette)* plate; **préparer la g. du chien** to prepare the dog's food **2** *Fam* **(se) ramasser** *ou* **(se) prendre une g.** to fall flat on one's face **3** *très Fam (baiser)* French kiss; **rouler une g. à qn** to French-kiss sb, *Br* to snog sb

gamète [gamɛt] NM *Biol* gamete

gamétocide [gametɔsid] NM *Méd* gametocide

gamétogénèse [gametoʒenɛz] NF *Biol* gametogenesis

gamin, -ine [gamɛ̃, -in] N *(enfant)* kid, child; **une gamine de dix ans** a girl of ten; **ce n'est qu'un grand g.** *(d'un adulte)* he's just a big kid ADJ **1** *(espiègle)* lively, mischievous **2** **elle est encore gamine** she's still just a child **3** *(puéril)* childish

gaminerie [gaminri] NF *(acte)* childish prank *or* trick; *(comportement)* childishness, childish behaviour; **il a passé l'âge de ces gamineries** he's too old to behave so childishly *or* in such a childish way

gamma [gama] NM *(lettre), Phot* gamma; *Nucl* **rayons g.** gamma rays

gammaglobuline [gamaglɔbylin] NF *Biol* gamma globulin

gamme [gam] NF **1** *(de couleurs, de services, d'articles etc)* range; **une vaste g. de produits** a vast range of products; **g. de prix** price range; **toute la g. des sensations** the whole gamut *or* range of sensations; **produit bas/haut de g.** bottom-of-the-range *or* downmarket/top-of-the-range *or* up-market product; **milieu de g.** middle-of-the-range; **un ordinateur d'entrée de g.** an entry level computer **2** *Mus* scale; **g. montante/descendante** rising/falling scale; **faire ses gammes** to do *or* practise scales; *Fig* **faire ses gammes** to learn the ropes

▸▸*Aut* **g. moyenne** mid-range; *Aut* **g. de transmission** driving range

gammée [game] ADJ F **croix g.** swastika

gamopétale [gamopetal] ADJ *Bot* gamopetalous

ganache [ganaʃ] NF **1** *Culin* ganache, = filling for cakes made from chocolate, butter and cream **2** *Fam (imbécile)* fool, idiot; **vieille g.** old codger, *Am* geezer **3** *(d'un cheval)* lower jaw, jowl

Gand [gã] N Ghent

gang¹ [gãg] NM gang; **guerre des gangs** gang warfare <small>VOIR GRAMMAIRE A11</small>

gang² [gɛg] NF *Can (bande)* band, group; **une g. de bandits** a gang

ganga [gãga] NM pintailed (sand) grouse

Gange [gãʒ] NM **le G.** the Ganges

ganglion [gãglijɔ̃] NM **1** *Anat* ganglion; **g. nerveux** ganglion cell; **ganglions lymphatiques** lymph nodes *or* glands; **j'ai des ganglions** my glands are swollen, I have swollen glands **2** *Vét* spavin

ganglionnaire [gãglijɔnɛr] ADJ *Anat* ganglionic; **fièvre g.** glandular fever

gangrené [gãgrəne] ADJ **1** *Méd* gangrenous, gangrened **2** *Fig* corrupt

gangrène [gãgrɛn] NF **1** *Méd* gangrene; **avoir la g.** to have gangrene; **g. gazeuse** gas gangrene; **g. des os** necrosis **2** *Fig* canker

gangrener [gãgrəne] (**il gangrène; il gangrènera**) VT **1** *Méd* to gangrene **2** *Fig* to corrupt
  VPR **se gangrener 1** *Méd* to become *or* go gangrenous **2** *Fig* to become corrupt

gangreneux, -euse [gãgrənø, -øz] ADJ *Méd* gangrenous

gangster [gãgstɛr] NM gangster

gangstérisme [gãgsterism] NM gangsterism

gangue [gãg] NF *(de pierre précieuse, de minerai)* gang(ue), matrix; *Fig (couche) (de boue, de glace etc)* layer; *Fig* **il n'a jamais pu sortir de la g. de son éducation/de la religion** he was never able to free himself from the straitjacket of his education/of religion

ganse [gãs] NF *(cordon)* braid, (plaited) cord, edging, piping

gansé [gãse] ADJ *(vêtement)* braided

ganser [gãse] VT *(vêtement)* to braid, to trim

gant [gã] NM *(de boxe)* *(armure)* gauntlet; **mettre ses gants** to put one's gloves on; **gants en daim/tissu** suede/fabric gloves; **gants fourrés** lined gloves; **gants de caoutchouc** rubber gloves; *Fig* **cela vous va comme un g.** *(de vêtement)* it fits you like a glove; *(de couleur)* it suits you down to the ground *or* to a T; **ce métier lui va comme un g.** the job suits her down to the ground, the job is tailor-made for her; *Fig* **il faut prendre ou mettre des gants pour l'approcher** *ou* **avec lui** you have to handle him with kid gloves (on); **tu as intérêt à prendre** *ou* **mettre des gants pour le lui dire** you'd do well to tell him gently; **jeter le g. à qn** to throw down the gauntlet to sb; **relever le g.** to take up the gauntlet, to accept the challenge; *Fig* **souple comme un g.** easygoing

▸▸**g. de boxe** boxing glove; **g. de crin** massage glove; **g. de Neptune** glove sponge; **g. de toilette** ≃ facecloth, (face) flannel, *Am* washcloth

gantelé [gãtle] ADJ gauntleted; **la main gantelée** the mailed fist

gantelet [gãtle] NM gauntlet

ganter [gãte] VT to glove
  VI **g. du sept** to take a (size) seven in gloves
  VPR **se ganter** to put one's gloves on

ganterie [gãtri] NF **1** *(industrie)* glove-making; *(commerce)* glove trade **2** *(fabrique)* glove factory; *(magasin)* glove shop; *(rayon)* glove counter *or* department

gantier, -ière [gãtje, -jer] N glover

gantois, -oise [gãtwa, -waz] ADJ of/from Ghent
  N **G.** *(natif)* native of Ghent; *(habitant)* inhabitant of Ghent

gapette [gapɛt] NF *Fam* (flat) cap

garage [garaʒ] NM **1** *(de voiture)* garage; **g. à plusieurs étages** multi-storey car park, *Am* tiered parking lot; **g. de** *ou* **à bicyclettes** bicycle *or* bike shed; **g. de canots** boathouse, boat shed; **g. d'autobus** bus depot; **g. d'avions** (aircraft) hangar; *Rail* **g. de machines** engine shed; **j'ai mis la voiture au g.** I've put the car in the garage; *Can* **vente de g.** garage sale **2** *(atelier)* garage; **ma voiture est au g. jusqu'à la semaine prochaine** my car is at the garage until next week **3** *Rail* shunting, sidetracking

garagiste [garaʒist] NM *Aut (propriétaire)* garage owner; *(mécanicien)* garage mechanic; **j'emmène la voiture chez le g.** I'm taking the car to the garage

garance [garãs] NF **1** *Bot* madder(wort); *Fam* **petite g., g. de chien** squinancy wort **2** *(teinture)* madder (dye)
  ADJ INV madder

garant, -ante [garã, -ãt] N guarantor; **se rendre** *ou* **se porter g. de qn** to answer for sb; *(devant la justice)* to go bail for sb; *(à la banque)* to stand guarantor for sb; **g. solidaire** joint and several guarantor; **tout sera fini en temps voulu, je m'en porte g.** everything will be finished on time, I can vouch for *or* guarantee it; **ça va marcher, j'en suis garante** it will work, I give you my word; **être g. de ses faits** to be answerable *or* accountable for one's actions; **les pays seront ga-**

rants du respect de l'accord the countries will be guarantors of the agreement

garantie [garãti] NF **1** *(précaution)* guarantee, safeguard (**contre** against); *(gage)* guarantee; **prendre des garanties contre le vol/les risques d'incendie** to take precautions against theft/fire risk

2 *(de l'exécution d'un contrat)* guarantee, pledge; *(d'un paiement)* security, guaranty; **fonds déposés** *ou* **détenus en g.** funds lodged *or* held as security for sb; **elle m'a donné toutes les garanties que...** she gave me every guarantee that ...

3 *Com (de qualité etc)* guarantee, warranty; **vendu avec g.** sold with a guarantee; **la voiture est encore sous g.** the car is still under guarantee; **il va essayer, mais c'est sans g.** he'll try, but there's no guarantee (that he'll succeed); **lettre de g. d'indemnité** letter of indemnity

4 *Fin* underwriting; **syndicat de g.** underwriters' syndicate

▸▸*Fin* **g. accessoire** collateral security; **g. bancaire** bank guarantee; *Fin* **g. de bonne exécution** *ou* **de bonne fin** performance bond; **g. contractuelle** contractual guarantee; **g. conventionnelle** contractual cover; *Bourse* **g. de cours** hedging; *Com* **g. de crédit acheteur** buyer credit guarantee; **g. de crédit à l'exportation** export credit guarantee; **g. d'exécution** contract bond; *Com* **g. illimitée** unlimited warranty; *Com* **g. légale** legal guarantee; *Com* **g. limitée** limited warranty; *Fin* **g. offre** bid bond; *Jur* **g. parlementaire** *(d'un député)* parliamentary privilege; *Com* **g. pièces et main d'œuvre** parts and labour warranty; *Com* **g. prolongée** extended warranty; *Com* **g. de remboursement** money-back guarantee; *Com* **g. retour atelier** return-to-base warranty *or* guarantee; *Com* **g. sur site** on-site warranty *or* guarantee; *Com* **g. totale** full warranty

garantir [garãtir] VT **1** *(dette, montre etc)* to guarantee; **créance garantie** secured debt; **pendule garantie (pour) deux ans** clock guaranteed for two years; **nous garantissons un délai de livraison d'une semaine** we guarantee delivery within seven days; **g. un fait** to vouch for a fact; **je vous en garantis le succès** I guarantee (you) success, I guarantee that you'll be successful; **je vous garantis qu'il viendra** I guarantee that he'll come; **je te garantis que je l'ai aperçu dans la foule** I can vouch for the fact that I spotted him in the crowd; **je peux te g. qu'il ne reviendra pas** I can guarantee you he won't come back, he won't come back, I warrant you; **elle m'a garanti qu'elle serait à l'heure** she gave me a guarantee that she'd be on time; **je te le garantis** I can vouch for it

2 *Fin (émission d'actions etc)* to underwrite; **g. un emprunt** to secure a loan

3 *(protéger)* to protect (**de** against, from); **ce double vitrage va vous g. du froid** this double-glazing will protect *or* shield you from the cold

4 *Jur* **g. qn contre qch** to indemnify sb from *or* against sth; **son assurance le garantit contre le vol** his insurance covers him against theft
  VPR **se garantir se g. contre le froid/le vent** to protect oneself from the cold/the wind

garce [gars] NF **1** *Fam Péj* bitch, cow; **g. de vie!** what a bitch of a life! **2** *Vieilli (prostituée)* whore, tart

garçon [garsɔ̃] NM **1** *(enfant mâle)* boy; **école de garçons** boys' school; **petit g.** small *or* little boy; **se sentir un petit g. à côté de qn** to feel like a child beside sb, to feel dwarfed by sb; **tu es un grand g. maintenant** you're a big boy now

2 *(fils)* boy, son

3 *(jeune homme)* young man; **un g. d'une**

vingtaine d'années a young man of about twenty; **un bon** *ou* **brave g.** a good lad; **un beau** *ou* **joli g.** a handsome young man; **il est assez beau g.** he's quite a good-looking *or* handsome young man; **un mauvais g.** a bad sort

  4 *(serveur)* waiter

  5 *Vieilli (célibataire)* bachelor; **il est encore g.** he's still single *or* still a bachelor; **vieux g.** confirmed bachelor; **des habitudes de vieux g.** bachelor habits *or* ways

  ▸▸ **g. d'ascenseur** liftboy, lift attendant, *Am* elevator operator; **g. boucher** butcher's boy; **g. de bureau** office boy; *Naut* **g. de cabine** (cabin) steward; **g. de café** *ou* **de restaurant** waiter; **g. coiffeur** hairdresser's assistant; **g. de courses** errand *or* message boy; **g. d'écurie** groom; **g. d'étage** floor waiter; **g. de ferme** farm hand; **g. d'honneur** best man; **g. manqué** tomboy; **g. de pont** deck steward; **g. de recette** bank messenger

garçonne [garsɔn] NF **1** **être coiffée à la g.** *(d'une femme)* to have an urchin cut; **style/vêtements à la g.** boyish style/clothes **2** *Vieilli* bachelor girl

garçonnet [garsɔnɛ] NM *(petit garçon)* little boy; *Com* **taille g.** small boy's size

garçonnier, -ière [garsɔnje, -jɛr] ADJ boyish

garçonnière [garsɔnjɛr] NF *Vieilli* bachelor flat *or Am* apartment

GARDE¹ [gard]

---

care **1** ▪ guarding **2** ▪ guard **3, 5, 6** ▪ to watch out *(prendre garde)* **3**

NF **1** *(protection)* *(d'une personne, chose)* care; **confier qch/qn à la g. de qn, confier la g. de qch/qn à qn** to entrust sb with (the care of); **c'est son oncle qui en a la g.** he's in the care of his uncle; **être sous bonne g.** to be in safekeeping; **avoir qch en g.** to have charge of sth; **que Dieu nous ait en g.** may God protect us; **je vous laisse les enfants en g.** I'm leaving the children in your care *or* safekeeping *or* charge; **droit de g.** (right of) custody

  2 *(surveillance)* *(d'une frontière, d'une machine etc)* guarding; **soldat de g. à la porte** soldier on guard at the door; **être de g.** to be on guard *or Naut* on duty; **monter la g.** to mount guard; **la police assurera la g. du tribunal** the police will guard the court, the court will be under police guard; **à la g.! guard turn out!; **assurer la g. de nuit** to be on night call *or* duty; *Mil* **poste de g.** guardroom; **chien de g.** guard dog, watchdog; **sentinelle de g.** duty sentry; **médecin de g.** doctor on duty; **pharmacie de g.** emergency *or* duty chemist

  3 *(méfiance)* **mettre qn en g. contre qch/qn** to put sb on his guard against sth/sb, to warn sb against sth/sb; **être** *ou* **se tenir sur ses gardes** to be on one's guard; **prendre g. à qn/qch** to watch out for sb/sth, to beware of sb/sth; **prenez g. aux orties!** mind *or* watch the nettles!; **prenez g.!** watch out!, look out!; *(menace)* watch out!

  4 *(attention)* **prendre g. à qch/qn** to attend to *or* pay attention to sth/sb; **un fait auquel on n'a pas pris g.** a fact that has been left out of consideration; **faire qch sans y prendre g.** to do sth without realizing it; **je n'y ai pas pris g.** I didn't notice anything; **prendre g. que ... (ne)** + *sub* to be careful *or* to take care that ...; **prenez g. qu'il (ne) vous voie** be careful *or* take care (that) he doesn't see you; **prendre g. à** *ou* **de ne pas faire qch** to be careful *or* take care not to do sth; **prenez g. à** *ou* **de ne pas vous perdre** mind you don't get lost, be careful *or* take care not to get lost; *Vieilli* **prendre g. de faire qch** to be careful *or* take care to do

sth; **prenez g. de tomber** mind you don't fall

  5 *(groupe de soldats)* **le corps de g., la g.** the guard; **relever la g.** to change the guard; **la g. à cheval** the Horseguards; **la g. à pied** the Footguards

  6 *Boxe, Escrime (position d'attente)* guard; **se mettre en g.** to take one's guard, to square up; *Escrime* **en g.!** en garde!; *Boxe, Fig* **baisser sa g.** to lower *or* drop one's guard

  7 *Aut* **g. au sol** ground clearance

  8 *Tech (partie d'une épée)* hilt; **gardes** *(d'une serrure)* wards

  9 *Cartes* covering card; **avoir une g. à cœur** to have a covering card in hearts

  ▸▸ *Fin* **g. en dépôt de titres** safe custody; *Mil* **g. descendante** old guard; *Mil* **g. du drapeau** colour *or Am* color guard; **g. d'enfants** child-minding; *Jur* **g. des enfants** *(après un divorce)* custody of the children; **g. d'honneur** guard of honour *or Am* honor; *Hist* **la G. impériale** the Imperial Guard *(of Napoleon)*; **la G. mobile** = the security police; *Mil* **g. montante** new *or* relieving guard; **la G. républicaine** the Republican Guard *(of Paris)*; *Jur* **g. à vue** police custody; **il a été mis/est resté en g. à vue** he was put/was kept in police custody

---

garde² NM **1** *(sentinelle)* guard **2** *(soldat d'une garde)* guardsman

NF *(pour les malades)* nurse; *(pour les enfants)* nanny

  ▸▸ **G. des Archives** *Br* ≃ Master of the Rolls; **g. champêtre** rural policeman; **g. du corps** bodyguard; *Mil* **gardes du corps** lifeguards; **g. forestier** forester, forest warden, *Am* ranger; **g. mobile** = member of the security police; **g. de nuit** *(pour un malade)* night nurse *(privately employed)*; *Mil* night watchman; *Hist, Admin* **G. des Sceaux** = Minister of Justice

gardé [garde] ADJ **1** *Cartes* **roi g.** guarded king; **dame gardée** guarded queen **2** **toute(s) proportion(s) gardée(s)** all things considered, making all due allowance

garde-à-vous NM INV *Mil* (position of) attention; **se mettre** *ou* **être** *ou* **se tenir au g.** to stand to attention; **au g.!** at attention; **g.!** attention!

garde-barrière,   *pl*   **gardes-barrière(s)** [gard(ə)barjɛr] N level-crossing, *Am* grade-crossing keeper

  NF *Ordinat* firewall

garde-boue [gardəbu] NM INV *(d'une bicyclette etc)* mudguard

garde-chasse, *pl* **gardes-chasse(s)** [gardəʃas] NM gamekeeper

garde-chiourme,   *pl*   **garde(s)-chiourme(s)** [gardəʃjurm] NM *Hist (de galériens)* warder; *Fig (personne autoritaire et brutale)* martinet, tyrant

garde-corps [gardəkɔr] NM INV *(mur)* parapet, balustrade; *Naut (corde)* guard rope; *Naut* **g. arrière** stern rail

garde-côte, *pl* **garde-côte(s)** [gardəkot] NM *(bateau)* coastguard vessel; *Vieilli (soldat)* coastguard

garde-feu [gardəfø] NM INV **1** fireguard **2** *Can (personne)* forest warden

garde-fou, *pl* **garde-fous** [gardəfu] NM *(mur)* parapet, balustrade; *(en fer) (d'un pont etc)* railing, guardrail; *Fig* safeguard

garde-frein, *pl* **gardes-frein(s)** [gardəfrɛ̃] NM *Rail* brakesman, *Am* brakeman

garde-frontière, *pl* **gardes-frontière(s)** [gardəfrɔ̃tjɛr] NM border guard

garde-ligne, *pl* **gardes-ligne(s)** [gard(ə)liɲ] NM *Rail* track watchman

garde-magasin, *pl* **gardes-magasin(s)** [gardəmagazɛ̃] NM warehouseman; *Mil* quartermaster

---

garde-malade,   *pl*   **gardes-malade(s)** [gard(ə)malad] N nurse

garde-manger [gardəmɑ̃ʒe] NM INV meat safe

garde-meuble,   *pl*   **garde-meuble(s)** [gardəmœbl] NM furniture repository, warehouse; **mettre une table au g.** to put a table into storage *or* store

gardénal® [gardenal] NM *Méd* ≃ Luminal®

gardénia [gardenja] NM gardenia

garde-pêche, *pl* **gardes-pêche** [gardəpɛʃ] NM *(personne)* water bailiff, *Am* fish warden NM INV *(bateau)* fisheries protection vessel

garde-place, *pl* **garde-place(s)** [gardəplas] NM *Rail* reservation ticket holder; *(ticket)* reservation ticket

garde-port, *pl* **gardes-port(s)** [gardəpɔr] NM wharfmaster *(on river)*

GARDER [garde]

VT to look after **1** ▪ to guard **1** ▪ to protect **2** ▪ to save **2, 6** ▪ to keep **3, 4, 6, 7** ▪ to stay in **5**
VPR to beware of *(se garder de)* **1** ▪ to take care not to do *(se garder de faire)* **2** ▪ to keep **4, 5**

VT **1** *(surveiller)* *(maison, boutique, sac, enfants)* to look after, to mind; *(prisonnier)* to guard, to watch over; **g. un troupeau** to tend a flock; *Fam* **nous n'avons pas gardé les cochons ensemble!** don't take liberties!; **comment peut-il me parler ainsi, nous n'avons pas gardé les cochons ensemble!** how can he talk to me like that, what a liberty!; *Jur* **g. qn à vue** to keep *or* hold sb in custody

  2 *(protéger)* to protect **(de** from); **si au moins cela pouvait te g. de faire des bêtises** if that could at least stop you (from) acting stupidly; **que Dieu nous garde de la souffrance!** may God protect *or* save *or* deliver us from suffering!

  3 *(conserver)* to keep; **g. un vêtement (sur soi)** to keep a garment on; **g. qn à dîner/pour le week-end** to get sb to stay for dinner/for the weekend; **g. qn en otage** to keep *or* hold sb hostage; **par cette chaleur il vaut mieux g. le lait au réfrigérateur** it's better to keep the milk in the fridge in this heat; **g. une pièce intacte** to keep a room as it was left *or* in its original state; *Journ* **g. la Une** to hold the front page

  4 *(continuer d'avoir)* to keep; *(somme d'argent)* to keep, to put by; **g. ses illusions/son innocence** to keep one's illusions/innocence; **g. son sang-froid** to keep cool (and collected); **g. rancune à qn** to harbour *or Am* to harbor resentment against sb, to bear a grudge against sb; **g. les yeux fermés** to keep one's eyes closed; **g. le sourire** to keep (on) smiling; **g. son sérieux** to keep a straight face; **g. la ligne** to keep *or* maintain one's figure; **je garde un bon/mauvais souvenir de mon séjour en Italie** I have (kept) a good/bad memory of my stay in Italy

  5 *(rester dans)* **g. la chambre** to keep to *or* stay in one's room; **être obligé de g. le lit** to have to stay in bed, to be laid up

  6 *(réserver)* to keep, to save; **garde-moi une place à côté de toi!** save *or* keep me a place next to you!; **je vous ai gardé du café** I've kept *or* saved you some coffee; *Fig* **g. une dent contre qn, g. un chien de sa chienne à qn** to hold a grudge against sb, to have it in for sb; *Fig* **g. une poire pour la soif** to keep something for a rainy day; *Fig* **g. qch pour la bonne bouche** to save sth up as a treat; **g. le meilleur pour la fin** to save *or* keep the best till last

  7 *(respecter)* **g. ses distances/son rang** to keep one's distance/one's rank; **g. un secret**

to keep a secret; **garde ça pour toi** *(je ne veux pas qu'on l'apprenne)* keep that to yourself

VPR se garder 1 *(se méfier de)* **se g. de qn/ qch** to beware of sb/sth

2 *(s'abstenir de)* **se g. de faire qch** to take care *or* be careful not to do sth; **gardez-vous (bien) de le perdre** mind you don't lose it!, take care *or* be careful not to lose it!; **je m'en garderai bien!** there's no chance of me doing that!, I'll do no such thing!, *Fam* no fear!

3 *Cartes* **se g. à trèfle** to keep a covering card in clubs

4 *Fam (conserver)* **tes réflexions, tu peux te les g.!** you can keep your opinions(s) *or* thoughts *or* comments to yourself!; **ses amis/ses soirées, elle peut se les g.!** she can keep *or* stick her friends/parties!

5 *(se conserver) (denrées)* to keep; **viande qui ne se garde pas bien** meat that does not keep well

---

garderie [gard(ə)ri] NF **1** *(pour enfants en bas âge)* day nursery, *Am* daycare center; *(dans magasin, université etc)* crèche, *Am* baby-sitting service; *(le soir, après l'école)* child-minding service **2** *(de garde forestier)* beat, domain

garde-rivière, *pl* **gardes-rivière(s)** [gard(ə)rivjer] NM river policeman

garde-robe, *pl* **garde-robes** [gard(ə)rɔb] NF wardrobe; **renouveler sa g.** to renew *or* replenish one's wardrobe

gardeur, -euse [gardœr, -øz] N *(d'animaux)* keeper; **g. de cochons** pig keeper, *Vieilli* swineherd; **g. de vaches** cowherd; **g. de moutons** shepherd

garde-voie, *pl* **gardes-voie** [gard(ə)vwa] NM *Rail* track watchman

gardian [gardjɑ̃] NM *(en Camargue)* herdsman

gardien, -ienne [gardjɛ̃, -jɛn] N *(concierge)* caretaker, *Am* janitor; *(de musée, de parking)* attendant; *Fig (de libertés, traditions etc)* guardian; **g. des intérêts publics** guardian *or* protector of the public interest; **se poser en g. de l'ordre** to set oneself up as a guardian *or* an upholder of public order

▸▸ *Sport* **g. (de but)** goalkeeper; **g. d'immeuble** caretaker, porter, *Am* janitor; **g. de nuit** night watchman; **g. de la paix** policeman; **g. de phare** lighthouse keeper; **g. de prison** prison warder *or Am* guard

gardiennage [gardjena3] NM *(de ponts)* guarding; *(d'un bâtiment)* caretaking; *(d'un port)* security; **société de g.** security firm

gardon [gardɔ̃] NM roach; *Fig* **frais comme un g.** fresh as a daisy, bright-eyed and bushy-tailed

gare¹ [gar] NF *Rail* (railway *or Am* railroad) station, train station; **(colis à prendre) en g.** *(parcel)* to be (left till) called for; **chef de g.** stationmaster, station manager; **g. d'arrivée/de départ** station of arrival/departure; **quelle est la g. d'arrivée à Londres?** what station does the train arrive at in London?; **entrer** *ou* **arriver en g.** *(d'un train)* to enter in *or* come into the station; **quai numéro 3, le train entre en g.** the train is now approaching platform 3; **café/hôtel de la g.** station café/hotel

▸▸ **g. aérienne** air terminal; *Naut* **g. (fluviale)** dock; **g. de fret** cargo terminal; **g. de marchandises** goods *or* freight station; **g. maritime** harbour *or Am* harbor station; **g. routière** bus *or* coach station, bus depot; **g. routière (de marchandises)** road haulage depot; **g. de triage** marshalling yard; **g. de voyageurs** passenger station

gare² INT **1** *(menace)* **g. à toi si on l'apprend** woe betide you if anyone finds out; *Fam* **si je te reprends à voler du gâteau, g. à tes fes-**

---

ses! if I catch you stealing cake again, you've had it *or Br* you're for it! **2** *(attention)* **g. à la casse!** mind you don't break it!; **g. à la peinture!** mind the paint!; *Vieilli* **g. les coups de fusil des chasseurs!** watch out *or* mind out for the hunters and their guns; **sans crier g.** without warning

garenne [garɛn] NF **1** *(rabbit)* warren; **lapin de g.** wild rabbit **2** *(réserve)* fishing preserve

garer [gare] VT *(voiture)* to park; *(train)* to shunt on to a siding; *(bateau)* to dock; **g. un avion** to park a plane; *(mettre à l'abri)* to put a plane in the hangar

VPR se garer 1 *Aut* to park; **la voiture s'est garée le long du trottoir** the car parked beside *or* drew in beside the pavement; **j'ai eu de la peine à me g.** I had trouble parking; **se g. facilement** to have no trouble parking; **tu trouveras à te g. dans le quartier** you'll find somewhere to park in the area **2 se g. de qch/qn** to avoid *or* steer clear of sth/sb

Gargantua [gargɑ̃tɥa] NM glutton, guzzler

gargantuesque [gargɑ̃tɥɛsk] ADJ gargantuan; **un appétit/repas g.** a gargantuan appetite/meal

gargariser (se) [səgargarize] VPR to gargle; *Péj* **se g. de formules pédantes** to delight *or* revel in pedantic expressions

gargarisme [gargarism] NM *(produit)* gargle; *(action de se gargariser)* gargling; **il doit (se) faire un g. par jour** he has to gargle once a day

gargote [gargɔt] NF *Péj* cheap restaurant

gargotier, -ière [gargɔtje, -jɛr] N *Péj* **1** *(patron d'une gargote)* owner of a cheap restaurant; **je vais aller dire deux mots au g.** I'm going to give the guy who runs this cheap place a piece of my mind **2** *(mauvais cuisinier)* poor cook

gargouille [garguj] NF **1** *Archit* gargoyle **2** *(d'un gouttière, d'une pompe)* (water)spout

gargouillement [gargujmɑ̃] NM **1** *(de l'eau)* gurgling **2** *(de l'estomac)* rumbling, gurgling; **j'ai eu des gargouillements pendant toute la réunion** my stomach rumbled *or* gurgled all through the meeting

gargouiller [garguje] VI **1** *(de l'eau)* to gurgle **2** *(de l'estomac)* to rumble, to gurgle **3 sol qui gargouille sous les pas** squelchy *or* squishy ground

gargouillis [garguji] NM = **gargouillement**

garnement [garnəmɑ̃] NM *(enfant)* scamp, rascal, imp

garni [garni] ADJ **1 bien g.** *(bourse)* well-lined; *(magasin)* well-stocked; *(maison)* well-appointed; **panier g.** food hamper, hamper of food **2** *Culin* garnished; *(plat, viande)* with vegetables; **choucroute garnie** sauerkraut with sausages **3** *Vieilli (meublé) (chambre)* furnished

NM *Vieilli (meublé)* furnished room(s)

garnir [garnir] VT **1** *(munir de ce qui protège, renforce etc)* to fit out **(de** with); *(commode, tiroir)* to line; *(fauteuil)* to stuff; **garni de feutre** felt-lined; **g. un mur de plaques de polystyrène** to cover *or* line a wall with polystyrene tiles

2 *(embellir, compléter) (robe, chapeau etc)* to trim **(de** with); **une robe garnie de dentelle** a dress trimmed with lace, a lace-trimmed dress; **la passementerie qui garnit cette veste est très colorée** the braid trimming on that jacket is very colourful

3 *Culin (plat)* to garnish; **une entrecôte garnie de pommes frites et de salade** a rib steak (served) with chips and salad

4 *(remplir)* to fill; *(cave)* to stock; **g. une étagère de disques** to fill a shelf with records

VPR se garnir la salle se garnit the hall *or Théâtre* the house is beginning to fill up *or* is filling up

---

garnison [garnizɔ̃] NF *Mil* garrison; **mettre une g. dans une ville** to garrison a town; **ville de g.** garrison town; **être en g.** *ou* **tenir dans une ville** to be garrisoned *or* stationed in a town

garnissage [garnisa3] NM **1** *(remplissage) (d'un coussin, d'une couette etc)* stuffing; *(décoration) (d'un manteau)* trimming; *Aut* **g. de plafond** headliner, headlining; *Aut* **g. de siège** seat trim **2** *Tech (d'un piston)* packing; *(d'une chaudière)* lagging **3** *(matériau)* packing, stuffing, *Métal (d'un fourneau)* lining **4** *Tex (d'un tissu)* napping, raising

garniture [garnityr] NF **1** *(d'un fusil)* mountings; *(d'un navire)* rigging; *(d'une commode)* (metal) furnishings; **garnitures d'une serrure** wards of a lock; **g. d'une pompe à incendie** hose of a fire engine; **g. intérieure d'une voiture** upholstery *or* interior trim of a car

2 *(ornement) (d'un chapeau, d'une robe etc)* trimming, decoration

3 *Culin (d'un plat)* garnish; *(légumes)* vegetables; *(d'un vol-au-vent)* filling; **pour la g., vous avez le choix entre des haricots verts ou des frites** to go with it, you have a choice of green beans or chips

4 *Tech (de joint)* packing; *(de piston)* stuffing *(piece)*; *(de chaudière)* lagging; *Typ* furniture

▸▸ **g. de bureau** desk set; **g. de cheminée** mantelpiece ornaments; **g. d'embrayage** clutch lining; **g. de feu** *ou* **de foyer** (set of) fire irons; *Aut etc* **g. de frein** brake lining; *(de disque de frein)* brake pad; **g. de lit** bedding; **g. de toilette** toilet set

Garonne [garɔn] NF **la G.** the Garonne

garrigue [garig] NF *Géog* garrigue

garrocher [garɔʃe] VT *Can Arg (pierres etc)* to throw

garrot¹ [garo] NM **1** *Méd* tourniquet; **appliquer un g. (à qn)** to put a tourniquet on (sb) **2** *Hist (supplice du)* **g.** gar(r)otting, gar(r)otte

garrot² NM *Zool (de cheval, de vache etc)* withers

garrottage [garɔta3] NM **g. d'une blessure** putting a tourniquet on a wound

garrotte [garɔt] NF *Hist* gar(r)otte, gar(r)otting

garrotter [garɔte] VT *(prisonnier etc)* to tie up; *Fig* **g. les opposants au régime/l'opinion publique** to muzzle *or* silence the régime's opponents/public opinion

gars [ga] NM *Fam (jeune homme)* lad, young man; *(homme)* guy, *Br* bloke; **un petit g.** a little boy; **un beau g.** a good-looking *or* handsome young man; **un brave g.** a good lad; **un drôle de g.** an odd guy *or Br* bloke; **allons-y, les g.!** come on, lads *or* boys!; **bonjour, mon petit g.!** *(à un enfant)* hello, young man!

Gascogne [gaskɔɲ] NF Gascony; **le golfe de G.** the Bay of Biscay

gascon, -onne [gaskɔ̃, -ɔn] ADJ Gascon

NM *Ling* Gascon

N **G.** Gascon; **offre** *ou* **promesse de G.** hollow *or* empty promise

gasconnade [gaskɔnad] NF boasting, bragging

gas(-)oil [gazɔjl, gazwal] NM diesel oil *or* fuel, *Am* gas oil, *Br* derv

gaspacho [gaspatʃo] NM gazpacho

gaspard [gaspar] NM *Arg* rat

gaspillage [gaspija3] NM *(d'argent)* wasting, squandering; *(de nourriture, temps)* wasting; **je n'admets pas le g. de nourriture** I won't allow food to be wasted; **c'est du g.** it's a waste, it's wasteful; **pas de g.!** don't be wasteful!; **quel g.!** what a waste!; **c'est un vrai g. de temps/d'argent** it's a real waste of time/ money

gaspiller [gaspije] **VT** *(argent, son talent, ses dons)* to waste, to squander; *(eau, papier, son énergie)* to waste, to waste, to squander; **g. son temps** to waste one's time (**à faire qch** doing sth)

gaspilleur, -euse [gaspijœr, -øz] **N** spend-thrift
▪ **ADJ** wasteful

gastéropode [gasteropod] **NM** *Zool* gast(e)ropod

gastralgie [gastralʒi] **NF** *Méd* stomach pains, *Spéc* gastralgia

gastralgique [gastralʒik] **ADJ** *Méd* gastralgic

gastrectomie [gastrektomi] **NF** *Chir* gastrectomy

gastrique [gastrik] **ADJ** gastric; **embarras g.** stomach upset, upset stomach

gastrite [gastrit] **NF** *Méd* gastritis

gastro-entérite, *pl* **gastro-entérites** [gastroãterit] **NF** *Méd* gastroenteritis

gastro-entérologie [gastroãterɔlɔʒi] **NF** *Méd* gastroenterology

gastro-entérologue, *pl* **gastro-entéro-logues** [gastroãterɔlɔg] **N** *Méd* gastro-enterologist

gastro-intestinal, -ale, -aux, -ales [gastroẽtestinal, -o] **ADJ** *Méd* gastrointestinal

gastronome [gastronom] **NM** gastronome, gourmet

gastronomie [gastronomi] **NF** gastronomy

gastronomique [gastronomik] **ADJ** gastronomic(al)

gastropode [gastropod] **NM** *Zool* gast(e)ropod

gâté [gate] **ADJ 1** *(pourri) (fruit)* damaged, spoilt; *(dents)* rotten, decayed; **viande gâtée** meat that has gone off *or* is bad, bad meat **2** *Fig* **enfant g.** spoilt *or* pampered child; **l'en-fant g. de la famille/de la littérature russe** the blue-eyed boy of the family/of Russian literature

gâteau, -eaux [gato] **NM 1** cake; **faire un g.** to make *or* bake a cake; **g. d'anniversaire** birthday cake; *Fam* **c'est du g.** it's a piece of cake, it's child's play; *Fam* **ce n'est pas du g. de la convaincre** it's no easy matter convin-cing her; *Fam* **avoir sa part du g.** to have one's slice *or* share of the cake; *Fam* **se par-tager le g.** to share out the cake **2** *(masse compacte, plate)* cake; *(de fulmicoton etc)* disc **3** *Suisse* tart
▪ **ADJ INV** *Fam* **papa g.** *(qui cède tout à ses en-fants)* indulgent father; **c'est un vrai papa g.** he's a real soft touch with his children; *Fam* **marraine g.** fairy godmother
▸▸ **g. de cire** honeycomb; **g. marbré** marble cake; **g. de miel** honeycomb; **g. de riz** ≃ rice pudding; **g. sec** biscuit, *Am* cookie; **g. de se-moule** ≃ semolina pudding

gâter [gate] **VT 1** *(paysage, plaisir)* to spoil, to ruin; **la grêle gâte le blé** hail damages wheat; **les mouches gâtent la viande** flies in-fect meat; **ce qui ne gâte rien** which is no bad thing **2** *(choyer) (enfant, mari)* to spoil, to pamper, to overindulge; **il a été très gâté à Noël** he was really spoilt at Christmas; **on n'est (vraiment) pas gâtés: de la pluie, du vent, le froid!** marvellous, isn't it: rain, wind, cold!; **la vie ne les avait pas gâtés** life hadn't treated them kindly; **il n'est pas gâté par la nature** nature hasn't been very kind to him
▪ **VPR se gâter** *(affaires, temps)* to take a turn for the worse, to deteriorate; **le poisson se gâte facilement** fish quickly goes bad *or* off

gâterie [gatri] **NF 1** *(petit cadeau)* treat, small present **2** *(friandise) (pour enfants)* treat, goody **3** *Euph Hum* **faire une petite g. à qn** to go down on sb

gâte-sauce [gatsos] **NM** kitchen boy; *Péj Vieilli (cuisinier)* bad cook

gâteux, -euse [gatø, -øz] *Fam* **N** doddering old man, *f* woman, old dodderer
▪ **ADJ** *(sénile)* senile; *Fam* gaga; **avec leurs petits-enfants, ils sont complètement g.** they're totally besotted with their grand-children, they absolutely dote on their grandchildren

gâtifier [gatifje] **VI** *Fam* to go gaga; **il commence à g. sérieusement, le grand-père** grandad's going gaga *or* soft in the head

gâtisme [gatism] **NM** *Méd* senility, senile de-cay; *Fig* **leurs épanchements sentimentaux ne sont rien moins que du g.** the way they bill and coo you'd think they were going soft in the head

GATT [gat] **NM** *Écon (abrév* **General Agree-ment on Tariffs and Trade)** GATT

gatter [gate] **VT** *Suisse Fam (cours)* to skip, to cut; **g. l'école** to play truant *or Am* hook(e)y

gauche [goʃ] **ADJ 1** *(maladroit) (personne, attitude, démarche, style etc)* awkward, clumsy; *(tentative)* clumsy, bungling; **attra-per un objet d'un geste g.** to catch an object awkwardly *or* clumsily **2** *Tech (déformé) (surface etc)* warped, crooked, out of true **3** *(par opposition à droit)* left; **main g.** left hand; *Fig* **mariage de la main g.** living toge-ther; *Fig* **se lever du pied g.** to get out of bed on the wrong side; **rive g.** left bank; **côté g.** *Aut (quand on conduit à gauche)* nearside; *(quand on conduit à droite)* offside; *Équita-tion* nearside
▪ **NF 1** *(côté)* left; **assis à ma g.** seated on my left; **mon voisin de g.** my left-hand neigh-bour; **le tiroir de g.** the left-hand drawer; **le magasin de g.** the shop on the left; **à g.** on the left(-hand side), to the left; **tournez à g.** turn left; **la première rue à g.** the first street on the left; **sur votre g., vous pouvez voir la tour Eiffel** on your left(-hand side) you can see the Eiffel Tower; **à g. de la porte d'en-trée/de Marie** on *or* to the left of the en-trance/of Marie; **en France, on double à g.** in France, you overtake on the left; **conduire à g.** to drive on the left; **lire de g. à droite** to read from left to right; *Fam* **mettre de l'ar-gent à g.** to put some money aside *or* away; **heureusement, elle avait de l'argent à g.** for-tunately she had some money put aside *or* tucked away; *Fam* **passer l'arme à g.** to kick the bucket; **vis/hélice à pas de g.** left-han-ded screw/left-hand propeller; *Fam* **jusqu'à la g.** to the end, to the last; **ils nous ont eus jusqu'à la g.** they cheated us left, right and centre
2 *Pol* **la g.** the left; **politique/gouverne-ment/**etc **de g.** left-wing politics/govern-ment/etc; **homme de g.** man of the left; **l'extrême g.** the far *or* extreme left; **être à g.** to be on the left, to be left-wing; **voter à g.** to vote for the left; **la g. plurielle** = the rainbow coalition of socialists, communists and eco-logists in the government of Lionel Jospin *(elected in 1997)*; *Fam* **la g. caviar** cham-pagne socialists
▪ **NM** *Boxe etc (poing gauche)* left; **feinter du g.** to feint with the left; **un crochet du g.** a left hook

gauchement [goʃmã] **ADV** awkwardly, clumsily

gaucher, -ère [goʃe, -ɛr] **ADJ** left-handed
▪ **N** left-hander; *Boxe* southpaw; **g. contrarié** = natural left-hander brought up to be right-handed

gaucherie [goʃri] **NF** awkwardness, clumsiness

gauchi [goʃi] **ADJ** *Tech* = **gauche 2**

gauchir [goʃir] **VI** *(du bois etc)* to warp; *(du fer)* to buckle
▪ **VT 1** *(déformer)* to warp; *(fer)* to buckle **2** *Aviat* **g. l'aileron** to bank **3** *Fig (idée, événe-*ment, témoignage, réalité)* to distort, to mis-represent
▪ **VPR se gauchir** *(de bois)* to warp; *(de fer)* to buckle

gauchisant, -ante [goʃizã, -ãt] **ADJ** écri-vain g. writer with left-wing sympathies
▪ **N c'est un g.** he has left-wing sympathies, *Fam* he's a bit of a lefty

gauchisme [goʃism] **NM** *Pol* leftism

gauchissement [goʃismã] **NM 1** *(de bois etc)* warping; *(de fer)* buckling **2** *Aviat* banking

gauchiste [goʃist] **ADJ** *Pol* left-wing, leftist
▪ **N** left-winger, leftist, *Fam* lefty

gaucho [goʃo] **NM** *(gardien de troupeaux)* gaucho
▪ **N** *Pol Fam* lefty

gaudriole [godrijol] **NF** *Fam Vieilli* **1** *(plai-santerie grivoise)* dirty *or* saucy *or* broad joke **2** **il/elle ne pense qu'à la g.** he's/she's only interested in one thing, he's/she's got a one-track mind

gaufrage [gofraʒ] **NM** *(du cuir, papier)* em-bossing; *(du lin)* goffering, fluting; *(d'une couverture)* blocking; **g. à froid** blind embossing

gaufre [gofr] **NF 1** *Culin* waffle; **moule à gau-fres** waffle iron **2** **g. de miel** honeycomb

gaufrer [gofre] **VT** *(cuir, velours, papier)* to emboss, to figure; *(lin)* to goffer, to flute; *(fer)* to corrugate; *(couverture)* to block

gaufrette [gofrɛt] **NF** wafer (biscuit)

gaufrier [gofrije] **NM** waffle iron

gaufrure [gofryr] **NF** *(sur cuir)* stamped de-sign; *(sur lin)* goffering

Gaule [gol] **NF** *Antiq* Gaul

gaule [gol] **NF 1** *(perche)* pole; *Pêche* fishing rod **2** *Vulg* **avoir la g.** to have a hard-on

gaulé [gole] **ADJ** *Fam* **être bien/mal g.** to have/not to have a great bod

gauler [gole] **VT 1** *(arbre fruitier, noyer)* to beat, to thrash; *(fruits, noix)* to bring down *(using a pole)* **2** *Fam (attraper)* **se faire g.** to get caught

gaullien, -ienne [goljẽ, -jɛn] **ADJ** de Gaulle-like

gaullisme [golism] **NM** *Pol* Gaullism

> **Gaullisme**
> The political ideology inspired by the ideas of General de Gaulle includes na-tionalism, independence from foreign powers, and a strong executive. Gaul-lists are strongly committed to the de-fence of France's prestige on the international scene.

gaulliste [golist] **ADJ, N** *Pol* Gaullist

gaulois, -oise [golwa, -waz] **ADJ** Gallic; es-prit g. (broad) Gallic humour; **contes g.** sau-cy *or* spicy stories
▪ **NM** *Ling* Gaulish
▪ **N G.** Gaul
▪ **NF Gauloise**® Gauloise *(popular brand of cigarette)*

gauloiserie [golwazri] **NF** *(plaisanterie)* broad *or* saucy joke; *(caractère)* sauciness

gausser (se) [sɔgose] **VPR** *Litt* **se g. de qn** to laugh at *or* make fun of *or* sneer at sb; **vous vous gaussez!** you jest!

gavage [gavaʒ] **NM** *(engraissement) (de la volaille)* force-feeding, cramming; *Méd* tube-feeding

gave [gav] **NM** *Géog* (mountain) torrent *(in the Pyrenees)*

gaver [gave] **VT** *(engraisser) (volaille)* to force-feed, to cram; *(personne) (de nourri-*ture)* to fill up, to stuff **(de** with); *Méd* to force-feed; *Fig* **g. qn de qch** to cram *or* stuff sb with sth; **j'ai été gavée de littérature classique** I had classical literature crammed into me; **la télévision gave les enfants de dessins animés** television feeds children a constant diet of cartoons

VPR se gaver *Fam (de chocolat, cacahuètes etc)* to gorge oneself (**de** on), to stuff oneself (**de** with); *Fig* **se g. de romans policiers/jeux vidéo** to read detective novels/play video games till they're coming out of one's ears

gavotte [gavɔt] NF *Mus* gavotte

gay [gɛ, ge] ADJ, NM *Fam (homosexuel)* gay

gaz [gaz] NM **1** gas; **gisement de g.** gas field; **faire la cuisine au g.** to cook by gas; **cuisinière à g.** gas cooker; *Culin* **sur le g.** on the gas; **allumer/couper le g.** to light/turn off the gas; **réchaud à g.** gas stove *(for camping)*; **usine à g.** gasworks; **chambre à g.** gas chamber; *Fam* **il y a de l'eau dans le g.** things aren't going too well, things are looking bad; *Fam* **être dans le g.** to be out of it **2** *Aut Fam* **mettre les g.** to put one's foot down, *Am* to step on the gas; *Aviat* to open up the throttle; **à pleins g.** *(rouler)* flat out; *(partir)* with the throttle full open **3** *Méd* **avoir des g.** to have wind *or Am* gas; **lâcher un g.** to break wind, *Am* to pass gas

▸▸**g. ammoniac** ammonia gas; **g. asphyxiant** poison gas; **g. carbonique** carbon dioxide; **g. de combat** poison gas; **g. comprimé** compressed gas; **g. domestique** domestic gas; **g. d'échappement** exhaust fumes *ou* gas; **g. d'éclairage** town gas; **g. hilarant** laughing gas; **g. inerte** inert gas; **g. lacrymogène** tear gas; **g. des marais** marsh gas; **g. naturel** natural gas; **g. de pétrole liquéfié** liquefied petroleum gas; **g. rare** rare gas; **g. toxique** poison gas; **g. de ville** town gas; **la cuisinière est-elle branchée sur le g. de ville?** is the kitchen connected to the mains gas?

Gaza [gaza] N **la bande de G.** the Gaza Strip

gazage [gazaʒ] NM *Mil* gassing

gaze [gaz] NF **1** gauze; *Méd* **g. oxygénée** antiseptic *or* sterilized gauze **2** *Vieilli (voile)* thin veil

gazé, -ée [gaze] ADJ gassed; **soldats gazés** soldiers killed by (poison) gas
N (poison) gas victim

gazéification [gazeifikasjɔ̃] NF *Chimie* gasification; *(des boissons)* carbonation

gazéifier [gazeifje] VT *(pr sub, impf* n. **gazéifiions**, v. **gazéifiiez)** *Chimie* to gasify; *(boissons)* to carbonate

gazelle [gazɛl] NF gazelle; **avoir des yeux de g.** to be doe-eyed

gazer [gaze] VT *Mil (troupes)* to gas
VI *Fam (aller vite)* to zoom along; **ça gaze!** everything's OK *or* fine!; **ça gaze?** all right?, everything OK?; **ça ne gaze pas très fort pour lui** things aren't going too well for him

gazetier [gaztje] NM *Arch* journalist

gazette [gazet] NF *Vieilli (journal)* gazette, newspaper; *Fam* **c'est une vraie g.** he/she knows all the local gossip; *Fam* **cette femme est la g. de l'immeuble** that woman can tell you *or* knows everything that goes on in the building

gazeux, -euse [gazø, -øz] ADJ **1** *Chimie* gaseous **2** *(eau)* carbonated, fizzy; *(boisson)* fizzy, sparkling

gazier, -ière [gazje, -jɛr] ADJ **l'industrie gazière** the gas industry
NM **1** *(dans une usine à gaz)* gas works employee; *(chargé des installations dans les immeubles etc)* gas fitter, gasman **2** *Arg (individu)* guy, *Br* bloke

gazinière [gazinjɛr] NF gas cooker

gazoduc [gazɔdyk, gaz-] NM gas pipeline, gas main

gazogène [gazɔʒɛn, gaz-] NM gas producer, gas generator; **gaz de g.** producer gas

gazole [gazɔl] NM = **gasoil**

gazoline [gazɔlin] NF gasoline, gasolene

gazomètre [gazɔmɛtr] NM gasometer, gas holder

gazon [gazɔ̃] NM **1** *(herbe)* grass, turf **2** *(surface)* lawn; **défense de marcher sur le g.** keep off the grass **3** *(motte de terre)* turf, sod **4** *Bot* **g. mousse** mossy saxifrage

gazonnage [gazɔnaʒ] NM turfing, planting with turf

gazonné [gazɔne] ADJ grass-covered, turfed

gazonnement [gazɔnmɑ̃] NM = **gazonnage**

gazonner [gazɔne] VT to cover with turf, to turf
VI *(d'un terrain)* to become covered with grass

gazouillant [gazujɑ̃] ADJ *(oiseau)* twittering, warbling, chirping; *(bébé)* babbling, gurgling; *(enfant)* prattling; **ruisseau g.** babbling brook

gazouillement [gazujmɑ̃] NM *(des oiseaux)* twittering, warbling, chirping; *(d'un bébé)* babbling, gurgling; *(des enfants)* prattle, prattling; *(de l'eau qui coule)* babbling, murmuring

gazouiller [gazuje] VI *(d'un oiseau)* to twitter, to warble, to chirp; *(d'un bébé)* to babble, to gurgle; *(d'un enfant)* to prattle; *(d'eau)* to babble, to murmur

gazouilleur, -euse [gazujœr, -øz] ADJ *(oiseau)* twittering, warbling, chirping; *(bébé)* babbling, gurgling; *(enfant)* prattling; **ruisseau g.** babbling brook

gazouillis [gazuji] NM = **gazouillement**

GB [ʒebe] NF *(abrév* **Grande-Bretagne**) GB

G-C [ʒese] *abrév* **grand-croix**

GDB [ʒedebe] NF *Fam (abrév* **gueule de bois**) hangover

GDF [ʒedeɛf] NM *abrév* **Gaz de France**

geai [ʒɛ] NM *Orn* jay

géant, -ante [ʒeɑ̃, -ɑ̃t] N **1** *Myth* giant, f giantess **2** *(personne anormalement grande)* giant; *Gym* **pas de g.** giant stride; *Fig* **avancer** *ou* **aller à pas de g.** to make great strides, to make spectacular progress; **la Chaussée des Géants** the Giant's Causeway **3** *(personne exceptionnelle)* giant; **les géants de la politique** the giants of politics, the political giants; **les géants de l'art** the great masters; **les géants du football** the football(ing) greats
ADJ **1** *(arbre, écran etc)* giant, gigantic; *Com* **carton g.** giant (-size) packet **2** *Fam (super)* **c'est g.** fantastic!, wicked!

gecko [ʒeko] NM gecko

gégène [ʒeʒɛn] NF *Fam* = torture by electric shock

géhenne [ʒeɛn] NF *Bible* Gehenna, Hell

geignard, -arde [ʒeɲar, -ard] *Fam* ADJ *(personne, voix)* whining, *Br* whingeing
N whiner

geignement [ʒeɲmɑ̃] NM *(action)* whining; *(résultat)* whine

geindre [ʒɛ̃dr] VI *(prp* **geignant**; *pp* **geint**; *pr ind* **je geins, il geint, n. geignons, ils geignent**; *impf* **je geignais**; *p hist* **je geignis**; *fu* **je geindrai)** **1** *(gémir)* to moan, to groan; **g. de douleur** to moan *or* groan with pain **2** *Fam (se plaindre constamment)* to whine, *Br* to whinge

geisha [geʃa] NF geisha

gel [ʒɛl] NM **1** *Météo* frost; *Fig* **g. des négociations** suspension of negotiations; **g. des subventions** freezing of subsidies; **g. des armements/des crédits** the arms/credit freeze **2** *(dans les produits cosmétiques) (pour les cheveux)* gel; **dentrifrice en g.** gel toothpaste; **se mettre du g.** to put gel on one's hair **3** *Chimie* gel
▸▸**g. douche** shower gel; *UE* **g. des terres** set-aside

gélatine [ʒelatin] NF gelatin(e); *Culin* **feuille de g.** sheet of gelatine

gélatiné [ʒelatine] ADJ gelatinized

gélatineux, -euse [ʒelatinø, -øz] ADJ gelatinous

gelé [ʒ(ə)le] ADJ *(lac, rivière)* frozen; *(nez, main etc)* frostbitten; *(plante)* frost-nipped; *Fig (assistance)* cold, indifferent; *Fin (bloqué) (fonds)* frozen; **mourir g.** to freeze to death; *Fam* **je suis complètement g.** I'm absolutely frozen *or* freezing; *Fam* **être g. jusqu'aux os** to be chilled to the marrow *or* bone; **ils ont eu les pieds gelés** they had frostbite in their feet

gelée [ʒ(ə)le] NF **1** *(gel)* frost; **forte g.** hard frost **2** *Culin* jelly; *(à base de fruits)* jelly, *Am* jello; **g. de veau/poulet** veal/chicken jelly; **œufs en g.** eggs in jelly; **g. de cassis** blackcurrant jelly *or Am* jello
▸▸**g. blanche** hoar (frost), white frost; **g. royale** royal jelly

geler [ʒ(ə)le] **(je gèle, n. gelons; je gèlerai)** VT **1** to freeze; *(lac, rivière)* to freeze (over); *(route)* to make icy; **froid qui gèle les conduites d'eau** cold that freezes the water pipes; **fleurs gelées par le froid** flowers nipped by the frost **2** *Fin (bloquer) (crédits, capital)* to freeze
VI *(d'un lac, d'une rivière)* to freeze (over); **l'étang a gelé d'un bout à l'autre** the pond has *or* is completely frozen over; **plantes qui gèlent facilement** plants easily damaged by frost; **on gèle dans cette salle** it's freezing in this room; **tu ne gèles pas, toi?** aren't you freezing *or* frozen?
V IMPERS **il gèle** it is freezing; **il gèle à pierre fendre** it's freezing hard; **il a gelé blanc cette nuit** there was a white frost last night
VPR **se geler** *(personne)* to freeze; *très Fam* **on se les gèle aujourd'hui** it's damned cold, *Br* it's brass monkey weather

gélifiant [ʒelifjɑ̃] NM gelling agent

gélifier [ʒelifje] *Chimie* VT *(transformer en gel)* to gel
VPR **se gélifier** to gel

gélinotte [ʒelinɔt] NF **g. (des bois)** hazel grouse; **g. des prairies** prairie chicken

gélose [ʒeloz] NF *Chimie* agar-agar

gélule [ʒelyl] NF *Pharm* capsule

gelure [ʒ(ə)lyr] NF frostbite

Gémeaux (les) [leʒemo] NMPL *Astron, Astrol* Gemini; **être (du signe des) G.** to be (a) Gemini

gémellaire [ʒemelɛr] ADJ twin

gémellité [ʒemelite] NF **taux de g.** incidence of twin births

gémination [ʒeminasjɔ̃] NF *Biol etc* gemination

géminé [ʒemine] ADJ **1** *Biol (feuilles)* geminate, twin; *Chimie* geminate; *Archit* **colonnes géminées** twin columns **2** *Ling* **consonnes géminées** doubled *or* geminate consonants

gémir [ʒemir] VI **1** *(d'une personne)* to groan, to moan; *(d'une porte)* to creak; *(du vent)* to moan; **g. de douleur** to groan *or* moan with pain; **g. sous le joug de la tyrannie** to groan under the yoke of tyranny **2** *(d'une colombe, tourterelle)* to coo

gémissant [ʒemisɑ̃] ADJ *(personne)* moaning, groaning; **voix gémissante** wailing voice; **essieu g.** creaking axle

gémissement [ʒemismɑ̃] NM **1** *(d'une personne)* groan, moan; *(de porte)* creaking; *(de vent)* moaning; **je ne supporte plus tes**

gémissements I can't bear your moaning or groaning any longer **2** (d'une colombe etc) cooing

gemmage [ʒɛmaʒ] **NM** tapping (of trees for resin)

gemme [ʒɛm] **NF 1** Minér gem (stone), precious stone **2** (sève) pine resin **3** Bot Arch (leaf) bud

ADJ pierre g. gem stone; **sel g.** rock salt

gemmé [ʒeme, ʒɛme] **ADJ** Litt gemmed, jewelled

gemmer [ʒeme, ʒɛme] **VT** to tap

gemmeur [ʒemœr] **NM** tapper

gémonies [ʒemɔni] **NFPL** Litt **traîner** ou **vouer qn aux g.** to hold sb up to public obloquy

gênant [ʒɛnɑ̃] **ADJ 1** (embarrassant) (personne) embarrassing; (situation, silence) embarrassing, awkward; (témoin) awkward; **j'ai trouvé extrêmement g. que tu abordes ce sujet** it was extremely embarrassing of you to mention the subject **2** (encombrant) (objet) cumbersome; **votre fils n'est pas g.** your son is no trouble or no bother; **il peut être très g. quand il nous interrompt** he can be a real nuisance when he interrupts us; **les jupes longues sont gênantes** long skirts are awkward or are a nuisance

gencive [ʒɑ̃siv] **NF 1** Anat gum; **abcès à la g.** abscess on the gum, gumboil **2** Fam **un coup dans les gencives** a punch on the jaw; Fig **prends ça dans les gencives!** take that!; **elle lui a envoyé dans les gencives tout ce qu'elle avait contre lui** she told him to his face everything she didn't like about him

gendarme [ʒɑ̃darm] **NM 1** gendarme, policeman, Br ≃ police constable; **gendarmes à cheval** mounted police; **gendarmes motocyclistes** motorcycle police; Fig **sa mère est un vrai g.** his mother is a real battle-axe; **jouer aux gendarmes et aux voleurs** to play (at) cops and robbers; Fam **faire le g.** to boss people about; Fam **la peur du g.** the fear of being caught; **chapeau de g.** paper hat **2** (d'une pierre précieuse) flaw **3** Géol rock pinnacle, gendarme **4** Culin Fam (hareng saur) red herring; (saucisson) = flat, dry sausage
▸▸ Aut Fam **g. couché** sleeping policeman

gendarmer (se) [səʒɑ̃darme] **VPR** (contre qn, une proposition etc) to kick up or create a fuss (**contre** about); **il n'y a pas de quoi se g.** there's nothing to get worked up about

gendarmerie [ʒɑ̃darməri] **NF 1** (corps) (en France) gendarmerie, police force; **g. nationale** = national police force, gendarmerie; **la G. royale du Canada** the Royal Canadian Mounted Police **2** (lieu) gendarmes' headquarters

gendre [ʒɑ̃dr] **NM** son-in-law

gène [ʒɛn] **NM** Biol gene; **g. terminator** terminator gene; **structure du g.** gene structure; **banque/famille de gènes** gene bank/family

gêne [ʒɛn] **NF 1** (confusion) embarrassment; **éprouver une certaine g. à parler en public** to feel rather ill at ease or embarrassed when speaking in public; **ressentir de la g. en présence de qn** to feel ill at ease or embarrassed in sb's presence; **elle a ressenti une certaine g. à le lui demander** she felt rather embarrassed or awkward about asking him; **je n'aurais aucune g. à le faire** I wouldn't be at all embarrassed about doing it; **où (il) y a de la g., (il n')y a pas de plaisir** there's no point in standing on ceremony **2** (dérangement) inconvenience; **nous prions nos clients de bien vouloir excuser la g. occasionnée par les travaux** we apologize to customers for the inconvenience caused by the work; **vous ne me causerez aucune g.** you won't inconvenience me in the least, you won't cause me any inconvenience

3 (difficulté physique) discomfort; **sentir une g. respiratoire** ou **pour respirer** to have difficulty (in) breathing; **elle éprouve une g. intense à avaler** she has great difficulty swallowing

4 (manque d'argent) **être dans la g.** to be short of money, to be in financial difficulties

5 Arch (physique, morale) torture

gêné [ʒene] **ADJ 1** (embarrassé) embarrassed, ill at ease; **je suis tellement gênée de tous ces cadeaux que vous me faites** I'm so embarrassed by all these presents you're giving me; Fam **il n'est pas g., lui!** he's got a nerve!; **elle avait l'air g. d'arriver si tard** she seemed embarrassed at arriving so late; **je serais trop g. de le lui dire** I'd be too embarrassed to tell him; **silence g.** embarrassed or awkward or uneasy silence; Fam **être g. aux entournures** to be ill at ease; **être g. par un vêtement** to be hampered by a garment **2** (qui manque d'argent) short of money, in financial difficulties; Fam **être g. aux entournures** to be short of money

généalogie [ʒenealɔʒi] **NF 1** (ascendance) genealogy, descent; (d'un cheval, d'un chien etc) pedigree **2** (science) genealogy

généalogique [ʒenealɔʒik] **ADJ** genealogical; **livre g.** (de chevaux) stud book; (du bétail) herd book

généalogiquement [ʒenealɔʒikmɑ̃] **ADV** genealogically

généalogiste [ʒenealɔʒist] **N** genealogist

gêner [ʒene] **VT 1** (perturber, empêcher) (activité) to interfere with; **g. la circulation** to hold up or block the traffic; **g. le passage** to be in the way; **g. la vue** to obstruct or block the view; **ma valise vous gêne-t-elle?** is my case in your way?; **pousse-toi, tu vois bien que tu gênes!** move along, you can see you're in the way!; **je veux bien venir avec vous mais je ne veux pas vous g.** I'd love to come with you but I don't want to be in the or your way; **les enfants me gênent quand je dois me concentrer** the children disturb or bother me when I have to concentrate; **ça me gêne dans mon travail** it disturbs me when I'm trying to work; **une bonne nous gênerait dans notre intimité** a maid would intrude on our privacy; **ce point de côté me gêne pour marcher** this stitch in my side makes it difficult for me to walk; **recule-toi, tu me gênes pour passer** move back, you're in my way or you're stopping me from getting past; **si tu pouvais te pousser, tu me gênes pour passer les vitesses** could you move over, I can't change gear with you there; **j'ai été gêné par le manque de temps/ma méconnaissance du milieu** I was hindered or hampered by the lack of time/my ignorance of the milieu; **j'ai été gêné par le bruit/la lumière/le monde** I was disturbed by the noise/the light/the people; **ça te gêne si je mets la musique plus fort?** do you mind if I turn up the music?; **cela vous gênerait-il que je revienne demain?** would it disturb you or bother you or put you out if I come back tomorrow?; **cela ne te gênerait pas de me prêter ta voiture?** would you mind lending me your car?; **ce qui me gêne, c'est que ...** what bothers me is that ...; **le froid ne me gêne pas** I don't mind the cold; **la fumée vous gêne-t-elle?** do you mind my smoking? **2** (serrer) **mes souliers me gênent** my shoes pinch or are too tight; **cette ceinture/ce col me gêne** this belt/this collar is too tight; **cette jupe trop étroite me gêne pour marcher** I find it hard to walk in this tight skirt **3** (mettre mal à l'aise) to embarrass; **cela me gênerait de le rencontrer** it would be awkward for me to meet him, I would feel uncomfortable meeting him; **sa présence me gêne** I feel awkward or embarrassed in his presence, his presence makes me feel ill at

ease; **ça me gêne qu'il écoute** I feel uneasy with him listening; Fam **et alors, ça te gêne?** what's it to you?, any objections?

VPR se gêner 1 je ne me suis pas gêné pour le lui dire I didn't hesitate to tell him so, I made no bones about telling him so; **ne te gêne pas pour le lui faire remarquer** go right ahead and point it out to him; **il trouve que le café ne vient pas assez vite? qu'il ne se gêne surtout pas pour le faire!** he thinks the coffee's taking too long? he can always make it himself!; **il ne se gêne pas avec nous** he doesn't stand on ceremony with us; **elle aurait tort de se g.** she has no need to feel embarrassed; Iron **il ne se gêne pas!** he's not backward in coming forward! Iron **ne vous gênez pas!** make yourself at home! Iron **faut pas se g.!** don't mind me!

2 (dans un lieu) to be in each other's way; **il y a beaucoup de place, nous ne nous gênerons pas** there's a lot of room, we won't be in each other's way

3 Suisse (être intimidé) to be shy

général, -ale, -aux, -ales [ʒeneral, -o] **ADJ** general; **assemblée/amnistie générale** general assembly/amnesty; **appeler à une grève générale** to call a general strike; **dans l'intérêt g.** in the general interest; **à la surprise générale** to everyone's surprise; **à la demande générale, nous allons rechanter la dernière chanson** by popular request we are going to sing the last song again; **satisfaire à la demande générale** to satisfy popular or general demand; Théâtre **répétition générale** dress rehearsal; **état g.** general or overall condition; **médecine générale** general medicine; **inspecteur g.** inspector general; **quartier g.** headquarters; Hist **états généraux** States General; **officier g.** Mil etc general officer; Naut flag officer; **le consentement g.** common consent; **d'une façon générale** generally speaking; **en règle générale** as a general rule, generally; **en g.** (globalement) in general; (habituellement) as a rule, generally; **la nature humaine en g.** human nature in general; **en g., elle se couche tôt** she goes to bed early as a rule, she generally goes to bed early

NM 1 (ce qui est universel) **le g.** the general; **passer du g. au particulier** to go from the general to the particular **2** Mil general

NF générale 1 Théâtre dress rehearsal **2** Mil (alerte) alarm call; **battre la générale** to call to arms, to sound the alarm; Naut to beat to quarters **3** **bonjour, madame la générale** (qui s'appelle Leclerc) hello, Mrs Leclerc
▸▸ **g. d'armée** (army) general; **g. d'armée aérienne** air chief marshal, Am major general; **g. de brigade** brigadier, Am brigadier general; **g. de brigade aérienne** air commodore, Am brigadier general; **g. de corps d'armée** lieutenant general; **g. de corps d'armée aérienne** air marshal, Am lieutenant general; **g. de division** major general; **g. de division aérienne** air vice-marshal, Am major general

généralement [ʒeneralmɑ̃] **ADV** generally; **il y a g. une trentaine d'élèves par classe** there are generally or usually about thirty pupils in a class

généralisable [ʒeneralizabl] **ADJ** that can be generalized

généralisateur, -trice [ʒeneralizatœr, -tris] **ADJ** (esprit, méthode) generalizing

généralisation [ʒeneralizasjɔ̃] **NF 1** (extension) generalization; **craindre la g. d'un conflit** to fear that a conflict will spread; Méd **g. d'un cancer** spread of a cancer **2** (de propos) generalization; **une g. hâtive** a sweeping generalization; **faire des généralisations** to make generalizations, to generalize; **tomber dans les généralisations** to lapse into generalization(s)

généraliser [ʒeneralize] **VT** to generalize; **g. une loi** to extend a law; **il a tendance à tout g.** he tends to generalize; *Méd* **un cancer généralisé** a generalized cancer

VT to generalize; **on ne peut pas g.** you can't generalize

VPR se généraliser *(d'une utilisation)* to become widespread; *(d'un usage, un conflit, une grève)* to spread; **la crise économique s'est généralisée** the economic crisis has spread

généralissime [ʒeneralisim] **NM** generalissimo, commander-in-chief

généraliste [ʒeneralist] **N** *Méd* general practitioner, GP, *Am* family practitioner

ADJ médecin g. general practitioner, GP, *Am* family practitioner; **radio/télévision g.** general-interest radio/television

généralité [ʒeneralite] **NF 1** *(majorité)* **dans la g. des cas** in the majority *or* generality of cases, in most cases **2** *(notion générale)* generality; **s'en tenir à des généralités** to confine oneself to generalities *or* to general remarks; **exposer quelques généralités dans un cours d'introduction** to present some general ideas in an introductory course

générateur, -trice [ʒeneratœr, -tris] **ADJ** *(machine etc)* generating; *(force, organe)* generative; **g. de** productive of; **un colorant alimentaire g. de troubles gastriques** a food colouring *or Am* coloring which causes gastric problems; *Fig* **une situation génératrice de conflits/d'idées** a situation that generates *or* produces conflict/ideas; **une situation peu génératrice d'emplois** a situation that generates *or* produces few jobs; **son discours a été g. de nombreuses questions** his speech threw up *or* raised a great many questions; *Élec* **station** *ou* **usine génératrice** generating station *or* plant; **chaudière génératrice** steam boiler

NM generator

NF génératrice generator, generating set; *Nucl* **génératrice nucléaire** nuclear power reactor

▸▸ *Ordinat* **g. de caractères** character generator; *TV* caption generator; *TV, Cin* **g. de couleur** colour synthesizer; *Ordinat* **g. d'écrans** screen generator; *Ordinat* **g. d'effets numériques** digital effects generator; *Ordinat* **g. d'effets spéciaux** (special) effects generator, SEG; *Élec* **g. d'électricité** electricity generator; *Ordinat* **g. d'états** report generator; *Ordinat* **g. graphique** graphics generator; *Électron* **g. d'impulsions** pulse generator; *Ordinat* **g. de menus** menu builder; **g. de signaux** *Électron* signal(ling) generator; *TV* colour coder; *Ordinat* **g. de son** sound generator; *TV etc* **g. de synchro** synchronizing generator, sync pulse generator, SPG; *TV, Cin* **g. de titres graphiques** graphic titler; **g. de vapeur** (steam) boiler, steam generator

génératif, -ive [ʒeneratif, -iv] **ADJ** generative

génération [ʒenerasjɔ̃] **NF 1** *(classe d'âge, degrés de filiation)* generation; **la g. actuelle** the present generation; **la jeune g.** the younger generation; **ils ne sont pas de la même g.** they are not (of) the same generation; **les gens de ma g.** the people of my generation; **de g. en g.** from generation to generation, through the generations; **immigrés de la deuxième g.** second-generation immigrants; **la g. pub/vidéo/etc** the advertising/video/etc generation; **la nouvelle g. d'ordinateurs/de machines à laver** the new generation of computers/washing machines VOIR GRAMMAIRE A11 **2** *(action de générer, produire)* generation; *(de vapeur etc)* generation, production; *(de métaux)* formation

▸▸ *Ordinat* **g. automatique de textes** automatic generation of texts; *Ordinat* **g. d'écrans** screen generation; *Biol* **g. spontanée** spontaneous generation

générer [ʒenere] **VT** (**je génère, n. générons; je générerai**) **1** *(faire naître)* *(idées, images, profits)* to generate; *Ordinat* **généré par ordinateur** computer-generated **2** *(produire)* *(électricité, vapeur etc)* to generate, to produce

généreusement [ʒenerøzmɑ̃] **ADV** generously; **il nous a servi g. à manger** he gave us a generous meal; **il nous a g. versé à boire** he gave us a generous amount to drink

généreux, -euse [ʒenerø, -øz] **ADJ** *(charitable)* generous; *Vieilli Fam (noble) (âme)* noble, generous; **il est très g. avec les enfants** he is very generous with (the) children; **un don g.** a generous gift; **terre généreuse** fertile soil; **vin g.** generous wine, wine with a fine bouquet; **elle a des formes généreuses** she has generous curves, she is a buxom woman

N generous person

générique [ʒenerik] **ADJ** generic; **produit g.** no-name *or* generic product; **médicament g.** generic drug

NM *TV, Cin* credits, titles; **faire le g.** to do the captions; **son nom ne figure pas au g.** his name doesn't appear in the credits, he doesn't get a credit; **g. de début** opening credits; **g. de fin** closing credits, end titles; **g. déroulant** rolling credits, rolling titles

générosité [ʒenerozite] **NF** *(libéralité)* generosity; **avec g.** generously; **g. de cœur** kindness of heart; **dans un élan de g.** in a sudden fit of generosity; **n'abuse pas de ma g.** don't abuse my generosity; **générosités** acts of generosity

Gênes [ʒɛn] **N** Genoa

genèse [ʒənɛz] **NF** genesis; *Bible* **la G.** (the Book of) Genesis

genet [ʒ(ə)nɛ] **NM** jennet

genêt [ʒ(ə)nɛ] **NM** *Bot* broom

généticien, -ienne [ʒenetisjɛ̃, -jɛn] **N** geneticist

génétique [ʒenetik] **ADJ** genetic; **code/empreinte/manipulation g.** genetic code/fingerprint/engineering; **fond g. commun** gene pool

NF genetics

génétiquement [ʒenetikmɑ̃] **ADV** genetically; **g. modifié** genetically modified

genette [ʒ(ə)nɛt] **NF** genet

gêneur, -euse [ʒɛnœr, -øz] **N** nuisance

Genève [ʒ(ə)nɛv] **N** Geneva

genevois, -oise [ʒənvwa, -waz] **ADJ** Genevan

N G. Genevan

genévrier [ʒənevrije] **NM** juniper

génial, -ale, -aux, -ales [ʒenjal, -o] **ADJ 1** *(inspiré par le génie)* *(invention, livre, tableau etc)* brilliant; **œuvre géniale** work of genius, brilliant work; **compositeur g.** composer of genius, brilliant composer **2** *Fam (extraordinaire)* *(idée, film, soirée etc)* brilliant, great; **c'est g.!** that's brilliant *or* great!; **un mec g.** a great guy; **tu es g.!** you're a genius!, you're brilliant!

> Il faut noter que l'adjectif anglais **genial** est un faux ami. Il signifie **cordial**.

génialement [ʒenjalmɑ̃] **ADV** brilliantly

génie [ʒeni] **NM 1** *(qualité, personne)* genius; **homme de g.** man of genius; **une idée/invention de g.** a brilliant idea/invention; **un trait de g.** a stroke of genius; **avoir le g. de qch/pour faire qch** to have a genius *or* gift for sth/for doing sth; *Iron* **tu as vraiment le**

g. pour te faire des ennemis you have a real genius *or* a real gift for making enemies VOIR GRAMMAIRE A14 **2** *(allégorie)* spirit; **g. d'une langue** genius *or* spirit of a language **3** *(être mythique)* genie; **son mauvais g.** his evil genius; **le petit g. de la forêt** the forest sprite; **les génies des contes arabes** the genies *or* the jinn of the Arabian Nights **4** *Tech* engineering; *Mil* **le (Corps du) G.** *Br* ≃ the Royal Engineers, the Engineers, *Am* ≃ the Corps of Engineers, the Engineer Corps; *Mil* **officier du g.** engineer officer; *Mil* **soldat du g.** engineer, *Br* sapper

▸▸ **g. aéroporté** airborne engineers; **g. de l'air** aviation engineers; **g. atomique** atomic *or* nuclear engineering; *(corps)* atomic *or* nuclear engineers; **g. civil** civil engineering; *(corps)* civil engineers; **g. électronique** electronic engineering; *Méd* **g. génétique** genetic engineering; **g. industriel** industrial engineering; **g. logiciel** systems engineering; *Tech* **g. maritime** marine *or* naval architecture; *(corps)* marine *or* naval architects

genièvre [ʒənjɛvr] **NM 1** *(fruit)* juniper berry; *(arbre)* juniper (tree); *Pharm* **essence de g.** juniper oil **2** *(alcool)* gin

génique [ʒenik] **ADJ** *Méd* **thérapie g.** gene therapy

génisse [ʒenis] **NF** heifer

génital, -ale, -aux, -ales [ʒenital, -o] **ADJ** genital; **les organes génitaux** the genitals, the genital organs; **appareil g.** genitalia

géniteur, -trice [ʒenitœr, -tris] **NM** *Zool* sire **N** *Hum* father, f mother; **nos géniteurs** our parents

génitif [ʒenitif] **NM** *Gram* genitive (case); **au g. in** the genitive VOIR GRAMMAIRE A15-16

génito-urinaire, *pl* **génito-urinaires** [ʒenitoyriner] **ADJ** *Anat* genito-urinary

génocide [ʒenɔsid] **NM** genocide

génois, -oise [ʒenwa, -waz] **ADJ** Genoese **N G.** Genoese

génoise [ʒenwaz] **NF** sponge cake

génome [ʒenom] **NM** *Biol* genome

génomique [ʒenomik] **NF** genomics VOIR GRAMMAIRE A10

génotype [ʒenotip] **NM** *Biol* genotype

genou, *pl* **genoux** [ʒ(ə)nu] **NM 1** *Anat* knee; **sa robe lui arrivait au-dessus du g./aux genoux** her dress came down to just above the knee/to her knees; **enfoncé jusqu'aux genoux dans la boue** knee-deep in mud, up to one's knees in mud; **avoir les genoux en dedans** to be knock-kneed; **à genoux** kneeling, on one's knees; **se mettre à genoux** to kneel (down), to go down on one's knees; *Fig* **être à genoux devant qn** to worship sb; *Fig* **se mettre à genoux devant qn** to go down on one's knees to sb; *Fig* **demander qch à genoux** to ask for sth on bended knee; **plier** *ou* **ployer** *ou* **fléchir le g. devant qn** to bend the knee to sb; *Fig* **être sur les genoux** to be on one's last legs, to be about to drop; **ce projet m'a mis sur les genoux** this project has worn *or* tired me out; **tenir un enfant sur ses genoux** to hold a child on one's knee *or* in one's lap; **sur les genoux des dieux** in the lap of the gods; **faire du g. à qn** to play footsie with sb

2 *Tech* **joint à g.** ball-and-socket joint

genouillère [ʒ(ə)nujer] **NF 1** *(protection du genou)* kneepad, knee guard; *Méd* knee bandage **2** *Tech* **articulation à g.** toggle joint

genre [ʒɑ̃r] **NM 1** *(sorte)* kind, sort, type; **quel g. de voitures/de livres?** what kind *or* sort of type of cars/books?; **quel g. de vie mène-t-il?** what kind *or* sort of (a) life does he lead?; **toutes les tentatives de ce g. ont échoué** all attempts of this kind *or* sort have failed; **c'est plus dans son g.** that's more in his line; **dans son g., c'est un artiste** he is glissé sur lui comme l'eau sur les plumes d'un canard I took him to task but it was like water off a duck's back; **rien ne l'émeut, tout glisse sur lui** nothing bothers him, it's all water off a duck's back; **glissons (là-dessus)** let's not dwell on that, let's skip over that **5** *(avoir une surface glissante)* to be slippery; **fais attention, ça glisse ce matin** watch out, it's slippery this morning; **la chaussée glisse beaucoup** the road is very slippery

VT *(introduire, passer etc)* to slip; **g. une lettre sous la porte** to slip a letter under the door; **g. qch dans la poche de qn** to slip sth into sb's pocket; **essaie de g. quelques citations dans ta dissertation** try to slip a few quotations into your essay; **g. un mot à l'oreille de qn** to drop a word in sb's ear; **g. un mot à qn** to have a quick word with sb; **j'ai glissé votre nom pendant le débat** I dropped your name into the debate

VPR se glisser to slip (**dans** into); **il s'est glissé discrètement dans la salle de conférence** he slipped discreetly into the lecture theatre; **se g. dans son lit** to slip *or* creep into bed; **retrouvez les erreurs qui se sont glissées dans le texte** locate the errors that have crept *or* slipped into the text

NM *Ordinat* g. d'icônes icon drag

glisser-lâcher, *pl* **glissers-lâchers NM** *Ordinat* drag and drop; **g. d'icônes** icon drag and drop

glissière [glisjɛr] **NF 1** *Tech* runner, slide; *Com* shelf strip; **à g.** sliding; **fermeture à g.** zip (fastener), *Am* zipper; **porte à glissières** sliding door; **banc à glissières** *(en aviron)* sliding seat **2 g. (de sécurité)** crash barrier **3** *Ind (pour le charbon)* chute

glissoir [gliswar] **NM 1** *(d'une machine)* slide, sliding block **2** *(pour le bois)* timber slide *or* chute

glissoire [gliswar] **NF** slide *(on ice or snow)*

global, -ale, -aux, -ales [glɔbal, -o] **ADJ** *(somme)* total, inclusive, global; *(paiement)* lump; **une vision globale des problèmes** an overall *or* a global view of the problems; *Scol* **méthode globale** word recognition method

globalement [glɔbalmã] **ADV** overall, all in all; **on peut g. s'estimer gagnant** overall *or* all in all we've come out on top

globalisation [glɔbalizasjɔ̃] **NF** globalization

globaliser [glɔbalize] **VT 1** *(problèmes)* to lump together; **essayez de g. vos réponses** try to give a general answer **2** *(mondialiser)* to globalize

VPR se globaliser *(phénomène, problème)* to become global

globalité [glɔbalite] **NF** **prendre un problème dans sa g.** to tackle a problem as a whole; **répondre à la g. des questions** to give an answer to cover all questions

globe [glɔb] **NM 1** *(sphère)* globe, sphere **2** *(terre)* globe; *(des insignes royaux)* orb; **la surface du g.** the surface of the globe; **une partie inhabitée du g.** an uninhabited part of the globe; **faire le tour du g.** to go round the world; **le g. du soleil** the orb of the sun **3** *(en verre) (d'une pendule)* glass dome *or* cover; **g. électrique** electric light globe; **statuette sous g.** statuette under glass; **c'est à conserver sous g.** it ought to be kept under glass; *Fig* **conserver qn/qch sous g.** to keep sb/sth under wraps **4** *Météo* **g. de feu** fireball, globe lightning
▸▸**g. oculaire** *ou* **de l'œil** eyeball; **g. terrestre** *(la terre)* earth; *(objet)* globe

globe-trotter, *pl* **globe-trotters** [glɔbtrɔtœr] **NM** globetrotter

globine [glɔbin] **NF** *Biol* globin

globulaire [glɔbylɛr] **ADJ** globular; *Méd* **numération g.** blood count

globule [glɔbyl] **NM** *(d'air, d'eau)* globule; *Physiol* (blood) corpuscle, blood cell; *Pharm* small pill; **globules blancs/rouges** white/red corpuscles *or* blood cells

globuleux, -euse [glɔbylø, -øz] **ADJ** globular; **yeux g.** protruding eyes

globuline [glɔbylin] **NF** *Biol, Chimie* globulin

glockenspiel [glɔkɛnʃpil] **NM** *Mus* glockenspiel

gloire [glwar] **NF 1** *(renom)* glory, fame; **se couvrir de g.** to cover oneself in glory; **être au sommet de la g.** to be at the height of one's fame; **elle a eu son heure de g.** she has had her hour of glory; **il est mort en pleine g.** he died at the height of his fame; **se faire** *ou* **tirer g. de qch** to glory in sth, to pride oneself on sth; **travailler pour la g.** to work for the glory (of it) *or* for nothing; **ce n'est pas la g.** it's not exactly brilliant

2 *(personne célèbre)* celebrity; **une g. oubliée** a forgotten celebrity; **il est la g. de notre école** he is the pride of our school

3 *(splendeur)* **la g. de Dieu** the glory of God; **la famille royale dans toute sa g.** the royal family in all its splendour

4 *(manifestation de respect)* glory, praise; **rendre g. à Dieu/qn** to glorify God/sb; **g. à Dieu!** glory (be) to God!; **g. aux soldats morts pour la France!** glory to the soldiers who died for France!; **à la g. de qn** in praise of sb

5 *Beaux-Arts (auréole)* glory, nimbus

glomérule [glɔmeryl] **NM** *Anat* glomerulus

gloria [glɔrja] **NM 1** *Rel* Gloria **2** *Fam Arch (café)* = coffee served with spirits

glorieusement [glɔrjøzmã] **ADV** gloriously

glorieux, -euse [glɔrjø, -øz] **ADJ 1** *(mémorable)* glorious; **ce n'est pas très g.** it's not exactly brilliant **2** *(illustre)* glorious; **porter un nom g.** to have an illustrious name; **il est promis à un avenir g.** he has a glorious future ahead of him; **un soldat g.** a renowned soldier **3** *Arch, Litt (fier)* proud (**de** of); *Péj* **g. de qch** vain *or* conceited about sth **NMPL** **les g.** the saints in glory

glorification [glɔrifikasjɔ̃] **NF** glorification

glorifier [glɔrifje] *(impf, pr sub n.* **glorifiions,** *v.* **glorifiiez)** **VT** to glorify, to praise **VPR se glorifier** to boast; **se g. de (faire) qch** to glory in (doing) sth, to boast of (doing) sth

gloriole [glɔrjɔl] **NF** **pour la g.** for the kudos of it; **faire qch par g.** to do sth in order to show off; **c'est une attitude de g.** he's just showing off

glose [gloz] **NF** *(explication)* gloss; *Péj* **gloses** gossip; **g. marginale** marginal note; **dire la vérité sans g.** to speak the plain *or* unvarnished truth

gloser [gloze] **VT** *(expliquer) (texte)* to gloss, to expound
VI to comment (**sur** on), *Péj* to gossip (**sur** about); *Vieilli* **g. sur qch/qn** *(critiquer)* to find fault with sth/sb

glossaire [glɔsɛr] **NM 1** *(pour termes spécifiques)* glossary **2** *(d'une langue)* vocabulary

glossine [glɔsin] **NF** tsetse fly

glossolalie [glɔsɔlali] **NF** glossolalia

glottal, -ale, -aux, -ales [glɔtal, -o] **ADJ** *Ling, Anat* glottal

glotte [glɔt] **NF** *Anat* glottis; *Ling* **coup de g.** glottal stop

glouglou [gluglu] **NM 1** *(bruit d'un liquide)* glug-glug, gurgle; **faire g.** to gurgle **2** *(cri de la dinde)* gobble

glouglouter [gluglute] **VI** *(de la dinde)* to gobble

gloussement [glusmã] **NM** *(de la poule)* clucking, cluck; *(de la dinde)* gobbling, gobble; *Fam (d'une personne)* chuckling, chuckle, chortle

glousser [gluse] **VI** *(d'une poule)* to cluck; *(d'une dinde)* to gobble; *Fam (d'une personne)* to chuckle, to chortle

glouteron [glutrɔ̃] **NM** *Bot* burdock, burr

glouton, -onne [glutɔ̃, -ɔn] **ADJ** greedy, gluttonous
N glutton
NM *Zool* wolverine

gloutonnement [glutɔnmã] **ADV** gluttonously, greedily

gloutonnerie [glutɔnri] **NF** gluttony, greed

glu [gly] **NF** *(pour prendre les oiseaux)* bird lime; *(colle)* glue; **prendre des oiseaux à la g.** to lime birds; *Fig Fam* **c'est une vraie g., ce type!** the guy clings like a limpet *or* sticks like glue

gluant [glyã] **ADJ** *(collant)* sticky; *(paroi, limace)* slimy

gluau, -aux [glyo] **NM** lime twig *(for catching birds)*

glucide [glysid] **NM** *Biol, Chimie* carbohydrate; **riche en glucides** *(aliment)* high *or* rich in carbohydrates

glucose [glykoz] **NM** glucose; **g. sanguin** blood sugar

glucosé [glykoze] **ADJ** containing glucose; **une solution glucosée** a glucose solution

glutamate [glytamat] **NM** glutamate

gluten [glytɛn] **NM** gluten; **sans g.** gluten-free

glutineux, -euse [glytinø, -øz] **ADJ** glutinous

glycémie [glisemi] **NF** *Méd* glycaemia

glycérine [gliserin] **NF** *Chimie* glycerin(e), glycerol

glycériner [gliserine] **VT** to put glycerin(e) on

glycérol [gliserɔl] **NM** *Chimie* glycerol, glycerin(e)

glycine¹ [glisin] **NF** wisteria, wistaria

glycine² **NF** *Biol, Chimie* glycine

glycogène [glikɔʒɛn] **NM** *Chimie* glycogen

glycol [glikɔl] **NM** *Chimie* glycol

glyphe [glif] **NM** *Archéol* glyph, groove, channel

glyptique [gliptik] **NF** glyptics

GM [ʒeɛm] **NM** *(abrév* **gentil membre)** = holidaymaker (at the Club Med)

GMS [ʒeɛmɛs] **NFPL** *(abrév* **grandes et moyennes surfaces)** = large and medium-sized commercial outlets

gnangnan [nɑ̃nɑ̃] *Fam* **ADJ INV** drippy; *(livre)* soppy; **elle est g.** she's a real drip
N drip

gnaule [nol] **NF** *Fam* rotgut

gneiss [gnɛs] **NM** *Géol* gneiss

gniac [njak] **NF** *Fam* fighting spirit, drive; **avoir la g., être plein de g.** to have plenty of drive

gniole [nol] **NF** *Fam* rotgut

gnocchi [nɔki] **NMPL** *Culin* gnocchi

gnognote, gnognotte [nɔnɔt] **NF** *Fam* **c'est de la g.** *(mauvaise qualité)* it's a load of rubbish; **c'est pas de la g., cette voiture** that car is quite something

gnole, gnôle [nol] **NF** *Fam* rotgut

gnome [gnom] **NM** gnome; *Fig Péj (homme)* dwarf, midget

gnomique [gnomik] **ADJ** gnomic

gnon [nɔ̃] **NM** *Fam (coup de poing)* thump, wallop; **se prendre un g.** to get thumped *or* walloped; **on lui a filé un g. dans le pif** he got a thump *or* he got thumped on the nose

gnose [gnoz] **NF 1** *Hist, Rel* gnosticism **2** *Vieilli* gnosis

gnosticisme [gnɔstisism] **NM** *Hist, Rel* gnosticism

gnostique [gnɔstik] **ADJ, N** *Rel* gnostic

gnou [gnu] **NM** gnu, wildebeest

gnouf [nuf] **NM** *Mil Arg* glasshouse

GO [ʒeo] **NFPL** *Radio* (*abrév* **grandes ondes**) LW

NM (*abrév* **gentil organisateur**) = activity organizer (at the Club Med)

go (tout de) [tud(ə)go] **ADV** straight away; **répondre tout de go** to answer straight off *or* straight out

Go NM *Ordinat* (**gigaoctet**) GB

goal [gol] **NM** *Sport* goalkeeper, *Fam* goalie

gobelet [gɔblɛ] **NM** (*en argent, étain, cristal*) tumbler; (**verre**) **g.** tumbler; **g. en plastique/carton** plastic/paper cup; **tour de g.** conjuring trick (*with tumblers*); *Vieilli Fig* trick

gobeletier [gɔblətje] **NM** (*fabricant*) glassware manufacturer; (*vendeur*) glassware dealer

gobe-mouches [gɔbmuʃ] **NM INV 1** *Orn* flycatcher **2** *Bot* **dionée g.** Venus's fly trap, Venus flytrap **3** *Fam* (*personne*) simpleton, dope

gober [gɔbe] **VT** (*nourriture*) to gulp down; *Fig* **g. le morceau** *ou* **l'hameçon** to swallow *or* rise to the bait; *Fam* **g. des mouches** to stand gaping; *Fig* **il gobe tout ce qu'on lui dit** he believes everything he's told, he'll swallow anything; *Fam* **je ne peux pas la g.** I can't stand her
VPR se gober *Fam* to think a lot of oneself, to fancy oneself

goberger (se) [səgɔbɛrʒe] **VPR** (**je me gobergeai(s); n. n. gobergeons**) *Fam* (*prendre ses aises*) to take things easy, to look after oneself; (*faire bombance*) to live it up, to have a ball

gobeur, -euse [gɔbœr, -øz] **N** gulper, swallower; *Fig Fam* **c'est un g.** he's very gullible, he'll swallow anything

gobie [gɔbi] **NM** goby

godailler [gɔdaje] **VI** = **goder**

godasse [gɔdas] **NF** *Fam* shoe

godelureau, -eaux [gɔdlyro] **NM** *Péj Vieilli* popinjay

godemiché [gɔdmiʃe] **NM** dildo

goder [gɔde] **VI** (*d'un vêtement*) to pucker (up), to ruck (up); **g. aux genoux** to bag at the knees

godet [gɔdɛ] **NM 1** (*récipient*) pot; **g. à couleur** saucer for mixing watercolours; **g. à huile** (*d'une machine*) waste oil cup; **g. d'une pipe** bowl of a pipe; *Fam* **viens boire un g.** come and have a jar **2** (*de noria*) scoop; (*d'un dragueur, d'un excavateur, d'une roue à eau*) bucket; *Tech* (*au pied d'une machine*) socket; *Min* skip; **roue à godets** overshot wheel **3** *Couture* (*ondulation*) flare; (*lé*) gore; **à godets** flared; (*à lés*) gored

godiche [gɔdiʃ] *Fam* **ADJ** (*empoté*) clumsy, hamfisted
NF **quelle g., cette fille!** what a lump (of a girl)!

godille [gɔdij] **NF 1** *Naut* scull; **aller à la g.** to (single-)scull **2** *Ski* wedeln; **faire de la g.** to wedeln

godiller [gɔdije] **VI 1** *Naut* to (single-)scull **2** *Ski* to wedeln

godilleur [gɔdijœr] **NM** *Naut* sculler

godillot [gɔdijo] **NM** *Mil* boot; *Fam* (*gros soulier*) clodhopper

goéland [gɔelɑ̃] **NM** gull; **g. argenté** herring gull

goélette [gɔelɛt] **NF** *Naut* (*navire*) schooner; (**voile**) **g.** trysail

goémon [gɔemɔ̃] **NM** wrack

goglu [gɔgly] **NM** *Can* (*oiseau*) bobolink

gogo[1] [gogo] **ADV** *Fam* **à g.** galore; **avoir de l'argent à g.** to have money galore *or* to burn

gogo[2] **NM** *Fam* sucker, mug

goguenard [gɔgnar] **ADJ** mocking

goguenardise [gɔgnardiz] **NF** mockery

goguenot [gɔgno] *Arg* **NM** *Vieilli* (*pot de chambre*) po, jerry
NMPL goguenots bog, *Am* john

gogues [gɔg] **NMPL** *Arg* = **goguenots**

goguette [gɔgɛt] **NF** *Fam* **être en g.** to be (a bit) tight *or* merry; (*faire la noce*) to be out for a good time

goï, *pl* **goïm** [gɔj, gɔjim] **NM** *Rel* goy, *pl* goyim

goinfre [gwɛ̃fr] *Fam* **N** greedyguts, pig
ADJ greedy, piggish

goinfrerie [gwɛ̃frəri] **NF** gluttony, guzzling

goinfrer (se) [səgwɛ̃fre] **VPR** *Fam* to guzzle, to gorge oneself; **se g. de qch** to gorge oneself on sth, to guzzle sth

goitre [gwatr] **NM** *Méd* goitre, *Am* goiter

goitreux, -euse [gwatrø, -øz] *Méd* **ADJ** (*cou, gonflement, personne*) goitrous
N goitrous person

golden [gɔldɛn] **NF INV** Golden Delicious (apple)

goldo [gɔldo] **NF** *Fam* = Gauloise® cigarette

golem [gɔlɛm] **NM** (*dans le folklore juif*) golem

golf [gɔlf] **NM** *Sport* golf; **on fait un g. demain?** how about a game of golf tomorrow?; (**terrain de**) **g.** golf course; **g. miniature** miniature golf; **jouer au g.** to play golf; **pantalon de g.** plus fours

golfe [gɔlf] **NM** gulf, bay; **le G. Persique** the Persian Gulf; **les États** *ou* **les pays du G.** the Gulf States; **la guerre du G.** the Gulf War

golfer [gɔlfe] **VI** *Can* to play golf

golfeur, -euse [gɔlfœr, -øz] **N** golfer

gomina® [gɔmina] **NF** hair cream, brilliantine

gominer (se) [səgɔmine] **VPR** to plaster down one's hair (*with brilliantine etc*); **cheveux gominés** plastered-down hair

gommage [gɔmaʒ] **NM 1** (*action d'enduire de gomme*) gumming **2** *Tech* (*des valves, des pistons*) sticking, gumming **3** (*pour effacer*) erasing, *Br* rubbing out **4** (*produit de beauté*) facial scrub; **se faire un g.** to give oneself a facial scrub; **g. pour le corps** body scrub

gommant [gɔmɑ̃] **ADJ** **crème gommante, soin g.** face scrub

gomme [gɔm] **NF 1** (*substance*) gum; **boule de g.** gum **2** (*pour effacer*) eraser, *Br* rubber; *Fam* **histoire à la g.** pointless story; **idée/soirée à la g.** pathetic idea/party; **individu à la g.** useless individual **3** *Fam* **mettre (toute) la g.** to get a move on, to get one's skates on; *Aut* to put one's foot down
▸▸ **g. arabique** gum arabic; **g. à crayon** eraser, *Br* rubber; **g. à encre** ink eraser; **g. laque** shellac; **g. à mâcher** chewing gum; **g. pour machine à écrire** typewriter eraser *or Br* rubber

gomme-gutte, *pl* **gommes-guttes** [gɔmgyt] **NF** gamboge

gomme-laque, *pl* **gommes-laques NF** shellac, lac

gommer [gɔme] **VT 1** (*enduire de gomme*) to gum **2** (*effacer*) to erase, *Br* to rub out; *Fig* **g. une partie de son passé/un souvenir pénible** to erase part of one's past/a painful memory **3** **g. les cellules mortes de la peau** to remove dead skin **4** *Tech* to stick, to gum; **piston gommé** gummed piston

gomme-résine, *pl* **gommes-résines NF** gum resin

gommette [gɔmɛt] **NF** coloured *or Am* colored sticker

gommeux, -euse [gɔmø, -øz] **ADJ** gummy, sticky; **plante gommeuse** gum-yielding plant
NM *Fam Vieilli* dandy, fop, *Am* dude

gommier [gɔmje] **NM** gum tree

gonade [gɔnad] **NF** *Biol* gonad

gond [gɔ̃] **NM** (*de porte*) hinge; **mettre une porte dans ses gonds** to hang a door; **sortir de ses gonds** (*d'une porte*) to come off its hinges; *Fig Fam* to fly off the handle, to lose one's temper

gondolage [gɔ̃dɔlaʒ] **NM** (*du bois*) warping; (*du papier*) curling; (*d'une plaque de fer*) buckling

gondolant [gɔ̃dɔlɑ̃] **ADJ** *Fam* (*histoire*) side-splitting, hilarious

gondole [gɔ̃dɔl] **NF 1** (*barque*) gondola **2** (*présentoir*) island, gondola

gondolement [gɔ̃dɔlmɑ̃] **NM** = **gondolage**

gondoler [gɔ̃dɔle] **VI** (*du bois*) to warp; (*du papier*) to curl; (*d'une plaque de fer*) to buckle
VPR se gondoler 1 (*du bois*) to warp; (*du papier*) to curl; (*d'une plaque de fer*) to buckle; **mon disque s'est gondolé à la chaleur** my record's warped in the sun, the sun's warped my record **2** *Fam* (*rire*) to fall about laughing, to split one's sides laughing

gondolier, -ière [gɔ̃dɔlje, -jɛr] **N** gondolier

gonfalon [gɔ̃falɔ̃], **gonfanon** [gɔ̃fanɔ̃] **NM** *Hist* gonfalon, gonfanon

gonflable [gɔ̃flabl] **ADJ** inflatable

gonflage [gɔ̃flaʒ] **NM 1** inflation; **vérifier le g. (des pneus)** to check the tyre *or Am* tire pressure **2** *Cin* blow-up printing

gonflant [gɔ̃flɑ̃] **ADJ 1** (*coiffure*) bouffant **2** *très Fam* (*énervant*) maddening, irritating
NM (*d'une coiffure*) bouffant; **mousse qui donne du g. à vos cheveux** mousse that gives body to your hair

gonfle [gɔ̃fl] *Suisse* **NF** (*congère*) snowdrift
ADJ (*enflé, gonflé*) swollen, puffy; (*ballonné*) bloated

gonflé [gɔ̃fle] **ADJ 1** (*boursouflé*) (*yeux*) swollen, puffy; (*visage*) bloated, swollen, puffy; (*estomac*) bloated, swollen; (*pieds, chevilles*) swollen; *Fig* **g. d'orgueil** puffed up with pride; **avoir le cœur g. de chagrin** to be heart-broken; **elle avait les yeux gonflés de larmes** her eyes were swollen with tears **2** *Naut* (*voile*) full **3** *Fam* **tu es g.** (*culotté*) you've got a nerve; **c'est g. ce qu'il a fait** that's what he did took some nerve; **g. à bloc** keyed up; (*en pleine forme physique*) full of beans; (*sûr de soi*) sure of oneself; *Aut Fam* **moteur g.** hotted-up *or* souped-up engine **4** (*exagéré*) **prix gonflés** excessive prices

gonflement [gɔ̃fləmɑ̃] **NM 1** (*des pneus, d'un ballon*) inflating, inflation; (*de l'estomac*) swelling **2** (*exagération*) (*de prix*) excessive increase; (*de résultats, statistiques*) exaggeration

gonfler [gɔ̃fle] **VT 1** (*pneu*) to blow up, to pump up, to inflate; (*ses joues*) to puff out, to blow out; **g. un ballon/un matelas pneumatique** to inflate *or* blow up a balloon/an airbed; **le vent gonfle les voiles** the wind fills the sails; **les bons résultats de son fils la gonflent d'orgueil** her son's good results make her as proud as a peacock; **cette bonne nouvelle gonfla son cœur de joie** the good news filled his heart with joy
2 (*faire augmenter de volume*) to swell; **torrent gonflé par les pluies** torrent swollen by the rains
3 *Fig* (*grossir*) (*résultats, conséquences*) to exaggerate; **g. les chiffres d'un sondage** to inflate *or* exaggerate the figures from a poll; **g. l'importance de qch/qn** to exaggerate *or* overstress the importance of sth/sb; **le prof a gonflé les notes** the teacher bumped up

the marks; **g. un événement** to hype an event

4 *Cin* to blow up, to enlarge

5 *Aut Fam (un moteur)* **g.** to hot up, to soup up

6 *très Fam (énerver)* **g. qn** to get on sb's nerves, to irritate sb; **il nous les gonfle avec ses matchs de foot** he really gets on our nerves *or* he's a real pain in the neck with his football matches

VI to swell; **le bois a gonflé** the wood has swollen; **laisser g. les haricots toute une nuit** to leave the beans to soak all night; **laisser de la pâte g.** to let dough rise

VPR se gonfler to swell; **les poumons se gonflent** the lungs fill; *Fig* **se g. d'orgueil** to swell up with pride; **se g. de colère** to be bursting with rage; **mon cœur s'est gonflé de joie à cette nouvelle** my heart filled with joy at the news

gonflette [gɔ̃flɛt] *NF Fam Péj* pumping iron; **faire de la g.** to pump iron

gonfleur [gɔ̃flœr] *NM (air)* pump

gong [gɔ̃(g)] *NM* **1** *Mus* gong **2** *Boxe* bell; *Fig* **sauvé par le g.** saved by the bell

goniomètre [gɔnjɔmɛtr] *NM Radio* goniometer, position finder, direction finder; *Mil* dial sight

goniométrie [gɔnjɔmetri] *NF* goniometry, position finding, direction finding

gonococcie [gɔnɔkɔksi] *NF Méd* gonorrhoea, *Am* gonorrhea

gonocoque [gɔnɔkɔk] *NM Méd* gonococcus

gonze [gɔ̃z] *NM Arg Vieilli (homme)* fellow, *Br* chap

gonzesse [gɔ̃zɛs] *NF très Fam (femme)* chick, *Br* bird, *Am* broad

gordien [gɔrdjɛ̃] *ADJ M Fig* **trancher le nœud g.** to cut the Gordian knot

gore [gɔr] *Fam* **ADJ INV** *(sanglant)* gory
NM *(genre)* gore (cinema); *(film)* gore film

goret [gɔrɛ] *NM* piglet; *Fam (enfant malpropre)* little pig; **manger comme un g.** to eat like a pig

goretex® [gɔrtɛks] *NM Tex* Gore-Tex

gorge [gɔrʒ] *NF* **1** *(gosier, cou)* throat; **avoir mal à la g., avoir un mal de g.** to have a sore throat; **un serrement de g.** a lump in one's throat; **avoir la g. serrée** to have a lump in one's throat; **parler avec la g. serrée par la peine/l'angoisse** to speak in a voice trembling with sorrow/anguish; **crier à pleine g.** *ou* **à g. déployée** to shout at the top of one's voice; **rire à pleine g.** *ou* **à g. déployée** to roar with laughter; *Fig* **faire des gorges chaudes de qch** to laugh sth to scorn; **trancher la g. à qn** to cut sb's throat; *Fig* **s'il s'en rend compte, il va me trancher la g.** if he finds out, he'll kill me; **le chien lui a sauté à la g.** the dog leapt at his throat; **ce n'est pas une raison pour me sauter à la g.** that's no reason to jump down my throat; *Fig* **avoir le couteau sous la g.** to have a gun at one's head; *Fig* **je le tiens à la g.** I've got him by the throat, I've got a stranglehold on him; *Fig* **prendre qn à la g.** to get sb in a stranglehold; **nous étions pris à la g., nous ne pouvions rien faire d'autre** we were in a stranglehold *or* we had a gun at our heads, we couldn't do anything else; **pris à la g. par ses créanciers, il ...** with his creditors holding a gun to his head, he ...; **faire rentrer à qn ses mots dans la g.** to make sb eat his/her words; *Fig* **cela m'est resté en travers de la g.** that stuck in my throat *or* gullet; *Fig* **rendre g.** to make restitution; **je lui ferai rendre g.** I'll make him pay it back

2 *(poitrine) (d'une femme)* bosom, breast; *(d'un pigeon)* breast

3 *Géog* gorge

4 *Tech* groove; *Archit* quirk; *(d'un écrou)* furrow; *(d'un pistolet, d'un étui à car-*

touches) neck; *(d'un verrou)* tumbler; *Archit* **moulure à g.** grooved moulding

gorgé [gɔrʒe] *ADJ* **une éponge gorgée d'eau** a sponge full of water; **sol g. d'eau** sodden soil; **champs gorgés d'eau** waterlogged fields; **des fruits gorgés de soleil** sun-kissed fruit; **g. de sang** gorged with blood

gorge-de-pigeon *ADJ INV* dove-coloured, *Am* dove-colored

gorgée [gɔrʒe] *NF (de vin)* mouthful; **petite g.** sip; **boire qch à petites gorgées** to sip sth; **avaler qch/finir son verre d'une g.** to swallow sth/finish one's glass in one (gulp)

gorgeon [gɔrʒɔ̃] *NM Fam* drink

gorger [gɔrʒe] **(je gorgeai(s), n. gorgeons)** *VT (oies)* to cram
VPR se gorger to stuff oneself **(de** with), to gorge oneself **(de** on, with); **la terre se gorgea d'eau** the ground became waterlogged; *Fig* **elle semblait se g. de sa présence** it seemed as if she couldn't see enough of him

Gorgone [gɔrgon] *NF Myth* Gorgon

gorgonzola [gɔrgɔ̃zɔla] *NM* Gorgonzola (cheese)

gorille [gɔrij] *NM* **1** *(mammifère)* gorilla **2** *Fig Fam* gorilla, bodyguard

gosier [gozje] *NM (pharynx)* throat, gullet; **avoir une arête dans le g.** to have a fishbone stuck in one's throat; *Fam* **avoir le g. sec** to be dry *or* thirsty; **rire à plein g.** to laugh loudly *or* heartily; *Fam* **avoir le g. en pente** to have a permanent thirst, to like one's drink

gospel [gɔspɛl] *NM* gospel (music)

gosse [gɔs] *N* **1** *Fam (enfant)* kid; **c'est encore une g.** she's just a kid; **elle est venue avec ses deux gosses** she came along with her two kids **2** *Fam (jeune)* **c'est une belle g.** she's a smashing girl; **il est plutôt beau g.** he's quite good-looking **3** *Can Arg* **gosses** balls
▸ ▸ **g. de riches** spoilt rich kid

gosser [gɔse] *VT Can Fam* to whittle

Goth [gɔt] *N Hist* Goth

gotha [gɔta] *NM* **le g. du show-business/de la finance** the show-business/financial elite; **le G. (almanach)** ≃ Burke's Peerage

gothique [gɔtik] *ADJ* Gothic
NM *Archit, Ling* Gothic
NF *Typ* Gothic, *Br* black letter; **écrire en g.** to write in Gothic script

gotique [gɔtik] *NM Ling* Gothic

gouache [gwaʃ] *NF Beaux-Arts* gouache; **peindre à la g.** to paint in gouache

gouailler [gwaje] *VI Vieilli* to joke

gouailleur, -euse [gwajœr, -øz] *Vieilli ADJ (ton)* joking, mocking, bantering
N joker

goualante [gwalɑ̃t] *NF Fam Vieilli* popular song

gouape [gwap] *NF Arg* lout

gouda [guda] *NM Culin* Gouda

goudron [gudrɔ̃] *NM* tar; **g. (de gaz** *ou* **de houille)** coal tar; **g. de bois** wood tar; **g. minéral** asphalt, bitumen

goudronnage [gudrɔnaʒ] *NM* tarring

goudronner [gudrɔne] *VT* to tar; **route goudronnée** tarred road; **toile goudronnée** tarpaulin; **papier goudronné** tar-lined paper

goudronneur [gudrɔnœr] *NM* tar sprayer *or* spreader

goudronneuse¹ [gudrɔnøz] *NF (machine)* tar sprayer; *(pour l'asphalte)* asphalt spreader

goudronneux, -euse² [gudrɔnø, -øz] *ADJ* tarry; *(huile)* gummy

gouffre [gufr] *NM* gulf, abyss, chasm; *(tourbillon)* whirlpool, vortex; *Géol* sinkhole, *Br* swallow hole; **g. béant** yawning gulf *or* chasm; **g. sous-marin** oceanic abyss; *Fig Litt*

le g. de l'oubli/du désespoir the depths of oblivion/despair; *Fig* **être au bord du g.** to be on the edge of the abyss; *Fig* **c'est un g. d'ignorance** the depths of his ignorance are unfathomable; *Fig* **cette voiture est un g.** this car just swallows up money, with this car it's like pouring money into a bottomless pit; *Mktg* **g. financier** *(produit)* financial disaster, dog

gouge [guʒ] *NF Tech* gouge, hollow chisel

gougère [guʒɛr] *NF Culin* gougère *(choux pastry with cheese)*

gougnafier [gupafje] *NM Fam* nerd

gouille [guj] *NF Suisse (flaque d'eau)* puddle; *(étang, mare)* pond

gouine [gwin] *NF Arg (lesbienne)* dyke, les

goujat [guʒa] *NM* boor, churl

goujaterie [guʒatri] *NF* boorishness, churlishness

goujon¹ [guʒɔ̃] *NM* gudgeon; *Fam* **taquiner le g.** to do a bit of fishing

goujon² *NM Constr (en maçonnerie)* gudgeon; *Menuis* tenon; *Tech* bolt, stud; *Menuis* **g. perdu, g. prisonnier** dowel (pin); *Tech* **g. de jonction** assembling pin, bolt; **g. de charnière** hinge pin; **g. d'arbre** shaft gudgeon

goujonner [guʒɔne] *VT Menuis* to dowel; *Constr* to joggle; *Tech* to pin, to bolt

goulache, goulasch [gulaʃ] *NF ou NM Culin* goulash

goulafre [gulafr] *Belg ADJ (glouton)* greedy
N *(glouton)* greedy person

goulag [gulag] *NM* Gulag

goulée [gule] *NF Fam* big mouthful, gulp; **j'ai besoin d'une bonne g. d'air pur** I need a good lungful of fresh air; **il tira sur ha vane, et aspira une grosse g.** he drew deeply on his cigar

goulet [gulɛ] *NM* **1** *Géog (défilé)* gully; **g. d'étranglement** bottleneck **2** *Naut (chenal) (d'un port)* gut, bottleneck, narrows; **le G. de Brest** the Brest Channel

gouleyant [gulɛjɑ̃] *ADJ (vin)* pleasant, easy-drinking

goulot [gulo] *NM (d'une bouteille)* neck; **boire au g.** to drink (straight) from the bottle; *Fig* **g. d'étranglement** bottleneck; *Fig Vulg* **refouler du g.** to have foul breath

goulotte [gulɔt] *NF Tech* chute; *(d'un wagonnet à charbon)* spout

goulu, -ue [guly] *ADJ* **1** *(glouton)* greedy, gluttonous; *(regards)* hungry, greedy **2 pois g.** sugar pea
N *(personne)* glutton

goulûment [gulymɑ̃] *ADV* greedily, voraciously; *(regarder)* hungrily, greedily

goupil [gupi] *NM Arch* fox

goupille [gupij] *NF Tech* pin; **g. fendue** split pin, cotter; **g. d'arrêt** stop bolt

goupiller [gupije] *VT* **1** *Tech* to pin; *(boulon)* to cotter **2** *Fam (arranger)* to fix (up); **bien/mal goupillé** well/badly organized; **je me demande ce qu'il est en train de g.** I wonder what he's up to
VPR se goupiller *Fam (d'une montre, un mécanisme)* to work; *Fig* **ça s'est bien goupillé** it worked out well; **ça s'est mal goupillé** it didn't work out

goupillon [gupijɔ̃] *NM* **1** *Rel (pour eau bénite)* sprinkler, aspergillum **2** *(pour biberons, bouteilles)* bottle brush

gourance [gurɑ̃s] *NF Fam* boob, bloomer, *Am* goof; **faire une g.** to (make a) boob, to make a bloomer, *Am* to goof

gourbi [gurbi] *NM* **1** *(cabane)* hut, shack **2** *Fam (taudis)* hovel

gourd [gur] *ADJ* numb (with cold); **avoir les doigts gourds** to have numb fingers

gourde¹ [gurd] *NF* **1** *Bot* gourd **2** *(récipient* *pour boissons)* flask; *(coloquinte)* gourd **3** *Fam (personne stupide)* dope, dimwit ▪ **ADJ** *Fam* dopey, dimwitted

gourde² NF *Fin (monnaie de Haïti)* gourde

gourdin [gurdɛ̃] NM club, cudgel, bludgeon

gourer (se) [səgure] VPR *Fam* to boob, to make a boob *or* bloomer, *Am* to goof; **se g. de route** to lose one's way; **se g. d'adresse** to get the wrong address

gourgandine [gurgɑ̃din] NF *Vieilli* loose woman

gourgane [gurgan] NF *Can* broad bean

gourmand, -ande [gurmɑ̃, -ɑ̃d] ADJ *(personne)* greedy; **être g. de** *(sucreries)* to be fond of; *Fig* to be greedy for; **ma voiture est vraiment gourmande en essence** my car really gobbles up the *Br* petrol *or Am* gas; **cet appareil est très g. d'électricité** this appliance gobbles up *or* consumes a lot of electricity; **pois g.** sugar pea, mangetout, *Am* snowpea ▪ **N** *(personne)* gourmand ▪ **NM** *(branche parasite)* sucker

gourmander [gurmɑ̃de] VT *Litt* to rebuke, to chide

gourmandise [gurmɑ̃diz] NF **1** greediness; **avec g.** greedily **2 gourmandises** delicacies, *Fam* goodies

gourme [gurm] NF **1** *Méd Vieilli* impetigo **2** *Vét* strangles **3** *Fig Vieilli* **jeter sa g.** to sow one's wild oats

gourmé [gurme] ADJ *Litt Péj* stiff, starchy, affected

gourmet [gurmɛ] NM gourmet; *Fig (connaisseur)* connoisseur; **un fin g.** a discerning gourmet

gourmette [gurmɛt] NF **1** *(d'une montre)* chain; *(bracelet)* chain (bracelet) **2** *(pour les chevaux)* curb (chain)

gourou [guru] NM *Rel, Fig* guru

gousse [gus] NF *(de légumineuses)* pod; **g. d'ail** clove of garlic; **g. de vanille** vanilla pod

gousset [gusɛ] NM **1** *(poche)* fob (pocket); **il a le g. bien garni** his pockets are well lined; **montre de g.** fob watch **2** *Tech (shoulder)* bracket, stay plate, gusset (plate)

GOÛT [gu]

taste **1–5** ▪ flavour **2** ▪ liking **4** ▪ style **6**	

NM **1** *(sens)* taste; *Fam* **faire passer le g. du pain à qn** *(le tuer)* to do away with sb; *(ôter l'envie de recommencer)* to put a stop to sb's little games

2 *(saveur)* taste, flavour, *Am* flavor; *(du vin)* bouquet; **g. amer/épicé** bitter/spicy taste; **avoir un g. de terroir** *(de pain)* to have a taste of the country; *(d'un accent)* to have a rural twang; **cela a le g. de la banane/du gin** it tastes like banana/gin; **donner du g. à un mets** to give a dish flavour; **manquer de g., ne pas avoir de g.** *(d'un plat)* to be tasteless, to have no taste; **sans g.** *(adjectif)* tasteless; *(adverbe)* tastelessly

3 *(préférence),* *Culin* **ajouter du sucre et du citron selon son g.** add sugar and lemon to taste; **chacun ses goûts, des goûts et des couleurs on ne discute pas, tous les goûts sont dans la nature** everyone to his (own) taste, there's no accounting for taste; **affaire de g.** matter of taste

4 *(prédilection, convenance)* taste, liking; **avoir des goûts de luxe** to have expensive tastes; **il a des goûts bizarres** he has strange tastes; **une maison/un homme à mon g.** a house/a man to my taste *or* liking; **elle n'est pas à mon g.** I don't care for her, she's not to my taste *or* liking; **trouver qch/qn à son g.** to find sth/sb to one's taste *or* liking; **le g. des affaires** a taste *or* liking for business; **g. pas-**

---

sager passing fancy; **avoir du g. pour** *ou* **le g. de qch** to have a taste or liking for sth; **faire qch par g.** to do sth from inclination, to do sth because one likes to; **je n'habite pas ici par g.** I don't live here from choice; **je le fais par g. du travail bien fait** I do it because I like to see work well done; **prendre g. à qch** to acquire a taste *or* develop a liking for sth; **avec le temps elle y a pris g.** it grew on her, she developed a liking for it; **elle n'a plus (de) g. à rien** she no longer wants to do anything; **reprendre g. à la lecture/à la musique** to regain one's taste for reading/music; **reprendre g. à la vie** to regain one's zest for living, to find life worth living again

5 *(discernement, jugement)* taste; **g. parfait** perfect taste; **il a du g.** he has (good) taste; **une femme de g.** a woman of taste; **remarque d'un g. douteux** remark in doubtful taste; **une plaisanterie/image de mauvais g.** a joke/picture in bad taste; **une robe de mauvais g.** a tasteless dress; **décoration de bon g.** tasteful decoration; **elle s'habille avec g.** she has (a) good dress sense, she has good taste in clothes

6 *Litt (style)* style, manner; **peint dans le g. de Watteau** painted in the style *or* manner of Watteau; **quelque chose dans ce g.-là** something like that, something of that sort

---

goûter [gute] NM snack; *(à quatre heures)* (afternoon) tea; **l'heure du g.** teatime; **elle est invitée pour le g.** *ou* **à un g.** she has been invited to tea

▪ VT **1** *(savourer) (nourriture)* to taste; *(pour la première fois) (nourriture, boisson)* to taste, to try **2** *Fig (aimer, apprécier) (la musique, la beauté de la nature etc)* to enjoy, to appreciate; **g. le silence de la nuit** to savour *or* relish the silence of night **3** *Belg, Can (avoir un goût de)* to taste; **ce fruit goûte le pourri** this fruit tastes rotten

▪ VI **1 g. à quatre heures** to have tea *or* a snack at four o'clock **2 g. de qch** to taste sth; *Fig* **elle a goûté de tous les petits boulots** she's had a go at all sorts of jobs; **g. à qch** to taste sth, to try sth **3** *Belg (avoir bon goût)* to taste nice

goûteur, -euse [gutœr, -øz] N taster

goutte [gut] NF **1** *(d'un liquide)* drop; **g. à g.** drop by drop; **tomber g. à g.** *(d'un liquide)* to drip; *Fig* **c'est la g. d'eau qui fait déborder le vase** it's the last straw, it's the straw that breaks/broke the camel's back; **se ressembler comme deux gouttes d'eau** to be as like as two peas in a pod; *Fig* **c'est une g. d'eau dans la mer** it's a drop in the ocean; **il suait à grosses gouttes** the sweat was pouring off him; **il n'y a pas eu une g. de pluie depuis trois mois** there hasn't been a drop of rain for three months; **il tombait quelques gouttes** it was spitting with rain; *Fam* **avoir la g. au nez** to have a runny *or* dripping nose; **g. d'eau** drop of water; *(bijou)* drop

2 *(petite quantité)* drop; **g. de cognac** *(dans une sauce)* dash *or* drop of brandy; **boire une g. de cognac après le repas** to have a drop *or* nip of brandy after one's meal; **encore une g. de café?** a drop more coffee?; *Fam* **boire la g.** to have a nip

3 *Pharm* **gouttes** drops; **prendre des gouttes** to take drops; **gouttes pour le nez** nose *or* nasal drops; **gouttes auriculaires** ear drops

4 *Méd* gout; **avoir la g.** to suffer from *or* have gout, to be gouty

▪ ADV *Arch, Hum* **je n'entends g. à ce que vous dites** I don't understand a word of what you're saying; *Litt* **je n'y vois g.** I can't see a thing

goutte-à-goutte NM INV *Méd* drip; **g. intraveineux** intravenous drip; **on lui fait un g.** he's on a drip; **on a dû lui faire** *ou* **mettre un g.** he had to be put on a drip

gouttelette [gutlɛt] NF droplet, tiny drop

---

goutter [gute] VI to drip

goutteux, -euse [gutø, -øz] *Méd* ADJ *(personne)* gouty ▪ N gout sufferer

gouttière [gutjɛr] NF **1** *(le long du toit)* gutter, guttering **2** *(le long du mur)* drainpipe, downpipe, *Am* downspout **3** *Anat (d'un os)* groove **4** *Méd* cradle, (cradle-like) splint **5** *Typ (de page)* gutter

gouvernable [guvɛrnabl] ADJ *(bateau, entreprise, équipe)* manageable; *(pays)* governable; **peu g.** *(entreprise, équipe)* unmanageable; *(pays)* ungovernable

gouvernail [guvɛrnaj] NM *Naut* rudder; **roue du g.** (steering) wheel; **tenir le g.** to be at the wheel *or* at the helm, to steer; *Fig* **tenir le g. de l'État/d'une affaire** to be at the helm of the state/a business

▪ ▸ *Aviat* **g. de direction** rudder; *Naut* **g. de plongée** *(d'un sous-marin)* horizontal rudder; **g. de profondeur** *Naut* diving rudder, plane, hydroplane; *Aviat* elevator

gouvernance [guvɛrnɑ̃s] NF **1** *(action de gouverner)* government **2** *(manière de gérer)* governance, government; **g. mondiale** global governance

gouvernant, -ante¹ [guvɛrnɑ̃, -ɑ̃t] ADJ *(classe, parti)* governing, ruling ▪ NMPL **les gouvernants** those in power

gouvernante² [guvɛrnɑ̃t] NF *(qui garde les enfants)* governess; *(qui s'occupe d'une personne, d'un hôtel)* housekeeper; **g. d'étage** *(d'un hôtel)* floor housekeeper; **g. du soir** *(d'un hôtel)* turndown housekeeper; **g. générale** *(d'un hôtel)* executive *or* head housekeeper

gouverne [guvɛrn] NF **1** *Naut* steering; *Fig* **pour votre g.** for your guidance **2** *Aviat* **gouvernes** control surfaces; **g. compensée** balanced surface; **g. de direction** rudder; **g. de profondeur** elevator

gouvernement [guvɛrnəmɑ̃] NM *Pol* government; **le g. français/britannique** the French/British government; **sous le g. Jospin** during Jospin's term of office, during Jospin's administration; **le chef du g.** the head of (the) government; **former un nouveau g.** to form a new government; **g. républicain/parlementaire** republican/parliamentary government; **g. central** central government; **g. de coalition** coalition government; **g. de cohabitation** = government in which the President and the parliamentary majority are from different parties; **g. fantoche** puppet government; **g. fédéral** federal government; **g. majoritaire** majority government; **g. minoritaire** minority government; **g. provisoire** provisional government; **g. représentatif** representative government; **g. de transition** interim government VOIR GRAMMAIRE A11

gouvernemental, -ale, -aux, -ales [guvɛrnəmɑ̃tal, -o] ADJ governmental; **politique gouvernementale** government(al) policy; **le parti g.** the governing *or* ruling party, the party in government; **un journal g.** a government newspaper

gouverner [guvɛrne] VT **1** *(diriger) (un pays)* to govern, to rule; *(dominer)* to control; **Dieu gouverne l'univers** God is the ruler of the universe; **g. ses passions/sa colère/sa jalousie** to control *or* govern one's passions/anger/jealousy; *Tech* **mouvement gouverné par un pendule** movement regulated *or* governed *or* controlled by a pendulum

2 *Naut (bateau)* to steer; **faire g.** to con; **g. sur un port** to steer *or* stand *or* head for a port, to bear in with a port; **g. à la lame** to steer by the sea; **gouvernez droit!** steady!

3 *Gram* **verbe qui gouverne l'accusatif** verb that governs *or* takes the accusative

4 *Vieilli* to manage, to administer; **bien g.**

gravillon [gravijɔ̃] NM (fine) gravel, grit; **gravillons** Br loose chippings, Am gravel

gravillonnage [gravijɔnaʒ] NM (fine-) gravelling

gravillonner [gravijɔne] VT to (fine-)gravel

gravimétrie [gravimetri] NF Phys gravimetry

gravimétrique [gravimetrik] ADJ Phys gravimetric

gravir [gravir] VT (montagne, escalier) to climb; (échelle) to climb, to mount; Fig **g. les échelons** to climb the ladder

gravissime [gravisim] ADJ extremely serious

gravitation [gravitasjɔ̃] NF Phys gravitation

gravitationnel [gravitasjɔnɛl] ADJ Phys gravitational; **force gravitationnelle** force of gravity

gravité [gravite] NF 1 Phys gravity; **g. spécifique** specific gravity; **centre de g.** centre of gravity; **alimentation par g.** gravity feed 2 (réserve, sérieux) gravity, seriousness 3 (danger) (d'une maladie, d'une opération) seriousness; **blessure sans g.** slight or minor wound; **accident/chute sans g.** minor accident/fall 4 (importance) (d'un problème) gravity, seriousness

graviter [gravite] VI 1 to revolve (**autour de** round); **g. autour de la terre** to orbit the earth; Fig **g. autour de qn** to hover around sb; **les flatteurs qui gravitent dans les hautes sphères du pouvoir** the flatterers who move in the higher echelons of power 2 Vieilli to gravitate (**vers** towards)

gravois [gravwa] NMPL Vieilli = gravats

gravure [gravyr] NF 1 (action) engraving; **g. à l'eau-forte** etching; **g. en creux** intaglio engraving; **g. en taille-douce** copperplate engraving; **g. sur bois** woodcutting, wood engraving 2 (ouvrage) engraving; **g. à l'eau-forte** etching; **g. en taille-douce, g. sur cuivre** copperplate (engraving); **g. sur bois** woodcut, wood engraving; **g. en couleurs** colour print; **g. hors texte** full-page plate; **g. avant la lettre** proof before letters; **g. de mode** fashion plate; Fig **cette fille est une g. de mode** that girl's a real fashion plate

grayé [greje] ADJ Can (pour faire qch) well-equipped; Arg (bien monté) well-hung

gré [gre] NM 1 (goût) à mon g., **selon mon g.** to my liking, to my taste; (à ma guise) as I please or like; **elle va et vient à son (bon) g.** she comes and goes as she pleases or likes; **je m'habille à mon g.** I dress to please myself; **trouver qch à son g.** to find sth to one's liking; **une chambre à mon g.** a room that I like or that suits me, a room to my liking 2 (volonté) **se marier contre le g. de son père** to get married against one's father's wishes; **elle a dû accepter contre son g.** she had to accept against her will; **bail renouvelable au g. du locataire** lease renewable at the option of the tenant; **de mon propre g., de mon plein g.** of my own free will, of my own accord; **de bon g.** willingly, gladly; **de mauvais g.** reluctantly; **bon g. mal g.** whether we/you/etc like it or not, willy-nilly; **il faut qu'il vienne de g. ou de force** he has to come whether he wants to or not, he has to come willy-nilly; **au g. des flots** at the mercy of the waves; **de g. à g.** by (mutual) agreement; **vendre de g. à g.** to sell by private contract, to sell privately; Fig **au g. des événements/circonstances** (agir, changer d'avis etc) according to how events turn out/to circumstances 3 Fml (gratitude) **savoir g. à qn de (faire) qch** to be grateful to sb for (doing) sth; **nous vous saurions g. de bien vouloir ...** we would be grateful if you would kindly ...; Vieilli **savoir mauvais g. à qn de qch** to be annoyed with sb about sth

grèbe [grɛb] NM grebe

grébiche [grebiʃ], **grébige** [grebiʒ] NF 1 Typ (d'un manuscrit etc) file number 2 (classeur) loose-leaf binder

grec, grecque [grɛk] ADJ Greek; **les orateurs grecs** the Greek orators; **tragédie grecque** Greek tragedy; **profil g.** Grecian profile
NM Ling Greek; **g. ancien/moderne** Ancient/Modern Greek
N **G.** Greek
NF **grecque 1** Culin **à la grecque** stewed with olive oil and herbs 2 Archit, Beaux-Arts Greek key pattern, Greek border

Grèce [grɛs] NF Greece

gréciser [gresize] VT to Hellenize; **g. un mot** to give a Greek form to a word

gréco-latin, pl gréco-latins [grekolatɛ̃] ADJ Ling Gr(a)eco-Latin

gréco-romain, pl gréco-romains [grekorɔmɛ̃] ADJ Gr(a)eco-Roman

gredin, -ine [grədɛ̃, -in] N Vieilli (vaurien) rascal, wretch; Fam **petit g.!** you little rascal or horror!

gredinerie [grədinri] NF Vieilli (acte) mean or underhand action; (conduite) mean or underhand behaviour

gréement [gremɑ̃] NM Naut 1 (ensemble des voiles) rigging; (équipement) gear 2 (disposition des mâts et des voiles) (d'un bateau) rig; **g. Marconi** Bermuda rig

gréer [gree] VT Naut (mât, bateau etc) to rig; (hamac, filets etc) to sling; **gréé en carré** square-rigged; **g. une vergue** to send up a yard

gréeur [greœr] NM Naut rigger

greffage [grɛfaʒ] NM Chir, Bot grafting

greffe [grɛf] NF 1 Chir (de peau, de tissu) graft; (d'organe) transplant; Bot graft, slip; **g. du cœur/du rein** heart/kidney transplant; **g. hépatique** liver transplant 2 Bot (action) **g. par œil détaché** budding; **g. en écusson** shield grafting or budding

greffe² NM 1 Jur clerk of the court's office 2 Fin (de société par actions) registry

greffé, -ée [grefe] N Méd **g. cardiaque** ou **du cœur** heart transplant patient

greffer [grefe] VT Chir, Bot (peau, tissu, bouture) to graft; Chir (organe) to transplant

greffeur [grefœr] NM Bot grafter, budder

greffier [grefje] NM 1 Jur clerk (of the court) 2 Admin, Fin registrar 3 Arg (chat) pussy(-cat), moggy

greffoir [grefwar] NM grafting knife

greffon [grefɔ̃] NM Chir (de tissu, de peau) graft; (d'organe) transplant; Bot graft, slip

grégaire [gregɛr] ADJ gregarious; **l'instinct g.** the herd instinct

> Il faut noter que lorsque l'adjectif anglais **gregarious** s'emploie à propos de personnes, il signifie **sociable**.

grégarisme [gregarism] NM gregariousness

grège [grɛʒ] ADJ 1 **soie g.** raw silk 2 (couleur) whitish-beige

grégeois [greʒwa] ADJ Antiq, Mil **feu g.** Greek fire

grégorien, -ienne [gregorjɛ̃, -jɛn] ADJ (rite, réforme) Gregorian; **chant g.** Gregorian chant
NM Gregorian chant

grêle¹ [grɛl] ADJ (jambe, membres, main) skinny; (tige, silhouette) slender; (voix, son) shrill; Anat **intestin g.** small intestine

grêle² NF hail; **orage de g.** hailstorm; Fig **g. de coups/balles** hail or shower of blows/bullets

grêlé [grele] ADJ (peau) pockmarked

grêler [grele] V IMPERS **il grêle** it's hailing
VT (cultures etc) to damage by hail; **la région a été complètement grêlée** the whole region has been hit by hail

grelin [grəlɛ̃] NM Naut hawser

grêlon [grɛlɔ̃] NM hailstone

grelot [grəlo] NM (small) bell; (de traîneau) sleigh bell; Fam **avoir les grelots** (avoir peur) to have the wind up

grelottement [grəlɔtmɑ̃] NM 1 (tremblement) shivering 2 (tintement) jingling, tinkling

grelotter [grəlɔte] VI 1 (trembler) **g. de froid/de peur** to shiver or tremble or shake with cold/fear 2 (tinter) to jingle, to tinkle

greluche [grəlyʃ] NF Péj très Fam chick, Br bird

Grenade [grənad] NF 1 (en Espagne) Granada 2 (aux îles du Vent) **la G.** Grenada

grenade [grənad] NF 1 Mil (projectile) grenade; **g. à main** hand grenade; **g. fumigène** smoke grenade; **g. lacrymogène** tear-gas grenade; Naut **g. sous-marine** depth charge 2 (fruit) pomegranate

grenadier¹ [grənadje] NM (arbre) pomegranate (tree)

grenadier² NM Mil grenadier; Fig tall and masculine woman; **boire comme un g.** to drink like a fish

grenadière [grənadjɛr] NF Mil (d'un fusil) band

grenadine [grənadin] NF 1 Culin grenadine 2 Tex grenadine

grenaillage [grənajaʒ] NM Tech shot blasting

grenaille [grənaj] NF 1 (en métal) shot; **g. de plomb** lead shot 2 (pour la volaille) refuse grain, tailings 3 Belg **grenailles errantes** (sur panneau) loose chippings, Am gravel

grenailler [grənaje] VT (métal) to granulate

grenat [grəna] NM garnet
ADJ INV garnet-red

grené [grəne] ADJ (dessin) stippled; (cuir) grainy
NM (de dessin) stipple; (de cuir) grain

greneler [grənle] VT (je grenelle, n. grenelons; je grenellerai) (papier, cuir) to grain

grener [grəne] VI (des céréales etc) to seed
VT 1 (réduire en grains) (poudre à canon) to granulate; (cire) to shred; (sel) to grain 2 (donner un aspect grené à) (papier, cuir) to grain

grènetis [grɛnti] NM (d'une pièce) milled edge

grenier [grənje] NM 1 (pour grain, fourrage) granary; **g. à foin** hayloft; **g. à blé** corn loft, Am wheat loft; Fig **l'Égypte était le g. du monde ancien** Egypt was the granary of the ancient world 2 (sous les combles) attic, garret; **chercher qch de la cave au g.** to hunt high and low for sth, to search the house from top to bottom for sth; **ranger la maison de la cave au g.** to tidy up the house from top to bottom

grenouillage [grənujaʒ] NM Fam Péj shady dealing, scheming

grenouille [grənuj] NF 1 (animal) frog 2 Fam (tirelire) ≃ piggy bank; **manger la g.** to make off with the cash
▸▸ Fig **g. de bénitier** Holy Joe; **g. taureau** ou **mugissante** bullfrog

grenouiller [grənuje] VI Fam Péj to go in for shady dealing, to scheme

grenouillère [grənujɛr] NF 1 (marécage) frog-pond 2 (pour bébé) sleepsuit

grenu [grəny] ADJ 1 (blé etc) grainy, full of grain 2 (cuir, peau etc) grained; (sel) coarse-grained, crystalline
NM graininess, granularity

grenure [grənyr] NF **1** Beaux-Arts stippling, stipple **2** (du cuir) grain(ing)

grès [grɛ] NM **1** Géol sandstone **2** (céramique) poterie de g., g. cérame stoneware; **cruche en g.** stoneware jug

gréseux, -euse [grezø, -øz] ADJ gritty, sandy; **roches gréseuses** sandstone rocks, sandstones

grésil [grezi(l)] NM fine hail

grésillement [grezijmã] NM (du feu) crackling; (de la flamme) sputtering; (d'une poêle à frire) sizzling

grésiller¹ [grezije] V IMPERS to hail

grésiller² VI (du feu) to crackle; (de la flamme) to sputter; (d'une poêle à frire) to sizzle

gressin [gresɛ̃] NM Culin bread stick

greubons [grøbɔ̃] NMPL Suisse Culin = leftover fat from cooked pork, fried and used as an ingredient in certain Swiss dishes

grève [grɛv] NF **1** (arrêt du travail) strike; **se mettre en g.** to go on or come out on strike, to strike, to take strike action or industrial action; **être en g., faire g.** to be on strike; **g. des trains/de la poste** train/postal strike; **briseur de g.** strike breaker; **piquet de g.** (strike) picket; **droit de g.** right to strike; **lancer un ordre de g.** to issue a strike order **2** (le long de la mer) (sea)shore, Litt strand; (d'un fleuve) (river) bank, Litt strand; **les grèves de la Loire** the sandbanks of the Loire; Hist **la (place de) G.** = open space on the banks of the Seine where dissatisfied workmen used to assemble

▸▸ **g. de la faim** hunger strike; **faire une g. de la faim** to be/go on hunger strike; **g. générale** general strike; **g. partielle** partial strike; **g. perlée** go-slow (strike), Am slowdown; **g. avec préavis** official strike; **g. de protestation** protest strike; **g. sauvage** wildcat strike; **g. de solidarité** sympathy strike; **g. surprise** lightning strike; **g. sur le tas** sit-down strike; **g. tournante** staggered strike; **g. du zèle** work-to-rule, go-slow; **faire la g. du zèle** to work to rule

grever [grəve] VT (je grève, n. grevons; je grèverai) **1** (alourdir) (succession) to burden, to encumber; (pouvoir d'achat) to restrict; **grevé d'impôts** weighed down or burdened with tax; **ce week-end aux sports d'hiver a grevé notre budget** this winter sports weekend has put a strain on our budget **2** Jur (propriété) to mortgage

gréviste [grevist] N striker; **g. de la faim** hunger striker

ADJ **mouvement g.** strike movement

GRH NF (abrév gestion des ressources humaines) HRM

gribiche [gribiʃ] ADJ **sauce g.** = flavoured mayonnaise with chopped hard-boiled egg and capers

NF Can (femme acariâtre) shrew

gribouillage [gribujaʒ] NM (écriture) scrawl, scribble; (dessin) doodle

gribouille [gribuj] NM Vieilli simpleton, nitwit, Br clot

NF Can (dispute) quarrel, fight

gribouiller [gribuje] VT & VI (écrire) to scribble, to scrawl; (dessiner) to doodle

gribouilleur, -euse [gribujœr, -øz] N scribbler

gribouillis [gribuji] NM = gribouillage

grief [grijɛf] NM grievance, ground for complaint; **faire g. à qn de qch** to hold sth against sb; **on lui a fait g. de ne pas se mêler aux autres** it was held against him that he didn't mix with the others

> Il faut noter que le nom anglais **grief** est un faux ami. Il signifie **chagrin**.

grièvement [grijɛvmã] ADV seriously, severely, badly

griffe [grif] NF **1** (d'animal) claw; (d'un faucon) claw, talon; **faire ses griffes** (d'un chat) to sharpen its claws; Fig to cut one's teeth; **coup de g.** scratch; **donner un coup de g. à qn** to claw or scratch sb; Fig to have a dig at sb; Fig **montrer les griffes** to show one's claws; Fig **arracher qn des griffes de qn** to snatch sb out of sb's clutches; Fig **tomber/ être sous** ou **entre les griffes de qn** to fall into/be in sb's clutches

2 Tech etc claw, clip, clamp; (outil) dog; (sur un bijou) claw; **accouplement/embrayage à griffes** claw coupling/clutch; **griffes de monteur** climbing irons

3 Bot (de la vigne) tendril; (d'asperge) crown **4** (empreinte) stamped signature; (ce qui sert à faire cette empreinte) (signature) stamp; (sur vêtements) label; Fig stamp; **g. de grande marque** designer label; **g. de réception** received stamp; **on reconnaît la g. de Zola dans ce roman** the novel bears Zola's stamp; **on reconnaît la g. de Saint-Laurent** you can recognize the Saint-Laurent style

griffé [grife] ADJ designer; **foulard g.** designer scarf

griffer [grife] VT **1** (d'un animal) to scratch, to claw **2** (signer) (vêtement) to put one's label on; **Chanel a griffé cette veste** this jacket bears the Chanel label

griffon [grifɔ̃] NM **1** Myth griffon, gryphon, griffin **2** (chien) griffon (terrier) **3** (oiseau) griffon (vulture)

griffonnage [grifɔnaʒ] NM (écriture) scrawl, scribble; (dessin) quick sketch

griffonnement [grifɔnmã] NM Beaux-Arts (en cire) wax model; (en terre) clay model

griffonner [grifɔne] VT (écrire) to scrawl, to scribble; (dessiner) to sketch quickly

griffu [grify] ADJ **patte griffue** clawed foot; **main griffue** claw-like hand

griffure [grifyr] NF scratch

grigner [griɲe] VI Tex to pucker, to crinkle up

grignotage [griɲɔtaʒ] NM nibbling; Fig (de libertés) erosion

grignotement [griɲɔtmã] NM nibbling

grignoter [griɲɔte] VT to nibble (at); Fig (libertés) to erode; Fig **g. son capital/ses économies** to eat into one's capital/one's savings; **les zones industrielles grignotent nos campagnes** industrial estates are gradually disfiguring our countryside

VI to nibble

grignoteur, -euse [griɲɔtœr, -øz] N nibbler

grigou [grigu] NM Fam skinflint, miser

gri-gri [grigri] NM amulet; (porte-bonheur) charm

gril [gril] NM **1** (de cuisine) grill, Am broiler; **faire cuire qch sur le g.** to grill sth, Am to broil sth; Fig Fam **être/mettre qn sur le g.** to be/keep sb on tenterhooks **2** Tech grating (protecting sluice gate); Rail, Naut gridiron; Théâtre grid, gridiron **3** Anat **g. costal** rib cage

grill [gril] NM **1** TV etc (pour l'éclairage) pipe grid **2** Culin steakhouse, grill

grillade [grijad] NF Culin grilled or Am broiled meat; **faire des grillades** to have a barbecue

grillage¹ [grijaʒ] NM **1** (de noix, de café etc) roasting **2** Métal (de minerais) calcining, roasting **3** Tex singeing

grillage² NM **1** (metal) grating, grill(e); **g. en fil de fer** wire netting; **poser un g. électrifié** to put up an electrified fence **2** Élec (plaque d'accumulateur) grid, frame

grillager [grijaʒe] VT (je grillageai(s); n. grillageons) **1** (garnir d'un grillage) to fit a grill(e) to; **fenêtre grillagée** window covered with wire mesh; **verre grillagé** wired glass **2** (entourer d'un grillage) to surround with wire netting

grille [grij] NF **1** (à l'entrée d'un parc, jardin etc) (entrance) gate; (clôture basse) (autour d'un monument etc) railings; **séparé de la rue par une g.** separated from the road by railings **2** (pour l'écoulement) (d'un évier, d'un égout etc) grating, grate **3** (à mailles fines) screen, netting; (du parloir d'un couvent) grill(e) **4** Élec (d'un accumulateur, d'un tube à électrons) grid; **courant de g.** grid current **5** (tableau quadrillé) (de mots croisés) grid

▸▸ **g. d'analyse par fonction** functional analysis chart; **g. d'avancement** career structure; **g. d'entrée d'air** air vent; **g. de gestion** managerial grid; **g. d'horaires** timetable, schedule; Compta **g. d'imputation** table of account codes; **g. indiciaire** salary structure or scale; **g. produit/marché** product/market grid; Radio, TV **g. des programmes** programme schedule or grid; Aut **g. de radiateur** radiator grille; **g. de réchauffeur** heater matrix; **g. de rémunération** salary scale; Ordinat **g. de saisie** input grid; **g. des salaires** salary scale

grille-calandre, pl **grilles-calandres** NF Aut grille

grille-pain NM INV toaster

griller¹ [grije] VT **1** (rôtir, passer au gril) (viande) to grill, Am to broil; (pain) to toast; (café, marrons) to roast **2** Métal (minerai) to roast, to calcine **3** Tex to singe **4** (brûler) to scorch, to burn; Élec Fam (ampoule, fusible, moteur etc) to burn out; **végétation grillée par le soleil** vegetation scorched by the sun; Fam **g. une cigarette** to smoke or have a cigarette; Arg **il est grillé** (dévoilé) his game's up; (rayé) he's had it; **g. un concurrent** to leave a competitor standing; Fam **g. un feu rouge** to jump the lights; Fam **g. les étapes** (dans sa carrière) to shoot up the ladder; (dans un travail) to cut corners

VI **1** Culin (d'un morceau de viande) to grill, Am to broil; (d'un morceau de pain) to toast; (de marrons) to roast; Fig **g. d'impatience** to be burning with impatience; Fig **g. d'envie de faire qch** to be bursting or itching to do sth **2** Élec (sauter) to burn out

VPR **se griller se g. au soleil** to roast in the sun; Fam **se g. auprès de qn** to blot one's copybook with sb

griller² VT (fenêtre) to cover with wire mesh

grilloir [grijwar] NM grill

grillon [grijɔ̃] NM cricket

grill(-room), pl **grill(-rooms)** [grilrum] NM grill (room)

grimaçant [grimasã] ADJ grimacing

grimace [grimas] NF grimace; **faire une g.** to make or pull a face, to grimace; **arrête de faire des grimaces au professeur** stop making faces at the teacher; **faire la g.** (avec dégoût) to pull a long face; **faire une g. de douleur** to wince; **faire des grimaces** (être maniéré) to put on airs; Prov **on n'apprend pas à un vieux singe à faire des grimaces** ≃ don't teach your grandmother how to suck eggs

grimacer [grimase] (je grimaçai(s), n. grimaçons) VI to grimace, to make or pull a face; **g. de douleur** to grimace or wince with pain

VT **g. un sourire** to force a smile, to give a wry smile

grimacier, -ière [grimasje, -jɛr] ADJ grimacing; Vieilli (maniéré) affected

grimage [grimaʒ] NM Théâtre (action) making up; (résultat) make-up

grimer [grime] Théâtre VT (un acteur, son visage) to make up

VPR **se grimer** (d'un acteur) to make up

grimoire [grimwar] NM **1** *(de sorcier)* book of spells **2** *(ouvrage confus et illisible)* piece of gibberish *or* mumbo-jumbo

grimpant [grɛ̃pɑ̃] ADJ *(animal)* climbing; **plante grimpante** climbing plant, climber; **rosier g.** climbing rose
▪ NM *Arg (pantalon)* trousers, *Am* pants

grimpe [grɛ̃p] NF rock-climbing; **faire de la g.** to go rock-climbing

grimpée [grɛ̃pe] NF *(stiff)* climb

grimper [grɛ̃pe] VI **1** *(monter)* to climb (up); *(faire de l'escalade)* to climb; **il a grimpé sur la muraille** he climbed (up) on to the wall; **la route grimpe jusqu'au col** the road climbs (up) to the pass; **ça grimpe** it's steep **2** *(de plantes)* to climb **3** *Fig (des prix)* to climb
▪ VT **1** *(montagne, échelons)* to climb (up); **g. l'escalier** to climb (up) *or* go up the stairs **2** *Vulg (posséder sexuellement)* to ride, to shaft, *Br* to shag

grimpette [grɛ̃pɛt] NF *Fam (chemin)* short, steep climb

grimpeur, -euse [grɛ̃pœr, -øz] ADJ *(oiseau)* climbing
▪ NM climber; *(de rocher)* rock-climber; *(en cyclisme)* hill climber; **c'est un bon/mauvais g.** *(d'un cycliste)* he's good/bad on hills

grinçant [grɛ̃sɑ̃] ADJ **1** *(qui grince)* creaking **2** *(caustique) (remarque)* caustic; **elle a un humour g.** she has a caustic wit

grincement [grɛ̃smɑ̃] NM *(d'une porte, de roues etc)* creaking; **g. de dents** grinding *or* gnashing of teeth; *Fig* **il y a eu des grincements de dents** there was much gnashing of teeth

grincer [grɛ̃se] VI (**je grinçai(s); n. grinçons**) *(d'une porte, de roues etc)* to creak; *(d'une chauve-souris)* to squeak; **g. des dents** to grind *or* gnash one's teeth; **cela fait g. des dents** it sets your teeth on edge; **porte qui grince sur ses gonds** creaking door

grinche [grɛ̃ʃ] ADJ *Suisse (grincheux)* grumpy, grouchy

grincheux, -euse [grɛ̃ʃø, -øz] ADJ grumpy, bad-tempered
▪ N grump, grumpy *or* bad-tempered person

gringalet [grɛ̃galɛ] NM *(homme, garçon)* (little) shrimp, weakling
▪ ADJ M puny

gringue [grɛ̃g] NM *Fam* **faire du g. à qn** to chat up sb, *Am* to sweet-talk sb

griotte [grijɔt] NF **1** *Bot* morello (cherry); **chocolats aux griottes** cherry liqueur chocolates **2** *Minér* griotte (marble)

grip [grip] NM *Sport* **1** *(position de la main au golf, au tennis)* grip **2** *(revêtement)* grip

grippage [gripaʒ], **grippement** [gripmɑ̃] NM *Tech (d'un palier, d'un piston etc)* seizing, jamming, binding

grippal, -ale, -aux, -ales [gripal, -o] ADJ *Méd* flu; **soulage les états grippaux** relieves flu symptoms; **virus g.** flu virus

grippe [grip] NF **1** *Méd* flu; *Fml* influenza; **se faire vacciner contre la g.** to be vaccinated against flu; **attraper/avoir la g.** to catch *or* get/have (the) flu; **g. intestinale** gastric flu **2** **prendre qn/qch en g.** to take a dislike to sb/sth

grippé [gripe] ADJ **1** *Méd* **être g.** to have (the) flu **2** *Tech (moteur, mécanisme etc)* seized(-up) **3** *Méd (visage)* pinched, drawn

gripper [gripe] VT *Tech (mécanisme)* to seize up, to jam
▪ VI *(d'une étoffe)* to crinkle (up), to wrinkle, to pucker **2** *(de paliers)* to seize (up), to bind, to jam
▪ VPR **se gripper** = VI **2**

grippe-sou, *pl* **grippe-sou(s)** NM skinflint, miser, Scrooge

gris [gri] ADJ **1** *(couleur)* grey, *Am* gray; *(temps)* cloudy, dull, overcast; **il fait g. ce matin** it's cloudy *or* dull *or* overcast this morning, it's a grey *or* dull morning; **g. de poussière** grey with dust; **robe g. clair** light grey dress; **aux cheveux g.** grey-haired; *Anat* **substance grise** grey matter; *Fam* **faire fonctionner sa matière grise** to get one's grey matter working; **vin g.** rosé wine; **faire grise mine** to look anything but pleased; **faire grise mine à qn** to give sb a cool welcome **2** *(ivre)* tipsy
▪ NM **1** *(couleur)* grey, *Am* gray; *Ordinat* **tons de g.** shades of grey; **s'habiller en g.** to dress in *or* wear grey **2** *(cheval)* grey, *Am* gray **3** *(tabac gris)* shag
▸▸ **g. acier** steel grey; **g. anthracite** charcoal grey; **g. ardoise** slate grey; **g.-bleu** blue-grey; **g. perle** pearl grey; **g. pommelé** *(cheval)* dapple-grey; **g. souris** soft grey; **g.-vert** greenish-grey

grisaille [grizaj] NF **1** *(caractère morne)* greyness, dreariness, *Am* grayness **2** *Beaux-Arts* grisaille; **peindre en g.** to paint in grisaille

grisailler [grizaje] VT *Beaux-Arts* **g. qch** to paint sth in grisaille
▪ VI to turn *or* go grey *or Am* gray

grisant [grizɑ̃] ADJ *Fig (succès, atmosphère)* intoxicating, exhilarating, heady; *(aventure, soirée)* exhilarating; **à une vitesse grisante** at (an) exhilarating speed

grisâtre [grizɑtr] ADJ greyish, *Am* grayish

grisbi [grizbi] NM *Arg (argent)* dosh, *Br* lolly

grisé [grize] NM *Ordinat* grey *or Am* gray tone; **en g.** *(article)* dimmed

griser [grize] VT **1** *(rendre gris)* to make grey *or Am* gray; *Ordinat* to shade **2** *(enivrer)* to make drunk *or* tipsy; *Fig* **grisé par le succès** carried away *or* intoxicated by *or* with success
▪ VPR **se griser se g. d'air pur** to get drunk on fresh air; **se g. des paroles de qn/de musique** to get carried away by sb's words/by music

griserie [grizri] NF **1** *(ivresse)* tipsiness **2** *Fig (exaltation)* exhilaration, excitement

grisette [grizɛt] NF *Arch* = young dressmaker, milliner, florist etc, usually of easy virtue

gris-gris NM amulet; *(porte-bonheur)* lucky charm

grisonnant [grizɔnɑ̃] ADJ *(cheveux)* greying, *Am* graying, touched with grey *or Am* gray; **avoir les tempes grisonnantes** to be greying at the temples; **un cinquantenaire g.** a greying fifty-year-old

grisonner [grizɔne] VI *(de cheveux, personne)* to go grey *or Am* gray

grisou [grizu] NM *Min* firedamp; **coup de g.** firedamp explosion

grive [griv] NF *(oiseau)* thrush; **soûl comme une g.** drunk as a lord; *Prov* **faute de grives on mange des merles** beggars can't be choosers, half a loaf is better than none

grivelé [grivle] ADJ *(plumage)* speckled

grivèlerie [grivɛlri] NF *Jur* = offence consisting of ordering a meal in a restaurant without having the money to pay for it

griveton [grivtɔ̃] NM *Fam* private (soldier), *Br* squaddie

grivois, -oise [grivwa, -waz] ADJ *(histoire, chanson, plaisanterie)* risqué, saucy, bawdy

grivoiserie [grivwazri] NF *(plaisanterie)* risqué *or* saucy joke; *(histoire)* risqué *or* saucy story; *(acte)* rude gesture

grizzli, grizzly [grizli] NM grizzly (bear)

Groenland [grɔɛnlɑ̃(d)] NM Greenland

groenlandais, -aise [grɔɛnlɑ̃dɛ, -ɛz] ADJ of *or* from Greenland
▪ NM *Ling* Greenlandic
▪ N **G.** Greenlander

grog [grɔg] NM grog, toddy

groggy [grɔgi] ADJ INV *Fam* groggy

grognard [grɔɲar] NM **1** *Hist* = soldier of Napoleon's Old Guard **2** *(militant traditionaliste)* member of the old guard **3** *Vieilli (grincheux)* grumbler

grognasse [grɔɲas] NF *Vulg Péj* old bag, old cow

grognasser [grɔɲase] VI *Fam* to grumble, to grouse, *Br* to whinge

grogne [grɔɲ] NF *Fam* grumbling; **c'est la g. chez les ouvriers/dans le milieu étudiant** the workers/the students are grumbling

grognement [grɔɲmɑ̃] NM **1** *(d'un cochon)* grunt(ing); *(d'un chien, ours)* growl(ing); **pousser des grognements** *(d'un cochon)* to grunt **2** *(d'une personne)* growl; **pousser un g.** to growl

grogner [grɔɲe] VI **1** *(d'un cochon)* to grunt; *(d'un chien)* to growl **2** *(d'une personne)* to grumble, to grouse, to moan; **g. contre qn** to grumble *or* complain about sb
▪ VT **g. un refus/une réponse** to growl out a refusal/an answer

grognon, -onne [grɔɲɔ̃, -ɔn] N grumbler, grouser, moaner
▪ ADJ *(f* **grognon** *or* **grognonne***)* grumpy, grumbling; **c'est une femme g.** *ou* **grognonne** she's always grumbling *or* moaning, she's a grumpy woman; **qu'est-ce que tu peux être g.!** what a grumbler *or* grouser *or* moaner you are!

grognonner [grɔɲɔne] VI *Fam* to grouse, to grumble, to moan

groin [grwɛ̃] NM *(d'un cochon)* snout; *Fig Péj (de personne)* ugly face

grole, grolle [grɔl] NF *très Fam (chaussure)* shoe

grommeler [grɔmle] (**je grommelle, n. grommelons; je grommellerai**) VI to mutter; *(d'un sanglier)* to snort, to grunt
▪ VT **g. un juron** to mutter an oath

grommellement [grɔmɛlmɑ̃] NM muttering

grondement [grɔ̃dmɑ̃] NM **1** *(d'un chien)* growl(ing), snarl(ing) **2** *(du tonnerre)* rumble, rumbling; *(d'un torrent de montagne, des vagues, d'un moteur)* roar(ing); *(des canons)* booming

gronder [grɔ̃de] VI **1** *(d'un chien)* to growl, to snarl **2** *(du tonnerre)* to rumble; *(des canons)* to boom; *(des vagues)* to roar; **la révolte/le mécontentement gronde** there are rumblings of rebellion/discontent
▪ VT *(réprimander)* to scold, to tell off; **attention, tu vas te faire g.!** watch out, or you'll get into trouble!

gronderie [grɔ̃dri] NF scolding

grondeur, -euse [grɔ̃dœr, -øz] ADJ **1** *(voix)* scolding, nagging; *(humeur, tempérament)* peevish **2** *(orage, torrent etc)* rumbling

grondin [grɔ̃dɛ̃] NM gurnard, gurnet

groom [grum] NM **1** *(dans un hôtel)* page, *Am* bellhop **2** *Équitation Arch* groom

GROS, GROSSE¹ [gro, gros]

ADJ big **1, 2, 5** ▪ large **1, 5** ▪ thick **1** ▪ heavy **1, 3, 6** ▪ stout **1, 2** ▪ fat **2** ▪ coarse **3, 4** ▪ serious **5**
ADV a lot
N fat man/woman
NM bulk **1** ▪ wholesale **2, 3**

ADJ 1 *(grand)* big, large; **g. morceau** big *or* large piece, lump; *Fig* **l'examen de statistiques, voilà le g. morceau** the statistics exam is the big one; **grosse corde** thick *or* stout rope; **g. pullover** thick *or* heavy *or* chunky sweater; **g. souliers** strong *or* stout shoes; **grosses chaussettes** thick *or* heavy socks;

g. moteur high-powered engine; **g. doigt de pied** big toe; **de grosses lèvres** thick lips; **avoir un g. ventre** (*être bien en chair*) to have a paunch, to have a pot(belly); **avoir une grosse tête** to have a large head; *Fig* **avoir la grosse tête** to be big-headed, to be swollen-headed; **prendre** *ou* **attraper la grosse tête** to get big-headed; **une orange grosse comme le poing** an orange the size of *or* as big as your fist; *Fig* **un mensonge g. comme une maison** *ou* **comme ça** a whopping lie, a whopper of a lie; *Fig* **faire les g. yeux** to glare, to glower; **yeux g. de larmes** eyes swollen with tears; **avoir le cœur g.** to have a heavy heart, to be sad at heart; **je suis parti le cœur g.** I left with a heavy heart; *Fig* **elle a un cœur g. comme ça** she's so big-hearted; *Péj* **g. nigaud** *ou* **bêta!** you big *or* great ninny *or Br* twit!; **écrire qch en g. caractères** to write sth in big *or* large letters; **g. utilisateur** heavy user; **g. mangeur** big *or* hearty eater; **g. buveur** heavy *or* big drinker; **g. appétit** big *or* hearty appetite; **g. rhume** heavy cold; **grosse fièvre** high fever; **un g. kilo** a good kilo; **avoir un g. chagrin** to be very upset; **une grosse récolte** a bumper harvest; *Naut* **grosse mer** heavy *or* rough sea; **g. temps** stormy *or* rough weather; **grosse averse/ pluie** heavy shower/rain; **g. vent** high wind; **grosse cavalerie** heavy cavalry

2 (*corpulent*) big, fat, stout; **un g. bébé** a big *or* fat baby; **un g. bonhomme** a fat gentleman

3 (*pas fin*) **grosse toile** coarse linen; **grosse voix** gruff voice; **faire la grosse besogne** to do the heavy work

4 (*grossier*) **un peu g.** not very subtle, a bit too obvious; **c'est un peu g.!** that's a bit much!; **g. rire** coarse laugh; **grosse indélicatesse** gross impropriety

5 (*important*) **grosse somme** large sum (of money); **ce n'est pas une grosse affaire** (*entreprise*) it's not a big company; (*préoccupation*) it's no big deal; **grosse commande** bulk order; **la plus grosse partie de nos affaires/ notre personnel** the bulk of our business/ our staff; **grosse faute** serious *or* gross mistake; **g. propriétaire** (**terrien**) big landowner; **grosse héritière** wealthy heiress

6 être g. de conséquences/menaces/etc to be heavy with consequences/threats/*etc*

ADV (*beaucoup*) **gagner g.** to earn a lot, to make big money; **ça peut rapporter g.** it can bring in a lot; **je donnerais g. pour savoir qui a fait ça** I'd give a lot to know who did that; **il y a g. à parier qu'il ne viendra pas** a hundred to one he won't come!; **il risque g.** he's taking a big risk, he's risking a lot; **jouer g.** *Cartes* to play for high stakes; *Fig* to take a big risk, to risk a lot

N (*personne corpulente*) large *or* fat man/ woman; **eh bien, mon g.!** well, old boy *or Br* old man!; (*à un enfant*) well, my boy!, well, son!; *Fam* **un g./une grosse plein(e) de soupe** a tub of lard

NM 1 (*partie la plus importante*) bulk; **le g. de la cargaison/du personnel** the bulk of the cargo/the staff; **le g. de l'armée** the main body *or* the bulk of the army; **le g. du peuple** the mass *or* bulk of the people; **le g. d'une mission** the main part of a mission; **le plus g. est fait** the biggest part of the job is done; **le plus g. du courrier** the bulk of the mail; **le g. de l'été/l'hiver** the height of summer/ depths of winter; **g. d'un mât** thick end of a mast

2 *Com* wholesale (trade); **marchand de g.** wholesaler; **vente de g.** wholesale; **ils ne vendent/font que du g.** they only sell/deal wholesale; **commerce de g.** wholesale business; **boucher de g.** wholesale butcher

3 **écrire en g.** to write in big *or* large letters; **raconter ce qui s'est passé en g.** to tell roughly what happened; **il y avait en g.**

---

quinze personnes there were roughly *or* about fifteen people there; **acheter en g.** to buy wholesale; (*en grosse quantité*) to buy in bulk; **vendre en g.** to sell wholesale

▸▸ *Fam* **g. bonnet** big shot, bigwig; *Typ* **g. corps** headings type, headline type; **g. gibier** big game; *Fam* **grosse légume** big shot, bigwig; **g. mot** swearword; *TV, Cin* **g. plan** tight shot; *TV, Cin* **en g. plan** in close-up; *TV, Cin* **en très g. plan** very close up; *TV, Cin* **g. plan d'objet/de tête** insert/head shot; **g. porteur** jumbo jet; **g. porteur polyvalent** multi-purpose large-capacity jet; **g. rouge** cheap red wine, *Br* plonk; **g. sel** cooking salt; *Ordinat* **g. système** mainframe; *Typ* **g. tirage** best-seller; *Journ* **g. titre** banner headline; **en g. titres** in banner headlines; *Journ* **g. titre de deuxième ordre** second lead, half lead

---

gros-bec, *pl* **gros-becs NM** hawfinch, grosbeak

gros-cul, *pl* **gros-culs NM** *Fam* lorry, *Am* truck

groseille [grozɛj] **NF g. (rouge)** redcurrant; **g. (blanche)** white currant; **g. à maquereau** gooseberry; **gelée de groseille(s)** redcurrant jelly

groseillier [grozeje] **NM** (red)currant bush; **g. à maquereau** gooseberry bush

gros-grain, *pl* **gros-grains NM** *Tex* grosgrain

Gros-jean [groʒɑ̃] **NM** *Prov* **se retrouver G. comme devant** to be back where one started

grosse² [gros] **NF 1** *Com* gross **2** *Jur* engrossment **3** *Arch* (*écriture*) roundhand (writing)

grossesse [grosɛs] **NF** pregnancy; **interruption volontaire de g.** termination (*of pregnancy*); **robe de g.** maternity dress; **pendant sa g.** during her pregnancy, while *or* when she was pregnant

▸▸ **g. extra-utérine** *or* **ectopique** ectopic pregnancy; **g. gémellaire** twin pregnancy; **g. nerveuse** false *or* phantom pregnancy; **g. à risque** high-risk pregnancy

grosseur [grosœr] **NF 1** (*taille, volume*) size; (*des lèvres*) thickness; **un objet de la g. d'un œuf** an object the size of an egg **2** *Méd* lump, growth

grossier, -ière [grosje, -jɛr] **ADJ 1** (*impoli*) (*personne*) rude (**envers** to); (*vulgaire*) (*personne, air*) uncouth, coarse; (*langage, plaisanterie*) coarse, crude; **un g. personnage** an uncouth individual; **il a été on ne peut plus g.** he was extremely rude; **parler d'un ton g.** to speak coarsely *or* crudely **2** (*commun, rudimentaire*) (*nourriture, tissu, vaisselle etc*) coarse, rough; (*méthode*) crude; (*dessin*) crude, rough; (*goûts, traits du visage*) unrefined, coarse; **c'est un esprit g.** he's ignorant, he's a Philistine **3** (*de taille*) **stupidité grossière** crass stupidity; **ignorance grossière** gross *or* crass ignorance; **faute grossière** gross mistake, blunder; **une ruse grossière** a very obvious trick

grossièrement [grosjɛrmɑ̃] **ADV 1** (*imparfaitement*) roughly, crudely; **table g. façonnée** roughly *or* crudely made table **2** (*approximativement*) roughly; **calculer g. un prix/le nombre de personnes** to roughly calculate a price/the number of people **3** (*de façon importante*) **se tromper g.** to be grossly mistaken **4** (*de façon impolie*) (*parler, répondre*) rudely

grossièreté [grosjɛrte] **NF 1** (*caractère rudimentaire*) (*d'un objet fabriqué*) coarseness, roughness **2** (*incorrection*) (*de manières, personne*) coarseness **3** (*parole grossière*) **dire des grossièretés à qn** to say crude *or* coarse things to sb

grossir [grosir] **VT objet grossi trois fois** object magnified three times; **torrent grossi**

---

par les pluies torrent swollen by the rain; **ce pantalon le grossit** those trousers make him look fatter; **g. les rangs des mécontents** to swell the ranks of the discontented; **g. sa voix** to raise one's voice; *Fig* **g. les faits/une histoire/une affaire** to exaggerate the facts/ a story/a matter; **g. l'importance de qch/le rôle de qn dans une action** to exaggerate the importance of sth/sb's part in an action

VI (*d'animaux, de fruits*) to get bigger *or* larger; (*de personne*) to put on weight, to get fatter; (*de mer*) to get rough, to rise; (*de rivière*) to swell; **elle a grossi de deux kilos** she has put on two kilos; **elle a beaucoup grossi** she has put on a lot of weight *or* has got fatter

grossissant [grosisɑ̃] **ADJ 1** (*qui devient plus gros*) (*foule, bruit*) growing, swelling **2** (*qui rend plus gros*) enlarging; **verre g.** magnifying glass

grossissement [grosismɑ̃] **NM 1** (*augmentation de taille*) increase in size **2** (*action de rendre plus gros*) (*d'un objet à travers un verre*) magnification, enlargement **3** (*capacité d'un instrument d'optique*) (*d'un verre*) magnification, magnifying power

grossiste [grosist] **N** wholesaler, wholesale dealer; **g. généraliste** general wholesaler; **g. importateur** import wholesaler

grosso modo [grosomɔdo] **ADV** roughly; **il y avait g. cinquante personnes** there were roughly fifty people; **g. c'est une comédie** roughly speaking *or* broadly speaking it's a comedy; **raconter l'affaire g.** to give a general account of the matter

grossoyer [groswaje] **VT** (**je grossoie, n. grossoyons; je grossoierai**) *Jur* (*document*) to engross

grotesque [grɔtɛsk] **ADJ** (*personne, allure, idée*) ludicrous, ridiculous; *Beaux-Arts* (*personnage*) grotesque

NM *Littér, Beaux-Arts* **le g.** the grotesque; **cet homme/cette situation est d'un g.!** the man's/the situation's ludicrous *or* ridiculous!

NFPL *Beaux-Arts* **grotesques** grotesques

grotesquement [grɔtɛskəmɑ̃] **ADV** ludicrously, ridiculously

grotte [grɔt] **NF** cave; **g. naturelle/préhistorique** natural/prehistoric cave; **g. artificielle** grotto

grouillant [grujɑ̃] **ADJ** swarming, crawling, alive (**de** with); **rue grouillante de monde** street swarming with people; **foule grouillante** teeming crowd

grouillement [grujmɑ̃] **NM** swarming; **le g. des asticots dans la viande avariée** the maggots swarming around in the rotten meat; **son esprit torturé n'était plus qu'un g. sans nom de pensées incohérentes** his tortured mind was nothing but a teeming mass of incoherent thoughts

grouiller [gruje] **VI 1** *Vieilli* (*bouger*) to move **2** (*de touristes, clients etc*) to swarm around; **la foule grouillait dans la rue** the street was teeming *or* swarming with people; **g. de** to swarm *or* crawl with; **fromage qui grouille de vers** cheese swarming *or* crawling *or* alive with maggots; **ce bouquin grouille de bonnes idées** this book is teeming with good ideas

VPR se grouiller *Arg* to get a move on, to get one's skates on; **grouille(-toi)!** get a move on!, get your skates on!

grouillot [grujo] **NM** *Bourse* messenger (boy); *TV, Cin* runner, best boy

groupage [grupaʒ] **NM 1** *Com* groupage, consolidation; (*de paquets*) bulking **2** *Méd* (blood) grouping

groupe [grup] **NM 1** (*de gens, choses*) group; (*d'arbres*) group, clump; (*musiciens*) group, proving housing conditions is one of the new mayor's priorities

habitation [abitasjɔ̃] NF **1** habitation; **impropre à l'h.** unsuitable or unfit for human habitation; **locaux à usage d'h.** premises for residential use **2** *(lieu)* dwelling (place), residence, abode; **une h. bien aménagée/située/chauffée** a well-equipped/well-situated/well-heated house; **changer d'h.** to change one's residence; **groupe (d'habitations)** *(lotissement)* housing estate
▸▸ **h. à loyer modéré** *Br* ≃ council flat/house, *Am* public housing unit

habiter [abite] VT *(maison, lieu)* to live in; **la région n'est pas habitée** the area is uninhabited; **c'est très peu habité par ici** very few people live around here; **cette pièce n'a jamais été habitée** this room has never been used; **Vénus est-elle habitée?** is there life on Venus?; **une planète habitée** an inhabited planet; **vaisseau spatial habité** manned spacecraft; *Fig* **la certitude qui m'habite** my personal conviction; **le calme qui l'habite depuis peu** the inner calm which he has recently acquired; **elle est habitée par la haine** she is full of hatred
VI to live (à in, at); **h. (à) Paris/la campagne** to live in Paris/in the country; **j'habite au 3, place des Cardeurs** I live at number 3, place des Cardeurs; **h. en Italie** to live in Italy; **vous habitez chez vos parents?** do you live with your parents?; **elle habite avec son frère/cet homme** she lives with her brother/this man

habitude [abityd] NF **1** habit, custom; **bonne/mauvaise h.** good/bad habit; **faire qch par h.** to do sth from or out of habit, to do sth from force of habit; **prendre l'h. de faire qch** to get into the habit of doing sth; **se faire une h. d'arriver en retard** to have a habit of being late; **avoir l'h. ou avoir pour h. de faire qch** to be in the habit of doing sth; **ça ne la gênera pas, elle a l'h.** that won't bother her or she won't mind, she's used to it; **je n'ai pas l'h. de mentir** I'm not in the habit of lying; **prendre de mauvaises habitudes** to get into bad habits, to pick up bad habits; **c'est une question d'h.** it's a question of habit; **avoir une longue h. du travail en commun** to have long experience of working together; **nous avons une longue h. de l'édition** we have long experience in the field of publishing; **ce n'est pas une h. chez moi, ce n'est pas dans mes habitudes** I don't make a habit of it; **à ou selon ou suivant son h.** as he usually does/did, as is/was his custom or *Fml* wont; **se défaire d'une h., perdre une h.** to get out of a habit, to break a habit; **faire perdre une h. à qn** to break sb of a habit; **d'h.** usually, ordinarily, normally; **meilleur que d'h.** better than usual; **comme d'h.** as usual; **plus tôt que d'h.** earlier than usual; **habitudes d'achat** shopping habits, buying habits; **habitudes d'écoute** listening habits; *TV* viewing habits
2 *(dextérité)* knack; **je n'en ai plus l'h.** I'm out of practice
3 habitudes ways, customs; **les habitudes du pays** the customs of the country

habitué, -ée [abitye] N *(d'une maison)* frequent or regular visitor; *(d'un restaurant, d'un magasin)* regular customer, regular; **c'est un h. de la maison** *(client)* he's a regular (customer)

habituel, -elle [abityɛl] ADJ usual, customary, regular; **cette attitude ne lui est pas habituelle** this is not his/her usual attitude, he/she doesn't usually take this attitude; **c'est le problème h. avec elle** it's the usual problem with her; *Fam* **c'est le coup h.** it's the same old story, it's par for the course; **elle nous a fait le coup h.** she's played the usual or the same old trick on us

habituellement [abitɥɛlmɑ̃] ADV usually, habitually, regularly; **elle arrive h. vers 18 heures 30** she usually arrives around half past six

habituer [abitɥe] VT to accustom, *Fml* to habituate; **h. qn à qch** to get sb used to sth, to accustom sb to sth; **il faut h. les enfants au rythme de l'école** you have to get the children used or accustomed to the pace of school; **h. des enfants à la politesse** to get children into the habit of being polite; **h. qn à la fatigue** to accustom sb to fatigue; **il faut h. son esprit à la concentration** you have to get used to concentrating; **maintenant j'y suis habitué** I'm used to it now; **elle est habituée à rester seule** she's used to being alone; **h. qn à faire qch** to get sb into the habit of doing sth, to get sb used to doing sth; **il faut les h. à manger peu de sucre** you must get them into the habit of or get them used to not eating much sugar
VPR **s'habituer** to get used, to get or grow accustomed (à to); **tu verras, tu vas t'y h.** you'll get used to it, you'll see; **s'h. à travailler très tôt le matin** to get used to working very early in the morning; **je n'arrive pas à m'y h.** I just can't get used to it; **je ne m'habituerai jamais à ...** I'll never get used to ...; **je ne m'y suis toujours pas habitué** I still haven't got used to it; **s'h. à une idée** to get used to an idea

*hâblerie [ɑbləri] NF **1** *(attitude)* bragging, boasting **2** *(propos)* boast

*hâbleur, -euse [ɑblœr, -øz] ADJ bragging, boasting, boastful
N boaster, braggart

*Habsbourg [apsbur] N *Hist* **la maison de H.** the House of Hapsburg

*hachage [aʃaʒ] NM *(de viande etc)* chopping (up), mincing; *(de la paille etc)* cutting

*hache [aʃ] NF axe, *Am* ax; **h. à main** hatchet; **fait ou taillé à coups de h.** roughhewn, hacked out; **visage taillé à coups de h.** angular face; **exécuter qn à la h.** to chop sb's head off; *Vieilli* **porter la h. dans les dépenses publiques** to axe or cut public spending
▸▸ *Arch* **h. d'abordage** scuttling axe; *Arch* **h. d'armes** battleaxe; **h. de guerre** tomahawk; *Fig* **enterrer la h. de guerre** to bury the hatchet

*haché [aʃe] ADJ **1** minced, chopped; **bifteck h.** minced beef, mince, *Am* ground beef; **steak h.** steak mince **2** *(style etc)* staccato, jerky; **un film h. par des publicités** a film interspersed with adverts **3** *(dessin)* (cross)hatched; *(carte)* hachured
NM = **hachis**

*hache-légumes NM INV *Culin* vegetable cutter

*hachement [aʃmɑ̃] NM = **hachage**

*hache-paille NM INV *Agr* chaffcutter

*hacher [aʃe] VT **1** to chop (up); *(viande)* to mince, *Am* to grind; **la grêle a haché les récoltes** the crops have been cut to shreds by the hail; **h. menu** to mince finely, to chop up small; *Fig* **h. qn menu comme chair à pâté** to make mincemeat of sb; *Fig* **se faire h.** *(se faire battre)* to be cut to pieces; **elle est prête à se faire h. pour lui** she'd do anything for him; **si tu reviens à cette heure, tu vas te faire h. menu** if you come home at this hour, you'll have your head in your hands!; *Fig* **plutôt me faire h. (menu) que de dire oui** I'd rather die than say yes **2** = **hachurer**

*hachette [aʃɛt] NF hatchet

*hache-viande NM INV *Culin* mincer

*hachis [aʃi] NM *Culin* *(à la viande)* minced or *Am* ground meat, mince; *(au poisson)* chopped fish; **h. de veau** minced veal; **h. Parmentier** *(au bœuf)* ≃ cottage pie; *(avec viande blanche)* = dish similar to cottage

pie, made with white meat; *(au mouton)* ≃ shepherd's pie; **h. d'herbes** chopped herbs

*hachisch [aʃiʃ] NM hashish; **fumer du h.** to smoke hash

*hachoir [aʃwar] NM *Culin* **1** *(couteau)* chopper **2** *(planche)* chopping board **3** *(électrique)* mincing machine, mincer

*hachurage [aʃyraʒ] NM *Ordinat* hatching

*hachurer [aʃyre] VT to (cross)hatch; *(carte)* to hachure

*hachures [aʃyr] NFPL (cross)hatching; *(sur une carte)* hachures; **carte en h.** hachured map

*hacienda [asjɛnda] NF hacienda

*hacker [akœr] NM *Ordinat* hacker

*haddock [adɔk] NM *Culin* smoked haddock

Hadrien [adrijɛ̃] N Hadrian; **le mur d'H.** Hadrian's wall

*Haendel [ɛndɛl] N Handel

*hagard [agar] ADJ *(visage)* haggard, drawn; *(expression, regard, yeux)* wild, distraught

hagiographe [aʒjɔgraf] N hagiographer

hagiographie [aʒjɔgrafi] NF hagiography

hagiographique [aʒjɔgrafik] ADJ hagiographic(al)

*haie [ɛ] NF **1** *(clôture)* hedge(row) **2** *Sport* hurdle; *Équitation* fence; *Sport* **course de haies** hurdle race, *Fam* hurdles; **400 mètres haies** 400 metre hurdles **3** *(d'arbres, de pieux, de curieux etc)* line, row; **faire ou former une h.** to line up
▸▸ **h. d'honneur** guard of honour or *Am* honor; **h. vive** quickset hedge

*haïku [aiku] NM haiku

*haillon [ɑjɔ̃] NM *(vêtements)* rag; **être en haillons** to be in rags (and tatters); **des enfants en haillons** children dressed in rags (and tatters)

*haine [ɛn] NF hatred **(pour** of, for), hate; **avoir de la h. pour qn/qch** to hate or detest sb/sth; **éprouver de la h. pour qn/qch** to feel hatred for sb/sth; **prendre qch/qn en h.** to take a strong aversion to sth/sb; **en haine ou par h. de qch** out of hatred of or for sth; *très Fam* **j'ai la h.!** I'm bloody furious; *très Fam* **les jeunes de la cité ont la h.** young people on the estate are full of rage

*haineusement [ɛnøzmɑ̃] ADV with (bitter) hatred

*haineux, -euse [ɛnø, -øz] ADJ full of hatred or hate; **regard h.** a look full of hatred; **d'un ton h.** with hate in his/her/*etc* voice; **une femme haineuse** a woman full of hatred

> Il faut noter que l'adjectif anglais **heinous** est un faux ami. Il signifie **atroce, abominable**.

*haïr [air] *(je hais [ɛ], tu hais, il hait, n. haïssons; imp hais; otherwise regular)* VT to hate, to detest, to loathe; **c'est ce que je hais le plus au monde** I hate or detest or loathe that more than anything else in the world; **h. qn d'avoir fait qch** to hate sb for doing or having done sth; *Can Fam* **h. qn à s'en confesser** to hate sb's guts
VPR **se haïr** *(soi-même)* to hate oneself; *(de deux personnes)* to hate each other; *Hum* **elles se haïssent cordialement** they cordially detest each other; **je me hais de lui avoir menti** I hate myself for lying to him

*haire [ɛr] NF *(chemise)* hairshirt

*haïssable [aisabl] ADJ hateful, detestable

*Haïti [aiti] NF Haiti

*haïtien, -ienne [aisjɛ̃, -jɛn] ADJ Haitian
N H. Haitian

*halage [alaʒ] NM towing; **chemin de h.** towpath; **corde de h.** towing line

halal [alal] ADJ INV (viande) halal, slaughtered according to Muslim law

*****hâle** [ɑl] NM (sun)tan

*****hâlé** [ɑle] ADJ (sun)tanned

haleine [alɛn] NF breath; **avoir l'h. fraîche** to have fresh breath; **avoir mauvaise h., avoir l'h. forte** to have bad breath; **à son h., j'ai compris qu'il avait bu** I could tell from his breath that he'd been drinking; **retenir son h.** to hold one's breath; **(tout) d'une h.** all in one breath, in the same breath; **reprendre h.** to get or catch one's breath, to get one's breath back; **sans avoir le temps de reprendre h.** without having time to get one's breath back; **perdre h.** to get out of breath, to lose one's breath; **courir à perdre h.** to run until one is out of breath; **discuter à perdre h.** to argue nonstop or Fam hammer and tongs; **hors d'h.** out of breath, breathless; **travail de longue h.** long and exacting task; **tenir qn en h.** to keep sb in suspense

*****haler** [ale] VT **1** (navire) to warp **2** (péniche etc) to tow **3 h. une embarcation au sec** to haul up a boat (onto the beach) **4** Naut (cordage etc) to pull, to haul in, to heave

VI Naut **h. sur une manœuvre** to haul or pull on a rope, to heave at a rope

*****hâler** [ɑle] VT (du soleil etc) to tan, to brown; **pour h. votre teint pâle** to tan your pale skin

*****haletant** [al(ə)tɑ̃] ADJ (coureur) panting, gasping, breathless, out of breath; (malade) panting, gasping; **respiration haletante** panting, gasping; **voix haletante** breathless or gasping voice

*****halètement** [alɛtmɑ̃] NM (d'un coureur) panting, gasping (for breath), puffing (and blowing); (d'un malade) panting, gasping; (d'une locomotive) puffing

*****haleter** [al(ə)te] VI (je halète; je halèterai) (d'un coureur) to pant, to gasp (for breath), to puff (and blow); (d'un malade) to pant, to gasp; Fig Litt (d'une locomotive) to puff; Fig **le cinéaste fait h. son public** the film-maker keeps his audience on the edge of their seats

*****haleur, -euse** [alœr, -øz] N (de bateaux) hauler, tower

*****half-track** [aftrak] NM Mil half-track

*****hall** [ol] NM entrance hall; (d'un hôtel) foyer, lobby; (d'un aéroport) lounge; **h. d'accueil** reception, lobby; **h. d'aéroport** airport lounge; **h. d'entrée** entrance hall; **h. d'entrée d'hôtel** hotel lobby; **h. d'exposition** exhibition hall; **h. de réception** foyer, lobby; **h. de gare** station concourse; **c'est un vrai h. de gare ici!** it's like Piccadilly Circus here!; **h. des départs** departure lounge

*****hallage** [alaʒ] NM Com market trader's dues

hallali [alali] NM mort; **sonner l'h.** to blow the mort

*****halle** [al] NF **1** (covered) market; (grande salle) hall; **h. aux poissons** fish market; **h. au blé** corn exchange; **les Halles (centrales)** the Halles (the central market in Paris) **2** Suisse (bâtiment) hall; **h. d'exposition** exhibition centre; **h. des fêtes** community centre; **h. de gymnastique** sports centre, sports hall; **h. polyvalente** community centre

*****hallebarde** [albard] NF Arch halberd, halbert; Fam **il pleut** ou **tombe des hallebardes** it's raining cats and dogs

*****hallebardier** [albardje] NM Arch halberdier

*****hallier** [alje] NM **1** thicket, copse **2** halliers brushwood

Halloween [alowin] NF Halloween

hallu [aly] NF Fam (abrév hallucination) hal-

lucination; **je dois avoir des hallus!** I must be seeing things!

hallucinant [alysinɑ̃] ADJ (drogue etc) hallucinatory; (pensée) haunting; (ressemblance etc) striking; **paysage h. de beauté** strikingly beautiful scenery; Fig Fam **c'est h.!** it's incredible!, I don't believe it!

hallucination [alysinasjɔ̃] NF hallucination, delusion; **avoir des hallucinations** (d'un malade, d'un ivrogne) to have hallucinations; Fig (se tromper) to imagine or see things; **une h. collective** a collective or mass hallucination

hallucinatoire [alysinatwar] ADJ hallucinatory

halluciné, -ée [alysine] ADJ hallucinating; Fig Fam mad

N person who suffers from hallucinations; Fig Fam madman, f madwoman; **il me regardait de son air d'h.** he looked at me like a madman or with that wild staring look in the eyes

halluciner [alysine] VT Rare to make hallucinate, to cause to hallucinate

VI (avoir des hallucinations) to hallucinate; Fig Fam **j'hallucine!** I don't believe it!

hallucinogène [alysinɔʒɛn] Pharm NM hallucinogen

ADJ hallucinogenic

*****halo** [alo] NM **1** Météo etc halo; Fig **un h. de gloire** a cloud of glory; **s'entourer d'un h. de mystère** to shroud oneself in mystery **2** Opt blurring **3** Phot fogging, Spéc halation

halogène [alɔʒɛn] ADJ halogenous

NM halogen; **lampe à h.** halogen lamp; **h. à quartz** quartz-halogen

*****halte** [alt] NF **1** (arrêt) stop, halt; **faire h.** to (make a) halt, to stop; **h.(-là)!** stop!, halt!; Fig **h.-là, je ne suis pas d'accord!** hold on or not so fast, I don't agree!; **h. à l'armement** stop the arms build-up!; **dire h. à l'inflation** to put a stop or an end to inflation **2** (lieu) stopping place, resting place; Rail halt; **h. routière** (roadside) rest area

*****halte-garderie,** pl **haltes-garderies** [alt(ə)gardəri] NF crèche

haltère [altɛr] NM dumb-bell; **des haltères de 3 kilos** 3-kilo dumb-bells; **faire des haltères** to do weightlifting or weight training

haltérophile [alterɔfil] N weightlifter

haltérophilie [alterɔfili] NF weightlifting; **elle fait de l'h.** she does weightlifting or weight training

*****halva** [alva] NM halva

*****hamac** [amak] NM **1** hammock; **accrocher/décrocher un h.** to sling/unsling a hammock **2** (fiche) suspension file

hamadryade [amadrijad] NF Myth hamadryad, dryad, wood nymph

hamamélis [amamelis] NM Bot witch hazel, Spéc hamamelis

*****Hambourg** [ɑbur] N Hamburg

*****hambourgeois, -oise** [ɑburʒwa, -waz] ADJ of Hamburg

N **H.** Hamburger

*****hamburger** [ɑburgœr] NM Culin hamburger

*****hameau, -eaux** [amo] NM hamlet

hameçon [amsɔ̃] NM (fish-)hook; **h. sans œillet** blind hook; Fig **mordre à l'h.** to swallow or rise to the bait

hameçonner [amsɔne] VT **1** (poisson) to hook **2** (ligne de pêche) to put hooks on

*****hammam** [amam] NM Turkish baths

*****hammerless** [amɛrlɛs] NM hammerless sporting gun

*****hampe¹** [ɑp] NF **1** (d'un drapeau etc) staff, pole; (d'une lance etc) stave, shaft; (d'un harpon) shank; Typ (de lettre) stem; (qui dépasse

vers le haut) ascender; **la h. du p** the stem of the p; Typ **h. montante** ascender **2** Bot flower spike

*****hampe²** NF Culin (de bœuf) = cut taken between the flank and the sirloin; (de la venaison) breast

*****hamster** [amster] NM Zool hamster; **h. doré** golden hamster

*****han** [ɑ̃] INT oof!; **pousser un h. à chaque coup** to (give a) grunt at every stroke

*****hanap** [anap] NM Arch goblet, tankard

*****hanche** [ɑ̃ʃ] NF **1** Anat hip; **déformation congénitale de la h.** congenital hip deformity; **les poings sur les hanches** (with his/her/etc) hands on (his/her/etc) hips, (with) arms akimbo; **il refusait d'avancer, les mains sur les hanches** hands on hips, he refused to go any further; **rouler les hanches** to swing one's hips; **être large des hanches** to have broad hips, Fam to be broad in the beam; **tour de hanches** hip measurement; **perdre quelques centimètres de tour de hanches** to lose a few centimetres from one's hips **2** (d'un cheval) haunch; **hanches** hindquarters **3** Naut (d'un navire) quarter; **par la h.** on the quarter

*****hand** [ɑ̃d] NM Fam handball

*****hand-ball** [ɑ̃dbal] NM Sport handball; **jouer au h.** to play handball; **ballon de h.** handball

*****handballeur, -euse** [ɑ̃dbalœr, -øz] N Sport handball player

*****handicap** [ɑ̃dikap] NM aussi Fig handicap; Fig **la Pologne part avec un h.** Poland is handicapped from the outset; **elle partait dans la vie avec un sérieux h.** she started out in life with a serious handicap or seriously disadvantaged

handicapant [ɑ̃dikapɑ̃] ADJ (maladie) disabling; Fam **ça peut être très h.** that can be a great handicap; Fam **ne pas avoir de voiture à la campagne est h.** being without a car in the countryside is a handicap

handicapé, -ée [ɑ̃dikape] ADJ handicapped; (physiquement) handicapped, disabled; **h. mental** mentally handicapped; **h. physique** physically handicapped, (physically) disabled

N handicapped person; (physique) handicapped or disabled person; **h. moteur** person with motor impairment; **les handicapés mentaux** the mentally handicapped; **les handicapés (physiques)** the disabled, the physically handicapped

*****handicaper** [ɑ̃dikape] VT to handicap

*****handicapeur** [ɑ̃dikapœr] NM Courses de chevaux handicapper

handisport [ɑ̃dispɔr] ADJ Sport tennis/équipement h. tennis/sports equipment for the disabled or handicapped; **jeux handisports** games for the handicapped or disabled

*****hangar** [ɑ̃gar] NM **1** shed, shelter; (grand) warehouse; (pour les trains, bus etc) depot; **h. à bateaux** boathouse **2** Aviat hangar

*****hanneton** [an(ə)tɔ̃] NM cockchafer, maybug, Am June beetle or bug; Fam **une dispute/un examen pas piqué(e) des hannetons** a stinker of an argument/exam; Fam **une réponse pas piquée des hannetons** an astounding answer; Fam **je vous ai amené un petit vin pas piqué des hannetons** I've brought you an unbelievable little wine

Hanoi [anɔj] N Hanoi

*****Hanovre** [anɔvr] N Hanover

*****hanovrien, -enne** [anɔvrijɛ̃, -ɛn] aussi Hist ADJ Hanoverian

N **H.** Hanoverian

*****hanse** [ɑ̃s] NF aussi Hist Hanse, Hansa; **la H.** the Hanseatic league

*hanséatique [ɑ̃seatik] **ADJ** *Hist* Hanseatic

*hanté [ɑ̃te] **ADJ** haunted; **maison hantée** haunted house; **être h. par un souvenir/une impression** to be haunted by a memory/a feeling

*hanter [ɑ̃te] **VT** *(d'un fantôme) (maison etc)* to haunt; **cette idée le hante** he is obsessed *or* haunted by the idea; **ce souvenir me hante** the memory haunts me; *Fig* **il passait ses nuits à h. les bistrots** he spent every night in the pub

*hantise [ɑ̃tiz] **NF** haunting memory *or* thought; **j'ai la h. de ce genre de réunion** I dread this kind of meeting

*happe [ap] **NF 1** *Menuis* cramp *or* clamp iron **2** *(anneau)* staple; **anneau à h.** ring and staple

*happement [apmɑ̃] **NM** snapping (up), snatching, seizing

*happening [apniŋ] **NM** happening

*happer [ape] **VT** *(des oiseaux etc) (insectes etc)* to snap up, to catch; **la voiture a été happée par un train** the car was hit by a train; **la machine a happé sa main** his hand got caught in the machine; *Fig* **happer qn** to buttonhole sb

happy end, happy ending [apiɛnd(iŋ)] **NM** happy ending; **j'aime les happy ends** I love happy endings

haptonomie [aptɔnɔmi] **NF** *Obst* = technique of communication with foetus through sensory stimulation

*haquenée [akne] **NF** *Arch* palfrey

hara-kiri, *pl* **hara-kiris** [arakiri] **NM** hara-kiri; **(se) faire h.** to commit hara-kiri

*harangue [arɑ̃g] **NF** harangue; *Fam* **nous avons eu droit à une de ses harangues** we were treated to one of his/her harangues *or* lectures

*haranguer [arɑ̃ge] **VT** to harangue, to lecture

*haras [ara] **NM** stud farm

*harassant [arasɑ̃] **ADJ** exhausting

*harassé [arase] **ADJ** worn out, exhausted; **h. de travail** overwhelmed with work

*harassement [arasmɑ̃] **NM** fatigue, exhaustion

*harasser [arase] **VT** to tire out, to exhaust

> Il faut noter que le verbe anglais **to harass** est un faux ami. Il signifie **harceler**.

*harcelant [arsəlɑ̃] **ADJ** harassing, pestering

*harcèlement [arsɛlmɑ̃] **NM** harassment, harassing; **le h. sexuel** sexual harassment

*harceler [arsəle] **VT** **(je harcèle; je harcèlerai)** *(personne)* to harass; *Mil* to harry, to harass; *(animal)* to bait; **h. qn de ses questions** to badger *or* pester *or* plague sb with one's questions; **h. qn pour obtenir qch** to pester sb for sth; **elle est harcelée de soucis** she's plagued by worries; **les remords/regrets le harcèlent** he's tormented *or* plagued by remorse/regrets

*harceleur, -euse [arsəlœr, -øz] **N** tormentor, pesterer; **h. téléphonique** phone pest

*hard [ard] *Fam* **ADJ la scène était un peu h.** the scene was a little risqué; **porno h.** hard *or* hard-core porn
  NM *Mus* hard rock; *Ordinat* hardware; *(porno)* hard-core porn

*harde [ard] **NF** *(de cerfs)* herd, bevy

*harde [ard] **NF** *(pour la meute)* leash

*hardes [ard] **NFPL** rags

*hardeur [ardœr] **NM** *Fam* hard-porn actor

*hardi [ardi] **ADJ** *(audacieux)* bold, daring; *(téméraire)* rash; *(osé)* impudent, brazen; **écriture hardie** bold hand(writing); **faire un**

commentaire h. to make a bold comment; **jugement h.** rash judgement; **mensonge h.** barefaced lie; **un décolleté h.** a daring neckline; **une interprétation hardie** a bold interpretation
  INT *Arch* go on!, go to it!; **h. les gars!** come on lads!

*hardiesse [ardjɛs] **NF** *(audace)* boldness, daring; *(effronterie)* impudence, effrontery; *(originalité)* boldness; **avoir la h. de faire qch** to be so bold as to do sth; **il a eu la h. de m'écrire** he had the audacity to write to me; **remarque la h. du style de ce peintre** note the boldness of this painter's style; **hardiesses** liberties; **se permettre des hardiesses envers qn** to take liberties with sb

*hardiment [ardimɑ̃] **ADV** *(avec audace)* boldly, audaciously, daringly; *(avec effronterie)* impudently; *(à la légère)* rashly; **vous avez agi bien h.** you acted very rashly

*hard-top, *pl* **hard-tops** [ardtɔp] **NM** *Aut* hard top

*hardware [ardwɛr] **NM** *Ordinat* hardware

*harem [arɛm] **NM** harem

*hareng [arɑ̃] **NM** herring; **h. (salé et) fumé** kipper; **h. saur** red *or* smoked herring; **h. bouffi** bloater; *Fam* **être sec comme un h.** to be as skinny *or* thin as a rake; *Fam* **on était serrés comme des harengs dans le bus** we were packed together like sardines in the bus **VOIR GRAMMAIRE A12**

*harengère [arɑ̃ʒɛr] **NF** fishwife

*harenguier [arɑ̃gje] **NM** herring boat

*harfang [arfɑ̃] **NM** *Can* snowy owl

*hargne [arɲ] **NF** bad temper, surly disposition; **parler/répondre/s'exprimer avec h.** to speak/answer/express oneself bad-temperedly *or* aggressively; **... dit-il avec h.** ... he snapped; **propos pleins de h.** aggressive remarks

*hargneusement [arɲøzmɑ̃] **ADV** bad-temperedly, aggressively

*hargneux, -euse [arɲø, -øz] **ADJ** *(personne)* bad-tempered, cantankerous, aggressive; *(femme)* nagging; *(chien)* snarling, vicious, fierce; **ton h.** aggressive tone

*haricot [ariko] **NM 1** bean; **haricots en grains** dried beans; *Fam* **des haricots!** not a sausage *or* bean!; *Fam* **c'est la fin des haricots** we've had it now; *très Fam* **courir sur le h. à qn** to tee sb off, *Br* to get on sb's wick *or* up sb's nose; *Fam* **travailler pour des haricots** to work for peanuts **2** *Culin* **h. de mouton** = Irish stew **3** *(bol)* kidney dish
  ▸▸ **h. beurre** butter bean; **h. blanc** haricot bean; **h. d'Espagne** scarlet runner; **h. mange-tout** mange-tout; **h. à rames** runner bean; **h. rouge** (red) kidney bean; **h. vert** French *or Am* string bean

*haridelle [aridɛl] **NF** old horse, nag

*harissa [arisa] **NF** *Culin* harissa

*harki [arki] **NM** *Mil* harki *(Algerian soldier who fought on French side during the War of Independence; also his descendants)*

*harle [arl] **NM** *Orn* merganser

harmonica [armɔnika] **NM** *Mus* harmonica, mouth organ; **jouer de l'h.** to play the mouth organ *or* harmonica

harmonie [armɔni] **NF 1** *Mus* harmony; **table d'h.** *(d'un piano)* sounding board **2** *(accord)* harmony; **être en h. avec qch** to be in keeping *or* in harmony with sth, to fit in with sth; **vivre en h.** to live in harmony *or* harmoniously; **l'h. qui règne dans cette famille** the harmony which reigns within this family **3** *(de l'orchestre)* wind section **4** *(fanfare)* brass band

harmonieusement [armɔnjøzmɑ̃] **ADV** harmoniously; **des couleurs qui s'unissent h.** colours which go well together

harmonieux, -euse [armɔnjø, -øz] **ADJ** *(son)* harmonious, melodious, tuneful; *(arrangement etc)* harmonious; **couleurs harmonieuses** harmonious colours

harmonique [armɔnik] **ADJ, NM** *Mus* harmonic

harmoniquement [armɔnikmɑ̃] **ADV** harmonically

harmonisation [armɔnizasjɔ̃] **NF** harmonization, harmonizing; **h. fiscale** tax harmonization; *Ling* **h. vocalique** vowel harmony

harmoniser [armɔnize] **VT 1** *Mus (mélodie etc)* to harmonize **2** *(mettre en accord)* to harmonize; *(couleurs)* to match
  VPR **s'harmoniser** to be in keeping *or* in harmony, to harmonize, to agree (**avec** with); **ces couleurs s'harmonisent très bien** these colours go very well together; **s'h. avec qch** *(de couleurs)* to match *or* go well with sth

harmoniseur [armɔnizœr] **NM** *Radio etc* harmonizer

harmonium [armɔnjɔm] **NM** harmonium

*harnaché [arnaʃe] **ADJ** *(d'un cheval)* harnessed; *Fam* **il part à la pêche tout h.** he goes off fishing all kitted out; *Fam* **curieusement h.** wearing the strangest gear *or* get-up

*harnachement [arnaʃmɑ̃] **NM 1** *(action)* harnessing **2** *(harnais)* harness; *(selles etc)* saddlery; *Fam (vêtements)* (absurd) rig-out, get-up; **sortir dans un curieux h.** to go out wearing the strangest gear *or* get-up

*harnacher [arnaʃe] **VT** *(cheval etc)* to harness; *Fam* **h. qn** to dress sb up, to rig sb out; **il fallait voir comment elle était harnachée** you should have seen the ridiculous outfit she was wearing
  VPR **se harnacher** to rig oneself out; **il faut toujours se h. pour aller en montagne** you must always get properly kitted out for the mountains

*harnais [arnɛ] **NM 1** *(sellerie)* harness; *Fig* **reprendre le h.** to get back into harness, to go back to work again; **blanchir sous le h.** to spend one's life in the same occupation, to grow grey in service; *Aut* **h. de sécurité** safety harness **2** *Arch (armure)* armour **3** *Tech* **h. d'engrenage** train of gear wheels, gearing

*harnois [arnwa] **NM** *Arch* = **harnais 2**

*haro [aro] **NM (clameur de) h.** outcry, hue and cry; **crier h.** to raise a hue and cry (**sur** about); **crier h. sur le baudet** to scream for blood

harpagon [arpagɔ̃] **NM** miser, skinflint, scrooge; **c'est un h.** he's a real miser

*harpe [arp] **NF** *Mus* harp; **jouer ou pincer de la h.** to play the harp; **h. éolienne** Aeolian harp

*harpie [arpi] **NF 1** *Myth* harpy; *Fig* harpy, shrew; **j'ai vu la concierge, cette h.** I've seen the caretaker, the old battleaxe **2** *Orn* harpy eagle

*harpiste [arpist] **N** *Mus* harpist

*harpon [arpɔ̃] **NM** *Pêche* harpoon; **pêche ou chasse (sous-marine) au h.** (underwater) spear fishing

*harponnage [arpɔnaʒ], **harponnement** [arpɔnmɑ̃] **NM** harpooning

*harponner [arpɔne] **VT 1** *Pêche* to harpoon **2** *très Fam (de la police) (personne)* to nab, to collar; *(personne)* to stop, to corner, to grab; **se faire h. par qn** to get cornered *or* nabbed by sb

*harponneur [arpɔnœr] **NM** *Pêche* harpooner

*hasard [azar] **NM 1** chance, luck; **coup de h.** stroke of luck, fluke; **c'est vraiment un coup de h., je ne m'y attendais pas du tout** it's a real stroke of luck, I wasn't expecting it at all; **par un coup de h.** by mere chance, by coincidence; **un heureux h. a fait qu'il a**

été muté dans la même région que moi by a stroke of luck he was transferred to the same area as me; **par un heureux h.** by a happy coincidence; **ne rien laisser au h.** to leave nothing to chance; **le h. a voulu** ou **a fait que je …** as luck would have it I …; **le h. fit que** + *ind,* **le h. voulut que** + *sub* (as) luck would have it; **le h. fait bien les choses!** what a stroke of luck!; **au h.** at random, *Péj* haphazardly; **j'en ai pris un au h.** I took one at random; **marcher au h.** to walk aimlessly; **au h. de ses voyages** in the course of his travels, as he travelled from one place to another; **au h. de mes lectures** in the course of my reading; **par h.** by accident, by chance; **par pur h.** quite by chance, entirely by accident; **par le plus grand des hasards** by the merest chance; **si par h. vous le voyez** if you (should) happen to see him; **sauriez-vous son adresse par h.?** do you happen to know his address?, do you know his address by any chance?; **et comme par h., il est tombé malade** and as if by chance, he fell ill; **à tout h.** on the off-chance, just in case; **je te le dis à tout h.** I'm telling you just in case; **à tout h., je vais lui demander** I'll ask him just in case or on the off-chance
2 *(danger)* risk, danger, hazard; **les hasards de la guerre** the hazards of war

> Il faut noter que le nom anglais **hazard** signifie uniquement **danger.**

*hasardé [azarde] ADJ *(entreprise etc)* hazardous, risky, foolhardy; *(paroles etc)* rash
*hasarder [azarde] VT *(sa vie etc)* to risk, to venture, to hazard; **h. une opinion** to hazard or venture an opinion; **h. 500 euros** to gamble 500 euros
▪ VPR **se hasarder** to take risks; **se h. à faire qch** to venture to do sth, to risk doing sth; **se h. dans la jungle** to venture (out) into the jungle
*hasardeux, -euse [azardø, -øz] ADJ hazardous, perilous, risky; **entreprise hasardeuse** risky business; **paroles hasardeuses** rash words
*hasch [aʃ] NM *Fam (drogue)* hash, pot
*haschisch [aʃiʃ] NM hashish; **fumer du h.** to smoke hashish
*hase [az] NF *Zool (d'un lièvre, d'un lapin de garenne)* doe
*hassidisme [asidism] NM *Rel* Chassidism, Hassidism
hast [ast] NM *Arch* shaft; **arme d'h.** shafted weapon
*hâte [ɑt] NF haste, hurry; **avoir h. de faire qch** to be in a hurry to do sth; *(avoir envie)* to be eager or to long to do sth, to look forward to doing sth; **j'ai h. de trouver un nouvel appartement** I can't wait to find a new flat; **j'ai h. de te revoir** I'm looking forward to seeing you again; **mettre trop de h. à faire qch** to be in too great a hurry or too much of a hurry to do sth; **il n'a qu'une h.: que tout soit fini** all he wants is to get it over with; **à la h.** in a hurry, in haste, hastily, hurriedly; **travail fait à la h.** slapdash work; **déjeuner à la h.** to hurry over one's lunch, *Fam* to bolt one's lunch; **en h.** hastily, in haste, hurriedly; **ils sont venus en h.** they came hurriedly or without delay; **en toute h.** post-haste, as quickly as possible; **sans h.** without haste, in a leisurely way
*hâter [ɑte] VT *(événement)* to hasten, to hurry along; *(fruit etc)* to force; **h. les choses** to hurry things up or along; **h. le pas** to quicken one's pace or step; **h. le mouvement** to hurry things up or along
▪ VPR **se hâter** to hurry, to hasten; **se h. de faire qch** to hurry to do sth, to lose or waste no time in doing sth; **je vais me h. de prendre rendez-vous** I'm going to waste no time in

making an appointment; **hâtez-vous lentement** more haste, less speed
*hâtif, -ive [ɑtif, -iv] ADJ **1** *(printemps, fruit etc)* early **2** *(mesure, décision etc)* hasty, hurried, ill-considered, premature
*hâtivement [ɑtivmɑ̃] ADV hastily, in a hurry, hurriedly; **se diriger h. vers …** to hurry towards …
*hauban [obɑ̃] NM **1** *Naut* shroud **2** *(corde, câble)* guy, stay
*haubaner [obane] VT *Naut* to guy, to stay, to brace
*haubert [obɛr] NM *Arch* coat of mail
*hausse [os] NF **1** *(de prix, de la température)* rise, increase; **h. de prix** price rise or increase or hike; **la h. des matières premières** the rise or increase in the price of raw materials; **baromètre en h.** rising barometer; *Com, Fin* **marché à la h.** rising or bull market; **h. de 4%** 4% rise; *Bourse* **h. des cours** stock market rise; **nous avons dû réviser nos prix à la h.** we've had to revise our prices upwards; **les cours sont orientés à la h.** there is an upward trend in share prices; **pousser les actions à la h.** to bull the market; **l'immobilier est en h.** house prices are going up; **le blé a subi une h. considérable** wheat has gone up considerably (in price); **h. à la pompe** rise in the price of petrol; *Bourse* **jouer à la h.** to speculate on a rising market, to bull the market; *Bourse* **spéculateur à la h.** bull **2** *Tech* prop, block, stand **3** *Mil (de fusil)* (back)sight, sighting gear
*haussement [osmɑ̃] NM **h. d'épaules** shrug (of the shoulders); **il accueillit la nouvelle par un h. d'épaules/avec un h. de sourcils** he welcomed the news with a shrug (of his shoulders)/with raised eyebrow(s)
*hausser [ose] VT *(lever)* to raise, to lift; *(élever)* to raise, to make higher, to heighten; *(augmenter) (prix)* to put up, to increase, to raise; **h. la voix** to raise one's voice; **h. les épaules** to shrug (one's shoulders); **h. les sourcils** to raise one's eyebrows
▪ VI *Naut (d'un terrain, d'un phare)* to rise (over the horizon)
▪ VPR **se hausser** to raise oneself (up); **se h. sur la pointe des pieds** to stand on tiptoe or one's toes; **se h. jusqu'à qn** to raise oneself to sb's level; **je me suis haussé jusqu'à la fenêtre** I hauled myself up to the window; **se h. jusqu'au poste de PDG** to climb to the position of Chairman, to rise to be Chairman
*haussier, -ière [osje, -jɛr] *Bourse* ADJ bullish
▪ N bull
*haussmannien, -ienne [osmanjɛ̃, -jɛn] ADJ Haussmannian

*HAUT, HAUTE [o, ot]

ADJ high **1, 3, 4, 6** ▪ tall **1** ▪ upper **2**		
▪ top **2** ▪ loud **4**		
ADV high **1** ▪ aloud **1** ▪ above **1, 2**		
▪ back **2**		
NM height **1** ▪ top **2**		
NF upper crust		

ADJ 1 high; *(herbe)* tall, long; *(édifice etc)* tall, high, lofty; **femme de haute taille** tall woman; **mur h. de six mètres** wall six metres high; **h. comme trois pommes** knee high to a grasshopper; **pièce haute de plafond** room with a high ceiling; **les pièces sont hautes de plafond** the rooms have high ceilings; **des talons hauts** high heels; **un front h.** a high forehead; **marcher la tête haute** or **le front h.** to hold one's head up; *Fig* to walk with one's head held high or one's head up; **h. sur pattes** long-legged; **la lune/Vénus était haute dans le ciel** the moon/Venus was high up in the sky; **les hautes latitudes** the high latitudes; **en haute montagne** high

in the mountains; **les hauts plateaux** the high plateaus or plateaux; **hautes terres** highlands, uplands; **les Hautes Terres (de l'Écosse)** the Highlands (of Scotland); **haute mer** open sea, high sea; **hautes eaux** high water; **à marée haute** at high tide, at high water; **la mer était haute** the tide was in or high; **je ne la tiens pas en haute estime** I don't hold her in very high regard or esteem; **avoir une haute idée de soi-même** to have a high opinion of oneself; *Fig* **avoir/garder la main haute sur ses affaires** to be in/to retain control of one's affairs
2 *(supérieur)* upper, higher; **les hautes branches** the upper branches, the top branches; **l'étage le plus h.** the top floor; **la plus haute branche** the topmost or uppermost branch; **ville haute** upper part of the town; **les hautes classes** *(de la société)* the upper classes; **les hautes mathématiques** higher mathematics; **le H.-Rhin** *(département)* the Haut-Rhin; **le h. Rhin** *(fleuve)* the upper Rhine; *Naut* **les hautes voiles** the upper sails
3 *(éminent)* exalted, important, great; **de la plus haute importance** of the greatest or utmost importance; **de h. rang** of high rank, high-ranking; **les plus hautes instances policières** the highest-ranking or most senior police authorities; **h. comique** high comedy
4 *(note de musique)* high; **voix haute** loud voice; *(aiguë)* high (-pitched) voice; **lire à haute voix** to read aloud; **elle parlait à haute voix** she spoke aloud or out loud; **pousser les hauts cris** to shout out loud; **elle n'a jamais une parole plus haute que l'autre** she never raises her voice; **avoir le verbe h.** to be high and mighty
5 *(ancien)* **la haute antiquité** remote or earliest antiquity; **le h. Moyen Âge** the Early Middle Ages
6 *(extrême)* **mécanisme de haute précision** precision device; **h. en couleurs** *(personnage, récit)* colourful; **haute pression** high pressure; **mécanisme de** ou **à haute sécurité** high security device; *Radio* **haute fréquence** high frequency; **à haute valeur ajoutée** high value added
▪ ADV **1** high (up), above, up; **h. les mains!** hands up!; **h. les cœurs!** cheer up!; **parler h.** to speak loudly; **parlez plus h.!** speak up!; **parle moins h.!** keep your voice down!; **une voix h. perchée** a high-pitched voice; **parler** ou **penser tout h.** to talk or think aloud or out loud; **dire tout h. ce que tout le monde pense tout bas** to say out loud what everyone else is thinking; **parler h. et clair** to speak one's mind; **je l'ai déjà dit h. et clair** I've already said it quite openly; **femme h. placée** woman in a high position; **des gens h. placés** highly placed people, people in high office; **viser h.** to aim or set one's sights high; **il la place très h. dans son estime** he has a very high opinion of her, he holds her in very high regard or esteem; *Naut* **l'ancre est h.** the anchor is up; **gagner h. la main** to win hands down; **ils ont remporté la course h. la main** they won the race hands down
2 *(en arrière)* back; **remonter plus h. (dans le temps)** to go further back; **comme il est dit plus h.** as indicated above or earlier; **ainsi que nous l'avons déjà vu plus h.** as we have already seen (above)
▪ NM **1** height; **le mur a six mètres de h.** the wall is six metres high; *Fig* **regarder qn du h. de sa grandeur** to look down one's nose at sb; **tomber de (son) h.** to fall flat on the ground, to fall headlong; *(être surpris ou déçu)* to fall flat on one's back, to be floored or flabbergasted
2 *(partie supérieure)* top, upper part; *Mktg (du marché)* high end, top end; **h.!** *(sur caisse)* this side up!; **la poste se trouve dans le h. du village** the Post Office is at the top end of the village; **le h. de la robe est en den-**

happily ever after; **h. comme un poisson dans l'eau** as happy as a sandboy; **vivre h.** to live happily; **je suis très h. de ce cadeau** I'm very happy or pleased with this gift; **je suis très h. de vous faire savoir que ...** I'm very happy or pleased to inform you that ...; **nous sommes très h. de vous annoncer le mariage de ...** we are very happy or pleased to announce the marriage of ...; **nous serions h. que vous acceptiez** we would be glad if you accepted; **je serais très heureuse si ...** I would be very happy or pleased if ...; **époque heureuse** happy times; **heureuse année!** Happy New Year!; **heureuse jeunesse!** the joys of youth!

2 (favorable) successful; (formulation etc) apt, Litt happy, felicitous; **avoir une heureuse façon de s'exprimer** to express oneself well; **la formulation n'est pas toujours très heureuse dans ce texte** this text is not always very well worded; **h. mariage** joyful wedding (ceremony); **mariage h.** happy marriage; **un h. mariage de couleurs** a successful blend of colours; **l'issue heureuse des négociations** the successful outcome of the negotiations; **une solution heureuse** a happy solution; **un choix h.** a good choice; Fig **début h.** auspicious beginning; **le résultat n'est pas très h.** it wasn't very successful, it didn't work out

3 (favorisé) fortunate, favoured, Am favored; **h. au jeu/en amour** lucky at cards/in love; **il peut s'estimer h.** he can think or consider himself lucky; **estime-toi h. d'avoir été sélectionné** think or consider yourself lucky to have been chosen; Bible **h. sont les pauvres en esprit** blessed are the poor in spirit

4 (chanceux) lucky, fortunate; **c'est fort h. pour vous** that's very lucky for you; **c'est h. que vous soyez libre** it's a good thing or a good job that you're free; Fam **encore h. qu'il ait gardé le ticket de caisse!** it's just as well that he held on to the receipt!; Fam **elle m'avait prévenu, encore h.!** it's a good thing she warned me!; **par un h. hasard** by a happy coincidence

N vous avez fait un h. you have made one man very happy; **si tu le lui donnes, tu vas faire un h.** if you give it to him, you will make him a happy man

▸▸ **h. événement** happy event

heuristique [œristik] ADJ heuristic
NF heuristics

***heurt** [œr] NM (des intérêts, des couleurs etc) clash; (des véhicules) collision; **leur collaboration ne va pas sans heurts** their collaboration has its ups and downs or its rough patches; **tout s'est fait sans h.** everything went smoothly or without a hitch

***heurté** [œrte] ADJ (style) abrupt, halting; (ton) abrupt; Beaux-Arts (couleurs) contrasting; **exécution ou jeu heurté(e) au piano** jerky style of playing the piano

***heurter** [œrte] VT **1** (personne, chose) to knock (against), to run into, to bump into; (personne) to collide with; Naut (rocher) to hit, to strike; **h. qch de la tête** to knock or bump one's head against sth
2 (sentiments etc) to shock, to offend; **ces théories vont h. de front un bon nombre d'idées reçues** these theories will clash head-on with a good number of received ideas; **h. toutes les idées reçues** to go against or run counter to convention
VI **h. à la porte** to knock at or on the door; **sa tête a heurté contre le pare-brise** he hit his head against the windscreen, his head struck the windscreen
VPR **se heurter 1** (se cogner) to collide (with each other); **se h. à ou contre qn/qch** to run (slap) into or collide with or bang into or bump into sb/sth; **les deux voitures se sont**

heurtées à 120 km/h the two cars crashed into each other at 120 kph; **je me suis heurtée contre un mur** I crashed into a wall; **se h. la tête à ou contre qch** to knock or bump one's head against sth; Fig **se h. à l'indifférence générale** to come up against general apathy or indifference; **se h. à une difficulté** to come up against a difficulty; **se h. aux idées reçues** to come into conflict with or to clash with received opinion
2 (de couleur, intérêt etc) to clash; **des couleurs/goûts qui se heurtent** clashing colours/tastes, colours/tastes which clash; Fig **au cours de la réunion, ils se sont heurtés violemment** during the meeting they clashed violently; **il est très fréquent qu'ils se heurtent** they're always clashing (with each other) or crossing swords

***heurtoir** [œrtwar] NM (de porte) (door) knocker; (amortisseur) catch, stop; Rail buffer

hévéa [evea] NM Bot hevea

hexacorde [ɛgzakɔrd] NM Mus hexachord

hexadécimal, -ale, -aux, -ales [ɛgzadesimal, -o] ADJ Ordinat hex, hexadecimal

hexaèdre [ɛgzaɛdr] ADJ hexahedral
NM hexahedron

hexagonal, -ale, -aux, -ales [ɛgzagɔnal, -o] ADJ hexagonal; Fig French

hexagone [ɛgzagɔn] NM hexagon; **l'H.** France

hexamètre [ɛgzamɛtr] ADJ hexametric(al)
NM hexameter

HF Radio etc (abrév **haute fréquence**) HF

hi INT (en riant) ha ha; (en pleurant) boo-hoo

hiatal, -ale, -aux, -ales [jatal, -o] ADJ Méd hiatal; **hernie hiatale** hiatus hernia

***hiatus** [jatys] NM (dans une narration etc) gap, break, hiatus; Ling, Anat hiatus; Fig **le h. entre la production et les besoins** the gap or discrepancy between production and needs

hibernal, -ale, -aux, -ales [ibɛrnal, -o] ADJ (germination, sommeil etc) winter, Spéc hibernal

hibernant [ibɛrnã] ADJ (animal) hibernating

hibernation [ibɛrnasjɔ̃] NF hibernation; Fig **la gauche sort de son h.** the left is coming in from the cold; **mettre un dossier en h.** to shelve a document; **h. artificielle** suspended animation, Spéc cryogenic suspension

hiberner [ibɛrne] VI to hibernate

hibiscus [ibiskys] NM Bot hibiscus

***hibou, -oux** [ibu] NM owl; **jeune h.** owlet; **des yeux de h.** eyes like saucers; Péj **quel vieux h.!** he is a real recluse!

***hic** [ik] NM Fam **voilà le h.!** that's the snag or the trouble!; **le h., c'est que ...** the trouble or snag is that ...

***hickory** [ikɔri] NM Bot hickory

hidalgo [idalgo] NM Fam Latin hunk

***hideur** [idœr] NF (qualité) hideousness

***hideusement** [idøzmã] ADV hideously

***hideux, -euse** [idø, -øz] ADJ hideous; **h. à voir** hideous-looking; **un crime h.** a hideous or heinous crime

hiémal, -ale, -aux, -ales [jemal] ADJ Litt winter

hier [jɛr] ADV yesterday; **h. matin, h. dans la matinée** yesterday morning; **h. (au) soir** yesterday evening, last night; **on s'en souvient comme si c'était h.** I/we/etc can remember it as if it were (only) yesterday; **le journal d'h.** yesterday's paper; Fig **cela ne date pas d'h.** that's nothing new; Fam **je ne suis pas né d'h.** I wasn't born yesterday
NM **tu avais tout h. ou toute la journée d'h. pour te décider** you had all (day) yesterday to make up your mind

***hiérarchie** [jerarʃi] NF hierarchy; **h. des valeurs sociales** scale of social values; **être en haut/bas de la h.** to be at the top/bottom of the hierarchy

***hiérarchique** [jerarʃik] ADJ hierarchical; **c'est mon supérieur h.** he's my immediate superior; **par (la) voie h.** through (the) official channels

***hiérarchiquement** [jerarʃikmã] ADV hierarchically; **il lui est h. supérieur** he is superior (in rank) to him

***hiérarchisation** [jerarʃizasjɔ̃] NF **h. des fonctions** grading of jobs; **h. des tâches** prioritization of tasks

***hiérarchisé** [jerarʃize] ADJ (système) hierarchical

***hiérarchiser** [jerarʃize] VT **1** (organiser) to form into a hierarchy; (régler) (état etc) to structure or to classify according to a hierarchical system; **pour fonctionner, il est nécessaire qu'une société soit hiérarchisée** a society must have a hierarchy in order to function; **h. les emplois** to grade jobs **2** (tâches) to prioritize

***hiératique** [jeratik] ADJ **1** (sacré) hieratic **2** (geste) solemn; **port de tête h.** regal carriage

***hiéroglyphe** [jerɔglif] NM hieroglyph(ic)

***hiéroglyphique** [jerɔglifik] ADJ hieroglyphic(al)

***hi-fi** [ifi] ADJ INV, NF INV hi-fi; **chaîne h.** hi-fi; **magasin de h.** hi-fi shop

***hi-han,** pl **hi-hans** [iã] INT, NM (d'âne) hee-haw

hi hi [ii, hihi] INT (rire nerveux) hee-hee!; (pleurs) boo-hoo!

hilarant [ilarã] ADJ hilarious; Chimie **gaz h.** laughing gas

hilare [ilar] ADJ (visage) beaming, grinning; **il était h.** he was beaming or grinning all over his face

hilarité [ilarite] NF hilarity, mirth; **provoquer l'h. générale** to cause general hilarity

***hile** [il] NM Anat, Bot hilum

Himalaya [imalaja] N **l'H.** the Himalayas

himalayen, -enne [imalajɛ̃, -jɛn] ADJ Himalayan; **la chaîne himalayenne** the Himalayan (mountain) range; Fig **les sommets himalayens de la bêtise** the (absolute) height of stupidity

***hindi** [indi] ADJ NM Ling Hindi

hindou, -oue [ɛ̃du] ADJ Hindu
N **H.** Hindu

hindouisme [ɛ̃duism] NM Hinduism

hindouiste [ɛ̃duist] ADJ, N Hindu

Hindoustan [ɛ̃dustã] N Géog Hindustan

hindoustani [ɛ̃dustani] NM Ling Hindustani

hinterland [interlãd] NM hinterland

***hippie** [ipi] ADJ, N hippie

hippique [ipik] ADJ relating to horses, equine; **concours h.** horse show

hippisme [ipism] NM horseriding; (courses) horseracing

hippocampe [ipɔkãp] NM Myth hippocampus; (poisson) sea horse

Hippocrate [ipɔkrat] N Antiq Hippocrates; **le serment d'H.** the Hippocratic oath

hippocratique [ipɔkratik] ADJ Hippocratic

hippodrome [ipɔdrom] NM racecourse; Antiq hippodrome, circus

hippomobile [ipɔmɔbil] ADJ horse-drawn

hippophagique [ipɔfaʒik] ADJ **boucherie h.** horsemeat butcher

hippopotame [ipɔpɔtam] NM hippopotamus, Fam hippo; **il avait une carrure d'h.** he was built like an ox VOIR GRAMMAIRE A14

hippopotamesque [ipɔpɔtamɛsk] ADJ

Fam Hum hippopotamus-like, of a hippopotamus; **une lourdeur/grâce h.** the weight/grace of a hippo

hippotechnie [ipɔtɛkni] **NF** (technique of) horse breeding and training

***hippy** [ipi] **ADJ, N** hippie

hirondelle [irɔ̃dɛl] **NF 1** *(oiseau)* swallow; *Prov* **une h. ne fait pas le printemps** one swallow doesn't make a summer; *Culin* **nid d'h.** bird's nest **2** *Fam Vieilli (agent de police)* cycle cop
▸▸ **h. de cheminée** swallow tern; **h. de fenêtre** house martin; **h. de mer** tern; **h. de rivage** sand martin

***hirsute** [irsyt] **ADJ** *(personne)* hairy, *Spéc* hirsute; *(barbe, ours)* shaggy

hispanique [ispanik] **ADJ** Hispanic, Spanish

hispanisant, -ante [ispanizɑ̃, -ɑ̃t] **N** student of/expert on Spanish

hispaniser [ispanize] **VT** to Hispanicize

hispanisme [ispanism] **NM** *Ling* Hispanicism

hispano-américain, -aine, *pl* **hispano-américain(e)s** [ispanɔamerikɛ̃, -ɛn] **ADJ** Hispano-American, Spanish-American
N H. Hispano-American, *Fam* Hispanic

hispano-arabe, *pl* **hispano-arabes** [ispanɔarab], **hispano-moresque** *pl* **hispano-moresques** [ispanɔmɔrɛsk] **ADJ** Hispano-Moorish, Hispano-Moresque

hispanophone [ispanɔfɔn] **ADJ** Spanish-speaking
N Spanish speaker

hispide [ispid] **ADJ** *Bot* hairy, *Spéc* hispid

***hisser** [ise] **VT** to hoist (up), to pull up; *Naut (embarcation)* to hoist in; **hissez!** hoist away!; *Naut* up sails!; **oh! hisse!** (yo-)heave-ho!; **h. une échelle par-dessus un mur** to haul a ladder over a wall; **h. qn vers soi** to lift sb up (towards one); **h. qn sur ses épaules** to hoist *or* lift sb onto one's shoulders
VPR se hisser se h. jusqu'à la fenêtre to pull *or* hoist oneself up to the window; **se h. sur la pointe des pieds** to stand on tiptoe; *Fig* **se h. jusqu'au pouvoir/gouvernement** to rise to a position of power/a position in government

histogramme [istɔgram] **NM** bar chart, histogram

HISTOIRE [istwar]

history 1 ▪ history book 2 ▪ story 3
▪ fib 3 ▪ trouble 3 ▪ fuss 3

NF 1 history; **l'h. seule jugera** history *or* posterity alone will be the judge; **h. du moyen âge/naturelle** medi(a)eval/natural history; **étudiant en h. de l'art** history of art student *or* art history student; **l'h. des sciences** the history of science; **la petite h.** sidelights on history, footnotes of history; **sachez, pour la petite h., qu'elle fut la maîtresse du roi** let me tell you, by the way *or* for the record, that she was the king's mistress; **l'h. de (la) France** the history of France, French history; *Fig* **tout cela, c'est de l'h. ancienne** that's all ancient history *or* dead and buried; **livre d'h.** history book
2 *(livre)* history book; **une h. d'Allemagne** a history of Germany
3 *(récit)* story, tale; *TV, Cin* story, narrative; *Fam (mensonge)* fib, story; **histoires pour enfants** children's stories; **auteur d'histoires pour enfants** children's author, author of children's stories; **j'ai l'impression que tu es en train de me raconter une h.** I have a feeling that you're pulling my leg *or* telling me a tall story; **je t'assure, je ne te raconte pas d'histoires!** I assure you, I'm not making it up!; **h. de marin** sailor's yarn; **livre d'histoires** story book; **c'est toujours la même h.** it's (always) the same old story; **c'est une autre**

h. it's quite a different matter *or* story; **tout ça, ce sont des histoires** that's all nonsense *or* rubbish; **tu crois encore ses histoires?** do you still believe his/her nonsense?; **le plus beau de l'h., c'est que ...** the best part of the story is that ...; **se fourrer dans une sale/drôle (d')h.** to get mixed up in a nasty/funny business; **il m'est arrivé une drôle d'h./une sale h.** a funny thing/a nasty thing happened to me; **figure-toi qu'il m'est arrivé une h. incroyable!** believe it or not, something incredible has happened to me!; *Fam* **il est sorti, h. de prendre un peu l'air** he went out just to get a breath of fresh air; **h. de rire un peu** just for a laugh, just for fun; **ce que j'en dis, c'est h. de parler** you can take or leave what I've said; **elle l'a dit, h. de dire quelque chose** she said it just for the sake of saying something; **c'est toute une h.** *(à raconter)* it's a long story; *(pour faire qch)* it's no end of a job, it's quite a business; **en voilà une h. pour pas grand-chose** what a fuss about nothing; *Fam* **en voilà une h.!** what a fuss!, what a song and dance!; *(c'est incroyable)* that's quite a story; **quelle h.!** that's quite a story!; *Fam* **faire des histoires** *ou* **un tas d'histoires** to make a fuss *or* a to-do; **tu fais bien des histoires!** you're making or kicking up such a fuss!; **s'attirer des histoires** to get oneself into trouble; **faire des histoires à qn** to make trouble for sb; **il faut éviter d'avoir des histoires** must keep out of trouble; *Fam* **pas d'histoires!** no fuss!; **au lit, et pas d'histoires** off to bed now, and I don't want any fuss
▸▸ **h. de fous** shaggy dog story; **c'est une h. de fous!** it's crazy!; **l'H. sainte** Biblical history

> Attention: ne pas confondre **history** et **story** lorsque l'on traduit **histoire**. Le terme **history** désigne la discipline, alors que **story** signifie **récit**.

histologie [istɔlɔʒi] **NF** histology

histologique [istɔlɔʒik] **ADJ** histological

historicité [istɔrisite] **NF** historicity

historié [istɔrje] **ADJ** that tells a story; *(initiales, bible)* illuminated

historien, -ienne [istɔrjɛ̃, -jɛn] **N** historian; **h. d'art** art historian

historiette [istɔrjɛt] **NF** anecdote, short story; **c'est une jolie petite h.** it's a nice little story

historiographe [istɔrjɔgraf] **N** historiographer

historiographie [istɔrjɔgrafi] **NF** historiography

historique [istɔrik] **ADJ** *(qui concerne l'histoire)* historical; *(important, décisif)* historic; *Gram* **présent h.** historic present; **être classé monument h.** *(d'un monument)* to be listed *or* classified as an ancient monument *or* as a place of historic interest; **liste des monuments historiques français** list of ancient French monuments; **c'est un événement h. dans la famille** it's a historic event *or* a red-letter day for the family
NM historical record *or* account; *Ordinat (de document)* log; **faire l'h. des événements** to give a chronological account of events; **faire l'h. d'une association/d'un gouvernement/d'un mot** to trace the history of an association/a government/a word; **h. d'entretien** *(d'une voiture etc)* service history

> Attention: ne pas confondre **historic** et **historical** lorsque l'on traduit **historique**. **Historic** signifie **important d'un point de vue historique**, alors que **historical** signifie **qui se rapporte à l'histoire**.

historiquement [istɔrikmɑ̃] **ADV** historically

histrion [istrijɔ̃] **NM** *Théâtre Arch* play actor; *Litt Péj* second-rate actor

hi-tech [aitɛk] **ADJ INV** hi-tech

hitlérien, -ienne [itlerjɛ̃, -jɛn] **ADJ** Hitlerite; **le gouvernement h.** the Hitler government
N Hitlerite

hitlérisme [itlerism] **NM** Hitlerism

***hit-parade** [itparad] **NM** charts; **chanteur n° 1 au h.** chart-topping singer; **chanson n° 1 au h.** chart-topper, number 1 in the charts; **être au h. de l'actualité** to be a big news item, to be headline news

***hittite** [itit] *Antiq* **ADJ** Hittite
N H. Hittite

HIV [aʃive] **NM** *(abrév* **human immunodeficiency virus)** HIV

hiver [ivɛr] **NM** winter; **l'h. sera doux/rude** it will be a mild/severe winter; **en h.** in winter; **temps d'h.** wintry weather; **depuis une semaine, il fait un temps d'h.** it's been like winter this last week; **vêtements/sports d'h.** winter clothes/sports; **jardin d'h.** winter garden; *Fam* **le bonhomme H.** Jack Frost VOIR GRAMMAIRE A7
▸▸ *Fig* **h. nucléaire** nuclear winter

hivernage [ivɛrnaʒ] **NM 1** *(du bétail, de navires, d'une expédition polaire etc)* wintering **2** *(endroit)* winter quarters; *Naut* winter harbour **3** *(fourrage)* winter fodder

hivernal, -ale, -aux, -ales [ivɛrnal, -o] **ADJ** *(froid etc)* winter; *(temps)* wintry; **station hivernale** winter sports resort, ski resort

hivernant, -ante [ivɛrnɑ̃, -ɑ̃t] **N** *(dans un lieu de vacances etc)* winter visitor *or* tourist

hiverner [ivɛrne] **VI** to winter; *(d'un navire)* to lie up (for the winter)
VT *(bétail)* to winter

HLM [aʃɛlɛm] **NF OU NM** *(abrév* **habitation à loyer modéré)** *Br* ≃ council flat/house, *Am* ≃ public housing unit; **vivre dans une** *ou* *Fam* **un H.** to live in a council flat/house

***ho** [o] **INT** *(appel)* hey!; *(surprise)* oh!

***hobby** [ɔbi] **NM** hobby

***hobereau, -eaux** [ɔbro] **NM 1** *souvent Péj* *(gentilhomme)* (country) squire **2** *Orn* hobby

***hochement** [ɔʃmɑ̃] **NM h. de tête** *(négatif)* shake of the head; *(affirmatif)* nod (of the head)

***hochepot** [ɔʃpo] **NM** *Culin* meat and vegetable stew

hochequeue [ɔʃkø] **NM** *Zool* wagtail

***hocher** [ɔʃe] **VT h. la tête** *(de dédain)* to toss one's head; *(pour dire non)* to shake one's head; *(pour dire oui)* to nod (one's head); *(d'un cheval)* to toss its head

***hochet** [ɔʃɛ] **NM** *(d'enfant)* (child's) rattle; *Fig* bauble, toy

***hockey** [ɔkɛ] **NM** *Sport (jeu)* (field) hockey; *Can (sur glace)* hockey; *Can (crosse)* (ice) hockey stick; **h. sur gazon** (field) hockey; **h. sur glace** ice hockey, *Am* hockey; **partie de h.** hockey game *or* match; **jouer au h.** to play hockey

***hockeyeur, -euse** [ɔkɛjœr, -øz] **N** hockey player

hoirie [wari] **NF** *Jur* avance *ou* avancement d'h. advancement

***holà** [ɔla] **INT** *(pour appeler)* stop!, hold on!; **h., on se calme, hein!** hey, quieten down, OK?; **h., je ne suis pas tout à fait d'accord avec vous, moi!** now hold on, I don't quite agree with you there!
NM **mettre le h. à qch** to put a stop to sth

***holding** [ɔldiŋ] **NM OU NF** *Fin* holding company

***hold-up** [ɔldœp] **NM INV** *Fam* hold-up, *surtout Am* stick-up; **faire un h.** to carry out a hold-up

---

The symbol * indicates that the initial **h** is aspirate and that hence there is no liaison, eg **les haricots** [leariko] and not [lezariko], or contraction in spelling, eg **la haine** and not **l'haine**.

*hollandais, -aise [ɔlɑ̃dɛ, -ɛz] **ADJ** Dutch
NM *Ling* Dutch
N H. Dutchman, *f* Dutchwoman; **les H.** the Dutch

*Hollande [ɔlɑ̃d] **NF** Holland

*hollande [ɔlɑ̃d] **NM** *(fromage)* Dutch cheese
NF *Tex* holland

*hollywoodien, -ienne [ɔliwudjɛ̃, -jɛn] **ADJ** *(acteur)* Hollywood; *(maison, cadre)* Hollywood-style

holmium [ɔlmjɔm] **NM** *Chimie* holmium

holocauste [ɔlɔkost] **NM 1** *(sacrifice)* sacrifice; *(avec immolation)* burnt offering; **l'H.** *(des Juifs)* the Holocaust **2** *(victime)* sacrifice

hologramme [ɔlɔgram] **NM** hologram

holographe [ɔlɔgraf] **ADJ** = olographe

holographie [ɔlɔgrafi] **NF** holography

holothurie [ɔlɔtyri] **NF** *Zool* sea cucumber, *Spéc* holothurian

*homard [ɔmar] **NM** lobster; **manger du h.** to eat lobster; **pinces de h.** lobster claws; **bisque de h.** lobster soup *or* bisque; *Fam* **rouge comme un h.** *(de honte, de gêne)* as red as a beetroot; *(après un coup de soleil)* as red as a lobster

*hombre [ɔ̃br] **NM** *Cartes Arch* (game of) ombre

*home [om] **NM** home; **h. d'enfants** residential leisure centre for children, summer camp; *Belg* **h. d'étudiants** student hall of residence *or Am* dormitory, student hostel; *Belg, Suisse* **h. pour personnes âgées** old people's home, retirement home

*home cinéma [omsinema] **NM** home cinema

homélie [ɔmeli] **NF** homily

homéopathe [ɔmeɔpat] *Méd* **ADJ** homeopathic
N homeopath

homéopathie [ɔmeɔpati] **NF** homeopathy; **se soigner à l'h.** to take homeopathic medicine, to have homeopathic treatment

homéopathique [ɔmeɔpatik] **ADJ** homeopathic

Homère [ɔmɛr] **N** Homer

homérique [ɔmerik] **ADJ** Homeric

homicide [ɔmisid] **ADJ** *Arch, Litt* homicidal; *(arme)* murderous
N *Litt (personne)* homicide, murderer, *f* murderess
NM *Jur (crime)* homicide; **commettre un h.** to commit homicide
▸▸ **h. involontaire** *ou* **par imprudence** manslaughter *(through negligence)*; **h. sans préméditation** culpable homicide; **h. volontaire** wilful homicide, murder

hominidés [ɔminide] **NMPL** hominids

hominoïdes [ɔminɔid] **NMPL** hominoids

hommage [ɔmaʒ] **NM 1** homage; **rendre h. à qn** to pay homage *or* (a) tribute to sb; **nous rendons h. à votre courage** we are paying tribute to your courage **2 hommages** respects, compliments; **présenter ses hommages à une dame** to pay one's respects to a lady; **transmettez-lui mes hommages** give him my respects *or* regards **3** *(de respect, d'estime)* tribute, token; **faire h. de qch à qn** to offer sth to sb as a token of (one's) esteem; **h. de l'éditeur** complimentary copy, presentation copy; **h. de l'auteur** with the author's compliments

hommasse [ɔmas] **ADJ** *Péj (femme)* masculine, mannish; **elle a des manières hommasses** she acts like a man

HOMME [ɔm]

| man **1–3** ▪ mankind **3** |

NM 1 man, *pl* men; **l'h. et la femme** man and woman; **jeune h.** young man; **je ne suis plus un jeune h.** I'm not as young as I was; **merci jeune h.** thank you, young man; **h. âgé** old man, elderly man; *Com* **rayon hommes** men's department, menswear; **parler à qn d'h. à h.** to talk to sb man to man, to have a man-to-man talk with sb; **un bel h.** a handsome man; **soyez un h.!** be a man!; *Fam* **mon h.** my man/husband VOIR GRAMMAIRE A13
2 *(individu)* (*pl* **hommes** *ou* **gens**) man, *pl* men; **j'ai trouvé ton h., je pense qu'il fera tout à fait l'affaire** I've found just the man for you, I think he'll do nicely; **trouver son h.** to meet one's match; **il n'est pas h. à laisser passer cela** he's not one to *or* the kind of man to let that happen; *Mil* **les officiers et les hommes** the officers and (the) men; **les hommes du président/du directeur** the President's/director's men; **les hommes (d'équipage)** the crew, the ship's company; **un h. de goût** a man of taste; **h. politique** politician; **un h. de droite/de gauche** a right-/left-winger; **c'est l'h. fort du parti** he's the strongman of the party; **l'abominable h. des neiges** the abominable snowman
3 *(genre humain)* man, mankind; **tous les hommes** all men, all mankind; **de mémoire d'h.** within living memory; **les droits de l'h.** human rights; **comme un seul h.** as one man, in unison; *Prov* **l'h. propose, Dieu dispose** man proposes, God disposes
▸▸ **h. d'affaires** businessman; *Naut* **h. de barre** helmsman; **h. de confiance** right-hand man; **h. d'église** man of the church; **h. d'entretien** maintenance man; **h. d'État** statesman; **h. à femmes** ladies' man; **h.-grenouille,** *pl* **hommes-grenouilles** frogman; **h. de journée** (day) labourer; **h. de lettres** man of letters; **h. de loi** man of law, lawyer; **h. de main** henchman; **h. de métier** professional; **h. du monde** gentleman; **h.-orchestre,** *pl* **hommes-orchestres** one-man band; **h. de paille** figurehead; **h. de parole** man of his word; **h. de peine** (day) labourer; *Litt* **h. de peu** worthless individual; *Naut* **h. de quart** watch; **h. de la rue** the man in the street; **h.-sandwich,** *pl* **hommes-sandwich(e)s** sandwich man; **h. à tout faire** odd-job man, handyman; **h. de troupe** ordinary soldier, private

---

Il faut noter que le terme anglais **man of the world** ne signifie pas **homme du monde** mais **homme d'expérience**.

---

homo [ɔmo] **ADJ, N** *Fam* gay

homocentrique [ɔmɔsɑ̃trik] **ADJ** *Math* homocentric

homogène [ɔmɔʒɛn] **ADJ** homogeneous

homogénéisation [ɔmɔʒeneizasjɔ̃] **NF** homogenization

homogénéiser [ɔmɔʒeneize] **VT** to homogenize; **lait homogénéisé** homogenized milk

homogénéité [ɔmɔʒeneite] **NF** homogeneousness, homogeneity

homographe [ɔmɔgraf] **NM** homograph
ADJ homographic

homologation [ɔmɔlɔgasjɔ̃] **NF** *Jur (d'un accord etc)* confirmation; *(d'un testament)* probate; *Sport (d'un record etc)* ratification

homologie [ɔmɔlɔʒi] **NF** homology

homologue [ɔmɔlɔg] **ADJ** *Biol etc* homologous
NM *Biol etc* homologue
N counterpart, opposite number

homologuer [ɔmɔlɔge] **VT** *Jur (accord etc)* to confirm, to endorse; *Jur (testament)* to prove; *(décision)* to ratify; *(comptes)* to approve; *Sport (record)* to ratify; *Admin* **prix homologués** authorized charges; *Sport* **record homologué** official record

homoncule [ɔmɔ̃kyl] **NM** = homuncule

homonyme [ɔmɔnim] **ADJ** *Ling* homonymous
NM *(mot)* homonym; *(personne)* namesake

homonymie [ɔmɔnimi] **NF** *Ling* homonymy

homoparental [ɔmɔparɑ̃tal] **ADJ** relating to gay parenting, *Spéc* homoparental

homoparentalité [ɔmɔparɑ̃talite] **NF** gay parenting

homophobe [ɔmɔfɔb] **ADJ** homophobic
N homophobe

homophobie [ɔmɔfɔbi] **NF** homophobia

homophone [ɔmɔfɔn] **ADJ** *Ling, Mus* homophonic, homophonous
NM *Ling* homophone

homophonie [ɔmɔfɔni] **NF** homophony

homosexualité [ɔmɔsɛksɥalite] **NF** homosexuality

homosexuel, -elle [ɔmɔsɛksɥɛl] **ADJ, N** homosexual

homuncule [ɔmɔ̃kyl] **NM** *Arch* homunculus; *Fig Péj* manikin, dwarf

*Honduras [ɔ̃dyras] **NM** le H. Honduras

*hondurien, -ienne [ɔ̃dyrjɛ̃, -jɛn] **ADJ** Honduran
N H. Honduran

*Hongkong, Hong-Kong [ɔ̃gkɔ̃g] **N** Hong Kong

*hongre [ɔ̃gr] **ADJ** *(cheval)* gelded, castrated
NM gelding

*hongrer [ɔ̃gre] **VT** *Vét* to geld, to castrate

*Hongrie [ɔ̃gri] **NF** Hungary

*hongrois, -oise [ɔ̃grwa, -waz] **ADJ** Hungarian
NM *Ling* Hungarian
N H. Hungarian

honnête [ɔnɛt] **ADJ 1** *(intègre) (personne etc)* honest, honourable; *Am* honorable; **ce n'est pas très h. de sa part** that isn't very honest of him; **homme h., h. homme** honest man, man of honour *or Am* honor; **h. homme** *(au XVIIIᵉ siècle etc)* man of culture, gentleman; **peu h.** dishonourable; **moyens honnêtes** fair *or* honest means; **être h. avec soi-même** to be honest with oneself
2 *(décent) (comportement etc)* decent, seemly, becoming; **attitude peu h.** unseemly *or* unbecoming attitude; **je suis une femme h., moi, monsieur!** I'm not that sort of woman!
3 *(acceptable) (prix etc)* reasonable, moderate, fair; **une note plus qu'h.** a more than reasonable mark; **un repas h. sans plus** a reasonable *or* an OK meal, but nothing more *or* nothing to write home about
4 *Arch* courteous, polite, well-bred

honnêtement [ɔnɛtmɑ̃] **ADV 1** *(avec intégrité)* honestly, honourably, *Am* honorably; **h., je pense que tu fais une erreur** honestly *or* to be honest, I think you're making a mistake; **conseiller qn h.** to give someone honest advice; **se comporter h. en affaires** to be an honest businessman/businesswoman
2 *(raisonnablement)* reasonably, fairly
3 *Arch (avec courtoisie)* courteously, politely

honnêteté [ɔnɛtte] **NF 1** *(intégrité)* honesty, integrity **2** *(décence)* decency, propriety, decorum **3** *(dans les rapports)* fairness, fair dealing **4** *Arch (courtoisie)* courtesy, politeness

honneur [ɔnœr] **NM 1** honour, *Am* honor; **homme d'h.** man of honour, honourable *or Am* honorable man; **mettre un point d'h. à faire qch, se faire un point d'h. de faire qch** to make it a point of honour to do sth; **déclarer/jurer sur l'h. que ...** to state/swear on one's honour that ...; **forfaire** *ou* **manquer à l'h.** to act dishonourably; **il faut sauver l'h.** honour must be saved; **l'h. est sauf** our/

his/*etc* honour is safe; **non, je ne l'ai pas vu, parole d'h.** no, I haven't seen him, I give you my word (of honour) *or* cross my heart; **se faire un h. de qch/de faire qch** to be proud of sth/to do sth; **en tout bien tout h.** *(proposition, affaire)* (fair and) aboveboard; **nous nous sommes vus en tout bien tout h.** it was all aboveboard, there was nothing underhand about it; **affaire d'h.** matter of honour; *(duel)* duel; **garçon d'h.** best man; **demoiselle d'h.** bridesmaid

2 *(hommage)* **réception en l'h. de qn** reception in honour *or Am* honor of sb *or* in sb's honour; **assis à la place d'h.** in the seat of honour; **cour d'h.** main courtyard; *Univ* main quadrangle; **escalier d'h.** main staircase, main stairs; *Mil etc* **garde d'h.** guard of honour, *Am* honor guard; **hôte d'h.** guest of honour; **président d'h.** honorary president; **faire h. à qn** to do honour to sb, to honour sb; **vous me faites un grand h.** you are doing me a great honour; **me ferez-vous l'h. de m'accompagner?** will you do me the honour of accompanying me?; **à qui ai-je l'h. (de parler)?** to whom have I the honour *or* the pleasure of speaking?; **j'ai l'h. de vous faire savoir que …** I beg to inform you that …; **j'ai l'h. de vous demander la main de votre fille** I have the honour of asking for the hand of your daughter; *Fam* **en quel h. vous voit-on ici?** to what do I/we *etc* owe the honour (of your visit)?; *Fam* **et en quel h. me demandes-tu ma voiture?** just who do you think you are, asking me for my car?; *Fam* **et en quel h. devrais-je t'aider?** give me one good reason why I should help you!; **à vous l'h.** after you; **jouer pour l'h.** to play for love; **être à l'h.** to have the place of honour; **le cricket est à l'h. en Angleterre** cricket holds a place of honour *or* holds pride of place in England; **les lignes floues sont en h. cette année en France** loose-fitting clothes are all the fashion in France this year

3 *Golf* **avoir l'h.** to have the honour *or Am* honor

4 *(gloire)* credit; **c'est à elle que revient tout l'h. de l'affaire** she must take all the credit for the matter; **être l'h. de son pays** to be an honour *or Am* honor *or* a credit to one's country; **son attitude lui fait h.** his attitude is a credit to him *or* does him credit; **on doit dire à leur h. que …** it must be said to their credit that …; **il en est sorti à son h.** he came out of it with flying colours; **son refus est tout à son h.** it speaks well for him *or* it is greatly to his credit that he did not accept; **avec h.** creditably

5 honneurs *(marques d'estime)* honours, *Am* honors; **rendre les derniers honneurs** *ou* **les honneurs suprêmes à qn** to pay a last tribute *or* one's last respects to sb; **rendre de grands honneurs aux vainqueurs** to hail the returning victors; *Mil* **rendre les honneurs à qn** to present arms to sb, to give *or* pay (military) honours to sb; **avec tous les honneurs de la guerre** with all the honours of war; **rechercher les honneurs** to be looking for honours; **avoir les honneurs de la première page** to appear on the front page; **faire (à qn) les honneurs de la maison** to (do the honours and) show sb round the house; **rendre les honneurs funèbres à qn** to bury sb with due ceremony; **honneurs militaires** military honours

6 faire h. à sa signature to honour *or Am* honor one's signature; **faire h. à ses engagements** to honour one's commitments; *Com* **faire h. à une traite** to honour *or* meet a bill; *Fam* **faire h. au dîner** to do justice to the dinner

7 *Cartes* **les honneurs** honours, *Am* honors; **quatre d'honneurs** four by honours; **honneurs partagés** honours even

*****honnir** [ɔnir] VT to disgrace, to dishonour, *Am* to dishonor; **honni soit qui mal y pense** honi soit qui mal y pense, evil be to him who evil thinks; **honni de tous** spurned by all

honorabilité [ɔnɔrabilite] NF honourableness, *Am* honorableness, worthiness; *(d'une famille, une profession etc)* respectability; **porter atteinte à l'h. de qn/qch** to bring dishonour on sb/sth; **l'h. de ses intentions ne fait aucun doute** his/her intentions are completely honourable; **c'est quelqu'un d'une très grande h.** he/she is a person of great integrity

honorable [ɔnɔrabl] ADJ **1** *(sentiments, personne)* honourable, *Am* honorable; *(famille, profession etc)* honourable, respectable; **mes intentions sont honorables** my intentions are honourable; **vieillesse h.** respected old age; *Euph* **un h. correspondant** a secret agent, a special operative **2** *(performance)* creditable; **doctorat avec mention h.** = doctorate awarded with distinction; **des résultats plus qu'honorables** more than satisfactory results

honorablement [ɔnɔrabləmɑ̃] ADV **1** honourably, *Am* honorably, with honour, *Am* with honor; **famille h. connue** family of good reputation; **gagner h. sa vie** to earn an honest living; **vivre h.** to lead a respectable life **2** *(correctement)* **s'acquitter h. de qch** to acquit oneself creditably in sth; **il s'en est h. tiré** he did quite creditably

honoraire [ɔnɔrɛr] ADJ *(fonction, membre etc)* honorary; **professeur h.** emeritus professor

NMPL **honoraires** fee(s); *(d'une profession libérale)* fee, *Spéc* honorarium; *(d'un avocat)* retainer; **honoraires d'agréé en douane** customs broker's fees; **honoraires fixes** fixed fees

honorariat [ɔnɔrarja] NM honorary membership

honoré, -ée [ɔnɔre] ADJ honoured, *Am* honored; **mon h. confrère** my respected colleague

NF **votre honorée du …** *(dans une lettre)* yours of the …

honorer [ɔnɔre] VT **1** to honour, *Am* to honor; *(qualités de qn etc)* to respect

2 *(gratifier)* *(personne)* to do honour *or Am* honor to; **h. qn de sa confiance** to honour sb with one's confidence; *aussi Iron* **une cérémonie de sa présence** to honour *or* grace a ceremony with one's presence

3 *Com (facture)* to honour, *Am* to honor, to meet; *Com, Jur* **refuser d'h. (un contrat)** to repudiate (a contract); **h. ses engagements** to honour one's commitments

4 *(valoir de l'estime à)* *(personne, chose)* to be an honour *or Am* honor to, to do credit to, to be a credit to; **c'est un sentiment qui vous honore** the sentiment does you credit **5** *(sexuellement)* *(d'un animal)* to mate with; *Hum (d'un homme)* to make love to

VPR **s'honorer s'h. de qch/d'avoir fait qch** to be proud of sth/of having done sth; **notre ville s'honore de ses peintres** our town is proud of its painters *or* takes pride in its painters

honorifique [ɔnɔrifik] ADJ *(titre, rang etc)* honorary; **président à titre h.** honorary president

honoris causa [ɔnɔriskoza] ADJ INV honoris causa; **docteur h.** doctor honoris causa, honorary doctor

*****honte** [ɔ̃t] NF **1** shame; **avoir perdu toute h.** *ou* **tout sentiment de h.**, **avoir toute h. bue** to have lost all sense of shame, to have no (sense) of shame, to be lacking in any sense of shame; **faire qch toute h. bue** to do sth quite shamelessly; **h. à vous!** shame on you!; **à ma grande h.** to my shame; **sans h.**

(comme adjectif) shameless; *(comme adverbe)* shamelessly; **avoir h.** to be ashamed (of oneself); **avoir h. de faire qch, avoir** *ou* **éprouver de la h. à faire qch** to be *or* feel ashamed to do sth *or* of doing something; **il ne faut pas avoir h. de le dire** you shouldn't be ashamed to say it; **avoir h. pour qn** to be ashamed of sb; **faire h. à qn** to make sb ashamed, to put sb to shame; **elle me faisait h.**, posant sans cesse ses questions ridicules she made me so ashamed, continually asking her ridiculous questions; **couvrir qn de h.**, **jeter la h. sur qn** to bring shame *or* disgrace (up)on sb; **fausse** *ou* **mauvaise h.** self-consciousness, bashfulness; **se cacher le visage de h.** to hide one's face in shame; **rougir de h.** to blush with shame

2 *(cause)* (cause of) shame, disgrace, dishonour, *Am* dishonor; **faire** *ou* **être la h. de qn** to be a disgrace to sb; **quelle h.!**, what a disgrace!; **c'est une h.** it's a disgrace; *Fam* **eh, t'as vu ses chaussures? la h.!** *ou* **oh là là, la h.!** have you seen his shoes? they're an absolute disgrace!

*****honteusement** [ɔ̃tøzmɑ̃] ADV shamefully, disgracefully; **il a fui h.** he fled in shame; **il a h. fui** to his shame, he fled

*****honteux, -euse** [ɔ̃tø, øz] ADJ **1** ashamed; **être h. de qch/d'avoir fait qch** to be ashamed of sth/having done sth **2** *(après une erreur)* shamefaced, sheepish **3** *Péj (conduite etc)* shameful, disgraceful, ignominious; *Vieilli* **maladie honteuse** venereal disease; **c'est h.!** it's a disgrace!, it's shameful!; **si c'est pas h. de voir des choses pareilles!** isn't it terrible!

*****hooligan** [uligan] NM hooligan

*****hooliganisme** [uliganism] NM hooliganism

*****hop** [ɔp] INT **allez h.!** *(saute!)* jump!; *(pars!)* off you go!; **allez h., tout le monde dehors!** come on, everybody out!; **h.-là!** oops(-a-daisy)!

hôpital, -aux [ɔpital, -o] NM hospital; **il est très bien soigné à l'h.** he is being very well cared for in hospital; **être emmené à l'h.** to be taken to hospital *or Am* the hospital; **chambre d'h.** hospital room; *Naut* **navire-h.** hospital ship

▸▸ **h. des armées** military hospital; **h. de campagne** field hospital; **h. militaire** military hospital; **h. psychiatrique** psychiatric hospital

*****hoquet** [ɔkɛ] NM **1** *Physiol* hiccup, hiccough; **avoir le h.** to have (the) hiccups; **que faire contre le h.?** how can you get rid of hiccups? **2** *(de surprise, de terreur etc)* gasp; **avoir un h. de surprise** to catch one's breath, to gasp in surprise; **le moteur eut un dernier h. et rendit l'âme** the engine gave a final splutter and died

*****hoqueter** [ɔk(ə)te] VI *(je hoquette, n. hoquetons; je hoquetterai)* to hiccup, to hiccough; **le moteur hoqueta puis se décida à partir** the engine spluttered into life

horaire [ɔrɛr] ADJ **1** *(qui correspond à une heure)* hourly; **salaire h.** hourly rate *or* wage; *Ind* **débit h.** hourly output, output per hour **2 fuseau h.** time zone

NM timetable, schedule; *(à l'école, pour les moyens de transport)* timetable, *Am* schedule; *(d'un magasin)* opening hours; **avoir un h. chargé** to have a busy schedule *or* full timetable; **être en retard sur l'h.** to be behind schedule; **horaires de bureau/de travail** office/working hours; **h. flexible** flexible hours, flexitime; **h. variable** flexible hours, flexitime; **h. fixe/flottant** fixed/variable working hours; **h. mobile** *ou* **à la carte** flexitime, flexible working hours; **horaires d'été** summer timetable; **horaires de départ** departure schedule; *(de bateau)* sailing schedule

The symbol * indicates that the initial **h** is aspirate and that hence there is no liaison, eg **les haricots** [leariko] and not [lezariko], or contraction in spelling, eg **la haine** and not **l'haine**.

ments binaires eight-bit **2** *(dans des séries)* eighth; **page/numéro h.** page/number eight; **Henri H.** Henry the Eighth

NM INV eight; **le h. mai** [ɥimɛ] (on) the eighth of May, (on) May the eighth, *Am* (on) May eight; *Cartes* **le h. de carreau** the eight of diamonds; **j'habite au h.** I live at number eight; *(figure de patinage)* figure of eight; **la route fait un h. dans les collines** the road snakes round the hills; **l'ivrogne avançait en faisant des h.** the drunk was reeling *or* staggering along; **le grand h.** rollercoaster

***huitain** [ɥitɛ̃] **NM** *Littér* octet

***huitaine** [ɥitɛn] **NF 1** (about) eight **2** *(une semaine)* week; **il faut compter une bonne h. (de jours) pour que le paquet arrive** you must allow a good week for the parcel to get there; **dans une h. de jours** in a week or so; **affaire remise à h.** case adjourned for a week

***huitante** [ɥitãt] **ADJ NUM INV** *Suisse* eighty

***huitantième** [ɥitãtjɛm] **ADJ NUM, N** *Suisse* eightieth

***huitième** [ɥitjɛm] **ADJ, N** eighth

NM *(fraction)* eighth; *Sport* **être en h. de finale** to be through to the last sixteen

NF *Scol Anciennement* **(classe de) h.** ≃ third form of junior school, *Am* ≃ eighth grade

***huitièmement** [ɥitjɛmmã] **ADV** eighthly, in eighth place

huître [ɥitr] **NF 1** oyster; **h. perlière** pearl oyster **2** *Fam (idiot)* fool, mug

***huit-reflets** [ɥir(ə)flɛ] **NM INV** top hat

huîtrier, -ère [ɥitrije, -ɛr] **ADJ industrie huî-trière** oyster farming

NM *Orn* oyster catcher
NF **huîtrière** oyster bed

***hulotte** [ylɔt] **NF** tawny owl

***hululement** [ylylmã] **NM** hoot; **le h. d'un hibou** the hoot *or* hooting of an owl; **des hululements** hooting

***hululer** [ylyle] **VI** *(du hibou)* to hoot

***hum** [œm] **INT** hem!, h'm!

humain [ymɛ̃] **ADJ 1** human; **il est h. après tout** he's only human; **c'est h.** it's only human; **le genre h.** mankind; **tu ne vas pas t'en prendre au genre h.** you can't put the blame on the whole human race; **les êtres humains** human beings, humans; **c'est un être h., après tout** he's a human being, after all; **des pertes humaines énormes** a huge loss of life; **à l'échelle humaine** on a human scale; **sciences humaines** social sciences; *Mus* **voix humaine** *(d'un orgue)* vox humana; **ressources humaines** human resources; **l'erreur est humaine** to err is human **2** *(compréhensif)* humane; **elle a toujours été très humaine avec moi** she has always treated me very considerately

NM human (being)

Attention: ne pas confondre **human** et **humane** lorsque l'on traduit **humain**. Human signifie qui se rapporte à l'être humain alors que **humane** signifie bienveillant.

humainement [ymɛnmã] **ADV 1** *(relatif à l'homme)* humanly; **si c'est h. possible** if humanly possible **2** *(avec bonté)* humanely

humanisation [ymanizasjɔ̃] **NF** humanization, humanizing

humaniser [ymanize] **VT 1** to humanize, to make human **2** *(rendre plus charitable)* **h. qn** to make sb more human *or* humane

VPR s'humaniser 1 to become more human **2** *(devenir plus charitable)* to become more human *or* humane

humanisme [ymanism] **NM** *Litt, Phil* humanism

humaniste [ymanist] **N** humanist
ADJ humanist(ic)

humanitaire [ymanitɛr] **ADJ** humanitarian; **organisation/aide h.** humanitarian organization/aid
N *(personne)* humanitarian (aid) worker

humanitarisme [ymanitarism] **NM** humanitarianism

humanité [ymanite] **NF 1** *(genre humain)* humanity, mankind; **tu rendrais service à l'h.** you'd be doing mankind *or* humanity a favour **2** *Rel (du Christ)* human nature **3** *(bonté)* humanity, humaneness; **traiter qn avec h.** to treat sb humanely **4 humanités** humanities, classics; **faire ses humanités** to study the classics

humanoïde [ymanɔid] **NM** humanoid

humble [œ̃bl] **ADJ** humble, lowly; **à mon h. avis** in my humble opinion

humblement [œ̃bləmã] **ADV** humbly

humectage [ymɛktaʒ] **NM** dampening, moistening

humecter [ymɛkte] **VT** to dampen, to moisten

VPR s'humecter s'h. les lèvres to moisten one's lips; *Fam* **s'h. le gosier** to wet one's whistle

***humer** [yme] **VT 1** *(aspirer)* to inhale; *(sentir)* to sniff; **h. l'air frais** to inhale *or* breathe in the fresh air; **h. le parfum d'une fleur** to smell a flower **2** *(liquide)* to suck in *or* up

huméral, -ale, -aux, -ales [ymeral, -o] **ADJ** *Anat* humeral

humérus [ymerys] **NM** *Anat* humerus

humeur [ymœr] **NF 1** *(disposition)* mood, spirits, humour, *Am* humor; **être de bonne h.** to be in a good mood *or* in good spirits; **un livre/film plein de bonne h.** a good-humoured book/film; **être de mauvaise h.** to be in a bad mood; **une personne de mauvaise h.** an ill-humoured person; **passer sa mauvaise h. sur qn/qch** to take one's bad mood out on sb/sth; **de méchante h.** in a (bad) temper; **être d'une h. massacrante** *ou* *Fam* **de chien** to be in a foul *or* filthy mood *or* temper; **être d'une h. noire** *(déprimé)* to be depressed; *(mécontent)* to be in a (bad) temper; **il est rentré d'h. noire** he came home in a bad temper; **être** *ou* **se sentir d'h. à refuser** to be in the mood to refuse

2 *(caractère)* temper, temperament; **avoir l'h. vive** to be quick-tempered; **il y a incompatibilité d'h. entre nous** we are temperamentally unsuited; **homme d'h. égale** even-tempered man

3 *Litt (mauvaise humeur)* ill humour *or Am* humor, bad mood; **mouvement d'h.** outburst of temper; **geste d'h.** ill-tempered gesture; **montrer de l'h.** to show (ill) temper; **avec h.** testily, irritably; **je redoute ses sautes d'h.** I dread his changes of mood; **épancher son h. sur qn** to vent one's spleen on sb

4 *Méd Arch* humour, *Am* humor

▸▸ *Anat* **h. aqueuse** aqueous humour; **h. vitrée** vitreous humour

Do not confuse with **humour**.

humide [ymid] **ADJ** *(maison, linge)* damp; *(climat)* damp, humid; **il fait h.** it *or* the weather is damp *or* humid; **couloir sombre et h.** dark, dank passage; **temps h. et chaud** muggy *or* close weather; **temps h. et froid** raw weather; **les yeux humides (de larmes)** eyes moist with tears; **elle me lançait des regards humides** she looked at me with moist eyes

humidificateur [ymidifikatœr] **NM** *(à usage domestique)* humidifier; *(pour les cigares)* humidor

humidification [ymidifikasjɔ̃] **NF** *(fait de rendre humide)* dampening, moistening; *(contre le dessèchement)* humidification; **pour l'h. des cigares** to prevent cigars drying out

humidifier [ymidifje] **VT** to dampen, moisten; *(contre le dessèchement)* to humidify

humidité [ymidite] **NF** *(d'une maison, du linge)* dampness; *(du climat)* humidity, dampness; **il faut beaucoup d'h. à cette plante** this plant needs a lot of moisture; **h. absolue/relative** absolute/relative humidity; **craint l'h.** *(sur un paquet)* keep dry, store in a dry place; **taches d'h.** damp patches, mildew; **teneur en h.** moisture content; **il y a de l'h. dans l'air** it's going to *or* it feels like rain; *(au bord de la mer)* there is moisture *or* dampness in the air

humiliant [ymiljã] **ADJ** humiliating, mortifying; **il lui fit des reproches humiliants** he upbraided him/her in a humiliating fashion

humiliation [ymiljasjɔ̃] **NF** humiliation, mortification; **elle en fut malade d'h.** she was totally mortified

humilier [ymilje] **VT** *(abaisser)* to humiliate; *Vieilli, Rel (rendre humble)* to humble

VPR s'humilier *(s'abaisser)* to humiliate oneself; *(devenir humble)* to humble oneself; **je ne veux pas m'h. devant eux** I'm not going to go grovelling to them; **s'h. jusqu'à faire qch** to stoop to doing sth

humilité [ymilite] **NF** humility, humbleness; **ton d'h.** humble tone, tone of humility; **ce fut une grande leçon d'h.** it was a lesson in humility

humoral, -ale, -aux, -ales [ymɔral, -o] **ADJ** *Méd* humoral

humoriste [ymɔrist] **ADJ** *(écrivain etc)* humorous
N humorist

humoristique [ymɔristik] **ADJ** *(orateur, écrivain etc)* humorous; **dessin h.** cartoon

humour [ymur] **NM** humour, *Am* humor; **faire preuve d'h.** to keep smiling, to keep one's sense of humour, *Fam* to grin and bear it; **avoir (le sens) de l'h.** to have a (good) sense of humour; **h. noir** sick humour, black humour; **h. anglais** English humour

Do not confuse with **humeur**.

humus [ymys] **NM** humus

***Hun** [œ̃] **NM** *Hist* Hun

***hune** [yn] **NF** *Naut* top; **h. de vigie** crow's nest

***hunier** [ynje] **NM** *Naut* topsail

***huppe** [yp] **NF 1** *Orn* hoopoe **2** *(d'un oiseau)* tuft, crest

***huppé** [ype] **ADJ 1** *(oiseau)* tufted, crested **2** *Fam* high-class, *Br Fam* posh; **les classes huppées** the upper classes, *Br Fam* the toffs; **des gens huppés** the upper crust, *Br Fam* toffs, posh folk; **ce quartier est des plus huppés** this is a very high-class *or Br Fam* posh area

***hure** [yr] **NF 1** *(de sanglier etc)* head **2** *Culin* brawn, *Am* headcheese

***hurlement** [yrləmã] **NM** *(d'un loup, d'un chien)* howl; *(d'une personne)* yell, scream; *(du vent)* howling; *(d'une sirène d'alarme)* shriek, wail; **hurlements** *(d'un loup etc)* howling; *(d'une personne)* yelling, screaming; **pousser un h.** to give a howl; **pousser des hurlements** to howl

***hurler** [yrle] **VI** *(d'un loup, d'un chien)* to howl; *(du vent, de la tempête)* to howl, to roar; *(d'une alarme)* to shriek, to wail; *(d'une personne)* to howl, to roar, to yell; **elle faisait h. sa radio dans la cuisine** she had her radio blaring in the kitchen; **h. de douleur** to howl *or* scream (out) with pain; **c'était à h. de rire** it was screamingly funny, it was a scream; **h. à la lune** to bay at the moon; **h. avec les loups** to follow the crowd; **couleurs qui hurlent** colours that clash (with one another)

VT *(chanson, discours etc)* to roar out, to

The symbol * indicates that the initial **h** is aspirate and that hence there is no liaison, eg **les haricots** [leariko] and not [lezariko], or contraction in spelling, eg **la haine** and not **l'haine**.

bawl out; **elle me hurlait une recette par téléphone** she bawled a recipe down the telephone at me

*hurleur, -euse [yrlœr, -øz] ADJ howling, yelling
N howler, yeller
NM *(singe)* howler (monkey)

hurluberlu [yrlybɛrly] NM eccentric (person); **cet h. de Michel** that oddball Michel; **quel h., celui-là!** he's really odd *or* strange

*huron, -onne [hyrɔ̃, ɔn] ADJ Huron; **le lac H.** Lake Huron
N H. Huron

husky [œski] NM husky

*hussard [ysar] NM *Mil* hussar

*hussarde [ysard] NF **à la h.** roughly, in a cavalier fashion, cavalierly; **partir à la h.** to leave unceremoniously

*hussite [ysit] NM *Hist, Rel* Hussite

*hutte [yt] NF hut

hyacinthe [jasɛ̃t] NF 1 *Arch (fleur)* hyacinth 2 *(pierre)* hyacinth, jacinth

hyalin [jalɛ̃] ADJ transparent, glassy; *Minér* **quartz h.** rock crystal

hybridation [ibridasjɔ̃] NF *Bot* hybridization; *Biol* cross-breeding

hybride [ibrid] ADJ hybrid; *(style de musique)* crossover
NM hybrid

hybrider [ibride] VT *Bot* to hybridize; *Biol* to cross(-breed)

hybridité [ibridite] NF hybridity, hybridism

hydracide [idrasid] NM *Chimie* hydracid

hydrante [idrãt] NF *Suisse* fire hydrant, *Am* fireplug

hydratant [idratã] ADJ *(crème)* moisturizing
NM moisturizer

hydratation [idratasjɔ̃] NF 1 *Chimie* hydration 2 *(de la peau)* moisturizing

hydrate [idrat] NM *Chimie* hydrate; **h. de potasse** caustic potash; **h. de carbone** carbohydrate

hydrater [idrate] VT 1 *Chimie* to hydrate 2 *(peau)* to moisturize
VPR **s'hydrater** to hydrate, to become hydrated *or* moisturized

hydraulicien [idrolisjɛ̃] NM hydraulic engineer

hydraulique [idrolik] ADJ hydraulic; **roue h.** waterwheel
NF 1 *(science)* hydraulics 2 *(technique)* hydraulic engineering

hydravion [idravjɔ̃] NM seaplane

hydre [idr] NF 1 *Zool* hydra; *Fig* **l'h. du chômage** the hydra of unemployment 2 *Myth* **H.** Hydra

hydrique [idrik] ADJ hydrous

hydrocarbure [idrokarbyr] NM *Chimie* hydrocarbon

hydrocéphale [idrosefal] *Méd* ADJ hydrocephalic, hydrocephalous
N hydrocephalic *or* hydrocephalous patient

hydrocortisone [idrokɔrtizɔn] NF hydrocortisone

hydrocracking, hydrocraquage [idrokrakiŋ, -kaʒ] NM *Pétr* hydrocracking

hydrocution [idrokysjɔ̃] NF immersion syncope

hydrodynamique [idrodinamik] ADJ hydrodynamic
NF hydrodynamics

hydro-électricité [idroelɛktrisite] NF hydroelectricity

hydro-électrique, *pl* **hydro-électriques** [idroelɛktrik] ADJ hydroelectric

hydrofoil [idrofɔil] NM hydrofoil

hydrofuge [idrofyʒ] ADJ *(vêtement, tissu)* waterproof

hydrofuger [idrofyʒe] VT **(j'hydrofugeai(s); n. hydrofugeons)** *(vêtement, tissu)* to waterproof

hydrogénation [idroʒenasjɔ̃] NF hydrogenation

hydrogène [idroʒɛn] NM *Chimie* hydrogen; **h. lourd** heavy hydrogen

hydrogéné [idroʒene] ADJ hydrogenated

hydrogéner [idroʒene] VT to hydrogenate

hydroglisseur [idroglisœr] NM jetfoil

hydrographe [idrograf] ADJ, NM **(ingénieur) h.** hydrographer

hydrographie [idrografi] NF hydrography

hydrographique [idrografik] ADJ hydrographic(al)

hydrologie [idrolɔʒi] NF hydrology

hydrologique [idrolɔʒik] ADJ hydrological

hydrologiste [idrolɔʒist], **hydrologue** [idrolɔg] N hydrologist

hydrolyse [idroliz] NF *Chimie* hydrolysis

hydrolyser [idrolize] VT *Chimie* to hydrolize, to hydrolyse

hydromel [idromɛl] NM mead

hydromètre [idromɛtr] NM hydrometer; *(d'océan)* depth gauge
NF *Entom* water spider

hydrométrie [idromɛtri] NF *Phys* hydrometry

hydrométrique [idromɛtrik] ADJ hydrometric

hydrominéralisme [idromineralism] NM water cures

hydrophile [idrofil] ADJ *(coton etc)* absorbent

hydrophobe [idrofɔb] ADJ hydrophobic
N *Méd* hydrophobic patient

hydrophobie [idrofɔbi] NF *Méd* hydrophobia

hydropique [idropik] *Méd* ADJ dropsical
N dropsical patient

hydropisie [idropizi] NF *Méd* dropsy

hydroponique [idroponik] ADJ hydroponic

hydroptère [idroptɛr] NM hydrofoil

hydroquinone [idrokinɔn] NF *Chimie, Phot* hydroquinone

hydrosol [idrosɔl] NM *Chimie* hydrosol

hydrosoluble [idrosɔlybl] ADJ water-soluble

hydrospeed [idrospid] NM *Sport* = type of water sport consisting of shooting the rapids on a board

hydrosphère [idrosfɛr] NF hydrosphere

hydrostatique [idrostatik] ADJ hydrostatic
NF hydrostatics

hydrothérapie [idroterapi] NF *Méd (traitement)* hydrotherapy, water cure; *(science)* hydrotherapeutics

hydrothérapique [idroterapik] ADJ hydrotherapeutic

hydrothermal, -ale, -aux, -ales [idrotɛrmal, -o] ADJ hydrothermal

hydrothermalisme [idrotɛrmalism] NM *Méd* water therapy

hydroxyde [idroksid] NM *Chimie* hydroxide

hydrure [idryr] NM *Chimie* hydride

hyène [jɛn] NF *(when aspirated* **la hyène,** *when silent* **l'hyène)** hyena

hygiaphone [iʒjafɔn] NM *(au guichet)* grill; **parlez dans l'h.** speak through the grill

hygiène [iʒjɛn] NF hygiene; **h. publique/mentale** public/mental health; **produits d'h. courante** cleaning *or* cleansing products; **prendre des mesures d'h.** to take steps to deal with a hygiene problem; **mauvaise h.**

alimentaire bad eating habits, poor diet; **vous devriez surveiller votre h. alimentaire** you should watch your diet *or* what you eat

hygiénique [iʒjenik] ADJ 1 *(sanitaire)* hygienic, sanitary; **peu h.** unhygienic; **papier h.** toilet paper; **serviette h.** sanitary towel *or Am* napkin 2 *(bon pour la santé)* healthy; **une promenade h.** a healthy walk, a constitutional

hygiéniquement [iʒjenikmã] ADV 1 hygienically 2 *(bon pour la santé)* healthily

hygrométrie [igrɔmetri] NF *Phys* hygrometry

hygroscope [igrɔskɔp] NM *Phys* hygroscope

hygroscopique [igrɔskɔpik] ADJ *Phys* hygroscopic

hymen [imɛn] NM 1 *Litt* marriage 2 *Anat* hymen

hyménée [imene] NM *Litt* marriage

hyménoptère [imenɔptɛr] *Entom* ADJ hymenopterous
NMPL **hyménoptères** Hymenoptera

hymne [imn] NM *(de louanges)* song (of praise); **un h. à la beauté** a hymn to beauty; **l'h. à la joie** the Ode to Joy; **h. national** national anthem
NM OU NF *Rel* hymn

hyoïde [jɔid] ADJ, NM *Anat* **(os) h.** hyoid (bone)

hyper [ipɛr] NM *Fam (abrév* **hypermarché)** hypermarket, superstore

hyper- [ipɛr] PRÉF 1 *(terme scientifique)* hyper- 2 *(en intensif)* **techniques h.-spécialisées** highly specialized techniques; *Fam* mega-; **h.-cool** hyper- *or* mega-cool; **h.-chiant** mega-boring

hyperacidité [iperasidite] NF *Méd* hyperacidity

hyperactif, -ive [iperaktif, -iv] ADJ hyperactive

hyperactivité [iperaktivite] NF hyperactivity

hyperbare [iperbar] ADJ *Tech* hyperbaric; **caisson h.** decompression chamber

hyperbole [iperbɔl] NF 1 *Littér* hyperbole 2 *Math* hyperbola

hyperbolique [iperbɔlik] ADJ *Littér, Math* hyperbolic(al)

hyperboliquement [iperbɔlikmã] ADV *Littér* hyperbolically

hyperboloïde [iperbɔlɔid] *Math* ADJ hyperboloidal
NM hyperboloid

hyperboréen, -enne [iperbɔreɛ̃, -ɛn] ADJ *Litt* hyperborean

hypercalorique [iperkalɔrik] ADJ hypercalorific

hypercritique [iperkritik] ADJ hypercritical, overcritical

hyperémotivité [iperemotivite] NF *Méd* hyperemotionalism, hyperemotivity

hyperfréquence [iperfrekãs] NF *Radio* ultra high frequency

hyperglycémie [iperglisemi] NF *Méd* hyperglyc(a)emia

hyperinflation [iperɛ̃flasjɔ̃] NF *Écon* hyperinflation

hyperlien [iperljɛ̃] NM *Ordinat* hyperlink

hypermarché [ipermarʃe] NM hypermarket, superstore

hypermédia NM *Ordinat* hypermedia

hypermétrope [ipermetrɔp] ADJ *Méd* hypermetropic

hypermétropie [ipermetrɔpi] NF *Méd* hypermetropia

hypernerveux, -euse [ipernervø, -øz] ADJ highly strung
N highly strung person

ILV [iɛlve] NF (abrév **information sur le lieu de vente**) point-of-sale information

image [imaʒ] NF **1** (dans l'eau, dans un miroir etc) reflection, image; Cin (de la pellicule) frame; Cin, TV (sur l'écran) picture; Opt **i. réelle/virtuelle** real/virtual image; Cin, TV **25 images par seconde** 25 frames per second; **nous avons le son mais pas l'i. ou pas les images** we've got the sound but no picture; **nous n'avons plus d'i.** the picture's gone; **à l'i.** on-camera; **être à l'i.** to be on camera; **images en direct** live pictures; **i. à l'écran** screen image; **soigner son i.** to cultivate one's image; **i. par i.** single frame **2** Fig image; **l'i. de son père** the image of his father; **Dieu créa l'homme à son i.** God created man in his own image; **ils sont l'i. du bonheur/de la réussite** they are the picture of happiness/success; **donner une bonne/mauvaise i. de qch** to present a good/bad image of sth **3** (dessin) picture; **livre d'images** picture book; **récit en images** pictorial record; **images pieuses** holy pictures; Scol **voici une i.** (récompense) ≃ here's a gold star; Mktg **images à compléter** picture completion **4** (représentation) image, picture; **i. visuelle forte** strong visual image or picture or impression; **garder l'i. d'une personne en mémoire** to keep an image or a picture of sb in one's memory; **la première i. qui vient à l'esprit** the first image that comes to mind; **i. fidèle** truthful account; Compta true and fair view **5** Littér image; **images** imagery ▸▸ TV, Cin **i. animée** moving picture; TV, Cin **i. d'archives** library picture; TV, Cin **images d'archives** library footage, found footage; TV, Cin **i. arrêtée** hold frame; Ordinat **i. bitmap** bitmap image; TV, Cin **i. chassée** pushover wipe; Ordinat **i. cliquable** image map; Ordinat **i. digitalisée** digitized image; TV, Cin **i. divisée en quatre** quad split; Mktg **i. de l'entreprise** corporate image; TV **i. fantôme** ghosting; TV, Cin **i. fixe** still frame, stop frame, photostill; **i. institutionnelle** corporate image; Ordinat **i. intégrée** inline image; **i. de marque** (d'un produit) brand image; (d'un homme politique, d'une société etc) (public) image; Ordinat **i. mémoire** dump; **prendre une i. mémoire** to take a hard copy, to dump; **i. en négatif** negative image; Mktg **i. du produit** product image; **i. publique** public image; Phot **i. de solarisation** solarized image; Ordinat **images de synthèse** computer-generated images, CGI; Ordinat **i. tramée** raster image; Ordinat **i. vectorielle** outline image

imagé [imaʒe] ADJ (style, langage) vivid, full of imagery; (expression) vivid

imager [imaʒe] VT (j'imageai(s); n. imageons) Litt (style, discours) to colour, Am to color

imagerie [imaʒri] NF **1** Littér imagery **2** Com colour or Am color print trade; (usine) colour or Am color print works **3** Méd **i. cérébrale** brain imaging or scanning; **i. par résonance magnétique** magnetic resonance imaging

imageur [imaʒœr] NM Ordinat imager; **i. documentaire** document imager

imagier [imaʒje] NM **1** (peintre) painter; (sculpteur) sculptor, carver **2** (dessinateur) drawer of pictures **3** (imprimeur) colour or Am color print maker; Com colour or Am color print seller **4** (livre d'images) picture book

imaginable [imaʒinabl] ADJ imaginable, conceivable; **cela n'était pas i. il y a quelques années** it was unimaginable or inconceivable a few years ago; **toutes les solutions possibles et imaginables** every conceivable solution, every solution imaginable

imaginaire [imaʒinɛr] ADJ (personnage, pays, animal etc) imaginary; Hum **malade i.** hypochondriac

NM imagination; **toute cette histoire relève de l'i.** the whole story is a product of the imagination, the story is entirely imaginary

imaginatif, -ive [imaʒinatif, -iv] ADJ imaginative

imagination [imaʒinasjɔ̃] NF imagination; **faire preuve d'i.** to show some imagination; **avoir de l'i.** to have imagination, to be imaginative; **avoir une i. débordante** to have a very active imagination; **tu manques d'i.!** you have no imagination!; **tu as vraiment trop d'i.!** you imagine things!; **ces histoires sortent de son i.** these stories are a product or Péj figment of his imagination; **voir qch en i.** to see sth in one's mind's eye or in one's imagination; **vivre qch en i.** to experience sth in one's imagination

imaginer [imaʒine] VT **1** (inventer) (méthode, système, stratagème) to devise, to think up; (machine, dispositif) to devise; **bien imaginé** well thought out; **les enfants imaginaient qu'ils étaient sur la lune** the children were pretending they were on the moon **2** (concevoir) to imagine; **imaginez un peu mon étonnement** just imagine my surprise; **tu l'imagines avec des enfants!** just think of or imagine or picture him/her with children!; **j'imagine qu'il viendra vers 9 heures** I imagine he'll come about 9 o'clock; **je n'imaginais pas que cela soit faisable** I didn't think it could be done; **tout ce qu'on peut i. de plus beau** the finest thing imaginable; **que vas-tu i. là?** how can you think such a thing?; **vous plaisantez, j'imagine** you must be joking! VPR **s'imaginer 1** (croire à tort) **elle s'imagine que tout le monde l'admire** she imagines or thinks (that) everyone admires her; **elle s'est imaginé qu'il allait tout lui dire** she imagined or got it into her head that he would tell her everything; **il s'imagine tout savoir** he thinks he knows everything **2** (se figurer) to imagine; **tu t'imagines la tête qu'il va faire** you can imagine how he'll take it; **comme on peut se l'i.** as you can (well) imagine; **je me l'imaginais bien plus grand** I imagined him much taller; **il est bien plus grand que je ne me l'imaginais** he's much taller than I imagined **3** (se voir) to picture or see oneself; **je m'imagine sur la scène/à quarante ans** I can (just) picture or see myself on the stage/at forty

imago [imago] NM Entom imago
NF Psy imago

imam [imam], **iman** [imã] NM imam

imbattable [ɛ̃batabl] ADJ (champion) invincible, unbeatable; (record) unbeatable, unbreakable; (prix) unbeatable

imbécile [ɛ̃besil] ADJ idiotic, stupid; Méd Vieilli imbecilic, idiotic
N idiot, fool, imbecile; Méd Vieilli imbecile, idiot; **le premier i. venu vous dira cela** any fool will tell you that; **c'est un i. heureux** he's a bit simple-minded; **faire l'i.** (faire des bêtises) to play or act the fool; (feindre de ne pas comprendre) to act stupid

imbécilement [ɛ̃besilmã] ADV idiotically, stupidly

imbécillité [ɛ̃besilite] NF **1** (stupidité) idiocy, stupidity; Méd Vieilli imbecility, idiocy **2** (parole, chose stupide) idiotic or stupid thing; **dire des imbécillités** to talk nonsense or rubbish

imberbe [ɛ̃bɛrb] ADJ beardless

imbibé [ɛ̃bibe] ADJ Fam smashed

imbiber [ɛ̃bibe] VT **i. qch (de qch)** to soak sth

(in or with sth); **imbibé d'eau** saturated (with water); (terrain) waterlogged; **chiffon imbibé d'huile** oil-soaked rag
VPR **s'imbiber 1** to become soaked (**de** with) **2** Fam **s'i. d'alcool** to hit the bottle; **s'i. d'alcool pour oublier ses problèmes** to drown one's sorrows (in drink)

imbit(t)able [ɛ̃bitabl] ADJ très Fam unfathomable, incomprehensible

imbrication [ɛ̃brikasjɔ̃] NF (de tuiles, d'écailles etc) overlap(ping); Ordinat embedding; (de commandes) nesting; **se dépêtrer d'une i. de problèmes** to extricate oneself from a mesh or web of problems; **je ne m'y retrouve pas dans cette i. de personnages** I can't get my bearings in this complex web of characters

imbriqué [ɛ̃brike] ADJ Ordinat embedded; (commande) nested

imbriquer [ɛ̃brike] VT to overlap; Ordinat to embed; (commandes) to nest
VPR **s'imbriquer** (de tuiles, d'écailles etc) to overlap; (de questions, problèmes, situations) to be interwoven; **tous ces problèmes s'imbriquent les uns dans les autres** all these problems are interwoven

imbroglio [ɛ̃brɔljo] NM imbroglio

imbu [ɛ̃by] ADJ **i. de sa personne** ou **de soi-même** full of one's own importance or of oneself

imbuvable [ɛ̃byvabl] ADJ undrinkable; Fig (personne) insufferable, unbearable; **je le trouve i., ce mec** I can't stand (the sight of) that guy, I can't stomach or Br stick that guy

IME [iɛmə] NM (abrév **Institut monétaire européen**) EMI

imitable [imitabl] ADJ imitable; **sa voix est facilement i.** his/her voice is easy to imitate or easily imitated

imitateur, -trice [imitatœr, -tris] N imitator; Théâtre impersonator
ADJ imitative

imitatif, -ive [imitatif, -iv] ADJ imitative

imitation [imitasjɔ̃] NF **1** (fait de copier) (de produit, style etc) imitation, imitating, copying; **à l'i. de qn/qch** in imitation of sb/sth **2** (de personne) imitation, mimicking, mimicry; Théâtre impersonation; (de cri d'animal, de chant d'oiseau) imitation; **elle fait d'excellentes imitations** she does excellent imitations, she is an excellent mimic **3** (de signature, de papier officiel etc) forgery, forging; (d'argent) counterfeiting **4** (copie) imitation, copy; **bijoux en i. argent** imitation silver jewellery; **manteau (en) i. loutre** imitation sealskin coat; Péj **une pâle i.** a pale imitation

imiter [imite] VT (personne) to imitate, to mimic, Fam to take off; Théâtre to impersonate; (faire comme) to imitate, to copy; (cri d'animal, chant d'oiseau) to imitate; (style) to imitate, to copy; (signature) to forge; (argent) to counterfeit; **il leva son verre et tout le monde l'imita** he raised his glass and everyone followed suit or did the same; **matière qui imite le cuir/le bois** material that simulates leather/wood; **je voudrais une table qui imite celle des bistrots parisiens** I'd like a table that looks like the ones in Parisian cafés

immaculé [imakyle] ADJ (draps, linge, blanc) spotless, immaculate; (réputation) spotless; Rel **l'Immaculée Conception** the Immaculate Conception

immanence [imanãs] NF immanence

immanent [imanã] ADJ immanent; **justice immanente** divine retribution

immangeable [ɛ̃mãʒabl] ADJ inedible, uneatable

immanquable [ɛ̃mãkabl] ADJ (événement,

conséquence etc) inevitable; *Vieilli (moyen, astuce etc)* infallible

immanquablement [ɛ̃mɑ̃kabləmɑ̃] ADV inevitably, without fail

immatérialité [imaterjalite] NF *Phil* immateriality

immatériel, -ielle [imaterjel] ADJ *Phil* immaterial; *Fin (actif)* intangible; *Litt (pâleur, minceur etc)* ethereal

immatriculation [imatrikylasjɔ̃] NF *(d'acte, de voiture etc)* registration, registering; *(d'étudiant)* registration, enrolment; *(à la Sécurité Sociale)* registration (**à** with); **numéro d'i.** registration number

---

Immatriculation

The last two numbers on French number plates refer to the "département" where the vehicle was registered. Vehicles from the Val-de-Marne, for example, bear the number 94.

---

immatriculer [imatrikyle] VT *(document, voiture etc)* to register; *(étudiant)* to register, to enrol; *(à la Sécurité Sociale)* to register (**à** with); **voiture immatriculée T 342 SPF/dans le Var** car with the registration number T 342 SPF/with a Var number plate *or Am* license plate; *Com* **i. des marchandises** to register goods

immature [imatyr] ADJ immature

immaturité [imatyrite] NF immaturity

immédiat [imedja] ADJ **1** *(cause, successeur etc)* immediate, direct; *(sentiment)* direct; *Chimie* **analyse immédiate** proximate analysis **2** *(proximité)* close; **être en contact i. avec le feu/le patron** to be in direct contact with the fire/the boss **3** *(dans le temps) (changement)* immediate, instant; *(résultat)* immediate; **la mort a été immédiate** death was instantaneous; **(mécanisme) à action immédiate** quick-acting (mechanism)
▪ NM **dans l'i.** for the moment, for the time being

immédiatement [imedjatmɑ̃] ADV immediately

immédiateté [imedjat(ə)te] NF *Phil* immediacy

immémorial, -ale, -aux, -ales [imemɔrjal, -o] ADJ *Litt* age-old; **de temps i.** from *or* since time immemorial; **en des temps immémoriaux** in ancient times

immense [imɑ̃s] ADJ *(maison, forêt, foule etc)* immense, vast, huge; *(tâche, sacrifice)* huge, immense; *(joie, soulagement)* tremendous, great; *(succès)* huge, great; **c'est un i. acteur/écrivain** he's a tremendous *or* great actor/writer

immensément [imɑ̃semɑ̃] ADV **i. grand/riche/généreux** immensely big/rich/generous; **ce cadeau me fait i. plaisir** this gift gives me tremendous *or* great pleasure, this gift pleases me greatly; **j'ai eu i. peur** I was terribly afraid

immensité [imɑ̃site] NF *(de parc, maison etc)* vastness, hugeness, immenseness; *(de tâche)* immensity, hugeness; **les yeux perdus dans l'i.** gazing into the far distance *or* into space

immergé [imɛrʒe] ADJ submerged; **plante immergée** aquatic plant; **bateau i. par 200 mètres de fond** boat lying 200 metres under(water)

immerger [imɛrʒe] (**j'immergeai(s); n. immergeons**) VT to immerse, to submerge (**dans** in); *(câble)* to lay underwater; *(déchets)* to get rid of *or* dispose of *or* dump at sea; *(mort)* to bury at sea
▪ VPR **s'immerger** *(d'un sous-marin)* to submerge, to dive

immérité [imerite] ADJ unmerited, undeserved

immersion [imɛrsjɔ̃] NF immersion; *(de câble)* laying underwater; *(de déchets)* disposal *or* dumping at sea; *(d'un sous-marin)* submersion, submergence; *(de mort)* burial at sea

immettable [ɛ̃metabl] ADJ unwearable

immeuble [imœbl] NM **1** *(bâtiment)* building; *(d'appartements)* block of flats, *Am* apartment block; **i. de bureaux** office block; **i. de 10 étages** 10-storey building; **i. de rapport, i. locatif** rental property **2** *Jur* real estate
▪ ADJ *Jur* real, fixed; **biens immeubles** real estate

immigrant, -ante [imigrɑ̃, -ɑ̃t] ADJ, N immigrant; *Can* **i. reçu** landed immigrant

immigration [imigrasjɔ̃] NF immigration; **agent du service de l'i.** immigration officer

immigré, -ée [imigre] ADJ, N immigrant

immigrer [imigre] VI to immigrate; **i. en Europe/aux États-Unis** to immigrate to Europe/the United States

imminence [iminɑ̃s] NF imminence

imminent [iminɑ̃] ADJ imminent, impending; **être i.** to be imminent

immiscer (s') [simise] VPR (**je m'immisçai(s); n. n. immisçons**) to interfere, to meddle (**dans** in); **il faut toujours qu'elle s'immisce dans les conversations** she always has to interrupt

immixtion [imikstjɔ̃] NF interference, meddling (**dans** in)

immobile [imɔbil] ADJ **1** *(personne, mer etc)* motionless, still; *(pièce de machine)* fixed, immobile; *(visage)* immobile, set; **rester complètement i.** to remain totally still **2** *Fig (institution, dogme etc)* unchanging, changeless

immobilier, -ière [imɔbilje, -jɛr] *Jur, Com* ADJ property, real-estate; **biens immobiliers** real estate, *esp Am* realty; **vente immobilière** sale of property; **société immobilière** property company; **agence immobilière** estate agency, *Am* real estate office; **agent i.** estate agent, *Am* real estate agent, realtor
▪ NM real estate, property, *Am* realty; **i. de loisir** holiday property; **l'i. locatif** *Br* the property *or Am* the real-estate rental business

immobilisation [imɔbilizasjɔ̃] NF **1** *(fait de ne plus bouger)* immobilization; **l'i. du malade est essentielle** it is essential to immobilize the patient; **attendre l'i. complète du train** wait until the train comes to a complete stop *or* standstill **2** *Jur* conversion into real estate **3** *Fin (de capital)* locking up, tying up, immobilization **4** *Compta* asset; **immobilisations** fixed *or* capital assets; **i. de capitaux** tied-up capital, capital assets; **immobilisations corporelles** tangible fixed assets; **immobilisations financières** long-term investments; **immobilisations incorporelles** intangible fixed assets; **immobilisations non financières** physical fixed assets

immobiliser [imɔbilize] VT **1** *(rendre immobile) (blessé)* to immobilize; *(train)* to bring to a standstill; **i. un véhicule** *(avec sabot)* to clamp a vehicle **2** *Jur* to convert into real estate **3** *Fin (capital)* to lock up, to tie up, to immobilize; *Fin* **i. des actifs** to freeze assets
▪ VPR **s'immobiliser** *(d'un véhicule)* to come to a stop *or* a standstill; *(d'un corps en mouvement)* to come to rest

immobilisme [imɔbilism] NM opposition to progress, ultra-conservatism

immobiliste [imɔbilist] ADJ opposed to progress, ultra-conservative
▪ N ultra-conservative

immobilité [imɔbilite] NF *(d'un animal, de l'eau, des feuilles, des arbres etc)* stillness, motionlessness; *(d'un visage)* immobility; **être condamné à l'i. pour une semaine** *(d'un malade)* to be kept immobile for a week

immodération [imɔderasjɔ̃] NF immoderation, immoderateness

immodéré [imɔdere] ADJ immoderate, excessive, inordinate

immodérément [imɔderemɑ̃] ADV immoderately, excessively, inordinately

immodeste [imɔdɛst] ADJ *Vieilli* immodest

immodestement [imɔdɛstəmɑ̃] ADV *Vieilli* immodestly

immodestie [imɔdɛsti] NF *Vieilli* immodesty

immolateur [imɔlatœr] NM *Arch, Litt* immolator, sacrificer

immolation [imɔlasjɔ̃] NF *Litt* immolation, sacrifice

immoler [imɔle] *Litt* VT to immolate, to sacrifice
▪ VPR **s'immoler** to immolate *or* sacrifice oneself; **s'i. par le feu** to die by setting fire to oneself

immonde [imɔ̃d] ADJ **1** *(sale) (quartier, maison etc)* foul, filthy, vile **2** *(ignoble) (acte, comportement etc)* foul, vile **3** *(laid) (personne, objet)* vile **4** *Rel* unclean

immondices [imɔ̃dis] NFPL refuse, rubbish

immoral, -ale, -aux, -ales [imɔral, -o] ADJ immoral

immoralement [imɔralmɑ̃] ADV immorally

immoralisme [imɔralism] NM *Phil* immoralism

immoraliste [imɔralist] ADJ, N *Phil* immoralist

immoralité [imɔralite] NF immorality

immortaliser [imɔrtalize] VT to immortalize
▪ VPR **s'immortaliser** to gain immortality, to win everlasting fame (**par** through, with)

immortalité [imɔrtalite] NF immortality; **entrer dans l'i.** to gain immortality, to win everlasting fame

immortel, -elle [imɔrtel] ADJ *(dieu, être)* immortal; *(réputation, amour etc)* everlasting, undying
▪ N *(membre de l'Académie française)* = member of the Académie Française
▪ NF **immortelle** *(plante)* everlasting (flower), immortelle

immotivé [imɔtive] ADJ *(action, renvoi)* unmotivated; *(peur)* groundless, baseless

immuabilité [imɥabilite] NF immutability

immuable [imɥabl] ADJ *(vérité)* unchanging, immutable; *(passion)* undying; *(opinion)* fixed, set; *(sourire)* fixed, perpetual

immuablement [imɥabləmɑ̃] ADV immutably, unalterably, perpetually

immun [imœ̃] ADJ immune

immunisant [imynizɑ̃] ADJ immunizing

immunisation [imynizasjɔ̃] NF *Méd* immunization

immuniser [imynize] VT *Méd* to immunize; **être immunisé contre qch** *Méd* to be immunized against sth; *Fig* to be immune to *or* from sth; *Fig* **je suis immunisé** I'm immune

immunitaire [imyniter] ADJ *Méd* **système i.** immune system; **réactions immunitaires** immune reactions *or* responses; **défenses immunitaires** immune defences

immunité [imynite] NF immunity; **i. diplomatique** diplomatic immunity; **i. fiscale** immunity from taxation; **i. naturelle/acquise** natural/acquired immunity; **i. parlementaire** parliamentary privilege *or* immunity

immunodéficience [imynɔdefisjɑ̃s] NF *Méd* immunodeficiency

immunodéficitaire [imynɔdefisitɛr] ADJ *Méd* immunodeficient

immunodépresseur [imynɔdepresœr] ADJ, NM *Méd* immunosuppressive

immunodépressif, -ive [imynɔdepresif, -iv] ADJ *Méd* immunosuppressive

immunodéprimé, -ée [imynɔdeprime] *Méd* ADJ with a weakened immune system N person with a weakened immune system

immunogène [imynɔʒɛn] ADJ *Méd* immunogenic

immunoglobuline [imynɔglɔbylin] NF *Méd* immunoglobulin

immunologie [imynɔlɔʒi] NF immunology

immunologique [imynɔlɔʒik] ADJ immunological

immunologiste [imynɔlɔʒist] N immunologist

immunosuppresseur [imynɔsypresœr] NM *Méd* immunosuppressive, immunosuppressant

immunothérapie [imynɔterapi] NF *Méd* immunotherapy

immutabilité [imytabilite] NF immutability

impact [ɛ̃pakt] NM impact; *Fig* avoir un i. sur qch to have an impact on sth, to impact on sth; point d'i. point of impact; étude d'i. impact study; i. sur les ventes sales impact, impact on sales

impair [ɛ̃pɛr] ADJ *(nombre, fonction etc)* odd, uneven; *(jour)* odd; *(côté de la rue)* odd-numbered; *(vers)* with an uneven number of syllables; *(organe)* unpaired NM 1 *(aux jeux)* odd numbers 2 *(gaffe)* blunder; faire *ou* commettre un i. to make a blunder, *Fam* to put one's foot in it

impala [ɛ̃pala] NM impala

impalpable [ɛ̃palpabl] ADJ impalpable, intangible

impaludation [ɛ̃palydasjɔ̃] NF infection with the malaria virus

impaludé [ɛ̃palyde] ADJ *(personne)* suffering from malaria; *(région)* infected with malaria

imparable [ɛ̃parabl] ADJ *(tir, coup, botte etc)* unstoppable; *Fig (argument, logique)* irrefutable, unanswerable

impardonnable [ɛ̃pardɔnabl] ADJ unforgivable, unpardonable; il serait i. de ne pas les aider it would be unforgivable not to help them; c'est vraiment i. d'avoir oublié l'anniversaire de ta femme it's really unforgivable of you to have forgotten your wife's birthday; j'ai encore pris votre parapluie, je suis i. I've taken your umbrella again, I'm hopeless

imparfait [ɛ̃parfɛ] ADJ 1 *Litt (qui n'est pas achevé)* unfinished, uncompleted; avoir une connaissance imparfaite de qch to have an imperfect knowledge of sth 2 *(qui a des défauts)* imperfect, defective NM *Gram* imperfect (tense); à l'i. in the imperfect (tense) SEE GRAMMAR B30

imparfaitement [ɛ̃parfɛtmɑ̃] ADV imperfectly

impartial, -iale, -iaux, -iales [ɛ̃parsjal, -jo] ADJ impartial, unbias(s)ed

impartialement [ɛ̃parsjalmɑ̃] ADV impartially, without bias

impartialité [ɛ̃parsjalite] NF impartiality, lack of bias

impartir [ɛ̃partir] VT *Jur, Litt (droit, faveur)* to grant (à to); *(tâche)* to assign (à to); *(don)* to bestow (à on); délai imparti time limit, time allowed; le temps qui vous est imparti the time allotted to you

impartition [ɛ̃partisjɔ̃] NF *Écon* subcontracting

impasse [ɛ̃pas] NF 1 *(cul-de-sac)* dead end, cul-de-sac; *(sur panneau)* no through road 2 *Fig* impasse, deadlock; être *ou* se trouver dans une i. to be at a dead end; il faut sortir de l'i. the deadlock has to be broken; les négociations sont dans l'i. the talks have reached an impasse *or* a deadlock *or* are deadlocked; aboutir à une i. to reach an impasse 3 *Fin Vieilli* i. budgétaire budget deficit 4 *Cartes* faire une i. to finesse; faire l'i. au roi to finesse against the king; *Scol* faire une i. sur un sujet to leave a subject a miss when revising for an exam; j'ai fait l'i. sur le Japon en géographie I gave Japan a miss in my geography revision

impassibilité [ɛ̃pasibilite] NF impassiveness, impassivity

impassible [ɛ̃pasibl] ADJ impassive

impassiblement [ɛ̃pasibləmɑ̃] ADV impassively

impatiemment [ɛ̃pasjamɑ̃] ADV impatiently

impatience [ɛ̃pasjɑ̃s] NF 1 impatience; avec i. impatiently; montrer des signes d'i. to show signs of impatience; elle brûle d'i. de te le dire she's dying to tell you; être dans l'i. de faire qch to be really impatient to do sth 2 *Litt* impatiences fits of impatience

impatient, -ente [ɛ̃pasjɑ̃, -ɑ̃t] ADJ impatient; d'un air i. impatiently; être i. de faire qch to be impatient *or* eager to do sth; être i. avec qn to be impatient with sb NF impatiente *(plante)* busy lizzie, *Spéc* impatiens

impatienter [ɛ̃pasjɑ̃te] VT *(personne)* to annoy, to irritate; tes questions m'impatientent I'm getting impatient with your questions, you're annoying *or* irritating me with your questions VPR s'impatienter to get impatient, to lose patience (de qch at sth; contre *ou* avec qn with sb)

impavide [ɛ̃pavid] ADJ *Fml* composed, unruffled, impassive

impayable [ɛ̃pɛjabl] ADJ *Fam (blague, histoire etc)* priceless; elle est i.! she's priceless!, she's a scream!

impayé [ɛ̃peje] ADJ *(dette, facture)* unpaid; *(paiement)* outstanding NM outstanding payment; j'ai un tas d'impayés I've got a stack of unpaid bills

impeachment [impitʃmɛnt] NM *Pol* impeachment

impec [ɛ̃pɛk] ADJ, ADV *Fam* = impeccable

impeccable [ɛ̃pekabl] ADJ *(propre) (costume, personne, chambre, voiture)* impeccable; *(parfait) (traduction, voiture, repassage)* impeccable, perfect; un travail i. an impeccable *or* a perfect piece of work; d'une propreté i. impeccably clean ADV *Fam* i.! great!

impeccablement [ɛ̃pekabləmɑ̃] ADV impeccably

impécunieux, -euse [ɛ̃pekynjø, -øz] ADJ *Litt* impecunious

impédance [ɛ̃pedɑ̃s] NF *Élec* impedance

impedimenta [ɛ̃pedimɛ̃ta] NMPL impedimenta

impénétrabilité [ɛ̃penetrabilite] NF 1 *(densité) (d'une forêt)* impenetrability; *(à l'eau)* imperviousness 2 *(mystère)* inscrutability

impénétrable [ɛ̃penetrabl] ADJ 1 *(forêt, citadelle, murs etc)* impenetrable; i. à l'eau impervious to water 2 *(visage, caractère)* inscrutable; *(mystère, secret, énigme)* unfathomable, impenetrable; *(texte)* impenetrable; prendre un air i. to adopt an inscrutable air; les voies du Seigneur sont impénétrables God works in mysterious ways

impénitence [ɛ̃penitɑ̃s] NF *Rel* impenitence

impénitent [ɛ̃penitɑ̃] ADJ *Rel* impenitent, unrepentant; *Fig* un fumeur/buveur i. an unrepentant *or* a confirmed smoker/drinker

impensable [ɛ̃pɑ̃sabl] ADJ unthinkable, inconceivable; il est i. de faire/que ... it's unthinkable *or* inconceivable to do/that ...

impense [ɛ̃pɑ̃s] NF *Fin* property improvement expense

imper [ɛ̃pɛr] NM *Fam* raincoat, *Br* mac

impératif, -ive [ɛ̃peratif, -iv] ADJ *(ton, geste etc)* imperious, imperative, peremptory; *(nécessité, besoin)* imperative; *Jur (loi, disposition)* mandatory; il est i. de connaître l'anglais pour ce poste knowledge of English is essential for this post NM 1 *(exigence)* requirement; savoir nager est un i. it is essential to be able to swim; les impératifs de la mode the dictates *or* demands of fashion; *Hum* ce sont les impératifs du direct that's what you have to contend with when you're broadcasting live 2 *Gram* imperative (mood); à l'i. in the imperative (mood) SEE GRAMMAR A40; B34–5

impérativement [ɛ̃perativmɑ̃] ADV imperatively; il faut i. que je la voie it is imperative that I see her

impératrice [ɛ̃peratris] NF empress

imperceptibilité [ɛ̃pɛrseptibilite] NF imperceptibility

imperceptible [ɛ̃pɛrseptibl] ADJ imperceptible; i. par l'oreille humaine imperceptible to the human ear; elle eut un sourire i. she gave a barely perceptible smile

imperceptiblement [ɛ̃pɛrseptibləmɑ̃] ADV imperceptibly; sourire i. to give a barely perceptible smile

imperdable [ɛ̃pɛrdabl] ADJ le match/le procès est i. the match/the case can't be lost; le match est i. pour la France France can't lose the match NF *Suisse (épingle de nourrice)* safety pin

imperfectible [ɛ̃pɛrfɛktibl] ADJ that cannot be perfected, imperfectible

imperfectif, -ive [ɛ̃pɛrfɛktif, -iv] ADJ *Gram* imperfective

imperfection [ɛ̃pɛrfɛksjɔ̃] NF *(état imparfait)* imperfection; *(défaut) (de texte)* imperfection, flaw; *(de peau)* imperfection, blemish; *(de prototype)* imperfection, defect, fault; *(d'une personne)* shortcoming, failing, fault

impérial, -ale, -aux, -ales [ɛ̃perjal, -o] ADJ 1 *(relatif à l'empire)* imperial; prendre un air i. to adopt an imperial *or* a magisterial air 2 *(de qualité supérieure)* imperial NF impériale 1 *(de bus, wagon etc)* top (deck), upper deck; autobus à i. double-decker (bus) 2 *(barbe)* imperial

impérialement [ɛ̃perjalmɑ̃] ADV imperially

impérialisme [ɛ̃perjalism] NM imperialism

impérialiste [ɛ̃perjalist] ADJ imperialist(ic) N imperialist

impérieusement [ɛ̃perjøzmɑ̃] ADV 1 *(avec autorité)* imperiously 2 *(de façon pressante)* urgently; il a i. besoin de manger he is urgently in need of *or* urgently needs something to eat

impérieux, -euse [ɛ̃perjø, -øz] ADJ 1 *(autoritaire)* imperious, domineering 2 *(impératif) (nécessité, désir etc)* urgent, pressing; j'ai un besoin i. de voir le patron I need to see the boss urgently

impérissable [ɛ̃perisabl] ADJ *(œuvre)* imperishable; *(gloire)* everlasting, eternal; *(vérité, valeur)* eternal, imperishable; *(souvenir)* unforgettable, enduring, indelible; cette aventure lui a laissé un souvenir i. this adventure made an unforgettable impression on him *or* stayed in his mind forever; ce film/mec ne me laissera pas un souvenir **i.** that film's/guy's pretty forgettable

imperméabilisant [ɛ̃permeabilizɑ̃] **ADJ** waterproofing
NM waterproofing agent

imperméabilisation [ɛ̃permeabilizasjɔ̃] **NF** waterproofing

imperméabiliser [ɛ̃permeabilize] **VT** to waterproof

imperméabilité [ɛ̃permeabilite] **NF** impermeability; *Fig* imperviousness (**à** to)

imperméable [ɛ̃permeabl] **ADJ** impermeable; *Fig* impervious (**à** to); **i. (à l'eau)** waterproof; **i. à la poussière** dustproof; *Fig* **être i. à la critique** to be impervious to criticism
NM raincoat, *Br* mackintosh

impersonnalité [ɛ̃persɔnalite] **NF** impersonality

impersonnel, -elle [ɛ̃persɔnel] **ADJ** impersonal SEE GRAMMAR A28; B29–30

impersonnellement [ɛ̃persɔnelmɑ̃] **ADV** impersonally

impertinemment [ɛ̃pertinamɑ̃] **ADV** impertinently

impertinence [ɛ̃pertinɑ̃s] **NF** impertinence; **dire des impertinences à qn** to speak impertinently to sb; **répondre avec i.** to answer impertinently

impertinent, -ente [ɛ̃pertinɑ̃, -ɑ̃t] **ADJ** impertinent
N impertinent person; **un petit i.** an impertinent little boy

imperturbabilité [ɛ̃pertyrbabilite] **NF** imperturbability

imperturbable [ɛ̃pertyrbabl] **ADJ** (*personne*) imperturbable; (*optimisme*) unshakeable; **il restait i.** he remained impassive *or* unruffled

imperturbablement [ɛ̃pertyrbabləmɑ̃] **ADV** imperturbably

impétigo [ɛ̃petigo] **NM** *Méd* impetigo

impétueusement [ɛ̃petɥøzmɑ̃] **ADV** *Litt* impetuously

impétueux, -euse [ɛ̃petɥø, -øz] **ADJ 1** (*fougueux*) (*personne*) impetuous, hotheaded, impulsive; (*tempérament*) fiery; (*amour*) impetuous **2** *Litt* (*torrent, flot etc*) raging, wild

impétuosité [ɛ̃petɥozite] **NF 1** (*fougue*) impetuosity, impetuousness **2** *Litt* **l'i. du torrent/des flots** the raging *or* wild torrent/waves

impie [ɛ̃pi] **ADJ** impious, ungodly
N impious *or* ungodly person

impiété [ɛ̃pjete] **NF 1** (*caractère impie*) impiety, ungodliness **2** (*acte, parole impie*) impiety

impitoyable [ɛ̃pitwajabl] **ADJ** pitiless, merciless, ruthless (**envers, pour** towards)

impitoyablement [ɛ̃pitwajabləmɑ̃] **ADV** pitilessly, mercilessly, ruthlessly

implacable [ɛ̃plakabl] **ADJ** (*personne*) implacable, unrelenting; (*haine, vengeance, logique*) implacable; (*avancée*) relentless

implacablement [ɛ̃plakabləmɑ̃] **ADV** implacably; (*avancer*) relentlessly

implant [ɛ̃plɑ̃] **NM 1** *Méd* implant; **i. dentaire** dental implant; **implants capillaires** hair transplant; **il s'est fait faire des implants** he had a hair transplant **2** (*bureau de voyages*) in-house travel agency, *Am* in-plant agency

implantation [ɛ̃plɑ̃tasjɔ̃] **NF** (*d'un système, d'une mode, d'une coutume*) introduction; (*d'une industrie, d'une filiale, d'un parti politique etc*) setting up, establishment; *Méd* implantation; (*des cheveux, des dents*) line; **i. commerciale** business operation

implanter [ɛ̃plɑ̃te] **VT** (*système, mode, coutume*) to introduce; (*idée*) to implant; (*industrie, filiale, parti politique etc*) to set up, to

establish; *Méd* to implant; **cette entreprise japonaise a plusieurs usines implantées en Europe** this Japanese company has a number of factories located in Europe; **cette habitude est bien implantée chez eux** this habit is well established with them; **solidement implanté** (*croyance*) firmly established
VPR s'implanter (*d'un usage, d'un sport, d'un parti etc*) to become established; (*d'une société, d'une industrie*) to set up, to become established (**dans** in); **s'i. à l'étranger** to set up overseas; **s'i. sur un marché** to establish oneself in a market

implémentation [ɛ̃plemɑ̃tasjɔ̃] **NF** *Ordinat* implementation

implémenter [ɛ̃plemɑ̃te] **VT** *Ordinat* to implement

implication [ɛ̃plikasjɔ̃] **NF 1** (*engagement*) involvement; *Jur* implication (**dans** in) **2** implications (*conséquences*) implications

implicite [ɛ̃plisit] **ADJ** implicit, implied

implicitement [ɛ̃plisitmɑ̃] **ADV** implicitly

impliquer [ɛ̃plike] **VT 1** (*compromettre*) to implicate (**dans** in); **véhicule impliqué (dans un accident)** vehicle involved (in an accident) **2** (*entraîner*) to involve, to entail, to mean; **la carrière de chanteur implique de nombreux déplacements** a singing career involves *or* entails *or* means a lot of travelling; **s'occuper d'enfants implique d'être très disponible** looking after children means having a lot of free time; **i. que ... + ind** to imply that ...; **je n'implique pas que vous deviez vous sentir responsable** I'm not implying that you should feel responsible **3** (*engager*) to involve (**dans** in)
VPR s'impliquer to become *or* get involved (**dans** in); **il s'est beaucoup impliqué** he became *or* got heavily *or* deeply involved

implorant [ɛ̃plɔrɑ̃] **ADJ** imploring; **d'un ton i.** imploringly

imploration [ɛ̃plɔrasjɔ̃] **NF** entreaty, plea; **i. de Dieu** entreaty *or* plea to God

implorer [ɛ̃plɔre] **VT** (*personne, Dieu, le Ciel*) to implore, to beseech, to entreat; **i. le pardon de qn** to beg sb's forgiveness; **i. qn du regard** to give sb an imploring look; **i. qn de faire qch** to implore *or* beseech *or* entreat sb to do sth

imploser [ɛ̃ploze] **VI** to implode

implosion [ɛ̃plozjɔ̃] **NF** implosion

impoli [ɛ̃pɔli] **ADJ** impolite, rude, *Fml* discourteous

impoliment [ɛ̃pɔlimɑ̃] **ADV** impolitely, rudely, *Fml* discourteously

impolitesse [ɛ̃pɔlites] **NF 1** (*caractère impoli*) rudeness, impoliteness, *Fml* discourtesy; **avec i.** rudely, impolitely, *Fml* discourteously **2** (*acte*) impolite act, act of rudeness; (*remarque*) rude *or* impolite remark; **dire des impolitesses** to be impolite *or* rude, to say impolite things; **dire une i. à qn** to make an impolite *or* rude remark to sb, to say something impolite *or* rude to sb; **c'est une i. de quitter la table avant la fin du repas** it is impolite *or* rude to leave the table before the end of the meal

impolitique [ɛ̃pɔlitik] **ADJ** impolitic, ill-advised

impondérabilité [ɛ̃pɔ̃derabilite] **NF** imponderability

impondérable [ɛ̃pɔ̃derabl] **ADJ** imponderable
NMPL les impondérables the imponderables

impopulaire [ɛ̃pɔpyler] **ADJ** unpopular

impopularité [ɛ̃pɔpylarite] **NF** unpopularity

import [ɛ̃pɔr] **NM 1** (*action d'importer*) import; *Ordinat* **i. de données** data import **2**

Belg (*montant*) amount; **une facture d'un i. de 3 000 euros** a bill for 3,000 euros

importable[1] [ɛ̃pɔrtabl] **ADJ** (*marchandises*) importable

importable[2] **ADJ** (*vêtement*) unwearable

importance [ɛ̃pɔrtɑ̃s] **NF 1** importance; **avoir de l'i.** to be important, to matter; **cela/ elle a beaucoup d'i. pour moi** it's/she's very important to me, it/she matters a lot to me; **sans i.** unimportant; **c'est sans i.** it's not important, it doesn't matter; **cela n'a pas d'i.** it's not important, it doesn't matter, it's of no importance *or Fml* of no consequence; **cela n'a aucune i.** it doesn't matter one bit *or* in the slightest, it's not at all important; **c'est d'une i. capitale** it's extremely important; **événement de la première ou de la plus haute i.** event of outstanding importance, all-important event; **attacher de l'i. à qch** to attach importance to sth; **tu attaches ou tu donnes trop d'i. à cela** you attach too much importance to it; **et alors? quelle i.?** so what?; **affaire d'i.** important matter; **l'affaire est d'i.** the matter is of some importance; **de peu d'i.** of little importance, of no great significance; **se donner de l'i.** to give oneself airs **2** (*d'une ville, d'un campus etc*) size; (*de dommages, d'une catastrophe etc*) extent; (*d'une somme, d'un projet*) size, magnitude; (*d'une blessure*) seriousness; **on ne connaît pas encore l'i. de ses blessures** the extent of his injuries is not yet known; **prendre de l'i.** (*d'une société etc*) to expand; **le mouvement prend de l'i.** the movement is gaining ground

important, -ante [ɛ̃pɔrtɑ̃, -ɑ̃t] **ADJ 1** (*qui compte*) important, significant; **ce n'est pas i.** it's not important, it doesn't matter; **cette maison est très importante pour moi** this house is very important to me; **il est très i. que vous le sachiez** it is very important that you (should) know; **ce qui est vraiment i., c'est que ...** what is really important *or* what really matters is that ...; **peu i.** unimportant, immaterial; **rien d'i.** nothing important, nothing of any importance *or* significance; **personnage i.** important *or* influential person; **c'est quelqu'un d'i.** he is (somebody) important; **se donner des airs importants** to give oneself airs **2** (*considérable*) (*ville, société, projet etc*) large, major; (*somme d'argent, dégâts etc*) considerable, significant; **la recette a atteint un chiffre i.** the takings reached a high *or* a considerable figure; **un retard i.** a considerable delay
N *Péj* **faire l'i.** to act important *or* big, to put on airs
NM l'i. the important thing, the main point; **l'i., c'est que tu sois satisfait** the important *or* main thing is for you to be satisfied; **ce n'est pas là le plus i.** that's not the most important thing, that's not what matters most

> Il faut noter que l'adjectif anglais **important** ne signifie jamais **considérable** et ne se rapporte donc jamais à des proportions ou à une quantité.

importateur, -trice [ɛ̃pɔrtatœr, -tris] **N** importer; **c'est l'i. exclusif de cette marque pour la France** they are the sole French importers of this brand
ADJ (*firme, pays etc*) importing; **les pays importateurs de pétrole** oil-importing countries, oil importers

importation [ɛ̃pɔrtasjɔ̃] **NF 1** (*de marchandises, de coutume*) import, importation, importing; **articles ou produits d'i.** imports; **licence d'i.** import licence; **i. en franchise** duty-free import **2** (*produit*) import; **i. grise** grey import; **importations invisibles** invisible imports; **importations parallèles** parallel imports served in full; **dépenses incompressibles** expenditure which cannot be reduced or pared down; **il existe un chômage i.** there is a level below which unemployment cannot be reduced

incompris, -ise [ɛ̃kɔ̃pri, -iz] ADJ misunderstood

N **je suis un i.** I am misunderstood, nobody understands me

inconcevable [ɛ̃kɔ̃s(ə)vabl] ADJ inconceivable, unthinkable, unimaginable; **il est i. que ...** it's inconceivable that ...; **c'est totalement i.** it's quite unthinkable

inconcevablement [ɛ̃kɔ̃s(ə)vabləmɑ̃] ADV inconceivably

inconciliable [ɛ̃kɔ̃siljabl] ADJ (théorie) irreconcilable (avec with); **le métier est i. avec une vie de famille** the profession is incompatible with family life

inconditionnalité [ɛ̃kɔ̃disjɔnalite] NF (d'un partisan) unwavering or unquestioning support

inconditionné [ɛ̃kɔ̃disjɔne] ADJ Psy (réflexe, stimulus) unconditioned

inconditionnel, -elle [ɛ̃kɔ̃disjɔnɛl] ADJ (soutien, retrait etc) unconditional; (obéissance) unquestioning, unconditional; (partisan) staunch, unwavering

N fan(atic), enthusiast; **c'est un i. de la pêche** he's a fishing fanatic, he's fanatical about fishing; **je suis une inconditionnelle de Prévert** I am a great fan of Prévert, I am mad about Prévert; **je suis une inconditionnelle de l'Espagne/des îles grecques** I am mad about or I adore Spain/the Greek islands

inconditionnellement [ɛ̃kɔ̃disjɔnɛlmɑ̃] ADV (soutenir qn) unconditionally, without question; (obéir) unquestioningly, without question; **être i. favorable à qn/qch** to support sb/sth wholeheartedly

inconduite [ɛ̃kɔ̃dɥit] NF Litt loose living; Jur misconduct

inconfort [ɛ̃kɔ̃fɔr] NM (manque de confort matériel) discomfort; (malaise moral) uncomfortableness

inconfortable [ɛ̃kɔ̃fɔrtabl] ADJ (siège, voiture), Fig (situation) uncomfortable

inconfortablement [ɛ̃kɔ̃fɔrtabləmɑ̃] ADV uncomfortably

incongru [ɛ̃kɔ̃gry] ADJ (remarque, réponse) incongruous, inappropriate, out of place; (question, comportement) inappropriate, improper, unseemly; (bruit) rude, unseemly; **il allait travailler dans une tenue des plus incongrues** he wore a really extravagant outfit to work

incongruité [ɛ̃kɔ̃grɥite] NF 1 (caractère déplacé) (d'une remarque, réponse) incongruity, inappropriateness; (d'un comportement, d'une question) inappropriateness, unseemliness, impropriety; (de vêtements) extravagance 2 (remarque déplacée) inappropriate or improper remark; (action qui choque) inappropriate or improper action

incongrûment [ɛ̃kɔ̃grymɑ̃] ADV Litt (répondre, parler) in an unseemly fashion

inconnaissable [ɛ̃kɔnɛsabl] ADJ, NM unknowable

inconnu, -ue [ɛ̃kɔny] ADJ (auteur, civilisation, destination) unknown (de, à to); **se retrouver dans un lieu i.** to find oneself in a strange place; **il m'était i.** I didn't know him, he was a stranger to me; **il était i. de tout le monde** nobody knew him, he was a stranger to everybody; **né de père i.** (sur document administratif) father unknown; **elle est née de père i.** she doesn't know who her father was; **visages inconnus** strange faces; **c'est un problème qui lui est totalement i.** the problem is totally foreign to him, it's a pro-

blem he knows absolutely nothing about; **i. à cette adresse** not known at this address; Fam **Durand? i. au bataillon!** Durand? never heard of him!

N (étranger) stranger; **c'est un i. qui a remporté le prix Nobel** someone no-one has ever heard of has won the Nobel prize

NM **l'i.** the unknown; **la peur de l'i.** the fear of the unknown; **faire un saut dans l'i.** to take a leap in the dark

NF Math **inconnue** unknown (quantity); Fig **il y a beaucoup trop d'inconnues dans cette affaire** there are two many unknowns in the matter

inconsciemment [ɛ̃kɔ̃sjamɑ̃] ADV 1 (dans l'inconscient) subconsciously 2 (sans réfléchir) without thinking, thoughtlessly; **il a signé un peu i.** he signed without giving it too much thought

inconscience [ɛ̃kɔ̃sjɑ̃s] NF 1 (physique) unconsciousness; **sombrer ou tomber dans l'i.** to lapse into unconsciousness, to become unconscious 2 (manque de jugement) recklessness, irresponsibility; **faire preuve d'i.** to be reckless or irresponsible; **c'est de l'i. pure et simple!** it's sheer madness!, how irresponsible can you get!

inconscient, -ente [ɛ̃kɔ̃sjɑ̃, -ɑ̃t] ADJ 1 (sans connaissance) (personne, blessé) unconscious 2 (irréfléchi) (personne) irresponsible; (geste) rash, Fml ill-considered; **c'est i. ce que tu as fait là** it was irresponsible of you 3 (non conscient) (acte) unconscious; **i. de ce qui se passe autour de lui** oblivious to or unaware of what is going on around him

N irresponsible person; **tu n'es qu'une inconsciente!** you really are irresponsible!

NM Psy **l'i.** the unconscious, the subconscious

▶▶ Psy **l'i. collectif** the collective unconscious

inconséquence [ɛ̃kɔ̃sekɑ̃s] NF (caractère inconséquent) thoughtlessness; (action inconséquente) rash or irresponsible act; **on me blâmait pour mes inconséquences** I was reproached for being rash or irresponsible

inconséquent [ɛ̃kɔ̃sekɑ̃] ADJ 1 (illogique, versatile) (argument, personne) inconsistent; **être i. dans ses propos** to contradict oneself, to speak illogically; **il dit des choses inconséquentes** he speaks incoherently 2 (irréfléchi) (personne, démarche) thoughtless, rash

inconsidéré [ɛ̃kɔ̃sidere] ADJ 1 (acte, remarque) thoughtless, rash, Fml ill-considered; (dépenses) rash, reckless; **faire des dépenses inconsidérées** to spend recklessly 2 Vieilli (personne) irresponsible

inconsidérément [ɛ̃kɔ̃sidiremɑ̃] ADV (agir, parler) thoughtlessly, without thinking, rashly; (dépenser) recklessly

inconsistance [ɛ̃kɔ̃sistɑ̃s] NF 1 (manque de consistance) (d'une pâte) runniness; (de la boue) softness; (du sol) looseness 2 (d'une personne, d'un acte) inconsistency; (d'une intrigue) thinness, flimsiness; (d'un film, d'un roman) thinness; (d'une accusation) flimsiness, insubstantial nature; **le film/roman était d'une i. telle que ...** the film/novel was so lacking in substance that ...

inconsistant [ɛ̃kɔ̃sistɑ̃] ADJ 1 (liquide) (pâte, crème) thin, runny; (boue) soft; (sol) loose 2 (intrigue) thin, flimsy, insubstantial; (film, roman) insubstantial; (accusation) flimsy, without substance; (personne) vacuous

Il faut noter que l'adjectif anglais **inconsistent** est un faux ami. Il signifie **incohérent**.

inconsolable [ɛ̃kɔ̃sɔlabl] ADJ (personne, chagrin, tristesse) inconsolable

inconsolé [ɛ̃kɔ̃sɔle] ADJ unconsoled

inconsommable [ɛ̃kɔ̃sɔmabl] ADJ unfit for consumption

inconstance [ɛ̃kɔ̃stɑ̃s] NF 1 (d'une personne) (de caractère) changeableness; (en amour) fickleness, Fml inconstancy 2 Litt (du temps, de la mode) fickleness, changeableness

inconstant [ɛ̃kɔ̃stɑ̃] ADJ 1 (personne) (caractère) changeable; (en amour) fickle, Fml inconstant; **être i. en amour** to be fickle 2 Litt (mode) fickle, changeable

inconstatable [ɛ̃kɔ̃statabl] ADJ unascertainable, unverifiable

inconstitutionnalité [ɛ̃kɔ̃stitysjɔnalite] NF Jur unconstitutionality

inconstitutionnel, -elle [ɛ̃kɔ̃stitysjɔnɛl] ADJ Jur unconstitutional

inconstitutionnellement [ɛ̃kɔ̃stitysjɔnɛlmɑ̃] ADV Jur unconstitutionally

inconstructible [ɛ̃kɔ̃stryktibl] ADJ (zone, terrain) that cannot be developed

incontestabilité [ɛ̃kɔ̃tɛstabilite] NF Jur incontestability

incontestable [ɛ̃kɔ̃tɛstabl] ADJ (fait, preuve, victoire) undeniable, indisputable, Fml incontestable; (vérité) undeniable, indisputable; **il est i. que ...** it is undeniable that ..., it cannot be denied that ...

incontestablement [ɛ̃kɔ̃tɛstabləmɑ̃] ADV undeniably, indisputably, beyond all doubt, Fml incontestably

incontesté [ɛ̃kɔ̃tɛste] ADJ (droit) uncontested, undisputed; (maître, victoire) undisputed

incontinence [ɛ̃kɔ̃tinɑ̃s] NF 1 Méd incontinence; **i. nocturne** bedwetting 2 Arch, Litt (luxure) incontinence, lack of restraint; **souffrir d'i. verbale** to have verbal diarrhoea

incontinent¹ [ɛ̃kɔ̃tinɑ̃] ADJ 1 Méd incontinent 2 Arch, Litt (pas chaste) incontinent, unrestrained; **être i. dans ses propos** to talk far too much; **un orateur complètement i. dans ses propos** an orator who goes on and on or who doesn't know when to stop

incontinent² ADV Arch, Litt at once, forthwith

incontournable [ɛ̃kɔ̃turnabl] ADJ **c'est i.** you can't get away from it; **son argument était i.** there was no getting away from his argument; **Harrods est un magasin i.** Harrods should not be missed, Harrods is a must; **son dernier film est absolument i.** his latest film is an absolute must

incontrôlable [ɛ̃kɔ̃trolabl] ADJ 1 (affirmation) difficult to verify or to check, unverifiable 2 (incendie, supporter) uncontrollable; **très vite, l'incendie fut i.** the fire very quickly got out of control or out of hand; **des éléments incontrôlables** rowdy elements

incontrôlé [ɛ̃kɔ̃trole] ADJ 1 (non vérifié) unchecked, unverified 2 (non surveillé) uncontrolled

inconvenance [ɛ̃kɔ̃v(ə)nɑ̃s] NF (caractère inconvenant) impropriety; **comme si j'avais dit/commis une i.** as if I had said/done something improper or out of place or out of turn

inconvenant [ɛ̃kɔ̃v(ə)nɑ̃] ADJ (propos, remarque, acte) improper, out of place, out of turn; **il est vraiment i.** he doesn't know how to behave, he has no manners; **il serait totalement i. d'aller à un enterrement habillé de rouge** it would be totally inappropriate to go to a funeral dressed in red

inconvénient [ɛ̃kɔ̃venjɑ̃] NM drawback, disadvantage; **les inconvénients qu'il y a à vivre si loin de la ville** the disadvantages or drawbacks or inconvenience of living so far from town; **le seul i., c'est que ...** the only drawback is that …; **l'i., c'est que …** the problem is that …; **je n'y vois pas d'i.** I can't see any objection(s) (to it), I've got nothing against it; **si vous n'y voyez aucun i., je voudrais …** if you have no objection, I'd like to …; **si je t'emprunte ta voiture, est-ce que tu y vois un i.?** would you have any objections if I borrowed your car?; **il n'y a pas d'i. à cela** that doesn't pose any problem; **nous pouvons sans i. modifier notre itinéraire** we can easily change our route

inconvertible [ɛ̃kɔ̃vɛrtibl] ADJ *(monnaie)* inconvertible, non-convertible

incoordination [ɛ̃kɔɔrdinasjɔ̃] NF lack of coordination; *Méd* ataxia

incorporable [ɛ̃kɔrpɔrabl] ADJ *Rare (appelé)* eligible for military service

incorporation [ɛ̃kɔrpɔrasjɔ̃] NF 1 *(mélange)* incorporation, blending, mixing (**de qch dans qch** of sth into *or* with sth); **opérer l'i. d'une poudre à un mélange** to incorporate a powder into a mixture; *Fin* **i. des réserves au capital** capitalization of reserves 2 *Mil* conscription; **sursis d'i.** deferment of call-up

incorporéité [ɛ̃kɔrpɔreite] NF incorporeity, incorporality

incorporel, -elle [ɛ̃kɔrpɔrɛl] ADJ *(qui n'a pas de corps)* incorporeal; *Jur* **biens incorporels** intangible property

incorporer [ɛ̃kɔrpɔre] VT 1 *(amalgamer)* **i. qch à** *ou* **avec qch** to incorporate *or* blend *or* mix sth into *or* with sth 2 *(intégrer)* *(terrain)* to incorporate (**dans un domaine** in(to) an estate); *(paragraphe)* to incorporate (**à** in(to)), to insert (**à** in); **le flash est incorporé à l'appareil photo** the flash is built into the camera; **un magnétophone avec micro incorporé** a tape recorder with a built-in microphone 3 *Mil (troupes)* to draft
▶ VPR **s'incorporer chercher à s'i. dans un groupe** to try to join a group

incorrect [ɛ̃kɔrɛkt] ADJ 1 *(impropre)* *(emploi d'un mot, réponse, traduction)* incorrect, wrong 2 *(défectueux)* *(montage)* defective, faulty; *(tracé)* incorrect, wrong 3 *(inconvenant)* contrary to etiquette; **tenue incorrecte** *(débraillée)* slovenly clothes; *(déplacée)* unsuitable clothes 4 *(personne)* impolite, ill-mannered, rude; *(attitude)* improper; **être i. en affaires** to be unscrupulous in business

incorrectement [ɛ̃kɔrɛktəmɑ̃] ADV 1 *(en faisant des erreurs)* *(employer, écrire, traduire)* incorrectly, wrongly 2 *(d'une façon défectueuse)* *(monté)* defectively; *(tracé)* incorrectly, wrongly 3 *(habillé)* *(de façon débraillée)* in a slovenly manner; *(de façon déplacée)* unsuitably 4 *(avec impolitesse)* *(agir, se comporter)* improperly; **se conduire i. avec qn, agir i. avec qn** to behave improperly towards sb

incorrection [ɛ̃kɔrɛksjɔ̃] NF 1 *(impolitesse)* rudeness, impoliteness, lack of (good) manners; **pour i. envers ses professeurs** for being rude to his teachers; **elle est d'une i. avec les gens!** she is incredibly rude to people! 2 *Gram* incorrect expression; **le mot était considéré comme une i.** the word used to be considered incorrect 3 *(action incorrecte)* impolite *or* rude action; *(propos incorrect)* impolite *or* rude remark; **à la suite d'une grave i. envers un professeur** after being extremely rude to a teacher

incorrigibilité [ɛ̃kɔriʒibilite] NF incorrigibility

incorrigible [ɛ̃kɔriʒibl] ADJ incorrigible; **d'une gourmandise i.** incorrigibly greedy

incorrigiblement [ɛ̃kɔriʒibləmɑ̃] ADV *Rare* incorrigibly; **elle est i. bavarde** she is an incorrigible chatterbox

incorruptibilité [ɛ̃kɔryptibilite] NF incorruptibility

incorruptible [ɛ̃kɔryptibl] ADJ incorruptible
N incorruptible person

incoté [ɛ̃kɔte] ADJ *Fin* unquoted

incoterms [ɛ̃kɔtɛrm] NMPL *Com* incoterms

incrédibilité [ɛ̃kredibilite] NF incredibility

incrédule [ɛ̃kredyl] ADJ *(sceptique)* incredulous; *Rel* unbelieving; **il hochait la tête d'un air i.** he shook his head in disbelief *or* incredulously; **je suis très i. quant à la véracité de ce qu'il raconte** I'm very sceptical *or* Am skeptical about what he says
N *(personne sceptique)*, *Rel* unbeliever

incrédulité [ɛ̃kredylite] NF incredulity; *Rel* unbelief; **avec i.** incredulously

incrémenter [ɛ̃kremɑ̃te] VT *Ordinat* to increment

increvable [ɛ̃krəvabl] ADJ 1 *(pneu)* puncture-proof 2 *Fam (personne)* full of energy *or Fam* beans, tireless; *(personne âgée, voiture, moteur)* indestructible; **les enfants sont increvables** children never seem to get tired

incriminé [ɛ̃krimine] ADJ *Jur (personne)* accused, charged

incriminer [ɛ̃krimine] VT *(personne)* *Jur* to accuse, to charge, to indict; *(tenir responsable)* to blame, to accuse; *(actions, paroles de qn)* to condemn

incrochetable [ɛ̃krɔʃtabl] ADJ *(serrure)* unpickable; *(coffre)* burglar-proof

incroyable [ɛ̃krwajabl] ADJ *(histoire, chance, paresse)* incredible, unbelievable, extraordinary; *(chapeau)* incredible, extraordinary; **une histoire tout à fait i.** an altogether incredible story; **il est d'une paresse i.** he's incredibly lazy; **j'ai eu une chance i.** I was incredibly lucky, I had incredible luck; **je trouve ça i. que …** I think it's incredible *or* extraordinary that …; **tu es vraiment i.!** you're the limit!, I don't believe you!; **c'est i. ça!** I don't believe it!
N *Hist* incroyable *(beau or belle of the French Directoire period)*

incroyablement [ɛ̃krwajabləmɑ̃] ADV *(beau, vulgaire)* incredibly, unbelievably, extraordinarily; *(vêtu, maquillé)* incredibly, extraordinarily; **il s'est i. bien comporté** he behaved incredibly well

incroyance [ɛ̃krwajɑ̃s] NF *Rel* unbelief

incroyant, -ante [ɛ̃krwajɑ̃, -ɑ̃t] ADJ unbelieving
N unbeliever, non-believer

incrustation [ɛ̃krystasjɔ̃] NF 1 *(action)* encrusting; *Menuis* inlaying 2 *(dépôt)* *(dans une chaudière, une bouilloire)* fur, scale 3 *(ornement)* encrustation, inlay, inlaid work; **i. de dentelle** lace inlay; **avec incrustations de nacre** inlaid with mother of pearl 4 *Couture* insertion 5 *TV* inlay, inset

incruste [ɛ̃kryst] NF *Fam* **si on l'invite, il va encore taper l'i.** if we invite him, we'll never get rid of him; **il a tapé l'i. à ma soirée** he gatecrashed my party

incruster [ɛ̃kryste] VT 1 *Menuis* to inlay (**de** with) 2 *(former un dépôt)* to encrust; *(d'une eau calcaire)* *(tuyaux, chaudière, bouilloire)* to scale, to fur (up) 3 *(pour orner)* to encrust 4 *TV* to inlay
▶ VPR **s'incruster** 1 *(adhérer)* to become encrusted 2 *(d'une chaudière, une bouilloire)* to fur up 3 *Fam (s'imposer)* **quand on l'invite, il s'incruste** once you invite him you can't get rid of him; **je ne voudrais pas m'i.** I wouldn't want to overstay my welcome; **ils font une fête, on s'incruste?** they're having a party, let's gatecrash

incubateur, -trice [ɛ̃kybatœr, -tris] ADJ *(appareil etc)* incubating
NM 1 *(couveuse)* incubator 2 *Écon* incubator

incubation [ɛ̃kybasjɔ̃] NF 1 *(d'œufs)* incubation; *(de poules)* sitting 2 *Méd* incubation; **période d'i.** incubation period

incube [ɛ̃kyb] NM incubus

incuber [ɛ̃kybe] VT *(œufs)* to incubate, to hatch (out)

inculcation [ɛ̃kylkasjɔ̃] NF *Litt* inculcating, inculcation

inculpation [ɛ̃kylpasjɔ̃] NF indictment; **depuis son i.** since his indictment, since he was indicted *or* charged; **le juge lui a notifié son i.** the judge informed him that he was being charged; **sous l'i. d'assassinat** charged with murder; **i. de trois responsables du club de football pour détournement de fonds** *(titre de journal)* three football club managers charged with embezzlement

inculpé, -ée [ɛ̃kylpe] N *Jur* **l'i.** the accused, the defendant

inculper [ɛ̃kylpe] VT to indict, to charge (**de, pour** with); **les trois hommes inculpés pour trafic de drogue** the three men charged with drug trafficking

inculquer [ɛ̃kylke] VT to instil, *Am* to instill, *Fml* to inculcate (**à qn** in sb)

inculte [ɛ̃kylt] ADJ *(non cultivé)* *(jardin)* uncultivated, wild; *(terre)* waste; *(non soigné)* *(barbe)* unkempt; *(ignorant)* *(personne)* uneducated

incultivable [ɛ̃kyltivabl] ADJ *(terre)* untillable, irreclaimable

incultivé [ɛ̃kyltive] ADJ *(terre)* untilled, uncultivated

inculture [ɛ̃kyltyr] NF lack of culture

incunable [ɛ̃kynabl] NM *Hist, Typ* incunabulum, *pl* incunabula

incurable [ɛ̃kyrabl] ADJ incurable; **d'une paresse/bêtise i.** incurably lazy/stupid
N person with an incurable disease

incurablement [ɛ̃kyrabləmɑ̃] ADV *(atteint, paresseux, bête)* incurably

incurie [ɛ̃kyri] NF *Fml* negligence; **faire preuve d'i.** to be negligent, to be guilty of negligence

incursion [ɛ̃kyrsjɔ̃] NF 1 *(invasion)* raid, foray, incursion 2 *Fig (entrée soudaine)* intrusion, interruption; **faire une i. dans une pièce/une réunion** to burst into a room/a meeting

incurvation [ɛ̃kyrvasjɔ̃] NF bend, curve

incurvé [ɛ̃kyrve] ADJ bent, curved

incurver [ɛ̃kyrve] VT to bend, to curve
▶ VPR **s'incurver** to bend, to curve

indatable [ɛ̃databl] ADJ that cannot be dated

Inde [ɛ̃d] NF India; *Vieilli* **les Indes** the Indies; *Hist* **les Indes occidentales** the West Indies; **les Indes orientales** the East Indies

inde [ɛ̃d] NM dark blue

indéboulonnable [ɛ̃debulɔnabl] ADJ *Fam* unbudgeable; **elle est i.** they just can't get rid of her *or* they're stuck with her

indébrouillable [ɛ̃debrujabl] ADJ *(situation)* inextricable, tangled; *(histoire)* tangled

indécemment [ɛ̃desamɑ̃] ADV indecently

indécence [ɛ̃desɑ̃s] NF indecency

indécent [ɛ̃desɑ̃] ADJ *(tenue, décolleté, jupe)* indecent; *(gaspillage)* sinful, immoral; *(luxe, étalage de richesses)* obscene

indéchiffrable [ɛ̃deʃifrabl] ADJ 1 *(qu'on ne peut pas lire)* *(inscription, message)* indecipherable; *(écriture)* illegible; *(partition)* impossible to sight-read 2 *(incompréhensible)* unintelligible, incomprehensible; *(personne)* impenetrable, inscrutable

indéchirable [ɛ̃deʃirabl] ADJ tearproof, impossible to tear

indécis, -ise [ɛ̃desi, -iz] ADJ 1 *(peu net)* *(question)* undecided, unsettled; *(victoire)* to brainwash sb; *Méd* **l. d'estomac** pumping out of the stomach; **faire un l. d'estomac à qn** to pump sb's stomach; *Fam* **l. de tête** dressing-down, telling-off

lavage-balayage, *pl* **lavages-balayages** NM *Aut* wash-wipe

lavallière [lavaljɛr] NF **(cravate) l.** necktie with a large bow, *Spéc* lavallière

lavande [lavɑ̃d] NF *Bot (fleur)* lavender; **(eau de) l.** lavender water; **bleu l.** lavender blue

lavandière [lavɑ̃djɛr] NF **1** *(blanchisseuse)* washerwoman, laundress **2** *(oiseau)* wagtail

lavaret [lavarɛ] NM *Région (poisson)* lavaret, pollan

lavasse [lavas] NF *Fam Péj (boisson)* dishwater; **son café, c'est de la l.** his coffee tastes like dishwater

lave [lav] NF *Géol* lava

lavé [lave] ADJ *(couleur)* pale, faint; *(délavé)* washed-out, faded; *Tech, Beaux-Arts* **dessin l.** wash drawing

lave-auto, *pl* **lave-autos** NM *Can* carwash

lave-dos [lavdo] NM INV back-scrubber

lave-essuie-phare, *pl* **lave-essuie-phares** NM *Aut* headlamp wash/wipe

lave-glace, *pl* **lave-glaces** NM *Aut* windscreen *or Am* windshield washer, screen wash

lave-linge NM INV washing machine

lave-mains NM INV (small) handbasin

lavement [lavmɑ̃] NM *Méd* enema; **l. baryté** barium enema

lave-phares NM INV *Aut* headlamp washer

laver [lave] VT **1** *(nettoyer avec un liquide)* to wash; **l. qch à l'eau froide** to wash sth in cold water; **l. à grande eau** *(plancher, bateau, voiture)* to swill down; *(cuisine, atelier)* to swill out, to sluice down; **l. à la brosse** to scrub; **l. qch à l'éponge** to sponge sth (down); **l. qch au jet** to hose sth (down); *(pièce, cuve etc)* to hose sth (out); **l. la vaisselle** to wash *or* do the dishes, *Br* to wash up, *Br* to do the washing-up; **l. une tache** to wash out a stain; **l. une plaie** to bathe *or* cleanse a wound; *Fig Fam* **l. la tête à qn** to tell sb off, to haul sb over the coals; *Fig* **il faut l. son linge sale en famille** one shouldn't wash one's dirty linen in public; *Fig* **l'affront a été lavé dans le sang** the insult was paid for *or* avenged in blood **2** *Fig Litt (disculper)* **l. qn d'une accusation/ de tout soupçon** to clear sb of an accusation/of all suspicion **3** *(mélanger d'eau) (peinture)* to dilute, to water down; **l. un dessin** to wash a drawing **4** *Tech* **l. un minerai** to wash an ore

VI **cette lessive lave très bien** this powder washes very well

VPR **se laver 1** *(se nettoyer)* to wash (oneself), to have a wash, *Am* to wash up; **se l. les dents** to clean *or* brush one's teeth; **se l. les cheveux** *ou* **la tête** to wash one's hair; **se l. les mains** to wash one's hands; *Fig* **je m'en lave les mains** I wash my hands of it **2** *(pouvoir être lavé)* **ce tissu ne se lave pas** this material won't wash *or* isn't washable; **comment ça se lave, la viscose?** how should viscose be washed?

laverie [lavri] NF **1** *Ind* washing plant, washery **2** **l. automatique** launderette, *Am* laundromat

lave-tête [lavtɛt] NM INV shampoo basin

lavette [lavɛt] NF **1** *(de vaisselle)* dishcloth **2** *Suisse (gant de toilette)* face cloth *or* flannel, *Am* washcloth **3** *Fig Fam (homme)* spineless creature, drip, wet

laveur, -euse [lavœr, -øz] N *(personne)* washer; **laveuse (de linge)** washerwoman; **l. de vaisselle** dishwasher, *Br* washer-up; **l. de vitres** window cleaner

NM scrubber

lave-vaisselle NM INV dishwasher

lave-vitre, *pl* **lave-vitres** NM *Aut* windscreen washer, *Am* windshield washer

lavis [lavi] NM **1** *(procédé) (de dessin)* washing, tinting **2** *(dessin)* wash drawing

lavoir [lavwar] NM **1** *(établissement)* **l. (public)** (public) washhouse **2** *(bassin)* (cement) washtub **3** *Tech, Ind (machine)* washer; *(atelier)* washing plant **4** *Belg (blanchisserie)* **l. (automatique)** self-service laundry

lavomatic [lavomatik] NM launderette, *Am* laundromat

laxatif, -ive [laksatif, -iv] ADJ, NM *Méd* laxative

laxisme [laksism] NM **1** *Rel* latitudinarianism **2** *(manque de fermeté)* laxness, laxity

laxiste [laksist] ADJ **1** *(qui manque de fermeté)* lax **2** *Rel* latitudinarian

N **1** *(qui manque de fermeté)* lax person **2** *Rel* latitudinarian

layette [lɛjɛt] NF baby clothes, layette; *Com* babywear; **bleu/rose l.** baby blue/pink

layon [lɛjɔ̃] NM forest track *or* trail; *(pour monter à cheval)* bridle path

lazaret [lazarɛ] NM lazaret(to)

lazariste [lazarist] NM Lazarist (priest)

lazulite [lazylit] NM *Minér* lazulite, blue spar

lazzi [lazi, ladzi] NMPL gibes

l/c NF *Fin (abrév* **lettre de crédit**) L/C

LCR [ɛlseɛr] NF *Fin (abrév* **lettre de change relevé**) bills of exchange statement

LDL-cholestérol [ɛldeɛlkɔlɛsterɔl] NM *Méd (abrév* **low-density lipoprotein-cholestérol**) LDL-cholesterol

LE¹, LA¹, LES¹ [lə, la, le] ART DÉF SEE GRAMMAR A5–8; B3–4 **(le** *and* **la** are elided to **l'** before a vowel or h mute; **le** *and* **les** contract with **à, de** *into* **au, aux, du, des) 1** *(précisant le nom ou pronom)* the; **ouvrez la porte** open the door; **il est venu la semaine dernière** he came last week; **j'apprends le français** I'm learning French; **j'étudie l'économie/la physique** I'm studying economics/physics; **la ville a perdu le quart/le tiers de ses habitants** the city has lost a quarter/a third of its inhabitants; **l'un ... l'autre** the one ... the other; **mon livre et le tien** my book and yours; **j'ai l'impression qu'il ne dit pas tout** I have the impression *or* a *or* the feeling that there's something he's not saying; **j'ai la certitude qu'il ment** I'm certain *or* sure that he's lying; **il est arrivé le lundi 12** he arrived on Monday the 12th; **ça s'est passé la veille de Noël** it happened on Christmas Eve; **oh! le beau chat!** what a beautiful cat!; **debout, les enfants!** time to get up, children!; **voilà le livre que j'ai préféré** this is the book that I liked best; **ce n'est plus la Claire que je connaissais** she's no longer the Claire I used to know; **le Paris de l'après-guerre/que nous aimions** post-war Paris/the Paris we knew and loved; **l'Amérique de Mark Twain n'existe plus** Mark Twain's America no longer exists

2 *(noms de lieux)* **la France** France; **l'Afrique** Africa; **le Mont Blanc** Mont Blanc; **les Alpes** the Alps; **la Seine** the Seine; **le lac de Constance** Lake Constance; **les Maldives** the Maldives; **la Réunion** Réunion (Island); **l'île de Pâques** Easter Island; **la vallée du Rhône** the Rhône Valley; **dans le Berry** in the Berry (region)

3 *(noms de personnes)* **l'empereur Guillaume** the Emperor William; **le roi Édouard** King Edward; **le cardinal Richelieu** Cardinal Richelieu; **le roi de France** the king of France; *Fam* **la Marie** Marie; *Fam* **le Pierre** Pierre

4 *(avec certains noms italiens, certains noms d'actrices et de cantatrices)* **le Tasse** Tasso; **la Callas** Callas; **le Caravage** Caravaggio

5 *(devant un nom déposé)* **la Renault®** de mon père my father's Renault

6 *(noms de villes)* **le Havre** Le Havre; **je reviens du Havre** I'm just back from Le Havre; **La Rochelle** La Rochelle; **Le Mans** Le Mans; **Le Caire** Cairo; **La Havane** Havana; **La Nouvelle-Orléans** New Orleans; **La Haye** The Hague

7 *(noms de famille)* **les tableaux de Le Brun** Le Brun's pictures; **les Curie** the Curies; **comment vont les Dupond?** how are the Duponds?

8 *(avec la plupart des jours de fête)* **la Toussaint** All Saints' Day; **quand tombe la Saint Simon?** what day does Saint Simon's day fall on?; *Fam* **la Noël** at Christmas

9 *(parties du corps)* **j'ai mal à la gorge** I've got a sore throat; **elle a les yeux bleus** she has blue eyes; **elle a les cheveux longs/blonds** she has long/blond hair; **elle a les hanches larges** she has wide hips; **hausser les épaules** to shrug one's shoulders; **elle ferma les yeux** she closed her eyes; **il s'est coincé le doigt dans la porte** he caught his finger in the door; **le bras me fait mal** my arm hurts

10 *Fam (environ)* **il a téléphoné vers les trois heures** he phoned (at) about *or* around three o'clock; **ça fera dans les 500 euros** it'll come to about *or* to something in the region of 500 euros

11 *(formant les superlatifs)* **les jours les plus longs** the longest days; **le meilleur vin de sa cave** the best wine in his cellar; **mon amie la plus intime** my closest friend; **c'est elle (qui est) la plus jolie** she's the prettiest; *(avec des adverbes)* **c'est elle qui travaille le mieux** she's the one who works (the) best; *(avec un superlatif absolu)* **c'est lorsqu'elle est seule qu'elle est le plus heureuse** she's happiest when she's by herself

12 *(généralisant le nom)* **je préfère le café au thé** I prefer coffee to tea; **aimer la musique/la littérature/le football** to like music/literature/football; **aller au théâtre/au cinéma** to go to the theatre/the cinema; **ils ne vont jamais au restaurant** they never go to a restaurant, they never eat out; **il méprise les pauvres** he scorns poor people *or* the poor; **l'homme est un animal social** man is a social animal; **le dauphin est un mammifère marin** the dolphin is a marine mammal; **il fume la pipe/la cigarette** he smokes a pipe/cigarettes; **je n'ai pas eu la patience d'attendre/le courage de refuser** I didn't have the patience to wait/the courage to refuse; **il a eu le culot de me réclamer de l'argent** he had the cheek to demand money from me; **j'ai le droit de vivre** I have a right to live; **donner l'exemple** to set an example; **la paresse est un des sept péchés capitaux** sloth is one of the seven deadly sins; **demander le divorce** to sue for (a) divorce; **belle excuse!** a fine excuse!

13 *(distributif)* **trois fois l'an** three times a year; **cinq euros la livre** five euros a pound; **il vient le jeudi/(tous) les jeudis** he comes on Thursdays/every Thursday; **il a passé le samedi chez ses parents** he spent Saturday at his parents' house; **il a passé la nuit dehors** he spent the night outdoors; **il a bu toute la nuit** he drank all night; **je n'ai pas mangé de la journée** I haven't eaten all day

14 *(avec un adjectif)* **je vous donne les livres neufs et je reprends les vieux** I'll give you the new books and take back the old ones; **tu préfères la rouge ou la jaune?** do you prefer the red (one) or the yellow (one)?

15 **à la française/l'italienne** in the French/Italian fashion *or* style *or* way; **champignons à la grecque** mushrooms à la grecque; **un**

travail fait à la va-vite *ou* à la hâte a piece of work done in a hurry; **encore une blague à la Marie** another one of Marie's little jokes **16** *(partitif)* **du, de la, des** *voir* **de**

le², **la²**, **les²** PRON PERS **1** *(remplaçant le nom)* *(pour un homme)* him; *(pour une femme)* her; *(pour un bébé, un animal)* it, him, her; *(pour une chose, une idée)* it; *(pour un navire)* it, her; *(au pluriel)* them; **je vous le/la présenterai** I'll introduce him/her to you; **je ne le lui ai pas donné** I didn't give it to him/her; **les voilà!** there they are!; **ne l'abimez pas!** don't spoil it!; **ce pays, je le connais** I know this country

2 *(remplaçant l'adjectif ou le nom utilisé adjectivement)* **malheureux, je l'étais certainement** I certainly was unhappy; **son frère est médecin, il voudrait l'être aussi** his brother is a doctor, he would like to be one too; **j'étais fatigué mais maintenant je ne le suis plus** I was tired, but now I'm not

3 *(remplaçant une proposition)* **il me l'a dit** he told me so; **je le pense aussi** I think so too; **il est plus riche que vous (ne) le pensez** he's richer than you think (he is); **tu le sais aussi bien que moi** you know (it) as well as I do

lé [le] NM *(de tissu)* width, breadth; *(de papier peint)* strip

leader [lidœr] NM **1** *Pol, Sp, Mktg* leader; **cette entreprise est le l. mondial de la micro-informatique** this company is the world leader in microcomputing; **l. sur le marché** market leader **2** *Journ* **(article) l.** editorial, *Br* leader, leading article

leasing [liziŋ] NM leasing; **acheter une auto en l.** to lease a car

léchage [leʃaʒ] NM licking; *Fam* **l. de bottes** bootlicking

lèche [lɛʃ] NF *très Fam* bootlicking; **faire de la l.** to be a bootlicker; **faire de la l. à qn** to suck up to sb, to lick sb's boots

lèche-bottes *Fam* ADJ INV **elle est l.** she's a bootlicker
  N INV bootlicker

lèche-cul NM INV *Vulg* arse-licker, *Am* ass-licker, brown-nose

lèchefrite [leʃfrit] NF **1** *Culin* dripping pan **2** *Can (moule à gâteau)* cake tin; *(moule à pain)* loaf tin **3** *Can (marmite)* maple syrup boiler

lécher [leʃe] (**je lèche, n. léchons; je lécherai**) VT **1** *(glace, cuiller, plaies etc)* to lick; **l. le beurre d'une tartine** to lick the butter off a slice of bread; *Fig* **l. les vitrines** to go window-shopping; *Péj* **l. les bottes** *ou Vulg* **le cul à qn** to lick sb's boots, *Vulg* to lick *or* kiss sb's arse *or Am* ass **2** *(fignoler) (travail, style)* to polish; **trop léché** overpolished, overdone **3** *(effleurer) (des vagues)* to lap against; *(des flammes)* to lick; **les vagues léchaient le sable** the waves were lapping on the sand
  VPR **se lécher** VT **les doigts** to lick one's fingers; *Fam* **il s'en léchait les doigts** *ou* **les babines** he licked his lips *or* his chops over it; *Fam* **quel beau gâteau, c'est à s'en l. les doigts** *ou* **les babines** what a lovely cake, it's really mouthwatering

lécheur, -euse [leʃœr, -øz] N *Fam Péj* bootlicker, toady

lèche-vitrines NM *Fam* window-shopping; **faire du l.** to go window-shopping

lécithine [lesitin] NF *Chimie* lecithin

leçon [ləsɔ̃] NF **1** *Scol (cours)* lesson, class; *(ce qu'on doit étudier, apprendre)* lesson; **il ne connaît pas sa/ses leçon(s)** he hasn't learned his lesson(s); **réciter sa l.** to recite one's lesson; *Fig* to recite one's answers/*etc* parrot-fashion; *Fig* **ils avaient bien appris leur l.** they had learnt their lines well, they

had rehearsed what to say very well; **leçons de chant** singing lessons; **le bricolage en dix leçons** DIY in ten (easy) lessons

2 *(conseil)* **leçon(s)** advice; **faire la l. à qn** *(le guider)* to give sb instructions, to tell sb what to do; *(le réprimander)* to lecture sb, to give sb a lecture; **faire une l.** *ou* **des leçons de morale à qn** to lecture sb (on his/her morals); **je n'ai pas de l. à recevoir de toi** I don't need your advice *or* (any) advice from you; **je n'ai de l. à recevoir de personne** I don't need anybody's advice *or* (any) advice from anybody

3 *(enseignement)* lesson; **donner une l. à qn** to teach sb a lesson; **espérons qu'il en aura tiré une l.** let's hope he's learnt his lesson; **que cela vous serve de l.** let that be a lesson *or* a warning to you

4 *(de manuscrit)* reading

5 *Rel* lesson

▸▸ **l. de choses** general science *(in primary school)*; **leçons particulières** private lessons, private tuition

lecteur, -trice [lɛktœr, -tris] N **1** *(personne qui lit)* reader; **c'est un grand l. de romans** he reads a lot of novels, he's a great novel reader **2** *(dans l'édition)* proofreader **3** *Univ* foreign language assistant, lector
  NM **1** *TV etc (dispositif)* player, playback deck, reproducer; **l. de badges** badge reader; **l. de carte** *Aut* map light, spot lamp; *(de cartes de crédit)* credit card reader; **l. de carte à puce** smartcard reader; **l. de cartes magnétiques** magnetic card reader; **l. de cartes à mémoire** smartcard reader, card reader; **l. de cartouche** cartridge player; **l. de cassettes** cassette deck, cassette player; **l. de codes barres** bar code reader *or* scanner; **l. de disques compacts** compact disc player, CD player; **l. de DVD** DVD player; **l. optique** optical reader; *Cin etc* **l. de ruban perforé** punchtape reader; **l. de son** sound head, sound reader; **l. de télé-cinéma** film scanner; **l. de vidéodisque** video disc player **2** *Ordinat* reader; **l. (de disquettes)** (disk) drive, floppy (disk) drive; **l. de bandes** tape drive *or* reader; **l. de bande audionumérique** DAT drive; **l. de CD-Rom** *ou* **de disque optique** CD-Rom drive; **l. de CD-ROM double vitesse** double-speed CD-ROM drive; **l. de courrier** mail reader; **l. DAT** DAT drive; **l. par défaut** default drive; **l. de destination** destination drive; **l. de disque dur** hard disk drive; **l. de lignes/de pages** line/page scanner; **l. de MP3** MP3 player; **l. OCR** OCR reader; **l. Zip®** Zip drive

lecteur-encodeur, *pl* **lecteurs-encodeurs** NM *Ordinat* reader-encoder

lectorat [lɛktɔra] NM **1** *Univ* assistantship **2** *(lecteurs)* readership

lecture [lɛktyr] NF **1** *(action de lire)* reading; **enseigner la l. à qn** to teach sb to read; **livre de l.** reading book, reader; **livre d'une l. agréable** book that makes pleasant reading; **salle de l.** *(de bibliothèque)* reading room; **méthode de l. rapide** rapid-reading method; *Mus* **l. à vue** sight-reading; **s'informer par la l. des journaux** to keep oneself informed by reading the newspapers; **l. à haute voix** *ou* **à voix haute** reading aloud; **faire la l. à qn** to read aloud to sb; **à la l. de sa lettre, j'ai souri** on reading his letter, I smiled; *Fml* **donner l. d'un document** to read out a document (**à qn** to sb); *Pol* **projet repoussé en deuxième l.** bill rejected at the second reading; **l. des épreuves** proofreading

2 *(ce qu'on lit)* reading, reading material; **l. pour la jeunesse** reading *or* books for young people; **Balzac fait partie de mes lectures** Balzac is part of my reading; **il m'a apporté de la l.** he brought me something to read; **avoir de saines/mauvaises lectures** to read the right/wrong things, to read wholesome/unwholesome books

3 *(interprétation)* reading, interpretation; **une nouvelle l. de Balzac** a new reading *or* interpretation of Balzac; **l. marxiste/psychanalytique** Marxist/psychoanalytic(al) reading *or* interpretation; **les sociologues n'ont pas la même l. des faits** not all sociologists read *or* interpret the facts in the same way; **grille de l.** interpretative framework

4 *Ordinat* read(ing); **en l. seule** in read-only mode; **mettre un fichier en l. seule** to make a file read-only; **l. optique** optical reading; **l. au scanneur** scan; **l. destructive** destructive read; **l. non destructive** non-destructive read; **l. sur disque** reading to disk

5 *Cin* **l. du son** sound reproduction

> Il faut noter que le nom anglais **lecture** est un faux ami. Il signifie **conférence**.

lecture-écriture NF *Ordinat* read-write (mode); **être en l.** to be in read-write (mode)

ledit, ladite, *pl* **lesdits, lesdites** [lədi, ladit, ledi, ledit] ADJ *(contractions avec* **à** *et* **de***: voir* **le¹**) the aforesaid, the aforementioned, the said

légal, -ale, -aux, -ales [legal, -o] ADJ legal; *(action)* legal, lawful; **avoir recours aux moyens légaux** to take legal action, to institute legal proceedings; **suivre la procédure légale** to follow the legal procedure; **par les voies légales** legally, by legal means; *Fin* **taux l.** official rate of interest; **monnaie légale** legal tender

légalement [legalmã] ADV legally, lawfully

légalisation [legalizasjɔ̃] NF legalization; *(de signature)* authentication, certification

légaliser [legalize] VT *(rendre légal) (pratique, drogue etc)* to legalize; *(authentifier) (signature, procuration)* to authenticate, to certify; **l. des documents** to certify documents

légalisme [legalism] NM legalism

légaliste [legalist] ADJ, N legalist

légalité [legalite] NF **1** *(de mesure, décision, licenciement etc)* legality, lawfulness **2** *(situation légale)* **la l.** the law; **rester dans/respecter la l.** to keep within/respect the law; **cet acte l'a fait sortir de la l.** this act has brought *or* put him/her outside the law; **agir en toute l.** to act within the law; **il l'a ainsi dépouillé de ses biens en toute l.** he thus stripped him of his possessions quite legally

légat [lega] NM *Rel, Antiq* legate; **l. du Pape** papal legate

légataire [legater] N *Jur* legatee, heir; **l. universel** sole legatee; **l. d'une succession** heir to an estate

légation [legasjɔ̃] NF legation

legato [legato] ADV *Mus* **jouer l.** to play legato

légendaire [leʒɑ̃dɛr] ADJ legendary

légende [leʒɑ̃d] NF **1** *(histoire, fable)* legend; *Fig (mensonge)* fairy tale *or* story; **entrer dans la l.** to become a legend; **entrer vivant dans la l.** to become a living legend *or* a legend in one's own lifetime; **la l. napoléonienne** the Napoleonic legend; **pays/personnage de l.** legendary country/character **2** *(sur une pièce, médaille)* inscription, legend; *(de dessin, photo)* caption; *(de diagramme, carte etc)* key, legend; **consulter la l.** to refer to the key

légender [leʒɑ̃de] VT *(photo, dessin etc)* to provide with a caption; *(plan, carte etc)* to provide with a key; **voir photo légendée** see photo with caption

LÉGER, -ÈRE [leʒe, -ɛr] ADJ **1** *(de peu de poids)* light; **l. comme une plume** as light as a feather; **armes légères** light weaponry; **un croiseur l.** a light cruiser; **industrie légère** light industry; **repas l.** light meal; **avoir le cœur l.** to be light-hearted; **partir le cœur l.** to leave with a light heart; **marcher d'un pas**

l. to walk with a light step *or* with a spring in one's step; *Fig* **je me sens plus l. depuis que je lui ai tout avoué** telling him everything has taken a (great) weight off my mind *or* shoulders

2 *(faible) (douleur, erreur, blessure)* slight; *(brise)* light, gentle; *(couche de peinture, vin, parfum)* light; *(tabac)* mild; *(thé, café)* weak; *(goût, odeur)* slight, light, faint; *(son, nuance)* faint; **avoir le sommeil l.** to be a light sleeper; **il y a eu quelques blessés légers** some people were slightly injured; *Jur* **peine légère** light sentence, mild punishment; **il y a un l. mieux** there is a slight improvement; **perte légère** slight *or* trivial loss; **une légère pointe d'ail/d'ironie** a slight *or* little touch of garlic/irony; **elle a eu un l. sourire** she gave a slight *or* little smile

3 *(insuffisant) (preuves, arguments)* thin, lightweight; **c'est un peu l.** it's a bit on the thin side; **c'est un peu l. comme résultat** there's not much to show for it; **la musique légère** light music, easy listening music; **c'est un film l.** it's a light film

4 *(désinvolte, frivole) (personne)* thoughtless; *(en amour)* fickle; **le responsable s'est montré un peu l.** the person in charge was quite offhand about it; **femme légère ou de mœurs légères** woman of easy virtue, loose woman; **avoir la cuisse légère** to sleep around; **propos légers** frivolous *or* idle talk

NF **agir à la légère** to act without due consideration *or* thoughtlessly; **parler à la légère** to speak unthinkingly *or* thoughtlessly; **ce nouveau parti est un danger pour la démocratie, je ne parle pas à la légère** this new party is a danger to democracy, and I'm not saying that lightly *or* I mean that very seriously; **prendre ou traiter qch à la légère** to make light of sth, not to take sth seriously, to treat sth lightly

ADV **manger l.** to eat lightly *or* light meals/a light meal; **s'habiller l.** to wear light clothes; *Fam* **il faut y aller l. avec les tranquillisants** you have to go easy with tranquillizers

légèrement [leʒɛrmã] **ADV 1** *(avec légèreté) (habillé, armé)* lightly; **manger l.** to eat lightly *or* light meals/a light meal **2** *(un peu) (ennuyeux, surpris, plus grand etc)* slightly, somewhat; *(blessé)* slightly; **ça sent l. le moisi** there's a slight smell of mildew; **pourrais-tu reculer l.?** could you go back slightly *or* a bit? **3** *(avec souplesse)* nimbly, gracefully; **elle se déplace l.** she moves gracefully **4** *(avec désinvolture)* **agir l.** to act without due consideration *or* thoughtlessly; **traiter qch l.** to make light of sth, not to take sth seriously, to treat sth lightly

légèreté [leʒɛrte] **NF 1** *(poids faible)* lightness; *(d'un danseur, sportif, cheval)* agility; **l. de main** *(d'un pianiste, d'une infirmière)* lightness of touch **2** *(faiblesse) (de blessure)* slightness; *(de brise)* lightness, gentleness; *(du tabac)* mildness; *(de vin)* lightness; *(du thé, café)* weakness; *(de son, nuance)* faintness **3** *(désinvolture)* thoughtlessness; **agir avec l.** to act without due consideration *or* thoughtlessly; **parler avec l.** to speak unthinkingly *or* thoughtlessly **4** *(en amour)* fickleness; *(des mœurs)* looseness

leggings [legiɲz] **NFPL** leggings

légiférer [leʒifere] **VI** (**je légifère, n. légiférons; je légiférai**) to legislate (**sur** on)

légion [leʒjõ] **NF** legion; **la L. (étrangère)** the Foreign Legion; **la L. d'honneur** the Legion of Honour *or Am* Honor; *Fig* **l. de moucherons/touristes** host *or* swarm of gnats/tourists; **elle a une l. d'oncles et tantes** she has a huge number of uncles and aunts; **ils sont l.** they are legion

légionnaire [leʒjɔnɛr] **NM 1** *Hist* legionary **2** *(à la Légion étrangère)* legionnaire, Foreign Legionary **3** *(membre de la Légion d'honneur)* member of the Legion of Honour *or Am* Honor **4** *Méd* **maladie du l.** legionnaire's disease

législateur, -trice [leʒislatœr, -tris] *Jur* **N** *(personne qui fait les lois)* legislator, lawmaker
NM *(corps législatif)* legislature
ADJ legislative, lawmaking; **puissance législatrice** legislative power

législatif, -ive [leʒislatif, -iv] **ADJ** *Jur* legislative; *Hist* **l'Assemblée législative** the Legislative Assembly; **élections législatives** parliamentary elections; **le pouvoir l.** the legislature
NM *Pol* **le l.** legislative power
NF 1 *Hist* **la Législative** the Legislative Assembly **2** *Pol* **législatives** parliamentary elections

législation [leʒislasjõ] **NF** *Jur* legislation, law(s); **l. criminelle/fiscale/du travail** criminal/tax/employment legislation *or* law; **l. française/anglaise** French/English legislation *or* laws; **l. antitrust** antitrust *or Br* antimonopoly legislation; **l. commerciale** commercial legislation *or* law; **l. sur la consommation** consumer legislation; **l. douanière** customs legislation; **l. européenne** EU legislation; **l. financière** financial legislation; **l. sur la sécurité** safety legislation

législature [leʒislatyr] **NF** *Jur* **1** *(durée)* term of office *(of legislative body)* **2** *(corps)* legislature, legislative body

légiste [leʒist] **NM** *Jur* jurist
ADJ **médecin l.** pathologist

légitimation [leʒitimasjõ] **NF 1** *(d'enfant)* legitimation **2** *(de délégué, titre etc)* official recognition **3** *Litt (de conduite)* justification

légitime [leʒitim] **ADJ 1** *(légal)* legitimate; *(action)* lawful; **propriétaire l.** legal owner; **union l.** marriage *(as opposed to living together)*; **héritier l.** rightful heir; **enfant l.** legitimate child; *Jur* **l. défense** self-defence, *Am* self-defense; **il était en état de l. défense** he was acting in self-defence **2** *(juste) (récompense, motif, désir etc)* legitimate, justified, justifiable; **il est tout à fait l. qu'il soit en colère, sa colère est tout à fait l.** he is quite justified in his anger, it's quite legitimate *or* justifiable for him to be angry, his anger is quite justified *or* legitimate
NF *Arg* **ma l.** my old lady, *Br* the wife, the missus

légitimement [leʒitimmã] **ADV** legitimately; *(en colère)* justifiably; *(appartenir à qn)* rightfully; *Jur* lawfully

légitimer [leʒitime] **VT 1** *Jur (enfant, union etc)* to legitim(at)ize, to legitimate **2** *(action, demande, titre)* to justify **3** *(titre, pouvoir)* to recognize

légitimiste [leʒitimist] **ADJ, N** *Hist* legitimist

légitimité [leʒitimite] **NF 1** *Jur (d'un enfant, d'une union etc)* legitimacy **2** *(bien-fondé) (de démarche, conduite etc)* legitimacy, justi-

fiability; **tes soupçons sont sans l.** your suspicions are unjustified *or* without foundation

legs [lɛ, leg] **NM 1** *Jur* legacy, bequest; **l. universel** universal bequest; **l. particulier** specific bequest; **faire un l. particulier à son neveu** to make a specific bequest to one's nephew; **faire un l. à qn** to leave sb a legacy, to make a bequest to sb **2** *Fig Litt (héritage)* **le l. du passé** the legacy of the past

léguer [lege] **VT** (**je lègue, n. léguons; je léguerai**) **1** *Jur* to bequeath, to leave (**à qn** to sb) **2** *(transmettre) (tradition, qualité etc)* to hand down, to pass on (**à** to)

légume [legym] **NM 1** vegetable; **légumes verts** green vegetables, greens; **soupe de légumes** vegetable soup; **légumes secs** pulses **2** *Fig Fam (personne végétative)* vegetable; **il est devenu un vrai l. après son accident** he's become a complete vegetable since his accident
NF *Fam* **grosse l.** bigwig, big shot

légumier, -ière [legymje, -jɛr] **ADJ** **culture légumière** vegetable growing
NM *(plat)* vegetable dish
N *Belg (commerçant)* greengrocer

légumineux, -euse [legyminø, -øz] *Bot* **ADJ** leguminous
NF **légumineuse** leguminous plant; **les légumineuses** Leguminosae

leitmotiv, *pl* **leitmotive** [lajtmɔtiv, lɛmɔtiv] **NM** *Mus, Fig* leitmotif, leitmotiv, recurring theme

lem [lɛm] **NM** *Astron* lunar exploration module, LEM, *Fam* moon buggy

Léman [lemã] **N** **le lac L.** Lake Geneva

lemme [lɛm] **NM** *Math, Phil* lemma

lemming [lemiŋ] **NM** lemming

lémure [lemyr] **NM** *Antiq* lemur

lémurien [lemyrjɛ̃] **NM** *Zool* lemur

lendemain [lãdmɛ̃] **NM 1** *(jour suivant)* **le l.** the next day, the following day; **le l. de la bataille** the day after the battle; **le l. matin** the next morning, the morning after; **le l. après-midi, (dans) l'après-midi du l.** the next afternoon, the afternoon after; **il devint célèbre du jour au l.** he became famous overnight; *Fam* **un l. de cuite ou de fête** the morning after (the night before) **2** *(avenir)* **il faut penser au l.** one must think of the future *or* of tomorrow; **des lendemains prometteurs** a promising future; *Hum* **des lendemains qui chantent** a better *or* bright(er) future; **avoir d'heureux lendemains** to have happy consequences; **des succès/aventures (amoureuses) sans l.** short-lived successes/(love) affairs **3** *(période qui suit)* **au l. de la guerre/de ce scandale** soon after *or* in the days following the war/this scandal

lénifiant [lenifjã] **ADJ** *Méd, Fig* soothing

lénifier [lenifje] **VT** (*pr sub, impf n.* **lénifiions, v. lénifiiez**) **1** *Méd* to soothe, to alleviate **2** *Fig (apaiser)* to soothe, to calm

Lénine [lenin] **N** Lenin

léninisme [leninism] **NM** *Pol* Leninism

léniniste [leninist] **ADJ, N** *Pol* Leninist

lénitif, -ive [lenitif, -iv] **ADJ, NM** lenitive

lent [lã] **ADJ** *(mouvement, développement etc)* slow; *(poison)* slow(-acting); *(tortue etc)* slow-moving; **mort lente** slow *or* lingering death; **être l. à faire qch** to be slow to do sth; **vous êtes l. à faire la vaisselle** you're slow at *or* taking your time doing the dishes; **vous êtes l. à manger** you're a slow eater, you eat slowly; **vous êtes l. à comprendre** you're slow to understand *or Fam* slow on the uptake; **avoir l'esprit l.** to be slow-witted, to be slow in understanding, *Fam* to be slow on the uptake

lente [lãt] **NF** nit

lentement [lãtmã] ADV slowly; **ruisseau qui coule l.** slow-flowing stream; **l. mais sûrement** slowly but surely

lenteur [lãtœr] NF **1** (développement lent) slowness; **avec l.** slowly **2 lenteurs** (actions lentes) slowness; **les lenteurs de la justice** the slowness of the law

lentigo [lãtigo] NM Méd lentigo

lentille [lãtij] NF **1** Culin, Bot lentil **2** Bot **l. d'eau** duckweed, Spéc lemna **3** Opt lens; **lentilles de contact** ou **cornéennes** contact lenses; **lentilles souples/dures** soft/hard lenses

lento [lɛnto] ADV, NM Mus lento

léonin [leɔnɛ̃] ADJ leonine; **partage l.** lion's share

léopard [leɔpar] NM **1** leopard; **manteau de l.** leopard skin coat **2** Hér leopard

LEP [ɛlɛpe, lɛp] NM **1** Anciennement (abrév Lycée d'enseignement professionnel) ≃ technical college **2** (abrév livret d'épargne populaire) = special tax-exempt savings account

lepeniste [ləpenist] N Pol = supporter of Jean-Marie Le Pen

lépidoptère [lepidɔptɛr] ADJ lepidopterous NM (insecte) lepidopteran; **les lépidoptères** Lepidoptera

lèpre [lɛpr] NF **1** Méd leprosy **2** Fig (pourriture, ce qui ronge) **mur rongé par la l.** peeling or flaking or crumbling wall **3** Litt (mal) canker, scourge; **l'envie le ronge comme une l.** envy eats away at him like a cancer

lépreux, -euse [leprø, -øz] ADJ **1** Méd leprous **2** Fig (mur) peeling, flaking, crumbling; (quartier) dilapidated, rundown N leper; **traiter qn comme un l.** to treat sb like a leper

léproserie [leprozri] NF leper hospital

leptine [lɛptin] NF leptin

LEQUEL, LAQUELLE, LESQUELS, LESQUELLES [ləkɛl, lakɛl, lekɛl] (contracted with à and de to auquel, auxquel(le)s, duquel, desquel(le)s) PRON REL (personne) who; (après prép) whom; (chose) which; **le père de cette jeune fille, l. est très riche** this girl's father, who is very rich; **le père de cette jeune fille, laquelle est très riche** the father of this girl, who is very rich; **ont comparu trois témoins, lesquels ont déclaré …** three witnesses appeared, who stated …; **la dame avec laquelle elle était sortie** the lady with whom she had gone out; **les deux officiers entre lesquels elle était assise** the two officers between whom she was sitting; **j'ai retrouvé mon parapluie, l. était sous mon lit** I've found my umbrella, which was under my bed; **l'adresse à laquelle il devait m'écrire** the address at which he was to write to me; **la farine avec laquelle j'ai fait ce gâteau** the flour (that) I used to make this cake or with which I made this cake; **l'actrice à laquelle je pense est plus jeune** the actress (that) I'm thinking of or of whom I'm thinking is younger; **la personne par laquelle il faut passer pour obtenir ce dossier** the person (that) you have to go through to get this file; **décision par laquelle …** decision whereby …; **n'importe l. fera l'affaire** any (one) of them will do; **il y avait beaucoup de gens, parmi lesquels mon cousin Paul** there were a lot of people, among whom was my cousin Paul; **la dame chez laquelle je l'ai rencontré** the lady at whose house I met him; **l'homme sans l'avis duquel on ne peut rien faire** the man without whose advice one can do nothing; **la maison sur la porte de laquelle vous trouverez une plaque** the house with a plaque on the door; **le roman d'après l. il a tiré son film** the novel from which or on which he based his film SEE GRAMMAR A32–3; B22
ADJ REL **voici cent euros, laquelle somme vous était due par mon père** here's a hundred euros, (which was) the sum my father owed you; **j'ai**

vu son adversaire, **l. adversaire est impressionnant** I've seen his opponent, (who is) an impressive one; **il écrira peut-être, auquel cas …** perhaps he will write, in which case … SEE GRAMMAR A31; B17
PRON INTERR which (one); **lesquel(le)s** which; **l. (de ces chapeaux) préférez-vous?** which (one) (of these hats) do you prefer?; **l. d'entre nous?** which (one) of us?; **de laquelle de ces deux régions êtes-vous originaire?** which (one) of these two regions do you come from?; **auquel de ces deux hommes faites-vous confiance?** which (one) of these two men do you trust?

lerch(e) [lɛrʃ] ADV Arg **pas l.** damn all, Br bugger all

lérot [lero] NM lerot, garden dormouse

les [le] voir **le**[1], **le**[2]

lesbianisme [lɛsbjanism] NM lesbianism

lesbien, -ienne [lɛsbjɛ̃, -jɛn] ADJ lesbian NF **lesbienne** lesbian

lèse-majesté [lɛzmaʒɛste] NF INV Jur high treason, lese-majesty

léser [leze] VT (je lèse, n. lésons; je léserai) **1** (désavantager) to wrong; (intérêts de qn) to harm, to damage; Jur **l. les droits de qn** to encroach or infringe upon sb's rights; **la partie lésée** the injured party **2** Méd (organe) to injure

lésine [lezin] NF Litt, Vieilli stinginess

lésiner [lezine] VI to skimp (sur on); **ils n'avaient pas lésiné sur le vin** they hadn't skimped on the wine; **ne pas l. sur les moyens** not to go in for penny-pinching; (pour une fête, en vacances etc) to really push the boat out

lésineur, -euse [lezinœr, -øz] N Vieilli niggard, miser

lésion [lezjɔ̃] NF Méd, Jur lesion

lessivable [lesivabl] ADJ (papier peint, tissus etc) washable

lessivage [lesivaʒ] NM (de linge, mur etc) washing; Chimie leaching; Fig **c'est le grand l. dans la compagnie** there's a big clear-out (of personnel) going on in the company

lessive [lesiv] NF **1** (produit) (en poudre) washing powder; (liquide) liquid detergent; Chimie lye **2** (action de laver) wash(ing); **faire la l.** to do the washing; **jour de l.** wash(ing) day; **j'ai fait trois lessives ce matin** I've done three washes this morning; **une l. de blanc et une l. de couleurs** one wash of whites and one wash of coloureds **3** (linge sale) (dirty) washing **4** (linge propre) (clean) washing; **une l.** a batch of washing **5** Fig (assainissement) shake-out, clear-out (operation); **il faut faire une grande l. dans cette famille** this family really needs sorting out

lessivé [lesive] ADJ Fam (fatigué) washed out, worn out, done in

lessiver [lesive] VT **1** (nettoyer) (sol, mur etc) to wash **2** Chimie to leach **3** Fig très Fam (battre) to lick, to wipe the floor with; **se faire l.** (au jeu) to be cleaned out **4** Fig Fam (fatiguer) to wear out, to do in; **ce match m'a lessivé** this match has worn me out or done me in

lessiveuse [lesivøz] NF **1** Anciennement boiler, Br copper **2** Belg (machine à laver) washing machine

lessiviel [lesivjɛl] ADJ detergent; **produit l.** detergent (product)

lest [lɛst] NM (de bateau, ballon) ballast; Naut **naviguer sur son l.** to sail in ballast or without a cargo; **jeter** ou **lâcher du l.** to discharge ballast; Fig (faire des concessions) to make concessions

lestage [lɛstaʒ] NM (de bateau, ballon) ballasting

leste [lɛst] ADJ **1** (agile) (personne, animal) nimble, agile; (mouvement) brisk, nimble **2**

Fig (grivois) (manières, gestes, mot) crude; (plaisanteries, roman etc) risqué

lestement [lɛstəmã] ADV nimbly, smartly; (avec une légèreté choquante) offhandedly, casually

lester [leste] VT **1** (bateau, ballon) to ballast **2** Fam (poche, portefeuille etc) to stuff, to fill; **l. son estomac** to fill one's stomach VPR **se lester 1** (plongeur etc) to weigh oneself down **2** Fam **se l. (l'estomac)** to stuff oneself; **se l. les poches de petite monnaie/de bonbons** to stuff or fill one's pockets with small change/sweets

létal, -ale, -aux, -ales [letal, -o] ADJ lethal; Biol **gène l.** lethal gene; **dose létale** lethal dose

letchi [lɛtʃi] NM Bot lychee, litchi

léthargie [letarʒi] NF lethargy; Méd coma; Méd **tomber en l.** to sink into a coma; Fig **en l.** in a state of lethargy

léthargique [letarʒik] ADJ lethargic

lette [lɛt] NM Ling Lettish, Latvian

letton, -onne [lɛtɔ̃, -ɔn] ADJ Latvian; (personne) Lett, Latvian NM Ling Lettish, Latvian N **L.** Latvian, Lett

Lettonie [lɛtɔni] NF Latvia

lettrage [lɛtraʒ] NM Typ lettering

LETTRE [lɛtr] NF **1** (de l'alphabet) letter; **l. majuscule/minuscule** capital/small letter; **mot de sept lettres** seven-letter word, word of seven letters; **écrire qch en toutes lettres** to write sth out in full; **écrire une somme en (toutes) lettres** to write an amount in words; Fig **c'est écrit en toutes lettres** it's there in black and white; **je l'ai vu écrit en toutes lettres dans les journaux** I saw it in black and white in the newspapers; Typ **le corps de la l.** the body of the letter; Fig Litt **c'est gravé en lettres d'or** it will remain in my/our/etc memory for all time; **c'est gravé en lettres de feu** it's written in letters of fire; **écrit/gravé en lettres de sang** written in blood

2 (missive) letter; **petite l.** note, short letter; **mettre une l. à la poste** ou **à la boîte** to mail or Br to post a letter; Vieilli **c'est pour moi lettres closes** it's a mystery to me; Fam **c'est passé comme une l. à la poste** it went off without a hitch, it went off smoothly; **ce couscous est passé comme une l. à la poste** this couscous went down with no trouble; **la nouvelle est passée comme une l. à la poste** the news was received without any fuss

3 selon la l. de la loi according to the letter of the law; **au pied de la l.** literally; **traduire à la l.** to translate word for word; **il prend les choses à la l.** he takes everything literally; **j'ai suivi vos instructions à la l.** I've followed your instructions to the letter; **il fut surréaliste avant la l.** he was a surrealist before the word had been invented

4 lettres (littérature) literature, Litt letters; Univ arts subjects, humanities; Litt **les belles lettres** literature; **homme/femme de lettres** man/woman of letters; **avoir des lettres** to be well read; Univ **faculté de lettres** faculty of arts or humanities

▸▸ **l. d'accompagnement** covering letter; **l. d'affaires** business letter; **l. d'amour** love letter; **l. anonyme** anonymous letter; **l. par avion** airmail letter; **l. d'avis** advice note; Hist **l. de cachet** = order under the King's private seal; Fin **l. de change** bill of exchange, B/E; Fin **l. de change relevé** bills of exchange statement; **l. circulaire** form letter; **lettres classiques** ≃ classics; **l. commerciale** business letter; **l. de confirmation** letter of confirmation; Pol **lettres de créance** credentials; Banque, Com **l. de crédit** letter of credit; Com **émettre une l. de crédit** to open a letter of credit; Com **l. de crédit docu-**

mentaire documentary letter of credit; *Com* **l. de crédit irrévocable** irrevocable letter of credit; **l. de démission** letter of resignation; **l. d'embauche** written offer of employment; **l. d'excuse** letter of apology; **l. exprès** express letter; **l. de félicitations** letter of congratulations, congratulatory letter; *Fin* **l. de gage** debenture bond; *(pour hypothèque)* mortgage bond; *Fin* **l. de garantie** letter of guarantee; *Fin* **l. de garantie bancaire** bank guarantee; **l. de grâce** reprieve; **l. d'injures** abusive letter; *Jur* **l. d'intention** letter of intent; **l. de licenciement** letter of dismissal; **l. de menace** threatening letter; *Jur* **l. missive** letter missive; **lettres modernes** *(section scolaire ou universitaire)* French; *Belg* **l. de mort** death announcement; **ce règlement est resté l. morte** this regulation was not enforced *or* stayed a dead letter; **ce projet est resté l. morte** this project was never put into operation; **toutes ses bonnes résolutions sont restées l. morte** he never put any of his good resolutions into practice; **l. de motivation** covering *or Am* cover letter *(in support of one's job application)*; **lettres de noblesse** letters patent of nobility; *Fig* **donner ses lettres de noblesse à qch** to establish *or* prove the worth of sth; *Fig* **conquérir *ou* gagner ses lettres de noblesse** to establish *or* prove its worth; *Journ* **l. ouverte** open letter *(à* to); *Hist* **lettres patentes** letters patent; **l. de poursuite** letter threatening legal action, chasing letter; **l. de rappel** reminder; **l. de réclamation** letter of complaint; **l. de recommandation** letter of recommendation, reference; **l. recommandée** registered letter; **l. recommandée avec accusé de réception** = registered letter with confirmation of receipt; **l. de relance** follow-up letter; **l. de relance des impayés** debt chasing letter; **lettres supérieures** = preparatory classes for the Normale Supérieure littéraire; **lettre-transfert,** *pl* **lettres-transferts** transfer *or Am* decal letter; *Com* **l. de transport aérien** air waybill; **l. type** *(pour mailing)* form letter; **l. de vente** sales letter; *Com* **l. de voiture** waybill, consignment note; *Com* **l. de voiture CIM** CIM waybill; *Com* **l. de voiture CMR** CMR waybill; *Com* **l. de voiture fluviale** inland waterway waybill

lettré, -ée [letre] ADJ **1** *(personne)* well-read, cultured **2** *Belg (sachant lire et écrire)* **il est l.** he can read and write
N **1** well-read person **2** *Belg (personne sachant lire et écrire)* = person who can read and write

lettrine [letrin] NF *Typ (au début des chapitres)* drop cap; *(dans un dictionnaire)* running head(line)

leu,[1] *pl* **lei** [lø, le] NM *(monnaie)* leu, *pl* lei

leu[2] NM **à la queue l. l.** in single file, in Indian file

leucémie [løsemi] NF *Méd* leukaemia, *Am* leukemia

leucémique [løsemik] *Méd* ADJ leukaemic, *Am* leukemic
N leukaemia *or Am* leukemia sufferer

leucocytaire [løkositɛr] ADJ *Physiol* leucocytic

leucocyte [løkosit] NM *Physiol* leucocyte, leukocyte

leucocytose [løkositoz] NF *Méd* leucocytosis

leucome [løkom] NM *Méd* leucoma, albugo

leucorrhée [løkɔre] NF *Méd* leucorrh(o)ea

leucose [løkoz] NF *Méd* leukaemia

leur[1] [lœr] ADJ POSS their; **l. oncle et l. tante** their uncle and (their) aunt; **l. père et l. mère,** *Litt* **leurs père et mère** their mother and father; **ils ont mis l. chapeau et leurs**

gants they put on their hat and (their) gloves; **elles ont pris l. sac** *(il n'y a qu'un sac)* they took their bag; *(chacune a son sac)* they took their bags; **elles ont pris leurs sacs** they took their bags; **un(e) de leurs ami(e)s** a teacher of theirs, one of their friends; **un professeur de leurs amis** a teacher friend of theirs; *Fam* **ils auront l. chambre à eux** *(il n'y a qu'une chambre)* they'll have their own room; *(chacun aura sa chambre)* they'll have their own rooms; *Fam* **l. imbécile de frère** their idiot of a brother; *Fam* **leurs artistes de mari** their artist husbands; *Fam* **ils ont eu l. vendredi** they got Friday off SEE GRAMMAR A30; B21

PRON POSS **le l., la l., les leurs** theirs; **ils me prêtent le l.** I can borrow theirs; **tu n'as qu'à prendre le l.** just take theirs; **il ressemble au l.** it looks like theirs; **ils veulent bien te donner du l.** you can have some of theirs; **ils n'en ont pas besoin, ils ont le l.** they don't need it, they've got their own; **je n'en ai pas besoin, j'ai le l.** I don't need it, I've got theirs; **les deux leurs** their two, the two *or* both of theirs; *(en insistant)* their own two; **ils nous ont laissé deux des leurs** they gave us two of theirs; *(ils en ont sacrifié deux)* they gave us two of their own; *très Fam* **le l. bébé est plus intelligent** their baby is more intelligent; *Fam* **à la l.!** *(en buvant)* let's drink to them! SEE GRAMMAR A30; B21–2
NM **le l.** *(ce qui leur appartient)* theirs; **ils devraient y mettre du l.** they should really do their share
NMPL **les leurs** *(leur famille)* their family, *Fam* their folks; *(leurs partisans)* their followers; *(leurs coéquipiers)* their team-mates; **ils font leurs vos principes** they have adopted these principles of yours; **ils font leurs les félicitations que je vous adresse** they join me in congratulating you

leur[2] PRON *voir* **lui**[1]

leurre [lœr] NM **1** *(pour faucons)* lure; *(pour gibier)* decoy; *(pour poissons)* (artificial) bait, lure **2** *(illusion)* illusion, delusion **3** *Mil* chaff

leurrer [lœre] VT **1** *(en fauconnerie) (faucon)* to lure **2** *(tromper)* to deceive, to delude; **l. qn par des promesses** to deceive sb with promises; **il se laisse facilement l.** he is easily taken in
VPR **se leurrer** to delude oneself *(sur* about)

lev, *pl* **leva** [lev, leva] NM *(monnaie)* lev, *pl* leva

levage [ləvaʒ] NM **1** *Tech* lifting (up), hoisting, raising; **câble de l.** hoisting cable; **appareil de l.** lifting apparatus; **cric de l.** lifting jack **2** *Culin (de pâte etc)* rising

levain [ləvɛ̃] NM leaven; **pain au/sans l.** leavened/unleavened bread; *Fig Litt* **ils furent le l. de la révolte/du changement** they sowed the seeds of revolt/change

levant [ləvɑ̃] ADJ **soleil l.** rising sun; **il est parti au soleil l.** he left at sunrise *or Am* at sun-up
NM **1** *Litt* **le l.** the east, the orient; **du l. au couchant** from East to West **2** *Vieilli* **le L.** the Levant

levantin, -ine [ləvɑ̃tɛ̃, -in] *Vieilli* ADJ Levantine
N **L.** Levantine

levé [ləve] ADJ **1** *(en l'air) (main, poing)* raised; **voter à mains levées** to vote by a show of hands; **dessin à main levée** freehand drawing; **pierre levée** standing stone **2** *Culin* **pâte bien levée** well-risen dough **3** *(debout)* up, out of bed; *(du soleil etc)* up; **je suis l. de bonne heure tous les jours** I'm up early every day **4** *Belg Fam* **bien/mal l.** in a good/bad mood
NM **1** *(de terrain)* plan, survey; **l. aérophotogrammétrique** aerial survey; **faire le l. d'un terrain** to survey a piece of land **2** *Mus* up beat

levée [ləve] NF **1** *(action de faire cesser)* *(d'embargo, de peine, d'interdiction, de sanctions etc)* lifting; *(de séance)* adjournment; *(d'immunité parlementaire)* stripping; *Mil (de siège)* raising; *(de scellés)* removal, breaking; *Jur* **demander la l. de la séance** to ask for an adjournment **2** *(enrôlement) (de troupes)* levy(ing) **3** *(collecte) (de lettres)* collection; **heures de l.** collection times; **la l. est faite** the post has been collected *or* has gone; **il y a trois levées par jour** there are three collections a day; *Vieilli* **la l. d'un impôt** the levying of a tax; **l. des impôts** tax collection, collection of taxes; *Fin* **l. des titres** taking delivery of shares; *Fin* **l. des actions** taking up of stock **4** *Cartes* trick; **faire une l.** to take a trick
► ► **l. de boucliers** general outcry; **levées de compte** personal withdrawals; **l. du corps** = removal of the coffin; **pendant la l. du corps la veuve s'est évanouie** the widow fainted as the coffin was being removed *or* carried out; *Jur* **l. d'écrou** release from prison; *Jur* **l. de jugement** transcript of the verdict; **l. en masse** levy *en masse*; *Jur* **l. d'option** exercising of an option; **l. de terre** levee

lève-glace(s) [levglas] NM INV *Aut* window winder

LEVER[1] [ləve] *(je lève, n.* **levons;** *je* **lèverai)** VT **1** *(objet)* to lift, to raise; *(filet de pêche)* to raise; *(store)* to open; *(vitre)* to wind up; **l. son verre (à qn/qch)** to raise one's glass (to sb/sth); **je lève mon verre à votre réussite/aux futurs époux** here's to your success/the happy couple; **l. un étendard** to raise a standard; *Fig Litt* **l. l'étendard de la révolte** to raise the standard of revolt; *Naut* **l. l'ancre** to weigh *or* lift anchor; *Fig Fam* to take off, to hit the road
2 *(parties du corps)* to raise, to lift; **l. la tête** to look up, to raise one's head; *Fig Litt (se montrer digne)* to hold one's head high; **l. les yeux (sur qn)** to look up (at sb); **lève les yeux quand je te parle!** look at me when I'm talking to you!; **l. les yeux au ciel** to raise one's eyes to heaven *or* the heavens; **l. les sourcils** to raise one's eyebrows; **l. les bras au ciel** to throw up one's hands; *Fig Fam* **l. le coude** to (be able to) knock it back; **l. la main droite** to raise one's right hand; *Fig* **l. la main sur qn** to raise *or* lift one's hand to sb; **l. le doigt** *(à l'école)* to put one's hand up; **il n'a pas levé le petit doigt** he didn't lift a finger, he didn't do a thing; **lève les pieds quand tu marches** lift your feet up when you walk; *Fam* **on conseille aux automobilistes de l. le pied ce soir** motorists are advised to drive slowly this evening; *Fam* **lève le pied** *(ralentis)* slow down; **ça me lève le cœur** it makes my stomach turn; *très Fam* **lève ton cul!** move your arse!; *Fam* **l. la patte** *(d'un chien)* to cock *or* lift its leg
3 *(faire cesser) (embargo, peine, interdiction)* to lift; *(difficulté, doute, ambiguïté, inhibitions)* to remove; *(audience)* to adjourn; *Mil (siège)* to raise; **l. la séance** to close a/the meeting; *Jur* to adjourn; **l. le camp** to strike *or* break camp; *Fig Fam* to take off, to hit the road, to go; *Fig* **cet article lève le voile sur l'affaire des diamants** this article reveals the truth about the affair of the diamonds
4 *Jur (enlever)* **l. les scellés** to break the seals
5 *(débusquer) (perdrix)* to flush; *Arg (femme)* to pick up, *Br* to pull; *(de prostituée) (client)* to pick up; **l. un lièvre** to start a hare; *Fig* to open a can of worms
6 *(faire sortir du lit) (enfant, malade)* to get up
7 *(collecter) (lettres, courrier)* to collect; *Fin (actions, titres, options)* to take up; **l. des impôts** to collect *ou Vieilli* levy taxes
8 *(enrôler) (troupes, armée)* to raise, to levy
9 *Cartes* **l. les cartes** to pick up a trick

10 *(plan)* to make, to draw
11 *Culin* **l. les filets** to remove the fillets
VI 1 *Litt (du blé, du grain)* to shoot
2 *(de la pâte)* to rise
3 *Cartes* to pick up a trick
VPR se lever 1 *(se mettre debout)* to stand up, to get up, to rise; **levez-vous** stand up, get up; **se l. de sa chaise** to get up (from one's chair), to rise (from one's chair), to stand up; *Jur* **accusé, levez-vous** the accused will rise; **va aider grand-mère à se l.** go and help grandma (to get) up; **se l. de table** to leave the table; **le peuple se leva en masse** *ou* **en foule contre l'oppresseur** the nation rose up as one against the oppressor
2 *(quitter le lit)* to get up, to get out of bed; **je me lève de bonne heure** I'm an early riser, I get up early; *Fam* **se l. du pied gauche** to get out of bed on the wrong side
3 *(apparaître) (du soleil, d'un astre, de la lune)* to rise; *(de la brise, du vent)* to rise, to get up; **le jour se lève** day is breaking *or* dawning; *Fig Litt* **le désespoir/la tristesse se lève dans mon cœur** despair/sadness is welling up inside me
4 *(s'éclaircir) (du temps)* to clear up; *(de la brume)* to lift, to clear up
5 *(se mouvoir vers le haut) (des mains)* to go up; *Théâtre (du rideau)* to go up, to rise; *(vitre)* to wind up

lever² **NM 1** *(du lit)* getting up, *Fml* rising; *Hist (du roi)* levee; **programme de la journée: l. 6h30, petit-déjeuner 7h30** today's schedule: get up 6.30, breakfast 7.30; **au l., il est bon de boire un jus d'orange** first thing in the morning, it's good to have a drink of orange juice
2 *(apparition)* **l. du soleil** sunrise; **l. du jour** daybreak **3** *(montée), Théâtre (du rideau)* rising, rise; **le l. du rideau est à 19h** the curtain rises at 7 pm; *Fig* **un l. de rideau** a curtain raiser **4** *(croquis)* = **levé** NM **1**

lève-tard [lɛvtar] **NM INV** *Fam* late riser
lève-tôt [lɛvto] **NM INV** *Fam* early riser
lève-vitre, *pl* **lève-vitres** [lɛvvitr] **NM** *Aut* window winder

levier [ləvje] **NM 1** *(outil)* crowbar, lever; **soulever/ouvrir qch avec un l.** to prize *or* prise *or* lever sth up/open
2 *Phys* lever; **bras de l.** lever arm; **force de l.** leverage; **faire l.** to act as a lever; **ce poids fait l. et permet de bouger la caisse** this weight acts as a lever and allows the crate to be moved
3 *(commande)* lever, handle; *Tech* **l. d'arrêt** shut-off lever; **l. de frein** brake lever; **l. de commande** control lever; *Fig* **être aux leviers de commande** to be in control *or* in command; **l. de dégagement du chariot** *(de machine à écrire)* carriage release arm; **l. de dégagement du papier** *(de machine à écrire)* paper release arm; *Aut* **l. (de changement) de vitesse** gear lever, gear stick, *Am* gearshift; *Aut* **l. de direction** steering lever; *Aut* **l. de débrayage** clutch release lever; *Aut* **l. de vitesses au plancher** floor shift; *Aut* **l. de vitesses sur colonne de direction** column change; *Aut* **l. sélecteur** selector lever; *Aut* **l. à fourche** forked lever
4 *Fig (motif d'action)* spur, lever
5 *Écon* **l. financier** financial leverage

lévitation [levitasjɔ̃] **NF** levitation; **être en l.** to be levitating
lévite [levit] **NM** *Rel* Levite
levraut [ləvro] **NM** leveret
lèvre [lɛvr] **NF 1** *Anat* lip; **avoir les lèvres charnues** *ou* **pleines/minces** to have thick *or* full/thin lips; **la l. inférieure** the lower lip; **se mettre du rouge à lèvres** to put on lipstick; **il avait un cigare aux lèvres** he had a cigar in his mouth; **le sourire aux lèvres** with a smile on his lips; **j'ai son nom sur les lèvres** *ou* **le bord des lèvres** his name is on the tip of

my tongue; **son nom est sur toutes les lèvres** his name is on everybody's lips; **manger du bout des lèvres** to nibble *or* pick at one's food; **il accepta, mais du bout des lèvres** he grudgingly accepted; **rire du bout des lèvres** to force a laugh; *Fig* **nous étions tous suspendus à ses lèvres** we were all hanging on his every word; **pincer les lèvres** *(pour ne pas rire, pour exprimer son dédain)* to purse one's lips **2** *Anat (de la vulve)* **lèvres** lips, labia; **les grandes/petites lèvres** the labia majora/minora **3** *(bord) (de plaie)* lip; *(de cratère)* rim **4** *Bot* lip, *Spéc* labium

levrette [ləvrɛt] **NF 1** greyhound bitch; **l. (d'Italie)** (small) Italian greyhound **2** *très Fam* en l. doggy fashion
lévrier [levrije] **NM** greyhound; **l. irlandais** *ou* **d'Irlande** Irish wolfhound; **l. d'Italie** Italian greyhound; **l. afghan** Afghan hound; **l. à poil long** borzoi; **courses de lévriers** greyhound racing
levure [ləvyr] **NF** yeast; **l. de boulanger** fresh *or* baker's yeast; **l. de bière** brewer's yeast; **l. chimique** = baking powder; **l. en sachet** yeast in a packet *or* sachet
lexème [lɛksɛm] **NM** *Ling* lexeme
lexical, -ale, -aux, -ales [lɛksikal, -o] **ADJ** lexical
lexicalisation [lɛksikalizasjɔ̃] **NF** lexicalization
lexicalisé [lɛksikalize] **ADJ** lexicalized
lexicographe [lɛksikɔgraf] **N** lexicographer
lexicographie [lɛksikɔgrafi] **NF** lexicography
lexicographique [lɛksikɔgrafik] **ADJ** lexicographical
lexicologie [lɛksikɔlɔʒi] **NF** lexicology
lexicologique [lɛksikɔlɔʒik] **ADJ** lexicological
lexicologue [lɛksikɔlɔg] **N** lexicologist
lexie [lɛksi] **NF** lexical unit
lexique [lɛksik] **NM 1** *(dictionnaire)* lexicon, small dictionary; *(glossaire)* glossary; **l. financier** financial glossary **2** *(à la fin d'un livre)* list of terms **3** *(mots d'un auteur)* vocabulary, *Spéc* lexis
lézard [lezar] **NM 1** *(reptile)* lizard; **l. gris/des murailles** grey/wall lizard; **l. vert** green lizard; *Fam* **faire le l.** to bask *or* lounge in the sun **2** *(cuir)* lizard skin **3** *Fam* **il y a un l.** there's a catch, there's something fishy about it; **il n'y a pas de l.** there's no catch, it's kosher
lézarde [lezard] **NF** crack
lézardé [lezarde] **ADJ** *(mur, plâtre)* cracked, full of cracks
lézarder [lezarde] **VT** *(plâtre, ciment)* to crack
  VI *Fam* to bask *or* lounge in the sun
  VPR se lézarder *(de mur)* to crack
LFAJ [ɛlɛfaʒi] **NF** *(abrév* **Ligue française des auberges de jeunesse***)* = French youth hostel association
liais [ljɛ] **NM** *Minér* hard limestone
liaison [ljɛzɔ̃] **NF 1** *(enchaînement logique)* connection; **il y a un manque de l. dans l'expression de vos idées** you express your ideas in a disjointed fashion; **des idées sans l.** unconnected ideas; **en l. avec ce qui a été dit** in connection with *or* leading on from what has been said
2 *Tél* communications link; **l. radio/téléphonique** radio/telephone link; **l. vidéo** video link; **l. par satellite** satellite link *or* linkup; **la l. est mauvaise** it's a bad connection; **la l. est coupée entre la plateforme et le continent** all shore contact with the rig has been lost; **établir une l. radio** to establish radio contact; *Ordinat* **l. alternat** half duplex; *Ordinat* **l. par modem** modem link; *Ordinat* **l. spécialisée** dedicated line

3 *(entre des personnes)* close contact *or* relationship; **assurer la l. entre deux personnes/services** to liaise between two people/departments; **les différents services sont en (étroite) l.** the various departments are in close contact *or* liaise closely (with each other); **les différents services sont en l. permanente** the various departments are constantly in touch with each other; **être en l. avec qn** to be in touch with sb; **rester en l.** to stay in touch; **se mettre en l. avec qn** to get in touch with sb; **travailler en l. (étroite) avec qn** to work (closely) with sb; *esp Mil* to liaise with sb; **l. (amoureuse)** (love) affair, *Fml* liaison; **agent de l.** go-between; *Mil* liaison officer
4 *(dans les transports)* **l. aérienne/maritime/ferroviaire/routière** air/sea/rail/road link; **toutes les liaisons Paris-Téhéran sont suspendues** all services between Paris and Tehran have been suspended; **une navette assure la l. entre l'aéroport et le centre-ville** there is a shuttle service between the airport and the town centre; **un avion hebdomadaire assure la l. entre Paris et Moscou** there is one flight a week between Paris and Moscow; **les liaisons sont bonnes entre ces deux villes, que ce soit par le train ou par la route** there are good rail and road services between the two towns
5 *Ling* liaison *(sounding of final consonant before initial vowel sound)*; **faire la l.** to make *or* sound the liaison; *Gram* **mot** *ou* **terme de l.** linkword
6 *Constr (de briques etc)* bonding; *(produit)* mortar, cement; **maçonnerie en l.** bonded masonry; *Tech* **l. élastique** rubber joint; *Aut* **l. transversale** cross-tie
7 *Mus (pour lier deux notes)* slur; *(pour lier une suite de notes)* tie, ligature
8 *Chimie* bond
9 *Culin (pour sauce)* thickening
liaisonner [ljɛzɔne] **VT** *Constr (briques)* to bond; *(en maçonnerie)* to grout, to point
liane [ljan] **NF** *Bot* creeper, *Spéc* liana
liant [ljɑ̃] **ADJ** sociable, friendly; **il est très l.** he's quick to make friends
  NM 1 *Tech* binder, binding agent **2** *Litt (sociabilité)* **avoir du l.** to be sociable **3** *(souplesse)* flexibility, pliability
liard [ljar] **NM** *Arch* half farthing; **il n'a pas un l.** he hasn't (got) a farthing, he hasn't (got) a penny to his name
lias [ljas] **NM** *Géol* lias
liasse [ljas] **NF** *(de lettres)* bundle, packet; *(de billets)* wad; *(de papiers)* bundle; **l. carbonée** print-through paper
libage [libaʒ] **NM** *Constr* bastard ashlar
Liban [libɑ̃] **NM** **le L.** (the) Lebanon
libanais, -aise [libanɛ, -ɛz] **ADJ** Lebanese
  N **L.** Lebanese; **les L.** the Lebanese
libanisation [libanizasjɔ̃] **NF** disintegration *(due to ethnic or religious strife)*
libation [libasjɔ̃] **NF 1** *Antiq, Rel* libation **2** *Fig* **faire des libations** to partake of libations
libelle [libɛl] **NM** *Litt* lampoon, scurrilous satire
libellé [libele] **NM** *(de document)* wording, terms used; **le l. du chèque/de la pièce comptable est incorrect** the cheque *or* Am check voucher is not made out correctly
libeller [libele] **VT** *Admin (document, acte, contrat)* to word, to draw up; *Fin* to denominate; **l. un chèque** to make out *or* write out a cheque; **chèque libellé à l'ordre de Y. Mourier** cheque made out *or* payable to Y. Mourier; **télégramme libellé comme suit ...** telegram worded as follows *or* that reads as follows ...; **l. une facture** to make out an invoice; **libellé au porteur** *(chèque)* made out to bearer; **libellé en** *(chèque)* made out in;

(cours) quoted *or* given in; *Fin* **libellé en dollars** denominated in dollars

libellule [libelyl] NF *(insecte)* dragonfly

libérable [liberabl] *Mil* ADJ *(soldat)* dischargeable, who can be demobbed; **congé** *ou* **permission l.** demob leave
　NM = soldier about to finish his military service

libéral, -ale, -aux, -ales [liberal, -o] ADJ **1** *(tolérant)* *(personne, éducation)* lenient, liberal; *(idées)* liberal **2** *(indépendant)* il exerce une profession libérale he's a professional man; **défendre la médecine libérale** to defend private medicine **3** *(généreux)* generous **4** *Pol* liberal; **le parti l.** the Liberal Party **5** *(économie, doctrine)* free-market
　N **1** *Pol* liberal **2** *Écon* free-marketeer

libéralement [liberalmɑ̃] ADV **1** *(généreusement)* liberally **2** *(avec tolérance)* leniently, liberally

libéralisation [liberalizasjɔ̃] NF **1** *Écon (de l'économie, des échanges commerciaux)* liberalization; **la l. de la presse** the liberalization of the press, the easing of restrictions on the press; **l. du commerce** liberalization of trade; **l. du cours de l'euro** freeing of the euro **2** *Jur* liberalization

libéraliser [liberalize] VT *(économie)* to liberalize

libéralisme [liberalism] NM *Pol, Écon* liberalism

libéralité [liberalite] NF **1** *(libéralisme)* liberality **2** *(générosité)* generosity **3** *(cadeau)* generous gift; *Litt* **faire des libéralités à qn** to give liberally *or* freely to sb; **vivre des libéralités de ses amis** to live off the generosity of one's friends

libérateur, -trice [liberatœr, -tris] ADJ *(soldats, force)* liberating; **guerre libératrice** war of liberation; **le pouvoir l. du rire** the liberating power of laughter
　N liberator

libération [liberasjɔ̃] NF **1** *(mise en liberté)* liberation, freeing, release; *(de prisonnier)* discharge, release; *(de soldat)* discharge; **l. conditionnelle** release of prisoner on parole **2** *(d'un joug)* liberation; **le mouvement de l. de la femme** the women's liberation movement, *Fam* women's lib; *Hist* **la L.** the Liberation *(from the Germans in 1944-45)* **3** *(dérèglement)* *(des prix, des échanges commerciaux)* freeing; *(de dette)* payment in full, discharge; *Fin* **l. d'une action** paying up of a share; **l. des échanges commerciaux** deregulation of trade **4** *Phys (émission)* liberation, release; **la l. de chaleur/d'hormones** the liberation *or* release of heat/hormones; *Astronaut* **vitesse de l.** escape *or* parabolic velocity

libératoire [liberatwar] ADJ *Jur* **paiement l.** payment in full discharge from debt

libéré [libere] ADJ **1** *(physiquement)* liberated, free; **jeune homme l. des obligations militaires** young man who has carried out his national service duties **2** *(moralement)* liberated **3** *Fin (action)* (fully) paid-up; **l. d'impôt** tax paid
　NM released prisoner

libérer [libere] *(je libère, n. libérons; je libérerai)* VT **1** *(rendre sa liberté à)* *(otage, prisonnier)* to free, to set free, to release; *(pays, peuple)* to liberate; *(soldat)* to discharge; **l. qn de ses chaînes** to free sb from his chains; **le prof a libéré les élèves plus tôt** the teacher let the children go *or* let the children out early; **l. qn de sa promesse** to release sb from his promise **2** *(soulager)* **l. sa conscience** to salve one's conscience; **cela me libérera d'un souci** *ou* **poids** that will take a load off my mind; **l. les jeunes des tabous sexuels** to free *or* liberate

young people from sexual taboos **3** *(rendre disponible)* *(appartement, chambre d'hôtel)* to vacate **4** *(débloquer)*, *Fin (prix, échanges commerciaux)* to free; *(cran de sûreté, mécanisme)* to release; *(instincts, passions)* to unleash; **l. le passage** to clear the way **5** *(décharger)* *(d'une dette)* to free; *(d'un engagement)* to release; **l. entièrement une action** to make a share fully paid-up, to pay up a share in full; **l. un débiteur** to discharge a debtor, to release a debtor **6** *(émettre)* *(gaz, hormone, énergie, chaleur)* to release
　VPR **se libérer 1** *(de liens, chaînes, oppresseur, passion)* to free oneself **2** *(se rendre disponible)* *(d'une personne)* to get away; **je n'ai pas pu me l. plus tôt** I couldn't get away any earlier; **se l. pour deux jours** to (arrange to) take two days off; **je viens juste de se l.** someone's just left a parking space; **il y a un poste qui vient de se l.** a job vacancy has just come up **3** *(se dégager)* **se l. (d'une dette)** to redeem *or* liquidate a debt; **se l. d'un engagement** to free oneself from a commitment

Liberia [liberja] NM Liberia

libérien, -ienne [liberjɛ̃, -jɛn] ADJ Liberian
　N **L.** Liberian

libéro [libero] NM *Ftbl* sweeper

libertaire [liberter] ADJ, N libertarian

liberté [liberte] NF **1** *(de personne, d'animal)* liberty, freedom; **l'assassin est toujours en l.** the murderer is still at large; **animaux en l.** animals in the wild, animals running free; **vivre en l.** *(d'un animal)* to live in the wild; **rendre sa l. à qn** *(fiancé etc)* to let sb go; **rendre sa l. à un animal** to let an animal go, to set an animal free; **reprendre sa l.** *(de conjoint)* to regain one's freedom; **être mis en l.** to be set free, to be released, to be allowed to go free; *(d'un inculpé)* to be discharged; **(re)mettre qn en l.** to set sb free, to free *or* release sb; *Jur* **mise en l.** *(d'un prisonnier)* release; *Jur* **(mise en) l. provisoire** *ou* **sous caution** (released on) bail; **mettre qn en l. provisoire** to release sb on bail; *Jur* **l. conditionnelle** parole; **mettre qn en l. conditionnelle** to release sb on parole; *Jur* **l. surveillée** probation; **mettre qn en l. surveillée** to release sb on probation **2** *Pol (droit de l'individu)* freedom, liberty; **la l. civile** civil liberty; **atteinte aux libertés individuelles** infringement of one's individual freedom; **l., égalité, fraternité** liberty, equality, fraternity **3** *(absence de contrainte)* freedom; **l. d'entreprise** free enterprise; **avoir toute** *ou* **pleine l. d'action** to have complete freedom of action, to have a free hand; **vous avez toute l. pour organiser la rencontre** you have a free hand *or* complete freedom to organize the meeting as you wish; **vous avez pleine (et entière) l. d'agir comme bon vous semble** you are quite free *or* you are completely at liberty to act as you see fit; **parler en toute l.** to speak freely *or* without restraint; **j'ai pris la l. de dire ...** I took the liberty of saying ...; **si je puis prendre une telle l.** if I may be so bold **4** *(temps libre)* **jour de l.** free day, day off; **un moment de l.** a spare *or* free moment; **avec tout ce travail je n'ai pas beaucoup de l.** with all this work I haven't (got) much spare *or* free time **5** *Fin, Écon (dérèglementation)* *(des échanges)* deregulation; *Aviat* **libertés commerciales** commercial freedoms; **l. des prix** freedom from price controls; **instaurer la l. des prix** to end *or* to abolish price controls **6** *(familiarités)* **prendre** *ou* **se permettre des libertés avec qn/un texte** to take liberties

with sb/a text; **se permettre des libertés de langage** to be rather free in one's use of language
　▸▸ **l. d'association** freedom of association; **libertés du citoyen** civil liberties; **libertés civiques** civil liberties; **l. de communication** freedom of communication; **l. de conscience** freedom of conscience; **l. du culte** freedom of worship; **l. d'enseignement** freedom of educational choice; **l. d'expression** freedom of expression *or* of speech; **l. d'information** freedom of information; **l. de mouvement** freedom of movement; **l. d'opinion** freedom of opinion; **l. de pensée** freedom of thought; **l. de la presse** freedom of the press; **libertés publiques** civil liberties; **l. de réunion** freedom of assembly; **l. syndicale** freedom of association

libertel [libertel] NF *Ordinat* freenet

libertin, -ine [libertɛ̃, -in] ADJ **1** *(aux mœurs libres)* *(personne)* libertine, dissolute; *(livre, propos)* licentious **2** *Hist* free-thinking
　N **1** *(de par ses mœurs)* libertine **2** *Hist* free-thinker

libertinage [libertinaʒ] NM **1** *(débauche)* licentiousness **2** *Hist* free-thinking

Liberty® [liberti] NM Liberty® fabric; **une housse de coussin en L.** a liberty cushion cover

libidineux, -euse [libidinø, -øz] ADJ libidinous, lustful; **des regards l.** lustful *or* lascivious glances

libido [libido] NF libido; **avoir une forte l.** to be highly sexed

libraire [librer] N *Com* bookseller

> Il faut noter que le nom anglais **librarian** est un faux ami. Il signifie **bibliothécaire**.

libraire-éditeur, *pl* **libraires-éditeurs** NM *Com* publisher and bookseller

librairie [libreri] NF **1** *(magasin)* bookshop, *Am* bookstore; **l. d'art** art bookshop; **l.-papeterie** bookshop and stationer's **2** *Com (activité)* bookselling; **ouvrages en l.** published books

> Il faut noter que le nom anglais **library** est un faux ami. Il signifie **bibliothèque**.

LIBRE [libr]

free **1, 2, 6, 11**	▪ vacant **2**	▪ spare **2**
▪ unrestrained **3**	▪ clear **5**	▪ open **5**
▪ independent **7**	▪ disengaged **8**	

ADJ **1** *(non soumis)* *(personne, pays)* free; **le monde l.** the free world; *Hist* **zone l.** unoccupied France; *Hist* **la France l.** Free France; **l'homme est l.** man is a free agent; **laisser qn l. d'agir** to leave sb a free hand, to leave sb free to act; **laisser qn l. de choisir** to leave sb free to choose; **il nous laisse libres de partir** he lets us go when we want; **vous êtes l. de le faire, à vous de le faire** you are quite free *or* at liberty to do it; **l. à vous d'essayer** you're free *or* welcome to try; **donner l. cours à son enthousiasme/sa curiosité/son imagination** to give one's enthusiasm/curiosity/imagination free rein; **être l. de tout souci** to be free from care, to be carefree; **l. de préjugés** free from prejudice; **l. d'impôt** tax-free **2** *(disponible)* *(personne)* free, not tied down; *(sentimentalement)* unattached; *(temps)* free, spare; *(appartement, maison, chambre)* available; *(toilettes)* *(sur la porte)* vacant; *(table, place de parking, fauteuil)* free, unoccupied; **vous êtes l.?** are you free?; **vous êtes l. ce soir?** are you free this evening?; **avoir du temps (de) l.** to have some free *or* spare time, to have some time free *or* to spare; **je suis l. de onze heu-**

res à midi I'm free between eleven and twelve; *Fam* le lundi est mon jour de l. Monday is my day off, I have Mondays free; je n'ai pas eu une minute de l. aujourd'hui I haven't had a spare minute today; être l. comme l'air to be as free as the air *or* a bird; j'ai les mains libres I'm not carrying anything; *Fig* I'm a free agent; *Fig* laisser les mains libres à qn to give sb a free rein *or* hand; studio à louer, l. de suite *(annonce)* one-room flat to rent, available immediately; j'ai trouvé une place l. pour me garer I found a place to park; *Tél* la ligne n'est pas l. the line is engaged *or esp Am* busy

3 *(non attaché) (mouvement etc)* unrestrained; robe qui laisse la taille l. dress which fits loosely round the waist; elle a les cheveux libres she wears her hair down *or* loose

4 être l. avec qn to be free with sb, to treat sb in a familiar way; allures *ou* manières libres free and easy manner

5 *(non bloqué) (route)* clear, open; laisser le champ l. to leave the field clear; je vous laisse le champ l. I'll leave you to it, you're free to do as you think best; *Fig* la voie est l. the coast is clear; *Rail* voie l. line clear

6 *(non imposé) (adaptation, traduction, vers)* free; *Scol* sujet l., texte l. free choice of subject

7 *(privé)* enseignement l. independent Catholic education system; école l. independent Catholic school; radio l. independent radio

8 *Tech* disengaged; roue l. *(de bicyclette, voiture)* freewheel; descendre une côte en roue l. to freewheel *or* coast down a hill; *Fig* être en roue l. to be coasting

9 *Com* entrée l. *(dans un magasin)* please come in and look around, no obligation to buy; *(entrée gratuite)* admission free

10 *Sport* free, freestyle; les figures libres freestyle skating; escalade l. free climbing

11 *(non réglementé) (prix)* free; le l. jeu de la concurrence the free play of competition; défendre la l. entreprise to defend free *or* private enterprise; il pratique les honoraires libres = he's in private practice; bibliothèque en l. accès public library; l. circulation des personnes freedom of movement; l. circulation des marchandises free movement of goods; l. échange international international free trade

▸▸ l. arbitre free will; *Écon* l.-échange free trade; *Écon* l.-échangisme free trade l. parole free speech; l. pensée free thinking, free thought; l. penseur/penseuse free thinker

libre-échangiste, *pl* **libre-échangistes** *Écon* **ADJ** *(politique, théorie)* free trade **N** free trader

librement [librəmɑ̃] **ADV** freely

libre-service, *pl* **libres-services NM 1** *(principe)* self-service; magasin/restaurant en l. self-service shop *or Am* store/restaurant; station-service en l. self-service petrol *or Am* gas station **2** *(magasin, restaurant)* self-service

librettiste [librɛtist] **N** *Mus* librettist

libretto, *pl* **libretti, librettos** [librɛto, librɛti] **NM** *Mus* libretto

Libreville [librəvil] **N** Libreville

Libye [libi] **NF** Libya

libyen, -yenne [libjɛ̃, -jɛn] **ADJ** Libyan **N L.** Libyan

lice [lis] **NF** *Hist (barrière, enclos)* lists; *Fig* entrer en l. to enter the lists *or* the fray; les athlètes français entreront en l. à 10 heures pour les épreuves de saut en hauteur the French high jumpers will enter the competition at 10 a.m.; trois concurrents sont en l. there are three competitors, three people are in contention

licence [lisɑ̃s] **NF 1** *(permis)* licence, *Am* license; accorder une l. à qn to license sb; accorder une l. sur un nom to license a name; l. d'utilisation user licence; l. de brevet patent licence; l. de fabrication manufacturing licence; l. de vente sales licence; l. exclusive exclusive licence; fabriqué sous l. made under licence; l. d'importation/d'exportation import/export licence; l. individuelle d'utilisation single user licence; l. de logiciel software licence **2** *Sport* permit, certificate *(giving right of entry into competition)* **3** *Univ* bachelor's degree; l. ès *ou* de lettres/ès *ou* de sciences/en droit bachelor's degree in arts/in science/in law, arts/science/law degree; passer sa l. to sit *or* take one's degree exams *or* one's finals; faire une l. to do a degree **4** *(liberté)* licence, *Am* license; l. poétique poetic licence; l. syntaxique syntactic licence; donner *ou* laisser à qn la l. de faire qch to give sb licence to do sth; je vous laisse toute l. pour la décoration du stand I leave the decoration of the stand entirely up to you, you can decorate the stand as you like; *Arch* prendre des licences avec qn to take liberties with sb **5** *Vieilli (dérèglement)* licentiousness

licencié, -ée [lisɑ̃sje] **ADJ 1** *Univ* il est l. he's a graduate; professeur l. graduate teacher **2** *(renvoyé)* (made) redundant; un ouvrier l. *(pour raisons économiques)* a redundant worker; *(pour faute professionnelle)* a dismissed worker

N 1 *Univ* l. ès lettres/ès *ou* en sciences/en droit bachelor of arts/of science/of law, arts/science/law graduate **2** *Sport* member

licenciement [lisɑ̃simɑ̃] **NM** *(pour raisons économiques)* redundancy; *(pour faute professionnelle)* dismissal; *Mil (de troupes)* disbanding; recevoir une lettre de l. to receive a redundancy notice/notice of dismissal; il y a eu beaucoup de licenciements many (people) were made redundant, there were a lot of redundancies; l. économique redundancy; l. collectif mass redundancies; l. abusif unfair dismissal; l. avec/sans préavis dismissal with/without notice

licencier [lisɑ̃sje] **VT** *(pr sub, impf n.* licenciions, *v.* licenciiez) *(pour raisons économiques)* to make redundant; *(pour faute professionnelle)* to dismiss; *Mil (troupes)* to disband

licencieusement [lisɑ̃sjøzmɑ̃] **ADV** *Litt* licentiously

licencieux, -euse [lisɑ̃sjø, -øz] **ADJ** *Litt* licentious

lichen [likɛn] **NM** lichen

lichette [liʃɛt] **NF** *Fam (de pain, fromage etc)* tiny bit, smidgen; *(de vin)* drop, smidgen

licite [lisit] **ADJ** licit, lawful, permissible

licitement [lisitmɑ̃] **ADV** licitly, lawfully

licol [likɔl] **NM** halter

licorne [likɔrn] **NF 1** *Myth, Hér* unicorn **2** *Zool* l. de mer sea unicorn, narwhal

licou [liku] **NM** halter

LICRA [likra] **NF** *(abrév* Ligue internationale contre le racisme et l'antisémitisme) = anti-racist movement

licteur [liktœr] **NM** *Antiq* lictor

lido [lido] **NM** *Géog* sand bar

lie [li] **NF** *(dépôt)* dregs; l. (de vin) lees *or* sediment of wine; *Fig* la l. de la société the dregs of society

ADJ INV l.(-)de(-)vin purplish red, wine-coloured

lié [lje] **ADJ 1** *(attaché)* bound; avoir les mains liées to have one's hands tied; *Fig* j'ai les mains liées my hands are tied **2** *(en relation étroite)* être (très) l. avec qn to be (great) friends *or* intimately acquainted with sb; nous sommes très liés we are great friends,

we are very close; avoir partie liée avec qn to be in league with sb **3** *Mus* notes liées slurred notes; *(deux notes différentes)* tied notes

lied, *pl* **lieder** [lid, lidœr] **NM** *Mus* lied, song

liège [ljɛʒ] **NM** *(matière naturelle)* cork; semelle de l. cork sole; cigarette à bout (de) l. cork-tipped cigarette; bouchon de l. cork

liégeois, -oise [ljeʒwa, -waz] **ADJ 1** of/from Liège **2** *Culin* café/chocolat l. coffee/chocolate ice cream topped with crème Chantilly **N L.** *(natif)* native of Liège; *(habitant)* inhabitant of Liège

lien [ljɛ̃] **NM 1** *(attache)* tie, *esp Litt* bond; il s'est libéré de ses liens he freed himself (from his bonds) **2** *Fig* liens du sang blood ties; l. de parenté *ou* de famille family relationship; il y a un l. de parenté entre ces deux familles the two families are related; des liens de famille avec le PDG expliquent sa nomination à ce poste the fact that he is related to the Chairman *or* is a relation of the Chairman accounts for his appointment; les liens du mariage the bonds of marriage *or* matrimony; je vous déclare unis par les liens du mariage = I now pronounce you man and wife; l. d'amitié bond of friendship; l. social civic bond **3** *Ordinat* link; l. hypertexte hypertext link **4** *(relation)* link, connection; j'ai du mal à faire le l. avec ce qu'il a dit avant I can't see the connection with what he said before; il y a un l. entre ces événements there's a connection *or* link between these events

lier [lje] *(pr sub, impf n.* liions, *v.* liiez) **VT 1** *(attacher)* to bind, to fasten, to tie, to tie up; *(d'un contrat)* to be binding on; l. qch avec une corde to bind sth *or* tie sth up with a rope; l. les pieds et les mains à qn to bind sb hand and foot; l. un fagot to tie up a bundle of sticks; on l'a lié à un arbre he's been tied (up) to a tree; vous êtes lié par ce contrat you are bound by this agreement, this agreement binds you *or* is binding on you; l'intérêt nous lie we have common interests; cela les a intimement liés that has formed a close bond between them; un même amour de l'art les lie they are united by a mutual love of art; l. les paragraphes to connect *or* link the paragraphs; tout est lié everything is connected; ce jardin est lié au souvenir de sa grand-mère the garden is linked to the memory of his grandmother; l. deux mots to link two words (in pronunciation), to sound the liaison; *Mus* l. deux notes to slur (two notes); *(deux notes différentes)* to tie two notes **2** *Culin (sauce)* to thicken **3** l. amitié/conversation avec qn to strike up a friendship/conversation with sb

VPR se lier **1** *(socialement)* se l. avec qn to form *or* strike up a friendship with sb; il se lie facilement he makes friends easily; je me suis lié d'amitié avec son père I have made friends with his father **2** *(se mélanger)* le lait et le jaune d'œuf se lient facilement milk and egg yolk blend easily

lierre [ljɛr] **NM** ivy; l. terrestre ground ivy

liesse [ljɛs] **NF** *Arch, Litt* jubilation, gaiety; *Litt* en l. jubilant, in celebratory mood

LIEU¹, *pl* **lieux** [ljø]

| place **1** ▪ premises *(lieux)* **3** ▪ scene *(lieux)* **3** ▪ to take place *(avoir lieu)* **4** ▪ instead of *(au lieu de)* **7** |

NM 1 *(endroit)* place; mettre qch en l. sûr to put sth in a safe place; *Litt* en tous lieux everywhere; *Litt* en aucun l. nowhere; visiter les lieux saints to visit the Holy Places; elle y a ses lieux de promenade she goes for walks there; c'est un drôle de l. de promenade it's a funny place for a walk; les mendiants se

mettent de préférence sur les lieux de passage beggars prefer busy areas *or* areas where there are lots of people going past; cette ville n'est qu'un l. de passage people merely pass through the town **2** *(dans l'espace ou le temps)* en premier l. in the first place, first of all, first(ly); c'est le saumon que je mettrais en premier l. I would put salmon first; peut-être devrais-tu lui poser la question en premier l. perhaps you should put the question to him first; en troisième l. third(ly); en dernier l. last of all, last(ly), finally; en temps et l. at the proper time and place; en son l. in due course **3** lieux *(local)* premises; *(d'un accident, d'un crime)* scene; avant de quitter ces lieux before leaving the premises; quitter *ou* vider les lieux to vacate the premises; la police est sur les lieux de l'accident the police are at the scene of the accident; quand je suis arrivé sur les lieux (du crime) when I arrived on the scene/at the scene of the crime; j'étais sur les lieux bien avant vous I was there well before you; rendez-vous immédiatement sur les lieux go there immediately; *Litt* il vous faut prendre congé du maître de ces lieux it's time to bid your host farewell; *Litt* ces lieux de tristesse this place of sorrow **4** avoir l. to take place; la réunion aura l. à ... the meeting will take place *or* be held at ... **5** *(raisons)* il y a (tout) l./j'ai tout l. de supposer que ... + *ind* there are/I have (good) grounds for supposing that ..., there is/I have (every) reason to suppose that ...; il y a l. d'attendre it would be advisable *or* as well to wait; je vous écrirai s'il y a l. I'll write to you if necessary; donner l. à *(une querelle, des problèmes)* to cause, to give rise to; son retour a donné l. à une réunion de famille his return was the occasion for a family gathering; donner l. à des désagréments to cause inconvenience; tout donne l. de croire que ... everything leads me/us/*etc or* there is every reason to believe that ... **6** *(fonction)* tenir l. de qch to take the place of sth; elle lui a tenu l. de mère she has been a mother to him **7** au l. de instead of, *Fml* in lieu of; au l. de te plaindre instead of complaining; au l. de cela, elle ... but instead she ...; *Litt* au l. que + *sub* instead of + *gerund*
▸▸ *Vieilli* lieux (d'aisances) lavatory; l. commun commonplace; l. de départ point of departure; l. de destination destination; l. d'émission place of issue; *Math* l. géométrique locus; l. de livraison point of delivery; l. de naissance place of birth; *Fin* l. de paiement place of payment; l. public public place; l. de rassemblement assembly point; l. de réception place of receipt; l. de rencontre meeting place; l. de rendez-vous meeting place; quel est le l. de rendez-vous? where are we/they/*etc* meeting?; *Cin* l. de tournage location; l. de travail place of work; sur le l. de travail in the workplace; l. de vacances holiday resort; l. de vente point of sale

lieu², *pl* lieus NM *(poisson)* l. jaune pollack, pollock; l. noir coalfish

lieu(-)dit, *pl* lieux(-)dits NM (named) place, locality

lieue [ljø] NF *(mesure)* league; *Naut* l. marine league; j'étais à cent *ou* mille lieues de penser/croire que ... I would never (in a million years) have dreamt/believed that ...

lieur, -euse [ljœr, -øz] *Agr*N *Arch (de gerbes, de bottes etc)* binder
NF lieuse *(machine)* (mechanical) sheaf binder

lieutenant [ljøtnɑ̃] NM **1** *Mil* lieutenant; *Aviat* flying officer, *Am* first lieutenant; *(dans la marine marchande)* mate; *Naut* premier l. second mate; *Naut* l. de vaisseau lieutenant **2** *(proche collaborateur)* right-hand man

lieutenant-colonel, *pl* lieutenants-colonels NM *Mil* lieutenant-colonel; *Aviat* wing commander

lièvre [ljɛvr] NM hare; *Fig* courir deux lièvres à la fois to try to do two things at once; *Culin* pâté de l. hare pâté

lift [lift] NM *Sport* topspin; faire un l. to give a ball topspin, to put topspin on a ball

lifter [lifte] VT **1** *Sport* l. une balle to give a ball topspin, to put topspin on a ball **2** *(faire un lifting à)* to perform a face lift on; *Fig (rénover)* to give a face lift to, to face-lift

liftier [liftje] NM lift attendant, *Am* elevator operator

lifting [liftiŋ] NM *Chir, Fig* face lift; elle s'est fait faire un l. she's had a face lift

ligament [ligamɑ̃] NM *Anat* ligament

ligature [ligatyr] NF **1** *(fait d'attacher)* tying, binding; la l. des greffes the binding of (the) grafts **2** *Élec (au moyen d'un fil, câble)* splice **3** *Chir, Typ* ligature; l. des trompes tying of tubes

ligaturer [ligatyre] VT *(attacher)* to bind; *Élec (câble, fil)* to splice; *Chir* to ligature, to tie; *Typ* to ligature

lige [liʒ] ADJ *Hist* liege

ligérien, -ienne [liʒerjɛ̃, -jɛn] ADJ from the Loire

light [lajt] ADJ INV *(plat, préparation)* light, low-fat; *(boisson)* light, slimline

lignage [liɲaʒ] NM **1** *Arch* lineage, descent **2** *Typ* linage, lineage

---
LIGNE [liɲ]

| line **1–10, 13** ▪ outline **3** ▪ route **6** |
| ▪ range **10** |

NF **1** *(trait)* line; l. droite straight line; l. brisée broken line; tracer une l. à main levée to draw a line freehand; les lignes de la main the lines of the hand; votre l. de vie/de cœur est courte you have a short life-/heart-line; avancer en l. droite to advance in a straight line; *Mus* l. supplémentaire ledger line; *Naut* la l. (équatoriale) the line, the Equator; passer la l. (équatoriale) to cross the line; l. de coke line of coke; *TV* définition de 625 lignes definition of 625 lines **2** *(d'écriture)* line; le prof m'a donné cent lignes *(en punition)* the teacher gave me a hundred lines; elle m'a juste envoyé deux lignes she just dropped me a line; je vous envoie ces quelques lignes pour vous donner les dernières nouvelles this is just a note to give you the latest news; *Fig* lire entre les lignes to read between the lines; aller à la l. to begin a new line *or* a new paragraph; à la l. *(en dictant)* new paragraph, new line; passer *ou* sauter une l. to leave a line; être payé à la l. to be paid by the line; tirer à la l. to pad (out) an article *(because it is being paid by the line)*; *Fig* mettre sur la même l. to compare; sa rapidité et son intelligence sont à mettre sur la même l. he is as quick as he is intelligent, his speed is matched by his intelligence; *Fig* entrer en l. de compte to be taken into consideration; les sentiments ne doivent pas entrer en l. de compte dans ton jugement feelings should not influence *or* enter into your decision; cela n'entre pas en l. de compte that doesn't come *or* enter into it; faire entrer un facteur en l. de compte to take a factor into account; c'est un facteur à faire entrer en l. de compte it's something to be considered *or* taken into account *or* consideration

3 *(contour, silhouette)* (out)line; la l. du nez the line *or* contour of the nose; la pureté des lignes purity of line; la l. élégante d'une voiture the elegant lines of a car; garder/soigner sa l. to keep/watch one's waistline *or* one's figure; avoir la l. to have a good figure; perdre la l. to lose one's figure **4** *(rangée)* line; se mettre en l. to line up; plantés en l. planted in a line *or* row; *Mil, Fig* en première l. in the front line; *Fig* sur toute la l. all along the line **5** *(direction, règle)* line; redéfinir sa l. d'action to adopt a different line *or* course of action; la l. du parti communiste the communist party line; *Fig* grandes lignes d'une œuvre broad *or* general outline(s) of a work; *Journ* l. éditoriale editorial policy, editorial line; je vais vous expliquer le projet dans ses grandes lignes I'll explain the broad outline(s) of the project to you **6** *(transports)*, *Aviat (destination)* route; *Rail* line; *Rail* grandes lignes main lines; l. maritime/aérienne shipping line/airline; *Aviat* lignes intérieures domestic services; *(destinations)* domestic routes; *Aviat* nous espérons vous revoir sur nos lignes we hope we will soon have the pleasure of welcoming you on board again; l. d'autobus bus service; *(parcours)* bus route; il n'y a que deux lignes de bus qui fonctionnent la nuit there are only two late-night bus services; l. de banlieue commuter service; *Aviat* l. radiale minor domestic air route; *Aviat* l. transversale domestic or international air route not serving the capital **7** *Élec* (power) line; l. télégraphique telegraph line **8** *Tél* line; l. téléphonique telephone line; être en l. *(téléphonique)* to be on a call; la l. est occupée the line is engaged *or esp Am* busy; la l. a été coupée I've/we've/*etc* been cut off; il y a quelqu'un sur la l. there's someone on the line; vous êtes en l. you're connected, you're through; il est déjà en l. he's on another line; l. commutée dial-up line; l. directe accessible 24 heures sur 24 twenty-four-hour hotline; l. extérieure outside line; l. ouverte open line; l. principale switchboard line, main line; l. privée private line; l. spécifique dedicated line; l. téléphonique directe direct dial telephone **9** *(fil)* line; *Pêche* (fishing) line; planter des arbres à la l. to plant trees straight by using a line *or* a cord **10** *Com* line, range; l. de produits line of products, product line; Lancôme lance une nouvelle l. de cosmétiques Lancôme are launching a new line *or* range of cosmetics; l. pour hommes range for men **11** *(filiation)* descendre en l. directe *ou* en droite l. de ... to be directly descended from ..., to be descended in a direct line from ... **12** *Can (mesure)* line, = 2.3 mm **13** *Ordinat* line; en l. on line; sur l. on line; hors l. off line; changer de l. to do a line feed; l. de commande command line; *(type de commande)* line command; l. d'état status line; l. louée leased line; l. ouverte open line; l. RNIS ISDN line; l. spécialisée dedicated line; l. vide blank line
▸▸ l. d'arrivée finishing line; l. d'attaque line of attack; l. de bataille line of battle, fighting line; *Aut* l. blanche white line, *Am* yellow line; l. de changement de date *ou* de jour International Date Line; *Naut* l. de charge load line; l. de combat line of battle; l. continue *(aussi sur la route)* continuous line; *Fin* l. de cotation line of quotation; *Fin* l. de crédit line of credit, credit line; l. de découvert line of credit, credit line; *Fin* l. de démarcation boundary; *Mil* demarcation line; l. de départ starting line; l. directrice keynote, thrust; l. discontinue *(sur la route)* broken line; *Aut* l. d'échappement exhaust sys-

tem; *Ordinat* **l.-écran**, *pl* **lignes-écran** screen line; *Naut* **l. de flottaison** waterline; **l. de fond** *Pêche* ledger line; *Tennis* base line; **lignes de force** *(grandes lignes)* dominating *or* guiding principles; *Phys* lines of force; *Mil* **l. de front** front line; **l. à haute tension** high-tension wire *or* line; **l. d'horizon** (line of the) horizon; *Aut* **l. jaune** white line, *Am* yellow line; *Hist* **L. Maginot** Maginot Line; **l. magnétique** magnetic *or* black strip; *Com* **l. maritime de conférence** conference line; **l. médiane** centre line; **l. de mire** line of sight; *Fam (d'un fusil à lunette)* sights; *Fig* **avoir qn dans sa l. de mire** to have sb in one's sights; **l. du partage des eaux** watershed; *Typ* **l. de pointillé** dotted line; *Mus* **l. de portée** stave line; **l. de sonde** plumb line; **l. de substitution** backup line; **l. de tir** line of fire; *Ftbl* **l. de touche** touch line; *Typ* **l. veuve** widow; *Mil* **l. de visée** line of sight

lignée [liɲe] NF (line of) descendants; *(origine)* line, lineage; **une nombreuse l.** a large number of descendants; **ce clan est très fier de sa nombreuse l. de combattants** the clan is very proud of its many warrior descendants; **de bonne l. allemande** of good German stock; *Fig* **un philosophe dans la l. de Russell** a philosopher in the tradition of Russell

ligneux, -euse [liɲø, -øz] ADJ ligneous, woody

lignite [liɲit] NM *Minér* lignite, brown coal

ligoter [ligɔte] VT to tie up; **être ligoté à qch** to be tied to sth

ligue [lig] NF league, confederacy; *Hist* **la (Sainte) L.** the (Holy Catholic) League; *Hist* **L. des droits de l'homme** = organization set up in 1898 to defend Dreyfus

liguer [lige] VT *(nations, clans etc)* to league together; **être ligué avec qn** to be in league with sb
▪ VPR **se liguer** to form a league (**avec** with, **contre** against); **ils se liguent contre moi** they're ganging up on me

ligueur, -euse [ligœr, -øz] N member of a league

lilas [lila] NM *Bot* lilac
▪ ADJ INV lilac

lilliputien, -ienne [lilipysjɛ̃, -jɛn] ADJ Lilliputian
▪ N **L.** Lilliputian

lillois, -oise [lilwa, -waz] ADJ of/from Lille
▪ N **L.** *(natif)* native of Lille; *(habitant)* inhabitant of Lille

Lima [lima] N Lima

limace [limas] NF **1** *(mollusque)* slug; *Fam* **c'est une vraie l.** he's such a slowcoach *or Am* slowpoke, *Am* he's as slow as molasses in winter **2** *Arg (chemise)* shirt

limaçon [limasɔ̃] NM **1** *Vieilli* snail **2** *Anat (de l'oreille)* cochlea

limage [limaʒ] NM filing (down)

limaille [limaj] NF filings; **l. de fer** iron filings

limande [limɑ̃d] NF *(poisson)* dab; **l.-sole** lemon sole; *Fam* **plate comme une l.** *(d'une femme)* as flat as a pancake

limbe [lɛ̃b] NM **1** *Astron, Math* limb **2** *Bot (de feuille)* lamina, limb **3** *Rel* **les Limbes** limbo; *Fig* **dans les limbes** in (a state of) limbo

lime[1] [lim] NF **1** *(outil)* file; **l. sourde** dead-smooth file; **l. à ongles** nail file; **l. émeri** emery board; **aiguiser un outil à la l.** to file up a tool **2** *(mollusque)* lima

lime[2] NF *Bot* lime

limer [lime] VT **1** *(réduire)* to file (down); *(polir)* to file (up); **l. les barreaux** to file through the bars **2** *Vulg* to screw
▪ VI *Vulg* to screw, to have one's end away
▪ VPR **se limer se l. les ongles** to file one's nails

limier [limje] NM *(chien)* bloodhound; *Fig* sleuth; *Bourse* investigator

liminaire [liminɛr] ADJ *(note, remarque etc)* introductory

limitatif, -ive [limitatif, -iv] ADJ limiting, restrictive, restricting; **dispositions limitatives** restrictions; **une liste non limitative** an open-ended list; **la liste n'est pas limitative** the list is not exhaustive

limitation [limitasjɔ̃] NF limitation, restriction; **l. des armements** arms limitation; **l. des naissances** birth control, family planning; **l. des salaires** imposition of wage restraints; *(volontaire)* (voluntary) wage restraint; **l. de vitesse** speed limit; **ce test se fait sans l. de temps** there is no time limit for the test; **l. de poids** weight limit; **l. des prix** price restrictions *or* controls; **l. de responsabilité** limitation of responsibility

limite [limit] NF **1** *(de pays, champ etc)* boundary; **les limites d'un terrain de football** the boundary (lines) of a football pitch; **marquer les limites du terrain** to mark out the ground; **à la l. du jardin, il y a une forêt** just beyond the garden there is a forest
2 *(de pouvoir, compréhension etc)* limit; **fixer** *ou* **imposer des limites à l'autorité de qn** to set limits *or* bounds on sb's authority; **son ambition/sa générosité/son amour pour elle ne connaît pas de limites** his ambition/his generosity/his love for her knows no bounds; **je connais mes limites** I know my limits; **il y a des limites!** there are limits!; **ma patience a des limites!** there are limits to my patience!, my patience is wearing thin!; **la bonté a des limites** there are limits to my/her/etc kindness; **mettre une l./des limites à qch** to set a limit/limits to sth, to limit sth; **franchir** *ou* **dépasser les limites** to go too far, to be out of line; **l'Irak a franchi les limites de l'horreur** the horror of what is happening in Iraq is beyond belief; **vous avez vraiment dépassé les limites du supportable** what you did is quite intolerable; **c'est à la l. de la vulgarité/du supportable** it's bordering on vulgarity/the unacceptable; **je vous aiderai dans les limites du possible** I'll do everything possible *or* everything I possibly can to help you, I'll help you as far as is humanly possible; **dans les limites du raisonnable** within reasonable limits; **dans les limites du sujet** within the limits of the subject; **veuillez rester dans les limites du sujet** please keep to the subject; **dans la l. des places disponibles** subject to availability; **dans la l. des stocks disponibles** while stocks last; **dans une certaine l.** up to a point, to a certain extent; **je suis prêt à vous prêter de l'argent dans une certaine l.** I am ready to lend you money up to a point; **à la l., j'accepterais de le voir** if pushed *or* if I have to, I'll agree to see him; **ça va? – oui, à la l.** is that OK? – yes, just about; **se battre/résister/travailler jusqu'à la dernière l.** to fight/resist/work to the last; **il est à la l. de ses forces** he's completely exhausted, he's at the limit of his endurance; **sans limites** unbounded, limitless; *Boxe* **gagner avant la l.** to win inside the distance
3 *Math* limit, limiting value
▪ ADJ **cas l.** borderline case; **vitesse l.** maximum speed; **charge l. d'un pont** maximum load of a bridge; **date l.** deadline; *(pour candidature etc)* deadline, closing date; *Fam* **50 euros, c'est le prix l. que j'accepterais de payer** 50 euros is my top price; *Fam* **je ne lui ai pas mis une claque, mais c'était l.** I didn't slap him but I came very close to it *or* but it was touch and go; *Fam* **elle est l., ta dissertation** your essay's a borderline case *or* only just this side of acceptable; *Fam* **je suis un peu l. financièrement** I'm a bit short (of cash), my bank account's not very healthy;

Fam **j'ai trouvé qu'il était l. avec elle** I thought he was a bit hard on her
▸▸ **l. d'âge** age limit; **l. de crédit** credit limit; *Tech* **l. d'élasticité** elastic limit; *Tech* **l. élastique** yield point; **l. d'endettement** borrowing limit; **l. de poids** weight limit; *Bourse* **l. de position** position limit; **l. de rupture** breaking *or* yield point

limité [limite] ADJ **1** limited; **vitesse limitée à 60 km/heure** speed restricted to 60km/hour; **en temps l.** in a limited amount of time; **n'avoir qu'une confiance limitée dans une machine/l'honnêteté de qn** to have a limited amount of confidence in a machine/a person's honesty; **avec lui, la conversation est limitée** conversation is limited with him, you can't have much of a conversation with him; *Fam* **il est un peu l. ce mec** the guy's a bit thick **2** *Can* Limited, Ltd; **Desrochers et Cie limitée** Desrochers and Co. Ltd.

limiter [limite] VT **1** *(délimiter) (pays, territoire etc)* to bound, to mark the bounds of **2** *(restreindre)* to limit, to restrict; *(pouvoir, droits etc de qn)* to set bounds *or* limits to; *Fam* **l. les dégâts** to limit the damage; **je ne connaissais pas vraiment le sujet de l'examen, mais j'ai limité les dégâts** I didn't really know anything about the exam subject but I managed to make something of it; **l. la production** to limit production
▪ VPR **se limiter il faut apprendre à se l.** you have to learn to limit yourself *or* to keep within limits; **quand il commence à boire, il est incapable de se l.** once he starts drinking he doesn't know when to stop; **se l. à ...** to limit *or* restrict *or* confine oneself to ...; **elle se limita à dire que ...** she confined herself to saying that ...; **son œuvre se limite à quelques essais** his works amount to no more than a few essays; **l'intérêt touristique de la ville se limite à un château en ruines** the only tourist attraction in the town is a ruined castle, all the town has to offer in the way of tourist attractions is a ruined castle

limiteur [limitœr] NM *Aut* limiter; **l. de freinage** *(correcteur)* pressure limiter; **l. de régime** over-run valve, rev limiter

limitrophe [limitrɔf] ADJ adjacent (**de** to), bordering (**de** on); **les pays limitrophes** the neighbouring *or Am* neighboring countries; **être l. d'un autre pays** to border on another country

limogeage [limɔʒaʒ] NM *(d'officier)* superseding; *(de fonctionnaire)* dismissal

limoger [limɔʒe] VT *(officier)* to supersede; *(fonctionnaire)* to dismiss

limon[1] [limɔ̃] NM **1** *(alluvion)* silt, *Spéc* alluvium; **le l. employé comme engrais** silt used as a fertilizer **2** *Géol* limon

limon[2] NM **1** *(brancard)* shaft **2** *Constr (d'escalier)* stringboard, stringer

limon[3] NM *Bot, Arch* lemon

limonade [limɔnad] NF *(boisson gazeuse)* (fizzy) lemonade

limonadier, -ière [limɔnadje, -jɛr] N **1** *Ind* soft drinks manufacturer **2** *Arch (cafetier)* café owner

limoner [limɔne] VI *Can Fam* **1** *(se plaindre)* to moan, to whinge; *(pleurnicher)* to whinge **2** *(hésiter)* to dither

limoneux, -euse [limɔnø, -øz] ADJ *(eau etc)* muddy, silty; *Géol* alluvial

limousin, -ine[1] [limuzɛ̃, -in] ADJ of/from (the province of) Limousin
▪ N **L.** *(natif)* native of (the province of) Limousin; *(inhabitant)* inhabitant of (the province of) Limousin
▪ NM *Ling* Limousin dialect

limousine[2] NF *Aut* limousine

limpide [lɛ̃pid] ADJ *(quartz, eau etc)* limpid, clear; *(explication)* clear, lucid; *(style)* limpid, lucid; **un regard l.** a clear *or Litt* limpid expression

limpidité [lɛ̃pidite] NF *(de quartz, eau)* clarity, limpidity; *(d'explication)* clarity, lucidity; *(de style)* limpidity, lucidity; *(de regard)* limpidity

lin [lɛ̃] NM **1** *(plante)* flax; **graine de l.** linseed; **huile de l.** linseed oil **2** *Tex* **(tissu/toile de) l.** linen

linceul [lɛ̃sœl] NM winding sheet, shroud

linéaire [lineɛr] ADJ **1** *Math* linear **2** dessin **l.** geometrical drawing **3** *Fig Litt* **récit l.** linear narrative
▪ NM *(dans un magasin)* shelf-space

linge [lɛ̃ʒ] NM **1** *(draps etc)* linen; **gros l.** household linen; **armoire à l.** linen cupboard **2** *(dessous)* **(petit) l.** underwear; *Fig Fam* **c'est du beau l.** they're society people **3** *(vêtements)* clothes **4** *(lessive)* washing; **corde à l.** clothesline; **corbeille à l.** laundry basket **5** *(morceau de tissu)* cloth **6** *Suisse (serviette de toilette)* towel
▸▸ **l. de corps** underwear; **l. de maison** household linen; **l. de table** table linen

lingère [lɛ̃ʒɛr] NF linen-keeper

lingerie [lɛ̃ʒri] NF **1** *(dessous féminins)* underwear, lingerie **2** *(pour rangement)* linen room; *(pour entretien)* laundry

lingette [lɛ̃ʒɛt] NF *(pour bébés)* baby wipe

lingot [lɛ̃go] NM **1** *(masse de métal)* ingot; **l. d'or** gold bar *or* ingot; *Fin* **or/argent en lingots** (gold/silver) bullion **2** *Typ* space, slug

lingual, -ale, -aux, -ales [lɛ̃gwal, -o] ADJ *Anat, Ling* lingual

linguiste [lɛ̃gɥist] N linguist

linguistique [lɛ̃gɥistik] ADJ linguistic; **un séjour l.** a stay in a foreign country *(for the purposes of learning the language)*; **une communauté l.** a speech community
▪ NF linguistics

linguistiquement [lɛ̃gɥistikmɑ̃] ADV linguistically

liniment [linimɑ̃] NM *Méd* liniment

lino [lino] NM *Fam (abrév* **linoléum**) lino

linoléum [linɔleɔm] NM linoleum

linon [linɔ̃] NM *Tex* lawn

linotte [linɔt] NF *(oiseau)* linnet; *Fam* **tête de l.** scatterbrain

linotype® [linɔtip] NF *Typ* Linotype®

linotypie [linɔtipi] NF *Typ* Linotype® setting

linotypiste [linɔtipist] N *Typ* linotypist

linteau, -eaux [lɛ̃to] NM *Constr* lintel

lion [ljɔ̃] NM **1** lion; **la part du l.** the lion's share; *Fam* **il a mangé** *ou Arg* **bouffé du l.** he's being all hyper; **tourner comme un l. en cage** to prowl around; **l. de mer** sea lion VOIR GRAMMAIRE A12 **2** *Arch, Litt* celebrity; *(littéraire)* lion **3** *Astron, Astrol* **le L.** Leo; **être (du signe du) L.** to be (a) Leo

lionceau, -eaux [ljɔ̃so] NM lion cub

lionne [ljɔn] NF lioness; *Vieilli Fig* **une l.** a handsome *or* elegant-looking woman

lipase [lipaz] NF *Biol, Chimie* lipase

lipide [lipid] NM *Biol, Chimie* lipid

liposome [lipozom] NM *Biol, Chimie* liposome

liposuccion [liposysjɔ̃] NF liposuction

lippe [lip] NF (thick) lower lip; **faire la l.** *(faire la moue)* to pout; *(bouder)* to sulk

lippu [lipy] ADJ *(personne)* thick-lipped; *(lèvre)* thick

liquéfaction [likefaksjɔ̃] NF liquefaction

liquéfiable [likefjabl] ADJ liquefiable

liquéfiant [likefjɑ̃] ADJ liquefactive, liquefying

liquéfier [likefje] [*pr sub, impf* n. **liquéfiions,** v. **liquéfiiez**) VT to liquefy

▪ VPR **se liquéfier** to liquefy; *Fig* to be drained (of energy); *(avoir peur)* to turn to jelly

liquette [likɛt] NF *Fam* shirt

liqueur [likœr] NF **1** *(spiritueux)* liqueur; **verre à l.** liqueur glass; **l. de cassis** blackcurrant liqueur **2** *Can* **l. (douce)** soft drink **3** *Chimie* solution; **l. titrée** standard solution; *Méd* **l. de Dakin** Dakin's solution

> Il faut noter que le terme **liquor**, utilisé en anglais américain, est un faux ami. Il signifie **alcool**.

liquidateur, -trice [likidatœr, -tris] N **1** *Jur* liquidator; **l. judiciaire** official liquidator **2** *Bourse* **l. officiel** official assignee

liquidation [likidasjɔ̃] NF **1** *Jur* liquidation; **l. forcée/volontaire** compulsory/voluntary liquidation; **l. judiciaire** official receivership; **l. des biens** liquidation of assets; **entrer en l.** to go into liquidation; **mettre en l.** to put into liquidation, to liquidate **2** *(de comptes)* settlement, clearing; *Bourse* settlement; *Bourse (d'une position)* liquidation; *Bourse* **l. en espèces** cash settlement; **chambre de l.** (bankers') clearing house; *Compta* **l. de fin de mois/de quinzaine** end-of-month/fortnightly settlement **3** *Com (de stocks)* selling off; **l. totale** *(sur panneau)* closing down sale, everything must go **4** *Fam (fait de tuer)* liquidation, elimination

liquide [likid] ADJ liquid; **la soupe est trop l.** the soup is too watery *or* too thin; **argent l.** cash, ready money, hard cash; *Fin* **actif l.** liquid asset; *Fin* **peu l.** illiquid
▪ NM **1** *(substance)* liquid, fluid; **il ne pourra prendre que des liquides pendant une semaine** he'll be on liquids for a week **2** *Fig (espèces)* (ready) cash; **je n'ai pas assez de l.** I haven't enough (ready) cash; **vous payez par chèque ou en l.?** are you paying by cheque or (in) cash?
▪ NF *Ling* liquid
▸▸ *Méd* **l. céphalo-rachidien** cerebrospinal fluid; **l. correcteur** correction fluid; *Aut* **l. de direction assistée** power steering fluid; *Aut* **l. de frein** brake fluid; *Aut* **l. hydraulique de frein** hydraulic brake fluid; **l. de nettoyage** cleaning fluid; **l. de refroidissement** coolant, coolant fluid; *Méd* **l. synovial** synovial fluid; *Aut* **l. pour transmission automatique** automatic transmission fluid

liquider [likide] VT **1** *Jur (affaire)* to liquidate, to wind up **2** *(compte)* to settle, to clear; *Bourse (une position)* to liquidate, to close out; **l. une dette** to pay off a debt **3** *Fam (tuer)* to liquidate, to eliminate; **l. une tâche** to get through a task, to get a task finished **4** *(stock)* to sell off; **ils liquident chez Martin** they're selling off stock at Martin's

liquidité [likidite] NF liquidity; *Fin* **liquidités** liquid assets; **liquidités excédentaires** excess liquidities; **liquidités obligatoires** mandatory liquid assets

liquoreux, -euse [likɔrø, -øz] ADJ *(vin)* liqueur-like

lire[1] [lir] *(prp* lisant; *pp* lu; *pr ind* je lis, il lit; *impf* je lisais; *p hist* je lus; *fu* je lirai) VT **1** *(livre, auteur, disquette, données, musique etc)* to read; *(bande son, image)* to reproduce; **elle sait l.** she can read; **l. tout haut** *ou* **à haute voix** to read aloud; **l. en diagonale** to scan, to cast a quick eye over, to skim through; **l. qch dans un livre** to read sth in a book; **l. qch à qn** to read sth (out) to sb; **avoir beaucoup lu** to be well read; **c'est un auteur qui est très lu** he's a widely read author; **lu et approuvé** read and approved; **dans l'attente de vous l.** *(dans une lettre)* hoping to hear from you soon; *Fig* **l. entre les lignes** to read between the lines; *Ordinat* **l. au scanneur** to scan; **l. les épreuves de tirage** to proof-read

2 *(interpréter)* to read; **on peut le l. de deux façons différentes** you can read it two different ways

3 *(déchiffrer)* **l. dans la pensée de qn** to read sb's thoughts; **l. dans le jeu de qn** to know sb's game, to know what sb is up to; **elle a voulu me l. les lignes de la main** she wanted to read my hand; **l. dans une boule de cristal** to read a crystal ball; **l. dans le marc de café** ≃ to read the tea leaves

4 *Fig (deviner) (sur un visage, dans un regard)* to read
▪ VPR **se lire 1** **ce livre se lit bien** *ou* **se laisse l.** it's a readable book, this book is very readable *or* a good read; **ce roman se lit en une soirée** this novel can be read in an evening; **ce genre de fautes se lit couramment** you read this sort of mistake a lot **2** *(se deviner)* **cela se lit sur votre visage/dans vos yeux** it shows in your face/in your eyes, it's written all over your face/you can read it in your eyes

lire[2] NF *(monnaie)* lira

lis [lis] NM lily; **l. blanc** white lily; **l. des vallées** lily of the valley; **l. d'eau** *ou* **d'étang** water lily; **teint de l.** lily-white complexion

Lisbonne [lizbɔn] N Lisbon

liseré [lizre], **liséré** [lizere] NM *Couture* border, edging

liseron [lizrɔ̃] NM bindweed, convolvulus

liseur, -euse [lizœr, -øz] N reader
▪ NF **liseuse 1** *(couverture amovible)* book cover **2** *(vêtement de femme)* (lady's) bed jacket **3** *(en train, en avion)* reading light

lisibilité [lizibilite] NF **1** *(d'une écriture)* legibility **2** *(d'un texte, fichier informatique)* readability

lisible [lizibl] ADJ **1** *(qu'on peut déchiffrer)* legible, readable; **l. par ordinateur** machine-readable **2** *(qu'on peut comprendre)* readable

lisiblement [liziblǝmɑ̃] ADV legibly

lisière [lizjɛr] NF **1** *(de champ, forêt)* edge, border **2** *(bande de tissu)* selvage, selvedge

lissage [lisaʒ] NM *(de pierre etc)* smoothing, polishing; *(de cuir)* sleeking; *(de papier etc)* glazing; *Ordinat* **l. de courbes/des caractères** curve/character smoothing

lisse[1] [lis] NF *Naut* **1** *(de coque)* ribband; **lisses de l'avant** harpings **2** *(du bastingage)* handrail

lisse[2] ADJ smooth; *(poli)* polished; *(pneu)* bald; **cheveux lisses** sleek hair

lisser [lise] VT *(cheveux)* to smooth down, to sleek down; *(pli)* to smooth out; *(pierre etc)* to smooth, to polish; *(cuir)* to sleek; *(papier etc)* to glaze
▪ VPR **se lisser se l. les plumes** *(d'un oiseau)* to preen its feathers *or* itself

lisseur [lisœr] NM **l. de fontes** font smoother

listage [listaʒ] NM *Ordinat* listing, printout

liste [list] NF list; **dresser/faire une l.** to draw up/make (out) a list; **être en tête/en fin de l.** to be at the top/the bottom of the list; **l. officielle des taux** schedule of charges; *Tél* **être sur (la) l. rouge** to be ex-directory, *Am* to have an unlisted number, to be unlisted
▸▸ **l. des actionnaires** list of shareholders; **l. d'adresses** mailing list, address list; **l. des arrivées** arrivals list; **l. d'attente** waiting list, waitlist; **l. bloquée** set list of candidates *(which electors cannot modify)*; **l. civile** civil list; **l. de clients** customer *or* client list; *(d'hôtel)* guest list; *Com* **l. de colisage** packing list; **l. commune** joint list (of candidates); **l. des correspondants** list of correspondents; **l. des départs** departure list; **l. de diffusion** mailing list; **l. électorale** electoral roll; **l. d'émargement** payroll; **l. d'envoi** mailing list; *Ordinat* **l. de fichiers à imprimer** print list, print queue; **l. de mariage** wedd-

ing list; **l. de naissance** = list of presents requested by the parents of a newborn baby; **l. noire** blacklist; **mettre qn sur la l. noire** to blacklist sb; **l. d'opposition** list of opposition candidates; *Pol* **l. panachée** = ballot paper in which a voter votes for candidates from different lists rather than for a list as a whole; *TV, Cin* **l. des prises de vue** shot list; **l. de prix** price list; *Ordinat* **l. à puces** bulleted list; *Ordinat* **l. rapide** draft; **l. récapitulative** checklist; **l. des réservations** reservations list; **l. des signatures autorisées** authorized signatory list; *Ordinat* **l. de signets** bookmark list; **l. des tarifs** price list, tariff; *(de transport)* fare list

listel, -els, listeau, -eaux [listɛl, -o] NM **1** *Archit etc* listel, fillet **2** *(de pièce de monnaie)* rim

lister [liste] VT to list

listériose [listerjoz] NF *Méd* listeriosis

listing [listiŋ] NM *Ordinat* listing, printout

lit [li] NM **1** *(meuble)* bed; **l. moelleux/dur** soft/hard bed *or* mattress; **l. de fer** iron bedstead; **aller au l.** to go to bed; **se mettre au l.** to get into bed; **l. pour deux personnes, grand l.** double bed; **mettre un enfant au l.** to put a child to bed; **au l. les enfants!** time for bed, children!, bedtime, children!; **au saut du l.** just after one has got up; **être au l.** to be in bed; **prendre le l.** to take to one's bed; **garder le l.** to stay in bed; **tirer qn du l.** to get sb out of bed; **je ne te tire** *ou* **sors pas du l. au moins?** I hope I didn't get you out of bed; **faire le l.** to make the bed; *Fig* **faire le l. de** to pave the way for; **faire l. à part** to sleep in separate beds; **un hôtel de 200 lits** a 200-bed hotel, a hotel with 200 beds; **chambre à un l./à deux lits** single-/twin-bedded room; **mourir dans son l.** to die in (one's) bed; **bois de l.** bedstead

2 *Jur* **enfant du second l.** child by one's second marriage

3 *(couche)* *(d'argile, de pierre etc)* bed, layer; **l. de cendres** bed of ashes; *Culin* **placer les filets sur un l. d'épinards** place the fillets on a bed of spinach

4 *(de rivière etc)* bed; **la rivière est sortie de son l.** the river has burst its banks

5 *Naut (de marée etc)* set; **être dans le l. de marée** to be in the tideway; **dans le l. du vent** in the wind's eye

▸▸ **l. à baldaquin** canopied four-poster (bed), tester bed; **l.-bateau,** *pl* **lits-bateaux** = bed with curved sides, higher at the ends; **l.-cage,** *pl* **lits-cages** cot, *Am* crib; **l. de camp** camp bed, *Am* cot; **l. en cathédrale** = bed placed upright with sleeper in it; **l. clos** box bed; **l. à colonnes** four-poster (bed); **l. conjugal** marital bed; *Litt* **l. de douleur** sick bed; **l. d'enfant** cot, *Am* crib; **l. escamotable** Murphy bed; **l. de long séjour** *(dans un hôtel)* long-stay bed; **l. majeur** *(d'un fleuve)* flood plain; *Tech* high water *or* bed; *Tech* **l. mineur** mean water *or* bed; *Vieilli* **l. de misère** childbed; **l. de mort: être sur son l. de mort** to be on one's death bed; **l.-nacelle,** *pl* **lits-nacelles** carry cot; **l. pliant** folding *or* foldaway bed; **l. en portefeuille** apple-pie bed; **l. de repos** couch; **l. une place** single bed; **lits gigognes** beds that fit into each other; **lits jumeaux** twin beds; **lits superposés** bunk beds, bunks

litanie [litani] NF **1** *Rel* **litanies** litany **2** *Péj (de griefs, plaintes)* litany; **c'est toujours la même l.** it's the same old story

litchi [litʃi] NM *(fruit)* lychee, litchi

liteau, -eaux [lito] NM **1** *Constr* batten, rail, ribband **2** *Tex (sur linge de table etc)* band, stripe

litée [lite] NF *(d'animaux)* litter

literie [litri] NF bedding

lithiase [litjaz] NF *Méd* lithiasis

lithine [litin] NF *Chimie* lithia

lithiné [litine] ADJ **eau lithinée** lithia water NMPL **lithinés** lithium salts

lithium [litjɔm] NM *Chimie* lithium

litho [lito] NF *Fam (abrév* **lithographie***)* litho

lithographe [litograf] N lithographer

lithographie [litografi] NF **1** *(technique)* lithography; **l. offset** offset lithography **2** *(estampe)* lithograph

lithographier [litografje] VT *(pr sub, impf* n. **lithographiions,** v. **lithographiiez***)* to lithograph

lithographique [litografik] ADJ lithographic

lithosphère [litɔsfɛr] NF *Géol* lithosphere

litière [litjer] NF **1** *(d'écurie)* litter; **la l. du chat** the cat's litter **2** *Hist (palanquin)* litter; **être porté en l.** to be carried in a litter

litige [litiʒ] NM dispute; *(poursuite)* lawsuit; *(recours à la loi)* litigation; **objet** *ou* **point de l.** bone of contention; *Jur* subject of the action; **être en l.** to be in dispute, to be disputed; **l. commercial** commercial dispute

litigieux, -euse [litiʒjø, -øz] ADJ *(affaire, héritage, contrat)* disputed, in dispute; *(question, cas)* contentious

litote [litɔt] NF *Littér* litotes, understatement

litre [litr] NM **1** *(mesure)* litre, *Am* liter **2** *(récipient d'un litre)* litre *or Am* liter bottle

litron [litrɔ̃] NM *Fam* litre *or Am* liter of wine

littéraire [literer] ADJ *(critique, prix, langue etc)* literary; **la vie l.** the literary world, literary life; **avoir l'esprit l.** to have a literary turn of mind

N **1** *(personne douée pour la littérature)* literary person **2** *(étudiant)* student of literature **3** *(professeur)* teacher of literature

littérairement [literɛrmɑ̃] ADV in literary terms; *(intéressant)* from a literary point of view

littéral, -ale, -aux, -ales [literal, -o] ADJ **1** *(traduction, sens etc)* literal; *Math* **coefficient l.** literal coefficient **2** *(par écrit)*, *Jur* **preuve littérale** documentary evidence; **arabe l.** written Arabic

littéralement [literalmɑ̃] ADV literally

littéralité [literalite] NF *Litt* literality, literalness

littérateur [literatœr] NM literary man, man of letters, *Péj* literary hack

littérature [literatyr] NF literature; **se lancer dans la l.** to embark on a literary career; **faire carrière dans la l.** to make a career in writing; **l. commerciale** sales literature; *Fig Péj* **tout ça c'est de la l.** all that's of trifling importance; **on a publié une importante l. sur le sujet** a considerable amount of literature has been published on the subject

littoral, -ale, -aux, -ales [litɔral, -o] ADJ coastal, *Spéc* littoral

NM coast(line), *Spéc* littoral

Lituanie [lityani] NF Lithuania

lituanien, -ienne [lityanjɛ̃, -jɛn] ADJ Lithuanian

NM *Ling* Lithuanian

N **L.** Lithuanian

liturgie [lityrʒi] NF *Rel* liturgy

liturgique [lityrʒik] ADJ *Rel* liturgical

livarde [livard] NF *Naut* sprit; **voile à l.** spritsail

livarot [livaro] NM *Culin* Livarot (cheese)

livide [livid] ADJ **1** *(teint)* pallid **2** *Litt (bleuâtre)* livid

lividité [lividite] NF pallor, pallidness; *Méd* **l. cadavérique** livor mortis, post-mortem lividity

living(-room), *pl* **living(-room)s** [liviŋ(-rum)] NM living room

livrable [livrabl] ADJ **1** *Com* that can be delivered; **marchandises livrables à domicile** goods delivered to your home **2** *Bourse* deliverable

livraison [livrɛzɔ̃] NF **1** *(de marchandises etc)* delivery; **l. gratuite,** *Spéc* **l. franco** free delivery, delivered free; **l. franco par nos soins** carriage paid; **payable à la l.** payable on delivery; **l. contre remboursement, paiement à la l.** *Br* cash on delivery, *Am* collect on delivery; **faire une l.** to make a delivery; **faire la l. de qch** to deliver sth; **faire la l. de pain/journaux** to deliver the bread/the newspapers; **prendre l. de qch** to take delivery of sth; **défaut de l.** non-delivery; **voiture de l.** delivery van; *Fin* **l. des titres** delivery of securities; *Com* **l. immédiate** available for delivery, ready delivery; **l. le jour même** same-day delivery; *Com* **l. à terme** future delivery, forward delivery; *Com* **l. à domicile** door-to-door delivery, home delivery; *(de journaux)* direct door delivery; **'l. à domicile'** home deliveries; **la l. est arrivée** *(marchandise)* the delivery has arrived **2** *(d'ouvrage publié en fascicules)* part

livre[1] [livr] NF **1** *(poids)* half kilo; ≃ pound; *Can* pound VOIR GRAMMAIRE A13 **2 l. (sterling)** pound (sterling) VOIR GRAMMAIRE A13 **3** *Hist (monnaie)* livre

livre[2] NM **1** *(objet)* book; **un l. sur les papillons** a book on *or* about butterflies; **connaître qch par les livres** to know sth from *or* through books; **elle a toujours le nez dans les livres** she's always got her nose in a book; **l. cartonné** *ou* **relié** hardback (book); **l. de classe** *ou* **scolaire** schoolbook; **l. de grammaire** grammar (book); **l. de lecture** reader, reading book; **l. de cuisine** cookery book, cookbook; **l. d'images/pour enfants** picture/children's book; **l. musical** musical book; **parler comme un l.** to talk like a book; **traduire un passage à l. ouvert** to translate a passage at sight; **il lit Cicéron à l. ouvert** he can read Cicero at sight

2 *(édition)* **l'industrie du l., le l.** the book trade; **les ouvriers du l.** printworkers

3 *Com (registre)* **grand l.** ledger; **tenir les livres** to keep the accounts *or* the books; **tenue des livres** book-keeping

4 *(de la Bible etc)* book; **le premier l. des 'Fables' de la Fontaine** the first book of La Fontaine's Fables

▸▸ *Compta* **l. d'achats** purchase ledger; **l. d'actionnaires** register of shareholders; **l. blanc** official report; **l. de bord** *Naut* log(-book); *Scol* (teacher's) record book; *(à la maison)* housekeeping book; **l. de caisse** cashbook; **l. de chevet** bedside book; **l. de commandes** order book; **l. de comptes** journal, ledger, account book; **l. de coupures de presse** cuttings book; *Compta* **l. des créanciers** accounts payable ledger; *Compta* **l. des débiteurs** accounts receivable ledger; *Compta* **l. de dépenses** cash book; **l. d'échéance** bill book; *Compta* **l. des effets à payer** bills payable ledger; *Compta* **l. des effets à recevoir** bills receivable ledger; **l. électronique** e-book; *Compta* **l. des entrées** purchase ledger; **l. électronique** e-book; **l. d'heures** book of hours; *Compta* **l. des inventaires** stock book; **l. journal** *Com* daybook, journal; *Compta* book of original entry; **l. de la Loi** book of the Law; **l. de messe** missal, prayer book; **l. numérique** e-book; **l. d'or** visitors' book; **l. de paie** payroll; *Compta* wages ledger; **l. de petite caisse** petty cash book; **l. de poche** paperback; **l. de prières** prayer book; **l. de prix** prize book; *Arch* **l. de raison** family record book; **l. des réclamations** claims book; *Compta* **l. des rendus** returns ledger; **l. de réservation** reservations book, hotel register; *Compta* **l. des sorties** sales ledger; *Compta* **l. de trésorerie géné-**

rale general cash book; **l. des ventes** sales ledger

livre-cassette, *pl* **livres-cassettes** NM spoken word cassette; *(pour les aveugles)* talking book

livrée [livʀe] NF **1** *(habit de domestique)* livery; **valet en l.** servant in livery, liveried servant **2** *(pelage)* coat; *(plumage)* plumage

livre-jeu, *pl* **livres-jeux** NM activity book

livrer [livʀe] VT **1** *(marchandises etc)* to deliver; **nous avons bien été livrés** we have received the delivery; **l. une commande** to fulfill an order; *Com* **l. à terme fixe** to deliver at a fixed term; **nous livrons à domicile** we deliver (anywhere) *or* to your door; **vous serez livrés dès demain** you'll receive delivery tomorrow; *Com* **livré franco domicile** delivered free at domicile

2 *(abandonner)* to abandon; *(remettre)* to deliver (à to); **l. un village au pillage/un pays à l'anarchie** to abandon a village to pillage/a country to anarchy; **l. qn à la justice** to deliver *or* hand over sb to justice *or* to the authorities; **il a finalement livré ses complices** he finally delivered up his accomplices; **l. une place forte à l'ennemi** to give up a fortress to the enemy; **l. qn à la mort** to send sb to his death; **l. qn/qch aux flammes** to commit sb/sth to the flames; *Litt* **un épouvantail livré aux vents** a scarecrow left to the mercy of the four winds; **bateau livré à la tempête** boat at the mercy of the storm; **livré à soi-même** left to oneself *or* to one's own devices

3 *(donner, dévoiler)* **l. un secret** to divulge a secret (à to); **je vous livre un secret … ** I'll let you in on a secret …; **l. ses secrets à qn** to confide one's secrets to sb; **l. un peu/beaucoup de soi-même** to reveal a little/a lot of oneself, to open up a bit/a lot; **elle livre peu d'elle-même au bureau** she doesn't reveal much of herself *or* doesn't open up much at the office

4 l. passage à qn to let sb pass; **l. bataille** *ou* **combat** to join battle (à with), to give battle (à to); *Fig* **l. bataille à la pauvreté/à la famine** to battle against poverty/famine

VPR **se livrer 1** *(se rendre)* to give oneself up (à to); **se l. à la justice** to surrender to the authorities, to give oneself up

2 *(se confier)* to open up; **se l. à qn** to confide in sb

3 *(s'abandonner à)* **se l. à un vice/à des pratiques ignobles** to indulge in a vice/disgraceful practices; **se l. à des spéculations/des plaisirs coupables** to indulge in *or* give oneself over to speculation/guilty pleasures; **se l. au désespoir** to give way to despair; **se l. à la violence** to behave violently, to turn violent; *Litt* **elle s'est livrée à son amant** she gave *or* offered herself (up) to her lover; *Arch, Litt* **se l. à la boisson** to take to drink

4 *(s'occuper à)* **se l. à des recherches** to be engaged in research; **se l. à ses occupations habituelles** to indulge in one's usual activities; **se l. à une enquête** to set up *or* hold an inquiry; **se l. à l'étude/à la lecture** to devote oneself to study/reading; **se l. à un sport** to practise a sport

livresque [livʀɛsk] ADJ **1** *(théorique)* acquired from books; **connaissances livresques** book learning **2** *Péj (esprit)* bookish

livret [livʀɛ] NM **1** *(petit livre)* booklet; **l. (de caisse) d'épargne** bankbook, passbook; **compte sur l.** savings account **2** *Mus (d'opéra)* libretto, book **3** *Suisse (table de multiplication)* multiplication table

► ► *Banque* **l. de compte** bankbook; *Banque* **l. de dépôts** deposit book, passbook; **l. d'épargne logement** *Br* ≃ building society passbook, *Am* ≃ savings and loan association passbook; *Admin* **l. de famille** = family record book for registration of births and deaths; **l. militaire** service record; **l. scolaire** school report book

livreur, -euse [livʀœʀ, -øz] N delivery man, *f* woman

LJM [ɛlʒiɛm] NF *Com (abrév* **livraison le jour même)** same-day delivery

LOA [ɛlɔa] NF *(abrév* **location avec option d'achat)** lease purchase

lob [lɔb] NM *Tennis* lob; **faire un l.** to hit a lob, to lob

lobby, *pl* **lobbies** [lɔbi] NM *Pol* lobby

lobbying [lɔbiiŋ] NM *Pol* lobbying; **faire du l.** to lobby

lobbyiste [lɔbiist] N *Pol* lobbyist

lobe [lɔb] NM **1** *Anat, Bot* lobe; **l. de l'oreille** ear lobe **2** *Archit* foil **3** *Radio* lobe

lobé [lɔbe] ADJ **1** *Bot* lobed, lobate **2** *Archit* foiled

lobectomie [lɔbɛktɔmi] NF *Chir* lobectomy

lobélie [lɔbeli] NF *Bot* lobelia

lober [lɔbe] VI *Tennis, Ftbl* to lob

VT *Ftbl* **l. le gardien de but** to lob the goalkeeper

lobotomie [lɔbɔtɔmi] NF *Chir* lobotomy; **on lui a fait une l.** he's had a lobotomy, he's been lobotomized

lobulaire [lɔbylɛʀ] ADJ *Anat* lobular

lobule [lɔbyl] NM *Anat* lobule

local, -ale, -aux, -ales [lɔkal, -o] ADJ *(autorité, radio, administration etc), Méd* local; **coutumes locales** local customs; **averses locales demain dans la matinée** scattered showers tomorrow morning; **le journal l.** the local paper; **anesthésie locale** local anaesthetic

NM **1** *(lieu, endroit) (de société, d'organisation)* premises; **l. d'habitation** dwelling; **l. professionnel** premises used for professional purposes; **locaux commerciaux** business premises; **ils cherchent un l. pour leur réunion** they need a place to hold their meeting **2** *(bureau, permanence)* office(s), premises; **rendez-vous au l. à dix heures pour préparer le matériel** meeting at the office at ten o'clock to prepare the equipment **3** *Can Tél* extension

NF *Journ* **locale** local column

> Il faut noter que le nom anglais **local** ne désigne jamais une pièce ou un bâtiment.

localement [lɔkalmã] ADV locally

localier [lɔkalje] NM *Journ* local reporter

localisable [lɔkalizabl] ADJ locatable; *(appel téléphonique)* traceable

localisation [lɔkalizasjõ] NF **1** *(circonscription)* localization, confinement **2** *(repérage)* location, locating; *(d'un appel téléphonique)* tracing; **l. de logiciel** software localization

localisé [lɔkalize] ADJ localized

localiser [lɔkalize] VT **1** *(circonscrire) (épidémie, incendie etc)* to localize, to confine **2** *(repérer) (bruit, gêne etc)* to locate; *(appel téléphonique)* to trace; **l. qch dans sa mémoire** to place sth; **ne quittez pas, je vais essayer de le l.** hold the line, I'll try and locate him *or* find out where he is

localité [lɔkalite] NF *(ville)* town; *(village)* village

locataire [lɔkatɛʀ] N *(de propriété louée, de locaux commerciaux)* tenant; *(chez le propriétaire)* lodger, *Am* roomer; *(avec bail)* lessee, leaseholder

locateur [lɔkatœʀ] NM *Jur* lessor

locatif¹, -ive [lɔkatif, -iv] ADJ concerning the renting of premises; **risques locatifs** = tenant's obligations and responsibilities *(as regards damage etc)*; **valeur locative** rental value; **réparations locatives** repairs incumbent upon the tenant; **le marché locatif** the property rental market

locatif², -ive *Gram* ADJ locative

NM locative (case)

location [lɔkasjõ] NF **1** *(de voiture, d'équipement, de costume etc) (par le locataire)* renting, *Br* hiring; *(par le propriétaire)* renting (out), rental, *Br* hiring (out); **prendre qch en l.** to rent sth, *Br* to hire sth; **donner qch en l.** to rent sth (out), *Br* to hire sth (out); **l. de voitures (sans chauffeur)** (self-drive) car rental *or Br* hire; **voiture de l.** rented *or* hire car, *Am* rental car; **vélos en l.** bikes for hire *or Am* rent **2** *(de logement) (par le locataire)* renting; *(par le propriétaire)* renting (out), *Br* letting (out); **prix de l.** rent; **dans cette agence ils ne font pas la l.** they don't rent (out) *or Br* let (out) property in this agency, they don't deal with rented property in this agency **3** *(propriété à louer)* rented property; *(pour y vivre uniquement)* rented accommodation; **nous n'avons pas trouvé de l. pour cet été** we haven't found anywhere to rent this summer **4** *(de places)* booking, reservation; **(bureau de) l.** box office, booking office

► ► **l.-bail,** *pl* **locations-bails** leasing, lease purchase; **l. gérance** rented business; **l. avec option d'achat** lease purchase; **l.-vente,** *pl* **locations-ventes** hire purchase, *Am* installment plan; **acheter qch en l.-vente** to buy sth on hire purchase *or Am* on the installment plan

> Il faut noter que le nom anglais **location** est un faux ami. Il signifie **endroit, emplacement.**

loch [lɔk] NM *Naut* (ship's) log; **ligne de l.** log line; **livre de l.** log

loche [lɔʃ] NF **1** *(poisson)* loach **2** *(mollusque)* grey slug **3** *Vulg (sein)* tit, boob

lock-out [lɔkawt] NM INV *Ind* lockout

lock-outer [lɔkawte] VT *Ind* to lock out

locks [lɔks] NFPL *Fam* dreadlocks

lock-up [lɔkœp] NM INV *Aut* lock-up

loco [loko] NF *Fam (abrév* **locomotive)** loco

locomoteur, -trice [lɔkɔmotœʀ, -tʀis] ADJ *(organe, troubles etc)* locomotor

NF *Rail* **locomotrice** electric engine

locomotion [lɔkɔmosjõ] NF locomotion; **moyens de l.** means of transport

locomotive [lɔkɔmotiv] NF **1** *Rail* locomotive, engine; **l. diesel (à transmission) électrique** diesel electric locomotive **2** *Fig (élément moteur)* motive force; *(leader)* pacemaker, pacesetter; *(en politique)* dynamic *or* forceful leader

locus [lɔkys] NM *Biol* locus

locuteur, -trice [lɔkytœʀ, -tʀis] N *Ling* speaker; **l. natif** native speaker

locution [lɔkysjõ] NF *(expression)* expression, phrase, locution; **l. figée** set phrase *or* expression; **l. vicieuse** incorrect expression; *Gram* **l. adverbiale** adverbial phrase; **l. conjonctive** complex conjunction

loden [lɔdɛn] NM *Tex* loden; *(manteau)* loden coat

lœss [løs] NM *Géol* loess

lof [lɔf] NM *Naut* windward side; **venir** *ou* **aller au l.** to sail into the wind, to luff; **virer l. pour l.** to wear

lofer [lɔfe] VI *Naut* to luff

loft [lɔft] NM converted warehouse/garage/ etc

logarithme [lɔgaʀitm] *Math* NM logarithm, log; **table de logarithmes** log(arithm) table; ADJ **fonction l.** logarithmic function

logarithmique [lɔgaʀitmik] ADJ *Math* logarithmic

loge [lɔʒ] NF **1** *(d'artiste)* dressing room **2** *(de spectateur)* box; **première l.** first-tier box; *Fig* **être aux premières loges** to have a ringside seat **3** *(maçonnique, de concierge)* lodge **4** *Beaux-Arts, Mus* individual exam room *(for the Prix de Rome)* **5** *Archit* loggia **6** *Bot* cell

logeable [lɔʒabl] ADJ *(habitable)* habitable, fit for occupation

logement [lɔʒmɑ̃] NM **1** *(habitation)* accommodation, *Am* accommodations; *(maison)* house; *(appartement)* flat, *Am* apartment; **chercher un l.** to look for somewhere to live, to look for accommodation; **l. garni** *ou* **meublé** furnished rooms *or* flat *or Am* apartment; **l. collectif** block of flats, *Am* apartment block; **l. à demeure** live-in accommodation; **l. locatif** rented accommodation **2** *(action) (de gens)* housing; *(de troupes)* quartering; *(dans maison privée)* billeting; *(de chevaux)* stabling; **crise du l.** housing shortage **3** *Mil (local)* quarters; *(dans maison privée)* billet **4** *(de pièce de machine)* seating; *(de manche)* housing

LOGER [lɔʒe] *(je logeai(s); n. logeons)* VI to live; *(de troupes)* to be quartered; *(dans maison privée)* to be billeted; **l. à l'hôtel** to stay *or* put up at *or* in a hotel; *Mil* **l. chez l'habitant** to be billeted in private houses; **je compte l. chez l'habitant pendant les vacances** I'm intending to stay in a private house when I go on holiday

VT **1** *(héberger) (étudiants, touristes etc)* to accommodate; *(troupes)* to quarter; *(dans maison privée)* to stable; **l. un ami pour la nuit** to put a friend up for the night; **l'auberge de jeunesse peut l. jusqu'à 200 personnes** the youth hostel can accommodate up to 200 people; **crois-tu qu'on arrivera à l. tous les invités dans la salle à manger?** do you think we'll manage to accommodate all the guests in the dining room?; **être logé et nourri** to have board and lodging *or* bed and board; **être bien/mal logé** to be well-/poorly-housed; **il est mal logé dans cet appartement** he's not very comfortable in that apartment

2 *(placer)* to put; **l. une balle dans qch** to put *or* lodge a bullet in sth; **j'ai réussi à l. ton sac entre les deux valises** I managed to put your bag between the two cases; **il faudra bien l. toutes nos affaires dans ce placard** we'll have to put all our belongings in that cupboard

3 *Fam (repérer)* to track down

VPR **se loger 1** *(pour s'installer)* to find accommodation, to find somewhere to live; *(pour la nuit)* to find accommodation, to find somewhere to stay; **nous avons trouvé à nous l.** we've found accommodation, we've found somewhere to live/stay

2 *(se placer)* **mon ballon est allé se l. entre l'antenne de télé et la cheminée** my ball got stuck *or* lodged itself between the television aerial and the chimney; **où a-t-il bien pu aller se l.?** where has it got to?; **la balle se logea dans le mur** the bullet embedded itself in the wall; **le malheureux s'est logé une balle dans la tête** the poor wretch put a bullet in *or* through his head; **la poignée repliée se loge dans un creux spécialement prévu à cet effet** the folded handle fits into a hollow specially designed for the purpose; **la jalousie s'est logée dans son cœur** jealousy filled his heart; **la souris s'est logée sous le lit** the mouse went and hid under the bed; **on a réussi à tous se l. dans son canapé** we all managed to fit *or* squeeze on to his sofa

logeur [lɔʒœr] NM landlord *(of furnished apartments)*

logeuse [lɔʒøz] NF landlady *(of furnished apartments)*

loggia [lɔdʒja] NF *Archit* loggia

logiciel [lɔʒisjɛl] NM *Ordinat* software; **un l.** a software package, a package; *(programme)* a piece of software, a computer program; **un l. très utile** a very useful software package; **l. d'application** application software; **l. auteur** authoring software; **l. bureautique** business software (package); **l. client** client software; **l. de communication** communications package, comms package, communications software; **l. de compression de données** data compression software; **l. de comptabilité** accounts package, accounts software; **l. de conception assistée par ordinateur** computer-aided design package; **l. contributif** shareware; **l. à contribution volontaire** shareware; **l. de conversion** conversion software; **l. de courrier électronique** e-mail software; **l. de cryptage** encryption software; **l. de décompression** decompression software, decompressor; **l. de dessin** art package, drawing program; **l. d'édition d'images** image editing program, image editor; **l. espion** spyware; **l. d'exploitation** operating system software; **l. de filtrage** filtering software; **l. grapheur** graphics package, graphics software; **l. graphique** illustration software; **l. de groupe** groupware; **l. intégré** integrated software; **l. de jeu** games software; **l. libre** freeware; **l. ludique** games software; **l. de mise en page** desktop publishing package; **l. monoposte** single-user software package; **l. multi-utilisateur** multi-user software; **l. de navigation** (Web) browser; **l. de PAO** DTP software; **l. de planification** scheduler; **l. de présentation** presentation software; **l. (du domaine) public** freeware; **l. de reconnaissance de caractères** OCR software, character recognition software; **l. de reconnaissance vocale** voice recognition software; **l. de récupération** recovery program; **l. de réseau** network software; **l. de SGBD** DBMS software; **l. système** system software; **l. de système d'exploitation** operating system software; **l. de télémaintenance** remote access software; *(pour base de données)* server software; **logiciels de traitement de texte** word-processing software, word-processing software packages, WP packages; **l. utilisateur** user software; **l. utilitaire** utility program

logicien, -ienne [lɔʒisjɛ̃, -jɛn] N logician

logique [lɔʒik] ADJ **1** *(cohérent) (raisonnement, déduction, esprit etc)* logical; **voyons, soyons logiques** come on, let's be logical about this; **il est tout à fait l. que tu n'aies pas envie de le revoir** it's quite natural that you don't want to see him again; **c'est l.** it stands to reason, it's only natural; **je trouve ça l.** it sounds logical to me; **tu n'es pas l.!** you're being illogical!; **il faut être l. avec soi-même** you have to be logical; **le candidat doit avoir l'esprit l.** the candidate must have a logical mind **2** *(analytique)* logical, methodical; *Ordinat* **analyseur l.** logic analyser; *Gram* **analyse l.** *(de phrase)* analysis

NF **1** *Phil, Math* logic; **faire de la l.** to do logic; **l. formelle/pure** formal/pure logic **2** *(cohérence, raisonnement)* logic; **la l. de la passion/de la folie** the logic of passion/madness; **la l. des enfants** children's logic, the way children's minds work; **nous sommes entrés dans une l. de guerre** war is inevitable, war is the next logical step; **en toute l., voilà ce qui devrait se passer** logically, that's what ought to happen; **c'est dans la l. des choses que les enfants ne vivent pas éternellement chez leurs parents** it's logical *or* natural that children shouldn't live with their parents for ever; **ça manque de l.** there's no logic in it, it's illogical; **là, vous manquez de l.** you're not being very logical

▸▸ *Ordinat* **l. câblée** wired logic; **l. floue** fuzzy logic

logiquement [lɔʒikmɑ̃] ADV *(rationnellement)* logically; *(normalement)* all going well, all things being equal; **l., il devrait déjà être là** he should already be here, there's no reason why he shouldn't already be here

logis [lɔʒi] NM *Vieilli, Litt (maison)* home, dwelling, abode; **trouver un l.** to find accommodation

logistique [lɔʒistik] ADJ logistic; **soutien l.** logistic(al) support
NF *Mil etc* logistics; *Mktg* **l. commerciale** marketing mix

logo [logo] NM *(abrév* **logotype***)* logo; *Radio etc* **l. audio/sonore** audio/sound logo; *Journ* **l. de page** page logo

logomachie [lɔgomaʃi] NF logomachy; *(assemblage de mots, vide de sens)* verbiage, verbosity; **une l.** a lot of verbiage

logopédiste [logopedist] N *Belg, Suisse (orthophoniste)* speech therapist

logorrhée [lɔgɔre] NF *Psy* logorrhea; *Hum* verbal diarrhoea; *Hum* **j'ai tendance à la l.** I tend to witter on

LOI [lwa] NF **1** *Jur* **la l.** *(le droit)* the law; **tomber sous le coup de la l.** to come under the law; **avoir la l. pour soi** to have the law on one's side; **je suis désolé mais c'est la l.** I'm sorry but that's the law *or* the law's the law; **respecter la l.** to respect *or* obey the law; **nul n'est censé ignorer la l.** ignorance is no defence in (a court of) law; **homme de l.** lawyer, legal practitioner

2 *(prescription de l'État)* **une l.** a law, an act *(of Parliament)*; **projet de l., proposition de l.** bill; **la l. anti-tabac n'est pas très respectée** not many people respect *or* abide by the anti-smoking laws; **l. fiscale** tax law, fiscal law; **l. bancaire** banking law

3 *(autorité individuelle)* law; **faire la** *ou* **sa l.** to lay down the law; **dicter sa l.** to lay down the law, to impose one's will; **faire la l. chez qn** to lay down the law *or* dictate to sb; **c'est lui qui fait la l.** he's the master *or Fam* the boss; **la l. du plus fort** might is right; **dans la cour de récréation c'est la l. du plus fort** it's the law of the jungle in the playground; *Litt* **ce qu'il dit fait l.** his word is law; **nécessité fait l.** needs must when the devil drives; *Litt* **se faire une l. de faire qch** to make a rule *or* a point of doing sth; *Litt* **subir la l. de qn** to be ruled by sb, to be under sb's thumb

4 *(règle qui s'impose)* law; **l. de la nature** law of nature; **l. de la jungle** law of the jungle; **les lois économiques** the laws of economics; **l. phonétique** law of phonetics; **l. de l'offre et de la demande** law of supply and demand; **lois tarifaires** tariff laws; **lois de l'esthétique** rules of aesthetics; **lois de la mode** dictates of fashion; **les lois de la politesse/de l'honneur** the rules of etiquette/the code of honour

5 *Phys, Math* law

6 *Rel* **la l. divine** divine law, the law of God; *Fig* **c'est la l. et les prophètes** its/his/*etc* word is law

▸▸ *Pol, Jur* **l. d'amnistie** amnesty law; **l. antitrust** antitrust *or Br* anti-monopoly law; **l. électorale** electoral law; **l. d'exception** emergency legislation; *Pol, Jur* **l. de finances** Finance Act; *Pol, Jur* **l. d'habilitation** enabling act; **L. Informatique et Libertés** ≃ Data Protection Act; **l. martiale** martial law; **l. naturelle** natural law; *Pol* **l. d'orientation** = act laying down the basic principles for government action in a given field; **l. sur les sociétés anonymes** public company law; **la l. du talion** an eye for an eye (and a tooth for a tooth)

loi-cadre, *pl* **lois-cadres** NF outline law

LOIN [lwɛ̃] ADV **1** *(dans l'espace ou le temps)* far (de from); **c'est encore l. le théâtre/Annecy?** is it far to the theatre/Annecy?; **est-ce l. d'ici?** is it far from here?; **ce n'est pas l.** it's not far; **la poste est l.** the post office is a long way off, it's a long way to the post office; **plus l.** farther *or* further (on); **moins l.** less far, not so far; **il y a l. d'ici à Paris** it's a long way to Paris; **l. de moi la prétention de vous apprendre quelque chose** far be it from me to tell you what to do; *Fig aussi Iron* **l. de moi cette idée!** I wouldn't dream of it!, the thought never entered my head!; **l. de moi l'idée d'insinuer que ...** far be it from me to insinuate that ..., I wouldn't dream of insinuating that ...; **le prisonnier s'est échappé mais il n'est pas allé très l.** the prisoner escaped but he didn't get very far; **la voiture est vieille, elle n'ira pas l.** the car is old and on its last legs; *Fig* **ce jeune homme ira l.** this young man will go far; *Fig* **tu n'iras pas l. avec des théories pareilles!** you won't get very far with theories like that!; *Fig* **on pourrait même aller plus l. et dire que ...** you could even go further and say that ...; *Fig* **ça va (très) l. ce que vous dites** that's taking things a bit far; *Fig* **vous allez trop l.** you're going too far; **ça peut aller très l.** you don't realize what you're getting into; **si je m'en mêle ça peut aller très l.** if I decide to do something about it they'd better watch out; **voir l.** to be far-sighted; *Fig* to be far-sighted *or* shrewd; **voir plus l.** *(dans un texte)* see below/see following pages; *Fig* to look further ahead, to look to the future; **l. derrière lui** far *or* way behind him; *Fig* **laisser ses souvenirs l. derrière soi** to leave one's memories far behind; **j'étais l. de la vérité, ça m'a coûté 2000 euros!** I was way out (in my calculations), it cost me 2,000 euros!; *Prov* **l. des yeux, l. du cœur** out of sight, out of mind; *Fig* **de là à l'accuser de mensonge il n'y a pas l.** that's not far from *or* it's close to calling him a liar; **il ne voit pas plus l. que le bout de son nez** he can't see any further than the end of his nose, he can't see beyond the end of his nose; *Prov* **il y a l. de la coupe aux lèvres** there's many a slip 'twixt the cup and the lip; **nous étions l. de penser/croire/d'imaginer que ...** we never thought/believed/imagined for a moment that ...; **je ne suis pas l. de penser que ...** I've more or less come to the conclusion that ...; **elle est l. d'être bête** she is far from stupid; **il est l. d'avoir compris** he still hasn't understood by a long chalk; **je suis encore l. d'avoir fini** I'm still far from finished; **ne pas être l. d'une découverte** to be on the brink of a discovery; **je ne suis pas fâché, l. de là!** I'm not angry, far from it *or* anything but!; **cette époque est bien l.** those days are long gone; **c'est l. tout ça** *(c'est du passé)* that all happened a long time ago; **ça remonte à l. maintenant** it happened a long time *or* years ago; **leur brouille remonte à l.** their quarrel is of long standing, they quarrelled a long time ago; **comme c'est l., tout ça!** that all happened such a long time ago!, that's ancient history!; **ce jour est encore l.** that day is still a long way off *or Fml* is still distant; **c'est encore l. les vacances?** is it still a long time (to go) till the holidays?; **il ne devait pas être l. de midi** it must have been getting on for twelve (o'clock); **ils ont payé pas l. de cent millions pour leur maison** they paid close to a hundred million *or* not far off a hundred million for their house **2** *(dans locutions)* **je l'ai reconnu de l.** I recognized him from a distance *or* from a long way off; **admirer qn de l.** to admire sb at *or* from a distance *or* from afar; **ils sont parents, mais de l.** they are only distantly related; *Litt* **d'aussi l. ou du plus l. qu'il se souvienne** as far back *or* for as long as he can remember; *Fig* **de l.** *(de beaucoup)* by

far; **il est de l. plus intelligent que moi** he is far more intelligent than I am; **c'est de l. son meilleur roman** it's by far his best novel; **l. de l'affoler** far from upsetting him; **de l. en l.** *(de temps en temps)* at long intervals, now and then

3 *Suisse (absent)* **il est l.** he's not here
NM **au l.** in the distance; **apercevoir qn au l.** to see sb a long way off *or* a long way away *or* in the distance

lointain [lwɛ̃tɛ̃] ADJ distant, far off, faraway; *(île)* remote; *(ressemblance)* vague; **mes souvenirs les plus lointains** my earliest recollections; **dans un avenir l.** in the distant future; **elle avait l'air l.** she looked as if she was miles away, she had a faraway look on her face; **elle écoutait la conversation, l'air l.** she was listening to the conversation with a faraway look on her face
NM distance; **dans le l.** in the distance; **regard plongé dans le l.** faraway look; *Beaux-Arts* **les lointains** the distances

loi-programme, *pl* **lois-programmes** NF *Fin, Pol* = law providing framework for long-term government programme

loir [lwar] NM *(mammifère)* dormouse; **dormir comme un l.** to sleep like a log

Loire [lwar] NF **la L.** the Loire; **le Val de L.** the Loire valley

loisible [lwazibl] ADJ *Litt* **il lui est l. de refuser** he is at liberty *or* entitled to refuse

loisir [lwazir] NM **1** *(temps libre)* leisure; **dans mes heures de l., pendant mes loisirs** in my spare time; **activités de l.** leisure *or* spare-time activities; **avoir des loisirs** to have some spare time **2** *(activité)* **le l., les loisirs** leisure *or* spare-time activities; **un professionnel du l.** = specialist travel agency; **le ski/la lecture est mon l. préféré** skiing/reading is my favourite pastime; **société de loisirs** leisure society; **les loisirs sportifs** sporting activities **3** *(possibilité, temps nécessaire)* opportunity; **je n'ai pas encore eu le l. de lui parler/de le lire** I haven't had a chance *or* (the) time to speak to him/to read it; *Litt* **donner ou laisser à qn le l. de faire qch** to give sb the opportunity to do sth, to allow sb to do sth; **on ne m'a pas laissé le l. de me reposer** I wasn't given the opportunity *or* any time to rest; **on ne m'a pas laissé le l. de donner mon avis** I wasn't given a chance *or* an opportunity to express my opinion; *Litt* **examiner qch à l.** to examine sth at one's leisure

lolette [lɔlɛt] NF *Suisse (tétine)* dummy, *Am* pacifier

lolo [lolo] NM *Fam* **1** *Enf (lait)* milk **2** *(sein)* booby

lombaire [lɔ̃bɛr] *Anat* ADJ *(douleur, région, vertèbre)* lower back, *Spéc* lumbar; **ponction l.** lumbar puncture
NF lumbar

lombalgie [lɔ̃balʒi] NF *Méd* lower back pain

lombard, -arde [lɔ̃bar, -ard] ADJ Lombard, of/from Lombardy; *Hist* **la ligue lombarde** the Lombard League
NM *Ling* Lombard dialect
N **L.** Lombard

Lombardie [lɔ̃bardi] NF Lombardy

lombes [lɔ̃b] NFPL *Anat* loins

lombric [lɔ̃brik] NM earthworm

Lomé [lɔme] N Lomé

londonien, -ienne [lɔ̃dɔnjɛ̃, -jɛn] ADJ London
N **L.** Londoner

Londres [lɔ̃dr] N London

londrès [lɔ̃drɛs] NM Havana cigar

LONG, LONGUE [lɔ̃, lɔ̃g]

ADJ long **1, 2** ▪ slow **3**
NM length **1** ▪ along *(le long de)* **2**

ADJ **1** *(dans l'espace)* long; **avoir un l. nez/de longues jambes** to have a long nose/long legs; **elle a les cheveux longs** she has long hair; **corde longue de 5 mètres** rope 5 metres long, 5-metre rope; **prendre le chemin le plus l.** to go the longest way (round); **un vieillard l. et maigre le regardait fixement** an old man, tall and slim, was staring at him; *Vieilli* **il est l. comme un jour sans pain** he's a real beanpole; **ce voyage/discours est l. comme un jour sans pain** this journey/speech seems to be lasting for ever *or* dragging on for ever; *Fig* **avoir le bras l.** to be able to pull strings, *Fam* to have pull; **phare longue portée** high-intensity light; **navigation au l. cours** deep-sea navigation **2** *(dans le temps)* long; **les jours sont de plus en plus longs** the days are getting longer (and longer); **dix jours, c'est l.** ten days is a long time; **pendant de longues années** for many years; **discours un peu l.** rather long *or* somewhat lengthy speech; **c'est une longue histoire** it's a long story; **je trouve le temps l.** time seems to drag; **je trouve les jours longs** I find the days long, time seems to drag; **l. soupir** long-drawn *or* lengthy sigh; **un ami de longue date** an old friend, a friend of long standing; **projet à longue échéance** long-term project; **à l. terme** long-term; **longue durée** *(chômage)* long-term; *(pile)* long-life; *(cassette)* extended play; *(disque)* long-playing; **à plus ou moins longue échéance, à plus ou moins l. terme** sooner or later **3** *(lent)* slow; **être l. à faire qch** to take a long time to do sth, to be slow to do sth; **qu'est-ce que tu es l.!** you're so slow!, you're taking forever!; **il est l. ce feu** these lights take forever to change; **être l. à réagir** to be slow to react; **j'ai été l. à comprendre** it took me a long time to understand; **je ne serai pas l.** I won't be long; **ce ne sera pas l.** it won't take long; **c'est un travail l. à faire** it's slow work, this work takes a long time; **il s'en sortira, mais ce sera l.** he'll recover but it'll take a long time *or* it will be a slow process **4** *Ling* **une voyelle longue** a long vowel; **'a' l.** long 'a' **5** *Culin (sauce)* thin
NM **1** *(dans l'espace)* length; **table qui a 2 mètres de l.** table 2 metres long *or* in length; **le l. de** along; **se faufiler/grimper le l. du mur** to creep along/to climb up the wall; **tout le l. du rivage** all along the shore; **en l.** *(couper, fendre)* lengthwise; **de l. en large** up and down, to and fro; **il arpentait la pièce de l. en large** he paced up and down the room; *Fam* **expliquer qch en l. et en large** *ou* **en l. en large et en travers** to explain sth in great detail *or* at great length; **étendu de tout son l.** stretched out (at) full length; **tomber de tout son l.** to fall flat on one's face **2** *(dans le temps)* **tout le l. du jour/de la nuit** all day/night long, throughout the day/night; **tout au** *ou* **du l. de l'entretien** throughout *or* all through the conversation
ADV **1** *(beaucoup)* **je crois qu'il est inutile que j'en dise plus l.** need I say more?; **regard qui en dit l.** meaningful *or* eloquent look, look that speaks volumes; **cette action en dit l. sur ...** this action speaks volumes for ...; **en savoir l./plus l./trop l.** to know a lot/more/too much; **j'en sais l./je pourrais en dire l. sur cette affaire** I know/I could say quite a lot about this business **2** **s'habiller l.** to wear long clothes
NF **longue 1** *Ling* long syllable **2** **à la longue** in time, in the end, eventually **3** *Mus* long note **4** *Cartes* **longue à pique/trèfles** long suit of spades/clubs

longanime [lɔ̃ganim] ADJ *Litt* forbearing

longanimité [lɔ̃ganimite] NF *Litt* forbearance

long-courrier, *pl* **long-courriers** ADJ *(navire)* ocean-going; *(avion)* long-haul, long-range
NM *Naut* ocean-going ship, ocean-goer, ocean liner; *Aviat* long-haul *or* long-range aircraft

longe[1] [lɔ̃ʒ] NF *(pour mener le cheval)* leading rein, halter; *(pour l'attacher)* tether; *(pour le dresser)* lunge, longe

longe[2] NF *Culin (de veau, porc)* loin

longer [lɔ̃ʒe] VT (**je longeai(s); n. longeons**) **1** *(suivre) (de personne, voiture) (route, rivière)* to follow, to go along; *(mur, côte)* to follow, to hug **2** *(s'étendre le long de) (de sentier, canal, voie ferrée)* to follow, to run alongside, to border; **la route longe un bois/la côte/la rivière** the road skirts a wood/follows *or* hugs the coastline/follows the river

longeron [lɔ̃ʒrɔ̃] NM **1** *Constr (de pont de chemin de fer)* stringer, longitudinal girder; *(maîtresse poutre)* beam, member **2** *Aut (de châssis)* side member, side sill **3** *Aviat (sur fuselage)* longeron; *(d'aile)* spar

longévité [lɔ̃ʒevite] NF *(durée de vie)* longevity; *(longue vie)* long life; *(de produit)* life; **table de l. d'une population** life-expectancy table of a population

longiligne [lɔ̃ʒiliɲ] ADJ willowy

longitude [lɔ̃ʒityd] NF *Géog* longitude; **par 10° de l. ouest** at 10° longitude west

longitudinal, -ale, -aux, -ales [lɔ̃ʒitydinal, -o] ADJ longitudinal, lengthwise

longitudinalement [lɔ̃ʒitydinalmɑ̃] ADV longitudinally, lengthwise, lengthways

long-métrage, *pl* **longs-métrages** NM *Cin* full-length movie *or Br* film, feature-length movie *or Br* film; **l. d'animation** feature-length cartoon

longrine [lɔ̃grin] NF **1** *Constr* longitudinal beam *or* girder *or* member **2** *Rail* longitudinal sleeper

LONGTEMPS [lɔ̃tɑ̃] ADV **1** *(pendant un long moment)* a long time; **attendre l.** to wait (for) a long time; **ça fait l. que tu attends?** have you been waiting long?; **Iron tu peux attendre l.** you'll have a long wait; **ça fait l. que ça va durer l.** it couldn't last (for) long; **est-ce que ça va durer l.?** will it take long?; **ça va durer encore l. ce vacarme?** is this racket going to go on for much longer?; **ça ne va plus durer l. maintenant** it won't be long now; **rester trop l.** to stay too long **2** *(long espace de temps)* **il y a l.** long ago, a long time ago; **il n'y a pas l.** not long ago; **il y a l. qu'il est mort** he has been dead (for) a long time *or Fam* for ages; **il y a l. que je ne l'ai vu** it's a long time *or Fam* ages since I saw him; **pendant l.** for a long time; **(pendant) l. j'ai cru qu'elle reviendrait** I believed for a long time that she would come back; **mettre l. à faire qch** to take a long time *or Fam* ages to do sth; **je n'en ai pas pour l.** I shan't be long, it won't take me long; **tu en as encore pour l.?** are you going to be much longer?; **il n'en a plus pour l.** he hasn't much longer (to live); **cela existe depuis l.** it has existed for a long time *or Fam* for ages; **l. avant/après** long before/after; **avant l.** before long; **cela ne se fera pas avant l.** it won't happen for a long time (to come); **je ne pensais pas vous revoir avant ou de l.** I didn't expect to see you again for a long time

longuement [lɔ̃gmɑ̃] ADV *(pendant longtemps) (attendre, réfléchir, s'attarder)* for a long time; *(parler)* for a long time, at great length; *(expliquer)* at great length, lengthily; **il la regarda l.** he gazed earnestly at her; **parler l. avec qn** to have a (good) long talk with sb; **il a l. insisté pour que je vienne** he kept

on insisting *or* was extremely insistent that I should come; **il faudrait analyser plus l. les personnages** the characters must be analysed in greater detail

longuet, -ette [lɔ̃gɛ, -ɛt] ADJ *Fam (livre, discours, spectacle, attente)* rather long, longish; **c'est un peu l.** it's a bit long
NM *Région* breadstick

longueur [lɔ̃gœr] NF **1** *(dimension)* length; **l. totale, l. hors tout** length over all, overall length; **mesures de l.** linear measures; **unité de l.** unit of length; **jardin de cent mètres de l. ou l. de cent mètres** garden a hundred metres long; **couper/scier qch en l. ou dans le sens de la l.** to cut/saw sth lengthwise; *Sport* **mener/gagner d'une l.** to lead/win by a length; **le cheval A prend une l. d'avance sur le cheval B** horse A is now one length ahead of horse B; *Fig* **la ville de Grenoble avait une l. d'avance sur les autres pour la prévention du sida** Grenoble had a clear lead over other cities as regards preventive measures against Aids; *Fig* **cette entreprise a plusieurs longueurs d'avance** this company has a good lead *or* is way ahead; *Péj* **traîner en l.** *(de discours, repas etc)* to drag (on), to drag on for ever; **faire traîner qch en l.** to drag sth out; *Typ* **l. de ligne** line width; *Typ* **l. de page** page length **2** *(état de ce qui est long)* **son discours/le film était d'une l.!** his speech/the film was incredibly long *or* dragged on for ever; **d'une l. incroyable/excessive** incredibly/excessively long **3** *Péj* **à l. de journée/de semaine/d'année** all day/week/year long; **je n'entends que ça à l. de journées** that's all I hear day after day **4** *Péj (développement trop long)* **roman plein de longueurs** novel full of long drawn-out passages **5** *(en nageant)* length; **faire des longueurs** to do lengths
▸▸ *Radio, Fig* **l. d'ondes** wavelength; *Fig* **nous ne sommes pas sur la même l. d'ondes** we're not on the same wavelength

longue-vue, *pl* **longues-vues** [lɔ̃gvy] NF telescope, field glass

look [luk] NM *Fam* look; **soigner son l.** to cultivate one's image; **changer de l.** to change one's look *or* image; *très Fam* **il a un l. d'enfer** he looks out of this world

looké [luke] ADJ *Fam* **être l. punk/grunge** to have a punky/grungy look *or* image

looping [lupiŋ] NM *Aviat* loop; **faire un l./des loopings** to loop the loop

lope [lɔp], **lopette** [lɔpɛt] NF **1** *Vulg (homosexuel)* poof, *Am* fag **2** *Fam (lâche)* wimp, wuss

lopin [lɔpɛ̃] NM **l. de terre** piece *or* patch *or* plot of ground

loquace [lɔkas] ADJ talkative, *Fml* loquacious

loquacité [lɔkasite] NF talkativeness, *Fml* loquacity; **elle a retrouvé sa l. d'antan** she's her old talkative self again

loque [lɔk] NF **1** rag; **être en loques** to be in rags *or* in tatters; **ses vêtements tombent en loques** his clothes are falling to pieces **2** *Fig (personne)* **l. (humaine)** wreck; **l'alcool a fait de lui une l.** alcohol has turned him into a human wreck **3** *Belg (serpillière)* mop

loquet [lɔkɛ] NM *(de porte)* latch; *Arch* **fermer la porte au l., pousser le l.** to put the latch on the door, to latch the door

loqueteau, -eaux [lɔkto] NM *(pour volet)* small latch, catch

loqueteux, -euse [lɔktø, -øz] ADJ *(personne)* in rags, in tatters; *(vêtements)* ragged, tattered; **un vieillard l.** an old man (dressed) in rags, a ragged old man
N ragamuffin

lord [lɔr(d)] NM lord; **la Chambre des lords** the House of Lords

lord-maire, *pl* **lords-maires** NM *(de Londres etc)* Lord Mayor

lordose [lɔrdoz] NF *Méd* hollow-back, *Spéc* lordosis

lorgner [lɔrɲe] VT **1** *(regarder indiscrètement) (personne, décolleté)* to eye; **l. une femme** to eye up *or* ogle a woman; **l. qch/qn du coin de l'œil** to keep eyeing sth/sb, to cast a sidelong glance at sth/sb **2** *(convoiter) (héritage, poste etc)* to have one's eye on

lorgnette [lɔrɲɛt] NF (pair of) opera glasses; *Fig* **regarder/voir qch par le petit bout de la l.** take a narrow-minded *or* blinkered view of sth

lorgnon [lɔrɲɔ̃] NM *(avec une tige)* lorgnette; *(avec ressort)* pince-nez

loriot [lɔrjo] NM **l. (jaune)** (golden) oriole

lorrain, -aine [lɔrɛ̃, -ɛn] ADJ from/of Lorraine
NM *Ling* Lorraine dialect
N **L.** *(habitant)* inhabitant of Lorraine; *(natif)* native of Lorraine
NF **la Lorraine** Lorraine

lorry [lɔri] NM *Rail* (platelayer's) trolley, pushcar

lors [lɔr] ADV **1** *Litt* **depuis l.** from that time, ever since then; **dès l.** *(à partir de ce moment-là)* from that moment on; **dès l. que tu refuses, tu es mis à la porte** should you *or* if you should happen to refuse, you're dismissed; **l. même qu'il souffre, il ne le dit pas** even though he is in pain, he says nothing; **espérez l. même qu'il n'y a plus d'espoir** you must hope against hope **2** **l. de** *(pendant)* during; **l. de mon séjour à Hawaï** during my stay in Hawaii, while I was in Hawaii; **l. de mon accident** at the time of my accident

lorsque [lɔrsk(ə)] CONJ *(becomes* **lorsqu'** *before* **il(s), elle(s), on, en, un(e)**) when SEE GRAMMAR B31–2

losange [lɔzɑ̃ʒ] NM **1** *(forme)* diamond; *Géom* rhomb(us) **2** *Hér* lozenge

losangé [lɔzɑ̃ʒe] ADJ *(boucle d'oreille etc)* diamond-shaped; *(frise)* with a diamond pattern; *Hér* lozengy

loser [luzœr] NM *Fam* loser

lot [lo] NM **1** *(à une loterie)* prize; **gros l.** first prize, jackpot; *Fig Fam* **en l'épousant, tu as gagné le gros l.** you've hit the jackpot marrying him; **l. de consolation** consolation prize; *Fin* **emprunt à lots** lottery loan **2** *(articles vendus ensemble) (de marchandises etc)* batch; *(de serviettes, casseroles)* set; *(de chaussettes, collants, savonnettes etc)* pack; *(aux enchères)* lot; **vendus par lots** *(casseroles, serviettes)* sold in sets; *(chaussettes, collants)* sold in packs; *Fig* **dans le l. il y en aura au moins un de bon** *(choses, personnes)* at least one out of this lot *or* batch should be some good; *Fig* **se détacher** *ou* **être au-dessus du l.** to stand out from the crowd **3** *(dans un partage)* share; **diviser un terrain en lots** to divide a piece of land into plots, to parcel up a piece of land **4** *Litt (sort)* lot, fate; **la souffrance est son l.** suffering is his lot; **son l. est d'être toujours seul** he is destined to remain alone all his life; **chacun son l.** we all have our cross to bear **5** *Ordinat* **traitement par lots** batch processing **6** *Bourse (d'actions)* parcel

loterie [lɔtri] NF lottery; **l. nationale** national lottery; **gagner à la l.** to win the lottery; *Fig* **c'est une l.** it's a lottery, it's the luck of the draw

loti [lɔti] ADJ **être bien/mal l.** to be well/badly off

lotion [losjɔ̃] NF lotion; **l. tonique** toning lotion, toner; **l. capillaire** hair lotion; **l. après-rasage** after-shave (lotion)

lotionner [losjɔne] VT *(épiderme, cuir chevelu)* to apply lotion to

lotir [lɔtir] **VT 1** (*diviser en lots*) (*terrain*) to divide into plots; (*immeubles*) to divide into lots; **terrains à l.** development site, building land **2** (*donner*) **l. qn de qch** to allot sth to sb

lotissement [lɔtismɑ̃] **NM 1** (*résidence*) housing estate *or* development **2** (*mise en lots*) (*de terrain*) parcelling out; (*de marchandises etc*) dividing into lots

loto [lɔto] **NM 1** (*jeu de hasard*) lotto; **un (jeu de) l.** (*matériel*) a lotto set; *Fig* **il me regarda avec des yeux en boules de l.** he looked at me with eyes like saucers **2** (*jeu national*) national lottery; **il joue au l. tous les mercredis** he buys a lottery ticket *or* takes part in *or* enters the national lottery every Wednesday; **le l. sportif** ≃ the pools; **il a gagné au l.** he won the lottery

lotte [lɔt] **NF** (*poisson*) burbot; (*de mer*) monkfish, anglerfish

lotus [lɔtys] **NM 1** (*plante*) lotus; **l. sacré** Indian lotus **2** (*arbre*) lotus tree **3** *Myth* Lotus

louable¹ [lwabl] **ADJ** (*acte, courage*) laudable, praiseworthy, commendable; (*intentions, efforts*) laudable; **c'est tout à fait l. de ta part** it is highly laudable of you, it is highly commendable on your part

louable² **ADJ** (*appartement, magasin etc*) rentable; **appartement difficilement l.** apartment that is difficult to rent

louage [lwaʒ] **NM** (*cession*) letting; (*jouissance*) renting; **prendre qch à l.** to rent sth; **contrat de l.** rental agreement *or* contract; **l. de services** contract of employment; **voiture de l.** hired carriage

louange [lwɑ̃ʒ] **NF** (*éloge*) praise; **digne de louange(s)** (*personne*) praiseworthy; (*action*) praiseworthy, commendable; **chanter les louanges de qn** to sing sb's praises; **couvrir qn de louanges** to shower sb with praise, to heap praise on sb; **faire un discours à la l. de qn** to make a speech in praise of sb; **c'est tout à sa l.** (*à son honneur*) it's to his credit, it's very commendable of him

louanger [lwɑ̃ʒe] **VT** *Litt* to sing the praises of

louangeur, -euse [lwɑ̃ʒœr, -øz] **ADJ** *Litt* (*poème, paroles*) laudatory

loubard, -e [lubar, -ard] **N** *Fam* yob(bo), lout, *surtout Am* hoodlum

louche¹ [luʃ] **ADJ 1** (*conduite, caractère, personne*) shady, suspicious, shifty; (*situation*) dubious; (*quartier, bar*) sleazy; (*passé*) shady; **c'est l.** there's something suspicious *or Fam* fishy about it; **il n'y a rien de l. là-dedans** it's all fair and above board, *Fam* there's nothing fishy about it **2** (*lumière, éclairage*) murky

NM il y a du l. dans cette affaire this business is a bit shady *or Fam* fishy

louche² **NF 1** (*ustensile de cuisine*) (soup) ladle **2** *Fam* (*main*) mitt, paw; **serrer la l. à qn** to shake hands with sb

loucher [luʃe] **VI** to squint; (*être atteint de strabisme*) to be cross-eyed, to have a squint; **l. de l'œil gauche** to have a squint in the left eye; *Fam* **l. vers** *ou* **sur qch** to eye *or* ogle sth; *Fig Fam* **l. sur l'héritage** to have one's eye on the inheritance

loucherie [luʃri] **NF** squint(ing)

loucheur, -euse [luʃœr, -øz] **N** cross-eyed *or* squint-eyed person

louer¹ [lwe] **VT 1** (*donner en location*) (*chambre, maison etc*) to rent (out), *Br* to let (out); (*équipement, véhicule, costume etc*) to rent (out), *Br* to hire (out) (**à** to); **maison à l.** house *Br* to let *or* for rent; **l. une ferme à bail** to lease out a farm **2** (*prendre en location*) (*chambre, maison etc*) to rent (**à** from); (*voiture, équipement, costume etc*) to rent, *Br* to hire; (*place de théâtre etc*) to reserve, to book; **l. une maison pour l'été** to take *or* rent a house for the summer

VPR se louer 1 (*être à louer*) (*de maison, chambre etc*) to be for rent, *Br* to be to let; (*d'équipement*) to be for rent *or Br* for hire; **cet appartement se loue très cher** this flat is very expensive to rent **2** *Arch* (*d'ouvrier agricole*) to hire oneself out

louer² **VT** (*personne, courage de qn*) to praise; (*officiellement*) to commend; **il n'a pas cessé de l. tes qualités** he has had nothing but praise for your qualities; **l. qn de** *ou* **pour qch** to praise sb for sth; **louons le seigneur!** praise the Lord!; **Dieu soit loué!** thank God!; **loués soient les philanthropes qui ...** praise be to the philanthropists who ...

VPR se louer 1 (*se féliciter*) **se l. de qch** to be pleased *or* well satisfied with sth; **je me loue chaque jour de notre collaboration** not a day goes by without my realizing the value of our collaboration; **je n'ai qu'à me l. de lui/de ses services** I have nothing but praise for him/for his services; **je n'ai qu'à me l. de mon choix** I must congratulate myself on my choice; **se l. d'avoir fait qch** to congratulate oneself on having done sth; **2** (*être loué*) **les locaux situés au centre de la capitale se louent à prix d'or** city centre premises are very expensive to rent

loueur, -euse [lwœr, -øz] **N** *Jur* lessor; **l. de bateaux/chevaux/costumes** person who rents (out) *or Br* hires (out) boats/horses/costumes

loufdingue [lufdɛ̃g] **ADJ** *Fam* crazy

loufiat [lufja] **NM** *Arg Vieilli* (*dans un café*) waiter

loufoque [lufɔk] *Fam* **ADJ** crazy
N crackpot, nut

loufoquerie [lufɔkri] **NF** *Fam* **1** (*absurdité*) craziness **2** (*acte*) crazy act; **loufoqueries** crazy behaviour

lougre [lugr] **NM** *Naut* lugger

louis [lwi] **NM** *Hist* **l. (d'or)** louis (d'or)

Louisiane [lwizjan] **NF** Louisiana

loukoum [lukum] **NM** (**rahat-)l.** Turkish delight; **j'ai mangé quatre loukoums** I've eaten four pieces of Turkish delight

loulou, -oute [lulu, -ut] **N** *Fam* **1** (*chéri, chérie*) dear, darling **2** *Fam* (*voyou*) lout, yob(bo), *Am* hoodlum

NM (*chien*) spitz; **l. de Poméranie** Pomeranian (dog), *Fam* pom

loup [lu] **NM 1** wolf; **une meute de loups** a pack of wolves; **à pas de l.** stealthily; **marcher à pas de l.** to creep along, to steal along, to walk stealthily; *Fig* **avoir une faim de l.** to be absolutely starving, to be ravenous; *Fig* **il fait un froid de l.** it's freezing (cold), it's bitterly cold; *Fig* **faire entrer le l. dans la bergerie** to set the fox to mind the geese; *Fig Fam* **se jeter dans la gueule du l.** to throw oneself into the lion's mouth; *Fig* **il est connu comme le l. blanc** everybody knows him; *Prov* **quand on parle du l. on en voit la queue** talk of the devil; *Fig* **avoir vu le l.** to have lost one's virginity; *Fig* **l'homme est un l. pour l'homme** it's dog eat dog in this world; *Prov* **les loups ne se mangent pas entre eux** there is honour among thieves; *Fig* **jeune l.** young go-getter; *Pol* **YoungTurk;** *Fig Fam* **mon petit l., mon gros l.** (*terme d'affection*) (my) darling, (my) pet VOIR GRAMMAIRE **A12 2** (*poisson*) sea perch, sea dace; **l. de mer** (*poisson*) sea perch, sea dace; *Fig Fam* (*marin*) old salt, seadog; (*tricot rayé*) striped tee-shirt **3** *Tech* (*dans le bois etc*) flaw; *Ind* defect **4** (*demi-masque*) eye mask, domino

loup-cervier, *pl* **loups-cerviers** [lusɛrvje] **NM** lynx

loupe [lup] **NF 1** *Opt* magnifying glass; **regarder qch à la l.** to look at sth through *or* with a magnifying glass; *Fig* to put sth under a *or* the microscope; **étudions-en tous les aspects à la l.** let's look at it very closely from every angle **2** *Méd* wen **3** (*sur arbre*) burr, burl; **un meuble en l. de noyer** a piece of furniture made of burr walnut

louper [lupe] *Fam* **VI** tu n'as pas voulu m'écouter et ça n'a pas loupé, tu t'es coupé you wouldn't listen to me and sure enough you've cut yourself; **je lui ai dit qu'il attraperait froid et ça n'a pas loupé** I told him he would catch cold and sure enough he did; **si tu continues comme ça tu vas tout faire l.** if you carry on like that you'll mess everything up *or* make a mess of everything

VT 1 (*ne pas réussir*) (*travail, discours, tarte etc*) to botch, to bungle, to make a botch *or* a mess of; (*examen*) to fail, *Am* to flunk; *Théâtre* **l. son entrée** to fluff one's entrance; **loupé!** missed!; **la soirée est loupée** the party's a flop; **la fin du film est complètement loupée** the end of the film is completely botched *or* bungled **2** (*ne pas prendre*) (*son tour, occasion, train*) to miss; **il n'en loupe pas une!** it's one stupid thing after another!; (*en parlant*) he's always opening his big mouth!; **je ne vais pas le l.** I won't let him get away with it

VPR se louper il a déjà fait plusieurs tentatives de suicide et cette fois-ci, il ne s'est pas loupé he's made several suicide attempts in the past and this time he didn't bungle it; **tu as vu son maquillage? – elle ne s'est pas loupée!** have you seen her make-up? – she's put it on with a trowel

loup-garou, *pl* **loups-garous** [lugaru] **NM 1** *Myth* werewolf **2** (*pour les enfants*) = bogeyman; **si tu ne manges pas ta soupe, attention au l.!** if you don't eat your soup, the bogeyman will get you!

loupiot [lupjo] **NM** *Fam* (*enfant*) kid

loupiote [lupjɔt] **NF** *Fam* (*lampe*) small light *or* lamp

LOURD, LOURDE [lur, lurd] **ADJ 1** (*objet, chargement, nourriture, repas etc*) heavy; (*sommeil*) heavy, deep; **démarche lourde** heavy gait; **artillerie/industrie lourde** heavy artillery/industry; **sol l.** heavy soil; **le terrain est l. aujourd'hui** *Sport* the ground is heavy *or* soft today; (*courses de chevaux*) the going is heavy *or* soft today; **marcher/quitter la pièce d'un pas l.** to walk/leave the room with a heavy tread *or* step; **yeux lourds de fatigue** eyes heavy with tiredness; **avoir le sommeil l.** to be a heavy *or* deep sleeper; **j'ai la tête lourde** I've got a thick head, my head feels fuzzy; **avoir l'estomac l.** to feel bloated; **c'est l. à digérer** it's difficult to digest, it's heavy on the stomach; **avoir le cœur l.** to feel very sad, *Litt* to have a heavy heart; **avoir la main lourde** (*punir*) to mete out punishment with a heavy hand; (*verser en quantité généreuse*) to be overgenerous; **ce travail est trop l. pour elle** this work is too much for her **2** (*à l'aspect pesant*) (*personne*) heavily-built; (*forme, silhouette, tentures etc*) heavy; **un visage aux traits lourds** a face with heavy features

3 (*qui manque de subtilité*) (*personne, comique, scène*) unsubtle, heavy-handed; (*plaisanterie*) unsubtle, obvious, clumsy; (*mouvement, style*) heavy, ponderous; **un gros garçon pataud aux mouvements lourds** a big fat lumbering oaf; **avoir l'esprit l.** to be slow(-witted) *or* dull-witted

4 (*sérieux, grave*) (*erreur*) serious, grave; (*perte*) heavy, severe, serious; (*dépenses, charges*) heavy; (*tâche, responsabilité*) heavy, weighty; **une lourde hérédité** a history of mental/physical illness in the family **5** (*temps*) close, sultry, muggy; **un parfum l.** a heavy *or* strong fragrance; **il fait l.** it's

close *or* sultry *or* muggy
6 incident/refus l. de conséquences incident/refusal fraught with consequences; **silence/nuages lourd(s) de menaces** ominous silence/clouds; **un discours l. de sous-entendus** a speech packed *or* loaded with innuendos
ADV peser l. to weigh a lot, to be heavy; *Fig* **peser l. (dans la balance)** to count for a lot; *Fig* **ça ne pèse pas l.** that doesn't count for much; **en avoir l. sur le cœur** to have a heavy heart, to feel very sad; *Fam* **il n'en reste pas l.** there isn't much left; *(dénombrable)* there aren't many left; **je n'en fais pas l.** I don't exactly overwork; **il n'en sait pas l. sur l'histoire de son pays** he doesn't know much about the history of his country; **il travaille beaucoup mais ne gagne pas l.** he works a lot but doesn't earn much; **ça ne fait pas l.** it's not much to show for it
NF *Arg* **lourde** door; **ferme la l.** put the wood in the hole

lourdaud, -aude [lurdo, -od] *Péj* **ADJ** *(maladroit)* awkward, clumsy; *(bête)* oafish
N oaf

lourdement [lurdəmã] **ADV 1** *(avec un matériel pesant)* heavily; **l. chargé/équipé** heavily laden/equipped **2** *(pesamment)* *(se déplacer)* heavily; **elle avance l.** she lumbers forward; **il est tombé l.** he fell heavily **3** *(grandement)* heavily; **se tromper l.** to be greatly mistaken; **ces changements vont peser l. sur notre budget** these changes will weigh heavily on our budget; **elle insistait l.** she *would* keep on insisting; **il insiste toujours l. sur les défauts de ses collègues** he always lays great stress on his colleagues' failings **4** *Péj (sans finesse) (rire)* coarsely

lourder [lurde] **VT** *Fam* **l. qn** to give sb the boot *or* the elbow; **se faire l. par sa petite amie** to get the boot *or* the elbow from one's girlfriend, to be given the boot *or* the elbow by one's girlfriend

lourdeur [lurdœr] **NF** *(d'objet, de charge etc)* heaviness; *(de bâtiment, d'architecture)* heaviness, massiveness; *(de traits de visage)* heaviness; *(d'administration, de bureaucratie)* unwieldiness, cumbersomeness; *(de personne) (dans les mouvements, de style)* clumsiness, awkwardness; *(manque de vivacité d'esprit)* slow (-witted)ness, dull-wittedness; *(de responsabilité)* weight; *(du temps)* sultriness, closeness; **l. d'esprit** slow(-witted)ness, dull-wittedness; *Vieilli* **avoir des lourdeurs de tête** to have fits of drowsiness, to feel heady; **j'ai des lourdeurs d'estomac** my stomach feels heavy

lourdingue [lurdɛ̃g] **ADJ** *Fam (style)* heavy; *(personne, plaisanterie)* unsubtle

loustic [lustik] **NM 1** *Fam (farceur)* joker; **il fait le l.** he's playing the fool, he's fooling around **2** *c'est un drôle de l.* *(louche)* he's a strange guy, he's an oddball

loutre [lutr] **NF** otter; *(fourrure)* otter (skin); **manteau de l.** otter-skin coat; **l. marine** *ou* **de mer** sea otter

louve [luv] **NF** she-wolf

louvet, -ette [luvɛ, -ɛt] **ADJ** dun

louveteau, -eaux [luvto] **NM 1** *Zool* wolf cub **2** *(jeune scout)* cub (scout)

louvoiement [luvwamã] **NM** *Naut* tacking; *Fig* hedging

louvoyer [luvwaje] **VI** (je louvoie, n. louvoyons; je louvoierai) *Naut* to tack, to beat about, to beat to windward; *Fig* to hedge, to beat about the bush

Louvre [luvr] **NM** **le (palais du) Louvre** the Louvre; **le Grand Louvre** the enlarged Musée du Louvre *(including all the new constructions and excavations)*; **l'école du Louvre** = art school in Paris

---

Louvre
This former royal palace became a museum in 1791–1793. It houses one of the richest art collections in the world. The museum was extended in 1989, with the construction of the glass "pyramide du Louvre" in the main courtyard, and again in 1993 when the Richelieu wing, formerly occupied by the ministry of finance, was inaugurated.

---

lover [lɔve] **VT** *(corde)* to coil; **lové dans un canapé** curled up on a couch
VPR se lover *(de serpent, d'anguille etc)* to coil up; **se l. dans un canapé moelleux** to curl up on a soft couch

loxodromique [lɔksɔdrɔmik] **ADJ** *Naut (courbe, navigation)* loxodromic; **navigation l.** plane sailing

loyal, -ale, -aux, -ales [lwajal, -o] **ADJ 1** *(honnête) (personne)* honest, fair, upright; *(procédés)* honest; *(combat)* clean; **être l. en affaires** to be straightforward *or* honest in one's business dealings; **il a été l. avec moi** he was honest *or* straight with me; **jeu l.** fair play; **ce n'est pas un adversaire l.** he doesn't play fair **2** *(serviteur, ami)* loyal, faithful, trusty; **après 25 ans de bons et loyaux services** after 25 years of good and faithful service
NF *Fam* **se battre à la loyale** to fight cleanly

loyalement [lwajalmã] **ADV 1** *(honnêtement) (agir)* honestly, fairly; *(se battre)* fairly **2** *(fidèlement) (servir)* loyally, faithfully

loyalisme [lwajalism] **NM** *Pol* loyalty

loyaliste [lwajalist] **ADJ, N** *Pol* loyalist

loyauté [lwajote] **NF 1** *(honnêteté)* honesty, fairness, uprightness **2** *(fidélité)* loyalty, faithfulness (**envers** to)

loyer [lwaje] **NM 1** rent; *Arch* **prendre une maison à l.** to rent a house; *Arch* **donner à l.** to rent (out); *Br* to let (out); *Can* **être à l.** to be a tenant, to be in rented accommodation; **vous êtes encore en retard pour payer votre l.** you're late with your rent again; **j'ai trois loyers de retard** I'm three months behind with my rent; **l. arriéré** rent arrears; **l. commercial** commercial rent; **l. nominal** nominal rent **2** *Fin* **l. de l'argent** cost of money

LP [ɛlpe] **NM** *(abrév* **lycée professionnel**) technical college

LSD [ɛlɛsde] **NM** *Chimie* LSD

LTA [ɛltea] **NF** *(abrév* **lettre de transport aérien**) AWB

lubie [lybi] **NF** whim, fad, craze; **il a des lubies, il lui prend des lubies** he has whims *or* fads *or* crazes; **il lui prit la l. de manger à 4 heures du matin** he took it into his head *or* got the crazy idea to have something to eat at 4 o'clock in the morning

lubricité [lybrisite] **NF** *(de personne, de regard)* lustfulness, lechery; *(de propos)* lewdness

lubrifiant [lybrifjã] **ADJ** lubricating
NM lubricant; **l. EP** EP lubricant; **l. extrême pression** extreme pressure lubricant

lubrification [lybrifikasjõ] **NF** lubrication

lubrifier [lybrifje] **VT** *(pr sub, impf* **n. lubrifiions, v. lubrifiiez**) to lubricate

lubrique [lybrik] **ADJ** *(homme, regard)* lustful, lecherous; *(propos)* lewd

lubriquement [lybrik(ə)mã] **ADV** *(regarder)* lustfully, lecherously; *(parler)* lewdly

Luc [lyk] **N** saint **L.** Saint Luke

lucane [lykan] **NM** *Entom* stag beetle

lucaniste [lykanist], **lucanophile** [lykanɔfil] **N** kite enthusiast *or* fan

lucarne [lykarn] **NF 1** *(fenêtre dans un toit)* dormer (window); *(tabatière)* skylight; **l.**

---

rampante dormer (window) **2** *Ftbl (de filet)* top corner

lucide [lysid] **ADJ 1** *(perspicace) (esprit, raisonnement etc)* lucid, clear; *(personne)* lucid, clear-headed; **il jette sur la société contemporaine un regard très l.** he casts a very lucid *or* clear gaze *or* eye on contemporary society; **elle ne se fait pas d'illusion sur ce qui l'attend, elle est l.** she has no illusions about what awaits her, she sees things clearly **2** *(conscient)* lucid

lucidement [lysidmã] **ADV** lucidly, clearly

lucidité [lysidite] **NF 1** *(perspicacité) (d'analyse, d'exposé)* lucidity, clearness; *(de personne)* lucidity, clear-headedness **2** *(état conscient)* lucidity; **elle a encore toute sa l.** she still has all her wits about her *or* all her faculties; **elle a des moments de l., puis se remet à délirer** she has lucid moments *or* moments of lucidity, then sinks back into delirium

Lucifer [lysifer] **N** Lucifer

luciférien, -ienne [lysiferjɛ̃, -jɛn] **ADJ** *(propre à Lucifer)* Luciferian
N *Hist* Satanist

luciole [lysjɔl] **NF** firefly, *Spéc* luciola

lucratif, -ive [lykratif, -iv] **ADJ** *(entreprise, opération)* lucrative, profitable; *(emploi)* well-paid, lucrative; **à but l.** profit-making; **sans but l.** non-profit-making, *Am* not-for-profit

lucrativement [lykrativmã] **ADV** lucratively

lucre [lykr] **NM** *Péj* lucre

ludiciel [lydisjɛl] **NM** *Ordinat* computer game

ludion [lydjõ] **NM** *Phys* Cartesian diver; *Fig (jouet des circonstances)* plaything, toy

ludique [lydik] **ADJ** play; **activité l.** play activity; **il doit y avoir une dimension l. dans ...** there has to be an aspect of play in ...

ludo-éducatif, -ive *pl* **ludo-éducatifs, -ives** [lydoedykatif, -iv] **ADJ** edutainment

ludothèque [lydɔtɛk] **NF** toy and game library

luette [lɥɛt] **NF 1** *Anat* uvula **2** *Can Fam* **se mouiller/se rincer la l.** *(prendre un verre)* to wet one's whistle, to have a drink; *(se soûler)* to get wasted *or* *Am* ratted

lueur [lɥœr] **NF 1** *(lumière faible) (de lampe, feu, allumette, soleil etc)* glow, glimmer; *(de couteau, épée)* gleam; **à la l. d'une bougie** by candlelight; **à la l. des étoiles** by starlight; **à la l. des derniers événements** in the light of recent events; **les premières lueurs de l'aube** the first light of dawn **2** *(lumière soudaine)* **l. soudaine** flash; **l'allumette jeta une dernière l. avant de s'éteindre** the match flared one last time, then went out **3** *Fig (moment bref)* *(de lucidité, colère)* flash; *(d'intelligence)* spark, glimmer; *(d'espoir)* glimmer, gleam

luge [lyʒ] **NF** toboggan, sledge, *Am* sled; *Sport* luge; **faire de la l.** to go tobogganing *or* sledging *or* *Am* sledding; *Sport* to luge

lugeur, -euse [lyʒœr, -øz] **N** *Sport* luger

lugubre [lygybr] **ADJ** *(atmosphère, humeur, personne, récit)* lugubrious, gloomy, dismal; *(endroit)* gloomy, grim; *(son, cri)* doleful, mournful

lugubrement [lygybrəmã] **ADV** lugubriously, gloomily

LUI [lɥi] **PRON PERS** *(pour un homme)* (to) him; *(pour une femme)* (to) her; *(pour un bébé, un animal)* (to) it, (to) him, (to) her; *(pour une chose, une idée)* (to) it; *(pour un pays, navire)* (to) it, (to) her; *(au pluriel)* (to) them; **je le l. donne** I give it (to) him/her, I give him/her it; **donnez-l.-en** give him/her some; **donnez-le-l.** give it (to) him/her, give him/her it; **cette maison leur appartient** this house belongs to them, this house is theirs; **je le leur ai reproché** I reproached them for it; **je l. trouve mauvaise mine** I think he/she looks ill; **je l. ai serré la main** I shook his/her hand; **je l. ai entendu dire …** I heard him/her say that …; **il l. vint une envie de tout l. dire** he/she felt a desire to tell him/her everything; **il leur jeta une pierre** he threw a stone at them; **montrez-le-leur** show it (to) them, show it

LUI² [lɥi] PRON PERS

> he/she/it *(subject)* **1** ▪ him/her/it *(object)* **2** ▪ himself/herself/itself *(reflexive)* **3**

1 *(sujet) (pour un homme)* he; *(pour un bébé, un animal)* it, he; *(pour une chose)* it; *(pour un pays, navire)* it, she; *(au pluriel)* they; **ce sont eux, c'est eux** it's them; **c'est l.** it's him; *(en le désignant)* that's him; **c'est l. qui nous a présentés** he's the one who introduced us, <u>he</u> introduced us; **c'est l. le coupable** <u>he's</u> the culprit *or* guilty one, <u>he's</u> guilty; **elle est blonde, l. est brun** she's blonde, he's dark-haired; **eux deux/tous** the two of/all of them; **Jacques et l. l'ont fait** he and Jacques did it, *Fam* Jacques and him did it; **l., au moins, il a fait un effort** he, at least, made an effort; **elle veut vendre la maison, mais est-ce que l. est d'accord?** she wants to sell the house, but does <u>he</u> agree to it?; **si j'étais l., je me méfierais** if I were him I'd be careful; **l.? il ne ferait jamais ça!** him? he'd never do that!; **mon frère, l., n'est pas venu** as for my brother, he didn't come; **il doit suivre un régime: il est malheureux, l. qui est si gourmand!** he has to go on a diet, and loving his food as he does, he's not happy about it; **ils jouent tous les deux au tennis, elle très bien, l. plutôt mal** they both play tennis, she very well, he rather badly; **elle aime le cinéma, l. non** she likes the cinema, he doesn't

2 *(objet) (pour un homme)* him; *(pour un bébé, un animal)* it, him; *(pour une chose)* it; *(pour un pays, un navire)* it, her; *(au pluriel)* them; **j'accuse son frère et l.** I accuse him and his brother; **l., je le connais, je le connais, l.** I know <u>him</u>; **l., je le connais, les autres non** him I know *or* I know <u>him</u> but not the others; **des deux frères, c'est l. que je connais le mieux** of the two brothers I know him *or* it's him I know best; **elle est plus grande que l.** she's taller than him *or* than he is; **elle gagne plus que l.** she earns more than him *or* than he does; **j'ai plus bu que l.** I've drunk more than him *or* than he has; **j'apprécie Marie plus que l.** *(plus qu'il ne l'apprécie)* I like Marie more than he does *or* than him; *(je préfère Marie)* I like Marie more than him; **elle m'a présenté à l.** she introduced me to him; **elle pense encore à l.** she still thinks about him; **ce livre est à l./à eux** this book is his/theirs; **à l. tout seul, il n'y arrivera pas** on his own he won't manage it; **à l. seul, il possède la moitié de la ville** he owns half of the town himself; **voilà une photo de l.** here's a photo of him; **c'est pour l.** it's for him; **c'est par l. que je l'ai su** it's *or* it was through him that I found out; **j'ai confiance en l.** I trust him; **c'est à l. de décider** it's for him to decide; **c'est un ami à l.** it's *or* he's a friend of his; **l'enfant n'est pas de l.** the child is not his; **maintenant tout le monde va vouloir faire comme eux** now everyone will want to do as they do

3 *(réfléchi) (pour un homme)* him(self); *(pour un bébé, un animal)* it(self), him(self); *(pour une chose)* it(self); *(pour un pays, un navire)* it(self), her(self); *(au pluriel)* them(selves); **il les rassembla autour de l.** he gathered them round him; **il ne pense qu'à l.** he thinks only of himself

lui-même PRON PERS *(pour un homme)* himself; *(pour un bébé, un animal)* itself, himself; *(pour un objet)* itself; **c'est l. qui me l'a dit** he told me so himself; **chacun d'eux travaille pour l.** each of them works for himself; *voir* **même** ADJ 3

luire [lɥir] VI *(prp luisant; pp lui, invariable in feminine; pr ind il luit, ils luisent; p hist il luit, ils luirent, parfois il luisit; fu il luira) (de métal, surface propre)* to gleam, to shine; *(de surface de l'eau, trottoirs mouillés etc)* to glisten; *(d'étoile, de soleil)* to shine; *(de feu, bougie)* to glow; *(d'yeux)* to gleam; *(de cheveux)* to be shiny, to shine; **l. au soleil** to gleam *or* shine in the sun

luisant [lɥizɑ̃] ADJ *(étoile, métal etc)* shining, bright; *(surface, pelage, peau)* shiny, glossy; *(yeux)* gleaming; *(peau)* glowing; **front l. de sueur** forehead glistening with sweat; **manteau l. d'usure** coat shiny with wear
> NM *(d'étoffe, de vernis)* shine, sheen

lumbago [lœbago] NM *Méd* lumbago

lumen [lymɛn] NM lumen

lumière [lymjɛr] NF **1** *(clarté)* light; **l. du jour** daylight; **l. du soleil** sunlight; **l. des étoiles** starlight; **l. électrique** electric light; **il n'y a plus de l.** the light's gone out; **la fenêtre donne de la l.** the window lets in (the) light; **à la l. de la lune** by moonlight; **allume la l., on n'y voit rien** put the light on, we can't see anything in here; **il y a de la l. chez lui** there's a light on *or* there are lights on at his place; **as-tu pensé à éteindre toutes les lumières?** did you remember to switch off all the lights?; **les lumières de la ville** the lights of the city, the city lights; *Aut Fam* **allume tes lumières, il y a du brouillard** put your lights on, it's foggy; **l. d'ambiance** floodlight; *Cin, TV* **l. ambiante** ambient light; *Cin, TV* **l. de base** key light; *Cin, TV* **l. diffuse** scattered light; **l. stroboscopique** strobe light; **l. tamisée** soft light

2 *Fig (compréhension)* light; **à la l. de son exposé, tout paraît évident** in the light of his presentation, everything seems clear; **mettre qch en l.** to bring sth out; **jeter une l. nouvelle sur qch** to throw *or* shed new light on sth; **faire (toute) la l. sur qch** to get (right) to the bottom of sth

3 *(connaissances rationnelles)* **les lumières de la raison** the light of reason; **avoir des lumières sur qch** to have some knowledge about sth; **j'ai besoin de tes lumières** I need the benefit of your knowledge; **le siècle des lumières** the Age of Enlightenment

4 *(homme de savoir)* **une des lumières de la science moderne/de son époque** one of the leading lights of modern science/of his age; *Fam* **ce n'est pas une l.** he's not very bright

5 *Tech (ouverture) (d'admission etc)* port; *(de mire)* aperture; **l. d'admission/d'échappement** inlet/exhaust port

6 *Phys, Astron* **l. oxhydrique** limelight; *Phys* **l. blanche** white light; **l. noire** *ou* **de Wood** black light; *Astron* **l. cendrée** earthlight, earthshine

lumignon [lymiɲɔ̃] NM **1** *(lampe)* dim light *or* lamp **2** *(bout de mèche)* candle end

luminaire [lyminɛr] NM **1** *(lampe)* light **2** *(dans une église)* lights

luminance [lyminɑ̃s] NF brightness

luminescence [lyminɛsɑ̃s] NF luminescence

luminescent [lyminɛsɑ̃] ADJ luminescent

lumineusement [lyminøzmɑ̃] ADV luminously, brightly; *Fig (expliquer)* lucidly, clearly

lumineux, -euse [lyminø, -øz] ADJ **1** *(corps, cadran)* luminous; *(pièce)* bright, filled with light; *(ciel)* bright, luminous; *Ordinat (bloc*

etc) highlighted; **montre à cadran l.** watch with a luminous dial, luminous watch; **enseigne lumineuse** illuminated sign; **couleur très lumineuse** very bright *or* intense colour; *Phys* **onde lumineuse** light wave **2** *Fig (explication, propos)* lucid, clear; **regard l.** radiant look *or* expression; **c'est une idée lumineuse** it's a brilliant idea *or* a brainwave *or Am* a brainstorm; **il est d'une intelligence lumineuse** he is extremely bright

luminosité [lyminozite] NF **1** *(de ciel)* brightness, luminosity; *(de regard)* radiance; **la l. est insuffisante pour prendre une photo** there is insufficient light (available) for taking a photo **2** *Phot (de l'objectif)* speed **3** *Ordinat* brightness; *(mise en relief)* highlighting

lump [lœp] NM lumpfish; **œufs de l.** lumpfish roe

lunaire [lynɛr] ADJ *(de la lune)* lunar; *(pareil à la lune)* moonlike; **paysage l.** lunar landscape; *Fig* **un visage l.** a moon-face
> NF *(plante)* honesty, moonwort, *Spéc* lunaria

lunaison [lynɛzɔ̃] NF *Astron* lunation, lunar month

lunatique [lynatik] ADJ *(personne)* moody

> Il faut noter que l'adjectif anglais **lunatic** est un faux ami. Il signifie **fou, dément**.

lunch, *pl* **lunches, lunchs** [lœntʃ] NM buffet lunch

lundi [lœdi] NM Monday; **le l. de Pâques/de la Pentecôte** Easter/Whit Monday *(voir aussi* **samedi)**

lune [lyn] NF **1** *Astron* moon; **la pleine l.** the full moon; **la nouvelle l.** the new moon; **les phases de la l.** the phases of the moon; **(au) clair de l.** (in the) moonlight; **nuit sans l.** moonless night; **la l. se lève** the moon is rising; **face de l., visage de pleine l.** moon-face, moonlike face; *Fig* **demander la l.** to ask for the moon; **je ne te demande pas la l.** I'm not asking for the moon; *Fig* **promettre la l.** to promise the moon; **je ne vous promets pas la l.** I can't promise you the moon; *Fig Fam* **être dans la l.** to be miles away, to be in the clouds; *Fig très Fam* **être con comme la l.** to be dead from the neck up, *Br* to be as thick as two short planks; *Fig Fam* **tomber de la l.** to look flabbergasted **2** *Arch, Litt (mois)* moon, month **3** *Fam (derrière)* bottom, backside **4** **vieilles lunes** old-fashioned *or* outmoded ideas **5** *Vieilli* **il est dans une bonne/mauvaise l.** *(humeur)* he is in one of his good/bad moods; **lunes** vagary, caprice, whim **6** **l. de mer, poisson l.** (ocean) sunfish **7** **pierre de l.** moonstone
> ▸▸*Bot* **l. d'eau** white water-lily; **l. de miel** honeymoon; **l. rousse** April moon

luné [lyne] ADJ *Fam* **être bien/mal l.** to be in a good/bad mood

lunetier, -ière [lyntje, -jɛr] N *(fabricant)* spectacle manufacturer
> ADJ **industrie lunetière** spectacle industry

lunette [lynɛt] NF **1** **(paire de) lunettes** (pair of) glasses *or* spectacles *or Fam* specs *or Am* eyeglasses; **porter des lunettes** to wear glasses *or* spectacles *or Fam* specs; *Fam* **c'est un type à lunettes, facile à reconnaître** he wears specs, he's easy to recognize; *Fam* **c'est le type à lunettes** he's the guy in specs; **lunettes de vue** corrective glasses; **lunettes d'écaille** horn-rimmed glasses VOIR GRAMMAIRE A10 **2** *Opt* **l. (d'approche)** telescope, field glass; *Mil* **l. de pointage** sighting telescope; **l. de fusil** gun sight(s); **fusil à l.** gun with sights; **l. astronomique** astronomical telescope **3** *Archit* lunette **4** *(de guillotine)* lunette **5** *(siège des W.-C.)* seat
> ▸▸*Aut* **l. arrière** rear window; **lunettes noir-**

es dark glasses, *Fam* shades; **lunettes de plongée** swimming goggles; **lunettes de protection** goggles; **lunettes de soleil,** *Belg* **l. solaires** sunglasses, *Fam* shades

lunetterie [lynɛtri] NF spectacle trade

lunule [lynyl] NF **1** *Math* lune **2** *Anat (d'ongle)* half-moon, *Spéc* lunula

lupanar [lypanar] NM *Litt Vieilli* brothel

lupin [lypɛ̃] NM *(plante)* lupin

lupus [lypys] NM *Méd* lupus

lurette [lyrɛt] NF *Fam* **il y a belle l.** ages ago; **il y a belle l. que je ne t'ai pas vu** I haven't seen you for ages, it's been ages since I saw you

luron, -onne [lyrɔ̃, -ɔn] N *Fam* **c'est un gai ou un joyeux l.** he's quite *or* a bit of a lad, *Vieilli* he's a gay dog; **c'est une sacrée luronne** she's quite a girl

lusitanien, -ienne [lyzitanjɛ̃, -jɛn] *Antiq* ADJ Lusitanian

N **L.** Lusitanian

lusophone [lysɔfɔn] ADJ Portuguese-speaking

N Portuguese speaker

lustrage [lystraʒ] NM *(de tissu, cuir)* glossing, glazing, lustring; *(de verre)* polishing; **l. des fourrures** lustring of furs

lustre[1] [lystr] NM **1** *(lampe)* chandelier **2** *(brillant)* lustre, *Am* luster, gloss **3** *Litt (éclat, prestige)* lustre, *Am* luster; **il faut redonner du l. à cette ancienne demeure** some of the lustre needs to be brought back to this stately old dwelling; **redonner du l. à un parti politique** to give a political party a facelift

lustre[2] NM *Litt (cinq ans)* lustrum; *Fig* **ça fait des lustres qu'on t'attend!** we've been waiting ages for you!; *Fig* **depuis des lustres** for ages

lustré [lystre] ADJ *(poterie)* glazed; *(fourrure, tissu, barbe, robe d'un cheval, cheveux)* glossy; **étoffe lustrée par l'usure** cloth shiny with wear

lustrer [lystre] VT *(glace, meuble, voiture)* to polish (up); *(par l'usure)* to make shiny; *Tech (tissu, cuir)* to glaze, to gloss, to lustre

VPR **se lustrer ce tissu se lustre facilement** this material gets shiny very quickly

lustrerie [lystrəri] NF *Ind, Com* lighting industry

lustrine [lystrin] NF cotton lustre

lut [lyt] NM *Cér, Ind* lute, luting

Lutèce [lytɛs] N *Antiq* Lutetia

lutéine [lytein] NF *Biol, Chimie* lutein

luter [lyte] VT *Cér, Ind* to lute, to seal with luting

luth [lyt] NM **1** *Mus* lute **2** *Zool* **l. ou tortue l.** leatherback (turtle)

luthéranisme [lyteranism] NM *Rel* Lutheranism

lutherie [lytri] NF *Mus* **1** *(fabrication)* stringed instrument making **2** *(instruments)* stringed instruments

luthérien, -ienne [lyterjɛ̃, -jɛn] ADJ, N *Rel* Lutheran

luthier [lytje] NM stringed instrument maker

luthiste [lytist] N *Mus* lutanist, lutenist, lute player

lutin [lytɛ̃] NM **1** *(créature de conte etc)* imp, elf, goblin; *(irlandais)* leprechaun **2** *(enfant)* imp

ADJ mischievous, impish

lutiner [lytine] VT **1** *(femme)* to fondle, to tickle **2** *(à la manière d'un lutin)* to plague, to torment; *(avec espièglerie)* to tease

lutrin [lytrɛ̃] NM **1** *Rel* lectern **2** *(pour soute-*

nir un livre, des feuilles) reading *or* book stand **3** *(endroit où se tient le chœur)* choir stall **4** *Belg, Can, Suisse Mus* music stand

lutte [lyt] NF **1** *Sport* wrestling; **l. libre** all-in *or* freestyle wrestling; **l. gréco-romaine** Graeco-Roman wrestling; **faire de la l.** to wrestle

2 *(combat, action violente)* fight, struggle; *(morale, de guerre)* conflict; **entrer/être en l. contre qn** to enter into/to be in conflict with sb; **après plusieurs années de l.** after several years of struggle; **la l. doit continuer!** the fight *or* struggle must go on!; **il faut soutenir les travailleurs en l.** we must support the workers in their fight *or* struggle; **les partis en l. pour le pouvoir** the opposing parties fighting for power; **luttes intestines** infighting; **l. d'influence** struggle for influence; **luttes parlementaires** parliamentary clashes; **l. armée** armed struggle; **se livrer à une l. acharnée pour qch** to be engaged in a desperate struggle for sth; **gagner de haute l.** to win by sheer force; **l. à mort** life-and-death struggle, fight to the death

3 *(pour venir à bout d'un mal)* **l. contre l'alcoolisme/le cancer** fight against alcoholism/cancer; **l. pour la liberté** struggle for freedom; **l. antipollution** fight against pollution

4 *Biol, Fig* **l. pour la vie** struggle *or* fight for survival; *(d'un malade)* fight for life

5 *(antagonisme)* conflict; **la l. entre le devoir et la passion/le bien et le mal** the conflict between duty and passion/good and evil; **l. d'intérêts** conflict *or* clash of interests; **la l. des classes** the class struggle *or* conflict

lutter [lyte] VI **1** *Sport* to wrestle (**avec, contre** with) **2** *(se battre)* to struggle, to fight; **l. contre la maladie** to fight (against) *or* to combat disease; **l. contre le vent** to battle with *or* against the wind; **l. contre un incendie** to fight a fire; **l. pour l'indépendance** to fight for independence; **l. contre le sommeil** to fight off sleep; **l. contre la tentation** to fight (against) temptation; **l. contre l'alcoolisme** to fight (against) alcoholism **3** *(rivaliser)* **l. de vitesse avec qn** to race sb; **elles luttent d'adresse** they're using all their skills to outdo each other

lutteur, -euse [lytœr, -øz] N **1** *Sport* wrestler **2** *(pour une cause etc)* fighter; **un tempérament de l.** a fighting *or* fighter's temperament

lux [lyks] NM *Phys* lux

luxation [lyksasjɔ̃] NF *Méd (d'articulation)* dislocation, *Spéc* luxation; **l. congénitale** congenital dislocation

luxe [lyks] NM **1** *(abondance, richesse)* luxury; *(de maison, pièce, ameublement etc)* luxuriousness, sumptuousness; **vivre dans le l.** to live in luxury; **goûts de l.** luxurious *or* extravagant tastes; **un l. tapageur** a flashy display of wealth; **étaler son l.** to flaunt one's wealth

2 *(qualité)* luxury, luxuriousness; **articles de l.** luxury articles; **édition de l.** de luxe edition; **voiture de l.** de luxe car, luxury car; **boutique de l.** luxury goods shop; **taxe (sur les produits) de l.** tax on luxury goods

3 *(bien superflu, coûteux)* luxury; **mon seul l., c'est d'aller au cinéma** my only luxury *or* indulgence is going to the cinema; **elle ne peut pas s'offrir le l. de refuser cet emploi** she can't afford the luxury of turning this job down; **je me suis payé le l. de le lui dire** I gave myself the pleasure of telling him so; **se payer le l. d'un cigare** to indulge in (the luxury of) a cigar; **je vais faire nettoyer ce vieil**

imperméable, ce ne sera pas du l. I'm going to have this old raincoat cleaned, it really needs it; **j'ai acheté un nouveau tapis, ce n'était pas du l.** I bought a new carpet, it had to be done *or* it was an essential purchase

4 *(profusion)* abundance; **un l. de précautions** a wealth of precautions; **l. de détails** wealth *or* abundance of details

Luxembourg [lyksɑ̃bur] NM *(pays, ville)* Luxembourg

luxembourgeois, -oise [lyksɑ̃burʒwa, -waz] ADJ of/from Luxembourg

N **L.** Luxembourger

luxer [lykse] VT *(articulation, coude etc)* to dislocate, *Spéc* to luxate

VPR **se luxer se l. un membre** to dislocate a limb; **se l. l'épaule** to dislocate one's shoulder, to put one's shoulder out

luxueusement [lyksyøzmɑ̃] ADV luxuriously, sumptuously

luxueux, -euse [lyksyø, -øz] ADJ luxurious, sumptuous

luxure [lyksyr] NF *Litt* lust

> Il faut noter que le nom anglais **luxury** est un faux ami. Il signifie **luxe**.

luxuriance [lyksyrjɑ̃s] NF luxuriance

luxuriant [lyksyrjɑ̃] ADJ *(végétation, forêt etc)* luxuriant, lush; *(chevelure)* luxuriant; *(imagination)* fertile; *Archit, Littér* **un style l.** a luxuriant style

luxurieux, -euse [lyksyrjø, -øz] ADJ lascivious, lewd, lustful, sensual

luzerne [lyzɛrn] NF *(plante)* lucerne, alfalfa

lycaon [likaɔ̃] NM wild dog

lycée [lise] NM **1** *Scol Br* ≃ secondary school, *Am* ≃ high school *(for pupils aged 15 to 18)*; *Anciennement* **l. (d'enseignement) professionnel** technical school; **l. technique** technical high school; **l. technique hôtelier** hotel school; **il se souvient du l. comme de ses meilleures années** he looks back on his schooldays as the best years of his life **2** *Antiq* **le L.** the Lyceum

lycéen, -éenne [liseɛ̃, -eɛn] N *Br* ≃ secondary school pupil, *Am* ≃ high school pupil

ADJ *Br* ≃ secondary school, *Am* ≃ high school

lycra® [likra] NM Lycra®; **pantalon en l.** Lycra® trousers

lymphatique [lɛ̃fatik] ADJ **1** *(glande etc)* lymphatic **2** *(personne)* lethargic, apathetic

NM lymphatic (duct)

lymphe [lɛ̃f] NF lymph

lymphocyte [lɛ̃fɔsit] NM lymphocyte

lymphoïde [lɛ̃fɔid] ADJ *(cellules, tissu)* lymphoid

lymphome [lɛ̃fɔm] NM lymphoma

lynchage [lɛ̃ʃaʒ] NM lynching

lyncher [lɛ̃ʃe] VT to lynch

lynx [lɛ̃ks] NM lynx; *Fig* **avoir des yeux de l.** to have eyes like a hawk, to be hawk-eyed

Lyon [ljɔ̃] N Lyons

lyonnais, -aise [ljɔnɛ, -ɛz] ADJ of/from Lyons

N **L.** *(natif)* native of Lyons; *(habitant)* inhabitant of Lyons

NM **le L.** *(région)* Lyonnais

lyophilisation [ljɔfilizasjɔ̃] NF *Tech* freeze-drying

lyophiliser [ljɔfilize] VT *Tech (café, soupe etc)* to freeze-dry; **café lyophilisé** freeze-dried coffee

lyre [lir] NF *Mus* lyre; *Fam* **toute la l.** the whole lot (of them), the whole shoot; **(oiseau-)l.** lyre bird

lyrique [lirik] ADJ **1** *Littér (poème, poète etc)* lyric **2** *(mis en musique)* **art l.** opera; **artiste l.** opera singer; **drame l.** lyric drama, opera; **comédie l.** comic opera, operetta; **théâtre l.** opera house **3** *(poétique, passionné)* lyrical; **des envolées lyriques** flights of lyricism; **parler de qch/qn d'une façon l.** *(avec lyrisme)* to wax lyrical about sth/sb

lyrisme [lirism] NM **1** lyricism; **parler avec l. de qch** to wax lyrical about sth; **s'exprimer avec l.** to wax lyrical **2** *(exaltation)* excessive NM lyric poet

M, m ¹ [ɛm] NM *(lettre)* M, m

m ² **1** *(abrév* **mètre)** m; **1 m 50** 1.5 m **2** *Gram* (*abrév* **masculin**) m

M. (*abrév* **Monsieur**) Mr

m' *voir* **me**

ma [ma] *voir* **mon**

maboul [mabul] *Fam* **ADJ** *(fou)* crazy, nuts ▪ N nut

mac [mak] NM *Arg (maquereau)* pimp

Macabées [makabe] NMPL *Bible* = Maccabées

macabre [makabr] **ADJ** *(découverte, histoire)* macabre, gruesome, grisly; *(humour)* macabre; **danse m.** dance of death, danse macabre

macache [makaʃ] **ADV** *Fam* **m. (bono)** *(absolument pas)* no way!, nothing doing!, not likely!; *(absolument rien)* not a sausage, *surtout Am* zilch

macadam [makadam] NM **1** *(revêtement)* macadam; **m. goudronné** tarmac(adam) **2** *(route)* road

macadamisage [makadamizaʒ] NM, **macadamisation** [makadamizasjɔ̃] NF *(de route)* tarmacking

macadamiser [makadamize] **VT** *(route)* to tarmac

macaque [makak] NM *(singe)* macaque; **m. rhésus** rhesus monkey ▪ N *Fam (personne)* ugly ape

macareux [makarø] NM puffin

macaron [makarɔ̃] NM **1** *Culin* macaroon **2 macarons** *(coiffure)* coils *(over the ears)*; *Fam* earphones **3** *(badge)* badge; *(décoration)* rosette; *(autocollant)* sticker; *Journ* **m. de presse** press badge

macaroni [makaroni] NM **1** *Culin* piece of macaroni; **des macaronis** macaroni VOIR GRAMMAIRE A14 **2** *Arg Péj (Italien)* wop, *Br* Eyetie, *Am* guinea

Maccabées [makabe] NMPL *Bible* Maccabees

macchabée [makabe] NM *très Fam (mort)* stiff, corpse

Macédoine [masedwan] NF **la M.** Macedonia

macédoine [masedwan] NF **1** *Culin* **m. de fruits** fruit salad; **m. de légumes** mixed vegetables, *Spéc* macedoine of vegetables **2** *Fam Vieilli (mélange)* medley, miscellany, *Péj* hotchpotch

macédonien, -ienne [masedɔnjɛ̃, -jɛn] **ADJ** Macedonian ▪ N **M.** Macedonian

macération [maserasjɔ̃] NF **1** steeping, soaking **2** *Rel* mortification

macérer [masere] (**je macère; je macérerai**) **VT 1** to steep, to soak; **laisser m. qch** to leave something to steep *or* soak **2** *Rel (chair)* to mortify

VI to steep, to soak; **la viande doit m. plusieurs jours** the meat should be left to steep *or* soak for several days; *Fig Fam* **laissons-le m. quelques jours** let's leave him stewing for a few days

Mach [mak] NM *Aviat* **(nombre de) M.** Mach (number)

mâche [maʃ] NF *Bot* corn salad, lamb's lettuce

mâchefer [maʃfɛr] NM *Tech* clinker, slag

mâchement [maʃmɑ̃] NM *Rare* chewing, *Fml* mastication

mâcher [maʃe] **VT** *(nourriture)* to chew, *Fml* to masticate; *(quelque chose qui croustille ou qui croque)* to munch; *(d'un animal) (fourrage)* to champ, to chomp; **m. le mors** *(d'un cheval)* to champ at the bit; **ne pas m. ses mots** not to mince (one's) words; **m. le travail ou la besogne à qn** to spoon-feed sb; **m. le bois** *(d'un outil émoussé etc)* to chew up the wood

machette [maʃɛt] NF machete

Machiavel [makjavɛl] N Machiavelli

machiavélique [makjavelik] **ADJ** *(ruse etc)* Machiavellian

machiavélisme [makjavelism] NM Machiavellianism

mâchicoulis [maʃikuli] NM *Archit* machicolation; **à m.** machicolated

machin [maʃɛ̃] NM *Fam* **1** *(objet)* thing(ummy), thingumajig, thingumabob, whatsit(sname), what-d'you-call-it; **qu'est-ce que c'est que ce m.-là?** what's that thing(ummy) *or* thingumajig *or* thingumabob? **2** *(personne)* **monsieur M.** Mr What's-his-name, what-d'you-call-him, Thingummy; **madame M.** Mrs What's-her-name, what-d'you-call-her, Thingummy; **j'ai vu m.-chouette aujourd'hui** I saw what's-his-name *or* what-d'you-call-him *or* thingummy today

machinal, -ale, -aux, -ales [maʃinal, -o] **ADJ** *(action, geste)* mechanical, unconscious; *(réaction)* automatic, instinctive; *(travail)* mechanical; **faire qch de façon machinale** to do sth mechanically *or* unconsciously

machinalement [maʃinalmɑ̃] **ADV** *(agir)* mechanically, unconsciously; *(réagir, répondre etc)* automatically

machination [maʃinasjɔ̃] NF plot, machination

machine [maʃin] NF **1** *(appareil)* machine; *Ind* **les machines** the machinery, the plant; **machines agricoles** agricultural machinery *or* machines; **écrire une lettre à la m.** to type a letter; **écrit à la m.** typed, typewritten; **travailler le métal à la m.** to machine metal; **fait à la m.** *(objets)* machine-made; *(opération)* done by machine; **laver qch en m.** to machine-wash sth, to wash sth in a machine; *Fig* **la m. administrative/judiciaire** the administrative/judicial machinery *or* machine;

Fig **la m. est usée/fatiguée** *(corps humain)* the old body has had it/is tired out; *Fig Péj* **il n'est qu'une m. à penser/à faire de l'argent** he's nothing but a thinking/money-making machine; *Théâtre* **pièce à machines** play with stage effects **2** *(locomotive)* locomotive, engine; *Fam (moto)* machine; **m. volante** flying machine **3** *Naut (moteur)* engine; **salle des machines** engine room; **stopper les machines** to stop the engines; **faire m. arrière** to reverse the engine; *Fig* to backtrack

▸▸ **m. à adresser** addressing machine; **m. à affranchir** franking machine; **m. agrafeuse** stapling machine, stapler; **m. à aléser** boring machine, fine borer; **m. à battre** threshing machine; **m. de bureau** office machine; **m. à café** coffee machine; **m. à calculer** calculator; *(plus grande)* adding machine, calculating machine; *Typ* **m. à composer** typesetting machine; **m. comptable** accounting machine; **m. à coudre** sewing machine; **m. à écrire** typewriter; **m. à écrire à mémoire** memory typewriter; *Aut* **m. d'équilibrage des roues** wheel-balancing machine; **m. à fraiser** milling machine; **m. de guerre** engine of war; **m. infernale** explosive device; **m. interprète de cartes perforées** punch card reader; **m. à laver**, *Belg* **m. à lessiver** washing machine, washer; **m. à laver la vaisselle** dishwasher; **m. à plier les documents** paper folding machine; **m. poinçonneuse** *(de cartes perforées)* punch; **m. à polycopier** duplicating machine; **m. à rayons X** X-ray machine; *Tech* **m. de rectification** grinding machine; **m. à repasser** ironing machine; **m. à sous** slot machine, *Fam* one-armed bandit, *Br* fruit machine; **m. de traitement de l'information** data processor; **m. à** *ou* **de traitement de texte** word processor; **m. à tricoter** knitting machine; **m. trieuse** sorter; **m. à vapeur** steam engine

machine-outil, *pl* **machines-outils** NF machine tool

machiner [maʃine] **VT** *Vieilli* to plot, to scheme; *(complot)* to hatch; **affaire machinée d'avance** put-up job; **qu'est-ce qu'il machine?** what's he plotting?; **c'est lui qui a tout machiné pour les faire accuser** he's the one who fixed *or* engineered everything so that they'd be blamed

machinerie [maʃinri] NF **1** *(machines)* machinery; *Ind* machinery, plant **2** *(salle), Ind* machine room; *Naut* engine room

machinisme [maʃinism] NM mechanization

machiniste [maʃinist] NM **1** *Théâtre* scenes-hifter, stagehand; *Cin, TV* grip; **m. de plateau** grip; **m. caméra** dolly operator; **m. de travelling** tracker **2** *(chauffeur) (d'autobus, de tramway)* driver; **'faire signe au m.'** 'request stop'

machisme [ma(t)ʃism] NM *Péj (virilité)* machismo; *(phallocratie)* male chauvinism

machiste [ma(t)ʃist] ADJ, NM *Péj* = macho

machmètre [makmetr] NM *Aviat* Mach-meter

macho [matʃo] *Péj* NM *(phallocrate)* male chauvinist (pig)

ADJ INV *(comportement, attitude)* male chauvinist, macho

mâchoire [maʃwar] NF **1** *Anat (d'une personne, d'un animal)* jaw; **rire à s'en décrocher la m.** to split one's sides (laughing); *Fam* **jouer** *ou* **travailler des mâchoires** *(manger avec appétit)* to get stuck in **2** mâchoires *(d'un étau, d'une tenaille, d'une pince)* jaws; *Tech* **m. d'une poulie** flange of a pulley; *Aut* **mâchoires de frein** brake shoes

mâchonnement [maʃɔnmā] NM chewing; *Méd* tooth-grinding, *Spéc* bruxism

mâchonner [maʃɔne] VT **1** *(nourriture, cigare)* to chew (on); *(d'un cheval)* to chew on, to munch; **m. son crayon** to chew (the end of) one's pencil **2** *(marmonner) (menace)* to mutter; *(prière)* to mumble, to mutter

mâchouiller [maʃuje] VT *Fam* to chew away at *or* on

mâchure [maʃyr] NF *Tex (dans velours, drap)* flaw

mâchurer[1] [maʃyre] VT *(noircir)* to soil, to dirty; *Typ (feuille)* to mackle, to blur

mâchurer[2] VT *Tech (partie métallique d'un étau)* to dent, to bruise

macis [masi] NM *Bot, Culin* mace

macle [makl] NF *Bot* water chestnut

maçon, -onne [masɔ̃, -ɔn] ADJ mason; **abeille maçonne** mason bee

NM **1** *(artisan)* bricklayer; *(avec des pierres)* (stone)mason **2** *(franc-maçon)* Mason, freemason

mâcon [makɔ̃] NM **m., vin de Mâcon** Mâcon (wine)

maçonnage [masɔnaʒ] NM *(action)* bricklaying; *(avec des pierres)* laying of stones; *(ouvrage)* masonry

maçonner [masɔne] VT *(construire)* to build; *(recouvrir de pierres) (mur)* to face with stone; *(condamner) (porte, fenêtre)* to wall up; *(avec des briques)* to brick up

maçonnerie [masɔnri] NF **1** *(avec des briques)* brickwork, masonry; *(avec des pierres)* masonry, stonework; **grosse m.** work on the superstructure; **petite m.** interior building work; **entreprise de m.** building *or* construction firm **2** *(organisation secrète)* (free)masonry

maçonnique [masɔnik] ADJ masonic

macramé [makrame] NM macramé; **faire du m.** to do macramé; **un set de table en m.** a set of macramé table mats

macre [makr] NF *Bot* water chestnut

macreuse [makrøz] NF **1** *(oiseau)* scoter (duck) **2** *Culin* shoulder of beef

macrobiotique [makrobjɔtik] ADJ macrobiotic

NF macrobiotics

macrocéphale [makrosefal] ADJ macrocephalic

macroclimat [makroklima] NM macroclimate

macro-commande, *pl* **macro-commandes** [makrokɔmād] NF *Ordinat* macro (command)

macrocosme [makrokɔsm] NM macrocosm

macroéconomie [makroekɔnɔmi] NF macroeconomics

macroéconomique [makroekɔnɔmik] ADJ macroeconomic

macroenvironnement [makroāvirɔnmā] NM macroenvironment

macroinstruction [makroɛ̃stryksjɔ̃] NF *Ordinat* macroinstruction

macrolangage [makrolāgaʒ] NM *Ordinat* macrolanguage

macromarketing [makromarketiŋ] NM, **macromercatique** [makromerkatik] NF macromarketing

macromolécule [makromɔlekyl] NF *Chimie* macromolecule

macroordinateur [makroordinatœr] NM mainframe

macrophotographie [makrofɔtografi] NF *Phot* macrophotography

macropode [makrɔpɔd] NM *(poisson)* paradise fish

macroscopique [makrɔskɔpik] ADJ macroscopic

macrostructure [makrostryktyr] NF macrostructure

macula [makyla] NF *Anat* macula

maculage [makylaʒ] NM *(action de salir)* soiling, staining; *Typ* off-setting, mackling; *(tache)* stain, spot

maculature [makylatyr] NF *Typ (pour l'emballage)* waste; *(feuille tachée)* smudged *or* mackled sheet; *(feuille intercalaire)* interleaf

macule [makyl] NF **1** *Typ (pour l'emballage)* waste sheet **2** *Arch, Litt (tache)* stain, spot **3** *Méd* macula **4** *Typ (salissure)* mackle, smudge; *(feuille tachée)* smudged *or* mackled sheet; *(feuille intercalaire)* interleaf

maculer [makyle] VT *Litt (de sang)* to stain, to spot; *(de boue)* to spatter, to spot **(de** with); *Typ* to mackle; **maculé de taches d'encre** smeared with ink stains

Madagascar [madagaskar] NM Madagascar; **aller à M.** to go to Madagascar

madame, *pl* **mesdames** [madam, medam] NF **1** *(titre)* Mrs; **M. Martin** Mrs Martin; **Mesdames Martin** the Mrs Martin; **M. Veuve Martin** Mrs Martin, widow of David/*etc* Martin; **M. la marquise/la comtesse de X** the Marchioness/the Countess of X; **je voudrais parler à m. la directrice** *(du magasin, d'un service)* I would like to speak to the manager; *(d'une école)* I would like to speak to the headmistress; *Fml* **comment va m. votre mère?** how is your mother?

2 *(utilisé seul)* **voici le chapeau de m.** here is your hat, madam; **M. se plaint que ...** *(dit par un vendeur)* the lady *or* this lady *or Fml* madam is complaining that ...; *(dit par un domestique)* the mistress *or Fml* madam is complaining that ...; **M. est sortie** Madam is not at home; **M. a sonné?** you rang, madam?; **M. est servie** dinner is served(, madam); **occupez-vous de M.** *(à un employé de magasin)* see to the *or* this lady

3 *(apostrophe)* madam, *surtout Am* ma'am; *(à une dame titrée)* your ladyship; *(dans la police, l'armée etc)* ma'am; **non/au revoir, m.** no/goodbye, *Fml* no/goodbye, madam; *(à une femme qui s'appelle Martin)* no/goodbye, Mrs Martin; **oui, m., la colonelle** yes, colonel; *(épouse du colonel Martin)* yes, Mrs Martin; **entrez, mesdames** come in, ladies; **m.?** *(dans un magasin)* can I help you?, *Fml* can I help you, madam?

4 *(dans une lettre) (always written in full)* **Madame** Dear Madam; **chère Madame** *(qui s'appelle Martin)* Dear Mrs Martin

5 *Fam (dame)* **jouer à la m.** to put on airs (and graces)

Madeleine [madlɛn] NF **1** *Bible* Magdalen(e); *Fam* **pleurer comme une M.** to cry one's eyes *or* heart out **2** *Culin* **m.** madeleine

mademoiselle, *pl* **mesdemoiselles** [madmwazɛl, medmwazɛl] NF **1** *(titre)* Miss; **M. Martin** Miss Martin; **Mesdemoiselles Martin et Durand** the Misses Martin and Durand, Miss Martin and Miss Durand; *Fml Vieilli* **comment va m. votre cousine?** how is your cousin? **2** *(utilisé seul)* **M. se plaint que ...**

(dans un magasin) the *or* this young lady is complaining that ... **3** *(apostrophe)* **merci m.** thank you, *Fml* thank you, miss; *(à une femme qui s'appelle Martin)* thank you, Miss Martin; **m. est servie** dinner is served(, madam); *Fml (à Caroline)* dinner is served, Miss Caroline; **m., avez-vous choisi?** *(au restaurant)* are you ready to order(, miss)?; **mesdemoiselles, un peu de silence je vous prie!** *(dans une classe)* let's have some quiet, girls, please! **4** *(dans une lettre) (always written in full)* **Mademoiselle** Dear Madam; **chère Mademoiselle** *(qui s'appelle Martin)* Dear Miss Martin

Madère [madɛr] N *Géog* Madeira
NM **m., vin de M.** Madeira (wine)

madone [madɔn] NF madonna; *Fig* **un visage de m.** a madonna-like face

madras [madra(s)] NM *(tissu)* madras (cotton); *(foulard)* (cotton) headscarf

madré, -ée [madre] *Litt* ADJ sly, crafty, wily
N sly fox, crafty devil

madrépore [madrepɔr] NM *Zool* madrepore

Madrid [madrid] N Madrid

madrier [madrije] NM (piece of) timber; *(façonné)* thick board *or* plank; *(poutre)* beam

madrigal, -aux [madrigal, -o] NM *Mus* madrigal

madrilène [madrilɛn] ADJ of/from Madrid
N **M.** *(natif)* native of Madrid; *(habitant)* inhabitant of Madrid

maelstrom [malstrɔm] NM maelstrom

maestria [maɛstrija] NF mastery; **avec m.** in a masterly manner, brilliantly

maestro [maɛstro] NM *Mus* maestro

maf(f)ia [mafja] NF **1** **la M.** the Mafia **2** *(groupe aux intérêts communs)* gang; **le monde du spectacle est une vraie m.** show business is a real Mafia

maf(f)ieux, -ieuse [mafjø, -jøz] ADJ Mafia
N mafioso

maf(f)ioso, *pl* **maf(f)iosi** [mafjozo, -zi] NM mafioso

mafflu [mafly] ADJ *Arch, Litt (personne)* chubby-cheeked, chubby-faced; *(visage)* chubby

maganer [magane] VT *Can (chose)* to spoil, to waste; *(personne)* to manhandle

magasin [magazɛ̃] NM **1** *(boutique)* shop, *surtout Am* store; **grand m.** department store; **chaîne de magasins** chain of shops *or* stores; **employé(e) de m.** shop assistant, *Am* (sales)clerk; **courir** *ou* **faire les magasins** to go shopping **2** *(entrepôt)* store, warehouse, storeroom; *TV etc* **m. de décors** scene dock; **marchandises en m.** stock in hand; **nous n'avons pas cet article en m.** we don't have that item in stock **3** *(de fusil, de projecteur)* magazine; **m. à papier** *(d'une imprimante etc)* paper tray

▸▸ **m. d'alimentation** grocery shop *or Am* store; **m. d'armes** armoury, *Am* armory; **m. de décors** scene dock; **m. détaxé** duty-free shop *or Am* store; **m. discompte** discount store; **m. électronique** on-line shop *or Am* store; **m. franchisé** franchise; *Can* **m. général** general store; **magasins généraux** (public) bonded warehouse(s); *Mktg* **m. laboratoire** = model test-shop used to monitor consumer behaviour; **m. à libre service** self-service store; **m. minimarge** discount store; **m. de proximité** convenience store; *Can* **m. à rayons** department store; **m. à succursales multiples** chain store; **m. d'usine** factory (retail) outlet, factory shop; **m. vidéo** video shop *or Am* store

magasinage [magazinaʒ] NM **1** *Com (de marchandises)* warehousing, storing **2** **(droits de) m.** warehouse dues, storage (charges) **3** *Can* **faire du m.** to go shopping

magasiner [magazine] **VI** *Can* to go shopping

magasinier [magazinje] **NM** warehouseman, storekeeper

magazine [magazin] **NM 1** *(journal)* magazine; **elle est dans tous les magazines en ce moment** her photo is in all the magazines at the moment; **m. féminin** women's magazine; **m. hebdomadaire/mensuel** weekly/monthly (magazine); **m. d'actualités** current affairs magazine; **m. électronique** ezine, e-zine; **m. d'information** news magazine; **m. littéraire** literary magazine *or* review; **m. people** celebrity magazine; **m. à sensation** trashy magazine; **m. télé, m. télévision** magazine programme; **m. en couleur** colour magazine **2** *Radio, TV* magazine (programme); **m. d'actualités** news programme; **m. d'information** current affairs (magazine) programme; **m. culturel** arts programme

magdalénien, -ienne [magdalenjɛ̃, -jɛn] **ADJ, NM** *Hist* Magdalenian

mage [maʒ] **NM 1** *Antiq* magus; *Bible* **les (trois) Rois Mages** the Three Wise Men, the (Three) Magi **2** *(voyant)* seer

magenta [maʒɛ̃ta] **ADJ INV, NM** magenta

Maghreb [magrɛb] **NM le M.** the Maghreb *(French-speaking North Africa)*

maghrébin, -ine [magrebɛ̃, -in] **ADJ** of/from the Maghreb
N M. person from the Maghreb

> **Maghrébin**
> This term usually refers to people from Algeria, Morocco and Tunisia, although it can also refer to Libyans and Mauritanians. It has a particular resonance in contemporary France, where immigrants from these countries constitute the largest ethnic minority.

magicien, -ienne [maʒisjɛ̃, -jɛn] **N 1** *(qui pratique la magie)* magician, sorcerer, *f* sorceress **2** *(illusionniste)*, *Fig* magician

magie [maʒi] **NF** magic; **c'est de la m.!** it's magic!; **comme par m.** as if by magic; *Fig* **la m. du verbe** the magic of language *or* words ▸▸ **m. blanche** white magic; **m. noire** black magic

magique [maʒik] **ADJ 1** *(pouvoirs)* magic, magical; *(mot, formule, baguette)* magic; **c'est m.!** it's magic! **2** *Fig (formidable) (spectacle, musique etc)* magical

magiquement [maʒikmɑ̃] **ADV** magically

magister [maʒistɛr] **NM 1** *Arch (maître d'école)* (village) schoolmaster **2** *Péj (pédant)* pedant

magistère [maʒistɛr] **NM 1** *Univ* post-graduate vocational qualification **2** *Fig (autorité)* authority **3** *(titre)* Grand Master; **M. de l'Ordre de Malte** Grand Master of the Order of Malta

magistral, -ale, -aux, -ales [maʒistral, -o] **ADJ 1** *(admirable) (œuvre, interprétation, démonstration)* masterly, authoritative; *(réussite)* brilliant, resounding; *Fig (rossée, engueulade)* sound, proper, thorough; *(gifle)* resounding; *(erreur)* colossal, monumental; **il s'est fait rembarrer de façon magistrale** he was told in no uncertain terms where to go; **réussir un coup m.** to pull off a master stroke **2** *(docte) (ton)* magisterial, authoritative **3** *Univ* **cours m.** lecture; **enseignement m.** lecturing **4** *Pharm* **préparation magistrale** prescribed medication specially made up by the pharmacist for the particular patient

magistralement [maʒistralmɑ̃] **ADV** authoritatively

magistrat [maʒistra] **NM 1** magistrate; **il est m.** he's a magistrate, he sits on the Bench; **m. du parquet** public prosecutor **2 premier m. de France** supreme judicial officer of France

magistrature [maʒistratyr] **NF 1** *(personnes)* magistrature; **la m. assise** = the judges, the Bench; **la m. debout** = the (body of) public prosecutors; **entrer dans la m.** *(devenir juge)* to be appointed a judge; *(devenir fonctionnaire public)* to be appointed a public prosecutor **2** *(période)* magistrature

magma [magma] **NM** *Chimie, Géol* magma; **un m. informe de boue et de pierres** a shapeless heap *or* pile of mud and stones; *Fig* **un m. d'idées confuses** a jumble of confused ideas

magnanerie [maɲanri] **NF 1** *(élevage)* silkworm breeding, *Spéc* sericulture **2** *(bâtiment)* silkworm house

magnanier, -ière [maɲanje, -jɛr] **N** silkworm breeder, *Spéc* sericulturist

magnanime [maɲanim] **ADJ** magnanimous; **se montrer m.** to show magnanimity, to be magnanimous

magnanimement [maɲanimmɑ̃] **ADV** magnanimously

magnanimité [maɲanimite] **NF** magnanimity

magnat [magna] **NM 1** *Com, Ind* magnate, tycoon; **m. des médias** media mogul; **magnats du pétrole** oil magnates *or* tycoons; **m. de la presse** press baron, press lord **2** *Hist (de Pologne, Hongrie)* magnate, grandee

magner (se) [s(ə)maɲe] **VPR** *Fam* to get a move on, to get one's skates on; *très Fam* **magne-toi le train!** get your backside *or* Am butt into gear!

magnésie [maɲezi] **NF** *Chimie, Pharm* magnesia, magnesium oxide; *Pharm* **sulfate de m.** Epsom salts

magnésite [maɲezit] **NF** *(carbonate de magnésium)* magnesite; *(silicate de magnésium)* meerschaum

magnésium [maɲezjɔm] **NM** *Chimie* magnesium; **éclair de m.** magnesium light *or* flash

magnétique [maɲetik] **ADJ** magnetic; **champ m.** magnetic field; **enregistrement sur bande m.** recording on magnetic tape, tape-recording; *Fig* **exercer un pouvoir m.** to exert a hypnotic *or* magnetic power (**sur** on, over)

magnétiquement [maɲetikmɑ̃] **ADV** magnetically

magnétisable [maɲetizabl] **ADJ** magnetizable; *(personne)* hypnotizable

magnétisation [maɲetizasjɔ̃] **NF 1** *Phys* magnetization **2** *(d'une personne)* hypnotizing, mesmerizing

magnétiser [maɲetize] **VT 1** *(fer etc)* to magnetize **2** *(personne)* to hypnotize, to mesmerize; *Fig* **auditoire magnétisé** hypnotized *or* spellbound audience; **orateur qui magnétise les foules** speaker who hypnotizes *or* mesmerizes the crowds, speaker who holds the crowds in his spell

magnétiseur [maɲetizœr] **NM** *(guérisseur)* healer; *(hypnotiseur)* hypnotist

magnétisme [maɲetism] **NM 1** *Phys* magnetism; **le m. terrestre** the earth's magnetism; **m. rémanent** residual magnetism **2** *(hypnotisme)* hypnotism, mesmerism; *Fig* **m. personnel** personal magnetism; **une personne qui a beaucoup de m.** a person with a great deal of charisma *or* personality; **m. animal** animal magnetism

magnétite [maɲetit] **NF** *Minér* magnetite, lodestone

magnéto [maɲeto] **NF** *Élec* magneto
NM *Fam (magnétophone)* tape recorder

magnétocassette [maɲetokasɛt] **NM** cassette deck *or* recorder; *Ordinat* **m. numérique** digital cassette recorder

magnétomètre [maɲetɔmɛtr] **NM** *Tech* magnetometer

magnétophone [maɲetɔfɔn] **NM** tape recorder; **m. (enregistreur) à cassettes** cassette recorder; **m. à bande** audio tape recorder; **m. à bobines** reel-to-reel tape recorder

magnétoscope [maɲetɔskɔp] **NM** video, video recorder, *Am* VCR; **enregistrer qch au m.** to video sth, to record sth on video; **m. d'enregistrement** recording deck; **m. de lecture** playback deck; **m. de standard professionel** video(tape) recorder, VTR; **m. à cassette** video cassette recorder, VCR; **m. à cassette vidéo numérique** digital video recorder

magnétoscoper [maɲetɔskɔpe] **VT** to videotape, to video, to record on video

magnificat [magnifikat] **NM INV** *Rel* magnificat

magnificence [maɲifisɑ̃s] **NF** *(richesse, éclat)* magnificence, *Br* splendour, *Am* splendor; *Litt (générosité)* munificence, lavishness

magnifier [maɲifje] **VT** *(pr sub, impf n.* **magnifiions, v. magnifiiez)** **1** *(exalter)* to magnify, to glorify **2** *(idéaliser)* to idealize

magnifique [maɲifik] **ADJ 1** *(château, palais, meubles etc)* magnificent, splendid; *(temps)* glorious, superb, splendid, magnificent; *(corps)* superb, magnificent; *(film, tableau, fruits, cadeau etc)* splendid, marvellous, wonderful; **on a une vue m. depuis le deuxième étage** there is a magnificent *or* superb view from the second floor; **(c'est) m.!** (it's) marvellous *or* great *or* fantastic!; **elle était m. dans sa robe de mariée** she looked magnificent *or* wonderful *or* superb in her wedding dress; **un bébé m.** a bonny (little) *or* lovely (little) baby; **il est m. dans le rôle** he is magnificent *or* superb *or* brilliant in the role **2** *Vieilli (généreux, prodigue) (personne)* liberal, munificent; **Laurent le M.** Lorenzo il Magnifico; **Gatsby le M.** the Great Gatsby

magnifiquement [maɲifikmɑ̃] **ADV** *(décoré, vêtu)* magnificently, splendidly; *(réussir)* brilliantly; **un morceau de musique m. exécuté** a brilliantly performed piece of music; **la soirée s'est m. passée** the party went splendidly *or* marvellously *or* wonderfully

magnitude [maɲityd] **NF** *Astron, Géol* magnitude; **un séisme de m. 5 sur l'échelle de Richter** an earthquake measuring 5 on the Richter scale

magnolia [maɲɔlja], **magnolier** [maɲɔlje] **NM** magnolia (tree)

magnum [magnɔm] **NM** magnum

magot¹ [mago] **NM** *Fam (d'argent)* hoard, pile; *(économies)* savings, nest egg; **il a dû amasser un joli m.** he must have built up a nice little nest egg *or* a nice little pile; **dis-nous où tu as mis le m.!** tell us where you've stashed the loot!

magot² **NM 1** *(singe)* Barbary ape **2** *(figurine)* magot

magouillage [maguja ʒ] **NM, magouille** [maguj] **NF** *Fam* scheming, shady dealing; **faire des magouillages** to scheme; **magouillages électoraux** pre-election scheming

magouiller [maguje] *Fam* **VT** to scheme; **il magouille un mauvais coup** he's cooking up a dirty trick
VI il est toujours en train de m. he's always wheeling and dealing, he's always scheming; **il magouille pour avoir des ordinateurs gratuits** he's trying to wangle some free computers, he's scheming to get some free computers; **il a dû m. pour avoir ce poste** he had to do some scheming to get the job

magouilleur, -euse [magujœr, -øz] **N** *Fam* schemer, wheeler-dealer

magret [magrɛ] **NM** *Culin (d'oie, de canard)* fillet, breast

magyar, -are [magjar] ADJ Magyar N **M.** Magyar

maharaja [maaradʒa] NM maharaja(h)

maharani [maarani] NF maharanee

mahatma [maatma] NM mahatma

mah-jong [maʒɔ̃g] NM mah-jong(g)

Mahomet [maɔmɛ] N Mohammed, Mahomet

mahométan, -ane [maɔmetɑ̃, -an] ADJ, N *Vieilli* Mohammedan, Mahometan

mahométisme [maɔmetism] NM *Vieilli* Mohammedanism

mai [mɛ] NM May; **en m.** in May; **au mois de m.** in (the month of) May; **le sept m.** (on) the seventh of May, (on) May the seventh, *Am* (on) May seventh; **le premier m.** the first of May; *Admin* May Day SEE GRAMMAR A81; B60–1

Mai 68
The events of May 1968 came about when student protests, coupled with widespread industrial unrest, culminated in a general strike and rioting. De Gaulle's government survived the crisis, but the issues raised made the events a turning point in French social history.

MAIF [maif] NF *abrév* Mutuelle assurance des instituteurs de France

maigre [mɛgr] ADJ *(personne, animal, bras, cou)* thin, *Péj* skinny; *(viande)* lean; *(revenu, récolte, résultats)* meagre, *Am* meager, poor; *(végétation)* sparse, scanty; *(barbe)* straggly, sparse; *(conclusions, explication)* thin; *(succès)* very limited; **m. comme un clou** as thin as a rake; *Can Fam* **m. comme un chicot** *ou* **un manche à balai** as thin as a rake; **homme grand et m.** tall, thin man; **fromage m.** low-fat cheese; **m. filet d'eau** thin trickle of water; **m. repas** scanty *or* frugal meal; **jour m.** day of abstinence; *Typ* **caractères maigres** light-face type
N *(personne)* **un grand m.** a tall, thin man; **c'est une fausse m.** she's not as thin as she looks
NM **1 maigres** *(de rivière)* shallows **2** *(viande)* **un morceau de m.** a piece of lean (meat)
ADV **manger** *ou* **faire m.** not to eat meat, to abstain from meat

maigréchine [mɛgreʃin] ADJ *Can Fam* scrawny, skinny

maigrelet, -ette [mɛgrəlɛ, -ɛt] *Péj* ADJ skinny
N skinny person

maigrement [mɛgrəmɑ̃] ADV meagrely, *Am* meagerly, poorly; **il est m. payé** he's poorly paid, he gets a meagre pay

maigreur [mɛgrœr] NF *(de personne)* thinness, *Péj* skinniness; *Fig (de végétation)* sparseness, scantiness; *(de récolte, salaire)* meagreness, *Am* meagerness, poorness; **d'une effrayante** frighteningly thin

maigrichon, -onne [mɛgriʃɔ̃, -ɔn], **maigriot, -otte** [mɛgrijo, -ɔt] ADJ, N *Fam* = **maigrelet**

maigrir [mɛgrir] VI to get thin(ner), to lose weight; **elle essaie de m.** she's trying to lose weight, she's slimming; **j'ai maigri de dix kilos** I've lost ten kilos; **régime pour m.** (weight-loss) diet
VT **1 m. qn** *(d'une maladie)* to make sb thin(ner); *(d'un vêtement)* to make sb look thin(ner) **2** *(pièce de bois)* to thin

mail [maj] NM **1** *Vieilli (allée)* mall, avenue, promenade **2** *Hist (jeu, lieu)* pall-mall **3** *Arch (marteau)* mallet

mailing [meliŋ] NM mailshot; **faire un m.** to do a mailshot

maillage [mɑjaʒ] NM **1** *Pêche (dimension des mailles d'un filet)* meshing **2** *(structuration en réseau)* **le m. de la région est insuffisant pour ce qui est des transports en commun** the region's public transport network *or* infrastructure is underdeveloped

maille [mɑj] NF **1** *(en tricot etc)* stitch; **m. (à l')endroit** plain (stitch); **m. (à l')envers** purl (stitch); **une m. à l'endroit, une m. à l'envers** knit one, purl one; **m. qui file** ladder, *Am* run **2** *(tissu tricoté)* knitwear; **une robe en m. de coton** a knitted cotton dress **3** *(d'une chaîne)* link; **j'aime la m. de son bracelet** I like the style of link in her bracelet; **cotte de mailles** coat of mail **4** *(de filet, de grillage etc)* mesh; **filet à larges mailles** wide-mesh net; **passer entre** *ou* **à travers les mailles du filet** to slip through the net

maille [mɑj] NF **avoir m. à partir avec qn** to have a set-to with sb; **avoir m. à partir avec la justice** to have a brush with the law

maillechort [mɑjʃɔr] NM nickel silver

mailler [mɑje] VT **1** *(fil)* to net, to mesh **2** *Naut* to shackle **3** *(organiser en réseau)* to network **4** *Suisse (tordre, fausser)* to warp
VI **1** *Pêche* to be netted **2** *Suisse (s'énerver, se mettre en colère)* to get worked up
VPR **se mailler** *Suisse (se tordre)* **se m. la cheville/le genou** to twist one's ankle/one's knee; *Fig* **se m. de rire** to kill oneself (laughing), to be in stitches

maillet [mɑjɛ] NM **1** *(outil)* mallet **2** *Sport (au polo)* stick, mallet; *(au croquet)* mallet

mailloche [mɑjɔʃ] NF **1** *(outil)* beetle, large mallet **2** *Mus* bass drumstick

maillon [mɑjɔ̃] NM **1** *(de chaîne)* link; **m. tournant** swivel; *Fig* **n'être qu'un m. de la chaîne** to be just one link in the chain **2** *Naut* shackle

maillot [mɑjo] NM **1** *(tee-shirt)* T-shirt, tee-shirt; *(pour la danse)* leotard; *Sport (de footballeur, d'équipe)* shirt, jersey; *(de coureur, rameur)* vest, singlet; **m. (de bain)** *(pour femme)* swimsuit, *Br* swimming *or* bathing costume; *(pour homme)* (swimming *or* bathing) trunks; **leur nouvelle collection de maillots** their new swimwear collection; **m. de corps** *(pour homme)* vest, *Am* undershirt; **m. une pièce/deux pièces** one-piece/two-piece swimsuit; **être m. jaune** to be the overall leader of the Tour de France; **m. de marin** striped teeshirt; *(pull)* striped sweater **2** *(pour bébé)* swaddling clothes

MAIN [mɛ̃] NF **1** hand; **faire qch de la m. droite/gauche** to do sth right-handed/left-handed *or* with one's right/left hand; **faire qch à la m.** to do sth by hand; *(fabriquer)* to make sth by hand; **fait à la m.** *(pull etc)* handmade; **travailler de ses mains** to work with one's hands; **écrire une lettre de sa propre m.** to write a letter in one's own hand; **notes écrites à la m.** handwritten notes; **d'une (seule) m.** with one hand; **je n'ai que deux mains** I only have one pair of hands; **prendre un plateau/son courage à deux mains** to take a tray/one's courage in both hands; *Fig* **signer qch des deux mains** to sign sth eagerly; *Fig* **souscrire à deux mains à qch** to subscribe unreservedly to sth; **je lui ai serré la m.** I shook hands with him, I shook his hand; **dire adieu de la m. à qn** to wave goodbye to sb; **donner la m. à qn** to hold sb's hand; **donne ta m. à Philippe** *(pour traverser la rue)* give Philippe your hand, take *or* hold Philippe's hand; **ils se tenaient (par) la m., ils se donnaient la m.** they were holding hands; *Fig* **se donner la m.** to give each other a helping hand; *Fig* **ces deux-là peuvent se donner la m.** they're two of a kind, those two are as bad as each other; **prendre qn par la m.** to take sb's hand, to take sb by the hand; *Fig* **tu n'as qu'à te prendre par la m.** just go

for it, just do it; **il n'a qu'à se prendre par la m. et le faire** he just has to do it; *Fig* **se prendre en m.** to take oneself in hand; **prendre qn en m.** to take sb in hand; **prendre une affaire/une situation en m.** to take a matter/a situation in hand; **il a sa voiture bien en m.** he's got the feel of his car; **j'ai la situation en m.** I've got the situation in hand *or* under control; **la m. dans la m.** hand in hand; **avoir/tenir qch dans la m.** to have/ hold sth in one's hand; **avoir une canne/une craie à la m.** to have a stick/a piece of chalk in one's hand; **mourir les armes à la m.** to die on the battlefield; **ne rien savoir faire de ses mains** to be hopeless with one's hands; **je ne suis pas très adroite de mes mains** I'm not very good with my hands; **la bouteille m'a échappé des mains** the bottle slipped out of *or* from my hands; **de m. en m.** from hand to hand; **passer de m. en m.** *(d'un objet)* to pass *or* be passed from hand to hand *or* from person to person; *Fig (d'une maison, d'un livre etc)* to go *or* pass through several hands; **passer aux mains de …** to pass *or* fall into the hands of …; **haut les mains!, les mains en l'air!** hands up!; **faire qch d'une m. habile** *ou* **experte** *ou* **exercée** to do sth with a skilled *or* an expert hand, to do sth skilfully; **en venir aux mains** to come to blows; **se battre à main(s) nue(s)** to fight with bare hands *or* fists; **combat à mains nues** bare-fisted *or* bare-knuckle fight; **attaque/vol à m. armée** armed attack/robbery; **venir/repartir les mains vides** to come/return empty-handed; *Fig* **arriver les mains dans les poches** to arrive unprepared; **donner d'une m. et reprendre de l'autre** to give with one hand and take back with the other; **demander la m. d'une jeune fille à ses parents** to ask a girl's parents for her hand (in marriage); **accorder/refuser sa m. à qn** *(d'une femme)* to give/refuse sb one's hand in marriage; **tendre la m.** to hold *or* stretch out one's hand (**à qn** to sb); *Fig (pour l'aider)* to hold *or* stretch out a hand (to sb); **tendre à qn une m. secourable** to hold *or* stretch out a helping hand to sb; *Fig* **on le soupçonna de vouloir tendre la m. aux protestants** he was suspected of making conciliatory moves towards the Protestants; *Fig* **passer la m. dans le dos à qn** to butter sb up; **porter la m. à son chapeau** *(pour saluer)* to touch one's hat, to tip one's hat; *Fig* **on ne le voit pas souvent mettre la m. à son portefeuille** you don't often see him putting his hand in his pocket; **porter** *ou* **lever la m. sur qn** to lift *or* raise one's hand to sb; *Fam* **tu veux ma m. sur la figure?** do you want my hand across your face?; **mettre la m. sur qn** *ou* **au collet de qn** *(de la police)* to catch sb, *Fam* to collar *or* nab sb; *(le trouver)* to find sb; **mettre la m. sur qch** *(trouver qch que l'on cherchait)* to lay one's hands on sth, to put one's hand on sth; *(trouver par hasard)* to come across sth, to find sth; **je n'en mettrais pas ma m. au feu** *ou* **à couper** I shouldn't like to swear to it; **j'en mettrais ma m. au feu** *ou* **à couper** I'd swear to it; **mettre la m. à la pâte** *ou* **à l'ouvrage** to lend a hand; **mettre la dernière m. à qch** to put the finishing touches to sth; *Arg* **mettre la m. au panier de qn** to grope sb's behind; **prendre qn la m. dans le sac** to catch sb red-handed; **ne pas y aller de m. morte** *(en frappant, insultant qn)* not to pull one's punches; *(exagérer)* to overdo it; **faire m. basse sur qch** to get one's hands on sth; **avoir qch sous la m.** *ou* **à portée de (la) m.** to have sth handy *or* within easy reach *or* close at hand; **le premier objet qui lui est tombé sous la m.** the first object that came to hand; **faire qch en sous-m.** to do sth in an underhand way; **ne pas laisser ce produit à portée de m. des enfants** keep out of the reach of children; *Fam* **donner un coup de m. à qn** to lend *or* give sb a hand; **prêter la m. à qn pour faire qch** to lend sb a hand to do sth; **prêter la m. à qch** to have a hand in sth; **se faire la m.** to get one's hand in; **pour garder la m.** in order to keep your hand in; **il avait gardé la m.** he hadn't lost the knack *or* his touch; **il a perdu la m.** he's lost the knack *or* his touch; *(d'un sportif, musicien)* he's out of practice; **avoir le coup de m. (pour faire qch)** to have the knack (of doing sth); **ce n'est pas à mettre entre toutes les mains** it mustn't fall into the wrong hands; **une m. de fer dans un gant de velours** an iron hand *or* fist in a velvet glove; **d'une m. de fer** with an iron hand; **il empoigna le kalachnikov à pleines mains** he grabbed the kalashnikov with both hands; **il puise à pleines mains dans la caisse** he's got his hand in the till; **il a puisé à pleines mains dans les caisses de l'État** he liberally helped himself from the state coffers; **donner de l'argent à pleine(s) main(s)** to dish out money by the handful; **prendre qch à pleines mains** to take handfuls of sth; **il prit le livre à pleines mains** he took the book in both hands; **payer de la m. à la m.** to pay cash in hand; **tomber entre les mains** *ou* **aux mains** *ou* **sous la m. de qn** to fall into sb's hands *or* clutches; **tomber aux mains de l'ennemi** to fall into enemy hands; **l'affaire est entre les mains du juge Martin** the case is in the hands of Mr Justice Martin; **mon avenir est entre vos mains** my future is in your hands; **la décision est entre vos mains** the decision is in your hands *or* is up to you *or* is yours; **être en** *ou* **entre (de) bonnes mains** to be in good hands; **remettre qch à qn en mains propres** to deliver sth to sb in person; **acheter qch en première/seconde m.** to buy sth first-hand/second-hand; **article de seconde m.** second-hand article; **renseignements de première m.** first-hand information; **avoir la m. verte** to have green fingers *or Am* a green thumb; **ça nous laisse les mains libres pour agir** that gives us a free hand; **garder les mains libres** to keep a free hand; **j'ai les mains liées** my hands are tied; **avoir la m. légère** to have a delicate touch; *Litt (être habile)* to be clever with one's hands; *(être délicat)* to act with restraint *or* discretion; *(ne pas faire sentir son autorité)* to rule with a light hand; *(ne pas assaisonner suffisamment)* to underseason; **tu as eu la m. légère avec la crème/le sucre** you haven't put enough cream/sugar in; **avoir la m. lourde** *(avec le poivre, le whisky etc)* to be over-generous, to be a bit heavy-handed (**avec** with); *(punir)* to mete out punishment with a heavy hand; **ce commerçant a la m. un peu lourde** this shopkeeper always gives you a bit over the weight; **avoir la m. leste** *(baladeuse)* to have wandering hands; *(être prompt à gifler)* to be a bit too quick with one's hands; **avoir la m. heureuse** to be lucky; **j'ai eu la m. heureuse** I was *or* got lucky, I had a lucky break; **mains criminelles/sacrilèges** criminal/sacrilegious hands; **dessin à m. levée** freehand drawing; **voter à m. levée** to vote by a show of hands; **gagner haut la m.** to win easily *or* hands down; *Vieilli* **de longue m.** for a long time (past); *Fig* **se laver les mains de qch** to wash one's hands of sth; *Fig* **se frotter les mains** to be rubbing one's hands with glee; **grand comme la m.** tiny; **leur maison est grande comme la m.** their house isn't big enough to swing a cat in; *Prov* **aux innocents les mains pleines** fortune favours fools, beginners have all the luck; *Mus* **morceau à quatre mains** piece for four hands, duet; **m. de maître** master hand; **de m. de maître** by a master('s) hand; **un concerto exécuté de m. de maître** a masterfully performed concerto; **la cérémonie a été organisée de m. de maître** the ceremony was a masterpiece of organiza-

tion; **c'est fait de m. de maître** it's a masterpiece; **on reconnaît la m. du maître** this is obviously the work of a master; **reconnaître la m. d'un peintre** to recognize a painter's style; **à m. droite/gauche** on the right-hand/left-hand side

2 *Cartes* lead; **avoir/perdre la m.** to have/lose the lead; **passer la m.** *Cartes* to pass the lead; *Fig* to stand aside, to give someone else a chance; **passer la m. à son fils** to hand over the reins to one's son

3 *Ordinat* pointing hand

4 *Couture* **petite m.** junior assistant

5 *Typ (de papier)* quire

ADV **tricoté/fait/cousu m.** hand-knitted/made/sewn

▸▸**m. d'accoucheur** claw-like hand; **m. courante** *(d'escalier)* handrail; *Com* day-book; *Com* **m. courante de caisse** counter cash book; *Com* **m. courante de dépenses** paid cash book; **m. courante de justice** *(dans un commissariat de police)* incident book; *Com* **m. courante de recettes** received cash book; **m. de Fatma** hand of Fatima; *Tél* **mains libres** *(appareil)* hands-free; **kit mains libres** hands-free kit

mainate [menat] **NM** myna(h) (bird)

main-d'œuvre [mɛ̃dœvr] **NF** *(personnes, travail)* manpower, workforce; *Écon* labour; *Am* labor; **embaucher de la m.** to take on workers; **m. étrangère** foreign labour(ers); **frais de m.** labour costs; **m. contractuelle** contract labour; **m. qualifiée** skilled labour; **m. temporaire** temporary labour

main-forte [mɛ̃fɔrt] **NF INV** **prêter m. à qn** to come to sb's assistance *or* aid

mainlevée [mɛ̃lve] **NF** *Jur (d'un acte)* lifting; **m. de saisie** restoration of goods *(taken in distraint)*

mainmise [mɛ̃miz] **NF** seizure (**sur** of); *Fig* **la m. du gouvernement sur les médias** the government's appropriation *or* takeover of the media

maint [mɛ̃] **ADJ** *Litt* many a; **m. auteur** many an author; **maintes et maintes fois, à maintes reprises, en maintes (et maintes) occasions** time and (time) again

maintenance [mɛ̃tnɑ̃s] **NF 1** *Ind (entretien)* maintenance, service; **m. sur site** on-site maintenance **2** *Mil* keeping up to strength

maintenant [mɛ̃tnɑ̃] **ADV** now; **vous devriez être prêt m.** you ought to be ready by now; **à vous m.** now it's your turn; **dès m., à partir de m.** from now on(wards), in future, *Fml* henceforth; **m. que tu es grand** now (that) you're a big boy; **je vous donne ce conseil, m. vous en faites ce que vous voulez** that's my advice to you, (now) take it or leave it; **m. reste à savoir si les employés voudront reprendre le travail** the question now is whether the employees will be willing to go back to work; **les jeunes de m.** young people today *or* nowadays, the young people *or* the youth of today **VOIR GRAMMAIRE A21**

mainteneur [mɛ̃tnœr] **NM** *Bourse* **m. de marché** market maker

MAINTENIR [mɛ̃tnir] *(conj like* **tenir**) **VT 1** *(soutenir, retenir, tenir fermement)* to keep *or* hold in position; **colonnes qui maintiennent la voûte** columns that hold up *or* support the vault; **m. la foule** to hold back the crowd; **m. son cheval** to keep one's horse under control **2** *(entretenir, garder) (tradition)* to maintain, to keep, to uphold; *(discipline)* to maintain, to keep; *(paix)* to keep, to maintain, to preserve; *(décision)* to abide by; **m. qn dans ses fonctions** to maintain *or* keep sb in office; **m. sa position** to maintain one's position; **je maintiens que c'est faux** I maintain that it's untrue; **les médecins font tout pour le m. en vie** the doctors are doing everything pos-

sible to keep him alive; **m. qch à température constante** to keep *or* maintain sth at a constant temperature; **nos programmes sont maintenus malgré la grève** the station is maintaining normal service despite the strike; **on accuse le gouvernement de m. cette entreprise en activité de façon artificielle** the government has been accused of using artificial means to keep the company operating

VPR **se maintenir** *(de prix, dollar, taux de change, cours de la Bourse)* to remain steady, to hold up *or* steady; **se m. dans les bonnes grâces de qn** to keep in favour with sb, to stay in sb's good books; *Fam* **comment ça va? – je me maintiens** how are you? – (I'm) bearing up; **cela ne peut pas se m. longtemps** it can't last long; **le temps se maintient** the weather is holding

maintien [mɛ̃tjɛ̃] **NM 1** *(fait de conserver dans le même état)* maintenance; *(de la loi, d'un principe)* upholding; *(de la discipline)* maintenance, keeping; **le m. du pouvoir d'achat des salariés doit être une priorité** maintaining wage-earners' purchasing power must be a priority; *Mil* **force de m. de la paix** peacekeeping force; **m. de l'ordre** policing, maintenance of law and order; *Jur* **m. dans les lieux** right(s) of occupancy, security of tenure; *Ordinat* **m. majuscule** caps lock **2** *(allure, posture)* bearing, deportment; **leçons de m.** lessons in deportment

maire [mɛr] **NM** mayor; *(en Écosse)* provost; **monsieur/madame le m.** the Mayor, His/Her Worship (the Mayor); *(en s'adressant à lui/elle)* Your Worship; *Hum* **passer devant (monsieur) le m.** to tie the knot, to get hitched

Maire

In France, the mayor has obligations not only to the community but also to national government. He or she is responsible for promulgating national law as well as supervising the local police and officiating at civic occasions. Mayors are elected by the "conseil municipal" (and thus indirectly by the town's residents).

mairesse [mɛrɛs] **NF** *Vieilli (femme du maire)* mayoress; *Rare (femme maire)* mayor

mairie [mɛri] **NF** *(lieu)* town hall, *Am* city hall; *(administration municipale)* town *or* city council, *Am* city hall; **la m. a organisé un voyage pour les personnes âgées de la ville** the council has organized a trip for the town's senior citizens; **c'est un employé de m.** he works for the council, he's a council worker

Mairie

Also called the "hôtel de ville", this is the centre of municipal government. The "mairie" serves as a vital information source for town residents. People go there to ask about taxes, to get married in a civil ceremony, to enrol in certain community-sponsored classes, etc.

mais [mɛ] **ADV** *Litt* **n'en pouvoir m.** to be unable to do anything about it

CONJ 1 *(marque l'opposition)* but; **famille riche m. honnête** rich but honest family; **il n'est pas très intelligent m. il est très travailleur** he's not very intelligent but he's a hard worker; **non seulement ..., m. aussi** *ou* **encore ...** not only ..., but also ... **2** *(emphatique)* **m. oui!** oh yes!, of course!; **m. non!** oh no!, not at all!, of course not!; **m. c'est vrai!** but it's true!, it really is true!; **m. enfin!**

well really!; **m. enfin je te l'avais bien dit!** I told you!; **elle ne fait rien de la journée, m. vraiment rien** she does nothing all day, absolutely nothing **3** *(transition)* **m. qu'avez-vous donc?** whatever's the matter?; **m. à quoi penses-tu?** whatever's got into you?; **m. tu l'as déjà vu?** what, you've already seen it?; **m. j'y pense, je ne l'ai pas encore appelé!** I've just thought, I haven't rung him yet!

NM il y a un m. there's one snag; **il n'y a pas de m. (qui tienne)** there are no buts about it

maïs [mais] **NM** *(plante)* maize, *Am* corn; *(légume)* (sweet) corn; **farine de m.** cornflour, *Am* cornstarch

maison [mɛzɔ̃] **NF 1** *(habitation)* house; **m. individuelle** detached house; **m. bourgeoise** luxurious house; **il porte des pantoufles dans la m.** he wears slippers indoors or around the house

2 *(foyer)* home; **tenir la m. de qn** to keep house for sb; **à la m.** at home; **retournons à la m.** let's go home, let's go back to the house; **elle travaille à la m.** she works at or from home; **ça fait longtemps que tu n'es pas venu à la m.** it's a long time since you came to our house; **dépenses de (la) m.** household expenses; **ça ne va pas fort à la m. en ce moment** things aren't too good at home just now; **toute la m. dort** the whole house is asleep; **le fils de la m.** the son of the house; **ami de la m.** friend of the family; **chez eux, c'est la m. du Bon Dieu** they keep open house, their door is always open

3 *(entreprise)* firm, company; **cela fait vingt ans qu'elle est dans la m., elle a vingt ans de m.** she's been with the firm or company for twenty years; **la m. décline toute responsabilité en cas de perte ou de vol** we accept no responsibility for loss or theft; **la m. ne fait pas crédit** we do not give credit; **la M. du Stylo** the Pen Shop; **l'esprit de la m.** the company spirit

4 *(lignée)* **la m. de Bourbon** the House of Bourbon

5 *(domestiques)* household, staff; **la m. du Roi** the Royal Household; **gens de m.** servants, (domestic) staff

6 *Astrol* house

ADJ INV 1 home-made; **spécialité m.** speciality of the house **2** *Fam (énorme)* colossal; **on s'est pris une engueulade m.** we got an almighty telling-off **3** *Fam (très réussi)* fantastic

▸▸ *Banque* **m. affiliée** affiliated company, *Am* affiliate; **m. d'acceptation** accepting house; **m. d'arrêt** ≃ remand centre; **m. de campagne** *(résidence secondaire)* house in the country, country house; *(de style campagnard)* country cottage; **m. centrale** prison; **m. close** brothel; **m. de commerce** business; **m. de convalescence** convalescent home; *Vieilli* **m. de correction** reformatory; **m. de courtage** brokerage house; **m. de couture** fashion house; **m. de la culture** ≃ arts centre; **m. de détail** retail business; **M. de Dieu** house of God; **m. de disques** record company; **m. d'édition** publisher, publishing house; **m. d'éducation surveillée** approved school, *Am* reformatory; **m. d'enfants** children's holiday centre, *Am* camp; **m. familiale** holiday or *Am* vacation home *(for families on low incomes)*; *Fig Fam* **m. de fous** madhouse; **m. de gros** wholesale business; **m. des jeunes et de la culture** ≃ youth club and arts centre; **m. de jeux** gambling club, gaming club; **m. de maître** large luxurious house; **m. mère** parent company; *Rel* mother house; **m. de passe** brothel; **m. de poupées** doll's house; **m. de la presse** newsagent's; **m. de prêt** loan office company; **m. de rapport** rental property; **m. de redressement** reformatory; **m. religieuse** convent; **m. de rendez-vous** love nest; **m. de repos**

rest home; **m. de retraite** old people's home; **m. de santé** *(établissement hospitalier)* nursing home; *(psychiatrique)* mental home; **M. du Seigneur** house of God; **m. à succursales multiples** multiple outlet company; *Fin* **m. de titres** securities firm; **m. de tolérance** brothel; **m. de vente par correspondance** mail order firm or house

Maison-Blanche (la) [lamɛzɔ̃blɑ̃ʃ] **NF** the White House

maisonnée [mɛzɔne] **NF** household, family

maisonnette [mɛzɔnɛt] **NF** small house; *(à la campagne)* cottage

maistrance [mɛstrɑ̃s] **NF** *Naut* petty officers

maître, maîtresse¹ [mɛtr, mɛtrɛs] **NM 1** *(personne qui contrôle)* master, *f* mistress; **je veux être m. chez moi** I insist on being master in my own house; **ce chien n'obéit qu'à son m.** the dog obeys nobody but its master; **agir/parler en m.** to act/speak authoritatively; **être m. de la situation** to be master of or in control of the situation; **un dictateur fou qui veut devenir le m. du monde** a mad dictator who wants to take over or rule the world; **trouver son m.** to meet one's match; **être/rester son propre m.** to be/remain one's own master; **être/rester m. de soi** to be/remain self-possessed, to be/remain in control of one's emotions; **il n'était plus m. de lui-même** he lost control (of himself); **être m. de son véhicule** to be in control of one's vehicle; **le conducteur n'était plus m. de son véhicule** the driver (had) lost control of the car; **se rendre m. de qch** to take possession of sth; **tableau de m.** masterpiece; **les grands maîtres de la peinture flamande/de la musique** the great masters of Flemish painting/the great composers; **coup de m.** masterstroke; **être passé m. dans l'art de (faire) qch** to be a past master at (doing) sth; *Naut* **second m.** petty officer; **premier m.** chief petty officer; **être le seul m. à bord** to be sole master on board; *Fig* to be free to choose, to be free to do whatever one wants; *Fig* **c'est toi le seul m. à bord** you're the boss, you're in charge

2 *Scol* (school)teacher

3 *Jur (forme d'adresse) (pour un avocat qui s'appelle Martin)* Mr/Mrs/Miss Martin, *Am* counselor; **M. Dupont s'occupera de l'affaire** Mr/Mrs/Miss Dupont will be dealing with the case

4 *(titre octroyé à un peintre etc)* Maestro

ADJ chief, principal, main; **m. mot** key word; **poutre maîtresse** *(en métal)* main girder; *(en bois)* main beam; **cheville maîtresse** kingpin; **idée maîtresse d'un ouvrage** governing or key idea of a work; **maîtresse femme** capable woman; **carte maîtresse** *Cartes, Ordinat* master card; *Fig (principal atout)* trump card

▸▸ **m. d'armes** fencing master; *Univ Anciennement* **m. assistant** ≃ assistant lecturer; *Rel* **m.-autel**, *pl* **maîtres-autels** high altar; *Scol Anciennement* **m. auxiliaire** supply or *Am* substitute teacher; **m. de cérémonies** master of ceremonies; **m. chanteur** blackmailer; **m. de chapelle** choirmaster; **m. charpentier** master carpenter; **m.-chien**, *pl* **maîtres-chiens** dog-handler; *Univ* **m. de conférence** ≃ (senior) lecturer, *Am* assistant professor; **m.-coq**, *pl* **maîtres-coqs** executive chef; *Aut* **m.-cylindre**, *pl* **maîtres-cylindres** master cylinder; **m. de danse** dancing master; **m. d'école** primary school or *Am* elementary school teacher; **m. d'équipage** boatswain; **m. de forges** ironmaster; **m. d'hôtel** *(dans une maison)* butler; *(dans un restaurant)* head waiter, *Am* maître d' ['mɛtr(ə)di:]; *Naut* **m.** chief steward; **m. d'internat** housemaster, *Am* house director; **m. maçon** master mason; **m. de maison** *(pour un invité)* host; **pourrais-je parler au m. de maison?** could I

speak to the man or the master of the house?; **m. de manège** riding instructor or master; **m. nageur** swimming instructor; **m. d'œuvre** prime contractor, project manager, master of works; **m. d'ouvrage** ou de **l'ouvrage** contracting authority; *Ordinat* **m. des postes** postmaster; *Culin* **m. queux** chef

maîtresse² **NF 1** *(personne qui contrôle)* voir **maître** **NM 2** *(d'un homme)* mistress; **avoir une m.** to have a mistress; **être la m. de qn** to be sb's mistress

▸▸ **m. d'école** primary school or *Am* elementary school teacher; **m. de maison** *(pour un invité)* hostess; *(ménagère)* lady of the house; **pourrais-je parler à la m. de maison?** could I speak to the lady of the house?

maîtrisable [mɛtrizabl] **ADJ** controllable

maîtrise [mɛtriz] **NF 1** *Univ* ≃ master's degree, MA; **une m. d'anglais** ≃ a master's degree in English, an MA in English **2** *(contrôle) (de ses passions, d'un art, un sujet etc)* mastery, command; **m. de soi** self-control; *Mil* **m. des mers** command or control of the seas **3** *Ind* supervisory staff **4** *(école)* choir school; *(chorale)* choir; *(poste)* post of choirmaster

maîtriser [mɛtrize] **VT** *(agresseur)* to overpower; *(élèves, animal)* to control; *(flammes, opposition)* to subdue; *(incendie, épidémie)* to control, to get under control; *(passion, impatience)* to control, to curb, to contain; *(ses nerfs)* to control; *(ses angoisses)* to master, to overcome; *(langue, sujet etc)* to master; **il ne maîtrise pas la langue** he has no command of the language

VPR se maîtriser to control oneself; **ne pas savoir se m.** to have no self-control

Maïzena® [maizena] **NF** *Culin* cornflour, *Am* cornstarch

majesté [maʒɛste] **NF 1** *(souverain)* majesty; **Sa M. le roi/la reine** His Majesty the King/Her Majesty the Queen; **Leurs Majestés** their Majesties; *Gram* **pluriel de m.** royal we **2** *(de port)* majesty, dignity, stateliness; *(de style, paysage)* majesty, grandeur

majestueusement [maʒɛstɥøzmɑ̃] **ADV** majestically

majestueux, -euse [maʒɛstɥø, -øz] **ADJ** *(port)* majestic, stately; *(silhouette)* majestic, imposing; **paysage m.** majestic or magnificent landscape

majeur, -eure [maʒœr] **ADJ 1** *(plus grand) (préoccupation, intérêt, difficulté)* major; **la majeure partie de** the greater part of, the major part of; **en majeure partie** for the most part; **prémisse majeure** major premise; *Rel* **les ordres majeurs** the major orders; **raison majeure de qch** chief reason for sth; **il n'y a pas de raison majeure pour que vous veniez** there's no real reason for you to come; **être absent pour raison majeure** to be unavoidably absent; *Cartes* **couleur majeure** major suit **2** *Jur* **être** to be of age; **le jour où il a été m.** the day he came of age; *Fig* **il est m., il sait ce qu'il fait** he's old enough or grown up, he knows what he's doing; *Hum* **je suis m. et vacciné** I'm old enough to look after myself; *Fig* **un peuple m.** a mature or responsible nation; *Jur* **m. incapable** mentally incompetent person **3** *Mus (clé etc)* major; **en sol bémol m.** in G flat major

N *(personne)* person who has come of age or reached the age of majority

NM *(doigt)* middle finger

NF *Cartes* **majeure** major suit

majolique [maʒɔlik] **NF** *Cér* majolica

major [maʒɔr] **NM 1** *Mil* regimental adjutant *(with administrative duties)*; **m. général** chief of staff *(of a commander-in-chief in the field)*; **m. du camp** camp commandant; *(médecin)* **m.** medical officer, MO **2** *Univ* **être m. de promotion** ≃ to be top of one's year

NF les **(grandes) majors** *Cin* the Majors; *(dans l'industrie de la musique)* major music conglomerates

majoration [maʒɔrasjɔ̃] **NF 1** *(surestimation)* *(de biens)* overestimation, overvaluation **2** *(augmentation) (d'une facture)* surcharge, additional charge (**de** on); *(d'un prix)* increase (**de** in); *(pour plus de bénéfices)* mark-up; **m. pour retard de paiement** additional charge *or* surcharge for late payment

majordome [maʒɔrdɔm] **NM** butler, major-domo

majorer [maʒɔre] **VT 1** *(surestimer) (biens)* to overestimate, to overvalue **2** *(augmenter) (facture)* to put a surcharge *or* an additional charge on; *(prix)* to raise, to put up, to increase; *(pour faire plus de bénéfices)* to mark up; *(salaires)* to increase; **m. les prix de dix pour cent** to raise *or* put up *or* increase prices by ten per cent; **m. une facture de dix pour cent** to put a surcharge of ten per cent on an invoice, to increase an invoice by ten per cent

majorette [maʒɔret] **NF** (drum) majorette

majoritaire [maʒɔriter] **ADJ** majority; *Pol* **vote/parti m.** majority vote/party; *Fin* **actionnaire m.** majority shareholder, *Am* majority stockholder; **être majoritaires** to be in the *or* a majority; **c'est un métier où les hommes ont toujours été largement majoritaires** it's a profession where men have always been in a large majority *or* where there has always been a large majority of men; **il a une participation m. dans la société** he has a majority interest *or* shareholding in the company

N *Pol* member of the majority (party); *Fin* majority shareholder *or* Am stockholder

majorité [maʒɔrite] **NF 1** *(supériorité en nombre)* majority; **la m. silencieuse** the silent majority; **la m. des personnes interrogées ...** the majority of (the) people *or* most of the people questioned ...; **être en m., avoir la m.** to be in a *or* the majority; **les citoyens pensent en m. que ...** the majority of citizens *or* most citizens think that ...; **dans la m. des cas** in the majority of cases, in most cases; **nous sommes une m. à vouloir combattre ce fléau** there *or* a majority of us want to fight against this scourge **VOIR GRAMMAIRE A11**

2 *(dans des élections)* majority; **remporter la m. des suffrages** to win a *or* the majority of the votes, to win a majority; **élu avec dix voix de m.** elected by a majority of ten; **m. relative/absolue** relative/absolute majority; **m. qualifiée** qualified majority; **m. simple** simple majority; **décision prise à la m. (des voix)** decision taken by a majority, majority decision

3 *Parl (parti)* majority party; **m. gouvernementale** parliamentary majority; **être dans la m.** to be a member of the majority party; **m. parlementaire** legislative majority; **m. plurielle** plural majority

4 *Jur* majority, coming of age; **atteindre la m.** to come of age, to attain one's majority; **m. légale** (minimum) voting age; **m. pénale** = minimum age in law at which a person is deemed capable of distinguishing between right and wrong

Majorque [maʒɔrk] **NF** Majorca

majorquin, -ine [maʒɔrkɛ̃, -in] **ADJ** Majorcan

N M. Majorcan

majuscule [maʒyskyl] **ADJ** *(lettre)* capital, upper-case; **les lettres majuscules** upper-case letters

NF capital (letter); *Typ* upper-case letter; **en majuscules** in capitals; **majuscules** caps; **majuscules d'imprimerie** block letters, block capitals

majuscule-clic, *pl* **majuscules-clics** **NM** *Ordinat* shift-click

majuscule-glisser, *pl* **majuscules-glisser** **NM** *Ordinat* shift-drag

making-of [mekinɔv] **NM** *Cin* featurette

MAL¹ *pl* **maux** [mal, mo]

pain **1** ▪ harm **2** ▪ evil **3**
▪ difficulty **4**

NM 1 *(douleur, sensation désagréable)* pain, ache; *(maladie)* illness, sickness; **souffrir d'horribles maux de ventre** to suffer from *or* to have terrible stomach pains; *Fam* **prendre** *ou* **attraper (du) m.** to catch cold, to catch a chill; **avoir m. à l'estomac/à la tête/au dos** to have stomach ache *or* a sore stomach/a headache *or* a sore head/backache *or* a sore back; **avoir m. à la gorge/au bras** to have a sore throat/arm; **avoir m. aux dents** to have toothache; *Fam* **avoir m. aux cheveux** to have a hangover; **où avez-vous m.?** where does it hurt?, where is the pain?; **vous me faites (du) m.** you're hurting me; **mon genou me fait m.** my knee hurts; **se faire m.** to hurt oneself; **spectacle qui fait m. (au cœur** *ou* **au ventre)** painful sight; **ça fait m. au ventre de voir des choses pareilles!** it makes you sick *or* it's sickening to see things like that!; *Fig Fam* **ça me ferait m. (au ventre)!** it would make me sick!; *très Fam* **ça me ferait m. aux seins!** it would really piss me off!; *Fam* **tu vas lui prêter ta robe? – ça me ferait m.!** are you going to lend her your dress? – no way!; **être en m. de qch** to be yearning *or* desperate for sth, to be badly in need of sth; **je ne me laisserai pas calomnier par des journalistes en m. de copie** I'm not going to be slandered by journalists with nothing better to write about *or* who are short of copy; **femme en m. d'enfants** woman desperate for children *or* to have children

2 *(préjudice, tort, souffrance)* harm, hurt; **faire du m.** to do harm; **faire du m. à qn** to harm sb, to do sb harm; **ne bougez pas et aucun m. ne vous sera fait** don't move and nobody will get hurt; **allez, un p'tit coup de gnôle, ça n'a jamais fait de m. à personne!** go on, a little tipple never did anyone any harm!; **mettre qch à m.** to damage sth; *Fig Vieilli* **il avait mis à m. toutes les servantes** he had ravished all the maidservants; **il fait plus de bruit que de m.** *(chien, personne)* his bark is worse than his bite; **s'en tirer sans aucun m.** to escape uninjured *or* unhurt *or* unscathed; **il ne ferait pas de m. à une mouche** he wouldn't hurt a fly; **je ne lui veux pas de m.** I mean him no harm; **cela fera plus de m. que de bien** it will do more harm than good; **le m. est fait** the harm *or* damage has been done; *Prov* **aux grands maux les grands remèdes** desperate situations call for desperate remedies; **souffrir de trois grands maux** to suffer from three great evils; **entre deux maux il faut choisir le moindre** you have to choose the lesser of two evils; **entre deux maux j'ai choisi le moindre** it was the lesser of two evils; **un m. nécessaire** a necessary evil; **il n'y a pas de m. à cela** there's no harm in that; **quel m. y a-t-il à cela?** what harm can that do?, what harm is there in it?; *Fam* **il n'y a pas de m.** *(à qn qui s'excuse)* there's no harm done; **m. lui en a pris** he has had cause to regret it *or* to rue it; **dire du m. de qn, parler en m. de qn** to speak ill of sb; **il a changé en m.** he has changed for the worse

3 *(contraire au bien)* wrong; *(vice)* evil; *(mauvaises actions)* wrongdoing; **le bien et le m.** right and wrong, good and evil; **faire la différence entre le bien et le m.** to know the difference between right and wrong; **rendre le m. pour le m.** to answer evil with

evil, to render evil for evil; **il ne pense à m.** he doesn't mean any harm; **voir le m. partout** to see bad in everything; *Rel* **délivrenous du m.** deliver us from evil; **les forces du m.** the forces of evil; **faire le m.** to do evil

4 *(difficulté)* **non sans m.** not without difficulty; **se donner du m. pour faire qch** to go to a lot of trouble to do sth, to take pains to do sth; **je me suis vraiment donné du m. pour que la soirée soit réussie** I really went to a lot of trouble *or* I took great pains to make the party a success; **je me suis donné beaucoup de m. pour faire cette traduction** I worked really hard on this translation; *Fam* **se donner un m. de chien** to go to a hell of a lot of trouble; **donner du m. à qn** to give sb (some) trouble; **avoir du m. à faire qch** to have difficulty *or* trouble (in) doing sth; **avoir le plus grand m. à faire qch** to have the utmost *or* a great deal of difficulty doing sth; **avoir de plus en plus de m. à faire qch** to find it harder and harder to do sth; **tu ne peux pas savoir le m. que j'ai eu pour trouver cet objet** you don't know the trouble I've had finding this thing; *Fam* **avoir un m. de chien à faire qch** to have a hell of a job to do sth; **prendre son m. en patience** to try to put up with it, to be patient; **on n'a rien sans m.** you don't get anything easily

▸ ▸ **m. de l'air** airsickness; **avoir le m. de l'air** to be airsick; **m. blanc** whitlow; **m. de cœur** sickness, nausea; **m. de dents** toothache; **m. de gorge** sore throat; **m. de mer** seasickness; **avoir le m. de mer** to be seasick; **m. des montagnes** altitude sickness; *Arch* **m. napolitain** pox; **m. du pays** homesickness; **avoir le m. du pays** to be homesick; **m. des rayons** radiation sickness; **m. de la route** carsickness; **avoir le m. de la route** to be carsick; *Litt* **m. du siècle** world-weariness; **la dépression est le nouveau m. du siècle** depression is the new scourge of the century; **m. de tête** headache; **m. des transports** travelsickness; **m. de vivre** weariness with life; **avoir le m. de vivre** to be tired of life

MAL²

badly **1** ▪ poorly **1** ▪ ill **2** ▪ wrong **4**
▪ bad **4**

ADV 1 *(jouer, nager, traiter qn, se conduire etc)* badly; *(payer)* poorly, badly; **tout cela finira m.** it will all end in tears; **leur histoire a m. fini** their story had a sad *or* an unhappy ending; **je n'aime pas ce livre, il finit m.** I don't like this book, it's got a sad *or* an unhappy ending; **si tu crois qu'elle va accepter, c'est m. la connaître!** if you think she's going to say yes, you don't know her very well!; **tout va m. en ce moment** everything's going wrong at the moment; **je dors très m. en ce moment** I'm sleeping very badly *or* I'm not sleeping at all well just now; **qu'est-ce qu'on mange m. ici** the food's really bad here; **cette cafetière verse m.** this coffee pot doesn't pour properly; **m. à l'aise** ill at ease; **vous avez m. agi** you did wrong, you acted badly; **je ne pensais pas m. faire** I didn't think I was doing anything wrong; **il se tient m. à table** he has bad table manners; **redresse-toi, tu te tiens m.** straighten up, you're not standing/sitting properly; *Prov* **bien m. acquis ne profite jamais** nobody ever profits by ill-gotten gains; **cette robe lui va m.** that dress doesn't suit her; **ça lui va m. de traiter les autres de paresseux** he's got a nerve calling other people lazy; **travail m. fait** badly done work, shoddy work; **tant bien que m.** as best one can/could; *(réussir)* after a fashion; **on a tout rangé tant bien que m.** we tidied everything up as best we could; **aller de m. en pis** to go from bad to worse; **s'y prendre m.** to go about it the wrong way; **s'y prendre**

foule s'est massée devant le tribunal the crowd gathered in front of the courtroom

masser² vt (frotter) to massage; **il m'a massé le dos** he massaged my back; **elle a massé le patient** she gave the patient a massage, she massaged the patient; **se faire m.** to have a massage, to be massaged

massette [masɛt] NF **1** (outil) two-handed hammer **2** Bot bulrush, reed mace, cat's tail

masseur, -euse [masœr, -øz] N (personne) masseur, f masseuse
NM (appareil) (vibro)massager

masseur-kinésithérapeute, pl **masseurs-kinésithérapeutes** N physiotherapist

massicot¹ [masiko] NM Chimie massicot

massicot² NM Tech guillotine, trimmer

massicoter [masikɔte] vt Tech to guillotine

massif, -ive [masif, -iv] ADJ **1** (gros, épais) massive, bulky; (homme) heavily built; **des traits massifs** heavy features **2** (plein) (argent, acajou etc) solid; **bijoux en or m.** solid gold jewellery **3** Fig (en masse, en grande quantité) (dose, bombardements) massive; **départs massifs** mass exodus; **un 'oui' franc et m.** a clear and overwhelming 'yes'
NM **1** (d'arbustes, d'arbres) clump; **m. de fleurs** bed of flowers, flowerbed **2** Géog massif; **le M. central** the Massif Central (mountain range in central France)

massique [masik] ADJ Phys mass; **puissance m.** power-to-weight ratio

massivement [masivmã] ADV (répondre, voter etc) en masse, in large numbers

mass media [masmedja] NMPL mass media

massue [masy] NF club, bludgeon; **coup de m.** blow with a club; Fig **ça a été le coup de m.** (prix excessif) it was a rip-off; (choc émotionnel) it was a bolt from the blue, it was a staggering blow; **quand on a reçu la facture, ça a été le coup de m.** when we got the invoice, we had a (very) nasty shock; **argument m.** sledgehammer argument

mastard [mastar] NM Fam hefty man

mastectomie [mastɛktɔmi] NF mastectomy

master [mastɛr] NM TV etc master; **m. monté** edited master

mastère [mastɛr] NM Univ (d'ingénieur) DEng; (de commerce) MBA

mastic [mastik] NM **1** (résine) mastic (resin); (pour fenêtres etc) putty; (pour bois etc) filler, mastic; **m. de colmatage** filler paste **2** Typ transposition; **faire un m.** to (accidentally) transpose characters
ADJ INV putty-coloured or Am -colored

masticage [mastikaʒ] NM (de fenêtre) puttying; (de bois) filling

masticateur, -trice [mastikatœr, -tris] ADJ masticatory

mastication [mastikasjɔ̃] NF chewing, Fml mastication

masticatoire [mastikatwar] ADJ, NM masticatory

mastiquer¹ [mastike] vt (mâcher) to chew, Fml to masticate

mastiquer² vt (fissures etc) to fill (in); (fenêtre, vitre) to putty
VI **couteau à m.** putty knife

mastite [mastit] NF Méd mastitis

mastoc [mastɔk] ADJ INV **1** Fam (personne) hulking, lumpish; (construction) cumbersome **2** Belg (fou) (personne) daft, dippy

mastodonte [mastɔdɔ̃t] NM **1** Zool mastodon **2** Fam (véhicule) juggernaut; (personne) colossus

mastoïde [mastɔid] NF Anat mastoid

mastoïdien, -ienne [mastɔidjɛ̃, -jɛn] ADJ Anat mastoid

mastose [mastoz] NF Méd mastosis

mastroquet [mastrɔkɛ] NM Vieilli **1** (cafetier) bar owner, Br publican **2** (bistro) bar, Br pub

masturbation [mastyrbasjɔ̃] NF masturbation; **c'est de la m. intellectuelle** it's intellectual self-indulgence or masturbation

masturbatoire [mastyrbatwar] ADJ masturbatory

masturber [mastyrbe] vt to masturbate
VPR **se masturber** to masturbate

m'as-tu-vu, -vue [matyvy] ADJ INV Fam show-off; **qu'est-ce qu'elle est m'as-tu-vue** what a show-off she is; **ce genre de voiture, ça fait très m.** it's a really flashy type of car

masure [mazyr] NF tumbledown cottage, Péj hovel

mat¹ [mat] ADJ (métal) mat(t), unpolished, dull; (couleur) mat(t), flat; **teint m.** mat(t) complexion; **son m.** dull sound, thud

mat² Échecs ADJ INV checkmated; **le roi est m.** the king is checkmated or in checkmate
NM INV (check)mate; **faire m. en trois coups** to mate in three

mat' [mat] NM Fam (abrév matin) **deux/trois heures du m.** two/three a.m. or in the morning

mât [mɑ] NM **1** Naut mast; **grand m.** mainmast; **m. d'artimon** mizzenmast; **m. de misaine** foremast; **m. de hune** topmast; **m. de charge** cargo boom, derrick; **navire à trois mâts** three-masted ship, three-master **2** (poteau) pole; **m. de tente** tent pole; **m. de cocagne** greasy pole; Rail **m. de sémaphore** signal post, signal mast

matador [matadɔr] NM matador

mataf [mataf] NM Arg (matelot) tar, sailor

matamore [matamɔr] NM braggart, boaster; **faire le m.** to boast, to brag

match, pl **matchs, matches** [matʃ] NM Sport match; **disputer un m.** to play a match; **on fait un m.?** shall we have or play a match?; **m. de barrage** relegation match; **m. de boxe** boxing match; Ftbl **m. de championnat (professionnel)** league match; **m. aller** first leg; **m. retour** return match, second leg; **m. amical** friendly (match); **m. nul** draw; **faire m. nul** to draw, to tie; **ils ont fait m. nul** they drew, the match ended in a draw

maté [mate] NM maté

matelas [matla] NM **1** mattress; **m. à ressorts** spring mattress; **m. pneumatique** inflatable mattress, air bed, Br Lilo®; **toile à m.** ticking; Constr **m. d'air** air space **2** Fam (fortune) pile (of money); **un m. de billets de banque** a wad of banknotes

matelassé [matlase] ADJ Tex quilted; **blouson m.** quilted or padded jacket; **enveloppe matelassée** padded envelope, Jiffy bag®
NM quilted material; **du m. de soie** quilted silk

matelasser [matlase] vt (meuble) to upholster; (tissu) to quilt; (recouvrir de tissu matelassé) to cover with quilted material

matelassure [matlasyr] NF (de matelas, selle etc) padding, stuffing

matelot [matlo] NM Naut **1** (personne) sailor; **m. (breveté) de première classe** leading seaman; **m. de deuxième classe** able seaman; **servir comme simple m.** to sail before the mast **2** (bateau) consort (ship); **m. d'avant/ d'arrière** next ship ahead/astern

matelotage [matlɔtaʒ] NM **1** (connaissances) seamanship **2** (paye) sailor's pay

matelote [matlɔt] NF Culin matelote, fish stew; **m. de morue** cod stew; **sauce m.** red wine and onion sauce

mater¹ [mate] vt **1** Échecs to (check)mate **2** Fig (dresser, dompter) (personne, chien) to bring to heel, to subdue, to tame

mater² vt **1** (métaux, verre etc) to mat(t), to dull **2** (joints de chaudière etc) to caulk, to hammer

mater³ Fam vt to ogle, to eye up; **mate un peu la gonzesse!** just take a look at or get an eyeful of that chick!; **se faire m.** to be ogled, to be eyed up
VI to eye up or ogle (the) women; **qu'est-ce que ça mate, ici!** all these men eyeing us up!

mâter [mate] vt (navire) to mast

matérialisation [materjalizasjɔ̃] NF (d'espoir, de projet) materialization, realization; **la m. de Dieu sur terre** the materialization of God on earth

matérialisé [materjalize] ADJ Admin **voie matérialisée** = section of road delimited by a white line

matérialiser [materjalize] vt (idée, espoir, projet), Fin to realize
VPR **se matérialiser** to materialize

matérialisme [materjalism] NM materialism

matérialiste [materjalist] ADJ materialistic
N materialist

matérialité [materjalite] NF **1** (caractère de ce qui est réel, matériel) materiality **2** (matérialisme) materialism

matériau [materjo] NM Constr material; **m. composite** composite

> Do not confuse with **matériel**.

matériaux [materjo] NMPL **1** Constr material(s); **m. de construction** building or construction material(s) **2** Fig material; **il n'a pas tellement de m. pour rédiger sa thèse** he doesn't have much material for his thesis

matériel, -ielle [materjɛl] ADJ (confort, besoins, aide etc) material; (financier) financial; **tu n'en as pas la preuve matérielle** you don't have material or solid or firm proof of it; **l'organisation matérielle de la fête a posé de gros problèmes** the practical organization of the party posed great problems; **je n'ai pas le temps m. de le faire** I simply don't have time to do it; **être dans l'impossibilité matérielle de bouger** to find it physically impossible to move
NM **1** equipment; (d'usine) plant; Mil equipment, Spéc matériel; Mil **service du m.** ordnance; **m. de camping/de laboratoire** camping/laboratory equipment; **m. d'exploitation** working plant; **m. de guerre** weaponry; **m. d'emballage** packaging; **m. de bureau** office equipment; **m. hi-fi** hi-fi equipment; **m. industriel** plant; Rail **m. roulant** rolling stock **2** Ordinat hardware; **m. de composition** film setting hardware; **m. informatique** computer hardware

> Do not confuse with **matériau**.

matériellement [materjɛlmã] ADV materially; (financièrement) financially; **avoir de quoi vivre m.** to have enough for one's material needs; **chose m. impossible** physical impossibility; **je ne peux m. pas accepter un travail à temps complet** it is physically impossible for me to take on a full-time job; **je n'ai m. pas le temps de venir te voir** I simply don't have time to come and see you

maternage [maternaʒ] NM mothering

maternel, -elle [maternɛl] ADJ maternal; (soins, gestes) motherly; **lait m.** mother's milk; **allaitement m.** breastfeeding; **l'instinct m.** the maternal instinct; **elle est très maternelle avec ses collègues** she acts in a very maternal or motherly way towards her colleagues; **un cousin du côté m.** a cousin on one's mother's side; **grand-père m.** maternal grandfather; **langue maternelle** mother tongue, native tongue; **centre de protection maternelle et infantile** mother-

and-baby clinic; **école maternelle** nursery (school)

NF **maternelle 1** *(école)* nursery (school) **2** *Fam (mère)* old lady, *Br* old dear *(mother)*

Maternelle

Nursery education for children from two to six years old is provided by the state and is available to all families in France. Although it is not compulsory, a vast majority of children attend nursery schools and are thus well-prepared for entry into primary school.

maternellement [matεrnεlmã] ADV maternally, in a motherly way

materner [matεrne] VT to mother

maternisé [matεrnize] ADJ **lait m.** milk suitable for infants

maternité [matεrnite] NF **1** *(fait d'être mère)* motherhood; **un corps déformé par des maternités successives** a body misshapen by one pregnancy after another; **en congé de m.** on maternity leave **2** *(hôpital)* maternity hospital **3** *Beaux-Arts* Madonna and Child

mateur, -euse [matœr, -øz] N *très Fam* ogler

mathématicien, -ienne [matematisjɛ̃, -jεn] N mathematician

mathématique [matematik] ADJ mathematical; *Fig (esprit)* (very) logical; *(rigueur)* mathematical; **c'est m.!** it's perfectly obvious!

NFPL **mathématiques** mathematics; **mathématiques pures/appliquées** pure/applied mathematics VOIR GRAMMAIRE A10

mathématiquement [matematikmã] ADV mathematically; **m., je ne pourrai pas être à l'heure** it's physically impossible for me to be on time

matheux, -euse [matø, -øz] N *Fam* mathematician; *(élève, étudiant)* maths *or Am* math student

math(s) [mat] NFPL *Fam* maths, *Am* math; *Univ* **m. sup/spé** = first/second-year maths class *(for candidates for the grandes écoles)*

Mathusalem [matyzalεm] NM **1** Methuselah; *Fam* **ça date de M.** *(objet)* it's as old as the hills; *(nouvelle)* it's ancient history **2 m.** *(bouteille)* Methuselah

matière [matjεr] NF **1** *(substance)* material; **en quelle m. est ton pantalon?** what material are your trousers made of?; **matière(s) plastique(s)** plastic(s); **sachet en m. plastique** plastic bag; **matières consommables** consumables

2 *Phys, Phil* matter; **m. inanimée** inanimate matter; **m. solide inflammable** flammable solid; **la désintégration de la m.** the disintegration of matter; *Biol* **m. vivante** living matter

3 *Fig (sujet, contenu) (de discours)* subject (matter); *(pour discussion)* subject, topic, theme; *(pour en faire un film, un livre, une étude etc)* material; *Scol* subject; **table des matières** (table of) contents; **faire une entrée en m.** to give an introduction; **il n'y a pas m. à rire** it's no laughing matter; **cela donne m. à réflexion** it's food for thought; **il y a m. à procès/dispute** there are grounds for going to court/for contesting it; **il n'y avait pas m. à discuter** there was nothing to be said about it; **en m. de** as regards; **être bon juge en m. de musique** to be a good judge of music; **être bon juge en la m.** to be a good judge of the subject

▸▸*Méd* **m. fécale** faecal *or Am* fecal matter; **matières grasses** fat; **fromage à 20% de matières grasses** cheese with a 20% fat content; **m. grise** grey matter; *Fin* **m. imposable** taxable income; *Ind* **matière(s) première(s)** raw material(s)

Matif [matif] NM *(abrév* **marché à terme des instruments financiers**) (French) international financial futures market

Matignon [matiɲɔ̃] N = French Prime Minister's offices; **M. a décidé que ...** the Prime Minister's office has decided that ...

Matignon

The name of the Prime Minister's offices is often used to refer to the Prime Minister and his or her administrative staff, for example "L'Élysée et Matignon ont fini par se mettre d'accord".

matin [matɛ̃] NM morning; **du m. au soir** from morning till night; **quatre heures du m.** four o'clock in the morning, 4 a.m.; **le jeudi deux au m.** on the morning of Thursday the second; **c'est le m. que je travaille le mieux** I work best in the morning; **elle travaille seulement le m.** she only works mornings, she only works in the morning; **demain m.** tomorrow morning; **tous les lundis m.** every Monday morning; **de grand** *ou* **bon m., le m. de bonne heure** early in the morning, in the early morning; **être du m.** to be an early bird *or* an early riser; **rentrer au petit m.** to come home in the small *or* early hours; **un de ces (quatre) matins, un beau m.** one of these (fine) days SEE GRAMMAR A80–1; B60

ADV early in the morning; **se lever très m.** to get up very early

mâtin, -ine [mɑtɛ̃, -in] NM *(chien)* mastiff, watchdog

N *Arch Fam (coquin)* sly dog, *f* minx
INT *Arch* by Jove!

matinal, -ale, -aux, -ales [matinal, -o] ADJ **1** *(brise)* morning; **à cette heure matinale** at this early hour; **promenade matinale** morning walk **2 être m.** to be an early riser; **comme tu es m. aujourd'hui!** you're an early bird!

N early riser

mâtiné [mɑtine] ADJ crossbred; *(chien)* mongrel, crossbred; **un teckel m. de caniche** a cross between a dachshund and a poodle; *Fig* **il parle un français m. d'anglais** his French is full of anglicisms; **un humour m. d'une touche de mépris** humour tinged with scorn

matinée [matine] NF **1** *(matin)* morning; **dans la m.** in (the course of) the morning; **en fin de m.** towards the end of the morning; **j'ai passé toute ma m. à l'attendre/au lit** I spent the whole morning waiting for him/in bed; **je ne l'ai pas vu de toute la m.** I haven't seen him all morning; **une m. de lecture** a morning (spent) reading; *Fam* **faire la grasse m.** to have a lie -in SEE GRAMMAR B61 **2** *Théâtre* matinee, afternoon performance; *Cin* matinee, afternoon showing *or* screening; **on joue ce film en m.** there's an afternoon performance *or* a matinee performance of this film

matines [matin] NFPL *Rel* matins

matir [matir] VT = **mater²**

matité [matite] NF *(de son)* dullness

matois, -oise [matwa, -waz] *Litt* ADJ sly, cunning, crafty

N crafty person; **fin m.** sly devil

maton, -onne [matɔ̃, -ɔn] N *Arg (de prison)* screw

matos [matos] NM *Fam* equipment

matou [matu] NM tom (cat)

matraquage [matrakaʒ] NM bludgeoning, *Br* coshing, *Am* blackjacking; *Fig* **m. idéologique** ideological brainwashing; **m. publicitaire** hype; **c'est vraiment du m. qu'ils font pour la sortie de ce film** they're really hyping *or* plugging the release of this film; **avec**

les élections, ça va être le m. à la télé! with the elections, it'll be total overkill on TV!

matraque [matrak] NF bludgeon, *Br* cosh, *Am* blackjack; *(d'agent de police)* surtout *Br* truncheon, *Am* billy (club); *Fig Fam* **c'est le coup de m.** it's a rip-off

matraquer [matrake] VT *(frapper)* to bludgeon, *Br* to cosh; *Fam (auditeur, consommateur)* to bombard; *(disque, chanson)* to plug; *Fig Fam* **m. le client** to rip off *or* fleece the customer; *Fig* **la radio matraque ses annonces/cette chanson toute la journée** the radio churns out its announcements/that song all day long

matriarcal, -ale, -aux, -ales [matrijarkal, -o] ADJ matriarchal

matriarcat [matrijarka] NM matriarchy

matricaire [matrikεr] NF *Bot* pineapple weed

matrice [matris] NF **1** *Math* matrix; *Tech* matrix, die; *Typ* matrix, type mould; *(de disque)* matrix VOIR GRAMMAIRE A14 **2** *Ordinat* array; **m. active/passive** active/passive matrix; **m. d'aiguilles** dot matrix; **m. de vérité** truth table **3** *Admin (du rôle des contributions)* original **4** *Anat* uterus, womb

matricide [matrisid] ADJ matricidal

N matricide

NM *(crime)* matricide

matriciel, -ielle [matrisjεl] ADJ *Math* matrix; *Ordinat* **imprimante matricielle** dot matrix printer

NF *Ordinat* **matricielle** dot matrix

matricule [matrikyl] ADJ *Mil, Admin* **numéro m.** number

NM *Mil, Admin* number; *Fam* **ça va chauffer pour ton m.** you'll be in hot water

NF **1** *(liste) (de prison, d'hôpital)* roll, register, list; *Mil* (regimental) roll; *(immatriculation)* registration **2** *(extrait)* registration certificate

matrimonial, -iale, -iaux, -iales [matrimɔnjal, -jo] ADJ matrimonial; **agence matrimoniale** dating agency; **régime m.** marriage settlement; **juge des affaires matrimoniales** divorce court judge

matrone [matrɔn] NF *Antiq* matron; *Péj (femme imposante)* stout *or* portly woman; **vieille m.** fat old woman

maturation [matyrasjɔ̃] NF maturation; *(de fruit, céréale, fromage)* ripening; *(de tabac)* maturing; *Physiol* **m. sexuelle** sexual maturation

mature [matyr] ADJ mature

mâture [mɑtyr] NF *Naut* masts (and spars); **dans la m.** aloft

maturité [matyrite] NF **1** *(de personne, d'animal)* maturity; *(de fruit, fromage)* ripeness; **arriver** *ou* **venir à m.** to come to maturity, to mature; **cette jeune femme ne manque pas de m.** that young woman is very mature; **elle manque totalement de m.** she's totally immature; **sa m. d'esprit est remarquable** he/she has a remarkably mature mind **2** *Suisse (baccalauréat)* **m. fédérale** school-leaving diploma *(from a gymnase, granting admission to university)*

matutinal, -ale, -aux, -ales [matytinal, -o] ADJ *Litt* morning

maudire [modir] VT *(prp* maudissant; *pp* maudit; *pr ind* je maudis, n. maudissons, v. maudissez, ils maudissent; *pr sub* je maudisse; *p hist* je maudis; *fu* je maudirai) to curse; *Litt* **maudit sois-tu!** a curse on you!

maudit, -ite [modi, -it] ADJ **1** *(crime, science)* accursed **2** *(avant nom) (voiture, ville etc)* damn(ed), blasted, cursed; **quel m. temps!** what filthy weather!

N **le M.** the Devil; **les maudits** the damned, the accursed

maugréer [mogree] **VI** to grumble, to grouse (**contre** about, at)

maure [mɔr] **ADJ** Moorish
  N M. Moor

mauresque [mɔresk] **ADJ** *(architecture, motif etc)* Moorish
  NF 1 M. Moorish woman **2** *(boisson)* = pastis with barley water and water

Maurice [mɔris] **N l'île M.** Mauritius

mauricien, -ienne [mɔrisjɛ̃, -jɛn] **ADJ** Mauritian
  N M. Mauritian

Mauritanie [mɔritani] **NF** Mauritania

mauritanien, -ienne [mɔritanjɛ̃, -jɛn] **ADJ** Mauritanian
  N M. Mauritanian

mausolée [mozɔle] **NM** mausoleum

maussade [mosad] **ADJ 1** *(de mauvaise humeur)* sullen, morose; *(triste)* glum; **ça l'a rendu m.** *(amer)* that disgruntled him **2** *(temps)* dull, gloomy; **paysage m.** gloomy countryside

maussaderie [mosadri] **NF** *Litt* sullenness, moroseness

MAUVAIS, -AISE [mɔvɛ, ɛz] **ADJ 1** *(repas, haleine, rêve, avis, organisation, qualité etc)* bad; **m. pour la santé/la digestion** bad for one's health/the digestion; **de plus en plus m.** worse and worse; **le plus m.** the worst; **m. temps** bad weather; **mauvaise mer** rough sea; **être en mauvaise posture** to be in a difficult situation; **cela a fait m. effet** it looked bad, it made a bad impression; **elle a reçu une mauvaise nouvelle** she has had some bad news; **ce n'est pas m.** *(c'est bon)* it's not bad; **je l'ai trouvé mauvaise** I didn't appreciate it; **il risque de la trouver mauvaise quand il apprendra** he's not going to be very happy when he finds out; **l'avoir m.** to be very put out, *Br Fam* to be miffed; **elle a mauvaise mine** she doesn't look well; **avoir une mauvaise santé** to be in bad *or* poor health; **mauvaise vue** bad *or* poor eyesight; **il a fait une mauvaise bronchite** he's had a bad attack of bronchitis; **faire de mauvaises affaires** to be involved in some bad business deals; **la récolte sera mauvaise** it will be a bad *or* poor harvest; **les freins sont m.** the brakes are defective; **c'est un m. banquier** he's a poor *or* bad banker; **m. en anglais** bad *or* poor at English; **une mauvaise excuse** a poor excuse

2 *(inapproprié)* wrong; **c'est la mauvaise clef** it's the wrong key; **arriver au m. moment** to come at a bad *or* an inconvenient time *or* at a bad *or* an awkward moment; *Tél* **m. numéro** wrong number

3 *(méchant) (personne)* bad, nasty; *(augure)* bad, ill; **être m. avec qn** to be nasty to sb; **qu'est-ce qu'elle est mauvaise aujourd'hui!** she's in a nasty mood today!; **mauvaise action** wrong(doing); **avoir l'air m.** *(de personne)* to look nasty; *(de chien)* to look fierce *or* vicious; **c'est un m. sujet** *or* **un m. garçon** he's a bad lot; **né sous une mauvaise étoile** born under an unlucky star; **elle n'a pas un m. fond** deep down she's not bad, she's not bad at heart; **elle a vraiment un m. fond!** she's a really nasty character!
  ADV sentir m. to smell (bad), to stink; **il fait m.** the weather's bad
  N villain; *Fam* baddie; **dans le film, il joue le rôle du m.** he plays the baddie in the film
  ▸▸ **mauvaise langue** (spiteful) gossip; **c'est vraiment une mauvaise langue** he's got a really spiteful *or* nasty tongue; **ce que tu peux être mauvaise langue, alors!** you can be a real gossip!; **m. œil** evil eye; **elle est persuadée d'avoir le m. œil** she's convinced that somebody has put the evil eye on her; **m. plaisant** practical joker

---

mauve [mov] **NM** *(couleur)* mauve
  NF *Bot* mallow
  ADJ mauve

mauviette [movjɛt] **NF** *Fam (physiquement)* wimp, *Br* weed; *(moralement)* wimp, drip; **quelle m. tu fais!** you're such a wimp!

MAV [emave] **NM** *(abrév* **marketing après-vente)** after-sales marketing

max [maks] **NM INV** *(abrév* **maximum)** **1** *(dans annonce)* max **2** *Fam* **un m.** loads, lots; **ça lui plaît un m.** he/she likes it loads *or* lots; **un m. de fric** loads of money; **on s'est éclaté un m. à la soirée de Caroline** we had a really fantastic time at Caroline's party

maxi [maksi] *Fam* **ADJ INV** maxi; **une m.(-) bouteille** a giant-size *or* jumbo-size bottle
  ADV on sera 20 m. there'll be 20 of us max *or* tops; **ça prendra deux heures m.** it'll take two hours max *or* tops
  NM *Vieilli (manteau)* maxi (coat); **la mode du m.** the maxi fashion
  NF *Vieilli (jupe)* maxi (skirt)

maxillaire [maksiler] *Anat* **ADJ** maxillary; **os m.** jawbone, *Spéc* maxilla
  NM jawbone, *Spéc* maxilla

maximal, -ale, -aux, -ales [maksimal, -o] **ADJ** *(effet, excitation, peine etc)* maximum; *(température)* maximum, top; **vitesse maximale autorisée: 60 km/h** speed limit: 60 kmph

maxime [maksim] **NF** maxim

maximisation [maksimizasjɔ̃] **NF m. du profit** profit optimization

maximiser [maksimize] **VT** to maximize

maximum [maksimɔm], *pl* **maximums** *ou* **maxima** [maksima] **NM** maximum; **faire le m. (pour faire qch)** to do one's utmost *or* one's best (to do sth); **m. de rendement** maximum output; **porter la production au m.** to increase production to a maximum, to maximize production; **je vais essayer de t'aider au m.** I'll try my very hardest *or* my very best to help you; **thermomètre à maxima** maximum thermometer; **on sera 20 au m.** there will be 20 of us at (the) most; **nous avons de la place pour 20 personnes au m.** we have room for a maximum of 20 (people) *or* for 20 (people) at (the) most; *Fam* **un m.** *(beaucoup)* loads, lots; *Fam* **ça lui plaît un m.** he likes it loads *or* lots
  ADJ SOUVENT INV maximum; **rendement m.** maximum *or* peak output

maya [maja] **ADJ** Maya, Mayan
  NM *Ling* Mayan
  N M. Maya, Mayan

Mayence [majɑ̃s] **N** Mainz

mayonnaise [majɔnɛz] **NF** *Culin* mayonnaise; *Fig Fam* **faire monter la m.** to stir things up; *Fig Fam* **la m. n'a pas pris** it didn't work; **la m. a pris** it worked

mazagran [mazagrɑ̃] **NM** *(en verre, faïence)* goblet

mazette [mazɛt] **INT** *Hum* my word!, *Br* goodness gracious!

mazout [mazut] **NM** *(fuel)* oil; **chauffage central au m.** oil-fired central heating; **poêle à m.** oil stove

mazouté [mazute] **ADJ** *(plage)* oil-polluted, polluted with oil; *(oiseau)* oil-covered, covered in oil, oiled

mazurka [mazyrka] **NF** mazurka

mb **NM** *Météo abrév* **millibar**

MBA [embea] **NF** *Compta (abrév* **marge brute d'autofinancement)** cashflow, funds generated by operations

Mbps *Ordinat (abrév* **mégabits par seconde)** mbps

MDD [emdede] **NF** *Com (abrév* **marque de distributeur)** distributor's brand name, own brand

---

me *(before a vowel sound* **m'**) [mə] **PRON PERS** SEE GRAMMAR A27; B18–19 **1** *(objet direct)* me; **il m'aime** he loves me; **me voici** here I am **2** *(objet indirect)* (to) me; **il m'a écrit** he wrote to me; **il me l'a dit** he told me (so); **donnez-m'en** give me some; *Fam* **tu veux bien m'éteindre la lumière?** would you switch off the light (for me)? **3** *(verbe pronominal)* myself; **je m'amusais** I was enjoying myself; **je ne m'en souviens plus** I don't remember any more; **je me suis dit que ...** I said to myself that ... SEE GRAMMAR A29; B28–9

mea-culpa [meakylpa] **NM INV** **faire** *ou* **dire son m.** to own up *or* to confess (to one's mistake)

méandre [meɑ̃dr] **NM** *(de rivière)* meander, loop; *(de route)* bend; *Fig* **se perdre dans les méandres d'un raisonnement** to get lost in the intricacies of an argument

mec [mɛk] **NM** *Fam* guy, *Br* bloke; **t'en fais pas, m.!** don't worry about it, mate *or* pal *or* surtout *Am* man!; **son nouveau m.** her new guy *or* man; **eh les mecs! venez voir!** hey guys! come and have a look!

mécanicien, -ienne [mekanisjɛ̃, -jɛn] **N 1** *Aut* (garage *or* motor) mechanic; *Naut* engineer; *Aviat* **m. de bord** *ou* **navigant** flight engineer; **c'est une bonne mécanicienne** she's a good mechanic; **ouvrier m.** mechanic; **ingénieur m.** mechanical engineer **2** *Rail* engine driver, *Am* engineer
  NF *Couture* **mécanicienne** machinist

mécanicien-dentiste, *pl* **mécaniciens-dentistes NM** *Vieilli* dental technician

mécanique [mekanik] **ADJ** *Tech etc (fonctionnement, système)* mechanical; *(dentelle, tuiles etc)* machine-made; **jouet m.** clockwork toy; **métier à tisser m.** power loom; **atelier(s) de constructions mécaniques** engineering works; **nous avons eu des ennuis mécaniques en route** we had mechanical problems on the way; **moyens mécaniques de contraception** barrier methods of contraception; *Fig* **un geste m.** a mechanical *or* an automatic movement; **c'est devenu m. pour lui** it's become automatic for him; **c'est un travail très m.** it's very mechanical work
  NF 1 *(science du mouvement)* mechanics; **m. des fluides** fluid mechanics; **m. quantique** quantum mechanics **2** *(des moteurs, machines)* mechanical engineering; *Aut* **il adore la m.** he likes fiddling about with cars/motorbikes; *Fam* **rouler les mécaniques** to walk with a swagger **3** *(mécanisme)* mechanism, piece of machinery; *(d'une imprimante laser)* engine; **c'est une belle m., cette moto** that motorbike's a lovely piece of machinery

> Il faut noter que le nom anglais **mechanic** est un faux ami. Il signifie **mécanicien**.

mécaniquement [mekanikmɑ̃] **ADV** mechanically

mécanisation [mekanizasjɔ̃] **NF** mechanization

mécaniser [mekanize] **VT** to mechanize

mécanisme [mekanism] **NM 1** mechanism; *(de montre)* works; **le m. du corps humain** the workings of the human body; **m. de défense** defence mechanism; *UE* **m. des taux de change** Exchange Rate Mechanism; **m. de l'offre et de la demande** supply and demand mechanism; **m. budgétaire** budgetary mechanism; **m. des prix** price mechanism; *Aut* **m. d'avance automatique** automatic advance mechanism; **m. d'avance centrifuge** centrifugal advance mechanism; *Aut* **m. de basculement** tipping gear; *Aut* **m. de direction** steering gear **2** *(de la pensée, parole)* mechanics

mécano [mekano] NM *Fam* mechanic, grease monkey

mécanographe [mekanɔgraf] N punch card operator

mécanographie [mekanɔgrafi] NF *(procédé)* (mechanical) data processing; *(service)* data processing department

mécanographique [mekanɔgrafik] ADJ **service m.** data processing department; **fiche m.** punch(ed) card

Meccano® [mekano] NM Meccano®

mécénat [mesena] NM sponsorship; *(des arts)* sponsorship, patronage; **m. d'entreprise** corporate or business sponsorship

mécène [mesen] NM sponsor; *(des arts)* sponsor, patron

méchamment [meʃamɑ̃] ADV **1** *(de façon méchante)* spitefully, nastily, maliciously **2** *Fam (vrai, bon etc)* damn(ed); *(trompé, déçu)* horribly, terribly; **il avait m. bu** he'd drunk a hell of a lot; **ça a m. cartonné hier au bar** there was one hell of a punch-up in the bar yesterday; **ce qu'il m'a dit m'a m. refroidi** what he said really put me off or *Br* didn't half put me off

méchanceté [meʃɑ̃ste] NF **1** *(de personne, remarque etc)* spitefulness, nastiness, maliciousness; *(d'enfant)* naughtiness; **faire qch par m.** to do sth out of spite or malice; **il l'a dit sans m.** he didn't mean to be unkind; **je dis ça sans m. aucune** I say that without any malice **2** *(action, parole)* spiteful or nasty action/remark; **quelle m.!** what a spiteful or nasty thing to do/say!

méchant, -ante [meʃɑ̃, -ɑ̃t] ADJ **1** *(personne, remarque etc)* spiteful, nasty, malicious; *(enfant)* naughty; *(animal)* vicious, bad-tempered; **attention chien m.** *(sur panneau)* beware of the dog; **il n'est pas si m. que ça!** he's not as bad as all that!; *Fam* **pas m.** harmless **2** *(désagréable) (affaire)* unpleasant, disagreeable; *(blessure, grippe)* nasty, bad; **être de méchante humeur** to be in a foul mood **3** *Fam (sacré)* terrific, incredible; **avoir une méchante dégaine** to look incredible; **j'avais une méchante envie de dormir/lui casser la figure** I had an incredible urge to sleep/to smash his face in **4** *(médiocre)* miserable, wretched, poor, sorry; **un m. billet de cinq euros** a paltry five-euro note; **une méchante excuse** a lame excuse **5** *Can Fam (mauvais)* bad, foul; **la soupe n'est pas méchante** the soup isn't at all bad, the soup is pretty good; **il fait m.** the weather is bad **6** *Can Fam (incorrect)* wrong; **le m. numéro** the wrong number
▪ N **petit m.!/petite méchante!** you naughty little boy/girl!; *Fam* **les bons et les méchants** the goodies and the baddies

mèche¹ [mɛʃ] NF **1** *(de bougie, lampe)* wick; *(pour mettre le feu à des explosifs)* match; *(de mine)* fuse; *Fam* **vendre la m.** to give the game away, to spill the beans; **éventer ou découvrir la m.** to uncover the plot **2** *(de cheveux)* lock; *(de laine)* wisp, tuft; **elle se fait faire des mèches tous les mois** she has streaks or highlights put in her hair every month; **m. postiche** hairpiece **3** *Chir* dressing **4** *(de câble etc)* core, heart; *Élec* **charbon à m.** cored carbon **5** *Menuis* auger, gimlet; **m. anglaise** ou **à trois pointes** centre bit; **m. hélicoïdale** twist bit, twist drill

mèche² NF INV *Fam* **1 être de m.** to be in cahoots (**avec qn** with sb) **2 il n'y a pas m.** nothing doing

méchoui [meʃwi] NM *Culin* spit-roasted lamb

mécompte [mekɔ̃t] NM **1** *Litt (désillusion)* disappointment; **il a eu un grave m.** he has had a serious disappointment, he has been badly let down **2** *Vieilli (erreur)* miscalculation, error

méconium [mekɔnjɔm] NM *Physiol* meconium

méconnaissable [mekɔnɛsabl] ADJ unrecognizable

méconnaissance [mekɔnɛsɑ̃s] NF **1** *Litt (du talent de qn)* lack of recognition; *(de faits, situation)* ignorance, lack of knowledge; **elle a toujours fait preuve d'une m. totale de la politique** she has never had any grasp or understanding of politics whatsoever **2** *(refus de reconnaître comme valable) (d'un droit, d'une loi)* disregard

méconnaître [mekɔnɛtr] VT *(conj like* **connaître***)* **1** *(talent de qn, écrivain etc)* to fail to appreciate, to fail to recognize; *(les faits)* to fail to take account of; *(l'importance d'une découverte)* to underrate, to misjudge **2** *(devoir)* to disregard

méconnu [mekɔny] ADJ *(talent, écrivain etc)* unrecognized, unappreciated

mécontent, -ente [mekɔ̃tɑ̃, -ɑ̃t] ADJ *(insatisfait)* displeased, dissatisfied, discontented (**de** with); *(fâché)* annoyed; **je ne suis pas m. de mon sort** I am not discontented with my lot; **être m. que ... + *sub*** to be annoyed that ...
▪ N grumbler, moaner; *Pol* **les mécontents** the discontented

mécontentement [mekɔ̃tɑ̃tmɑ̃] NM *(insatisfaction)* discontent, dissatisfaction; *(contrariété)* annoyance; **c'est un sujet de m.** it's a source of discontent or dissatisfaction; **marquer** ou **exprimer son m.** to show or express one's annoyance or displeasure

mécontenter [mekɔ̃tɑ̃te] VT to displease

Mecque (La) [lamɛk] NF Mecca; **pendant le festival, Juan-les-Pins est La M. des amateurs de jazz** during the festival, Juan-les-Pins becomes a Mecca for jazz fans

mécréant, -ante [mekreɑ̃, -ɑ̃t] *Vieilli* ADJ infidel, unbelieving
▪ N unbeliever, heathen

Il faut noter que le nom anglais **miscreant** est un faux ami. Il signifie **scélérat**.

mecton [mɛktɔ̃] NM *Fam* guy, *Br* bloke

MÉDAF [medaf] NM *Fin (abrév* **modèle d'évaluation des actifs***)* CAPM

médaille [medaj] NF **1** *(récompense)* medal; *Sport* **la m. d'or/d'argent/de bronze** the gold/silver/bronze (medal); **détenir la m. du 60 mètres** to hold the medal for the 60 metres; **être m. d'or** *(de sportif)* to be a gold medallist, to be a gold medal winner; **m. du travail** medal for long service, long-service medal; *Fig* **le revers de la m.** the other side of the coin; *Fig* **je ne lui donnerais pas la m. du courage!** he wouldn't win any medals for bravery! **2** *(en hommage à qn)* medal; **m. pieuse** holy medal **3** *(insigne)* (official) badge; *(plaque d'identité) (de chat, chien)* identity disc or tag

médaillé, -ée [medaje] ADJ holding a medal; *(soldat)* decorated
▪ N *Mil* medal-holder; *Sport* medallist; **le m. du 400 mètres nage libre** the 400 metres freestyle medallist; **un m. du travail** a holder of a long-service medal

médaillier [medaje] NM medal collection *(in cabinet)*

médaillon [medajɔ̃] NM **1** *(médaille)* medallion **2** *Culin* medallion **3** *(bijou)* medallion; *(avec photo)* locket **4** *TV, Cin, Journ* inset

médecin [medsɛ̃] NM doctor, *Fml* physician; **aller chez le m.** to go to the doctor('s); **femme m.** woman doctor
▪▪ **m. de bord** ship's doctor; **m. de campagne** country doctor; **m.-conseil,** *pl* **médecins-conseils** medical consultant or adviser; **m. consultant** consultant; **m. de famille** fa-

mily doctor; **m. généraliste** general practitioner, GP, *Am* family practitioner; **m. légiste** forensic pathologist, *Am* medical examiner; **m. militaire** army medical officer, MO; **Médecins sans frontières** = charitable organization providing medical aid, especially to Third World countries; **m. traitant** consulting physician; **qui est votre m. traitant?** who is your (regular) doctor?; **m. du travail** = doctor who carries out the annual examination, required by law, of a company's employees

médecine [medsin] NF **1** *(science)* medicine; *Fam* **elle fait m.** she's doing medicine; **docteur en m.** doctor of medicine, MD; **étudiant en m.** medical student, *Fam* medic; **école de m.** medical school **2** *(profession du médecin)* medicine; **exercer la m.** to practise medicine
▪▪ **m. douce** alternative medicine; **m. générale** general medicine; **m. légale** forensic medicine, *Fam* forensics; **service de m. légale** forensic department, *Fam* forensics; **m. naturelle** natural medicine; **m. parallèle** alternative medicine; **m. préventive** preventive medicine; **m. sportive** sports medicine; **m. du travail** industrial medicine

Il faut noter que le nom anglais **medicine** signifie également **médicament, remède**.

Medef [medɛf] NM *(abrév* **Mouvement des entreprises de France***)* French employers' association, *Br* ≃ CBI

média [medja] NM medium, *pl* media; **le pouvoir des médias** the power of the media; **faire campagne dans tous les médias** to carry out a media-wide advertising campaign; **la télévision est un m. privilégié** television is the most efficient medium; **m. grand public** mass media; **m. planneur** media planner; **médias de télécommunication** telecommunications media; **médias numériques interactifs** interactive digital media; **médias électroniques** electronic media **VOIR GRAMMAIRE A11**

médial, -iale, -iaux, -iales [medjal, -jo] ADJ *Ling (lettre)* medial
▪ NF **médiale** *(en statistique)* median

médian, -iane [medjɑ̃, -jan] ADJ *(nerf, ligne etc)* median
▪ NF **médiane 1** *Ling* mid vowel **2** *(en statistique)* median

médiateur, -trice [medjatœr, -tris] ADJ mediating, mediatory
▪ N *(personne) Ind* mediator; *Admin* ≃ ombudsman; **agir en tant que m., servir de m.** to act as (a) mediator; **m. d'entreprises** arbitrator; **le M. européen** the European Ombudsman; **le M. de la République** *Br* ≃ the Parliamentary Commissioner, the Ombudsman

médiathèque [medjatɛk] NF media library

médiation [medjasjɔ̃] NF mediation

médiatique [medjatik] ADJ *(couverture, personnalité etc)* media; **d'un intérêt m.** newsworthy; **événement m.** media event; **c'est quelqu'un de très m.** he/she is well suited to or comes over well in the media

médiatisation [medjatizasjɔ̃] NF **la m. d'un événement** the media coverage or attention given to an event; **la m. à outrance des faits et gestes des hommes politiques** the excessive media coverage given to politicians' behaviour, the media hype surrounding politicians' behaviour

médiatiser [medjatize] VT *(événement)* to give media coverage to; **m. la guerre** to turn the war into a media event

médiator [medjatɔr] NM *Mus* plectrum

médiatrice [medjatris] NF *Géom* median

médical, -ale, -aux, -ales [medikal, -o] ADJ medical; **examen m. (complet)** medical dain; **m. des richesses** contempt for wealth; **avoir le m. de l'argent/des conventions** to scorn *or* despise money/convention; **avoir du m. pour qn** to despise sb; **je n'éprouve que du m. à son égard** I have nothing but contempt for him/her; **au m. de qch** regardless of sth; **avec m.** scornfully, contemptuously; **sourire de m.** contemptuous *or* scornful smile

méprisable [meprizabl] ADJ contemptible, despicable

méprisant [meprizɑ̃] ADJ contemptuous, scornful

méprise [mepriz] NF mistake; **il y a m. sur le destinataire** it has been delivered to the wrong person; **par m.** by mistake

mépriser [meprize] VT *(personne, argent)* to despise, to scorn; *(conseil, offre, danger)* to scorn

mer [mɛr] NF **1** *(étendue d'eau)* sea; **en haute ou pleine m.** (out) at sea; **m. fermée ou intérieure** inland sea, landlocked sea; **la m. Rouge/Noire** the Red/Black Sea; **la m. Baltique** the Baltic (Sea); **la m. du Nord** the North Sea; **m. d'huile** sea as calm as a millpond; **au bord de la m.** at *or* by the seaside; **aller à la m.** to go to the seaside; **une maison à la m.** a house by the sea(side); **grosse m.** heavy sea; **par grosse m.** when the sea is heavy; **il y a de la m.** the sea is running high, there's a heavy sea; **essuyer un coup de m.** to be struck by a heavy sea; **un homme à la m.!** man overboard!; **servir sur m.** to serve afloat *or* at sea; **voyager par m.** to travel by sea; **prendre la m.** to set sail, to put (out) to sea; **ce capitaine/navire n'a pas pris la m. depuis vingt ans** this captain/boat hasn't been to sea for twenty years; **mettre une embarcation à la m.** to get out a boat; *(d'un navire)* to lower a boat; **tenir la m.** *(rester au large)* to remain at sea; *(la contrôler)* to hold the seas, to rule the waves; **navire qui tient bien la m.** ship that behaves well in a heavy sea; **droit de la m.** maritime law; *Fam* **ce n'est pas la m. à boire** it's no big deal; *Fig* **m. de sable** vast expanse of sand **2** *(marée)* tide; **m. haute, pleine m.** high tide; **basse m.** low tide

mer-air ADJ INV *Mil* **missile m.** sea-to-air missile

mercanti [mɛrkɑ̃ti] NM *(marchand)* bazaar-keeper, *Péj* profiteer, shark

mercantile [mɛrkɑ̃til] ADJ **1** *Péj* **esprit m.** money-grabbing mentality **2** *Arch (opération etc)* mercantile, commercial

mercantilisme [mɛrkɑ̃tilism] NM **1** *Péj* money-grabbing, profiteering **2** *Écon, Hist* mercantilism

mercaphonie [mɛrkafɔni] NF *Mktg* telemarketing, telephone marketing

mercaticien, -ienne [mɛrkatisjɛ̃, -jɛn] N *Mktg* marketeer, marketer, marketing expert

mercatique [mɛrkatik] NF marketing; **m. après-vente** after-sales marketing; **m. ciblée** niche *or* target marketing; **m. commerciale** trade marketing; **m. de contact** direct marketing; **m. défensive** defensive marketing; **m. écologique** green marketing; **m. expansionniste** rollout marketing; **m. de grande consommation** mass marketing; **m. indifférenciée** undifferentiated marketing; **m. non lucrative** not-for-profit marketing; *(résultats insatisfaisants)* unprofitable marketing; **m. de relance** remarketing; **m. relationnelle** relationship *or* direct marketing; **m. de stimulation** stimulation *or* incentive marketing; **m. stratégique** strategic marketing; **m. sur mesure** customized marketing; **m. test dirigé** controlled test marketing; **m. téléphonique** telephone marketing; **m. de la valeur** value marketing

mercenaire [mɛrsənɛr] ADJ, N mercenary

mercerie [mɛrsəri] NF **1** *(marchandise)* haberdashery, *Am* notions **2** *(magasin)* haberdasher's (shop), *Am* notions store

merceriser [mɛrsərize] VT *Tex* to mercerize; **coton mercerisé** mercerized cotton

merchandising [mɛrʃɑ̃dajziŋ] NM *Écon* merchandising

merci [mɛrsi] INT thank you, thanks; *(refus)* no thank you, no thanks; **dire m.** to say thank you *or* thanks; **il ne m'a pas dit m.** he didn't say thank you to me; **m. bien, m. beaucoup** thank you very much, thanks a lot; **m. de** *ou* **pour votre offre** thank you for your offer; *Fam* **m. qui? m. mon chien!** don't bother to say thank you!; **grand m.!** no thank you!; *Iron* **m'excuser? m. bien, après ce qu'il m'a fait!** apologize? no way *or* no thanks, not after what he did to me!; *Iron* **m. du compliment!** thanks for the compliment!; **mille mercis de** *ou* **pour votre invitation** thank you so much *or* many thanks for your invitation

▸ thank you; **il a pris le livre sans un m.** he took the book without a word of thanks *or* without saying thank you *or* without so much as a thanks

▸ NF mercy; **être à la m. de qn/qch** to be at the mercy of sb/sth; **tenir qn à sa m.** to have sb at one's mercy; **crier m.** to cry for mercy; **sans m.** *(adjectif)* merciless, pitiless, ruthless; *(adverbe)* mercilessly, pitilessly, ruthlessly

mercier, -ière [mɛrsje, -jɛr] N haberdasher, *Am* notions dealer

Mercosur [mɛrkɔsyr] NM *Écon* Mercosur

mercredi [mɛrkrədi] NM Wednesday; **le m. des Cendres** Ash Wednesday *(voir aussi* **samedi** SEE GRAMMAR A81–2; B61

▸ INT *Euph* sugar!

mercure [mɛrkyr] NM **1** *Chimie* mercury **2** *Myth* **M.** Mercury

▸ NF *Astron* **M.** Mercury

mercuriale¹ [mɛrkyrjal] NF *Bot* mercury

mercuriale² NF *Litt (réprimande)* reprimand, rebuke

mercuriale³ NF *Com* commodity price list

mercuriel, -ielle [mɛrkyrjɛl] ADJ *Pharm* mercurial

Mercurochrome® [mɛrkyrɔkrɔm] NM mercurochrome®

merde [mɛrd] *très Fam* NF *(excrément)* shit, crap; *(étron)* turd; **j'ai marché dans une m. de chien** I've trodden in a dog turd *or* in some dog shit; **il y a une m. d'oiseau sur le pare-brise** there's some bird shit on the windscreen; **il ne se prend pas pour de la m.** he thinks he's God's gift to the world, *Br Vulg* he thinks the sun shines out of his arse; **c'est de la m.** *(ce qu'il vient de dire)* that's a load of shit *or* crap; *(ce tissu, ce film etc)* it's crap; **c'est une vraie m.** it's a right load of crap; **une m. à 5 euros** some cheap rubbish costing 5 euros; **de m.** *(voiture, idée etc)* shitty, crappy; **c'est la m.** things are shitty, *Am* this sucks; **c'est la m. dans le pays en ce moment** the country's a *Br* bloody *or* *Am* goddamn mess *or* shambles at the moment; **foutre la m.** to create havoc; **être dans la m.** to be in the shit, to be up shit creek; **il a de la m. dans les yeux** he never sees a thing, he can't see what's going on right in front of him; **il m'est arrivé une m.** something shit's happened; **traîner qn dans la m.** to drag sb's name through the mud

▸ INT shit!; **m. alors, je ne m'attendais pas à ça** oh shit, I didn't expect that; **et m., j'en ai marre!** to hell with it *or Br* sod it, I've had enough!; **et m. au boulot, je vais au ciné** to hell with work *or Br* sod work, I'm off to the cinema; **t'es d'accord, oui ou m.?** are we agreed or not, for Christ's sake?; **dire m. à**

qn to tell sb to piss off *or Br* bugger off; **je te dis m.!** *(bonne chance!)* ≃ break a leg!; **avoir un œil qui dit m. à l'autre** to have a squint

merder [mɛrde] VI *très Fam* **ma bagnole merde depuis huit jours** my car's been playing up for the past week; **j'ai envie de partir en vacances, mais j'ai l'impression que ça va m.** I want to go on holiday, but I've a feeling it'll all come to nothing; **j'ai complètement merdé dans les explications que je t'ai données** I made a real hash *or* mess of the instructions I gave you; **ils ne savent pas trop ce qui a merdé entre eux** they don't really know what screwed things up between them

merdeux, -euse [mɛrdø, -øz] *Vulg* ADJ *(linge etc)* shitty; *Arch* **c'est un bâton m.** he's a shit; **elle se sent merdeuse** she feels shitty ▸ N **1** *(personne)* jerk; **un petit m.** a jerk *or* prat **2** *(enfant)* brat

merdier [mɛrdje] NM *Vulg (désordre)* mess; **je ne sais pas par quel bout ranger, tellement c'est le m.** it's such a mess *or* pigsty I don't know where to start tidying up; **c'est le m. dans ma vie** my life's (in) a real mess; **je suis dans un sacré m.** I'm really in the shit

merdique [mɛrdik] ADJ *Vulg* shitty, crappy

merdouiller [mɛrduje], **merdoyer** [mɛrdwaje] VI *(je merdoie, n. merdoyons; je merdoierai) Vulg* to make a cockup *or* balls-up *or Am* ball-up, *Br* to cock up

mère [mɛr] NF **1** *(parent)* mother; *Zool* dam; **elle est m. de famille** she is a wife and mother; **elle est m. de trois enfants** she is the mother of three children, she is a mother of three; **elle a été une vraie m. pour son frère** she's been like a mother to her brother; **sœur par la m.** half-sister on the mother's side; *Fam* **la m. Martin** old Mrs Martin; *Fam* **et dites donc, la petite m.!** well, missus!

2 *(source, origine)* **l'oisiveté est (la) m. de tous les vices** the devil finds work for idle hands (to do)

3 *Beaux-Arts, Cér (pour moules en plâtre etc)* mould, *Am* mold, matrix

4 **langue m.** mother tongue; *Biol* **cellule m.** mother cell; *Com* **maison m.** parent company; **la reine m.** the Queen Mother

▸▸ *Rel* **m. abbesse** abbess; **m. biologique** natural *or* biological mother; **m. célibataire** single *or Vieilli* unmarried mother; **m. d'emprunt** surrogate mother; **m. génétique** natural *or* biological mother; **m. nourricière** foster mother; **m. patrie** mother country, motherland; **m. porteuse** surrogate mother; **m. poule** mother hen; **m. de substitution** surrogate mother; *Rel* **M. supérieure** Mother Superior *(of convent)*; **m. de vinaigre** mother of vinegar

merguez [mɛrgɛz] NF merguez *(spicy North African sausage)*

méridien, -ienne [meridjɛ̃, -jɛn] ADJ *(ligne etc)* meridian, meridional; **chaleur méridienne** midday heat; **ombre méridienne** shadow at noon

▸ NM meridian; **sous le m. de vingt degrés à l'ouest de Greenwich** twenty degrees west of Greenwich

▸ NF **méridienne 1** *Astron* meridian line; *(altitude)* meridian altitude **2** *Arch (sieste)* midday siesta *or* nap **3** *(canapé)* day bed

méridional, -ale, -aux, -ales [meridjɔnal, -o] ADJ *(du Sud)* southern; *(du Sud de la France)* Southern French

▸ N *(du Sud)* southerner; *(du Sud de la France)* Southern Frenchman, f Frenchwoman; **méridionaux** *(du Sud de la France)* Southern French people

meringue [mərɛ̃g] NF *Culin* meringue

meringuer [mərɛ̃ge] VT *Culin* to cover with meringue; **tarte à la rhubarbe meringuée** rhubarb meringue pie

mérinos [merinos] NM *(mouton, laine, tissu)* merino; *Arg* **laisse pisser le m.!** don't let it get to you!

merise [məriz] NF *(fruit)* wild cherry

merisier [mərizje] NM *(arbre)* wild cherry (tree); *(bois)* cherry (wood)

méritant [meritɑ̃] ADJ deserving; **peu m.** undeserving

mérite [merit] NM *(qualité estimable)* merit; *(honneur)* credit; *(valeur)* worth; **ses remarques avaient le m. d'être franches** his/her remarks had the merit of being frank; **tu n'as même pas le m. de l'avoir fait tout seul** you can't even take credit for doing it yourself; **je n'ai aucun m.** I deserve no credit, I can't take any credit (for it); **s'attribuer le m. de qch** to take the credit for sth; **tout le m. lui revient** the credit is all his, all the credit is due to him/her; **son m. est grand d'avoir tout accepté, il a le grand m. d'avoir tout accepté** it is greatly to his credit that he accepted everything; **au seul m.** on merit alone; **augmentation au m.** merit increase; **par ordre de m.** in order of merit; **selon ses mérites** according to one's merits; **homme de m.** man of merit *or* talent *or* ability

mériter [merite] VT **1** to deserve, to merit; **il mérite des baffes** he deserves to be slapped; **il n'a que ce qu'il mérite** he's got what he deserves, it serves him right; **livre qui mérite d'être lu** book worth reading; **cela mérite réflexion** it's worth thinking about; **tu mérites qu'on te fasse la même chose** you deserve to have the same thing happen to you; **tu mériterais que je te laisse là tout seul** it would serve you right if I left you there on your own **2 voilà ce qui lui a mérité cette renommée** this is what earned him this fame; **bien m. de la patrie** to deserve well of one's country

méritocratie [meritokrasi] NF meritocracy

méritoire [meritwar] ADJ commendable, praiseworthy, meritorious

merlan [merlɑ̃] NM **1** *(poisson)* whiting; *Fam* **faire des yeux de m. frit à qn, regarder qn avec des yeux de m. frit** *(parce qu'on n'a pas compris)* to gape at sb; *(parce qu'on est amoureux de lui)* to make sheep's eyes at sb **2** *Arg (coiffeur) (pour hommes)* barber, hairdresser; *(pour femmes)* hairdresser

merle [merl] NM *(oiseau)* blackbird; *Fig* **vilain m.,** *Iron* **beau m.** nasty customer, *Br* nasty piece of work; **m. blanc** rare bird; **chercher le m. blanc** to ask for the moon

merlin¹ [merlɛ̃] NM *Naut* marline

merlin² NM *(hache)* axe, *Am* ax; *(pour abattre les arbres)* felling axe; *(pour abattre le bétail)* poleaxe

merlu [merly] NM hake

merluche [merlyʃ] NF **1** *(poisson)* hake VOIR GRAMMAIRE A12 **2** *Culin* dried (unsalted) cod, stockfish

mer-mer ADJ INV *Mil* **missile m.** sea-to-sea missile

mérou [meru] NM *(poisson)* grouper

mérovingien, -ienne [merɔvɛ̃ʒjɛ̃, -jɛn] *Hist* ADJ Merovingian
N **M.** Merovingian

mer-sol ADJ INV *Mil* **missile m.** sea-to-ground missile

merveille [mervej] NF **1** marvel, wonder; **les merveilles de la technologie** the marvels *or* wonders of technology; **les sept merveilles du monde** the seven wonders of the world; **ma nouvelle machine à laver est une m.** my new washing machine is a marvel; **faire m.** to work *or* do wonders (sur with, for); **faire des merveilles** to work *or* do *or* perform wonders; **c'est m. que vous soyez à l'heure** it's a wonder that you're on time; **à m.** per-

---

fectly, wonderfully (well); **se porter à m.** to be in excellent health *or* in the best of health; **ce chèque tombe à m.** this cheque has arrived at exactly the right moment **2** *Culin* = sweet fritter

merveilleusement [mervejøzmɑ̃] ADV marvellously, wonderfully; **il fait m. beau** it's marvellous *or* wonderful weather, the weather's marvellous *or* wonderful; **aller m. bien** to be wonderfully well, to be in excellent health; **elle a m. réussi son examen** she passed her exam with excellent results

merveilleux, -euse [mervejø, -øz] ADJ marvellous, wonderful; **il a fait un temps m.** it was marvellous *or* wonderful weather, the weather was marvellous *or* wonderful; **c'est m. ce qu'il a changé** it's marvellous how he's changed
NM **le m.** the supernatural
NF *Hist* **merveilleuse** merveilleuse, fine lady

mes [me] *voir* **mon**

mésadapté, -ée [mezadapte] *Can* ADJ maladjusted
N misfit, maladjusted person; **m. social** social misfit

mésalliance [mezaljɑ̃s] NF unsuitable marriage; **faire une m.** to marry beneath oneself

mésallier (se) [səmezalje] VT *(conj like allier)* to marry beneath oneself

mésange [mezɑ̃ʒ] NF tit; **m. bleue** bluetit; **m. charbonnière** great tit; **m. noire** coaltit

mésaventure [mezavɑ̃tyr] NF misadventure, mishap, misfortune

mescal [meskal] NM mescal

mescaline [meskalin] NF mescalin(e)

mésentente [mezɑ̃tɑ̃t] NF disagreement; **climat de m.** coolness

mésestimation [mezestimasjɔ̃] NF *Litt* underestimation, underrating, undervaluing

mésestime [mezestim] NF *Litt* low esteem; **tenir qn en m.** to hold sb in low esteem

mésestimer [mezestime] VT to underestimate

mésintelligence [mezɛ̃teliʒɑ̃s] NF *Litt* disagreement; **être en m. avec qn** to be at loggerheads with sb

mesmérisme [mesmerism] NM mesmerism

Mésopotamie (la) [lamezɔpɔtami] NF Mesopotamia

mésopotamien, -ienne [mezɔpɔtamjɛ̃, -jɛn] ADJ Mesopotamian
N **M.** Mesopotamian

mésothérapie [mezoterapi] NF *Méd* mesotherapy *(method of treatment involving intradermal injections with mini-needles)*

mésozoïque [mezɔzɔik] ADJ, NM *Géol* Mesozoic

mesquin [meskɛ̃] ADJ *(méchant)* mean, petty; *(avare)* mean, stingy, niggardly; *(excuse)* paltry, petty; **un coup m.** a mean *or* shabby trick; **il a vraiment un esprit m.** he's really small-minded *or* mean *or* petty

mesquinement [meskinmɑ̃] ADV meanly

mesquinerie [meskinri] NF *(de caractère, procédé)* meanness, pettiness; *(avarice)* meanness, stinginess, niggardliness; **je ne te savais pas capable de telles mesquineries** I would never have thought you capable of such meanness *or* pettiness, I didn't think you could be so mean *or* petty

mess [mes] NM *Mil* mess; **m. des officiers** officers' mess

message [mesaʒ] NM message; **prendre un m.** to take a message; **veuillez laisser un m. après le signal sonore** please leave a message after the tone; **chanson/pièce à m.** song/play with a message; **m. codé** coded message; **m. électronique** e-mail; **envoyer**

---

un m. électronique à qn to e-mail sb; **m. enregistré** recorded message; **m. subliminal** subliminal message; **m. télex** telex (message); **m. téléphonique** telephone message; *Tél* **m. texte** text message; **envoyer un m. texte à qn** to text sb, to text-message sb; **m. de détresse** distress message; **m. publicitaire** advertisement, advertising message; *Ordinat* **messages publicitaires** *(envoyés par e-mail)* junk mail, spam; *Ordinat* **m. d'accueil** welcome message; *Ordinat* **m. d'aide** help message; *Ordinat* **m. d'alerte** warning message, alert box; *Ordinat* **m. d'attente (du système)** (system) prompt; *Ordinat* **m. d'erreur** error message; *Ordinat* **m. d'invite (du système)** prompt; *Ordinat* **m. guide-opérateur** prompt

messager, -ère [mesaʒe, -er] N messenger; **m. de malheur** bearer of bad news; *Litt* **m. du printemps** harbinger of spring
NM *(de colis, cargaison)* carrier

messagerie [mesaʒri] NF service de messageries parcel delivery service; *Ordinat* **m. de dialogue en direct** chat; **m. électronique** electronic mail service, e-mail; **m. instantanée** instant messaging; **m. de presse** newspaper distributing service; **m. rose** = interactive Minitel services enabling individuals seeking companionship to make contact; **m. vocale** voice mail; **messageries maritimes** shipping line; **messageries aériennes** air freight company; **bureau de(s) messageries** *Naut* shipping office; *Rail* parcel(s) office; *Hist* stagecoach office

messe [mes] NF *Rel* mass; **aller à la m.** to go to mass; **célébrer** *ou* **dire la m.** to celebrate *or* say mass; **faire dire une m. pour qn** to have a mass said for sb; *Mus* **m. en si mineur** mass in B minor; *Fig* **la m. est dite** the die is cast; *Can Fig* **il y a du monde à la m.!** the place is jam-packed!
▸▸**m. basse** low mass; *Fig Fam* **pas de messes basses!** stop whispering!; **m. de minuit** midnight mass; **m. des morts** requiem mass; **m. noire** black mass

messeigneurs [mesɛɲœr] NMPL *voir* **monseigneur**

messeoir [meswar] VI *(prp* messeyant; *no pp; pr ind* il messied, ils messeyent; *pr sub* il messeye; *impf* il messeyait; *no p hist; fu* il messiéra) *Arch, Litt* to be unbecoming *or* unseemly; **il lui messied de …** it ill becomes him to …

messianique [mesjanik] ADJ Messianic

messianisme [mesjanism] NM Messianism

messidor [mesidɔr] NM *Hist* = tenth month of the French Republican calendar *(19-20 June – 19-20 July)*

Messie [mesi] NM Messiah; **on l'a attendu comme le M.** we were waiting eagerly for him

messin, -ine [mesɛ̃, -in] ADJ of/from Metz
N **M.** *(natif)* native of Metz; *(habitant)* inhabitant of Metz

messire [mesir] NM *Arch* Sir, Master

mestrance [mestrɑ̃s] NF *Naut* petty officers

mesurable [məzyrabl] ADJ measurable, *Spéc* mensurable

mesurage [məzyraʒ] NM measuring, measurement

mesure [məzyr] NF **1** *(dimension)* measurement; *(action)* measurement, measuring; **appareil de m.** measuring apparatus; **prendre les mesures de qn** to take sb's measurements, to measure sb; **prendre les mesures de qch** to measure sth; *Fig* **prendre la m. de qn** to size sb up, to get the measure of sb; **sur m.** made to measure, tailor-made; **complet (fait) sur mesure(s)** made-to-measure *or Am* custom-made suit; **faire faire un complet sur m.** to have a suit made to measure or tailor-made; *Fig* **être en m. de faire qch** to be in a position to do sth; **le producteur lui a trouvé un rôle sur m.** the producer found him a role that was tailor-made for him; *Fig* **donner toute sa m.** to show what one is capable of; *Fig* **être à la m. de qn/qch** to measure up to sb/sth; *Sp, Fig* **trouver un adversaire à sa m.** to meet one's match SEE GRAMMAR B59

2 dans une certaine m. to some or a certain extent or degree; **dans une large m.** to a large extent or degree, in large measure; **dans la m. où** insofar as; **je vous aiderai dans la m. de mes forces** ou **du possible** I'll help you to the best of my ability or as much as I can or as best I can; **ces dépenses ne sont pas dans la m. de mes moyens** this expenditure is beyond my means

3 (au fur et) à m. as one goes along; **je vérifie les chiffres (au fur et) à m.** I check the figures as I go along; **à m. que** as; **à m. que je reculais, il s'avançait** as I retreated, he advanced

4 *(action)* measure, step, action; **m. de sécurité** safety measure or precaution; **par m. de sécurité/d'hygiène** for reasons of safety/hygiene, as a safety/hygiene measure; **par m. d'économie** as a cost-saving measure, for reasons of economy; **prendre des mesures** to take measures or steps or action; **prendre des mesures pour faire qch/pour que ...** to take measures or steps to do sth/so that ...; **prendre des mesures contre qch** to take action against sth; **prendre ses mesures** to make arrangements; **j'ai pris mes mesures pour que les enfants soient gardés** I've made arrangements for the children to be looked after; **mesures d'austérité** austerity measures; **m. conservatoire** protective measure; **m. fiscale** fiscal measure; **m. incitative** incentive (measure); **mesures protectionnistes** protectionist measures; **mesures protectrices** protective measures; **mesures provisoires** temporary measures; **m. de rétorsion** retaliatory measure, reprisal; **m. d'urgence** emergency measure

5 *(quantité, unité)* measure; **verser une m. de vin à qn** to pour sb out a measure of wine; **faites-moi bonne m.** give me good measure; *Fig* **il n'y a pas commune m. entre ces deux vins** there is no comparison between the two wines; **sans commune m.** unrivalled; **m. de longueur** measure of length; **m. de surface** ou **de superficie** square measure; **m. de volume** cubic measure; **poids et mesures** weights and measures

6 pièces qui ne sont pas de m. pieces that are not the right size or that are not to size; **rester dans la juste m.** to keep within bounds; **elle n'a pas le sens de la m.** she has no sense of moderation; **(dé)passer la m.** to overstep the mark, to go too far; **ne garder aucune m., oublier toute m.** to fling aside all restraint, to lose all sense of moderation or proportion; **ambition sans m.** unbounded or limitless ambition

7 *Escrime* measure, reach, distance

8 *Mus (temps)* time; *(division)* bar; **m. à quatre temps** four-four time, common time; **battre la m.** to beat time; **barre de m.** bar line; **en m.** in (strict) time; **aller en m.** to keep time; **deux mesures plus loin** two bars further on

9 *Littér (de vers)* metre, *Am* meter

mesuré [məzyre] ADJ *(pas)* measured; *(langage, personne)* moderate, restrained

mesurément [məzyremɑ̃] ADV in moderation

mesurer [məzyre] VT **1** *(dimensions, taille)* to measure; *(farine, sucre etc)* to measure out; *(bois, terre)* to measure (up); *(tissu)* to measure off; *(carburant)* to meter; *Fig (personne, chose)* to size up; **m. deux mètres** *(de personne)* to be two metres tall; **la colonne me-**

sure **dix mètres** the column measures ten metres or is ten metres high; **on mesure le travail au résultat** the work is measured by results; **m. la nourriture à qn** to ration sb's food; **le temps vous sera mesuré pour cette épreuve** you will have a limited amount of time for this test; **m. sa dépense sur ses profits** to cut one's coat according to one's cloth; **m. la distance à la vue** to judge or estimate or gauge the distance with one's eyes **2** *(ménager, régler)* **m. le châtiment à l'offense** to make the punishment fit the crime; **m. ses paroles** ou **son vocabulaire** to moderate one's language; **il ne mesure pas la portée de ses paroles** he says things without thinking

VPR **se mesurer se m. avec** ou **à qn** to measure one's strength against sb, to measure or pit oneself against sb; **vous n'êtes pas de force** ou **de taille à vous m. avec lui** you're no match for him; **les adversaires se mesurèrent des yeux** the opponents sized each other up

mesurette [məzyrɛt] NF **1** *(pour doser)* measuring spoon **2** *(décision sans grande portée)* petty reform

mesureur [məzyrœr] NM *(personne, appareil)* measurer; **m. de pression** pressure gauge

mésuser [mezyze] VI **m. de son bien** to misuse one's wealth; **m. de son pouvoir** to abuse one's power

métabolique [metabɔlik] ADJ metabolic

métabolisme [metabɔlism] NM metabolism

métacarpe [metakarp] NM *Anat* metacarpus

métacarpien, -ienne [metakarpjɛ̃, -jɛn] ADJ, NM *Anat* metacarpal

métairie [meteri] NF small farm *(worked by share-cropper)*

métal, -aux [metal, -o] NM **1** metal; **métaux précieux** precious metals; **m. blanc** white metal; **m. antifriction** Babbit metal, bearing metal **2** *Fin* **m. en barres** bullion

métalangage [metalɑ̃gaʒ] NM metalanguage

métalangue [metalɑ̃g] NF metalanguage

métallifère [metalifɛr] ADJ metal-bearing, metalliferous

métallique [metalik] ADJ metallic; **câble m.** wire rope; **plume m.** metal nib; **rendre un son m.** to clang, to clank; *Fin* **réserve m.** bullion reserve

métallisation [metalizasjɔ̃] NF metallization

métallisé [metalize] ADJ *surtout Aut (peinture)* metallic; **voiture bleu m.** metallic blue car

métalliser [metalize] VT to metallize

métallo [metalo] NM *Fam* metalworker

métallurgie [metalyrʒi] NF metallurgy; **crise dans la m.** crisis in the metallurgical industry

métallurgique [metalyrʒik] ADJ metallurgical

métallurgiste [metalyrʒist] NM **1** *(scientifique)* metallurgist **2** *(ouvrier)* metalworker

métamorphique [metamɔrfik] ADJ *Géol* metamorphic

métamorphiser [metamɔrfize] VT *Géol* to metamorphose

métamorphisme [metamɔrfism] NM *Géol* metamorphism

métamorphose [metamɔrfoz] NF transformation, metamorphosis; *Fig* transformation; *Fig* **quelle m.!** what a transformation!

métamorphoser [metamɔrfoze] VT to transform, to metamorphose; *Fig* to transform

VPR **se métamorphoser** to change completely, to be transformed

métaphore [metafɔr] NF metaphor; **parler par métaphores** to speak in metaphors; **elle parle beaucoup par métaphores** she is very metaphorical in her speech, she uses a lot of metaphor(s) when she speaks

métaphorique [metafɔrik] ADJ *(expression, style)* metaphorical, figurative; **cela n'a qu'une valeur m.** it's purely metaphorical or figurative

métaphoriquement [metafɔrikmɑ̃] ADV metaphorically, figuratively

métaphysicien, -ienne [metafizisjɛ̃, -jɛn] N metaphysician, metaphysicist

métaphysique [metafizik] ADJ metaphysical
NF metaphysics

métaphysiquement [metafizikmɑ̃] ADV metaphysically

métapsychique [metapsiʃik] ADJ *(phénomène)* psychic
NF parapsychology

métastase [metastaz] NF *Méd* metastasis, secondary cancer; **former des métastases** to metastasize

métatarse [metatars] NM *Anat* metatarsus

métatarsien, -ienne [metatarsjɛ̃, -jɛn] ADJ, NM *Anat* metatarsal

métathèse [metatɛz] NF *Ling* metathesis

métayage [metejaʒ] NM *Agr* sharecropping

métayer, -ère [meteje, -ɛr] N *Agr* sharecropper

métazoaire [metazɔer] NM *Biol* metazoan; **métazoaires** Metazoa

métempsycose [metɑ̃psikoz] NF transmigration of the soul, *Spéc* metempsychosis

météo [meteo] *Fam* NF **1** weather forecast or report; **la m. est mauvaise pour toute la semaine** the weather forecast is bad for the whole week; **je n'ai pas eu le temps d'écouter/de regarder la m.** I didn't have time to listen to/to look at the weather (forecast) **2** *(bureau)* weather office, *Br* ≃ Met Office, *Am* ≃ Weather Bureau
NM **Monsieur M.** the weather man
ADJ weather, meteorological; **bulletin m.** weather report or forecast; **station m.** meteorological or weather station; **frégate** ou **navire m.** weather ship

météore [meteɔr] NM meteor

météorique [meteɔrik] ADJ meteoric

météorite [meteɔrit] NM OU F meteorite

météorologie [meteɔrɔlɔʒi] NF meteorology; **le bureau central de m.** = the meteorological or weather office

météorologique [meteɔrɔlɔʒik] ADJ = météo ADJ

météorologiste [meteɔrɔlɔʒist], **météorologue** [meteɔrɔlɔg] N meteorologist

métèque [metɛk] NM *très Fam (terme injurieux)* = racist term used to refer to any dark-skinned foreigner living in France, especially one from the Mediterranean

méthadone [metadɔn] NF methadone

méthane [metan] NM *Chimie* methane

méthanier [metanje] NM *Naut* methane tanker

méthanol [metanɔl] NM methanol

méthode [metɔd] NF **1** *(démarche)* method, way; **m. pour faire qch** method or way of doing sth; **une bonne m. pour apprendre les langues** a good method for or way of learning languages; **c'est quoi ta m. pour rester aussi mince?** how do you manage to stay so slim?; **elle a sa m.** she has her own method or way of doing things; **je vais changer de m.** I'm going to change my methods; **tu as suivi quelle m.?** which method did you use?; **c'est**

la seule m. à suivre it's the only way to do it; **il n'y a pas 36 méthodes** it's the only way; *Fam* **je n'ai pas la m. avec lui** I don't know how to handle him; **tu as vraiment la m. avec les enfants!** you really have a way with *or* know how to handle children!; *Fam* **trouver la m. pour faire qch** to find out how to do sth, to find a way of doing sth; **m. de lecture** reading method; **m. de financement** funding method; **m. de gestion** management technique; **m. de travail** work method; *UE* **m. communautaire** Community method; *Compta* **m. par** *ou* **à échelles** daily balance interest calculation; **m. des coûts variables** direct costing; **m. des coûts marginaux** cost pricing; **m. du coût de revient complet** full costing, full cost accounting (method); **m. de vente** sales *or* selling technique

2 *(ordre)* method; **il a beaucoup de m.** he's very methodical *or* systematic; **avec m.** methodically, systematically; **sans m.** unmethodically, without method, unsystematically

3 *(livre)* primer, grammar; **m. de piano** piano tutor

méthodique [metɔdik] **ADJ** methodic(al), systematic

méthodiquement [metɔdikmɑ̃] **ADV** methodically, systematically

méthodisme [metɔdism] **NM** *Rel* Methodism

méthodiste [metɔdist] **ADJ, N** *Rel* Methodist

méthodologie [metɔdɔlɔʒi] **NF** methodology

méthodologique [metɔdɔlɔʒik] **ADJ** methodological

méthyle [metil] **NM** *Chimie* methyl

méthylène [metilɛn] **NM** *Chimie* methylene

méthylique [metilik] **ADJ** *Chimie* methyl(ic)

méticuleusement [metikyløzmɑ̃] **ADV** meticulously

méticuleux, -euse [metikylø, -øz] **ADJ** meticulous; **par trop m.** over-meticulous; **elle est d'une propreté méticuleuse** she keeps everything immaculate *or* everything spotless(ly clean)

méticulosité [metikylozite] **NF** *Litt* meticulousness; **d'une m. exaspérante** exasperatingly meticulous

métier [metje] **NM 1** *(travail)* trade, profession, occupation; **les métiers artistiques** the artistic professions; **j'ai fait tous les métiers** I've done a bit of everything; **quel est votre m.?** what do you do (for a living)?, what's your job?; **exercer** *ou* **faire un m.** to carry on a trade *or* a profession; **j'exerce le m. de journaliste** I'm a journalist (by profession); **quel m. veux-tu faire plus tard?** what do you want to be when you grow up?; **il n'est pas** *ou* **il n'y a pas de sot m.** a job's a job; **m. de banquier** banking profession, banking; **les métiers de bouche** the food and catering trade; *Euph* **le plus vieux m. du monde** the oldest profession in the world; **il est charpentier de son m.** he's a carpenter by trade; **elle a un bon m.** she has a good job; **il sent qu'il est temps de changer de m.** he feels it's time he changed his job; **ils sont du m.** they're in the business *or* trade; *Fig* **ce n'est pas mon m.** it's not my job; **il connaît son m.** he knows what he's doing; **ce n'est pas toi qui vas m'apprendre mon m.** don't teach me my business, I know what I'm doing; **ils font leur m.** they're only doing their job; **parler m.** to talk shop; *Fam* **quel m.!** what a life!; **quel m. de fou!** you don't have to be crazy to do this job, but it helps!; **chacun son m. (et les vaches seront bien gardées)** you do your job and I'll do mine; **terme de m.** technical term SEE GRAMMAR B5

2 *(savoir-faire, expérience)* experience; **il a**

du m. he has experience, he is experienced; **elle a plusieurs années de m.** she has several years' experience; **homme de m.** professional; **gens de m.** experts, professionals; **ficelles** *ou* **trucs du m.** tricks of the trade; *Fig* **c'est le m. qui rentre** put it down to experience, that's how you learn

3 *Tex* **m. à tisser** loom; **m. mécanique** power loom; **m. à filer** spinning frame; **m. à tapisserie** tapestry frame; **m. à broder** embroidery frame, tambour frame; *Fig* **avoir un ouvrage sur le m.** to have a piece of work in hand

métis, -isse [metis] **ADJ 1** *(personne)* half-caste; *(animal)* crossbreed; *(chien)* mongrel; **plante métisse** hybrid plant **2** *Tex* **tissu m.** linen-cotton mixture

N *(personne)* halfcaste, *Péj* halfbreed; *(animal)* crossbreed; *(chien)* mongrel

NM *Tex* linen-cotton mixture

métissage [metisaʒ] **NM** crossbreeding

métisser [metise] **VT** to cross(breed); **une population très métissée** a highly intermixed population

métonymie [metɔnimi] **NF** *Ling* metonymy

métrage [metraʒ] **NM 1** *(action)* measuring, measurement; *Constr* quantity surveying **2** *(longueur)* (metric) length; **grand/petit m.** *(tissu)* cut lengthways/crossways; **des métrages de lin** lengths of linen; **vous le voulez en quel m.?** what width would you like? **3** *Cin* footage; **long m.** feature film; **moyen m.** medium length film; **court m.** short

mètre [mɛtr] **NM 1** *metre, Am* meter; **m. carré/cube** square/cubic metre; *Sport* **elle se prépare à courir un 200 mètres (haies)** she's training for the 200 metres (hurdles); **l'épreuve du 400 mètres** the 400 metres (race) **2** *(pour mesurer)* tape measure; *(en bois)* rule; **m. pliant** folding rule; **m. à ruban** tape measure **3** *Littér* metre, *Am* meter

métré [metre] **NM** *Constr (de terrain à construire etc)* measurement(s); *(devis)* bill of quantities

métrer [metre] **VT** (**je mètre; je métrerai**) **1** to measure (by the metre *or Am* meter) **2** *Constr* to survey (for quantities)

métreur, -euse [metrœr, -øz] **N m. (vérificateur)** quantity surveyor

métrique [metrik] **ADJ 1** metric; **adopter le système m.** to adopt the metric system, *Fam* to go metric **2** *Littér* metric(al)

NF *Littér* prosody, metrics

métro [metro] **NM** underground, *Am* subway; **le m. de Paris/de Montréal** the Paris/Montreal metro; **le m. de Londres** the London underground (system), *Fam* the tube; **aller quelque part en m.** to go somewhere by metro/underground/tube/subway; **il y a un m. direct de la gare jusque chez moi** you can get a metro/tube/subway directly from the station to my place; **au m. Charonne** at Charonne metro (station); *Fam* **avoir un m. de retard** to be behind the times; *Fam* **m., boulot, dodo** the daily grind, the daily routine; **depuis que j'habite à Paris, ma vie c'est vraiment m., boulot, dodo** life has become very humdrum *or* routine since I moved to Paris

métrologie [metrɔlɔʒi] **NF** metrology

métrologique [metrɔlɔʒik] **ADJ** metrological

métrologiste [metrɔlɔʒist] **N** metrologist

métronome [metrɔnɔm] **NM** *Mus* metronome

métropole [metrɔpɔl] **NF 1** *(grande ville)* metropolis; **faire de Marseille une m. d'équilibre** to turn Marseilles into a second capital **2** *(État)* mother country; **les Français de la M.** the French of Metropolitan France **3** *Rel* metropolis; *(d'archevêque)* see

métropolitain, -aine [metrɔpɔlitɛ̃, -ɛn] **ADJ 1** *Admin* metropolitan; **armée métropoli-**

taine home army **2** *Rel* metropolitan; *(église etc)* archiepiscopal

NM 1 *Admin* underground (railway), *Am* subway **2** *Rel* archbishop; *(de l'Église orthodoxe)* metropolitan

mets [mɛ] **NM** food

mettable [metabl] **ADJ 1** *(vêtements etc)* wearable; **pas m.** not fit to wear; **elle dit n'avoir plus rien de m.** she says she has nothing to wear **2** *Vulg (personne)* fuckable, *Br* shaggable

metteur, -euse [metœr, -øz] **N** *Typ* compositor, comp; **m. en scène** *Cin* director; *Théâtre, Radio* director, *Br* producer; *Radio* **m. en ondes** producer; *Typ* **m. en pages** layout artist; **m. en œuvre** *(de bijoux etc)* mounter

METTRE [mɛtr] *(prp* **mettant;** *pp* **mis;** *pr ind* **je mets, il met, n. mettons, ils mettent;** *p hist* **je mis;** *fu* **je mettrai)**

VT ■ to put **1, 8** ■ to put on **2, 5, 6** ■ to take **3** ■ to spend **4** ■ to wear **5** ■ to turn on **6** ■ to lay **7** ■ to put up **7** ■ to suppose **9** ■ to write **10**
VPR ■ to go **1** ■ to start + ing *(se mettre à faire)* **3** ■ to put on **4**

VT 1 *(placer)* to put; **ne mets pas les coudes sur la table!** don't put your elbows on the table!; **m. qn au lit/dans le train** to put sb to bed/on the train; **il a mis le pied sur une peau de banane** he stepped on a banana skin; **il mit la main sur mon épaule** he put *or* laid his hand on my shoulder; **m. genou à terre** to go down on one knee; **mettez tout cela par terre** put all that on the floor; **m. qch debout** to stand sth upright; **mets les livres debout** stand the books on end; **m. qch à plat** to put *or* lay sth down flat; **m. un manche à un balai** to put a handle on *or* fit a handle to a broom; **m. une annonce dans les journaux** to put an advertisement in the (news)papers; **il a mis de la boue sur le tapis** he's got mud on the carpet; **m. une lettre à la poste** to post a letter; **m. de l'argent sur un compte** to put money into an account; **qu'est-ce qui vous a mis cela dans la tête?** what put that into your head?; **il met ses parents avant tout le reste** he puts his parents first; *Sport* **m. le ballon au fond des filets** to put the ball in the back of the net; **nous avons mis 3 km entre nous et nos poursuivants** we put 3 km between us and our pursuers

2 *(appliquer) (fond de teint, maquillage, parfum, pansement, couche de peinture etc)* to put on

3 *(consacrer)* **m. du temps à faire qch** to take time to do sth; **j'ai mis deux ans à faire cela** I took *or* it took me two years to do that; *Fam* **tu y as mis le temps, pour comprendre** it took you a while to catch on; **combien de temps met-on pour aller de Paris à Marseille en voiture?** how long does it take to get from Paris to Marseilles by car?; **le train met deux heures pour le trajet** the trip takes two hours by train, it takes the train two hours to do the trip; **m. toute son énergie/tout son enthousiasme à faire qch** to put all one's energy/enthusiasm into doing sth; **j'y mettrai tous mes soins** I'll give it my full attention

4 *(dépenser une somme d'argent)* to spend; *(investir)* to sink; **m. 500 euros dans qch** to spend 500 euros on sth; **il faudra m. dans les 2000 euros** you'll have to spend about 2,000 euros; **m. 20 000 euros dans une affaire** to sink 20,000 euros into a business venture; **je serais prêt à m. tout ce que j'ai dans cette entreprise** I'd be willing to put everything I have into this venture; *Fam* **y m. le prix** to pay for it; **mais il faudra que vous y mettiez le prix** but it'll cost you; **m. un enjeu** to lay a stake; **m. de l'argent sur**

micro-onde, *pl* **micro-ondes** [mikrɔ5d] NF microwave; **four à micro-ondes** microwave oven

micro-ondes NM INV microwave (oven); **faire cuire qch au m.** to cook sth in the microwave, to microwave sth

micro-ordinateur, *pl* **micro-ordinateurs** NM *Ordinat* micro(computer)

micro-organisme, *pl* **micro-organismes** NM micro-organism

micropaiement [mikropɛmɑ̃] NM *Ordinat* micropayment

microphone [mikrɔfɔn] NM microphone; *(de téléphone)* mouthpiece; **m. à condensateur** condenser microphone; **m. sur girafe** sound-boom microphone; **m. sur pied** stand microphone

microphotographie [mikrɔfɔtografi] NF **1** *(activité)* microphotography, photomicrography **2** *(résultat)* microphotograph, photomicrograph

microphotographique [mikrɔfɔtografik] ADJ microphotographic, photomicrographic

microphysique [mikrofizik] NF microphysics

micropilule [mikropilyl] NF *Pharm* minipill

microplaquette [mikroplakɛt] NF *Électron* chip

microprocesseur [mikroprɔsesœr] NM *Ordinat* microprocessor; **m. en tranches** bit slice microprocessor

microprogramme [mikroprɔgram] NM *Ordinat* microprogram

microscope [mikrɔskɔp] NM microscope; **regarder au m.** to look through a microscope; **regarder qch au m.** to look at sth through *or* under a microscope; **visible au m.** visible under the microscope; **m. électronique** electron microscope; **m. électronique à balayage** electron scanning microscope; **m. optique** light microscope

microscopie [mikrɔskɔpi] NF microscopy

microscopique [mikrɔskɔpik] ADJ microscopic

microseconde [mikrosəg5d] NF microsecond

microserveur [mikrosɛrvœr] NM *Ordinat* bulletin board service

microsillon [mikrɔsij5] NM **1** *(sillon)* microgroove **2** *(disque)* **m.** long-playing record, LP

microsociété [mikrosɔsjete] NF miniature society, society in miniature

microsociologie [mikrosɔsjɔlɔ3i] NF = sociology of small groups

microtome [mikrɔtɔm] NM microtome

micro-trottoir, *pl* **micros-trottoirs** NM street interview, *Br Fam* vox pop

miction [miksj5] NF urination, *Spéc* micturition

MidCAC [midkak] NM *Bourse* **le M., l'indice M.** = Paris stock exchange index comprised of 100 medium-range shares, ≃ MidCap

midi [midi] NM **1** *(heure)* midday, (twelve) noon, twelve o'clock; **il est m.** it's twelve o'clock; **avant/après m.** before/after twelve (o'clock); **m. et demi** half-past twelve; **entre m. et deux** at lunch time; *Fig* **chercher m. à quatorze heures** to look for difficulties where there are none, to complicate matters **2** *(moment du déjeuner)* lunch time; **tu fais quoi, ce m.?** what are you doing at lunch time *or* for lunch?; **à m.** at lunch time; **à m., j'ai mangé des frites** I had chips at lunch time *or* for lunch; **repas de m.** midday meal **3** *(milieu du jour)* **en plein m.** at the height of noon **4** *(sud)* south; **chambre au m.** room facing south; **le M. (de la France)** the South of France

ADJ INV *(de taille moyenne)* **chaîne m.** midi system

midinette [midinɛt] NF **1** silly young girl; **des lectures de m.** slushy novels **2** *Vieilli (ouvrière)* shop girl; *(couturière)* young dressmaker

mi-distance (à) ADV halfway, midway; **nous sommes à m. de notre but** we are halfway to our goal

midship, *pl* **midships** [midʃip] NM midshipman

mie¹ [mi] NF crumb *(of loaf, as opposed to crust)*; **pain de m.** sandwich loaf

mie² NF *Arch, Litt* truelove, ladylove; **ma m.** my beloved

miel [mjɛl] NM honey; **une tartine de m.** a slice of bread and honey; **m. rosat** rose honey; *Fig* **faire son m. de qch** to make capital out of sth; *Fig* **elle était (tout sucre et) tout m.** she was all sweetness and light INT *Fam* **et m.!** oh, sugar!

miellé [mjele] ADJ *Litt (parfum)* honeyed; *(boisson)* tasting of honey

mielleusement [mjeløzmɑ̃] ADV *Péj (dire)* in honeyed tones; **sourire m.** to give a sweet, sugary smile

mielleux, -euse [mjelø, -øz] ADJ **1** *(boisson, bonbon etc)* tasting of honey **2** *Péj (discours, sourire etc)* sugary; *(personne)* sugary, smooth

mien, mienne [mjɛ̃, mjɛn] PRON POSS **le m., la mienne, les miens, les miennes** mine; **je te prête le m.** you can borrow mine; **tu n'as qu'à prendre la mienne** just take mine; **il ressemble au mien.** it looks like mine; **je veux bien te donner du m.** please have some of mine; **tu n'en as pas besoin, tu as le m.** you don't need it, you've got mine; **les deux miens** my two, both of mine; *(en insistant)* my own two; **je lui ai laissé deux des miens** I gave him two of mine; *très Fam* **le m. de bébé est plus intelligent** my baby is more intelligent; *Fam* **à la mienne!** *(en buvant)* here's to me! SEE GRAMMAR A30; B21–2

NM **le m.** *(ce qui m'appartient)* mine; **je devrais y mettre du m.** I should really do my share

NMPL **les miens** *(ma famille)* my family, *Am* my folks; *(mes partisans)* my followers; *(mes coéquipiers)* my team-mates

ADJ POSS *Litt* mine; **un m. cousin** a cousin of mine; **je fais miens tes principes** I've adopted your principles as my own; **je fais miennes les félicitations qu'il vous adresse** I join (with) him in congratulating you

miette [mjɛt] NF *(de pain)* crumb; *(morceau)* morsel, scrap; **miettes de crabe/thon** flaked crab/tuna; **elle m'a laissé quelques miettes de son gâteau** she left me a few crumbs of her cake; **ils n'en ont pas laissé une m.** they didn't leave a crumb, they scoffed the lot; **mettre** *ou* **réduire qch en miettes** *(objet)* to smash sth to pieces *or* bits *or* smithereens; **je n'en prendrai qu'une m.** I'll just have a morsel *or* a very little *or* *Fam* a smidgeon; *Fig* **elle n'a pas perdu une m. de la conversation** not one scrap of the conversation escaped her *or* passed her by

MIEUX [mjø]

ADV	better **1** ▪ best **2**
ADJ	better ▪ best
NM	best

ADV **1** *(comp)* better; **elle danse m. que moi** she dances better than I do; **j'avais espéré m.** I had hoped for better *or* more; **je ne peux pas m. dire** *ou* **dire m.** that's all I can say, what more can I say?; **il ne parle pas m. l'italien que l'espagnol** his Italian isn't any *or* is no better than his Spanish, he speaks Italian no better than he does Spanish; **on va vivre**

ensemble, m. on va se marier! we're going to live together, better still, we're getting married!; **je ne demande pas m.!** I'd be delighted!, there's nothing I'd like better!; **je ne demande pas m. que (de) te rendre service** I'd be delighted to help, there's nothing I'd like better than to help; **il vaut m. les surveiller** you should watch them more closely; **vous feriez m. de m'écouter** you'd do better to *or* you'd be well advised to listen to me, you'd better listen to me; *Prov* **m. vaut tard que jamais** better late than never; *Prov* **m. vaut prévenir que guérir** prevention is better than cure; **elle va m. que jamais** she has never been better; **il va m.** he's (feeling) better; **il ne va pas m.** he is no better, he isn't any better; **ça va m.** things are improving; *Fam* **ça va m.?** feeling better?; *Fam* **j'ai l'impression que, Bernard, ça va m. aujourd'hui** I'm under the impression that Bernard is feeling better today; **comment ça va, la santé/l'école/avec ton mari? – ça va m.** how are you/things at school/things with your husband? – better; **ça ira m. demain** it'll *or* things'll be better tomorrow; *Hum* **je vois que ça ne va pas m.!** you've not improved one bit!, there hasn't been any change for the better!; *Scol* **'peut m. faire'** 'can do better'; **moins je travaille, m. je me porte** the less I work, the better I feel; **plus je le vois, m. je l'apprécie** the more I see of him, the more I appreciate him *or* the better I like him; **de m. en m.** better and better; **au bureau, ça va de m. en m.** it's getting better and better at the office, things are improving all the time at the office; **m. encore ...** better still ...; **m. encore, je dirais que c'est un artiste** I'd go even further and describe him as an artist; **on dirait m. 'pallier les inconvénients'** 'pallier les inconvénients' is more correct; **qui dit m.?** *(pour faire monter les enchères)* any advance?; **elle va on ne peut m.** she's in the best of health; **ce travail est on ne peut m. fait** no one could have done better, he has/you have/*etc* done a perfect job; **elle coud on ne peut m.** no one sews better than she does; **faire qch à qui m. m.** to vie with one another in doing sth; **ils criaient à qui m. m.** it was a case of who could shout the loudest VOIR GRAMMAIRE A41

2 le m., la m., les m. (the) best; **la femme la m. habillée de Paris** the best-dressed woman in Paris; **c'est à Paris que les femmes sont le m. habillées** you find the best-dressed women in Paris; **c'est à ce bureau que je travaille le m.** I work best at this desk; **le plus tôt sera le m.** the sooner the better; **il s'en est acquitté le m. du monde** nobody could have done it better; **un service des m. organisés** an extremely well-organized department; **fais du m. que tu peux** do the best you can

ADJ **vous serez m. dans ce fauteuil** you'll be more comfortable *or* better in this armchair; **il est m.** he's (feeling) better; **vous ne trouverez pas m. comme hôtel** you won't find a better hotel; **tu ne trouveras rien de m.** you won't find anything better; *Fam* **c'est ce qu'il y a de m., c'est ce qu'on fait de m.** it's the best there is; **ce qu'il y a de m. sur le marché** the best (there is) on the market; **c'est ce qu'il y a de m. si ...** it's ideal if ...; **c'est ce qu'il y a de m. (à faire) dans votre cas** that's the best thing (to do) in your case; **ce que vous avez de m. à faire, c'est de ...** the best thing you can do is to ...; **si tu n'as rien de m. à faire** if you've nothing better to do; **tu ne crois pas que tu as m. à faire que ...?** don't you think there are better things to do than ...?; *Iron* **elle n'a rien trouvé de m. que d'aller le répéter à sa mère** what did she do but go and tell her mother; **c'est m. comme ça** its better like that; *Fam* **c'était la m. des trois sœurs** she was the best of the three sisters; *(la plus jo-*

lie) she was the best-looking of the three sisters

NM **le m. est l'ennemi du bien** leave well (enough) alone, *Fam* if it ain't broke, don't fix it; **faute de m.** for want *or* lack of anything better; **il y a un m.** *ou* **du m.** there's been a change for the better, there's been an improvement; **faire** *ou* **agir pour le m.** to act for the best; **mais on fera pour le m.** but we'll do our best, but we'll do the best we can; **le m. serait de ...** the best thing would be to ..., it would be best to ...; **le m. serait qu'il se désiste de lui-même** it would be best if he withdrew his own accord; **(en mettant les choses) au m., je ferai ce travail en deux mois** I can do the job in two months at best; **(en mettant les choses) au m., je ne pourrai pas être là avant six heures** I can't be there before six o'clock at the earliest; **au m., il la vendra 100 euros** he'll get 100 euros at most for it; **agir au m. des intérêts de qn** to act in sb's best interests; **être au m. avec qn** to be on the best of terms with sb; **faire de son m.** to do one's best, to do the best one can

mieux-disant, *pl* **mieux-disants** [mjødizɑ̃] **NM** elite

mieux-être NM improved condition; **les progrès techniques doivent servir au m. des hommes** technical progress must improve the human condition

mieux-vivre NM better *or* higher standard of living; **la lutte pour le m.** the struggle for a better *or* higher standard of living

mièvre [mjɛvr] **ADJ** *Péj (fille)* insipid; *(ton)* simpering; **des trucs mièvres à la télé** stupid things on TV

mièvrerie [mjɛvrəri] **NF** *Péj* insipidness; **d'une m. exaspérante** exasperatingly insipid; **ces mièvreries qu'on nous sert à la télé** these stupid programmes *or* the pap they show on TV

mi-fin, *pl* **mi-fins ADJ** *Com* medium

mignard [miɲar] **ADJ** **1** = **mignon** **2** *Péj* affected

mignardise [miɲardiz] **NF** **1** *(caractère mignon)* charm, *Péj* affectedness **2** *(œillet)* **m.** garden pink

mignon, -onne [miɲɔ̃, -ɔn] **ADJ** delightful, charming; *(enfant)* darling, *surtout Am* cute; **un mec super m.** a great-looking guy; **est-elle mignonne!** isn't she a darling!; **c'est m. comme tout chez eux** they have a delightful *or* charming home; **sois m., va me chercher mes cigarettes** be a dear *or* an angel and get my cigarettes

N 1 *(terme d'affection)* pet, darling, dear **2** *Arch (favori)* minion

mignonnet, -ette [miɲɔnɛ, -ɛt] **ADJ** pretty-pretty

mignonnette [miɲɔnɛt] **NF 1** *(plante) (saxifrage ombreuse)* London pride; *(chicorée sauvage)* wild chicory; *(œillet mignardise)* garden pink **2** *Tex* mignonette lace **3** *(poivre)* coarse-ground pepper **4** *(gravier)* gravel **5** *(flacon)* miniature

migraine [migrɛn] **NF** migraine; *Fam (mal de tête)* headache; **elle a des migraines** she has migraines; **elle a la m.** she has a headache; **m. ophtalmique** headache caused by eyestrain

migraineux, -euse [migrɛnø, -øz] **N** migraine sufferer

migrant, -ante [migrɑ̃, -ɑ̃t] **ADJ** migrant

N migrant; **m. économique** economic refugee

migrateur, -trice [migratœr, -tris] **ADJ** *(animaux)* migrating, migratory; *(personnes)* migrant

migration [migrasjɔ̃] **NF** *Orn* migration; *Fig* exodus; **au moment des vacances, les migra-**

---

tions sont impressionnantes the number of people on the move at holiday time is staggering

migratoire [migratwar] **ADJ** migratory

migrer [migre] **VI** to migrate (**vers** to); *Ordinat* **faire m.** to transmit

mi-jambe(s) (à) **ADV** halfway up the leg(s)

mijaurée [miʒɔre] **NF** *Péj* conceited *or* affected woman; **ne fais pas la** *ou* **ta m.!** don't give yourself such airs!

mijoter [miʒɔte] **VT** *Culin* to simmer, to let simmer; *Fig (projet, vengeance)* to mull over; **elle mijote avec amour de bons petits plats à son mari** she lovingly prepares wonderful meals for her husband; **m. un complot** to hatch a plot; **qu'est-ce que vous mijotez encore?** now what are you scheming *or* up to?

VI to simmer; *Fig* **je vois bien que ça mijote dans sa tête** I know he's up to something

VPR **se mijoter** *Fig* **il se mijote quelque chose** there's something in the wind, something's brewing

mikado [mikado] **NM** mikado

mil¹ [mil] **ADJ** thousand *(used only in writing out dates AD)*; **l'an m. neuf cent quatre-vingt-un** (the year) nineteen hundred and eighty-one

mil² [mij, mil] **NM** *(céréale)* millet

milady, *pl* **miladys** [miledi] **NF** *(titre)* my Lady; *(noble)* titled (English) lady

milan [milɑ̃] **NM** *(oiseau)* kite

milanais, -aise [milanɛ, -ɛz] **ADJ** Milanese **N M.** Milanese; **les M.** the Milanese

mildiou [mildju] **NM** mildew; *(de la vigne)* brown rot; **atteint de m.** mildewed

mildiousé [mildjuze] **ADJ** *(vigne etc)* mildewed

mile [majl] **NM** *(mesure)* mile *(= 1.609 m)*

miliaire [miljɛr] *Méd* **ADJ** *(glande, fièvre etc)* miliary

NF prickly heat, *Spéc* miliaria

milice [milis] **NF 1** militia **2** *Belg (service militaire)* military service; **la m.** the army

milicien, -ienne [milisjɛ̃, -jɛn] **N** member of a/the militia, *m* militiaman

milieu, -ieux [miljø] **NM 1** *(centre)* middle; **couper/plier qch en son m.** to cut sth through/to fold sth in the middle; **il est entré en plein m. d'une discussion** he came in right in the middle of a discussion; **au m. de** in the middle of, *Litt* amid(st), in the midst of; **au beau m. de la rue/la cour** right in the middle of the street/the yard; **au m. du courant** in midstream; **au m. de l'été** in the middle *or* at the height of summer; **au m. de l'hiver** in the middle *or* depth(s) of winter; **au m. de la nuit** in the middle of the night, *Litt* at dead of night; **vers le m. du mois** about the middle of the month; **la table du m.** the middle table

2 *(environnement) (physique)* environment, surroundings, milieu; *(social)* (social) sphere, circle; *Phys* medium; **le m. familial** the home environment, family surroundings; **dans les milieux financiers** in financial circles; **les animaux dans leur m.** animals in their environment *or* natural surroundings; **je n'appartiens pas à leur m., je ne suis pas de leur m.** I don't belong to or I'm not part of their set *or* circle, I don't move in their circles; **dans les milieux bien informés** in well-informed circles *or* quarters; **elle ne tient pas à changer de m.** she's not keen on a change of surroundings; **c'est parce qu'elle n'est pas dans son m.** it's because she's not in her usual surroundings

3 le m., les gens du m. the underworld; **c'est un type du m.** he's a member of the underworld

4 *(moyenne)* middle course; **il n'y a pas de**

---

m. there's no middle course; **le juste m.** the happy medium, the golden mean; **tenir le m. entre ... et ...** to steer a middle course between ... and ...

militaire [militɛr] **ADJ** *(discipline, service, hôpital, opération etc)* military; **véhicule m.** military *or* army vehicle; **à huit heures, heure m.** at eight o'clock sharp; **la marine m.** the Navy; **port m.** naval port

NM serviceman, soldier; **les militaires** the military, the armed forces, the services; **m. de carrière** career *or* professional soldier

militairement [militɛrmɑ̃] **ADV** militarily; **saluer m.** to give a military salute; **occuper une ville m.** to occupy a town by force of arms

militance [militɑ̃s] **NF** militancy

militant, -ante [militɑ̃, -ɑ̃t] **ADJ** militant **N** militant; *(d'un parti)* member; **m. de base** grassroots member; **m. syndical** trade union militant *or* activist

militantisme [militɑ̃tism] **NM** militancy

militarisation [militarizasjɔ̃] **NF** militarization

militariser [militarize] **VT** to militarize

militarisme [militarism] **NM** militarism

militariste [militarist] **ADJ, N** militarist

militer [milite] **VI** to militate (**pour, en faveur de** in favour of; **contre** against); **m. au PS** to be a member of the Socialist Party

milk-shake, *pl* **milk-shakes** [milkʃɛk] **NM** milk shake; **m. à la vanille** vanilla milk shake

millage [milaʒ] **NM** *Can* mileage

mille¹ [mil] **ADJ INV 1** thousand; **m. hommes** a thousand men, one thousand men; **deux m.** two thousand; **trois cent m. hommes** three hundred thousand men; **m. un** a thousand and one, one thousand and one; **Les M. et une Nuits** the Arabian Nights, the Thousand and One Nights; **l'an m.** the year one thousand; **l'an m. neuf cent avant J.C.** (the year) nineteen hundred BC **2** *Fig (beaucoup de) (exemples, raisons)* countless, numerous, many; **je vous l'ai dit m. fois** I've told you a thousand times, I've told you time and time again; **vous avez m. fois raison** you are so right; **m. baisers** much love; **m. mercis** many thanks, thank you so much; **je vous pardons** *ou* **regrets** I am so sorry; **c'est m. fois trop grand** it's miles *or* way too big; **casser qch en m. morceaux** to smash sth to smithereens; **souffrir** *ou* **endurer m. morts** *(physiquement)* to suffer agonies, to go through hell; *(moralement)* to go through hell, to die a thousand deaths; **j'étais à m. lieues de me douter que ...** I never for a moment suspected that ...; **je te le donne en m.** you'll never guess in a million years **SEE GRAMMAR A12–13; B58–9**

NM INV 1 *(chiffre)* thousand; **m. plus m.** a thousand plus a thousand, one thousand plus one thousand; **par m. de briques vendu(es)** per thousand bricks sold, for every thousand bricks sold; **un habitant sur m.** one inhabitant in a thousand; **les chances de guérison sont de dix pour m.** there's a one in a hundred chance of a cure; **un taux de natalité de 5 pour m.** a birth rate of 0.5 per cent; **ils sont morts par centaines de m.** they died in (their) hundreds of thousands **2** *Fig* mettre *ou* donner dans le m. to hit the bull's-eye; *Fam* il gagne des m. et des cents he makes a mint

mille² **NM** *(mesure)* mile *(= 1.609 m)*; **m. (marin** *ou* **nautique)** nautical mile

mille-feuille, *pl* **mille-feuilles** [milfœj] **NF** *Bot* milfoil, yarrow

NM *Culin* millefeuille, *Am* napoleon

millénaire [mil(l)enɛr] **ADJ** *(arbre, monument)* a thousand years old; **cette superstition est plusieurs fois m.** the superstition has existed for several thousands of years

NM thousand years, millennium; *(anniversaire)* millennium, millenary; **dater du premier m. av. J.-C.** to date from the first millennium BC; **cette tradition est vieille d'au moins un m.** the tradition has existed for at least a thousand years VOIR GRAMMAIRE A13

millénarisme [milenarism] **NM** millenarianism

millénariste [milenarist] **ADJ, N** millenarian, millenary

millénium [milenjɔm] **NM** millennium VOIR GRAMMAIRE A13

mille-pattes [milpat] **NM INV** centipede, millipede

mille-pertuis, millepertuis [milpɛrtɥi] **NM INV** *Bot* St John's wort

mille-raies [milrɛ] **NM INV** needlecord **ADJ INV velours m.** needlecord

millésime [milezim] **NM** *(de voiture)* year of manufacture; *(de vin)* year, vintage; *(sur pièce, timbre)* date; **il ne boit que de grands millésimes** he only drinks vintage wine

millésimé [milezime] **ADJ** *(vin)* vintage; *(pièce)* dated

millet [mijɛ] **NM** *Bot* millet; **(grains de) m.** birdseed, canary seed

milliampère [miliɑ̃pɛr] **NM** milliamp(ere)

milliard [miljar] **NM** billion, *Br Vieilli* thousand million, milliard VOIR GRAMMAIRE A76

milliardaire [miljardɛr] **ADJ, N** billionaire

milliardième [miljardjɛm] **ADJ, N** billionth, *Br Vieilli* thousand millionth

millibar [milibar] **NM** *Météo* millibar

millième [miljɛm] **ADJ, N** thousandth

millier [milje] **NM** thousand; **un m. de personnes** a thousand people; **des milliers de personnes** thousands of people; **les gens sont venus par milliers** people came in their thousands; **ils en vendent par milliers** they sell them by the thousand

milligramme [miligram] **NM** milligram(me)

millilitre [mililitr] **NM** millilitre, *Am* milliliter

millimètre [milimɛtr] **NM** millimetre, *Am* millimeter

millimétré [milimetre], **millimétrique** [milimetrik] **ADJ** **échelle millimétrée** millimetre *or Am* millimeter scale; **papier m.** graph paper

million [miljɔ̃] **NM** million; **quatre millions d'hommes** four million men; **riche à millions** worth millions; **il n'y en a pas des millions à s'appeler comme ça** there can't be too many people with a name like that VOIR GRAMMAIRE A12–13

millionième [miljɔnjɛm] **ADJ, N** millionth

millionnaire [miljɔnɛr] **ADJ, N** millionaire

milliseconde [milis(ə)gɔ̃d] **NF** millisecond

millivolt [milivɔlt] **NM** millivolt

milliwatt [miliwat] **NM** milliwatt

milord [milɔr] **NM 1** *(titre)* my Lord; *(noble)* (English) nobleman; *Fig* immensely wealthy man **2** *Arch (voiture)* victoria

mi-lourd, *pl* **mi-lourds ADJ, NM** *Boxe* **(poids) m.** light heavyweight (boxer)

mime [mim] **NM** mime, (art of) miming; **faire du m.** to mime, to do mime; **spectacle de m.** mime show
N *(personne)* mime; *(imitateur)* mimic

mimer [mime] **VT 1** to mime; **m. une scène** to mime a scene, to act a scene in dumb show **2** *(imiter)* to mimic

mimétique [mimetik] **ADJ** *Zool* mimetic; **le pouvoir de sa voix** his ability to imitate other people's voices

mimétisme [mimetism] **NM** *Zool* mimicry, *Spéc* mimesis; **par m., elle a fini par faire aussi de la peinture** taking the attitude that

'if you can't beat 'em, join 'em', she ended up doing painting too; **ils le font tous par m.** they can't help copying each other, they can't help mimicking each other

mimi [mimi] **NM** *Enf* **1** *(chat)* pussy (cat), kitty; **mon petit m.** my darling, my pet **2** *(baiser)* kiss; **fais m. à ta sœur** give your sister a kiss; **faire un gros m. à qn** to give sb a big kiss; **elle adore faire des mimis à son petit frère** she loves cuddling her little brother
ADJ INV *Fam (mignon)* lovely, cute

mimique [mimik] **ADJ** **langage m.** sign language
NF *(expression)* expression; *(grimace)* grimace; *(de sourd-muet)* sign language; **il s'exprime beaucoup par m.** he uses his face to convey his feelings

mimodrame [mimɔdram] **NM** *Théâtre* mime

mimolette [mimɔlɛt] **NF** *Culin* = type of firm cheese

mimosa [mimoza] **NM** mimosa

mi-moyen, *pl* **mi-moyens ADJ, NM** *Boxe* **(poids) m.** welterweight (boxer)

min *(abrév* **minimum)** min

minable [minabl] *Péj* **ADJ** *(appartement, apparence)* shabby, seedy; *(personne)* pathetic; **salaire m.** mere pittance (of a wage), miserable *or* pathetic wage; **c'est m., ce que tu lui as fait** that was a rotten trick you played on him
N failure, loser; **quelle bande de minables** what a pathetic *or* useless bunch

minaret [minarɛ] **NM** minaret

minauder [minode] **VI** to simper

minauderie [minodri] **NF** simpering; **minauderies** simpering (manner)

minaudier, -ière [minodje, -jɛr] **ADJ** *(personne)* simpering, affected

mince [mɛ̃s] **ADJ 1** *(fin)* *(planche, étoffe, tranche, mur etc)* thin; *(personne)* slim, slender **2** *(insuffisant)* *(prétexte)* slim, thin; *(preuves)* slim, thin, scant; *(profit)* small, slight; *(chance)* slight; **mes connaissances dans ce domaine sont trop minces** I know too little about this field, my knowledge in this field is too scanty; **d'un intérêt un peu m.** of little interest; **m. revenu** slender *or* small *or* scanty income; **tes arguments sont un peu minces** your arguments are a bit poor *or* feeble; **Fam ce n'est pas une m. affaire** it's not an easy job, it's not easy
INT *Fam* **m. (alors)!** *(surprise)* well, I'm blowed!; *(déception)* blast (it)!
ADV thinly

minceur [mɛ̃sœr] **NF 1** *(de couche, de peau)* thinness; *(de personne)* slimness, slenderness; **elle est d'une m. extraordinaire** she is extraordinarily slim **2** *(insuffisance)* scantiness; **étant donné la m. de mes revenus** since my income is so small

mincir [mɛ̃sir] **VI** to get thinner *or* slimmer, to lose weight

mine¹ [min] **NF 1** *(gisement)* mine; **travailler à la m.** to work in the mine, to be a miner; **exploitation des mines** mining; **m. de charbon** coalmine, colliery, pit; **m. d'or** goldmine; *Fig* **ce travail est loin d'être une m. d'or** you won't get rich doing this job; **m. à ciel ouvert** opencast mine; *Fig* **une m. de renseignements** a mine of information
2 *Admin* **les Mines** = government department responsible for supervising all construction projects involving tunnelling; **École des Mines,** *Fam* **les Mines** = grande école of engineering studies; **ingénieur des Mines** = engineer (who has graduated from the École des Mines); **service des Mines** = government department which verifies the roadworthiness of cars which have been involved in accidents
3 m. (de crayon) (pencil) lead; **crayon à m.**

grasse/dure soft/hard pencil; **m. de plomb** graphite, blacklead
4 *Mil, Constr etc* mine; **poser** *ou* **mouiller une m.** to lay a mine; **faire jouer une m.** to fire a blast *or* a mine; **coup de m.** blast; **attention aux coups de m.!** *(sur panneau)* danger, blasting; **m. flottante** floating mine; **mouilleur de mines** minelayer; **champ de mines** minefield; **m. terrestre** landmine

mine² **NF** *(de personne)* appearance, look; **mines** *(de bébé)* gestures, expressions; **avoir bonne/mauvaise m.** to look well/ill; *Iron* **nous avons bonne m. maintenant!** we do look good *or* silly!; **plat qui a bonne m.** dish that looks good *or* appetizing; **sa bonne m. fait plaisir à voir** it's a pleasure to see him looking so well; **avoir une m. resplendissante** to look in the best of health; **vous avez meilleure m.** you're looking better; **il en a une (sale) m.!** he does look ill!; **avoir une m. de papier mâché** *ou* **de déterré** to look like death warmed up; **m. boudeuse** sulky expression; **elle a toujours une m. réjouie** she always looks happy; **prendre une m. contrite** to look offended; **ne fais pas cette m.** don't look like that; **faire** *ou* **avoir triste m.** to look down in the dumps; **faire bonne m.** to put a good face on it *or* on things; **faire bonne m. à** *ou* **devant qn** to be pleasant to sb, to greet sb pleasantly *or* with a smile; **faire grise m.** to look miserable *or* po-faced; **faire grise m. à qn** to give sb a cool reception; **juger les gens sur la m.** to judge people by *or* on appearances; **sous sa m. d'homme rangé** behind that sober exterior of his; **il ne faut pas vous fier à sa m. de petite fille sage** don't trust that butter-wouldn't-melt-in-my-mouth expression of hers; *Fig* **ça/il ne paie pas de m.** it/he isn't much to look at; **faire m. d'être fâché** to pretend to be angry; **il a fait m. de me suivre** he made as if to follow me; *Fam* **m. de rien, essaie de vérifier** try to check on it without letting on (what you're up to); *Fam* **m. de rien, l'affaire progresse** the work is progressing, though you wouldn't think so to look at it; *Péj* **faire des mines** to simper; **elles font des mines devant le miroir** they're making faces in the mirror

miner [mine] **VT 1** *(saper)* *(forteresse etc)* to mine; **la mer mine les falaises** the sea is undermining the cliffs *or* is eating the cliffs away **2** *Fig* **la fièvre l'a miné** fever has undermined *or* sapped his strength; **ses soucis la minent** her worries are wearing him down; **miné par l'envie** eaten up *or* consumed with envy **3** *(poser des mines dans)* to mine

minerai [minrɛ] **NM** ore; **m. de fer** iron ore

minéral, -ale, -aux, -ales [mineral, -o] **ADJ** mineral
NM mineral

minéralier [mineralje] **NM** ore tanker

minéralisation [mineralizasjɔ̃] **NF** mineralization

minéraliser [mineralize] **VT** to mineralize

minéralogie [mineralɔʒi] **NF** mineralogy

minéralogique [mineralɔʒik] **ADJ 1** *Géol* mineralogical **2** *Aut, Admin* **numéro m.** registration number, *Am* license *or* Can licence number; **plaque m.** numberplate, *Am* license *or* Can licence plate

minéralogiste [mineralɔʒist] **N** mineralogist

Minerve [minɛrv] **N** *Myth* Minerva

minerve [minɛrv] **NF** *Méd* (surgical) collar

minestrone [minɛstrɔn] **NM** *Culin* minestrone

minet, -ette [minɛ, -ɛt] **N** *Fam* **1** *(chat)* pussy (cat), kitty; **mon m./ma minette** *(terme d'affection)* my darling, my pet **2** *Péj (jeune)* *(garçon)* trendy young guy, pretty boy; *(fille)* trendy chick, babe

mineur¹ [minœr] NM **1** *(ouvrier)* (coal) miner, collier; **m. de fond** underground worker **2** *Mil* sapper

mineur², **-eure** ADJ **1** *(inférieur)* minor, lesser; **Asie Mineure** Asia Minor **2** *Jur* under age **3** *Mus (note, gamme etc)* minor; **en ut m.** in C minor **4** *(de moindre importance)* minor; **ce sont des soucis mineurs** these are minor worries

   N *Jur* minor; **ce film est interdit aux mineurs** this film is restricted to over-18s; **cet établissement est interdit aux mineurs** these premises are banned to persons under 18
   NM *Mus* minor key

mini [mini] *Fam* ADJ INV mini; **la mode m. est de retour** the mini is back (in fashion)
   NF mini(skirt)
   ADV **s'habiller m.** to wear miniskirts

miniature [minjatyr] NF miniature; **peintre de miniatures** miniature painter, miniaturist; **en m.** in miniature, on a small scale; **c'est tout sa mère en m.** she's a miniature version of her mother
   ADJ INV miniature

miniaturisation [minjatyrizasjɔ̃] NF miniaturization; **la m. de l'informatique** computer (circuitry) miniaturization

miniaturiser [minjatyrize] VT to miniaturize; **un téléviseur miniaturisé** a mini or miniature television
   VPR **se miniaturiser** to become miniaturized; **la hi-fi se miniaturise** sound systems are getting much smaller

miniaturiste [minjatyrist] N miniaturist, miniature painter

minibar [minibar] NM **1** *(dans le train)* trolley; **un service de m. est assuré dans ce train** there is a trolley service on this train **2** *(à l'hôtel)* minibar; **avez-vous consommé au m.?** did you have anything from the minibar?

minibus [minibys] NM minibus

minicassette [minikasɛt] NF mini-cassette
   NM portable tape recorder

minichaîne [miniʃɛn] NF mini system

minidisc® [minidisk] NM MiniDisc®

mini-disquette, *pl* **mini-disquettes** NF minidisk, mini-floppy

minier, **-ière** [minje, -jɛr] ADJ *(industrie, région etc)* mining
   NF **minière** surface or opencast mine

minigolf [minigɔlf] NM crazy golf

minijupe [miniʒyp] NF miniskirt

minima [minima] *voir* **minimum**

minimal, **-ale**, **-aux**, **-ales** [minimal, -o] ADJ *(température, durée)* minimum; *(art)* minimal; *Ling* **paire minimale** minimal pair

minimalisme [minimalism] NM *Beaux-Arts* minimalism

minimaliste [minimalist] ADJ, N *Beaux-Arts* minimalist

minime [minim] ADJ *(dégâts, implication)* minimal; *(rôle)* minor; *(perte)* trivial; *(valeur)* trifling
   N *Sport* junior *(to 15 years old)*
   NM *Rel, Hist* Minim friar

mini-message, *pl* **mini-messages** NM *Tél* text message; **envoyer un m. à qn** to text sb, to send sb a text message

minimisation [minimizasjɔ̃] NF minimization; **ce n'est pas la m. de nos problèmes qui va les résoudre** we won't solve our problems by minimizing them or *Fam* by playing them down

minimiser [minimize] VT to minimize, to reduce to the minimum; *Fig (rôle, situation, problème)* to play down, to downplay

minimum [minimɔm], *pl* **minima** [minima] *ou* **minimums** NM minimum; **avec un m. d'ef-**forts with a minimum of effort; **un m. de temps** a minimum amount of time; **en un m. de temps** in as short a time as possible; **nous exigeons un m. de garanties** we demand the minimum guarantees; **trois mois, c'est un m. pour s'habituer au climat** three months is the minimum it takes or it takes at least three months to get used to the climate; **c'est vraiment le m. que tu puisses faire pour elle** it's the least you can do for her; **il ne fait même plus le m. pour donner le change à sa femme** he's stopped making even the slightest attempt to keep his wife in the dark; **m. vital** minimum living wage; **m. vieillesse** basic old-age pension; **les minima sociaux** = basic income support; **réduire les frais au m.** to reduce expenses to a minimum; *Fam* **je n'y resterai que le m. de temps** I'll make it as brief as I can; **dépenser le m.** to spend as little as possible; *Fam* **bouger le** *ou* **au m.** to move as little as possible; **au m. 200 euros/cinq ans d'expérience** at least 200 euros/five years' experience, a minimum of 200 euros/five years' experience; **m. imposable** tax threshold

   ADJ minimum; **les largeurs minimums** *ou* **minima** the minimum widths; **vitesse m.** minimum speed; **prix m.** *(à une vente aux enchères)* reserve price; *Élec* **charge m.** *(de génératrice)* base load

mini-ordinateur, *pl* **mini-ordinateurs** NM minicomputer, mini

minipilule [minipilyl] NF minipill

mini-séjour, *pl* **mini-séjours** NM minibreak, short break

mini-série, *pl* **mini-séries** NF *TV* miniseries

mini-slip, *pl* **mini-slips** NM tanga

ministère [ministɛr] NM **1** *(département)* government department; **m. des Affaires étrangères** *Br* ≃ Foreign (and Commonwealth) Office, *Am* ≃ State Department, *Can* ≃ External Affairs Department; **m. de l'Agriculture** Ministry or Department of Agriculture; **m. du Commerce** Ministry of Trade, *Br* ≃ Department of Trade and Industry; **m. du Commerce extérieur** Foreign Trade Department; **m. de la Communication** Ministry for Communications; **m. de la Culture** Ministry of Culture, Ministry for the Arts; **m. de la Défense (nationale)** *Br* ≃ Ministry of Defence, *Am* ≃ Department of Defense; **m. de l'Économie et des Finances** Treasury; **m. de l'Éducation nationale** ≃ Department of Education; **m. de l'Environnement** ≃ Department of the Environment; **m. des Finances** Ministry of Finance, *Br* Exchequer; **m. de l'Intérieur** *Br* ≃ Home Office, *Am* ≃ Department of the Interior; **m. de la Justice** Department of Justice; **m. de la Santé et de la Sécurité sociale** *Br* ≃ Department of Social Security, *Am* ≃ Department of Health and Human Services; **m. du Tourisme** Ministry of Tourism; **m. du Travail** *Br* ≃ Department of Education and Employment, *Am* ≃ Department of Labor; **m. des Travaux publics** *Can* ≃ Department of Public Works, *Br Hist* ≃ Ministry of Public Works **2** *(gouvernement)* government; **entrer dans un m.** to take office; **former un m.** to form a government; **sous le m. Raffarin** under Raffarin's government **3** *Jur* **le m. public** *Br* ≃ the (Department of the) Director of Public Prosecutions, *Am* ≃ the District Attorney's Office **4** *Rel* **le (saint) m.** the ministry **5** *Arch, Litt (aide)* agency; **user du m. de qn** to make use of sb's services; *Jur* **l'accusé a droit au m. d'un avocat** the accused has the right to counsel or *Am* a lawyer

ministériel, **-ielle** [ministerjɛl] ADJ *(arrêté, décret, entourage)* ministerial; *(crise, rema-*niement)* cabinet; *Vieilli* **journal m.** newspaper supporting the government, government organ; *Jur* **officier m.** *(avoué, huissier, notaire)* officer of the court

ministrable [ministrabl] *Pol* ADJ likely to become a minister
   N likely candidate for minister, ministerial hopeful

ministre [ministr] NM **1** *(de gouvernement)* minister; **Premier m.** Prime Minister; *Can (d'une province)* Premier; **m. des Affaires étrangères** *Br* ≃ Foreign Secretary, *Am* ≃ Secretary of State, *Can* ≃ Secretary of State for External Affairs; **m. de l'Agriculture** Agriculture Minister, Minister for Agriculture; **m. du Commerce** *Br* ≃ Secretary of State for Trade and Industry, *Am* ≃ Secretary of Commerce; **m. de la Communication** Minister for Communications; **m. de la Culture** Minister for Culture, Arts Minister; **m. de la Défense (nationale)** ≃ Secretary of State for Defence, Minister of Defence; **m. de l'Éducation nationale** ≃ Secretary of State for Education; **m. de l'Environnement** ≃ Secretary of State for the Environment; **m. des Finances** *Br* ≃ Chancellor of the Exchequer, *Am* ≃ Secretary of the Treasury, *Can* ≃ Minister of Finance; **m. de l'Intérieur** *Br* ≃ Home Secretary, *Am* ≃ Secretary of the Interior; **m. de la Justice** *Br* ≃ Lord Chancellor, *Am* ≃ Attorney General, *Can* ≃ Minister of Justice and Attorney General; **m. de la Santé et de la Sécurité sociale** *Br* ≃ Secretary of State for Social Security, *Am* ≃ Secretary for Health and Human Services; **m. du Tourisme** Minister for Tourism; **m. des Transports** *Br* ≃ Secretary of State for Transport, *Am* ≃ Transportation Secretary; **m. du Travail** *Br* ≃ Secretary of State for Education and Employment, *Am* ≃ Labor Secretary; **m. des Travaux publics** *Br Hist, Can* ≃ Minister of Public Works; **m. sans portefeuille** minister without portfolio; **papier m.** ≃ official foolscap **2** *Rel* (Protestant) minister, clergyman **3** *Arch, Litt (de Dieu, d'un prince etc)* servant, agent

Minitel® [minitɛl] NM = viewdata service, *Am* ≃ Minitel®; **sur M.** on viewdata, *Am* on Minitel®; **m. rose** = erotic viewdata service

> **Minitel®**
> The domestic viewdata service run by France Télécom has become a familiar part of French life. The basic monitor and keyboard are provided free of charge, and the subscriber is charged for the services used on his or her ordinary telephone bill. The subscriber dials a four-figure number (typically 3615); a code word then gives access to the particular service required. Some Minitel® services are purely informative (the weather, road conditions, news etc); others are interactive (enabling users to carry out bank transactions, book tickets for travel, register for and obtain the results of nationwide examinations, for example). The Minitel® also serves as an electronic telephone directory. Nowadays the services offered by Minitel® are increasingly available on the Internet.

minitéliste [minitelist] N Minitel® user

mini-tour, *pl* **mini-tours** NF *Ordinat* mini tower

minium [minjɔm] NM *Chimie* red lead, minium; *(antirouille)* red lead paint

minivague [minivag] NF body wave

minois [minwa] NM *(d'enfant, de jeune*

femme) (pretty) face; **une jeune fille au frais m.** a fresh-faced young girl

minoration [minɔrasjɔ̃] NF (*de tarifs, temps de travail*) reduction, decrease

minorer [minɔre] VT (*minimiser*) (*incident*) to downplay, (*faire baisser*) (*chiffre, somme, prix, impôt etc*) to lower, to reduce

minoritaire [minɔritɛr] ADJ (*parti, participation*) minority; **ils sont minoritaires à l'Assemblée** they are in the minority in the Assembly; **très minoritaires** very much in the minority

N member of a minority

minorité [minɔrite] NF minority; *Jur* minority, infancy, nonage; **le service ne fonctionne qu'avec une m. de gens** the department is run by a skeleton staff; **être en m.** to be in the *or* in a minority; **mettre en m.** to defeat; **la gauche a été mise en m. lors des dernières élections** the left became the minority party at the last elections; **m. ethnique** ethnic minority; **m. de blocage** blocking minority vote; **m. agissante** active minority VOIR GRAM-MAIRE A11

Minorque [minɔrk] NF Minorca

minorquin, -ine [minɔrkɛ̃, -in] ADJ Minorcan
N **M.** Minorcan

minoterie [minɔtri] NF (*moulin*) (large) flour mill; (*activité*) flour-milling

minotier [minɔtje] NM (flour) miller

minou [minu] NM 1 *Fam* (*chat*) pussy (cat), kitty; **mon m.** my darling, my pet 2 *très Fam* (*sexe de la femme*) pussy, beaver, snatch

minuit [minɥi] NM midnight, twelve (o'clock) (at night); **m. et demi** half-past twelve (at night)

minus [minys] NM *Fam* 1 (*nabot*) midget, shortie, runt 2 (*incapable*) no-hoper, nobody 3 **m. habens** half-wit, moron

minuscule [minyskyl] ADJ 1 (*très petit*) tiny, minute, minuscule 2 *Typ* lower-case; **lettre m.** small letter; *Typ* lower-case letter
NF small letter; *Typ* lower-case letter; **en minuscules** (in) lower case

minutage [minytaʒ] NM timing; **faire un m. exact de qch** to time something to the minute

minute [minyt] NF 1 (*d'heure, de degré*) minute; **à deux minutes près, vous le ratiez** a couple of minutes later and you would have missed him; **toutes les vingt minutes** every twenty minutes; **de dernière m.** last-minute; **faire qch à la m.** to do sth at a minute's *or* a moment's notice; *Fam* **on n'est pas à la m.** we've got plenty of time, there's no rush; **il sera là d'une m. à l'autre** he'll be here any minute now; *Fam* **m. (papillon)!** just a minute!, hold on! SEE GRAMMAR A80; B60 2 (*court moment*) minute; **ne pas avoir une m. à perdre/de répit** not to have a moment *or* minute to lose/a moment's *or* minute's rest; **ne pas avoir une m. à soi** not to have a minute *or* a moment to oneself; **une m. de silence** a moment's silence; **la m. de vérité** the moment of truth; **nettoyage-m.** dry-cleaning while you wait; **talons/clés m.** heel/key bar; **réparations (à la) m.** repairs while you wait; **repas-m.** convenience meal; **steak m.** minute steak 3 (*de contrat etc*) minute, draft; (*d'acte, de jugement*) record; **faire la m. d'un acte** to draft an act; **faire la m. d'une réunion** to draw up the minutes of *or* to minute a meeting

minuter [minyte] VT 1 (*dans le temps*) to time; **sa journée est soigneusement minutée** every minute of his day is carefully planned *or* accounted for 2 (*accord etc*) to minute, to draw up, to draft; (*acte, jugement*) to record, to enter

minuterie [minytri] NF 1 (*appareil*) (*de lumière*) timer, (automatic) time switch 2 (*méca-*)

nisme) (*d'une horlogerie*) motionwork, train of wheels; **as-tu mis en route la m. du four?** did you set the oven timer?

minuteur [minytœr] NM timer

minutie [minysi] NF 1 (*caractère*) meticulousness, attention to detail; **avec m.** meticulously; **d'une m. remarquable** remarkably meticulous 2 *Vieilli* (*détail*) minute detail; **minuties** trifles, petty details, *Fml* minutiae

minutieusement [minysjøzmɑ̃] ADV meticulously, with attention to detail; **très m.** very meticulously, with great attention to detail; **examiner qch m.** to examine sth minutely, to scrutinize sth

minutieux, -ieuse [minysjø, -jøz] ADJ (*personne*) meticulous; (*inspection, examen*) close, thorough, minute, detailed; (*dessin, sculpture*) detailed; **la broderie est un travail très m.** embroidery demands close work *or* attention to detail

miocène [mjɔsɛn] ADJ, NM *Géol* Miocene

mioche [mjɔʃ] N *Fam* kid(die), tot, *Péj* brat

mi-pente (à) ADV halfway up/down the hill

MIPS [mips] NM *Ordinat* (*abrév* million d'instructions par seconde) MIPS

mirabelle [mirabɛl] NF mirabelle plum

mirabellier [mirabelje] NM mirabelle plum tree

miracle [mirakl] NM 1 miracle; **ne t'attends pas à un m.** don't expect any miracles; **faire un m.** to perform *or* work a miracle; *Fig* **faire des miracles** to work miracles *or* wonders; **croire aux miracles** to believe in miracles; **cela tient du m.** it's miraculous; **m. d'architecture** marvel *or* miracle of architecture; **m. économique** economic miracle; **le m. industriel français** the French industrial miracle; **par m.** miraculously, by a miracle; **échapper par m.** to have a miraculous escape; **c'est (un) m. que ... + *sub*** it's a miracle *or* a wonder that ...; **crier (au) m.** to go into raptures 2 *Hist, Littér* miracle (play)
ADJ INV *Fam* **produit m.** miracle *or* wonder product; **une crème m.** contre la cellulite a cream that works miracles *or* wonders on cellulite; **je ne crois pas aux solutions m.** I don't believe in miracle cures; **elle a toujours des solutions m.** she can always come up with a solution

miraculé, -ée [mirakyle] ADJ (*personne*) miraculously cured/saved, cured/saved by a miracle
N **je suis un m.** I'm lucky to be alive; **l'explosion n'a laissé que quelques miraculés** only a few people escaped death in the explosion; **les miraculés de Lourdes** the miracle cures of Lourdes

miraculeusement [mirakyløzmɑ̃] ADV by a miracle, miraculously; **m. vite** miraculously quickly

miraculeux, -euse [mirakylø, -øz] ADJ miraculous, wonderful; **remède m.** miracle cure; **cette crème est miraculeuse contre les rides** this cream works miracles *or* wonders on wrinkles

mirador [miradɔr] NM 1 *Archit* mirador, belvedere 2 *Mil* (*dans un arbre etc*) observation post; (*de camp de prisonniers*) watchtower

mirage [miraʒ] NM mirage

miraud [miro] ADJ *Fam* = miro

mire [mir] NF 1 (*de fusil*) foresight 2 (*signal*) sighting mark; *TV* test pattern, *Br* test card; **m. de réglage** test pattern, *Br* test card 3 (*piquet*) (surveyor's) ranging pole

mirer [mire] VT 1 *Vieilli* (*viser*) to aim at, to take aim at 2 *Littér* (*refléter*) to reflect, to mirror 3 (*œufs*) to candle
VPR **se mirer** (*dans un miroir, l'eau etc*) to

look *or* gaze at oneself; *Littér* **les arbres se mirent dans l'eau** the trees are reflected in the water

mirettes [mirɛt] NFPL *Fam* (*yeux*) peepers, *Am* baby blues; **on s'en est pris plein les m.** we feasted our eyes on it

mirifique [mirifik] ADJ *Fam* wonderful, fabulous

mirliflor(e) [mirliflɔr] NM *Hum, Fig Vieilli* dandy, fop

mirliton [mirlitɔ̃] NM (*sifflet*) kazoo, mirliton; **des vers de m.** doggerel, bad verse

mirmidon [mirmidɔ̃] NM *Vieilli* whippersnapper, pipsqueak, little runt

miro [miro] ADJ *Fam* short-sighted; **il est complètement m.** he's as blind as a bat

mirobolant [mirɔbɔlɑ̃] ADJ *Fam* fabulous, wonderful, marvellous; **son travail n'est vraiment pas m.** his work is not exactly brilliant

miroir [mirwar] NM mirror, *Fml* (looking) glass; **m. (pliant) à trois faces** triple mirror; **m. grossissant** magnifying mirror; **m. déformant** distorting mirror; *Fig* **le m. d'une société** the mirror of a society; **ce journal est-il réellement le m. de ce que pensent les gens?** does this newspaper really mirror *or* reflect what people think?
▸ ▸ **m. aux alouettes** = lure for attracting birds; *Fig* snare, delusion; **m. de courtoisie** vanity mirror

miroitant [mirwatɑ̃] ADJ (*argent*) glistening, gleaming, flashing; (*lac, soie*) shimmering; (*bijou*) sparkling

miroité [mirwate] ADJ (*cheval*) dappled bay

miroitement [mirwatmɑ̃] NM (*d'argent*) glistening, gleam(ing), flash(ing); (*de lac, de soie*) shimmer(ing); (*de bijou*) sparkle, sparkling

miroiter [mirwate] VI (*d'argent*) to glisten, to gleam, to flash; (*de lac, de soie*) to shimmer; (*de bijou*) to sparkle; *Fig* **faire m. l'avenir à qn** to lure sb with bright prospects, to hold out *or* dangle the prospect of a bright future in front of sb; **ils m'ont fait m. une promotion/un voyage** they dangled the prospect of promotion/a trip in front of me

miroton [mirɔtɔ̃], *Fam* **mironton** [mirɔ̃tɔ̃] NM *Culin* (**bœuf**) **m.** = beef boiled in sauce with onions

mis [mi] ADJ *Vieilli* **être bien/mal m.** to be well/badly attired

misaine [mizɛn] NF *Naut* (**voile de**) **m.** (square) foresail; **mât de m.** foremast

misanthrope [mizɑ̃trɔp] NM misanthropist, misanthrope
ADJ misanthropic

misanthropie [mizɑ̃trɔpi] NF misanthropy

misanthropique [mizɑ̃trɔpik] ADJ *Litt* misanthropic

miscible [misibl] ADJ miscible

mise [miz] NF 1 (*placement*) placing, putting in place; **m. à l'eau** (*d'un bateau*) launch, launching; **m. en bouteilles** bottling; **m. en boîtes** canning; **m. à terre** (*de marchandises*) landing; **m. en pratique** carrying out, putting into practice; **m. en musique d'un poème** setting a poem to music; **m. en eau** (*d'un barrage*) filling (of a reservoir); **m. au net** (*d'un document etc*) finalizing; **m. à exécution** (*d'une mesure*) implementation; **toute une série de mesures avec m. à exécution immédiate** a whole series of measures to be implemented immediately; **on craint la m. à exécution des menaces** there is concern that the threats will be carried out; **m. en italiques** italicization; **m. en valeur** (*d'un terrain, d'arguments*) development; **pour assurer la m. en valeur de sa collection** to show his collection off to better advantage *or* better effect; **m. en vigueur** implementation; **m. en application** *(d'un règlement, d'une décision)* implementation, application; **la m. en application du règlement avait connu quelques difficultés** there had been some difficulties in implementing *or* applying the regulation; **m. en place** setting up, putting into place; **nous avons dû retarder la m. en place du nouveau système** we have had to postpone setting up the new system; **la m. en place du nouveau réseau demandera plusieurs mois** it will take several months to set up the new system *or* to get the new system up and running; **m. en vente** putting up for sale, putting on the market; **elle attend la m. en vente de sa maison pour commencer à en chercher une autre** she's waiting for her house to go on the market before she starts looking for another; **j'ai confié la m. en vente de la maison à un notaire** I put the sale of the house in the hands of a notary; **m. en exploitation** *(d'une machine)* commissioning; **m. en veille** putting on standby; *Tél* **m. en attente d'appels** call holding; *Ordinat* **m. en attente des fichiers à imprimer** printer spooling; *Ordinat* **m. en ligne** putting on-line; *Ordinat* **m. en mémoire** saving; **la m. en mémoire n'a pas été faite** it hasn't been saved; *Ordinat* **m. en relief** highlighting; *Ordinat* **m. en réseau** networking; **m. sur pied** setting up

2 *(habillement)* dress, clothing, *Fml* attire; **elle est simple dans sa m.** she dresses simply; **on voit à sa m. qu'elle n'est pas très riche** you can see from the way she dresses *or* the clothes she wears that she's not very rich

3 *Cartes* stake; *(à une vente aux enchères)* bid; **m. à prix** reserve price, upset price; *Fig* **son arrivée m'a sauvé la m.** his arrival got me out of a tight spot

4 être de m. to be obligatory; **le tutoiement n'est pas de m.** it's not the done thing to say 'tu'; **si tu y vas, sache que la cravate est de m.** if you go, you'll have to wear a tie, mind

▸▸ **m. en accusation** committal (for trial); *Fig* **on a assisté à une véritable m. en accusation du président du club** accusations were hurled at the club chairman; **m. bas** *(d'animal)* dropping *(of young)*; **assister à la m. en bière** to be present when the body is placed in the coffin; **m. en cause** *(de l'honnêteté etc de qn)* questioning; *(dans une affaire)* involvement; **m. en circulation** *(de billets)* issue; **m. en demeure** summons; *Journ* injunction; *(de paiement)* formal demand; **m. en dépôt** warehousing; **m. en disponibilité** leave of absence; *Can Ind* layoff; **demander sa** *ou* **une m. en disponibilité** to ask for leave of absence; **m. sur écoutes (téléphoniques)** bugging; **c'est pourquoi ils ont décidé de la m. sur écoutes** that's why they decided to bug his/her/*etc* phone; *Jur* **m. en examen** indictment; **m. à feu** *(de fusée etc)* firing; *Com* **m. de fonds** investment; *Typ, Ordinat* **m. en forme** formatting; **m. en gage** pawning, pledging; **m. en garde** warning, caution; **m. hors** *(action)* disbursement; *(somme)* sum advanced; **m. hors tension** power-down; **m. en jeu** *(au début)* *Ftbl, Rugby* kick off; *Hockey* bully-off; *(à la touche)* *Ftbl* throw-in; *Rugby* line-out; **m. à jour** *(réactualisation)* *(action)* updating, update, bringing up to date; *(résultat)* update, updated version; *(d'un secret etc)* bringing to light; *Ordinat* updating; **m. en liberté** release; *Jur* **m. en liberté provisoire** release on bail; **m. en marche** *(de moteur etc)* starting, start up; **m. à mort** killing; *Ordinat* **m. à niveau** upgrade; *Scol* **faire une m. à niveau en maths** = to catch up in maths *(after switching to another specialization)*; **m. en œuvre** *(d'un projet)* implementation; *Radio* **m. en ondes** production; *Astronaut* **m. en orbite** putting into

orbit; **depuis sa m. en orbite** since it was put into orbit; **la m. en orbite est prévue pour 15 h** the satellite is scheduled to be sent into orbit at 3 pm; *Typ* **m. en pages** page make-up *or* design *or* layout; **m. en pension** borrowing against securities, pledging; **m. à pied** *(disciplinaire)* *(permanent)* dismissal; *(temporaire)* suspension; *Can (chômage)* layoff; **donner trois jours de m. à pied à qn** to give sb three days' suspension, to suspend sb for three days; **m. en plis** set; **faire une m. en plis à qn** to set sb's hair, to give sb a set; **shampooing et m. en plis** shampoo and set; **m. au point** *(d'un objectif)* focusing; *(d'une technique)* perfecting; *(d'un moteur)* tuning; *(d'un mécanisme)* adjustment; *(d'un document, d'un rapport)* finalization, finalizing; *Journ* correction; **je voudrais faire une m. au point** I'd like to clarify something; *Ordinat* **m. en relation** *(avec un service)* logon; *Typ* **m. en retrait** indent; **m. à la** *ou* **en retraite** pensioning (off), retirement on a pension; **il y aura 50 mises en retraite** 50 people will be retired; **m. en route** start-up; **m. à sac** *(par des soldats)* sacking; *(par des voleurs)* ransacking; **après la m. à sac de la maison** after the house was ransacked; **se livrer à une m. à sac** *(de voyous)* to go on a looting spree; **m. en scène** *(d'une pièce)* staging, production; *(d'un film)* direction; **c'est elle qui fera la m. en scène** she'll be responsible for staging the play; *Fig* **toute cette histoire n'était en fait qu'une vaste m. en scène** the entire story was just one big set-up; **m. en service** *(d'une machine)* commissioning; **mais sa m. en service ne se fera qu'en septembre** but it won't come into service until September; *Ordinat, Élec* **m. sous tension** *(d'un ordinateur, d'une turbine)* power-up; **m. en train** *(d'un projet etc)* start-up; **quelques minutes d'exercice pour assurer sa m. en train** a few minutes' exercise to get oneself started *or* going in the morning

miser [mize] **VT** to stake (**sur** on)
VI **m. sur un cheval** to back a horse, to (put a) bet on a horse; *Fig* **m. sur les deux tableaux** to try to have it both ways; *Fam* **m. sur qn** to count *or* bank on sb; *Bourse* **m. sur une hausse/une baisse** to speculate on a rising/falling market

misérabilisme [mizerabilism] **NM** sordid realism

misérabiliste [mizerabilist] **ADJ** sordidly realistic

misérable [mizerabl] **ADJ 1** *(indigent)* poor, wretched, impoverished, miserable; *(condition, existence)* wretched; **quartier m.** poor *or* poverty-stricken district **2** *(insignifiant)* wretched, miserable, worthless; **un m. salaire** a miserable wage, a mere pittance (of a wage); **pour la m. somme de 20 euros** for a paltry 20 euros **3** *Vieilli (action etc)* despicable, mean

N *Arch (malheureux)* poor wretch; *Vieilli (fripouille)* scoundrel, wretch, villain; **comment as-tu pu faire une chose pareille, m.?** how could you have done such a thing, you scoundrel *or* wretch?

Il faut noter que l'adjectif anglais **miserable** est un faux ami. Il signifie le plus souvent **malheureux, triste.**

misérablement [mizerabləmɑ̃] **ADV** miserably

misère [mizer] **NF 1** *(indigence)* extreme poverty, destitution; **être dans la m.** to be poverty-stricken *or* destitute; **ils sont dans une m. noire** they have nothing, they are quite destitute; **vivre dans la m.** to live in poverty; **tomber dans la m.** to become destitute; **réduire qn à la m.** to reduce sb to penury; **crier** *ou* **pleurer m.** to plead poverty;

salaire de m. starvation wage **2** *(ennui)* trouble, misfortune; **les misères de l'âge** the afflictions of old age; **faire des misères** *ou* **Can de la misère à qn** to tease sb unmercifully **3** *Vieilli (malheur)* misery; **reprendre son collier de m.** to get back to the treadmill; **c'est vraiment une m. de la voir si malheureuse!** it is dreadful to see her so unhappy!; **lit de m.** sick bed **4** *(vétille)* **une m.** a trifle; **cent euros? une m.!** a hundred euros? a mere nothing!; **je l'ai eu pour une m.** I got it for a song **5** *Cartes* misère **6** *Bot* tradescantia **INT m.!** damn!, blast!

Il faut noter que le nom anglais **misery** est un faux ami. Il signifie **malheur** ou **tristesse.**

miserere, miséréré [mizerere] **NM INV** *Rel, Mus* miserere

miséreux, -euse [mizerø, -øz] **ADJ** poverty-stricken, destitute
N poverty-stricken *or* destitute person

miséricorde [mizerikɔrd] **NF** mercy
INT *Vieilli* mercy on us!

miséricordieux, -ieuse [mizerikɔrdjø, -jøz] **ADJ** merciful (**envers** to)

misogyne [mizɔʒin] **ADJ** misogynous
N misogynist, woman-hater

misogynie [mizɔʒini] **NF** misogyny; **d'une m. invraisemblable** incredibly misogynous

miss, *pl* **miss(es)** [mis] **NF 1** *(reine de beauté)* beauty queen; **M. Monde/France** Miss World/France **2** *Fam* **voilà, m.** there you are(, miss); **et comment va m. Martin?** and how is Miss Martin?; *(en s'adressant directement à la personne)* and how are we today, Miss Martin? **3** *Arch (gouvernante)* (English) governess

missel [misel] **NM** *Rel* missal

missile [misil] **NM** *Mil* missile; **m. à tête chercheuse à infrarouge** heat-seeking missile; **m. ballistique de moyenne portée** *ou* **de portée intermédiaire** intermediate-range ballistic missile; **m. de courte/longue portée** short-/long-range missile; **m. de croisière** cruise missile; **m. stratégique** strategic missile; **m. tactique** tactical missile; **m. anti-sous-marins** anti-submarine missile

mission [misjɔ̃] **NF 1** *(tâche)*, *Pol, Mil etc* mission; *(d'employé)* job, task, assignment; **j'ai (pour) m. de faire qch** my job *or* task is to do sth; **ministre en m. spéciale à Paris** minister on a special mission to Paris; **chargé de m.** representative; **envoyer qn en m. aux États-Unis** to send sb to the United States; **partir en m.** *(d'un cadre)* to go away on business; *(d'un diplomate)* to go off on a mission; *Mil* **en m. de reconnaissance** on a reconnaissance mission, on reconnaissance; **m. accomplie** mission accomplished; **m. vous avait été confiée de faire ...** you were given the job of doing ..., *Fml* you were assigned the task of doing ...; **il s'était donné pour m. de sauver les enfants** he had taken it upon himself to save the children; *Hum* **viens ici, j'ai une m. à te confier** *(à un enfant)* come here, there's something I'd like you to do for me

2 *(groupe)* delegation; *Pol* delegation, mission; **m. scientifique** scientific expedition; **partir en m. au pôle Nord** to go on an expedition to the North Pole

3 *Rel (vocation, organisation)* mission; *(bâtiment)* mission (station)

4 *(rôle)* *(de l'art etc)* task, rôle, function; **la m. civilisatrice de l'école** the civilizing mission of schools

▸▸ **m. de bons offices** goodwill mission; **m. commerciale** business assignment; *(gouvernementale)* trade mission; **m. diplomatique** diplomatic mission

missionnaire [misjɔnɛr] ADJ, N missionary

Mississippi [misisipi] NM le M. *(le fleuve)* the Mississippi (River); *(l'État)* Mississippi

missive [misiv] NF *Litt, Hum* missive, letter

mistigri [mistigri] NM *Fam (chat)* puss

mistoufle [mistufl] NF *Fam Vieilli* **1** être dans la m. to be broke *or* hard up *or* skint **2** faire des mistoufles à qn to annoy *or* tease *or* plague sb

mistral [mistral] NM *Météo* mistral

mitaine [mitɛn] NF *Can (moufle)* mitten; *(qui laisse les doigts nus)* fingerless glove

mitan [mitã] NM *Fam Vieilli* le m. the underworld, gangland

mitard [mitar] NM *Fam* disciplinary cell; **se retrouver au m.** to end up in solitary

mite [mit] NF **1** mite; **m. du fromage** cheese mite **2** *(petit papillon)* moth; **mangé des** *ou* **aux mites, troué aux mites** moth-eaten

mité [mite] ADJ moth-eaten

mi-temps NF INV *Ftbl etc* half-time; **première/seconde m.** first/second half; **la police craint la troisième m.** the police fear after-match trouble *or* violence
▷ NM part-time job; **l'emploi à m.** part-time work *or* employment; **travailler** *ou* **être à m.** to work part-time, to have a part-time job; *Scol* **m. pédagogique** part-time teaching position; **l'avantage d'un m.** the advantage of a part-time job *or* of working part-time

miter (se) [səmite] VPR to become motheaten

miteux, -euse [mitø, -øz] ADJ *(vêtements, quartier, boîte)* seedy, shabby, tatty; *(personne)* seedy-looking, shabby, down-at-heel
▷ N *Fam* shabby *or* down-at-heel *or* seedy-looking person; **tes amis, c'est une bande de m.!** your friends are a seedy lot!

Mithridate [mitridat] N Mithridates

mithridatiser [mitridatize] VT **m. qn** to make sb immune (to poison)

mitigation [mitigasjɔ̃] NF *Jur* mitigation

mitigé [mitiʒe] ADJ *(enthousiasme)* moderate, *Fml* mitigated; *(sentiments, impressions)* mixed; **le public était assez m.** the public was quite mixed in its reaction; **morale mitigée** lax morals; *Jur* **peine mitigée** reduced sentence

mitiger [mitiʒe] VT (**je mitigeai(s), n. mitigeons**) *Vieilli (mal)* to mitigate; *(peine)* to reduce, to mitigate; *(règlement, loi)* to relax

mitigeur [mitiʒœr] NM mixer tap

mitochondrie [mitokɔ̃dri] NF mitochondrion

mitonner [mitɔne] VT **1** *Culin* to prepare, to cook; *(cuire à feu doux)* to simmer; **sa femme lui mitonne de bons petits plats** his wife cooks nice little meals for him **2** *Fig (projet etc)* to concoct, to cook up **3** *Litt (enfant)* to coddle, to pamper, to cosset
▷ VI *Culin* to simmer

mitose [mitoz] NF *Biol* mitosis

mitoyen, -enne [mitwajɛ̃, -ɛn] ADJ intermediate; **mur m.** party wall; **cloison mitoyenne** dividing wall *(between two rooms)*; **maisons mitoyennes** semi-detached houses; *(plus de deux)* terraced houses

mitoyenneté [mitwajɛnte] NF *Jur (de mur, de haie)* joint ownership

mitraillade [mitrajad] NF (volley of) shots, machine-gun fire; **une m.** a burst of machine-gun fire

mitraillage [mitrajaʒ] NM machinegunning

mitraille [mitraj] NF **1** *Mil (projectiles)* case shot, canister shot, grapeshot; *(décharge)* hail of bullets **2** *Fam (monnaie)* small change

mitrailler [mitraje] VT to machine-gun; *Phot Fam* to click away at, to snap away at,

---

to take snaps of; **les vedettes ont été abondamment mitraillées** lots of photographs were taken of the film stars; *Fig* **m. qn de questions** to fire questions at sb, to bombard sb with questions

mitraillette [mitrajɛt] NF submachine gun, *Fam* tommy gun

mitrailleur [mitrajœr] NM machine-gunner; *Mil, Aviat* **m. arrière** rear gunner
▷ ADJ **fusil m.** Bren gun

mitrailleuse [mitrajøz] NF machine gun

mitral, -ale, -aux, -ales [mitral, -o] ADJ *Anat* mitral

mitre [mitr] NF **1** *(d'évêque)* mitre, *Am* miter **2** *Tech (de cheminée)* cowl

mitré [mitre] ADJ *(abbé)* mitred, *Am* mitered

mitron [mitrɔ̃] NM baker's boy

mi-voix (à) ADV in an undertone, under one's breath

mix [miks] NM *Mktg (marchéage)* mix; **m. de produits** product mix

mixage [miksaʒ] NM *Cin, Radio (procédé)* mixing; *(résultat)* (sound) mix; **m. magnétique final** master soundtrack

mixer [mikse] VT **1** *Cin, Radio* to mix **2** *Culin* to blend, to liquidize

mixe(u)r [miksœr] NM mixer; *(pour rendre liquide)* liquidizer

mixité [miksite] NF *Scol* co-education

mixte [mikst] ADJ **1** *(des deux sexes)* mixed; **école m.** mixed *or* co-educational school; *Tennis* **double m.** mixed doubles **2** *(combiné)* **train m.** composite train *(goods and passengers)*; **commission m.** joint commission; **billet m.** combined rail and road ticket; **mariage m.** mixed marriage; **cuisinière m.** gas and electric cooker

mixtion [mikstjɔ̃] NF *Pharm (action) (de drogues etc)* compounding; *(médicament)* mixture

mixture [mikstyr] NF **1** *Pharm* mixture **2** *Culin, Fig* concoction

MJC [ɛmʒise] NF *(abrév* **maison des jeunes et de la culture**) = youth club and arts centre

ml *(abrév* **millilitre(s)**) ml

MLF [ɛmɛlɛf] NM *abrév* **Mouvement de libération de la femme**

Mlle *(abrév* **mademoiselle**) Miss

Mlles *(abrév* **mesdemoiselles**) Misses

MM *(abrév* **Messieurs**) Messrs

mm *(abrév* **millimètre(s)**) mm

Mme *(abrév* **Madame**) Mrs

Mmes *abrév* **Mesdames**

MMS [ɛmɛmɛs] NM *Tél (abrév* **multimedia messaging service**) MMS

mnémonique [mnemɔnik] ADJ, NF mnemonic

mnémotechnie [mnemɔtɛkni] NF mnemonics

mnémotechnique [mnemɔtɛknik] ADJ mnemonic; **un moyen m.** a mnemonic
▷ NF mnemonics

Mo [ɛmo] NM *Ordinat (abrév* **méga-octet**) Mb

mob [mɔb] NF *Fam* = **Mobylette®**

mobile [mɔbil] ADJ **1** *(qui peut être bougé) (cloison)* mobile, movable; *(feuillets)* loose; **album à feuilles mobiles** loose-leaf album **2** *(expression, regard)* shifting, changing; *(visage)* lively, expressive; *(organe, cartilage)* mobile, having freedom of movement; *(cible)* moving; *(personne âgée)* mobile; *(employé, main d'œuvre)* willing to move *or* relocate; *(population)* mobile, shifting; **dans les pays pauvres les populations ont tendance à être plus mobiles** people in poor countries tend to move around more; **le boxeur est très m.** the boxer is very nimble, the boxer is very quick on his feet; *Tech* **organes mobi-**

---

les sliding *or* working *or* moving parts **3** *Mil* **gendarmerie m.** ≃ flying squad; **gendarme** *ou* **garde m.** ≃ member of the flying squad; *Hist* **garde nationale m.** *(de 1848, de 1868-71)* militia; *Hist* **la garde républicaine m.** = the (State) security police **4** *Vieilli (humeur)* changeable
▷ NM **1** *(motif) (du crime)* motive (**de** for); *Mktg* **m. d'achat** buying inducement, purchasing motivator **2** *(téléphone portable)* mobile (phone) **3** *Phys etc* moving body, body in motion **4** *(en décoration)*, *Beaux-Arts* mobile; *Mktg* **m. publicitaire** advertising mobile

mobile home, *pl* **mobile homes** [mɔbilom] NM mobile home

mobilier, -ière [mɔbilje, -jɛr] ADJ *Jur* movable, personal; **biens mobiliers** personal property, chattels; *Fin* **valeurs mobilières** stocks and shares, transferable securities
▷ NM *(ameublement)* furniture; **m. de bureau** office furniture; **m. de présentation** display stands
▷ ▷ **m. national** government property; **m. urbain** street furniture

┌─────────────────────────────────────┐
│ Do not confuse with **meuble**. │
└─────────────────────────────────────┘

mobilisable [mɔbilizabl] ADJ **1** *Mil (troupes)* which can be mobilized; **les jeunes de moins de 18 ans ne sont pas mobilisables** young people under 18 are not eligible for call-up **2** *(créance)* discountable

mobilisateur, -trice [mɔbilizatœr, -tris] ADJ motivating; **slogan m.** rallying cry; **un appel m.** a call to rally the troops

mobilisation [mɔbilizasjɔ̃] NF *(de troupes)* mobilization; *Fin (de capital)* raising; **m. de fonds** raising of funds; *Mil* **ordre de m. générale** general mobilization order; **les syndicats comptent beaucoup sur la m. des enseignants contre ce projet de réforme** the unions are relying heavily on the teachers rallying to fight this proposed reform; **nous avons besoin d'une m. des électeurs/consommateurs pour dire non à ...** we need voters/consumers to mobilize *or* rally and say no to ...; **on sent un manque de m. total chez les étudiants en faveur de/contre ces nouvelles mesures** students seem to be totally unwilling to rally in order to support/fight these new measures

mobilisé, -ée [mɔbilize] ADJ *(troupes)* mobilized; *(réservistes)* called up
▷ N serviceman, *f* servicewoman; **un m. de la guerre de 14** a soldier in the First World War; **les mobilisés de la dernière guerre** those who served in the last war

mobiliser [mɔbilize] VT *(troupes)* to mobilize; *(réserviste)* to call up; *(syndicat, électorat)* to rally; *(ressources)* to mobilize; *(créances)* to discount; *(capital, argent)* to raise; **m. toute son énergie** to summon up all one's energy; *(de son travail, ses enfants)* to use up all one's energy; **il faut m. les énergies** we'll have to mobilize people
▷ VPR **se mobiliser** to mobilize; **se m. contre/en faveur de qch** to rally against/in support of sth

mobilité [mɔbilite] NF *(de la population etc)* mobility; *(dans le travail)* willingness to move *or* relocate; *(des organes)* freedom of movement; *Fig (de caractère, d'humeur)* changeability; **la m. de son visage est remarquable** he has a remarkably lively face; **personnes à m. réduite** people of reduced mobility; **la m. de la mâchoire inférieure est affectée** the movement of the lower jaw is affected; *Écon* **m. sociale** upward mobility

Mobylette® [mɔbilɛt] NF moped; **faire de la M.** to ride a moped; **elle y va en** *ou* **à M.** she goes there on her moped

mocassin [mɔkasɛ̃] NM moccasin

moche [mɔʃ] ADJ *Fam* **1** *(individu, chose)* hideous, ugly; **qu'est-ce qu'elle est m. aujourd'hui!** she looks a real sight today!; **c'est m. ces rideaux bleus avec ce canapé rose!** those blue curtains look really hideous with that pink sofa!; **je ne trouve pas qu'il soit m.** I don't think he's bad-looking **2** *(appréciation morale)* rotten, nasty; **c'est m. ce qu'ils t'ont fait** it's rotten what they did to you; **c'est trop m. de mourir à vingt ans** it's terrible to die at twenty

mocheté [mɔʃte] NF *Fam (laideur)* ugliness; **c'est d'une m.!** what an eyesore!, it's absolutely hideous!; **la mode de cet été est d'une m.!** this summer's fashions are hideous!; **quelle m., cette fille!** that girl's such a dog!

modal, -ale, -aux, -ales [mɔdal, -o] ADJ, NM *Ling* modal SEE GRAMMAR A57–61; B39–40

modalité [mɔdalite] NF **1** method, mode; *(d'application d'une loi)* mode; *Jur* **modalités** *(restrictive)* clauses; **modalités de paiement** *(liquide, chèque etc)* methods of payment; *(conditions)* terms or conditions of payment; **modalités d'examen** examination procedure; *Fin* **modalités d'une émission** terms and conditions of an issue; **modalités de financement** financing terms or conditions **2** *Phil, Mus, Gram* modality

mode[1] [mɔd] NF **1** fashion; **la m. est aux couleurs pastel** pastels are in (fashion); **la m. des pantalons pattes d'éléphant est revenue** flares are back (in fashion); **la m. du long est passée** long skirts are out (of fashion); **lancer la m. de qch** to set the fashion for sth, to make sth fashionable; **être à la m.** to be in fashion or in vogue, to be all the rage; **ta sœur est très à la m.** your sister's very fashionable or *Fam* trendy; **robe à la m.** fashionable or stylish dress; **revenir à la m.** to come back (into fashion); **passer de m.** to go out of fashion; **tu ne trouves pas que c'est un peu passé de m.?** don't you think it's a bit old-fashioned?; **à l'ancienne m.** in the old style; **journal de m.** fashion magazine; **un professionnel de la m.** a fashion professional; **à la m. de …** after the style or manner of …; **neveu/nièce à la m. de Bretagne** first cousin once removed **2** *Arch* **modes** *(vêtements)* fashions; **gravures de modes** fashion plates; **magasin de modes** milliner's shop
ADJ INV **le coloris m.** fashionable shades or colours, the shades or colours in fashion; **elle est toujours habillée très m.** she's always dressed very fashionably; **c'est très m.** it's very fashionable, it's very much in fashion

mode[2] NM **1** *(d'éducation etc)* method, mode; **m. d'emploi** instructions; **m. de vie** lifestyle, way of life; **m. de cuisson** cooking instructions; **m. opératoire** modus operandi; **m. de gestion** management method or style; **m. d'expression** means of expression; **m. d'expédition** method of delivery; **m. de classement** filing system; **m. de codification** coding method; **m. de paiement** ou **de règlement** method of payment; *Pol* **m. de scrutin** voting system; **m. de transport** method of transport; *Aut* **m. de conduite hiver** winter driving mode; *Aut* **m. de sélecteur de vitesses** gear selector; *Aut* **m. dégradé** limp-home mode **2** *Gram* mood; *Mus, Ordinat* mode SEE GRAMMAR A40; B32–5
▸▸ *Ordinat* **m. ajout** append mode; **m. amélioré** enhanced mode; **m. brouillon** draft mode; **m. caractère** character mode; **m. continu** continuous mode; *(de transmission)* burst mode; **m. conversationnel** *(d'un modem)* conversation mode; **m. dialogue** *(d'un modem)* dialog(ue) mode; **m. différé** non real-time mode, off-line mode; **m. direct** real-time mode; *Typ* **m. 'à la française'** portrait mode; **m. insertion** insert mode; *Typ* **m.**

'à l'italienne' landscape mode; **m. lecture seule** read-only mode; **m. linéaire** straight-line method; **m. machine à écrire** typewriter mode; **m. multitâche** multitask(ing) mode; **m. paysage** landscape mode; **m. point** bit-map; **m. portrait** portrait mode; **m. de prévisualisation** preview mode; **m. survol** browse mode; **m. sélectif** veto mode; **m. texte** text mode

modelage [mɔdlaʒ] NM *(action) (de l'argile etc)* modelling; *(résultat)* model

modèle [mɔdɛl] NM **1** *(exemple)* model; **m. d'écriture** handwriting copy; **m. de lettre** standard letter; **machines toutes bâties sur le même m.** machines all built to one pattern or on or along the same lines; **faites un résumé de ce texte en vous aidant du m.** summarize this text along the same lines; **prendre qn pour m.** to take sb as one's (role) model, to model oneself on sb; **Anne n'est pas un m. (à suivre)** don't follow Anne's example or lead; **le m. américain/japonais** the American/Japanese model; **m. de générosité/fidélité** model of generosity/fidelity; **m. de vertu** paragon or model of virtue
2 *Com (version)* model; **m. sport/deux portes** sports/two-door model; **voiture dernier m.** car of the latest design; **ils ont présenté leur nouveau m. au salon de l'auto** they unveiled their new model at the car show; **ce m. existe aussi en rouge** this model also comes in or is also available in red
3 *Couture (de robe)* style; *(de tricot)* pattern; *Beaux-Arts (artist's)* model; **vous n'auriez pas un plus grand m.?** do you have it in a larger size?; **dessiné d'après m.** drawn from life; **servir de m. à un artiste** to sit or model for an artist
4 *Écon, Math, Ling etc (représentation schématique)* model; **m. de décision** decision model; **m. de décision en arborescence** decision-tree model; **m. du chemin critique** critical path model; **m. décisionnel** ou **déterministe** decision model; **m. mathématique** mathematical model
ADJ époux **m.** model or exemplary husband; **l'employé m.** the model employee; **adopter une conduite m.** to behave in an exemplary manner; **appartement/maison m.** show flat/house
▸▸ *Com, Ind* **m. déposé** registered pattern or model; **m.-phare** flagship; **m. réduit** scale model; **m. réduit de yacht/d'avion** model yacht/airplane; **amateurs de modèles réduits** model enthusiasts

modelé [mɔdle] NM **1** *Beaux-Arts* relief; *(de sculpture)* contours **2** *Géog* relief

modeler [mɔdle] (**je modèle; je modèlerai**) VT *(argile, cire)* to model, to mould, *Am* to mold; *Fig (caractère)* to shape, to mould; *(destinée)* to shape; **il avait un corps d'athlète, modelé par l'exercice physique** he had the body of an athlete, shaped by physical exercise; **un lobe d'oreille délicatement modelé** a delicately shaped earlobe; **l'eau/l'érosion a modelé le relief de la côte** water/erosion has shaped the coastline; **m. sa personnalité sur celle de qn** to model oneself on sb
VPR **se modeler se m. sur qn** to take sb as one's model, to model oneself on sb

modeleur, -euse [mɔdlœr, -øz] N *Beaux-Arts* modeller; *Tech, Ind* pattern maker

modélisation [mɔdelizasjɔ̃] NF modelling

modélisme [mɔdelism] NM model-making; **un passionné de m.** a keen model-maker

modéliste [mɔdelist] N **1** *(de maquette)* model-maker **2** *(de vêtements)* dress designer

modem [mɔdɛm] NM *Ordinat* modem; **carte m.** modem card; **m. externe** external modem; **m. fax** fax modem; **m. interne** internal modem; **m. longue distance** long-haul

modem; **m. nul** null modem; **m. RNIS** ISDN modem; **envoyer qch à qn par m.** to modem sth to sb, to send sth to sb by modem

modem-câble, *pl* **modems-câbles** NM cable modem

modem-télécopieur, *pl* **modems-télécopieurs** NM fax-modem

modérateur, -trice [mɔderatœr, -tris] ADJ moderating, restraining
N moderating influence
NM **1** *(de moteur etc)* regulator, governor; *Nucl* moderator **2** *(dans un forum Internet)* regulator

modération [mɔderasjɔ̃] NF **1** *(retenue)* moderation, restraint; **sa réponse était pleine de m.** his answer was very restrained; **tu devrais faire preuve d'un peu plus de m. dans tes propos** you should curb your tongue a bit more; **avec m.** in or with moderation **2** *(réduction) (de prix)* restriction; *(fiscale)* reduction; **promettre une m. des impôts** to promise lower taxes

modéré, -ée [mɔdere] ADJ *(personne, propos)* moderate, restrained; *(ton, attitude)* restrained; *(température)* moderate; *(prix etc)* reasonable, moderate; *(acclamations)* subdued
N *Pol* moderate

modérément [mɔderemɑ̃] ADV moderately, in moderation; **j'aime m. le whisky** I'm moderately fond of whisky; **il fume, mais m.** he smokes, but in moderation; *Iron* **j'ai m. apprécié sa conduite** I was less than overwhelmed by his behaviour; **j'ai m. apprécié qu'il dise que je ronflais!** I didn't exactly appreciate his saying I snored!; **j'apprécie m. qu'on mette le nez dans mes affaires** I'm not very keen on people sticking their noses into my business

modérer [mɔdere] (**je modère; je modérerai**) VT **1** *(passions, désirs, envies)* to moderate, to restrain, to curb; *(vitesse)* to reduce, to slacken; *Ind* **m. les cadences** to reduce or lower production rates; **m. ses ambitions** to lower one's sights, to be less ambitious; **je te prie de m. ton langage!** please mind your tongue! **2** *(réduire) (prix)* to restrict
VPR **se modérer** *(s'apaiser)* to control oneself, to calm down; *(faire preuve de sobriété)* to restrain oneself

moderne [mɔdɛrn] ADJ *(concept, monde, médecine, musique, danse)* modern; *(équipement, méthode, technologie, idée, pensée)* modern, up-to-date; **studio équipé de tout le confort m.** studio flat with all modern conveniences; **découverte m.** recent discovery; **la femme m. travaille** the modern woman goes out to work; *Hist* **la période m.** the modern period, recent history; **grec m.** modern Greek; **étudier les lettres modernes** *(en France)* to study French language and literature
NM **le m.** *(style)* (the) modern style; **nous avons tout meublé en m.** all our furniture is modern; **mélanger le m. et l'ancien** to mix old and new
N *(personne)* modern

modernisation [mɔdɛrnizasjɔ̃] NF modernization; **les efforts de m. de l'enseignement** the attempts to modernize education

moderniser [mɔdɛrnize] VT to modernize, to bring up to date

modernisme [mɔdɛrnism] NM modernism

moderniste [mɔdɛrnist] ADJ, N modernist

modernité [mɔdɛrnite] NF modernity; **on est tout d'abord frappé par sa m.** the first thing that strikes you is how modern it is; **il a toujours été un défenseur de la m.** he has always defended what is modern

modern style [mɔdɛrnstil] NM art nouveau

ADJ INVart nouveau; **balcon m.** art nouveau balcony

modeste [mɔdɛst] **ADJ 1** (sans orgueil) (personne) modest, unassuming, self-effacing **2** (sans faste) (revenu, hôtel, appartement, repas) modest; (milieu) modest, humble; (personne) humble, simple; **avoir un train de vie m.** to have a modest lifestyle or way of life; **être d'une origine m.** to be of humble origin; **une pièce aux dimensions modestes** a small room, a room of modest dimensions **3** Litt Vieilli (pudique) modest ▶**N**ne faites pas le/la **m.** don't be (so) modest; **elle joue les modestes** she's acting modest

modestement [mɔdɛstəmɑ̃] **ADV** (sourire, parler) modestly; **être m. logé** to live in modest surroundings

modestie [mɔdɛsti] **NF 1** (de personne, revenu) modesty; **fausse m.** false modesty **2** Litt Vieilli (pudeur) modesty

modicité [mɔdisite] **NF** (de moyens, revenus) slenderness; (de prix) moderateness, lowness, reasonableness; **la m. de ses revenus l'empêchait de partir en vacances** his income was too small or low to allow him to go on holiday; **malgré la m. du loyer** despite the low rent

modifiable [mɔdifjabl] **ADJ** modifiable; **jouet m.** Transformer®; **après cela, le texte ne sera plus m.** after that, the text cannot be amended

modificateur, -trice [mɔdifikatœr, -tris] **ADJ** modifying ▶**NM** modifier

modificatif, -ive [mɔdifikatif, -iv] **ADJ** modifying

modification [mɔdifikasjɔ̃] **NF** (à un discours, un texte, une déclaration) alteration, change, amendment, modification; (à une loi, une convention, un contrat) amendment; (à un plan, un programme, une carte) alteration, change; (physique) change; **apporter** ou **faire une m. à qch** to make an alteration to or modify sth

modifier [mɔdifje] (pr sub, impf n. modifiions, v. modifiiez) **VT 1** (texte, discours, déclaration) to alter, to change, to amend, to modify; (projet de loi, convention) to amend; (plan, programme, façon de faire) to alter, to change; **ne modifiez rien** don't change anything, don't make any changes or alterations; **j'ai modifié la disposition des meubles** I've moved or changed the furniture around; Naut **m. la route** to alter course **2** Gram (verbe) to qualify, to modify ▶**VPR se modifier** to alter, to be modified or altered

modique [mɔdik] **ADJ** (coût, prix etc) moderate, modest, reasonable; (revenu) modest, slender; **pour la m. somme de 50 euros** for the modest sum of 50 euros, for a mere 50 euros; Iron **sa voiture a coûté la m. somme de 50 000 euros** his car cost a cool 50,000 euros

modiquement [mɔdikmɑ̃] **ADV m. payé** poorly paid

modiste [mɔdist] **NF** milliner

modulable [mɔdylabl] **ADJ** (horaires, tarif) flexible; (salle) multi-purpose; (espace intérieur) adjustable

modulaire [mɔdyler] **ADJ** modular

modulateur, -trice [mɔdylatœr, -tris] Radio etc **ADJ** (valve etc) modulating ▶**NM** modulator; **m. de fréquence** converter

modulation [mɔdylasjɔ̃] **NF 1** Mus modulation, transition; Fig **une m. des paiements serait souhaitable pour les nouveaux adhérents** it would be desirable to adjust the rate of payment for new members **2** (de la voix) modulation, inflexion **3** Radio etc modulation, mod; **m. d'amplitude** ampli-

tude modulation; **m. de fréquence** frequency modulation **4** Ling modulation

module [mɔdyl] **NM** (élément constitutif d'un tout) unit; Archit, Astronaut, Ordinat module; Math, Tech, Phys modulus; Univ **m. (d'enseignement)** module; Astronaut **m. lunaire/de commande** lunar/command module; Ordinat **m. d'aide** help module; Ordinat **m. d'extension** plug-in

moduler [mɔdyle] **VT** (des sons), Phys (amplitude etc) to modulate; (sa voix) to inflect, to modulate; Fig **m. des paiements** to adjust the rate of payment; **m. la thérapeutique en fonction des résultats obtenus** to adjust the treatment in the light of results ▶**VI** Mus to modulate

modus vivendi [mɔdysvivɛ̃di] **NM INV** modus vivendi

moé [mwe] **PRON** Can Fam me

moelle [mwal] **NF 1** (d'os) marrow, Spéc medulla; **m. épinière** spinal cord; **m. osseuse** bone marrow; **greffe de m. osseuse** bone marrow transplant; **os à m.** marrowbone; Fig **anglais jusqu'à la m.** English to the core; Fig **glacé jusqu'à la m.** frozen to the bone or to the marrow; Fig **corrompu** ou **pourri jusqu'à la m.** rotten to the core **2** Bot pith

moelleusement [mwaløzmɑ̃] **ADV** snugly; **s'enfoncer m. dans un coussin de plumes** to snuggle down into a feather cushion; **être m. installé dans son lit** to be snuggled up in bed, to be snugly tucked up in bed; **être m. installé dans un fauteuil/sous une couette** to be snuggled up in an armchair/under an eiderdown

moelleux, -euse [mwalø, -øz] **ADJ** (tapis, étoffe, pull) (velvety) soft; (coussin, lit) soft; (couverture, couette) soft, downy; (caramel, substance) smooth; (gâteau) moist; (vin, voix) mellow, smooth ▶**NM** (d'un tapis, d'une étoffe, d'un pull) (velvety) softness, velvetiness; (d'un lit, de coussins) softness; (d'une couverture) softness, downiness; (d'une voix, d'un vin) mellowness, smoothness; **un vin qui a du m.** a mellow or smooth wine

moellon [mwalɔ̃] **NM** quarry stone; **m. brut** rubble(stone); **m. d'appareil** ashlar

mœurs [mœr(s)] **NFPL 1** (coutumes) (de gens) manners, customs; (de pays, d'époque etc) customs, Fml mores; (d'animaux) habits; **vivre avec les m. de son temps** to be in tune with the times; **il a de drôles de m.!** he's got some funny habits or ways!; **entrer** ou **passer dans les m.** to become part of everyday life **2** (conduite en matière sexuelle) Jur **certificat de bonne vie et m.** certificate of good character; **la brigade des m.**, Fam **les M.** ≃ the vice squad; **attentat aux m.** sexual offence; **affaire de m.** sex case; **il a des m. spéciales** ou **particulières** he's the other way inclined; **femme de m. légères** ou **faciles** woman of easy virtue **3** (sens moral) morals; **gens sans m.** unprincipled people; Arch **bonnes m.** morality; **c'est contraire aux bonnes m.** it is immoral or indecent; Arch **avoir des m.** to be of good moral character

mofette [mɔfɛt] **NF** (mammifère) skunk

moffler [mɔfle] **VT** Belg Fam **j'ai été mofflé** I failed my exam

mogette [mɔʒɛt] **NF** Région bean

mohair [mɔer] **NM** Tex mohair; **laine m.** mohair wool; **un pull en m.** a mohair sweater

Mohican [mɔikɑ̃] **NM** Mohican

moi [mwa] **PRON PERS** VOIR GRAMMAIRE A27; B20–1 **1** (sujet) I; **c'est m.** it's me, Fml it is I; **il est plus âgé que m.** he is older than me or than I am; **elle est invitée et m. aussi** she's invited and so am I; **qui vient avec nous?** – **m.** who's coming with us? – I am or me; **m. m'sieur, m. m'sieur, je connais la réponse!** me sir,

me sir, I know the answer; **m., je veux bien (le faire)** I don't mind (doing it); **m. qui vous parle** I'm telling you; **m., quand je serai grand** when I grow up; très Fam **m., les femmes, c'est fini** I've had it with women **2** (objet) me; **il nous accuse mon frère et m.** he's accusing my brother and me; **et m.? vous m'oubliez?** what about me? have you forgotten me?; **vous me soupçonnez, m.!** you suspect me!; **avec m.** with me; **venez à m.** come to me; **à m.!** help!; **à m., au secours!** help! help!; **ce livre est à m.** this book is mine or belongs to me; **un ami à m.** a friend of mine; **ces vers ne sont pas de m.** these verses are not mine; **de vous à m.** between you and me, between ourselves, Fam between you, me and the gatepost; **c'est pour m.** (quand on apporte l'addition) I'll get this or it **3** (après impératif) **laissez-moi tranquille** leave me alone; **donnez-le-moi** give it to me; **dis-moi, où est-ce que tu as mis le dossier bleu?** (by the way or by the by or Am say,) where have you put the blue file?; **dites-moi, Jérôme, si nous allions à la mer cet été?** how about going to the seaside this year, Jérôme?, Am say, Jérôme, how about going to the seaside this year? ▶**NM** ego, self; **culte du m.** egoism; **la psychanalyse nous aide à découvrir notre vrai m.** psychoanalysis helps us discover our true selves VOIR GRAMMAIRE A12

moignon [mwaɲɔ̃] **NM** (de membre amputé etc) stump

moi-même **PRON PERS** myself; voir même

moindre [mwɛ̃dr] **ADJ 1** (comp) less(er); (prix) lower; (quantité) smaller; (vitesse) slower, lower; **question de m. importance** question of less(er) importance or of minor importance; **deux sur dix c'est un m. mal** two out of ten is not as bad as it might have been; **ce qui est un m. mal** so things aren't as bad as they might have been; **s'il arrive à s'en sortir avec seulement une jambe cassée, ce sera un m. mal** if he comes out of it with just a broken leg he'll be lucky VOIR GRAMMAIRE A26 **2** (superl) **le/la m.** the least; **pas la m. chance** not the slightest or remotest or faintest chance; **c'est la m. des choses** ou **politesses** it's the least I/he/etc can do; **au m. reproche, il se met à pleurer** he bursts into tears at the slightest reproach; **au m. sourire il s'imagine qu'on s'intéresse à lui** the least little smile and he thinks you're interested in him; **il n'y a pas le m. espoir de les retrouver vivants** there isn't the slightest hope of finding them alive; **je ne lui ai pas fait le m. reproche** I didn't reproach him in the slightest or in the least **3** Suisse Fam (malade) ill; **se sentir m.** to feel ill or sick ▶**N de deux maux il faut choisir le m.** you have to choose the lesser of two evils; **un expert, et non des moindres** no mean expert

moindrement [mwɛ̃drəmɑ̃] **ADV** Litt, Can (souvent avec nég) **sans être le m. intéressé/gêné** without being in the least bit interested/embarrassed; **je vous dérange?** – **pas le m.** am I disturbing you? – not at all or not in the slightest or not in the least

moine [mwan] **NM 1** Rel monk, friar; Prov **l'habit ne fait pas le m.** clothes do not make the man; Fig **être gras comme un m.** to be fat, esp Am to be a real butterball; **mener une vie de m.** to live like a monk **2** Arch (bassinoire) bed warmer

moineau, -eaux [mwano] **NM** (oiseau) sparrow; Fam **c'est un vilain m.** he's a bad lot or a nasty piece of work; Com **têtes de m.** nuts (of coal)

moinillon [mwaniɲɔ̃] **NM** Fam young monk

MOINS [mwɛ̃]

ADV less **1** ▪ fewer **1** ▪ unless *(à moins que)* **2** ▪ the least **3** ▪ at least *(du moins, au moins)* **4**
PRÉP minus ▪ to

ADV 1 *(comparatif)* less; **je gagne m. que vous** I earn less than you (do); **elle gagne peu et lui m. encore** she doesn't earn much and he earns even less *or Fml* still less; **elle est m. intelligente que sa sœur** she's not as intelligent as her sister, she's less intelligent than her sister; **il est m. pingre qu'économe** he's not so much stingy as thrifty; **beaucoup m. long** much shorter; **m. d'argent** less money, not so much money, not as much money; **m. d'hommes/d'occasions** fewer *or* not so many men/opportunities; **j'ai eu m. de remords** I felt less remorse; **un peu m. de fierté** a little less pride; **plus on le punit, m. il travaille** the more he's punished, the less he works; **plus il vieillit, m. il a de cheveux** the older he gets, the less hair he has; *Fam* **m. je le vois, mieux je me porte** the less I see of him the better; **il travaille de m. en m.** he's working less and less; **m. de dix euros** less than *or* under ten euros; **celui-ci coûte dix euros de m. que l'autre** this is ten euros less than the other one; **il y a eu 20% de visiteurs de m.** *ou* **en m.** there have been 20% fewer visitors; **je ne peux pas vous le laisser à m.** I can't let you have it for less; **il a m. de trente ans** he's less than *or* under thirty; **les m. de trente ans** the under-thirties; **les jeunes et les m. jeunes** the young and the not so young; **vous compterez cela en m.** you can deduct that, you can take that off the total; **il est revenu avec un œil/un bras/une jambe en m.** he came back minus an eye/an arm/a leg; **nous étions à m. d'un kilomètre de l'église** we were less than a kilometre from the church, we were within one kilometre of the church; **en m. de dix minutes** in less than ten minutes; **en m. de temps qu'il ne faut pour le dire**, *Fam* **en m. de deux** in no time (at all); *Fam* **c'était m. une** it was a close shave, it was a close *or* near thing; **il est on ne peut m. soigneux/honnête** he is extremely untidy/dishonest, *Fml* he is untidy/dishonest in the extreme; **je n'en suis pas m. décidée à le faire** I'm still going to do it nonetheless; **il est gentil mais il n'en est pas m. vrai que ...** he's very nice but it's true nonetheless that ...; **pas m. de 200 personnes** no fewer than 200 people, *Fam* no less than 200 people; **pas m. de 2 000 euros/trois jours** no less than 2,000 euros/three days; **rien m. que** nothing less than; **ce n'est rien m. qu'un héros** he's nothing less than a hero; **ce n'est rien (de) m. qu'un miracle** it's nothing short of a miracle; **elle mérite des éloges non m. que son frère** she deserves no less praise than her brother, she deserves praise quite as much as her brother VOIR GRAMMAIRE A26

2 à m. d'avis contraire unless I/you/*etc* hear to the contrary; **à m. d'un imprévu/un miracle/une catastrophe** barring something unforeseen/a miracle/a catastrophe, unless something unforeseen happens/a miracle happens/there's a catastrophe; **à m. de partir tout de suite** unless I/you/*etc* leave at once; **à m. que ... + *sub*** unless ...; **à m. que vous (ne) l'ordonniez** unless you order it **3** *(superlatif)* **le m.** the least; **les élèves les m. appliqués** the least industrious pupils; **le m. de gens possible** the smallest possible number of people, as few people as possible; **pas le m. du monde** not in the least *or* slightest, by no means; *Prov* **qui peut le plus peut le m.** you've/he's/*etc* done much more complicated things in your/his/*etc* time

4 du m. at least, that is to say, at all events;

c'est (tout) du m. ce qu'il dit that's what he says, at least; **au m.** at least; **gagner 20 000 euros par an au m.** to earn 20,000 euros a year at (the very) least; *Fam* **tu as fait ton travail, au m.?** you've done your work, I hope?; **c'est pour le m. surprenant** it's surprising, to say the least
PRÉP minus, less; **une heure m. cinq** five (minutes) to *or Am* of one; **six m. quatre égale deux** six minus four equals two; **il fait m. dix (degrés)** it's minus ten (degrees)
NM *Math* minus (sign)
N *Fam* **un/une m. que rien** a rat

> Attention: ne pas confondre **fewer** et **less** lorsque l'on traduit **moins**. **Fewer** s'utilise uniquement avec des termes dénombrables; **less** s'utilise avec des termes indénombrables ou dénombrables (bien que ce dernier emploi soit contesté).

moins-disant, *pl* **moins-disants** [mwɛ̃dizɑ̃] **NM** lowest bidder

moins-perçu, *pl* **moins-perçus NM** *Fin* outstanding amount, amount due *or* owing

moins-value, *pl* **moins-values** [mwɛ̃valy] **NF** *Fin* depreciation, drop in value; *(après une vente)* capital loss

moirage [mwaraʒ] **NM** *(de soie etc) (action de moirer)* watering

moire [mwar] **NF 1** *Tex* moire, moiré; **m. de soie** watered silk **2** *(reflet)* shimmer

moiré [mware] **ADJ 1** *Tex (soie etc)* watered, moiré **2** *(aux reflets changeants)* shimmering **NM** = moirure

moirer [mware] **VT 1** *Tex (soie etc)* to water **2** *Litt* to make shimmer

moirure [mwaryr] **NF 1** *Tex* watered effect, moiré **2** *Litt* shimmer, shimmering

mois [mwa] **NM 1** month; **au m. d'août** in (the month of) August; **louer qch au m.** to hire sth by the month; **pendant deux m.** for two months; **cent euros par m.** a hundred euros a month; **un m. de vacances/salaire** a month's holiday/wages; **le treizième m.** = one month's salary paid as a bonus; *Bourse* **m. d'échéance** trading month VOIR GRAMMAIRE A81; B60–1 **2** *(de paie)* month's wages *or* salary; **je n'ai pas encore touché mon m.** I still haven't received this month's wages *or* salary; **je dois deux m. à l'épicier** I haven't paid the grocer for two months

Moïse [mɔiz] **N** *Bible* Moses

moïse [mɔiz] **NM** *(berceau)* Moses basket

moisi [mwazi] **ADJ** *(pain, gâteau, fromage)* mouldy, *Am* moldy; *(mur, tissu etc)* mildewed, mildewy; *(goût)* musty; *(odeur)* musty, fusty
NM *(sur pain, confiture, fromage)* mould, *Am* mold; *(sur mur, tissu)* mildew; **odeur de m.** musty *or* fusty smell; **avoir un goût de m.** to taste mouldy *or* musty; **sentir le m.** to smell musty *or* fusty

moisir [mwazir] **VI** *(de pain)* to go mouldy *or Am* moldy; *(de raisins)* to go mouldy, to mildew; *(de linge)* to mildew; *Fig* **j'avais l'impression de m. dans cette ville** I felt I was mouldering away in that town; **il m'a laissé m. deux heures** he left me cooling my heels for two hours; *Fig Fam* **on ne va pas m. ici** *(partons)* let's not hang about here
VT *(pain)* to make mouldy *or Am* moldy; *(raisins, linge)* to mildew

moisissure [mwazisyr] **NF 1** *(partie moisie)* mould, *Am* mold; **moisissures** mouldy bits, mould **2** *(processus)* (formation of) mould *or Am* mold; **une forte odeur de m.** a strong musty smell

moisson [mwasɔ̃] **NF 1** *(action) (de céréales)* harvest(ing); *(époque)* harvest time; **faire la m.** *ou* **les moissons** to harvest; *Fig* **une m. de**

documents a pile *or* sheaf of documents; **une m. d'idées** a wealth of ideas **2** *(récolte)* crop, harvest; **rentrer la m.** to bring in the crops *or* the harvest

moissonnage [mwasɔnaʒ] **NM** harvesting, reaping

moissonner [mwasɔne] **VT 1** *(céréales)* to reap, to harvest; *(champ)* to reap; *(récoltes)* to harvest, to gather (in); **lundi prochain, on commence à m.** we'll start harvesting next Monday; *Litt Fig* **m. des informations** to gather a wealth of information; **m. des lauriers** to reap *or* win laurels **2** *Litt* la guerre moissonne les vies humaines war cuts short many lives

moissonneur, -euse [mwasɔnœr, -øz] **N** harvester, reaper
NF **moissonneuse** *(machine)* reaper, reaping machine

moissonneuse-batteuse, *pl* **moissonneuses-batteuses NF** combine (harvester)

moissonneuse-lieuse, *pl* **moissonneuses-lieuses NF** reaper-binder

moite [mwat] **ADJ** *(mains, front)* sweaty, clammy; *(atmosphère, air)* muggy; *(chaleur)* moist; **j'avais les mains moites de sueur** my hands were sweaty, my hands were damp with sweat

moiteur [mwatœr] **NF** *(de mains, du front)* sweatiness, clamminess; *(de terre)* wetness; *(d'atmosphère, d'air)* mugginess

moitié [mwatje] **NF 1** half; **quelle est la m. de dix?** what is half of ten?; **la m. de la production** half (of) the production; **qui veut la m. d'une banane?** who wants half (of) a banana?; **la bouteille était à m. pleine/vide** the bottle was half full/empty; **deux moitiés** two halves; **partagé en deux moitiés** divided into two halves, halved; **vendre qch à m. prix** to sell sth (at) half price; **réduit de m.** reduced by half; *Fam* **m.-m.** fifty-fifty; **faire m.-m.** to go halves *or* fifty-fifty; **ça devrait faire à peu près m.-m.** that should be us just about even; **se mettre** *ou* **être de m. avec qn** to go halves with sb, to go fifty-fifty with sb; **il est pour m. responsable** he is equally *or* just as much to blame, half the responsibility is his; **à m. half;** **à m. mort/cuit/nu/endormi** half-dead/-cooked/ -naked/-asleep; **faire les choses à m.** to do things by halves; **elle ne fait pas les choses à m.** she doesn't do things by halves VOIR GRAMMAIRE A5; A12 **2** *Hum Fam (époux, épouse)* **ma (chère) m.** my better half
ADV half; **m. riant, m. pleurant** half laughing, half crying; **m. anglaise, m. écossaise** half English, half Scottish; **m. plus** half as much again; **il y a m. de plus de monde que l'année dernière** there are half as many people again as there were last year; **m. moins gros/cher** fifty per cent smaller/cheaper; **c'est m. moins gros que l'autre** it's half the size of the other one; **ça m'a coûté m. moins cher** it cost me half the price; **m. moins de monde** fifty per cent fewer people; **il y a m. moins de monde qu'à la première représentation** there are half the people there were at the first performance

moitir [mwatir] **VT** *Vieilli Tech (papier etc)* to moisten

moka [mɔka] **NM** *(café)* mocha (coffee); *(gâteau)* mocha *or* coffee cake; **glace au m.** coffee ice cream
N *Géog* **M.** Mocha, Mokha

mol *voir* mou¹

molaire¹ [mɔlɛr] **NF** molar

molaire² **ADJ** *Phys* molar

molasse [mɔlas] **NF** *Géol* molasse

moldave [mɔldav] **ADJ** Moldavian
N M. Moldavian

Moldavie [mɔldavi] **NF** Moldavia

mole [mol] NF *Phys* mole

môle [mol] NM *(brise-lames)* breakwater, mole; *(quai)* pier

moléculaire [molekylɛr] ADJ molecular

molécule [molekyl] NF molecule

molécule-gramme, *pl* **molécules-grammes** NF *Phys* gram(me) molecule

molène [molɛn] NF *Bot* mullein

moleskine [moleskin] NF imitation leather; *(coton)* moleskin

molester [moleste] VT **m. qn** to rough sb up; **se faire m. par la police** to be roughed up by the police

> Il faut noter que le verbe anglais **to molest** est un faux ami. Il signifie le plus souvent **faire subir des sévices sexuels.**

moletage [moltaʒ] NM milling, knurling

moleter [molte] VT **(je molette; je moletterai)** to mill, to knurl

molette [molɛt] NF 1 *(d'éperon)* rowel; *(de briquet)* wheel; *(de jumelles)* focus wheel; **m. de réglage** control knob 2 *(pour le verre etc)* cutting wheel 3 *Ordinat* **m. de défilement** scroll wheel

Molières [moljɛr] NMPL **les M.** *(cérémonie)* = French theatre awards ceremony

moliéresque [moljɛrɛsk] ADJ *(situation, verve)* reminiscent of Molière

mollah [mola] NM *Rel* mullah

mollard [molar] NM *Vulg* gob of spit

mollarder [molarde] VI *Vulg* to spit, *Br* to gob

mollasse [molas] ADJ flabby; *Fig Fam (personne) (physiquement)* lethargic; *(moralement)* spineless
  N *Fam* **un/une m.** a lazy lump (of a man/woman)

mollasson, -onne [molasõ, -on] *Fam* ADJ *(personne) (physiquement)* lethargic; *(moralement)* spineless
  N **un m./une mollassonne** a lazy lump (of a man/woman)

molle *voir* **mou**[1]

mollement [molmã] ADV 1 *(avec abandon)* languidly; *(avec lenteur)* gently; **les barques se balançaient m. sur l'eau** the small boats were bobbing gently on the water; **m. étendu sur sa couche** stretched out languidly on his couch 2 *(sans énergie)* *(répondre, se déplacer)* feebly, weakly; *(serrer la main)* limply; *(protester, réagir)* feebly

mollesse [molɛs] NF 1 *(manque d'énergie)* lethargy; *(de tissus, muscles)* flabbiness; *(de style)* flabbiness, limpness; *(de gouvernement)* laxity, laxness; *Beaux-Arts* **la m. du trait** the lack of vigour in the brushstrokes 2 *(de coussin, matelas, chaise etc)* softness

mollet[1] [molɛ] ADJ M *(œuf)* soft-boiled; **pain m.** (soft) bread roll

mollet[2] NM *Anat* calf; **des mollets de coq** spindly legs VOIR GRAMMAIRE A12

molletière [moltjɛr] ADJ F **bandes molletières** puttees
  NF puttee

molleton [moltõ] NM *(en coton)* flannelette; *(en laine)* flannel; *(de table)* table felt

molletonné [moltone] ADJ *(gants, veste)* fleece-lined

molletonner [moltone] VT to line with fleece

mollir [molir] VI *(du vent)* to die down, to abate; *(de courage, d'enthousiasme)* to flag, to slacken; **je sentis mes jambes m.** I felt my legs give way (beneath me); **le sol mollissait sous mes pieds** the ground was giving way beneath my feet
  VT *Naut (cordage)* to slacken, to ease, to slack off; *(barre)* to ease

mollo [molo] ADV *Fam* **y aller m.** to take it easy

mollusque [molysk] NM 1 *Zool* mollusc, *Am* mollusk 2 *Fam (personne)* lazy lump

molosse [molos] NM watchdog, guard dog

molybdène [molibdɛn] NM *Minér* molybdenum

môme [mom] N *Fam (enfant)* kid
  NF *Arg (femme, fille)* chick; *(petite amie)* girl
  ADJ *Fam* **quand j'étais (tout) m.** when I was (just) a kid

moment [momã] NM 1 *(espace de temps)* moment; **le m. venu** *(passé)* when the time came; *(futur)* when the time comes; **à ce m.-là** then; *Fig (dans ces conditions)* if that's the case, in that case; **s'il ne peut pas te ramener, à ce m.-là tu m'appelles et je passerai** if he can't bring you back, then ring me and I'll come and get you; **à un m. donné** at one point; **c'est le bon m. pour …** now is the (right) time to …; **c'est le m. ou jamais** it's now or never; **c'est le m. ou jamais de lui dire ce que tu penses** now's the time (if ever there was one) to tell him what you think; **un m.!** one moment!, just a moment!; **je suis à vous dans un m.** I'll be with you in a moment; **en ce m.** at the moment, just now, at present; **à quel m. de l'année/la semaine?** at what time of the year/the week?; **à quel m. de l'histoire/sa vie?** at what stage of or point in the story/his life?; **il ne me faut rien pour le m.** I don't need anything at the moment or for the moment or for the time being; **sur le m.** at the time; **dans ces moments,** on ne réfléchit pas at times like that, you don't think; **passer un bon m.** to have a good time; **attendre le m. opportun** to wait for an opportune moment or the right moment; **arriver au bon m.** to arrive at just the right time; **ce n'est qu'un mauvais m. à passer** it'll soon be over with; **j'ai eu un m. de honte** for a moment I felt ashamed; **elle n'a pas eu un m. de repos aujourd'hui** she hasn't had a moment's rest today; **elle n'a pas un m. à elle** she hasn't a moment or minute to herself; **elle en a pour un m. avec ce travail** the work'll keep her busy for a (good) while; **par moments** at times, now and again; **d'un m. à l'autre** (at) any moment or time or minute; **à tout m., à tous moments** *(sans cesse)* constantly; *(n'importe quand)* at any moment; **il vaut mieux lui demander dans un de ses bons moments** it's better to ask him when he's in one of his good moods; **dans un m. de bonté** in a moment of kindness; **au m. de partir** just as I/he/*etc* was leaving or was about to leave; **il attend toujours le dernier m. pour nous dire ce qu'il a décidé** he always waits till the last moment or minute to tell us what he's decided; **les derniers moments de sa vie** the last moments of his life; **au m. de sa naissance/de l'accident/des élections** at the time of his birth/of the accident/of the elections; **jusqu'au m. où … until …**
  2 **du m. que …** seeing that …, since …
  3 *(temps présent)* **le m.** the moment; **c'est le disque/la star du m.** it's the record/she's the star of the moment
  4 *Phys (de force, d'inertie etc)* moment

momentané [momãtane] ADJ *(effort, coup de cafard)* brief; *(absence, interruption)* brief, temporary; *(panne)* temporary; **je suis bloqué chez moi mais c'est m.** I'm stuck at home, but it won't be for long; **je prends ce bureau mais ce n'est que m.** I'm taking this office, but it's only a temporary measure

momentanément [momãtanemã] ADV *(perdre connaissance, s'assoupir)* momentarily, for a moment, briefly; *(être absent, arrêter de fumer)* temporarily; *TV* **nos programmes sont m. interrompus** there is a temporary break in transmission

momerie [momri] NF *Litt Vieilli* mummery; *(pratique insincère)* insincerity

mômerie [momri] NF *(enfantillage)* childishness, childish behaviour; **cesse tes mômeries** stop being so childish

momie [momi] NF mummy

momification [momifikasjõ] NF mummification

momifier [momifje] *(impf, pr sub* **n. momifiions, v. momifiiez**) VT to mummify
  VPR **se momifier** to become mummified; *Fig* to become fossilized

mon, ma, mes [mõ, ma, me] ADJ POSS ‎SEE GRAMMAR A30; B21‎ (**mon** *is used instead of* **ma** *before f words beginning with vowel or mute* h) 1 my; **m. ami/amie** my friend; **m. meilleur ami/ma meilleure amie** my best friend; **m. oncle et ma tante** my uncle and (my) aunt; **m. père et ma mère,** *Litt* **mes père et mère** my mother and father; **j'ai mis m. chapeau et mes gants** I put on my hat and (my) gloves; **un(e) de mes ami(e)s** one of my friends, a friend of mine; **un professeur de mes amis** a teacher friend of mine; *Fam* **j'aurai ma chambre à moi** I'll have my own room; *Fam* **m. imbécile de frère** my idiot of a brother; *Fam* **m. artiste de mari** my husband, the artist; *Fam* **alors, tu veux le rencontrer, m. artiste?** do you want to meet this artist of mine, then?; *Fam* **et voilà m. Simon qui se met à rouspéter** then old Simon starts grumbling; *Fam* **j'ai eu m. vendredi** I got Friday off
  2 *(pour s'adresser à qn)* **non, m. général/capitaine** no, General/Captain; *Rel* **oui, ma sœur/ma mère/m. père** yes, Sister/Mother/Father; *Fml* **m. oncle, je vous écris pour demander …** I'm writing to you, uncle, to ask you …; **viens, m. enfant** come here, child

monacal, -ale, -aux, -ales [monakal, -o] ADJ *(vie, calme)* monastic

monachisme [monaʃism] NM monasticism

Monaco [monako] N **(la principauté de) M.** (the principality of) Monaco

monade [monad] NF *Phil* monad

monarchie [monarʃi] NF monarchy; **m. constitutionnelle/absolue** constitutional/absolute monarchy; **m. parlementaire** parliamentary monarchy

monarchique [monarʃik] ADJ monarchic(al)

monarchisme [monarʃism] NM monarchism

monarchiste [monarʃist] ADJ, N monarchist

monarque [monark] NM monarch

monastère [monastɛr] NM *(de moines)* monastery; *(de religieuses)* convent

monastique [monastik] ADJ monastic

monaural, -ale, -aux, -ales [monoral, -o] ADJ monaural

monceau, -eaux [mõso] NM heap, pile

mondain, -aine [mõdɛ̃, -ɛn] ADJ 1 *(lieu)* fashionable; **réunion/soirée mondaine** society gathering/evening; *Journ* **carnet m., rubrique** *ou* **chronique mondaine** society news, gossip column; **écrivain/chroniqueur m.** society writer/columnist; **la brigade mondaine** ≃ the vice squad 2 *Péj (qui aime les mondanités)* **il est très m.** he likes moving in fashionable circles, he's a great socialite 3 *Rel (plaisirs etc)* worldly, earthly
  N socialite
  NF *Fam* **la Mondaine** ≃ the vice squad

> Il faut noter que l'adjectif anglais **mundane** est un faux ami. Il signifie **terre-à-terre.**

mondanité [mõdanite] NF 1 society life; **je ne supporte pas sa m.** I can't bear his love of society 2 **mondanités** social gatherings; *(politesses, conversations superficielles)* social niceties; *Journ* society news, gossip column 3 *Rel* worldliness

monde [mɔ̃d] NM **1** (univers, humanité) world; **le m. entier** the whole world; **dans le m. entier** (connu, en vente) worldwide, all over the world, the world over; **(que) le m. est petit!** it's a small world!; **faire le tour du m.** to go round the world; **faire le tour du m. à la voile** to sail round the world; **les quatre coins du m.** the four corners of the world or globe; **il est allé/a travaillé aux quatre coins du m.** he's been/worked all over the world; **parcourir** ou **courir le m.** to travel the world; **mettre qn au m.** to bring sb into the world, to give birth to sb; **être seul au m.** to be alone in the world; **il est encore de ce m.** he is still with us, he is still alive; **je ne te ferais souffrir pour rien au m.** I wouldn't hurt you for (anything in) the world; Fam **c'est un m.!**, **c'est quand même un m.!** that's a bit much!; Fam **c'est tout de même** ou **quand même un m. de ne pas pouvoir faire ce qu'on veut chez soi!** it's a bit much if you can't do what you want in your own home!; Fam **elle se fait toujours un m. de tout** she always gets worked up about everything; Fam **il n'y a pas de quoi s'en faire un m.** it's not worth getting worked up about, it's no big deal; **personne au m. ne me fera changer d'avis** no one in the world will make me change my mind; **un des seuls êtres en ce m. qui ...** one of the few people in the world who ...; **les meilleurs amis du m.** the best friends in the world; **vieux comme le m.** (as) old as the hills; **depuis que le m. est m.** since time began, since the beginning of time; **elle a volé à la face du m.** she stole things right under everybody's nose; Fig **c'est le m. à l'envers** the world's gone mad, the whole world's topsy-turvy; **le bout du m.** the ends of the earth; **ils habitent au bout du m.** they live at the back of beyond; Fig Fam **ce n'est pas le bout du m.!** (c'est faisable) it's not the end of the world!, it's no big deal!; Fig Fam **c'est le bout du m. s'il me faut deux jours pour terminer ce travail** I'll finish the job in two days at the outside or at the very most; **il faut de tout pour faire un m.** it takes all sorts (to make a world); **ainsi va le m.** it's the way of the world; **refaire le m.** to put the world to rights; Iron **tout est pour le mieux dans le meilleur des mondes** everything is for the best in the best of all possible worlds; **l'autre m.** the next world; **il vit dans un autre m.** he lives in another world; **elle est dans son m.** she's in her own little world; **en ce bas m.** here on earth

2 (milieu) world; **le m. de la haute finance** the world of high finance; **je ne suis pas de leur m.** I'm not in their set or crowd; **le (beau) m.** (fashionable) society, Fam the glitterati; **le grand m.** high society; **aller (beaucoup) dans le m.** to go out a great deal, to move in fashionable circles; **homme du m.** society man; Iron **embarquez-moi tout ce joli m. dans le panier à salade** throw this bunch or crew into the back of the van

3 (gens) people; **tout le m.** everybody, everyone; **il y a du m.** (le lieu n'est pas désert) there are some people; (il y a foule) there are a lot of people; très Fam **il y a du m. au balcon** she's well-endowed; **il y a trop de m.** it's too crowded, there are too many people; **peu de m., pas grand m.** not many people, not a large crowd; **avoir du m. à dîner** to have people to dinner; **tu te moques du m.?** je te demande d'arriver à 9 h et ... what do you take me for? I asked you to be here by 9 o'clock and ...; Fam **les politiciens se fichent vraiment du m.** politicians really must think we're stupid; très Fam **je n'aime pas qu'on se foute du m.! quand on me dit une chose un jour ...** I don't like being taken for a bloody idiot! if I'm told one thing one day ...; **il connaît son m.** he knows the people he has to deal with; **comment va tout votre m.?** how is your or the family?

4 Arch (domestiques) servants, men, hands **5** (vie séculière) **se retirer du m.** to withdraw from the world

mondial, -iale, -iaux, -iales [mɔ̃djal, -jo] ADJ (crise, conflit, problème, ampleur) worldwide, global; **à l'échelle mondiale** on a world(wide) scale, on a global scale; **la première/seconde guerre mondiale** the First/Second World War, World War One/Two ▪ NM Ftbl **le M.** the World Cup

mondialement [mɔ̃djalmɑ̃] ADV throughout the world, universally; **m. reconnu pour son génie** known throughout the world or universally for his genius; **m. célébré** world-famous, celebrated throughout the world

mondialisation [mɔ̃djalizasjɔ̃] NF globalization; **la m. libérale** liberal globalization

mondialiser [mɔ̃djalize] VT to globalize ▪ VPR **se mondialiser** to become globalized; **la crise s'est rapidement mondialisée** the crisis has rapidly taken on an international dimension

mondovision [mɔ̃dovizjɔ̃] NF TV world television

monégasque [mɔnegask] ADJ Monacan, Monegasque ▪ N **M.** Monacan, Monegasque

monème [mɔnɛm] NM Ling moneme

MONEP [mɔnɛp] NM (abrév **marché des options négociables de Paris**) MONEP

monétaire [mɔnetɛr] ADJ (unité, système, questions) monetary; **quelle est l'unité m. du Pérou?** what is the currency of Peru?; **marché m.** money market; **masse m.** money supply; UE **le serpent m.** the (currency) snake

monétarisme [mɔnetarism] NM Écon monetarism

monétariste [mɔnetarist] ADJ, N Écon monetarist

Monétique® [mɔnetik] NF Fin electronic money, e-money; Banque electronic banking

monétisation [mɔnetizasjɔ̃] NF Écon monetization

monétiser [mɔnetize] VT Écon to monetize

mongol, -ole [mɔ̃gɔl] ADJ **1** (de Mongolie) Mongol, Mongolian **2** Fam Péj moronic ▪ NM Ling Mongolian ▪ N **1** Géog **M.** Mongol, Mongolian **2** Fam Péj moron

Mongolie [mɔ̃gɔli] NF Mongolia

mongolien, -ienne [mɔ̃gɔljɛ̃, -jɛn] Méd ADJ **bébé m.** Down's syndrome baby, Vieilli mongol baby ▪ N (bébé) Down's syndrome baby, Vieilli mongol (baby); (personne) person with Down's syndrome, Vieilli mongol

mongolique [mɔ̃gɔlik] ADJ Mongol(ian)

mongolisme [mɔ̃gɔlism] NM Méd Down's syndrome, Vieilli mongolism

mongoloïde [mɔ̃gɔlɔid] Méd ADJ (traits) mongoloid; (individu) affected by Down's syndrome ▪ N Vieilli mongoloid

moniteur, -trice [mɔnitœr, -tris] N **1** Sport instructor, f instructress, coach; **m. d'auto-école/de ski** driving/ski instructor **2** (dans une colonie de vacances) assistant, Am (camp) counselor ▪ NM Tech, Méd, TV monitor; Ordinat (écran) display unit; Méd **m. cardiaque** cardiac or heart monitor; Ordinat **m. SVGA** SVGA monitor; Ordinat **m. basse radiation** low-radiation monitor; **m. couleur** colour monitor; Ordinat **m. pleine page** A4 monitor; **m. à cristaux liquides** liquid crystal monitor; Ordinat **m. à tube cathodique** cathode ray tube monitor; **m. à écran plat** flat screen monitor

monitorage [mɔnitɔraʒ] NM monitoring; **écran de m.** monitor

monitorat [mɔnitɔra] NM (fonction) instructorship; (période de formation) instructor training; **m. sportif** sports instruction

monitoring [mɔnitɔriŋ] NM monitoring

monnaie [mɔnɛ] NF **1** Fin (argent) money; (d'un pays) currency; **pièce de m.** coin; **m. électronique** electronic money, e-money; **m. légale** legal tender; **m. scripturale** bank money, deposit money; **fausse m.** counterfeit money; **frapper la m., battre m.** to coin or mint money; **(l'hôtel de) la M.** = the French Mint, Br ≃ the Royal Mint; **m. de papier** paper money; **m. de compte (convertible)** (convertible) money of account; UE **m. commune** common currency; **m. faible** soft currency; **m. fiduciaire** fiduciary money or issue, paper money, Am fiat money; **m. forte** hard currency; **m. de réserve** reserve currency; **m. unique** single currency; Fam **m. de singe** worthless currency; Fam **c'est de la m. de singe!** it's worthless!; Fam **payer qn en m. de singe** to fob sb off, to let sb whistle for his/her money; **c'est m. courante dans ce milieu** it's common in these circles **2** (pièces etc) change; **petite m.** small change; **vous auriez de la m. pour le parcmètre?** do you have some change for the parking meter?; **vous auriez la m. de cent euros?** could you give me change for a hundred-euro note, could you change a hundred-euro note for me?; **faire de la m.** to get some change; **pourriez-vous me faire de la m.?** could you give me some change?; **faire la m. de 50 euros** to get change for a 50-euro note; (du commerçant) to give change for a 50-euro note; Fig **rendre à qn la m. de sa pièce** to pay sb back in his/her own coin or in kind

> Il faut noter que le nom anglais **money** est un faux ami. Il signifie **argent**.

monnaie-du-pape, pl **monnaies-du-pape** NF Bot honesty

monnayable [mɔnɛjabl] ADJ convertible into money; Fig **cette formation/son expérience est m.** this training/his experience is worth money; **ce diplôme n'est pas m.** this diploma is of no value financially

monnayage [mɔnɛjaʒ] NM minting, coining

monnayer [mɔnɛje] (je monnaye, je monnaie; je monnayerai, je monnaierai) VT **1** (argent) to coin, to mint **2** Fig (son influence, son talent etc) to capitalize on, to cash in on; **il refusa de m. son silence** he refused to put a price on his silence ▪ VPR **se monnayer** **ça se monnaye** there's money to be made out of it, there's money in it; **je veux bien faire ce que vous me demandez mais ça se monnaye** I'm happy to do what you ask, but it'll cost you; **ici tout se monnaye** money can buy (you) anything here, everything here has its price

monnayeur [mɔnɛjœr] NM coiner, minter; **faux m.** counterfeiter

mono¹ [mɔno] ADJ INV Fam (disque) mono; **en m.** in mono

mono² N Fam = **moniteur**

monoacide [mɔnoasid] ADJ Chimie monoacid(ic)

monobloc [mɔnoblɔk] ADJ INV (cylindres, châssis) made in one piece, cast solid

monocaméra [mɔnokamera] NF single camera

monocaméral, -ale, -aux, -ales [mɔnokameral, -o] ADJ Pol unicameral

monocamérisme [mɔnokamerism], **monocaméralisme** [mɔnokameralism] NM Pol unicameralism

monochrome [mɔnokrom] ADJ mono-chrome; *Ordinat* **écran m.** monochrome screen
  NM *Beaux-Arts* monochrome

monochromie [mɔnokromi] NF monochromaticity

monocle [mɔnɔkl] NM monocle

monocoque [mɔnokɔk] ADJ **avion m.** monocoque; **carrosserie m.** *(de voiture)* monocoque body; **bateau m.** monohull
  NM *(bateau)* monohull

monocorde [mɔnokɔrd] ADJ 1 *Mus (instrument)* single-stringed 2 *(son, ton, voix)* monotonous
  NM monochord

monocorps [mɔnokɔr] ADJ *Aut* monobox

monocotylédone [mɔnokɔtiledɔn] NF *Bot* monocotyledon

monoculaire [mɔnokylɛr] ADJ *(jumelles, vision, microscope)* monocular; **cécité m.** blindness in one eye

monoculture [mɔnokyltyr] NF *Agr* monoculture

monocycle [mɔnosikl] NM unicycle, monocycle

monocylindre [mɔnosilɛ̃dr] NM *Aut* single-cylinder engine

monocylindrique [mɔnosilɛ̃drik] ADJ *Aut (moteur)* single-cylinder

monoéthylèneglycol [mɔnoetilɛnglikɔl] NM monoethylene glycol

monogame [mɔnɔgam] ADJ monogamous

monogamie [mɔnɔgami] NF monogamy

monogamique [mɔnɔgamik] ADJ monogamous

monogramme [mɔnɔgram] NM monogram

monographie [mɔnɔgrafi] NF monograph

monoï [mɔnɔj] NM scented coconut oil

mono-insaturé, *pl* **mono-insaturés** [mɔnoɛ̃satyre] ADJ *(lipide)* mono-unsaturated

monokini [mɔnokini] NM monokini; **faire du m.** to wear a monokini, to go topless

monolingue [mɔnolɛ̃g] ADJ monolingual

monolinguisme [mɔnolɛ̃gɥism] NM monolingualism

monolithe [mɔnolit] ADJ monolithic
  NM monolith

monolithique [mɔnolitik] ADJ monolithic; *Fig (organisation, parti)* monolithic; *(caractère, personne)* uncompromising

monologue [mɔnolɔg] NM monologue; *Théâtre (de Hamlet etc)* soliloquy, monologue; **m. intérieur** interior monologue

monologuer [mɔnolɔge] VI *(parler seul)* to talk to oneself; *Théâtre* to soliloquize, to talk to oneself

monomaniaque [mɔnomanjak] ADJ monomaniacal
  N monomaniac

monomanie [mɔnomani] NF monomania

monôme [mɔnom] NM *Math* monomial, single term

monométallisme [mɔnometalism] NM *Fin* monometallism

monomoteur [mɔnomotœr] ADJ M single-engined
  NM single-engined aircraft

mononucléose [mɔnonykleoz] NF *Méd* mononucleosis; **m. infectieuse** glandular fever, *Spéc* infectious mononucleosis

monoparental, -ale, -aux, -ales [mɔnoparãtal, -o] ADJ *(famille)* single-parent, one-parent

monoparentalité [mɔnoparãtalite] NF single parenthood

monophasé [mɔnofɑze] *Élec* ADJ *(courant)* single-phase
  NM single-phase current

monophonique [mɔnofɔnik] ADJ monaural

monoplace [mɔnoplas] ADJ *(avion, voiture)* single-seater
  NM OU F *Aut* single-seater (car)
  NM *Aviat* single-seater (plane)

monoplan [mɔnoplã] NM *Aviat* monoplane

monopole [mɔnopɔl] NM monopoly; **m. d'État** State monopoly; *Écon* **m. d'achat** buyer's monopoly; **m. bilatéral** bilateral monopoly; **m. d'émission** issuing monopoly; **m. d'exploitation** operating monopoly; **m. de fabrication** manufacturing monopoly; **m. naturel** natural monopoly; **m. de vente** sales monopoly; **avoir le m. de qch** *Écon* to have the monopoly of sth, to have a monopoly on sth; *Fig* to have a monopoly on sth; **exercer un m. sur un secteur** to monopolize a sector

monopoleur [mɔnopolœr] NM monopolist

monopolisateur, -trice [mɔnopolizatœr, -tris] N monopolizer, monopolist
  ADJ monopolizing

monopolisation [mɔnopolizasjɔ̃] NF monopolization

monopoliser [mɔnopolize] VT to monopolize; **m. la parole** not to let anyone else speak

monoposte [mɔnopɔst] NM *Ordinat* stand-alone

monorail [mɔnorɑj] ADJ INV monorail
  NM monorail

monoski [mɔnoski] NM *Sport* monoski; **faire du m.** to monoski

monospace [mɔnospas] NM *Aut* people carrier

monosyllabe [mɔnosilab] ADJ monosyllabic
  NM monosyllable

monosyllabique [mɔnosilabik] ADJ monosyllabic

mono-tâche ADJ INV *Ordinat* single-tasking

monothéisme [mɔnoteism] NM monotheism

monothéiste [mɔnoteist] ADJ monotheistic
  N monotheist

monotone [mɔnotɔn] ADJ monotonous; *(existence)* monotonous, humdrum

monotonie [mɔnotɔni] NF monotony; **rompre la m.** to break the monotony

Monotype® [mɔnotip] NF *Typ* Monotype® (machine)

monovalent [mɔnovalã] ADJ *Chimie* monovalent, univalent

monoxyde [mɔnoksid] NM **m. de carbone** carbon monoxide

monseigneur [mɔ̃sɛɲœr] NM 1 *pl* **nosseigneurs** *ou* **messeigneurs** *(référence à un prince)* His Royal Highness; *(à un cardinal)* His Eminence; *(à un duc, archevêque)* His Grace; *(à un évêque)* His Lordship; **m. l'évêque de …** the Lord Bishop of … 2 *pl* **messeigneurs** *(en s'adressant au prince)* Your Royal Highness; *(au cardinal)* Your Eminence; *(au duc, à l'archevêque)* Your Grace; *(à l'évêque)* My Lord (Bishop), Your Lordship

monsieur [məsjø] *pl* **messieurs** [mesjø] NM 1 **M. Robert Marceau** Mr Robert Marceau; **Messieurs Marceau et Cie** Messrs Marceau and Co; **m. le duc/le comte de Montignac** the Duke/the Earl of Montignac; **m. le duc/le comte est servi** dinner is served, your Grace/my Lord

  2 *Vieilli (à un petit garçon)* **M. Robert** Master Robert

3 *Fml (utilisé seul)* **voici le chapeau de m.** *(en s'adressant à lui)* here's your hat, sir; *(sans s'adresser à lui)* here's the gentleman's hat; *(à quelqu'un qui s'appelle Martin etc)* here's Mr Martin's/*etc* hat; **m. n'est pas là** Mr Martin/*etc* is out; **m. a sonné?** you rang, sir?

4 *(à un homme)* sir; *(à un duc)* sir, Your Grace; *(à un comte)* sir, Your Lordship; **au revoir, m.** goodbye, *Fml* goodbye sir; **bonsoir, messieurs** goodnight, gentlemen; **que prendront ces messieurs?** what will you have, gentlemen?; **Mesdames, Messieurs** ladies and gentlemen; **bonjour, Messieurs-Dames!** good morning/afternoon!

5 *(dans une lettre)* **M.** *(à un étranger)* (Dear) Sir; **M. et cher Confrère, M. et cher Collègue** *(qui s'appelle Martin etc)* Dear Mr Martin/*etc*; **Cher M.** *(à une connaissance qui s'appelle Martin etc)* Dear Mr Martin/*etc*

6 *(sur enveloppe)* **M. T. Marceau** Mr T. Marceau, *Fml* T. Marceau Esq

7 *(homme)* (gentle)man; *Enf* **dis bonjour au m.** say hello (to the gentleman); **il y a un m. qui veut vous parler** there is a (gentle)man here who wants to speak to you; **c'est un vilain m.** he's a nasty piece of work

▸▸ **m. je-sais-tout** Mr Know(-it)-all; **il va encore nous jouer son m. je-sais-tout** here he goes again, the know(-it)-all; *TV etc* **M. Météo** the weatherman; **m. tout-le-monde** the man in the street, *Am* Joe Public, Joe Blow

monstre [mɔ̃str] NM *Myth, Fig* monster; **les monstres marins** the monsters of the deep; *Fig* **m. d'ingratitude/d'égoïsme** ungrateful/selfish monster *or* brute, *Fml* monster of ingratitude/selfishness; *Fig Fam* **petit m.!** you little monster *or* horror!
  ADJ *Fam* huge, colossal, mammoth; *(succès)* enormous, huge, wild; **un travail m.** a mammoth task; **j'ai eu une chance m.** I was incredibly lucky; **elle avait une trouille m.** she was scared stiff *or* to death
  ▸▸ **m. sacré** *(du cinéma, de la danse etc)* giant, idol

monstrueusement [mɔ̃stryøzmã] ADV *(laid, gros)* monstrously, hideously; *(égoïste)* horrendously, outrageously

monstrueux, -euse [mɔ̃stryø, -øz] ADJ 1 *(malformé)* monstrous, deformed 2 *(énorme) (erreur, gaffe)* huge, colossal; *(prix)* extortionate, exorbitant 3 *(scandaleux)* monstrous; **elle est d'un égoïsme m.** she is a selfish monster

monstruosité [mɔ̃stryozite] NF 1 *(difformité)* monstrosity 2 *(de crime, criminel etc)* monstrousness, monstrosity

mont [mɔ̃] NM 1 mountain; **le m. Sinaï/Everest** Mount Sinai/Everest; **le m. des Oliviers** the Mount of Olives; **le m. Blanc** Mont Blanc; *Fig* **par monts et par vaux** up hill and down dale; *Fig* **être toujours par monts et par vaux** to be always on the move; *Fig* **promettre monts et merveilles à qn** to promise sb the earth *or* the moon 2 *Anat* **m. de Vénus** mons veneris

montage [mɔ̃taʒ] NM 1 *(pose) (de bijou)* setting, mounting; *(de pneu)* fitting (on); *(d'appareil, de meuble etc)* assembling, assembly; *(d'atelier etc)* fitting out; *(de porte)* hanging; *Ind* **chaîne de m.** assembly line; *Ind* **atelier de m.** assembly shop; *Tech* **m. serré** push fit; *Tech* **m. à la presse** press fit 2 *Cin, Radio, TV* editing; *Phot, Cin, TV (image truquée)* montage; *Typ* make-up; **couper qch au m.** to edit sth out; **m. original** edited master; **m. vidéo** video(tape) editing, tape editing; *Cin, TV, Radio* **m. sonore** sound editing; *(avec truquage)* sound montage; *Cin* **salle de m.** cutting room; *Cin* **film de m.** film montage 3 *Écon* **le m. financier d'un projet** the financial arrangements for a project; **le m. financier a été difficile** it wasn't easy getting the money together; **le m. financier du projet**

sera le suivant money for the project will be provided as follows **4** *Élec* connecting (up), wiring (up) **5** *(de matériaux de construction etc)* taking up, carrying up

montagnard, -arde [mɔ̃taɲar, -ard] **ADJ** mountain, highland

N 1 *(habitant)* mountain dweller, highlander **2** *Hist* member of the Mountain

montagne [mɔ̃taɲ] **NF 1** mountain; *(région)* mountains, mountain region; **la haute m.** the high mountains; **la moyenne m.** the uplands; **passer ses vacances à la m.** to spend one's holiday in the mountains; **aimer les paysages de montagnes** to like mountain scenery; *Fig* **une m. de choux/repassage** a huge pile of cabbages/ironing; *Fig* **se faire une m. de qch** to make a great song and dance *or* a great to-do about sth; **tu t'en fais une m.!** you're making a mountain out of a molehill!; *Fig* **c'est la m. qui accouche d'une souris** what a lot of fuss for nothing, *Litt* the mountain laboured and brought forth a mouse

2 *Sport* **faire de la m.** *(alpinisme)* to go mountain climbing; *(randonnée)* to go hill walking; **sports de m.** mountain sports

3 *Hist* **la M.** the Mountain

► ► *UE* **m. de beurre** butter mountain; **montagnes russes** *(à la foire)* big dipper, roller coaster; *Fig* **faire des montagnes russes** *(d'une route)* to switchback; **m. à vaches** hills

montagneux, -euse [mɔ̃taɲø, -øz] **ADJ** mountainous

montant [mɔ̃tɑ̃] **ADJ** rising; **chemin m.** uphill road; **marée montante** rising tide, flood tide; **col m.** high *or* stand-up collar; *Rail* **train/quai m.** up train/platform; **m. garde montante** new guard, relieving guard

NM 1 *(somme)* amount, sum; **cinq versements d'un m. de 500 euros** five payments of 500 euros (each); **j'ignore le m. de mes dettes** I don't know what my debts amount to; **m. brut/total** gross/total (amount); **m. du retour net** net return; **m. exonéré de TVA** VAT exempt amount; **m. forfaitaire** lump sum; **m. maximum/minimum** maximum/minimum (amount); **m. net** net (total); **m. prévisionnel des ventes** forecast sales level; *UE, Écon* **montants compensatoires (monétaires)** subsidies, *Spéc* compensatory amounts; **m. à reporter** amount brought forward

2 *(partie verticale)* *(d'échelle)* upright; *(de lit)* post; *(de fenêtre)* jamb; *(de portail)* post; *(de bride)* cheek strap; *Sport* **les montants** *(de but)* the goalposts; *Aut* **m. de pare-brise** screen pillar, windscreen pillar, A-pillar; *Aut* **m. de porte** door pillar, B-pillar

mont-de-piété, *pl* **monts-de-piété NM** *Arch* pawnshop; **mettre qch au m.** to pawn sth

monte [mɔ̃t] **NF 1** *Courses de chevaux (action)* mounting; **jockey qui a eu trois montes dans la journée** jockey who has ridden three times *or* who has had three mounts *or* rides in the day **2** *(façon de monter à cheval)* horsemanship; **m. à l'obstacle** jumping **3** *(accouplement)* covering; *(époque de l'accouplement)* breeding *or* mating season

monté [mɔ̃te] **ADJ 1** *(à cheval) (police, troupes)* mounted **2** *(bijou)* set, mounted; **m. sur or** gold-mounted; **médaille montée en pendentif** medal mounted as a pendant; **photographies non montées** unmounted photographs **3** *(approvisionné)* **cave/boutique bien montée** well-stocked cellar/shop; **être bien monté en vaisselle** to be well supplied with crockery **4** *Fam* **il était m.** *ou* **il avait la tête montée contre elle** he had it in for her; **il est drôlement m., ce matin, le patron!** the boss is really worked up *or* wound

up this morning! **5** *Vulg* **bien m.** *(homme)* well-hung

monte-charge, *pl* **monte-charges NM** hoist, *Br* goods lift, *Br* service lift, *Am* goods elevator

montée [mɔ̃te] **NF 1** *(mouvement)* rise, rising; *(ascension)* ascent; *Fig (du nationalisme, fascisme etc)* rise, growth, increase; **pendant la m. du col** as he was/we were/*etc* going uphill; *Tech etc* **tuyau de m.** uptake pipe, riser; **m. des eaux** *(dans un réservoir)* inflow; **la m. des prix** the rise in prices, rising prices; *Physiol* **m. de lait** onset of lactation **2** *Aut, Aviat* **essai de m.** climbing test; **vitesse en m.** *Aviat* climbing speed; *Aut, Rail* speed on a gradient **3** *(côte) (sur une route)* slope, hill; **en haut de la m.** at the top of the slope *or* hill; **il y a une méchante m. avant d'arriver chez lui** there's a stiff climb before you reach his house

monte-en-l'air NM INV *Fam Vieilli* cat burglar

monte-plats NM INV *(au restaurant)* dumbwaiter

MONTER [mɔ̃te]

VI = to go up **1, 4, 5** = to climb on/in **1, 2, 4** = to get on/in **2** = to rise **3–5**	
VT = to go up **1** = to bring up **2** = to set **3** = to fit **3** = to set up **3** = to edit **3** = to ride **5**	
VPR to come to *(se monter à)* **1** = to equip oneself **2** = to be ridden **4**	

VI *(aux souvent* **être,** *parfois* **avoir)* 1** *(se déplacer vers le haut)* to go up, to climb (up); *(vu d'en haut)* to come up; *(en haut de l'escalier)* to go up(stairs); *(vu d'en haut)* to come up(stairs); *(d'un oiseau)* to soar, to fly up; *(d'un avion)* to climb, to fly up; **m. à** *ou* **sur un arbre/une échelle** to climb (up) (into) a tree/(on to) a ladder; **m. en haut d'une colline** to climb *or* go up (right) to the top of a hill; **m. en courant/en rampant** to run/crawl up; **m. se coucher** to go (up) to bed; **faire m. qn** to show sb up; **montez chez moi** come up to my place; **après ses études, il est monté à Paris** after college, he moved up to Paris; **elle monte souvent à Paris pour voir sa sœur** she often goes up to Paris to see her sister; *Aut* **m. en régime** to rev; *Mil* **m. en ligne** to go to the front (line); **m. à l'assaut** to go into the attack; *Tennis* **m. au filet** to come up/go up to the net; *Naut* **faire m. tous les hommes** to order all hands on deck

2 *(pour s'installer etc)* to climb *or* get on/in; *(dans le train, l'autobus etc)* to get on; **où êtes-vous monté?** where did you get on?; **m. sur une chaise** to stand *or* get on a chair; **m. en chaire** to ascend the pulpit; **m. à cheval** to get on a horse, to mount (a horse); *(faire de l'équitation)* to ride, to go riding; **montez-vous (à cheval)?** do you ride?; *Fam* **m. sur ses grands chevaux** to get on one's high horse; **m. à** *ou* **en bicyclette** to ride a bicycle; **m. en voiture** to get into a car; *Naut, Aviat* **m. à bord** to go on board, to board; **faire m. qn (en voiture) avec soi** to give sb a lift; *Théâtre* **m. sur les planches** to go on the stage

3 *(d'un ballon, du soleil etc)* to rise; *(d'un prix, du baromètre etc)* to rise, to go up; *(de la marée)* to rise, to come in; **les frais montent** the costs are mounting (up); **la somme monte à cent euros** the total amounts to *or* comes to a hundred euros; **m. en flèche** *(de prix)* to soar; **faire m. les prix** to put up *or* increase *or* raise prices; **empêcher les prix de m.** to keep prices down, to stop prices rising; **le sang lui monta à la tête** the blood rushed to his head; **faire m. les larmes aux yeux de qn** to bring tears to sb's eyes

4 *(d'une route etc)* to climb, to go up, to rise;

la rue va en montant the street climbs

5 m. dans l'estime de qn to go up *or* rise in sb's estimation; **faire m. qn dans l'estime de qn** to raise sb in sb's estimation

VT *(aux* **avoir) 1** *(colline, escalier etc)* to go/come up, to climb (up); **m. la rue en courant** to run up the street

2 *(porter)* to bring up; *(vu d'en bas)* to take up; **m. du vin de la cave** to fetch *or* bring wine up from the cellar; **m. le courrier** to bring the post; **m. le son** to turn up the volume; *Fig* **m. (la tête à) qn contre qn** to set sb against sb

3 *(bijou)* to set, to mount; *(photo, hameçon etc)* to mount; *(pneu)* to fit (on); *(appareil, machine)* to set up, to erect; *(porte)* to hang; *(atelier)* to fit out, to equip; *Théâtre (scène)* to set; *(pièce)* to put on, to stage, to produce; *Cin (film)* to edit; *Couture (vêtement)* to make up; *(en imprimerie)* to paste up; **m. une entreprise** to set up a business; **m. un magasin** to set up *or* open a shop; **elle commence à m. son trousseau** she's beginning to put her trousseau together; **m. un complot/un coup** to hatch a plot/plan a job; *Fam* **m. le coup à qn** to take sb in, to take sb for a ride; *Fam* **m. qch en épingle** to blow sth up out of all proportion; *Tricot* **m. les mailles** to cast on (the stitches)

4 *Mil etc* **m. la garde** to mount *or* keep guard **5** *(cheval)* to ride

6 *Élec* to connect up, to wire (up)

VPR se monter 1 *(d'un prix etc)* **se m. à** to come to, to add up to, to amount to; **à combien se monte tout cela?** how much does all this come to *or* add up to *or* amount to?

2 *(s'équiper)* to equip oneself, to fit oneself out (**en** with); **se m. en vaisselle** to supply oneself with crockery; **se m. en affaires** to set up (in business) on one's own

3 *Fam (s'énerver)* to get worked up *or* wound up; **elle s'est montée contre lui** she's got it in for him

4 *(d'un cheval)* to be ridden; **Flicka se monte facilement** Flicka is easy to ride

---

monteur, -euse [mɔ̃tœr, -øz] **N** *(de bijoux)* setter; *(d'images)* mounter; *Cin* editor; *Tech* fitter; *Aut* engine fitter; *TV, Cin* **m. vidéo** videotape editor, VT editor

Montevideo [mɔ̃tevideo] **N** Montevideo

montgolfière [mɔ̃gɔlfjɛr] **NF** hot-air balloon

monticule [mɔ̃tikyl] **NM** *(petite colline)* hillock, mound; *(plus petit)* hummock; *Can Baseball* mound

montoir [mɔ̃twar] **NM** *(de cheval)* mounting block; **côté (du) m.** nearside; **côté hors (du) m.** offside

montrable [mɔ̃trabl] **ADJ** presentable, fit to be seen

montre [mɔ̃tr] **NF 1** *(instrument)* watch; **m. (de poignet)** (wrist)watch; **m. de plongée** diver's watch; **m. à quartz** quartz watch; **à ma m., il est midi** by my watch, it's twelve o'clock; **cela lui a pris dix minutes m. en main** it took him exactly ten minutes; **course contre la m.** race against the clock; *Fig* **on est dans une course contre la m.** we're racing against time *or* the clock; *Fig* **jouer la m.** to play for time **2** *(preuve)* show, display; **faire m. de patience/d'un grand courage** to show *or* display patience/great courage; *Litt* **faire qch pour la m.** to do sth merely for show **3** *(vitrine)* shop window, display window; *(dans meuble)* showcase; **mettre qch en m.** to put sth in the window *or* on show *or* on display

Montréal [mɔ̃real] **N** Montreal

montréalais, -aise [mɔ̃realɛ, -ɛz] **ADJ** (of/from) Montreal

N M. Montrealer

montre-bracelet, *pl* **montres-bracelets** NF wristwatch

montrer [mɔ̃tre] VT *(révéler)* to show; *(désigner)* to show, to point out; *(faire preuve de)* to show, to display; **elle nous a montré où nous allions dormir** she showed us *or* pointed out to us where we were to sleep; **il a montré un grand courage** he showed *or* displayed great courage; **il faudrait que tu montres ta fille/cette vilaine blessure à un médecin** you should let a doctor have a look at *or* see your daughter/that nasty wound; **une robe décolletée qui montre les épaules** a low-cut dress which leaves the shoulders bare *or* which exposes the shoulders; **elle a montré une jolie paire de jambes en s'asseyant** she showed a pretty pair of legs as she sat down; **elle adore m. ses charmes** she loves showing off *or* displaying her charms; **il n'y montre jamais le nez** he never shows his face there; **m. qn/qch du doigt** to point sb/sth out, to point to *or* at sb/sth; *Fig* to point the finger at sb/sth; **m. le chemin à qn** to show sb the way; **m. la ville à qn** to show sb round the town; **il a réussi à ne pas m. qu'il était au courant** he managed not to show that he knew about it; **cela te montre qu'il faut être prudent** that (just) shows that you have to be careful; **montre-lui la manière de le faire** *ou* **comment le faire** show him how to do it *or* how it's done; **peux-tu me m. comment ça marche?** can you show me how it works?; **m. le poing à qn** to shake one's fist at sb; **m. les dents** to show *or* bare one's teeth; **m. la porte à qn** to show sb the door

VPR **se montrer 1** *(se présenter)* to show oneself, to appear; **il n'ose plus se m.** he doesn't dare show himself *or* his face **2** *(se révéler)* **il s'est montré très gentil/courageux** he was very kind/courageous, he showed great kindness/courage; **il s'est montré incapable de faire face à la situation** he proved (to be) *or* he was incapable of facing up to the situation

montreur, -euse [mɔ̃trœr, -øz] N *(dans une foire etc) (de bêtes sauvages)* exhibitor; **m. d'ours** bear leader; **m. de marionnettes** puppeteer

montueux, -euse [mɔ̃tɥø, -øz] ADJ hilly

monture [mɔ̃tyr] NF **1** *(de bijou)* setting; *(de scie, parapluie, lunettes etc)* frame; *(de fusil, revolver)* stock; *(d'épée)* guard; **lunettes sans m.** rimless spectacles **2** *(cheval etc)* mount

monument [mɔnymɑ̃] NM **1** *(statue etc)* monument, memorial; **élever un m. à la mémoire de qn** to erect a monument in memory of *or* to the memory of sb; **m. funéraire** monument *(over a tomb)*; **m. aux morts** war memorial **2** *(édifice public)* monument; **m. historique** historic monument *or* building; **être classé m. historique** to be a listed building **3** *Fam* **cette armoire est un m.** this cupboard's enormous; **être un m. d'absurdité** to be monumentally absurd **4** *Fig (livre, film)* masterpiece

monumental, -ale, -aux, -ales [mɔnymɑ̃tal, -o] ADJ monumental; **une erreur monumentale** a monumental blunder; **elle est d'une bêtise monumentale** she's monumentally stupid

mooniste [munist] N *(membre de la secte Moon)* moonie

mope [mɔp] NF *Can (balai)* mop

moque [mɔk] NF **1** *Naut* cringle **2** *Suisse Fam (morve)* snot

moquer [mɔke] VT *Arch* to mock
VPR **se moquer 1** *(railler)* **se m. de qn/qch** to make fun of *or* laugh at *or* poke fun at *or* mock sb/sth; **vous vous moquez?** what are you laughing at?, what's so funny? **2** *(ne pas faire cas)* **se m. de qch** not to care *or* not to

give a damn about sth; **je me moque de ce que les gens pensent** I don't care *or* I don't give a damn what people think; **je m'en moque** I don't care, I don't give a damn; **elle s'en moque éperdument** she doesn't give a damn, she just couldn't care less; **il se moque du tiers comme du quart** he doesn't care *or* give a damn about anybody or anything; *Fam* **je m'en moque comme de l'an quarante** *ou* **comme de ma première chemise** I don't give a damn, I don't care two hoots *or* a tinker's cuss **3** *(tromper)* **vous vous moquez** *ou* **c'est se m. du monde!** you've got a nerve!

moquerie [mɔkri] NF mockery, jeering, ridicule; **leurs moqueries continuelles** their constant mockery *or* jeering *or* ridicule

moquette [mɔkɛt] NF **1** fitted carpet, wall-to-wall carpet; **faire poser une** *ou* **de la m.** to have a (fitted *or* wall-to-wall) carpet laid **2** *Tex* moquette

moquetter [mɔkete] VT to carpet

moqueur, -euse [mɔkœr, -øz] ADJ **1** *(remarque, rires etc)* mocking, jeering, derisive **2** *(personne)* given to mockery
N *(personne)* mocker, scoffer
NM *(oiseau)* mockingbird

moqueusement [mɔkøzmɑ̃] ADV mockingly

moraillon [mɔrajɔ̃] NM *(de serrure)* hasp

moraine [mɔrɛn] NF *Géol* moraine

moral, -ale, -aux, -ales [mɔral, -o] ADJ **1** *(conduite, sens, certitude, courage, victoire)* moral; **cette histoire n'est pas morale** this is not a very edifying story; **facultés morales** ability to distinguish between right and wrong; **je me fais une obligation morale de le faire** I'm under a moral obligation *or* I'm morally obliged to do it **2** *Jur* **personne morale** legal entity, corporation
NM **morale**; **c'est bon pour le m.** it's good for morale; **le m. est bas** morale is low; **son m. est bas** his spirits are low, he's in low spirits; **je n'ai pas le m. en ce moment** I'm feeling down just now; **avoir le m. au beau fixe** to be in fine spirits; **elle a un m. d'acier** nothing gets her down; *Fam* **avoir le m. à zéro** to feel down in the dumps; **remonter le m. de** *ou* **à qn** to raise sb's spirits, to cheer sb up; **il se marie avec elle? il a le m.!** he's marrying her? he's got guts *or* he's a brave chap!

morale [mɔral] NF **1** *(bien)* morals, morality; **contraire/conforme à la m.** immoral/moral **2** *(règles)* morality, ethics; **tu ne vas quand même pas me faire une leçon de m.?** you're not going to start lecturing me, are you now?; **faire la m. à qn** to lecture sb; **adopter une m. d'ascète** to adopt an ascetic philosophy *or* way of life **3** *(d'une histoire)* moral

moralement [mɔralmɑ̃] ADV morally; **m., tu ne peux pas lui faire ça** morally (speaking), you can't do that to him

moralisant [mɔralizɑ̃] ADJ moralizing

moralisateur, -trice [mɔralizatœr, -tris] ADJ **1** *(personne)* moralizing **2** *(principes)* elevating, edifying
N moralizer

moralisation [mɔralizasjɔ̃] NF moralization

moraliser [mɔralize] VI to moralize
VT **1** *(politique, le marché financier etc)* to clean up **2** *(personne)* to lecture

moraliste [mɔralist] ADJ moralistic
N moralist

moralité [mɔralite] NF **1** *(mérite)* morality, (good) moral conduct; **certificat de m.** character reference **2** *(attitude)* morals, morality; **elle est d'une m. douteuse** her morals are dubious, she has dubious morals, she is of dubious morality; **quelqu'un d'une haute m./d'une m. au-dessus de tout soupçon** some one with high/impeccable moral

standards **3** *(d'une histoire)* moral; **m.: rien ne sert de courir, il faut partir à point** the moral of the story is that it's better to start on time than to try to catch up later; **il n'a pris aucune précaution, m.: il est mort** he didn't take any precautions and as a result he's dead **4** *Hist, Littér* morality (play)

morasse [mɔras] NF *Typ (de journal)* brush proof

moratoire [mɔratwar] *Jur* ADJ *(accord etc)* moratory; *(paiement)* delayed by agreement; **intérêts moratoires** interest on overdue payments
NM moratorium

moratorium [mɔratɔrjɔm] NM *Jur* moratorium

morbide [mɔrbid] ADJ morbid

morbidement [mɔrbidmɑ̃] ADV morbidly

morbidité [mɔrbidite] NF morbidness, morbidity

morbier [mɔrbje] NM **1** *(fromage)* Morbier (cheese) **2** *Suisse (horloge)* grandfather clock

morbleu [mɔrblø] INT *Arch* 'sdeath!, zounds!

morce [mɔrs] NF *Suisse (bouchée)* mouthful; **manger une m.** to have a bite to eat

morceau, -eaux [mɔrso] NM **1** *(de nourriture)* piece, bit; **m. de choix** choice morsel; **bas morceaux** *(de viande)* cheap(er) cuts; **aimer les bons morceaux** to like good things (to eat); *Fam* **manger** *ou* **prendre un m.** to have a bite to eat *or* a snack; *Fig Fam* **emporter le m.** to win (the day) *(in deal, court case etc)*; *Fig Fam* **lâcher** *ou* **cracher le m.** to spill the beans **2** *(de savon, tissu, laine, ficelle etc)* piece, bit; *(de papier)* piece, bit, scrap; *(de sucre)* lump; *(de terre)* piece, patch; *Mus* piece; **en morceaux** in pieces; **sucre en morceaux** lump sugar, cube sugar; **mettre qch en morceaux** to pull *or* tear sth to pieces *or* to bits; **il va me mettre en morceaux** he'll tear me limb from limb; **tomber en morceaux** to fall to pieces *or* bits; *Mus* **m. pour trombone** piece for trombone; *Littér* **morceaux choisis** selected passages *or* extracts; **m. d'anthologie** anthology piece; **m. de bravoure** purple passage, purple patch; *Fam* **cette fille, c'est un beau m.** she's a bit of all right, that girl

morceler [mɔrsəle] VT (**je morcelle; je morcellerai**) to divide (up); **m. une propriété** to break up *or* parcel out *or* divide (up) an estate

morcellement [mɔrsɛlmɑ̃] NM division

mordacité [mɔrdasite] NF *Litt (de critique)* mordancy

mordant [mɔrdɑ̃] ADJ *(esprit, ironie, discours)* biting, caustic, scathing, *Fml* mordant; *(remarque, ton)* cutting, caustic, scathing; *(personne)* scathing; **froid m.** biting cold
NM *(d'esprit, d'ironie)* bite, *Litt* mordancy; *(d'analyse)* scathing nature; *(de troupes, d'équipe etc)* keenness; *(d'outil)* bite; *(pour teinture)* mordant; **le m. de son ton** his cutting *or* caustic *or* scathing tone

mordée [mɔrde] NF *Can (bouchée)* bite; **prendre une m. dans qch** to take a bite out of sth, to bite sth

mordicus [mɔrdikys] ADV *Fam* stubbornly, doggedly; **elle l'affirme m.** she's quite stubborn *or* dogged about it

mordieu [mɔrdjø] INT *Arch* 'sdeath!, zounds!

mordillage [mɔrdijaʒ] NM, **mordillement** [mɔrdijmɑ̃] NM nibbling

mordiller [mɔrdije] VT to nibble

mordoré [mɔrdore] ADJ, NM *(couleur)* bronze

mordorer [mɔrdore] VT *Litt* to bronze

mordorure [mɔrdoryr] NF *(couleur)* bronze

mordre [mɔrdr] VT **1** (d'une personne, d'un chien etc) to bite; **m. une pomme** to bite into an apple; **m. qn au bras** to bite sb's arm, to bite sb on the arm; **elle s'est fait m. par un rat** she was bitten by a rat; **approche, je ne vais pas te m.** come here, I won't bite you; **le froid lui mordait les doigts** the cold was nipping or biting his fingers; Fig Fam **m. la poussière** to bite the dust **2** (accrocher) to bite into; **acide qui mord les métaux** acid that eats into metals **3** Beaux-Arts **m. une planche** to etch a plate

VI **1** (d'une personne, d'un chien etc) to bite; **m. dans une pomme** to bite into or take a bite out of an apple; Fig **m. sur qch** to encroach (up)on sth; **la route mord sur mon terrain** the road encroaches on my land; Tennis **m. sur la ligne** to have one's foot (just) over the line; Pêche, Fig **m. à l'appât** ou **à l'hameçon** to rise to or swallow the bait; **le public a bien mordu** the public responded well; Fam **il mord au latin** he's taking to Latin; Pêche **ça mord** I've got a bite; **ça mord?** are they biting? **2** (accrocher) to bite; **lime/ vis qui mord** file/screw that bites or has a good bite; **l'ancre ne mord pas** the anchor won't hold or grip

VPR **se mordre** to bite oneself; **se m. la langue** to bite one's tongue; **se m. la langue d'avoir parlé** to regret bitterly having spoken; **se m. les lèvres pour ne pas rire/pour ne pas hurler** to bite one's lip so as not to laugh/scream; Fig **il s'en mord les doigts** he's kicking himself; **si vous outrepassez mes ordres, vous vous en mordrez les doigts** if you exceed my orders, you'll be sorry or you'll regret it

mordu, -ue [mɔrdy] ADJ bitten; Fig Fam madly in love; Fig Fam **elle est m. de ski/tricot** she's been bitten by the skiing/knitting bug, she's mad on skiing/knitting

N Fam enthusiast; **m. du bridge/du cinéma** bridge/film fanatic or enthusiast

more [mɔr] ADJ, N = **maure**

morelle [mɔrɛl] NF Bot nightshade

moresque [mɔrɛsk] ADJ, NF = **mauresque**

morfal, -ale, -als, -ales [mɔrfal] N Fam greedy-guts, Br Fam gannet; **il a un appétit de m.** he eats like a horse

morfler [mɔrfle] Fam VT **1** (recevoir) to get; **il a morflé une claque dans la tronche** he got a slap in the face **2** (se voir infliger une peine de) to get, to cop

VI **1** (être abîmé) to get smashed up; (être blessé) to get injured **2** (être sévèrement puni) to catch it, Br to cop it

morfondre (se) [sɔmɔrfɔdr] VPR **1** (s'ennuyer) to be bored to death; (être triste) to mope; **la fillette était là à se m. en attendant son père, qui avait déjà deux heures de retard** the little girl was waiting dejectedly for her father, who was already two hours late **2** Can (s'épuiser) to wear oneself out

morfondu [mɔrfɔdy] ADJ gloomy, dejected

morganatique [mɔrganatik] ADJ morganatic

morgue[1] [mɔrg] NF (insolence) pride, haughtiness, arrogance; **regard plein de m.** haughty or arrogant look

morgue[2] NF (dans un hôpital) mortuary, morgue

moribond, -onde [mɔribɔ, -ɔd] ADJ dying, Fml moribund

N dying man, f woman; **les moribonds** the dying

moricaud, -aude [mɔriko, -od] Fam Péj ADJ dark-skinned, dusky, swarthy

N dark-skinned person; (terme raciste) darky, darkie

morigéner [mɔriʒene] VT (je morigène; je morigénerai) to lecture, to take to task, to give a good talking-to

morille [mɔrij] NF Culin morel

morillon [mɔrijɔ] NM **1** (oiseau) tufted duck **2** (pierre précieuse) rough emerald

mormon, -one [mɔrmɔ, -ɔn] ADJ, N Mormon

mormonisme [mɔrmɔnism] NM Mormonism

morne [mɔrn] ADJ (personne, regard) gloomy, glum; (silence) gloomy; (temps, vacances) dismal, dreary, dull; **parler d'un ton m.** to speak drearily or in a dreary voice

mornifle [mɔrnifl] NF Fam clout, slap

morose [mɔroz] ADJ (personne, humeur) morose, sullen, glum; (temps, année) miserable

morosité [mɔrozite] NF (de personne) moroseness, sullenness; (de climat) miserableness; (du paysage) gloominess

Morphée [mɔrfe] N Morpheus; **dans les bras de M.** in the arms of Morpheus

morphème [mɔrfɛm] NM Ling morpheme

morphine [mɔrfin] NF morphine, morphia

morphing [mɔrfiŋ] NM Cin morphing

morphinisme [mɔrfinism] NM Méd morphinism

morphinomane [mɔrfinɔman] ADJ addicted to morphine

N morphine addict

morphinomanie [mɔrfinɔmani] NF addiction to morphine

morphologie [mɔrfɔlɔʒi] NF morphology

morphologique [mɔrfɔlɔʒik] ADJ morphological

morphologiquement [mɔrfɔlɔʒikmɑ] ADV morphologically

morphopsychologie [mɔrfɔpsikɔlɔʒi] NF = study of the relationship between people's morphology and their psychological make-up

morpion [mɔrpjɔ] NM **1** Arg (pou du pubis) crab **2** Arg (gamin) kid **3** (jeu) noughts and crosses, Am tick-tack-toe

mors [mɔr] NM **1** (d'un étau) jaw **2** (de livre) joint **3** (de harnais) bit; **prendre le m. aux dents** (d'un cheval) to take the bit in its teeth; Fig (d'une personne) to take the bit between one's teeth

morse[1] [mɔrs] NM Zool walrus

morse[2] NM (code) Morse (code)

morsure [mɔrsyr] NF **1** bite; **une m. de chien** a dog bite **2** (d'acide) biting

mort[1]**, morte** [mɔr, mɔrt] ADJ **1** (personne, peau, feuille, langue etc) dead; **m. et enterré** dead and buried, dead and gone; **je le veux m. ou vif** I want him dead or alive; **plus m. que vif** (à demi mort) more dead than alive; (très effrayé) half-dead with fright; **il est m.** he's dead; **il est m. hier** he died yesterday; **si tu fais un geste, tu es un homme m.** one move and you're a dead man; **il est m. pour la France** he died for France; Prov **morte la bête, m. le venin** dead men tell no tales; **m. de peur/d'inquiétude/de froid** frightened/ worried/frozen to death; Fam **je n'en peux plus, je suis m. (de fatigue)** I can't go on, I'm dead tired; Fam **être m. de rire** to be killing oneself (laughing); **elle avait le regard m.** her eyes were lifeless; **la mer Morte** the Dead Sea; **au mois d'août, la ville semble morte** in August the town seems dead **2 temps m.** Sport (dans un match) injury time, stoppage time; (dans le travail, la conversation) lull; **poids m.** Tech dead weight; Constr dead load; **point m.** (de la course d'un piston) dead centre; (d'un levier etc) neutral position; Aut neutral; Aut **mettre le levier au point m.** to put the (gear) lever into neutral; Fig **arriver à un point m.** to come to a standstill; **angle m.** (dans une voiture etc)

blind spot; **eau morte** stagnant water; Beaux-Arts **nature morte** still life; **balle morte** spent bullet

3 Fam (hors d'usage) (piles, appareil etc) finished; **ma voiture est morte** my car's had it

N dead person, dead man, f woman; **les morts** the dead; **le nombre des morts sur la route** the number of deaths on the roads; **cet accident a fait trois morts** the accident claimed three lives, three people died or were killed in the accident; **la drogue fait de nombreux morts chaque année** drugs claim many lives each year, many people die from drugs each year; Rel **jour** ou **fête des Morts** All Souls' Day; **l'office des morts** the burial service; **faire le m.** to pretend to be dead, to play dead; **je lui ai écrit il y a trois semaines, mais depuis, il fait le m.** I wrote to him three weeks ago, but since then he's been as silent as the grave or I haven't heard a thing; Aut **la place du m.** the passenger or Am Fam the death seat; Fig **c'est un m. vivant** he's half dead, he's more dead than alive; Fig **les morts vivants** the walking dead, the zombies

NM Cartes dummy; **faire le m.** to be dummy

mort[2] NF death; **m. accidentelle/violente/ clinique** accidental/violent/clinical death; **trouver la m. dans un accident** to die in an accident; **se donner la m.** to take one's (own) life; Fam **vous allez attraper la m.!** you'll catch your death (of cold)!; Fam **c'est pas la m.!** it won't kill you/him/etc!; **mourir de sa belle m.** ou **de m. naturelle** to die a natural death, to die of natural causes; **mourir de m. violente** to die a violent death; **être à la m.** ou **à l'article de la m.** to be at death's door; **à la m. de son père** on his father's death; **pâle comme la m.** as pale as death, deathly pale; **il n'y a pas eu m. d'homme** there was no loss of life; **mettre qn à m.** to put sb to death; **condamner qn à m.** to condemn or sentence sb to death; **sentence ou arrêt de m.** death sentence, sentence of death; **à m. les traîtres!** death to the traitors!; Arg **m. aux vaches!** down with the cops!; **blessé à m.** fatally or Litt mortally wounded; **lutte à m.** fight to the death or the end; Fam **freiner à m.** to jam on the brakes; **haïr qn à m.** to hate sb's guts, to loathe and detest sb; Arg **s'emmerder à m.** to be bored to death or out of one's mind, to be bored rigid; **nous sommes fâchés à m.** we are at daggers drawn; **en vouloir à qn à m.** to have a huge grudge against sb; **je lui en veux à m. d'avoir dit ça** I'll never forgive him for saying that; **ennemis à m.** deadly enemies; **silence de m.** deadly or deathlike silence or hush; **il avait la m. dans l'âme** he was sick at heart, he had a heavy heart; **partir la m. dans l'âme** to leave with a heavy heart; **souffrir m. et passion** to suffer agonies; **je m'en souviendrai jusqu'à la m.** I'll remember it until my dying day; **à la vie, à la m.** for ever, for life; **jamais je ne t'abandonnerai, à la vie, à la m.** I'll never leave you, we're in this together; **le monopole est la m. de l'industrie** monopoly means the end or is the ruin of industry; **ce fut un arrêt de m. pour notre entreprise** it spelt the end or was the death knell for our company

▸▸ Bot **m. aux loups** wolfsbane; Bot **m. aux poules** henbane; Méd, Sp **m. subite** sudden death; Méd **m. subite du nourrisson** cot death, Spéc sudden infant death syndrome

mortadelle [mɔrtadɛl] NF mortadella

mortaise [mɔrtɛz] NF Menuis mortise; **assemblage à tenon et à m.** mortise (and tenon) joint

mortaiser [mɔrteze] VT Menuis to mortise

mortalité [mɔrtalite] NF **1** mortality, death

rate; **taux de m.** mortality *or* death rate; **m. infantile** child *or* infant mortality **2** *Arch (condition mortelle)* mortal nature

mort-aux-rats [mɔrora] NF INV rat poison

mort-bois, *pl* **morts-bois** NM underwood, brushwood

morte-eau, *pl* **mortes-eaux** NF neap tide

mortel, -elle [mɔrtɛl] ADJ **1** *(sujet à la mort)* mortal **2** *(qui tue) (blessure, maladie, accident)* fatal; *(coup)* fatal, lethal; *Fml* mortal; *(dose)* lethal; *(champignon)* poisonous, deadly; **poison m.** deadly poison; **rayon m.** death ray; **il a fait une chute mortelle de 100 mètres** he fell 100 metres to his death; *Fam* **il fait un froid m. dans cette chambre!** it's freezing in this bedroom!, you could freeze to death in this bedroom! **3** *(haine, péché)* deadly; *(silence)* deathly; **ennemi m.** deadly enemy, mortal enemy; **d'une pâleur mortelle** deathly pale **4** *Fam (ennuyeux)* deadly dull, dead boring; **je l'ai attendu deux mortelles heures** I waited two solid *or* whole hours for him; **le sport, je trouve ça m.** I find sport deadly dull; **d'un ennui m.** deadly dull, dead boring **5** *Fam (excellent)* wicked, awesome
▪ N mortal

mortellement [mɔrtɛlmɑ̃] ADV *(blessé)* fatally, *Fml* mortally; **m. pâle** deathly pale; **m. offensé** mortally offended; *Fam* **s'ennuyer m.** to be bored to death, to be bored rigid; **m. ennuyeux** deadly dull, dead boring; *Rel* **pécher m.** to commit a mortal sin

morte-saison, *pl* **mortes-saisons** NF *Com* slack period, off season

mortier [mɔrtje] NM **1** *Culin* mortar; **pilon et m.** mortar and pestle **2** *Mil* mortar; **obus/tirs de m.** mortar shell/fire; **attaque au m.** mortar attack **3** *Constr* mortar; **m. liquide** *ou* **clair** grout(ing); **planche à m.** mortarboard

mortifiant [mɔrtifjɑ̃] ADJ mortifying, humiliating

mortification [mɔrtifikasjɔ̃] NF **1** *(de la chair, des passions etc)* mortification **2** *(humiliation)* mortification, humiliation; **il a subi une terrible m.** he felt mortified *or* humiliated; **infliger une m. à qn** to mortify *or* humiliate sb **3** *Culin (de gibier)* hanging **4** *Méd Vieilli (de membre)* gangrene, mortification

mortifié [mɔrtifje] ADJ **1** mortified, humiliated **2** *Méd Vieilli* gangrenous

mortifier [mɔrtifje] *(pr sub, impf* n. **mortifiions,** v. **mortifiiez)** VT **1** *(chair, passions)* to mortify **2** *(humilier)* to mortify, to humiliate; **elle en a été mortifiée** she was mortified **3** *Culin (gibier etc)* to hang **4** *Méd Vieilli (membre)* to make gangrenous
▪ VPR **se mortifier** to mortify oneself

mortinatalité [mɔrtinatalite] NF **(taux de) m.** stillbirth rate, number of stillbirths

mort-né, -née, *pl* **mort-né(e)s** ADJ *(enfant, animal)* stillborn; *Fig* **projet m.** plan destined to fail
▪ N stillborn child

mortuaire [mɔrtɥɛr] ADJ **drap m.** pall; **masque m.** death mask; **registre m.** register of deaths; **la maison m.** the house of the deceased; **chambre m.** death chamber; **dépôt m.** mortuary; **cérémonie m.** funeral; **couronne m.** funeral wreath

morue [mɔry] NF **1** *(poisson)* cod; **huile de foie de m.** cod-liver oil VOIR GRAMMAIRE A12 **2** *Vulg (prostituée)* tart

morutier, -ière [mɔrytje, -jɛr] ADJ *(industrie)* cod-fishing
▪ NM **1** *(bateau)* cod-fishing boat **2** *(pêcheur)* cod-fisher(man)

morve [mɔrv] NF **1** *(de nez)* (nasal) mucus, *Fam* snot; **ce gamin a toujours la m. qui lui**

coule du nez that kid has always got a snotty nose **2** *Vét* glanders

morveux, -euse [mɔrvø, -øz] ADJ **1** *(enfant etc)* runny-nosed; *Fam* snotty-nosed; *(nez)* runny, *Fam* snotty; *Prov* **qui se sent m. se mouche** if the cap fits, wear it **2** *Vét* glandered
▪ N *Fam (gamin)* kid, *Péj* brat; *(plus âgé)* snot, (little) jerk, snotty-nosed kid

MOS [mɔs] NM *(abrév* **métal-oxyde-semiconducteur)** *Ordinat* **M. complémentaire** complementary MOS

mosaïque[1] [mɔzaik] ADJ *Bible (loi)* Mosaic

mosaïque[2] NF **1** *Beaux-Arts, Fig* mosaic; **dallage en m.** mosaic flooring; *Fig* **une m. de couleurs** a kaleidoscope of colours **2** *TV (procédé)* pixellation

mosaïste [mɔzaist] N *Beaux-Arts* worker in mosaic

Moscou [mɔsku] N Moscow

moscovite [mɔskɔvit] ADJ Muscovite
▪ N **M.** Muscovite

mosquée [mɔske] NF mosque

mot [mo] NM word; **les mots me manquent pour t'exprimer ma gratitude** I cannot find the words to express my gratitude; **les mots me manquent!** words fail me!; **manger** *ou* **avaler ses mots** to mumble; **répéter qch m. pour m.** to repeat sth word for word *or* verbatim; **traduire m. à m., faire du m. à m.** to translate word for word *or* literally; **prendre qn au m.** to take sb at his/her word; **groupe de mots** word group; **sans m. dire** without (saying) a word; **il n'a pas dit un m. de toute la soirée** he didn't say a (single) word the entire evening; **qui ne dit m. consent** silence is tantamount to consent; **ne pas souffler m. de qch** not to breathe a word about sth; **dire un m.** *ou* **deux mots à qn** to have a word with sb; **il n'a pas dit un seul m. en ta faveur** he didn't put in a single good word for you; **avoir des mots avec qn** to have words with sb; **lâche? en effet, je crois que c'est le m. a** coward? yes, I think that's just the word for him; **avoir le dernier m.** to have the last word; **je ne sais pas un (traître) m. de russe** I don't know a word of Russian; **sur ces mots, il se leva** and with these words *or* so saying, he got up; **en un m./quelques mots** in a word/a few words; **en un m. comme en cent** in a nutshell; **il faut compter au bas m. trois heures/500 euros** you'll have to allow at least three hours/500 euros; **gros m.** swearword; **ne dis pas de gros mots!** don't swear!; **des mots doux, des mots d'amour** loving words, *Fam* sweet nothings; **il ne dit jamais un m. plus haut que l'autre** he never raises his voice, he never utters a cross word; **voilà le fin m. de l'affaire!** so that's what's at the bottom of it!; **on ne saura jamais le fin m. de l'affaire** we'll never get to the bottom of it, we'll never know the truth of the matter; **dire qch à mots couverts** to hint at sth, to say sth in a roundabout manner; **faire comprendre qch à qn à mots couverts** to give sb to understand sth in a roundabout manner; **se donner le m.** to pass *or* give the word; **ils ont dû se donner le m.** they must have agreed on it, they must have passed the word around; **envoyer** *ou* **écrire un (petit) m. à qn** to drop sb a line, to write sb a note; **il m'a laissé un m. sur mon bureau** he left a note on my desk; **un m. d'excuse pour l'institutrice** a note for the teacher; **je lui en toucherai un m.** I'll have a word with him about it, I'll mention it to him; **avoir son m. à dire** to have one's say; **tu n'as qu'un m. à dire** just say the word, you just have to say the word; **je ne pouvais pas placer un m.** I couldn't get a word in edgeways; **il a toujours le m. pour rire** he's always ready with a joke; **m. historique** historic remark, mem-

orable saying; **bon m.** witty remark, witticism; *Ordinat* **m. de 6 bits** 6-bit byte; *Ordinat* **m. binaire** binary word
▪ ▪ *aussi Ordinat* **mot-clé,** *pl* **mots-clés** keyword; **mots croisés** crossword puzzle, crossword; **faire des mots croisés** to do crosswords *or* crossword puzzles; **m. d'ordre** *Mil* password; *(de politique)* keynote; *(de parti politique, d'organisation)* watchword, slogan; **m. de passe** password; *Mil* **m. de ralliement** password

motard [mɔtar] NM *Fam* **1** biker **2** *(de police)* motorcycle policeman

motel [mɔtɛl] NM motel

motet [mɔtɛ] NM *Mus* motet

moteur, -trice [mɔtœr, -tris] ADJ **1** *Tech* **arbre m.** drive shaft, main shaft; *Tech* **unité motrice** power pack *or* unit; **force motrice** driving force; **roue motrice** driving wheel; **voiture à roues avant motrices** car with front-wheel drive; **temps m.** power stroke **2** *Anat (nerve)* motor; **troubles moteurs** motor deficiencies; **un handicapé m.** a person with motor deficiencies
▪ NM **1** motor, engine; *Cin* **m.!** camera!; **à m.** motor(-driven), power(-driven); **bateau à m.** motorboat; **caméra à m.** motor-driven camera; **commandé par m.** motor(-driven), power(-driven); **à moteurs multiples, à plusieurs moteurs** *(aircraft etc)* multi-engine(d) **2** *Fig* **c'est lui le m. de l'entreprise** he's the driving force behind the undertaking; *Fig* **le m. principal de la pensée hégélienne** the mainspring of Hegelian thought; **sans autre m. que l'amour de la gloire** for no other reason than love of glory
▪ NF **Rail motrice** motor coach, *surtout Am* motor car
▪ ▪ **m. ACT** ohc engine; **m. à allumage par bougie** spark-ignition engine; **m. à allumage par compression** compression-ignition engine; **m. alternatif à combustion interne** internal combustion (reciprocating) engine; **m. d'avion** aero-engine; **m. carré** square engine; **m. à combustion interne** internal combustion engine; **m. à cylindres à plat** boxer engine; **m. à deux temps** two-stroke engine; **m. diesel** diesel engine; **m. électrique** electric motor; **m. à explosion** internal combustion engine; **m. à gaz** gas engine; **m. à hydrogène** hydrogen engine; **m. d'impression** *(d'une imprimante laser)* printer engine; **m. à injection** fuel-injected engine; **m. 'lean burn'** lean-burn engine; **m. en ligne** in-line engine; **m. multicylindre** multi-cylinder engine; **m. multisoupape** multi-valve engine; **m. pas à pas** stepper motor; **m. à pistons** piston engine; **m. à plat** flat engine; **m. polycarburant** multi-fuel engine; **m. polycylindre** multi-cylinder engine; **m. à quatre temps** four-stroke engine; **m. à réaction** jet engine; *Ordinat* **m. de recherche** search engine; **m. à refroidissement par air** air-cooled engine; **m. rénové** reconditioned engine, recon; **m. seize soupapes** sixteen-valve engine; **m. turbocompressé** turbocharged engine; **m. turbodiesel** turbo-diesel engine; **m. en V** vee engine; **m. V6** V6 (engine); **m. à vapeur** steam engine

motif [mɔtif] NM **1** motive, reason; **un m. valable** a valid reason; **m. de licenciement** grounds for dismissal; **m. de mécontentement** cause *or* grounds for discontent; **m. de réclamation** reason for claim; **avoir un m. pour faire qch** to have a motive *or* a reason for doing sth; **c'est un faux m.** that's not the real reason; **pour quel m. a-t-il été puni?** what was the reason for punishing him?, why was he punished?; *Fam Vieilli* **courtiser qn pour le bon m.** to court sb with honourable intentions; **quel est le m. de ce coup de téléphone?** what is the reason for *or* behind this telephone call?; **quel m. avez-vous de vous plaindre?** what cause *or* grounds have you for complaint?; **soupçons sans m.** groundless *or* unfounded suspicions; **il s'est fâché sans m.** he got angry for no reason at all *or* without any reason; **insulter qn sans m.** to insult sb for no reason at all *or Fml* gratuitously; **il semble que l'individu ait agi sans m.** it seems that he acted without any motive; **le crime avait-il un m.?** did the crime have a motive?, was there a motive to the crime?; *Jur* **motifs d'un jugement** grounds upon which a judgment has been delivered **2** *Beaux-Arts* motif; *Couture (pour la broderie)* design, pattern, motif; *Mus* theme, motif, motto; **m. à fleurs** flower(ed) pattern; **papier peint à m. à fleurs** flowered wallpaper; **une veste avec des motifs noirs et blancs** a jacket with a black and white design

motion [mosjɔ̃] NF motion; **proposer une m.** to propose a motion, to move a proposal; **la m. a été adoptée** the motion was carried; **présenter une m.** to table a motion; **m. de censure** motion of censure

motivant [mɔtivɑ̃] ADJ *(travail)* motivating; *(salaire, rémunération)* worthwhile

motivation [mɔtivasjɔ̃] NF *Psy* motivation; **quelles sont vos motivations?** what motivates you?; **joindre une lettre de m. à votre CV** send a covering letter with your CV telling us why you're interested in the job *or* what prompted you to apply; **m. d'achat** buying motivation

motivé [mɔtive] ADJ **1** *(personne)* motivated; **élève très m.** very keen *or* motivated pupil **2** *(action)* justified; **refus m.** justifiable refusal; **non m.** unjustified, unwarranted; *Jur* **sentence arbitrale motivée** = award stating the reasons on which it is based; *Jur* **avis m.** counsel's opinion

motiver [mɔtive] VT **1** *(causer, stimuler)* *(action, personne)* to motivate; **l'ambition les motive** they are motivated by ambition; **des crimes motivés par l'argent** crimes motivated by money *or* with money as the motive **2** *(justifier)* to justify, to warrant; *(refus etc)* to state the reason for; **la situation motive nos craintes** the situation gives us (just) cause for concern

moto [moto] NF *Fam* motorbike; **aller au travail à** *ou* **en m.** to go to work on a motorbike, to ride a motorbike to work; **faire de la m.** to ride a motorbike; **m. tout terrain** motocross bike

motocross [motokrɔs] NM *Sport* motocross

motoculteur [motokyltœr] NM *Agr* motor cultivator

motoculture [motokyltyr] NF mechanized farming

motocycle [motosikl] NM *Admin* motorcycle

motocyclette [motosiklɛt] NF motorcycle, *Fam* motorbike

motocycliste [motosiklist] N motorcyclist, *Fam* biker; *Mil* dispatch rider

motomarine [motomarin] NF *Can* jet ski

motonautique [motonotik] ADJ **sport m.** motorboating

motonautisme [motonotism] NM motorboating

motoneige [motonɛʒ] NF snowmobile, *surtout Can* skidoo

motopompe [motopɔ̃p] NF motor(-driven) pump

motorisation [mɔtorizasjɔ̃] NF mechanization

motorisé [mɔtorize] ADJ mechanized; *Mil* **troupes motorisées** mechanized troops; *Fam* **vous êtes m.?** have you got a car or

transport *or Am Fam* wheels?, are you mobile?

motoriser [mɔtorize] VT to mechanize

motoriste [mɔtorist] NM engine manufacturer

mot-outil, *pl* **mots-outils** NM *Ling* form word, link word

motrice [mɔtris] ADJ, NF *voir* **moteur**

motricité [mɔtrisite] NF *Physiol* motor function

motte [mɔt] NF **1** *(de terre)* clod, clump; *(sur les racines d'un arbre)* root ball; **m. de gazon** sod, turf; **m. de tourbe** (turf of) peat; **m. de beurre** pat *or* block of butter; **du beurre à la m.** butter in blocks **2** *Archéol* motte

motteux [mɔtø] NM *(oiseau)* wheatear, stonechat

motus [mɔtys] INT **m. (et bouche cousue)!** mum's the word!

mou¹, molle [mu, mɔl] ADJ *(the masc form* **mol** *is used before vowel or h mute)* *(beurre, matelas, substance)* soft; *(personne)* spineless; *(gouvernement, chef)* spineless, lax, soft; *(geste)* lifeless, limp; *(corde)* slack; *(pédale)* slack, spongy; *(chair, main, ventre)* flabby, soft; *(poignée de main)* limp, flabby, feeble; *(muscle)* soft, *Fml* flaccid; *(style)* feeble, flabby; **ce que tu peux être m.!** God you're feeble *or* useless!; **j'ai les jambes molles** my legs are like cotton wool; **m. au toucher** soft to the touch; **un mol (et doux) oreiller** a (soft and) downy pillow; **des collines molles, des collines au relief m.** rolling hills; *Fam* **il est m. comme une chiffe** *ou* **comme une chique** he's an absolute wimp; *Fam* **je ne me sens pas bien, je suis** *ou* **je me sens tout m.** I'm not well, I feel like a wet rag; **il m'a fait de molles excuses** he gave me some lame *or* feeble excuses

▸ N *Fam* wimp

▸ NM *(de corde, fil)* slack; **donne-moi un peu de m.** give me some slack; **donner du m. à un cordage** to slacken a rope; **prendre du m.** *(d'une corde)* to slacken

▸ ADV **1** **elle joue trop m.** she doesn't put enough verve into her playing **2** *très Fam* **vas-y m.!** go easy!, take it easy!; **vas-y m. avec le whisky** go easy on the whisky

mou² NM *(abats)* lights, lungs ; *Fig Fam* **il est en train de te bourrer le m.** he's spinning you a yarn *or* handing you a line; *Fig Fam* **je vais lui rentrer dans le m.** I'll punch him one

mouais [mwɛ] ADV *Fam* well, yeah; **alors, t'as aimé le film? – m., j'ai vu pire** did you like the movie, then? – well, yeah, I've seen worse

mouchage [muʃaʒ] NM **1** *(de nez)* wiping, blowing **2** *(de chandelles)* snuffing (out)

mouchard, -arde [muʃar, -ard] N *Fam (informateur)* grass, informer, stool pigeon; *Scol* sneak

▸ NM **1** *Tech (tachymètre)* spy in the cab **2** *(contrôleur)* watchman's clock **3** *Aviat* observation plane **4** *(dans une porte)* peephole **5** *Ordinat* **m. électronique** cookie

moucharder [muʃarde] VT *Fam (personne)* to grass *or* squeal on, to grass up; *Scol* to sneak on; **tu n'as pas intérêt à m.** you'd better not grass *or* squeal

mouche [muʃ] NF **1** *(insecte)* fly; **on aurait entendu une m. voler** you could have heard a pin drop; **gober les mouches, regarder les mouches voler** to gaze *or* stare into space; *Fam* **prendre** *ou* *Suisse* **piquer la m.** to fly off the handle; *Fam* **quelle m. vous pique?** what's up with you?, what's bitten you?, who rattled your cage?; **elle ne ferait pas de mal à une m.** she wouldn't hurt a fly; **tomber comme des mouches** to be dropping like flies; **c'est une fine m.** he's a sharp customer, he's a fly one; **j'ai des mouches devant les**

yeux I've got spots before my eyes; *Pêche* **m. mouillée** wet fly; *Pêche* **m. à saumon** salmon fly; **pêche à la m. sèche** dry-fly fishing; *Boxe* **poids m.** flyweight **2** *(de cible)* bull's-eye; **faire m.** to hit the bull's-eye, to score a bull; *Fig* **il a fait m. avec cette proposition** he hit the jackpot *or* he scored with that suggestion **3 bateau m.** river bus, bateau mouche **4** *Hist (faux grain de beauté)* patch; *(sur menton)* tuft of hair **5** *Escrime* button **6** *Arch (tache)* spot, speck; *(sur vêtement etc)* stain

▸▸ **m. bleue** bluebottle, blowfly; **m. domestique** housefly; *Can* **m. à feu** firefly; *très Fam* **m. à merde (bleue)** bluebottle; *(verte)* greenbottle; **m. à miel** honey bee; **m. tsé-tsé** tsetse fly; **m. de la viande** blowfly, bluebottle

moucher [muʃe] VT **1** *(nez)* to wipe, to blow; **m. un enfant** to wipe a child's nose; **je mouche du sang** there's blood on my handkerchief when I blow my nose **2** *(chandelle)* to snuff (out); *Fam* **m. qn** to put sb in his/her place

▸ VPR **se moucher** to blow one's nose; *Fam* **il ne se mouche pas du coude** *ou* **du pied** he thinks a lot *or* he's got a high opinion of himself

moucheron [muʃrɔ̃] NM gnat, midge

moucheronner [muʃrɔne] VI *(de poisson)* to be rising, to be on the rise

moucheté [muʃte] ADJ **1** *(poisson, œuf)* speckled; *(robe de cheval)* dappled; **mer mouchetée d'écume** foam-flecked sea; **nez m. de taches de rousseur** freckled nose; **une écharpe blanche mouchetée de noir** a white scarf flecked *or* specked with black, a white scarf with black flecks **2** *Escrime (fleuret)* buttoned

moucheter [muʃte] VT *(je mouchette; je mouchetterai)* **1** *(étoffe, papier)* to speckle, to fleck **2** *Escrime* to button, to put a button on

mouchettes [muʃɛt] NF **1** mouchettes *(pour chandelles)* (pair of) snuffers **2** *Archit (de larmier)* outer fillet

moucheture [muʃtyr] NF speck, speckle; **une écharpe blanche avec des mouchetures noires** a white scarf with black flecks, a white scarf specked *or* flecked with black

mouchoir [muʃwar] NM handkerchief; *(autour du cou)* kerchief; **m. en papier** paper handkerchief, tissue; **m. en tissu** handkerchief; *Fig* **je vais faire un nœud à mon m.** I'll tie a knot in my handkerchief; **jardin grand comme un m. (de poche)** pocket handkerchief (of a) garden; **arriver dans un m. de poche** to come in neck and neck

mouchure [muʃyr] NF *(du nez)* mucus

moudjahidin [mudʒaidin] NMPL mujaheddin, mujahedeen

moudre [mudr] VT *(prp* **moulant;** *pp* **moulu;** *pr ind* **je mouds, il moud, n. moulons, ils moulent;** *pr sub* **je moule;** *p hist* **je moulus;** *fu* **je moudrai)** **1** *(grain)* to grind, to mill; *(café, poivre)* to grind; *Fig* **m. qn de coups** to beat sb to a pulp **2** *Vieilli (air) (sur orgue de Barbarie)* to grind out

moue [mu] NF pout; **faire la m.** to pout, to look sulky; **faire une m.** to purse one's lips; **m. boudeuse** sulk; **il eut une m. désapprobatrice** he looked disapproving; *Fig* **le public fit la m. et la pièce fit un four** the public stayed away in droves and the play flopped; **les critiques firent la m.** the critics turned up their noses

mouette [mwɛt] NF (sea)gull

mouf(f)ette [mufɛt] NF skunk

moufle [mufl] NF *(gant)* mitten, mitt

▸ N *Tech* **1** tackle block, pulley block **2** *(palan)* (block and) tackle

mouflet, -ette [muflɛ, -ɛt] N *Fam (enfant)* kid, *Péj* brat

mouflon [muflɔ̃] NM mouf(f)lon, wild sheep

moufter [mufte] VI *Fam* **ne pas m.** to keep shtum, to keep one's mouth shut

mouillage [mujaʒ] NM **1** *(de tissu, linge)* moistening, damping; *(du vin)* (fraudulent) watering down **2** *Naut (de bateau)* anchoring; *(de mine)* laying; *(de bouée)* putting down **3** *Naut (emplacement)* anchorage, moorage; **être au m.** to be riding at anchor; **prendre son m.** to anchor

mouillé [muje] ADJ **1** wet; **tout m.** soaked; **m. jusqu'aux os** wet through, soaked to the skin; **elle avait les yeux mouillés de larmes** her eyes were wet with tears **2** *Ling (consonne)* palatalized

mouillement [mujmɑ̃] NM *Ling* palatalization

mouiller [muje] VT **1** *(rendre humide)* to wet; *(linge à repasser)* to moisten, to damp(en); *Culin (ragoût)* to add liquid to; *(vin, boisson alcoolisée, lait)* to dilute, to water down; **il a mouillé le bas de son pantalon en traversant la rivière à gué** he got the bottom of his trousers wet wading across the river; **l'averse a mouillé le linge** the clothes got wet in the rain; **on s'est fait m. par l'averse** we got soaked in the downpour; *Fig* **m. sa chemise** to put one's back into it, to work up a sweat, to get stuck in; **ce n'est pas avec le travail qu'il fournit qu'il risque de m. sa chemise** *ou* **son maillot** he's not likely to break into a sweat with the amount of work that he does **2** *Naut (ancre)* to cast, to drop **3** *Naut (mine)* to lay; *(bouée)* to put down **4** *Fam (compromettre)* to involve, to drag in **5** *Ling (consonne)* to palatalize **6** *Can Fam (fêter)* **il va falloir m. ça!** we'll have to have a drink to celebrate!, this calls for a celebration!
▶ VI **1** *Naut* to anchor; *(de navire)* to lie at anchor; **mouillez!** let go (the anchor)! **2** *Fam (avoir peur)* to wet oneself **3** *très Fam (être excitée sexuellement)* to be wet **4** *Can Fam (pleuvoir)* to rain; **m. à siau** *ou* **à verse** *ou* **à boire debout** to rain buckets
▶ VPR **se mouiller 1** to get wet; *(des yeux)* to fill with tears; **se m. les pieds** to get one's feet wet **2** *Fam (dans un crime, une affaire louche)* to get involved; **il ne veut pas se m.** *(prendre parti)* he doesn't want to stick his neck out

mouillette [mujɛt] NF *(de pain)* finger, *surtout Br* soldier

mouilleur [mujœr] NM **1** *Naut* **m. de mines** minelayer **2** *(pour timbres)* damper

mouillure [mujyr] NF **1** *(marque)* damp mark, stain **2** *Ling (de consonne)* palatalization

mouise [mwiz] NF *Arg (misère)* poverty; *(ennuis)* hassle; **être dans la m.** to be hard up *or* in dire straits; **tirer qn de la m.** to get sb out of a hole

moujik [muʒik] NM moujik

moujingue [muʒɛ̃g] N *Arg (enfant)* kid, *Péj* brat

moukère [mukɛr] NF *(femme maghrébine)* Maghrebi woman; *Arg (femme)* female; *(prostituée)* pro

moulage¹ [mulaʒ] NM *(du grain)* grinding, milling

moulage² NM **1** *(fait de mouler)* casting, moulding, *Am* molding; *(de fer)* founding; **m. à cire perdue** lost wax process **2 m. au** *ou* **en plâtre** plaster cast

moule¹ [mul] NM **1** mould, *Am* mold; *Tech* mould, *Spéc* matrix; **m. à gelée** jelly mould; **m. à gâteaux** cake tin; **m. à beurre** butter mould *or* print **2** *Fig* **on n'en fait plus des comme lui, on a cassé le m.** they broke the mould when they made him; **elle a rejeté le m. de son éducation** she has broken out of the mould of her upbringing; **ils ont été coulés dans le même m.** they're cast in the same mould, they're out of the same mould;

l'école est un m. qui étouffe la créativité de l'enfant school stifles children's creativity by forcing them into a mould; **une fille faite au m.** a girl with a great figure

moule² NF **1** *Zool, Culin* mussel **2** *Arg (personne molle)* wimp, drip; *(idiot)* fool, idiot **3** *Vulg (sexe de femme)* pussy, cunt

moulé [mule] ADJ cast, moulded, *Am* molded; **statue de plâtre m.** plaster cast; **pain m.** tin loaf; **écriture moulée** copperplate handwriting; **lettres moulées** printing; **je me trouve trop moulée dans cette robe** this dress clings too much

mouler [mule] VT to mould, *Am* to mold; *Métal* to cast; **robe qui moule la taille** tightly fitting *or* figure-hugging dress; *Fig* **m. sa conduite sur qn** to model one's behaviour on sb
▶ VPR **se mouler** *Fig (prendre pour modèle)* to model oneself (**sur** on)

moules-frites [mulfrit] NM INV *Belg* **1** *Culin* mussels and chips *or Am* French fries **2** *(restaurant)* = restaurant specializing in mussels and chips *or Am* French fries

mouleur [mulœr] NM caster, moulder, *Am* molder

moulière [muljɛr] NF mussel bed

moulin [mulɛ̃] NM **1** mill; **roue de m.** millwheel; **on y entre comme dans un m.** people *or* all and sundry can just walk in; **ce n'est pas un m. ici!** you can't just walk in *or* breeze in as if you own the place! **2** *Fam (de voiture)* engine
▶ **m. à café** coffee grinder; *(manuel)* coffee mill; **m. à eau** watermill; **m. à légumes** food mill; **m. à minerai** ore crusher; *Fig* **m. à paroles** chatterbox, gasbag; **m. à poivre** pepper mill; *Rel* **m. à prières** prayer wheel; **m. à vent** windmill; *Fig* **se battre contre des moulins à vent** to tilt at windmills

mouliner [muline] VT **1** *Culin* to pass through a food mill **2** *Pêche (ligne)* to reel in

moulinet [mulinɛ] NM **1** *Tech* winch; *Pêche* reel **2 faire des moulinets (avec sa canne)** to twirl one's (walking) stick; **faire des moulinets (avec les bras)** to wave one's arms around

Moulinette® [mulinɛt] NF food mill; **passer la viande à la M.** to put the meat through the food mill; *Fig* **il m'a passé à la M.** he put me through it *or* through the mill; *Fig* **passer qch à la M.** to tear sth to shreds

moult [mult] ADV *Hum, Vieilli* a multitude of; **avec m. remerciements** with many thanks

moulu [muly] ADJ *(café, poivre)* ground; *Fig (personne)* shattered, worn-out, dead-beat; **m. (de coups)** black and blue

moulure [mulyr] NF *Archit, Menuis* (ornamental) moulding *or Am* molding

moulurer [mulyre] VT *Constr* to cut a moulding *or Am* molding on; **profils moulurés** mouldings

moumoute [mumut] NF **1** *(veste)* fleece (jacket) **2** *Fam (perruque)* wig, rug, *Br* syrup

mourant, -ante [murɑ̃, -ɑ̃t] ADJ dying; *(voix)* faint
▶ N dying man, f woman; **les mourants** the dying

mourir [murir] *(prp* **mourant**; *pp* **mort**; *pr ind* **je meurs, il meurt, n. mourons, ils meurent**; *pr sub* **je meure, n. mourions**; *p hist* **il mourut**; *fu* **je mourrai** [murre]; *aux* **être**) VI **1** *(de personne, d'animal, de plante)* to die; **il est mort hier** he died yesterday; **il est mort assassiné** he was murdered; **il est mort de vieillesse** he died of old age; **m. de faim** to die of starvation, to starve to death; *(avoir très faim)* to be starving; **m. de soif/de chaleur/d'épuisement** to die of thirst/heat/exhaustion; **m. de froid** to freeze to death; **m.**

accidentellement to die in an accident; **elle l'aimait à en m.** she was desperately in love with him; **m. avant l'âge** to die before one's time; **m. à la tâche** to die in harness, *Fam* to die with one's boots on; **au moment de m.** in the hour of death; **au moment de m., il a fait venir toute sa famille** just before he died, he sent for his entire family; **faire m. qn** to put sb to death; **faire m. qn à petit feu** to kill sb by inches; *Fam* **il me fera m.** he'll be the death of me; **vous me faites m. d'impatience** the suspense is killing me; **je mourais de peur** I was dying of fright, I was frightened to death; **m. d'inquiétude** to be worried to death; **elle me fera m. d'inquiétude** she'll worry me to death, she'll be the death of me; **m. de chagrin** to be weighed down with grief, to be grief-stricken; *(littéralement)* to die of grief; **m. d'ennui** to die of boredom; **ennuyer qn à m.** to bore sb to death; **être à m. d'ennui** *(de film, roman, conversation)* to be deadly boring; **m. d'envie de faire qch** to be dying to do sth; **j'ai cru m. de rire** I thought I would die laughing, I nearly died laughing; **être à m. de rire** *(de film, roman, personne)* to be uproariously funny; *très Fam* **plus bête/avare que lui, tu meurs** there's nobody on God's earth who's as stupid/mean as he is; *Fig* **tu ne vas pas en m., tout de même!** it won't kill you, you know!
2 *(d'un feu, d'une coutume, d'une industrie, d'une civilisation)* to die out; *(d'une région)* to die; **la plainte s'enfla, envahit l'espace, puis finit par m.** the wailing grew, filled the whole space, then finally died away *or* faded away; **les vagues qui viennent m. sur la plage** the waves which break and spend themselves on the beach
▶ V IMPERS **il meurt des milliers d'enfants chaque jour** thousands of children die every day
▶ VPR **se mourir** *Litt* to be dying; *(d'une habitude)* to die out; *(d'un feu)* to die away; **je sens que je me meurs** I feel that I am dying; **la lampe se mourait** the lamp was fading *or* giving out

mouroir [murwar] NM *Fam Péj* old people's home; **ces foyers de personnes âgées sont des mouroirs** these homes are just places where old people are left to die

mouron [murɔ̃] NM *Fam* **se faire du m.** to worry; **je commence à me faire du m.** I'm beginning to worry *or* get worried

mousquet [muskɛ] NM musket

mousquetaire [muskətɛr] NM musketeer; **gants (à la) m.** gauntlets

mousqueterie [muskətri] NF musketry; **feu de m.** musket fire

mousqueton [muskətɔ̃] NM **1** *Mil (fusil court)* carbine **2** *(d'escalade etc) (anneau)* karabiner; *(système d'accrochage)* snaphook

moussage [musaʒ] NM

moussaillon [musajɔ̃] NM *Fam* ship's boy

moussaka [musaka] NF *Culin* moussaka

moussant [musɑ̃] ADJ *(gel)* foaming; **être très m.** to produce a lot of lather; **il est peu m.** it doesn't produce *or* give much of a lather

mousse¹ [mus] NF **1** *Bot* moss; **couvert de m.** covered with moss, moss-grown, mossy; *Prov* **pierre qui roule n'amasse pas m.** a rolling stone gathers no moss; *Tricot* **point m.** moss stitch **2** *(de mer, dans cours d'eau pollué, de cappuccino)* froth, foam; *(sur verre de bière)* head; *(de savon)* lather; *Culin* mousse; **les assiettes sont encore pleines de m.** the plates are still covered in suds; **les vêtements sont encore pleins de m.** the clothes are still full of soap; *Fam* **une m.** *(bière)* a beer; *Fam* **se faire de la m.** to fret, to worry; *Culin* **m. au chocolat/de saumon** chocolate/salmon mousse; **m. à raser** shaving foam **3** **(caoutchouc)** M.® foam rubber; **matelas en M.** foam rubber mattress

mousse² NM **1** *(dans la marine)* ship's boy **2** *Can Fam (terme d'affection)* darling, sweetheart

mousse³ ADJ *Tech (lame, pointe etc)* blunt

mousseline [muslin] NF **1** *Tex* muslin; **m. de soie** chiffon **2** *Culin* **pommes (de terre) m.** puréed potatoes

mousser [muse] VI *(de bière)* to froth, to foam; *(d'eau savonneuse, de savon, de lessive)* to lather; *(de vin, d'eau gazeuse)* to sparkle, to fizz; **ce savon/cette lessive ne mousse pas beaucoup** this soap/washing powder doesn't lather very well *or* doesn't give much of a lather; **ce champagne mousse beaucoup** there are a lot of bubbles in this champagne, this champagne is very fizzy; *Arg* **faire m. qn** *(mettre en colère)* to make sb lose his/her temper *or* flare up; *(faire valoir)* to boast about sb, to sing sb's praises; **se faire m.** to show off

mousseron [musrɔ̃] NM edible mushroom, *surtout* St George's agaric

mousseux, -euse [musø, -øz] ADJ **1** *(écumeux) (eau)* frothy, foaming; *(chocolat, cappuccino, crème)* frothy; *(bière)* frothy, with a lot of head **2** *(vin, cidre)* sparkling
NM sparkling wine

moussoir [muswar] NM whisk

mousson [musɔ̃] NF monsoon

moussu [musy] ADJ mossy, mossgrown

moustache [mustaʃ] NF **1** m., **moustaches** moustache; **m. à la gauloise** walrus moustache; **m. en brosse** toothbrush moustache; **porter la m., avoir une m.** to have a moustache **2** *(de chat, rongeur)* whiskers

moustachu [mustaʃy] ADJ *(homme)* with a moustache; **être m.** to have a moustache
NM man with a moustache

moustiquaire [mustiker] NF mosquito net; *Can (à la fenêtre)* screen

moustique [mustik] NM **1** *(insecte)* mosquito VOIR GRAMMAIRE A12 **2** *Fam (personne maigrichonne)* weed; *(enfant)* kid, nipper

moût [mu] NM *(de raisins)* must; *(de bière)* wort

moutard [mutar] NM *Arg (enfant)* kid, nipper

moutarde [mutard] NF mustard; **m. forte** *ou* **de Dijon** strong *or* Dijon mustard; **graine de m.** mustard seed; *Fig* **la m.** lui est montée au nez he lost his temper *or* flared up; **je sens la m. qui me monte au nez** I'm beginning to lose my temper
ADJ INV **gaz m.** mustard gas; **(jaune) m.** mustard (yellow)

moutardier [mutardje] NM **1** *(fabricant)* mustard maker; *(vendeur)* mustard seller; *Fam* **il se croit le premier m. du pape** he thinks he's the cat's pyjamas *or* the bee's knees **2** *(pot)* mustard pot

moutier [mutje] NM *Arch* monastery

mouton, -onne [mutɔ̃, -ɔn] NM **1** *Zool* sheep; *Culin* mutton; **(peau de) m.** sheepskin; *Culin* **ragoût de m.** mutton stew; **éleveur de moutons** *(pour la viande)* sheep farmer; *(pour la laine)* woolgrower; **être frisé comme un m.** as meek as a lamb; **être frisé comme un m.** to have curly hair; *Fig* **revenons à nos moutons** let's get back to the subject; **ils ont tous suivi comme des moutons** they all followed like sheep; **compter les moutons** *(pour s'endormir)* to count sheep; *Fig* **c'est un m. à cinq pattes** he's a rare breed; **vous recherchez le m. à cinq pattes** you're looking for something that doesn't exist, you want the impossible VOIR GRAMMAIRE A12 **2** *Fam (dans les prisons)* grass **3 moutons** *(sur les vagues)* white horses; *(dans le ciel)* fluffy *or* fleecy white clouds; **la mer fait des moutons**

there are white horses on the sea **4 moutons** *(sous les meubles)* fluff, *Am* dust bunnies **5** *Constr* drop hammer
ADJ *Fig* sheeplike

moutonnant [mutɔnɑ̃] ADJ *(mer)* covered with white horses

moutonné [mutɔne] ADJ *(ciel)* dotted with fleecy clouds; **tête moutonnée** curly head of hair

moutonnement [mutɔnmɑ̃] NM *(de la mer)* breaking into white horses, frothing; **m. du ciel** dotting of fleecy clouds in the sky

moutonner [mutɔne] VI *(de la mer)* to break into white horses, to froth; *(du ciel)* to become dotted with fleecy clouds

moutonneux, -euse [mutɔnø, -øz] ADJ **1** *(mer)* foam-flecked, covered with white horses **2** *(ciel)* dotted with fleecy clouds

moutonnier, -ière [mutɔnje, -jɛr] ADJ *(élevage)* sheep; *Fig (foule)* sheeplike; *(personne)* easily led

mouture [mutyr] NF **1** *(de blé)* grinding, milling; *(de café)* grinding; **avec ce moulin à café, la m. est excellente** this mill grinds the coffee really well; **si la m. était plus fine** if it were ground more finely; **vous voulez quelle m.?** how would you like it ground?; *Fig Vieilli* **tirer deux moutures d'un sac** to profit twice over from sth **2** *(d'un ouvrage, d'un livre)* version, *Péj* rehash; **c'est la deuxième m. du texte** this is the second version of *or* draft of *or* Fam go at the text

mouv' [muv] NM *Fam (abrév* **mouvement)** **c'est dans le m.** it's dead hip, it's totally cool

mouvance [muvɑ̃s] NF **1** *(de pays)* sphere of influence; **elle a été dans la m. surréaliste pendant un temps** she moved in surrealist circles for a time; **il se situe davantage dans la m. du Parti socialiste** he is closer to *or* tends more towards the Socialist Party **2** *Litt (instabilité)* flux, constant change; **tout est en m.** everything is in a state of flux

mouvant [muvɑ̃] ADJ *(terrain)* unstable; *(cible)* moving; *(feuillage, herbe)* swaying; **les blés mouvants sous le ciel d'orage** the swaying corn under the stormy sky; *Fig* **être sur un terrain m.** to be on shifting *or* unsteady ground

mouvement [muvmɑ̃] NM **1** *(déplacement)* movement, motion; *(geste)* gesture; **m. vers l'arrière** backward movement *or* motion; **il tomba du cheval et resta sans m.** he fell from his horse and lay motionless on the ground; **il y eut un m. de panique dans la foule** the crowd panicked; **il y eut un m. de foule** a ripple ran through the crowd; **il y eut un m. de foule et je perdis mon frère de vue** I lost sight of my brother in the crush; **un m. de panique à la Bourse** panic *or* a panicky reaction on the Stock Exchange; **faire un m.** to move; **faire un faux m.** *(qui provoque une douleur)* to move the wrong way; **j'ai fait un faux m. et j'ai renversé le verre de vin** I clumsily knocked the glass of wine over; **surveiller les mouvements de qn** to monitor sb's movements; **il aime le m.** *(voyager)* he likes to move around, he can't stay in one place; **être toujours en m.** *(d'une personne)* to be always on the move; **répondre d'un m. de tête** *(pour dire non)* to answer with a shake of the head, to shake one's head; *(pour dire oui)* to answer with a nod, to nod; **elle me fit signe d'entrer d'un m. de tête** she signalled to me to come in; **avoir un m. de dégoût** to recoil in disgust; **il a eu un m. de recul** he recoiled, he started backwards; **mettre un mécanisme en m.** to set a machine in motion, to start a machine; **se mettre en m.** to start off, to move off; **c'est une ville toujours en m.** it's a bustling *or* very lively city; **quelques mouvements de gymnastique** a few exercises; **des mouvements**

pour soulager son mal de dos exercises to relieve one's backache; **on ne pouvait pas faire un m.** you couldn't move; **un film d'action où il y a beaucoup de m.** an action film with lots going on; **pièces en m.** *(de machine)* moving parts; **contrôler le m. des marchandises/des capitaux** to monitor the flow *or* movement of goods/capital; *Aut* **m. de caisse** body roll; *Mil* **m. de troupes** troop movement; **guerre de m.** mobile warfare; **amorcer un m. de repli** to start falling back; *Fam* **il faut accélérer le m.** we'll have to get a move on; **m. perpétuel** perpetual motion

2 *(changement)* **m. de terrain** undulation; **un m. de personnel** staff changes; **suivre le m.** to go with the flow; **le m. des idées** evolution of ideas; **le m. des naissances** the trend in the birth rate; *Fam* **être dans le m.** to be with it, to be abreast of the times *or* up to date; *Bourse* **connaître un m. à la hausse/à la baisse** to move up/down; **m. ascensionnel** upward movement; **m. de baisse** downward movement; **m. boursier** Stock Market movement; **mouvements de compte** account transactions; **m. des capitaux** movement of capital; **m. des cours/des prix** price fluctuation; **m. des devises** currency fluctuation; **m. des valeurs** share movements; **mouvements monétaires** monetary fluctuations

3 *(élan)* **mon premier m. fut de …** my first impulse was to …; **m. d'humeur** outburst (of temper); **dans un m. de colère** in a fit of anger; **de son propre m.** of one's own accord; **avoir un bon m.** to act on a kindly impulse; **allez! un bon m.!** be a good sort!

4 *Pol etc* movement; **le m. syndical/ouvrier** the union/labour movement; **M. de libération de la femme** Women's Liberation Movement, *Fam* Women's Lib; **m. pacifiste** peace movement; **m. de contestation** protest movement; **m. de défense des consommateurs** consumer movement; **les cheminots vont reconduire leur m. de grève** the railwaymen want to extend their strike action; **lancer un m. de grève/révolte** to instigate a strike/revolt; **m. indépendantiste** independence *or* separatist movement; **m. insurrectionnel** uprising; **m. ouvrier** labour movement; **m. séparatiste** separatist *or* independence movement; **mouvements sociaux** workers' protest movements; **m. syndical** trade-union *or* Am labor-union movement

5 *(aspect)* *(de draperies, cou, reins)* line(s); *(de terrain)* contours

6 *(dans un port, un aéroport, une gare)* traffic; **un quartier où il y a toujours beaucoup de m.** a very busy area, an area with a lot of traffic; *Rail* **mouvements des trains** train arrivals and departures; *Rail* **chef de m.** traffic manager; **mouvements des navires** shipping intelligence

7 *Mus* movement; **symphonie à trois mouvements** symphony in three movements; **presser/ralentir le m.** to quicken/slow the tempo

8 *(d'horloge)* works, movement; **m. d'horlogerie** clockwork

mouvementé [muvmɑ̃te] ADJ **1** *(discussion, débat)* animated, lively; *(journée, voyage, traversée, vie)* eventful; **une partie mouvementée** an exciting game **2** **terrain m.** undulating ground

mouvoir [muvwar] *(prp* **mouvant;** *pp* **mû,** *f* **mue;** *pr ind* **je meus, il meut, n. mouvons, ils meuvent;** *pr sub* **je meuve, n. mouvions, ils meuvent;** *p hist* **je mus** *(rare); fu* **je mouvrai)** VT **1** *(machine)* to drive, *Fml* to actuate; *(bateau)* to propel; **mû par la vapeur** steam-driven; **mû par un ressort** spring-loaded; *Fig* **mû par la colère** moved *or* prompted by anger; **mû par l'intérêt** prompted by interest **2** *(objet)* to move
VPR **se mouvoir** to move

moyen¹, -enne [mwajɛ̃, -ɛn] **ADJ 1** *(du milieu)* middle; **les classes moyennes** the middle class(es); *Scol* **cours m.** intermediate class; **cours m. première/deuxième année** *Br* ≃ primary IV/V, *Am* ≃ fourth/fifth grade; *Géog* **le cours m. d'un fleuve** the middle reaches of a river; **moyenne saison** *(en tourisme)* shoulder period **2** *(coût, prix, durée, consommateur, élève, altitude etc)* average; *(pression, vitesse, température, temps de réaction)* average, *surtout Spéc* mean; *(qualité)* average, medium; **la durée moyenne de travail du Français** the average hours of work in France; **le Français m.** the average Frenchman, the man in the street; **à m. terme** in the medium term; **choisir un m. terme** to choose a middle course; **entre la passivité et la guerre, il doit y avoir un m. terme** there must be a middle ground between passiveness and war; **de taille** *ou* **grandeur moyenne** medium-sized; **femme de taille moyenne** woman of average height; *Péj* **travail/vin d'une qualité très moyenne** very average work/wine, work/wine of a very indifferent quality; **il est trop m. en physique** his physics marks aren't good enough

MOYEN² **NM** VOIR GRAMMAIRE A13 **1** means; *Prov* **la fin justifie les moyens** the end justifies the means; *Prov* **qui veut la fin veut les moyens** you can't make an omelette without breaking eggs; **par tous les moyens** any way I/you/*etc* can/could, *Péj* by fair means or foul; **j'emploierai tous les moyens** I'll use whatever means I have to, I'll do whatever I have to; **employer les grands moyens** to take extreme measures; **au m.** *ou* **par (le) m. de qch** by means of *or* with the help of sth; **il a calé la table au m. d'un ticket de métro** he used a metro ticket as a wedge for the table, he wedged the table with a metro ticket; **y a-t-il m. de le faire?** is there any way it can be done?, is it possible (to do it)?; **y a-t-il m. d'éviter le centre-ville?** is there any way of avoiding the centre of town?; **y aurait-il m. de s'arrêter cinq minutes?** would it be possible to *or* could we stop for five minutes?; **y aurait-il m. d'avoir un vol moins cher/d'avoir un peu de pain avec mon fromage?** is there any chance of a cheaper flight/a bit of bread with my cheese?; **il y a m. de la contacter par l'intermédiaire de ses parents** she can be contacted through her parents; **il n'y a pas m.** it can't be done, it's impossible; **j'ai essayé d'ouvrir le pot, il n'y a pas m.** I've tried to open the jar but it's impossible, *Fam* I've tried but no way can I get the jar open; **il n'y a pas m. de le lui faire comprendre** there's no way of making him understand, it's impossible to *or Fam* no way can you make him understand; **j'ai essayé de le convaincre mais il n'y a pas eu m.** I tried to convince him but it was impossible *or* but I couldn't budge him; *Fam* **j'ai essayé de lui faire entendre raison/de le faire changer d'avis: pas m.!** I tried to make him see reason/change his mind, but no way!; *Fam* **j'ai essayé de joindre au téléphone tout l'après-midi: pas m.!** I tried all afternoon to get him on the phone but it was impossible *or* but nothing doing; *Fam* **y'a m.!** can do!; **trouver un m. de faire qch** to find a way *or* means of doing sth; **trouver le m. de faire qch** to discover *or* find out how to do sth; **il a encore trouvé le m. de se faire dispenser** he's managed to get out of it again; *Iron* **elle a trouvé le m. de se mettre mal avec tous ses collègues** she's managed to get *or* she's succeeded in getting on bad terms with all her colleagues; **inventer un m. de s'échapper** to come up with a way of escaping; **faire qch par ses propres moyens** to

do sth on one's own *or* unaided; **elle est venue par ses propres moyens** she came under her own steam; **m. de transport** means of transport; **disposes-tu d'un m. de transport?** do you have transport?; **moyens de production** means of production; **moyens de communication** means of communication; **avec les moyens du bord** with the means at one's disposal; **nous avons fait avec les moyens du bord** we made do with what we had; **si tu veux réussir, il faut t'en donner les moyens** if you want to succeed, you have to equip yourself to do so; **dans la mesure de mes moyens** to the best *or* to the utmost of my ability, as best I can; **enfant qui a des moyens** bright *or* talented child; **il a peu de moyens** he's not very bright; **perdre tous ses moyens** to lose one's head, to go to pieces; **faire perdre tous ses moyens à qn** to make sb lose his/her head

2 *Fin* **moyens** means; **moyens de paiement** means of payment; **moyens financiers** financial means; **moyens liquides** liquid resources; **vivre au-dessus de ses moyens** to live beyond one's means; **il a largement les moyens de faire construire** he can well afford to build; **je n'en ai pas les moyens** I can't afford it; **ils ont les moyens** *(ils ont de l'argent)* they're well off; *(ils peuvent se le permettre)* they can afford it; **dans la mesure de mes moyens** as best I can, as far as my finances permit

Moyen Âge [mwajɛnaʒ] **NM le M.** the Middle Ages; **le haut M.** the early Middle Ages; **coutumes du M.** medieval customs

moyenâgeux, -euse [mwajɛnaʒø, -øz] **ADJ** medieval; *Fig Péj* medieval, old-fashioned, outdated

moyen-courrier, *pl* **moyens-courriers** **ADJ, NM (avion)** m. medium-range *or* medium-haul aircraft

moyen-métrage, *pl* **moyens-métrages** **NM** *Cin* medium-length film

moyennant [mwajɛnɑ̃] **PRÉP** (in return) for; **louer qch m. cent euros par jour** to hire sth for *or* at (a charge of) a hundred euros a day; **m. paiement** in exchange for payment, subject to payment; **faire qch m. finance** to do sth in return for payment *or* for a consideration; **je veux bien nettoyer ton jardin, mais m. finance** I'm willing to tidy up your garden, but I'll want to be paid for it; **m. dix euros** for ten euros, on payment of ten euros; **m. quoi** in return for which, *Fml* in consideration of which; **je l'ai aidé à faire son devoir d'anglais, m. quoi il …** I helped him with his English homework, and in return he …

moyenne [mwajɛn] **NF** average; *Math* mean; *Scol* pass mark; **j'ai 8/20 de m. en mathématiques** I averaged 40% in maths; *Scol* **améliorer sa m. de français** to improve one's average (mark) in French; **en m.** on (an) average; **m. (horaire)** (hourly) average; *Aut* average (speed); **faire du 100 de m.** to do an average of *or* to average 100 kilometres per hour; **supérieure/inférieure à la m.** above/below average, higher/lower than average; **enfant d'une intelligence au-dessus/au-dessous de la m.** child of above/below average intelligence; **m. de temps entre deux pannes** mean time between failures, MTBF; *Compta* **m. mobile** moving average; **m. pondérée** weighted average

moyennement [mwajɛnmɑ̃] **ADV** moderately, fairly; **travailler m.** to work fairly well

Moyen-Orient [mwajɛnɔrjɑ̃] **NM le M.** the Middle East

moyen-oriental, -ale, -aux, -ales [mwajɛnɔrjɑ̃tal, -o] **ADJ** Middle Eastern

moyette [mwajɛt] **NF** *Agr (de blé)* shock

moyeu, -eux [mwajø] **NM** *(de roue de voiture)* hub; *(de roue de charrette)* nave; *(d'hélice)* boss

mozambicain, -aine [mɔzãbikɛ̃, -ɛn] **ADJ** Mozambican

N M. Mozambican

Mozambique [mɔzãbik] **NM** Mozambique

mozzarella [mɔdzarɛla], **mozzarelle** [mɔdzarɛl] **NF** mozzarella

MRAP [mrap] **NM** *(abrév* **Mouvement contre le racisme, l'antisémitisme et pour la paix)** = French antiracist pacifist movement

MS-DOS [ɛmɛsdɔs] **NM** *Ordinat (abrév* **Microsoft Disk Operating System)** MS-DOS

MST¹ [ɛmɛste] **NF** *Méd (abrév* **maladie sexuellement transmissible)** STD

MST² **NF** *(abrév* **Maîtrise de Sciences et Techniques)** M. hôtellerie-restauration = higher vocational qualification in hotel management and catering

mû *voir* **mouvoir**

muance [mɥɑ̃s] **NF** *Arch (à la puberté)* breaking of the voice

mucilage [mysilaʒ] **NM** mucilage, gum

mucilagineux, -euse [mysilaʒinø, -øz] **ADJ** mucilaginous, viscous

mucosité [mykozite] **NF** mucus, mucosity

mucoviscidose [mykovisidoz] **NF** *Méd* cystic fibrosis

mucus [mykys] **NM** mucus

mue [my] **NF 1** *(d'oiseaux, de mammifères, de crustacés)* moult(ing), *Am* molt(ing); *(de cerf)* shedding *or* casting of the antlers; *(de reptiles)* sloughing; *(époque)* moulting season; *(dépouille) (d'oiseau)* discarded feathers; *(de crustacé)* discarded shell; *(de cerf)* discarded antlers; *(de serpents)* slough; **serin en m.** moulting canary **2** *Physiol (à la puberté)* breaking of the voice **3** *(cage) (pour faucons)* mew; *(pour volaille)* coop

muer [mɥe] **VT** *Litt* **m. sa tête** *(de cerf)* to shed *or* cast its antlers

VI 1 *(d'oiseau, de mammifère, de crustacé)* to moult, *Am* to molt; *(de cerf)* to shed *or* cast its antlers; *(de reptile)* to slough, to cast its skin **2** *(de voix) (à la puberté)* to break; **il commence à m.** his voice is breaking

VPR se muer se m. en to change (in)to

muesli [mɥɛsli, mysli] **NM** muesli

muet, -ette [mɥɛ, -ɛt] **ADJ** *(personne) (privé de l'usage de la parole)* dumb; *(silencieux)* silent, dumb, mute; *(film, cinéma, complicité)* Ling silent; *(rôle, acteur)* non-speaking, walk-on; *(carte géographique)* blank; *(clavier de machine à écrire)* blank, unmarked; **m. de naissance** born dumb, dumb from birth; *Fig* **la stupeur m'a rendu m.** I was struck dumb with astonishment; **j'écoutais, m. d'étonnement** I listened, speechless with astonishment *or* in mute astonishment; **m. de colère** speechless with anger; **rester m.** to remain silent; **m. comme une tombe** (as) silent as the grave; **il est resté m. comme une carpe** *(il n'a pas répondu à la question)* he didn't say a word, he clammed up; **tu es resté m. comme une carpe toute la soirée** you didn't open your mouth *or* say a word all evening; **les grandes douleurs sont muettes** great sorrow is often silent; **le cinéma m.** silent cinema *or* films

N mute

NM *Cin* **le m.** silent films

muezzin [mɥedzin] **NM** muezzin

mufle [myfl] **NM 1** *(du bœuf, bison etc)* (hairless part of) muzzle, muffle; *(de lion, taureau etc)* nose, *Fam* snout **2** *Fam (malotru)* boor, lout

muflée [myfle] **NF** *Fam* **prendre une m.** to get wrecked *or* wasted *or Br* legless; **il tenait une sacrée m.** he was totally wrecked *or* wasted *or Br* legless

muflerie [myflǝri] NF *Fam* **1** *(caractère)* boorishness **2** *(action)* boorish behaviour; **lassée de ses mufleries** tired of his boorish behaviour *or* boorishness **3** *(parole)* boorish remark

muflier [myflije] NM *Bot* antirrhinum, snapdragon

mufti [myfti] NM *Rel* mufti

muge [myʒ] NM *(poisson)* mullet

mugir [myʒir] VI **1** *(de vache)* to low, to moo; *(de taureau)* to bellow **2** *(du vent)* to moan, to howl; *(d'un torrent)* to roar; *(d'une sirène)* to wail

mugissement [myʒismã] NM **1** *(de vache)* lowing, mooing; *(de taureau)* bellowing **2** *(du vent)* moaning, howling; *(d'un torrent)* roaring; *(d'une sirène)* wailing

muguet [mygε] NM **1** *(plante)* lily of the valley **2** *Méd* thrush

Muguet
On May Day in France, bunches of lily of the valley are sold in the streets and given as presents. The flowers are supposed to bring good luck.

mulâtre [mylɑtr] ADJ mulatto, half-caste N *(f* **mulâtre, mulâtresse** [mylɑtrεs]*)* mulatto

mule¹ [myl] NF **1** *Zool* mule **2** *Fam (passeur de drogue)* mule

mule² NF *(pantoufle)* mule; **la m. du Pape** the Pope's slipper; **baiser la m. du Pape** to kiss the Pope's toe

mulet¹ [mylε] NM *Zool* mule

mulet² NM *(poisson)* grey mullet

muletier, -ière [myltje, -jεr] ADJ *(chemin, sentier)* mule; **équipage m.** mule train ■ NM mule driver, muleteer

mulot [mylo] NM field mouse

multibancarisation [myltibãkarizasjɔ̃] NF growth in the number of banks

multicantonal, -ale, -aux, -ales [myltikãtɔnal, -o] ADJ *Suisse* involving many cantons

multicarte [myltikart] ADJ, N **(représentant) m.** rep for several companies

multicellulaire [myltiselylεr] ADJ multicellular

multicolonnage [myltikɔlɔnaʒ] NM *Ordinat* multicolumn working

multicolore [myltikɔlɔr] ADJ multicoloured, *Am* multicolored

multicoque [myltikɔk] NM *Naut* multihull

multicritère [myltikritεr] NM *Ordinat* multicriterion

multiculturalisme [myltikyltyralism] NM multiculturalism

multiculturel, -elle [myltikyltyrεl] ADJ multicultural

multidevise [myltidǝviz] ADJ multicurrency

multidimensionnel, -elle [myltidimã- sjɔnεl] ADJ multidimensional; *Fig (expérience, compétence etc)* multifaceted

multidisciplinaire [myltidisiplinεr] ADJ multidisciplinary

multidistribution [myltidistribysjɔ̃] NF multidistribution

multi-écran, *pl* **multi-écrans** [myltiekrã] NM *TV* multiscreen, split screen

multiemploi [myltiãplwa] NM = holding several jobs at the same time

multiflore [myltiflɔr] ADJ *Bot* multiflora

multifonctions [myltifɔ̃ksjɔ̃] ADJ multifunctional; *Ordinat* **clavier m.** multi-functional keyboard

multiforme [myltifɔrm] ADJ multiform; *Fig (pays, problème etc)* multifaceted

multigrade [myltigrad] ADJ *(huile)* multigrade

multi-image, *pl* **multi-images** [myltiimaʒ] ADJ *TV etc* multi-image

multilatéral, -ale, -aux, -ales [myltilateral, -o] ADJ *(accord)* multilateral

multimarque [myltimark] NF *Mktg* multibrand

multimédia [myltimedja] ADJ, NM multimedia

multimilliardaire [myltimiljarder], **multimillionnaire** [myltimiljɔner] ADJ, N multimillionaire

multimode [myltimɔd] ADJ *Ordinat* multimode

multinational, -ale, -aux, -ales [myltinasjɔnal, -o] ADJ multinational
■ NF **multinationale** multinational (company)

multinorme [myltinɔrm] ADJ *TV* multistandard

multipare [myltipar] ADJ multiparous ■ NF multipara

multipartisme [myltipartism] NM *Pol* multiparty system

multipartite [myltipartit] ADJ *Pol* multiparty, multipartite

multipassage [myltipasaʒ] ADJ *Ordinat* multistrike

multipiste [myltipist] ADJ multitrack

multiplace [myltiplas] ADJ, NM **(avion) m.** passenger aircraft

multiplateforme [myltiplatfɔrm] ADJ *Ordinat* cross-platform

multiple [myltipl] ADJ **1** *(raisons, résidences, talents, dangers)* many, numerous; *Psy (personnalité)* multiple; **les causes sont multiples** the reasons are many *or Fml* manifold; **à usages multiples** multipurpose; **maison à succursales multiples** multiple store, chain store; *Scol* **question à choix multiples** multiple-choice question; **nous avons essayé de vous joindre à de multiples reprises** we tried repeatedly to contact you; *Ordinat* **à accès m.** multi-access **2** *(complexe) (monde, âme etc)* complex, multifaceted
■ NM *Math* multiple; **le plus petit commun m.** the lowest common multiple

multiplex [myltiplεks] ADJ INV, NM *Radio, TV* multiplex

multiplexage [myltiplεksaʒ] NM multiplexing

multiplexe [myltiplεks] NM multiplex (cinema)

multiplexé [myltiplεkse] ADJ multiplex

multiplexer [myltiplεkse] VT to multiplex

multiplexeur [myltiplεksœr] NM multiplexer, multiplexor

multipliable [myltiplijabl] ADJ multipliable; **tout nombre est m.** any number can be multiplied

multiplicande [myltiplikãd] NM *Math* multiplicand

multiplicateur, -trice [myltiplikatœr, -tris] ADJ multiplying; **engrenage m.** step-up gear ■ NM *Math, Élec* multiplier

multiplicatif, -ive [myltiplikatif, -iv] ADJ multiplicative, multiplying

multiplication [myltiplikasjɔ̃] NF **1** *Math* multiplication; **la m. des vols de voitures/ des clubs sportifs** the increase in car theft/ in the number of sports clubs; *Bible* **la m. des pains** the miracle of the loaves and fishes **2** *Tech* gear (ratio); **grande/petite m.** high/low gear; **m. du levier** leverage

multiplicité [myltiplisite] NF multiplicity

multiplier [myltiplije] *(pr sub, impf* n. **multipliions,** v. **multipliiez)** VT **1** *Math* to multiply

(par by) **2** *(répéter)* **m. les mises en garde** to issue repeated warnings; **m. les erreurs** to make mistake after mistake; **le chef de l'État a multiplié les appels au calme** the head of state has called repeatedly for calm; **ses erreurs/efforts multiplié(e)s** his repeated mistakes/efforts **3** *Tech* **m. la vitesse de révolution** to gear up
VPR **se multiplier 1** to increase; **les crimes se multiplient** crime is on the increase; **les lapins se multiplient rapidement** rabbits multiply rapidly **2** *Fig (être partout à la fois)* to be in half a dozen places at once; **se m. pour aider qn** to bend over backwards to help sb

multipolaire [myltipɔlεr] ADJ **1** *Élec, Biol* multipolar **2** *Pol* multipolar

multipostage [myltipɔstaʒ] NM volume mailing

multiposte [myltipɔst] ADJ *Ordinat* multistation

multiprocesseur [myltiprɔsesœr] NM *Ordinat* multiprocessor

multiprogrammation [myltiprɔgramasjɔ̃] NF *Ordinat* multiprogramming

multipropriété [myltiprɔprijete] NF timeshare, multi-ownership; **acheter un appartement/une maison en m.** to buy a timeshare (flat/house)

multiracial, -iale, -iaux, -iales [myltirasjal, -jo] ADJ multiracial

multirécidiviste [myltiresidivist] N persistent offender, repeat offender

multirisque [myltirisk] ADJ **assurance m.** comprehensive insurance

multisalles [myltisal] ADJ INV **complexe m.** multiplex (cinema)
■ NM INV multiplex (cinema)

multisectoriel, -ielle [myltisektɔrjεl] ADJ multisector

multisoupape [myltisupap] NM *Aut* multivalve (engine)

multistandard [myltistãdar] ADJ INV *TV* multistandard

multitâche [myltitaʃ] ADJ *Ordinat* multitasking

multithérapie [myltiterapi] NF *Méd* combination therapy

multitraitement [myltitrεtmã] NM *Ordinat* multiprocessing

multitude [myltityd] NF **1** multitude (**de** of); **une m. de gens** hosts *or* crowds *or* swarms of people; **il y avait sur la cheminée une m. de bibelots** the mantelpiece was crowded with ornaments **2** *Litt Péj* **la m.** the masses

multi-utilisateur, *pl* **multi-utilisateurs** [myltiytilizatœr] ADJ *Ordinat* multi-user

multivision [myltivizjɔ̃] NF *TV* multivision

munichois, -oise [mynikwa, -waz] ADJ of/ from Munich
■ N **1 M.** *(natif)* native of Munich; *(habitant)* inhabitant of Munich **2** *Hist, Pol (partisan des accords de Munich)* Munich supporter **3** *(capitulard)* defeatist

municipal, -ale, -aux, -ales [mynisipal, -o] ADJ *(élection, employé)* municipal, localgovernment; *(bibliothèque, stade, patinoire, piscine)* municipal, local; **conseil m.** town council, local council; **arrêté m.** bylaw; *Hist* **la garde municipale** the military police *(of Paris)*
■ NFPL **les municipales** municipal *or* local (-government) elections

Municipales
These are the elections where residents choose the town councils. Electors vote for a list of council members whose leader or "tête de liste" will become the mayor, a ceremonial and political post.

municipalisation [mynisipalizasjɔ̃] NF municipalization; **la m. des sols a été votée** there has been a vote in favour of placing land under municipal control

municipaliser [mynisipalize] VT to municipalize

municipalité [mynisipalite] NF **1** *(ville)* municipality, town **2** *(région)* local administrative area **3** *(maire et conseillers municipaux)* (local) council, corporation

munificence [mynifisɑ̃s] NF *Litt* munificence

munificent [mynifisɑ̃] ADJ *Litt* munificent

munir [mynir] VT *(personne)* to supply, to provide, *Fml* to furnish (**de** with); *(voiture, chambre)* to fit, to equip (**de** with); **muni des sacrements de l'Église** fortified with the rites of the Church

    VPR **se munir se m. de** *(vêtements chauds, cartes routières, provisions)* to equip or provide oneself with; *(crème solaire, parapluie)* to take; **il faut se m. d'un passeport** you need (to take) a passport

munition [mynisjɔ̃] NF **1 munitions (de guerre)** ammunition, munitions; **des armes et des munitions** arms and ammunition **2** *Arch (d'armée)* munitioning, provisioning; **munitions de bouche** provisions

munster [mœ̃stɛr] NM Munster (cheese)

muon [myɔ̃] NM *Phys* muon

muphti [myfti] NM *Rel* mufti

muqueux, -euse [mykø, -øz] ADJ *(membrane)* mucous
    NF **muqueuse** mucous membrane

mur [myr] NM *Constr, Fig (d'eau, de policiers)* wall; **m. de clôture** surrounding wall; **m. d'appui** low wall; **m. de soutènement** retaining wall; **m. de refend** partition (wall); **m. mitoyen** party wall; **m. porteur** load-bearing wall; **m. d'escalade, m. de varappe** climbing wall; **gros murs** main walls; *Fam* **les cambrioleurs n'ont laissé que les (quatre) murs** the burglars took everything but the kitchen sink, the burglars stripped the place bare; **rester entre quatre murs** *(en prison)* to be inside; **j'en ai marre de rester entre quatre murs toute la journée** I'm tired of being cooped up all day; *Fig* **mettre qn au pied du m.** to put sb on the spot, to drive sb into a corner, to have sb with his back to the wall; **être au pied du m.** to have one's back to the wall; **l'ennemi est dans nos murs** the enemy is within the gates; *Fig* **il est à présent dans nos murs** *(en visite dans notre ville)* he is in town at the moment; *(dans nos locaux)* he is on the premises at the moment; *Fig* **c'est à se taper la tête contre les murs** it's enough to drive or send you up the wall; *Fig* **se heurter à un m.** to come up against a brick wall; **se heurter à un m. d'incompréhension** to come up against a wall or a barrier of incomprehension; *Fig* **j'ai l'impression de parler à un m.** it's like talking to a brick wall; *Fig* **les murs ont des oreilles** walls have ears; **faire le m.** to sneak out
    ▸▸ *Hist* **le m. de Berlin** the Berlin Wall; *Ordinat* **m. coupe-feu** firewall; **le m. des Lamentations** the Wailing Wall; **m. du son** sound barrier; **franchir le m. du son** to break the sound barrier

mûr [myr] ADJ **1** *(fruit)* ripe; *(vin)* mellow; *(personne, esprit)* mature; **trop m.** *(fruit)* overripe; **il est très m. pour son âge** he is very mature for his age; **l'abcès est m.** the abscess has come to a head; **l'âge m.** maturity; **homme d'âge m.** man of mature years; **après mûre réflexion** after careful or *Fml* mature consideration; **m. pour qch** ripe or ready for sth; *Litt* **les temps sont mûrs** the time has come, the time is ripe **2** *Arg (saoul)* plastered, canned

murage [myraʒ] NM *(de porte, fenêtre)* walling up, blocking up

muraille [myraj] NF **1** *(mur)* (high) wall; **la Grande M. de Chine** the Great Wall of China; **les murailles de la ville** the town walls **2** *(de bateau)* side

mural, -ale, -aux, -ales [myral, -o] ADJ wall; **peinture murale** mural; **pendule murale** wall clock; **carte murale** wall map; *Archit* **console murale** wall bracket

mûre [myr] NF **1 m. (sauvage** *ou* **de ronce)** blackberry **2** *(fruit du mûrier)* mulberry

mûrement [myrmɑ̃] ADV **après avoir m. réfléchi** after careful or *Fml* mature consideration; **un plan m. réfléchi** a carefully thought-out plan; **tout cela a été m. préparé** it was all very carefully planned

murène [myrɛn] NF *(poisson)* moray (eel)

murer [myre] VT **1** *(entourer de murs) (ville, cité)* to wall in **2** *(bloquer) (porte, fenêtre)* to wall up, to block up; *(personne)* to wall up
    VPR **se murer** to shut oneself away; **elle se mure dans le silence/la solitude** she has retreated or withdrawn into silence/solitude; **muré chez soi** shut away at home

muret [myrɛ] NM, **murette** [myrɛt] NF low wall; *(de pierres posées les unes sur les autres)* dry-stone wall

murge [myrʒ] NF *Fam* **prendre une m.** *(s'enivrer)* to get wasted or *Br* legless

mûrier [myrje] NM *Bot* mulberry (tree or bush); **m. (sauvage)** blackberry bush, bramble

mûrir [myrir] VT *(fruit)* to ripen; *Fig (projet, pensées)* to nurture; **les épreuves l'ont beaucoup mûri** his hardships have made him much more mature; **laisser m. un abcès** to let an abscess come to a head
    VI *(de fruit)* to ripen; *(d'abcès)* to come to a head; *(de projet, processus)* to evolve, to develop; *(de sentiment)* to ripen; **cet enfant a beaucoup mûri** the child has become much more mature or has greatly matured

mûrissant [myrisɑ̃] ADJ *(fruit)* ripening; *(personne)* of mature years

mûrissement [myrismɑ̃] NM *(de fruits)* ripening; *Fig (de projet)* development

murmure [myrmyr] NM *(à voix basse)* murmur, murmuring; *(de ruisseau)* babbling; **murmures** murmuring, murmurs; *(plaintes)* murmuring, muttering, grumbling; **un m. d'approbation** a murmur of approval; **ce fut accepté sans un m. (de réprobation)** this was accepted without a murmur

murmurer [myrmyre] VT to murmur; **on murmure qu'il va démissionner** rumour has it or there are rumours that he's going to resign
    VI *(à voix basse)* to murmur; *(se plaindre)* to grumble, to complain; *(cancaner)* to say things, to talk; *(de ruisseau)* to babble; **m. entre ses dents** to mutter

mûron [myrɔ̃] NM *Bot* wild raspberry

musaraigne [myzarɛɲ] NF *Zool* shrew

musard, -arde [myzar, -ard] *Fam Vieilli* ADJ dawdling
    N dawdler

musarder [myzarde] VI to dawdle, to amble; *(fainéanter)* to dither

musc [mysk] NM musk

muscade [myskad] NF **1** *Bot* **(noix) m.** nutmeg; **fleur de m.** mace **2** *(d'escamoteur)* vanishing ball; **passez m.!** hey presto!

muscadier [myskadje] NM *Bot* nutmeg (tree)

muscadin [myskadɛ̃] NM *Arch* dandy, fop

muscardin [myskardɛ̃] NM *Zool* dormouse

muscat [myska] ADJ muscat; **raisin m.** muscat grape, muscatel grape; **vin m.** muscatel (wine)

    NM *(raisin)* muscat or muscatel grape; *(vin)* muscatel (wine)

muscle [myskl] NM muscle; **avoir des muscles** to be muscular, to be brawny; **il est tout en muscles** he's all muscle; **m. antagoniste** antagonistic muscle; **m. biceps** biceps

musclé [myskle] ADJ *(personne, bras, jambes)* muscular, brawny; **il est bien m.** he is very muscular, he has well-developed muscles; *Fig* **cet écrivain écrit dans un style m.** this author has a sinewy or robust style; **un café m.** a good strong coffee; **une campagne électorale musclée** a punchy electoral campaign; **un discours m.** a punchy or forceful speech; **l'intervention musclée de la police** the strong-arm tactics of the police; **un régime m.** a strong-arm regime; **politique musclée** hardline or tough policy

muscler [myskle] VT to develop the muscles of; **il faut te m. les jambes** you must develop your leg muscles; *Fig* **tout faire pour m. l'industrie française** to do everything to give French industry some muscle or to beef up French industry
    VI *Fam* **le sport, ça muscle** sport builds up your muscles
    VPR **se muscler** to develop one's muscles

muscu [mysky] NF *Fam* = **musculation**

musculaire [myskylɛr] ADJ *(système, tissu, force)* muscular; **fibre m.** muscle fibre

musculation [myskylasjɔ̃] NF body-building; **faire de la m.** to do body-building

musculature [myskylatyr] NF musculature; **il a une belle m.** he has a fine set of muscles

musculeux, -euse [myskylø, -øz] ADJ *aussi Anat* muscular

muse [myz] NF muse; *Myth* **les Muses** the Muses; **invoquer sa m.** to invoke or call on one's muse; **taquiner la M.** to write the odd bit of verse

museau, -eaux [myzo] NM **1** *(d'animal)* muzzle, snout; *Culin* **m. vinaigrette** = brawn in vinaigrette **2** *Fam (visage)* face; **vilain m.** ugly mug

musée [myze] NM museum; **m. (de peinture ou d'art)** art gallery; **m. des arts et traditions populaires** folk museum; **m. des transports** transport museum; **Venise, ville-m.** the historical city of Venice; *Fam* **chez eux, c'est le m. des horreurs!** their place is full of things I wouldn't give house room to!; **tu as vu le m. des horreurs!** *(ce groupe)* what an ugly looking crew!

muséifier [myzeifje] VT *Péj (quartier, ville)* to museumify

museler [myzle] VT (**je muselle; je musellerai**) *(animal)* to muzzle; *Fig (personne, la presse, l'opposition)* to muzzle, to gag

muselière [myzəljɛr] NF muzzle; **mettre une m. à** *(un chien), Fig (la presse)* to muzzle

musellement [myzɛlmɑ̃] NM *(d'animal)* muzzling; *(de personne, la presse)* muzzling, gagging

muséographie [myzeɔgrafi] NF museography

muser [myze] VI **1** *Arch, Litt* to idle (about); *(flâner)* to dawdle, to amble **2** *Belg (fredonner)* to hum

muserolle [myzrɔl] NF *Équitation* noseband

musette [myzɛt] NF **1** *Mus (instrument)* musette *(type of bagpipe)*; **orchestre m.** accordion band; **bal m.** dance to an accordion band; *(lieu)* dance hall with an accordion band **2** *(de cheval)* **m. (mangeoire)** nosebag **3** *(sac)* bag; *Mil* haversack; *Arch (d'écolier)* satchel
    NM *Mus Fam* **le m.** accordion music

muséum [myzeɔm] NM natural history museum

musical, -ale, -aux, -ales [myzikal, -o] ADJ *(son, soirée)* musical; **l'art m.** music; **avoir l'oreille musicale** to have an ear *or* a good ear for music

musicalement [myzikalmɑ̃] ADV musically

musicalité [myzikalite] NF musicality, musical quality

music-hall, *pl* **music-halls** [myzikol] NM *(spectacle)* variety, *Br* music hall, *Am* vaudeville; *(salle)* variety theatre, *Br* music hall, *Am* vaudeville theater; **faire du m.** to do variety *or Br* music hall *or Am* vaudeville; **numéros de m.** variety turns

musicien, -ienne [myzisjɛ̃, -jɛn] ADJ musical
N musician

musicographe [myzikɔgraf] N musicographer

musicologie [myzikɔlɔʒi] NF musicology

musicologue [myzikɔlɔg] N musicologist

musicos [myzikos] NM *Fam* muso

musicothérapie [myzikoterapi] NF music therapy

musique [myzik] NF music; **mettre des paroles en m.** to set words to music; **instrument de m.** musical instrument; **boîte à m.** music(al) box; **chef de m.** bandmaster; **m. classique** classical music; **m. légère** light music; **m. folklorique** folk music; **m. pop** pop music; **m. religieuse** church music; **m. de chambre** chamber music; **m. d'ambiance** *ou* **de fond** background music; **m. de supermarché** Muzak®, piped music; **m. militaire** *(formation)* military band; *(composition)* military music; **faire de la m.** to make music, to play; **lire la m.** to read music; *Fig Fam* **je connais la m.** I've heard it all before, it's the same old story; **il veut acheter la m. du film** he wants to buy the soundtrack of the film; *Fam* **en avant la m.!** let's get started!; *Can* **faire face à la m.** to face the music; *TV* **m. d'archives** library music; *TV etc* **m. de générique** title music, theme tune; *TV etc* **m. (de générique) de fin** playout music; *TV etc* **m. d'ouverture** introductory music

musiquette [myzikɛt] NF *Péj* piped music, Muzak®

musoir [myzwar] NM pierhead, jetty head

musqué [myske] ADJ 1 *(odeur, parfum)* musky 2 **bœuf m.** musk ox; **rat m.** muskrat, musquash; **canard m.** muscovy duck, musk duck 3 *Arch (poète, style etc)* affected

must [mœst] NM *Fam* must

mustang [mystɑ̃g] NM mustang

musulman, -ane [myzylmɑ̃, -an] ADJ, N Muslim, Moslem

mutabilité [mytabilite] NF mutability

mutable [mytabl] ADJ mutable

mutant, -ante [mytɑ̃, -ɑ̃t] ADJ, N mutant

mutation [mytasjɔ̃] NF 1 *(de personnel)* transfer; **il a demandé/obtenu sa m. pour raison de santé** he asked for/obtained a transfer for health reasons 2 *(changement)* change, alteration; *Biol* mutation; *Ling (de voyelle)* gradation; *(de consonne)* shift; *Jur* change of ownership; *(de propriété)* transfer; **l'Europe de l'Est est en pleine m. politique** Eastern Europe is undergoing profound political change; **le secteur sidérurgique a subi de profondes mutations** the steel industry has undergone extensive change(s)

muter [myte] VT *(personnel)* to transfer
VI *Biol* to mutate

mutilateur, -trice [mytilatœr, -tris] N mutilator
ADJ *Fig (expérience)* crippling

mutilation [mytilasjɔ̃] NF *(de personne)* mutilation, maiming; *(de statue, d'objet d'art)*

mutilation, defacement; *(de texte)* mutilation; **m. volontaire** self-mutilation

mutilé, -ée [mytile] ADJ *(personne)* mutilated, maimed; **il est m. du bras** he's lost an arm; **m. au visage** disfigured
N disabled person; **mutilés de guerre** disabled ex-servicemen

mutiler [mytile] VT *(personne)* to mutilate, to maim; *(statue, objet d'art)* to mutilate, to deface; *(arbre, texte)* to mutilate; *(paysage)* to disfigure; **il a eu les deux jambes mutilées à la guerre** he lost both legs in the war; **il a eu la main mutilée dans un accident du travail** his hand was badly injured in an industrial accident
VPR **se mutiler** to mutilate oneself

mutin [mytɛ̃] ADJ 1 *(malicieux)* mischievous, impish, playful 2 *Arch (désobéissant)* disobedient, unruly, unbiddable
NM *(rebelle)* mutineer

mutiné [mytine] ADJ rebellious; *(troupes)* mutinous
NM mutineer

mutiner (se) [səmytine] VPR to rebel (**contre** against); *Naut, Mil* to mutiny

mutinerie [mytinri] NF rebellion; *Naut, Mil* mutiny

mutique [mytik] ADJ *Méd (personne)* suffering from mutism

mutisme [mytism] NM 1 silence; **les responsables observent un m. absolu** the officials are maintaining (a) total silence; **s'enfermer dans le m.** to maintain a stubborn silence 2 *Méd* mutism

mutité [mytite] NF *Méd* mutism

mutualisme [mytɥalism] NM 1 *Biol* symbiosis, mutualism 2 *Écon* mutual insurance

mutualiste [mytɥalist] ADJ 1 *Biol* symbiotic, mutualistic 2 *Écon* **pharmacie m.** = chemist associated with a private insurance company, which may offer reduced rates on certain items to members of the company
N *Écon* member of a mutual insurance company

mutualité [mytɥalite] NF *Écon* mutual insurance; **société de m.** mutual insurance company, *Br* friendly society

mutuel, -elle [mytɥɛl] ADJ *(amour etc)* mutual; **société d'assurance mutuelle** mutual insurance company, *Br* friendly society
NF **mutuelle** *(société)* mutual insurance company, *Br* friendly society; *(assurance)* private insurance; **prendre une mutuelle** to take out private insurance

---

Mutuelle
A "mutuelle" is a non-profit-making health insurance company which provides insurance complementary to that of the **"Sécurité sociale".** Often these companies are set up for a particular profession: there is a "mutuelle" for students, one for teachers etc.

---

mutuellement [mytɥɛlmɑ̃] ADV each other, one another; **ils se sont aidés/critiqués m.** they helped/criticized each other *or* one another

Myanmar [mjanmar] NM Myanmar

Mycènes [misɛn] N *Hist* Mycenae

mycénien, -ienne [misenjɛ̃, -jɛn] ADJ *Hist* Mycenaean

mycologie [mikɔlɔʒi] NF *Bot* mycology

mycose [mikoz] NF *Méd* fungal infection, *Spéc* mycosis; *(sur les pieds)* athlete's foot

myéline [mjelin] NF *Anat* myelin

myélite [mjelit] NF *Méd* myelitis

myélome [mjelom] NM *Méd* myeloma

mygale [migal] NF trapdoor spider

myocarde [mjɔkard] NM *Anat* myocardium

myocardite [mjɔkardit] NF *Méd* myocarditis

myologie [mjɔlɔʒi] NF *Anat* myology

myome [mjom] NM *Méd* myoma

myopathe [mjɔpat] N *Méd* person with muscular dystrophy

myopathie [mjɔpati] NF *Méd* muscular dystrophy

myope [mjɔp] ADJ shortsighted, *Spéc* myopic; *Fig* **m. comme une taupe** as blind as a bat
N shortsighted person, *Spéc* myope

myopie [mjɔpi] NF *Méd* shortsightedness, *Spéc* myopia; *Mktg* **m. mercatique** marketing myopia

myosotis [mjɔzɔtis] NM *(fleur)* forget-me-not, *Spéc* myosotis

myriade [mirjad] NF myriad; **des myriades d'étoiles** myriads of stars, a myriad stars

myrmidon [mirmidɔ̃] NM *Fam* pipsqueak

myrrhe [mir] NF myrrh

myrte [mirt] NM *(plante)* myrtle; **m. des marais** bog myrtle

myrtille [mirtij] NF *(baie)* bilberry, whortleberry

Mystère® [mistɛr] NM *Culin* = ice-cream dessert coated with hazelnuts and with a meringue centre

mystère [mistɛr] NM 1 mystery; **rester un m.** to remain a mystery; **on n'a jamais pénétré ce m.** no one has ever got to the bottom of this mystery; **si tu veux réussir, il faut travailler, il n'y a pas de m.!** if you want to succeed, you have to work, there's no mystery about it *or* it's as simple as that!; **ce garçon est un m. pour moi** that boy's a mystery to me; *Fam* **m. et boule de gomme** *(je n'en ai aucune idée)* I've no idea, search me; *Fig* **ne fais pas tant de mystères!** don't be so mysterious!; **je n'en fais pas m.** I make no secret of it 2 *Hist, Littér* mystery (play); **m. de la Passion** Passion play 3 *Antiq, Myth* mystery

mystérieusement [misterjøzmɑ̃] ADV mysteriously

mystérieux, -ieuse [misterjø, -jøz] ADJ mysterious; *(secret)* secret; **un rendez-vous m.** a secret rendezvous
NM 1 **jouer le(s) m.** to behave very mysteriously 2 **le m.** the mysterious

mysticisme [mistisism] NM mysticism

mystifiable [mistifjabl] ADJ gullible

mystifiant [mistifjɑ̃] ADJ deceiving

mystificateur, -trice [mistifikatœr, -tris] ADJ *(coup de téléphone, lettre, annonce)* hoax; **avoir un côté m.** to have a mischievous streak
N hoaxer

mystification [mistifikasjɔ̃] NF *Péj (tromperie)* deception; *(farce)* hoax; **m. collective** mass deception

mystifier [mistifje] VT *(pr sub, impf* **n. mystifiions, v. mystifiiez)** **m. qn** *(faire marcher)* to pull sb's leg; *(leurrer)* to fool sb, to take sb in; **se laisser m. par qch** to (let oneself) be taken in *or* fooled by sth

---

Il faut noter que le verbe anglais **to mystify** est un faux ami. Il signifie **déconcerter, laisser perplexe.**

---

mystique [mistik] ADJ mystical
N *(personne)* mystic
NF mystique

mystiquement [mistikmɑ̃] ADV mystically

mythe [mit] NM myth

mythique [mitik] ADJ mythical

mytho [mito] N *Fam (abrév* **mythomane)** compulsive liar

mythologie [mitɔlɔʒi] NF mythology

mythologique [mitɔlɔʒik] ADJ mythological

mythologiquement [mitɔlɔʒikmã] ADV mythologically

mythologue [mitɔlɔg] N mythologist

mythomane [mitɔman] ADJ **être m.** to be a compulsive *or* pathological liar ▸ N compulsive *or* pathological liar; *Psy* mythomaniac

mythomanie [mitɔmani] NF *Psy* mythomania

mytiliculteur, -trice [mitilikyltœr, -tris] N mussel farmer

mytiliculture [mitilikyltyr] NF mussel farming

myxœdème [miksedɛm] NM *Méd* myxoedema, *Am* myxedema

myxomatose [miksɔmatoz] NF myxomatosis

N¹, n [ɛn] **NM** *(lettre)* N, n

N² *(abrév* **Nord**) N

na [na] **INT** *Fam* **(et) na!** so there!

nabab [nabab] **NM** nabob

nabot, -ote [nabo, -ɔt] *Péj* **N** dwarf, midget
▪ **ADJ** *(personne)* dwarfish, tiny

Nabuchodonosor [nabykɔdɔnɔzɔr] **NM 1**
Bible, Hist Nebuchadnezzar **2** *(bouteille de champagne)* n. Nebuchadnezzar

nacelle [nasɛl] **NF 1** *(de montgolfière)* basket;
(de dirigeable) gondola, car; *(d'avion)* na-
celle; *(de moteur d'avion)* pod; *(de laveur de carreau)* cradle, aerial work platform **2** *(de landau, poussette)* *(détachable)* carrycot;
(fixe) carriage **3** *Vieilli (bateau)* skiff, wherry

nacre [nakr] **NF** mother-of-pearl; **un collier de** *ou* **en n.** a mother-of-pearl necklace

nacré [nakre] **ADJ** pearlescent

nacrer [nakre] **VT 1 n. qch** to give sth a pearly
finish **2** *Litt* to cast a pearly glimmer onto

nadir [nadir] **NM** *Astron* nadir

nævus [nevys] **NM** *Méd* naevus, *Am* nevus

nage [naʒ] **NF 1** swimming; *(style)* stroke; **atteindre le rivage à la n.** to swim to the shore;
traverser une rivière à la n. to swim across a
river; **je pratique trois nages** I can do three
strokes; **épreuve du 100 m quatre nages** 4 x
100 m relay; **n. libre** freestyle; **n. sur le dos**
backstroke; **n. (à l')indienne** overarm stroke
2 être (tout) en n. to be bathed in perspiration **3** *(aviron)* rowing, sculling; **banc de
n.** thwart; **chef de n.** stroke **4** *Culin* **à la n.**
poached in white wine

nageoire [naʒwar] **NF 1** *(de poisson)* fin; *(de
dauphin, cétacé etc)* flipper; **n. caudale** caudal fin, tail fluke; **n. dorsale** dorsal fin; **n.
anale** anal fin; **n. pelvienne** pelvic fin; **n. pectorale** pectoral fin **2** *(d'hydravion)* fin

nager [naʒe] (**je nageais, nous nageons**) **VI 1**
to swim; *(de bois, bouchon etc)* to float; **on va
n.?** shall we go for a swim?; **tu sais n.?** can
you swim?; *Fig* **savoir n.** to know one's way
around, to know how to take care of oneself;
n. sous la côte to swim for the shore; **n. sous
l'eau/sur le dos** to swim underwater/on
one's back; **n. comme un poisson** to swim
like a fish; **n. comme un fer à repasser** to swim
like a brick; **n. entre deux eaux** to be floating
beneath the surface; *Fig* not to commit oneself; **légumes qui nagent dans le beurre** vegetables swimming in butter; *Fig* **n. dans son
sang** to be bathed in blood; **n. dans l'abondance** to be rolling in money; **on ne peut
pas dire que la région nage dans l'abondance** the region is not exactly well-off *or*
blessed with prosperity; **n. dans le bonheur**
to be blissfully happy; *Fam* **tu nages dans ce
costume** the suit drowns you; **tu nages vraiment trop dans ce short** the shorts really are
far too big for you; **depuis qu'il a perdu 20 kg
il nage dans tous ses vêtements** his clothes
just hang on him since he lost 20 kilos; *Fig*

Fam **je nage** I'm all at sea; **je nage complètement!** I'm totally at sea *or* lost!

2 *Fig Litt (de vapeurs, nuages, effluves)* to
drift

3 *Naut* to row; **nagez partout!** pull away!; **n.
en arrière** *ou* *Spéc* **à culer** to back water; **n.
plat** to feather; **n. à** *ou* **en couple** to (double)
scull; **n. en pointe** to row
▪ **VT 1** *(la brasse, le crawl etc)* to do, to swim **2**
(disputer) **n. le 100 mètres/le quatre fois 100
mètres** to swim (in) the 100 metres/the 4 x
100 metres relay

nageur, -euse [naʒœr, -øz] **N 1** swimmer;
être bon/mauvais n. to be a good/bad
swimmer, to swim well/badly; *Mil* **n. de
combat** frogman **2** *Naut (rameur)* oarsman,
f oarswoman, rower; **n. de l'arrière** stroke;
n. de l'avant bow (oar)
▪ **NM** *(maillot de bain une pièce)* one-piece
swimsuit *or* swimming costume
▪ **ADJ** *(animal)* swimming

naguère [nagɛr] **ADV** *Litt* not long ago, a
short time ago, lately; *(autrefois)* formerly

naïade [najad] **NF** naiad, water nymph

naïf, -ïve [naif, -iv] **ADJ** *(innocent)* naive, ingenuous, innocent; **elle était assez naïve
pour croire ses mensonges** she was naive
enough to believe his lies; *Beaux-Arts* **un
peintre n.** a naive painter
▪ **N 1 vous me prenez pour un n.!** what sort of
a fool do you take me for?; **jouer les naïfs/les
naïves** to act *or* play the innocent **2** *Beaux-
Arts* naive (painter)

nain, naine [nɛ̃, nɛn] VOIR GRAMMAIRE A12 **N 1**
dwarf, midget **2** *Arg (enfant)* kid, brat
▪ **NF naine** *(étoile)* dwarf
▪ **ADJ** *(personne, étoile)* dwarf; **haricots nains**
dwarf beans; **poule naine** bantam; **caniche
n.** toy poodle; **rosier n.** miniature rosebush
▸▸ **n. de jardin** garden gnome; *Cartes* **n.
jaune** Pope Joan

Nairobi [nerobi] **N** Nairobi

naissain [nɛsɛ̃] **NM** *(d'huître, de moule)*
spawn, spat

naissance [nɛsɑ̃s] **NF 1** *aussi Fig* birth; **date
de n.** date of birth; **lieu de n.** birthplace; **acte
de n.** birth certificate *(original)*; **extrait de n.**
birth certificate *(copy of original)*; **contrôle**
ou **limitation** *ou* **régulation des naissances**
birth control; **donner n. à un enfant** to give
birth to a child; **à sa n.,** il avait les cheveux
blonds his hair was blond when he was
born; **sourd/aveugle de n.** deaf/blind from
birth, born deaf/blind; **paresseux de n.**
bone idle; **qu'est-ce que tu es paresseuse! –
oui, je sais, chez moi, c'est de n.** you're so
lazy! – I know, I was born that way *or* I've been
like that since the day I was born; **français
de n.** French by birth; **n. de haute/d'obscure
n.** of high *or* noble/humble birth; *Fig Litt* **la
n. du printemps** the birth of spring; *Litt* **la n.
du jour** dawn, daybreak, the break of day;
donner n. à une rumeur/de nouvelles habi-

tudes de vie to give rise to a rumour/new
lifestyles **2** *(de langue, d'ongle etc)* root; *(de
rivière)* source; *Archit (de pilier, d'arche)*
spring; **n. du cou** base of the neck; **cicatrice
à la n. des cheveux** scar just where the hair
begins *or* at the hairline; **à la n. des seins** at
the top of one's cleavage; **prendre n.** to originate, to start; *(d'une rivière)* to rise

naissant [nɛsɑ̃] **ADJ 1** *(jour)* dawning;
(beauté) nascent; **à l'aube naissante** at
break of day; **une barbe naissante** the beginnings of a beard; **ses seins naissants** her
budding breasts; **les rondeurs naissantes de
sa gorge** the blossoming curves of her
breasts **2** *Chimie* **à l'état n.** nascent

naître [nɛtr] **VI** *(prp* **naissant;** *pp* **né;** *pr ind* **je
nais, il naît, nous naissons, ils naissent;** *pr
sub* **je naisse;** *p hist* **je naquis;** *fu* **je naîtrai;**
aux **être**) **1** to be born; **il naquit** *ou* **est né
en 1880** he was born in 1880; **enfant/pous-
sin qui vient de n.** newly born child/newly
hatched chick; **je l'ai vu n.** I have known
him *from* birth *or* since he was a baby; **né
de parents anglais** born of English parents,
of English parentage; **né de parents inconnus** of unknown parentage; **enfant à n.** unborn child; **il naît plus de filles que de
garçons** more girls are being born than
boys, there's a higher level of female births
than male births; **Casanova était né pour
l'amour** Casanova was destined to be a
great lover; **il est né pour être musicien/ré-
ussir/diriger** he was born *or* destined to be a
musician/to succeed/to be a manager; **elle
est née pour emmerder le monde** it seems to
be her mission in life to get up people's
noses; *Litt* **n. à l'amour** to know love for the
first time, to awaken to love; **il est né poète/
bricoleur** he is a born poet/handyman; **je ne
suis pas né d'hier** *ou* **de la dernière pluie** I
wasn't born yesterday; **il n'est pas encore
né, celui qui me fera manger les escargots!**
the man who can make me eat snails hasn't
been born yet! **2** *(d'espoirs)* to spring up, to
(a)rise, to be born; *(de peur)* to (a)rise; *(de
projet, d'idée)* to originate (**de** in), to arise
(**de** out of); **faire n.** *(espoir, doute)* to give rise
to, to raise; *(soupçon)* to give rise to, to
arouse, to cause; *(sourire)* to provoke, to
raise; **cette peur du noir est née du fait
qu'enfant, il avait été laissé seul** his fear of
the dark originates *or* arises from his being
left alone as a child; **l'espoir de paix est né
de la rencontre des deux présidents** the
meeting between the two presidents has
given rise to hopes of peace **3** *(de plantes)*
to begin to grow *or* come up, to appear; *(du
jour)* to dawn

naïvement [naivmɑ̃] **ADV** naively

naïveté [naivte] **NF 1** *(innocence)* naivety;
elle a eu la n. de croire à ses promesses she
was naive enough to believe his promises **2**
(remarque) naive remark

Namibie [namibi] NF Namibia

namibien, -ienne [namibjɛ̃, -jɛn] ADJ Namibian
  N **N.** Namibian

nana [nana] NF Fam **1** (jeune fille) girl, bird, Am chick; **une n. qu'elle a rencontrée cet été** a girl she met last summer; **c'est là qu'on trouve les plus belles nanas** that's where the best-looking birds or chicks are; **c'est plein de nanas, mais il n'y a pas un seul mec** it's full of women/girls but there isn't a single man **2** (petite amie) girlfriend

nanar [nanar] NM Fam **1** (marchandise sans valeur) junk, trash, garbage **2** (mauvais film) lousy film, Am turkey

nandou [nãdu] NM Zool rhea

nanisme [nanism] NM Méd dwarfism

Nankin [nɑ̃kɛ̃] N Nanking

nankin [nɑ̃kɛ̃] ADJ INV, NM Tex nankeen

nanomètre [nanɔmɛtr] NM nanometre, Br, nanometer

nanoseconde [nanos(ə)gɔ̃d] NF nanosecond

nansouk [nãzuk] NM Tex nainsook

nanti, -ie [nãti] ADJ (personne, pays) well-off, rich
  N rich person; **les nantis** the well-off, the rich

nantir [nɑ̃tir] VT **1 n. qn de qch** to provide sb with sth; **être bien nanti** to be well-off or well provided for **2** Jur (créancier) to give security to; **n. des valeurs** to deposit shares as security; **n. un prêt** to secure a loan
  VPR **se nantir** Litt **se n. d'un parapluie** to provide oneself or arm oneself with an umbrella

nantissement [nɑ̃tismɑ̃] NM security; (pour prêt) collateral, security; **déposer des titres en n.** to lodge stock as security; Banque **n. flottant** ou **général** floating charge; Bourse **n. d'actions** lien on shares

napalm [napalm] NM napalm; **bombe au n.** napalm bomb

naphtaline [naftalin] NF naphthalene; Can Fig **sortir qch de la n.** to take sth out of mothballs; **boules de n.** mothballs

naphte [naft] NM naphtha, mineral oil; **n. de goudron** coal-tar naphtha

Napoléon [napɔleɔ̃] NM **1** Napoleon **2** Anciennement **n.** (pièce) twenty-franc piece (bearing the effigy of Napoleon)

napoléonien, -ienne [napɔleɔnjɛ̃, -jɛn] ADJ (guerre, empire) Napoleonic

napolitain, -aine [napɔlitɛ̃, -ɛn] ADJ Neapolitan
  NM (dialecte) Neapolitan
  N **N.** Neapolitan

nappage [napaʒ] NM Culin coating, covering

nappe [nap] NF **1** (de table) tablecloth; **mettre/ôter la n.** to lay/remove the cloth; **n. à thé** tea cloth; Rel **n. d'autel** altar cloth **2** Fig (vaste étendue) (de glace) sheet; **n. de feu** sea of flames
  ▸▸**n. d'armature** belt; **n. de brouillard** fog patch; **n. carcasse** casing ply; **n. croisée** cross-ply; Géog **n. d'eau** water table; **n. éruptive** lava flow; **n. de pétrole** oil slick; **n. pétrolifère** oil layer; Géog **n. phréatique** water table

napper [nape] VT **1** Culin to coat, to cover (**de** with); **glace à la vanille, nappée de chocolat** vanilla ice cream topped with chocolate or with chocolate topping **2** Vieilli (recouvrir) (table) to cover with a cloth

napperon [naprɔ̃] NM mat

Narcisse [narsis] N Myth Narcissus

narcisse [narsis] NM **1** (plante) narcissus; **n. des poètes** pheasant's eye; **n. sauvage** ou **des prés** daffodil **2** Psy narcissist

narcissique [narsisik] ADJ Psy narcissistic

narcissisme [narsisism] NM Psy narcissism

narcodollars [narkodɔlar] NMPL drug money

narcolepsie [narkolɛpsi] NF Méd narcolepsy

narcose [narkoz] NF Méd narcosis

narcotique [narkɔtik] Méd ADJ narcotic
  NM narcotic, drug; **faire prendre un n. à qn** to give sb a narcotic, to drug sb

narcotrafic [narkotrafik] NM drug trafficking

narcotrafiquant, -ante [narkotrafikɑ̃, -ɑ̃t] N drug trafficker

nard [nar] NM Bot, Pharm spikenard, nard

narguer [narge] VT to taunt, to scoff at; (la mort, le danger) to flout

narguilé, narghilé, narghileh [nargile] NM hookah, narghile

narine [narin] NF nostril

narquois [narkwa] ADJ (ton, sourire) taunting, mocking

narquoisement [narkwazmɑ̃] ADV tauntingly, mockingly

narrateur, -trice [naratœr, -tris] N (de roman, de film) narrator; (conteur) storyteller

narratif, -ive [naratif, -iv] ADJ (style, contenu) narrative

narration [narasjɔ̃] NF **1** narration; Gram **présent de n.** historic present **2** (d'événement) narrative, account; Scol Vieilli narrative composition

narrer [nare] VT Litt to narrate, to relate

narval, -als [narval] NM narwhal, unicorn whale

nasal, -ale, -aux, -ales [nazal, -o] ADJ (os, son, cloison) nasal
  NF Ling **nasale** nasal

nasaliser [nazalize] VT (son) to nasalize

Nasdaq® [nasdak] NM Écon Nasdaq®

nase [naz] Fam ADJ **1** (fatigué) (personne) shattered, whacked, dead beat; (voiture etc) clapped out **2** (idiot) thick; **il est tout n., ce mec** the guy's a complete idiot **3** (nul) bloody useless or hopeless
  N **c'est un n., ce mec** this guy's rubbish, this guy's bloody useless

naseau, -eaux [nazo] NM (de cheval, bœuf) nostril; Fam **les naseaux** (nez) the hooter, the conk

nasillard [nazijar] ADJ nasal; (vieux disque etc) tinny; **ton n.** (nasal) twang; **parler d'une voix nasillarde** to talk through one's nose

nasillement [nazijmɑ̃] NM (son nasillard) (nasal) twang

nasiller [nazije] VI to speak through one's nose or with a twang; (de radio, vieux disque) to make a tinny sound; (du canard) to quack

nasique [nazik] NM (singe) proboscis monkey

nasse [nas] NF lobster pot; (pour oiseaux) hoop net; (pour rats) trap; Fig Vieilli **tomber dans la n.** to fall into the trap

natal, -ale, -als, -ales [natal] ADJ (village) native; **ville natale** birthplace, Fam home town; **mon pays n.** my native land; **mon Écosse/ma France natale** my native Scotland/France; **ma maison natale** the house where I was born

> Do not confuse with **natif**.

nataliste [natalist] ADJ **politique n.** policy to increase the birth rate, pro-birth policy

natalité [natalite] NF **(taux de) n.** birth rate; **forte n.** high birth rate; **courbe de n.** birth rate

natation [natasjɔ̃] NF swimming; **club de n.**

swimming club; **faire de la n.** to swim; **n. synchronisée** synchronized swimming

natatoire [natatwar] ADJ Zool (organe, membrane) natatory, natatorial; **vessie n.** (de poisson) swim bladder, air bladder

Natel [natɛl] NM Suisse (abrév **Nationales Autotelefon**) mobile (phone), Am cellphone

natif, -ive [natif, -iv] ADJ **1** native; **je suis n. de Londres** I'm a native Londoner, I'm a Londoner (by birth) **2** Minér (or etc) native, virgin **3** Litt (inné) natural, inborn; **bon sens n.** mother or native wit
  N native

> Do not confuse with **natal**.

nation [nasjɔ̃] NF nation; **n. commerçante** mercantile nation; **Nations unies** United Nations

national, -ale, -aux, -ales [nasjɔnal, -o] ADJ (équipe, gloire) national; **l'hymne n.** the national anthem; **à l'échelle nationale et internationale** nationally and internationally
  NMPL **nationaux** nationals
  NF Aut **nationale** main road, Br ≃ A road, Am ≃ highway

nationalement [nasjɔnalmɑ̃] ADV nationally

nationalisation [nasjɔnalizasjɔ̃] NF nationalization

nationaliser [nasjɔnalize] VT (industrie) to nationalize; **nationalisé** nationalized

nationalisme [nasjɔnalism] NM Pol nationalism

nationaliste [nasjɔnalist] N Pol nationalist
  ADJ nationalist, Péj nationalistic; **la Chine n.** Nationalist China

nationalité [nasjɔnalite] NF nationality; Naut **acte de n.** (ship's) certificate of registry; **les personnes de n. française** people of French nationality, French nationals; **il est de quelle n.?** what nationality is he?; **n. à la naissance** nationality at birth; **code de la n.** = rules and regulations defining entitlement to French nationality VOIR GRAMMAIRE A19; B11–12

national-populisme NM Pol national populism

national-socialisme NM Hist, Pol National Socialism

national-socialiste Hist, Pol ADJ National Socialist
  N National Socialist

nativité [nativite] NF Rel nativity; Beaux-Arts nativity (scene)

natron [natrɔ̃] NM, **natrum** [natrɔm] NM Minér natron

natte [nat] NF **1** (de cheveux, fil d'or etc) plait, surtout Am braid; **porter des nattes** to wear one's hair in plaits or pigtails, to have plaits or pigtails; **porter** ou **avoir une n.** to have a pigtail **2** (de jonc, paille) mat

natter [nate] VT **1** (cheveux, paille etc) to plait, to braid **2** (mur etc) to cover with mats

naturalisation [natyralizasjɔ̃] NF **1** Admin naturalization **2** (de plante, d'animal) naturalization; (de mot) adoption, naturalization **3** (de spécimen botanique etc) preservation, mounting; **n. d'animaux** taxidermy

naturalisé, -ée [natyralize] ADJ naturalized
  N naturalized subject or citizen

naturaliser [natyralize] VT **1** Admin to naturalize; **se faire n. français** to take French citizenship **2** (plante, animal) to naturalize, to acclimatize; (mot) to adopt, to naturalize **3** (préserver) (spécimen botanique etc) to preserve, to mount; (empailler) (animal) to stuff

naturalisme [natyralism] NM naturalism

naturaliste [natyralist] N **1** (savant) naturalist **2** (artisan) taxidermist
  ADJ naturalistic

nature [natyr] NF 1 *(univers)* nature; **les lois de la n.** the laws of nature; **une merveille de la n.** a wonder of nature; **une force de la n.** a force of nature; **laisser faire la n.** to let nature take its course; **tous les goûts sont dans la n.** everyone to his own taste; **vice contre n.** unnatural vice; **c'est contre n. qu'une femme ait des enfants après la ménopause** it's unnatural *or* it's against nature for a woman to have children after the menopause; **la n. fait bien les choses** *ou* **est bien faite** Mother Nature does wonderful things, isn't nature wonderful?; *Fam* **la pauvre fille n'est pas gâtée par la n.** nature hasn't been kind to the poor girl; **à l'état de n.** in the natural state
2 *(milieu végétal et animal)* nature; **une n. luxuriante s'offrit à nos yeux** a luxuriant landscape opened up before us; **les amoureux de la n.** nature lovers; **protection de la n.** protection of the environment; **maison en pleine n.** house deep in the country; **se promener dans la n.** to go for a walk in the country; *Fig* **se perdre** *ou* **disparaître dans la n.** to vanish into thin air; *Aut Fam* **partir dans la n.** to run into a ditch/a field; *Beaux-Arts* **n. morte** still life
3 *(caractère)* nature; **n. du climat/du sol** nature of the climate/the soil; **ce n'est pas dans ma n.** it's not in my nature; **c'est dans la n. des choses** it's in the nature of things; **une découverte de n. à révolutionner la science** a discovery likely to revolutionize science; **ce genre de détail n'est pas de n. à les inquiéter** that kind of detail is unlikely to bother them; **faits de n. à nous étonner** facts of an astonishing nature, astonishing facts; **un programme de cette n.** a programme of this kind *or* nature; **être d'une n. douce** to have a gentle nature; **être timide de** *ou* **par n., être d'une n. timide** to be naturally shy, to be shy by nature; **c'est une bonne n.** he's/she's a kind soul *or* a kindly (sort of) man/woman; **c'est une n. violente** he's/she's a violent sort; **c'est une n. petite n.** *(n'a pas une santé solide)* he's/she's got a weak constitution
4 *(réalité)* **plus grand que n.** larger than life; **peindre d'après n.** to paint from nature *or* from life; **payer en n.** *(avec des marchandises)* to pay in kind
ADJ INV **1** *Culin* (yaourt, omelette) plain; **riz n.** (plain) boiled rice; **thé n.** tea without milk **2** *(conforme à la réalité)* **grandeur n.** full-scale, life-size(d) **3** *Fam (personne)* natural, unaffected

naturel, -elle [natyrɛl] ADJ **1** *(inhérent à la nature)* (phénomène, loi, frontière, gaz) natural; *(besoin, fonction)* bodily; **mort naturelle** death from natural causes; **il est mort de mort naturelle** he died from natural causes; **les défenses naturelles de l'organisme** the body's natural defences **2** *(inné)* (don, tendance) natural, innate; **il a des dispositions naturelles pour la peinture** painting comes naturally to him; **il a une grâce naturelle** he is naturally graceful **3** *(non artificiel)* (procréation, couleur de cheveux, jus de fruit etc) natural; **soie naturelle** pure *or* real silk **4** *(normal)* natural; **son inquiétude est tout à fait naturelle** it's only natural that he should be worried; **c'est n. de le faire** it's only natural *or* reasonable to do so; **mais c'est tout n.** don't mention it, you're welcome **5** *(non affecté)* (personne, air, style) natural, unaffected; *(réponse)* simple, straightforward; **vin n.** unfortified wine **6** *Mus* **note naturelle** natural
NM **1** *(tempérament)* nature, character, disposition; **d'un bon n.** kind, of a kind disposition; **elle est d'un n. généreux/peureux/jaloux** she has a generous/timid/jealous

nature, she is generous/timid/jealous by nature; *Prov* **chassez le n., il revient au galop** what's bred in the bone (will come out in the flesh) **2** *(simplicité, spontanéité)* naturalness; **elle joue la comédie avec beaucoup de n.** she's a natural (as a) comic actor; **parler avec n.** to speak naturally **3** *Culin* **thon au n.** tuna (packed) in brine; **poires au n.** pears in natural fruit juice

naturellement [natyrɛlmã] ADV naturally; **n. timide** naturally shy, shy by nature; **se conduire n.** to behave naturally *or* without affectation; **vous vous en êtes fâché? – n.!** you resented it? – naturally! *or* of course (I did)!

naturisme [natyrism] NM naturism; **adepte du n.** naturist, nudist

naturiste [natyrist] N naturist, nudist
ADJ naturist; **centre n.** nudist colony *or* camp

naufrage [nofraʒ] NM (ship)wreck; *Fig (d'entreprise)* failure; **lors du n. du Titanic** when the Titanic sank; **faire n.** *(de bateau)* to be wrecked; *(de marin)* to be shipwrecked; *Fig (d'entreprise, de mariage)* to collapse; **périr dans un n.** to be lost at sea; *Fig* **le pays va vers le n.** the country is heading for disaster; *Fig* **le n. de ses ambitions** the collapse of his ambitions

naufragé, -ée [nofraʒe] ADJ *(bateau)* wrecked; *(marin)* shipwrecked, castaway
N castaway, shipwrecked man/woman

naufrageur, -euse [nofraʒœr, -øz] N *(de bateaux)* wrecker; **bateau n.** wrecker

naupathie [nopati] NF *Méd* seasickness

nauséabond [nozeabɔ̃] ADJ *(odeur)* nauseating, foul; *(personne, pièce)* foul-smelling; *Fig (thèses etc)* sickening, nauseating

nausée [noze] NF **1** *(envie de vomir)* nausea; *(chez la femme enceinte)* morning sickness; **avoir la n.** *ou* **des nausées** to feel sick *or* nauseous; **avoir des nausées** *(d'une femme enceinte)* to have morning sickness; **donner des nausées à qn** to make sb feel sick **2** *Fig* disgust; **l'hypocrisie me donne la n.** hypocrisy makes me sick *or* nauseates me

nauséeux, -euse [nozeø, -øz] ADJ **1** *(odeur)* nauseating; **se sentir n.** to feel sick *or* nauseous **2** *Fig (hypocrisie etc)* nauseating, sickening

nautile [notil] NM *Zool* nautilus

nautique [notik] ADJ *(terme, instrument etc)* nautical; **sports nautiques** water sports; **carte n.** (sea) chart; **salon n.** boat show

nautisme [notism] NM *Sport* water sports

naval, -ale, -als, -ales [naval] ADJ *(architecture, base, combat)* naval; **termes navals** nautical *or* sailing terms; **construction navale** shipbuilding; **chantier n.** shipyard; **les forces navales** the navy; **l'École navale** the Naval College
NF *Fam* **faire Navale** to attend Naval College

navarin [navarɛ̃] NM *Culin* lamb stew *or* casserole

navel [navɛl] NF navel orange

navet [navɛ] NM **1** turnip **2** *Fam (film, pièce de théâtre)* **c'est un n.** it's a load of rubbish *or* nonsense

navette¹ [navɛt] NF **1** *Tex* shuttle **2** *Aviat etc* shuttle (service); **navettes fréquentes entre la gare et la ville** frequent (shuttle) service between station and town; **faire la n. entre deux endroits/services** *(de véhicule, personne, dossier etc)* to shuttle back and forth between two places/two departments; **je fais la n. entre Glasgow et Édimbourg tous les jours** I commute between Glasgow and Edinburgh; **n. de transfert** transfer bus; **n. gratuite** courtesy bus; **n. parlementaire** =

successive readings of bills by the Assemblée nationale and the Sénat **3** *(fusée)* shuttle **4** *Rel* incense box
► ► **n. spatiale** space shuttle

navette² NF *Bot* rape; **(huile de) n.** rape (seed) oil, colza oil

navetteur, -euse [navɛtœr, -øz] N *Belg* commuter

navigabilité [navigabilite] NF **1** *(de rivière etc)* navigability **2** *(état de)* n. *(de bateau)* seaworthiness; *(d'avion)* airworthiness; **en (bon) état de n.** *(bateau)* seaworthy; *(avion)* airworthy

navigable [navigabl] ADJ **1** *(rivière, voie)* navigable **2** *(bateau)* seaworthy; *(avion)* airworthy

navigant [navigã] ADJ **personnel n.** navigation crew, flight crew
NMPL **les navigants** the navigation crew, the flight crew

navigateur, -trice [navigatœr, -tris] N **1** *(de bateau, d'avion etc)* navigator **2** *(voyageur sur mer)* navigator, seafarer; **n. solitaire** lone *or* single-handed yachtsman *or* sailor
NM *Ordinat* (Web) browser
ADJ **peuple n.** seafaring people

navigation [navigasjɔ̃] NF **1** *Naut, Aviat* navigation; **école de n.** *(de la marine marchande)* nautical school; **compagnie de n.** shipping company; **compagnie de n. aérienne** airline; **permis de n.** ship's passport, sea letter; **après un mois de n.** after a month at sea **2** *Ordinat* **n. sur (l')Internet** browsing the Web, Internet surfing; **n. rapide/sécurisée** rapid/secure browsing
► ► **n. côtière** coastal navigation; **n. à l'estime** dead reckoning; **n. extérieure** deep-sea navigation; **n. fluviale** inland navigation; **n. hauturière** deep-sea *or* ocean navigation; *Aviat* **n. aux instruments** instrument flying; **n. intérieure** inland navigation; **n. au long cours** deep-sea *or* ocean navigation; **n. maritime** deep-sea *or* maritime navigation; **n. de plaisance** sailing, yachting, pleasure cruising; *Astronaut* **n. spatiale** space navigation, astronautics; **n. à voile** sailing; *Aviat* **n. à vue** visual flying

naviguer [navige] VI **1** *(de bateau, marin)* to sail (**vers** to); **navire qui navigue bien** ship that handles well at sea *or* that behaves well; **n. au compas** to sail *or* navigate by the compass; *Fig Fam* **savoir n.** to know the ropes **2** *(se déplacer)* *(de personne, dossier)* to move around; **le dossier a navigué entre les différents responsables du projet** the file moved around from *or* was passed from project manager to project manager **3** *Ordinat* **n. sur (l')Internet** to surf the Net, to browse the Web
VT *(bateau, avion)* to navigate

navire [navir] NM ship, vessel; **les navires du port** the ships *or* shipping in the harbour
► ► **n. amiral** flagship; **n.-citerne** tanker; **n. de combat** battleship; **n. de commerce** merchant ship, merchantman; **n. de conférence** conference ship; **n.-école** training ship; **n. frigorifique** refrigerated vessel; **n. de guerre** warship; **n.-hôpital** hospital ship; **n.-jumeau** twin ship; **n. au long cours** ocean-going ship; **n. marchand** merchant ship, merchantman; **n. mixte** mixed passenger and cargo ship; **n. porte-conteneurs** container ship; **n.-usine** factory ship; **n. à voiles** sailing ship

navrant [navrã] ADJ *(nouvelle, attitude etc)* distressing, upsetting; **un film n. de bêtise** an incredibly stupid film; **un contretemps n.** an unfortunate *or* regrettable mishap

navré [navre] ADJ *(personne, expression, ton)* distressed; **être n.** *(désolé)* to be very *or* terribly sorry; **je suis n. (de l'apprendre)** I'm terribly or very sorry (to hear that); **n. de vous avoir fait attendre** sorry to have kept you waiting

navrer [navʀe] VT to distress, to upset

nazaréen, -enne [nazaʀeɛ̃, -ɛn] ADJ, N Bible Nazarene

naze [naz] ADJ, N Fam = nase

nazi, -ie [nazi] ADJ, N Hist, Pol Nazi

nazillon, -onne [nazijɔ̃, -ɔn] N Fam little Nazi

nazisme [nazism] NM Hist, Pol Nazism

NB [ɛnbe] (abrév nota bene) NB

NbP Typ (abrév note de bas de page) footnote

NC [ɛnse] NM (abrév network computer) NC

NCM NFPL [ɛnseɛm] (abrév négociations commerciales multilatérales) multilateral trade negotiations

NDLR (abrév note de la rédaction) Ed

NdT (abrév note du traducteur) translator's note

NE, N¹ [n(ə)] ADV SEE GRAMMAR B62–3 **1** (forming neg verb with pas) **je ne la connais pas** I don't know her; (emphatique) I do not know her; **il ne m'avait pas vu** he hadn't seen me (**NOTE** for the use of ne in conjunction with **aucun, aucunement, goutte, guère, jamais, mot, personne, plus, point, que, rien** see these words) **2** (used alone, chiefly in literary style, with **cesser, oser, pouvoir, savoir, importer** and often as an archaism with other verbs) **il ne cesse de parler** he is forever or always talking, he doesn't stop or never stops talking; **je n'ose lui parler** I dare not speak to him; **je ne puis vous le promettre** I cannot promise you that; **je ne sais que faire** I do not know what to do; **je ne saurais vous le dire** I cannot tell you **3** (in the following constructions) **qui ne connaît cette œuvre célèbre?** who does not know this famous work?; **que ne ferait-elle pour vous?** what would she not do for you?; **je n'ai d'autre désir que celui de vous plaire** I have no other desire than to please you; **si je ne me trompe** ou **m'abuse** if I am not mistaken, unless I am mistaken; **voilà six mois que je ne l'ai vue** it is now six months since I (last) saw her, I haven't seen her for six months; **il n'y a personne à qui il ne se soit adressé** there is no one whom he didn't speak to; **il n'eut garde d'y aller** he took good care not to go, he made quite sure he did not go; **qu'à cela ne tienne!** never mind (about) that!, that's no problem!; **je n'ai que faire de votre aide** I have no need of your help **4** (used optionally in literary style with a vague negative connotation) **je crains qu'elle (ne) prenne froid** I am afraid she may catch cold; **évitez** ou **prenez garde qu'on (ne) vous voie** take care not to be seen; **peu s'en fallut qu'elle (ne) tombât** she very nearly fell; **je ne nie pas que cela (ne) soit vrai** I don't deny that it's true; **il est plus vigoureux qu'il n'y paraît** he is stronger than he looks; **elle agit autrement qu'elle ne parle** her actions belie or don't match her words

né [ne] ADJ born; Litt **c'est un conteur/conducteur né** he's a born story-teller/driver; **enfant né d'un premier mariage** child from a first marriage; **né d'une famille bourgeoise** born into a middle-class family; Fig **un film né de la rencontre d'un réalisateur et d'une actrice** a film born of or that grew out of a meeting between a director and an actress; **Mme Martin, née Dupond** Mrs Martin, née Dupond; Arch **être bien né** to be well born or of noble birth

néanmoins [neɑ̃mwɛ̃] ADV nevertheless, nonetheless, yet; **il est sérieux mais n. décontracté** he's serious but nevertheless or but nonetheless or yet relaxed

néant [neɑ̃] NM **1** (ce qui n'existe pas) nothingness, void; **sortir du n.** to rise from nothing; **réduire qch à n.** to reduce sth to nothing, to destroy sth; **tous ses espoirs furent réduits à n.** all his hopes were dashed **2** (sur formulaire, feuille de déclaration d'impôts etc) none, nil; **signes particuliers: n.** distinguishing marks: none

nébuleux, -euse [nebylø, -øz] ADJ (ciel, vue) cloudy, hazy, misty; (idées, raisonnement, explications) vague, hazy, nebulous; (écrivain, théorie, propos) obscure
  NF Astron **nébuleuse** nebula; Fig **toute une nébuleuse de sociétés-écrans** a whole cluster of umbrella companies

nébuliseur [nebylizœʀ] NM nebulizer

nébulosité [nebylozite] NF **1** Météo (nuage très fin) wispy cloud; (ciel couvert) cloud cover; **forte n.** heavy cloud cover **2** (d'une idée etc) vagueness, haziness

nécessaire [neseseʀ] ADJ **1** necessary; **cela ne sera pas n.** that won't be necessary; **n. à** ou **pour qn/qch** necessary or required for sb/sth; **n. pour faire qch** necessary to do sth; **avoir l'argent/le temps/la patience n.** to have the necessary money/time/patience; **il est n. de bien lire les instructions** the instructions need to be read properly, it is necessary to read the instructions properly; **il n'est pas n. d'être impoli** there is no need to be rude; **il n'est pas n. de passer par le standard** there is no need or it is not necessary to go through the switchboard; **ils n'ont pas jugé n. de venir s'excuser** they didn't think or consider it necessary to come and apologize; **il est n. que vous teniez compte de cela/procédiez de cette manière** you need to or you must take notice of this/proceed like this; **peu n.** unnecessary, needless **2** Phil necessary
  NM **le strict n.** the bare necessities or essentials; **il ne fait que le strict n.** he does no more than that which is strictly necessary; **manquer du n.** to lack the necessities or basics of life; **faire le n.** to do what is necessary, Fam to do the necessary; **je vais faire le n.** I'll see to it; **pour les billets ne t'inquiète pas, je ferai le n.** don't worry about the tickets, I'll see to them; **merci de faire le n. pour qu'il soit accueilli à l'aéroport** thank you for arranging for him to be met at the airport
  ▸▸ **n. à chaussures** shoe-cleaning kit; **n. de couture** sewing kit; **n. à ongles** manicure set; **n. de toilette** (set of) toiletries; **n. de voyage** overnight bag

nécessairement [neseseʀmɑ̃] ADV necessarily; **ce n'est pas n. une mauvaise idée** it's not necessarily a bad idea; **mais c'est complètement idiot! – pas n.** but it's completely stupid! – not necessarily

nécessité [nesesite] NF **1** (caractère nécessaire), Phil necessity; **être dans la n. de faire qch** to have no choice but to do sth; **c'est une n.** it's essential; **quelle n. y avait-il de faire cela?** what need was there to do that?; **faire qch par n.** to do sth out of necessity, to be compelled to do sth; **faire de n. vertu** to make a virtue (out) of necessity; Vieilli **de (toute) n.** necessarily, of necessity; **il est de toute n. de faire quelque chose** it is essential that we do something, we simply must do something; **objets** ou **articles de première n.** essential items, essentials; **denrées de première n.** essential commodities; **être dans la n.** (être pauvre) to be in need **2** (chose nécessaire) necessity; **les nécessités de la vie** the necessities of life; **à cause des nécessités du service** due to operational requirements

nécessiter [nesesite] VT to require, to need, to necessitate; **une telle question nécessite qu'on prenne le temps de réfléchir** such a

question requires or needs time to be considered

nécessiteux, -euse [nesesitø, -øz] ADJ needy, in need
  NMPL **les n.** the needy, the poor, the destitute

nec plus ultra [nɛkplyzyltʀa] NM INV **le n.** the best there is; **le n. des voitures** the best car in comfort/luxury; **le n. du confort/luxe** the last word in comfort/luxury

nécrologe [nekʀɔlɔʒ] NM necrology, death roll

nécrologie [nekʀɔlɔʒi] NF (notice) obituary (notice); Journ (rubrique) obituary column

nécrologique [nekʀɔlɔʒik] ADJ **avis/rubrique n.** obituary notice/column

nécromancie [nekʀɔmɑ̃si] NF necromancy

nécromancien, -ienne [nekʀɔmɑ̃sjɛ̃, -jɛn] N necromancer

nécrophage [nekʀɔfaʒ] ADJ necrophagous

nécrophile [nekʀɔfil] ADJ necrophiliac

nécrophilie [nekʀɔfili] NF necrophilia

nécrophore [nekʀɔfɔʀ] NM carrion beetle

nécropole [nekʀɔpɔl] NF necropolis

nécrose [nekʀoz] NF Biol necrosis

nécroser [nekʀoze] Biol VT (tissu) to necrose
  VPR **se nécroser** to necrose

nectaire [nɛktɛʀ] NM Bot nectary

nectar [nɛktaʀ] NM (jus de fruit, Litt boisson exquise), Myth, Bot nectar; **n. de poire/d'abricot** pear/apricot nectar

nectarine [nɛktaʀin] NF (fruit) nectarine

néerlandais, -aise [neɛʀlɑ̃dɛ, -ɛz] ADJ Dutch, (of the) Netherlands; **le gouvernement n.** the Dutch government, the government of the Netherlands
  NM Ling (aux Pays-Bas) Dutch; (en Belgique) Flemish
  N N. Dutchman, f Dutchwoman; **les N.** the Dutch

nef [nɛf] NF **1** (d'église) **n. (centrale)** nave; **n. latérale** aisle **2** Litt (navire) ship

néfaste [nefast] ADJ (effet, conséquence, influence) harmful; **jour n.** ill-fated or evil day

nèfle [nɛfl] NF (fruit) medlar; Fig Fam **des nèfles!** no fear!, nothing doing!; **n. du Japon** loquat

néflier [neflije] NM medlar (tree); **n. du Japon** loquat (tree)

négateur, -trice [negatœʀ, -tʀis] Litt ADJ **une doctrine négatrice** a negative doctrine
  N denier

négatif, -ive [negatif, -iv] ADJ negative; Phot **épreuve négative** negative
  NM Phot negative
  NF Gram **négative** negative; **je réponds par la négative** my answer is in the negative
  ADV Fam **n.!** negative!

négation [negasjɔ̃] NF **1** (fait de nier) negation, denial **2** Gram negative SEE GRAMMAR A47–8; B62–3

négationnisme [negasjɔnism] NM revisionism (denying that the Holocaust ever happened)

négationniste [negasjɔnist] ADJ revisionist (denying that the Holocaust ever happened)
  N revisionist (who denies that the Holocaust ever happened)

négativement [negativmɑ̃] ADV (réagir) negatively; (répondre) in the negative

négativisme [negativism] NM negativism

négligé [negliʒe] ADJ **1** (peu soigné) (tenue, apparence, personne) slovenly, untidy, scruffy; (travail, devoir, style) slovenly, careless **2** (auquel on ne porte pas assez d'attention) (enfant, femme etc) neglected
  NM **1** (caractère) slovenliness, untidiness **2** (vêtement) negligee, negligée

négligeable [negliʒabl] ADJ (détail, risque,

quantité) negligible, insignificant; **un avantage non n.** a not inconsiderable advantage; **une quantité non n. de** a significant quantity of; **il me traite comme (une) quantité n.** he treats me as if I'm not there *or* as if I don't exist

négligemment [negliʒamã] ADV **1** *(habillé)* carelessly, untidily, scruffily **2** *(répondre, lire)* casually, nonchalantly; *(pour feindre l'inattention)* casually; **elle était n. installée dans le canapé** she was draped over the sofa

négligence [negliʒãs] NF **1** *(manque de soin)* negligence, carelessness; *(de quelqu'un, d'un devoir)* neglect; **avec n.** *(travailler)* carelessly; **par (pure) n.** through (sheer) carelessness *or* negligence **2** *(insouciance)* casualness, nonchalance; **il me répondit avec n. qu'il viendrait peut-être** he casually *or* nonchalantly replied that he would perhaps come **3** *(acte négligent)* act of carelessness, careless act; *(oubli)* oversight; **l'accident est dû à une n.** the accident was due to carelessness; **je reconnais que c'est une n. de notre part** I admit that it is an oversight on our part; **n. de style** stylistic error, error of style; *Jur* **n. coupable** *ou* **criminelle** criminal negligence

négligent [negliʒã] ADJ *(parent, touriste, campeur)* negligent, careless; *(remarque, attitude, coup d'œil)* casual

négliger [negliʒe] *(je négligeai(s); nous négligeons)* VT **1** *(délaisser)* *(sa santé, son devoir, ses enfants)* to neglect, to be neglectful of; *(son apparence, sa tenue)* not to care about **2** *(omettre, oublier)* *(avis, conseil)* to disregard; *(occasion)* to miss; *(élément, détail)* to overlook, to disregard; **il ne faut jamais rien n.** you must never leave anything to chance; **n. de faire qch** to neglect *or* fail to do sth ▸ VPR **se négliger** to neglect one's appearance, to let oneself go

négoce [negɔs] NM trade; *Arch* **faire du n.** to be in trade; **le n. international** international trade *or* trading; *Bourse* **n. de titres** share dealing

négociabilité [negɔsjabilite] NF *Fin* negotiability

négociable [negɔsjabl] ADJ *(salaire, prix, conditions d'emploi)* negotiable; *Fin (bon, traite)* negotiable, transferable, trad(e)able; **n. en banque** bankable; **n. en Bourse** negotiable on the Stock Exchange

négociant, -ante [negɔsjã, -ãt] N **1** *(de commerce)* merchant, dealer; **n. en gros** wholesaler; **n. en vins** wine merchant; **n. exportateur** export merchant **2** *Bourse* trader; **n. courtier** broker-dealer

négociateur, -trice [negɔsjatœr, -tris] N *(de traité, marché etc)* negotiator

négociation [negɔsjasjɔ̃] NF **1** *(de traité, paix)* negotiation; **entamer des négociations** to enter into negotiations; *UE* **négociations d'adhésion** accession negotiations; **négociations collectives** joint negotiations; *(au sein d'une entreprise)* collective bargaining; **négociations commerciales multilatérales** multilateral trade negotiations; **négociations pour la paix** peace negotiations; **négociations précontractuelles** precontractual negotiations; **en n.** *(conditions etc)* under negotiation; **nous sommes en n. avec la direction** we are negotiating *or* we are in negotiation with management **2** *Com* negotiation, transaction; **n. d'un effet** negotiation of a bill of exchange; **négociations au comptant** spot trading; **négociations à prime** options trading; **négociations à terme** futures trading

négocier [negɔsje] *(impf, pr sub nous négociions)* VI **1** *(traiter, discuter)* to nego-

tiate (**avec** with) **2** *Arch (faire du commerce)* to trade ▸ VT **1** *(prêt, traite, salaire, paix)* to negotiate; *Bourse* to trade; **modalités du contrat: à n. terms** negotiable **2** *Aut* **n. un virage** to negotiate a bend

nègre [negr] NM **1** *Péj (Noir)* Negro; **la traite des nègres** the slave trade; *Fam* **travailler comme un n.** to work like a slave VOIR GRAMMAIRE A12 **2** *Fig (écrivain)* ghost (writer); **être le n. de qn** to ghost for sb ▸ ADJ **1** *(art)* Negro **2** *Péj (race)* Negro **3** *inv (couleur)* nigger(-brown)
▸ ▸ **n. blanc** White Negro; **propos n. blanc** double talk; *Culin* **n. en chemise** = chocolate dessert with whipped cream

négresse [negres] NF *Péj* Negress

négrier [negrije] NM **1** *(trafiquant d'esclaves)* slave trader; *(employeur, surveillant)* slave driver **2** *(bateau)* slave ship, slaver ▸ ADJ **vaisseau n.** slave ship, slaver

négrillon, -onne [negrijɔ̃, -ɔn] N *Péj* piccaninny

négritude [negrityd] NF negritude

négro [negro] NM *très Fam (terme raciste)* Negro, nigger

négroïde [negrɔid] ADJ *(traits, type)* Negroid

neige [neʒ] NF **1** snow; **tempête de n.** blizzard, snowstorm; *Can* **banc de n.** snow bank; **être bloqué par la n.** to be snowed up *or* snowbound; **aller à la n.** to go on a skiing holiday; **sports de n.** winter sports; **fondre comme n. au soleil** to melt away (like snow in the sun); **blanc comme (la) n.** white as snow, snow-white; *Fig* **être blanc comme n.** to be as pure as the driven snow; *Culin* **blancs d'œufs battus en n.** stiffly beaten egg whites **2** *Arg (cocaïne)* snow
▸ ▸ **n. artificielle** artificial snow; **n. carbonique** dry ice, (carbon dioxide) snow; **neiges éternelles** perpetual snow; **n. fondue** *(qui tombe)* sleet; *(par terre)* slush; **n. fraîche** freshly fallen snow; **n. poudreuse** powdery snow; *Ski* **n. pourrie** hazardous *or* crumbly snow; *Ski* **n. tôlée** crusted snow

neiger [neʒe] V IMPERS *(il neigeait)* to snow

neigeux, -euse [neʒø, -øz] ADJ **1** *(pic, temps)* snowy; *(toit, pente etc)* snow-covered **2** *Fig (barbe)* snow-white, snowy

nem [nem] NM *Culin* spring roll

nématode [nematɔd] NM *Zool* nematode (threadworm)

néné [nene] NM *Fam* tit, boob

nénette [nenet] NF *Fam* **1** *(jeune fille)* bird, *Am* chick **2** *(petite amie)* girl **3** *(tête)* **se casser la n. (à faire qch)** to go to a lot of bother (to do sth); **tu ne t'es pas trop cassé la n. pour faire ta rédaction** you didn't exactly strain yourself *or* exert yourself over your essay; **te casse pas la n.** don't worry about it, don't let it bother you

nénuphar [nenyfar] NM waterlily; **n. des étangs, n. jaune** yellow pond lily

néo- [neo] PRÉF neo-

néo-calédonien, -ienne, *pl* **néo-calédoniens, -iennes** ADJ New Caledonian ▸ N **N.-C.** New Caledonian

néocapitalisme [neokapitalism] NM neo-capitalism

néocapitaliste [neokapitalist] ADJ, N neo-capitalist

néoclassicisme [neoklasisism] NM neo-classicism

néoclassique [neoklasik] ADJ *(style, architecture)* neoclassical

néocolonial, -iale, -iaux, -iales [neokolɔnjal, -jo] ADJ neocolonial

néocolonialisme [neokolɔnjalism] NM neocolonialism

néofascisme [neofasism, -ʃism] NM neofascism

néofasciste [neofaʃist] ADJ, N neofascist

néogothique [neogɔtik] ADJ, NM *Archit* neogothic

néo-hébridais, -aise, *pl* **néo-hébridais, -aises** [neoebride, -ɛz] ADJ of the New Hebrides ▸ N **N.-H.** *(natif)* native of the New Hebrides; *(habitant)* inhabitant of the New Hebrides

néo-impressionnisme NM *Beaux-Arts* neo-impressionism

néolibéralisme [neoliberalism] NM neo-liberalism

néolithique [neolitik] ADJ, NM Neolithic

néologisme [neolɔʒism] NM neologism

néon [neɔ̃] NM *Chimie* neon; **tube au n.** neon tube

néonatal, -ale, -als, -ales [neonatal] ADJ *Méd* neonatal

néonazi, -ie [neonazi] ADJ, N neo-Nazi

néonazisme [neonazism] NM neo-Nazism

néophyte [neofit] N **1** *Rel (converti)* neophyte **2** *Fig (novice)* novice, tyro; **je suis totalement n.** I'm a complete novice

Néoprène® [neopren] NM *Tech* neoprene

néoréalisme [neorealism] NM *Cin* neo-realism

néoréaliste [neorealist] ADJ *Cin (film, cinéaste)* neorealist

néorural, -ale, -aux, -ales [neoryral] ADJ neo-rural

néo-zélandais, -aise, *pl* **néo-zélandais, -aises** [neozelãde, -ɛz] ADJ New Zealand ▸ N **N.-Z.** New Zealander

Népal [nepal] NM Nepal

népalais, -aise [nepalɛ, -ɛz] ADJ Nepalese, Nepali ▸ NM *Ling* Nepali ▸ N **N.** Nepalese, Nepali

népérien, -ienne [neperjɛ̃, -jɛn] ADJ *(logarithmes)* Napierian

néphrétique [nefretik] ADJ **colique n.** renal colic ▸ N sufferer from nephritis

néphrite [nefrit] NF **1** *Méd* nephritis; **n. chronique** Bright's disease **2** *Minér* nephrite, jade

néphrologie [nefrolɔʒi] NF *Méd* nephrology

néphron [nefrɔ̃] NM *Méd* nephron

népotisme [nepɔtism] NM nepotism

Neptune [neptyn] NM *Myth* Neptune *m* ▸ NF *Astron* Neptune *f*

néréide [nereid] NF nereid, sea nymph

nerf [nɛr] NM **1** *(optique, spinal)* nerve; **viande pleine de nerfs** meat full of gristle, gristly meat; *Fam* **il a les nerfs en pelote** *ou* **à vif** *ou* **en boule** his nerves are *or* he is on edge; *Fam* **porter** *ou* **taper** *ou* *Can* **tomber sur les nerfs à qn** to get on sb's nerves; **avoir les nerfs à fleur de peau** to be all on edge; **je suis à bout de nerfs** I'm at the end of my tether; *Fam* **c'est un paquet** *ou* **une boule de nerfs** he is a bundle *or* bag of nerves; **être** *ou* **vivre sur les nerfs** to live on one's nerves; **passer ses nerfs sur qn/qch** to take it out on sb/sth; **guerre des nerfs** war of nerves; *Fam* **avoir les nerfs** to be really fed up; **avoir les nerfs solides** to have strong *or* steady nerves, to have nerves of steel; **être malade des nerfs** to suffer from nerves, to have bad nerves; *Fam* **foutre les nerfs à qn** to hack sb off, to get sb's back up **2** *Vieilli (tendon)* sinew, tendon, ligament; **un grand athlète tout en n.** a tall sinewy athlete **3** *(force)* **un peu de n.!, du n.!** put some energy into it!; **avoir du n.** *(d'un moteur, d'une voiture)* to be responsive *or* lively; *(d'une personne)* to have some go about one; **l'argent est le n. de la guerre** money is the sinews of war

4 *(de reliure)* band, cord

▸▸ **n. de bœuf** cosh, *Am* blackjack; *Anat* **n. crânien** cranial nerve; *Anat* **n. sciatique** sciatic nerve

nerprun [nɛrprœ̃] NM *Bot* buckthorn

nervation [nɛrvasjɔ̃] NF *Bot, Zool* nervation, venation

nervé [nɛrve] ADJ *Bot* nervate, veined

nerveusement [nɛrvøzmɑ̃] ADV **1** nervously **2** *(avec énergie)* energetically

nerveux, -euse [nɛrvø, -øz] ADJ **1** *(relatif aux nerfs) (système, maladie)* nervous; **centre n.** nerve centre; **dépression nerveuse** nervous breakdown; **influx n.** nerve impulse **2** *(émotif) (personne, tempérament)* nervous, excitable, highly-strung, *Br Fam* nervy; *(en un moment précis, avant un examen etc)* nervous, tense; *(rire, toux)* nervous; **être d'une nature nerveuse** to be of a nervous disposition; **rendre qn n.** to make sb nervous; **le café me rend n.** coffee makes me hyper **3** *(aux tendons apparents) (corps, mains)* sinewy; *(viande)* stringy **4** *(dynamique) (personne)* dynamic, energetic; *(style)* vigorous, terse; *Aut (conduite)* dynamic; **votre conduite est trop nerveuse** your driving is jerky; **moteur n.** responsive *or* lively engine

▸ N nervous person

nervi [nɛrvi] NM henchman, thug

nervosité [nɛrvozite] NF nervousness; *(irritabilité)* irritability; **donner des signes de n.** to show signs of agitation

nervure [nɛrvyr] NF *(de feuille, d'aile d'insecte)* nervure, vein, rib; *Tech* flange, rib; *(de radiateur etc)* gill; *Aviat (d'aile)* rib; *(au dos d'un livre)* rib, raised band; *Archit* **voûte à nervures** ribbed vault; **plafond à nervures** filleted ceiling; *Couture* **nervures** pin tucks

nervuré [nɛrvyre] ADJ *(feuille, aile)* veined; *(vêtement)* ribbed

n'est-ce pas [nɛspa] ADV **tu viendras, n.?** you'll come, won't you?; **tu l'as déjà vue, n.?** you've already seen her, haven't you?; **n. qu'elle est mignonne?** she's cute, isn't she?; **le problème, n., c'est qu'elle est un peu prude** the problem, you see, is that she's something of a prude VOIR GRAMMAIRE A47

Net [nɛt] NM **le N.** the Net, the Internet

NET, NETTE [nɛt] ADJ **1** *(propre) (assiette, pièce, miroir, mains)* clean; *Fig (conscience)* clear; **j'ai la conscience nette** I have a clear conscience, my conscience is clear; *Fig* **j'ai les mains nettes** my hands are clean; **faire place nette** to clear everything out; *Cartes etc* **faire tapis n.** to sweep the board

2 *(clair, précis) (vue, idée, style)* clear; *(contour)* sharp; *(réponse)* plain, straight; **je n'ai pas les idées très nettes aujourd'hui** I'm not quite with it today; **écriture nette** neat handwriting; **il fait plus froid ici, c'est très n.** it's noticeably *or* definitely colder here; *Phot, TV, Opt* **image nette** sharp image; **cassure nette** clean break; **division nette** clear-cut division; **elle a gardé des souvenirs très nets de sa petite enfance** she remembers her childhood quite clearly *or* vividly

3 *(différence, amélioration, refroidissement etc)* clear, marked, distinct

4 *Fam* **il n'est pas n.** *(un peu dérangé)* he's not all there; *(louche)* he's a bit shady

5 *(poids, prix, salaire)* net; *(profit)* net, clear; **n. d'impôt** net of tax; **le montant n.** the net amount, the net

ADV **1** *(de manière précise, brutale) (parler)* plainly, frankly; **refuser (tout) n.** to refuse point-blank *or* flatly; **je lui ai dit tout n. ma façon de penser** I told him plainly *or* frankly what I thought; **s'arrêter n.** to stop dead; **se**

casser n. to break clean through; **coupé n.** cut clean through; **tué n.** killed outright; **mets ton exercice au n.** copy the exercise out neatly

2 *Com* **cent euros n.** a hundred euros net; **gagner mille euros n.** to earn a thousand euros net, to net a thousand euros

▸▸ *Compta* **n. commercial** net profit; **n. financier** net interest income; *(à payer)* net interest charges; **n. à payer** net payable

netéconomie [nɛtekɔnɔmi] NF *Écon, Ordinat* Internet economy

netiquette [netikɛt] NF *Ordinat (sur l'Internet)* netiquette

netsurfer [nɛtsœrfœr] NM *Ordinat* net surfer

nettement [nɛtmɑ̃] ADV **1** *(distinctement) (voir, se dessiner)* clearly, distinctly; **profil n. découpé** clear-cut profile **2** *(incontestablement)* distinctly, markedly; **ce livre est n. pacifiste** this book is distinctly *or* markedly pacifist **3** *(beaucoup)* much, distinctly; **ça va n. mieux comme ça** it's a lot *or* much better like this; **elle est n. moins bonne que lui** she's not nearly as good as him; **il est arrivé n. en retard** he was more than a little late, he arrived quite late

netteté [nɛtte] NF **1** *(propreté)* cleanliness, cleanness **2** *(précision) (de rupture)* cleanness; **s'exprimer avec n.** to express oneself clearly **3** *(clarté) (de pensée, style)* clearness, clarity; *(de vision, d'objet)* distinctness; *(d'image)* sharpness; *(de mémoire)* vividness; *(de refus)* flatness; **l'image manque de n.** the picture isn't very sharp; *Phot* **régler la n.** to focus

nettoiement [nɛtwamɑ̃] NM *(de rues)* cleaning; *(du sol)* cleaning, clearing; *(de forêt)* clearing; **service du n.** refuse collection service

nettoyage [nɛtwajaʒ] NM **1** cleaning; **faire le n.** to do the cleaning; **grand n. de printemps** spring-cleaning; **produit de n.** cleaning product; **entreprise de n.** cleaning firm **2** *(par la police)* cleaning *or* clearing out; **les policiers ont opéré un véritable n. du quartier** the police officers really cleaned out *or* cleared out the district; *Mil* **opérations de n.** mopping-up operations

▸▸ *Pol* **n. ethnique** ethnic cleansing; **n. à sec** dry-cleaning; **n. par le vide** vacuum cleaning; *Fig* **faire le n. par le vide** to throw everything out

nettoyant [nɛtwajɑ̃] ADJ cleaning

NM cleaning product

nettoyer [nɛtwaje] *(je nettoie; je nettoierai)* VT **1** *(pièce, vêtements, casserole, blessure)* to clean; *(bouteille)* to wash out; *Naut (pont)* to swab; **n. à sec** to dry-clean **2** *Fig Fam (de cambrioleur) (maison)* to strip, to clean out; **se faire n. au jeu** to be *or* get cleaned out gambling; **la police est en train de n. le quartier** the police are cleaning out *or* clearing out the district; *Mil* **n. les poches de résistance** to mop up **3** *Fam (tuer)* to wipe out; **se faire n.** to be *or* get wiped out

VPR **se nettoyer se n. les oreilles/les mains** to clean one's ears/hands; **le four se nettoie automatiquement** the oven cleans itself automatically *or* is self-cleaning

nettoyeur, -euse [nɛtwajœr, -øz] N *(personne)* cleaner

NF **nettoyeuse** *(machine)* cleaning machine, cleaner

neuf[^1] [nœf, *before* ans *and* heures nœv] ADJ **1** nine; **à n. heures** at nine o'clock; **n. fois sur dix** nine times out of ten **2** *(dans séries)* ninth; **page/numéro n.** page/number nine; **Louis N.** Louis the Ninth

NM INV nine; **le n. mai** (on) the ninth of May, (on) May the ninth, *Am* (on) May ninth; *Cartes* **le n. de carreau** the nine of diamonds;

j'habite au n. I live at number nine; *Math* **faire la preuve par n.** to cast out the nines

neuf[^2]**, neuve** [nœf, nœv] ADJ new; **à l'état n.** in new condition, as new; *(timbre postal, livre)* in mint condition, unused; **'état n.'** *(dans petite annonce)* 'as new'; **tout n.** brand new; **comme n.** as good as new; **aborder/considérer/regarder qch d'un œil n.** to approach/consider/look at sth with a fresh eye; **la curiosité (toute) neuve d'un enfant** a child's newly awakened curiosity; **être n. dans un métier** to be new to a job; **quoi de n.?** what's new?; **il n'y a rien de n.** there's nothing new

NM **vendre du n. et de l'occasion** to sell new and second-hand goods; **habillé de n.** wearing new clothes; **meublé en n.** newly furnished; **acheter du n.** *(dans l'immobilier)* to buy new; **refaire/repeindre une maison à n.** to redo/repaint a house completely; **remettre qch à n.** to make sth as good as new; *(machine)* to recondition sth, to renovate sth; **tu as du n. pour ton visa?** any developments on the visa front?, have you heard anything about your visa?

neurasthénie [nørasteni] NF *Méd* neurasthenia; *Vieilli* **faire de la n.** *(dépression)* to be depressed

neurasthénique [nørastenik] ADJ *Vieilli* depressed; *Méd* neurasthenic

N *Vieilli* depressive, depressed person; *Méd* neurasthenic

neurobiologie [nørobjɔlɔʒi] NF neurobiology

neuroblaste [nøroblast] NM *Biol* neuroblast

neurochirurgie [nøroʃiryrʒi] NF *Chir* neurosurgery

neurochirurgien, -ienne [nøroʃiryrʒjɛ̃, -jɛn] N *Chir* neurosurgeon

neuroleptique [nøroleptik] *Méd* ADJ *(médicament)* neuroleptic

NM neuroleptic, *Fam* tranquillizer; **être sous neuroleptiques** to be on tranquillizers

neurologie [nørolɔʒi] NF *Méd* neurology

neurologiste [nørolɔʒist] N, **neurologue** [nørolɔg] N *Méd* neurologist, nerve specialist

neuromusculaire [nøromyskylɛr] ADJ neuromuscular

neuronal, -ale, -aux, -ales [nørɔnal, -o] ADJ neuronal; **réseau n.** neural net

neurone [nørɔn, -ron] NM *Biol, Ordinat* neuron, neurone

neuronique [nørɔnik] ADJ neuronic

neuropathologie [nøropatɔlɔʒi] NF neuropathology

neuropsychiatrie [nøropsikjatri] NF neuropsychiatry

neuropsychologie [nøropsikɔlɔʒi] NF neuropsychology

neurovégétatif, -ive [nørovɛʒetatif, -iv] ADJ *Anat (système)* neurovegetative

neutralisation [nøtralizasjɔ̃] NF *(de pays, d'acide etc)* neutralization, neutralizing; *Mil* **tir de n.** neutralizing fire

neutraliser [nøtralize] VT *(pays, acide)* to neutralize; *(efforts, concurrence, agents ennemis etc)* to thwart; *(agresseur)* to overpower; *(circulation)* to stop

VPR **se neutraliser** *(s'annuler réciproquement)* to cancel each other out

neutralisme [nøtralism] NM *Pol* neutralism

neutraliste [nøtralist] ADJ, N *Pol* neutralist

neutralité [nøtralite] NF *Pol, Chimie, Élec etc* neutrality; **garder la n.** to remain neutral; **sortir de sa n.** to take sides; *Pol* to abandon one's neutrality *or* one's neutral position; **violer la n. d'un État** to violate a state's neutrality

neutre [nøtr] ADJ **1** *(ni masculin, ni féminin)*

neuter; *Gram* **pronom** n. neuter pronoun; **abeille** n. neuter *or* worker bee **2** *(qui n'a pas pris position) (nation, navire, position, article de presse)* neutral; *Mil* **la zone** n. no-man's land; **rester** n. to remain neutral, not to take sides **3** *(sans caractéristique distinctive) (ton de voix, couleur)* neutral **4** *Chimie, Élec (sel, fil)* neutral

NM 1 *Gram* neuter; **au** n. in the neuter **2** *Can Aut* neutral; **se mettre sur le** n. to go into neutral

neutrino [nøtrino] **NM** *Phys* neutrino

neutron [nøtrɔ̃] **NM** *Phys* neutron; **bombe à neutrons** neutron bomb

neuvaine [nøvɛn] **NF** *Rel* novena

neuvième [nœvjɛm] **ADJ** ninth; **le** n. **art** *(la bande dessinée)* cartoons

N *(personne, chose)* ninth; **la** n. **de Beethoven** Beethoven's Ninth

NM *(fraction)* ninth

NF *Mus* ninth; *Scol Anciennement (d'école primaire) Br* ≃ third year of primary school, *Am* ≃ third grade

neuvièmement [nœvjɛmmɑ̃] **ADV** ninthly

névé [neve] **NM** *Géol* névé, firn

neveu, -eux [nœvø] **NM** nephew; *Fam* **un peu mon** n.**!** [nvø] you bet!

névralgie [nevralʒi] **NF** neuralgia; **avoir des névralgies** to suffer from neuralgia

névralgique [nevralʒik] **ADJ** neuralgic; *Fig* **point** n. *(d'une situation)* sensitive area

névrite [nevrit] **NF** *Méd* neuritis

névritique [nevritik] **ADJ** neuritic

névropathe [nevrɔpat] **N** *Vieilli* neuropath

névrose [nevroz] **NF** *Méd* neurosis; n. **post-traumatique** post-traumatic stress disorder

névrosé, -ée [nevroze] **ADJ, N** neurotic

névrotique [nevrɔtik] **ADJ** *Psy (désordre etc)* neurotic

new-look [njuluk] **NM INV, ADJ INV** New Look

newsgroup [njuzgrup] **NM** *Ordinat* newsgroup

new-yorkais, -aise, *pl* **new-yorkais, -aises** [njujɔrkɛ, -ɛz] **ADJ** *(of/from)* New York; **un bar/théâtre** n. a bar/theatre in New York

N N.-Y. New Yorker

nez [ne] **NM 1** nose; **parler/respirer du** n. to speak/breathe through one's nose; **j'ai le** n. **bouché** my nose is stuffed up *or* blocked; **se casser le** n. to break one's nose; *Fig (trouver porte close)* to find nobody at home; *(échouer)* to come a cropper; **le bout du** n. the tip of the nose; *Fig* **elle ne voit pas plus loin que le bout de son** n. she can't see beyond the *or* further than the end of her nose; **montrer (le bout de) son** n. to show oneself *or* one's face, to put in an appearance; **mener qn par le bout du** n. to have sb wrapped round one's little finger; **se laisser mener par le bout du** n. to let oneself be manipulated; **avoir le** n. **en l'air** to look up in the air; *Fig (rêvasser)* to have one's head in the clouds; **partir/se promener le** n. **au vent** to stroll *or* dawdle off/along; **où est mon dictionnaire? – il est sous ton** n. *ou* **tu as le** n. **dessus** where's my dictionary? – it's (right) under your nose; **avoir le** n. **dans son journal/ses bouquins** to have one's nose in one's newspaper/one's books; **sans lever le** n. *(lire, travailler)* without a break; **ça se voit comme le** n. **au milieu de la figure** it's as plain as the nose on your face; **se trouver** n. **à** n. **avec qn** to find oneself face to face with sb; **fourrer** *ou* **mettre son** n. **dans les affaires d'autrui** to poke one's nose *or* pry into other people's affairs; **je n'aime pas qu'on mette le** n. **dans mes affaires** I don't like people poking their noses *or* prying into my affairs; **baisser le** n. to hang one's head, to look sheepish; **cela lui pend au** n. he's got

it coming (to him); *Arg* **je l'ai dans le** n. I can't stand him, *Br* he gets up my nose; **avoir un verre** *ou* **un coup dans le** n. to be a bit merry *or* tipsy; **ça m'est passé sous le** n. it slipped through my fingers; **regarder qn sous le** n. to stare sb in the face; **dire qch au** n. **de qn** to say sth to sb's face; **rire au** n. **de qn** to laugh in sb's face; **raccrocher au** n. **de qn** to hang up on sb, to put the phone down on sb; **s'évader au** n. **et à la barbe des gendarmes** to escape right under the police's noses; **dérober qch au** n. **et à la barbe de qn** to steal sth from right under sb's nose; *Fam* **se manger** *ou* **se bouffer le** n. to be at each other's throats; **fermer** *ou* **claquer la porte au** n. **de qn** to shut the door in sb's face; **je n'ai pas mis le** n. **dehors de la journée** I didn't set foot outside the door all day; **il fait un temps à ne pas mettre le** n. **dehors** it's not the kind of weather to be out in; **ton** n. **remue** *ou* **s'allonge!** *(tu mens)* your nose is getting longer!; **sentir l'ail à plein** n. to smell strongly of garlic; **sentir le renfermé à plein** n. to smell very musty; *Fig* **ça sent le discours préparé à plein** n. you can tell it's a well-rehearsed speech; *Fig* **ça sent l'entourloupe à plein** n. there's some dirty business going on **2** *(odorat)* sense of smell; *(de chiens)* scent; **avoir le** n. **fin** *(avoir un bon odorat)* to have a good nose *or* a keen sense of smell; *Fig* **avoir le** n. **fin** *ou* **creux, avoir du** n. *(avoir de l'intuition)* to be shrewd

3 *(de bateau)* nose, bow, head; *(d'avion)* nose; *(de marche)* nosing; *(de moteur)* nose-piece; *Com* n. **de caisse** checkout display; **piquer du** n. *(d'un avion)* to nosedive; *(s'endormir)* to nod off, to doze off

▸▸ n. **en pied de marmite** bulbous nose; n. **en trompette, n. retroussé** turned-up *or* snub nose

NF [ɛnɛf] **NF** *(abrév* **norme française***)* = label indicating compliance with official French standards, *Br* ≃ BS, *Am* ≃ US standard

NfD *Typ (abrév* **note de fin de document***)* endnote

NGP **NF** [ɛnʒepe] *Com (abrév* **nomenclature générale des produits***)* customs nomenclature

ni [ni] **CONJ** (**ne** *is either expressed or implied)* nor; **ni moi** nor me (either); *Fml* **nor l,** *Fam* me neither; **sans argent ni bagages** without money or luggage, with neither money nor luggage; **il ne mange ni ne boit** he neither eats nor drinks; **il est parti sans manger ni boire** he left without (either) eating or drinking; **ni … ni** neither … nor; **ni Pierre ni Henri ne sont** *ou* **n'est là** neither Pierre nor Henri is there; **je n'ai ni femme ni enfant ni amis** I have neither wife nor child nor friends; **ni l'un ni l'autre ne se souvient** neither (of them) remembers; **lequel a été pris sur les deux? – ni l'un ni l'autre** which of the two was taken? – neither of them *or* neither one nor the other; **ni plus ni moins** neither more nor less **SEE GRAMMAR B62–3**

niacoué, -ée [njakwe] **N** *très Fam (terme raciste)* slant-eye, *Am* gook

niais, -aise [njɛ, -ɛz] **ADJ** *(personne, réponse, air)* simple, foolish, silly; *(sourire)* inane, silly

N fool, simpleton; **espèce de** n.**!** you silly fool!

niaisage [njɛzaʒ] **NM** *Can* idleness

niaisement [njɛzmɑ̃] **ADV** foolishly; **rire** n. to give a silly laugh, to laugh inanely

niaiser [njɛze] *Can* **VT** n. **qn** *(faire tourner en bourrique)* to drive sb crazy; *(se moquer de)* to laugh at sb; *(raconter des histoires à)* to pull sb's leg

VI *(ne rien faire)* to hang around doing nothing

niaiserie [njɛzri] **NF 1** *(caractère stupide)* sil-

liness, foolishness **2** *(une bêtise, une ânerie)* silly thing; **dire des niaiseries** to talk nonsense

niaiseux, -euse [njɛzø, -øz] *Can Fam* **ADJ** idiotic, stupid

N idiot

nibard [nibar] **NM** *Fam (sein)* tit, knocker, jug

Nicaragua [nikaragwa] **NM** Nicaragua

nicaraguayen, -enne [nikaragwajɛ̃, -ɛn] **ADJ** Nicaraguan

N N. Nicaraguan

Nicée [nise] **NF** *Antiq* Nicaea; **le symbole de N.** the Nicene Creed

niche¹ [niʃ] **NF 1** *(renfoncement)* niche, recess, alcove **2** *(de chien)* kennel **3** *Mktg* niche (market)

niche² **NF** *Fam Vieilli (farce)* trick, prank

nichée [niʃe] **NF** *(d'oisillons)* nest(ful), brood; *(de souris, de chiots)* litter; *Hum (d'enfants)* brood

nicher [niʃe] **VI** *(d'oiseaux)* to nest, to build a nest (**dans** in); *Fam (de personnes)* to hang out; **maison nichée dans la montagne** cottage nestling in *or* hidden away in the mountains; **niché dans un fauteuil** curled up in an armchair

VPR se nicher 1 *(d'oiseaux)* to nest, to build a nest **2** *(se cacher)* **où est-il allé se n.?** where's he hiding (himself)?, where's he got to?; **où ce chat a-t-il bien pu se n.?** where's the cat got to?

VT *(blottir)* n. **sa tête au creux de l'épaule de qn** to nuzzle *or* nestle one's head against sb's shoulder

nichet [niʃɛ] **NM** *(œuf factice)* nest egg

nichoir [niʃwar] **NM** nesting box

nichon [niʃɔ̃] **NM** *Fam (sein)* boob, tit

nickel [nikɛl] **NM** *Métal* nickel

ADJ INV *Fam (propre)* clean as a whistle

ADV *Fam* **faire qch** n. *ou* n. **chrome** to do something really well

nickelage [niklaʒ] **NM** nickel plating

nickelé [nikle] **ADJ** nickel-plated, nickelled; *Vieilli* **avoir les pieds nickelés** to sit tight, to refuse to budge

nickeler [nikle] **VT** (**je nickelle, nous nickelons; je nickellerai**) to nickel

nickélifère [nikelifɛr] **ADJ** nickel-bearing

niçois, -oise [niswa, -waz] **ADJ** of/from Nice

N N. *(natif)* native of Nice; *(habitant)* inhabitant of Nice

nicotine [nikɔtin] **NF** *Chimie* nicotine

nictation [niktasjɔ̃] **NF, nictitation** [niktitasjɔ̃] **NF** nictation, nictitation

nictitant [niktitɑ̃] **ADJ** *Zool (membrane)* nictitating

nid [ni] **NM 1** *(d'oiseaux, de souris, de fourmis etc)* nest; *aussi Fig* n. **d'aigle** eyrie; *Fig* n. **de brigands/d'espions** den of ruffians/of spies; *Mil* n. **de mitrailleuses** nest of machine guns; *Prov* **petit à petit l'oiseau fait son** n. slow and steady wins the race **2** *(logis confortable)* nest; **un petit** n. **douillet** a cosy little nest; n. **d'amour(eux)** love nest

▸▸ *Couture* **nid(s) d'abeilles** smocking, honeycomb stitch; **un torchon nid(s) d'abeilles** a honeycomb cloth; n. **d'ange** *(pour les bébés)* (baby's) sleeping bag, *Am* bunting (bag); n. **à poussière** dust trap

nid-de-pie, *pl* **nids-de-pie NM** *Naut* crow's nest; *Mil (retranchement)* lodg(e)ment

nid-de-poule, *pl* **nids-de-poule NM** pothole

nièce [njɛs] **NF** niece

nielle¹ [njɛl] **NF 1** *(maladie du blé)* smut, blight **2** *(fleur)* n. **des blés** corncockle

nielle² **NM** *Beaux-Arts* niello

niellé [njele] **ADJ blé** n. blighted wheat

nieller [njele] VT *Beaux-Arts* to inlay with niello

niellure [njelyr] NF *Beaux-Arts* niello work

nier [nje] (*impf, pr sub* **nous niions**) VT (*un fait, l'existence de qch*) to deny; **je nie l'avoir vue** I deny having seen her; **je nie qu'il m'ait vu** I deny that he saw me; **n. l'évidence** to deny the obvious *or* what's obvious; **je ne nie pas que j'ai parfois tort** I don't deny that I'm sometimes wrong; **on ne peut pas n. que …** there's no denying *or* one can't deny *or* it's undeniable that …

◇ VI **l'accusé nie** the accused denies the charge

niet [njɛt] INT *Fam* no way!, not a chance!

nigaud, -aude [nigo, -od] N ninny, fool; **gros n.!** you great *or* big ninny!
◇ ADJ (*sourire, réponse*) silly

nigelle [niʒɛl] NF (*fleur*) nigella, love-in-a-mist

Niger [niʒer] NM Niger

Nigeria [niʒerja] NM Nigeria

nigérian, -ane [niʒerjɑ̃, -an] ADJ Nigerian
◇ N **N.** Nigerian

nigérien, -ienne [niʒerjɛ̃, -jɛn] ADJ of/from Niger, Nigerien
◇ N **N.** Nigerien

nihilisme [niilism] NM *Phil* nihilism

nihiliste [niilist] *Phil* ADJ nihilist(ic)
◇ N nihilist

Nil [nil] NM **le N.** the Nile; **vert N.** (*couleur*) eau-de-nil

nilgaut [nilgo] NM (*mammifère*) nilgai

nilotique [nilɔtik] ADJ of the Nile, Nilotic

nimbe [nɛ̃b] NM halo, nimbus

nimbé [nɛ̃be] ADJ haloed

nimbus [nɛ̃bys] NM *Météo* nimbus

ninas [ninas] NM INV small cigar

nipper [nipe] *Fam* VT (*habiller*) to deck out; **bien nippé** well turned out
◇ VPR **se nipper** (*s'habiller*) to dress; **je me nippe chez Tati** I get my clothes at Tati's

nippes [nip] NFPL *Fam* (*vêtements*) gear, togs; **à part les n., rien ne l'intéresse** he isn't interested in anything apart from clothes

nippon, -one [nipɔ̃, -ɔn] ADJ Japanese
◇ N **N.** Japanese; **les Nippons** the Japanese

nique [nik] NF *Fam* **faire la n. à qn** to cock a snook at sb

niquer [nike] VT **1** *Vulg* (*posséder sexuellement*) to screw, to shag **2** *très Fam* (*duper*) to shaft, to screw; **c'est un faux, tu t'es fait n.!** it's a fake, you've been shafted *or* screwed! **3** *Fam* (*endommager*) to knacker, to bugger

niquet [nikɛ] NM *Belg Fam* snooze, nap

nirvana [nirvana] NM Nirvana

nissart [nisar] NM = dialect of occitan spoken in the Nice region of France

nitrate [nitrat] NM *Chimie* nitrate

nitre [nitr] NM *Chimie* nitre, saltpetre, *Am* niter, saltpeter

nitré [nitre] ADJ *Chimie* nitrated; **composé n.** nitro compound

nitrer [nitre] VT *Tech* to nitrate

nitreux, -euse [nitrø, -øz] ADJ *Chimie* nitrous

nitrifier [nitrifje] VT *Chimie* to nitrify

nitrique [nitrik] ADJ *Chimie* (*acide*) nitric

nitrobenzène [nitrobɛ̃zɛn] NM *Chimie* nitrobenzene

nitroglycérine [nitrogliserin] NF *Chimie* nitroglycerine

nitrure [nitryr] NM *Chimie* nitride; **n. de fer** iron nitride

nitrurer [nitryre] VT *Métal* to nitride

niveau, -eaux [nivo] NM **1** (*hauteur*) level; **n. d'eau/d'huile** water/oil level; **n. de l'eau/**
de la mer water/sea level; **au n. de la mer** at sea level; **n. des basses/hautes eaux** low-water/high-water mark; **elle a une cicatrice au n. de la cuisse** she has a scar on her leg at about thigh-level; **l'eau nous arrivait au n. de la taille** the water came up to our waists; **les deux encadrements ne sont pas au même n.** the two frames are not level (with each other) *or* are not on the same level; **la Saône n'avait jamais atteint un n. aussi haut** the Saône had never reached such a high level *or* had never been so high; **quand tu arrives au n. de la place des Jacobins, prends à gauche** when you get to the Place des Jacobins, turn left; **au n. régional/local** at regional/local level; **au n. matériel/du travail** on the financial/work front, financewise/workwise, where finance/work is concerned; **au n. sentimental** as far as one's love life is concerned; *aussi Fig* **se mettre au n. de qn** to come down to sb's level; **être de n.** to be level; **mettre qch de n.** to make sth level

2 (*étage*) level; **jardin à trois niveaux** garden on three levels; **immeuble à dix niveaux** ten-storey building; **le supermarché se trouve au troisième n.** the supermarket is on the third level; **n. arrivée** (*d'un aéroport*) arrivals level; **n. départ** (*d'un aéroport*) departures level

3 (*degré*) level; *Scol* standard; **n. de pollution** pollution level; **n. sonore** noise level; *Radio* **n. de transmission** transmission level; **n. scolaire** academic standard; **tous les élèves ne sont pas du ou n'ont pas le même n.** not all the pupils are of *or* have reached the same (academic) standard, not all the pupils are of the same level of ability; **quel est son n. en anglais?** what is his standard in English?; **il a un très bon n. en physique** his physics is of a very high standard; **avoir le n. (requis), être au n.** to be up to standard, *Fam* to be up to scratch; **votre fils n'a pas le n. pour passer le concours** your son is not of a high enough standard to take the examination; **évaluer le n. des candidats** to evaluate the candidates' level of ability; **test de n.** assessment; **être au n. de qn/qch, être de n. avec qn/qch** to be on a level *or* on a par with sb/sth; **nous recherchons un candidat n. baccalauréat/maîtrise** we are looking for a candidate of baccalauréat/master's degree standard; **ils sont d'un n. social différent** they are from different social backgrounds; **au plus bas n. de l'échelle** at the very bottom of the ladder; **au plus haut n. de la hiérarchie** at the highest level of the hierarchy, at the very top; **les salaires augmentent régulièrement à tous les niveaux** there are regular salary increases for all grades *or* at all levels; **la production n'avait jamais atteint un n. aussi haut** production had never reached such a high level *or* had never been so high; **n. d'occupation** (*d'un hôtel*) occupancy level; **n. des prix** price levels; **n. des salaires** salary levels; **n. des stocks** inventory *or* stock level; **n. record** record level

▸▸ *Ordinat* **n. d'accès** (*dans un réseau*) access level; **n. à bulle d'air** spirit level; *Bourse* **n. de cours des actions** stock price level; *Bourse* **n. de dépôt requis** margin requirement; *Ordinat* **n. de gris** greyscale; *Ling* **n. de langue** register, language level; *Tech* **n. à lunette** surveyor's level; *Tech* **n. de maçon** vertical *or* plumb level; *Tech* **n. à plomb** vertical *or* plumb level; **n. tarifaire** fare level; *Écon* **n. de vie** standard of living

nivelage [niv(ə)laʒ] NM *Constr* levelling

niveler [nivle] VT (**je nivelle**; **je nivellerai**) **1** (*aplanir*) (*sol, terrain*) to level, to make level **2** (*les fortunes*) to level, to even out *or* up; **n. les prix** to level prices; **n. par le bas** to level down

niveleur, -euse [nivlœr, -øz] N leveller
◇ NM *Hist* Leveller
◇ NF *Constr* **niveleuse** grader

nivellement [nivɛlmɑ̃] NM (*de terrain, des classes sociales*) levelling; **n. par le bas** levelling down; **repère de n.** (*dans l'arpentage*) bench mark

nivéole [niveɔl] NF (*plante*) snowflake

nivôse [nivoz] NM *Hist* = fourth month of the Republican calendar (*December-January*)

NNTP [ɛnɛntepe] NM *Ordinat* (*abrév* **Network News Transfer Protocol**) NNTP

nobélisable [nobelizabl] ADJ (*chercheur, écrivain*) potential Nobel prizewinning
◇ N potential Nobel prizewinner

nobiliaire [nobiljer] ADJ **titre n.** title; **particule n.** nobiliary particle
◇ NM peerage (list)

noble [nobl] ADJ **1** (*famille, origine*) noble **2** (*imposant*) (*air, allure*) noble, stately **3** (*hautement apprécié*) (*cause, motif, entreprise*) noble; **il n'est animé que par de nobles sentiments** he is acting out of noble sentiments; **le n. art** (*boxe*) the noble art **4** (*précieux*) noble; **la soie est une matière n.** silk is a noble fabric
◇ N noble, nobleman, f noblewoman; **les nobles** the nobility, the nobles

noblement [nobləmɑ̃] ADV nobly

noblesse [nobles] NF **1** (*par la descendance*) nobility; **famille de n. récente** recently ennobled family; **la haute et la petite n.** the nobility and the gentry; **se marier dans la n.** to marry into nobility, to marry a title; **n. oblige** noblesse oblige **2** (*de style, de conduite*) nobility, nobleness; **agir avec beaucoup de n.** to act very nobly

▸▸ *Hist* **n. d'épée** old nobility; *Hist* **n. de robe** noblesse de robe

nobliau, -iaux [noblijo] NM *Péj* lesser noble(man)

noce [nos] NF **1** (*cérémonie du mariage*) wedding; (*fête*) wedding festivities; (*ensemble des assistants*) wedding party; **repas de n.** wedding breakfast; **noces d'argent/de vermeil/d'or/de diamant** silver/ruby/golden/diamond wedding; **il l'avait épousée en secondes noces** she was his second wife **2** *Fam* **faire la n.** to go on a binge, to live it up; **être à la n.** to have the time of one's life, to have a whale of a time; **je n'étais pas à la n.** it was no picnic

noceur, -euse [nosœr, -øz] N *Fam* fast liver, *Br* raver

nocif, -ive [nosif, -iv] ADJ (*produit, émanation*) harmful, noxious

nocivité [nosivite] NF harmfulness, noxiousness

noctambule [noktabyl] N (*qui aime sortir la nuit*) night owl, night bird

noctuelle [noktɥɛl] NF *Entom* noctua, owlet moth

nocturne [noktyrn] ADJ (*animal*) nocturnal; (*attaque, visite*) night; *Bot* night-flowering; **évasion n.** escape by night
◇ NM **1** (*rapace*) nocturnal bird (of prey) **2** *Rel* nocturn **3** *Beaux-Arts, Mus* nocturne
◇ NF (*d'un magasin etc*) late-night opening; *Sport* **match (disputé) en n.** evening game

nodal, -ale, -aux, -ales [nodal, -o] ADJ (*point, ligne*) nodal
◇ NM *TV* master control room

nodosité [nodozite] NF *Bot, Méd* (*nodule*) node, nodule; (*état*) nodosity

nodule [nodyl] NM *Géol, Méd etc* nodule

Noé [noe] N *Bible* Noah

Noël [noɛl] NM **1** (*fête*) Christmas; **à N., Région à la N.** at Christmas (time); **le jour de N.** Christmas Day; **la nuit ou la veillée de N.**

Christmas Eve; **bûche de N.** yule log; **vacances de N.** Christmas holidays, *Am* Christmas vacation; **arbre** *ou* **sapin de N.** Christmas tree; **joyeux N.!** Happy *or* Merry Christmas! **2** *(chanson)* (Christmas) carol **3** *(cadeau)* **offrir qch à qn pour son (petit) n.** to give sb sth for Christmas *or* as a Christmas present

nœud [nø] **NM 1** *(entrecroisement)* knot; *Naut* hitch, bend; **corde à nœuds** knotted rope; **faire** *ou* **serrer un n.** to make *or* tie a knot; *Fig* **faire un n. à son mouchoir** to tie a knot in one's handkerchief; *Fig* **avoir un n. dans l'estomac** to have a knot in one's stomach; *Fig* **avoir un n. dans la gorge** to have a lump in one's throat; *Fig* **le n. du problème** the crux of the problem *or* matter; *Fig* **quel sac de nœuds!** what a muddle! **2** *(ornement)* bow; **faire un n.** to tie a bow; **mettre un n. dans ses cheveux** to put a bow in one's hair; **n. de diamants** diamond cluster **3** *(de serpent)* coil **4** *(d'orbite, de courbe, d'oscillation)*, *Ordinat* node **5** *(sur un arbre, une planche)* knot, knur(l) **6** *(carrefour de grandes lignes)* **n. autoroutier/ferroviaire** major road/rail junction *or* intersection **7** *Naut (vitesse)* knot; **filer** *ou* **faire vingt nœuds** to do *or* make twenty knots **8** *Littér, Théâtre* knot, crux **9** *Vulg (pénis)* prick, dick, cock; **à la mords-moi le n.** lousy, crappy, *Br* poxy

▸▸ **n. coulant** *(pour serrer)* slipknot; *(pour étrangler)* noose; **n. de cravate** tie knot; **faire son n. de cravate** to knot one's tie; **n. gordien** Gordian knot; **trancher le n. gordien** to cut the Gordian knot; *Tech* **n. de grappin** fisherman's bend; *Anat* **n. lymphatique** lymph node; **n. papillon**, *Fam* **n. pap** bow tie; **n. plat** reef knot; *Tech* **n. de vache** carrick bend; **n. de vipères** nest of vipers

noir, noire [nwar] **ADJ 1** *(couleur)* black; **n. comme de l'encre** as black as ink, inky black; *Litt* **n. comme (de) l'ébène** as black as ebony, ebony black; *Litt* **n. comme (du) jais** jet black; *Litt* **n. comme de la poix** pitch-black; **n. d'ivoire** ivory black; **la place était noire de monde** the square was thick *or* swarming with people

2 *(très sombre)* *(cheveux, yeux, ciel, lunettes)* dark; **il est rentré n. de ses vacances** he was incredibly brown when he came back from his holidays

3 *(relatif à la race)* *(peau, race, origine, quartier, chanteuse)* black

4 *(plongé dans l'obscurité)* *(nuit, cellule)* dark; **il fait n.** it's dark; **il faisait nuit noire** *ou* **n. comme dans un four** it was pitch-dark *or* pitch-black

5 *(pessimiste)* *(pensées, vision)* black, gloomy; **avoir des idées noires** to be down in the dumps; **il m'a fait un tableau très n. de la situation** he painted a very black *or* gloomy picture of the situation; **le lundi/jeudi n.** Black Monday/Thursday; **rien n'est tout blanc ou tout n.** nothing is completely black and white

6 *(sale)* *(visage, mains, ongles, linge)* black, filthy, dirty; **tu es tout n.** you're all black *or* filthy *or* dirty; **être n. de crasse** to be black with grime; **être n. comme du charbon** to be as black as soot

7 *(inspiré par la colère)* *(regard)* black; *Litt (crime)* heinous, foul; *(ingratitude)* utter; *(calomnie)* wicked; **regarder qn d'un œil n.** to give sb a black look; *Litt* **de noirs desseins** evil designs; **être d'une humeur noire** to be in a black *or* foul mood

8 *(illicite)* **le marché n.** the black market

9 *(intense)* **colère noire** towering rage; **se mettre dans une colère noire** to fly into a towering rage; **misère noire** dire *or* abject poverty, utter destitution; **être dans une misère noire** to be utterly destitute

10 *Arg (ivre)* blind drunk

11 *Cin, Littér* **film n.** film noir, gangster thriller; **roman n.** gangster novel

N **N.** Black (man), *f* Black (woman); **il est N.** he's (a) Black; *Hist* **traite des Noirs** slave trade

NM 1 *(couleur)* black; **j'aime le n.** I like black; **le n. et blanc** *Cin* black and white; *Phot* black-and-white photography; *TV* black-and-white television; **en n. et blanc** *(film, photographie)* black-and-white; **être vêtu de n.**, **être en n.** to be dressed (all) in black; *Fam* **se mettre du n. aux yeux** to put eyeliner on; **d'un n. d'ébène** as black as ebony, ebony black; **c'était écrit n. sur blanc** it was there in black and white

2 *(obscurité)* dark, darkness; **avoir peur du n.** *ou* **dans le n.** to be afraid of the dark

3 *(trace de salissure)* **tu as du n. sur le visage** you've got a black mark on your face; **j'ai mis plein de n. sur mon pantalon** I've got black marks all over my trousers

4 *(pessimisme)* **voir tout en n.** to look on the black side of everything; **broyer du n.** to be down in the dumps

5 *(travail illicite)* **le travail au n.** moonlighting, work on the side; **travailler au n.** to moonlight; **il a été engagé au n.** he was employed illegally; **il est chauffeur de taxi au n.** he moonlights *or* works on the side as a taxi driver; **faire des petits boulots au n.** to do some little jobs on the side

6 *(d'une cible)* bull's-eye

7 *(café)* **un (petit) n.** a (small) black coffee **NF** *Mus* **noire** crotchet, *Am* quarter note

▸▸ *Typ* **n. au blanc** reverse printing, white-on-black; **n. de Chine** Indian ink, *Am* India ink; **n. de fumée** lampblack; *Typ* **n. au gris** black-on-tone

noirâtre [nwarɑtr] **ADJ** blackish

noiraud, -aude [nwaro, -od] **ADJ** dark, swarthy

N dark *or* swarthy person, *Péj* darky, darkie

noirceur [nwarsœr] **NF 1** *(d'encre etc)* blackness; *Litt (d'un crime)* heinousness, foulness **2** *Can (obscurité)* dark, darkness; **dans la n.** in the dark *or* darkness; **avoir peur dans la n.** to be afraid of the dark

noircir [nwarsir] **VI** to turn *or* go black, to darken

VT *(mur, pierres etc)* to blacken, to make black; *Fig* **n. du papier**, **n. des pages et des pages** to write page after page; **il a noirci trois feuilles sans s'interrompre** he covered three sheets of paper without stopping; **tout ce qu'il est capable de faire, c'est n. du papier** the only thing he's good at is putting ink on paper; **n. qn** *ou* **la réputation de qn** to blacken sb's reputation; **n. le tableau** *ou* **la situation** to paint things blacker than they are

VPR **se noircir** *(de métal, pierre, mur etc)* to turn *or* go black, to darken; *(du ciel)* to darken, to become overcast; *Fig Fam (se soûler)* to get blind drunk (**à la vodka**/*etc* on vodka/*etc*); **se n. le visage** to black one's face; *Théâtre* to black up

noircissement [nwarsismɑ̃] **NM** blackening

noircissure [nwarsisyr] **NF** black mark

noise [nwaz] **NF** *Litt* **chercher n.** *ou* **des noises à qn** to try to pick a quarrel with sb

noisetier [nwaztje] **NM** hazel (tree *or* bush); *(bois)* hazel (wood)

noisette [nwazɛt] **NF 1** *Bot, Culin* hazel(nut) **2** *(petite quantité)* *(de beurre)* knob; *(de mousse coiffante)* small ball **3** *Culin* **n. d'agneau** noisette of lamb **4** *(café)* espresso coffee with milk

ADJ INV **yeux n.** hazel eyes

noix [nwa] **NF 1** *(fruit)* walnut **2** *Fam* **quelle n.!** *(imbécile)* what a twerp!; **comment vas-tu, vieille n.?** how are you, old thing?; *Fig Fam* **à la n. (de coco)** rubbishy, lousy; **excu-**

ses à la n. paltry *or* trivial excuses **3** *Culin* **n. de bœuf**, **n. de côtelette**, **n. de gigot** pope's eye; **rôti dans la n.**, **n. de veau** cushion *or* topside of veal **4** *(petite quantité)* **n. de beurre** knob of butter

▸▸ **n. d'acajou** cashew nut; **n. du Brésil** Brazil nut; **n. de cajou** cashew nut; **n. de coco** coconut; **n. de pécan** pecan; **n. vomique** nux vomica

nolisation [nɔlizasjɔ̃] **NF** chartering

nolisement [nɔliz(ə)mɑ̃] **NM** chartering

noliser [nɔlize] **VT** to charter

nom [nɔ̃] **NM 1** *(de personne)* name; **quel est votre n.?** what's your name?; **n. ..., prénom ... (sur formulaire)** surname ..., first name ...; **n. et prénoms** full name; **vos n., prénoms et adresse** your full name and address; **quelqu'un dont je tairai le n.** someone who shall remain nameless; **je porte le n. de ma grand-mère** I'm called after my grandmother; **tu porteras le n. de ton mari ou pas?** will you take your husband's name or not?; **je la connais de n. seulement** I only know her by name; **je n'arrive pas à mettre un n. sur sa tête/sur sa voix** I can't put a name to him; **voyager sous un faux n.** to travel under a false name *or* an alias; **on le connaissait sous le n. de Leduc** he was known by *or* was known by the name of Leduc; **se faire un n.** to make a name for oneself; **un grand n. de la musique** one of the great names of music; **les grands noms de la littérature russe** the great names of Russian literature; **il est médecin que de n.** he's a doctor in name only; **faire une proposition au n. de qn** to make a proposal for sb *or* on behalf of sb; **parler en son n.** to speak for oneself; **je parlerai en votre n.** I'll speak for you *or* in your name; **un homme du n. de Pierre** a man by the name of *or* named Pierre; **Louis, treizième du n.** Louis, thirteenth king of that name; **traiter qn de tous les noms** to call sb names; **je lui ai donné tous les noms d'oiseaux** I called him every name under the sun; *Fam* **avoir un n. à coucher dehors** to have a totally unpronounceable name **SEE GRAMMAR B8**

2 *(de plantes, d'animaux, d'objets etc)* name; **c'est quoi le n. de ta rue?** what's the name of your street?; **appeler les choses par leur n.** to call a spade a spade; **impolitesse sans n.** unspeakable rudeness; *Fam* **n. de n.!**, **n. d'une pipe!**, **n. d'un chien!**, **n. de Dieu!** hell!; **au n. de la loi** in the name of the law; **faire qch au n. de l'amitié/la justice** to do sth in the name of friendship/justice

3 *Gram* noun **SEE GRAMMAR A9–17; B5–8**

▸▸ **n. de baptême** first name, Christian name, *Am* given name; *Ordinat* **n. de champ** field name; **n. commercial** company *or* trade name; *Gram* **n. commun** common noun; *Gram* **n. composé** compound (noun); *Com* **n. déposé** (registered) trademark; *Ordinat* **n. de domaine** domain name; **n. d'emprunt** assumed name; *Bourse* nominee name; **n. de famille** surname; *Mktg* **n. de famille global** blanket family name; *Ordinat* **n. de fichier** file name; *Mktg* **n. générique** generic name; **n. de guerre** assumed name, pseudonym; *(d'un écrivain, d'un journaliste)* pseudonym, pen name; *(d'un acteur)* stage name; **n. de jeune fille** maiden name; **n. de marque** brand name; **n. à particule** = name with a nobiliary particle; **n. de plume** nom de plume, pen name, pseudonym; *Gram* **n. propre** proper noun; **SEE GRAMMAR B8** *Fam* **n. à rallonges** long aristocratic surname, double-barrelled name; **n. de scène** stage name; **n. de théâtre** stage name; *Fam* **n. à tiroirs** long aristocratic surname, double-barrelled name

nomade [nɔmad] **ADJ** *(vie, tribu)* nomadic, wandering

N *(du désert)* nomad; *Jur (gitan)* traveller; *Ordinat, Tél* road warrior

nomadisme [nɔmadism] **NM** nomadism

nombre [nɔ̃br] **NM 1** number; **(bon) n. de gens, un certain n. de gens, un assez grand n. de gens** a number of people, a good many people; **le plus grand n. est de cet avis** the majority are of this opinion; **un grand/petit n. d'entre nous** many/a few of us; **ils finirent par succomber sous le n. des assaillants** they were finally overcome by the sheer number of their attackers; *Ordinat, Typ* **n. de caractères** character count; *Journ* **n. de lecteurs** readership; *Ordinat, Typ* **n. de mots** word count; *Typ* **n. de pages** extent; *Litt* **surpasser en n.** to outnumber; **supérieur en n.** superior in number(s); **nous sommes en n. suffisant** there are enough of us; *(dans une réunion)* we have a quorum; **sans n.** *(foule)* huge, vast; **venez pour faire n.** come and make up the numbers; **venir/se précipiter en n.** to come/rush in large *or* great numbers; **les voitures/manifestants convergeaient en (très) grand n. vers le centre de la ville** the cars/demonstrators were converging in huge numbers on the town centre; *Litt* **en n. écrasant** by an overwhelming majority; **ils sont au n. de huit** there are eight of them; **être au n.** *ou* **du n. des élus** to be one of *or* be among the elect; *Fml* **mettre** *ou* **compter qn au n. de ses intimes** to number sb among one's friends; **sur le n.** among *or* out of (all) those; *Bible* **Le Livre des Nombres** (the Book of) Numbers SEE GRAMMAR A76–7; B58–60 **2** *Gram* number; **s'accorder en genre et en n.** to agree in gender and number
▸▸**n. atomique** atomic number; *Phys* **n. d'Avogadro** Avogadro number; *Math* **n. complexe** complex number; *Math* **n. décimal** decimal (number); *Math* **n. entier** whole number, integer; **n. d'or** golden section; *Math* **n. premier** prime number

nombreux, -euse [nɔ̃brø, -øz] **ADJ** *(membres, objets)* numerous, many; *(famille, armée, groupe)* large; **auditoire peu n.** small audience; **pendant de nombreuses générations** for many generations; **nous sommes peu n.** there are not many of us, there are very few of us; **n. sont ceux qui …** there are/were many who …; **venir (très) n.** to come in (very) large numbers; **venez n.!** all (are) welcome!, everyone (is) welcome!

nombril [nɔ̃bri(l)] **NM 1** *Anat* navel; *Fam Hum* **être décolletée jusqu'au n.** to be showing a lot of cleavage; **il avait une chemise ouverte jusqu'au n.** his shirt was open to the waist; *Fam* **il se prend pour le n. du monde** *ou* **de la terre** he thinks the whole world revolves around him; *Fig* **se regarder le n.** to contemplate one's navel; *Can* **ne pas avoir le n. sec** to be (still) wet behind the ears, to be green **2** *Bot* hilum

nombrilisme [nɔ̃brilism] **NM** self-absorption, self-centredness; **faire du n.** to contemplate one's navel

nombriliste [nɔ̃brilist] **ADJ** self-absorbed, self-centred

nomenclature [nɔmãklatyr] **NF** *(ensemble de termes techniques)* nomenclature; *(liste des objets d'une collection etc)* list, catalogue; *(d'un dictionnaire)* word list; *(d'une voiture etc)* parts list; **n. douanière** *ou* **générale des produits** customs nomenclature

nominal, -ale, -aux, -ales [nɔminal, -o] **ADJ 1** *(prix, puissance en chevaux, autorité)* nominal; *Fin* nominal, par; *Fin* **valeur nominale** face value; *Élec* **courant n.** *(d'une machine)* rated current **2** *(relatif au nom de famille)* appel n. roll call; **liste nominale** list of names, name list; **vérification** *ou* **contrôle nominal(e)** name check **3** *Gram (emploi, fonction)* nominal

NM *Fin (d'une action)* nominal value; *(d'une obligation)* par value

nominalement [nɔminalmã] **ADV 1** *(appeler qn)* by name; **rester n. propriétaire d'un immeuble** to remain the owner of an apartment block in name only **2** *Gram (comme un nom)* nominally, as a noun

nominalisme [nɔminalism] **NM** *Phil* nominalism

nominatif, -ive [nɔminatif, -iv] **ADJ 1** *(qui comporte un nom) (carte d'adhérent, billet)* nontransferable; **état n.** list of names, name list; **votre carte bancaire est nominative** *(inscription sur carte)* this banker's card may be used only by the authorized signatory *or* by the person whose name it bears; **les places de concert ne sont pas nominatives** the seats for the concert are transferable **2** *Fin* **titres nominatifs** registered securities
NM 1 *Gram* nominative (case); **au n.** in the nominative (case)
2 *Fin* **dividende au n.** dividend on registered securities

nomination [nɔminasjɔ̃] **NF 1** *(à un poste)* appointment *(à* to); **attendre sa n.** to expect to be appointed; **n. à un grade supérieur** promotion **2** *(pour une récompense)* nomination; **ce film a trois nominations pour les Césars** this film has received three César nominations **3** *Phil* naming

nominativement [nɔminativmã] **ADV** by name

nominé [nɔmine] **ADJ** *(film, acteur)* nominated (**à** une récompense for an award)

nominer [nɔmine] **VT** to nominate

nommage [nɔmaʒ] **NM** *Ordinat (de site Internet)* designation

nommé, -ée [nɔme] **ADJ** *(personne, objet)* named
N **le n. Antoine** the man named *or* called Antoine; **la nommée Chantal** the woman named *or* called Chantal; **un n. Bertrand a appelé** someone named *or* called Bertrand rang

nommément [nɔmemã] **ADV 1** **accuser/ dénoncer/désigner qn n.** to accuse/denounce/refer to sb by name **2** *(spécialement)* especially, in particular

nommer [nɔme] **VT 1** *(appeler)* to name, to give a name to; **on le nomma Paul** they named *or* called him Paul; **on nomme aumôniers les prêtres attachés à un régiment** priests attached to a regiment are called chaplains **2** *(désigner) (personne)* to name, to mention by name; **un homme que je ne nommerai pas** a man who shall remain nameless *or* whom I won't (mention by) name; *Hum* **M. Dutronc, pour ne pas le n.** without mentioning any names *or* naming no names, Mr Dutronc; *Vieilli* **à jour nommé** on the appointed day; **elle est arrivée à point nommé** she arrived just at the right moment *or* just when she needed **3** *(à un poste)* to appoint (**à** to); *Mil (un officier)* to commission; **n. qn directeur** to appoint sb manager; **n. des experts** to appoint experts; **elle a été nommée responsable des ventes** she was appointed sales director; **être nommé au grade supérieur** to be promoted; **être nommé à Lille** to be posted to Lille
VPR **se nommer 1** *(avoir pour nom)* to be called *or* named; **comment vous nommez-vous?** what is your name? **2** *(s'identifier)* to give one's name

non [nɔ̃] SEE GRAMMAR B62–3 **ADV 1** *(en réponse)* no; **répondre par oui ou n.** to answer yes or no; **n., n. et n.!** no, no, no!; **c'est dégoûtant, n.?** it's disgusting, isn't it?; **il est pas mal, n.(, tu ne trouves pas)?** he's not bad-looking, is he?; **il a commencé comme éboueur – n.!** *(c'est pas*

possible!) he started as a dustman – no! *or* really?; **alors, ton augmentation? – c'est n.** what about your pay rise? – I didn't get it; **mais n.!, dame n.!, mon Dieu n.!,** *Hum* **que n.!** certainly not!, definitely not!; **n. mais! je ne te permets pas** no, really! I can't allow that; **tu es content? – ma foi n.!** *ou* **certes n.!** are you happy? – certainly not! *or* far from it!; *Litt* **n. pas!** not so!, not at all!; **n., je vous en prie** please don't; **je pense que n.** I don't think so, I think not; **je dis que n.** I say no; **faire signe que n.** *(de la tête)* to shake one's head; *(avec le doigt)* to indicate no; **il voulait traverser la rue, mais sa mère lui fit signe que n.** he was about to cross the road, but his mother signalled to him not to; **tu viens, oui ou n.?** are you coming, yes or no?; **qu'elle vienne ou n.** whether she comes or not SEE GRAMMAR B64 **2** *(pas)* not; **n. loin de la ville** not far from the town; **n. sans raison** not without reason; **n. seulement …, mais encore** *ou* **aussi …** not only …, but also …; **moi n. plus** me neither; **le problème est cette fois n. plus d'ordre économique mais social** the problem is now not economic but social; **ton frère est studieux, toi n.** your brother is studious, but you're not *or* unlike you; **il faut que ce soit toi qui lui parles et n. l'inverse** it's you who have to talk to him and not the other way round; **n. content de conduire sans permis, l'individu était ivre** not content with driving without a licence, the man was also drunk; **n. coupable** not guilty; **n. solvable** insolvent; **n. (pas) que je le craigne** not that I fear him; **n. que je ne vous plaigne** not that I don't pity you VOIR GRAMMAIRE A23–4
NM INV no; **répondre par un n.** to answer with a no *or* in the negative; **les n. l'emportent** the noes have it; **se fâcher/pleurer pour un oui, pour un n.** to flare up/cry at the least (little) thing

non-acceptation [nɔ̃akseptasjɔ̃] **NF** *Banque (d'une lettre de change)* non-acceptance

non-accomplissement [nɔ̃akɔ̃plismã] **NM** *(d'un contrat)* non-fulfilment

non-activité [nɔ̃aktivite] **NF** *Admin* **mettre en n.** *(employé)* to suspend; *Mil (officier)* to put on half pay; **mise en n.** *(d'un employé)* suspension; *Mil (d'un officier)* putting on half pay

nonagénaire [nɔnaʒenɛr] **ADJ, N** nonagenarian, ninety-year-old

non-agression [nɔnagresjɔ̃] **NF** non-aggression; **pacte de n.** non-aggression pact

non-alcoolisé [nɔnalkɔlize] **ADJ** non-alcoholic

non-aligné, *pl* **non-alignés** [nɔnaliɲe] *Pol* **ADJ** *(pays)* nonaligned
NMPL **les non-alignés** the nonaligned countries

non-alignement [nɔnaliɲ(ə)mã] **NM** *Pol* nonalignment

nonantaine [nɔnãtɛn] **NF** *Belg, Suisse* **1** *(quantité)* **une n.** around *or* about ninety, ninety or so; **une n. de voitures** around *or* about ninety cars **2** *(âge)* **avoir la n.** to be around *or* about ninety

nonante [nɔnãt] **ADJ, NM INV** *Belg, Suisse* ninety

nonantième [nɔnãtjɛm] **ADJ, N** *Belg, Suisse* ninetieth

non-assistance [nɔnasistãs] **NF** *Jur* **n. à personne en danger** failure to render assistance to a person in danger

non-autorisé [nɔnotorize, nɔ̃-] **ADJ** *Ordinat (nom de fichier etc)* illegal

non-banque **ADJ** non-bank

non-belligérance **NF** nonbelligerence

non-belligérant, -ante **ADJ, N** non-belligerent

nonce [nɔ̃s] **NM n. du Pape** Papal Nuncio

non-cessible **ADJ** *(billet etc)* not transferable

nonchalamment [nɔ̃ʃalamɑ̃] **ADV** nonchalantly; **marcher n.** to saunter along

nonchalance [nɔ̃ʃalɑ̃s] **NF** nonchalance

nonchalant [nɔ̃ʃalɑ̃] **ADJ** nonchalant

nonciature [nɔ̃sjatyr] **NF 1** *(charge d'un nonce)* nunciature **2** *(résidence)* nuncio's residence

non-combattant, *pl* **non-combattants** **ADJ, NM** non-combatant

non-comparution **NF** non-appearance

non-conciliation **NF** failure to settle out of court

non-confirmé **ADJ** unconfirmed

non-conformisme **NM** *Rel, Fig* nonconformism

non-conformiste, *pl* **non-conformistes** **ADJ, N** *Rel, Fig* nonconformist

non-conformité **NF** **n. d'un produit** nonconformity of a product

non-connecté **ADJ** *Ordinat* off-line

non-consigné **ADJ** non-returnable

non-coté [nɔ̃kɔte] **ADJ** *Bourse* unquoted

non-cumul **NM n. des peines** concurrence of sentences; *Pol* **les règles de n. des mandats** = the laws prohibiting politicians from holding more than one post at a time

non-dit, *pl* **non-dits** **NM le n.** what is unspoken *or* unvoiced; **non-dits** unspoken *or* unvoiced comments; **un film riche en non-dits** a film full of meaningful silences

non-droit **NM zone de n.** area in which law and order have/had broken down; **état de n.** situation in which law and order have/had broken down

none [nɔn] **NF** *Antiq (heure)* ninth hour; **nones** *(jour)* nones

non-encaissé [nɔnɑ̃kese] **ADJ** *(chèque)* uncashed

non-engagé, *pl* **non-engagés** [nɔnɑ̃gaʒe] *Pol* **ADJ** neutral
NM neutral country

non-engagement [nɔnɑ̃gaʒmɑ̃] **NM** *Pol* neutrality

non-être [nɔnɛtr] **NM** *Phil* nonbeing, nonexistence

non-événement [nɔnevenmɑ̃] **NM** nonevent

non-exécution [nɔnegzekysjɔ̃] **NF** *(d'un accord)* non-fulfilment; *(d'un contrat)* non-performance

non-existence [nɔnegzistɑ̃s] **NF** nonexistence

non-ferreux, -euse **ADJ** *Métal* nonferrous

non-figuratif, -ive *Beaux-Arts* **ADJ** nonfigurative
N nonfigurative artist

non-formaté **ADJ** *Ordinat* unformatted

non-fumeur, -euse **ADJ** nonsmoking; **fumeur ou n.?** smoking or nonsmoking?
N nonsmoker

non-gage **NM** *Aut* **certificat de n.** certificate of ownership

non-ingérence [nɔnɛ̃ʒerɑ̃s] **NF** noninterference

non-initialisé [nɔninisjalize, nɔ̃-] **ADJ** *Ordinat* uninitialized

non-initié, -ée [nɔninisje] **ADJ** uninitiated
N uninitiated person; **les non-initiés** the uninitiated

non-inscrit, -ite [nɔnɛ̃skri] **N** *Pol* independent

non-intervention [nɔnɛ̃tervɑ̃sjɔ̃] **NF** nonintervention

non-interventionniste, *pl* **non-inver-**

ventionnistes [nɔnɛ̃tervɑ̃sjɔnist] **ADJ, N** noninterventionist

non-jouissance **NF** *Jur (d'un bien)* nonenjoyment

non-justifié **ADJ** *Typ* ragged, unjustified; **n. à droite** ragged right; **n. à gauche** ragged left

non-lieu, *pl* **non-lieux** **NM** *Jur* **bénéficier d'un n.** to be discharged through lack of evidence; **ordonnance** *ou* **arrêt de n.** nonsuit

non-livraison **NF** *Com* non-delivery

non-modifiable **ADJ** *(billet etc)* not alterable

nonne [nɔn] **NF** *Rel* nun

non-négociable **ADJ** non-negotiable

nonnette [nɔnɛt] **NF 1** *Rel Fam* young nun **2** *Culin* small iced gingerbread cake **3** *(oiseau)* tit

non-nuisible **ADJ n. à l'environnement** environmentally friendly, environment-friendly

nono, -ote [nɔno, -ɔt] **N** *Can Fam* idiot

nonobstant [nɔnɔpstɑ̃] **PRÉP, ADV** *Vieilli* notwithstanding; **ce n.** this notwithstanding

non-paiement **NM** nonpayment

nonpareil, -eille [nɔ̃parɛj] **ADJ** *Vieilli* peerless

non-partant, *pl* **non-partants** **NM** *(cheval)* nonstarter

non-polluant **ADJ** environmentally friendly

non-prolifération **NF** nonproliferation

non-recevoir **NM opposer une fin de n. à une réclamation** to refuse; *Jur* to put in a plea in bar of a claim

non-récupérable **ADJ** *Ordinat* nonrecoverable

non-relationnel, -elle **ADJ** *Ordinat* nonrelational

non-remboursable **ADJ** non-refundable

non-représentation **NF** *Jur* **n. d'enfant** refusal to comply with the access *or* visiting rights of a child

non-résident, -ente **N** nonresident

non-respect **NM** failure to respect; **le n. de la loi** failure to respect the law

non-retour **NM point de n.** point of no return

non-salarié, -ée **ADJ** unsalaried
N self-employed person; **les non-salariés** the self-employed

non-sens **NM INV 1** *Scol (dans une traduction)* meaningless word *or* phrase **2 c'est un n.** it's (a) nonsense

non-spécialiste, *pl* **non-spécialistes** **N** nonspecialist

non-stop [nɔnstɔp] **ADJ INV, ADV** *Fam* nonstop

non-structuré **ADJ** *Ordinat* unstructured

non-suspendu **ADJ** *Aut (freins)* outboard

non-syndiqué, -ée **ADJ** *(employé)* non-union, *Am* non-unionized
N non-union *or Am* non-unionized worker

non-taxable **ADJ** non-dutiable

non-tissé [nɔ̃tise] **NM** *Tex* nonwoven material

non-trié [nɔ̃trije] **ADJ** *Ordinat* unsorted

non-usage [nɔnyzaʒ] **NM** non-use

non-valeur, *pl* **non-valeurs** **NF** *Jur (état)* unproductiveness; *(bien)* unproductive asset; *Fin* bad debt; *(créance)* worthless amount; **terres en n.** unproductive land

non-vérifié [nɔ̃verifje] **ADJ** *Compta* unaudited

non-viable **ADJ** *Méd* nonviable

non-violence **NF** nonviolence

non-violent, -ente **N** supporter of non-violence
ADJ nonviolent

non-voyant, -ante **N** unsighted person; **les non-voyants** the unsighted

nopal, -als [nɔpal] **NM** *Bot* nopal

noquette [nɔkɛt] **NF** *Belg (petite quantité)* **une n. de beurre** a knob of butter

noradrénaline [nɔradrenalin] **NF** *Biol, Chimie* noradrenalin(e)

nord [nɔr] **NM** *(no pl)* **1** *(point cardinal)* north; **au n., dans le n.** in the north; **où est le n. ?** which way is north?; **la partie la plus au n. de l'île** the northernmost part of the island; **le vent vient du n.** it's a north *or* northerly wind, the wind is coming from the north; **un vent du n.** a northerly wind; **le vent du n.** the north wind; **aller au** *ou* **vers le n.** to go north *or* northwards; **les trains qui vont vers le n.** trains going north, north-bound trains; **rouler vers le n.** to drive north *or* northwards; **aller droit vers le n.** to head due north; **la cuisine est plein n.** *ou* **exposée au n.** the kitchen faces due north; **n. géographique** true *or* geographic north; **n. magnétique** magnetic north; *Fig Fam* **perdre le n.** to go bonkers, to lose it **2** *(partie d'un pays, d'un continent)* north, northern area *or* regions *(partie d'une ville)* north; **la mer du N.** the North Sea; **le Grand N.** the Far North; **le n. de l'Italie** northern Italy, the north of Italy; **dans le n. de l'Espagne** in northern Spain, in the north of Spain; **elle habite dans le n.** she lives in the north; **il habite dans le n. de Paris** he lives in the north of Paris; **elle est du n.** she's from the north; **les gens du n.** people who live in the north
ADJ INV *(côté, face)* north; *(banlieue, partie, région)* northern; **le pôle N.** the North Pole; **la façade n. d'un immeuble** the north-facing wall of a building; **la chambre est côté n.** the bedroom faces north; **dans la partie n. de la France** in the north of France, in northern France; **suivre la direction n.** to head *or* to go northwards

nord-africain, -aine, *pl* **nord-africains, -aines** **ADJ** North African
N N.-A. North African

nord-américain, -aine, *pl* **nord-américains, -aines** **ADJ** North American
N N.-A. North American

nord-coréen, -enne, *pl* **nord-coréens, -ennes** **ADJ** North Korean
N N.-C. North Korean

nord-est [nɔrɛst] **NM INV** *(point cardinal)* north-east
ADJ INV north-east

nordicité [nɔrdisite] **NF** *Can* northerliness

nordique [nɔrdik] **ADJ** Nordic; *Hist* Norse; **langues nordiques** Nordic *or* Scandinavian languages
NM *Ling* Norse
N N. Scandinavian

nordir [nɔrdir] **VI** *Naut (du vent)* to veer north(ward)

nordiste [nɔrdist] **ADJ 1** *Am Hist* Northern **2** *Sport (club)* northern
NM *Am Hist* Northerner

nord-nord-est **NM INV** north-north-east
ADJ INV north-north-east

nord-nord-ouest **NM INV** north-north-west
ADJ INV north-north-west

nord-ouest **NM INV 1** *(point cardinal)* north-west **2** *(vent)* north-west wind, north-wester, nor'wester
ADJ INV north-west

nord-vietnamien, -ienne, *pl* **nord-vietnamiens, -iennes** **ADJ** North Vietnamese
N N.-V. North Vietnamese

NOREX [nɔrɛks] *Com* = source of information on standards and rules governing goods for export

noria [nɔrja] **NF 1** *(machine)* noria **2** *(de véhicules qui vont et viennent)* endless stream

normal, -ale, -aux, -ales [nɔrmal, -o] **ADJ 1** *(dans la norme) (état, cours)* normal; **elle n'est pas dans son état n.** she's not her normal *or* usual self; **en temps n.** in *or* under normal circumstances **2** *(naturel)* normal; **c'est tout à fait n. que la jeunesse se rebelle** it's only normal *or* natural for young people to rebel; **c'est bien n.** it's quite normal *or* natural; **tu trouves ça n. toi?** do you think that's all right *or* OK?; **ce n'est pas n.** it's not right (**que** that) **3** *(moyen) (poids, taille)* standard; **cet enfant n'a pas encore atteint la taille normale pour son age** this child is still below the average height for his age; **vitesse normale** normal *or Spéc* rated speed **4** *(intellectuellement) (personne)* normal **5** *Typ* roman ▪ **NF normale 1** la normale normal, the norm; **la température est revenue à la normale** the temperature is back to normal; **intelligence/température au-dessus/au-dessous de la normale** above-/below-average intelligence/temperature; **température au-dessous des normales saisonnières** temperature below the seasonal norm *or* average **2** *Univ Fam* **Normale Sup** = École normale supérieure

normalement [nɔrmalmɑ̃] **ADV 1** *(de façon normale)* normally; **depuis un certain temps, il ne se comporte plus n.** for some time, he's not been behaving normally **2** *(habituellement)* usually, normally; **n. il passe nous voir le dimanche** he usually *or* normally calls to see us on Sundays **3** *(si tout va bien)* n., **nous devrions arriver pour le déjeuner** all being well *or* if all goes well, we should arrive in time for lunch; **n. elle devrait déjà être arrivée** she should be here by now

> Il faut noter que l'adverbe anglais **normally** ne s'emploie jamais dans le sens "si tout va bien".

normalien, -ienne [nɔrmaljɛ̃, -jɛn] **N** *Scol* student/former student of a teacher training college; *Univ* student/former student of the École normale supérieure

normalisation [nɔrmalizasjɔ̃] **NF 1** *Pol* normalization **2** *Ind* standardization

normalisé [nɔrmalize] **ADJ** *(produit)* standard

normaliser [nɔrmalize] **VT** *(relations)* to normalize; *(équipement)* to standardize

normalité [nɔrmalite] **NF** normality

normand, -ande [nɔrmɑ̃, -ɑ̃d] **ADJ 1** *(de Normandie)* Norman, (of) Normandy; **armoire normande** large rustic wardrobe **2** *Hist* Norman; **la conquête normande** the Norman Conquest ▪ **N N.** Norman; **c'est un fin N.** he's shrewd; **réponse de N.** non-committal *or* equivocal *or* evasive answer **2** *Hist* **les Normands** the Normans

Normandie [nɔrmɑ̃di] **NF** Normandy

norme [nɔrm] **NF 1** *(règle)* norm, standard; **échapper à la n.** to be an exception; **être d'une intelligence qui échappe à la n.** to be exceptionally intelligent **2** *Ind, Com* standard; **normes européennes** European standards; **n. française** French standard, *Br* ≃ British standard, *Am* ≃ US standard; **jouet conforme aux normes de sécurité** toy which conforms to safety standards; **n. de production** production norm; **n. de productivité** productivity norm; **n. de travail** work standard; **n. technique** technical standard; **n. d'application** relevant standard; **normes d'application obligatoires** compulsory standards; **normes d'application volontaires** voluntary standards; **normes publicitaires** advertising standards **3** *Math* norm

normographe [nɔrmɔgraf] **NM** stencil

norois, noroît [nɔrwa] **NM** *(vent)* northwest wind, northwester, nor'wester

Norvège [nɔrvɛʒ] **NF** Norway

norvégien, -ienne [nɔrveʒjɛ̃, -jɛn] **ADJ** Norwegian ▪ **NM** *Ling* Norwegian ▪ **N N.** Norwegian ▪ **NF norvégienne** round-stemmed boat

nos *voir* **notre**

nosocomial, -ale, -aux, -ales [nozokɔmjal, -o] **ADJ** *Méd (maladie, infection)* nosocomial

nostalgie [nɔstalʒi] **NF** nostalgia; *(mal du pays)* homesickness; **j'ai la n. de ces temps-là** I look back on that time with nostalgia, I feel nostalgia for that time; **avoir la n. de son foyer** to long *or* yearn for home, to be homesick; **avoir la n. du pays** to be homesick; **penser à qch avec n.** to think of sth nostalgically *or* with nostalgia

nostalgique [nɔstalʒik] **ADJ** *(humeur, souvenirs, sentiments, personne)* nostalgic ▪ **N** nostalgic person; **les nostalgiques des années 80** people who pine for the 1980s, people who are nostalgic for the 1980s

nostalgiquement [nɔstalʒikmɑ̃] **ADV** nostalgically

nota [nɔta] **NM INV** *(en bas de texte)* footnote; *(en marge)* marginal note; **nota bene** [nɔtabene] nota bene, NB

notabilité [nɔtabilite] **NF** *(personne, caractère)* notability

notable [nɔtabl] **ADJ 1** *(remarquable)* notable, worthy of note; **sans variation n.** without appreciable change **2** *(personne)* notable, distinguished ▪ **NM** notable (person), distinguished person, person of note *or* distinction; **les notables de la ville** the leading citizens, *Hum* the local worthies

notablement [nɔtabləmɑ̃] **ADV** notably, appreciably

notaire [nɔtɛr] **NM** *Jur* notary (public); **par-devant n.** before a notary

notamment [nɔtamɑ̃] **ADV** notably

notarié [nɔtarje] **ADJ** *Jur* certified by a notary; **acte n.** notarized deed

notation [nɔtasjɔ̃] **NF 1** *Scol (d'un travail, d'un élève)* marking **2** *(par des symboles)* notation; *Ordinat* **n. hexadécimale** hex *or* hexadecimal code **3** *Fin* rating; *Bourse* **n. AAA** triple-A rating

note [nɔt] **NF 1** *(mots, phrases)* note; **prendre des notes** to take (down) notes; **jeter quelques notes sur le papier** to jot down a few notes; **prendre n. de qch, prendre qch en n.** to note sth, to make a note of sth; **prendre bonne n. de qch** to take due note of sth; *Typ* **n. de bas de page** footnote; **n. de couverture** cover note; **n. marginale** note in the margin; **n. de renvoi** cross reference; *Journ* **n. de la rédaction** editor's note; **notes prises en sténo(graphie)** shorthand notes **2** *Scol, Univ (appréciation)* mark, *Am* grade; **bonne/mauvaise n.** good/bad mark; **notes trimestrielles** (end-of-term) report; **carnet** *ou* **relevé de notes** school report **3** *Mus* note; **fausse n.** wrong note; *Fig* false note; **donner la n.** *(aux chanteurs etc)* to sound the keynote; *Fig* **forcer la n.** to exaggerate; *(faire du zèle)* to overdo it; **sa robe n'était pas/ses blagues n'étaient pas dans la n.** her dress/his jokes struck the wrong note; **une n. d'originalité/de gaieté** a touch *or* note of originality/gaiety **4** *(facture), Com* bill; *(dans un hôtel etc)*

bill, *Am* check; **n. de téléphone** phone bill; *Fin* **n. de commission** commission note, fee note; **n. de crédit** credit note; **n. de débit** debit note; **n. de rappel** reminder
▸▸ **n. diplomatique** diplomatic note; *Ordinat, Typ* **n. de fin de document** end note; **n. de frais** expense account; *(présentée après coup)* expenses; **mettre qch sur sa n. de frais** to put sth on one's expense account; *Admin* **n. de service** memorandum, memo

noté [nɔte] **ADJ 1** **être bien/mal n.** *(d'élève, d'employé)* to have a good/bad record; *(de devoir)* to have received a good/poor mark **2** *Bourse* **n. triple A** triple-A rated

notebook [nɔtbuk] **NM** *Ordinat* notebook

noter [nɔte] **VT 1** *(mettre par écrit)* to note *or* put *or* jot down, to make a note of; **vas-y, je note** go ahead, I've got something to write with; **n. un passage** to mark a passage; **n. une commande** to log *or* note an order; **n. que** to note down *or* make a note that **2** *(remarquer)* to note, to take notice of; **à n.: les bus ne circulent pas le dimanche** note: there are no buses on Sundays; **notez bien cela** take good note of this, note this well; **il est à n. que ...** it is to be noted that ...; **c'est bon à n.** it's worthy noting *or* making a note of; **notez bien ce que je vous dis** mark my words; **note bien que cela n'a pas d'importance/je pourrais faire autrement** but it really doesn't matter/I could always do something else; **très bien, chef, c'est noté** *ou* **je note** OK boss, I've got it **3** *Scol, Univ (travail)* to mark, *Am* to grade

notice [nɔtis] **NF 1** *(notes sommaires)* note; **n. bibliographique** bibliographical note **2** *(préface de livre)* note **3** *(mode d'emploi)* instructions, directions; *(livret)* instruction book(let), handbook, manual; **n. explicative** directions for use, explanatory leaflet; **n. du constructeur** manufacturer's instructions; **n. technique** technical specification

> Il faut noter que le nom anglais **notice** est un faux ami. Il signifie le plus souvent **avertissement, écriteau** ou **attention**, selon le contexte.

notification [nɔtifikasjɔ̃] **NF** *Jur* notification, notice; **recevoir n. de qch** to receive notification *or* be notified of sth

notifier [nɔtifje] **VT** *(impf, pr sub* **n. notifiions, v. notifiiez)** *(faire savoir)* **n. qch à qn** to notify sb of sth; *Jur* **n. son consentement** to signify one's consent (**à qn** to sb); **on lui notifia qu'il aurait à déménager dans les vingt-quatre heures** he received notice to quit within twenty-four hours

notion [nosjɔ̃] **NF 1** *(concept)* notion, concept; **l'amitié est une n. abstraite** friendship is an abstract notion *or* concept; **perdre la n. du temps/de la réalité** to lose track of time/all sense of reality **2** *(connaissance succincte)* **des notions de** a smattering of, the basics of; **avoir des notions de chimie/russe** to have a smattering of *or* know the basics of chemistry/Russian

notoire [nɔtwar] **ADJ** *(connu de tous)* well-known, *Péj* notorious; **son avarice est n.** his miserliness is notorious *or* legendary

> Il faut noter que l'adjectif anglais **notorious** signifie "tristement célèbre".

notoirement [nɔtwarmɑ̃] **ADV** manifestly, *Péj* notoriously; **fait n. faux** manifestly false fact; **un malfrat n. connu** a notorious gangster

notoriété [nɔtɔrjete] **NF 1** *(d'un fait, d'une personne)* reputation; **avoir de la n.** to be well known, to have a (good) reputation; **cela lui a valu une certaine n.** that brought *or* earned him a certain reputation; **il est de**

n. publique que … it is public *or* common knowledge that …; *Mktg* n. de la marque brand awareness **2** *Jur* acte de n. attested affidavit

> Il faut noter que le nom anglais **notoriety** signifie uniquement "mauvaise réputation".

notre, nos [nɔtr, no] ADJ POSS our; *(de roi, de reine)* Our; **n. oncle et n. tante** our uncle and (our) aunt; **n. père et n. mère,** *Litt* **nos père et mère** our father and mother; **ils ont mis n. chapeau et nos gants** they put on our hats and (our) gloves; **nous avons pris n. sac** *(il n'y a qu'un sac)* we took our bag; *(chacun a son sac)* we took our bags; **nous avons pris nos sacs** *Fam* **nous aurons n. chambre à nous** *(il y a une chambre)* we will have our own room; *Fam* **n. imbécile de frère** our idiot of a brother; *Fam* **nos artistes de maris** our artist-husbands; **nous retrouvons n. héros dix ans plus tard** … we meet our hero again ten years later …; *Fam* **nous avons n. vendredi** we've got Friday off SEE GRAMMAR A30; B21–2

nôtre [notr] PRON POSS **le n., la n., les nôtres** ours; **il ressemble au n.** it looks like ours; **nous voulons bien te donner du n.** you can have some of ours; **nous n'en avons pas besoin, nous avons le n.** we don't need it, we've got our own; **tu n'en as pas besoin, tu as le n.** you don't need it, you've got ours; **les deux nôtres** our two, the two of ours, both of ours; *(en insistant)* our own two; **nous devrions y mettre du n.** we should do our share; *Fam* **le n. de bébé est plus intelligent!** our baby is more intelligent!; *Fam* **à la n.!** *(en buvant)* here's to us! SEE GRAMMAR A30; B21 ▸ NMPL **les nôtres** *(notre famille)* our family, *Am* our folks; *(nos partisans)* our followers; *(nos coéquipiers)* our team-mates; **est-il des nôtres?** *(de notre côté)* is he one of us?; **vous serez des nôtres, n'est-ce pas?** *(pour dîner)* you will join us, won't you? ▸ ADJ POSS *Litt* **un n. cousin** a cousin of ours; **nous ferons nôtres ses principes** we shall adopt these principles of his; **nous faisons nôtres les félicitations qu'ils vous adressent** we join them in congratulating you

Notre-Dame [nɔtrədam] NF *Rel* Our Lady; **la fête de N.** the feast of the Assumption

nouba [nuba] NF **1** *Fam* party; **faire la n.** to party **2** *(musique)* (Algerian) military band

noue¹ [nu] NF *(terre grasse)* marshy meadow, water meadow

noue² NF *Constr* **1** *(arête)* valley **2** *(tuile)* gutter tile; *(bande de plomb)* flashing

nouer [nwe] VT *(ficelle, corde, ruban)* to tie, to knot; **n. qch serré** to knot sth tightly, to make a tight knot in sth; **n. ses cheveux** to tie up one's hair; **n. sa cravate** to knot one's tie; **n. ses lacets** to tie (up) one's laces; **n. son tablier** to tie one's apron; **elle noua ses bras autour du cou de son ami** she wrapped her arms around her friend's neck; **avoir la gorge nouée** to have a lump in one's throat; **avoir l'estomac noué** to have a knot in one's stomach; **n. conversation avec qn** to enter into conversation with sb; **n. des relations avec qn** to establish relations with sb; **n. l'intrigue d'un roman** to bring the action of a novel to a head *or* climax ▸ VI *(de fleur)* to set ▸ VPR **se nouer 1 se n. les cheveux** to tie up one's hair **2** *(se faire)* **des amitiés qui se nouent** friendships which are formed *or* which form **3** *Littér, Théâtre, Cin* to take shape; **l'intrigue se noue dès le premier acte** the plot takes shape right from Act One

noueux, -euse [nwø, -øz] ADJ *(ficelle, bois)* knotty; *(tronc d'arbre, mains, doigts)* gnarled

nougat [nuga] NM **1** *(confiserie)* nougat **2** *Fam* **nougats** *(pieds)* feet

nougatine [nugatin] NF nougatine

nouille [nuj] NF **1** *Culin* noodle **2** *Fam (personne molle)* drip; *(bébête)* dimwit, noodle

noumène [numɛn] NM *Phil* noumenon

nounou [nunu] NF *Fam* nanny

nounours [nunurs] NM *Enf* teddy (bear)

nourri [nuri] ADJ **1** *(alimenté)* fed; **bien n.** well fed; **mal n.** undernourished, underfed; **être logé (et) nourri (blanchi)** to get (one's) bed and board; **avoir 500 euros par mois logé et nourri** to get 500 euros a month with board and lodging **2** *(riche) (style)* rich; *(ligne en dessin)* broad, firm; *(ton, son)* full; *(applaudissements)* sustained, prolonged; **discussion nourrie** heated debate, lively discussion; *Mil* **feu n.** heavy *or* sustained fire

nourrice [nuris] NF **1** *(assistante maternelle)* child-minder; **n. agréée** registered child-minder **2** *(personne qui allaite)* (wet) nurse; **mettre un enfant en n.** to put a child out to nurse **3** *Tech* auxiliary tank, service tank; *Aut (de carburant)* spare can

nourricier, -ière [nurisje, -jɛr] ADJ *Bot (sève, suc)* nutritive; *Anat (artère, canal)* nutrient; *Litt (terre)* nourishing ▸ N **père n.** foster father; **mère nourricière** foster mother

nourrir [nurir] VT **1** *(donner à manger à) (personnes, animaux)* to feed (**de, avec** with, on); **nourri au biberon/sein** bottle-/breast-fed; **n. sa famille** to provide for *or* feed one's family; **j'ai cinq personnes à n.** I've five mouths to feed; **travail qui nourrit son homme** job that provides a living; **le lait nourrit** milk is nourishing; *Fig* **lectures qui nourrissent l'esprit** reading that improves the mind; *Mus* **n. le son** to give fullness *or* body to the tone **2** *(de crème, lotion) (peau, visage, cuir)* to nourish; *(feu)* to feed **3** *Litt (entretenir) (haine)* to foster; *(idées de vengeance, illusion etc)* to harbour, *Am* to harbor; *(espoir)* to cherish, to harbour, to entertain; *(projet)* to nurse; **je nourris l'espoir de le revoir** I cherish the hope of seeing him again ▸ VPR **se nourrir** *(manger)* to eat; **il refuse de se n.** he won't eat; **chasser pour se n.** to hunt for one's food; **il gagne juste de quoi se n.** he earns just enough to live on; **se n. de lait/fruits** to live on milk/fruit

nourrissant [nurisɑ̃] ADJ *(repas, aliments)* nourishing, nutritious; *(crème pour le visage, le cuir)* nourishing

nourrisseur [nurisœr] NM **1** *(de bétail, de boucherie)* stockbreeder; *(de vaches laitières)* dairyman **2** *Tech (pour l'alimentation des animaux)* feed roll

nourrisson [nurisɔ̃] NM young baby, infant

nourriture [nurityr] NF *(aliments)* food; **retrouver une n. saine et équilibrée** to get back to a healthy and balanced diet; **priver qn de n.** to starve sb, to deprive sb of food; **il refuse toute n. depuis trois jours** he has been refusing food *or* refusing to eat for three days; **n. de l'esprit** food for the mind; **les nourritures terrestres** the fruits of the earth

nous [nu] PRON PERS SEE GRAMMAR A27; B18–19 **1** *(sujet)* we; *Fam* **n. sommes allés au restaurant avec mon mari** *(lui et moi)* me and my husband went to the restaurant **2** *(objet direct)* us; *(objet indirect)* to us; **il ne n. connaît pas** he does not know us; **lisez-le-n.** read it to us; **elle n. en a parlé** she spoke to us about it **3** *(réfléchi)* **n. n. réchauffons** we are warming ourselves; **n. n. sommes versé du vin** we poured ourselves some wine; **n. n. battions avec l'ennemi** we were fighting the enemy SEE GRAMMAR A29–30; B28–9 **4** *(réciproque)* n. n.

connaissons we know each other **5 n. deux/tous** *(sujet)* both/all of us, we two/all; *(objet)* both/all of us, us two/all; **c'est n. qui sommes fautifs** we are to blame, it is us *or* surtout *Fml* we who are to blame; **n. autres Anglais** we English; **un ami à n.** a friend of ours; **ce livre est à n.** that book is ours *or* belongs to us; **bon, à n. maintenant** so, we can have a talk now; **à n. deux** *(sur ton menaçant)* let's have a little talk; *(avant de se battre)* let's fight it out; **c'est à n. de jouer** it's our turn; **il était avec n.** he was with us; **entre n. (soit dit)** (this is) between ourselves **6** (**nous de majesté ou de modestie, employé pour je**) we; **n. sommes désolés de l'apprendre** we are grieved to hear it

nous-même PRON PERS *(après nous de majesté, de modestie)* ourself; *voir* **même**

nous-mêmes PRON PERS ourselves; **nous l'avons fait n.** we did it ourselves; *voir* **même**

nouveau, -el, -elle, -eaux [nuvo, -ɛl] ADJ (**nouvel** is used before m sing nouns beginning with a vowel or h mute) **1** *(récent)* new; **nouvelles voitures** new cars; **livres nouveaux** new books; **il est n., ce manteau?** is this coat new?; **techniques nouvelles** new *or* up-to-date techniques; **je suis n. dans ce métier** I'm new to this business; *Fam* **tu sais ce que c'est, tout n. tout beau, ça lui passera** you know what it's like, it's all new and exciting at first, but she'll get over it; **il n'y a rien de n.** there's nothing new, there are no new developments; **il y a quelqu'un de n. au bureau** there's someone new in the office; **c'est n. ça!** that's new!; **il n'y a rien de n. sous le soleil** there's nothing new under the sun; **nouvel utilisateur** first-time user

2 *(qui succède à un autre) (télévision, directeur, épisode, gouvernement, adresse, collection)* new; **les nouveaux pères** modern(-day) fathers; **nouvelle technologie** new technology; *Fin* **nouvelle émission** *(d'actions)* new issue; **nouveaux emprunts** new borrowings; *Cin etc* **nouvelle version** remake; **faire une nouvelle version de** to do a remake of, to reversion; **jusqu'à nouvel ordre** until further notice; **que font-ils au sujet des enfants? – jusqu'à nouvel ordre, rien** what are they doing about the children? – they haven't decided yet; **la nouvelle Marilyn Monroe** the new Marilyn Monroe; **la nouvelle mode** the latest fashion; **la nouvelle génération** the new *or* rising generation; **j'ai besoin d'une nouvelle voiture** I need a new car; **il met tous les jours une nouvelle chemise** he wears a clean *or* different shirt every day; **n. et amélioré** *(sur emballage)* new improved

3 *(autre)* new; **sous un jour n.** in a new light; **un n. chapitre** a new *or* fresh chapter; **une nouvelle raison/hausse des prix** a further *or* an additional *or* another reason/price rise; **se faire de nouveaux amis** *(supplémentaires)* to make new friends; **elle a eu un nouvel enfant** she has had another child; **faire de nouveaux efforts** to make new *or* fresh efforts; *Jur* **n. procès** retrial

4 *(nouvellement produit) (carotte, pomme de terre)* new; **du vin n.** new *or* young wine; **le beaujolais n.** the new Beaujolais *or* Beaujolais nouveau; **herbe nouvelle** young grass

5 *(avec une fonction adverbiale)* **le nouvel arrivé** the newcomer; **les nouveaux arrivés** the newcomers; **les nouveaux élus** those newly elected; **les nouveaux convertis** the new converts, the newly converted; **n. pays industrialisé** newly industrialized country **6** **à n., de n.** *(once or over)* again; **recommencer à n.** to start afresh; **elle est de n. malade** she is ill again; **la terre a à n. ou de n. tremblé en Californie** there has been another earthquake in California ▸ NM **il y a du n.** there's been a new development; **j'ai du n. au sujet de ...** I've got news about ...; **tu as du n. pour ton billet d'avion?** have you heard anything more about your plane ticket?

N *(personne)* new person; *Scol* new pupil

▶▶ **Nouvel An** New Year; **passer le Nouvel An chez des amis** to spend New Year's Eve at friends'; **nouvelle cuisine** nouvelle cuisine; *Pol* **la nouvelle droite** the New Right; **nouvelle économie** new economy; *Anciennement* **n. franc** new franc; *Pol* **la nouvelle gauche** the New Left; **les nouveaux médias** the new media; **Nouveau Monde** New World; **nouveaux pauvres** new poor; *Beaux-Arts* **n. réalisme** New Realism; **n. réaliste** New Realist; *Péj* **n. riche** nouveau riche; **n. roman** nouveau roman, new novel; **Nouveau Testament** New Testament; *Cin* **la nouvelle vague** the New Wave, the Nouvelle Vague

Nouveau-Brunswick [nuvobræzvik] **NM** New Brunswick

Nouveau-Mexique [nuvomɛksik] **NM** New Mexico

nouveau-né, -née, *pl* **nouveau-nés, -nées** **ADJ** newborn

N newborn child

nouveauté [nuvote] **NF 1** *(caractère nouveau)* newness, novelty; **recherche constante de la n.** constant search for something new *or* for novelty **2** *(produit récent)* *(livre)* new publication; *(invention)* new invention; **le cinéma n'est plus une n.** the cinema is no longer a novelty *or* anything new; **vous trouverez ce disque/livre au rayon des nouveautés** you'll find that record in the new releases rack/that book on the new titles shelf; *Fam* **tu sais qu'il trompe sa femme? – c'est pas une n.!** do you know he's cheating on his wife? – that's nothing new! **3** **les nouveautés de printemps** *(vêtements)* the new spring fashions; *Vieilli* **magasin de nouveautés** draper's shop, *Am* dry goods store

nouvelle [nuvɛl] **NF 1** *(annonce d'un événement)* (piece of) news; **bonne/mauvaise n.** good/bad news; **j'ai une bonne n.!** (I've) good news!; **une n. plutôt décevante** a rather disappointing piece of news; **première n.!** that's news to me!, that's the first I've heard of it!; **la n. de sa mort** the news of his death; **la n. a été confirmée par le gouvernement** the news *or* report was confirmed by the government; **vous connaissez la n.?** have you heard the news *or* the latest? VOIR GRAMMAIRE A10

2 *(informations)* **nouvelles (de qn/qch)** news (of *or* about sb/sth); **demander** *ou* **(aller) prendre des nouvelles de (la santé de) qn** to inquire *or* ask about sb('s health); **j'ai eu des nouvelles de Pierre** *(par lui-même)* I've had news from *or* I've heard from Pierre; *(par qn d'autre)* I've had news about *or* of Pierre; **envoyez-moi de vos nouvelles** let me know how you're doing; **on n'eut plus jamais de leurs nouvelles** they were never heard of again; **je suis sans nouvelles de lui** *(directement)* I've had no news from him, I've not heard from him; *(indirectement)* I've had no news of *or* about him; **aux dernières nouvelles, il était à Lima** he was last heard of in Lima; **les nouvelles vont vite!** news travels fast!; **goûtez cela, vous m'en direz des nouvelles** taste this, I'm sure you'll like it; **vous aurez de mes nouvelles!** you'll be hearing from me!; **pas de nouvelles, bonnes nouvelles** no news is good news

3 *Journ* news item; **les nouvelles** the news; **les dernières nouvelles** the latest news; **à quelle heure sont les nouvelles?** when's the news on?

4 *Littér* short story

Il faut noter que le nom anglais **novel** est un faux ami. Il signifie **roman**.

Nouvelle-Angleterre **NF** New England

Nouvelle-Calédonie [nuvɛlkaledɔni] **NF** New Caledonia

Nouvelle-Écosse **NF** Nova Scotia

Nouvelle-Galles du Sud **NF** New South Wales

Nouvelle-Guinée **NF** New Guinea

nouvellement [nuvɛlmã] **ADV** newly, recently

Nouvelle-Orléans [nuvɛlɔrleã] **NF La N.** New Orleans

Nouvelles-Hébrides [nuvɛlzebrid] **NFPL** New Hebrides

Nouvelle-Zélande [nuvɛlzelãd] **NF** New Zealand

nouvelliste [nuvelist] **N** short story writer

nova, *pl* **novæ** [nɔva, -e] **NF** *Astron* nova

novateur, -trice [nɔvatœr, -tris] **ADJ** innovative

N innovator

novélisation [nɔvelizasjõ] **NF** novelization

novembre [nɔvãbr] **NM** November; **en n.** in November; **au mois de n.** in (the month of) November; **le premier n.** (on) the first of November, **(on)** November the first SEE GRAMMAR A81–2; B60–2

novice [nɔvis] **N** *(personne sans expérience)* novice, beginner; *(au couvent)* novice

NM *(jeune marin)* junior seaman

ADJ **être n. à** *ou* **dans qch** to be new to *or* inexperienced in sth

noviciat [nɔvisja] **NM** *Rel* noviciate, novitiate

noyade [nwajad] **NF 1** drowning; **sauver qn de la n.** to save sb from drowning; **mort par n.** death by drowning **2** *Hist* execution by drowning

noyau, -aux [nwajo] **NM 1** *(de fruit)* stone, *Am* pit; **fruit à n.** stone fruit; **enlever** *ou* **retirer le n. d'un fruit** to stone *or Am* pit a fruit; **n. de cerise** cherry stone *or Am* pit **2** *(centre)* *(d'atome, de cellule, de comète)* nucleus; *(de la terre)* core; **n. de bombe nucléaire** nuclear bomb core VOIR GRAMMAIRE A14 **3** *(petit groupe)* **un n. de joueurs** a small group of players; **un n. d'opposants/d'irréductibles** a small group of opponents/hardliners; **un n. d'amis** a small circle of friends; **le n. dur** the hard core; *Bourse* = group of stable shareholders chosen for a company by the government on its flotation; **noyaux de résistance** pockets of resistance **4** *Archit* *(d'escalier)* newel; **escalier à n. plein** winding staircase **5** *Él* *(d'armature), Métal (de moule)* core; *Ordinat* node; *Géol* **n. volcanique** volcanic bomb

noyautage [nwajotaʒ] **NM** *Pol* infiltration

noyauter [nwajote] **VT** *Pol* *(syndicat, parti, organisation)* to infiltrate

noyé, -ée [nwaje] **ADJ** *(par noyade)* **mourir n.** to die by drowning; *Fig* **être n.** to be out of one's depth

N drowned person; **secours aux noyés** first aid for the drowning; **on a repêché un n. dans la rivière** a drowned man was fished out of the river

noyer¹ [nwaje] **NM** *(arbre)* walnut (tree); *(bois)* walnut; **n. (blanc) d'Amérique** hickory

noyer² [nwaje] *(je noie, nous noyons; je noierai)* **VT** **1** *(personne, animal)* to drown; *(la terre etc)* to swamp, to inundate, to deluge; *(soute)* to flood; **les polders ont été noyés sous des mètres cubes d'eau** the polders were submerged under several cubic metres of water; **n. une rébellion dans le sang** to quash a rebellion with bloodshed; *Fig* **n. son chagrin (dans l'alcool)** to drown one's sorrows (in drink); **noyé dans la foule** lost in the crowd; **n. le poisson** *(à la ligne)* to play the

---

fish; *Fig* to confuse the issue deliberately, to muddy the waters

2 *Aut* **n. le moteur** to flood the engine

3 *(mouiller abondamment)* **les larmes noyaient son visage/ses joues** his face was/his cheeks were drenched with tears, tears poured down his face/cheeks; **yeux noyés de larmes** eyes brimming with tears; **elle avait les yeux noyés de larmes** her eyes were brimming with tears; **n. la sauce** to make the sauce too thin; **n. le vin** to drown the wine

4 *(recouvrir entièrement)* *(de brouillard, brume)* to shroud, to envelop; **le village était noyé dans la brume** *ou* **noyé de brume** the village was shrouded *or* enveloped in mist; **la chambre était noyée dans la pénombre/de lumière** the room was shrouded in darkness/bathed in light; **les points essentiels sont noyés dans le détail** the essential points are buried *or* lost in too many details

5 *(contours, couleurs)* to blend, to blur

6 *Constr* to sink in cement; *(vis)* to countersink; *(clou)* to drive in flush

VPR se noyer *(mourir par noyade)* *(accidentellement)* to be drowned, to drown; *(volontairement)* to drown oneself; *Fig* **se n. dans les détails/des explications** to get bogged down in details/in explanations; **elle se noierait dans un verre d'eau** she makes a mountain out of a molehill

NPI [ɛnpei] **NM** *(abrév* **nouveau pays industrialisé)** NIC

NTI [ɛntei] **NFPL** *(abrév* **nouvelles technologies de l'information)** NIT

nu [ny] **ADJ 1** *(dévêtu)* *(personne)* naked; *(épaules, bras, jambe)* bare; *Beaux-Arts* nude; **mettez-vous torse nu** strip to the waist; **il était torse nu** *ou* **nu jusqu'à la ceinture** he was stripped to the waist; **être tout nu** to be stark naked; **se baigner tout nu** to bathe in the nude, *Fam* to go skinny-dipping; **avoir les seins nus** to be topless, to have bare breasts; **nu comme la main** *ou* **comme un ver** stark naked, *Fam* in the buff; **danseuse nue** striptease artist; (**NOTE** nu *before the noun that it qualifies is invariable and is joined to the noun by a hyphen)* **aller tête nue** *ou* **nu-tête** to go bareheaded *or* without anything on one's head; **aller pieds nus** *ou* **nu-pieds** to go barefoot; **se battre à main(s) nue(s)** to fight with bare fists; **la boxe à main(s) nue(s)** bare-knuckle boxing **2** *Fig* *(style)* plain, unadorned; *(épée)* unsheathed, naked; **la vérité (toute) nue** the plain *or* naked truth; *Élec* **fil nu** bare wire **3** *(dégarni)* *(paysage, arbre, pièce, mur)* bare

NM *Beaux-Arts* *(personne, œuvre)* nude; **le nu** *(genre)* the nude; **mettre à nu** to lay bare, to expose, to uncover; *(fil électrique)* to strip; **il a mis son cœur à nu** he laid bare his heart; *Équitation Vieilli* **monter un cheval à nu** to ride (a horse) bareback

nuage [nɥaʒ] **NM** cloud; **nuages pommelés** fleecy *or* fluffy clouds; **nuages en flocons** fluffy clouds; **ciel couvert** *ou* **chargé de nuages** overcast *or* cloudy sky; **n. de poussière/fumée/sauterelles** cloud of dust/smoke/locusts; **n. radioactif** cloud of radioactive dust; **sans nuages** *(ciel)* cloudless; *Fig (vie, avenir)* unclouded; *Fig* **bonheur sans nuages** perfect bliss; *Fig* **un n. de tristesse assombrissait son front** his face was clouded with sadness; *Fig* **être dans les nuages** to have one's head in the clouds, to be daydreaming; **n. de lait** drop *or* dash of milk

nuageux, -euse [nɥaʒø, -øz] **ADJ** *(temps)* cloudy; *(ciel)* overcast, cloudy; **masse nuageuse** cloud mass

nuance [nɥãs] **NF 1** *(de couleur)* shade, hue; **toutes les nuances de bleu** all shades of blue **2** *(légère trace)* **une n. d'amertume/de mépris/de regrets** a touch *or* hint *or* suggestion of bitterness/contempt/regret **3** *(subtilité)* nuance; *(légère différence)* slight *or* subtle difference; **les nuances de la langue** the nuances of the language; **récit tout en nuances** story full of nuances; **je ne saisis pas la n.** I don't quite see the difference; **il y a une n.!** there's a slight difference!; **j'ai dit peut-être, pas oui, n.!** I said perhaps, not yes, there's a slight difference!; *Fig* **il est sans nuances** he sees everything in black and white **4** *Mus* nuance; **il joue sans nuances** he plays without any light and shade

nuancé [nɥɑ̃se] **ADJ** *(couleur, ton)* subtle; *Fig (discours, propos, attitude)* full of nuances; **ses réponses sont toujours très nuancées** he always qualifies his answers a lot

nuancer [nɥɑ̃se] **VT** (**je nuançai(s); nous nuançons**) **1** *(en dessin, peinture) (couleurs)* to shade; *(mélanger)* to blend (**de** with); **n. une couleur avec une autre** to shade one colour into another **2** *(modérer) (pensée, jugement, propos)* to qualify **3** *Mus* **n. son jeu** to introduce light and shade into one's playing

nuancier [nɥɑ̃sje] **NM** *(de couleurs)*, *Com* sample card *or* chart; *Phot* colour chart; *Typ* swatch; *Aut* graduated tint shadeband

nubile [nybil] **ADJ** nubile, marriageable; **âge n.** *(en sociologie)* age of nubility

nubilité [nybilite] **NF** nubility

nucléaire [nykleɛr] **ADJ 1** *Phys, Mil (énergie, fission, armes)* nuclear; **particule n.** elementary particle **2** *Biol (membrane)* nuclear **3** *(en sociologie)* **la famille n.** the nuclear family
NM le n. nuclear power

nucléarisation [nyklearizasjɔ̃] **NF** *Ind* = introduction of nuclear power to replace conventional energy sources; *Mil* nuclearization

nucléariser [nyklearize] **VT** to supply with nuclear power; *Mil* to supply with nuclear weapons, to nuclearize
VPR se nucléariser 1 *(choisir l'énergie nucléaire)* to go nuclear **2** *Mil (se doter d'armes nucléaires)* to go nuclear, to nuclearize

nucléé [nyklee] **ADJ** *Biol (cellule)* nucleate

nucléique [nykleik] **ADJ** *(acide)* nucleic

nucléole [nykleɔl] **NM** *Biol* nucleolus

nucléon [nykleɔ̃] **NM** *Phys* nucleon

nucléonique [nykleɔnik] *Phys* **ADJ** nucleonic
NF nucleonics

nucléus [nykleys] **NM** *Biol* nucleus

nudisme [nydism] **NM** nudism; **faire du n.** to be a nudist, to practise nudism

nudiste [nydist] **N** nudist; **camp de nudistes** nudist camp

nudité [nydite] **NF 1** *(de personne)* nudity, nakedness; *(de rocher, de mur)* bareness; *Fig* **l'horreur étalée dans toute sa n.** the horror displayed in all its starkness **2** *Beaux-Arts* nude (figure)

nue [ny] **NF** *Arch, Litt* high cloud(s); **nues** skies; **l'oiseau fendait les nues** the bird was cleaving its way through the skies; *Fig* **porter qn/qch aux nues** to laud *or* praise sb/sth to the skies; *Litt* **se perdre dans les nues** to have one's head (completely) in the clouds, to be lost in the clouds *or* in daydreams; *Fig* **tomber des nues** to be flabbergasted, to be thunderstruck

nuée [nɥe] **NF** *Litt* cloud, storm cloud; *(d'insectes, de criquets)* cloud, swarm; *Fig* **une n. de journalistes/touristes** a horde *or* swarm of journalists/tourists; **n. ardente** nuée ardente *(cloud of ash, gas etc)*

nue-propriété, *pl* **nues-propriétés NF** reversionary ownership

nuire [nɥir] (*ppr* **nuisant**; *pp* **nui**; *pr ind* **je nuis, nous nuisons**; *pr sub* **je nuise**; *p hist* **je nuisis**; *fu* **je nuirai**) **VI** *(desservir)* **n. à qn/à**

qch *(de personne)* to harm sb/sth; *(de chose)* to harm *or* be harmful to sb/sth; **cela ne nuira en rien** it won't do any harm; **cela nuira à sa réputation** it will damage *or* harm his reputation, it will be harmful to his reputation; **n. aux intérêts de qn** to prejudice *or* harm *or* damage sb's interests; **le tabac nuit gravement à la santé** smoking seriously damages your health; **dans l'intention de n.** maliciously; *Prov* **abondance de biens ne nuit pas** you can't have too much of a good thing; *Prov* **trop parler nuit** too much talking is harmful
VPR se nuire to do oneself (a great deal of) harm

nuisance [nɥizɑ̃s] **NF** nuisance; **nuisances acoustiques** noise pollution; **nuisances chimiques** chemical pollution

nuisette [nɥizɛt] **NF** baby doll (nightie)

nuisibilité [nɥizibilite] **NF** harmfulness

nuisible [nɥizibl] **ADJ** harmful (**à** to); **plantes nuisibles** noxious plants; **animaux nuisibles** vermin, pests
NM pest; **les nuisibles** vermin, pests

nuit [nɥi] **NF 1** night; **la n. dernière** last night; **cette n.** tonight; *(passée)* last night; **cela s'est passé dans la n. de samedi à dimanche** it happened during Saturday night *or* the night of Saturday to Sunday; **la n. où il est mort** the night (when) he died; **bonne n.!** good night!; **as-tu passé une bonne n.?** did you have a good night?; **veiller jusqu'à une heure avancée de la n.** to sit up far into the night; **passer la n. à faire qch** to stay up *or* spend all night doing sth; **on a passé la n. à faire la fête** we made a night of it; **passer la n. chez des amis** to stay overnight *or* the night with friends; **passer la n. à l'hôtel** to spend *or* stay the night at a hotel; **une chambre à 100 euros la n.** a room at 100 euros a *or* per night; **le train/bateau/voyage de n.** the night train/boat *or* ferry/journey; **vêtements de n.** nightwear; **médecin de n.** night doctor; *Beaux-Arts* **effet de n.** night effect; **être de n.** to be on night shift *or* night duty *or Fam* nights; **voyager de n.** *ou* **la n.** to travel by night *or* at night; **conduire de n.** to drive at night *or* in the dark; **n. et jour** [nɥitəʒur] night and day; **il ne passera pas la n.** he won't last the night; **je n'ai pas dormi de la n.** I didn't sleep a wink all night; **le bébé fait ses nuits** the baby sleeps through the night; **il commence à faire n.** night is falling, it is growing *or* getting dark; **il fait déjà n.** it is dark already; **à la n. tombante** at nightfall, at dusk; **une fois la n. tombée, à (la) n. tombée** after dark; **la n. porte conseil** it would be best to sleep on it; *Prov* **la n., tous les chats sont gris** all cats are grey in the dark
2 *Fig* darkness; *Litt* **la n. de l'ignorance** the darkness of ignorance; **perdu dans la n. des temps** lost in the mists of time; **c'est le jour et la n.** they're (like) chalk and cheese
▸▸ *Cin* **n. américaine** day for night; **tourné en n. américaine** shot in day for night; **n. blanche** sleepless night; **passer une n. blanche** *(par insomnie)* to spend a sleepless night; *(volontairement)* to stay up all night; **n. bleue** night of bomb attacks; **n. d'hôtel** *(dans l'hôtellerie)* bed-night; **payer une n. d'hôtel** to pay for a night at a hotel; *Hist* **la N. des longs couteaux** the Night of the Long Knives; **n. de noces** wedding night; **la n. de la Saint-Jean** Midsummer Night

nuitamment [nɥitamɑ̃] **ADV** *Litt* by night

nuitée [nɥite] **NF** *(dans l'hôtellerie)* overnight stay, bed-night; **deux nuitées pour quatre personnes** two nights for four people; **la n. va de midi à midi le lendemain** a night runs from noon to noon the next day

nul, nulle [nyl] **ADJ 1** *(inexistant) (différence, risques, écart, récolte)* nil; *(élection)* null and void, invalid; **rendre n.** to nullify, to annul;

Sport **score n. zéro (à) zéro** *(en fin de match)* match drawn nil-nil; *(à la mi-temps)* score nil-nil; **le score est n.** *(en fin de match)* the game is drawn, the result is a draw; *(à la mi-temps)* neither team has scored yet, the game so far is drawn; **match n.** draw, drawn match; **faire match n.** to draw, to tie; **bulletin (de vote) n.** spoilt (ballot) paper; **le solde est n.** the balance is nil; *Phys* **tension nulle** zero tension; *Jur* **n. et non avenu** invalid, null and void **2** *Fam (qui ne vaut rien)* *(réponse, personne)* useless, hopeless; *(film, livre, chanson, blague)* rubbish, *très Fam* crap; *(argument)* useless; *Vulg* **c'est n. à chier!** it's a load of crap! **3** *Fam (incompétent)* *(élève, employé)* hopeless, useless; **être n. en qch** to be hopeless *or* useless at sth
ADJ INDÉF *(avec* **ne** *exprimé ou compris)* no; *Litt* **n. espoir** no hope; **il n'a nulle raison de se plaindre** he has no reason to complain; **sans nulle vanité** without boasting; **n. doute qu'il y serait parvenu** there's no doubt that he would have managed it; *Litt* **à nul(le) autre pareil(le)** unparalleled; **n. autre que moi ne le sait** I alone know of it SEE GRAMMAR B63
PRON INDÉF no one, nobody; *Prov* **n. n'est prophète en son pays** no man is a prophet in his own country; **à l'impossible n. n'est tenu** you can't be expected to do the impossible
N *Fam* useless idiot, prat

nullard, -arde [nylar, -ard] *très Fam* **ADJ** *(personne)* useless, hopeless
N dimwit, *Br* plonker

nullement [nylmɑ̃] **ADV** *(avec* **ne** *exprimé ou compris)* not at all, by no means; **cela vous dérange-t-il? – n.!** does that bother you? – not at all! *or* by no means!; **nous ne sommes n. surpris** we are not in the least *or* at all surprised; **je n'ai n. l'intention d'y aller** I haven't the slightest *or* least intention of going; **il n'est n. sot** he is no fool

nulle part ADV nowhere; **je ne les vois n.** I can't see them anywhere; **je n'ai vu ça n. (ailleurs)** I've not seen that anywhere (else), I've seen that nowhere (else)

nullification [nylifikasjɔ̃] **NF** nullification

nullissime [nylisim] **ADJ** *Fam* totally useless, pathetic

nullité [nyl(l)ite] **NF 1** *Jur (de contrat, de mariage etc)* nullity, invalidity; **frapper une clause de n.** to render a clause void; **lors d'un mariage, la bigamie est une cause de n.** bigamy is grounds for the annulment of a marriage **2** *(stupidité) (de personne)* uselessness, hopelessness; *(de remarque, plaisanterie)* crassness; **elle est d'une n.!** she's totally useless!; **cette blague est d'une n. totale** that joke is completely pathetic **3** *Fam (personne incompétente)* dead loss

nûment [nymɑ̃] **ADV** *Litt* frankly, without embellishment

numéraire [nymerɛr] **ADJ** *(monnaie)* legal; **valeur n.** cash value
NM specie, (current) coin; **payer en n.** to pay in cash *or* *Spéc* in specie

numéral, -ale, -aux, -ales [nymeral, -o] **ADJ, NM** numeral

numérateur [nymeratœr] **NM** *Math* numerator

numération [nymerasjɔ̃] **NF** *Math* numeration, notation; *Méd* **n. globulaire** blood count; **n. et formule sanguine** full blood count

numérique [nymerik] **ADJ 1** *(valeur, supériorité etc)* numerical **2** *Ordinat (ordinateur, donnée)* digital; **balance à affichage n.** digital scales; **enregistrement/disque n.** digital recording/record
NM digital (broadcasting); **n. hertzien** *ou* **terrestre** digital terrestrial (broadcasting)

numériquement [nymerikmã] ADV **1** numerically **2** Ordinat digitally

numérisation [nymerizasjɔ̃] NF Ordinat digitization; **n. en lots** batch capture

numériser [nymerize] VT Ordinat to digitize

numériseur [nymerizœr] NM Ordinat digitizer; **n. d'image** image digitizer

numéro [nymero] NM **1** (chiffre) number; **tirer le bon n.** to draw the lucky or winning number; Fig to strike (it) lucky; **le n. gagnant** the winning number; **n. de page** page number; Typ folio; **le n. un/deux du parti** the number one/two in the party; **j'habite au n. 10** I live at number 10; **l'ennemi public n. un** public enemy number one; **la chambre n. 20** room (number) 20; **n. de téléphone** telephone number; **est-ce que tu as son n.?** have you got his number?

2 (de périodique) issue (sur on, about); (d'émission) edition; **le n. du jour/de la semaine/du mois, le dernier n.** the current issue; **ancien n., n. déjà paru** back issue or number; **deux numéros en un** double issue; **n. spécial** special issue; **n. zéro** zero edition; **vente au n.** single copies sold; **acheter un magazine au n.** to buy a magazine as it appears; **il faudra chercher dans de vieux numéros** we'll have to look through some back issues; **la suite au prochain n.** (dans un magazine) (to be) continued in the next issue, to be continued; Fig Fam watch this space

3 (d'artiste) spot; **n. de cirque** circus act; Fam **il aime faire son petit n.** he likes doing his little act

4 (personne) **quel n.!** what a character!

▸▸ **n. d'appel** telephone number; **n. d'appel gratuit** Freefone® number, Am toll-free number; Tél **n. azur** = type of Freefone® number in which costs are shared between caller and company; **n. de chambre** room number; Aut **n. de châssis** chassis or commission number; **n. de commande** order number; Journ **n. de commission paritaire** publication registration number; **n. de compte** account number; **n. d'enregistrement** booking number; **n. d'identification** identification number; **n. d'identité bancaire** bank sort code; **n. d'immatriculation** registration number; Ordinat **n. Internet** Internet number; Ordinat **n. IP** IP number; Ordinat **n. de licence** registration number; **n. d'ordre** running or serial or order number; Belg, Suisse **n. postal** postcode, Am zip code; Tél **n. de poste** extension number; **n. de référence** reference number; **n. de sécurité sociale** social security number; **n. de série** serial number; **n. de sociétaire** (d'une assurance) insurance or policy number; Tél **n. surtaxé** premium rate number; **n. de téléphone** telephone number; VOIR GRAMMAIRE A77 Tél **n. d'urgence** hot-line; Tél **n. vert** Br ≃ Freefone® number, 0800 number, Can ≃ Zenith number, Am ≃ 0800 number, toll-free number; **n. de vol** flight number

numérologie [nymerɔlɔʒi] NF numerology

numérotage [nymerɔtaʒ] NM numbering; **n. de pages** page numbering, pagination

numérotation [nymerɔtasjɔ̃] NF numbering; (téléphone) dialling, Am dialing; Tél **n. abrégée** short code dialling; Ordinat **n. alphanumérique** alphanumeric numbering; Ordinat **n. décimale** decimal numbering

numéroter [nymerɔte] VT (maisons, pages de livre etc) to number; **les places ne sont pas numérotées** the seats are not numbered; Mil **numérotez-vous (à partir de la droite)!** (from the right) number!
VI Tél to dial

numéroteur [nymerɔtœr] NM numbering device

numismate [nymismat] N numismatist

numismatique [nymismatik] ADJ numismatic
NF numismatics, numismatology

nummulaire [nymylɛr] NF Bot moneywort, creeping Jenny

nunuche [nynyʃ] ADJ Fam silly

nu-pieds NM INV sandal
ADV barefoot

nu-propriétaire, nue-propriétaire, pl **nu(e)s-propriétaires** N reversionary owner

nuptial, -iale, -iaux, -iales [nypsjal, -jo] ADJ wedding; **anneau n.** wedding ring; **marche nuptiale** wedding march; **chambre nuptiale** bridal suite; **cortège n.** bridal procession; **robe nuptiale** wedding dress, bridal gown; **messe nuptiale** nuptial mass

nuptialité [nypsjalite] NF marriage rate

nuque [nyk] NF nape or back of the neck; **elle veut une coupe de cheveux qui dégage bien la n.** she wants her hair cut short at the back; **saisir qn par la n.** to catch hold of sb by the scruff of the neck

nurse [nœrs] NF Vieilli nanny, (children's) nurse

nursery, pl **nurseries** [nœrsəri] NF (d'hôpital) nursery

nutation [nytasjɔ̃] NF nutation

nu-tête ADV bare-headed

nutritif, -ive [nytritif, -iv] ADJ nutritive; (aliment) nutritious, nourishing; **valeur nutritive** food or nutritional value

nutrition [nytrisjɔ̃] NF nutrition; **une mauvaise n.** a bad or an unbalanced diet

nutritionniste [nytrisjɔnist] N nutritionist

nyctalope [niktalɔp] ADJ day-blind, Spéc hemeralopic

Nylon® [nilɔ̃] NM nylon; **des bas (de) N.** nylon stockings, nylons

nymphe [nɛ̃f] NF **1** Myth nymph **2** Entom nymph, pupa, chrysalis

nymphéa [nɛ̃fea] NM Bot nymphea, white waterlily

nymphette [nɛ̃fɛt] NF nymphet

nympho [nɛ̃fo] NF Fam (abrév **nymphomane**) nympho

nymphomane [nɛ̃fɔman] ADJ, NF nymphomaniac

nymphomanie [nɛ̃fɔmani] NF nymphomania

O¹, o [o] NM (*lettre*) O, o

O² (*abrév* **Ouest**) W

ô [o] INT *Litt* O!

OAA [oaa] NF (*abrév* **Organisation de l'alimentation et l'agriculture**) FAO

OACI [oasei] NF (*abrév* **Organisation de l'aviation civile internationale**) ICAO

OAS [oaɛs] NF *Hist abrév* **Organisation de l'armée secrète**

oasien, -ienne [oazjɛ̃, -jɛn] ADJ oasis
N oasis dweller

oasis [ɔazis] NF (*parfois m*) oasis; *Fig* **une o. de calme/bonheur** a haven of peace/happiness **VOIR GRAMMAIRE A14**

OAT [oate] NF (*abrév* **obligation assimilable du Trésor**) = French government bond

obédience [ɔbedjɑ̃s] NF **1** (*appartenance*) **musulman/catholique de stricte o.** strict *or* devout Muslim/Catholic; **pays d'o. communiste** countries under Communist rule; **des communistes d'o. trotskiste** Communists of the Trotskyist tendency **2** *Rel* obedience

Il faut noter que le nom anglais **obedience** signifie le plus souvent **obéissance**.

obéir [ɔbeir] VI to obey; **o. à qn** to obey sb; **o. à qn au doigt et à l'œil** to be at sb's beck and call; **mes enfants m'obéissent peu** my children aren't very obedient; **il est obéi de ses enfants** he is obeyed by his children; **un prof pas du tout obéi de ses élèves** a teacher with no control over his pupils; **se faire o.** to command obedience; **o. à un règlement/une loi** to obey a rule/a law, to abide by a rule/a law; **o. à un ordre** to obey an order, to comply with an order; **o. à la force/une contrainte** to yield to force/a constraint; **o. à son instinct** to follow *or* obey one's instinct; **o. à une impulsion** to act on *or* follow an impulse; **o. à une envie très forte** to give in to a very strong desire; **o. à sa conscience** to follow the dictates of *or* to obey one's conscience; **o. à la mode** to follow (the dictates of) fashion; *Naut* **o. à la barre** to answer the helm; *Aviat* **o. aux commandes** to respond to the controls

obéissance [ɔbeisɑ̃s] NF obedience (**à** to); **refus d'o.** insubordination; **devoir o. à qn** to owe sb obedience *or* allegiance; **jurer o. au roi** to swear allegiance to the king

obéissant [ɔbeisɑ̃] ADJ obedient

obélisque [ɔbelisk] NM *Archit* obelisk

obérer [ɔbere] VT (**j'obère; j'obérerai**) *Fml* (*personne, secteur etc*) to burden with debt; **très** *ou* **fort obéré** heavily burdened with debt, deeply in debt, debt-ridden

obèse [ɔbɛz] ADJ obese
N obese person

obésité [ɔbezite] NF obesity

obier [ɔbje] NM guelder rose, snowball tree

objecter [ɔbʒɛkte] VT (*rétorquer*) to raise as an objection; **je n'ai rien à o. à la proposition** I have no objection to the proposal, I have nothing (to say) against the proposal; **qu'avait-il à o.?** what was his objection?, what did he have against it?; **o. des arguments à une théorie** to put forward arguments against a theory; **o. qch à qn** to put sth forward as an argument to sb; **que puis-je lui o.?** how can I answer him?, what can I say in response?; **tout ce qu'il m'a objecté, j'y avais déjà réfléchi** I'd already given some thought to what arguments he might use; **o. que ...** to object that ...; **on vous objectera que ...** they will object that ...; **on lui objecta sa jeunesse** they took exception to his youth, his youth counted *or* was held against him

objecteur [ɔbʒɛktœr] NM **o. de conscience** conscientious objector

objectif, -ive [ɔbʒɛktif, -iv] ADJ (*impartial*) objective; **observateur o.** neutral *or* objective observer
NM **1** (*but*) object(ive), aim; *Mil* objective; (*cible*) target; **atteindre son o.** to attain one's object(ive); **o. de chiffre d'affaires** sales target; **o. de vente** sales target *or* objective; **o. à terme** short-term objective **2** *Phot, Cin, TV* lens; *Phys* (*d'un microscope*) object glass, objective; **régler l'o.** to adjust the focus; **braquer son o. sur qch** to train one's camera on sth; **fixer l'o.** to look into the camera; **devant l'o.** in front of the camera; **o. fish-eye** fish-eye lens; **o. grand angle** wide-angle lens; **o. normal** normal-angle lens; **o. ultra grand angle** fish-eye lens; **o. zoom** zoom lens; *TV, Cin* **o. à courte focale** short-focus lens; *TV, Cin* **o. à distance focale variable** zoom lens; *TV, Cin* **o. à focale fixe** prime lens

objection [ɔbʒɛksjɔ̃] NF objection; **faire** *ou* **formuler** *ou* **soulever une o.** to make *or* raise an objection, to object (**à qch** to sth); **on me fit l'o. que ...** they objected *or* argued that ...; **voyez-vous une o. à son départ/à ce que je lui en parle?** do you have any objection to his leaving/to my talking to him about it?; *Jur* **o. (votre honneur)!** objection *or* I object, m'lud *or Am* your honor!
▸▸ **o. de conscience** conscientious objection

objectivement [ɔbʒɛktivmɑ̃] ADV objectively

objectiver [ɔbʒɛktive] VT to objectivize

objectivisme [ɔbʒɛktivism] NM objectivism

objectivité [ɔbʒɛktivite] NF objectivity, objectiveness

objet [ɔbʒɛ] NM **1** (*chose*) object, thing; **o. de luxe** luxury article *or* item; **o. de première nécessité** essential *or* basic item; **objets trouvés** lost-property office, *Am* lost and found
2 *Gram* object; **o. direct/indirect** direct/indirect object **SEE GRAMMAR A78–9; B52–3**
3 *Phil* object; **femme-o.** woman as an object

4 (*sujet*) (*d'une dispute, d'un colloque*) subject; (*d'une conversation*) topic, subject; **l'o. du litige** the matter at issue; **o. d'un contrat** subject matter of a contract; **quel est l'o. de l'anthropologie?** what does anthropology cover?; **les enfants sont l'o. de nombreux soins** children receive a lot of care; **votre requête sera l'o. de toute notre attention** your request will receive our full attention; **cela fera l'o. de ma conférence/d'une recherche approfondie** this will be the subject of my lecture/of a thorough investigation; **o. de pitié/haine** object of pity/hatred
5 (*but*) (*d'une action*) object, aim, purpose; **l'o. de ma visite** the purpose of my visit; **remplir son o.** to achieve *or* fulfil its object *or* aim *or* purpose; **cet appareil/cette nouvelle mesure remplit tout à fait son o.** the device/the new measure does exactly what it's supposed to; **sans o.** (*remarque, réclamation, préoccupation*) unjustified
6 *Ordinat* object
▸▸ **o. d'art** objet d'art; **objets de valeur** valuable items, valuables; **aucun o. de valeur n'a disparu** nothing valuable was taken; **ne laissez pas d'o. de valeur dans votre voiture** don't leave valuables in your car; *Astron* **o. volant non identifié** unidentified flying object

objurgation [ɔbʒyrgasjɔ̃] NF objurgation

oblat, -ate [ɔbla, -at] N *Rel* oblate

oblation [ɔblasjɔ̃] NF *Rel* oblation, offering

obligataire [ɔbligatɛr] *Fin* N bondholder, debenture holder
NM (*obligation*) debenture bond
ADJ **emprunt/marché o.** debenture *or* bond loan/market

obligation [ɔbligasjɔ̃] NF **1** (*contrainte, devoir*) obligation; **tu viens si tu veux, mais ce n'est pas une o.** you can come if you want, but you're not obliged to *or* you don't have to; **avoir l'o. de faire qch** to be under an obligation to do sth, to be obliged to do sth; **être dans l'o. de faire qch** to be obliged to do sth; **je me sens dans l'o. de vous avertir** I feel obliged to warn you; **je me vois dans l'o. de me taire** I find myself obliged to keep silent; **sans o. d'achat** no purchase necessary; **sans o. de votre part** without any obligation (on your part); **tu manques à toutes tes obligations** you're not facing up to any of your responsibilities; *Fin* **honorer ses obligations** to honour *or* meet one's obligations; **remplir ses obligations** to meet one's obligations; **avoir/se sentir des obligations envers qn** to be/feel under an obligation to sb; **avoir des obligations (familiales)** to have (family) obligations; **obligations militaires** liability to military service; **ayant rempli ses obligations militaires** having completed one's military service; **o. contractuelle** contractual obligation **SEE GRAMMAR A60–1; B39**
2 *Jur* (*acte*) recognizance, bond; **o. alimen-**

taire maintenance order; **contracter une o. irrévocable** to enter into a binding agreement

3 *Fin* bond, debenture; **obligations** bonds, loan stock *or* notes; **o. assimilable du Trésor** = French government bond; **o. cautionnée** secured bond; **o. convertible** *ou* **échangeable** convertible bond; **o. garantie** guaranteed bond; **o. hypothécaire** mortgage bond; **o. indexée** index-linked bond; **o. à intérêt variable** floating rate bond; **o. nominative** registered bond; **o. au porteur** bearer bond; **o. à revenu fixe** fixed rate bond; **o. à revenu variable** floating rate bond; **o. à taux progressif** step-up bond; **o. à taux variable** variable-income bond, floating-rate bond; **o. transférable**, **o. transmissible** transferable bond

obligatoire [ɔbligatwaʀ] ADJ obligatory, compulsory, mandatory; **école laïque, gratuite et o.** free, compulsory and non-religious education; **l'uniforme est o.** uniform is compulsory *or* obligatory *or* must be worn; *Fam* **c'était o.** *(c'était forcé)* it had to happen, it was bound to happen, it was inevitable

obligatoirement [ɔbligatwaʀmɑ̃] ADV **vous devez o. montrer votre passeport** you are required to show your passport; *Fam* **elle lui demandera o. des comptes sur ce qui s'est passé** she's bound to ask him for an explanation of what happened; **est-ce qu'il faut porter une robe habillée? – pas o.** do you have to wear an evening dress? – not necessarily

obligé, -ée [ɔbliʒe] ADJ **1** *(contraint)* obliged, compelled (**de faire qch** to do sth); **tu y es allé? – (bien) o.!** did you go? – I had to! **2** *(indispensable)* necessary; **c'est un passage o.** it's something that has to be done **3** *Fam (inévitable)* inevitable; **c'est o.** it's inevitable; **c'est o. qu'il rate son examen** he's bound to fail his exam **4** *Fml (reconnaissant)* obliged, grateful (**de** for); **je vous serais très o. de …** *(dans une lettre)* I would be most obliged *or* grateful (to you) if you would … **5** *Mus* **récitatif o.** recitative ob(b)ligato
▪ N person under an obligation; *Jur* obligee; *Vieilli* **je suis votre o.** I am in your debt

obligeamment [ɔbliʒamɑ̃] ADV obligingly; **il m'a o. aidé à porter ma valise** he obligingly helped me to carry my suitcase

obligeance [ɔbliʒɑ̃s] NF obligingness; **ayez** *ou* **veuillez avoir l'o. de fermer la porte** would you oblige me by closing the door, would you be so kind as to close the door

obligeant [ɔbliʒɑ̃] ADJ obliging, helpful, kind

obliger [ɔbliʒe] (**j'obligeai(s); n. obligeons**) VT **1** *(contraindre)* **o. qn à faire qch** *(d'une personne)* to compel *or* force sb to do sth, to make sb do sth; *(d'une situation etc)* to force *or* oblige sb to do sth; **ce travail m'oblige à me lever à cinq heures tous les matins** this job means I have to get up at five o'clock every morning; **ne m'oblige pas à me mettre en colère** don't make me lose my temper; **personne ne t'oblige à aller travailler à l'étranger** nobody's forcing you to go and work abroad; **son état de santé l'oblige à de longs moments de repos** the state of his health means he has to rest for long periods; **le temps nous oblige à rester enfermés** the weather is keeping us indoors; **ma signature m'y oblige** my signature binds me *or* holds me to it; **la loi m'y oblige** I'm required to by law, the law requires me to; **votre devoir/honneur vous y oblige** you are duty-/honour-bound to do it; **être obligé de faire qch** to be obliged *or* compelled to do sth, to have to do sth; **ne te sens pas obligé de le faire** don't feel obliged *or* compelled to do

it, don't feel you have to do it; **ne te crois pas obligé de tout manger** don't feel you have to eat everything; **rien ne t'y oblige** you don't have to, nobody's forcing you **2** *Fml (rendre service à)* **o. qn** to oblige sb; **vous m'obligeriez en fermant la porte** I'd be obliged if you would close the door, you would oblige me by closing the door
▪ VPR **s'obliger s'o. à faire qch** *(ne pas manquer de)* to make a point of doing sth; *(se forcer à)* to force oneself to do sth

oblique [ɔblik] ADJ *(ligne)* oblique; *(rayon)* slanting, oblique; **regard o.** sideways *or* sidelong glance; **manœuvre o.** *(malhonnête)* underhand move; *Gram* **cas o.** oblique case
▪ NF *Anat* oblique muscle
▪ NF oblique (line); *Typ* slash; **en o.** diagonally; **stationner en o.** to angle-park

obliquement [ɔblikmɑ̃] ADV obliquely, slantwise; **regarder qn o.** to look sideways *or* sidelong at sb

obliquer [ɔblike] VI **obliquez à gauche/à droite!** bear left/right!

obliquité [ɔblikɥite] NF obliqueness

oblitérateur, -trice [ɔbliteratœʀ, -tʀis] ADJ *Tech* cancelling
▪ NM *(pour timbres)* franker

oblitération [ɔbliterasjɔ̃] NF **1** *Méd* obstruction **2** *(de timbres)* cancellation, cancelling; **(cachet d')o.** postmark

oblitérer [ɔblitere] (**j'oblitère, n. oblitérons; j'oblitérerai**) VT **1** *(timbre)* to cancel, to frank; **timbre oblitéré** used stamp; **la lettre n'a pas été oblitérée** the letter hasn't been postmarked **2** *Méd (obstruer)* to obstruct **3** *Litt Fig (souvenirs, le passé etc)* to obliterate
▪ VPR **s'oblitérer** *Litt* **peu à peu le passé s'oblitérait dans sa mémoire** little by little, every trace of the past disappeared from his memory

oblong, -ongue [ɔblɔ̃, -ɔ̃g] ADJ **1** oblong; **un coquillage de forme oblongue** an oblong shell **2** *Typ* **format o.** oblong format

obnubiler [ɔbnybile] VT *(obséder)* to obsess; **elle est obnubilée par l'idée que …** she is obsessed by the idea that …

obole [ɔbɔl] NF **1** *(argent)* small offering; *(dans la Bible)* widow's mite; **apporter** *ou* **verser son o. (à qch)** to make a contribution (to sth); *esp Litt* **il ne m'a pas fait l'o. d'un sourire** he didn't deign to smile at me **2** *Hist (monnaie grecque)* obol(us); *(monnaie française)* obole

OBSA [ɔpsa] NF *Fin (abrév* **obligation avec bon de souscription d'actions)** bond with share warrant attached

obscène [ɔpsɛn] ADJ *(langage, livre)* obscene; *(geste)* obscene, lewd

obscénité [ɔpsenite] NF *(d'un langage, d'un livre)* obscenity, smuttiness; *(d'un geste)* obscenity, lewdness; **dire des obscénités** to make obscene remarks

obscur [ɔpskyʀ] ADJ **1** *(sombre) (nuit, chambre)* dark **2** *(inexplicable, confus)* obscure **3** *(vague) (pressentiment)* vague, dim; *(impression)* vague **4** *(inconnu) (écrivain, peintre etc)* obscure; *(humble) (naissance)* lowly, humble

obscurantisme [ɔpskyʀɑ̃tism] NM obscurantism

obscurantiste [ɔpskyʀɑ̃tist] ADJ, N obscurantist

obscurcir [ɔpskyʀsiʀ] VT **1** *(assombrir) (lumière)* to obscure; *(chambre, ciel)* to darken; **yeux obscurcis par les larmes** eyes misty *or* dim with tears **2** *(rendre confus)* **il avait le jugement/les idées obscurci(es) par l'alcool/la douleur** his judgment/thinking was clouded by alcohol/pain
▪ VPR **s'obscurcir** *(d'une pièce, du paysage)* to darken, to grow dark; *(du ciel)* to darken, to grow dark, to cloud over; *(de l'esprit, de la*

vue) to grow dim; **son regard s'obscurcit** his face clouded over *or* darkened

obscurcissement [ɔpskyʀsismɑ̃] NM *(du sens)* obscuring; *(d'une chambre, du ciel)* darkening; *(de l'esprit, de la vue)* dimming

obscurément [ɔpskyremɑ̃] ADV obscurely, dimly; *(sentir)* vaguely; **j'ai o. l'impression que …** I've a vague impression that …; **mourir o.** to die in obscurity

obscurité [ɔpskyrite] NF **1** *(noirceur)* darkness; **dans l'o.** in the dark; **j'ai peur dans l'o.** I'm scared in the dark; **elle doit rester dans l'o.** she has to stay in darkness *or* in a darkened room; **soudain, l'o. se fit** everything suddenly went dark **2** *(caractère complexe, confusion)* obscurity; **la solution de cette énigme restera à jamais dans l'o.** the answer to this enigma will for ever remain shrouded in obscurity **3** *(anonymat)* obscurity; **vivre dans l'o.** to live in obscurity; **sortir de l'o.** to emerge from obscurity, to become known

obsédant [ɔpsedɑ̃] ADJ *(souvenir, musique)* haunting; *(pensée)* obsessive

obsédé, -ée N fanatic; **un o. du cinéma/du rangement** a film/tidiness fanatic *or* freak; **un o. (sexuel)** a sex maniac

obséder [ɔpsede] VT (**j'obsède; j'obséderai**) *(d'une pensée, d'un souvenir)* to obsess; **son souvenir m'obsède** I'm obsessed by his memory; **être obsédé par qch** to be obsessed by *or* with sth; **elle est obsédée par ses enfants** she is obsessed with her children; **c'est un problème, mais ne te laisse pas o.** it's a problem, but don't become obsessed by it *or* don't let it become an obsession

obsèques [ɔpsɛk] NFPL funeral; **avoir droit à des o. nationales** to be given a state funeral; **les o. se feront dans la plus stricte intimité** the funeral will be strictly private

obséquieusement [ɔpsekjøzmɑ̃] ADV obsequiously

obséquieux, -ieuse [ɔpsekjø, -jøz] ADJ obsequious

obséquiosité [ɔpsekjozite] NF obsequiousness

observable [ɔpsɛrvabl] ADJ observable; **un fait o. uniquement dans certaines couches de la population** a phenomenon that can be observed only in certain segments of the population

observance [ɔpsɛrvɑ̃s] NF *(d'un règlement)* observance; **communiste de stricte o.** hardline communist; **un bénédictin d'ancienne o.** a Benedictine of the old school

observateur, -trice [ɔpsɛrvatœr, -tris] N **1** *(d'événements, d'un phénomène, des mouvements de l'ennemi etc)* observer; *Mil (qui règle les tirs)* spotter; **o. des Nations unies** United Nations observer **2** *(des règlements, des lois)* observer, keeper
▪ ADJ observant

observation [ɔpsɛrvasjɔ̃] NF **1** *(surveillance)* observation; **être en o.** to be under observation; **mettre/(main)tenir qn en o.** to put/keep sb under observation; **malade en o.** patient under observation; **poste d'o.** observation *or* lookout post; **avion d'o.** spotter plane; **observations par satellite** satellite observations; **il a l'esprit d'o.** he is very observant **2** *(remarque)* observation, remark, comment; *(critique)* remark; **faire des observations** to make observations *or* remarks *or* comments; *(critiques)* to make *or* pass remarks; **je peux faire une petite o.?** can I make one tiny remark?; **si je puis me permettre une o.** if I may make an observation *or* say something; **il faisait toujours des observations à ses élèves** he was always finding fault with his pupils; **à la moindre o. de ma part, elle se met en colère** the slightest remark from me and she gets angry, she gets angry if I make the slightest remark **3** *(respect)* *(des lois)* observance, keeping **4** *(étude)* *(des étoiles, des insectes, des oiseaux etc)* observation

observatoire [ɔpsɛrvatwar] **NM** *Astron* observatory; *Mil* observation post

observer [ɔpsɛrve] **VT 1** *(surveiller, regarder)* *(personne, chose)* to watch, to observe; **on nous observe** we are being watched; **se sentir observé** to feel one is being watched; **elle adore o. les gens dans le métro** she loves watching people *or* she loves to people-watch in the metro **2** *(remarquer)* to notice; **nous observons un retour à …** we are seeing *or* witnessing a return to …; **faire o. qch à qn** to draw sb's attention to sth, to point sth out to sb; **faire o. à qn que …** to point out to sb that …; **je vous ferai o. que …** I must point out to you that … **3** *(suivre, respecter)* *(règlements, lois etc)* to observe, to keep (to), to comply with; *(promesse)* to keep; **o. le silence** to keep silent; **o. une minute de silence** to observe a minute's silence; **o. la loi** to observe the law; **faire o. la loi** to enforce (obedience to) the law; **o. un contrat** to comply with a contract **4** *(étudier)* *(les étoiles, les insectes, les peuplades etc)* to observe; *(un angle)* to take, to read; **il passait des heures à o. les oiseaux** he spent hours bird-watching; *Naut* **o. le soleil** to take the sun, to take a sight at the sun

VPR s'observer 1 *(d'un phénomène, d'une attitude)* to be seen; **ce phénomène ne s'observe que dans les pays tropicaux** this phenomenon can be seen only in tropical countries **2** *(de deux personnes)* to watch *or* observe each other **3** *(d'une personne)* to keep a check on oneself

obsession [ɔpsɛsjɔ̃] **NF** obsession; **mais c'est une o. ou de l'o.!** you're/he's/*etc* obsessed (with the idea)!; **il ne faudrait pas en faire une o.,** il ne faudrait pas que cela devienne de l'o. it shouldn't become an obsession; **avoir l'o. de qch** to be obsessed with sth

obsessionnel, -elle [ɔpsɛsjɔnɛl] *Psy* **ADJ** obsessional; **névrose obsessionnelle** obsessional neurosis

N c'est un o. he's obsessive, he has *or* is an obsessive personality

obsidienne [ɔpsidjɛn] **NF** *Minér* obsidian

obsolescence [ɔpsɔlesɑ̃s] **NF** obsolescence; **o. calculée ou planifiée** built-in *or* planned obsolescence

obsolescent [ɔpsɔlesɑ̃] **ADJ** obsolescent

obsolète [ɔpsɔlɛt] **ADJ** obsolete; **un mot devenu o.** a word that has become obsolete, an obsolete word

obstacle [ɔpstakl] **NM** obstacle; *Courses de chevaux* fence, jump; *Sport* hurdle; *Fig* obstacle, hindrance, impediment; **il continua sa route/il a atteint son but sans rencontrer d'o.** he continued on his way/he achieved his aim without meeting any obstacles; **se heurter à un o.** to come up against an obstacle; **venir à bout d'un o.** to overcome an obstacle; **faire o. à qch** to be an obstacle to sth, to stand in the way of sth; **plus rien ne faisait o. à mon départ** *ou* à ce que je parte there was no longer any reason for me not to go; **je n'y vois pas d'o.** I don't see any difficulty *or* problem (about it); **course d'obstacles** *Courses de chevaux* steeplechase; *Sport* hurdle race

obstétrical, -ale, -aux, -ales [ɔpstetrikal, -o] **ADJ** obstetric

obstétricien, -ienne [ɔpstetrisjɛ̃, -jɛn] **N** obstetrician

obstétrique [ɔpstetrik] **NF** obstetrics

obstination [ɔpstinasjɔ̃] **NF** obstinacy, stubbornness, *Fam Péj* pigheadedness

obstiné [ɔpstine] **ADJ** *(personne, caractère)*

obstinate, stubborn, *Fam Péj* pigheaded; *(résistance)* stubborn, dogged; *(travail)* determined, dogged

obstinément [ɔpstinemɑ̃] **ADV** obstinately, stubbornly; *(travailler, avancer)* determinedly, doggedly; *(répondre)* stubbornly

obstiner (s') [ɔpstine] **VPR** to persist; **obstine-toi!** be persistent!, don't give up!; **s'o. à faire qch** *(continuer)* to persist in doing sth; *(vouloir)* to be set *or Fml* bent on doing sth; **elle s'obstine sur cette question** she won't let go, she won't give up, *Fam* she's like a dog with a bone; **s'o. dans son silence** to remain stubbornly *or* obstinately silent; **s'o. dans ses idées/convictions** to cling stubbornly *or* doggedly to one's ideas/convictions

obstruction [ɔpstryksjɔ̃] **NF** *(d'une rue, d'un passage)* blocking, obstruction; *(d'un égout)* blocking; *Méd* **o. intestinale** obstruction of the bowels; **faire de l'o.** *Pol* to be obstructive, to use obstructive tactics; *Sport* to obstruct

obstructionnisme [ɔpstryksjɔnism] **NM** *Pol* obstructionism

obstructionniste [ɔpstryksjɔnist] **ADJ, N** *Pol* obstructionist

obstruer [ɔpstrye] **VT** *(rue, passage)* to block, to obstruct; *(tuyau)* to block; **il a des artères obstruées** he has blocked arteries; **le tuyau est obstrué par des cheveux** the pipe is clogged up with hair

obtempérer [ɔptɑ̃pere] **VI** (j'obtempère, n. obtempérons; j'obtempérerai) **o. à** *(ordre, assignation)* to obey, to comply with; *Jur* **refus d'o.** obstruction

obtenir [ɔptənir] *(conj like* **tenir)** **VT** *(biens, permission, réponse etc)* to obtain, to get; *(promesse)* to secure, to get; *(le consentement de qn)* to obtain, to gain, to get; *(résultat)* to obtain, to achieve, to get; **o. la libération des otages** to obtain the release of the hostages; **si on mélange ces deux substances, qu'obtient-on?** what do you get if you mix these two substances?; **si on ajoute les deux, on obtient 500** if you add the two together, you get 500; **j'ai travaillé sur ce dossier pendant trois mois et qu'ai-je obtenu? – rien!** I've worked on this case for three months and what have I got to show for it *or* what have I achieved? – nothing!; **o. qch de qn** to obtain *or* get sth from sb; **n'espère plus rien o. de moi** don't expect *(to get)* anything else from me; **c'est lui qui m'a fait o. ces renseignements** he's the one who got (hold of) *or* obtained the information for me; **j'ai obtenu de le voir** I obtained *or* got permission to see him; **j'ai obtenu d'elle qu'elle vérifie tout** I got her to agree to check everything; **j'ai obtenu qu'elle revienne** I arranged for her to come back

VPR s'obtenir où cela s'obtient-il? where can you get it?

obtention [ɔptɑ̃sjɔ̃] **NF** obtaining; **depuis l'o. de son diplôme** since obtaining his diploma, since he got his diploma; **ajoutez du blanc jusqu'à o. de la couleur désirée** add white until the desired colour is obtained; **pour l'o. de qch** (in order) to obtain sth; **o. d'un prêt** obtaining of a loan

obturateur, -trice [ɔptyratœr, -tris] **ADJ** closing; *Anat (membrane, muscle)* obturator

NM 1 *Anat, Chir (d'une ouverture)* obturator **2** *(clapet)* shutter, stop valve; *Aut* throttle; *Phot* shutter; **armer/déclencher l'o.** to set/to release the shutter; *Phot* **o. de plaque** focal-plane shutter; *Phot* **o. au diaphragme** diaphragm shutter; *Aut* **o. de bloc** core plug; *Aut* **o. papillon** throttle valve

obturation [ɔptyrasjɔ̃] **NF** *(d'un tuyau, d'une ouverture)* sealing; *(d'une dent)* filling

obturer [ɔptyre] **VT** *(tuyau, ouverture)* to seal; *(dent)* to fill

obtus [ɔpty] **ADJ 1** *(angle)* obtuse **2** *(personne)* obtuse, dim-witted

obus [ɔby, oby] **NM** *Mil* shell; **o. à balles** *ou* à mitraille shrapnel (shell); **o. de mortier** mortar shell; **o. traçant** tracer shell

obusier [ɔbyzje] **NM** *Mil* howitzer

obvier [ɔbvje] **VI** (impf, pr sub n. obviions, v. obviiez) *Litt* **o. à qch** to obviate sth; **o. à un accident** to take precautions *or* to guard against an accident

OC [ose] **NFPL** *Radio (abrév* **ondes courtes)** SW

oc [ɔk] **ADV** *Hist, Ling* **langue d'oc** langue d'oc *(language of southern France)*

ocarina [ɔkarina] **NM** *Mus* ocarina

occase [ɔkaz] **NF** *Fam* **1** *(affaire)* bargain **2** *(article de seconde main)* second-hand item; **elle est neuve, ta voiture? – non, c'est une o.** is your car new? – no, it's second-hand; **je cherche une o. pas trop chère** I'm looking for a second-hand one, not too expensive; **acheter qch d'o.** to buy sth second-hand

occasion [ɔkazjɔ̃] **NF 1** *(circonstance favorable)* opportunity, chance; *(moment)* occasion; **saisir l'o.** to take *or* seize the opportunity; *Fam* **sauter sur l'o.** to jump at the chance *or* the opportunity; *Fam* **c'est l'o. ou jamais** it's now or never; *Fam* **c'est l'o. ou jamais de le faire** now's the time to do it; *Fam* **c'était l'o. ou jamais de changer de boulot!** if ever there was a time to change jobs, it was then!; **avoir l'o. de faire qch** to have the opportunity *or* chance of doing *or* to do sth; **tout le monde n'a pas l'o. de faire ça** not everybody has the chance *or* opportunity to do that; **je n'ai jamais eu l'o. de le regretter** I've never had cause *or* reason to regret it, I've never had any cause for regret; **donner à qn l'o. de faire qch** to give sb the *or* an opportunity *or* a *or* the chance to do sth; **si l'o. se présente** if you get the chance, if the opportunity arises, *Fml* should the opportunity arise; **laisser passer l'o.** to let the opportunity slip (by); **profiter de l'o. pour faire qch** to take the opportunity to do sth; *Iron* **tu as encore perdu l'o. de te taire** why can't you keep your mouth shut?; *Iron* **il ne perd jamais une o. d'être désagréable/de se faire remarquer** he never misses an opportunity to be unpleasant/to get himself noticed; **attendre l'o.** to bide one's time; **à l'o.** when the opportunity presents itself; **voir qn à l'o.** to see sb occasionally *or* from time to time; **venez boire un coup à l'o.** come for a drink when you get a *or* the chance; **elle sait être très virulente à l'o.** she can be very harsh on occasions; **il faudra que je m'en assure, à l'o.** I'll have to check it myself, when I get the chance; **à la première o.** at the first *or* earliest opportunity; **je m'en débarrasserai à la première o.** I'll get rid of it the first chance I get; **à** *ou* **en plusieurs occasions** on several occasions; **s'habiller pour l'o.** to dress for the occasion; **on a bu du champagne pour l'o.** we drank champagne to celebrate, we drank champagne to mark the occasion; **à l'o. de son mariage** on the occasion of his marriage; **je l'ai rencontré à l'o. d'un concert** I met him at a concert; **je m'en suis rendu compte à l'o. d'une visite de routine** I realized it during a routine visit; **à l'o. de sa venue** upon his arrival; **en pareille o.** in circumstances like these, in similar circumstances; **à cette o.** on that occasion; **dans/pour les grandes occasions** on/for great occasions; *Prov* **l'o. fait le larron** opportunity makes the thief; **être l'o. de qch** to be the occasion of sth; **ce sera l'o. de faire la fête** that will be a good excuse for a party; *Fin* **o. de profit** profit opportunity

2 *(affaire)* bargain; **le marché de l'o.** the

second-hand market; **faire le neuf et l'o.** to sell new and second-hand goods; **marchandises/voitures/livres/meubles d'o.** second-hand goods/cars/books/furniture; **elle est neuve, ta voiture? – non, c'est une o.** is your car new? – no, it's secondhand; **je l'ai acheté d'o.** I bought it secondhand; **ça, c'est une o.!** it's a bargain!

occasionnel, -elle [ɔkazjɔnɛl] ADJ occasional; *(rencontre)* chance; *(aide)* casual; **je vais parfois au restaurant mais cela reste très o.** I sometimes go to the restaurant but only very occasionally; **cause occasionnelle d'une révolte** event that triggered *or Fml* occasioned a revolt

occasionnellement [ɔkazjɔnɛlmɑ̃] ADV occasionally

occasionner [ɔkazjɔne] VT to cause, to give rise to, *Fml* to occasion; **un bébé occasionne de nombreux frais** having a baby is a costly business

occident [ɔksidɑ̃] NM west, *Fml* occident; *Pol* **l'O.** the West

occidental, -ale, -aux, -ales [ɔksidɑtal, -o] ADJ west, western; **côte occidentale** west coast; **l'Europe occidentale** Western Europe; **les Indes occidentales** the West Indies ▸ N Westerner, *Fml* Occidental

occidentalisation [ɔksidɑtalizasjɔ̃] NF westernization

occidentaliser [ɔksidɑtalize] VT to westernize
▸ VPR **s'occidentaliser** to become westernized

occipital, -ale, -aux, -ales [ɔksipital, -o] *Anat* ADJ occipital
▸ NM occipital (bone)

occiput [ɔksipyt] NM *Anat* occiput

occire [ɔksir] VT *(used only in inf & pp occis) Arch, Hum* to slay; **se faire o.** to be slain

occitan [ɔksitɑ̃] ADJ of the langue d'oc
▸ NM *(langue)* langue d'oc *(dialect spoken in parts of southern France)*

occlusif, -ive [ɔklyzif, -iv] *Ling* ADJ occlusive
▸ NF **occlusive** occlusive consonant, stop

occlusion [ɔklyzjɔ̃] NF occlusion; *Méd* **o. intestinale** intestinal obstruction, *Spéc* ileus

occultation [ɔkyltasjɔ̃] NF *Astron* occultation; *Fig* concealment

occulte [ɔkylt] ADJ *(surnaturel)* occult; *(secret) (comptabilité)* secret; *(cause)* hidden; *(rôle)* clandestine, covert; **les sciences occultes** the occult, the occult sciences

occulter [ɔkylte] VT *Astron* to occult; *(signal lumineux)* to block out, *Spéc* to occult; *Fig (informations, intentions etc)* to conceal

occultisme [ɔkyltism] NM occultism

occupant, -ante [ɔkypɑ̃, -ɑ̃t] ADJ *(locataire, armée)* occupying
▸ N *(d'une maison)* occupier, occupant; *(d'un poste)* occupant; *Jur* **premier o.** occupant; *Mil* **l'o.** the occupying forces

occupation [ɔkypasjɔ̃] NF 1 *(fait d'être ou de rester quelque part)* occupancy, occupation; *(fait de posséder ou d'entrer en possession) (d'une maison)* possession; *(d'un territoire conquis)* occupation; **armée d'o.** army of occupation; *Hist* **l'O.** the Occupation; **grève avec o. des lieux** sit-down strike, sit-in; **manifestation estudiantine avec o. des locaux** student sit-in; **o. des chambres/des lits** *(dans un hôtel)* room/bed occupancy; **o. double** double occupancy; **o. maximale** capacity occupancy 2 *(besogne, ouvrage)* occupation; **avoir de l'o.** to be busy, to have things to do; **être sans o., ne pas avoir d'o.** to have nothing to do; **j'ai bien assez d'occupations comme cela!** I've got enough to do *or* enough on my plate already!; **vaquer à ses**

occupations to go about one's business; *Admin* **o. principale** main occupation

occupé [ɔkype] ADJ 1 *(personne) (travaillant)* busy; *(avec un autre client)* busy, engaged; **o. aux préparatifs du départ** busy with the preparations for departure, busy getting ready to leave; **o. à relire le texte** busy rereading the text; **c'est un homme fort o.** he's a very busy man; **elle a des journées/semaines très occupées en ce moment** her days/weeks are very full at present 2 *(place)* taken; *Tél (ligne)* engaged, *Am* busy; *(sur la porte des toilettes)* engaged; *Ordinat (imprimante)* busy; **en territoire o.** in occupied territory

occuper [ɔkype] VT 1 *(maison)* to occupy; *(place)* to take up, to occupy; **ce lit occupe beaucoup trop de place** this bed takes up *or* occupies far too much room; **les livres d'art occupent trois étagères de la bibliothèque** the art books take up *or* occupy *or* fill three shelves of the bookcase; **le magasin n'occupe que le rez-de-chaussée** the shop takes up *or* occupies only the ground floor
2 *Mil etc (par la force) (ville, bâtiment)* to occupy; **les ouvriers ont décidé d'o. l'usine** the workers have decided to occupy the factory; **o. le terrain** *Mil* to hold the field; *Com* to make one's presence felt in the market
3 *(remplir) (temps)* to fill, to occupy; **faire qch pour o. le temps** to do sth to fill *or* occupy the time; **o. ses loisirs** to fill *or* occupy one's free time; **les enfants occupent la majeure partie de mon temps** the children take up the greater part of my time; **o. sa journée à faire qch** to spend one's day doing sth
4 *(poste etc)* to have, to hold
5 **o. qn** *(employer)* to employ sb; *(donner une activité à)* to keep sb busy *or* occupied, to give sb something to do, to occupy sb; **la lecture de ce livre m'a occupé toute la soirée** reading this book took up my entire evening *or* kept me busy all evening; **ces problèmes m'ont occupé pendant un certain temps** these problems have kept me busy *or* kept me occupied *or* given me something to think about for some time; **fais un peu de ménage, ça occupe!** *ou* **ça t'occupera!** do a bit of housework, that'll pass *or* fill the time!
▸ VPR **s'occuper 1** to keep oneself busy *or* occupied; **s'o. à faire qch** to be busy doing sth, to be occupied in doing sth; **s'o. en lisant** to spend one's time reading; **on a toujours de quoi s'o.** there's always something to keep you busy *or* occupied, there's always something that needs doing; **je trouverai bien de quoi m'o. en attendant** I'll find something to keep me busy *or* to occupy myself with while I wait
2 **s'o. de** *(être intéressé par) (photographie, littérature etc)* to be interested in; *(se charger de) (quelque chose)* to deal with, to take care of, to attend to; *(personnes, enfants)* to take care of, to look after; **s'o. de faire qch** to see about doing sth; **cette mai son son s'occupe surtout d'argenterie** this firm specializes in silverware; **nous allons maintenant nous o. du bilan** we will now turn (our attention) to the balance sheet; **ce n'est pas la peine de vous o. de cela pour l'instant** it's not worth worrying *or* bothering about that at the moment; **il s'occupe de trop de choses** he takes on too much, he has too many irons in the fire; **je m'en occuperai** I'll see to it, I'll deal with it, I'll take care of it; *Fam* **occupe-toi de ce qui te regarde** *ou* **de tes affaires** *ou* **de tes oignons!** mind your own business!; **de quoi tu t'occupes?** what business is it of yours?, what's it got to do with you?; *Fam* **t'occupe (pas)!** keep your nose out!, mind your own business!; *Iron* **je vais m'o. de lui** I'll take care of him; *Com* **est-ce qu'on s'occupe de**

vous? are you being attended to *or* being served?

occurrence [ɔkyrɑ̃s] NF 1 *(circonstance)* **en l'o.** in this case, as it happens/happened; **et en l'o., il s'agissait d'une ville romaine** and as it happened *or* as it turned out, it was a Roman town; **mais en l'o., tu as tort** but in this case *or* but this time *or* but as it happens, you're wrong 2 *Ling (apparition)* occurrence

OCDE [osede] NF *(abrév* **Organisation de coopération et de développement économique)** OECD

océan [ɔseɑ̃] NM ocean; **l'o. Atlantique** the Atlantic (Ocean); **l'o. Indien** the Indian Ocean; **l'o. Pacifique** the Pacific (Ocean); **l'o. Antarctique** *ou* **Austral** the Antarctic Ocean; **l'o. Arctique** the Arctic Ocean; **d'un o. à l'autre** from coast to coast; *Fig* **un o. de fleurs/couleurs** a sea of flowers/colour

océane [ɔsean] ADJ F 1 *Culin (salade, sauce)* seafood 2 *Litt (de l'Océan)* **une brise o.** a sea breeze
▸ NF **l'O.** *(autoroute)* = the Paris-Nantes motorway

Océanie [ɔseani] NF Oceania

océanien, -ienne [ɔseanjɛ̃, -jen] ADJ Oceanian
▸ N **O.** Oceanian; *(de Polynésie, Mélanésie)* South Sea Islander

océanique [ɔseanik] ADJ *(courant, climat)* ocean, oceanic

océanographe [ɔseanɔgraf] N oceanographer

océanographie [ɔseanɔgrafi] NF oceanography

océanographique [ɔseanɔgrafik] ADJ oceanographic(al)

océanologie [ɔseanɔlɔʒi] NF oceanology

ocelle [ɔsɛl] NM *Zool (d'un insecte)* simple eye, *Spéc* ocellus; *(d'une plume, de l'aile d'un insecte)* eye, *Spéc* ocellus

ocelot [ɔslo] NM ocelot

ocre [ɔkr] NF, ADJ INV ochre, *Am* ocher

ocré [ɔkre] ADJ ochre(-coloured), *Am* ocher(-colored)

ocreux, -euse [ɔkrø, -øz] ADJ ochreous

octaèdre [ɔktaɛdr] ADJ octahedral
▸ NM octahedron

octaédrique [ɔktaedrik] ADJ octahedral

octal, -ale, -aux, -ales [ɔktal, -o] ADJ *Ordinat* octal

octane [ɔktan] NM *Chimie* octane; **essence à haut indice d'o.** high-octane petrol *or Am* gasoline

octante [ɔktɑ̃t] ADJ INV *Région* eighty

octave [ɔktav] NF octave; **jouer à l'o.** *(plus haut)* to play an octave higher; *(plus bas)* to play an octave lower

octet [ɔktɛ] NM *Ordinat* (eight-bit) byte; **milliard d'octets** gigabyte; **o. de contrôle** check byte

octobre [ɔktɔbr] NM October; **en o.** in October; **au mois d'o.** in (the month of) October; **le premier o.** (on) October the first, (on) the first of October, *Am* (on) October first SEE GRAMMAR A81–2; B60–2

octogénaire [ɔktɔʒenɛr] ADJ, N octogenarian

octogonal, -ale, -aux, -ales [ɔktɔgɔnal, -o] ADJ octagonal

octogone [ɔktɔgɔn] NM octagon

octopode [ɔktɔpɔd] ADJ, NM octopod

octosyllabe [ɔktɔsilab] ADJ octosyllabic
▸ NM octosyllable

octosyllabique [ɔktɔsilabik] ADJ octosyllabic

octroi [ɔktrwa] NM 1 *(concession) (d'une faveur)* concession, granting; *Com* **o. de licence** licensing 2 *Hist (impôt)* town dues, city toll; *(bureau)* tollhouse

octroyer [ɔktrwaje] (**j'octroie, n. octroyons; j'octroierai**) **VT o. qch à qn** to grant *or* concede sth to sb; **o. du temps à qn** to allow sb time; **o. une permission à qn** to give *or* grant sb leave; **o. sa grâce à un condamné à mort** to reprieve a condemned man; **o. des faveurs à qn** to bestow favours on sb; **o. un prêt** to grant a loan
  VPR s'octroyer il s'est octroyé un jour de vacances supplémentaire he gave himself *or* awarded himself an extra day's holiday

octuor [ɔktɥɔr] **NM** *Mus* octet

octuple [ɔktypl] **ADJ** octuple; *(montant)* eightfold
  NM octuple

oculaire [ɔkylɛr] **ADJ 1** *(visuel)* **témoin o.** eyewitness **2** *(de l'œil)* **hygiène o.** eye care, care of the eyes; **globe o.** eyeball
  NM *Opt* eyepiece; *Spéc* ocular; *Phot* viewfinder; **o. de visée** *(d'une caméra)* eyepiece

oculiste [ɔkylist] **N** eye specialist, ophthalmologist

odalisque [ɔdalisk] **NF** odalisque, odalisk

ode [ɔd] **NF** ode

odeur [ɔdœr] **NF** *(généralement désagréable)* smell, odour, *Am* odor; *(agréable)* scent, smell; **il a une drôle d'o., ce poisson** this fish has a funny smell *or*, smells funny; **o. de brûlé** smell of burning; **je sentais une o. de brûlé** I could smell something burning; **sans o.** odourless, *Am* odorless; **bonne o.** lovely *or* pleasant smell; **mauvaise o.** bad *or* unpleasant smell, *Fam* stink; *Fig* **mourir en o. de sainteté** to die in the odour of sanctity; *Fig* **être en o. de sainteté auprès de qn** to be in sb's good books; **ne pas être en o. de sainteté auprès de qn** to be in sb's bad books; **je ne suis pas en o. de sainteté** I'm not popular, *Fam* I'm in the doghouse, *Fam* I'm not flavour of the month; *Prov* **l'argent n'a pas d'o.** money has no smell

odieusement [ɔdjøzmã] **ADV** odiously, hatefully

odieux, -ieuse [ɔdjø, -jøz] **ADJ** *(personne)* odious, hateful; *(crime, vice)* odious, abominable

odomètre [ɔdɔmɛtr] **NM** *(pour véhicule)* odometer; *(pour piéton)* pedometer

odontologie [ɔdɔ̃tɔlɔʒi] **NF** *Méd* odontology

odorant [ɔdɔrã] **ADJ** *(agréable)* sweet-smelling, fragrant; *(désagréable)* strong-smelling, *Fam* smelly

odorat [ɔdɔra] **NM** (sense of) smell; **avoir l'o. développé** to have a keen sense of smell

odoriférant [ɔdɔriferã] **ADJ** sweet-smelling, *Litt* odoriferous

odyssée [ɔdise] **NF 1** *Littér* **l'O.** the Odyssey **2** *Fig* odyssey; **ce voyage a été une véritable o.** it was a truly epic journey

OEA [ɔəa] **NF** *(abrév* **Organisation des États américains**) OAS

œcuménique [ekymenik, ø-] **ADJ** *Rel* ecumenical

œcuménisme [ekymenism, ø-] **NM** *Rel* ecumenicalism

œcuméniste [ekymenist, ø-] **N, ADJ** *Rel* ecumenist

œdème [edɛm, ø-] **NM** *Méd* oedema, *Am* edema; **avoir un o. aux poumons** to have pulmonary oedema

Œdipe [edip, ø-] **N** *Littér* Oedipus; *Psy* **complexe d'O.** Oedipus complex

œil, *pl* **yeux** [œj, jø] **NM 1** *Anat* eye; **avoir de grands/petits yeux** to have large/small eyes; **avoir les yeux bleus** to have blue eyes; **avoir les yeux globuleux/enfoncés** to have protruding/deep-set eyes; **j'ai le soleil dans les yeux** *ou* **dans l'o.** the sun's in my eyes, I've got the sun in my eyes; **se maquiller** *ou* **se faire les yeux** to do one's eyes, to put on one's eye make-up; **visible à l'o. nu** visible to the naked eye; **voir qch de ses (propres) yeux** to see sth with one's own eyes; **je l'ai de mes yeux vu** I saw it with my (very) own eyes; *Fam* **avoir un o. qui dit zut** *ou* **merde à l'autre, avoir un o. qui joue au billard et l'autre qui compte les points, avoir les yeux qui se croisent les bras** to be cross-eyed, to have a squint; **avoir un o. de verre** to have a glass eye; *Fam* **avoir une coquetterie dans l'o.** to have a cast in one's eye; **avoir les yeux injectés de sang** to have bloodshot eyes; **fermer/ouvrir les yeux; je n'ai pas fermé l'o. de la nuit** I didn't sleep a wink all night; **ne dormir que d'un o.** to sleep with one eye open; **j'étais tellement inquiète que je n'ai pu dormir que d'un o.** I was so worried I couldn't sleep properly; *Fig* **je pourrais le faire les yeux fermés** I could do it with my eyes shut *or* closed; **chez eux, j'achète les yeux fermés** I buy things from them with complete confidence; **ouvrir un o.** to half-open one's eyes; **ouvrir de grands yeux** to look surprised; **faire les gros yeux (à qn)** to glare (at sb); **lever les yeux au ciel** to raise one's eyes heavenward *or* to heaven; **baisser les yeux** to lower one's eyes *or* gaze, to look down; **avoir de petits yeux** to look tired; **j'ai les yeux qui se ferment (tout seuls), je ne peux plus garder les yeux ouverts** I can't keep my eyes open; **avoir un o. au beurre noir** *ou* **un o. poché** to have a black eye; **regarder qn dans les yeux** to look sb in the eye; *Fam* **entre quat'z'yeux** [katzjø] in private; *(avec franchise)* man to man/woman to woman, frankly; **les yeux dans les yeux** face to face, facing each other; *(amoureusement)* gazing into each other's eyes; **n'avoir d'yeux que pour une personne** to have eyes for only one person; *Prov* **o. pour o., dent pour dent** an eye for an eye, a tooth for a tooth; **épouser une femme pour ses beaux yeux** to marry a woman for her (good) looks; **je ne travaille pas pour les beaux yeux de mon patron!** I don't do this job for the love of it!; **je ne le fais pas pour ses beaux yeux** I'm not doing it just to please him; *Fam* **avoir des yeux de merlan frit** to look like a lovesick calf; **coûter les yeux de la tête** to cost a fortune *or* an arm and a leg; **tu as les yeux plus gros** *ou* **grands que le ventre** your eyes are bigger than your belly; **n'avoir plus que les** *ou* **ses yeux pour pleurer** to have nothing left apart from the clothes on one's back; **ça saute aux yeux** it's glaringly obvious; **ça crève les yeux qu'il est amoureux d'elle** it's glaringly obvious that he's in love with her; *Fam* **je m'en bats l'o.** I don't give a damn, I couldn't care less; *Fam* **mon o.!** my eye!; **tourner de l'o.** to keel over, to faint; *Fam* **à l'o.** free, gratis, for nothing; **le mauvais o.** the evil eye; **porter un o. critique sur qch** to be critical about sth; **nous voyons ça du même o.** we see eye to eye (with each other) about it; **nous ne voyons pas du tout les choses de cet o.-là** we don't see things in that light at all; **voir** *ou* **regarder qn/qch d'un bon o.** to look favourably *or* approvingly on sb/sth; **voir** *ou* **regarder qn/qch d'un mauvais o.** to look unfavourably *or* disapprovingly on sb/sth, to frown on sb/sth; **je n'en croyais pas mes yeux** I couldn't *or* didn't believe my eyes; **faire les yeux doux à qn** to make eyes at sb; *Fam* **faire de l'o. à qn** to give sb the eye; *Fam* **taper dans l'o. à qn** to take sb's fancy

2 *(vue)* (eye)sight, eyes; **avoir de bons/mauvais yeux** to have good/bad (eye)sight; **je n'ai plus mes yeux de 20 ans** I can't see as well as I used to; **s'user** *ou* **s'abîmer les yeux** to ruin one's eyes *or* eyesight; **fatiguer les yeux** to strain one's eyes; **cette lumière me fatigue les yeux** I'm straining my eyes in this light; **dès que j'eus jeté les yeux sur lui** as soon as I had set eyes on him; **chercher qn des yeux** to look around for sb; **suivre qn des yeux** to follow sb with one's eyes; **couver** *ou* **manger** *ou* **dévorer qn des yeux** to look lovingly *or* fondly at sb; **regarder qn avec les yeux de l'amour** to look at sb through the eyes of love; *Fam* **se rincer l'o.** to get an eyeful; **elle n'a pas froid aux yeux** she's not afraid of anything; **aux yeux de la loi** in the eyes of the law; **aux yeux de Dieu** in the eyes *or* sight of God; **à mes yeux** in my eyes, in my opinion; **l'accident s'est déroulé sous mes yeux** the accident happened right before my eyes; **sous l'o. jaloux/inquisiteur/bienveillant de qn** under the jealous/inquisitive/kindly eye of sb; **avoir qch sous les yeux** to have sth right in front of one *or* one's eyes; **je n'ai pas encore eu leur projet sous les yeux** I haven't had sight of *or* I haven't seen their plan yet

3 *(attention)* **avoir** *ou* **garder l'o. ouvert** *ou* **les yeux ouverts** to keep one's eyes open; **avoir l'o. sur qch** to keep an eye on sth; **avoir l'o. sur qn, avoir qn à l'o.** to keep an eye on sb; **avoir l'o. à tout** to keep an eye on everything; *Fam* **ouvrir l'o. (et le bon)** to keep one's eyes open *or* peeled *or* skinned; **ne pas avoir les yeux en face des trous** to be half-asleep; *Fam* **elle n'a pas les yeux dans sa poche** she keeps her eyes open, she's very observant; **fermer les yeux sur qch** *(par indulgence)* to turn a blind eye to sth; *(par refus de la réalité)* to close one's eyes to sth; **ouvrir les yeux à qn sur qch** to open sb's eyes to sth; **coup d'o.** glance; **au** *ou* **du premier coup d'o., d'un seul coup d'o.** at a glance; **jeter un coup d'o. sur qch** to have a quick look at sth, to have a glance at sth; **il y a un joli coup d'o. d'ici** there's a lovely view from here; **avoir le coup d'o.** to have a good eye (for things); **ça vaut** *ou* **ça mérite le coup d'o.** it's worth a look

4 *(d'une aiguille etc)* eye; *(d'une charnière)* (screw-)hole; *(sur une corde)* eye (splice); *(dans du pain, du gruyère)* hole; *(dans la soupe)* globule *or* speck of fat; **piton à o.** eye bolt

5 *Typ* *(pl* **œils)** typeface

6 *Élec, TV* **o. électrique** electric eye; *Radio* **o. magique, o. cathodique** magic eye

7 *Météo* *(d'un cyclone)* eye

œil-de-bœuf, *pl* **œils-de-bœuf NM** bull's-eye (window)

œil-de-chat, *pl* **œils-de-chat NM** *Minér* cat's-eye

œil-de-perdrix, *pl* **œils-de-perdrix NM** *(au pied)* (soft) corn

œillade [œjad] **NF** glance; **lancer** *ou* **jeter une o. à qn** to give sb the eye; **lancer des œillades à qn** to make eyes at sb, to give sb the eye

œillère [œjɛr] **NF 1** *(pour un cheval)* blinker, *Am* blinder; *Fig* **avoir des œillères** *(être borné)* to be narrow-minded; *(ignorer la réalité)* to wear blinkers **2** *Méd* eyebath, *Am* eyecup

œillet [œjɛ] **NM 1** *(fleur)* carnation; **o. des fleuristes** carnation, clove pink; **o. de poète** sweet william; **o. des prés** ragged robin; **o. d'Inde** French marigold **2** *(trou)* *(d'une botte, d'une voile etc)* eyelet **3** *(en papeterie)* (gummed) reinforcement

œilleton [œjtɔ̃] **NM 1** *Opt* *(d'un viseur)* eyepiece **2** *(d'une plante)* eye (bud)

œillette [œjɛt] **NF** oil poppy, opium poppy; **huile d'o.** poppy seed oil

œnologie [enɔlɔʒi, ø-] **NF** wine-making, *Spéc* oenology, *Am* enology; **cours d'o.** wine appreciation course

œnologique [enɔlɔʒik, ø-] **ADJ** wine, *Spéc* oenological, *Am* enological; **croisière o.** wine-tasting cruise

œnologue [enɔlɔg, ø-] **N** wine expert, *Spéc* oenologist, *Am* enologist

œsophage [ezɔfaʒ, ø-] **NM** *Anat* oesophagus, *Am* esophagus

œstre [ɛstr] **NM** *(mouche)* gadfly, warble fly

œstrogène [ɛstrɔʒɛn, ø-] **ADJ, NM** *Physiol* oestrogen, *Am* estrogen

œstrus [ɛstrys] **NM** *Physiol* oestrus, *Am* estrus

œuf, *pl* **œufs** [œf, ø] **NM 1** egg; **blanc/jaune d'o.** egg white/yolk; **o. du jour** freshly laid egg; **o. frais** fresh egg; **œufs battus** *ou* **montés en neige** beaten egg whites; **en forme d'o.** egg-shaped; *Fig* **mettre tous ses œufs dans le même panier** to put all one's eggs in one basket; *Fig Fam* **marcher sur des œufs** to tread warily; **il tondrait un o.** he's a skinflint; *Prov* **qui vole un o. vole un bœuf** he that will steal a penny will steal a pound; **tuer la poule aux œufs d'or** to kill the goose that lays the golden egg(s); *Fam* **quel o.!** what an idiot *or* fool!; *Fam* **une tête d'o.** an egghead; *Fam* **va te faire cuire un o.!** take a running jump!, go jump in the lake!; **c'est comme l'o. de Christophe Colomb, il fallait y penser** it's easy when you know how **2** *Biol* egg; *(d'écrevisse, de homard)* berry; *(d'insecte)* egg; **œufs** *(de grenouille)* spawn; *(de poisson)* spawn, hard roe; *Fam* **étouffer** *ou* **tuer qch dans l'o.** to nip sth in the bud **3** *Ski (télécabine)* cable car

▸▸ **œufs brouillés** scrambled eggs; **o. en chocolat** chocolate egg; **o. à la coque** boiled egg; **o. dur,** *Belg* **o. cuit dur** hard-boiled egg; **œufs au lait** egg custard; **œufs à la liqueur** small liqueur-filled Easter eggs; **œufs de lump** lumpfish roe; **œufs mimosa** eggs mimosa *(egg whites filled with mayonnaise and crushed egg yolk)*; **o. (au) miroir** fried egg; **o. mollet** soft-boiled egg; **œufs à la neige** floating islands; **o. de Pâques** Easter egg; **o. au plat** *ou* **sur le plat** fried egg; *Péj Fig Fam* **elle n'a que des œufs sur le plat** she's as flat as a pancake; **o. poché** poached egg; **o. en poudre** dried *or* dehydrated *or* powdered egg; *Couture* **o. à repriser** darning egg

œufrier [œfrije] **NM** egg holder *or* stand *(for boiling eggs)*

œuvre [œvr] **NF 1** *(travail)* work; **faire o. utile** to do useful work; **leur rencontre était son o.** *(grâce à lui)* it was thanks to him that they met; *(à cause de lui)* it was because of him that they met; **être à l'o.** to be at work; **mettre qn à l'o.** to set sb to work; **se mettre à l'o.** to get down to *or* set to work; **quand le médecin arriva, la mort avait déjà fait son o.** by the time the doctor arrived, the patient had already died; **la maladie/cette idée néfaste a déjà fait son o.** the disease/this dangerous idea has already done its work; **mettre en o.** to use, to make use of; *(traité, loi, système)* to implement; **mettre tout en o.** to do everything possible; **les bonnes œuvres** charitable work; **quête au profit d'une o.** collection in aid of a charity **2** *(création)* work; **œuvres d'un peintre** works of a painter; **œuvres complètes/choisies** complete/selected works

NM *Constr* **gros o.** *(d'un bâtiment)* fabric (of a building); **à pied d'o.** on site; *Fig* ready to start work

NM *ou* **F** *Beaux-Arts, Littér (ensemble de créations)* works; **l'o. entière** *ou* **entier de Beethoven** the complete works of Beethoven

▸▸ **o. d'art** work of art; **o. de bienfaisance** charity, charitable institution; **o. cinématographique** cinematic work; **o. de charité** charity, charitable institution; *Naut* **œuvres mortes** dead works, upper works, topsides; *Naut* **œuvres vives** quick works, vitals

œuvrer [œvre] **VI** *Litt* to work

off [ɔf] **ADJ INV 1** *Cin (hors champ)* off-screen; **voix o.** voice off **2** *(festival)* fringe
NM fringe festival

offensant [ɔfɑ̃sɑ̃] **ADJ** offensive, insulting

offense [ɔfɑ̃s] **NF 1** *(affront)* insult; **faire (une) o. à qn** to offend sb; **o. envers un chef d'État** insult to a head of state; **soit dit sans o.** with all due respect; *Fam* **il n'y a pas d'o.** no offence taken **2** *Rel* transgression, trespass; **pardonne-nous nos offenses** forgive us our trespasses

offensé, -ée [ɔfɑ̃se] **ADJ** offended, insulted
N offended *or* injured party

offenser [ɔfɑ̃se] **VT 1 o. qn** to offend sb, to give offence *or Am* offense to sb; **sans (vouloir) vous o., monsieur le ministre** with all due respect, Minister; **sans vouloir t'o., Jean-Pierre, j'ai bien l'impression que ...** no offence (intended), Jean-Pierre *or* I don't wish to offend, Jean-Pierre, but I get the feeling that ... **2** *Litt (bon goût, délicatesse etc)* to offend against; **o. les regards** to be an eyesore, *Litt* to offend the eye
VPR **s'offenser** to be offended **(de** by), to take offence *or Am* offense **(de** at)

offenseur [ɔfɑ̃sœr] **NM** offending person *or* party

offensif, -ive [ɔfɑ̃sif, -iv] **ADJ** *(guerre, arme)* offensive
NF **offensive** offensive; **passer à l'o.** to go on the *or* over to the offensive; *Fig* **l'o. de l'hiver est particulièrement précoce cette année** winter has come particularly early this year; **o. du froid** sudden cold spell, cold snap; **o. diplomatique** diplomatic offensive; **o. de paix** peace offensive

offertoire [ɔfɛrtwar] **NM** *Rel, Mus* offertory

office [ɔfis] **NM 1** *(charge)* office; **le secrétaire n'a pas rempli son o.** the secretary didn't carry out his duties; **la pénicilline a rempli son o.** the penicillin did its job; **faire o. de secrétaire/témoin** to act as secretary/witness; **une robe blanche toute simple a fait o. de robe de mariée** a simple white dress served as a wedding gown; **d'o.** automatically, as a matter of course; *Jur* **nommé** *ou* **commis d'o.** appointed by the court; **être mis à la retraite d'o.** to be automatically retired **2** *(assistance)* **accepter les bons offices de qn** to accept sb's good offices; **proposer ses bons offices** to offer to act as mediator; *Fam* **monsieur bons offices** mediator **3** *Rel* service, office; **l'o. des morts** the burial service, the Office for the Dead; **livre d'o.** prayer book; **aller à l'o.** to go to church
NM *ou* **F** *Vieilli (pièce)* back kitchen, scullery

▸▸ **O. du commerce extérieur** foreign trade office; **O. national de la navigation** French national shipping and inland waterways office; *Suisse* **o. de poste** post office; **o. de publicité** advertising agency; **o. du tourisme(syndicat d'initiative)** tourist information centre *or Am* center

officialisation [ɔfisjalizasjɔ̃] **NF** officialization, officializing

officialiser [ɔfisjalize] **VT** to officialize

officiant [ɔfisjɑ̃] *Rel* **ADJ** *(prêtre)* officiating
NM officiant

officiel, -ielle [ɔfisjɛl] **ADJ** *(déclaration, langage, visite, source)* official; **la version officielle est le suicide** the official version is suicide; **c'est o., il est officiel** it's official; **à titre o.** officially, formally; **le Journal o.** = French government publication giving information to the public about new laws, *Br* ≃ Hansard, *Am* ≃ Federal Register
NM 1 official; **les officiels du Parti** the Party officials **2 l'O.** *Br* ≃ Hansard, *Am* ≃ Federal Register

officiellement [ɔfisjɛlmɑ̃] **ADV** officially; **o., il a donné sa démission** officially, he re-

signed; **il a donné sa démission o.** he formally resigned

officier [1] [ɔfisje] **NM 1** *(fonctionnaire)* official, officer **2** *Mil* officer; **o. de marine** naval officer
▸▸ **o. d'état civil** ≃ registrar (of births, marriages and deaths); **o. général** *Mil* general officer; *Naut* flag officer; **O. de la Légion d'honneur** Officer of the Legion of Honour *or Am* Honor; *Jur* **o. ministériel** *(notaire)* notary (public); *(huissier)* officer of the court; *Naut* **o. de pont** deck officer; **o. de port** harbour *or Am* harbor master; *Mil* **o. supérieur** field officer

officier [2] **VI** *(impf, pr sub* n. officiions, v. officiiez)* to officiate; *Hum, Fig* to do the honours *or Am* honors

officieusement [ɔfisjøzmɑ̃] **ADV** unofficially

officieux, -ieuse [ɔfisjø, -jøz] **ADJ** unofficial; *Journ* **note d'origine officieuse** inspired piece; **à titre o.** unofficially

officinal, -ale, -aux, -ales [ɔfisinal, -o] **ADJ** *Pharm (plante)* medicinal; **préparation officinale** patent medicine

officine [ɔfisin] **NF 1** *Pharm* dispensary, pharmacy **2** *Fig (d'une intrigue)* hotbed; *(d'espions)* nest

off-line [ɔflajn] **ADJ** *Ordinat* off-line

offrande [ɔfrɑ̃d] **NF 1** offering, gift; **apporter son** *ou* **une o.** to make a donation (à to) **2** *Rel (don)* offering; *(cérémonie)* offertory; **o. votive** votive offering

offrant [ɔfrɑ̃] **NM** **le plus o.** the highest bidder; **vendre au plus o.** to sell to the highest bidder; **on me propose deux emplois et j'ai décidé de dire oui au plus o.** I've got two job offers and I've decided to accept the one offering the most money

offre [ɔfr] **NF** offer; *(dans un appel d'offres)* tender, bid; *(dans une vente aux enchères)* bid; **faire o. de qch** to offer sth; **recevoir/accepter une o.** to receive/accept an offer; **faire des offres de service à qn** to offer to help sb; *Com* to solicit orders from sb; *Écon* **l'o. et la demande** supply and demand
▸▸ *Mktg* **o.-ami** introduce-a-friend scheme; **o. de base** basic offer; **o. de bon de réduction** coupon offer; **o. commerciale** bid; **o. d'emploi** job offer, offer of employment; *Journ* **offres d'emploi** situations vacant; **o. d'essai** trial offer; **o. excédentaire** excess supply; **o. export** export bid; **o. globale** aggregate supply; **o. de lancement** introductory offer; **o. promotionnelle** promotional offer; *Fin* **o. publique** takeover bid; *Fin* **o. publique d'achat** takeover bid; **faire** *ou* **lancer une o. publique d'achat** to make a takeover bid (sur for); *Fin* **o. publique d'échange** takeover bid for shares; *Fin* **o. publique de vente** public offering, public share offer; **o. de remboursement** money-back offer; **o. de service** offer of services; **o. spéciale** special offer, bargain offer; **o. de vente** offer for sale

offreur, -euse [ɔfrœr, -øz] **N** *Écon* seller

OFFRIR [ɔfrir] *(prp* offrant; *pp* offert [ɔfɛr], *pr ind* j'offre, n. offrons; *p hist* j'offris; *fu* j'offrirai)* **VT 1** *(cadeau)* to give; *(sacrifice)* to offer up; **c'est pour o.** it's a gift *or* present; **c'est pour o.?** would you like it giftwrapped?; **o. à déjeuner à qn** to offer sb lunch; **essaie de te faire o. un repas au restaurant** try to get yourself invited out for a meal; **je t'offre un verre** I'll buy *or* stand you a drink **2** *(proposer)* to offer; **o. de faire qch** to offer to do sth; **o. mille euros (pour** *ou* **de qch)** to offer a thousand euros (for sth); *(aux enchères)* to bid a thousand euros (for sth); **combien t'en a-t-il offert?** how much did he offer you for it?; **o. des marchandises** to offer goods for sale; **o. un prix** to offer a price; **on lui a offert une place de mécanicien** he was offered a job as a mechanic; **o. la main de sa fille à qn** to offer one's daughter's hand in marriage to sb

3 (présenter) **o. une résistance acharnée** to put up stiff or fierce resistance; **la campagne offre des vues splendides** the countryside offers or Fml affords magnificent views; **l'histoire en offre plusieurs exemples** history gives or Fml affords several examples of it **VPR s'offrir 1 s'o. comme guide** to offer to act as a guide, to offer oneself or one's services as a guide; **s'o. pour faire qch** to offer to do sth; **s'o. à faire qch** to offer or volunteer to do sth; **s'o. aux regards** (d'un spectacle, d'une vue) to meet or greet the eyes; (d'une personne) to expose oneself to the public gaze, Péj to flaunt oneself

2 s'o. un bon cigare/une semaine de vacances to treat oneself to a good cigar/a week's holiday; **tu ne peux vraiment pas t'o. une soirée au cinéma?** can you really not afford a night out at the cinema?; **je ne peux pas m'o. une secrétaire** I can't afford (the luxury of) a secretary

offset [ɔfsɛt] Typ ADJ offset
NM offset (process)
NF offset (printing) machine

off-shore [ɔfʃɔr] ADJ **1** Sport **bateau o.** speedboat, powerboat; **course o.** speedboat or powerboat race; Pétr **plate-forme/forage o.** offshore oil rig/drilling **2** Fin **placement o.** offshore investment
NM (bateau) speedboat, powerboat; (course) speedboat or powerboat racing

offusquer [ɔfyske] VT (personne) to offend, to shock
VPR s'offusquer **s'o. de qch** to take offence or Am offense at sth; **il s'offusque d'un rien** he takes offence at the slightest thing

ogival, -ale, -aux, -ales [ɔʒival, -o] ADJ Archit ogival

ogive [ɔʒiv] NF **1** Archit (diagonal) rib; **voûte d'ogives** ribbed vault **2** Mil (d'un obus) head; (d'une roquette) nose cone; **o. nucléaire** nuclear warhead

OGM [ɔʒeɛm] NM (abrév organisme génétiquement modifié) GMO

ogre [ɔgr] NM ogre; **manger comme un o.** to eat like a horse

ogresse [ɔgrɛs] NF ogress

oh [o] INT oh!; oh! hisse! (yo-)heave-ho!

ohé [ɔe] INT hey!; **o. du bateau!** ahoy!

ohm [om] NM Élec ohm

ohmique [omik] ADJ Élec ohmic

ohmmètre [ommɛtr] NM Élec ohmmeter

oie [wa] NF goose; **o. sauvage** wild goose; Culin **confit d'o.** = goose preserved in goose fat; **graisse d'o.** goose fat; **conte de ma mère l'O.** Mother Goose story; **pas de l'o.** goose step; **jeu de l'o.** ≃ snakes and ladders
▶▶ Fam **o. blanche** naive young girl; **je ne suis pas une o. blanche** I'm no innocent

oignon [ɔɲɔ̃] NM **1** (légume) onion; **petits oignons** (pour les salades) spring onions; (pour les conserves) pickling onions; **aux petits oignons** Culin with baby onions; Fig Fam (parfait) first-rate; Fig Fam **chez eux, je suis toujours soigné aux petits oignons** I always get the VIP treatment when I stay with them; **en rang d'oignons** in a row or line; **se mettre en rang d'oignons** to form up in a row or line, to line up; Fam **occupe-toi** ou **mêle-toi de tes oignons** mind your own business; Fam **ce ne sont pas tes oignons** it's none of your business **2** Bot bulb; **oignons de tulipe** tulip bulbs **3** Méd bunion **4** (montre) turnip (watch)

oïl [ɔjl] ADV Hist, Ling **langue d'o.** langue d'oïl (language of northern France)

oindre [wɛ̃dr] VT (conj like **craindre**) **1** Vieilli (enduire) to (rub with) oil **2** Rel (roi etc) to anoint

oint, ointe [wɛ̃, wɛ̃t] ADJ, N anointed; **l'O. du Seigneur** the Lord's anointed

oiseau, -eaux [wazo] NM bird; Prov **petit à petit, l'o. fait son nid** slow and steady wins the race; **avoir un appétit d'o., manger comme un o.** to eat like a bird; **à vol d'o.** as the crow flies; Fig Fam **l'o. s'est envolé** the bird has flown; Fig Fam **c'est un drôle d'o.** he's an odd type or sort or customer, he's a funny old bird; **mon petit o.** my pet; **donner à qn des noms d'o.** to call sb names
▶▶ **oiseaux de basse-cour** poultry; Fig **o. de malheur, o. de mauvais augure** bird of ill omen; **o. de nuit** nocturnal bird; Fig night owl; **o. de passage** bird of passage; **o. de proie** bird of prey; **c'est l'o. rare** he's/she's a rare bird; **elle cherche l'o. rare** (comme époux) she's looking for the ideal man; (comme employé) she's looking for the ideal employee

oiseau-lyre, pl **oiseaux-lyres** NM lyrebird

oiseau-mouche, pl **oiseaux-mouches** NM hummingbird

oiseleur [wazlœr] NM bird catcher

oiselier [wazəlje] NM bird seller

oiselle [wazɛl] NF hen bird; Fig Fam naive young girl

oisellerie [wazɛlri] NF (élevage) bird breeding; (vente) bird selling

oiseux, -euse [wazø, -øz] ADJ (conversation) idle; (débat) pointless; **explication oiseuse** unsatisfactory explanation

oisif, -ive [wazif, -iv] ADJ idle, unoccupied; (capital) idle; **vie oisive** idle life, life of idleness
N person of leisure

oisillon [wazijɔ̃] NM fledgling

oisivement [wazivmɑ̃] ADV idly

oisiveté [wazivte] NF idleness; Prov **l'o. est (la) mère de tous les vices** the Devil finds work for idle hands to do

oison [wazɔ̃] NM gosling

OIT [oite] NF (abrév Organisation internationale du travail) ILO

OK [ɔkɛ] Fam ADV OK, okay
ADJ OK, okay; **c'est OK en ce qui me concerne!** that's OK or fine by me!

okapi [ɔkapi] NM okapi

olé [ɔle] INT olé!

oléagineux, -euse [ɔleaʒinø, -øz] ADJ oleaginous, oil-yielding; **graines oléagineuses** oilseeds
NMPL oleaginous or oil-yielding plants

oléiculteur, -trice [ɔleikyltœr, -tris] N olive grower

oléiculture [ɔleikyltyr] NF olive growing

oléifère [ɔleifɛr] ADJ oil-producing

oléine [ɔlein] NF olein, triolein

oléique [ɔleik] ADJ Chimie (acide) oleic

oléoduc [ɔleɔdyk] NM pipeline

olé olé ADJ INV Fam (propos, spectacle) risqué; (robe) daring; (gens, soirée) wild; **elle est très o. depuis qu'elle a divorcé** she's been leading a pretty wild life since her divorce; **il y a quelques scènes o.** some of the scenes are a bit close to the bone or risqué or Br near the knuckle

oléopneumatique [ɔleopnømatik] ADJ air/hydraulic

olfactif, -ive [ɔlfaktif, -iv] ADJ (nerfs, sens, bulbe) olfactory

olibrius [ɔlibrijys] NM Fam Péj oddball

olifant [ɔlifɑ̃] NM (ivory) horn

oligarchie [ɔligarʃi] NF oligarchy

oligarchique [ɔligarʃik] ADJ oligarchic(al)

oligarque [ɔligark] NM oligarch

oligoélément [ɔligoelemɑ̃] NM Biol trace element

oligopole [ɔligopɔl] NM Écon oligopoly

oligopolistique [ɔligopolistik] ADJ Écon oligopolistic

oligopsone [ɔligopsɔn] NM Écon oligopsony

oliphant [ɔlifɑ̃] NM (ivory) horn

olivaie [ɔlivɛ] NF olive grove or plantation

olivâtre [ɔlivatr] ADJ olive-greenish; (teint) sallow

olive [ɔliv] NF **1** olive; **huile d'o.** olive oil **2** Élec switch
ADJ INV olive (green)

oliveraie [ɔlivrɛ] NF olive grove or plantation

olivette [ɔlivɛt] NF **1** (raisin) = variety of grape; (tomate) plum tomato **2** (olivaie) olive plantation or grove

olivier [ɔlivje] NM **1** (arbre) olive (tree); Bible **le mont des Oliviers** the Mount of Olives; **se présenter un rameau d'o. à la main** to hold out the olive branch **2** (bois) olive (wood); **saladier en o.** olive-wood salad bowl

olographe [ɔlograf] ADJ Jur **testament o.** holograph will

OLP [ɔɛlpe] NF (abrév Organisation de libération de la Palestine) PLO

Olympe [ɔlɛ̃p] NM Myth **l'O.** (Mount) Olympus; **les dieux de l'O.** the gods of Olympus

olympiade [ɔlɛ̃pjad] NF Olympiad

olympien, -ienne [ɔlɛ̃pjɛ̃, -jɛn] ADJ Olympian; Fig **calme o.** Olympian calm
N O. Olympian

olympique [ɔlɛ̃pik] ADJ (jeux, champion, flamme) Olympic; **Comité international o.** International Olympic Committee; **stade/ piscine o.** Olympic stadium/pool

ombelle [ɔ̃bɛl] NF Bot umbel; **en o.** umbellate

ombellifère [ɔ̃belifɛr] Bot ADJ umbelliferous
NFPL **ombellifères** Umbelliferae, umbellifers

ombilic [ɔ̃bilik] NM Anat navel, Spéc umbilicus

ombilical, -ale, -aux, -ales [ɔ̃bilikal, -o] ADJ umbilical; Obst, Astronaut **cordon o.** umbilical cord; Fig **couper le cordon o.** to cut the apron strings

omble [ɔ̃bl] NM **o.(-chevalier)** char

ombrage [ɔ̃braʒ] NM **1** (des arbres) shade **2** Ordinat shading **3** Fig **prendre o. de qch** to take umbrage or offence or Am offense at sth; **porter** ou **faire o. à qn** to give offence to sb

ombragé [ɔ̃braʒe] ADJ shaded, shady

ombrager [ɔ̃braʒe] VT (il ombrageait) (d'un arbre) to shade

ombrageux, -euse [ɔ̃braʒø, -øz] ADJ (personne) touchy, easily offended, quick to take offence or Am offense; (cheval) skittish

ombre¹ [ɔ̃br] NF **1** (forme) shadow; **projeter une o.** to cast a shadow; Fig **suivre qn comme son o.** to stick to sb like glue; (espionner) to shadow sb; **avoir peur de son o.** to be afraid of one's own shadow; **lâcher la proie pour l'o.** to catch at shadows

2 (d'un arbre) shade; **se reposer à l'o. d'un arbre** to rest in the shade of a tree; **quarante degrés à l'o.** forty degrees in the shade; **elle a grandi à l'o. de la tour Eiffel** she grew up in the shadow of or within a stone's throw of the Eiffel Tower; Fig Fam **mettre qn à l'o.** to put sb inside, to put sb behind bars; Fig **jeter une o. sur la fête** to cast a shadow or a gloom over the festivities; Fig **vivre dans l'o. de qn** to live in sb's shadow, to be (always) overshadowed by sb; **faire de l'o. à qn** to be in sb's light; *Fig* to put sb in the shade; *Fam* **marche à l'o.!** *(conseil)* keep a low profile!; *(menace)* stay out of my sight!

3 *(obscurité)* darkness; *Fig (anonymat)* obscurity; **ils disparurent dans l'o. de la nuit** they were swallowed up by the darkness; **leurs agissements délictueux se faisaient dans l'o. de la nuit** their criminal schemes were carried out under cover of darkness; *Fig* **rester dans/sortir de l'o.** to remain in/emerge from obscurity; *Fig* **laisser qch dans l'o.** to keep sth dark; *Fig* **travailler dans l'o.** to work behind the scenes

4 *(être de l'au-delà)* ghost, *Litt* shade; **le royaume des ombres** the nether world; *Fig* **n'être plus que l'o. de soi-même** to be a mere shadow of one's former self

5 *(trace)* **vous n'avez pas l'o. d'une chance** you haven't the ghost of a chance; **il n'y a pas l'o. d'un doute** there isn't the *or* a shadow of a doubt; **elle n'a pas l'o. d'un scrupule!** she's totally unscrupulous *or* without scruples!; **une o. de méchanceté/jalousie** a hint of malice/jealousy

6 *Astron* umbra

7 *Beaux-Arts* **l'o. et la lumière** light and shade; *Fig* **il y a une o. au tableau** there's a fly in the ointment

▸▸ **ombres chinoises** shadow play; **théâtre d'ombres chinoises** shadow theatre; **o. à paupières** eye shadow

> Attention: ne pas confondre **shadow** et **shade** lorsque l'on traduit **ombre**. **Shadow** décrit une forme projetée par un objet se trouvant dans une source de lumière, alors que **shade** s'applique simplement à un lieu se trouvant à l'abri du soleil.

ombre² NF terre d'o. umber

ombre³ NM *(poisson)* o.(-chevalier) char; **o. de rivière** grayling

ombré [ɔ̃bre] NM *Ordinat* shading

ombrelle [ɔ̃brɛl] NF sunshade, parasol; *Zool (d'une méduse)* umbrella

> Il faut noter que le nom anglais **umbrella** est un faux ami. Il signifie **parapluie**.

ombrer [ɔ̃bre] VT *(serre, dessin)* to shade; **o. ses paupières de bleu** to put blue eye shadow on

ombreux, -euse [ɔ̃brø, -øz] ADJ *Litt (promenade, bosquet)* shady

Ombrie [ɔ̃bri] NF Umbria

ombudsman, *pl* **ombudsmans** [ɔ̃bydsman] NM ombudsman

OMC [oɛmse] NF *(abrév* **Organisation mondiale du commerce)** WTO

OMCI [oɛmsei] NF *(abrév* **Organisation de la navigation maritime consultative et intergouvernementale)** IMCO

oméga [ɔmega] NM omega

omelette [ɔmlɛt] NF omelette, *Am* omelet; **o. au jambon** ham omelette; **o. norvégienne** baked Alaska; *Prov* **on ne fait pas d'o. sans casser des œufs** you can't make an omelette without breaking eggs

omettre [ɔmɛtr] VT *(conj like* **mettre)** *(mot, détail)* to omit, to miss out, to leave out; **o. de faire qch** to fail *or* omit *or* neglect to do sth

OMI [oɛmi] NF *(abrév* **Organisation maritime internationale)** IMO

omission [ɔmisjɔ̃] NF *(d'un mot, détail)* omission; *(oubli)* oversight; **péché/mensonge par o.** sin/lie of omission; *Typ* **signe d'o.** caret

omnibus [ɔmnibys] NM **1** *(train)* slow train, *Br* stopping train **2** *Arch (bus)* omnibus
ADJ INV **train o.** slow train, *Br* stopping train; *Élec* **barre o.** busbar

omnidirectionnel, -elle [ɔmnidirɛksjɔnɛl] ADJ *(microphone, antenne, transmetteur)* omnidirectional

omnipotence [ɔmnipɔtɑ̃s] NF omnipotence

omnipotent [ɔmnipɔtɑ̃] ADJ omnipotent, all-powerful

omnipraticien, -ienne [ɔmnipratisjɛ̃, -jɛn] N *Méd* general practitioner, GP

omniprésence [ɔmniprezɑ̃s] NF omnipresence

omniprésent [ɔmniprezɑ̃] ADJ omnipresent

omniscience [ɔmnisjɑ̃s] NF omniscience

omniscient [ɔmnisjɑ̃] ADJ omniscient

omnisports [ɔmnispɔr] ADJ INV **stade/centre o.** sports stadium/centre

omnium [ɔmnjɔm] NM **1** *Écon* combine; *Bourse* **o. de valeurs** = type of investment trust **2** *Sport* open; *Courses de chevaux* open handicap **3** *Belg* comprehensive insurance

omnivore [ɔmnivɔr] ADJ omnivorous
NM omnivore

omoplate [ɔmɔplat] NF shoulder blade, *Spéc* scapula

OMS [oɛmɛs] NF *(abrév* **Organisation mondiale de la santé)** WHO

on [ɔ̃] PRON INDÉF *(sometimes becomes* **l'on**, *especially after vowel sound)* **1** *(indéterminé)* you, people, *Fml* one; *(quelqu'un)* someone, somebody; **on ne sait jamais** you never know, *Fml* one never knows, you *or Fml* one never can tell; **on n'en sait rien** nobody knows anything about it; **on n'aime pas être traité comme ça** people don't like to be treated like that; **on dit qu'elle est folle** it's said *or* they say *or* people say that she's mad, she's said to be mad; **on le dit dans les milieux autorisés** that's what is being said in official circles; **partout où l'on trouve de ces fossiles** wherever these fossils are found; **on ne connaît jamais son bonheur** you never know how lucky you are, *Fml* one never knows how lucky one is; **quand on demande à une femme de vous épouser** when a man asks a woman to marry him, when you ask a woman to marry you; **on était le sept mars** it was the seventh of March; **on frappe à la porte** someone's *or* somebody's (knocking) at the door, there's a knock at the door; **on sonne** there's the (door)bell, there's someone *or* somebody at the door; **on a enfoncé la porte** the door was burst open; **on m'a volé mon sac** my bag has been stolen, someone's stolen my bag; **on demande une bonne cuisinière** *(annonce)* wanted, good cook

2 *(précisé) (a following adj, noun or pp agrees in gender and number as the sense requires)* **on parlait très peu au déjeuner** we didn't talk much over lunch; **on ne s'était jamais séparés** we had never been separated; **on n'est pas toujours jeune et belle** women can't be young and beautiful forever; **où va-t-on?** where are we going?; **alors, on s'en va comme ça?** are you really leaving just like that?; **on est dix en tout** there are ten of us in all; *Fam* **nous, on est tous égaux** we're all equal here; *Fam* **on est allés au cinema avec les parents** we went to the pictures with our parents

onagre¹ [ɔnagr] NF *Bot* evening primrose

onagre² NM *Zool* onager, wild ass

onanisme [ɔnanism] NM onanism

once¹ [ɔ̃s] NF *(mesure)* ounce; **il n'a pas une o. de bon sens** he doesn't have an ounce of common sense

once² NF *Zool* ounce, snow leopard

oncle [ɔ̃kl] NM uncle; **o. à la mode de Bretagne** first cousin once removed; **o. d'Amérique** rich uncle; **o. à héritage** rich uncle *(from whom one expects to inherit)*; **O. Sam** Uncle Sam

oncogène [ɔ̃kɔʒɛn] ADJ *Méd* oncogenic

onction [ɔ̃ksjɔ̃] NF *Rel, Fig* unction; *Méd Vieilli* = massage or rubbing with oil

onctueusement [ɔ̃ktɥøzmɑ̃] ADV *Péj* unctuously

onctueux, -euse [ɔ̃ktɥø, -øz] ADJ *(yaourt, sauce)* smooth, creamy; *Péj (manières, paroles)* smooth, unctuous

onctuosité [ɔ̃ktɥozite] NF *(de yaourt, d'une sauce)* smoothness, creaminess

onde [ɔ̃d] NF **1** *Phys* wave; **o. calorifique/lumineuse/sonore** heat/light/sound wave; *Radio* **ondes** airwaves; **sur les ondes** on the air; **passer sur les ondes** *(d'une émission)* to be broadcast; *(d'une personne)* to be on air; **mettre en ondes** to produce; **petites ondes** short wave; **grandes ondes** long wave; **sur grandes ondes** on long wave; *Fig Fam* **nous ne sommes pas sur la même longueur d'o.** we're not on the same wavelength **2** *Métal* corrugation **3** *Litt (eau)* waters; **sur la terre et sur l'o.** on land and water

▸▸ **o. de choc** shock wave; **ondes courtes** short wave; **ondes hertziennes** airwaves, hertzian waves, radio waves; **ondes longues** long wave; **ondes moyennes** medium wave; **ondes radio** radio waves; **ondes très courtes** very high frequency; **ondes ultra-courtes** ultrashort waves

ondé [ɔ̃de] ADJ *Litt (cheveux)* wavy; *(soie)* watered

ondée [ɔ̃de] NF sudden downpour

ondemètre [ɔ̃dmɛtr] NM *Radio* wavemeter

ondin, -ine [ɔ̃dɛ̃, -in] N *Myth* water sprite

on-dit NM INV rumour, *Am* rumor, hearsay; **il ne faut pas croire à ces o.** you shouldn't believe these rumours; **ce ne sont que des o.** it's only hearsay

ondoiement [ɔ̃dwamɑ̃] NM **1** *(des roseaux, du maïs etc)* swaying, undulation **2** *Rel* summary baptism *(conducted in cases of emergency)*

ondoyant [ɔ̃dwajɑ̃] ADJ **1** *(sol)* undulating; *(cheveux)* wavy; *(foule, mouvement)* swaying; *(roseaux)* swaying, undulating **2** *Litt (personne, caractère)* changeable

ondoyer [ɔ̃dwaje] *(j'ondoie; j'ondoierai)* VI *(des blés)* to sway, to undulate; *(d'un drapeau)* to wave; *(de la surface de l'eau)* to undulate; *(de flammes)* to flicker
VT *Rel* to baptize summarily *(in cases of emergency)*

ondulant [ɔ̃dylɑ̃] ADJ *(courbe, ligne)* undulating; *(plaine)* rolling, undulating; *(roseaux)* swaying, undulating; *(crinière)* flowing; **avoir une démarche ondulante** to swing one's hips

ondulation [ɔ̃dylasjɔ̃] NF *(de l'eau, du sol etc)* undulation; *(dans les cheveux)* wave; *TV* **o. de l'image** picture weave

ondulatoire [ɔ̃dylatwar] ADJ undulatory; *Phys* **mouvement o.** wave motion

ondulé [ɔ̃dyle] ADJ *(sol)* undulating; *(cheveux)* wavy; *(tôle, carton)* corrugated; **route ondulée** switchback road; **trait o.** wavy line

onduler [ɔ̃dyle] VI to undulate; *(de cheveux)* to be wavy
VT *(cheveux)* to wave

onduleur [ɔ̃dylœr] NM *Ordinat* uninterruptible power supply, UPS

onduleux, -euse [ɔ̃dylø, -øz] ADJ = **ondulant**

onéreux, -euse [ɔnerø, -øz] ADJ *(dépense)* heavy; *(achat)* expensive, costly; **à titre o.** subject to payment

> Il faut noter que l'adjectif anglais **onerous** est un faux ami. Il signifie **lourd, pénible**.

ONF [ɔɛnɛf] NM (abrév **Office national des forêts**) Br ≃ Forestry Commission, Am ≃ National Forestry Service

ONG [ɔɛnʒe] NF (abrév **organisation non gouvernementale**) NGO

ongle [ɔ̃gl] NM (finger)nail; (des orteils) (toe)nail; (d'un animal) claw; (d'un oiseau de proie) talon, claw; **coup d'o.** scratch; **se faire les ongles** to do one's nails; Fam **avoir les ongles en deuil** to have dirty nails; Méd **o. incarné** ingrowing nail; **se ronger les ongles** to bite one's nails; Fig **avoir les ongles crochus** to be mean or tight-fisted; **connaître** ou **savoir qch sur le bout des ongles** to know sth perfectly; **il est français jusqu'au bout des ongles** he's French to his fingertips, he's every inch a Frenchman

onglée [ɔ̃gle] NF tingling, aching (of numbed fingertips); **j'ai l'o.** my fingers are numb with cold

onglet [ɔ̃glɛ] NM **1** (d'un répertoire) tab; (d'un canif) thumbnail groove; **dictionnaire à onglets** thumb-indexed dictionary; **o. à fenêtre** (d'une fiche etc) window tab **2** Typ (béquet) tab; (d'un livre) guard **3** Menuis mitre, Am miter; **boîte à onglets** mitre box; **tailler à o.** to mitre **4** Culin flank of beef

onglier [ɔ̃glije] NM manicure set

onguent [ɔ̃gɑ̃] NM Litt ointment, unguent

ongulé [ɔ̃gyle] ADJ, NM Zool ungulate

onirique [ɔnirik] ADJ Litt dreamlike

onirisme [ɔnirism] NM (state of) hallucination

onirologie [ɔnirɔlɔʒi] NF interpretation of dreams

ONN [ɔɛnɛn] NM (abrév **Office national de la navigation**) = French national shipping and inland waterways office

onomasiologie [ɔnɔmazjɔlɔʒi] NF Ling onomasiology

onomastique [ɔnɔmastik] Ling NF onomastics
ADJ onomastic

onomatopée [ɔnɔmatɔpe] NF onomatopoeia

onomatopéique [ɔnɔmatɔpeik] ADJ onomatopoeic

Ontario [ɔ̃tarjo] NM **l'O.** Ontario; **le lac O.** Lake Ontario

ontogenèse [ɔ̃tɔʒənɛz] NF ontogenesis, ontogeny

ontogénétique [ɔ̃tɔʒenetik] ADJ ontogenetic, ontogenic

ontogénie [ɔ̃tɔʒeni] NF = **ontogenèse**

ontologie [ɔ̃tɔlɔʒi] NF Phil ontology

ontologique [ɔ̃tɔlɔʒik] ADJ Phil ontological

ONU, Onu [ɔny, ɔɛny] NF (abrév **Organisation des Nations unies**) UN

ONUDI, Onudi [ɔnydi] NF (abrév **Organisation des Nations unies pour le développement industriel**) UNIDO

onusien, -ienne [ɔnyzjɛ̃, -jɛn] ADJ (of the) UN; **la politique onusienne** UN policy
N UN official

onyx [ɔniks] NM Minér onyx

onze [ɔ̃z] (the e of **le** and **de** is not, as a rule, elided before **onze** and its derivatives) ADJ INV eleven; **o. cent trente** eleven hundred and thirty; **nous n'étions que o.** [kɔ̃z], **nous n'étions qu'o.** there were only eleven of us; **le o. avril** the eleventh of April, Am April eleventh; **Louis O.** Louis the Eleventh
NM INV Ftbl **le o. de France** the French team, the French eleven

onzième [ɔ̃zjɛm] ADJ eleventh; **le o. jour** the eleventh day
N (personne, chose) eleventh
NM (fraction) eleventh
NF Mus eleventh

onzièmement [ɔ̃zjɛmmɑ̃] ADV in the eleventh place

oolithe [ɔɔlit] NM Minér oolite

oolithique [ɔɔlitik] ADJ Minér oolitic

OPA [opea] NF (abrév **offre publique d'achat**) takeover bid; **lancer une O.** to make a takeover bid (**sur** for); **O. amicale/inamicale** friendly/hostile takeover bid; **être l'objet d'une O.** to be the subject of a takeover bid

opacification [ɔpasifikasjɔ̃] NF making opaque

opacifier [ɔpasifje] VT to make opaque

opacité [ɔpasite] NM (d'un corps, d'un liquide) opacity, opaqueness; (d'une forêt) darkness, denseness; (d'un texte) opaqueness, impenetrability; Typ opacity

opale [ɔpal] NF opal
ADJ INV **verre o.** opal glass; Élec **ampoule o.** pearl bulb

opalescence [ɔpalɛsɑ̃s] NF opalescence

opalescent [ɔpalɛsɑ̃] ADJ opalescent

opalin, -ine [ɔpalɛ̃, -in] ADJ (nuance, reflet) opaline
NF **opaline** opaline

opaque [ɔpak] ADJ opaque; (forêt) dark, dense; Fig (texte, explications) opaque, impenetrable; Typ (papier) opaque; **collant o.** opaque tights; **o. aux rayons X** impervious to X-rays; Ling **mot o.** opaque word

op art [ɔpart] NM op art

OPCVM [opeseveɛm] NM Bourse (abrév **organisme de placements collectifs en valeurs mobilières**) unit trust, Am mutual fund; **O. actions** equity-based unit trust

OPE [opeə] NF abrév **offre publique d'échange**

opéable [opeabl] ADJ ripe for takeover

opeamania [opeamanja] NF Fin takeover fever

open [ɔpɛn] ADJ INV open; **une compétition o.** an open competition; **un billet o.** an open ticket
NM Sport open; **un o. de tennis** a tennis open

OPEP [ɔpɛp] NF (abrév **Organisation des pays exportateurs de pétrole**) OPEC

opéra [ɔpera] NM **1** (genre, œuvre) opera; **il aime beaucoup l'o.** he loves opera; **c'est une chanteuse d'o.** she's an opera singer; **grand o.** grand opera **2** (lieu) opera house; **je vais rarement à l'o.** I rarely go to the opera; **l'O. (de Paris)** the Paris Opera House; **les petits rats de l'O.** = the ballet pupils at the Paris Opera House
▸▸ **o. bouffe** comic opera, opera buffa

opérable [operabl] ADJ Chir (tumeur) operable; (malade) who can be operated on, operable

opéra-comique, pl **opéras-comiques** NM opéra comique (opera with spoken dialogue)

opérande [operɑ̃d] NM Ordinat operand

opérant [operɑ̃] ADJ effective; **les mesures ont été opérantes** the measures (taken) were effective

opérateur, -trice [operatœr, -tris] N (personne) (machine) operator; Typ machine setter; Journ copytaker; Fin trader; Tél telecommunications company; Cin cameraman, f camerawoman
NM **1** Math operator **2** (d'une machine) working piece
▸▸ TV, Cin **o. banc-titre** rostrum cameraman, f rostrum camerawoman; Ordinat **o. booléen** Boolean operator; Fin **o. boursier** stock-exchange dealer; Ordinat **o. de comparaison** comparator; Bourse **o. en couverture** hedger; Ordinat **o. logique** logical operator; TV, Cin **o. magnétoscope** video-

tape operator, VT operator; TV, Cin **o. de prise de vue** camera operator; **o. de radio** radio operator; Ordinat **o. relationnel** relational operator; Ordinat **o. de saisie** keyboard operator, keyboarder; TV, Cin **o. steadicam** steadicam operator; Ordinat **o. système** systems operator, SYSOP; Com **o. de transport multimodal** multi-modal operator; **o. vidéo** video operator, VT operator; TV, Cin **o. de la vision** video control operator

opération [operasjɔ̃] NF **1** Chir **o. (chirurgicale)** operation; **subir une o.** to have or undergo an operation; **salle d'o.** operating theatre or Am room
2 Math, Mil, Ordinat operation; Com, Fin, Banque transaction; **o. de change** exchange transaction; **o. financière** financial transaction; **o. imposable** taxable transaction; **opérations militaires** military operations; **o. de police** police operation; **o. publicitaire** advertising campaign; Fin **opérations fermes** firm transactions; Scol **j'ai des opérations à faire pour demain** I've some sums to do for tomorrow
3 (démarche) operation, process; **par l'o. du Saint-Esprit** by the working of the Holy Ghost; Fig Fam by magic
▸▸ Bourse **o. blanche** break-even transaction; **opérations de Bourse** Stock Exchange dealings or business or transactions; Banque **opérations de caisse** counter transactions; Compta **o. en capital** capital transaction; Méd **o. à chaud** emergency operation (for appendicitis etc); Compta **o. de clearing** clearing transaction; Chir **o. à cœur ouvert** open-heart surgery; Com **opérations en commun** joint ventures; **la police a effectué une o. coup de poing contre les revendeurs de drogue du quartier** the police launched a crackdown on drug pushers in the area; **'o. coup de poing sur les chaînes hi-fi'** 'hi-fi prices slashed'; Compta **o. courante** normal business transaction; Compta **opérations courantes** ordinary activities; Bourse **opérations de couverture** hedging; **o. escargot** go-slow or Am slow-down by lorry/bus/car drivers; Bourse **o. de journée** day trade; Bourse **o. jumbo** jumbo trade; Ordinat **o. 'si-alors'** if-then operation; Bourse **opérations à terme** futures trading

opérationnel, -elle [operasjɔnɛl] ADJ operational

opératoire [operatwar] ADJ Chir (procédure) operating; **médecine o.** surgery; **choc o.** post-operative shock

opercule [operkyl] NM Tech cover, lid, cap; Biol (d'un poisson, d'un mollusque) operculum; Naut **o. de hublot** deadlight

operculé [operkyle] ADJ Biol operculate(d)

opéré, -ée [opere] N patient (who has/had had an operation)

opérer [opere] (j'opère; j'opérerai) VT **1** (accomplir, faire) (réforme) to carry out; (multiplication), Chimie (synthèse) to perform; **o. une retraite** to (effect a) retreat; **o. un sondage** Tech to sink a borehole; (d'opinion) to carry out or conduct an opinion poll; Banque **o. un virement** to make a transfer **2** Chir to operate on; **être opéré de l'appendicite** to be operated on for appendicitis, to have an operation for appendicitis; **o. qn des amygdales** to take sb's tonsils out; **se faire o.** to have or undergo an operation; **se faire o. des amygdales** to have one's tonsils taken out; **tu t'es déjà fait o.?** have you been operated on or had an operation before?
VI (d'un médicament) to take effect, to work; **laisser o. la nature** to let nature take its course; **laissons les choses o. par elles-mêmes** let's allow things to take their own course; **son éloquence/charme opéra sur la foule** his eloquence/charm had an effect on

or worked on the crowd; **la façon dont les cambrioleurs ont opéré** the way the burglars went to work; **je ne sais pas comment il opère en de telles circonstances** I don't know how he proceeds in such circumstances ▶ **VPR s'opérer** *(d'un changement, d'une transformation)* to come about, to take place; **un changement complet s'est opéré dans sa vie** there's been a complete change in his life, his life has changed completely

opérette [ɔperɛt] **NF** operetta; **chanteuse d'o.** operetta singer; *Fig* **héros d'o.** cardboard *or* two-dimensional hero

ophidien, -ienne [ɔfidjɛ̃, -jɛn] **ADJ, NM** ophidian

ophite [ɔfit] **NM** *Minér* ophite, serpentine

ophrys [ɔfris] **NM** *Bot* ophrys; **o. abeille** bee orchid; **o. araignée** spider orchid

ophtalmie [ɔftalmi] **NF** *Méd* ophthalmia; **o. des neiges** snow blindness

ophtalmique [ɔftalmik] **ADJ** *Méd* ophthalmic

ophtalmo [ɔftalmo] **N** *Méd Fam* ophthalmologist

ophtalmologie [ɔftalmɔlɔʒi] **NF** *Méd* ophthalmology

ophtalmologiste [ɔftalmɔlɔʒist], **ophtalmologue** [ɔftalmɔlɔg] **N** *Méd* ophthalmologist

ophtalmoscope [ɔftalmɔskɔp] **NM** *Méd* ophthalmoscope

opiacé [ɔpjase] *Pharm* **ADJ** containing opium, opiate ▶ **NM** opiate

opiner [ɔpine] **VI** **o. pour/contre qch** to come down in favour of/against sth; **o. du chef** *ou* **de la tête** *ou* **du bonnet** to nod (one's) assent, to nod in agreement

opiniâtre [ɔpinjɑtr] **ADJ** *(tenace) (personne)* obstinate, stubborn; *(toux)* stubborn, persistent; *(opposition)* stubborn, unyielding; *(résistance)* stubborn, dogged

opiniâtrement [ɔpinjɑtrəmɑ̃] **ADV** obstinately, stubbornly; *(résister)* stubbornly, doggedly

opiniâtreté [ɔpinjɑtrəte] **NF** *Vieilli (obstination)* obstinacy, stubbornness; *(persévérance)* perseverance, determination

opinion [ɔpinjɔ̃] **NF** opinion (**de** of; **sur** about, on); **opinions politiques/religieuses** political/religious opinions *or* views; **liberté d'o.** freedom of thought *or* opinion; **journal d'o.** = political weekly/monthly (with a particular stance); **créer un mouvement d'o.** to create a groundswell of opinion; **sondage d'o.** opinion poll; **se faire une o. sur qch** to make up one's mind about sth, to form an opinion about sth; **mon o. est faite** I've made up my mind; **émettre** *ou* **exprimer une o.** to express an opinion; **sans o.** *(dans un sondage)* don't know; **les opinions sont partagées** opinion is divided; **partager l'o. de qn** to agree with sb, to share sb's opinion; **partager les opinions de qn** to share sb's opinions *or* views, to think the same way as sb; **avoir le courage de ses opinions** to have the courage of one's convictions; **amener qn à son o.** to bring sb round to one's way of thinking; **avoir bonne/mauvaise o. de qn/qch** to have a good/bad opinion of sb/sth; **donner bonne o. de soi** to make a good impression ▸▸ **o. publique** public opinion

opiomane [ɔpjɔman] **N** opium addict

opium [ɔpjɔm] **NM** opium; *Fig* **la religion est l'o. du peuple** religion is the opium of the people; *Hist* **guerre de l'o.** opium war

opossum [ɔpɔsɔm] **NM** opossum

opportun [ɔpɔrtœ̃] **ADJ** *(arrivée)* timely, opportune, well-timed; *(moment, jour)* right; **arriver au moment o.** to come at the right time *or* an opportune moment

opportunément [ɔpɔrtynemɑ̃] **ADV** at the right time, opportunely

opportunisme [ɔpɔrtynism] **NM** opportunism

opportuniste [ɔpɔrtynist] **ADJ** opportunist; *(maladie)* opportunistic ▶ **N** opportunist

opportunité [ɔpɔrtynite] **NF** *(d'une arrivée)* timeliness, *Fml* opportuneness; *(d'un projet, d'une décision)* advisability; **o. commerciale** market opportunity; **o. mercatique** marketing opportunity

opposable [ɔpozabl] **ADJ** opposable (**à** to); **rien n'est o. à ses arguments** there is no answer to his arguments, nothing can be said against his arguments

opposant, -ante [ɔpozɑ̃, -ɑ̃t] **ADJ** *(minorité)* opposing ▶ **N** opponent (**à** of); *Pol* member of the Opposition

opposé [ɔpoze] **ADJ 1** *(armées, caractères etc)* opposing; *(côtés, rivage, direction)* opposite; *(intérêts, conseil)* conflicting; **angles opposés par le sommet** vertically opposite angles; **leurs opinions sont diamétralement opposées** their views are poles apart *or* diametrically opposed; **elle est plutôt artiste, lui est diamétralement o.** she is rather artistic, he is the exact opposite; **tons opposés** contrasting colours **2** **être o. à une mesure** to oppose *or* be opposed to *or* be against a measure; **je suis o. à ce qu'une centrale soit construite dans cette région** I'm opposed to *or* I'm against a power station being built in this area ▶ **NM 1** *(contraire)* **l'o.** the opposite, the reverse; **à l'o.** *(dans l'espace)* opposite, on the other side; *Fig* on the other hand; **le deuxième film de ce réalisateur est vraiment l'o. du premier** the director's second film is the complete opposite of *or* is in complete contrast to his first; **mon avis est à l'o. du sien** my opinion is the opposite of his; **à l'o. de ce que nous attendions** contrary to expectation *or* to what we expected; **cela va à l'o. de ce que l'on m'avait promis/de notre politique** that goes against what I was promised/our policy **2 à la gare est à l'o.** the station is in the opposite direction; **à l'o. de la gare** opposite the station

opposer [ɔpoze] **VT** *(deux adversaires)* to bring into conflict (with each other); **o. des arguments valables à une théorie** to put forward valid arguments against a theory; **je n'ai rien à o. à ce raisonnement** I cannot counter this argument; **que peut-il t'o.?** what objection can he have to that?, what can he say against that?; **o. une résistance vigoureuse** to put up *or* offer vigorous resistance, *Fam* to resist tooth and nail; **o. un farouche refus à qch** to be fiercely opposed to sth; **o. son veto** to exercise one's veto; **o. des idées/théories l'une à l'autre** to contrast ideas/theories; **o. Mozart à Debussy** to contrast Mozart with Debussy; **cette course oppose les meilleurs athlètes de toute l'Europe** this race brings together Europe's finest athletes; **ce match opposera le joueur français au joueur américain** this match will pit the French player against the American; **la finale opposera la France à l'Italie** France will meet Italy *or* come up against Italy in the final ▶ **VPR s'opposer** **s'o. à qch** to oppose sth, to be opposed to sth, to be against sth; **nous nous opposons à ce que la centrale soit construite** we oppose the building of the power station, we are opposed to *or* are against the power station being built; **nous nous opposons à ce qu'il arrête ses études** we are

against *or* we are opposed to the idea of him giving up his studies; **il n'y a pas de loi qui s'y oppose** there is no law against it; **rien ne s'oppose à votre succès** nothing stands between you and success; **rien ne s'oppose à votre projet** nothing stands in the way of your plan; **rien ne s'oppose à ce que vous fassiez ce que vous souhaitez** there's nothing to stop you doing what you want to; **les meilleurs joueurs d'échecs s'opposent dans ce tournoi** this tournament pits the best chess players against one another, the best chess players come up against each other in this tournament

opposite [ɔpozit] **NM à l'o. de** opposite, facing; *Fig* opposed to

opposition [ɔpozisjɔ̃] **NF 1** *(résistance)* opposition; *Pol* **l'o.** the Opposition; **faire o. à un chèque** to stop a cheque, to stop payment of a cheque; **à chaque fois qu'on parle d'un nouveau projet, il fait de l'o.** every time there is talk of a new plan, he is opposed to it *or* against it **2** *Jur* caveat; **o. sur titre** attachment against securities; **jugement susceptible d'o.** judgment liable to stay of execution **3** *(contraste)* contrast; **c'est en o. totale avec les principes qu'il expose dans ses livres** it is in complete contrast to *or* is totally at odds with *or* totally contradicts the principles that he puts forward in his books; **tout cela est en o. totale avec ce que je pense** all that is the complete opposite of what I think; **par o. à qch** as opposed to sth; **couleurs en o.** contrasting colours **4** *Astron (des planètes)* opposition

oppositionnel, -elle [ɔpozisjɔnɛl] *Pol* **ADJ** oppositional, opposition ▶ **N** oppositionist

oppressant [ɔpresɑ̃] **ADJ** *(chaleur, sentiment)* oppressive

oppresser [ɔprese] **VT 1** *(d'une situation, d'une atmosphère etc)* to oppress **2** *(de problèmes, de responsabilités)* to weigh down **3** *Litt* = **opprimer**

> Do not confuse with **opprimer**.

oppresseur [ɔpresœr] **NM** oppressor ▶ **ADJ M** oppressive

oppressif, -ive [ɔpresif, -iv] **ADJ** *(gouvernement, autorité etc)* oppressive

oppression [ɔpresjɔ̃] **NF 1** *(d'un peuple)* oppression **2** *Méd* **o. de la poitrine** tightness of the chest, difficulty in breathing

opprimé [ɔprime] **ADJ** oppressed, downtrodden ▶ **NMPL les opprimés** the oppressed

opprimer [ɔprime] **VT** *(peuple, nation)* to oppress; *(liberté)* to suppress

> Do not confuse with **oppresser**.

opprobre [ɔprɔbr] **NM** *Litt* opprobrium; **jeter l'o. sur qn** to cast opprobrium on sb; **accabler** *ou* **couvrir qn d'o.** to heap opprobrium on sb

optatif, -ive [ɔptatif, -iv] **ADJ, NM** *Ling* optative

opter [ɔpte] **VI** **o. entre deux choses** to choose between two things; **o. pour qch** to opt for sth

opticien, -ienne [ɔptisjɛ̃, -jɛn] **N** optician

optimal, -ale, -aux, -ales [ɔptimal, -o] **ADJ** optimum, optimal

optimalisation [ɔptimalizasjɔ̃] **NF** optimization; *Fin* **o. des profits** profit optimization

optimisation [ɔptimizasjɔ̃] **NF** *aussi Ordinat* optimization

optimiser [ɔptimize] **VT** *Ordinat, Mktg etc* to optimize

optimiseur [ɔptimizœr] **NM** *Ordinat* optimizer

optimisme [ɔptimism] NM optimism; **avec o.** optimistically

optimiste [ɔptimist] ADJ optimistic; **sois un peu o.** try to be optimistic, try to look on the bright side; **nous ne sommes pas très optimistes quant à la guérison de ce malade** we're not very optimistic about the patient's chances of recovery or that the patient will recover
N optimist

optimum [ɔptimɔm], pl **optimums,** parfois **optima** [ɔptima] ADJ (conditions) optimum; **la température o. ne dépasse pas 5 degrés** the optimum temperature does not exceed 5 degrees
NM optimum

option [ɔpsjɔ̃] NF option, choice (**de** of; **entre** between); **prendre une o. sur qch** to take (out) an option on sth; **le flash est en o.** the flash is optional or is an optional extra; Bourse **jour d'o.** option day; Scol **matières à o.** optional or elective subjects; **il avait le latin en o. au baccalauréat** he took Latin as an option an optional subject or an elective subject for the baccalauréat

▸▸ Bourse **o. d'achat** call (option), option to buy; Bourse **o. sur actions** options on shares; Bourse **o. américaine** American-style option; Fin **o. de change** foreign currency option; **o. cotée** traded option; **o. d'échange** swap option; Bourse **o. européenne** European-style option; Ordinat **o. d'impression** print option; Bourse **o. sur indice** index option; Ordinat **o. de menu** menu option; Bourse **o. négociable** traded option; Ordinat **o. de sauvegarde** save option; Bourse **o. de vente** put (option), option to sell; Pol **o. zéro** zero option

optionnel, -elle [ɔpsjɔnɛl] ADJ optional

optique [ɔptik] ADJ (nerf) optic; (angle) visual; (verre) optical; **télégraphie o.** visual signalling
NF **1** (science) optics; **instruments d'o.** optical instruments; **o. électronique** electron optics; **transmettre par o.** to communicate by visual signals **2** (perspective) perspective; **nous ne travaillons pas dans la même o.** we're working towards different aims; **o. du théâtre** stage perspective; Mktg **o. mercatique** marketing orientation; Mktg **o. produit** product orientation; Mktg **o. vente** sales orientation, sales philosophy **3** (d'un projecteur) optical system

optométrie [ɔptɔmetri] NF optometry

optométriste [ɔptɔmetrist] N optometrist

opulence [ɔpylɑ̃s] NF opulence, affluence; Fig (de la poitrine, des formes etc) fullness, ampleness; **nager** ou **être dans l'o.** to be rolling in money; **vivre dans l'o.** to have an opulent lifestyle, to live in opulence

opulent [ɔpylɑ̃] ADJ (mobilier, environs) opulent; (personne) opulent, wealthy, affluent; Fig (moisson, pâturage) abundant; **une poitrine opulente** an ample or full bosom

opus [ɔpys] NM opus

opuscule [ɔpyskyl] NM opuscule

OPV [ɔpeve] NF Fin (abrév **offre publique de vente**) public offer for sale

or¹ [ɔr] NM **1** (métal) gold; **or pur/fin** pure/fine gold; **la ruée vers l'or** the gold rush; **chercheur d'or** gold-prospector; Min, Fig **mine d'or** gold mine; Fig **cette boutique est une véritable mine d'or pour les collectionneurs** this shop is a real gold mine or treasure trove for collectors; **or en barre** ou **en lingots** (gold) bullion; Fig **c'est de l'or en barre** it's as safe as the Bank of England or as houses; Fin **étalon or** gold standard; **poudre d'or** gold dust; **montre en or** ou **d'or** gold watch; **bracelet doré à l'or fin** a fine gold-

(-plated) bracelet; **en or massif** (in) solid gold; **or en feuille(s)** gold leaf or foil; **feuille d'or** gold leaf; **payer qch à prix d'or** to pay a fortune for sth; **revendre qch à prix d'or** to resell sth for a fortune; **affaire en or** (achat) excellent bargain; (commerce, combine) lucrative line of business; Fam **j'ai une femme en or** I've a wonderful wife; **il/ça vaut son pesant d'or** he's worth his/it's worth its weight in gold; **pour tout l'or du monde** for all the money in the world, for all the tea in China; **l'âge d'or** the golden age; **cœur d'or** heart of gold; **parler d'or** to speak words of wisdom; **livre d'or** (official) visitors' book; **rouler sur l'or, être (tout) cousu d'or** to be rolling in money, to have money coming out of one's ears; **il ne roule pas sur l'or** he isn't exactly rolling in it; Prov **tout ce qui brille n'est pas or** all that glitters or glistens is not gold; **le silence est d'or** silence is golden

2 (couleur) gold; Hér or; **vieil or** old gold; **murs/voiture vieil or** old gold walls/car; **chevelure d'or** golden hair

▸▸ **or blanc** ou **gris** white gold; **or noir** black gold, oil; **or rouge** red gold

or² CONJ now; (pour conclure) well; **or, pour revenir à ce que nous disions** now, to come back to what we were saying; **or ..., donc ...** now ..., therefore ...; **avant de la lire, je pensais que le livre était bon – or, il ne l'était pas** before reading it, I thought the book was good – well, it wasn't; **il n'achète jamais de chocolats, or ...** he never buys chocolates, but ...

oracle [ɔrakl] NM oracle; **parler d'un ton d'o.** to speak with assurance

orage [ɔraʒ] NM (thunder)storm; **temps d'o.** thundery or stormy weather; **le temps est à l'o.** there's thunder in the air, there's a storm brewing; Fig **l'atmosphère est à l'o. au bureau** there's trouble or a storm brewing in the office; **il va faire de l'o., il y a de l'o. dans l'air** there's a storm brewing; Fig there's trouble or a storm brewing, there's trouble in the air; Fig **laisser passer l'o.** to let the storm blow over

▸▸ **o. magnétique** magnetic storm

orageusement [ɔraʒøzmɑ̃] ADV stormily

orageux, -euse [ɔraʒø, -øz] ADJ (temps) thundery, stormy; (saison, mer) stormy; Fig (vie) stormy, tempestuous; (discussion) stormy, heated

oraison [ɔrɛzɔ̃] NF prayer; **faire** ou **dire** ou **réciter une o.** to say a prayer; **o. funèbre** funeral oration

oral, -ale, -aux, -ales [ɔral, -o] ADJ (tradition, enseignement, examen) oral; (déposition, communication) oral, verbal; Anat (cavité) oral; **par voie orale** orally; Psy **stade o.** oral stage
NM oral examination; surtout Univ oral or viva voce examination, Fam oral, viva

oralement [ɔralmɑ̃] ADV orally

orange [ɔrɑ̃ʒ] NF (fruit) orange; **peau d'o.** orange peel; Fig orange-peel skin
NM (couleur) orange; Aut **passer à l'o.** to go through (the lights) on amber; **le feu était à l'o.** the lights were at amber
ADJ INV orange; Aut **feu o.** amber light; **carte o.** (pour les transports parisiens) = combined monthly pass for the underground, bus and suburban train

▸▸ **o. amère** bitter orange, Seville orange; **o. givrée** orange sorbet; **o. pressée** freshly-squeezed orange juice; **o. sanguine** blood orange

orangé [ɔrɑ̃ʒe] ADJ orange-coloured or Am -colored
NM orange colour or Am color

orangeade [ɔrɑ̃ʒad] NF orangeade

oranger [ɔrɑ̃ʒe] NM orange tree; **fleur d'o.**

orange blossom; **eau de fleur d'o.** orange-flower water

orangeraie [ɔrɑ̃ʒrɛ] NF orange grove

orangerie [ɔrɑ̃ʒri] NF orangery

orangiste [ɔrɑ̃ʒist] N **1** (en Irlande du Nord) Orangeman, f Orangewoman **2** Hist Orangist
ADJ Orange

orang-outan(g) [ɔrɑ̃utɑ̃], pl **orangs-outan(g)s** NM orang-outang, orang-utan

orateur, -trice [ɔratœr, -tris] N orator; (dans un dîner) speaker

oratoire¹ [ɔratwar] ADJ oratorical; **l'art o.** (the art of) oratory, public speaking; **il a pris des précautions oratoires** he chose his words carefully; **joutes oratoires** verbal sparring matches

oratoire² NM Rel **1** (chapelle) oratory, chapel for private prayer **2** **l'O.** the Oratory

oratorio [ɔratɔrjo] NM Mus oratorio

orbe¹ [ɔrb] NM orb

orbe² ADJ **mur o.** blind wall

orbitaire [ɔrbitɛr] ADJ Anat orbital

orbital, -ale, -aux, -ales [ɔrbital, -o] ADJ Astron orbital

orbite [ɔrbit] NF **1** (d'une planète, d'un vaisseau spatial, d'un électron) orbit; **en** ou **sur o.** in orbit; **mettre** ou **placer un satellite en** ou **sur o.** to put a satellite into orbit **2** (sphère d'influence) orbit, (sphere of) influence **3** Anat (de l'œil) socket, orbit

orbiter [ɔrbite] VI to orbit

Orcades [ɔrkad] NFPL **les O.** the Orkneys, the Orkney Islands

orchestral, -ale, -aux, -ales [ɔrkestral, -o] ADJ orchestral

orchestration [ɔrkestrasjɔ̃] NF **1** Mus orchestration; **faire une nouvelle o. d'un morceau** to re-orchestrate a piece **2** Fig (d'une campagne électorale ou commerciale) orchestration, organization

orchestre [ɔrkestr] NM Mus orchestra; **diriger un o.** to conduct an orchestra; **chef d'o.** conductor; **o. de jazz** jazz band; **o. de chambre** chamber orchestra; Théâtre **(fauteuil d')o.** seat in the stalls or Am orchestra; **deux fauteuils d'o., deux orchestres** two stalls, two stall or Am orchestra seats ▸VOIR GRAMMAIRE A11

orchestrer [ɔrkestre] VT Mus to orchestrate; Fig (organiser) (campagne électorale ou commerciale etc) to orchestrate, to organize

orchidée [ɔrkide] NF orchid

ordalie [ɔrdali] NF Hist ordeal; **o. par l'eau/le feu** ordeal by water/fire

ordinaire [ɔrdinɛr] ADJ (habituel) ordinary, usual, normal; **vêtements ordinaires** ordinary or everyday clothes; **vin o.** table or Am jug wine; **peu** ou **pas o.** unusual, uncommon, out of the ordinary; **gens ordinaires** ordinary people; **elle est vraiment o.** she's so ordinary; Fam **voilà une chose qui n'est pas o.!** that's not something you see every day!; Math **fractions ordinaires** vulgar fractions; Fin **actions ordinaires** ordinary shares, Am common stock; **votre fournisseur o.** your normal or regular or usual supplier; **votre médicin o.** your usual doctor; **médecin o. du roi** physician in ordinary to the king; **évêque o.** diocesan bishop; **de taille o.** ordinary-sized, normal-sized, Am regular-sized; (personne) of average height; **vin très o.** very ordinary wine; **une vie très o.** a very ordinary or run-of-the-mill life

NM **1** (habitude) **d'o., à l'o.** usually, as a rule; **plus en forme qu'à l'o.** fitter than usual; **comme à l'o., comme d'o.** as usual **2** (moyenne) **cela sort de l'o.** it's unusual, it's out of the ordinary; **beauté/intelligence qui sort de l'o.** exceptional beauty/intelligence **3** *(au restaurant)* standard fare; *Mil* (company) mess; **auberge où l'o. est excellent** inn where the food is excellent; *Mil* **fonds d'o.** mess fund **4** *Cathol* **l'o. de la messe** the ordinary of the Mass

ordinairement [ɔrdinɛrmã] ADVordinarily, usually, as a rule

ordinal, -ale, -aux, -ales [ɔrdinal, -o] ADJ ordinal SEE GRAMMAR A76; B59

ordinateur [ɔrdinatœr] NM **1** *(machine)* computer; **o. autonome** stand alone (computer); **o. bloc-notes** notebook (computer); *Aut* **o. de bord** trip computer; **o. de bureau** business computer, desktop (computer); **o. central** mainframe (computer); **o. domestique** home computer; **o. à écran tactile** touch-screen computer; **o. familial** family computer; **o. final** front-end processor; **o. frontal** front end computer *or* processor, front end; **o. individuel** personal computer; **o. multimédia** multimedia computer; **o. numérique** digital computer; **o. de poche** palmtop (computer), pocket computer; **o. portable** *ou* **portatif** portable (computer), laptop (computer); **o. de réseau** network computer; **o. sans clavier** keyboardless computer; **o. serveur** host computer, server; **o. de table** desktop (PC) **2** *Rel* ordainer

ordination [ɔrdinasjõ] NF *Rel* ordination

ordinogramme [ɔrdinɔgram] NM flow chart

ordonnance [ɔrdɔnãs] NF **1** *(disposition)* *(d'un bâtiment)* layout, (general) arrangement; *(d'un tableau)* organization **2** *(ordre)* order; *Jur* order, ruling; **o. d'amnistie** amnesty order; *Fin* **o. de paiement** order *or* warrant for payment, order to pay **3** *Méd* prescription; **délivré seulement sur o.** available only on prescription **4** *Mil* orderly; **bottes d'o.** standard issue boots; **revolver d'o.** service revolver; **officier d'o.** aide-de-camp; *Naut* flag lieutenant

ordonnancement [ɔrdɔnãsmã] NM **1** *Fin* order to pay **2** *Ind* *(de production)* scheduling

ordonnancer [ɔrdɔnãse] VT *(j'ordonnançai(s); n. ordonnançons)* *Fin* to authorize; **o. un paiement** to order *or* authorize a payment

ordonnancier [ɔrdɔnãsje] NM *(du pharmacien)* prescription book; *(du médecin)* prescription pad

ordonnateur, -trice [ɔrdɔnatœr, -tris] N **1** organizer; *(d'un spectacle)* master of ceremonies; **o. des pompes funèbres** funeral director *(at the funeral itself)* **2** *Admin* person authorized to pass accounts; *Fin* payer; *Bourse* giver *or* placer of an/the order

ordonné, -ée [ɔrdɔne] ADJ **1** *(vie, rangement)* orderly, (well-) ordered; *Ordinat* **traitement non o.** random processing **2** *(personne)* tidy, orderly

NF *Math* **ordonnée** ordinate; **axe des ordonnées** Y-axis

ordonner [ɔrdɔne] VT **1** *(mettre de l'ordre dans)* to organize, to arrange; *Math* to arrange in order; **il faut davantage o. votre argumentation** you need to organize your arguments a bit more, you need to get more order into your arguments **2** *(commander)* to order; **o. à qn de faire qch** to order sb to do sth; **o. à qn de se taire** to tell sb to be quiet; **o. une grève** to call a strike; **o. une enquête** to order an enquiry; *Méd* **o. un remède à qn** to prescribe a remedy for sb **3** *Jur* *(statuer)* to ordain, to rule; *Rel* **o. qn prêtre** to ordain sb

ORDRE [ɔrdr] NM **1** *(organisation)* order; **o. alphabétique/chronologique** alphabetical/chronological order; **par o. alphabétique** in alphabetical order; **o. croissant/décroissant** ascending/descending order; **rangé par o.**

de grandeur arranged in order of size; **procéder par o.** to do things in order; *Théâtre* **distribution par o. d'entrée en scène** *ou Cin, TV* **par o. d'apparition à l'écran** cast in order of appearance; **numéro d'o.** serial number; **l'o. de classement des livres/dossiers est le suivant** books/files are arranged as follows; *Fig* **c'est dans l'o. des choses** it's in the nature of things; **avec o.** *(travailler)* methodically; **manque d'o.** untidiness; **manquer d'o.** to be untidy; **en bon o.** *(de façon réglée)* in an orderly manner; *(comme cela doit être)* in good order; **mettre bon o. à qch** to sort sth out; **homme d'o.** orderly man; *(qui est pour l'ordre public)* law-and-order man; **avoir de l'o.** *(ranger ses affaires)* to be tidy; *(être méthodique)* to be methodical; **(re)mettre de l'o. dans sa vie** to put *or* get one's life (back) in order; **(re)mettre de l'o. dans ses souvenirs** to get one's memories into some kind of order; **mettre de l'o. dans sa chambre, mettre sa chambre en o.** to tidy (up) one's room; **laisser une maison en o.** to leave a house tidy; **mettre de l'o. dans ses affaires, mettre ses affaires en o.** *(arranger, régler)* to put one's affairs in order, to settle one's affairs; *Fig* to set one's house in order; **tout est en o.** everything is in order; **en o. de marche** *(machine etc)* in working order

2 *(discipline)* order; **assurer l'o.** to preserve (law and) order; **maintenir l'o.** to maintain order; **rétablir l'o.** to restore order; **les forces de l'o.** the police, the forces of law and order *(especially at demonstration etc)*; **rappeler qn à l'o.** to call sb to order; **tout est rentré dans l'o.** everything has returned to normal; *(après une émeute etc)* order has been restored; **idées qui renversent l'o. établi** ideas that upset the established order (of things); **retour à l'o. moral** return to traditional moral values

3 *(catégorie)*, *Biol, Archit* order; **o. des carnivores** order of carnivores; **ordres grecs** classical orders; *Hist* **les trois ordres (de l'État)** the three orders *or* classes (of the State); **de premier o.** first-class, first-rate; **tireur de premier o.** crack shot; **un crétin de premier o.** a first-class cretin; **hôtel de troisième o.** third-rate hotel; **renseignements/idées d'o. général** general information/ideas; **d'o. privé** of a private nature; **dans un tout autre o. d'idées** in a quite different connection; **du même o.** of the same order; **de l'o. de dix tonnes** in the order *or* region of ten tonnes

4 *(communauté)* order; **o. religieux** religious *or* monastic order; *Rel* **les ordres** holy orders; **entrer dans les ordres** to take holy orders

5 *(acte d'autorité)* order; *Mil* order, command; **o. d'exécution** death warrant; *Ind etc* instruction to proceed; **donner l'o. à qn de faire qch** to order sb to do sth; **donner des ordres à qn** to give sb orders, to order sb about; **recevoir des ordres** to be given orders; **je n'ai d'ordres à recevoir de personne** I don't take orders from anyone; **je ne reçois** *ou* **prends mes ordres que de mes supérieurs** I only take orders from my superiors; **se mettre aux ordres de qn** to put oneself at sb's disposal; **être aux ordres de qn** to be at sb's disposal; **je ne suis pas à tes ordres!** I don't take orders from you!; **à vos ordres, mon général!** yes sir!; *Hum* **à vos ordres!** yes sir!; **c'est un o.!** that's an order!; **par o.** *ou* **sur l'o. de qn** on the order of sb; **jusqu'à nouvel o.** until further notice; *(pour le moment)* for the time being; **sauf o. contraire** unless otherwise stated; **mot d'o.** watchword

6 *Fin, Com* order; **à l'o. de ...** payable to (the order of) ...; **payez à l'o. de J. Martin** pay to the order of J. Martin; **faites votre chèque à l'o. de ...** make your cheque out to ..., make your cheque payable to ...; **c'est à quel o.?**

who should I make it out to?, who should I make it payable to?; **billet à o.** bill of exchange payable to order

▸▸ **o. d'achat** *Com* purchase order; *Bourse* buy order; *Mil* **o. d'appel (sous les drapeaux)** call-up papers, *Am* draft notice; **o. des avocats** Bar Association; *Mil* **o. de bataille** battle order *or* array; *Bourse* **o. de Bourse** Stock Exchange order; **o. de chevalerie** order of knighthood; *Jur* **o. de comparaître** summons; *Fin* **o. au comptant** cash order; *Bourse* **o. conditionnel** contingent order; *Bourse* **o. environ** discretionary order; *Fin* **o. ferme** firm order; **O. de la Jarretière** Order of the Garter; **o. du jour** *(du comité etc)* agenda; *Mil* general orders, order of the day; *Mil* **cité à l'o. du jour** mentioned in dispatches; *Fig* **le mariage de la princesse est à l'o. du jour** the princess's marriage is very much in the news; **o. de la Légion d'honneur** Order of the Legion of Honour; *Bourse* **o. lié** straddle; **l'o. des médecins** *Br* ≃ the British Medical Association, *Am* ≃ the American Medical Association; *Bourse* **o. au mieux** market order; *Bourse* **o. de négociation** trading order; *Fin* **o. de paiement** payment order; *Banque* **o. permanent** standing order; *Banque* **o. de prélèvement automatique** direct debit mandate; **o. public** law and order, public order; **atteinte à l'o. public** breach of the peace; **troubler l'o. public** to cause a breach of the peace; *Bourse* **o. à révocation** good-till-cancelled order; *Bourse* **o. stop à cours limité** stop-limit order; *Fin* **o. à terme** futures order; *Bourse* **o. 'tout ou rien'** all-or-none order; **o. de transfert permanent** banker's order, *Br* standing order; **o. de vente** order to sell; *Fin* **o. de virement** transfer order

ordré [ɔrdre] ADJ *Suisse (ordonné)* tidy, orderly, neat

ordure [ɔrdyr] NF **1** *(saleté)* dirt, filth, muck; **faire ses ordures sur le trottoir** *(d'un chien)* to make a mess on the pavement **2** *(objets)* **ordures** refuse, *Br* rubbish, *Am* garbage; **boîte à ordures** dustbin, *Am* garbage can *or* trash can; **jeter** *ou* **mettre qch aux ordures** to throw sth in the dustbin *or Am* garbage *or* trash can; **c'est bon à mettre aux ordures** it's fit for the dustbin *or Am* garbage can *or Am* the trash **3** *(dans un échange)* filth, dirt, smut; **dire/écrire des ordures** to talk/write filth *or* dirt *or* smut; *Litt* **se vautrer dans l'o.** to wallow in filth **4** *Fig Péj très Fam* **il exploite tout le monde, c'est vraiment une o.** he exploits everybody, he's a real shit *or* bastard

▸▸ **ordures ménagères** household refuse *or Br* rubbish *or Am* garbage

ordurier, -ière [ɔrdyrje, -jɛr] ADJ *(livre, chanson, langage)* filthy, dirty, smutty

orée [ɔre] NF **à l'o. de la forêt/du bois** on the edge of the forest/wood

oreillard [ɔrejar] NM **1** *Zool* long-eared bat **2** *(d'un fauteuil)* wing

oreille [ɔrɛj] NF **1** *(d'une personne, d'un animal)* ear; **il a les oreilles décollées** his ears stick out, he has protruding ears; *Fam* **avoir les oreilles en feuilles de chou** to have huge protruding ears; **avoir mal à l'o./aux oreilles** to have earache; **chien aux oreilles courtes/longues** short-eared/long-eared dog; **mettre** *ou* **porter son chapeau sur l'o.** to wear one's hat over one ear; *Fig* **baisser l'o., avoir l'o. basse** to be crestfallen; **il partit l'o. basse** he went off with his tail between his legs; **coucher les oreilles** *(d'un cheval)* to set *or* lay its ears back; **tirer les oreilles à qn** to pull *or* tweak sb's ears; *Fig* to give sb a telling off; *Fig* **tu vas te faire tirer les oreilles** you'll get told off, you'll get a telling off; *Fam* **il s'est (bien) fait tirer l'o.** he took a lot of coaxing; *Fam* **il ne s'est pas fait tirer l'o.** he didn't have to be asked twice; *Fig* **montrer le bout de l'o.**

to show one's true colours; **rougir jusqu'aux oreilles** to go as red as a beetroot; **n'écouter que d'une o.**, **écouter d'une o. distraite** to listen with half an ear; *Fam* **ça lui entre par une o. et ça sort par l'autre** it goes in one ear and out the other; **dire** *ou* **souffler qch à l'o. de qn** *ou* **dans le creux de l'o. de qn** to whisper sth in sb's ear; **dresser** *ou* **tendre l'o.** to prick up one's ears; **être tout oreilles** to be all ears; **prêter l'o.** to lend an ear; **je n'en crois pas mes oreilles** I can't believe my ears *or* what I'm hearing; **faire la sourde o. (à qch)** to turn a deaf ear (to sth); *Fig* **il doit avoir les oreilles qui sifflent** his ears must be burning; **ce n'est pas tombé dans l'o. d'un sourd** it did not fall on deaf ears; **il n'entend pas de cette o.-là** he is deaf in that ear; *Fig* **il ne l'entend pas de cette o.** he won't hear of it; *Fam* **(é)chauffer les oreilles à qn** to get on sb's nerves, to annoy sb; **casser les oreilles à qn** *(en faisant du bruit)* to deafen sb; *(en posant des questions ennuyeuses)* to drive sb crazy; **c'est le bouche à o. qui a fait le succès de ce film** it was word of mouth that made the film a hit; **quand ça m'est venu** *ou* **arrivé aux oreilles** when I got to hear of it; **mettre la puce à l'o. à qn** to set sb thinking, to make sb suspicious; **rebattre les oreilles à qn de qch** to go on and on to sb about sth; **être dur d'o.** to be hard of hearing; *Fig* **vous pouvez dormir sur vos deux oreilles** you can sleep easy in your bed; **avoir de l'o.** *(pour la musique)* to have a good ear, to have an ear for music; **avoir l'o. absolue** to have perfect pitch
2 *(d'un fauteuil)* wing; *(d'un plat, d'un vase)* handle; *(d'une casquette)* ear flap; **écrou à oreilles** wing *or* butterfly nut
3 *Journ* position to right/left of headline
▸▸ *Anat* **o. externe** outer ear; **o. interne** inner ear; **o. moyenne** middle ear

oreiller [ɔrɛje] NM pillow; **taie d'o.** pillowcase, pillowslip; **sur l'o.** in bed; **confidences sur l'o.** pillow talk

oreillette [ɔrɛjɛt] NF **1** *Anat (du cœur)* auricle, atrium **2** *(écouteur)* earpiece **3** **fauteuil à oreillettes** wing chair; **casquette à oreillettes** cap with ear flaps

oreillons [ɔrɛjɔ̃] NMPL *Méd* mumps VOIR GRAMMAIRE A10

Orénoque (l') [ɔrenɔk] NM the Orinoco

ores [ɔr] ADV **d'o. et déjà** already

orfèvre [ɔrfɛvr] NM *(qui travaille l'or)* goldsmith; *(qui travaille l'argent)* silversmith; *Fig* **être o. en la matière** to be an expert in the matter

orfèvrerie [ɔrfɛvrəri] NF *(métier) (de l'or)* goldsmith's trade; *(de l'argent)* silversmith's trade; *(magasin) (d'objets d'or)* goldsmith's shop *or Am* store; *(d'objets d'argent)* silversmith's shop *or Am* store

orfraie [ɔrfrɛ] NF *Orn* sea eagle; *Fam* **pousser des cris d'o.** to shriek at the top of one's voice

organdi [ɔrgɑ̃di] NM *Tex* organdie

organe [ɔrgan] NM **1** *Physiol* organ; **les organes génitaux** the genital organs, the genitals, the genitalia **2** *(élément) (d'une machine)* part, component; **organes de transmission** transmission system; *Ordinat* **o. d'entrée** input unit; *Ordinat* **o. périphérique** peripheral device **3** *Fig (instrument)* organ; **o. de publicité** advertising agency; **o. de presse** *(publication)* organ of the press; **l'o. officiel du parti** the official organ of the party **4** *(voix)* voice; **o. mâle et sonore** manly voice; *Hum* **il a un bel o.** he has a fine voice

organigramme [ɔrganigram] NM organization chart; *Ordinat* (data) flow chart; **o. de production** production flow chart

organique [ɔrganik] ADJ *(maladie, chimie, loi)* organic

organiquement [ɔrganikmɑ̃] ADV organically

organisateur, -trice [ɔrganizatœr, -tris] ADJ organizing
N organizer; *(d'une rencontre sportive)* promoter, organizer; **o. de conférences** *ou* **de congrès** conference organizer; **o. de voyages** tour operator

organisation [ɔrganizasjɔ̃] NF **1** *(planification)* organization; **qualités d'o.** organizing *or* organizational ability; *Ordinat* **o. des données** data organization **2** *(groupement)* organization; **o. à but non lucratif** non profit-making organization, *Am* not-for-profit organization; **o. politique/syndicale** political/trade-union organization **3** *Biol (du corps humain)* structure
▸▸ **O. de l'alimentation et l'agriculture** Food and Agriculture Organization; *Hist* **O. de l'armée secrète** Secret Army Organization *(right-wing group opposed to Algerian independence)*; **O. de l'aviation civile internationale** International Civil Aviation Authority; **O. de coopération et de développement économique** Organization for Economic Cooperation and Development; **o. humanitaire** aid agency; **O. internationale de normalisation** International Standards Organization; **O. internationale du travail** International Labour Organization; **O. de libération de la Palestine** Palestine Liberation Organization; **O. maritime internationale** International Maritime Organization; **O. mondiale de la santé** World Health Organization; **O. des Nations unies** United Nations Organization; **O. des Nations unies pour le développement industriel** United Nations Industrial Development Organization; **O. des Nations unies pour l'éducation, la science et la culture** United Nations Educational, Scientific and Cultural Organization; **O. de la navigation maritime consultative et intergouvernementale** Intergovernmental Maritime Consultative Organization; **o. non gouvernementale** non-governmental organization; **O. des pays exportateurs de pétrole** Organization of Petroleum Exporting Countries; **o. scientifique du travail** organization and methods, time and motion studies; **O. du traité de l'Atlantique Nord** North Atlantic Treaty Organization; **O. de l'unité africaine** Organization of African Unity

organisationnel, -elle [ɔrganizasjɔnɛl] ADJ organizational

organisé [ɔrganize] ADJ **1** *(planifié)* organized; **voyage o.** package tour; *Fam* **c'est du vol o.** it's a rip-off, *Br* it's daylight robbery; **il est bien o.** he is (well-)organized; **les manifestants n'étaient pas organisés** the demonstrators were not organized **2** *Biol (être)* organic

organiser [ɔrganize] VT *(réunion, affaires, fête, voyage etc)* to organize, to arrange; *(temps, emploi du temps)* to organize, to plan
VPR **s'organiser** to get organized

organiseur [ɔrganizœr] NM **o. personnel** *(logiciel)* personal organizer; **o. électronique** electronic organizer

organisme [ɔrganism] NM **1** *Biol* organism; *Anat* system; **le tabac est mauvais pour l'o.** tobacco is bad for the system; **o. génétiquement modifié** genetically modified organism **2** *(organisation)* organization, body; **o. d'aide** aid organization; **o. de contrôle** watchdog; **o. de crédit** credit institution; **o. de défense des consommateurs** consumer organization; **o. international** international organization; **o. de normalisation** standards committee; **o. professionnel** professional body; **o. de surveillance** watchdog

organiste [ɔrganist] N *Mus* organist

organoleptique [ɔrganolɛptik] ADJ organoleptic

orgasme [ɔrgasm] NM orgasm

orge [ɔrʒ] NF barley; **sucre d'o.** barley sugar
NM **o. mondé** hulled barley; **o. perlé** pearl barley

orgeat [ɔrʒa] NM **sirop d'o.** barley water

orgelet [ɔrʒəlɛ] NM *Méd* sty(e)

orgiaque [ɔrʒjak] ADJ orgiastic

orgie [ɔrʒi] NF *(sexuelle)* orgy; *(avec excès de boissons)* drunken feast; *Fig* **j'ai fait une o. de foie gras** I gorged myself on foie gras; **une o. de couleurs** a riot of colour; **une o. de lumières** a profusion of lights

orgue [ɔrg] NM *(pl souvent f)* **1** *Mus* organ; **un bel o., de belles orgues** a fine organ; **tenir l'o.** *ou* **les orgues** to be at *or* be playing the organ; **o. électrique/électronique** electric/electronic organ; **joueur d'o.** organ grinder; **point d'o.** pause; *Fig* **le point d'o. de la réunion** the climax *or* high point of the meeting **2** *Géol* **orgues de basalte** basalt columns
▸▸ **o. de Barbarie** barrel organ

orgueil [ɔrgœj] NM pride; *Péj* pride, arrogance; **péché d'o.** sin of pride; **être gonflé** *ou* **bouffi d'o.** to be puffed up *or* swollen with pride; **tirer o. de qch** to take pride in sth; **être l'o. (et la joie) de qn** to be sb's pride and joy; **par o.** out of pride; **par o., il ne veut pas admettre son erreur** he is too proud to admit his error

orgueilleusement [ɔrgœjøzmɑ̃] ADV proudly; *Péj* proudly, arrogantly

orgueilleux, -euse [ɔrgœjø, -øz] ADJ proud; *Péj* proud, arrogant
N proud person; *Péj* arrogant person

oriel [ɔrjɛl] NM oriel (window), bay window

orient [ɔrjɑ̃] NM **1** *(est)* east, *Litt* orient; **l'O.** the East, the Orient; **en O.** in the East; **pays/peuples d'O.** Oriental nations/peoples; **tapis d'O.** oriental carpet; *Hist* **l'Empire d'O.** the Eastern (Roman) Empire **2** *(dans la franc-maçonnerie)* **Grand-O.** Grand Lodge

orientable [ɔrjɑ̃tabl] ADJ *(grue)* swivelling; *(lampe, antenne)* adjustable

oriental, -ale, -aux, -ales [ɔrjɑ̃tal, -o] ADJ *(région)* eastern; *(côte)* east; *(langue)* oriental; *Hist* **les Indes orientales** the East Indies
N **O.** Oriental

orientalisme [ɔrjɑ̃talism] NM Orientalism

orientaliste [ɔrjɑ̃talist] N Orientalist

orientateur, -trice [ɔrjɑ̃tatœr, -tris] N = **orienteur**

orientation [ɔrjɑ̃tasjɔ̃] NF **1** *(détermination de position)* orientation; **table d'o.** orientation *or* panoramic table; **avoir le sens de l'o.** to have a (good) sense of direction; **course d'o.** orienteering course **2** *Scol* **choisir une o.** to choose a course of study; **o. en fin de cinquième** = determination of future course of studies at the end of one's second year; **conseiller d'o.** course and careers adviser **3** *(d'une grue, d'une antenne)* positioning; **o. d'un canon** training of a gun; **à o. libre** free-moving, adjustable; *Aut* **o. de la roue** wheel alignment, tracking **4** *(d'une maison)* aspect, orientation; *(d'une politique)* thrust; **o. des voiles** set *or* trim of the sails; **o. de la Bourse** Stock Market trend; **o. du marché** market orientation; **o. stratégique de la société** corporate strategic orientation
▸▸ **o. politique** *(d'un journal, d'une personne)* political leanings *or* tendencies; *(d'un parti)* political direction; **o. professionnelle** careers advice *or* guidance

orienté [ɔrjɑ̃te] ADJ **1** *(disposé)* **maison/pièce orientée au sud** house/room facing south, house/room with a southerly aspect; **le jardin est mal o.** the garden is badly positioned; *Bourse* **o. à la baisse** *(marché)* falling;

o. à la hausse *(marché)* rising **2** *(peu objectif)* bias(s)ed, slanted; **ouvrage o. politiquement** work with a political bias *or* slant **3** *Ordinat* **o. bloc** block-orientated; **o. ligne** line-orientated; **o. objet** object-orientated; **o. problème** problem-orientated; **o. procédure** procedure-orientated

orienter [ɔrjɑ̃te] **VT 1** *(bâtiment)* to orient(ate); *(canon, fusil)* to train (**vers** on); *(télescope)* to point, to direct; *(voile)* to trim **2** *(mener)* to direct, to guide; *Scol* **o. un élève vers la chimie** to steer a pupil towards chemistry, to advise a pupil to take up chemistry; *Scol* **on l'a mal/bien orienté** he was given the wrong/right academic advice; **o. la conversation vers d'autres sujets** to steer *or* turn the conversation to other topics; **j'ai essayé d'o. la conversation sur toi** I tried to bring *or* steer the conversation round to you **3** *(carte)* to orient(ate) **4** *Math* **o. une droite** to indicate the direction of a straight line

VPR s'orienter 1 *(déterminer sa position)* to get *or* find one's bearings, to orientate oneself; *(avec une boussole)* to take one's bearings **2** *(se destiner)* **elle veut s'o. vers le droit** she wants to go in for *or* specialize in law; **il a décidé de s'o. vers la carrière diplomatique** he has decided on a career in the diplomatic service; **cette politique s'oriente vers le communisme** this policy is tending *or* moving towards Communism; **s'o. vers la vente de produits écologiques** to specialize in the sale of environmentally friendly products; **s'o. en fonction des cours** to move in relation to prices

orienteur, -euse [ɔrjɑ̃tœr, -øz] **N** careers adviser

NM *(instrument)* orientator

ADJ *Mil* **officier o.** interviewing officer *(for candidates for military service)*

orifice [ɔrifis] **NM** opening, aperture; *(du corps)* orifice; *(d'un puits, d'une galerie)* mouth; *Tech* port; *Aut* **o. d'admission** inlet port; *Aut* **o. d'air** air port; *Aut* **o. d'alimentation** feed hole; *Aut* **o. d'arrivée d'essence** petrol port; *Aut* **o. d'écoulement d'huile** oil drain hole; *Aut* **o. de sortie** outlet port

oriflamme [ɔriflam] **NF 1** *Hist* oriflamme **2** *(bannière)* banner

origami [ɔrigami] **NM** origami

origan [ɔrigɑ̃] **NM** oregano

originaire [ɔriʒinɛr] **ADJ 1 o. de** *(personne)* originating from, coming from; **il est o. de Russie/du Havre** he is a native of *or* he comes from Russia/Le Havre; **le haggis est o. d'Écosse** haggis originates in *or* comes from Scotland **2** *(initial)* *(membre)* original, founding

originairement [ɔriʒinɛrmɑ̃] **ADV** originally

original, -ale, -aux, -ales [ɔriʒinal, -o] **ADJ 1** *(premier)* *(texte, manuscrit)* original; *(bande etc)* master; **édition originale** first edition; *Cin* **copie originale (du film)** master print **2** *(nouveau)* *(style, idée)* original **3** *(excentrique)* odd, eccentric

NM *(œuvre, document)* original; *(d'un fichier, d'une disquette)* master copy; **copier qch d'après l'o.** to copy sth from the original

N *(excentrique)* eccentric; **c'est un o.** he's (quite) a character, he's an eccentric

Do not confuse with **originel**.

originalité [ɔriʒinalite] **NF 1** *(nouveauté)* originality **2** *(excentricité)* eccentricity, oddness **3** *(trait original)* original feature; *(de personne)* eccentricity

origine [ɔriʒin] **NF 1** *(création, début)* origin; **l'o. de l'univers** the origin of the universe; **dès l'o.** from the very beginning, from the

outset; **à l'o.** originally, in the beginning, at first; **à l'o. de** at the origin of; **des origines à nos jours** from the earliest times to the present day **2** *(ascendance)* origin; **être d'o. illustre/ouvrière** to be of noble/working-class descent; **être d'o. modeste** to be of humble origin *or* descent; **il est d'o. anglaise, il est anglais d'o.** he is English by birth; **il a des origines anglaises** he is of English extraction *or* has English origins; **d'o. française** *(produit, mot)* of French origin; **la colonie devait son o. aux baleiniers** the colony was founded by *or* owed its origins to whalers **3** *(source)* origin, source; *(d'un mot)* origin, derivation; *(d'une tradition)* origin; **l'o. de cette coutume est ...** the custom has its origins in ...; **tirer son o. de qch** to originate from sth, to have its origins in sth; **le mot tire son o. du latin** the word originates *or* derives from the Latin; **bureau d'o.** office of dispatch; **certificat d'o.** certificate of origin; **vins d'o.** vintage wines; **appellation d'o. contrôlée d'un vin** = official quality guarantee of a wine **4** *Math* **(point) o.** zero point

originel, -elle [ɔriʒinɛl] **ADJ** *(péché, forme)* original; *(cause, sens)* original, primary

Do not confuse with the French adjective **original**.

originellement [ɔriʒinɛlmɑ̃] **ADV** *(à l'origine)* originally; *(dès l'origine)* from the outset

orignal, -aux [ɔriɲal, -o] **NM** *Zool* moose

oripeaux [ɔripo] **NMPL** *(haillons)* rags, tatters; *(vêtements voyants)* loud *or* gaudy clothes

ORL [oɛrɛl] **N** *Méd* *(abrév* **oto-rhino-laryngologiste)** ENT specialist

orléaniste [ɔrleanist] **ADJ, N** *Hist* Orleanist

Orlon® [ɔrlɔ̃] **NM** Orlon®

ormaie [ɔrmɛ] **NF** elm grove

orme [ɔrm] **NM 1** *(arbre)* elm (tree); **o. blanc, o. de(s) montagne(s)** wych elm; **o. champêtre** *ou* **à petites feuilles** common elm, English elm; **maladie des ormes** Dutch elm disease **2** *(bois)* elm (wood)

ormeau, -eaux [ɔrmo] **NM** *(arbre)* (young) elm

orné [ɔrne] **ADJ** *(style)* ornate, florid; **lettre ornée** illuminated letter

ornement [ɔrnəmɑ̃] **NM** ornament; *(détail)* embellishment; *(parure)* adornment; **sans o.** plain, unadorned; **plantes d'o.** ornamental plants; *Rel* **ornements sacerdotaux** vestments; *Mus* **notes d'o.** grace notes, ornaments

ornemental, -ale, -aux, -ales [ɔrnəmɑ̃tal, -o] **ADJ** ornamental

ornementation [ɔrnəmɑ̃tasjɔ̃] **NF** ornamentation, decoration

ornementer [ɔrnəmɑ̃te] **VT** to ornament, to decorate

orner [ɔrne] **VT** to decorate (**de** with); **o. une robe de dentelles** to trim a dress with lace

ornière [ɔrnjɛr] **NF** rut; *Fig* **sortir de l'o.** to get out of trouble; *Fig* **tirer qn de l'o.** to get sb out of trouble

ornithologie [ɔrnitɔlɔʒi] **NF** ornithology

ornithologique [ɔrnitɔlɔʒik] **ADJ** ornithological

ornithologiste [ɔrnitɔlɔʒist], **ornithologue** [ɔrnitɔlɔg] **N** ornithologist

ornithorynque [ɔrnitɔrɛ̃k] **NM** *Zool* duck-billed platypus, *Spéc* ornithorhynchus

orogenèse [ɔrɔʒənɛz] **NF** *Géol* orogenesis

orogénie [ɔrɔʒeni] **NF** *Géol* orogeny

orogénique [ɔrɔʒenik] **ADJ** *Géol* orogenic

orographie [ɔrɔgrafi] **NF** orography

oronge [ɔrɔ̃ʒ] **NF** *Bot* royal agaric, Caesar's mushroom; **fausse o.** fly agaric

orpaillage [ɔrpajaʒ] **NM** gold washing *or* panning

Orphée [ɔrfe] **N** *Myth* Orpheus

orphelin, -ine [ɔrfəlɛ̃, -in] **N** orphan

ADJ orphan(ed); **o. de père** fatherless; **o. de mère** motherless

NF *Typ* **orpheline** orphan

orphelinat [ɔrfəlina] **NM** orphanage

orphéon [ɔrfeɔ̃] **NM 1** *(fanfare)* band **2** *Arch* *(chorale)* choral society

orphéoniste [ɔrfeɔnist] **N 1** *(d'une fanfare)* band member **2** *Arch* *(d'une chorale)* choral society member

orphie [ɔrfi] **NF** *Zool* garfish, garpike

orphisme [ɔrfism] **NM** orphisme

orpiment [ɔrpimɑ̃] **NM** *Tech* orpiment

orque [ɔrk] **NF** *Zool* killer whale, orc, grampus

Orsay [ɔrsɛ] **N le Quai d'O.** = the French Foreign Office

ORSEC [ɔrsɛk] *(abrév* **organisation des secours)** **le plan O.** = disaster contingency plan

Le plan ORSEC

This scheme is set in motion whenever there is a major disaster in France, such as flooding or forest fires. Under the provisions of the scheme, the "préfet", or chief of police, is empowered to mobilize both public and private resources to deal with a civil emergency.

orteil [ɔrtɛj] **NM** toe; **gros o.** big toe; **petit o.** little toe

ORTF [oɛrteɛf] **NM** *Anciennement* *(abrév* **Office de la radiodiffusion et télévision française)** = publicly owned broadcasting organization, divided into seven autonomous organizations in 1974

orthochromatique [ɔrtokrɔmatik] **ADJ** *Phot* orthochromatic

orthodontie [ɔrtodɔ̃ti] **NF** orthodontics

orthodontique [ɔrtodɔ̃tik] **ADJ** orthodontic

orthodontiste [ɔrtodɔ̃tist] **N** orthodontist

orthodoxe [ɔrtodɔks] **ADJ** *(église, doctrine, opinion)* orthodox; **peu o.** unorthodox, unconventional

N *Rel* person of orthodox beliefs; *(de l'Église orthodoxe)* member of the Orthodox Church; *Pol* follower of the (official) party line

orthodoxie [ɔrtodɔksi] **NF** orthodoxy

orthogénie [ɔrtoʒeni] **NF** *Méd* birth control, family planning

orthogonal, -ale, -aux, -ales [ɔrtogɔnal, -o] **ADJ** orthogonal

orthogonalement [ɔrtogɔnalmɑ̃] **ADV** orthogonally, at right angles

orthographe [ɔrtograf] **NF** spelling; **je ne connais pas l'o. de ce mot** I don't know how to spell this word *or* how this word is spelt; **mot qui a deux orthographes** word that has two spellings, word that can be spelt in two ways; **faute d'o.** spelling mistake; **réforme de l'o.** spelling reform; **o. d'usage/d'accord** literal/grammatical spelling; **être bon en o., avoir une bonne o.** to be good at spelling **VOIR GRAMMAIRE A79-80**

orthographier [ɔrtografje] **VT** *(impf, pr sub* **n. orthographiions, v. orthographiiez)** to spell; **mal o. un mot** to spell a word incorrectly, to misspell a word

orthographique [ɔrtografik] **ADJ** *Gram* orthographic(al); **réforme o.** spelling reform

orthopédie [ɔrtɔpedi] NF orthopaedics, *Am* orthopedics

orthopédique [ɔrtɔpedik] ADJ orthopaedic, *surtout Am* orthopedic; **chaussures orthopédiques** orthopaedic shoes; **semelles orthopédiques** built-up soles

orthopédiste [ɔrtɔpedist] N **1** *(médecin)* orthopaedist, *surtout Am* orthopedist; **chirurgien o.** orthopaedic *or surtout Am* orthopedic surgeon **2** *(fabricant)* maker of orthopaedic *or surtout Am* orthopedic apparatus

orthophonie [ɔrtɔfɔni] NF speech therapy

orthophoniste [ɔrtɔfɔnist] N speech therapist

orthoptie [ɔrtɔpsi] NF orthoptics

orthoptiste [ɔrtɔptist] N orthoptist

ortie [ɔrti] NF nettle; **o. brûlante** stinging nettle; **o. blanche** dead nettle

ortolan [ɔrtɔlɑ̃] NM *Orn* ortolan (bunting)

orvet [ɔrvɛ] NM *Zool* slow-worm, blindworm

oryx [ɔriks] NM oryx

OS [ɔɛs] NM *abrév* **ouvrier spécialisé**

os [ɔs, *pl* o] NM bone; **avoir de gros/petits os** to be big-boned/small-boned; **viande avec os** meat on the bone; **viande sans os** meat off the bone, boned meat; **cuiller en os** bone spoon; **n'avoir que la peau sur les os, n'être qu'un sac** *ou* **un paquet d'os** to be nothing but skin and bone, to be just a bag of bones; **elle est tellement maigre qu'on lui voit les os** she's a bag of bones; **voir qn en chair et en os** to see sb in the flesh; **mouillé** *ou* **trempé jusqu'aux os** soaked to the skin, wet through; **pourri jusqu'à l'os** thoroughly corrupt; **se rompre les os** to break one's neck; **il ne fera pas de vieux os** he's not long for this world, he won't make old bones; *Fig* **donner** *ou* **jeter un os à ronger à qn** to give sb something to keep him/her happy; *Fam* **tomber sur un os** to run up against *or* hit a snag; *Fam* **il y a un os** there's a snag *or* hitch; *très Fam* **je l'ai dans l'os** I've been shafted *or* screwed
▸▸ *Anat* **os malaire** cheek bone; **os à moelle** marrowbone; **os de seiche** cuttlebone

oscar [ɔskar] NM *Cin* Oscar; **elle a reçu l'o. du meilleur second rôle** she won the Oscar for best supporting actress

OSCE [ɔɛsseə] NF *(abrév* **Organisation pour la sécurité et la coopération en Europe)** OSCE

oscillant, -ja ADJ *(pendule)*, *Élec (décharge)* oscillating; *(tige)* rocking; *Radio* **circuit o.** oscillatory circuit; *Méd* **fièvre oscillante** irregular fever

oscillateur [ɔsilatœr] NM *Radio, Électron* oscillator

oscillation [ɔsilasjɔ̃] NF **1** *(d'un pendule)* swing, oscillation; *Phys, Élec* oscillation; *Phys* **oscillations amorties/entretenues** damped/sustained oscillations **2** *(d'un bateau)* rocking **3** *Tech* vibration **4** *Fig (du marché, de l'opinion etc)* fluctuation; **oscillations saisonnières** seasonal fluctuations

oscillatoire [ɔsilatwar] ADJ *(mouvement, circuit)* oscillatory

osciller [ɔsile, -je] VI **1** *(d'un pendule)* to swing, to oscillate; *(de l'aiguille d'un compteur de vitesse)* to flicker; *(d'un bateau)* to rock; *Phys, Élec* to oscillate **2** *(hésiter)* **o. entre deux opinions/positions** to waver between two opinions/positions **3** *Fin (du marché)* to fluctuate

oscillogramme [ɔsilɔgram] NM oscillogram

oscillographe [ɔsilɔgraf] NM oscillograph; **o. cathodique** cathode ray tube

oscilloscope [ɔsilɔskɔp] NM oscilloscope

osé [oze] ADJ *(tentative, démarche, geste)* dar-

ing, bold, audacious; *(plaisanterie, scène d'un film)* daring, risqué; *(demande)* bold; **c'est vraiment o. de sa part** that's really daring *or* bold *or* audacious of him

oseille [ozɛj] NF **1** *Bot* sorrel **2** *Arg (argent)* dough, bread, *Br* lolly; **avoir de l'o.** to have bags *or* pots of money, to be loaded

oser [oze] VT **1 o. faire qch** to dare (to) do sth; **elle n'ose (pas) le faire** she daren't do it, she doesn't dare (to) do it; **les mots qu'il n'a jamais osé dire** the words he never dared (to) say; **comment osez-tu répondre à ton père!** how dare you answer your father back!; **je voudrais qu'il vienne mais je n'ose l'espérer** I'd like him to come but I daren't hope *or* I don't dare hope that he will; **si j'ose dire** if I may *(venture to)* say so; *Litt* **o. qch** to dare sth; **il faut o.** nothing ventured, nothing gained; **comment osez-vous?** how dare you!; **approchez si vous osez!** come over here if you dare!; **il veut me parler? qu'il ose un peu!** he wants to talk to me? just let him dare!; **vous n'oseriez pas!** you wouldn't dare! SEE GRAMMAR A40-1; A61; B35 **2** *Suisse (avoir la permission de)* **est-ce que j'ose entrer?** may I come in?

oseraie [ozrɛ] NF osier bed

osier [ozje] NM **1** *Bot* osier; **brin d'o.** withy **2** *(en vannerie)* wicker; **panier d'o.** wicker basket

Oslo [oslo] N Oslo

osmonde [ɔsmɔ̃d] NF *Bot* **o. royale** royal fern

osmose [ɔsmoz] NF *aussi Fig* osmosis; *Fig (entre des personnes)* total empathy

ossature [ɔsatyr] NF **1** *Biol (d'un homme, d'un animal)* frame, skeleton; **d'une o. puissante** powerfully built, of powerful build **2** *Fig (structure) (d'un bâtiment)* frame(work); *(d'un pont)* main girders; *(d'un texte)* framework, structure

osselet [ɔslɛ] NM *(de mouton)* knucklebone; **jouer aux osselets** to play at knucklebones; *Anat* **les osselets de l'oreille** the ossicles of the ear, the otic bones

ossements [ɔsmɑ̃] NMPL bones

osseux, -euse [ɔsø, -øz] ADJ *(visage, main)* bony; *(tissu)* bone, *Spéc* osseous; **système o.** bone structure; **greffe osseuse** bone graft

ossification [ɔsifikasjɔ̃] NF *Méd* ossification

ossifier [ɔsifje] VT to ossify
VPR **s'ossifier** to ossify, to become ossified

ossu [ɔsy] ADJ big-boned, raw-boned

ossuaire [ɔsɥɛr] NM ossuary, charnel house

OST [ɔɛste] NF *Com (abrév* **organisation scientifique du travail)** organization and methods, time and motion studies

ostensible [ɔstɑ̃sibl] ADJ open; *(mépris)* clear, patent

Il faut noter que le terme anglais **ostensible** est un faux ami. Il signifie **prétendu, apparent**.

ostensiblement [ɔstɑ̃sibləmɑ̃] ADV openly

Il faut noter que le terme anglais **ostensibly** est un faux ami. Il signifie **prétendument, en apparence**.

ostensoir [ɔstɑ̃swar] NM *Rel* monstrance

ostentation [ɔstɑ̃tasjɔ̃] NF ostentation, show, display; *Litt* **faire o. de sa misère** to parade one's poverty; **agir par** *ou* **avec o.** to act ostentatiously; **sans o.** unostentatiously

ostentatoire [ɔstɑ̃tatwar] ADJ ostentatious

ostéologie [ɔsteɔlɔʒi] NF osteology

ostéomyélite [ɔsteɔmjelit] NF *Méd* osteomyelitis

ostéopathe [ɔsteɔpat] N *Méd* osteopath

ostéoporose [ɔsteɔpɔroz] NF *Méd* osteoporosis

ostracisme [ɔstrasism] NM **1** *(exclusion)* ostracism; **frapper qn d'o.** to ostracize sb **2** *(hostilité, attitude de rejet)* hostility

ostréicole [ɔstreikɔl] ADJ **l'industrie o.** oyster farming; **parc o.** oyster bed; **la région est l'une des plus grands parcs ostréicoles de la France** it is one of the largest oyster-producing regions in France

ostréiculteur, -trice [ɔstreikyltœr, -tris] N oyster farmer

ostréiculture [ɔstreikyltyr] NF oyster farming

ostrogot(h), ostrogot(h)e [ɔstrɔgo, -ɔt] N *Hist* **O.** Ostrogoth
NM *(homme malappris)* boor

OT NM *(abrév* **Office du Tourisme)** tourist office

otage [ɔtaʒ] NM hostage; **prendre qn en o.** to take sb hostage; **une prise d'o.** a hostage-taking

otalgie [ɔtalʒi] NF *Méd* earache, *Spéc* otalgia

OTAN [ɔtɑ̃] NF *(abrév* **Organisation du traité de l'Atlantique Nord)** NATO

otarie [ɔtari] NF sea lion, *Spéc* otary, eared seal

OTASE [ɔtaz] NF *(abrév* **Organisation du traité de l'Asie du Sud-Est)** SEATO

ôter [ote] VT to remove, to take away; *(vêtement)* to take off; *(tache)* to remove, to take out; *(assiettes)* to clear away; **ô. le couvert** to clear away, to clear the table; **ô. qch à qn** to take sth away from sb; **il faudrait leur ô. ces armes des mains** these weapons should be taken away from them; **ô. ses illusions à qn** to rid sb of his/her illusions; **ça lui a ôté ses illusions** that shattered his illusions; **cela lui a ôté l'appétit** it has taken away his appetite; **cela lui a ôté toute sa force** it has drained him of all his strength; **ô. à qn l'espoir/l'envie de faire qch** to deprive sb of all hope/all desire of doing sth; **tu ne m'ôteras pas de l'idée que ...** I'm quite convinced that ...; **cela n'ôte rien à sa valeur/à notre amitié** that in no way detracts from its value/from our friendship; **ô. qch à** *ou* **de qch** to remove sth from sth; **ôtez trois de cinq** take (away) *or* subtract three from five; **10 ôté de 30 égale 20** 30 minus 10 equals 20, 10 taken away from 30 leaves 20; **cela me l'a ôté tout à fait de l'esprit** that drove *or* put it right out of my head; **ô. le pain de la bouche à qn** to take the bread out of sb's mouth; **ô. la vie à qn** to take sb's life
VPR **s'ôter** *Fam* **ôtez-vous de là!** get out of the way!, move (yourself)!; **ôte-toi de mon chemin!** get out of my way!; **ôte-toi de là que je m'y mette!** get out and make room for me!; **il faut qu'il ôte cette idée de la tête** he has to get that idea out of his head; **elle ne peut pas s'ô. de l'idée que ...** she can't get it out of her head that ...

otique [ɔtik] ADJ *Anat* otic

otite [ɔtit] NF *Méd* otitis

OTM [ɔteɛm] NM *Com (abrév* **opérateur de transport multimodal)** multi-modal operator

otologie [ɔtɔlɔʒi] NF otology

oto-rhino, pl oto-rhinos [otorino] N *Méd Fam* ENT specialist

oto-rhino-laryngologie NF *Méd* ear, nose and throat medicine, *Spéc* otolaryngology, otorhinolaryngology

oto-rhino-laryngologiste, pl oto-rhino-laryngologistes N *Méd* ear, nose and throat specialist, *Spéc* otolaryngologist

otoscope [ɔtɔskɔp] NM *Méd* otoscope, ear speculum

OTSI [oteɛsi] **NM** (*abrév* **Office du tourisme-syndicat d'initiative**) tourist office

Ottawa [ɔtawa] **N** Ottawa

ottoman, -ane [ɔtɔmɑ̃, -an] **ADJ** *Hist* Ottoman
▸ **N** *Hist* **O.** Ottoman
▸ **NM** (*étoffe*) ottoman
▸ **NF ottomane** (*meuble*) ottoman

ou [u] **CONJ** or; **voulez-vous du bœuf ou du jambon?** would you like beef or ham?; **trois ou quatre fois par jour** three or four times a day; **l'un ou l'autre** one or the other; **entrez ou sortez** either come in or go out; **qu'il vienne ou non, nous irons** whether he comes or not, we'll go; **vous ou moi, nous lui en parlerons** (either) you or I will speak to him about it; **lui ou son frère va** *ou* **vont vous aider** he or his brother will help you; **l'un ou l'autre devait forcément être le chef** one or the other was bound to be leader; **j'appelle tout de suite ou j'attends demain?** shall I call straight away or wait till tomorrow?; **ou ... ou (bien) ...** either ... or (else) ...; **ou vous payez ou j'appelle la police** either you pay up or (else) I call the police; *Ordinat* **circuit OU** OR circuit

où [u] **ADV 1** (*dans l'espace*) (*interr*) where; **où habite-t-il?** where does he live?; **où allez-vous?** where are you going?; **où en êtes-vous?** how far have you got (with it)?; **par où est-il passé?** which way did he go?; **jusqu'où les a-t-il suivis?** how far did he follow them?; **qui peut dire où nous vivrons dans dix ans** who can tell where we'll be living in ten years' time?

2 (*dans l'espace*) (*rel*) where; **j'irai où vous voudrez** I'll go where(ever) you wish; **partout où il va** wherever he goes, everywhere he goes; **vous le trouverez là où vous l'avez laissé** you'll find it where you left it; **d'où on conclut qu'il est coupable** from which one concludes that he is guilty; **d'où sa tristesse** hence her sadness; **où que vous soyez** wherever you may be; **mettez-le n'importe où** put it down anywhere; **nous cherchons un studio où passer quelques jours** we're looking for a studio flat for a few days *or* where we can spend a few days; **dans l'état où elle est** in the state she's in; **au train où vont les choses** at this rate, at the rate things are going SEE GRAMMAR B23

3 (*temps*) when; **à l'époque où il était jeune** in the days when he was young

4 (= *dans lequel, auquel etc*) **la maison où il habite** the house he lives in, the house in which he lives

OUA [oya] **NF** (*abrév* **Organisation de l'unité africaine**) OAU

ouache [waʃ] **NF** *Can* bear's den

ouah [wa] **INT** woof!

ouaille [waj] **NF** *Bible, Litt* sheep; **le pasteur et ses ouailles** the minister and his flock

ouais [wɛ] **INT** *Fam* yeah!, yep!; (*sceptique*) oh yeah?

ouananiche [wananiʃ] **NF** *Can* freshwater salmon

ouaouaron [wawarɔ̃] **NM** *Can* bullfrog

ouate [wat] **NF** (*souvent* **la ouate**, *parfois* **l'ouate**) **1** (*pour rembourrage*) padding, wadding; **doublé d'o.** quilted **2** (*pour soins*) cotton wool, *Am* absorbent cotton; **o. hydrophile** absorbent cotton wool *or* cotton; *Fig* **avoir été élevé dans la o.** to have been brought up in cotton wool

ouaté [wate] **ADJ** (*vêtement*) quilted; *Fig* (*bruit de pas*) muffled, soft; (*contours*) vague, fuzzy

ouater [wate] **VT** to quilt

ouatine [watin] **NF** *Tex* quilting (material)

ouatiné [watine] **ADJ** (*tissu*) quilted

oubli [ubli] **NM 1** (*acte d'oublier*) forgetting; (*défaillance de la mémoire*) forgetfulness; (*négligence*) (*du devoir*) neglect; **l'o. de soi** selflessness **2** (*général*) oblivion; **tomber dans l'o.** to sink *or* fall into oblivion, to be forgotten; **sortir de l'o.** to emerge from oblivion **3** (*trou de mémoire*) oversight; (*lacune*) omission; **réparer un o.** to rectify an oversight/omission; **je suis désolée de ne pas l'avoir fait, c'est un o.** I'm sorry I've not done it, it's an oversight on my part

oublier [ublije] (*impf, pr sub n.* **oubliions,** *v.* **oubliiez**) **VT 1** (*ne pas se rappeler*) to forget; **j'ai oublié son nom** I've forgotten his name, his name has slipped my mind; **j'ai oublié son visage** I've forgotten what he looks like; **o. où/quand/qui ...** to forget where/when/who ...; **j'ai complètement oublié que nous avions rendez-vous aujourd'hui** I completely forgot that we'd agreed to meet today; **o. le passé** to forget the past; **oublions le passé** let's let bygones be bygones; **faire o. son passé** to live down one's past; **o. de faire qch** to forget to do sth; **on ne nous le laissera pas o.** we'll never hear the last of it *or* be allowed to forget it, we'll never live it down; **il mourut oublié de tous** he died forgotten by all, he died in obscurity; **n'oubliez pas à qui vous vous adressez** remember who you're talking to; *Hum* **il a oublié d'être bête** he's not lacking in brains, he's as clever as they come VOIR GRAMMAIRE A44

2 (*ne pas prendre*) to forget, to leave (behind); (*omettre*) to leave out; (*rendez-vous*) to overlook; (*devoir*) to neglect; **j'ai oublié mes lunettes chez toi** I've left my glasses (behind) at your place; **o. l'heure** to forget the time, to lose track of the time

▸ **VPR s'oublier 1** (*se relâcher*) to forget oneself, to forget one's manners; **le chien s'est oublié sur le tapis** the dog's made a mess on the carpet

2 (*s'exclure*) to forget oneself; *Fam* **il ne s'oublie pas** he always looks after himself, he always takes care of number one

3 (*sortir de la mémoire*) **les langues étrangères s'oublient facilement quand on ne les pratique pas** foreign languages are easily forgotten when you don't use them; **des choses pareilles ne doivent jamais s'o.** things like that must never be forgotten; **c'est comme le vélo, ça ne s'oublie pas** it's like riding a bike, once you learn you never forget

oubliette [ublijɛt] **NF** dungeon, oubliette; *Fig Fam* **mettre qch aux oubliettes** to shelve sth indefinitely; **cet homme politique fut mis aux oubliettes pendant dix ans** this politician was condemned to ten years in the wilderness

oublieux, -ieuse [ublijø, -jøz] **ADJ** forgetful; **o. de** forgetful of; (*devoir*) neglectful of, forgetful of

oued [wɛd] **NM** *Géog* wadi

Ouessant [wɛsɑ̃] **NM** Ushant

ouest [wɛst] **NM** (*no pl*) **1** (*point cardinal*) west; **à l'o., dans l'o.** in the west; **où est l'o.?** which way is west?; **la partie la plus à l'o. de l'île** the westernmost part of the island; **le vent vient de l'o.** it's a west *or* westerly wind, the wind is coming from the west; **un vent d'o.** a westerly wind; **le vent d'o.** the west wind; **aller au** *ou* **vers l'o.** to go west *or* westwards; **les trains qui vont vers l'o.** trains going west, westbound trains; **rouler vers l'o.** to drive west *or* westwards; **aller droit vers l'o.** to head due west; **la cuisine est plein o.** *ou* **exposée à l'o.** the kitchen faces due west; **le soleil se couche à l'o.** the sun sets in the west **2** (*partie d'un pays, d'un continent*) west, western area *or* regions; (*partie d'une ville*) west; **l'o. de l'Italie** western Italy, the west of Italy; **dans l'o. de l'Espagne** in western Spain, in the west of Spain; **elle habite dans l'o.** she lives in the west; **il habite dans**

l'o. de Paris he lives in the west of Paris; **elle est de l'o.** she's from the west; **les gens de l'o.** people who live in the west
▸ **ADJ INV** (*côte, face*) west; (*banlieue, partie, région*) western; **la façade o. d'un immeuble** the west-facing wall of a building; **la chambre est côté o.** the bedroom faces west; **dans la partie o. de la France** in the west of France, in western France; **suivre la direction o.** to head *or* go westwards

ouest-allemand, -ande, *pl* **ouest-allemand(e)s** *Anciennement* **ADJ** West German
▸ **N O.** West German

ouf [uf] **INT** whew!, phew!; *Fam* **il n'a pas eu le temps de dire o.!** he didn't even have time to catch his breath!
▸ **NM pousser un o. de soulagement** to heave a sigh of relief

ouf [uf] **ADJ** *Fam* crazy, *Br* mental, barking, *Am* nutso

Ouganda [ugɑ̃da] **NM** Uganda

ougandais, -aise [ugɑ̃dɛ, -ɛz] **ADJ** Ugandan
▸ **N O.** Ugandan

ougrien, -ienne [ugrijɛ̃, -jɛn] *Ling* **ADJ** Ugric
▸ **NM** Ugric

oui [wi] **ADV** yes; **vient-il? – o.** is he coming? – yes (he is); **je crois que o.** I think so; **faire signe que o., faire o. de la tête** to nod (one's head); **mais o., bien sûr que o.** (yes,) of course; **o., o., allez-y** yes, (yes,) get on with it; **êtes-vous content de partir? – o. et non** are you happy to be leaving? – yes and no; **eh o.! c'est encore moi!** yes! it's me again!; *Naut* **o., commandant!** aye, aye, sir!; **ah, o.?** really?, is that so?; *Fam* **tu viens, o.?** you're coming, aren't you?; *Fam* **tu viens, o. ou non** *ou très Fam* **o. ou merde?** are you coming or not?, are you coming or aren't you?, are you coming, yes or no? SEE GRAMMAR B64
▸ **NM INV** *Pol* **deux cents o. et trois cents non** two hundred ayes and three hundred noes; *Fam* **se quereller/pleurer pour un o. pour un non** to quarrel/cry over the slightest thing; **changer d'avis pour un o. pour un non** to change one's mind at the drop of a hat

ouï-dire [widir] **NM INV** hearsay; **ce sont des o.** it's hearsay; **je ne le sais que par o.** I know it only by *or* from hearsay

ouïe [wi] **NF 1** (*sens*) (sense of) hearing; **avoir l'o. fine** to have keen *or* sharp ears, to have excellent hearing; **avoir l'o. défectueuse** to be hard of hearing; **à portée de l'o.** within earshot, within hearing distance; **être tout o.** to be all ears *or* all attention **2** *Mus* **ouïes** (*de violon*) sound holes **3** *Tech* (*d'un ventilateur*) ear **4** *Zool* **ouïes** gills

ouille [uj] **INT** ouch!, ow!

ouïr [wir] **VT** (*only used in inf, pp* **ouï,** *compound tenses, prp* **oyant** *and imp* **oyez;** *p hist* **j'ouïs** *and fu* **j'ouïrai** *sometimes used*) *Arch* to hear; **nous l'avons ouï dire à notre père** we have heard our father say so; **j'ai souvent ouï dire que ...** I have often heard it said that ...; *Jur* **o. les témoins** to hear the witnesses; *Arch* **oyez, oyez braves gens ...** oyez, oyez *or* now hear this, good people ...

ouistiti [wistiti] **NM** *Zool* marmoset; *Fig Fam* **un drôle de o.** an odd character

ouragan [uragɑ̃] **NM** hurricane; **entrer comme un o. dans une pièce** to burst into a room; **sa déclaration a déclenché un o. de protestations** his statement caused a storm of protest *or* an uproar

Oural (l') [lural] **NM 1** (*fleuve*) the Ural **2** (*montagnes*) the Urals, the Ural Mountains

ourdir [urdir] **VT 1** *Tex* (*lin, tissu*) to warp **2** (*paille*) to plait **3** *Fig* (*complot*) to hatch, to weave

ourdissage [urdisaʒ] NM *Tex* warping

ourdou [urdu] NM *Ling* Urdu

ourlé [urle] ADJ *Couture* hemmed; **des oreilles délicatement ourlées** delicately shaped ears

ourler [urle] VT **1** *Couture* to hem; **o. à jour** to hemstitch **2** *(border)* to edge (**de** with) **3** *Tech (feuilles de métal)* to lap-joint

ourlet [urlɛ] NM **1** *Couture* hem; **o. à jour** hemstitched hem; **faux o.** false hem; **point d'o.** hemstitch **2** *(repli, rebord) (d'un cratère)* edge; *(de l'oreille)* rim, *Spéc* helix **3** *Tech (de feuilles de métal)* lap joint, hem

ours, ourse [urs] N *Zool* bear; *f* she bear; **il vit comme un o.** he's a grumpy, unsociable sort; *Fig* **quel o.!** what a boor!; *Prov* **il ne faut pas vendre la peau de l'o. avant de l'avoir tué** don't count your chickens before they're hatched; *Arg* **avoir ses o.** *(d'une femme)* to have the curse, to have one's period
  NM *Journ* credit pages *(where contributors to a book or newspaper are acknowledged)*
  NF *Astron* **la Grande Ourse** *(constellation)* the Great Bear; *(sept étoiles)* the Plough, *Am* the Big Dipper; **la Petite Ourse** the Little Bear, *Am* the Little Dipper
  ▸▸ **o. blanc** polar bear; **o. brun** brown bear; **o. gris d'Amérique** grizzly bear; *Fam* **o. mal léché** uncouth individual; **o. marin** sea bear, fur seal; **o. en peluche** teddy bear; **o. polaire** polar bear

oursin [ursɛ̃] NM sea urchin; *Fam* **avoir des oursins dans le porte-monnaie** to be tightfisted

ourson [ursɔ̃] NM bear cub

oust(e) [ust] INT *Fam* **allez o.!** *(avance!)* get a move on!; *(va-t'en!)* scram!, *Br* hop it!

out [awt] ADJ INV **1** *(personne)* out (of fashion); **ce chanteur est déjà o.** that singer is already out of fashion **2** *Tennis* out

outarde [utard] NF *Orn* **1** bustard **2** *(bernache du Canada)* Canada goose

outil [uti] NM **1** *(d'un ouvrier, artisan)* tool; *(d'un jardinier)* tool, implement; **o. coupant** *ou* **de coupe** *ou* **tranchant** cutting tool; *(pour bords ou bordures)* edging tool **2** *(moyen)* tool; **outils pédagogiques** teaching aids; *Bourse* **o. de spéculation** trading instrument; **o. de travail** tool, work instrument; **o. d'aide à la décision** decision-making tool; *Ordinat* **o. auteur** authoring tool; *Ordinat* **o. de création de pages Web** web authoring tool; **o. de gestion** management tool; *Ordinat* **o. de navigation sur le Web** web browser; **o. de production** production tool; **o. de recherche** research tool

outillage [utijaʒ] NM **1** *(ensemble d'outils)* (set of) tools **2** *(équipement) (d'une usine)* plant, equipment

outiller [utije] VT *(ouvrier)* to equip *or* supply with tools; *(usine)* to equip, to fit out, to tool up; **nous ne sommes pas outillés pour ce genre de réparation** we're not equipped *or* we don't have the tools for that sort of repair
  VPR **s'outiller** *(d'une usine)* to equip itself; *(d'un bricoleur)* to equip oneself with tools

outrage [utraʒ] NM *(injure) (au bon goût etc)* insult (**à** to); **c'est un o. aux convenances/à la morale** it offends against propriety/against morality; *Euph* **faire subir les derniers outrages à une femme** to violate a woman; *Litt* **l'o. des ans** *ou* **du temps** the ravages of time
  ▸▸ *Jur* **o. à agent** insulting behaviour; **o. aux bonnes mœurs** affront to public decency; **o. à magistrat** contempt of court; **o. à la pudeur** public indecency

outrageant [utraʒɑ̃] ADJ *(proposition, refus)* insulting; *(plaisanterie, propos)* offensive; *(accusation)* outrageous

outrager [utraʒe] VT **(j'outrageai(s))** **1** *(insulter)* to insult; **o. un homme dans son honneur/sa dignité** to offend against a man's honour/dignity **2** *Vieilli (porter atteinte à) (la vérité)* to violate; *(la raison, le bon sens, le bon goût)* to offend against

outrageusement [utraʒøzmɑ̃] ADV **1** *(excessivement)* excessively, outrageously **2** *Vieilli* insultingly

outrageux, -euse [utraʒø, -øz] ADJ *Vieilli* insulting

outrance [utrɑ̃s] NF excess; *(d'une tenue, d'une attitude, de propos)* extravagance; **agressif/méfiant à o.** excessively aggressive/mistrustful; **combat à o.** fight to the death; **industrialisation à o.** all out industrialization; **travailler à o.** to work excessively *or* to excess

outrancier, -ière [utrɑ̃sje, -jɛr] ADJ *(personnalité, propos)* extreme

outre¹ [utr] NF wine skin; *(en peau de chèvre)* goatskin bottle

outre² PRÉP **1** **o. mesure** *(travailler)* excessively; *(se soucier, s'exposer etc)* unduly, excessively; **se fatiguer o. mesure** to tire oneself out unduly, to overtire oneself; **je ne me sens pas fatigué o. mesure** I don't feel unduly *or* overly tired; **il n'est pas scrupuleux o. mesure** he's not excessively *or* overly scrupulous **2** *(en plus de)* besides, in addition to; **o. cette somme** besides *or* in addition to that sum; **o. cela** besides that, in addition to that
  ADV **passer o., aller o.** to go on *or* further; *Fig* **passer o.** to carry on regardless; **passer o. à une interdiction/la loi** to disregard *or* take no notice of *or* ignore a ban/the law; **en o.** besides, moreover; **j'ai, en o., deux neveux** I have two nephews besides
  CONJ **o. (le fait) qu'il est riche** apart from the fact that he's rich, apart from *or* besides *or* in addition to being rich; **o. qu'il est riche, il est extrêmement aimable** he's not only rich, he's also very nice

outré [utre] ADJ **1** *(indigné)* outraged, indignant; **je suis o. de voir que ...** I'm outraged to see that ... **2** *Litt (excessif) (éloge)* exaggerated, extravagant, overdone; **comédien dont le jeu est o.** actor who overacts, actor whose acting is overdone

outre-Atlantique ADV on the other side of the Atlantic, across the Atlantic

outrecuidance [utrəkɥidɑ̃s] NF **1** *(orgueil)* presumptuousness **2** *(insolence)* impertinence, effrontery; **il a eu l'o. de me dire que ...** he had the impertinence *or* effrontery to tell me that ...

outrecuidant [utrəkɥidɑ̃] ADJ **1** *(orgueilleux)* presumptuous **2** *(insolent)* impertinent

outre-Manche [utrəmɑ̃ʃ] ADV on the other side of the Channel, across the Channel

outremer [utrəmɛr] NM **1** *Minér* lapis lazuli **2 (bleu d')o.** ultramarine
  ADJ INV ultramarine

outre-mer [utrəmɛr] ADV overseas; **commerce d'o.** overseas trade; *Admin* **territoires d'o.** overseas territories

outrepasser [utrəpase] VT *(une limite, ses droits)* to exceed, to go beyond

outrer [utre] VT **1** *(exagérer)* to exaggerate; *(rôle)* to overdo **2** *(mettre en colère)* to outrage, to infuriate; **j'ai été outré par son attitude** I was outraged by *or* at his attitude

outre-Rhin [utrərɛ̃] ADV beyond *or* across the Rhine

outre-Sarine [utrəsarin] ADV *Suisse* in German-speaking Switzerland

outre-tombe (d') [dutrətɔ̃b] ADV from beyond the grave; *Fig* **une voix d'o.** a sepulchral voice

outsider [awtsajdœr] NM *Courses de chevaux, Fig* outsider

ouvert [uvɛr] ADJ **1** *(porte, fenêtre, tiroir)* open; **entre, la porte est ouverte** *ou* **c'est o.** come in, the door's open; **porte grande ouverte** wide-open door; **plaie ouverte** open *or* gaping wound; **fracture ouverte** open fracture; **il a le crâne/le genou o.** he has a gaping wound in his skull/knee, his skull/knee has been split open; *Chir* **opérer qn à cœur o.** to perform open-heart surgery on sb; **accueillir qn à bras ouverts** to welcome sb with open arms; **il était dans son lit, les yeux ouverts** he was lying in bed with his eyes open; **tu ne peux pas les recevoir chemise ouverte** you can't greet them with your shirt open *or* undone; **manteau qui se porte le col o.** coat that is worn with the collar open *or* undone; **voyelle ouverte** open vowel; *Ftbl* **jeu o.** open play; **traduire à livre o.** to translate at sight *or* off the cuff; **elle lit le grec à livre o.** she can read Greek at sight; **ville ouverte** open *or* unfortified town; **o. de 10 heures à 5 heures** open (from) 10 to 5; *Fam* **l'épicier du coin reste o. jusqu'à minuit** the grocer on the corner stays open till midnight; **collection ouverte au public** collection open to the public; **o. à la navigation** open to navigation; *Banque* **compte o.** open account; **c'est la guerre ouverte contre les fumeurs** it's open war on smokers; **être en guerre ouverte avec qn** to be openly at war with sb; **le gaz/robinet est o.** the gas/tap is on; **la séance est ouverte** I declare the meeting open; **la chasse/la campagne électorale est ouverte depuis ce matin** the hunting season/the election campaign began *or* started this morning; **les paris sont ouverts** *Courses de chevaux* bets are being taken; *Fig* it's anyone's guess **2** *Fig (franc, sans préjugé) (personne, caractère)* open, frank; **être o. à toute proposition** to be open to suggestions; **avoir l'esprit o.** to be open-minded; **parler à cœur o.** to speak openly *or* frankly **3** *Suisse (en pichet)* **du vin o.** wine in a carafe

ouvertement [uvɛrtəmɑ̃] ADV openly; *(parler)* openly, frankly

ouverture [uvɛrtyr] NF **1** *(d'une porte, d'un livre, d'une séance etc)* opening; *(de la saison de chasse, d'une campagne)* opening, start; **pour ne pas faire la queue, j'étais là avant même l'o.** to avoid queuing, I was there even before it *or* the doors opened; **elle travaille dans cette boutique depuis l'o.** she has worked in the shop since it opened; **j'ai fait l'o. de la galerie** I was at the opening of the gallery; *Bourse* **à l'o., le dollar était à 5,98 euros** at the start of trading, the dollar was at 5.98 euros, the dollar opened at 5.98 euros; **l'o. des portes du musée est prévue pour janvier** the museum is scheduled to open (its doors) in January; **l'o. des portes du lycée se fait tous les jours à huit heures** the school doors are opened every day at eight o'clock; **o. d'un compte** opening of an account; *Fin* **o. d'un crédit** granting of a loan; **o. des hostilités** outbreak of hostilities; *Ordinat* **o. de session** logon; *Aut* **o. sans clé** keyless entry; **conférence/discours d'o.** opening lecture/speech; *Bourse* **cours d'o.** opening price; **heures d'o.** opening hours; *Rugby* **il est demi d'o.** he plays stand-off *or* fly-half
  2 ouvertures *(avances)* overtures; **faire des ouvertures à qn** to make overtures to sb; **des ouvertures de paix** peace overtures
  3 *Mus* overture
  4 *(accès) (dans un mur etc)* opening, aperture; *(d'une caverne)* mouth; *(d'une haie)* gap, break
  5 *(écartement) (d'une voûte etc)* width, span; *(des branches d'un compas)* spread; *Élec* **o. d'induit** armature gap

6 *Phot* aperture, f-stop; **réduire l'o.** to stop down; **o. du diaphragme** aperture, f-stop
7 *Fig* o. de cœur openness, frankness; **o. d'esprit** open-mindedness; *Pol* **le Président pratique une politique d'o.** the President is following a policy of conciliation
8 *Cartes, Échecs* opening
9 *Mktg* window of opportunity; **l'o. de nouveaux marchés** the opening up of new markets

ouvrable [uvrabl] **ADJ jour o.** working day; **heures ouvrables** business hours, working hours

ouvrage [uvraʒ] **NM 1** *(travail)* work; **se mettre à l'o.** to set to work, to get down to work; **avoir du cœur à l'o.** to put one's heart into one's work, to work with a will; **je n'ai pas le cœur à l'o. aujourd'hui** I'm not in the mood for work today, I don't feel like working today
2 *Constr* work; **entreprise spécialisée dans les ouvrages de maçonnerie** firm specializing in masonry work; **ouvrages d'art** civil engineering works **3** *(livre)* work, book; **o. en prose** prose work; **un o. de philosophie** a work of philosophy, a philosophy book; **un o. de géographie** a geography book; **o. de référence** reference work *or* book; **ouvrages de fonds** backlist titles **4** *(résultat)* piece of work, product; *(tricot, broderie)* work; *Vieilli* **o. de dames** needlework; **corbeille à o.** workbasket; **boîte à o.** workbox; **une rencontre qui est l'o. du hasard** a meeting which is due to chance, a chance meeting; **l'o. du temps** the work of time
NF *Fam* **c'est de la belle o.** that's a nice bit of work

ouvragé [uvraʒe] **ADJ = ouvré**

ouvrager [uvraʒe] **VT (j'ouvrageai(s))** *(métal, bijou)* to work; *(orner) (brocart)* to figure

ouvrant [uvrã] **ADJ** *Aut* **toit o.** sun roof, sliding roof
NM *Beaux-Arts (d'un triptyque)* panel

ouvré [uvre] **ADJ 1** *Tech (fer)* wrought; **produits ouvrés et semi-ouvrés** finished and semi-finished products **2** *Litt (orné)* decorated; *(nappe)* embroidered

ouvre-boîte(s), pl ouvre-boîtes [uvrəbwat] **NM** can opener, *Br* tin opener; **o. électrique** electric can *or Br* tin opener

ouvre-bouteille(s), pl ouvre-bouteilles [uvrəbutɛj] **NM** bottle opener

ouvre-huître(s), pl ouvre-huîtres [uvrɥitr] **NM** oyster knife

ouvrer [uvre] **VT 1** *Tech (bois, cuivre etc)* to work **2** *(orner) (nappe etc)* to work, to embroider

ouvreur, -euse [uvrœr, -øz] **N** *Cartes* opener
NF *Théâtre, Cin* usherette

ouvrez-moi [uvremwa] **NM INV** *Ordinat* read-me document

ouvrier, -ère [uvrije, -ɛr] **ADJ 1** *(prolétaire) (quartier, tradition)* working-class; **la classe ouvrière** the working class(es); **agitation ouvrière** industrial unrest, labour unrest; **syndicat o.** trade union **2** *Zool* **abeille ouvrière** worker bee; **fourmi ouvrière** worker ant
N worker; *(prolétaire)* working man, *f* woman; *(de réparation, de travaux publics)* workman; *(d'une machine)* operative; **o. en bois** woodworker; **o. sur métaux** metalworker; **une famille d'ouvriers** a working-class family; *Litt Fig* **il est l'o. de sa fortune** he is a self-made man
NF *Zool* **ouvrière** worker
▸▸ **o. agricole** farm worker *or* hand, agricultural labourer; **o. non qualifié** unskilled manual worker; **o. qualifié** skilled worker; **o. spécialisé** semi-skilled worker

ouvriérisme [uvrijerism] **NM** *Pol (autogestion)* worker control; *(syndicalisme)* trade unionism

---
OUVRIR [uvrir] *(prp ouvrant; pp ouvert; pr ind j'ouvre; p hist j'ouvris)*

VT to open **1, 2, 4** ▪ to unfasten **1** ▪ to unlock **1** ▪ to turn on **1** ▪ to broaden **2** ▪ to cut through **3** ▪ to open up **4** ▪ to start **4**	
VI to open	
VPR to open **1** ▪ to open up **1** ▪ to cut open **2**	

VT 1 *(porte, fenêtre, boîte, bouteille etc)* to open; *(verrou)* to draw; *(loquet)* to unfasten; *(avec une clef)* to unlock; *(rideaux)* to open, to draw (back); **o. sa maison** *ou* **sa porte à qn** to throw open one's house to sb; *Fig* **o. la porte à qch** to open the door to sth; **il n'a pas ouvert la bouche,** *Fam* **il ne l'a pas ouverte** he didn't open his mouth; *Fam* **tu ferais mieux de ne pas l'o.!** you'd better keep your mouth *or* trap shut!; **o. le lit** to turn down the bed(clothes); **o. un robinet/le gaz** to turn on a tap/the gas; **o. l'électricité** to switch on (the electricity); *Fam* **o. le poste** to put on *or* switch on the radio; *Élec* **o. le circuit** to switch off *or* break the current
2 *Fig (découvrir)* **o. son cœur à qn** to open one's heart to sb, to unburden oneself to sb; **cette expérience lui a ouvert l'esprit** the experience broadened his mind; **cela ouvre l'appétit** it sharpens *or* whets the appetite
3 *(percer) (mur)* to cut through; *(mine)* to open up; *(canal)* to cut; *Méd (abcès)* to lance; **le chirurgien lui a ouvert l'estomac** the surgeon opened (up) his/her stomach
4 *(commencer, lancer) (une école, une boutique)* to open; *(un débat, une discussion)* to open, to start; **o. un compte chez qn** to open an account with sb; **o. un col en montagne** to open up a pass through *or* in the mountains; **cette discussion m'a ouvert de nouvelles perspectives** the discussion opened (up) new horizons for me; **ce sont des professions que nous voulons o. aux femmes** they are professions that we want to open up to women; **o. le bal** to open the ball; **o. boutique** to set up shop; **o. la marche** to lead the way; *Fin* **o. un crédit** to grant a loan; *Com* **o. un débouché à un produit** to open up a new outlet for a product; *Ordinat* **o. une session** to log in, to log on
VI to open; *(ouvrir la porte)* to open the door; **o. à qn** to open the door to sb, to let sb in; **les magasins n'ouvrent pas les jours de fête** the shops don't open *or* aren't open on public holidays; **la fenêtre n'ouvre plus** the window doesn't *or* won't open any more; **la porte n'ouvre que de l'intérieur** the door can only be opened from the inside, the door only opens from the inside; **la scène ouvre par un chœur** the scene opens with a chorus; **le salon/la fenêtre ouvrait sur le jardin** the drawing room/the window opened on(to) the garden; *TV, Cin* **o. en fondu** to fade in; *TV, Cin* **o. par un volet** to wipe on
VPR s'ouvrir 1 *(devenir ouvert) (d'une porte, d'une fenêtre, des yeux etc)* to open; *(d'une fleur)* to come out, to open; **la porte s'ouvrit en coup de vent** the door flew open; **les fenêtres s'ouvrent sur le jardin** the windows open on(to) the garden; *Fig* **un gouffre s'ouvrait sous mes pieds** a chasm opened up *or* yawned under my feet; **les possibilités/nouvelles perspectives qui s'ouvrent aux jeunes diplômés** the possibilities/new horizons that are opening up for young graduates; **carrières qui s'ouvrent de plus en plus aux femmes** careers that are opening up more and more to women; **s'o. à de nouvelles technologies** to open (up) one's mind to new technologies; **tu ne peux pas ne pas**

t'o. à l'informatique you can't afford to close yourself off to computer technology, you have to be open to computer technology; **la séance s'ouvre par un discours** the meeting opens with a speech; **le bal s'ouvrit par une valse** the ball opened *or* began *or* started with a waltz
2 *(se couper)* **s'o. la main/le menton** to cut open one's hand/chin; **s'o. les veines** to slash one's wrists; **s'o. un chemin à travers la foule** to push one's way through the crowd
3 *(se confier)* **s'o. à qn** to unburden oneself to sb, to confide in sb; **s'o. à qn de qch** to open one's heart to sb about sth, to confide in sb about sth

ouvroir [uvrwar] **NM** workroom, sewing room

ouzbek [uzbɛk] **ADJ** Uzbek
N O. Uzbek

Ouzbékistan [uzbekistã] **NM** Uzbekistan

ovaire [ovɛr] **NM** *Anat, Bot* ovary; **kyste de l'o.** ovarian cyst

ovale [oval] **ADJ** oval; *Sport* **ballon o.** rugby ball; **le ballon o.** *(le rugby)* rugby; **les adeptes du ballon o.** rugby fans
NM oval; **en o.** oval

ovalisation [ovalizasjõ] **NF** *Tech (des cylindres)* ovalization

ovalisé [ovalize] **ADJ** *Tech (cylindre)* ovalized

ovaliser [ovalize] **VT** *Tech* **l'usure ovalise les cylindres** cylinders become ovalized through wear

ovariectomie [ovarjɛktɔmi] **NF** *Méd* ovariectomy, oophorectomy

ovarien, -ienne [ovarjɛ̃, -jɛn] **ADJ** *Anat, Bot* ovarian

ovation [ovasjõ] **NF** ovation; **faire une o. à qn** to give sb an ovation

ovationner [ovasjone] **VT o. qn** to give sb an ovation

ové [ove] **ADJ** *(fruit)* egg-shaped, ovate

overdose [ovɛrdoz] **NF** *Méd, Fig* overdose; **mourir d'une o.** to die of *or* from an overdose; *Fig* **j'ai fait une o. de films japonais** I've overdosed on *or* I've had an overdose of Japanese films

overdrive [ovɛrdrajv] **NM** *Aut* overdrive

ovidés [ovide] **NMPL** *Zool, Agr* Ovidae

oviducte [ovidykt] **NM** oviduct

ovin [ovɛ̃] *Agr* **ADJ** ovine
NMPL ovins sheep

ovipare [ovipar] *Zool* **ADJ** oviparous
NM oviparous animal

ovni [ovni] **NM** *(abrév objet volant non identifié)* UFO

ovocyte [ovɔsit] **NM** oocyte

ovoïde [ovɔid] **ADJ** ovoid, egg-shaped; *Élec* **maillon o.** egg insulator

ovovivipare [ovovivipar] *Zool* **ADJ** ovoviviparous
NM ovoviviparous animal

ovulaire [ovylɛr] **ADJ** ovular

ovulation [ovylasjõ] **NF** ovulation

ovule [ovyl] **NM 1** *Biol* ovum **2** *Pharm* **ovules gynécologiques** (vaginal) pessaries

ovuler [ovyle] **VI** to ovulate

oxalate [ɔksalat] **NM** *Chimie* oxalate

oxalide [ɔksalid] **NF, oxalis** [ɔksalis] **NM** *Bot* oxalis, wood sorrel

oxalique [ɔksalik] **ADJ** *Chimie* **acide o.** oxalic acid

oxford [ɔksfɔrd] *Tex* **NM une chemise en o.** an Oxford shirt
ADJ de la flanelle o. Oxford

oxhydrique [ɔksidrik] **ADJ** oxyhydrogen

oxyacétylénique [ɔksjasetilenik] **ADJ** *Tech (gaz, soudure)* oxyacetylene

oxycoupage [ɔksikupaʒ] NM *Métal* oxygen cutting

oxydable [ɔksidabl] ADJ **1** *Chimie* oxidizable **2** *(d'un métal)* liable to rust

oxydant [ɔksidɑ̃] ADJ oxidizing NM oxidizer, oxidizing agent

oxydation [ɔksidasjɔ̃] NF *Chimie* oxidization, oxidation

oxyde [ɔksid] NM *Chimie* oxide; **o. de carbone** carbon monoxide; **o. d'azote** nitrogen oxide; **o. nitrique** nitric oxide

oxyder [ɔkside] VT to oxidize VPR **s'oxyder** to oxidize

oxygénation [ɔksiʒenasjɔ̃] NF **1** *Chimie* oxygenation **2** *(application d'eau oxygénée)*

les méfaits de l'o. sur les cheveux the damaging effects of bleach on the hair

oxygéné [ɔksiʒene] ADJ *Chimie* oxygenated; **eau oxygénée** hydrogen peroxide; **cheveux oxygénés** peroxide blonde hair, bleached hair

oxygène [ɔksiʒɛn] NM **1** *Chimie* oxygen; *Méd* **tente à o.** oxygen tent **2** *Fam* **j'ai besoin d'o.** I need a change of air

oxygéner [ɔksiʒene] (**il oxygène; il oxygénera**) VT **1** *Chimie (liquide, tissu vivant)* to oxygenate, to oxygenize; *(élément, produit chimique)* to oxidize **2** *(cheveux)* to bleach, to peroxide

VPR **s'oxygéner** *Fam (respirer)* to take *or* get a breath of fresh air; **partir à la campagne**

pour une quinzaine pour s'o. to go off to the countryside for two weeks to get some good clean air (in one's lungs)

oxymore [ɔksimɔr], **oxymoron** [ɔksimɔrɔ̃] NM *Ling* oxymoron

oxyton [ɔksitɔ̃] NM *Ling* oxytone

oxyure [ɔksjyr] NM *Méd* oxyuris

oyat [ɔja] NM *Bot* marram grass

Ozalid® [ɔzalid] NM *Typ* Ozalid®

ozone [ɔzon] NM *Chimie* ozone; **couche d'o.** ozone layer

ozonisation [ɔzɔnizasjɔ̃] NF *Chimie, Tech* ozonization

ozoniser [ɔzɔnize] VT to ozonize

P, p [pe] NM *(lettre)* P, p

PAC [pak] NF *(abrév* **Politique Agricole Commune)** CAP

PACA [paka] NF *(abrév* **Provence-Alpes-Côte d'Azur)** = region of southeastern France

pacage [pakaʒ] NM *Agr* **1** *(champ)* pasture(-land); **p. d'été** summer pasture **2** *(action de faire paître)* pasturing, grazing; *Jur* **droit(s) de p.** grazing rights

pacager [pakaʒe] *(je pacageai(s); n. pacageons)* VT *(troupeau)* to pasture, to graze
VI *(d'un troupeau)* to graze

pacane [pakan] NF pecan (nut); *Culin* **tarte aux pacanes** pecan pie

pacemaker [pɛsmekœr] NM *Sport, Méd* pacemaker

pacha [paʃa] NM pasha; *Fam* **mener une vie de p.** to live like a lord; **tu ne vas pas faire le p. tout le week-end!** don't expect to be waited on hand and foot all weekend!

pachyderme [paʃidɛrm] NM pachyderm; *Fig Fam (personne)* great *or* fat lump, tub of lard; **de p.** *(allure, démarche)* elephantine, lumbering; *(grâce)* elephantine

pacificateur, -trice [pasifikatœr, -tris] ADJ pacifying
N peacemaker

pacification [pasifikasjɔ̃] NF pacification

pacifier [pasifje] VT *(impf, pr sub* n. **pacifiions,** v. **pacifiiez)** to pacify

pacifique [pasifik] ADJ *(coexistence, manifestation etc)* peaceful; *(qui aime la paix)* peace-loving; **mesure à but p.** measure intended to bring about peace; **mener une existence p.** to lead a quiet *or* peaceful life; **l'océan P.** the Pacific (Ocean); *Jur* **possesseur p.** uncontested owner
N *Bible* **bienheureux les pacifiques** blessed are the peacemakers
NM **le P.** *(océan)* the Pacific

pacifiquement [pasifikmɑ̃] ADV peacefully; **le meeting s'est déroulé p.** the meeting went off peacefully *or* quietly

pacifisme [pasifism] NM *Pol* pacifism

pacifiste [pasifist] ADJ, N *Pol* pacifist

pack [pak] NM **1** *(des mers polaires)* pack ice, ice pack **2** *Rugby* pack **3** *(lot)* pack; **des cannettes de bière en p. de six** a six-pack (of beer); **lait vendu en p.** milk sold in multipacks

package [pakɛdʒ] NM *Com, Ordinat* package

packaging [pakedʒiŋ] NM packaging

pacotille [pakɔtij] NF *Péj* **(marchandises de) p.** shoddy goods; **c'est de la p.** it's junk; **de p.** shoddy, third-rate; **bijoux de p.** paste jewellery; **exotisme de p.** third-rate exoticism

Pacs [paks] NM *(abrév* **Pacte civil de solidarité)** civil solidarity pact *(law introduced in France in 1999 extending the legal rights of married couples to unmarried heterosexual couples and to homosexual couples, particu-* larly with regard to inheritance and taxation); **faire** *ou* **conclure un P.** to enter into a Pacs agreement

pacser [pakse] *Fam* VI to sign a Pacs contract, to enter into a civil solidarity pact
VPR **se pacser** to sign a Pacs contract, to enter into a civil solidarity pact

pacson [paksɔ̃] NM *Fam (argent, paquet)* packet; **toucher le p.** to win a fortune

pacte [pakt] NM pact; **conclure** *ou* **faire** *ou* **sceller un p. avec/contre qn** to enter into a pact with/against sb; **signer un p. avec le diable** to sign a pact with the Devil
▸▸ **p. pour l'emploi** = job creation scheme for young people; **p. de non-agression** non-aggression pact; **p. à quatre** four-power pact; *UE* **p. de stabilité** stability pact; *UE* **p. de stabilité et de croissance** stability and growth pact; **le P. de Varsovie** the Warsaw Pact

pactiser [paktize] VI **p. avec qn** to come to terms with sb; **p. avec le diable** to make a pact with the Devil; *Fig* **p. avec sa conscience** to come to terms with one's conscience

pactole [paktɔl] NM **1** *Litt (qui enrichit)* gold mine; **ce travail est un vrai p.** this type of work is a real gold mine **2** *Fam (argent mis en jeu)* kitty; **il rêvait de gagner le p.** *(au loto)* he dreamt of winning the lottery; **son job lui rapporte un sacré p.** his job brings in megabucks; **elle a touché un joli p. quand son grand-père est mort** she came in for a nice little sum when her grandfather died

paddle [padœl] NM *Sport* paddle tennis

paddock [padɔk] NM paddock; *Fam (lit)* bed; *Fam* **se mettre** *ou* **aller au p.** *(se coucher)* to hit the sack *or* hay

paddy [padi] NM INV paddy

Padoue [padu] N Padua

paella [paɛla, paeja] NF *Culin* paella

PAF [paf] NM *(abrév* **paysage audiovisuel français)** **le P.** the broadcasting scene *or* set-up in France

paf [paf] INT slap!, bang!
ADJ INV *Fam* **être p.** *(saoul)* to be pissed; **il est complètement p.** he's as pissed as a newt

PAG [peaʒe] NF *Com (abrév* **procédure accélérée générale de dédouanement)** accelerated customs clearance procedure

pagaie [page] NF *(rame)* paddle

pagaïe, pagaille [pagaj] NF *Fam (d'objets)* disorder, clutter; **il y a une drôle de p. dans ce bureau** this office looks as if a bomb has hit it *or* is in a fine old mess; **c'est la p. dans les rues de Paris** the streets of Paris are completely snarled up; **quelle p.!** what a mess!, what a shambles!; *(à cause des embouteillages)* **p.** he's snarl-up!; **quelle p. dans cette pièce!** this room's (in) a real mess!; **en p.** *(maison, chambre)* in a mess; *(affaires, papiers)* all jumbled up, in a mess; **ses affaires étaient en p. avec les miennes/dans le sac** his/her things were jumbled up with mine/ in the bag; **j'ai mis mes papiers en p. dans mon cartable** I stuffed my papers into my briefcase any old how; **je les ai mis en p.** *(ces livres etc)* I've just bundled them up, they're not in any particular order; **évite de mettre tout en p.** don't get things all jumbled up *or* mixed up; **avec des cadeaux en p.** with presents galore, with masses *or* loads of presents; **il y en a en p.** there's masses *or* lots *or* loads of it; *(nombre)* there are masses *or* lots *or* loads of them; **semer la p.** to cause trouble *(parmi* among; *dans* in); **il adore semer la p.** he likes causing trouble, *Br Fam* he's a real stirrer

paganisme [paganism] NM paganism

pagayer [pageje] VI *(je pagaie, je pagaye)* to paddle

pagayeur, -euse [pagejœr, -øz] N paddler

page¹ [paʒ] NF *(de journal, de livre, de site Web)* page; **feuilleter les pages d'un magazine** to flick through a magazine; **un livre de 250 pages** a 250-page book; **être payé à la p.** to be paid by the page; **je gagne quatre euros de la p.** I earn four euros a page; **en première p. des journaux** on the front page of the newspapers; **faire la première p. des journaux** to hit the headlines; *Journ* **photo sur une double p.** two-page photo spread; *Journ* **article sur une double p.** two-page spread; **ouvrez vos livres à la p. 10** open your books at page 10 *or* turn to page 10; **j'ai perdu la p.** I've lost my place; **je voudrais finir la p.** I'd like to finish the page I'm on; *Typ* **mettre en page(s)** to make up; *Typ* **mise en page(s)** pagination, page make-up; *Ordinat* **logiciel de mise en p.** desktop publishing package; *Typ* **belle p.** right-hand page, recto (page); *Typ* **fausse p.** dummy; **une des plus belles pages de Victor Hugo** one of Victor Hugo's finest passages; *Fig* **une des plus célèbres pages de l'histoire** one of the most famous pages *or* chapters in history; **une nouvelle p. de l'histoire de France était tournée** a new chapter had begun in the history of France; *Fam* **être à la p.** to be up to date; **je ne suis plus vraiment à la p. en matière de musique** I'm pretty out of touch with what's happening in music; **ne pas être à la p.** to be behind the times; **tu n'es plus du tout à la p.** you're totally behind the times *or* out of it; **il faut te mettre à la p.** you're going to have to get with it; **rester à la p.** to keep up to date
▸▸ *Ordinat* **p. d'accueil** home page; *Journ* **p. d'actualités** news page; *Journ* **p. centrale** centre page; *Journ* **p. centrale dépliante** centre spread, centrefold; **p. de couverture** cover page; *Typ* **pages de départ** prelims; *Ordinat* **p.-écran** screen page; *Journ* **p. féminine** women's page; *Journ* **pages financières** financial *or Br* City pages; **p. de garde** *Typ* endpaper; *Ordinat* splash page; *(d'un fax)* cover(ing) sheet; **les pages jaunes (de l'an-**

nuaire) the yellow pages; *Journ* **p. de mode** fashion page; *Ordinat* **p. perso, p. personelle** personal home page; *Ordinat* **p. précédente** page up; **p. de publicité** *Journ* full-page advert; *Radio, TV* commercial break; *Ordinat* **p. suivante** page down; *Typ* **p. de titre** title page; **p. volante** slip page; *Ordinat* **p. Web** Web page

page² NM *Hist* page(boy)

page³ NM *Fam* = **pageot**

pageot [paʒo] NM *Fam* bed; **se mettre** *ou* **aller au p.** to hit the sack *or* hay

pageur [paʒœr] NM pager

pageux [paʒø] NM *Typ* compositor, comp

pagination [paʒinasjɔ̃] NF pagination, page numbering; **il y a une erreur de p.** the pages have been numbered wrongly

paginer [paʒine] VT to paginate, to number the pages of

pagne [paɲ] NM loincloth; *(en paille)* grass skirt

pagnoter (se) [səpaɲɔte] VPR *Fam (se coucher)* to hit the sack *or* hay

pagode [pagɔd] NF **1** *Archit* pagoda; **toit en p.** pagoda roof; **manches pagodes** pagoda sleeves **2** *(figurine à tête mobile)* mandarin

Pagsi [paksi] NM *(abrév* **Programme d'action gouvernemental pour la société de l'information)** = government scheme to promote the use of the Internet in education and in public services

paie [pɛ] NF pay; *(par semaine)* wages; **feuille** *ou* **bulletin de p.** pay (advice) slip; **jour de p.** pay day; **faire la p.** to pay (out) the wages; **toucher sa p.** to get paid, to get one's pay; *Fig Fam* **ça fait une p. que je ne l'ai pas vu** I haven't seen him for ages; **quand vous êtes-vous rencontrés? – ça fait une p.!** when did you meet? – donkey's years ago!

paiement [pemɑ̃] NM payment; **p. mensuel** monthly payment; **p. du solde** payment of the balance; **demander des délais de p.** to ask for time to pay; *aussi Fig* **c'est tout ce qu'il reçut en p. de son travail** that's all he got for his work; *Fig* **voilà donc le p. de mon aide!** so that's what I get (in return) for helping you!
▸▸ **p. par accomptes** payment by *or* in instalments *or Am* installments; **p. anticipatif** *ou* **anticipé** advance payment, payment in advance, prepayment; **p. par anticipation** payment in advance; **p. arriéré** payment in arrears; **p. d'avance** payment in advance, advance payment, prepayment; *TV* **p. à la carte** *(des programmes)* pay per view; *Banque* **p. par carte** card payment, payment by card; *Tél* **p. par carte prépayée** pay-as-you-go; **p. par chèque** payment by cheque; **p. à la commande** cash with order, CWO; **p. (au) comptant** cash payment, payment in cash; *TV* **p. à la consommation** pay per view; **p. contre documents** payment against documents; **p. différé** deferred payment; **p. échelonné** staged *or* staggered payment; **p. électronique** electronic payment, payment by electronic transfer; **p. en espèces** payment in cash, cash payment; **p. intégral** payment in full; **p. libératoire** payment in full discharge from debt; **p. à la livraison, p. contre livraison** *Br* cash on delivery, COD, *Am* collect on delivery; **p. en nature** payment in kind; **p. partiel** partial *or* part payment; **paiements périodiques** periodic payments; **p. préalable** prepayment; **p. progressif** graduated *or* increasing payments; **p. au prorata** payment pro rata; *TV* **p. à la séance** pay per view; *Ordinat* **p. sécurisé** secure (electronic) transaction; **p. en souffrance** overdue *or* outstanding payment; **p.**

à tempérament payment by *or* in instalments; **p. à termes** payment by *or* in instalments

païen, -ïenne [pajɛ̃, -jɛn] ADJ, N pagan, heathen; **jurer comme un p.** to swear like a trooper

paierie [pɛri] NF local government finance office

paillage [pajaʒ] NM *Agr* mulching

paillard, -arde [pajar, -ard] ADJ *(personne, chanson, plaisanterie)* bawdy, ribald; **regard p.** leer
▸ N debauchee; *(homme)* debauchee, rake

paillardise [pajardiz] NF **1** *(d'une personne, chanson etc)* bawdiness, ribaldry **2** *Vieilli (histoire)* bawdy story

paillasse [pajas] NF **1** *(matelas)* straw mattress, paillasse, palliasse **2** *(de l'évier)* draining board; *(de laboratoire)* (laboratory) bench **3** *Fam* **crever** *ou* **trouer la p. à qn** to stab sb in the stomach (and kill him/her) **4** *Fam Vieilli (prostituée)* floozy, tart
▸ NM clown, buffoon

paillasson [pajasɔ̃] NM *(tapis-brosse)* (door)mat; *Agr* straw matting; *Fig (personne)* doormat; *Fig* **mettre la clef sous le p.** to clear out, *Br Fam* to scarper

paille [paj] NF **1** straw; **p. de litière** loose straw; **menue p., p. d'avoine** chaff; **p. de riz** *ou* **d'Italie** rice straw; **chapeau de p.** straw hat; **chaise de p.** straw-bottomed chair; **vin de p.** straw wine *(wine made from grapes dried on straw mats before pressing)*; *Fig* **homme de p.** man of straw, *Am* straw man; **il leur fallait un homme de p.** they needed a front man *or* a figurehead; *Fig* **feu de p.** flash in the pan; **ce ne fut qu'un feu de p.** *(leur amour)* it was just a flash in the pan; *(ce scandale)* it was just a nine days' wonder; **cela leur passera comme un feu de p.** they'll soon get over it, it'll be a flash in the pan; **sur la p. humide des cachots** behind bars; *Fig* **sur la p.** destitute, *Fam* on one's uppers, down and out; **voilà ce qui t'a mis sur la p.** that's what put you on your uppers; **mourir sur la p.** to die destitute; **vieillir sur la p.** to be old and destitute; **c'est facile de voir la p. dans l'œil du voisin (et ne pas voir la poutre dans le sien)** it's easy to criticize, you/he/*etc* should take the mote out of your/his/*etc* own eye first; **c'est la p. et la poutre** you/he/*etc* should take the mote out of your/his/*etc* own eye first; **tirer à la courte p.** to draw lots; **on tira à la courte p. qui irait faire du café** we drew lots to see who would make the coffee; **on tira à la courte p. le nom du gagnant** the winner was chosen by lot, the name of the winner was drawn out of a hat; *Fam* **une p.!** *(peu de chose)* chickenfeed!, peanuts! **2** *(pour boire)* (drinking) straw; **boire qch avec une p.** to drink sth through *or* with a straw; **tirer sur une p.** to suck on a straw **3 p. de fer** steel wool **4** *(défaut) (dans une pierre précieuse etc)* flaw
▸ ADJ INV **1** straw-coloured *or Am* -colored; **jaune p.** pale yellow **2** *Culin* **pommes p.** thinly cut chips *or surtout Am* (French) fries

paillé¹ [paje] NM stable litter

paillé² ADJ **1** *(couleur)* straw-coloured *or Am* -colored **2** *(chaise)* straw-bottomed **3** *(métal, pierre précieuse etc)* flawed

pailler¹ [paje] NM *(hangar)* farmyard, straw yard; *(meule)* straw stack

pailler² VT **1** *(arbuste)* to protect *or* mulch with straw **2** *(chaise)* to put a straw bottom in

paillet [paje] NM *Naut* mat, fender; **p. d'abordage, p. makarov** collision mat

pailleté [pajte] ADJ spangled (**de** with), sequined

pailleter [pajte] VT (**je paillette; je pailletterai**) to sequin, to spangle

paillette [pajet] NF **1** *(sur des vêtements)* sequin, spangle; **à paillettes** sequined **2** *(de maquillage)* **des paillettes** glitter **3** *(de mica etc)* flake; **p. d'or** grain of gold dust; **savon en paillettes** soap flakes **4** *(d'une pierre précieuse)* flaw

pailleux, -euse [pajø, -øz] ADJ **1** *Agr* **fumier p.** = manure which has not rotted down sufficiently **2** *Tech (acier)* flawed

paillis [paji] NM *Agr* mulch

paillote [pajɔt] NF straw hut

pain [pɛ̃] NM **1** *(aliment)* bread; *(unité)* loaf, *pl* loaves; **achète deux pains** buy two loaves; **quelle sorte de p. devrais-je acheter?** what kind of bread should I buy?; *Rel* **le p. et le vin** the bread and wine; *Rel* **le/notre p. quotidien** our daily bread; **mettre qn au p. (sec) et à l'eau/au p. sec** to put sb on bread and water/on dry bread; **bon comme du bon p.** *ou* **comme le p.** extremely kind-hearted; **long comme un jour sans p.** interminable; *Fig* **c'est p. bénit** it serves him/her/them right but it's a godsend for us; **acheter qch pour une bouchée de p.** to buy sth for a song *or* for next to nothing; **il ne vaut pas le p. qu'il mange** he isn't worth his salt; **avoir du p. sur la planche** to have a lot on one's plate, to have plenty of work to do; **gagner son p. (à la sueur de son front)** to earn one's living *or* make a living (by the sweat of one's brow); **ôter le p. de la bouche à qn** to take the bread out of sb's mouth; **je ne mange pas de ce p.-là** I'm not getting involved in that, I'm not having any of that; **ça ne mange pas de p.** it won't cost you/him/*etc* anything; **du p. et des jeux** bread and circuses; *Bot* **arbre à p.** breadfruit tree **VOIR GRAMMAIRE A12**
2 petit p. (bread) roll; *Fig* **ça part** *ou* **se vend comme des petits pains** it sells/it's selling like hot cakes; **ces foulards sont partis comme des petits pains** those scarves went *or* sold like hot cakes; *Culin* **p. de poisson** fish loaf
3 *(de savon)* bar, cake; *(de cire)* stick
4 *Fam (coup de poing)* punch; **flanque-lui un p.** sock him one, *Br* give him a bunch of fives; **il a pris un p. dans la gueule** he got socked in the kisser
▸▸ **p. azyme** unleavened bread; **p. bis** brown bread/loaf; *Fig* **p. blanc: il a mangé son p. blanc le premier** he was lucky to start with; **fais attention à ne pas manger ton p. blanc le premier** remember that tomorrow always comes, always keep something to fall back on; **p. brioché** = bread closely resembling brioche in texture; **p. de campagne** farmhouse loaf; **p. au chocolat** pain au chocolat *(chocolate-filled pastry)*; **p. complet** wholemeal bread/loaf; **p. d'épices** ≃ gingerbread; **p. de Gênes** Genoa cake; **p. grillé** toast; **p. au lait** sweet roll; **p. au levain** sourdough bread/loaf; **p. de ménage** homemade bread/loaf; **p. de mie** sandwich loaf; **p. noir** black bread; **p. parisien** short French stick; **p. paysan** farmhouse loaf; **p. perdu** *(cuit à la poêle)* French toast; *(cuit au four)* bread-and-butter pudding; **p. aux raisins** = circular pastry made from sweetened dough and raisins; **p. de seigle** rye bread/loaf; **p. au** *ou* **de son** bran bread/loaf; **p. de sucre** sugar loaf; *Géog (montagne en)* **p. de sucre** sugar loaf (mountain); **p. viennois** Viennese bread/loaf

pair [pɛr] ADJ *(nombre)* even; **jours pairs** even dates; *Ordinat* **parité paire** even parity; **organes pairs** paired organs
▸ NM **1** *(égal)* equal, peer; **être jugé par ses pairs** to be judged by one's peers; *Litt* **être avec qn** *ou* **traiter qn de p. à compagnon** to treat sb as an equal; **hors (de) p.** *(habileté, talent, efficacité etc)* unequalled, unrivalled,

beyond compare; *(personne)* unequalled; **c'est un traducteur hors p.** as a translator, he's second to none *or* in a class by himself; **pour ce qui est de l'informatique, elle est hors p.** there is no one to equal *or* match her *or* she is unequalled when it comes to computers; **aller de p.** *(de deux choses)* to go together, to go hand in hand; **aller de p. avec qch** to go hand in hand with sth; **le chômage va de p. avec les crises économiques** unemployment and economic crises go hand in hand; **ça va de p.** the two go hand in hand **2** *(noble)* peer (of the realm); *Br* **Chambre des Pairs** House of Lords; *Br* **p. à vie** life peer **3** *Fin* par; *Com* **p. commercial** par; *Com* **p. du change** par of exchange; **au-dessous/au-dessus du p.** below/above par; **au p.** at par **4 travailler au p.** to work au pair, to do au pair work; **jeune fille au p.** au pair (girl); **elle est au p. dans une famille bordelaise/chez un médecin** she's working (as an) au pair for a family in Bordeaux/for a doctor; **elle envoie des jeunes filles au p. aux États-Unis** she sends girls to work au pair in the United States **5 jouer p./impair** to bet on the even/odd numbers

paire [pɛr] NF *(de chaussures, de lunettes, de ciseaux etc)* pair; *(de draps)* set; *(de gibier à plumes, de pistolets)* brace; **p. de bœufs** yoke of oxen; **une belle p. de seins** a great pair, *Arg* great boobs *or* tits; *Fam* **une belle p. de fesses** a nice arse *or Am* ass; **il a reçu une p. de claques** he got his face slapped; *Fig Fam* **ça, c'est une autre p. de manches** that's another matter, that's a different kettle of fish; **quant à lui faire comprendre cela, c'est une autre p. de manches** it's another matter *or* a different kettle of fish getting him to understand; *Fam* **ils font la p.** they're two of a kind; *Fam* **se faire la p.** to clear out, to beat it, *Br* to scarper; *Tech* **p. torsadée** twisted pair VOIR GRAMMAIRE A10

pairesse [pɛrɛs] NF *Br* peeress

pairie [pɛri] NF peerage; **p. à vie** life peerage

paisible [pɛzibl] ADJ peaceful; *(silence, sommeil)* peaceful, undisturbed; *(personne)* quiet; *(eau)* calm; *Jur* **p. possesseur d'un bien** uncontested owner of a piece of property; **dormir d'un sommeil p.** to sleep peacefully; **retrouver un sommeil p.** to sleep peacefully again

paisiblement [pɛzibləmã] ADV peacefully

paître [pɛtr] *(prp* **paisant**; *pr ind* **je pais, il pait**, n. **paissons**; *pr sub* **je paisse**; *impf* **je paissais**; *fu* **je paîtrai**; *no p hist)* VT *(des animaux) (feuilles etc)* to feed on; *(herbe)* to crop; *Arch, Litt (bétail)* to feed, to graze ▸ VI *(des animaux)* to feed; *(manger de l'herbe)* to graze, to pasture; *(manger des feuilles)* to browse; *Fig Fam* **je l'ai envoyé p.** I sent him packing, I sent him off with a flea in his ear

paix [pɛ] NF **1** *(entre États)* peace; **en temps de p.** in peacetime, in times of peace; **demander la p.** to sue for peace; **troubler la p.** to break the peace; **faire la p.** to make peace (**avec** with); *Fig* **faire la p. avec qn** to make one's peace with sb, to make it up with sb; *Fig* **on fait la p.?** let's make up, let's be friends again; *Fig* **faire la p. avec son passé** to come to terms with one's past; **rester en p. avec un pays** to remain at peace with a country; **vivre en p. avec ses voisins** to live at peace with one's neighbours; *Fig* **je souhaite vivre en p. avec ma conscience/mon passé** I want to be able to live with my conscience/my past; *Jur* **juge de p.** magistrate, justice of the peace; **climat de p. sociale** *(absence de grève)* climate of industrial peace **2** *Rel (sérénité)* peace; **la p. du tombeau** the quiet of the grave; **p. à son âme** may his/her soul rest in peace; **qu'il repose en p.** may he rest in peace; **allez en p.** go in peace

3 *(tranquillité)* peace; **dormir en p.** to sleep peacefully; **avoir besoin de p. pour se concentrer** to need peace and quiet to concentrate; **troubler la p. de qn** to disturb sb; *(moralement)* to disturb sb's peace of mind; **troubler la p. de ce petit matin** to break the peace of the early morning; **il ne m'a pas laissé en p. tant que ...** he gave me no peace until ...; **laissez-moi en p.** leave me alone *or* in peace; **je suis pour la p. des ménages** I'm a great believer in marital harmony; *Fam* **avoir la p.** to get peace (and quiet); **impossible d'avoir la p. quand il est là** it's impossible to get any peace (and quiet) when he's around; **je peux avoir la p. cinq minutes?** can I have five minutes' peace (and quiet)?, can't I be left alone for five minutes?; *Fam* **je veux qu'on me fiche** *ou* **foute la p.** I want to be left alone; *Fam* **il faut lui ficher** *ou* **foutre la p. avec tes questions** stop pestering him with your damn questions; *Fam* **fiche-moi** *ou* **fous-moi la p.!** leave me alone!, stop pestering me!, get off my back!; *Fam* **bloody leave him alone!**; *Fam* **la p.!** hush!, be quiet!

▸▸ **p. armée** armed peace; **p. séparée** separate peace; **p. universelle** universal peace

Pakistan [pakistã] NM Pakistan

pakistanais, -aise [pakistanɛ, -ɛz] ADJ Pakistani ▸ N **P.** Pakistani

PAL [pal] ADJ TV *(abrév* **Phase Alternation Line**) PAL

pal, -als [pal] NM **1** *(pieu)* pale, stake; *Arch* **le (supplice du) p.** impalement **2** *(plantoir)* planter, dibber

palabre [palabr] NM OU NF *(souvent pl)* palabres palaver, (endless) discussion; **après de long(ue)s palabres** after a long discussion; **s'éterniser en palabres** to drag on forever

palabrer [palabre] VI to palaver, to talk endlessly

palace [palas] NM luxury hotel; **tu verrais sa maison, c'est un vrai p.** you should see his house, it's palatial *or* luxurious

> Il faut noter que le terme anglais **palace** est un faux ami. Il signifie **palais**.
>
> Do not confuse with **palais**.

paladin [paladɛ̃] NM paladin; *(itinérant)* knight-errant

palais¹ [palɛ] NM **1** *(d'un roi etc)* palace **2** *Jur* **le p. de Justice, le p.** the law courts; **les gens du** *ou* **de p., le p.** the legal profession; **terme de p.** legal term; **le style du p.** legal language *or* jargon, the language of the courts

▸▸ **le P. Bourbon** = home of the French Parliament; **le P. Brongniart** = the Paris Stock Exchange; **p. des congrès** convention centre; **le p. de l'Élysée** the Élysée (Palace) *(official residence of the French President)*; **le p. Garnier** = the Paris Opera House; **le Grand P.** = science museum in Paris, originally built as part of the 1900 World Fair; **le P. du Luxembourg** = home of the French Senate in Paris; **le P. des Papes** = papal palace in Avignon, now the centre of a large arts festival; **le Petit P.** = art museum in Paris, originally built as part of the 1900 World Fair; **p. des sports** sports centre

> Do not confuse with the French word **palace**.

palais² NM **1** *Anat* palate; **voûte du p., p. dur** hard palate; **voile du p., p. mou** soft palate; **p. fendu** cleft palate **2** *(goût)* (sense of) taste; **avoir le p. fin** to have a fine palate; **flatter le p.** to please the palate

palan [palã] NM *Tech* hoist, hoisting gear;

Naut pulley block, purchase tackle, whip; *Com* **sous p.** under ship's tackle

palanche [palãʃ] NF *(pour porter des seaux etc)* yoke

palanque [palãk] NF (timber) stockade

palanquée [palãke] NF *(multitude)* **une p. de...** a raft of...

palanquer [palãke] VT to stockade

palanquin [palãkɛ̃] NM palanquin

palatal, -ale, -aux, -ales [palatal, -o] ADJ **1** *Ling (consonne)* palatal; *(voyelle)* front **2** *Anat (os etc)* palatal ▸ NF *Ling* **palatale** *(consonne)* palatal (consonant); *(voyelle)* front vowel

palatalisation [palatalizasjõ] NF *Ling* palatalization

palataliser [palatalize] *Ling* VT to palatalize ▸ VPR **se palataliser** to be palatalized

palatin, -ine [palatɛ̃, -in] ADJ **1** *Hist* palatine; **comte p.** Count Palatine **2** *Géog* **le mont P.** the Palatine Hill ▸ N *Hist* palatine ▸ NF *Hist* **La Palatine** the Princess Palatine

Palatinat (le) [ləpalatina] NM *Hist* the Palatinate

pale¹ [pal] NF **1** *(d'une rame, d'une hélice, d'un ventilateur etc)* blade; **hélice à trois/quatre pales** three-/four-bladed propeller **2** *(vanne)* sluice (gate)

pale² NF *Rel* chalice cover, pall(a)

pâle [pal] ADJ **1** *(livide, blafard)* pale; *Litt, Méd* pallid; **p. comme un linge** as white as a sheet; **p. comme la mort** deathly pale; ashen, as pale as death; **p. de colère** livid with rage; **p. de jalousie** green with envy; *Mil Fam* **se faire porter p.** to report sick; **les Visages pâles** the Palefaces **2** *(couleur, ciel)* pale; *(lumière)* pale, faint; *(sourire)* wan, faint; *(style)* colourless, *Am* colorless; **une p. imitation de Vermeer** a pale *or* poor imitation of Vermeer; **mes aventures semblent bien pâles auprès des vôtres** my adventures pale in comparison with yours; *Fam* **c'est un p. crétin** he's a complete idiot *or* fool

palefrenier [palfrənje] NM groom; *Arch (d'auberge)* ostler

palefroi [palfrwa] NM *Arch* palfrey

paléoanthropologie [paleoãtropɔlɔʒi] NF palaeoanthropology, *surtout Am* paleoanthropology

paléoanthropologue [paleoãtropɔlɔg] N palaeoanthropologist, *surtout Am* paleoanthropologist

paléographe [paleograf] N palaeographer, *surtout Am* paleographer

paléographie [paleografi] NF palaeography, *surtout Am* paleography

paléographique [paleografik] ADJ palaeographic, *surtout Am* paleographic

paléolithique [paleolitik] ADJ Palaeolithic, *surtout Am* Paleolithic ▸ NM Palaeolithic age, *surtout Am* Paleolithic age

paléontologie [paleõtɔlɔʒi] NF palaeontology, *surtout Am* paleontology

paléontologique [paleõtɔlɔʒik] ADJ palaeontological, *surtout Am* paleontological

paléontologiste [paleõtɔlɔʒist], **paléontologue** [paleõtɔlɔg] N palaeontologist, *surtout Am* paleontologist

paléozoïque [paleozoik] *Géol* ADJ Palaeozoic, *surtout Am* Paleozoic ▸ NM **le p.** the Palaeozoic *or surtout Am* Palezoic (era)

Palerme [palɛrm] N Palermo

paleron [palrõ] NM *(de cheval, de bœuf etc)* shoulder blade, blade bone; *Culin* neck, *Am* chuck; *Culin* **p. de bœuf** chuck

Palestine [palɛstin] NF *Géog* Palestine

palestinien, -ienne [palɛstinjɛ̃, -jɛn] ADJ Palestinian
N **P.** Palestinian

palet [palɛ] NM **1** *(anneau)* quoit; **jouer au(x) palet(s)** to play quoits **2** *(pour hockey sur glace)* puck; *(pour curling)* stone

paletot [palto] NM (short) overcoat; *Fig Fam* **tomber sur le p. à qn** *(l'attaquer)* to jump sb; *(d'un voleur)* to mug sb; *(pour lui parler)* to buttonhole sb, to nab sb

palette [palɛt] NF **1** *(de peintre)* palette; *Fig (éventail) (d'activités, de produits etc)* range; *Fig* **la p. de Matisse** the range of colours used by Matisse, Matisse's palette; *Ordinat* **p. d'outils** tool palette; **p. graphique** graphics palette **2** *(pour la manutention)* pallet; **p. (en) bois** wooden pallet; *Com* **p.-avion** air freight pallet **3** *Culin (de mouton, de porc)* shoulder **4** *(d'une roue à aubes)* paddle **5** *Sport (raquette de bois)* (wooden) battledore **6** *(pour le linge)* (washerwoman's) beetle

palettisation [palɛtizasjɔ̃] NF *Tech* palletization

palettiser [palɛtize] ADJ *Tech* to palletize

palettiseur [palɛtizœr] NM *Com* palletizer

palétuvier [paletyvje] NM mangrove

pâleur [palœr] NF *(du teint)* paleness, pallor; *(de la lumière)* faintness; *(du style)* colourlessness, *Am* colorlessness; **d'une p. mortelle** deathly pale

pâlichon, -onne [paliʃɔ̃, -ɔn] ADJ *Fam* pale, green around the gills

palier [palje] NM **1** *Archit (d'escalier)* landing; **nous sommes voisins de p.** we live on the same floor; **tu connais tes voisins de p.?** do you know the people who live on the same floor as you?, do you know your next-door neighbours?; **p. intermédiaire** half-landing **2** *(étape)* stage; **par paliers** in stages **3** *Aut, Rail etc* level stretch; *Math etc (d'un graphique)* plateau; **atteindre un p.** *(devenir plat)* to reach a plateau; **le taux des naissances a atteint un p.** the birth rate has reached a plateau *or* has levelled off; **à partir d'un certain p., le taux change** the rate changes at a certain point; *Aut, Rail etc* **vitesse en p.** speed on the level *or* on the flat; *Aviat* **voler en p.** to fly level **4** *Tech* bearing; **p. d'arbre** shaft bearing; **p. d'appui** mounting; **p. de tête de bielle** big-end bearing

palière [paljer] ADJ **porte p.** landing door, door opening onto the landing; **marche p.** top step

palimpseste [palɛ̃psɛst] NM palimpsest

palindrome [palɛ̃drom] NM *Ling* palindrome

palinodie [palinɔdi] NF **1** *Littér* palinode **2** *Péj (revirement)* volte-face

pâlir [palir] VI *(d'une personne)* to turn *or* become *or* grow pale, to pale; *(d'une lumière, d'une étoile etc)* to fade, to grow dim; *(d'une couleur, d'un souvenir)* to fade; **ses joues ont pâli** his/her cheeks have lost their colour; **p. d'horreur/de peur** to turn pale *or* go white with horror/fright; **p. de rage/de colère** to become livid with rage/anger; **p. de jalousie** to turn green with envy; **faire p. qn de jalousie** to make sb green with envy; **à faire p.** *(cauchemar, histoire)* terrifying; *(revenus, succès, maison)* amazing, unbelievable; **ils ont une maison à faire p. (d'envie)** they have a house that would make you green with envy; *Fig* **p. sur un travail** to slave over a piece of work
VT *Littér* **p. qn** *(d'une couleur, un maquillage etc)* to make sb look pale

palis [pali] NM **1** *(clôture)* (picket) fence **2** *(espace clôturé)* enclosure **3** *(pieu)* picket

palissade [palisad] NF **1** *(clôture)* fence; *Mil* palisade **2** *(haie)* hedge

palissader [palisade] VT to fence in, to rail in, to enclose; *Mil* to palisade

palissandre [palisɑ̃dr] NM *(bois)* Brazilian rosewood

pâlissant [palisɑ̃] ADJ *(visage)* turning pale; *(lumière)* fading, waning; *(couleur)* fading

palladium [paladjɔm] NM *Chimie* palladium

palliatif, -ive [paljatif, -iv] ADJ palliative
NM *Méd* palliative; *Fig* stopgap measure, *Litt* palliative

pallier [palje] *(impf, pr sub* **n. palliions,** *v.* **palliiez)** VT *(atténuer) (douleur, maladie)* to alleviate, *Fml* to palliate; *(faute, erreur)* to lessen the impact of
VI **p. à** *(un manque de qch)* to compensate for, to make up for; *(conséquences, problèmes)* to lessen the impact of

palmarès [palmarɛs] NM *Scol etc* honours *or Am* honors list; *(à une distribution de prix)* (list of) prize winners; *Sport* (list of) winners; *Mus, Radio etc* **le p. (de la chanson)** the charts; **être** *ou* **figurer au p.** to be among the (prize) winners; *Mus* to be in the charts; **une chanteuse qui ne figure plus au p.** a singer who's dropped out of the charts; **être premier au p.** to be number one, to top the charts; **il est au p. des hommes les plus séduisants de France** he's been voted one of the most attractive men in France; **avoir un beau p.** *(d'un sportif)* to be having a good season *or* year; **il a** *ou* **compte 50 victoires à son p.** he has fifty wins to his credit, he has notched up fifty wins

palme [palm] NF **1** *(de palmier)* palm (branch); *Fig (symbole de la victoire)* palm; **le dimanche des Palmes** Palm Sunday; **p. du martyre** martyr's crown, crown of martyrdom; **avec p.** *(décoration)* ≃ with bar; **décerner la p. de qch** to award the prize for sth; **remporter la p.** to win, to be victorious, *Litt* to carry off the palm of victory; **la p. lui revient** he's the winner, the victory goes to him; *Fig* **pour ce qui est de la cuisine, c'est lui qui remporte la p.** when it comes to cooking, there's no one to beat him; *Hum* **on peut lui décerner la p. de la paresse** he takes the biscuit for sheer laziness **2** *Arch (arbre)* palm (tree); **huile/vin de p.** palm oil/wine **3** *(pour nager)* flipper
▸▸ **la P. d'or (du festival de Cannes)** the Palme d'or (of the Cannes Film Festival) *(top prize awarded to a film)*; *Admin* **les palmes (académiques)** = decoration awarded to teachers; **décerner les palmes académiques à qn** to decorate sb for services to teaching

palmé [palme] ADJ **1** *Bot (feuille)* palmate **2** *Orn* web-footed; **pied p.** webbed foot; *Fam* **les avoir palmées** to be bone idle *or* a complete layabout

palmer [palmɛr] NM *Tech* micrometer

palmeraie [palmərɛ] NF palm grove

palmier [palmje] NM **1** *(arbre)* palm (tree); **p. dattier** date palm; **cœur de p.** palm (tree) heart **2** *Culin* = small sweet heart-shaped pastry

palmipède [palmipɛd] *Orn* ADJ web-footed, *Spéc* palmiped(e)
NM web-footed bird, *Spéc* palmiped(e)

palmiste [palmist] NM *(plante)* cabbage palm *or* tree; **chou p.** palm tree heart

palombe [palɔ̃b] NF *Région* ringdove, wood pigeon

palonnier [palɔnje] NM *Aviat* rudder bar; *Aut* **p. de freinage** compensator

palot [palo] NM *très Fam* French kiss; **rouler un p. à qn** to French kiss sb, *Br* to snog sb

pâlot, -otte [palo, -ɔt] ADJ rather pale, peaky

palourde [palurd] NF *(mollusque)* clam

palpable [palpabl] ADJ **1** *(que l'on peut toucher)* palpable, tangible **2** *(réel, vérifiable) (erreur, mensonge)* palpable; *(vérité etc)* obvious, plain

palpation [palpasjɔ̃] NF *Méd* palpation

palper [palpe] VT **1** *(objet)* to feel (with one's hands); *Méd* to palpate **2** *Fam (somme)* to be paid, to get
VI *Fam* to get one's money, to get paid; **qu'est-ce qu'il a dû p.!** he must have made a mint!
NM *Méd* palpation

palpeur [palpœr] NM (heat) sensor; *Ordinat* sensor; *Aut* **p. de détonation** knock sensor

palpitant [palpitɑ̃] ADJ *(cœur, pouls)* fluttering; *(plus fort)* throbbing; *Méd* palpitating; *(personne) (d'émotion etc)* quivering; **p. (d'intérêt)** *(roman, film etc)* exciting, thrilling
NM *Arg (cœur)* ticker

palpitation [palpitasjɔ̃] NF *(du cœur, pouls)* fluttering; *(plus fort)* throbbing; *Méd* palpitation; *(d'une paupière)* fluttering; **avoir des palpitations** to have palpitations

palpiter [palpite] VI *(du cœur, pouls)* to flutter; *(plus fort)* to throb; *Méd* to palpitate; *(d'une paupière)* to flutter; *(d'une lumière etc)* to flicker; *(d'une personne) (de peur, rage)* to quiver **(de** with); **p. de froid** to tremble with cold

paltoquet [paltɔkɛ] NM *Fam Vieilli* jackanapes

paluche [palyʃ] NF *très Fam (main)* mitt, paw

paludéen, -enne [palydeɛ̃, -ɛn] ADJ *(plante, terrain etc)* marsh; *Méd* malarial

paludisme [palydism] NM malaria

palustre [palystr] ADJ *(plante etc)* marsh; *Méd* malarial

PAM [pam] NM *(abrév* **programme alimentaire mondial)** WFP

pâmer (se) [səpame] VPR *Vieilli (s'évanouir)* to swoon, to faint; *Fig Hum* to (practically) swoon; *Fig* **se p. devant qn** to practically swoon over sb; **se p. (d'aise)** to be blissfully happy; **se p. de rire** to be convulsed with laughter; **ça la faisait se p. de rire, cette histoire** the story sent her into hysterics; **se p. d'admiration** to be in raptures **(sur** over), to be overcome with admiration **(sur** for); **se p. d'amour** to be head over heels in love

pâmoison [pamwazɔ̃] NF *Vieilli* swoon; *Iron* **tomber en p.** to swoon; **tomber en p. devant qch** to go into raptures *or* to swoon over sth

pampa [pɑ̃pa] NF *(d'Amérique du Sud)* pampas

pamphlet [pɑ̃flɛ] NM lampoon, satirical tract

> Il faut noter que le terme anglais **pamphlet** est un faux ami. Il désigne le plus souvent une brochure.

pamphlétaire [pɑ̃fletɛr] ADJ *(ton, esprit)* pamphleteering
N lampoonist, pamphleteer

pamplemousse [pɑ̃pləmus] NM *(fruit)* grapefruit

pampre [pɑ̃pr] NM *Litt* vine branch *(with grapes)*

Pan [pɑ̃] N *Myth* Pan

pan¹ [pɑ̃] NM **1** *(de chemise, manteau)* tail; *(de jupe)* panel; **relever les pans de son manteau** to hitch up one's coat; **il l'a enveloppée des pans de son manteau** he wrapped his coat around her; **se promener en p. de chemise** to wander about in one's shirt-tails **2** *(morceau)* section, piece; *Fig (d'enfance, d'une époque)* section, portion; **p. de mur** section of wall; **p. de ciel** patch of sky **3** *(d'un* *polyèdre etc)* face, side; **tour à huit pans** eight-sided *or* octagonal tower; **p. coupé** cant; **en p. coupé** with the corner cut off

pan² INT **1** bang!, crash!, wham!; **et p.! je te tue!** bang! bang! you're dead!; **et p., le voilà qui entre!** and then, would you believe it, in he comes! **2** *Enf* **je vais te faire p. p. (cucul)!** I'll smack you!

panacée [panase] NF panacea

panachage [panaʃaʒ] NM **1** *(de couleurs etc)* mixing **2** *Pol* **p. électoral** splitting one's vote between candidates from different parties

panache [panaʃ] NM **1** *(aigrette)* plume, panache; *(de plumes etc)* plume, tuft; **p. de fumée** plume *or* wreath *or* trail of smoke **2** *(brio, éclat)* panache; **avec p.** with panache; **il avait le goût du p.** he did things in style *or* with panache

panaché [panaʃe] ADJ **1** *(oiseau, fleur)* multicoloured, *Am* multicolored; *(feuillage)* variegated; *(foule)* motley; **p. de blanc** streaked with white, with white streaks; *Culin* **salade panachée** mixed salad; **glace panachée** = selection of various flavours of ice cream; **demi p.** shandy **2** *Pol* **liste (électorale) panachée** = ballot paper in which votes are split among candidates from different parties
NM shandy

panacher [panaʃe] VT **1** *(bigarrer) (couleurs)* to mix; **p. un bouquet** to put together a mixed bouquet **2** *Pol* **p. une liste électorale** to split one's votes *(among candidates from different parties)*

panade [panad] NF *Culin* = soup made from bread; *Fig Fam* **être dans la p.** to be in the soup *or* in a real fix; *(ne pas avoir d'argent temporairement)* to be short of cash; **ça m'a mise dans la p.** I was really up the creek; **quelle p.!** what a mess!

panafricain [panafrikɛ̃] ADJ *Pol* Pan-African

panafricanisme [panafrikanism] NM *Pol* Pan-Africanism

panais [panɛ] NM *(légume)* parsnip

Panama [panama] NM **1** *Géog* Panama; **le canal de P.** the Panama Canal **2** **p.** *(chapeau)* panama hat

Paname [panam] N *Géog Fam* = nickname given to Paris

panaméen, -enne [panameɛ̃, -ɛn] ADJ Panamanian
N **P.** Panamanian

panaméricain [panamerikɛ̃] ADJ *Pol* Pan-American

panaméricanisme [panamerikanism] NM *Pol* Pan-Americanism

panarabe [panarab] ADJ *Pol* Pan-Arab

panarabisme [panarabism] NM *Pol* Pan-Arabism

panard [panar] ADJ *(cheval)* knock-kneed
NM *très Fam (pied)* foot; **panards** feet, *Br* plates (of meat); *Fig* **quel p.!** great!, terrific!, fantastic!; **tu imagines, vivre au bord de la mer, quel p.!** just imagine how great *or* terrific *or* fantastic it would be to live at the seaside!; **ce n'est pas le p.** it's not exactly a load of laughs *or* a barrel of fun

panaris [panari] NM *Méd* whitlow

panavision [panavizjɔ̃] NF panavision

pan-bagnat, *pl* **pans-bagnats** [pɑ̃baɲa] NM = filled roll sliced and filled with salade niçoise

pancarte [pɑ̃kart] NF sign, notice; *(affiche)* placard

pancréas [pɑ̃kreas] NM *Anat* pancreas

pancréatique [pɑ̃kreatik] ADJ *Anat* pancreatic

panda [pɑ̃da] NM panda

pandémie [pɑ̃demi] NF *Méd* pandemic

pandémique [pɑ̃demik] ADJ *Méd* pandemic

pandémonium [pɑ̃demɔnjɔm] NM *(lieu de corruption)* den of vice *or* iniquity; *(lieu de désordre)* pandemonium

pandit [pɑ̃di] NM *(titre indien)* pandit, pundit

Pandore [pɑ̃dɔr] N *Myth* Pandora; **boîte de P.** Pandora's box

pané [pane] ADJ *Culin* coated with breadcrumbs, breaded

panégyrique [paneʒirik] NM eulogy, *Litt* panegyric; **faire le p. de qn** to extol sb's virtues *or* merits, to eulogize sb

panégyriste [paneʒirist] NM eulogist, *Litt* panegyrist

panel [panɛl] NM *(groupe)* panel; *(échantillon)* sample (group); *Mktg* **p. de consommateurs** consumer panel, shopping panel; *Mktg* **p. de distributeurs** distributor panel; *Mktg* **p. de détaillants** retail panel; *Mktg* **p. d'essayeurs de produits** product testing panel; **p. de téléspectateurs** television viewing panel

panéliste [panelist] N *Mktg* panellist, panel member

paner [pane] VT *Culin* to cover *or* coat with breadcrumbs, to bread

panetière [pantjer] NF bread bin

paneuropéanisme [panørɔpeanism] NM *Pol* Pan-Europeanism

paneuropéen, -enne [panørɔpeɛ̃, -ɛn] ADJ *Pol* Pan-European

pangermanisme [pɑ̃ʒermanism] NM *Pol* Pan-Germanism

pangermaniste [pɑ̃ʒermanist] ADJ, N *Pol* Pan-Germanist

panier [panje] NM **1** *(corbeille)* basket; *(de fruits etc)* basket(ful); **p. à anse(s)** basket; **un plein p. de fruits** a basketful of fruit; **mettre** *ou* **jeter qch au p.** to throw sth in the wastepaper basket; *Fig* to throw sth away *or* out, *Br Fam* to bin sth; **ton pantalon est bon à mettre au p.** your trousers aren't fit to be seen, your trousers should be thrown out; *Fig* **mettre tous ses œufs dans le même p.** to put all one's eggs in one basket; *Fig* **moi, les hommes, je les mets tous dans le même p.** men are all alike *or* the same, as far as I'm concerned; *Fig* **il ne faut pas tous les mettre dans le même p.** you can't lump them all together, they're not all tarred with the same brush; *Fig* **le dessus du p.** the elite; *Scol, Univ* the pick of the bunch, the cream of the crop; **il ne fréquente que le dessus du p.** he only mixes with the very best people; **faire partie du dessus du p.** to be out of the top drawer; *Scol, Univ* to be one of the best
2 *Mktg (présentoir)* dump bin; **p. de présentation en vrac, p. présentoir** dump bin; **p. à la sortie** check-out display; **p. vrac** dump bin
3 *Ordinat* shopping basket, *Am* shopping cart; **ajouter au p.** add to shopping basket *ou Am* shopping cart
4 *(nasse)* lobster pot
5 *Sport (au basketball)* basket; **réussir** *ou* **marquer un p.** to score (a basket)
6 *(de tondeuse)* grass box
7 *(pour diapositives)* slide magazine
8 *(de crinoline)* hoop
9 *Fam* **il a mis la main au p. de la serveuse** he groped the waitress's behind
▸▸ *Bourse* **p. d'actions** basket of shares; **p. à bouteilles** bottle carrier; *Fig* **p. de crabes: c'est un p. de crabes** they're constantly at each other's throats, they're always trying to stick knives in each other's backs; *Fin* **p. de devises** basket of currencies; **p. à légumes** *(pour cuisson vapeur)* steamer insert; *(de Cocotte-Minute®)* food basket; **p. à linge** linen basket; *Écon* **le p. de la ménagère** the shopping basket; **avec des conséquences sur le p. de la ménagère** with consequences

for the food bill; *Écon* **p. de monnaies** basket of currencies; **p. à ouvrage** sewing basket; *Fam* **p. percé** *(dépensier)* spendthrift; *Can (indiscret)* blabbermouth; **p. à provisions** shopping basket; **p. à salade** salad shaker; *Fam (convoi cellulaire)* police van *or Am* wagon, *Br Vieilli* Black Maria

panier-repas, *pl* **paniers-repas** NM *(panier)* lunch basket; *(repas)* packed lunch

panifiable [panifjabl] ADJ *(céréale)* suitable for making bread; **farine p.** bread flour

panifier [panifje] VT *(impf, pr sub* **n. panifiions, v. panifiiez)** **p. de la farine** to make bread

panique [panik] ADJ **peur p.** panic
NF panic; **pris de p.** panic-stricken; **pris de p., ils s'enfuirent** they fled in (a) panic; **pris de p., je ne trouvais plus mes mots** I was panic-stricken and couldn't say a word; **être pris de p.** to panic; **p. boursière** stock market panic; **ne pas céder à la p.** not to let oneself be panicked, not to give way to panic; **la police recommande à la population de ne pas céder à la p.** the police are urging people not to panic; *Fam* **pas de p., ce n'est pas la fin du monde!** don't panic, it's not the end of the world!; **c'était la p. totale** it was panic stations; **il y a eu un début de p.** people started to panic; **il y a eu un mouvement de p.** there was a stampede, there was panic; **la p. était générale** there was a general state of panic

paniqué [panike] ADJ *Fam* in a panic, panicky; **complètement p.** in a complete panic

paniquer [panike] *Fam* VT **p. qn** to get sb into a panic, to panic sb, to put the wind up sb
VI to (get into a) panic, to get panicky

panislamique [panislamik] ADJ *Pol* Pan-Islamic

panislamisme [panislamism] NM *Pol* Pan-Islamism

panne¹ [pan] NF **1** *Tex* panne, plush **2** *(gras)* fat, *Fig (d'une personne)* flab; *Fig* **tu prends/tu as de la p.** you're getting/you're flabby

panne² NF **1** *(arrêt de fonctionnement)* (mechanical) breakdown; *Aut* breakdown; *Élec* (power) failure, outage; *Ordinat* failure, crash; **p. de courant** *ou* **d'électricité** power failure *or* cut, blackout; *Radio, TV* **p. d'émission** technical fault *or* hitch; **p. de moteur** engine failure; **nous avons eu plusieurs pannes de moteur avec cette auto** the engine on the car has failed several times; **p. de secteur** power failure *or* outage, mains failure; *Ordinat* **p. du système** system crash; *Ordinat* **p. matérielle** hardware crash; **tomber en p.** *(d'une voiture, une machine)* to break down; *(d'un automobiliste)* to break down, to have a breakdown; **tomber en p. d'essence, tomber en p. sèche** to run out of petrol *or Am* gas; **en p.** *(ascenseur etc)* out of order; **je suis en p.** *(d'automobiliste)* I've broken down; *Fam* **rester en p. devant une difficulté** to be put off *or* floored by a difficulty; *Fam* **laisser qn en p.** to leave sb in the lurch, to let sb down; *Fam* **je suis en p. d'allumettes/de café/d'idées** I've run out of matches/coffee/ideas; **trouver la p.** to find the problem, to find the cause of the problem; **soudain, ce fut la p.** suddenly, we/they/it/etc broke down; *Fam Hum* **j'ai eu une p. d'oreiller** I overslept; *Fam* **il m'a fait le coup de la p.** he pretended we'd run out of petrol, he tried to pull the old 'we've run out of petrol' trick **2** *Naut* **en p.** hove to; **mettre un navire en p.** to bring a ship to

panne³ NF *Constr (d'un toit)* purlin

panne⁴ NF *Tech (d'un marteau)* peen, pane

panneau, -eaux [pano] NM **1** *(pour afficher)* board **2** *(élément plan) (de bois, contre-plaqué etc)* panel; **panneaux** panelling, panels; **porte à panneaux** panelled door; **p.**

vitré glass panel; **p. mobile/coulissant** movable/sliding panel **3** *(pour le gibier)* snare, net; *Fig* **tomber** *ou* **donner dans le p.** to fall into the trap **4** *Aut* signpost, direction sign **5** *Ordinat (d'écran d'ordinateur)* pane
▸▸ **p. d'affichage** notice *ou Am* bulletin board; *Ordinat* bulletin board; *Naut* **p. de cale** hatch cover; *Aut* **p. de carrosserie** body panel; *Ordinat* **p. de configuration** control panel; *Mktg* **p. à crochets** *(présentoir)* pegboard; *Naut* **p. d'écoutille** hatch cover; **panneaux électoraux** noticeboards for election posters; *Aut* **p. indicateur** signpost; **p. publicitaire** hoarding, *Am* billboard; **p. de signalisation (routière)** roadsign; **p. solaire** solar panel

panneton [pantɔ̃] NM *(d'une clé)* web, bit

pano [pano] NM *(abrév* **panoramique***) TV, Cin* **p. de poursuite** following pan; **p. filé** whip *or* zip pan

panonceau, -eaux [panɔ̃so] NM **1** *(de notaire etc)* plaque **2** *(pancarte)* sign **3** *Hist* escutcheon

panoplie [panɔpli] NF *(armure)* panoply; *(assortiment) (d'outils)* set; *Fig (de raisons)* array, multitude; *(d'arguments)* battery; *(de dettes)* multitude, *Fam* pile; **p. de soldat/d'infirmière** *(pour enfants)* soldier's/nurse's outfit *or* costume; **toute la p. du parfait bricoleur** a whole array of DIY equipment; *Iron* **j'ai eu droit à toute la p.** I got the works

panorama [panɔrama] NM panorama; *Fig* overview

panoramique [panɔramik] ADJ *(écran etc)* panoramic; *(restaurant)* with panoramic views; *Méd (radiographie)* all-over, total; **voiture avec carrosserie p.** car with panoramic *or* wrap-round windows; **vue p.** panoramic view; *Fig* overview; *Cin* **prise p.** panning shot ▪ NM *Cin, TV* pan (shot); **faire un p.** to pan; **p. horizontal** pan (shot); **faire un p. horizontal** to pan; **faire un p. vers le bas/le haut** to pan down/up; **p. vertical** tilt, tilted shot; **faire un p. vertical** to tilt

panoramiquer [panɔramike] VI *TV, Cin* to pan; **p. vers le bas/le haut** to pan down/up

panosse [panɔs] NF *Suisse (serpillière)* mop

panosser [panɔse] VT *Suisse (passer à la serpillière)* to mop

pansage [pɑ̃saʒ] NM *(d'un cheval etc)* grooming

panse [pɑ̃s] NF **1** *Fam (ventre)* belly, paunch, pot; **s'en mettre plein la p.** to gorge *or* stuff oneself; **manger à s'en faire crever la p.** to stuff oneself *or* one's face, to eat until one is fit to burst **2** *(d'un ruminant)* first stomach, paunch, rumen **3** *(d'une bouteille etc)* belly, bulge

pansement [pɑ̃smɑ̃] NM *Méd* **1** *(action) (d'une blessure)* dressing **2** *(élément protecteur)* dressing; *(enroulé autour d'une blessure)* bandage; **p. (adhésif)** (sticking) plaster; **faire un p.** to dress a wound, to apply a dressing; **refaire un p.** to change a dressing; **faire/refaire un p. à qn** to dress sb's wound(s)/change sb's dressing(s); **il est couvert de pansements** he's all bandaged up; **il faut mettre un p.** it needs a plaster
▸▸ **p. gastrique** *(liquide)* ≃ milk of magnesia; *(poudre)* stomach powder

panser [pɑ̃se] VT **1** *(blessure)* to dress, to put a dressing on; *(membre)* to bandage; *(avec un sparadrap)* to put a plaster on; **p. qn** to dress sb's wounds; *Fig* **p. ses blessures** to lick one's wounds; **six mois lui suffiront pour p. ses blessures** six months will be long enough for him to get over it **2** *(cheval)* to groom, to rub down

panslavisme [pɑ̃slavism] NM *Pol* Pan-Slavism

pansu [pɑ̃sy] ADJ *(personne)* potbellied, paunchy; *(bouteille)* potbellied

pantagruélique [pɑ̃tagryelik] ADJ *(repas, appétit)* enormous, gigantic

pantalon [pɑ̃talɔ̃] NM **1** (pair of) trousers *or Am* pants; **mettre un p.** to put on a pair of trousers; **mettre son p.** to put on one's trousers; **un p. neuf** a new pair of trousers, some new trousers; **p. cigarette** drainpipes; **p. fuseau** tapered trousers *or Am* pants, ski pants; **p. de golf** plus-fours; **p. à pattes d'éléphant** flared trousers *or Am* pants, flares; **p. à pinces** pleated trousers *or Am* pants; **p. de pyjama** pyjama trousers *or Am* pants; **p. de ski** ski pants; **p. de toile** canvas trousers *or Am* pants; **p. de velours côtelé** corduroy trousers *or Am* pants, cords; **elle porte un p.** *ou Vieilli* **des pantalons** she wears trousers; *Fig* **c'est elle qui porte le p.** she wears the trousers *or Am* pants VOIR GRAMMAIRE A10 **2** *Théâtre* **P.** Pantaloon

pantalon-jupe, *pl* **pantalons-jupes** NM palazzo pants

pantalonnade [pɑ̃talɔnad] NF **1** *Hist, Théâtre* burlesque farce **2** *(hypocrisie)* piece of hypocrisy

pantelant [pɑ̃tlɑ̃] ADJ **1** panting, gasping (**de** with); **tout p.** gasping for breath, out of breath; **la nouvelle m'a laissé p.** the news left *or* had me gasping **2** *(homme ou animal à l'agonie)* quivering, twitching; **chair pantelante** *(d'un animal à l'agonie)* twitching flesh

panteler [pɑ̃tle] VI (**je pantelle,** n. **pantelons; je pantellerai**) *Vieilli (respirer)* to pant; *Fig (d'émotion)* to gasp (**de** with); *(palpiter)* to quiver

panthéisme [pɑ̃teism] NM *Phil* pantheism

panthéiste [pɑ̃teist] *Phil* ADJ pantheistic(al) ▪ N pantheist

panthéon [pɑ̃teɔ̃] NM pantheon; **faire partie du p. des hommes célèbres** to have a place in the hall of fame; **le p. cinématographique** the film industry's hall of fame; **elle fait partie du p. cinématographique** she is one of the all-time movie greats; **mettre qn au p. des musiciens** to consider sb a great musician, to rank sb among the best musicians

panthère [pɑ̃tɛr] NF **1** *Zool* leopard; **p. des neiges** snow leopard; **p. noire** panther **2** *Pol* **les Panthères noires** the Black Panthers

pantin [pɑ̃tɛ̃] NM *(poupée)* jumping jack; *Péj (fantoche)* puppet, stooge; **elle a fait de son époux un p.** she has turned her husband into a puppet

pantographe [pɑ̃tɔgraf] NM *Rail* pantograph; *Aut* scissor jack

pantois [pɑ̃twa] ADJ astounded, *Fam* flabbergasted; **j'en suis tout p.** I'm astounded *or* speechless *or Fam* flabbergasted; **en rester p.** to be speechless *or Fam* flabbergasted

pantomime [pɑ̃tɔmim] NF **1** *Théâtre (art)* mime; *(spectacle)* mime show **2** *Péj (comédie)* scene; **que signifie cette p.?** what is all this nonsense?

> Il faut noter que le terme anglais **pantomime** est un faux ami. Il désigne un spectacle de Noël inspiré d'un conte de fées.

pantouflard, -arde [pɑ̃tuflar, -ard] ADJ, N *Fam* stay-at-home; **ils sont très pantouflards** they're real homebodies, they never go out; **ce qu'il est p.!** he's a real stay-at-home!

pantoufle [pɑ̃tufl] NF slipper; **il était en pantoufles** he was wearing slippers, he was in his slippers; **les pantoufles de vair** *ou* **de verre de Cendrillon** Cinderella's glass slippers; *Fig* **passer sa vie dans ses pantoufles** to live a quiet life; *Fig Fam* **raisonner comme une p.** to talk through one's hat

pantoufler [pɑ̃tufle] VI *Fam (d'un fonctionnaire)* to join the private sector

pantoute [pɑ̃tut] ADV *Can Fam (pas du tout)* absolutely not, no way; *(jamais de la vie)* never

panure [panyr] NF *Culin* breadcrumbs

Panurge [panyrʒ] N **agir comme les moutons de P.** to follow the herd

panurgisme [panyrʒism] NM herd mentality

PAO [peao] NF *Ordinat (abrév* **publication assistée par ordinateur***)* DTP

paon [pɑ̃] NM **1** *(oiseau)* peacock; **pousser des cris de p.** to screech like a peacock; *Fig* **se parer des plumes du p.** to take all the credit; **être vaniteux comme un p.** to be as vain as a peacock; **faire le p.** to strut about **2** *(insecte)* peacock butterfly

paonne [pan] NF peahen

paonneau, -eaux [pano] NM peachick

PAP [pap] NM *(abrév* **prêt d'accession à la propriété***)* = loan for first-time homebuyers

papa [papa] NM dad, *surtout Enf* daddy, *surtout Am* pop; **jouer au p. et à la maman** to play mummies and daddies; **c'est un fils à p.** he's a daddy's boy; *Fam* **faire qch à la p.** to do sth in a leisurely fashion; *Fam* **l'amour à la p.** boring sex; **nous allons faire ça à la p.** we'll take it easy, we won't rush things; **aller à la p.** *(en voiture)* to potter along; *Fam Péj* **de p.** old-fashioned, behind the times; *Fam* **le cinéma/l'armée de p.** the films/army of the past; **p. gâteau** indulgent father; **p. poule** doting father

papal, -ale, -aux, -ales [papal, -o] ADJ papal

paparazzi [paparadzi] NMPL paparazzi

paparazzo [paparadzo] NM paparazzo

papauté [papote] NF papacy

papaye [papaj] NF pawpaw, papaya

papayer [papaje] NM pawpaw *or* papaya (tree)

pape [pap] NM **1** *Rel* pope; *Fam* **heureux comme un p.** happy as a sandboy, happy as Larry; *Fam* **sérieux comme un p.** deadly serious, very solemn; **le P. Jean-Paul II** Pope John Paul II **2** *(d'une association, d'un mouvement etc)* leading light

papelard¹, -arde [paplar, -ard] *Péj* ADJ *(voix etc)* sanctimonious; **il a un air p.** he looks as if butter wouldn't melt in his mouth; **dit-il d'un air p.** he said sanctimoniously ▪ N sanctimonious *or* self-righteous person, hypocrite

papelard² NM *Fam (petit papier)* (piece of) paper; *(journal)* (news)paper; *Journ (article)* article, piece; **j'ai oublié mes papelards** I've forgotten my (identity) papers *or Fam* my ID

paperasse [papras] NF *Péj* papers, *Br Fam* bumf, bumph; *(fiches à remplir)* forms; **il y a plein de p. sur mon bureau** my desk is covered in paper; **c'est de la p.!** it's just a load of bumph!; **j'ai horreur de toutes ces paperasses** I hate all this red tape; **je passe mon temps à m'occuper de paperasses** I spend all my time doing paperwork

paperasserie [paprasri] NF *Péj (accumulation of)* papers, *Br Fam* bumf, bumph; *(à remplir)* forms; **la p. (administrative)** red tape; **il y a trop de p.** *(dans ce travail)* there's too much paperwork; *(pour obtenir un visa etc)* there's too much paperwork *or* red tape (involved)

paperassier, -ière [paprasje, -jɛr] *Péj* ADJ *(personne)* fond of paperwork; *(procédure)* cluttered up with red tape ▪ N **1** *(personne qui amasse les papiers)* hoarder of (old) papers, *Am Fam* pack rat **2** *(fonctionnaire)* bureaucrat

papet [papɛ] NM *Suisse Culin* = Swiss dish made with potatoes, leeks and sausages

papeterie [papetri] NF **1** *(fabrication)* paper manufacturing; *(usine)* paper mill; **la p.** *(industrie)* the paper industry **2** *(magasin)* stationer's (shop); *(articles)* stationery

papetier, -ière [pap(ə)tje, -jɛr] N **1** *Ind* paper manufacturer **2** *Com* stationer
ADJ paper

papetier-libraire, *pl* **papetiers-libraires** NM *Com* bookseller and stationer

papi [papi] NM grandpa, granddad

papier [papje] NM **1** *(matière)* paper; **pâte à p.** pulp; **un p.** a sheet *or* piece of paper; **notez plutôt cela dans votre carnet que sur un p.** write it down in your notebook rather than on a scrap of paper; **son bureau est couvert de papiers** his desk is covered in paper(s); **classer ses papiers** to put one's papers in order; **jeter des idées sur le p.** to put some ideas down on paper; **ça n'est pas ce qui est dit sur le p.** that's not what it says here; *Fig* **sur le p.** on paper, in theory; **gratter du p.** *(comme métier)* to be a pen-pusher; *(en utiliser beaucoup)* to use a lot of paper; *Fig Fam* **être dans les petits papiers de qn** to be in sb's good books; *Fig Fam* **rayez cela de vos papiers** don't count on it, (you can) forget it **2** **papiers** *(documents)* papers, documents; *Jur* **papiers d'une affaire** documents relating to a case; **les papiers de la vente/de la voiture** the sale/car documents; *Admin* **papiers (d'identité)** identity papers, *Fam* ID; **mes papiers sont en règle** my papers are in order; **vos papiers, s'il vous plaît!** can I see your identity papers, please?; *Aut* can I see your driving licence *or Am* driver's license, please?; **faux papiers** false ID **3** *Jur* **p. timbré** stamped paper *(for official and legal documents)* **4** *Fin* bill(s); **p. de commerce** commercial *or* trade paper; **p. long** *ou* **à long terme** long(-dated) bill **5** *Journ* article, piece; **faire un p. sur qch** to do a piece *or* an article on sth
▸▸ *Fam* **p. alu** (kitchen *or* aluminium) foil; **p. d'aluminium** aluminium foil, tinfoil; **p. d'argent** silver foil *or* paper; **p. avion** airmail paper; *Fin* **p. bancable** bankable paper; *Ordinat* **p. à bandes perforées** perforated paper; **p. bible** Bible paper; **p. de bonbon** sweet wrapper; **p. buvard** blotting paper; **p. cadeau** gift wrap, wrapping paper; **mettre un p. cadeau à qch** to giftwrap sth; **p. calque** tracing paper; **p. carbone** carbon paper; *Ordinat* **p. Caroll** perforated paper; **p. à cigarettes** cigarette paper; **fin comme du p. à cigarettes** *(usé)* like tissue paper; **un voile fin comme du p. à cigarettes** a gossamer-thin veil; *Fin* **p. commercial** commercial paper; *Fin* **p. commercial de premier ordre** prime bill; *Ordinat* **p. continu** continuous paper *or* stationery; *Ordinat* **p. continu plié en accordéon** fanfold paper; **p. couché** coated paper; *Beaux-Arts* art paper; *Vulg* **p. cul** bog paper; **p. à dessin** drawing paper; **p. d'emballage** wrapping *or* packing paper; **p. émeri** emery paper; **p. à en-tête** headed notepaper; **p. d'étain** tinfoil; **p. à étiquettes** sheets of labels; *Fin* **p. sur l'étranger** foreign bill; **p. filtre** filter paper; **p. glacé** glazed paper; **papiers gras** litter; **p. hygiénique** toilet paper, *Br Fam* loo paper; *Ordinat* **p. d'impression** printer paper; **p. journal** newsprint; *(vieux journaux)* newspaper; **p. kraft** manila paper; **p. à lettres** notepaper, writing paper; *Ordinat* **p. listing** listing paper; **p. mâché** papier mâché; **poupée en p. mâché** papier mâché doll; **avoir une mine de p. mâché** to look green about the gills; **p. machine** typing paper; **p. ministre** foolscap; *Fin* **p.-monnaie** paper money; *Ordinat* **p. multiple** multi-part stationery; **p. à musique** music paper, manuscript paper; **être réglé comme du p. à musique** to be as regular as clockwork; **une vie réglée comme du p. à musique** a very orderly life; **un emploi du temps réglé comme du p. à musique** a very strict routine; **chez nous, le matin, c'est réglé comme du p. à musique** there's a strict routine in our house in the morning; *Fin* **p. négociable** negotiable paper; *Fin* **p. à ordre** instrument to order; **p. parcheminé** greaseproof paper; *aussi Ordinat* **p. peint** wallpaper; **p. pelure** onion skin; *Phot* **p. photo** photographic paper; *Fin* **p. au porteur** bearer paper; **p. réglé** ruled *or* lined paper; *Phot* **p. sensible** sensitized paper; **p. de soie** tissue paper; *Ordinat* **p. thermique** thermal paper; **p. toilette** toilet paper, *Br Fam* loo paper; *Fin* **papiers valeurs** securities; **p. vélin** vellum paper; **p. de verre** glasspaper, sandpaper; *Fin* **p. à vue** sight paper

papillaire [papilɛr] ADJ *Anat etc* papillary

papille [papij, -il] NF *Anat, Bot* papilla; **p. gustative** taste bud

papillon [papijɔ̃] NM **1** *(insecte)* butterfly; **p. de nuit** moth; *Fig* **être un p.** to be flighty; *Fam* **minute p.!** just a minute!, hold on a minute!; *Natation* **(brasse) p.** butterfly (stroke); **nager le p.** to do the butterfly **2** *(dans un livre)* inset; *(prospectus)* handbill; *(sur document)* flag; **p. publicitaire** advertising leaflet, flier **3** *Fam (contravention)* (parking) ticket **4** *Tech (de réglage)* butterfly valve, throttle; *(écrou)* thumb screw, butterfly *or* wing nut; *Aut* **p. des gaz** throttle

papillonnant [papijɔnɑ̃] ADJ fluttering, flitting; *Fig (personne)* flighty, fickle

papillonnement [papijɔnmɑ̃] NM fluttering; *(d'un lieu à un autre, d'une personne à une autre)* flitting; *Fig (d'une personne)* flightiness, fickleness

papillonner [papijɔne] VI *(des paupières)* to flutter; *(d'une personne à une autre)* to flit about; *(d'un sujet à un autre)* to pass rapidly; **les yeux des enfants papillonnaient devant le spectacle** the children blinked (in astonishment) at the sight

papillotage [papijɔtaʒ] NM **p. des yeux** blinking (of the eyes)

papillote [papijɔt] NF **1** *Culin (pour faire cuire les côtelettes etc)* buttered paper; *(en papier alu)* silver foil; **cailles en papillotes** quails en papillote **2** *(papier)* twist of paper; *(autour d'un jambon etc)* frill; *Fig* **tu peux en faire des papillotes** you can throw it away; *Fig* **ta dissertation, tu peux en faire des papillotes** your essay is rubbish, your essay isn't worth the paper it's written on **3** *Arch (pour les cheveux)* paper **4** *Région (bonbon)* = special kind of sweet with shiny wrapper, available at Christmas

papillotement [papijɔtmɑ̃] NM *(des yeux)* blinking; *(d'une lumière)*, *Cin, TV* flicker

papilloter [papijɔte] VI **1** *(des yeux)* to blink; *(d'une lumière)*, *Cin, TV* to flicker **2** *(scintiller)* to glitter; *(plus brillamment)* to dazzle
VT *Arch* **p. ses cheveux** to put one's hair in curl papers

papisme [papism] NM (Roman) Catholicism, *Péj* popery, papistry

papiste [papist] N (Roman) Catholic, *Péj* papist

papoter [papɔte] VI *Fam* to chat, to have a natter; **nous avons passé la journée à p.** we spent the day nattering *or Am* shooting the breeze

papou, -oue [papu] ADJ Papuan
NM *Ling* Papuan
N **P.** Papuan

Papouasie-Nouvelle-Guinée [papwazi-nuvɛlgine] NF Papua New Guinea

papouille [papuj] NF *Fam* **faire des papouilles à qn** to cuddle *or* squeeze sb; **se faire des papouilles** to have a bit of a cuddle *or Br* a bit of slap and tickle; **il aime les papouilles** he likes a little cuddle

paprika [paprika] NM *Bot, Culin* paprika

papule [papyl] NF pimple; *Méd* papule; *(d'urticaire)* weal

papy [papi] NM granpa, granddad

papy-boom [papibum] NM *Hum (augmentation de la proportion du troisième âge dans la population)* grey *or Am* gray boom

papyrus [papirys] NM papyrus; *(feuille)* sheet of papyrus; **écrire sur des p.** to write on papyrus VOIR GRAMMAIRE A14.

paqson [paksɔ̃] NM *Fam* = **pacson**

pâque [pɑk] NF *Rel* **P., la P. juive** Passover
NFPL **pâques** Easter; **faire ses pâques** to take the sacrament at Easter
NM *(contraction of* **jour de Pâques,** *used without article)* **Pâques** Easter; **le lundi de Pâques** Easter Monday; **œufs de Pâques** Easter eggs; *Fig Fam* **remettre qch à Pâques ou à la Trinité** to put sth off indefinitely; **il le fera, enfin, à Pâques ou à la Trinité** he'll never do it in a month of Sundays; **île de Pâques** Easter Island

Pâques
In France, Easter is traditionally symbolized not only by eggs but also by bells; according to legend, church bells fly to Rome at Easter. At this time of the year, people offer each other chocolate eggs, bells, fish or hens.

paquebot [pakbo] NM *Naut* (steam)ship; *(gros)* liner; **p. de ligne** liner; **p. de haute mer** ocean liner

paquégique [pakeʒik] NF *Mktg* packaging

pâquerette [pɑkrɛt] NF daisy; *Fam* **voler au ras des pâquerettes** *(conversation, plaisanterie)* to be a bit on the basic side

paquet [pakɛ] NM **1** *(de thé, pâtes)* packet; *(de café, sucre, riz)* bag, packet; *(de cigarettes)* packet, *Am* pack; *(postal)* parcel, package; *(ballot, liasse)* bundle; **expédier** *ou* **envoyer un p.** to send (off) a parcel; **faire un p.** to make up a parcel; **faire son p.** *ou* **ses paquets** to pack one's bags; **p. de billets** wad of notes; *Fam* **il a touché un joli p.** he's made a packet; **du riz/du café en p.** prepacked *or* packaged rice/coffee; **il fume un p. (de cigarettes) par jour** he smokes twenty *or* a packet *or Am* a pack a day; **il est tombé un p. de neige** it snowed heavily, there was a lot of snow; **des paquets d'eau tombaient** the rain was coming down in sheets; **c'est un p. d'os** he's/she's all skin and bone; **c'est un p. de nerfs** he's/she's a bag *or* bundle of nerves; *Fig Fam* **mettre le p.** to go all out, to pull out all the stops; *Fig Fam* **risquer le p.** to risk *or* chance everything one's got *or* the lot; *Fig Fam* **lâcher le p.** to spill the beans **2** *Ordinat* packet **3** *Rugby* **p. (d'avants)** pack
▸▸ *Fin* **p. d'actions** parcel *or* block of shares; *Com* **p. économique** economy pack; *Com* **p. familial** family-size packet; **p. fiscal** tax package; **p. de mer** *(vague)* big wave; **embarquer des paquets de mer** *(d'un bateau)* to take on a lot of water; **p. postal** parcel; *Com* **p. de présentation** display pack; *Fin* **p. de valeurs** parcel *or* block of shares

paquetage [paktaʒ] NM *Mil etc* (soldier's) pack; **faire son p.** to get one's kit ready

paquet-cadeau, *pl* **paquets-cadeaux** NM gift-wrapped parcel; **je vous fais un p.?** would you like it gift-wrapped?; **dans un joli p.** prettily gift-wrapped

paquet-poste, *pl* **paquets-poste** NM mailing box

PAR [par]

PRÉP by **4, 6** ▪ through **1** ▪ round here *(par ici)* **2** ▪ on **3** ▪ in **3** ▪ at **4** ▪ out of **5** ▪ with **6** ▪ according to **7** ▪ per **8**

PRÉP SEE GRAMMAR B56 **1** *(à travers) (porte, hall, trou de la serrure)* through; **il entra p. la fenêtre** he came in through *or* by the window; **regarder p. la fenêtre** *(de l'intérieur)* to look out (of) the window; *(de l'extérieur)* to look (in) through the window; **passer p. Calais** to travel *or* go through *or* via Calais *or* by way of Calais; **venez p. ici** come this way; **allez p. là** go that way; **p. ici la sortie** this is the way out, it's this way out; **p. où est-il passé?** which way did he go?; **p. où passe ce cordon électrique?** where does this wire go?; **p. où est-il entré?** how did he get in?; **il court p. les rues** he runs through the streets; **de p. le monde** all over the world

2 *(position)* **p. ici** round (about) here; **p. 10° de latitude nord** at a latitude of 10° North; **j'ai mal p. ici** it hurts round about here; **ça doit être p. là quelque part** it must be over there somewhere

3 *(pendant, durant)* **p. un jour d'hiver** on a winter's day; **p. cette chaleur/ces temps de pluie** in this heat/rainy weather; **p. le passé** in the past; **je l'ai averti p. trois fois** I warned him three times; *Litt* **p. trois fois, il fut blessé** he was wounded on three separate occasions

4 *(agent)* by; **tu as été appelé p. M. Alain** Mr Alain called you, you had a call from Mr Alain; **accablé p. l'inquiétude** overcome by *or* with anxiety; **soulagé p. cette nouvelle** relieved by *or* at the news; **faire qch p. soi-même** *(seul)* to do sth by oneself *or* on one's own; *(de sa propre volonté)* to do sth on one's own initiative; **examiner/juger/voir qch p. soi-même** to examine/judge/see sth for oneself; **elle est remarquable p. sa beauté** she is remarkable for her beauty; **elle est unique p. sa générosité/son intelligence** there is no one to equal her for generosity/intelligence; **j'ai appris p. les Martin que vous étiez malade** I heard through *or* from the Martins that you were ill; *Fam* **tu le sais p. qui, toi?** who did you get that from?, who told you that?; **faire faire qch p. qn** to have sth done by sb; **as-tu vu Don Juan p. Planchon?** have you seen Planchon's Don Juan?

5 *(motif) (habitude, négligence, curiosité, amitié etc)* out of; **j'ai fait cela p. amitié/respect pour vous** I did it out of friendship/respect for you; **p. pitié!** for pity's sake!; **p. hasard/erreur** by chance/mistake; **p. malheur** unfortunately, as bad luck would have it

6 *(au moyen de) (clou, chaîne etc)* with, by (means of); *(train, avion, voiture, bateau)* by; **il fut salué p. des acclamations** he was hailed with *or* by cheers; **remercié p. un bouquet** thanked with a bouquet; **conduire/ prendre qn p. la main** to lead/take sb by the hand; **tenir qn p. la taille** to hold sb round the waist; **envoyer qch p. la poste** to send sth by post *or* through the post; **répondre p. oui ou p. non** to answer yes or no; **commencer** *ou* **débuter/finir** *ou* **achever** *ou* **terminer p. qch/faire qch** to begin/end with sth/by doing sth; **se terminer p. un divorce/ une dispute** to end in divorce/an argument; **commençons p. le commencement** let's begin at the beginning; **il a essayé p. tous les moyens** he tried (by) every possible means, he tried everything; **il est monté p. l'escalier** he took the stairs up; **il a dû monter p. l'échelle** he must have climbed the ladder; **mon cousin p. alliance** my cousin by marriage; **société p. actions** joint-stock company; **obtenir qch p. la force** to obtain sth by

force; **p. la seule volonté** by sheer force of will; **appeler qn p. son nom** to call sb by his/her name; *Fig* **appeler les choses p. leur(s) nom(s)** to call a spade a spade; **p. route** by road

7 *(selon)* according to; **p. taille, p. ordre de grandeur** according to size; **p. ordre alpha-bétique/chronologique** in alphabetical/chronological order

8 *(distributif)* **entrer deux p. deux** to come in two by two, to come in in twos; **deux jours p. semaine** two days a week; **il gagne 200 euros p. semaine** he earns 200 euros a *or* per week; **10 000 euros p. an** 10,000 euros a year *or* per annum; **un siège p. personne** one seat per person; **un guide p. groupe de six** one guide per group of six *or* for each group of six; **actualité transmise heure p. heure** hourly news broadcasts

9 *Arch (au nom de)* **de p. le Roi** by order of the King, in the name of the King

ADV *Litt* **p. trop** far too, much too; **vous êtes p. trop aimable** you are much too kind

para [para] NM *Fam (abrév* **parachutiste**) para

parabole [parabɔl] NF **1** *(allégorie)* parable; **parler par paraboles** to speak in parables **2** *Géom* parabola **3** *Tél, TV (antenne)* satellite dish, dish aerial, *Am* dish antenna

parabolique [parabɔlik] ADJ *(miroir), Géom (courbe)* parabolic; *Tél, TV* **antenne p.** satellite dish, dish aerial, *Am* dish antenna; **radiateur p.** electric fire *(with parabolic reflector)* NM electric fire *(with parabolic reflector)*

paracétamol [parasetamɔl] NM paracetamol; **prendre du p.** to take some paracetamol; **deux cachets de p.** two paracetamol

parachèvement [paraʃɛvmɑ̃] NM completion, finishing; *(perfectionnement)* perfecting, perfection

parachever [paraʃ(ə)ve] VT *(conj like* **achever**) to complete, to finish off; *(perfectionner)* to perfect

parachutage [paraʃytaʒ] NM parachuting, dropping (by parachute); *Pol Fam (d'un candidat)* parachuting in; *Fig Fam* **son p. dans le bureau** the way he was foisted on *or* parachuted into the office

parachute [paraʃyt] NM *(appareil de saut)* parachute, *Fam* chute; **p. dorsal/ventral** back-(pack)/lap-pack parachute; **saut en p.** parachute jump; **sauter en p.** to make a parachute jump; **faire du p.** to go parachuting; **p. ascensionnel** parascending

parachuter [paraʃyte] VT *(vivres)* to drop by parachute, to parachute in; *(soldats)* to parachute in; *Pol Fam (nommer)* to parachute in; *Fig Fam* **la façon dont il s'est fait p. dans le service** the way he was foisted on *or* parachuted into the department; *Fig Fam* **j'ai été parachuté à ce poste** I've been pitchforked into this job

parachutisme [paraʃytism] NM parachuting, parachute jumping

parachutiste [paraʃytist] N parachutist, parachute jumper
NM *Mil* paratrooper; **parachutistes** *(corps d'armée)* paratroops
ADJ parachute

parade [parad] NF **1** *(défilé)* parade; **faire la p.** to parade; **comme à la p.** *(facilement)* like clockwork; **p. de cirque** circus parade **2** *(exhibition)* show, ostentation; **faire p. de** *(ses bijoux, ses connaissances)* to parade, to display, to show off; *(sa beauté)* to flaunt; **habits de p.** full-dress *or* ceremonial clothes; *Fig* **de p.** *(sourire, air etc)* insincere, forced **3** *Équitation (de cheval)* stopping, pulling up **4** *Zool* display; **p. nuptiale** *(des animaux)* courtship dance *or* ritual **5** *Escrime* parade, parry; *Boxe* parry **6** *(réplique)* riposte; **faire**

une p. to riposte, to parry; **je n'ai pas encore trouvé la p.** I haven't come up with a way of handling it/them yet

parader [parade] VI to show off; *(en se promenant)* to strut about; *Zool* to display

paradigmatique [paradigmatik] *Ling* ADJ paradigmatic
NF study of paradigmatic relationships

paradigme [paradigm] NM *Ling* paradigm

paradis [paradi] NM paradise, heaven; *Fig* paradise; **un p. terrestre** heaven on earth, an earthly paradise; **les p. artificiels** drug-induced euphoria; **l'enfer et le p.** heaven and hell; **aller au** *ou* **en p.** to go to heaven *or* paradise; **il ne l'emportera pas au** *ou* **en p.** he won't get away with it, he'll be sorry; **un p. pour les enfants** a paradise for children; **c'est le p. des pêcheurs** it's a fisherman's paradise *or* idea of heaven; *Théâtre Fam* **le p.** the gods; **oiseau de p.** bird of paradise
▸▸ **p. fiscal** tax haven; **le P. terrestre** the Garden of Eden

paradisiaque [paradizjak] ADJ of paradise, *Fml* paradisiac(al), paradisaical; *Fig (vacances, lieu)* heavenly

paradisier [paradizje] NM *(oiseau)* bird of paradise

paradoxal, -ale, -aux, -ales [paradɔksal, -o] ADJ paradoxical; **c'est complètement p.** it's totally illogical

paradoxalement [paradɔksalmɑ̃] ADV paradoxically

paradoxe [paradɔks] NM paradox

parafe [paraf] NM = **paraphe**

parafer [parafe] VT = **parapher**

paraffinage [parafinaʒ] NM paraffining, waxing

paraffine [parafin] NF *Chimie* paraffin; *Com* paraffin (wax); *Méd* **huile de p.** liquid paraffin

paraffiner [parafine] VT to paraffin

parafiscal, -ale, -aux, -ales [parafiskal, -o] ADJ *(taxe)* exceptional, special

parafiscalité [parafiskalite] NF indirect taxation, special taxation

parage¹ [paraʒ] NM *Arch* **de haut p.** of high lineage, high-born

parage² NM **1** *Naut (souvent pl)* **parages** waters, region(s); **les parages du cap Horn** the waters off Cape Horn; **se trouver dans les parages du cap Horn** to be off Cape Horn **2** *(toujours pl)* **dans les parages de ...** in the vicinity of ..., near ...; **que faites-vous dans ces parages?** what are you doing here *or* in this neck of the woods?; **est-ce qu'il est dans les parages?** is he around?; **il est dans les parages** he's around somewhere; **elle habite dans les parages** she lives round about here

paragraphe [paragraf] NM **1** paragraph; *Journ* par; *(d'un texte de loi)* subsection **2** *Typ* section mark, paragraph

Paraguay [paragwɛ] NM Paraguay

paraguayen, -enne [paragwɛjɛ̃, -ɛn] ADJ Paraguayan
N **P.** Paraguayan

para-hôtellerie NF serviced accommodation industry

paraître¹ [parɛtr] NM **l'être et le p.** appearance and reality; **s'intéresser davantage au p.** to be more interested in appearances; **juger sur le p.** to judge by appearances

PARAÎTRE² *(prp* **paraissant**; *pp* **paru**; *pr ind* **je parais, il paraît, n. paraissons**; *impf* **je paraissais**; *p hist* **je parus**; *fu* **je paraîtrai**)

| **VI** to appear **1–3** ▪ to come out **2** ▪ to look **3** ▪ to seem **3** |
| **V IMPERS** to seem **1, 2** ▪ to appear **2** |

VI 1 *(se montrer)* to appear; *(d'une étoile, de la lune etc)* to appear, to come out; *(d'un acteur)* to appear, to come on; **le jour commençait à p.** day was dawning; **il n'a pas** *ou* **n'est pas paru de la journée** he hasn't appeared all day; **lorsque l'enfant paraît** when the baby arrives; **laisser p. ses sentiments/sa déception** to show one's feelings/disappointment, to let one's feelings/disappointment show; **il ne pouvait pas s'empêcher de laisser p. un certain agacement** he couldn't help showing *or* betraying a degree of annoyance; **un faible sourire a paru sur ses lèvres** he/she smiled weakly; **p. en public** to appear in public; *Théâtre* **c'est alors qu'elle parut sur la scène** it was at that moment that she appeared on stage *or* she came on (stage); **elle aime un peu trop p.** she likes to show off; **elle ne pense qu'à p.** all she thinks about is impressing people

2 *(d'un livre etc)* to come out, to appear, to be published; *(d'un périodique)* to appear, to come out; **faire p. un livre** to publish a book, to bring out a book; **vient de p.** just out; *(livre)* just published; **le dernier San Antonio vient de p.** the latest San Antonio has just come out

3 *(sembler)* to seem, to look, to appear; **il paraissait furieux** he looked furious; *(à l'entendre)* he sounded furious; **cette décision me paraît bizarre** it seems a strange decision to me, it strikes me as a strange decision; **cela me paraît (être) une très bonne idée** it sounds to me like *or* strikes me as a very good idea; **ça ne te paraît pas une bonne idée?** don't you think that's a good idea?; **l'endroit lui parut familier** the place seemed familiar to him; **il ne paraît pas remarquer leur présence** he doesn't seem *or* appear to notice their presence; **il paraît (avoir) trente ans** he looks about thirty; *(d'une personne plus âgée)* he looks no more than thirty; **elle a quarante ans, mais elle ne les paraît pas** she's forty, but she doesn't look it; **p. son âge** to look one's age; **il veut p. ce qu'il n'est pas** he wants to pass for *or* he wants to appear to be something that he isn't; **pourquoi ce besoin de p.?** why this need to appear to be what you're/he's/*etc* not?

V IMPERS SEE GRAMMAR B29 **1** *(sembler)* **je suis très mal – il n'y paraît pas** I'm very ill – you don't look it *or* it doesn't look as if you are; **demain, il n'y paraîtra plus** there'll be no trace of it tomorrow; **sans qu'il n'y paraisse** without it *or Fml* its being apparent; **il faut l'aider sans qu'il n'y paraisse** we must help him/her without making it obvious *or* without making it look as if we are doing; **il me paraît que …** it seems to me *or* it strikes me that …; **il me paraît utile de …** I think it would be useful to …

2 il paraît que *(on dit que)* it seems *or* appears that; **il paraît qu'elle s'en va, elle s'en va, paraît-il** it seems *or* appears *or* would appear that she's leaving, she's leaving apparently; **il paraît que ça fait maigrir** apparently it helps you lose weight; **à ce qu'il paraît** apparently, it would seem so; **à ce qu'il paraît, c'est plus rapide par la route que par avion** apparently *or* seemingly *or* it would appear that it's quicker by road than by air; **il paraît (que oui)** so it appears *or* would appear, it appears *or* seems so, apparently; **il paraît que non** it appears *or* would appear not, it seems not, apparently not

---

paralangage [paralɑ̃gaʒ] NM paralanguage

paralinguistique [paralɛ̃gɥistik] ADJ paralinguistic
  NF paralinguistics

paralittéraire [paraliterɛr] ADJ œuvre **p.** work of popular literature; **écriture p.** popular writing

paralittérature [paraliteratyr] NF popular literature

parallaxe [paralaks] NF *Astron etc* parallax; *Opt etc* **erreur de p.** parallax error

parallèle [paralɛl] ADJ *Géom* parallel (**à** to, **with**); *Fig (expériences, destinées, carrières etc)* very similar; *Ordinat* **imprimante/interface p.** parallel printer/interface; *Gym* **barres parallèles** parallel bars; **faire des barres parallèles** to do exercises on the parallel bars; **rue qui est p. à la rivière** street that is *or* runs parallel to *or* with the river; **droites parallèles à l'infini** parallel straight lines extending into infinity; **mener une action p.** to take parallel *or* similar action; **mener une vie p.** to lead a secret life; **circuits parallèles de vente** parallel sales networks; **police p.** illegally constituted police force; *Écon* **marché p.** unofficial *or* illegal market
  NF parallel (line)
  NM *Géog (d'une latitude)* parallel; *(comparaison)* comparison, parallel; **en p.** *(employé adjectivement)* parallel; *(employé adverbialement)* in parallel; **mettre qch en p. avec qch** to compare sth with sth; **mettre deux événements/réactions en p.** to compare two events/reactions, to set two events/reactions side by side; **établir un p. entre … et …** to establish *or* draw a parallel between … and …

parallèlement [paralɛlmɑ̃] ADV parallel (**à** to, with); *(en même temps)* at the same time, *Fml* concurrently; *(de la même façon)* in the same way; **p. à la route** parallel to the road, alongside the road

parallélépipède [paralelepipɛd] NM *Géom* parallelepiped

parallélisme [paralelism] NM parallelism; *Aut* **p. (des roues)** (wheel) alignment; *Aut* **il y a un défaut de p.** there's something wrong with the alignment, the wheels aren't properly aligned

parallélogramme [paralelogram] NM *Géom* parallelogram

paralympique [paralɛ̃pik] ADJ *voir* jeu

paralysant [paralizɑ̃] ADJ *Méd, Fig (peur)* paralysing; *(timidité)* crippling, paralysing

paralysé, -ée [paralize] ADJ *Méd* paralysed; *Fig (pays)* crippled; *Fig* **p. de peur** paralysed with fear; *Fig* **je suis resté p.** I was paralysed *or* petrified; **nous sommes paralysés par l'absence de fonds suffisants** we are hamstrung by a lack of funds
  NF person who is paralysed; **les paralysés** the paralysed

paralyser [paralize] VT *(rendre infirme)* to paralyse; *Fig (empêcher d'agir, de fonctionner)* to paralyse, to incapacitate; *Fig (économie, pays)* to cripple; *Fig (circulation)* to bring to a standstill; **paralysé des deux jambes** paralysed in both legs; **le froid paralyse ses mains** his/her hands are numb with the cold; **ce genre de situation me paralyse** I'm petrified in that kind of situation; **paralysé par la peur** paralysed *or* helpless with fear

paralysie [paralizi] NF *Méd (d'une partie du corps)* paralysis; *Fig* state of paralysis; **p. agitante** Parkinson's disease; **p. générale (progressive)** creeping paralysis; **p. cérébrale** cerebral palsy; **p. faciale** facial palsy

paralytique [paralitik] ADJ paralytic
  NF person who is paralysed, paralytic

paramédical, -ale, -aux, -ales [paramedikal, -o] ADJ paramedical; **personnel p.** paramedics
  NM **emplois du p.** jobs in paramedics, paramedic jobs

paramétrable [parametrabl] ADJ *Ordinat* configurable; **p. par l'utilisateur** user-definable

paramétrage [parametraʒ] NM *Ordinat* configuration

paramètre [parametr] NM *Math, Fig* parameter; *Ordinat* parameter, setting; *(du DOS)* switch

paramétrer [parametre] VT *Ordinat* to configure

paramilitaire [paramiliter] ADJ paramilitary
  N paramilitary

parangon [parɑ̃gɔ̃] NM *Litt* paragon; **p. de vertu** paragon of virtue

parano [parano] *Fam* ADJ paranoid
  NF *(paranoïa)* paranoia; **elle fait de la p.!** she's being paranoid!; **tu es en pleine p.!** you're being completely paranoid!; **arrête ta p.!** stop being paranoid!
  N *(personne)* **c'est un/une p.!** he's/she's paranoid!

paranoïa [paranɔja] NF *Psy* paranoia; *Fig* **tu es en pleine p.** you're being completely paranoid

paranoïaque [paranɔjak] ADJ, N *Psy* paranoiac

paranoïde [paranɔid] ADJ paranoid

paranormal, -ale, -aux, -ales [paranormal, -o] ADJ paranormal

parapente [parapɑ̃t] NM *(activité)* paragliding; *(parachute)* paraglider; **faire du p.** to go paragliding

parapet [parapɛ] NM parapet

parapharmacie [parafarmasi] NF **1** *(produits)* = personal hygiene products and cosmetics **2** *(rayon, boutique)* = chemist's selling personal hygiene products and cosmetics, *Am* ≃ drugstore

paraphe [paraf] NM **1** *(ajouté à la signature)* flourish **2** *(de son nom)* initials

parapher [parafe] VT to initial; *(signer)* to sign

parapheur [parafœr] NM signature book

paraphrase [parafraz] NF paraphrase; **faire de la p.** to paraphrase

paraphraser [parafraze] VT to paraphrase

paraplégie [parapleʒi] NF *Méd* paraplegia

paraplégique [parapleʒik] ADJ, N *Méd* paraplegic

parapluie [paraplɥi] NM umbrella, *Br Fam* brolly; **p. de golf** golf umbrella; *Fig* **p. nucléaire** *ou* **atomique** nuclear umbrella

parapsychologie [parapsikɔlɔʒi] NF parapsychology

parapublic, -ique [parapyblik] ADJ *(entreprise)* part government-owned

parasciences [parasjɑ̃s] NFPL sciences of the paranormal

parascolaire [paraskɔlɛr] ADJ extra-curricular

parasismique [parasismik] ADJ anti-earthquake

parasitaire [paraziter] ADJ parasitic(al)

parasite [parazit] NM *Biol* parasite; *Fig* parasite, *Fam* sponger, freeloader; **un p. social** a social parasite; *Radio, TV* **parasites** interference, static, *Br* atmospherics
  ADJ *Biol (insecte, plante etc)* parasitic; *Fig (mot)* unnecessary, superfluous; *Radio, TV* **bruits parasites** interference

parasiter [parazite] VT *Biol* to parasitize; *Radio, TV* to cause interference in; *Fig Fam* **p. la société** to be a parasite on society

parasitique [parazitik] ADJ parasitic(al)

parasitisme [parazitism] NM parasitism

parasitologie [parazitɔlɔʒi] NF *Méd* parasitology

parasitologique [parazitɔlɔʒik] ADJ *Méd* parasitological

parasitose [parazitoz] NF *Méd* disease caused by a parasite

parasol [parasɔl] NM parasol, sunshade; *(sur la plage)* beach umbrella; **pin p.** parasol *or* umbrella pine

parasympathique [parasɛ̃patik] ADJ *Anat* parasympathetic

parataxe [parataks] NF parataxis

paratonnerre [paratɔnɛr] NM lightning conductor

paratyphoïde [paratifɔid] ADJ, NF *Méd* **(fièvre) p.** paratyphoid fever

paravalanche [paravalɑ̃ʃ] ADJ **mur** *ou* **installation p.** avalanche barrier *or* wall
▪ NM avalanche barrier *or* wall

paravent [paravɑ̃] NM screen; *Fig* **ce n'est qu'un p.** it's just a smoke screen *or* a front; **cette société leur sert de p. pour d'autres activités** the company is a screen *or* front for their other activities

parbleu [parblø] INT *Vieilli* good Lord!

parc [park] NM **1** *(jardin)* park; *(d'un château etc)* grounds, park **2** *(pour enfant)* playpen **3** *(ensemble) (de bus, de voitures etc)* fleet; *Rail* rolling stock; **p. automobile** number of cars on the roads; **le p. automobile français** the number of cars in France; **le p. des téléviseurs couleurs** the total number of colour televisions owned by the population; *Ordinat* **p. de micros** computer park; *Ordinat* **p. informatique** computer park; **p. immobilier** housing stock; **le p. nucléaire de la France** France's nuclear power stations
▸▸ **p. aquatique** water park; **p. d'attractions** theme park; **p. à bestiaux** cattle pen; *Aut* **p. d'exposition** forecourt; **p. des expositions** exhibition centre; **p. à huîtres** oyster bed; **p. industriel** industrial park; *Br* industrial estate; **p. de loisirs** leisure park; **p. à moules** mussel bed; **p. à moutons** sheep pen, sheepfold; **p. national** national park; **p. naturel** nature reserve; **p. régional** regional park; **p. résidentiel de loisirs** chalet park, holiday camp; **p. de stationnement** car park, *Am* parking lot; **p. de stationnement à plusieurs niveaux** multi-storey car park, *Am* multi-story parking garage; **p. technologique** technology park; **p. à thème** theme park; **p. zoologique** zoo, *Fml* zoological gardens

parcage [parkaʒ] NM **1** *(du bétail, de moutons)* penning, enclosing **2** *Tél* hold; **mettre en p.** *(correspondant)* to put on hold; *Ordinat (disque dur)* to park

parcellaire [parselɛr] ADJ *(terrain)* divided into small portions *or* into parcels; **travail p.** work divided into sections

parcelle [parsɛl] NF (small) fragment, morsel; *(de terrain)* piece, parcel; *Fig* **pas la moindre p. de jugement/d'intelligence/de vérité** not an ounce of common sense/intelligence/truth; **il n'a pas la moindre p. de générosité** he doesn't have a generous bone in his body; **il ne cédera pas la moindre p. de son indépendance/sa liberté** he will not give up the least little bit of his independence/freedom

parcellisation [parselizasjɔ̃] NF *(du terrain)* parcelling up; **p. du travail** breaking work down into sections

parcelliser [parselize] VT *(terrain)* to divide into small portions, to parcel up; *(travail)* to break down into sections

parce que [pars(ə)kə] CONJ because; **p. c'est vrai** because it's true; **ce n'est pas p. tu n'aimes pas la cervelle que …** just because you don't like brains doesn't mean that …; **parce qu'on lui dit de le faire, il le fait** he does it (just) because he's told to do it; **pourquoi ne viens-tu pas? – p.** why aren't you coming? – (just) because (I'm not); **mais pourquoi pleures-tu comme ça? – p.** why are you crying? – just because; **ce chandelier vous in-**téresse? **p. je pourrais …** are you interested in the chandelier? because if you are *or* if so, I could …; **je le ferai, mais p. c'est vous!** I'll do it, but only because it's you!

parchemin [parʃəmɛ̃] NM parchment; *(de livre)* vellum; **papier p.** parchment paper; **un p.** a parchment; *Univ* a diploma; **des parchemins** *(titres de noblesse)* titles of nobility

parcheminé [parʃəmine] ADJ parchment-like; *Fig (visage)* wizened, wrinkled

parcheminer [parʃəmine] VT *(papier)* to give a parchment finish to
▪ VPR **se parcheminer** *(de la peau)* to shrivel up, to become shrivelled

parcimonie [parsimɔni] NF thrift; **avec p.** sparingly; **elle distribue les conseils avec p.** she is sparing with her advice

parcimonieusement [parsimɔnjøzmɑ̃] ADV sparingly; **distribuer les compliments p.** to be sparing with one's compliments

parcimonieux, -ieuse [parsimɔnjø, -jøz] ADJ *(personne, action)* thrifty; **une distribution parcimonieuse du pain** a sparing distribution of bread

par-ci, par-là ADV *(dans l'espace)* here and there; *(dans le temps)* now and then, from time to time; **une virgule par-ci, un point d'exclamation par-là** a comma here, an exclamation mark there

parcmètre [parkmɛtr], **parcomètre** [parkɔmɛtr] NM *(parking)* meter; **ma voiture est au p.** I'm on a meter

parcourir [parkurir] VT *(conj like* **courir***)* **1** *(région, quartier)* to roam, to travel through; *(les rues)* to roam, to wander (through); **p. les mers** to sail the seas; **le p. de long en large** to travel the length and breadth of the country; **p. un endroit à la recherche de qn** to scour a place for sb; **p. une distance de plusieurs kilomètres** to cover a distance of several kilometres; **il reste deux kilomètres/un long chemin à p.** there are two kilometres/there is a long way to go; **le pays est parcouru de canaux** the country has a network of canals; **mesurer le chemin parcouru** to measure the distance covered; *Fig* to measure one's progress; *Fig* **un frisson me parcourut** a shiver went through me; *Fig* **un frisson me parcourut l'échine** *ou* **le dos** a shiver ran down my spine; *Fig* **un murmure a parcouru la foule** a murmur ran through the crowd
2 *(regarder) (texte, document)* to look at briefly, to read *or* run through *or* over; *(lettre, journal)* to skim, to glance at; *(livre)* to skim (through), to glance through; *Ordinat* to scroll through; **p. qch des yeux** *ou* **du regard** to glance at *or* over sth, to run one's eyes over sth; **p. ses notes avant une réunion** to go over *or* look over one's notes before a meeting

parcours [parkur] NM *(d'un défilé, de bus etc)* route; *(d'un fleuve)* course; *Sport (de voitures, motos etc)* circuit; *(de chevaux)* Golf course; *(distance)* distance covered; *(voyage en avion)* leg; *(itinéraire)* route; *Aviat* **p. à vide** deadhead flight, empty leg; **les chevaux font un p. de 20 kilomètres** the horses run over a distance of 20 kilometres; *Golf* **un p. dix-huit trous** an eighteen-hole course; **le car fait le p. entre la ville et la côte** the bus runs between the town and the coast; **elle fait plusieurs fois le p. dans la journée** she does the journey several times a day; **je fais le p. à pied dans les deux sens** I walk both ways; **payer le p.** *(dans un taxi)* to pay the fare; **le prix du p.** the fare; **je ne connais pas le prix du p. pour aller à l'aéroport** I don't know the fare to the airport *or* how much it costs to get to the airport; *Courses de chevaux* **reconnaître le p.** to walk the course; **faire un p. sans faute** *(d'un cheval)* to have a clear round; *Fig (dans une carrière)* to have a copybook career; *Mil, Fig* **p. du combattant** obstacle course; **faire le p. du combattant** to do an obstacle course

par-delà PRÉP, ADV beyond

par-derrière ADV *(attaquer qn)* from behind; *(se boutonner)* at the back; **entrer p.** to come in the back way, to come in the back door; **des coups p.** underhand tricks; **elle a toujours fait des coups p.** she's always been underhand; **dire des choses p.** to say things behind people's backs; **mais p. je suis sûr qu'il dit autre chose** but I'm sure he says something quite different behind my back
▪ PRÉP behind

par-dessous PRÉP under, beneath, underneath
▪ ADV underneath; **je suis passé p.** I crept underneath; **prendre qch p.** to get hold of sth underneath

pardessus [pardəsy] NM overcoat

par-dessus PRÉP over (the top of); **sauter p. la table** to leap over the table; **jeter qch p. bord** to throw sth overboard; *Fig* **p. le marché** into the bargain; **p. tout** above all; *(le comble)* to crown it all, on top of it all; *Fig Fam* **j'en ai p. la tête** I've had just about enough; **regarder p. l'épaule de qn** to look over sb's shoulder
▪ ADV over

par-devant PRÉP in front of; **passer p. la maison** to pass the house; *Jur* **acte signé p. (le) notaire** deed signed in the presence of a lawyer
▪ ADV in front

par-devers [pardəver] PRÉP **1 p. soi** in one's possession **2 p. le juge** before the judge

pardi [pardi] INT *Fam* of course!, naturally!

pardieu [pardjø] INT *Arch* zounds!

pardon [pardɔ̃] NM **1** *(grâce)* forgiveness; **accorder son p. à qn** to forgive *or* pardon sb; **demander p. à qn** to apologize to sb, to say sorry to sb; **demander p. à Dieu pour ses péchés** to ask God's forgiveness for one's sins; **mille pardons** a thousand apologies; **arrête de toujours (me) demander p.** stop apologizing; **c'est à lui de te demander p.** it's up to him to apologize, he should apologize to you; **(je vous demande) p.** (I'm) sorry, I beg your pardon; *(pour passer, avertir, attirer l'attention de qn)* excuse me; **j'ai fait une grosse bêtise, je vous demande p.** I'm sorry *or* I do apologize, I've done something very stupid; **je vous demande p., quel est votre nom?** I'm sorry, what is your name?; **p., ce n'est pas ce que j'ai dit!** *(pour contredire)* excuse me *or* pardon me, but that's not what I said!; **p. (qu'as-tu dit)?** what did you say?, excuse me?, (I beg your) pardon?; *Fam* **on dit qu'il n'est pas très malin, mais son fils, p.!** he's not very bright, it seems, but his son is even worse!; *Fam* **la mère est jolie, mais la fille, p.!** the mother's pretty, but the daughter, wow! **2** *Rel (en Bretagne)* religious festival; *Rel juive* **le Grand P., le jour du P.** the Day of Atonement, Yom Kippur

pardonnable [pardɔnabl] ADJ *(faute, erreur)* forgivable, excusable, pardonable; **il s'est trompé mais c'est p.** he made a mistake, but he can be forgiven *or* excused *or* it's excusable; **tu es p. d'avoir oublié** you can be forgiven for forgetting; **vous n'êtes pas p.!** it's unforgivable *or* inexcusable of you!

pardonner [pardɔne] VT *(erreur, faute)* to forgive, to excuse, to pardon; *(personne)* to forgive; **est-ce que tu me pardonnes?** do you forgive me?, am I forgiven?; **p. qch à qn** to forgive sb sth; **elle m'a pardonné d'avoir oublié** she forgave me for forgetting; **pardonnez-moi si je vous contredis** I'm sorry to contradict you, excuse *or* forgive *or* pardon me for contradicting you; **pour me/te**/etc **faire p.** to make it up; **pour se faire p. son retard** as a way of saying sorry for being late; **tu es tout pardonné** you are forgiven

VI to forgive; **elle pardonne vite** she is quick to forgive; **maladie/faute qui ne pardonne pas** fatal illness/mistake; **ça ne pardonne pas** you don't get a second chance

VPR se pardonner je ne me le pardonnerai jamais I'll never forgive myself (for it); **c'est une erreur qui ne se pardonne pas** it's an unforgivable mistake; **ils se sont pardonné leurs paroles de colère** they forgave each other for being angry

paré [pare] **ADJ 1** (prêt) ready (à for); **être p. contre** (le froid, les attaques etc) to be prepared for; **vous voilà p.!** you're all set!; Naut **p. à virer!** ready about! **2** (orné) decorated, ornamented (de with); (personne) (vêtu) dressed (up) (de in); (couvert de bijoux) wearing jewels, covered in jewels **3** Culin (viande) dressed

pare-avalanches [paravalɑ̃ʃ] **NM INV** avalanche barrier or wall

pare-balles [parbal] **ADJ INV** bullet-proof; **gilet p.** bullet-proof vest

pare-boue [parbu] **NM INV** mudflap

pare-brise [parbriz] **NM INV** Aut etc windscreen, Am windshield; **p. feuilleté** laminated windscreen

pare-chocs [parʃɔk] **NM INV** Aut bumper; **on roulait p. contre p.** it or the traffic was bumper to bumper; **p. bouclier** bumper; **p. circonférenciel** ou **enveloppant** wrap-around bumper; **p. à absorption d'énergie** energy-absorbing bumper

pare-éclats [parekla] **NM INV** Mil splinter-proof shield (on trench parapet etc)

pare-étincelles [paretɛ̃sɛl] **NM INV** fireguard

pare-feu [parfø] **NM INV 1** (dans la forêt) firebreak **2** (de cheminée) fireguard; **porte p.** fire door; Aut **p. de moteur** engine bulkhead, Am firewall **3** Ordinat firewall

pare-flammes [parflam] **NM INV** Aut flame arrester

parégorique [paregɔrik] **ADJ** Pharm paregoric

pareil, -eille [parɛj] **ADJ 1** (semblable) alike, similar; **elles sont presque pareilles** they are almost the same; **ce n'est pas p.** it's not the same (thing); **une erreur et un oubli, ce n'est pas p.** a mistake and an oversight are not the same (thing); **ce n'est pas p. que l'année dernière** it's not the same as last year; **en voici un tout p.** here's one exactly the same or exactly like it; **il est vraiment p.** it's very similar; **l'an dernier à pareille époque** this time last year; Litt **à nul autre p.** without equal, unparalleled; **p. que** ou **à** the same as, just like; **et lui, qu'est-ce qu'on lui donne? – p., une orange** and what will we give him? – the same (thing), an orange; **ses deux chaussettes ne sont pas pareilles** his socks don't match; **ces bougeoirs ne sont pas pareils** these candlesticks aren't alike or the same; **il n'y en a pas deux (de) pareils** no two are alike; **les gens sont partout pareils** people are the same the world over; Fam **si ça ne te plaît pas, c'est p.** too bad if you don't like it; **toujours p. à lui-même** the same as always; **c'est toujours p. avec lui** it's always the same with him

2 (tel) such, like this/that; **en p. cas** in a case like this, in such cases; **dans de pareils moments, dans des moments pareils** at times like these; **dans** ou **une pareille situation** in a similar situation; **par un temps p.** in weather like this; **comment a-t-elle pu faire une chose pareille!** how could she do such a thing!; **je n'ai jamais vu (une) chose pareille**

I've never seen anything like it; **mais je n'ai jamais dit une chose pareille!** but I never said any such thing!; **tu ne vas pas croire une chose pareille!** you're not going to believe something like that!; **qu'a-t-il donc fait pour avoir une chance pareille?** how did he manage to get so lucky?; **j'ignorais que tu y portais un p. intérêt** I didn't realize you were so interested; **a-t-on idée de rentrer à des heures pareilles!** what kind of time is this to come home at?

N (pair) **il n'a pas son p. au monde** there's no one like him, he's second to none; **un cuisinier qui n'a pas son p. au monde** a chef in a class of his own; **cet endroit n'a pas son p. au monde** there's nowhere else like this; **comme sage-femme, elle n'a pas sa pareille** there's no one to equal or match her as a midwife; **elle n'a pas son p. pour faire le cassoulet** nobody can make cassoulet like her or the way she can; **sans p.** (occasion, méchanceté) unparalleled; (richesse, beauté) unparalleled, unrivalled, unequalled; (gentillesse, imagination) unparalleled, unequalled; **une soirée sans pareille** a wonderful evening; **c'est une cuisinière sans p.** she's a superb cook, no one can match her when it comes to cooking; **mes pareils** my equals; **lui et ses pareils** him and people like him

NF rendre la pareille à qn (se venger) to get one's own back on sb; (faire preuve de reconnaissance) to repay sb, to pay sb back; **elle ne manquera pas de lui rendre la pareille** she'll get her own back (on him/her); **si on me frappe, je rends la pareille** if anyone hits me, I hit back

NM Fam **c'est du p. au même** it's six of one and half a dozen of the other, it comes (down) to the same thing

ADV Fam **faire p.** to do the same thing; **je ne fais pas p.** that's not how I do it; **ils s'habillent/écrivent p.** they dress/write the same (way); **ils mangent/lisent p.** they eat/read the same kind of things; **elles se coiffent p.** they have the same hairdo, they do their hair the same way; **elle se coiffe p. depuis 10 ans** she's had the same hairdo for the past 10 years

pareillement [parɛjmɑ̃] **ADV 1** (de la même manière) in a similar manner, in the same way; **p. habillé** dressed the same **2** (aussi) also, likewise; **p!** (en réponse à des vœux) the same to you!; **et moi p.!** same here!; **ravi de vous rencontrer – et moi p.!** pleased to meet you – likewise!

parement [parmɑ̃] **NM 1** (décoration) ornament, decoration; Couture (de manche, col) facing; Rel **p. d'autel** (altar) frontal **2** Constr (d'un mur) facing; (de la pierre) (dressed) face

parent, -ente [parɑ̃, -ɑ̃t] **NM 1** (always pl) **parents** (père et mère) parents, mother and father; **les parents sortent ce soir** my parents or surtout Am my folks or Fam (my) mum and dad are going out this evening; **tu as prévenu les parents?** have you told mum and dad?; **la relation parents-enfant** the parent-child relationship **2** Litt (always pl) **parents** (ancêtres) forefathers, forebears **3** Biol parent

N (personne appartenant à la proche famille) relative, relation; **c'est mon seul p.** he's my only living relative; Jur **le p. survivant** the last surviving relative; **proche p.** close relative; **p. éloigné** distant relative; **être (proches) parents** to be (closely) related; **être p. avec qn, être un p. de qn** to be related to sb; **nous sommes parents par alliance/par mon père** we are related by marriage/on my father's side; Fig **p. pauvre** poor relation; Fig **traiter qn en p. pauvre** to treat sb like a poor relation

ADJ related; (semblable) similar; **sciences parentes** related sciences; **leurs œuvres révèlent des intelligences/sensibilités parentes** their work shows a similar intelligence/sensitivity

▸▸ **parents adoptifs** adoptive parents; **parents biologiques** biological parents; **parents d'élèves: association de parents d'élèves** parent teacher association, PTA

parental, -ale, -aux, -ales [parɑ̃tal, -o] **ADJ** (autorité etc) parental

parenté [parɑ̃te] **NF 1** aussi Fig (rapport) relationship; Spéc (en sociologie) kinship; **il n'y a entre eux aucune p.** they are not related in any way; **quel est le lien de p. entre eux?** what relation are they to each other?, how are they related?; **as-tu un lien de p. avec …?** are you related to or any relation of …?; **liens de p.** family connections **2** (famille) family, relations

parenthèse [parɑ̃tɛz] **NF** parenthesis, Br bracket; Fig (dans un discours) digression; **entre parenthèses** in parentheses, Br in brackets; Fig incidentally, by the way; **mettre qch entre parenthèses** to put sth in parentheses, Br to put sth in brackets; Typ **p. fermante/ouvrante** closing/opening bracket; Fig **cette époque a été une p. dans sa vie** that period was an interlude in his life; Fig **c'est une p. dans ma routine quotidienne** it's a break from my daily routine; **ouvrir/fermer une p.** to open/to close the brackets; Fig **je voudrais ouvrir une p.** (pour aborder cette question) I would like to digress for a moment; **je voudrais vous dire, dans une p.** ou **par p., que …** I would like to say by way of digression that …; **il est temps de fermer la p. et de revenir à notre sujet** enough of this digression, let's get back to our subject **VOIR GRAMMAIRE A14**

paréo [pareo] **NM** pareo; **jupe-p.** sarong (skirt)

parer[1] [pare] **VT 1** (éviter) (attaque, coup) to fend off, to ward off; Escrime, Boxe, Fig (question) to parry; (en esquivant) (coup) to dodge; Naut (abordage) to avoid, to fend off; Fig **ils savaient qu'une OPA se préparait et ils ont réussi à p. le coup** they knew a takeover was in the offing and managed to ward it off; Naut **p. un cap** to clear or double a headland **2** (protéger) to protect (contre against); **je suis paré contre le froid/l'hiver** I'm ready for or to face the cold/the winter

VI p. à (accident) to prevent, to guard against; (difficulté, problème) to avoid; (défaite, désastre) to ward off, to stave off; **pour p. à toute difficulté/à tout retard** in order to guard against any difficulties/delay; **p. à toute éventualité** to be prepared for anything; **on ne peut pas p. à tout** you can't guard against everything; **p. au plus pressé** to attend to the most urgent things first; **nous devons p. au plus pressé** first things first

parer[2] **VT 1** (arranger) (viande, cuir) to dress; Naut (câble, ancre etc) to clear **2** (vêtir) (personne) to deck out, to adorn (de with); (décorer) to decorate with taste; **p. la mariée** to dress the bride; Fig **p. qn de toutes les vertus/qualités** to endow sb with every virtue/quality

VPR se parer 1 to dress oneself up; **se p. de bijoux** to deck oneself out in jewels, to adorn oneself with jewels; **elle ne sort pas sans s'être parée de bijoux** she never goes out without her jewellery on; **se p. d'un faux titre** to assume a false title; **je me suis paré contre le froid** I've made sure that I'm not going to feel the cold **2** Can (se préparer) to get ready

pare-soleil [parsɔlɛj] **NM INV** Aut sun visor; Phot lens hood

paresse [parɛs] **NF 1** (indolence) laziness,

idleness; **par pure p.** out of sheer laziness; **d'une p. incroyable/incurable** incredibly/incurably lazy **2** (*lenteur*) **p. d'esprit** *ou* **intellectuelle** sluggishness of mind; *Méd* **p. intestinale** sluggishness of the bowels

paresser [paʀɛse] **VI** to laze (about *or* around)

paresseusement [paʀɛsøzmɑ̃] **ADV** lazily; **le fleuve coule p.** the river moves slowly *or* sluggishly

paresseux, -euse [paʀɛsø, -øz] **ADJ 1** (*nonchalant*) lazy, *Fml* indolent; **p. comme une couleuvre** *ou* **un loir** bone idle; **il est p. le matin** he moves at a snail's pace in the morning **2** (*lent*) (*intestins*) sluggish; (*geste*) lazy; (*fleuve*) sluggish, slow-moving; **c'est un esprit p.** he won't use the brains God gave him, he's mentally lazy
▶ **N** lazy person, *Fam* lazybones
▶ **NM** *Zool* sloth

parfaire [paʀfɛʀ] **VT** (*conj like* **faire**; *used chiefly in inf and pp*) (*travail etc*) to finish off, to complete; (*technique, compétences etc*) to perfect

parfait [paʀfɛ] **ADJ 1** (*irréprochable*) perfect; (*performance*) faultless, perfect; (*diamant*) flawless; (*réputation*) unsullied; **en ordre p.** in perfect order; **le tout était rangé dans un ordre p.** there was not a thing out of place; **il est p. en toute occasion** he always knows what to do; **personne n'est p.** nobody's perfect; **il est loin d'être p.** he's far from perfect, he's no saint; **vous avez été p.** you were wonderful *or* splendid *or* marvellous; *Iron* you were just great; **(c'est** *ou* **voilà qui est) p.!** (that's) splendid! *or* fine! *or* wonderful!, *Fam* great!; *Iron* (that's just) great!; **p., passons à autre chose** fine *or* good, let's go on to something else
2 (*complet*) (*bonheur*) perfect, complete; (*réussite*) complete; (*ressemblance*) exact; **un p. orateur** an accomplished speaker; **un p. meneur d'hommes** a wonderful leader; *Fam* **un p. imbécile** a perfect *or* complete idiot, an utter fool; **en p. accord** in full *or* perfect agreement; **je suis en p. accord avec ce qu'il a dit** I quite *or* totally agree with what he said; **nous travaillons en p. accord** *ou* **en parfaite harmonie l'un avec l'autre** we work in perfect harmony with each other; **être dans l'ignorance la plus parfaite de qch** to be completely ignorant of sth; *Mus* **accord p.** perfect chord
▶ **NM 1** *Gram* perfect (tense) SEE GRAMMAR A50; B30 **2** *Culin* parfait; **p. au café** coffee parfait

parfaitement [paʀfɛtmɑ̃] **ADV 1** (*admirablement*) perfectly, to perfection; **cela m'ira p.** that will suit me perfectly *or* just fine; **elle s'occupe p. de ses enfants** she looks after her children wonderfully well; **un vin qui accompagne p. le poisson** a wine that is the perfect accompaniment for fish; **elle parle p. (l')anglais** she speaks English perfectly, she speaks perfect English
2 (*totalement*) completely, thoroughly; (*compréhensible, clair, heureux*) perfectly; **elle est p. qualifiée pour faire le travail** she's perfectly *or* ideally qualified for the job; **il connaît p. son domaine** he knows his field thoroughly; **je comprends p.** I quite *or* perfectly understand; **il est p. idiot** he's a perfect idiot; **il a p. le droit de le dire** he has a perfect right *or* he is perfectly entitled to say so; **ceci m'est p. égal** it's really all the same to me; **j'ai p. conscience de …** I'm fully aware of …; **il a p. raison** he's perfectly right
3 (*tout à fait*) certainly, exactly; **vous dites que vous l'avez vu? – oui, p.** you say you saw it? – indeed I did *or* yes, I most definitely did; **oui, p., j'y étais** yes indeed, I was there

parfois [paʀfwa] **ADV** sometimes, at times; (*moins souvent*) occasionally, (every) now

and then; **p. elle lit, p. elle tricote** sometimes she reads, other times she knits

parfum [paʀfœ̃] **NM 1** (*senteur, odeur*) (*de fleurs*) perfume, fragrance, scent; (*d'un vin*) bouquet, aroma; *Fig* **un p. de scandale** a whiff of scandal **2** (*à base d'essences*) perfume, *Br* scent **3** *Culin* (*de glace, yaourt*) flavour, *Am* flavor **4** *Fig Fam* **être au p.** to be in the know; **il n'était pas au p.** he didn't know anything (about it); **mettre qn au p.** to fill sb in, to put sb in the picture

parfumé [paʀfyme] **ADJ** (*fleur*) scented, fragrant, sweet-smelling; (*savon*) perfumed, scented; (*vin, air*) fragrant; (*au goût*) sweet-tasting; **des fruits très parfumés** fruit that is full of flavour *or Am* flavor; **glace parfumée au café** coffee-flavoured *or Am* -flavored ice cream; **l'air p. du soir** the balmy evening air; **elle est trop parfumée** she's wearing too much perfume

parfumer [paʀfyme] **VT 1** (*embaumer*) to scent, to perfume; **les fleurs parfument la pièce** the flowers scent the room; **un potpourri pour p. votre maison** potpourri to scent *or* fragrance your house; **le gâteau parfume la cuisine** the kitchen smells of cake **2** *Culin* to flavour, *Am* to flavor (**à** with) **3** (*mettre du parfum sur*) (*mouchoir*) to scent; (*armoire à linge*) to perfume; (*eau de bain*) to scent, to fragrance; **je vous parfume?** (*à une cliente*) would you like to try some (perfume)?
▶ **VPR se parfumer** to wear *or* use perfume; (*mettre du parfum*) to put perfume on

parfumerie [paʀfymʀi] **NF** (*magasin*) perfume shop, perfumery; (*rayon*) perfume counter; (*produits*) perfumes, perfumery; (*industrie*) perfume industry

parfumeur, -euse [paʀfymœʀ, -øz] **N** perfumer

pari [paʀi] **NM 1** (*convention*) bet, *Fml* wager; **faire un p.** to make *or* lay a bet; **faire un p. avec qn** to make a bet with sb; **je suis prêt à faire le p. que …** I'm willing to bet that …; **tenir un p.** to take a bet; *Fig* **les paris sont ouverts** it's anyone's guess **2** (*jeu*) betting; **p. mutuel** *Br* ≃ totalizator system, *Fam* tote, *Am* ≃ pari-mutuel

paria [paʀja] **NM** (*en Inde*) pariah; *Fig* pariah, (social) outcast

parier [paʀje] (*impf, pr sub n. pariions, v. pariiez*) **VT** to bet, *Fml* to wager; **je parie une bouteille de vin qu'il ne viendra pas** I bet a bottle of wine he won't come; **je parie qu'il viendra** I bet he'll come, it's my bet he'll come; **tu veux p. qu'il te le reprochera?** what's the betting he'll blame you?; **il y a gros** *ou* **fort à p. que …** it's virtually certain that …, the odds are that …, it's odds on that …; **je te parie tout ce que tu veux …** I bet you anything (you like) …; **je l'aurais parié** I might have known (it) *or* guessed; *Fam* **tu en as assez, je parie?** I bet you've had enough
▶ **VI** to bet; **p. avec qn/sur qch** to bet with sb/ on sth; **p. sur un cheval** to bet on *or* back a horse; **on a parié gros** the betting ran high; **je te dis qu'il viendra – on parie?** he'll come, I tell you – (do you) want to bet?

pariétal, -e, -aux, -ales [paʀjetal, -o] **ADJ 1** *Anat* (*os*) parietal **2** *Beaux-Arts* **art p.** cave painting
▶ **NM** *Anat* parietal bone

parieur, -ieuse [paʀjœʀ, -jøz] **N** better, *Fam* punter; *Sport, surtout Courses de chevaux* backer; **c'est un p.** he'll bet on anything

parigot, -ote [paʀigo, -ɔt] *Fam Péj* **ADJ** Parisian
▶ **N P.** Parisian

Paris [paʀi] **N** Paris

parisianisme [paʀizjanism] **NM** *Ling* ≃ expression particular to Paris

parisien, -ienne [paʀizjɛ̃, -jɛn] **ADJ** Parisian; *Péj* **esprit p.** superior Parisian outlook; **le Bassin p.** the Paris Basin; **la banlieue parisienne** the Paris suburbs
▶ **N P.** Parisian

paritaire [paʀitɛʀ] **ADJ** *Ind* with parity of representation; **commission p.** = board on which management and unions are equally represented

parité [paʀite] **NF 1** (*égalité*) parity; (*de rang, de valeur*) equality; *Fin* **p. des monnaies** monetary parity; *Fin* **p. euro-dollar** euro-dollar parity; *Bourse* **à p.** at the money; *Bourse* **au voisinage de la p.** close to par; **p. du pouvoir d'achat** purchasing power parity; **parités du change** exchange rate parity; **p. fixe** fixed parity **2** *Math, Ordinat* parity; **p. paire/impaire** even/odd parity; **pas de p.** no parity

parjure [paʀʒyʀ] **NM** perjury; **commettre un p.** to commit perjury, to perjure oneself
▶ **N** (*personne*) perjurer
▶ **ADJ** (*personne*) who does not keep his/her word

parjurer (se) [səpaʀʒyʀe] **VPR** to perjure oneself, to be guilty of *or* to commit perjury

parka [paʀka] **NM** *OU* **NF** parka

parking [paʀkiŋ] **NM** (*stationnement*) parking; (*emplacement*) car park, *Am* parking lot; **place de p.** parking place *or* spot, place to park; **il y a encore des places de p. derrière le restaurant** there's more parking space behind the restaurant; **mettre sa voiture au p.** to put one's car in the car park
▶ ▶ **p. courte durée** short-stay car park; **p. gratuit** free car park; **p. longue durée** long-stay car park; **p. payant** paying car park; **p. privé** private car park; **'p. privé'** 'private parking'

parkinsonien, -ienne [paʀkinsɔnjɛ̃, -jɛn] *Méd* **ADJ** Parkinson's
▶ **N** person with Parkinson's (disease), Parkinson's sufferer

parlant [paʀlɑ̃] **ADJ 1** (*doué de parole*) speaking; (*portrait*) lifelike; (*geste*) eloquent, meaningful; (*description*) vivid; **cinéma p.** talking pictures, *Fam* talkies; **film p.** talking picture, *Fam* talkie; *Tél* **l'horloge parlante** the speaking clock; **être p.** (*d'une réaction, de preuve*) to speak for itself **2** *Fam* (*bavard*) talkative

parlé [paʀle] **ADJ** **l'anglais/le français p.** colloquial English/French; **ça se dit dans la langue parlée** it's a colloquial term, it's used colloquially; *TV, Radio* **journal p.** news (broadcast *or* programme); **présenter le journal p.** to present the news
▶ **NM** (*dans un opéra*) spoken part

parlement [paʀləmɑ̃] **NM 1 le P.** Parliament; **au P.** in Parliament VOIR GRAMMAIRE A11 **2** *Hist, Jur* high judicial court (*in Paris and provinces*)
▶ ▶ **p. bicaméral** bicameral *or* two-chamber parliament; **le P. européen** the European Parliament; **membre du P. européen** member of the European Parliament, MEP, Euro-MP

parlementaire [paʀləmɑ̃tɛʀ] **ADJ** *Pol* (*gouvernement, immunité, débat etc*) parliamentary
▶ **N 1** *Pol* member of Parliament, *Am* Congressman, *f* Congresswoman; **p. européen** member of the European Parliament, Euro-MP, MEP **2** *Mil* negotiator, mediator

parlementarisme [paʀləmɑ̃taʀism] **NM** *Pol* parliamentary government

parlementer [paʀləmɑ̃te] **VI** (*négocier*) to negotiate (**avec** with), *Vieilli* to parley, to hold a parley (**avec** with); **nous avons dû p. avant de pouvoir quitter le poste de police** we had to talk our way out of the police station

PARLER¹ [parle] VI **1** to speak, to talk; (avouer) to talk; **je ne peux pas le faire p.** I can't get him to talk, I can't get a word out of him; **parlons peu mais parlons bien** let's be brief and to the point; **elle a perdu sa voix à force de p.** she lost her voice from talking so much; **s'enrouer à force de p.** to talk oneself hoarse; **son fils ne parle pas encore** her son isn't talking yet; **est-ce que ton perroquet parle?** can your parrot talk?; **le président va p.** the president is about to speak; **laissez-le p.** (ne l'interrompez pas) let him speak or have his say or say what he has to say; (ne faites pas attention à ce qu'il dit) let him talk; **elle aime s'écouter p.** she likes the sound of her own voice; **il parle bien/avec style** (d'un orateur) he's a good/stylish speaker; **p. haut/bas** to talk or speak loudly/quietly; **parlez plus haut ou plus fort!** speak up!; **il faut p. moins haut** don't speak so loud; **parle plus bas** lower your voice; **p. par signes** to sign, to use sign language; **p. avec les mains** to gesticulate, to talk with one's hands; **p. par gestes** (des muets) to use sign language; (pour éviter de parler) to gesture (à qn to sb); **p. entre ses dents** to mumble; **p. du nez** to talk through one's nose; **parlez-vous sérieusement?** are you serious?, do you really mean it?; **p. pour ne rien dire** to talk for the sake of talking, Br Fam to rabbit on; **p. en l'air** to make empty promises; **p. à tort et à travers** to talk drivel; **parlons franc** let's talk frank, let's talk frankly; **généralement parlant** generally speaking; **on parlait très peu au petit déjeuner** there was very little talking over breakfast; **ils parlent très peu entre eux** they don't talk much to each other, they don't do much talking; **elle parle peu, ta sœur** your sister isn't very talkative, your sister doesn't have much to say for herself; **(c'est une) façon de p.** so to speak; **enfin, c'est une façon de p.** well, that's one way of putting it; **elle connaît six langues étrangères, enfin c'est une façon de p.** she can speak six languages more or less; Fam **tu peux (bien) p.!** you can talk!, you're a fine one to talk!; Fam **ses ambitions? parlons-en!** his ambitions? who are you kidding? or you've got to be joking!; Fam **tu parles!** you're telling me!, you bet!; (pas question) you must be joking!, no way!; Fam Iron **des progrès? tu parles!** progress? you must be joking!; Fam Iron **tu parles comme c'était intéressant!** talk about interesting!; Fam **tu parles d'une occasion/d'un idiot!** talk about an opportunity/an idiot!; Fam **parle pour toi!** speak for yourself!; Fam **tu parles d'un athlète!** some athlete!; Fam **que tu m'aides, tu parles!** you? help me? you must be joking!; Fam **tu parles si je te la prêterai!** no way will I lend it to you!, you must be joking if you think I'll lend it to you!; Fam **tu parles si c'est utile!** a fat lot of use that is!; Fam **voilà qui est parlé!** now you're talking!; **il trouvera à qui p.** he'll get more than he bargained for; **mais je parle, je parle, qu'en pense notre cher ami?** but I'm talking too much or I really mustn't go on so much, what do you think about it?; **je parle en toute connaissance de cause** I know what I'm talking about

2 p. to talk or speak to sb; **p. de qn/qch** to talk about sb/sth; **je ne lui parle plus** (je me suis disputé avec lui) I'm not talking to him, I'm not on speaking terms with him; **je ne lui parle plus depuis cette date** I haven't said a word to him since; **je l'avais déjà rencontré, mais je ne lui avais jamais parlé** I'd met him but I'd never spoken to him; Fam **moi qui vous parle, je peux vous aider** I'm the one who can help you; **moi qui vous parle, j'ai fait trois guerres** listen, I've been in three wars; **c'est (comme) p. à un mur** it's like talking to a brick wall; Fig **cette peinture parle à l'imagination** this painting fires the imagination; Fig Fam **cette peinture ne me parle pas beaucoup/du tout** this painting doesn't do much/does absolutely nothing for me; **il est temps que nous parlions de ta conduite** it's time we had a talk about your behaviour; **je sais de quoi je parle** I know what I'm talking about; **nous avons dû p. de cette question une douzaine de fois!** we must have gone over this point a dozen times!; **son dernier film/livre parle de la guerre** his latest film/book is about the war; **ce tableau parle de …** the subject of the painting is …; **ça parle de quoi?** what's it about?; **on ne parle que de cela** everyone's talking about it, that's all people are talking about; **les journaux ne parlent que de ça** the newspapers are full of it; **faire p. de soi** to become famous; **il a beaucoup fait p. de lui dans les années 50** he was very much to the fore in the 50s; **tu lui en as parlé?** have you talked or spoken to him about it?, have you mentioned it to him?; **ne lui en parle surtout pas!** don't mention it to him!, don't say a word about it to him!; **nous en parlerons après déjeuner** we'll talk about it or discuss it after lunch; **toute la ville en parle** the whole town is talking about it, it's the talk of the town; Fig **ici, tout me parle de toi** everything here reminds me of you; **il n'en parle jamais** he never talks about or refers to or mentions it; **n'en parlez à personne** don't tell anyone about it, don't mention it to anyone; Fam **ne m'en parlez pas!** you're telling me!; **les voisins? ne m'en parlez pas!** the neighbours? don't mention them or their name to me!; **n'en parlons plus** let's drop the subject, let's say no more about it; **vacances, n'en parlons plus** let's drop the subject of holidays, let's say no more about holidays; **cela ne vaut pas la peine d'en p.** it isn't worth talking about, it's nothing to speak of; **on parle d'organiser une fête** there's some talk about or they're talking about (organizing) a party; **elle parle de déménager** she's talking about moving; **sans p. de …** to say nothing of …, not to mention …; **pour ne p. que des …** to mention only the …; **les résultats/faits parlent d'eux-mêmes** the results/facts speak for themselves; **mal p. de qn** to criticize sb, to run sb down; **p. pour/contre qn** to speak for/against sb; **j'entends beaucoup p. de lui** I hear a lot about him; **mon père ne veut pas en entendre p.** my father won't hear of it; **on m'a beaucoup parlé de vous** I've heard a lot about you; **elle ne veut pas entendre p. d'informatique** she doesn't want to hear a word about computers; **il veut p. de moi à son patron** he's going to mention or recommend me to his boss; **je n'en ai jamais entendu p.** I've never heard of it/him/her/etc

VT **p. (le) français** to speak French; **p. le langage des sourds-muets** to know (how to use) sign language or how to sign; **elle parlait français** she was speaking French or talking (in) French; **ici on parle français** (dans un magasin) French spoken; **p. chiffons/cuisine/vacances** to talk about or discuss clothes/cooking/holidays; **p. affaires/boutique/politique** to talk business/shop/politics

VPR **se parler 1** (d'une langue) to be spoken; **l'anglais se parle partout** English is spoken everywhere

2 se p. à soi-même to talk to oneself; **ils ne se parlent plus** (ils se sont disputés) they're not speaking or talking to each other, they're not on speaking terms; **nous ne nous parlons plus** (de conjoints) we've stopped communicating, we don't talk any more; **ils ne s'étaient jamais parlé** they had never spoken (to each other)

parler² NM speech; (régional) dialect; **il a un p. rude** he's got a coarse way of speaking

parler-vrai, pl **parlers-vrai** NM straight talking

parleur, -euse [parlœr, -øz] N Péj **beau p.** smooth talker; **c'est un beau p.** he's all talk, Fam he's got the gift of the gab; (il est enjôleur) he's a smooth talker, Fam he's got the gift of the gab

parloir [parlwar] NM **1** visiting room; Rel parlour, Am parlor **2** Belg (salon) parlour

parlot(t)e [parlɔt] NF Fam gossip, Br natter; **faire la p.** to gossip, to chat; **faire la p. avec qn** to have a chat or Br natter with sb; **j'en ai assez de ces parlottes** I've had enough of this chitchat or gossiping or chattering

Parme [parm] N Parma; **jambon de P.** Parma ham

parmentier [parmɑ̃tje] NM Culin (au bœuf) ≃ cottage pie; (avec de la viande blanche) = dish similar to cottage pie, made with white meat; (au mouton) ≃ shepherd's pie

parmesan [parməzɑ̃] NM Culin Parmesan (cheese)

parmi [parmi] PRÉP among; **p. la foule** among or in the crowd; **nous souhaitons vous voir bientôt p. nous** we hope that you'll soon be with us; **c'est une solution p. d'autres** that's one solution; **il figure p. les meilleurs** he's one of the best, he's among the best **SEE GRAMMAR A68; B56**
ADV Suisse (mutuellement, les uns les autres) **on s'invite p.** we invite each other or one another

Parnasse (le) [ləparnas] NM **1** Antiq Parnassus **2** Hist, Littér the Parnassian School (of poetry)

parnassien, -ienne [parnasjɛ̃, -jɛn] ADJ, NM Hist, Littér Parnassian

parodie [parɔdi] NF (pastiche) parody; (simulacre) parody, mockery; **c'est une p. de procès** this trial is a mockery or Fam a joke

parodier [parɔdje] VT (impf, pr sub n. parodiions, v. parodiiez) (personne, pièce de théâtre) to parody

parodique [parɔdik] ADJ Littér parodic(al)

parodiste [parɔdist] N Littér parodist

paroi [parwa] NF **1** (cloison) (entre des pièces) partition (wall) **2** (mur) (d'une tente etc), Biol (d'une cellule) wall; (d'une maison) (inner) wall; (d'une falaise) face; **p. artérielle** artery wall **3** (face intérieure) (d'un tunnel) lining; (de l'estomac) lining, wall; (d'un vase etc) inner side or surface; Aut **p. des cylindres** cylinder wall

paroisse [parwas] NF **1** (territoire) parish; **il n'est pas de la p.** he's not from here **2** (habitants) parishioners

paroissial, -iale, -iaux, -iales [parwasjal, -jo] ADJ parish; **église paroissiale** parish church; **salle paroissiale** church hall

paroissien, -ienne [parwasjɛ̃, -jɛn] N parishioner; Fam Vieilli **un drôle de p.** a queer bird
NM (livre) prayer book

parole [parɔl] NF **1** (mot) word; **paroles** (d'une chanson) lyrics, words; **elle n'a pas dit une p. de la journée** she hasn't said a word or spoken all day; **c'est la seule p. qu'il a prononcée** that's all he said; **ce sont ses propres paroles** those are his very words; **assez de paroles! des actes!** that's enough talk(ing)! let's see some action!; **être courageux en paroles** to be all talk, to talk big; **histoire sans paroles** cartoon without a caption; TV, Cin short silent film; **la p. de Dieu** the word of God; **p. blessante** hurtful remark; Iron **belles paroles** fine words; **ce sont encore de belles paroles, mais …** that's all very well and good, but …; **sur ces belles paroles …** on this note …; **voilà une bonne p.!** well said!, Am Fam right on!

2 *Fig (engagement)* promise, word; **tenir (sa) p.** to keep one's promise *or* word; **nous vous obligerons à tenir p.** we'll keep you to that *or* to your word; **manquer à sa p.** to break one's promise *or* word; **il est (homme) de p., il a sa p., il n'a qu'une p.** he's a man of his word; **donner sa p. d'honneur à qn que ...** to give sb one's word that ..., to promise sb that ...; **(ma) p. d'honneur!** (on) my word of honour!; **non, je ne l'ai pas vu, p. d'honneur** no, I haven't seen him, I give you my word (of honour); **je vous en donne ma p.** I give you my word, (you can) take my word for it; **je vous crois sur p.** I'll take your word for it; **il a promis de m'aider et je l'ai cru sur p.** he promised to help me and I took him at his word; **c'est votre p. contre la sienne** it's your word against his; **prisonnier sur p.** prisoner on parole

3 la p. *(faculté de parler)* speech; *(manière, diction)* delivery; **avoir le don de la p.** to be a good speaker; **perdre la p.** to lose the power of speech; **usage de la p.** power of speech; **si les animaux avaient l'usage de la p.** if animals could speak *or* talk *or* had the power of speech; **retrouver l'usage de la p.** to be able to speak again; *Hum* **tu as perdu l'usage de la p.?** cat got your tongue?; **il ne lui manque que la p.** *(d'un chien)* the only thing he can't do is talk; **retrouver l'usage de la p.** to be able to speak again; **adresser la p. à qn** to speak to sb, to address sb; **elle ne m'a pas adressé la p. de toute la soirée** she didn't say a word to me *or* speak to me the entire evening; **couper la p. à qn** to interrupt sb, to cut sb short; **prendre la p.** to speak; **je vous rends la p.** *(dans un débat)* the floor is yours again; *Radio, TV* back *or* over to you; *Radio, TV* **nous passons maintenant la p. à ...** we now hand over *or* go over to ...; **taisez-vous, vous n'avez pas la p.** be quiet, it's not your turn to speak; *(dans un débat)* be quiet, you don't have the floor; **la p. est à M. Renault** Mr Renault will now speak, Mr Renault has the floor

4 *Cartes* **p.!** pass!; *(au bridge)* no bid!

parolier, -ière [parɔlje, -jɛr] N *(de chanson)* lyricist; *(d'opéra)* librettist

paronyme [parɔnim] NM paronym

paronymie [parɔnimi] NF paronymy

paroxysme [parɔksism] NM *(de colère, violence, plaisir)* height, peak; *Méd (d'une maladie)* crisis (point); **être au p. de la joie** to be ecstatically happy; **être au p. de la douleur** to be in agony; **il était au p. de la colère** he was blazingly angry *or Fml* in a paroxysm of rage; **être au p. de la solitude** to be agonizingly lonely; **être au p. de l'angoisse** to be in anguish; **l'incendie était à son p.** the fire was at its height; **cela va pousser la crise à son p.** that's going to take the crisis to breaking point; **atteindre son p.** to reach a climax, to peak *or* climax; **la crise/la douleur a atteint son p.** the crisis/the pain is at its height *or* its worst

parpaing [parpɛ̃] NM *Constr* breeze block

Parque [park] NF *Myth* **les Parques** the Fates

parquer [parke] VT *(voiture)*, *Ordinat (disque)* to park; *(bétail, moutons)* to pen; *(prisonniers)* to confine, to pack in; **on nous a parqués comme des moutons dans la salle d'attente** we were herded into the waiting room; **des étudiants parqués dans des salles de cours trop petites** students packed into lecture theatres that are too small

parquet [parkɛ] NM **1** *Jur* public prosecutor's office; **(membres du) p.** public prosecutor and his deputies; **déposer une plainte au p.** to lodge a complaint in court **2** *Bourse* **le P.** the (trading) floor, *Am* the pit **3** *Constr* (wooden *or* parquet) floor *or* flooring; **lame de p.** floorboard

parquetage [parkətaʒ] NM **1** *(installation)* laying of wooden *or* parquet floors **2** *(sol)* wooden *or* parquet flooring *or* floor

parqueter [parkəte] VT (**je parquette, n. parquetons; je parquetterai**) **p. une pièce** to lay a wooden *or* parquet floor in a room, to parquet a room

parqueterie [parkɛtri, -kətri] NF *(installation)* laying of (wooden *or* parquet) floors; *(fabrication)* making of (wooden *or* parquet) floors

parqueteur [parkətœr] NM *(fabricant)* parquet maker; *(installateur)* parquet layer

parrain [parɛ̃] NM *Rel, Fig* godfather; *(d'un enfant du tiers-monde, d'un sportif, d'une manifestation sportive)* sponsor; *(d'un nouveau membre d'un club)* sponsor, proposer; *(d'une fondation)* patron; *Mktg* promoter, sponsor; *Rel* **être p.** to be *or* stand godfather (**de** to); **être le p. d'un navire** to name a ship

parrainage [parɛnaʒ] NM *(d'un enfant du tiers-monde)* sponsorship, sponsoring; *(d'un nouveau membre)* sponsorship, sponsoring, proposing; *(d'un navire)* naming; *(d'une fondation)* patronage; *Mktg* **p.** sponsorship; **p.-partenariat** partnership sponsoring; **p.-télévision** television sponsorship *or* sponsoring

parrainer [parene] VT *Rel (enfant)* to act as godfather/godmother to; *(enfant du tiers-monde)* to sponsor; *(nouveau membre)* to sponsor, to propose; *(navire)* to name; *(fondation)* to act as patron of; *Mktg* to sponsor

parraineur [parɛnœr] NM sponsor

parricide [parisid] N parricide

  NM *(crime)* parricide; **commettre un p.** to commit parricide

  ADJ parricidal

parsemé [parsəme] ADJ **ciel p. d'étoiles** sky studded *or* spangled with stars; **champ p. de pâquerettes** field dotted with daisies; **texte p. de coquilles** text littered with misprints; **un visage p. de taches de rousseur** a freckled face; **ses affaires sont parsemées sur le sol de sa chambre** his things are scattered *or* strewn all over the floor of his room

parsemer [parsəme] VT *(conj like* **semer***) (de papiers)* to strew (**de** with); *(de sucre)* to sprinkle (**de** with); *(de graines)* to scatter (**de** with); **des feuilles parsemaient le chemin** the path was scattered *or* strewn with leaves, leaves were scattered *or* strewn all over the path

parsi, -ie [parsi] ADJ, N *Rel* Parsee

PART [par]

> share **1, 2** ▪ nowhere *(nulle part)* **3**
> ▪ from *(de la part de)* **4** ▪ apart *(à part)*
> **5**

NF **1** *(portion)* share, part, portion; **diviser un gâteau en parts égales** to divide a cake into equal portions; **combien de parts de gâteau faut-il faire?** how many pieces should I cut (the cake into)?; **une p. de gâteau** a piece of cake; *Fig* **avoir/vouloir sa p. du gâteau** to have/want one's share of the cake *or* slice of the cake; **sa p. des bénéfices** his/her share of the profits; **elle a eu sa p. de malheurs** she's had her share of misfortune; **professeur à p. entière** fully qualified teacher, *Fam* fully fledged *or Am* full-fledged teacher; **ils viennent pour une bonne p. des environs de Lille** a good many of them come from *or* they come very largely from the Lille area; **une grande/petite p. d'entre elles** a large/ small proportion *or* number of them; **pour ma p.** for my part, as for me, as far as I am concerned, speaking for myself; *Fig* **prendre qch en bonne/mauvaise p.** to take sth in good/bad part, to take sth the right/wrong way, to take sth well/badly; *Fig* **ne le prends pas en mauvaise p. mais ...** don't take this

the wrong way but ...; *Fig* **comment veux-tu que je ne le prenne pas en mauvaise p.?** how else should I react?

2 *(participation)* share, part; **avoir p. à qch** to have a hand *or* a share in sth; **avoir p. aux bénéfices** to have a share of the profits; **prendre p. à** to take part in; *(conversation, débat, jeu)* to take part in, to join in; *(honneurs)* to share (in); *(la joie, la douleur, la déception de qn)* to share; **je n'y ai pris aucune p.** I had nothing to do with it, I had no part in it; **faire p. de qch à qn** to inform sb of sth, to tell sb about sth; **qui t'a fait p. de cette information?** who gave you this information?; **je tenais à vous faire p. de notre joie** I wanted to let you know how happy we are; **lettre de faire-p.** *(de mariage, de décès)* announcement; **faire la p. de qch** to take sth into account *or* into consideration, to make allowance(s) for sth; **faire la p. des choses** to make allowances

3 nulle p. nowhere; **je ne les ai vus nulle p.** I couldn't see them anywhere; **nulle p. ailleurs** nowhere else; **elle ne veut partir nulle p. ailleurs** she doesn't want to go anywhere else; **autre p.** somewhere else, *Fml* elsewhere; **quelque p.** somewhere; **de p. et d'autre** here and there; **faire des concessions de p. et d'autre** to make concessions on both sides; **de toute(s) part(s)** on all sides; **de p. en p.** through and through, right through; **d'une p. ... d'autre p. ...** on the one hand ... on the other hand ... ▫SEE GRAMMAR B63▫

4 de la p. de from; **je viens de la p. de Madame Dubol** *(c'est elle qui m'envoie)* I've come on behalf of Madame Dubol; *(c'est elle qui m'a parlé de vous)* Madame Dubol gave me your name; **une indiscrétion de la p. de ...** an indiscretion on the part of ...; *Tél* **c'est de la p. de qui?** who's speaking *or* calling?; **dites-lui de ma p. que ...** tell him from me that ...; **ce serait bien aimable de votre p.** it would be very kind of you; **cela m'étonne de sa p.** that surprises me, coming from him; **je n'aurais jamais cru ça de sa p.** I would never have believed it of him/her

5 à p. apart, separately; **prendre qn à p.** to take sb aside; **il m'en a parlé à p.** he spoke to me about it in private; **mettre de l'argent à p.** to put money by *or* aside; **plaisanterie à p.** joking apart; **c'est une femme à p.** she's an exceptional woman, she's one of a kind; **un cas à p.** a special case, a case apart; **et à p. lui?** who besides him?, who apart from him?; **tu aimes le foot, et à p. ça?** what else do you like apart from *or* besides football?; **je me disais à p. moi que ...** I was saying to myself that ...; **à p. quelques exceptions/ quelques pages** with a few exceptions/the exception of a few pages; **à p. quelques fautes d'inattention** apart from *or* except for a few careless mistakes; **à p. cela, tout va bien** apart from that, everything is fine; *Fam* **à p. que ...** apart from the fact that ...

  ▸▸ *TV* **p. d'audience** audience share; **p. du feu: faire la p. du feu** to cut one's losses; *Fin* **p. de fondateur** founder's share(s); **la p. du lion** the lion's share; *Com* **p. de marché** market share, share of the market; **p. patronale** employer's contribution; **p. salariale** employee's contribution; *Fin* **p. sociale** share of capital, capital share

partage [partaʒ] NM **1** *(action)* *(d'une fortune, d'un domaine, d'une propriété etc)* division, sharing out; *Pol, Jur (d'un pays, de biens)* partition; **faire le p. de qch** to divide sth up, to share sth out; **sans p.** *(amour, engagement etc)* total; **il y a p. d'opinions** opinions are divided; *Géog* **ligne de p. des eaux** watershed, *Am* divide **2** *(lot)* share, portion; **donner qch en p.** to give sth away *(as part of one's fortune)*; **recevoir qch en p.** to receive sth *(as part of one's inheritance)*;

il leur donna cet argent en p. he gave them the money (as their share of his fortune); **ce que les hommes reçurent en p. de la nature** nature's gifts to mankind; **la pauvre n'a pas reçu la beauté en p.** the poor girl isn't one of nature's beauties; **la souffrance est le p. du genre humain** suffering is the lot of mankind; **cela fait partie du p. de chacun** it's something we all have to put up with

▸▸*Ordinat* **p. des données** data sharing; *Ordinat* **p. de fichiers** file sharing; *Ordinat* **p. d'imprimantes** printer sharing; **p. du pouvoir** power sharing; **p. de temps** time sharing; **p. du (temps de) travail** job-sharing; **p. des voix** distribution of votes; **regardons le p. des voix** let's look at how people voted; **en cas de p. des voix** in the event of a tied vote

partagé [partaʒe] **ADJ 1** *(incertain)* **elle est partagée** *(elle a du mal à décider, à choisir)* she's torn; **je suis très p. sur ce point** I have very mixed feelings on the subject; **je suis partagée entre la tristesse et la joie** I don't know whether to feel sad or happy; **être p. entre son devoir et ses sentiments** to be torn between one's duty and one's feelings; **les avis sont partagés** opinions are divided **2** *(entre plusieurs personnes)* *(convictions, sentiments, impressions)* shared; **amour p.** mutual love; *Ordinat* **travail en temps p.** timesharing

partageable [partaʒabl] **ADJ** divisible, which can be divided

partager [partaʒe] (**je partageai(s); n. partageons**) **VT 1** *(terrain, groupes etc)* to divide (up); *(biens etc)* to divide (up), to apportion; *(butin etc)* to divide (up), to share (out); **p. son temps entre deux occupations** to divide *or* split one's time between two occupations; **p. qch en deux** to divide sth in two, to halve sth; **le fleuve partage le pays en deux** the river divides *or* splits *or* cuts the country in two; **ce débat partage l'opinion** people are divided *or* split over the issue **2** *(avoir ou mettre en commun)* to share; **nous partageons la même chambre** we share a room; **je partage un appartement avec mon amie** I share a flat *or* I flat-share with a friend; **je ne partage vraiment rien avec ces gens-là** I really have nothing in common with those people; **p. l'avis de qn** to share sb's opinion; **p. la joie/la douleur de qn** to share (in) sb's joy/sorrow; **p. le repas de qn** to share sb's meal, to share a meal with sb; **je lui ai proposé de p. mon croissant** I offered him/her a share of my croissant **VI** to share; **elle n'aime pas p.** she doesn't like sharing

VPR se partager 1 *(être partagé)* to divide, to be divided; **le gâteau peut se p. en quatre morceaux** the cake can be cut into four portions **2** *(se communiquer)* **ces expériences ne se partagent pas si facilement** it's not very easy to share such experiences; **ça ne se partage pas** it's not something you can share **3** *(faire un partage entre soi)* to share; **ils se sont partagé les bénéfices** they shared *or* divided the profits between them **4** *(partager son temps)* to divide one's time; **elle se partage entre ses enfants et son travail** she divides her time between her children and her work

partageur, -euse [partaʒœr, -øz] **ADJ** willing to share; **il n'est pas p.** he doesn't like sharing, he's not very good at sharing; **on ne lui a jamais appris à être p.** he's never been taught to share

partagiciel [partaʒisjel] **NM** *Ordinat* shareware

partance [partɑ̃s] **NF en p.** *(train)* about to leave; *(avion)* about to take off; *(navire)* about to sail; **en p. pour Bordeaux** bound for Bordeaux; **train en p. pour Londres** train for London, London train

partant¹ [partɑ̃] **ADV** *Litt* consequently, therefore

partant², -ante [-ɑ̃t] **ADJ** departing; *Fam* **je suis p.** you can count me in, I'm game; *Fam* **êtes-vous toujours p?** are you still game?, can I/we/*etc* still count you in?; *Fam* **elle est toujours partante pour aller au restaurant** she's always game for a meal out

N *Sport* starter; *(en athlétisme)*, *Courses de chevaux* runner, starter

partenaire [partənɛr] **N** partner; *(dans une affaire)* (business) partner; *(dans un film)* co-star; **partenaires commerciaux** trading partners; **les partenaires sociaux** employers and trade unions *or Am* labor unions, workers and management; **je suis son p. au tennis** I partner him at tennis, I'm his tennis partner

partenariat [partənarja] **NM** partnership; **p. public-privé** public-private partnership, private finance initiative; *Mktg* **p. télévision** television tie-in

parterre [partɛr] **NM 1** *Fam (sol)* floor **2** *(de fleurs)* (flower)bed; *(plate-bande)* border **3** *Théâtre (places, le public)* pit

Parthe [part] **NM la flèche du P.** the Parthian shot

parthénogénèse [partenoʒenez] **NF** *Biol* parthenogenesis

parthénogénétique [partenoʒenetik] **ADJ** *Biol* parthenogenetic

Parthénon [partenɔ̃] **NM** *Antiq* **le P.** the Parthenon

PARTI¹ [parti]

party **1, 2** ▪ side **1** ▪ to side with someone *(prendre parti pour quelqu'un)* **1** ▪ to resign oneself *(en prendre son parti)* **4** ▪ to take advantage of *(tirer parti de)* **5** ▪ bias *(parti pris)* **7**

NM 1 *(camp)* party, side; **prendre le p. de qn, se mettre** *ou* **se ranger du p. de qn** to take sb's side *or* part, to take sides with sb, to side with sb; **prendre p. pour qn** to side with sb, to take sb's side; **prendre p. contre qn** to side *or* take sides against sb; **je ne prends p. pour ou contre personne** I'm not taking sides; **j'hésite à prendre p.** I'm reluctant to come down on one side or the other; **il faut que tu prennes p. pour ou contre l'un ou l'autre** you're going to have to make your mind up one way or the other; **il ne faut pas que tu prennes p. contre l'un ou l'autre** you mustn't take sides

2 *Pol* party; **prendre sa carte du** *ou* **au p.** to join the party, to become a card-carrying member; **les partis de droite** the parties of the right, the right-wing parties; **les partis de gauche** the parties of the left, the left-wing parties; **le P. (communiste)** the Communist Party; **le P. communiste français** the French Communist Party; **le P. conservateur** *(en Grande-Bretagne)* the Conservative Party, the Tory Party; *(au Canada)* the Progressive Conservative Party; **le P. démocrate** the Democratic Party; **p. majoritaire** majority party; **p. minoritaire** minority party; **p. politique** political party; **le P. républicain** the Republican Party; **le P. socialiste** = left-of-centre French political party; **le P. travailliste** *(en Grande-Bretagne)* the Labour Party; **un p. unique** a single party

3 *(personne bonne à marier)* **un bon** *ou* **beau p.** a good match *or Fam* catch

4 *(choix, décision)* **prendre un p.** to decide, to make up one's mind, to come to a decision; **prendre le p. de faire qch** to decide *or* resolve to do sth; **il ne savait quel p. prendre** he didn't know what course to take; **en prendre son p.** to resign oneself, to make the best of it *or Fam* the best of a bad job

5 *(profit)* **tirer p. de qch** to take advantage of sth, to make (good) use of sth, to turn sth to (good) account; **il n'a jamais cherché à tirer p. de cet avantage** he's never tried to take advantage of it; **tirer le meilleur p. possible de ...** to make the best possible use of ...

6 faire un mauvais p. à qn to treat sb badly; **la presse lui fit un mauvais p.** he got rough treatment from the press

7 p. pris *(pour ou contre un concurrent etc)* bias; *(préjugé)* prejudice; **avoir un p. pris contre qn/qch** to be prejudiced about sb/sth, to have a prejudice towards sb/sth; **avoir un p. pris pour qn** to be bia(s)ed in sb's favour; **faire preuve de p. pris** to show bias; **sans p. pris** unbias(s)ed; **sans p. pris, elle est vraiment mauvaise dans son domaine, non?** speaking impartially, she's really bad in her field, isn't she?

parti² **ADJ** *Fam (ivre)* wasted, plastered; *(sous l'effet de la drogue)* high, spaced out; **il est complètement p.** *(ivre)* he's plastered; *(sous l'effet de la drogue)* he's totally spaced out

partial, -iale, -iaux, -iales [parsjal, -jo] **ADJ** *(personne)* bias(s)ed, partial; *(opinion, article)* bias(s)ed, one-sided

Do not confuse with **partiel**.

partialement [parsjalmɑ̃] **ADV** in a bias(-s)ed way, with bias

partialité [parsjalite] **NF** bias (**envers** in favour of; **contre** against), partiality (**envers** for, to); **il juge toujours avec p.** he's always bia(s)ed in his judgments; **s'exprimer avec p.** to be bia(s)ed

participant, -ante [partisipɑ̃, -ɑ̃t] **ADJ** participating; **les personnes participantes** the participants, the people taking part

N *(à une réunion, une action)* participant *(à in)*; *(à un concours)* participant, contestant; *(d'un club)* member; *Sport etc* competitor; **les participants à la manifestation** those taking part in the demonstration; **le nombre croissant des participants aux manifestations sportives** the increase in the number of people taking part in sporting activities

participation [partisipasjɔ̃] **NF 1** *(collaboration)* participation *(à in)*; *(aux élections)* turnout; *(à un cadeau)* contribution; **cela s'est fait sans ma p.** I didn't take any part in it, I had no part *or* hand in it; **cela s'est fait avec ma p.** I was involved in it; *Cin, TV* **avec la p. de Jean Martin (dans le rôle de ...)** with *or* featuring Jean Martin (as ...); **nous avons pu réaliser ce film grâce à la p. des Transports Dubout** our thanks to the Dubout Transport Company for helping us make this film; **sans la p. de M. Martin, rien de tout cela n'aurait vu le jour** none of this would have been possible without the help of Mr Martin; **représentation avec la p. de plusieurs vedettes** show with appearances by several stars; *Scol* **mauvaise p. d'un élève en classe** poor level of participation by a pupil; *Scol* **doit faire des efforts de p.** must try to take part more; **p. aux frais** (financial) contribution; **la p. aux frais est de 200 euros par personne** each person will contribute 200 euros; **taux de p.** level of participation; *(à un marathon, un jeu télévisé)* entries; **taux de p. électorale** voter turnout **2** *Com* share, interest *(à in)*; *Fin* share, interest, holding *(à in)*

▸▸**p. active** active participation; **p. aux bénéfices** profit sharing; **p. croisée** cross-holding; **p. majoritaire** major shareholding, majority holding; **p. minoritaire** minority interest; **p. ouvrière** worker participation; **p. des salariés aux bénéfices** profit-sharing scheme

participe [partisip] **NM** *Gram* participle **A44-6; 837-9**

participer [partisipe] VI **1 p. à** *(réunion, jeu etc)* to take part in; *(discussion etc)* to take part in, to participate in; *(concours)* to take part in, to enter; *(marathon)* to take part in, to enter, to run in; *(complot etc)* to be involved in, to be (a) party to; *(d'un acteur) (spectacle)* to appear in; **p. à la joie/au chagrin de qn** to share (in) sb's joy/sadness; **elle participe activement au projet** she is taking an active part in the project **2 p. à** *(financièrement)* to contribute (money) to **3 p. à** *(partager) (bénéfices etc)* to share in, to have a share in; *Fin* **p. à une entreprise** to have an interest in a business **4** *Fml* **p. de qch** to partake of sth, to have some of the characteristics of sth; **sa théorie participe plus de la philosophie que des sciences exactes** his theory bears more of a resemblance to philosophy than to the exact sciences

participial, -iale, -iaux, -iales [partisipjal, -jo] *Gram* ADJ *(proposition etc)* participial **NF participiale** participial clause

particularisation [partikylarizasjɔ̃] NF particularization

particulariser [partikylarize] VT *(définir par ses particularités)* to particularize
VPR se particulariser to stand out; **il se particularise par ses cheveux roux** his red hair makes him stand out, he stands out by virtue of his red hair; **il s'habille toujours en noir pour se p.** he always wears black to make himself different *or* to make himself stand out

particularisme [partikylarism] NM *Pol, Rel etc* particularism

particularité [partikylarite] NF **1** *(spécificité) (de quelque chose)* particularity, special nature **2** *(trait caractéristique)* characteristic, (distinctive) feature; *(qui sort de l'ordinaire)* peculiarity; **la p. de cette imprimante, c'est que ...** what distinguishes this printer (from all the rest) *or* what is special about this printer is that ... **3** *Litt (détail)* detail, particular

particule [partikyl] NF **1** *(de poussière, sable etc)*, *Nucl* particle; **panneau de particules** particle board; *Nucl* **p. élémentaire** elementary particle; *Nucl* **p. alpha/bêta** alpha/beta particle; *Nucl* **physique des particules** particle physics **2** *Gram* particle; **avoir un nom à p.** ≃ to have a double-barrelled name

particulier, -ière [partikylje, -jer] ADJ **1** *(spécial)* particular, special; *(propre)* characteristic (**à** of), peculiar (**à** to); **signes particuliers** *(sur passeport)* distinguishing features; **il a un humour qui lui est p.** he has his own special brand of humour; **sa démarche bien particulière** his own particular way of walking; **la saveur très particulière du citron vert** the very distinctive taste of the lime; **les besoins particuliers à l'enfant** the special *or* specific *or* particular needs of children; **revenir sur un point p.** to come back to a specific *or* particular point **2** *(remarquable)* unusual, exceptional; *(soin, attention, patience, intérêt)* particular; *Péj (style, gens, mœurs etc)* peculiar; **le médecin s'est occupé de lui avec une patience toute particulière** the doctor was particularly patient with him; **cas p.** special case; *Hum* **elle, c'est un cas p.** she's a real oddball **3** *(privé) (maison, voiture etc)* private; *(compte)* personal; *(salle de bain)* en-suite; **secrétaire p./particulière** private secretary; **cours particuliers, leçons particulières** private lessons *or* tuition; **j'ai des raisons particulières pour le désirer** I have my own (private *or* particular) reasons *or* I have reasons of my own for wishing it; **à titre p.** in a private capacity; **il a pris la voiture de l'entreprise pour s'en servir à titre p.** he took the company car for his own personal use

4 en p. *(spécialement)* in particular, particularly; **ses frères et en p. son frère cadet** his brothers, particularly his younger brother, his brothers and his younger brother in particular; **ce livre en p.** this book in particular **5 en p.** *(en privé)* privately, in private; **recevoir qn en p.** to see sb privately *or* in private; **demander à être reçu en p.** to ask for a private meeting; **prendre qn en p.** to take sb aside; **je ne pourrai pas m'occuper de vous en p.** I won't be able to deal with you in person

N *(private)* individual; *Fam Péj Vieilli* individual; **simple p.** ordinary person, private citizen; *Vieilli* **que veut cette particulière?** what does she *or* that woman want?; **vente de p. à p.** private sale

NM **le p. ne l'intéresse pas** he's not interested in details; **aller du p. au général** to go from the specific to the general

> Attention: ne pas confondre **particular** et **peculiar** lorsque l'on traduit **particulier**. **Particular** signifie **spécifique**, alors que **peculiar** signifie **bizarre**.

particulièrement [partikyljɛrmɑ̃] ADV **1** *(surtout)* particularly, (e)specially; **il aime tous les arts et p. la peinture** he is fond of all the arts, especially painting *or* and painting in particular **2** *(spécialement) (intelligent, beau, bête etc)* particularly, outstandingly, exceptionally; **j'attire tout p. votre attention sur cette question** I would particularly like to draw your attention to this question; **cela ne me fait pas p. plaisir** I'm not particularly happy about it; **je sais que cela lui fera p. plaisir** I know it will give him particular pleasure; **pas p.** not particularly **3** *(d'une façon intime)* intimately; **je ne la connais pas p.** I don't know her very *or* particularly well

PARTIE [parti]

| part 1, 6 | ▪ partly *(en partie)* 2 | ▪ to be part of *(faire partie de)* 3 | ▪ field 5 | ▪ party 7, 10, 11 | ▪ game 8 | ▪ to tell somebody off *(prendre quelqu'un à partie)* 12 |

NF **1** *(morceau) (d'un tout)* part; **certaines parties ne sont pas mauvaises** it's not bad in parts, parts *or* bits of it aren't bad; **une p. de la maison est à louer** part of the house is to let; **une bonne p. du papier est abîmée** a good *or* great deal of the paper is damaged; **une bonne p. du personnel est en grève** a good portion of the staff *or* a good many of the employees are on strike; **une bonne p. des pistes de ski** a good many of the ski runs; **la plus grande p. du chemin** the best part of the way; **la plus grande p. de mon temps/du travail** the greatest part of *or* most of *or* the majority of my time/the work; **il dépense la plus grande p. de son argent** he spends most of *or* the best part of his money; **les parties communes** *(d'une maison)* the communal areas; **les parties du corps** the parts of the body SEE GRAMMAR B21 ; **les parties génitales**, *Fam Vieilli* **les parties honteuses**, *Fam* **les parties** the genitals, *Fam* the private parts; *Fam* **les parties** the privates; **une dissertation en trois parties** a dissertation in three parts *or* sections; *Hum* **je ne vais pas te faire une démonstration en trois parties** I won't go into the sordid details; **parties par million** parts per million

2 en p. partly, in part; **en p. responsable** partly responsible, responsible in part; **refait en p.** *(appartement)* partly redecorated; **nous avons été en p. remboursés** we got a part refund, we were partially refunded; **j'étais en p. surprise/déçue** I was slightly surprised/disappointed; **en grande** *ou* **majeure p.** largely, to a great extent, for the

most part; **ce sont en grande p. des adolescents** most of them are teenagers, they are teenagers for the most part

3 faire p. de qch to be *or* form part of sth; **cela fait p. de mes intentions** that's one of the things I intend to do; **cela ne fait pas p. de mes responsabilités** that isn't part of *or* one of my responsibilities; **cela ne fait pas p. des choses qui nous occupent aujourd'hui** that's not one of the things that concern us today; **je ne fais plus p. de ce cercle** I don't belong to this club any longer; **elle ne fait plus p. de nos amis** she is no longer a friend of ours; **faire p. de la famille** to be part of *or* one of the family; **tu fais un peu p. de la famille, maintenant** you're like one of the family now; **je n'ai pas l'impression de faire p. de cette famille** I don't feel like (I'm) part *or* a member of this family; *Fam* **faire p. des meubles** to be part of the furniture

4 *Fin* **p. double** double entry; **comptabilité en p. simple/double** single-/double-entry book-keeping

5 *(domaine)* field, subject; *(d'une entreprise, d'une profession)* line, particular branch; **ce n'est pas (de) ma p., je ne suis pas de la p.** that's not (in) my line, that's not up my street **6** *Mus (d'une voix, d'un instrument)* part; **parties d'orchestre** orchestral parts

7 *(fête, réunion)* party; *Fig* **voulez-vous être de la p.?** will you join us?; *Fig* **s'il voulait être de la p., nous pourrions bénéficier de ses conseils** if he was willing to come in with us we could benefit from his advice; **je n'étais pas de la p.** I wasn't invited; **elle ne pouvait pas être de la p. car ...** she couldn't be here *or* join us because ...

8 *(jeu) (de cartes, d'échecs, de tennis)* game; *(de golf)* game, round; **faire une p. de cartes/d'échecs** to have *or* play a game of cards/chess; **p. nulle** draw; **gagner la p.** to win the game; **après 30 minutes de jeu, elle avait la p. gagnée** the match was hers *or* she had the match won after 30 minutes; *Fig* **ce n'est que p. remise** we'll do it soon, *Am* let's take a rain check

9 *(combat)* struggle; *(pour un point d'honneur)* duel; **p. inégale** uneven struggle

10 *Jur (d'un litige, dans un contrat etc)* party; **la p. adverse** the other side; **entendre les avocats des deux parties** to hear counsel on both sides; *Fig* **être juge et p.** to be judge and jury; **p. prenante** party concerned; *(dans un projet)* participant

11 *(adversaire)* opponent; **les parties belligérantes** the belligerent parties, the belligerents; **avoir affaire à forte p.** to have a tough opponent on one's hands

12 prendre qn à p. to tell sb off; **il nous a pris à p. en nous reprochant de faire trop de bruit** he told us off for making too much noise **13 avoir p. liée avec qn** to have joined forces with sb

▸▸ **parties annexes** *(dans l'édition)* end matter; **p. de campagne** picnic; *Fam* **p. carrée** foursome *(in bed)*; **p. de chasse** shooting party; *Jur* **p. civile** plaintiff claiming damages *(in criminal case)*; **se constituer** *ou* **se porter p. civile** to take civil action, to sue; *Gram* **parties du discours** parts of speech; *Fam* **p. fine** orgy; *Fam* **p. de jambes en l'air** roll in the hay; **ils commencent à m'énerver avec leurs parties de jambes en l'air en pleine nuit** they're beginning to get on my nerves doing it in the middle of the night; **p. de plaisir: ce n'est pas une p. de plaisir!** it's no picnic!, it's not my idea of fun!

partiel, -ielle [parsjɛl] ADJ partial; **paiement p.** part payment; *Pol* **élection partielle** by-election; *Univ* **épreuve partielle** class exam
NM *Univ* class exam
NF *Pol* **partielle** by-election

passavant [pasavɑ̃] NM **1** Naut (fore-and-aft) gangway, catwalk **2** Jur transire; Com transire, transit bill

passe [pas] NF **1** Ftbl pass; Escrime pass, thrust; Escrime, Fig **p. d'armes** passage of arms; Ftbl **p. en avant/en retrait** forward/back pass **2** (manipulation) **passes magnétiques** mesmeric or hypnotic passes **3** Métal (sur un tour) cut **4** (d'une prostituée) trick; **c'est combien la p.?** how much is it a time?; **j'ai fait dix passes** I've had ten clients or Br punters; **maison de p.** brothel; **hôtel de p.** = hotel used by prostitutes and their clients **5** (à la roulette) passe (any number above 18) **6** Naut (chenal) pass, channel; **p. étroite** narrows **7** Fig **être en p. de faire qch** to be on the way to doing sth; **être dans une mauvaise p.** to be in a fix or a tight corner; **tirer qn/se sortir d'une mauvaise p.** to get sb out of/get out of a tight corner; **elle est dans une bonne p.** everything's going right for her **8** Typ (main de) **p.** overs, overplus; **exemplaires de p.** surplus copies, over copies **9** Fin **p. de caisse** cashier error allowance
NM Fam (clé) skeleton or master or pass key

passé [pase] ADJ **1** (écoulé) (temps) past; **la semaine/l'année passée** last week/year; **lundi p.** last Monday; **il est quatre heures passées** it's gone four, it's after four; **il a quarante ans passés** he's over forty; **à quinze ans passés, il ne savait toujours pas lire** he was over fifteen and he still couldn't read; **ça fait deux ans passés que je ne l'ai pas vu** it's over two years now since I saw him; **p. de mode** out of fashion **2** (fini) over; **l'orage/la crise est passé(e)** the storm/the crisis is over; **penser à son enfance/sa beauté passée** to think of one's vanished childhood/beauty **3** (éteint, décoloré) (couleur, tissu etc) faded; **mon salon est tout p.** my living room is looking old and drab
NM **1** (temps révolu) **le p.** the past; **dans le p.** in the past; **comme par le p.** as in the past; **tout ça, c'est du p.** that's all in the past; **avoir un p. chargé** ou **un lourd p.** to have a shady past; **oublier le p.** to forget the past; **oublions le p.** let's let bygones be bygones; **avoir honte/être fier de son p.** to be ashamed/proud of one's past **2** Gram past (tense); **les temps du p.** the past tenses; **p. simple** preterite, past historic; **p. composé** perfect (tense); **au p.** in the past (tense); **p. progressif** past continuous SEE GRAMMAR A49–50; B30–1
PRÉP after; **p. les arbres ...** after or beyond the trees ...; **p. cette date** after this date; **p. la première impression** once or after the first impression has worn off

passe-crassane [paskrasan] NF INV passe crassane (type of pear)

passe-droit, pl **passe-droits** NM (undeserved) privilege, favour, Am favor; **le fils du patron a eu un p., on a fait un p. au fils du patron** the boss's son got preferential treatment

passéisme [paseism] NM Péj attachment to the past, backward-looking attitude

passéiste [paseist] Péj ADJ backward-looking
N backward-looking person

passe-lacet, pl **passe-lacets** NM bodkin; Fig Fam **raide comme un p.** stony broke, Am stone broke

passement [pasmɑ̃] NM braid, braiding

passementer [pasmɑ̃te] VT to braid

passementerie [pasmɑ̃tri] NF **1** Com haberdashery trade, Am notions trade **2** (accessoire décoratif) braid

passementier, -ière [pasmɑ̃tje, -jer] ADJ (commerce, industrie) haberdashery, Am notions
N haberdasher, Am dealer in notions

passe-montagne, pl **passe-montagnes** NM balaclava (helmet)

passe-partout NM INV **1** (clef) skeleton or master or pass key **2** (scie) cross-cut saw **3** (cadre) passe-partout **4** Journ filler
ADJ INV all-purpose; **réponse p.** stock or all-purpose reply or answer; **tenue p.** all-purpose outfit

passe-passe NM INV **tour de p.** (conjuring or magic) trick; Fig (tromperie) trick

passe-plat, pl **passe-plats** NM serving hatch

passepoil [paspwal] NM (pour vêtements) piping

passepoiler [paspwale] VT (vêtement) to pipe; **poche passepoilée** welted pocket

passeport [paspɔr] NM Admin, Fig passport; Naut passport, sea letter; **les enfants sont sur le p. de leur mère** the children are on their mother's passport

---

PASSER [pase]

VI to pass **1, 8, 9, 13** ▪ to go by **1, 9** ▪ to go through (passer par) **4, 7** ▪ to be on **5** ▪ to call on somebody (passer chez quelqu'un) **6** ▪ to disappear **8** ▪ to fade **8** ▪ to pass for (passer pour) **10** ▪ to be accepted **11** ▪ to filter **14**
VT to cross **1** ▪ to go over **1** ▪ to go through **1** ▪ to carry across **2** ▪ to pass **3, 4** ▪ to give **4** ▪ to put **5** ▪ to show **6** ▪ to excuse **8** ▪ to leave out **9** ▪ to enter into **10** ▪ to take **12** ▪ to sit **12**
VPR to happen **1** ▪ to take place **1** ▪ to go by **2** ▪ to pass **2** ▪ to go **2** ▪ to come to an end **2** ▪ to do without (se passer de) **3**

VI (aux être) **1** (se déplacer, circuler) to pass, to go/come past, Fml to proceed; **par où est-il passé?** which way did he go?; **je regardais p. la procession** I was watching the procession go by; **p. sur un pont** to cross (over) a bridge; **il est passé devant le magasin** he went/came by or passed (by) the shop; **p. par-dessus/par-dessous qch** to get over/under sth; **la voiture lui est passée** ou **lui a passé sur les jambes** the car ran over his legs; Fig **p. sur le corps de qn pour parvenir à qch** to trample all over sb to attain sth; **il faudrait me p. sur le corps pour que je dise oui** if you get me to say yes it'll be over my dead body; **la bouteille est passée** ou **a passé de main en main** the bottle was passed round; **faire p. les gâteaux/photos** to hand round or pass round the cakes/photos; **p. sur une difficulté** to pass over a difficulty; **passons!** let's leave it at that!; **en passant** in passing; **dire qch en passant** to mention sth in passing; **soit dit en passant** by the way, incidentally

2 (aller d'un lieu à un autre, changer) **p. à l'ennemi** to go over to the enemy; (d'un espion) to defect; **le chiffre d'affaires est passé de deux à trois millions** the turnover has gone up from two to three million; **p. à table** to come to or sit up at the table; **passons à table!** come to the table, everybody!; **passons à la salle à manger** let's go into the dining room; **il nous fit p. dans le bureau** he showed us into the office; Scol **p. dans la classe supérieure** to move up or be moved up (a class); Sport **p. en seconde division** (être promu) to go up to the second division; (être relégué) to go down to the second division; **passons à autre chose** let's move on to other matters; (changeons de sujet) let's change the subject; Aut **p. en seconde/troisième** to go or change into second/third (gear); **il est passé du rire aux larmes** his laughter turned to tears

3 (se transmettre) **p. à la postérité** to go

down to posterity; **l'héritage est passé à sa fille** the inheritance went to his daughter; **le mot est passé dans l'usage/dans le vocabulaire général** the word passed into common usage/into the general vocabulary; **c'est passé dans la tradition/les coutumes** it passed into tradition/custom; **c'est passé dans la langue** it's entered the language; **l'alcool passe très rapidement dans le sang** alcohol goes or gets into the bloodstream very quickly

4 (traverser) **la route passe par le village** the road runs or goes through the village; **passez par la fenêtre** go through the window; **on est passé par Bourges/la Belgique** we went through or via Bourges/Belgium; **mon dîner ne passe pas** my dinner won't go down; Fig **ce qu'il m'a dit, ça ne passe pas** what he told me sticks in my throat; **je ne peux pas p.** I can't get by or past; **empêcher qn de p.** to stop sb from getting by or past; **on ne passe pas** you're not allowed through; **laisser p.** (lumière, air etc) to let in; (personne etc) to let through; Fig **laisser p. une erreur** to overlook a mistake; **faire p. un tuyau à travers le mur** to run a pipe through the wall; **faire p. des gens d'un pays à un autre** to smuggle people out of one country and into another; Fig **il est passé par l'université** he did a university course; **il dit tout ce qui lui passe par la tête** he says anything or the first thing that comes into his head; **la première chose qui m'est passée** ou **m'a passé par la tête** the first thing that came into my head; **une idée m'est passée par la tête ...** an idea has occurred to me ..., I've had an idea ...; Can **j'ai passé tout droit** I overslept

5 Cin to be on, to be showing; Radio, TV to be on; **p. à la radio** (d'une émission, personne) to be on the radio or the air; **p. à la télévision** (de personne) to be or appear on television; (de film) to be on television; **son documentaire n'est jamais passé** her documentary was never shown; **ça ne passe jamais à la radio/télévision** it's never on the radio/on television; **ce film est passé la semaine dernière** the film was on last week; **qu'est-ce qui passe ce soir?** what's on this evening?

6 (aller) **p. chez qn** to call on sb; **p. au pressing/à la boucherie** to call (in) at or Fam pop in at the dry cleaner's/butcher's; **je passerai chez vous ce soir** I'll come round or drop round this evening; **je passerai vous prendre vers 18 h** I'll pick you up or call for you or fetch you at about 6 o'clock; **en passant, je suis entré dire bonjour** I just looked in or dropped in on my way past; **il est passé prendre le courrier** he dropped by to pick up the mail; **je ne fais que p.** I'm not stopping; **est-ce que le facteur est passé?** has the postman been?, has the post come?

7 (subir) **elle est passée par des périodes vraiment difficiles** she has been or gone through some really difficult periods; **je suis passé par là** I've been through it, it's happened to me; Fam **quand il se met en colère, tout le monde y passe** when he gets angry, everybody bears the brunt of it; Fam **il a failli y p.** he nearly died; **toute sa fortune y est passée** he spent his entire fortune on it

8 (disparaître, finir) to disappear; **la douleur est passée** the pain has gone or passed or disappeared; **cela fera p. la douleur** that will get rid of the pain; **cela a fait p. mon mal de tête** it has cured my headache; **le vert est passé de mode** green is out of fashion; **le plus dur est passé** the worst is over; **ça lui passera (avec l'âge)** he'll grow out of it; **j'ai été un peu déprimé mais maintenant c'est passé** ou **ça m'a passé** I was a bit down but it's over now or I've got over it now or that's all in the past now; **couleurs qui passent** colours that fade; **le soleil a fait p. les couleurs**

the sun faded the colours; **il faut laisser p. l'orage** we must let the storm blow over; **la crise est passée** the crisis is over or past; **il fallait bien laisser p. cette période difficile** we just had to get through that difficult period; **laisser p. sa dernière chance** to miss one's last chance; **laisser p. une occasion** to miss or let slip an opportunity

9 (s'écouler) to go by, to pass; **des ou les années ont passé depuis …** years have passed or it's been years since …; **à mesure que les années passent** as the years go by; **comme le temps passe (vite)!** how time flies!; **faire p. le temps** to pass the time; **tout passe, tout lasse, tout casse** nothing lasts, everything comes to an end

10 (être considéré) **p. pour riche** to be considered rich, to pass for rich; **p. pour avoir fait qch** to be credited with having done sth; **ceci passe pour vrai** everyone believes this is true; **se faire p. pour …** to pass oneself off as …; **tu veux me faire p. pour un imbécile ou quoi?** do you want me to be taken for a fool or what?

11 (être accepté) to be accepted; **la loi est passée** the law has been passed or has gone through; **passe encore qu'il revienne demain, mais …, qu'il revienne demain, passe encore mais …** if he comes back tomorrow that's one thing or (that's all) well and good, but …; **cela peut p./ne passe pas** it will/won't do; Fam **cette excuse ne passera pas** that excuse won't wash; **alors, c'est passé, il a accepté?** well, did it work, did he accept?, Fam well, any joy, did he accept?

12 Jur **p. en jugement** to come up for judgment; **l'affaire passera demain/en janvier** the case will be heard tomorrow/in January

13 Cartes **passe!** pass!; (au bridge) no bid!

14 (de café, liquide) to filter

VT (aux **avoir**) **1** (pont, rivière, frontière) to cross, to go over; (porte, barrière) to go through, to pass through; (douanes) to go through, to clear; Fig (limite) to pass, to go beyond, to exceed; **vous avez passé la maison** you've gone past the house; Fig **il a passé la soixantaine** he's in his sixties; Fig **cela passe les limites ou les bornes** that's going too far; Fig **le vieux ne passera pas l'hiver** the old man won't last the winter (out); **p. son chemin** to carry on one's way

2 (transporter) to convey across, to carry across; **p. des marchandises en fraude** to smuggle goods

3 (mettre en circulation) to pass; **p. des faux billets** to pass forged banknotes

4 (donner) **p. qch à qn** to pass or give sth to sb; **voulez-vous me p. l'eau, s'il vous plaît?** would you pass me the water, please?; **est-ce que tu peux me p. ton stylo?** (prêter) could you lend me your pen?; **voulez-vous me p. le volant?** do you want me to drive?; **p. un message (à qn)** to pass on a message (to sb); **il m'a passé son rhume** he gave me his cold, I caught his cold; Sport **p. le ballon** to pass the ball; **p. la parole à qn** to hand over to sb; Tél **allô, je vous passe Paris/M. Robert** hello, I'm putting you through to Paris/Mr Robert; Tél **passez-moi M. Robert** put me through to or give me Mr Robert; Tél **passez-moi un coup de fil demain** call me tomorrow, give me a call or Br a ring tomorrow; **p. son tour** (en jouant) to miss one's go; (exprès) to pass

5 (mettre, faire aller) **p. l'éponge sur le tableau** to wipe the blackboard; Fig **passons l'éponge là-dessus** let's say no more about it; **p. l'aspirateur sur le tapis** to vacuum or Br hoover the carpet; **p. un coup de chiffon sur les meubles** to give the furniture a quick dust; **p. sa tête par la fenêtre** to put or stick one's head out of the window; **p. sa main dans qch** to put or slip one's hand in sth; **je lui ai passé mon bras autour de la taille** I

put or slipped my arm round his/her waist; **p. une chemise/une robe** to slip on a shirt/a dress; Aut **p. la seconde/la troisième** to go into or change into second/third (gear); Naut **p. une manœuvre** to reeve a rope; **p. sa colère sur qn** to vent one's anger on sb; **p. ses nerfs sur qn** to take it out on sb; **qu'est-ce que je vais lui p.!** I won't half tell him off!, he won't half catch it!; Fam **il s'est fait p. un savon** he got a telling off; **je l'ai senti p.** I really caught it; **p. un couteau à la meule** to sharpen a knife; **p. un parquet à la cire** to polish a (parquet) floor; **p. des troupes en revue** to inspect or review troops

6 Cin, TV (film) to show, to screen; Radio (émission) to broadcast; **p. un disque** to put on or play a record; **p. une vidéo** to put on a video; **qu'est-ce qu'ils passent au cinéma cette semaine?** what's on or showing at the cinema this week?, what are they showing at the cinema this week?

7 (temps, sa vie, vacances) to spend; **p. l'après-midi à faire qch** to spend the afternoon doing sth; **la secrétaire qui passe son temps à ne rien faire** the secretary who sits there doing nothing; **on y passera le temps nécessaire** we'll spend as much time on it as necessary; **pour p. le temps** (in order) to while away or pass the time

8 (pardonner) to excuse; **on ne lui passe rien** he doesn't get away with anything; **elle lui passe tout** she lets him get away with everything; **passez-moi l'expression** (if you'll) pardon the expression

9 (omettre) to leave out, to omit; **p. qch sous silence** to make no mention of sth; (fait gênant, secret inavouable) to keep quiet about sth; **(et) j'en passe, et des meilleures** and that's not all, and that's not the half of it; **il est beau, intelligent, instruit, et j'en passe** he's handsome, intelligent, cultured, and that's not all

10 Jur (accord, contrat) to enter into, to sign; **p. un marché** to sign a deal; Fin **p. un montant** to post an amount; **p. une commande** to place an order (**de qch à qn** for sth with sb); **p. une loi** to pass a law

11 Compta **p. un article en compte** to post an entry; **p. par pertes et profits** to transfer to profit and loss

12 p. un examen to take or sit an exam; **p. le permis de conduire** to take one's driving test

13 (liquide) to strain; (farine) to sift; **p. le café** to filter the coffee

14 (devenir) **p. capitaine** to be promoted to captain; **elle est passée maître dans l'art du collage/l'art de mentir ou du mensonge** she's a past master at collage/lying

VPR se passer 1 (se produire, arriver) to happen, to take place; **cela s'est passé il y a dix ans** it happened ten years ago; **que se passe-t-il?, qu'est-ce qui se passe?** what's going on?, what's happening?; **tout s'est bien passé** everything went (off) smoothly; **comment ça c'est passé?** how did it go?; **mon histoire se passe en France** my story is set in France; Fam **ça ne se passera pas comme ça** I won't stand for it SEE GRAMMAR B29

2 (cesser) (du temps) to go by, to pass; **nos ennuis finiront par se p.** our troubles will come to an end eventually; **mon mal de tête se passe** my headache is going

3 se p. de qn/qch to do without sb/sth, to dispense with sb/sth; **je m'en passerai** I'll do or manage without it/them; **je m'en passerais** I can well do without it/them; **ces faits se passent de commentaires** these facts need no comment

4 se p. la main dans les cheveux to run one's fingers through one's hair; **se p. un mouchoir sur le visage** to wipe one's face with a handkerchief

5 se p. une fantaisie to indulge a whim

Il faut noter que l'expression **passer un examen** se traduit par **to sit an exam** ou **to take an exam**. To pass an exam signifie **réussir un examen**.

passereau, -eaux [pasro] NM Orn passerine; Arch (moineau) sparrow

passerelle [pasrɛl] NF **1** (au-dessus d'une rue, d'un ruisseau) footbridge **2** Naut boarding bridge; (escalier) boarding steps; (de ferry) linkspan, boarding ramp; **p. (de commandement)** bridge; **p. de navigation** navigation bridge **3** (pont incliné) **p. de débarquement ou d'embarquement** Naut gangway, gangplank; Aviat (amovible) steps; (fixe) passenger bridge **4** Fig (intermédiaire) link; **ce cours est une p. entre les deux niveaux** this course bridges the two levels **5** Ordinat **p. (de connexion)** gateway (**avec** to)

passe-temps NM INV pastime, hobby

passe-thé NM INV tea strainer

passeur, -euse [pasœr, -øz] N ferryman, f ferrywoman; **il est p.** (de marchandises) he's a smuggler; (de gens) he smuggles people across the border

passe-vite NM INV Belg, Suisse (moulin à légumes) vegetable mill

passible [pasibl] ADJ liable (**de** to, for); **p. d'une amende** liable to a fine; **p. de l'impôt** liable for tax; **p. de taxe** liable to tax

passif, -ive [pasif, -iv] ADJ passive; **rester p.** to remain passive; Pol **faire de la résistance passive** to offer passive resistance; Gram **forme passive** passive form; Com **dettes passives** liabilities; Mil **défense passive** civil defence

NM **1** Gram passive; **au p.** in the passive SEE GRAMMAR A54–5; B39 **2** Fin liabilities; **l'actif et le p.** assets and liabilities; **p. reporté** deferred liabilities; **p. exigible ou circulant** current liabilities

passiflore [pasiflɔr] NF Bot passionflower

passing-shot, pl **passing-shots** [pasiŋʃɔt] NM Sport passing shot; **faire un p.** to play a passing shot

passion [pasjɔ̃] NF **1** passion; **avoir une p. pour la musique** to have a passion for music; **il a la p. des voitures** he has a passion for cars; **la moto est sa p., la moto est une p. chez lui** he's mad about motorbikes; **vivre une p.** to have a passionate love affair, to be passionately in love; **avec p.** passionately; **aimer qn à la ou avec p.** to love sb passionately; **parler avec/sans p.** to speak passionately/dispassionately; **lutter contre ses passions** to struggle against one's passions; **déchaîner les passions** to unleash passions or strong emotions **2** Rel **la P.** the Passion (of Christ); **la semaine de la P.** Passion Week; Mus **la P. selon saint Jean** the St John Passion

passionnant [pasjɔnɑ̃] ADJ (histoire, livre, film) gripping, fascinating; (aventure) thrilling, exciting; (personne) fascinating; **ce boulot n'est vraiment pas très p.** this job's really not very exciting

passionné, -ée [pasjɔne] ADJ passionate; **débat p.** heated or impassioned debate; **p. de ou pour qn/qch** passionately fond of sb/sth

N enthusiast; **c'est une passionnée de moto(s)** she's mad about motorbikes, she's a motorbike fanatic

passionnel, -elle [pasjɔnɛl] ADJ passionate; **état p.** state of passion, passionate state; **crime p.** crime of passion

passionnément [pasjɔnemɑ̃] ADV passionately

passionner [pasjɔne] VT **1** (inspirer un intérêt très vif à) (d'un livre, film etc) to fascinate, to grip; **ce livre m'a passionné** I found this book fascinating or gripping, this book fascinated *or* gripped me; **le sport/travailler avec les enfants la passionne** sport/working with children is a passion with her; **son métier le passionne** he finds his job fascinating **2** *(animer) (débat)* to inflame

VPR se passionner se p. de *ou* **pour qch** to be passionately fond of sth, to have a passion for sth

passivement [pasivmɑ̃] ADV passively

passivité [pasivite] NF passivity, passiveness

passoire [paswar] NF *Culin* sieve; *(pour liquides)* strainer; **p. (à légumes)** colander; **sa mémoire est une (vraie) p., il a la tête comme une p.** he's got a memory *or* a head like a sieve; **cette frontière est une vraie p.** this border doesn't keep anyone in or out; *Fam* **ce gardien est une vraie p.!** this goalkeeper is really useless *or* lets everything in!; *Fam* **transformer qn en p.** to pump sb full of lead, to riddle sb with bullets

pastel [pastɛl] NM **1** *Beaux-Arts* pastel; *(dessin)* pastel (drawing); **tableau au p.** picture in pastels **2** *Bot* woad

ADJ INV pastel; **bleu p.** pastel blue; **tons p.** pastel shades

pastelliste [pastelist] N *Beaux-Arts* pastellist

pastèque [pastɛk] NF watermelon; *Fam* **j'ai la tête comme une p.** my head's buzzing

pasteur [pastœr] NM **1** *Litt (berger)* shepherd; **peuple p.** pastoral people; *Rel* **le bon P.** the Good Shepherd **2** *Rel* pastor, minister

pasteurisation [pastœrizasjɔ̃] NF pasteurization

pasteuriser [pastœrize] VT to pasteurize

pastiche [pastiʃ] NM parody

pasticher [pastiʃe] VT to parody

pasticheur, -euse [pastiʃœr, -øz] N writer of pastiches

pastille [pastij] NF **1** *(bonbon, pilule) (molle)* pastille; *(dure)* lozenge; **p. contre la toux** cough drop *or Br* sweet; **p. de menthe** (pepper)mint; **p. pour purifier l'eau** water sterilizing tablet **2** *(motif)* circle **3** **p. verte** = green label on a low-emission vehicle indicating that it may be driven on days when restrictions are placed on traffic due to high levels of atmospheric pollution

pastis [pastis] NM **1** *(boisson)* pastis **2** *Fig Fam* **être dans le p.** to be in a fix; **quel p.!** what a mess!

pastoral, -ale, -aux, -ales [pastoral, -o] ADJ pastoral

NF pastorale *Littér* pastoral; *Mus* pastorale

pastorat [pastora] NM pastorate

pastoureau, -elle, -eaux, -elles [pasturo, -ɛl] N *Arch, Litt* shepherd lad, *f* shepherd lass

NF pastourelle *Mus* pastourelle; *(danse)* fourth figure of the quadrille

pat [pat] NM INV *Échecs* stalemate; **les Noirs sont p.** Black is stalemated

patachon [pataʃɔ̃] NM *Arg* **mener une vie de p.** to lead a wild life

Patagonie (la) [lapatagoni] NF Patagonia

patapouf [patapuf] INT flop!

NM *Enf* gros p. fat lump

pataquès [patakɛs] NM **1** *(faute de liaison)* incorrect liaison **2** *(faute de langage)* serious mistake *(in pronunciation etc)* **3** *Fam (gaffe)* boo-boo, *Br* boob

patata [patata] INT *voir* **patati**

patate [patat] NF **1** *Fam (pomme de terre)* spud; *Can* **patates frites** French fries, *Br* chips; **la corvée de patates** peeling the spuds; *Mil* spud-bashing **2 p. (douce)** sweet potato **3** *Fam (imbécile)* clot, idiot **4** *Anciennement Fam (dix mille francs)* ten thousand francs **5** *Math* set diagram **6** *Fam* **en avoir**

gros sur la p. to be down in the mouth *or* down in the dumps **7** *Can Fam (cœur)* heart, *Br* ticker; **monter les escaliers, c'est dur pour la p.** going up the stairs is hard on the old ticker

patati [patati] INT *Fam* **et p. et patata** and so on and so forth

patatras [patatra] INT *Fam* crash!

pataud, -aude [pato, -od] NM *(chiot)* puppy with big paws

N *Vieilli* lump

ADJ *Fam (personne)* lumpish, clumsy; *(apparence, démarche)* clumsy, awkward

Pataugas® [patogas] NM = canvas walking shoe

pataugeoire [patoʒwar] NF paddling pool

patauger [patoʒe] VI (**je pataugeai(s); n. pataugeons**) **1** *(dans la boue)* to squelch; *(dans l'eau)* to paddle **2** *Fig Fam (s'empêtrer)* to flounder; **il patauge dans ses réponses** he's getting more and more bogged down trying to answer; **p. (dans la semoule)** to be totally lost **3** *Fam (ne pas progresser) (d'une enquête)* to get bogged down

patch [patʃ] NM **1** *Pharm* (skin) patch **2** *Élec* jackfield

patchouli [patʃuli] NM patchouli

patchwork [patʃwœrk] NM patchwork

pâte [pat] NF **1** *Culin (à tarte)* pastry; *(à pain)* dough; *(à gâteau)* mixture; **pâtes (alimentaires)** pasta; **pâtes fraîches** fresh pasta; *Fig* **c'est une bonne p.** he's a good sort; *Fig* **mettre la main à la p.** to lend a hand; *Fig* **être comme un coq en p.** to be in clover; *Fig* **une p. molle** a drip, a wimp **2** *(mélange, composition)* **fromage à p. dure/molle** hard/soft cheese **3** *Beaux-Arts* paint, colours, *Am* colors; *(plus épais)* paste **4** *Typ* (printer's) pie; **caractères tombés en p.** pied type

▸▸ **p. d'amandes** marzipan, almond paste; **p. brisée** short(crust) pastry; **p. à choux** choux pastry; **p. à crêpes** pancake batter; **p. dentifrice** toothpaste; **p. feuilletée** flaky pastry; **p. à frire** batter; **p. de fruits** fruit jelly; **p. à modeler** modelling *or Am* modeling clay; **p. à pain** bread dough; **p. à papier** pulp; **p. sablée** rich shortcrust pastry; **p. à tarte** pastry

pâté [pate] NM **1** *Culin (terrine)* pâté; **p. de foie** liver pâté; **p. de campagne** pâté de campagne *(coarse pâté made with pork)*; **p. en croûte** pâté en croûte, *Br* raised (crust) pie; **p. impérial** spring roll **2 p. (de sable)** sandpie **3** *(tache d'encre)* blot; **faire un p. sur sa copie** to blot one's paper **4** *(bloc)* **p. de maisons** block of houses **5** *Belg (gâteau)* cake

pâtée [pate] NF **1** *(pour volaille, cochon)* mash; *(pour chat/chien)* cat/dog food **2** *Fam (défaite)* **prendre la p.** to get a thrashing *or* a good hiding; **on leur a mis** *ou* **foutu la p.** they got a thrashing, they were thrashed

patelin [patlɛ̃] ADJ *Litt Péj (personne, manière, air)* unctuous

NM *Fam* village; **quel sale p.!** what a dump!, what a hole!

patelle [patɛl] NF **1** *(mollusque)* limpet **2** *Archéol* patella

patène [patɛn] NF *Rel* paten

patenôtre [patnotr] NF *Fam* prayer, *Arch* paternoster; *Fig (paroles incompréhensibles)* gibberish

patent [patɑ̃] ADJ **1** *(clair) (erreur, injustice)* obvious, patent; **il est p. que ...** it is patently obvious that ... **2 lettres patentes** letters patent

patentable [patɑ̃tabl] ADJ *Admin* subject to a licence, requiring a licence

patente [patɑ̃t] NF **1** *Com (licence)* licence *(to exercise a trade or profession)*; *Anciennement (impôt)* tax *(paid by traders and profes-*

sional men); **payer p.** to be duly licensed **2** *Naut* **p. (de santé)** bill of health

patenté [patɑ̃te] ADJ *Com* licensed; *Fig Fam* **spécialiste/graphiste p.** recognized specialist/graphic designer; **imbécile/menteur/voleur p.** out-and-out fool/liar/thief

patenter [patɑ̃te] VT *Com* to license

pater [pater] NM INV **1** *Rel* Paternoster **2** *Fam (père)* old man; **le p.** the old man, *Am* pop, *Br* Vieilli, *Hum* pater

patère [patɛr] NF (coat) peg

paternalisme [paternalism] NM paternalism

paternaliste [paternalist] ADJ paternalistic

paterne [patɛrn] ADJ *Litt* benevolent

paternel, -elle [patɛrnɛl] ADJ paternal; *(protecteur, bienveillant) (ton, conseil)* fatherly, kindly; *(attention)* fatherly; **du côté p.** on the father's side; **ma grand-mère paternelle** my grandmother on my father's side; **le domicile p.** (the family) home; **image paternelle** father figure; **l'amour p.** paternal *or* fatherly love

NM *Fam (père)* old man; **le p.** the old man, *Br* Vieilli, *Hum* pater, *Am* pop

paternellement [patɛrnɛlmɑ̃] ADV paternally, in a fatherly way

paternité [patɛrnite] NF paternity, fatherhood; *Jur* **p. légitime/naturelle** legitimate/natural paternity; *Jur* **recherche de p.** affiliation; **il vit mal sa p.** he's finding fatherhood difficult, he's finding it difficult being a father; *Fig* **revendiquer/désavouer la p. d'un livre** to claim/repudiate authorship of a book; **la p. d'une découverte/d'une invention** the paternity of a discovery/an invention

pâteux, -euse [patø, -øz] ADJ **1** *(substance, crème)* pasty; *(pain)* doughy; **j'ai la langue pâteuse** my tongue is all furry; **j'ai la bouche pâteuse** my mouth is all dry *or Fam* is like the bottom of a parrot's cage *(trop épais)* *(encre)* thick; *Péj* **style p.** woolly style

pathétique [patetik] ADJ **1** *Litt (histoire, situation, ton)* pathetic, touching, moving **2** *Anat* **nerf p.** pathetic nerve

NM *Litt* pathos

> Il faut noter que l'adjectif anglais **pathetic** est un faux ami. Il signifie souvent **lamentable**.

pathétiquement [patetikmɑ̃] ADV pathetically, movingly

pathétisme [patetism] NM *Litt* pathos

pathogène [patoʒɛn] ADJ *Méd* pathogenic

pathologie [patoloʒi] NF *Méd* pathology

pathologique [patoloʒik] ADJ *Méd* pathological; **c'est un cas p.** he/she's a pathological case; *Fam* **c'est p. chez lui** it's a neurosis with him, it's pathological

pathologiquement [patoloʒikmɑ̃] ADJ *Méd* pathologically

pathologiste [patoloʒist] N *Méd* pathologist

pathos [patos] NM *Litt* pathos

patibulaire [patibylɛr] ADJ **1** *(sinistre)* **avoir une mine p.** to have a sinister look, to look sinister **2** *Vieilli* **fourches patibulaires** gibbet

patiemment [pasjamɑ̃] ADV patiently

patience¹ [pasjɑ̃s] NF **1** patience; **avoir de la p., prendre p.** to be patient, to have patience; **avoir de la p. avec qn** to be patient with sb; **prendre son mal en p.** to suffer patiently; **faire preuve de p.** *ou* **montrer de la p. envers qn** to be patient with sb; **avoir une p. d'ange** to have the patience of a saint *or* of Job; **avec p.** patiently; **ma p. est à bout, je suis à bout de p.** my patience is exhausted *or* is at an end; **ma p. a des limites!** there are limits to my patience!; **s'armer de p.** to be as patient as one can; **(prenez) p.!** be patient!; **perdre p.** to lose patience; *Prov* **p. et longueur de temps (font plus que force ni que rage)** all things must take their time; **jeu de p.** (jigsaw) puzzle; *Fig* test of patience **2** *Cartes* patience, *Am* solitaire; **faire des patiences** to play patience *or Am* solitaire

patience² NF *Bot* patience (dock)

patient, -ente [pasjɑ̃, -ɑ̃t] ADJ patient; *(qui endure une épreuve)* long-suffering

N *Méd* patient

patienter [pasjɑ̃te] VI to wait; **faire p. qn** to ask sb to wait; *Tél* to ask sb to hold; **pour vous faire p., je vais vous passer un film** I'll show you a film while you're waiting *or* to pass the time for you; **p. en lisant le journal** to read the newspaper to while away *or* pass the time

patin [patɛ̃] NM **1** *(de patineur)* skate; *(de traîneau)* runner; **patins à glace/à roulettes** ice/roller skates; **nous allons faire du p. à glace** we're going (ice)skating; **sais-tu faire du p. à glace/à roulettes?** can you (ice)skate/(roller)skate?; *Can Fam* **être vite sur ses patins** to be quick off the mark; *Can Fam* **accrocher ses patins** to hang up one's hat, to retire; *(d'un sportif)* to hang up one's boots, to retire **2** *(sur parquet)* cloth pad; *Arch (chaussure)* patten **3** *Tech* shoe; **p. (de frein)** (brake) shoe; *Aut* **p. amortisseur** damping slipper; *Fam* **donner** *ou* **filer un coup de p.** *(un coup de frein)* to slam on the brakes **4** *très Fam (baiser)* French kiss; **rouler un p. à qn** to French-kiss sb; **ils n'ont pas arrêté de se rouler des patins toute la soirée** they had their tongues down each other's throats the whole evening

patinage [patinaʒ] NM **1** *Sport* skating; **p. artistique** figure skating; **p. de vitesse** speed skating **2** *(d'une roue)* spinning; *Aut* **p. de l'embrayage** clutch slip; **p. des roues** wheel spin **3** *Tech* patination

patine [patin] NF patina; *Fig* **la p. du temps** the patina of age *or* time

patiner [patine] VI **1** *(faire du patinage)* to skate **2** *Aut* to skid; *(d'une roue)* to spin; *(d'une courroie, de l'embrayage)* to slip; *Fig (stagner)* to get nowhere; **ça patine!** it's slippery!; **faire p. l'embrayage** to slip the clutch VT *Tech* to give a patina to; **une table patinée par les ans** a table that has acquired a patina with age

VPR **se patiner** to develop a patina

patinette [patinɛt] NF scooter

patineur, -euse [patinœr, -øz] N skater

patinoire [patinwar] NF skating *or* ice rink; **cette route est une vraie p.** this road is like a skating rink *or* an ice rink

patio [patjo] NM patio

pâtir [patir] VI to suffer (**de** because of); **c'est moi qui vais en p.** I'm the one that's going to suffer

pâtis [pati] NM *Agr* grazing ground, pasture

pâtisserie [patisri] NF **1** *Culin (gâteau)* pastry, (small) cake; *(gâteaux)* pastries **2** *(confection de gâteaux)* pastry-making; **apprendre à faire de la p.** to learn pastry-making; **elle fait de la bonne p.** she makes good cakes **3** *(magasin)* cake shop; **p.-confiserie** confectioner's

pâtissier, -ière [patisje, -jɛr] N *(de restaurant)* pastrycook; *(commerçant)* confectioner; **Papa est très bon p.** Dad makes very good cakes

ADJ **crème pâtissière** confectioner's custard

patois [patwa] NM patois, (local) dialect

ADJ patois

patoisant, -ante [patwazɑ̃, -ɑ̃t] ADJ *(personne)* patois- *or* dialect-speaking; **histoire patoisante** story in patois *or* dialect

N patois *or* dialect speaker

patouiller [patuje] *Fam* VI to flounder
VT to paw

patraque [patrak] ADJ *Fam (personne)* out of sorts, under the weather

pâtre [patr] NM *Litt (pour bétail)* herdsman; *(pour moutons)* shepherd

patriarcal, -ale, -aux, -ales [patriarkal, -o] ADJ patriarchal

patriarcat [patriarka] NM **1** patriarchy **2** *Rel* patriarchate

patriarche [patriarʃ] NM patriarch

patricien, -ienne [patrisjɛ̃, -jɛn] ADJ, N patrician

patrie [patri] NF *(nation)* homeland; *(localité de naissance)* birthplace; **mère p.** mother country; **mourir pour la p.** to die for one's country; **une seconde p.** my/his/*etc* second home; *Fig* **la p. des arts/de la musique** the cradle of the arts/of music

patrimoine [patrimwan] NM heritage; *(d'un ancêtre)* patrimony, inheritance; *Fin* property, wealth, personal assets; *(actif net)* net worth; **faire partie du p.** to be part of our/one's/*etc* heritage; **p. familial** family wealth *or* heritage; *Fig* family heritage; *Banque* **p. social** social assets; **p. artistique** artistic heritage; **p. culturel** cultural heritage; *Biol* **p. génétique** gene pool; **p. héréditaire** genetic inheritance; **p. immobilier** property assets, *Am* real-estate assets

patrimonial, -iale, -iaux, -iales [patrimɔnjal, -jo] ADJ *Jur* patrimonial

patriotard [patriɔtar] *Péj* ADJ jingoistic
NM jingoist

patriote [patriɔt] ADJ *(personne)* patriotic
N patriot

patriotique [patriɔtik] ADJ patriotic

patriotisme [patriɔtism] NM patriotism

patron, -onne [patrɔ̃, -ɔn] N **1** *(d'une usine, d'une entreprise, d'un hôtel) (personne qui dirige)* boss; *(propriétaire)* owner; *Fam* **c'est moi le p.!** I'm the boss!, I'm in charge!; **eh la patronne, une bière!** a beer please, landlady!; **être son propre p.** to be one's own boss; **oui, p.** yes, boss, *Am* yes, chief; **il faut en parler au p.** you'll have to speak to the boss about it; **p. de presse** publisher *(newspaper owner)*; *Univ* **p. de thèse** thesis supervisor **2** *Fam (conjoint)* old man; *(conjointe)* old lady **3** *(protecteur) (d'une association, des arts, d'un artiste)* patron, *f* patroness; **le p. d'un club** the patron of a club **4** *Rel* patron saint; **le saint p.** the patron saint; **la patronne des musiciens** the patron saint of musicians **5** *Méd (dans un hôpital universitaire)* senior consultant; **les grands patrons** the leading specialists *or* consultants

NM *Couture* pattern; **p. (ajuré)** stencil (plate)

> Il faut noter que le terme anglais **patron** est un faux ami. Il signifie le plus souvent **client**.

patronage [patrɔnaʒ] NM **1** *(parrainage)* patronage; *Com* sponsoring; **placé sous le p. de ...** sponsored by ...; **sous le p. de** under the sponsorship of **2** *(organisation, siège)* youth club; *Fig Péj* **roman de p.** moralizing *or Fam* preachy novel

patronal, -ale, -aux, -ales [patrɔnal, -o] ADJ **1** *(de l'employeur)* employers', of employers; **syndicat p.** employers' association **2** *(relatif au saint patron)* patronal

patronat [patrɔna] NM employers; *(syndicat)* employers' organization, *Br* ≃ Confederation of British Industry, CBI; **le p. français** French employers

patronner [patrɔne] VT *(hôpital, charité etc)* to support; *(artiste, candidat)* to sponsor; **p. une candidature** to support a candidacy;

(avec aide financière) to sponsor a candidacy; **p. une entreprise** to back a business

patronnesse [patrɔnɛs] ADJ, NF *souvent Iron* **(dame) p.** patroness

patronyme [patrɔnim] NM patronymic

patronymique [patrɔnimik] ADJ patronymic

patrouille [patruj] NF *Mil etc* patrol; **aller en p.** to go on patrol; **être de p.** to be on patrol; *Aviat* **p. de chasse** fighter patrol

patrouiller [patruje] VI to patrol, to be on patrol

patrouilleur [patrujœr] NM **1** soldier/guard/*etc* on patrol; *Aviat* patrol plane; *Naut* patrol boat **2** *Suisse* **p. scolaire** school patroller

patte [pat] NF **1** *(de chien, chat etc)* paw; *(d'oiseau)* foot; *(d'insecte)* leg; *Fam (jambe)* pin, leg; *Fam (main)* hand, *Péj* paw; **se dresser sur ses pattes** to sit up and beg; **pattes de devant** forelegs; *(partie griffue)* forepaws; **pattes de derrière** hind legs; *(partie griffue)* back paws; **marcher/se mettre à quatre pattes** to walk/get down on all fours; *Fig* **retomber sur ses pattes** to land on one's feet; *Fig* **tirer dans les pattes de qn** to give sb a hard time; **court/haut sur pattes** short-/long-legged; **coup de p.** blow with the paw; *Fig* cutting remark, *Fam* dig; *Fam* **pattes (de lapin)** *(cheveux)* sideboards, sideburns; *Fam* **avoir le coup de p.** *(d'un peintre)* to have talent; *Fam* **tomber dans les pattes de qn** to fall into sb's clutches; *Fam* **bas les pattes!** hands off!; *Fig Fam* **graisser la p. à qn** to grease sb's palm **2** *(rabat) (d'une poche, d'une enveloppe)* flap; *(d'un portefeuille, d'une chaussure)* tongue **3** *(attache)* clamp, clip, fastening; *Naut (d'une ancre)* fluke, palm; *(d'un grappin)* claw **4** *Couture (sur un vêtement)* strap; **pattes d'épaule** shoulder straps **5** *Suisse (torchon)* cloth

▸▸ **p. blanche:** *Fig* **montrer p. blanche** to show one's credentials; **pattes d'éléphant: pantalon à pattes d'éléphant** bell-bottom(ed) *or* flared trousers; **p. folle: avoir une p. folle** to have a gammy *or Am* gimpy leg; **p. de lapin** rabbit foot; *Fam* **pattes de mouche(s)** cramped handwriting; **p. de velours: faire p. de velours** *(d'un chat)* to draw in its claws; *Fig* to be all sweetness and light

patte-d'oie, *pl* **pattes-d'oie** NF **1** *(carrefour)* crossroads **2** *(ride)* crow's-foot **3** *Bot* goosefoot

pattemouille [patmuj] NF damp cloth *(for ironing clothes)*

pâturage [patyraʒ] NM **1** *(action)* grazing; *Jur (droit)* grazing rights **2** *(endroit)* pasture; **pâturages** pasture land

pâture [patyr] NF **1** *(nourriture) (pour animaux)* food, feed, fodder; *Fig* **p. intellectuelle** food for the mind; *Fig* **donner qn/qch en p. au public** to serve sb/sth up for public consumption **2** *(pâturage)* pasture; *Jur* **vaine p.** (right of) common

pâturer [patyre] VI *(du bétail)* to graze

paturon [patyrɔ̃] NM **1** *(du cheval)* pastern **2** *Fam (pied)* foot

paume [pom] NF **1** *Anat (de la main)* palm **2** **(jeu de) p.** real tennis; **jeu de p.** *(terrain)* real-tennis court

paumé, -ée [pome] *Fam* ADJ *(perdu)* lost; *(dans une explication)* all at sea, lost; *Fig* **il est complètement p.** he hasn't got a clue; **un bled complètement p.** a godforsaken hole

N *(personne)* loser

paumelle [pomɛl] NF **1** *Naut* (sailmaker's) palm **2** *(des gonds d'une porte)* plate

paumer [pome] *Fam* VT to lose
VPR **se paumer** to get lost

paupérisation [poperizasjɔ̃] NF impoverishment

paupériser [poperize] VT to impoverish

paupérisme [poperism] NM pauperism

paupière [popjɛr] NF *Anat* eyelid

paupiette [popjɛt] NF *Culin* (meat) olive; **paupiettes de veau** veal olives

pause [poz] NF 1 *(arrêt) (dans une activité)* break; *(en parlant)* pause; *(pour déjeuner)* meal break; **faire une p.** to have a break; *(en parlant)* to pause; **p. de midi** lunch break 2 *Mus* semibreve *or Am* whole-note rest ▸▸ **p.-café** coffee break; **p.-cigarette** cigarette break; **p.-repas** meal break

pause-carrière, *pl* **pauses-carrière** NF *Belg* sabbatical year *(on reduced pay)*

pauvre [povr] ADJ SEE GRAMMAR B10 1 *(qui manque de biens)* poor; **p. comme Job** poor as a church mouse; **minerai p. en métal** ore with a low metal content; **p. en vitamine C** with a low vitamin C content; *Aut* **mélange p.** weak mixture 2 *(malheureux)* poor, unfortunate; **le p. homme!** poor chap!; **p. de moi!** poor old me!; **p. Pierre** poor (old) Pierre; **p. vieux/vieille** poor old thing 3 *(misérable) (robe, meubles etc)* shabby; *(excuse)* paltry, poor, weak; *(sourire)* weak, thin; *(argument)* pathetic, weak, poor; *(orateur)* poor, bad; **c'est un p. type** he's pathetic, *Br très Fam* he's a poor sod; **p. idiot!** silly fool!; *très Fam* **p. con!** poor bastard!, *Br* poor sod! 4 *(stérile) (sol)* poor; **des terres pauvres** barren lands N poor man, *f* woman; **les pauvres et les riches** the poor and the rich; *Fig* **p. d'esprit** half-wit; *Rel* **les pauvres d'esprit** the poor in spirit; **le p., il n'a pas de chance** poor chap, he doesn't have much luck!; **la p., elle a encore loupé son examen** poor thing, she's failed her exam again; **mon p.!** you poor thing!

pauvrement [povrəmã] ADV poorly; **p. vêtu/meublé** poorly *or* shabbily dressed/furnished

pauvresse [povrɛs] NF poor girl/woman

pauvret, -ette [povrɛ, -ɛt] N *Fam* **le p./la pauvrette** the poor little thing

pauvreté [povrəte] NF poverty; *Fig (du langage)* poverty, poorness; *(d'un style)* poverty, baldness; *Rel* **vœu de p.** vow of poverty; **p. du sol** poorness of the soil

pavage [pavaʒ] NM 1 *(action)* paving; *(aux pavés ronds)* cobbling 2 *(revêtement)* paving; *(rond)* cobbles, cobblestones

pavane [pavan] NF *Mus* pavan(e)

pavaner (se) [səpavane] VPR to strut about

pavé [pave] N 1 *(morceau de grès)* paving stone; *(rond)* cobblestone; *Journ (encart)* block (of text); *Journ Fam (article)* prominent article; *Fam Péj (livre, thèse)* massive tome; *Fig* **un p. dans la mare** a bombshell; **jeter un p. dans la mare** to drop a bombshell; *Fig* **avoir un p. sur l'estomac** to have a weight on one's stomach; *Culin* **p. (de bœuf)** slab of beef; *Journ* **p. publicitaire** (large) display advertisement 2 *(revêtement)* pavement, paving; *(rond)* cobbles; *Fig* **le p. (rues)** the street, the streets; **brûler le p.** to tear along; *Fig* **tenir le haut du p.** to be at the top; *Fig* **céder le haut du p. à qn** to give pride of place to sb; **battre le p.** to loaf about the streets; **être sur le p.** to be on the street; **sous les pavés, la plage** = slogan dating from the 1968 student riots and referring both to the paving stones thrown at the police and to the ideal of a more fulfilling life beyond the confines of drab conformity 3 *Ordinat* keypad; **p. numérique** numeric keypad 4 *Typ* box 5 *Fam (dent)* tooth

pavement [pavmã] NM paving

paver [pave] VT to pave; *(avec des pavés ronds)* to cobble; **cour pavée** paved/cobbled

yard; *Fig* **l'enfer est pavé de bonnes intentions** the road to hell is paved with good intentions; *Can* **être pavé de monde** to be full of *or* packed with people

paveur [pavœr] NM paver

pavillon [pavijɔ̃] NM 1 *(petite maison)* (small) bungalow; **p. d'entrée** (gate) lodge; **p. de jardin** summerhouse, pavilion; **p. de chasse** hunting *or* shooting lodge 2 *(d'un hôpital)* pavilion, block, wing 3 *(partie évasée) (d'un Klaxon®, d'un haut-parleur, d'une sirène)* horn; *(d'un entonnoir)* mouth; *Mus (de cuivres)* bell; *Tél* **p. d'écouteur** earpiece; *Anat* **p. de l'oreille** auricle, pinna, external ear 4 *Naut (drapeau)* flag; **hisser** *ou* **arborer son p.** to hoist one's colours; **battre p. britannique** to fly the British flag; **baisser p.** to strike one's flag, to surrender; *Fig (céder)* to admit defeat, to give in 5 *Mil Arch* pavilion, tent 6 *Aut* roof, roof panel ▸▸ **p. de complaisance** flag of convenience; **p. de départ** Blue Peter; **p. de détresse** flag of distress; **p. noir** Jolly Roger; **p. de partance** Blue Peter; **p. de quarantaine** yellow flag

pavillonnaire [pavijɔnɛr] ADJ **banlieue p.** suburbia

pavois [pavwa] NM 1 *Naut (d'un navire)* bulwark 2 *Naut* **petit/grand p.** flags *(for dressing ship)*, dressing; **mettre** *ou* **hisser le grand p.** to dress over all 3 *Hist (grand bouclier)* (body) shield, pavis(e)

pavoiser [pavwaze] VT *(décorer) (rue, maison)* to deck with flags *or* bunting; *Naut (navire)* to dress VI *(décorer)* to put out the flags; *Naut* to dress ship; *Fam (se réjouir)* to crow; *Fam* **il n'y a vraiment pas de quoi p.!** there's nothing to crow about!

pavot [pavo] NM *(fleur)* poppy; **p. somnifère** opium poppy; **tête de p.** poppyhead; **graine(s) de p.** poppy seed

payable [pɛjabl] ADJ payable; *Com* **p. à la livraison** payable on delivery; **p. à vue** payable at *or* on sight; **p. comptant** payable in cash; **p. à l'arrivée** payable on arrival; **p. à l'échéance** payable at maturity; **p. à la banque** payable at the bank; **p. à la commande** payable with order; **p. au porteur** payable to bearer

payant [pɛjã] ADJ *(qui paie) (hôte, élève)* paying; *(où il faut payer)* with charge for admission; **spectateur p.** ticket-holder who pays/paid (for admission); **spectacle p.** show with charge for admission; **l'entrée est payante** there is an admission charge *or* a charge for admission; *Fig* **affaire payante** *(bénéfique)* paying proposition; *Fig* **ça s'est avéré p.** it turned out to be worth it

paye [pɛj] NF = **paie**

payement [pɛjmã] NM = **paiement**

PAYER [pɛje] *(je paye, je paie; je payerai, je paierai)* VT 1 *(somme)* to pay; **p. qn** to pay sb; **payez au porteur** pay to bearer; **tu l'as payé combien pour qu'il fasse tout cela?** how much did you pay him to do all that?; **je ne suis pas payé pour ça** that's not my job; **combien vous a-t-il fait p.?** how much did he charge you?; **elle ne nous/m'/etc a pas fait p. cher** she didn't charge a lot; **p. qn de ses services** to pay sb for his/her services; **trop payé** overpaid; **trop peu payé** underpaid; **bien/mal payé** well-/badly paid; **ce travail est peu payé** this work isn't paid *or* doesn't pay very well; **se faire p.** to get *or* be paid; **il a accepté de nous aider mais il veut se faire p.** he has agreed to help us but he wants paying *or* he wants to be paid; **p. qn de paroles** *ou* **de mots** to put sb off with fine words; **il les méprise et il est payé de retour** he despises them and the feeling is mutual

2 *(acquitter, régler) (dette)* to pay, to settle, to discharge; **p. son loyer** to pay one's *or* the rent; **p. la note** to pay the bill; *Com* **p. un effet** to honour *or Am* honor a bill; **la prime de déplacement ne me paie pas tous les frais de voyage** the relocation allowance doesn't cover all the travel costs; **congés payés** paid holidays; *Admin* paid leave; **tu as les congés payés?** do you get holiday pay?

3 *(acquérir contre de l'argent)* to pay for; **la viande a été payée** the meat's (been) paid for; **combien tu l'as payé?** how much did you pay for it?; **elle ne l'a pas payé très cher** she didn't pay a lot for it; **je ne vous fais pas p. le transport** I'm not charging you for transport; **je le lui ai payé cent euros** I paid him a hundred euros for it; **p. qch à qn** *(lui offrir)* to buy sth for sb; **ses parents lui paient tout ce qu'il veut** his parents pay for everything he wants, his parents buy him anything he wants; **elle va se le faire p. par son mari** she's going to get her husband to buy it for her; **p. le dîner à qn** to treat sb to dinner; **c'est moi qui paie la tournée** it's my round; **payé d'avance** prepaid; **port payé** post(age) paid; *Tél* **réponse payée** answer prepaid

4 *Fig (expier)* to pay for; **il a payé sa témérité de sa vie** he paid for his rashness with his life; **faire p. ses méfaits à qn** to bring sb to account; **vous me le paierez!** you'll pay for it!; *Fam* **je suis payé pour le savoir** I've learnt (it) the hard way; **il l'a payé cher** he paid dearly for it; **il paya cher son insolence** he paid dearly for his rudeness, his rudeness cost him

VI 1 *(verser de l'argent)* to pay; **vous payez comment?** how are you paying?, how would you like to pay?; **p. cash** *ou* **comptant** to pay cash; **p. en liquide/par carte (de crédit)** to pay (in) cash/by credit card; **p. par chèque** to pay by cheque *or Am* check; **p. à vue** to pay at sight; **p. de sa poche** to pay out of one's own pocket; **c'est toujours moi qui paie** I'm always the one who pays, it's always me who pays; **p. rubis sur l'ongle** to pay on the nail

2 **p. de ses dernières économies** to sacrifice the last of one's savings; *Fig* **p. de sa personne** to put oneself out; **il lui fallut p. d'audace** he had to be bold; **il ne paie pas de mine, mais il est doué** he doesn't look it, but he's very clever, he doesn't look very clever but he is

3 *(rapporter)* to pay; **le crime ne paie pas** crime doesn't pay; **la traduction en free-lance, ça ne paie pas** freelance translation doesn't pay; **ça a payé** *(cette affaire)* it was worth it

VPR **se payer 1 voilà monsieur, payez-vous** here you are, take it out of that; *Fig* **se p. de mots** to talk a lot of fine words

2 *(s'offrir)* **je me suis payé une glace/une semaine de vacances** I treated myself to an ice cream/a week's holiday; **se p. le luxe de sortir deux fois par semaine** to treat oneself to two nights out a week; *Fig* **se p. le culot de partir sans régler ses dettes** to have the nerve to leave without paying one's debts; *Fig* **se p. la tête de qn** to make fun of sb; **je n'aime pas qu'on se paie ma tête** I don't like being made fun of; *Fam* **se p. un arbre/un mur** to crash into a tree/a wall; *Fam* **je me suis payé un bon rhume** I got a nasty cold; *Fam* **s'en p. (une tranche)** to have a good time; *Fam* **si il continue à m'énerver, celui-là, je vais me le p.!** if he carries on annoying me, I'm going to swing for him *or* thump him one!

payeur, -euse [pɛjœr, -øz] N payer; *Admin* pay clerk; *Mil* paymaster; **mauvais p.** bad payer

pays¹ [pei] NM 1 *(nation)* country; **un p. lointain** a faraway country *or* land; **l'Espagne, p.**

de la corrida Spain, land of the bullfight; **vi-siter des p. étrangers** to visit foreign countries *or* lands VOIR GRAMMAIRE A8; A28 **2** *(région)* region, district, locality; **voir du p.** to travel around; **p. du rêve** dreamland; **vous n'êtes donc pas du p.?** so you're not from these parts *or* from round here?; **être en p. de connaissance** to be among friends; *(sur un sujet)* to be on familiar *or* home ground; **vin de p.** *ou* **du p.** local wine; **miel/fruits du p.** locally produced honey/fruit; **c'est un gars/une coutume du p.** he's a local lad/it's a local custom; **revenir au p.** to go back home; **avoir le mal du p.** to be homesick; **p. de montagne(s)/lacs** mountain/lake country; **p. de chasse/pêche** hunting/fishing country **3** *Admin* = group of neighbouring communes which have joined together to promote distinctive aspects of the locality

▸▸ *UE* **p. candidat** applicant country; **p. de destination** country of destination; **p. développé** developed country; **p. émergent** newly industrialized country; **p. d'Europe centrale et orientale** Central and East European country; **p. d'Europe de l'Est** Eastern European country; **p. exportateur** exporting country; **p. hors communauté** non-EC country; **p. importateur** importing country; *UE* **p. in** = EU member state that has adopted the euro; **p. industrialisé** industrialized *or* developed country; **p. membre** member state; **p. d'origine** country of origin; *UE* **p. out** = EU member state that has not adopted the euro; *UE* **p. pré-in** = EU member state that has not adopted the euro; **p. de provenance** country of export; **p. riche** affluent country; **p. signataire** *(d'un accord)* signatory country; **p. sous-développé** developing country; *UE* **p. tiers** third *or* non-EU country; **p. du tiers-monde** Third World country; **p. en voie de développement** developing country; **p. en voie d'industrialisation** industrializing country

pays², **payse** [pei, peiz] **N** *Région* fellow-countryman, *f* fellow-countrywoman; **nous sommes p.** we're from the same area *or* place

paysage [peizaʒ] **NM 1** landscape; *(vue)* scenery; *Fig (ensemble)* scene, set-up; **cette région offre de merveilleux paysages** this area has marvellous scenery; *Fam* **cela fait bien dans le p.** it looks good; *Fig* **le p. urbain** the urban landscape; *Fig* **le p. audiovisuel français** the broadcasting scene *or* set-up in France; *Fig* **le p. politique** the political scene **2** *Beaux-Arts* landscape (painting) **3** *Ordinat* **mode** *ou* **format p.** landscape mode; **imprimer qch en p.** to print sth in landscape

paysager, -ère [peizaʒe, -ɛr] **ADJ** *(jardin, espace)* landscaped; **bureau p.** open-plan office

paysagiste [peizaʒist] **N 1** *(peintre)* landscape painter **2** *(jardinier)* **p.** landscape gardener

paysan, -anne [peizɑ̃, -an] **ADJ** *(vie, famille)* peasant; *(façon de vivre, manières)* rustic, country
▪ **N** (small) farmer, *Péj* peasant; *Hum Péj* rustic; *Hist* peasant; *Agr* **p. (propriétaire)** farmer; *Hist* **les paysans** the peasants, the peasantry

paysannerie [peizanri] **NF** *Hist* peasantry

Pays-Bas (les) [lepeibɑ] **NMPL** the Netherlands

PC [pese] **NM 1** *(abrév* **parti communiste***)* CP **2** **poste de commandement 3** *Ordinat* PC
▪ **NF** *Fin (abrév* **pièce de caisse***)* cash voucher

PCC, Pcc [pesese] *abrév* **pour copie conforme**

PCF [peseɛf] **NM** *(abrév* **parti communiste français***)* French Communist Party

PCG [peseʒe] **NM** *Compta (abrév* **plan comptable général***)* chart of accounts

PCS [peseɛs] **NFPL** *(abrév* **professions et catégories sociales***)* socio-economic categories

PCV [peseve] **NM** *Tél (abrév* **payable chez vous***)* **(appel en) P.** reverse-charge call, *Am* collect call; **appeler en P., faire un appel en P.** to make a reverse-charge call, *Am* to call collect

pd *Com abrév* **port dû**

PDG [pedeʒe] **NM INV** *(abrév* **Président-directeur général***)* chairman and managing director, CEO, chief executive officer, *Am* President

PDM [pedeɛm] **NF** *(abrév* **part de marché***)* market share

PDV [pedeve] **NM** *(abrév* **point de vente***)* POS

PEA [peøa] **NM** *Fin (abrév* **plan d'épargne en actions***)* investment trust, *Br* ≃ PEP

péage [peaʒ] **NM 1** *(droit)* toll; **pont à p.** toll bridge; *Hist* **barrière de p.** turnpike, tollgate **2** *(installation) Aut* tollbooth; *Hist* tollhouse **3** *TV* **chaîne (de télévision) à p.** pay channel; **p. à la consommation** pay per view, PPV

péagiste [peaʒist] **N** *Aut* tollbooth attendant

peau, peaux [po] **NF 1** *(derme)* skin; **avoir la p. blanche/noire** to be white/black; **une belle p.** a beautiful skin *or* complexion; **avoir la p. grasse/sèche/mixte** to have greasy/dry/combination skin; **peaux mortes** dead skin; *Fig* **p. de pêche** (soft and) velvety skin; **avoir une p. de pêche** to have (soft and) velvety skin; *Fig* **avoir la p. dure** *(d'une personne)* to have a thick skin, to be thick-skinned; **ce genre de croyances stupides a la p. dure** this sort of stupid belief takes a long time to die out; *Fig* **attraper** *ou* **prendre qn par la p. du cou** *ou* **du dos** *ou* *Fam* **des fesses** *ou* *Vulg* **du cul** to grab *or* take sb by the scruff of the neck; *Fig* **faire p. neuve** *(d'une personne)* to turn over a new leaf; *(d'une entreprise, d'un parti etc)* to get a new image, to modernize itself; **elle n'a que la p. et les os** she's nothing but skin and bone; **je ne voudrais pas être dans sa p.** I wouldn't like to be in his shoes; **se mettre dans la p. de qn** to put oneself in sb's shoes; *Théâtre* **entrer dans la p. d'un personnage** to get right inside a character, to get under the skin of a character; *Fig* **j'ai ça dans la p.** it's in my blood; *Fig Fam* **avoir qn dans la p.** to be crazy about sb; *Fam* **se sentir bien/mal dans sa p.** to feel/not to feel good about oneself; *Fam* **craindre pour/tenir à sa p.** to fear for/value one's life; *Fam* **risquer sa p.** to risk one's neck *or* one's life; *Fam* **sauver sa p.** to save one's skin *or* bacon; *Fam* **se faire trouer** *ou* **crever la p.** to get bumped off, to get killed; *Fam* **recevoir** *ou* **prendre douze balles dans la p.** to be shot by a firing squad; *Fam* **faire la p. à qn** to kill sb; *Fam* **j'aurai sa p.!** I'll get *or* have him!; *Fam* **la p.!, p. de balle** *ou* *Vulg* **de zébi!** nothing doing!, no way!; *Fam* **ce qu'on nous a donné? p. de balle!** what did we get? *Br* bugger all! *or* *surtout Am* zilch!; *Arg Vieilli* **vieille p.** old hag **2** *(dépouille) (d'un animal)* skin, hide; *(d'un animal à fourrure)* pelt, fur; **p. de lapin** rabbit skin, cony(skin); **vêtu de peaux de bête** dressed in (animal) skins

3 *(cuir)* hide, leather; **p. de chamois** shammy (leather), chamois leather; **p. de chevreau** kid; **p. de daim** buckskin; **p. de mouton** sheepskin; **p. de requin** shagreen; **p. de serpent** snakeskin; **p. de veau** calfskin, box calf

4 *(de fruit)* skin, peel; **enlever la p. d'un fruit** to peel a fruit; *aussi Fig* **p. de banane** banana skin; **p. d'orange** orange peel; *Fig* orange-peel skin

5 *(pellicule) (du lait)* skin

6 *(autour des ongles)* hangnail

▸▸ *Fam* **p. d'âne** diploma; *Fig Fam* **p. de cha-**

grin diminishing asset; **diminuer comme une p. de chagrin** to dwindle away; *Arg* **p. de vache: c'est une p. de vache** *(cet homme)* he's a bastard; *(cette femme)* she's a cow *or* a bitch

peaucier [posje] **ADJ, NM** *Anat* **(muscle) p.** platysma

peaufiner [pofine] **VT** to clean with a shammy leather; *Fig Fam (fignoler) (texte)* to polish up, to add the final touches to

Peau-Rouge, *pl* **Peaux-Rouges ADJ, N** *Vieilli (amérindien)* Red Indian, redskin

peausserie [posri] **NF 1** *(commerce)* skin trade **2** *(marchandise)* leatherwear

peaussier [posje] **NM** skinner, skin dresser

pébroc, pébroque [pebrɔk] **NM** *Fam* umbrella, *Br* brolly

pécari [pekari] **NM** peccary

peccadille [pekadij] **NF** peccadillo

pechblende [peʃblɛ̃d] **NF** *Minér* pitchblende

pêche¹ [peʃ] **NF 1** *(fruit)* peach; **p.-abricot, p. jaune** yellow peach; **p. blanche** white peach; **p. Melba** peach Melba **2** *Fam (coup)* clout, blow; **se prendre une p.** to get a clout **3** *Fam* **se fendre la p.** *(rire)* to split one's sides (laughing); *(s'amuser)* to have a good laugh **4** *Fam (forme)* feeling of being on top of the world; **avoir la p.** to be feeling on top of the world, to be on top form; **ça va te donner la p.** it'll make you feel on top of the world
▪ **ADJ INV** peach(-coloured), *Am* peach(-colored)

pêche² **NF 1** *(activité)* fishing; **aller à la p.** to go fishing; **p. à la truite** trout fishing; **p. aux crevettes** shrimping; **grande p.** deep-sea fishing; **canne à p.** fishing rod **2** *(produits pêchés)* catch; **faire une heureuse** *ou* **bonne p.** to get a good haul **3** *(endroit)* fishing ground(s); **p. gardée** restricted fishing area; **p. privée** private fishing ground
▸▸ **p. côtière** coastal *or* inshore fishing; **p. au large** deep-sea fishing; **p. à la ligne** angling; **la p. miraculeuse** *Bible* the miraculous draught of fishes; *(à la fête foraine)* ≃ the lucky dip; **p. à la mouche** fly fishing

péché [peʃe] **NM** sin, *Fml* transgression; **les sept péchés capitaux** the seven deadly sins; **vivre dans le p.** *Rel* to live in a state of sin, to lead a sinful life; *Hum (de concubins)* to live in sin; **à tout p. miséricorde** there is no sin that cannot be forgiven; *Fam* **ce n'est pas un p.!** it's not a crime!
▸▸ **p. de jeunesse** youthful indiscretion; **p. mignon: les éclairs au chocolat, c'est son p. mignon** chocolate éclairs are his weakness; **p. mortel** mortal sin; **le p. originel** original sin

pécher [peʃe] **VI** (*je pèche, n. péchons; je pécherai*) to sin, *Fml* to transgress; **p. par orgueil** to commit the sin of pride; **il pèche par excès de timidité/trop d'humilité** he is excessively shy/humble; **p. par manque de confiance** to lack sufficient confidence; **cette enquête pèche sur un point** the inquiry falls down on one point; **p. par excès/défaut** to exceed/fall short of what is required; **p. par omission** to sin by omission; **p. contre l'honnêteté** to act dishonestly; **p. contre le bon goût** to break the rules of good taste

pêcher¹ [peʃe] **NM** peach tree

pêcher² **VT 1** *(truite etc)* to fish for; **p. le corail** to dive for coral; **p. la baleine** to hunt whales, to go whaling **2** *Fam (trouver)* **où avez-vous (été) pêché cela?** where did you pick that up?, where did you get hold of that?; **je ne sais pas où elle a (été) pêché que nous allions nous marier** I don't know where she got hold of the idea that we're getting married
▪ **VI** to fish, to go fishing; **p. à la ligne** to go

angling; **p. à la mouche** to go fly-fishing; **p. en mer** to go sea fishing; *Fig* **p. en eau trouble** to fish in troubled waters

pêcherie [peʃri] NF fishery, fishing ground

pécheur, pécheresse [peʃœr, peʃrɛs] *Rel* N sinner, *Fml* transgressor
ADJ sinful

pêcheur, -euse [pɛʃœr, -øz] N fisherman, *f* fisherwoman; **p. à la ligne** angler; **p. de baleines** whaler; **p. de perles** pearl diver
ADJ **bateau p.** fishing boat

pêchu [peʃy] ADJ *Fam* on (top) form, full of go

pécloter [peklɔte] VI *Suisse Fam* **1** *(être en mauvaise santé)* to be in a bad way **2** *(mal fonctionner)* to play up

PECO [peko] NM *(abrév* **pays d'Europe centrale et orientale)** CEEC

pécore [pekɔr] *Fam* N *(paysan)* yokel, peasant, *Am* hick
NF *Fam* silly stuck-up girl/woman

pectine [pɛktin] NF pectin

pectique [pɛktik] ADJ *(acide)* pectic

pectoral, -ale, -aux, -ales [pɛktɔral, -o] ADJ *(muscle, nageoire etc)* pectoral; *Méd* **sirop p.** expectorant; *Méd* **pâte pectorale** cough lozenge
NM *Anat* pectoral muscle; **travailler ses pectoraux** to work on one's pecs

pécule [pekyl] NM **1** *(économies)* savings, nest egg **2** *Mil, Naut* gratuity *(on discharge)*

pécuniaire [pekynjɛr] ADJ *(avantage)* financial, *Fml* pecuniary; *(position)* financial

pécuniairement [pekynjɛrmã] ADV financially

PED [peəde] NM *(abrév* **pays en voie de développement)** DC

pédagogie [pedagɔʒi] NF pedagogy, pedagogics; **manquer de p.** to lack teaching skills

pédagogique [pedagɔʒik] ADJ *(voyage, sortie etc)* educational; *(méthode)* teaching, *Fml* pedagogical

pédagogiquement [pedagɔʒikmã] ADV pedagogically

pédagogue [pedagɔg] N educationalist, *Fml, Arch* pedagogue

pédale [pedal] NF **1** *(de vélo, de voiture, de piano etc)* pedal; *Tech (de tour)* pedal, treadle; **appuyer sur les pédales** *(à vélo)* to pedal hard; **p. d'embrayage** clutch pedal; **p. d'accélérateur** accelerator pedal; **p. de frein** brake pedal; *Fam* **perdre les pédales** to get all mixed up; *(s'affoler)* to lose one's head, to get in a tizzy; *Fam* **s'emmêler les pédales** to get all mixed up, to get hopelessly lost **2** *Mus* **(note de) p.** pedal (note); *Fig Fam* **mettre la p. douce** to go easy **3** *Fam Péj (homosexuel)* queer, poof(ter); **il est de la p.** he's queer

pédaler [pedale] VI **1** to pedal **2** *Fam* **p. dans la choucroute** *ou* **la semoule** to get nowhere

pédaleur, -euse [pedalœr, -øz] N pedaller

pédalier [pedalje] NM **1** *(de vélo)* crank gear **2** *(clavier d'orgue)* pedal board

Pédalo® [pedalo] NM pedal boat, pedalo

pédant, -ante [pedã, -ãt] N pedant
ADJ pedantic

pédanterie [pedãtri] NF pedantry

pédantesque [pedãtɛsk] ADJ pedantic

pédantisme [pedãtism] NM pedantry

pédé [pede] *Fam Péj* ADJ queer, *Br* bent; **p. comme un phoque** as bent as a nine-bob note *or* as a three-pound note, *Am* as queer as a three-dollar bill
NM *(homosexuel)* queer, poof(ter)

pédégé [pedeʒe] NM *Hum* MD, *Am* CEO

pédéraste [pederast] NM **1** pederast **2** *(homosexuel)* homosexual

pédérastie [pederasti] NF **1** pederasty **2** *(homosexualité)* homosexuality

pédestre [pedɛstr] ADJ *(voyage)* on foot; **chemin p.** footpath; **randonnée p.** hike

pédiatre [pedjatr] N *Méd* paediatrician, *Am* pediatrician

pédiatrie [pedjatri] NF *Méd* paediatrics, *Am* pediatrics

pedibus [pedibys] ADV *Fam Hum* **p. (cum jambis)** on foot, on Shanks's pony *or Am* mare

pédicelle [pedisɛl] NM *Biol, Bot* pedicel, pedicle

pédicule [pedikyl] NM *Biol, Anat* pedicle, peduncle

pédicure [pedikyr] N chiropodist

pédieux, -ieuse [pedjø, -jøz] ADJ *Anat* pedal

pedigree [pedigre] NM *(d'un animal), Fig (d'une personne)* pedigree

pédomètre [pedɔmɛtr] NM pedometer

pédoncule [pedɔkyl] NM *Biol* peduncle

pédophile [pedɔfil] ADJ paedophile, *Am* pedophile

pédophilie [pedɔfili] NF paedophilia, *Am* pedophilia

pedzouille [pɛdzuj] NM *Fam* peasant, country bumpkin, yokel, *Am* hick

PEE [peəə] NM *Fin (abrév* **plan d'épargne d'entreprise)** employee share *or Am* stock ownership plan

peeling [piliŋ] NM *(gommage)* facial scrub; *Méd* exfoliation treatment; **se faire un p.** to give oneself a facial scrub; *Méd* **se faire faire un p.** to have one's skin peeled

pègre [pɛgr] NF **la p.** the underworld

peignage [pɛɲaʒ] NM *Tex* carding, combing

peigne [pɛɲ] NM **1** *(démêloir, barrette)* comb; **p. fin** fine-tooth comb; *Fig* **passer qch au p. fin** to go through sth with a fine-tooth comb; **se donner un coup de p.** to run a comb through one's hair, to give one's hair a comb; **sale comme un p.** filthy **2** *Tex (pour la laine)* card, comb; *(pour le chanvre)* hackle; **p. de métier à tisser** reed **3** *(mollusque)* pecten, scallop
ADJ *Can Fam Péj (avare)* stingy

peigné [pɛɲe] ADJ **1** *(personne)* combed; **bien p.** *(personne)* well-groomed; *(cheveux)* tidy; **mal p.** *(personne)* unkempt; *(cheveux)* tousled **2** *Tex (fil)* worsted
NM worsted (yarn)

peigne-cul, *pl* **peigne-culs** NM *très Fam Péj* creep

peignée [pɛɲe] NF **1** *Tex (de laine, de lin, de chanvre)* cardful **2** *Fam (raclée)* thrashing, good hiding

peigner [pɛɲe] VT **1** *(coiffer) (cheveux)* to comb; **p. un enfant** to comb a child's hair; *Fig Fam* **p. la girafe** to waste one's time **2** *Tex (laine)* to card, to comb; *(chanvre)* to hackle
VPR **se peigner** to comb one's hair

peignoir [pɛɲwar] NM **1** *(vêtement d'intérieur)* housecoat; *(robe de chambre)* dressing gown; **p. (de bain)** bath robe **2** *(chez le coiffeur)* cape, overall

peinard [pɛnar] ADJ *Fam (poste, situation)* cushy; **rester p.** to take it *or* things easy; **tiens-toi p.** keep quiet, keep your nose clean; **il est bien p.** he's having an easy time of it; **ils sont peinards dans leur nouvelle baraque** they're nice and comfortable in their new place; **il a trouvé un coin p. pour pioncer** he found a quiet corner to crash out
ADV *Fam (tranquillement)* in peace, peacefully; **inutile de se presser, on va y aller p.** there's no point in hurrying, we'll take our time

peindre [pɛdr] *(prp* **peignant;** *pp* **peint;** *pr ind* **je peins, il peint,** n. **peignons;** *impf* **je peignais;** *p hist* **je peignis;** *fu* **je peindrai)** VT to paint; **p. qch en vert** to paint sth green; **p. au pinceau/au rouleau/à la brosse** to paint with a brush/a roller/a brush; **papier peint** wallpaper; *Fig* **elle peint la situation avec justesse** she portrays *or* depicts the situation accurately; *Fig* **p. tout en rose** to paint everything in rosy colours; *Suisse* **p. le diable sur la muraille** to be pessimistic
VI to paint
VPR **se peindre** *Fig* **l'innocence se peint sur son visage** innocence is written on his face

PEINE [pɛn]

| punishment **1** ▪ penalty **1** ▪ sorrow **2** ▪ trouble **3** ▪ difficulty **4** ▪ hardly *(à peine)* **5** |

NF **1** *(sanction)* punishment, penalty; **p. capitale** capital punishment; **la p. de mort** the death penalty; **condamné à la p. capitale** *ou* **de mort** sentenced to death; **p. de prison** prison sentence; **p. incompressible** sentence without remission; **p. de substitution** non-custodial sentence; **double p.** double punishment *(in the form of a prison sentence followed by expulsion from the country)*; **défense d'entrer sous p. d'amende** *ou* **de poursuites** trespassers will be prosecuted; **pour la** *ou* **ta p., tu vas descendre la poubelle** (just) for that, you can take the bin down
2 *(chagrin)* sorrow, sadness; *(tourment)* distress; **j'ai beaucoup de p.** I feel very upset, I'm very distressed; **faire de la p. à qn** to upset *or* distress sb, to cause sb distress; **je m'en suis séparé avec beaucoup de p.** I was very sorry to part with it; **cela fait p. à voir** it's painful *or* distressing to see; **elle fait p. à voir** she's a pitiful sight; **être dans la p.** to be in distress; **p. de cœur** heartache; **raconter ses peines de cœur à qn** to tell sb about one's troubled love life
3 *(effort)* trouble, pains; **se donner de la p. pour faire qch** to take the trouble *or* take pains to do sth; **se donner beaucoup de p. pour faire qch** to go to a lot of trouble *or* take great pains to do sth; **ils se sont donné beaucoup de p. pour leurs enfants** they went to a lot of trouble *or* they really put themselves out for their children; **ils se sont donné beaucoup de p. pour la décoration** they took a lot of trouble with *or* over the decoration; **en vous donnant un peu de p., vous y arriverez** with a little effort, you'll manage it; **donnez-vous** *ou* **prenez la p. d'entrer** please come in; **si au moins tu te donnais la p. de lui en parler** if you at least made the effort to talk to him about it; **ne vous donnez pas cette p.** don't bother; **se mettre en p. pour qn/qch** to put oneself out *or* put oneself to a lot of trouble for sb/sth; **c'est p. perdue** it's a waste of time; **elle n'est pas au bout de ses peines** her troubles aren't over yet; **en être pour sa p.** to have nothing to show for one's trouble; **il lui a donné 15 euros pour sa p.** he gave him 15 euros for his trouble; **cela vaut la p. d'essayer** it's worth trying; **cela vaut la p. que tu viennes** it's (well) worth your while coming; **ça ne vaut pas la p. qu'on y aille à trois** it's not worth all three of us going; **cela ne vaut pas la p.** it's not worth it, it's not worth the trouble; **non, ce n'est pas la p.** no, don't bother; **ce n'est pas la p. d'aller voir cette pièce/de lui en parler** it's not worth *or* it's a waste of time going to see that play/talking to him about it; **ce n'est pas la p. de changer de robe** you needn't bother to change *or* it's not worth changing your dress; *Iron* **c'était bien la p. de venir!** we might just as well have stayed at home!; *Iron* **c'était bien la p. que je me dérange!** I'm glad I went to so much trouble!

4 *(difficulté)* difficulty; **j'ai eu toutes les peines du monde à le trouver** I had a real *or* terrible job finding it; **elle a de la p. à parler** *(après une opération)* she has difficulty speaking, she finds it difficult to speak; **elle a de la p. à en parler** it's difficult for her to talk about it, she finds it difficult to talk about; **j'ai (de la) p. à croire que ... +** *sub* I find it hard to believe that ...; **avoir p. à retenir ses larmes** to have difficulty holding back one's tears; **ne jamais être en p. de trouver une excuse** never to be at a loss for an excuse; **elle serait bien en p. de t'expliquer comment ça marche** she'd be hard put *or* she'd have great difficulty explaining to you how it works; **elle n'est pas en p. pour trouver des amis avec qui sortir** she has no trouble *or* difficulty finding friends to go out with; **avec p.** with difficulty; **à grand-p.** with great difficulty; **faire qch sans p.** to do sth without difficulty *or* easily; **l'anglais sans p.** English made easy, English without tears; **cela n'a pas été sans p.** it was no easy matter; **sans p. aucune** without any difficulty *or* trouble

5 à p. hardly, barely, scarcely; **on tient à p. debout, tellement il y a de vent!** it's so windy, we can hardly *or* barely *or* scarcely stay on our feet!; **c'est à p. si je le connais** I hardly know him; **il est à p. 3 heures** it's barely 3 o'clock; **à p. étions-nous sortis qu'il se mit à pleuvoir** we had only just gone out when it began to rain, we were scarcely out of the door before it started to rain; **j'arrive à p.** I've only just arrived, I've arrived just this minute; **à p. arrivée, elle se mit à se plaindre** no sooner had she arrived than she began to complain; *Iron Fam* **à p.!** hardly!, not much! SEE GRAMMAR B62

peiner [pene] **vт** *(quelqu'un)* to upset, to sadden, to distress; **cette nouvelle m'a beaucoup peiné** I was very upset *or* saddened by the news; **d'un ton peiné** in a sad tone ▪ **vi** to toil, to labour, *Am* to labor; *Aut (d'un moteur)* to labour; **il peinait sur son travail** he was toiling at *or* over his work; **p. à marcher** to have trouble *or* difficulty walking; **je peine à comprendre son point de vue** I find it hard to understand his point of view

peintre [pɛ̃tr] **nм 1 (artiste) p.** painter, artist; **une femme p.** a woman artist **2** *(ouvrier, artisan)* **p. en bâtiment(s)** (house) painter; **p.(-)décorateur** painter and decorator; *TV etc* scenic artist **3** *Fig* portrayer; **cet auteur est un p. de la société parisienne** this author is a portrayer of *or* portrays Parisian society

peinture [pɛ̃tyr] **nf 1** *(art, action)* painting; **musée de p.** art *or* picture gallery; **faire de la p.** to paint **2** *(tableau)* painting, picture; *Fig* **p. des mœurs de l'époque** portrayal *or* description of the customs of the period; *Fig* **je ne peux pas le voir en p.** I can't stand the sight of him **3** *(matière)* paint; **attention p. fraîche!, attention à la p.!** wet paint; **p. à la colle** size; **p. en détrempe** distemper; **p. mate** matt emulsion (paint); **p. brillante** *ou* **laquée** gloss (paint); *Péj* **c'est un vrai pot de p.!** she wears make-up an inch thick! **4** *(surface peinte)* paintwork; **il faudra refaire les peintures** the paintwork will have to be done; **c'est moi qui ai fait la p. de la cuisine** I did the paintwork in the kitchen

▸▸ **p. en bâtiments** (house) painting; **p. à l'eau** watercolour *or Am* watercolor (painting); **p. figurative** figurative painting; **p. à l'huile** oil painting; **p. au pistolet** spray painting

peinturer [pɛ̃tyre] **vт** *Can* to paint

peinturlurer [pɛ̃tyrlyre] **vт** *Fam (toile, mur, morceau de papier etc)* to daub (with paint)

péjoratif, -ive [peʒɔratif, -iv] **adj** *(mot, sens)* pejorative; *(remarque, ton)* disparaging ▪ **nм** pejorative

péjoration [peʒɔrasjɔ̃] **nf** pejoration

péjorativement [peʒɔrativmɑ̃] **adv** pejoratively

Pékin [pekɛ̃] **n** Peking, Beijing

pékin [pekɛ̃] **nм 1** *Tex* Pekin (fabric) **2** *Mil Fam* civilian; **être en p.** to be in civvies **3** *Fam (individu)* guy, *Br* bloke

pékinois, -oise [pekinwa, -waz] **adj** of/from Peking *or* Beijing ▪ **nм 1** *(chien)* pekin(g)ese, *Fam* peke **2** *(dialecte)* Mandarin (Chinese), Pekinese ▪ **n P.** Pekin(g)ese

PEL **nм** *(abrév* **plan épargne-logement)** *Br ≃* building society account, *Am ≃* savings and loan association account

pelade [pəlad] **nf** *Méd* alopecia

pelage [pəlaʒ] **nм** *(d'un animal)* coat, fur

pélagique [pelaʒik] **adj** pelagic, pelagian

pelant [pəlɑ̃] **adj** *Belg Fam (agaçant)* annoying; *(assommant)* boring; **c'est p.!** *(agaçant)* it's a real pain in the neck *or* a real nuisance!; *(assommant)* it's a real drag!

pélargonium [pelargɔnjɔm] **nм** pelargonium, *Fam* geranium

pelé, -ée [pəle] **adj** *(personne, fourrure)* bald; *Fig (paysage)* bare; *(tissu)* threadbare ▪ **n** *Fam* baldie; **il n'y avait que trois pelés et un tondu** there was hardly anyone there

pêle-mêle [pɛlmɛl] **adv** higgledy-piggledy; **tout est entassé p.** everything is piled up higgledy-piggledy *or* any old how; **mettre tout p.** to jumble everything up ▪ **nм inv** jumble; *(cadre)* multiple (photo) frame

peler [pəle] **vт** *(légumes, fruit)* to peel, to skin ▪ **vi** *(de la peau etc)* to peel; **j'ai le nez qui pèle** my nose is peeling; *Fig Fam* **je pèle (de froid)** I'm freezing (cold) ▪ **vpr se peler** to peel; **la pêche se pèle facilement** peaches peel easily *or* are easy to peel; *Fig Fam* **on se pèle (de froid)** it's freezing (cold)

pèlerin, -ine¹ [pɛlrɛ̃, -in] **n** pilgrim ▪ **nм 1 (requin) p.** basking shark **2 (faucon) p.** peregrine falcon **3** *Fam (individu)* guy, *Br* bloke

pèlerinage [pɛlrinaʒ] **nм** *(action)* pilgrimage; *(lieu)* place of pilgrimage; **faire un p.** to go on a pilgrimage

pèlerine² [pɛlrin] **nf** cape; *(à capuche)* hooded cape

pélican [pelikɑ̃] **nм** pelican

pelisse [pəlis] **nf** pelisse

pellagre [pelagr] **nf** *Méd* pellagra

pelle [pɛl] **nf** *(d'enfant, de jardinier)* spade; *(pour charbon, cendres)* shovel; *(pour céréales, noix etc)* scoop; **ramasser qch à la p.** to shovel sth up; *Fig* **à la p.** by the bucketful; *Fig* **il y en a à la p., on les ramasse à la p.** there's masses *or* loads (of it); *(nombre)* there are masses *or* loads (of them); **remuer/ramasser l'argent à la p.** to be rolling in money/raking it in; **ça ne se trouve pas à la p. des mecs comme lui** guys like him are few and far between; *Fam* **ramasser** *ou* **se prendre une p.** to fall flat on one's face; *Fam* **rouler une p. à qn** to French-kiss sb; **ils étaient en train de se rouler une p.** they had their tongues down each other's throats

▸▸ **p. à charbon** coal shovel; *Constr etc* **p. mécanique** mechanical shovel; *(drague)* shovel dredger; **p. à ordures** dustpan; **p. à tarte** cake *or* tart slice

pelle-pioche, *pl* **pelles-pioches nf** combined pick and shovel

pelletée [pɛlte] **nf** shovelful, spadeful; *Fig Fam* **une p. d'injures** a stream of insults

pelleter [pɛlte] **vт (je pellette** [pɛlt]**, n. pelletons; je pelletterai** [pɛltre]**)** to shovel (up); *Can* **p. des nuages** to dream up idle schemes

pelleterie [pɛltri] **nf 1** *(fourrure)* pelt **2** *(confection)* fur making; *(commerce)* fur trade, furriery

pelleteuse [pɛltøz] **nf** *Constr* mechanical shovel

pelletier, -ière [pɛltje, -jer] **n** furrier

pellicule [pelikyl] **nf 1** *(de glace, peinture)* thin layer; *(sur un liquide)* film **2** *(enveloppe du raisin)* grape skin **3** *Cin, TV, Phot* film; **p. en bobine** roll film; **p. inversible** reversal film **4** *(dans les cheveux)* **pellicules** dandruff; **avoir des pellicules** to have dandruff; **shampooing contre les pellicules** (anti-)dandruff shampoo

pelloche [pelɔʃ] **nf** *Fam* film *(for camera)*

pélo [pelo] **nм** *Fam (individu)* guy, *Br* bloke

Péloponnèse (le) [lepelɔpɔnɛz] **nм** the Peloponnese

pelotage [p(ə)lɔtaʒ] **nм** *Fam* petting

pelotari [p(ə)lɔtari] **nм** pelota player

pelote [p(ə)lɔt] **nf 1** *(de laine, de ficelle)* ball; **p. (à épingles)** pincushion; *Fig Fam* **faire sa p.** to make one's pile; *(aux dépens d'autrui)* to feather one's nest; *Fig* **avoir les nerfs en p.** to be on edge, to be nervy; *Vieilli Fam* **envoyer qn aux pelotes** to send sb packing **2** *Can (boule)* **p. de neige** snowball **3** *Sport* **p. (basque)** pelota

peloter [p(ə)lɔte] *Fam* **vт** to feel up, to touch up; **elle s'est fait p. dans le métro** somebody groped her in the metro ▪ **vpr se peloter** to pet

peloteur, -euse [p(ə)lɔtœr, -øz] **n 1** *Fam* **c'est un sacré p.** he's got wandering hands, he can't keep his hands to himself **2** *Tex (ouvrier)* ball winder ▪ **nf** *Tex* **peloteuse** *(machine)* balling machine

peloton [p(ə)lɔtɔ̃] **nм 1** *(de laine, de ficelle etc)* (small) ball **2** *(de gens)* group; *(d'abeilles, de chenilles)* cluster; *Sport* **le p.** the pack, the bunch; **le p. de tête** *Sport* the leaders, the leading bunch, the front pack; *Fig* the front runners, the leaders **3** *Mil (de cavalerie)* troop; *(de tanks)* platoon

▸▸ **p. de discipline** punishment squad; **p. d'exécution** firing squad; **p. d'instruction** training unit; **p. de punition** punishment squad

pelotonner [p(ə)lɔtɔne] **vт** *(laine, ficelle etc)* to wind into a ball ▪ **vpr se pelotonner** to curl up; *(pour avoir chaud)* to huddle up; **se p. dans un fauteuil** to curl up in an armchair; **se p. contre la cheminée** to huddle up to the fire; **se p. dans les bras de qn** to snuggle up in sb's arms

pelouse [p(ə)luz] **nf** lawn; *Courses de chevaux* **la p.** the public enclosure; **'p. interdite'** *(sur panneau)* 'keep off the grass'

peluche [p(ə)lyʃ] **nf 1** *Tex* plush; **un jouet en p., une p.** a soft *or* cuddly toy **2** *(flocon, poil)* (piece of) fluff; **mon pull est plein de peluches** my sweater is all pilled

peluché [p(ə)lyʃe] **adj** *(tissu)* pilled

pelucher [p(ə)lyʃe] **vi** *(d'un tissu usé)* to pill

pelucheux, -euse [p(ə)lyʃø, -øz] **adj** fluffy

pelure [p(ə)lyr] **nf 1** *(peau) (de fruit)* peel, skin; *(de légumes)* peelings; **p. d'oignon** *(vin)* dark rosé wine; **(papier) p.** onion skin **2** *Fam (vêtement)* coat

pelvien, -ienne [pɛlvjɛ̃, -jɛn] **adj** *Anat* pelvic

pelvis [pɛlvis] **nм** *Anat* pelvis

pénal, -ale, -aux, -ales [penal, -o] **adj** *(code)* penal; **clause pénale** penalty clause

pénalement [penalmɑ̃] **adv** penally

(pince) perforatrice ticket punch **3** *Ordinat* card punch, (key) punch; **perforatrice de bande** tape punch
NM *Chir* perforator

perforation [pɛrfɔrasjɔ̃] NF *(action)* perforation, perforating; *Ordinat* punching **2** *(trou)* perforation; *Ordinat* punch (hole); *Méd* **p. intestinale** perforation of the intestine

perforer [pɛrfɔre] VT **1** *(trouer) (papier)* to perforate; *(bois, mur)* to bore (through), to drill; *(cuir)* to punch **2** *Ordinat (carte, bande)* to punch; **carte perforée** punch card; **bande perforée** punched tape

perforeuse [pɛrfɔrøz] NF perforator; *Ordinat* card punch

performance [pɛrfɔrmɑ̃s] NF *Sport* performance; *Fig (exploit)* feat, achievement; *Tech* **les performances d'une voiture/d'un ordinateur** a car's/computer's performance; **il faut améliorer les performances de notre entreprise** we must improve our company's performance; **moteur (à) haute p.** high-performance engine; **la p. éblouissante d'un acteur** the dazzling performance of an actor

performant [pɛrfɔrmɑ̃] ADJ *(machine)* high-performance; *(entreprise)* high-performance, efficient; *(investissement)* profitable, high-yield; **des résultats performants** outstanding *or* impressive results

perfuser [pɛrfyze] VT *Méd* to put on a drip; *(organe)* to attach a drip to

perfusion [pɛrfyzjɔ̃] NF *Méd* drip, *Spéc* perfusion; **être sous p.** to be on a drip

pergola [pɛrgɔla] NF pergola

péricarde [perikard] NM *Anat* pericardium

péricardite [perikardit] NF *Méd* pericarditis

péricliter [periklite] VI *(d'une affaire, d'une entreprise)* to be in jeopardy; **ses affaires périclitent** his business is about to collapse

péridot [perido] NM *(pierre)* peridot, chrysolite

péridural, -ale, -aux, -ales [peridyral, -o] *Méd* ADJ epidural; **anesthésie péridurale** epidural anaesthesia *or Am* anesthesia
NF **péridurale** epidural; **accoucher sous péridurale** to give birth under an epidural

périf [perif] NM *Fam (abrév* **boulevard périphérique) le p.** = the ring road around Paris

périgée [periʒe] NM *Astron* perigee

périglaciaire [periglasjer] ADJ *Géog* periglacial

périhélie [perieli] NM *Astron* perihelion

péri-informatique [periɛ̃fɔrmatik] NF *Tech* computer peripherals

péril [peril] NM peril, danger; *(particulier)* risk, hazard; **au p. de sa vie** at the risk of one's life; **en p.** in peril, in danger; **il y aurait p. à sortir en mer aujourd'hui** it would be unsafe to go out to sea today; **mettre qch en p.** to imperil *or* endanger *or* jeopardize sth; **les périls de cette affaire** the risks involved in this affair; **à ses risques et périls** at one's own risk; **il y a p. en la demeure** it's a matter of great urgency; **il n'y a pas p. en la demeure** there's no urgency about it; *Péj* **le p. jaune** the yellow peril

périlleusement [perijøzmɑ̃] ADV perilously

périlleux, -euse [perijø, -øz] ADJ perilous, dangerous, hazardous; **saut p.** somersault

périmé [perime] ADJ *(billet, passeport, coupon)* out of date, no longer valid; *(mandat)* lapsed; *(nourriture, marchandise)* past its sell-by date; **votre passeport est p.** your passport has expired *or* is out of date *or* is no longer valid; *Fig* **conceptions périmées** outdated *or* outmoded concepts

périmer [perime] VI laisser p. un passeport to let a passport expire; **laisser p. de la nourriture** to let food go off *or* bad
VPR **se périmer** *Jur* to lapse; *(d'un passeport, d'un billet)* to expire

périmètre [perimɛtr] NM *Géom* perimeter; **dans un p. de 50 km** within a 50-km radius; **p. de vision** zone of vision

périnatal, -ale, -als *ou* **-aux, -ales** [perinatal, -o] ADJ *Méd* perinatal

périnatologie [perinatɔlɔʒi] NF *Méd* perinatal medicine

périnée [perine] NM *Anat* perineum

période [perjɔd] NF **1** *(de temps)* period; **p. de changements sociaux** period of social change; **longue p. de beau temps** long spell of fine weather; **la p. bleue de Picasso** Picasso's Blue Period; **elle a eu sa p. jazz** she went through a jazz period; *Beaux-Arts* **la p. classique** the Classical Period *or* Age; **première p. de l'existence** early stages of life; *Mil* **p. (d'instruction)** training; **pendant la p. électorale** during the elections; **aller en France en pleine p. électorale** to go to France in the middle of elections; **pendant la p. de Noël** *ou* **des fêtes** during the Christmas period; **p. de fêtes** holiday period; **p. estivale** summer season; **p. de pointe** peak period **2** *(d'un phénomène récurrent, d'un cycle)* period; **nombre de périodes par seconde** *(d'une onde sonore etc)* frequency; *Math* **p. d'une fraction décimale** repetend of a (recurring) decimal; *Phys* **p. d'une onde** period of a wave **3** *Gram* period, complete sentence; *Mus* **p. (musicale)** phrase
▸▸ *Fin* **p. d'amortissement** depreciation period; *Rail* **p. blanche/bleue** = moderately busy/slackest period on the French rail system; *Fin* **p. comptable** financial *or Am* fiscal period; *UE* **p. de double circulation** *(de la monnaie nationale et de l'euro)* double circulation period; **p. d'essai** trial period; **p. d'essai gratuit** free trial period; *Biol* **p. d'incubation** incubation period; *Chimie* **p. de radioactivité** half-life; **p. de référence** reference period; **p. de réflexion** *(après signature d'un contrat)* cooling-off period; *Rail* **p. rouge** = busiest period on the French rail system; **p. de sûreté** minimum period of imprisonment

périodicité [perjɔdisite] NF periodicity; *(d'un périodique)* frequency of publication; *(d'une émission)* frequency of broadcast

périodique [perjɔdik] ADJ **1** periodic; **phases périodiques de récession et de progrès** periodic *or* cyclical phases of recession and economic progress; *Journ* **presse p.** periodical publications; *Math* **fraction p.** recurring decimal; *Math* **fonction p.** periodic function; *Méd* **fièvre p.** recurrent fever **2** *(hygiénique)* **tampons périodiques** tampons; **serviettes** *ou* **garnitures périodiques** sanitary towels *or Am* napkins
NM *Journ* periodical

périodiquement [perjɔdikmɑ̃] ADV periodically

périoste [perjɔst] NM *Anat* periosteum

péripatéticien, -ienne [peripatetisjɛ̃, -jɛn] ADJ *Phil* peripatetic
N *Phil* peripatetic
NF *Fam* **péripatéticienne** streetwalker, prostitute

péripétie [peripesi] NF *Litt* **1** *(dans un roman, dans la vie)* sudden change of fortune **2** **péripéties** adventures, incidents; *(de la vie)* ups and downs, vicissitudes

périph [perif] NM *Fam* = **périf**

périphérie [periferi] NF **1** periphery; *Géom* circumference **2** *(banlieue)* outskirts; **vivre à la p. de Paris** to live on the outskirts of Paris

périphérique [periferik] ADJ **1** *(situé autour)* peripheral; **boulevard p.** ring road, *Am* beltway; *Radio* **radio p.** = radio station broadcasting from outside national territory; *Anat* **système nerveux p.** peripheral nervous system **2** *Ordinat* peripheral
NM **1** *(ceinture routière)* ring road, *Am* beltway **2** *Ordinat* peripheral; **p. d'entrée** input device; **p. externe** external device; **p. d'impression** printer peripheral; **p. série** serial device; **p. de sortie** output device

périphrase [perifraz] NF circumlocution; *Gram* periphrasis, periphrase

périphrastique [perifrastik] ADJ circumlocutory; *Gram* periphrastic

périple [peripl] NM *(voyage)* (long) tour, journey; *(par mer)* (sea) voyage

périr [perir] VI *(aux avoir) (d'une personne)* to perish, to die; *(de la gloire, d'une réputation)* to be destroyed; *(d'un empire)* to fall; **p. dans un incendie/accident** to die or perish in a fire/an accident; **p. noyé** to drown, to be drowned; *Fig Litt* **p. d'ennui** to die of boredom; *Fig Litt* **s'ennuyer à p.** to be bored to death; **son nom ne périra pas** his name will live (on); **la démocratie ne peut p.** democracy cannot be destroyed

périscolaire [periskɔler] ADJ extra-curricular

périscope [periskɔp] NM periscope

périscopique [periskɔpik] ADJ periscopic

périssabilité [perisabilite] NF perishability

périssable [perisabl] ADJ perishable; **denrées périssables** perishable foodstuffs

périssoire [periswar] NF canoe

péristaltique [peristaltik] ADJ *Physiol (mouvement)* peristaltic

péristaltisme [peristaltism] NM *Physiol* peristalsis

péristyle [peristil] NM *Archit* peristyle

péritel® [peritɛl] ADJ INV **prise p.** SCART plug; *(qui reçoit)* SCART socket

péritéléphonie [peritelefɔni] NF *Tech* peripheral telephone equipment

péritoine [peritwan] NM *Anat* peritoneum

péritonite [peritɔnit] NF *Méd* peritonitis

périurbain [periyrbɛ̃] ADJ *(cité, lotissement)* suburban; *(parking, shopping)* out-of-town

perle [pɛrl] NF **1** *(naturelle)* pearl; *(de verre, de métal etc)* bead; *Fig (personne)* gem, treasure; **rang de perles** row *or* string of pearls; *Fig* **jeter des perles aux pourceaux** to cast pearls before swine; **c'est la p. des frères** he's the best brother in the world; **ma bonne est une p. (rare)** my maid is a (real) gem *or* treasure; *Fig Fam* **enfiler des perles** to waste one's time on trivia; **p. de rosée** dewdrop; **perles de sang** drops of blood; **perles de sueur** beads of sweat **2** *Scol* howler
▸▸ **p. de culture** cultured pearl; **p. fine** real pearl

perlé [pɛrle] ADJ **1** *(orné de perles)* set with pearls; *(de perles de verre)* beaded; **riz p.** husked *or* polished rice; **orge p.** pearl barley; **coton p.** pearl cotton; *Fig* **rire p.** rippling laughter **2** *(travail)* exquisitely done; *Mus* clear-cut

perler [pɛrle] VT *(travail)* to execute to perfection; *Mus* to play in clear-cut fashion
VI *(des larmes, de la sueur etc)* to form in beads; **la sueur perlait sur son front** sweat beaded his forehead; **des perles de sueur perlaient sur son front** beads of sweat stood out on his forehead

perlier, -ière [pɛrlje, -jer] ADJ **huître perlière** pearl oyster; **industrie perlière** pearl industry

perlimpinpin [pɛrlɛ̃pɛ̃pɛ̃] NM **poudre de p.** magic *or* miracle powder

perlingual, -ale, -aux, -ales [pɛrlɛ̃gwal,

-o] **ADJ** *Méd* **à prendre par voie perlinguale** place under the tongue

perlouse, perlouze [pɛrluz] **NF 1** *Arg* pearl **2** *Vulg (pet)* fart; **lâcher une p.** to fart

perm [pɛrm] **NF** *Fam* **1** *Mil* leave **2** *Scol* study room; **aller en p.** to go to the study room; **avoir deux heures de p.** to have two hours' private study

permanence [pɛrmanɑ̃s] **NF 1** *(continuité)* permanence; **en p.** permanently, continuously **2** *(service d'accueil d'un organisme)* reception; **la p. est assurée le dimanche** there is someone on duty on Sundays; **être de p.** to be on duty; **p. électorale** committee rooms **3** *Scol* study room; **aller en p.** to go to the study room; **avoir deux heures de p.** to have two hours' private study

permanent, -ente [pɛrmanɑ̃, -ɑ̃t] **ADJ** *(ordre, commission)* standing; *(spectacle)* continuous; *(tribunal)* permanent; **en direct de notre envoyé p. à New York** live from our New York correspondent *or* from our permanent correspondent in New York; *Ordinat* **mémoire permanente** permanent memory; **cinéma p.** *(concept)* continuous showings; *(bâtiment)* cinema *or Am* movie theater with continous showings
NF permanente perm, permanent wave; **se faire faire une permanente** to have a perm, to have one's hair permed
N *Pol* official

permanenter [pɛrmanɑ̃te] **VT** to perm; **se faire p.** to have a perm, to have one's hair permed

permanganate [pɛrmɑ̃ganat] **NM** *Chimie* permanganate

perméabilité [pɛrmeabilite] **NF** permeability, perviousness; *Fig (à une influence)* susceptibility

perméable [pɛrmeabl] **ADJ** permeable, pervious (**à** to); *Fig* susceptible (**à** to)

PERMETTRE [pɛrmɛtr] *(conj like* **mettre)** **VT** to allow, to permit; **p. qch à qn** to allow sb sth; **les médecins ne lui permettent pas l'alcool/ le sport** the doctors don't allow *or* permit him to drink/to do sport; **p. à qn de faire qch** to allow *or* permit sb to do sth, to let sb do sth; **mes moyens ne me le permettent pas** I can't afford it; **est-il permis d'entrer?** may I come in?; **s'il est permis de s'exprimer ainsi** if I/we may (be allowed to) say so; **il n'est pas permis de stationner là** you're not allowed *or* permitted to park there, parking there isn't allowed *or* permitted; **est-ce qu'il est permis de rapporter six bouteilles de vin?** am I allowed to bring back six bottles of wine?, are six bottles of wine allowable?; **cela ne devrait pas être permis** it shouldn't be allowed; *Hum* **être aussi beau/riche que ça, ça ne devrait pas être permis** nobody's got a right to be that good-looking/rich; **est-il permis de se montrer aussi insolent?** how can anyone be so insolent?; *Fam* **il est égoïste comme ce n'est pas permis!** he's incredibly selfish!; *Fam* **il boit comme c'est pas permis!** he drinks like there's no tomorrow!; **autant qu'il est permis d'en juger** as far as one can tell; **il se croit tout permis** he thinks he can do anything he likes *or* whatever he likes; **il n'est pas permis à tout le monde de …** not everyone can …; **permettez-moi de vous dire que vous avez tort** excuse me, but you're wrong; **permettez-moi de vous présenter ma sœur** allow me to introduce you to my sister, may I introduce you to my sister?; **permettez!** excuse me!, if you don't mind!; **vous permettez?** may I?, do you mind?; **si le temps le permet** weather permitting; **si mon emploi du temps le permet** if my schedule allows it
VPR se permettre 1 se p. de faire qch to take the liberty of doing sth; **je me permets d'attirer votre attention sur …** may I draw your

attention to …; **tu ne t'es pas servi un verre? – je ne me serais pas permis!** didn't you get yourself a drink? – I didn't like to!
2 se p. qch to allow oneself sth; **il se permet bien des choses** he takes a lot of liberties

permis [pɛrmi] **ADJ** allowed, permitted
NM *Admin* permit, licence, *Am* license; *Aut Fam* driving licence, *Can* driver's licence, *Am* driver's license; *(examen)* driving test
▸▸ **p. de chasse** hunting permit; *Aut* **p. de conduire** driving licence, *Can* driver's licence, *Am* driver's license; *(examen)* driving test; **p. de conduire international** international driving licence; **p. de construire** planning permission; **p. de débarquement** unloading note *or* permit; **p. de douane** customs permit; **p. d'embarquement** shipping note *or* permit; **p. d'exportation** export licence; **p. d'importation** import licence; **p. d'inhumer** burial certificate; **p. provisoire** = temporary licence issued after passing driving test; **p. de séjour** residence permit; **p. tous véhicules** full licence; **p. de travail** work permit

permissif, -ive [pɛrmisif, -iv] **ADJ** permissive

permission [pɛrmisjɔ̃] **NF 1** *(autorisation)* permission; *Jur* leave; **demander/donner la p. à qn de faire qch** to ask/give sb permission to do sth; **il n'a pas même demandé la p.** he didn't even ask permission; **avec votre p.** with your permission, if I/we may SEE GRAMMAR A58–9; B40 **2** *Mil (congé)* leave (of absence); *(certificat)* pass; **en p.** on leave; **il s'est marié pendant sa p.** he got married during his leave *or* while (he was) on leave

permissionnaire [pɛrmisjɔnɛr] **NM 1** *Mil* man on leave; *Naut* liberty man **2** *(détenteur d'un permis)* permit holder
ADJ officier p. officer on leave

permissivité [pɛrmisivite] **NF** permissiveness

permutabilité [pɛrmytabilite] **NF** permutability, interchangeability

permutable [pɛrmytabl] **ADJ** permutable, interchangeable

permutation [pɛrmytasjɔ̃] **NF 1** *(échange)* exchange of posts; *Mil* transfer **2** *(de lettres, de chiffres)* transposition; *Math* permutation **3** *Ling* metathesis

permuter [pɛrmyte] **VT 1** *(lettres, chiffres)* to transpose; *Math* to permute **2** *Vieilli (poste)* to exchange (**avec qn** with sb)
VI to exchange posts

pernicieusement [pɛrnisjøzmɑ̃] **ADV** perniciously

pernicieux, -ieuse [pɛrnisjø, -jøz] **ADJ** pernicious, harmful; *Méd* **anémie pernicieuse** pernicious anaemia *or Am* anemia

péroné [perɔne] **NM** *Anat* fibula

péronnelle [perɔnɛl] **NF** *Fam Péj* silly goose

péroraison [perɔrɛzɔ̃] **NF** peroration

pérorer [perɔre] **VI** *Péj* to hold forth, to speechify, to spout

Pérou [peru] **NM** Peru; *Fig Fam* **ce n'est pas le P., on peut se l'offrir** it doesn't cost a fortune, we can afford it

peroxyde [perɔksid] **NM** *Chimie* peroxide

peroxydé [perɔkside] **ADJ** peroxide; **une blonde peroxydée** a peroxide blonde

perpendiculaire [pɛrpɑ̃dikylɛr] **ADJ** perpendicular (**à, sur** to)
NF *Géom* perpendicular; **tirer une p.** to drop *or* draw a perpendicular (**à, sur** to)

perpendiculairement [pɛrpɑ̃dikylɛrmɑ̃] **ADV** perpendicularly; **p. à** perpendicular to

perpète [pɛrpɛt] **ADV** *Fam* **1** *(perpétuité)* **condamné à p.** sentenced to life; **il a pris p.** he got life; **je ne vais pas t'attendre jusqu'à p.!** I'm not going to wait for you for ever! **2**

(distance) **envoyer qn à p.** *(très loin)* to send sb miles away; **vivre à P.(-les-Oies)** to live at the back of beyond *or* in the sticks *or Am* in the boonies

perpétration [pɛrpetrasjɔ̃] **NF** *Jur* perpetration

perpétrer [pɛrpetre] **VT** (**je perpètre; je perpétrerai**) to perpetrate

perpette [pɛrpɛt] = **perpète**

perpétuation [pɛrpetɥasjɔ̃] **NF** perpetuation

perpétuel, -elle [pɛrpetɥɛl] **ADJ** perpetual; *(Dieu, amour)* everlasting; *(secrétaire, membre)* permanent; **rente perpétuelle** perpetuity; **mouvement** *m.* perpetual motion; **crainte perpétuelle** perpetual *or* constant fear; **de perpétuels reproches** perpetual *or* constant *or* endless reproaches

perpétuellement [pɛrpetɥɛlmɑ̃] **ADV** perpetually

perpétuer [pɛrpetɥe] **VT** *(nom, réputation)* to perpetuate; *(tradition)* to carry on, to perpetuate; **p. le souvenir de qn** to perpetuate sb's memory, to keep sb's memory alive
VPR se perpétuer to survive; *Fig (d'un problème)* to survive, to live on; **se p. dans son œuvre** to live on in one's work

perpétuité [pɛrpetɥite] **NF** perpetuity; **à p.** *(concession)* in perpetuity; *(emprisonnement)* for life; **être condamné à la réclusion à p.** to be sentenced to life (imprisonment)

perplexe [pɛrplɛks] **ADJ** perplexed, puzzled; **laisser qn p.** to perplex *or* puzzle sb

perplexité [pɛrplɛksite] **NF** perplexity; **être dans la plus grande p.** to be completely baffled *or* utterly perplexed; **plonger qn dans la plus grande p.** to completely baffle *or* utterly perplex sb; **avoir un air de p.** to look confused; **la p. se lisait sur son visage** you could see that he was confused

perquisition [pɛrkizisjɔ̃] **NF** *Jur* search; **mandat de p.** search warrant; **faire une p. chez qn** to search sb's premises; **procéder à une p.** to carry out a search

perquisitionner [pɛrkizisjɔne] **VI** *Jur* to make *or* conduct *or* carry out a search; **p. au domicile de qn** to search sb's house
VT to search

perré [pere] **NM** *Constr (d'une route, d'une digue)* stone pitching *or* facing

perron [perɔ̃] **NM** *Archit* (flight of) steps *(leading to building)*, *Spéc* perron

perroquet [perɔkɛ] **NM 1** *Orn* parrot; **p. de mer** puffin; **répéter qch comme un p.** to repeat sth parrot-fashion **2** *(boisson)* pastis with mint **3** *Naut (voile)* topgallant **4** *(crochet)* hook

perruche [peryʃ] **NF 1** *(oiseau)* budgerigar, *Fam* budgie; *Vieilli Fam (femelle du perroquet)* hen parrot; *Fam (femme bavarde)* chatterbox, chatterer **2** *Naut* mizzen topgallant sail

perruque [peryk] **NF 1** *(postiche)* wig; *Hist* periwig, peruke **2** *Pêche* tangled line, *Fam* bird's nest

perruquier, -ière [perykje, -jɛr] **N** wig maker

pers [pɛr] **ADJ** *Litt* blue-green

persan, -ane [pɛrsɑ̃, -an] **ADJ** Persian; **chat p.** Persian cat; **tapis p.** Persian carpet *or (plus petit)* rug
NM *Ling* Farsi; *Hist* Persian

perse [pɛrs] **NF 1** *Géog* **la P.** Persia; **tapis de P.** Persian carpet *or (plus petit)* rug **2** *Tex* chintz
ADJ of/from ancient Persia, (ancient) Persian
N *P.* Persian
NM *Hist, Ling* Persian

persécuté, -ée [pɛrsekyte] **ADJ** *(personne)* persecuted

N 1 *Psy* sufferer from persecution mania **2** *(victime)* victim of persecution

persécuter [pɛrsekyte] **VT** *(minorité, peuple)* to persecute; *(harceler)* to harass; *(élève, enfant)* to bully; **se sentir persécuté** to feel persecuted

persécuteur, -trice [pɛrsekytœr, -tris] **N** persecutor
ADJ persecuting

persécution [pɛrsekysjɔ̃] **NF** persecution; *Psy* **manie** *ou* **délire de p.** persecution mania *or* complex; *Psy* **avoir la manie de la p.** to have a persecution complex

persévérance [pɛrseverɑ̃s] **NF** perseverance

persévérant [pɛrseverɑ̃] **ADJ** persevering

persévérer [pɛrsevere] **VI** *(je persévère, n. persévérons; je persévérerai)* to persevere *(dans* in); **p. dans une attitude de refus** to remain stubbornly opposed; **il persévère dans l'erreur** he refuses to admit that he is wrong; **il n'a guère persévéré** he didn't show much perseverance; *Litt* **p. à faire qch** to persevere in doing sth

persicaire [pɛrsiker] **NF** *Bot* persicaria, lady's thumb

persienne [pɛrsjɛn] **NF** (slatted) shutter

persiflage [pɛrsiflaʒ] **NM** mockery

persifler [pɛrsifle] **VT** to mock, to ridicule

persifleur, -euse [pɛrsiflœr, -øz] **N** mocker
ADJ mocking, derisive

persil [pɛrsi] **NM** parsley

persillade [pɛrsijad] **NF** *Culin* persillade, = finely chopped garlic, parsley and lemon zest; *(plat)* beef seasoned with persillade

persillé [pɛrsije] **ADJ** *Culin* **1 fromage à pâte persillée** veined cheese **2** *(viande)* marbled **3** *(assaisonné de persil)* sprinkled with chopped parsley

persique [pɛrsik] **ADJ** (ancient) Persian; **le golfe P.** the Persian Gulf

persistance [pɛrsistɑ̃s] **NF 1** *(constance)* persistence, persistency *(à faire qch* in doing sth); **avec p.** persistently; **p. dans le mensonge** persistent lying **2** *(continuité)* *(de la fièvre etc)* persistence, continuance; **p. rétinienne** persistence of vision

persistant [pɛrsistɑ̃] **ADJ** *(parfum, toux, fièvre etc)* persistent; *Bot (feuilles)* persistent, indeciduous

persister [pɛrsiste] **VI 1** *(persévérer)* to persist; **il faut p.** you must persevere, you must keep at it; **p. dans sa résolution** to persist in one's resolve; **p. dans sa décision/son choix** to stick to one's decision/choice; **p. à faire qch** to persist in doing sth; **p. à croire qch** to persist in thinking sth, to continue to believe sth; **je persiste et signe** I'm sticking to it **2** *(continuer)* *(de fièvre, mécontentement etc)* to persist, to continue; **(il) persiste un doute/une interrogation** there remains a doubt/question

perso [pɛrso] *Fam* **ADJ INV** personal; **pour un ailier, il est trop p.** for a winger, he hogs the ball too much *or* he is too much of a solo artist
ADV *(dans les jeux de ballon)* **il joue trop p.** he hogs the ball too much

persona [pɛrsɔna] **ADJ INV p. grata/non grata** persona grata/non grata; **déclarer qn p. grata/non grata** to declare sb persona grata/non grata

personnage [pɛrsɔnaʒ] **NM 1** *(personne importante)* important person, *Fml* personage; **p. connu** *ou* **célèbre** celebrity; **p. officiel** VIP; **un grand p.** a great figure; **un grand p. de l'État** a State dignitary; **les grands personnages de l'histoire** the great names of history; **c'est devenu un p.** he's become an important person *or Fam* a big shot **2** *(individu)* indivi-

dual, character; **un curieux p.** an odd (sort of) character; **c'est un triste p.** he's a poor specimen; **cet homme-là, c'est un p.!** he's quite a character, that man! **3** *(image publique)* (public) image, persona; **il s'est construit un p.** he's created an image for himself **4** *Théâtre, Cin, TV, Littér* character; **p. principal** main *or* principal character; **jouer un p.** to play a part *or* role; *Fig* to play a part *or* role, to put on an act **5** *Beaux-Arts (de tableau)* figure

personnalisation [pɛrsɔnalizasjɔ̃] **NF** personalization; *Mktg* customization

personnalisé [pɛrsɔnalize] **ADJ** personalized; *(voiture, crédit)* customized; **nous vous promettons un accueil p.** we promise you a welcome with a personal touch

personnaliser [pɛrsɔnalize] **VT** to personalize; *(chambre, appartement, bureau etc)* to give a personal touch to; **p. une voiture** to customize a car; **p. sa retraite** to adapt one's pension to one's personal needs; **p. l'image de marque du personnel** to give the staff a corporate identity; **nous devons p. l'accueil** we must welcome our guests/clients/*etc* in a more personal manner

personnalité [pɛrsɔnalite] **NF 1** *(caractère)* personality; **trouble de la p.** personality disorder; **avoir de la p.** to be full of personality; **manquer de p.** to have no personality; **elle ne manque pas de p.** she's got plenty of personality, she doesn't lack personality; **c'est une forte p.** he/she has a strong personality; *Fam* **il a une sacrée p.** he's got one hell of a personality; **culte de la p.** personality cult **2** *(personnage important)* personality, VIP; **les personnalités politiques** the key political figures; **c'est une p.** he's/she's an important man/woman **3** *Jur* **p. juridique** legal personality *or* status

---
PERSONNE [pɛrsɔn]
NF person **1, 4, 5** ■ people **1** ■ in person (en personne) **3**
PRON INDÉFINI anybody **1** ■ nobody **2**

NF 1 *(individu)* person; **trois personnes** three people; **le respect de la p. (humaine)** respect for the individual's rights; **une tierce p.** a third party; **par p. interposée** through a third person *or* party; **toute p. intéressée doit** *ou* **toutes les personnes intéressées sont priées de me contacter au …** all interested parties *or* all those interested should contact me at …; **p. interrogée** respondent; **cela coûte 20 euros par p.** it costs 20 euros a head *or* per head *or* per person; **il y a deux oranges par p.** there are two oranges per person *or* each; **une p. âgée** an elderly person; **les personnes âgées** the elderly, elderly people, senior citizens; **p. handicapée** disabled person; **une grande p.** a grown-up; **une jeune p.** a young lady; **il y a erreur sur la p.** you've got the wrong person; **personnes à charge** dependants

2 *Jur* **p. morale** body corporate, corporate body, legal entity; **p. physique** natural person; **personnes physiques ou morales** individual and legal persons

3 *(soi-même)* **être satisfait/faire grand cas de sa (petite) p.** to be self-satisfied/full of (one's own) self-importance; **prendre soin de sa (petite) p.** to look after oneself; **il ne pense qu'à sa petite p.** he only thinks about number one, he's all self; **en p.** in person, personally; **le roi est venu en p.** the king came in person, the king himself came; **il est la bonté en p.** he is kindness itself, he is kindness personified; **elle est bien de sa p.** she's got a good figure; **il est bien/mal fait de sa p.** he's well/badly proportioned; **exposer sa p.** to expose oneself to danger, to risk one's life; **y aller** *ou* **donner**

de sa p. to give everything one has

4 *(personnalité)* person; **la gentillesse émane de toute sa p.** his/her whole person *or* being radiates kindness; **j'apprécie le cinéaste, mais je n'aime pas la p.** I like him as a film maker, but not as a person

5 *Gram* person; **écrire à la troisième p. du singulier** to write in the third person singular

PRON INDÉF SEE GRAMMAR B16 **1** *(quiconque)* anyone, anybody; **il le sait aussi bien** *ou* **mieux que p.** nobody knows it better than he does; **il est exclu que p. parle** nobody is allowed to speak; **elle danse comme p.** no one dances *or* can dance like her, she dances *or* can dance better than anyone; **sans nommer p.** without naming anybody, naming no names, without naming names

2 *(with* ne *expressed or understood)* no one, nobody; **p. n'est venu, il n'est venu p.** no one *or* nobody has come; **qui est là? – p.** who's there? – no one *or* nobody; **que p. ne sorte** no one *or* nobody is to leave; **il n'y a p. de blessé** no one *or* nobody has been injured, there are no casualties; **il n'y avait p. d'intéressé** no one *or* nobody was interested; **p. d'autre n'était à bord** there was no one else *or* nobody else on board; **je ne peux le dire à p. d'autre** I can't tell anyone *or* anybody else; **je ne dois rien à p.** I don't owe anyone anything; **dans cette maison p. ne se connaissait** in this house no one knew anyone else *or* nobody knew anybody else; **je n'y suis pour p.** I'm not at home to anybody *or* anyone, if anybody *or* anyone calls, I'm not at home; **je ne connais p. de plus hypocrite** I don't know anybody *or* anyone (who is) more hypocritical; **ne connaissez-vous p. qui puisse nous aider?** do you *or* don't you know anybody who could help us?; *Fam* **dès qu'il s'agit de travailler, il n'y a plus p.** as soon as there's work to be done, you can't see anyone for dust SEE GRAMMAR B62

personnel, -elle [pɛrsɔnɛl] **ADJ 1** *(lettre, entreprise, idées etc)* personal; *(titre de transport)* non-transferable; **objets personnels** personal belongings; **fortune personnelle** personal *or* private fortune; *Gram* **pronom p.** personal pronoun SEE GRAMMAR A27–9; B18–21 **2** *(égoïste)* selfish; *Sport* **joueur p.** selfish player; **il avait un intérêt p. à voir se détériorer les choses** he had a personal *or* vested interest in seeing things get worse; **elle a des intérêts personnels dans cette affaire** she has a vested interest in the matter

NM *(d'une institution, d'une firme)* personnel, staff, employees; *(d'une école)* staff; *(d'une usine, dans l'industrie)* workforce, employees; *Mil* personnel, manpower; *Naut* complement; **faire partie du p. de …** to be on the staff of …; **p. réduit** reduced *or* skeleton staff; **manquer de p.** to be understaffed; **un membre du p.** a member of staff, *surtout Am* a staffer; **directeur du p.** personnel manager; **service du p.** personnel (department); **le p. politique/artistique** the political/artistic staff VOIR GRAMMAIRE A11

▸ **p. administratif** administrative staff; *Banque* **p. de back-office** back-office staff; **p. de bureau** office *or* clerical staff; *Aviat* **p. de cabine** flight personnel, cabin staff; **p. d'encadrement** management; *(animateurs)* activity organizers; *(moniteurs)* instructors; **p. extra** relief staff; *Aviat* **p. navigant** flight personnel *or* staff *or* crew; *TV etc* **p. de plateau** floor crew; **p. saisonnier** seasonal staff; *Aviat* **p. au sol** ground personnel *or* staff *or* crew; *Mktg* **p. de soutien commercial** sales support staff; **p. à temps partiel** part-time staff; **p. titulaire** permanent staff; **p. de vente** sales personnel

personnellement [pɛrsɔnɛlmɑ̃] **ADV** personally

personnification [pɛrsɔnifikasjɔ̃] NF personification, embodiment

personnifier [pɛrsɔnifje] VT (*impf, pr sub* **n. personnifiions, v. personnifiiez**) (*objet, vertu, vice etc*) to personify; **elle personnifie toute la bonté humaine** she is the embodiment *or* personification of all human kindness; **il est la bêtise personnifiée** he is stupidity personified, he is stupidity itself; **il personnifie son pays** he typifies his country

perspectif, -ive[1] [pɛrspɛktif, -iv] ADJ (*plan*) perspective

perspective[2] [pɛrspɛktiv] NF **1** (*avenir, idée*) prospect; **en p.** in prospect; **avoir qch en p.** to have sth in prospect *or* in view; **quels sont les projets en p.?** what projects are there lined up *or* in prospect?; **perspectives de reprise** outlook for recovery; **elle était très excitée à la p. de faire ce voyage** she was very excited at the prospect of going on the journey; **j'envisage avec plaisir la p. de le revoir** I am looking forward to seeing him again; **des perspectives d'avenir** future prospects **2** *Beaux-Arts* etc perspective; **p. à vol d'oiseau** bird's-eye view; **dessin en p.** drawing in perspective **3** (*point de vue*) viewpoint, point of view; **ce roman est analysé sous des perspectives différentes** this novel is analysed from several different viewpoints *or* points of view; **dans une p. marxiste** from a Marxist viewpoint *or* point of view

perspicace [pɛrspikas] ADJ shrewd, perspicacious

perspicacité [pɛrspikasite] NF shrewdness, insight, perspicacity

persuader [pɛrsɥade] VT **1 p. qn** to persuade *or* convince sb; **p. qn de qch/de faire qch** to persuade *or* convince sb of sth/persuade sb to do sth; **j'ai fini par les p.** I convinced *or* persuaded them in the end, I talked them round in the end; **être persuadé de qch** to be convinced of sth; **être persuadé que ...** to be sure *or* convinced that ...; **j'en suis tout à fait persuadé** I'm quite convinced (of it); **je n'en suis pas persuadé** I'm not convinced (of it) **2** *Vieilli* **p. qch à qn** to persuade sb of sth, to make sb believe sth
▸ VPR **se persuader** (*se convaincre*) to persuade *or* convince oneself; **ils se sont persuadé(s) que ...** they have persuaded *or* convinced themselves that ...

persuasif, -ive [pɛrsɥazif, -iv] ADJ persuasive

persuasion [pɛrsɥazjɔ̃] NF **1** (*fait ou action de persuader*) persuasion; **à force de p.** through (the use of) persuasion; **agir par (la) p.** to use persuasion, to persuade; **avoir un grand pouvoir de p.** to have great powers of persuasion **2** (*conviction, certitude*) conviction, belief

perte [pɛrt] NF **1** (*d'argent, d'un proche, d'un procès, de la vue, de la raison etc*) loss; **des pertes importantes** considerable *or* significant losses; **de lourdes pertes en hommes et en matériel** heavy losses of men and equipment; *Fig Fam* **elle a été renvoyée avec p. et fracas** she was thrown out of her job; *Fig Fam* **il est sorti avec p. et fracas** he made a big scene when he left; **à p. de vue** as far as the eye can see; **ce n'est pas une grosse p.** it's no great loss; **p. de pouvoir d'achat** loss of purchasing power; **pertes et profits** profit and loss; **pertes et profits exceptionnels** extraordinary items; *aussi Fig* **passer qch par pertes et profits** to write sth off; **vendre qch à p.** to sell sth at a loss; **travailler** *ou* **fonctionner à p.** to operate at a loss
2 (*gaspillage*) waste; **une p. de temps** a waste of time; **en pure p.** to no purpose, fruitlessly; **expliquer qch à qn en pure p.** to

waste one's time *or* one's breath trying to explain sth to sb; **une dépense en pure p.** wasteful expenditure
3 (*déperdition*) loss; (*de tuyau, récipient*) leakage; **p. de chaleur** heat loss, loss of heat; *Élec* **p. de charge** drop in voltage; *Élec* **p. à la terre** earth *or* Am ground leakage; *Aviat* **avion en p. de vitesse** plane that is losing speed; *Fig* **le président/le cinéma semble en p. de vitesse** the President/the film industry seems to be running out of steam; **pertes de mémoire** memory losses; *Méd* **pertes de sang** bleeding
4 (*destruction*) ruin; **jurer la p. de qn** to swear to ruin sb; **il/l'entreprise court à sa p.** he/the company is heading for disaster
▸▸ **p. de bénéfice** loss of profit; **p. brute** gross loss; **p. en capitaux** capital loss; *Fin* **p. de change** (foreign) exchange loss; **p. de connaissance** loss of consciousness; *Ordinat* **p. de données irréparable** irretrievable data loss; **p. envisagée** estimated loss; *Fin* **p. d'intérêts** loss of interest; *Fin* **p. latente** unrealized loss; *Fin* **p. nette** net loss; *Fin* **p. sèche** dead loss; *Compta* **p. supportée** loss attributable; *Fin* **p. totale** total loss; *Compta* **p. transférée** loss transferred; *Méd* **pertes blanches** vaginal discharge, *Spéc* leucorrhoea, *surtout Am* leukorrhea; **pertes humaines** loss of life

pertinemment [pɛrtinamã] ADV **1** *Litt* (*s'exprimer*) pertinently, to the point **2 savoir qch p.** to know sth for a fact

pertinence [pɛrtinãs] NF pertinence, pertinency, relevance

pertinent [pɛrtinã] ADJ pertinent, relevant

pertuis [pɛrtɥi] NM **1** (*canal*) sluice **2** (*d'un fleuve*) narrows; (*détroit*) strait(s), (narrow) channel

perturbant [pɛrtyrbã] ADJ disturbing, upsetting

perturbateur, -trice [pɛrtyrbatœr, -tris] ADJ disruptive
N troublemaker

perturbation [pɛrtyrbasjɔ̃] NF (*de services publics*) disruption; *Astron* perturbation; **p. (atmosphérique)** (atmospheric) disturbance; **perturbations du service aérien** disruption of air travel

perturber [pɛrtyrbe] VT (*services publics, trains, métro*) to disrupt; (*personne*) to perturb, to upset; *Astron* to perturb

péruvien, -ienne [peryvjɛ̃, -jɛn] ADJ Peruvian
N **P.** Peruvian

pervenche [pɛrvãʃ] NF **1** (*plante*) periwinkle; **(bleu) p.** periwinkle blue **2** *Fam* (*contractuelle*) (female) traffic warden, *Am* meter maid

pervers, -erse [pɛrvɛr, -ɛrs] ADJ (*idée*) perverse; (*esprit, pratiques sexuelles*) perverted; **goûts p.** unnatural *or* perverted tastes; **conseils p.** evil advice; **effet p.** perverse effect
N twisted person, (*vicieux*) pervert

> Il faut noter que l'adjectif anglais **perverse** signifie également **contrariant**.

perversion [pɛrvɛrsjɔ̃] NF (*des goûts, de la morale*) perversion; (*de l'esprit*) warping; *Fam* **c'est de la p.!** that's twisted *or* perverted!; **p. sexuelle** sexual perversion

perversité [pɛrvɛrsite] NF perversity, depravity

perverti, -ie [pɛrvɛrti] ADJ (*personne*) perverted, depraved
N pervert

pervertir [pɛrvɛrtir] VT (*goût, sens*) to pervert; (*personne*) to pervert, to deprave, to corrupt; (*morale*) to corrupt
▸ VPR **se pervertir** (*d'un goût, d'un sens*) to be-

come perverted; (*d'une personne*) to become perverted *or* depraved *or* corrupt(ed); (*d'une morale*) to become corrupt(ed)

pesage [pəzaʒ] NM **1** (*pesée*) weighing **2** *Courses de chevaux* weigh-in; (*lieu*) weighing room

pesamment [pəzamã] ADV heavily; **marcher p.** to walk with a heavy tread *or* heavily

pesant [pəzã] ADJ (*valise, pas*) heavy; (*style, écrivain*) heavy, ponderous; (*esprit*) slow, sluggish; (*sommeil*) deep; (*ambiance*) oppressive; **silence p.** heavy silence; **marcher à pas pesants** to walk with a heavy step *or* heavily; **le temps me semble p.** time hangs heavy on my hands
NM **cela vaut son p. d'or** *ou Fam* **de moutarde** *ou Fam* **de cacahuètes** it's worth its weight in gold

pesanteur [pəzãtœr] NF **1** *Phys* gravity; **p. spécifique** specific gravity **2** (*lourdeur*) heaviness; (*d'un mouvement, d'une démarche*) inelegance, unwieldiness; (*de l'esprit*) slowness, sluggishness; **j'ai une p. d'estomac** there's something lying heavy on my stomach; *Fig* **pesanteurs intellectuelles** intellectual baggage *or* impedimenta; *Fig* **pesanteurs économiques** economic impedimenta

PESC [peɛsse] NF *UE* (*abrév* **politique étrangère et de sécurité commune**) CFSP

pèse-alcool [pɛzalkɔl] NM INV alcoholometer

pèse-bébé, *pl* **pèse-bébés** [pɛzbebe] NM baby scales

pesée [pəze] NF **1** weighing; *Boxe, Courses de chevaux* weigh-in; **faire la p. de qch** to weigh sth; **cette balance a une p. de 150 kilos** these scales can weigh up to 150 kilos **2** (*pression*) force, effort; **exercer une p. sur une porte** to try to force a door

pèse-lait [pɛzlɛ] NM INV lactometer

pèse-lettre, *pl* **pèse-lettre(s)** [pɛzlɛtr] NM letter scales

pèse-personne, *pl* **pèse-personnes** [pɛzpɛrsɔn] NM scales

peser [pəze] (**je pèse, n. pesons; je pèserai**) VT to weigh; **p. à vide** to tare; *Fig* **p. ses mots** *ou* **ses paroles** to weigh one's words, to think before one speaks; **et je pèse mes mots!** and I don't say it lightly!; **réponse bien pesée** considered *or* careful answer; *Fig* **tout bien pesé** all things considered; **p. tous les éléments** to weigh (up) all the facts; **p. une décision** to weigh up *or* ponder a decision; **p. le pour et le contre** to weigh (up) the pros and cons; *Sport* **se faire p.** to weigh in
▸ VI **1** (*faire ou avoir comme poids*) to weigh; (*être lourd*) to be heavy; (*d'un argument*) to carry weight; **ce paquet pèse deux kilos** this parcel weighs two kilos; **il ne pèse pas lourd** he doesn't weigh much, he's not very heavy; *Fig* he doesn't carry much weight *or* count for much; **mon avis ne pèse pas lourd** my opinion doesn't carry much weight *or* count for much; **cela me pèse de vous le demander** it isn't easy for me to ask you; **le temps lui pèse** time hangs heavy on his hands; **l'isolement/votre absence me pèse** this isolation/your absence gets me down *or* is a strain; **cette ambiance me pèse un peu** I'm finding this atmosphere a bit oppressive; **toutes ces discussions lui pèsent** all these discussions are a strain on him; **p. sur qch** to press on sth; **p. sur un levier** to press down *or* push down on a lever; *Can* **p. sur un bouton** to push a button; **aliment qui pèse sur l'estomac** food that lies heavy on the stomach; **p. sur le cœur à qn** to give sb a heavy heart; **un silence pesait sur l'assemblée** a heavy silence hung over the meeting; **une lourde responsabilité pèse sur lui** he is weighed

down by a heavy responsibility; **une menace qui pèse sur nous** a threat that is hanging over us; **ça lui pèse sur la conscience** it lies heavy on his conscience; **p. sur un choix** to weigh up *or* mull over a choice; **p. sur** *ou* **dans une décision** to carry weight in a decision; **p. sur un mot** to lay stress on a word, to stress a word
2 (*valoir*) (*d'une entreprise, d'une personne*) to be worth; **cette entreprise pèse 20 millions de dollars** this company is worth 20 million dollars
VPR se peser to weigh oneself

peseta [pezeta] NF *Anciennement* peseta

pèse-vin [pεzvɛ̃] NM INV oenometer

peso [pezo] NM peso

peson [pəzɔ̃] NM balance

pessaire [pesεr] NM *Méd* pessary

pesse [pεs] NF, **pessereau** [pεsro] NM (*plante*) horse tail, *Spéc* equisetum

pessimisme [pesimism] NM pessimism

pessimiste [pesimist] ADJ pessimistic
N pessimist

peste [pεst] NF **1** *Méd* plague, *Litt, Arch* pestilence; **être atteint de la p.** to have the plague, to be stricken with the plague; *Fam* **fuir qn/qch comme la p.** to avoid sb/sth like the plague; **je me méfie de lui/ça comme de la p.** I don't trust him/it one little bit, I wouldn't trust him/it as far as I could throw him/it; *Litt, Vieilli* **p.!** good gracious!, heavens!; *Litt, Arch* **(la) p. soit du vieux fou!** a plague on the old fool!; *Vieilli* **que la p. t'étouffe!** a plague on you! **2** *Fig Péj* (*enfant*) pest, nuisance; **une petite p.** a little devil *or* pest
▸▸ **p. bovine** cattle plague; **la p. bubonique** *ou* **noire** the bubonic plague; *Hist* the Black Death; **p. porcine** swine fever

Il faut noter que le terme anglais **pest** est un faux ami. Il ne désigne jamais une maladie.

pester [pεste] VI **p. contre qn/qch** to curse sb/sth, to rave at sb/sth; **il pestait** he was cursing

pesticide [pεstisid] ADJ pesticidal
NM pesticide

pestiféré, -ée [pεstifere] ADJ plague-stricken
N plague victim; **fuir qn comme un p.** to avoid sb like the plague

pestilence [pεstilɑ̃s] NF stench, stink

pestilentiel, -ielle [pεstilɑ̃sjεl] ADJ stinking, fetid

pet [pe] NM **1** *Fam* (*vent*) fart; **faire** *ou* **lâcher un p.** to fart; **ça ne vaut pas un p. (de lapin)** it isn't worth a monkey's fart *or* a damn; *Fig* **il a toujours un p. de travers** there's always something wrong with him *or* the matter with him **2** *Arg Vieilli* (*grabuge*) **il va y avoir du p.** there's going to be trouble **3** *Fam* **faire le p.** (*faire le guet*) to keep watch *or* a lookout **4** *Fam* (*choc*) [pεt] **ta voiture a pris un p.** your car's had a bash; **j'ai fait un p. à la voiture** I've put a dent in the car; **plein de pets** all bashed up, full of dents

pétage [petaʒ] NM *Fam* **p. de plombs** (*fait de se mettre en colère*) going ballistic, hitting the roof *or Am* ceiling; (*fait de craquer nerveusement*) cracking up; **le patron nous a fait un p. de plombs maison quand il s'est aperçu de ce qui s'était passé** the boss went totally ballistic *or* totally hit the roof *or Am* ceiling when he saw what had happened; **il faut que je prenne des vacances parce que là je suis au bord du p. de plombs** I need to take a holiday because I'm on the verge of cracking up

pétainiste [petenist] *Hist* ADJ Pétainist
N follower of Pétain, Pétainist

pétale [petal] NM petal

pétanque [petɑ̃k] NF ≃ bowls (*played in the South of France*)

Pétanque
Originally invented in the South of France, where it has become a local institution, this bowling game is equally popular with tourists. The game, which requires two teams and is played up to a score of thirteen points, is played outdoors on a flat sandy or earth surface. Each team consists of two to three players, each of whom has three steel "boules". Each player tosses or rolls their "boule" so that it ends up as near as possible to the "cochonnet" (a small wooden ball thrown from a distance of 6 to 10 metres), at the same time trying to hit the other team's "boules" so as to scatter them. Players take turns, and whoever ends up closest to the "cochonnet" when all balls are played, wins.

---

pétant, -ante [petɑ̃, -ɑ̃t] ADJ *Fam* **à neuf heures pétantes** at nine o'clock sharp *or* on the dot, on the stroke of nine

Pétaouchnock [petauʃnɔk] N *Fam* = imaginary distant place; **ils l'ont envoyé à P.** they sent him to some place in the back of beyond

pétaradant [petaradɑ̃] ADJ (*moto, camion etc*) spluttering, sputtering

pétarade [petarad] NF **1** (*d'un cheval*) (succession of) farts **2** (*de feux d'artifice, d'armes à feu*) crackling **3** (*de voiture, Mobylette® etc*) backfiring, backfire

pétarader [petarade] VI **1** (*d'un cheval*) to let off a succession of farts **2** (*de feux d'artifice, d'armes à feu*) to crackle **3** (*de voiture, Mobylette® etc*) to backfire

pétard [petar] NM **1** (*feu d'artifice*) (fire)cracker, *Br* banger; *Min* shot, blast; *Mil* explosive charge, *Arch* petard; *Rail* fog signal; **faire partir** *ou* **claquer un p.** to let off a (fire)cracker *or Br* banger; *Fig* **p. mouillé** damp squib **2** *Fam* (*grabuge*) **il va y avoir du p.** there's going to be a hell of a row; **être en p.** (*en colère*) to be raging (**contre** against), to be in a flaming temper; **se mettre en p.** to fly off the handle **3** *Fam* (*pistolet*) shooter, *Am* gat **4** *Fam* (*derrière*) bum, *Am* ass, fanny **5** *Fam* (*joint*) joint, *Br* spliff

pétasse [petas] NF *Vulg* (*terme injurieux*) bitch, slut; (*prostituée*) whore, hooker

pétaudière [petodjεr] NF bedlam, bear garden; **la réunion a tourné en p.** the meeting turned into a bear garden

pet-de-nonne [pεtdənɔn], *pl* **pets-de-nonne** NM *Culin* fritter

pété [pete] ADJ *Fam* (*ivre*) smashed, plastered

péter [pete] (**je pète, n. pétons; je péterai**) VI **1** *Fam* (*d'une personne*) to fart; *Fig* **il l'a envoyé p.** he told him to piss off; *Fig* **p. dans la soie** to be stinking rich, to be loaded; *Fig* **il pète plus haut que son derrière** *ou* **son cul** he thinks he's really somebody *or* really it, he thinks he's God's gift to humanity **2** *Fam* (*exploser*) to blow up; **faire p. des pétards** to set off (fire)crackers; *Fig* **il faut que ça pète** let's have it all out in the open; **si les relations entre les deux pays continuent à se détériorer**, ça va finir par p. if relations between the two countries continue to deteriorate, all hell will break loose; **ça va p. entre eux** they're going to have one hell of a row **3** (*de bois qui brûle*) to crack, to crackle; (*d'un bouchon*) to pop **4** *Fam* (*casser*) to

break; (*d'une ficelle, d'une branche, d'un câble*) to snap, to break; **ça va lui p. entre les mains** it'll break in his hands; **tous les boutons étaient prêts à p.** all the buttons were about to pop off **5** *Fam* **p. de joie/santé** to be jumping for joy/bouncing with health; **et je veux que ça pète!** chop, chop!, *Arg* and get your finger out!; **on a enfin l'impression que ça pète!** things seem to be moving at last!, we're seeing a bit of action at last!
VT *Fam* **1 p. le feu** *ou* **la forme** to be bursting with energy *or* vitality; **ça va p. des flammes** there's going to be a hell of a row **2** (*casser*) to bust; **je vais lui p. la gueule** I'll smash his face in **3 p. sa frime** to show off, to pose **4 la p.** (*avoir très faim*) to be starving *or* ravenous
VPR **se péter** *Fam* **1** (*d'une machine etc*) to break; **il s'est pété la gueule** (*il est tombé*) he came a cropper; (*il s'est saoulé*) he got smashed *or* plastered **2 se la p.** to show off, to pose; *Can* **se p. les bretelles** to brag, to be full of oneself

pète-sec [pεtsεk] *Fam* NM INV snappy person
ADJ INV curt

péteux, -euse [petø, -øz] *Fam Péj* N **1** (*lâche*) yellowbelly, coward; **c'est un petit p.** he's yellow **2** (*prétentieux*) upstart
ADJ **1** (*lâche*) cowardly **2** (*prétentieux*) stuck-up, snooty

pétillant [petijɑ̃] ADJ (*feu*) crackling; (*vin*) sparkling; (*eau*) fizzy, *Fig* (*yeux*) sparkling; *Fig* **esprit p.** sparkling wit

pétillement [petijmɑ̃] NM (*du bois qui brûle*) crackling; (*du champagne*) sparkling, fizzing, bubbling; (*des yeux*) sparkling

pétiller [petije] VI (*de bois qui brûle*) to crackle; (*d'une boisson*) to sparkle, to fizz, to bubble; *Fig* (*des yeux*) to sparkle; *Fig* **p. d'esprit** to sparkle with wit; **elle pétillait de joie** she was bubbling over with joy; **un regard qui pétille de joie/d'intelligence** a look that sparkles with joy/with intelligence

pétiole [pesjɔl] NM *Bot* petiole

petiot, -ote [pətjo, -ɔt] *Fam* ADJ tiny, wee
N tiny child; **ma petiote** my little girl; **viens ici, p.** come here, little fellow

PETIT, -ITE [p(ə)ti, -it]

ADJ	small **1, 5, 7** ▪ little **1–3, 6**
	▪ insignificant **5** ▪ young **6** ▪ mean **8**
	▪ petty **8**
N	(little) boy/girl
NM	young

ADJ **1** (*de taille réduite*) small, little; **un p. homme** a small *or* short *or* little man; **c'est un homme p.** he's small *or* short *or* little; **jouer avec des petits soldats/des petites voitures** to play with toy soldiers/toy cars; **une toute petite maison/boîte/entreprise** a tiny little house/box/firm; **petite distance** short distance; **un p. nombre de gens** a small number of people; **ces chaussures sont trop petites (pour moi)** these shoes are too small (for me); **faire de petits profits** to make a small profit; **rouler à petite vitesse** to drive slowly; **pendant un p. moment** for a little while; *Fam* **nous avons attendu un bon p. moment** we waited quite a time; *Fam* **j'y suis resté une petite demi-heure** I stayed there just under half an hour; *Fig* **se faire tout p.** to make oneself as inconspicuous as possible; **il s'est fait tout p. devant elle** he tried to do everything to please her; *Fig* **comme le monde est p.** it's a small world
VOIR GRAMMAIRE A17

2 (*méprisant*) **p. crétin/con!** little idiot/bastard!

3 (*affectueux*) little; **mais ma petite Louise ...** but my dear Louise ...; **Ma chère petite maman** (*dans une lettre*) Dear Mummy; **un**

p. coup de rouge a drop of red wine; **et si on se regardait une petite cassette vidéo?** how about watching a video?; **je prendrais bien une petite cigarette** I'd love a cigarette; **on s'en fume une petite?** shall we have a quick smoke *or Br* fag?

4 *(de niveau inférieur)* lesser, minor; *Scol* **les petites classes** the lower classes; **le p. personnel** the junior staff; **la petite industrie** light industry; **les petits propriétaires** the small landowners; *Com* **petite caisse** petty cash

5 *(de moindre importance) (problème, erreur etc)* small, minor, insignificant; *(fait)* insignificant, unimportant; *Péj (plainte, affaire)* petty; *(événement)* minor; **petites routes** minor roads; **entrer par la petite porte** to start off at the bottom; **ce n'est pas une petite affaire** it's no small matter; **p. accident** minor accident; **j'ai un p. rhume** I've a slight cold *or* a bit of a cold; **les petites gens** ordinary people

6 *(jeune)* little, young; **p. enfant** little *or* young child; **petite fille** little girl; **mon p. frère** my little brother; **tu es trop p. pour ça** you're too young for that; **quand tu étais p.** when you were little *or* small *or* young; **un p. Anglais** an English boy; **les petits Thomas** the Thomas children

7 *(faible)* **il a une petite santé** he's delicate; **une petite voix** a small voice

8 *(borné)* narrow-minded; *(mesquin)* petty; *(remarque, acte)* mean, petty; *(dans ses compliments, ses défaites)* ungenerous; **c'est vraiment p.** that's really mean *or* petty; **c'est un p. esprit** he's petty-minded

N *(enfant)* (little) boy, *f* (little) girl; **pauvre petit(e)** poor little thing; *Scol* **les petits** the juniors; **le p.** *(dans une famille)* the youngest (boy); *Fam* **bonjour, mon p.** *(à une femme, un enfant)* good morning, my dear

NM *(d'un animal)* young; **petits du chien** (dog's) puppies; **petits du chat** (cat's) kittens; **faire** *ou* **avoir des petits** to have young; *(d'une chienne)* to have pups, *Spéc* to pup, to whelp; *(d'une lionne)* to have cubs, *Spéc* to whelp; *(d'une truie)* to have piglets, *Spéc* to farrow; *(d'une chatte)* to have kittens, *Spéc* to kitten; *(d'une louve)* to have cubs, *Spéc* to cub; *Fig Fam* **faire des petits** *(de l'argent)* to increase, to multiply

ADV **p. à p.** little by little, bit by bit, gradually; **en p.** on a small scale, in miniature; **le même mais en plus p.** the same only smaller ▸▸ **p. ami** boyfriend; **petite amie** girlfriend; *Journ* **petite annonce** classified ad, small ad; *Journ* **petites annonces personnelles** personal column; **p. bois** kindling wood; *Typ* **petite capitale** small cap; *Fam* **le p. coin** the toilet, *Br* the loo, *Am* the john; **p. commerçant** shopkeeper; **p. commerce** *(secteur)* small retail trade; *(endroit)* small shop; *Fam* **p. copain** boyfriend; *Fam* **petite copine** girlfriend; *Typ* **petits corps** small type; **p. cousin/petite cousine** second cousin; **p. déjeuner** breakfast; **p. déjeuner américain** American breakfast; **p. déjeuner à l'anglaise** English breakfast; **p. déjeuner continental** continental breakfast; **p. doigt** little finger, *Am, Scot* pinkie; **le p. écran** television, the small screen; **la petite enfance** early childhood, infancy; **petits-fours** petits fours; **la petite mort** orgasm; **petites et moyennes entreprises** small (and medium-sized) businesses; **petites et moyennes industries** small (and medium-sized) industries; *Fam* **p. nom** first name; *Fig* **petites phrases** *(des hommes politiques)* soundbites; **il est connu pour ses petites phrases très médiatiques** he's the master of the soundbite; **petits pois** (garden) peas; *Fin* **p. porteur** small investor *or* shareholder; *Culin* **p. salé** = type of streaky bacon; **petits salariés** low wage-earners

petit-beurre, *pl* **petits-beurre NM** *Culin* butter biscuit *or Am* cookie

petit-bourgeois, **petite-bourgeoise,** *pl* **petit(e)s-bourgeois(es) ADJ** *aussi Péj* lower middle class, petit-bourgeois **N** member of the lower middle class; **les petits-bourgeois** the petty bourgeoisie

petit-déj' [p(ə)tideʒ] **NM** *Fam* breakfast

petite-fille, *pl* **petites-filles** [p(ə)titfij] **NF** granddaughter

petitement [pətitmɑ̃] **ADV 1** *(dans la pauvreté)* poorly **2** *(à l'étroit)* **elle est logée p.** she lives in cramped accommodation **3** *(bassement)* meanly, pettily

petite-nièce, *pl* **petites-nièces** [p(ə)titnjɛs] **NF** great-niece

petitesse [p(ə)titɛs] **NF 1** *(d'un objet)* smallness, small size; *(d'une silhouette)* slenderness **2** *Péj (mesquinerie)* meanness, pettiness; *(d'un repas, d'une somme d'argent)* paltriness; **p. d'esprit** narrow-mindedness; **p. de cœur** small-mindedness **3** *Péj (action mesquine)* shabby deed

petit-fils, *pl* **petits-fils NM** grandson

petit-gris, *pl* **petits-gris NM 1** *(écureuil)* Siberian squirrel; *(fourrure)* squirrel (fur) **2** *Culin* = edible brown snail

pétition [petisjɔ̃] **NF 1** petition; **adresser une p. à qn** to petition sb; **faire signer une p. à qn** to get sb to sign a petition **2** **p. de principe** begging the question, *Spéc* petitio principii

pétitionnaire [petisjɔnɛr] **N** petitioner

pétitionner [petisjɔne] **VI** to petition

petit-lait, *pl* **petits-laits NM** whey; **cela se boit comme du p.** it goes down *or* slips down a treat; *Fig* **boire du p.** to lap it up

petit-maître, *pl* **petits-maîtres NM** *Arch* fop, dandy

petit-nègre NM *Ling Fam* **1** *(mauvais français)* bad French; **c'est du p.** it's gibberish **2** *Vieilli (français parlé dans les colonies)* pidgin French

petit-neveu, *pl* **petits-neveux NM** great-nephew

petits-enfants [p(ə)tizɑ̃fɑ̃] **NMPL** grandchildren

petit-suisse, *pl* **petits-suisses NM** *Culin* petit-suisse *(small cream cheese dessert)*

pétochard, -arde [petɔʃar, -ard] **N** *Fam* yellowbelly, coward

pétoche [petɔʃ] **NF** *Fam* jitters; **avoir la p.** to have the jitters, to be scared stiff; **ficher** *ou* **flanquer** *ou très Fam* **foutre la p. à qn** to give sb the jitters, to scare sb stiff

pétocher [petɔʃe] **VI** *Fam* to be scared stiff *or* witless

pétoire [petwar] **NF 1** *(sarbacane)* peashooter **2** *(mauvais fusil)* popgun **3** *(moto)* motorbike; *(Mobylette®)* moped

pétole [petɔl] **NF** *Suisse (crotte de chèvre)* goat shit

peton [pətɔ̃] **NM** *Enf* tootsy(-wootsy); **petons** tootsies, tootsy-wootsies

pétoncle [petɔ̃kl] **NM** scallop

pétouiller [petuje] **VI** *Suisse Fam (traînasser)* to loaf around

Pétrarque [petrark] **N** Petrarch

pétrel [petrɛl] **NM** petrel; **p. tempête** storm(y) petrel

pétri [petri] **ADJ** kneaded, moulded, *Am* molded *(de* out of); **un homme p. d'orgueil** a man puffed up with pride; **p. d'ignorance** steeped in ignorance; **p. de contradictions** riddled with contradictions

pétrifiant [petrifjɑ̃] **ADJ** *(eau)* petrifying, petrifactive; *(nouvelle)* stupefying

pétrification [petrifikasjɔ̃] **NF** petrification,

petrifaction; *Fig* **p. du cœur** hardening of the heart; **p. de l'esprit** sclerosis of the mind

pétrifier [petrifje] *(impf, pr sub* **n. pétrifiions, v. pétrifiiez)* **VT 1** *Minér* to petrify; *Fig* **pétrifié de peur** petrified, paralysed *or Am* paralyzed with fear; **pétrifié de froid** frozen stiff **2** *(couvrir de calcaire)* to encrust with lime

VPR se pétrifier *Minér* to petrify, to become petrified; *Fig* **son sourire se pétrifia** his smile froze; **son esprit se pétrifiait** he was developing sclerosis of the mind; **en entendant son nom, elle s'est pétrifiée** hearing his name, she froze

pétrin [petrɛ̃] **NM** kneading trough; **p. mécanique** kneading machine; *Fam* **mettre qn/se mettre dans le p.** to get sb/get into a mess *or* a fix; *Fam* **laisser qn dans le p.** to drop sb in it, to leave sb in a mess; *Fam* **être dans le p.** to be in a mess *or* a fix; **nous voilà dans un beau** *ou* **joli** *ou* **sale p.** that's a fine *or* right mess we're in

pétrir [petrir] **VT** *(brasser) (pâte à pain)* to knead; *(façonner) (argile)* to knead, to shape, to mould, *Am* to mold; *Fig* **p. l'esprit de qn** to mould *or* shape sb's mind; **il lui pétrissait le bras** he was kneading her arm; **il pétrissait son chapeau avec nervosité** he was nervously fiddling *or* toying with his hat; *Méd* **p. un muscle** to knead a muscle

pétrissage [petrisaʒ] **NM** kneading

pétrisseur, -euse [petrisœr, -øz] **N** *(ouvrier)* **p.** dough mixer

NF **pétrisseuse** *(machine)* kneading machine

pétrochimie [petroʃimi] **NF** petrochemistry

pétrochimique [petroʃimik] **ADJ** petrochemical

pétrochimiste [petroʃimist] **N** petrochemist

pétrodollar [petrodɔlar] **NM** *Fin* petrodollar

pétrographie [petrografi] **NF** *Géol* petrography

pétrole [petrɔl] **NM** oil, petroleum; **p. brut** crude (oil); **p. lampant** paraffin (oil), *Am* kerosene; **gisement de p.** oil deposit, oilfield; **puits de p.** oil well; **lampe à p.** oil lamp; **bleu p.** *inv* petrol blue; **vert p.** *inv* deep turquoise

> Il faut noter que le terme anglais britannique **petrol** est un faux ami. Il signifie **essence.**

pétrolette [petrɔlɛt] **NF** *Fam* moped

pétroleuse [petrɔløz] **NF** activist; *Hist* female incendiary *(during the Paris Commune of 1871)*

pétrolier, -ière [petrɔlje, -jɛr] **ADJ** **l'industrie pétrolière** the oil *or* petroleum industry; **société pétrolière** oil company; **pays p.** oil-producing country; **navire p.** (oil) tanker; **choc p.** oil crisis

NM 1 *(financier, industriel)* oil magnate, oilman; *(technicien)* petroleum engineer **2** *(navire)* (oil) tanker

> Do not confuse with **pétrolifère.**

pétrolifère [petrolifɛr] **ADJ** oil-bearing, *Spéc* petroliferous; **gisement p.** oilfield

> Do not confuse with **pétrolier.**

pétromonarchie [petromɔnarʃi] **NF** oil kingdom

pétulance [petylɑ̃s] **NF** liveliness, exuberance

pétulant [petylɑ̃] **ADJ** lively, exuberant

> Il faut noter que l'adjectif anglais **petulant** est un faux ami. Il signifie **irascible.**

pétunia [petynja] **NM** petunia

PEU [pø]

| **ADV** little **1** ▪ few **2** ▪ not very **3** |
| **NM** little **1** ▪ a little (un peu) **2, 3** ▪ a bit (un peu) **2, 3** |

ADV 1 ((en) petite quantité) little; **très/trop p.** very/too little; **de l'instruction, il en avait p. ou pas** he had little or no education, he had precious little education; **p. ou point** little or none; **manger p. (ou point)** to eat little (or nothing); **p. à p.** bit by bit, little by little, gradually; **c'est p. dire** that's an understatement; **c'est p. dire qu'il était content** it's an understatement to say that he was content; **ce n'est pas p. dire** that's saying a good deal or a lot; **il a p. fait pour nous** he has done (very) little for us; **quelque p.** somewhat, rather; **je suis quelque p. surpris** I am somewhat or rather surprised; **si tu m'aimais tant soit p.** if you loved me at all or even a little; **si tu es tant soit p. fatigué** if you're at all or the least bit tired; **p. s'en faut ou il s'en faut de p. pour que je me mette en colère** I'm on the verge of losing my temper, it won't take much to make me lose my temper; **p. s'en est fallu qu'il fasse tout rater, il s'en est fallu de p. qu'il fasse tout rater** he very nearly ruined everything; **pour p. qu'il soit de mauvaise humeur, on va passer une sacrée soirée** if he's in a bad mood at all, we're in for one hell of an evening; **il ne s'est pas découragé pour si p.** he didn't get discouraged by such a small thing; **p. de viande** not much meat, very little meat; **c'est p. de chose** it's nothing; **nous en savons p. de choses** we know little about it, we don't know much about it; **il suffirait de p. de choses pour que ça fonctionne** it wouldn't need much or it would take very little to get it to work; **nous sommes bien p. de choses** life is so fragile; **fort p. (de sucre etc)** very little, not much; Fam **très p. pour moi!** not for me!

2 (nombre) few; **p. en garderont un souvenir** few (people) will remember it; **p. de gens ou monde** few people; **très p. de gens** very few people, not very many people; **p. d'entre eux avaient voyagé** few of them had travelled; **en p. de mots** in a few words VOIR GRAMMAIRE A6

3 (pas, pas très) not very; **p. utile** not very useful; **p. intelligent** unintelligent, not very intelligent; **p. enviable** unenviable; **p. honnête** dishonest; **p. profond** shallow; **p. souvent** not very often, infrequently; **elle n'est pas p. séduisante** she's more than a little seductive

4 (de temps) **il reste p. de temps** there's not much time left; **très p. de temps** very little time, not very much time; **en très p. de temps** very quickly, in no time at all; **p. après** shortly after(wards), not long after(wards); **sous p., dans p., avant p., d'ici p.** soon, shortly, before long; **depuis p.** lately, recently; **j'ai manqué le train de p.** I (only) just missed the train; **il y a p.** not (very) long ago, recently; **j'ai p. de temps à vous accorder** I don't have much time

NM 1 (petite quantité) little; **le p. qu'il y a est à votre disposition** you are welcome to the little there is; **le p. que je sais de lui** the little I know about him; **le p. d'argent qu'il me reste** what little money I have left; **finis le plat, pour le p. qu'il reste** finish the dish, there's only a little bit left; **son p. d'instruction** what little education he has had

2 un p. a little, a bit; **un p. de** a little, a bit of; **il nous reste un p. de temps/sucre** we still have a little time/sugar left or a little more/sugar left; **elle a un p. moins/un p. plus de quarante ans** she's a little under/over forty; **j'en veux un p. plus/moins** I want a little or a bit more/less; **un tout petit p.** a tiny bit, a

very little; **un tout petit p. de beurre** a tiny bit of butter, a very little butter; **encore un p.** a bit more, a little more; (encore quelques-uns) a few more; **encore un p. de lait** a bit or a little more milk; **j'ai besoin d'un petit p. de temps avant de donner une réponse** I need a little bit of time before giving an answer; **il sait un p. d'anglais** he knows a little English or a bit of English, he has a smattering of English; **vous êtes allé un p. loin!** you went a bit far!; **il est un p. en retard** I'm a bit or a little late; **il est un p. artiste** he's something of an artist; Fam **ça, c'est un p. fort!** that's a bit much!; **un p. plus et il tombait dans l'eau** he very nearly fell in the water; **pour un p. je l'aurais jeté dehors** I all but or I very nearly threw him out; **écoutez un p.** just listen; **viens un p. ici** come here a minute; **regarde un p. ce que tu as fait!** just look what you've done!; **il m'aime un p., beaucoup, passionnément, à la folie, pas du tout** (en effeuillant une marguerite) ≃ he loves me, he loves me not; très Fam **t'as vu un p. comment il m'a parlé?** did you see the way he spoke to me?; Fam **je vous demande un p.!** I ask you!; Fam **tu ferais ça? – un p.!** you'd do that? – you bet!; Fam **un p. mon neveu!** you bet!, sure! VOIR GRAMMAIRE A6

3 (de temps) **restez encore un p.** stay a bit longer, stay a little (while) longer; **j'aurais voulu prolonger encore un p. mon séjour** I would have liked to extend my stay a bit or a little

peuchère [pøʃɛr] **INT** Région heavens!, Br strewth!

peuh [pø] **INT** pooh!, bah!

peuplade [pœplad] **NF** (small) tribe

peuple [pœpl] **NM** VOIR GRAMMAIRE A11 **1** (nation) people, nation; **le p. français** the French people; **le p. élu** the chosen people **2** (ensemble des citoyens) people (considered as a political entity); **dans une démocratie, le p. gouverne** in a democracy, it is the people who govern; **le roi et son p.** the king and his people or subjects; **les gens du p.,** Vieilli **le bas ou petit p.** the lower classes; Fam **que demande le p.?** what more could you ask for? **3** Fam (foule) crowd (of people); Fam **quel p.!** what a crowd!, what a lot of people!; Fam **ça fait du p.** that's a lot of people; Fam **elle se fiche ou se fout ou se moque du p.** who does she think she is!

ADJ INV Fam Péj common, vulgar; **ça fait p.** that's common, that's vulgar

peuplé [pœple] **ADJ** inhabited; **p. de** inhabited by; **très/peu p.** densely/sparsely populated

peuplement [pœpləmã] **NM** (d'une région) populating; (d'un vivier, d'un parc à gibier etc) stocking; (d'une forêt) planting (with trees); **régions à faible p.** sparsely populated areas

peupler [pœple] **VT 1** (pourvoir d'habitants) (pays) to populate, to people; (vivier, parc à gibier etc) to stock; (forêt) to plant (with trees) **2** (occuper) to inhabit; **rue peuplée de gens** street crowded with people, crowded street; Fig **ville peuplée de souvenirs** town full of memories

VPR se peupler (d'une région, ville) to become populated; **la rue s'est peuplée peu à peu** the street gradually filled (up) with people

peupleraie [pøplərɛ] **NF** poplar grove or plantation

peuplier [pøplije] **NM** poplar; **p. tremble** aspen

peur [pœr] **NF** fear; (subite) fright; **avoir p. to** be afraid or frightened; **avoir p. des chiens** to be afraid or frightened of dogs; Fig **n'ayons pas p. des mots** let's call a spade a spade,

let's not mince our words; **ne pas avoir p. de mourir** not to be afraid or frightened of dying; **il ne faut pas avoir p. de le lui dire** you mustn't be afraid or frightened of telling him so; **j'avais p. de vous gêner** I was afraid I might be in your way; **elle n'a pas p. de déplaire** she doesn't care if she's not liked; **j'ai p. pour lui** I'm afraid or frightened for him; **n'ayez pas p.!** don't be afraid!; **n'aie pas p., tout va s'arranger** don't worry, everything will be all right; Fam **vous n'avez pas p.!** you've got a or some nerve!; **prendre p.** to take fright; **je n'avais qu'une p., qu'il dise oui** my only fear was that he might say yes; Fam **avoir une p. bleue** to be scared to death; **avoir une p. bleue des abeilles/de parler en public** to be scared to death of bees/of speaking in public; **avoir une p. panique des voyages en avion** to be terrified of flying; **avoir la p. au ventre** to be terrified or petrified; **en être quitte pour la p.** to get off with a fright; **il a eu plus de p. que de mal** he was more frightened than hurt; **il me fait p.** he frightens me; **tu m'as fait p.!** you frightened or startled me!, you gave me a fright!; **il m'a fait une de ces peurs!** he gave me such a fright!; **être laid à faire p.** to be as ugly as sin; **c'était d'un ennui à faire p.** it was dreadfully boring; **sans p.** (employé comme adj) fearless; (employé comme adv) fearlessly; **un chevalier sans p. et sans reproche** ≃ a very parfit gentle knight; **j'en ai bien p.** I'm afraid so; **j'ai p. qu'il (ne) soit en retard** I'm worried in case he is or Fml should be late; **la p. des élèves (devant leur professeur)** the children's fear (of their teacher); Fam **la p. du gendarme** the fear of being caught; **c'est par p. des représailles que ...** it's for or through fear of reprisals that ...; **la p. de s'engager** the fear of committing oneself; **de p. de faire qch** for fear of doing sth; **de p. que ... (ne) + sub** in case ..., for fear that ...; **elle ne t'en a pas parlé de p. que tu ne t'offenses** she didn't tell you about it in case you took or for fear that you should take offence

peureusement [pørøzmã] **ADV** fearfully

peureux, -euse [pørø, -øz] **ADJ** (personne, regard) timid, fearful, Fml timorous

N fearful or timid person; **quel p.!** what a coward!, Fam what a wimp!

peut-être [pøtɛtr] **ADV** perhaps, maybe, possibly; **p. que oui, p. que non** perhaps or perhaps not, maybe, maybe not; **elle est p. rentrée chez elle** perhaps or maybe she has gone home, she may have gone home; **je ne suis p. pas riche, mais j'ai mon honneur** I may not be rich or perhaps I'm not rich, but I have my honour; **p. bien qu'il viendra** he may (very) well come; Iron **tu le sais mieux que moi, p.?** you think you know better, do you?; **je ne sais pas faire la cuisine, p.?** you think I can't cook? SEE GRAMMAR B62

p. ex. (abrév par exemple) eg

pèze [pɛz] **NM** Arg (argent) dough, cash

pff [pf], **pfft** [pft], **pffut** [pfyt] **INT** pooh!

PgPr Ordinat (abrév page précédente) PgUp

PgSv Ordinat (abrév page suivante) PgDn

pH [peaʃ] **NM** Chimie pH

phacochère [fakɔʃɛr] **NM** warthog

phaéton [faetɔ̃] **NM** phaeton

phagocyte [fagɔsit] **NM** Biol phagocyte

phagocyter [fagɔsite] **VT 1** Biol to phagocytose **2** Fig to swallow up, to engulf; **les zones industrielles phagocytent la banlieue** the suburbs are being swallowed up or engulfed by industrial estates

phagocytose [fagɔsitoz] **NF** Biol phagocytosis; Fig swallowing up

phalange [falãʒ] **NF 1** Antiq, Mil phalanx; Litt (armée) host, army; Hist, Pol **la P.** the Falange, the Falangist party **2** Anat phalanx

phalangette [falɑ̃ʒɛt] NF *Anat (du doigt, de l'orteil)* top joint, *Spéc* ungual phalanx

phalangien, -ienne [falɑ̃ʒjɛ̃, -jɛn] ADJ *Anat* phalangeal

phalangiste [falɑ̃ʒist] N *Hist, Pol* Falangist

phalanstère [falɑ̃stɛr] NM *Hist, Écon* phalanstery; *Fig* **un p. de philosophes** a community of philosophers

phalène [falɛn] NF *(parfois nm en poésie)* geometrid (moth)

phallique [falik] ADJ phallic

phallo [falo] NM *Fam Péj (abrév* **phallocrate***)* male chauvinist (pig)

phallocrate [falɔkrat] NM *Péj* male chauvinist (pig)

phallocratie [falɔkrasi] NF male chauvinism

phalloïde [falɔid] ADJ *Biol* phalloid; **amanite p.** *(champignon vénéneux)* death cap, *Spéc* amanita phalloides

phallus [falys] NM phallus

phantasme [fɑ̃tasm] NM = **fantasme**

pharamineux, -euse [faraminø, -øz] ADJ *Fam* phenomenal, staggering

pharaon [faraɔ̃] NM **1** *Hist* Pharaoh **2** *Cartes* faro

pharaonique [faraɔnik], **pharaonien, -ienne** [faraɔnjɛ̃, -jɛn] ADJ **1** *Hist* Pharaonic **2** *Fig (gigantesque)* huge, enormous

phare [far] NM **1** *(tour lumineuse)* lighthouse; **p. à éclats** flashing light; **p. à feu fixe/à feu tournant** fixed/revolving light; **gardien de p.** lighthouse keeper **2** *Aviat* beacon; **p. d'atterrissage** landing light **3** *Aut* headlight, headlamp; **faire un appel de phares** to flash one's headlights; **mettre ses phares** to switch on one's headlights; **se mettre en phares** to dip *or Am* dim one's headlights; **rouler (en) pleins phares** to drive on full headlights *or Br* on full beam *or Am* on high beams; **p. anti-brouillard** foglight; **p. de recul** reversing *or Am* backup light

-phare [far] SUFF **personnalité-p.** leading light; **film-p.** seminal film

pharisaïque [farizaik] ADJ **1** *Péj (hypocrite)* hypocritical, *Litt* pharisaic(al) **2** *Hist, Rel* Pharisaic(al)

pharisien, -ienne [farizjɛ̃, -jɛn] N **1** *Péj (hypocrite)* hypocrite, *Vieilli, Litt* pharisee **2** *Hist, Rel* Pharisee
▪ ADJ **1** *Péj (pointilleux)* self-righteous **2** *Hist, Rel* Pharisaic(al)

pharmaceutique [farmasøtik] ADJ pharmaceutical

pharmacie [farmasi] NF **1** *(science)* pharmacy, pharmaceutics **2** *(magasin)* pharmacy, chemist's (shop), *Am* drugstore; *(dispensaire)* dispensary; **la p. de l'hôpital** the hospital dispensary **3** *(médicaments)* pharmaceuticals; **(armoire à) p.** medicine chest *or* cabinet; **p. de premiers soins** first-aid kit; **p. de voyage** travelling *or Am* traveling first-aid kit

pharmacien, -ienne [farmasjɛ̃, -jɛn] N *(vendeur)* pharmacist, *Br* (dispensing) chemist, *Am* druggist; *(d'un laboratoire pharmaceutique, dans l'industrie)* pharmacist, *Br* chemist

pharmacodépendance [farmakodepɑ̃dɑ̃s] NF drug dependency

pharmacologie [farmakɔlɔʒi] NF pharmacology

pharmacologique [farmakɔlɔʒik] ADJ pharmacological

pharmacopée [farmakɔpe] NF pharmacopoeia

pharmacorésistance [farmakorezistɑ̃s] NF resistance to drugs

pharmacovigilance [farmakoviʒilɑ̃s] NF drug testing and control

pharyngé [farɛ̃ʒe], **pharyngien, -ienne** [farɛ̃ʒjɛ̃, -jɛn] ADJ *Méd, Anat* pharyng(e)al

pharyngite [farɛ̃ʒit] NF *Méd* pharyngitis

pharynx [farɛ̃ks] NM *Anat* pharynx

phascolome [faskɔlɔm] NM *Zool* wombat

phase [fɑz] NF *(période)* phase, stage; *Astron, Chimie, Phys* phase; **cancer en p. terminale** terminal cancer; **cancéreux en p. terminale** terminal cancer patient; *Ind* **p. de production** stage of production; **p. de croissance** growth phase; **être en p. de croissance** to be growing; *Phys* **en p.** in phase; *Fig* **être en p.** to be on the same wavelength; *Phys* **décalage de p.** difference of phase, phase displacement; *Élec* **(conducteur de) p.** phase conductor

phatique [fatik] ADJ *Ling* **fonction p.** phatic function

Phébus [febys] N *Myth* Phoebus

Phèdre [fɛdr] N *Myth* Phaedra

Phénicie [fenisi] NF Phoenicia

phénicien, -ienne [fenisjɛ̃, -jɛn] *Hist* ADJ Phoenician
▪ NM *Ling* Phoenician
▪ N P. Phoenician

phénix [feniks] NM *Myth* phoenix; *Fig Litt (personne unique en son genre)* paragon

phénol [fenɔl] NM *Chimie* phenol; *Com* carbolic acid

phénoménal, -ale, -aux, -ales [fenɔmenal, -o] ADJ *Phil, Fam (incroyable)* phenomenal

phénoménalement [fenɔmenalmɑ̃] ADV phenomenally

phénomène [fenɔmɛn] NM *(expérience, fait, personne)* phenomenon, *pl* phenomena; *(dans les foires)* freak; **quel p.!** *(excentrique)* what a character!; **c'est un drôle de p.!** he's quite a character!

phénoménologie [fenɔmenɔlɔʒi] NF *Phil* phenomenology

Philadelphie [filadɛlfi] N Philadelphia

philanthrope [filɑ̃trɔp] N philanthropist

philanthropie [filɑ̃trɔpi] NF philanthropy

philanthropique [filɑ̃trɔpik] ADJ philanthropic

philatélie [filateli] NF philately, stamp collecting

philatélique [filatelik] ADJ philatelic

philatéliste [filatelist] N philatelist, stamp collector

philharmonie [filarmɔni] NF philharmonic society

philharmonique [filarmɔnik] ADJ *(société, orchestre etc)* philharmonic

philhellène [filelɛn] NM philhellene
▪ ADJ philhellenic

philhellénisme [filelenism] NM philhellenism

philippin, -ine [filipɛ̃, -in] ADJ Filipino, Philippine
▪ N P. Filipino

Philippines (les) [lefilipin] NFPL the Philippines VOIR GRAMMAIRE A8

philistin [filistɛ̃] ADJ M, NM *Péj* philistine

philo [filo] NF *Scol Fam* philosophy

philodendron [filɔdɛ̃drɔ̃] NM philodendron

philologie [filɔlɔʒi] NF philology

philologique [filɔlɔʒik] ADJ philological

philologiquement [filɔlɔʒikmɑ̃] ADV philologically

philologue [filɔlɔg] N philologist

philosophale [filɔzɔfal] ADJ F **la pierre p.** the philosophers' stone

philosophe [filɔzɔf] N philosopher; **prendre les choses en p.** to take things philosophically

▪ ADJ philosophical; **se montrer p. face à une déception** to react philosophically to a disappointment

philosopher [filɔzɔfe] VI to philosophize

philosophie [filɔzɔfi] NF *(science)* philosophy; **la p. de l'histoire/des sciences** the philosophy of history/science; **supporter une épreuve avec p.** to suffer a hardship philosophically; *Fam* **c'est ma p.** that's my philosophy, that's my outlook on life; *Scol Vieilli* **(classe de) p.** final-year arts and humanities class

philosophique [filɔzɔfik] ADJ philosophical

philosophiquement [filɔzɔfikmɑ̃] ADV philosophically

philtre [filtr] NM philtre, *Am* philter; **p. d'amour** love potion

phlébite [flebit] NF *Méd* phlebitis

phlébologie [flebɔlɔʒi] NF *Méd* phlebology

phlébologue [flebɔlɔg] N *Méd* vein specialist

phlébotomie [flebɔtɔmi] NF *Méd* phlebotomy

phlegmon [flɛgmɔ̃] NM *Méd* phlegmon

phlox [flɔks] NM phlox

pH-mètre [peaʃmɛtr] NM *Tech* pH-meter

phobie [fɔbi] NF *Psy, Méd* phobia, morbid fear; **avoir la p. de qch** to have a phobia about sth

phobique [fɔbik] ADJ, N *Psy, Méd* phobic

phocéen, -enne [fɔseɛ̃, -ɛn] ADJ Marseilles

phonation [fɔnasjɔ̃] NF *Physiol, Ling* phonation

phonatoire [fɔnatwar] ADJ phonatory

phone [fɔn] NM *Phys* phon

phonématique [fɔnematik] ADJ *Ling* phonemic

phonème [fɔnɛm] NM *Ling* phoneme

phonémique [fɔnemik] ADJ *Ling* phonemic

phonéticien, -ienne [fɔnetisjɛ̃, -jɛn] N phonetician

phonétique [fɔnetik] ADJ phonetic
▪ NF phonetics

phonétiquement [fɔnetikmɑ̃] ADV phonetically

phoniatre [fɔnjatr] N *Méd* speech therapist

phoniatrie [fɔnjatri] NF *Méd* speech therapy

phonie [fɔni] NF *Radio, Électron* wireless telegraphy, radiotelegraphy

phoning [fɔniŋ] NM *Mktg* telesales

phonique [fɔnik] ADJ acoustic, *Vieilli* phonic; **isolation p.** soundproofing, sound insulation

phono [fono] NM *Fam Vieilli* = **phonographe**

phonographe [fɔnɔgraf] NM *(gramophone)* gramophone, *Am, Arch* phonograph

phonographique [fɔnɔgrafik] ADJ phonographic

phonologie [fɔnɔlɔʒi] NF *Ling* phonology

phonologique [fɔnɔlɔʒik] ADJ *Ling* phonological

phonologue [fɔnɔlɔg] N *Ling* phonologist

phonothèque [fɔnɔtɛk] NF sound archives, audio library

phoque [fɔk] NM **1** *(animal)* seal; **souffler comme un p.** to (puff and) wheeze *or* (puff and) blow like a grampus; *Vulg* **il est pédé comme un p.** he's a real queer *or Br* poofter **2** *(fourrure)* sealskin

phosgène [fɔsʒɛn] NM *Chimie* phosgene (gas)

phosphatage [fɔsfataʒ] NM *Agr* treating with phosphates

phosphate [fɔsfat] NM *Chimie* phosphate; **sans phosphates** phosphate-free

phosphaté [fɔsfate] ADJ *Chimie* phosphatic, phosphated; *(engrais etc)* phosphate-enriched

phosphater [fɔsfate] VT to treat with phosphates, to phosphate

phosphène [fɔsfɛn] NM *Physiol* phosphene

phosphore [fɔsfɔr] NM *Chimie* phosphorus

phosphoré [fɔsfɔre] ADJ *Chimie* phosphorated

phosphorer [fɔsfɔre] VI *Fam* to have one's thinking cap on; **alors, ça phosphore?** working hard, are we?

phosphorescence [fɔsfɔresɑ̃s] NF phosphorescence

phosphorescent [fɔsfɔresɑ̃] ADJ phosphorescent

phosphoreux, -euse [fɔsfɔrø, -øz] ADJ *Chimie* phosphorous

phosphorique [fɔsfɔrik] ADJ *Chimie* phosphoric

phosphure [fɔsfyr] NM *Chimie* phosphide

phot [fɔt] NM *Phys* phot

photo [foto] NF *(activité)* photography; *(cliché)* photo, shot; *(tirée d'un film, du tournage)* still, photostill; **faire de la p.** *(en professionnel)* to be a photographer; *(en amateur)* to be an amateur photographer; **prendre qn en p., prendre une photo de qn** to take sb's photo, to take a photo of sb; **prendre qch en p., prendre une p. de qch** to take a photo of sth; **se faire prendre en p. par qn** to have one's photo taken by sb; **il est bien en p.** he photographs well; *Fam* **tu veux ma p.?** who do you think you're staring at?, what are you staring at?; **appareil p.** camera; **p. d'identité** identity photo, passport-sized photograph; **p. souvenir** souvenir photo; **p. de mode** fashion photo

photobiologie [fotobjɔlɔʒi] NF photobiology

photochimie [fotoʃimi] NF photochemistry

photochimique [fotoʃimik] ADJ photochemical

photocomposer [fotokɔ̃poze] VTI to photocompose, to photoset, *Br* to filmset

photocomposeur [fotokɔ̃pozœr] NM = **photocompositeur**

photocomposeuse [fotokɔ̃pozøz] NF *(machine)* photocomposer, photosetter, *Br* filmsetter

photocompositeur, -trice [fotokɔ̃pozitœr, -tris] N photocomposer, photosetter, *Br* filmsetter

photocomposition [fotokɔ̃pozisjɔ̃] NF photocomposition, photosetting, *Br* filmsetting

photoconducteur, -trice [fotokɔ̃dyktœr, -tris] ADJ photoconductive

photoconductivité [fotokɔ̃dyktivite] NF photoconductivity

photocopie [fotokɔpi] NF photocopy

photocopier [fotokɔpje] VT *(conj like co-pier)* to photocopy

photocopieur [fotokɔpjœr] NM, **photocopieuse** [fotokɔpjøz] NF photocopier

photocopillage [fotokɔpijaʒ] NM = infringement of copyright through excessive use of photocopiers

photodiode [fotodjɔd] NF photodiode

photoélectricité [fotoelɛktrisite] NF photoelectricity

photoélectrique [fotoelɛktrik] ADJ *(cellule, effet)* photoelectric

photo-finish, *pl* **photos-finish** NM *Sport* photo finish; *(appareil)* photo-finish camera; **l'arrivée a dû être vérifiée au p.** it was a photo finish

photogénique [fotoʒenik] ADJ photogenic

photogramme [fotogram] NM *Cin* frame

photogrammétrie [fotogrametri] NF photogrammetry

photographe [fotograf] N *(professionnel de la photo)* photographer; **reporter p.** photojournalist; **p. de mode** fashion photographer; *Cin* **p. de plateau** still photographer, unit photographer; **p. de presse** press photographer; **p. indépendant(e)** freelance photographer

Il faut noter que le terme anglais **photograph** est un faux ami. Il signifie **photographie, cliché.**

photographie [fotografi] NF **1** *(technique, hobby etc)* photography; **p. numérique** digital imaging; **p. journalistique** press photography; **p. par téléobjectif** long-lens photography; **faire de la p.** *(en professionnel)* to be a photographer; *(en amateur)* to be an amateur photographer **2** *(cliché)* photograph, photo, shot; **prendre qn en p., prendre une p. de qn** to take sb's photo, to take a photo of sb; **p. qch en p., prendre la p. de qch** to take a photo of sth; **p. aérienne** aerial photograph

photographier [fotografje] VT *(impf, pr sub n.* **photographiions,** *v.* **photographiiez)** to photograph, to take a photograph of; **se faire p.** to have one's photograph taken

photographique [fotografik] ADJ *(reproduction, description etc)* photographic; **appareil p.** camera

photographiquement [fotografikmɑ̃] ADV photographically

photograveur [fotogravœr] NM photoengraver

photogravure [fotogravyr] NF *(procédé, épreuve)* photogravure, photoengraving

photo-interprétation NF *Tech* photointerpretation

photojournalisme [fotoʒurnalism] NM photojournalism

photojournaliste [fotoʒurnalist] N photojournalist

photolithographie [fotolitɔgrafi] NF photolithography

photolyse [fotoliz] NF *Chimie* photolysis

Photomaton® [fotomatɔ̃] NM (automatic) photo machine *or* booth

photomécanique [fotomekanik] ADJ *Tech* *(procédé)* photomechanical

photomètre [fotomɛtr] NM *Tech* photometer

photométrie [fotometri] NF *Phys* photometry

photométrique [fotometrik] ADJ *Phys* photometric

photomontage [fotomɔ̃taʒ] NM photomontage

photon [fotɔ̃] NM photon

photopériode [fotoperjɔd] NF *Bot* photoperiod

photopériodique [fotoperjɔdik] ADJ *Bot* photoperiodic

photopériodisme [fotoperjɔdism] NM *Bot* photoperiodism

photophobie [fotofɔbi] NF *Méd* photophobia

photophore [fotofɔr] NM **1** *(lampe)* reflective lamp *(esp of miner)* **2** *(pour bougie)* candle holder with glass shade

photopile [fotopil] NF *Tech* solar cell

photoreportage [fotorəpɔrtaʒ] NM **1** *(discipline)* photojournalism **2** *(reportage)* photo report

photo-robot, *pl* **photos-robots** NF Identikit® *or* Photofit® (picture)

photosensible [fotosɑ̃sibl] ADJ photosensitive

photosphère [fotosfɛr] NF *Astron* photosphere

photostat [fotosta] NM *Tech* photostat

photostoppeur, -euse [fotostɔpœr, -øz] N street photographer

photostyle [fotostil] NM *Ordinat* light pen

photosynthèse [fotosɛ̃tez] NF *Biol* photosynthesis

photothèque [fototɛk] NF photo *or* picture library; **p. électronique** electronic still store

photothérapie [fototerapi] NF *Méd* phototherapy

phototransistor [fototrɑ̃zistɔr] NM phototransistor

phototypie [fototipi] NF *Tech* phototype (process)

photovoltaïque [fotovɔltaik] ADJ photovoltaic; **cellule p.** photovoltaic cell; **effet p.** photovoltaic effect

phragmite [fragmit] NM **1** *Bot* reed **2** *Orn* sedge warbler

phrase [frɑz] NF *Gram* sentence; *Mus* phrase; **p. toute faite** stock phrase; *Fig* **faire des phrases, faire de grandes phrases** to use high-flown language; **phrases à compléter** sentence completion; **sans phrases** straight out, without mincing one's words; *Gram* **membre de p.** phrase SEE GRAMMAR A78–9; B62–4

Il faut noter que le nom anglais **phrase** est un faux ami. Il signifie **expression.**

phrasé [frɑze] NM *Mus* phrasing

phraséologie [frɑzeɔlɔʒi] NF *(syntaxe)* phraseology; *Péj (verbiage)* flowery *or* high-flown language

phraser [frɑze] VT *Mus* to phrase VI to use high-flown language

phraseur, -euse [frɑzœr, -øz] N *Péj* phrasemonger

phrastique [frastik] ADJ *Gram* sentence

phréatique [freatik] ADJ *Géol* **nappe p.** ground water

phrénologie [frenɔlɔʒi] NF phrenology

phrénologique [frenɔlɔʒik] ADJ phrenological

phrénologiste [frenɔlɔʒist] NM phrenologist

Phrygie [friʒi] NF *Antiq* Phrygia

phrygien, -ienne [friʒjɛ̃, -jɛn] ADJ *Antiq* Phrygian; *Hist* **bonnet p.** Phrygian cap *(in French Revolution)* N *Antiq* **P.** Phrygian

phtisie [ftizi] NF *Méd Arch* consumption, *Spéc* phthisis; **p. galopante** galloping consumption

phylactère [filaktɛr] NM **1** *Rel juive* phylactery **2** *Beaux-Arts* scroll **3** *(de bande dessinée)* bubble, balloon

phylloxéra, phylloxera [filɔksera] NM *Entom* phylloxera

phylogénèse [filoʒenɛz] NF phylogenesis, phylogeny

physicien, -ienne [fizisjɛ̃, -jɛn] N physicist; **p. de l'atome** nuclear physicist

Il faut noter que le terme anglais **physician** est un faux ami. Il signifie **médecin.**

physicochimie [fizikoʃimi] NF physical chemistry

physicochimique [fizikoʃimik] ADJ physicochemical

physicomathématique [fizikomatematik]

NF mathematical physics
ADJ relating to mathematical physics

physiocrate [fizjɔkrat] **NM** *Écon, Hist* physiocrat

physiocratie [fizjɔkrasi] **NF** *Écon, Hist* physiocracy

physiologie [fizjɔlɔʒi] **NF** physiology

physiologique [fizjɔlɔʒik] **ADJ** physiological

physiologiquement [fizjɔlɔʒikmɑ̃] **ADV** physiologically

physiologiste [fizjɔlɔʒist] **N** physiologist

physionomie [fizjɔnɔmi] **NF 1** *(traits du visage)* facial appearance, features, *Litt, Hum* physiognomy; **il a une p. joviale** he has a jolly face; **il ne faut pas juger les gens sur leur p.** you shouldn't judge by appearances **2** *(aspect)* face; **la p. de l'Europe va changer** the face of Europe will change

physionomiste [fizjɔnɔmist] **ADJ je ne suis pas p.** I've no memory for faces; **elle est très p.** she has a very good memory for faces ▪ **N c'est un p.** he's got a good memory for faces

physiopathologie [fizjopatɔlɔʒi] **NF** *Méd* physiopathology

physiothérapie [fizjɔterapi] **NF** *Méd* natural medicine

physique [fizik] **ADJ** physical; **culture p.** physical training; *Scol* **éducation p.** physical education; **le monde p.** the physical *or* material world; *Fam* **je ne le supporte pas, c'est p.** I can't stand him, it's a physical thing ▪ **NF** *(science)* physics; *Scol Vieilli (livre)* physics (text)book; **p. nucléaire** nuclear physics; *Géog* **p. du globe** geophysics VOIR GRAMMAIRE A10 ▪ **NM** *(d'une personne)* physique; *(apparence)* external appearance; **avoir un p. avantageux** to have a fine physique; **soigner son p.** to take care of *or* look after oneself; **il a le p. de l'emploi** he looks the part; **le p. et le moral** the mind and the body; **au p.** physically

physiquement [fizikmɑ̃] **ADV** physically

phytobiologie [fitobjɔlɔʒi] **NF** phytology

phytogéographie [fitoʒeɔgrafi] **NF** phytogeography

phytoplancton [fitoplɑ̃ktɔ̃] **NM** phytoplankton

phytosanitaire [fitosaniter] **ADJ produits phytosanitaires** plant-care products

phytothérapie [fitoterapi] **NF** herbal medicine

pi [pi] **NM** *(lettre)*, *Math* pi

piaf [pjaf] **NM** *Fam* sparrow

piaffement [pjafmɑ̃] **NM** *(d'un cheval)* pawing (the ground)

piaffer [pjafe] **VI** *(d'un cheval)* to paw the ground; *Fig (trépigner)* to stamp one's feet; **p. d'impatience** to fidget impatiently

piaillard, -arde [pjɑjar, -ard] **ADJ, N** *Fam voir* piailleur

piaillement [pjɑjmɑ̃] **NM** *Fam (d'un oiseau)* cheeping; *Fig (d'un enfant)* squealing, squalling

piailler [pjɑje] **VI** *Fam (de petits oiseaux)* to cheep; *Fig (des enfants)* to squeal, to squall

piaillerie [pjɑjri] **NF** *Fam* = piaillement

piailleur, -euse [pjɑjœr, -øz] *Fam* **ADJ** *(oiseau)* cheeping; *(enfant)* squealing, squalling ▪ **N** cheeping bird; *Fig Péj (enfant)* squealer, squaller

piane-piane [pjanpjan] **ADV** *Fam* **allez-y p.** gently does it, go easy

pianiste [pjanist] **N** pianist; **un p. (de) jazz** a jazz pianist

piano¹ [pjano] **NM** *(instrument)* piano; **jouer ou faire du p.** to play the piano
▸▸ *Fam* **p. à bretelles** squeezebox; **p. de concert** concert grand; **p. crapaud** boudoir grand; **p. demi-queue** baby grand; **p. droit** upright piano; **p. mécanique** player piano; **p. quart de queue** miniature grand; **p. à queue** grand piano

piano² **ADV** *Mus* piano; *Fig Fam* **allez-y p.** gently does it, go easy; **allez-y p. avec lui** go easy with *or* on him; **vas-y p. avec le café** go easy with *or* on the coffee

piano-bar, *pl* **pianos-bars NM** piano bar

pianoforte [pjanoforte] **NM** *Mus Arch* fortepiano

pianotage [pjanotaʒ] **NM** *Fam (sur le piano)* tinkling (away); *(des doigts)* drumming

pianoter [pjanɔte] **VI** *Fam* **1** *(mal jouer du piano)* to tinkle away (on the piano) **2** *(tapoter)* to drum one's fingers; **ses doigts pianotent sur la nappe** he's drumming his fingers *or* his fingers are drumming on the tablecloth

piastre [pjastr] **NF** piastre; *Can Arg (dollar)* buck

piaule [pjol] **NF** *Fam (logement)* pad

piaulement [pjolmɑ̃] **NM** *(des poussins)* cheeping; *Fig Fam (des enfants)* whimpering, whining

piauler [pjole] **VI** *(des poussins)* to cheep; *Fig Fam (des enfants)* to whimper, to whine

PIB [peibe] **NM** *Écon (abrév produit intérieur brut)* GDP

PIBOR [pibɔr] **NM** *Bourse (abrév Paris interbank offered rate)* PIBOR; **P. trois mois** three-month PIBOR

pic¹ [pik] **NM 1** *(pioche)* pick, pickaxe, *Am* pickax; **p. pneumatique** pneumatic drill; **p. de mineur** miner's pick; **p. à glace** ice pick **2** *(sommet)* (mountain) peak; *(d'une courbe)* peak; **à p.** *(chute, falaise)* sheer; *(tomber)* straight down; **sentier à p.** steep path; **promontoire à p.** sheer headland, bluff; **couler à p.** to sink like a stone; *Fig Fam* **tomber à p.** to come at just the right moment

pic² **NM** *(oiseau)* woodpecker

pica [pika] **NM** *Typ* pica

picador [pikadɔr] **NM** picador

picaillons [pikajɔ̃] **NMPL** *Arg (argent)* dough, bread

picard, -arde [pikar, -ard] **ADJ** *(of/from)* Picardy; *Culin* **ficelle picarde** = ham and cheese pancake ▪ **NM** *Ling* Picardy dialect ▪ **N P.** *(natif)* native of Picardy; *(habitant)* inhabitant of Picardy

Picardie [pikardi] **NF** Picardy

picaresque [pikaresk] **ADJ** *(roman)* picaresque

piccolo [pikɔlo] **NM** *Mus* piccolo

pichenette [piʃnet] **NF** flick (of the finger), flip; *(avec le pied)* flick

pichet [piʃe] **NM** (small) jug, *Am* pitcher

pickles [pikœlz] **NMPL** pickles

pickpocket [pikpɔket] **NM** pickpocket

pick-up **NM INV 1** *(bras de lecture)* pick-up (arm); *Vieilli (électrophone)* record player **2** *(véhicule)* pick-up (truck)

picoler [pikɔle] **VI** *Fam* to booze, to knock it back; **qu'est-ce qu'il peut p.!** he's a real boozer!; **ici, ça picole dur** they're real boozers here!

picoleur, -euse [pikɔlœr, -øz] **N** *Fam* boozer

picolo [pikɔlo] **NM** *Mus* piccolo

picorer [pikɔre] **VI** *(d'un oiseau)* to pick *or* scratch about; *Fig (manger à peine)* to pick at one's food ▪ **VT** *(d'un oiseau)* to peck (at); *(par manque*

d'appétit) (nourriture) to pick at; *(grignoter)* to nibble; **on a eu des olives à p.** we had olives to nibble, that's all

picoseconde [pikos(ə)gɔ̃d] **NF** picosecond

picot [piko] **NM 1** *(pointe)* splinter (of wood) **2** *Tech (de roue d'entraînement)* pin **3** *Couture* picot **4** *Pêche* fishing net *(for flatfish)*

picotement [pikɔtmɑ̃] **NM** *(dans la gorge, le nez)* tickle, tickling; *(dans les yeux)* stinging, smarting; *(sur la peau)* prickling; **j'ai des picotements dans les yeux** my eyes are stinging *or* smarting; **j'ai des picotements dans le nez** my nose is tickling, I've got a tickle in my nose

picoter [pikɔte] **VT 1** *(faire de petits trous dans)* to prick tiny holes in **2** *(d'un oiseau)* to peck (at) **3** *(irriter) (quelque chose)* to produce a tingling sensation in; *(gorge)* to tickle; *(peau)* to prickle; **la fumée me picotait les yeux** the smoke made my eyes sting *or* smart; **j'ai les yeux qui (me) picotent** my eyes are stinging *or* smarting; **j'ai la gorge qui (me) picote** I've a tickle in my throat, my throat is tickling; **j'ai la peau qui (me) picote** my skin is prickling

picotin [pikɔtɛ̃] **NM** *Agr (d'avoine) (mesure)* peck; *(ration)* feed, ration

picrate [pikrat] **NM 1** *Arg (vin)* cheap red wine, *Br* plonk **2** *Chimie* picrate

Pictes [pikt] **NMPL** *Hist* Picts

pictogramme [piktɔgram] **NM** pictogram, pictograph

pictographe [piktɔgraf] **NM** pictogram, pictograph

pictographie [piktɔgrafi] **NF** pictography

pictographique [piktɔgrafik] **ADJ** *Ling* pictographic

pictural, -ale, -aux, -ales [piktyral, -o] **ADJ** pictorial

pic-vert, *pl* **pics-verts** [piver] **NM** green woodpecker

Pie [pi] **N** Pius

pie¹ [pi] **NF** magpie; *Fam (personne bavarde)* chatterbox; *Fam* **être bavard comme une p.** to be a real chatterbox; *Naut* **nid de p.** crow's nest
▪ **ADJ INV cheval/jument p.** piebald (horse/mare), *Am* pinto (horse/mare); **vache p.** black and white cow; *Vieilli* **voiture p.** patrol car, *Br* Panda car

pie² **ADJ œuvre p.** good deed, act of charity

PIÈCE [pjes]

> room **1** ▪ pièce **2, 5, 9, 11, 12** ▪ coin **3** ▪ play **4** ▪ part **7** ▪ patch **8** ▪ bit **9** ▪ document **10**

NF 1 *(salle, chambre)* room; **un appartement de trois pièces, un trois-pièces** a three-room(ed) flat *or Am* apartment; **un trois-pièces cuisine** a three-room(ed) flat with kitchen, *Am* a three and a half
2 *(élément)* piece; **p. de musée** museum piece; **p. de bétail/gibier** head of cattle/game; **p. de blé** wheatfield; **un service complet de trente-six pièces** a complete thirty-six-piece dinner service; **les pièces d'un uniforme** the items of a uniform; **costume deux-pièces/trois-pièces** two-piece/three-piece suit; **un (maillot de bain) une-p./deux-pièces** a one-piece/two-piece swimsuit; **ils coûtent dix euros (la) p.** they cost ten euros each *or* apiece; **ils se vendent à la p.** they are sold singly *or* separately; **travailler aux pièces** to do piece work; *Fam* **on n'est pas aux pièces** there's no hurry *or* rush
3 *Fin* coin; **p. de deux euros** two-euro piece; **donner la p. à qn** to give sb a tip, to tip sb; **je ne vous demanderai qu'une petite p.** *(d'un mendiant)* have you got any loose change you don't need?

4 *Théâtre* play; **monter une p.** to put on *or* stage a play; **p. radiophonique** radio play, radio drama

5 *Mus, Littér* piece; **une p. de Couperin/en vers** a piece by Couperin/of verse

6 tout d'une p. all in one piece; *Fig* **être tout d'une p.** to be straightforward and uncompromising; **une histoire inventée de toutes pièces** a completely made-up story, a complete fabrication; **ce qu'il raconte est forgé de toutes pièces** he's making the whole thing up; **mensonge fait de toutes pièces** out-and-out lie

7 *(d'une machine, d'une horloge etc)* part, component; **pièces de rechange, pièces détachées** replacement parts, spare parts, spares; **p. de charpente** beam; *(sous le plancher)* joist; *Tech* **p. en croix** crosspiece; *Tech* **p. en mouvement** moving part; *Tech* **p. matricée** pressing

8 *(raccord)* patch; **mettre** *ou* **poser une p. à un vêtement** to put a patch on *or* to patch a garment

9 *(morceau, débris)* piece, bit, fragment; **être en pièces** to be in pieces; *(de vêtements)* to be in tatters; **mettre en pièces** *(vase)* to smash to bits *or* to pieces; *(livre)* to pull *or* tear to pieces; *(vêtement)* to tear to pieces; **tailler l'ennemi en pièces** to cut the enemy to pieces; *Fig* **se faire tailler en pièces** to be torn to pieces

10 *Jur, Admin etc (document)* document, paper; **p. justificative** *Admin* written proof; *Jur* relevant document; *Com* voucher (copy); *Compta* **p. de caisse** cash voucher; **p. à l'appui** supporting document; **juger sur pièces** to judge on the evidence; **p. jointe** *(à une lettre)* enclosure; **p. à joindre** *(à une lettre)* enclosure

11 *(quantité déterminée)* **p. de bœuf** cut *or* piece of beef; **p. d'étoffe** length *or* piece of material

12 *Échecs* piece; *(aux dames)* draught(s-man), *Am* checker

13 *Mil* **p. (d'artillerie)** gun, *Spéc* piece of ordnance; **p. de campagne** field gun; **chef de p.** number one, squad leader, *Am* chief of (piece) section

▸▸ *Jur* **p. à conviction** exhibit *(in criminal case)*; **p. détachée** component; *(de rechange)* spare part; **p. d'eau** ornamental lake; *(plus petite)* water feature, ornamental pond; **p. d'identité** identity paper(s), proof of identity; **p. de monnaie** coin; *Culin* **p. montée** ornamental cake; **p. rapportée** insert; *Couture* patch; *Fig (dans une famille)* in-law; **p. de résistance** *Culin* pièce de résistance, main dish; *Fig* pièce de résistance; **p. de théâtre** play; **p. de vin** barrel *or* cask of wine

---

Pièce

Flats in France are referred to in terms of the total number of rooms they have (excluding the kitchen and bathroom). "Un deux-pièces" is a flat with a living room and one bedroom; "un cinq-pièces" is a flat with five rooms.

---

piécette [pjesɛt] **NF** small coin

PIED [pje] **NM 1** *(d'une personne)* foot; **p. bot/ plat** club/flat foot; **doigts de p.** toes; **sauter à pieds joints/sur un p.** to jump with (one's) feet together/hop (on one foot); **être/marcher pieds nus** to be/walk barefoot(ed), to be/walk in one's bare feet; **elle s'est mise pieds nus** she took off her shoes (and stockings); **il n'avait pas de chaussures aux pieds** he had no shoes on (his feet); **se jeter aux pieds de qn** to throw oneself at sb's feet; **avoir bon p. bon œil** to be hale and hearty; **se lever du p. gauche** to get out of bed on the

wrong side; **il ne peut pas mettre un p. devant l'autre** he can hardly put one foot in front of the other; **de la tête aux pieds, de p. en cap** [dəpjetɑ̃kap] from head to toe *or* foot, from top to toe; *Fig* **faire des pieds et des mains pour faire qch** to move heaven and earth to do sth; *Fam* **être bête comme ses pieds** to be unbelievably stupid, *Br* to be as thick as two short planks; *Fam* **faire du p. à qn** to play footsie with sb; *Fam* **ça lui fera les pieds!** that'll teach him a lesson!; *Fam* **c'est bien fait pour tes pieds!** it serves you right!; *Fam* **elle me casse les pieds** *(elle m'ennuie)* she bores the pants off me; *(elle m'agace)* she gets on my nerves *or* *Br* my wick; **ça fait deux mois qu'elle me casse les pieds pour que je t'en parle** she's been on at me for two months now to talk to you about it; **mettre p. à terre** [pjetaʀ] *(d'un cheval, d'un vélo)* to dismount; *(sans descendre de vélo)* to put one's foot down; *aussi Fig* **tomber sur ses pieds** to fall *or* land on one's feet; **je ne remettrai jamais les pieds chez lui** I'll never set foot in his house again; *Fam* **mettre les pieds dans le plat** to put one's foot in it; **attention où vous mettez les pieds!** mind where you're treading!, watch your step!; **avoir un p. dans la tombe** to have one foot in the grave; **marcher sur les pieds de qn** to tread on sb's toes; *Fig* **tu ne vas pas te laisser marcher sur les pieds par ton chef de service?** you're not going to let your head of department walk all over you *or* take advantage of you?; *Fam* **lever le p.** *(partir)* to run off, *Br* to scarper, to do a runner; *(en voiture)* to ease off; **faire qch au p. levé** to do sth at a moment's notice; **répondre au p. levé** to answer off the cuff; *Fig* **pieds et poings liés** bound hand and foot; **frapper du p.** to stamp (one's foot); **pousser qch du p.** to kick sth; **coup de p.** kick; **donner** *ou* **envoyer un coup de p. à qn** to kick sb, to give sb a kick; **il faut te donner un bon coup de p. (au derrière)** you need a good kick (up the backside); **recevoir un coup de p.** to be kicked, to get a kick; **chasser qn à coups de p.** to kick sb out; **enfoncer une porte à coups de p.** to kick a door in *or* down; **se prendre les pieds dans un tapis** to trip over a carpet; *Belg Fam* **jouer avec les pieds de qn** *(se moquer de)* to make fun of sb, *Br* to take the mick *or* the mickey out of sb; *(duper)* to take sb for a ride

2 à p. on foot; **aller à p.** to walk, to go on foot; **faire deux kilomètres à p.** to walk two kilometres; **vous en avez pour vingt minutes à p.** it will take you twenty minutes to walk (there) *or* twenty minutes on foot; **course à p.** (running) race; **mettre qn à p.** to suspend sb, *Can* to lay sb off

3 mettre une affaire sur p. to set up *or* start a business; **il est de nouveau sur p.** he's up and about again, he's getting about again; **portrait en p.** full-length portrait

4 *Fam* **jouer/chanter/conduire comme un p.** to be a lousy *or* terrible player/singer/driver; **je m'y suis pris comme un p. pour le réparer** I made a real mess of repairing it

5 *Fig* **elle a le p. marin** she's a good sailor, she never gets seasick; *aussi Fig* **perdre p.** to get out of one's depth; **prendre p.** *(sur un marché/un territoire)* to get a foothold (in a market/a territory); **lâcher p.** to give in, to give way; **faire un p. de nez à qn** to cock a snook at sb; **faire un p. de nez au destin** to thumb one's nose at fate

6 *Fam* **prendre son p.** to get one's kicks; *(sexuellement)* to come; **c'est le p.!** it's fantastic!, it's great!; **ce n'est pas (vraiment) le p.** it's not much fun

7 *Fig (rang)* **être sur un p. d'égalité avec qn** to be on an equal footing with sb; **vivre sur un grand p.** to live on a grand scale

8 *(patte) (de cheval)* hoof; *(à la chasse)*

(trace) footprint; *(piste)* track(s); *Culin* **p. de veau/mouton/porc** knuckle of veal/leg of mutton/pig's trotter

9 *(partie inférieure)* *(d'un bas, d'un arbre, d'un escalier, d'un lit)* foot; *(d'une colonne, d'un mur)* foot, base; *(d'une montagne)* foot, bottom; *Math (d'une perpendiculaire)* foot; *Typ (d'une lettre)* foot; *Typ* **p. de page** footer; **à p. d'œuvre** *Constr etc* on site; *Fig* ready to get on with the job

10 *(support)* *(d'une chaise, d'une table etc)* leg; *(de télescope)* stand, rest; *(d'un verre)* stem; *Phot* foot; **p. (à trois branches)** tripod; **p. de lampe** *ou* **de lampadaire** lampstand; *TV, Cin* **p. de sol** *(d'une caméra)* high-hat

11 *(tige)* stalk; *(de vigne)* stock; **p. de céleri/ d'asperges/de salade** head of celery/asparagus/lettuce

12 *Naut (du mât)* step, heel

13 *(mesure), Littér* foot; **p. carré/cube** square/cubic foot; **au petit p.** (in) miniature; **p. à p.** [pjeapje] inch by inch; **six pieds sous terre** six foot under; **p. à coulisse** calliper VOIR GRAMMAIRE A13

Pied noir

This is the name given to the French settlers who settled in North Africa (most notably in Algeria) during the period of French colonial expansion. Most of them resettled in France (mainly on the south coast) after the colonies regained their independence. The largest wave of these settlers to arrive in France was in 1962, following the Algerian war.

---

pied-à-terre [pjetatɛʀ] **NM INV** pied-à-terre

pied-bot, *pl* **pieds-bots NM** *(personne)* club-footed person; *(infirmité)* club foot

pied-d'alouette, *pl* **pieds-d'alouette NM** *Bot* larkspur, delphinium

pied-de-biche, *pl* **pieds-de-biche NM** *(poignée de sonnette)* bell pull; *(outil)* nail claw, nail extractor; *(d'une machine à coudre)* presser foot; *(d'une chaise, d'une table etc)* cabriole leg

pied-de-coq, *pl* **pieds-de-coq ADJ, NM** *Tex* hound's-tooth

pied-de-poule, *pl* **pieds-de-poule ADJ, NM** *Tex* hound's-tooth

pied-de-roi, *pl* **pieds-de-roi NM** *Can* folding rule

pied-droit, *pl* **pieds-droits NM** *Constr* *(d'une voûte, d'un pont)* pier

piédestal, -aux [pjedɛstal, -o] **NM** pedestal

pied-noir, *pl* **pieds-noirs** *Fam* **N** Algerian-born Frenchman, *f* Frenchwoman

ADJ French Algerian, Algerian French

piédouche [pjeduʃ] **NM** small pedestal

piédroit [pjedʀwa] **NM** = **pied-droit**

piège [pjɛʒ] **NM 1** *(pour les animaux)* trap, snare; **p. à souris** mousetrap; **p. à rats** rat trap; **dresser** *ou* **tendre un p.** to set a trap *(à* for); **prendre un animal au p.** to trap an animal, to catch an animal in a trap **2** *Fig (embuscade)* trap; **attirer l'ennemi dans un p.** to draw the enemy into a trap; **donner** *ou* **tomber dans un p.** to fall into a trap; **tendre un p. à qn** to set a trap for sb; **être pris à son propre p.** to be caught in one's own trap, *Prov* to be hoist by one's own petard; **dictée pleine de pièges** dictation full of pitfalls; *très Fam* **p. à cons** con, scam

piégeage [pjeʒaʒ] **NM** *(d'animaux)* trapping

piéger [pjeʒe] **VT** (**je piège, n. piégeons; je piégeai(s); je piégerai**) **1** *(attraper)* *Fig* to trap; **se laisser p.** to fall into a trap, to get trapped **2** *(munir de pièges) (cour, forêt)* to set a trap/traps in **3** *(placer un explosif dans)* to booby-trap; **voi-**

ture piégée car bomb, booby-trapped car; **colis piégé** parcel bomb; **lettre piégée** letter bomb

piégeur [pjeʒœr] NM trapper

pie-grièche, *pl* **pies-grièches** [pigrijɛʃ] NF *Orn* shrike

pie-mère, *pl* **pies-mères** NF *Anat* pia mater

Piémont [pjemɔ̃] NM Piedmont

piémontais, -aise [pjemɔ̃tɛ, -ɛz] ADJ Piedmontese
NM *Ling* Piedmont (dialect)
N P. Piedmontese

piercé [pirse] ADJ *Fam (partie du corps)* pierced

piercing [pirsiŋ] NM piercing

piéride [pjerid] NF pierid; **p. du chou** cabbage white (butterfly)

pierraille [pjɛraj] NF loose stones

Pierre [pjɛr] N **P. le Grand** Peter the Great

pierre [pjɛr] NF **1** *(matière, caillou, bloc rocheux)* stone; *(rocher)* rock, boulder; **pierres de gué** stepping stones; *Prov* **p. qui roule n'amasse pas mousse** a rolling stone gathers no moss; **attaquer qn à coups de pierres** to pelt sb with stones, to throw stones at sb; **on le fit partir à coups de pierres** they drove him away by throwing stones (at him); **jeter une p. à qn** to throw a stone at sb; *Fig* **jeter la p. à qn** to reproach sb; *Fig* **je ne serai pas le premier à lui jeter la p.** I will not be the one to throw the first stone; *Fig* **c'est une p. dans votre jardin** that's a dig at you; *Fig* **faire d'une p. deux coups** to kill two birds with one stone; *Fig* **être malheureux comme les pierres** to be bitterly unhappy; *Fig* **avoir un cœur de p.** to have a heart of stone; **mur de p.** stone wall; **mur en pierres sèches** drystone wall; **maison de** *ou* **en p.** stone(-built) house; **investir (son argent) dans la p.** to invest in bricks and mortar; **aimer les vieilles pierres** to like old buildings; **p. à p.** stone by stone; *Fig (progressivement)* bit by bit, little by little; **ils n'ont pas laissé p. sur p.** they didn't leave a stone standing; *Fig* **apporter sa p. à l'édifice** to make a contribution; **poser la première p.** to lay the foundation stone; *Fig* **to lay the foundation (de for);** *Hist* **âge de p.** Stone Age; **âge de la p. taillée/polie** Old/New Stone Age; **outils en p.** stone implements

2 *(en bijouterie)* stone; **p. précieuse** precious stone, gem; **p. fine** *ou* **semi-précieuse** semi-precious stone

3 *(concrétion)* piece of grit; **des fruits pleins de pierres** fruit full of grit

▸▸**p. d'achoppement** stumbling block; *Tech* **p. à aiguiser** whetstone, grindstone; *Constr, Fig* **p. angulaire** cornerstone; *Constr* **p. à bâtir** building stone; **p. à briquet** (lighter) flint; **p. à chaux** limestone; **p. à fusil** gun flint; **p. de lune** moonstone; **p. philosophale** philosopher's stone; **p. ponce** pumice (stone); **p. de taille** dressed stone; *Minér, Fig* **p. de touche** touchstone

pierreries [pjɛr(ə)ri] NFPL precious stones, jewels, gems

pierreux, -euse [pjɛrø, -øz] ADJ **1** *(couvert de pierres)* (sol, route etc) stony; *(lit de rivière)* gravelly **2** *(qui contient des concrétions)* *(poire)* gritty **3** *Méd (formation)* calculous

pierrot [pjero] NM **1** *Théâtre* **P.** Pierrot **2** *Fam (oiseau)* sparrow

pietà [pjeta] NF INV pietà

piétaille [pjetaj] NF *Mil Vieilli* rank and file, infantrymen; *Fig* rank and file; *(piétons)* pedestrians

piété [pjete] NF **1** *(ferveur religieuse)* piety; **articles de p.** devotional objects **2** *(affection)* **p. filiale** filial devotion

piétinement [pjetinmã] NM *(bruit)* stamp-

ing; *(marche sur place)* standing around; *Fig (stagnation)* lack of progress; **à cause du p. de l'enquête** because the enquiry is at a standstill *or* is marking time

piétiner [pjetine] VT **1 p. qch** *(en trépignant)* to stamp on sth; *(en marchant)* to trample on sth; *(écraser)* to trample sth underfoot; **ils sont morts piétinés par la foule** they were trampled to death by the crowd **2** *Fig (malmener) (les convictions de qn, les souhaits de qn, la mémoire de qn etc)* to have no respect for, to trample underfoot

VI *(frapper des pieds)* **p. d'impatience** to stamp (one's feet) impatiently *or* with impatience; **p. (sur place)** to stand around; *Fig* **l'instruction piétine** the investigation is marking time *or* is making no headway *or* is at a standstill; **je piétine depuis deux mois** I've been marking time for two months

piétisme [pjetism] NM *Hist, Rel* Pietism

piétiste [pjetist] ADJ, N *Hist, Rel* Pietist

piéton, -onne [pjetɔ̃, -ɔn] N pedestrian; **passage (pour) piétons** pedestrian crossing, *Br* ≃ zebra crossing, *Am* crosswalk
ADJ rue piétonne pedestrianized street; **zone piétonne** pedestrian precinct

piétonnier, -ière [pjetɔnje, -jɛr] ADJ pedestrian; **rue piétonnière** pedestrianized street; **zone piétonnière** pedestrian precinct

piètre [pjɛtr] ADJ *Litt (compagnon)* wretched, poor; *(excuse)* lame, paltry; **faire p. figure** to cut a poor *or* sorry figure; **p. consolation** cold *or* small comfort

piètrement [pjɛtrəmã] ADV wretchedly, poorly

pieu¹, pieux [pjø] NM **1** *(piquet)* stake, post; *Constr* pile; **enfoncer** *ou* **battre un p.** to drive (in) a pile; **p. creux** tubular pile; **p. de fondation** foundation pile **2** *Fam (lit)* bed; **se mettre au p., aller au p.** to hit the hay *or* the sack

pieusement [pjøzmã] ADV *(dévotement)* piously, devoutly; *(avec grand respect)* reverently

pieuter [pjøte] *Fam* VI *(passer la nuit)* to crash (out)
VPR se pieuter to hit the hay *or* the sack

pieuvre [pjœvr] NF *(animal)* octopus; *Fig Péj (personne)* leech; *Fig* **la p. bureaucratique** the tentacles of bureaucracy; **la p.** *(la Mafia)* the Mob

pieux, -euse [pjø, -øz] ADJ **1** *(religieux)* pious, devout; *Fig* **p. mensonge** white lie; **c'est un vœu p.** it's wishful thinking **2** *Litt (dévoué) (silence)* reverent; *(fils)* devoted

pif¹ [pif] INT bang!, smack!; **p., paf!** pow!; **p., paf, boum!** slap! bang! wallop!

pif² NM *Fam* **1** *(nez)* conk, *Br* hooter; **je l'ai dans le p.** I can't stand the sight of him, *Br* he gets right up my nose **2** *Fig* **faire qch au p.** to do sth by guesswork; **j'ai dit ça au p.** I was just guessing; **j'ai fait ça au p.** it was sheer guesswork, I made it up as I went along; **répondre à une question au p.** to guess at the answer to a question; **au p., je dirais qu'il y en a vingt** at a rough guess I'd say there are twenty; **au lieu d'y aller au p., tu ferais mieux de consulter un plan!** instead of just following your nose, you'd do better to consult a map!

pif(f)er [pife] VT *Fam* **je peux pas le p.** I can't stand (the sight of) him, I can't stomach him

pifomètre [pifɔmɛtr] NM *Fam* intuition; **en politique, il n'y a que le p. qui compte** in politics, having a nose for things *or* having intuition is all-important; **au p.** *voir* **pif² 2**

pige [piʒ] NF **1** *(mesure)* measuring rod; *Typ* take *(amount of copy to be set up in a given time)*; *Journ* freelance contribution; **être payé à la p.** to be paid by the line; **faire des piges,** *Can* **travailler à la p.** to work freelance **2** *Fam (année)* **il a 45 piges** he's 45; **à 60 piges**

at 60 **3** *Fam* **faire la p. à qn** to go one better than sb

pigeon [piʒɔ̃] NM **1** *(oiseau)* pigeon; **p. mâle/femelle** cock/hen pigeon; **p. voyageur** carrier pigeon, homing pigeon; **p. colombin** *ou* **bleu** stock dove; **p. ramier** ring dove, wood pigeon; **p. paon** fantail (pigeon); **p. d'argile** clay pigeon; **tir aux pigeons d'argile** *(sport)* clay-pigeon shooting; *(événement)* clay-pigeon shoot; **p. vole** = children's game consisting of giving a yes or no answer to the question 'does X fly?' **2** *Fam Péj (dupe)* sucker, mug, *Am* fall guy **3** *Constr* builder's plaster; *(morceau de pierre dans la chaux)* hard lump

pigeonnant [piʒɔnã] ADJ *Fam* **poitrine pigeonnante** high bust; **soutien-gorge p.** uplift bra

pigeonne [piʒɔn] NF hen pigeon

pigeonneau, -eaux [piʒɔno] NM young pigeon, *Spéc* squab

pigeonner [piʒɔne] VT *Fam* **p. qn** to take sb in; **je me suis laissé** *ou* **fait p.** I've been had, I've been taken for a ride *or* taken in

pigeonnier [piʒɔnje] NM **1** dovecot(e) **2** *Fig Fam (logement très petit)* garret, attic

piger [piʒe] (**je pigeai(s); n. pigeons**) VT *Fam (comprendre)* to get; **tu piges la combine?** do you get what they're/we're/etc up to?; **je ne pige rien aux mathématiques** I haven't got a clue about mathematics; **je n'ai rien pigé à ce qu'il a raconté** I didn't get any of what he was on about, I didn't have a clue what he was on about
VI tu piges? get it?; **il a pigé** he's got it, *Br* he's twigged, the penny's dropped; **il ne pige pas** *(chaque fois)* he doesn't get it; *(cette fois-ci)* he hasn't got it

pigiste [piʒist] N **1** *(journaliste)* freelance journalist, freelancer; **travailler comme p.** to freelance, to work as a freelancer **2** *Can (free-lance)* freelancer

pigment [pigmã] NM pigment

pigmentaire [pigmãtɛr] ADJ pigmentary

pigmentation [pigmãtasjɔ̃] NF pigmentation

pigmenter [pigmãte] VT to pigment

pigne [piɲ] NF pine cone; *(graine)* pine nut *or* kernel

pignocher [piɲɔʃe] VI *Vieilli* to pick at one's food

pignon¹ [piɲɔ̃] NM *Constr* gable; **avoir p. sur rue** to have premises in a desirable location; *Fig* to be of some standing

pignon² NM *Tech* gear(wheel); *(la plus petite de deux roues)* pinion; **p. de chaîne** sprocket wheel, chain sprocket; **grand p.** *(d'une bicyclette)* front chain wheel; *Tech* **p. conique** bevel gear; **p. d'attaque** *(de différentiel)* driving pinion; **p. de distribution** timing gear; **p. fou** idler; **p. planétaire** planet gear, planet wheel; **p. satellite** (intermediate) planet gear, = gearing between sun gear and planet gear

pignon³ NM *Bot* pine nut *or* kernel

pignoratif, -ive [piɲɔratif, -iv] ADJ *Fin* with a repurchase option

pignouf [piɲuf] NM *Fam* slob, *Br* yob(bo)

pilaf [pilaf] NM *Culin* pilaf, pilau; **riz p.** pilau rice

pilage [pilaʒ] NM pounding, crushing, grinding

pilaire [pilɛr] ADJ of the hair

pilastre [pilastr] NM *Archit* pilaster; *(au bout d'une rampe)* newel

Pilate [pilat] N *Hist* **Ponce P.** Pontius Pilate

pilchard [pilʃar] NM pilchard

pile¹ [pil] NF **1** *(tas)* pile, stack; **mettre en p.** to stack (up), to pile (up) **2** *(pilier) (d'un pont)* pier **3** *Élec* battery, *Spéc* cell; **p. sèche** dry cell; **p. plate/ronde** square/round battery; **p. bouton** *(pour montre/appareil photo/calculatrice)* watch/camera/calculator battery; **la radio marche aussi avec des piles** the radio also works on *or* off batteries **4** *Nucl Vieilli* **p. atomique** atomic pile, nuclear reactor

pile² NF *Fam* **1** *(volée de coups)* belting, beating, thrashing; **flanquer** *ou* **donner une p. à qn** to give sb a thrashing *or* belting *or* beating **2** *(défaite)* hammering; **recevoir** *ou* **prendre une p.** to take *or* get a hammering, to get hammered; **flanquer une p. à une équipe** to hammer a team, to walk all over a team

pile³ NF *(d'une pièce)* reverse; **p. ou face?** heads or tails?; **jouer** *ou* **tirer à p. ou face** to toss for it; **on tira à p. ou face qui irait chercher de l'eau** we tossed (up) *or* tossed a coin to decide who was going to get some water
ADJ **côté p.** *(d'une pièce)* reverse side
ADV *Fam* **s'arrêter p.** to stop dead, to come to a dead stop; **vous tombez p.** you've come just at the right moment; **ça tombait p.** that's just what was wanted *or* just what the doctor ordered, that came just at the right time; **tu seras p. à l'heure** you'll be (there) right on time, you'll be (there) on the dot; **à six heures p.** at six on the dot, bang on six; **ma montre est p. à l'heure** my watch is dead on *or* bang on; **elle est arrivée p. le même jour que moi** she arrived on exactly the same day as I did; **nous étions p. dix à table** there were exactly ten of us at the table

pile-poil INT *Fam* wicked!, great!

piler [pile] VT **1** *(broyer)* to pound, to crush, to grind; *(amandes)* to grind **2** *Fam (battre)* to thrash, to hammer; **notre équipe s'est fait p.** our team got a good thrashing *or* hammering
VI *Fam* to slam on the brakes

pilet [pilɛ] NM **(canard) p.** pintail (duck)

pileux, -euse [pilø, -øz] ADJ *Anat* hair, *Spéc* pilose; **follicule p.** hair follicle; **système p.** hair

pilier [pilje] NM **1** *(colonne)* pillar, column; *(poteau, pieu)* post **2** *Rugby* prop (forward) **3** *Fig (soutien)* **ce point est le p. de notre théorie** that point is the mainstay of our theory, our theory rests on that point; **p. de l'Église/de la démocratie** *(personne, journal)* bastion *or* pillar of the Church/of democracy; *Fam Péj* **c'est un p. de bar** *ou* **de bistrot** he's always propping up the bar

pili-pili [pilipili] NM INV bird-pepper

pillage [pijaʒ] NM **1** *(ravage)* pillaging, looting, plundering; **mettre une ville au p.** to sack a town **2** *Fig (d'œuvre)* plagiarism

pillard, -arde [pijar, -ard] ADJ pillaging, looting
N pillager, plunderer; *(lors d'une émeute)* looter

piller [pije] VT **1** *(dévaster, ravager) (village)* to pillage, to plunder; *(magasin)* to loot; *(Rome etc)* to sack; *(maison, pièce)* to ransack **2** *Fig (livre, film)* to plagiarize; **p. un auteur** to plagiarize an author, to steal from an author; **p. les idées de qn** to steal sb's ideas

pilleur, -euse [pijœr, -øz] ADJ pillaging, plundering, looting
N pillager, plunderer; *(lors d'une émeute)* looter; **c'est un p. d'idées** he's always stealing ideas from people; *Naut* **p. d'épaves** plunderer of wrecks

pilon [pilɔ̃] NM **1** *Pharm etc* pestle; *Tech* (earth) rammer; **p. mécanique** power hammer; *Fig* **mettre un livre au p.** to pulp a book; **tous ces livres iront au p.** all these books will be pulped **2** *(cuisse de poulet)* drumstick **3** *(jambe de bois)* wooden leg

pilonnage [pilɔnaʒ] NM *(de produits phar-*

maceutiques etc) pounding; *(de terre, béton etc)* ramming; *Mil* bombardment, shelling

pilonner [pilɔne] VT **1** *(écraser) (produits pharmaceutiques etc)* to pound; *(papier)* to pulp; *(terre, béton etc)* to ram **2** *Mil* to bombard, to shell

pilori [pilɔri] NM pillory; *aussi Fig* **clouer** *ou* **mettre qn au p.** to pillory sb

pilosébacé [pilosebase] ADJ *Anat* pilosebaceous

pilosité [pilozite] NF *Anat* hairiness, *Spéc* pilosity; **p. normale/excessive** normal/excessive hair growth; **p. faciale** facial hair

pilot [pilo] NM **1** *Constr* pile; **p. de pont** bridge pile **2** *Tech (chiffons)* = cloth used in paper-making

pilotage [pilɔtaʒ] NM **1** *Naut* piloting; **(droits** *ou* **frais de) p.** pilotage (dues) **2** *Aviat* piloting, flying; **le p. d'un jumbo-jet ne s'apprend pas en un mois** you can't learn to fly a jumbo jet in the space of a month; **poste de p.** cockpit; *(dans un avion plus important)* flight deck; **p. automatique** automatic piloting; **école de p.** flying school **3** *Ordinat* control

pilote [pilɔt] NM **1** *Aviat, Naut* pilot; *(conducteur) (de voiture de course)* driver; *(de moto de course)* rider; *Aviat* **p. d'essai** test pilot; *Aviat* **p. de ligne** airline pilot; **p. breveté** *Aviat* licensed pilot; *Mil, Aviat* certified pilot; **p. automatique** automatic pilot, autopilot, *Br Fam* George; *Fig* **je vais lui servir de p.** I'll show him/her round, I'll act as his/her guide **2** *(poisson)* pilot fish **3** *Ordinat* driver; **p. d'affichage** display driver; **p. d'imprimante** printer driver; **p. de logiciel** software driver; **p. de périphérique** device driver; **p. de mise en attente des fichiers à imprimer** printer spooler **4** *TV* pilot
ADJ pilot; **étude p.** pilot study; **usine/installation p.** pilot factory/plant; **université p.** experimental university; **bateau(-)p.** pilot boat

piloter [pilɔte] VT **1** *(navire)* to pilot; *(avion)* to pilot, to fly; *(conduire) (voiture de course)* to drive; *(moto de course)* to ride; *Fig (projet)* to be in charge of; *Fig* **p. qn dans Londres** to guide *or* show sb round London **2** *Ordinat* to drive; **piloté par menu** menu-driven

pilotis [pilɔti] NM *Constr* piling, piles; **bâti sur p.** built on piles

pilou [pilu] NM *Tex* flannelette, cotton flannel

pils [pils] NF *Belg (bière blonde)* lager

pilulaire [pilylɛr] ADJ *Pharm* pilular

pilule [pilyl] NF *Pharm* pill, tablet; **la p. (contraceptive** *ou* **anticonceptionnelle)** the (contraceptive) pill; **prendre la p.** to be on the pill; **p. abortive** abortion pill; **p. du lendemain** morning-after pill; *Fig* **avaler la p.** to grin and bear it; *Fig* **vous aurez du mal à leur faire avaler la p.** you'll have a hard time getting them to accept that; *Fig* **la p. était amère** it was a bitter pill to swallow; *Fig* **dorer la p. (à qn)** to sugar the pill (for sb); *Fig très Fam* **on va prendre la p.** *ou* **une de ces pilules!** we'll get a hammering!, we'll get hammered!

pimbêche [pɛ̃bɛʃ] NF stuck-up girl/woman
ADJ stuck-up

piment [pimɑ̃] NM *Bot* pimento, capsicum; *Fig (piquant)* spice, piquancy; *Culin* **p. rouge** chilli; **p. doux** pepper, *Am* bell pepper, capsicum; **une histoire/vie qui ne manque pas de p.** a story/life that is anything but dull; **donner du p. à une histoire/une soirée** to add spice to a story/a party

pimenté [pimɑ̃te] ADJ *Culin* spicy, highly spiced, hot; *Fig (histoire)* spicy

pimenter [pimɑ̃te] VT *Culin* to spice up; *Fig (relever) (histoire)* to spice up, to add spice to

pimpant [pɛ̃pɑ̃] ADJ *(personne)* smart, spruce, trim

pimprenelle [pɛ̃prɔnɛl] NF *Bot* burnet

pin [pɛ̃] NM **1** *(arbre)* pine (tree); **p. maritime** maritime pine; **p. d'Écosse** *ou* **sylvestre** Scots pine; **p. pignon** *ou* **parasol** umbrella pine; **p. de montagne** silver pine, white pine; **p. de Virginie** scrub pine; **pomme de p.** pine cone; *(de sapin)* fir cone **2** *(bois)* pine(wood)

pinacle [pinakl] NM pinnacle; *Fig* **porter qn au p.** to praise sb to the skies; **être au p.** to be at the top

pinacothèque [pinakɔtɛk] NF picture gallery, art gallery

pinaillage [pinajaʒ] NM *Fam* quibbling, hair-splitting, nitpicking

pinailler [pinaje] VI *Fam* to quibble, to split hairs, to nitpick; **p. sur qch** to quibble over sth

pinailleur, -euse [pinajœr, -øz] *Fam* ADJ nitpicking
N quibbler, nitpicker

pinard [pinar] NM *Fam* vino, wine; *(de qualité inférieure)* cheap wine, *Br* plonk

pinasse [pinas] NF *Naut* pinnace, shallop

pinçage [pɛ̃saʒ] NM *(de bourgeons)* pinching off, nipping off

pince [pɛ̃s] NF **1** *(outil)* pliers; *(aux mâchoires recourbées)* pincers; *(de forgeron)* tongs; *Chir* forceps VOIR GRAMMAIRE A10 **2** *(patte) (de crabe etc)* pincer, claw **3** *Fam (main)* paw, mitt; **serrer la p. à qn** to shake hands with sb **4** *(d'un animal herbivore)* incisor **5** *(du sabot d'un cheval)* toe, point; *Fam* **aller à pinces** *(à pied)* to hoof it; *Fam* **il est parti à pinces** he left on foot **6** *Couture* dart
▸ ▸ **p. alligator** alligator clip; **p. à becs fins** needle-nosed pliers; **p. à becs pointus** pointed-nose pliers; **p. à circlip** circlip pliers; **pince(s) coupante(s)** cutting pliers, wire cutters; **pince(s) coupante(s) d'électricien** electrician's side cutters; **p. de cravate** tie clip; **p. crocodile** crocodile clip; **p. à épiler** tweezers; *Élec* **p. pour fil terminal** terminal clamp; *Chir* **p. hémostatique** artery clip; **p. à linge** clothes peg; **p. multiprise** combination pliers; **p. à ongles** nail clippers; *TV, Cin* **p. pour projecteur** gaffer grip; *Élec* **p. de raccordement** connecting clamp, connector; **p. à sucre** sugar tongs; **p. universelle** (universal) pliers, combination pliers; **p. à vélo** bicycle clip

pincé [pɛ̃se] ADJ *(air)* stiff, starchy; **sourire p.** tight-lipped smile; **répondre d'un ton p.** to answer stiffly *or* starchily; **nez p.** thin nose; **les lèvres pincées** with pursed lips *or* lips pursed, tight-lipped; **instrument à cordes pincées** plucked stringed instrument

pinceau, -eaux [pɛ̃so] NM **1** *(brosse)* (paint)brush; **p. en poils de martre** sable brush; **coup de p.** brush stroke; **on reconnaît facilement le coup de p. de l'artiste** the artist's brushwork is easily recognizable; **elle a un bon coup de p.** she paints well **2** *Fig (technique, manière)* brushwork **3** *Fam (pied)* foot; **s'emmêler les pinceaux** *(trébucher)* to trip up, to stumble; *(s'embrouiller)* to tie oneself in knots **4** *Opt* **p. de lumière** pencil of light

pincée [pɛ̃se] NF *(de sel, de tabac à priser etc)* pinch

pince-fesses NM INV *Fam Vieilli* knees-up, shindig, bash

pincement [pɛ̃smɑ̃] NM **1** *(fait de pincer)* pinching, nipping **2** *Fig (sensation vive, douloureuse) (de regret etc)* pang, twinge; **il a eu un p. au cœur** his heart missed a beat **3** *Mus (des cordes de guitare etc)* plucking **4** *(des bourgeons)* pinching off, nipping off

pince-monseigneur, *pl* **pinces-monsei-**

gneur NF jemmy, *Am* jimmy; **forcer une porte à la p.** to jemmy *or Am* jimmy a door

pince-nez NM INV pince-nez

pincer [pɛ̃se] (**je pinçai(s); n. pinçons**) VT **1** (*serrer*) to pinch, to nip; **son grand-père lui pinça la joue** his grandfather pinched his cheek; **p. les lèvres** to purse one's lips; **non mais pince-moi, je rêve!** pinch me, I'm dreaming!; *Fam* **ça pince dur ce matin!** it's pretty nippy this morning! **2** (*bourgeons*) to pinch off, to nip off; (*plante*) to top **3** *Mus* (*cordes de harpe etc*) to pluck **4** *Couture* (*vêtement*) to put darts in **5** *Fam* (*attraper*) (*personne*) to catch; **se faire p.** to be *or* get caught, to cop it; *Fam* **en p. pour qn** to be crazy about sb, to be gone on sb

▪ VPR **se pincer se p. le doigt dans la porte** to catch one's finger in the door; **fais attention, tu vas te p.** watch out, you'll catch yourself; **se p. le nez** to hold one's nose

pince-sans-rire N INV person with a dry sense of humour

▪ ADJ INV dry, deadpan; **répondre d'un air p.** to answer drily *or* deadpan

pincette [pɛ̃set] NF **1** (*petite pince*) tweezers; **pincettes** (*fire*) tongs, pair of (fire) tongs; *Fig Fam* **il n'est pas à prendre avec des pincettes** (*il est sale*) he's absolutely filthy; (*il est de très mauvaise humeur*) he's like a bear with a sore head VOIR GRAMMAIRE A10 **2** *Suisse* (*pince à linge*) clothes peg

pinçon [pɛ̃sɔ̃] NM pinch mark

pindarique [pɛ̃daʁik] ADJ *Littér* Pindaric

pine [pin] NF *Vulg* dick, prick, cock

pinéal, -ale, -aux, -ales [pineal, -o] ADJ *Anat* pineal

Pineau [pino] NM Pineau (*apéritif made from unfermented grape juice and brandy*)

pinède [pinɛd], **pineraie** [pinʁɛ] NF pine forest *or* wood

pinglot [pɛ̃glo] NM *Fam* foot, *Br* plate, *Am* dog

pingouin [pɛ̃gwɛ̃] NM penguin; (*de la famille des macareux*) auk; **p. royal** king penguin

ping-pong [piŋpɔ̃g] NM ping-pong, table tennis

pingre [pɛ̃gʁ] *Péj* ADJ stingy, niggardly, miserly

▪ N miser, skinflint, *Am* tightwad

pingrerie [pɛ̃gʁəʁi] NF *Péj* stinginess, niggardliness, miserliness

pinot [pino] NM Pinot grape

pin's [pinz] NM INV lapel badge *or* pin

pinson [pɛ̃sɔ̃] NM chaffinch; **être gai comme un p.** to be as happy as a lark

pintade [pɛ̃tad] NF guinea fowl; **p. mâle** guinea cock; **p. femelle** guinea hen

pintadeau, -eaux [pɛ̃tado] NM young guinea fowl, guinea poult

pinte [pɛ̃t] NF **1** *Arch* (*mesure*) pint (*0.93 litres*); *Br, Am* pint; *Can* quart **2** *Fam Vieilli* **se payer une p. de bon sang** to have a good time *or* a good laugh **3** *Suisse* café-bar **4** *Can* **se faire une p. de mauvais sang** to worry oneself sick

pinter [pɛ̃te] *très Fam* VI to booze

▪ VPR **se pinter** to booze; (*s'enivrer*) to get sozzled *or* plastered; **il s'est pinté (la gueule)** he got plastered, *Am* he tied one on

pinteur, -euse [pɛ̃tœr, -øz] N *Belg, Suisse Fam* (*alcoolique*) boozer, alky

pin up [pinœp] NF INV (*photo*) pin-up; (*jolie fille*) sexy-looking girl

pinyin [pinjin] NM *Ling* Pinyin

pioche [pjɔʃ] NF **1** (*outil*) pick, pickaxe, *Am* pickax; *Agr* mattock; *Fig Fam* **tête de p.** pigheaded person **2** (*aux dominos*) stock, pile

piocher [pjɔʃe] VT **1** (*creuser*) to dig (with a pick) **2** *Scol Fam* **p. son allemand** to swot up *or* mug up one's German

▪ VI **1** (*fouiller*) to dig, to delve (**dans** into) **2** (*aux dominos*) to draw from the stock

piocheur, -euse [pjɔʃœr, -øz] *Fam* ▪ ADJ hardworking

▪ N *Scol Vieilli* slogger, *Péj* swot, *Am* grind

piolet [pjɔlɛ] NM **1** ice axe, *Am* ice ax **2** *Suisse* (*bâton de ski*) ski stick, ski pole

pion, -onne [pjɔ̃, -ɔn] N *Scol Fam* supervisor (*paid to supervise pupils outside class hours*)

▪ NM **1** *Échecs* pawn; (*aux dames*) draught(s-man), *Am* checker; (*dans d'autres jeux*) piece; *Fig* **n'être qu'un p. (sur l'échiquier)** to be only a pawn in the game **2** *Tech* peg

> ### Pion
> In French lycées, the "pions" (officially called "surveillants") are responsible for supervising pupils outside class hours; they are often university students who do the job to make a little extra money.

pioncer [pjɔ̃se] VI (**je pionçai(s); n. pionçons**) *Fam* to sleep, *Br* to kip

pionnier, -ière [pjɔnje, -jɛr] N *aussi Fig* pioneer

▪ ADJ pioneering; **son esprit p.** his pioneering spirit

pipe¹ [pip] NF **1** (*de fumeur*) pipe; **p. de bruyère/en terre** briar/clay pipe; **fumer la p.** to smoke a pipe; *Fig Fam* **casser sa p.** to kick the bucket; **nom d'une p.!** heavens above!; *Fam* **20 euros par tête de p.** 20 euros a head; *Fam* **se fendre la p.** (*rire*) to split one's sides (laughing); (*s'amuser*) to have a good laugh; *Vulg* **faire *ou* tailler une p. à qn** to give sb a blow job **2** (*contenu*) pipe(ful) **3** *Arg Vieilli* (*cigarette*) ciggy, *Br* fag **4** *Région* (*futaille*) (*large*) cask, barrel

pipe² [pajp] NM (*tuyau*) pipe(line) (*for liquid, gas*)

pipeau, -eaux [pipo] NM *Mus* (reed) pipe; **p. de chasse** bird call; **pipeaux** (*pour prendre les oiseaux*) limed twigs; *Fam* **c'est du p.** it's all claptrap

pipée [pipe] NF bird snaring, bird catching (*with bird calls and limed twigs*)

pipelet, -ette [piplɛ, -ɛt] *Fam* ▪ N *Vieilli* concierge, porter, *Am* janitor

▪ NF **pipelette** (*personne bavarde*) gossip, chatterbox

pipe(-)line, *pl* **pipe(-)lines** [piplin, pajplajn] NM pipeline

piper [pipe] VT **1** (*attraper avec des appeaux*) (*oiseaux*) to lure by means of bird calls **2** (*truquer*) (*dés*) to load; (*cartes*) to mark; *Fig* **les dés sont pipés** the dice are loaded **3** *Fam* **ne pas p. (mot)** not to say a word, to keep silent, to keep mum

piperade [pip(ə)rad], **pipérade** [piperad] NF *Culin* piperade, = rich stew of tomatoes and sweet peppers, mixed with beaten eggs and slightly scrambled

pipette [pipɛt] NF pipette; *Suisse* **ça ne vaut pas p.** (*ça ne vaut rien*) it's not worth a bean *or Am* a red cent

pipi [pipi] NM *Fam* pee, *Enf* wee(-wee); **faire p.** to pee, *Enf* to wee(-wee), to have a wee(-wee); **aller faire p.** to go to the loo *or Am* john, to go for a pee; **faire p. au lit** to wet the bed; **le chien a fait p. sur le tapis** the dog's made a puddle on the carpet; *Fam Péj* **c'est du p. de chat** (*boisson*) it's dishwater; (*argument, discours etc*) it's tripe

pipi-room, *pl* **pipi-rooms** [pipirum] NM *Fam* loo, *Am* rest room; **où sont les pipi-rooms?** where's the loo?

pipistrelle [pipistrɛl] NF *Zool* pipistrelle

piquage [pika3] NM *Couture* (machine) stitching; (*d'une surface métallique*) pitting

piquant [pikɑ̃] ADJ **1** (*pointu*) (*objet*) pointed; (*plante*) prickly, thorny; (*ortie*) stinging; (*barbe*) bristly, prickly; (*sensation*) prickling **2** (*vent*) biting **3** (*goût*) spicy, hot, piquant; (*moutarde, radis*) hot **4** *Fig* (*caustique*) (*remarques etc*) cutting, caustic **5** *Fig* (*qui stimule la curiosité, l'intérêt*) (*beauté*) piquant, striking; **une petite brune piquante** a striking little brunette

▪ NM **1** (*épine*) (*d'une plante*) prickle, thorn; (*d'un porc-épic*) quill, spine; (*d'un hérisson*) bristle; (*de fil de fer barbelé*) spike, barb **2** *Fam* (*agrément*) (*d'un style, d'une situation*) piquancy; (*d'une histoire*) spice; **cette fille a du p.** that girl is rather striking *or* is strikingly attractive; **le changement donne du p. à la vie** variety is the spice of life; **c'est ce qui fait tout le p. de la situation** it's what makes the situation so piquant

pique¹ [pik] NF (*arme*) pike; (*d'un picador*) lance

▪ NM *Cartes* (*carte*) spade; (*couleur*) spades; **valet de p.** jack of spades; **jouer (un) p.** to play spades *or* a spade; **il me reste encore trois piques** I still have three spades left (in my hand)

pique² NF **1** (*méchanceté*) taunt, spiteful remark, *Fam* dig; **envoyer *ou* lancer des piques à qn** to get at sb, *Fam* to have a dig *or* a go at sb **2** *Vieilli* (*brouille*) tiff

piqué, -ée [pike] ADJ **1** (*dessus-de-lit, vêtement*) quilted; **p. à la machine** machine-stitched; (*matelassé*) machine-quilted **2** (*marqué par les vers*) (*bois, livre*) worm-eaten; (*marqué par l'humidité*) (*miroir*) tarnished; (*page, gravure*) foxed; (*métal*) pitted; *Fig* **ciel p. d'étoiles** sky studded with stars; *Fam* **une histoire/recette qui n'est pas piquée des hannetons *ou* des vers** one heck of a story/recipe **3** *Fam* (*fou*) crazy, mad **4** (*acide*) (*vin*) sour, tart **5** *Mus* (*notes*) staccato

▪ NM **1** *Aviat* **descente en p.** vertical dive, nose dive; **bombardement en p.** dive bombing **2** *Tex* piqué

▪ N *Fam* (*fou, folle*) nutter, loony

pique-assiette, *pl* **pique-assiettes** N *Fam* scrounger, sponger, freeloader

pique-bœuf, *pl* **pique-bœufs** NM *Orn* oxpecker

pique-feu NM INV poker

pique-fleurs NM INV flower holder, frog

pique-nique, *pl* **pique-niques** NM picnic; **faire un p.** to have a picnic

pique-niquer VI to have a picnic, to picnic

pique-niqueur, -euse, *pl* **pique-niqueurs, -euses** [piknikœr, -øz] N picnicker

pique-notes NM INV spike

piquer [pike] VT **1** (*percer avec une pointe*) to prick; (*d'une guêpe, d'un moustique etc*) to sting; (*d'une puce*) to bite; (*aiguillonner*) (*cheval*) to spur on; (*bœuf*) to goad; *Fam* **quelle mouche vous a piqué?** what's eating *or* biting you?, what's got into you?, who rattled your cage?; **se faire p. par un insecte** to be bitten by an insect; **p. un cheval de l'éperon** to prick *or* spur a horse; **la fumée me pique les yeux** the smoke makes my eyes sting *or* smart; **ça me pique la gorge/le nez** it tickles my throat/nose

2 *Méd* **p. qn** to give sb an injection *or Br Fam* a jab; *Fam* **se faire p. contre qch** to be vaccinated against sth; *Fam* **p. un chien** to put a dog down, to put a dog to sleep; *Fam* **faire p. un chien** to have a dog put down *or* put to sleep

3 (*offenser, froisser*) to offend, to pique; **p. qn au vif** to cut sb to the quick

4 *(exciter)* **p. l'attention de qn** to arouse sb's attention; **p. la curiosité de qn** to arouse *or* excite sb's curiosity

5 *(trouer)* *(d'acide, de vers)* to eat into; *(tacheter)* to spot, to mark; **mains piquées de taches de rousseur** freckled *or* freckly hands

6 *(coudre)* to (back)stitch; *(dessus-de-lit etc)* to quilt; **p. (à la machine)** to machine (stitch); **p. du cuir** to stitch leather

7 *Culin* **p. de la viande** to lard meat; **rôti piqué d'ail** joint stuck with garlic

8 *Mus* **p. une note** to play a note staccato; *Naut* **p. l'heure** to strike the hour

9 *Fam (voler)* to pinch, to swipe (**qch à qn** sth from sb); **ils m'ont piqué ma voiture** they pinched *or* swiped my car; **je me suis fait p. mon stylo** my pen got pinched *or* swiped

10 *(enfoncer)* to stick (**dans** into)

11 *Fam* **p. un cent mètres** to sprint off; **p. une tête** to take a header, to dive; **p. un roupillon** to have forty winks *or* a nap *or* a snooze; **p. une crise** *ou* **une colère** to throw a fit; **p. une crise de nerfs** to have hysterics; **p. un soleil** *ou* **un fard** to go bright red, to blush

VI 1 *Aviat* **p. (du nez)** to nosedive; *Fig* **p. du nez** to nod off, to doze off; *(baisser les yeux)* to look down; *Naut* **p. de l'avant** to go down by the bows

2 *(picoter)* *(de plat)* to be hot *or* spicy; *(de vin)* to be sour *or* tart; **moutarde qui pique** hot mustard; *Fam* **eau qui pique** fizzy water; **vent qui pique** keen *or* biting wind; **ça pique** it stings; **tu piques!** *(à un homme mal rasé)* you're all bristly!

3 *(d'une abeille, d'un moustique, d'une plante)* to sting; *(d'une puce)* to bite

4 **p. des deux** to spur on one's horse; *(s'en aller à cheval)* to gallop off; *Fig* to rush *or* dash off

VPR se piquer 1 *(se blesser)* to prick oneself; **il s'est piqué le doigt en cousant un bouton** he pricked his finger sewing on a button

2 *(se faire une piqûre)* *(de malade, drogué)* to give oneself an injection, to inject oneself; **il se pique** he shoots up

3 *(se froisser)* to take offence *or Am* offense

4 se p. de faire qch to pride oneself on doing sth; **se p. de littérature** to pride oneself on one's knowledge of literature; **se p. au jeu** to get into it **5** *(se couvrir de taches)* *(de miroir)* to tarnish; *(de métaux)* to pit; *(du bois)* to become wormeaten, to get woodworm; *(des vêtements etc)* to become motheaten, *(de livres)* to become foxed; *(devenir acide)* *(du vin)* to turn acid, to (turn) sour

piquet[1] [pikɛ] **NM 1** *(pieu)* stake, post; *(plus petit)* peg; **mettre** *ou* **attacher les chevaux au p.** to tether the horses; **droit/raide comme un p.** as straight as a ramrod/stiff as a poker; **rester planté comme un p.** to stand there doing nothing, *Br Fam* to stand there like a lemon **2** *Scol* **mettre** *ou* **envoyer qn au p.** to send sb to stand in the corner; **être au p.** to stand in the corner

▸▸ *Ind* **p. de grève** strike picket, picket line; **p. d'incendie** fire picket; **p. de tente** tent peg

piquet[2] **NM** *Cartes* piquet; **faire un p.** to play a hand of piquet

piquetage [piktaʒ] **NM** *Tech* staking (out)

piqueter [pikte] **VT** (**je piquette, n. piquetons; je piquetterai**) **1** *(jalonner)* to stake out, to mark out **2** *(marquer)* to spot, to dot; **piqueté de noir** spotted *or* dotted with black

piquette [pikɛt] **NF 1** *Péj (vin)* cheap wine, *Br Fam* plonk **2** *Fam (défaite)* hammering, thrashing; **prendre une** *ou* **la p.** to get *or* take a hammering, to get a good thrashing

piqueur, -euse [pikœr, -øz] **NM 1** *(à la chasse)* whipper-in; *Équitation* groom **2** *Min* hewer, pickman **3** *Rail* platelayer, *Am* tracklayer

N *Ind* stitcher

ADJ *Zool* **insecte p.** stinging insect

piquouse [pikuz] **NF** *Fam* shot, *Br* jab; **se faire une p.** to have a jab

piqûre [pikyr] **NF 1** *(petite blessure)* *(de guêpe etc)* sting; *(de puce)* bite; **p. d'épingle** pinprick **2** *Méd* injection, *Fam* shot, *Br Fam* jab; **faire une p. à qn** to give sb an injection **3** *(trou)* (small) hole; *(dans le métal)* pit; **p. de vers** *(dans bois, livre)* wormhole; **p. d'aiguille** *(dans le cuir)* pinhole **4** *Couture (d'un tissu, du cuir)* (back)stitching; **(point de) p.** *(d'une machine à coudre)* lockstitch **5** *(tache)* *(de rouille, de poussière, de moisi)* spot, speck; **piqûres** *(dans le métal)* pitting

piranha [pirana] **NM** piranha

piratage [pirataʒ] **NM** piracy; **p. informatique** (computer) hacking, cracking

pirate [pirat] **NM 1** *(des mers)* pirate **2** *(voleur, filou)* crook

ADJ *Fig* pirate; *Radio* **station p.** pirate station; **enregistrement p.** pirate *or* bootleg recording

▸▸ **p. de l'air** hijacker, skyjacker; *Ordinat* **p. informatique** hacker, cracker; **p. de la route** robber *(who preys on motorists)*

pirater [pirate] **VT** *(enregistrement, cassette)* to pirate; *Ordinat* to hack; **p. un film** to make a pirate copy of a film

piraterie [piratri] **NF 1** *(sur les mers)* piracy; *(acte)* act of piracy; *Aviat* **p. aérienne** hijacking, skyjacking **2** *Fig (escroquerie)* swindling; *Ordinat* hacking; **p. audiovisuelle** unauthorized copying *or* reproduction, *Fam* bootlegging; **p. informatique** hacking; **p. commerciale** illegal copying of brand-name goods, counterfeiting

pire [pir] **ADJ 1** *(comp)* worse; **cela est bien p.** that's much worse; **c'est p. qu'avant** it's worse than before; **p. que jamais** worse than ever; **le remède est p. que le mal** the cure is worse than the disease; *Prov* **il n'est p. eau que l'eau qui dort** still waters run deep; *Prov* **il n'est p. sourd que celui qui ne veut pas entendre** there is none so deaf as he who will not hear; **rien n'est p. que ...** nothing is worse than ..., there is nothing worse than ...; **ce qui est p.** what is worse; **c'est de p. en p.** it's getting worse and worse **2** *(superl)* worst; **le p./la p./les pires** the worst; **un voyou de la p. espèce** a lout of the worst kind; **nos pires erreurs** our worst mistakes; **c'est mon p. ennemi** he's my worst enemy

NM le p. de l'histoire, c'est que ... the worst thing about it is that ...; **pour le meilleur et pour le p.** for better or for worse; **il est capable du meilleur comme du p.** he can be extremely good or extremely bad; **craindre le p.** to fear the worst; **s'attendre au p.** to expect the worst; **(en mettant les choses) au p.** if the worst comes to the worst, at worst

Pirée (le) [ləpire] **NM** Piraeus

piriforme [piriform] **ADJ** pear-shaped, *Spéc* pyriform

pirogue [pirɔg] **NF** pirogue, dugout (canoe)

piroguier [pirɔgje] **NM** boatman *(in a pirogue)*

pirouette [pirwɛt] **NF 1** *(de danseuse)*, *Équitation* pirouette; *Fig Fam* **répondre par une p.** *ou* **des pirouettes** to give a flippant answer **2** *Fig (revirement)* about-turn, volte-face

pirouetter [pirwɛte] **VI** to pirouette

pis[1] [pi] **NM** *(d'une vache etc)* udder

pis[2] **ADV** **aller de mal en p.** to go from bad to worse

ADJ *Litt* **1** *(comp)* worse; **cela serait encore p.** that would be worse still *or* even worse; **qui p. est** what is worse; **son état est p. que jamais** his condition is worse than ever **2** *(superl)* **ce qu'il y a de p.** what is worst

NM 1 *(comp)* worse; **il y a p.** there is/are

worse; **il a fait tout cela et p.** he did all that and (something even) worse; **dire p. que pendre de qn** to call sb every name under the sun, not to have a good word to say for sb; **on m'a dit p. que pendre de cet homme-là** I've been told the most dreadful things about that man **2** *(superl)* **le p.** the worst; **en mettant les choses au p.** if the worst comes to the worst, at worst; **au p. aller** at the very worst

pis-aller [pizale] **NM INV** *(solution temporaire)* stopgap (solution); **on va l'engager mais c'est un p.** we'll take him on but we're scraping the bottom (of the barrel), we'll take him on as the best of a bad lot; **j'ai pris ce travail, mais pour moi, c'est un p.** I took the job as the best thing available in the circumstances *or* although it's far from ideal

piscicole [pisikɔl] **ADJ** fish-breeding, *Fml* piscicultural

pisciculteur, -trice [pisikyltœr, -tris] **N** fish breeder, *Fml* pisciculturist

pisciculture [pisikyltyr] **NF** fish breeding, *Fml* pisciculture

pisciforme [pisifɔrm] **ADJ** pisciform

piscine [pisin] **NF 1** *(bassin de natation)* (swimming) pool; **p. couverte/en plein air** indoor/open-air *or* outdoor pool; **p. d'eau de mer** sea-water pool; **p. d'eau douce** freshwater pool; **p. intérieure** indoor pool; **p. publique** (public) swimming pool, *Br* swimming baths **2** *Arg* **la p.** = the French secret service

piscivore [pisivɔr] **ADJ** fish-eating, *Spéc* piscivorous

Pise [piz] **N** Pisa

pissaladière [pisaladjɛr] **NF** *Culin* = (open) onion, olive and anchovy tart, a speciality of Nice

pissat [pisa] **NM** *(de cheval, d'âne etc)* urine

pisse [pis] **NF** *Vulg* piss, pee; **c'est de la p. d'âne, ta bière!** your beer's like (gnat's) piss!

pisse-copie **N INV** *Fam* hack

pisse-froid **NM INV** *Fam (personne morose)* wet blanket

pissenlit [pisɑ̃li] **NM 1** dandelion; *Fam* **manger les pissenlits par la racine** to be pushing up the daisies, to be six feet under **2** *Can Fam (enfant souffrant d'énurésie)* bedwetter, child who wets his/her bed

pisser [pise] **VI 1** *très Fam* to (have a) piss, to (have a) pee; **il a pissé dans sa culotte** he's pissed in *or* peed in *or* wet his pants; **c'est comme si je pissais dans un violon** it's a complete waste of time, it's like pissing in the wind; **laisse p. (le mérinos)!** leave it!, forget it!, don't let it get to you!; **p. de rire** to piss oneself (laughing); **ça n'ira pas loin** it's/he's not up to much; **ça l'a pris comme une envie de p.** he felt a sudden urge to do it, the urge suddenly took him to do it; **je pisse sur les intellectuels** I despise these fucking intellectuals; **ton patron, je lui pisse dessus!** I don't give a shit about your boss!; **je te pisse à la raie!** up yours! **2** *Fam (fuir)* *(d'un récipient)* to leak; *(d'un liquide)* to squirt out; **tonneau qui pisse** leaky barrel

VT *Fam* **son bras pissait le sang** there was blood gushing *or* pouring from his arm, his arm was pouring with blood; **elle pissait le sang** blood was pouring out of her; *Méd très Fam* **p. du sang** to pass blood; **le robinet pisse de l'eau continuellement** the tap is continually leaking

pissette [pisɛt] **NF 1** *Chimie* wash(ing) bottle **2** *Can Fam (pénis)* dick, prick

pisseur, -euse[1] [pisœr, -øz] *Vulg* **N 1** **c'est un p.** he's always going for a piss *or* pee, he's got a weak bladder **2** *Journ Péj* **p. de copie** writer who churns/churned out rubbish

NF pisseuse *(petite fille)* little girl, *Péj* brat

pisseux, -euse² [pisø, -øz] ADJ *Fam* **1** *(qui sent l'urine)* smelling of piss; *(taché par l'urine)* stained with piss, piss-stained **2** *Fig (couleur)* washed out, wishy-washy, yellowy

pisse-vinaigre NM INV *Fam (avare)* skinflint, tightwad; *(rabat-joie)* killjoy

pissoir [piswar] NM, **pissotière** [pisɔtjɛr] NF *Fam* (public) urinal; *(dans la rue)* street urinal

pissou [pisu] NM *Can Fam* wimp, wuss

pistache [pistaʃ] NF pistachio (nut); *Culin* **glace à la p.** pistachio ice cream
ADJ INV pistachio (green)

pistachier [pistaʃje] NM pistachio (tree)

pistage [pistaʒ] NM *(d'animal)* tracking, trailing; *(de personne)* tailing

pistard, -arde [pistar, -ard] N *Cyclisme* track racer

piste [pist] NF **1** *(trace)* track, trail; **suivre la p.** to follow the track *or* the trail; **être sur la p. de qn/qch** to be on the track of sb/sth; **la police a plusieurs pistes** the police have several leads; **brouiller les pistes** to cover one's tracks; *Fig* to confuse the issue; **suivre une fausse p.** to be on the wrong track; **être sur la bonne p.** to be on the right track
2 *Sport* track; *Courses de chevaux* (race)-track; *(course automobile)* (racing) track; *Fig Fam Dial* **aller en p.** to go clubbing; **p. cendrée** cinder track; **tour de p.** lap; *Aut etc* **p. de vitesse** racing track; **p. d'essai** test track; **p. de patinage** skating rink; **p. de ski** (ski) run, piste; **p. de luge** toboggan run; *Ski* **p. artificielle** artificial *or* dry ski slope; **p. de danse** dance floor; **p. (de cirque)** (circus) ring; **en p.!** into the ring!; *Fig (au travail)* get cracking!
3 *Aviat* runway; **p. d'envol** take-off runway; **p. d'atterrissage** landing runway; *(dans la brousse etc)* airstrip; **p. de fortune** airstrip, landing strip
4 *(chemin)* track, trail; **p. cyclable** cycle path; *Tech* **p. des billes** ball race; **p. en terre** dirt track
5 *(de magnétophone)*, *Ordinat (de disque)*, *Cin* track; **magnéto 4 pistes** 4-track tape recorder; *Cin* **p. sonore** soundtrack; **p. audio** sound track; *Ordinat* **p. d'amorçage** boot track; *TV etc* **p. de fond** backing track; **p. magnétique** magnetic track; *Ordinat* **magnetic stripe**; **p. optique** optical track; *TV, Cin* **p. pilote** control track; *TV, Cin* **p. son** sound track, audio track; **p. son non synchrone** wild track; *TV, Cin* **p. vidéo** video track; *Ordinat* **pistes par pouce** tracks per inch

pister [piste] VT *(animal)* to track, to trail; **p. qn** to tail *or* shadow *or* follow sb

pisteur [pistœr] NM ski-run attendant *or* supervisor

pistil [pistil] NM *Bot* pistil

pistoche [pistɔʃ] NF *Fam* (swimming) pool

pistole [pistɔl] NF pistole

pistolet [pistɔlɛ] NM **1** *(arme à feu)* pistol, gun; *Tech* **peinture au p.** spray painting, spraying **2** *Culin (petit pain au lait)* (milk) roll; *Belg (petit pain)* (bread) roll; **3** *(de dessinateur)* French curve **4** *Fam (urinal)* bottle **5** *(type bizarre)* **un drôle de p.** a queer *or* an odd sort *or* *Fam* fish **6** *Can Fam* **être en p.** *(être en colère)* to be hopping mad *or* fuming
▸▸ **p. à air comprimé** air pistol *or* gun; *Hist* **p. d'arçon** horse pistol; **p. à bouchon** popgun; **p. à eau** water pistol; *Tech* **p. à peinture** paint gun, spray gun; *Sport* **p. de starter** starting pistol; *Mil etc* **p. de tir** firing pistol; *Tech* **p. vaporisateur** paint gun, spray gun

pistolet-mitrailleur, *pl* **pistolets-mitrailleurs** NM submachine gun, tommy gun, sten gun

pistoleur [pistɔlœr] NM *Tech* spray(-gun) painter

piston [pistɔ̃] NM **1** *Tech (de machine, de pompe, de cric etc)* piston; **p. à air/eau** air/water piston; **tête de p.** piston head; **p. plongeur** *(d'une pompe refoulante etc)* plunger; *(d'une presse hydraulique)* ram; **p. de servo** booster piston **2** *Fam (recommandation)* string-pulling; **avoir du p.** to have friends in the right places; **il a eu la place par p.** someone pulled strings to get him the job; **faire jouer le p.** to pull strings **3** *Mus* valve; **(cornet à) p.** cornet

pistonné, -ée [pistɔne] N **c'est un p.** he got where he is thanks to a bit of string-pulling

pistonner [pistɔne] VT *Fam* **p. qn** to pull strings for sb; **il s'est fait p.** he got someone to pull strings for him

pistou [pistu] NM *Culin* pesto; **soupe de** *ou* **au p.** vegetable soup with pesto

pita [pita] NM pitta bread

pitance [pitɑ̃s] NF **1** *Arch (dans un couvent)* allowance (of food) **2** *Péj Vieilli* sustenance

> Il faut noter que le terme anglais **pittance** est un faux ami. Il désigne une somme dérisoire.

pit-bull, *pl* **pit-bulls** [pitbul] NM pit bull (terrier)

pitchoun, -oune [pitʃun] N *Région (enfant)* little one

pitchpin [pitʃpɛ̃] NM *Bot* pitch pine

piteusement [pitøzmɑ̃] ADV pitifully, miserably

piteux, -euse [pitø, -øz] ADJ **1** *Vieilli (qui suscite la pitié)* pitiful **2** *(médiocre)* **p. résultat** poor *or* miserable *or* pitiful result; **en p. état** in a sorry *or* pitiful state **3 faire une mine piteuse, faire piteuse mine** to look crestfallen; **il annonça d'un air p. que ...** he announced shamefaced that ...

pithécanthrope [pitekɑ̃trɔp] NM pithecanthropus

pithiviers [pitivje] NM *Culin* = cake made of puff pastry containing rum and almond-flavoured cream

pitié [pitje] NF **1** *(compassion)* pity, compassion; **avoir p. de qn** to pity sb; *(s'apitoyer)* to take *or* have pity on sb; *(épargner)* to have mercy on sb; **prendre p. de qn, prendre qn en p.** to take pity on sb; **être sans p.** to be pitiless *or* merciless *or* ruthless; **il les a jugés sans p.** he judged them pitilessly *or* mercilessly *or* ruthlessly; **par p.** out of pity; *(en implorant)* for pity's sake; **p.!** *(grâce)* (have) mercy!, have pity on me!; *(arrête ça)* for pity's sake!; **faire p.** to arouse pity; **il me faisait p.** I felt sorry for him; **cela faisait p. à voir** it was pitiful *or* *Fml* pitiable to see (it); *Vieilli* **c'est p. qu'il soit resté seul** it's pitiful *or* sad that he should have been left alone **2** *(commisération mêlée de mépris)* pity; **c'est (une) p. de voir des choses pareilles** it's pitiful to see such things

piton [pitɔ̃] NM **1** *Tech* eye (bolt); **p. (d'alpiniste)** piton, peg; **p. à vis** screw eye; **p. à boucle** ring bolt **2** *(sommet de montagne)* **p. (rocheux)** (rocky) peak **3** *Can Fam (d'une sonnette)* button; *(d'un clavier)* key

pitoune [pitun] NF *Can* **1** *(bille de bois)* pulpwood bolt **2** *Fam (femme bien en chair)* plump woman; **grosse p.** fat lump (of a woman) **3** *Fam Péj (femme de mœurs légères)* tramp, tart **4** *Fam (terme d'affection)* darling, sweetheart

pitoyable [pitwajabl] ADJ **1** *(digne de pitié)* *(récit, condition etc)* pitiful; *Fml* pitiable, piteous **2** *Péj (lamentable)* *(excuse, plaisanterie etc)* pathetic, pitiful

pitoyablement [pitwajabləmɑ̃] ADV pitifully; **échouer p.** to fail miserably

pitre [pitr] NM *(clown)* clown; **faire le p.** to clown (around), to play *or* act the fool

pitrerie [pitrəri] NF clowning around, tomfoolery

pittoresque [pitɔrɛsk] ADJ picturesque; *(description, style)* colourful, *Am* colorful, vivid
NM picturesqueness; *(d'un style, d'une description)* vividness

pituitaire [pitɥitɛr] ADJ *Anat* pituitary

pituite [pitɥit] NF *Anat (vomissement)* bile, *Arch* phlegm

pive [piv] NF *Suisse (pomme de pin)* pine cone

pivelé [pivle] ADJ *Can (moucheté)* spotted; *(couvert de taches de rousseur)* freckled

pivert [pivɛr] NM green woodpecker

pivoine [pivwan] NF *Bot* peony; *Fig* **rouge comme une p.** red as a beetroot

pivot [pivo] NM **1** *(axe)* pivot; *(de fusil)* swivel; *(de levier)* fulcrum; *(en dentisterie)* post; *(de compas, de boussole)* centre pin; **p. à rotule** ball pivot; **à p., monté sur p.** pivoted, swivelling; **canon à p.** swivel gun; *Tech* **p. de fusée** swivel pin, king pin **2** *Fig (élément central)* *(d'un drame)* mainspring, pivot **3** *Bot* tap root **4** *(au basket)* centre, *Am* center

pivotant [pivotɑ̃] ADJ **1** *(qui tourne)* pivoting, swivelling, revolving; **fauteuil p.** swivel chair; **base pivotante** swivel base **2** *Bot* **racine pivotante** tap root

pivoter [pivote] VI **1** *(tourner)* to pivot, to swivel, to turn (**sur** (up)on); *Mil (des troupes)* to wheel; **pivoter** *ou* **qch** to turn *or* swivel sth round; **p. sur ses talons** to swing round *or* pivot on one's heels **2** *Bot (d'une plante)* to form a tap root

pixel [piksɛl] NM *Ordinat* pixel

pixélisé [pikselize] ADJ *Ordinat* pixellated

pizza [pidza] NF pizza

pizzeria [pidzerja] NF pizzeria

pizzicato [pidzikato], *pl* **pizzicati** [pidzikati] NM *Mus* pizzicato

PJ¹ *(abrév* **pièce jointe**) encl

PJ² [peʒi] NF *Fam (abrév* **Police Judiciaire**) *Br* ≃ CID, *Am* ≃ FBI

placage [plakaʒ] NM **1** *(fait de recouvrir)* *(de bois)* veneering; *(de métal)* plating; **p. au chrome** chrome *or* chromium plating **2** *(matériau) (bois)* veneer; *(métal)* plating; **bois de p.** veneer **3** *Rugby* tackle

placard [plakar] NM **1** *(armoire murale)* cupboard; *Fig Fam* **mettre qn au p.** to sideline sb; *Fam* **mettre un projet au p.** to put a plan on ice *or* into cold storage, to shelve a project **2** *(affiche)* poster; *Journ* **p. publicitaire** *ou* **de publicité** display advertisement **3** *Typ (format)* broadsheet; **(épreuve en) p.** galley *(proof)* **4** *Naut (sur une voile)* patch **5** *Tech (d'une porte)* panel **6** *Fam (prison)* clink, *Br* nick; **faire 20 ans de p.** to do 20 years inside *or* in the clink

> Il faut noter que le terme anglais **placard** est un faux ami. Il signifie **pancarte**.

placarder [plakarde] VT **1** *(affiche)* to stick up, to put up; **p. un mur de posters** to stick *or* put posters (up) on a wall **2** *Typ* to set in galleys

placardisation [plakardizasjɔ̃] NF *Fam (de personnes)* sidelining

placardiser [plakardize] VT *Fam (personnes)* to sideline

PLACE [plas]

place **1, 2, 5, 10** ▪ room **3** ▪ seat **4** ▪ job **6** ▪ square **7** ▪ market **8**

NF **1** *(lieu, endroit)* place; **changer sa chaise**

de p. to move or shift one's chair; **mettre qch en p.** to put sth in place; **tout est à sa p.** everything's in its place; **p. de parking** parking place or space; **je n'ai pas trouvé de p. en ville** I couldn't find any parking places or spaces in town; **remettez vos livres à leur p.** put your books away; **voulez-vous prendre ma p.?** would you like to take my place?; **il ne peut pas rester en p.** he can't keep still; **il ne tient pas en p. aujourd'hui** he is very fidgety today; **sur p.** on the spot; Constr on site; Fam **faire du sur p.** to mark time, to stand still; (en voiture) to crawl along; Fam **dans cette affaire, j'ai l'impression de faire du sur p.** I've a feeling I'm getting nowhere with this matter; **il lut la lettre sur p.** he read the letter there and then or on the spot; **personnel engagé sur p.** staff hired locally; **rester sur p.** to stay put; **la police sera sur p. dans quelques minutes** the police will be on the scene or spot in a few minutes; **on trouve tout sur p.** everything we need is here/will be there; **son nom a pris p. dans l'histoire** his name has found a place in history

2 Fig (condition, situation) place; **avoir sa p. au soleil** to have one's place in the sun; **il finira par trouver sa p. dans ce milieu** he'll eventually find his place or a niche among those people; **prendre sa p. dans la société** to take one's place in society; **je viens à la p. de mon père** I've come instead of my father, I've come in my father's place or Fml stead; **parler à la p. de qn** to speak for sb; **remettre qn à sa p.** to put sb in his/her place; **rester à sa p.** to know one's place; **à votre p., je …** in your place or if I were you, I …; **mets-toi à sa p.** put yourself in his position, look at things from his point of view

3 (espace) room, space; **prendre** ou **occuper beaucoup de p.** to take up a great deal of room or space; **nous n'avons pas de p. pour mettre un piano** we have no room or space for a piano; **gagner de la p.** to gain some (extra) room or space; **faire p. à qn/qch** to make way for sb/sth; Vieilli **(faites) p.!** stand aside!, make way!; **faites-lui un peu de p.** make room for him; Fig **céder la p. aux jeunes** to make way for the younger generation; Aut **p. aux pieds** footwell; Aviat **p. pour les jambes** legroom

4 (siège) seat; **céder sa p. à qn** to give up one's seat to sb, to give sb one's seat; **à vos places!** take your seats!; **restez à votre p.** stay in your seat, remain seated; **louer deux places au théâtre** to book two seats at the theatre; **prendre p.** (s'asseoir) to take a seat, to sit down; (debout) to take up one's place; **il n'y avait pas une p.** there wasn't a seat to be found or to be had; **voiture à deux/à quatre places** two-/four-seater (car); Aut **une deux places** a two-seater; **prix des places** (transports publics) fares; (spectacles) seats; **payer p. entière** (transports publics) to pay full fare; (spectacles) to pay full price; **p. assise** seat; **places debout 15** (sur un écriteau) standing room for 15 passengers; **p. côté couloir** aisle seat; **p. côté fenêtre** window seat; **p. fumeur** smoking seat; **p. non-fumeur** no-smoking seat; **p. du mort** (front) passenger seat

5 (appartenance, rôle) place; **la p. de l'homme dans le monde** man's place in the world; **sa famille tient une grande p. dans sa vie** his family has an important place in his life; **il aura toujours une p. dans mon cœur** he'll always have a place in my heart

6 (emploi, poste) job, post; **quitter/perdre sa p.** to leave/lose one's job; **le gouvernement en p.** the government in office or power; Fig **une personne en p.** a person in high office; Fig **les gens en p.** people in high places, people with influence

7 (lieu public) square; **la p. Rouge** Red Square; **p. du marché** market place; Suisse **p. de jeu(x)** playground

8 Com, Fin market; **achats sur p.** local purchases; **prix sur p.** loco price; **être bien connu sur la p.** to be a well-known player in the market; **avoir du crédit sur la p.** to have credit (facilities) locally; **affaires sur la p. de Paris** business on the Paris market

9 Mil **p. (forte** ou **de guerre)** fortified place; (ville) fortress or fortified town; **p. d'armes** parade ground, drill ground

10 (rang) place, placing; **il a eu une bonne p. au concours** he was well placed in the competition; **une p. d'honneur** a place of honour

11 Suisse **p. de parc** parking space

12 Belg (pièce d'habitation) room

▸▸ **p. bancaire** banking centre; **p. boursière** stock market; **p. commerciale** trade centre; **p. financière** financial centre or marketplace; **p. marchande** market place; **p. monétaire** money market

placé [plase] Courses de chevaux ADJ placed; **arriver p.** to be placed
   NM placed horse

placebo [plasebo] NM placebo

placement [plasmɑ̃] NM **1** (fait de donner un emploi) placement, placing; (fait d'attribuer un siège) seating; **bureau** ou **agence de placement(s)** employment bureau or agency, Am placement bureau **2** Jur (d'un mineur dans une famille d'accueil ou dans un organisme) placement **3** Fin (d'argent) investment, investing; (argent) investment; **faire des placements** to invest (money), to make investments; **faire un bon p.** to make a good investment; **p. avantageux** good investment; **p. en actions** equity investment; **p. éthique** ethical investment; Fam **p. de père de famille** blue chip (investment), gilt-edged investment; **p. à court terme** short-term investment; **p. obligataire** bond investment; **p. temporaire** temporary investment; **p. à revenus fixes** fixed income investment; **p. à revenus variables** variable income investment **4** Mktg **p. de produit** product placement

placenta [plasɛ̃ta] NM Obst placenta; (expulsé après accouchement) afterbirth, placenta

placentaire [plasɛ̃tɛr] ADJ Obst placental

PLACER [plase] (je plaçai(s); n. plaçons) VT **1** (mettre à sa place) to place, to put; (spectateurs, invités etc) to seat; **p. qn** (au spectacle) to show sb to his/her seat; Fig **vous êtes mieux placés que moi pour en juger** you're better placed than I (am) to judge; Fig **vous êtes bien placés pour le savoir** you're in a position to know, you ought to know; **p. une sentinelle** to post a soldier on sentry duty; **maison bien placée** well-situated house; **p. l'honnêteté au plus haut rang** to put or set or place a high value on honesty; **je place le courage au-dessus de toutes les valeurs** I put or set or place courage above all other values; **confiance mal placée** misplaced confidence; TV etc **p. les bandes-son** to lay tracks

2 (procurer un emploi à) to find a job for; **p. qn comme apprenti chez qn** to apprentice sb to sb

3 (vendre) (marchandises) to sell; Fin **valeurs difficiles à p.** bills difficult to negotiate

4 (situer) to set; **c'est ici que l'auteur a placé son roman** this is where the author set his/her novel

5 (dire) to get in; **il voulait à tout prix p. son histoire** he was determined to get his anecdote in (in the conversation etc); Fam **avec elle, on ne peut pas en p. une!** you can't get a word in edgeways or Am edgewise with

her!; **je n'ai pas pu p. un mot** I couldn't get a word in edgeways or Am edgewise

6 Fin (argent) to invest; **p. à court terme** to invest short-term; **p. à intérêts** to invest at interest

VPR **se placer 1** (prendre sa place) to take one's seat or one's place (at table etc); Mil, Sp etc to take up one's position; **dites-moi où me p.** tell me where to sit/stand; **il faut se p. dans son optique** you have to look at things from his point of view; **se p. sous la protection de qn** to place oneself under sb's protection; **marchandises qui se placent facilement** goods that sell readily

2 (trouver un emploi) to get or find a job; **se p. comme vendeuse** to get a job as a sales assistant or Am clerk

placet [plasɛ] NM **1** Arch petition, address **2** Jur (plaintiff's) claim

placette [plasɛt] NF (small) square

placeur, -euse [plasœr, -øz] N **1** (personne qui tient un bureau de placement) employment agent or consultant **2** (dans des réunions publiques) steward; Cin, Théâtre usher, f usherette

placide [plasid] ADJ placid, calm

placidement [plasidmɑ̃] ADV placidly, calmly

placidité [plasidite] NF placidity, calmness

placier, -ière [plasje, -jɛr] N Com **1** (représentant) travelling salesman, f saleswoman, traveller **2** (forain) = person who allocates stall space in a market

Placoplâtre® [plakoplɑtr] NM plasterboard

placoter [plakɔte] VI Can Fam to chat

plafond [plafɔ̃] NM **1** Archit ceiling; **p. à caissons** coffered ceiling; **chambre haute/basse de p.** high-/low-ceilinged room; Fig Fam **avoir une araignée au p.** to have bats in the belfry; Fig Fam **être bas de p.** to be a bit slow on the uptake **2** (toit) (de voiture, de caverne) roof **3** (maximum) ceiling; **prix p.** maximum price, ceiling (price); **fixer un p. à un budget** to fix or put a ceiling on a budget; **p. des charges budgétaires** spending limit, budgetary limit; Fin **p. du crédit** credit ceiling; **Banque p. d'autorisation** ou **de retrait** withdrawal limit; **Banque p. de découvert** overdraft limit **4** Aviat (d'avion) ceiling, maximum flying height; Aut top or maximum speed; Météo **p. (nuageux)** (cloud) ceiling

plafonnage [plafɔnaʒ] NM Constr ceiling work

plafonnement [plafɔnmɑ̃] NM **p. des salaires/cotisations** (fait de limiter) fixing or putting a ceiling on wages/contributions; (fait d'atteindre un plafond) peaking or levelling or Am leveling off of wages/contributions

plafonner [plafɔne] VT **1** (pièce) to put a ceiling in **2** (salaire etc) to put a ceiling on; Fin **être plafonné à** to have a ceiling of
   VI **1** Aviat to fly at the ceiling; Aut to go at maximum or top speed **2** Fig to peak, to level out, to level off; **la production plafonne** output has reached its ceiling; **cette année, l'inflation a plafonné à 3%** inflation this year peaked at 3%

plafonneur [plafɔnœr] NM Tech plasterer of ceilings

plafonnier [plafɔnje] NM ceiling light; Aut courtesy or interior light

plage [plaʒ] NF **1** (grève) beach; **p. de sable/de galets** sandy/pebble beach; **sac/robe de p.** beach bag/robe **2** (lieu touristique) seaside resort **3** Naut (d'un cuirassé) freeboard deck; **p. arrière** Naut quarterdeck; Aut window shelf, (rear) parcel shelf **4** (surface) area; Opt **p. lumineuse** light area, high light **5** (laps de temps) time, period; TV, Radio (d'émissions) (time) segment; **p. horaire** time slot; **p. horaire très écoutée/regardée** peak listening/viewing time or period; *Can* **p. fixe** *(dans un horaire variable)* core time **6** *Fig (éventail)* range; *Radio* **p. de réception** tuning range; *Com* **p. de prix** price range; *Aut* **p. de régime** engine speed range, rev range **7** *(d'un disque)* track

plagiaire [plaʒjɛr] **N** plagiarist, plagiarizer

plagiat [plaʒja] **NM** plagiarism

plagier [plaʒje] **VT** *(impf, pr sub* **n. plagiions, v. plagiiez)** to plagiarize

plagiste [plaʒist] **N** beach attendant

plaid [plɛd] **NM** travelling rug

plaidable [plɛdabl] **ADJ** *Jur* pleadable

plaidant [plɛdã] **ADJ** *Jur* **avocat p.** ≃ lawyer, *Br* barrister; **les parties plaidantes** the litigants

plaider [plede] **VT** to plead; **p. la cause de qn** *Jur* to plead sb's case, to defend sb; *Fig* to speak in favour of or defend sb, to plead sb's cause; **p. sa propre cause** *Jur* to conduct one's own defence; *Fig* to speak in one's own defence; **son défenseur va p. la folie** his counsel will plead insanity or will put forward a plea of insanity; **p. le faux pour savoir le vrai** to lie in order to get at the truth; **p. coupable/non coupable** to plead guilty/ not guilty

VI *(d'un avocat)* to plead (**pour** for; **contre** against); *(d'un plaignant)* to go to court, to litigate; **p. contre qn** to take sb to court, to take proceedings against sb; *Fig* **p. pour** ou **en faveur de qn/qch** to speak for sb/sth, to defend sb/sth

VPR se plaider la cause s'est plaidée hier the case was heard yesterday

plaideur, -euse [plɛdœr, -øz] **N** *Jur* litigant

plaidoirie [plɛdwari] **NF** *Jur* speech for the defence or Am defense

plaidoyer [plɛdwaje] **NM** *Jur* speech for the defence or Am defense; *Fig (défense passionnée)* plea

plaie [plɛ] **NF 1** *(blessure)*, *Fig* wound; *(coupure)* cut; *Fig* **rouvrir d'anciennes plaies** to reopen old wounds; **retourner** ou **remuer le couteau** ou **le fer dans la p.** to twist or turn the knife in the wound; **mettre le doigt sur la p.** to put one's finger on the source of the trouble **2** *(fléau)* affliction, scourge; *(personne, chose)* pest, nuisance; **quelle p.!** what a pest or nuisance!; *Bible* **les dix plaies d'Égypte** the ten plagues of Egypt; *Prov* **p. d'argent n'est pas mortelle** money isn't everything

plaignant, -ante [plɛɲã, -ãt] *Jur* **ADJ partie plaignante** plaintiff, complainant

N plaintiff, complainant

plain [plɛ̃] **ADJ** *Vieilli (terrain, surface)* flat, level, even

NM le p. high tide

plain-chant, *pl* **plains-chants NM** *Mus* plainsong, plainchant

plaindre [plɛ̃dr] *(prp* **plaignant;** *pp* **plaint;** *pr ind* **je plains, il plaint, n. plaignons, ils plaignent;** *pr sub* **je plaigne;** *impf* **je plaignais;** *p hist* **je plaignis;** *fu* **je plaindrai) VT 1** *(témoigner de la compassion à)* to pity, to feel sorry for; **je vous plains de voyager dans ces conditions** I pity you or I feel sorry for you having to travel in those conditions; **il est fort à p.** he is greatly to be pitied; **elle n'est pas à p.** she hasn't anything to worry about, she's got it made; **il est plus à p. qu'à blâmer** he is more to be pitied than blamed **2** *Région, Arch (donner parcimonieusement à)* to (be)grudge; **on n'a pas plaint l'argent** there was no stinting of money, no expense was spared; **il ne plaint pas sa peine** he spares himself no trouble

VPR se plaindre to complain (**à** to); *(se lamenter)* to moan, to groan; **se p. de qn/qch**

to complain about sb/sth; **se p. de maux d'estomac** to complain of stomach pains; **il n'y a pas de quoi vous p., vous n'avez pas à vous p.** you've nothing to complain about, you shouldn't grumble; **se p. (de ce) que ...** + *sub* to complain (about the fact) that ...

plaine [plɛn] **NF 1** *Géog* plain **2** *Hist* **la P.** the Plain *(moderate deputies during the French Revolution)* **3** *Belg* **p. de jeux** playground; **p. de(s) manœuvres** exercise ground; **p. de(s) sports** sports field or ground

plain-pied **ADV de p.** on the same level, on a level; *(au même étage)* on one floor; **salon de p. avec le jardin** sitting room on a level with or on the same level as the garden; **deux surfaces de p.** two surfaces flush with each other; *Fig* **nous sommes de p.** we are on an equal footing (with each other)

plainte [plɛ̃t] **NF 1** *(cri, gémissement)* moan, groan **2** *(revendication, protestation)* complaint; **un sujet de p.** the subject of a complaint **3** *Jur* complaint; **porter p.** ou **déposer une p. contre qn** to lodge a complaint against sb (**auprès de** with); **p. en diffamation** action for libel; **p. contre X** complaint against a person or persons unknown

plaintif, -ive [plɛ̃tif, -iv] **ADJ** *(ton)* plaintive

plaintivement [plɛ̃tivmã] **ADV** plaintively

plaire [plɛr] *(prp* **plaisant;** *pp* **plu;** *pr ind* **je plais, il plaît, n. plaisons, ils plaisent;** *pr sub* **je plaise;** *impf* **je plaisais;** *p hist* **je plus;** *fu* **je plairai) VI 1** **cet homme me plaît** I like this man; **ce livre/film m'a plu** I liked or enjoyed this book/film; **elle te plaît, ta nouvelle voiture?** do you like your new car?; **la nouvelle robe lui plaît beaucoup** she's very pleased with or she really likes the new dress; **cette offre devrait lui p.** the offer should appeal to him; **il ne plaît pas aux femmes** women don't like him; *(physiquement)* women don't find him attractive; **cela ne me plaît pas du tout** I don't like that at all; **c'est ce qui plaît en ce moment** it's what people seem to like just now; **il plaît** people like him, he's popular; **ça plaît beaucoup** it's very popular; **tu devrais faire une tarte aux pommes, ça plaît toujours** you ought to make an apple tart, that's always popular or welcome or that always goes down well; **je le ferai, si cela me plaît** I'll do it if I want to or if I feel like it; *Fam* **si ça ne te plaît pas, c'est pareil!** if you don't like it, tough!; **que cela te plaise ou non** whether you like it or not; *Fam Iron* **tu commences à me p.!** you're beginning to annoy or irritate me!

2 *(se rendre agréable)* **p. à qn** to please sb; **chercher à p. à qn** to try to please sb; **elle veut p.** *(elle veut qu'on l'aime)* she wants to be liked

V IMPERS s'il vous plaît please, *Vieilli* if you please; *Fam (pour insister)* if you please; **s'il te plaît please; et pas n'importe qui, s'il vous plaît** and not just anybody, if you please or if you don't mind; **elle passe ses vacances à Saint-Tropez, s'il vous plaît** she goes to St-Tropez for her holidays, if you please or don't you know; **vous plairait-il de nous accompagner?** would you like to come with us?; *Vieilli, Région* **plaît-il?** I beg your pardon?, what did you say?; **comme il vous plaira** (just) as you like or please; **plaise à Dieu qu'il vienne!** please God let him come!, *Fml* God grant that he may come!; **à Dieu ne plaise (que ...)** God forbid (that ...); **plût au ciel que ...!** would to heaven that ...!

VPR se plaire 1 *(s'aimer soi-même)* to admire oneself, *Fam* to fancy oneself; **elle se plaît dans cette robe** she likes wearing that dress, she likes herself in that dress **2** *(de deux personnes)* to be attracted to each other, *Fam* to fancy each other **3** *(se trouver bien)* **je me plais beaucoup à Paris** I'm very happy in Paris; **se p. à faire qch** to enjoy or like doing sth;

il ne se plaît pas ici he doesn't like it here, he's unhappy here; **la vigne se plaît sur les coteaux** the vine does well or thrives on hillsides

plaisamment [plɛzamã] **ADV 1** *(agréablement)* pleasantly **2** *(drôlement)* funnily, amusingly **3** *Litt (d'une façon ridicule)* ridiculously

plaisance [plɛzãs] **NF 1 bateau de p.** pleasure boat; **port de p.** marina; **navigation de p., la p.** boating **2** *Arch (plaisir)* pleasure

plaisancier, -ière [plɛzãsje, -jɛr] **N** (amateur) yachtsman, *f* yachtswoman

plaisant [plɛzã] **ADJ 1** *(agréable)* pleasant, agreeable; **p. à l'œil** pleasing to or for *Fam* easy on the eye, pleasing to look at **2** *(drôle)* funny, amusing; *(d'un humour sec ou ironique)* droll **3** *(always before the noun)* *Vieilli (ridicule) (personne, réponse)* ridiculous, absurd, ludicrous

NM 1 le (plus) p. de l'affaire, c'est que ... the funniest thing about it is that ... **2** *Arch (farceur)* wag, joker; **faire le p.** to play or act the comedian; **mauvais p.** malicious joker

plaisanter [plɛzãte] **VI 1** *(s'amuser, rire)* to joke, *Fml* to jest; **elle aime bien p.** she enjoys a joke; **il faut bien p., n'est-ce pas?** we all have to have a joke from time to time, don't we?; **dire qch en plaisantant** to say sth as a joke or in jest; **il n'est pas d'humeur à p.** he's not in a joking mood **2** *(dire par jeu)* to joke; **vous plaisantez!** you're joking!, you're kidding!, you don't mean it!; **je ne plaisante pas** I'm serious, I'm not joking; **c'est un homme avec qui on ne plaisante pas** he is not a man to be trifled with; **on ne plaisante pas avec la justice** the law is not to be trifled with; **on ne plaisante pas avec la santé** health is a serious matter; **il ne plaisante pas là-dessus** ou **sur ces choses-là** he doesn't joke about things like that; **dans leur famille, on ne plaisante pas avec la religion** you don't joke about religion in their family, religion isn't a joking matter in their family

VT to tease (**sur qch** about sth), to poke fun at, to make fun of

plaisanterie [plɛzãtri] **NF** *(blague)* joke, *Fml* jest; *(activité)* joking, *Fml* jesting; **une fine p.** a subtle joke; **une mauvaise p.** *(blague)* a bad joke; *(farce)* a nasty trick; **faire des plaisanteries** to tell or crack jokes; **les plaisanteries les plus courtes sont les meilleures** brevity is the soul of wit; **tourner qch en p.** to laugh sth off, to make a joke out of sth; **entendre la p.** to know how to take a joke; **par p.** for fun, for a joke; *Fig* **c'est une p.!** it's a joke!, it's ridiculous or laughable!; **ce sera une p. pour toi** it'll be child's play for you; **pousser trop loin la p.** to take the joke too far, to go too far

plaisantin [plɛzãtɛ̃] **NM** joker; *Fig Péj* **c'est un (petit) p.** *(on ne peut pas lui faire confiance)* he's (a bit of) a joker

plaisir [plɛzir] **NM 1** *(sensation plaisante)* pleasure, delight; **j'apprends avec p. que vous êtes de mon avis** I'm pleased or delighted or glad to hear you agree with me; **c'est avec p. que j'ai appris la nouvelle** I was pleased or delighted or glad to hear the news; **faire p. à qn** to please sb; **ça me ferait vraiment p. que tu acceptes ce travail** I would be really pleased or delighted if you accepted the job; **fais-moi p., viens danser** do me a favour, come and dance; **cela m'a fait p. de le revoir** I was pleased or delighted to see him again, it gave me great pleasure to see him again; **si cela peut te faire p., s'il n'y a que ça pour te faire p.** if it will make you happy; **je viens avec toi, mais c'est bien pour te faire p.!** I'll come with you just to keep you happy!; **cela me fait grand p. de vous voir** I'm delighted to see you; **cela fait p. à voir** it's a pleasure to see; *Iron* **ça fait**

(toujours) p.! charming!; **faire à qn le p. de venir** to do sb the pleasure of coming; **voulez-vous me faire le p. de vous taire!** will you please be quiet!; **ils vous prient de leur faire le p. de dîner avec eux** they request the pleasure of your company at dinner; **j'ai le p. de vous apprendre que ...** I have pleasure in informing *or* I am pleased to inform you that ..., I'm pleased to be able to tell you that ...; **tout le p. est pour moi** the pleasure is all mine; **gâcher le p. de qn** to spoil sb's pleasure; **car tel est le bon p. du roi** because that is what His Majesty wishes; **le p. d'offrir/de recevoir** the pleasure of giving/receiving; **au p. de vous revoir** goodbye, I hope we'll meet again; *Fam* **au p.!** goodbye!, see you (again)!; **pour le plus grand p. de l'assistance/de ses collègues** to the great delight of the audience/of one's colleagues; **prendre (grand) p. à qch** to (really) enjoy sth; **prendre p.** *ou* **avoir du p. à faire qch** to enjoy doing sth; **prendre un malin p. à faire qch** to take a malicious pleasure in doing sth; **il va se faire un p. de te téléphoner demain** he'll be only too pleased to phone you tomorrow; **rougir/frissonner/gémir de p.** to flush/quiver/moan with pleasure; **avec p.!** with pleasure!

2 (*agrément*) pleasure, fun; **c'est par p. que vous faites cela?** are you doing that because you like it *or* for the fun of it?; **parler pour le p. de parler** to talk for talking's sake *or* for the sake of it; **elle le dit pour le p. de te faire souffrir** she said it because she wants to make you suffer; **elle travaille pour le p.** she works because she enjoys *or* likes it; **se tourmenter à p.** to worry for the sake of worrying *or* for the sake of it; **faire durer le p.** to make the pleasure last; *Iron* to prolong the agony; *Iron* **je vous souhaite bien du p.!** the best of luck (to you)!

3 (*distraction*) pleasure, enjoyment, amusement; **son plus grand p. est de faire des photos** what he likes doing most *or* best is taking photos; **les plaisirs de la table** fine food; **chaque âge a ses plaisirs** every age has its pleasures; **on prend son p. comme on peut** you take your pleasure where you find it; **s'accorder** *ou* **s'offrir un petit p.** to indulge oneself; **faire qch pour le p.** *ou* **pour son p.** to do sth for pleasure *or* for fun; **le planeur est un p. coûteux** gliding's an expensive pastime *or* hobby; *Iron* **ce n'est pas une partie de p.** it's no picnic

4 *Litt* (*sensuel*) **le p., les plaisirs** dissipation; **lieu de p.** place of amusement; (*où l'on s'amuse la nuit*) night haunt **5 le p.** (*sexuel*) (sexual) pleasure; **il y prit du p.** he got a (sexual) thrill out of it; **p. solitaire** self-abuse

PLAN¹ [plã] **ADJ** (*terrain, surface*) flat, level, even; *Géom* (*surface etc*) plane
NM 1 *Math etc* plane

2 *Cin, TV* shot; *Beaux-Arts* **premier p.** foreground; **second p.** middle ground; **au second p.** in the middle distance; *Fig* **ce problème occupe le premier p.** this question is very much to the fore *or* is very much in the foreground; *Fig* **reléguer qn au second p.** to push sb into the background; *Fig* **un artiste de premier p.** an artist of the first rank, a first-rate artist; *Cin, TV* **hors p.** off-shot; **sur le même p.** on the same level; **sur le p. politique/économique, au p. politique/économique** on the political/economic level; *Phot, Cin* **faire un gros p.** to take *or* shoot a close-up

3 *Aviat* **p. de sustentation** aerofoil, *Am* airfoil; **p. fixe horizontal** tail plane; **p. supérieur** (*d'un biplan*) upper wing *or* plane

▶▶ *TV, Cin* **p. accéléré** time-lapse shot; *TV, Cin* **p. américain** American shot, two-shot; *TV, Cin* **p. d'archives** stock shot; *TV, Cin* **p. de buste** bust shot; *TV, Cin* **p. ceinture** waist

shot; *TV, Cin* **p. en contre-plongée** periscope shot; **p. de cuisson** hob; *TV, Cin* **p. de détail** detail *or* insert shot; **p. d'eau** stretch of water; (*d'une rivière*) reach; *TV, Cin* **p. éloigné** long shot; *TV, Cin* **p. d'ensemble** wide shot; *TV, Cin* **p. fixe** static shot; *Opt* **p. focal** focal plane; *TV, Cin* **p. général** full-length shot, long shot; **p. incliné** inclined plane; *Tech* ball ramp; *TV, Cin* **p. en intérieur** interior (shot); *TV, Cin* **p. de longue durée** continuous film sequence; *TV, Cin* **p. moyen** medium shot; *TV, Cin* **p. en plongée** high-angle shot, overhead shot; *TV, Cin* **p. rapproché** medium close-up, close-up, close shot; *TV, Cin* **p. de réaction** reaction shot; *TV, Cin* **p. refilmé** retake; *TV, Cin* **p. séquence** sequence shot; *TV, Cin* **p. serré** close-up, tight shot; *TV, Cin* **p. à la taille** waist shot; **p. de travail** (*d'une cuisine*) work(ing) surface, worktop; *TV, Cin* **p. travelling** travelling shot; *TV, Cin* **p. très éloigné** extra *or* extreme long shot; *TV, Cin* **p. très rapproché** extreme close-up; *TV, Cin* **p. très serré** big close-up; *TV, Cin* **p. de visage** face shot

PLAN² **NM 1** (*relevé*) plan; *Constr, Tech* blueprint; (*de ville*) plan, map; **tracer un p.** to draw a plan; **relever le p. d'une région** to map out *or* survey an area; **p. de classement** filing method; **p. d'étage** floor plan; **p. géométral** ground plan; *Typ* **p. de maquette** layout card; **p. de mise en page** page plan

2 (*projet*) plan, scheme, project; **faire** *ou* **arrêter le p. de qch** to plan sth; **quels sont vos plans pour les années à venir?** what are your plans for the future?; *Fig* **tirer** *ou* **faire des plans sur la comète** to build castles in Spain *or* in the air; *Fam* **t'as un p. pour ce soir?** got any plans for tonight?; *Fam* **il a de bons plans pour bouffer à l'œil** he's got good ideas when it comes to finding cheap places to eat; **sans p. arrêté** without any set plan; **p. de carrière** career plan; **p. d'études** study plan *or* programme; **p. économique** economic plan, plan for the economy; **p. d'un roman/d'un devoir** plan for a novel/an essay

3 *Fam* **laisser qn en p.** to leave sb in the lurch; (*sans moyen de transport*) to leave sb stranded; **laisser son travail en p.** to leave one's work unfinished; **il a tout laissé en p. et il est rentré** he dropped everything and went home

▶▶ *Mktg* **p. d'activité** business plan; *Compta* **p. d'amortissement** depreciation schedule; *Ordinat* **p. calcul** = plan to establish a computer industry in France; *Compta* **p. comptable** chart of accounts; *Compta* **p. comptable général** chart of accounts; *Compta* **p. de comptes** chart of accounts; *TV, Cin* **p. des décors** floor plan; *Fin* **p. d'épargne** savings scheme *or* plan; *Fin* **p. d'épargne en actions** personal equity plan, PEP; *Fin* **p. d'épargne entreprise** employee share *or* Am stock ownership plan; *Fin* **p. d'épargne retraite** retirement savings plan *or* scheme; **p. d'évacuation** escape route; *Compta* **p. de financement** funding plan, financial plan; *Mktg* **p. de marchéage** marketing mix; *Mktg* **p. (des) médias** media planning; *Mktg* **p. de mercatique (stratégique)** (strategic) marketing plan; *Ordinat* **p. de navigation** site map; **p. d'occupation des sols** land-use plan; *TV, Cin* **p. de positionnement sur le plateau** staging plan; *Cin, TV* **p. de production** production schedule; **p. quinquennal** five-year plan; **p. de redressement** recovery plan; *Constr* **p. de référence** datum plane *or* level; **p. social** (*du gouvernement*) social plan; *Com* = corporate restructuring plan, usually involving job losses; *Mktg* **p. stratégique d'entreprise** strategic business plan; *Mktg* **p. des supports** media planning; **p. de travail créatif** (*publicité*) creative brief; *Aviat* **p. de vol** flight plan

planage [planaʒ] **NM** *Tech* (*de bois*) planing; (*de métal*) planishing

planant [planã] **ADJ** *Fam* (*drogue*) relaxing; (*musique*) mellow

planche [plãʃ] **NF 1** (*pièce de bois*) plank; (*plus large*) board; (*étagère*) shelf; *Fam* (*ski*) plank; *Fig* **c'est ma p. de salut** it's my sheet anchor; (*dernier espoir*) it's my last hope; *Natation* **faire la p.** to float on one's back; *Fig Fam* **c'est une p. à pain, elle est plate comme une p. à pain** she's as flat as a pancake; *Fig* **avoir du pain sur la p.** to have a lot on one's plate **2** *Naut* **p. (de débarquement)** gangplank; **passer à la p.** to walk the plank; **jour de p.** lay day **3** *Théâtre* **les planches** the stage, the boards; **monter sur les planches** to go on the stage, to tread the boards; **être sur les planches** to be on the stage; **l'amour des planches** love of the stage **4** (*d'imprimerie, de gravure etc*) plate, block; **planches en couleurs** colour plates **5** (*de jardin potager*) bed **6** *Sport* (*de surf*) surfboard; (*à voile*) sailboard **7** **les planches** (*sur une plage*) the boardwalk

▶▶ **p. à billets** printing press (*for printing banknotes*); *Fig* **faire fonctionner la p. à billets** to print money; *Aut* **p. de bord** dashboard, fascia panel; **p. à découper** chopping board; **p. à dessin** drawing board; **p. à fromage** cheeseboard; **p. à hacher** chopping board; **p. à laver** washboard; *Can* **p. des neiges** (*objet*) snowboard; (*sport*) snowboarding; **p. à pain** breadboard; **p. à pâtisserie** pastry board; **p. à repasser** ironing board *or* Am table; **p. à roulettes** skateboard; **faire de la p. à roulettes** to go skateboarding, to skateboard; **p. de surf** surfboard; **p. à voile** sailboard; **faire de la p. à voile** to go windsurfing, to windsurf

planchéiage [plãʃejaʒ] **NM** (*de cloison, de plancher*) boarding, planking; (*d'une pièce*) flooring

planchéier [plãʃeje] **VT** (*impf, pr sub* n. **planchéiions**, v. **planchéiiez**) (*cloison*) to board, to plank; (*plancher*) to board over, to plank over; (*pièce*) to floor

plancher¹ [plãʃe] **NM 1** (*sol*) floor; *Fam* **le p. des vaches** dry land, terra firma; *Fam* **débarrassez-moi le p.!** get out!, clear out!, beat it!; *Fam* **avoir un feu de p.** = to be wearing trousers that are too short **2** *Fig* (*minimum*) minimum, lower limit; **le p. des versements** the minimum deposit; **prix p.** bottom price **3** *Tech* (*de pont*) planking; (*de la salle des machines*) floorplates; (*de tranchée*) flooring; *Aut* floor, floorpan; *Aut* **p. de chargement** load floor; *Aut, Fig* **mettre le pied au p.** to put one's foot down **4** *Tech* (*de serrure*) bottom **5** *Anat* (*d'une cavité*) floor; **p. pelvien** pelvic floor

plancher² **VI** *Scol Fam* to be tested, to have a test; **les ministres planchent sur ce problème** the ministers are working on the problem

planchette [plãʃet] **NF** (*petite planche*) (small) board; (*étagère*) (small) shelf; *Spéc* (*de topographe*) plane table; *Phot* **p. d'objectif** lens panel

planchiste [plãʃist] **N** *Sport* windsurfer

plançon [plãsõ] **NM** (*jeune arbre*) sapling; (*plante*) set, slip

plan-concave, pl **plan-concaves ADJ** *Opt* (*lentilles*) plano-concave

plan-convexe, pl **plan-convexes ADJ** *Opt* (*lentilles*) plano-convex

plancton [plãktõ] **NM** plankton

plané [plane] **ADJ** *Aviat* **vol p.** gliding; **descendre en vol p.** to glide down; *Fam* **faire un vol p.** (*tomber*) to go flying

planéité [planeite] **NF** flatness, evenness

planer¹ [plane] **VT** *Tech* (*bois*) to plane; (*métal*) to planish

planer² vi **1** *(d'un oiseau)* to glide, to soar; *(voltiger)* to hover; *(d'un ballon)* to float; *(d'un planeur)* to glide; *(de la brume, fumée)* to hover, to hang; *Fig* **p. sur qn/qch** to hang or hover over sb/sth; **la menace plane** there's a sense of threat in the air **2** *Litt* **son regard planait au-delà des montagnes** he gazed out beyond the mountains; **son esprit planait au-dessus de la ville** his mind soared above the city **3** *Fig Fam (se sentir particulièrement bien)* to be on cloud nine, to be or feel on top of the world; *(perdre le sens des réalités)* to have one's head in the clouds; *(après s'être drogué)* to be high; *(penser à autre chose)* to be miles away, to have one's head in the clouds

planétaire [planetɛr] ADJ **1** *Astron (système)* planetary **2** *Tech* **engrenage p.** planetary gear **3** *Phys (électrons)* orbital, orbiting **4** *(expansion, action)* on a worldwide or global scale
▸ NM *Aut* sun gear

planétairement [planetɛrmɑ̃] ADV **voir les choses p.** to look at things on a worldwide or global basis

planétarisation [planetarizasjɔ̃] NF globalization; **la p. économique** the growth of a world economy

planétarium [planetarjɔm] NM *Astron* planetarium

planète [planɛt] NF *Astron* planet; **planètes inférieures/supérieures** inferior/superior planets; **sur toute la p.** over the whole planet, all over the planet

planétisation [planetizasjɔ̃] NF = **planétarisation**

planétoïde [planetɔid] NM *Astron* planetoid

planétologie [planetɔlɔʒi] NF planetology

planeur¹ [planœr] NM *Aviat* glider; **faire du p.** to go gliding

planeur², **-euse** [planœr, -øz] *Tech* N *(ouvrier)* planisher
▸ NF **planeuse** *(machine)* planing machine; *(pour métal)* planishing machine

planifiable [planifjabl] ADJ *Écon* that can be planned

planificateur, -trice [planifikatœr, -tris] *Écon* ADJ *(autorité, mesures)* planning
▸ N planner

planification [planifikasjɔ̃] NF *Écon* planning; **p. budgétaire** budget planning; **p. à court terme** short-term planning; **p. économique** economic planning; *Mktg* **p. de l'entreprise** corporate planning; **p. à long terme** long-term planning; **p. des naissances** population control; **p. nationale** state planning; **p. stratégique** strategic planning

planifier [planifje] VT *(impf, pr sub* **n. planifiions, v. planifiiez)** *Écon* to plan

planigramme [planigram] NM *Mktg* flowchart

planisme [planism] NM *Écon* planning

planisphère [planisfɛr] NM planisphere

planning [planiŋ] NM **1** plan, schedule; *(programme d'activités, de travail)* schedule; **p. Whitney** *(dans un hôtel)* Whitney rack; **p. d'occupation journalière** *(dans un hôtel)* daily occupancy chart; **p. de fabrication** manufacturing plan or schedule; *Compta* **p. des charges** expenditure plan; **p. à gouttières** slot-in planner; **nous avons un p. très chargé cette semaine** we have a very busy schedule this week **2 p. familial** family planning; *(lieu)* family planning clinic

plan-plan [plɑ̃plɑ̃] ADJ INV *Fam* routine, humdrum

planque [plɑ̃k] NF *Fam* **1** *(cachette) (pour une personne)* hideout, hideaway, hiding place; *(pour quelque chose)* hiding place; **la police est en p. devant la maison** the police

are staking out the house **2** *(travail facile)* cushy job or number; **vraiment, ce boulot, c'est la p.!** this job is really cushy!

planqué, -ée [plɑ̃ke] N *Fam Péj* person with a cushy job; *Mil* dodger, shirker; **quelle planquée!** what a cushy job she's got!

planquer [plɑ̃ke] *Fam* VT to hide (away), to stash (away); *(personne)* to hide
▸ VI *(de la police)* **p. devant la maison** to stake out the house
▸ VPR **se planquer** to hide; *(se mettre à l'abri)* to take cover

plant [plɑ̃] NM **1** *(pépinière) (d'arbres, d'arbustes)* nursery **plantation 2** *(carré)* patch, bed; **p. de choux** cabbage patch **3** *(bouture) (d'un arbre)* sapling; *(d'une plante)* set, slip; **jeunes plants** seedlings

plantage [plɑ̃taʒ] NM *Fam (échec)* flop; *Ordinat* crash

plantain [plɑ̃tɛ̃] NM *Bot* plantain

plantaire [plɑ̃tɛr] ADJ *Anat* plantar; **voûte p.** plantar arch

plantard [plɑ̃tar] NM = **plançon**

plantation [plɑ̃tasjɔ̃] NF **1** *(fait de planter) (d'arbres, de graines)* planting **2** *(exploitation) (de sucre, thé)* plantation; **p. d'oranges** orange grove

plante¹ [plɑ̃t] NF *Anat* **p. du pied** sole (of the foot); **la p. des pieds** the soles (of the feet)

plante² NF *Bot* plant; **le Jardin des Plantes** = botanical gardens and zoo in Paris; *Fig Fam* **cette fille, quelle belle p.!** she's a stunner, that girl!
▸ ▸ **p. d'appartement** pot or house plant; **p. à fleurs** flowering plant; **p. grasse** succulent (plant); **p. marine** seaweed; **p. potagère** *(herbe)* herb; *(légume)* vegetable; **p. de serre** hothouse plant; **plantes vertes** house plants, foliage

planté [plɑ̃te] ADJ **1 enfant bien p.** sturdy or healthy child; **bien p. sur ses jambes** sturdily built; **avoir les dents bien/mal plantées** to have straight/crooked teeth **2** *(debout)* standing; **il était p. au milieu de la pièce** he had planted himself or he was standing right in the middle of the room; *Fam* **ne la laissez pas plantée là** don't leave her standing there; **tu ne vas pas rester p. devant nous à ne rien faire** you're not just going to stand there doing nothing **3** *Ordinat Fam* **être p.** *(réseau, ordinateur)* to be down

planter [plɑ̃te] VT **1** *(graines, fleurs, arbres)* to plant; *(bouture)* to plant, to set out; **colline plantée d'arbres** hill planted with trees **2** *(clou)* to knock in, to hammer in; **p. un pieu dans le sol** to drive a stake into the ground; **p. un drapeau** to put up or hoist or raise a flag; **p. une échelle contre le mur** to stand a ladder (up) against the wall; **p. sa tente** to put up or pitch one's tent; *Fig* **p. les personnages** to build up the characters, to give substance to the characters; *Fam* **p. son chapeau sur la tête** to stick or put one's hat on one's head; **p. un baiser sur la joue de qn** to plant a kiss on sb's cheek; *Fig Fam* **p. son regard sur qn** to fix one's gaze on sb; *Fam* **p. là qn** to dump sb; **il veut tout p. là** he wants to drop everything or give it all up; *Can Fig* **p. des clous** to doze off (in one's chair)
▸ VI *Ordinat Fam (ordinateur)* to crash
▸ VPR **se planter 1** *(se tenir immobile)* to plant oneself, to stand; **se p. devant qn** to plant oneself or stand in front of sb **2** *Fam (se tromper)* to get it wrong; **se p. dans ses calculs** to get one's calculations wrong **3** *Fam (en voiture)* to crash, to have an accident **4** *Fam (tomber)* to fall

planteur [plɑ̃tœr] NM **1** *(exploitant dans un pays tropical)* planter **2** *(cocktail)* planter's punch

planteuse [plɑ̃tøz] NF *Agr, Tech* potato planting machine

plantigrade [plɑ̃tigrad] ADJ, NM *Zool* plantigrade

plantoir [plɑ̃twar] NM dibble, dibber

planton [plɑ̃tɔ̃] NM *Mil* orderly; **être de p.** to be on orderly duty; *Fam* **faire le p.** to kick one's heels, to hang around

plantureusement [plɑ̃tyrøzmɑ̃] ADV copiously

plantureux, -euse [plɑ̃tyrø, -øz] ADJ **1** *(copieux) (repas)* copious, lavish; *(femme)* buxom; **poitrine plantureuse** ample bosom **2** *(fécond) (région)* fertile

plaquage [plakaʒ] NM = **placage 3**

plaque [plak] NF **1** *(feuille rigide) (de métal)* plate, sheet; *(de marbre)* slab; *(de chocolat)* block; *(de glace)* patch, sheet; *(de neige)* layer; *Phot* **appareil à plaques** plate camera **2** *Radio* anode; **tension de p.** plate voltage, anode voltage **3** *(portant une inscription)* plaque; *(insigne) (d'un bureau)* badge; *(d'un ordre)* star; **p. de porte** door plate; *(avec nom)* nameplate; **p. de rue** street nameplate, street sign **4** *Méd (sur la peau)* patch, *Spéc* plaque; **p. (dentaire)** (dental) plaque; **plaques muqueuses** mucous plaque; **sclérose en plaques** multiple sclerosis **5** *Fig Fam* **être à côté de la p.** to be off-target, to be wide of the mark **6** *Suisse (à gâteau)* cake tin
▸ ▸ *Élec* **p. d'accumulateur** accumulator plate; **p. d'auto-école** ≃ L-plate; **p. de blindage** armour or Am armor plate; **p. chauffante** hotplate; **p. de cheminée** fireback; **p. commémorative** commemorative plaque; *Com* **p. CSC** CSC plate; **p. d'égout** manhole cover; *Tech* **p. de fond** base plate; **p. de four** baking sheet or tray, *Am* cookie sheet; **p. funéraire** church brass; *Suisse* **p. à gâteau** cake tin; **p. à grille** grid plate; **p. d'identification** *(d'une machine)* model identification plate; *(avec nom)* nameplate; *(avec numéro)* numberplate; **p. d'identité** *(de soldat)* identity disc, *Am Fam* dog tag; *Aut* **p. d'immatriculation** ou **minéralogique** numberplate, *Am* license plate; **p. mortuaire** church brass; *Typ* **p. offset** offset plate; *Aut* **p. oscillante** *(de pompe d'injection rotative)* cam plate; **p. photographique** photographic plate; **p. de propreté** *(sur une porte)* fingerplate; **p. stéréoscopique** stereo slide; *Typ* **p. de tirage** printing plate; *Rail* **p. tournante** turntable; *Fig* **c'est la p. tournante du projet** the plan hinges on it; **cet aéroport est une p. tournante pour les industries régionales** this airport is the hub of industrial activity in the region; **cette ville deviendra la p. tournante de l'Europe** this city will become the hub of Europe

plaqué [plake] NM **1 p. or** gold plate; **montre en p. or** gold-plated watch; **c'est du p.** it's plated **2** *(bois)* veneered wood
▸ ADJ **p. or/argent** gold-/silver-plated

plaquemine [plakmin] NF *Bot* persimmon

plaqueminier [plakminje] NM *Bot* persimmon (tree)

plaquer [plake] VT **1** *(appliquer une plaque sur) (bois)* to veneer; *(métal)* to plate; *(appliquer) (plâtre)* to lay on **2** *(mettre à plat) (cheveux)* to plaster down; **le vent lui plaquait son manteau sur les jambes** the wind blew or flattened his coat against his/her legs; **p. qn contre un mur** to pin sb to a wall; **il avait les épaules plaquées au mur** he had his shoulders pinned or pressed to the wall **3** *Rugby (adversaire)* to tackle, to bring down **4** *Mus* **p. un accord** to strike (and hold) a chord **5** *Fam (abandonner) (amant, petit ami)* to ditch, to chuck; **j'ai envie de tout p.** I feel like chucking it all in **6** *Belg (coller)* to stick
▸ VPR **se plaquer se p. au sol/contre un mur** to

lie flat on the ground/flatten oneself against a wall

plaquette [plakɛt] NF **1** *(petite plaque) (de métal)* (small) plate; *(portant un nom, une inscription etc)* (small) plaque; *(bloc) (de métal)* block; *Ordinat* circuit board; **p. de circuits imprimés** printed circuit board, PCB; *Aut* **p. de frein** brake pad **2** *(petit livre)* booklet; **p. publicitaire** advertising brochure **3 plaquettes (sanguines)** (blood) platelets

plaqueur [plakœr] NM **1** *(sur métaux)* plater **2** *(sur bois)* veneerer

plasma [plasma] NM **1** *Biol* plasma; **p. sanguin** blood plasma **2** *Phys* **p. gazeux** gas plasma

plastic [plastik] NM plastic explosive

plasticage [plastikaʒ] NM bomb attack (**de** on)

plasticien, -ienne [plastisjɛ̃, -jɛn] N **1** *Tech* plastics technician **2** *Méd* plastic surgeon

plasticité [plastisite] NF plasticity

plastie [plasti] NF *Méd* plastic surgery

plastifiant [plastifjɑ̃] NM plasticizer

plastifier [plastifje] VT *(impf, pr sub* n. **plastifiions, v. plastifiiez)* **1** *(recouvrir de plastique)* to laminate; **jaquette plastifiée** laminated jacket **2** *Tech* to plasticize

plastiquage [plastikaʒ] NM = **plasticage**

plastique [plastik] ADJ **1** *(malléable)* plastic, malleable **2 arts plastiques** plastic arts; **chirurgie p.** plastic surgery; **statue aux formes plastiques** finely formed statue; **beauté p.** fine forms ▸ NF **1** *Beaux-Arts* plastic art, art of modelling **2** *(harmonie des formes) (d'une actrice, d'un danseur)* figure, physique ▸ NM plastic

plastiquement [plastikmɑ̃] ADV from the viewpoint of form; **cet athlète est p. très beau** this athlete has a very fine physique

plastiquer [plastike] VT to bomb *(using plastic explosive)*

plastiqueur, -euse [plastikœr, -øz] N bomber *(using plastic explosive)*

plastoc [plastɔk] NM *Fam* plastic

plastron [plastrɔ̃] NM **1** *(pièce d'armure)* breastplate, plastron; *(d'escrimeur)* plastron **2** *(de vêtement)* front; *(de chemise) (fixe)* shirt front; *(amovible)* dick(e)y, false shirt front

plastronner [plastrɔne] VT *(personne)* to put a plastron on ▸ VI to throw out one's chest; *Fig* to strut around, to swagger around

PLAT [pla] ADJ **1** *(qui a peu de relief)* flat, level; **pays p.** flat country; **chaussure plate** low-heeled *or* flat shoe; **avoir la poitrine plate/les pieds plats** to be flat-chested/-footed; *Fam* **elle est plate comme une limande** she's as flat as a pancake; **cheveux plats** flat hair; **mer plate** smooth *or* still sea; *Naut* **calme p.** dead calm; **c'est le calme p.** there's a dead calm; *Fig* things are dead quiet; **eau plate** still water; **vis à tête plate** flat-head(ed) screw; **assiette plate** dinner plate; *Ordinat* **écran p.** flat screen **2** *Fig (ennuyeux) (style, livre, film, intrigue)* flat, dull, *Fml* insipid; **vin p.** wine that lacks body **3 à p.** *(pneu, batterie)* flat; **mettre qch à p.** to lay sth (down) flat; *Fig* **mettre un problème à p.** to look at a problem from all sides; **couché à p. sur le sol** lying flat on the ground; **dormir à p.** to sleep without a pillow; *Fig* **tomber à p.** *(d'une proposition, d'un projet etc)* to fall flat; **se mettre à p. ventre** to lie flat on one's stomach; *Péj Fig* **se mettre à p. ventre (devant qn)** to crawl *or* grovel *or* kowtow (to sb); *Fam* **être à p.** *(épuisé)* to be exhausted *or* all in; *(en mauvaise santé)* to be run down; *Aut* to

have a flat; **cette maladie l'a mis à p.** the illness has taken it out of him ▸ NM **1** *(partie plate) (de la main)* flat; *(d'un aviron)* blade; *(d'un marteau)* face **2** *Sport* **course de p.** flat race; *Natation* **faire un p.** to do a bellyflop **3** *Fam* **faire du p. à qn** *(chercher à séduire)* to make advances to sb; *(flatter)* to crawl to sb, *Br* to suck up to sb; *Fam* **il en fait un p.** *(il fait très chaud)* it's a scorcher, *Br* it's roasting **4** *Culin (contenant)* dish; **p. (de service)** serving dish; **p. à barbe** shaving dish; **p. de quête** *(dans une église)* collection plate; *Fig* **mettre les petits plats dans les grands** to put on a marvellous spread; *Fig* **mettre les pieds dans le p.** to put one's foot in it; *Fam* **en faire tout un p.** to make a great fuss about it **5** *Culin (mets)* dish; *(partie du menu)* course; **p. cuisiné** ready-cooked dish; *(à emporter)* takeaway dish; **p. du jour** today's special, dish of the day; **p. principal** main course; **p. de résistance** main course; *Fig* pièce de résistance

platane [platan] NM plane tree; *Fam* **rentrer dans un p.** to crash into a tree

plat-bord, *pl* **plats-bords** NM *Naut* gunwale, gunnel; **hauteur au-dessus du p.** height above the hull

plate [plat] NF *Naut* punt, flat-bottomed boat

plateau, -eaux [plato] NM **1** *(plat)* tray; **p. d'argent** silver tray *or* salver; **p. à fromages** *(objet)* cheeseboard; **p. de fromages** *(choix de fromages)* cheeseboard; **p. de fruits de mer** seafood platter; **p. petit déjeuner** breakfast tray; **p. de courtoisie** hospitality tray; *Fig* **(servi) sur un p.** on a plate; *Fig* **ça ne va pas t'arriver servi sur un p.** you're not going to get it handed to you on a plate **2** *(d'une balance)* pan; *(d'une platine, d'un four micro-ondes)* turntable; *(de table)* top; **p. tournant** *(de tourne-disque)* turntable **3** *Géog* plateau; **haut p.** high plateau; **p. continental** continental shelf **4** *Méd* plateau **5** *Théâtre* stage; *Cin, TV* set; *Cin, TV* **sur le p.** on set; **p. de tournage** film set; **p. fermé** closed set; **p. sonorisé** sound stage; **p. tournant** revolving stage **6** *Rail* flat truck *or* wagon *or Am* car **7** *Tech* plate, disc, *Am* disk; **p. absorbeur de couple** torque plate; **p. de chargement** load bed, load platform; **p. d'embrayage** clutch plate; **p. de friction** friction plate; *Aut* **p. menant** driving plate; *Aut* **p. mené** driven plate; *Aut* **p. oscillant** wobble-plate, swashplate; *Cyclisme* **p. de pédalier** front chain wheel; **p. de pression** pressure plate; *Aut etc* **raccordement à plateaux** flange assembly

plateau-repas, *pl* **plateaux-repas** NM meal on a tray

plate-bande, *pl* **plates-bandes** NF flowerbed; *Fig Fam* **marcher sur les plates-bandes de qn** to trespass on sb's patch; **ne marchez pas sur mes plates-bandes** keep off my patch

plate-forme, *pl* **plates-formes** NF **1** *(partie ouverte) (d'un bus)* platform; *(d'une locomotive)* footplate; **toit en p.** flat roof; **p. de chargement** loading platform; *Aut* load deck; **p. de déchargement** unloading *or* offloading platform; *TV, Cin* **p. de prise de vue** camera platform **2** *Géog* **p. continentale** continental shelf **3** *Rail (wagon)* flat truck *or* wagon *or Am* car **4** *Mil* **p. de tir** gun platform; **p. tournante** turntable **5** *Pol* platform; **p. électorale** electoral platform **6** *Ordinat* platform **7** *Pétr* **p. pétrolière** *ou* **de forage** oil rig

plate-longe, *pl* **plates-longes** NF *(longe)* leading rein

platement [platmɑ̃] ADV *(s'exprimer, écrire)* in a dull *or* flat way, dully, flatly; **s'excuser p.** to apologize humbly

platinage [platinaʒ] NM platinum plating

platine¹ [platin] NF *Tech (d'une serrure)* plate; *(d'une presse à imprimer, d'une machine à écrire)* platen; *(d'un microscope)* stage; *(tourne-disque)* (record) deck, (record) turntable; **p. cassettes** cassette *or* tape deck; **p. laser** CD player

platine² [platin] NM platinum ▸ ADJ INV platinum; **cheveux (blonds) p.** platinum blond hair

platiné [platine] ADJ **1** *(recouvert de platine)* platinum-plated; *Aut* **vis platinées** points **2 cheveux platinés** platinum blond hair; **une blonde platinée** a platinum blonde

platiner [platine] VT to plate with platinum

platitude [platityd] NF **1** *(de personnalité, style, discussion)* dullness; **ce film est d'une p.!** this film is so dull! **2** *(propos)* platitude, trite remark; **débiter des platitudes** to talk in platitudes, *Fml* to platitudinize; *Arch* **faire des platitudes à qn** to grovel to sb

Platon [platɔ̃] N Plato

platonicien, -ienne [platɔnisjɛ̃, -jɛn] ADJ *(école, philosophe)* Platonic ▸ N Platonist

platonique [platɔnik] ADJ **1** *(amour)* platonic **2** *(vain)* futile, vain

platoniquement [platɔnikmɑ̃] ADV *(aimer)* platonically

platonisme [platɔnism] NM Platonism

plâtrage [plɑtraʒ] NM *Constr (action)* plastering; *(ouvrage)* plasterwork

plâtras [plɑtra] NM *(débris)* (plaster) rubble; *(morceau)* lump of plaster

plâtre [plɑtr] NM **1** *Constr* plaster; **les plâtres** the plasterwork; *Fig Fam* **essuyer les plâtres** *(d'une maison)* to be the first occupant; *(subir des conséquences fâcheuses)* to put up with the teething problems; *Fig Fam* **ce camembert, c'est du p.** this Camembert is like chalk **2** *Beaux-Arts* plaster; *(ouvrage)* plaster cast; **p. de moulage** plaster of Paris **3** *Méd* plaster; *(moule)* plaster cast; **poser un p.** to put a plaster cast on; **avoir la jambe dans le p.** to have one's leg in plaster

plâtrée [plɑtre] NF *Fam* huge helping; **une p. de nouilles** a huge helping of noodles

plâtrer [plɑtre] VT **1** *(enduire de plâtre) (mur, plafond)* to plaster; *(trou, fissure)* to plaster over *or* up **2** *Méd* to put in plaster **3** *Agr (sol)* to dress with sulphate

plâtrerie [plɑtrəri] NF *(usine)* plasterworks; **travaux de p.** plasterwork, plastering

plâtreux, -euse [plɑtrø, -øz] ADJ *(mur)* covered with plaster; *Fig (camembert)* chalky; **teint p.** pasty *or* chalky complexion

plâtrier [plɑtrije] NM plasterer

plâtrière [plɑtrijɛr] NF *(carrière)* gypsum quarry; *(four)* plaster kiln, gypsum kiln

plausibilité [plozibilite] NF plausibility

plausible [plozibl] ADJ plausible

plausiblement [plozibləmɑ̃] ADV plausibly

Plaute [plot] N Plautus

play-back [plɛbak] NM INV miming; **chanter en p.** to mime; **c'est du p.** he's/she's/*etc* miming

play-boy, *pl* **play-boys** [plɛbɔj] NM playboy

plèbe [plɛb] NF **1** *Antiq* **la p.** the plebs **2** *Litt Péj* **la p.** the hoi polloi, the plebs, the common people

plébéien, -ienne [plebejɛ̃, -jɛn] ADJ, N plebeian

plébiscite [plebisit] NM plebiscite

plébisciter [plebisite] VT **1** *(élire par plébiscite)* **p. qn/qch** to vote for sb/sth by plebiscite **2** *(élire à une très forte majorité)* **p. qn** to elect sb by a large majority **3** *Fig* to heartily approve of, to endorse

plectre [plɛktr] NM plectrum

pléiade [plejad] NF 1 *Astron* **les Pléiades** the Pleiades 2 *Littér* **la P.** the Pleiad; *Fig* **une p. de gens célèbres** a galaxy of famous people

PLEIN [plɛ̃]

> **ADJ** full **1–5** ▪ complete **2** ▪ right in the middle of *(en plein)* **5** ▪ pregnant *(pleine)* **6** ▪ drunk **7**
> **ADV** lots of *(plein de)*
> **NM** full tank (of petrol) **1** ▪ right in the middle of *(en plein dans)* **3**

ADJ 1 *(rempli)* full (**de** of); **une bouteille pleine** a full bottle; **une pleine bouteille** a whole bottle, a bottleful; **p. comme un œuf** chock-full, chock-a-block; **salle pleine à craquer** room full to bursting; **avoir le ventre p.** to be full (up), to have eaten one's fill; **ne parle pas la bouche pleine** don't speak with your mouth full; **suffit, j'ai la tête pleine!** that's enough, I've had it up to here!; **être p. de courage** to have a lot of courage; **être p. d'espoir** to be full of hope, to be hopeful; **une entreprise pleine de dangers/risques** an enterprise fraught with danger/risk; **il a les doigts pleins d'encre** his fingers are covered with ink; **être p. de certitudes** to be sure of things

2 *(complet)* *(accord, adhésion)* full, complete; **pleine lune** full moon; **p. sud** due south; **la chambre est (en) p. ouest** the room faces due west; **pleine mer** *(marée haute)* high tide; **en pleine mer** out at sea, on the open sea; **gagner la pleine mer** to reach the open sea; **p. tarif** full price; *(de transports)* full fare; *(dans un hôtel)* rack rate; **trois jours pleins** three full days; **reliure pleine peau** full leather binding; **p. format** *(de journal)* text-size format, broadsheet format; **p. pouvoir** full power; *Jur* power of attorney; **avoir les pleins pouvoirs** to have full powers; **de son p. gré** of one's own free will, of one's own accord

3 *(solide, qui occupe toute la masse)* *(pneu, essieu etc)* solid; *(ligne)* continuous, unbroken; *(visage)* full; **joues pleines** full *or* plump cheeks

4 *(intense)* **respirer à pleins poumons** to breathe deeply; **crier à pleine gorge** to shout at the top of one's voice; **rire à pleine gorge** to roar with laughter; **ça sent le brûlé à p. nez** there's a strong smell of burning; **apporter des fleurs à pleines brassées** to bring armfuls of flowers; **être en pleine forme** to be on top form; **être en pleine possession de ses moyens** to be in full possession of one's faculties; **à p. temps** full-time; **travailler à p. temps** to work full-time; **un p. temps** a full-time job

5 *(au milieu de)* **en p.** *(milieu du)* **cours** (right) in the middle of the lesson; **en pleine réunion/messe** (right) in the middle of the meeting/of Mass; **s'arrêter en p. milieu de la place** to stop right in the middle of the square; **en pleine figure**, *très Fam* **en pleine gueule** right *or* bang in the face; **il a reçu la balle en p. cœur/en pleine poitrine** he got the bullet right *or* bang in the heart/in the chest; **en p. hiver** in the depths *or* the middle of winter; **en p. air** in the open (air); **restaurant/piscine en p. air** open-air restaurant/swimming pool; **en p. soleil** in the full heat of the sun; **marché en p. vent** open-air market; **planté en pleine terre** planted in open ground; **en p. jour** in broad daylight; **en pleine nuit** in the middle of the night, at dead of night; **en pleine lumière** in the full light; **en pleine saison** at the height of the season; **prix de la pleine saison** high-season prices; **en p. tribunal** in open court; **être en p. travail** to be hard at work; **être en pleine croissance** to be growing fast; **à pleines**

voiles with all sails set, under full sail

6 *(animal)* pregnant; **jument pleine** mare in foal; **brebis pleine** ewe with lamb; **chèvre pleine** goat in kid

7 *Fam* **être p. (comme une barrique)** *(ivre)* to be (dead) drunk, to be plastered, to have had a skinful

ADV il avait des larmes p. les yeux his eyes were full of tears; **il a des billes/livres p. ses poches** his pockets are full of marbles/stuffed with books; **avoir de l'argent p. les poches** to have plenty of money; **elle avait de la colle p. les mains** her hands were covered with *or* in glue; **elle a des vêtements p. ses armoires** her cupboards are full of *or* stuffed with clothes; **elle en a p. la bouche** she's full of him/it/*etc*, she never shuts up about him/it/*etc*, *Fam* **en avoir p. le dos** *ou* *très Fam* **le cul** to be sick of it, to be fed up with it, *Fam* **to have had a bellyful; *Fam* **en avoir p. les jambes** *ou* **les bottes** to be on one's last legs; *Fam* **en mettre p. la vue à qn** to dazzle sb, to impress sb; *Fam* **s'en mettre p. la lampe** to have a good blowout; **à p.** *(travailler, fonctionner etc)* at full capacity; **l'avion part à p.** the plane is leaving with a full passenger load; **l'argument/la remarque a porté à p.** the argument/remark has had the desired effect; **elle est mignonne tout p.** she's awfully sweet; *Fam* **p. de gens/magasins/journaux** lots *or* loads of people/shops/newspapers; *Naut* **porter p.** to keep her full

NM 1 *(de carburant)* full tank; **faire le p. d'un réservoir** to fill up a tank; *Aut* **faire le p. (d'essence)** to fill up (with petrol *or Am* gas); **(faites) le p., s'il vous plaît** fill her up, please; *Fig* **faire le p. d'air pur/de soleil** to get a good dose of fresh air/sunshine; **on fait le p. une fois par semaine chez Casino** *(de courses)* we do a big shop *or* stock-up once a week at Casino; **avoir son p.** *(d'un bateau)* to be fully laden

2 *(phase maximale)* **le p. (de la mer)** high tide; **battre son p.** *(de la marée)* to be at the full; *Fig* **la saison bat son p., c'est le p. de la saison** the season is at its height *or* is in full swing; **la fête battait son p.** the party was in full swing

3 en p. dans le centre full *or* right in the middle, *Fam* slap bang in the middle; **en p. dans le mille** right in the bull's-eye; *Fig* spot on, *Fam* bang on

4 *(trait épais)* downstroke; *Typ* thick stroke

pleinement [plɛnmɑ̃] ADV fully; **je veux en profiter p.** I want to make the most of it *or* to take full advantage of it

plein-emploi [plɛnɑ̃plwa] NM INV full employment

pléistocène [pleistɔsɛn] ADJ, NM *Géol* Pleistocene

plénier, -ière [plenje, -jɛr] ADJ plenary

plénipotentiaire [plenipɔtɑ̃sjɛr] ADJ, NM plenipotentiary

plénitude [plenityd] NF *(d'une émotion, d'une expérience etc)* fullness, plenitude; *(d'une victoire etc)* completeness; *(d'un son)* fullness, richness

plénum [plenɔm] NM plenum

pléonasme [pleɔnasm] NM pleonasm

pléonastique [pleɔnastik] ADJ pleonastic

plésiosaure [plezjɔzɔr] NM plesiosaurus

pléthore [pletɔr] NF plethora (**de** of)

pléthorique [pletɔrik] ADJ 1 *Méd Vieilli* full-blooded, plethoric 2 *(très abondant)* superabundant; *(trop)* excessive

pleur [plœr] NM *Litt* tear; **verser des pleurs** to shed tears; **fondre en pleurs** to dissolve into tears; **cessez vos pleurs** dry your tears; **être (tout) en pleurs** to be (bathed) in tears; *Bible* **il va y avoir des pleurs et des grince-**

ments de dents there will be wailing and gnashing of teeth

pleurage [plœraʒ] NM *Tech* wow; **niveau de p.** wow level

pleural, -ale, -aux, -ales [plœral, -o] ADJ *Anat* pleural

pleurant, -ante [plœrɑ̃, -ɑ̃t] ADJ *Litt* weeping, crying
▸ N *Beaux-Arts* weeper, mourner *(on a tomb)*

pleurard, -arde [plœrar, -ard] *Péj Vieilli* ADJ *(enfant)* whimpering, fractious; *(voix)* whining, whimpering, tearful
▸ N whiner, *Fam* crybaby

pleurer [plœre] VT 1 **p. qn** to mourn (for) sb; **p. la mort de qn** to mourn sb's death; **p. sa jeunesse, p. ses vingt ans** to weep for *or* over one's lost youth; **mourir sans être pleuré** to die unmourned

2 *(laisser couler)* to cry, to shed, to weep; **p. toutes les larmes de son corps** to cry one's eyes out; **p. des larmes de sang** to weep bitterly, to shed bitter tears; **p. des larmes de bonheur** to cry *or* weep for joy; **p. misère** to bemoan one's lot

3 *Fig Fam Vieilli (ménager) (argent)* to stint; **elle ne pleure pas ses efforts** *ou* **sa peine/ses conseils** she spares no effort/is generous with her advice

▸ VI 1 *(verser des larmes)* to cry, to weep (**sur** over; **pour** for); **et puis j'ai vu que je m'étais trompé et j'en aurais pleuré** when I saw I had made a mistake, I could have cried *or* wept; **elle pleure de ne pas avoir eu son examen** she's crying because she hasn't passed her exam; **p. sur soi-même** *ou* **sur son sort** to bewail *or* bemoan one's fate; **p. de joie** to cry *or* weep for joy; **p. à chaudes larmes** *ou Fam* **comme une madeleine** *ou Fam* **comme un veau** to sob *or* cry one's heart out; **s'endormir en pleurant** to cry oneself to sleep; **il était sentimental, c'était à en p.** he was ridiculously sentimental; **c'est à (faire) p.** it's enough to make you weep *or* cry; **bête/méchant à faire p.** terribly stupid/nasty

2 **j'ai les yeux qui pleurent** my eyes are watering *or* running

3 *Fig Péj (supplier)* to beg; **aller p. auprès de qn** to go begging to sb; *Fam* **et qu'il ne vienne pas me p. dans les bras!** and he needn't come begging to me!; **p. après une faveur** to beg for a favour

pleurésie [plœrezi] NF *Méd* pleurisy

pleurétique [plœretik] ADJ, N *Méd* pleuritic

pleureur, -euse [plœrœr, -øz] N *Péj Vieilli* whimperer
▸ NF **pleureuse** *(dans un cortège funèbre)* (hired) mourner, *Arch* mute
▸ ADJ *Péj* whimpering; **saule p.** weeping willow

pleurite [plœrit] NF *Méd* dry pleurisy

pleurnichard, -arde [plœrniʃar, -ard] N, ADJ = pleurnicheur

pleurnichement [plœrniʃmɑ̃] NM = pleurnicherie

pleurnicher [plœrniʃe] VI *Fam* to whine, to snivel, *Br (surtout d'un jeune enfant)* to grizzle

pleurnicherie [plœrniʃri] NF *Fam* whining, snivelling, *Br (surtout d'un jeune enfant)* grizzling

pleurnicheur, -euse [plœrniʃœr, -øz] *Fam* N whiner, sniveller; *(qui pleure facilement)* cry baby
▸ ADJ whining, snivelling

pleurote [plœrɔt] NM oyster mushroom

pleutre [pløtr] *Litt Péj* ADJ craven, cowardly
▸ NM craven, coward

pleuvasser [pløvase], **pleuviner** [pløvine] V IMPERS to drizzle

pleuvoir [pløvwar] *(prp* **pleuvant**; *pp* **plu**; *pr* *ind* **il pleut, ils pleuvent**; *impf* **il pleuvait**; *p hist* **il plut**; *fu* **il pleuvra**) **v IMPERS** to rain; **il pleut** it's raining; **il pleut à verse** *ou* **à seaux** it's pouring (down) (with rain); **les jours où il pleut** on wet *or* rainy days; *Fam* **il pleut des cordes** *ou* **des hallebardes, il pleut comme vache qui pisse** it's raining cats and dogs, it's coming down in buckets, *Br* it's tipping it down; *Can* **il pleut à boire debout** it's pouring; **des cadeaux comme s'il en pleuvait** presents galore; **dépenser de l'argent comme s'il en pleuvait** to spend money as if there's no tomorrow *or* as if it's going out of fashion **vI faire p. des coups sur qn** to rain blows (down) on sb, to shower sb with blows; **les invitations pleuvent sur lui** invitations are pouring in to him, he's being inundated with invitations; **ce ne sont pas exactement les compliments qui pleuvent** I'm not exactly being showered with compliments

pleuvoter [plœvɔte] **v IMPERS** = **pleuvasser**

plèvre [plɛvr] **NF** *Anat* pleura, pleural membrane

Plexiglas® [plɛksiglas] **NM** Perspex®, *Am* Plexiglas®

plexus [plɛksys] **NM** *Anat* plexus; **p. solaire** solar plexus

pli [pli] **NM 1** *(rabat) (de rideaux, tissu)* fold; *Couture* pleat; **(faux) p.** crease; *Couture* **p. creux** *ou* **rentré** *ou* **inverti, double p.** box pleat, inverted pleat; **p. couché** knife pleat; **petit p.** tuck; **jupe à plis** pleated skirt; **faire** *ou* **marquer le p. d'un pantalon** to put a crease in a pair of trousers; **faire des plis à une robe** to put pleats in a dress, to pleat a dress; *(la froisser)* to crease a dress
2 mise en plis set; **faire une mise en plis à qn** to set sb's hair
3 *Aut (d'un pneu)* ply; **p. diagonal** diagonal ply; **p. radial** radial ply
4 *Fig* **ça ne fait pas un p.** (there's) no doubt about it; **j'étais sûr qu'il allait se tromper, et ça n'a pas fait un p.!** I was sure he'd make a mistake, and I was right!; *Fig* **prendre le p. (de faire qch)** to get into the habit (of doing sth); **il a pris le p.** he got used to it, he got into the habit; **le p. était pris** I/he/*etc* had got used to it; *Fig* **prendre un mauvais p.** to get into a bad habit
5 *(du bras, de la jambe)* bend; *(de peau)* fold; *(petit)* wrinkle; **p. du jarret** hollow of the knee; **les plis du front** the lines on the forehead; **elle a de gros plis sur le ventre** she has big folds of skin on her stomach; **il a de petits plis autour des yeux** he has wrinkles round his eyes
6 *(enveloppe)* envelope; *(lettre)* letter; **sous p. séparé** under separate cover; **sous p. discret** under plain cover, *aussi Hum* in a plain brown wrapper; **nous vous envoyons sous ce p. ...** we are sending you herewith ..., please find enclosed ...; **p. cacheté** sealed envelope; *Naut* sealed orders; **envoyer qch sous p. cacheté** to send sth in a sealed envelope; **p. chargé** registered and insured letter; **p. recommandé** registered letter; **par p. recommandé** by registered mail
7 *Cartes* trick; **faire un p.** to take a trick
8 *Géol* **p. de terrain** fold

pliable [plijabl] **ADJ** *(chaise, lit)* foldable; **canot p.** folding boat

pliage [plijaʒ] **NM** *(d'un tissu)* folding; *(origami)* paper folding; *(objet)* folded-paper model

pliant [plijã] **ADJ** *(chaise, table)* folding, collapsible; **pied p.** folding tripod
NM folding *or* collapsible stool

plie [pli] **NF** plaice

plié [plije] **NM** *(en danse)* plié

plier [plije] *(impf, pr sub* **n. pliions, v. pliiez)* **vT 1** *(mettre en double) (draps, vêtements)* to fold; *(page)* to turn down; *(voile)* to furl; *(rabattre) (parapluie)* to fold up *or* away; *Fig* **p. bagage** to pack one's bags **2** *(courber) (branche, genou etc)* to bend; **plié en deux** *(personne)* bent double, doubled up; *Fig Fam* **être plié (de rire)** to be doubled up *or* bent double with laughter; **p. qn à la discipline/une règle/une contrainte** to impose discipline/a rule/a constraint on sb; **p. qn à une habitude** to get sb into a habit **3** *Fam (détruire)* to smash up, to wreck
vI 1 *(se courber)* to bend (over); **p. sous le poids de qch** *(d'une poutre, de branches etc)* to bend *or* give *or* sag under the weight of sth **2** *(se soumettre)* to submit, to yield; *(des troupes dans une bataille)* to give way; **elle ne pliera pas devant lui** she will not submit to him *or* give in to him
vPR se plier *(d'un parapluie, d'une chaise)* to fold (up); **se p. aux circonstances** to yield *or* bow *or* submit to circumstances; **se p. à la discipline** to submit to discipline; **se p. aux lois** to obey the law; **se p. aux caprices/volontés de qn** to give in to sb's whims/wishes

plieur, -ieuse [plijœr, -jøz] *Tech* **N** *(personne)* folder
NF plieuse folding machine

Pline [plin] **N P. l'Ancien/le Jeune** Pliny the Elder/the Younger

plinthe [plɛ̃t] **NF 1** *(lame de bois)* skirting (board), *Am* baseboard **2** *Archit (de colonne)* plinth

pliocène [plijɔsɛn] **ADJ, NM** *Géol* Pliocene

plioir [plijwar] **NM** *(coupe-papier)* paper knife

plissage [plisaʒ] **NM** *(d'un tissu)* pleating

plissé [plise] **ADJ 1** *Couture* pleated **2 front p.** wrinkled brow; **visage tout p.** creased *or* wrinkled face
NM *Couture* pleats; **p. soleil** sunray *or* *Am* sunburst pleats

plissement [plismã] **NM 1** *(fait de plier) (d'un tissu)* pleating; *(de papier)* folding; *(de métal, de carton)* corrugation **2** *(froissement) (de papier, de tissu)* creasing, crumpling, crinkling **3** *(froncement) (des yeux)* screwing up **4** *Géol* fold; **le p. hercynien** the Armorican *or* Hercynian fold

plisser [plise] **vT 1** *(plier) (vêtement)* to pleat; *(papier)* to fold; *(métal, carton)* to corrugate **2** *(froisser) (papier, tissu)* to crease, to crumple, to crinkle **3** *(froncer) (front)* to wrinkle; *(lèvres)* to pucker; **p. les yeux** to screw up one's eyes
vI *(d'un vêtement)* to crease
vPR se plisser *(d'une étoffe)* to crease; *(d'une bouche)* to pucker; **la soie se plisse facilement** silk creases easily; **ses yeux se plissent quand elle sourit** her eyes go all crinkly when she smiles; **son front se plissa** he frowned

plisseur, -euse [plisœr, -øz] *Tex* **N** *(personne)* pleater
NF plisseuse pleating machine

plissure [plisyr] **NF** pleats

pliure [plijyr] **NF** *(action) (du papier)* folding; *(résultat) (d'un tissu)* fold; *(du genou)* bend

ploc [plɔk] **INT** plop!

ploiement [plwamã] **NM** bending

plomb [plɔ̃] **NM 1** *(métal)* lead; **p.-étain** lead-tin; **p. laminé** *ou* **en feuilles** sheet lead; **tuyau de p.** lead pipe; **blanc de p.** white lead; *Fig* **sommeil de p.** deep *or* heavy sleep; **dormir d'un sommeil de p.** to sleep like a log; **ciel de p.** leaden sky; **teint de p.** livid complexion; **soleil de p.** blazing (hot) sun; *Fig* **n'avoir pas de p. dans la tête** to be scatterbrained; **espérons que cela lui mettra un peu de p. dans la tête** *ou* **dans la cervelle** let's hope that will knock some sense into him; **années de p.** dark years; **les années de p. de l'Occupation** the dark years of the Occupation **2** *(poids)* lead (weight); *Pêche* sinker; *Naut* **jeter** *ou* **lancer le p. (de sonde)** to heave the lead; **fil à p.** plumb line; **à p.** upright, vertical **3** *Archit* **plombs** *(de fenêtre)* leadwork, leads; **mise en p.** leading **4** *Typ* type, metal; *(de chasse)* shot; **petit** *ou* **menu p.** small shot; **gros p.** buckshot; *Fig* **avoir du p. dans l'aile** to be in a bad way **5** *(sceau)* lead seal *(on meter etc)*; *Élec* **p. (fusible)** fuse; **faire sauter les plombs** to blow the fuses; *très Fam* **j'ai pété les plombs** I blew my top

plombage [plɔ̃baʒ] **NM 1** *(fait de garnir avec du plomb)* covering with lead; *Cér* lead glazing **2** *(fait de mettre des plombs)* weighting with lead **3** *(d'une dent)* filling

plombagine [plɔ̃baʒin] **NF** *Minér* black lead, graphite

plombe [plɔ̃b] **NF** *Arg* hour; **quatre plombes, ce n'est pas une heure à rentrer** four o'clock is no time to come home; **on ne va pas attendre pendant des plombes** we're not going to wait for him for ever

plombé [plɔ̃be] **ADJ** *(fenêtre)* leaded; *(toit)* lead(-covered); *Fig (teint)* livid; *(ciel)* leaden

plomber [plɔ̃be] **vT 1** *(couvrir de plomb)* to cover with lead; *Cér* to glaze **2** *(mettre des plombs à)* to weight with lead **3** *Fig (rendre livide) (teint, ciel)* to turn livid **4** *(dent)* to fill, to stop; **le dentiste m'a plombé une dent** the dentist gave me a filling **5** *(handicapper, compromettre)* to jeopardize, to undermine **6** *Constr (mur)* to plumb **7** *très Fam (transmettre une maladie vénérienne à)* **plomber qn** to give sb a dose
vPR se plomber *(du teint)* to become livid; *(du ciel)* to become leaden

plomberie [plɔ̃bri] **NF** *(installations, métier)* plumbing; *(atelier)* plumber's shop

plombier [plɔ̃bje] **NM** *(technicien)* plumber; *Fig Fam Péj (policier spécialiste de l'écoute clandestine)* snooper, eavesdropper; *(au téléphone)* phone-tapper

plombières [plɔ̃bjɛr] **NF** *Culin* tutti-frutti (ice cream)

plonge [plɔ̃ʒ] **NF** *Fam (dans un restaurant)* dishwashing, *Br* washing up; **faire la p.** *(dans un restaurant)* to be a dishwasher; *(at home)* to wash the dishes, *Br* to do the washing up

plongeant [plɔ̃ʒã] **ADJ** *(tir, décolleté)* plunging; **vue plongeante** bird's-eye view (**sur** onto), view from above

plongée [plɔ̃ʒe] **NF 1** *(de nageur)* diving; **faire de la p.** to dive; **partir en p.** to go diving; **p. sous-marine** skin *or* scuba diving **2** *(de sous-marin)* dive, diving, submersion; **effectuer sa p.** to dive, to submerge; **p. raide** crash-dive **3** *Cin, TV* elevated shot; *(verticale)* bird's-eye view **4** *Aut* **p. (au freinage)** dive

plongeoir [plɔ̃ʒwar] **NM** diving board

plongeon [plɔ̃ʒõ] **NM 1** *(fait de plonger)* dive; **p. de haut vol** high dive; **faire un p.** *(d'un nageur, gardien de but)* to dive; *Fig Fam* **faire le p.** *(dans les affaires)* to suffer heavy losses, *Am* to take a bath **2** *(oiseau)* diver, *Am* loon

plonger [plɔ̃ʒe] (**je plongeai(s)**; *n.* **plongeons**) **vI 1** *(s'immerger) (d'un nageur, sous-marin, avion etc)* to dive (**dans** into) **2** *Fig (descendre)* to plunge; **les murs plongent dans le fossé** the walls plunge into *or* run steeply down into the moat; **son regard plongea sur nous** he gazed down at us; **d'ici, on plonge sur la cathédrale** from here, you look down on the cathedral *or* you have a view down onto the cathedral; **p. dans le sommeil** to fall into a deep sleep; **p. dans la décadence** to sink rapidly into decline; **p. dans le travail pour oublier** to throw oneself into work *or* immerse oneself in work to take one's mind off things **3** *Fam (être envoyé en prison)* to be put inside *or* away, *Br* to be sent down

VT to plunge, to thrust (**dans** in(to)); **p. la main dans sa poche/un couteau dans le cœur de qn** to plunge *or* thrust one's hand into one's pocket/a knife into sb's heart; **il plongea son regard sur nous** he stared at us **VPR se plonger** to immerse oneself (**dans** in); *Fig* **être plongé dans ses pensées** to be immersed *or* lost *or* deep in thought; **être plongé dans le silence** to be plunged in silence; **être plongé dans le noir/l'angoisse** to be plunged in darkness/overcome by anguish; **se p. dans son travail/l'étude** to throw oneself into *or* to immerse *or* bury oneself in one's work/one's studies; **se p. dans Proust** to become absorbed *or* engrossed in Proust; **se p. dans le vice** to plunge into the world of vice

plongeur, -euse [plɔ̃ʒœr, -øz] **N 1** *(personne qui plonge dans l'eau)* diver; **cloche à plongeurs** diving bell; **p. sous-marin** skin *or* scuba diver **2** *Fam (dans un restaurant)* dishwasher, *Br* washer-up

NM 1 *Orn* diver, diving bird **2** *Tech (d'une pompe)* plunger

plot [plo] **NM** *Élec* contact (stud)

plouc [pluk] *Péj* **ADJ** *Fam* naff; **ça fait p.!** that's really naff!

NM yokel, (country) bumpkin

plouf [pluf] **INT** plop!; *(objet plus lourd)* splash!

ploutocrate [plutɔkrat] **N** plutocrat

ploutocratie [plutɔkrasi] **NF** plutocracy

ploutocratique [plutɔkratik] **ADJ** plutocratic

ployable [plwajabl] **ADJ** pliable, flexible

ployer [plwaje] (**je ploie, n. ployons; je ploierai**) **VI** *(courber)* to bend; *(d'un plancher, d'une poutre)* to sag; *(se casser, s'effondrer)* to give (way); *(sous un joug, un fardeau)* to bend, to bow; *(de troupes)* to give way, to submit, to yield

VT *(branche, genou)* to bend

pluches [plyʃ] **NFPL** *Mil Fam* **(corvée de) p.** potato-peeling, *Br* spud-bashing; **je suis de p.** I'm on potato-peeling *or Br* spud-bashing (duty)

pluie [plɥi] **NF 1** rain; **pluies acides** acid rain; **p. battante** driving *or* pelting *or* lashing rain; **p. diluvienne** pouring rain; **p. torrentielle** torrential rain; **p. fine** drizzle; **p. d'orage** cloudburst; **goutte de p.** raindrop; **il n'y a pas eu une goutte de p. dans la région depuis deux mois** the region hasn't had a drop of rain for two months; **eau de p.** rainwater; **le temps est à la p.** it looks like rain; **temps de p.** rainy *or* wet weather; **jour sans p.** dry day; **sous la p.** in the rain; **sous une p. diluvienne** in the pouring rain; **la saison des pluies** the rainy season; **ajoutez la farine en la versant en p.** sprinkle in the flour; *Fig* **parler de la p. et du beau temps** to talk about nothing in particular, to talk of this and that, *Am* to shoot the breeze; *Fig Fam* **il n'est pas tombé de la dernière p.** he wasn't born yesterday; *Prov* **après la p., le beau temps** it's a long road that has no turning; *Fam* **faire la p. et le beau temps** to rule the roost, to be the boss **2** *Fig (de coups, balles, pierres)* hail, shower; *(de reproches, compliments)* stream; **p. d'or** shower of gold

plumage [plymaʒ] **NM** *(ensemble des plumes)* plumage, feathers; *(fait de plumer)* plucking

plumard [plymar] **NM** *Fam* bed; **aller au p.** to hit the sack *or* the hay, to crash (out)

plume¹ [plym] **NF 1** *(d'oiseau)* feather; **oiseau sans plumes** unfledged bird; **gibier à plumes** game birds; *Fig Fam* **il y a laissé des plumes** he didn't come out of it unscathed, he didn't get off lightly; *Fig Fam* **on lui a volé dans les plumes** they laid into him; **léger comme une p.** (as) light as a feather; *Prov* **la belle p. fait le bel oiseau** fine feathers make fine birds; **lit de plume(s)** feather bed; **couette en plumes d'oie** goose-feather duvet; *Fig Hum* **perdre ses plumes** to go thin on top, to go bald; **poids p.** *Boxe* featherweight; *Fig* lightweight; **un poids p. en politique** a political lightweight **2** *(de stylo)* (pen) nib; **p. (d'oie)** quill (pen); **p. à dessin** drawing pen; **les idées se pressent sous sa p.** he can't write his ideas down quickly enough, his ideas are coming thick and fast; **écrire des mots/ses idées au courant** *ou* **au fil de la p.** to write down words/one's ideas as they come into one's head; **dessin à la p.** pen (and ink) drawing; **trait de p.** stroke of the pen; **prendre la p.** to put pen to paper; **j'ai pris ma plus belle p. pour écrire cette lettre** I made this the most beautiful letter I could; **vivre de sa p.** to make one's living by writing, to live by one's pen; **avoir la p. facile** to have a gift for writing **3** *Méd* **p. à vaccin** vaccine point

plume² **NM** *Fam* = **plumard**

plumeau, -eaux [plymo] **NM** feather duster

plumer [plyme] **VT** *(volaille)* to pluck; *Fam (personne)* to fleece

VPR se plumer *Fam* to hit the sack *or Am* the hay, to crash (out)

plumet [plymɛ] **NM** plume

plumetis [plymti] **NM** *Couture* **1** broderie au **p.** raised *or* satin stitch **2** *(étoffe)* Swiss muslin

plumeux, -euse [plymø, -øz] **ADJ** feathery

plumier [plymje] **NM** *(ouvert)* pen tray; *(à couvercle)* pencil box, pencil case

plumitif [plymitif] **NM** *Péj (employé de bureau)* penpusher; *(mauvais écrivain)* scribbler

plum-pudding, *pl* **plum-puddings** [plumpudiŋ] **NM** Christmas pudding, *Vieilli* plum pudding

plupart (la) [laplypar] **NF** most, the majority, *Fml* the greater part; **la p. des gens** most people, the majority of people; **la p. de mes clients** most of my customers, the majority of my customers; **la p. d'entre eux** most of them, the majority of them; **la p. du temps** most of the time; *(en général)* in most cases, generally; **il passe la p. du temps à lire** he spends most of his time reading; **dans la p. des cas** in most cases, in the majority of cases; **pour la p.** for the most part, mostly

plural, -ale, -aux, -ales [plyral, -o] **ADJ** **vote p.** plural voting

pluralisme [plyralism] **NM** *Pol, Phil* pluralism

pluraliste [plyralist] **ADJ** pluralist; **élections pluralistes** multi-party elections

N pluralist

pluralité [plyralite] **NF** *(multiplicité)* plurality, multiplicity; *Rel* **p. des bénéfices** pluralism; *Arch* **élu à la p. des voix** elected by a majority

pluriannuel, -elle [plyriannɥɛl] **ADJ** **récolte pluriannuelle** crop harvested every few years; **contrat p.** contract valid for a number of years

pluridisciplinaire [plyridisiplinɛr] **ADJ** *(approche, études)* multidisciplinary

NM **le technicien doit être un p.** the technician must possess a range of skills; **des pluridisciplinaires** people with a range of skills

pluridisciplinarité [plyridisiplinarite] **NF** multidisciplinary approach; **favoriser la p. dans les études universitaires** to encourage students to take up a range of subjects; **nous**

visons à une certaine p. dans nos services we're aiming to widen the range of tasks undertaken in our departments

pluriel, -ielle [plyrjɛl] **ADJ** plural SEE GRAMMAR A9–15; B8; B10

NM plural; **au p.** in the plural

pluriethnique [plyriɛtnik] **ADJ** multiethnic

plurilingue [plyrilɛ̃g] **ADJ** multilingual

plurilinguisme [plyrilɛ̃gɥism] **NM** multilingualism

plurinational, -ale, -aux, -ales [plyrinasjɔnal, -o] **ADJ** multinational

plurinominal [plyrinɔminal] **ADJ** *Pol* **scrutin p.** = voting for more than one candidate

pluripartisme [plyripartism] **NM** *Pol* multiparty system

PLUS [ply] *(often* [plys] *at the end of a word group;* [plyz] *before a vowel* **plus on est de fous, plus on rit** [plyzɔ̃nɛdfuplyzɔ̃ri])

> more **1, 6** = most **2** = not any more **3** = either *(non plus)* **4** = plus **5** = in addition *(en plus)* **7** = more or less *(plus ou moins)* **8**

ADV 1 *(davantage)* more; **p. de** *(davantage)* more; *(au-delà de)* more than; **soyez p. réaliste!** be more realistic!; **p. courageux** braver, more courageous; **p. clair/fort** clearer/stronger; **ils sont (beaucoup) p. nombreux** there are (far) more of them; **c'est sa mère, en p. jeune** she's a younger version of her mother, she looks just like her mother, only younger; **le même, en p. petit** the same, only smaller; **il est p. grand que moi** he's taller than I am *or* than me; **je ne suis pas p. grand que lui** I'm no taller than he is *or* than him; **elle écoute p. attentivement** she listens more attentively; **une fenêtre p. haute que large** a window higher than it is wide; **elle est p. jolie que belle** she is pretty rather than beautiful; **deux fois p. grand/rapide (que)** twice as big/fast (as); **c'est mille fois p. adapté pour ce que tu fais** it's a thousand times more suitable for what you're doing; *Fam* **c'est p. que bien** it's more than just good; **des résultats p. que satisfaisants** more than satisfactory results; **je gagne p. que vous** I earn more than you (do); **p. qu'à moitié** *(souvent* [plyskamwatje]*) (fait etc)* more than half; **en vouloir toujours p.** to be always wanting more; **il a p. de patience/temps que moi** he has more patience/time than I have *or* than me; **p. d'une fois** more than once; **p. de dix hommes** more than ten men; **il a p. de vingt ans** he's over twenty; **pendant p. d'une heure/d'un kilomètre** for over *or* for more than an hour/a kilometre; **p. loin** further *or* farther (on); **p. tôt** earlier; **je n'étais pas p. tôt arrivé que le téléphone sonnait** no sooner had I arrived than the telephone rang; **p. … (et) p. …** the more …, the more …; **p. on est de fous, p. on rit** the more the merrier; **p. je lis, moins je retiens** the more I read, the less I remember; **et qui p. est** [plyzɛ] and what is more, and moreover; **j'en ai trois fois p. qu'il ne m'en faut** I've (got) three times as much/as many as I need; **il y en a tant et p.** there's an awful lot (of it); *(nombre)* there are an awful lot (of them); **c'est d'autant p. facile/compliqué que …** it's all the easier/the more complicated since …, it's particularly easy/complicated since …; **c'est d'autant p. vrai qu'il l'a dit lui-même** it must be true, he said so himself SEE GRAMMAR A24–6; B11; B13–14

2 (le) p. (the) most; **la p. longue rue** *ou* **la rue la p. longue de la ville** the longest street in the town; **la p. belle femme que j'aie jamais vue** the most beautiful woman I've ever seen; **c'est la femme la p. capable de le faire** she's the woman most capable of doing it;

c'est vous qui avez fait le p. de fautes you've made (the) most mistakes; **le p. vite possible** as quickly as possible; **c'est à trente ans qu'elle a été la p. belle** she was at her most beautiful at thirty; **ce que je désire le p.** what I most desire, what I desire (the) most; **le p. drôle, ce qu'il y a de p. drôle** the funniest thing; **crier le p. fort** to shout (the) loudest; **faites le p. que vous pourrez** do the most you can or as much as you can; **(tout) au p.** at the (very) most, at the (very) outside; **c'est tout au p. s'il est midi** it's twelve o'clock at the latest; **c'est tout ce qu'il y a de p. simple** nothing could be simpler; **c'était des p. réussis** (extrêmement) it was most successful; **un gâteau des p. délicieux** a most delicious cake SEE GRAMMAR A24–6; B11; B13–14

3 (négation) **ne ... p.** not any more, not any longer, no more, no longer; **je ne les vois p.** I don't see them any more or any longer, I no longer see them; **je ne le ferai p.** I won't do it again or any more; **tu n'iras p.** you won't go again or any more; **je ne la verrai p. (jamais)** I'll never see her again; Litt **il n'est p.** (mort) he is no more; **je ne veux p. de cela** I don't want any more of that; **je n'ai** ou Fam **j'ai p. d'argent** I haven't any money left or any more money, I've (got) no more money; **nous n'avons p. d'espoir de la retrouver** we no longer have any hope or we have no hope any more of finding her; **il n'y a p. aucun espoir** I've/they've/etc given up hope; **sans p. attendre** without further ado; **(il n'y a) p. de doute** there is no longer any doubt about it; **il n'y a p. de jeunesse!** young people aren't what they used to be!, honestly, young people nowadays!; **p. de potage, merci** no more soup, thank you; **il (n')y en a p.** there is/are no more (left), there is/are none left; **il (n')y a p. rien** there's nothing left; **p. que dix minutes!** only ten minutes left!; **on procède non p. par ordre alphabétique, mais par thème** we shall no longer proceed in alphabetical order, but according to theme; **pas p. que** no more than; **pas p. qu'on ne doit voler, on ne doit mentir** it is no more acceptable to lie than it is to steal SEE GRAMMAR B62

4 non p. either (in negative sentences); **je n'en ai pas non p.** I haven't got any either; **(ni) moi non p.** neither do I/did I/etc, I don't/didn't/etc either, Fam me neither; **jamais non p. je n'avais songé à ... nor** had I ever thought of ...; **vous n'en avez guère non p.** you haven't got much/many either

5 [plys] surtout Math plus; **sept p. neuf** seven plus nine; **il fait p. 20 (degrés)** it's plus 20 (degrees); **500 euros d'amende, p. les frais** 500 euros fine and or plus costs; Golf **p. quatre** [plyskatr] plus four

6 de p. more; **une journée de p.** one day more, one more day; **il a trois ans de p. que moi** he's three years older than I am or than me; **rien de p., merci** nothing else, thank you; **de p. en p.** more and more; **de p. en p. froid** colder and colder

7 en p. in addition, into the bargain; (en sus) extra; **la même maison, avec un balcon en p.** the same house, but with a balcony; (avec un autre balcon) the same house, but with an extra or additional balcony; **le vin est en p.** wine is extra; **il y en a trois en p. de lui** there are three more besides him; **en p. de ce qu'il me doit** over and above or in addition to or besides what he owes me; **sans p.** but no more than that; **elle a été aimable, sans p.** she was pleasant, but no more than that

8 p. ou moins [plyzumwɛ̃] more or less; **elle joue p. ou moins bien** she plays fairly well, she's not a bad player; **c'est un mensonge, ni p. ni moins** it's nothing more nor less than a lie, it's purely and simply a lie

NM [plys] **1** Prov **qui peut le p. peut le moins**

you have/he has/etc done more difficult things than that before **2** Math (signe) plus (sign) **3** Golf **le p.** the odd **4** Fig (atout) plus; **c'est un p. pour vous** that's a plus for you

---

plusieurs [plyzjœr] ADJ, PRON several; **p. personnes l'ont remarqué** several people or a number of people have noticed it; **de p. manières** in more ways than one, in several ways; **j'en ai p.** I have several; **on s'y est mis à p.** several of us or a number of us got together (to do it) SEE GRAMMAR B15–16

plus-que-parfait, pl **plus-que-parfaits** [plyskəparfɛ] NM Gram pluperfect, past perfect SEE GRAMMAR A50; B30

plus-value, pl **plus-values** [plyvaly] NF Écon, Fin (de biens, de terrains etc) capital gain, appreciation, increase in value; (excédent) (d'impôts) surplus, excess yield; **les recettes présentent une p. de ...** the receipts show an increase of ...; **impôt sur les plus-values** capital gains tax; **p. sur titres** paper profit

Pluton [plytɔ̃] N (dieu) Pluto
NF (planète) Pluto

plutonium [plytɔnjɔm] NM Chimie plutonium

plutôt [plyto] ADV **1** (de préférence) rather; **p. que de faire les choses en cachette** rather than do things in secret; **p. la mort que l'esclavage** death before slavery, rather or sooner death than slavery; **p. souffrir que mentir** it is better to suffer than to lie; **il récite p. qu'il ne chante** he recites rather than sings; **p. que de partir** rather than leave, instead of leaving; **demande p. à ta mère** ask your mother instead; **ne te plains pas, travaille p.!** don't complain, just work!; **il faudrait p. en rire** it's best to laugh
2 (pour préciser) rather; **il faisait p. froid (que chaud)** the weather was cold if anything, it was cold rather than anything (else); **elle n'est pas bête, p. étourdie** she's absent-minded rather than stupid, she's not so much stupid as absent-minded, she's not stupid, just absent-minded; **ses parents, ou p. son père** his parents, or rather or or more precisely his father; **il n'est pas satisfait, mais p., soulagé** he's relieved rather than satisfied
3 (assez) fairly, quite, rather, Fam pretty, surtout Fml somewhat; **son discours était p. long** his speech was fairly or quite or rather long or was on the long side; Fam **il est p. bien, ce type!** he's not bad-looking at all, that guy!; **c'est p. une bonne idée, tu ne trouves pas?** it's rather a good idea, isn't it?; **je suis en retard? – oui, p.!** am I late? – you can say that again! or Br not half! VOIR GRAMMAIRE A5
4 Litt (à peine) hardly, scarcely; **il ne nous avait pas p. annoncé la venue de son frère ...** hardly or scarcely had he announced the arrival of his brother before ..., no sooner had he announced his brother's arrival than ... VOIR GRAMMAIRE A78

pluvial, -iale, -iaux, -iales [plyvjal, -jo] ADJ Géog pluvial; **eau pluviale** rainwater

pluvier [plyvje] NM Orn plover

pluvieux, -ieuse [plyvjø, -jøz] ADJ wet, rainy

pluviner [plyvine] VI = **pleuvasser**

pluviomètre [plyvjɔmɛtr] NM Météo rain gauge, Spéc pluviometer

pluviôse [plyvjoz] NM Hist = fifth month of the French Republican calendar (January-February)

pluviosité [plyvjozite] NF Météo rainfall

PLV [peɛlve] NF (abrév **publicité sur le lieu de vente**) point-of-sale promotion

---

PMA [peɛma] NF (abrév **procréation médicalement assistée**) artificial or assisted reproduction

NMPL (abrév **pays les moins avancés**) LDCs

PME [peɛmə] NF(PL) (abrév **petite(s) et moyenne(s) entreprise(s)**) small business(es), small and medium-sized businesses(es); **une P.** a small business

PMI [peɛmi] NF (abrév **petite et moyenne industrie**) small (and medium-sized) industries

PMU [peɛmy] NM (abrév **Pari mutuel urbain**) = state-run betting system, Br ≃ tote

PNB [peɛnbe] NM Écon (abrév **Produit national brut**) GNP

pneu [pnø] NM **1** Aut tyre, Am tire; **avoir des pneus lisses** to have worn tyres; **avoir un p. à plat/crevé** to have a flat/a puncture **2** (lettre exprès) express letter (sent through a pneumatic despatch system)
▸ ▸ **p. à architecture radiale** radial-ply tyre; **p. à ceinture** braced or belted tyre; **p. à clous, p. clouté** studded tyre; **pneus jumelés** twin tyres; **p. neige** snow tyre; **p. pluie** wet-weather tyre; **p. sans chambre** tubeless tyre; **p. à structure diagonale** cross-ply tyre; **p. à structure radiale** radial tyre; **p. taille basse** low-profile tyre; **p. temps sec** dry-weather tyre; **p. tout-temps** all-weather tyre; **p. tout-terrain** all-terrain tyre; **p. à usage mixte** town-and-country tyre

pneumatique [pnømatik] ADJ pneumatic; (canoë) inflatable; **canot p.** rubber dinghy; **matelas/pistolet p.** air mattress/gun
NM = **pneu**

pneumocoque [pnømɔkɔk] NM Biol pneumococcus

pneumologie [pnømɔlɔʒi] NF Méd pneumology

pneumologue [pnømɔlɔg] N Méd lung specialist

pneumonie [pnømɔni] NF Méd pneumonia; **p. atypique** atypical pneumonia; (SRAS) SARS

pneumothorax [pnømotɔraks] NM Méd pneumothorax

PNUD [pnyd] NM (abrév **programme des Nations unies pour le développement**) UNDP

Pô (le) [ləpo] NM Géog the (River) Po

PO 1 Com (abrév **par ordre**) by order **2** Radio (abrév **petites ondes**) MW

pochade [pɔʃad] NF quick sketch

pochard, -arde [pɔʃar, -ard] N Fam drunk(ard)

poche [pɔʃ] NF **1** (partie de vêtement) pocket; **p. intérieure** inside pocket; **p. plaquée** patch pocket; **p. de poitrine** breast pocket; **p. revolver** hip pocket; Fam **faire les poches à qn** to go through or rifle sb's pockets; **argent de p.** pocket money; **calculatrice de p.** pocket calculator; **carnet de p.** pocketbook; **livre de p.** paperback; **j'en suis de ma p.** I'm out of pocket (by it); **payer de sa p.** to pay out of one's own pocket; Fig **connaître qn/qch comme sa p.** to know sb/sth inside out or like the back of one's hand; Fig Fam **se remplir les poches, s'en mettre plein les poches** to make a packet; **j'ai cent euros en p.** I've got a hundred euros on me; **mettre qch dans sa p.** to put sth in one's pocket, to pocket sth; Fam **mettez ça dans votre p. (et votre mouchoir dessus)** put that in your pipe and smoke it; Fig **les mains dans les poches** without a care in the world; **il n'a pas sa langue dans sa p.** he's got plenty to say for himself; **ne pas avoir les yeux dans sa p.** to keep one's eyes open; **elle l'a mis dans sa p.** she's got him eating out of her hand; Fam **c'est dans la p.** it's in the bag.
2 (sac) bag; **p. à cartes** map case or holder; **p. à tabac** tobacco pouch; Fig **acheter chat**

en p. to buy a pig in a poke **3** *(amas de substance)* pocket; **p. de pétrole** pocket of oil; **p. d'air** *Aviat* air pocket; *(dans une pipe)* airlock **4** *(déformation)* bag; **pantalon qui fait des poches aux genoux** trousers that are baggy *or* that bag at the knees; **poches sous les yeux** bags under the eyes **5** *Biol, Méd, Anat* sac; *(d'un kangourou etc)* pouch **6** *(filet de chasse)* purse *or* bag net; **p. de chalut** purse seine **7** *Fig (secteur)* pocket; **p. de résistance/pauvreté** pocket of resistance/deprivation **8** *Suisse (louche)* ladle
▸ *NM Fam (livre)* paperback; **paru en (collection de) p.** published in paperback
▸▸ *Tech* **p. à couler** *ou* **de coulée** casting ladle; *Culin* **p. à douille** piping bag; *Méd* **p. des eaux** amniotic sac

poché [pɔʃe] **ADJ 1** *Culin* **œuf p.** poached egg **2** *Fam* **œil p.** black eye

pocher [pɔʃe] **VT 1** *Culin (œuf, poisson)* to poach **2** *Beaux-Arts* to dash off **3** *Fam* **p. l'œil à qn** to give sb a black eye; **la ferme, ou je te poche un œil!** shut up, or I'll give you one!
▸ **VI** *(de vêtements)* to go *or* get baggy, to bag; **mon pantalon poche aux genoux** my trousers are going *or* getting baggy at the knees

pochetron [pɔʃtrɔ̃] **NM** *Fam* alky, boozer

pochette [pɔʃɛt] **NF 1** *(enveloppe)* pouch; *(pour papiers)* envelope; *(pour stylos, articles de toilette)* case; *(d'un disque)* sleeve; *(pour protéger un document)* document cover; **p. d'expédition de disquette** disk mailer; **p. matelassée** Jiffy bag®, padded envelope; **p. d'allumettes** book of matches; **p.-surprise** lucky bag; *Fam* **il a eu son permis dans une p.-surprise** he's a lousy driver **2** *(petit mouchoir)* (breast) pocket handkerchief

pochoir [pɔʃwar] **NM** stencil; **passer qch au p.** to stencil sth; **motifs au p.** stencils, stencil(led) patterns; **brosse à p.** stencil(ling) brush

pochon [pɔʃɔ̃] **NM** *Région* **1** *(sac)* bag **2** *(grande louche)* ladle

pochothèque [pɔʃɔtɛk] **NF** paperback shop; *(rayon)* paperback section

podagre [pɔdagr] *Vieilli* **NF** *(goutte)* gout
N gout sufferer
ADJ suffering from gout

podiatre [pɔdjatr] **N** *Can Méd* chiropodist, *Am* podiatrist

podium [pɔdjɔm] **NM** podium; **monter sur le p.** to mount the *or* take to the podium

podologie [pɔdɔlɔʒi] **NF** *Méd* chiropody, *Am* podiatry

podologue [pɔdɔlɔg] **N** *Méd* chiropodist, *Am* podiatrist

podomètre [pɔdɔmɛtr] **NM** pedometer

poêle[1] [pwal] **NF** frying pan, *Am* skillet; **passer qch à la p.** to fry sth

poêle[2] **NM** *(appareil de chauffage)* stove; **p. à feu continu** slow-burning stove; **p. à bois/à mazout** wood(-burning)/oil stove

poêle[3] **NM 1** *Hist (dans un mariage catholique)* canopy **2** *(drap)* pall; **tenir les cordons du p.** to be a pallbearer

poêlée [pwale] **NF** panful

poêler [pwale] **VT** to fry

poêlon [pwalɔ̃] **NM** casserole (dish)

poème [pɔɛm] **NM** poem; **p. symphonique/en prose** symphonic/prose poem; *Fam* **c'est tout un p.** *(personne)* he's quite a character; *(situation)* it's quite a business *or* a palaver *or Br* a carry-on

poésie [pɔezi] **NF 1** *(art)* poetry; **écrire** *ou* **faire de la p.** to write poetry; *Fig* **la p. du** **style/film** the poetry of the style/film; **tu manques de p.** you don't have any soul; **une région pleine de p.** a region full of (poetic) charm; **la p. des grandes villes américaines** the romance of the great American cities **2** *(poème)* poem, piece of poetry

poète [pɔɛt] **NM** *aussi Fig* poet; **elle est devenue le grand p. de son temps** she became the greatest poet of her age

poétesse [pɔetɛs] **NF** woman poet, poetess

poétique [pɔetik] **ADJ** *(inspiration, licence etc)* poetic; **l'art p.** the art of poetry
NF poetics

poétiquement [pɔetikmã] **ADV** poetically

poétiser [pɔetize] **VT** to poeticize

pogne [pɔɲ] **NF** *Arg (main)* paw, mitt

pognon [pɔɲɔ̃] **NM** *Fam (argent)* dough, bread, *Br* dosh

pogrom(e) [pɔgrɔm] **NM** *Hist* pogrom

POIDS [pwa] **NM 1** weight; *(lourdeur)* weight, heaviness; **de tout son p.** with all one's weight, with the whole of one's weight; **surveiller son p.** to watch one's weight; **perdre du p.** to lose weight; **vendre au p.** to sell by weight; **être plié sous le p. d'un sac** to be weighed down by a sack; **ajouter qch pour faire le p.** to put sth in to make up the weight; **ne pas faire le p.** to fail to come up to weight *or* to make the (minimum) weight; *Fig Fam* **il ne fait pas le p.** he's not up to the job *or* up to scratch *or* up to it; **faire le p. face à la concurrence** to measure up to the competition; **le parti ne fait pas le p. devant le problème** the party does not measure up to the problem **2** *(charge)* *(dans une horloge, sur une balance)* weight; *Sport* shot; **un p. de 20 kilos** a 20-kilo weight; *Admin* **p. et mesures** weights and measures; **étalonnage des p.** standardization of weights; *Sport* **lancer le p.** to put the shot **3** *Fig (charge pénible, écrasante)* burden; *Litt* **le p. des ans** the weight of the years; **le p. des impôts** the burden of taxation; **p. de la fiscalité** tax burden; **le p. de ses soucis** the burden of his worries **4** *Fig (importance)* weight; **donner du p. à qch** to give weight to sth; **cette région finira par avoir autant de p. que Paris** this region will eventually carry as much weight as Paris; **son opinion a un certain p.** his opinion carries a certain weight
▸▸ **p. atomique** atomic weight; **p. brut** gross weight; **p. en charge** laden weight; *Boxe* **p. coq** bantamweight; **p. embarqué** shipped weight; *Boxe* **p. léger** lightweight; **p. lourd** *Aut* heavy goods vehicle, HGV, heavy lorry *or Am* truck; *Boxe* heavyweight; *Fig* **un p. lourd de la politique** a political heavyweight; *Boxe* **p. mi-moyen** welterweight; *Mktg* **p. mort** cash trap, dog, dodo; *Fig* **c'est un p. mort** he's a dead weight; *Boxe* **p. mouche** flyweight; *Boxe* **p. moyen** middleweight; **p. net** net weight; *Aut* **p. en ordre de marche** kerb weight; **p. plume** *Boxe* featherweight; *Fig* lightweight; **p. remorqué** tow weight; *Com* **p. rendu** delivered weight; **p. spécifique** *Phys* specific weight; *Chimie* specific gravity; *Com* **p. de taxation** chargeable weight; **p. total autorisé** maximum permissible weight; **p. utile** live weight; *Aviat* payload; **p. à vide** *Aut* unloaded weight, kerb weight; *Com* tare; *Boxe* **p. welter** welterweight

poignant [pwaɲã] **ADJ** *(moment, pensée)* poignant; *(expérience, spectacle, lecture etc)* harrowing

poignard [pwaɲar] **NM** dagger; **coup de p.** stab; **donner un coup de p. à qn** to stab sb; *Fig* **recevoir un coup de p. dans le dos** to get stabbed in the back

poignarder [pwaɲarde] **VT** to stab, *Fam* to knife; **se faire p.** to get stabbed *or Fam* knifed

poigne [pwaɲ] **NF** grip, grasp; *Fig* **homme à p.** *ou* **qui a de la p.** strong *or* forceful man; **un chef d'État à p.** a strong head of state, a head of state with a firm grip

poignée [pwaɲe] **NF 1** *(quantité contenue dans une main)* (de farine, de bonbons etc) handful; *(de billets de banque)* fistful; **à** *ou* **par poignées** by the handful, in handfuls **2** *(petit nombre)* handful; **p. d'hommes** handful of men **3** *(de porte, sac)* handle; *(de pistolet)* grip; *(d'épée)* hilt; *Aut* **p. de maintien** passenger assist handle, grab handle; *Aut* **p. de portière** door handle **4** **p. de main** handshake; **donner une p. de main à qn** to shake hands with sb, to shake sb's hand **5** *Fam* **poignées d'amour** love handles

poignet [pwaɲe] **NM 1** *Anat* wrist; *Fig* **faire qch à la force du p.** to do sth by sheer strength *or* brute force; *(à force de travail)* to do sth by sheer hard work **2** *(d'un vêtement)* cuff; *(bracelet, brassard)* wristband

poil [pwal] **NM 1** *(d'un animal)* hair; *(pelage)* coat; **poils de chat** cat hairs; **p. de chameau** camelhair; **à p. long/ras** long-/short-haired; **cheval d'un beau p.** sleek horse; **chien au p. rude/à p. dur** wire-haired/rough-coated dog; *Fig* **caresser qn dans le sens du p.** to rub sb up the right way; *Fig Fam* **tomber sur le p. à qn** to lay into *or* go for sb; *Arch* **monter un cheval à p.** to ride a horse bareback; **les poils d'une brosse** the bristles of a brush **2** *Tex (d'un tissu)* nap; *(du velours)* pile **3** *(d'une personne)* hair; **poils du visage** facial hair; **poils follets** down; *Fam* **à p.** stark naked, *Br* starkers; *Fam* **se mettre à p.** to strip off; *Fam* **avoir un p. dans la main** to be bone idle *or* workshy; *Fam* **ne pas avoir un p. sur le caillou** to be as bald as a coot; *Fam* **avoir du p. aux pattes** to have hairy legs; *Fig* **reprendre du p. de la bête** to regain (one's) strength, to pick up, *Fam* to perk up; *Fig Fam* **de tous poils** of all sorts *or* kinds; *Fam* **être de bon/mauvais p.** to be in a good/bad mood; *Fam* **au quart de p.** perfectly; **démarrer au quart de p.** to start right away *or* first time; *Fam* **à un p. près** very nearly; **à un p. près, il ratait son examen** he very nearly failed his exam; **nous avons payé la même chose à un p. près** we paid more or less the same, we paid the same, or as near as makes no difference; *Fam* **un p. plus haut/moins vite** a fraction *or* a touch higher/slower; *Fam* **au (petit) p.** great, fantastic; **il est arrivé au p.** he turned up at just the right moment **4** *(d'une plante)* hair **5** **p. à gratter** itching powder

poilant [pwalã] **ADJ** *Fam* hilarious, screamingly funny

poiler (se) [səpwale] **VPR** *Fam* to kill oneself *or* die laughing

poilu [pwaly] **ADJ** *(qui a des poils)* hairy; **p. comme un singe** hairy as an ape
NM *Fam* poilu *(French soldier 1914-1918)*

poinçon [pwɛ̃sɔ̃] **NM 1** *(pointeau)* *(de graveur)* style, burin; *(de cordonnier)* awl, bradawl; *Couture* bodkin; **p. à glace** ice pick **2** *(matrice)* die, stamp; **p. à chiffrer** number punch **3** *(marque)* stamp; **p. de contrôle** hallmark *(stamp)*

poinçonnage [pwɛ̃sɔnaʒ], **poinçonnement** [pwɛ̃sɔnmã] **NM** *(de métal, cuir)* punching; *(contrôle par perforation)* punching, clipping; *(estampillage)* stamping; *(d'or, d'argent)* hallmarking

poinçonner [pwɛ̃sɔne] **VT** *(métal, cuir)* to punch; *(contrôler)* to punch, to clip; *(estampiller)* to stamp; *(or, argent)* to hallmark

poinçonneur, -euse [pwɛ̃sɔnœr, -øz] **N**

(personne) Ind puncher; *(à la gare)* ticket puncher

NF **poinçonneuse** punching machine

poindre [pwɛdr] VI *(prp* poignant; *pp* point; *pr ind* il point, ils poignent; *imp* il poignait; *p hist* il poignit; *fu* il poindra; *used esp in third person and in inf) (du jour)* to dawn, to break; *(des plantes, des étoiles)* to appear, to come out; **le jour point à l'horizon** day is breaking; **p. à l'horizon** *(apparaître)* to come into view

poing [pwɛ̃] NM fist; **se battre poings nus** to fight with one's bare fists; **sabre/revolver au p.** sword/revolver in hand; **serrer les poings** to clench one's fists; **menacer qn du p.,** montrer le **p. à qn** to shake one's fist at sb; **les poings sur les hanches** hands on hips, arms akimbo; **dormir à poings fermés** to sleep soundly *or* like a log; **coup de p.** punch; **coup de p. (américain)** knuckleduster; **donner un coup de p. à qn** to punch sb; **recevoir un coup de p.** to be punched; *Fam* **envoyer son p. dans la figure de qn,** *très Fam* **mettre son p. sur** *ou* **dans la gueule de qn** to give sb a punch in the face, to bash *or* smash sb's face in; **taper du p. sur la table** to bang one's fist (down) on the table, to pound the table; *Fig* to put one's foot down; **lever le p.** to give a raised-fist salute; **ils défilaient le p. levé** they marched past with their fists raised *or* with raised fists; *Suisse* **faire le p. dans sa poche** to swallow one's anger

POINT¹ [pwɛ̃]

point **1-3, 11, 13, 14** ▪ spot **1, 10** ▪ place
1 ▪ stitch **4, 6** ▪ dot **9, 10** ▪ full stop
9 ▪ period **9** ▪ stage **11** ▪ extent **11**

NM **1** *(dans l'espace)* point, spot, place; *aussi Fig* **p. de départ** starting point, point of departure; **p. de vue** *(panorama)* view; *Fig (opinion)* point of view, viewpoint, standpoint; **au** *ou* **du p. de vue international/économique** from an international/economic point of view *or* viewpoint; *Fam* **du** *ou* **au p. de vue caractère/rapidité** as far as character/speed is concerned, character-/speed-wise; **en tous points** in every way, in all respects; *Tech, Fig* **p. critique** critical point; *Aviat* **essai au p. fixe** ground run

2 *(dans le temps)* point; **le p. du jour** daybreak, dawn; **être sur le p. de faire qch** to be about to do sth, to be on the point *or* verge of doing sth; **sur le p. de mourir** at *or* on the point of death; **arriver à p. nommé** *ou* **juste à p.** to arrive just at the right moment; **tout vient à p. à qui sait attendre** everything comes to him who waits

3 *(question)* point; **p. de droit** point of law; **le p. capital** the main point; **traiter un problème en trois points** to deal with a problem in three stages; **mettre son** *ou* **un p. d'honneur à ne pas céder** to make it a point of honour not to yield; **n'ayez aucune crainte sur ce p.** don't worry on that score *or* on that count; **je suis d'accord avec vous sur ce p.** I agree with you on that point; **exécuter un ordre p. par p.** to carry out an order exactly *or* to the letter

4 *Couture* stitch; **faire un p. à un vêtement** to put a few stitches in a garment; **p. arrière** backstitch; **p. de Bruxelles** Brussels lace; **p. de chaînette** chainstitch; **p. de chausson** herringbone stitch; **p. de croix** cross-stitch; **p. devant** *ou* **glissé** *ou* **coulé** running stitch; **p. de feston** buttonhole stitch; **p. de languette** blanket stitch; **p. noué** knot stitch; **p. perdu** blind *or* slip stitch; **coudre qch à points perdus** to blindstitch *or* slipstitch sth; **p. roulé** whipping

5 *Tricot* stitch; **p. de riz** moss stitch; **p. mousse** garter stitch

6 p. de côté *(douleur)* stitch (in one's side);

avoir un p. au dos to have a stabbing pain in one's back

7 *Naut, Aviat* **p. estimé** dead reckoning (position); **faire le p.** to take bearings, to find one's position

8 *Opt* **au p.** in focus; **mettre au p.** *(lentilles, objectif, caméra etc)* to focus; *(moteur)* to tune; *(mécanisme)* to adjust; *(technique)* to perfect; *(projet, stratégie)* to finalize; **mise au p.** *(de lentilles, d'objectif etc)* focusing; *(d'un moteur)* tuning; *(d'un mécanisme)* adjusting; *(d'une technique)* perfecting; *(d'un projet, d'une stratégie)* finalization, finalizing; **leur organisation n'est pas vraiment au p.** their organization is really not up to scratch; **faire le p.** to take stock; **faire le p. sur l'affaire Martin** to take stock of the Martin affair; *Vieilli* **recherche et mise au p.** research and development

9 *(marque), Typ* dot; *(sur les dés)* pip; *(dans une adresse électronique)* dot; **p. (final)** full stop, *Am* period; **mettre les points sur les i** to dot one's i's; *Fig* to make one's meaning perfectly plain; **deux points** colon; **(trois) points de suspension** suspension points; *(en parlant ou en dictant)* dot, dot, dot; *Fam* **tu restes ici, un p., c'est tout!** *ou* **p. final!** *ou* **p. à la ligne!** *ou* **p. barre!** you're staying here and that's final *or* that's that!, *Am* you're staying here, period!; *Tél* **points et traits** *(de l'alphabet Morse)* dots and dashes; *Typ* **caractères de huit points** eight-point type; *Typ* **points par pouce** dots per inch; *Ordinat* **gdupont arrobas transex, p., co, p., uk** *(adresse électronique)* gdupont at transex, dot, co, dot, uk

10 *(marque visible)* speck, spot, dot; **le navire n'est qu'un p. à l'horizon** the ship is a mere speck on the horizon

11 *(phase, degré)* point, stage; *(étendue)* degree, extent; *Culin* **(cuit) à p.** done to a turn; *(steak)* medium-rare; **jusqu'à un certain p.** to a certain extent, up to a (certain) point; **au p. où en sont les choses** as matters stand, as things are; **au p. où j'en suis** the way things are at the moment (for me); **à ce p. que ..., à tel p. que ..., au p. que ...** to such a point *or* an extent that ..., so much so that ...; **ils étaient déçus au p. qu'ils ont préféré rentrer directement** they were so disappointed that they preferred to return right away; **vous n'êtes pas malade à ce p.-là** you're not as ill as all that; **au dernier p.** to *or* in the last degree

12 mal en p. in a bad way

13 *(de jeux)* point; *Scol* mark; **marquer les points** to keep (the) score; **elle a marqué 10 points** she scored 10 points; *Fig* **là, tu marques un p.!** that's one up to you!; *Boxe* **gagner aux points** to win on points; **rendre des points à qn** to give sb points; *Fig* to be more than a match for sb; *Scol* **bon p.** good mark

14 *(unité)* point; **l'indice des prix gagne/perd deux points** the retail price index has gone up/down (by) two points

15 *Ordinat* **en mode p.** bitmap, bitmapped
► ► *Aut* **p. allumage** firing point; *Aut* **p. d'ancrage** anchor(age) point; **p. d'appui** *Mil etc* base of operations; *Méd* pressure point; *Tech (de levier)* fulcrum; *Fig (d'un argument, d'une théorie)* basis; *Naut* **p. d'attache** mooring (post); *Géog* **points cardinaux** cardinal points, points of the compass; *Ordinat* **p. de césure** breakpoint, hyphenation point; **p. chaud** *(pendant une guerre)* hot spot, trouble spot; *Fig* **les points chauds de l'actualité** the most topical issues of the day; *Typ* **points de conduite** dotted leader; **p. de congélation** freezing point; *TV, Cin* **p. diffus** soft focus; *Mktg* **p. de distribution** distribution outlet; **p. d'eau** *(dans le désert)* waterhole; *(dans un camping)* water supply point; **p. d'ébullition à sec** dry boiling point;

p. d'éclair flash point; *TV etc* **p. d'entrée** *(d'une bande)* inpoint; **p. d'exclamation** exclamation mark *or Am* point; **p. faible** weak point; *TV, Cin* **p. focal** focus; **p. fort** strong point; **p. de fusion** melting point; **p. de graissage** lubricating point; *Aut* **p. d'inflammation** point of ignition; **p. d'interrogation** *Typ, Fig* question mark; *Mktg (produit)* question mark; *Fig* **ce qu'il lui a dit? on ne sait pas, c'est la p. d'interrogation** what did he say to him? we don't know, that's the question we're all asking; **p. d'intersection** (point of) intersection; *Aut* **p. de levage** *(au cric)* jacking *or* jack point; *Math* **points limites** limit points; **p. de mire** target; *Fig* **p. de mire de tous les yeux** *(critiqué)* target for criticism; *(admiré)* focus of attention, *Fml* cynosure; *TV, Cin* **p. de montage** edit point; **p. mort** *Aut* neutral; *Fin* breakeven (point); *Fig* **être au p. mort** to be at a standstill; **p. noir** *(comédon)* blackhead; *Fig* problem; *(à l'avenir)* cloud on the horizon; *Aut* accident blackspot; *(embouteillage)* blackspot; *Mus* **p. d'orgue** pause, fermata; *Fig* climax, highpoint; *Aut* **p. de prise** *(d'embrayage)* take-up point; **p. prix** price point; **p. de référence** benchmark; **p. retrait** cashpoint; *Com* **p. de saturation** saturation point; *Tech* **p. de soudure** weld spot; **p. de tabulation** *Ordinat* tab marker; *Typ* tab set; *Aut* **p. talon** accelerator heel point; *Com* **p. de vente** point of sale; *(magasin)* sales outlet; **disponible dans votre p. de vente habituel** available at your local stockist; *Com* **p. de vente au détail** retail outlet; *Com* **p. de vente électronique** electronic point of sale, EPOS

point² ADV *Vieilli, Litt, Dial* = **pas²**; **peu ou p.** little or not at all; **le connaissez-vous? – p.** do you know him? – not at all; **depuis plusieurs semaines, p. de nouvelles** there's been no news (at all) for several weeks **SEE GRAMMAR B62**

pointage [pwɛ̃taʒ] NM **1** *(contrôle) (de noms sur une liste)* checking, ticking off; *(de votes)* counting; *Naut (d'une carte marine)* pricking; *(d'une position sur une carte)* plotting; *(à l'usine)* timekeeping; *(à l'arrivée)* clocking in; *(au départ)* clocking out; **p. des salariés** signing-in of employees **2** *Mus (d'une note)* dotting **3** *(d'un télescope)* pointing, levelling, training; *(de fusil)* aiming, training

pointe [pwɛ̃t] NF **1** *(extrémité) (d'aiguille, de couteau etc)* point; *(de flèche)* tip, head; *(de balle)* nose; *(de chaussure)* toe; *(d'une flèche d'église)* top; *(de sein)* nipple; *Rail* **p. d'une aiguille** point of a switchblade; **à la p. de l'épée** at the point of a sword; *Fig Vieilli* **j'ai obtenu mon contrat à la p. de l'épée** I had to fight hard to get my contract; **en p.** pointed; **partir en p.,** *former* **une p.** to taper to a point; **tailler en p.** to cut (in)to a point; *(crayon)* to sharpen; *Fam* **je vais te tailler les oreilles en p.!** I'll box your ears!; **p. de lance** spearhead; **marcher/se tenir sur la p. des pieds** to walk/stand on tiptoe; **entrer sur la p. des pieds** to tiptoe in; **faire des pointes** *(en danse)* to go up on points

2 *(moment d'intensité), Math, Élec, Méd (d'une courbe, d'une charge, de la fièvre)* peak; *Sport* **p. de vitesse** burst of speed, spurt; **faire une p. de vitesse** to put on a burst of speed *or* a spurt; **avec des pointes de vitesse de 160 km/h** with a top speed of 160 km/h; **dans les pointes de vitesse, on peut faire du 200 km/h** at top speed you can do 200 km/h; **vitesse de p.** top *or* highest speed; **heure de p.** rush hour; **période de p.** peak period; *Litt* **p. du jour** daybreak, dawn

3 *Mil (d'une sentinelle avancée)* point; **nous avons poussé une p. jusqu'à** *ou* **sur Paris** we pressed on *or* pushed on to Paris; *Naut* **tir en p.** firing ahead; **être à la p. du progrès/de la**

recherche to be in or at the forefront of progress/of research, to be at the cutting or leading edge of progress/of research; **à la p. de l'actualité** in the headlines, very much in the news; *Fig* **les secteurs de p.** the high-tech industries, the most advanced sectors of industry; **industrie de p.** high-tech or state-of-the- art industry; **technologie de p.** state-of-the-art technology, leading-edge technology; **c'est de la technologie de p.** it's very state-of-the-art

4 (petite quantité, trace) hint, touch, tinge; **parler avec une p. d'accent** to speak with a hint of an accent; **p. d'ironie** touch or hint or tinge of irony; **p. d'ail** touch of garlic; **p. de vanille** dash of vanilla

5 (raillerie) barb, pointed remark; **lancer des pointes à qn** to make digs at sb
6 *Géog* **p. (de terre)** headland, foreland
7 (outil) (de maçon) point; *Menuis* **p. carrée** bradawl; **p. à tracer** scribe
8 (clou) nail; (pour tapis) tack; *Sport* (sur une chaussure) spike; **chaussures à pointes** spiked shoes, spikes; **casque à p.** spiked helmet
9 (lange) nappy, *Am* diaper; (écharpe, foulard) (triangular) scarf
▸▸**p. d'asperge** asparagus tip; **p. Bic®** ballpoint (pen), *Br* Biro®; *Méd* **pointes de feu** ignipuncture; *Beaux-Arts* **p. sèche** (dry) point; (procédé) dry-point (engraving); *Élec* **p. de tension** surge, spike

pointeau, -eaux [pwɛ̃to] NM **1** *Tech* centre or *Am* center punch; (de carburateur) needle **2** *Vieilli* (personne) timekeeper **3** (sur un autocuiseur) pressure valve

pointer¹ [pwɛ̃te] VT **1** (vérifier) (noms sur une liste) to check, to tick off; (votes) to count; *Naut* (carte marine) to prick; (position sur une carte) to plot
2 (dresser) **p. les oreilles** to prick up its ears; **le chien arriva en pointant le bout de son museau** the dog arrived with its muzzle in the air; *Fig* **il pointa son nez à la porte** his face appeared around the door, he peeped around the door; **s'il pointe son nez ici, je lui donne une gifle!** if he shows his face here, I'll give him one!; **il n'a pas pointé le bout de son nez depuis longtemps** he hasn't looked in or been round for a long time
3 (diriger) (télescope) to point (sur at), to train (sur on); (fusil) to aim, to level (sur at), to train (sur on); (spot, projecteur) to train (sur on); *Ordinat* (curseur) to position (sur on); *Ordinat* **pointé** (mot, page) where the cursor is/was; **j'ai pointé le doigt vers lui** I pointed (my finger) at him
4 (signaler, révéler) to point to
5 *Mus* (note) to dot; **note pointée** dotted note
6 *Vieilli* (piquer) (avec une épée) to stab; (avec une aiguille) to prick
VI **1** (d'employé) (en arrivant) to sign in; (en partant) to sign out; **p. (à l'arrivée/à la sortie)** (à l'usine) to clock in/out; **p. à l'ANPE ou au chômage** to register unemployed
2 (apparaître) to appear; (d'une plante) to come up; (d'un oiseau) to soar; (d'un cheval) to rear up; (du jour) to dawn; **ses seins pointaient sous son corsage** her firm breasts were clearly outlined beneath her bodice; **ses os pointaient** his bones were sticking out; **le clocher de l'église pointait vers un ciel d'azur** the church steeple soared into or rose towards a bright blue sky
3 (au jeu de boules) = to get one's ball nearest to the jack
VPR **se pointer** *Fam* to turn up, to show up

pointer² [pwɛ̃tœr] NM (chien) pointer

pointeur, -euse [pwɛ̃tœr, -øz] N (contrôleur) *Ind* timekeeper; *Sport* scorer, marker
NF **pointeuse** (horloge) (time)clock
NM *Ordinat* pointer; **p.-balle** beachball

pointer; **p.-croix** crosshair pointer; **p.-montre** watch pointer; **p. de pile** stack pointer; **p. en I** I-beam

pointillage [pwɛ̃tijaʒ] NM *Beaux-Arts* dotting; (plus serré) stippling

pointillé [pwɛ̃tije] ADJ (ligne) dotted; (gravure) stippled; *Tex* (tissu) pinhead
NM **1** (trait) dotted line; (sur une feuille détachable) perforations; **détacher suivant les pointillés** tear along the dotted line/the perforations **2** (technique de dessin) stippling; **dessin en p.** stippled design; **ligne en p.** dotted line; *Fig* **on pouvait lire en p. des allusions à son passé glorieux** reading between the lines, we saw certain allusions to his glorious past

pointiller [pwɛ̃tije] VT **1** (percer de petits trous) to dot **2** *Beaux-Arts* to stipple
VI *Péj Arch* to cavil (over trifles), to split hairs

pointilleux, -euse [pwɛ̃tijø, -øz] ADJ particular, fussy, finicky, *Fam* pernickety (sur about)

pointillisme [pwɛ̃tijism] NM *Beaux-Arts* pointillism

pointilliste [pwɛ̃tijist] ADJ, N *Beaux-Arts* pointillist

pointu [pwɛ̃ty] ADJ **1** (en forme de pointe) pointed; (aigu) (couteau) sharp, pointed; (voix) shrill **2** *Fig* (susceptible) (ton de la voix, humeur) touchy; **prendre un air p.** to bridle **3** *Fig* (spécialisé) specialized, specialist
ADV *Région Fam* **parler p.** to speak with a Parisian accent

pointure [pwɛ̃tyr] NF (de chaussures, de gants, de coiffure) size; **quelle est votre p. (de gants/de chaussures)?, quelle p. faites-vous?** what size (gloves/shoes) do you take?, what's your (glove/shoe) size?; *Fig Fam* **une (grosse) p. du cinéma français/de la physique nucléaire** a big name in French cinema/in nuclear physics

point-virgule, pl **points-virgules** NM semicolon

poire [pwar] NF **1** (fruit) pear; **entre la p. et le fromage** at the end of the meal; *Fig* **garder une p. pour la soif** to put something by for a rainy day; *Fig* **couper la p. en deux** to compromise; (faire la moyenne entre deux quantités) to split the difference; **en forme de p.** pear-shaped **2** (objet en forme de poire) (d'un appareil photo) (pear-shaped) bulb; (d'un interrupteur électrique) (pear-shaped) switch; **p. à lavement** enema bag **3** *Fam* (tête) mug, face; **il a une bonne p.** he's got a nice enough face, he looks nice enough; **en pleine p.** right in the face **4** *Fam* (idiot) sucker, *Br* mug; **je ne suis pas une p.!** I'm no sucker or *Br* mug!; **je suis vraiment trop bonne p., je lui pardonne toujours tout** I'm a real sucker or *Br* mug, I let him get away with everything; **et moi, bonne p., j'ai accepté** and like the sucker or *Br* mug that I am, I accepted

poiré [pware] NM perry

poireau, -eaux [pwaro] NM (légume) leek; *Fam* **faire le p.** to be kept hanging around or waiting, to kick or cool one's heels

poireauter [pwarote] VI *Fam* to be kept hanging around or waiting, to kick or cool one's heels; **faire p. qn** to keep sb hanging around or waiting, to leave sb to kick or cool his/her heels

poirée [pware] NF *Bot* white beet

poirier [pwarje] NM **1** (arbre) pear tree; *Gym* **faire le p.** to do a headstand, to stand on one's head **2** (bois) pear-tree wood

pois [pwa] NM **1** (plante) pea; *Culin* **petits p.** (garden) peas; **purée de p.** thick pea soup; *Fam* (brouillard) peasouper **2** (rond) spot, (polka) dot; **cravate bleue à p. blancs** blue tie with white spots, blue polka-dot tie; **tis-**

su/robe à p. spotted or polka-dot material/dress
▸▸**p. carré** marrowfat pea; **p. cassés** split peas; **p. chiche** chickpea; **p. de senteur** sweet pea

poiscaille [pwaskɑj] NF *Fam* fish

poison [pwazɔ̃] NM **1** (substance fatale) poison **2** *Fig Fam* **quel p.!** what a drag or bind!, how boring!
N *Fam* (personne, chien etc) pest, horror

poissard, -arde [pwasar, -ard] ADJ vulgar, coarse
NF *Vieilli Péj* **poissarde** fishwife

poisse [pwas] NF *Fam* bad luck; **c'est la p.!** just my/our luck!; **porter la p. (à qn)** to bring (sb) bad luck

poisser [pwase] VT **1** (engluer) to pitch; **fil poissé** waxed thread **2** (salir avec une matière gluante) to make sticky **3** *Fam Vieilli* (personne) to nab, to collar
VI (d'une substance) to be sticky

poisseux, -euse [pwasø, -øz] ADJ sticky

poisson [pwasɔ̃] NM **1** fish; **p. d'eau douce/de mer** freshwater/saltwater fish; **prendre un/du p.** to catch a/some fish; **je n'aime pas le p.** I don't like fish; **manger du p.** to eat fish; **p. d'avril!** April fool!; **c'est un p. d'avril** it's an April fool's trick; **être (heureux) comme un p. dans l'eau** to be really in one's element; *Fam* **engueuler qn comme du p. pourri** to give sb a real mouthful; *Fam* **se faire engueuler comme du p. pourri** to get a real mouthful; *Prov* **petit p. deviendra grand** great oaks from little acorns grow VOIR GRAMMAIRE A12 **2** *Astron, Astrol* **les Poissons** Pisces; **être (du signe des) Poissons** to be (a) Pisces
▸▸*Entom* **p. d'argent** silverfish; **p.-chat** catfish; **p. lune** sunfish; **p. pilote** pilot fish; **p. plat** flatfish; **p. rouge** goldfish; **p. volant** flying fish

---

Poisson d'avril
In France and in French-speaking countries, on the first of April, children cut fish shapes out of paper and stick them on their unsuspecting classmates' backs, and people play practical jokes on one another before crying out "Poisson d'avril!" ("April fool!"). This custom is referred to in Quebec as "courir le poisson d'avril".

---

poissonnerie [pwasɔnri] NF (magasin) fish shop, *Br* fishmonger's; (marché) fish market

poissonneux, -euse [pwasɔnø, -øz] ADJ full of fish

poissonnier, -ière [pwasɔnje, -jer] N *Com* fishmonger, *Am* fish merchant
NM (bateau) = small boat used to buy fish direct from fishing boats
NF **poissonnière** (ustensile) fish kettle

poitevin [pwatvɛ̃] ADJ (de Poitiers) of/from Poitiers; (du Poitou) of/from Poitou
N (de Poitiers) = inhabitant of or person from Poitiers; (du Poitou) = inhabitant of or person from Poitou

poitrail [pwatraj] NM **1** (partie du corps de certains animaux) breast; *Fig Fam* (poitrine) chest; **un homme au p. découvert** a man with a bare chest **2** (partie de harnais) breast strap, breastplate

poitrinaire [pwatriner] ADJ, N *Vieilli* consumptive

poitrine [pwatrin] NF **1** (poumons) chest; **chanter à pleine p.** to sing at the top of one's voice; **être fragile de la p.** to have a weak chest; *Arch* **s'en aller de la p.** to be dying of consumption; *Mus* **voix de p.** chest voice **2** (thorax) chest, *Litt* breast; (de femme) bosom, bust, chest; **serrer qn contre** ou **sur sa p.** to hold or press or clasp sb to one's breast; **tour de p.** (d'un homme, d'un enfant) chest *(measurement)*; *(d'une femme)* bust *(measurement)*; **avoir une belle/forte p.** to have a shapely bosom/be well-endowed; **ne pas avoir de p.** to be flat-chested, to have no bust; **ne pas avoir beaucoup de p.** to be small-chested, to have a small bust; **elle n'a pas encore de p.** her bust hasn't started to develop yet **3** *Culin (de veau)* breast; *(de bœuf)* brisket; *(de porc)* belly

poivrade [pwavrad] NF *Culin (sauce)* = sauce made by reducing a heavily peppered mixture of wine and vinegar; **manger des artichauts à la p.** to eat artichokes (raw) with salt and pepper

poivre [pwavr] NM pepper; **p. blanc/noir** *ou* **gris** white/black pepper; **p. vert/rouge** green/red pepper; **p. de Cayenne** cayenne (pepper); *Culin* **steak au p.** pepper steak; **grain de p.** peppercorn; **des cheveux p. et sel** pepper-and-salt hair; **une femme p. et sel** a woman with pepper-and-salt hair

poivré [pwavre] ADJ **1** *(nourriture)* peppery; *(odeur)* pungent, spicy **2** *Fig (grivois) (histoire)* spicy, juicy **3** *Fam (ivre)* wasted, *Br* sloshed

poivrer [pwavre] VT to put pepper on/in, to season with pepper
▪ VPR **se poivrer** *Fam (boire)* to get plastered *or* smashed

poivrier [pwavrije] NM **1** *Bot* pepper plant **2** *(petit pot)* pepper pot; *(moulin)* pepper mill

poivrière [pwavrijɛr] NF **1** *(plantation)* pepper plantation **2** *(boîte)* pepper pot **3** *Archit* pepperpot (turret)

poivron [pwavrɔ̃] NM *Bot* (sweet) pepper, capsicum, *Am* bell pepper; **p. vert/rouge/ jaune** green/red/yellow pepper

poivrot, -ote [pwavro, -ɔt] N *Fam* drunk, alky

poix [pwa] NF pitch; **p. sèche** resin; **p. liquide** tar; **noir comme (de la) p.** pitch black; **collant comme de la p.** sticky as glue

poker [pɔkɛr] NM *Cartes* poker; **faire un p.** to have a game of poker; **p. d'as** *(cartes)* four aces; *(dés)* poker dice; **le menteur** liar poker; *Fig* **une partie de p.** a poker game, a game of bluff (and counter-bluff); *Fig* **c'est un coup de p.** it's a game of bluff

Polac, Polack [pɔlak] N *Fam Péj (Polonais)* Polack

polaire [pɔlɛr] ADJ polar; **l'étoile P.** the Pole Star; **froid p.** intense *or* Arctic cold; **expédition p.** polar expedition, expedition to the (North/South) Pole; **laine p.** fleece, fleecy material; **fourrure p.** fleecy jacket
▪ NF *Math* polar; *Astron* **la P.** the Pole Star

polar [pɔlar] NM *Fam (livre, film)* whodunnit

polard, -arde [pɔlar, -ard] *Arg* N swot
▪ ADJ **être p.** to be a swot

polarimètre [pɔlarimɛtr] NM *Phys* polarimeter

polarisable [pɔlarizabl] ADJ polarizable

polarisant [pɔlarizɑ̃] ADJ polarizing

polarisation [pɔlarizasjɔ̃] NF **1** *Phys (de la lumière, d'électrodes)* polarization, polarizing; *Électron* **p. de grille** grid bias; **résistance de p. de grille** bias resistor **2** *Fig (focalisation) (d'attention, d'énergies etc)* focusing

polariscope [pɔlariskɔp] NM *Opt* polariscope

polariser [pɔlarize] VT *Phys, Électron* to polarize; *Fig (attention)* to attract; **ce phénomène polarise l'attention de tous** this phenomenon is the focus of everybody's attention; **cette décision a polarisé le mécontentement des masses salariales** this decision has become the focus of the workers' discontent; **p. qn** *ou* **p. l'attention de qn sur qch** to focus sb's attention on sth
▪ VPR **se polariser** *Fam (de l'attention)* to focus;

se p. sur qch *(d'une personne)* to focus one's attention on sth

polariseur [pɔlarizœr] NM *Opt* polarizer

polarité [pɔlarite] NF polarity

Polaroïd® [pɔlarɔid] NM *Phot (appareil)* Polaroid® (camera)

polatouche [pɔlatuʃ] NM *Zool* flying squirrel

polder [pɔlder] NM *Géog* polder

pôle [pol] NM **1** *Géog* pole; **p. Nord/Sud** North/South Pole; *Phys* **pôles semblables** like poles; **pôles contraires** opposite poles; **pôles magnétiques** magnetic poles **2** *Fig* **p. d'intérêt** focus of interest; **p. d'attraction** centre of attention; **un p. d'attraction économique/touristique** a centre of economic/tourist development; *Écon, Pol* **les pôles de croissance** the main centres of economic growth; **p. de reconversion** development *or* reconversion zone

polémique [pɔlemik] ADJ polemical
▪ NF argument, controversy, *Fml* polemic; **faire de la p.** to provoke arguments, to be controversial; **chercher la p.** to look for an argument; **une vive p. s'ensuivit** a heated argument ensued

polémiquer [pɔlemike] VI to argue

polémiste [pɔlemist] N polemicist

polémologie [pɔlemɔlɔʒi] NF study of war

polenta [pɔlɛnta] NF *Culin* polenta

pole position [polpozisjɔ̃] NF *(dans une course automobile)* **être en p.** to be in pole position

poli¹ [pɔli] ADJ **1** *(lisse) (métal)* polished, burnished, buffed; *(pierre)* polished **2** *(élégant) (style)* polished, elegant
▪ NM shine, polish, gloss

poli² ADJ *(courtois) (personne, réponse, manières)* polite, civil; **être très p. avec qn** to be very polite *or* very courteous to sb; **il est trop p. pour être honnête** he's so polite that I'm suspicious of him; **peu p.** impolite, rude, discourteous

police¹ [pɔlis] NF **1** *(maintien de l'ordre)* maintenance of law and order; *(par la police)* policing; **exercer** *ou* **faire la p.** to maintain law and order, to keep order; *(au bureau, dans une classe etc)* to keep order; *Aut Vieilli* **numéro de p.** registration *or Am* license number; **intervention des forces de p.** police intervention, intervention by the police; *Jur* **tribunal de (simple) p.** magistrate's court; *Mil* **salle de p.** guardroom
2 *(institution)* **la p.** the police (force); **appeler la p.** to call the police; **appeler p. secours** ≃ to dial *Br* 999 *or Am* 911 (for the police); **être de** *ou* **dans la p.** to be in *or* to be a member of the police (force); *Fig Hum* **tu n'es pas de la p. à ce que je sache!** what is this, the Spanish Inquisition?, what is this, Twenty Questions?; **p.!, les mains en l'air!** police!, hands up!; **remettre qn entre les mains de la p.** to give sb up to the police; **la p. est à vos trousses** the police are after you *or* are (hot) on your heels; **la guerre des polices** = rivalry between different police departments; **toutes les polices de France sont à ses trousses** the entire French police force are hot on his heels; **p. de la circulation** traffic police; **p. administrative** = administrative branch of the police; **p. judiciaire** *Br* ≃ Criminal Investigation Department, *Am* ≃ Federal Bureau of Investigation; **p. municipale** local police; **la p. nationale** = national police force; **p. mondaine** *ou* **des mœurs** ≃ vice squad; **p. de l'air et des frontières** airport and border police; **p. de l'immigration** immigration police; **p. secrète** secret police; *Fam* **la p. des polices** *Br* ≃ Complaints Investigation Bureau, *Am* ≃ Internal Investigation Board; **p. montée** mounted police; **p.**

parallèle secret police; **agent de p.** police officer; *(de circulation)* traffic policeman; **inspecteur de p.** (police) inspector; **commissaire de p.** *Br* ≃ (police) superintendent, *Am* ≃ (police) captain; **préfet de p.** ≃ chief commissioner of police VOIR GRAMMAIRE A11

> ## Police nationale
> The "Police nationale" operates under the authority of the Ministry of the Interior, unlike the "Gendarmerie", which is an army corps.

police² NF **1** *Jur* (insurance) policy; **prendre une p.** to take out a policy; **p. d'assurance (sur la) vie/(contre l')incendie** life insurance/fire insurance policy; **p. d'assurance maritime** marine insurance policy; *Com* **p. de chargement** bill of lading; **p. individuelle crédit acheteur** individual buyer credit policy; **p. individuelle crédit fournisseur** individual supplier credit policy; *Com* **p. ouverte** open policy; **p. tous risques** comprehensive policy, all-risks policy; **p. universelle** worldwide policy; **p. au voyage** travel insurance policy **2** *Typ, Ordinat* **p. (de caractères)** font; **p. bâton** sans serif font; **p. bitmap** *ou* **pixélisée** bitmap font; **p. par défaut** default font; **p. proportionnelle** proportional font; **p. de taille variable** scalable font; **p. vectorielle** outline font

policé [pɔlise] ADJ civilized

policeman [pɔlisman] NM (British) policeman

policer [pɔlise] VT (je poliçai(s); n. poliçons) **1** *Arch (gouverner)* **p. un pays** to bring a country under orderly government **2** *Arch, Litt (civiliser)* to civilize

polichinelle [pɔliʃinɛl] NM **1** *(marionnette)* Punch; **théâtre de p.** ≃ Punch and Judy show; **secret de p.** open secret; *Fig Fam* **avoir un p. dans le tiroir** *(être enceinte)* to have a bun in the oven, to be in the pudding club **2** *Fig Péj* buffoon; **faire le p.** to act *or* play the fool

policier, -ière [pɔlisje, -jɛr] ADJ *(enquête, État, chien etc)* police; *(roman, film)* detective
▪ NM **1** *(officier de police)* policeman, police officer; **femme p.** woman police officer VOIR GRAMMAIRE A11 **2** *(roman)* detective novel; *(film)* detective film

policlinique [pɔliklinik] NF outpatients' clinic *or* department

poliment [pɔlimɑ̃] ADV politely

polio [pɔljo] *Méd* NF *(maladie)* polio
▪ N polio victim

poliomyélite [pɔljɔmjelit] NF *Méd* poliomyelitis

poliomyélitique [pɔljɔmjelitik] *Méd* ADJ *(vaccin)* polio; *(personne)* suffering from polio
▪ N polio victim

polir [pɔlir] VT **1** *(poncer) (métal)* to polish, to burnish, to buff; *(pierre)* to polish; **poli par l'usage** shiny with use; **poli par l'érosion/le temps** made smooth by erosion/the passage of time **2** *(perfectionner) (style, discours etc)* to polish (up); *(manières)* to refine
▪ VPR **se polir** **se p. les ongles** to polish *or* buff one's nails

Polisario [pɔlisarjo] N *Pol* **le Front P.** the Polisario

polissage [pɔlisaʒ] NM *(de métal)* polishing, burnishing, buffing; *(des ongles)* polishing, buffing

polisseur, -euse [pɔlisœr, -øz] N polisher
▪ NF **polisseuse** *(machine)* polishing machine, polisher

polissoir [pɔliswar] NM *Tech* buffing wheel; *(de graveur)* grinding disc; *(pour les ongles)* nail buffer

polissoire [pɔliswar] NF **1** *(brosse) (pour chaussures)* (polishing) brush **2** *Ind (atelier)* polishing shop

polisson, -onne [pɔlisɔ̃, -ɔn] N **1** *(enfant espiègle)* rascal, scamp **2** *Vieilli Fam (gamin des rues)* street urchin
▸ ADJ **1** *(méchant) (enfant)* naughty, mischievous **2** *(coquin, grivois)* smutty; **regard p.** leer

polissonner [pɔlisɔne] VI *Vieilli (d'un enfant)* to be mischievous *or* naughty

polissonnerie [pɔlisɔnri] NF **1** *(espièglerie)* mischievous trick **2** *Vieilli (parole)* smutty remark; *(plaisanterie)* smutty joke

politesse [pɔlitɛs] NF politeness, courtesy; **il est toujours d'une grande p. avec les gens** he is always very polite *or* courteous to people; **dire/faire qch par p.** to say/do sth out of politeness *or* to be polite; **brûler la p. à qn** to leave sb abruptly, to leave without saying goodbye to sb; **faire des politesses à qn** to be polite to sb; **faire échange de politesses** to exchange compliments; **ce serait la moindre des politesses de le prévenir** it's only polite to warn him; **il m'a rendu la p.** he returned the favour *or Am* favor; *(invitation)* he returned my invitation; *(mauvais tour)* he paid me back

politicaillerie [pɔlitikajri] NF *Fam Péj* political scheming

politicard, -arde [pɔlitikar, -ard] *Fam Péj* N political schemer
▸ ADJ scheming

politicien, -ienne [pɔlitisjɛ̃, -jɛn] N politician, *Am Fam* politico
▸ ADJ *Péj* politicking; **politique politicienne** politicking; **faire de la politique politicienne** to politick

politique [pɔlitik] ADJ **1** *(de la société, du gouvernement)* political; **homme/femme p.** politician; **ambitionner une carrière p.** to have political ambitions; **le corps p.** the body politic; **détenu p.** political prisoner; **économie p.** economics, political economy **2** *Arch, Litt (réponse, choix, conduite)* politic
▸ NF **1** *(de gouvernement, d'entreprise)* policy; **p. intérieure/extérieure** domestic/foreign policy; **suivre** *ou* **adopter une nouvelle p.** to follow *or* adopt a new policy; **la p. de l'autruche** burying one's head in the sand; **pratiquer la p. de l'autruche** to bury one's head in the sand; **pratiquer la p. de la chaise vide** to make a political point by not attending meetings; **p. de la main tendue** policy of the outstretched hand; **pratiquer la p. de la main tendue** to make friendly overtures, to be conciliatory; **la p. du pire** = deliberately worsening the situation to further one's ends; *Écon* **p. de la porte ouverte** open-door policy; **p. de droite/gauche** right-wing/left-wing policy; *UE* **la p. agricole commune** the Common Agricultural Policy; **p. d'apaisement** policy of appeasement; **p. d'austérité** austerity policy; **p. budgétaire** budgetary *or* fiscal policy; **p. commerciale** trade policy; *UE* **p. communautaire** EU policy; *UE* **p. commune de la pêche** Common Fisheries Policy; *Mktg* **p. de communication** promotional policy; **p. conjoncturelle** economic policy *(responding to changes in the business cycle)*; *Pol* **p. conventionnelle** = policy relating to union-management agreements; *Fin* **p. de crédit** credit policy; **p. économique** economic policy; *Journ* **p. éditoriale, p. de la rédaction** *(principe)* editorial policy; **p. étrangère** foreign policy; *UE* **p. étrangère et de sécurité commune** Common Foreign and Security Policy; **p. fiscale** fiscal policy; **p. industrielle** industrial policy; **p. de libre-échange** free-trade policy; **p. monétaire** monetary policy; **p. d'ouverture** consensus politics; **p. de plein emploi** policy of full em-

ployment; **p. politicienne** party politics; *Mktg* **p. de vente** sales policy; **p. des prix** pricing policy; **p. de relance** reflationary policy; **p. de rigueur** policy of austerity; **p. des salaires** wages policy; **p. sécuritaire** repressive law-and-order policy **2** *(affaires publiques)* politics; **parler/discuter p.** to talk/discuss politics; **se lancer dans la p.** to go into politics; **faire de la p.** to be in politics; **tu sais, moi, je ne fais pas de p.** I'm not politically inclined; *Fig* **p.-fiction** political fiction; **scénario de p.-fiction** scenario belonging to the realms of political fiction; **un roman de p.-fiction** a political novel VOIR GRAMMAIRE A10
▸ NM **1** *(personne)* politician **2** *Fig (domaine)* politics; **le p. français** French politics

> Attention: ne pas confondre **politics** et **policy** lorsque l'on traduit **politique**. **Politics** est un terme indénombrable qui désigne la politique en tant que discipline, alors que le terme **policy** est un terme dénombrable qui désigne un ensemble de mesures.

politiquement [pɔlitikmɑ̃] ADV *Pol* politically; *Fig Litt* politically, diplomatically; **p. correct** politically correct

politiquer [pɔlitike] VI *Arch Fam* to talk politics

politisation [pɔlitizasjɔ̃] NF politicization

politiser [pɔlitize] VT *(chose)* to politicize, to bring politics into; *(personne)* to politicize; **plus/moins/très politisé** more/less/very politically inclined *or* political

politologie [pɔlitɔlɔʒi] NF political science

politologue [pɔlitɔlɔg] N political scientist

polka [pɔlka] NF polka

pollen [pɔlɛn] NM pollen

pollinisation [pɔlinizasjɔ̃] NF pollination

polliniser [pɔlinize] VT to pollinate

polluant [pɔlɥɑ̃] ADJ polluting; **produit p.** pollutant
▸ NM pollutant

pollué [pɔlɥe] ADJ polluted; **région fortement polluée** highly polluted region, region with a high level of pollution

polluer [pɔlɥe] VT to pollute

pollueur, -euse [pɔlɥœr, -øz] N polluter; **le principe du p.-payeur** 'the polluter pays' principle
▸ ADJ polluting

pollution [pɔlysjɔ̃] NF **1** *(dégradation de l'environnement)* pollution; **p. atmosphérique** atmospheric *or* air pollution; **p. automobile** traffic pollution **2** *Méd* **pollutions nocturnes** wet dreams, *Spéc* nocturnal emissions

polo [pɔlo] NM **1** *Sport* polo **2** *(chemise)* polo shirt

polochon [pɔlɔʃɔ̃] NM *Fam* bolster; **bataille de polochons** pillow fight; **se battre à coups de polochons** to have a pillow fight

Pologne [pɔlɔɲ] NF Poland

polonais, -aise [pɔlɔnɛ, -ɛz] VOIR GRAMMAIRE A19 ADJ Polish
▸ NM *Ling* Polish
▸ N **P.** Pole; *Fam* **soûl comme un P.** as drunk as a lord
▸ NF *Mus* **polonaise** polonaise

polonium [pɔlɔnjɔm] NM *Chimie* polonium

poltron, -onne [pɔltrɔ̃, -ɔn] ADJ cowardly
▸ N coward

poltronnerie [pɔltrɔnri] NF cowardice

polyacide [pɔliasid] ADJ, NM *Chimie* polyacid

polyamide [pɔliamid] NM *Chimie* polyamide

polyandre [pɔljɑ̃dr] ADJ polyandrous

polyandrie [pɔljɑ̃dri] NF polyandry

polyarthrite [pɔliartrit] NF *Méd* polyarthritis

polycentrisme [pɔlisɑ̃trism] NM *Pol* polycentrism

polychrome [pɔlikrom] ADJ polychrome, polychromatic

polychromie [pɔlikromi] NF polychromy

polyclinique [pɔliklinik] NF *Méd* polyclinic

polycopie [pɔlikɔpi] NF *(procédé)* duplicating, duplication; *(document)* duplicate

polycopié [pɔlikɔpje] ADJ duplicated
▸ NM duplicate; *Scol, Univ* (duplicated) course material; *(plus petit)* handout

polycopier [pɔlikɔpje] VT to duplicate

polyculture [pɔlikyltyr] NF *Agr* mixed farming

polydactyle [pɔlidaktil] ADJ polydactyl

polyèdre [pɔliɛdr] *Géom* ADJ polyhedral
▸ NM polyhedron

polyédrique [pɔliedrik] ADJ *Géom* polyhedral

polyester [pɔliɛstɛr] NM *Chimie* polyester

polyéthylène [pɔlietilɛn] NM polythene, *surtout Am* polyethylene

polygame [pɔligam] ADJ polygamous
▸ N polygamist

polygamie [pɔligami] NF polygamy

polyglotte [pɔliglɔt] ADJ, N polyglot

polygonal, -ale, -aux, -ales [pɔligɔnal, -o] ADJ polygonal

polygone [pɔligon] NM **1** *Géom* polygon **2** *Mil* shooting range

polygraphe [pɔligraf] N versatile writer

polyinsaturé [pɔliɛ̃satyre] ADJ *(lipide)* polyunsaturated

polymère [pɔlimɛr] *Chimie* ADJ polymeric
▸ NM polymer

polymérisation [pɔlimerizasjɔ̃] NF *Chimie* polymerization

polymorphe [pɔlimɔrf] ADJ polymorphous, polymorphic

polymorphie [pɔlimɔrfi] NF, **polymorphisme** [pɔlimɔrfism] NM polymorphism

Polynésie [pɔlinezi] NF Polynesia

polynésien, -ienne [pɔlinezjɛ̃, -jɛn] ADJ Polynesian
▸ N **P.** Polynesian

polynôme [pɔlinom] NM *Math* polynomial

polynucléaire [pɔlinykleɛr] ADJ *Biol* polynuclear

polype [pɔlip] NM *Méd, Zool* polyp

polypétale [pɔlipetal] ADJ *Bot* polypetalous

polypeux, -euse [pɔlipø, -øz] ADJ *Méd* polypous

polyphasé [pɔlifaze] ADJ *Élec (système)* polyphase, multiphase

polyphonie [pɔlifɔni] NF *Mus* polyphony

polypropylène [pɔliprɔpilɛn] NM polypropylene

polysémie [pɔlisemi] NF *Ling* polysemy

polysémique [pɔlisemik] ADJ *Ling* polysemous

polysoc [pɔlisɔk] NM *Agr* multiple plough *or Am* plow

polystyle [pɔlistil] ADJ *Archit (salle, temple)* polystyle

polystyrène [pɔlistirɛn] NM *Chimie* polystyrene; **boîte en p.** polystyrene box

polysyllabe [pɔlisilab] ADJ *(mot)* polysyllabic
▸ NM polysyllable

polysyllabique [pɔlisilabik] ADJ polysyllabic

polytechnicien, -ienne [pɔliteknisjɛ̃, -jɛn] N student at the École polytechnique; *(diplômé)* graduate of the École polytechnique

polytechnique [politɛknik] **ADJ** École p. = grande école specializing in technology
NF P. = grande école specializing in technology

Il faut noter que le nom anglais **polytechnic** est un faux ami. Il désigne un établissement d'enseignement supérieur comparable à un IUT.

École polytechnique

Founded in 1794, this prestigious engineering college has close connections with the Ministry of Defence. Formerly situated in the heart of the 5th arrondissement, the college moved to Palaiseau, near Paris, in the 1970s. It is popularly known as "l'X". Students are effectively enlisted in the army and must repay their education through government service.

polythéisme [politeism] **NM** polytheism
polythéiste [politeist] **N** polytheist
ADJ polytheistic
polythène [politɛn] **NM** *Chimie* polythene
polytransfusé, -ée [politrãsfyze] *Méd* **ADJ** who has/had received multiple blood transfusions
N person who has/had received multiple blood transfusions
polytraumatisé [politromatize] **ADJ** *Méd* suffering from multiple injuries
polyuréthane [poliyretan] **NM** *Chimie* polyurethane
polyvalence [polivalãs] **NF** *Chimie* polyvalency, multivalency; *Fig (d'une personne)* versatility
polyvalent [polivalã] **ADJ 1** *Chimie* polyvalent, multivalent **2** *Fig (salle)* multipurpose; *(outil)* versatile, multipurpose; *(personne)* versatile; *Admin* inspecteur p. tax inspector
NM *Admin* tax inspector
polyvinyle [polivinil] **NM** *Chimie* polyvinyl; **chlorure de p.** polyvinyl chloride
polyvinylique [polivinilik] **ADJ** *Chimie* polyvinyl
pomélo [pomelo] **NM** pomelo
Poméranie [pomerani] **NF** *Géog* Pomerania; **loulou de P.** Pomeranian, *Fam* Pom
pommade [pomad] **NF** *Méd* ointment; *Arch (pour les cheveux)* pomade; **p. pour les lèvres** lip salve; *Fig Fam* **passer de la p. à qn** to butter sb up
pommader [pomade] **VT** *Arch (cheveux)* to pomade
pomme [pom] **NF 1** *(fruit)* apple; **p. à cuire** cooking apple, *Br* cooker; **p. à couteau** eating apple; **p. à cidre** cider apple; **compote de pommes** stewed apples, *Am* applesauce; *Fig Fam* **c'est toujours pour ma p.** it's always yours truly that gets it; *Fam* **je ne veux pas voir sa p. ici** I don't want to see him/her here; *Fam* **ramener sa p.** to turn up, to roll up; *Fam* **haut comme trois pommes** knee-high to a grasshopper; *Fam* **tomber dans les pommes** to pass out, to faint; *Fam* **aux pommes** super, great; *Myth* **les pommes d'or du jardin des Hespérides** the golden apples of Hesperides **2** *(cœur)* *(de salade, de chou)* heart **3** *(partie arrondie)* *(de bois de lit, de canne etc)* knob; *(d'arrosoir)* rose; *Naut (de mât)* truck; **canne à p. d'or** gold-headed stick; **p. de douche** shower head **4** *Fam (personne naïve)* sucker, *Br* mug, *Am* patsy **5** *Suisse (eau de vie de pomme)* apple brandy
▸▸ *Anat* **p. d'Adam** Adam's apple; **pommes allumettes** matchstick chips *or Am* potatoes; **p.**

d'amour *(tomate)* love apple; **p. d'api** = type of small red and white apple; **p. cannelle** custard apple; **p. de chêne** oak apple; **pommes chips** (potato) crisps *or Am* chips; **pommes dauphine** dauphine potatoes; *Fig* **p. de discorde** bone of contention; **pommes duchesse** duchesse potatoes; **p. épineuse** thorn apple; **pommes frites** (French) fries, *Br* chips; **pommes noisette** = small potato croquettes; **p. de pin** pine cone; *(de sapin)* fir cone; **p. reinette** pippin; **p. sauvage** crab apple; **p. de terre** potato; **pommes de terre à l'eau** boiled potatoes; **p. de terre au four** *ou* **en robe de chambre** *ou* **en robe des champs** baked potato, jacket potato; **pommes de terre frites** (French) fries, *Br* chips; **pommes vapeur** steamed potatoes
pommé [pome] **ADJ 1** *(laitue, chou)* hearty, firm (and round) **2** *Fam Vieilli (idiot, gaffe)* complete, downright
pommeau, -eaux [pomo] **NM** *(d'un sabre, d'une selle)* pommel; *(d'une canne à pêche)* butt; *(d'une canne, d'un levier de vitesse)* knob; **p. de douche** shower head
pommelé [pomle] **ADJ** dappled, mottled; **gris p.** *(cheval)* dapple-grey; **ciel p.** mackerel sky
pommeler (se) [səpomle] **VPR** (**il se pommelle; il se pommellera**) **1** *(du ciel)* to become covered *or* dappled with small fleecy clouds **2** *(d'un chou, d'une laitue)* to form a head *or* heart
pommelle [pomɛl] **NF** grating *(over drain-pipe etc)*
pommer [pome] **VI** *(d'un chou, d'une laitue)* to form a head *or* heart
pommeraie [pomrɛ] **NF** apple orchard
pommette [pomɛt] **NF** *Anat* cheekbone; **avoir les pommettes saillantes** to have high cheekbones
pommier [pomje] **NM** apple tree; **p. sauvage** crab (apple) tree
pompage [pɔ̃paʒ] **NM** pumping; *Aut (de moteur)* hunting; *TV, Radio (d'une bande)* flutter; **station de p.** pumping station
pompe¹ [pɔ̃p] **NF** *(cérémonie)* pomp, ceremony; **en grande p.** with great (pomp and) ceremony; **las de la cour et de ses pompes** tired of all the pomp and ceremony
pompe² **NF 1** *(machine)* pump; **puiser l'eau à la p.** to pump out the water; **prendre de l'eau à la p.** to get water from the pump; *Fam* **avoir le** *ou* **un coup de p.** to feel done in *or* shattered all of a sudden; **une barre de chocolat pour le coup de p. de onze heures** a chocolate bar for when you need an energy boost; *Fam* **à toutes pompes** like lightning, at top speed; *Sport Fam* **faire des pompes** to do push-ups *or Br* press-ups **2** *Mus* **p. d'accord** *(d'un instrument à vent)* (tuning) slide **3** **serrure à p.** high security lock **4** *Fam* **pompes** *(chaussures)* shoes; **ça, c'est de la p.!** those are some shoes!; *Fig* **être bien/mal dans ses pompes** to have got it together/be mixed up; *Fig* **il est à côté de ses pompes** he's not with it, he's not himself **5** *Mil Arg* **(soldat de) deuxième p.** squaddie, *Am* grunt
▸▸ **p. à air** air pump, pneumatic pump; **p. d'alimentation** *ou* **alimentaire** feed pump; **p. aspirante** suction pump, lift pump; **p. aspirante et foulante** lift-and-force pump; **p. de bicyclette** bicycle pump; **p. à bière** beer pump; **p. à carburant** fuel pump; **p. à chaleur** heat pump; *Aut* **p. distributrice** distributor pump; *Aut* **p. à eau** water pump; **p. à essence** *(de moteur)* fuel pump; *(distributeur)* petrol *or Am* gas pump; *(station-service)* petrol *or Am* gas station; **p. foulante** force pump; **pompes funèbres** undertaker's, funeral di-

rector's, *Am* mortician's; **ordonnateur** *ou* **entrepreneur de pompes funèbres** undertaker, funeral director, *Am* mortician; *Aut* **p. de graissage** grease gun; *Tech* **p. à graisse** grease gun; *Aut* **p. à huile** oil pump; **p. à incendie** water pump *(on a fire engine)*; *Aut* **p. d'injection** injection pump, injector pump; **p. pneumatique** air *or* pneumatic pump; **p. refoulante** force pump; *Aut* **p. de refoulement** *ou* **de relevage** lift pump; *Aut* **p. de reprise** accelerator *or* acceleration pump; *Fam* **p. à vélo** bicycle pump; **p. à vide** vacuum pump; *Aut* exhauster
pompé [pɔ̃pe] **ADJ** *Fam (épuisé)* bushed, *Br* knackered
Pompée [pɔ̃pe] **N** Pompey
Pompéi [pɔ̃pei] **N** Pompeii
pompéien, -ienne [pɔ̃pejɛ̃, -jɛn] **ADJ** Pompeiian
N P. Pompeiian
pomper [pɔ̃pe] **VT 1** *(puiser)* *(eau, air)* to pump; *(faire monter)* to pump up; *(évacuer)* to pump out; **p. de l'eau du puits** to pump (up) water from the well; **p. de l'air dans un pneu** to pump air into a tyre; **des parasites qui pompent le sang** parasites that suck blood; *Fig Fam* **p. qn** *(épuiser)* to do sb in, to wear sb out; *Fam* **être pompé** to be done in *or* shattered; *Fam* **tu me pompes l'air** you're getting on my nerves **2** *Fam (boisson)* to knock back **3** *Scol Fam* to copy (**sur qn** from sb)
VI 1 *(faire marcher une pompe)* to pump **2** *Scol Fam* to copy (**sur qn** from sb)
pompette [pɔ̃pɛt] **ADJ** *Fam* tipsy, *Br* merry
pompeusement [pɔ̃pøzmã] **ADV** *Péj* pompously
pompeux, -euse [pɔ̃pø, -øz] **ADJ** *Péj* pompous
pompier [pɔ̃pje] **NM 1** fireman, fire fighter; **p. de service** fire officer; **appeler les pompiers** to call the fire brigade *or Am* the fire fighters; *Fam* **fumer comme un p.** to smoke like a chimney **2** *Vulg (fellation)* blow job; **faire un p. à qn** to give sb a blow job
pompier, -ière [pɔ̃pje, -jɛr] *Beaux-Arts Péj* **ADJ** *(art, style, tableau)* pompous
NM artist with a pompous style
pompiste [pɔ̃pist] **N** *Aut* (petrol *or Am* gas) pump attendant, forecourt attendant
pom-pom girl, *pl* **pom-pom girls** [pɔ̃pɔ̃mgœrl] **NF** cheerleader
pompon [pɔ̃pɔ̃] **NM** pompom, bobble; **bonnet à p.** bobble hat; *Fam* **ça, c'est le p.!** that's the limit!, that's the last straw!; *Iron* **avoir le p.** to be the limit, to take the biscuit *or Am* cake; *Fam Vieilli* **avoir son p.** to be tipsy
pomponner (se) [səpɔ̃pɔne] **VPR** *Fam* to doll oneself up
ponçage [pɔ̃saʒ] **NM 1** *(action de poncer)* *(à la pierre ponce)* pumicing; *(au papier de verre)* sandpapering; *(de peinture)* rubbing down, sanding down; *(avec une ponceuse)* sanding **2** *Beaux-Arts* pouncing
ponce [pɔ̃s] **NF (pierre) p.** pumice (stone)
Ponce Pilate [pɔ̃spilat] **N** *Bible* Pontius Pilate
poncer [pɔ̃se] **VT** (**je ponçai(s); n. ponçons**) **1** *(passer à la pierre ponce)* to pumice; *(au papier de verre)* to sandpaper; *(peinture)* to rub down, to sand down; *(avec une ponceuse)* to sand **2** *Beaux-Arts* to pounce
ponceur [pɔ̃sœr] **NM** polisher
ponceuse [pɔ̃søz] **NF** sander, sanding machine
poncho [pɔ̃tʃo] **NM** poncho
poncif [pɔ̃sif] **NM 1** *Beaux-Arts* pouncing pattern **2** *(banalité, évidence)* cliché, commonplace

ponction [pɔ̃ksjɔ̃] NF *Méd* puncture; *(de poumon)* tapping; **p. lombaire** lumbar puncture; *Fig* **faire une p./des ponctions dans ses économies** to draw on one's savings; *Admin* **p. fiscale** taxation; **c'est une p. importante sur mes revenus** it makes a big hole *or* dent in my income

ponctionner [pɔ̃ksjɔne] VT *Méd* to puncture; *(poumon, malade)* to tap; *Fig Fam (argent)* to draw on; **on nous ponctionne un tiers de notre salaire en impôts** a third of our salary goes in tax

ponctualité [pɔ̃ktɥalite] NF punctuality

ponctuation [pɔ̃ktɥasjɔ̃] NF punctuation

ponctuel, -elle [pɔ̃ktɥɛl] ADJ **1** *(à l'heure)* punctual **2** *Phys* **source ponctuelle de chaleur** pinpoint flame; **source lumineuse ponctuelle** point source; **projecteur p.** spotlight **3** *Fig (qui ne concerne qu'un point)* (opération, aide) ad hoc; **intervention ponctuelle du gouvernement** exceptional action by the government; **nous n'avons fait que des changements ponctuels** we have made only selective changes; **débrayage p.** one-off stoppage; **les terroristes ne se livraient qu'à des actions ponctuelles** the terrorists made only sporadic attacks

ponctuellement [pɔ̃ktɥɛlmɑ̃] ADV *(de façon limitée)* on an ad hoc basis

ponctuer [pɔ̃ktɥe] VT *(phrase)* to punctuate; **elle ponctua ses explications de silences** her explanation was punctuated with silences

pondaison [pɔ̃dɛzɔ̃] NF egg-laying time

pondérable [pɔ̃derabl] ADJ *Tech* weighable

pondéral, -ale, -aux, -ales [pɔ̃deral, -o] ADJ weight; **surcharge pondérale** excess weight

pondérateur, -trice [pɔ̃deratœr, -tris] ADJ stabilizing, balancing

pondération [pɔ̃derasjɔ̃] NF **1** *(d'une personne)* level-headedness; *(symétrie, équilibre)* balance; **parler/agir avec p.** to speak/act level-headedly **2** *Écon (d'un indice)* weighting; *Math* **coefficient de p.** weighting

pondéré [pɔ̃dere] ADJ **1** *(équilibré, calme)* (esprit) well-balanced; *(personne)* level-headed **2** *Écon* **indice p.** weighted index; **moyenne pondérée** weighted average

pondérer [pɔ̃dere] VT **(je pondère; je pondérerai) 1** *(équilibrer)* to balance **2** *Écon (indice, moyenne)* to weight

pondéreux, -euse [pɔ̃derø, -øz] *Tech* ADJ *(marchandises etc)* heavy
NMPL **les p.** heavy goods

pondeur, -euse [pɔ̃dœr, -øz] ADJ (egg-)laying; **poule pondeuse** laying hen
NF **pondeuse** *(poule)* (good) layer; *Fig Péj* **quelle pondeuse!** *(femme)* she's like a battery hen!
NM *Péj* **p. de prose** prolific scribbler; **p. de tableaux** prolific dauber; **c'est un p. d'articles/de romans** he just churns out articles/novels

pondoir [pɔ̃dwar] NM nest box

pondre [pɔ̃dr] VT **1** *(œuf)* to lay; **œuf frais pondu** new-laid *or* newly laid *or* freshly laid egg **2** *Fam (mettre au monde)* (enfant) to produce **3** *Fig Fam (texte, solution)* to come up with; *(articles, romans)* to churn out; **elle a pondu une de ces traductions!** she came up with a great translation!; **p. une lettre tous les jours** to churn out a letter every day

poney [pɔnɛ] NM pony

pongiste [pɔ̃ʒist] N *Sport* table tennis player

Pont (le) [lǝpɔ̃] NM *Antiq* **1** the (Kingdom of) Pontus **2** **le P.-Euxin** the Euxine Sea, the Black Sea

pont [pɔ̃] NM **1** *Constr* bridge; *Admin* **les Ponts et Chaussées** Department of Civil En-

gineering; **École des Ponts et Chaussées** = specialist institute of Civil Engineering; *Mil* **tête de p.** bridgehead; **vivre sous les ponts** to be a tramp; *Fig* **il est passé de l'eau sous les ponts** a lot of water has passed *or* flowed under the bridge; *Fig* **faire le p.** = to take the intervening day or days off; *Fig* **le p. de la Pentecôte** the (long) Whitsun Bank Holiday weekend
2 *Naut* deck; **faux p.** orlop deck; **navire à un p.** single-decker (ship), single-deck ship; **navire à deux/trois ponts** two-/three-decker; **homme** *ou* **matelot de p.** deck hand; *(dans la marine)* upper-deck rating; **sur le p.** on deck; **tout le monde sur le p.!** all hands on deck!; *(dans la marine)* clear lower deck!; *Com* **sur p.** free on board, fob
3 *Tech* live axle; *Aut* drive axle
4 *Fig* link; **assurer un p. entre Paris et la province** to provide a link between Paris and the provinces; **couper les ponts** to break off all relations *or* sever all links *or* sever all ties (**avec qn** with sb)
► ► **p. aérien** airlift; **p. aux ânes** *Géom* pons asinorum; *Fig* (piece of) common knowledge; **p. arrière** *Aut* rear *or* back axle; *Naut* afterdeck; **p. autoroutier** motorway bridge, overpass; **p. avant** foredeck; **p. basculant** *ou* **à bascule** drawbridge, bascule bridge; **p. de bateaux** floating *or* pontoon bridge; **p. cantilever** cantilever bridge; *Ind* **p. à chariot culbuteur** tipping stage; **p. à consoles** cantilever bridge; *Ind* **p. de décharge** tipping stage; **p. élévateur** *(dans un garage)* (repair) ramp; **p. des embarcations** boat deck; **p. des emménagements** saloon deck; **p. en encorbellement** cantilever bridge; **p. d'envol** *(d'un porte-avions)* flight deck; **p. des gaillards** upper deck; **p. de graissage** *(dans un garage)* ramp; **p. inférieur** lower deck; **p. de manœuvre** hurricane deck; **p. d'or** golden hello; **faire un p. d'or à qn** to offer a golden hello to sb; **p. pour piétons** footbridge; **p. pivotant** swing bridge; **p. des premières** saloon deck; **p. principal** main deck; **p. promenade** promenade deck; *(sur un paquebot)* sun deck, hurricane deck; *Ind* **p. roulant** travelling crane; *(support)* gantry; *Ordinat* **p. routeur** routing node; **p. supérieur** upper deck; **p. suspendu** suspension bridge; **p. tournant** swing bridge; **p. tubulaire** box (girder) bridge; **p. volant** flying bridge; *Élec* **p. de Wheatstone** Wheatstone bridge

pontage [pɔ̃taʒ] NM **1** *Constr* bridge building; *(travaux)* bridging **2** *Naut* decking **3** *Méd* bypass (operation); **p. coronarien** heart bypass (operation); **on lui a fait un p.** he's had a bypass, he's had bypass surgery

pont-bascule, *pl* **ponts-bascules** NM drawbridge, bascule bridge; *(pour peser les poids lourds)* weighbridge

ponte¹ [pɔ̃t] NF *(action)* (egg) laying; *(œufs)* eggs (laid); **p. ovulaire** ovulation

ponte² NM **1** *(aux jeux de hasard)* punter **2** *Fam (personnage important)* big shot; **un grand p. de la médecine** a big shot in medicine

ponté [pɔ̃te] ADJ decked; **non p.** open

pontée [pɔ̃te] NF *Naut* deck load, deck cargo

ponter¹ [pɔ̃te] VT *Naut (navire)* to lay the deck(s) of, to deck

ponter² VI *(aux jeux de hasard)* to punt

pontier [pɔ̃tje] NM *Tech* swing-bridge keeper

pontife [pɔ̃tif] NM *Rel* pontiff; *Fig Fam* big shot, bigwig; **le souverain p.** the Supreme Pontiff; *Fig Fam* **les pontifes de l'hôpital** the bigwigs *or* top brass at the hospital

pontifiant [pɔ̃tifjɑ̃] ADJ *Fam Péj* pontificating

pontifical, -ale, -aux, -ales [pɔ̃tifikal, -o]

ADJ pontifical, papal
NM pontifical

pontificat [pɔ̃tifika] NM pontificate; **sous le p. de Jean-Paul II** during the pontificate of John Paul II

pontifier [pɔ̃tifje] VI *(impf, pr sub n. pontifiions, v. pontifiiez)* to pontificate

pont-l'évêque [pɔ̃levɛk] NM INV Pont-l'Évêque (cheese)

pont-levis, *pl* **ponts-levis** [pɔ̃l(ǝ)vi] NM drawbridge; **p. à fléau** *ou* **à balancier** lever drawbridge

Pont-Neuf [pɔ̃nœf] NM *Fig* **être solide comme le P.** to have the constitution of an ox, to be as fit as a fiddle

ponton [pɔ̃tɔ̃] NM **1** *(construction flottante)* pontoon; **p. d'incendie** fire float; **p. d'atterrissage** (floating) landing stage **2** *Naut Vieilli (prison flottante)* hulk, prison ship

pontonnier [pɔ̃tɔnje] NM **1** *Mil* pontoneer, pontonier **2** *(gardien)* swing-bridge keeper

pool [pul] NM **1** *Écon* pool; **p. d'assurances** insurance pool; **p. bancaire** banking pool **2** *(équipe)* **p. de dactylos** typing pool; **p. de secrétaires** secretarial pool

pop [pɔp] ADJ INV, NF **(musique) p.** pop (music); **chanteur p.** pop singer

pop art [pɔpart] NM *Beaux-Arts* pop art

pop-corn [pɔpkɔrn] NM INV popcorn; **on a mangé du p./des p.** we ate (some) popcorn

pope [pɔp] NM *Rel* pope (of the Orthodox Church)

popeline [pɔplin] NF *Tex* poplin

popote [pɔpɔt] NF **1** *Fam (cuisine)* cooking; **faire la p.** to do the cooking **2** *Mil* canteen; *(mess)* officers' mess
ADJ INV *Fam souvent Péj (personne)* stay-at-home

popotin [pɔpɔtɛ̃] NM *Fam* bum, *Am* butt; **se manier le p.** to get a move on

populace [pɔpylas] NF *Péj* rabble, riff-raff, mob

populacier, -ière [pɔpylasje, -jɛr] ADJ *Péj* vulgar, common

populage [pɔpylaʒ] NM *Bot* marsh marigold

populaire [pɔpylɛr] ADJ **1** *(du peuple)* popular; **démocratie p.** popular *or* people's democracy; **manifestation p.** mass demonstration **2** *(pour le peuple)* **chanson p.** popular song; **expression p.** vernacular expression; **un roman p.** a low-brow novel; **bal p.** (local) dance *(open to the public)*; **la soupe p.** the soup kitchen **3** *(ouvrier)* working-class; **les classes populaires** the working classes; **quartier p.** working-class district **4** *(qui plaît)* popular; **se rendre p.** to make oneself popular

populairement [pɔpylɛrmɑ̃] ADV *(s'exprimer, parler)* in the vernacular

populariser [pɔpylarize] VT to popularize

popularité [pɔpylarite] NF popularity; **cote de p.** popularity rating

population [pɔpylasjɔ̃] NF population
► ► **p. active** working population, labour force; *Mktg* **p. cible** target population; **p. inactive** non-working population; **p.-mère** basic population; **p. prévue** projected population

populationnisme [pɔpylasjɔnism] NM policy of population growth

populationniste [pɔpylasjɔnist] ADJ **politique p.** policy of population growth; **gouvernement p.** government in favour of population growth

populeux, -euse [pɔpylø, -øz] ADJ populous, densely populated

populisme [pɔpylism] NM *Littér* populism

populiste [pɔpylist] ADJ, N *Littér* populist

populo [pɔpylo] NM *Fam* **1** le p. ordinary people, *Péj* the riffraff, the rabble **2** *(foule)* crowd (of people)

poquet [pɔkɛ] NM *Agr* seed hole

porc [pɔr] NM **1** *(animal)* pig, *Am* hog; *Fam (homme grossier)* pig, slob; **gardeur de porcs** pig keeper, pigman, *Arch* swineherd; **p. sauvage** wild boar; **(peau de) p.** pigskin; **sale comme un p.** filthy (dirty); **manger comme un p.** to eat like a pig **2** *Culin* pork; **côtelette de p.** pork chop

porcelaine [pɔrsəlɛn] NF **1** *Cér (matière)* porcelain, china; *(objet)* piece of porcelain *or* china; **p. de Chine** china; **p. de Saxe** Dresden china; **p. tendre (anglaise)** bone china **2** *(mollusque)* cowrie

porcelainier, -ière [pɔrsəlɛnje, -jɛr] ADJ **industrie porcelainière** porcelain *or* china industry
▪ N porcelain *or* china manufacturer

porcelet [pɔrsəlɛ] NM piglet, young pig

porc-épic [pɔrkepik], *pl* **porcs-épics** [pɔrkepik] NM porcupine; *Fam (personne)* prickly person; **c'est un vrai p.** *(il pique)* his face is all bristly

porche [pɔrʃ] NM porch

porcher, -ère [pɔrʃe, -ɛr] N pig keeper, *Arch* swineherd

porcherie [pɔrʃəri] NF piggery; *(enclos)* pigsty, *Am* pigpen; *Fig Péj* **quelle p.!** what a pigsty *or* pigpen!

porcin [pɔrsɛ̃] ADJ pig, *Fml* porcine; **élevage p.** pig breeding; **peste porcine** swine fever, *Am* hog cholera; *Fig Péj* **un visage p.** a piggy face; **yeux porcins** piggy eyes
▪ NMPL **porcins** pigs, swine, *Am* hogs

pore [pɔr] NM *(de peau, de plante, de pierre)* pore; **avoir les pores dilatés** to have open pores; *Fig* **il sue la couardise par tous les pores** he exudes cowardice from every pore

poreux, -euse [pɔrø, -øz] ADJ porous

porno [pɔrno] *Fam* ADJ *(abrév* **pornographique***) (film, magazine, scène)* porn, porno; **des photos pornos** dirty pictures
▪ NM *(abrév* **pornographie***)* **1** le p. *(genre)* porn; *(industrie)* the porn industry **2** *(film)* blue movie, *Br* porno film

pornographe [pɔrnɔgraf] N pornographer

pornographie [pɔrnɔgrafi] NF pornography

pornographique [pɔrnɔgrafik] ADJ pornographic

porosité [pɔrozite] NF porosity, porousness

porphyre [pɔrfir] NM *Minér* porphyry

porreau [pɔro] NM *Suisse (poireau)* leek

porridge [pɔridʒ] NM *Culin* porridge

port¹ [pɔr] NM **1** *(abri)* harbour, *Am* harbor; *(plus important)* port; **capitaine de p.** harbour master; **droits de p.** harbour dues, port charges; **entrer dans le p.** to enter harbour; **entrer au p.** to come into port; **quitter le p.** to leave port, to clear the harbour; *Fig* **arriver à bon p.** to arrive safe and sound; **Dunkerque est le premier p. de France** Dunkirk is the largest port in France; *Naut* **les ports de la métropole** the home ports **2** *Ordinat* port; *(pour Internet)* socket; **p. de communication** comms port, communications port; **p. d'entrée/sortie** input/output port; **p. d'E/S** I/O port; **p. d'extension** expansion port; **p. d'imprimante** printer port; **p. (de connexion pour) jeux** games port; **p. modem** modem port; **p. parallèle** parallel port; **p. SCSI** SCSI port; **p. série** serial port; **p. série universel** USB, universal serial bus; **p. souris** mouse port; **p. USB** USB port
▪▪ **p. d'armement** port of registry, *Am* port of documentation; **p. d'arrivée** port of arrival, port of entry; **p. artificiel** artificial port; **p. d'attache** home port, port of commission-ing; *Com* port of registry; *Fig* home base; **p. de commerce** commercial port; **p. pour conteneurs** container port; *Com* **p. de départ** port of departure; *Com* **p. d'embarquement** port of loading, port of embarkation; **p. d'entrée** port of entry; **p. d'escale** port of call; **p. pour ferry** ferry port; **p. fluvial** river port; **p. franc** free port; **p. de guerre** naval port, naval base; **p. lacustre** lakeside port; **p. maritime** *ou* **de mer** seaport; *Com* **p. militaire** naval port, naval base; **p. naturel** natural harbour; **p. de pêche** fishing port; **p. de plaisance** marina; **p. de transit** port of transit

port² NM **1** *(fait de porter)* carrying; **permis de p. d'armes** permit for carrying firearms; *Mil* **se mettre au p. d'armes** to shoulder arms **2** *(fait de revêtir) (de vêtement, lunettes, barbe)* wearing; **le p. du casque est obligatoire** *(sur panneau)* safety helmets must be worn; *(en moto)* crash helmets must be worn **3** *(transport payant) (de marchandises)* carriage; *(de paquet, de lettre, de télégramme)* delivery; **ports de lettres, frais de p.** postage, postal charges; **en p. dû** carriage forward, freight collect; **p. avancé** carriage forward, freight collect, freight forward; **p. compris** postage included; **p. débours** carriage forward paid against invoice; **p. en lourd** deadweight, dwt; **p. et emballage** postage and packing, p&p; **p. forfait** = carriage forward paid in a lump sum in advance; **p. franc, p. payé, franc(o) de p.** *(de revue, de journal)* postage paid; *(de marchandise)* carriage paid *or* free, freight collect; **p. payé, assurance comprise** carriage insurance paid **4** *(allure) (d'une personne)* bearing, carriage; **un p. de reine** a regal *or* queenly bearing; **un gracieux p. de tête** a graceful manner of holding one's head **5** *Bot (d'une plante)* habit **6** *Naut (d'un navire)* burden, tonnage

port³ NM *(dans les Pyrénées)* pass

portabilité [pɔrtabilite] NF *Ordinat* portability

portable [pɔrtabl] ADJ **1** *(facilement transportable) (machine à écrire, ordinateur etc)* portable; *(ordinateur)* laptop; *Ordinat (programme)* portable; **téléphone p.** mobile (phone), *Am* cellphone **2** *(mettable) (vêtement)* wearable, presentable **3** *Jur* payable at the address of the payee
▪ NM *Ordinat* laptop; *Tél* mobile (phone), *Am* cellphone

portage [pɔrtaʒ] NM **1** *(transport) (de marchandises)* porterage, conveyance, transport; *(de bateau)* portage; **frais de p.** porterage **2** *(partie d'un fleuve)* portage **3** *Banque* piggybacking

portager [pɔrtaʒe] VI *Can* to portage

portail [pɔrtaj] NM *aussi Ordinat* portal

portance [pɔrtɑ̃s] NF *Aviat* lift (per unit area)

portant [pɔrtɑ̃] ADJ **1** *(qui soutient)* **mur p.** load-bearing wall; **à bout p.** at point-blank range, point-blank; *Aviat* **surface portante** aerofoil, *Am* airfoil; *Naut* **vent p.** fair wind **2** **être bien p.** to be in good health, to be well; **être mal p.** to be in poor health, to be unwell; **enfants bien/mal portants** healthy/unhealthy children
▪ NM **1** *Tech* upright; *(support)* stay, strut **2** *Vieilli (anse)* handle **3** *(chenille) (d'une roue)* tread **4** *(présentoir) (dans un magasin de vêtements)* rack

portatif, -ive [pɔrtatif, -iv] ADJ *(machine à écrire, radio)* portable; *(ordinateur)* laptop; **armes portatives** small arms
▪ NM *Ordinat* laptop

Port-au-Prince [pɔropɛ̃s] N Port-au-Prince

porte [pɔrt] NF **1** *(de maison, de placard etc)* door; **à ma p.** on my doorstep; **aller ouvrir la p.** to answer the door; **le musée ouvrira ses portes (au public) en juin** the museum will open its doors to the public in June; **le théâtre fermera ses portes à la fin du mois** the theatre will close at the end of the month; *Fam* **ce n'est pas la p. à côté** it's hardly just around the corner; **il y a deux kilomètres/on met deux heures de p. à p.** it's two kilometres/it takes two hours door to door; *Fam* **je lui ai parlé entre deux portes** I spoke to him for a brief moment *or* briefly, I had a quick word with him; *Fam* **on s'est vus entre deux portes** we saw each other briefly; **trouver p. close** to find nobody in; **j'ai voulu aller au musée mais j'ai trouvé p. close** I wanted to go to the museum but it was closed; **être à la p.** to be locked out; **mettre qn à la p.** to throw *or* kick sb out; *(d'un emploi)* to fire *or Br* sack sb; *Fam* **tais-toi ou tu vas prendre la p.** be quiet or you're out; **qu'il prenne la p. s'il n'est pas content** let him leave *or* he doesn't have to stay if he's not happy; **elle m'a fermé/claqué la p. au nez** she closed/slammed the door in my face; **refuser *ou* fermer *ou* défendre sa p. à qn** not to allow sb in, to refuse sb admission; *Fig* **vous avez frappé *ou* sonné à la bonne/mauvaise p.** you've come to the right/wrong person; *Fam* **entrer dans une profession par la petite p.** to start at the bottom; *Fig* **c'est la p. ouverte à toutes les atrocités** it leaves the door wide open to all sorts of atrocities; *Fig* **journée portes ouvertes** open day *or Am* house; *Prov* **il faut qu'une p. soit ouverte ou fermée** it has to be either one way or the other; **chassez-le par la p., il reviendra par la fenêtre** get rid of him one way and he'll come back another **2** *(voie d'entrée) (d'un parc)* gate(way); *(d'un immeuble)* doorway, entrance; *(dans un aéroport)* gate; **portes d'une ville** gates of a town; **l'entreprise est installée aux portes de Paris** the company is situated on the outskirts of Paris; **l'ennemi est à nos portes** the enemy is at our gates; **la guerre est à nos portes** the war is on our doorstep; *(temporel)* war is around the corner; **la campagne est à vos portes** the countryside is on your doorstep; **aux portes du désert** at the gateway to the desert; **être aux portes de la mort** to be at death's door; **les portes de l'enfer** the gates of hell; *Hist* **la (Sublime-)P., la P. ottomane** the (Sublime) Porte **3** *(portière) (de voiture, de train)* door; **attendre l'ouverture complète des portes** wait until the doors are fully open; **(voiture) deux/quatre/cinq portes** two-/four-/five-door car **4** *Ski* gate **5** *(fente) (d'une agrafe)* eye **6** *(usu pl)* **portes** *(dans la roche)* gorge; *(passage étroit)* defile, pass **7** *Ordinat* gate; **p. logique** logic gate
▪▪ **p. d'aérage** air gate, trap door; **p. battante** swing door; **p. cochère** carriage entrance; **portes communicantes** inter-connecting doors; **p. coulissante** sliding door; **p. de débarquement** (disembarkation) gate; **p. de derrière** back door; **p. à deux battants** double door; *Tech* **p. d'écluse** (lock) gate; **p. d'embarquement** (boarding) gate; **p. d'entrée**, *Belg* **p. de rue** front door; **p. roulante** sliding door; **p. de secours** emergency exit; **p. de service** *(de maison, d'appartement) (de derrière)* back door; *(sur le côté)* side door; *Vieilli* tradesman's entrance; **p. de sortie** way out, exit; *Fig* way out, means of escape; **p. tournante, p. à tambour** revolving door; *Tech* **p. de visite** inspection door; *(d'égout)* manhole cover; **p. vitrée** glass door

porté [pɔrte] ADJ **être p. à l'indulgence/la compréhension** to be inclined to be indulgent/understanding; **être p. à la discussion** to be inclined or prone to argue; **être p. à la colère** to be quick-tempered; **p. à faire qch** inclined to do sth, given to doing sth; **être p. à oublier** to be apt or inclined to forget; **p. sur qch** fond of sth; Fam **être p. sur la chose** to be sex-mad, to have a one-track mind

porte(-)à(-)faux [pɔrtafo] NM INV overhang; Constr cantilever; **en p.** overhanging; Fig **être en p.** to be awkwardly placed; **il est en p. avec la ligne officielle du parti** he's at odds with or out of step with the official party line

porte-affiche(s), pl **porte-affiches** NM notice or Am bulletin board

porte-aiguille, pl **porte-aiguille(s)** NM Chir needle holder

porte-aiguilles NM INV Couture needle case

porte-amarre, pl **porte-amarre(s)** NM Naut line-throwing apparatus; **flèche p.** line-throwing rocket

porte-à-porte NM INV door-to-door selling; **faire du p.** (pour vendre) to sell from door to door, to do door-to-door selling; (faire des enquêtes etc) to go from door to door

porte-avions NM INV Naut aircraft carrier

porte-bagages NM INV luggage rack; (de bicyclette) carrier; (de voiture) roof rack

porte-baïonnette, pl **porte-baïonnette(s)** NM bayonet frog

porte-balai, pl **porte-balai(s)** NM Élec brush holder

porte-bébé, pl **porte-bébés** NM baby carrier

porte-billets NM INV notecase, Am billfold

porte-bombes NM INV Mil, Aviat bomb rack

porte-bonheur NM INV (lucky) charm; (animal, enfant) mascot; **couleur/petit cochon p.** lucky colour/pig

porte-bouteilles NM INV (pour stocker le vin) wine rack, bottle rack; (pour porter) bottle carrier

porte-brosses [pɔrt(ə)brɔs] NM INV **p. (à dents)** toothbrush holder

porte-cartes [pɔrtəkart] NM INV **1** (pour cartes de crédit, de visite) card holder or wallet **2** (pour cartes géographiques) map case or holder

porte-chapeaux NM INV hat stand

porte-chars [pɔrtəʃar] NM INV Mil tank transporter

porte-chéquier, pl **porte-chéquiers** NM cheque or Am check book holder

porte-cigares NM INV cigar case

porte-cigarettes NM INV cigarette case

porte-clefs, porte-clés [pɔrtəkle] NM INV key ring

porte-conteneurs NM INV Tech container ship

porte-copie, pl **porte-copie(s)** NM Typ copy holder

porte-couteau, pl **porte-couteau(x)** NM knife rest

porte-croix [pɔrtəkrwa] NM INV Rel cross bearer

porte-documents NM INV briefcase

porte-drapeau, pl **porte-drapeau(x)** NM Mil, Fig standard bearer

portée [pɔrte] NF **1** (petits) litter, brood; (d'une truie) farrow

2 (amplitude) (des bras) reach; (de la flèche d'une grue) radius; (d'un fusil, d'un émetteur) range; (d'un traité) scope; (de voix) range, compass; **(à) courte p., (à) petite p.** (at) short range; **(à) grande p., (à) longue p.** (at)

long range; **canon à longue p.** long-range gun; **à p. (de tir)** within range; **à p. de fusil** within rifle range, within gunshot; **à p. de canon** within gun range; **à p. de (la) voix** within earshot; **à p. de (la) vue** (with)in sight; **des chaussures à la p. de toutes les bourses** shoes to suit every pocket or budget; **ce sport est maintenant à la p. de toutes les bourses** this sport is now within everyone's means, everyone can now afford this sport; **des chaussures à ce prix ne sont pas à la p. de tout le monde** not everyone can afford shoes at that price; **c'est à ma p.** (cet objet) it's within my reach; (ce livre) I can understand it; (ce travail) I can do it; **hors de ma p.** (dans l'espace) beyond my reach; Fig (de compréhension) beyond my understanding, Fam beyond me; **hors de p.** out of reach, beyond reach; **à mettre hors de (la) p. des enfants** keep out of the reach of children; **à p. de (la) main** within reach, to hand; **j'ai toujours un tube d'aspirine à p. de la main** I always have some aspirin handy; **livre à la p. de tout le monde** (facile à lire) book that anyone can understand; **cette musique/ce roman n'est pas à la p. de tout le monde** this music/novel is not accessible to everyone

  3 Mus stave, staff

  4 Radio, TV reach

  5 Fig (force) (d'une déclaration, des mots) (full) significance or Fml import; **conséquences d'une p. incalculable** far-reaching consequences; **un changement/une décision d'une très grande p.** a very significant or a far-reaching change/decision

  6 Constr (charge) bearing; (distance) span; Naut **p. en lourd** ou **en poids** deadweight (capacity)

  7 Tech bearing surface; (point d'appui) (d'un arbre) boss; **portées** (d'un arbre) (main) journals

porte-étendard NM INV Hist (dans la cavalerie) standard bearer

portefaix [pɔrtəfɛ] NM Hist (street) porter

porte-fenêtre, pl **portes-fenêtres** NF French window or Am door

portefeuille [pɔrtəfœj] NM **1** (pour l'argent) wallet, Am billfold; Fig **avoir un p. bien garni** to be well off, to be rich; **lit en p.** apple-pie bed; **jupe p.** wrapover or wraparound skirt **2** (cartable) portfolio; Com **p. d'assurances** (d'un assureur) portfolio; **p. d'actions** share portfolio; Fin **effets en p.** bills in hand, holdings; **p. (titres)** investments, securities; **p. de titres** securities portfolio; Mktg **p. d'activité** business portfolio, portfolio mix; **p. d'investissements** investment portfolio **3** Pol (fonction de ministre) portfolio; **ministre sans p.** minister without portfolio **4** Aut (de semi-remorque) jackknifing

porte-greffe(s) [pɔrtəgrɛf] NM INV Bot stock

porte-hélicoptères [pɔrtelikɔptɛr] NM INV Naut helicopter carrier

porte-jarretelles NM INV suspender or Am garter belt

porte-journaux NM INV newspaper rack

porte-jupe, pl **porte-jupe(s)** [pɔrtəʒyp] NM skirt hanger

porte-malheur NM INV bringer of bad luck, jinx; **les plumes de paon sont considérées comme un p.** peacock feathers are thought to bring bad luck

portemanteau, -eaux [pɔrtmãto] NM **1** (accroché au mur) coat rack; (sur pied) coat stand **2** Arch (malle) portmanteau

portement [pɔrtəmã] NM **p. de croix** (Christ's) bearing of the Cross

porte-menu NM INV menu holder

portemine [pɔrt(ə)min] NM propelling pencil

porte-monnaie NM INV purse; **p. électronique** electronic purse or wallet

porte-musique NM INV music case

porte-objet, pl **porte-objet(s)** NM (de microscope) (object) slide; (platine) stage

porte-outil, pl **porte-outil(s)** NM (d'un machine-outil) tool holder; (d'une perceuse) chuck; (d'un tour) slide rest

porte-papier NM INV **p. (hygiénique)** toilet paper holder; (pour rouleau) toilet roll holder

porte-parapluies NM INV umbrella stand

porte-parole NM INV spokesperson, spokesman, f spokeswoman; (organe d'un parti politique) organ; **se faire le p. de qn** to speak on sb's behalf

porte-pipes [pɔrtəpip] NM INV pipe rack

porte-plat, pl **porte-plat(s)** [pɔrtəpla] NM (dish) stand

porte-plume [pɔrtəplym] NM INV penholder

PORTER [pɔrte]

VT to carry **1** ▪ to produce **2** ▪ to wear **3** ▪ to take **4** ▪ to bring **4, 9** ▪ to direct **5** ▪ to enter **6** ▪ to bear **7** ▪ to incite **8** ▪ to have **10**	
VI to rest **1** ▪ to hit **2** ▪ to have effect **2**	
VPR to go **1** ▪ to turn to **3** ▪ to be well (bien se porter) **4** ▪ to be worn **6**	

VT 1 (soutenir) (valise, enfant etc) to carry; (poids, charge) to bear, to carry; **p. qn en triomphe** to carry sb in triumph or shoulder high (in triumph); **p. la tête haute** to hold or carry one's head high; **ces abus portent en eux leur propre châtiment** these abuses carry their own punishment; **une réforme qui porte en elle tous les abus** a reform that carries or has within it the seed of all sorts of abuse; **elle porte bien son âge** she's wearing well; **elle porte/ne porte pas son âge** she looks/doesn't look her age; **elle a 30 ans? elle ne les porte pas du tout** she's 30? she doesn't look it at all; **mes jambes ne me portent plus** my legs won't carry me any further; **je ne le porte pas dans mon cœur** he's not exactly my favourite or Am favorite person; Mil **portez armes!** shoulder arms!; Naut **p. tout dessus** (d'un voilier) to have all sails set

  2 (produire) to produce; **p. des fruits** to bear fruit; **terres qui portent du blé** wheat-producing land; **p. intérêt** to yield interest; **argent qui porte intérêt** money that brings in or bears interest; **cela vous portera bonheur/malheur** that will bring you luck/bad luck; Prov **la nuit porte conseil** sleep on it

  3 (avoir avec ou sur soi) (vêtement, chapeau) to wear; **p. des lunettes/une bague/du noir** to wear glasses/a ring/black; **p. une moustache/la barbe** to have or wear a moustache/a beard; **p. les cheveux courts/longs** to wear one's hair short/long, to have short/long hair; **il portait une cicatrice à la joue droite** he had a scar on his right cheek; Fig **p. la soutane** to be a priest; Fig Fam **faire p. le chapeau à qn** to make sb take the rap or Br carry the can, Am to leave sb holding the bag; Fig Fam **c'est elle qui porte la culotte** she wears the trousers in their house; **il porte le nom de son oncle** he's called after his uncle; **ce produit porte le nom de son inventeur** this product is named after its inventor, this product bears the name of its inventor; **p. le même prénom que qn** to have the same name as sb; **qu'est-ce qu'elle porte comme prénom?** what's her first name?; **elle porte bien/mal son nom/prénom** her name suits/doesn't suit her; **le chameau porte deux bosses** the camel has two humps

4 *(transporter)* *(là-bas)* to take; *(ici)* to bring; **p. qch dans la maison/dehors** to take/bring sth into the house/outside; **p. une chaise d'une pièce à une autre** to take *or* carry a chair from one room to another; **p. une lettre à la poste** *ou Fam* **boîte** to post *or Am* mail a letter; **je suis allée lui p. un message** I took him a message; **je suis allé lui p. la nouvelle** I went to give *or* to tell him the news; **p. à domicile** to deliver to domicile; **p. le lait à domicile** to deliver milk to the door; **il porta le verre à ses lèvres** he raised *or* lifted the glass to his lips; **p. qn en terre** to carry sb to his/her grave
5 *(diriger)* **p. un coup à qn, p. la main sur qn** to strike *or* hit sb; **s'il porte la main une seule fois sur toi, dis-le-moi** if he ever lays a hand on you *or* strikes you, tell me; **p. la main à sa nuque** to touch the back of one's neck; **il porta la main à sa casquette** he touched his cap; **p. la main à son front** to hold one's hand to one's forehead; **p. ses regards sur qn** to direct one's gaze towards sb, to look at sb; **p. son attention sur qch** to turn one's attention to sth, to give sth one's attention; *Fig* **p. qch devant un tribunal/les tribunaux** to take sth to court; **p. plainte** to make a complaint; *Fig* **p. un toast à qn** to drink *or* offer a toast to sb, to toast sb; **p. témoignage** to testify, to give evidence, to bear witness; **p. qch à la connaissance de qn** to bring sth to sb's attention, to make sth known to sb, to let sb know about sth
6 *(inscrire)* *(noms, chiffres)* to enter, to write; **p. une position sur une carte** to mark a position on a map; **p. une somme au crédit/au débit de qn** to credit/debit sb with a sum; **p. une somme au crédit/débit d'un compte** to credit/debit a sum to an account; **se faire p. malade** *ou Fam* **pâle** to report sick; *Mil etc* **p. qn manquant à l'appel** to report sb absent from roll call; **p. qn absent** to report sb absent; **p. qn déserteur** to declare sb a deserter; **être porté disparu** to be reported missing; *Naut* **p. un homme au rôle de l'équipage** to enter a seaman on the ship's books
7 *(être revêtu ou marqué de)* to bear; **la lettre porte la date du 2 juin** the letter is dated 2 June; **p. une signature** to bear a signature; **p. le titre de ...** *(d'un livre)* to be entitled *or* called ...
8 *(inciter à)* **p. qn à qch** to incite sb to sth; **p. qn à faire qch** to induce *or* prompt sb to do sth; **tout me porte à croire que ...** everything leads *or* inclines me to believe that ...
9 *(monter, transformer)* to bring; **p. la température à 100°** to raise the temperature to 100°; **p. qn au pouvoir** to bring sb to power; **p. une pièce classique à l'écran** to bring *or* transfer a classical drama to the screen; **p. la production au maximum** to raise *or* increase production to a maximum; **portez le liquide à ébullition** bring the liquid to the boil; **ça porte à dix le nombre des victimes** that brings the number of victims to ten; **cela portera à cent euros le prix du billet** that will bring the price of the ticket up to a hundred euros
10 *(avoir)* *(intérêt)* to have (**à** in); *(affection, amour)* to have, to feel (**à** for, towards)
11 *(donner)* **p. secours à un bateau en détresse/à qn** to come to the aid of a boat in distress/of sb; **p. assistance à qn** to come to sb's assistance, to offer assistance to sb
12 *(mentionner)* **le rapport ne porte aucune mention de tout cela** the report makes no mention of any of that; **la loi porte que cet usage est interdit** this practice is expressly forbidden by law; *Mil etc* **la décision porte que ...** it is stated in orders that ...

vi 1 *(appuyer)* to rest, to bear; **tout le poids porte sur cette poutre** all the weight rests *or* bears on this beam; **croyez-vous que la glace porte?** do you think the ice will hold?;

la discussion porte toujours sur le même sujet the discussion always deals with *or* turns on the same subject; **les questions ont porté sur un chapitre que je n'avais pas revu** the questions dealt with *or* were about a chapter that I hadn't revised; **faire p. son attention sur qch** to turn one's attention to sth, to focus one's attention on sth; **faire p. sa thèse sur qch** to choose sth as the subject for one's thesis
2 *(atteindre)* **sa tête a porté sur le rebord du trottoir/contre le volant** his/her head hit *or* struck the kerb/the wheel; **aucun des coups n'a porté** none of the blows struck home *or* hit their target; **ses attaques/critiques n'ont pas porté** his attacks/criticisms had no effect; **chaque mot a porté** every word hit home; **coup qui porte/qui a porté** telling blow; **sa voix porte bien** his voice carries well; **courant qui porte au sud** current that sets to the south; *Fam* **ce bruit me porte sur les nerfs** that noise gets on my nerves
3 *Naut (d'une voile)* to fill, to draw
4 *Naut* **laisser p.** to bear away; **laisser p. sur un navire** to bear down upon *or* run down a ship
5 *(être en gestation)* **les juments portent onze mois** the gestation period of a mare is eleven months
VPR se porter 1 *(aller)* to go, *Fml* to proceed; **se p. au secours de qn** to go to sb's assistance; **se p. au-devant de tout besoin** to anticipate every need; **la foule s'est portée vers la gare** the crowd made for *or* went towards the station
2 *(se livrer à)* **se p. à des voies de fait/à des extrémités** to commit assault/to go to extremes
3 *(se diriger)* **son regard se portait vers son frère** his gaze fell on his brother; *Mil* **se p. en avant** to advance; **la conversation s'est portée sur l'Extrême-Orient** the conversation turned to the Far East; **la conversation se porte toujours sur les mêmes sujets** the conversation always turns on *or* revolves around *or* is always about the same subjects
4 **se p. bien** to be well, to be in good health; **se p. à merveille** to be in the best of health; **comment vous portez-vous?** how are you?; **je ne m'en porte pas plus mal** I'm none the worse for it; **moins je le vois, mieux je me porte** the less I see him, the better I feel
5 *(se présenter comme)* **se p. acquéreur de qch** to offer to buy sth; **se p. candidat** to put oneself forward *or* up as a candidate, *Br* to stand as a candidate; **se p. caution** to stand surety; **se p. garant envers** to stand guarantor for, to stand surety for
6 *(devoir être porté)* to be worn; *(être à la mode)* to be fashionable; **le nœud papillon se porte de plus en plus** more and more people are wearing bow ties, bow ties are becoming more and more fashionable; **le bleu se porte beaucoup cette année** blue is being worn a lot *or* is very fashionable this year

porte-raclette, *pl* **porte-raclettes NM** *Aut* wiper arm
porte-revues NM INV magazine rack
porterie [pɔrtəri] **NF** *(d'un couvent etc)* gatehouse
porte-satellites NM INV *Aut* planet carrier
porte-savon, *pl* **porte-savon(s) NM** soapdish
porte-serviettes NM INV towel rail
porte-skis [pɔrt(ə)ski] **NM INV** *Aut* ski carrier, ski rack
porte-toasts [pɔrtətost] **NM INV** toast rack
porteur, -euse [pɔrtœr, -øz] **N 1** *(d'un message)* bearer; **p. de nouvelles** bearer *or* bringer of news; **j'arrivais p. d'heureuses nouvelles** I arrived bringing *or* bearing good

news; **par p.** by messenger **2** *(de gare, d'aéroport etc)* porter; **p. d'eau** water carrier; **chaise à porteurs** sedan chair **3** *Méd* carrier; **p. de germes** (germ) carrier; **p. sain** unaffected carrier **4** *(détenteur)* holder; *Fin (d'un chèque)* bearer, payee, endorsee; **p. d'actions** shareholder; **les petits/gros porteurs** small/big shareholders; **p. de papiers volés/de faux papiers** person carrying stolen/false identity papers; **il était p. de faux papiers** he was carrying false papers; **p. d'une procuration** holder of a power of attorney, holder of a proxy; **p. de titres** holder of stock, stockholder; **p. d'une traite** bearer of a bill, holder of a bill; **payable au p.** payable to bearer; **effets au p.** bearer stock(s)
ADJ 1 *Tech* **essieu p.** bearing axle, carrying axle; **câble p.** suspension cable; *Élec* **fréquence porteuse** carrier frequency; **onde porteuse** carrier wave **2** *Méd* **les individus porteurs du virus** individuals who carry the virus, (individuals who are) carriers of the virus **3** *Fig (industrie, marché, créneau)* buoyant, flourishing
NF porteuse 1 *Tél* carrier **2** *Can (marraine)* godmother

> Do not confuse with **portier**, which means **doorman**.

porte-vélo, *pl* **porte-vélos NM** *Aut* bike carrier
porte-vent [pɔrtəvã] **NM INV** *Tech* air duct
porte-voix [pɔrtəvwa] **NM INV** megaphone; *(électrique)* loudhailer, *Am* bullhorn; **mettre ses mains en p.** to cup one's hands round one's mouth
portfolio [pɔrtfoljo] **NM** portfolio
portier, -ière [pɔrtje, -jɛr] **NM 1** *(gardien)* porter, doorman, doorkeeper; *(dans un hôtel)* commissionaire; **p. de nuit** night porter **2** *Litt (d'un domaine, monastère etc)* gatekeeper
N Rel (frère) p. porter; **(sœur) portière** portress

> Do not confuse with **porteur**.

portière [pɔrtjɛr] **NF 1** *(d'une voiture, d'un wagon)* door **2** *(rideau)* door curtain, portière
portillon [pɔrtijɔ̃] **NM** wicket (gate); *Rail (dans un passage à niveau)* side gate; *(dans une gare)* gate, barrier; *Fam* **cela se bouscule au p.** *(il y a foule)* people are turning up in droves; *(il s'exprime difficilement)* he can't get his words out; *Fam* **ça ne se bouscule pas au p.** people are staying away in droves
portion [pɔrsjɔ̃] **NF** *(d'argent)* portion, share; *(de gâteau, fromage etc)* portion; *(de viande)* portion, helping; *(d'un groupe, d'une population etc)* portion, section; *(d'un livre)* section, part
portique [pɔrtik] **NM 1** *Archit* portico **2** *Gym (pour accrocher des agrès)* (cross)beam **3** *Rail* **p. à signaux** signal gantry **4** *Tech* **grue à p.** travelling gantry crane
portland [pɔrtlãd] **NM** *Tech* Portland cement
Porto [pɔrto] **N** *Géog* Oporto
porto [pɔrto] **NM** *(vin)* port
portoricain, -aine [pɔrtɔrikɛ̃, -ɛn] **ADJ** Puerto Rican
N P. Puerto Rican
Porto Rico [pɔrtoriko] **NM** *Géog* Puerto Rico
portos [pɔrtos] **N INV** *Fam Péj* Dago *(from Portugal)*
portrait [pɔrtrɛ] **NM 1** *(représentation)* portrait; *(photo)* portrait(-sized photo); **p. en pied/buste** full-/half-length portrait; **faire le p. de qn** to do *or* paint a portrait of sb; *(au crayon)* to do *or* draw a portrait of sb;

Fig **c'est le p. vivant de son père, c'est tout le p. de son père** he's the spitting image of his father; *Fam* **se faire tirer le p.** to have one's photo taken; **p. littéraire** character sketch **2** *(description)* description, portrayal; **faire le p. de qn/qch** to paint a picture of sb/sth, to describe *or* portray sb/sth; **il nous a fait un p. flatteur de la situation/de sa future femme** he painted a flattering picture of the situation/his future wife **3** *Fam (visage)* face, mug; **il s'est fait abîmer** *ou* **arranger le p.** someone's made a real mess of *or Fam* someone's rearranged his face **4** *Beaux-Arts* **le p.** *(genre)* portrait painting, portraiture; *Ordinat* **mode p.** portrait mode; **imprimer qch en p.** to print sth in portrait

portraitiste [pɔrtretist] **N** portrait painter, portraitist

portrait-robot, *pl* **portraits-robots** **NM** Photofit® (picture), Identikit® picture; *Fig* **faire le p. du candidat idéal** to draw up a profile of the ideal candidate

portraiturer [pɔrtretyre] **VT** *Rare* to portray

portuaire [pɔrtɥer] **ADJ** port, harbour, *Am* harbor; **installations portuaires** port facilities *or* installations

portugais, -aise [pɔrtygɛ, -ɛz] **ADJ** Portuguese
▪ **NM** *Ling* Portuguese
▪ **P.** Portuguese
▪ **NF portugaise 1** *(huître)* Portuguese oyster **2** *Fam (oreille)* ear; **tu as les portugaises ensablées ou quoi?** are you deaf or what?

Portugal [pɔrtygal] **NM** *Géog* Portugal

pose [poz] **NF 1** *(de rideaux)* putting up, hanging; *(d'un tableau)* hanging; *(de briques, de moquette etc)* laying; *(de pierres précieuses)* setting; *(de bombe)* planting; *(de verre de montre etc)* fitting; *(d'appareils)* installation; **p. de câbles** cable laying; *Typ* **p. de marges** margin setting; **p. de tabulations** tabbing, setting of tabs **2** *(attitude)* pose, posture; *Beaux-Arts, Phot etc* pose; **garder la p.** to hold the pose; **prendre une p.** to assume *or* strike a pose **3** *Péj (airs)* posing, posturing, affectation; **sans p.** *(adverbe)* unaffectedly; *(adjectif)* unaffected **4** *Golf (d'une balle)* lie **5** *Phot (cliché, durée)* exposure; **temps de p.** exposure time; **p. instantanée** instantaneous exposure; **pellicule de 24 poses** 24-exposure film

posé [poze] **ADJ 1** *(réfléchi, calme)* self-possessed, composed, calm; *Mus* **voix bien posée** even *or* steady voice **2** *(en train de couver) (oiseau)* sitting

posément [pozemã] **ADV** calmly, with composure; *(avancer, bouger)* steadily, deliberately

posemètre [pozmɛtr] **NM** *Phot* light meter

POSER [poze]

VI to rest **1** ▪ to lie **1** ▪ to pose **2, 3** ▪ to show off **3**	
VT to put **1** ▪ to place **1** ▪ to put down **1** ▪ to ask **2** ▪ to lay down **2, 6** ▪ to write down **3** ▪ to lay **4** ▪ to put up **4** ▪ to put forward **6**	
VPR to land **1** ▪ to arise **2** ▪ to claim to be *(se poser en)* **3**	

VI 1 *(d'une poutre)* to rest, to lie (**sur** on) **2** *(comme modèle)* to pose; *(pour qu'on fasse son portrait)* to sit, to pose; **p. pour la postérité** to have one's portrait painted for posterity; **p. nu** to pose (in the) nude **3** *Péj (prendre des airs)* to show off, to pose; **p. pour la galerie** to play to the gallery; *Fam* **je ne pose pas à l'ange** I don't pretend to be an angel; **il pose au grand connaisseur** he plays *or* acts the great connoisseur
▪ **VT 1** *(mettre)* to put, to place; **pose-le sur la table** put it (down) on the table; **p. les armes** to lay down one's arms; **p. un avion** to land an aircraft; **p. sa candidature** *(aux élections)* to put oneself forward (as a candidate), *Br* to stand (as a candidate); *(à un poste)* to apply; **à peine avais-je posé la tête sur l'oreiller que …** no sooner had my head hit *or* touched the pillow than …; **l'examen est terminé, posez les stylos** the exam is over, put your pens down
2 *(formuler)* **p. une question** to ask a question; **p. une question à qn** to ask sb a question, to put a question to sb; *Pol* **p. la question de confiance** to table a motion of confidence; **p. un problème** to pose a problem (**à qn** for sb); **bien/mal p. le problème** *(dans une dissertation)* to identify the problem well/poorly; **p. une règle de conduite** to lay down a rule of conduct
3 *Math (écrire) (opération, équation)* to write down; **p. un chiffre** to put down *or* set down a number; **je pose deux et je retiens un** put down two (and) carry one
4 *(rideau, papier peint)* to put up, to hang; *(tableau)* to hang; *(briques, moquette, pierre de fondation, rails etc)* to lay; *(pierres précieuses, rivets)* to set; *(bombe)* to plant; *(chaudière)* to install; *(verre de montre etc)* to fit; **p. une vitre** to put in a pane of glass; **faire p. le téléphone** to have a telephone put in *or* installed; *Typ* **p. des tabulations dans** to tab; *Fig* **p. les jalons** to prepare the ground (**de** for); **p. la première pierre de qch** to lay the foundation stone for sth; *Fig* **to lay the foundation(s) for sth**
5 **p. qn** to establish sb's reputation; **une telle expérience, ça vous pose un homme** an experience like that sets you up for life
6 *(supposer, établir) (hypothèse)* to put forward; **p. des principes** to lay down principles; **posons le cas que cela soit** supposing *or* assuming *or* let's suppose *or* let's assume that that is the case; **cela posé** assuming this to be true
7 *Mus* **bien p. la voix** to pitch (one's voice) correctly
8 **p. son regard sur qn/qch** to look at sb/sth; **il posa sur elle son regard de myope** he peered at her shortsightedly
9 *Can (photographier)* to photograph, to take a photograph *or* picture of; **il s'est fait p. avec sa copine** he had his picture taken with his girlfriend
▪ **VPR se poser 1** *(d'un oiseau)* to land, to settle, to alight (**sur** on); *(d'un avion)* to land
2 *(apparaître) (d'une question, d'un problème)* to arise, to come up, to crop up; **un nouveau problème se pose** we are faced with a new problem, a new problem has arisen; **la question se posera toujours** it's a perennial question; **la question qui se pose est la suivante** the question we are faced with is the following
3 *(se prétendre)* **se p. en réformateur/redresseur de torts** to set oneself up as *or* to claim to be a reformer/a righter of wrongs
4 *(devoir être posé)* **cette potiche se pose par terre/dans un coin** this vase should be (placed) *or* this vase goes on the ground/in a corner; **ça se pose comme du papier peint** you put it up *or* it goes on like wallpaper
5 **se p. des questions** to ask oneself questions; **je finis par me p. des questions** I'm beginning to have my doubts; **il se pose la question de savoir si …** he is wondering whether …
6 *Fam* **il se pose un peu là, comme bricoleur/cuisinier!** some handyman/cook(, I don't think)!; **comme enquiquineur, il se pose là!** he's a real pain in the neck!

poseur, -euse [pozœr, -øz] **N 1** *Tech (de câble etc)* layer; **p. d'affiches** billsticker, billposter; *Rail* **p. de rails** platelayer, *Am* tracklayer; *Naut* **p. de mines** minelayer; **p.**

de bombes bomb planter; **la police recherche activement les poseurs de bombes** the police have launched a manhunt for the people who planted the bombs **2** *Péj (pédant)* show-off, poser, poseur; **il est p.** he's always putting on airs, he's affected

posidonie [pozidɔni] **NF** posidonia

positif, -ive [pozitif, -iv] **ADJ 1** *(sûr, certain)* *(résultat, fait)* positive, actual, real; *Méd (réaction, test)* positive **2** *Math, Élec etc (nombre, pôle etc)* positive; *Phot* **épreuve positive** positive **3** *(pratique) (personne, esprit)* practical, pragmatic **4** *(enthousiaste) (remarque, attitude, personne)* positive **5** *Jur* **droit p.** statute law
▪ **NM** *Phot* positive; **p. (en) couleur** colour positive; **p. transparent** transparency

POSITION [pozisjɔ̃] **NF 1** *(emplacement) (de navire, d'avion etc)* position; *Golf (de la balle)* lie; **le coureur français est en première/deuxième p.** the French runner is in the lead *or* in first place *or* position/in second place *or* position; **prendre la première p.** to take the lead, to go into first place *or* position; **il est arrivé en troisième p.** he came third; *Aut* **feux de p.** sidelights; **p. d'atterrissage** *(d'un avion)* landing attitude; *Aut* **p. nuit anti-éblouissement** *(de rétro intérieur)* anti-glare position; **p. clé** key position; **p. défensive** *ou* **de défense** defensive position; *Mil, Fig* **p. de repli** fall-back position
2 *(attitude corporelle)* position, posture, attitude; *(debout)* stance; *(des pieds)* position; **s'endormir dans une mauvaise p.** to fall asleep in an uncomfortable *or* awkward position; **être/se mettre en p.** to be in/get into position; **la p. du missionnaire** the missionary position; **première/troisième p.** *(en danse)* first/third position; **en p. debout/assise** in a standing/sitting position; **trois cents passagers en p. debout** three hundred standing passengers
3 *(opinion, avis)* position; **quelle est votre p. sur la guerre?** what is your position on the war?, what position do you take on the war?; **expliquer sa p.** to explain one's position; **elle est restée sur ses positions** she refused to back down, she stood her ground, she stood firm; **prendre p.** to take a stand; **prise de p.** stand; **la prise de p. de notre pays** our country's stand, the stand taken by our country; **une prise de p. devient nécessaire** it's becoming necessary to take a stand; **p. politique** political stance; **p. sociale** *(d'un journal)* social stance
4 *(dans la société)* position; **p. sociale** social standing *or* position *or* status
5 *(situation)* position, situation; **voici ma p.** this is how things stand with me, this is my position *or* situation; **être en p. de faire qch** to be in a position to do sth; *Fam* **être dans une p. intéressante** to be pregnant, *Vieilli* to be in an interesting situation; **p. gênante** embarrassing position *or* situation; **p. concurrentielle** competitive position; **p. sur le marché** market position
6 *Fin* balance; **demander sa p.** to ask for one's balance; **p. d'un compte** balance of an account; *Fin* **p. de compte** balance; **p. créditrice** credit balance; **p. débitrice** debit balance; **p. financière** financial position
7 *Bourse* **p. acheteur** long position; **p. (courte) couverte** covered (short) position; **p. élémentaire** simple position; **p. longue** long position; **p. non couverte** uncovered position; **p. vendeur** short position

positionnement [pozisjɔnmã] **NM 1** *Tech* positioning **2** *Fin (d'un compte)* calculation of the balance **3** *Com* positioning; *Mktg* **p. concurrentiel** competitive positioning; **p. de la marque** brand positioning; **p. de prix** price positioning; **p. du produit** product positioning; **p. stratégique** strategic position-ing

positionner [pozisjɔne] **VT 1** *Tech, Ordinat (curseur, graphique etc)* to position **2** *Fin (compte)* to calculate the balance of **3** *Mktg (produit)* to position
VPR se positionner se p. à la hausse sur le marché to move upmarket; **se p. par rapport à la concurrence** to position oneself in relation to the competition

positivement [pozitivmɑ̃] **ADV** positively; **je ne le sais pas p.** I don't know for certain, I can't be positive about it; *Élec* **chargé p.** positively charged

positiver [pozitive] **VI** *Fam* to be positive, to look on the bright side; **arrête donc de te morfondre comme ça, essaye de p.!** stop moping around like that, try to look on the bright side!

positivisme [pozitivism] **NM** *Phil* positivism
positiviste [pozitivist] **ADJ, N** *Phil* positivist
positivité [pozitivite] **NF** *Élec, Phil, Méd* positivity

positon [pozitɔ̃] **NM, positron** [pozitrɔ̃] **NM** *Nucl* positron

posologie [pɔzɔlɔʒi] **NF** *Méd (de produit pharmaceutique)* dosage; *(science)* posology

possédant, -ante [posedɑ̃, -ɑ̃t] **ADJ, N les possédants, les classes possédantes** the propertied *or* moneyed classes, the wealthy

possédé, -ée [posede] **ADJ** *(par la passion, la jalousie etc)* gripped, dominated (**par** by); **p. du diable** *ou* **du démon** possessed by the devil
N person possessed; *Fig* maniac, madman, *f* madwoman; **hurler comme un p.** to wail like a banshee, *Fml* to scream like one possessed

posséder [posede] (**je possède; je posséderai**) **VT 1** *(avoir)* to possess, to own, to have; **p. un titre** to have a title; **p. un million** to be a millionaire; **je ne possède pas un centime** I don't have a penny (to my name); **p. un grand talent/sens de l'humour** to possess *or* have a great talent/sense of humour; *Fig* **p. le cœur d'une femme** to have won a woman's heart **2** *(connaître) (sujet)* to have a thorough knowledge of, to be master of; *(langue, technique)* to have mastered, to have a good mastery of; **tu ne possèdes pas la vérité, tu sais** you don't know everything, you know; **p. son métier** to know one's job inside out; **elle possède maintenant tous les automatismes** now it comes automatically to her **3** *(dominer) (d'un démon, du diable etc)* to possess; **ils étaient tous possédés de la même illusion** they all laboured under the same delusion **4** *Fam (tromper) (personne)* to take in, to fool; **je me suis fait p.** I've been taken in *or* had **5 p. une femme** to possess a woman
VPR se posséder to control oneself; **elle ne se possédait plus de joie/rage** she was beside herself with joy/rage; **elle ne se possède plus!** she's out of her mind!

possesseur [posesœr] **NM** owner; *(de titre)* holder, possessor; **il se croit le p. de la vérité** he thinks he knows everything; **p. de valeurs** share owner

possessif, -ive [posesif, -iv] **ADJ 1** *Gram* possessive **2** *Psy (mère, mari)* possessive
NM *Gram* possessive SEE GRAMMAR A30; B21–2

possession [posesjɔ̃] **NF 1** *(fait de détenir, d'avoir)* ownership; *(de titre)* holding, possession; **être en p. de qch** to be in possession of sth, to possess sth; *Jur, Fml* to be possessed of sth; *Com* **nous sommes en p. de votre lettre du 4 mars** we are in receipt of *or* have received your letter of 4 March; **avoir qch en sa p.** to have sth in one's possession; **entrer en p. d'un héritage** to enter

into possession of an inheritance; **entrée en p. d'un patrimoine** accession to an estate; **prendre p. de qch** to take possession of sth; **rentrer en p. de qch** to gain possession of sth; **comment ce manuscrit est-il tombé en votre p.?** how did this manuscript come into your possession?; **p. vaut titre** possession is nine points *or* nine-tenths of the law; **p. de fait** de facto possession
2 *(bien) (surtout bien immobilier, domaine)* possession; **avoir quelques possessions** to have a few possessions; *Fin* **possessions d'une société** assets of a company
3 *Psy, Rel* possession *(by evil spirit)*
4 *(maîtrise)* self-control, self-possession; **reprendre p. de soi-même** to regain *or* recover one's self-control *or* composure; **être en pleine p. de ses facultés, être en p. de toutes ses facultés** to be in (full) possession of one's faculties; **elle était en pleine p. de ses moyens** she was at the peak of her powers *or* her abilities

possessivité [posesivite] **NF** possessiveness

possessoire [poseswar] *Jur* **ADJ intenter une action p.** to undertake an action for possession (of land)
NM right of possession

possibilité [posibilite] **NF 1** *(éventualité)* possibility; *(d'un projet, d'une opération)* feasibility; **voir la p. de faire qch** to see the possibility of doing sth; **nous ne voyons aucune p. de changement** we can't see any possibility of change; **il faut prendre en compte la p. du rejet (de greffe)** we have to allow for the possibility of rejection *or* for the possibility that the transplant will be rejected SEE GRAMMAR A58–60; B40
2 *(cas)* possibility; **c'est une p. que je n'avais pas envisagée** it's a possibility that I hadn't envisaged
3 *(moyen, occasion)* opportunity, chance; **c'est la première fois qu'elle a la p. de le faire** this is the first opportunity *or* chance she's had to do it *or* of doing it; **on ne m'en a jamais donné la p.** I was never given the opportunity *or* chance; **si j'ai la p. de lui écrire** if it's possible for me *or* if I can manage to write to him; **p. d'emprunter** borrowing power; *Ordinat* **possibilités d'extension** upgradeability
4 possibilités *(d'une personne)* capabilities; *(financières)* means; **connaître ses possibilités** to be aware of one's (own) capabilities; **chacun doit payer selon ses possibilités** from each according to his means; **la région dispose de nombreuses possibilités de vacances** the region offers many holiday possibilities; **le nombre de touristes dépasse largement les possibilités de l'hôtel** the number of tourists easily exceeds the capacity of the hotel; **quelles sont vos possibilités d'embauche?** what are your plans for taking people on?; **quelles sont vos possibilités de logement?** how many people can you put up?

POSSIBLE [posibl] **ADJ 1** *(faisable)* possible; *(projet, opération)* feasible; **c'est (bien) p.** it's (quite) possible, (very) possibly; **est-ce p.?, ce n'est pas p.!,** *Fam* **pas p.!** it's not possible!, impossible!, I don't believe it!; *Fam* **c'est pas Dieu p.** it's unbelievable; **si (c'est) p.** if (it's) possible; **est-il p. de faire des fautes pareilles?** how can people make such mistakes?; **il leur est p. de vous héberger** it's possible for them to put you up; **est-ce qu'il serait p. de travailler demain?** would it be possible for you to work tomorrow?, could you possibly work tomorrow?; **il ne m'est pas p. de le faire** it's impossible *or* not possible for me to do it, I can't possibly do it; **il ne m'est guère p. de le faire** it's a bit difficult for me to do it; **cela lui est tout à fait p.** it's no trouble at all

for him; **il est p. qu'il soit mort** it's possible that he's dead, he may *or* might be dead; **il n'est pas p. que j'y aille** *(je ne peux pas)* it's impossible *or* not possible for me to go; *(il n'est pas question)* there's no possibility of my going; **il est bien p. que …** it's quite possible that …; **aussitôt que p., dès que p.** as soon as possible; *Fml* **le plus tôt qu'il vous sera p.** at your earliest convenience; **est-ce que tu viens? – p.** are you coming? – possibly; **il faut absolument qu'il nous conduise à l'aéroport, ce n'est pas p. autrement** he'll have to drive us to the airport, otherwise we'll never make it
2 *(existant, maximum, minimum)* **le moins souvent p.** as infrequently as possible; **le moins de détails possible(s)** as few details as possible; **elle nous en parle le moins p.** she talks to us about it as little as possible; **tous les détails possibles** every possible detail; **toutes les informations possibles** all available information; **la boîte la plus grande p.** the largest box possible, the largest possible box; **elle a eu tous les ennuis possibles et imaginables** she's had every problem you can think of; **dans la plus large mesure p.** as far as possible
3 *(éventuel)* possible; **danger p.** possible *or* potential danger; **il est p. qu'il y pense à la dernière minute** he may well think of it at the last minute; *Fam* **c'est dans les choses possibles** it's a possibility
4 *Fam (supportable)* **cette fille/situation n'est pas p.!** that girl/this situation is impossible!; **ça n'est plus p.** I can't take (it) any more, I've had enough
NM 1 *(ce qui est possible)* what is possible; **dans la mesure du p.** as far as possible; **faire tout son p. pour …** to do all *or* everything one can (possibly) to …, to do one's utmost *or* best to …, to try one's hardest to …; **il s'est montré aimable au p.** he couldn't have been nicer, he was extremely pleasant
2 *(chose réalisable)* possibility; **envisageons tous les possibles** let's consider all the possibilities

post-achat [postaʃa] **ADJ** *Mktg* post-purchase
post-acheminement, *pl* **post-acheminements** [postaʃ(e)minmɑ̃] **NM** transfer from main airport
postal, -ale, -aux, -ales [postal, -o] **ADJ** *(tarif)* mail, *Br* postal; *(train, camion, wagon)* mail; **code p.** postcode, postal code, *Am* zip code; **sac p.** mailbag, *Br* postbag; **carte postale** postcard; **colis p.** parcel sent by post; **les services postaux** the postal *or Am* mail services; **les services postaux sont assez fiables dans ce pays** the postal service is quite reliable in this country

postcombustion [postkɔ̃bystjɔ̃] **NF** *Tech (d'une fusée, d'un turboréacteur)* afterburning, reheat; **dispositif de p.** afterburner
postcommunion [postkomynjɔ̃] **NF** *Rel* postcommunion
postcommunisme [postkomynism] **NM** postcommunism
postcure [postkyr] **NF** *Méd* aftercare; **elle est en p.** she's in aftercare
postdater [postdate] **VT** to postdate
poste[1] [post] **NF 1** *(service)* mail, *Br* post; **la P.** the mail *or Br* postal service, *Br ≃* the Post Office, *Am ≃* the US Postal Service; **envoyer une lettre par la p.** to send a letter by mail *or Br* post; **mettre une lettre à la p.** to mail *or Br* post a letter; **(bureau de) p.** post office; **p. principale, grande p.** main post office; **aller à la p.** to go to the post office; **receveur/receveuse des postes** postmaster/postmistress; **grève des postes** mail *or Br* postal strike **2** *Arch (relais de chevaux)* post, relay; **chevaux de p.** posthorses; **maître de p.** postmaster;

aller en p. to travel post; **courir la p.** to go posthaste

▸▸**p. aérienne** airmail; **p. restante** poste restante, *Am* general delivery

poste² NM **1** *(fonction)* job, position, post; **il y a des postes vacants** there are (job) vacancies; **présenter sa candidature à un p. de technicien** to apply for a job as a technician; **un p. clé** a key position; **occuper un p. de confiance** to hold a position of trust; *Ind* **p. de jour/nuit** day/night shift; **p. à pourvoir** vacancy

2 *Radio, TV* **p. (de) radio** radio set; **p. de télévision** television set; *Fam* **ouvrir/fermer le p.** to switch the radio/television on/off; *Radio* **p. émetteur** *(endroit)* broadcasting station; *(équipement)* transmitter

3 *Tél* extension; **je voudrais le p. 35, s'il vous plaît** I'd like extension 35, please; **le p. est occupé** the extension *or* line is *Br* engaged *or Am* busy; **je vous passe le p.** I'm putting you through

4 *(bureau)* post; *(de police)* station; **passer la nuit au p.** to spend the night at the station; **p. de la Croix-Rouge** Red Cross station

5 *(salle)* quarters; **p. d'équipage** crew's quarters; *(dans la marine marchande)* forecastle; *Naut* **p. des maîtres** warrant officers' wardroom; **p. des aspirants** gunroom

6 *Compta* entry, item; **p. créditeur/débiteur** credit/debit item; **p. de bilan** balance sheet item; **p. extraordinaire** extraordinary item

7 *Mil (d'un soldat)* post, station; *Mil* **p. avancé** advanced *or* outlying post; *Mil, Naut* **chef de p.** guard commander; **à vos postes!** to your posts!, stand by!; **postes de combat** action stations; **être à son p.** to be at one's post; *Fig* **être solide** *ou* **fidèle au p.** to be still going strong

8 *Naut (emplacement)* berth; **p. de mouillage** anchoring berth; **p. d'amarrage** mooring berth, mooring(s); **mettre les ancres à p.** to stow the anchors

9 *Ordinat* **p. autonome** stand-alone; **p. terminal** terminal; **p. de travail** workstation

▸▸*Rail* **p. d'aiguillage** signal box; **p. de commandement** headquarters, command post; *Naut* control room; **p. de contrôle** checkpoint; *Mil* **p. d'écoute** listening station; **p. d'essence** petrol *or Am* gas station, filling station; *Mil* **p. de garde** guardroom; **p. d'incendie** fire point; *Mil* **p. d'observation** observation post; **p. de péage** toll booth; *Aviat* **p. de pilotage** cockpit; *(dans un avion plus important)* flight deck; **p. de police** (police) station; *Mil* guardroom; **p. de secours** first-aid post

posté, -ée [pɔste] ADJ **travail p.** shift work; **ouvrier p.** shift worker
  N shift worker

poster¹ [pɔste] VT *(sentinelle)* to post; *(hommes, troupes)* to station
  VPR **se poster** to take up a position, to station oneself

poster² VT *(courrier)* to mail, *Br* to post

poster³ [pɔstɛr] NM poster

postérieur [pɔsterjœr] ADJ **1** *(dans le temps)* later, subsequent; **p. à son décès** after his death; **la rechute est très postérieure à son opération** the relapse came a long time after his operation; **avoir lieu à une date postérieure** to be held at a later date; **être remis à une date postérieure** to be postponed to a later date; **à une date postérieure à notre coup de téléphone** at a date some time after our phone call **2** *(dans l'espace) (pattes)* back, hind, rear; *Anat* posterior; **partie postérieure** back part
  NM *Fam (derrière)* behind, backside, *Hum* posterior

postérieurement [pɔsterjœrmã] ADV later, subsequently, at a later date; **p. à** after

postériorité [pɔsterjorite] NF posteriority

postérité [pɔsterite] NF posterity; *(famille, descendance)* posterity, descendants; **mourir sans (laisser de) p.** to die without issue; **nous travaillons pour la p.** we are working for posterity; *Fig* **la p. du nouveau-roman** the legacy of the nouveau roman; **entrer dans la p., passer à la p.** *(d'une personne)* to go down in history; *(d'une œuvre, d'un mot etc)* to be handed down to posterity

postface [pɔstfas] NF postscript

postglaciaire [pɔstglasjer] ADJ *Géol* postglacial

posthume [pɔstym] ADJ posthumous

postiche [pɔstiʃ] ADJ *(cheveux, cils etc)* false
  NM hairpiece

postier, -ière [pɔstje, -jer] N postal worker, post office employee

postillon [pɔstijõ] NM **1** *Hist (cocher)* postilion **2** *(salive)* postillons shower(s) of spit; **envoyer des postillons** to splutter, to sputter

postillonner [pɔstijone] VI *(en parlant)* to splutter, to sputter

postindustriel, -ielle [pɔstẽdystrijel] ADJ postindustrial

postmoderne [pɔstmɔdern] ADJ postmodern

postmodernisme [pɔstmɔdernism] NM postmodernism

postnatal, -ale, -als, -ales [pɔstnatal] ADJ postnatal

postopératoire [pɔstɔperatwar] ADJ *Méd* postoperative

postpartum [pɔstpartɔm] NM INV *Méd* postpartum period

postposer [pɔstpoze] VT **1** *Gram* **p. un adjectif/un verbe** to place *or* put an adjective/a verb after; **adjectif postposé** adjective placed after the noun, postpositive adjective **2** *Belg (remettre à plus tard)* to postpone

postposition [pɔstpozisjõ] NF *Gram* postposition

post-production [pɔstprɔdyksjõ] NF *TV etc* postproduction

postscolaire [pɔstskɔler] ADJ *(cours)* continuation; **enseignement p.** further *or* continuing education

post-scriptum [pɔstskriptɔm] NM INV postscript, PS

postsonorisation [pɔstsɔnɔrizasjõ] NF *Cin* post-synchronization, dubbing

postsonoriser [pɔstsɔnɔrize] VT *Cin* to post-synchronize, to dub

post-synchro [pɔstsẽkro] NF *Cin* post-synching

postsynchronisation [pɔstsẽkrɔnizasjõ] NF *Cin* post-synchronization, ADR

postsynchroniser [pɔstsẽkrɔnize] VT *Cin* to post-synchronize, to dub

postulant, -ante [pɔstylã, -ãt] N **1** *(à un emploi)* applicant, candidate **2** *Rel* postulant

postulat [pɔstyla] NM *Phil* postulate, assumption

postuler [pɔstyle] VT **1** *(demander) (poste, emploi)* to apply for **2** *Phil* to postulate
  VI **1** *Jur* **p. pour un client** *(d'un avocat)* to act on behalf of *or* represent a client **2** **p. à** *ou* **pour un emploi** to apply for a job

posture [pɔstyr] NF **1** *(attitude du corps)* posture, position, attitude **2** **être en p. de faire qch** to be in a position to do sth; **être en bonne/mauvaise p. (pour faire qch)** to be in a good/bad position *or* well/badly placed (to do sth); **être en fâcheuse p.** to be in an awkward situation

pot [po] NM **1** *(récipient)* pot; **p. de terre**

earthenware pot; **p. à tabac** tobacco jar; *Fig Fam (personne petite et grosse)* tubby person; **p. à eau** water jug; **p. de fleurs** *(récipient)* flowerpot, plant pot; *(plante)* pot of flowers; **p. à lait, p. au lait** milk jug; *(en métal)* milk can; **p. de confiture** jam jar; *Fam* **le p.** *(pour enfant)* the potty; **aller sur le p.** to use the potty; **mettre en p.** *(plante)* to pot; **p. de colle** pot of glue; *Fig Fam* **quel p. de colle!** he sticks to you like glue!, you can't shake him off *or* get rid of him!; **quel p. de colle tu fais aujourd'hui!** stop annoying *or* bugging me!; **il est gentil mais c'est un p. de colle** he's nice but he tends to cling; *Fig* **payer les pots cassés** to take the rap, *Br* to carry the can; *Fig* **découvrir le p. aux roses** [potoroz] to find out what's been going on; *Fam* **c'est le p. de terre contre le p. de fer** he doesn't stand a chance, he's more than met his match

2 *(contenu)* pot; **finir un p. de confiture** to finish a jar *or* pot of jam; **un p. d'eau** a jug of water; **petit p.** *(pour bébé)* (jar of) baby food; **p. d'accueil** welcoming drink; *Fam* **allons prendre un p.** let's go for a drink *or Br* jar; *Fam* **faire un p. (d'adieu/d'anniversaire)** to have a (farewell/birthday) drink

3 *Culin (marmite)* (cooking) pot; **manger à la fortune du p.** to take pot luck; **en trois coups de cuiller à p.** in less than no time, in no time (at all), in two shakes (of a lamb's tail); *Fig* **tourner autour du p.** to beat about the bush; **sourd comme un p.** as deaf as a post

4 *Fam (chance)* **avoir du p.** to be lucky; **avoir un coup de p.** to have a stroke of luck; **manque de p., pas de p.** just his/your/*etc* luck; **elle n'a vraiment pas de p.!** she has no luck at all!

5 *Fam* **plein p.** *(à toute vitesse)* like the clappers, *Am* like sixty; **ils croyaient qu'ils auraient droit à une réduction mais finalement ils ont payé plein p.** they thought they would be entitled to a discount but they ended up paying the full whack; **elle met toujours la musique à pleins pots** she always puts music on at full blast

▸▸**p. à absorption** absorption silencer; **p. à catalyseur** catalytic converter; **p. catalytique** catalytic converter; **p. de chambre** chamber pot; **p. d'échappement** silencer, *Am* muffler; *(ensemble du système)* exhaust (system); *(tuyau)* exhaust (pipe), *Am* tail pipe; *Naut* **p. au noir** doldrums; *Aut* **p. de résonance** resonance chamber

potable [pɔtabl] ADJ **1** *(que l'on peut boire)* drinkable, fit to drink; **eau p.** drinking water **2** *Fam (correct)* passable, reasonable; *(tenue)* acceptable, decent

potache [pɔtaʃ] NM *Scol Fam* schoolboy *(attending a collège or lycée)*

potage [pɔtaʒ] NM **1** *(soupe)* soup; **p. aux légumes** vegetable soup; *Fam* **être dans le p.** *(être évanoui)* to be out cold; *(être dans une situation pénible)* to be in the soup **2** *Arch, Litt* **pour tout p.** all told, (all) in all

potager, -ère [pɔtaʒe, -er] ADJ **herbes potagères** herbs for cooking, pot herbs; **plante potagère** vegetable; **jardin p.** vegetable *or* kitchen garden
  NM vegetable *or* kitchen garden

potasse [pɔtas] NF *Chimie* potash; **chlorate de p.** potassium chlorate

potasser [pɔtase] *Fam* VT to bone up on, *Br* to swot up
  VI to bone up, *Br* to swot

potassique [pɔtasik] ADJ *Chimie* potassium; *(sel)* potassic

potassium [pɔtasjɔm] NM *Chimie* potassium

pot-au-feu [potofø] NM INV *Culin* = boiled beef with vegetables
  ADJ INV *Fam Vieilli (personne)* stay-at-home

pot-de-vin, *pl* **pots-de-vin** NM bribe, *Fam* backhander; **donner un p. à qn** to bribe sb, *Fam* to give sb a backhander

pote [pɔt] NM *Fam* pal, chum

poteau, -eaux [pɔto] NM **1** post; *Min* pit prop; *Sport (de but)* (goal)post; **p. indicateur** signpost; **p. télégraphique** telegraph pole; **p. électrique** electricity pylon; *Sport* **p. de départ** starting post; *Sport* **p. d'arrivée** finishing post, winning post; **rester au p.** to be left at the post; **être coiffé sur le p.** to be pipped at the post, *Am* to be beaten by a nose; *Fam* **avoir des jambes comme des poteaux** to have legs like tree-trunks **2 p. (d'exécution)** execution post *or* stake *(for sb about to be shot)*; **mettre qn au p.** to put sb up against a wall and shoot him/her; **le général au p.!** down with the general! **3** *Fam (ami)* pal, chum

potée [pɔte] NF *Culin* stew *(especially cabbage and carrots with pork)*

potelé [pɔtle] ADJ chubby, plump

potence [pɔtɑ̃s] NF **1** *(gibet)* gallows, gibbet; **échapper à la p.** to cheat the gallows; **gibier de p.** gallows bird VOIR GRAMMAIRE A13 **2** *(charpente)* bracket, arm, support; *(de grue)* jib; *(d'un guidon de bicyclette)* stem; *(d'une perfusion)* stand; **en p.** bracket-shaped, L-shaped **3** *Naut, Mil* davit

potentat [pɔtɑ̃ta] NM potentate

potentialisation [pɔtɑ̃sjalizɑsjɔ̃] NF *Pharm* potentiation

potentialiser [pɔtɑ̃sjalize] VT **1** *Pharm* to potentiate **2** *Fig* to maximize
VPR **se potentialiser** to maximize one's potential

potentialité [pɔtɑ̃sjalite] NF potentiality; **une p. inutilisée** unused potential

potentiel, -ielle [pɔtɑ̃sjɛl] ADJ potential; *Gram* **préfixe/sens p.** potential prefix/ meaning; *Tech* **énergie potentielle** potential energy
NM **1** potential; **avoir un bon/fort p.** to have good/strong potential; **p. de croissance** growth potential; **p. de guerre** establishment; **p. industriel** industrial potential; **p. de vente** sales potential; **p. du marché** market potential **2** *Élec* potential; *Radio* **p. de grille** grid potential **3** *Gram* potential *(mood)*

potentiellement [pɔtɑ̃sjɛlmɑ̃] ADV potentially

potentille [pɔtɑ̃tij] NF *Bot* **p. (rampante)** cinquefoil

potentiomètre [pɔtɑ̃sjɔmetr] NM *Électron* potentiometer; *Cin (de son)* fader; **p. de micro** microphone fader; **p. vidéo** video fader

poterie [pɔtri] NF **1** *(usine)* pottery (works); *(atelier)* potter's workshop *or* studio; *(art, techniques)* pottery; **cours de p.** pottery class; **faire de la p.** to do *or* make pottery **2** *(objet)* piece of pottery; *(objets)* pottery; **elle achète souvent de la p./des poteries** she often buys pottery; **p. (de terre)** earthenware; **p. de grès** stoneware **3** *Tech* **p. d'étain** pewter(ware)

poterne [pɔtɛrn] NF postern (gate)

potiche [pɔtiʃ] NF **1** *(vase)* (large) vase *(especially of Chinese or Japanese porcelain)* **2** *Fig* figurehead

potier, -ière [pɔtje, -jɛr] N potter

potin [pɔtɛ̃] NM *Fam* **1** potins gossip, tittle-tattle; **s'intéresser aux petits potins** to take an interest in idle gossip **2** *(bruit)* row, din, rumpus; **faire du p.** to kick up a row *or* rumpus, to make a din

potiner [pɔtine] VI to gossip

potion [posjɔ̃] NF *Méd* potion; **p. magique** magic potion

potiron [pɔtirɔ̃] NM pumpkin

pot-pourri, *pl* **pots-pourris** NM *Mus* potpourri, medley; *(fleurs séchées)* potpourri

potron-minet [pɔtrɔ̃minɛ] NM INV *Arch Fam* **dès p.** at daybreak, at the crack of dawn

pou, *pl* **poux** [pu] NM louse, *pl* lice; **p. du pubis** pubic louse, *Fam* crab (louse); *Fam* **laid comme un p.** as ugly as sin; **fier** *ou* **orgueilleux comme un p.** as proud as a peacock; **sale comme un p.** filthy dirty; **elle est vexée comme un p.** she's really really upset, *Br* she's really got the hump; *Fam* **chercher des poux dans la tête à qn** to pick a quarrel with sb (about nothing)

pouah [pwa] INT ugh!

poubelle [pubɛl] NF **1** *(pour les ordures)* (dust)bin, *Am* garbage *or* trash can; *Ordinat* wastebasket, *Am* trash; **p. à pédale** pedal bin; **jeter** *ou* **mettre qch à la p.** to throw *or* put sth in the (dust)bin, to throw sth away; *Fig Fam* to think sth is a load of rubbish; **c'est bon à jeter** *ou* **mettre à la p.** it should be thrown out, it's fit for the dustbin; *Fig* it's a load of rubbish; **qu'est-ce que j'en fais? – p.!** what do I do with this? – just bin it!; **descendre la p.** to take the rubbish *or Am* garbage down; **faire les poubelles** to scrounge in dustbins **2** *Fam (voiture)* heap, banger, rustbucket

pouce [pus] NM **1** *(doigt)* thumb; **sucer son p.** to suck one's thumb; *Fam* **donner un coup de p. à qn/qch** to help sb/sth along (a bit); **elle/le projet n'a besoin que d'un coup de p.** she/ the project just needs to be helped along a bit; *Fam* **manger sur le p.** to have a (quick) snack; **se tourner les pouces** to twiddle one's thumbs; **dire p.** to give up; *Scol* **p.! truce!**, *Br* **pax!**; *Suisse Fam* **tenir les pouces à qn** to keep one's fingers crossed for sb; *Can* **faire du p.** to thumb a lift *or Am* ride; *Can* **avoir les mains pleines de pouces** to be all thumbs, to be clumsy with one's hands **2** *(gros orteil)* big toe **3** *(mesure)* inch; **disquette de 3,5/5,25 pouces** 3.5-/5.25-inch disk; *aussi Fig* **ne pas bouger d'un p.** not to move an inch; *aussi Fig* **ne pas céder un p. de terrain** not to yield *or* budge an inch

poucer [puse] VI *Can Fam (faire de l'autostop)* to thumb a lift *or Am* ride

Poucet [pusɛ] NM **le Petit P.** Tom Thumb

poucettes [pusɛt] NFPL *Arch* = metal rings attached to the thumbs of prisoners

poucier [pusje] NM *(doigtier)* thumbstall

pouding [pudiŋ] NM = **pudding** ²

poudingue [pudɛ̃g] NM *Géol* pudding stone

poudrage [pudraʒ] NM *Tech* powdering

poudre [pudr] NF **1** *(substance)* powder; **réduire qch en p.** to reduce sth to powder, to pulverize sth, to powder sth; **café en p.** instant coffee; **chocolat en p.** chocolate powder; **lait en p.** powdered milk; **sucre en p.** caster sugar; **lessive en p., p. à laver**, *Belg* **p. à lessiver** washing powder; **savon en p.** soap powder; **p. compacte/libre** *(maquillage)* pressed/loose powder; *Fam* **prendre la p. d'escampette** to make off, *Br* to do a bunk **2** *(explosif)* (explosive) powder; **p. à canon** gunpowder; *Fig* **être vif comme la p.** to flare up easily; *Fig* **mettre le feu aux poudres** to spark off a crisis; **la nouvelle s'est répandue comme une traînée de p.** the news spread like wildfire; **faire parler la p.** to let one's guns do the talking; *Fig* **ça sent la p.** there's trouble brewing **3** *Arch (poussière)* dust; *Fig* **jeter de la p. aux yeux de qn** to dazzle *or* impress sb **4** *Arg (héroïne)* smack; *(cocaïne)* coke, charlie

▸▸ **p. dentifrice** tooth powder; **p. d'encre** toner; **p. à éternuer** sneezing powder; *Suisse* **p. à lever** *(levure)* baking powder; **p. d'or** gold dust; **p. de perlimpinpin** magic *or* mira-cle powder; **p. à récurer** scouring powder; **p. de riz** face powder

poudrer [pudre] VT to powder; **p. ses cheveux** to powder one's hair, to put powder on one's hair; **une femme poudrée** a woman with a powdered face
V IMPERS *Can* **il poudre** it's snowing slightly
VPR **se poudrer** to powder one's face *or* nose; **se p. le visage** to powder one's face

poudrerie [pudrəri] NF **1** *(fabrique de poudre)* (gun)powder factory **2** *Can (neige)* drifting snow

poudreux, -euse [pudrø, -øz] ADJ **1** *(qui a la consistance de la poudre)* powdery; **neige poudreuse** powder snow **2** *Vieilli (couvert de poussière)* dusty
NF **poudreuse 1** *(neige)* powder snow **2** *(sucrier)* sugar sprinkler *or* caster

poudrier [pudrije] NM powder box; *(porté dans un sac à main etc)* (powder) compact

poudrière [pudrijɛr] NF *(entrepôt)* powder magazine; *Fig (région)* powder keg

poudrin [pudrɛ̃] NM spindrift

poudroiement [pudrwamɑ̃] NM dust haze

poudroyer [pudrwaje] VI *Litt* (**il poudroie; il poudroiera**) *(du soleil)* to pick out the dust in the air; **la route poudroie** the dust whirls up from the road

pouf [puf] INT bump!, thud!
NM **1** *(meuble)* pouf(fe) **2** *Belg* **à p.** *(à crédit)* on tick; **taper à p.** *(au hasard)* to make a wild guess

pouffer [pufe] VI **p. (de rire)** to burst out laughing

pouffiasse [pufjas] NF *Vulg Vieilli (prostituée)* whore, tart; *Péj Vulg* **une grosse p.** a (great) fat cow, *Br* a fat slag; **quelle p.!** what a slag!

pouillerie [pujri] NF squalor; *(lieu)* filthy place, lousy hole

pouilleux, -euse [pujø, -øz] ADJ **1** *(couvert de vermine)* lousy, flea-ridden, verminous **2** *(misérable)* wretched, miserable; *(quartier, maison)* squalid, shabby **3** *Géog* **la Champagne pouilleuse** = the barren part of the Champagne region
N **1** *(personne couverte de vermine)* louse-ridden *or* flea-ridden person **2** *(clochard)* tramp, *Am* bum

pouillot [pujo] NM *Orn* warbler

poujadisme [puʒadism] NM *Hist, Pol* Pouja-dism *(lower-middle-class, populist movement in the 1950s and 60s)*; *Fig Péj* narrow-minded *or* shopkeeper mentality

poujadiste [puʒadist] N *Hist, Pol* Poujadist; *Fig Péj* narrow-minded person

poulaille [pulaj] NF *Fam* **la p.** the cops, the pigs, *Br* the fuzz

poulailler [pulaje] NM **1** *(basse-cour)* hen house, hen roost **2** *Théâtre Fam* **le p.** the gods; **places de p.** seats in the gods

poulain [pulɛ̃] NM **1** *(cheval)* foal **2** *Fig* protégé **3** *Tech* **p. (de chargement)** *(pour décharger les tonneaux etc)* skid

poulaine [pulɛn] NF **1** *Naut* (ship's) head; **les poulaines** the latrines *(for crew)* **2** **soulier à la p.** long pointed shoe

poulamon [pulamɔ̃] NM *Can* tomcod

poularde [pulard] NF *Culin* fattened pullet

poulbot [pulbo] NM street urchin (of Montmartre)

poule¹ [pul] NF **1** *Zool* hen; *Culin* (boiling) fowl; **p. pondeuse** laying hen; **p. au pot** boiled chicken; *Fig* **ma (petite) p.!** my dear!, my pet!; *Fig* **la p. aux œufs d'or** the goose that lays the golden eggs; *Fig* **mère p.** mother hen; *Fig Péj* **p. mouillée** *(personne)* softie, wimp; *surtout Br Pol* wet; **se coucher comme** *ou* **avec les poules** to go to bed early; **lait de**

p. (non-alcoholic) egg flip *or* egg nog; *Fig* **quand les poules auront des dents** when pigs can fly; **p. d'eau** moorhen; **p. faisane** hen pheasant; **petite p. de bruyère** grey hen; **nid de p.** *(sur la route)* pothole **2** *Arg Péj (femme légère)* floozy, tart; *(maîtresse)* mistress; **p. de luxe** high-class call girl

> Do not confuse with **poulet**.

poule² NF **1** *(enjeu)* pool, kitty **2** *Escrime* pool, tournament; *Rugby* group **3** *Courses de chevaux* **p. d'essai** = early-season race for three-year-olds

poulet [pulɛ] NM **1** *Zool, Culin* chicken; *Culin* **p. fermier** *ou* **de grain** free-range chicken; **p. élevé en batterie** battery(-farmed) chicken; *Culin* **aile de p.** chicken wing; **cuisse de p.** chicken leg; **p. rôti** roast chicken; *très Fam* **et mon cul, c'est du p.?** oh come on, don't give me that crap! **2** **mon (petit) p.** my darling, my pet, *Hum* my little chickadee **3** *Fam (policier)* cop **4** *Arch Fam (billet doux)* billet-doux

> Do not confuse with **poule**.

poulette [pulɛt] NF **1** *Vieilli (jeune poule)* pullet, young hen; *Culin* **sauce (à la) p.** = rich white sauce *(with onions, mushrooms, white wine etc)* **2** *Fam Vieilli (fille)* girl, *Am* dame **3** *Fam* **ma p.** my darling, my pet

pouliche [puliʃ] NF filly

poulie [puli] NF pulley; **p. simple/double** single/double block; **p. fixe** fixed pulley, standing block; **p. d'entraînement** drive pulley; **p. folle** loose pulley, idler

pouliner [puline] VI *(d'une jument)* to foal

poulinière [pulinjɛr] ADJ, NF **(jument) p.** brood mare

pouliot¹ [puljo] NM *Bot* pennyroyal

pouliot² NM *(sur charrette)* windlass

poulot, -otte [pulo, -ɔt] N *Enf* sweetheart, sweetie

poulpe [pulp] NM octopus

pouls [pu] NM pulse; **tâter le p. de qn** to feel sb's pulse; **prendre le p. à qn** to take sb's pulse; *Fig* **tâter** *ou* **prendre le p. de l'économie** to take the pulse of the economy; *Fig* **tâter** *ou* **prendre le p. de l'opinion** to sound out public opinion

poumon [pumɔ̃] NM *Anat* lung; **p. d'acier** iron lung; **respirer à pleins poumons** to breathe deeply, to take deep breaths/a deep breath; **crier à pleins poumons** to shout at the top of one's voice; **avoir de bons poumons** *ou* **des poumons** *(d'un chanteur etc)* to have good lungs; *Fam* **cracher ses poumons** to cough one's guts up *or* out; *Fig* **cette région était jadis le p. économique du pays** in days gone by this region was the economic lung of the country

poupard [pupar] NM **1** *Vieilli (gros bébé)* chubby baby **2** *Arch (poupée)* baby doll
ADJ *Vieilli* chubby(-cheeked); **visage p.** baby face

poupe [pup] NF *Naut* stern, poop; **avoir le vent en p.** to have the wind aft; *Fig* to have the wind in one's sails

poupée [pupe] NF **1** *(jouet)* doll, *Enf* dolly; **p. mannequin** doll for dressing up; **poupées gigognes** *ou* **russes** Russian dolls; **p. gonflable** inflatable doll; **maison de p.** doll's house; *Fig* **doll's house, shoebox; **jouer à la p.** to play with dolls **2** *Fam (jolie fille)* doll **3** *(pansement au doigt)* finger bandage; *(le doigt lui-même)* bandaged finger; **faire une p. à qn** to bandage sb's finger **4** *Naut* **p. de cabestan** capstan head

poupin [pupɛ̃] ADJ *(personne)* chubby(-cheeked); *(air)* baby-like; **visage p.** baby face

poupon [pupɔ̃] NM **1** *(enfant)* (tiny) baby **2** *(poupée)* doll; **il a un visage de p.** he's baby-faced

pouponner [pupɔne] VI to play the doting mother/father

pouponnière [pupɔnjɛr] NF nursery *(for children up to three years old)*

poupoune [pupun] NF *Can Fam* sweetie, honey

POUR [pur]

> **PRÉP** for **1–8, 18** • on behalf of **1** • as **2** • in favour of **7** • in my/his opinion *(pour moi/lui)* **8** • to **3, 9, 10, 12** • in order to **10** • if *(pour peu que)* **17**
> **NM INV** the pros and cons *(le pour et le contre)*

PRÉP **1** *(à la place de)* for; **dis-le-lui/allez-y p. moi** tell him/go for me; **agir p. qn** to act for sb *or* on sb's behalf; **p. le Président, son secrétaire ...** on behalf of the President, his secretary ...; *Fin* **p. acquit** received with thanks

2 *(comme)* for; **il la veut p. femme** he wants her for *or* as his wife; **tenir qn p. fou** to regard sb as mad, to consider sb mad; **prendre qn p. un autre** to take sb for somebody else; **laisser qn p. mort** to leave sb for dead; **une attitude p. le moins étrange** a somewhat strange attitude, a strange attitude to say the least; *Fam* **c'est p. de bon** *ou* **p. de vrai** I mean it, I'm serious; *Fam* **ça compte p. du beurre, on rejoue** that doesn't count, let's play again; **avec p. tout bagage ...** with only ... as luggage, taking only ...

3 *(direction)* for; **je pars p. la France** I'm off to France, I'm leaving for France; **le train/l'avion p. Paris** the Paris train/plane, the train/plane to *or* for Paris

4 *(temps)* for; **je vais en Suisse p. quinze jours** I'm going to Switzerland for two weeks; **p. dans trois jours** in three days, in three days' time; **p. toujours** for ever, for good; **p. le moment** for the moment; **il sera ici p. quatre heures** he'll be here for four hours; *(à quatre heures)* he'll be here by four o'clock; **j'en ai p. une heure** it'll take me an hour, I'll be an hour SEE GRAMMAR A70; B56–7

5 *(contre)* for; **il a acheté son vélo p. 50 euros** he bought his bike for 50 euros; **il me l'a vendu p. trois fois rien** he sold it to me for next to nothing; **trente p. cent** thirty per cent; **10 p. 1000** one percent; **mot p. mot** word for word; **jour p. jour** to the (very) day; **donnez-moi p. 50 euros d'essence** give me 50 euros' worth of petrol; **j'en ai p. mon argent** I've got my money's worth; **être p. beaucoup/peu dans qch** to play a large part/not to play much of a part in sth, to have a great deal to do/not to have much to do with sth; **je n'y suis p. rien!** it's got nothing to do with me!, I've got nothing to do with it!

6 *(cause, but)* for; **vêtements p. hommes** men's clothes, clothes for men; **livres p. enfants** children's books, books for children; **j'épargne p. quand je serai vieux** I'm saving for my old age *or* for when I'm old; **je le mets de côté p. ce soir** I'm putting it aside for tonight; **je suis ici p. affaires** I'm here on business; **voyager p. le plaisir** to travel for pleasure; **je viens p. la machine à laver** I've come about the washing machine; **je vous téléphone p. l'annonce parue dans le journal** I'm calling about the advertisement in the newspaper; **pommade p. les démangeaisons** ointment to relieve itching; **shampooing p. cheveux secs** shampoo for dry hair; *Ordinat* **moniteur p. graphismes** graphics monitor; **c'est p. cela qu'il est venu** that's why he came, that's the reason he came; **p. l'amour de Dieu** for God's sake, for heaven's sake; **faites-le p. moi** do it for me *or*

my sake; **nous devons y réfléchir p. les générations futures** we should think about it for the sake of future generations; **j'avais peur p. lui** I was afraid for him, I feared for him; **elle s'inquiète p. toi** she's worried about you; **il est bon p. les animaux** he's kind to animals; **l'art p. l'art** art for art's sake; **p. la forme** for form's sake; **beaucoup de bruit p. rien** a lot of fuss about *or* over nothing, *Litt* much ado about nothing; **tant pis p. moi** it's just hard luck on me; **tant mieux p. elle** good for her; **p. quoi faire?** what for?; *Fam* **c'est fait p.** that's what it's there for; *Fam* **c'est p. quoi?** what's that for?

7 *(en faveur de)* for, in favour *or Am* favor of; **parler p. qn** to speak in favour of sb; **je suis p. la libération de la femme** I'm (all) for *or* in favour of women's liberation; **moi, je suis p.** I'm (all) for it, I'm in favour of it

8 *(quant à, en ce qui concerne)* for; **p. mon compte (personnel)** for my part, as far as I'm concerned; **il est grand p. son âge** he's tall for his age; **p. ce qui est de ...** as regards ..., with regard to ...; **p. (ce qui est de) moi** as for me, for my part, as far as I'm concerned; **p. moi, c'est absurde** in my opinion it's ridiculous, I think it's ridiculous; **ce ne sera une surprise p. personne** it will come as no surprise to anybody; **il n'en est pas plus intelligent p. cela** he's none the cleverer for all that; **et p. cela ...** and so ...; **en tout et p. tout** all in all, altogether, in total; *Fam* **p. de la chance, c'est de la chance** you're in luck and no mistake; **p. une surprise, c'est une surprise!** that's a surprise and no mistake!; **p. une déception/un anniversaire, ce fut une déception/un anniversaire!** it was some disappointment/birthday!, *Fam* it was one hell of a disappointment/birthday!

9 p. + inf (in order) to; **il faut manger p. vivre** one must eat (in order) to live; **p. ainsi dire** so to speak; **p. bien faire** to do things properly; **c'était p. rire** it was just for fun *or* for a laugh; **il s'en va p. ne jamais revenir** he's going away for good, he's leaving never to return; **nous nous sommes dépêchés p. ne pas être en retard** we hurried so as not to be late

10 p. que + sub so that, in order that; **je vous dis cela p. que vous soyez sur vos gardes** I'm telling you this in order to put you on your guard *or* so that you'll be on your guard; **il est trop tard p. qu'elle sorte** it is too late for her to go out; **mettez-le là, p. qu'on ne l'oublie pas** put it there so that it won't be forgotten

11 *(ayant pour résultat)* **p. notre grand malheur, il nous a quittés bien tôt** most unfortunately for us, he died very young; **cela n'est pas p. me surprendre** that doesn't come as a surprise to me; **cette amitié n'était pas p. lui plaire** the friendship was not to his liking; **de telles remarques ne sont pas p. me déplaire** such remarks are not unwelcome

12 assez intelligent p. comprendre intelligent enough to understand; **être trop faible p. marcher** to be too weak to walk; **trop beau p. être vrai** too good to be true

13 *Litt (étant donné que)* **il est bien ignorant p. avoir étudié si longtemps** he's very ignorant considering how long he's studied

14 *Litt (concession)* (a)lthough; **p. être petit, il n'en est pas moins brave** though small, he is none the less brave

15 *Fam* **être p. partir** to be about to start out *or* set off, to be on the point of starting out *or* setting off

16 mourir p. mourir if I/we/*etc* must die; **ennuis p. ennuis, je préfère les miens** as troubles go, I prefer my own

17 p. peu que vous hésitiez, vous êtes fichu if you hesitate at all, you've had it; **p. peu qu'il se trompe, il est mis à la porte** if he makes any sort of mistake, he's out

18 (*à cause de*) for; **on l'apprécie p. sa gentillesse** he is liked for *or* on account of his kindness; **fermeture p. raisons familiales** closed for family reasons; **congé p. maladie** sick leave; **p. un rien** over nothing; **p. un peu, c'était trop tard** it was very nearly too late; **merci p. tout** thank you for everything; **être puni p. avoir désobéi** to be punished for having disobeyed *or* for disobeying *or* for disobedience; **je le sais p. l'avoir vu** I know from having seen it *or* from seeing it; **il est mort p. avoir trop travaillé** he died from overwork(ing) *or* from working too hard

NM INV peser le p. et le contre to weigh (up) the pros and cons; **entendre le p. et le contre** to hear both sides; **il y a du p. et du contre** there are pros and cons

pourboire [purbwar] NM tip, *Fml* gratuity; **donner un p. au porteur** to tip the porter, to give the porter a tip; **laisser 5 euros/10% de p.** to leave a 5-euro/10% tip; **être payé au p.** to depend on tips for one's pay

pourceau, -eaux [purso] NM pig, swine, *Am* hog

pourcentage [pursãtaʒ] NM percentage; (*d'intérêts*) rate; (*pour représentant*) percentage, commission; **au p.** on a percentage basis, on a commission basis; **un p. fixe** a fixed percentage; **p. de grisé** shading percentage

pourchasser [purʃase] VT to pursue; (*criminel*) to pursue, to hunt (down); (*de créanciers, journalistes*) to harry; **pourchassé de rue en rue** hounded from street to street

> Il faut noter que le verbe anglais **to purchase** est un faux ami. Il signifie **acheter**.

pourfendeur, -euse [purfãdœr, -øz] N *Litt, Iron* **p. d'injustices** fighter against injustice

pourfendre [purfãdr] VT *Litt, Iron* (*injustices, crime etc*) to combat, to fight against

pourlécher (se) [səpurleʃe] (**je me pourlèche; je me pourlécherai**) VPR **se p.** (**les babines**) to lick one's lips; **ça sent bon, d'avance, je m'en pourlèche les babines** that smells good, my mouth is watering already

pourliche [purliʃ] NM *Fam* tip (*in bar, restaurant*)

pourparlers [purparle] NMPL talks, discussions, negotiations; **entrer en p.** to enter into *or* begin talks *or* discussions *or* negotiations (**avec** with); **nous sommes en p. avec le Japon** we're having talks *or* discussions with Japan, we're in negotiation with Japan; **p. de paix** peace talks

pourpier [purpje] NM *Bot* purslane

pourpoint [purpwɛ̃] NM *Hist* pourpoint, doublet

pourpre [purpr] NF **1** (*teinte naturelle*) purple (dye) **2** *Fig* (*symbole de haute dignité*) purple; **né dans la p.** born in *or* to the purple **NM 1** crimson, rich red; **le p. (de la honte) lui monta au visage** he/she turned crimson (with shame); *Physiol* **p. rétinien** visual purple **2** (*animal*) murex **ADJ** crimson; (*personne*) crimson, purple (**de rage** with rage)

pourpré [purpre] ADJ *Litt* crimson

pourquoi [purkwa] ADV, CONJ why; **p. cela?** why?; **p. êtes-vous venu?** why have you come?, what have you come for?; **dis-moi p. tell me why; mais p. donc?** but what on earth for?; **je voulais savoir p. (il était parti)** I wanted to know why (he had left); **voilà p.** that's (the reason) why; **c'est p. ...** and that's why ..., and so ...; **p. pas?, p. non?** why (ever) not?; **il a trouvé du travail, p. pas toi?** he's found a job, why haven't you?; **et p. ne pas aller voir un film?** why don't we go to see a film? VOIR GRAMMAIRE A41

NM INV (*raison*) reason (**de** for); **je ne sais**

pas le p. I don't know the reason why; **le p. et le comment** the whys and wherefores; **les p. des enfants** the questions that children ask

pourri [puri] ADJ **1** (*fruit*) rotten, bad; (*bois*) rotten; (*dent*) rotten, decayed; (*chair*) putrid; (*œufs*) bad; *Fam* (*corrompu*) (*chef, gouvernement etc*) corrupt; *Fam* **il est p. de vices** he's rotten to the core; *Fam* **ils sont pourris de fric** they're stinking rich, they're rolling in money; *Fam* **il est p. de talent** he's amazingly talented, he's bursting with talent **2** *Fam* (*insupportable*) (*ville, boulot, été, temps etc*) rotten; **cet enfant est p. gâté** that kid is spoiled rotten

NM 1 (*décomposition*) (*d'un fruit*) rotten *or* bad part; **sentir le p.** to smell rotten **2** *très Fam* (*terme injurieux*) bastard; **bande de pourris!** you bastards! **3** *Belg* (*paresseux*) lazy so-and-so

pourriel [purjɛl] NM *Ordinat* spam e-mail

pourrir [purir] VI to rot; (*d'un corps*) to putrefy, to decompose; (*de fruits, de la nourriture, d'œufs*) to go rotten, to go bad; **faire p.** to rot; *Fig* **p. en prison** to rot in prison; *Fig* **laisser p. les choses/la situation** to allow things/the situation to deteriorate; **laisser p. une grève** to allow a strike to drag on

VT **1** (*gâter*) (*fruits, bois*) to rot **2** *Fam* (*corrompre*) to spoil; **elle pourrit ses enfants en leur donnant tant d'argent** she's spoiling her children by giving them so much money; **elle me pourrit la vie** she's ruining my life **3** *Fam* (*dire du mal de*) to bad-mouth, *Br* to slag off

pourrissement [purismã] NM (*d'une situation*) deterioration

pourrissoir [puriswar] NM *Litt* muck heap

pourriture [purityr] NF **1** (*décomposition*) rotting, rot, decay; **p. sèche (du bois)** dry rot **2** (*état de décomposition*) rottenness; *Fig Fam* corruption **3** *très Fam* (*terme injurieux*) bastard

pour-soi NM INV *Phil* pour-soi

poursuite [pursɥit] NF **1** (*chasse*) pursuit; (*d'un criminel*) hunt (**de** for), pursuit, hunting, tracking (**de** of); **se mettre ou se lancer à la p. de qn** to set off in pursuit of sb, to chase after sb; **être à la p. de qch** (*bonheur, paix etc*) to be in pursuit *or* search of sth; (*travail, livre etc*) to be looking for sth; *Fig* **la p. du bonheur/de la sagesse** the pursuit of happiness/wisdom; *Cyclisme* (*course*) **p.** pursuit; *Cin* **scènes de p.** chase scenes **2** (*continuation*) continuation; **p. d'un travail** carrying on (with) a piece of work; **nous avons décidé de la p. de la grève** we've decided to continue the strike **3** *Électron* (*d'un avion, d'un missile etc*) tracking; **radar de p.** tracking radar **4** *Jur* **poursuites (judiciaires)** (legal) proceedings; (*en droit pénal*) prosecution; **engager** *ou* **entamer ou intenter des poursuites (judiciaires) contre qn** to start *or* institute (legal) proceedings against sb, to take legal action against sb; (*en droit pénal*) to prosecute sb; **s'exposer à des poursuites** to lay oneself open to prosecution **5** *Théâtre* (*projecteur*) follow spot

poursuiteur, -euse [pursɥitœr, -øz] N *Cyclisme* pursuit cyclist

poursuivant, -ante [pursɥivã, -ãt] ADJ *Jur* (*partie*) prosecuting

N **1** *Jur* plaintiff **2** (*personne qui poursuit*) pursuer

poursuivre [pursɥivr] (*conj like* **suivre**) VT **1** (*pourchasser*) (*personne, animal*) to pursue, to go after, to chase, to hunt (down); (*d'un songe, d'une idée, d'une crainte*) to haunt; **poursuivi par la malchance** dogged by bad luck **2** (*chercher à atteindre*) (*idéal, rêve, but*) to pursue, to chase (after) **3** (*harceler*) to pester, to plague (**de** with); (*débiteur*) to

hound, to harry; *Mil* (*ennemi*) to harry; **p. une femme de ses assiduités** to force one's attentions on a woman; **p. qn de sa colère** to vent *or* unleash one's anger on sb **4** *Jur* **p. (en justice)** to sue, to bring proceedings against, to take legal action against; (*en droit pénal*) to prosecute **5** (*continuer*) to pursue, to continue, to go on with, to proceed with; **p. un travail** to carry on (with) a piece of work

VI to go on, to continue; **poursuivez** (*votre histoire etc*) go on, continue; **bien, je poursuis ...** well, to continue ...

VPR **se poursuivre** (*de préparatifs, négociations etc*) to continue, to go on

pourtant [purtã] ADV yet, all the same; **un homme malade, et p. plein d'optimisme** a man who, though ill, is full of optimism; **il t'aime bien et p. s'il savait ...** he likes you and yet if he knew ...; **vous n'allez p. pas nous quitter?** you're surely not going to leave us?, you're not going to leave us though, are you?; **je ne peux p. pas l'empêcher de venir** all the same *or* even so, I can't stop him from coming; **je fume encore, p. j'aimerais bien m'arrêter** I still smoke, but I'd really like to stop; **tout avait p. bien commencé** and yet it all started so well; **ça n'est p. pas compliqué!** it's hardly complicated!; **on t'avait p. bien dit de ne pas y aller!** we *did* tell you not to go!; **les instructions étaient p. claires** the instructions were quite clear; **je sais que j'ai bien fait, et p. ...!** I know I did the right thing, and yet *or* but still ...!

pourtour [purtur] NM circumference, perimeter; **les pays du p. méditerranéen** the countries around the Mediterranean; **avec des rosiers sur le p.** with rose bushes around the edges

pourvoi [purvwa] NM *Jur* appeal; **p. en grâce** appeal for clemency; **p. en cassation** appeal to the Supreme Court

pourvoir [purvwar] (*prp* **pourvoyant**; *pp* **pourvu**; *pr ind* **je pourvois**, **n. pourvoyons**; *pr sub* **je pourvoie**; *impf* **je pourvoyais**; *p hist* **je pourvus**; *fu* **je pourvoirai**) VI **p. aux besoins de qn** to provide for *or* cater for *or* supply sb's needs; (*de façon plus immédiate*) to attend to *or* see to sb's needs; **p. à un emploi** to fill a job; **il y a un poste à p. à la comptabilité** there is a vacancy in Accounts; **on n'y a pas pourvu** no provision has been made for it

VT **p. qn de** to supply *or* provide *or Fml* furnish sb with; (*outils*) to equip sb with; **p. qn d'une charge** to appoint sb to an office; **être pourvu de tout l'équipement nécessaire** to be supplied *or* provided with all the necessary equipment; **nous étions bien pourvus pour la montagne** we were well equipped for the mountains; **p. une maison du chauffage central** to fit out *or* equip a house with central heating; **il est pourvu d'un grand talent** he is endowed with great talent; **la nature l'a pourvu d'une intelligence hors du commun** nature has endowed him with exceptional intelligence

VPR **se pourvoir 1** (*se munir*) to provide oneself (**de** with) **2** *Jur* to appeal, to lodge an appeal; **se p. en grâce** to appeal for clemency; **se p. en cassation** to take one's case to the Supreme Court of Appeal

pourvoyeur, -euse [purvwajœr, -øz] N supplier, provider, *Fml* purveyor; *Constr* contractor; **p. de drogue** drug dealer

pourvu que [purvykə] CONJ (+ *sub*) **1** (*exprimant une condition*) provided (that), so *or* as long as; **tu peux y aller p. tu sois rentré pour le dîner** you can go provided (that) *or* so long as *or* as long as you're back for dinner **2** (*exprimant un souhait*) **pourvu qu'il ne fasse pas de gaffes!** I just hope/let's just hope he won't make any blunders!; **p. ça dure!** let's just hope it lasts!

poussage [pusaʒ] NM *Tech* pushing

poussa(h) [pusa] NM *(jouet)* tumbler; *Fig (gros homme)* potbellied man

pousse [pus] NF **1** *(croissance) (des feuilles, des cheveux, des plumes)* growth; *(des dents)* cutting **2** *Bot (bourgeon)* (young) shoot, sprout; **p. de bambou** bamboo shoot; **cette plante a des pousses** this plant is putting out shoots **3** *Com* **jeune p. (d'entreprise)** start-up

poussé [puse] ADJ *(ornementation etc)* elaborate; *(étude)* thorough, searching, extensive; *(connaissances)* extensive; *(interrogatoire)* intensive; **il aboutit à un scepticisme assez p.** he carries scepticism to some lengths *or* rather far; **un pessimisme assez p.** a fairly deep pessimism; **faire des études très poussées** to pursue one's studies to a very advanced level; **des recherches très poussées** very advanced research; **des critiques très poussées** thoroughgoing criticism; *Aut* **moteur p.** hotted-up *or* souped-up engine

pousse-au-crime *Fam* ADJ INV that invites crime

NM INV **1 c'est du p.** it's an invitation to crime **2** *(eau-de-vie)* firewater, rotgut

pousse-café NM INV (glass of) liqueur *(after coffee)*

poussée [puse] NF **1** *(pression)*, *Phys* thrust; *(de liquide)* buoyancy; *(de la mer)* heave; **p. du vent** wind pressure; *Phys* **centre de p.** aerodynamic centre, centre of pressure; *(de liquide)* centre of buoyancy; *Phys* **axe de p.** aerodynamic axis; *Phys* **force de p.** upward thrust; **la p. de la foule** the pushing and shoving of the crowd **2** *(geste, fait de pousser qn)* push, shove; **écarter qch d'une p.** to push *or* shove sth aside **3** *(fait de croître)* growth; *Méd (accès) (de boutons, d'herpès)* eruption, outbreak; **p. de croissance** spurt of growth; **faire une p. de croissance** to shoot up; **p. de fièvre** sudden rise of *or* in temperature **4** *Fig (augmentation soudaine) (des prix, de l'inflation etc)* upsurge (**de** in)

pousse-pousse NM INV **1** rickshaw; **en p.** by rickshaw **2** *Suisse (poussette)* pushchair, *Am* stroller

POUSSER [puse]

| VT to push **1, 2** ▪ to shove **1** ▪ to urge on **2** ▪ to pursue **3** ▪ to grow **4** |
| VI to push **1** ▪ to push on **2** ▪ to grow **3** |
| VPR to move over **2** |

VT **1** *(soumettre à une force)* to push; *(rudement)* to shove; *(bétail)* to drive; *(bicyclette)* to push, to wheel; *(charrette, brouette)* to push (along); *(du vent) (embarcation)* to blow, to drive; **p. qn du coude/du genou** to nudge sb (with one's elbow/knee); **p. la porte/les volets** *(ouvrir)* to push the door/the shutters open; *(fermer)* to push the door/the shutters to; **on a poussé tous les meubles et on a dansé** we pushed all the furniture out of the way *or* aside and danced; **pousse un peu la chaise, je ne vois plus rien** push the chair out of the way *or* move the chair a bit, I can't see anything; **il poussa le moteur encore un peu plus** he pushed the engine a little harder, he squeezed a bit more out of the engine; **p. un pion** *(aux échecs)* to move a pawn; *Fig* **p. l'aiguille** to sew; *Fig Fam* **p. le bouchon trop loin** to go too far; *Fig Fam* **faut pas p. Mémé** *ou* **Mémère dans les orties!** don't push your luck!; *Fig Fam* **à la va comme je te pousse** slipshod; **fait à la va comme je te pousse** done in a slipshod way; *Fam* **pousse tes fesses** *ou* **très**

Fam **ton cul!** shift yourself!, shove over!

2 *(inciter) (quelqu'un)* to push, to urge on; *(cheval)* to urge on; **des élèves qu'il faut p.** pupils who need pushing *or* to be pushed; **il n'a pas fallu le p. beaucoup pour qu'il accepte** he didn't need much pushing *or* convincing to accept; **nous avons dû le p. à la roue pour qu'il …** we had to push him a bit to get him to …; **p. qn à faire qch** *(de la faim, la jalousie etc)* to drive sb to do sth, to lead sb to do sth; *(d'une personne) (contre son gré)* to push sb into doing sth; *(encourager)* to urge *or* encourage sb to do sth, to egg sb on to do sth; **p. qn à la dépense** to encourage sb to spend money; **les publicités sont faites pour p. à la consommation** advertisements are designed to encourage *or* stimulate consumption; **poussé par la pitié/la curiosité** prompted by pity/curiosity; *très Fam* **p. qn au cul** to give sb a kick up the back side **3** *(continuer) (études)* to pursue, to continue; **p. trop loin une plaisanterie** to take *or* carry a joke too far; **si l'on pousse encore plus loin cette explication/hypothèse** if we take this explanation/hypothesis further still; **p. qch jusqu'au bout** *ou* **jusqu'à l'extrême** to push *or* take sth to the limit; **il a même poussé la générosité jusqu'à …** he was so generous that he even …; **p. les enchères** to push up the bidding; **p. le chauffage/le son** to turn up the heating/volume; **p. le feu** to poke the fire; *Tech* **p. les feux** to raise steam, to stoke up

4 *(produire) (feuilles, racines)* to put out, to grow; *(d'un enfant) (dents)* to cut

5 *(exprimer)* **p. un cri** to shout, to give a shout; **p. des cris** to shout; **p. un cri de joie/de douleur** to shout with joy/pain, to give *or Fml* utter a shout of joy/pain; **p. un soupir** to sigh, to give *or* heave a sigh; **p. un gémissement** to groan, to moan, to give a groan *or* moan; **p. des acclamations** to cheer; **p. un juron** to swear; *Fam* **p. la chansonnette** *ou* **la romance, en p. une** to sing a song; *Fam* **il nous en a poussé une** he gave us a song; *très Fam* **p. une gueulante** to raise the roof, to kick up one hell of a stink

VI **1** *(faire un effort pour expulser qch)* to push; **ne poussez pas!** don't push!, don't shove!; *Fig* **p. à la roue** to do some pushing; *Fig Fam* **faut pas p.!** don't push your luck!; *Fam* **partir sans prévenir, vraiment, tu pousses!** going without saying anything, really, it's a bit much *or* you're taking things a bit too far!

2 *(continuer, avancer)* to push on; *Mil* to push forward; **p. jusqu'au bois** to push on as far as the wood

3 *(croître) (d'une plante, des cheveux, des ongles, d'une ville)* to grow; *(d'un bourgeon)* to sprout; *(des dents)* to come through; **laisser p. sa barbe** to grow a beard; **ses dents commencent à p.** his teeth are beginning to come through, he's beginning to cut his teeth; **p. comme du chiendent** to grow like a weed; **des villes qui ont poussé comme des champignons** towns that sprang up like mushrooms, towns that mushroomed; **tous ces enfants poussent** *(grandissent)* these children are all shooting up; **qu'est-ce qu'elle a poussé!** hasn't she grown!

4 *(inciter)* **p. à** to press *or* push for; **p. au changement** to press *or* push for change; **p. à la manifestation/la grève** to press *or* push for a demonstration/a strike; *Écon* **p. à la hausse/la baisse** to have an inflationary/a deflationary effect; **poussé par les profits** profit-driven

VPR **se pousser 1** *(se mettre en vue)* to push oneself forward; *(dans la société etc)* to make one's way

2 *(se presser) (pour faire de la place)* to move *or* shift over *or* up

3 *Can Fam (s'enfuir)* to take off, *Br* to scarper

poussette [pusɛt] NF *(voiture d'enfants)* pushchair, *Am* stroller; *(Caddie®)* shopping trolley *or Am* cart

pousseur [pusœr] NM **1** *(bateau)* tug **2** *Astronaut* booster rocket

poussier [pusje] NM coal dust, *Spéc* screenings; *(charbon)* slack

poussière [pusjɛr] NF dust; **une p.** a speck of dust; **p. d'or** gold dust; **enlever la p. des meubles** to dust the furniture; *Fam* **faire la p.** *ou* **les poussières** to do the dusting, to dust; **couvert de p.** covered in dust; **s'en aller** *ou* **tomber en p.** to crumble (away) to dust; **réduire qch en p.** to reduce sth to dust; *Fig* to demolish sth; **mordre la p.** to bite the dust; **je lui ferai mordre la p.** I'll wipe the floor with him; *Fam* **dix euros/jours et des poussières** ten and a bit euros/days, ten euros/days and a bit; **poussières radioactives** radioactive dust

poussiéreux, -euse [pusjerø, -øz] ADJ dusty; *Fig (terne)* dull, humdrum; *(dépassé)* outmoded

poussif, -ive [pusif, -iv] ADJ *(personne)* wheezy, short-winded; *(cheval)* broken-winded; *(moteur)* wheezy

poussin [pusɛ̃] NM *Zool* chick; *Culin* spring chicken; *Fam* **mon p.** pet

poussivement [pusivmɑ̃] ADV wheezily

poussoir [puswar] NM *(d'une sonnerie électrique)* (push) button; *Tech (d'une valve)* push rod; *Aut* tappet, cam follower; *Ordinat (de souris)* button; **p. à ressort** trigger

poutou [putu] NM *Fam (baiser)* kiss

poutrage [putraʒ] NM, **poutraison** [putrɛzɔ̃] NF *Constr* framework of beams

poutre [putr] NF *(en bois)* beam; **grosse p.** ba(u)lk; **p. de faîte** ridge piece, roof tree; **p. de plancher** ceiling joist; **poutres apparentes** exposed beams **2** *(en métal)* girder; **p. à âme pleine** plate girder; **p. à caisson** box girder; **p. maîtresse** main girder *or* beam

poutrelle [putrɛl] NF *Constr* girder

poutser [putse] VT *Suisse Fam* to clean

POUVOIR¹ [puvwar] NM **1** *(possibilité)* power, ability; **il n'est pas en mon p. de …** it is not within *or* it is beyond my power to …; **je ferai tout ce qui est en mon p.** I'll do everything (that's) in my power; **avoir le p. de faire qch** to have the power to do sth; **il a des pouvoirs surnaturels** he has supernatural powers

2 *Chimie, Phys etc (propriété)* **p. calorifique** calorific value; **p. rayonnant** radiating capacity; *Aut* **p. antidétonant** anti-knock rating; **p. absorbant** absorbency

3 *(puissance)* power; **p. politique** political power; **p. absolu** absolute power; **avoir un p. absolu sur qn** to have complete power over sb; **avoir un certain p. sur qn** to have (a certain) power over sb; **tenir qn en son p.** to have sb in one's power; **le p. des sens/des images/des mots** the power of the senses/of images/of words; **abuser de son p.** *ou* **de ses pouvoirs** to abuse one's power; **vouloir prendre le p.** to aim for power; **prendre le p.** to assume power; **arriver au p.** to come to power; **le parti au p.** the party in power; **quand les Libéraux sont au p.** when the Liberals are in (power); *Fig* **dans les milieux proches du p.** in the corridors of power; *Fig* **une affaire qui concerne le p.** a government matter; **huit ans de p.** eight years in power; **avoir un p. de décision** to have decision-making power *or* ability; **en vertu des pouvoirs qui me sont conférés …** by virtue of the powers invested in me …

4 *Jur (procuration)* power of attorney; **avoir/recevoir plein(s) pouvoir(s) pour agir** to have full powers/to be (fully) empowered *or* authorized to act; **se présenter sans pou-**

voirs réguliers to come without full credentials; **bon pour p.** good for proxy

▸▸ *Écon* **p. d'achat** purchasing power, buying power; **p. exécutif** executive power; **p. judiciaire** judicial power; *(les juges)* judiciary; **p. législatif** legislative power; **les pouvoirs publics** the authorities, the public authorities

---

POUVOIR² *(prp* **pouvant;** *pp* **pu;** *pr ind* **je peux, je puis** *(always* **puis-je** [pɥiʒ]*),* **tu peux, il peut, n. pouvons, ils peuvent;** *pr sub* **je puisse, n. puissions;** *impf* **je pouvais;** *p hist* **je pus;** *fu* **je pourrai** [pure]*)*

VT	to be able to **1** ▪ to be allowed to **2**
	▪ can **1–3** ▪ may **2–4** ▪ might **3**
V IMPERS	can, may, might

VT SEE GRAMMAR A58–60; B39–40 **1** *(être capable)* to be able; **faire tout ce qu'on peut** to do one's best, to do the best or all or everything one can; **si je peux** if I can, if I'm able to; **je ne peux pas** I can't, I'm unable to; **je ne peux (pas) le faire** I can't or cannot do it, I'm unable or not able to do it; **cela ne peut (pas) se faire** it can't or cannot be done; **comment a-t-il pu dire cela?** how could he say that?; **comment a-t-il pu?** how could he?; **il aurait pu le faire s'il avait voulu** he could have done it if he had wanted to; **si vous aviez pu le voir** if you could have seen him, if you'd been able to see him; **il ne pouvait pas l'accompagner** he couldn't go with him, he wasn't able or he was unable to go with him; **j'ai fait toutes les démarches que j'ai pu** I took every step that I possibly could; **j'ai pu le revoir** I managed or got or was able to see him again; **je n'y peux rien** I can't help it; **on n'y peut rien** it can't be helped, there's nothing that can be done about it; **il a été on ne peut plus grossier** he couldn't have been ruder, he was extremely rude; **des gens on ne peut plus aimables** extremely kind people; **il travaille on ne peut mieux** he's as good a worker as it's possible to be; **il n'en peut plus (de fatigue)** he's quite exhausted or worn out or tired out; **je n'en peux plus (de ses scènes/des voisins)** I've had enough or I can't take any more (of his scenes/the neighbours); **il n'en peut plus** *(d'impatience)* he can't take any more; **elle peut beaucoup** she's very capable; **sauve qui peut** every man for himself; **on ne peut pas ne pas l'admirer** you can't not admire him, you can't help but admire him, you have to admire him; **je viendrai aussitôt que je pourrai** I'll come as soon as I can or I'm able; **qu'est-ce qu'il peut bien me vouloir?** what(ever) can he want?; **où pouvait-il bien être à cette heure?** where(ver) could he be at this time?; **la loi ne peut rien contre lui** the law can't touch him; **nous ne pouvons rien pour vous** we can't do anything for you

2 *(avoir le droit, la permission (de))* to be allowed to; **vous pouvez partir** you can or *Fml* may go; **elle ne peut pas sortir seule** she can't go out alone, she isn't allowed out alone; **puis-je entrer?** can or *Fml* may I come in?; **quand pourrai-je emménager?** when can I move in?, when will I be able to move in?

3 *(être possible)* **la porte a pu se fermer toute seule** the door may have or could have closed on its own; **on peut se tromper, n'est-ce pas?** after all, we may or could be wrong; **nous pourrions le trouver si nous nous dépêchions** we might or could find him if we hurry; **elle pourrait le rencontrer, si elle le voulait** she could meet him if she wanted to; **elle peut bien s'excuser, je ne lui pardonnerai pas** she can apologize all she likes, but I shan't forgive her; **tout de même, vous auriez (bien) pu faire moins de bruit** all the

same, you could have or might have made less noise; **tu peux (bien) me raconter tout ce que tu veux ...** you can say what you like ...; **il pouvait être trois ou quatre heures du matin** it might have been three or four in the morning; *Fam* **qu'est-ce que ça peut (bien) te faire?** what's that got to do with you?

4 *Litt* **puisse-t-il défendre nos lois!** may he defend our laws!

V IMPERS **cela se peut (bien)** it may be or it could well be (the case), it's quite possible, maybe, possibly; **cela ne se peut pas** that's impossible, that's not possible; **ça se pourrait (bien)** that's quite possible; **advienne que pourra** come what may; **autant que faire se peut** as much as can/could be done; **il peut se faire** *ou* **il peut arriver que ... + *sub*** it may be or may happen that ...; **il se peut qu'il vienne** he may or might come; **il se peut qu'il ne soit pas coupable** he may not or might not be guilty

pp [pepe] **1** *abrév* **port payé 2** *(abrév* **par procuration)** *(à la fin d'une lettre)* pp

PPCM [pepeseɛm] NM *Math (abrév* **plus petit commun multiple)** LCM

ppm [pepeɛm] **1** *(abrév* **parties par million)** ppm **2** *(abrév* **pages par minute)** ppm

ppp [pepepe] NMPL *Ordinat (abrév* **pixels par pouce)** ppi

PQ [peky] NM **1** *Can Pol (abrév* **Parti Québécois)** PQ **2** *très Fam (papier hygiénique)* toilet paper, *Br* loo paper, *Br* bog roll

PR¹ [peɛr] *abrév* **poste restante**

PR² NM *abrév* **Parti Républicain**

pragmatique [pragmatik] ADJ pragmatic

pragmatisme [pragmatism] NM pragmatism

pragmatiste [pragmatist] ADJ, N pragmatist

Prague [prag] N Prague

praire [prɛr] NF clam

prairial [prɛrjal] NM *Hist* = ninth month of the French Republican Calendar (May-June)

prairie [preri] NF *(pré, champ)* meadow; *(large étendue)* grassland, *Am* prairie; **p. artificielle** cultivated grassland; *Géog* **la P.** the Prairies

pralin [pralɛ̃] NM *Culin* praline

praline [pralin] NF **1** *Culin* praline; *Péj Fam* **cucul la p.** silly, idiotic **2** *Fam (balle d'arme à feu)* bullet, slug

praliné [praline] ADJ *Culin (chocolat)* praline-filled; *(crème, glace)* praline-flavoured; **amandes pralinées** = almonds coated in caramelized sugar

praticable [pratikabl] ADJ *(possible, réalisable)* practicable; *Théâtre (porte, fenêtre)* practicable; *(projet, idée)* feasible, practicable; *(route etc)* passable, negotiable

▪ NM *Théâtre (décor)* practicable scenery; *Cin, TV* dolly

praticien, -ienne [pratisjɛ̃, -jɛn] N **1** *Jur (legal)* practitioner; *Méd (medical)* practitioner **2** *(technicien)* practitioner **3** *Beaux-Arts (ouvrier)* sculptor's assistant

praticité [pratisite] NF *(caractère pratique)* practicality

pratiquant, -ante [pratikã, -ãt] *Rel* ADJ practising; **catholique p.** practising Catholic; **il est très p.** he's very religious, he's a strong believer; *(d'un chrétien)* he's a regular churchgoer, he goes to church regularly

▪ N religious person; *(chrétien)* (regular) churchgoer

pratique [pratik] ADJ *(méthode, personne etc)* practical; *(gadget, outil etc)* practical, handy; *(date, heure, jour)* convenient; **avoir l'esprit p.** to have a practical turn of mind, to be practically minded; **sens p.** practical

common sense; **c'est très p. d'avoir l'école si près de la maison** it's very practical or handy to have the school so close to the house; **cette crème n'est pas p. à appliquer** this cream isn't easy to apply

▪ NF **1** *(application)* practice; **mettre qch en p.** to put sth into practice; **c'est une p. courante** it's common practice, it's quite usual; **la théorie et la p.** theory and practice; **en p.** in practice

2 *(expérience)* (practical) experience; *Litt (de la vertu)* practice; **p. du théâtre** theatrical experience; **la p. du football m'a valu une jambe cassée** I got a broken leg or I broke my leg (through) playing football; **la p. d'un sport est encouragée** sporting activity or practising a sport is encouraged; **perdre la p. de qch** to lose the knack of sth; *(d'un sport, d'une activité)* to get out of practice at sth; **avoir une grande** *ou* **longue p. de qch** to have a lot of (practical) experience of sth

3 *Jur (de la loi)* practice; **terme de p.** legal term

4 *(action)* practice; **pratiques clandestines** underhand practices; **pratiques religieuses** religious practices; *Com* **pratiques restrictives** restrictive practices; **la p. de ce genre de vente est illégale en France** this kind of sales practice is illegal in France; *Jur* **libre p.** *(de sa religion etc)* free exercise; *Naut* **avoir libre p.** to be out of quarantine

5 *(d'avocat, de médecin)* practice; *(de fournisseur)* custom, business; *Vieilli (clientèle) (d'un avocat)* clients; *(d'un médecin)* patients; *(d'un fournisseur)* customers

6 *Arch* **il avait vécu dans la p. des hauts fonctionnaires** he had associated with high-ranking civil servants

pratiquement [pratikmã] ADV *(dans l'expérience)* in practice; *(en fait)* in actual fact; *(presque)* practically, virtually; **il ne vient p. jamais plus** he practically never comes any more

pratiquer [pratike] VT **1** *(exercer) (activité, sorcellerie, vertu, charité, religion etc)* to practise; *(méthode)* to employ, to use; *(langue)* to use; **il pratique le football** he plays football; **elle pratique la natation** she's a (keen) swimmer, she swims; **elle ne pratique aucun sport** she doesn't do or take part in or practise any sport; **il a appris le piano mais ne pratique plus beaucoup** he learnt the piano but doesn't play it much any more; *Com* **les cours pratiqués** the ruling prices; **les prix pratiqués ici** the prices being asked here **2** *Méd* **p. une intervention** to carry out an operation, to operate; **p. une petite incision** to make a small incision **3** *(ménager)* to make; **p. une ouverture dans un mur** to make an opening in a wall; **p. un sentier** to make a path, to open up a path **4** *(livre, auteur)* to study **5** *Arch (fréquenter)* to frequent, to associate with

▪ VI **1** *(travailler) (d'un médecin, avocat, conseiller)* to practise; **il ne pratique plus** he's no longer in practice, he no longer practises **2** *Rel* to observe the practices of one's religion; **ils sont catholiques mais ne pratiquent pas** they're Catholics but not practising Catholics

▪ VPR **se pratiquer** to be practised; **le commerce de l'ivoire se pratique encore** ivory trading still goes on or is still practised; **les mariages arrangés ne se pratiquent plus** arranged marriages no longer take place; **voilà comment ça se pratique** that's how it's done

praxis [praksis] NF praxis

pré [pre] NM meadow; *Arch* **aller sur le p.** to fight a duel

pré-acheminement, *pl* **pré-acheminements** [preaʃ(ə)minmã] NM transfer to main airport

préadhésion [preadezjɔ̃] NF *UE* pre-accession

préadolescence [preadɔlesɑ̃s] NF preadolescence

préadolescent, -ente [preadɔlesɑ̃, -ɑ̃t] N preadolescent, preteen

préalable [prealabl] ADJ previous, prior (**à** to); *(accord)* prior; **formalités préalables au débat** formalities that precede the debate; **mais il y a quelques formalités préalables** but there are a few formalities to be gone through first ▪ NM **1** *(condition)* prerequisite, precondition; **préalables d'un accord** pre-contract conditions; **au p.** first, beforehand **2** *Arch (préparation)* preliminary

préalablement [prealabləmɑ̃] ADV first, beforehand; **p. à …** prior to …

pré-allumage [prealymaʒ] NM *Aut* pre-ignition

Préalpes (les) [leprealp] NFPL the foothills of the Alps

préalpin [prealpɛ̃] ADJ of the foothills of the Alps

préambule [preɑ̃byl] NM *(d'un discours)* preamble (**de** to); *(d'une action)* prelude (**de** to); **il a abordé le sujet sans p.** he (dispensed with preliminaries and) came straight to the point; **sans p., elle lui a demandé son âge** she asked him straight off how old he was

préamplificateur [preɑ̃plifikatœr] NM *Électron* preamplifier

PréAO [preao] NF *Ordinat (abrév présentation assistée par ordinateur)* computer-assisted presentation

préapprentissage [preaprɑ̃tisaʒ] NM pre-apprenticeship training

préau, -aux [preo] NM **1** *(cour intérieure)* (court)yard **2** *(partie couverte)* covered part (of the playground)

préavis [preavi] NM (previous or advance) notice; **exiger un p. de trois mois** to require three months' notice; **sans p.** without notice or warning; **p. de licenciement** notice (of dismissal); **p. de paiement** payment advice; **p. de grève** strike notice; **déposer un p. de grève** to give notice of strike action

prébende [prebɑ̃d] NF *Rel* prebend; *Fig (profit)* sizeable income

prébendé [prebɑ̃de] ADJ *Rel* prebendal

prébendier [prebɑ̃dje] NM *Rel* prebendary

précaire [prekɛr] ADJ *(position, état de santé)* precarious; *(santé)* delicate; *(abri)* precarious, rickety; *(emploi)* insecure; **être dans un équilibre un peu p.** to be rather precariously balanced

précairement [prekɛrmɑ̃] ADV precariously

précambrien, -ienne [prekɑ̃brijɛ̃, -jɛn] ADJ *Géol* Precambrian, Pre-Cambrian

précarisation [prekarizasjɔ̃] NF jeopardizing; **p. de l'emploi** casualization of labour

précariser [prekarize] VT to jeopardize

précarité [prekarite] NF precariousness; **p. de l'emploi** lack of job security

précaution [prekosjɔ̃] NF **1** *(mesure)* precaution; **prendre des** *ou* **ses précautions** to take precautions (**pour** for); *Euph* **prendre ses précautions** to go *(to the toilet)*; **mesures de p.** precautionary measures; **par (mesure de) p.** as a precaution; **précautions oratoires** carefully chosen remarks; *Prov* **deux précautions valent mieux qu'une** you can never be too sure, better safe than sorry **2** *(soin)* caution, wariness, care; **avec p.** cautiously, warily, carefully; **pour plus de p.** to be extra safe, to be on the safe side, to err on the side of caution

précautionner [prekosjɔne] VT *Arch* to warn, to caution (**contre** against) ▪ VPR **se précautionner** to take precautions; **se p. contre qch** to take precautions *or* guard against sth

précautionneusement [prekosjɔnøzmɑ̃] ADV carefully

précautionneux, -euse [prekosjɔnø, -øz] ADJ careful

précédemment [presedamɑ̃] ADV previously, before

précédent [presedɑ̃] ADJ previous; **le jour/mois p.** the day/month before, the previous day/month ▪ NM precedent; **créer un p.** to create *or* set a precedent; **sans p.** unprecedented, without precedent

précéder [presede] *(conj like* **céder***)* VT to precede; **la musique précède les troupes** the band marches in front of *or* precedes the troops; **il me précédait pour me guider** he went in front of *or* preceded me in order to guide me; **l'antichambre qui précède le salon** the antechamber leading to the drawing room; **je l'ai précédé de 10 minutes** I got there ten minutes before he did *or* before him *or* ahead of him; **nous serons précédés de quelques jours par nos enfants** our children will get there a few days before we do *or* before us *or* ahead of us; **le scandale a précédé la révélation de l'affaire** the scandal occurred before the affair came to light; **sa réputation le précédait** his reputation went before *or* preceded him; **p. qn (en dignité)** to have precedence over sb; **faire p. un concert d'un discours** to preface a concert with a speech ▪ VI **la page qui précède** the preceding *or* previous page, the page before; **dans les jours qui précèdent** in the days before, in the preceding days; **ce qui précède** the foregoing

précepte [presɛpt] NM precept

précepteur, -trice [preseptœr, -tris] N (private) tutor

préceptorat [preseptɔra] NM tutorship

précession [presesjɔ̃] NF precession

préchambre [preʃɑ̃br] NF *Tech (d'un moteur diesel)* precombustion chamber

précharge [preʃarʒ] NF *Aut* pre-load

préchargé [preʃarʒe] ADJ *(logiciel)* pre-loaded

préchauffage [preʃofaʒ] NM pre-heating; *(d'un appareil)* warm-up; **p. moteur diesel** pre-heating

préchauffer [preʃofe] VT to pre-heat

prêche [prɛʃ] NM sermon

prêcher [preʃe] VT *(enseigner)* to preach (**à** to); **p. qn** to preach to sb; **p. l'économie** to preach economy; *Iron* **p. la bonne parole** to spread the good word; **p. un converti** to preach to the converted *or Am* to the choir ▪ VI *(prononcer un sermon)* to preach; *Fig (moraliser)* to preach, to preachify, to sermonize; *Rel, Fig* **p. dans le désert** to be a voice crying in the wilderness; **p. d'exemple** *ou* **par l'exemple** to practise what one preaches; *Fig* **p. pour sa paroisse** to look after one's own interests

prêcheur, -euse [preʃœr, -øz] ADJ **1** *(moine)* preaching **2** *(moralisateur) (personne)* sermonizing ▪ N *Fig Péj* sermonizer, preacher

prêchi-prêcha [preʃipreʃa] NM INV *Fam Péj* preaching, preachifying, sermonizing

précieusement [presjøzmɑ̃] ADV **1** *(avec soin)* very carefully; **garder** *ou* **conserver qch p.** to treasure sth **2** *(avec préciosité)* preciously, affectedly

précieux, -ieuse [presjø, -jøz] ADJ **1** *(d'une grande valeur)* precious; **pierre précieuse** precious stone **2** *(conseil, temps etc)* valuable (**à** to) **3** *Litt (style)* precious, affected, mannered ▪ NF *Hist, Littér* **précieuse** = pedantic, over-refined woman

préciosité [presjozite] NF *Litt* affectation, affectedness, preciosity

précipice [presipis] NM chasm, abyss; *(bord d'une falaise, d'un ravin etc)* precipice; *Fig* abyss; **au bord d'un p.** on the edge of a precipice; *Fig* **être au bord du p.** to be on the brink, to be on the edge of a precipice

précipitamment [presipitamɑ̃] ADV hurriedly, hastily, *Fml* precipitately; **entrer/sortir p.** to rush *or* hurry *or* dash in/out; **agir trop p.** to be too hasty *or Fml* precipitate, to be overhasty, to act too hastily *or Fml* precipitately

précipitation [presipitasjɔ̃] NF **1** *(grande hâte)* haste, great hurry, *Fml* precipitation; **avec p.** hurriedly, hastily, *Fml* precipitately; **entrer/sortir avec p.** to hurry *or* rush *or* dash in/out **2** *Chimie, Phys* precipitation **3** *Météo* **précipitations** precipitation

précipité [presipite] ADJ *(action, décision)* hasty, hurried, *Fml* precipitate; *(départ)* hasty, hurried, abrupt; *(pouls)* racing; **s'avancer à pas précipités** to rush forward; **un bruit de pas précipités** (the sound of) hurried *or* quick footsteps ▪ NM *Chimie* precipitate

précipiter [presipite] VT **1** *(entraîner)* to throw down, to hurl down; *Fig* to plunge; **p. qn contre un mur/dans le vide** to hurl sb against a wall/over the edge; *Fig* **p. qn dans le désespoir/le malheur** to plunge sb into despair/misfortune; **p. un peuple dans la guerre** to plunge a nation into war **2** *(dépêcher, hâter) (un achat, une embauche, un mariage etc)* to speed up; *(événements)* to precipitate; *(la mort de qn, la perte de qn)* to hasten; **il ne faut rien p.** we mustn't rush things, we mustn't be overhasty **3** *Chimie (substance)* to precipitate ▪ VI *Chimie (d'une substance)* to precipitate, to form a precipitate ▪ VPR **se précipiter 1** *(se hâter)* to rush, to hurry **2** *(s'accélérer)* **les événements se sont précipités** things started happening quickly **3** *(se jeter)* to rush (**sur** at; **vers** towards); **se p. à la fenêtre** to rush to the window; **se p. aux pieds de qn** to throw oneself at sb's feet; **dès qu'il rentre à la maison, il se précipite devant la télévision** as soon as he gets home, he throws himself down in front of the television; **le fleuve se précipite dans la mer** the river rushes into the sea **4** *Chimie* to precipitate

précis [presi] ADJ *(description, vocabulaire, plan, but etc)* precise, exact; **à cet instant p.** at this precise *or* exact moment; **exiger d'une façon précise que …** to call unambiguously for …; **à deux heures précises** at two o'clock precisely *or* exactly *or* sharp; **je suis parti sans raison précise** I left for no definite reason *or* for no particular reason; **en termes p.** in precise terms, precisely; **il est très p. dans son travail** he's very meticulous *or* precise *or* exact in his work; **des gestes p.** precise movements; **pensez-vous à quelque chose de p.?** do you have something specific in mind?; **pour être plus p.** to be more precise ▪ NM précis, summary, abstract; *(livre)* handbook; **p. d'histoire de France** short history of France

précisément [presizemɑ̃] ADV **1** *(exactement)* precisely, exactly; **ou plus p. …** or more precisely …, or to be more precise …; **ce n'est pas p. une réussite** it's not exactly a success, it's not (exactly) what you'd call a success; **a-t-il dit cela? – oui, p.** did he say that? – yes, those were his very words **2**

(justement) **c'est p. l'homme que je cherche** he's just the man I'm looking for; **c'est p. ce que je lui disais** that's just *or* exactly what I said to him/her; **p. il m'en fallait un aujour-d'hui** as it happens *or* as a matter of fact, I needed one today

préciser [presize] VT **1** *(déterminer) (prix, date, informations)* to specify; **il faut p. vos affirmations/arguments** you must be (more) explicit *or* specific in your state-ments/arguments **2** *(rendre plus net)* to clarify; **je tiens à p. que ...** I wish to make it clear that ...; **p. la date de la réunion** to give the exact *or* precise date of the meeting; **la circulaire ne précise pas où aura lieu la réu-nion** the circular doesn't specify where the meeting will take place; **il n'a pas été précisé qu'il fallait être en tenue de soirée** it wasn't specifically stated that evening dress was to be worn, evening dress wasn't specified
   VI to be (more) precise *or* explicit
   VPR **se préciser** to become clear(er); *(des idées, d'un contrat)* to take shape; **les vacan-ces se précisent** the holiday plans are taking shape

précision [presizjɔ̃] NF **1** *(exactitude) (d'in-formation, d'une description, d'un travail)* ac-curacy; *(de mouvements)* preciseness, pre-cision; **avec p.** accurately, precisely; **p. de tir** accuracy of fire; *Typ* **p. de frappe** key-ing accuracy; **instruments de p.** precision instruments **2 une p.** a (precise) detail, a (point of) clarification; **donner** *ou* **apporter des précisions sur qch** to give precise details about sth; **demander des précisions sur qch** to ask for more *or* further information *or* de-tails about sth; **merci de ces précisions** thank you for this information

précité [presite] ADJ aforesaid, aforemen-tioned; *(plus haut sur une page, dans un document)* above(-mentioned)

préclassique [preklasik] ADJ *Hist* preclas-sical

précoce [prekɔs] ADJ *(enfant)* precocious; *(fruit, gel)* early; *(sénilité, calvitie)* prema-ture; **l'été est p. cette année** summer is early this year; **enfant p. pour son âge** child who is advanced *or* precocious for his age; **se-xuellement p.** sexually precocious

précocement [prekɔsmɑ̃] ADV *Litt* preco-ciously

précocité [prekɔsite] NF precociousness, precocity; *(de fruits, d'une saison etc)* earliness; **p. sexuelle** sexual precocious-ness

précolombien, -ienne [prekɔlɔ̃bjɛ̃, -jɛn] ADJ *Hist* pre- Columbian

précombustion [prekɔ̃bystjɔ̃] NF *Tech* precombustion

précommercialisation [prekɔmɛrsjali-zasjɔ̃] NF *Mktg* pre-marketing

précomptabilisation [prekɔ̃tabilizasjɔ̃] NF preparation of accounting entries

précompte [prekɔ̃t] NM *(d'un compte, d'un salaire)* (advance) deduction

précompter [prekɔ̃te] VT to deduct, to with-hold (**sur** from)

préconception [prekɔ̃sɛpsjɔ̃] NF precon-ception; *(contre quelqu'un, quelque chose)* prejudice

préconçu [prekɔ̃sy] ADJ preconceived; *Péj* **idée préconçue** preconceived idea

préconditionné [prekɔ̃disjɔne] ADJ pre-packed, pre-packaged

préconditionner [prekɔ̃disjɔne] VT to pre-pack, to pre-package

préconfiguré [prekɔ̃figyre] ADJ *Ordinat* preconfigured

préconisation [prekɔnizasjɔ̃] NF recom-mendation

préconiser [prekɔnize] VT to recommend, to advocate; *(remède)* to recommend

précontraint [prekɔ̃trɛ̃] ADJ, NM *Tech* **(bé-ton) p.** prestressed concrete

précouche [prekuʃ] NF precoating

précuit [prekɥi] ADJ pre-cooked, ready-cooked

précurseur [prekyrsœr] NM precursor, fore-runner
   ADJ precursory; **signe p.** forewarning, portent

prédateur, -trice [predatœr, -tris] ADJ pre-datory
   NM predator

prédécesseur [predesesœr] NM predeces-sor

prédécoupé [predekupe] ADJ pre-cut, rea-dy-cut

prédéfinition NF *Ordinat* **p. des secteurs** hard sectoring

prédélinquant, -ante [predelɛ̃kɑ̃, -ɑ̃t] N potential delinquent

prédestination [predɛstinasjɔ̃] NF predes-tination

prédestiné [predɛstine] ADJ predestined, fated (**à faire qch** to do sth); **p. à qch** predes-tined for sth

prédestiner [predɛstine] VT to predestine (**à faire qch** to do sth; **à qch** sth)

prédétermination [predetɛrminasjɔ̃] NF predetermination

prédéterminer [predetɛrmine] VT to prede-termine

prédicant [predikɑ̃] NM *Rel* preacher

prédicat [predika] NM *Gram* predicate

prédicateur, -trice [predikatœr, -tris] N preacher

prédicatif, -ive [predikatif, -iv] ADJ *Gram* predicative

prédication [predikasjɔ̃] NF **1** *Rel* preaching; *(sermon)* sermon **2** *Gram* predication

prédiction [prediksjɔ̃] NF **1** *(action de pré-dire)* prediction, predicting, foretelling **2** *(ce qui est prédit)* prediction, forecast

prédigéré [prediʒere] ADJ predigested

prédilection [predilɛksjɔ̃] NF predilection, partiality, fondness; **auteur/restaurant de p.** favourite *or Am* favorite author/restaur-ant; **avoir une p. pour qch** to be partial to sth, to have a predilection *or* fondness for sth

prédire [predir] VT *(conj like* **dire** *except pr ind & imp* (v.) **prédisez**) to predict, to proph-esy, to foretell; **p. qch à qn** to predict sth for sb; **p. que** to predict that

prédisposer [predispoze] VT to predispose (**à qch** to sth; **à faire qch** to do sth)

prédisposition [predispozisjɔ̃] NF predis-position (**à** to)

prédominance [predɔminɑ̃s] NF predom-inance

prédominant [predɔminɑ̃] ADJ predominant

prédominer [predɔmine] VI to predomi-nate; *(d'une préoccupation)* to be upper-most; **ce qui prédomine chez lui, c'est la générosité** generosity is his chief quality

préélectoral, -ale, -aux, -ales [preelɛkt-ɔral, -o] ADJ *Pol* pre-electoral, pre-election

préemballé [preɑ̃bale] ADJ pre-packed

préemballer [preɑ̃bale] VT to pre-pack, to pre-package

pré-embarquement [preɑ̃barkəmɑ̃] NM *(à un aéroport)* pre-boarding

pré-embarquer [preɑ̃barke] VI *(à un aéro-port)* to pre-board

prééminence [preeminɑ̃s] NF pre-emin-ence

prééminent [preeminɑ̃] ADJ pre-eminent

préempter [preɑ̃pte] VT *Jur* to pre-empt

préemption [preɑ̃psjɔ̃] NF *Jur* pre-emption

préencollé [preɑ̃kɔle] ADJ *(papier peint)* pre-pasted, ready-pasted

préenregistré [preɑ̃r(ə)ʒistre] ADJ *TV, Radio* pre-recorded

préenregistrement [preɑ̃rəʒistrəmɑ̃] NM *(à un aéroport)* pre-registration; *TV, Radio* pre-recording

préétablir [preetablir] VT to pre-establish

préexistant [preɛgzistɑ̃] ADJ pre-existing, pre-existent

préexistence [preɛgzistɑ̃s] NF pre-existence

préexister [preɛgziste] VI to pre-exist; **p. à qch** to exist *or* be in existence before sth

préfabrication [prefabrikasjɔ̃] NF prefab-rication

préfabriqué [prefabrike] ADJ prefabricated; *Fig Péj* **sourire p.** artificial smile; **candidat p.** packaged candidate
   NM *(maison)* prefabricated house, *Fam* prefab

préface [prefas] NF **1** *(avant-propos)* pre-face, foreword (**à, de** to) **2** *Rel* preface

préfacer [prefase] VT to write a preface to *or* for, to preface

préfacier [prefasje] NM preface writer

préfacturation [prefaktyrasjɔ̃] NF *Compta* prebilling

préfectoral, -ale, -aux, -ales [pre-fɛktɔral, -o] ADJ *Admin* prefectorial

préfecture [prefɛktyr] NF *Admin* prefecture; **la P. de police** police headquarters; **p. mari-time** = area under command of a port admi-ral; *(bureau)* naval superintendent's office, port admiral's office

---

Préfecture

This refers to the main administrative office of each "département". The word has also come to refer to the town where the office is located. One goes to the "préfecture" to obtain a driving licence or a "carte de séjour", for example.

---

préférable [preferabl] ADJ preferable (**à** to); **il serait p. de le revoir** *ou* **qu'on le revoie** it would be preferable *or* better to see him again

préférablement [preferabləmɑ̃] ADV preferably

préféré, -ée [prefere] ADJ, N favourite, *Am* favorite

préférence [preferɑ̃s] NF preference; **de p.** preferably; **de p. à ...** in preference to ...; **donner** *ou* **accorder la p. à qn** to give sb pre-ference (**sur** over); **il n'a pas de p.** he has no (particular) preference; **par ordre de p.** in order of preference; *Jur* **droits de p.** priority rights; *Fin* **actions de p.** preference shares, *Am* preferred stock; **la p. nationale** policy of discrimination in favour of a country's own nationals *(as opposed to immigrants)*; *Ordi-nat* **préférences** preferences

préférentiel, -ielle [preferɑ̃sjɛl] ADJ prefe-rential; *Jur* **vote p.** preferential voting (sys-tem); **tarif p.** preferential rate

préférer [prefere] VT (**je préfère; je préfére-rai**) to prefer (**à** to); **je préférerais du thé** I'd prefer tea, I'd rather have tea; **je préférerais que vous veniez** I'd prefer it if you came, I'd rather you came; **p. faire qch** to prefer to do sth; **il préféra mourir plutôt que de se ren-dre** he preferred to die rather than surren-der, he died rather than surrender; **je préfère ne pas y aller** I'd rather not go, I'd prefer not to go

préfet [prefɛ] NM *Admin* prefect; **p. de police** = chief commissioner of police; *Naut* **p. maritime** port admiral, commander-in-chief of the port

préfète [prefɛt] NF *Admin* prefect; *(épouse)* prefect's wife

préfiguration [prefigyrasjɔ̃] NF prefiguration, foreshadowing

préfigurer [prefigyre] VT to prefigure, to foreshadow

préfinancement [prefinɑ̃smɑ̃] NM *Fin* advance funding, pre-financing

préfixal, -ale, -aux, -ales [prefiksal, -o] ADJ *Gram* prefixal

préfixation [prefiksasjɔ̃] NF *Gram* prefixation

préfixe [prefiks] NM *Ling, Tél* prefix

préfixer [prefikse] VT to prefix

préformaté [preformate] ADJ *Ordinat* preformatted

préformater [preformate] VT *Ordinat* to preformat

pré-gardiennat [pregardjɛna] NM *Belg (jardin d'enfants)* nursery school, *Am* kindergarten

préglaciaire [preglasjɛr] ADJ *Géol* preglacial

préhellénique [preelenik] ADJ pre-Hellenic

préhenseur [preɑ̃sœr] ADJ M prehensile

préhensile [preɑ̃sil] ADJ prehensile

préhension [preɑ̃sjɔ̃] NF gripping, *Spéc* prehension

préhistoire [preistwar] NF prehistory

préhistorique [preistɔrik] ADJ prehistoric

préimpression [preɛ̃presjɔ̃] NF *Typ* pre-press

préimprimé [preɛ̃prime] NM preprinted form

préimprimée [preɛ̃prime] NF preprinted form

préimputation [preɛ̃pytasjɔ̃] NF *Compta* pre-input preparation

préindustriel, -ielle [preɛ̃dystrijɛl] ADJ pre-industrial

préinscription [preɛ̃skripsjɔ̃] NF pre-check-in

préinstallé [preɛ̃stale] ADJ *Ordinat* preinstalled

préinstaller [preɛ̃stale] VT *Ordinat* to preinstall

préjudice [preʒydis] NM *(à une cause, à la situation de qn etc)* prejudice, detriment; *(à une personne)* harm, wrong, injury; *(aux perspectives de qn)* damage; *Jur* tort; **subir un p. (matériel)** to sustain damage; **subir un p. (moral)** to be wronged; **porter p. à qn** to do sb harm; *(d'une action, d'une déclaration)* to be prejudicial to sb's interests; **p. financier** financial harm; **au p. de qn** to the prejudice or detriment of sb; **au p. de la justice** at the expense of justice; **sans p. de …** without prejudice to …

> Il faut noter que le terme anglais **prejudice** est un faux ami. Il signifie le plus souvent **préjugé**.

préjudiciable [preʒydisjabl] ADJ prejudicial, detrimental, harmful (**à** to)

préjudiciel, -ielle [preʒydisjɛl] ADJ *Jur (question)* interlocutory; *(action)* prejudicial

préjudicier [preʒydisje] VI *(pr sub, impf n. préjudiciions) Arch, Litt* to be detrimental or prejudicial (**à** to)

préjugé [preʒyʒe] NM *(opinion toute faite)* prejudice, bias; **p. de classe** class prejudice; **préjugés raciaux** racial prejudice; **avoir un p. pour** ou **envers/contre qn/qch** to be prejudiced or bias(s)ed in favour or *Am* favor

of/against sb/sth; **elle avait un p. favorable à son égard** he had created a favourable or *Am* favorable impression upon her; **bénéficier d'un p. favorable** *(dans une course)* to look a likely winner; *(avoir bonne réputation)* to be well thought of

préjuger [preʒyʒe] VI *(conj like juger)* **p. de qch** to prejudge sth; **autant qu'on peut en p.** as far as one can judge beforehand or in advance; **il ne faut jamais p. de l'avenir** you can't tell what the future has in store

prélart [prelar] NM tarpaulin

prélasser (se) [səprelase] VPR to lounge, to loll; *(au soleil)* to bask

prélat [prela] NM prelate

prélature [prelatyr] NF prelacy

prélavage [prelavaʒ] NM prewash

prèle, prêle [prɛl] NF *Bot* horsetail

prélèvement [prelɛvmɑ̃] NM **1** *Fin (action)* deduction, withholding (**sur** from); **p. sur le capital** ou **sur la fortune** capital levy; **faire un p. sur un compte** to debit an account; **p. fiscal** tax deduction; **p. de l'impôt à la source** taxation at source; **p. salarial** deduction from wages; **prélèvements sociaux** social security contributions **2** *Ind (action)* sampling; *(échantillon)* sample; **nous procéderons ensuite à un p. d'échantillons** next we shall proceed to take some samples **3** *Méd (action)* sampling; *(échantillon)* sample; *(d'un organe)* removal; *(de sécrétion)* swab; **faire un p. à qn** to take a sample from sb; **faire un p. de sang** ou **sanguin à qn** to take a blood sample from sb
▸▸ **Banque p. automatique** direct debit; **prélèvements obligatoires** = tax and social security contributions

prélever [prelve] VT *(conj like lever)* **1** *(somme d'argent)* to deduct, to withhold (**sur** from); *(impôt)* to levy; **p. des taxes** to withhold taxes, to deduct taxes; **p. une commission de deux pour cent** to deduct or charge a commission of two per cent; **p. qch à la source** to deduct sth at source **2** *(organe)* to remove; **p. un échantillon** to take a sample; **p. du sang** to take a blood sample; **p. un morceau de tissu organique** to take a sample of organic tissue

préliminaire [preliminɛr] ADJ preliminary
NMPL **préliminaires** preliminaries; *(discussions)* preliminary talks; *Typ* prelims

prélude [prelyd] NM *Mus, Fig* prelude (**de, à** to)

préluder [prelyde] VI *Mus* to warm up; *(jouer un prélude)* to play a prelude; *Fig* **p. à qch** to serve as or be a prelude to sth

prémaquette [premakɛt] NF rough layout

prématuré, -ée [prematyre] ADJ premature; *(mort)* premature, untimely; **il est p. de l'annoncer** it's too early to announce it, an announcement would be premature; **être p. de six semaines** *(de bébé)* to be six weeks premature or early
N premature baby

prématurément [prematyremɑ̃] ADV prematurely

prématurité [prematyrite] NF prematureness, prematurity

prémédication [premedikasjɔ̃] NF *Méd* premedication, *Fam* premed

prémédiquer [premedike] VT *Méd* to premedicate

préméditation [premeditasjɔ̃] NF premeditation; *Jur* **avec p.** *(agir, tuer)* with premeditation, with malice aforethought; **meurtre avec p.** premeditated murder; **meurtre sans p.** unpremeditated murder, murder without premeditation

préméditer [premedite] VT to premeditate; **elle n'avait pas prémédité de lui demander**

de rester she hadn't planned or intended to ask him to stay

prémenstruel, -elle [premɑ̃stryɛl] ADJ premenstrual; **syndrome p.** premenstrual tension or syndrome, PMT

prémices [premis] NFPL **1** *Hist (fruits)* first fruits **2** *Litt (début)* early beginnings

> Il faut noter que le nom anglais **premises** est un faux ami. Il signifie **locaux**. Do not confuse with **prémisse**.

PREMIER, -IÈRE [prəmje, -jɛr] ADJ **1** *(initial)* first; **le p. jour du mois** the first day of the month; **les trois premières années** the first three years; **les premières heures du matin** the early hours (of the morning), the (wee) small hours; **enseignement du p. degré** primary education; **professeurs du p. degré** primary(-school) teachers; **les premiers temps, elle n'osait pas parler** at first she didn't dare speak; **en p. (lieu)** in the first place, first, firstly; **la première fois** the first time; **il y a toujours une première fois** there's always a first time, there's a first time for everything; **dès le p. jour** from the first day, from the beginning or the outset; **du p. coup** at the first attempt; **les premiers arrivés** the first to arrive; **le p. venu vous dira cela** anybody or anyone will tell you that; **je ne vais pas coucher avec le p. venu** I'm not going to sleep with the first man that comes along; **ce n'est pas le p. venu** he isn't just anybody or anyone; **il n'a pas le p. sou** *Br* he hasn't (got) two halfpennies to rub together, *Am* hasn't a cent; *Typ* **première épreuve** first proof; **première diffusion** *(d'un film)* first run; *Journ* **première page** front page **SEE** GRAMMAR B59

2 *(original)* primary, original; **sens p. d'un mot** primary or original meaning of a word; **cause première** prime or primary cause; **vérité première** basic truth; *Ind* **matières premières** raw materials

3 *(dans un ordre)* first; **habiter au p. étage** to live on the first or *Am* second floor; **p. plan** foreground; *Fig* forefront; **une personnalité de tout p. plan** a leading personality; **première marche** bottom stair; *Théâtre* **premières loges** first-tier boxes; *Fig* **être aux premières loges** to have a ringside seat; **s'asseoir au p. rang** to sit in the front row; **ce pays est au p. rang mondial pour l'exportation du nickel** this country is one of the world leaders in the export of nickel; **au tout p. rang** in the forefront; **prendre la première place** to take the lead

4 *(placé au sommet de la hiérarchie)* **le p. chirurgien de Paris** the leading or top surgeon in Paris; **la première dame de France** the First Lady of France; **capitaine en p.** senior captain; *Culin* **du p. choix** prime cuts (of meat); **un morceau de p. choix** a prime cut (of meat); **de première importance** of the highest importance, of prime importance; **de première nécessité** essential; **je suis concerné au p. chef** it affects me first and foremost; **je suis le p. intéressé/concerné** I'm the one with most at stake/the one most affected; **billet de première classe** first-class ticket; **voyager en première classe** to travel first-class; *Théâtre* **p. rôle** leading part, lead

5 *(en logique) (terme)* given; **nombre p.** prime number

N **1** *(dans un classement)* first; **il/elle est le p./la première de sa classe** he's/she's (the) top of his/her class; **arriver le p./la première** ou **en p.** to arrive first; **elle était la première à arriver** she was the first to arrive; **nous sommes arrivés les premiers** we were the first to arrive, we arrived first; **arriver bon p.** to come in an easy first; **être le p. à faire qch** to be (the) first to do sth; **au p. de ces messieurs** next, please

2 *Théâtre* **jeune p./première** (young) romantic lead; *Fig* **il a des airs de jeune p.** he looks like a matinée idol *or* film star

NF première 1 *Couture* head seamstress **2** *Théâtre* first *or* opening night, première; *Cin* première; *Fig* **c'est une première!** it's a first!; *Journ* **première de couverture** *ou Arg* **de couve** front cover **3** *(ascension)* first ascent **4** *Aviat, Rail etc* first class; **billet de première** first-class ticket; **voyager en première** to travel first-class **5** *Scol Br* ≃ lower sixth (form), *Am* ≃ eleventh grade **6** *(vitesse)* first (gear), bottom (gear); **passer en première** to go into first (gear) **7** *(de chaussure)* inner sole, insole **8** *Fin* **première de change** first of exchange **9** *Fam* **de première** first-rate, first-class

NM 1 *(date)* **le p. janvier** the first of January, January (the) first; **le p. de l'an** New Year's Day **2** *(premier étage)* first floor, *Am* second floor; **les gens du p.** the people on the first *or Am* second floor

▸▸ **p. commis** principal clerk, head clerk; *Sport* **p. de cordée** leader; **p. cycle** *Scol* = first three years of secondary school; *Univ* = first two years of undergraduate course; **première danseuse** leading dancer; *Cin* **première exclusivité** first showing; *Naut* **p. maître** chief petty officer; **P. ministre** Prime Minister; *Can (d'une province)* Premier; *TV, Cin* **p. montage** rough cut; **p. numéro** first issue; *Cin, TV* **p. rôle** leading part; **p. tirage** first run; *(presse)* early edition; **p. violon** first violin; *(qui dirige)* leader, *Am* concertmaster

premièrement [prəmjɛrmɑ̃] ADV first, firstly, in the first place

premier-né, première-née, *pl* **premiers-nés, premières-nées** [prəmjene, prəmjɛrne] ADJ, N firstborn

prémilitaire [premilitɛr] ADJ premilitary

prémisse [premis] NF *Phil* premise, premiss

> Do not confuse with **prémices**.

prémix [premiks] NM alcopop

prémolaire [premɔlɛr] NF *Anat* premolar

prémonition [premɔnisjɔ̃] NF premonition

prémonitoire [premɔnitwar] ADJ premonitory

prémunir [premynir] VT *Vieilli* **p. qn contre qch** *(protéger)* to protect sb against sth; *(mettre en garde)* to put sb on his/her guard against sth
• VPR **se prémunir se p. contre qch** *(être vigilant)* to be on one's guard against sth; **se p. contre le rhume** to take precautions against (catching) a cold

prenable [prənabl] ADJ *(ville, fort)* pregnable

prenant [prənɑ̃] ADJ **1** *Fin* **partie prenante** payee; *(d'argent, de biens)* recipient **2** *Zool (queue)* prehensile **3** *(voix)* captivating; *(livre, film, travail)* fascinating, absorbing

prénatal, -ale, -als, -ales [prenatal] ADJ antenatal, prenatal

PRENDRE [prɑ̃dr] *(prp* **prenant;** *pp* **pris;** *pr ind* **je prends, il prend, n. prenons, ils prennent;** *pr sub* **je prenne, n. prenions;** *impf* **je prenais, n. prenions;** *p hist* **je pris, n. prîmes;** *fu* **je prendrai)**

VT to take **1, 3–6, 12, 18, 22, 23** ▪ to take away **4** ▪ to charge **5** ▪ to catch **8, 20** ▪ to collect **10** ▪ to get **11, 20** ▪ to take on **15, 21** ▪ to have **18**
VI to set **1** ▪ to take **2, 3** ▪ to catch **3** ▪ to work **4** ▪ to go **6**
VPR to get caught **1** ▪ to attack *(s'en prendre à)* **6** ▪ to go about it *(s'y prendre)* **7**

VT 1 *(saisir)* to take; **p. qch dans un tiroir** to take *or* get sth from *or* out of a drawer; **p. qch sur la table** to take sth from *or* off the table; **p. brusquement qch** to snatch sth (up), to seize sth; **je suis allé p. mon parapluie** I went to get my umbrella; **il l'a prise par le bras/la main** he took her (by the) arm/hand; **p. qn par la taille** to put one's arm round sb's waist; **p. qn par les cheveux** to take *or* grab sb by the hair; **je l'ai prise dans mes bras** I took her in my arms; **p. les armes** to take up arms; **il faut savoir le p.** you have to know how to handle him; **où avez-vous pris cela?** where did you get that (from)?; *(cette idée)* where did you get that idea (from)?; *Tech* **p. en étau** to clamp

2 p. qch sur soi to take responsibility for sth; **p. sur soi de faire qch** to take it upon oneself to do sth

3 *(accepter, recevoir)* to take; *(pensionnaire)* to take (in); **vous avez mal pris mes paroles** you took me *or* what I said the wrong way; **il a très mal pris la chose** he took it very badly; **p. une commande** to take an order; **p. qch à bail** to take out a lease on sth, to lease sth

4 *(enlever)* to take (away); **p. qch à qn** to take sth (away) from sb; *(voler)* to steal sth from sb, to rob sb of sth; *(priver)* to deprive sb of sth; **cela me prend tout mon temps** it takes (up) all my time; **ça m'a pris deux heures** it took me two hours; **mon temps est entièrement pris** I haven't a free minute, my time is completely taken up; **toute sa semaine est déjà prise** his whole week is already taken up; **c'est toujours ça de pris** that's something at least; **j'ai dû p. sur mes économies** I had to draw on my savings

5 *(en argent)* **prenez ce que je vous offre** take what I'm offering you; **dites-moi ce que vous prenez pour cela** how much do you charge for that?; **il prend combien?** how much does he charge?; *Fam* **il prend cher** he charges a lot, he's expensive

6 *(s'approprier)* to take; **c'est à p. ou à laisser** take it or leave it; **il y a à p. et à laisser** there are good things and bad things; **il y a à p. et à laisser dans ce qu'elle dit** some of what she says is right and some of it isn't

7 *(considérer)* **à tout p.** on the whole, all in all

8 *(s'emparer de)* *(fugitif, voleur)* to catch, to capture; *(ville, région)* to take, to capture, to seize; *(marchandises illégales)* to seize; *(poisson, lièvre etc)* to catch; **p. une ville d'assaut** to take a town by storm, to storm a town; *Prov* **tel est pris qui croyait p.** it's a case of the biter bit; **se faire p.** to be *or* get caught; **se laisser p.** to let oneself be *or* get caught; *Fig* to let oneself be taken in; **il s'y est laissé p.** he fell into the trap; **p. qn à voler** to catch sb stealing; **être pris à faire qch** to be caught doing sth; **p. qn sur le fait** to catch sb in the act *or* red-handed; **que je vous y prenne!** just *or* don't let me catch you (at it) again!; **on ne m'y prendra plus** I won't be caught (out) *or* taken in again; **être pris par le brouillard/la tourmente** to be caught in the fog/the gale; **il s'est pris le pied dans une racine** he caught his foot on a root

9 **pris de panique** panic-stricken; **pris d'un sentiment d'angoisse** overcome by a feeling of anxiety; **être pris d'une faiblesse** to feel suddenly faint; **elle a été prise d'un fou rire** she got (a fit of) the giggles; **l'envie lui a pris** *ou* **il lui a pris l'envie de partir** he got a sudden urge to leave, he was seized with a desire to leave; **si jamais l'envie vous en prenait** if ever you should feel so inclined; *Fam* **ça te prend souvent?** do you get like that often?; **qu'est-ce qui lui prend?** what's come over him?, what's up with him?; **bien lui en a pris** it was lucky for him that he did; *Fig très Fam* **ça/il me prend la tête** it/he really gets on my nerves

10 *(emmener)* to call for, to collect, to fetch; **prends ton frère avec toi** take your brother with you; **le taxi s'est arrêté pour p. un client** the taxi stopped to pick up a fare; **passe me p. vers six heures** call for *or* come for *or* fetch me at about six o'clock; **p. des marchandises** *(d'un bateau)* to take in cargo; **le bateau prend l'eau** the boat is leaking, the boat is letting in water; **les murs prennent l'humidité** the walls are getting damp

11 *(acheter)* to get, to buy; *(réserver)* to book, to reserve; **p. une chambre** *(dans un hôtel)* to take a room; *(réserver)* to book a room; **j'ai pris un petit studio** I took a little studio flat; **p. une police d'assurance** to take out an insurance policy

12 p. sa retraite to retire; **il n'a pas pris de vacances l'année dernière** he didn't take *or* have any holidays last year; **tu devrais p. quelques jours (de vacances)** you ought to take a few days off; **p. du repos** to take *or* have a rest

13 *(s'informer de)* **p. des renseignements** to make enquiries; **tous renseignements pris ...** after (making) thorough enquiries ...

14 *(noter)* **p. des notes** to take (down) notes; **p. le pouls/la température de qn** to take sb's pulse/temperature

15 *(embaucher)* *(personnel)* to take on, *Fml* to engage

16 p. qn/qch comme exemple to take sb/sth as an example; **p. qn comme modèle** to model oneself on sb

17 p. qn/qch pour ... to take sb/sth for ...; **on le prenait pour un colonel** we/they/etc took him for a colonel, we/they/etc took him to be a colonel

18 *(nourriture, boisson)* to have; *(médicament)* to take; *(bain)* to take, to have; **qu'est-ce que vous pren(dr)ez?** what will you have (to drink)?; **il prend du sucre dans son thé** he takes sugar in his tea; **il prend toujours un petit verre d'aller se coucher** he always has a small glass of something before going to bed

19 *Fam (recevoir)* **qu'est-ce que tu vas p.!** you're for it!, you'll catch it!; **elle a pris une sacrée raclée** she got a real good hiding *or* thrashing

20 *(attraper)* *(maladie)* to get; *(accent, habitudes)* to acquire; **p. froid** to catch cold

21 *(se mettre à avoir)* *(apparence)* to take on, to assume; *(attitude)* to strike, to assume; **elle prit un ton sévère** her voice took on a severe tone; **p. du poids** to put on *or* gain weight; **p. de l'âge** to be getting old *or* on; **p. un coup de vieux** to age

22 *Méd* **p. du sang** to take a blood sample

23 *(utiliser)* *(train, bus etc)* to take; **j'ai pris l'avion** I flew, I took the plane; **prenez une chaise** take *or* have a seat, sit down; **p. la route de** *ou* **pour Paris** to take the road to Paris; **il est temps de p. la route** it's time to set off *or Fam* to hit the road; *Aut* **p. un virage** to take a bend; *Naut* **p. le large** to take to the open sea; **p. le trot** *(d'un cheval)* to break into a trot; *TV, Radio* **p. l'antenne** to go on the air

VI 1 *(du mortier, de la gelée, du ciment, d'un flan etc)* to set

2 *(d'une plante)* to take (root)

3 *(du feu)* to take, to catch; *(d'une allumette)* to strike, to light; **le feu a pris à sa robe** her dress caught fire; **le feu a pris vite et s'est propagé** the fire took hold quickly and spread

4 *(réussir, marcher)* **le vaccin a pris** the vaccine has taken (effect); **cette mode ne prendra pas** this fashion won't catch on; *Fam* **ce truc-là prend toujours** this trick always works *or* is always successful; *Fam* **ça ne prend pas avec moi!** you can't fool me!, it won't wash with me!

5 p. sur soi to restrain *or* contain oneself

6 (aller) **p. à gauche** to bear (to the) left, to go left; **p. par la vieille ville** to go via the old town; **p. à travers champs** to strike across the fields

VPR se prendre 1 (s'accrocher) **son manteau s'est pris dans la porte/à un clou** her coat (got) caught in the door/on a nail; **ils se sont pris par la taille/le cou** they put their arms around each other('s waists/necks); **se p. par la main** to hold hands, to take each other by the hand

2 (se saisir) to be held; (être attrapé) to be caught; **le verre se prend par son pied** the glass is held or you hold the glass by the stem; **un médicament qui se prend le soir** a medicine which is (to be) taken in the evening

3 (se considérer) **se p. au sérieux** to take oneself seriously; **il se prend pour un héros** he thinks he's a hero

4 se p. d'amitié pour qn to take a liking to sb; (devenir ami) to form a friendship with sb; **se p. de dégoût pour qch** to take a (strong) dislike to sth

5 Litt (commencer) **se p. à faire qch** to begin or start to do sth, to begin or start doing sth

6 s'en p. à qn (physiquement, verbalement) to attack sb; (moralement) to blame sb, to put or lay the blame on sb; (passer sa colère sur) to take it out on sb; **ne t'en prends qu'à toi-même** you've only (got) yourself to blame

7 il sait comment s'y p. he knows how to go or set about it; **je sais comment m'y p. avec lui** I know how to deal with him or handle him; **vous vous y prenez mal** you're going about it (in) the wrong way; **il s'y prend bien** he sets or goes about it (in) the right way; **elle s'y prend bien pour le faire** she's going or setting about it (in) the right way; **s'y p. à deux fois** to make two attempts, to have two goes

8 très Fam **se p. la tête** to make life difficult for oneself

---

preneur, -euse [prənœr, -øz] N **1** Com, Fin buyer, purchaser; (d'un chèque) payee; **je suis p.** I'll take it; **trouver p.** to find a buyer; Fin **p. de lettre de change** payee of a bill of exchange **2** Jur (locataire) lessee, leaseholder **3 p. de son** sound engineer, sound technician **4 p. d'otages** hostage taker

prénom [prenɔ̃] NM first or Am given name; (dans les pays chrétiens) Christian name

prénommé, -ée [prenɔme] ADJ called, named; Jur said, above-named, aforesaid; **le p. Victor** the man called or named Victor

N Jur **le p./la prénommée** the above-named, the aforesaid

prénommer [prenɔme] VT to call, to name; **on la prénomma Irma** she was called or named Irma

VPR **se prénommer il se prénomme Adam** his first or Am given name is Adam, he is called Adam

prénuptial, -iale, -iaux, -iales [prenypsjal, -jo] ADJ premarital; **examen p.** premarital medical check

préoccupant [preɔkypɑ̃] ADJ worrying

préoccupation [preɔkypasjɔ̃] NF **1** (priorité) concern, preoccupation; **ma seule p. a été d'assurer …** my sole concern has been to ensure …; **j'ai d'autres préoccupations** I have other things to worry about **2** (tourment) worry

préoccupé [preɔkype] ADJ preoccupied; (inquiet) worried; **tu as l'air p.** you look worried; **d'un ton p.** (pensant à autre chose) absentmindedly; (inquiet) in a worried tone; **d'un air p.** with a worried look (on his/her face)

préoccuper [preɔkype] VT (tracasser) to worry; (obséder) to preoccupy; **être préoc-**

cupé par qch to be concerned or preoccupied with sth; **sa santé me préoccupe** I'm worried or anxious or concerned about his health; **elle a quelque chose qui la préoccupe** she's got something on her mind, something's worrying her; **le foot est tout ce qui le préoccupe** football is all he thinks about

VPR **se préoccuper se p. de qn/qch** to concern oneself with sb/sth; **il ne s'est pas beaucoup préoccupé de savoir si j'allais bien** he didn't bother himself much to find out if I was all right

préopératoire [preɔperatwar] ADJ Méd preoperative

prépa [prepa] NF Scol Fam preparatory class (for the entrance exam to the grandes écoles); **faire une p., être en p.** to be studying for the entrance exam to the grandes écoles

prépaiement [prepemɑ̃] NM prepayment

préparamétré [preparametre] ADJ Ordinat (logiciel) preconfigured

préparateur, -trice [preparatœr, -tris] N (assistant) assistant (in laboratory); Ind demonstrator; **p. en pharmacie** pharmacist's or Br (dispensing) chemist's assistant

préparatifs [preparatif] NMPL preparations (de for); **faire ses p. de départ** to prepare to or get ready to leave, to make one's preparations for departure; **j'étais en plein p. de départ quand …** I was in the middle of preparing or getting ready to leave when …

préparation [preparasjɔ̃] NF **1** (fait de préparer, de se préparer) preparation (à for); (des repas) preparation, esp Am Fam fixing; **faire un discours sans p.** to make an ad-lib or impromptu speech; **annoncer une nouvelle sans p.** to blurt out a piece of news; **tu ne peux pas le lui dire sans p.** you can't tell him without any preparation, you can't blurt it out; **faire une p. militaire** to do a training course in preparation for military service; **p. au mariage** preparation for marriage **2** Scol (à un examen) preparation (de for); (composition, exercice préparé) preparation; **faire une p. aux grandes écoles** to prepare for the entrance exam to the grandes écoles **3** Pharm preparation; Culin **p. pour gâteau/sauce** cake/sauce mix **4** (organisation) preparation, planning

préparatoire [preparatwar] ADJ preparatory, preliminary; Scol **cours p.** Br ≃ first year infants' class, Am ≃ nursery school; **classes préparatoires** preparatory classes (for the entrance exam to the grandes écoles); **école p.** = school that prepares students for higher education

préparer [prepare] VT **1** (organiser, apprêter) to prepare, to get ready; (réunions) to make preparations or arrangements for, to arrange; (lit) to make (up); (repas) to prepare, surtout Am Fam to fix; (poisson, poulet) to prepare, to dress; Pharm (ordonnance) to make up; **elle prépare le déjeuner** she's getting lunch ready, she's preparing lunch; **plats (tout) préparés** ready-cooked meals

2 p. qn à qch to prepare sb for sth; (entraîner) to train or coach sb for sth; **p. qn à une nouvelle** to prepare sb for a piece of news; **rien ne m'y avait préparé** nothing had prepared me for this

3 Univ (examen) to prepare for, to study for

4 (prévoir, ébaucher) to plan, to prepare; **p. un coup** to be hatching something, to be cooking something up; **p. ses vacances** to plan or arrange one's holidays; **p. un discours** to prepare a speech; **p. son avenir** to prepare for one's future; **cette découverte a été préparée par toute une tradition scientifique** a whole scientific tradition prepared the ground or paved the way for this dis-

covery; **je suis sûr qu'il nous prépare quelque chose** I'm sure he's up to something

VPR **se préparer 1** (être imminent) to be in the offing; **un orage se prépare** a storm is brewing; **il se prépare quelque chose** there's something in the air; (mauvais coup) there's something fishy going on

2 (s'apprêter) **se p. à qch/à faire qch** to prepare (oneself) or to get ready for sth/to do sth; **se p. à ou pour un voyage** to get ready for a journey, to make preparations for a journey; **se p. au combat** to prepare for action or combat; **il est dans la salle de bain, il se prépare** he's in the bathroom getting ready

3 (se faire) **se p. un café** to make oneself a coffee; **tu te prépares bien des ennuis/des désillusions** you're in for trouble/a surprise

prépasserelle [prepasrɛl] NF pre-boarding bridge

prépayé [prepeje] ADJ prepaid

préplanification [preplanifikasjɔ̃] NF pre-planning

prépondérance [prepɔ̃derɑ̃s] NF predominance (sur over)

prépondérant [prepɔ̃derɑ̃] ADJ predominant; **sa voix sera prépondérante** he will have the casting vote

préposé, -ée [prepoze] N (employé, agent) employee; Admin official; (dans un vestiaire) attendant; **p. (des postes)** postman, f postwoman, Am mailman, f mailwoman; **p. à la caisse** cashier; **p. des douanes** customs officer; Jur **commettant et p.** principal and agent; **p. aux réservations** reservations clerk

préposer [prepoze] VT **p. qn à une fonction** to appoint sb to an office; **il a été préposé au poste de chargé des relations publiques** he was put in charge of public relations, he was appointed public relations officer

prépositif, -ive [prepozitif, -iv] ADJ Gram (locution) prepositional

préposition [prepozisjɔ̃] NF Gram preposition SEE GRAMMAR A66–73; B54–7

prépositionnel, -elle [prepozisjɔnɛl] ADJ Gram prepositional

préproduction [preprɔdyksjɔ̃] NF preproduction

préprogrammé [preprɔgrame] ADJ Ordinat preprogrammed

prépubère [prepybɛr] ADJ prepubescent

prépublication [prepyblikasjɔ̃] NF prepublication

prépuce [prepys] NM Anat foreskin, Spéc prepuce

préraphaélisme [prerafaelism] NM Beaux-Arts Pre-Raphaelitism

préraphaélite [prerafaelit] ADJ, N Beaux-Arts Pre-Raphaelite

prérentrée [prerɑ̃tre] NF Scol = day before school begins, used by teachers for preparation

prérequis [prerəki] NM prerequisite

préretraite [prer(ə)trɛt] NF early retirement; (pension) early retirement pension; **partir en p.** to take early retirement; **être en p.** to have taken early retirement; **être mis en p.** to be given early retirement, to be pensioned off, Fam to be put out to grass

préretraité, -ée [prer(ə)trete] N = person who has taken early retirement; (mis en préretraite) = person who has been given early retirement

prérogative [prerɔgativ] NF prerogative

préromantique [prerɔmɑ̃tik] ADJ Hist, Littér pre-Romantic

préromantisme [prerɔmɑ̃tism] NM Hist, Littér pre-Romanticism

PRÈS [prε]

ADV 1 ▪ near **1** ▪ close **1** ▪ nearly (*à peu près*) **2** ▪ closely (*de près*) **4**
PRÉP near (to) **1** ▪ close to **1**

ADV 1 (*dans l'espace*) near, close; (*dans le temps*) close; **il habite tout p.** he lives very near here *or* very close by; **c'est tout p.** it's very near *or* close; **vous êtes trop p.** you're too close *or* near; **plus p.** nearer, closer; **moins p.** farther away; **à un détail p.** except for *or* apart from one detail; **à cela p. que …** except that …; **à quelques exceptions p.** with a few exceptions; **à cinq centimètres p.** to within five centimetres; **il devinerait votre poids à un milligramme p.** he would guess your weight to the nearest milligram; **nous n'en sommes pas à un ou deux jours/ dix euros p.** a day or two/ten euros more or less doesn't matter; **je l'ai raté à deux minutes p.** I missed him by two minutes; **à peu de choses p.,** *Fam* à **quelque chose p.** more or less **2 à peu p.** (*pas tout à fait*) nearly, almost; (*approximativement*) about, approximately; **le travail est à peu p. achevé** the work is nearly *or* almost *or* just about *or* more or less finished; **il était à peu p. certain que …** it was fairly certain that … **3** *Naut* **courir au plus p.** to sail on a wind *or* close to the wind *or* on a bowline **4 de p.** closely; (*voir quelqu'un*) close to, close up; **tirer de p.** to fire at close range; **examiner qch de p.** to examine sth closely; **suivre qn de p.** (*ne pas être loin derrière*) to follow sb closely, to follow close behind sb, to follow hard *or* close on sb's heels; (*d'un médecin, professeur etc*) to follow sb's progress closely; **de p., elles sont très différentes** (*seen*) close to *or* up, they are very different
PRÉP 1 p. de (*dans l'espace*) near (to), close to; (*dans le temps*) close to; **p. de là** nearby, close by; **p. de chez eux** near (to) *or* close to where they live; **tout p. de moi** very close *or* near to me; *Naut* **courir p. du vent** to sail close to the wind; **il est p. de midi** it's close on *or* nearly *or* almost twelve (o'clock); **il y a p. de dix ans** close on *or* nearly *or* almost ten years ago; **il a fallu p. de deux heures pour …** we needed close on *or* nearly *or* almost two hours to …; **être p. de faire qch** to be about to do sth, to be on the point *or* verge of doing sth; **elle était p. d'éclater en sanglots** she was about to burst into tears, she was close to tears *or* on the brink *or* the verge of tears; *Iron* **nous ne sommes pas p. de le revoir** we won't see him again in a hurry; **est-il p. d'avoir fini?** is he anywhere near finished?; *Fam* **être p. de ses sous** to be tight-fisted, to be mean **2** *Admin* **ambassadeur p. le gouvernement français** ambassador to France

présage [preza3] NM omen, sign, *Litt* presage, portent; (*de malheur*) foreboding; **mauvais p.** bad *or* ill omen

présager [preza3e] VT (**je présageai(s); n. présageons**) **1** (*annoncer*) to be an omen of, *Litt* to presage, to portend; (*malheur*) to (fore)bode; **cela ne présage rien de bon** bodes no good, nothing good will come of it **2** (*prédire*) (*d'une personne*) to predict; **ces gros nuages noirs laissent p. un orage** those big black clouds are a sure sign of a storm

présalaire [presalεr] NM (student) grant

pré-salé, *pl* **prés-salés** NM (*mouton*) salt-meadow sheep; (*viande*) salt-meadow lamb

presbyte [prεzbit] ADJ long-sighted, *Spéc* presbyopic

presbytère [prεzbitεr] NM presbytery

presbytérianisme [prεzbiterjanism] NM Presbyterianism

presbytérien, -ienne [prεzbiterjε̃, -jεn] ADJ, N Presbyterian

presbytie [prεsbisi] NF long-sightedness, *Spéc* presbyopia

prescience [presjɑ̃s] NF (*de l'avenir*) foreknowledge, *Fml* prescience

prescient [presjɑ̃] ADJ prescient

préscolaire [preskɔlεr] ADJ preschool

préscolarisation [preskɔlarizasjɔ̃] NF preschool education

prescripteur, -trice [preskriptœr, -tris] N (*médecin*) prescriber; **le p. d'une ordonnance** the writer of a prescription NM *Mktg* influencer

prescription [preskripsjɔ̃] NF **1** *Jur* prescription; **invoquer la p.** to raise a defence under the statute of limitations; **après 50 ans, il y a p.** the statute of limitations runs out after 50 years; *Fin* **p. acquisitive** acquisition of a right due to the passage of time; *Fin* **p. extinctive** lapse of a right due to the passage of time **2** *Méd* prescription, direction(s) (for treatment) **3** (*instruction*) rule, regulation

prescrire [preskrir] (*conj like* **écrire**) VT **1** (*ordonner*) (*conditions*) to stipulate, to lay down, to specify; (*remède*) to prescribe; **à la date prescrite** on the date laid down, on the prescribed date **2** *Jur* to prescribe, to bar by the statute of limitations **3** (*réclamer*) to demand, to require; **ce que l'honneur prescrit** the demands *or* dictates of honour
VPR **se prescrire** *Jur* **ces dettes se prescrivent par cinq ans** these debts are barred at the end of five years; *Méd* **ce médicament se prescrit en cas de …** this medicine is prescribed for …

préséance [preseɑ̃s] NF precedence, priority (**sur** over); **avoir la p. sur qn** to have precedence over sb

présélecteur [preselεktœr] NM *Tech* preselector

présélection [preselεksjɔ̃] NF **1** (*premier choix*) preselection, preselecting; (*pour un emploi*) shortlisting **2** *Aut* **boîte de vitesses à p.** preselector gearbox

présélectionner [preselεksjɔne] VT *Tech* to preselect; (*candidats*) to shortlist

présence [prezɑ̃s] NF **1** (*fait d'être dans un lieu*) presence; (*aux cours etc*) attendance; **je désire sa p.** I want him to be here; **il ignore votre p.** he doesn't know you're here; **faire acte de p., faire la p.** to put in an appearance; **feuille de p.** attendance sheet; *Ind* time card; **p. policière** police presence **2** (*personnalité*) presence; **avoir de la p.** to have great presence; **elle n'a aucune p. sur scène** she has no stage presence **3 en p.** face to face, facing one another; **mettre les deux parties en p.** to bring the two parties face to face *or* together; **en p. de toute la famille** in front of *or* in the presence of the whole family; **je ne parlerai qu'en p. de mon avocat** I'll only speak with my lawyer present; **en p. de la mort** in the presence of death; **en p. de ces faits/cette situation** faced with these facts/this situation, in view of these facts/this situation; **en p. du virus …** when the virus is present …; **mis en p. du réactif …** when placed in the vicinity of the reagent …; **cela s'est fait en ma p.** it was done in my presence; **cela s'est dit en ma p.** it was said in my presence *or* hearing **4** (*existence*) presence; **la p. de sang dans les urines** the presence of blood in the urine; **expliquez-moi la p. de cette arme ici** explain to me how this weapon comes to be here; **j'ai senti une p. à côté de moi** I felt a presence beside me
▸▸**p. d'esprit** presence of mind; **je n'ai pas eu la p. d'esprit de lui dire** I didn't have the

presence of mind to tell him; *Rel* **p. réelle** real presence

PRÉSENT, -ENTE [prezɑ̃, -ɑ̃t] ADJ **1** (*qui est dans le lieu dont on parle*) present; **les personnes présentes** those present; **être p. à un spectacle/un mariage** to be present at a performance/a wedding; **Jacques Martin, ici p., vous le dira** Jacques Martin, who is here with us, will tell you; *Scol* **Tardi? – p!** Tardi? – here! *or* present!; *Hum* **dès qu'il s'agit de manger, tu peux être sûr qu'il répond p.** as soon as there's food on the go, you can be sure he'll be there; **cela m'est toujours p. à l'esprit** it's always in my mind; (*d'un conseil, d'un danger etc*) I always keep it in mind; **p. par la pensée** here/there in spirit **2** (*actuel*) (*situation, moment*) present; **vivre dans l'instant p.** to live for the moment; **la présente convention** this convention; *Jur* **par la présente lettre** hereby, by these presents **3** *Gram* present; **le temps p.** the present (tense)
N (*témoin*) person present; **le nom des présents à la réunion** the names of those present at the meeting
NM **1** *Gram* present (tense); **le p. du subjonctif/de l'indicatif** the present subjunctive/indicative; **mettre le texte au p.** to put the text into the present (tense) SEE GRAMMAR A49; B30 **2** (*partie du temps*) present; **vivre dans le p.** to live for the moment *or* in the present **3** *Litt* (*cadeau*) present, gift; **faire p. de qch à qn** to make a present of sth to sb
NF *Jur, Admin* **par la présente** *ou* **les présentes** (*par cette lettre, ce texte*) hereby, by these presents
ADV **à p.** at present, (just) now; **jusqu'à p.** up to now, up to the present (time), until now; (*de qch qui ne s'est pas encore produit*) as yet; **dès à p.** from now on, *Fml* henceforth; **à p. que …** now that …

présentable [prezɑ̃tabl] ADJ presentable

présentateur, -trice [prezɑ̃tatœr, -tris] N *Radio, TV* presenter; (*d'un spectacle télévisé*) master of ceremonies, MC; **p. télé** TV presenter; **p. de journal télévisé** newscaster, newsreader; *TV, Radio* **p. principal** anchor

présentation [prezɑ̃tasjɔ̃] NF **1** (*de faits, d'un travail, d'un titre de transport etc*) presentation; **10% de réduction sur p. de la carte** 10% discount on presentation of this card; *Banque* **p. à l'encaissement d'un chèque** paying in, *Br* encashment; *Admin Fml* presentation for collection; *Com* **payable à p.** payable on demand *or* on presentation *or* at sight; **p. au paiement** presentation for payment; *Fin* **p. à l'acceptation** presentation for acceptance **2** (*apparence*) (*d'une personne*) appearance; (*d'un document etc*) presentation; **soigner la** *ou* **sa p.** to take care over one's appearance *or* over how one looks; **recherche hôtesses, excellente p.** hostesses required, must have smart, attractive appearance; **livre de bonne p.** well-produced book; **la p. des objets dans une vitrine** the presentation *or* display of items in a shop window; **p. assistée par ordinateur** computer-aided presentation **3** *Obst* presentation; **p. par les pieds** breech presentation **4** (*dans un groupe etc*) introduction (**à qn** to sb); (*à la cour*) presentation; **lettre de p.** letter of introduction; **je vous laisse faire les présentations** I'll leave you to make the introductions **5** *Rel* **la P. de la Vierge** (the Feast of) the Presentation (of the Blessed Virgin Mary) **6** (*à un public*) (*d'un film*) showing, presentation; *Mil* **p. du drapeau** trooping the colour; *Com* **p. de collections, p. de mode**

fashion show; **la p. du nouveau modèle diesel** the unveiling *or* presentation of the new diesel model

7 *Tél* **p. du numéro de l'appelant** caller display

présentement [prezātmā] **ADV** at present, *Am* presently

Il faut noter que le terme anglais britannique **presently** est un faux ami. Il signifie **bientôt** ou **peu de temps après**, selon le contexte.

PRÉSENTER [prezāte]

VT to show **1** ▪ to present **1, 3–5** ▪ to offer **2, 3**
VPR to arise **1** ▪ to apply **2** ▪ to come **3** ▪ to introduce oneself **4** ▪ to present **5**

VT 1 *(montrer) (passeport, billet etc)* to show, to produce, to present; *(spectacle, film, émission)* to present; *(bulletin d'informations)* to present, to read; *(jeu télévisé)* to host; **p. son passeport au douanier** to show one's passport to the customs officer; **p. une pièce d'identité** *(au commissariat etc)* to show *or* produce *or* present proof of identity; **p. des factures** to present invoices; **p. à l'encaissement** to present for collection; **p. sa main à qn** to hold out one's hand to sb; **il m'a présenté son dos** he turned his back on *or* to me; **je lui ai présenté le meilleur fauteuil/des cacahuètes** I offered him the best chair/some peanuts; *Mil* **p. les armes** to present arms; **présentez armes!** present arms!

2 *(dire, exprimer)* **je vous présente mes excuses** I do apologize; **p. ses condoléances** to offer one's condolences; **p. ses hommages à qn** to pay one's respects to sb; **p. ses arguments/raisons** to present *or* set out one's arguments/reasons; **p. ses craintes** to express one's fears

3 *(soumettre) (facture, addition)* to present, to submit; **p. sa candidature à un poste** to apply for a job; *Scol* **p. le français (à un examen)** to take *or* offer French (as one of one's exam subjects)

4 *(faire connaître) (motion)* to table; *(spectacle)* to present, to compere, *Am Fam* to emcee; **il m'a présenté tous les faits** he set out *or* put *or* laid all the facts before me; **p. des conclusions** to submit conclusions; **p. un projet de loi** to bring in *or* introduce a bill; **son travail est bien présenté** his work is well presented *or* set out; **vitrine joliment présentée** attractively dressed window; **les chocolats sont présentés dans une très belle boîte** the chocolates are presented *or* packaged in a very attractive box

5 *(comporter)* **son projet présente des inconvénients** there are drawbacks to his plan, his plan has got drawbacks; **ceci ne présente aucun intérêt** it's totally pointless; **le produit présente de nombreux défauts** there are a lot of problems with this product; *Méd* **p. un symptôme** to present a symptom

6 p. qn à qn to introduce sb to sb; *(à la cour)* to present sb to sb; **nous n'avons pas été présentés** we haven't been introduced; **je voudrais vous p. ma cousine** I'd like you to meet my cousin, *Fml* allow me to introduce my cousin (to you); **p. qn comme candidat** to put sb forward as a candidate; **il a été présenté pour ce poste** he has been put forward *or* proposed for this post; **p. les meilleurs élèves pour le concours d'entrée** to enter the best pupils *or* put the best pupils forward for the entrance examination

VI *Fam* **il présente bien** he has a good appearance

VPR se présenter 1 *(se produire)* to arise; **si l'occasion se présente** if the opportunity

presents itself *or* arises (**de faire qch** to do sth); **si le cas se présente** if the case arises; **un beau spectacle s'est présenté à mes yeux** a beautiful sight met my eyes; **attendre que quelque chose se présente** to wait for something to turn up; **la chose se présente bien** things look promising; **l'affaire se présente sous un jour nouveau** the matter appears in a new light

2 *(se porter candidat)* to apply; **est-ce que beaucoup de gens se sont présentés?** did many people apply?, were there many applications?; **se p. à un examen** to take *or Br* sit an examination; **se p. aux élections** to be a candidate *or Br* stand (as a candidate) at the elections; **se p. comme candidat** to come forward as a candidate

3 *(se rendre) (au commissariat), Mil* to report; **se p. chez qn** to call on sb; **elle s'est présentée ivre chez son nouvel employeur** she arrived drunk at her new employer's; **prière de vous p. chez Monsieur Troc** please go to see Mr Troc, *Fml* please report to Mr Troc; **si vous êtes intéressé, présentez-vous à nos bureaux** if you're interested, come along to our office

4 *(se faire connaître)* **se p.** to introduce oneself (à to); **permettez-moi de me p.** may I introduce myself?

5 *Méd, Obst* to present; **l'enfant se présente mal** the child is presenting badly; **le bébé s'est présenté par la tête/les pieds** the baby was in a normal/breech position

présentoir [prezātwar] **NM** *Com* display unit, display shelf; **p. de caisse** check-out display; **p. au sol** floor display, floor stand

présérie [preseri] **NF** *Tech* test series, pilot series

préservateur, -trice [prezervatœr, -tris] **ADJ** *Arch* preservative; *(mesures)* preventive **NM** *(dans la nourriture)* preservative

préservatif, -ive [prezervatif, -iv] **ADJ** *Vieilli (épaisseur, vêtement)* protective; **des mesures préservatives contre l'épidémie** steps to ward off the epidemic

NM *(condom)* condom, sheath; **p. féminin** female condom, Femidom®; *(diaphragme)* diaphragm, cap

Il faut noter que le terme anglais **preservative** est un faux ami. Il signifie **agent de conservation**.

préservation [prezervasjɔ̃] **NF** *(de l'environnement, des traditions etc)* preservation, protection; *(d'une personne, des récoltes)* protection

préserver [prezerve] **VT** to preserve; *(protéger)* to protect (**de** from); **le ciel m'en préserve!** heaven forbid!; **à p. de l'humidité** to be kept dry

VPR se préserver to protect oneself (**de** from); **se p. de l'ennui/de la solitude** to guard against boredom/loneliness

présidence [prezidās] **NF 1** *Pol* presidency; **sous sa p.** under *or* during his presidency; **un candidat à la p.** a presidential candidate, a candidate for the presidency; **p. d'une société** chairmanship of a company, *Am* presidency of a company; *UE* **p. tournante** rotating presidency **2** *(de club etc)* chairmanship; **prendre la p.** *(à une réunion)* to take the chair **3** *(habitation)* presidential residence

président, -ente [prezidā, -āt] **N 1** *Pol* president; **le P.** the President; **la Présidente** the President; *Vieilli (femme du Président)* the President's wife, *Am* the First Lady **2** *(d'assemblée, d'un club etc)* chairperson, chairman, *f* chairwoman; **être élu p.** to be voted into the chair, to be elected chairperson; **Monsieur le p./Madame la présidente**, per-

mettez-moi de ... Mr Chairman/Madam Chairwoman, allow me to ... **3** *(magistrat)* presiding judge

▸ ▸ **p. de l'Assemblée Nationale** President of the National Assembly; **p. de la Commission européenne** President of the European Commission; *Hist, Pol* **p. du Conseil** Prime Minister; *Com* **P. du conseil d'administration** Chairman of the Board; *Ind, Com* **p.-directeur général** chairman and managing director, chief executive officer, CEO; **p. du jury** *Jur* foreman of the jury; *(dans un concours)* chairman of the adjudicating committee; **p. du Parlement européen** President of the European Parliament; **p. du Sénat** President of the Senate; **p. à vie** life president

présidentiable [prezidāsjabl] **N** presidential hopeful

présidentialisme [prezidāsjalism] **NM** presidential (government) system

présidentiel, -ielle [prezidāsjel] **ADJ** presidential; **l'élection présidentielle** the presidential election, the election for president; **régime p.** presidency, presidential system of government

NFPL présidentielles presidential elections

Présidentielles

In France, since 1873, the president has been traditionally elected for a renewable seven-year term ("le septennat"). However, as a result of a referendum held in September 2000 the French parliament ruled that the seven-year term of office was to be replaced in 2002 by a five-year term ("le quinquennat"). Candidates are usually nominated by the main political parties, but anyone who collects the requisite number of sponsors can run. If no candidate wins an outright majority in the first round of voting, a runoff between the two frontrunners is held two weeks later.

présider [prezide] **VT 1** *(diriger) (conseil)* to preside over; *(réunion)* to chair **2** *(être à la place d'honneur de) (banquet)* to be the guest of honour *or Am* honor at

VI 1 *(diriger)* to preside, to be in the chair; **p. à une réunion** to preside at *or* over a meeting **2** *(veiller)* **p. à** to preside over; **p. aux destinées de ...** to preside over the destinies of ...; **les codes qui président à ces cérémonies** the codes that govern these ceremonies

présomptif, -ive [prezɔ̃ptif, -iv] **ADJ** héritier **p.** heir presumptive; *(fils aîné)* heir apparent

présomption [prezɔ̃psjɔ̃] **NF 1** *(supposition), Jur* presumption; **de fortes présomptions pèsent sur lui** he is under great suspicion; **ce ne sont que des présomptions de votre part** these are just presumptions *or* assumptions of yours; *Jur* **p. de responsabilité** presumption of liability **2** *(suffisance)* presumption, presumptuousness

présomptueusement [prezɔ̃ptɥøzmā] **ADV** presumptuously

présomptueux, -euse [prezɔ̃ptɥø, -øz] **ADJ** presumptuous

N un jeune p. a presumptuous young man

présono [presono] **NF** *TV, Radio* playback

présonorisation [presonorizasjɔ̃] **NF** *TV etc* playback

presque [presk(ə)] **ADV 1** *(à peu près)* almost, nearly; **c'est p. impossible** it's almost *or* next to *or* all but *or* well-nigh impossible; **c'est p. sûr** it's almost *or* nearly *or* well-nigh certain; **ça n'est pas sûr mais p.** it's not certain, but just about *or* but as good as; **je les ai p. tous** I have nearly *or* almost all of them; **c'est p. de la folie/la répression** it's little short of madness/repression; **il est sourd ou p.** he's deaf or as good as *or* just about; **j'ai vu tout le monde ou p.** I saw everybody or almost *or* nearly *or* just about everybody

2 (+ *nég*) scarcely, hardly; **p. jamais** scarcely *or* hardly ever, almost never; **p. rien** scarcely *or* hardly anything, next to nothing; **je ne dors p. pas** I hardly *or* scarcely get any sleep; **je ne dors p. plus** I hardly *or* scarcely get any sleep any more; **p. personne** hardly *or* scarcely anyone; **je ne connais p. personne** I hardly *or* scarcely know anyone; **rien ou p.** nothing, or hardly *or* scarcely anything, nothing, or as good as (nothing)

3 (*devant un nom*) **la p. totalité de son œuvre** nearly *or* almost all (of) his/her works, the near totality of his/her works; *Litt* **la p. obscurité** the near darkness; **c'est une p. certitude** it's virtually certain, it's well-nigh certain

presqu'île [preskil] **NF** peninsula

pressage [presaʒ] **NM** (*des raisins, du linge, de disques etc*) pressing

pressant [presã] **ADJ** (*besoin*) pressing, urgent; (*créancier, demande*) insistent; **cas p.** urgent case; **il se faisait p.** he was very insistent; *Euph Fam* **avoir un besoin p.** to need to go (*to the toilet*)

press-book, *pl* **press-books** [presbuk] **NM** press book; (*d'un mannequin, d'un artiste etc*) portfolio

presse [pres] **NF 1** (*ensemble des imprimés, des textes*) press; **la grande p.** large-circulation newspapers and magazines; **la liberté de la p.** the freedom of the press, press freedom; **délits de p.** infringements of press laws; **je l'ai lu dans la p.** I read it in the papers; **c'est dans toute la p.** it's in all the papers; **photographe de p.** press photographer; **attaché de p.** press attaché; **service de p.** publicity (department); **agence de p.** news *or* press agency; **conférence de p.** press conference; **avoir bonne/mauvaise p.** to have a good/bad press; *Fig* to be well/badly thought of (**auprès de** by); **la p. affaires** business press; **la p. de charme** soft porn magazines; **la p. clandestine** underground press; **la p. du cœur** romance magazines; **la p. de distribution professionnelle** trade press; **la p. économique** the financial press; **la p. écrite** print media, press; **la p. féminine** women's magazines; **la p. généraliste** general(-interest) press; **la p. grand public** general press; **la p. d'information** newspapers and magazines; **la p. d'information professionnelle** trade press; **la p. magazine** news magazines; **la p. de midinette** romance press; **la p. musicale** music press; **la p. d'opinion** quality press; **la p. parlée/télévisée** radio/television news; **la p. people** celebrity magazines; **la p. périodique** periodical press; **la p. professionnelle** trade press; **la p. de qualité** quality press; **la p. régionale** *ou* **de province** the regional press; **p. à scandale, p. à sensation** popular press, gutter press; ≃ tabloids; **la p. du soir** the evening newspapers; **la p. spécialisée** specialist press; **la p. sportive** sports press

2 *Tech* press; **p. mécanique** power press; **p. à copier** letter press, copying press; **travailler du métal à la p.** to stamp metal; **p. étoupe** gland; **p. à pantalon** trouser-press; **p. monétaire** minting press

3 *Typ* (printing) press; **p. à imprimer** *ou* **d'imprimerie** printing press; **p. à bras** hand press; **p. à rogner** guillotine; **p. rotative** rotary press; **livre sous p.** book that has gone to press; **être mis sous p.** to go to press; **prêt à mettre sous p.** (*livre*) ready for press; (*journal*) ready to put to bed; **le livre sera**

mis sous p. fin septembre the book will go to press at the end of September; **à l'heure où nous mettons sous p.** at the time of going to press

4 *Arch, Litt* (*foule*) press, throng, crowd; **fendre la p.** to force one's way through the crowd

5 *Naut Arch* press (gang)

6 *Can* (*urgence*) **il n'y a pas de p.** there's no hurry *or* rush; **dans les moments de p.** at busy periods

pressé [prese] **ADJ 1** (*comprimé*) pressed; **citron p.** freshly squeezed lemon juice; **p. à froid** cold-pressed **2** (*serré*) **il était p. contre le mur** he was pressed *or* squashed up against the wall; **pressés les uns contre les autres** pressed *or* crowded *or* packed *or* squashed together; (*objets*) pressed *or* packed *or* squashed together **3** (*qui a hâte*) in a hurry *or* rush; **je suis très p.** I'm in rather a hurry, I'm very pressed for time; **p. de faire qch** in a hurry to do sth; **être p. par le temps** to be pushed for time; **aller** *ou* **marcher d'un pas p.** to walk hurriedly; **avoir un air p.** to look as though one is in a hurry; **on n'est pas p.** there's no rush, we're not in a hurry **4** (*urgent*) urgent; **ce n'est pas p.** it's not urgent, there's no hurry *or* rush; **si vous n'avez rien de plus p. à faire** if you've got nothing more urgent to do

  NM aller *ou* **parer au plus p.** to deal with the most urgent thing(s) first

presse-agrumes [presagrym] **NM INV** juice extractor, juicer

presse-ail [presaj] **NM INV** garlic press

presse-bouton [presbutɔ̃] **ADJ INV** push-button

presse-citron [presitrɔ̃] **NM INV** lemon squeezer

pressentiment [presɑ̃timɑ̃] **NM** presentiment; (*d'un malheur*) foreboding; **j'ai comme un p. que ...** I have a (funny) feeling that ...; **avoir le p. que quelque chose va se passer** to have the *or* a feeling that something is going to happen

pressentir [presɑ̃tir] **VT** (*conj like* sentir) **1** (*prévoir*) to have a presentiment *or* premonition of, to sense; (*malheur*) to have a foreboding of; **p. que quelque chose va se passer** to have a (funny) feeling that something is going to happen; **faire** *ou* **laisser p. qch** to foreshadow *or* portend sth; (*malheur*) to forebode sth; **son attitude me fait p. que ...** I get the feeling from his attitude that ...; **rien ne laissait p. une rage pareille** nothing could have prepared me/us/*etc* for such a rage **2 p. qn** (*sur* **ou pour qch**) to sound sb out *or* approach sb (about sth); **le candidat pressenti** the likely candidate (for the job)

presse-papiers [prespapje] **NM INV** paperweight; *Ordinat* clipboard

presse-purée [prespyre] **NM INV** potato masher

presser [prese] **VT 1** (*citron, éponge etc*) to squeeze; (*raisin, pommes*), *Tech* (*disque*) to press; **p. à froid** to cold-press; **p. qn contre son cœur** to clasp sb in one's arms, to hug sb; **p. le bras à qn** to squeeze sb's arm; **il m'entraînait en me pressant le bras** he dragged me off clutching me by the arm; *Fam* **ici on vous presse comme un citron** they get as much out of you as they can here

2 (*appuyer sur*) (*commutateur, bouton*) to press, to push; *Ordinat* to hit

3 (*harceler*) to press; **pressé par ses créanciers** pressed by his creditors; **p. l'ennemi** to press the enemy; **p. qn de questions** to ply *or* bombard sb with questions; **p. qn de faire qch** to press *or* urge sb to do sth

4 (*dépêcher*) (*quelqu'un*) to hurry (up); (*travail, mouvement*) to speed up, to accelerate;

p. le pas *ou* **l'allure** to speed up, to quicken one's pace; **p. le départ de qn** to speed up *or* hasten sb's departure; **qu'est-ce qui vous presse?** why are you in such a hurry?, what's the hurry *or* rush?; **rien ne nous presse** we're not in any hurry *or* rush; **allons, pressons!** come on, let's get a move on!

VI le temps presse there isn't much time (left), time is short *or* is pressing; **le temps ne presse pas** there's plenty of time (left), there's no need to hurry; **l'affaire presse** the matter is urgent; **il n'y a rien qui presse, rien ne presse,** *Fam* **ça ne presse pas** there's no hurry *or* rush

VPR se presser 1 (*s'entasser*) to press, to crowd; (*contre des grilles*) to squash up, to crush; **on s'y presse toujours à six heures** there's always a crowd there at six o'clock

2 (*se serrer*) **elle s'est pressée contre lui** she pressed (herself) against him; (*de façon affectueuse*) she snuggled (up) against him, she snuggled up to him; **les badauds se pressaient autour de la victime** the onlookers crowded *or* clustered around the victim; **on se pressa pour entrer** there was a crush to get in; **les mots se pressaient dans sa bouche** he had so much to say he could not express himself clearly

3 (*se dépêcher*) to hurry (up); **pressez-vous!** hurry (up)!; **presse-toi de répondre à l'annonce** hurry up and reply to the advertisement; **faire qch sans se p.** to take one's time over doing sth; **répondre sans se p.** to answer deliberately *or* leisurely, to give an unhurried answer; **il faut se p. d'oublier** we must forget as quickly as we can

4 *Fam* **se p. le citron** to rack one's brains

presse-raquette [presraket] **NM INV** racket press

pressing [presiŋ] **NM 1** (*repassage à la vapeur*) (steam) pressing **2** (*magasin*) dry cleaner's **3** *Fig Fam* pressure; **faire le p.** to put on pressure

pression [presjɔ̃] **NF 1** *Fig* (*action insistante*) pressure; **faire p. sur qn,** *Fam* **mettre la p. sur qn** to put pressure on sb, to pressure *or* pressurize sb; **ils vont faire p. sur lui pour qu'il signe** they're going to put pressure on him to sign, they're going to pressure *or* pressurize him into signing; **être soumis/céder à des pressions** to be subjected to/to give in to pressure; **faire monter la p.** to pile on *or* increase the pressure; **être sous p.** to be under pressure; **sous la p. des événements, il dut démissionner** the pressure of events was such that he had to resign; **je travaille mieux sous p.** I work better under pressure; **groupe de p.** pressure group; **p. sociale/démographique** social/demographic pressure; **p. fiscale** tax burden

2 (*action de presser*) pressure; **exercer une p. sur qch, faire p. sur qch** to exert pressure on sth; **faire monter** *ou* **augmenter la p.** to increase the pressure; **en exerçant une simple p. du doigt** by simply pressing with one's finger; **un bouton (à) p., une p.** a press stud, *Am* a snap fastener, *Fam* a popper

3 *Tech* pressure; **vis de p.** binding screw; **p. d'huile** oil pressure; *Aut* **p. de gonflage** tyre pressure; *Aut* **p. des pneumatiques** tyre pressure; *Aut* **p. du carburant** fuel pressure; *Aut* **jauge de p.** pressure gauge; *Tech* **machine à haute/basse p.** high-/low-pressure engine; **mettre sous p.** to get up steam; **mettre la chaudière sous p.** to get up steam; **cabine sous p.** pressurized cabin

4 *Phys* pressure; **p. atmosphérique/artérielle** atmospheric/blood pressure; *Météo* **zone de hautes/basses pressions** area of high/low pressure

5 bière (à la) p. draught *or Am* draft beer; **une p., s'il vous plaît** ≃ half a pint of lager *or Am* a beer, please

pressographe [presɔgraf] NM credit card machine, imprinter machine

pressoir [preswar] NM **1** (presse) (pour faire du vin) wine press; (pour faire du cidre) cider press; (pour huile) oil press **2** (lieu) press house, press room

pressurage [presyraʒ] NM pressing

pressurer [presyre] VT (fruits) to press; Fig (exploiter) to squeeze

pressurisation [presyrizasjɔ̃] NF pressurization

pressuriser [presyrize] VT to pressurize

prestance [prestɑ̃s] NF presence; **avoir de la p.** to have (great) presence; **il faut une certaine p. pour porter ces vêtements** you need a certain style to wear these clothes; **un homme de belle p.** a fine-looking man

prestataire [prestatɛr] NM **1** Admin person receiving benefits or allowances; **p. de service** service provider, service supplier **2** TV facilities man

prestation [prestasjɔ̃] NF **1** (allocation) benefit; Admin allowance; **prestations services**; **prestations familiales** family benefits; **prestations sociales** social security benefits; **p. compensatoire** (en cas de divorce) compensation; **prestations maladie** sickness benefit; **p. en nature** payment or allowances in kind; **recevoir des prestations** to receive benefits **2** Com service; **p. de service** provision of a service; **p. de capitaux** provision of capital **3** (résultat, performance) performance; **la p. d'un homme politique à la télévision** the performance of a politician on television **4** Jur **p. de serment** oath taking; Hist **p. de foi** oath of fealty

preste [prest] ADJ nimble; **avoir la main p.** to have nimble fingers

prestement [prestəmɑ̃] ADV promptly

prestidigitateur, -trice [prestidiʒitatœr, -tris] N conjurer, magician

prestidigitation [prestidiʒitasjɔ̃] NF conjuring, magic; **tour de p.** conjuring trick, magic trick; Fig **c'est de la p.!** it's magic!

prestige [prestiʒ] NM **1** (d'une personne, d'une société importante etc) prestige; (séduction, attrait) (d'une star de cinéma, d'une façon de vivre etc) glamour, Am glamor; **sans p.** undistinguished; **publicité/magazine de p.** prestige advertising/magazine; **le p. de l'uniforme** the glamour of the uniform **2** Arch (chose étonnante) marvel

prestigieux, -ieuse [prestiʒjø, -jøz] ADJ **1** (qui a du renom) (artiste, nom etc) prestigious, famous, great; **produits p.** prestige products **2** Litt (étonnant) marvellous, wonderful, amazing

presto [presto] ADV **1** Mus presto **2** Fam double-quick, at the double

présumable [prezymabl] ADJ presumable

présumer [prezyme] VT (supposer) to presume, to assume; **tu viens aussi, je présume?, je présume que tu viens aussi?** you're coming too, I presume or assume?, I presume or assume that you're coming too?; **p. qn innocent** to presume sb (to be) innocent; **le coupable présumé, le présumé coupable** the alleged culprit; **le voleur présumé** the alleged thief; **il est l'auteur présumé de cette œuvre** he is presumed to be the author or he is the presumed author of this work; **on présume qu'il est mort** he is assumed or presumed (to be) dead

VI **trop p. de soi** to presume too much, to be overconfident; **trop p. de ses forces** to overestimate or overrate one's strength

présupposé [presypoze] ADJ presupposed

NM presupposition

présupposer [presypoze] VT to presuppose

présupposition [presypozisjɔ̃] NF presupposition

---

présure [prezyr] NF rennet

prêt¹ [prɛ] ADJ ready; **p. à l'emploi** ready for use; **p. à servir** ready to serve; **se tenir p.** to hold oneself in readiness, to be ready; **être p. à tout** to be ready for anything; (pour parvenir à son but) to be prepared to do anything; **je le sens p. à tout** I think he will stop at nothing; **être p. à faire qch** to be ready to do sth, to be all set to do sth; **p. à partir** ready to leave or go, Fam ready for the off; **toujours p. à rendre service** always willing or ready to help

prêt² NM **1** (action) lending; (somme) loan; **p. de 1000 euros** loan of 1,000 euros; **faire/consentir/obtenir un p.** to make/grant/get or obtain a loan; **demander un p.** to ask for or apply for a loan; **p. à court/moyen/long terme** short-/medium-/long-term loan; **le service du p.** (d'une bibliothèque) the lending department **2** Mil pay **3** (avance sur salaire) advance

▸▸ Banque **p. pour l'accession à la propriété** home loan; **p. bancaire** bank loan; **p. bonifié** loan at reduced rate of interest, soft loan; **p. à la consommation** consumer loan; **p. à découvert** overdraft loan; **p. d'épargne-logement** home loan; **p. à fonds perdus** without security, unsecured loan; **p. sur gage(s)** pawnbroking; **p. garanti** guaranteed loan; **p. d'honneur** loan on trust; **p. hypothécaire** mortgage loan; **p. immobilier** Br property or Am real-estate loan; **p. à intérêts** loan at interest; **p. participatif** equity loan; **p. en participation** syndicated loan; **prêts aux particuliers** personal loans; **p. personnalisé** ou **personnel** personal loan; **p.-relais** bridging loan, Am bridge loan; **p. sans intérêt** interest-free loan; **p. en souffrance** non-performing loan; **p. sur titres** loan against securities; **p. à vue** loan at call, loan repayable on demand

prêt-à-diffuser, pl **prêts-à-diffuser** [pretadifyze] NM master tape

prêt-à-porter, pl **prêts-à-porter** [pretaporte] NM **1** ready-to-wear clothes; **en p.** off the peg or Am rack; **acheter du p.** to buy ready-to-wear or Br off-the-peg or Am off-the-rack clothes **2** (secteur) ready-to-wear (clothing business)

prêté [prete] ADJ borrowed

NM **c'est un p. pour un rendu** it's tit for tat

prétendant, -ante [pretɑ̃dɑ̃, -ɑ̃t] N applicant, candidate (à for); (à un bien, à un titre) claimant (à to); (au trône) pretender (à to)

NM suitor, admirer; Mktg challenger

prétendre [pretɑ̃dr] VT **1** (déclarer) to maintain, to assert, to claim; **je prétends que ce n'est pas vrai** I maintain that it is not true; **on prétend que …** people say that …, it is said that …; **à ce qu'il prétend** according to him; **elle prétend pouvoir guérir le cancer** she claims to be able to cure cancer; **il ne prétend pas être artiste** he doesn't pretend to be artistic, he lays no claim to being an artist; **je ne prétends pas lui faire comprendre** I don't pretend to be able to make him understand; **on le prétend fou** they say he's mad **2** (vouloir) to mean; **je prétends être obéi** I mean to be obeyed **3** Vieilli (exiger) to require, to want; **que prétendez-vous de moi?** what do you require or want of me? **4** Belg (avoir l'intention de) **il ne prétend pas le faire** he doesn't intend to do it

VI **p. à qch** to lay claim to sth; **p. aux honneurs** to aspire to honours; Litt **p. à la main de qn** to aspire to marry sb

VPR **se prétendre** to claim to be; **elle se prétend trompée sur la qualité du produit** she claims to have been misled about the quality of the product

Il faut noter que le verbe anglais **to pretend** est un faux ami. Il signifie **faire semblant**.

---

prétendu, -ue [pretɑ̃dy] ADJ (coupable, voleur etc) alleged; (héros, cantatrice etc) would-be; **un p. baron** a self-styled baron; **prétendus progrès** so-called progress

N Arch, Région **mon p.** my fiancé; **ma prétendue** my fiancée

prétendument [pretɑ̃dymɑ̃] ADV supposedly; **cet individu p. architecte nous avait construit une horreur** this so-called architect built us a monstrosity

prête-nom, pl **prête-noms** [pretnɔ̃] NM Fig figurehead; Fin (société) nominee company

prétenseur [pretɑ̃sœr] NM Aut **p. de ceinture** seatbelt pre-tensioner

prétentaine [pretɑ̃tɛn] NF Vieilli **courir la p.** to chase (after) women

prétentieusement [pretɑ̃sjøzmɑ̃] ADV pretentiously

prétentieux, -ieuse [pretɑ̃sjø, -jøz] ADJ (écrivain, personne, style) pretentious; (tenue, apparence) showy

N pretentious person; **un jeune p.** a conceited young idiot; **regarde-la, quelle prétentieuse!** look at her, she's so full of herself or she really fancies herself!

prétention [pretɑ̃sjɔ̃] NF **1** (revendication, ambition) pretension, claim (à to); **je n'ai pas la p. d'avoir réponse à tout** I don't claim to know the answer to everything; **renoncer à ses prétentions** to renounce one's claims **2** (fait d'être prétentieux) pretentiousness, pretension; **homme sans prétention(s)** unassuming or unpretentious man; **repas sans p.** simple meal; **un style plein de p.** a very pretentious style **3** (salaire demandé) **envoyer curriculum vitae et prétentions** send curriculum vitae and state salary required; **quelles sont ses prétentions?** what sort of salary does he want?

PRÊTER [prete] VT **1** (fournir temporairement) to lend, surtout Am to loan; **p. qch à qn** to lend sth to sb, to lend sb sth; **p. sur gage(s)** to lend against security; **p. de l'argent à 6%** to lend money at 6%; Prov **on ne prête qu'aux riches** only lend to those who can repay; Fig people are judged according to their reputation; **p. sur titres** to lend against securities; **p. à intérêt** to lend at interest

2 (donner) to lend, to give; **p. son appui** ou **son concours à qn** to give or lend sb one's support; **p. assistance** ou **secours à qn** to lend or give assistance to sb; **p. main forte à qn** to lend or give sb a hand; **p. l'oreille** to listen, to lend an ear; **p. attention à qch** to pay attention to sth; **p. serment** to take an oath; **p. le flanc à la critique** to lay oneself open or expose oneself to criticism; **p. son nom à qch** to lend one's name to sth, to allow one's name to be used for sth; Vieilli **si Dieu me prête vie** God willing

3 (attribuer) (propos, intentions etc) to attribute, to ascribe (à to); **on me prête des discours que je n'ai jamais tenus** I am credited with speeches which I never made

VI **1 p. à confusion/la critique** to give rise to confusion/to criticism; **privilège qui prête aux abus** privilege that lends itself to or that is open to or that invites abuse; **cela prête à rire** that's laughable

2 (des gants, d'un tissu etc) to give, to stretch

VPR **se prêter 1** (consentir) to lend oneself, to be a party (à to); **se p. à un accommodement** to fall in with or consent to an arrangement

2 (permettre) to lend itself (à to); **roman qui se prête à des interprétations différentes** novel which lends itself to different interpretations; **domaine d'étude qui se prête à des développements variés** area of study that can be developed in different ways; **j'aurais voulu lui parler de ses enfants, mais la situation ne s'y prêtait pas** I'd have liked to talk to him about his children, but it was neither the time nor the place; **attends que la situation s'y prête** wait until the situation is right; **j'aimerais faire une grande fête mais mon appartement ne s'y prête guère** I'd like to have a big party but my flat is hardly the right place

prétérit [preterit] NM *Gram* preterite (tense); **au p.** in the preterite VOIR GRAMMAIRE A39

prétériter [preterite] VT *Suisse (faire du tort à) (personne)* to wrong

pré-test, *pl* **pré-tests** [pretest] NM **p. publicitaire** pre-testing advertisement; **pré-tests publicitaires** copy testing; **pré-tests** pretesting

pré-tester [preteste] VT to pre-test

préteur [pretœr] NM *Antiq* praetor

prêteur, -euse [pretœr, -øz] N lender; **p. sur gages** pawnbroker
◊ ADJ ready *or* willing to lend things; **je ne suis pas p.** I don't like lending things

prétexte [pretɛkst] NM pretext, excuse; **ce n'est qu'un p.** it's just a pretext *or* an excuse; **bon/mauvais p.** good/poor excuse; **se chercher des prétextes** to look for excuses; **sous p. de faire qch** on *or* under the pretext of doing sth; **sous p. d'amitié** on *or* under the pretext of friendship; **sous p. que ...** on *or* under the pretext that ...; **sous aucun p.** on no account, under no circumstances; **prendre p. de qch pour faire qch** to use sth as a pretext *or* an excuse for doing sth; **prendre** *ou* **saisir le premier p. pour ...** to take advantage of the first pretext one can to ...; **donner p. à** to provide an excuse for
    NF *Antiq* toga praetexta
    ADJ *Antiq* **toge p.** toga praetexta

prétexter [pretɛkste] VT to use *or* give as a pretext *or* an excuse; **il a prétexté qu'il était malade** he gave the excuse that he was ill; **p. la fatigue** to plead fatigue, to give fatigue as a pretext *or* an excuse

prétoire [pretwar] NM **1** *Jur* court **2** *Antiq* praetorium

Pretoria [pretɔrja] N Pretoria

prétorien, -ienne [pretɔrjɛ̃, -jɛn] ADJ *Antiq* praetorian
    NM *Antiq* praetorian; *Fig (de dictature)* praetorian guard, military bodyguard

prêtre [prɛtr] NM priest; **grand p.** high priest; **se faire (ordonner) p.** to be ordained (a priest), to become a priest

prêtre-ouvrier, *pl* **prêtres-ouvriers** NM worker priest

prêtresse [prɛtrɛs] NF priestess

prêtrise [prɛtriz] NF priesthood; **recevoir la p.** to take (holy) orders

preuve [prœv] NF **1** *(d'innocence, d'amitié, de courage etc)* proof, evidence; **une p. de mauvaise organisation** evidence *or* proof of poor organization; **ce n'est pas une p.** that proves nothing *or* doesn't prove anything; **il nous faut des preuves** we need proof *or* evidence; **faire la p. de qch** to prove sth; **avoir la p. que/de ...** to have proof that/of ...; **faire p. d'intelligence/de générosité**/*etc* to show intelligence/generosity/*etc*; **faire ses preuves** *(d'un élève, employé etc)* to prove oneself, to show what one can do; **cette méthode a fait ses preuves** this method has proved itself *or* has stood the test of time; **jusqu'à p. du contraire** until there's proof to the contrary; **comme p.** by way of proof, as proof; *Fam* **le directeur est un incapable, à p. le déficit de la maison** the manager is incompetent, witness the firm's deficit; *Fam* **on ne peut pas compter sur lui, la p. il est encore absent** you can't count on him, as you can see he's absent again; **à p. que ...** which (just) goes to show that ...; **j'en veux pour p. ...** the proof of it is ...; **être la p. vivante que ...** to be living proof that ...; **p. d'achat** proof of pur-

chase **2** *Math* **faire la p. d'une opération** to prove *or* test the validity of a mathematical operation; **faire la p. par neuf** to cast out nines **3** *Jur* evidence; **p. directe** direct evidence; **p. indirecte** circumstantial evidence; **preuves testimoniales** (witnesses') evidence; **le soin** *ou* **l'obligation de faire la p.** the onus *or* burden of proof

preux [prø] *Arch, Litt* ADJ M gallant, valiant
    NM gallant *or* valiant knight

prévalence [prevalɑ̃s] NF *Méd* prevalence

prévaloir [prevalwar] *(conj like* valoir *except pr sub* je prévale*)* VI to prevail (**sur** over; **contre** against); **ce principe prévaut sur tous les autres** this principle takes precedence over all others; **faire p. ses droits** to assert one's rights; **faire p. son opinion** to win acceptance for one's opinion
    VPR **se prévaloir 1 se p. de** *(profiter de)* to take advantage of **2 se p. de qch** *(s'enorgueillir)* to pride oneself on sth

prévaricateur, -trice [prevarikatœr, -tris] *Jur* ADJ *(fonctionnaire, magistrat)* dishonest
    N dishonest official; *(dans une gestion)* betrayer of trust

prévarication [prevarikasjɔ̃] NF *Jur* breach of trust; *(dans une organisation)* maladministration

prévariquer [prevarike] VI *Jur* to be guilty of a breach of trust

prévenance [prevnɑ̃s] NF kindness, consideration; *(d'un geste, d'une bonne idée)* thoughtfulness; **une p.** a thoughtful *or* kind act *or* deed; **entourer qn de prévenances** to show sb great kindness *or* consideration; **avoir des prévenances pour qn** to show sb kindness *or* consideration

prévenant [prevnɑ̃] ADJ *(personne)* kind (**envers, avec** to), considerate (**envers, avec** towards); *(geste)* thoughtful (**envers, avec** towards); *(manière, apparence)* pleasing, prepossessing

prévenir [prevnir] VT *(conj like* venir *but with aux* avoir*)* **1** *(informer)* to inform, to tell, to let know (**de qch** about sth, of sth); *(avertir)* to warn; *(à l'avance)* to forewarn; **les personnes à p. en cas d'accident** those to be informed *or* notified in case of an accident; **je vais le p. que vous êtes ici** I'll tell him *or* let him know that you're here; **on m'avait prévenu que la police était à mes trousses** I had been warned that the police were after me; **vous auriez dû m'en** *ou* **me p.** you should have told me (about it) beforehand; **je l'ai prévenue, si ça ne s'améliore pas, c'est la porte!** I've warned her, if there's no improvement she'll be out of a job!; **tu es prévenu!** you've been warned!; **partir sans p.** to leave without telling anyone *or* without warning **2** *(empêcher) (maladie)* to prevent, to ward off, to avert; *(danger, accident)* to avert; *Prov* **mieux vaut p. que guérir** prevention is better than cure **3** *(devancer) (les désirs de quelqu'un)* to anticipate; *(question, objection)* to forestall **4** *Litt (agir, influencer)* **p. qn en faveur de qn** to predispose sb *or* bias sb in favour of sb; **p. qn contre qn** to prejudice sb against sb, to bias sb *or* make sb bias(s)ed against sb; **son visage prévient en sa faveur** he has a prepossessing face

préventif, -ive [prevɑ̃tif, -iv] ADJ preventive; **à titre p.** as a preventive (measure); **médecine préventive** preventive medicine; *Cartes* **ouverture préventive** pre-emptive bid; *Jur* **détention préventive** detention awaiting trial; **être en détention préventive** to be in custody

prévention [prevɑ̃sjɔ̃] NF **1** *(d'une maladie etc)* prevention; **p. routière** road safety; **p. des accidents du travail** prevention of industrial accidents **2** *Jur* **mettre qn en p.** to

commit sb for trial; **mise en p.** committal for trial **3** *Litt (opinion, avis)* predisposition, bias (**en faveur de** in favour of), prejudice, bias (**contre** against); **observateur sans p.** unprejudiced *or* unbias(s)ed observer

préventivement [prevɑ̃tivmɑ̃] ADV **1** as a preventive (measure) **2** *Jur* **arrêter qn p.** to arrest sb on suspicion; **détenu p.** committed for trial

préventorium [prevɑ̃tɔrjɔm] NM tuberculosis sanatorium

prévenu, -ue [prevny] ADJ **1** *(qui a une opinion)* prejudiced, bias(s)ed **2** *Jur* **p. de vol** charged with theft
    N *Jur* **le p./la prévenue** the accused

prévisibilité [previzibilite] NF foreseeability

prévisible [previzibl] ADJ foreseeable; **c'était difficilement p.** it was hard to foresee

prévision [previzjɔ̃] NF forecast; *(activité)* forecasting; *(description d'un événement futur)* forecast, prediction; **en p. de qch** in expectation *or* anticipation of sth; **dépasser les prévisions** to exceed all expectations; **au-delà de toute p.** beyond all expectation; **selon nos prévisions** according to our forecast; **prévisions météorologiques** *ou* **du temps** weather forecast; *Mktg* **prévisions aléatoires** probability forecasting; *Mktg* **p. de la base** grass-roots forecast; *Mktg* **p. depuis la base** bottom-up forecast; *Fin* **p. boursière** stock-exchange forecast; **prévisions budgétaires** budget estimates *or* forecasts; **prévisions de l'entreprise** company forecasting; *Mktg* **p. événementielle** hazard forecast; *(activité)* hazard forecasting; **prévisions hiérarchisées** top-down forecasting; **p. du marché** market forecast; *(activité)* market forecasting; **p. des ventes** sales forecast; *(activité)* sales forecasting; **p. des ventes et profits** sales and profit forecast; *(activité)* sales and profit forecasting

prévisionnel, -elle [previzjɔnɛl] ADJ forecast; *(budget, coûts)* estimated, provisional; *(analyse, étude)* preliminary; **la gestion prévisionnelle des entreprises** management by objectives; **étude prévisionnelle des ventes** sales forecast *or* projection

prévisionner [previzjɔne] VT *TV, Cin* to preview

prévisionniste [previzjɔnist] N *Écon* forecaster

prévisualisation [previzɥalizasjɔ̃] NF *Ordinat* print preview

prévoir [prevwar] VT *(conj like* voir *except in fu and cond* je prévoirai, je prévoirais*)* **1** *(penser, imaginer) (futur, désastre)* to foresee; *(météo, prix etc)* to forecast; *(réaction)* to anticipate; *(difficultés, retards)* to foresee, to anticipate; **il est difficile de p. ce qui va arriver** it's difficult to foresee *or* forecast what will happen; **nous n'avions pas prévu toutes ces dépenses** we didn't foresee *or* allow for *or* plan on all this expense; **tout laisse p. que ...** everything indicates that ...; **rien ne laisse p. un changement de temps** there appears to be no prospect of a change in the weather; **rien ne laissait p. qu'ils prendraient la fuite** there was nothing to indicate *or* suggest that they would run away; **comment aurais-je pu p. que ça n'allait pas me plaire?** how could I have foreseen *or* known in advance *or* anticipated that I wouldn't like it?; **cela n'était pas prévu au programme** that wasn't on the agenda; **ces incidents n'étaient pas prévus au programme** these incidents were totally unplanned; **heureusement qu'on avait prévu le coup!** luckily, we had anticipated this! **2** *(organiser) (quelque chose)* to provide for; **p. des mesures** to take measures; **p. des changements** to make changes; **dépenses prévues au budget** expenses provided for *or* included in the budget; **la loi n'a pas prévu un cas semblable** the law makes no provision for a case of this kind; **les seuls cas prévus par la loi** the only cases covered by *or* provided for by the law; **le personnel prévu dans le contrat** the personnel provided for *or* laid down *or* stipulated in the contract; **l'argent que nous avions prévu pour le voyage n'a pas suffi** the money we allowed for *or* budgeted for *or* set aside for the trip wasn't enough; **la réunion est prévue pour demain** the meeting is arranged *or* planned *or* scheduled for tomorrow; **on ne peut pas tout p.** you can't think of everything; **elle prévoit de demander une augmentation** she's planning to ask for *or* planning on asking for a rise; **comme prévu** as (was) planned, as expected; **cela s'est passé comme prévu** it went according to plan; **plus tôt/tard que prévu** sooner/later than expected; **vitesse prévue** *(d'un bateau)* designed speed; **charge prévue** *(d'un poids lourd etc)* specified load

3 *(préparer)* *(repas, pique-nique)* to provide, to arrange; **il faudra p. des vêtements de pluie** we'll have to take waterproof clothes; **on a prévu une tente en cas de pluie** we've brought a tent in case it rains

prévôt [prevo] NM **1** *Escrime* **p. de salle** *ou* **d'armes** assistant fencing master **2** *Mil* assistant provost marshal; **grand p.** provost marshal **3** *Hist, Jur* provost

prévoyance [prevwajãs] NF *(précaution)* precaution; *(dans le futur)* foresight, forethought; *Fin* contingency, provision for the future; **elle a manqué de p. en achetant cette voiture** it was rather short-sighted *or* unwise of her to buy the car; **il ne manque pas de p.** he thinks well ahead, he doesn't lack foresight; **faire preuve de p.** to show foresight, to be far-sighted, to look ahead; **fonds** *ou* **caisse de p.** contingency fund, reserve fund; **société de p.** provident society; **p. sociale** social security provisions

prévoyant [prevwajã] ADJ far-sighted, *Fml* provident; **un homme p. aurait ...** a man with foresight would have ...; **en bon père p., il avait prévu de ...** as a prudent father should, he had made arrangements to ...

priapisme [prijapism] NM priapism

prie-Dieu [pridjø] NM INV prie-dieu, prayer stool

prier [prije] *(impf, pr sub n. priions, v. priiez)* VT **1** *Rel (Dieu etc)* to pray to; **je prie Dieu qu'il en soit ainsi** I pray (to) God that it may be so **2** *(supplier)* to beg, *Fml, Litt* to beseech, to entreat; **se faire p.** to need a lot of persuasion *or* persuading *or* coaxing; **après s'être fait un peu p.** after a bit of persuasion *or* persuading *or* coaxing; **il ne s'est pas fait p. pour venir** he didn't need *or* take much persuading to come, he didn't need to be asked twice to come; **sans se faire p.** readily, willingly; **il est parti sans se faire p.** it didn't need any coaxing *or* persuasion to get him to go **3** *Fml (demander)* to ask, to request; **p. qn de faire qch** to ask sb to do sth; **je te prie de ne pas t'occuper de ça!** I'd be obliged if you minded your own business!, kindly *or* please mind your own business!; **taisezvous, je vous prie!** please be quiet!; **puis-je vous p. de fermer la porte?** would you be so kind as to *or* be kind enough to close the door?; **dites-moi, je vous prie** would you mind telling me; **je te prie de croire qu'elle a été très surprise** she was very surprised, believe you me *or* let me tell you; **je vous en prie!** *(faites-le)* please do!, of course!; *(ne le faites pas)* please don't!; *(il n'y a pas de quoi)* it's/it was a pleasure!, you're welcome!, not at all!; *Fml* **je vous prie de bien vouloir recevoir l'assurance de mes sentiments les meilleurs** *(dans une lettre)* yours sincerely *or*

truly; **Monsieur et Madame Hugo prient Monsieur et Madame Adam de leur faire l'honneur d'assister à ...** Mr and Mrs Hugo request the pleasure of Mr and Mrs Adam's company at ...; *Arch, Litt* **p. qn à dîner** to invite sb to dine

VI to pray (**pour qn/qch** for sb/sth); **nous avons prié pour qu'il revienne vivant** we prayed that he might return alive, we prayed for his safe return

prière [prijer] NF **1** *(formule)* prayer; **faire** *ou* **dire ses prières** to say one's prayers; *Hum* **tu peux faire ta p.** *ou* **tes prières** you can say your prayers **2** *(acte de prier)* **faire** *ou* **dire la p.** to offer prayer; **c'est l'heure de la p.** it's time for prayers; **être en prières** to be praying *or* at prayer; **aller à la p.** to go to prayers **3** *(demande)* request, *Fml, Litt* entreaty; **à la p. de qn** at sb's request; **céder aux prières de qn** to give in to sb, *Fml* to give way to sb's entreaties; **p. de ne pas fumer** no smoking please, thank you for not smoking, you are requested not to smoke; **p. de fermer la porte** please close the door

prieur, -eure [prijœr] N prior, *f* prioress

prieuré [prijœre] NM *Rel* priory

prima donna [primadɔna], *pl* **prime donne** [primedɔne] NF prima donna

primage [primaʒ] NM *Tech* priming

primaire [primɛr] ADJ **1** *(école, couleur etc)*, *Géol (ère)* primary; *Élec, Tech* **circuit p.** primary; *Écon* **secteur p.** primary sector **2** *Péj (simpliste)* *(personne)* narrow (in outlook), unsophisticated; *(réaction, attitude)* narrow-minded, unsophisticated; *(racisme)* narrow-minded

NM **1** *Scol* primary education; **être en p.** to be at primary school; **les classes du p.** primary school classes **2** *Géol* primary era **3** *Élec* primary (winding) **4** *Écon* primary sector **5** *Péj (personne)* person of narrow outlook

NF *Am Pol* primary (election); **les primaires** the primaries

primat [prima] NM **1** *Rel* primate **2** *Phil* primacy

primate [primat] NM *Zool* primate

primauté [primote] NF **1** *Rel etc* primacy **2** *(supériorité)* supremacy; **avoir la p.** to have priority, to come first; **donner à qch la p. sur qch** to give sth priority over sth

prime¹ [prim] ADJ *Arch, Litt* first; **de p. abord** at first sight; **de p. abord, il a l'air très sympathique** he seems very nice; **dès sa p. jeunesse** since his/her early youth; **elle n'est plus dans sa p. jeunesse!** she's no spring chicken!

NF **1** *Rel* prime; **chanter p.** to sing the prime **2** *Math* **B p.** B prime

prime² NF **1** *Fin (d'assurance)* premium; *Bourse* **marché à p.** option market; *Fig* **faire p.** to come first, to take precedence over everything else; **faire p. sur qch** to come before sth, to take precedence over sth **2** *Com, Admin etc (allocation)* grant; *(sur salaire)* bonus **3** *Com (cadeau)* free gift; **et vous aurez droit à une cafetière en p.** and you will get a free coffee maker *or* a coffee maker as a free gift; *Fig* **en p.** into the bargain

▸▸**p. acheteur** buyer's option; **p. d'ancienneté** long service award; **p. annuelle** annual premium; **p. d'assurance** insurance premium; *Mktg* **p. auto-payante** self-liquidator; **p. du change** agio; **p. à la construction** construction grant *(for people building their own homes)*; **p. contenant** *(pour bouteille etc)* container premium; **p. de conversion** conversion premium; **p. de déménagement** relocation allowance; *Mil* **p. de démobilisation** demobilization gratuity; **p. de départ** severance pay, golden handshake; **p. d'éloignement** isolated post allowance; *Bourse* **p.**

d'émission bond discount; **p. pour l'emploi** = tax credit awarded to low wage-earners, as an incentive to continue working and not claim benefit instead; **p. à l'exportation** export subsidy; **p. familiale** family allowance; **p. de fusion** merger premium; **p. d'intéressement** reversionary bonus; **p. à l'investissement** investment subsidy; **p. de licenciement** severance allowance; **p. de remboursement** premium on redemption, redemption fee; **p. de rendement** *Ind* productivity bonus, performance bonus; *(suite à une mission réussie)* success fee; **p. de renouvellement** renewal premium; **p. de risque** danger money; **p. de transport** transport allowance; **p. de vie chère** cost of living allowance

primer¹ [prime] VT *(avoir la priorité sur)* to take precedence over; **considération qui prime toutes les autres** consideration of the first importance, consideration that outweighs all others

VI *Fig* to come first, to take precedence; **le travail prime avant tout** work takes precedence over *or* comes before everything else; **il faut savoir ce qui prime pour toi** you have to know what comes first with you *or* matters most to you, you have to know what your priorities are; **le courage prime sur toutes les autres qualités** courage is the most important quality; **ce qui prime chez lui, c'est l'honnêteté** honesty is his outstanding quality *or* trait

primer² VT *(donner un prix honorifique à)* to award a prize to; **primé** *(taureau)* prize; *(roman, film)* prizewinning, award-winning; **vous avez été primé deux fois à Cannes** you have twice won an award *or* you have won two awards at Cannes

primerose [primroz] NF *(fleur)* hollyhock

primesautier, -ière [primsotje, -jɛr] ADJ *(personne, réaction, réponse)* spontaneous; *(esprit)* ready, quick; **au risque de paraître un peu trop p.** at the risk of appearing a little impulsive; **répondre de façon primesautière** to answer spontaneously

prime time [prajmtajm] NM *TV, Radio* prime time

primeur [primœr] NF **1 primeurs** (early) fruit and vegetables; **marchand de primeurs** greengrocer *(selling early produce)* **2** *Journ* scoop; **avoir la p. d'une nouvelle** to be the first to hear a piece of news; *Journ, TV* **avoir la p. du reportage/de l'information** to be first with *or* to scoop the report/news; *Journ, TV* **c'est un mariage dont le chanteur nous a réservé la p.** the singer gave us a scoop on his forthcoming marriage; **je vous en réserverai la p.** you'll be the first to know; **nous réservons à nos lecteurs la p. de l'interview** this interview is exclusive to our readers

primevère [primvɛr] NF *(fleur)* primula; **p. à grandes fleurs** primrose; **p. commune** cowslip; **p. des jardins** polyanthus

primipare [primipar] ADJ primiparous

NF primipara

primitif, -ive [primitif, -iv] ADJ **1** *(qui est le plus près de l'origine)* *(instinct, l'homme)* primitive; *Opt* **couleurs primitives** primary colours; *Géol* **terrains primitifs** primitive strata, primitive terrain; *Gram* **temps primitifs** primary tenses **2** *(premier)* *(forme, couleur)* original; **la forme primitive d'une société** the earliest form of a society; **économie primitive** primitive economic system **3** *Péj (rudimentaire)* *(société, coutumes etc)* primitive; *(outil, méthodes)* primitive, crude

NM **1** *Beaux-Arts* primitive, early master **2** *(membre d'une tribu)* primitive tribesman

primitivement [primitivmã] ADV originally

primitivisme [primitivism] NM primitivism

primo [primo] ADV *Fam* first(ly), in the first place

primogéniture [primoʒenityr] NF *Jur* primogeniture

primo-infection, *pl* **primo-infections** NF *Méd* primary infection

primordial, -iale, -iaux, -iales [primɔrdjal, -jo] ADJ **1** *(premier)* primordial; *(instinct, besoin)* primal; **c'est un besoin p. que de communiquer** we have a primal need to communicate, communication is one of our most basic needs **2** *(capital) (question, rôle, point, caractéristique)* of the utmost importance, essential; *(souci, nécessité, importance)* prime; **d'une nécessité/importance primordiale** of prime necessity/importance; **il est p. que tu sois là** you must be there, your presence is essential; **il est p. de s'inscrire à temps** it is of prime or the utmost importance to register in time; **l'eau est un élément p. de la vie** water is essential to life

prince [prɛ̃s] NM prince; **p. héritier** *ou* **royal** *ou* **impérial** crown prince; **le fait du p.** highhanded government action; **c'est le fait du p., que pouvons-nous y faire?** that's what the government's decided or how the government wants it, so what can we do?; *Fig* **comme un p.** *(traité, élevé)* like a prince, like royalty; **il est habillé comme un p.** he's dressed like a prince; *Fig* **être bon p., se montrer bon p.** to be very decent; **il s'est montré bon p. en t'accordant un délai supplémentaire** it was very decent or good of him to give you more time; **allez, montre-toi bon p.** be a good sort; **je vais me montrer bon p. et …** I'm going to be very generous or kind and …
▸▸**le p. charmant** Prince Charming; **p. consort** prince consort; **le p. des ténèbres** the Prince of Darkness

prince de Galles [gal] ADJ, NM INV *Tex* Prince of Wales check

princeps [prɛ̃sɛps] ADJ INV **édition p.** first edition

princesse [prɛ̃sɛs] NF princess; **p. royale** princess royal

princier, -ière [prɛ̃sje, -jer] ADJ princely

princièrement [prɛ̃sjɛrmɑ̃] ADV *(dîner)* like a prince, in princely fashion; *(accueilli)* like royalty; **nous avons été reçu p.** we were treated like royalty or given the red carpet treatment

principal, -ale, -aux, -ales [prɛ̃sipal, -o] ADJ *(personne)* main, principal, chief, leading; *(question, bâtiment, but)* main, principal; *(agent)*, *Gram (proposition)* main; *(actionnaire)* main, major; **associé p.** senior partner; **principale compétence** core competence; **les principaux intéressés** those most concerned
NM **1 le p.** the main thing, the most important thing **2** *Fin* principal, capital sum; *(de l'impôt)* = original amount of tax payable (before surcharges); **p. et intérêts** principal and interest **3** *Mus* principal
N principal, chief; *Scol (d'un collège etc)* principal, *Br* head (teacher), headmaster, *f* headmistress

principalement [prɛ̃sipalmɑ̃] ADV mainly, principally

principauté [prɛ̃sipote] NF principality

principe [prɛ̃sip] NM **1** *(fondement, loi)* principle; **les principes de la géométrie** the principles of geometry; **un accord de p.** an agreement in principle; **poser qch en p.** to lay sth down as a principle; **le p. de nos actions** the principle governing our actions, the mainspring of our actions; **partir du p. que …** to assume that …, to take it as given that …; **p. de précaution** precautionary

principle; **p. de solidarité** solidarity principle; *Pol* **p. de subsidiarité** subsidiarity principle; *Compta* **p. de la partie double** double-entry method; *Bourse* **p. mark to market** mark-to-market principle
2 *Chimie (d'une substance)* element, constituent; **p. actif** active principle or constituent
3 principes *(rudiments)* rudiments; **avoir des principes de philosophie** to have a rudimentary knowledge of philosophy
4 *(règle de conduite)* principle; **déclaration de principes** statement or declaration of principle; **ne serait-ce que pour le p.** if only for the principle of the thing; **c'est une question de p.** it's a matter of principle; **par p.** on principle, as a matter of principle; **en p.** in principle, theoretically, in theory; **avoir pour p. de …** to make it a matter of principle to …
5 principes (moraux) *(moral)* principles; **avoir des principes** to have (high) principles; **manquer à ses principes** to fail to live up to one's principles; **sans principes** unprincipled

printanier, -ière [prɛ̃tanje, -jer] ADJ *(fleurs etc)* spring; *(température, couleur etc)* spring-like; **comme tu es printanière dans cette robe!** how (fresh and) spring-like you look in that dress!

printemps [prɛ̃tɑ̃] NM spring; **au p.** in (the) spring(time); *Can Fam* **avoir la fièvre du p.** to have spring fever; *Fig* **le p. de la vie** the springtime of one's life; **fêter ses 26 p.** to celebrate one's 26th birthday; *Litt* **ses 26 p.** her 26 summers; *Fig* **elle n'a que 26 p.** she's only 26; *Fig* **le p. de la démocratie** the flowering of democracy VOIR GRAMMAIRE A7

prion [prijɔ̃] NM prion

prioritaire [prijoriter] N *(automobiliste)* person with priority
ADJ *(that has)* priority; **être p.** to have priority; **droits prioritaires** priority rights; *Fin* **actions prioritaires** preference shares, *Am* preferred stock; **le véhicule venant de la droite est p.** the vehicle coming from the right has (the) right of way or has priority; **le véhicule p.** the vehicle with the right of way or with priority; **votre demande sera p. sur toutes les autres** your application will have priority over the others; **route p.** main road, road which has priority

priorité [prijorite] NF **1** priority; **donner la p. à qn/qch** to give sb/sth priority; **une question qui vient en p.** a question which has priority; **régler une question en p.** to settle a question as a (matter of) priority; **leur dossier sera traité en p.** their file will get priority treatment; **la p. des priorités** top priority; **ce dossier a la p. absolue** this file is top priority; **avoir la p. sur** to have or take priority or precedence over; **réclamer la p.** to claim the right to speak first; **droits de p.** priority rights; *Fin* **actions de p.** preference shares, *Am* preferred stock; **carte de p.** = pass entitling its holder to move to the head of a queue **2** *Aut* **p. (de passage)** right of way, priority; **avoir p.** to have priority or right of way; **accorder** *ou* **laisser la p. à une voiture** to give way or *Am* to yield to a car; **refuser la p.** to refuse to give way; **p. à droite** *(sur panneau)* ≃ give way to vehicles coming from the right; **route à p.** major road

pris [pri] ADJ **1** *(siège)* occupied, taken; **tout est p.** everything is taken; **avoir les mains prises** to have one's hands full; **tu ne vois donc pas que j'ai les mains prises!** can't you see my hands are full? **2** *(personne)* busy; **je suis très p. ce matin** I'm very busy this morning, I've got a lot on this morning; **je suis déjà p. ce jour-là** I've already got something on that day, that day's booked already; **désolé, toute ma journée est prise** sorry, I'm tied up

all day; **désolé, je suis p.** sorry, I'm tied up **3 p. de peur** seized with fear; **p. de panique** panic-stricken, in a panic; **p. de remords** smitten with remorse; **p. de rage** in a rage; **p. de colère, il a déchiré la lettre** he angrily tore up the letter; **p. de boisson** *(ivre)* the worse for drink or *Fam* wear; *Fml, Jur* under the influence (of alcohol) **4** *(flan, gelée etc)* set; *(rivière etc)* frozen (over); **avoir le nez p.** to have a blocked nose; **avoir la gorge prise** to have a sore throat **5 bien p.** *(taille)* trim **6** *(attrapé)* caught, captured

prise [priz] NF **1** *(fait de prendre) (d'une ville, de prisonniers etc)* taking, capture, seizure; *(de minerai etc)* sample; **la p. de la Bastille** the fall or storming of the Bastille; **de nombreuses prises de guerre** numerous war trophies; *Échecs* **la p. de la dame par le fou** the capture of the queen by the bishop; *Méd* **faire une p. de sang** to take a blood sample; *Tech* **faire une p. à une rivière/sur un câble** to tap a river/a cable; **la p. du médicament doit se faire à heures régulières** the medication must be taken regularly; **la p. de cette substance peut provoquer des hallucinations** (taking) this substance may cause hallucinations; **p. de conscience** awareness, realization; **sa première p. de conscience de la situation réelle** the first time he realized or grasped the truth of the situation; **la p. en considération de facteurs importants** the taking into consideration or account of important factors; **la p. de voile se fit à 39 ans** she took the veil at the age of 39; *Fam* **quelle p. de tête!** what a pain (in the neck)!
2 *(quantité) (de poissons)* catch; *(de médicament) (dose)* dose; *(de tabac à priser)* pinch
3 *Élec* socket, *Am* outlet; *(mâle)* plug; **p. pour rasoir électrique** shaver socket
4 *Phot, Cin, TV (cliché)* shot; *(de filmage continu)* take; *TV, Cin* **p. non-utilisée** outtake; *Cin* **entre les prises** between takes
5 *Tech* engagement, mesh(ing); **en p.** in gear, engaged; **mettre en p.** to engage, to put into gear; *Tech* **p. constante** constant mesh; **p. câblée** cable connection; **p. directe** direct drive; *Aut* **en p. (directe)** in top gear; *Fig* **en p. (directe) sur** *ou* **avec qch** in touch or in contact with sth; **hors de p.** out of gear
6 *(solidification)* **faire p.** *(du ciment)* to set; **ciment à p. rapide** fast-setting cement
7 *(pour se retenir)* hold; *(plus ferme)* grasp, grip; *(en escalade)* hold; *(pour le pied)* foothold; **trouver (une) p. à** *ou* **sur qch** to get a grip or a hold on or of sth; *Tech, Fml* to gain a purchase on sth; **il faut trouver de bonnes prises** you have to get a good grip; **je n'avais pas de p. (pour me hisser)** I didn't have a good enough grip (to pull myself up); *Fig* **avoir p. sur qn** to have a hold on or over sb; **la morale n'a aucune p. sur ce garçon** preaching has no effect or makes no impression on that boy; **ce film n'a eu aucune p. sur moi** the film didn't grip me; **lâcher p.** to lose one's grip; *Fig* to give up, to throw in the towel; **donner p. aux reproches/critiques** to lay oneself open to reproach/criticism
8 *(de judo, de lutte)* hold; **faire une p. de judo à qn** to use a judo throw on sb; *Fig* **être aux prises avec qch** to grapple with sth; **elle est aux prises avec son chef de service** she is at odds with her boss; **leurs intérêts se sont trouvés aux prises** their interests have clashed
▸▸**p. d'air** air intake; *Tech* **p. d'alimentation** input socket; *Fin* **p. de bénéfices** profit-taking; **p. en charge** *(par taxi) (d'un passager)* picking up; *Admin (par Sécurité sociale)* (guaranteed) reimbursement; **p. de contact** contact; *Com* **p. de contrôle** takeover; *Ordinat* **p. de contrôle à distance** remote control; **p. de corps** *Jur* arrest; *Fin* charge; **p. de cou-**

rant *(mâle)* plug; *(femelle)* socket, plug *or* power point, outlet; **p. de décision** decision-making; *Com* **p. à domicile** receipt at domicile; **p. d'eau** *Tech* intake of water; *(dispositif)* cock, tap, valve; *(à incendie)* (fire) hydrant; *(point d'alimentation) (d'un canal, à partir d'une rivière etc)* offtake; *Jur, Pol* **p. illégale d'intérêt** = misuse of public office; *TV, Cin* **p. des marques** blocking; *Élec* **p. multiple** adapter; **p. de notes** note-taking; **p. d'otages** hostage-taking; **p. de participation** *(dans une entreprise)* acquisition of an interest in a company; *Ordinat* **p. péri-informatique** connector; **p. Péritel®** scart connector; **p. de position** stance, position; *Bourse* position taking; **une p. de position est nécessaire** we must take a stand; **p. de possession: la p. de possession de qch** taking possession of sth; **p. de pouvoir** *(légale)* (political) takeover; *(illégale)* seizure of power; *TV, Cin* **p. de repères** camera blocking; *TV, Cin* **p. de son** sound recording; **effectuer une p. de son** to shoot sound; *Élec* **p. de terre** earth *or Am* ground (connection); *Élec* **avoir une p. de terre** to be earthed *or Am* grounded; **p. de vue** *Phot* photography; *TV, Cin (technique)* shooting; *(cliché)* (camera) shot; **p. de vue de couverture** cover shot; *TV* **p. de vue(s) en direct** live broadcast

prisée [prize] NF *Jur (de biens)* valuation

priser[1] [prize] VT **p. du tabac** to take snuff; **p. de la cocaïne** to sniff cocaine
VI to take snuff; **tabac à p.** snuff

priser[2] VT *1 Litt (estimer)* to prize, to value *2 Arch (biens)* to appraise, to value

priseur, -euse [prizœr, -øz] N snuff-taker

prismatique [prismatik] ADJ prismatic

prisme [prism] NM prism; *Fig* **elle voit la situation à travers un p.** she has a distorted view of the situation; **jumelles à p.** prismatic binoculars; *TV, Cin* **p. diviseur (de faisceau)** (prism) beam splitter

prison [prizɔ̃] NF *1 (lieu de détention)* prison, jail; **être/aller en p.** to be in/to go to prison *or* jail; **mettre qn en p.** to put sb in prison *or* jail, *Fml* to imprison sb; **sortir de p.** to come *or* get out (of prison *or* jail), to be released (from prison *or* jail); **s'échapper de p.** to escape from *or* break out of prison *or* jail; *Fig* **cette école est une vraie p.** this school is like a prison; *Péj Fam* **aimable comme une porte de p.** extremely unpleasant; **gardien de p.** prison officer, prison warder VOIR GRAMMAIRE A6-7 *2 (peine)* imprisonment; **il risque la p.** he risks going to prison *or* jail; **faire de la p.** to be in prison *or* jail, to serve a prison *or* jail sentence; **cinq ans de p.** five years' imprisonment; **elle a fait deux ans de p.** she spent two years in prison *or* inside; *Fam* **il a été condamné à cinq ans de p. ferme/avec sursis** he was given a five-year prison *or* jail sentence/a five-year suspended prison sentence; **p. à vie** *ou* **à perpétuité** life imprisonment; **on l'a condamné à la p. à vie** *ou* **à perpétuité** he was sentenced to life imprisonment, he received a life sentence, he was sent to prison for life

prisonnier, -ière [prizɔnje, -jɛr] N prisoner; **faire qn p.** to take sb prisoner; **se constituer p.** to give oneself up; **camp de prisonniers** prison camp; **p. condamné à perpétuité** prisoner serving a life sentence, *Fam* lifer
ADJ imprisoned, in prison; *(pris, attrapé)* captive; **ils sont encore prisonniers sous les décombres** they are still trapped in the rubble; *Fig* **être p. de ses principes** to be a slave to one's principles; **être p. de ses habitudes** to be a creature of habit; **je suis p. du confort** I can't do without my creature comforts; **on est toujours p. de son milieu** you can never break free of your environment

▸▸ *Jur* **p. de droit commun** prisoner; **p. de guerre** prisoner of war, POW; *Pol* **p. d'opinion** prisoner of conscience; **p. politique** political prisoner

Prisunic® [prizynik] NM = low-priced department store; *Péj* **il m'a donné un truc de P.** he gave me a real cheapo present; **le genre Marilyn des P.** the dyed blonde dollybird type

privatif, -ive [privatif, -iv] ADJ *1 Gram* privative *2 (particulier)* private
NM *Gram* privative prefix

privation [privasjɔ̃] NF *1 (perte, manque)* deprivation; **p. d'un droit/de la liberté** loss of a right/of freedom *2* **privations** hardship, privation; **une vie de privations** a life of hardship; **s'imposer des privations** to deprive oneself, to go without

privatique [privatik] NF home video equipment

privatisable [privatizabl] ADJ which can be privatized, privatizable

privatisation [privatizasjɔ̃] NF privatization

privatiser [privatize] VT to privatize

privautés [privote] NFPL (undue) familiarity; **prendre** *ou* **se permettre des p. avec qn** to be over-familiar with sb

privé [prive] ADJ *1 (individuel) (vie, entreprise, chemin, propriété etc)* private; **se réunir en séance privée** to sit in private *or* closed session; **visite privée** *(d'un président etc)* private *or* unofficial visit; **nous avons eu droit à une visite privée du château** we were given a private tour of the castle; *Hist* **le Conseil p.** the Privy Council; *Fig* **c'est un peu son domaine p.** it's his own private domain *2 (libre) (école, patient etc)* private
NM *1 (vie)* private life; **en p.** *(parler à qn, voir qn)* in private; **connaître qn dans le p.** to know sb in private life; **dans le p., cet acteur est très modeste** off stage he's a very modest man *2 Ind, Scol, Méd* **le p.** *(secteur libre)* the private sector; **dans le p., les médecins sont plus attentifs** private doctors are more attentive; *Scol* **elle a mis ses filles dans le p.** she sent her daughters to a private school *3 Fam (détective privé)* private eye, *Am* dick, shamus

priver [prive] VT **p. qn de qch** to deprive sb of sth; **on l'a privé de sortie, il a été privé de sortie** *(à cause de ce qu'il a fait)* he wasn't allowed to go out, *Am Fam* he was grounded; **tu seras privé de dessert** you'll go without pudding, there'll be no pudding for you; **j'ai été privé de sommeil** I didn't get any sleep; **je suis privée de télévision depuis un mois** I've been without television for a month; **je ne vous en prive pas?** can you spare it?, I'm not depriving you, am I?; **ça te prive beaucoup si je te l'emprunte pour la nuit?** would it be too much to ask to borrow it overnight?; **ça ne le prive pas du tout de ne plus fumer** he doesn't find it a hardship not to smoke any more; **ce genre de situation me prive de tous mes moyens** I completely lose my head *or* I go completely to pieces in that kind of situation
VPR **se priver** to do *or* go without; **se p. de** *(nourriture etc)* to do *or* go without; *(plaisir etc)* to deprive oneself of, to deny oneself; **toi, tu n'aimes pas te p.!** you certainly don't like to go *or* do without, do you?; **il ne se prive pas de le lui dire** he never misses a chance *or* an opportunity to tell him/her so; **je ne me suis pas privé de lui dire ce que je pensais** I didn't hesitate to tell him/her what I thought; **tu peux te reposer cinq minutes, elle ne s'en est pas privée!** you can have a rest for five minutes, she did!

privilège [privilɛʒ] NM *1 (avantage, droit)* privilege; **jouir du p.** *ou* **avoir le p. de faire qch** to have the privilege of doing sth, to be

privileged to do sth; **cette méthode a le p. d'être très rapide** this method has the advantage of being very fast; **le p. de l'âge/de la beauté/de la naissance** the privileges of age/beauty/birth; **c'est le p. de l'âge que de pouvoir dire ce qu'on pense** speaking your mind is one of the privileges of age; **la raison fait partie des privilèges de l'homme** the ability to reason is one of the advantages enjoyed by man; **c'est un triste p.** it's a dubious privilege; *Iron* **il a le p. de me déplaire** I have a particular dislike for him; *Iron* **elle a le p. de nous agacer** we find her particularly annoying; *Hist* **abolition des privilèges** abolition of privilege *2 (exclusivité)* licence, grant; *(d'une banque)* charter *3 Jur* preferential claim

privilégié, -ée [privileʒje] ADJ *(favorisé)* *(classe)* privileged; *(situation)* privileged, favourable; **entretenir des relations privilégiées avec un pays** to have a special relationship with a country; **elle est privilégiée par son expérience** she is at *or* has an advantage on account of her experience; **jouir d'un climat p.** to be privileged *or* blessed in its climate; **le moyen d'expression p. de cet artiste** the artist's favourite *or* preferred means of expression, the means of expression favoured by the artist; **banque privilégiée** chartered bank; **créancier p.** preferential *or* preferred creditor; **action privilégiée** preference share
N privileged person; **quelques privilégiés l'ont vu** a privileged few have seen it; **nous faisons partie des privilégiés** we are among the privileged; **c'est un p.** *(d'un milieu favorisé)* he comes from a privileged background; **tu es un p.** *(tu as de la chance)* you're one of the privileged

privilégier [privileʒje] VT *(pr sub, impf n.* **privilégiions,** v. **privilégiiez)** *(personne, groupe)* to privilege; *(facteur, aspect)* to prioritize; **c'est l'objectif à p.** it's the objective to be prioritized

prix [pri] NM *1 (valeur)* value, worth; *(coût)* cost; *Fig* **à tout p.** at all costs, whatever the cost, at any price; **faire qch à p. d'argent** to do sth for money; **se vendre à p. d'or** *(de biens)* to fetch huge prices; **acheter qch à p. d'or** to pay a huge amount *or Fam* a fortune for sth; **à aucun p.** not on any terms, not at any price; **elle n'ira à aucun p.** she won't go on any terms *or* at any price, nothing will make her go; **à n'importe quel p.** no matter what it costs; **à tout p.** at all costs; **elle veut changer de travail à tout p.** she wants to change jobs no matter what it costs *or* takes; *Fig* **au p. de** at the cost of; **attacher beaucoup de p.** *ou* **un grand p. à qch** to set great store by sth, to set a lot of value on sth; **il attache beaucoup de p.** *ou* **un grand p. à l'apparence de sa voiture** he sets great store by his car's appearance, he prizes his car's appearance *2 (en argent)* price; **acheter qch à juste p.** to buy sth at a fair price, to pay a fair price for sth; **je l'ai acheté à bas p.** I didn't pay very much for it, I paid a low price for it; *Fam* **faire un p. à qn** to give sb a good deal; **vous nous faites un p. si on en prend deux?** will you give us a good price if we take two?; **je vous ferai un p. (d'ami)** I'll let you have it cheap; **une voiture dans mes p.** a car I can afford *or* within my means *or* within my price range; **ce n'est pas du tout dans mes p.** I can't afford it, it's way beyond my means *or* well outside my price range; **c'est plus dans mes p.** that's more in my price range *or* my line; *Bourse* **actions cotées au p. de ...** shares quoted at the rate of ...; **articles de p.** expensive goods; **coûter un p. fou** to cost the earth *or Fam* an arm and a leg; **hors de p.** prohibitively expensive; **ne pas avoir de p.** to be priceless; **la santé/le bonheur, ça n'a pas de p.**

minimum skeleton programme; *TV, Radio* **p. phare** top-rating programme, banker; **p. radiodiffusé** radio programme; **p. radiophonique** radio programme; *TV, Radio* **p. de stock** programme with re-run potential; **p. télé**TV programme

2 *Scol* **p. (d'études)** curriculum; *(d'un cours)* syllabus; **être** *ou* **figurer au p.** to be on the syllabus; **ne pas sortir du p.** not to depart from the syllabus; **les auteurs au** *ou* **du p.** the set books; **des auteurs hors p.** books that are not on the syllabus; **une question hors p.** a question not covered by the syllabus VOIR GRAMMAIRE A13

3 *(d'un parti politique, d'une entreprise commerciale)* programme, *Am* program, platform; **p. de réformes sociales** programme of social reform; **p. électoral** (election) platform; *Fig* **c'est tout un p.** it's quite a job *or* a business *or* an undertaking; **P. alimentaire mondial** World Food Programme; *Mktg* **p. d'amélioration de la qualité** quality improvement programme, QIP; **p. de fidélisation** frequent user programme; **p. de formation** training programme; **p. marketing** marketing programme; *Mktg* **p. marketing de fidélisation** frequency marketing programme, FMP; *Mktg* **p. de stimulation** incentive scheme; *Mktg* **p. de vente pyramidale** pyramid selling scheme; **p. de voyage de stimulation** incentive travel programme

4 *Ordinat* program; **p. d'amorçage** boot program; **p. antivirus** antivirus program; **p. d'arrière-plan** background program; **p. assembleur** assembler program; **p. d'autotest** self-test program; **p. de césure** hyphenation program; **p. de commande** driver; **p. de commande d'impression** printer driver; **p. de commande de la souris** mouse driver; **p. de configuration** configuration program; **p. de conversion** conversion program; **p. de courrier électronique** e-mail program; **p. en cours d'éxécution** active program; **p. de création de pages Web** web authoring program; **p. de dessin** drawing program, paint program; **p. détecteur de virus** virus detection program; **p. de diagnostic** malfunction routine; **p. éditeur de liens** link program, linker; **p. d'évaluation (de performance)** benchmark program; **p. de formatage** formatter; **p. de gestion** driver; **p. d'initialisation** initialization program; **p. d'installation** setup program, installer; **p. maître** master program; **p. objet** object program; **p. pilote** driver; **p. prioritaire** foreground program; **p. de publipostage** mailmerge program; **p. en recouvrement** overlay program; **p. résident** resident program; **p. de routage** router; **p. sentinelle** watchdog program; **p. source** source program; **p. système** system program; **p. de test** test program; **p. traducteur** interpreter; **p. de traitement par lots** batch program; **p. utilitaire** utility program; **p. virus** virus program

programmer [prɔgrame] *VT* **1** *Ordinat* to program; **p. en assembleur** to program in assembly language **2** *TV, Radio (émission)* to schedule **3** *(organiser, mettre au point) (vacances, changements)* to plan, to schedule *VI* **1** *TV, Radio* to schedule, to draw up a schedule **2** *Ordinat* to program

programmeur, -euse [prɔgramœr, -øz] *N Ordinat* programmer; **analyste-p.** systems analyst

progrès [prɔgrɛ] *NM* **1** *(avance)* progress; *(d'une armée)* progress, advance; *(d'une épidémie)* progress, spread; *(d'un incendie, d'une inondation)* spread

2 *(d'un élève, d'un malade)* progress, improvement; *(d'une enquête)* progress; **faire des p.** *(d'un élève, d'un malade)* to make progress, to improve; *(dans une enquête)* to make progress *or* headway; *Scol* **il n'a pas**

---

fait beaucoup de p. he hasn't made much progress *or* hasn't improved much; **le malade fait des p. satisfaisants** the patient is making satisfactory progress *or* is progressing satisfactorily; **on guette les moindres p. du malade** the patient is being watched for the slightest signs of progress *or* improvement; **suivre les p. d'un malade/d'un élève** to follow *or* monitor a patient's/pupil's progress; **la science a fait de grands p.** science has made great progress *or* great strides (forward); **suivre les p. d'une science** to keep abreast of a science; **suivre les p. d'une affaire** *Jur* to monitor *or* keep track of a case; *Com* to monitor *or* keep track of a transaction; **être en p.** to be making progress; **il y a un net p. par rapport à l'an dernier** it's a distinct improvement over last year; **un p. sensible vers la démocratie** a significant step *or* advance towards democracy; *Fam* **il y a du p.** there's been an improvement

3 le p. progress; **croire au p.** to believe in progress; **c'est ça, le p.!** that's progress for you!; *Pol* **un parti de p.** a party of progress, a progressive party; **le parti du p.** the party of progress

progresser [prɔgrese] *VI* **1** *(avancer) (d'une armée)* to advance, to progress; *(d'un marcheur)* to make progress; **p. lentement/rapidement** to make slow/rapid progress **2** *(évoluer) (d'une épidémie, d'un incendie)* to spread, to gain ground; **son cancer progresse** his cancer is spreading **3** *(faire des progrès) (d'un élève, d'un malade)* to make progress, to make headway, to improve; *(d'un projet)* to progress, to make progress; *(d'une enquête, d'un policier)* to make progress *or* headway; **p. lentement/rapidement** *(dans une étude/des recherches)* to make slow/rapid progress; **p. lentement/rapidement dans la lecture d'un livre** to make slow/rapid progress with a book, to get through a book slowly/quickly

progressif, -ive [prɔgresif, -iv] *ADJ* progressive; *(amélioration, expansion)* gradual; *(taux)* graduated, increasing; *Ling* **la forme progressive en anglais** the progressive *or* continuous form in English; **impôt p.** progressive *or* graduated tax VOIR GRAMMAIRE A49–52

progression [prɔgresjɔ̃] *NF* **1** *(avance) (d'une armée)* advance, progress; **la p. des marcheurs** the walkers' progress **2** *(évolution) (d'une incendie, d'une maladie, d'un cancer, d'une épidémie, du sida)* spread; *(de la délinquance, du chômage)* rise; *(d'un secteur économique)* expansion; *Bourse (des actions)* rise, improvement; *(dans une carrière)* progress, advancement; *(dans la société)* advancement; *(amélioration)* upturn; **être en p.** *(d'un secteur économique)* to be growing *or* expanding; *(d'une maladie)* to be spreading; *(du chômage, de la criminalité)* to be increasing *or* rising, to be on the increase *or* rise

▸▸ *Math* **p. arithmétique** arithmetical progression; *Mus* **p. harmonique** harmonic progression

progressiste [prɔgresist] *ADJ, N Pol* progressive

progressivement [prɔgresivmɑ̃] *ADV* progressively

progressivité [prɔgresivite] *NF* progressiveness; *(d'impôt)* graduation

prohiber [prɔibe] *VT* to prohibit, to forbid; **l'alcool est prohibé là-bas** alcohol is prohibited *or* forbidden there; **marchandises prohibées** illegal goods; **le port d'armes est prohibé** it is illegal to carry weapons, people are forbidden to carry weapons

prohibitif, -ive [prɔibitif, -iv] *ADJ* **1** *(prix)* prohibitive **2** *(loi etc)* prohibitory

prohibition [prɔibisjɔ̃] *NF* prohibition; **la p.**

---

du port d'armes the ban on carrying weapons; *Hist* **pendant la p.** during Prohibition; **p. d'importation** import ban

prohibitionnisme [prɔibisjɔnism] *NM Écon etc* prohibitionism

prohibitionniste [prɔibisjɔnist] *ADJ, N Écon etc* prohibitionist

proie [prwa] *NF* prey; *(à la chasse)* quarry; **oiseau de p.** bird of prey; **faire sa p. de qch** *(d'un animal)* to prey on sth; *Fig* **une p. facile/des proies faciles** easy prey *or* meat; **être la p. de qn** to be the prey *or* victim of sb; **une partie de la population est la p. de cette maladie** part of the population has fallen victim *or* prey to the disease; **les enfants sont la p. de la publicité** children are the victims of advertising; **la maison fut vite la p. des flammes** the house was soon devoured *or* consumed by the flames; **être en p. aux remords/au doute** to be racked *or* tormented by remorse/doubt, *Litt* to be prey to remorse/doubt; **une personne en p. à des obsessions/des hallucinations** a person prey to obsessions/hallucinations; **tomber en p. à la tentation** to fall prey to temptation

projecteur [prɔʒɛktœr] *NM* **1** *Cin, Phot* projector; **p. de diapositives** slide projector; *TV, Cin* **p. de décors** scenic projector; **p. de films** film projector; **p. de télévision** telejector; **p. à arc** brute, arc light; **p. à faisceau concentré** spotlight **2** *(lampe)* searchlight; *(sur un bâtiment, sur un monument)* floodlight; *Théâtre* spotlight; *Aut* headlamp, headlight; **illuminé par des projecteurs** floodlit; *Fig* **sous les projecteurs de l'actualité** in the limelight *or* news; *Aut* **p. antibrouillard** fog lamp; **p. halogène** halogen headlight; **p. polyéllipsoïde** poly-ellipsoid headlight; **p. de poursuite** follow spot

projectif, -ive [prɔʒɛktif, -iv] *ADJ Géom, Psy* projective

projectile [prɔʒɛktil] *NM* projectile; *(autoguidé)* missile

projection [prɔʒɛksjɔ̃] *NF* **1** *(fait de projeter)* projection; *(d'un liquide)* splashing; *(de boue)* splashing, splattering; *(de graisse)* spattering; **des projections de boue** splashes *or* splatters of mud; *Géol* projections volcaniques volcanic ash, *Spéc* (volcanic) ejecta; *Aut* **p. de gravillons** loose chippings **2** *Cin, Phot* projection; *Cin (d'un film)* screening, showing; **une p. de diapositives** a slide show; *Cin* **la p. durera 45 minutes** it will take 45 minutes to show the film, the screening will last 45 minutes; **nous avons vu le film en p. privée** we were given a private screening *or* showing (of the film); **appareil de p.** projector; **cabine de p.** projection booth; **par transparence** rear projection; **conférence avec projections** lecture (illustrated) with slides **3** *(de lumière)* beam **4** *Math, Archit etc* projection, plan; **p. horizontale** ground plan **5** *(image)* (outward) manifestation; *Psy* projection (**dans** onto); **cette expression est la p. de sa pensée** that expression reveals what he is thinking; *Psy* **faire une p. sur qn** to project oneself onto sb **6** *(prévision)* projection; **p. des ventes** sales projection

projectionniste [prɔʒɛksjɔnist] *N Cin* projectionist

projet [prɔʒɛ] *NM* **1** *(plan)* plan, project, scheme; *(travaux)* Scol, Univ project; **quels sont vos projets pour cet été?** what are your plans for the summer?; **avoir d'autres projets** to have other plans; **faire des projets** to make plans; **faire des projets d'avenir** to plan *or* make plans for the future; **faire** *ou* **former le p. de faire qch** to plan to do sth; **nous avons fait le p. de partir en Norvège l'an prochain** we're planning on *or* thinking about going to Norway next year; **p. d'entre-**

prise business plan; **p. d'OPA sur ...** planned takeover of ...; **p. de budget** draft budget; *Jur* **p. de contrat** draft agreement; *Jur* **p. de convention** draft treaty; *Jur* **p. de loi** bill; **mettre un p. de loi au vote** to vote on a bill; **adopter/repousser un p. de loi** to pass/reject a bill; **à l'état de p., en p.** at the planning stage; **ça n'est resté qu'à l'état de p.** it never got off the ground **2** *(d'un bâtiment)* plan; *(d'une machine)* blueprint

projeter [prɔʒte] *(conj like* **jeter***)* **VT 1** *(lancer)* to project; *(graisse)* to spatter; *(liquide)* to splash; *(boue)* to splatter, to splash; *(d'un volcan) (cendres)* to eject, to spew out; **le train projette des gravillons en passant** the train throws up loose stones as it passes; **la poêle chaude projette de la graisse** grease is spattering from the hot frying pan; **être projeté au sol/contre la vitre** to be thrown *or* flung *or* hurled to the ground/against the windscreen **2** *(ombre)* to cast, to throw **3** *Cin (film)* to show, to screen **4** *(voyage, expédition etc)* to plan, to think about; **p. de faire qch** to plan to do, to plan on doing sth **5** *Psy* to project (**sur** onto) **6** *Math* to project
VPR se projeter une ombre s'est projetée sur le mur a shadow fell *or* was cast on the wall; *Psy* **il se projette sur son fils** he's projecting himself onto his son

projeteur [prɔʒtœr] **NM** *Tech* planner; *(d'une machine etc)* designer

projo [prɔʒo] **NM** *Fam* projector

prolapsus [prɔlapsys] **NM** *Méd* prolapse

prolétaire [prɔletɛr] **ADJ, N** proletarian

prolétariat [prɔletarja] **NM** proletariat   VOIR
GRAMMAIRE A11

prolétarien, -ienne [prɔletarjɛ̃, -jɛn] **ADJ** proletarian

prolétarisation [prɔletarizasjɔ̃] **NF** proletarianization

prolétariser [prɔletarize] **VT** to proletarianize

prolifération [prɔliferasjɔ̃] **NF** proliferation; **p. des armes** arms proliferation

prolifère [prɔlifɛr] **ADJ** *Biol* proliferous

proliférer [prɔlifere] **VI** (**il prolifère; il proliférera**) to proliferate; **les affichages illégaux prolifèrent** flyposting is on the increase

prolifique [prɔlifik] **ADJ** prolific

prolixe [prɔliks] **ADJ** wordy, verbose, *Fml* prolix

prolixement [prɔliksəmɑ̃] **ADV** at great length

prolixité [prɔliksite] **NF** verbosity, *Fml* prolixity

prolo [prɔlo] *Péj Fam* **ADJ** *(accent, goûts)* plebby, working-class
N pleb, prole, oik

prologue [prɔlɔg] **NM** prologue (**de** to)

prolongation [prɔlɔ̃gasjɔ̃] **NF** *(de discussions)* prolongation, protraction; *(de congé, séjour)* extension, prolongation; *Ftbl* **jouer les prolongations** to play extra time *or Am* overtime

Do not confuse with **prolongement**, which conveys the idea of physical extension.

prolonge [prɔlɔ̃ʒ] **NF** *Mil* ammunition wagon; **p. d'artillerie** gun carriage *(at military funeral)*

prolongé [prɔlɔ̃ʒe] **ADJ** *(absence, séjour)* prolonged, lengthy; **visite très prolongée** very lengthy visit; **soupir p.** long-drawn-out sigh; **applaudissements prolongés** prolonged *or* sustained applause; **éviter tout séjour p. au soleil** do not stay in the sun too long, avoid prolonged exposure to the sun; **rue Crinas prolongée** = continuation of rue Crinas

prolongement [prɔlɔ̃ʒmɑ̃] **NM 1** *(d'une rue etc)* prolongation, continuation; *(d'un mur, d'une voie de chemin de fer)* extension; **je veux installer le Frigidaire® dans le p. de l'évier** I want the fridge in line with the sink; *Fig* **ce départ était dans le p. de sa toute première décision** the departure was in line with *or* consistent with his original decision **2 prolongements** *(d'une action etc)* ramifications (**de** of)

Do not confuse with **prolongation**, which only has to do with duration.

prolonger [prɔlɔ̃ʒe] *(***je prolongeai(s); n. prolongeons***)* **VT** *(la vie)* to prolong; *(séjour, absence)* to prolong, to extend; *(débat, discours, repas)* to prolong, to draw *or* spin out; *(mur, route, voie ferrée etc)* to extend *(***jusqu'à** to, as far as)*; *Rail* **p. un billet** to extend a ticket; **des écuries prolongent les murs de la maison** stables are built on to the house; *Math* **p. une droite** to continue *or* produce a line
VPR se prolonger *(d'une absence, une réunion)* to be prolonged; *(d'une rue etc)* to continue, to extend; *(d'une guerre, d'un film etc)* to go *or* carry on, to continue; **leur visite s'est prolongée jusqu'à minuit** they stayed until midnight; **la soirée ne s'est pas prolongée très tard** the party didn't go on till very late *or* finished quite early; **mais il ne faudrait pas que cela se prolonge** but it mustn't be for too long

promenade [prɔmnad] **NF 1** *(balade)* walk; *(courte)* stroll; *(en voiture)* drive, outing, trip; **faire une p. (à pied)** to go for a walk; **faire une p. en voiture** to go for a drive *or* a run; **faire une p. à bicyclette** to go for a bike ride; **faire une p. à cheval** to go (horse)riding, to go for a ride; **faire une p. en bateau** *(en canot)* row; *(en voilier)* sail; **être en p.** *(à pied)* to be out walking, to be out for a walk; *(à bicyclette)* to be out on a bike ride; *(à cheval)* to be out riding, to be out for a ride; **ils ne sont pas chez eux, ils sont en p.** they've gone out; **faire faire une p. à qn** to take sb (out) for a walk; **l'heure de la p.** *(d'un détenu)* exercise time; *Mil* **p. militaire** route march; *Mus* **concert p.** promenade concert, *Br* prom **2** *(avenue) (au bord de la mer)* promenade

promener [prɔmne] *(***je promène; je promènerai***)* **VT 1** *(faire aller, conduire)* **p. qn** *(à pied)* to take sb (out) for a walk; *(en voiture)* to take sb (out) for a drive; **p. le chien** to take the dog for a walk, to walk the dog, to take the dog out; **p. son cheval** to exercise one's horse; **p. des amis à travers Paris** to show *or* take friends round Paris; *Fam* **cela vous promènera un peu** it'll get you out (of the house) a bit; **ça te tristesse** to parade one's sadness; **je promenais toujours les mêmes idées sombres** I couldn't shake off my dark thoughts, the same dark thoughts were always with me; *Fig* **il m'a promené de musée en musée** he dragged me from museum to museum; *Fig Fam* **j'ai vraiment l'impression qu'il me promène** I really get the impression that he's having me on *or* taking me for a ride; **j'en ai assez qu'on me promène** I've had enough of being taken for a ride **2** *(faire aller) (sa main)* to run (**sur** over); **p. ses yeux sur** *(liste, texte)* to run one's eye(s) over, to scan; *(salle, foule)* to scan
VPR se promener 1 *(se balader)* to walk; *Ordinat* to browse; **je vais me p.** I'm going (out) for a walk *or* stroll; **se p. en Auvergne** to tour Auvergne; *Ordinat* **se p. dans** *(texte)* to scroll through; *(base de données)* to browse through; *(se omitted)* **mener p. les enfants** to take the children (out) for a walk; *Fam* **envoyer p. qn** to send sb packing, to send sb off with a flea in his/her ear; **va te p.!** get out!, *Fam* get lost!, *Am* take a hike!

2 *(des yeux, des pensées etc)* to wander; *Fig Fam* **cette vieille chaise s'est promenée dans toute la maison** that old chair has found its way into *or* has been in every room in the house; *Fam* **il laisse se p. ses affaires partout** he leaves his things lying about *or* around all over the place
3 *Fam (éprouver de la facilité)* **il se promène en anglais** he finds English a pushover

promeneur, -euse [prɔmnœr, -øz] **N** *(dans un parc etc)* stroller, walker; *(randonneur)* walker, rambler

promenoir [prɔmnwar] **NM** promenade, (covered) walk; *(dans une cour de justice etc)* lobby; *Théâtre Vieilli* promenade

promesse [prɔmɛs] **NF 1** *(serment)* promise; *Mktg* claim; **faire une p.** to make a promise; **je vais te faire une p.** I'm going to make you a promise; **tu pourrais me faire une p.?** will you promise me something?; **elle m'a fait la p. de ne plus en parler** she has promised me not to speak of it again; **elle m'avait fait de grandes promesses** she promised me great things; **tenir sa p.** to keep one's promise; **tu as ma p.** you have my word *or* promise; **manquer à sa p.** to break one's promise; *Com* **p. écrite** written promise, written undertaking; **p. de Gascon** empty *or* hollow promise; *Fig* **la p. d'un avenir meilleur** the promise of a better future; *Fig* **ces réunions sont la p. d'une paix future** these meetings hold out the hope of peace; *Fig* **plein de promesses** full of promise, that shows a great deal of promise, very promising; **un avenir plein de promesses** a very promising *or* bright future; *Pol* **p. électorale** electoral promise; *Mktg* **p. mensongère** false claim **2** *Com etc* undertaking to pay; **p. d'achat/de vente** agreement *or* undertaking to purchase/undertaking *or* promise to sell

Prométhée [prɔmete] **N** Prometheus

prométhéen, -enne [prɔmeteɛ̃, -ɛn] **ADJ** *Litt* Promethean

prometteur, -euse [prɔmetœr, -øz] **ADJ** *(artiste, premier roman etc)* promising, full of promise; *(sourire)* full of promise; **des débuts prometteurs** a promising start; **c'est très p.!** it's very promising!

promettre [prɔmetr] *(conj like* **mettre***)* **VT 1** to promise; **p. qch à qn** to promise sb sth, to promise sth to sb; **je ne peux rien te p.** I can't promise (you), I can't make any promises, I can't guarantee it; **tu (me) le promets?** (do you) promise?; **je (te) le promets!** I promise (you)!; **je te promets de lui en parler** I promise you that I'll talk to him/her about it, I promise to talk to him/her about it; **il m'a promis qu'il le ferait** he promised (me) he'd do it; **on promet une forte récompense** a handsome reward is being offered; **le médecin promet un prompt rétablissement** the doctor predicts a speedy recovery; **je te rembourserai, c'est promis** I'll pay you back, I promise; *Fam* **tu le regretteras, je te le promets!** you'll regret it, mark my words *or* take my word for it!; *Fam* **je m'en souviendrai du 1er mai, je te le promets!** you can take it from me *or* you can take my word for it that I won't forget the first of May!; *Fam* **je vous promets qu'on s'est amusé** we had a really great time **2** *(faire espérer)* **il promet d'éclipser tous ses rivaux** he looks set *or* he promises to eclipse all his rivals; **la soirée promet d'être amusante** it promises to be an amusing evening; **ça nous promet de gros orages** it looks as if we're in for some violent storms; **ce vent nous promet une mer agitée** we're in for rough seas judging from this wind; **la hausse des taux d'intérêt ne promet rien de bon pour l'industrie** the rise in interest rates does not look good *or Fml* does not augur well for industry

vi *(d'un projet etc)* to look promising; **un enfant qui promet** a child with promise; *Fam* **ça promet!** *(avant, au début d'une affaire)* that looks promising!; *Iron* great!, terrific!; *Iron* **eh bien, ça promet pour la fin de la semaine!** well then, it looks as if we're in for a great weekend!; *Iron* **vraiment, ça promet pour le reste de la soirée!** well now, the rest of the evening promises to be rather interesting!

vpr se promettre 1 *(mutuellement)* to promise (to) each other; **ils se sont promis de ne plus se disputer** they promised (each other) not to *or* that they wouldn't quarrel any more **2 se p. qch** to promise oneself sth **3** *(décider)* **se p. de travailler** to make up one's mind *or* to resolve to work; **je me suis promis de ne pas pleurer devant lui** I made up my mind *or* I promised myself that I wouldn't cry in front of him

promis, -ise [prɔmi, -iz] **adj** promised; **la Terre promise** the Promised Land; **p. à destined for**; **il est p. à un grand avenir** he is destined for a great future, he has a great future ahead of him

n *Vieilli, Région* fiancé, *f* fiancée, betrothed

promiscuité [prɔmiskɥite] **nf** overcrowding; **vivre dans la p.** to live in crowded accommodation; **je ne supportais plus la p. de cet appartement** I couldn't take the overcrowding in the flat any more; **je déteste la p. des transports en commun** I hate the crowding *or* the crowds on public transport; **je ne supporte pas la p.** I can't bear having people around me, I need lots of space; **la p. des plages en été** the overcrowding of beaches in summer

> Il faut noter que le terme anglais **promiscuity** est un faux ami. Il désigne uniquement **un changement fréquent de partenaires sexuels**.

promo [prɔmo] **nf** *Fam* promo; **en p.** on special offer

promontoire [prɔmɔ̃twar] **nm** promontory, headland; *(plus grand)* cape

promoteur, -trice [prɔmɔtœr, -tris] **n 1** *Com* promoter; **p. (immobilier)** property developer **2** *(créateur)* originator *(de* of)

promotion [prɔmosjɔ̃] **nf 1** *(avancement)* promotion; *Rel* preferment; **p. à l'ancienneté** promotion by seniority; **p. interne** internal promotion, promotion from within the company; **p. sociale** upward mobility, *Fml* social advancement

2 *Univ* (students of the same) year, *Am* class; **camarade de p.** fellow student; **le premier de sa p.** the first in his year

3 *Com* promotion; **articles en p.** items on promotion *or Am* on special; **notre p. de la semaine** this week's special offer *or Am* special; **faire une p. sur un produit** to promote a product; **faire la p. de** to sell, to promote; **faire de la p. immobilière** to go in for property development; **contrat de p. immobilière** property development contract; **p. (en quatrième de couverture)** (back-cover) blurb; *Mktg* **p. auprès des intermédiaires** trade promotion order; *Mktg* **p. collective** tie-in promotion; *Mktg* **p. d'entreprises** corporate identity; *Mktg* **p. par une personnalité** personality promotion; *Mktg* **p. sur le lieu de vente** point-of-sale promotion; *Mktg* **p. sur point d'achat** point-of-purchase promotion; **p. spéciale** special promotion; **p. des ventes** sales promotion

nfpl *Suisse* **promotions** *(remise de diplômes)* = school prizegiving ceremony marking the move up to the next class

promotionnel, -elle [prɔmosjɔnɛl] **adj**

Com (brochure) promotional; *(tarif)* special; **vente promotionnelle** special offer

promouvoir [prɔmuvwar] **vt** *(conj like* **mouvoir) 1** *(donner un avancement à)* to promote; **être promu** to be promoted, to get promotion; **elle a été promue chef du personnel** she's been promoted *or* moved up to personnel manager **2** *Fig (favoriser)* *(recherche, création d'entreprise, relations entre États)* to promote, to further **3** *Com* to promote; *(à prix réduit)* to put on special offer *or Am* on special

prompt [prɔ̃] **adj** *(réaction, condamnation)* prompt, quick, swift; *(vengeance)* swift, speedy; **avoir la main prompte** to be quick with one's hands *or* to raise one's hand; **avoir la repartie prompte** to be always ready with an answer, *Fml* to have a ready wit; **nous vous souhaitons un p. rétablissement** we wish you a speedy recovery, get well soon; **esprit p.** quick mind; *(sens de l'humour)* ready wit; **être d'humeur prompte** to be quick-tempered; **il est p. à la colère** *ou* **à se fâcher** he loses his temper *or* flares up easily, *Fml* he is quick to anger; **p. à agir** quick *or* prompt to act; **p. à décider** decisive; **p. à la riposte** quick with a riposte

promptement [prɔ̃tmɑ̃, prɔ̃ptəmɑ̃] **adv** *Litt* promptly, quickly, swiftly

prompteur [prɔ̃ptœr] **nm** teleprompt(er), Autocue®; **p. déroulant** roller prompter

promptitude [prɔ̃tityd] **nf** *Litt (d'une réaction etc)* promptness, quickness, swiftness; **avec toute la p. possible** with all possible dispatch

promu, -ue [prɔmy] **adj** (who has been) promoted

n person who has been promoted; *Univ* **les nouveaux promus** = this year's graduates *(of a grande école)*

promulgation [prɔmylgasjɔ̃] **nf** *(d'une loi)* promulgation; *(d'un décret)* publication

promulguer [prɔmylge] **vt** *(loi)* to promulgate; *(décret)* to publish, to issue

prône [pron] **nm** *Rel* sermon, homily

prôner [prone] **vt** *(patience, indulgence, tolérance)* to strongly recommend, to advocate, to urge; *(méthode)* to strongly recommend, to advocate

pronom [prɔnɔ̃] **nm** *Gram* pronoun; **p. défini/indéfini/interrogatif** definite/indefinite/interrogative pronoun **SEE GRAMMAR A27–38; B14–23**

pronominal, -ale, -aux, -ales [prɔnɔminal, -o] **adj** *Gram* pronominal

pronominalement [prɔnɔminalmɑ̃] **adv** pronominally

prononçable [prɔnɔ̃sabl] **adj** pronounceable

prononcé [prɔnɔ̃se] **adj** *(traits)* strong; *(forme)* strong, definite; *(tendance)* marked; *(accent)* broad, strong, pronounced; **courbe prononcée** sharp curve; **avoir un goût p. pour qch** to have a strong *or* distinct taste for sth; **peu p.** *(accent)* faint, slight; *(forme)* indefinite, vague; *(relief)* flattish; **avoir un goût peu p. pour qch** to have little taste for sth

nm *Jur* decision; **p. du jugement** verdict

prononcer [prɔnɔ̃se] (**je prononçai(s); n. prononçons**) **vt 1** *(dire) (mot)* to say, to utter; **il a prononcé quelques paroles sur ...** he said a few words about ...; **c'est à peine s'il prononça quelques paroles** he hardly said a word; **sans p. un mot** without (uttering) a word; **il a prononcé quelques mots entre ses dents** he muttered a few words; **il ne faut jamais p. son nom** you must never mention him *or* his name

2 *(déclarer) (discours)* to deliver, to make; *Jur (arrêt)* to deliver; **p. une sentence** to pass *or* pronounce sentence; **p. un divorce** to

pronounce *or* declare a couple divorced; *Rel* **p. ses vœux** to take one's vows

3 *(articuler) (mot)* to pronounce; **mal p. un mot** to mispronounce a word

vi 1 *(articuler)* to pronounce (one's words); **apprendre à p.** to learn to pronounce one's words properly, to learn proper pronunciation; **p. bien/mal** to have good/bad pronunciation

2 *Jur (s'exprimer)* to give one's verdict (**sur qch** on sth); **p. en faveur de qn** to decide *or* declare in favour of sb; **p. sur une question** to adjudge *or* adjudicate a question

vpr se prononcer 1 *(être articulé)* to be pronounced; **ça s'écrit comme ça se prononce** it is written as it is pronounced; **comment se prononce ...?** how do you pronounce ...?; **le s ne se prononce pas** the s isn't pronounced, the s is silent

2 *(apparaître) (de différences)* to become more pronounced; *(de rides)* to become more marked

3 *(s'exprimer)* to give an opinion; *(d'un juge)* to give a decision; **le médecin ne s'est pas encore prononcé** the doctor has not yet given his prognosis; **j'ai mis longtemps avant de me p.** it took me a long time to make up my mind; **50 pour cent ne se prononcent pas** *(dans un sondage)* 50 per cent are undecided; **se p. pour** *ou* **en faveur de qn/qch** to express one's support for sb/sth; **ils se sont prononcés pour** *ou* **en faveur de/contre la construction du barrage** they said they were in favour of/against the dam being built; **se p. contre qn/qch** to express one's opposition to sb/sth

prononciation [prɔnɔ̃sjasjɔ̃] **nf 1** *(articulation)* pronunciation; **défaut de p.** speech defect; **faute de p.** mispronunciation, mistake in pronunciation; **elle a une très bonne/mauvaise p.** her pronunciation is very good/bad **2** *(d'un discours)* delivery; *Jur (d'une condamnation)* passing; *(d'un divorce)* pronouncement; *(d'un arrêt)* delivering

pronostic [prɔnɔstik] **nm 1** *(prévision)* forecast, prediction, prognosis; **quel est votre p. pour le match/la course?** what's your forecast for the match/race?, who do you tip to win the match/race? **2** *Méd* prognosis

pronostiquer [prɔnɔstike] **vt 1** *(prévoir)* to forecast, to predict; **je lui pronostique la première place** I predict that he'll come in first, I tip him for first place; **on pronostique qu'elle prendra la première place** she's being tipped for first place **2** *Méd* **un p. prompt rétablissement** to predict a speedy recovery

pronostiqueur, -euse [prɔnɔstikœr, -øz] **n** forecaster, pundit; *Sport* tipster

pronunciamiento [prɔnunsjamjɛnto] **nm** *Pol* pronunciamiento

propagande [prɔpagɑ̃d] **nf** *Péj* propaganda; *Pol* **faire de la p. pour qn** to electioneer on behalf of sb; **c'est de la p.!** it's propaganda!; **p. électorale** electioneering

propagandiste [prɔpagɑ̃dist] **adj, n** propagandist

propagateur, -trice [prɔpagatœr, -tris] **n** *(de nouvelles)* spreader; *(d'idées)* disseminator

propagation [prɔpagasjɔ̃] **nf** *(d'une plante, d'une espèce)* propagation; *(d'une épidémie, d'une rumeur, d'une nouvelle)* spreading; *(d'idées, d'une doctrine)* spreading, dissemination, *Fml* propagation; *Phys* **la vitesse de p. d'une onde** the velocity of propagation of a wave

propager [prɔpaʒe] (**je propageai(s); n. propageons**) **vt** *(plante, espèce)* to propagate; *(épidémie)* to spread; *(rumeur, nouvelle)* to spread, *Litt* to spread abroad; *(idées, doctrine)* to spread, *Fml* to propagate; **p. une mode** to spread *or* popularize a fashion

VPR se propager 1 (d'une épidémie etc) to spread **2** Phys (de la lumière, du son) to be propagated **3** Biol (d'une plante etc) to propagate, to reproduce

propane [prɔpan] NM Chimie propane

propanier [prɔpanje] NM Naut propane tanker

propédeutique [prɔpedøtik] NF **1** (enseignement préparatoire) propaedeutics **2** Univ Anciennement = first year of university course

propène [prɔpɛn] NM Tech propene

propension [prɔpɑ̃sjɔ̃] NF propensity, tendency, inclination (à to)

propergol [prɔpergɔl] NM Tech (rocket) propellant

prophète, prophétesse [prɔfɛt, prɔfetɛs] N prophet, f prophetess, Litt seer; **parler en p.** to prophesy; **p. de malheur** prophet of doom, Jeremiah; **nul n'est p. en son pays** no man is a prophet in his own country

prophétie [prɔfesi] NF prophecy

prophétique [prɔfetik] ADJ prophetic

prophétiquement [prɔfetikmɑ̃] ADV prophetically

prophétiser [prɔfetize] VT to prophesy, to foretell

prophylactique [prɔfilaktik] ADJ Méd prophylactic

prophylaxie [prɔfilaksi] NF Méd prophylaxis

propice [prɔpis] ADJ propitious (à to); (signe, commencement) auspicious; (conditions) favourable, Am favorable; **attendre le moment p. pour faire qch** to wait for the right moment to do sth; **cet endroit est p. au repos** it's a restful spot; **un climat p. à la guérison des malades** a good climate for people who are ill; **ce festival est p. aux rencontres** the festival is a good place to meet people; **si la fortune nous est p.** if Fortune smiles on us; **peu p.** unpropitious; (signe, commencement) inauspicious; **c'est arrivé à un moment peu p.** it did not come at a very good time

propitiation [prɔpisjasjɔ̃] NF Rel propitiation

propitiatoire [prɔpisjatwar] ADJ Rel propitiatory

proportion [prɔpɔrsjɔ̃] NF **1** proportion; Math ratio; **il a bien respecté les proportions** he got the proportions right; **la p. du tronc et des jambes** the size of the trunk (as) compared with the legs; **varier en p. directe/inverse** to vary in direct proportion or ratio/in indirect proportion or inverse ratio (de to); **p. d'alcool dans un vin** percentage of alcohol in a wine, alcohol content of a wine; **les bénéfices ont augmenté dans une p. de 30 pour cent** profits have risen by 30 per cent; **à p., en p.** proportionally, proportionately, in proportion; **à p. de, en p. de** in proportion to; **payé en p. du travail fourni/des heures passées** paid in proportion to or according to the amount of work done/the number of hours; **tout augmente, et les salaires à p.** everything is going up, and salaries are keeping pace; **hors de (toute) p. avec** out of (all) proportion to; Fig **cette dispute est sans p. avec son objet** the argument is out of all proportion to the issue; **des travaux hors de p.** work of huge proportions; **toute(s) proportion(s) gardée(s)** up to a point, in certain respects SEE GRAMMAR 859

2 proportions size, proportions; **salle de vastes proportions** hall of vast proportions or dimensions; **dans de plus vastes proportions** on a much larger scale; **si les commandes diminuent dans de sérieuses proportions** if orders should decrease to any great

extent; **cette histoire a pris de sérieuses proportions** this business has assumed serious proportions; **pourquoi les choses ont-elles pris de telles proportions?** why have things escalated to such an extent?

proportionnalité [prɔpɔrsjɔnalite] NF **1** Math proportionality **2** (rapport) balance, (good) proportions **3** (répartition) equal distribution **4** Écon **p. de l'impôt** fixed rate system of taxation

proportionné [prɔpɔrsjɔne] ADJ **1 bien/mal p.** (corps etc) well/badly proportioned **2** proportionate, proportional (à to); (de la même échelle, du même degré) commensurate (à with); **la cotisation est proportionnée à vos revenus** payment is in proportion or proportional or proportionate to your income; **salaire p. aux qualifications** salary commensurate with qualifications

proportionnel, -elle [prɔpɔrsjɔnɛl] ADJ proportional (à to); Pol **représentation proportionnelle** proportional representation; Ordinat **espacement p.** proportional spacing; **inversement p.** inversely proportional, in inverse ratio (à to); **impôt p. (au revenu)** fixed-rate or fixed-percentage income tax
NF **proportionnelle 1** Math proportional **2** Pol proportional representation; **élu à la proportionnelle** elected by proportional representation

proportionnellement [prɔpɔrsjɔnɛlmɑ̃] ADV proportionally, proportionately, in proportion (à to)

proportionner [prɔpɔrsjɔne] VT to adapt, to adjust, to proportion (à to); **p. les dépenses aux ressources** to adjust expenditure to suit resources, Fam Prov to cut one's coat according to one's cloth

propos [prɔpo] NM **1** (sujet) subject, matter; **à ce p.** talking of which, while we're on the subject, in connection with that; **à p., avez-vous lu ce livre?** by the way or by the by or incidentally, have you read this book?; **à tout p.** constantly, at every turn; **dire qch à p.** to say sth to the point, to say sth suitable or appropriate; **elle n'est pas du tout intervenue à p.** what she had to say was entirely irrelevant; **vous avez réagi tout à fait à p.** you reacted quite appropriately; **jeté à p., fait à p.** (mot, remarque) timely; **faire qch à p.** to do sth at the right moment; **arriver fort à p.** to arrive at just the right moment or in the nick of time; **juger à p. de faire qch** to consider it advisable to do sth, to see fit to do sth; **mal à p.** at the wrong time or moment, Fml inopportunely; **tu ne pouvais pas tomber plus mal à p.** you couldn't have come at a worse time or Fml a more inopportune moment; **hors de p.** (remarque) irrelevant; **il est intervenu tout à fait hors de p.** what he had to say was entirely irrelevant; **à p. de** about, in connection with, with regard to, on the subject of; **à p. de rien** (se disputer, se chamailler, s'agiter) about nothing, for nothing at all, for no reason whatever; **à p. de tout et de rien** about anything and everything; **à p. de quoi?, à quel p.?** what about?; **à quel p. t'a-t-elle dit cela?** what did she say that to you for?; **c'est à quel p.?** what's it about?; **elle veut te voir – à quel p.?** she wants to see you – what about or what for?

2 (intention) purpose, intention, resolution; **avoir la ferme p. de faire qch** to firmly intend to do sth, to have the firm intention of doing sth; **de p. délibéré** deliberately, on purpose; **tel n'est pas mon p.** that is not my intention; **ce n'est pas le p.** that's not the point

3 (parole) des **p.** talk, words; **p. méchants/désagréables** nasty/unpleasant remarks; **les p. qu'ils échangèrent sont restés confidentiels** their talk or conversation has remained confidential; **des p. de table**

table talk; **changer de p.** to change the subject

proposer [prɔpoze] VT (projet, solution, idée, plan d'action etc) to propose, to suggest; (théorie) to propose, to suggest, Fml to propound; (définition, interprétation, lecture d'un texte) to suggest, to offer, to propose; (appartement, somme d'argent, travail) to offer; Parl (amendement, décret, loi) to table, to propose, to move, to put forward; **mais que propose-t-il d'autre?** but what else does he have to suggest?; **c'est tout ce que tu proposes comme idée?** is that all you have to offer by way of an idea?; **écoutez, voilà ce que je vous propose** listen, this is what I suggest; **'allons boire une bière', proposa-t-elle** 'let's go for a beer', she suggested; **ils (vous) proposent deux semaines aux Seychelles pour une misère** they're offering two weeks in the Seychelles for next to nothing; **le cinéma le César vous propose cette semaine ...** this week at le César: ...; **aujourd'hui le restaurant vous propose comme plat du jour ...** today's special is ...; **p. ses services à qn** to offer or volunteer one's services to sb; **je vous en propose 6000 euros/un bon prix** I'll give you 6,000 euros/a good price for it; **il m'a proposé un bon prix pour la voiture** he offered me a good price for the car; **p. un candidat** to put forward or put up or propose a candidate; **être proposé pour un emploi** to be suggested or proposed or recommended for a job; **son nom a été proposé plusieurs fois** his name has been suggested or put forward several times; **puis-je vous p. mon parapluie?** would you like or can I offer you my umbrella?; **p. que l'on fasse qch** to suggest or propose that sth should be done; **je propose que l'on passe d'abord au marché** I suggest going or that we go to the market first; **je propose que nous commencions par le problème du Brésil** (en ouverture de discours) I propose to start with the problem of Brazil; **je lui ai proposé de venir avec moi** I suggested (to him) that he should come with me; **je vous propose d'attendre jusqu'à ce que ...** I suggest waiting or that you should wait until ...; **elle m'a proposé de m'aider** she offered to help me
VI to propose; **je le laisse p.** I leave him to make the suggestions; **l'homme propose et Dieu dispose** man proposes and God disposes
VPR se proposer 1 (se présenter) to come forward, to offer one's services; **se p. comme secrétaire** to offer to act as secretary, to offer one's services or oneself as secretary; **se p. pour faire qch** to offer or volunteer to do sth **2** il s'est proposé cet objectif he set himself this objective; **se p. de faire qch** to propose to do sth

> Il faut noter que le verbe anglais **to propose to somebody** signifie **demander quelqu'un en mariage**.

proposition [prɔpozisjɔ̃] NF **1** (suggestion) proposal, suggestion, proposition; (d'emploi) offer; **faire une p.** to make a suggestion or proposal; (dans une assemblée) to put or propose a motion; **si vous voulez acheter l'appartement, faites-moi une p.** if you want to buy the flat, make me an offer; **il a fait une p. pour l'appartement à 60 000 euros** he made an offer or he offered 60,000 euros for the flat; **si quelqu'un a une p. à faire** if anyone has any suggestions; **je vais vous faire une p.: vous vous occupez de ...** I've got a proposition for you: you deal with ...; **de nombreux réalisateurs lui ont fait des propositions (de film)** lots of directors have offered him films, he's had lots of offers from directors; **faire des propositions à une femme** to proposition a woman; **mettre**

une **p. aux voix** to put a motion to the vote; **sur la p. de** at the suggestion of; **dernière p.** final offer; **p. de loi** *Br* ≃ private member's bill, *Am* ≃ private bill; **propositions de paix** peace proposals; **p. d'assurance** insurance proposal; *Mktg* **p. d'idées** ideation; **p. de paiement** payment proposal; **p. de prix** price proposal; **p. ferme** firm offer; **p. unique** unique proposition; *Mktg* **p. unique de vente** unique selling proposition, USP **2** *Phil, Math etc* proposition **3** *Gram* clause; **p. principale/subordonnée/relative** main/subordinate/relative clause; **p. circonstancielle de temps/lieu/but** adverbial clause of time/place/purpose SEE GRAMMAR A4; B2

PROPRE [prɔpr]

ADJ proper **1** ▪ characteristic **2** ▪ own **3** ▪ appropriate **4** ▪ clean **5** ▪ neat **5** ▪ tidy **5**
NM characteristic **1**

ADJ SEE GRAMMAR B10 **1** *(exact)* proper; **signification p. d'un mot** proper meaning of a word; **le mot est ici employé au sens p.** the word is used literally here; **un débile, au sens p. du mot** a mental defective in the true sense of the word; **chercher le mot p.** to try to find the right *or* appropriate word
2 *(particulier)* characteristic (à of), *Fml* peculiar (à to); **c'est une technique qui lui est p.** it's a technique that is characteristic of him; **une façon de marcher à lui p.** his own particular *or* characteristic way of walking
3 *(personnel)* own; **mon p. argent** my own money; **ses idées lui sont propres** his ideas are his own; **c'est par ta p. faute que ...** it's your own fault if ...; **de son p. chef** on one's own, *Fam* off one's own bat; **voir/entendre qch de ses propres yeux/oreilles** to see/hear sth with one's own eyes/ears; **je le lui ai remis en main(s) propre(s)** I delivered it to him/her personally; **à remettre en main p.** to be delivered to the addressee in person; **dans votre p. intérêt** in your own interest; **ce sont là ses propres paroles** those are his very words
4 *(convenable)* appropriate, suitable, proper, fitting; **p. à qch** adapted *or* fitted *or* suited to sth; **un lieu p. aux rencontres** a good place for meeting people; **l'endroit le plus p. au camping** the best *or* most suitable place for camping; **des conditions peu propres à la discussion** conditions that are not very conducive to a discussion; **exercice p. à aiguiser l'intelligence** exercise calculated to sharpen the wits; **p. à rien** good for nothing
5 *(impeccable)* *(linge, maison, hôtel), Scol (copie)* clean; *(bureau, apparence)* neat; *(soigné, bien présenté) (travail)* neat, tidy; *(non polluant) (moteur, voiture)* clean, non-polluting; **n'utilise pas la serviette de ton frère, ce n'est pas p.!** don't use your brother's towel, it's not hygienic!; **une énergie p.** a clean form of energy; **chambre p. et nette** clean and tidy room; **je n'ai plus rien de p.** I haven't (got) anything clean to wear; **habillé de p.** wearing clean clothes; **p. comme un sou neuf** as clean as a new pin, spick and span; *(personne)* spick and span; **être p. sur soi** to be clean, to have clean habits; *Fam* **nous voilà propres!** we're in a fine *or* nice mess!; **le chat est un animal très p.** the cat is a very clean animal; **mon bébé était p. à vingt mois** my baby was potty-trained at twenty months; **la pianiste a un jeu très p.** the pianist has a very clean style
6 *Fig (réputation)* spotless; *(conscience)* clear; *Fam* **elle n'est pas p., son affaire** there's something shady *or Fam* not quite kosher about the business; **ça ne me paraît pas très p., tout ça** it all seems a bit shady *or* dodgy to me; **ce n'est pas très p., tout ça** *(du point de vue moral)* that's a bit tacky

NM 1 *(d'une nation, d'une personne etc)* property, attribute, characteristic; *(caractère, nature)* nature; **le p. de l'homme** man's distinguishing feature
2 *(sens propre)* **au p.** in the literal sense; **employer un mot au p.** to use a word in its literal sense *or* literally
3 avoir qch en p. to possess sth in one's own right; **la maison m'appartient en p.** the house is mine, the house belongs to me; **il a un exemplaire en p.** he has a copy of his own
4 *Scol* **mettre qch au p.** to make a neat copy of sth, to copy sth out neatly; **recopier qch au p.** to make a fair *or* clean copy of sth, to copy sth (neatly)
5 c'est du p.! *(saleté)* what a mess!; *(action immorale)* that's not right!, *Fam* that's a bit tacky!
6 ça sent le p. it smells clean; **ça sent le p. dans toute la maison** the whole house smells clean

Il faut noter que l'adjectif anglais **proper** est un faux ami. Il ne se rapporte jamais à la propreté.

propre-à-rien, *pl* **propres-à-rien** N good-for-nothing, *Vieilli* ne'er-do-well

proprement [prɔprəmɑ̃] **ADV 1** *(d'une manière propre)* cleanly; **une maison p. tenue** a well-kept house; **p. vêtu** correctly *or* properly dressed; **manger p.** not to make a mess when eating; **mange tes brochettes p.!** don't make a mess with your kebabs!; **tu ne sais pas encore manger p.!** you still can't eat without making a mess!
2 *Fam (convenablement)* well; *(de façon efficace)* efficiently; *(odieux, ridicule)* thoroughly, altogether, absolutely; **assez p.** tolerably well; *Iron* **se faire renvoyer p.** to be sent packing, to be sent off with a flea in one's ear; **il l'a p. ridiculisée** he made an absolute fool of her; **ils se sont fait p. battre par les concurrents** they were thoroughly *or* well and truly beaten *or Fam* they were hammered by the other side; **c'est p. scandaleux!** it's an absolute disgrace!
3 *(avec honnêteté) (se conduire)* decently, honourably, fairly; **se tirer d'affaire p.** to get out of a difficult situation with one's honour intact
4 à p. parler strictly speaking; **pas à p. parler** not exactly; **p. dit** actual; **pierres précieuses p. dites** precious stones according to the strictest definition of the term
5 *(strictement)* strictly (speaking); **c'est un problème p. urbain** it's purely *or* strictly an inner-city problem

Il faut noter que l'adverbe anglais **properly** est un faux ami. Il signifie **correctement**.

propret, -ette [prɔprɛ, -ɛt] **ADJ** neat, tidy
propreté [prɔprəte] **NF 1** *(hygiène, soin)* cleanliness; *(des vêtements, de la vaisselle)* cleanness; *(d'une pièce, d'un travail)* neatness, tidiness **2** *(de moteur etc)* cleanness
propriétaire [prɔprietɛr] **N 1** *(d'une voiture, d'une propriété etc)* owner; *(d'une entreprise, d'un hôtel)* proprietor, *f* proprietress, owner; **devenir** *ou* **se rendre p. de qch** to acquire sth; **p. (de maison)** householder; **qui est le p. de cette terre?** who owns this land?; **p. foncier** landowner; **être p.** to be a man/woman of property *or* a landowner; *(de maison)* to be a property owner, to have a house *or* home of one's own; **maintenant que vous êtes p.** now that you're a homeowner, now that you own your own home; **vous voulez faire le tour du p.?** would you like a guided tour? **2** *(qui loue)* landlord, *f* landlady
propriété [prɔpriete] **NF 1** *(fait de posséder)*

ownership, proprietorship; *(chose possédée)* property; *(terres)* property, estate; **une p. de 20 hectares** a 20-hectare estate; **p. privée/publique** private/public property; **titres de p.** title deeds; **p. littéraire** literary property; *(droit)* copyright; **p. artistique** copyright; **p. collective** social ownership; **p. de l'État** government *or* state property; **p. industrielle** patent rights, industrial property; **p. intellectuelle** intellectual property; **p. foncière** landed property, landed estate; **p. foncière (perpétuelle et) libre** freehold; **p. immobilière** property; **propriétés immobilières** real estate, *surtout Am* realty; **p. de l'État** government property; *Fin* **p. allégée, p.-loisirs, p.-vacances** = timeshare taken on a lease basis converting to ownership after a certain period **2** *(d'un métal, d'une plante etc)* property, characteristic, peculiar quality **3** *(de mot etc)* correctness, appropriateness **4** *Ordinat* **propriétés** *(de fichier)* properties

Il faut noter que le terme anglais **propriety** est un faux ami. Il signifie **bienséance**.

proprio [prɔprio] N *Fam* landlord, *f* landlady
propulser [prɔpylse] **VT** to propel
VPR se propulser *Fam* to shoot; **il s'est propulsé dans le bureau du patron** he shot off to the boss's office; **se p. au sommet de la gloire** to shoot to the heights of fame; **se p. en tête du peloton** to shoot to the front of the pack
propulseur [prɔpylsœr] **ADJ** propellent, propulsive, propelling; **gaz p.** propellant, propellent
NM 1 *Aviat etc* propeller; **p. à hélice** screw propeller **2** *(gaz)* propellant, propellent
propulsif, -ive [prɔpylsif, -iv] **ADJ = propulseur ADJ**
propulsion [prɔpylsjɔ̃] **NF** propulsion, propelling; **réacteur de p.** propulsion jet; **sous-marin à p. nucléaire** nuclear-powered submarine; **véhicule à p. électrique** electrically powered vehicle; *Aut* **p. arrière** rear-wheel drive
propylène [prɔpilɛn] **NM** *Chimie* propylene
prorata [prɔrata] **NM INV** proportional part, proportion; **paiement au p.** payment pro rata; **au p. de qch** in proportion to sth
prorogatif, -ive [prɔrɔgatif, -iv] **ADJ** proroguing
prorogation [prɔrɔgasjɔ̃] **NF 1** *surtout Jur* extension; *(de séance)* adjournment **2** *(de parlement)* prorogation
proroger [prɔrɔʒe] **VT** (**je prorogeai(s); n. prorogeons**) **1** *(contrat, bail)* to extend; **p. une échéance** to extend payment terms **2** *(parlement)* to prorogue; *(séance)* to adjourn
prosaïque [prozaik] **ADJ** prosaic, commonplace, pedestrian
prosaïquement [prozaikmɑ̃] **ADV** prosaically
prosaïsme [prozaism] **NM** prosaic nature *or* quality, prosaicness
prosateur [prozatœr] **NM** prose writer
proscenium [prosɛnjɔm] **NM 1** *Théâtre (avant-scène)* proscenium, apron **2** *Antiq* proscenium (arch)
proscription [prɔskripsjɔ̃] **NF** *(d'une personne)* outlawing, *Fml* proscription; *(d'un mot, d'un usage)* outlawing, banning
proscrire [prɔskrir] **VT** *(conj like* **écrire**) *(personne)* to outlaw, *Fml* to proscribe; *(mot, usage)* to outlaw, to ban, *Fml* to proscribe; **p. qn de la société** to ostracize sb; **p. un mot de son vocabulaire** to banish a word from one's vocabulary
proscrit, -ite [prɔskri, -it] **ADJ** *(personne)* outlawed, *Fml* proscribed; *(mot, usage)*

outlawed, banned, *Fml* proscribed
N outlaw

prose [proz] **NF** prose; **en p.** *(écrire)* in prose; *(texte, poème)* prose; *Fam Hum* **j'ai lu sa p.** I've read his literary masterpiece

prosélyte [prozelit] **N** proselyte; *Fig* convert; *Fig* **faire des prosélytes** to make *or* gain converts

prosélytisme [prozelitism] **NM** proselytism, proselytizing; **faire du p.** to proselytize

prosodie [prozodi] **NF** prosody

prosodique [prozodik] **ADJ** prosodic

prospect [prospɛ] **NM** prospective customer, prospect; *Mktg* **prospects à forte potentialité** hot prospect pool

prospecter [prospɛkte] **VT 1** *Min* to prospect **2** *Com (client)* to canvass; *(marché)* to explore; **p. la clientèle** to canvass for new business

prospecteur, -trice [prospɛktœr, -tris] **N 1** *Min* prospector **2** *Com* canvasser

prospectif, -ive [prospɛktif, -iv] **ADJ** prospective; **analyse prospective** *(en affaires)* forecast

prospection [prospɛksjɔ̃] **NF 1** *Min* prospecting **2** *Com* canvassing; *Mktg* prospecting; **faire de la p.** to explore the market; **p. téléphonique** telephone marketing; **p. sur le terrain** field research

prospectus [prospɛktys] **NM 1** *Bourse* prospectus **2** *(de publicité)* leaflet; *(de plusieurs pages)* brochure; *(donnant renseignements de base)* factsheet

prospère [prospɛr] **ADJ** *(ville, région)* prosperous, thriving, flourishing; *(personne, année)* prosperous; *(santé)* glowing; **les années prospères de sa vie** the prosperous period in his life, his/her years of prosperity

prospérer [prospere] **VI** *(je prospère; je prospérerai)* *(d'une personne)* to prosper, to do well; *(d'une société, d'un pays)* to prosper, to thrive, to do well

prospérité [prosperite] **NF** prosperity, prosperousness; *Com* **vague de p.** boom; **en période de p.** in times of prosperity, in prosperous times; **cette industrie est en pleine p.** the industry is thriving

prostaglandine [prostaglɑ̃din] **NF** *Méd* prostaglandin

prostate [prostat] **NF** *Anat* prostate (gland)

prostatique [prostatik] **ADJ** *Anat* prostatic
NM prostate sufferer

prosternation [prosternasjɔ̃] **NF** *Litt* prostration; *Fig Péj* kowtowing

prosterné [prosterne] **ADJ** prostrate

prosternement [prosternəmɑ̃] **NM** prostration; *(état)* prostrate attitude

prosterner (se) [səprosterne] **VPR** *(se courber)* to prostrate oneself (**devant** before); *Fig Péj (s'abaisser)* to grovel, to kowtow (**devant** to)

prostitué, -ée [prostitɥe] **N** *(homme)* male prostitute; *(femme)* prostitute

prostituer [prostitɥe] **VT** *(personne, talent etc)* to prostitute
VPR se prostituer to prostitute oneself

prostitution [prostitysjɔ̃] **NF** prostitution; *Fig* **c'est de la p.** *(ton attitude)* you're just prostituting yourself

prostration [prostrasjɔ̃] **NF 1** prostration **2** *Méd* (nervous) exhaustion

prostré [prostre] **ADJ** prostrate

protagoniste [protagonist] **N** protagonist

protal [protal] **NM** *Fam* head, headmaster, *f* headmistress, *Am* principal

prote [prot] **NM** *Typ* foreman

protecteur, -trice [protɛktœr, -tris] **N 1** *(personne)* protector; *Can Admin* **Bureau du**

p. du citoyen Office of the Ombudsman **2** *(des arts etc)* patron, *f* patroness
NM protector, shield; *(pour machine-outil etc)* guard
ADJ *(appareil, tarif, vêtements etc)* protective; *Péj (ton etc)* patronizing, condescending; **il est très p. avec ses enfants** he is very protective towards his children; **crème protectrice** barrier cream; **société protectrice des animaux** = society for the prevention of cruelty to animals; **des mesures économiques protectrices** measures designed to protect the economy

protection [protɛksjɔ̃] **NF 1** protection (**contre** from, against); *(de l'environnement etc)* protection, conservation; **p. civile** civil defence; **p. du consommateur** consumer protection; **p. de l'enfance** child welfare; **ne t'inquiète pas, tu es sous ma p.** don't worry, I'll protect *or* shield you; **assurer la p. rapprochée de qn** to act as a bodyguard for sb; **p. sociale** social welfare (system); **seul le préservatif assure une bonne p.** only condoms provide real protection; **sous la p. de la police** under police protection; **de p.** *(écran, visière, vernis)* protective; **dispositif de p.** safety device, protective device; *Can Admin* **Commissaire à la p. de la vie privée** Privacy Commissioner; *Ordinat* **p. d'accès logique** logical access protection; *Ordinat* **p. de bloc** block protection; *Ordinat* **p. contre l'écriture** *ou* **en écriture** write-protection; *Ordinat* **p. contre la copie** copy protection; *Ordinat* **p. de fichiers** file protection; *Ordinat* **p. de l'information** data protection; *Ordinat* **p. mémoire** protected location; *Ordinat* **p. par mot de passe** password protection; *Aut* **p. de phare** lamp guard **2** *(patronage)* patronage; *(mécénat) (des arts etc)* patronage, sponsorship; **prendre qn sous sa p.** to take sb under one's wing; *Péj* **par p.** through patronage *or* influence

protectionnisme [protɛksjɔnism] **NM** *Écon* protectionism

protectionniste [protɛksjɔnist] **ADJ, N** protectionist

protectorat [protɛktora] **NM** protectorate

protégé, -ée [proteʒe] **ADJ** protected; **p. contre l'inflation** inflation-proof; *Ordinat* **p. contre la copie** copy-protected; *Ordinat* **p. en écriture** write-protected; *Ordinat* **p. par mot de passe** password-protected; *Aut* **'passage p.'** = priority (over vehicles entering from minor road ahead)
N *(jeune artiste, sportif etc)* protégé, *f* protégée

protège-cahier, *pl* **protège-cahiers** [proteʒkaje] **NM** exercise-book cover

protège-dents [proteʒdɑ̃] **NM INV** *Boxe* gum shield

protéger [proteʒe] *(je protège, n. protégeons; je protégeai(s); je protégerai)* **VT 1** *(personne, peau, mains)*, *Écon (industrie etc)* to protect (**contre** from); *Bourse (position)* to hedge; **p. une maison du froid/de l'humidité** to protect a house against *or* from the cold/dampness; **les arbres protègent la maison du vent** the trees shelter the house from the wind; **c'est pour p. son frère qu'elle a dit cela** she said it in order to protect *or* shield her brother; **p. qn contre un danger** to shield sb from danger; **p. une invention par un brevet** to patent an invention; **les verres fumés protègent bien les yeux** tinted lenses offer good protection for the eyes; **cet écran total vous protégera parfaitement** this sun block will provide complete protection; **on la protège en haut-lieu** she has friends in high places; **p. les droits acquis** to protect *or* defend hard-won rights; **que Dieu vous protège!** God keep you!; *Ordinat* **p. contre l'écriture** *ou* **en**

écriture to write-protect; *Ordinat* **p. contre la copie** to copy-protect **2** *(arts etc)* to patronize, to be a patron of; *(artiste)* to be a patron of
VPR se protéger to protect oneself; **l'usage du préservatif est le seul moyen de se p.** a condom is the sole means of protection *or* the only way you can protect yourself; **ils doivent absolument prendre l'habitude de se p.** *(du sida etc)* they must get into the habit of taking precautions *or* into the habit of safe sex; **se p. de** *ou* **contre** *(intempéries, soleil)* to protect *or* shield oneself from; *(maladie, excès de confiance en soi)* to guard against

protège-slip, *pl* **protège-slips** [proteʒ(ə)slip] **NM** panty-liner

protège-tibia, *pl* **protège-tibias** [proteʒtibja] **NM** *Sport* shin guard

protège-tympan [proteʒtɛ̃pɑ̃] **NM INV** earplug

protéiforme [proteiform] **ADJ** protean

protéine [protein] **NF** protein; **surveiller les protéines dans son alimentation** to watch one's protein intake; **alimentation faible/riche en protéines** food that is low/high in protein, low-/high-protein food

protéique [proteik] **ADJ** *Chimie* proteinic, proteinous, proteinaceous

protestable [protɛstabl] **ADJ** *Jur* which may be protested; *Fin* protestable

protestant, -ante [protɛstɑ̃, -ɑ̃t] **ADJ, N** *Rel* Protestant

protestantisme [protɛstɑ̃tism] **NM** *Rel* Protestantism; *(ensemble des protestants)* Protestant churches, Protestant community

protestataire [protɛstatɛr] **ADJ** *(lettre etc)* of protest
N protester, protestor

protestation [protɛstasjɔ̃] **NF 1** *(affirmation)* protestation, declaration, affirmation; **protestations** protestations; **faire une p.** *ou* **des protestations d'innocence/d'amour** to protest *or* declare one's innocence/love; **ses protestations d'amour** his protestations *or* declaration of love **2** *(reproche, déclaration opposée)* protest; **voulez-vous signer notre p.?** will you sign our protest?; **émettre des protestations** to protest; **élever des protestations énergiques** to protest strongly; **paroles/geste de p.** words/gesture of protest; **réunion/manifestation/vote de p.** protest meeting/demonstration/vote; **démissionner en signe de p.** to resign in protest

protester [protɛste] **VI** to protest; **p. contre** *(une injustice, une décision) (en manifestant)* to protest *or* make a protest about *or* against, *Am* to protest; **p. contre une décision** *(devant la justice)* to challenge a ruling; **elle a protesté auprès du directeur** she complained to the manager; **p. de** *(son innocence, sa bonne foi)* to protest
VT *(affirmer)* to protest

protêt [protɛ] **NM** *Com, Jur* protest; **dresser un p.** to make a protest

prothèse [protɛz] **NF 1** *Chir* prosthetics, prosthesis **2 (appareil de)** p. prosthesis; **p. auditive** hearing aid; **p. dentaire** *(complète)* false teeth, denture(s); *(partielle)* bridge, *Spéc* dental prosthesis

prothésiste [protezist] **N** prosthesis maker

prothétique [protetik] **NF** prosthetics

protide [protid] **NM** protein

protocolaire [protokolɛr] **ADJ** formal, pertaining to protocol *or* etiquette; **clauses protocolaires d'accord** formal provisions of agreement

protocole [protokol] **NM 1** *(procédés diplomatiques)* protocol; *(usage)* etiquette, formalities, social conventions; **le chef du p.**

the chief of protocol; **p. d'accord** protocol of agreement; *(contrat)* outline agreement **2** *Typ* list of proofreading symbols **3** *Ordinat* protocol; *(de réseau)* frame format; *(de traitement etc)* procedure; **p. Internet** Internet protocol; **p. multivoie/univoie** multi-channel/single-channel protocol; **p. de téléchargement** download protocol; **p. de transfert anonyme** anonymous FTP; **p. de transfert de fichiers** file transfer protocol; **p. de transmission** transmission protocol

protoétoile [prɔtoetwal] NF *Astron* protostar

protohistoire [prɔtoistwar] NF protohistory

proton [prɔtɔ̃] NM *Nucl* proton

protoplasma [prɔtɔplasma] NM, **protoplasme** [prɔtɔplasm] NM *Biol* protoplasm

prototype [prɔtɔtip] NM prototype

protoxyde [prɔtɔksid] NM *Chimie* protoxide; **p. d'azote** nitrous oxide

protozoaire [prɔtɔzɔɛr] NM *Zool* protozoan, protozoon; **les protozoaires** the Protozoa

protractile [prɔtraktil] ADJ protractile

protrusion [prɔtryzjɔ̃] NF protrusion

protubérance [prɔtyberɑ̃s] NF protuberance; *(sur bâton etc)* knob; *Anat (sur le crâne)* bump

protubérant [prɔtyberɑ̃] ADJ protuberant

protuteur, -trice [prɔtytœr, -tris] N *Jur (d'un mineur)* acting guardian

prou [pru] ADV **peu ou p.** more or less

proue [pru] NF *(de navire)* prow, stem, bow(s)

prouesse [prues] NF **1** *Litt (acte héroïque)* deed of valour *or Am* valor **2** *(en sport etc)* feat, achievement; *Iron* **quelle p.!** that's quite a feat *or* an achievement!; **faire des prouesses** to do the impossible, to work miracles; **j'ai dû faire des prouesses pour le convaincre** it took everything I had *or* I had to work very hard to convince him

proustien, -ienne [prustjɛ̃, -jɛn] ADJ Proustian

prout [prut] NM *Fam (pet)* fart; **faire un p.** to fart

prout-prout ADJ *Fam* snobby, up oneself; **qu'est-ce qu'elle peut être p., sa copine!** his girlfriend can be so up herself

prouvable [pruvabl] ADJ provable; **c'est facilement/difficilement p.** it's easy/difficult to prove

prouver [pruve] VT **1** *(établir comme vrai) (fait)* to prove; **la police n'a rien pu p.** the police couldn't prove anything; **p. le bien-fondé d'une réclamation** to substantiate a claim, to prove the merits of a claim; **cela reste à p.** it still has to be proved; **elle dit qu'elle est experte mais cela reste à p.** she says she's an expert but that remains to be seen; **son dévouement n'est plus à p.** he has proved his devotion; **p. qch par A plus B** to prove sth in a logical fashion; **p. qch à qn** to prove sth to sb, to give sb proof of sth; **il y était aussi – prouve-le-moi!** he was there too – prove it!; **peux-tu me p. le contraire?** can you convince me otherwise *or* any differently? **2** *(être la preuve de)* to prove, to show; **ce qui prouve qu'on aurait dû écouter ce que je disais** which only goes to show that you should have listened to me
▪ VPR **se prouver 1** *(à soi-même)* to prove to oneself; **que cherche-t-il à se p.?** what's he trying to prove to himself? **2** *(mutuellement)* **nous nous sommes prouvé que les deux versions étaient correctes** we proved to each other that both versions were correct **3** *(pouvoir être prouvé)* **ça ne se prouve pas** *(c'est une intuition)* you can't prove it, it's not the sort of thing you can prove

provenance [prɔvnɑ̃s] NF source, origin; **de p. anglaise** of English origin, English in origin; **marchandise de p. italienne** Italian merchandise, merchandise from Italy; **pays de p.** country of origin; **train en p. de Bordeaux** train from Bordeaux

provençal, -ale, -aux, -ales [prɔvɑ̃sal, -o] ADJ Provençal, of Provence
▪ NM *Ling* Provençal
▪ N **P.** person from Provence

provende [prɔvɑ̃d] NF *(pour élevage)* fodder, provender

provenir [prɔvnir] VI *(conj like* **venir***)* **p. de** to come from; *(tirer son origine de)* to originate in; **d'où provient cet argent?** where does this money come from?; **des produits provenant du Japon** products from Japan; **des vins provenant des meilleurs crûs** wines from the best vintages; **les difficultés qui proviennent de cette situation** the difficulties arising from *or* out of the situation; *Jur* **les enfants provenant ou provenus de ce mariage** the children issuing from this marriage, the children of this marriage

proverbe [prɔvɛrb] NM proverb; **passer en p.** to become a proverb

proverbial, -iale, -iaux, -iales [prɔvɛrbjal, -jo] ADJ proverbial; *(beauté, sagesse, bonté, intelligence etc)* legendary, proverbial

proverbialement [prɔvɛrbjalmɑ̃] ADV proverbially

providence [prɔvidɑ̃s] NF providence; **c'est un secret de la p.** it's in the hands of providence; **être la p. de qn** *(d'une personne)* to be sb's guardian angel; **cette auberge est la p. des marcheurs** the inn is a godsend for walkers; **ce centre de conseils fut notre p.** the advice centre was a godsend *or* was heaven-sent; **l'État P.** the Welfare State

providentiel, -ielle [prɔvidɑ̃sjɛl] ADJ *(aide, rencontre etc)* providential, heaven-sent; **par une circonstance providentielle** by an act of providence

providentiellement [prɔvidɑ̃sjɛlmɑ̃] ADV providentially

province [prɔvɛ̃s] NF **1 la p.** the provinces; *(la campagne)* the country; **sa p. (d'origine)** the part of the country where he was born, *Litt, Hum* his native heath; **ça n'arriverait jamais dans ma p.** that type of thing would never happen where I come from; **elle s'est perdue dans le métro, elle arrive de sa p.** she got lost in the metro, she's new in town; **en p.** in the provinces; **aller en p.** to go to the country; **de p.** provincial; **vie de p.** provincial life, life in the provinces; *Péj* **mentalité de p.** small-town *or* provincial mentality **2** *Admin* province; *Can Géog* **les Provinces Maritimes** the Maritime Provinces, *Fam* the Maritimes; **la Belle P.** *(le Québec)* the Beautiful Province
▪ ADJ INV *Fam Péj (attitude, personne)* provincial, parochial; *(air)* provincial

provincial, -iale, -iaux, -iales [prɔvɛ̃sjal, -jo] ADJ provincial; *Péj (manières)* provincial, countrified; *(mentalité, attitude)* provincial, parochial; **la vie provinciale** provincial life, life in the provinces; **manières provinciales** small-town *or* provincial ways
▪ N provincial; **une jeune provinciale** a small-town girl, a girl from the provinces

provincialisme [prɔvɛ̃sjalism] NM *Ling* provincialism

provirus [prɔvirys] NM *Méd* provirus

proviseur [prɔvizœr] NM *Scol (d'un lycée)* headmaster, *f* headmistress

provision [prɔvizjɔ̃] NF **1** *(de pain, bois, nourriture)* supply, stock, store; *(d'eau)* supply; **faire des provisions ou faire p. de qch** to stock up on sth, to lay in a supply *or* stock

of sth; **nos provisions d'eau/de bois** our water/wood supply; **faire ses provisions** to go shopping; **provisions de guerre** munitions; *Vieilli* **provisions de bouche** food; **placard à provisions** store cupboard; **sac à provisions** shopping bag **2** *Com* funds; **verser une p. ou des provisions** to pay a deposit; **faire p. pour une lettre de change** to provide for a bill; **insuffisance de p.** *(pour honorer un chèque etc)* insufficient funds; **chèque sans p.** bad *or Fam* dud *or* rubber cheque, cheque that bounces/bounced; **faire un chèque sans p.** to write out a bad *or Fam* dud *or* rubber cheque; **il m'a fait un chèque sans p.** his cheque bounced; **un demi-mois de loyer par p.** a deposit of two weeks' rent; *Compta* **p. pour dépréciation** provision for depreciation, allowance for depreciation; **p. pour risques et charges** contingency and loss provision; *Fin* **provisions réglementées** regulated provisions **3** *Jur* retainer

provisionnel, -elle [prɔvizjɔnɛl] ADJ *Jur* provisional, interim; **tiers p.** = thrice-yearly income tax payment based on estimated tax due for the previous year

provisionnement [prɔvizjɔnmɑ̃] NM *Banque* funding

provisoire [prɔvizwar] ADJ *(arrêt)* temporary, provisional; *(arrangement, solution etc)* temporary, provisional, interim; **elle gère le centre, mais c'est p.** she manages the centre but it's a temporary arrangement, she's managing the centre but it's only on a temporary basis; **nommé à titre p.** appointed provisionally; **dividende p.** interim dividend; **habitation p.** emergency *or* temporary accommodation; *Jur* **détention p.** *(temporary)* custody; *Jur* **être en liberté p.** to be (out) on bail, to have been released on bail; **mis en liberté p.** released on bail
▪ NM **ça n'est que du p.** it's only temporary, it's only for the time being; **il s'est installé dans le p.** he's got used to living on a day-to-day basis; **je ne veux plus vivre dans le p.** I'm tired of living in uncertainty

provisoirement [prɔvizwarmɑ̃] ADV provisionally, temporarily

provitamine [prɔvitamin] NF *Biol, Chimie* provitamin

provoc [prɔvɔk] NF *Fam (abrév* **provocation***)* provocation

provocant [prɔvɔkɑ̃] ADJ **1** *(agressif) (paroles, langage, attitude)* provocative **2** *(sourire, robe)* provocative; **d'une manière provocante** provocatively

provocateur, -trice [prɔvɔkatœr, -tris] ADJ *(sourire)* provocative; *(attitude)* provocative, challenging; **agent p.** agent provocateur
▪ N troublemaker, agitator

provocation [prɔvɔkasjɔ̃] NF **1** *(défi)* provocation; **un ton/air de p.** a challenging tone/look, a tone/look of provocation; **elle le fait par p.** she does it to provoke, she's being provocative; **il te l'a dit par p.** he said it to provoke you; **c'est de la p.!** it's deliberate provocation!; **p. en duel** challenge to a duel **2** *Jur* instigation; **p. au crime** incitement to crime

provoquer [prɔvɔke] VT **1** *(défier, sexuellement)* to provoke; **p. qn en duel** to challenge sb to a duel; *Fam* **tu me provoques, toi!** you're starting to get up my nose! **2** *(inciter) (crime, violence)* to instigate; **p. les jeunes à la violence/au crime** to incite young people to violence/to crime **3** *(effet)* to have; *(stupeur, incendie, mort)* to cause; *(malaise, crise cardiaque)* to cause, *Fam* to bring on; *Méd (sommeil, des vomissements)* to induce; *(critique)* to provoke, to give rise to, to generate; *(réaction)* to provoke, to produce; *(jalousie, ressentiment)* to arouse; *(courant d'air)* to cause, to create; **un coma provoqué par la**

drogue a drug-induced coma; **il faut p. l'accouchement** we'll have to induce you/her or labour
VPR se provoquer to provoke each other

proxénète [prɔksenet] N pimp, Litt, Arch pander; Jur procurer, f procuress

proxénétisme [prɔksenetism] NM pimping; Jur procuring

proximité [prɔksimite] NF proximity, nearness, closeness; (d'un événement) imminence, proximity; **j'apprécie la p. de la ville** I appreciate the fact that the town is nearby or is within easy reach; **la p. du départ rend la famille nerveuse** the family are becoming apprehensive as the day of departure draws near; **p. de parenté** near relationship; **à p.** close by, near at hand; **à p. de qch** near sth, close to sth, in the vicinity of sth; **police de p.** community policing; **justice de p.** = legal system in which the judiciary have closer links with the community they serve; **commerce de p.** neighbourhood shop or store

proyer [prwaje] NM (oiseau) (bruant) p. bunting

prude [pryd] Péj ADJ prudish
NF prude; **ne fais pas la p.!** don't be so prudish!, don't be such a prude!

prudemment [prydamɑ̃] ADV prudently, carefully, cautiously

prudence [prydɑ̃s] NF prudence, carefulness, cautiousness, caution; (d'un conducteur) cautiousnessness; **avec p.** (agir) cautiously, prudently; (conduire) carefully; **on conseille la p.** caution is advised; **son excès de p. l'exaspérait** she was sick of his overcautiousness; **donner des conseils de p. à qn** to advise sb to be cautious; **par (mesure de) p.** as a precaution; **par p., je n'ai pas voulu lui en parler tout de suite** I thought it wiser not to speak of it to him right away; Prov **p. est mère de sûreté** discretion is the better part of valour; Litt **des prudences** precautionary measures

prudent [prydɑ̃] ADJ (personne) careful, cautious, prudent; (conducteur) careful, cautious; (décision etc) wise, sensible, prudent; (ligne de conduite) prudent, advisable; **on n'est jamais trop p.** you can't be too careful; **vous avez raison, c'est plus p.** you're right, it's wiser or more sensible; **j'ai jugé c. de le prévenir tout de suite** I thought it wise or sensible to let him know right away; **un homme très p. en affaires** a very cautious businessman; **il faut être p. de ne pas décider trop vite** we must be careful not to decide too quickly; **attention brouillard, soyez prudents** fog warning, drive cautiously

pruderie [prydri] NF Péj prudery, prudishness

prud'homme [prydɔm] NM Ind, Jur industrial arbitrator; **conseil des prud'hommes** ≃ industrial tribunal; **aller aux** ou **devant les prud'hommes** ≃ to go before an industrial tribunal

prudhommerie [prydɔmri] NF Péj pomposity, sententiousness

pruine [prɥin] NF (sur fruit) bloom

prune [pryn] NF **1** (fruit) plum; (liqueur) plum brandy; **p. de Damas** damson; Fig Fam **pour des prunes** for nothing; **travailler pour des prunes** to work for nothing or for peanuts; **si j'y suis allée, ce n'est pas pour des prunes!** I didn't go just for the fun of it!; FigFam **tu crois qu'elle m'en donnerait? – des prunes!** do you think she'll let me have some? – no way! or no fear! or not bloody likely!; **et qu'est-ce que j'ai reçu en remerciements? des prunes!** and what did I get by way of thanks? not a bloody thing! **2** Fam (coup de poing) punch, thump, clout **3** Fam (contravention) fine
ADJ INV plum(-coloured orAm -colored)

> Il faut noter que le terme anglais **prune** est un faux ami. Il signifie **pruneau**.

pruneau, -eaux [pryno] NM **1** (fruit) prune **2** Suisse (prune) red plum **3** Arg (balle d'arme à feu) slug, bullet

prunelle [prynɛl] NF **1** (fruit) sloe; **(liqueur de) p.** sloe gin **2** Anat (des yeux) pupil; Fig **j'y tiens comme à la p. de mes yeux** it's the apple of my eye, it's my pride and joy; Fam **jouer de la p.** to flutter one's eyelashes

prunellier [prynelje] NM blackthorn, sloe (bush)

prunier [prynje] NM plum tree; Fam **secouer qn comme un p.** to give sb a good shaking, Fam to shake sb till his/her teeth rattle; Fig to give sb a good telling-off, to tear sb off a strip; Fam **arrête de me secouer comme un p.** stop shaking me like that

prunus [prynys] NM (arbre) prunus, Japanese flowering cherry

prurigineux, -euse [pryriʒinø, -øz] ADJ Méd which causes itching, Spéc pruritic

prurit [pryrit] NM Méd itching, Spéc pruritus

Prusse [prys] NF Hist Prussia; **bleu de P.** Prussian blue; FigFam **travailler pour le roi de P.** to work for nothing orfor peanuts

Prusse-Orientale [prysɔrjɑ̃tal] NF Ancien-nement la P. East Prussia

prussiate [prysjat] NM Chimie cyanide

prussien, -ienne [prysjɛ̃, -jɛn] Hist ADJ Prussian
N P. Prussian

prytanée [pritane] NM military school (for sons of officers)

PS [pees] NM **1** abrév **Parti socialiste 2** (abrév **post-scriptum**) P.S.

psallette [psalɛt] NF choir school

psalmiste [psalmist] NM psalmist

psalmodie [psalmɔdi] NF **1** Rel psalmody **2** (déclamation, formule monotone) droning

psalmodier [psalmɔdje] (pr sub, impf n. psalmodiions, v. psalmodiiez) VT **1** Rel (office etc) to intone, to chant **2** (dire avec monotonie) to drone out, to recite monotonously
VI 1 Rel to intone, to chant **2** (parler avec monotonie) to drone (on or away)

psaltérion [psalterjɔ̃] NM Mus psaltery

psaume [psom] NM psalm

psautier [psotje] NM Mus psalter, psalm book

pseudo [psødo] NM Fam (abrév **pseudonyme**) alias

pseudo- [psødo] PRÉF pseudo-; **des p.-intellectuels** pseudo-intellectuals; **un p.-médecin** a quack, a bogus orfake doctor

pseudo-membrane, pl **pseudo-membranes** NF Méd pseudomembrane, false membrane

pseudonyme [psødɔnim] NM pseudonym; **prendre un p.** to adopt a pseudonym; **elle a pris un p.** (cette écrivain) she writes under a pseudonym

pseudo-rubis NM INV Minér rose quartz

pseudo-saphir, pl **pseudo-saphirs** NM Minér blue quartz

psi [psi] NM psi

psitt [psit] INT psst!

psittacose [psitakoz] NF Méd, Vét psittacosis

psoriasis [psɔrjazis] NM Méd psoriasis

pst [pst] INT psst!

psy [psi] Fam ADJ = **psychiatrique, psychologique, psychanalytique**
NF = **psychiatrie, psychologie, psychanalyse**
N (psychologue, psychanalyste) shrink

psychanalyse [psikanaliz] NF (domaine) psychoanalysis; (traitement) (psycho)analysis; **faire une p.** to be in or undergoing (psycho)analysis; **commencer une p.** to start analysis, to go into (psycho)analysis; **il a fait une p. pendant cinq ans** he was in (psycho)analysis for five years; **faire de la p.** to psychoanalyse people

psychanalyser [psikanalize] VT (personne, rêves etc) to (psycho)analyse; **se faire p.** to be (psycho)analysed

psychanalyste [psikanalist] N psychoanalyst

psychanalytique [psikanalitik] ADJ psychoanalytical; **école p.** school of psychoanalysis

psyché [psiʃe] NF **1** Myth P. Psyche **2** Phil psyche **3** (miroir) cheval glass

psychédélique [psikedelik] ADJ psychedelic; Fam **la mode p.** the fashion for psychedelia

psychiatre [psikjatr] N psychiatrist

psychiatrie [psikjatri] NF psychiatry

psychiatrique [psikjatrik] ADJ psychiatric

psychique [psiʃik] ADJ psychic

psychisme [psiʃism] NM psyche, inner mind

psycho [psiko] NF = **psychologie**

psychodrame [psikodram] NM role-playing, Spéc psychodrama

psychographie [psikografi] NF psychographics

psychographique [psikografik] ADJ psychographic

psycholinguistique [psikolɛ̃gɥistik] NF psycholinguistics

psychologie [psikɔlɔʒi] NF psychology; Univ **faire de** ou **étudier la p.**, Fam **faire p.** to do or study psychology; Univ **études de p.** psychology (studies); **étudiants en p.** psychology students; **faire preuve de p.** to be a good psychologist, to use psychology; **tu manques de p.** you're not much of a psychologist, you don't have much idea of how people's minds work; **il a réellement manqué de p.** he showed a great lack of insight; **la p. des descriptions chez Proust** the psychological insights offered by Proust's descriptions; **une p. très fragile** a very fragile personality; **il faut comprendre sa p.** you have to understand the way his/her mind works

psychologique [psikɔlɔʒik] ADJ (roman, film etc) psychological; **le moment p.** the psychological moment; **son état p.** his psychological state, his state of mind; **son état p. n'était pas bon du tout** he wasn't in a good state of mind orframe of mind at all; **c'est p.!** it's psychological!

psychologiquement [psikɔlɔʒikmɑ̃] ADV psychologically

psychologue [psikɔlɔg] N psychologist; Fig **c'est un fin p.** he's a good psychologist
ADJ elle n'est pas très p. she's not much of a psychologist, she doesn't understand how people's minds work

psychonévrose [psikonevroz] NF psychoneurosis

psychopathe [psikɔpat] N psychopath

psychopathie [psikɔpati] NF psychopathy

psychopathologie [psikopatɔlɔʒi] ADJ psychopathology

psychopédagogie [psikopedagɔʒi] NF application of experimental psychology to education

psychopharmacologie [psikofarmakɔlɔʒi] NF psychopharmacology

psychophysiologie [psikofizjɔlɔʒi] NF psychophysiology

psychose [psikoz] NF **1** Psy psychosis; Mil **p.**

traumatique post-combat stress syndrome, shellshock; **p. maniaco-dépressive** manic depression; **souffrir de p. maniaco-dépressive** to be a manic-depressive **2** *(obsession) (d'une maladie, une crise, une guerre)* psychosis (**de** about), fear (**de** of)

psychosociologie [psikosɔsjɔlɔʒi] **NF** social psychology

psychosomatique [psikosɔmatik] **ADJ** *Méd* psychosomatic

psychotechnique [psikotɛknik] **ADJ** psychological testing, *Spéc* psychotechnical **NF** psychological testing, *Spéc* psychotechnology, psychotechnics

psychothérapeute [psikoterapøt] **N** psychotherapist

psychothérapie [psikoterapi] **NF** (psycho)-therapy; **p. analytique** analytical (psycho)-therapy; **p. familiale** family therapy; **faire une p. de groupe** to go to *or* do group therapy

psychothérapique [psikoterapik] **ADJ** psychotherapeutic; **intervention p.** psychotherapeutic treatment

psychotique [psikɔtik] **ADJ, N** psychotic

psychotonique [psikotɔnik] **ADJ** *Pharm* psychoactive, psychotropic

psychotrope [psikɔtrɔp] **NM** *Pharm* psychotropic drug
ADJ *Anat* psychotropic

ptérodactyle [pterɔdaktil] **NM** pterodactyl

ptérosaurien [pterɔsɔrjɛ̃] **NM** pterosaur

Ptolémée [ptɔleme] **N** *Antiq* Ptolemy; *Astron* **système de P.** Ptolemaic system

ptomaïne [ptɔmain] **NF** *Biol, Chimie* ptomaine

PTT [petete] **NFPL** *Anciennement (abrév* **Postes, Télécommunications et Télédiffusion)** = former French post office and telecommunications network

PU [pey] **NM** *Com (abrév* **prix unitaire)** UP

puant [pyɑ̃] **ADJ 1** *(qui sent mauvais)* stinking, foul-smelling; *Chimie Fam* **gaz p.** hydrogen sulphide, *Fam* stink bomb gas; **boule puante** stink bomb **2** *Fig (odieux)* cocky

puanteur [pyɑ̃tœr] **NF** stink, stench, *Br Fam* pong

pub¹ [pyb] **NF** *Fam* = **publicité 1, 2**

pub² [pœb] **NM** pub

pubère [pybɛr] **ADJ** pubescent

puberté [pybɛrte] **NF** puberty

pubescent [pybesɑ̃] **ADJ** *Bot* pubescent

pubien, -ienne [pybjɛ̃, -jɛn] **ADJ** *Anat* pubic

pubis [pybis] **NM** *Anat* pubis, pubes; *(os)* pubic bone

publiable [pybliabl] **ADJ** fit for publication, publishable

public, -ique [pyblik] **ADJ** public; *(assemblée)* public, open (to the public); **la séance est publique** the meeting is open to the public; **la chose publique** res publica; **service p.** public utility (service), *Am* utility; **travailler pour le bien p.** to work for the common good; **la voie publique** the public highway; **il est de notoriété publique que ...** it is public *or* common knowledge that ...; *Admin* **ministère p.** = public prosecutor
NM *(d'un spectacle, d'une émission)* audience; **cette émission a été enregistrée en p.** this programme was recorded before a live audience; **un p. cultivé** a cultured *or* an educated audience; *(lecteurs)* cultured *or* discerning readers; **cette chanteuse a encore son p.** this singer still has a following; **le p.** the public; **'interdit au p.'** 'no admittance *or* admission to the public', 'keep out'; **le grand p.** the general public; **un film pour le grand p.** a family film, a film (suitable) for

everybody; **électronique grand p.** consumer electronics; **en p.** in public, publicly; **faire une déclaration en p.** to make a public statement; **p. cible** target audience; **p. en studio** studio audience **VOIR GRAMMAIRE A11**

publicain [pyblikɛ̃] **NM** *Antiq* tax gatherer; *Bible* publican

publication [pyblikasjɔ̃] **NF 1** *(fait de rendre public)* publication, publishing; **p. en feuilleton** serialization; **p. de vente aux enchères** notice of sale by auction; **date de p.** publication date, date of publication; **p. assistée par ordinateur** desk-top publishing **2** *(magazine etc)* publication; **p. périodique** periodical; **p. trimestrielle** quarterly (publication); **p. spécialisée** specialist journal; **p. interne** in-house publication

publiciste [pyblisist] **N** *Com Fam* person who works in advertising, *(homme)* adman

publicitaire [pyblisiter] **ADJ** (concerned with) publicity; *Com* (concerned with) advertising; **campagne p.** publicity campaign; *Com* advertising campaign; **agence p.** advertising agency; **vente p.** promotional sale; *TV, Radio* **spot/message p.** commercial, ad(vert)
N person who works in advertising; *Fam (homme)* adman

publicité [pyblisite] **NF 1** *(notoriété)* publicity; *Com* advertising; **être dans la p.** to be in advertising; **faire de la p. pour un savon** *(d'un acteur)* to advertise a soap; *(d'une agence)* to do the advertising for a soap; **l'animateur a fait de la p. pour cet album** the disc jockey plugged the album; **ça lui fait de la p.** it's publicity for him; **la p. paie** it pays to advertise; **une agence de p.** an advertising agency
2 *(affiche)* **Journ** ad(vert); *TV, Radio* ad(vert), commercial; **une pleine page de p. dans le journal** a full page ad(vert) *or* advertisement in the paper; **il y a trop de p. à la télévision** there are too many ads *or* there's too much advertising on television
3 *(caractère public) (d'un débat)* public nature
▸▸ **p. associé** cooperative advertising; **p. clandestine** underhand advertising; **p. commerciale** commercial advertising; **p. comparative** comparative advertising; *(activité)* comparative *or* comparison advertising; **p. par correspondance** direct mail advertising; **p. directe** direct advertising *or* mail, below-the-line advertising; **p. d'entreprise** corporate advertising; **p. par l'événement** event advertising; **p. extérieure** outdoor advertising; **p. hors-médias** below-the-line promotion; **p. d'intérêt général** government advertisement; *(activité)* government advertising; **p. sur le lieu de vente** point-of-sale promotion; **p. média** *(publicité directe)* above-the-line *or* media advertising; **p. mensongère** false *or* misleading advertising; **p. sur panneau** billboard advertisement; *(activité)* billboard advertising; **p. plein page** full page advertisement; **p. par publipostage** direct mail advertising; **p. pure** above-the-line advertising; **p. de rappel** follow-up advertisement; *(activité)* follow-up publicity; **p. rédactionnelle** advertorial; **p. télévisée** television advertisement *or* commercial, TV ad; *(activité)* television advertising

public-relations [pœblikrilefɔnz] **NF** public relations, PR; **le service de p.** the public relations department, the PR department
N public relations officer, PR man, *f* woman

publier [pyblije] **VT** *(pr sub, impf* n. **publiions, v. publiiez)* **1** *(rendre public) (chiffres du commerce etc)* to publish, to make public, to make known; *(décret etc)* to proclaim; *(règlement)* to issue; **les bans ont-ils été pu-**

bliés? have the banns been published?; **p. la nouvelle que ...** to release the news that ... **2** *(livre)* to publish, to bring out; **ce journal est publié sur seize pages** the paper runs to sixteen pages

publi-information, *pl* **publi-informations** [pybliɛ̃fɔrmasjɔ̃] **NF** advertorial

Publiphone® [pyblifɔn] **NM** card phone

publipostage [pyblipostaʒ] **NM** mailshot; **logiciel de p.** mail merge software; **faire un p.** to do a mailshot; **p. groupé** volume mailing

publi-promotion, *pl* **publi-promotions** [pyblipromosjɔ̃] **NF** promotional offer

publiquement [pyblikmɑ̃] **ADV** publicly, in public; *(ouvertement)* openly; **se faire ridiculer p.** to be publicly insulted, to be insulted in public

publireportage [pyblir(ə)portaʒ] **NM** advertorial, advertising feature, promotional article

puce [pys] **NF 1** *(insecte)* flea; **p. de mer** sand hopper *or* flea; **herbe aux puces** fleawort; **jeu de p.** tiddlywinks; **piqûre de p.** fleabite; **le marché aux puces, les puces** the flea market; **les puces de Paris** the Paris flea market; *Fig* **mettre la p. à l'oreille à qn** to make sb suspicious, to arouse sb's suspicions; *Fam* **secouer les puces à qn** to give sb a good telling off; *Fam* **elle est excitée comme une p.** she can't sit still, she's jumping up and down with excitement; **elle est rentrée de l'école excitée comme une p.** she came home jumping up and down with excitement; *Fam* **mais oui, ma p.** yes, (my) dear *or* (my) love *or* (my) pet **2** *Ordinat* (micro)chip; **p. à ADN** DNA chip; **p. antiviolence** V-chip; **p. logique** logic chip; **p. mémoire** memory chip; **p. de reconnaissance vocale** voice recognition chip
ADJ INV puce(-coloured *or Am* -colored)

puceau, -eaux [pyso] **NM, ADJ M** *Fam* virgin

pucelage [pyslaʒ] **NM** *Hum* virginity; **perdre son p.** to lose one's virginity

pucelle [pysɛl] **ADJ F** virgin
NF virgin, *Arch, Euph* maid(en); *Hist* **la P. d'Orléans** the Maid of Orleans

puceron [pysrɔ̃] **NM** greenfly, aphid

pucier [pysje] **NM** *Arg (lit)* bed

pudding [pudiŋ] **NM** *Culin* **1** steamed pudding; *(pour Noël)* (plum) pudding, Christmas pudding **2** *(gâteau)* = filling type of cake made from stale bread

puddlage [pydlaʒ] **NM** *Métal* puddling

puddler [pydle] **VT** *Métal* to puddle

pudeur [pydœr] **NF** *(réserve)* modesty; **sans p.** *(adjectivement)* unblushing, shameless; *(adverbialement)* unblushingly, shamelessly; **avec p.** modestly; **rougir de p.** to blush with shame; **par p., il n'a pas abordé le sujet** out of a sense of decency *or* propriety, he did not mention the subject; **avoir la p. de faire qch** to have the decency to do sth

pudibond [pydibɔ̃] **ADJ** easily shocked, prudish

> Do not confuse with **pudique**.

pudibonderie [pydibɔ̃dri] **NF** prudishness

pudicité [pydisite] **NF** *Litt* modesty

pudique [pydik] **ADJ** modest; **une allusion p.** a discreet reference

> Do not confuse with **pudibond**.

pudiquement [pydikmɑ̃] **ADV** modestly

puer [pɥe] **VI** to stink, to reek; **ça pue!** what a stink *or Br Fam* pong!
VT **ça pue le poisson** it stinks *or* reeks of fish; **il pue des pieds** his feet stink

puériculteur, -trice [pɥerikyltœr, -tris] N nursery nurse

puériculture [pɥerikyltyr] NF child care, infant welfare

puéril [pɥeril] ADJ childish, *Fml* puerile

puérilement [pɥerilmã] ADV childishly

puérilité [pɥerilite] NF childishness, *Fml* puerility

puerpéral, -ale, -aux, -ales [pɥɛrperal, -o] ADJ *Obst* puerperal

puffin [pyfɛ̃] NM *(oiseau)* shearwater

pugilat [pyʒila] NM **1** *(combat de boxeurs)* boxing, *Fml* pugilism **2** *(dispute, bataille)* fight, brawl, *Fam* set-to

pugiliste [pyʒilist] NM boxer, *Fml* pugilist

pugnace [pygnas] ADJ *Litt* pugnacious

pugnacité [pygnasite] NF *Litt* pugnacity, pugnaciousness

puîné, -ée [pɥine] *Vieilli* ADJ *(de deux)* younger; *(de plusieurs)* youngest
N *(frère)* younger/youngest brother; *(sœur)* younger/youngest sister

puis [pɥi] ADV then; **tourner à droite p. à gauche** turn right (and) then left; **et p.** and then; *(d'ailleurs)* moreover, (and) besides; **et p. qu'est-ce qui s'est passé?** then what happened?, what happened then *or* next?; **et p., c'est tout** and that's all there is to it; **et p. (quoi)?, et p. après?** then what?, what next?; *Fam (qu'est-ce que ça peut faire)* so what?

puisage [pɥizaʒ] NM *(d'eau)* drawing (up)

puisard [pɥizar] NM *(pour ordures)* cesspool, sink; *Min, Tech etc* sump, well

puisatier [pɥizatje] NM *(ouvrier)* well maker, well sinker; *Min* shaft sinker

puisement [pɥizmã] NM = **puisage**

puiser [pɥize] VT *(eau)* to draw (**à, dans** from); *Fig (inspiration, idée)* to derive, to get, to take (**dans, chez** from); **p. aux sources** to draw on the original sources, to go to the source, *Litt, Hum* to go to the fountainhead
VI **elle puise dans ses réserves** she's drawing on her reserves; **elle ne s'est pas gênée pour p. dans ma trousse de maquillage** she felt no embarrassment about using my make-up *or* dipping into my make-up bag; **p. dans son porte-monnaie** to dip *or* put one's hand in one's wallet

puisque [pɥisk(ə)] CONJ since, as, seeing that; **je le ferai, puisqu'il le faut** I'll do it, since I must; **p. tu veux savoir, je vais te le dire** since *or* seeing that you want to know, I'll tell you; **p. c'est comme ça** if that's how you feel/he feels/*etc*, if that's how things are; **d'accord, p. c'est ce que tu veux!** all right, if that's what you want!; **p. je te dis que je l'ai vu!** but I'm telling you I did see it!; **tu es sûr que tu peux y aller? – mais p. je te le dis!** are you sure you can go? – I said so, didn't I?

puissamment [pɥisamã] ADV powerfully; *Fam* **p. riche** exceedingly rich

puissance [pɥisãs] NF **1** power; *(du vent)* force, strength; *(d'une armée)* strength; **p. d'une machine** power of an engine; *Mil* **p. de** *ou* **du feu** fire power; **p. en chevaux** horsepower; **p. au frein** brake horsepower; *Aut* **p. de traction** pulling power; **p. effective** power output; **p. nominale** rated power; **p. utile** usable brake horsepower, usable bhp; *Admin* **p. fiscale d'une voiture** = engine rating of a car for road tax purposes; **p. administrative** taxable horsepower; *Radio* **p. d'antenne** aerial capacity; **poste émetteur de haute p.** high-power radio transmitter **2** *Math* power; **élever un nombre à la nième p.** to raise a number to the nth power; **dix (à la) p. quatre** ten to the fourth, ten to the power of four **3** *(autorité)* power; **avoir qn en sa p.** to

have sb in one's power; **la volonté de p.** the desire for power; **être en p. de mari** to be under a husband's control *or* authority; **p. paternelle** paternal authority **4** *Pol* **les grandes puissances** the great powers; *Fig* **les puissances célestes** the powers above; **les puissances des ténèbres** the powers of darkness **5** **en p.** *(assassin, meurtrier)* potential

puissant [pɥisã] ADJ **1** *(qui a du pouvoir) (armée, moteur, voiture, pays etc)* powerful **2** *(qui a de la force physique, fort) (homme, vent, musculature)*, *Fig (envie)* strong; *(voix)* powerful; *(remède)* powerful, strong, potent **3** *Fam (remarquable)* wicked, *Br* fab, *Am* awesome
NMPL **les puissants** the powerful, the mighty (ones)

puits [pɥi] NM **1** *(pour l'eau)* well; **p. de sondage** borehole; **p. artésien** artesian well; **p. absorbant, p. perdu** cesspool; *Fig* **c'est un p. de science** he's a mine of information; *(d'un esprit plus profond)* he's a fount of knowledge **2** *(de mine)* shaft, pit; **p. d'aération** *ou* **d'aérage** air shaft, ventilation shaft; **p. d'extraction** winding shaft **3** *Mil* **p. de lancement** launching silo **4** *Culin* **p. d'amour** = small round of puff pastry filled with pastry cream

pull [pyl] NM *Fam* jumper, sweater, pullover

pullman [pulman] NM *Rail* Pullman (car)

pull-over, *pl* **pull-overs** [pylɔvœr] NM jumper, sweater, pullover

pullulation [pylylasjɔ̃] NF, **pullulement** [pylylmã] NM **1** *(d'organismes etc)* rapid multiplication, *Fml* pullulation **2** *(d'enfants etc)* swarm

pulluler [pylyle] VI **1** *(se reproduire)* to multiply rapidly, *Fml* to pullulate **2** *(être en profusion)* to abound, to be found in profusion; *(en mouvement)* to swarm; **la rue pullule de monde** the street is swarming with people; **les marchands de chaussures pullulent dans ce coin de la ville** there are lots of shoe shops in this part of town, this part of town is full of *or* swarming with shoe shops

pulmonaire [pylmɔnɛr] ADJ pulmonary; **congestion p.** pulmonary congestion
NF lungwort

pulpe [pylp] NF **1** *(de fruit)* pulp; **yaourt à la p. de fruits** yoghurt with pieces of fruit in it; **réduire qch en p.** to reduce sth to a pulp, to pulp sth **2** *(partie molle) (des doigts ou des orteils)* pad; *(des dents)* pulp

pulpeux, -euse [pylpø, -øz] ADJ *(lèvres)* fleshy; **une fille pulpeuse** a sexy female

pulsar [pylsar] NM *Astron* pulsar

pulsation [pylsasjɔ̃] NF *(fait de battre) (du cœur)* beating, throbbing; *(battement)* throb

pulsative [pylsativ] ADJ F *Méd* **douleur p.** throbbing pain, *Spéc* pulsatory pain

pulser [pylse] VT *(air) (dans une pièce, dans un moteur)* to force

pulsion [pylsjɔ̃] NF *Psy* impulse; **p. sexuelle** sex drive; **p. de mort** death wish

pulsionnel, -elle [pylsjɔnɛl] ADJ impulsive, impulse; **phénomène p.** impulsive action, instinctive action; **c'était plus p. que réfléchi** it was more of a reflex *or* an impulse than a conscious act

pulsoréacteur [pylsoreaktœr] NM *Aviat* pulse jet

pulvérisable [pylverizabl] ADJ *(poudre etc)* which can be crushed; *(liquide)* that can be sprayed

pulvérisateur [pylverizatœr] NM **1** *(de matières solides)* pulverizer **2** *(de liquide)* spray; *Tech* vaporizer, atomizer

pulvérisation [pylverizasjɔ̃] NF **1** *(de matières solides)* pulverizing, crushing **2** *(de li-*

quides) spraying; *Tech* vaporization; **p. métallisée** metal-spraying

pulvériser [pylverize] VT **1** *(roche)* to crush, to pulverize; **p. une matière** to grind *or* reduce a substance to powder **2** *(liquide, parfum)* to spray; *Ind* to vaporize **3** *Fig Fam (record)* to smash, to shatter; **la voiture a été pulvérisée lors de l'accident** the car was completely smashed up *or* was smashed to pieces in the accident; **p. qn** to beat the hell out of sb, to pulverize sb

pulvériseur [pylverizœr] NM *Agr* disc *or Am* disk harrow

pulvérulence [pylverylãs] NF powderiness, dustiness

pulvérulent [pylverylã] ADJ powdery, dusty

puma [pyma] NM puma, cougar, mountain lion

punaise [pynɛz] NF **1** *(insecte)* bug; **p. des lits** bed bug; *Fam* **p. de sacristie** fervent churchgoer; *Fam* **oh p.!** golly!, goodness!, gosh! **2** *(pour accrocher)* drawing pin, *Am* thumbtack

punaiser [pynɛze] VT *Fam* to pin (up); **p. des affiches au mur** to pin posters to the wall

punch¹ [pɔ̃ʃ] NM *Culin* punch; **bol à p.** punchbowl

punch² [pœnʃ] NM *Boxe, Fig Fam* punch; *Fig* **elle ne manque pas de p.** *(elle a de l'énergie)* she's full of energy; **ça vous donnera du p. pour la suite!** it'll give you energy *or* set you up for what's to come!; **un slogan qui a du p.** a punchy *or* catchy slogan; **cette aide de l'État a donné du p. à notre organisation** the government's assistance was a shot in the arm for our organization

punching-ball, *pl* **punching-balls** [pœnʃiŋbol] NM *Boxe* punchball

punique [pynik] ADJ *Hist (guerres etc)* Punic

punir [pynir] VT *(personne, crime)* to punish; **p. qn de mort/prison** to punish sb with death/imprisonment; **p. qn d'un crime/ pour un mensonge** to punish sb for a crime/for lying; **être puni de ses crimes** to be punished *or* pay the penalty for one's crimes; **ça te punira de ta curiosité!** that'll teach you to be nosy!; **me voilà puni de ma gourmandise!** it serves me right for being greedy!, that'll teach me to be greedy!; **être puni par où l'on a péché** to reap what one has sown

punissable [pynisabl] ADJ punishable

punitif, -ive [pynitif, -iv] ADJ *(expédition, mesure etc)* punitive

punition [pynisjɔ̃] NF punishment; **p. corporelle** corporal punishment; **donner une p. à un enfant** to punish a child; **en p. de qch** as (a) punishment for sth; **par** *ou* **pour p.** for punishment, by way of punishment, as a punishment

punk [pœnk] ADJ INV *(musique etc)* punk
N punk

pupe [pyp] NF **1** *(enveloppe)* pupa case **2** *(chrysalide)* pupa, chrysalis

pupillaire¹ [pypilɛr] ADJ *Jur* pertaining to a ward, *Spéc* pupil(l)ary

pupillaire² [pypilɛr] ADJ *Anat (membrane etc)* pupil(l)ary

pupillarité [pypilarite] NF *Jur* wardship, *Spéc* pupil(l)age

pupille¹ [pypil, -ij] N *Jur* ward; **pupilles de la Marine/de l'Air** = children whose fathers have died while serving in the Navy/Air Force; **p. de l'État** child in (state) care; **pupilles de la Nation** war orphans

pupille² NF *Anat (de l'œil)* pupil

pupillomètre [pypijɔmɛtr] NM pupillometer

pupitre [pypitr] NM **1** *(d'écolier etc)* desk; *(d'où s'adresse un orateur)* lectern; **p. à musique** music stand **2** *Mus (d'instruments)* group; **chef de p.** front desk player **3** *TV, Radio* console; **p. de mixage** mixing desk; **p. de mélange vidéo** switcher; **p. de régie** studio control console, studio desk, control board; **p. son** audio (control) console **4** *Ordinat* **p. (de commande)** console (desk); **p. de visualisation** visual display unit

pupitreur, -euse [pypitrœr, -øz] N *Ordinat* console operator

pur, pure [pyr] ADJ **1** *(pas mélangé)* *(or, laine, jus de fruits, style etc)* pure; *(air)* clean, pure; *(ciel)* clear; *(whisky, gin etc)* straight, neat; **un peu d'air p. nous fera du bien** a bit of fresh air will do us good; **elle boit son whisky p.** she drinks her whisky straight *or* neat; **de l'eau de Javel pure** undiluted bleach; **liquide p. de tout mélange** liquid free from all admixture; **biscuits p. beurre** all-butter biscuits; **elle parle un italien très p.** her Italian is very pure; **cheval p. sang** thoroughbred horse; **c'est un p. produit de mai 68/du catholicisme** he's a true child of May 68/of the Catholic church; **être un p. produit de la bourgeoisie** to be middle-class through and through, to be a hundred per cent middle-class; **un p. produit du féminisme** a one hundred per cent red-blooded feminist; **c'est un p. produit de Polytechnique** he's a typical Polytechnique graduate **2** *(total)* pure; **p. hasard** pure chance, mere chance; **c'est un p. hasard qu'il se soit trouvé là** it was pure *or* sheer chance that he was there; **par p. hasard, il y avait un médecin dans le car** by sheer chance there was a doctor on the bus; **la pure vérité** the simple *or* plain *or* honest *or* unvarnished truth; **la vérité pure et simple** the plain and simple truth; **c'est de la folie pure (et simple)** it's sheer madness, it's pure folly; **un socialiste/trotskiste p. et dur** a hard-line Socialist/Trotskyist; **un bouddhiste p. et dur** a strict Buddhist; **c'est un Breton p. et dur** he's extremely proud of being a Breton; **l'invitation est de pure forme** the invitation is purely for form's sake; **par pure malice** out of pure *or* sheer malice; **travailler en pure perte** to work for nothing *or* to no purpose; **elle l'a fait en pure perte** she did it all for nothing, it was a sheer waste of her time **3** *Fig (moralement)* pure; *(esthétiquement)* *(lignes)* pure, clean, clean-cut; *(visage)* clean-cut; **conscience pure** clear conscience; **p. d'esprit** pure-minded **4** *(théorique)* *(science, mathématiques etc)* pure
▪ N *Pol etc* diehard

purée [pyre] NF *Culin* purée; **p. (de pommes de terre)** mashed *or* creamed potato(es), *Br Fam* mash; **p. de carottes** puréed carrots; **p. de pois** thick pea soup; *Fam* peasouper; *Fam* **être dans la p.** *(dans la gêne financière)* to be hard up, to be down on one's luck; *(dans une situation difficile)* to be up the creek
▪ INT *Fam (colère etc)* hell!, blast (it)!; *(surprise)* wow!

purement [pyrmɑ̃] ADV purely

pureté [pyrte] NF purity; *(du ciel)* clearness; *(de lignes)* purity, cleanness

purgatif, -ive [pyrgatif, -iv] *Méd* ADJ purgative
▪ NM purgative, purge

purgation [pyrgasjɔ̃] NF *Méd* purging

purgatoire [pyrgatwar] NM *Rel* purgatory

purge [pyrʒ] NF **1** *Méd* purge, purgative **2** *Pol* purge **3** *(d'un liquide)* draining; *Aut (des freins)* bleeding; **robinet de p.** drain *or* bleed cock; *Aut* **p. de carburant** fuel bleed; **vis de**

▪ **p. bleed screw 4** *Jur (d'une hypothèque)* redemption, paying off

purgeoir [pyrʒwar] NM *(d'une réserve d'eau etc)* purifying tank, filtering tank

purger [pyrʒe] *(je purgeai(s); n. purgeons)* VT **1** *Méd* to purge; **p. les intestins** to clean out *or* cleanse *or* purge the system; *Fig* **p. un pays de voleurs** to rid *or* purge a country of bandits; **p. une société des fainéants** to get rid of the shirkers in a company **2** *Jur (hypothèque)* to redeem, to pay off; *(dettes)* to pay off, to clear; **p. sa peine** to serve one's sentence **3** *Tech (freins)* to bleed; *(radiateur)* to bleed, to drain
▪ VPR **se purger 1** *Méd* to take a purgative *or* a laxative **2** *Fig* **se p. d'une accusation** to clear oneself of an accusation

purgeur [pyrʒœr] NM *Tech* drain cock, bleed cock; *Aut* bleeder valve

purifiant [pyrifjɑ̃] ADJ purifying, cleansing

purificateur, -trice [pyrifikatœr, -tris] ADJ purifying, cleansing
▪ NM purifier, cleanser; **p. d'air** *ou* **d'atmosphère** air purifier

purification [pyrifikasjɔ̃] NF purification; *(de métaux)* refining; *(du sang)* cleansing; **p. ethnique** ethnic cleansing

purifier [pyrifje] *(pr sub, impf n.* **purifiions***, v.* **purifiiez***)* VT *aussi Fig* to purify, to cleanse; *(langue)* to purify; *(métal)* to refine; *(sang)* to cleanse; **lotion qui purifie la peau** skin cleanser
▪ VPR **se purifier** to become pure, to be purified

purin [pyrɛ̃] NM *Agr* slurry, liquid manure

purisme [pyrism] NM *(du langage etc)* purism

puriste [pyrist] N purist

puritain, -aine [pyritɛ̃, -ɛn] N puritan; *Hist* Puritan
▪ ADJ puritan(ical); *Hist* Puritan

puritanisme [pyritanism] NM puritanism

purotin [pyrɔtɛ̃] NM *Arg Vieilli* down-and-out

purpura [pyrpyra] NM *Méd* purpura

purpurin [pyrpyrɛ̃] ADJ *Litt* deep crimson

pur-sang NM INV thoroughbred (horse)

purulence [pyrylɑ̃s] NF *Méd* purulence

purulent [pyrylɑ̃] ADJ *Méd* suppurating, *Spéc* purulent; **foyer p.** abscess

pus [py] NM *Méd* pus, matter

push-pull [puʃpul] NM INV, ADJ INV *Élec* push-pull

pusillanime [pyzilanim] ADJ *Litt* pusillanimous, faint-hearted

pusillanimité [pyzilanimite] NF *Litt* pusillanimity, faint-heartedness

pustule [pystyl] NF blister, pustule; *(de crapauds)* wart

pustuleux, -euse [pystylø, -øz] ADJ pus-filled, pustulous

put [put] NM *Bourse* put (option)

putain [pytɛ̃] *Arg Vulg* NF **1** prostitute, whore, *Am* hooker; **faire la p.** *(se prostituer)* to prostitute oneself; *Fig (chercher à plaire)* to prostitute oneself; *(renoncer à ses principes)* to sell out **2** **cette p. de guerre/machine** this bloody *or* *Vulg* fucking war/machine
▪ INT *(colère etc)* shit!; *(surprise)* Christ!

putassier, -ière [pytasje, -jɛr] ADJ *Vulg* **a** *(tenue, manières)* tarty **2** *(servile, obséquieux)* ingratiating

putatif, -ive [pytatif, -iv] ADJ putative, supposed, presumed

pute [pyt] NF *Arg Vulg* = **putain** NF **1**; **la p.!** *(elle m'a menti etc)* the bitch!; **fils de p.!** bastard!, son of a bitch!

---

putois [pytwa] NM *(animal)* polecat; *(fourrure)* polecat (fur); **p. (d'Amérique)** skunk; *Fam* **crier comme un p.** to scream blue murder

putréfaction [pytrefaksjɔ̃] NF putrefaction; **matière en p.** putrefying matter

putréfier [pytrefje] VT to putrefy, to rot
▪ VPR **se putréfier** to putrefy, to become putrid

putrescence [pytresɑ̃s] NF putrescence

putrescent [pytresɑ̃] ADJ putrescent

putrescible [pytresibl] ADJ liable to putrefy

putride [pytrid] ADJ putrid

putridité [pytridite] NF *Litt* putridness

putsch [putʃ] NM *Pol* putsch

putschiste [putʃist] *Pol* ADJ putsch
▪ NM person involved in a putsch, putschist

puzzle [pœzl] NM (jigsaw) puzzle; *Fig* puzzle; *Fig* **le p. commence à prendre forme dans son esprit** the pieces of the puzzle are beginning to fall into place

PV [peve] NM *Fam (abrév* **procès-verbal***)* (parking) ticket; **j'ai eu un P. ce matin** I got a ticket this morning

PVC [pevese] NM *Tech (abrév* **polyvinyl chloride***)* PVC; **siège en P.** PVC seat

PVD [pevede] NM *(abrév* **pays en voie de développement***)* developing country

pygmée [pigme] N pygmy, pigmy

pyjama [piʒama] NM pyjamas, *Am* pajamas; **un p.** a pair of pyjamas; **elle était encore en p.** she was still in her pyjamas; **c'est un vrai p.** *(ce vêtement)* it's loose and comfortable; **j'y suis comme dans un p.** it's really comfortable VOIR GRAMMAIRE A10

pylône [pilon] NM **1** *Élec* pylon; *(pour fils télégraphiques)* lattice mast; **p. électrique** electricity pylon; **grue à p.** tower crane **2** *Archit (de temples égyptiens)* pylon

pylore [pilɔr] NM *Anat* pylorus

pyorrhée [pjɔre] NF *Méd* pyorrhoea, *Am* pyorrhea

pyramidal, -ale, -aux, -ales [piramidal, -o] ADJ pyramidal

pyramide [piramid] NF pyramid; **p. des âges** age pyramid; **p. des salaires** wage pyramid; **entasser des oranges en p.** to pile up oranges in a pyramid; **structure en p.** pyramid-like *or* pyramidal structure

pyrénéen, -enne [pireneɛ̃, -ɛn] ADJ Pyrenean
▪ N P. Pyrenean

Pyrénées (les) [lepirene] NFPL the Pyrenees

pyrèthre [pirɛtr] NM *(plante)* feverfew, pyrethrum; **poudre de p.** insect powder

Pyrex® [pirɛks] NM Pyrex®; **plat en P.** Pyrex® dish; **c'est du P., ton plat?** is your dish (made of) Pyrex®?

pyrexie [pirɛksi] NF *Méd* pyrexia, fever

pyrite [pirit] NF *Minér* pyrites

pyrograveur, -euse [pirogravœr, -øz] N *Beaux-Arts* pyrographer

pyrogravure [pirogravyr] NF *Beaux-Arts* poker work, pyrography; *(gravure)* pyrograph

pyrolyse [piroliz] NF pyrolysis; **four à p.** self-cleaning oven

pyromane [piroman] N *Psy* pyromaniac; *Jur (incendiaire)* arsonist

pyromanie [piromani] NF *Psy* pyromania

pyromètre [pirometr] NM *Phys, Tech* pyrometer

pyrosis [pirozis] NM *Méd* heartburn, *Spéc* pyrosis

pyrotechnie [pirotɛkni] NF pyrotechnics

pyrotechnique [piroteknik] ADJ pyrotechnic(al)

Pythagore [pitagɔr] N Pythagoras; **théorème de P.** Pythagoras' theorem

pythagoricien, -ienne [pitagɔrisjɛ̃, -jɛn] *Phil* ADJ Pythagorean ▸ N **P.** Pythagorean

pythagorisme [pitagɔrism] NM *Phil*

Pythagoreanism

Pythie [piti] NF **1** *Myth* **P. de Delphes** Pythia of Delphi **2** *Litt* prophetess, oracle

python [pitɔ̃] NM python

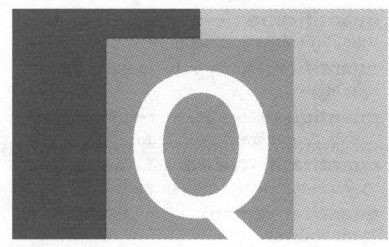

Q, q [ky] NM *(lettre)* Q, q

Qatar [katar] NM Qatar

QCM [kyseɛm] NM INV *(abrév* **questionnaire à choix multiple)** multiple-choice questionnaire

QG [kyʒe] NM INV *Mil Fam (abrév* **quartier général)** HQ

QI [kyi] NM INV *(abrév* **quotient intellectuel)** IQ

quad [kwad] NM **1** *(moto)* quad bike **2** *(patin à roulettes)* quad (roller) skate

quadra [kwadra] N *Fam* = quadragénaire

quadragénaire [kwadraʒenɛr] ADJ, N forty-year-old, quadragenarian; **elle est q.** she's in her forties

Quadragésime [kwadraʒezim] NF *Rel* **(le dimanche de) la Q.** Quadragesima (Sunday)

quadrangulaire [kwadrãgylɛr] ADJ quadrangular, four-angled; *(bâtiment)* four-cornered, four-sided

quadrant [k(w)adrã] NM *Géom* quadrant

quadratique [kwadratik] ADJ **1** *Math* quadratic **2** *Minér* quadratic, tetragonal

quadrature [kwadratyr] NF **1** *Géom* quadrature, squaring; *Fig* **c'est la q. du cercle** it's like trying to square the circle **2** *Astron, Phys* quadrature; **marées de q.** neap tides, neaps

quadriceps [kwadrisɛps] NM *Anat* quadriceps

quadrichromie [kwadrikrɔmi, kadrikromi] NF four-colour processing *or* printing

quadriennal, -ale, -aux, -ales [kwadrijenal, -o] ADJ *(plan, période)* quadrennial, four-year; **les Jeux olympiques sont quadriennaux** the Olympic Games take place every four years

quadrifolié [kwadrifɔlje] ADJ *Bot* four-leaved, quadrifoliate

quadrijumeaux [kwadriʒymo] NMPL quadruplets

quadrilatère [k(w)adrilatɛr] NM *Géom, Mil etc* quadrilateral

quadrillage [kadrijaʒ] NM **1** *(action) (d'un papier, d'une carte)* ruling in squares, cross-ruling; **la police a établi un q. du quartier** the police have the district under tight surveillance **2** *(motif)* squares; *(sur une carte)* grid

quadrille [kadrij] NM quadrille; **q. des lanciers** lancers

quadrillé [kadrije] ADJ *(papier)* squared, cross-ruled; **carte quadrillée** grid map

quadriller [kadrije] VT **1** *(papier)* to rule in squares, to cross-rule; **le quartier est quadrillé par un réseau de ruelles** the district is criss-crossed by a network of alleys **2** *(quartier)* to put under tight surveillance; **tout le quartier est quadrillé** the whole district is under tight surveillance

quadrimoteur [k(w)adrimɔtœr] ADJ, NM **(avion) q.** four-engined plane

quadriparti [kwadriparti], **quadripartite** [kwadripartit] ADJ *(corolle, traité)* quadripartite; *(conférence, commission) (de partis)* four-party; *(de pays)* four-power

quadriphonie [kwadrifoni] NF quadraphony

quadriplégie [kwadriplezi] NF *Méd* quadriplegia

quadriréacteur [k(w)adrireaktœr] NM *Aviat* four-engined jet

quadrisyllabe [kwadrisilab] NM quadrisyllable

quadrisyllabique [kwadrisilabik] ADJ quadrisyllabic

quadrumane [k(w)adryman] *Zool* ADJ *(animal)* quadrumanous, four-handed
NM quadrumane

quadrupède [k(w)adrypɛd] *Zool* ADJ *(animal)* quadruped, four-footed
NM quadruped

quadruple [k(w)adrypl] ADJ quadruple, fourfold
NM quadruple; **au q.** fourfold; **payer le q. du prix** to pay four times the price; **elle gagne le q. de ce que je gagne** she earns four times as much as I do

quadrupler [k(w)adryple] VTI to quadruple, to increase fourfold

quadruplés, -ées [k(w)adryple] NPL quadruplets, *Fam* quads

quai [kɛ] NM **1** *Naut* quay; *(d'embarquement, de débarquement)* wharf; *(construit au-dessus de l'eau)* pier; **amener un navire à q.** to bring a ship alongside, to berth a ship; **se mettre à q.** to berth; **navire à q.** berthed ship; **q. des pétroliers** oil wharf; **droits de q.** wharfage; *Com* **livrable à q.** *(marchandises)* ex-quay, ex-wharf VOIR GRAMMAIRE A12 **2** *(le long d'une rivière, d'un fleuve)* embankment **3** *Rail* platform; **accès aux quais** ≃ to the trains; **le train est à q.** the train is in
▸▸**q. d'arrivée** *Naut* arrival quay; *Rail* arrival platform; *Naut* **q. de chargement** loading quay; *Naut* **q. de déchargement** unloading quay; **q. de départ** *Naut* departure quay; *Rail* departure platform; **le Q. des Orfèvres** Police Headquarters *(in Paris)*; **le Q. d'Orsay** the French Foreign Office

quaker, -eresse [kwɛkœr, -(ə)rɛs, kwa-] N Quaker, *f* Quakeress

quakerisme [kwɛkœrism, kwak(ə)rism] NM Quakerism

qualifiable [kalifjabl] ADJ *(que l'on peut qualifier)* definable; **sa conduite n'est pas q.** his/her behaviour is indescribable

qualificatif, -ive [kalifikatif, -iv] *Gram* ADJ *(adjectif etc)* qualifying
NM qualifier, modifier; *Fig* **il n'y a pas de q. assez fort pour la décrire** there's no word strong enough to describe her

qualification [kalifikasjõ] NF **1** *(formation)* qualification; **q. professionnelle** professional qualification **2** *Sport* qualification; **obtenir sa q.** to qualify; **obtenir sa q. pour la** *ou* **en finale** to qualify for the final; **match de q.** qualifying match; **il court les épreuves de q.** he's running in the heats; **leur q. est assurée** they are sure to qualify **3** *(nom)* designation, name; **s'attribuer la q. de colonel** to call oneself colonel; **elle n'est pas médecin spécialiste, mais elle en a pris la q.** she's not a specialist doctor, but she's given herself that title **4** *Gram (d'un nom etc)* qualifying; *Jur (d'un crime etc)* legal definition **5** *Bourse* qualification *(by acquisition of shares)*

qualifié, -ée [kalifje] ADJ **1** *(compétent)* qualified; **q. pour faire qch** qualified to do sth; **je suis certainement q. pour en parler** I am certainly qualified to speak about it; **ouvrier q./non q.** skilled/unskilled worker **2** *Jur (délit, vol)* aggravated **3** *Sport* **cheval/coureur q.** qualifier; **équipe qualifiée** qualifying team
N *Sport* qualifier

qualifier [kalifje] *(impf, pr sub* **n. qualifiions)** VT **1** **q. qn pour qch/pour faire qch** to qualify sb for sth/to do sth **2** *(appeler)* to describe; **q. qn/qch de ...** to call sb/sth ..., to describe sb/sth as ...; **q. qn de charlatan** to call sb a quack, to describe sb as a quack; **acte qualifié de crime** action termed a crime; **conduite qu'on ne saurait q.** unspeakable behaviour **3** *Gram* to qualify
VPR **se qualifier 1** *Sport* to qualify; **il s'est qualifié pour la finale** he qualified for *or* got through to the final **2** **se q. de génie/d'artiste/etc** to call oneself a genius/an artist/etc

qualitatif, -ive [kalitatif, -iv] ADJ qualitative; *Chimie* **analyse qualitative** qualitative analysis

qualité [kalite] NF **1** *(de produit etc)* quality; **bonne/mauvaise q.** good *or* high/bad *or* poor quality; **produit de (bonne) q.** (good-)quality product; **produit de mauvaise q.** poor-quality product, product of poor quality; **de première q.** top-quality; **blé/viande de première q.** prime wheat/meat; **vin de première q.** choice wine; **chocolat de q. supérieure** extra fine chocolate; **minerai de q. inférieure** low-grade ore; *Ordinat* **q. brouillon, q. liste rapide, q. listing** draft quality; *Ordinat* **q. courrier** (near) letter quality; **garantie de q.** guarantee of quality; **améliorer la q. de la vie** to improve the quality of life; **q. de l'environnement** quality of the environment; *Ordinat* **q. d'impression** print quality **2** *(de personne)* quality; **homme qui a beaucoup de qualités** man with many good qualities *or* points; **qualités de gestionnaire** management *or* managerial qualities; **elle n'a pas que des qualités** she isn't all good; **cet ordinateur a beaucoup de qualités** this computer has many good points; **les quali-**

tés littéraires d'un texte the literary qualities of a text

3 *(propriété)* quality, property; **c'est une des qualités de cette plante** it's one of the properties of this plant; **qualités fébrifuges** antifebrile properties

4 *(occupation)* occupation; *(fonction)* capacity; **décliner ses titres et qualités** to state one's titles and qualifications; *Admin* **nom, prénom et q.** surname, forename and occupation; **il nous révéla sa q. de prêtre** he disclosed the fact that he was a priest; **agir en q. de tuteur** to act (in one's capacity) as guardian; **en (ma) q. de citoyen, je voudrais ...** (in my capacity) as a citizen, I would like ...; **ès qualités** in one's official capacity; **avoir q. pour agir** to have authority to act; **avoir les qualités requises pour un emploi** to have the necessary qualifications or to be qualified for a job

5 *Vieilli* **gens de q.** people of quality, gentlefolk

QUAND [kɑ̃]

CONJ when **1** ■ even if *(quand bien même)* **2** ■ anyway *(quand même)* **3** ■ still *(quand même)* **3**
ADV when

CONJ 1 when; **je lui en parlerai q. je le verrai** I'll mention it to him when I see him; **q. je lui téléphone, elle est toujours pressée** when I ring her she's always in a hurry, whenever I ring her she's in a hurry; *Fam* **je me souviens de q. tu as commencé à travailler ici** I remember when you started working here; *Fam* **q. je pense que le voyage devait être annulé** when I think that they were going to cancel the trip; *Fam* **q. je vous le disais!** I told you so!, didn't I tell you so! SEE GRAMMAR B31–2
2 *Litt* **q. (même), q. (bien même)** even if, even though; **q. (bien même) il me l'affirmerait, je n'en croirais rien** even if he assured me, I wouldn't believe it; **je n'en voudrais pas q. (bien) même on me le donnerait** I wouldn't have it (even) as a gift
3 *Fam* **je le ferai q. même** I'll do it anyway; **q. même, ça serait plus gentil d'aller la chercher à la gare** still or even so, it would be nicer to meet her at the station; **c'est q. même gentil de sa part** still or even so, it's nice of him; **tu aurais pu me le dire q. même!** you might have told me!; **elle ne sait pas compter – q. même!** she can't count – come on!
ADV when; **q. viendra-t-il?** when will he come?; **dites-moi q. il viendra** tell me when he will come; **n'importe q.** no matter when, at any time; **jusqu'à q. serez-vous à Paris?** how long will you be in Paris?; **depuis q. êtes-vous à Paris?** how long have you been in Paris?; **à q. le mariage?** when will the wedding be?, when is the wedding?; **de q. est ce journal?** what is the date of this paper?; **pour q. est la réunion?** when is the meeting?; *Fam* **c'est prévu pour q.?** when is this supposed to be happening?

quant à [kɑ̃ta] **PRÉP** as for; **q. moi** as for me, for my part, as far as I am concerned; **q. cela ...** as for or to that ..., as far as that is concerned ...; **q. l'avenir ...** as for or to the future ..., as far as the future is concerned ...; **s'inquiéter q. à l'avenir** to be worried about the future; **q. le demander, je n'y aurais pas songé** as for asking for it, I wouldn't have dreamt of it

quant-à-soi [kɑ̃taswa] **NM INV** reserve; **rester sur** ou **se tenir sur son q.** to keep oneself to oneself

quantième [kɑ̃tjɛm] **NM** *Litt* day of the month; **quel q. (du mois) sommes-nous?** what day of the month is it?, what is the date?

quantifiable [kwɑ̃tifjabl] **ADJ** quantifiable; **données non-quantifiables** unquantifiable data

quantification [kwɑ̃tifikasjɔ̃] **NF** *Phil* quantification; *Phys* quantization

quantifier [kɑ̃tifje] **VT** to quantify; *Phys* to quantize

quantique [kɑ̃tik] **ADJ** *Phys etc (théorie, mécanique, nombre etc)* quantum

quantitatif, -ive [kɑ̃titatif, -iv] **ADJ** *(analyse, changement etc)* quantitative

quantitativement [kɑ̃titativmɑ̃] **ADV** quantitatively

quantité [kɑ̃tite] **NF 1** *(somme, dose)* quantity, amount; **en grande/petite q.** in large/small quantities or amounts; **dans la q. prescrite** in the prescribed dose; **en q.** in quantity; **nous en avons en q.** we have plenty of them; **q.** ou **des quantités de gens/réponses** a lot of or a great number of or a great many people/replies; **il n'en reste pas des quantités** there are not a lot left; **q. négligeable** negligible quantity or amount; *Fam* **il faut la considérer comme q. négligeable** what she thinks is of no consequence, her opinion is neither here nor there SEE GRAMMAR B59–60 **2** *Phys etc* quantity; *Math* **q. variable** variable quantity; *Phys* **q. de mouvement** momentum, impulse

quantum, *pl* **quanta** [k(w)ɑ̃tɔm, -a] **NM 1** *Phys* quantum; **théorie des quanta** quantum theory **2** *(quantité)* amount; **fixer le q. des dommages-intérêts** to fix the amount of damages, to assess the damages

quarantaine [karɑ̃tɛn] **NF 1** *(environ quarante)* about forty, forty or so; **une q. de personnes/jours** about forty or forty or so people/days **2** *(âge)* about forty, forty or so; **approcher de la q.** to be getting on for forty, to be almost forty; **avoir la q.** to be in one's forties; **elle doit avoir une petite q. d'années** she must be just over forty; **les problèmes typiques de la q.** the typical problems of the fortysomething generation **3** *(isolement)* quarantine; **pavillon de q.** quarantine flag; **mettre un navire en q.** to quarantine a ship, to put a ship in quarantine; **mettre qn en q.** to quarantine sb, to put sb in quarantine; *Fig Fam* to send sb to Coventry; **être en q.** to be in quarantine **4** *Ordinat* **mettre un fichier en q.** to quarantine a file

quarante [karɑ̃t] **ADJ INV, NM INV** forty; **page q.** page forty; **habiter au (numéro) q.** to live at number forty; **la semaine de q. heures** the forty-hour week; *Fam* **je m'en fiche comme de l'an q.** I couldn't care less, I don't give a damn; *Tennis* **q. à** ou **partout** deuce; **les années q.** the forties; **les Q.** the Académie française

quarante-cinq **ADJ INV** **q. tours** *(disque)* single, 45

quarantenaire [karɑ̃tnɛr] **ADJ 1** *(régulations etc)* quarantine **2** *Jur* forty-year, lasting for forty years

quarantième [karɑ̃tjɛm] **ADJ, N** fortieth

quark [kwark] **NM** quark

quart¹ [kar] **ADJ** **le q.-monde** *(pays)* the Fourth World; *(pauvres des pays riches)* the underclass *(of a developed country)*

quart² **NM 1** *(fraction)* quarter; **donner un q. de tour à une vis** to give a screw a quarter turn; **partir au q. de tour** *(d'une voiture)* to start first time; *Fig (d'une personne)* to fly off the handle; **il est parti** ou **a démarré au q. de tour** *(d'un moteur)* it started first time or right away; *Fam (d'un débat etc)* it got off to a great start, it took off right away; *Fam* **il est parti au q. de tour** he hit the roof, he blew up; *Fam* **il part au q. de tour** *(il est coléreux)* he's got a short fuse; *Fam* **elle a compris au q. de tour** she understood straight off or right

away; *Com* **remise du q.** 25% discount, discount of 25%; **un q. de siècle** a quarter (of a) century, twenty-five years; **un q. d'heure** a quarter of an hour; **dans un petit q. d'heure** in ten minutes or so; *Fam* **passer un mauvais q. d'heure** to have a bad time of it; **je vais lui faire passer un mauvais q. d'heure** I'm going to give him a bad time; **un q. de beurre** a quarter (of a) kilo of butter; **trois quarts** three quarters; **la mode du trois quarts** the fashion for three-quarter-length skirts and coats; **manteau trois quarts** three-quarter-length coat; *Fam* **les trois quarts du temps** most of the time; *Fam* **être aux trois quarts ivre/mort** to be three parts drunk/all but or as good as dead; *Fam* **elle était décidée aux trois quarts** she had all but or as good as decided; **il est deux heures et q.** ou **deux heures un q.** it's (a) quarter past or Am after two; **six heures moins le q., cinq heures trois quarts** (a) quarter to or Am of six

2 *(bouteille, pichet)* quarter litre or Am liter; *Mil (gobelet)* quarter litre or Am liter mug

3 *Naut* **q. (de vent)** point of the compass; **nord-est q. est** north-east by east

4 *Naut (veille)* watch; **officier de q.** officer of the watch; **homme de q.** watch keeper; **être de q.** to be on watch; **faire le q.** to keep watch; *Fam (d'une prostituée)* to walk her beat

5 *Arg (poste de police)* cop shop, police station

▸▸ *Fam* **q. de brie** *(nez)* beak, *Br* conk, hooter; **q. de cercle** quadrant; *Sport* **q. de finale** quarter final; **l'équipe va jouer en q. de finale** the team will play in the quarter final; *Mus* **q. de soupir** semiquaver or Am sixteenth rest

quarte [kart] **NF 1** *Mus* fourth **2** *Escrime* quarte, quart, carte; **parer en q.** to parry in carte

quarté [karte] **NM** = system of betting on four horses in the same race

quarteron, -onne [kart(ə)rɔ̃, -ɔn] **N** *(métis)* quadroon
NM *(petit nombre)* bunch; **un q. de manifestants** a bunch of demonstrators

quartette [kwartet] **NM** jazz quartet

quartier [kartje] **NM 1** *(quart)* quarter, *Fml* fourth part; **bois de q.** quartered logs; **la lune est au premier q.** the moon is in the first quarter; *Culin* **q. d'agneau/de bœuf** quarter of lamb/of beef; **cinquième q.** offal; *Hér* **quartiers de l'écusson** quarters or quarterings of the shield; **avoir quatre quartiers de noblesse** to belong to the established nobility

2 *(morceau)* *(d'un gâteau)* portion; *(d'une orange)* segment; *(d'une pomme)* piece; *(d'une terre)* plot; **q. de lard** side of bacon; **q. de chevreuil** haunch of venison

3 *(d'une ville)* district, area, neighbourhood, *Am* neighborhood; *Admin* district; **les beaux quartiers** the fashionable districts or areas; **les quartiers nord de la ville** the north side of (the) town; **le q. des spectacles** theatreland, the theatre district; **je ne suis pas du q.** I'm not from around here, I'm not local; **demandez aux gens du q.** ask the locals or the local people; **médecin/cinéma de q.** local doctor/cinema or Am movie theater; **tout le q. en parle** the whole neighbourhood is talking about it

4 *Mil* **quartier(s)** quarters; **rentrer au q.** ou **aux quartiers** to return to quarters; **avoir q. libre** to be off duty; *Fig* **vous avez q. libre jusqu'à dix-huit heures** you're free until six o'clock, take a break until six o'clock, your time's your own till six o'clock; **quartiers d'hiver** winter quarters; *Fig* **un endroit idéal pour prendre nos quartiers d'hiver** an ideal place to spend the winter

5 *Vieilli* **demander q.** to ask for quarter;

faire q. à qn to give sb quarter; **ne pas faire de q.** to give no quarter; **pas de q.!** no quarter!; **il ne fait de q. à personne** he spares nobody

▸▸**q. général** headquarters VOIR GRAMMAIRE A13 ; **grand q. général** general headquarters; **q. de haute sécurité** *(dans une prison)* top- *or* maximum-security wing; **q. réservé** red-light district

quartier-maître, *pl* **quartiers-maîtres** NM *Naut* leading seaman

quartile [kwartil] NM quartile

quartz [kwarts] NM *Minér, Électron* quartz; **piloté par q.** crystal-controlled; **horloge/ montre à q.** quartz clock/watch

quartzeux, -euse [kwartsø, -øz] ADJ *Minér* **sable q.** quartz sand

quartzite [kwartsit] NM *Minér* quartzite

quasar [kazar] NM *Astron* quasar

quasi [kazi] NM *Culin (de veau, de bœuf)* chump end

quasi [kazi] ADV almost, virtually; **q. aveugle** almost *or* virtually blind; **j'en ai la q.-certitude** I am practically *or* virtually certain of it; **une q.-collision** a near miss; **la q.-totalité du budget** almost the whole *or* entire budget; **la q.-totalité des femmes** almost all (the) women; **une q.-dispute/un q.-divorce** a sort of argument/divorce; *Jur* **q.-contrat** implied contract; **q.-délit** technical offence

quasiment [kazimɑ̃] ADV almost, nearly, as good as; **q. guéri** almost *or* nearly *or* as good as cured; **je n'ai q. rien senti** I hardly *or* barely *or* scarcely felt a thing

Quasimodo [kazimɔdo] NF *Rel* Low Sunday; **le lundi de (la) Q.** Low Monday

quaternaire [kwatɛrnɛr] ADJ *Chimie etc* quaternary; *Géol* Quaternary

NM Quaternary

quatorze [katɔrz] ADJ INV, NM INV fourteen; **le q. juillet** the fourteenth of July, Bastille Day; **page q.** page fourteen; **Louis Q.** Louis the Fourteenth; **habiter au (numéro) q.** to live at number fourteen; **la guerre de q.** the First World War, World War I, the 1914-18 War

quatorzième [katɔrzjɛm] ADJ, N fourteenth

NM *(fraction)* fourteenth

quatorzièmement [katɔrzjɛmmɑ̃] ADV in the fourteenth place, fourteenthly

quatrain [katrɛ̃] NM *Littér* quatrain

quatre [katr] ADJ INV **1** four; **à q. heures** at four o'clock; *Fam* **ton q. heures** your afternoon snack; **trèfle à q. feuilles** four-leaf(ed) clover; **q. barré** *(à l'aviron)* coxed four; **par q.** in fours; **se mettre par q.** to get into *or* form fours; **manger comme q.** to eat like a horse; **monter l'escalier q. à q.** to go upstairs four at a time, to rush upstairs; *Sport Fam* **il est arrivé q. ou cinquième** he came in fourth *or* fifth; *Fig* **se mettre** *ou* **se couper en q. pour faire qch** to do one's utmost to do sth; *Fig* **clair comme deux et deux font q.** as clear as daylight *or* crystal; *Fig* **je me tenais à q. pour ne pas rire** it was all I could do not to laugh; *Fig* **plié en q.** doubled up with laughter; *Fig* **pull/livre de q. sous** cheap *or* inexpensive sweater/book; *Fig* **il a fait les q. cents coups dans sa jeunesse** he sowed his wild oats when he was young; *Fig* **les q. coins du monde** the four corners of the world; **il n'y est pas allé par q. chemins** he came straight to the point *or* he didn't beat about the bush; **être tiré à q. épingles** to be dressed to the nines; *Fam* **un de ces q.** one of these days; **dire ses q. vérités à qn** to tell sb a few home truths; *Mus* **jouer à q. mains** to play a duet; **se mettre à q. pattes** to go down on all fours **2** *(dans des séries)* fourth; **page/ numéro q.** page/number four; **Henri Q.** Henry the Fourth

NM INV four; **le q. août** (on) the fourth of Au-

gust, (on) August the fourth, *Am* (on) August fourth; *Cartes* **q. de carreau** four of diamonds; **j'habite au q.** I live at number four

Quatre-Cantons [katr(ə)kɑ̃tɔ̃] NMPL **le lac des Q.** Lake Lucerne

quatre-cent-vingt-et-un [katsɑ̃vɛ̃teɛ̃] NM INV = dice game in which the aim is to throw 4-2-1

quatre-mâts [katrəma] NM INV *Naut* fourmasted ship, four master

quatre-quarts [kat(rə)kar] NM INV *Culin* ≃ pound cake

quatre-quatre [katkatr] NM OU NF INV *Aut* four-wheel drive

quatre-saisons [kat(rə)sɛzɔ̃] NFPL **marchand des q.** street merchant *(selling fresh fruit and vegetables)*, *Br Vieilli* costermonger

NF INV *(fraise)* perpetual-fruiting strawberry

Quatre-Temps [katrətɑ̃] NMPL *Rel* Ember days

quatre-vingt-dix [katrəvɛ̃dis] ADJ INV, NM INV ninety

quatre-vingt-dixième [katrəvɛ̃dizjɛm] ADJ, N ninetieth

quatre-vingtième [katrəvɛ̃tjɛm] ADJ, N eightieth

quatre-vingts [katrəvɛ̃] ADJ, NM INV *(omits the final s when followed by another number or when used as an ordinal)* eighty; **ils étaient q.** there were eighty of them; **page quatre-vingt** page eighty; **quatre-vingt-un** eighty-one; **quatre-vingt-onze** ninety-one; **ça fait q.** that comes to eighty; **habiter au (numéro) quatre-vingt** to live at number eighty; **les années q.** the eighties

quatrième [katrijɛm] ADJ fourth; **habiter au q. étage** to live on the fourth *or Am* the fifth floor; **le q. âge** *(personnes)* the over-75s; *(état)* life after the age of 75

NF **1** *Cartes* sequence of four; **q. de couverture** *(d'un livre)* outside back cover **2** *Scol* **(classe de) q.** *Br* ≃ third form, *Am* ≃ seventh or eighth grade

NM **monter au q.** to go up to the fourth *or Am* fifth floor

quatrièmement [katrijɛmmɑ̃] ADV fourthly, in the fourth place

quattrocento [kwatrɔtʃɛnto] NM *Beaux-Arts* quattrocento

quatuor [kwatɥɔr] NM *Mus* quartet, quartette; **q. à cordes** string quartet

quat'zyeux [katzjø] *Fam* **entre q.** in private

QUE [k(ə)] PRON REL **1** *(souvent omis en anglais)* *(personne)* that, *Fml* whom; *(chose)* that, which; **l'homme q. vous voyez** the man (that) you see, *Fml* the man whom you see; **montrez-moi les livres q. vous avez achetés** show me the books (that *or* which) you have bought; **la tarte q. j'ai fait cuire** the tart (that) I baked; **c'est le meilleur q. nous ayons** it is the best (that) we have; **il n'est venu personne q. je connaisse** no one I know has come; **il faut attendre le temps qu'elle se prépare** you'll need to wait till she's ready SEE GRAMMAR A32-3; B22

2 *(attribut)* **il mourut en brave soldat qu'il était** he died like the gallant soldier he was; **idiot q. je suis** fool that I am; **menteur q. tu es!** you liar!; **couvert qu'il était de poussière** covered with dust as he was; **purs mensonges q. tout cela!** that's all a pack of lies!; **le garçon/livre q. voilà** that boy/book (there); **c'est une théorie intéressante q. la vôtre** yours is an interesting theory

3 *(de temps)* **depuis trois mois q. j'habite Paris** for the three months I have been living in Paris; **un jour q. j'étais de service** one day when I was on duty; **il y a trois jours q. je ne l'ai vue** it's been three days since I saw her; *Vieilli* **les jours qu'il fait chaud** on hot days;

Vieilli **du temps q. les automobiles n'existaient pas** (in the time) before cars existed; *Vieilli* **les trois ans q. j'ai habité à Paris** the three years (during which) I lived in Paris

PRON INTERR what; **q. voulez-vous?** what do you want?; **q. dit Jean?** what does Jean say?; **qu'y a-t-il à voir dans cette ville?** what is there to see in this town?; **q. faire?** what can I/we/one do?, what's to be done?; **q. dire?** what can/could I say?; **il ne savait q. penser** he didn't know what to think; **je n'ai q. faire de vos souhaits** you can keep your good wishes; **qu'en sait-elle?** what does she know (about it)?; **q. prendrez-vous, du lait ou de la crème?** what *or* which would you like, milk or cream?; **qu'est-il arrivé?, q. s'est-il passé?** what has happened?; *Litt* **qu'est-ce?** what is it?; *Litt* **q. ne le disiez-vous?** why didn't you say so? SEE GRAMMAR A31-2; B17

PRON EXCLAMATIF **qu'il est beau!** how handsome he is!; **q. c'est vrai!** how true!; **q. de déceptions!** what a lot of disappointments!

CONJ SEE GRAMMAR B58 **1** that *(souvent omis en anglais)*; **je vois qu'il se trompe** I see (that) he's mistaken; **je pense qu'il a raison** I think (that) he's right; **je ne doute pas qu'elle y consente** I have no doubt (that) she will consent; **je désire qu'il vienne** I want him to come; **j'ai peur qu'il ne vienne** I'm afraid he will come; **je pense q. non** I think not; **il faut qu'elle le fasse** she has to *or* must do it; **peut-être qu'il est venu ce matin** perhaps he came this morning, he may have come this morning; **c'est q. je ne savais pas q. ...** it's because I didn't know (that) ...; **l'ennui est q. je n'ai rien préparé pour lui** the trouble is (that) I haven't prepared anything for him

2 *(pour exprimer un souhait)* **qu'elle entre!** let her come in!; **q. Dieu lui pardonne!** (may) God forgive him!; **q. je vous y reprenne!** don't let me *or* just let me catch you at it again!

3 *(pour exprimer une hypothèse)* **q. la machine chauffe, et il y aura un accident** let the machine get hot and there will be an accident; **qu'il essaie encore une fois, et il ...!** just let him try again and he'll ...!

4 *(dans une alternative)* **qu'il pleuve ou qu'il fasse du vent** whether it rains or blows; **q. tu le veuilles ou non** whether you like it or not

5 *(reliant deux conditionnels)* **il l'affirmerait q. je ne le croirais pas** even if he said it was true, I would not believe it

6 *(équivalent de où)* *Litt* **il ne se passe jamais une année qu'il ne nous écrive** a year never goes by without his writing to us

7 *(équivalent de afin que, alors que, avant que, depuis que, puisque, sans que, tant que, etc)* **approchez qu'on vous entende** come nearer so that we can hear you; *Litt* **ne partez pas q. je ne vous aie parlé** don't go before I have had a talk with you

8 *(pour ne pas répéter une autre conjonction)* **quand il entrera et qu'il vous trouvera ici** when he comes in and finds you here; **c'est pour quand tu iras mieux et q. tu voudras sortir** it's for when you're better and you want to go out; **quoiqu'il pleuve et qu'il fasse froid** although it is rainy and cold; **si on vient et qu'on veuille me consulter** if anyone comes and wants to consult me

9 *(dans les comparaisons)* **plus grand/ moins rapide q. moi** taller/slower than me; **aussi grand q. moi** as tall as I (am) *or* me; **c'est moins bien q. l'année dernière** it's not as good as last year; **il y a plus de monde q. la semaine dernière** there are more people than last week; **tout autre q. moi** anyone but me; **un autre parapluie q. celui-là** another umbrella besides that one; **vous écrivez plus correctement q. vous (ne) parlez** you write more correctly than you speak; **il habite la même maison q. moi** he lives in the same house as I do *or* as me

10 ne … **q.** only; **il n'est q. blessé** he is only wounded; **il n'a qu'une jambe** he has only one leg, he only has one leg; **il n'a fait qu'entrer et sortir** he just slipped in and out again; **je ne fais q. passer** I'm not stopping, I won't stay; **elle ne fait q. (de) sortir** she has only just gone out; **je n'en ai q. trop** I have all too many; **je ne le connais q. trop** I know him only *or* all too well; **il n'y a pas qu'elle qui le sache** she is not the only one who knows it; **l'homme ne vit pas q. de pain** man does not live by bread alone; **il ne me reste plus q. vingt euros** I have only twenty euros left; **je ne bois jamais q. de l'eau** I never drink anything but water, I only ever drink water SEE GRAMMAR A22; B62–3

11 *Arch, Litt* **q. si vous savez la vérité, il est de votre devoir de la révéler** if you know the truth, it is your duty to reveal it

12 *Fam* **ah! q. non!/q. si** *ou* **oui!** ah! surely not!/yes indeed!; **il va au cercle – qu'il dit!** he goes to the club – so he says!; **ton manteau est dans un état, q. c'est une horreur!** your coat is in a terrible state!

Québec [kebɛk] NM *Géog* Quebec

québécisme [kebesism] NM *Ling* = word or expression peculiar to Quebec French

québécitude [kebesityd] NF Quebec identity

québécois, -oise [kebekwa, -waz] ADJ (of *or* from) Quebec
▪ NM *Ling* Quebec French
▪ N **Q.** Quebec(k)er

QUEL, QUELLE [kɛl] ADJ INTERR *(personne)* which; *(chose)* which, what; **q. livre avez-vous pris?** which *or* what book did you take?; **q. homme?** which man?; **quelle réponse a-t-elle faite?** what was her reply?; **quelle heure est-il?** what time is it?, what's the time?; **dites-moi quelle heure il est** tell me the time, tell me what time it is; **q. genre d'homme est-ce?** what sort of a man is he?; **si tu savais à q. point il tient à cette montre** if you knew how fond he is of this watch; **de quels hommes parlez-vous?** which men are you talking about?; **à q. projet faites-vous référence?** which project are you referring to?; **quels sont ces messieurs?** who are these gentlemen?; **quels sont ces livres?** what are these books? SEE GRAMMAR A31–2; B16

▪ ADJ EXCLAMATIF **q. homme!** what a man!; **quelle surprise!** what a surprise!; **quelle bonté!** how kind!; **q. dommage que personne n'en ait rien su** what a shame no one knew anything about it; **quelle bêtise d'avoir oublié le tire-bouchon** how stupid to have forgotten the corkscrew SEE GRAMMAR A5; B17

▪ ADJ REL *(personne)* whoever; *(chose)* whatever; **q. que soit le résultat** whatever the result may be; **quelle que soit mon affection pour vous** however great my affection for you, much as I love you; **quels que soient ces hommes** whoever these men may be; **q. que soit l'endroit où …** wherever …, no matter where …; **il l'a rendu tel q.** he gave it back the way (it was when) he got it; **mettez-moi à n'importe quelle table** put me at any table you like VOIR GRAMMAIRE A33

▪ PRON INTERR which (one); **de vous trois, q. est le plus rapide?** which (one) of you three is the fastest?

quelconque [kɛlkɔ̃k] ADJ **1** *(n'importe lequel)* any, some … or other; **s'il y a un q. problème** if there is any problem (whatever); **si pour une raison q. tu …** if for some reason or other *or* for any reason you …; **je prends un prétexte q. pour sortir** I go out on some pretext or other; **décrire un cercle passant par trois points quelconques** to describe a circle passing through any three points; **le projet peut échouer pour une raison q.** the plan

can fail for any (of a) number of reasons

2 *(insignifiant, médiocre)* ordinary, mediocre; **parler de choses quelconques** to talk about one thing and another; **une femme très q.** a very nondescript *or* average sort of woman; *(physiquement)* a very plain-looking woman; **on ne peut pas lui donner un emploi q.** we can't give him an ordinary job *or Fam* any old job; **son travail est q.** his work isn't up to much; **un q. général Alain** some General Alain or other

QUELQUE [kɛlk(ə)] ADJ **1** some; **quelques** some, a few; **pendant q. temps** for some time; **si j'avais q. argent** if I had some money; **je ressentais q. inquiétude** I felt some *or* a slight uneasiness; **avec quelques amis** with some friends, with a few friends; **il y a quelques jours** a few days ago; **cent et quelques mètres** a hundred metres plus, a hundred metres and a bit; *Fam* **nous étions quarante et quelques** there were forty or so of us, there were rather more than forty of us SEE GRAMMAR A34–5; B15

2 *(correlative to qui, que + sub)* **q. ambition qui l'agite** whatever ambition moves him; **quelques erreurs qu'elle ait commises** whatever mistakes she has made; **je vous interdis de sortir sous q. prétexte que ce soit** I forbid you to go out for any reason whatsoever; **tout traité de q. nature qu'il soit** every treaty, whatever its nature; **de q. côté que vous regardiez** whichever way you look

3 *(un)* some; **avez-vous q. ami qui puisse vous aider?** have you some *or* a friend who can help you?

▪ ADV **1** *(environ)* some, about; **q. dix ans** some *or* about ten years; **les q. mille euros qu'il m'a prêtés** the thousand euros or so *or* or thereabouts that he lent me

2 *(correlative to que + sub)* **q. grandes que soient ses fautes** however great his faults (may be); **q. méchant qu'il fût** wicked as he was

quelque chose [kɛlkəʃoz] PRON INDÉF INV SEE GRAMMAR A34; B16 something; *(dans les phrases interrogatives ou conditionnelles)* *(chose indéfinie)* anything, something; *(chose définie)* something; **q. me dit qu'elle viendra** something tells me she will come; **avez-vous q. à dire?** do you have anything *or* something to say?; **est-ce que je peux te dire q. ?** can I tell you something?; **si je te dis q., est-ce que tu promets de ne pas te mettre en colère?** if I tell you something, do you promise not to get angry?; **q. de nouveau/plus moderne** something new/more modern; **q. d'autre** something else; **tu veux q. à manger/boire?** would you like something to eat/drink?; **il y a q. entre eux** there's something between them; **il y est pour q.** he has something to do with it; **il se doute de q.** he suspects something; **cela m'a fait q.** it had an effect on me; **ça te ferait vraiment q. si je m'en allais?** would it really matter to you if I went away?; **c'est déjà q.** that's something (anyhow); *Fam* **il a q.** there's something the matter with him; *Fam* **ah mais c'est q., ça!** that's a bit much!; *Fam* **q. comme deux ans** something like two years; *Fam* **je lui ai offert un petit q. (cadeau)** I gave him a little something; *Fam* **il tenait q. comme cuite!** he was totally plastered!; *Fam* **il lui a passé un savon, q. de bien** he gave him an almighty telling-off

quelquefois [kɛlkəfwa] ADV sometimes, at times

quelque part [kɛlkəpar] ADV **1** somewhere; **on ira q. où tu n'es jamais allé** we'll go somewhere you've never been before; **cela doit bien venir de q.** it must come from somewhere; *Euph* **je lui ai donné un coup**

de pied q. I kicked him in an unmentionable part of his anatomy; **son contrat, il peut se le mettre q.** he can shove his contract you know where **2** *Litt, Vieilli (correlative to que + sub)* **q. qu'il fouillât** wherever he searched

quelqu'un, quelqu'une [kɛlkœ̃, kɛlkyn], *pl* **quelques-uns, -unes** [kɛlkəzœ̃, -yn] PRON INDÉF **quelques-uns, quelques-unes** some, a few; **quelques-uns des magasins** some *or* a few of the shops; **j'ai lu quelques-unes des lettres** I have read some *or* a few of the letters; **quelques-un(e)s d'entre nous** some *or* a few of us SEE GRAMMAR A34; B16
▪ NM someone, somebody; *(dans les phrases interrogatives ou conditionnelles)* anyone, anybody, someone, somebody; **q. me l'a dit** someone *or* somebody told me; **de la part de q. qui pense à vous** from someone *or* somebody who is thinking of you; **si q. vient** if anyone *or* anybody *or* someone *or* somebody comes; **q. de plus** someone *or* somebody extra; **q. de trop** one too many; **y a-t-il eu q. de blessé?** was anyone *or* anybody *or* someone *or* somebody hurt?; **il faudra q. d'assez fort** it will need someone *or* somebody fairly strong; **c'est q. de très généreux** he's a very generous person; **ce doit être q. d'important** he must be someone *or* somebody important, he must be an important person; *Fam* **ça t'intéresse q.?** anyone *or* anybody interested?; *Fam* **je veux vraiment devenir q.** I really want to be somebody; *Fam* **c'est q., tu sais!** *(c'est un homme remarquable)* he's quite something, you know!; *Fam* **on ne me parle pas comme ça! je suis q., moi, monsieur!** don't talk to me like that! I'm not just anybody, you know!

quémander [kemɑ̃de] VT **q. qch à qn** to beg for sth from sb
▪ VI to beg

quémandeur, -euse [kemɑ̃dœr, -øz] N *Litt* beggar

qu'en-dira-t-on [kɑ̃diratɔ̃] NM INV gossip, tittle-tattle; **se moquer du q.** not to care what people say; **par souci du q.** for fear of what people might say

quenelle [kənɛl] NF *Culin* quenelle

quenotte [kənɔt] NF *Enf (dent)* toothy-peg, tooth

quenouille [kənuj] NF **1** *Tex* distaff; *Fig* **tomber en q.** *(d'une succession)* to fall to the distaff side; *(d'une entreprise, d'un projet etc)* to fall to pieces **2** *(d'un lit à baldaquin)* bedpost

quéquette [keket] NF *Fam* willy, *Am* peter

querelle [kərɛl] NF quarrel, dispute, *Fam* row; **chercher q. à qn** to try to pick a quarrel with sb; **avoir une q. avec qn** to have a quarrel *or Fam* a row with sb; **q. d'argent** quarrel over money; **querelles de famille** family squabbles
▪ ▸ ▸ **q. d'Allemand** quarrel over nothing; **q. d'amoureux** lovers' tiff; **q. de clocher** petty feud; **q. d'ivrognes** drunken brawl

quereller [kərele] VT *Vieilli (quelqu'un)* to scold
▪ VPR **se quereller** to quarrel (with each other); *(d'amoureux)* to have a tiff

querelleur, -euse [kərɛlœr, -øz] N quarreller
▪ ADJ quarrelsome

quérir [kerir] VT *Vieilli, Litt (used only in the inf after aller, venir, envoyer)* **aller q. qn/qch** to go and fetch sb/sth

qu'est-ce que [kɛskə] PRON INTERR what; **q. vous voulez?** what do you want?; **q. la grammaire?** what is grammar?; **q. c'est que ça?** what's that?; **q. c'est que ce petit garçon qui ne veut pas se coucher?** what's all this about some little boy not wanting to go to bed?; *Fam* **q. tu avais besoin d'aller lui dire ça?**

what did you have to go and tell him that for? SEE GRAMMAR A31–2; B17

PRON EXCLAMATIF qu'est-ce qu'il fait beau! what lovely weather!; **qu'est-ce qu'on a rigolé!** we had such a good laugh!

qu'est-ce qui [kɛski] **PRON INTERR** what; **q. est arrivé?** what (has) happened? SEE GRAMMAR A31–2; B17

questeur [kɛstœr] **NM 1** *Antiq* quaestor **2** *Pol* parliamentary administrator

QUESTION [kɛstjɔ̃] **NF 1** *(interrogation)* question; *(demande de précisions)*, query (**sur** about, on); *Ordinat* query; **faire** *ou* **poser** *ou* **adresser une q. à qn** to ask sb a question, to put a question to sb; **sa fidélité ne fait pas q.** there is no doubt *or* no question about his/her loyalty; **quelle q.!** what a question!, what a thing to ask!; **tu te poses trop de questions** you worry too much; **je commence à me poser des questions sur son honnêteté** I'm beginning to wonder about *or* have my doubts about his/her honesty; **être en q.** to be called into question; **mettre en q.** to question, to call into question; *(affirmation)* to challenge; **elle ne cesse de tout remettre en q.** she questions absolutely everything; **le voyage est remis en q.** there's a question mark hanging over the trip; **voici un point qui fait q.** this is a debatable *or* moot point; **il n'y a pas de q.** there is no question *or* doubt about it SEE GRAMMAR A46–7; B63–4

2 *(affaire)* question, matter, issue; **je voudrais vous consulter sur une q. d'affaires** I would like to consult you on a business matter; **questions d'actualité** current affairs; **ce n'est qu'une q. d'argent/de temps** it is simply a question *or* matter of money/of time; **c'est une q. de minutes/d'habitude** it's a matter of minutes/of habit; **de quoi est-il q.?** what is it all about?; **il est q. de l'affaire de détournement de fonds** it's about this matter of embezzlement; **il est q. de lui élever une statue** there is some talk of putting up a statue to him/her; **il n'en est pas q.** it's out of the question; **il n'est pas q. de leur en parler** talking to them about it is out of the question; **il n'est pas q. que tu y retournes** it is out of the question for you to go back; **il ne saurait être q. de les inviter** we couldn't think of *or* there can be no question of inviting them; **la personne/l'affaire en q.** the person/the business in question; **sortir de la q.** to wander from the point; **ce n'est pas là la q., là n'est pas la q., la q. n'est pas là** that is not the point; *Iron* **c'est bien la q.!** that's completely beside the point!; **qu'il n'en soit plus q.** let us say no more about it, let's drop the subject; *Fam* **q. argent, ce n'est pas rose** moneywise *or* as far as money goes, things are pretty grim; *Fam* **q. vacances, ça pourrait être mieux** as far as holidays go, it could be better; *Fam* **pas q. no way, no chance

3 *Jur* (point at) issue; **q. de fait/droit** issue of fact/law

4 *Hist* **appliquer la q. à qn, mettre qn à la q.** to put sb to the question, to torture sb

▸▸ *Mktg* **q. cafétéria** multiple choice question; **q. à choix multiple** multiple choice question; *Pol* **q. de confiance** vote of confidence; **q. de contrôle** check question; **q. fermée** closed question; **q. fermée à choix unique** dichotomous question; *Mktg* **q. filtre** check question; **q. majeure** leading question; **q. ouverte** open question; **q. piège** trick question; *Mktg* **q. ricochet** boomerang question; **q. subsidiaire** *(d'un jeu)* tiebreak, tiebreaker

questionnaire [kɛstjɔnɛr] **NM** questionnaire; **q. à choix multiple** *(à l'école etc)* multiple choice question paper; *(sondage)* multiple choice questionnaire; **q. d'évalua-**

tion *(remis aux clients)* customer satisfaction questionnaire; **q. pilote** pilot questionnaire

questionnement [kɛstjɔn(ə)mɑ̃] **NM** questioning; *Ordinat* **q. logique** logical querying

questionner [kɛstjɔne] **VT** *(quelqu'un)* to question (**sur** about)

VPR se questionner to question each other

questionneur, -euse [kɛstjɔnœr, -øz] **ADJ** *(enfant, air)* inquisitive

N *Rare* questioner

questure [kɛstyr] **NF 1** *Antiq* quaestorship **2** *Pol* = treasury and administrative department of the French Parliament

quête [kɛt] **NF 1** *(recherche)* quest, search (**de** for); **se mettre en q. de qn/qch** to set out *or* go in search of sb/sth, to go looking for sb/sth; **gens en q. de plaisirs** people in search of pleasure, pleasure-seekers **2** *(pour trouver du gibier)* beating; *(de la meute)* tracking, scenting **3** *(collecte)* collection; **faire la q.** *(pour amasser des fonds)* to make a collection, *Fam* to pass the hat round; *Rel* to take the collection

quêter [kɛte] **VT 1** *(argent etc)* to collect **2** *(approbation, louanges)* to seek; *(compliments)* to fish for, to angle for; *(de la meute) (gibier)* to seek

VI 1 *(faire la quête)* to collect money, to make a collection **2** *(de la meute)* to quarter

quêteur, -euse [kɛtœr, -øz] **N** collector; *Rel* collection taker, person taking the collection

quêteux [kɛtø] **NM** *Can* beggar

quetsche [kwɛtʃ(ə)] **NF 1** *(prune)* dark-red plum **2** *(eau-de-vie)* = plum liqueur similar to kirsch

queue [kø] **NF 1** *(d'animal)* tail; **couper la q. à un cheval** to dock a horse *or* a horse's tail; **cheval à longue q.** long-tailed horse; **cheval à q. écourtée** bobtail (horse); **q. de renard** fox's brush; **elle a des queues de rat** her hair is like rats' tails; *Fam* **il est parti la q. entre les jambes** he went off with his tail between his legs; *Fam* **pas la q. d'un** *ou* **d'une** not a blessed one

2 *(d'une comète, d'un cerf-volant)* tail; *(d'un météore)* trail; *(d'une noire, d'une croche)* stem; *(d'une casserole)* handle; *(d'un fruit, d'une fleur)* stalk; *Typ (d'une lettre)* stem, descender; *Typ (d'une page)* tail, foot; **habit à q.** tail coat; **piano à q.** grand piano; *Typ* **lettre à q. inférieure** descending letter

3 *(d'une procession)* (tail) end, rear; **venir en q.** *(d'un cortège etc)* to bring up the rear; **être en q.** *(d'un cortège etc)* to be at the rear; **Courses de chevaux arriver en q.** to come in at the tail end; **être à la q. de la classe, être en q. de classe** to be at the bottom of the class; *Fig* **une histoire/un film sans q. ni tête** a story/a film one can't make head or tail of, an incomprehensible story/film; **voiture en q. de train** *ou* **du train** carriage *or Am* car in the rear of the train; **wagon de** *ou* **en q.** end carriage, *Am* end car; **attaquer une armée en q.** to attack an army in the rear

4 *(de gens)* queue, *Am* line; **ce sont les premiers de la q.** they are (the) first in the queue *or Am* line; **faire la q.** to queue (up), *Am* to stand in line; **se mettre dans** *ou* **prendre la q.** to get in *or* join the queue *or Am* line; **faire une heure de q.** to queue *or* to stand in a queue *or Am* to stand in line for an hour

5 *Billard* cue; **faire fausse q.** to miscue

6 *Vulg (pénis)* prick, cock, dick

▸▸ **q. de cheval** *(coiffure)* ponytail; **avoir une q. de cheval** to have a ponytail, to wear one's hair in a ponytail; **q. de poisson: le conducteur m'a fait une q. de poisson** the driver cut in (front of me); *Fam* **finir en q. de poisson** *(d'une pièce de théâtre, d'un projet etc)* to fizzle out; *Suisse Fam* **ne pas se prendre pour la q. de la poire** to think one is the bee's knees

queue-d'aronde, *pl* **queues-d'aronde NF** *Menuis* dovetail; **assemblage à q.** dovetail(ed) joint

queue-de-cochon, *pl* **queues-de-cochon NF** *(outil)* auger bit, gimlet

queue-de-morue, *pl* **queues-de-morue NF 1** *(basques)* tail; **(habit à) q.** tail coat, *Fam* tails **2** *(brosse)* flat (paint)brush

queue-de-pie, *pl* **queues-de-pie NF = queue-de-morue**

queue-de-rat, *pl* **queues-de-rat NF 1** *(lime)* rat tail, rat-tailed file **2** *(pour les trous)* reamer

queuter [køte] **VI** *Fam (échouer)* to fail; **q. à un examen** to flunk an exam

QUI [ki] **PRON REL** SEE GRAMMAR A32–3; B22 **1** *(personne)* who, that; *(animal, chose)* which, that; **homme/femme q. parle français** man/woman who *or* that speaks French; **phrases q. ne sont pas françaises** sentences which *or* that are not French; **vous q. êtes libres** you who are free; **c'est la plus âgée q. a répondu** it was the eldest who *or* that answered; **il y a peu de gens q. savent cela,** *Litt* **il est peu de gens q. sachent cela** there are few people who *or* that know that; **il n'y a personne q. ne comprenne cela** there is no one who *or* that does not understand that; **dans ce match, q. était son premier, l'équipe a fait preuve de résistance** in this their first match, the team showed great staying power; **je le vois q. vient** I can see him coming; **la voici q. arrive** she's coming (now), here she is (now); **le voilà q. râle à présent** there he goes, moaning; **c'est une femme charmante, et q. a du talent** she is a charming woman, and talented

2 (= celui qui) **q. vivra verra** time will tell; **tout vient à point à q. sait attendre** all things come to him who waits; **sauve q. peut** every man for himself; **adressez-vous à q. vous voudrez** apply to anyone you like; *Fam* **comme q. dirait** so to speak, as it were

3 (= ce qui) **q. plus est** what is more; **q. pis est** what is worse; **voilà q. me plaît** that's what I like

4 **ce q.** *voir* **ce**

5 *(après prép) (peut être omis en anglais)* who, *Fml* whom; **voilà l'homme à q. je pensais** there is the man (who) I was thinking of *or Fml* the man of whom I was thinking; **il cherche quelqu'un avec q. jouer** he is looking for someone to play with

6 *(indéf)* some; **on se dispersa, q. d'un côté, q. d'un autre** we scattered, some going one way, some another

7 **q. que ce soit** *(sujet)* whoever; *(objet)* anyone; **je défie q. que ce soit de le prouver** I challenge anyone to prove it

PRON INTERR who; *(complément d'objet ou après prép)* who, *Fml* whom; **q. a dit cela?** who said that?; **savez-vous q. a dit cela?** do you know who said that?; **q. désirez-vous voir?** who *or Fml* whom do you wish to see?; **q. vient à la réunion?** who is coming to the meeting?; **devinez q. est arrivé le premier** guess who was here first; **à q. est ce canif?** whose knife is this?, whose is this knife?; **de q. parlez-vous?** who are you talking about?, *Fml* of whom are you speaking?; **de q. êtes-vous le fils?** whose son are you?; **je me demande de q. il tient son mauvais caractère** I wonder who *or* where he gets his bad temper from; **q. d'autre?** who else?; **q. de vous me suivra?** which of you will follow me?; *Fam* **q. ça?** who's that?; **c'est à q. entrera le premier** it's a question of who comes in first; **c'était à q. l'aiderait** they vied with *or* outdid each other in helping him; *Fam* **il est là – q. donc?** he's here – who? SEE GRAMMAR A31; B17

quia (à) [akɥija] **ADV** *Vieilli* **être à q.** to be at a loss for an answer; **réduire** *ou* **mettre qn à q.** to nonplus sb

quiche [kiʃ] NF *Culin* quiche; **q. lorraine** quiche lorraine

quiconque [kikɔ̃k] PRON INDÉF **1** *(relatif)* whoever, anyone who, anybody who; **q. désobéira sera puni** whoever disobeys *or* anyone who *or* anybody who disobeys will be punished **2** *(n'importe qui)* anyone, anybody; **q. de mes amis** any of my friends

quid [kwid] PRON *Hum* **q. de …?** what about …?

quidam [kidam] NM *Fam* fellow, individual

qui est-ce que [kiɛskə] PRON INTERR *(objet)* who, *Fml* whom; **q. vous désirez voir?** who *or Fml* whom do you wish to see?

qui est-ce qui [kiɛski] PRON INTERR *(sujet)* who

quiet, -ète [kjɛ, -ɛt] ADJ *Arch* calm

quiétisme [kjetism] NM *Hist, Rel* quietism

quiétiste [kjetist] ADJ, N *Hist, Rel* quietist

quiétude [kjetyd] NF peace(fulness); **en toute q.** quite calmly

quignon [kiɲɔ̃] NM *(de pain) (morceau)* chunk, hunk; *(bout)* end crust

quillard [kijar] NM *Anciennement Fam* = soldier about to be discharged *or* nearing the end of his national service

quille¹ [kij] NF **1** skittle, ninepin; **jouer aux quilles** to play skittles *or* ninepins; *Fig* **être reçu comme un chien dans un jeu de quilles** to be treated as an intruder; *Fig* **se tenir droit comme une q.** to hold oneself as straight as a ramrod **2** *très Fam (jambe)* pin, leg; **il ne tient pas sur ses quilles** he's shaky on his pins **3** *Anciennement Fam (fin du service militaire)* discharge, *Br* demob; **à nous la q.!** civvy street, here we come!; **la q., c'est dans cent cinquante jours** we'll be back in civvy street in a hundred and fifty days

quille² NF *Naut* keel; **fausse q.** false keel, outer keel; **q. de roulis, q. latérale** bilge keel; **poser la q. d'un navire** to lay down a ship; **la q. en l'air** bottom up

quilleur, -euse [kijœr, -øz] N *Can* skittle player

quillier [kije] NM set of skittles

quincaillerie [kɛ̃kajri] NF **1** *(ustensiles)* hardware, *Br* ironmongery; *Fig Fam* **elle a mis toute sa q.** she's wearing every bit of jewellery she's got **2** *(commerce)* hardware business; *(magasin)* hardware shop, *Br* ironmonger's **3** *Fam (armes)* weapons; **il ne sort jamais sans toute sa q.** he's always armed to the teeth when he goes out

quincaillier, -ière [kɛ̃kaje, -jɛr] N hardware dealer, *Br* ironmonger

quinconce [kɛ̃kɔ̃s] NM quincunx; **arbres disposés en q.** trees arranged in staggered rows; **rivetage en q.** staggered *or* zigzag riveting

quinine [kinin] NF quinine

quinqua [kɛ̃ka] *(abrév* **quinquagénaire)** ADJ INV fifty-something
N fifty-something

quinquagénaire [kɛ̃kaʒenɛr] ADJ, N fifty-year-old, quinquagenarian; **elle est q.** she is in her fifties

Quinquagésime [kɛ̃kaʒezim] NF *Rel* Quinquagesima (Sunday)

quinquennal, -ale, -aux, -ales [kɛ̃kenal, -o] ADJ quinquennial; *(plan)* five-year; **une exposition quinquennale** a five-yearly exhibition

quinquennat [kɛ̃kena] NM five-year term; **pendant son premier q.** during his first term of office

quinquet [kɛ̃kɛ] NM **1** *Fam Vieilli* quinquets eyes; **ouvrez/fermez les quinquets!** open/close your eyes! **2** *(lampe)* oil lamp

quinquina [kɛ̃kina] NM **1** *Pharm* cinchona **2** *(vin de)* q. *(apéritif)* tonic wine

quint [kɛ̃] ADJ *Arch* fifth

quintal, -aux [kɛ̃tal, -o] NM quintal

quinte [kɛ̃t] NF **1** q. **de toux** coughing fit, fit of coughing **2** *Mus* fifth; **q. juste** perfect fifth **3** *Cartes* straight; **q. flush** straight flush **4** *Escrime* quinte **5** *Vieilli (accès de mauvaise humeur)* fit of bad temper

quintefeuille [kɛ̃tfœj] NF *Hér, Bot* cinquefoil
NM *Archit* cinquefoil

quinter [kɛ̃te] VI *Suisse (se mettre en colère)* to flare up, to lose one's temper

quintessence [kɛ̃tesɑ̃s] NF quintessence

quintette [k(ɥ)ɛ̃tɛt] NM *Mus* quintet(te)

quinteux, -euse [kɛ̃tø, -øz] ADJ *(personne)* crotchety, testy; *(cheval)* restive; *(toux)* fitful

quintuple [kɛ̃typl] ADJ fivefold, quintuple
NM quintuple; **au q.** fivefold; **trente est (le) q. de six** thirty is five times (as much as) six

quintupler [kɛ̃typle] VT & VI to increase fivefold, to quintuple

quintuplés, -ées [kɛ̃typle] NPL quintuplets, *Fam* quins, *Am* quints

quinzaine [kɛ̃zɛn] NF **1** *(environ quinze)* about fifteen, fifteen or so, some fifteen; **une q. d'euros/personnes** about fifteen *or* fifteen or so *or* some fifteen euros/people **2** *(deux semaines)* **une q. (de jours)** two weeks, *Br* a fortnight; **remettre une cause à q.** to adjourn a case for two weeks *or Br* a fortnight **3** *(salaire)* two weeks' *or Br* a fortnight's pay

quinze [kɛ̃z] ADJ INV **1** fifteen; **Louis Q.** Louis the Fifteenth; **numéro q.** number fifteen **2** q. **jours** two weeks, *Br* a fortnight; **tous les q. jours** every other *or* second week, *Br* every fortnight, once a fortnight, fortnightly
NM INV **1** fifteen; **le q. mai** (on) the fifteenth of May, (on) May the fifteenth, *Am* (on) May fifteenth; **habiter au q.** to live at number fifteen; *Tennis* **q. partout** fifteen all **2 demain en q.** two weeks *or Br* a fortnight (from) tomorrow, *Br* tomorrow fortnight **3** *Rugby* **le q. de France** the French fifteen **4** *UE* **les Q.** = the fifteen member states of the European Union from 1995 to 2004

quinzième [kɛ̃zjɛm] ADJ, N fifteenth
NM *(fraction)* fifteenth

quinzièmement [kɛ̃zjɛmmɑ̃] ADV in the fifteenth place, fifteenthly

quiproquo [kiproko] NM *(en prenant une personne pour une autre)* case of mistaken identity, mix-up; *(en prenant une chose pour une autre)* mix-up; **il y a eu un q.** there's been a mix-up

quittance [kitɑ̃s] NF receipt; **q. de loyer** rent receipt; **q. pour solde** receipt in full; *Banque* **q. pour solde de compte** closing account balance; *Fin* **q. finale** final payment *or* discharge; **q. comptable** accountable receipt

quittancer [kitɑ̃se] VT *(je quittançai(s))* *(facture, dette)* to receipt

quitte [kit] ADJ **1** *(libéré)* **je suis q. envers vous** I'm no longer in debt to you; **nous sommes quittes** we're quits *or* all square; **tenir qn q. de qch** to let sb off (with) sth; **je vous tiens q. du reste** I'll let you off (with) the rest, never mind the rest; **il en a été q. pour la peur** he got off *or* escaped with a fright; **ils en ont été quittes à bon compte** they got off lightly; **jouer (à) q. ou double** to play double or quits; *Jur* **être q. de dettes** to be out of debt, to be clear of debts **2 q. à** even if it means; **je le ferai, q. à être grondé/m'ennuyer** I'll do it even if it means being scolded/getting bored; **il abandonne ce travail, q. à le reprendre plus tard** he's giving up this work but may resume it later
NM **un q. ou double** double or quits

quitter [kite] VT *(endroit, personne)* to leave;

(métier) to leave, to quit; *(fonction, chambre d'hôtel)* to vacate; **q. la grande route** to turn off *or* leave the main road; **la voiture a quitté la route** *(par accident)* the car went off *or* left the road; *(délibérément)* the car turned off (the road); **q. les rails** *(d'un train)* to jump *or* leave the rails, to derail; *Naut* **q. la jetée** *ou* **le quai** to cast off; **q. l'hôtel** to check out (of the hotel); *Ordinat* **q. le système** to quit (the system); **q. le théâtre** to give up the stage; **q. les affaires** to retire from business; **q. une mauvaise habitude** to give up a bad habit; **q. la vie** to depart this life; **un ami très cher vient de nous q.** we have just lost a very dear friend, a very dear friend has just passed away; **quel plaisir de tout q.!** how nice to get away from it all!; **sa main n'a pas quitté la mienne** his/her hand didn't leave mine; **il ne l'a pas quittée des yeux** he didn't take his eyes off her; **ne le quittez pas des yeux** keep your eye on him, don't let him out of your sight, don't take your eyes off him; **c'est une idée qui ne me quitte pas** I can't get the idea out of my head; **elle veut q. son mari** she wants to leave her husband; **elle ne quitte pas sa mère** *(elle n'est pas indépendante)* she won't leave her mother, she never leaves her mother's side; **je dois vous q., il est tard** I must leave you, it's late; **vous ne quittez pas votre veste?** won't you take off your jacket?; **tu vas adorer ce pull, tu ne le quitteras plus** you'll love this sweater, you won't want to take it off; *Tél* **ne quittez pas (l'écoute)!** hold on!, hold the line!; **q. la partie** to give up
VPR **se quitter** *(des amis etc)* to part, to say goodbye; *(d'un couple)* to part, to split up, to break up; **il est tard, nous devons nous q.** it's late, we have to say goodbye now; **ils se sont quittés bons amis** they parted good friends

quitus [k(ɥ)itys] NM *Jur (d'une dette, d'une responsabilité etc)* quietus, final discharge; **q. fiscal** tax clearance

qui-vive NM INV **être** *ou* **se tenir sur le q.** to be on the alert *or* the qui vive

QUOI [kwa] PRON REL **1** what; **ce sur q. l'on discute** what is being discussed; **ce à q. je m'oppose** what I object to; **c'est en q. vous vous trompez** that is where you are wrong; **après q.** after which; **c'est ce pour q. il s'est battu ces années durant** this is what he's been fighting for for years; **travaille, sans q. tu ne mangeras pas** work, otherwise you won't eat; **il a de q. vivre** he has enough to live on; **il a bien autre chose à q. penser!** he has other things to think about! SEE GRAMMAR A32–3; B22–3
2 il y a de q. vous faire enrager it's enough to drive you mad; **il n'y a pas de q. être fier/se réjouir** there's nothing to be proud of/to get excited about; **je suis en colère – je vous comprends, il y a de q.** I'm angry – I understand, you've every right *or* reason to be; **il n'y a pas de q.** *(en réponse à des remerciements, des excuses)* don't mention it, not at all; *Fam* **il a de q.** he's well *or* comfortably off; **avez-vous de q. écrire/manger?** have you anything *or* something to write with/to eat?; **il faut trouver de q. allumer le feu** we must find something to light the fire with
3 *(dans une exclamation) Fam* **comme q. ça n'était pas la peine de s'énerver!** so it wasn't worth getting worked up about!
4 *(correlative à* **qui, que** *+ sub)* **q. qui survienne, restez calme** whatever happens, keep calm; **q. qu'il en soit** be that as it may, however that may be; **q. qu'on fasse, il n'est jamais content** no matter what you do *or* whatever you do, he's never satisfied; **q. que ce soit** anything (whatever); **puis-je vous être utile en q. que ce soit?** can I be of use to you in any way?; **avez-vous dit que ce soit?** did you say anything (at all)?; **q. que ce soit qui l'en empêche** whatever

may be preventing him

PRON INTERR what; **q. d'autre?** what else?; **q. de nouveau** *ou* **neuf?** what's new?; **q. de plus simple?** what could be simpler *or* easier?; **je ne sais q. penser/lui dire** I don't know what to think/to say to him; **à q. pensez-vous?** what are you thinking of *or* about?; **de q. parlez-vous?** what are you talking about?; **en q. puis-je vous être utile?** how can I help you?; **à q. bon (faire qch)?** what's the use *or* good (of doing sth)?; **en q. est-ce?, c'est en q.?** what's it made of?; *Fam* **eh bien! q.?** well, what about *or* of it?; *Fam* **tu es sourd ou q.?** are you deaf or what?; *Fam* **q.? je n'entends rien!** what? I can't hear you!; *très Fam* **vous désirez q.?** what is it you want?; *très Fam* **de q.?** what!, what's that? SEE GRAMMAR A31–2; B17

INT (mais) q.! what!; **q. donc!** what's that?; **q., c'est vous!** what, is it you?; **mais alors q.? tout est annulé?** don't tell me it's all off!; **enfin q.!** il ne peut pas se désister comme ça! wait a minute, he can't back out like that!; **on ne va pas y passer la nuit, q.!** we're not going to spend the night there!

quoique [kwak(ə)] **CONJ 1** *(+ sub)* (al)-though; **quoiqu'il soit pauvre, il est généreux** (al)though he is poor, he is generous; **je suis heureux q. malade** I am happy (al)though I'm ill; **q. jeune, il avait une certaine expérience** (al)though young, he had some experience **2** *(+ ind) (à la réflexion)* **nous recevons souvent des coups, q., vous savez, nous en donnons aussi** we often receive blows, but then, of course, we hit back

quolibet [kɔlibɛ] **NM** gibe, jeer; **poursuivre qn de ses quolibets** to gibe *or* jeer at sb

quorum [k(w)ɔrɔm] **NM** quorum; **atteindre le q.** to have a quorum

quota [k(w)ɔta] **NM** quota; **q. d'exportation** export quota; **q. d'importation** import quota; **quotas volontaires à l'export** voluntary export restraint; *Can Fig* **avoir son q.** to be fed up

quote-part, *pl* **quotes-parts** [kɔtpar] **NF** share, quota, portion

quotidien, -ienne [kɔtidjɛ̃, -jɛn] **ADJ** *(tra-vail, promenade, journal, émission)* daily; *(ennuis)* everyday; **la vie quotidienne** everyday *or* daily life

NM 1 *(journal)* daily (paper); **un grand q.** a (major) national daily **2 au q.** on a day-to-day basis; **la science-fiction au q.** science fiction in the everyday world

quotidiennement [kɔtidjɛnmɑ̃] **ADV** daily, every day

quotidienneté [kɔtidjɛnte] **NF** everyday nature

quotient [kɔsjɑ̃] **NM** *Math etc* quotient
  ▶▶ **q. électoral** electoral quota; *Admin* **q. familial** family allowance; **q. intellectuel** intelligence quotient, IQ; **son q. intellectuel est de 120** he/she has an IQ of 120

quotité [kɔtite] **NF** quota, share, proportion; *Jur* **q. disponible** disposable portion of estate; **impôt de q.** proportional tax; **q. garantie** *(en assurance)* guaranteed cover limit

QWERTY [kwɛrti] **ADJ INV clavier Q.** QWERTY keyboard

R, r [εr] NM (*lettre*) R, r; **rouler les r** to roll one's r's; **ne mangez des fruits de mer que pendant les mois en r** only eat seafood when there's an r in the month

r. (*abrév* **route**) Rd

rab [rab] NM *Fam* (*nourriture*) extra (food); (*temps*) overtime; **un r. de poulet** a second helping *or* seconds of chicken; **un r. de cigarettes** extra cigarettes; **faire du r.** to put in a bit of overtime; **avoir un r. de cinq minutes** to have an extra five minutes, to have five more minutes; **un r. de sommeil, c'est toujours agréable** it's always nice to get some extra sleep; **il reste du poulet en r.** there's some chicken going spare *or* up for grabs; **j'en ai encore en r.** I still have some left over

rabâchage [rabɑʃaʒ] NM (tedious) repetition

rabâcher [rabɑʃe] VI to say the same thing over and over again

▸ VT (*conseils, recommandations*) to keep on repeating; (*leçon*) to repeat parrot-fashion; **ils rabâchent toujours la même chose** they're always (harping) on about the same old thing; **elle nous a rabâché qu'il fallait faire attention au verglas** she kept on at us about being careful of the ice; **c'est ce qu'elle a passé son temps à me r.** that was what she kept on at me about; **le prof rabâche le même cours depuis dix ans** the teacher's been regurgitating *or* churning out the same old course for ten years

rabâcheur, -euse [rabɑʃœr, -øz] ADJ repetitive; **il est très r.** he's always repeating himself *or* harping on about the same thing; **elle devient un peu rabâcheuse** she's starting to repeat herself

▸ N repetitive person

rabais [rabε] NM discount, reduction; **r. en cas de paiement comptant** cash discount; **r. différé** deferred rebate; **faire un r. (sur qch)** to give a discount (on sth); **faire un r. de 50 euros/de 15%** to give a 50-euro/15% discount, to take 50 euros/15% off the price; **vendre qch au r.** to sell sth at a discount *or* at a reduced price; **il m'a fait un r. de 20 pour cent** he gave me 20 percent off *or* a 20 percent discount; *Fig* **au r.** (*travail*) poorly *or* badly paid; (*système éducatif*) second-rate; **formation au r.** second-rate training, training on the cheap

rabaissement [rabεsmɑ̃] NM *Rare* **1** (*de store*) lowering **2** (*critique*) disparagement

rabaisser [rabese] VT **1** (*store*) to lower; (*prix*) to reduce, to lower **2** (*personne, talents etc*) to belittle, *Fam* to put down

▸ VPR **se rabaisser** to belittle oneself, *Fam* to put oneself down; **se r. devant qn** to put oneself down with sb

rabane [raban] NF *Tex* raffia (fabric); **rabanes** (raffia) mats

rabat [raba] NM **1** (*de sac à main, d'une enveloppe*) flap; (*d'un costume officiel*) bands **2** (*pour gibier*) beating

rabat-joie [rabaʒwa] NM INV killjoy, *Fam* spoilsport, *Fam* wet blanket

▸ ADJ INV **elle est r.** she's such a killjoy *or* spoilsport *or* wet blanket

rabattable [rabatabl] ADJ (*siège, dossier*) folding, fold-down; *Aut* **capote r.** folding roof, drophead

rabattage [rabataʒ] NM (*du bois*) beating; (*du gibier*) beating

rabatteur, -euse [rabatœr, -øz] N **1** (*à la chasse*) beater **2** (*de clients*) tout; (*de partisans*) canvasser

rabattre [rabatr] (*conj like* **battre**) VT **1** (*capote*) to fold down; (*couvercle, siège de toilettes*) to close, to shut, to put down; (*store*) to lower, to pull down, to shut; (*col*) to turn down; (*siège*) (*vers le haut*) to fold up, to put up; (*vers le bas*) to fold down, to put down; (*remettre en place*) to fold *or* put back; **r. une couture** to press down *or* flatten a seam; **r. le bord d'une tôle** to flange a plate; **le vent rabat la fumée** the wind is blowing *or* driving the smoke in this direction; **le vent rabattait la fumée vers nous** the wind was blowing *or* driving the smoke in our direction; *Sport* **r. la balle** to smash the ball; **r. la foule vers la place** to drive the crowd back towards the square

2 (*diminuer*) (*prix*) to reduce, to cut; (*arbre, branche*) to cut back; **r. 100 euros du prix** to take *or Fam* knock 100 euros off the price; **je n'en rabattrai pas un sou** I won't take a penny less for it; **r. l'orgueil de qn** to humble sb; *Fam* **r. le caquet à qn** to shut sb up, to put sb in his/her place; *Fam* **se faire r. le caquet** to get put in one's place; **r. de ses prétentions, en r.** to lower one's sights; *Tricot* **r. les mailles** to cast off

3 (*gibier*) to drive; (*fugitifs*) to herd

▸ VPR **se rabattre 1** (*de siège de voiture*) to fold down; **table qui se rabat** folding *or* drop-leaf table **2 l'armée se rabattit sur la ville** the army fell back on the town; **la fumée s'est rabattue sur nous** the smoke was blown *or* driven in our direction **3 se r. sur** (*se contenter de*) (*un sujet*) to fall back on; (*un film, une personne*) to fall back on, to make do with; **elle finira par se r. sur ce qu'on lui propose** she'll end up accepting *or* making do with what she's offered **4** *Aut* to pull back in; (*s'écarter*) to move over

---

Do not confuse with **rebattre**.

---

rabattu [rabaty] ADJ **col r.** turn(ed)-down collar; **couture rabattue** run and fell seam

rabbin [rabε̃] NM rabbi; **grand r.** Chief Rabbi

rabbinique [rabinik] ADJ rabbinical

rabbinisme [rabinism] NM rabbinism

rabbiniste [rabinist] N rabbinist

rabdomancie [rabdɔmɑ̃si] NF dowsing, *Spéc* rhabdomancy

rabelaisien, -ienne [rablεzjε̃, -jεn] ADJ *Littér* Rabelaisian

rabibochage [rabibɔʃaʒ] NM *Fam* patching up, repairing, mending; *Fig* (*entre amis*) making up, reconciliation

rabibocher [rabibɔʃe] *Fam* VT *Fig* **j'ai réussi à les r.** I managed to patch things up between them

▸ VPR **se rabibocher** to patch things up, to make it up (**avec** with)

rabiot [rabjo] NM *Fam Vieilli* = **rab**

rabioter [rabjɔte] *Fam* VI to scrounge, to cadge; (*de commerçant*) to give short measure; **elle rabiote sur la nourriture** she skimps on the food

▸ VT (*nourriture*) to snaffle; (*de commerçant*) to skimp on; **r. quelques centimes** ≃ to skim off a few pennies *or Am* cents; **j'ai réussi à r. cinq minutes** I managed to snatch *or* steal an extra five minutes

rabique [rabik] ADJ (*virus*) rabies

rabistoquer [rabistɔke] VT *Belg Fam* (*réparer*) to patch up; (*remonter le moral à*) to buck up

râble[1] [rɑbl] NM (*de lièvre, lapin*) back; *Culin* **r. de lièvre** saddle of hare; *Fam* **il m'a sauté sur le r.** he jumped on me; *Fam* **je ne pouvais pas me douter de ce qui allait me tomber sur le r.** I didn't suspect what was waiting for me round the corner

râble[2] NM fire rake

râblé [rɑble] ADJ (*personne*) stocky, stockily built

rabot [rabo] NM *Menuis* plane; **r. à languette** grooving plane, tongue plane; **passer le r. sur qch, donner un coup de r. à qch** to plane sth

rabotage [rabɔtaʒ] NM *Menuis* planing

raboter [rabɔte] VT *Menuis* (*avec un rabot*) to plane; (*avec un autre outil*) to scrape, to rub; *Fig Vieilli* **r. son style** to polish one's style

raboteur [rabɔtœr] NM *Menuis* (*personne*) planer

raboteuse [rabɔtøz] NF *Menuis* planing machine, planer

raboteux, -euse [rabɔtø, -øz] ADJ (*surface*) rough, uneven; (*bois*) knotty; (*route*) bumpy, uneven; *Fig* (*style*) unpolished

rabougri [rabugri] ADJ (*plante, personne*) stunted

rabougrir [rabugrir] VT & VI (*plante, fruit etc*) to shrivel up; (*personne*) to become shrivelled

▸ VPR **se rabougrir** to shrivel up

rabouter [rabute] VT to join end to end

rabrouer [rabrue] VT to berate

racaille [rakɑj] NF (*voyous*) scum; *Fam Vieilli* (*populace*) riff-raff, rabble

raccommodable [rakɔmɔdabl] ADJ which can be mended

raccommodage [rakɔmɔdaʒ] NM **1** (*action*)

(de vêtements) mending; *(de bas, chaussettes)* darning; **faire du r.** to do some mending **2** *(résultat)* mend; *(de bas)* darn

raccommodement [rakɔmɔdmɑ̃] NM *Fam* reconciliation

raccommoder [rakɔmɔde] VT **1** *(vêtement)* to mend; *(bas, chaussette)* to darn **2** *Fam (personnes)* to patch things up between ▸ VPR **se raccommoder** *Fam* to make it up, to patch things up; **se r. avec qn** to make it up *or* to patch things up with sb

raccommodeur, -euse [rakɔmɔdœr, -øz] N mender

raccompagner [rakɔ̃paɲe] VT **r.** qn to accompany sb back; **je vais vous r.** *(à pied)* I'll take you back, I'll go back with you, I'll see you home; *(en voiture)* I'll drive *or* take you home; **je te raccompagne jusqu'à ta voiture** I'll see *or* walk you to your car; **r. qn à la porte** to see *or* show sb to the door

raccord [rakɔr] NM **1** *(de papier peint)* join; **papier peint sans raccords** (wall)paper with no pattern repeat; **faire des raccords de peinture** to touch up the paintwork; **faire un r. à une bande magnétique** to splice a tape; *Fam* **faire un r.** *(de maquillage)* to touch up one's make-up; **j'ai eu du mal avec les raccords** *(de papier peint)* I had trouble matching up the pattern **2** *Tech* union; *(pièce d'assemblage)* connection, coupling, joint; *Élec* **r. mâle et femelle** plug and socket connection; **bouchon de r.** adapter; **r. de lampe** lamp adapter *or* connector; **r. de graissage** grease nipple **3** *Cin (liaison de scènes)* continuity; *(plan)* link shot; **faux r.** jump cut

raccordement [rakɔrdəmɑ̃] NM **1** *(en ajustant)* adjusting **2** *(pour relier)* joining, linking (up), connecting; **pièces de r.** *(de canalisations etc)* making-up lengths; *Rail* **voie de r.** junction line, loop line; *(vers une usine etc)* service siding; *Élec* **boîte de r.** *(pour câbles etc)* junction box **3** *Ordinat* link

raccorder [rakɔrde] VT **1** *(relier)* to join (up), to connect; *(bâtiments, routes)* to link up; *Ordinat* to connect; **r. qn au réseau téléphonique** to connect sb to the telephone system; **nous ne sommes toujours pas raccordés au réseau électrique** we still don't have mains electricity; *Élec* **r. à la masse** *ou* **à la terre** to earth, *Am* to ground **2** *(pièces)* to connect **3** *(bande magnétique)* to splice ▸ VPR **se raccorder** *aussi Fig* to fit together, to link up; *Ordinat* **se r. à** to link up to

raccourci [rakursi] NM **1** *(route plus courte)* short cut; **prendre un r.** to take a short cut; *Ordinat* **r. clavier** keyboard shortcut **2** *(résumé)* abridg(e)ment, shortened version; **en r.** briefly, in brief; **par un r. saisissant on a facile way; c'est un r. saisissant que d'affirmer que …** it is facile to say that … **3** *Beaux-Arts* foreshortening; **bras en r.** foreshortened arm

raccourcir [rakursir] VT **1** *(discours, texte, chemin etc)* to shorten (**de** by); *Couture (manches, jupe etc)* to shorten, to take up (**de** by); **r. ses cheveux** to have a bit taken off one's hair; *Fig Fam* **tomber à bras raccourcis sur qn** to pitch into sb **2** *Beaux-Arts* to foreshorten **3** *Fam* **r. qn** *(guillotiner)* to chop sb's head off

▸ VI to grow shorter, to shorten; **les jours raccourcissent** the days are growing shorter *or* drawing in; **son tee-shirt a raccourci au lavage** his/her tee-shirt has shrunk in the wash; *Fam* **les jupes raccourcissent encore cet hiver** skirts are getting even shorter this winter

raccourcissement [rakursismɑ̃] NM **1** *(action de raccourcir)* shortening **2** *Beaux-Arts* foreshortening **3** *(des jours)* drawing in; *(de vêtement)* *(au lavage)* shrinking; **le r. des ju-**

pes shortening hemlines, the rise in hemlines

raccroc [rakro] NM fluke, lucky stroke; **par r.** by a fluke, by a stroke of luck

raccrocher [rakroʃe] VT **1** **r. qch** to hang sth up again, to put sth back on the hook; **elle ne pouvait pas r. la scie sur son crochet** she couldn't get the saw back on its hook; *Tél* **r. l'appareil** *ou* **le téléphone** to hang up; **ce boxeur devrait r. les gants** it's time this boxer hung up his gloves **2** *Fam (récupérer) (commande, contrat, affaire)* to salvage **3** *(personne dans la rue)* to accost, to stop; *(d'une prostituée)* to accost, to solicit

▸ VI **1** *Tél* to hang up; *Fam* **il m'a raccroché au nez** he hung up on me, he put the phone down on me; **je n'ai pas envie de me faire r. au nez** I don't want to have the phone put down on me **2** *Sport Fam* to retire; *(d'un boxeur)* to hang up one's gloves, to retire

▸ VPR **se raccrocher 1 se r. à qch** to catch hold of sth, to catch on to sth; **se r. à une espérance** to cling to a hope; *Fig Fam* **se r. aux branches** to clutch at straws **2** *(se rapporter)* to be linked, to be connected; **cette idée ne se raccroche pas du tout au sujet** that idea has nothing to do with *or* is totally unrelated to the subject

race [ras] NF **1** *(famille)* ancestry, descent; **de r. noble** of noble blood *or* descent *or* extraction; *Fig* **être de la r. des gagnants** to be a born winner; **être fin de r.** to be decadent; **elle a de la r.** she's very distinguished-looking **2** *(ethnie)* race; **la r. blanche/noire** whites/blacks; **la r. humaine** the human race; **sans distinction de r.** without discrimination on the grounds of race, regardless of race; *Fam (injurieux)* **quelle sale r.!** what filth!; **les banquiers, quelle sale r.!** those bankers are nothing but bastards! **3** *Zool* breed; **la r. chevaline** the horse species; **améliorer/croiser les races** to improve/to cross breeds; **chien/taureau de r.** pure-bred dog/bull, pedigree dog/bull; **cheval de r.** thoroughbred (horse); **avoir de la r.** to be pure-bred; *(de cheval)* to be a thoroughbred

racé [rase] ADJ *(animal)* pure-bred; *(cheval)* thoroughbred; *(personne)* patrician, tall and aristocratic-looking; *Fam* **profil r.** *(d'une voiture, d'un bateau)* clean *or* elegant lines

racème [rasɛm] NM *Bot* raceme

rachat [raʃa] NM **1** repurchase, buying back; **ils ont convenu du r. des captifs** they came to an agreement over the prisoners' ransom; *Jur* **pacte de r.** covenant of redemption; *Jur* **avec faculté de r.** with option of repurchase *or* redemption; *Bourse* **r. gagnant** repurchase at a profit **2** *(de police d'assurance)* surrender; *(de valeur, police etc)* redemption; **valeur de r.** surrender value; *Compta* **r. forfaitaire des créances** lump-sum purchase of accounts receivable **3** *(de société)* buy-out; *Fin* **r. d'entreprise avec un fort levier financier** leveraged buy-out; **r. d'une société par la direction** management buy-out **4** *Rel* **r. d'un péché** atonement for a sin

rachetable [raʃtabl] ADJ **1** *(stock)* redeemable **2** *(péché)* for which atonement can be made

racheter [raʃte] *(conj like* **acheter***)* VT **1** *(objet perdu, objet cassé)* to replace; **je pourrai le r., je pourrai en r. un** I can replace it, I can buy another; **r. qch à qn** to replace sth for sb **2** *(au propriétaire)* to buy back, to repurchase *(de qn* from**);** to buy out; **r. les parts de qn** to buy sb out; **je te le rachèterai si tu ne l'aimes pas** I'll buy it from you or *Fam* I'll take it off your hands if you don't like it **3** *(acheter davantage de)* to buy some more; **je n'ai plus de café, je dois en r.** I've no coffee left, I'll have to buy some more; **je vais r. de la lessive** I'm going to buy some

more soap powder **4** *(en assurances) (police)* to surrender; *Jur (rente, dette, gage)* to redeem; *(otage, prisonnier)* to pay a ransom for, to ransom; *Compta* **r. une créance** to purchase an account receivable; **r. une obligation** to retire *or* redeem a bond **5** *Fig (faute)* to make up for, to compensate for; **Jésus-Christ est mort pour r. les hommes** Christ died to redeem mankind; **r. ses péchés** to atone for one's sins; **r. son honneur/son nom** to retrieve one's honour/reputation; **la profusion de détails ne rachète pas la faiblesse du plan** the wealth of detail does not make up for *or* atone for the lack of planning ▸ VPR **se racheter** to redeem oneself; **que puis-je faire pour me r.?** what can I do to make up for it?, how can I redeem myself?

racheteur [raʃtœr] NM purchaser

rachicentèse [raʃisɛtɛz] NF *Méd* lumbar puncture

rachidien, -ienne [raʃidjɛ̃, -jɛn] ADJ *Anat (bulbe, canal)* rachidian

rachis [raʃis] NM *Anat, Bot* rachis, spinal column, spine; *Anat* **r. cervical** cervical vertebrae; *Anat* **r. coccygien** coccyx; *Anat* **r. dorsal** dorsal vertebrae; *Anat* **r. lombaire** lumbar vertebrae; *Anat* **r. sacré** sacrum; *Anat* **r. thoracique** thoracic vertebrae

rachitique [raʃitik] ADJ *Méd* rickety, *Spéc* rachitic; *Fam (très maigre)* scrawny

rachitisme [raʃitism] NM *Méd* rickets, *Spéc* rachitis; **faire du r.** to have rickets VOIR GRAMMAIRE A10

racho [raʃo] ADJ *Fam (abrév* **rachitique***) (personne)* weedy, scrawny; *(portion)* mean, stingy

racial, -iale, -iaux, -iales [rasjal, -jo] ADJ racial

racine [rasin] NF **1** *(de plante, de cheveu, d'ongle, de dent etc)* root; *Bot* **r. pivotante** tap root; **r. de gingembre** root ginger; **prendre r.** *(d'une plante)*, *Fig (d'une personne)* to take root; *Fig* **attaquer** *ou* **couper le mal à la r.** to strike at the root of the evil; *Fig Fam* **manger les pissenlits par la r.** to be pushing up (the) daisies; *Fam* **se faire faire les racines** *(chez le coiffeur)* to have one's roots done **2** *Math* **r. carrée/cubique** square/cube root **3** *Ling (d'un mot)* root **4** *Fig (origine)* root; **être à la recherche de ses racines** to be searching for one's roots **5** *Ordinat* root

raciner [rasine] VT *(couvertures de livre)* to marble

racisme [rasism] NM rac(ial)ism; *Fig Fam* **c'est du r. anti-vieux** that's ageism; **r. anti-jeunes** prejudice *or* bias against young people

raciste [rasist] ADJ, N rac(ial)ist

racket [rakɛt] NM *Fam* racket; **faire du r.** to run a racket

racketter [rakɛte] VT *Fam* **r. qn** to extort money from sb; **se faire r.** to pay protection money

racketteur, -euse [rakɛtœr, -øz] N *Fam* racketeer

raclage [raklaʒ] NM scraping

raclée [rakle] NF *Fam* thrashing, hiding; **flanquer** *ou* **administrer une r. à qn** to give sb a thrashing *or* hiding; *Fig* **son parti/son équipe a pris une belle r.** his party/team got a good thrashing *or* hiding *or* licking

raclement [rakləmɑ̃] NM scraping (noise)

racler [rakle] VT *(frotter) (peau, semelle)* to scrape; *(pour faire partir) (peinture, vernis etc)* to scrape off; *(pour nettoyer)* to scrape (out); **ce vin racle la gorge** this wine's (a bit) rough on the throat; *Péj* **r. du** *ou* **le violon** to scrape *or* saw on the fiddle; *Fig Fam* **r. les (fonds de) tiroirs** to scrape (the bottom of) the barrel

vpr se racler se r. la gorge to clear one's throat

raclette [raklɛt] **nf** **1** (racloir) scraper; Aut (de balai) wiper blade **2** (de jardin) hoe **3** Culin raclette, = Swiss speciality consisting of melted cheese prepared at the table using a special heater or grill, served with potatoes and cold meats

racloir [raklwar] **nm** **1** scraper **2** Phot etc squeegee

raclure [raklyr] **nf** très Fam (homme méprisable) bastard, Am son-of-a-bitch; (femme méprisable) bitch

racolage [rakɔlaʒ] **nm** (d'une prostituée) soliciting, accosting; (d'un publicitaire) touting for business or custom; Hist (pour l'armée, la marine) press-ganging; **faire du r.** (d'une prostituée) to solicit; (d'un publicitaire) to tout for business or custom; (pour un parti) to tout for votes; **r. de partisans** enlisting of supporters

racoler [rakɔle] **vt** (d'une prostituée) to solicit, to accost; (clients) to tout for; (électeurs, partisans) to canvass; Hist (hommes pour l'armée, la marine) to press-gang; **r. des clients** to tout for custom or business **vi** (d'une prostituée) to solicit; (d'un publicitaire) to tout for custom or business; (pour un parti) to canvass votes

racoleur, -euse [rakɔlœr, -øz] **adj** (publicité, affiche) eye-catching; (titre, journal) sensationalist; (campagne électorale) vote-catching
n (politicien) = canvasser who attempts to recruit party members using unscrupulous means; (commerçant) tout
nm Hist, Mil crimp
nf racoleuse street walker

racontable [rakɔ̃tabl] **adj** relatable, tellable; **cette plaisanterie n'est pas r. devant des enfants** it's not the kind of joke you can tell in front of children

racontar [rakɔ̃tar] **nm** story, piece of gossip; **ce ne sont que des racontars** it's just gossip or tittle-tattle

raconter [rakɔ̃te] **vt** to tell, Fml to relate, to narrate, to recount; **r. une histoire à qn** to tell sb a story; **j'ai l'impression qu'elle m'a raconté une histoire ou des histoires** I have a feeling she wasn't telling me the truth; **r. sa vie à qn** to tell sb the story of one's life or one's life story; **raconte-nous tes dernières vacances** tell us about your last holiday; **on m'a raconté beaucoup de choses sur toi** I've heard a lot about you; **il en a raconté de belles** he told some pretty incredible stories; **on en raconte de belles sur toi!** I've heard quite a few tales about you!; **qu'est-ce qu'il raconte (là)?** what is he talking about?; **alors qu'est-ce que tu racontes (de beau ou de neuf)?** so what's new?; **est-ce que tu as quelque chose de beau à nous r.?** (pour nous distraire) haven't you got anything interesting to tell us?; (à qn qu'on revoit) so what's new?; **on raconte que ...** apparently, ..., people are saying that ...; **à ce qu'on raconte** judging by or from what people say; Fam **je te raconte pas!** you can't imagine!; **on s'est pris une de ces cuites, je te raconte pas ...** you can't imagine how plastered we got
vi r. bien/mal to be a good/bad storyteller; **il faut toujours qu'elle nous raconte!** she always has to tell us all about it!; **je vais tenter de vous r. en quelques mots** I'll try to tell you in a few words; **allez, raconte!** come on, out with it!
vpr se raconter to talk about oneself; **je ne tiens pas à me r. devant tout le monde** I'm not keen on talking about myself in front of lots of people; **ce sont des choses qui ne se racontent pas** it's not the type of thing you

can talk about; Fam **se r. des histoires** to fool or delude oneself; **elle se raconte des histoires si elle s'imagine qu'elle va avoir une augmentation** she's living in cloud-cuckoo-land if she thinks that she's going to get a rise; Fam **se la r.** to show off

raconteur, -euse [rakɔ̃tœr, -øz] **n** storyteller; (d'un film, d'une pièce de théâtre) narrator

racornir [rakɔrnir] **vt** **r. qch** to shrivel sth (up), to dry sth out
vpr se racornir (des ongles) to grow horny; (du papier) to grow brittle; (de plante, chair) to shrivel up, to dry out

racornissement [rakɔrnismɑ̃] **nm** hardening, toughening (up)

racrapoter (se) [sərakrapɔte] **vpr** Belg (confortablement) to curl up; (dans l'inconfort) to huddle up; Fig to retreat into or turn in on oneself

radar [radar] **nm** radar; **r. à ondes entretenues** continuous-wave radar; **balayage r.** radar scan; **écho r.** radar echo; **r. d'autoguidage** homing radar; Fig Fam **ce matin je suis ou j'avance au r.** I'm like a zombie this morning, I'm on autopilot this morning

radariste [radarist] **n** radar operator

rade¹ [rad] **nf 1** Naut roadstead; **r. foraine** ou **ouverte** open roadstead; **r. fermée** sheltered roadstead; **navire en r.** ship in the roads; **mettre un navire en r.** to lay up a ship; **en r. de Toulon** off Toulon **2** Fam **laisser en r.** (personne) to leave in the lurch; (projet) to jettison; Fam **tomber en r.** to break down

rade² **nm** Arg (comptoir) bar, counter; (bistro) bar

radeau, -eaux [rado] **nm** raft; **r. de sauvetage** life raft

radial, -iale, -iaux, -iales [radjal, -jo] **adj** **1** radial; **pneumatique à carcasse radiale** radial(-ply) tyre **2** Anat (muscle, nerf) radial
nf radiale 1 radial road, urban motorway **2** Anat radial

radian [radjɑ̃] **nm** Math radian

radiance [radjɑ̃s] **nf** Litt radiance

radiant [radjɑ̃] **adj** (chaleur), Vieilli (beauté) radiant; **pouvoir r.** radiating capacity
nm Astron radiant (point)

radiateur [radjatœr] **nm** radiator; **r. à accumulation** storage heater; **r. à ailettes** fin radiator; **r. à bain d'huile** oil-filled radiator; **r. à eau chaude** hot-water radiator; **r. électrique** electric fire; **r. à** ou **en nid d'abeilles** honeycomb radiator, cellular film-type radiator; **r. soufflant** fan heater; **r. transversal** cross-flow radiator; **r. vertical** vertical-flow radiator

radiation¹ [radjasjɔ̃] **nf** (d'une liste) striking out, crossing out; (de dette) cancellation; (d'un avocat) disbarment; (d'un médecin) striking off; (d'un sportif) banning; **vous risquez la r.** you risk being disbarred/struck off/banned

radiation² **nf** Phys radiation; **r. cosmique** cosmic radiation; Électron **r. (de) haute fréquence** high-frequency radiation; Nucl **r. alpha/bêta** alpha/beta radiation, alpha-ray/beta-ray emission

radical, -ale, -aux, -ales [radikal, -o] **adj** radical; Pol left of centre; Math **signe r.** radical or root sign; **c'est r.** (d'un médicament, d'une méthode) it does the trick, it works like magic (**contre** on)
n radical; Pol person who is left of centre; **être r. de droite/de gauche** to be right/left of centre
nm Ling root, radical; Math radical or root sign; Chimie radical; **radicaux libres** free radicals

radicalement [radikalmɑ̃] **adv** radically

radicalisation [radikalizasjɔ̃] **nf** Pol radicalization; **la r. du conflit** the heightening of the conflict

radicaliser [radikalize] Pol **vt** to make more radical, to radicalize
vpr se radicaliser to become more radical, to radicalize

radicalisme [radikalism] **nm** Pol radicalism

radical-socialisme **nm** Pol liberalism; Hist, Pol radical socialism

radical-socialiste, pl **radicaux-socialistes** **adj, n** Pol liberal; Hist, Pol radical socialist

radicelle [radisɛl] **nf** Bot rootlet, Spéc radicel

radicule [radikyl] **nf** Bot radicle

radier¹ [radje] **nm** Constr frame, floor, bed; (de porte d'écluse) sill; (de bassin) apron; **r. de fondation** foundation raft

radier² **vt** (impf, pr sub **n. radiions**) to strike or cross out; **r. qn/qch d'une liste** to strike or cross sb/sth off a list

radiesthésie [radjɛstezi] **nf** dowsing, divination

radiesthésiste [radjɛstezist] **n** dowser, diviner

radieux, -ieuse [radjø, -jøz] **adj** (soleil) radiant, dazzling; (temps) glorious; (personne) radiant; **elle avait un regard r., son regard était r.** she was radiant or glowing

radin, -ine [radɛ̃, -in] Fam **n** skinflint, tightwad
adj stingy

radiner [radine] Fam **vi** to turn up, to show up, to roll up
vpr se radiner to turn up, to show up, to roll up; **c'est à cette heure-ci que tu te radines?** what kind of time do you call this?; **alors tu te radines?** are you coming or not?

radio [radjo] **nf 1** (poste) radio (set); **à la r.** on the radio; **écouter la r.** to listen to the radio; **passer à la r.** (personne) to be on the radio; (chanson) to be played on the radio; (concert) to be broadcast (on the radio); **travailler à la r.** to work on the or for (the) radio; **faire de la r.** to be or work as a radio presenter **2** (station) radio station; **sur toutes les radios** on all stations **3** (radiotéléphonie) radiotelephony **4** Méd X-ray (photograph); **passer une r.** ou **à la r.** to be X-rayed
nm Vieilli **1** (télégramme) radio(gram) **2** (opérateur) radio operator
adj inv radio
▸ ▸ **r. commerciale** commercial radio; (station) commercial radio station; **r. communautaire** community radio; (station) community radio station; **r. K7** radio-cassette player; **r. libre** independent local radio (station); **r. locale** local radio; **r. périphérique** = any independent radio broadcasting organization based outside France; **r. pirate** pirate radio (station); **r. scolaire** schools radio

radioactif, -ive [radjoaktif, -iv] **adj** radioactive

radioactivité [radjoaktivite] **nf** radioactivity

radioalignement [radjoaliɲ(ə)mɑ̃] **nm** Aviat, Naut radio-beacon route; **voler par r.** to fly airways

radioamateur **nm** radio ham

radioastronomie [radjoastrɔnɔmi] **nf** radio astronomy

radiobalisage [radjobalizaʒ] **nm** radio-beacon navigation; Aviat airways navigation

radiobalise [radjobaliz] **nf** radio beacon, marker beacon

radiocassette [radjokasɛt] **nf** radio cassette (player)

radiocommunication [radjokɔmynikasjɔ̃] **nf** radiocommunication

radiocompas [radjokɔ̃pa] NM *Aviat* radio compass

radioconducteur [radjokɔ̃dyktœr] NM *Phys* radio conductor

radiodermite [radjodɛrmit] NF *Méd* radiodermatitis, X-ray dermatitis

radiodiagnostic [radjodjagnɔstik] NM *Méd* X-ray diagnosis

radiodiffuser [radjodifyze] VT *Radio* to broadcast; **un concert radiodiffusé** a broadcast concert

radiodiffusion [radjodifyzjɔ̃] NF *Radio* broadcasting

radioélectricien, -ienne [radjoelɛktrisjɛ̃, -jɛn] N radio (and television) technician

radiogénique [radjoʒenik] ADJ *Fam* il a une voix r. he has a good broadcasting voice; elle est très r. she has a good voice for radio

radiogoniomètre [radjogonjomɛtr] NM direction finder, *Spéc* radiogoniometer

radiogoniométrie [radjogonjometri] NF direction finding, *Spéc* radiogoniometry

radiogramme [radjogram] NM *(message)* radio telegram, radiogram

radiographie [radjografi] NF *Méd* **1** *(technique)* radiography, X-ray photography **2** *(cliché)* X-ray (photograph), radiograph

radiographier [radjografje] VT *(impf, pr sub n. radiographiions) Méd* to X-ray

radiographique [radjografik] ADJ *Méd* X-ray, radiographic; **examen r.** X-ray (examination)

radioguidage [radjogidaʒ] NM *Aviat, Naut* radio control or direction or guidance; *(de missile etc)* homing; *Radio (pour automobilistes)* traffic news or information

radioguidé [radjogide] ADJ radio-controlled; *(missile)* guided

radio(-)journal, *pl* **radio(-)journaux** NM *Radio* radio news, news bulletin

radiologie [radjolɔʒi] NF *Méd* radiology

radiologique [radjolɔʒik] ADJ *Méd* radiological; **examen r.** X-ray (examination)

radiologue [radjolɔg], **radiologiste** [radjolɔʒist] N *Méd* radiologist

radiomètre [radjomɛtr] NM *Phys* radiometer

radionavigant [radjonavigɑ̃] NM *Naut, Aviat* radio officer

radionavigation [radjonavigasjɔ̃] NF navigation by radar

radiophare [radjofar] NM *Naut, Aviat* radio beacon

radiophonie [radjofoni] NF radio(tele)phony, wireless telephony, broadcasting

radiophonique [radjofonik] ADJ radio

radiorepérage [radjorəperaʒ] NM radiolocation

radioreportage [radjorəpɔrtaʒ] NM *Radio* radio reporting; **un r.** a report

radioreporter [radjorəpɔrtɛr] NM *Radio* radio reporter

radioréveil [radjorevɛj] NM radio-alarm (clock)

radioscopie [radjoskɔpi] NF *Méd* radioscopy, X-ray (examination)

radioscopique [radjoskɔpik] ADJ *Méd* **examen r.** X-ray (examination)

radiosondage [radjosɔ̃daʒ] NM *Météo* radiosonde exploration

radiosonde [radjosɔ̃d] NF **1** *Météo* radiosonde **2** *Aviat* radio altimeter

radio-taxi, *pl* **radio-taxis** NM radio taxi

radiotechnique [radjotɛknik] NF radiotechnology

radiotélégramme [radjotelegram] NM radio telegram

radiotélégraphie [radjotelegrafi] NF radio telegraphy, wireless telegraphy

radiotélégraphier [radjotelegrafje] VT *(conj like **télégraphier**) (télégramme)* to radio

radiotéléphone [radjotelefon] NM radio-telephone

radiotéléphonie [radjotelefoni] NF radio-telephony, radio communication

radiotélescope [radjoteleskɔp] NM radio telescope

radiotélévisé [radjotelevize] ADJ simulcast, broadcast simultaneously on radio and television

radiotélévision [radjotelevizjɔ̃] NF radio and television

radiothérapeute [radjoterapøt] N *Méd* radiotherapist

radiothérapie [radjoterapi] NF *Méd* radiotherapy, X-ray treatment

radis [radi] NM radish; **r. noir** black radish; *Fig Fam* **ne pas/plus avoir un r.** to be (stony) broke, not to have a bean; **sans un r.** broke, *Br* skint

radium [radjɔm] NM radium

radius [radjys] NM *Anat* radius

radon [radɔ̃] NM radon

radotage [radotaʒ] NM twaddle, drivel; *(d'une vieille personne etc)* rambling talk

radoter [radote] VI *(divaguer)* to ramble on; *(rabâcher)* to keep on repeating oneself; **il commence à r.** *(par sénilité)* he or his mind is starting to wander; *(il se répète)* he's starting to repeat himself all the time
▸ VT *Fam* **tu radotes toujours les mêmes histoires!** you keep on coming out with the same old thing!; **mais qu'est-ce qu'il radote?** what's he (rabbiting) on about?

radoteur, -euse [radotœr, -øz] N dotard; **c'est un (vieux) r.** he's always rambling on

radoub [radu] NM *(d'un bateau)* refitting, graving; **navire au r.** ship under repair or in dry dock; **bassin de r.** graving dock, dry dock

radouber [radube] VT **1** *(bateau)* to repair the hull of **2** *(filet)* to mend, to repair; *Fam Vieilli (vêtement)* to patch up

radoucir [radusir] VT *(personne)* to calm down, to mollify; *(caractère)* to soften; **r. le temps/la température** *(de la pluie, du vent)* to bring milder weather/temperatures
▸ VPR **se radoucir** *(d'une personne)* to calm down; *(d'une voix)* to soften; *(du temps)* to become milder

radoucissement [radusismɑ̃] NM **1** *(de la voix)* softening; *(d'une personne)* calming down **2** *Météo* milder spell; **on prévoit un net r. de la température** distinctly milder temperatures are forecast

rafale [rafal] NF **1** *(de vent)* squall, strong gust, blast; *(de pluie)* burst; **vent à rafales** blustering or gusty wind; **temps à rafales** blustery or squally weather; **le vent soufflait par ou en rafales** the wind was blowing in strong gusts; **la pluie tombait par rafales** the rain was falling in great bursts **2** *(de coups de feu)* burst

raffermir [rafɛrmir] VT **1** *(chair)* to firm up, to make firm(er); *(peau, tissus)* to tone up **2** *(autorité)* to reinforce, to strengthen; *(courage)* to strengthen; **l'équipe gouvernementale est sortie raffermie du conflit** the government team came out of the conflict stronger or strengthened
▸ VPR **se raffermir** *(du sol, des muscles, de la peau etc)* to firm up, to get firmer; *(des prix)* to steady; *(du gouvernement) (devenir plus intransigeant)* to take a stronger or firmer or tougher line; *(devenir plus fort)* to become stronger; **ses jambes se raffermissent** his/her legs are growing stronger again; **son au-**

torité se raffermit he is recovering or regaining his authority; **il se raffermit dans ses intentions** he is more determined than he used to be

raffermissement [rafɛrmismɑ̃] NM **1** *(du sol)* firming (up), making firm(er); *(des tissus, de la peau)* toning **2** *(des prix)* steadying **3** *(de l'autorité, du pouvoir)* strengthening

raffinage [rafinaʒ] NM *(du pétrole, du sucre etc)* refining

raffiné [rafine] ADJ **1** *(pétrole, sucre etc)* refined **2** *(esprit)* subtle, refined; *(goût)* refined; *(manières, style)* refined, polished

raffinement [rafinmɑ̃] NM *(des manières, de langage, de luxe)* refinement; *(de la pensée, d'une politique)* subtlety, refinement; **le comble du r.** the height of refinement; **avec des raffinements de cruauté** with sophisticated cruelty

raffiner [rafine] VT *(sucre, huile etc)* to refine; *(ses manières)* to refine, to polish
▸ VI to be overmeticulous or fussy (**sur** about); **r. sur la propreté** to carry cleanliness to extremes; **on ne va pas r. sur les détails!** we won't be too fussy about the details!; **vous raffinez!** you're getting too hung up on detail!

raffinerie [rafinri] NF refinery; **r. de pétrole** oil refinery

raffineur, -euse [rafinœr, -øz] N refiner

raffoler [rafole] VI *Fam* **r. de qn/qch** to adore sb/sth, to be mad about or dote on sb/sth

raffut [rafy] NM *Fam (bruit)* din, racket, row; **faire du r.** *(bruit)* to make a din or racket or row; *(scandale)* to set tongues wagging; *(pour protester)* to kick up a fuss

raffûter [rafyte] VT *(outil)* to (re)sharpen, to (re)set

rafiau, rafiot [rafjo] NM *Naut* skiff *(with lateen sail)*; **vieux r.** old tub

rafistolage [rafistolaʒ] NM *Fam* patching up; **ça n'ira pas loin, c'est du r.** it won't last long, it's just a makeshift or patched-up job; **ces changements ne sont que du r.** these changes will do nothing more than patch things up

rafistoler [rafistole] VT *Fam* to patch up

rafle [rafl] NF **1** *(par la police)* raid; **la police a fait une r. dans le club** the police raided the club; *Hist* **la r. du Vel'd'Hiv** = the rounding-up of Jews in the Velodrome d'Hiver in Paris on 16 July, 1942 **2** *Vieilli* thieving; *Fam (par des voleurs etc)* clean sweep; **r. d'étalage avec bris de devanture** smash-and-grab raid

rafler [rafle] VT *Fam (de cambrioleurs)* to swipe, to nick; **ils m'ont tout raflé** they've totally cleaned me out, they've swiped the lot; **les enfants ont tout raflé dans la cuisine** the children have made off with everything in the kitchen; **le film qui a raflé tous les oscars** the film which made a clean sweep of the Oscars, the film which walked off with all the Oscars

rafraîchir [rafrɛʃir] VT **1** *(rendre frais) (personne)* to cool (down); *(pièce)* to air; **pour r. l'atmosphère** to cool the air (down) **2** *(couleur, maquillage)* to freshen up; *(peintures)* to freshen up, to do up, to renovate; *Fig* **r. sa coupe à qn** to trim sb's hair, to give sb('s hair) a trim; *Fig Fam* **r. la mémoire à qn** to refresh sb's memory; *Fig Fam* **je vais te r. les idées** I'll refresh your memory for you
▸ VI **1** *Météo* to get cooler or colder; **le temps rafraîchit** it's getting colder **2** *Culin* to chill; **mettre qch à rafraîchir** to chill sth; **mettre le vin à r. à la cave** to put the wine to cool in the cellar **3** *Ordinat* to refresh
▸ VPR **se rafraîchir 1** *(du temps)* to grow or turn cooler **2** *(d'une personne) (se laver)* to freshen up; *Fam (en buvant)* to have a refreshing drink

rafraîchissant [rafrɛʃisɑ̃] ADJ *(brise, boisson)* refreshing, cooling; *Fig (simplicité, spontanéité)* refreshing; **d'une simplicité/spontanéité rafraîchissante** refreshingly simple/spontaneous

rafraîchissement [rafrɛʃismɑ̃] NM **1** *(de la température, d'un liquide etc)* cooling; **on prévoit un r. des températures ce week-end** temperatures are expected to drop *or* things are expected to be a bit cooler this weekend **2** *(boisson)* cold drink; **rafraîchissements** refreshments **3** *Ordinat* refresh

rafting [raftiŋ] NM rafting

raga [raga] NM INV *Mus* raga

ragaillardir [ragajardir] VT **r. qn** *(physiquement)* to revive sb, to make sb feel better; *(encourager)* to cheer sb up
 VPR **se ragaillardir** to cheer up, *Fam* to buck up

rage [raʒ] NF **1** *Méd, Vét* rabies **2** *Fig* rage, fury, frenzy; *(passion)* passion (**de qch** for sth); **la tempête fait r.** the storm is raging; **l'incendie faisait r.** the fire was blazing *or* raging (furiously); **avoir la r. du jeu/d'écrire** to have a passion for gambling/writing; **avoir la r. au cœur** to be bitterly angry; **fou de r.** furious, hopping mad; **se mettre en r.** to get into a rage, to get furious (**contre qn** with sb; **contre qch** about sth); **ça me met en r.** it infuriates me, it makes me furious *or* my blood boil; **r. de dents** raging toothache; *Fam* **ce n'est pas de l'amour, c'est de la r.** that's not love, it's madness

rageant [raʒɑ̃] ADJ *Fam* infuriating

rager [raʒe] VI (**je rageai(s); n. rageons**) *Fam* to rage, to be in a rage, to fume; **ça me fait r. de voir ça!** it makes me hopping mad to see that!, seeing that makes my blood boil!

rageur, -euse [raʒœr, -øz] ADJ *(ton, voix)* furious, infuriated; **dit-elle d'un ton r.** she said furiously; **'va au diable!', dit-il, r.** 'go to hell!', he said furiously

rageusement [raʒøzmɑ̃] ADV furiously

raglan [raglɑ̃] NM raglan coat
 ADJ INV **manches r.** raglan sleeves

ragondin [ragɔ̃dɛ̃] NM *Zool* coypu; *(fourrure)* nutria

ragot¹ [rago] NM *(sanglier)* boar in its third year
 ADJ *Vieilli* dumpy, squat

ragot² NM *Fam (commérages)* piece of gossip *or* tittle-tattle; **faire des ragots** to gossip, to tittle-tattle

ragoût [ragu] NM *Culin* stew, ragout; **r. de mouton** mutton stew; **(faire) cuire qch en r.** to stew sth

ragoûtant [ragutɑ̃] ADJ *(with neg)* **peu** *ou* **pas r.** *(plat)* unappetizing, uninviting; *(personne)* disgusting; **des choses peu ragoûtantes** some rather unpleasant *or* nasty things

ragréer [ragree] VT **1** *(maçonnerie, boiserie)* to finish off; *(jointure etc)* to clean up, to trim up **2** *(façade d'un bâtiment)* to clean

ragtime [ragtajm] NM *(danse)*, *Mus* ragtime

rahat-lokoum [raatlokum], **rahat-loukoum** [raatlukum] NM piece of Turkish delight; **des rahat-lo(u)koums** Turkish delight

rai [rɛ] NM *(de lumière)* ray; *(d'étoile)* point

raï [raj] NM INV *Mus* = North African popular music influenced by music from the West

raid [rɛd] NM **1** *Mil* raid; **r. aérien** air raid; **lancer un r.** to launch *or* mount a raid (**contre** on) **2** *Sport* endurance test; *(en automobile)* long-distance rally; *(en avion)* long-distance flight **3** *Fin* raid; **lancer/financer un r.** to mount/to finance a raid

raide [rɛd] ADJ **1** *(membre, articulation)* stiff; *(câble etc)* taut, tight; **corde r.** tightrope; *Fig* **être sur la corde r.** to be walking a tightrope; **cheveux raides** straight hair; **mettre un**

---

câble au r. to take up the slack in a cable; **assis r. sur sa chaise** sitting bolt upright on his chair; **r. comme un piquet** as stiff as a ramrod, ramrod straight; *Fig Fam* **r. (comme un passe-lacet)** *(sans le sou)* (stony) broke **2** *(manières, mouvement, démarche)* stiff; *(caractère)* inflexible, unbending, unyielding **3** *(escalier, pente)* steep; **ça descend en pente r.** it slopes steeply **4** *Fam* **ça, c'est un peu r.!** that's a bit thick *or* a bit much!; **il en a vu de raides** he's had a tough life; **elle m'en a dit de raides sur toi** she told me some pretty nasty things about you **5** *très Fam (drogué)* stoned, wasted; *(ivre)* plastered, *Br* legless
 ADV **1** *(monter)* steeply **2 tomber r.** to collapse; **tomber r. (par terre)** to fall to the ground; **r. mort** dead as a doornail; **tomber r. mort** to drop dead; **il y avait une odeur à tomber r. mort** it stank to high heaven, the smell was enough to kill you; *Fam Vieilli* **il faut travailler r.** we're going to have to work like galley slaves

raider [rɛdœr] NM *Fin* (corporate) raider

raideur [rɛdœr] NF **1** *(d'un membre, d'une articulation, d'un mouvement)* stiffness; *(d'une corde)* tautness; **donne plus de r. à ta démarche** be a little bit more dignified; **avoir une r. dans le cou** to have a stiff neck **2** *(de manières)* stiffness, starchiness; *(de caractère)* inflexibility, rigidity; **répondre avec une certaine r.** to answer rather stiffly **3** *(d'une pente)* steepness, abruptness

raidillon [rɛdijɔ̃] NM steep path; *(sur une route)* (short and steep) rise

raidir [rɛdir] VT *(corde, câble etc)* to tighten, to pull tight *or* taut; *(tissu)* to stiffen; **r. les bras/jambes** to brace one's arms/legs; **un cadavre raidi par la mort** a body in rigor mortis
 VPR **se raidir 1** *(des membres, des articulations)* to stiffen up, to grow stiff(er); *(de câble)* to grow taut, to tauten **2** *(d'une personne)* to tense up, to grow tense; *Fig* **se r. contre le malheur** to steel *or* brace oneself against misfortune

raidissement [rɛdismɑ̃] NM stiffening; *(de corde)* tautening; *Fig* **r. des rapports internationaux** increase of tension in international relations; **il y a un net r. de la position des ouvriers face à la direction** the workers are quite clearly standing their ground with the management

raidisseur [rɛdisœr] NM *Tech* stiffener; *(pour fils de fer)* wire stretcher

raie¹ [rɛ] NF **1** *(motif)* stripe **2** *Opt* **raies du spectre, raies spectrales** spectrum lines **3** *(dans les cheveux)* parting, *Am* part; **porter la r. à droite** to part one's hair on the right; **porter la r. sur le** *ou* **de côté/au milieu** to part one's hair at the side/in the centre, to have a side/centre parting; **je ne porte pas de r.** I don't have a parting; **où portez-vous la r.?** where do you part your hair?; **avoir une coiffure sans r.** to wear one's hair without a parting **4** *Agr* furrow

raie² NF *(poisson)* skate, ray; **r. bouclée** thornback; *Culin* **r. au beurre noir** skate in brown butter sauce

raifort [rɛfɔr] NM horseradish

rail [raj] NM **1** rail; **rails mobiles** movable rails, switch rails; **r. conducteur** *(d'une voie ferrée électrifiée)* conductor rail, live rail; **quitter les rails, sortir des rails** *(d'un train)* to be derailed, to go off the rails; *Fig* to go off the rails; *Fig* **remettre l'économie sur les rails** to get the economy back on the rails *or* (back) on its feet again; *Fig* **il faut le remettre sur les rails** we'll have to put him back on the rails *or* straighten him out **2** *(chemins de fer)* railways, *Am* railroads; **travailleurs du r.** railwaymen, *Am* railroaders; **le r. est un moyen de locomotion très développé en**

France the railway is a much-used means of transport in France **3** *(glissière)* **r. (de sécurité)** crash barrier **4** *(itinéraire)* lane; **les bateaux se déplacent sur quatre rails au large d'Ouessant** boats sail along four sea lanes off Ushant; **le respect des rails aériens** the respect of air (traffic) lanes *or* air corridors

railler [raje] *Litt* VT *(personne)* to mock, to make fun of; **elle le raille sur sa timidité** she mocks *or* makes fun of his shyness
 VI to jest; **il me répondit en raillant** he answered me in jest
 VPR **se railler se r. de qn/qch** to mock sb/sth, to make fun of sb/sth

raillerie [rajri] NF *(plaisanterie)* jest; **sans r.** jesting apart; **recueillir des railleries** to be scoffed *or* mocked at; **il décida d'ignorer leurs railleries** he decided to ignore their scoffing; *Litt* **il n'entend pas r. sur les choses religieuses** he will not have jokes made about religion

railleur, -euse [rajœr, -øz] ADJ *(ton, voix, commentaire etc)* mocking, derisive
 N scoffer

railleusement [rajøzmɑ̃] ADV mockingly, derisively

rainer [rene] VT to groove

rainette [rɛnɛt] NF **1** *(grenouille)* tree frog **2** *(pomme)* pippin; **r. grise** russet

rainure [rɛnyr] NF **1** groove; **r. de clavette** keyway, key slot; **à rainure(s)** grooved **2** *Astron* rille

rainurer [rɛnyre] VT to groove

raiponce [rɛpɔ̃s] NF *Bot* rampion

raisin [rɛzɛ̃] NM **1 du r.** (some) grapes; **manger du r.** to eat grapes; **(grain de) r.** grape; **grappe de r.** bunch of grapes; **raisin(s) de table** dessert grapes; **raisins secs** raisins; **raisins de Corinthe** currants; **raisins de Smyrne** sultanas **2** *Bot* **r. de renard** herb Paris; *Bot* **r. d'ours** bearberry **3** *(mollusque)* **r. de mer** sea grapes, cuttlefish eggs **4 grand r.** *(papier)* ≃ royal

> Il faut noter que le terme anglais **raisin** est un faux ami. Il signifie **raisin sec**.

raisiné [rɛzine] NM **1** fruit preserved in grape jelly **2** *Arg (sang)* blood

raisinet [rɛzinɛ] NM *Suisse (groseille)* redcurrant

raison [rɛzɔ̃] NF **1** *(motif)* reason, ground (**de** for); **mais ce n'est pas une r. pour venir me déranger** but there's no reason to disturb *or* for disturbing me; **pour des raisons de convenance personnelle** for personal reasons; **pour quelle r.?** for what reason?; **sans r.** without (any) reason, for no reason; **elle s'est inquiétée sans r.** she worried needlessly; **en r. de qch** because of *or* on account of sth; **en r. d'un deuil récent** owing to a recent bereavement; **je me rends à vos raisons** I concede defeat; **rendre r. de qch** to give a reason for sth, to give an explanation of sth, to account for sth; **à plus forte r. puisqu'il suit un traitement** particularly since he's being given treatment; **à plus forte r. si elle est invitée** particularly if she's invited too; **r. de plus** all the more reason (**pour venir** to come); **r. de plus pour qu'elle fasse un effort** all the more reason for her to make an effort; **la r. pour laquelle il est venu** the reason (why) he came

 2 *(entendement)* reason; **il n'a pas toute sa r.** he is not quite sane, he's not quite in his right mind; **il n'a plus toute sa r.** he's losing his faculties; **recouvrer la r.** to regain one's sanity; **heureusement, il a recouvré la r. et le mariage n'a pas eu lieu** luckily he came to his senses and the wedding was called off; **ramener qn à la r.** to make sb see reason *or* sense; **revenir à la r.** to come to one's senses, to see reason; **se rendre à la r.** to see sense, to come to one's senses; **rends-toi à la r.!** see sense!, be sensible!; **vous perdez la r.!** have you taken leave of your senses?; **entendre r.** to listen to reason; **l'âge de r.** the age of reason; **mariage de r.** marriage of convenience **3 avoir r.** to be right; **avoir r. de faire qch** to be right to do or in doing sth; **elle a bien r. de ne pas lui demander son avis** she's quite right not to ask his/her opinion; **donner r. à qn** to admit that sb is right; **les événements lui donnèrent r.** events proved him/her right; **se faire une r.** to accept the inevitable, to resign oneself; **le travail n'était pas bon, mais il a bien fallu se faire une r.** the work wasn't well done but we just had to accept it as it was; **avec r.** rightly; **elle s'est mise en colère avec r.** she was right to get angry, she got angry and rightly so; **boire plus que de r.** to drink too much or more than is reasonable; **il avait bu, et plus que de r.** he had drunk too much, he had been drinking more than was reasonable; **il est inquiet plus que de r.** he is unreasonably concerned, his concern is slightly irrational; **gourmand plus que de r.** more than reasonably greedy; **comme de r.** as a matter of course, as one might expect **4** *(satisfaction)* satisfaction, reparation; **demander r. d'un affront** to demand satisfaction for an insult; **avoir r. de qn/qch** to get the better of sb/sth; **elle ne partira pas tant qu'elle n'aura pas eu r. de cet appareil** she won't leave until she's sorted that machine out **5** *Math* ratio; **r. géométrique/arithmétique** geometrical/arithmetical ratio; **r. directe/ inverse** direct/inverse ratio or proportion; **le poids est en r. directe du volume** the weight is directly proportional or in direct proportion to the volume; **travail payé à r. de cinquante euros l'heure** work paid at the rate of fifty euros an hour; **je suis payé à r. de cinquante euros de l'heure** I am paid fifty euros an hour; **à r. de deux par minute** at the rate of two per or a minute; **à r. de huit mots par ligne** on the basis of eight words to a line ▸▸ *Com* **r. commerciale** trade name; **la r. d'État** reasons of State, raison d'état; **le gouvernement a invoqué la r. d'État pour justifier cette mesure** the government said that it had done this for reasons of State; **r. d'être: r. d'être de qch** raison d'être of or object of or reason for sth; **c'est ma seule r. d'être** it's my whole life or raison d'être; **sa petite fille est sa r. d'être** his granddaughter is his entire reason for living or his only raison d'être, he lives for his granddaughter; **c'est la r. d'être de cet organisme** that's the whole point of or reason for the institution, that's what the institution is there for; **cela n'a plus aucune r. d'être** there's no longer any need for it; *Com* **r. sociale** (company) name

raisonnable [rɛzɔnabl] ADJ **1** *(sensé)* reasonable; **tu n'es pas r.** you're not being reasonable; **soyez r.!** be sensible or reasonable!, listen to reason!; **tu n'es pas r. de tellement fumer** you're silly to smoke so much, you're not being sensible smoking so much; **à son âge il devrait être plus r.** he is old enough to know better; **ce n'est pas r. de sortir avant la fin** it's silly to leave before the end; **tu ne peux pas sortir et travailler, ce n'est pas r.!** you can't go out (all the time) and work, it's stupid! **2** *(doué de raison)* rational; **l'homme est un animal r.** man is a rational or reasoning animal **3** *(condition, frais etc)* reasonable; **prix r.** reasonable or moderate or fair price; **à un prix r.** reasonably priced, at a reasonable price

raisonnablement [rɛzɔnabləmɑ̃] ADV **1** *(avec bon sens)* reasonably, rationally; **tout ce qu'on pouvait r. demander** all that one

could reasonably ask for **2** *(assez) (grand etc)* reasonably, fairly; *(manger etc)* moderately, in moderation; *Fam (travailler etc)* fairly well, reasonably well

raisonné [rɛzɔne] ADJ *(argumentation)* reasoned; *(grammaire)* rational, analytical; **voilà qui est bien r.!** well worked out!; *Com* **catalogue r.** descriptive catalogue

raisonnement [rɛzɔnmɑ̃] NM *(pensée etc)* reasoning; **homme de r. juste** man of sense; **je comprends ton r.** I understand your reasoning or (line of) argument; **on ne peut pas tenir un tel r. avec lui** you can't take that line with him; **pas de raisonnements!** don't argue!

raisonner [rɛzɔne] VI **1** *(penser)* to reason (**sur** about); **r. par induction/déduction** to reason by induction or inductively/by deduction or deductively **2** *(discuter)* to argue (**sur** about); **on ne peut r. avec ce genre de personnes** you can't reason with people like that; **ne raisonnez pas tant!** don't be so argumentative!
▪ VT *(personne)* to reason with; **je vais essayer de le r.** I'll try and reason with him or make him see sense; **il faut absolument la r.** she must be made to see sense
▪ VPR **se raisonner** to see reason; **raisonne-toi donc!** <u>try</u> to be reasonable!, <u>do</u> see reason!; **la jalousie ne se raisonne pas** jealousy cannot be reasoned with or knows no reason

raisonneur, -euse [rɛzɔnœr, -øz] ADJ **1** reasoning, rational **2** *(qui discutaille)* argumentative
▪ N **1** reasoner **2** *(discutailleur)* arguer

raja(h) [raʒa] NM raja(h)

rajeunir [raʒœnir] VT **1** *(personne)* to rejuvenate; **ce chapeau te/la rajeunit (de dix ans)** that hat makes you/her look (ten years) younger; **ça me rajeunit** it makes me feel younger or feel young again; **ça ne nous rajeunit pas!** it brings it home or makes you realize that we're not getting any younger!; **tu la rajeunis, elle a passé la trentaine** she's not as young as you think, she's over thirty; **vous me rajeunissez, j'ai cinq ans de plus!** I'm five years older than that!, add five years to that figure!; **elle me rajeunit de cinq ans** she's taking five years off my age **2** *(robe, veste etc)* to update; *(organisation, bureau)* to modernize; **r. une équipe** to bring new blood into a team; **une équipe rajeunie** a younger team; **le comité a besoin d'être rajeuni** the committee needs new blood
▪ VI to get younger, to grow young again; **je ne rajeunis pas** I'm not getting any younger; **il a rajeuni de dix ans** he's ten years younger
▪ VPR **se rajeunir** *(pour paraître plus jeune)* to make oneself look younger; *(se dire, prétendre plus jeune)* to make oneself out to be younger than one is; **elle se rajeunit de quelques années** she's taking a few years off her age

rajeunissant [raʒœnisɑ̃] ADJ *(traitement, crème)* rejuvenating

rajeunissement [raʒœnismɑ̃] NM rejuvenation

rajout [raʒu] NM addition; **on ne peut plus faire de r.** nothing else can be added, we can't add anything else

rajouter [raʒute] VT to add; **r. du sel** add (more) salt, put in more salt

rajustement [raʒystəmɑ̃] NM readjustment, adjustment

rajuster [raʒyste] VT *(vêtement, chapeau, cravate)* to adjust, to straighten; *(chignon)* to fix, to tidy; *(prix)* to adjust; **r. les salaires** to bring wages into line with the cost of living; **il faut r. les salaires des femmes** women's wages have to be brought into line with men's

▪ VPR **se rajuster** to tidy or smarten or straighten oneself up

râle [ral] NM *(oiseau)* **r. d'eau** water rail; **r. des genêts** corncrake

râle², **râlement** [ralmɑ̃] NM *(venant de la gorge)* rattle; **le r. (de la mort)** the death rattle; *Méd* **un r. au poumon** a rale or *Fam* rattle in the lung

ralenti [ralɑ̃ti] ADJ slow(er); **au trot r.** at a slow trot
▪ NM **1** *Cin* slow motion; *Cin* **scène au ou en r.** scene in slow motion; *Aut* **prendre un virage au r.** to take a corner slowly; **l'usine tourne au r.** the factory's not working at full capacity, the factory's just ticking over; **elle travaille au r.** she's slowed right down; **la ville tourne au r.** things are pretty quiet in the city; **la malade a l'impression de vivre au r.** the patient feels he's living in slow motion or hardly living at all **2** *(de moteur)* idling, slow running, idle; **r. accéléré** fast idle; **tourner au r.** to idle, to tick over

ralentir [ralɑ̃tir] VT *(circulation, progression)* to slow (down); *(production, progrès, économie)* to slow (down or up); **r. la marche** to slow down, to walk a bit more slowly; **r. le pas** to slow down; **r. l'allure** to slow down; **r. ses efforts** to ease up
▪ VI to slow down; *(d'un train, véhicule, convoi etc)* to slow (down), to reduce speed; *(de la progression)* to slow (down); *(de la production, des progrès, de l'économie)* to slow (down or up); **le train ralentit quand il entre en gare** the train slows down or reduces its speed when it pulls into a station; **ralentis, il y a du verglas!** slow down, there's black ice on the road!
▪ VPR **se ralentir** *(de mouvements, de la circulation etc)* to slow (down); *(de la production, des progrès, de l'économie)* to slow (down or up)

ralentissement [ralɑ̃tismɑ̃] NM *(de la circulation, d'un rythme, de l'économie etc)* slowdown, slowing down, slowing up; *(des exportations, de la production, des ventes)* slowdown (**de** in); **des ralentissements** *(de la circulation)* hold-ups, delays; **périodes de r. dans les affaires** slow or slack periods in business; **il comptait sur un r. de la progression de l'armée allemande** he was counting on the German army's advance slowing down

ralentisseur [ralɑ̃tisœr] NM *Aut* speed bump, ramp, *Br Fam* sleeping policeman; *Tech, Élec* retarder; *Nucl* moderator

râler [rale] VI **1** *Fam (se plaindre)* to moan, to grouse, to grumble; **elle râle contre notre retard** she's moaning about us being late; **ça me fait r.!** it gets up my nose!; **ça me fait r. de perdre du temps comme ça!** wasting time like that really bugs me!; **laisse-le r.** let him moan; **mais qu'est-ce qu'elle a encore à r.?** what is she moaning about now? **2** *(de douleur)* to moan, to groan; *(d'un mourant)* to give a or the death rattle **3** *(d'un tigre)* to growl

râleur, -euse [ralœr, -øz] *Fam* ADJ grumbling, moaning, grousing; **elle est très râleuse** she's a real moaner or grumbler
▪ N moaner, grumbler

ralliement [ralimɑ̃] NM **1** *(des troupes)* rallying; **mot de r.** *Mil* password; *Fig* rallying cry; **point de r.** rallying point, meeting place; **ce bar est un bon point de r.** the bar is a good meeting place; **Paris est le point de r. de tous les comédiens français** Paris is a magnet for all French actors; **signe de r.** rallying sign; **en signe de r., ils portent tous le même tee-shirt** they all wear the same tee-shirt as a kind of badge or so they can recognize each other **2** *(d'un avion)* homing **3** *(d'adhérents)* winning over; **son r. à notre**

parti fut immédiat he/she immediately came over or was won over to our party

rallier [ralje] (*impf, pr sub n.* **ralliions**) VT **1** (*troupes, navires etc*) to rally; *Fig* **r. l'opinion autour d'une idée commune** to mobilize or rally public opinion around a common idea **2** *Mil etc (d'un soldat etc) (unité)* to rejoin; (*base*) to return to, to make one's way back to; *Naut* **r. le bord** to rejoin one's ship **3 r. qn** (*à un parti, mouvement*) to win sb over; (*à une opinion*) to win sb over, to bring sb round; *Fig* **les groupuscules ont rallié le groupe majoritaire** the small groups have united with or joined the majority group; *Fig* **r. tous les suffrages** to win unanimous approval or support

▸ VPR **se rallier 1** (*des troupes etc*) to rally; *Hum* **ralliez-vous à mon panache blanc!** follow me! **2** (*des opposants, dissidents*) to rally; **se r. à** (*une opinion, un point de vue*) to come round to; (*un parti*) to join; (*une cause*) to rally to

rallonge [ralɔ̃ʒ] NF **1** (*d'une table*) (extension) leaf; *Can* (*d'un bureau*) runoff; *Tech* extension bar or piece; **table à rallonge(s)** extending table **2** (*électrique*) extension cord or lead **3** *Fam* additional or extra time/payment/*etc*; **r. budgétaire** addition to the budget; **obtenir une r. de 30 000 euros** to get an extra 30,000 euros; **une r. de trois jours** an additional or an extra or another three days

rallongement [ralɔ̃ʒmɑ̃] NM lengthening, extension

rallonger [ralɔ̃ʒe] (**je rallongeai(s); n. rallongeons**) VT (*prolonger*) to make longer; (*vacances, journée de travail, route*) to extend (**de** by); (*vêtement*) to let down, to lengthen; **r. qch de dix centimètres/de deux heures** to make sth ten centimetres/two hours longer; *Fam* **ça me rallongerait de 20 minutes** it would add 20 minutes onto my journey; **ils ont rallongé le câble d'un mètre** they lengthened the cable by a metre, they made the cable a metre longer; **tu devrais r. ce paragraphe** you should make this paragraph longer; **j'ai fait r. cette jupe de dix centimètres** I had this skirt let down or taken down ten centimetres

▸ VI (*des jours*) to get longer, to draw out; (*des nuits*) to get longer, to draw in

rallumer [ralyme] VT (*appareil électrique*) to turn on or switch on again; (*avec une allumette*) to light again; *Fig* (*querelle, colère, espoir etc*) to rekindle, to revive; **r. l'électricité** *ou* **la lumière** *ou* **les lumières** to turn on or switch on the light(s) again

▸ VI **rallume, s'il te plaît** switch or turn the light/television/*etc* on again, please

▸ VPR **se rallumer** (*de la lumière, d'un appareil électrique*) to come back or go back on; (*d'un feu*) to flare up or blaze up again; *Fig* (*d'une guerre, dispute*) to flare up again; (*de l'espoir etc*) to rekindle, to revive; **il tira sur la pipe, qui se ralluma** he puffed on the pipe, which got going again

rally [rali] NM *Bourse* rally

rallye [rali] NM **1** *Sport* (car) rally **2** = series of dances held for young, upper-class people, ≃ the débutantes' season

RAM [ram] NF *Ordinat* RAM; **R. sur carte** onboard RAM

Ramadan [ramadɑ̃] NM *Rel* Ramadan; **respecter le R., faire le R.** to observe Ramadan

ramage [ramaʒ] NM **1** *Vieilli* (*feuillage*) foliage; (*motif*) floral design **2** (*des oiseaux*) song, twittering, chirping

ramas [rama] NM *Vieilli* = **ramassis**

ramassage [ramasaʒ] NM **1** (*des ordures, de vêtements, de vieux journaux*) collection; (*de fruits, noix etc*) gathering, picking; **r. scolaire** school bus service; **car de r. scolaire** school

bus; **il n'existe pas de service de r. scolaire** there isn't a school bus **2** *Bourse* (*d'actions*) buying up

ramassé [ramase] ADJ **1** (*trapu*) thickset, stocky **2** (*recroquevillé*) (*person, village etc*) huddled; **village r. autour de son église** village huddled or clustering round its church **3** (*machine, style*) compact

ramasse-miettes [ramasmjɛt] NM INV table tidy (*a small brush and pan for clearing the crumbs off the table*)

ramasse-monnaie [ramasmɔnɛ] NM INV change tray

ramasse-poussière [ramaspusjɛr] NM INV **1** *Belg* dustpan **2** dust-trap; **ces bibelots sont de véritables r.** these ornaments just gather or collect the dust

RAMASSER [ramase]

> VT to pick up **1, 2** ▪ to collect **1, 2** ▪ to gather **1, 2** ▪ to dig up **1** ▪ to get **3** ▪ to catch **3**
> VPR to gather oneself **1** ▪ to crouch **1** ▪ to fail **2**

VT **1** (*prendre par terre*) (*objet tombé*) to pick up; (*fruits, noix, coquillages*) to gather, to collect, to pick up; (*champignons*) to pick, to gather, to collect; (*pommes de terre*) to dig up, to lift; **r. qch avec une pelle et une balayette** to sweep sth up (with a brush and dustpan); **r. qch avec un chiffon** to wipe sth up; **r. des feuilles avec un râteau** to rake up leaves; **r. ses jupes** (*pour ne pas se salir*) to gather one's skirts up; *Cartes* **r. la mise** to win the kitty; **r. qn** to help sb up or to his/her feet, to pick sb up; *Fam* (*de la police*) to pick sb up; *Fig* **r. qn dans le ruisseau** to pick sb up out of the gutter; *Fig* **être à r. à la petite cuillère** to be worn to a frazzle, to be fit to drop; *Fam* **se faire r.** (*par la police*) to be run in or picked up

2 (*regrouper*) (*des assiettes, copies, feuilles etc*) to collect, to gather (up); (*de l'argent*) to collect; (*informations*) to gather, to collect; (*des enfants, ouvriers, courrier*) to pick up, to collect; (*actions*) to buy up; **r. les cartes** to pick up the cards; **r. ses affaires** to collect one's belongings; **r. ses cheveux dans une natte/sur le dessus de la tête** to put one's hair (up) in a pigtail/to pile one's hair on top of one's head; **r. (toutes) ses forces** to gather or muster all one's strength; **les quelques informations/connaissances qu'il a pu r.** the scraps of information/knowledge he was able to pick up; **le tigre ramasse son corps avant de bondir** the tiger crouches before springing; *Fam* **il a dû r. pas mal d'argent avec cette affaire** he must have made quite a pile or a fair old whack out of the business

3 *Fig Fam* (*recevoir*) (*engueulade, gifle, râclée, procès-verbal*) to get; (*rhume*) to catch; **r. une bûche** *ou* **une pelle** to fall flat on one's face, to come a cropper

▸ VPR **se ramasser 1** (*pour faire un effort*) to gather oneself; (*d'un tigre*) (*avant de bondir*) to crouch

2 (*après une chute*) to pick oneself up; *Fig Fam* (*échouer, tomber*) to fail, to fall flat on one's face, to come a cropper

ramassette [ramasɛt] NF *Belg* dustpan

ramasseur, -euse [ramasœr, -øz] N (*de champignons etc*) picker, collector, gatherer; *Tennis* **r./ramasseuse de balles** ball boy/girl; **r. de lait** milk collector (*who collects milk from farms*)

ramassis [ramasi] NM *Péj* (*de choses*) heap, pile, jumble; (*de gens*) bunch; (*d'idées*) collection, hotchpotch

ramassoire [ramaswar] NF *Suisse* (*pelle à poussière*) dustpan

rambarde [rɑ̃bard] NF *Naut etc* (guard)rail

ramdam [ramdam] NM *Fam* row, racket; **faire du** *ou* **un sacré r.** to make a heck of a din or racket

rame¹ [ram] NF (*pour faire pousser des pois etc*) stick, cane; **haricots à rames** stick beans

rame² NF (*aviron*) oar; **aller à la r.** to row; **nous avons rejoint le port à la r.** we rowed into port; **faire force de rames** to row hard; *Fam* **elle n'en fiche pas une r.** she does damn all, she never does a stroke (of work)

rame³ NF **1** (*de papier*) ream **2** *Rail* train; *Naut* (*de péniches*) string, tow; *Rail* **la r. directe pour Tours** the through coach(es) for Tours; **r. (de métro)** (underground or Am subway) train

rameau, -eaux [ramo] NM **1** (*d'arbre*) (small) branch or bough; **un r. d'olivier** an olive branch; *Rel* **le dimanche des Rameaux, les Rameaux** Palm Sunday **2** (*de familles, de langues*) branch **3** *Anat* ramification

ramée [rame] NF **1** *Litt, Vieilli* (*d'un arbre*) green or leafy boughs **2** (*branches coupées*) cut branches **3** *Fam* **il n'en fiche pas une r.** he does damn all, he never does a stroke (of work)

ramener [ramne] (*conj like* **mener**) VT **1** (*reconduire*) (*personne*), *Fam* (*objet*) (*vers le point de référence choisi*) to bring back; (*en s'éloignant du point de référence choisi*) to take back; (*l'ordre, la paix*) to restore; **ramenez-nous-le vite!** bring him back quickly!; **on peut maintenant r. les enfants à l'école** we can take the children back to school now; **il a fallu la r. d'urgence à l'hôpital** we had to rush her back to hospital; **c'est lui qui est chargé de r. le journal** it's his job to fetch or get the newspaper; **r. qn chez lui en voiture** to drive sb home; **je peux vous r.?** can I give you a lift or Am ride back?; **la faim/la fatigue/le froid le ramènera** he'll come back when he's hungry/tired/cold; **la curiosité le ramènera** curiosity will bring him back; **la faim/la fatigue/le froid le ramena** he came back because he was hungry/tired/cold; **r. qn à la vie** to bring sb back to life, to resuscitate sb; **r. qn à la raison** to make sb see reason or sense; **r. la conversation sur un sujet** to lead or bring the conversation back to a subject; *Fam* **r. le compteur à zéro** to reset the counter to zero, to zero the counter; **ça me ramène des années en arrière!** that really takes me back!; **ça me ramène au temps de mon enfance/au temps où ...** that takes me back to my childhood/to when ...; *Fam* **r. sa fraise** *ou* *très Fam* **sa gueule, la r.** (*s'immiscer*) to stick or shove one's oar in; **ramène ta fraise, ramène-la** (*viens ici*) get yourself over here a minute

2 (*réduire*) (*nombre de chômeurs, prix, inflation etc*) to reduce (**à** to); **r. l'inflation à un taux inférieur** to bring down inflation

3 (*remettre*) (*couverture*) to pull up (**sur** over); (*baisser*) (*chapeau, jupe*) to pull down (**sur** over); **r. ses cheveux sur le côté** to sweep one's hair to the side; *Fig* **elle ramène tout à elle/à ses propres problèmes** she always drags the conversation round to herself/her own problems

▸ VPR **se ramener 1** voici à quoi se ramène son raisonnement this is what his/her argument boils down to **2** *Fam* (*arriver*) to roll up; **c'est à cette heure-ci que tu te ramènes?** what kind of time do you call this!

ramequin [ramkɛ̃] NM *Culin* ramekin

ramer¹ [rame] VT (*pois etc*) to stake

ramer² VI **1** (*pagayer*) to row, *Litt* to pull (at the oar/oars); **r. en couple** to scull; **r. à rebours** to back water **2** *Fig Fam* to sweat blood; **qu'est-ce qu'on a ramé!** we sweated blood!, we worked like dogs or like galley slaves!; **j'ai ramé pendant des années avant de trouver ce travail** I had a hard time of it for years before I found this job; **j'ai ramé pendant des années pour restaurer cette maison** it took years of hard graft to restore this house

rameur, -euse [ramœr, -øz] N (à l'aviron) rower, oarsman, f oarswoman; **r. de couple** sculler

rameux, -euse [ramø, -øz] ADJ branching, Spéc ramose

rami [rami] NM Cartes rummy

ramie [rami] NF Bot ramie

ramier [ramje] ADJ INV, NM **(pigeon) r.** ring dove, wood pigeon

ramification [ramifikasjɔ̃] NF Bot ramification, branching (out); Fig (d'une secte, famille, science etc) branch; Fig **ramifications** (d'une affaire, d'un scandale) ramifications

ramifier (se) [səramifje] VPR to branch out (en into); Fig **cette organisation se ramifie dans plusieurs pays** this organization has branches in several countries

ramille [ramij] NF twig

ramolli, -ie [ramɔli] ADJ (beurre) soft; Fam (personne) (physiquement) limp, washed out; (mentalement) soft in the head; **je suis ou je me sens tout r.** I feel like a wet rag or as if I've had all of the stuffing knocked out of me

N Fam wimp; **c'est un r. du cerveau** he's going soft in the head

ramollir [ramɔlir] VT (cire, beurre) to soften; Fig (volonté) to sap; **ces vacances m'ont ramolli** this holiday has left me without any energy

VPR **se ramollir** (du beurre, goudron) to go soft, to soften; Fig (physiquement) to go downhill; (moralement) to have no energy, Fam to have no get up and go; Fam **son cerveau se ramollit** he's going soft in the head

ramollissement [ramɔlismã] NM softening

ramollo [ramɔlo] Fam ADJ (inv in f) (physiquement) limp, washed out; **je me sens tout r.** I feel like a wet rag or as if I've had all of the stuffing knocked out of me; **son grand-père est un peu r.** his grandfather's a bit soft in the head

N **c'est un r.** he's a wimp

ramon [ramɔ̃] NM Belg (balai) broom

ramonage [ramɔnaʒ] NM (chimney) sweeping or cleaning; (en alpinisme) climbing a chimney, chimneying

ramoner [ramɔne] VT (cheminée) to sweep, to clean

VI to sweep or clean the chimney; (en alpinisme) to (climb a) chimney

ramoneur [ramɔnœr] NM (chimney) sweep

rampage [rãpaʒ] NM Aut (d'une boîte automatique) creep

rampant, -e [rãpã] ADJ **1** (plante) creeping; (animal) crawling; Aviat **personnel r.** ground staff **2** Péj (personne, caractère) crawling, grovelling **3** (inflation) rampant; Hér **lion r.** lion rampant

rampe [rãp] NF **1** (d'escalier) ban(n)isters, handrail; **faire des glissades sur la r.** to slide down the banisters; Fam **tenir bon la r.** to be still going strong; Arg **lâcher la r.** to kick the bucket, to snuff it **2** (pente) slope, incline, rise; (d'une route) gradient; Aut **vitesse en r.** speed when (hill) climbing or going uphill; Aut **ralentir dans la r.** to slow down on the incline **3** (passerelle etc) ramp, gangway **4** (de projecteurs etc) bank **5** Théâtre footlights; Fig **être sous les feux de la r.** to be in the limelight; **pièce/acteur qui ne passe pas la r.** play that/actor who doesn't come across

▸▸ **r. d'accès** access ramp; **r. de graissage** lubricating rack, oil distributor; **r. de lance-**

ment (de projectile) launching ramp; Aviat **r. (lumineuse) d'atterrissage** illuminated landing strip; **r. mobile** portable ramp, movable gangway

rampement [rãpmã] NM creeping, crawling

ramper [rãpe] VI (d'un animal, d'une personne) to crawl; (d'une plante) to creep; **entrer/sortir en rampant** to crawl in/out; Péj **r. devant les chefs** to crawl or grovel to the bosses; **je n'aime pas les gens qui rampent!** I don't like crawlers!

rampon [rãpɔ̃] NM Suisse (mâche) lamb's lettuce

ramponneau, -eaux [rãpɔno] NM Fam clout, thump

ramure [ramyr] NF **1** (d'arbre) branches, boughs **2** (d'un cerf) antlers

rancard [rãkar] NM **1** Fam (rendez-vous) (avec son petit ami) date; (chez le médecin, le dentiste etc) appointment; **j'ai r. avec lui à deux heures** (ami) I'm meeting him at two o'clock; (petit ami) I've got a date with him at two o'clock; (médecin) I've got an appointment with him at or for two o'clock; **on s'est filé un r. pour la semaine prochaine** we arranged to meet next week, we made a date for next week **2** Arg (renseignement) tip

rancarder [rãkarde] VT Arg **r. qn sur qch** to put sb on to sth; **on a dû les r.** they must have been tipped off

rancart [rãkar] NM Fam **mettre au r.** (objet) to discard; (projet) to shelve; (personne) to put on the sidelines, to sideline; **on a finalement décidé la mise au r. du projet** we finally decided to shelve the project

rance [rãs] ADJ rancid, rank

NM **sentir le r.** (du beurre) to smell rancid; (d'un placard) to smell fusty; **un goût de r.** a rancid taste; **avoir un goût de r.** to taste rancid

ranch [rãtʃ] NM ranch; **exploiter un r.** to ranch

rancidité [rãsidite] NF rancidness

rancir [rãsir] VI to become or grow rancid

rancœur [rãkœr] NF resentment, bitterness, rancour; **j'ai de la r. contre lui** I feel resentment towards him, I resent him; **plein de r.** (personne, ton) resentful, bitter

rançon [rãsɔ̃] NF ransom; Litt **mettre qn à r.** to hold sb to ransom; Fig **la r. du progrès/de la gloire** the price of progress/fame; **c'est la r. du progrès!** that's the price you pay for progress!

rançonner [rãsɔne] VT **r. qn** to hold sb to ransom; Fig Fam to fleece sb; **r. un voyageur** to hold up (and rob) a traveller

rancune [rãkyn] NF spite; **garder r. à qn, avoir de la r. contre qn** to have a grudge against sb, to bear sb a grudge; **plein de r.** spiteful; **par r.** out of spite; **sans r.!** no hard feelings!; **il y a de vieilles rancunes entre eux** there is bad blood between them

rancunier, -ière [rãkynje, -jɛr] ADJ vindictive, spiteful

N vindictive or spiteful person

randomisation [rãdɔmizasjɔ̃] NF randomization

randomiser [rãdɔmize] VT to randomize

randonnée [rãdɔne] NF ramble, hike; (sport) rambling, trekking; (en voiture) outing, trip; (à vélo) run, ride; (en montagne) hill-walking, climbing; (à ski de fond) cross-country skiing; (avec peau de phoque) ski-mountaineering; **r. à pied** ou **pédestre** hike; **r. équestre** pony trek; **chemin de grande r.** long-distance footpath; **faire de la r.** (à pied) to go hiking; (en petite montagne) to go hill-walking; (en moyenne montagne) to go climbing; (en haute montagne) to go moun-

taineering; **r. en VTT** mountain biking; **une r. en montagne** a hill-walk, a climb; **r. sac au dos** backpacking (tour); **r. à dos de poney** pony-trekking

randonneur, -euse [rãdɔnœr, -øz] N (à pied) rambler, hiker, walker; (en petite montagne) hill-walker; (en moyenne montagne) climber; (en haute montagne) mountaineer; (à ski) cross-country skier; (avec peau de phoque) ski-mountaineer

rang [rã] NM **1** (d'arbres, de sièges etc) row, line; (d'oignons, de tricot) row; (d'avirons) bank; Mil rank; **fauteuil au premier r.** front-row seat; Scol **être (assis) au premier/dernier r.** to sit in the front/back row, to sit at the front/back of the class; Fig **je le sais, j'étais au premier r. (pour le voir)** I should know, I have first-hand experience; **se mettre en r./rangs** to line up; Hum **se mettre en r. d'oignons** to stand (close together) in a line; **(un collier avec) trois rangs de perles** a triple strand of beads; **machine à quatre rangs de touches** four-bank typewriter; **sur deux rangs** in two ranks, two deep; **par rangs de trois** three abreast, three in a row; Mil **homme du r.** private; Mil **formez les rangs!** fall in!; Mil, Fig **serrer les rangs** to close ranks; Mil **en rangs serrés** in close order; Fig **nous sommes arrivés en rangs serrés dans le bureau du directeur** we trooped into the manager's office; Fig **s'il le faut, nous irons en rangs serrés lui en parler** we'll talk to him about it all together or as a group or en masse if necessary; Mil, Fig **rompre les rangs** to break ranks; Mil **sortir des rangs** to fall out (of line), to break rank; **officier sorti du r.** officer promoted from the ranks; Fig **un ancien ouvrier sorti du r.** a former worker who came up or rose through the ranks

2 (classement) rank, place; (social) station; Mil, Fin (d'une créance) rank; **r. élevé** high rank; **dame de haut r.** lady of rank; **un militaire de haut r.** a high-ranking or senior officer; **r. social** social status; **il faut tenir notre r.** we have to keep up our position (in life); **avoir r. de colonel** to hold the rank of colonel; **de premier/second r.** first-/second-class, first-/second-rate; **il est au r. des meilleurs** he ranks amongst the best; **il est au premier r. de sa profession** he is at the top of (the tree in) his profession; **par r. de** (taille, ancienneté, âge) by, according to; **occuper un r. supérieur à qn** to rank above or outrank sb; **prendre** ou **avoir r. avant/après qn** to come before/after sb (in rank); **il a pris r. parmi les grands poètes** he has taken his place or is counted among the great poets; **prendre r. dans un parti** to join a party; **sortir d'une École avec un bon r.** = to graduate near the top of one's class; **venir au** ou **en troisième r.** to rank third; **arriver au premier r.** to be in the forefront; **le chômage arrive au premier r. des préoccupations des Français** unemployment is one of the main concerns of the French; Fig **se mettre sur les rangs** to enter the lists, to join the fray, to put one's name forward; **il y avait déjà quelqu'un sur les rangs** there was already someone in the field; Fig **grossir les rangs des révoltés/des chômeurs** to swell the ranks of the rebels/the unemployed

3 Can concession road; (quartier) concession, rural district

rangé [rãʒe] ADJ **1** (en ordre) tidy, orderly; (vie) well-ordered, orderly; (personne) steady; **une jeune fille rangée** a well-behaved girl; **c'était un homme très r.** he was a very quiet kind of man; **une maison très bien rangée** a very tidy or well-kept house; **ce n'est pas bien r. chez elle** her place isn't very tidy; **ma petite vie bien rangée** my quiet or unexciting little life; Fig Fam **être r. des voitures** to be a reformed character, to have settled or steadied down **2 bataille rangée** pitched battle

rangée [rɑ̃ʒe] NF *(de personnes, boutons, sièges, d'arbres)* row, line; *(de gradins)* tier; **r. de cylindres** cylinder bank

rangement [rɑ̃ʒmɑ̃] NM **1** *(action)* tidying, putting in order; *Ordinat* storage; **avoir la manie du r.** to have a mania for tidiness, to be fanatically tidy; **volume de r.** storage space; **faire du r. (dans son bureau)** to do some tidying up (in one's office); **faire du r. dans ses affaires** to tidy up one's things **2** *(placard)* **(meuble de) r.** storage unit; **cette cuisine manque de rangements** this kitchen lacks storage space; **r. de cuisine** kitchen cabinet **3** *(disposition)* arrangement

ranger [rɑ̃ʒe] (je **rangeai(s)**; n. **rangeons**) VT **1** *(pièce, maison)* to tidy (up), to put away; **tout est si bien rangé dans cette maison** this house is so beautifully tidy

2 *(affaires, vêtements)* to put *or* tidy away; *(par ordre alphabétique, de taille etc)* to arrange; *Com (marchandises)* to stow; *(voiture)* to park; **où as-tu rangé les fourchettes/ton livre?** where have you put the forks/your book?; **tu devrais r. tes classeurs (à leur place)** you should put your files away *or* put your files back where they belong; **tout est si bien rangé** everything is arranged so neatly *or* tidily; *Ordinat* **r. en mémoire** to store

3 r. qn parmi les grands écrivains to rank *or* count sb amongst the great writers; **on le range parmi les meilleurs médecins/psychanalystes** he is said to be one of the best doctors/psychoanalysts

4 *Mil (troupes)* to draw up, to marshal
VPR **se ranger 1** *(s'écarter)* **se r. (de côté)** *(d'un piéton)* to get out of the way, to stand aside; *(d'une voiture)* to pull over; **on se rangea pour nous laisser passer** they stood aside for us, they made way for us; **la voiture s'est rangée contre le mur** the car pulled in alongside the wall; *Naut* **se r. à quai** to berth **2** *Fig* **se r. du côté de qn** to side with sb, to take sb's side; **se r. à l'opinion de qn** to come round to sb's point of view

3 *Fam (s'assagir)* to settle down; **se r. des voitures** to settle down; *(criminel)* to go straight

rani [rani] NF ranee

ranimation [ranimasjɔ̃] NF resuscitation, reanimation

ranimer [ranime] VT *(personne qui s'évanouit)* to bring round; *Méd (après un arrêt cardiaque)* to resuscitate; *Fig (ville, industrie)* to revive, to put new life into; *(couleurs)* to brighten, to revive; *(feu)* to rekindle; *(colère, désir)* to reawaken, to rekindle; *(espoir)* to revive, to reawaken, to rekindle; *(souvenir, enthousiasme, débat)* to rekindle, to revive; *(conversation)* to liven up; **r. le courage de qn** to put new heart into sb; **un simple mouvement du bras suffit à r. la douleur** just moving the arm is enough to make the pain flare up
VPR **se ranimer** *(d'un feu)* to flicker into life; *(d'une conversation)* to pick up again, to come to life again; **son visage se ranima** his/her face lit up

rap [rap] NM *Mus* rap

rapace [rapas] ADJ predatory; *Fig (personne)* grasping, *Fml* rapacious; **oiseau r.** bird of prey
NM bird of prey

rapacité [rapasite] NF rapacity; *Fig* rapaciousness, rapacity; **avec r.** greedily, *Fml* rapaciously

râpage [rɑpaʒ] NM *(du métal, du bois)* rasping

rapatrié, -ée [rapatrije] N person who has been repatriated, repatriate; **les rapatriés**

d'Algérie the people repatriated from Algeria

rapatriement [rapatrimɑ̃] NM repatriation; **r. sanitaire** repatriation for health reasons

rapatrier [rapatrije] VT *(personne), Fig (capitaux)* to repatriate; **se faire r.** to get *or* be repatriated

râpe [rɑp] NF **1** *(de cuisine)* grater; **r. à muscade/à fromage** nutmeg/cheese grater **2** *Tech* rasp **3** *Suisse Fam (avare)* miser

râpé [rɑpe] ADJ **1** *(fromage, carotte etc)* grated **2** *(usé) (vêtement)* worn out, threadbare **3** *Fam (raté)* **c'est r. pour ce week-end** this weekend's had it; **pour le pique-nique, c'est r.** the picnic's out, the picnic's had it
NM **1** *(vin)* rape wine **2** *(fromage)* grated cheese

râper [rɑpe] VT *(carotte, noix de muscade etc)* to grate; *(bois, métal)* to rasp; **ce vin râpe la gorge** this wine is rough *or* harsh on the throat

rapetassage [raptasaʒ] NM *Fam* patching up

rapetasser [raptase] VT *Fam (vêtement)* to patch up

rapetissement [raptismɑ̃] NM *(d'un objet) (dû à la distance)* reduction (in size); *(d'un vieillard)* shrinking

rapetisser [raptise] VT *(chose)* to make smaller, to reduce in size; *(vêtement)* to shrink; *Fig (succès)* to belittle; **la distance rapetisse les objets** distance makes things look smaller; **r. les mérites de qn** to belittle sb
VI *(d'un vêtement, d'une personne)* to shrink; **au pied de cet immeuble, on a l'impression de r.** you feel very small in front of this building, you feel dwarfed by this building; **j'aurais voulu r. pour qu'il ne me voie pas** I wanted to make myself invisible so that he didn't see me
VPR **se rapetisser** to make oneself shorter; **elle portait des talons plats pour essayer de se r.** she wore flat shoes in an attempt to make herself look shorter

râpeux, -euse [rɑpø, -øz] ADJ *(langue)* raspy; *(vin)* harsh; *(voix)* grating, rasping

raphia [rafja] NM *(fibre)* raffia; *(arbre)* raffia (palm)

rapiat, -ate [rapja, -at] *Fam* ADJ *(avare)* stingy, miserly, tight-fisted
N miser, skinflint, *Am* tightwad

rapide [rapid] ADJ **1** *(coureur, itinéraire, voiture etc)* fast; *(pouls, progrès, changement, récit etc)* rapid, fast; *(décision)* rapid, speedy; *(courant)* rapid, swift, fast; **être r. à la course** to be a fast *or* quick runner, to run fast; **il est r. dans son travail** he's a fast *or* quick worker; **il a l'esprit très r.** *(il comprend vite)* he's quick to grasp things, he has a quick mind; **la voiture la plus r. de sa catégorie** the fastest car in its category; **c'est plus r. si tu passes par là** it's faster *or* quicker if you go that way; **faire une lecture trop r. de qch** to read sth too quickly *or* fast; **une décision trop r.** a hasty decision; **r. comme une flèche, r. comme l'éclair** as swift as an arrow; *(réponse, coureur)* quick as lightning; **il est r. en affaires** he doesn't waste any time, he's a fast worker; **fusil à tir r.** quick-firing *or* rapid-fire rifle **2** *(abrupt) (pente)* steep
NM **1** *(de rivière)* rapid; **descendre les rapides** to shoot the rapids **2** *(train)* express (train)
N *(personne)* **c'est une r.** *(compréhension)* she's quick on the uptake; *(travail)* she's a fast worker

rapidement [rapidmɑ̃] ADV quickly, fast, rapidly; **le temps passe r.** time flies; **trop r.** too fast, too quick(ly); **je l'ai lu r.** I read through it quickly, I had a quick read through it; **parcourir r. le journal** to skim the newspaper

rapidité [rapidite] NF **1** *(d'actions)* speed, swiftness, rapidity; *(d'une décision)* speediness; *(d'une réponse)* swiftness; **célèbre pour sa r. à la course** famous for being a fast runner; **grâce à sa r. d'esprit** because of the speed with which he/she grasps things; **faire preuve d'une grande r.** *(dans son travail, dans un jeu)* to be very quick *or* fast; **le poison agit avec une r. fulgurante** the poison is incredibly fast-acting; *Ordinat* **r. d'impression** print speed; **r. de traitement** processing speed **2** *(d'une pente)* steepness

rapido [rapido], **rapidos** [rapidos] ADV *Fam* quickly; **boire un coup r.** to have a quick drink

rapiéçage [rapjesaʒ], **rapiècement** [rapjesmɑ̃] NM *(d'un vêtement)* patching (up), mending

rapiécer [rapjese] VT (je **rapièce**, n. **rapiéçons**; je **rapiécerai**) *(vêtement)* to patch, to put a patch on

rapière [rapjer] NF rapier

rapin [rapɛ̃] NM *Fam Péj (peintre)* dauber

rapine [rapin] NF *Litt* rapine, pillage; *(butin)* spoils; **habitudes de r.** predatory habits

raplapla [raplapla] ADJ INV *Fam (personne)* washed out; *(pneu, coussin)* flat as a pancake; **je me sens tout r. aujourd'hui** I don't have any go in me at all today

rappareiller [raparεje], **rapparier** [raparje] VT *(impf, pr sub n.* **rappariions**) *Rare* to match, to find a match for; *(chaussettes)* to pair

rappel [rapεl] NM **1** *(d'un incident etc)* calling to mind, recalling; *(pour se souvenir)* reminder; **(lettre de) r.** (letter of) reminder; *Fin* **r. de compte** reminder of account outstanding; **r. de traitement/de solde/de salaire** back pay; *Radio, TV* **voici le r. des titres (de l'actualité)** here's a reminder of the headlines; **et les coussins sont assortis aux rideaux, quel joli r. de couleurs** the colour of the cushions is nicely picked up *or* repeated in the curtains

2 *(d'un général, ambassadeur, de réservistes)* recall; **lettres de r.** *(d'un ambassadeur)* letters of recall; *Mil* **battre le r.** to call *or* beat to arms; *Fig* to rally the troops, to send out a call to arms

3 *Com (d'une somme déjà avancée)* calling in; *(de marchandises défectueuses)* recall

4 *Méd* **(injection de) r.** booster (injection); **faire un r.** to have a booster

5 r. à l'ordre *(à un membre d'une assemblée)* call to order; *(à un employé)* warning; **un simple r. au bon sens suffira à le faire changer d'avis** an appeal to his common sense will make him change his mind

6 *Théâtre* curtain call; *(à un concert)* encore; **il y a eu plusieurs rappels** *Théâtre* he/she/*etc* took several curtain calls *or* was called back several times; *Mus* there were several encores

7 *Sport* abseil; **faire une descente** *ou* **descendre en r., faire du r.** to abseil down

8 *Ordinat (de texte)* restore; *Tech* **vis de r.** adjusting screw; **fil de r.** bracing *or* straining wire; **ressort de r.** return spring, drawback spring; **tige de r.** stay rod; *Aut* **r. latéral de clignotant** side repeat indicator

---

RAPPELER [rap(ə)le] *(conj like* **appeler**)

VT to call again **1** ▪ to ring again **1** ▪ to ring back **1** ▪ to recall **2, 3, 5** ▪ to remind sb of sth *(rappeler qch à qn)* **3**		
VPR to remember **1** ▪ to recollect **1**		

VT **1** *(oralement) (personne)* to call back; *Tél (pour rendre un coup de téléphone)* to call *or* phone *or Br* ring back; *(quelqu'un que l'on a des difficultés à joindre)* to call *or* phone *or Br* ring again; *Tél* **je l'ai rappelé plusieurs fois** mais je n'ai jamais réussi à lui parler I called or phoned or Br rang (him) several times but I didn't get to speak to him; *Tél* **je l'ai rappelé une cinquième fois** I called or phoned or Br rang him for the fifth time; **je (le) rappelle dans une minute** I'll call (him) back/again in a minute

2 *(faire revenir)* to recall, to call or summon back; *(ambassadeur)*, *Ordinat* to recall; *Mil* **r. qn (sous les drapeaux)** to call sb up; **être rappelé trois fois** *(d'un comédien)* to take three curtain calls; *(d'un musicien, chanteur)* to give three encores; **r. son chien** to call off one's dog; **r. qn à l'ordre** *(membre d'une association)* to call sb to order; *(élève)* to warn sb; **tu vas te faire r. à l'ordre** you're going to get a warning, you're going to be pulled up; **r. qn à la vie** *ou* **à lui** *(personne évanouie)* to bring sb round; *(blessé, noyé)* to resuscitate sb; *Fig* to bring sb back to life; **r. qn à son** *ou* **au devoir** to remind sb of their duty or where their duty lies; **r. qn à la raison** to make sb see reason or sense; **être rappelé au chevet de qn** to be called to sb's bedside; **Dieu l'a rappelée à lui** God called her to Him

3 *(pour se souvenir de)* *(quelque chose)* to recall; **r. qch à qn** to remind sb of sth; **rappelez-moi votre nom** what was your name again?; **vous me rappelez mon oncle** you remind me of my uncle; **cela me rappelle mon enfance** it brings back my childhood, it reminds me of my childhood; **ça me rappelle quelque chose** it reminds me of something, it rings a bell; **cela ne me rappelle rien** it doesn't ring a bell or any bells; **puis-je te r. que tu me dois 200 euros?** may I remind you that you owe me 200 euros?; **rappelez-moi à son bon souvenir** remember me (kindly) to him; **ce sont des choses qu'il vaut autant ne pas r.** these things are best forgotten; **il n'est pas nécessaire de r. que vous devez tous être ponctuels au cours** there's no need to remind you that you all have to be on time for class; *Com* **prière de r. ce numéro** in reply please quote this number

4 *Tech (pièce d'une machine etc)* to draw back; *Typ* **r. le chariot** to return the carriage; *(de quelques espaces)* to backspace

5 *(marchandises défectueuses)* to recall

VPR se rappeler 1 se r. qch, *Fam* **se r. de qch** to remember or recall or recollect sth, to call sth to mind; **je ne me le rappelle plus**, *Fam* **je ne m'en rappelle plus** I can't remember it; **un rêve dont je ne me rappelle presque plus rien** a dream I remember almost nothing about; **se r. (d')avoir promis qch** to remember promising sth; **rappelez-vous que ce n'est qu'une enfant** remember that or bear in mind that she's only a child

2 *Tél Fam* **on se rappelle la semaine prochaine** *(au téléphone)* we'll talk again next week; **on se rappelle, hein?** talk to you on the phone

---

Attention: ne pas confondre les verbes **to remember** et **to remind** lorsque l'on traduit le verbe **rappeler**.
Se rappeler quelque chose se traduit **to remember something**, alors que **rappeler quelque chose à quelqu'un** se dit **to remind somebody of something**.

---

rappeur, -euse [rapœr, -øz] N *Mus* rapper

rappliquer [raplike] VI *très Fam* to turn or roll up, to show (up); **r. à la maison** to roll back home; **je n'ai aucune envie de le voir r. ici** I don't want him turning up here

---

| relationship **1** | relation **2** |
| connection **2** | ratio **3** | report **4** |
| return **5** |

NM **1** *(relation humaine)* **mettre qn en r. avec qn** to put sb in touch with sb; **quelle est la nature de vos rapports avec elle?** what is the nature of your relationship with her?, what exactly is your relationship with her?; **nos rapports sont purement professionnels** our relationship is purely professional; **nous avons maintenu des rapports amicaux** we've stayed on friendly terms; **nous ne sommes plus en r. depuis des années** we lost touch years ago, we haven't been in touch for years; **rapports commerciaux** business relations; **avoir des rapports avec qn** *(officiels)* to have dealings or relations with sb; *(sexuels)* to have sex with sb, *Fml* to have sexual intercourse with sb; **les couples qui n'ont plus de rapports** couples who no longer have sex or sexual relations; **à quand remontent vos derniers rapports?** when did you last have intercourse?; **avoir de bons rapports avec qn** to be on good terms with sb; **les rapports qu'elle a avec son père sont très tendres/tendus** she and her father have a very loving/tense relationship; **les rapports qu'elle a avec son père sont très amicaux** she and her father have a very friendly relationship or are on very friendly terms; **ses difficultés relationnelles trouvent leur origine dans son r. à sa mère** her difficulties in forming relationships stem from her own relationship with her mother; **un r. de forces** a battle of wills; **entretenir des rapports d'affaires avec qn** to have a business relationship with sb; **cesser tout r. avec qn** to break off all contact or relations with sb; *Pol* **les rapports Est-Ouest** East-West relations; **entretenir des rapports de bon voisinage avec les pays européens** to maintain good relations with European countries

2 *(lien)* relation, connection (**avec** with); **sans r. avec le sujet** without any bearing on or unconnected with or irrelevant to the subject; **la question est sans r. avec ce que nous disions** the question has no bearing on or is not relevant to what we were saying; **ce n'est pas sans r. avec ce que je disais** it is not unrelated to what I was saying; **sa décision est sans r. avec ce qui se passe ici** his/her decision has no bearing on or relevance to what's happening here; **avoir r. à qch** to be about sth, to have to do with sth, to relate to sth; **mais ça n'a aucun r. avec ce que je disais!** but that's got nothing to do with what I was saying!; **question qui a un r. très étroit avec une autre** question that is closely connected with another; **un métier en r. avec ses goûts** a trade that suits his/her tastes; **un travail (plus) en r. avec vos capacités** a job (more) in keeping with your abilities; **il a un mode de vie parfaitement en r. avec ses revenus** he has a lifestyle well within his means; **une histoire en r. avec votre vie quotidienne** a story about or that has to do with your daily life; **parlez-lui de choses qui sont peut-être moins en r. avec votre passé** talk to him about things that maybe have a bit less to do with your past; **établir un r. entre deux choses** to establish or make a connection between two things; **elle n'a pas fait le r.** she didn't make the connection; **je ne vois pas le r.** I can't see the connection or link; **où est le r.?** where's the link or connection?; **par r. à qch** *(en ce qui concerne)* with regard to sth; *(en comparaison)* compared or in comparison with sth; *Fin* **par r. au dollar** against the dollar; *Fam* **je suis venu vous voir r. à mes allocs** I've come to see you about my dole money; **sous ce r.** in this respect; **analyser un texte sous le r. de la sémiologie** to analyse a text from a semiotic angle; **sous le r. de l'efficacité** from the performance point of view; **sous tous les rapports** in all respects, in every respect; **un homme bien sous tous rapports** a fine

man in every respect or in every way; **cherche jeune femme bien sous tous rapports pour garder deux enfants** *(dans petite annonce)* wanted: respectable young woman to look after two children

3 *(proportion)* ratio, proportion; *Math* ratio; *(vitesse)* gear; **en r. avec** in proportion or proportional to; **dans le r. de un à trois** in a ratio of one to three; **le r. maître-élèves est de 1 pour 20** the staff-student ratio is 1 to 20; **le r. des forces entre le Nord et le Sud** the balance of power between North and South; *Com* **r. qualité-prix** quality-price ratio; **ce produit est d'un bon r. qualité-prix** this product is good value for money; **r. valeur-prix** value-price ratio; *Aut* **r. des engrenages** gear ratio; **changer de r.** to change gear; **r. avant** forward gear ratio; **r. course-alésage** stroke-bore ratio; **r. de boîte** gearbox ratio; **r. inférieur** low (gear); **r. intermédiaire** intermediate gear

4 *(écrit etc)* report; *(des dépenses etc)* return; **faire** *ou* **rédiger un r. sur qch** to make a report on sth, to draw up a report on sth; **r. d'activité** progress report; *Com, Fin* **r. annuel** annual report; **r. commercial** market report; **r. d'expertise** valuation, expert's report; *Compta* **r. d'exploitation** operating statement; **r. d'intelligence mercatique** market intelligence report; **r. d'étude de marché** market study report; **r. de gestion** management report; *Com* **r. de situation journalière** daily trading report; *Com* **r. de situation mensuelle** monthly trading report; **r. des affaires sociales** social report; **r. des commissaires aux comptes** government auditors' report; **r. financier** financial report; **r. récapitulatif** summary report

5 *Fin* yield, return, profit; *Agr* yield; **vivre du r. d'une terre** to live off the money that a piece of land brings in; **capital en r.** interest-bearing or productive capital; **arbre fruitier en plein r.** fruit tree in full yield; *Agr* **terre en plein r.** extremely productive land; **immeuble de r.** rental property; **d'un bon r.** profitable, that brings in a good return, that pays well; **d'un mauvais r.** unprofitable, that brings in a poor return, that does not pay well; **les rapports du tiercé** winnings on the horse races

6 *Mil* daily assembly for issue of orders; **salle des rapports** orderly room

rapportage [rapɔrtaʒ] NM *Scol Fam* tale-telling, sneaking

rapporté [rapɔrte] ADJ *Couture* **manche rapportée** set-in sleeve; **poches rapportées** patch pockets

rapporter [rapɔrte] VT **1** *(pour rendre)* *(vers le locuteur)* to bring back, to return; *(en s'éloignant du locuteur)* to take back, to return; *(d'un chien)* *(gibier)* to retrieve; **rapportez-moi un kilo de sucre** bring me back a kilo of sugar; **j'espère que tu nous rapportes de bonnes nouvelles!** I hope you've brought us some good news!; **je t'ai rapporté l'aspirateur** I've brought back the or your vacuum cleaner; *(en le présentant)* here's the vacuum cleaner that I borrowed; **veux-tu r. ce livre à la bibliothèque?** will you take this book back to the library?, will you return this book to the library?; **il n'en a rapporté que la déception** all he got out of it was disappointment; **allez! rapporte!** *(à un chien)* fetch!; *Journ* **r. une copie** to file copy

2 *(relier à)* **r. qch à une cause** to attribute or ascribe sth to a cause; **il faut r. l'événement à l'époque où il a eu lieu** one must look at or consider the event in context; **r. tout à soi** to relate everything to oneself; *(parler de soi)* to drag the conversation round to oneself

3 *(faire le compte rendu de)* to report, to give an account of; **tu me rapporteras sa réponse/ce qu'il dit de notre proposition** let me know his answer/what he says about our proposal; **le journal rapporte l'anecdote suivante ...** the newspaper carries this story ...; **l'histoire rapporte que ...** history relates that ...; **on rapporte qu'il avait des pouvoirs surnaturels** he is said or reported to have had supernatural powers; **je vous rapporte ses paroles** I'm telling you what he said; **il rapporte tous les faits et gestes de ses collègues à son patron** he reports to his boss on everything that his colleagues do; **vous n'auriez pas dû le r.** you shouldn't have repeated it; **ce petit fayot est allé tout r. à l'instituteur** the little sneak has gone and told the teacher

4 *Couture (poche, pièce)* to sew on

5 *Fin* to bring in, to bear, to yield; *Agr* to yield; **r. de l'argent** to be profitable; **r. des bénéfices** to be profitable; **r. des intérêts** to yield interest; **placement qui rapporte dix pour cent** investment that brings in or yields ten per cent; **arbres qui rapportent beaucoup** trees that yield well; **cela ne rapporte rien** it doesn't pay; *Fig* **est-ce que tu crois que ça va te r. quelque chose?** do you think you're going to get anything out of it?, do you think it will do you any good?

6 *Jur etc (décret)* to rescind, to revoke; *(ordre)* to withdraw, to cancel; **r. un ordre de grève** to call off a strike, *Fml* to rescind a strike order

7 *Géom (angle)* to plot, to set off, to lay off; **r. des mesures à une autre échelle** to plot measurements on a different scale

8 *Compta (écriture)* to post

VPR se rapporter 1 *(avoir rapport avec)* **se r. à qch** to refer to sth, to relate to sth; **les documents qui se rapportent à l'affaire** the relevant documents, the documents relating to or connected with the case; **la réponse ne se rapporte pas à la question posée** the answer has nothing to do with or is irrelevant to the question asked; **les souvenirs qui se rapportent à cette expérience** the memories connected with the experience

2 s'en r. à qn/au témoignage de qn to rely on or to put one's faith in sb/sb's evidence; **je m'en rapporte à vous pour ce qui est des invitations** I can rely on you to arrange the invitations; **je m'en rapporte à votre jugement** I have every faith in your judgement

3 *Tech (d'une pièce)* to fit (**avec** with)

VI1 *(être rentable)* to pay; **c'est un métier qui rapporte** it's a profitable career; **une affaire qui rapporte** a profitable business, a business that pays; **ça ne rapporte pas** it doesn't pay, there's no money in it; **vous croyez que ça rapporte?** do you think there's any money in it?; **ça peut r. gros** it can be very profitable

2 *(en secret)* to tell tales, to sneak; **r. sur le compte de qn** to tell on sb; **je n'aime pas les enfants qui rapportent** I don't like telltales

3 *Litt (ressembler à)* to be on a level or a par with

rapporteur, -euse [rapɔrtœr, -øz] **ADJ** telltale, sneaky

N telltale, sneak

NM 1 *Admin, Pol* reporter, recorder; **r. officiel** official recorder; **r. de la commission =** committee member who acts as spokesman **2** *Mil* judge advocate *(at court martial)* **3** *Math* protractor; **r. à limbe complet** circular protractor

rapprendre [raprɑ̃dr] **VT** *(conj like* **prendre**) **1** *(apprendre)* to learn (over) again; **elle a dû r. à marcher après son accident** she had to learn to walk (all over) again after her accident; **r. le bonheur** to learn how to be happy again **2** *(enseigner)* to teach again; **il faut leur r. sans cesse le code de la route** you

have to keep teaching them the Highway Code

rapproché [raprɔʃe] **ADJ** *(dans l'espace, dans le temps)* near; *(yeux)* close-set; **maisons très rapprochées** houses very close together, houses very close or near to one another; **des examens très rapprochés** *ou* **qui ont lieu à des dates très rapprochées** exams coming very close together or very close to each other; **j'ai trois réunions très rapprochées dans la journée** I've got three meetings one right after the other; **faits rapprochés dans le temps** events occurring close together (in time); *Phot, Cin* **plan r. sur un visage** close-up of a face; *(sur script)* close-up on a face

rapprochement [raprɔʃmɑ̃] **NM 1** *(de faits, d'idées)* comparison, setting side by side, putting together; **il n'a pas fait le r.** he didn't make the connection; **je ne peux m'empêcher de faire un r. entre ces deux faits** I can't help making a connection between or linking the two facts **2** *(de deux objets)* bringing or placing together; *Fig (de deux personnes)* reconciliation, bringing together; *Pol* rapprochement; *Typ* **r. de caractères** kerning; **un r. israélo-palestinien** an Israeli-Palestinian rapprochement; **le r. qui s'est opéré entre elles** their reconciliation; *Compta* **r. bancaire** bank reconciliation

rapprocher [raprɔʃe] **VT1** *(mettre plus près)* *(objet)* to move or bring nearer or closer; *(deux objets)* to move nearer or closer together; **rapproche ta chaise de la table** move your chair closer to the table; **r. une chaise du feu** to draw a chair up to the fire; **le vent rapproche les nuages de la côte** the wind is blowing the clouds inshore; **et si on rapprochait les deux cousins à table?** how about sitting the two cousins closer to each other at the table?; **r. les lèvres d'une plaie** to draw together or join the lips of a wound; **une lunette rapproche les objets** a field glass makes objects look nearer; **il va falloir r. les rendez-vous** we'll have to meet more often; *(en affaires)* we'll have to have more frequent meetings; **chaque jour les rapproche de la fin** each day brings them nearer the end; **je te déposerai sur la place, ça te rapprochera (de chez toi)** I'll drop you off in the square, that'll get you a bit nearer home **2** *(réconcilier) (deux personnes)* to bring together; **un intérêt commun les rapproche** they are united or brought together or drawn together by a common interest; **cette épreuve nous a rapprochés** the ordeal drew or brought us closer together; **elle essaie de r. le père et le fils** she is trying to reconcile father and son

3 *(lier) (des faits, des idées)* to put together or side by side, to compare

VPR se rapprocher 1 se r. de *(sa destination, un lieu)* to get closer to, to approach; *(la télévision, la table)* to move closer to; **rapproche-toi de lui, il n'entend pas** move closer (to him), he can't hear; *Fig* **se r. de son idéal** to come close to one's ideal; **son costume se rapprochait d'un uniforme** his clothes looked almost like or came near to being a uniform; **se r. de la vérité** to get close to the truth; **ça n'est pas tout à fait ça, mais ça s'en rapproche** that's not quite it but it's close; **à mesure que nous nous rapprochons du premier anniversaire de sa mort ...** as we near or approach the first anniversary of his/her death ...; **plus on se rapprochait de la fin du trimestre, plus les enfants devenaient espiègles** the closer or nearer we got to the end of the term, the more mischievous the children became

2 *Fig* **se r. de qn** to become closer to sb; *(après une brouille)* to become reconciled with sb, to make it up with sb; **la France et**

l'Espagne s'étaient rapprochées a rapprochement had taken place between France and Spain

rapsodie [rapsɔdi] **NF** rhapsody

rapt [rapt] **NM** abduction, kidnapping

râpure [rɑpyr] **NF** *Tech* raspings, gratings, filings

raqué [rake] **ADJ** *Can Fam (en panne, en ruine)* broken-down, wrecked; *Fig (épuisé)* knackered, *Am* bushed

raquer [rake] **VT** *Fam* to fork out, to cough up, to stump up

raquette [raket] **NF1** *(de tennis, badminton, squash)* racket, racquet; *(de ping-pong)* bat; *Aut Fam* **coups de r.** jolts; *Fig* **une des meilleures raquettes du monde** one of the best (tennis/squash/table tennis/etc) players in the world **2** *(pour marcher dans la neige)* snowshoe; **ils sont montés en raquettes** they snowshoed up **3** *Bot Fam* prickly pear

rare [rar] **ADJ 1** *(peu courant) (livre, plante, insecte etc)* rare; **lors d'une de ses rares visites** on one of his/her rare or few visits; **elle ne nous fait plus que de rares visites** she rarely or seldom visits us now; **je n'ai que de rares visites** I seldom or rarely get visitors; **je suis un des rares à aimer la pluie** I'm one of the few people who like rain; **vous devenez r. comme les beaux jours** you're quite a stranger, we seldom see you (these days); **se faire r.** to be becoming rare; **il se faisait r. dans le quartier** he was rarely seen around the area; **la main-d'œuvre/l'argent était r.** there was a shortage of labour/money; **les denrées de base se font rares** basic food items are becoming scarce; **c'est (bien) r. qu'il pleuve ici** it (very) rarely rains here; **cela n'avait rien de r. à cette époque** it was quite common at that time; **il n'est pas r. qu'elle rentre au petit matin** it's not uncommon for her to go home in the small hours; *Litt* **rares sont ceux que la famine épargne** rare are they who are spared by the famine **2** *(exceptionnel) (mérite, beauté, intelligence, talent etc)* rare, uncommon, exceptional

3 *(clairsemé) (végétation etc)* thin, sparse, scanty; *(jour, lumière)* dim, poor; *(oxygène)* rare; **avoir le cheveu r.** to have thinning hair

raréfaction [rarefaksjɔ̃] **NF 1** *Phys (de gaz, d'air)* rarefaction **2** *(d'un produit, de l'argent)* growing scarcity

raréfier [rarefje] **VT1** *Phys* to rarefy **2** *Rare (rendre rare)* to deplete, to make scarce

VPR se raréfier 1 *Phys* to become rarefied, to rarefy **2** *(animal, plante)* to become scarce

rarement [rarmɑ̃] **ADV** rarely, seldom

rareté [rarte] **NF 1** *Phys (de gaz etc)* rarity **2** *(d'objets)* scarceness, scarcity, *Fml* dearth; *(de visites)* infrequency; *(d'un phénomène)* novelty, singularity, unusualness; *(d'un mot, d'une maladie etc)* rare occurrence, rareness **3** *(objet rare)* **cabinet plein de raretés** cabinet full of rare objects or of rarities or curiosities

RAS [ɛraɛs] *Fam (abrév* **rien à signaler***) (à l'écrit)* everything OK; **quoi de neuf? – R.!** what's new? – nothing much!

ras [rɑ] **ADJ 1** *(cheveux, tête)* close-cropped; *(menton)* close-shaven; *(barbe)* short; *(tapis)* short-pile; **chien à poil r.** short-haired dog; **pull r. du cou** crew-neck (sweater), round-neck sweater

2 mesure rase full (level) measure; **deux cuillerées rases de sucre** two level spoonfuls of sugar; **verser du vin à qn à r. bord** to fill sb's wineglass to the brim; **à** *ou* **au r. de** (on a) level or flush with; **vaisseau chargé au r. de l'eau** vessel laden to the water line; **voler au r. du sol/de l'eau** to fly close to the ground/water, to skim (along) the ground/

water; *Fam* **voler** *ou* **rester au r. des pâque-rettes** *(d'un livre, d'un film, d'une conversa-tion)* to be very lowbrow; **son humour vole** *ou* **reste au r. des pâquerettes** his/her sense of humour is pretty basic *or* lowbrow; *Fam* **elle portait une minijupe qui lui arrivait au r. des fesses** she was wearing a mini-skirt which was more like a belt; **en rase cam-pagne** in the open country

3 *Fam* **en avoir r. le bol** *ou* **la casquette** *ou* *Vulg* **le cul** to have had it up to here, to be fed up (to the back teeth); **j'en ai** *ou* **il y en a r. le bol (de tes histoires)** I'm fed up *or* I've had it up to here (with your nonsense), I'm sick to the back teeth (of your nonsense); **j'en ai r. le bol de ne pas pouvoir lui parler directement** I'm fed up with not being able to talk to him/her directly; **r. le bol!** enough is enough!

ADV se faire couper les cheveux r. to have one's hair cropped

rasade [razad] NF *(de vin)* glassful

rasage [razaʒ] NM shaving; *Tex* shearing; **lo-tion après-r.** aftershave lotion

rasant [razɑ̃] ADJ **1** tir r. grazing fire; **trajec-toire rasante** flat trajectory; **vol r.** flight that skims the ground; **lumière rasante** oblique *or* (almost) horizontal light **2** *Fam (per-sonne, discours, film etc)* boring

rascasse [raskas] NF scorpion fish

rasé [raze] ADJ shaven; **r. de près** close-shaven; **(entièrement) r.** *(visage)* (clean-)shaven; *(tête)* shaven; **des enfants rasés** children with shaven heads

rase-mottes [razmɔt] NM INV *Aviat Fam* **faire du** *ou* **voler en r.** to hedgehop, to skim the ground; **le vol en r.** hedgehopping

raser [raze] VT **1** *(tête)* to shave; *(moustache, barbe, cheveux)* to shave off; **r. un homme** to shave a man, to give a man a shave; **r. une femme/un enfant/un prisonnier** to shave a woman's/a child's/a prisoner's head; **se faire r.** to be given a shave **2** *(bâtiment, ville)* to raze to the ground **3** *(frôler) (surface de qch)* to graze, to brush; *(sol, eau)* to skim (over); *Fig Fam* **r. les murs** to hug the walls **4** *Fam (ennuyer)* to bore

VPR se raser 1 to shave, to have a shave; **je dois me r.** I need a shave; **se r. les jambes/les aisselles** to shave one's legs/armpits **2** *Fam (s'ennuyer)* to be bored; **qu'est-ce qu'on se rase chez eux!** they're really boring

raseur, -euse [razœr, -øz] N *Fam* bore

rasibus [razibys] ADV *Fam* **couper les che-veux** *ou* **tondre le crâne r. à qn, tondre qn r.** to scalp sb; **la balle est passée r.** the bullet whizzed past very close; **le couteau lui est passé à côté du doigt r.** the knife only just missed his/her finger; **il est passé en termi-nale mais r.** he made it into the sixth form but only by the skin of his teeth

rasif [razif] NM *Fam* razor; **ils se sont battus à coups de r.** they were going at each other with open razors

ras-le-bol [ralbɔl] NM INV *Fam (sentiment)* discontent, dissatisfaction; **le r. généralisé qui s'empare des professeurs** the wide-spread feeling among teachers that they've had as much as they can take *or Fam* that they've had it up to here; **le r. des jeunes** *ou* **de la jeunesse** the feeling among young people that they've had it up to here

rasoir [razwar] NM **1** razor; **r. de sûreté** safety razor; **r. électrique** electric razor *or* shaver; **pierre à r.** hone; **cuir à r.** strop; **couper comme un r.** to be as sharp as a razor; **le feu du r.** razor burn **2** *Fam (personne)* bore
ADJ INV boring

rassasié [rasazje] ADJ *(repu)* satisfied; *Fig Fam* full, sated (**de** with); **ah non, plus de films d'horreur, je suis r.!** no more horror

films, I've had enough *or* my fill!; **les Français sont rassasiés de discours électoraux** the French have had their fill of political speeches

rassasiement [rasazimɑ̃] NM *Rare (de la faim)* satisfaction; *Fig* satiety, surfeit

rassasier [rasazje] VT *(faim)*, *Fig (curiosité, soif d'apprendre, passion pour qch)* to satis-fy; **r. qn** to satisfy sb's hunger; *Fig* **r. son re-gard à contempler qch** to feast one's eyes on sth; **les fruits ne rassasient pas** fruit isn't very filling *or* doesn't satisfy your hunger; *Fam* **je suis rassasiée de toutes vos histoires** I've had more than enough *or* than my fill of your stories
VPR se rassasier to eat one's fill; **se r. d'un mets** to eat one's fill of *or* take one's fill on a dish; *Fig* **se r. de plaisirs** to take one's fill of pleasure; **je ne me rassasie pas de cette vue/sa présence** I never tire of this view/his presence

rassemblement [rasɑ̃bləmɑ̃] NM **1** *(de documents, de troupes, d'outils)* assembling, collecting, gathering; *Mil* fall in, parade; *Mil* **sonner le r.** to sound the assembly; *Mil* **r.!** fall in!, form up!; *Pol* **œuvrer au r. de la gauche** to work towards the union of the left **2** *(foule)* crowd, gathering; **provoquer un r.** to draw *or* attract a crowd; **disperser les rassemble-ments** to disperse the crowd; **r. pour la paix** peace rally

rassembler [rasɑ̃ble] VT *(personnes, choses, etc)* to collect, to gather together, to get to-gether, to assemble; *(troupes)* to assemble, to muster; **r. ses affaires** to collect one's things, to get one's things together; **r. les gens qui partagent la même opinion** to bring together the people who share the same viewpoint; **ce qui nous rassemble ici ce soir, c'est la passion du théâtre** it is a pas-sion for the theatre which has brought us here this evening; **nous sommes rassemblés ici pour fêter …** we are gathered here this evening to celebrate …; **c'est pourquoi nous avons voulu vous r. aujourd'hui** that's why we wanted to gather you all together here today; **c'est le besoin qui les rassemble** they are brought together by need; **r. toutes les pièces d'un procès** to bring together all the documents in a case; **r. ses idées** to collect *or* gather together one's thoughts; **r. ses es-prits** to collect oneself, to regain one's composure; *Fig* **r. son courage/toutes ses forces** to muster *or* summon up one's cou-rage/all one's strength; *Équitation* **r. un che-val** to gather a horse
VPR se rassembler *(s'assembler)* to assemble, to get together, to gather; *(d'une foule)* to col-lect, to gather; *Mil* to fall in, to muster; **les ou-vriers se rassemblent sous l'égide du syndicat** the workers are gathering *or* band-ing together under the aegis of the union; **nous nous rassemblons tous les jeudis dans ce bar** we meet *or* get together in this bar every Thursday

rasseoir [raswar] *(conj like* **asseoir***)* VT **r. qn** *(qui était debout)* to sit sb down again; *(qui était couché)* to sit sb up again; **faire r. qn** to make sb sit down again; **r. une statue sur sa base** to replace a statue on its base; *Fig* **r. l'école dans la démocratie** to re-establish the educational system as one of the funda-mental institutions of democracy; **il faut r. la psychanalyse dans la pratique hos-pitalière** psychoanalysis must be restored to its former prominence in hospital medi-cine
VPR se rasseoir 1 *(de personne)* to sit down again, to sit back down **2** *(de liquide)* to settle; **laisser r. le vin** to let the wine settle

rasséréner [raserene] *(je* **rassérène,** *n.* **ras-sérénons; je rassé15rérai)** VT **r. qn** to put sb's mind at rest; **je suis rasséréné** my mind's at rest

VPR se rasséréner 1 *(du ciel)* to clear (up) **2** *(d'une personne)* to calm down

rassir [rasir] VI to go *or* get stale; **j'ai laissé r. mon pain** I've let my bread go stale
VPR se rassir to go *or* get stale

rassis [rasi] ADJ **1** pain r. stale bread **2** *Fig (personne, caractère, disposition)* calm, sedate

rassortir [rasɔrtir] VT = **réassortir**

rassurant [rasyrɑ̃] ADJ *(personne)* reassur-ing; *(nouvelle, paroles)* reassuring, hearten-ing; **peu r.** disquieting; **c'est une nouvelle peu rassurante** that's not very reassuring news

rassurer [rasyre] VT *(d'une personne)* to reas-sure; *(d'une nouvelle, paroles)* to reassure, to cheer, to hearten; **je ne suis pas trop rassuré de la savoir seule** I have my worries about her being alone; **il n'a pas l'air très rassuré** he's not looking too cheery; **cela me rassure (de savoir que …)** it reassures me (to know that …); **ce n'est pas ça qui va me r.** that's not enough to reassure me, that doesn't do anything to calm my misgivings; **je te ras-sure tout de suite, je n'irai pas poser la ques-tion!** I can assure you, I won't be the one who asks the question!; **eh bien, me voilà rassuré!** that's a relief!; **ah, tu me rassures!** well, that's a relief!, you've taken a weight off my mind!
VPR se rassurer to feel reassured; **rassurez-vous là-dessus** set your mind at rest on that point; **rassurez-vous** rest assured; **vous pou-vez vous r., ça ne fait pas mal du tout** you can relax, it doesn't hurt at all

rasta [rasta] ADJ, N Rasta(farian)

rastaquouère [rastakwer] NM *Fam* **un drôle de r.** a queer bird

rat [ra] NM **1** *(animal)* rat; *Fig* **c'est un r. d'église** he's never out of church; *Fig* **les rats quittent le navire** the rats are leaving the sinking ship; *Fam* **être fait comme un r.** to be caught like a rat in a trap; *Fam* **s'ennuyer comme un r. mort** to be bored out of one's mind *or* skull, to be bored to death; **petit r. (de l'Opéra)** ballet pupil; *Fam* **mon petit r.** darling; *Fam* **ah le r., il ne m'a pas téléphoné!** the rat didn't call me; **Fam face de r.!** ratface! **2** *(avare)* miser, skinflint, *Am* tightwad; *Fam* **c'est un r.** he's stingy *or* a miser **3** *Can (sour-nois)* sly customer
ADJ INV *Fam* **1** *(avare)* stingy, tight; **ce qu'il est r.!** what a skinflint *or Am* tightwad! **2** *Can (sournois)* wily, sly
▸▸ **r. d'Amérique** coypu; *Fig* **r. de biblio-thèque** bookworm; **r. des champs** field mouse; **r. d'eau** water vole; **r. d'Égypte** mon-goose; **r. géant (des Indes)** bandicoot; *Fig* **r. d'hôtel** hotel thief; **r. musqué** muskrat, mus-quash; **r. noir** black rat; **r. de Pharaon** mon-goose; **r. surmulot** brown *or* Norway rat

rata [rata] NM *Mil Fam Vieilli* grub, *Péj* pigswill

ratafia [ratafja] NM *(boisson)* ratafia

ratage [rataʒ] NM *Fam* botching, bungling, messing up

rataplan [rataplɑ̃] NM *(d'un tambour)* rat-a-tat

ratatiné [ratatine] ADJ **1** *(à cause de l'âge, du dessèchement, du feu)* shrivelled; **petite vieille ratatinée** little old wizened *or* shrun-ken woman **2** *Fam (accidenté)* smashed-up

ratatiner [ratatine] VT **1** *(pomme, visage etc)* to shrivel (up) **2** *Fam (écraser)* to scrunch up **3** *très Fam* **r. qn** *(tuer)* to bump sb off; *(battre)* to beat sb up; **se faire r. par l'équipe adverse** to get thrashed *or* hammered by the other side
VPR se ratatiner *(de cuir, d'une plante, d'un parchemin)* to shrivel up; **une vieille dame qui se ratatine** a shrunken little old lady; **je commence à me r.** I'm beginning to shrink;

Fam **tu vas te faire r.** *(dans un concours, match)* you're going to get slaughtered; *(à un examen)* you're going to fail abysmally

ratatouille [ratatuj] NF *Culin* ratatouille

rate¹ [rat] NF *Anat* spleen; *Fam* **se dilater la r.** to laugh one's head off, to split one's sides laughing; *Fam* **ne pas se fouler la r.** not to strain oneself

rate² NF *(animal)* female rat

raté, -ée [rate] N *(personne)* failure, loser; **comme écrivain, je suis un r.** I'm a failure *or* a washout as a writer

NM *(d'un fusil, d'un moteur)* misfire; *Fig* hitch, minor problem; *TV, Radio etc* fluff; **le moteur avait des ratés** the engine was misfiring; **avoir un r. (d'allumage)** to backfire, to misfire

râteau, -eaux [rato] NM **1** *(de jardin)* rake; **r. mécanique** raker; **r. faneur** tedder; **donner un coup de r. à l'allée** to give the path a rake; **ramasser les feuilles mortes avec un r.** to rake up the dead leaves

2 *Naut* **r. de pont** squeegee
3 *(de croupier)* rake
4 *(de métier à tisser)* comb
5 *Fam (peigne)* comb
6 *Fam* **se prendre un r.** *(être rejeté)* to get turned down, *Br* to get a knockback
7 *Suisse Fam (avare)* stingy, tight-fisted

râteler [ratle] VT *(* **je râtelle, n. râtelons; je râtellerai** *) (foin etc)* to rake up

râtelier [ratəlje] NM **1** *(dans une étable)* rack; *Fig* **manger au r. de qn** to live off sb; **il mange à tous les râteliers** he serves more than one master, he has his foot in more than one camp; *Fig Fam* **quand il n'y a plus de foin dans le r.** when I'm/we're/*etc* broke, when there's nothing left in the kitty **2** *(support)* **r. d'armes/à outils/à pipes** weapon/tool/pipe rack **3** *Fam (dents)* (set of) choppers

rater [rate] VI *(d'un fusil)* to misfire, to fail to go off; *(d'un moteur)* to misfire; *Fig (d'une entreprise, d'une expérience)* to fail; **c'est raté, la plaie s'infecte** it hasn't worked, the wound is becoming infected; **si tu voulais lui parler, c'est raté, il vient de partir** if you wanted to talk to him, you're too late, he's just gone; *Fam* **j'étais sûr qu'elle allait être en retard et ça n'a pas raté** I was convinced she was going to be late and, sure enough *or* right enough, she was; *Fam* **tu as tout fait r.!** you've ruined everything!

VT **1** *(échouer à)* *(examen, bac, permis de conduire)* to fail; **le dîner était super mais j'ai raté mon gâteau** the dinner was great but I made a mess of the cake *or* my cake was a flop; **r. sa vie** to make a mess of one's life; **r. son coup** *(aux fléchettes etc)* to miss (one's shot *or* the target); *Golf* to foozle one's shot; *Fig Fam* to make a mess of it; **j'ai raté mon coup, maintenant elle ne viendra pas** I blew it, she won't be coming now; **elle n'a pas raté son coup, tout le monde l'a entendue** she got what she wanted, everybody heard her; *Aviat* **atterrissage raté** bad landing

2 *(manquer)* *(train, avion, personne)* to miss; **j'ai raté l'occasion** *ou* **ma chance** I missed my opportunity *or* chance; **tu n'as pas raté grand-chose** you didn't miss much; **tu as raté un film extraordinaire** you missed *or* missed out on a great film; *Fam* **je ne vais pas le r.** I'm really going to let him have it; *Fam* **le coiffeur ne t'a pas raté, dis donc!** the hairdresser really did a job on you!; *Fam* **elle n'en rate pas une!** she's always putting her foot in it!

VPR **se rater 1** *(manquer son suicide)* to make a failed suicide attempt

2 *Fam* **on avait rendez-vous à l'Arc de triomphe mais on s'est ratés** we were supposed to meet at the Arc de Triomphe but we missed each other

ratiboiser [ratibwaze] VT *très Fam* **1 r. qn** *(au jeu, en Bourse, dans une entreprise)* to clean sb out; **je suis complètement ratiboisé** I'm flat broke *or Br* stony broke *or* skint; **j'ai été complètement ratiboisé dans cette affaire** that business cleaned me out totally; **se faire r. la colline** to get scalped **2** *Fam Vieilli* **r. qch à qn** to do *or* swindle sb out of sth

ratiche [ratiʃ] NF *Fam* tooth

raticide [ratisid] NM rat poison

ratier [ratje] ADJ, NM **(chien) r.** ratter

ratière [ratjɛr] NF rat trap

ratification [ratifikasjɔ̃] NF ratification; **accord sous réserve de r.** agreement subject to ratification *or* confirmation

ratifier [ratifje] VT *(traité, acte)* to ratify; *(décision)* to confirm

ratio [rasjo] NM ratio; **r. de capitalisation** p/e ratio, price/earnings ratio; **r. capital-travail** capital-labour ratio; **r. cours-bénéfices** price-earnings ratio; *Compta* **r. d'exploitation** performance ratio, operating ratio; **r. de gestion** financial ratio, financial management ratio; **r. de levier** leverage; **r. de liquidités** quick ratio, acid test ratio; **r. de situation** financial ratio; **r. de solvabilité** solvency ratio; **r. de trésorerie** cash ratio; **r. des ventes** sales ratio

ratiocination [rasjɔsinasjɔ̃] NF *Litt* mulling *or* brooding over

ratiociner [rasjɔsine] VI *Litt* to brood over; **r. sur qch** to mull *or* brood over sth

ration [rasjɔ̃] NF *(d'eau, de sucre etc)* ration; *(pour bête)* feed; *Fig (de critiques, de difficultés, de malheurs)* share; **r. alimentaire** food ration, ration of food; **r. calorique** calorie intake; **r. de combat** iron rations; **rations de survie** survival rations; **rations imposées en temps de guerre** wartime rations

rationalisation [rasjɔnalizasjɔ̃] NF rationalization, rationalizing, streamlining

rationaliser [rasjɔnalize] VT to rationalize, to streamline

rationalisme [rasjɔnalism] NM rationalism

rationaliste [rasjɔnalist] ADJ, N rationalist

rationalité [rasjɔnalite] NF rationality

rationnel, -elle [rasjɔnɛl] ADJ rational

rationnellement [rasjɔnɛlmã] ADV rationally

rationnement [rasjɔnmã] NM rationing

rationner [rasjɔne] VT *(population, malade, approvisionnement)* to ration
VPR **se rationner** to ration oneself

ratissage [ratisaʒ] NM **1** *(du jardin)* raking **2** *Fam (au casino) (des mises)* raking in **3** *Fam (d'un quartier, par la police etc)* combing, thorough search

ratisser [ratise] VT **1** *(allée, sol)* to rake (over); *(feuilles)* to rake (up) **2** *Fam* **r. les mises** *(au casino)* to rake in the stakes **3** *Fam (quartier)* to comb, to search, to make a thorough search of **4** *Fam (voler) (personne)* to clean out; **se faire r.** *(au jeu)* to be cleaned out
VI **r. large** to cast one's net wide

raton [ratɔ̃] NM **1** *(animal)* young rat; **r. laveur** raccoon **2** *Fam (terme injurieux)* = racist insult directed at Arabs from North Africa, *Br* ≃ wog

ratonnade [ratɔnad] NF *(contre des Maghrébins)* attack on North African Arabs, *Br* ≃ Paki-bashing

ratoureux, -euse [raturø, -øz] *Can* ADJ wily, devious; **parfois le bonheur est un peu r.** sometimes happiness is not all it seems
N shady customer

RATP [ɛratepe] NF *(abrév* **Régie autonome des transports parisiens** *)* = Parisian municipal transport system

rattachement [rataʃmã] NM *(d'un objet à un autre)* re-attachment; **le r. de l'Alsace à la France** the return of Alsace to France; **la société a décidé votre r. au bureau de Londres** the company has decided that you should report to the London office

rattacher [rataʃe] VT *(attacher de nouveau) (lacets)* to do up *or* fasten *or* tie (up) again; *(cheveux)* to put up again; *(chien, objet)* to tie up again (**à** to); **r. un sac sur un vélo** to tie *or* fasten a bag onto a bike again; **r. l'Alsace à la France** to (re)unite Alsace with France; **nous sommes rattachés à l'Hôpital Broussais** we're attached to the Broussais Hospital; **il est rattaché au service de M. Benoît** he reports to Monsieur Benoît's department; *Fig* **les liens qui vous rattachent à la famille** the ties that bind you to your family; *Fig* **c'était la seule chose qui nous rattachait l'un à l'autre** it was the only thing that bound us together; **c'est tout ce qui le rattache à la vie** it's the only thing keeping him alive; **r. une idée à une autre** to link (up) *or* connect one idea with another; **r. un mot à un autre par son étymologie** to establish the origin of a word through its etymology; *Mil* **unité rattachée** attached unit
VPR **se rattacher se r. à qch** to be connected with sth; **voici le rapport et toutes les pièces qui s'y rattachent** here is the report and its related documents

rattachiste [rataʃist] N = Belgian who supports the integration of French-speaking parts of Belgium into France

rattrapage [ratrapaʒ] NM *Scol* **cours de r.** remedial course; **être admis au r.**, **être admis à passer les épreuves de r.** = to be allowed to sit further oral examinations to gain a pass mark in the baccalauréat; **l'oral de r.** = further oral examination to gain a pass mark in the baccalauréat; **j'ai eu mon bac au r.** I passed my bac at the oral; **r. des salaires/des prix** the catching up of wages/prices

rattraper [ratrape] VT **1** *(reprendre) (prisonnier, chien)* to recapture, to catch; *Tricot* **r. une maille qui file** to pick up a dropped stitch; **se faire r. par la police** to get caught by the police

2 *(attraper) (objet ou personne qui tombe)* to catch

3 *(rejoindre) (personne, voiture)* to catch up (with); **je vous rattraperai à l'angle de la rue** I'll catch you up *or* catch up with you at the corner

4 *(regagner) (argent)* to recover, to get back; **r. le temps perdu** to make up for lost time; **nous avons rattrapé notre retard** we made up the time; **j'ai du sommeil à r.** I have to catch up on some sleep; **ce que tu perds d'un côté, tu le rattrapes de l'autre** what you lose on the swings, you gain on the roundabouts

5 *(rétablir) (faute d'orthographe, de calcul etc)* to correct; *(situation)*, *Culin (mayonnaise)* to salvage; **j'aurais voulu r. l'énorme gaffe que je venais de faire** if only I could have taken back the huge gaffe I'd just made; **ça, tu ne pourras pas le r.** you'll never be able to make up for it; **dis-moi comment r. le mal que je t'ai fait** tell me how I can make up for the hurt I've caused you

6 *Scol* **r. un élève** = to award a borderline candidate a pass in the baccalauréat
VPR **se rattraper se r. à qch** to catch hold of sth; *Fig Fam* **se r. aux branches** to clutch at straws; **se r. de justesse** to just stop oneself falling; **se r. (avant de faire une erreur)** to stop oneself (before making a mistake); ... **mais je me suis rattrapé de justesse** ... but I caught *or* stopped myself just in time; **je me suis rattrapé en l'invitant** I made up for it *or* I made amends by inviting him/her; **pas de soleil depuis trois mois, je vais me r.!** no

sun for three months, I'm going to make up for it now *or* I'm going to make up for lost time!; **elle s'est bien rattrapée depuis** she's really made up for it since; **elle ne peut pas parler pendant le travail, mais le soir, elle se rattrape avec son mari** she can't talk at work but she makes up for it in the evening with her husband; **se r. de ses pertes** to make good *or* recoup one's losses

vi *Fam* to catch up

rature [ratyr] **nf** crossing-out, deletion; **faire une r.** to cross out *or* delete a word; **sans ratures ni surcharges** without deletions or additions

raturer [ratyre] **vt** *(mot, phrase etc)* to cross *or* score out, to delete; **les devoirs raturés ne seront pas corrigés** homework with too many crossings-out in it will not be marked

raucité [rosite] **nf** *Litt (enrouement)* hoarseness; *(caractère voilé)* huskiness; *(de rire)* raucousness

raugmenter [rɔgmɑ̃te] **vi** *Fam (d'un prix)* to go up again

rauque [rok] **adj** *(voix) (enroué)* hoarse; *(voilé)* husky; *(rire, cri)* raucous

ravage [ravaʒ] **nm** *(often pl)* **ravages** havoc, devastation; *(d'une guerre, d'une maladie)* ravages; **les ravages du feu/de la tempête** the devastation *or* destruction caused by the fire/the storm; **faire des ravages** to wreak *or* cause havoc; *Fig* **cette mode fait des ravages parmi les jeunes** this fashion is all the rage among the young; *Fam* **elle va faire des ravages avec son bronzage parfait** with that perfect suntan of hers, she'll have them queuing up at her door

ravagé [ravaʒe] **adj 1** *(pays)* ravaged, devastated; *(visage)* ravaged, haggard; **visage r. par la petite vérole** face pitted with *or* ravaged by smallpox; **un visage r. par la colère** a face disfigured *or* contorted by anger **2** *Fam (fou)* bonkers, crazy; **il n'est pas un peu r., ton copain?** your mate's got a screw *or* slate loose; **c'est un r. du cerveau** he's off his rocker *or* trolley

ravager [ravaʒe] **vt** *(je ravageai(s); n. ravageons)* *(ville, région etc)* to ravage, to devastate, to lay waste; *(récoltes)* to ravage, to devastate, to play havoc with; *(visage)* to ravage

ravageur, -euse [ravaʒœr, -øz] **adj** ravaging; *(orage)* devastating; *(oiseaux)* destructive

n ravager, destroyer

ravalement [ravalmɑ̃] **nm 1** *Constr (de la maçonnerie)* repointing; *(en recrépissant)* roughcasting; *(enduit)* (coat of) roughcast **2** *(d'un arbre)* pruning, cutting back **3** *Vieilli (d'une personne)* disparagement **4** *Fig Fam* **r. de façade** facelift

ravaler [ravale] **vt 1** *(avaler de nouveau)* *(salive)* to swallow; *Fig (sanglot, larmes)* to swallow, to choke (back); *(colère, indignation, rancunes)* to swallow, to suppress, to stifle; *(réplique)* to bite back; **je lui ferai r. ses paroles** I'll make him eat his words **2** *(abaisser) (personne)* to degrade, to lower; *(dévaluer) (personne, talents, qualités etc)* to run down, to disparage; **l'assistante du directeur s'est sentie ravalée au rang de secrétaire** the manager's assistant felt she was being effectively demoted to secretary **3** *(arbre)* to prune, to cut back **4** *Constr (maçonnerie)* to repoint; *(mur)* to roughcast; *Fig Fam* **se faire r. la façade** to have a facelift

vpr se ravaler 1 to degrade *or* lower *or* debase oneself; **vous ne vous ravaleriez pas jusque-là** you wouldn't stoop to that, you wouldn't lower yourself to that extent; **ce ne serait pas se r. que d'accepter** you wouldn't be demeaning yourself if you agreed

2 *Fam* **se r. la façade** to touch up one's warpaint

ravaleur [ravalœr] **nm** roughcaster, plasterer

ravaudage [ravodaʒ] **nm 1** *(action) (de vêtements)* mending, repairing; *(de chaussettes)* darning, mending; *Fig* **ce n'est que du r. mais ça fait de l'effet** it's just a quick repair job but it looks good **2** *(résultat) (d'un vêtement)* mend, repair; *(de chaussettes)* darn, mend; **mon r. ne dura pas longtemps** my makeshift repair *or* my bit of make-do and mend didn't last long

ravauder [ravode] **vt 1** *(vêtements)* to mend, to repair; *(chaussettes)* to darn, to mend **2** *Can (errer)* to wander about; *(faire l'idiot)* to fool *or* clown around **3** *Can (faire du bruit)* to make a racket

ravaudeur, -euse [ravodœr, -øz] **n** *(de vêtements)* mender; *(de chaussettes)* darner

rave¹ [rav] **nf** *(colza)* rape; *(radis)* radish; *(navet)* turnip; **céleri r.** celeriac

rave² [rɛv] **nf** *Fam* rave

ravi [ravi] **adj** delighted (**de** with); **je suis r. de vous voir** I'm delighted to see you; **r. de vous rencontrer** pleased to meet you; **d'un air r.** delightedly; **eh bien, tu m'en vois r.!** I'm positively delighted!; *Iron* oh great!, terrific!; *Iron* **r. de le savoir** *ou* **de l'apprendre** thanks for telling me

ravier [ravje] **nm** hors d'œuvres dish

ravigotant [ravigɔtɑ̃] **adj** *Fam* invigorating; **un verre de calva, c'est r.** a glass of calvados will put new life into you/him/*etc or* blow your/his/*etc* cobwebs away

ravigote [ravigɔt] **nf** *Culin* = hard-boiled eggs served with ravigote sauce and herbs; **sauce r.** ravigote sauce *(highly seasoned oil and vinegar dressing)*

ravigoter [ravigɔte] **vt** *Fam* **r. qn** to put new life into sb; **se sentir tout ravigoté** to feel rejuvenated; **après ce bon chocolat chaud, je me sens tout ravigoté!** that nice hot chocolate has really perked me up!

ravin [ravɛ̃] **nm** ravine

ravine [ravin] **nf 1** *(petit ravin)* gully **2** *(rivière)* (mountain) torrent

ravinement [ravinmɑ̃] **nm** gullying, channelling *(by running water)*

raviner [ravine] **vt** *(d'orage, de torrent) (sol)* to gully, to channel; *(route)* to furrow, to cut up; *Fig (visage)* to crease

ravioli, *pl* **ravioli** *ou* **raviolis** [ravjɔli] **nm** *Culin* piece of ravioli; **des ravioli(s)** ravioli

ravir [ravir] **vt 1** *(plaire)* to delight; **sa gentillesse me ravit** I am delighted by his/her kindness; **ce film m'a ravi** I thought the film was delightful; **à r.** *(jouer, chanter)* delightfully, charmingly, beautifully; **belle à r.** ravishing, ravishingly beautiful; **elle est douce à r.** she is extremely gentle; **cela te va à r.** it suits you beautifully, you look delightful in it

2 *Litt (femme)* to carry off, *Arch* to ravish; *(enfant)* to abduct; **r. qch à qn** to rob sb of sth, to steal sth from sb; **la mort nous l'a ravi bien trop tôt** death took him from us *or* snatched him away from us far too soon; **ceux que la mort a ravis** those whom death has taken from our midst

raviser (se) [səravize] **vpr** to change one's mind

ravissant [ravisɑ̃] **adj** delightful, entrancing, ravishing

ravissement [ravismɑ̃] **nm 1** *(extase)* rapture, ecstasy, delight; **être dans le r.** to be in raptures *or* in ecstasies; **ce qui la plongeait dans le r. le plus total** which sent her into raptures; **avec r.** *(écouter, contempler qch)* with delight; **c'est ce que nous**

avons découvert avec r. that's what we found out to our delight **2** *Litt (d'une femme)* carrying off, *Arch* ravishment

ravisseur, -euse [ravisœr, -øz] **adj** predatory

n abductor, kidnapper, *Arch* ravisher

ravitaillement [ravitajmɑ̃] **nm 1** *Mil etc (action)* supplying (**en** with); **r. (en carburant)** refuelling; **r. en munitions** ammunition supply; **convoi de r.** supply column; **r. à la mer** replenishment *or* refuelling at sea; *Aviat* **r. en vol** in-flight refuelling; **le r. des grandes villes est un des problèmes de la guerre** maintaining supplies in large cities is one of the problems of war; *Fam* **aller au r.** to go shopping **2** *(denrées)* supplies; **distribution du r.** issue of supplies

ravitailler [ravitaje] **vt** *(armée, camp, refuge)* to supply; *(avion, navire)* to refuel; **r. un avion en vol** to refuel an aircraft in flight

vpr se ravitailler to take in (fresh) supplies; *Fam (faire des courses)* to stock up, to do a big shop; **se r. (en carburant)** to refuel

ravitailleur [ravitajœr] **nm** *Mil etc (camion)* supply truck; *(bateau)* supply ship; *(avion)* supply aircraft

adj **navire/avion r.** supply ship/aircraft

ravivage [ravivaʒ] **nm** *(de couleur)* brightening up; *(de surfaces métalliques)* cleaning

raviver [ravive] **vt** *(feu)*, *Fig (colère)* to rekindle; *(couleur)* to brighten up; *(douleur)* to revive; *(surfaces à souder)* to clean; *Fig (souvenir, querelle)* to rekindle, to revive; *Fig* **r. une plaie** to reopen an old wound

vpr se raviver *(d'une conversation)* to revive, to pick up; *(de la colère, de l'inquiétude)* to flare up again

ravoir [ravwar] **vt** *(only in inf)* **1** *(récupérer)* **r. qch** to have *or* get sth back again **2** *Fam (nettoyer)* to clean (up); **je n'arrive pas à r. cette casserole** I can't get this pan clean, I can't get the marks off this pan

vpr se ravoir *Belg (reprendre haleine)* to get one's breath back; *(retrouver ses esprits)* to come to one's senses

rayage [rɛjaʒ] **nm** *(d'arme à feu)* rifling

rayé [rɛje] **adj 1** striped, stripy; **tablier r. rouge et bleu** red and blue striped *or* stripy apron; **un animal r. noir et blanc** an animal with black and white stripes **2** *(papier)* lined, ruled **3** *(fusil)* rifled, grooved **4** *(disque, verre, parquet, carrosserie de voiture)* scratched

rayer [rɛje] **vt** *(je raie, je raye, n. rayons; je raierai, je rayerai)* **1** *(verre, parquet, carrosserie de voiture, disque etc)* to scratch; *(surface)* to score

2 *(papier)* to rule, to line

3 *(tissu)* to stripe

4 *(fusil)* to rifle; *(cylindre)* to groove

5 *(mot etc)* to strike out, to cross out, to delete; **on vous a rayé** *ou* **on a rayé votre nom de la liste** you have *or* your name has been struck off *or* crossed off *or* deleted from the list; **rayez les mentions inutiles** delete as appropriate; **on peut r. les articles que l'on a déjà achetés** we can cross off the things we've already bought; *Fig* **tu ne peux pas r. cet événement de ta vie** you can't banish *or* blot out the event from your life; *Fig* **il voudrait me r. de sa vie** he'd like to forget he ever knew me; *Fig* **une ville qui fut rayée de la carte** a town that was wiped off the map; *Mil* **r. qn des contrôles** to strike sb off the strength

rayon¹ [rɛjɔ̃] **nm 1** *(faisceau) (de lumière)* ray, beam, shaft; *Fig (d'espoir)* ray; **un faible r. de lumière** a faint gleam of light; **r. de soleil** sunbeam; *Fig* **c'est un peu mon r. de soleil** he/she has brought a ray of sunshine into my life; *Opt* **r. visuel** line of sight; **rayons X** X-rays; **passer qn/qch aux rayons X** to X-ray sb/sth; *Méd* **mal des rayons** radiation sickness; **r. électronique** *ou* **cathodique** electron beam; **r. laser** laser beam

2 *(périmètre)* range; *(d'un cercle)* radius; *Aut* **r. de braquage** turning circle; **dans un r. de deux kilomètres** within a radius of two kilometres (**autour de** of); **r. d'action** *(d'un avion)* range (of action *or* operation); **avion à grand r. d'action** long-range aircraft; *Fig* **r. d'action d'une campagne publicitaire** scope *or* coverage *or* range of an advertising campaign; **cette société a étendu son r. d'action** the firm has extended the scope of its operations

3 *(de roue)* spoke

rayon ² NM **1** *(dans un magasin)* department; **r. hommes/femmes** menswear/ladies' wear (department); **r. jardinage** gardening department; **chef de r.** head of department, department manager; **magasin à rayons multiples** department store; **r. des soldes** bargain counter; *Fig Fam* **ce n'est pas mon r.** *(ça ne me concerne pas)* that's nothing to do with me, that's none of my business; *(ça n'est pas dans mes compétences)* that's not my department; *Fig Fam* **elle en connaît un r.** (**sur la question**) she's well clued up (on the subject), she knows all there is to know (about the subject)

2 *(de placard etc)* shelf; **rayons** shelves, shelving

3 r. de miel honeycomb

rayon ³ NM *Agr* drill; **r. d'oignons** row of onions

rayonnage [rεjɔnaʒ] NM shelving, shelves

rayonnant [rεjɔnɑ̃] ADJ *(chaleur, soleil, lumière)* radiant; *Fig (visage)* radiant, beaming; **r. de joie** radiant (with joy); **r. de santé/bonheur** glowing with health/radiant with happiness

rayonne [rεjɔn] NF *Tex* rayon

rayonnement [rεjɔnmɑ̃] NM **1** *Phys* radiation **2** *(du soleil etc)* radiance; *Fig* influence; **un r. émanait de toute sa personne** his/her entire being was radiant with joy

rayonner ¹ [rεjɔne] VI **1** *Phys* to radiate **2** *(du soleil)*, *Fig (du visage)* to beam, to shine; **il rayonnait (de joie)** he was radiant *or* beaming (with joy); **r. de bonheur** to radiate happiness; **son visage rayonnait de plaisir** his/her face *or* he/she was glowing *or* aglow with pleasure **3** *(à partir d'un centre)* to radiate; *Fig* **r. dans le monde** *(d'une culture, d'une école de pensée, d'art etc)* to have worldwide influence; **une douleur qui rayonne** a spreading pain; **r. autour d'Avignon** to use Avignon as a base *(for excursions)*

rayonner ² VT *(pièce etc)* to fit with shelves, to put shelves up in

rayure [rεjyr] NF **1** *(bande)* stripe; **tissu à rayures** striped *or* stripy material; **à rayures rouges et jaunes** with red and yellow stripes; **les rayures noires et blanches du zèbre** the black and white stripes *or* markings of the zebra **2** *(éraflure)* scratch; *TV, Cin (sur l'écran)* line **3** *(d'un fusil)* groove

raz [ra] NM **r. (de courant)** strong current, *Spéc* race *(in estuary)*; **r. de marée** tidal wave; *Fig* **cette nouvelle a eu l'effet d'un r. de marée** the news caused great upheaval; *Pol Fig* **ce fut un r. de marée (électoral) pour les** *ou* **en faveur des socialistes** it was a landslide (victory) for the Socialists, it was a Socialist landslide

razzia [razja] NF *(attaque)* incursion, raid; *Hist* razzia; *Fam* **faire une r. sur les articles en solde** to make a clean sweep of *or* to snap up the bargains; **faire une r. dans le frigo** to raid the fridge

RD [εrde] NF *abrév* **route départementale**

RDA [εrdea] NF *Anciennement (abrév* **République démocratique allemande)** GDR

rdc *abrév* **rez-de-chaussée**

RDS [εrdeεs] NM *(abrév* **Remboursement de la dette sociale)** = contribution paid by every taxpayer towards the Social Security deficit

ré [re] NM INV *Mus* **1** *(note)* D **2** *(en solfège)* re

réa [rea] NF *Fam abrév* **réanimation**

réabonnement [reabɔnmɑ̃] NM subscription renewal

réabonner [reabɔne] VT **r. qn** to renew sb's subscription (**à** to)
VPR **se réabonner** to renew one's subscription (**à** to)

réabsorber [reapsɔrbe] VT to reabsorb

réabsorption [reapsɔrpsjɔ̃] NF reabsorption

réac [reak] ADJ, N *Pol Fam Péj* reactionary

réaccoutumer [reakutyme] VT to reaccustom (**à** to)
VPR **se réaccoutumer se r. à qch** to get used to sth again, to become reaccustomed to sth; **j'aurais du mal à me r.** I would find it hard to get used to things again

réachat [reaʃa] NM repurchase

réacheminement [reaʃ(ə)minmɑ̃] NM *(de marchandises)* rerouting; *Ordinat (de message)* redirecting

réacheminer [reaʃ(ə)mine] VT *(marchandises)* to reroute; *Ordinat (message etc)* to redirect

réacheter [reaʃte] VT to repurchase

réactance [reaktɑ̃s] NF *Élec* reactance

réacteur [reaktœr] NM **1** *(moteur)* jet engine **2** *Nucl* reactor, pile; **r. propulseur de navire** ship-propulsion reactor; **r. nucléaire** nuclear reactor; *Tech* **r. thermique** thermal reactor

réactif, -ive [reaktif, -iv] ADJ reactive; **non r.** non-reactive; *Chimie* **papier r.** reagent paper, test paper; *Élec* **courant r.** reactive current
NM *Chimie* reagent; **r. à base de mercure** mercury reagent

réaction [reaksjɔ̃] NF **1** *Chimie, Phys* reaction; **r. en chaîne** chain reaction; **r. nucléaire** nuclear reaction
2 *Élec* reaction, feedback
3 *(de machines etc)* reaction; *(de fusil)* kick; **moteur à r.** jet engine; **propulsion par r.** jet propulsion; **avion à r.** jet(-propelled) aircraft, jet plane, jet; *Fam* **la voiture a de très bonnes réactions (sur la glace)** the car responds well *or* handles well (on ice); **r. du moteur** engine response
4 *Physiol (d'un organe etc)* reaction, response; **r. cutanée** skin reaction, *Spéc* cutaneous reaction; **temps de r.** response time; **il y a toujours un temps de r. avant qu'elle ne réponde** she always takes a while to answer; **avoir des réactions lentes** to be slow to react; *Physiol* **r. auditive** response to auditory stimulus
5 *(à une remarque, à un incident, au stress etc)* reaction; **elle eut une r. de peur/de colère** her reaction was one of fear/anger; **faire qch par r.** to do sth as a reaction; **elle s'y oppose, simplement par r.** she is opposed to it as a matter of principle; **en r. à sa famille** in reaction to his/her family; **la décision a été prise en r. à ...** the decision was taken in response to ...; **je suis resté sans r.** I didn't react; **qu'a-t-il répondu? – rien, il n'a eu aucune r.** what did he reply? – nothing, he didn't react at all; **provoquer des réactions** to cause a reaction
6 *Pol* **la r.** reaction, reactionary attitudes; *(personnes)* reactionaries

réactionnaire [reaksjɔnεr] ADJ, N *Pol* reactionary

réactiver [reaktive] VT *(catalyseur, sérum)* to reactivate; *Fig (vieilles colères, anciens sentiments)* to rekindle, to arouse again, to stir up; **r. le feu** to revive *or* poke the fire; **cela a réactivé la douleur** it caused the pain to flare up again

réactivité [reaktivite] NF reactivity

réactualisation [reaktɥalizasjɔ̃] NF updating

réactualiser [reaktɥalize] VT to bring up to date, to update

réadaptation [readaptasjɔ̃] NF **1** *(d'un invalide, d'un prisonnier)* rehabilitation **2** *(de projets etc)* readjustment

réadapter [readapte] VT **1** *(invalide, prisonnier)* to rehabilitate **2** *(projets)* to readjust
VPR **se réadapter** to readjust, to become readjusted; **il n'a pas eu de mal à se r.** he didn't have any problem readjusting

réadmettre [readmεtr] VT *(conj like* **mettre)** to readmit

réadmission [readmisjɔ̃] NF readmission

réaffectation [reafεktasjɔ̃] NF *(d'un employé)* reassignment; *aussi Ordinat* reallocation; *Ordinat (d'une touche)* reassignment

réaffecter [reafεkte] VT *(personnel)* to reassign; *(crédits)*, *Ordinat* to reallocate; *Ordinat (touche)* to reassign; **r. qn à son premier emploi** to reinstate sb in his/her former job; **r. une subvention à sa destination première** to reallocate funds to their original use

réafficher [reafiʃe] VT *Ordinat* to redisplay

réaffirmer [reafirme] VT to reaffirm

réagir [reaʒir] VI to react (**sur** on; **contre** against; **à** to); **on verra comment il réagira** we'll see how he reacts; **ça ne l'a pas du tout fait r.** he/she didn't react at all, it didn't provoke any reaction; **allez, secoue-toi, il faut r.!** come on, wake up, <u>do</u> something!; **elle a très fortement réagi à son vaccin** she had a very strong reaction to the vaccination; **tu réagis trop violemment** you're overreacting; **r. contre qch** to take a stand against sth, to stand up to sth

réajuster [reaʒyste] VT = **rajuster**

réal, -aux [real, -o] NM *(monnaie)* real

réalésage [realezaʒ] NM *Aut* rebore

réaléser [realeze] VT *Aut* to rebore

réalignement [realiɲmɑ̃] NM *(des taux de change)* realignment; **r. monétaire** realignment of currencies

réaligner [realiɲe] VT to realign

réalisable [realizabl] ADJ *(projet, proposition)* feasible, practical, workable; *Fin (avoirs)* realizable; *Fig (rêve)* attainable

réalisateur, -trice [realizatœr, -tris] N *Cin (film)* director; *Radio, TV* producer; *(d'une pièce, d'un feuilleton)* director

réalisation [realizasjɔ̃] NF **1** *(d'un projet)* implementation, carrying out, realization; *(d'une œuvre d'art)*, *Culin (d'une pièce montée)* creation; *(d'un bâtiment)* construction; **la dernière r. de Picasso** Picasso's final *or* last creation; **les autres projets sont en cours de r.** the other projects are still in progress; **la rénovation du quartier est en cours de r.** the renovation of the area is an ongoing project
2 *(d'un rêve)* attainment; **tu verras s'accomplir la r. de ton rêve/ton souhait** you'll see your dream/wish come true
3 *Radio, TV* production; *(d'un film, d'une pièce télévisée ou radiodiffusée)* direction; **r.: Claudine Rébersat** directed by Claudine Rébersat
4 *Fin* realization; **r. d'un bénéfice** making a profit

réaliser [realize] VT **1** *(ambition)* to achieve, to realize; *(projet)* to carry out, to implement, to put into effect; *(œuvre d'art)*,

Culin (pièce montée) to create
2 *(rêve)* to attain; **elle a mis 30 ans avant de r. son rêve** her dream took 30 years to come true
3 *Cin* to direct; *Radio, TV* to produce
4 *Fin* **r. un capital** to realize an asset, to convert an asset into cash; **r. un profit** to make a profit; **r. un chiffre d'affaires de 10 millions d'euros** to have a turnover of 10 million euros, to have a 10 million euro turnover
5 *Fam (erreur, situation)* to realize, to understand; **elle n'arrive pas à r. que cela est vrai** she can't take it in, it hasn't sunk in *or* registered yet; **j'ai mis un certain temps avant de le r.** it was some time before I realized
VPR se réaliser 1 *(d'une prédiction, d'un rêve)* to come true
2 *(d'une personne)* to fulfil oneself
VI *Fam* to realize, to twig; **laisse-lui le temps de r.** give him time for it to sink in *or* register

réalisme [realism] **NM** realism; **faire preuve de r.** to be realistic; **faire preuve de r. politique** to demonstrate political realism *or* pragmatism; **décrire qch avec r.** to describe sth realistically; **décrire qn avec r.** to give a realistic portrayal of sb, to give a true-to-life description of sb

réaliste [realist] **ADJ** *(attitude, personne, proposition, description)* realistic; *(portrait)* lifelike
N realist

réalité [realite] **NF** reality; **la r. de la situation fait que nous ne pouvons ...** the situation being what it is, we can't ...; **il faut prendre en compte la r. de la situation** you/we/*etc* have to face facts *or* to look at the situation realistically; **c'est une r.** it's a reality *or* fact; **elle n'a pas le sens des réalités** she has no sense of reality, she doesn't live in the real world; **en r.** in reality, really, actually; **en r., ce n'est pas du tout comme cela que ça s'est passé** that's not really what happened, actually that's not what happened at all; **lorsque la r. dépasse la fiction** when truth is stranger than fiction; *Ordinat* **r. virtuelle** virtual reality

reality show [realitiʃo] **NM** reality show

realpolitik [realpɔlitik] **NF** *Pol* realpolitik

réaménagement [reamenaʒmã] **NM 1** *(d'un bâtiment)* refitting; **r. urbain** urban redevelopment **2** *(d'un horaire, d'un projet)* reorganization; *(d'une politique)* reshaping **3** *Fin (d'une dette)* rescheduling

réaménager [reamenaʒe] **VT 1** *(bâtiment)* to refit **2** *(horaire, projet)* to reorganize; *(politique)* to reshape **3** *Fin (dette)* to reschedule

réamorcer [reamɔrse] *Ordinat* **VT** to reboot
VPR se réamorcer to reboot

réanimation [reanimasjɔ̃] **NF** *Méd* resuscitation; **service de r.** intensive care (unit); **mettre qn en r.** to put sb in intensive care

réanimer [reanime] **VT** *Méd (patient)* to resuscitate

réapparaître [reaparetr] **VI** *(conj like* **apparaître***; aux often* **être***)* to reappear; *(d'une douleur)* to come back, to recur, to return; *Mus (d'un thème)* to be repeated, to recur, to return

réapparition [reaparisjɔ̃] **NF** *(d'une personne)* reappearance; *(d'une douleur)* recurrence; *(du nationalisme, d'une tendance, du choléra etc)* resurgence; *Mus (d'un thème)* recurrence, return

réapprovisionnement [reaprɔvizjɔnmã] **NM** restocking; **assurer le r.** to restock

réapprovisionner [reaprɔvizjɔne] **VT** *(magasin)* to restock a shop (**en** with); **r. qn** to replenish sb's supplies (**en** of)
VPR se réapprovisionner *(d'un magasin)* to stock up again, to restock (**en** with); *(d'une*

personne) to replenish one's supplies (**en** of), to stock up (**en** on)

réargenter [rearʒãte] **VT** to resilver

réarmement [rearməmã] **NM 1** *Pol* rearmament, rearming; *Pol, Rel* **r. moral** moral rearmament **2** *Naut* refitting, recommissioning

réarmer [rearme] **VT 1** *Pol* to rearm **2** *(arme à feu)* to recock; *(appareil photo)* to reset **3** *Naut* to refit, to recommission
VI *Pol* to rearm
VPR se réarmer *Pol* to rearm

réassort [reasɔr] **NM** *(d'une boutique)* restocking

réassortiment [reasɔrtimã] **NM 1** *(de couleurs)* matching **2** *(d'une boutique)* restocking; *(stock)* new stock

réassortir [reasɔrtir] *(conj like* **assortir***)* **VT 1** *(tissu, parure de lit etc)* to match **2** *(magasin)* to restock
VPR se réassortir to restock

réassurance [reasyrãs] **NF** reinsurance

réassurer [reasyre] **VT** to reinsure

réassureur [reasyrœr] **NM** reinsurer

rebaptiser [rəbatize] **VT** *(rue etc)* to rename

rébarbatif, -ive [rebarbatif, -iv] **ADJ** *(sujet, tâche)* daunting; *(visage, mine)* forbidding, unprepossessing; *(style)* off-putting; *(logiciel, écran)* not user-friendly

rebâtir [rəbatir] **VT** *(maison)* to rebuild

rebattre [rəbatr] **VT** *(conj like* **battre***)* **1** to beat again **2** *Cartes* to reshuffle **3** *Fam* **r. les oreilles à qn de qch** to shove sth down sb's throat; **il me rebat les oreilles de ses vacances au Maroc** he keeps shoving his holiday in Morocco down my throat, he keeps bending my ear about his holiday in Morocco

Do not confuse with **rabattre**.

rebattu [r(ə)baty] **ADJ** *(histoire, thème)* hackneyed, trite; *(conversation)* trite; **c'est un sujet r.** it's a trite subject, *Fam* it's (a subject that's) been done to death; **avoir les oreilles rebattues de qch** to have had sth shoved down one's throat, to have had one's ear bent about sth

rebelle [rəbɛl] **ADJ** *(personne, esprit etc)* rebellious; *(camp, armée, troupes)* rebel; *(fièvre)* stubborn, obstinate; **pour les mèches rebelles** for unruly *or* unmanageable hair; **r. à toute discipline** unamenable to discipline; **r. aux antibiotiques** resistant to antibiotics
N rebel; **le chef des rebelles** the rebel leader

rebeller (se) [sərəbɛle] **VPR** to rebel, to revolt (**contre** against); *Fig (protester)* to protest

rébellion [rebɛljɔ̃] **NF** rebellion, (up)rising, revolt; **armer une r.** to arm a rebellion; **mater une r.** to curb a rebellion; **en état de r.** *(pays, jeunes)* in a state of rebellion; *(armée)* insurgent; **acte de r.** act of rebellion, rebellious act

rebelote [rəbəlɔt] **NF 1** *(aux cartes)* rebelote *(said when playing the second card of a pair of king and queen of trumps while playing belote)* **2** *Fam* **r.!** here we go again!

rebeu [rəbø] **NM** *Fam* = person born and living in France of North African immigrant parents

rebibes [rəbib] **NFPL** *Suisse (de fromage)* = thin slices of cheese; *(de viande)* = small pieces of cured meat

rebiffer (se) [sər(ə)bife] **VPR** *Fam* to hit back (**contre** at)

rebiquer [r(ə)bike] **VI** *Fam (de cheveux, col de chemise etc)* to stick up

reblochon [rəblɔʃɔ̃] **NM** Reblochon *(type of cheese from Savoie)*

reboire [rəbwar] **VT** *(conj like* **boire***)* to drink

again; **jamais je ne reboirai de ce vin** I'll never drink *or* touch that wine again

reboisement [rəbwazmã] **NM** reforestation, *Br* (re)afforestation

reboiser [rəbwaze] **VT** to reforest, *Br* to (re)afforest

rebond [rəbɔ̃] **NM 1** *(d'un ballon)* bounce; *(ricochet)* rebound; **faux r.** spin; **saisir la balle au r.** to catch the ball on the rebound; *Fig* to seize the opportunity; *Aut* **r. des roues** wheel hop **2** *Fin (d'actions, de marché, de monnaie)* recovery

rebondi [rəbɔ̃di] **ADJ** *(joues)* round, chubby; *(personne)* plump, chubby; **ventre r.** paunch; **aux formes rebondies** with generous curves

rebondir [rəbɔ̃dir] **VI 1** *(d'un ballon)* to bounce; *(ricocher)* to rebound; **r. contre** *ou* **sur qch** to bounce off sth **2** *Fig* to flare up again; **faire r. l'intrigue/la conversation** to get the plot/conversation moving again; **c'est ça qui a fait r. toute l'affaire** that was what started the whole business up again; *Can* **son chèque a rebondi** his cheque bounced **3** *(se remettre) (économie)* to recover, to pick up again; **le dollar a rebondi** the dollar has bounced back, the (value of the) dollar has shot back up again; **il n'a jamais vraiment rebondi après cet échec** he never really recovered from that setback

rebondissement [rəbɔ̃dismã] **NM 1** rebound, bounce; **les rebondissements de la balle sur le parquet** the bouncing of the ball on the floor **2** *Fig (dans une affaire etc)* development

rebord [rəbɔr] **NM 1** *(d'une table, d'un puits)* edge; *(d'une assiette)* rim, edge; **r. d'une fenêtre** window sill *or* ledge **2** *Tech (surélevé)* raised edge, flange

reborder [rəbɔrde] **VT 1** *(vêtement)* to put a new edging *or* border *or* hem on **2 r. qn dans son lit** to tuck sb up (in bed) again

reboucher [rəbuʃe] **VT 1** *(fermer de nouveau) (bouteille)* to recork, to put the cork back in; *(tube de colle, de dentifrice)* to put the top back on **2** *(obturer de nouveau) (évier)* to block *or* stop up again; *(trou)* to fill in again
VPR se reboucher 1 *(d'un évier, des W.-C.)* to get blocked up again **2 la bouteille se rebouche mal** it's not easy to get the cork back in (the bottle); **la bouteille se rebouche hermétiquement** once the cork is back in, the bottle is hermetically sealed

rebours [rəbur] **NM** **prendre qn à r.** to rub sb up the wrong way; **compter à r.** to count backwards; **compte à r.** countdown; **prendre à r. une rue à sens unique** to go the wrong way along a one-way street; **prendre tout à r.** to take everything the wrong way; **faire/commencer qch à r.** to do/start sth back to front *or* the wrong way round; **tu as compris à r.** you've got hold of the wrong end of the stick

rebouter [rəbute] **VT** *Fam (membre fracturé)* to set; *(articulation démise)* to put back

rebouteur, -euse [rəbutœr, -øz] **N** *Fam* bonesetter

reboutonner [rəbutɔne] **VT** to rebutton, to button up again
VPR se reboutonner to do oneself up, to do up one's buttons again

rebrancher [rəbrãʃe] **VT** to reconnect

rebrousse-poil (à) [arəbruspwal] **ADV** **brosser un chapeau à r.** to brush a hat against the nap *or* the wrong way; **caresser un chat à r.** to stroke a cat the wrong way *or* against its fur; *Fig Fam* **prendre qn à r.** to rub sb up the wrong way

rebrousser [rəbruse] **VT** **r. chemin** to turn back, to go back the way one came, to retrace one's steps

rebuffade [rəbyfad] NF rebuff, snub; **essuyer une r.** to be snubbed or rebuffed, to meet with a rebuff

rébus [rebys] NM rebus; Fig enigma, puzzle

rebut [rəby] NM **(article de) r.** reject; **habits de r.** cast-off clothing, cast-offs; Ind **pièces de r.** rejects, throw-outs; **marchandises de r.** rejects; **mettre au r.** (voiture, ordinateur etc) to discard, to scrap; **bon à mettre au r.** fit for the scrapheap; **bureau des rebuts** (à la poste) dead-letter office; Fig **le r. de la société/du genre humain** the dregs of society/of the human race

rebutant [rəbytɑ̃] ADJ **1** (tâche) disagreeable, Fam off-putting; **j'ai trouvé l'administration particulièrement rebutante dans ce pays** I found having to deal with the administration in that country particularly disheartening **2** (manière, personne) disagreeable, unprepossessing, Fam off-putting

rebuter [rəbyte] VT **1** (déplaire fortement) (d'une situation, de conditions de travail) to put off; **ce qui me rebutait dans ce travail, c'est que …** what I found disagreeable about the job was that …; **son mauvais caractère l'a rebutée** she was disgusted by how nasty he was **2** (dégoûter) to disgust, to repulse
▪ VPR **se rebuter** to be put off; **c'est pour cela que je me suis rebuté** that's what put me off

recacheter [rəkaʃte] VT to reseal

recadrage [rəkadraʒ] NM Phot cropping; Cin framing

recadrer [rəkadre] VT Phot to crop; Cin to frame

recalage [rəkalaʒ] NM Fam (à un examen) failure

recalcification [rəkalsifikasjɔ̃] NF recalcification, recalcifying

recalcifier [rəkalsifje] VT to (re)calcify

récalcitrant, -ante [rekalsitrɑ̃, -ɑ̃t] ADJ (personne, cheval) recalcitrant, obstinate
▪ N recalcitrant

recalé, -ée [rəkale] N Fam failure; **il y a cinq recalés dans cette classe** five people in this class have failed

recaler [rəkale] VT Fam (personne) (à un examen) to fail; **être recalé, se faire r. (au baccalauréat/en maths)** to fail or Fam to flunk (the baccalauréat/(in) maths)

recapitalisation [rəkapitalizasjɔ̃] NF Fin recapitalization

recapitaliser [rəkapitalize] VT to recapitalize

récapitulatif, -ive [rekapitylatif, -iv] ADJ recapitulatory, recapitulative; Ordinat **carte récapitulative** summary card

récapitulation [rekapitylasjɔ̃] NF **1** recap, summing up, Fml recapitulation; **faire la r. des points importants** to recap or sum up the important points **2** (résumé) recap, summary, résumé

récapituler [rekapityle] VT to recap, to sum up, Fml to recapitulate
▪ VI to recap, to sum up; **alors, je récapitule** so, I'll recap

recapoter [rəkapote] VI Aut to put up the hood

recaser [rəkaze] Fam VT **1** (dans une entreprise) to find another job for **2** (dans un logement) to rehouse
▪ VPR **se recaser** (retrouver du travail) to find a new job; (se remarier) to get hitched again

recel [rəsɛl] NM Jur (de biens volés) receiving (and concealing), Fam fencing; (d'un criminel) harbouring, Am harboring

receler [rəs(ə)le] VT (pr ind **je recèle**, n. **recelons**; fu **je recèlerai**) **1** Jur (biens volés) to receive; Fam to fence; (criminel) to harbour, Am to harbor **2 la terre recèle de grands tré-

sors** great treasures lie hidden in the earth; Litt **r. un grand secret** to harbour or conceal a deep secret

recéler [rəsele] VT (**je recèle, n. recélons; je recélerai**) = receler

receleur, -euse [rəs(ə)lœr, -øz] N Jur (de biens volés) receiver, Fam fence

récemment [resamɑ̃] ADV recently, lately, Fml of late; **je le constatai encore r.** I noticed it again recently; **un livre r. publié** ou **publié r.** a recently published book; **encore r., elle me disait que …** she was saying to me only the other day that …

recensement [rəsɑ̃smɑ̃] NM (de voitures, d'appartements libres etc) count, inventory; Admin (de la population) census; Pol (des votes) counting; Fin stocktake; **r. du contingent** registration of those eligible for military service; **faire un r.** to make a count or an inventory; (de la population) to take a census; **agent chargé du r.** census official; **r. de la population** population census; **r. de la production** census of production; **r. des distributeurs** census of distribution; **r. des entreprises** company census

recenser [rəsɑ̃se] VT (livres, disques etc) to count, to make an inventory of; Admin (ville, habitants etc) to take a census of; Pol (votes) to count; Mil to register; **r. des marchandises** to inventory goods, to check off goods

recenseur, -euse [rəsɑ̃sœr, -øz] N Admin census taker; Pol (des votes) counter, teller

récent [resɑ̃] ADJ recent

recentrage [rəsɑ̃traʒ] NM **1** Pol move towards the centre or Am center; **le r. du Parti socialiste s'est opéré lentement mais sûrement** the Socialist party has moved slowly but surely towards the centre **2** (d'activités) **l'entreprise a décidé d'opérer un r. sur les activités multimédia** the company has decided to concentrate on the multimedia sector

recentrer [rəsɑ̃tre] VT (parti politique) to move towards the centre or Am center; Sport (balle) to centre again
▪ VPR **se recentrer** to refocus; **nous devons nous r. de façon à être plus compétitifs** we need to refocus our activities in order to be more competitive

recéper [rəsepe] VT (**je recèpe, n. recépons; je recéperai**) (arbre, pied de vigne) to cut back to the stump

récépissé [resepise] NM (d'un dépôt, d'un envoi) receipt; **r. aérien** airfreight consignment note; **r. de dépôt** deposit receipt; **r. de versement** receipt of payment; **r. des chemins de fer** rail consignment note

réceptacle [resɛptakl] NM **1** receptacle; **la mer est le r. des déchets de la ville** the sea is the receptacle or dumping ground for the city's waste; Fig **cette région ne peut pas devenir le r. de tous les gangsters du pays** the region cannot become a meeting place for all the gangsters of the country **2** Bot receptacle **3** Ordinat **r. pour extension** extension slot

récepteur, -trice [resɛptœr, -tris] ADJ Radio (appareil, poste) receiving
▪ NM **1** Physiol (de stimuli) receptor; **r. olfactif/auditif/tactile** olfactory/auditory/tactile receptor **2** (de radar), Tél, Radio, TV receiver; (de frein) slave cylinder; **r. d'embrayage** clutch slave cylinder; **r. de poche** pager; Tél **décrocher le r.** to lift the receiver; Tél **r. Morse** Morse receiver; **r. de liaison terre/satellite** uplink receiver; Ordinat **r. de données** data receiver

réceptif, -ive [resɛptif, -iv] ADJ receptive, responsive (**à** to)
▪ NM Mktg **r. précoce** early adopter

réception [resɛpsjɔ̃] NF **1** (d'une lettre, d'une commande, de biens) receipt; **prévoir quelqu'un pour la r. des marchandises** to ar-

range for somebody to take delivery (of the goods); Com **à payer à la r.** cash on delivery, COD; Com **r. définitive** final hand-over, final acceptance; Com, Ind **r. des travaux** acceptance of work; **accuser r. de qch** to acknowledge receipt of sth
2 (accueil) welcome; **faire une bonne r. à qn** to give sb a good reception or warm welcome, to receive or welcome sb warmly; **séance de r. de M. Yourcenar à l'Académie française** ceremony admitting M. Yourcenar to the Académie Française, Fml M. Yourcenar's induction into the Académie Française; **discours de r.** induction speech
3 (soirée) reception, function; **salle de r.** reception room
4 (dans un hôtel) reception (desk); **passer à la r.** to go to reception; **prière de laisser les clefs à la r.** please leave your keys at reception or the (front) desk
5 Tél, Radio, TV, Électron reception; **appareil** ou **poste de r.** receiving set; **la r. est bonne/mauvaise ici** the reception is good/bad here, you get good/bad reception here; **cet appareil n'a pas une bonne r.** the reception on this set isn't very good; **r. hertzienne** terrestrial signal reception
6 Sport (de gymnaste, sauteur) landing; Ftbl, Rugby (de ballon) take; **il s'est blessé à la r.** (d'un sauteur etc) he hurt himself on landing; **mauvaise r. de Zidane** Zidane fumbles the pass; **et Zidane à la r.** to Zidane

réceptionnaire [resɛpsjɔner] N (de marchandises) consignee; Com, Ind receiving agent or clerk; (dans un hôtel) receptionist, Am desk clerk

réceptionner [resɛpsjɔne] VT **1** Com, Ind (marchandises livrées) to check and sign for, to take delivery of **2** TV, Radio to receive

réceptionniste [resɛpsjɔnist] N receptionist, Am desk or reception clerk; **r. de nuit** night porter

réceptivité [resɛptivite] NF (à des sensations, impressions) receptiveness, responsiveness; (à une infection) susceptibility; **dans un état de r.** in a receptive or responsive mood

récessif, -ive [resesif, -iv] ADJ Biol recessive

récession [resesjɔ̃] NF Écon recession; **r. économique** economic recession

recette [rəsɛt] NF **1** Fin takings, receipts; Sport gate money; **dépenses et recettes** expenditure and receipts, outgoings and incomings; **les recettes de la boutique sont en hausse cette semaine** the shop's takings are or Fam take is up this week; **r. annuelle** annual income or receipts or revenue; **r. brute** gross income or receipts or earnings; **recettes en devises** foreign currency earnings; **r. des douanes** customs office; **recettes de l'État** public revenue, state revenue; **recettes fiscales** tax revenue; **r. journalière** daily takings; **r. nette** net income or receipts; **recettes publiques** government revenue; **faire r.** to be profitable or a success; Théâtre, Cin to be a (box-office) success, to be a hit at the box office; Cin **recettes en salles** box-office takings
2 (d'argent dû) collection; (bureau) tax collector's office; **garçon de r.** bank messenger; **faire la r. de l'argent/des contributions** to collect the money/contributions
3 Culin recipe; Pharm formula; **r. de cuisine** recipe; **livre de recettes** cookery book, recipe book; Fig **la r. du succès/bonheur** the recipe for success/happiness, the secret of success/happiness

recevable [rəsəvabl] ADJ (excuse) admissible, acceptable; Com, Ind (marchandises) fit for acceptance; Jur (témoignage) admissible; Fml **être r. dans une demande** to be entitled to proceed with a claim

recevant [rəsəvã] ADJ *Can (hospitalier)* hospitable, who likes to entertain

receveur, -euse [rəsəvœr, -øz] N 1 *(d'une lettre, d'une transfusion sanguine)* recipient; *Méd* **r. universel** universal recipient 2 *(des impôts)* collector; **r. des douanes** excise officer; **r. des Finances** district tax collector; **r./receveuse des Postes** postmaster/postmistress; **r. municipal** = collector of municipal taxes; **r. des contributions directes** tax collector; **r. buraliste** tobacconist 3 *Vieilli* (bus) conductor, *f* (bus) conductress
NM *Can* 1 *Base-ball* receiver 2 *Am Ftbl (éloigné)* wide receiver; *(rapproché)* tight end; *(inséré)* slotback

RECEVOIR [rəsəvwar] *(prp recevant; pp reçu; pr ind je reçois, il reçoit, n. recevons, ils reçoivent; pr sub je reçoive, n. recevions; impf je recevais; p hist je reçus; fu je recevrai)*

> **VT** to receive **1–3, 5, 7** ▪ to get **1, 2, 6, 7** ▪ to deal with **3** ▪ to entertain **4** ▪ to admit **5**

VT 1 *(entrer en possession de) (lettre)* to receive, to get; *(cadeau, conseil, fleurs)* to get, to receive (**de** from); *(prix, récompense)* to get, to be awarded, to receive; *Rel (communion, absolution)* to receive; **r. des nouvelles de qn** *(directement)* to hear from sb, to have news from sb; *(indirectement)* to have news of sb; **j'ai reçu de tes nouvelles par ton père** I had news of you through your father; **j'ai reçu une lettre d'elle** I've had *or* received a letter from her; **nous avons bien reçu votre lettre** we have received *or Com Fml* are in receipt of your letter; **vous avez reçu un appel de Londres** you've had *or* received a call from London; *Com* **reçu pour solde de tout compte** received in full settlement; **r. des ordres de qn** to take orders from sb; **je n'ai de conseils à r. de personne!** I don't need advice from anybody!; **elle ne sait pas r. les compliments** she doesn't know how to take *or* accept compliments; *Com, Admin* **recevez, Monsieur, l'assurance de ma considération distinguée** yours faithfully; *(quand la formule de salutation comprend le nom du destinataire)* yours sincerely; *Rel* **r. la confession de qn** to hear *or* receive sb's confession 2 *(se voir infliger) (blâme)* to receive, to get; *(fessée)* to get, to receive; **il a reçu une balle dans l'épaule** he got a bullet *or* he was shot in the shoulder; **il a reçu le ballon en pleine poitrine** the ball hit him right in the chest, he got the ball right in the chest; **j'ai dû r. un coup** something must have hit me; **il a reçu un coup sur la tête** he got hit on the head, he received a blow to the head; *Fam (il est fou)* he must have got dropped on the head; **r. un choc** to get *or* receive a shock; **laisse-le tranquille, il a reçu un choc** leave him alone, he's had a shock; **r. une blessure (au bras)** to get wounded (in the arm); **la blessure que j'ai reçue (au bras) me fait toujours souffrir** the wound I received *or* got (in the arm) still causes me pain; *Fam* **arrête ou tu vas r. une gifle** stop it or you'll get a slap; *Fam* **arrête ou tu vas r. ma main sur la figure** stop it or you'll feel the back of my hand; *Fam* **qu'est-ce que j'ai reçu quand il est rentré!** he really gave me what for when he got home!; *Fam* **ça ne te ferait pas de mal de r. un coup de pieds aux fesses de temps en temps!** a kick up the backside wouldn't do you any harm from time to time!
3 *(accueillir) (personne)* to receive, to welcome; *(clients)* to deal with; **être mal/bien reçu** to get a poor/good reception; *Iron* **je vais demander une augmentation et je sens que je vais être bien reçu!** I'm going to ask for a rise and I'm sure I'll be in for a warm reception!; **ils vous reçoivent comme un chien** they treat you like a dog; **r. qn à bras ouverts** to welcome sb with open arms; **je ne peux pas le r. aujourd'hui** I can't see him today; **le projet/la proposition n'a pas été bien reçu(e)** the project/proposal was not well received; **ils ont bien reçu la proposition** they gave the proposal a good reception; **r. la visite de qn** to have a visit from sb; **je pense r. de la visite cet été** I think I'll be having visitors this summer; **tu as reçu la visite d'un monsieur** you had a visit from a gentleman 4 *(inviter) (amis)* to entertain; **r. des amis à dîner** to have friends (round) to dinner; **r. qn à sa table** to receive sb for dinner/lunch; **elle reçoit des pensionnaires** she takes (in) boarders *or* lodgers; **cet hôtel peut r. jusqu'à 200 clients** this hotel can take *or* accommodate up to 200 guests
5 *(admettre)* to receive, to admit; **elle a été reçue à l'Académie française** she was admitted to the Académie Française; *Scol* **élèves reçus en terminale** pupils admitted to the top form; **être reçu à un examen** to pass an exam(ination); **être reçu premier** to be *or* come (out) first *or* top; **incroyable! je suis reçu!** unbelievable! I've passed!; *Naut* **être reçu capitaine** to get one's captain's certificate 6 *(prendre) (pluie, soleil, lumière)* to get; **le Rhône reçoit l'Isère et la Sorgue** the Isère and the Sorgue flow into the Rhone; **la plante ne doit pas r. trop de lumière** the plant shouldn't have *or* get too much light; **r. des radiations** to be exposed to radiation, to receive a dose of radiation 7 *Radio (transmission)* to receive; *(chaîne)* to get; **ce poste ne reçoit pas les radios étrangères** the radio doesn't pick up foreign stations

VI 1 *(donner des réceptions)* to entertain; **aimer r.** to enjoy entertaining; **savoir r.** to be a good host/hostess; **ils reçoivent très peu** they don't do much entertaining, they don't have friends round much *or* often 2 *(consulter)* to be available for consultation; **le docteur ne reçoit que sur rendez-vous** the doctor will only see patients by appointment; **le médecin reçoit à 6 heures** the doctor is available for consultation at 6 o'clock, the doctor's surgery is at 6 o'clock 3 *(se voir offrir)* **mieux vaut donner que r.** it is better to give than to receive

VPR **se recevoir 1** *Sport* to land 2 *(s'inviter)* to entertain *or* visit one another, to go to one another's houses

rechange [rəʃãʒ] NM *(vêtements)* change of clothes, spare set of clothes; *Aut* spare; **linge ou vêtements de r.** spare clothes; **trousse de r.** *(d'outils etc)* spare *or* duplicate set; *Aut etc* **pièces de r.** spare parts; **pile de r.** *(pour torche)* spare battery; **solution/politique de r.** alternative solution/policy

rechanger [rəʃãʒe] VT *(conj like* **changer***)* to change again

rechanter [rəʃãte] VT to sing again

rechapage [rəʃapaʒ] NM *(des pneus)* retreading, remoulding

rechaper [rəʃape] VT *(pneu)* to retread, to remould; **pneu rechapé** retread, remould

réchappé, -ée [reʃape] N *Litt (d'un désastre, d'un naufrage etc)* survivor

réchapper [reʃape] VI *(aux* **avoir** *or* **être***)* **r. de** *(naufrage, accident, maladie etc)* to survive; **il en a** *ou* **est réchappé** he survived; **il n'en réchappera pas** *(de naufrage, accident, maladie)* his chances of survival are nonexistent; **si j'en réchappe** if I get out of this, if I survive; **il ne réchappera pas à ce scandale** his reputation won't survive the scandal; **r. à une crise** to come through *or* survive a crisis

recharge [rəʃarʒ] NF 1 *(pour stylo à bille, briquet, rouge à lèvres etc)* refill; **r. d'encre** ink refill 2 *(d'une batterie)* recharging; **mettre l'accumulateur en r.** to put the battery on charge 3 *(de téléphone portable)* top-up card

rechargeable [rəʃarʒabl] ADJ *(briquet, vaporisateur de parfum)* refillable; *(pile)* rechargeable; *(arme)* reloadable

rechargement [rəʃarʒəmã] NM 1 *(de briquet, vaporisateur de parfum)* refilling; *(d'un accumulateur)* recharging; *(d'un véhicule, d'un fusil, d'un bateau)* reloading 2 *(d'une route)* remetalling; *(d'une voie ferrée)* reballasting

recharger [rəʃarʒe] VT *(conj like* **charger***)* 1 *(accumulateur)* to recharge; *Fig Fam* **r. ses batteries** *ou* **ses accus** to recharge one's batteries 2 *(camion, fusil, appareil photo)* to reload; *(stylo, briquet, vaporisateur de parfum)* to refill 3 *(route)* to remetal; *(voie ferrée)* to reballast
VPR **se recharger** *Ordinat* to reload

réchaud [reʃo] NM 1 stove; **r. à gaz** gas ring; **r. à alcool** spirit stove 2 *(chauffe-plat)* hotplate, plate warmer

réchauffage [reʃofaʒ] NM *(de la nourriture)* reheating, warming up

réchauffé [reʃofe] ADJ 1 *(plat)* reheated, warmed-up, *Péj* rehashed 2 *Fig Fam (plaisanterie)* stale, old
NM *Fig Fam* **c'est du r.** *(plaisanterie)* that's an old *or* a stale joke; *(nouvelles)* that's stale news *or* old hat; *(politique)* it's the same old thing; *(livre, discours)* it's a rehash; **rien de nouveau dans le journal sur l'affaire, il n'y a que du r.** there's nothing new in the paper about the business, just a rehash of what's been said already

réchauffement [reʃofmã] NM warming (up); **r. de la planète** *ou* **de l'atmosphère** global warming; **un soudain r. de la température** a sudden rise in temperature

réchauffer [reʃofe] VT *(plat)* to reheat, to warm up; *(personne)* to warm up; **ça réchauffe, hein?** it really warms you up *or* gives you a nice warm glow inside, doesn't it?; **on ne réchauffe pas les artichauts** artichokes are no good reheated; *Fig* **r. le cœur à qn** to put new heart into sb; **cela me réchauffe le cœur** it does my heart good, it's heart-warming; **ces paroles m'ont réchauffé le cœur** these were heart-warming words
VPR **se réchauffer** *(d'une personne)* to warm up, to get warm (again); **alors, tu t'es réchauffé?** have you warmed up?, are you warm again?; **se r. les pieds** to warm one's feet; **l'atmosphère se réchauffe** the atmosphere is getting warmer *or* warming (up)

réchauffeur [reʃofœr] NM *Tech* heater; **serpentin r.** heating coil

rechausser [rəʃose] VT 1 **r. qn** to put sb's shoes/boots on again (for them); **r. ses skis** to put one's skis on again; *(après une longue interruption)* to start skiing again; **ce marchand de chaussures m'a rechaussé de neuf** I got my new shoes in that shop; **il était rechaussé de neuf** he was wearing new shoes 2 *Aut* **r. une voiture** to fit a car with new tyres 3 *(consolider) (structure, mur)* to underpin
VPR **se rechausser** to put one's shoes on again; *(acheter de nouvelles chaussures)* to buy (oneself) new shoes

rêche [rɛʃ] ADJ *(surface, vin, matière)* rough; *(cheveux)* coarse; *Fig (personne, attitude)* forbidding

recherche [rəʃɛrʃ] NF 1 search (**de** for); *Fig Litt, Fml* quest (**de** for); **la r. de la vérité** the search for *or Litt, Fml* after the truth; **la r. des plaisirs** pleasure-seeking, the pursuit of pleasure; **la r. de la gloire/du bonheur** quest for *or* pursuit of glory/happiness; **ils se sont joints aux recherches pour retrouver l'enfant** they joined in the search *or* hunt for the child; **dans l'affaire Mennesson, la police continue les** *ou* **ses recherches** the police are continuing their enquiry into the Mennesson affair; **les recherches pour retrouver l'otage sont demeurées vaines** the hunt for the hostage has been to no avail; **r. de débouchés** search for markets; **r. d'informations** information search, fact-finding; *Minér* **r. de filons** prospecting; **r. pétrolière** oil prospecting; *Élec* **r. de dérangements** locating of faults; **être à la r. de** *(objet difficile à trouver)* to be looking for; *(objet ou personne qui a disparu)* to be looking for, to be searching for; **ils ont fait tout Paris à la r. d'un vase identique** they went round the whole of Paris in search of an identical vase; **j'ai couru à la r. d'un médecin** I ran for *or* to find a doctor; *Naut* **droit de r.** *(en mer)* right of search

2 *(scientifique, universitaire etc)* research (**sur** on, into); **faire de la r., être dans la r.** to do research, to be engaged in research; **faire des recherches sur qch** to do research on sth, to research sth; **la r. sur le cancer** cancer research; **r. commerciale** marketing research; **r. et développement** research and development, R&D; **r. documentaire** desk research; **r. expérimentale** experimental research; **laboratoire/équipe de r.** research laboratory/team; **r. mercatique** marketing research; *Mktg* **recherches par panel** panel research; **r. par sondage** survey research; **recherches sur les besoins des consommateurs** consumer research; **r. sur les prix** pricing research; **r. sur le terrain** fieldwork

3 *(effort)* sophistication; **avec r.** with style; **sans r.** *(style)* straightforward, down to earth **4** *Ordinat* find, search; *(de données, d'un fichier)* retrieval; **faire une r.** to do a search; **r. arrière** backward search; **r. avant, r. vers le bas** forward search; **r. booléenne** Boolean search; **r. documentaire** information retrieval; **r. de données** data retrieval; **r. globale** global search; **r. logique** logic seeking; **r. et remplacement** search and replace; **r. et remplacement global** global search and replace; **r. vers le haut** backward search

recherché [rəʃɛrʃe] **ADJ 1** *(que l'on recherche)* *(criminel)* wanted; *(objet)* sought-after, in demand; **être très r.** to be much sought after, to be in great demand; **ce style de fauteuil est très r.** there's a lot of demand for this type of chair; **sa compagnie est très recherchée** he *or* his company is much in demand *or* much sought after **2** *(robe, écriture)* elegant, exquisite; *(style)* refined, elegant; *(discours)* elegantly phrased, well-turned; **d'un travail r.** of exquisite workmanship; **trop r.** *(style)* affected, mannered, *Fml* recherché; *(écriture)* elaborate, fancy

rechercher [rəʃɛrʃe] **VT 1** *(objet ou personne qui a disparu)* to look *or* search for; *(causes, raisons etc)* to look *or* search for, to inquire into; *(un emploi)* to look for, to seek; **j'ai laissé ma bicyclette chez Paul, il va falloir que j'aille la r.** I left my bike at Paul's place, I'll have to go and get it back; **je viendrai te r. plus tard** I'll come back to pick you up later; *Ordinat* **r. qch** to search *or* do a search for sth; *Ordinat* **r. et remplacer** to search and replace; *Ordinat* **r. vers le bas/haut** to search forwards/backwards; *Tél etc* **r. un dérangement** to try to locate a fault; **un homme recherché par la police/pour meurtre** a man wanted by the police/for murder; **nous recherchons cette femme, vous la connaissez?** we are attempting to locate *or* find this woman, do you recognize her?; **h. 35 ans recherche j. f. pour sorties** *(dans petite annonce)* male, 35, seeks *or* seeking female for nights out; **r. l'origine d'un mot** to look up the origin of a word

2 *(chercher de nouveau)* to look again for; **il va falloir r. l'information dans tous les dossiers** we'll have to go through all the files again and have another look for the information

3 *(faveurs, perfection)* to look for, to seek; *(gloire, plaisirs, honneurs)* to seek, to be in pursuit of; *(louanges)* to court; **elle recherche la solitude** she's looking for solitude *or* for a place where she can be alone; **r. la difficulté** *(compliquer les choses)* to look for difficulties; *(aimer les défis)* to like a challenge

rechigner [rəʃiɲe] **VI** *Fam* to grimace, to look sour; **il a rangé sa chambre en rechignant** moaning and groaning, he tidied his bedroom; **faire qch sans r.** to do sth without (making) a fuss; **r. à la besogne** *ou* **au travail** to be unwilling to do it; **r. à faire qch** to make a fuss about doing sth

rechute [rəʃyt] **NF 1** *Méd* relapse; **faire une r.** to suffer *or* have a relapse, to have a setback **2** *Écon* slump; **on craint une r. de l'activité économique** there are fears of another slump in economic activity

rechuter [rəʃyte] **VI** *Méd* to have a relapse

récidivant [residivɑ̃] **ADJ** *Méd (maladie)* recurring, recurrent

récidive [residiv] **NF 1** *Jur* repeat offence *or Am* offense; **c'est sa première r.** it's his first repeat offence; **… et depuis il a fait plusieurs récidives** … and he's had several repeat offences since; **à la première r., tu es renvoyé** do it one more time and you're sacked; **en cas de r., une peine de prison est inévitable** a repeat offence will lead to a mandatory prison sentence **2** *Méd (d'une maladie)* recurrence

récidiver [residive] **VI 1** *Jur* to repeat an offence *or Am* offense; **il a récidivé** he has relapsed into crime, *Fam* he's done it again **2** *(d'une maladie)* to recur

récidiviste [residivist] **N** repeat offender, habitual criminal, *Fml* recidivist

récidivité [residivite] **NF** *Méd (d'une maladie)* recurrent nature

récif [resif] **NM** reef; **r. (en) barrière** barrier reef; **r. de corail** *ou* **corallien** coral reef

récipiendaire [resipjɑ̃dɛr] **N** *Littr (d'honneur, de diplôme)* recipient

récipient [resipjɑ̃] **NM** container

> Il faut noter que le terme anglais **recipient** est un faux ami. Il signifie **destinataire** ou **bénéficiaire**.

réciprocité [resiprɔsite] **NF** reciprocity

réciproque [resiprɔk] **ADJ 1** *(amour, confiance, tolérance, sentiments etc)* mutual; *(bénéfices, accord, concessions)* reciprocal, mutual; **elle ne veut plus me voir, et c'est r.** she doesn't want to see me again and the feeling is mutual **2** *Gram* reciprocal; *Math (proportion)* reciprocal, inverse; *(en logique), Math (propositions)* converse

NF 1 **rendre la r. à qn** to get one's own back on sb, to get even with sb; **et la r. est vraie** and the reverse is true; **elle le déteste, et la r. est vraie** she hates him and vice versa **2** *(en logique), Math (proposition)* converse; *Math (proportion)* reciprocal

réciproquement [resiprɔkmɑ̃] **ADV** *(mutuellement)* mutually; **et r.** and vice versa

réciproquer [resiprɔke] *Belg* **VI** **je vous souhaite une bonne année! – je réciproque!** happy New Year! – same to you! **VT** *(vœux)* to return

récit [resi] **NM 1** account; *(histoire)* story; *Littér* narrative; **il nous fit le r. de ses aventures** he gave us an account of his adventures **2** *Mus* solo; **jeux de r.** solo organ

récital, -als [resital] **NM** recital

récitant, -ante [resitɑ̃, -ɑ̃t] **N 1** *Mus (voix, instrument)* solo **2** *(lecteur)* narrator

récitatif [resitatif] **NM** *Mus* recitative

récitation [resitasjɔ̃] **NF** *(action)* recitation, reciting; *Scol (texte)* recitation

réciter [resite] **VT** *(poème etc)* to recite; **on dirait qu'il récite ses remerciements** his thanks sound rehearsed

reck [rɛk] **NM** *Suisse* **1** *Sport* horizontal bar **2** *(pente)* steep slope

réclamant, -ante [reklamɑ̃, -ɑ̃t] **N** *Jur* claimant; *(en droit civil)* plaintiff

réclamation [reklamasjɔ̃] **NF 1** *(plainte)* complaint, objection, protest; **faire une r.** to complain; **r. de client** customer complaint; **pour toute r., veuillez vous adresser au patron** please refer any complaints to the manager; *Tél* **le service des réclamations, les réclamations** complaints *or* service (department); **il y a r.** *(à l'issue d'une course hippique)* a steward's enquiry is taking place **2** *(pour recevoir un dédommagement)* claim; **faire** *ou* **déposer une r.** to make *or* put in a claim; **r. de dommages-intérêts** claim for damages; **prouver le bien-fondé d'une r.** to substantiate a claim; **r. d'indemnité** claim for compensation

réclame [reklam] **NF** *(publicité)* advertising; *(panneau)* advertisement; *TV, Radio* commercial; **faire de la r. pour qch** to advertise sth; *Fig* **faire de la r. pour qn** to sing sb's praises; *Fig* **cela ne lui fera pas de r.** it's not a very good advertisement for him; **article (en) r.** special offer; **c'était en r.** it was a special offer, *Am* it was on special; **vente r.** sale; **r. lumineuse** illuminated sign

réclamer [reklame] **VI** to complain; **r. auprès de** to make a claim against; *(se plaindre)* to lodge a complaint with; **r. contre** *(quelque chose)* to protest against, to object to; *(décision)* to appeal against; *Fam* **cet enfant ne cesse de r.** that child's never satisfied

VT 1 *(demander)* *(livre, cotisation, pourboire, silence)* to ask for; *(droit, allocation)* to claim; *(bien perdu)* to reclaim; **r. de l'argent à qn** to ask sb for money; **l'enfant réclame ses parents** the child is calling for his/her parents; **il va finir par te r. une augmentation de salaire** he'll end up asking you for a pay rise

2 *(exiger)* *(secours, aide, intervention, réformes etc)* to demand; **il réclame son argent** he wants his money back; **r. des dommages et intérêts** to claim damages; **r. le paiement** to demand payment; **mon client me réclame les épreuves pour mardi** my customer's clamouring to have the proofs back by Tuesday; **les enfants réclament leur dessert** the children are clamouring for *or* demanding their dessert; **Monsieur le Président, je réclame la parole** Mr President, may I say something?; **il me le réclame sans cesse** he keeps nagging me about it; **je ne fais que r. mon dû** I am merely claiming what is mine; **r. qch à cor et à cri** to clamour for sth; **r. qn/qch à grands cris** to clamour for sb/sth

3 *(avoir besoin de)* *(soins, attention)* to require, to need

VPR se réclamer **il se réclame de la droite/du mouvement écologiste** he proclaims to be right-wing/an environmentalist; **elle se réclama du Maire pour se faire nommer** she used the Mayor's name to secure her appointment

> Il faut noter que le verbe anglais **to reclaim** est un faux ami. Il signifie **récupérer**.

reclassement [rəklasmɑ̃] **NM 1** *(réarrangement)* reordering, rearrangement **2** *(dans une catégorie différente)* reclassifying, reclassification; *(du personnel)* regrading; **r. professionnel** redeployment

reclasser [rəklase] VT **1** *(réarranger)* to reorder, to rearrange **2** *(dans une catégorie différente)* to reclassify; *(personnel, salaires)* to regrade; *(poste)* to reassign

reclus, -use [rəkly, -yz] ADJ *Rel* cloistered N recluse; *Rel* cloistered monk or f nun; *Fig* recluse; **vivre en r.** to live like a hermit, to live the life of a recluse, to be a recluse

réclusion [reklyzjõ] NF *Jur* imprisonment; **r. criminelle à perpétuité** life imprisonment **2** *(solitude)* seclusion; **il vit dans la r. la plus totale** he lives totally secluded or cut off from the world

réclusionnaire [reklyzjɔnɛr] N *Jur* long-term prisoner

récognition [rekɔɲisjõ] NF *Phil* recognition, identification

recoiffer [rəkwafe] VT **r. qn** to redo sb's hair; *(remettre un chapeau à)* to put sb's hat on again
VPR **se recoiffer 1** to redo one's hair **2** *(remettre son chapeau)* to put one's hat on again

recoin [rəkwɛ̃] NM nook, recess; **maison pleine de recoins** rambling house, house full of nooks and crannies; **les coins et les recoins** the nooks and crannies; **je l'ai cherché dans les coins et les recoins** *ou* **jusque dans les moindres recoins** I've searched high and low or every nook and cranny for it; *Fig* **les recoins de la mémoire** the deepest recesses of the memory

récollection [rekɔleksjõ] NF *Rel* meditation

recoller [rəkɔle] VT *(vase cassé)* to glue or stick back together again; *(timbre)* to stick back on; *(enveloppe)* to stick back down; *Fig* **il recolla son front à la vitre glacée** he pressed his forehead back against the frosted windowpane; *Fig Fam* **r. les morceaux** to put the pieces back together again; *Fam* **r. une amende/mauvaise note à qn** to dole out another fine/bad mark to sb
VI *Sport* **r. au peloton** to catch up with the pack
VPR **se recoller 1** *(d'un os cassé)* to knit; **ça s'est recollé comme par miracle!** as if by magic, it's back in one piece! **2** *Fam* **ils se sont recollés (ensemble)** they're back together again, they've patched things up

récoltable [rekɔltabl] ADJ ready for harvesting

récoltant, -ante [rekɔltɑ̃, -ɑ̃t] ADJ apiculteur r. honey producer; **propriétaire** *ou* **viticulteur r. =** winegrower who harvests his own grapes
N **mis en bouteille chez le r.** estate-bottled

récolte [rekɔlt] NF **1** *Agr (des cultures, fruits, pommes de terre, miel)* harvesting, gathering; **nous avons fait une bonne/mauvaise r.** we got a good/bad crop; **pendant la r.** during harvesting, at harvest time; **faire la r.** to harvest (the crops); **faire la r. du blé** to harvest the wheat; **partir faire les récoltes** to go harvesting; *Fig Fam* **la r. a été bonne** *(au marché aux puces, chez l'antiquaire etc)* I/we/*etc* came back with a good haul **2** *Bot (de spécimens etc)* collecting, gathering **3** *(produits) (céréales, fruits, pommes de terre)* harvest, crop(s); *(miel)* harvest; **une belle r.** a good harvest or crop; **donner une bonne r.** *(d'une terre, une variété de pomme de terre etc)* to give a good crop, to crop well; **rentrer la r.** to get in or bring in or gather in the harvest or the crops; *Fig* **une bonne r. de renseignements** a good crop of information

récolter [rekɔlte] VT *(cultures)* to harvest, to gather in, to get in; *Fig Fam (renseignements, documents etc)* to collect, to gather, to garner; **si tu arrives à r. des informations sur ...** if you should happen to come up with any information on ...; **elle a récolté toute**

une série de mauvaises notes she got a whole crop or series of bad marks; **et finalement, je n'ai récolté que des injures** and in the end, all I got was insults; **il récolte ce qu'il a semé** it's his own fault, he's reaping what he sowed; *Prov* **qui sème le vent récolte la tempête** sow the wind and reap the whirlwind
VPR **se récolter** *Agr* **ces fraises se récoltent en juin** these strawberries are ready for picking or are harvested in June

recombinaison [rəkõbinɛzõ] NF *Biol* recombination

recombinant [rəkõbinɑ̃] ADJ *Biol* recombinant

recombustion [rəkõbystjõ] NF *(des imbrûlés)* recombustion

recommandable [rəkɔmɑ̃dabl] ADJ **1** commendable; **en tous points r., r. à tous égards** *(personne)* highly respectable; **le seul restaurant r. du quartier** the only decent restaurant in the area, the only restaurant in the area worth recommending; **peu r.** *(personne)* undesirable; **hôtel peu r.** disreputable hotel **2** *(que l'on conseille)* advisable

recommandation [rəkɔmɑ̃dasjõ] NF **1** recommendation; **(lettre de) r.** letter of recommendation or of introduction; **avez-vous des recommandations?** do you have references?; **je viens sur la r. d'un de vos clients** I've come on the recommendation of one of your customers, one of your customers recommended you to me; **suivre les recommandations de qn** to follow sb's advice; **maman nous a fait mille recommandations sur la façon de se bien conduire** Mum told us a thousand things to do and not to do **3** *(d'une lettre)* registration

recommandé [rəkɔmɑ̃de] ADJ *(lettre)* registered
NM **un envoi en r.,** *Fam* **un r.** a registered letter/parcel; **envoyer qch en r.** to send sth registered (post)

recommander [rəkɔmɑ̃de] VT **1** *(hôtel, produit, film, employé, médecin etc)* to recommend; **je peux vous la r.** I can recommend her; **est-ce qu'elle est recommandée?** does she have references?; **r. son âme à Dieu** to commend one's soul to God
2 *(conseiller) (discrétion, prudence etc)* to advise, to urge; **r. à qn de faire qch** to advise or urge sb to do sth; **je vous recommande de rester** I advise you to stay, my advice is to stay, I recommend that you stay; **r. la prudence à qn** to advise or urge sb to be cautious; **je te le recommande fortement** I would strongly advise it; **il est recommandé aux clients de réserver à l'avance** customers are advised to book in advance; **il n'est pas recommandé de boire de l'alcool pendant le traitement** it is inadvisable to drink alcohol during the treatment; **ce n'est pas très recommandé** it's not very advisable, I wouldn't recommend it
3 *(lettre, paquet)* to register
4 *(passer une nouvelle commande)* **r. un café/une bière** to order another coffee/beer
VPR **se recommander 1 se r. à Dieu** to commend oneself to God
2 se r. de qn *(pour un emploi)* to give sb or use sb's name as a reference; **il se recommande du docteur Martin** he's been referred by Dr Martin
3 se r. par qch to have sth in one's favour; **elle se recommande par son efficacité** efficiency is a strong point in her favour; **ce restaurant se recommande par ses poissons** the restaurant is to be recommended for its fish

4 *Suisse (insister)* **je me recommande pour que vous fermiez bien la porte à la clé** I'd just like to remind you to make sure you lock the door

recommencement [rəkɔmɑ̃smɑ̃] NM beginning or starting again; *(d'un débat, de pourparlers)* reopening; **la vie est un éternel** *ou* **perpétuel r.** life is a constant succession of new beginnings

recommencer [rəkɔmɑ̃se] (**je recommençai(s); n. recommençons**) VT *(une tâche, un jeu, un récit etc)* to start or begin again, *Fml* to recommence; **r. sa vie** to make a new or fresh start (in life), to start life afresh; **r. à faire qch** to start or begin to do or doing sth again; **tout est à r.** we'll have to start or begin all over again; *Fam* we'll have to go back to square one; **si c'était à r., j'accepterais le poste en Martinique** if I could do it all over again, I'd accept the job in Martinique
VI *(d'une personne)* to start or begin again, to start afresh, *Am* to start over; *(d'une guerre, de la pluie)* to start (up) again; *(de combats)* to break out again; **ça fait trois fois que je recommence** I've started this three times; **ne recommencez pas!** don't do it again!; **le voilà qui recommence!** he's at it again!; **je vous garantis qu'il ne recommencera pas de sitôt** I can guarantee he won't do that again in a hurry; **qui parle? alors, ça recommence?** who's talking? that chatter's not going to start again, is it?; **l'orage a recommencé en fin de soirée** there was another storm late in the evening; **il recommence à pleuvoir** it's starting to rain again

recommercialiser [rəkɔmɛrsjalize] VT to remarket

récompense [rekõpɑ̃s] NF reward; **mille euros de r.** a thousand euro reward; **et en r. elle a reçu ...** and as a reward or in reward or in return she was given ...; **on ne peut pas les laisser sans r.** they can't go unrewarded; **en r. de vos services** as a reward for your services, in return for your services; **en r. de votre bonté** in return for your kindness, to repay you for your kindness; **c'est une modeste r. pour votre bonté** it's a small recompense or return for your kindness; **et c'était là la r. de mes efforts** and that was how you/he/*etc* repaid me, and that was all the thanks I got; **la juste r. de ses crimes** just retribution for his/her crimes

récompenser [rekõpɑ̃se] VT to reward; **r. qn de qch** to reward sb for sth; **r. qn de sa bonté** to repay sb for their kindness; **son travail a été bien récompensé** his/her work was well or amply rewarded; *Iron* **me voilà récompensé d'avoir tant travaillé** that's all the thanks I get for working so hard; **film récompensé au Festival de Venise** film that won an award at the Venice Film Festival

recomposer [rəkõpoze] VT **1** *Chimie (éléments)* to recompose, to recombine **2** *Typ (texte)* to reset **3** *Tél (numéro)* to redial

recomposition [rəkõpozisjõ] NF **1** *Chimie* recombining **2** *Typ* resetting **3** *Tél* redialling, *Am* redialing

recompter [rəkõte] VT to recount, to count again

reconcevoir [rəkõs(ə)vwar] VT to redesign

réconciliateur, -trice [rekõsiljatœr, -tris] N reconciler

réconciliation [rekõsiljasjõ] NF reconciliation; **amener une r. entre deux personnes** to bring about a reconciliation or to heal the breach between two people; **en signe de r.** as a sign of reconciliation; **pour sceller notre r.** to show that we've made it up

réconcilier [rekõsilje] VT *(personnes, aspects différents d'une personnalité etc)* to reconcile; **r. qn avec ses parents** to reconcile sb with his/her parents, to heal the breach between sb and his/her parents; **ce voyage m'a réconcilié avec la marche** the trip renewed my appetite for walking; **ça m'a réconcilié avec la vie** it renewed my appetite for life, it made life seem worth living again; **la famille s'en trouva réconciliée** it brought the family together again; **réconcilié avec lui-même** at peace with himself

VPR se réconcilier to be or become reconciled; **se r. avec qn** to be reconciled with sb, to make it up or be friends again with sb, to patch things up with sb; **se r. avec soi-même** to be or feel at peace with oneself; **se r. avec la vie** to renew one's appetite for life, to find life worth living again; **se r. avec le sport/son travail** to renew one's appetite for sport/one's job; **c'est ainsi que j'ai pu me r. avec la vie/le sport** that's what made life/sport seem worthwhile again

> Do not confuse with **concilier**.

reconditionner [rəkɔ̃disjɔne] VT to repackage

reconductible [rəkɔ̃dyktibl] ADJ (contrat, bail) renewable

reconduction [rəkɔ̃dyksjɔ̃] NF **1** Jur (d'un bail, contrat) renewal; **r. tacite** (d'un accord) tacit renewal **2** Admin, Pol (de budget, mesures, politique etc) continuation; **voter la r. de la grève** to vote for the continuation of the strike or for continued strike action or for the strike to continue

reconduire [rəkɔ̃dɥir] VT (conj like conduire) **1 r. qn** (à son hôtel etc) (en voiture) to take or drive sb back; (à pied) to see or walk sb back; (chez lui) (en voiture) to drive or take sb home; (à pied) to see or walk sb home; **r. qn** (jusqu'à la porte) to see or show sb out, to see or walk sb to the door; **r. qn à la frontière** to escort sb back over the border **2** (renouveler) (bail, contrat etc) to renew; Admin, Pol (mesure temporaire, politique, grève) to continue

reconfiguration [rəkɔ̃figyrasjɔ̃] NF **1** (d'une société) reengineering **2** Ordinat reconfiguration

reconfigurer [rəkɔ̃figyre] VT Ordinat to reconfigure

reconfirmation [rəkɔ̃firmasjɔ̃] NF reconfirmation

réconfort [rekɔ̃fɔr] NM comfort, reassurance; **le r. qu'apporte la religion** the comfort or consolation that religion brings; **le r. procuré par ces paroles** the comfort that these words brought; **avoir besoin de r.** to need cheering up; **paroles de r.** words of comfort, comforting or reassuring words; **vous m'êtes toujours d'un grand r.** you're a great comfort to me

réconfortant [rekɔ̃fɔrtɑ̃] ADJ **1** (physiquement) (médicament, traitement) tonic **2** (moralement) (personne, attitude) comforting; (paroles, nouvelle) comforting, cheering, cheery; **c'est une idée peu réconfortante** it's not a very comforting idea, there's not much comfort in that idea

réconforter [rekɔ̃fɔrte] VT **1** (physiquement) to build up; **cette soupe te réconfortera** the soup will help build you or your strength up **2** (moralement) to comfort; **ces paroles l'ont réconforté** these words brought him some comfort; **elle a su nous r. dans ces moments difficiles** she was a great comfort to us in those difficult times; **cela me réconforte de voir que je ne suis pas la seule** it cheers me up or I'm glad to see I'm not the only one
VPR se réconforter to cheer oneself up

reconnaissable [rəkɔnesabl] ADJ (parfum, odeur, style, allure etc) recognizable (à by, from); **r. entre tous** (style, personne etc) un-

mistakable; **c'est difficilement r. sur la photo** it's hardly or scarcely recognizable in the photo, it's hard to recognize in the photo; **il n'est plus r.** he's unrecognizable, you wouldn't recognize or know him, he's changed beyond all recognition

reconnaissance [rəkɔnesɑ̃s] NF **1** (action de reconnaître) recognition; **je porterai un canotier, ce sera notre signe de r.** I'll be wearing a boater, that's how you'll recognize me; **de la main, elle lui fit un signe de r.** she waved to show she'd seen him; Mil **signal de r.** recognition signal
2 (acte formel) (d'une promesse, dette, d'un enfant né hors mariage etc) acknowledgement; (d'un gouvernement) recognition, acknowledgement; (d'une erreur) acknowledgement, admission; **en r. de son courage** in recognition of his courage
3 (gratitude) gratitude; **r. de ou pour qch** gratitude or thankfulness for sth; **témoigner de la r. à qn** to show gratitude to sb; **je n'éprouve ou je n'ai aucune r. pour eux** I feel no gratitude towards them; **avoir une profonde r. pour qch** to be deeply grateful or thankful for sth; **en r. de votre invitation** in gratitude for your invitation; **avec r.** gratefully; **parler de qch avec r.** to speak of sth with gratitude; Fam **c'est la r. du ventre** that's cupboard love
4 Com note of hand, promissory note; **r. (de dépôt de gage)** pawn ticket
5 Mil reconnaissance, reconnoitring, Fam recce; **détachement/avion de r.** reconnaissance party/aircraft; **faire une r. rapide du village** to do a quick reconnaissance or Fam recce of the village; **être en r.** to be on (a) reconnaissance, to be reconnoitring; **partir en r.** to go off on reconnaissance; Fig Fam **je pars en r.** I'll go and check things out; Fam **j'y suis allé en r.** I went to check it out
6 (d'un terrain, d'un site) inspection, exploration, examination; Min prospecting; (topographie) surveying, charting; **levé de r.** exploratory survey
▸▸ **r. de dette** IOU, promissory note; Ordinat **r. de l'écriture manuscrite** handwriting recognition; Ordinat **r. optique des caractères** optical character recognition, OCR; Ordinat **r. de la parole, r. vocale** speech recognition

reconnaissant [rəkɔnesɑ̃] ADJ grateful; **être r. à qn de qch/de faire qch** to be grateful to sb for sth/for doing sth; **je vous en suis très r.** I'm very grateful, I'm in your debt; **je vous serais r. de ne plus en parler** I'd thank you not to mention it again, I'd be grateful if you didn't mention it again; Fml **votre fils r.** (dans une lettre) your grateful or loving or devoted son

reconnaître [rəkɔnɛtr] (conj like connaître) VT **1** (identifier) (personne, lieu, air) to recognize; **r. qn à sa démarche** to recognize or know or tell sb by his/her walk; **j'ai eu beaucoup de mal à le r.** I hardly knew or recognized him; **je la reconnaîtrais n'importe où** I'd know or recognize her anywhere; **est-ce que vous le reconnaîtriez?** would you know him again?, would you recognize him?; **ils se ressemblent tant qu'on ne peut les r.** they're so alike that you can't tell them apart; **je te reconnais bien là!** that's just like you!, that's you all over!
2 Naut **r. la terre** to sight land
3 (admettre) (vérité, droit, gouvernement) to recognize, to acknowledge; (erreur, faute) to acknowledge, to admit; Jur (enfant) to acknowledge, to own; **r. les qualités de qn** to acknowledge sb's qualities; **tu peux au moins lui r. cette qualité** you could at least acknowledge that or Fam at least give him/her that; **r. qn pour chef** to acknowledge sb as leader; **r. qch comme vrai** to acknowledge

the truth of sth; **reconnu comme (étant) le plus grand chef de France** recognized as the or acknowledged to be the greatest chef in France; **r. qu'on s'est trompé, r. s'être trompé** to admit or acknowledge that one was mistaken; **je suis allée trop vite, je le reconnais** I went too fast, I admit it
4 Mil etc (examiner) (position etc) to reconnoitre, to make a reconnaissance of; (terrain) to explore
5 Min to prospect
VPR se reconnaître 1 (soi-même) to recognize oneself; **je ne me reconnais pas sur cette photo** I don't recognize myself in that photo; **se r. vaincu/coupable** to acknowledge defeat/one's guilt; **elle se reconnaît tout à fait dans son rôle** she recognizes herself in the part
2 (se retrouver) to find one's way about or around; **ce n'est pas facile de se r. dans Tokyo** it's not easy to find your way about or to get your bearings in Tokyo; **je n'arrive plus à m'y r.** I can't find my way around any more; Fig I'm lost, I'm confused; Fig **c'est à ne pas s'y r.** it's all very confusing
3 gaz qui se reconnaît à son odeur gas recognizable by its smell; **un vrai gentleman se reconnaît à ...** you can tell a real gentleman by ...
4 (entre personnes) to recognize or know each other

reconnecter (se) [sərəkɔnɛkte] VPR to reconnect

reconquérir [rəkɔ̃kerir] VT (conj like conquérir) (province, royaume, pays) to reconquer; (territoire, liberté, droit) to win back, to regain, to recover; (l'estime, l'amitié de qn) to win back, to regain; **r. une femme/un homme** to get or win a woman/man back

reconquête [rəkɔ̃kɛt] NF (d'un royaume) reconquest; (d'un droit, de la liberté) recovery, winning back

reconsidérer [rəkɔ̃sidere] VT (conj like considérer) to reconsider

reconstituant [rəkɔ̃stitɥɑ̃] ADJ Méd tonic; **c'est un aliment r.** it's nourishing
NM pick-me-up, tonic

reconstituer [rəkɔ̃stitɥe] VT (armée, gouvernement) to reconstitute; (société, parti) to revive; (bâtiment abîmé, quartier) to restore; (d'un archéologue) (vase, crâne) to piece or put back together; (forces) to build up; (crime) to reconstruct; (faits) to piece together; (fortune) to restore, to build up again; **deux steaks hachés reconstitués** two beef patties; **r. des stocks** to replenish stocks, to restock

reconstitution [rəkɔ̃stitysjɔ̃] NF (d'un gouvernement) reconstitution; (d'une société, d'un parti) revival; (d'un bâtiment, d'une danse d'époque etc) restoration; (d'un crime, d'une bataille) reconstruction; Admin **r. de carrière** employment record or history; **r. historique** (spectacle) historical reconstruction; **la r. du squelette/vase sera bientôt complète** the task of putting or piecing the skeleton/vase back together will soon be completed

reconstruction [rəkɔ̃stryksjɔ̃] NF (d'une ville), Fig (d'un parti) reconstruction, rebuilding

reconstruire [rəkɔ̃strɥir] VT (conj like construire) (édifice, structure) to reconstruct, to rebuild; **r. le monde** to change the world, Fam to put the world to rights; **r. sa vie** to put one's life back together, to rebuild one's life; **essayons de r. notre bonheur passé** let's try to be happy again the way we used to be

reconventionnel, -elle [rəkɔ̃vɑ̃sjɔnɛl] ADJ Jur **demande reconventionnelle** counterclaim

reconversion [rəkɔ̃vɛrsjɔ̃] NF **1** (d'une

usine) conversion; **r. économique** economic restructuring; **r. industrielle** industrial redeployment **2** *(du personnel)* retraining

reconvertir [rəkɔ̃vɛrtir] **VT 1** *(usine)* to convert **2** *(personnel)* to retrain
VPR se reconvertir *(se recycler)* to retrain; **se r. dans** *(industrie)* to move into, to diversify into; **se r. dans la publicité** *(d'une personne)* to start a new career in advertising; **ils se sont reconvertis dans le bâtiment** *(d'une entreprise)* they changed over *or* converted to construction work

recopier [rəkɔpje] **VT** *(conj like copier)* **1** *(en double) (document, information etc)* to recopy, to take another copy of; *Ordinat* to recopy; *Ordinat* **r. à l'identique** to replicate **2** *(au propre) (brouillon, devoir, manuscrit)* to copy out, to make a fair *or* clean copy of

record [rəkɔr] **NM** *Sport etc* record; **établir un r.** to set a record; **détenir le r.** to hold the record, to be the record holder; **battre le r.** to break *or* beat the record; **une performance qui bat tous les records** a record-breaking performance; *Fig* **il bat tous les records d'impolitesse, son impolitesse bat tous les records** he takes some beating when it comes to rudeness
ADJ INV *(chiffre, vitesse etc)* record; **dans** *ou* **en un temps r.** in record time; **attirer une affluence r.** to draw record crowds

recorder [rəkɔrde] **VT** *(raquette)* to restring

recordman, *pl* **recordmen** [rəkɔr(d)man, -mɛn] **NM** *(men's)* record holder

recordwoman, *pl* **recordwomen** [rəkɔr(d)-wuman, -mɛn] **NF** (women's) record holder

recors [rəkɔr] **NM** *Jur Arch Fam* bailiff's man; **les r. de la justice** the minions of the law

recouche [rəkuʃ] **NF** *(dans un hôtel)* stay-(over); **liste des clients en r.** stay list

recoucher [rəkuʃe] **VT 1** *(au lit)* **r. qn** to put sb to bed again **2** *(bouteille)* to lay down again
VI *Fam* **r. avec qn** to sleep with sb again
VPR se recoucher to go back to bed

recoudre [rəkudr] **VT** *(conj like coudre)* to sew again; *(bouton)* to sew on again, to sew back on; *(déchirure, blessure)* to sew *or* stitch up; *Fam* **il a fallu me r.** they had to stitch me up

recoupement [rəkupmɑ̃] **NM** *(de renseignements)* crosschecking; **faire un** *ou* **le r.** to crosscheck, to do a crosscheck; **je l'ai compris par r.** I found out by crosschecking *or* by doing a crosscheck

recouper [rəkupe] **VT 1** *(couper à nouveau) (vêtement)* to recut; **je vous recoupe une tranche de gâteau?** shall I cut you another slice *or* piece of cake? **2** *(vins etc)* to (re)blend **3** *(faire coïncider)* to confirm, to support; **r. des témoignages** to crosscheck testimony **4** *Cartes* to reshuffle
VPR se recouper *(de cercles)* to intersect again; *Fig (de témoignages, de résultats)* to tally, to agree

recouponnement [rəkuponmɑ̃] **NM** *Bourse* renewal of coupons

recouponner [rəkupɔne] **VT** *Bourse* to renew the coupons of

recourbé [rəkurbe] **ADJ** bent, curved; *(bec)* curved, hooked; **nez r.** hook nose

recourber [rəkurbe] **VT** to bend
VPR se recourber to bend, to curve

recourir [rəkurir] *(conj like courir)* **VI 1** *(courir de nouveau)* to run again; **r. jusque chez soi** to run back home; *Sport* **elle n'a pas recouru depuis les Jeux olympiques** she hasn't run since the Olympic Games **2** *(employer)* **r. à (l'aide de) qn** to appeal to sb for help, to turn to sb; **r. à qch** to use *or Fml* have recourse to sth; **r. à la violence** to resort to violence; **r. à la justice** to take legal proceedings **3** *Jur* **r. en cassation** to appeal

VT *Sport* to rerun, to run again; **je recourrai le marathon l'an prochain** I'll be running in the marathon again next year

recours [rəkur] **NM 1** recourse, resort; **c'est son seul r.** it's his/her only option *or* recourse; **en dernier r.** as a last resort; **c'est sans r.** there's nothing else for it, there's no other option; **avoir r. à qn** to go *or* turn to sb; **avoir r. à un spécialiste/un avocat** to consult *or* see *or* go to a specialist/a lawyer; **avoir r. à** *(la violence)* to resort to; *(une agence immobilière)* to go to, to use **2** *Jur* **r. en cassation** appeal; **r. en grâce** petition for reprieve; **s'assurer contre le r. des tiers** to insure against a third party claim; **r. contentieux** litigation, legal recourse; **r. contre l'endosseur** recourse against the endorser; *Can* **r. collectif** class action

recouvrable [rəkuvrabl] **ADJ** *(dette, facture)* recoverable, collectable; *(impôt)* collectable, collectible

recouvrement¹ [rəkuvrəmɑ̃] **NM 1** *(des dettes, d'une facture)* recovery, collection; *(de l'impôt)* collection; **r. de créances** debt collection; **r. d'impôts** tax collection; **r. du coût total** full cost recovery; **recouvrements outstanding debts 2** *Vieilli (de la santé, des forces etc)* recovery

recouvrement² **NM 1** *(action de recouvrir)* re-covering; *(pour la première fois)* covering; **tôle de r.** covering plate **2** *(fait de chevaucher)* (over)lapping; *(surface recouverte)* overlap; **à r.** lapped, lap-jointed; **en r.** overlapping; **planches à r.** weatherboarding **3** *Tech (ce qui couvre)* cover; *Ordinat* overlay

recouvrer [rəkuvre] **VT 1** *(ses biens, son argent)* to recover, to retrieve, to get back; *(santé, vue)* to recover, to get back; *(forces, liberté)* to regain, to get back; *(courage, enthousiasme)* to get back **2** *(percevoir) (dettes, impôts)* to recover, to collect; **créances à r.** outstanding debts

recouvrir [rəkuvrir] *(conj like couvrir)* **VT 1** *(couvrir de nouveau) (cahier, toit)* to re-cover; *(enfant)* to cover up again **2** *(couvrir complètement)* to cover **(de** in, with) **3** *(tapisser)* to cover **(de** with); **fauteuil recouvert de velours** armchair covered in velvet **4** *(masquer) (défauts)*, *Fig (angoisse, égoïsme)* to cover up, to hide **5** *(englober)* to cover **6** *Tech (ardoises etc)* to (over)lap
VPR se recouvrir *(du ciel)* to cloud over (again); **le champ s'est recouvert d'eau** the field was covered with *or* in water

recracher [rəkraʃe] **VT** *(bonbon, vin etc)* to spit out; **on lui a fait r. la pièce qu'il avait avalée** they made him bring up the coin he had swallowed
VI to spit again

récré [rekre] **NF** *Scol Fam* break, *Am* recess; *(pour les plus jeunes)* playtime; **pendant la r., à la r.** during *or* at break/playtime

récréatif, -ive [rekreatif, -iv] **ADJ** *(activité)* entertaining, amusing; **lecture récréative** light reading; **séance récréative** *(à la maternelle)* playtime

récréation [rekreasjɔ̃] **NF 1** *(détente)* recreation, amusement, relaxation; **le tricot/la télé, c'est ma r.** knitting/watching TV is how I relax, I relax by knitting/watching TV **2** *Scol* recreation, break, *Am* recess; *(pour les plus jeunes)* playtime; **cour de r.** playground; **pendant la r., à la r.** during *or* at break/playtime

recréer [rəkree] **VT** *(conditions, climat, œuvre etc)* to re-create

recrépir [rəkrepir] **VT** *(mur)* to renew the roughcast of

recrépissage [rəkrepisaʒ] **NM** renewal of the roughcast

recreuser [rəkrøze] **VT** *(trou)* to dig again; *Fig (question etc)* to dig deeper *or* go deeper into

récrier (se) [sərekrije] **VPR** *(conj like crier)* *(de mécontents)* to protest, to complain (**contre** about); *(de la meute)* to be in full cry

récriminateur, -trice [rekriminatœr, -tris] **ADJ** recriminatory

récrimination [rekriminasjɔ̃] **NF** recrimination

récriminer [rekrimine] **VI** to make recriminations; **r. contre qn/qch** to make representations about sb/sth

récrire [rekrir] *(conj like écrire)* = **réécrire**

récriture [rekrityr] **NF** rewriting

recroquevillé [rəkrɔkvije] **ADJ 1 r. dans un fauteuil** curled up in an armchair **2** *(feuille, papier etc)* shrivelled, curled up

recroqueviller (se) [sərəkrɔkvije] **VPR 1** *(d'une personne)* to curl up **2** *(d'une feuille)* to shrivel (up), to curl up

recru [rəkry] **ADJ** *Litt* **r. (de fatigue)** tired out, worn out; *Arch* **être r. d'amour** to be replete with love

recrudescence [rəkrydesɑ̃s] **NF** *(du feu, d'une épidémie)* renewed *or* fresh outbreak; *(de la délinquance)* upsurge; **la r. de la violence/des bombardements** the renewed violence/bombing

recrudescent [rəkrydesɑ̃] **ADJ** *Litt* fast-growing

recrue [rəkry] **NF** *(dans un parti, dans une équipe)*, *Mil* recruit; *Can Sport* rookie; **le parti fait de nouvelles recrues** the party is gaining new recruits; **jeune r.** raw recruit

recrutement [rəkrytmɑ̃] **NM** *(de soldats, de personnel etc)* recruiting, recruitment; **nous sommes en plein r.** we are recruiting (staff) at the moment, we are taking on staff at the moment; *Pol* **campagne de r.** recruitment *or* membership drive; **agence de r.** recruiting *or* recruitment agency

recruter [rəkryte] **VT** *(soldats, employés)* to recruit; *(supporters)* to enlist, to recruit (**dans** from); **nous recrutons un secrétaire** we are looking for a secretary, we have a vacancy for a secretary; **notre directeur a été recruté par un chasseur de têtes** our director was headhunted
VI to recruit; **r. par voie de concours** to recruit by competition
VPR se recruter *(d'employés)* to be recruited (**parmi** from among); *(de supporters)* to be enlisted, to be recruited

recruteur, -euse [rəkrytœr, -øz] **ADJ** *(officier)* recruiting

recta [rɛkta] **ADV** *Fam Vieilli* **payer r.** to pay on the nail; **arriver r.** to arrive punctually *or* on the dot

rectal, -ale, -aux, -ales [rɛktal, -o] **ADJ** *Anat (toucher, température)* rectal; **prendre la température de qn par voie rectale** to take sb's temperature using a rectal thermometer

rectangle [rɛktɑ̃gl] **ADJ** right-angled
NM rectangle; *TV* **r. blanc** 'for adults only' sign; *Ordinat* **r. de sélection** selection box

rectangulaire [rɛktɑ̃gylɛr] **ADJ** rectangular; *Math (coordonnées)* right-angled

recteur, -trice [rɛktœr, -tris] **NM** *Rel* rector; *Scol* chief education officer
ADJ *Orn* **penne rectrice** tail feather
NF *Orn* **rectrice** tail feather

rectificateur [rɛktifikatœr] **NM** *Chimie* rectifier; *Élec (current)* rectifier

rectificatif, -ive [rɛktifikatif, -iv] **ADJ** *(lettre)* of amendment; *(texte, facture)* amended
NM correction

rectification [rɛktifikasjɔ̃] **NF 1** *(d'un docu-*

ment, texte) amendment, correction; *(d'un calcul)* correction, adjustment; *(d'une erreur)* rectification, correction; *(d'un compte, instrument)* adjustment; *(d'une courbe, frontière)* adjustment, rectification; *(d'un alignement)* straightening; **je voudrais faire** *ou* **apporter une r.** I'd like to make a correction **2** *Chimie (de l'alcool, du pétrole)* rectifying, redistilling **3** *Élec (du courant)* rectification

rectifier [rɛktifje] **VT 1** *(document, texte)* to amend, to correct; *(calcul)* to correct, to adjust; *(erreur)* to rectify, to correct, to put right; *(prix, instrument)* to adjust; *(compte)* to amend, to adjust; *(frontière, courbe)* to rectify, to adjust; *(alignement)* to straighten; *Mil* **r. l'alignement** to dress the ranks; **r. le tir** *Mil* to adjust the range; *Fig* to take a slightly different tack; **'il est banquier', rectifia-t-elle** 'he's a banker', she corrected him/me/*etc* **2** *Chimie (alcool, pétrole)* to rectify, to redistil **3** *Élec (courant)* to rectify **4** *Arg (tuer)* **r. qn** to bump sb off; **se faire r.** to get bumped off

rectiligne [rɛktiliɲ] **ADJ** *(mouvement)* in a straight line; *(figure)* rectilinear; *(avenue)* straight

rectilinéaire [rɛktilineɛr] **ADJ** *Phot (objectif)* rectilinear

rectitude [rɛktityd] **NF 1** *(d'une ligne)* straightness **2** *Fig (honnêteté)* rectitude, uprightness, integrity; *(d'un jugement, du raisonnement)* correctness, soundness; **agir avec r.** to behave correctly *or* with integrity

recto [rɛkto] **NM** *(d'effet)* face; *(d'une feuille de papier)* front, face, *Spéc* recto; **cinq feuilles r. verso** five sheets written on both sides; **voir au r.** see over; *Typ* **impression r.-verso** double-sided printing

rectorat [rɛktɔra] **NM** *Admin* rectorship, rectorate

rectum [rɛktɔm] **NM** *Anat* rectum; **cancer du r.** rectal cancer, cancer of the rectum

reçu, -ue [rəsy] **ADJ** *(usages)* accepted, recognized; *(opinion)* received; **idées reçues** preconceived ideas; **cela fait partie des usages reçus** it's standard *or* accepted practice **NM** *(pour des marchandises, de l'argent)* receipt; **je vous fais un r.?** would you like a receipt?; **r. d'espèces** cash receipt; **r. libératoire** receipt in full discharge

N *(à un examen)* successful candidate; **il n'y a que dix reçus** only ten people passed

recueil [rəkœj] **NM** *(de poèmes, chansons, recettes etc)* collection, compilation; *(de lois)* compendium, body; **r. de morceaux choisis** selection, anthology; **r. des données** data collection

recueillement [rəkœjmɑ̃] **NM** meditation, contemplation; *(gravité)* gravity; **avec r.** contemplatively; **pensons avec r. à cet homme à qui nous devons tant de choses** let us meditate a little about this man to whom we owe so much

recueilli [rəkœji] **ADJ** meditative, contemplative; *(grave)* grave, sober

recueillir [rəkœjir] *(conj like* **cueillir***)* **VT 1** *(récolter) (argent, fonds)* to collect; *(anecdotes, renseignements, miel etc)* to collect, to gather; *(pour conserver)* to collect, to make a collection of; *(eau de pluie)* to collect, to catch; *(sous-produits)* to recover; *(votes)* to win, to collect; *(louanges)* to win, to attract; *(déposition)* to take; *Journ* **r. le témoignage des passants** to listen to what the passers-by have to say; *Journ* **propos recueillis par Daniel Renault** (story by) Daniel Renault; **r. le fruit de ses travaux** to reap the fruit of one's labours; **r. un héritage** to inherit; **r. des données** to collect data **2** *(recevoir)* **r. qn** to take sb in, to give sb a home

VPR **se recueillir** to meditate; **se r. sur la tombe d'un ami** to meditate beside a friend's

grave; **se r. pour prier** to gather one's thoughts before praying

recuire [rəkɥir] **VT** *(conj like* **cuire***)* **1 il faut r. ce steak** this steak needs to be cooked longer **2** *(acier)* to anneal, to temper; *(verre)* to anneal

recuisson [rəkɥisɔ̃] **NF** *(de l'acier)* annealing, tempering; *(du verre)* annealing

recuit [rəkɥi] **NM** *(de l'acier)* annealing, tempering; *(du verre)* annealing

recul [rəkyl] **NM 1** *(action) (d'un glacier, d'une armée)* retreat; *(d'un cheval)* backing; *(d'un levier de commande)* backward movement, return; *(d'un canon)* recoil; *(d'un fusil)* recoil, kick; *(baisse) (des valeurs, des exportations)* drop *(* **de** *in)*; **il eut un brusque mouvement de r.** he recoiled, he started back; **le r. de la mortalité** the downturn *or* decline in the death rate; *Aut* **phare de r.** reversing light **2** *(distance)* **on n'a pas assez de r. dans cette galerie** there's not enough room in this gallery to get a decent look at the pictures; **il faut un certain r. pour juger le tableau** you need to stand back a bit to judge the painting; **manquer de r.** to be too close for a proper view; *Fig* **je manque de r. pour juger** I'm too closely involved *or* too close to be able to judge; *Fig* **considérer la situation avec r.** to consider the situation with detachment; *Fig* **avec le r. (du temps), la situation ne semble pas si désespérée** in retrospect *or* with hindsight *or* looking back (on it), the situation doesn't seem so desperate; *Fig* **tu devrais prendre du r.** you ought to stand back a bit from things; *Fig* **es-tu sûr d'avoir assez de r. pour juger?** are you sure you're objective enough to judge?

reculade [rəkylad] **NF** *(d'une armée)* retreat; *Fig Péj* climbdown

reculé [rəkyle] **ADJ** *(endroit)* remote, distant; *(époque)* remote

reculer [rəkyle] **VI 1** *(aller en arrière) (d'une personne)* to move back, to step back, to draw back; *(d'un glacier, des eaux)* to recede; *Mil* to fall back, to retreat; *(d'une épidémie)* to lose ground; *(du taux de mortalité, natalité, chômage etc)* to decline; *(du cours de Bourse)* to drop; *(d'un fusil, canon)* to recoil; *(d'un automobiliste, d'une voiture)* to reverse; *Ordinat* to backspace; **elle recula de dégoût** she recoiled *or* drew back in disgust; **reculez ou je tire!** back off *or* get back or I'll shoot!; **faire r. un cheval** to back a horse; **la police a fait r. la foule** the police moved *or* pushed the crowd back; *Fig* **faire r. la maladie** to get the disease under control; **le yen recule par rapport au dollar** the yen is falling against the dollar; **faire r. la pauvreté** to reduce (the level of) poverty; *Fig Fam* **r. pour mieux sauter** to put off the evil day

2 *Fig (renoncer)* to give in; **r. devant des menaces** to give way in the face of threats; **r. devant une obligation** to shirk an obligation; **il ne recule devant rien** nothing daunts him; **elle ne recule devant rien pour le satisfaire** she'll do anything to satisfy him; **comme d'habitude, elle recule devant lui** as usual, she gave in *or* gave way to him; **il est trop tard pour r.** it's too late to draw back *or* pull out; **cela en a fait r. plus d'un** that's put off *or* daunted more than one person; **r. à l'idée de faire qch** to recoil at the idea of doing sth

VT 1 *(chaise)* to move back; *(cheval)* to back; *(voiture)* to back (up), to reverse; *Fig* **r. les frontières de la science** to push *or* roll back the frontiers of science

2 *(remettre) (paiement, décision)* to postpone, to defer, to put off; **r. le moment de décider** to put off (making) a decision

VPR **se reculer** to stand *or* step *or* move *or* draw back

reculons (à) [ar(ə)kylɔ̃] **ADV** **marcher** *ou* **al-**

ler à r. to walk backwards; *Fig* **aller à r.** to go *or* move backwards; **sortir à r.** to back out; *Fig Fam* **aller au travail à r.** to force oneself to go to work

récup [rekyp] **NF** *Fam (abrév* **récupération***)* **1 de la r.** *(des matériaux de récupération)* scrap **2** *(récupération idéologique)* exploitation

récupérable [rekyperabl] **ADJ** *(déchets)* recoverable; **ferraille r.** scrap metal; **les heures supplémentaires sont récupérables** additional time off may be taken in lieu of overtime pay; **ce garçon-là est r./n'est pas r.** there's hope for that boy/that boy's a hopeless case

récupérateur [rekyperatœr] **NM** *Ind* regenerator, recuperator

récupération [rekyperasjɔ̃] **NF 1** *(de dette, livre, vaisseau spatial, TVA etc)* recovery; **la r. des heures supplémentaires** time off in lieu (of overtime pay); **deux jours de r. pour les heures supplémentaires que j'ai faites** two days off to make up for the overtime I've done

2 *Ind (de déchets de fabrication)* recovery, salvage; **r. de chaleur** heat recovery

3 *(de sportif)* recovery

4 *Pol Péj* hijacking; **la r. d'une manifestation par un parti politique** the hijacking of a demonstration by a political party; **c'est de la r.** it's sheer exploitation

5 *Ordinat* **r. de données** data recovery

récupérer [rekypere] *(* **je récupère, n. récupérons; je récupérerai***)* **VT 1** *(objet prêté ou perdu) (livre etc)* to get back, to retrieve, to recover; *(bagages, TVA)* to retrieve, to reclaim; *Ordinat (fichier, données)* to retrieve; *Aviat (boîte noire)* to recover, to retrieve; *Fam (personne)* to collect, to pick up; **elle est passée r. ses affaires** she dropped by to pick up her things; **r. ses forces** to recover (one's strength), to regain one's strength

2 *(recycler) (déchets de fabrication)* to recover, to salvage; *(vieux papiers, canettes etc)* to salvage; *Fig Fam (employé)* to find alternative employment for; *(délinquant)* to rehabilitate; **r. de la ferraille** to collect scrap; **je ne jette rien, je récupère tout** I don't throw anything away, I save everything

3 *Pol Péj (personne, mouvement)* to co-opt, to hijack, to use for one's own ends; *(proposition)* to hijack, to take over; **se faire r.** to be co-opted *or* hijacked

4 *Fin (pertes)* to recoup, to retrieve; *Fin* **r. ses débours** to recoup one's expenditure; *Admin* **r. des heures supplémentaires (en prenant des congés)** to take time off in lieu

VI *(après une maladie, après un choc)* to recover; **j'ai besoin de r.** *(prendre des vacances)* I need to get my breath back, I need to relax; **j'ai de plus en plus de mal à r.** *(reprendre mon souffle)* it takes me longer and longer to get my breath back

récurage [rekyraʒ] **NM** scouring

récurer [rekyre] **VT** *(casseroles, évier, baignoire etc)* to scour; **poudre/tampon à r.** scouring powder/pad

récurrence [rekyrɑ̃s] **NF** recurrence

récurrent [rekyrɑ̃] **ADJ** *Anat (nerf, veine)* recurrent; *(thème, son, mot)* recurrent, recurring; *Méd (fièvre)* recurrent; *Math (série)* recurrent; *Ordinat* **processus r.** recursive process

récusable [rekyzabl] **ADJ** *Jur (juré, témoin)* challengeable; *(témoignage)* impugnable; **son témoignage n'est pas r.** it will be impossible to challenge his/her testimony; **c'est une affirmation r.** that statement is open to challenge

récusation [rekyzasjɔ̃] **NF** *(d'une thèse), Jur (d'un témoin)* challenging; *Jur* **r. de juré/d'arbitre** challenge of *or* exception to *or* objection to a juryman/an arbitrator; **r. de témoignage** impugnment of evidence

récuser [rekyze] **VT** *(témoin, juré, arbitre etc)* to challenge, to take exception to, to object to; *(témoignage)* to impugn; *(autorité, thèse)* to challenge

VPR se récuser *Jur* to decline to give an opinion, to disclaim competence

recyclable [rəsiklabl] **ADJ** *(papier, verre etc)* recyclable

recyclage [rəsikla3] **NM 1** *(de matériaux)* recycling; *Aut* **r. des gaz d'échappement** exhaust gas recirculation **2** *Ind (du personnel)* retraining

recycler [rəsikle] **VT 1** *(papier, verre etc)* to recycle **2** *Ind (personnel)* to retrain

VPR se recycler *Ind* to retrain; **se r. en comptabilité** to retrain as an accountant

rédacteur, -trice [redaktœr, -tris] **N 1** *(d'un acte, communiqué)* writer, drafter; *(d'un dictionnaire)* editor, compiler **2** *Journ* editor; **r. en chef** editor-in-chief, (chief) editor; **r. en chef actualités** news editor; **r. en chef adjoint** deputy editor; **r. en chef de nuit** night editor; **r. en chef des affaires financières** financial editor, *Br* City editor; **r. en chef sportif** sports editor; **r. en chef technique** production editor; **r. aux actualités** news editor; **r. d'actualités** news writer; **r. artistique** art editor; **r. juridique** legally responsible editor; **r. politique** political editor; **r. sportif** sports editor; **r. permanent** staff writer; **r. pigiste** freelance writer; **r. publicitaire** copy writer

rédaction [redaksjõ] **NF 1** *(d'un acte, communiqué)* drafting, drawing up, writing; *(d'un article de dictionnaire)* compiling, writing; *(révision)* editing; **la r. de cet article a demandé l'intervention de plusieurs rédacteurs** it took several editors to write the article; **r. de questionnaire** questionnaire design **2** *Journ* editing; *(poste)* editorship; *(personnel)* editorial staff; *(département)* editorial department; **(salle de) r.** editorial office; **note de la r.** editor's note; **secrétaire de r.** subeditor **3** *Scol* essay, composition

rédactionnel, -elle [redaksjɔnɛl] **ADJ** *(décision, politique etc)* editorial; **publicité rédactionnelle** advertorial

reddition [redisjõ] **NF 1** *(d'une ville, armée)* surrender; **r. sans conditions** unconditional surrender **2** *Fin (d'un compte)* rendering; **r. de comptes** presentation of accounts for audit, reporting

redécoupage [rədekupa3] **NM r. électoral** redrawing of the electoral boundaries; **procéder à** *ou* **effectuer un r. électoral** to redraw the electoral boundaries

redécouverte [rədekuvɛrt] **NF** rediscovery

redécouvrir [rədekuvrir] **VT** *(conj like* **couvrir**) **1** *(auteur, œuvre)* to rediscover **2** *(enfant)* to take the covers off

redéfinir [rədefinir] **VT** *Ordinat (touche)* to redefine

redéfinissable [rədefinisabl] **ADJ** *Ordinat* redefinable

redemander [rəd(ə)mãde] **VT 1** *(en reposant une question)* to ask again; **r. pourquoi/quand/qui** to ask why/when/who again; **je lui ai redemandé de fermer la porte** I asked him/her again to close the door; **il a dû oublier, il faut le lui r.** he must have forgotten, we'll have to ask him again; **j'ai redemandé qu'il nous écrive un article** I asked again if he would write an article for us; **r. de l'aide à qn** to ask sb again for help
2 *(pour en avoir plus)* **r. de la soupe/des enveloppes** to ask for more soup/envelopes; **r. un litre de vin** to ask for another litre of wine; **je lui ai redemandé un article,** *Fam* **j'ai redemandé qu'il écrive un article** I asked

him for another article, I asked him to write another article; *Fig Fam* **des traducteurs comme ça, on en redemande!** translators like that are much in demand!; **tout le monde en redemande** everybody is clamouring *or* keeps asking for more, they can't get enough of it; *Iron* **elle en redemande** she's still asking for it, she hasn't had enough
3 *(pour récupérer)* **r. qch** to ask for sth back (again); **redemande-le-moi dès que tu en as besoin** ask for it back (again) when you need it, ask me for it when you need it
VI to ask again

redémarrage [rədemara3] **NM 1** *(d'une machine)* starting up again; *Ordinat* reboot, restart; **r. à chaud** warm boot, warm start **2** *(de l'économie, des ventes)* recovery; **attendre le r. de l'économie/des ventes** to wait for the economy/sales to pick up *or* take off again *or* recover

redémarrer [rədemare] **VI** *(d'une voiture)* to start again; *(de l'économie, des ventes)* to recover, to pick up, to take off again; *Ordinat* to reboot; **faire r. une voiture** to start a car again; **faire r. l'économie** to get the economy started again

rédempteur, -trice [redãptœr, -tris] **ADJ** redeeming
N redeemer

rédemption [redãpsjõ] **NF** redemption

redéploiement [rədeplwamã] **NM 1** *Mil (d'une armée)* redeployment **2** *Écon (d'une entreprise, de ressources)* reorganization, restructuring

redéployer [rədeplwaje] **VT 1** *Mil (armée)* to redeploy **2** *Écon (entreprise, ressources)* to reorganize, to restructure
VPR se redéployer *(armée)* to redeploy; *(entreprise)* to reorganize its operations

redescendre [rədesãdr, -dɛ-] *(conj like* **descendre**) **VI** *(du point de vue de qn qui est en haut)* to go down again, to go back down; *(du point de vue de qn qui est en bas)* to come down again, to come back down; *(d'un alpiniste)* to climb back down; *Naut (du vent)* to back; **quand tu redescendras, veux-tu …** *(nous sommes au même étage)* when you go down again *or* go back down, will you …; *(je suis à l'étage inférieur)* when you come down again *or* come back down, will you …; **je suis redescendu en télécabine** *(je viens de le faire)* I came back down by cable car; *(en racontant plus tard)* I went *or* came back down by cable car; **vous pouvez r. par ce sentier-là** you can get back down by that path over there; **r. de voiture** to get out of the car (again)
VT 1 *(apporter) (du point de vue de qn qui est en haut)* to take down again, to take back down; *(du point de vue de qn qui est en bas)* to bring down again, to bring back down; **veux-tu r. la valise?** *(nous sommes au même étage)* will you take the suitcase back down(stairs)?; *(je suis à l'étage inférieur)* will you bring the suitcase back down(stairs)?; **r. des affaires du grenier** to get things back down from the attic
2 *(descendre à nouveau) (escalier, rivière) (du point de vue de qn qui est en haut)* to go down again, to go back down; *(du point de vue de qn qui est en bas)* to come down again, to come back down

redevable [rəd(ə)vabl] **ADJ être r. de qch à qn** to be indebted to sb for sth; **je vous suis r. de cent euros** I still owe you a hundred euros; **être r. de l'impôt** to be liable to tax
N person liable for tax

redevance [rəd(ə)vãs] **NF** *TV* licence fee; *(de téléphone)* rental fee; **r. pétrolière** oil royalty; **redevances d'auteur** author's royalties

redevenir [rədəv(ə)nir] **VI** *(conj like* **devenir**)

r. jeune to become *or* grow young again; **j'ai l'impression d'être redevenu moi-même** I feel like my old self again; **r. silencieux** to fall silent again; **la situation est redevenue normale** the situation is back to normal; **le temps est redevenu maussade** the weather's turned gloomy again

redevoir [rəd(ə)vwar] **VT** *(conj like* **devoir**) *(somme d'argent)* to owe a balance of; *Fam* **il me redoit dix euros** he still owes me ten euros

rédhibition [redibisjõ] **NF** *Com* cancellation of sale due to a material defect

rédhibitoire [redibitwar] **ADJ 1** vice **r.** *Com* material defect; *Jur* redhibitory defect **2** **dans ce métier, être petit est r.** being small is a bar to entering the profession; **des conditions de travail réhibitoires** appalling working conditions; **être d'un égoïsme r.** to be appallingly selfish

rediffuser [rədifyze] **VT** *Radio (émission)* to repeat, to broadcast again; *TV (émission)* to repeat, to show again, to rerun; *(film)* to show again, to rerun

rediffusion [rədifyzjõ] **NF** *Radio (d'une émission)* repeat; *TV, Cin* repeat, rerun

rédiger [redi3e] **VT** *(je rédigeai(s); n. rédigeons)* **1** *(contrat, lettre etc)* to draw up, to draft, to write; *(article)* to write; *Méd (ordonnance)* to write out; *(bon de commande)* to make out; **savoir r.** to be a good writer, to write well; **être bien/mal rédigé** to be well/badly written **2** *Journ (périodique)* to edit

redimensionnable [rədimãsjɔnabl] **ADJ** *Ordinat (fenêtre)* resizable

redimensionnement [rədimãsjɔnmã] **NM** *Ordinat* resizing

redimensionner [rədimãsjɔne] **VT** *Ordinat (fenêtre)* to resize

redingote [rədɛ̃gɔt] **NF** *(pour femmes)* fitted coat; *Vieilli (pour hommes)* redingote

redire [rədir] **VT** *(conj like* **dire**) **1** to say again, to repeat; **tu redis toujours la même chose** you say the same thing over and over again, you constantly repeat yourself; **pourrais-tu lui r. que …?** could you tell him/her again that …?; **je ne le redirai jamais assez** I can never say it often enough; **elle te l'a dit et redit cent fois!** she's told you time and time again!; **elle ne se l'est pas fait r. deux fois** she didn't need asking twice, she didn't need any persuading; **j'espère qu'elle n'ira pas lui r. ce que je lui ai confié** I hope she won't go and tell him *or* repeat to him what I said to her in confidence **2 trouver à r.** to complain; **trouver à r. à qch** to find fault with *or* to pick holes in sth; *Fam* **il n'y a rien à r. à cela** there's nothing wrong with that

redirection [rədirɛksjõ] **NF** *Tél* **r. d'appel** call forwarding, call redirection

rediriger [rədiri3e] **VT** *Tél* to redirect

rediscuter [rədiskyte] **VT** to have further discussions on, to discuss again

redistribuer [rədistribɥe] **VT** to redistribute, to re-allocate; *Cartes* to redeal

redistribution [rədistribysjõ] **NF** redistribution, re-allocation; *(de personnel)* redeployment

redite [rədit] **NF** (useless) repetition

redondance [rədõdãs] **NF** *(de style, mot),* *Ordinat* redundancy; **de nombreuses redondances** a lot of redundancy

redondant [rədõdã] **ADJ** *(mot, style, information),* *Ordinat* redundant

redonner [rədɔne] **VT 1** *(donner de nouveau)* to give again; *Cartes* to redeal; *Théâtre* **on redonne Hamlet** Hamlet is on again; **r. un coup d'œil/un coup de pied à qn** to glance at/kick sb again **2** *(donner davantage de)* to give more of; **tu veux bien m'en r. un peu plus?**

will you give me *or* can I have a bit more? **3** *(pour rendre)* to give back, to return; **r. de l'appétit à qn** to restore sb's appetite, to give sb back his/her appetite; **cela m'a redonné du courage** that put new heart into me *or* restored my courage; **ça m'a redonné envie de voyager** that made me want to travel again; **ce médicament va vous r. des forces** the medicine will give you back your strength *or* will get your strength back; **ces vacances lui ont redonné bonne mine** the holiday put the colour back in his/her cheeks

vi *Littr* **r. dans des excès** to fall back into excess; **r. dans l'exagération** to exaggerate again

redorer [rədɔre] vt *Tech* to regild; *(société, image)* to repackage; *Fig* **r. son blason** *(d'un noble qui se remarie)* to restore the family fortunes by marrying money; *(d'une personne) (par un succès etc)* to restore one's reputation

redormir [rədɔrmir] vi *(conj like* **dormir**) to go to sleep again, to go back to sleep; **je n'ai pas pu r.** I couldn't get back to sleep; **je suis allée r. quelques heures** I went to get a few more hours' sleep

redoublant, -ante [rədublɑ̃, -ɑ̃t] n *Scol* = pupil who repeats a year

redoublé [rəduble] adj *Littér (rime)* double; **frapper** *ou* **battre qn à coups redoublés** to thrash sb soundly; **frapper à une porte à coups redoublés** to hammer at a door

redoublement [rədubləmɑ̃] nm **1** *(de joie, chagrin, violence, douleur etc)* increase; *(d'une tempête)* worsening; **avec un r. de zèle** with renewed *or* redoubled zeal **2** *Ling (d'une syllabe, lettre)* reduplication **3** *Scol* repeating a year *or* class; **dans son cas, le r. n'est pas justifié** there's no need for him to repeat the year

redoubler [rəduble] vt **1** *(sentiment d'injustice, chagrin)* to add to; *(dose)* to double again, to redouble; *Fam (doubler)* to double; *(film)* to re-voice; **r. ses efforts** to redouble one's efforts; *Scol* **r. une classe** to repeat a year *or* class **2** *(vêtement)* to reline

vi **1** *Scol* to repeat a year *or Am* grade **2** *(augmenter) (du chagrin, froid)* to intensify, to increase; **la pluie/le vent redoubla de violence** the rain came down/the wind blew harder than ever, the rain came down/the wind blew twice as hard as before; **r. d'efforts** to redouble one's efforts; **r. de prudence/d'attention/de douceur** to be twice as cautious/attentive/gentle

redoutable [rədutabl] adj *(personne, adversaire)* formidable; *(ennemi)* formidable, dangerous, *Fml* redoubtable; *(hiver)* fierce; *(odeur)* dreadful; **il fait un froid r.** it's dreadfully cold

redoute [rədut] nf *(fortification)* redoubt

redouter [rədute] vt *(chose, événement)* to dread, to fear; *(personne)* to be in awe of; **je redoute la journée de lundi** I'm dreading Monday; **ce jour si redouté se passa sans incident notable** the dreaded day passed off without incident; **un prof redouté de tous les élèves** a much-dreaded teacher; **r. d'apprendre qch** to dread hearing sth; **je redoute surtout de devenir aveugle** the thing *or* what I fear *or* dread most is going blind; **elle redoute que tu ne lui en parles** she's terrified that you'll mention it to him/her

redoux [rədu] nm *Météo* milder weather; **on attend le r.** we're expecting a return to milder weather

redresse [rədrɛs] nf *très Fam* **c'est un type à la r.** he's no soft touch

redressement [rədrɛsmɑ̃] nm **1** *(d'un objet renversé)* righting, setting up again; *(d'un*

bateau, avion) righting; *(de la tête)* raising; *(des épaules)* straightening **2** *(rectification) (d'un compte, d'une erreur)* rectification, correction; *Compta* adjustment; *(d'un tort)* righting; *Tech (d'une surface)* tru(e)ing; *Écon* **plan de r.** recovery plan; *Vieilli* **maison de r.** ≃ approved school, reformatory **3** *Élec (du courant alternatif)* rectification; **valve de r.** rectifying valve

▶▶ **r. économique** economic recovery; **plan de r. économique** recovery plan; **r. financier** gearing adjustment; *Admin* **r. fiscal** tax adjustment, demand for tax arrears; **r. judiciaire** receivership; **être mis en r. judiciaire** to go into receivership

redresser [rədrɛse] vt **1** *(objet renversé)* to right, to set upright again; *(bateau)* to right; *(avion)* to right, to straighten up, to lift the nose of **2** *(rectifier) (grief)* to redress, to right; *(erreur, situation)* to rectify, to correct; *(compte)* to adjust; *(bois courbé, tôle cabossée)* to straighten (out); *(surface)* to true; **r. les épaules** to straighten one's shoulders; **r. la tête** to hold up one's head; *(la lever)* to raise *or* lift one's head, to look up; *Fig* **il peut r. la tête maintenant** he can hold his head up now, he can look people in the eye now; **tu n'es pas là pour r. les torts** you're not there to right wrongs; **r. l'équilibre des forces** to redress the balance of power; **pour r. l'économie** in order to bring about an economic recovery; **r. une entreprise** to put a company back on its feet **3** *Élec (courant)* to rectify

vpr **se redresser 1** *(d'une personne)* to straighten up, to straighten one's back; *(avec fierté)* to draw oneself up, to hold one's head up; **se r. sur son séant** to sit up straight (again) **2** *(de l'économie, d'un pays, des ventes etc)* to recover

redresseur, -euse [rədrɛsœr, -øz] n **r. de torts** righter of wrongs; *(chevalier), Hum* knight errant; **r. d'entreprise** company doctor

nm *Élec (du courant)* rectifier
adj *Élec (appareil)* rectifying

redû [rədy] nm balance due

réduc [redyk] nf *Fam (abrév* **réduction**) discount

réducteur, -trice [redyktœr, -tris] adj *Péj (explication, point de vue etc)* reductive, simplistic; *Chimie* **agent r.** reducing agent; *Tech* **ensemble r.** reduction gear assembly

nm *Chimie* reducing agent; *Tech* reduction gear *or* unit; *Théâtre* **r. d'éclairage** dimmer; **r. de têtes** head shrinker

réductible [redyktibl] adj *Méd (fracture)* which can be set, *Spéc* reducible; *(dislocation), Math (fraction)* reducible

réduction [redyksjɔ̃] nf **1** *(de prix, salaires, personnel)* reduction, cut (**de** in); *(de dépenses, de la production)* reduction, cutting back (**de** in); *(d'un budget)* cutting back (**de** of); *(de la pression)* reduction, lowering (**de** of); *(d'une pénalité)* reduction (**de** of); *Chir (d'une fraction)* reduction; *(de gravure)* small reproduction; *Fin (d'un capital)* writing down; *Méd (d'une fracture)* setting; *(d'une dislocation)* reduction; *Élec (du voltage)* stepping down; **réductions de salaires/de personnel** reductions *or* cutbacks in wages/staff, wage/staff cuts; **on nous a demandé d'accepter une r. de salaire** we were asked to take a cut in (our) wages; **r. de 60 euros** 60 euros off; **faire une r. de 15%** to give 15% off; **r. de capital** decrease in capital; **r. des impôts** tax cut; **la r. du temps de travail** = reduction of the working week in France from 39 to 35 hours, introduced by the government of Lionel Jospin in 1998 and phased in from 2000 onwards; **carte de r.** discount card; **cette carte donne droit à**

une r. this card entitles the holder to a reduction; **une r. de 15% sur la literie** a 15% reduction on bedding; **faire une r. à qn** to give sb a reduction; **r. des bruits** noise reduction; *Mus* **r. pour piano** *(d'un opéra etc)* short score; **un bateau en r.** a scale model of a ship **2** *(d'une ville)* capture

réduire [reduir] *(prp* **réduisant**; *pp* **réduit**; *pr ind* **je réduis, il réduit,** n. **réduisons**; *impf* **je réduisais**; *p hist* **je réduisis**; *fu* **je réduirai**) vt *(montant, vitesse, photographie, dessin), Math (fractions), Culin (sauce)* to reduce; *(prix, taux d'intérêt)* to reduce, to lower, to bring down; *(dépenses, frais)* to reduce, to cut (down *or* back), to curtail; *(chômage, taux de mortalité, de natalité)* to reduce, to lower, to bring down; *(personnel, salaires)* to reduce, to cut (back); *(texte)* to shorten, to cut; *(pression)* to reduce, to lower, to relieve; *Fin (capital)* to write down; *Élec (voltage)* to step down; *Méd (fracture)* to set, *Spéc* to reduce; *(dislocation)* to reduce; **r. un texte de 200 pages** to shorten a text by 200 pages; **on a nettement réduit les dépenses d'armement** arms spending has been cut right back *or* sharply reduced; **la société réduit progressivement ses opérations en Allemagne** the company is winding down its operations in Germany; *Com, Ind* **r. ses effectifs** to reduce the size of the workforce, to downsize; **r. le personnel** to cut staff, to make staff cutbacks; **billet à prix réduit** cheap *or* cutprice ticket, *Br Fam* concession; **voyager à prix réduit** to travel at reduced rates; **réduit de moitié** half size; *Mus* **r. une partition** to arrange a score for the piano; **r. qch en cendres/poussière** to reduce sth to ashes/dust; **r. des euros en cents/des kilogrammes en grammes** to convert *or* reduce euros to cents/kilograms to grams; **r. qn à la misère/au silence/à la mendicité** to reduce sb to poverty/silence/begging; **r. qn au désespoir** to drive sb to despair; **nous en sommes réduits à ça!** is this what we're *or* we've been reduced to?; **j'en suis réduit à le faire moi-même** I'm reduced to doing it myself

vi *Culin* to reduce; **faire r. un sirop** to reduce a syrup

vpr **se réduire 1 se r. à** to amount to; **leurs différences se réduisent à peu de choses** their differences don't amount to much; **à quoi se réduit tout cela?** what does it all amount to *or* boil down to? **2** *Culin (d'une sauce)* to reduce; **se r. en poussière** to crumble into dust **3** *Fam Vieilli (faire des économies)* to cut down *or* back

réduit [redqi] nm *(petite pièce)* cubbyhole; **elle habite une sorte de r. sale et humide** she lives in a damp and dirty little cubbyhole

réduplication [redyplikasjɔ̃] nf *Ling* reduplication

rééchelonnement [reeʃ(ə)lɔnmɑ̃] nm *Fin (d'une dette)* rescheduling

rééchelonner [reeʃ(ə)lɔne] vt *Fin (dette)* to reschedule

réécrire [reekrir] *(conj like* **écrire**) vt *(rédiger à nouveau) (lettre, texte, annonce etc)* to rewrite; *(devoir etc qui contenait des fautes)* to write (out) again; **j'ai dû lui r. tout son article** I had to rewrite his entire article for him, I had to write his entire article all over again

vi **r. à qn** to write to sb again, to send sb another letter

réécriture [reekrityr] nf *(d'un texte, d'une annonce etc)* rewriting

réédification [reedifikasjɔ̃] nf rebuilding, reconstruction

réédifier [reedifje] vt *(conj like* **édifier**) to rebuild, to reconstruct

rééditer [reedite] vt *(livre)* to republish, to re-issue; *Fig Fam (exploit)* to give a repeat performance of

réédition [reedisjɔ̃] NF (d'un livre etc) re-issue; Fig Fam repeat; **c'est une r. de leur dispute de la semaine dernière** it's a repeat or rerun of the argument they had last week, it's last week's argument all over again

rééducatif, -ive [reedykatif, -iv] ADJ **thérapie rééducative** occupational therapy

rééducation [reedykasjɔ̃] NF 1 Méd (de muscles après accident etc) re-education; (d'un handicapé, accidenté) rehabilitation; **r. de la parole** speech therapy; **centre de r. (professionnelle)** rehabilitation centre; **faire de la r.** (chez un kinésithérapeute) to have physio(-)therapy or Am physical therapy **2** Psy re-education; (de délinquants) rehabilitation

rééduquer [reedyke] VT (handicapé, accidenté, délinquant) to rehabilitate; Méd (muscle), Psy to re-educate

réel, -elle [reɛl] ADJ **1** (avantage, coût, monde), Math (nombre) real; (personnage) real(-life), actual; (fait) actual; Opt (image) true; **grandeur réelle** actual size; **salaire r.** real salary; **en termes réels** in real terms; **offre réelle** cash offer; **ce film nous rend la personne de Charlie Chaplin plus réelle** this film brings Charlie Chaplin to life **2** (before noun) (plaisir, sentiment de bonheur etc) real, great; **connaître enfin un r. sentiment de bonheur** to know real or true happiness at last; **prendre un r. plaisir à faire qch** to take real or great pleasure in doing sth
▪ NM **1** Math real number **2 le r.** reality

réélection [reelɛksjɔ̃] NF re-election

rééligible [reeliʒibl] ADJ re-eligible

réélire [reelir] VT (conj like élire) to re-elect

réellement [reelmɑ̃] ADV (drôle, déçu, incroyable etc) really; **cela s'est r. passé** it really or actually happened; **des choses qui existent r.** things that really or actually exist

réembarquer [reɑ̃barke] VT (passagers) to re-embark; (marchandises) to reload, to re-embark
▪ VI to re-embark, to go back on board
▪ VPR **se réembarquer** to re-embark, to go back on board; Fig **se r. dans qch** to get involved in sth again

réembaucher [reɑ̃boʃe] VT **r. qn** to take sb on again, to rehire sb

réémetteur [reemetœr] NM TV, Radio relay transmitter

réemploi [reɑ̃plwa] NM (du personnel d'une autre entreprise) employment

réemployer [reɑ̃plwaje] VT (ancien employé) to re-employ, to employ again; (produit) to use again

réemprunter [reɑ̃prœ̃te] VT to borrow again

réencoder [reɑ̃kɔde] VT Ordinat to recode

réentendre [reɑ̃tɑ̃dr] VT (disque, cassette etc) to listen to or hear again

réentraînement [reɑ̃trɛnmɑ̃] NM retraining

rééquilibrage [reekilibraʒ] NM (de pneus) balancing; **le r. des forces politiques** the restoration of the balance of power; Pol **tout faire pour le r. de la gauche** to do everything to restore the balance within the parties of the left

rééquilibrer [reekilibre] VT (pneus) to balance; **r. les forces politiques** to restore the balance of power

réescompte [reɛskɔ̃t] NM Fin rediscount

réescompter [reɛskɔ̃te] VT Fin to rediscount

réessayer [reeseje] VT & VI to retry

réévaluation [reevalyasjɔ̃] NF revaluation

réévaluer [reevalye] VT (monnaie) to revalue; (prix) to reassess

réexamen [reɛgzamɛ̃] NM (d'une politique, situation) re-examination, reappraisal, reassessment; (d'une décision) reconsideration; (d'un dossier, d'une question, d'un malade) re-examination

réexaminer [reɛgzamine] VT (politique, situation) to re-examine, to reappraise, to reassess; (décision) to reconsider; (dossier, question, malade) to re-examine, to examine again

réexpédier [reɛkspedje] VT (conj like expédier) **1** (lettres, marchandises) to send on, to forward, to redirect **2** (pour rendre) (à l'expéditeur) to send back, to return

réexpédition [reɛkspedisjɔ̃] NF **1** (d'une lettre, de marchandises) forwarding, redirection; **frais de r.** fee for redirection; **ordre de r. du courrier** request for mail to be redirected **2** (à l'expéditeur) return

réexportation [reɛkspɔrtasjɔ̃] NF (action) re-export, re-exportation; **les réexportations** re-exports

réexporter [reɛkspɔrte] VT to re-export

réfaction [refaksjɔ̃] NF Com, Jur (de biens endommagés ou de qualité inférieure) allowance, rebate

refaire [rəfɛr] (conj like faire) VT **1** (faire à nouveau) (travail, traduction), Théâtre (scène) to do (all over) again, to redo, Am to do over; (voyage, robe etc) to make (all over) again; (film) to remake; **j'ai dû r. du riz** I had to make (some) more rice; **tu nous referas du bœuf bourguignon comme l'autre fois?** will you make us some bœuf bourguignon like you did last time?; **r. ses lacets** to tie one's laces again; **r. la conclusion d'une dissertation** to change an essay's conclusion; **on a dépassé le budget, il faut qu'on refasse la fin** (d'un film) we've gone over the budget, we'll have to rewrite the ending; **refais le calcul, tu as dû te tromper** do the sum again, you must have made a mistake; **c'est trop serré, il faut r. le pansement** the bandage is too tight, you'll have to redo it; **nous avons refait à pied les vingt kilomètres qui nous séparaient du village** we walked the twenty kilometres back to the village; Fam **elle nous a refait sa crise** she gave us another bout of hysterics; Fam **tu ne vas pas nous r. ta crise!** you're not going to go into hysterics again!; **tu ne vas pas me r. une scène!** you're not going to start again!; **je refais de la fièvre** my temperature's up again; **c'est à r.** it will have to be done (all over) again; **et si c'était à r.?** and if you had to do it all over again?; **ton éducation est à r.** your education has been sadly neglected; **r. le monde** to put or set the world to rights; **r. sa vie** to make a new life for oneself; **r. sa vie avec qn** to make or start a new life with sb; Tél **r. le numéro** to redial

2 (réparer) to repair, to mend; (remettre en état) (maison, appartement) to do up, to redo; **r. la peinture** ou **les peintures** to redo or do up the paintwork; **r. la décoration d'une maison** to redecorate a house; **r. à neuf** (moteur) to recondition; (appartement, peintures) to redo completely; (fauteuil) to renovate; **r. les talons de ses souliers** to have one's shoes reheeled; **r. l'installation électrique d'une maison** to rewire a house, to redo the wiring in a house; **r. le revêtement de qch** to resurface sth

3 Fam (personne) (d'un marchand) to do, to diddle; (duper) to fool, to take in; **on vous a refait** you've been had; **on vous a refait de plusieurs centaines d'euros** you've been done or diddled out of several hundred euros
▪ VPR **se refaire 1 se r. une santé** to recover one's health, to get one's health back; **une soirée comme ça, ça ne se refera pas** a party like that doesn't happen twice or only happens once in a lifetime; Fam **elle se refait une beauté** she's doing her face again

2 (se changer) to change one's ways; **on ne se refait pas** I/you/etc can't change the way I am/you are/etc (made), a leopard can't change its spots

3 Fam (financièrement) to be solvent again; (au jeu) to win back the money one has lost; **après mes vacances, j'ai mis trois mois pour me r.** after my holiday it was three months before I was solvent again or before I had two pennies to rub together
▪ V IMPERS **il refait soleil** it's sunny again

réfection [refɛksjɔ̃] NF (réparation) (d'un bâtiment, appartement, d'une maison) (extensive) repair; **travaux de r.** repair work; **route en r.** road under repair

réfectoire [refɛktwar] NM refectory, dining hall

référé [refere] NM Jur summary procedure; **(ordonnance de) r.** provisional order

référence [referɑ̃s] NF **1** reference; Mktg (produit) benchmark; **ouvrage/livre de r.** reference work/book; **faire r. à un texte/auteur** to refer to a text/an author; **il n'a pas fait une seule fois r. à notre conversation** he didn't refer to or mention our conversation once; **références au bas des pages** footnotes; **r. de page** page reference; Fam **ce n'est pas une r.** don't take my/his/etc word for it, don't go by what I/he/etc say(s); **le film a été primé à Cannes mais ce n'est pas une r.** the film won a prize at Cannes but that's no recommendation **2** (sur une lettre, sur un document) reference; **r. à rappeler** in replying please quote, please quote reference; **en r. à** with reference to **3 références** (employee's) reference, Vieilli testimonial; **références exigées** (sur offre d'emploi) references required; **une lettre de r.** a reference
▪▪ **références bancaires** bank references; **références commerciales** trade references; Ordinat **r. croisée** cross reference; **r. topographique** map reference

référencé [referɑ̃se] ADJ Com **être r.** to have a reference number; **votre lettre référencée … your letter reference number …**

référencer [referɑ̃se] VT Ordinat to reference

référencié [referɑ̃sje] ADJ (quotation) with a reference

référendaire [referɑ̃dɛr] ADJ referendum

referendum, référendum [referɛ̃dɔm] NM referendum; **faire un r.** to hold a referendum; **les Français ont décidé par r. de …** the French have decided in a or by referendum to …

référent [referɑ̃] NM Ling referent

référer [refere] (je réfère, n. référons; je référerai) VI **r. à qn d'une question** to refer a matter to sb; **en r. à la cour** to report or submit the case to the court; **en r. à son supérieur** to refer to or consult one's superior
▪ VPR **se référer se r. à qch** to refer to sth; **tout ce qui ne se réfère pas directement à notre affaire** anything that is not directly connected with or related to our business; **se r. à** ou **s'en r. à qn d'une question** to refer a matter to sb

refermer [rəfɛrme] VT to shut or close again; **il referma la porte sur lui** he closed the door behind or after him
▪ VPR **se refermer** (d'une porte) to close or shut (again); (d'une fleur) to close up; (d'une blessure) to close up, to heal; Fig **le piège se referme sur l'espion** the net is closing in around the spy

refiler [rəfile] VT Fam **r. qch à qn** (objet de mauvaise qualité) to palm sth off on sb, to foist or unload sth on sb; (objet utile) to pass sth on to sb; **ils vont nous r. les enfants pour le week-end** they're palming the kids off on us *or* dumping the kids on us for the weekend; **il m'a refilé son rhume** he's given me his cold

refinancement [rəfinãsmã] **NM** *(d'un crédit)* refinancing

refinancer [rəfinãse] **VT** to refinance

réfléchi [refleʃi] **ADJ 1** *(personne)* thoughtful, reflective; *(action, opinion)* deliberate, considered; **d'un air r.** thoughtfully; **elle est très réfléchie** she doesn't do anything without thinking it over first; **c'est tout r.** that's settled; **tout bien r.** all things considered, after due consideration **2** *Gram (verbe, pronom)* reflexive SEE GRAMMAR A29–30; B28–9

réfléchir [refleʃir] **VT 1** *(image)* to reflect; *(lumière, son)* to reflect, to throw back **2 r. que ... + ind** to realize that ...; **il réfléchit que son argent ne suffirait pas** it occurred to him that he wouldn't have enough money **VI** to think; **je réfléchis** I'm thinking; *(avant de décider)* I'm thinking about it; **prends le temps de r.** (take time to) think about it; **donne-moi le temps de r.** give me time to think; **r. à qch** to think about sth, to consider sth, to turn sth over in one's mind; **j'ai beaucoup réfléchi au problème** I've given the problem a great deal of thought; **j'ai réfléchi à ce que vous m'avez dit** I've thought about what you told me; **réfléchissez-y** think about it, think it over; **je demande à r.** I'd like to think about it *or* think it over; **donner à r. à qn** to give sb food for thought, to make sb think twice; **parler sans r.** to speak without thinking *or* hastily
VPR se réfléchir *(d'une image, d'une lumière, de la chaleur, du son etc)* to be reflected

réfléchissant [refleʃisɑ̃] **ADJ** *(miroir, surface)* reflective

réflecteur, -trice [reflɛktœr, -tris] **ADJ** *(miroir, panneau)* reflecting
NM *Aut* reflector; *(miroir)* reflecting mirror; *(télescope)* reflector, reflecting telescope; *TV* **r. parabolique** parabolic reflector

réflectif, -ive [reflɛktif, -iv] **ADJ 1** *(de la réflexion)* reflective **2** *Physiol* reflex

réflectorisé [reflɛktɔrize] **ADJ** *(panneau routier, casque)* reflective

reflet [rəflɛ] **NM** *(dans un miroir, sur l'eau)* reflection; *(de la soie etc)* sheen, shimmer; **r. des eaux** gleam on the waters; **les reflets de la lune sur le lac** the reflection *or* shimmer of the moon on the lake; **chevelure à reflets d'or** hair with glints of gold; **reflets changeants** play of colours; *Fig* **être le r. de qch** to reflect sth; **ce n'est que le r. du temps des colonies** it's a pale reflection of colonial times

refléter [rəflete] (**je reflète, n. reflétons; je refléterai**) **VT** *(lumière, image), Fig (gêne, jalousie, sentiments de qn)* to reflect; **son attitude ne reflète pas ses sentiments** his feelings are not reflected in his attitude
VPR se refléter to be mirrored *or* reflected

refleurir [rəflœrir] **VI** to flower *or* blossom again; *Fig (de l'art, de la littérature, de l'économie etc)* to flourish again
VT *(tombe)* to put fresh flowers on

reflex [reflɛks] **ADJ, NM** *Phot* **(appareil) r.** reflex (camera)

réflexe [reflɛks] **ADJ** *Phys, Physiol* reflex
NM *Physiol* reflex; *(réaction)* reflex, reaction; **r. rotulien** knee reflex *or* jerk; **avoir de bons réflexes** to have good reflexes, to react quickly; **ça a été un r.** it was a reflex (action), it was automatic; **c'est devenu un r.** it's become automatic; **je n'ai pas eu le r. de le lui faire remarquer** I wasn't quick-witted enough to point it out to him/her

réflexif, -ive [reflɛksif, -iv] **ADJ** *Phil, Math* reflexive

réflexion [reflɛksjɔ̃] **NF 1** *(pensée)* reflection, thought; **plongé dans une profonde r.**

deep in thought; **après mûre r.** after much thought; **donner matière à r.** *(d'un film, livre etc)* to provide food for thought; **agir sans r.** to act hastily *or* without thinking; **(toute) r. faite, à la r.** *(finalement)* on reflection; *(après avoir changé d'avis)* on further consideration, on second thoughts; **voilà qui mérite r.** there's food for thought **2** *(remarque)* remark; **elle ne supporte pas qu'on lui fasse la moindre r.** she can't stand the slightest criticism; **faire une r. à qn** to make a remark *or* comment to sb; **on ne m'a jamais fait de r. à ce sujet** nobody's ever made any remarks to me about it *or* remarked on it to me; **s'il te fait la moindre r.** if he says the least little thing to you **3** *Phys (d'une image, de la lumière, du son)* reflection; **angle de r.** angle of reflection; *TV, Cin* **r. parasite** blooming

refluer [rəflye] **VI 1** to flow back; *(de la marée)* to ebb; **le sang lui reflua au visage** the blood surged to his/her cheeks; **la foule a reflué vers la ville** the crowd swept *or* surged back towards the town; **faire r. des gens** to push people back, to make people move back **2** *Fin* **faire r. le dollar/le yen** to keep down the value of the dollar/yen

reflux [rəfly] **NM** *(de la marée)* ebb(ing); *(d'une foule)* surging back

refondation [rəfɔ̃dasjɔ̃] **NF** *(d'un parti politique)* radical reform; **les militants ont réclamé une r. du parti** the militants have called for radical reform of the party

refonder [rəfɔ̃de] **VT** *(parti politique)* to radically reform

refondre [rəfɔ̃dr] **VT 1** *(métal, cloche)* to recast; *(monnaie)* to recoin, to remint **2** *(texte, ouvrage)* to revise, to rewrite, *Fml, Litt* to recast
VI *(de la neige)* to melt again

refonte [rəfɔ̃t] **NF 1** *(du métal)* recasting; *(de la monnaie)* recoinage **2** *(d'un texte)* rewriting, revision

réformable [refɔrmabl] **ADJ** reformable

reformatage [rəfɔrmataʒ] **NM** *Ordinat* reformatting

reformater [rəfɔrmate] **VT** *Ordinat (page, disque)* to reformat

réformateur, -trice [refɔrmatœr, -tris] **ADJ** *(mesure, initiative)* reforming
N reformer

réformation [refɔrmasjɔ̃] **NF** reformation, reform; *Hist, Rel* **la R.** the Reformation

réforme [refɔrm] **NF 1** *(politique, de l'orthographe, d'un abus, du calendrier etc)* reform; *Hist, Rel* **la R.** the Reformation; **r. constitutionnelle** constitutional reform; **r. électorale** electoral reform; **r. monétaire** monetary reform; **réformes sociales** social reforms **2** *Mil (d'un homme) (pour mauvaise condition physique)* discharge on medical grounds, invaliding out; *(d'une recrue)* rejection; *(de matériel)* scrapping; **r. temporaire** deferment; **commission de r.** special medical board; **matériel en r.** scrapped equipment; *Fam Vieilli* **mettre à la r.** *(objets)* to scrap

réformé, -ée [refɔrme] **ADJ 1** *Rel* Protestant; *(église)* reformed **2** *Mil (exempté)* discharged for unfitness *or* on medical grounds, invalided out; *(recrue)* rejected; *(matériel)* scrapped; **être r. P4** to be rejected/discharged for reasons of mental health
N 1 *Rel* Protestant **2** *Mil* **r. temporaire** deferred recruit

reformer [rəfɔrme] **VT** to form again, to re-form; **r. les rangs** to fall into line again
VPR se reformer to re-form

Do not confuse with **réformer**.

réformer [refɔrme] **VT 1** *(abus, loi etc)* to reform; *Jur (décision)* to reverse **2** *Mil, Naut (homme, officier)* to discharge as unfit *or* on

medical grounds, to invalid out (of the service); *(recrue)* to reject; *(matériel)* to scrap, to condemn; **se faire r.** *(avant l'incorporation)* to be rejected from military service; *(après l'incorporation)* to get oneself discharged

Do not confuse with **reformer**.

réformisme [refɔrmism] **NM** *Pol* reformism

réformiste [refɔrmist] **ADJ, N** reformist

reformulation [rəfɔrmylasjɔ̃] **NF** rewording

reformuler [rəfɔrmyle] **VT** to reformulate, to reword

refoulé, -ée [rəfule] *Psy* **ADJ** *(sentiments, instincts, pulsions)* repressed; *(personne)* repressed, inhibited
N repressed *or* inhibited person
NM le retour du r. a Freudian slip

refoulement [rəfulmã] **NM 1** *Psy* (unconscious) repression, suppression **2** *Tech (d'une canalisation)* delivery, discharge, output; **soupape de r.** *(d'une pompe)* delivery valve; **tuyau de r.** exhaust pipe **3** *(renvoi)* **il faut instaurer un r. systématique des hooligans** *(à la frontière)* we must start systematically refusing entry to hooligans; **la police tentait d'organiser le r. des supporters** the police were trying to push *or* drive back the supporters

refouler [rəfule] **VT 1** *(faire reculer) (manifestants, foule)* to drive back, to force back, to press back; *Admin (étranger)* to refuse entry to, to turn back; *(train)* to back up; **le nombre des étrangers refoulés aux frontières** the number of foreigners turned back at the borders; **on nous a refoulés à l'entrée** we got turned away at the door
2 *(sentiments, colère)* to repress, to suppress, to contain; *(larmes)* to force *or* choke *or* fight back; *(agressivité, souvenir), Psy (pulsion, instinct)* to repress; *(désirs)* to suppress; **il ne faut pas r. ses sentiments** you mustn't bottle up your feelings
3 *Tech (eau)* to deliver, to discharge; **pompe refoulante** force pump
VI 1 *(de l'évier)* to back up; **la cheminée/la machine à laver refoule** the chimney's not drawing/the washing machine's not draining properly
2 *Vulg (sentir mauvais)* to stink

réfractaire [refrakter] **ADJ** rebellious, insubordinate, *Fml* refractory; *Tech, Méd (minerai, maladie)* stubborn, *Spéc* refractory; *(brique, argile)* fireproof, fire; *Hist* **prêtre r.** non-juring priest; **r. à** *Tech* resistant to; *(la loi, des conseils, une proposition)* unwilling *or* loath to accept; **il est r. à l'opéra** opera goes straight over his head; **r. aux acides** acid-proof; **être r. à l'autorité** to reject authority; **elle est r. aux sciences** science is a closed book to her
N rebel; *Mil, Jur* defaulter

réfracter [refrakte] **VT** *(rayons etc)* to refract, to bend

réfracteur, -trice [refraktœr, -tris] **ADJ** refracting
NM refractor

réfraction [refraksjɔ̃] **NF** *(de rayons)* refraction, bending; **indice de r.** index of refraction, refractive index

refrain [rəfrɛ̃] **NM** *(d'une chanson)* chorus, refrain; **chanter de vieux refrains** to sing old songs *or* old ditties; **reprendre le r. en chœur** to sing the chorus; *Fam* **c'est toujours le même r.** it's (always) the same old story *or* thing; *Fam* **change un peu de r.!** change the record! VOIR GRAMMAIRE A14

réfrangible [refrãʒibl] **ADJ** *Phys* refrangible

refrappe [rəfrap] **NF** *Ordinat* rekeying

refrapper [rəfrape] **VT** *Ordinat* to rekey

refréner [rǝfrene] VT (**je refrène, n. refré-nons; je refrénerai**) (*sentiments, colère, impatience etc*) to curb, to restrain, to control

réfrigérant [refriʒerã] ADJ (*action, appareil*) refrigerating, cooling; (*produit*) freezing; *Fig* (*accueil, personne*) chilly; **mélange r.** refrigerant
  NM (*mélange*) refrigerant, coolant; (*d'un alambic*) refrigerator, condenser; **r. à cheminée** cooling tower

réfrigérateur [refriʒeratœr] NM refrigerator, fridge, *Am* icebox; **conserver au r.** keep refrigerated; **conserver au r. après ouverture** refrigerate after opening; *Fig Fam* **mettre qn au r.** to sideline sb; *Fam* **mettre un projet au r.** to shelve a plan, to put a plan on ice *or* in cold storage; *Fam* **sortir qn du r.** to bring sb in out of the cold; **ils ont sorti le projet du r.** they took the project down off the shelf *or* out of cold storage

réfrigération [refriʒerasjõ] NF (*de la viande, de boissons etc*) refrigeration, chilling; **appareils de r.** refrigeration appliances; **r. industrielle** industrial refrigeration

réfrigéré [refriʒere] ADJ refrigerated

réfrigérer [refriʒere] VT (**je réfrigère, n. réfrigérons; je réfrigérerai**) to refrigerate; **viande réfrigérée** chilled meat; **camion réfrigéré** refrigerated van, reefer; *Fig* **son accueil me réfrigéra** I received a chilly welcome; **ma question l'a réfrigéré** my question met with a chilly response *or* lowered the temperature quite considerably; *Fam* **je suis réfrigérée** I'm freezing

réfringence [refrɛ̃ʒãs] NF *Phys* refringency

réfringent [refrɛ̃ʒã] ADJ *Phys* refringent

refroidi [rǝfrwadi] NM *Fam* (*cadavre*) stiff

refroidir [rǝfrwadir] VT **1** (*eau*) to cool (down); (*moteur, fluide*) to cool; (*métal*) to quench; **refroidi par (l')air/huile** air-/oil-cooled; **refroidi par eau** water-cooled **2** *Fig* (*amitié, passion, amour etc*) to cool; (*ardeur*) to cool, to quench; (*enthousiasme*) to dampen, to dash, to quench; *Fam* **r. qn** (*d'un accueil, d'une réaction, question*) to dampen sb's enthusiasm **3** *Arg* **r. qn** (*tuer*) to bump sb off, to ice sb
  VI (*d'un liquide ou d'un plat qui devrait être chaud*) to get cold; (*d'un liquide ou d'un plat qui est trop chaud*) to cool down; **laisser r. son thé** (*exprès*) to let one's tea cool down; (*si l'on attend trop*) to let one's tea get cold; **dépêchez-vous! ça va r.!** hurry up! it's getting cold!; **le temps a refroidi** it *or* the weather has got *or* grown colder; *Fam* **tu refroidis!** (*tu devines mal*) you're getting colder!
  VPR **se refroidir 1 le temps** *ou* **la température se refroidit** it's *or* the weather's getting colder; **la soupe se refroidit** the soup's getting cold **2** *Fig* (*d'une amitié, de relations*) to cool; **nos relations se sont refroidies depuis cette dispute** things have cooled between us since the argument **3** *Méd* to catch a chill

refroidissement [rǝfrwadismã] NM **1** (*de l'eau, d'un moteur*) cooling; (*du métal*) quenching; *Météo* drop in temperature; **agent de r.** cooling agent, coolant; *Aut* **r. intermédiaire** intercooling; **r. par air** air cooling; **r. par eau** water cooling **2** *Méd* chill **3** *Fig* (*d'une amitié, de relations*) cooling off

refroidisseur [rǝfrwadisœr] NM cooler, refrigerator unit; *Nucl* cooler, coolant; **système r.** cooling system

refuge [rǝfyʒ] NM **1** refuge, shelter; (*lieu de*) **r.** place of refuge; **r. anti-bombe** air-raid shelter; **pays de r.** country of refuge; **valeur r.** safe investment; **trouver/chercher r.** to find *or* take/seek refuge; *Fig* **le sport/l'alcool est son r.** he takes refuge in sport/alcohol; **Dieu est mon r.** God is my refuge **2** (*en montagne*)

(mountain) hut, refuge; (*d'oiseaux*) (bird) sanctuary; (*sur la route*) traffic island

réfugié, -ée [refyʒje] N refugee; **r. politique** political refugee

réfugier (se) [sǝrefyʒje] VPR to take refuge, to find shelter, to shelter; **se r. dans le mensonge/le sport** to take refuge in lying/sport

refus [rǝfy] NM (*d'une invitation, offre*), *Équitation* refusal; (*d'une proposition*) rebuff, rejection; (*d'un candidat, manuscrit, de marchandises*) rejection; **son r. d'obéir** his/her refusal to obey; **essuyer un r.** to meet with a refusal; **se heurter à un r. de la part de qn** to meet with a refusal from sb; **opposer un r. à qn/qch** to turn sb/sth down; **il opposa un r. catégorique à ma proposition** he turned my suggestion down flat; *Fam* **ce n'est pas de r.** I won't say no
  ▸▸ **r. d'acceptation** non-acceptance; **r. d'obéissance** insubordination; *Jur* contempt of court; *Jur* **r. d'obtempérer** obstruction; **r. de paiement** non-payment; (*de traite*) dishonour, *Am* dishonor; *Aut* **r. de priorité** failure to give way *or Am* to yield

---

Il faut noter que le terme anglais **refuse** est un faux ami. Il signifie **ordures**.

---

refuser [rǝfyze] VT **1** (*offre, invitation*) to refuse, to decline, to turn down; (*proposition*) to turn down; (*demande*) to deny; (*marchandises, manuscrit*) to reject; **r. qch à qn** to refuse *or* deny sb sth; **on ne peut rien lui r.** you can't refuse him anything; **on lui refuse jusqu'au droit de voir sa femme** he's even being refused *or* denied the right to see his wife; **se voir r. sa demande** to have one's request turned down *or* denied; **r. toute qualité à qn** to refuse to see any good in sb; **r. sa porte à qn** to refuse to see sb, *Fml* to deny sb admittance; **r. l'obstacle** (*d'un cheval*) to refuse; **r. le combat** to refuse to fight
  2 r. qn to turn sb down; *Mil* **r. un homme** to reject a man; **r. du monde** to turn people away; *Scol* **être refusé** (*à un examen*) to fail
  VI to refuse; (*d'un cheval*) to refuse, to ba(u)lk; **r. tout net** to refuse point blank, to give a point-blank refusal; **r. de faire qch** to refuse to do sth; **r. d'accepter un effet** to dishonour a bill by non-acceptance; **r. de payer une traite** to dishonour a bill by non-payment; *Naut* **r. de virer** not to obey the helm; **l'ordinateur refuse de s'allumer** the computer refuses to *or* won't turn on
  VPR **se refuser cela ne se refuse pas** it's not the kind of thing to pass up; **un petit verre, ça ne se refuse pas** (*en proposant une boisson*) I wouldn't say no to a drink; (*en acceptant une boisson*) you can't say no to a drink; **on ne se refuse rien!, tu ne te refuses rien!** you don't stint yourself!, you don't believe in self-denial!; **se r. à l'évidence** to shut one's eyes to the facts; **se r. à tout commentaire** to refuse *or* decline to comment; **se r. à faire qch** to refuse to do sth; **je me refuse à ce genre de pratique** I refuse to get involved in that kind of thing

réfutable [refytabl] ADJ (*argument*) refutable; **c'est difficilement r.** it's hard to refute

réfutation [refytasjõ] NF rebuttal, refutation

réfuter [refyte] VT to refute, to rebut

refuznik [rǝfyznik] N refusenik

rég *Mil* (*abrév* **régiment**) Rgt

regagner [rǝɡaɲe] VT **1** (*confiance, affection, estime, amitié de qn*) to regain, to win *or* get back; **r. le temps perdu** to make up for lost time; **r. le terrain perdu** to make up lost ground; **r. aux courses l'argent perdu à la Bourse** to win back on the horses the money lost on the Stock Exchange; **c'est en 1999 qu'il s'est mis à r. de l'argent** it was in 1999 that he started earning money again **2** (*en-*

droit) to get back to; **r. son foyer** to go back *or* return home; **r. sa place** to go back *or* return to one's place; **r. la côte à la nage** to swim back to shore; **r. la capitale en hélicoptère** to go back to the capital by helicopter; **ils purent r. l'Espagne après la mort de Franco** they were able to go back *or* return to Spain after Franco's death; **vous êtes maintenant autorisés à r. vos bureaux** you may now go back to your offices

regain [rǝɡɛ̃] NM (*d'intérêt, activité*) renewal, revival; **un r. d'espoir** renewed hope; **ce r. d'activité/d'intérêt nous a surpris** this renewed activity/interest surprised us; **on constate un r. d'activité sur les marchés boursiers** we can see renewed activity *or* a renewal of activity on the Stock Market; **connaître un r. de vie** to have a new lease of life

régal, -als [regal] NM treat; **les marrons glacés, c'est mon r.** I adore marrons glacés, marrons glacés are my favourite treat; **cette tarte aux pommes est un r.** this apple tart is delicious; **c'est un vrai r. de l'écouter** it's a treat *or* a pleasure to listen to him; **c'est un r. pour les yeux** it's a sight for sore eyes

régalade [regalad] NF *Fam* **boire à la r.** to pour a drink down one's throat without the bottle touching one's lips

régale [regal] ADJ *Chimie* **eau r.** aqua regia

régaler¹ [regale] VT (*sol*) to level

régaler² VT *Fam* **r. qn** to give sb an excellent meal; **r. qn de qch** to regale sb with sth
  VI *Fam* **c'est moi qui régale** it's on me, (it's) my treat
  VPR **se régaler on s'est (bien) régalés!** we had an absolute feast!; **se r. de qch** to adore sth; *Fig* **elle se régale avec ses petits-enfants** she's having the time of her life with her grandchildren

regard [rǝɡar] NM **1** (*des yeux*) look; (*coup d'œil*) glance; **un r. tendre/amusé/intelligent** a tender/an amused/an intelligent look *or* expression in one's eyes; **r. appuyé** fixed *or* intent gaze *or* look; **ses regards appuyés me dérangent** I don't like the way he looks at me so intently *or* stares at me; **r. de côté** sidelong glance *or* look; **r. vitreux** glassy stare, glazed look; **porter son r. sur qn/qch** to look at sb/sth; **détourner le r.** to look away, to avert one's eyes *or* gaze; **avoir un beau r.** to have beautiful eyes; **nous eûmes un r. complice** we exchanged a knowing look; **avant tout, Lauren Bacall, c'était un r.** the first thing you noticed about Lauren Bacall was the way she looked at you; **je sentis son r. se poser sur moi** I felt him/her looking at me, I felt his/her gaze on me; **tourner son r. vers qn/qch** to turn one's gaze *or* eyes to sb/sth; **jeter un r. à qn** to glance at sb; **jeter** *ou* **lancer un r. à** *ou* **sur qch** to (cast a) glance at sth; **jeter un r. autour de soi** to glance round; **lancer un r. furieux à qn** to glare at sb; **lancer un r. noir à qn** to give sb a black look; **chercher qn du r.** to look round for sb; **interroger qn du r., lancer à qn un r. interrogateur** to give sb a questioning look, to look at sb inquiringly; **j'ai compris au premier r.** I realized at a glance *or* immediately *or* right away; **exposé aux regards** exposed to view; **la jeune fille que l'on avait cachée aux regards des hommes** the young girl who had been kept out of the sight of men; **soustraire qn/qch aux regards de qn** to keep sb/sth out of sb's sight; **à l'abri des regards indiscrets** away from prying eyes; **attirer le(s) regard(s)** to attract attention, to be conspicuous; **elle attire tous les regards** everyone turns to look at her; **nous attirions des regards très étonnés** we were getting some very strange looks; **sous les regards de la foule** while the crowd looked on; **en r. de**

qch opposite *or* facing sth; *(comparé à)* compared with sth; **texte avec illustration en r.** text with illustration opposite *or* on the opposite page; **au r. de nos livres de comptabilité** on looking at *or* examining our accounts; **au r. de la loi, elle est coupable** she is guilty in the eyes of the law; *Fig* **porter un nouveau r./un r. critique sur qch** to take a fresh/critical look at sth

2 *(ouverture)* *(d'une porte)* peephole; **r.** **(d'accès** *ou* **de visite)** inspection hole; *(d'un égout)* manhole

3 *(contrôle)* *Jur* **droit de r.** right of inspection; **je demande un droit de r. sur tous les textes qui sortent de ce bureau** I demand the right to check all texts leaving this office

> Il faut noter que le terme anglais **regard** est un faux ami. Il ne correspond jamais au français **regard**.

regardant [rəgardã] ADJ **1** *(avare)* careful with one's money; **être r. à la dépense/sur l'argent que l'on donne** to be careful how one spends one's money/gives one's money away **2** *(exigeant)* **elle n'est pas regardante sur la présentation** she's not concerned *or* bothered about the presentation

REGARDER [rəgarde]

> VT to look at **1** ▪ to watch **1** ▪ to consider **2** ▪ to concern **3**
> VI to look **1** ▪ to face **2**

VT **1** *(personne, chose)* to look at; *(émission, film etc)* to watch; **r. qn dans les yeux** to look sb in the eye *or* eyes; **r. qn dans le blanc des yeux** to look sb straight in the eye; **r. qn fixement** to stare at sb; **r. qn avec méfiance** to look at *or* eye sb suspiciously; **regarde où tu marches** *ou* **où tu mets les pieds!** look *or* watch where you're going *or* where you're putting your feet!; **r. qn faire qch** to watch sb doing *or* do sth; **elle le regardait partir** she watched him leaving *or* leave; **elle veut être regardée** she wants people to look at her, she wants to attract attention; **r. une définition dans le dictionnaire** to look up a word in the dictionary; *Fam* **regarde voir si ce n'est pas cuit** (check and) see if it's cooked yet; *Fam* **regarde-moi ça!** *(viens voir)* (come and) look at this!; *Fam* **regarde-moi ça, c'est ce que tu appelles du travail fini!** just look at this, that's what you call a job well done!; *Fam* **non, mais tu ne m'as pas regardé!** what do you take me for? SEE GRAMMAR A41; B35

2 *(considérer)* *(personne, chose)* to regard, to consider (**comme** as); **r. la vie en face** to face up to life; **r. les choses en face** to face (up to) things; **il faut r. les choses telles qu'elles sont** you've got to see things as they are; **elle regardait cela d'un mauvais œil** she was far from keen on the idea, *Fml, Litt* she took a jaundiced view of it; **ne r. que ses intérêts** to consider only one's own interests

3 *(concerner)* *(personne)* to concern; **cela ne regarde que moi** that's nobody's business but mine; **cela ne vous regarde pas** that doesn't concern you, that's no concern of yours, that's none of your business

VI **1 puis-je r.?** can I look?, can I have a look?; **je regarde seulement, merci** *(dans un magasin)* I'm just looking *or* having a look, thank you; **r. en bas/en arrière/autour de soi** to look down/back/round; **r. vers l'avenir** to look to the future; **r. par** *ou* **à la fenêtre** *(du dedans)* to look out of the window; *(du dehors)* to look in (through) the window; **r. par le trou de la serrure** to peep *or* look through the keyhole; **r. dans le dictionnaire** to look in the dictionary; **je ne suis pas sûr de l'orthographe, je vais r. dans le dictionnaire** I'm not sure of the spelling, I'll look it up in the dictionary

2 r. sur *ou* **vers** *(jardin, rue etc)* to look on to, to face

3 r. à qch to pay attention to sth; **sans r. à la dépense** regardless of expense; **je ne regarde pas à vingt euros** I'm not worried about twenty euros; **à y bien r.** on thinking it over; **y bien r.** *ou* **y r. à deux fois avant de faire qch** to think twice before doing sth; **je n'y regarde pas de si près** I'm not as fussy as all that

VPR **se regarder** *(d'une seule personne)* to look at oneself; *(de deux personnes)* to look at each other; **mais regarde-toi donc!** just look at you!; **se r. dans les yeux** to gaze *or* look into each other's eyes; **ils se regardaient en chiens de faïence** they were glaring at each other; **nos deux maisons se regardent** our houses face each other *or* are opposite each other; **ça se regarde dans les deux sens** there are two ways of looking at that; *Fam* **elle ne s'est pas regardée!**, **elle s'est regardée, elle?** she's got a cheek to talk!, she can talk!

> Il faut noter que le verbe anglais **to regard** est un faux ami. Il ne signifie jamais **regarder**.

regarnir [rəgarnir] VT *(garde-manger, étagères)* to restock; **r. une trousse de maquillage** to stock up on make-up; **il faut que je regarnisse mon portefeuille** I must get some money *or* cash

régate [regat] NF *Naut* regatta; **faire de la r.** to race; **faire une r.** to have *or* hold a regatta; **r. à voiles** yacht races; **r. à l'aviron** boat races

régater [regate] VI *Naut* to race

régatier, -ière [regatje, -jɛr] N *Naut* racing yachtsman, *f* racing yachtswoman; *(à l'aviron)* racing oarsman, *f* racing oarswoman

regazonner [rəgazɔne] VT to returf

regel [rəʒɛl] NM renewed frost

regeler [rəʒ(ə)le] VI (**il regèle**; **il regèlera**) to freeze again

régence [reʒãs] NF regency; *Hist* **la R.** the Regency *(1715-1723)*
ADJ INV **style R.** Regency (style); **meubles style R.** Regency furniture; *Fam* **elle est très r.** she's very genteel

régénérateur, -trice [reʒeneratœr, -tris] ADJ regenerating, regenerative; *Rel* **eau régénératrice** baptismal water; *Nucl* **pile régénératrice** breeder reactor
NM *Ind* regenerator, regenerating plant *or* furnace

régénération [reʒenerasjɔ̃] NF **1** *(d'une cellule, de la peau etc)* regeneration **2** *Ind* reconditioning; *Nucl* breeding; *Ordinat* **r. de l'écran** screen refresh

régénérer [reʒenere] (**je régénère, n. régénérons; je régénérerai**) VT **1** *Biol* *(cellule, épiderme)* to regenerate; *Fig (d'une douche, des vacances)* to refresh; **cette discussion/rencontre m'a régénérée** I feel alive again *or* regenerated after that talk/meeting **2** *(catalyseur)* to reactivate
VPR **se régénérer** *Biol (de cellule)* to regenerate (itself); *Fig (de l'enthousiasme, l'intérêt)* to reawaken

régent, -ente [reʒã, -ãt] N **1** *Pol* regent **2** *Fin Anciennement* director **3** *Belg Scol* (secondary) schoolmaster **4 le R.** *(diamant)* the Regent diamond
ADJ **reine régente/prince r.** Queen/Prince Regent

régenter [reʒãte] VT *(personne)* to dictate to; **il veut tout r.** he wants to run everything *or* the show

reggae [rege] NM, ADJ INV reggae; **un chanteur de r.** a reggae singer

régicide [reʒisid] N regicide
NM *(crime)* regicide
ADJ regicidal

régie [reʒi] NF **1** *Admin* management, control; *(d'un domaine)* administration, stewardship; **en r.** in the hands of trustees **2** *(entreprise publique)* public corporation, state-owned company **3** *Hist* **la R.** = collection of taxes by state functionaries, *Br* ≃ Customs and Excise; **employé de la r.** exciseman **4** *Théâtre* management; *Cin* production; *Radio* control room; *TV* control room, gallery; *TV, Cin* **r. de contrôle** video control room; **r. de diffusion** broadcast suite; **r. d'exploitation** control room; **r. de montage** edit suite; **r. mobile** mobile control centre, mobile control room; **r. publicitaire** advertising sales agency, space selling organization; **r. vidéo** video centre
▸▸ **r. du dépôt légal** copyright department; *Admin* **r. des impôts indirects** excise (administration), *Br* ≃ Customs and Excise department; *Can* **R. des Loyers** ≃ rental board

regimber [rəʒɛ̃be] VI *(d'une personne)* to jib, to ba(u)lk (**contre** at), to kick (**contre** against); *(d'un cheval)* to kick (**contre** at, against); **il est toujours à r.** he's always protesting about something; **il est inutile de r.** there's no point protesting

régime [reʒim] NM **1** *Pol, Admin* (form *or* system of) government, regime; **le r. féodal** the feudal system; *Hist* **l'Ancien R.** the old regime, the Ancien Régime; **le r. actuel** the present government; **sous le r. de Chirac/Blair** during the Chirac/Blair administration; **la chute du r.** the fall of the regime or the government; **r. militaire/parlementaire/totalitaire** military/parliamentary/totalitarian regime

2 *(règlements)* **r. des hôpitaux/des prisons** hospital/prison regulations *or* rules; **le r. du travail** the organization of labour; **nous nous sommes mariés sous le r. de la communauté/de la séparation de biens** our marriage was on the basis of a joint settlement of property/of separate ownership of property; **r. douanier** customs system; **r. électoral** electoral system; **r. de faveur** preferential treatment; **r. fiscal** tax system; *Fin* **r. du forfait** standard assessment system, fixed rate tax assessment system; **r. d'imposition** tax system; *Écon* **r. préférentiel** special arrangements; **r. de protection sociale** social welfare system; *Fin* **r. du réel** full assessment system; *Fin* **r. du réel simplifié** simplified full assessment system; **r. de retraite** pension plan; **r. de retraite par capitalisation** funded pension scheme; *Fin* **r. simplifié** simplified system; *Com* **r. de transit** transit system

3 *Aut* (engine) speed; **à haut r.** at high speed; **à moyen r.** at average speed; *Tech* **r. (nominal)** *(d'une machine, d'un moteur, groupe électrogène)* rating; **r. de marche normal** normal working *or* operating conditions; **charge de r.** rated load; **puissance de r.** normal power; *Aviat, Naut, Aut* **r. de croisière** cruising speed; *Aut* **r. moteur** engine speed; **elle fait trois litres au cent en r. de ville** she does 100 km to three litres in town *or* on an urban cycle; **aller à plein r.** to go full throttle; *Fig* **à ce r., on aura fini dans trois jours** at this rate, we'll be finished in three days; *Élec* **r. de charge** *(d'un accumulateur)* charging rate; **variations de r.** load variations

4 *Géog* *(d'une rivière etc)* (rate of) flow; **r. climatique** climatic conditions; **r. thermique** temperature pattern

5 *(alimentaire)* diet; **être au r.** to be on a diet, to be dieting; **se mettre au r.** to go on a diet; **je dois faire** *ou* **suivre un r.** I must go on a diet; **mettre qn au r.** to put sb on a diet; **r.**

lacté/sans sel/équilibré/sec milk/salt-free/balanced/alcohol-free diet; **r. amincissant** slimming diet; **r. dissocié** food-combining diet, Hay diet; *Fam* **le r. jockey** a starvation diet; *Méd* **r. hyposodé** low-salt diet, low-sodium diet

6 *Gram* object; **cas r.** objective case; **r. direct/indirect** direct/indirect object

7 *(de bananes)* bunch, stem, hand; *(de dattes)* bunch, stem

régiment [reʒimɑ̃] NM *Mil* regiment; *Fig (d'admirateurs, créanciers)* host, swarm; *Fam* **aller au r.** to join the army; **quand j'étais au r.** when I was in the army, when I was doing my military service; **la musique/le drapeau du r.** the regimental band/colours; *Fam* **il y en a pour un r.** there's enough for a whole army

régimentaire [reʒimɑ̃tɛr] ADJ regimental

région [reʒjɔ̃] NF *(d'un pays)* region, area; *Admin* region; **r. militaire** military district, command; **dans la r. de Nantes** in the Nantes area, in the region of Nantes; **en r.** in the provinces, in provincial areas; **je ne connais pas la r.** I don't know the area; **si jamais tu passes dans la r. …** if you're ever in the area …; **les régions polaires** the polar regions; **dans nos régions** in these regions; **la r. parisienne** Paris and its suburbs; **j'habite dans la r. parisienne** I live in the Paris area; *Admin* **la r. Nord-Pas-de-Calais** the Nord-Pas-de-Calais Region; **je suis financé par la R.** I get funding from the region; **r. productrice de coton** cotton-growing area; **r. du vin** wine-producing area; **r. minière** mining area *or* district; *Anat* **la r. lombaire/du cœur** the lumbar/heart region; **r. cible** target area; *Com* **r. test** test area

régional, -ale, -aux, -ales [reʒjɔnal, -o] ADJ *(expressions, cuisine, développement etc)* regional; *(conseil)* local
▪ NM **1** *Tél* area telephone system **2** *Suisse (train omnibus)* local train

régionalisation [reʒjɔnalizasjɔ̃] NF regionalization

régionaliser [reʒjɔnalize] VT **1** *(décentraliser)* to regionalize **2** *(organiser au niveau régional)* **r. un programme d'investissements** to break down an investment programme by region

régionalisme [reʒjɔnalism] NM regionalism

régionaliste [reʒjɔnalist] ADJ regional
▪ N **1** *(écrivain)* regional writer **2** *Pol* regionalist

régir [reʒir] VT *(d'une loi, d'un principe physique), Gram (cas, nom)* to govern; *(domaine)* to manage; **r. des biens** to manage assets

régisseur [reʒisœr] NM *(d'un domaine)* agent, manager; *Vieilli* steward; *(d'une ferme)* bailiff; *Théâtre* stage manager; *Cin* assistant director; *TV* **r. de plateau** floor manager, FM; **r. de plateau adjoint** assistant floor manager, AFM; **r. général** location manager

registre [reʒistr] NM **1** *(livre)* register, record; *(de comptes)* account book; *(des délibérations)* minute book; *Tech (de machine)* log book; **rapporter un article sur un r.** to post *or* enter an item in a register; **s'inscrire au r. du commerce** to enter oneself in the trade register; **signer le r.** *(d'un hôtel)* to sign the register; **les registres de l'état civil** the registers of births, marriages and deaths **2** *Mus* register; *(étendue totale)* compass **3** *Typ* register **4** *Tech* regulator lever, throttle (valve) **5** *Ordinat* register **6** *(d'une œuvre)* tone, style; **changer de r.** *(d'un écrivain)* to change one's style; **il choisit ses images dans un r. poétique** he uses poetic images **7** *Ling* register

▸▸ *Ordinat* **r. d'accès mémoire** memory access register; **r. des actionnaires** register of shareholders, shareholders' register; *Tech* **r. d'aérage** ventilation flap; **r. des arrivées** *(d'un hôtel)* arrivals register; **r. de cheminée** *(d'un fourneau, d'une cheminée)* register, damper; **r. des chevaux** stud book; **r. de comptabilité** account book, ledger; **r. des départs** *(d'un hôtel)* departures book; **r. électoral** electoral register; **r. à feuillets rechargeables** loose-leaf register; **r. d'index** index register; *Com* **r. international des marques** international trademark register; **r. de présence** attendance register; **r. des procès-verbaux** minutes book; **r. des salaires** payroll

réglable [reglabl] ADJ adjustable

réglage [reglaʒ] NM **1** *(d'un siège)* adjustment; *(d'un appareil)* adjustment, regulating, setting; *(dispositif)* adjuster; *(d'un chronomètre)* rating; **r. automatique** automatic control; **à r. automatique** self-adjusting; **vis de r.** set screw; **r. de la vitesse** speed control; *Aut* **r. de distribution** valve timing; *Aut* **r. de pression** pressure setting; **r. des phares** headlamp adjustment; *Aut* **r. programmable** *(des sièges)* memory setting; **r. en hauteur** height adjustment; *Mil* **r. du tir** ranging **2** *Radio, TV* tuning; **réglages** dial readings; **r. de la luminosité** brightness control; *TV, Ordinat* **r. du contraste** contrast control; *TV, Ordinat* **r. du volume** volume control **3** *(du papier)* ruling

règle [regl] NF **1** *(de conduite, de grammaire etc), Rel (d'un ordre)* rule; **les règles de l'honneur** the code of honour; **les règles de la politesse exigent que …** courtesy demands that …; **c'est la première des règles de politesse** it's common courtesy; **les règles du jeu** the rules of the game; *Fig* **c'est la r. du jeu** that's the rule of the game; *Fig* **le gouvernement a encore changé les règles du jeu** the government have moved the goalposts again; **se faire une r. de se coucher de bonne heure** to make it a rule to go to bed early; **en r.** *(passeport, papiers)* in order; **reçu en r.** formal receipt; **bataille en r.** *Mil* battle according to the rules; *Fig* regular set-to; **je suis en r. avec lui** I'm all square with him; **être en r. avec sa conscience** to have a clear conscience; **mettre qch en r.** to sort sth out; **tout est en r.** everything is in order *or* is correct; **en r. générale** as a general rule; **agir dans les règles** to behave properly, to play by the rules; **jouer selon les règles** to play by the rules; *Fig* **dans** *ou* **selon les règles de l'art** by *or* according to the book; *Fig* **elle fait la bouillabaisse selon les règles de l'art** makes a classic *or* traditional bouillabaisse; **c'est la r.** that's the rule; **comme c'est la r., comme de r.** as is the rule

2 *(pour tracer des lignes)* ruler; *Tech* rule; *(d'arpenteur)* measuring rod; *Ordinat (sur écran)* ruler line; **r. graduée** ruler; **tirer des traits à la r.** to draw lines with a ruler

3 *Physiol* **règles** period; **avoir ses règles** to have one's period; **règles abondantes** heavy periods; **absence de règles** amenorrhoea

▸▸ *Sport* **r. de l'avantage** advantage rule; **r. à calcul** slide rule; *Compta* **r. du décalage d'un mois** one month in arrears rule; *Typ* **r. d'encadrement** panel rule; **r. d'or** golden rule; *Naut* **règles de route** *(en mer)* rule of the road; *Math* **r. de trois** rule of three

réglé [regle] ADJ **1** *(papier)* ruled; **papier non r.** plain paper **2** *(organisé)* regular, well-ordered, fixed, steady; **vie réglée (comme du papier à musique)** well-ordered life; *Fam* **r. comme du papier à musique** as regular as clockwork; **elle a un emploi du temps r. comme du papier à musique** she has a very strict routine, *Fam* you could set your watch by her **3** *(jeune fille)* who has started having

periods; **elle est mal réglée** she's not very regular

règlement [reglǝmɑ̃] NM **1** *(d'un compte)* settlement; *(paiement)* payment; **faire un r. par chèque** to pay by cheque; **pour r. de tout compte** in full settlement; **r. au comptant** payment in cash, cash payment; **en cours de r.** being settled, under discussion **2** *(statut)* regulation(s); *(d'université)* statutes; *(d'une société)* rules; **le r. intérieur** *(d'une école)* school rules; *(d'un bureau)* staff *or* company regulations; **c'est le r.** that's the rule; **les règlements militaires** army regulations; **règlements douaniers** customs regulations; **règlements et usages** code of practice

▸▸ **r. à l'amiable** amicable settlement; *Fig* **r. de compte(s)** settling of scores; *UE* **r. européen** piece of European legislation; *Jur* **r. judiciaire** compulsory liquidation; **se mettre en r. judiciaire** to go into liquidation *or* receivership; *Admin* **règlements de police** by(e)-laws

réglementaire [reglǝmɑ̃tɛr] ADJ statutory, regulation; **tenue r.** regulation uniform; **ce n'est pas r.** it's against the rules; **faire qch dans le temps r.** to do sth in the prescribed time; **le score était de 0-0 à l'issue du temps r.** the full-time score was nil-nil; **dispositions réglementaires** regulations

réglementariste [reglǝmɑ̃tarist] ADJ *(attitude, professeur etc)* pernickety, nit-picking; **un fonctionnaire r.** a civil servant who goes by the book
▪ N nit-picker, pernickety person

réglementation [reglǝmɑ̃tasjɔ̃] NF **1** *(action)* regulating, regulation; **r. du trafic des changes** exchange control; **r. douanière** customs regulations; **r. du change** exchange control regulations; **r. du travail** labour legislation; **r. sur l'hygiène** health regulations; **r. sur l'hygiène alimentaire** food hygiene regulations; **r. sur l'hygiène et la sécurité** health and safety regulations; **r. sur la sécurité** safety regulations **2** **la r.** *(règles)* the regulations, the rules

réglementer [reglǝmɑ̃te] VT *(ventes, importations)* to regulate, to make rules for; **r. le droit de grève** to control the right to strike

régler [regle] (**je règle, n. réglons; je réglerai**) VT **1** *(papier)* to line

2 *(mécanisme, montre, siège, boussole), Aut (allumage, freins, ceinture de sécurité), TV (image)* to adjust; *(radio), Aut (moteur)* to tune; **r. sa journée** to plan one's day; **jeune homme, il faut r. ta conduite** young man, it's about time you mended your ways; **r. ses dépenses sur ses revenus** to cut one's coat to suit one's cloth; **les obligations qui règlent des échanges commerciaux** the obligations that govern trade; *Tech, Aut etc* **r. qch avec précision** to fine-tune sth; *Sport* **r. l'allure** to set the pace; **r. son allure sur celle de son compagnon** to adjust one's pace to that of one's companion; *Mil* **r. le tir** to range; **la pendule est bien réglée** the clock keeps good time; **il a réglé sa montre sur la mienne** he set his watch by mine; **r. les livres** to balance the books

3 *(résoudre) (question, dispute)* to settle; **r. ses affaires** to put one's affairs in order; **r. à l'amiable** to settle out of court

4 *(payer) (compte)* to settle; *(facture)* to settle, to pay; *(épicier, femme de ménage, note, loyer etc)* to pay; **est-ce que j'ai réglé tout ce que je vous devais?** are we square?, have I paid you everything I owed you?; **je peux vous r. par chèque?** will you take a cheque?, can I pay by cheque?; **r. au comptant** to pay in cash; **r. le gaz** to pay the gas bill; **r. son compte à qn** *(se venger)* to settle accounts with sb; **je vais lui r. son compte** I'll settle his/her hash *or* score, I'll sort him/her out; **r. de vieux comptes** to pay off *or* settle old scores

vi to pay; **r. en espèces** to pay (in) cash; **c'est moi qui règle** I'm paying, this is on me

vpr se régler 1 *(d'un mécanisme)* to be adjustable; **son pas finit par se r. sur celui de son compagnon** he finished up walking at the same rhythm as his companion **2** *(se finir)* to be concluded *or* settled; **ça s'est réglé à l'amiable** it was settled amicably

réglette [reglɛt] **NF** small ruler; *Aut (d'une boîte de vitesses)* control rod; *Mktg (sur rayon de magasin)* shelf strip; *Ordinat* **r. de clavier** keyboard template

réglisse [reglis] **NF** *Bot* liquorice

NM OU NF liquorice; **bâton de r.** stick of liquorice; **bonbon à la** *ou* **au r.** liquorice-flavoured *or Am* -flavored sweet

réglo [reglo] **ADJ INV** *Fam (contrat, proposition)* kosher; **ça n'est pas très r.** that's a bit dodgy; **elle a été très r.** she played by the rules; **c'est un type très r.** he's as straight as a die *or* as they come, *Am* he's a regular guy; **il n'a pas été très r. avec moi** he wasn't very straight with me

réglure [reglyr] **NF** *(sur ou du papier)* ruling; **r. fine** feint; **à r. fine** feint-ruled

régnant [reɲɑ̃] **ADJ** *(prince, famille)*, *Fig (idéologie)* reigning; *Fig (opinion)* prevailing

règne [rɛɲ] **NM 1** *(d'un roi, d'une reine)*, *Fig (d'un champion, de la démocratie)* reign; **sous le r. de Louis XIV** in the reign of Louis XIV; **c'est le r. de l'argent/de la technologie** money/technology reigns supreme **2** *(végétal, animal)* kingdom

régner [reɲe] **vi** (je **règne**, n. **régnons**; je **régnerai**) **1** *(d'un monarque)* to reign, to rule; *Fig (de conditions)* to exist, *Fml* to prevail; *(d'une opinion)* to be prevalent, to hold sway; **r. (pendant) dix ans** to reign *or* rule for ten years; **r. sur un pays** to reign over *or* rule (over) a country; **r. sur l'opinion** to be predominant, to hold sway; **r. en maître sur qch** to reign supreme over sth; **diviser pour mieux r.** divide and conquer; **s'efforcer de faire r. la paix** to try to keep the peace; **la police est chargée de faire r. l'ordre** the police are there to keep law and order; **la terreur qu'ils faisaient r. a pris fin** their reign of terror is at an end; **la suspicion qui règne au bureau** the climate of suspicion in the office *or* which pervades the office; **il règne une ambiance très étrange dans la ville** a very strange atmosphere prevails in the town; **il régnait, dans la maison, une atmosphère de paix et de tranquillité** peace and quiet reigned in the house; *Iron* **la confiance règne!** there's trust *or* confidence for you!, confidence reigns supreme!

2 *Vieilli* **une galerie règne le long du bâtiment** a gallery runs *or* extends along the building

regonfler [rəgɔ̃fle] **vt** *(ballon)* to reinflate, to blow up again; *(pneus)* to blow up, to pump up; *Fam* **r. (le moral à) qn** to cheer sb up; *Fam* **je suis regonflé à bloc!** I'm back on form!

vi *(d'une rivière)* to swell, to rise (again); **son pied a regonflé** his/her foot has swollen up again *or* is swollen again

regorger [rəgɔrʒe] **vi** (je **regorgeai(s)**; n. **regorgeons**) **r. de qch** to have an abundance of sth, to abound in sth; **r. de monde** *(d'un train, magasin, d'une pièce)* to be packed (with people), to be packed to overflowing; *(des rues)* to be packed, to be teeming *or* swarming with people; **la ville regorge de musées** the town has an abundance of museums

régresser [regrese] **vi 1** *(diminuer)* *(de la criminalité, d'une théorie, d'un style)* to decline; *(d'un parti politique)* to lose ground; *(de la douleur)* to improve; *(de la production,*

du chiffre d'affaires) to drop; **j'ai régressé en maths** my maths has deteriorated; **l'industrie textile régresse** the textile industry is in decline **2** *Psy* to regress

régressif, -ive [regresif, -iv] **ADJ** regressive; *(impôt, tarif)* tapering; *Biol* **forme régressive** throwback

régression [regresjɔ̃] **NF 1** regression; *Math* **coefficient de r.** regression coefficient **2** *Biol* retrogression; *Psy* regression; **être en r.** to be regressing **3** *(des affaires, ventes etc)* decline, drop; **être en r.** *(d'une épidémie)* to be on the decline, to be losing ground; *(du chômage, de la production etc)* to be on the decline, to be declining

regret [rəgrɛ] **NM** regret (**de** for); **rongé de regrets** eaten up with regret; **avoir des regrets** to feel regret, to be sorry; **j'avais des regrets de ne l'avoir pas vu davantage** I was sorry not to see more of him, I regretted not seeing more of him; **tu as déjà des regrets?** are you regretting it already?; **exprimer ses regrets** to express one's regret; **exprimer le r. de ne pouvoir être présent** to express regret at not being able to be present; **faire qch à r.** to do sth with regret *or* reluctantly; **j'ai dû le faire à r.** I was reluctant to do it, I did it reluctantly; **... dit-elle avec r. ...** she said with regret *or* regretfully; **nous nous en sommes séparés avec r.** we were sorry to part with it; **je suis parti sans r., c'est sans r. que je suis parti** I left without regret, I had no regrets about leaving; **je n'ai aucun r.** I have no regrets; **je n'ai qu'un r., c'est que ...** my only regret is that ...; **j'ai r. à vous quitter** I'm sorry to leave you; **j'ai le r.** *ou* **je suis au r. de vous annoncer que ...** I regret *or* am sorry to inform you that ...; **je suis au r. de ne pouvoir vous répondre favorablement** I regret that I cannot give you a favourable answer; **à mon (grand) r.** (much) to my regret; *Fam* **sans r.?** (you have) no regrets?, you're quite happy about it?; *Fam* **tous mes regrets!** sorry!, my apologies!; **un ton plein de r.** a regretful *or* sorrowful tone of voice; **mourir sans laisser de regrets** to die unmourned; **le r. du pays natal** homesickness; **éprouver le r. du pays natal** to be *or* feel homesick

regrettable [rəgrɛtabl] **ADJ** *(erreur, retard, incident etc)* regrettable, unfortunate; **il est tout à fait r. que vous n'ayez pas été prévenu** it is most unfortunate that you were not informed

regrettablement [rəgrɛtabləmɑ̃] **ADV** *Rare* regrettably

regretter [rəgrɛte] **vt 1** *(sa naïveté, son imprudence etc)* to regret; **vous le regretterez** you'll regret it, you'll be sorry, you'll rue the day; **tu ne le regretteras pas!** you won't regret it!, you won't be sorry!; **je ne regrette rien** I have no regrets; **je regrette le jour où je l'ai rencontré** I rue the day I met him; **il me ferait presque r. ma gentillesse** I'm almost sorry I was so kind to him; **je regrette de vous annoncer que ...** I regret to inform you that ...; **r. d'avoir fait qch** to regret *or* be sorry for having done sth; **je ne regrette pas d'avoir dit cela** I'm not sorry I said it, I don't regret saying it; **je regrette qu'elle soit partie si tôt** I'm sorry that she left so early, I wish she hadn't left so early; **il est à r. que ... il** it is to be regretted that ..., it is unfortunate *or* regrettable that ...; **son absence est à r.** his/her absence is unfortunate *or* regrettable *or* is to be regretted; **je regrette!** (I'm) sorry!; **je regrette, je ne pourrai pas y assister** I'm sorry, I won't be able to attend, *Fml* regretfully, I will be unable to attend

2 *(personne, endroit)* to miss; **mourir regretté de tous** to die mourned by all; **il sera regretté de tous** he'll be greatly *or* sorely missed; **r. sa jeunesse/son enfance** to wish

one was young/a child again; **r. son argent** to wish one had one's money back

regrèvement [rəgrɛvmɑ̃] **NM** *Fin* tax increase

regrimper [rəgrɛ̃pe] **vt** *(escalier, pente)* to climb (up) again

vi to climb again; *Fam (de la fièvre)* to go up again; **r. à l'arbre** to climb the tree again

regrossir [rəgrosir] **vi** to put on weight again

regroupement [rəgrupmɑ̃] **NM 1** grouping; *(d'animaux, d'enfants)* rounding up, round-up; *(de sociétés)* amalgamation; *(de comptes)* consolidation; *Mil* regrouping **2** *(groupe)* grouping

regrouper [rəgrupe] **vt** *(personnes)* to gather *or* bring together; *(animaux, enfants)* to round up; *(objets)* to gather *or* put together; *Mil (hommes)* to regroup; *(sections, sociétés)* to merge, to amalgamate; *(comptes)* to consolidate; **les dernières œuvres de Dali ont été regroupées** *(pour cette exposition)* Dali's last paintings have been brought together; **regroupons le parti autour d'une idée-force** let us unite the party around a key idea; **nous avons regroupé nos économies pour lui faire un beau cadeau** we pooled our savings to get him/her a nice present

vpr se regrouper *(de gens)* to gather *or* get together; *Mil (d'hommes)* to regroup; *(de sociétés)* to merge, to amalgamate

régularisation [regylarizasjɔ̃] **NF 1** *(d'une situation, d'un litige)* regularizing, regularization; *Fin (d'un compte, des stocks, charges)* adjustment; *(de papiers d'identité)* putting in order; **ses papiers sont en voie de r.** his/her papers are (in the process of) being put in order **2** *(d'une rivière, d'un mécanisme)* regulation, regulating; **r. de la circulation** traffic control

régulariser [regylarize] **vt 1** *(document)* to put into proper form; *(papiers d'identité)* to put in order; *Fin (compte)* to adjust; **r. une situation** to regularize *or Fam* sort out a situation; **est-ce qu'il va r. la situation?** *(en se mariant)* is he going to make an honest woman out of you/her? **2** *(fleuve, fonctionnement d'une machine)* to regulate; *(circulation)* to regulate, to control

régularité [regylarite] **NF 1** *(de traits, forme, habitudes)* regularity; *(d'un mouvement)* steadiness, evenness, regularity; **faire qch avec une r. infaillible** to do sth with unfailing regularity; **faire preuve de r.** to be reliable; **avec une r. d'horloge** as regular as clockwork **2** *(conformité aux règles)* *(d'une élection, d'un vote etc)* legality; *Fin* **r. et sincérité des charges** true and fair nature of expenses

régulateur, -trice [regylatœr, -tris] **ADJ** *(mécanisme, hormone etc)* regulating; **soupape régulatrice** governor valve; **le travail est un élément r.** having a job brings a degree of order to your life

NM 1 *(dispositif)* *Tech* regulator; *(d'une horloge)* regulator, governor, balance wheel; *(d'une turbine)* regulator, governor; *(d'une machine à vapeur)* throttle valve, regulator, governor; **r. de marge** margin stop; *Théâtre* **r. d'éclairage de scène** stage dimmer; *Tech* **r. de tension** voltage smoother; *Tech* **r. de vitesse** speed governor **2** *(personne)*, *Rail* controller, *Am* dispatcher; *(de taxis)* dispatcher; **r. aérien** air traffic controller

régulation [regylasjɔ̃] **NF 1** *(action de régler)* *(d'un compas)* regulation, readjustment **2** *(contrôle)* *(de la circulation)*, *Tech (du carburant, de la pression)* control; **r. des naissances** birth control; *Élec* **r. de la tension** voltage regulation *or* control

régulier, -ière[1] [regylje, -jɛr] **ADJ 1** *(service de bus, examens, visites)* regular; *(augmentation, mouvement, progrès)* steady; *(pouls, res-*

piration, coups, revenu) regular, steady; *(vie) (pleine d'habitudes)* ordered; *(morale)* honourable, *Am* honorable; *(résultats)* consistent, steady; *(écriture, couche, pression)* even; *(paroi)* smooth; **avoir un visage r.** *ou* **des traits réguliers** to have regular features; **il fit avec le pinceau un trait bien r.** he painted an even line; **son travail n'est pas r.** his/her work isn't consistent *or* is patchy, he/she doesn't work consistently; **c'est un employé r.** he's a steady worker; **c'est un élève r.** he's a consistent pupil; **se lever et se coucher à heures régulières** to keep regular hours; **être r. dans ses habitudes** to be regular in one's habits; **son humeur régulière** his/her even temper; **d'une humeur régulière** even-tempered; **à intervalles réguliers** at regular intervals

2 *(conforme)* legitimate; *(honnête)* straight, on the level; **ce n'est pas r.** that's not above board; **le coup n'était pas r.** it was a bit of a dirty trick, it was a low blow; **il n'a pas été très r. dans cette affaire** he didn't altogether play by the rules *or* go by the book; **être r. en affaires** to be an honest person to deal with; **il n'a pas été très r. avec moi** he didn't play fair with me, he wasn't straight with me; **être en situation régulière** to have one's official papers in order; *Gram* **verbe r.** regular verb SEE GRAMMAR A38; B24 ; **quittance régulière** receipt in due form, proper receipt

3 *(soldat, clergé)* regular; **troupes régulières** regular troops, regulars

4 *Can (standard) (format, prix etc)* standard, *surtout Am* regular

▸ **N** regular (customer); **un r. du bar** a regular (at the bar)

régulière² NF **1** *Vieilli, Hum Fam (épouse)* old lady, *Br* missus; *(petite amie)* steady **2** *Fam* **à la r.** fair and square

régulièrement [regyljɛrmɑ̃] ADV **1** *(avec constance) (aller à un endroit, rendre visite à qn etc)* regularly; *(respirer)* steadily, evenly; *(réparti, étalé)* evenly; **j'entendais des coups frappés r. contre le mur** I heard a steady knocking on the wall; **le son vous fera aller r. à la selle** bran will keep you regular; **elle va r. se plaindre chez le directeur** she regularly goes to the boss to complain **2** *(selon la loi)* legitimately, lawfully; **membres r. désignés** properly *or* duly elected members; **je ferai en sorte que les choses se passent r.** I'll make sure that things happen as they should

régurgitation [regyrʒitasjɔ̃] NF regurgitation

régurgiter [regyrʒite] VT *(nourriture)* to regurgitate

réhabilitation [reabilitasjɔ̃] NF **1** *(d'un délinquant)* rehabilitation; *(d'une faillite)* discharge; **obtenir la r. de qn** to clear sb's name **2** *(remise en état) (d'un quartier déshérité)* rehabilitation, renovation

réhabilité, -ée [reabilite] N rehabilitated person; *Fin* discharged bankrupt

réhabiliter [reabilite] VT **1** *(délinquant, politicien)* to rehabilitate; *(personne accusée d'un crime, nom de qn)* to clear; *(personne qui a fait faillite)* to discharge; **r. qn dans ses droits** to restore sb's rights **2** *(bâtiment, quartier)* to rehabilitate, to renovate; *(friche industrielle)* to reclaim

▸ **VPR se réhabiliter** to rehabilitate oneself, to restore one's reputation

réhabituer [reabitɥe] VT to reaccustom (**à** to); **r. qn à (faire) qch** to get sb used *or* accustomed to (doing) sth again

▸ **VPR se réhabituer se r. à (faire) qch** to get used *or* accustomed to (doing) sth again; **on va avoir du mal à se r.** we'll have trouble getting used to it again

rehaussement [rəosmɑ̃] NM *(d'un mur)* raising, heightening; *(d'un tableau sur un mur)* raising; **r. fiscal** tax increase

---

rehausser [rəose] VT **1** *(mur, bâtiment)* to make higher, to heighten **2** *(faire valoir) (couleur, teint)* to enhance, to set off; *(détail)* to enhance, to accentuate; **r. une veste de jalons** to liven up *or* brighten up a jacket with braid

réhausseur [reosœr] NM *Aut* child booster cushion

rehaut [rəo] NM *Beaux-Arts (sur un tableau)* highlight

réhydratation [reidratasjɔ̃] NF *Méd* rehydration

réimperméabiliser [reɛ̃pɛrmeabilize] VT *(imperméable)* to reproof

réimplantation [reɛ̃plɑ̃tasjɔ̃] NF **1** *(d'une société, usine)* relocation **2** *Chir* reimplantation; *(d'une dent)* reimplant

réimplanter [reɛ̃plɑ̃te] VT *Chir (une dent)* to reimplant

réimportation [reɛ̃pɔrtasjɔ̃] NF **1** reimport, reimportation **2** *(marchandise)* reimport

réimporter [reɛ̃pɔrte] VT to reimport

réimposer [reɛ̃poze] VT *Fin (produit)* to reintroduce tax on, to retax

réimposition [reɛ̃pozisjɔ̃] NF *Fin* retaxation

réimpression [reɛ̃presjɔ̃] NF **1** *(action)* reprinting; **en cours de r.** *(sur catalogue)* being reprinted, new edition pending; **c'est en cours de r.** it's being reprinted, there's a new edition pending **2** *(livre etc)* reprint

réimprimer [reɛ̃prime] VT to reprint

Reims [rɛ̃s] N Rheims

rein [rɛ̃] NM **1** *Anat* kidney; **r. artificiel** kidney *or* dialysis machine **2 reins** *(partie inférieure du dos)* (lower) back; *Litt (taille)* waist; **la chute** *ou* **le creux des reins** the small of the back; **douleur** *ou* **mal aux reins** backache, lower back pain; **avoir mal aux reins** to have a pain in the small of one's back; **les cheveux lui tombaient jusqu'aux reins** her hair went down to the small of her back; **donner un coup de reins** to heave; **j'ai dû donner un coup de reins pour soulever l'armoire** I had to heave the wardrobe up; *Fam* **se faire un tour de reins** to rick one's back; *Fig* **casser les reins à qn** to ruin *or* break sb; *Fig* **il a les reins solides** he's tough, he's made of pretty stern stuff; *(financièrement)* he's well-heeled

réincarcération [reɛ̃karserasjɔ̃] NF reimprisonment, *Fml* reincarceration

réincarcérer [reɛ̃karsere] VT to reimprison, *Fml* to reincarcerate

réincarnation [reɛ̃karnasjɔ̃] NF reincarnation

réincarner (se) [səreɛ̃karne] VPR to be reincarnated (**en qn/qch** as sb/sth); **je voudrais me r. en aigle** I want to be reincarnated *or* come back as an eagle

reine [rɛn] NF **1** *(monarque)*, *Fig* queen; **un port** *ou* **un maintien de r.** a queenly *or* regal bearing; **la r. Anne** Queen Anne; **la r. mère** the Queen Mother; *Fam (belle-mère)* the mother-in-law; *Fam* **je suis la r. des pommes!** what a total idiot I am! **2** *Entom (abeille)* queen (bee) **3** *Échecs* queen **4** *(femme)* **r. de beauté** beauty queen; **la r. du bal** the belle of the ball **5** *Sport* **la petite r.** cycling

reine-claude, *pl* **reines-claudes** [rɛnklod] NF greengage

reine-des-prés, *pl* **reines-des-prés** NF *Bot* meadowsweet

reine-marguerite, *pl* **reines-marguerites** NF *Bot* China aster

reinette [rɛnɛt] NF pippin; **r. grise** russet

réinfecter [reɛ̃fɛkte] VT to reinfect

▸ **VPR se réinfecter** to become reinfected

réinfection [reɛ̃fɛksjɔ̃] NF reinfection

réinitialisation [reinisjalizasjɔ̃] NF *Ordinat* restart; *(de la mémoire)* reinitialization; **sim-**

---

ple r. soft reset; **r. totale de la machine** hard reset

réinitialiser [reinisjalize] VT *Ordinat* to reset; *(mémoire)* to reinitialize

réinjecter [reɛ̃ʒɛkte] VT *(liquide)* to reinject; *(argent, fonds)* to reinject, to make a fresh injection of

réinscriptible [reɛ̃skriptibl] ADJ *Ordinat* rewritable

réinscription [reɛ̃skripsjɔ̃] NF registration

réinscrire [reɛ̃skrir] VT *(conj like* **inscrire***)* to re-register

▸ **VPR se réinscrire** to sign up again, to re-register (**à un cours** for a class)

réinsérer [reɛ̃sere] VT *(dans la société etc)* to reintegrate (**dans** into); *Ordinat (bloc)* to re-insert

▸ **VPR se réinsérer** to be reintegrated (**dans** into)

réinsertion [reɛ̃sɛrsjɔ̃] NF reintegration; **r. sociale** rehabilitation

réinstallation [reɛ̃stalasjɔ̃] NF relocation; *Ordinat* reinstallation; **depuis sa r. au premier** since she moved to the first floor; *(pour la deuxième fois)* since she moved back to the first floor

réinstaller [reɛ̃stale] VT *(changer de place)* to move; *(pour la deuxième fois)* to move back; *Ordinat* to reinstall

▸ **VPR se réinstaller** to settle down again; **il s'est réinstallé à Reims** he has moved back to Rheims

réintégration [reɛ̃tegrasjɔ̃] NF **1** *(d'un fonctionnaire etc)* reinstatement; *(dans un parti)* readmission; **r. des démobilisés dans la vie civile** rehabilitation of ex-servicemen (in civilian life) **2** *Jur* **r. de domicile** resumption of residence; **r. du domicile conjugal** restitution of conjugal rights **3** *Fin* add-back

réintégrer [reɛ̃tegre] VT *(conj like* **intégrer***)* **1 r. qn** *(dans un parti)* to readmit sb; **r. qn (dans ses fonctions)** to reinstate sb **2 r. son domicile** to return to one's home; *Jur* to resume possession of one's domicile

réintroduction [reɛ̃trɔdyksjɔ̃] NF reintroduction

réintroduire [reɛ̃trɔdɥir] VT *(conj like* **introduire***)* to reintroduce

réinvestir [reɛ̃vɛstir] VT to reinvest

réitératif, -ive [reiteratif, -iv] ADJ reiterative

réitération [reiterasjɔ̃] NF *(d'une demande, promesse)* repetition, reiteration; *(d'une démarche)* repetition

réitérer [reitere] VT (**je réitère, n. réitérons;** **je réitérerai**) *(demande, promesse, question)* to repeat, to reiterate; *(démarche)* to repeat

rejaillir [rəʒajir] VI to gush out, to spurt *or* splash up *or* out; *Fig* **r. sur qn** *(d'un scandale, du mérite de qn)* to reflect on sb; **tout ceci rejaillit sur moi** it all reflects on me; **sa honte a rejailli sur nous** we suffered disgrace too, the mud stuck to us too

rejaillissement [rəʒajismɑ̃] NM **1** *(d'un liquide)* gushing (out), spurting (up *or* out) **2** *Fig (de la gloire)* reflection

rejet [rəʒɛ] NM **1** *(action)* throwing out *or* away; *(de substances toxiques)* dumping; *(terre)* spoil (earth); *Géol* **r. horizontal** heave **2** *(d'une proposition, candidature, personne)*, *Méd (d'une greffe)* rejection; *(d'une requête)* rejection, refusal; *(d'une doctrine)*, *Jur (d'une réclamation, d'un appel)* dismissal; *Fig Fam* **faire un r. de l'école/du sport** to hate school/sports; **ne lui parle pas de sport, il fait un r.** don't talk to him about sport, he can't stand it; **un phénomène de r.** rejection; **être victime d'un phénomène de r.** to be rejected; **il a été traumatisé par ces réactions de r.** he was traumatized by this display of rejection **3** *(de plante)* shoot; *(émise par une souche)* sucker **4** *(en poésie)* enjambment

rejeté [rəʒte] ADJ *Journ (article)* on the spike

rejeter [rəʒte] *(conj like* jeter*)* VT **1** *(relancer, remettre) (balle, tête)* to throw *or* toss back; *(déchets, gaz toxiques etc)* to release, to discharge; *(de la mer, d'une rivière) (épaves, poissons etc)* to cast up, to wash up; **r. un poisson à l'eau** to throw *or* toss a fish back; **r. ses cheveux en arrière** to toss one's hair back; **épaves rejetées sur la plage** wreckage cast up *or* washed up on the beach; **la lave rejetée par le volcan** the lava thrown out *or* spewed out by the volcano; **la terre rejetée venait s'amonceler derrière eux** the earth which had been dug up was piling up behind them; **les envahisseurs furent rejetés à la mer** the invaders were driven back over the sea; *Fig* **r. le blâme/la responsabilité de qch sur qn d'autre** to shift the blame/the responsibility for sth on to sb else; **en allemand, le verbe est rejeté en fin de phrase** in German, the verb goes to the end of the sentence; **rejette l'idée en fin de paragraphe pour lui donner plus de poids** move this idea to the end of the paragraph in order to give it more weight

2 *(ne pas admettre) (enfant, conseil), Méd (greffe)* to reject; *(candidat, candidature)* to turn down, to reject; *(offre, proposition)* to reject, to turn down, to dismiss; *Jur (témoignage)* to disallow; *(doctrine, réclamation, accusation), Jur (pourvoi)* to dismiss; *Journ (un article)* to spike, to kill; **r. un projet de loi** to reject a bill, to throw out *or* vote out a bill; **elle croit qu'on la rejette** she feels rejected; **ceux que la société rejette** the outcasts of society; **elle rejette toute nourriture** she won't take any food

VPR **se rejeter 1** *(se satisfaire de)* to fall back (**sur** on)

2 *(sauter à nouveau)* to throw oneself again; **se r. en arrière** to jump back; *(d'un cheval)* to shy

3 elles se rejettent la responsabilité de cet échec they're laying the blame for this failure on each other

rejeton [rəʒtɔ̃] NM **1** *(de plante)* shoot, sucker **2** *Fam (progéniture)* offspring; *(enfant)* sprog; **il avait amené ses rejetons avec lui** he'd brought his offspring (with him)

rejoindre [rəʒwɛ̃dr] *(conj like* joindre*)* VT **1** *(mettre bord à bord)* to join (together); *(lèvres d'une plaie)* to close

2 *(aboutir à) (d'une rue, rivière)* to join (up with), to meet; **la rue rejoint le boulevard cinq cents mètres plus bas** the street joins (up with) the avenue five hundred metres further down; **nous rejoindrons bientôt l'autoroute** we'll soon join (up with) *or Fam* hit the motorway *or Am* freeway

3 *(ressembler à)* to be along the same lines as; **ses propos rejoignent les miens** he echoes what I say; **cela rejoint ce que je disais tout à l'heure** that fits in with what I was saying just now

4 *(retrouver) (personne) (pour un rendezvous)* to meet; *(rattraper)* to catch up (with); *Mil, Naut (son régiment, son bâtiment)* to (re)join; **le nageur eut du mal à r. le rivage** the swimmer had difficulty reaching the shore

5 *Pol (adhérer à)* to join; **il rejoignit le parti communiste en 1955** he joined the Communist Party in 1955; **elle a fini par rejoindre le parti socialiste** she ended up joining the Socialist Party

VPR **se rejoindre** *(d'amis)* to meet (up); *(de rivières, routes, lignes)* to join (up), to meet (up); **les droites se rejoignent au point P** the straight lines meet at (the point) P

rejouer [rəʒwe] VT *Sport (match, point)* to replay; *(morceau de musique)* to play again; *(pièce de théâtre)* to do again

VI to play again; **on rejoue?** shall we have another game?

réjoui [reʒwi] ADJ joyful; **je voyais à sa mine réjouie que les nouvelles étaient bonnes** I could see from the joyful expression on his/her face *or* from his/her joyful expression that it was good news; **la mine réjouie, il annonça sa promotion** he delightedly announced his promotion

réjouir [reʒwir] VT *(personne)* to delight, to cheer, to gladden; **toutes ces bonnes nouvelles ne peuvent que nous r.** we can only be glad of all this good news; **cela me réjouit le cœur de l'entendre** it does my heart good *or* it makes my heart glad *or* it gladdens my heart to hear it; **r. l'œil** to delight the eye; **savoir qu'il va partir me réjouit** I'm thrilled to know that he's leaving; **cette nouvelle ne me réjouit pas spécialement** I'm less than thrilled to hear the news

VPR **se réjouir 1** to rejoice (**de** at, in), to be glad (**de** of), to be delighted (**de** at); **je me réjouis à la pensée de le revoir** I'm delighted at the thought of seeing him again; **il faut se r. que tout se passe bien** we must be glad that everything is going well; **je me réjouis de te savoir guéri** I'm delighted that you're better **2** *Vieilli (s'amuser)* to enjoy oneself **3** *Suisse* **se réjouir de qch/de faire qch** to look forward to sth/to doing sth

réjouissance [reʒwisɑ̃s] NF rejoicing; **en signe de r.** to mark the occasion; **réjouissances publiques** public festivities; **le programme des réjouissances** the programme of festivities; *Iron* the list of treats in store; *Iron* **quel est le programme des réjouissances?** so what treats have you got in store for me?, what fun things have you got lined up for me to do?

réjouissant [reʒwisɑ̃] ADJ *(nouvelles, perspective etc)* delightful; **cela n'a rien de r.** it's a gloomy prospect; **la nouvelle n'est pas réjouissante** it's not exactly the most cheerful of news

relâche [rəlaʃ] NF **1** *(arrêt)* respite, rest; **travailler sans r.** to work without a break *or* a let-up *or Fml* without respite; **elle le répète sans r.** she repeats it continually, she keeps on repeating it; **prendre un peu de r., se donner r.** to have a brief respite; *Théâtre* **il y a ce soir** there is no performance this evening; *Théâtre* **faire r.** to be closed; *Théâtre* **r.** *(sur panneau)* closed **2** *(d'une corde)* slackening, loosening **3** *Naut (arrêt)* call; *(port)* port of call; **faire r. dans un port** to call at *or* put into a port

relâché [rəlaʃe] ADJ *(corde)* slack, loose; *(mœurs, conduite)* loose, lax

relâchement [rəlaʃmɑ̃] NM **1** *(d'une corde)* slackening, loosening; *(de la discipline)* relaxation; *(des mœurs)* looseness, laxity, laxness; *(des efforts)* let-up; *(dans le travail)* slacking off; **le r. de l'attention des élèves** the wavering of the pupils' attention; **il y a du r.** people are slacking off **2** *(de prisonniers)* release

relâcher [rəlaʃe] VT **1** *(corde)* to loosen, to slacken; *(son étreinte, les intestins)* to loosen; *(muscle, discipline, efforts)* to relax; **j'ai relâché mon attention pendant un instant** my attention slackened *or* wavered for a moment **2** *(prisonnier, oiseau en cage)* to release, to let go; *Fig* **je vous relâche** I'll let you go

VI *Naut* to put into port

VPR **se relâcher** *(de corde)* to slacken; *(d'un lacet)* to come loose; *(d'un employé, de la discipline)* to become slack; *(du zèle)* to flag, to fall off; *(des mœurs)* to grow lax; *(de l'attention)* to slacken, to waver; *(d'une étreinte)* to relax, to loosen; **cet élève s'est relâché** this pupil has slackened off; **se r. dans son tra-**

vail to slacken *or* ease off; **la discipline s'est un peu trop relâchée ces jours-ci** discipline is a bit too relaxed these days

relais [rəlɛ] NM **1** *(d'ouvriers)* shift; **ouvriers de r.** shift workers; **travail sans r.** unrelieved (spell of) work; **ville-r.** stopover (town); *Sport* **(course de) r.** relay (race); *Sport* **r. 4 fois 100 mètres** 4 x 100-metre relay; **passer le r. à qn** *Sport* to hand over the baton to sb; *Fig* to hand over to sb; **il est temps que je passe le r.** it's time I handed over (control); *Sport* **passage du r.** handover; **prendre le r.** to take over (**de qn** from sb); **l'homéopathie prend le r. de la médecine traditionnelle** homeopathy is taking over from traditional medicine; **tu prendras le r. avec le bébé** you take over with the baby, you have a spell with the baby; *Vieilli* **chevaux de r.** post horses

2 *(auberge) Vieilli* coaching inn, post house; **r.-château** country house hotel; **r. gastronomique** gourmet restaurant; **r. de tourisme** country house hotel; *Aut* **r. routier** service station (with café); **prochain r. routier: 10 km** *(sur panneau)* ≈ services: 10 km

3 *Tech, Élec* relay; *Radio* **r. de radio-diffusion** relay *(broadcasting)* station; **r. de télévision** television relay station

4 je leur sers de r. quand ils ont quelque chose à se dire they communicate with each other through me; **le graphiste sert de r. entre le client et l'imprimeur** the graphic artist is the link between the customer and the printer

relais-bébé NM INV baby changing room *(in shopping centre etc)*

relance [rəlɑ̃s] NF **1** *(de l'économie, de la production, des ventes, du commerce)* revival; *(d'un produit)* relaunch; **plan de r.** recovery plan; **des mesures pour la r. de l'économie** measures to revive *or* boost the economy *or* to get the economy going again; **r. de la natalité** upturn in the birth rate **2** *Com (d'un client)* follow-up; **lettre de r.** follow-up letter; **r. téléphonique** telephone follow-up **3** *Cartes* raise; **poker sans maximum de r.** poker with no ceiling

relancement [rəlɑ̃smɑ̃] NM **1** *(d'un engin spatial)* relaunch **2** *(d'une machine)* restarting; *(de la production)* boosting; *(d'un produit)* relaunching

relancer [rəlɑ̃se] *(conj like* lancer*)* VT **1** *(ballon)* to throw again; *(pour le rendre)* to throw back **2** *(économie)* to boost, to revive; *(commerce, ventes, production)* to boost; *(moteur)* to restart; *Ordinat (programme)* to rerun; *(logiciel)* to restart; **r. un projet** to relaunch a project **3** *Com (produit)* to relaunch **4 r. qn** *(harceler)* to badger sb, to pester sb; *Com* **r. un débiteur** to chase up a debtor; **r. un client** to follow up *or* to chase up a customer; **je l'ai relancée plusieurs fois pour qu'elle vienne dîner chez nous** I pestered her several times to come to dinner; **et pourtant, elle continue à lui téléphoner plusieurs fois par semaine pour le r.** and she still badgers him on the telephone several times a week

VI *Cartes etc* to increase the stake, to raise the bid

relaps, -apse [rəlaps] ADJ relapsed; **être laps et r.** to have abandoned the Catholic faith

N relapsed heretic

relater [rəlate] VT *(faits)* to relate, to state

relatif, -ive [rəlatif, -iv] ADJ *(position, valeur, calme, liberté etc), Gram (pronom, proposition)* relative; *Pol* **avoir la majorité relative** to have a relative majority; *Mus* **tons relatifs** related keys; **r.** à relating *or* related to, connected with; **vivre dans un luxe r.** to live in comparative luxury; **cette notion est très relative** it is a very relative concept; **tout est r.** everything is relative

NM 1 *Gram* relative pronoun `SEE GRAMMAR` A32–3; B22–3 **2 le r.** the relative

relation [rəlasjɔ̃] **NF 1** *(rapports entre personnes)* relationship; **entamer des relations ou se mettre ou entrer en relation(s) avec qn** to enter into a relationship with sb; **avoir ou entretenir des relations avec qn** to be in touch with sb; **être en r. avec qn** to be in touch *or* in communication with sb; **je vais les mettre en r.** I'll put them in touch (with each other); **avoir de bonnes/mauvaises relations avec qn** to be on good/bad terms with sb, to have a good/bad relationship with sb; **nos relations sont assez tendues** relations between us are rather strained; **nos relations sont très chaleureuses** we are on very good terms (with one another); **relations d'affaires ou commerciales** business relations; **nos relations sont purement professionnelles** our relationship is purely professional; **être en relation(s) d'amitié avec qn**, **entretenir des relations amicales avec qn** to be on friendly terms with sb, to have a friendly relationship with sb; **entretenir des relations de bon voisinage avec les pays d'Europe/sa belle-famille** to be on neighbourly *or* good terms with European countries/on good terms with one's in-laws; **les relations humaines** human relationships; **des relations épistolaires** correspondence; **il avait eu une r. épistolaire avec cette femme** he had corresponded with this woman; **relations sociales** labour relations; **les relations culturelles/diplomatiques/internationales** cultural/diplomatic/international relations; **nos relations avec la Hollande** our relations with Holland; **cesser ses relations avec qn/un pays** to break off relations with sb/a country; **les deux pays ont cessé toute r.** the two countries have broken off all relations **2** *(lien entre deux idées, deux faits etc)* relationship, connection; **r. entre la cause et l'effet**, **r. de cause à effet** relationship between cause and effect; **il n'y a aucune r. entre ces deux faits** the two facts are not related *or* connected; **c'est sans r. avec le sujet** it bears no relation to the subject; **ce n'est pas sans r. avec ce que nous avons dit plus tôt** it is not unconnected with *or* unrelated to what we said earlier; **en r. avec …** in relation to … **3** *(d'amour)* relationship; **r. (amoureuse)** love affair; **avoir une r. avec qn** to have a relationship with sb; **elle a eu une r. avec un homme marié** she had an affair with a married man; **avoir des relations sexuelles avec qn** to have (sexual) intercourse with sb **4** *(connaissance)* acquaintance; **r. d'affaires** business acquaintance; **elle a des relations (mondaines)** she is well connected, she has influential friends; **sans relations, on ne peut rien faire** you can't do anything unless you know (the right) people *or* unless you have contacts *or* connections; **faire jouer ses relations** to pull strings; **c'est une r. de travail** he's a colleague **5** *(récit)* account, report; **faire la r. de qch** to give an account of sth ▸▸*Mktg* **relations clientèle** customer relations; *Pol* **relations extérieures** foreign affairs; **relations presse** press relations; **relations publiques** public relations, PR; **il travaille dans les relations publiques**, *Fam* **il est relations publiques** he's in *or* works in public relations *or* PR

relationnel, -elle [rəlasjɔnɛl] **ADJ** relational; *Ordinat* **base de données relationnelles** relational database

relativement [rəlativmɑ̃] **ADV 1** *(d'une façon relative) (rare, fréquent, bien payé etc)* relatively, comparatively **2** *(en relation)* **r. à** relating to, concerning **3** *(en comparaison)* **plus**

petit, **r. au premier** smaller compared *or* by comparison with the first

relativiser [rəlativize] **VT r. un problème** to put a problem into perspective; **il faut r.** you have to look at things in perspective

relativisme [rəlativism] **NM** *Phil* relativism

relativiste [rəlativist] **ADJ, N** *Phil* relativist

relativité [rəlativite] **NF** relativity; **théorie de la r.** theory of relativity, relativity theory

relaver [rəlave] **VT 1** to wash again

relax [rəlaks] *Fam* **ADJ** *(personne)* laid-back, easy-going; *(soirée, entretien)* laid-back; **fauteuil r.** reclining chair; **baby-r.** baby chair

ADV on va réviser, mais r., OK? we'll do some revision, but we'll take it easy, OK?; **vas-y r.** take it easy

INT r. Max! chill out!

relaxant [rəlaksɑ̃] **ADJ** relaxing; **bain r. (aux plantes)** herbal foam bath

relaxation [rəlaksasjɔ̃] **NF** relaxation; **faire de la r.** to practise relaxation; **cours de r.** relaxation class, stress management class

relaxe¹ [rəlaks] **NF** *(d'un accusé)* release, discharge

relaxe² **ADJ** *Fam* **= relax ADJ**

relaxer [rəlakse] **VT 1** to relax; **ce bain m'a bien relaxé** I feel really relaxed after my bath **2** *Jur (prisonnier)* to release, to discharge **VPR se relaxer** to relax

relayer [rəlɛje] **(je relaie, je relaye, n. relayons; je relaierai, je relayerai) VT 1** *(personne)* to take over from, to relieve **2** *TV, Radio* to relay **3** *(transmettre)* **r. l'information** to relay *or* transmit information **VI** *Arch* to relay, to change horses **VPR se relayer** to take turns *(pour faire qch* doing sth); *Sport* **les coureurs se relaient tous les cent mètres** the runners take over from each other every hundred metres; **ils se relaient au volant** they take turns at the wheel, they take it in turns to drive; **on se relaie toutes les trois heures** we change over every three hours

relayeur, -euse [rəlɛjœr, -øz] **N** *Sport* relay runner

relecture [rəlɛktyr] **NF** *(d'épreuves)* proofreading; *(d'un livre)* rereading; **faire de la r. en free-lance** to be a freelance proofreader; **la r. de Stendhal m'a pris deux mois** it took me two months to reread Stendhal

relégation [rəlegasjɔ̃] **NF** *Hist, Jur* transportation

reléguer [rəlege] **VT** *(conj like* **léguer)** **1** *Sport (équipe), Fig* to relegate; **r. un tableau au grenier** to relegate *or* consign a picture to the attic; *Fig* **relégué au second plan** pushed into the background; **mes projets de vacances sont relégués au second plan pour le moment** my holiday plans have been pushed into the background *or* are having to take a back seat for the moment **2** *Hist, Jur (détenu)* to exile, to relegate

relent [rəlɑ̃] **NM** *(odeur)* stale smell; **des relents de graillon** a smell of stale fat; *Fig* **un r. de scandale entoure ce politicien** there is a whiff of scandal about this politician; *Fig* **ces histoires ont un r. de calomnie** these stories smack of slander

relevable [rəlvabl] **ADJ** *(siège, dossier, appuie-tête etc)* adjustable; *Aviat* **train d'atterrissage r.** retractable undercarriage; **accoudoir r.** folding armrest

relevage [rəlvaʒ] **NM** raising, lifting

relevailles [rəlvaj] **NFPL** *Vieilli (d'une femme qui vient d'accoucher)* churching; **faire ses r.** to be churched

relevé [rəlve] **ADJ 1** *(tête)* raised; *(sourcils) (après chirurgie esthétique)* lifted; *(manches)* turned up, rolled up; *(col)* turned up; **cha-**

peau **r.** off-the-face hat; **pantalon à bords relevés** turn-up trousers, turn-ups, *Am* pants with cuffs; *Aut* **virage r.** banked turn **2** *Fig (sentiment)* noble; *(style)* lofty; **dans des milieux plus relevés** in higher circles **3** *(sauce)* highly seasoned; **un plat très/peu r.** a hot *or* spicy/mild dish

NM 1 summary, statement; **r. de consommation (du gaz)** meter reading; **r. de communications téléphoniques** telephone call sheet **2** *(en topographie)* survey; **faire le r. d'un terrain** to plot a piece of land ▸▸**r. d'achat** purchase report; *Mktg* **r. (d'achat) journalier** diary; **r. de caisse** cash statement; **r. de compte** bank statement, statement of account; **r. de factures** statement of invoices; **r. de fin de mois** end-of-month statement; **r. d'identité bancaire** = document giving details of one's bank account, bank details; **r. d'identité postale** = document giving details of one's post office account; **r. des naissances** table *or* summary of births; **r. de vente** sales report

---

Relevé d'identité bancaire

A "RIB" is a small slip of paper with all of a person's bank details. Employers, utility companies and other financial institutions may ask for one to effect standing orders.

---

relève [rəlɛv] **NF 1** *(des troupes, de la sentinelle)* relief; *Ind (d'une équipe)* changing, changeover; *Mil* **la r. de la garde** the changing of the guard; **(troupes de) r.** relieving troops; **prendre la r. de qn** to take over from sb; *Mil, (au travail)* to relieve sb, to take over from sb; **prendre la r.** to take over **2** *(de personnel)* relief (driver/etc)

relèvement [rəlɛvmɑ̃] **NM 1** *(action) (d'un objet renversé)* picking up, righting; *(d'un mur)* raising, heightening; *(des affaires, d'une économie, d'un pays)* recovery, revival; *(des salaires, d'une impôt)* raising, increasing; **contribuer au r. d'un pays/d'une économie** to help a country/an economy recover **2** *(de terrain), Naut* position; *(au compas)* bearing; **r. radio(goniométrique)** radio bearing *or Fam* fix; **faire ou prendre un r.** to take a bearing, to take bearings

---

`RELEVER` [rəlve] *(conj like* **lever)**

| **VT** to pick up **1** ▪ to collect **2** ▪ to raise **3** ▪ to increase **3** ▪ to turn up **3** ▪ to note **4** ▪ to record **4** ▪ to enhance **5** ▪ to relieve **6** |
| **VI** to be a matter for *(relever de)* **2** |
| **VPR** to get up **1** ▪ to get up again **1** ▪ to lift **1** ▪ to recover **2** |

VT 1 *(remettre à la verticale) (objet renversé, personne)* to pick up; *(bateau)* to right; *(mur démoli)* to rebuild; **veuillez r. votre tablette** please fold away your tables; **relevez votre dossier** *(d'avion)* return your seats to an upright position; *(de cabriolet)* pull your seat back up; **r. la tête** to look up, to raise one's head; *Fig* to hold one's head up (again) **2** *(ramasser), Scol (compositions, copies)* to collect, to take in; **r. ses cheveux** to put one's hair up; *Fig* **r. le gant** to take up the gauntlet *or* challenge, to accept the challenge; **r. le défi** to accept *or* take up the challenge **3** *(hausser) (niveau de vie, niveau d'eau)* to raise; *(col)* to turn up; *(manches, bas de pantalon)* to turn up, to roll up; *(voilette)* to raise, to lift; *(jupe)* to lift (up), *Fam* to hoick up; *Tricot (maille)* to pick up; *(navire coulé)* to refloat; *(salaires, prix)* to increase, to raise; *(notes d'examen)* to put up; **r. les yeux** to look up again *(* **de** *from)*; **il releva les yeux pour regarder les horaires** he looked up

again at the timetables; **r. l'économie** to revive the economy; **r. une industrie** to revive an industry; **les richesses minières ont permis de r. le pays** mineral wealth contributed to the country's economic revival; *Fam* **cela l'a relevé aux yeux des électeurs** it boosted him in the eyes of the electorate

4 *(noter) (contradiction, faux sens etc)* to pick out; *(adresse, numéro de téléphone)* to take down; *(température)* to note, to record; *(traces)* to uncover; *(compte)* to make out; *(compteur)* to read; **r. le gaz** to read the gas meter; **r. des empreintes digitales** *(reporter)* to take fingerprints; **la police n'a pas relevé d'empreintes** the police haven't found any fingerprints; **on n'a relevé aucune preuve contre elle** no evidence has been found against her; **r. l'allusion** to respond, to react, to rise to the bait; **je n'ai pas relevé ce qu'il a dit contre moi** I ignored what he said about me; **il a affirmé l'ignorer et moi, je n'ai pas relevé** he claimed not to know about it and I didn't challenge him

5 *(mettre en valeur) (couleur, beauté etc)* to enhance, to heighten, to set off; *(sauce)* to season; *(plat)* to liven *or* perk up; *(histoire)* to liven up, to enliven

6 *(remplacer) (troupes, sentinelle)* to relieve; **r. qn** to take sb's place, to take over from sb; **r. la garde** to change the guard

7 *(libérer)* **r. qn d'un vœu** to release sb from a vow; **r. qn de ses fonctions** to relieve sb of his duties

8 *Naut (endroit)* to take the bearings of; *Naut (terre)* to sight; *(d'un arpenteur) (terrain)* to survey, to plot; *Math (graphique)* to plot

VI 1 r. de maladie to be recovering from an illness, to be convalescing

2 r. de qn to be answerable *or* responsible to sb, to report to sb; **r. de l'article 7** to come under article 7; **cette affaire ne relève pas de notre département** the matter is not our department's responsibility; **cette affaire relève de la justice** this is a matter for the courts; **son cas relève de la folie** he can be diagnosed as insane; **de telles décisions relèvent d'un manque de responsabilité coupable** decisions like that indicate a culpable lack of responsibility; **tout ce qui relève de la culture étrusque le passionne** everything relating to Etruscan culture fascinates him

VPR se relever 1 *(de son siège)* to get up; *(après être tombé)* to get up, to pick oneself up; *(après avoir été à genoux)* to get up from one's knees; *(du lit)* to get up again, to get out of bed again; *(d'un navire)* to right itself; **l'accoudoir se relève** the armrest lifts up; **aide-le à se r.** *(dans son lit)* help him to sit up; *(debout)* help him up

2 *(d'un pays, d'une économie)* to recover; **se r. d'une maladie** to recover from *or* get over an illness; **il aura du mal à se r. de cette déception** he'll have difficulty recovering from *or* getting over this disappointment; **il ne s'en relèvera pas** he'll never get over it

releveur, -euse [rəlvœr, -øz] **N** *(personne)* meter reader

relief [rəljɛf] **NM 1** *Beaux-Arts, Archit, Géog* relief; *Ordinat* highlight; **mettre en r.** to highlight; **en r.** *Beaux-Arts* in relief; *(caractère)* raised; *(carte)* relief; **cinéma/photographie en r.** stereoscopic cinema/photography; *Fig* **mettre en r., donner du r. à** *(idées, qualité)* to bring out; *(beauté)* to set off, to emphasize; *(taille fine, yeux)* to emphasize, to draw attention to; *(avantage)* to highlight; **mets ce paragraphe en r. en faisant des marges plus larges** make this paragraph stand out by making the margins wider; **l'état de ses finances met en r. son piètre sens de l'économie** the state of his finances emphasizes *or* throws into relief his

lack of financial sense; **sans r.** *(paysage, style)* flat; **r. acoustique** stereophonic sound **2** *Litt* **reliefs** *(d'un repas)* remains; *Fig (de la gloire)* shreds, tatters

> Il faut noter que le nom anglais **relief** signifie le plus souvent **soulagement** ou **aide**, selon le contexte.

relier [rəlje] **VT** *(impf, pr sub* **n. reliions)** **1** *(objets, points, personnes)* to connect, to link, to join *(à* to); *(idées)* to link together; **le cordon ombilical relie la mère à l'enfant** the umbilical cord attaches *or* connects the mother to the baby; **c'est la seule chose qui les relie** it's the only thing they have in common; **vos idées sont bien/mal reliées entre elles** your ideas are well/badly linked together **2** *(livre)* to bind; **relié en veau** bound in calf, calf-bound

VPR se relier *Ordinat* to link up

relieur, -ieuse [rəljœr, -jøz] **N** (book)binder

religieusement [rəliʒjøzmɑ̃] **ADV 1** *(selon la religion)* piously, religiously; **se marier r.** to get married in church, to have a church wedding **2** *(avec révérence) (écouter)* reverently; **conservé r. dans un écrin en velours** kept reverently in a velvet case; **il lit l'Humanité r. tous les jours** he reads l'Humanité with reverence every day **3** *(scrupuleusement)* religiously; **elle allait r. à la gym deux fois par semaine** she went to the gym religiously twice a week

religieux, -ieuse [rəliʒjø, -jøz] **ADJ** *(éducation, communauté, fanatique)* religious; *(musique, art)* sacred; **n'avoir aucun sentiment r.** to have no religious inclinations; **école religieuse** church school; **mariage r.** church wedding; *Fig* **soin r.** religious *or* scrupulous care; **elle prépare ses gâteaux avec un soin r.** she takes (an almost) religious care over her cakes; **conservé avec un soin r. dans du coton** reverently wrapped up in cotton wool; **mettre un soin r. à faire qch** to be religious about doing sth; **silence r.** respectful silence

NM *(moine)* monk, friar

NF religieuse 1 *(nonne)* nun **2** *(gâteau)* cream puff

religion [rəliʒjɔ̃] **NF 1** religion; **avoir de la r.** to be religious; **mourir en r.** to die in the faith; **entrer en r.** to take one's vows; **guerre de r.** war of religion; **la r. chrétienne/juive/bouddhiste** the Christian/Jewish/Buddhist religion *or* faith; **je ne connais pas sa r.** I don't know what religion he is; **est-ce que vous pratiquez une r.?** are you a practising Catholic/Muslim/*etc*? **2** *Fig* religion; **le football est une r. pour certains** football is a religion with some people, some people make a religion out of football; *Arch* **se faire une r. de qch** to make a religion of sth, to make sth a point of conscience; **se faire une r. sur qch** to have made up one's mind about sth

religiosité [rəliʒjozite] **NF** religiousness, *Péj* religiosity

reliquaire [rəlikɛr] **NM** reliquary, shrine

reliquat [rəlika] **NM 1** *(reste) (d'argent)* remainder; **r. de compte** account balance; **r. de caisse** cash balance; *Fig Litt* **un r. du passé** a relic of the past **2** *Méd Vieilli (d'une maladie)* aftereffects

relique [rəlik] **NF** *(d'un saint), Fig* relic; **garder qch comme une r.** to treasure sth, to keep sth like a relic; *Litt* **les reliques de sa gloire** the relics *or* remnants of his/her glory

relire [rəlir] *(conj like* **lire)** **VT** *(livre, auteur, ce qu'on a écrit)* to reread, to read (over) again; *(épreuves)* to read; *(vérifier)* to proofread

VPR se relire to read (over) what one has written; **j'ai du mal à me r.** I'm having trouble reading *or* deciphering my own handwriting

reliure [rəljyr] **NF 1** *(activité, art)* bookbinding; **atelier de r.** bindery; **donner un livre à la r.** to send a book for binding *or* to be bound **2** *(couverture)* **r. anglaise** *ou* **en toile** cloth binding; **r. pleine** full leather binding

relocalisation [rələkalizasjɔ̃] **NF** relocation

relogement [rələʒmɑ̃] **NM** rehousing

reloger [rələʒe] **VT** *(conj like* **loger)** to rehouse

relooker [rəluke] *Fam* **VT** to revamp

VPR se relooker to change one's image

relouer [rəlue] **VT 1** *(donner en location) (maison etc)* to rent (out) again, *Br* to relet, *Br* to let (out) again *(à* to) **2** *(prendre en location) (maison etc)* to rent again; **nous relouons chaque année le même appartement** we rent *or* take the same flat every year

réluctance [relyktɑ̃s] **NF** *Aut* reluctance

reluire [rəlɥir] **VI** *(conj like* **luire)** *(du parquet, d'un meuble, des chaussures)* to shine, to gleam; *(du métal)* to shine, to gleam, to glitter; **faire r. qch** to polish *or* shine sth (up); **brosse à r.** shoebrush; *Fig Fam* **manier la brosse à r.** to do some soft-soaping *or* buttering-up; **elle sait manier la brosse à r.** she's good at soft-soaping people *or* buttering people up

reluisant [rəlɥizɑ̃] **ADJ** *(parquet, meuble, chaussures)* shining, gleaming; **r. de propreté** *(sol, parquet)* gleaming; *Fig Fam* **ce qu'il a fait n'est pas très r.** *(moralement)* what he did was a bit off; **c'est une perspective peu reluisante** it's hardly a glowing prospect

reluquer [rəlyke] **VT** *Fam (personne, l'argent de qn etc)* to eye; **r. les filles** to eye (up) *or* ogle the girls; **il reluque ta fortune** he's got his eyes on your money, he's only after your money

relutif, -ive [rəlytif, -iv] **ADJ** *Fin* **avoir un effet r.** to strengthen the equity capital of a company

relution [rəlysjɔ̃] **ADJ** *Fin* strengthening of equity capital

rem [rɛm] **NM** *(abrév* **Röntgen equivalent man)** rem

remâcher [rəmɑʃe] **VT** to chew again; *Fig (le passé, une déception)* to brood over *or* about, to chew over

remailler [rəmaje] **VT** *(filet, bas)* to mend; *(pull, chaussette etc)* to darn

remake [rimɛk] **NM** *Cin* remake; **faire un r.** to do a remake

rémanence [remanɑ̃s] **NF** remanence, residual magnetism; *Ordinat (de l'affichage)* afterglow; *Opt* **r. des images visuelles** persistence of vision

rémanent [remanɑ̃] **ADJ** *(en magnétisme), Élec* residual, remanent; *Opt* **image rémanente** after-image

remanger [rəmɑ̃ʒe] **VT** *(conj like* **manger)** to eat again; **j'en ai remangé** I had some more; **je n'en ai jamais remangé** I've never eaten any since *or* again

remaniement [rəmanimɑ̃] **NM 1** *(d'un texte, discours, d'une politique)* reworking, revising, rejigging; **procéder au r. d'un texte** to rework *or* revise *or* rejig a text **2** *(changement)* alteration, modification; **apporter des remaniements à un ouvrage** to make changes to a work; *Pol* **r. ministériel** cabinet reshuffle; **r. du personnel** staff reshuffle

remanier [rəmanje] **VT** *(impf, pr sub* **n. remaniions)** *(texte, discours etc)* to rework, to revise, to rejig; *(équipe)* to make changes in, to reshuffle, to rejig; *Pol (gouvernement)* to reshuffle

remaquiller [rəmakije] **VT r. qn** to make sb up again

VPR se remaquiller *(de nouveau)* to make oneself up again; *(en retouchant)* to touch up one's make-up; **depuis peu, je me remaquille** I've started wearing make-up again recently

remarcher [rəmarʃe] **VI 1** *(d'une personne)* to walk again; **elle ne remarchera plus** she won't walk again **2** *(d'une machine etc)* to work again; *Fam* **ça a l'air de bien r. entre eux** they seem to have worked things out

remariage [rəmarjaʒ] **NM** remarriage

remarier [rəmarje] **VT r. sa fille** to marry off one's daughter again; **ils espéraient bien r. leur fille** they really hoped to see their daughter married again
VPR se remarier to remarry, to marry *or* get married again; **se r. avec qn** to remarry sb

remarquable [rəmarkabl] **ADJ** *(changement, résultat, progrès, invention, personne etc)* remarkable; *(événement, livre)* remarkable, noteworthy (**par** for); **les faits remarquables de la semaine** the highlights *or* outstanding events of the week; **d'un courage r.** remarkably brave; **elle est r. par sa** *ou* **de patience/beauté** she is remarkably patient/beautiful; **il est r. qu'il n'ait rien entendu** it's remarkable *or* strange that he heard nothing

remarquablement [rəmarkabləmã] **ADV** *(bon, mauvais, bien, changer, progresser etc)* remarkably; **danser/cuisiner r.** to dance/ cook remarkably well, to be a remarkably good *or* an outstanding dancer/cook

remarque [rəmark] **NF** *(observation)* remark; **faire une r.** to make *or* pass a remark; *(critique)* to pass a remark; **cette r. t'était destinée** that was aimed at you, that was a dig at you; **elle a fait la r. que ...** she remarked that ...; **faire la r. de qch** to remark on sth; **je dois lui en faire la r.** I must point it out *or* remark on it to him; **tu sais, je m'en étais fait la r.** it had crossed my mind, you know; **texte avec remarques** text with notes *or* comments; *Litt* **digne de r.** noteworthy

remarqué [rəmarke] **ADJ entrée/absence très remarquée** conspicuous entrance/absence; **discours très r.** speech that attracted considerable attention; **c'est un fait souvent/ peu r.** it's a well-known/little-known fact

remarquer [rəmarke] **VT 1** *(constater, voir)* to notice; **r. qn dans la foule** to notice *or* spot sb in the crowd; **il est entré sans que je le remarque** he came in without me noticing (him); **elle a été remarquée par un réalisateur de télévision** she was spotted *or* noticed by a television director; **je n'ai pas remarqué son absence** I didn't notice his/ her absence, I didn't miss him/her; **je remarque que personne n'en a parlé** I notice *or* note that no one has spoken about it; **faire r. qch à qn** to point sth out to sb, to call sb's attention to sth; **je te ferai juste r. que tu devais être là à sept heures** you should have been here at seven o'clock, you know; **je vous ferai r. que ...** I'll have you know that ...; **je te ferai r. que c'est encore moi qui ai fait la vaisselle!** just in case you hadn't noticed, it was me that did the dishes again!; **se faire r.** to attract attention, to get noticed; **il est entré sans se faire r.** he came in unobtrusively *or* without attracting attention, he came in without anybody noticing; **je ne voudrais pas me faire r.** I don't want to attract attention *or* to make myself conspicuous; *Fam* **remarque, il n'est pas le seul** he's not the only one, mind (you)
2 *(dire)* to remark, to observe
VPR se remarquer *(d'une tache, d'une cicatrice, d'un sentiment etc)* to show, to be noticeable; **sa déception se remarquait** his/her disappointment showed, he/she was noticeably disappointed; **cela se remarque à**

peine it hardly shows, you hardly notice it; **elle était amoureuse de lui, ça a fini par se r.** she was in love with him and it became obvious; **ça ne se remarquera pas** it won't show, it won't be noticed

---

Il faut noter que le verbe anglais **to remark** est un faux ami. Il ne signifie jamais **s'apercevoir de**; il signifie uniquement **faire remarquer**.

---

remastériser [rəmasterize] **VT** to remaster

remballage [rãbalaʒ] **NM** repacking

remballer [rãbale] **VT** *(marchandises)* to repack, to pack (up) again; *(cadeau)* to wrap (up) again, to rewrap; *Fig Fam* **r. la marchandise** to take off, to clear out; *Fig Fam* **tu peux r. les compliments** you can keep your compliments to yourself

rembarquement [rãbarkəmã] **NM** *(des passagers, des troupes)* re-embarking, re-embarkation; *(de marchandises)* reshipping, reshipment

rembarquer [rãbarke] **VT** *(passagers, troupes)* to re-embark; *(marchandises)* to reship; *(bateau)* to hoist in
VI to re-embark, to go on board again
VPR se rembarquer to re-embark, to go on board again

rembarrer [rãbare] **VT** *Fam* **r. qn** to tell sb where to go, to put sb (firmly) in his/her place; **se faire r.** to get told where to go, to get put (firmly) in one's place

remblai [rãblɛ] **NM** *Constr* **1** *(action) (avec de la terre etc)* backfilling; *(pour levée de terre)* embanking, banking (up) **2** *(terre etc)* backfill **3** *(levée de terre)* embankment, bank; **route en r.** (em)banked road

remblayage [rãblɛjaʒ] **NM** = **remblai 1**

remblayer [rãblɛje] **VT** (**je remblaie, je remblaye, n. remblayons; je remblaierai, je remblayerai**) *Constr* **1** *(partie effondrée du sol)* to fill (up), to pack **2** *(pour levée de terre)* *(route, voie ferrée)* to embank, to bank (up)

rembobinage [rãbobinaʒ] **NM** *(de film etc)* rewinding

rembobiner [rãbobine] **VT** *(film, ruban de machine à écrire, cassette)* to rewind
VPR se rembobiner to rewind

remboîtage [rãbwataʒ] **NM** *(d'un livre)* recasing

remboîtement [rãbwatmã] **NM 1** *(d'un livre)* recasing **2** *Chir (d'un os déplacé)* putting back into place, *Spéc* reduction

remboîter [rãbwate] **VT 1** *(livre)* to recase **2** *(pièces etc)* to reassemble, to fit together again **3** *Chir (os déplacé)* to put back into place, *Spéc* to reduce

rembourrage [rãbura3] **NM** *(action, matériau)* stuffing

rembourrer [rãbure] **VT** *(chaise, matelas, coussin etc)* to stuff; *(épaulettes)* to pad; **bien rembourré** *(coussin, fauteuil), Fig Fam (personne)* well-padded

remboursable [rãbursabl] **ADJ** *(dépenses, billet)* refundable; *(rente, obligation)* redeemable; *(crédit)* repayable; **les coupons sont remboursables en espèces** coupons are redeemable for cash

remboursement [rãbursəmã] **NM** *(des dépenses)* reimbursement, refund; *(d'une rente, d'une obligation)* redemption; *(d'un crédit)* repayment; **procéder au r. des frais** to refund *or* reimburse expenses; **obtenir le r. de ses frais de déplacement** to get one's travelling expenses reimbursed *or* refunded *or* paid; **r. anticipé** early repayment; **r. garanti** satisfaction or your money back; **r. in fine** bullet repayment; **emprunt de r.** refunding loan; **livraison contre r.** payment *or* cash on delivery, COD

rembourser [rãburse] **VT** *(dépenses)* to reimburse, to refund; *(achat)* to refund; *(rente, obligation)* to redeem, to pay off; *(crédit, dettes, prêt)* to repay, to pay back; *(coupon)* to redeem; **ce médicament est remboursé à 70%** 70% of the cost of this medicine will be refunded; **est-ce que vous êtes remboursé à 100%?** are you entitled to a full refund?; **r. qn de qch** to reimburse sb for sth; **r. qn de ses frais** *ou* **dépenses** to reimburse *or* refund *or* pay sb's expenses; **je peux te r. demain?** can I pay you back tomorrow?; **puis-je être remboursé?** *(dans un magasin etc)* can I have *or* get my money back *or* a refund?; **je me suis fait r., on m'a remboursé** I got my money back, I got a refund; *Théâtre Fam* **remboursez!** give us our money back!
VPR se rembourser to get one's money back; **elle s'est remboursée dans la caisse** she paid herself back out of the till

rembrunir [rãbrynir] **VT** *Litt (assemblée)* to cast a gloom over
VPR se rembrunir 1 *(d'un visage)* to cloud over; **elle s'est rembrunie** her face darkened, she scowled **2** *Litt (du ciel)* to cloud over, to grow dark

remède [rəmɛd] **NM** *Méd, Fig* remedy, cure (**à, de, contre** for); **c'est un bon r. contre la douleur** it's a good painkiller; **le r. est pire que le mal** the cure is worse than the disease; **r. de bonne femme** old wives' remedy; **r. de cheval** kill-or-cure remedy; **c'est sans r.** it is beyond remedy; **porter r. à qch** to find a remedy *or* cure for sth; *Prov* **aux grands maux les grands remèdes** desperate times call for desperate measures; *Fig Fam* **c'est un r. contre l'amour** she's/he's/it's a real turn-off

remédier [rəmedje] **VI** *(impf, pr sub* **n. remédiions**) **r. à** *(erreur, situation)* to remedy, to put right; *(problème)* to remedy, to cure; *(manque)* to remedy; *Méd (maladie)* to cure; *(inconvénient)* to compensate for, to make up for; *(abus)* to right

remembrement [rəmãbrəmã] **NM** *Admin (de terres)* re-allocation, regrouping

remembrer [rəmãbre] **VT** *Admin (terres)* to re-allocate, to regroup

remémorer [rəmemore] **VT r. qch à qn** to remind sb of sth
VPR se remémorer se r. qch to remember sth, to recall sth

remerciement [rəmɛrsimã] **NM** remerciements thanks; *(dans un livre)* acknowledgements; **avoir quelques paroles de r.** to say a few words of thanks; **lettre de r.** thank-you letter, letter of thanks; **faire ses remerciements à qn pour qch** to thank sb for sth; **tous mes remerciements à vos parents** (give) my thanks to your parents; **remerciements anticipés** with thanks in advance; **je crois que j'ai droit à un r.** *ou* **des remerciements** I think I deserve a thank-you VOIR GRAMMAIRE A10

remercier [rəmɛrsje] **VT** *(impf, pr sub* **n. remerciions**) **1** *(dire merci à)* to thank (**de, pour** for); **je vous remercie de m'avoir aidé** thank you for helping me; **je remercie Dieu/le ciel de m'avoir épargné la souffrance** I thank God/Heaven for having spared my suffering; **il me remercia d'un sourire** he smiled his thanks, he thanked me with a smile; **remerciez-les bien de ma part** thank them very much for me; **comment vas-tu? — très bien, je te remercie** how are you? — very well, thank you; **(non,) je vous remercie** no thank you; *Iron* **c'est ainsi qu'il nous remercie!** that's how he thanks us!, that's all the thanks we get! **2** *(congédier) (employé)* to dismiss; **se faire r.** to be dismissed, *Iron* to be thanked for one's services

réméré [remere] **NM** *Com* repurchase

remetteur, -euse [rəmɛtœr, -øz] *Fin* ADJ *(banque etc)* remitting
N remitter

REMETTRE [rəmɛtr] *(conj like* **mettre)**

> **VT** to put back **1** ▪ to put back on **4** ▪ to add **5** ▪ to deliver **6** ▪ to submit **6** ▪ to hand in **6** ▪ to hand over **6** ▪ to postpone **8** ▪ to put off **8**
> **VPR** to start again **2** ▪ to recover **3** ▪ to rely on *(s'en remettre à)* **4**

VT 1 *(replacer)* to put back; **r. qch à sa place** *ou* **en place** to replace sth, to put sth back in its place *or* where it belongs; **n'oublie pas de le r. à sa place** don't forget to put it back (again); *Fig Fam* **r. qn à sa place** to put sb in his/her place; **se faire r. à sa place** to get put in one's place; **r. un os en place** to put a bone back in place, *Spéc* to reduce a bone; *Fam* **r. les idées en place à qn** to bring sb to their senses; *Ftbl* **r. le ballon en jeu** to throw the ball (back) in(to play); *Tennis* **balle à r.** let (ball); **r. un manche à un balai** to put a new handle on a broom; **r. un bouton à un manteau** to sew a button on a coat; **r. une doublure à un habit** to reline a coat; *Fam* **je n'y ai plus jamais remis les pieds** I never set foot in there again; **qu'il ne remette jamais les pieds ici!** I don't want him ever setting foot in here again!; **r. qn sur le trône** to restore sb to the throne; **r. qn sur son chemin** *ou* **sur la bonne voie** to set sb on his/her way *or* on the right path; **r. qch en cause** *ou* **en question** to question sth, to raise questions *or* doubts about sth, to call sth into question; **r. qn en liberté** to set sb free; **on l'a remis en liberté, il a été remis en liberté** he was set free, he was freed *or* released; **r. qn à l'école/en prison** to send sb back to school/prison; **r. un malade à l'hôpital** to readmit a patient to hospital; *Fam* **on ne pourra r. l'eau/le gaz/le téléphone avant demain** we can't connect the water/gas/telephone (up) again until tomorrow; *Ordinat* **r. en forme** *(texte)* to reformat

2 *(rappeler)* to recall, to recollect; **il faut le lui r. en mémoire** he'll have to be reminded of it; *Fml* **je ne vous remets pas** I can't quite place you

3 *(dans un état antérieur)* **r. qn de bonne humeur** to put sb in a good mood again, to bring sb round; **r. à zéro** to reset, to zero; **r. qch en usage** to bring sth back; **r. en ordre** *(dossiers, maison)* to tidy (up); **r. de l'ordre dans sa chambre** to tidy (up) one's bedroom; **r. de l'ordre dans sa vie** to get one's life straightened out; **r. qch en service** to repair sth; **l'ascenseur sera remis en service demain** the lift will be back in service tomorrow; **r. en état** *(auto, machine)* to repair; *(maison)* to restore; **r. à neuf** to do up (like new); **r. en marche** *(moteur, machine)* to restart; **r. le contact** to start the engine again; **r. qn en forme** to get sb back on form; **r. qn sur pied** to restore sb to health, to get sb back on his/her feet again; **r. qn à flot** to put sb back on his/her feet again; *Couture* **r. un vêtement à plat** to alter a garment by unpicking and laying all the pieces out flat before restitching; *Arch Fig* **r. l'esprit de qn** to assuage sb

4 *(mettre de nouveau)* *(vêtement)* to put back on, to put on again; *(chauffage)* to turn *or* put back on *or* on again; *(télévision, radio)* to turn *or* switch back on *or* on again; *(disque, chanson, musique)* to put back on *or* on again; **ne remets pas cette veste demain** don't put that jacket on *or* don't wear that jacket again tomorrow; **nous avons décidé de r. de la moquette dans le salon** we've decided to carpet the living room again

5 *(ajouter)* *(sel, eau)* to add (**dans** to); **je remets quelques pommes de terre** I'll add

some potatoes, I'll put in some more potatoes; **r. de l'argent sur un compte** to pay money into an account; *Fam* **tu devrais r. un peu d'eau à cette plante** you should give that plant a bit more water

6 *(donner)* *(lettre, télégramme, colis etc)* to deliver; *(formulaire)* to send in; *(rapport)* to submit; **r. sa démission** to hand in *or Fml* tender one's resignation; **r. qch en mains propres** to deliver sth in person; **r. qn à la justice** *ou* **entre les mains de la police** to hand *or* turn sb over to the police; **r. son âme à Dieu** to commit one's soul to God; **je remets mon sort entre vos mains** my fate is in your hands; **r. sa charge à qn** to hand over one's duties to sb; **r. une somme à qn** to send *or Fin Fml* to remit a sum to sb; **r. à l'encaissement** to remit for collection; **r. à l'escompte** to remit for discount

7 *(faire grâce de, pardonner)* *(dette)* to cancel; *(peine)* to remit; *(faute)* to pardon, to forgive

8 *(différer)* *(réunion etc)* to postpone, to put off (**à** to, till); **r. une dette** *(à plus tard)* to defer (payment of) a debt; *Jur* **r. une cause à huitaine** to adjourn *or* remand a case for a week; **r. qch à plus tard** to put sth off (till later); *Échecs etc* **partie remise** draw, drawn game; *Fig* **ce n'est que partie remise** we'll do it some other time, there'll be another time for it; **il ne faut jamais r. à plus tard ce qu'on peut faire le jour même** never put off till tomorrow what you can do today; **arrête de r. les choses au lendemain** stop putting things off till tomorrow, stop procrastinating

9 *Fam (recommencer)* **on remet ça?** how about another (one)?; **garçon, remettez-nous ça!** (the) same again!; **il faudra r. ça** we must do it again sometime; **tu ne vas pas r. ça!** you're not going to start that again, are you?

10 *Fam* **en r.** to lay it on (a bit) thick

11 *Belg, Suisse (céder)* to sell; **ils ont remis leur boutique** they gave up their shop

12 *Belg (vomir)* to vomit

13 *Belg (rendre)* *(monnaie)* **il m'a remis trois euros** he gave me three euros change

VPR se remettre 1 *(se mettre de nouveau dans un endroit, dans un état)* **se r. au lit** to go back to bed; **se r. en route** to set off again; **le temps se remet (au beau)** the weather is clearing up (again); **se r. en selle** to get back in the saddle; **se r. en cause** *ou* **en question** to question oneself; *Fam* **se r. avec qn** to go back to sb again; *Fam* **se r. ensemble** *(d'époux, amants)* to get back together again

2 *(recommencer)* **se r. au travail** *ou* **à travailler** to start *or* set to work again; **elle s'est remise à boire** she's (started) drinking again; **se r. au français/au tennis** to take up French/tennis again; **se r. au régime** to go back on one's diet

3 *(d'une maladie, d'un choc)* to recover; **il lui faudra un certain temps pour se r.** it will take her some time to recover *or* to get over it; *Fig* **voyons, remettez-vous!** come on, pull yourself together!; *Fig* **elle ne s'en est pas remise** she couldn't get over it

4 *(se reposer sur)* **s'en r. à qn de qch** to rely on sb for sth; **s'en r. à la discrétion/au jugement de qn** to rely on sb's discretion/judgement; **je m'en remets à vous** I'll leave it to you, it's up to you; **je m'en remets totalement à vous** I have complete confidence *or* faith in you; **je m'en remets à votre avis** I'm leaving the decision entirely to you

remeubler [rəmœble] VT *(maison etc)* to refurnish
VPR **se remeubler** to refurnish one's house/flat

remilitarisation [rəmilitarizasjɔ̃] NF remilitarization

remilitariser [rəmilitarize] VT to remilitarize
VPR **se remilitariser** to become remilitarized

réminiscence [reminisɑ̃s] NF **1** *Phil, Psy* reminiscence **2** *(souvenir vague)* vague recollection; **il y a des réminiscences de Mozart dans ce morceau** there are echoes of Mozart in this piece, this piece is reminiscent of Mozart

remise [rəmiz] NF **1** *(dans son lieu ou son état d'origine)* *Ftbl* **r. en jeu** throw-in; *Rugby* **r. en jeu à la touche** line-out; **r. en état** *(d'une maison)* restoration; **r. à neuf** *(d'appareils ménagers, d'une voiture etc)* reconditioning; **r. en ordre** *(de dossiers, d'une maison)* tidying up, putting in order; *Ordinat* **r. en forme** *(de texte)* reformatting; *Ordinat* **r. à blanc** *(d'une disquette)* reformatting; **r. en marche** *(d'un moteur)* restarting; *(d'un projet)* relaunching; **r. en question** doubting, questioning; **ses remises en question continuelles** his/her constant doubts *or* questioning

2 *(fait de donner)* *(d'une lettre, rançon etc)* delivery; **payable contre r. du coupon** payable on presentation of the coupon; **r. des clefs** *(d'un appartement etc)* handing over of the keys; *Scol* **r. des prix** prizegiving

3 *(fait de pardonner)* *(d'une dette, d'un impôt)* cancellation; *(de peine)* reduction; **faire r. d'une dette** to cancel a debt; **bénéficier d'une r. de peine** to be granted a reduction in one's sentence, to have one's sentence reduced

4 *Fin* remittance; **faire une r. (de fonds) à qn** to send sb a remittance; *Com* **r. d'effets** remittance of bills; **r. de fonds** remittance of funds; **r. documentaire** documentary remittance; **r. à vue** demand deposit

5 *(rabais)* discount, reduction, allowance; *(pour paiement anticipé)* settlement discount; **r. sur marchandises** trade discount; **r. de caisse** cash discount, cash rebate; **r. de fidélité au client** loyal-customer discount; **r. pour quantité** quantity discount; **r. promotionnelle** promotional allowance; **r. de marchandisage** merchandising allowance; *Mktg* **r. psychologique** psychological discount; **r. quantitative** bulk discount; **r. saisonnière** seasonal discount; **r. sur les prix** price discount; **faire une r. sur un article** to allow a discount *or* make a reduction on an article; **r. d'usage** trade discount

6 *(appentis)* shed, outhouse; *Rail* engine shed; *(pour carrosses)* coach house; **voiture de (grande) r.** hired car (with chauffeur); **(voiture de) r.** *(carrosse)* hired *or* livery carriage

7 *(ajournement)* postponement; **faire qch sans r.** to do sth without fail; **r. d'une dette** deferment of (payment of) a debt

remiser [rəmize] VT **1** *(voiture, valise, vélo etc)* to put away **2** *Fam (rembarrer)* **r. qn** to put sb in his/her place, to take sb down a peg or two; **se faire r.** to get put in one's place, to get taken down a peg or two

remisier [rəmizje] NM *Bourse* half-commission man, intermediate broker

rémissible [remisibl] ADJ remissible

rémission [remisjɔ̃] NF **1** *(d'un péché, d'une dette)* remission; *Fig* **sans r. (travailler)** unremittingly; *(payer, punir qn)* without delay **2** *Méd (d'une maladie)* remission; *(de la douleur)* abatement; *(de la fièvre)* remission, abatement; **être en r.** to be in remission

rémittent [remitɑ̃] ADJ *Méd* remittent

remix [rəmiks] NM *(disque)* remix

remixer [rəmikse] VT *(disque)* to remix

remmailler [rɑ̃maje] VT = **remailler**

remmener [rɑ̃mne] VT *(conj like* **mener)** *(au point de départ)* to take back; **il fut remmené en prison** he was taken back to prison; **r. un**

enfant au zoo to take a child to the zoo again or back to the zoo; **r. qn en voiture** to drive sb back

remodelage [rəmɔdlaʒ] NM **1** remodelling **2** (réorganisation) restructuring

remodeler [rəmɔdle] VT (conj like **modeler**) **1** (refaçonner) to remodel **2** (réorganiser) to restructure

rémois, -oise [remwa, -waz] ADJ (population, architecture, école) of Rheims; (écrivain) from Rheims

N **R.** (natif) native of Rheims; (habitant) inhabitant of Rheims

remontage [rəmɔ̃taʒ] NM **1** (d'une horloge, montre) winding up; **montre à r. automatique** self-winding watch **2** (assemblage) (des pièces d'un mécanisme etc) reassembly

remontant [rəmɔ̃tɑ̃] ADJ **1 une boisson remontante** a tonic, Fam a pick-me-up **2** (rose) repeat-flowering
NM tonic, Fam pick-me-up

remonte [rəmɔ̃t] NF **1** (d'un poisson qui fraie) run; (d'un bateau qui remonte le courant) ascent **2** Mil (de la cavalerie) remounting; **cheval de r.** remount

remontée [rəmɔ̃te] NF **1** (d'une colline, rivière etc) ascent; (d'un sportif), Fin (d'une monnaie), Fig recovery; Sport, Fin, Fig **faire une belle r.** to make a good recovery **2** Ski **r. mécanique** ski lift **3** Min raising (to the surface)

remonte-pente, pl **remonte-pentes** NM T-bar, ski lift, ski tow

remonter [rəmɔ̃te] VI (aux usu **être**, sometimes **avoir**) **1** (dans l'espace) (d'une personne) to go/come up again, to go/come back up; (d'une route, ruelle etc) to rise again, to climb again; (d'un soutien-gorge, d'une jupe) to ride up; (de la marée) to flow; **je suis remonté lui parler** I went upstairs again or back upstairs to speak to him/her; **je suis remonté pour vous dire que …** I've come back upstairs to tell you that …; **r. dans sa chambre** to go back up to one's room; **r. sur son cheval** to remount one's horse, to get back up on one's horse; **je ne suis jamais remonté sur un cheval depuis** I've never been on a horse again since; **r. (à cheval)** (après en être descendu) to remount one's horse, to get back up on one's horse; (refaire du cheval) to ride again, to go riding again; **r. à bicyclette** to get back on one's bike, to remount (one's bicycle); **je n'étais pas remontée sur des skis depuis dix ans** I hadn't been on skis for ten years; **r. en voiture** to get back in one's car, to get into one's car again; **r. à la surface** to resurface, to come back up to the surface; **r. vers la source de la rivière** to go upstream; **r. dans l'estime de qn** to go up or rise again in sb's estimation; **r. dans les sondages** to improve one's position or go up in the polls; **r. au classement** to go up in the ranking; Ftbl to move up the league or division; Naut **r. au** ou **dans le vent** to beat up to windward

2 (dans le temps) to go back (à to); **cette dette remonte à plusieurs années** this debt dates back or goes back several years; **une amitié qui remonte au déluge** a friendship that is as old as the hills

3 (s'accroître de nouveau) (des actions, d'une monnaie, de la température) to go up again, to rise again, to climb again; (d'un baromètre) to rise again; Fig Fam **ses actions remontent** things are looking up for him/her, his/her stock is rising

VT (aux **avoir**) **1** (colline, escaliers etc) to go/come or climb back up, to go/come or climb up again; **j'ai remonté la colline/l'escalier** (je suis en bas) I went or climbed back up the hill/the stairs, I went or climbed up the hill/stairs again; (je suis en haut) I came or

climbed back up the hill/the stairs, I came or climbed up the hill/stairs again; **r. la rue** to go back up the street; **r. la rivière** to go upstream; (d'un poisson) to run upstream; **r. une rivière en canoë** to canoe up a river; **r. une pente en canard** to herringbone up a slope; Fig **r. la pente** (financièrement) to get back on one's feet (again); **il a eu du mal à r. la pente** (moralement) he found it difficult to pull himself out of it

2 (hausser etc) (étagère, poster) to move up; (pantalon, jupe) to pull up, to hitch up; (pull, manche, chaussettes) to pull up; (fermeture à glissière) to do up, to pull up; (vitre de voiture) to close, to wind or roll up; Min (mineurs, charbon) to raise; **puisque tu es à la cave, peux-tu r. une bouteille de vin?** since you're in the cellar, can you bring up a bottle of wine?; **peux-tu m'aider à r. cette malle à la cuisine?** can you help me take this trunk up to the kitchen?; **peux-tu m'aider à r. ma fermeture?** help me with my zip, will you?

3 Mil (cavalerie) to remount, to provide fresh mounts for

4 r. une horloge/montre to wind (up) or rewind a clock/watch; **r. le moral à qn** to cheer sb up, to lift or raise sb's spirits; **ça m'a remonté le moral** it cheered me up or made me feel a bit more cheerful or gave me a lift; **un verre de vin vous remontera** a glass of wine will cheer you up or do you good

5 (assembler) (pièces d'une machine etc) to put together again, to reassemble

6 (magasin) to restock; (garde-robe) to replenish

7 Théâtre (pièce) to put on again, to revive
VPR **se remonter 1 se r. en vin/café/linge de maison** to stock up on wine/coffee/household linen; **j'ai dû me r. en vêtements** I had to buy a whole new wardrobe **2** (moralement) to cheer up, to recover one's spirits; (physiquement) to recover one's strength; **j'ai pris un petit whisky pour me r.** I had a small whisky to revive my spirits or cheer me up

remontoir [rəmɔ̃twar] NM (de montre) winder

remontrance [rəmɔ̃trɑ̃s] NF remonstrance; **elle ne me fait jamais aucune r.** she never admonishes me; **remontrances** remonstrations, admonishments; **faire des remontrances à qn** to remonstrate with sb, to admonish sb

remontrer [rəmɔ̃tre] VT **1 r. qch** to show sth again **2 en r. à qn** to give sb a lesson or two; **il en remontrerait à ses professeurs** he could teach or show his teachers a thing or two
VPR **se remontrer** to show oneself or one's face again

rémora [remɔra] NM (poisson) remora

remordre [rəmɔrdr] VT to bite again
VI **r. à qch** to take another bite of sth; Fig to have another go or stab at sth; Fig Fam **r. à l'hameçon** to take the bait again, to fall for it again, to be taken in again by the same trick

remords [rəmɔr] NM remorse; **plein de r.** full of or filled with remorse; **avoir du** ou **des r.** to feel remorse; **j'ai des r. de l'avoir laissé partir à pied** I feel bad about leaving him to walk; **une pointe de r.** a twinge of remorse; **j'en ai qu'un r.: celui de ne pas le lui avoir dit** my only regret is that I didn't tell him/her; **des r. de conscience** twinges of conscience; **j'ai des r. de conscience** my conscience is troubling or bothering me; **être bourrelé de r.** to be stricken with remorse; **je n'ai aucun r.!** I'm not the slightest bit sorry!

remorquage [rəmɔrkaʒ] NM (d'une voiture, remorque, péniche etc) towing; (d'un train) pulling, hauling; **barre de r.** tow bar

remorque [rəmɔrk] NF **1** (traction) towing;

prendre un navire/une voiture en ou **à la r.** to take a ship/a car in tow, to tow a ship/a car; **vous pourriez me prendre en r.?** could you tow me or give me a tow?; **être en** ou **à la r.** to be in or on or under tow; **sortir du port à la r.** to be towed out of harbour; Fig Péj **être à la r. de qn** to follow where sb leads; Fam **il est toujours à la r.** he's always lagging or trailing behind; **croc de r.** tow hook; **timon de r.** tow bar

2 (câble de) r. towline, towrope; Naut **donner la r.** to give or pass the tow line

3 (bateau) tow, vessel under tow or being towed

4 (véhicule) trailer; **r. de plaisance, r. (de) camping** caravan, Am (camping) trailer

5 Rail **rame r.** slip portion; **voiture r.** slip coach

remorquer [rəmɔrke] VT (voiture, remorque, péniche etc) to tow; (train) to pull, to haul; **et puis on m'a remorqué jusqu'au garage** and then I was towed or taken in tow to the garage; **le dépanneur a remorqué la voiture** the breakdown man towed the car away; **se faire r.** to get towed; Fig **elle remorque toujours un groupe de fans avec elle** she always has a group of fans in tow or following in her wake

remorqueur, -euse [rəmɔrkœr, -øz] ADJ (bateau etc) towing; Rail (machine) relief
NM tug(boat); (avion) towplane

rémoulade [remulad] NF Culin **(sauce) r.** remoulade (sauce) (mayonnaise sauce with mustard, herbs etc); **céleri r.** celeriac in a remoulade (sauce)

remoulage [rəmulaʒ] NM (farine) bran

rémouleur [remulœr] NM knife grinder

remous [rəmu] NM (d'une rivière) eddy; (d'un bateau) wash, backwash; (de la marée) swirl; Fig (de la foule) ripple; **il y eut des r. dans la foule** a ripple ran through the crowd; **r. d'eau** whirlpool; Aviat **r. d'air** eddy; Fig **provoquer des r.** to cause a stir

rempaillage [rɑ̃pajaʒ] NM (de vieilles chaises) reseating, rebottoming

rempailler [rɑ̃paje] VT (vieille chaise) to reseat, to rebottom

rempailleur, -euse [rɑ̃pajœr, -øz] N upholsterer

rempaqueter [rɑ̃pakte] VT (conj like **paqueter**) to rewrap, to wrap up again

rempart [rɑ̃par] NM rampart; **remparts** walls; **faire un r. de son corps à qn** to shield sb with one's body; Fig **le dernier r. de la démocratie** the last bastion of democracy; Fig **le r. de nos libertés** the bulwark or bastion of our liberties

rempiéter [rɑ̃pjete] VT (**je rempiète, n. rempiétons; je rempiéterai**) Constr (mur) to underpin

rempiler [rɑ̃pile] VT to stack or pile up again
VI Mil Fam Hum to re-enlist; **il a rempilé pour cinq ans** he signed up for five more years

remplaçable [rɑ̃plasabl] ADJ replaceable

remplaçant, -ante [rɑ̃plasɑ̃, -ɑ̃t] N (personne) substitute, replacement, stand-in; Sport (dans une équipe) reserve, substitute, Fam sub; (d'un médecin, d'un pasteur) locum (tenens); Scol supply teacher, Am substitute teacher

remplacement [rɑ̃plasmɑ̃] NM **1** replacement, substitution; **le r. du beurre par la margarine** the replacement of butter by margarine, the substitution of margarine for butter; **en r. de qn/qch** in place of sb/sth, as a replacement or substitute for sb/sth; **en r. des heures supplémentaires** in lieu of overtime; **assurer** ou **faire un r.** to act as a replacement, to stand in, to cover (**de** for); **dactylo qui fait des remplacements** temporary typist, Fam temp; Scol **je fais des rem-**

placements I do supply teaching, I'm a supply teacher *or Am* a substitute teacher **2 de r.** *(pneu)* spare; *(valeur, pile)* replacement; **produit de r.** substitute

remplacer [rɑ̃plase] *(conj like* **placer***)* VT **1** *(succéder à, tenir lieu de) (personne)* to take the place of, to replace, to take over from; *(chose)* to take the place of, to replace; *(temporairement) (personne)* to stand in for, to substitute for, to act as a substitute for; **si je pouvais me faire r.** if I could get somebody to stand in *or* cover for me *or* to take my place; **je la remplace pendant les vacances** I'm standing in *or* filling in (for her) while she's on holiday **2** *(changer) (vieille voiture, pneu etc)* to replace, to renew; *(objet cassé)* to replace; **r. qch par qch d'autre** to replace sth with *or* by sth else, to put sth else in place of sth; **r. le beurre par de la margarine** to replace butter with margarine, to substitute margarine for butter; **r. un mot par un autre** to replace one word with another

VPR **se remplacer** to be replaceable; **cette pièce se remplace facilement** the part is easy to replace; **un ami comme toi, ça ne se remplace pas** friends like you are irreplaceable *or* can't be replaced, friends like you are hard to come by; **une mère, ça ne se remplace pas** there's no substitute for a mother

remplage [rɑ̃plaʒ] NM *Archit (d'une fenêtre gothique)* tracery

rempli [rɑ̃pli] ADJ full; **visage (bien) r.** full face; **avoir l'estomac bien r.** to have a full stomach; **r. de qch** full of sth, filled with sth; **tout r. de son importance** full of his/her own importance

NM *Couture* tuck

remplir [rɑ̃plir] VT **1** to fill (**de** with); *(verre etc)* to fill (up); *(à nouveau)* to refill; *(espace, trou)* to fill in; *(formulaire etc)* to fill in *or* out, to complete; **elle a déjà rempli dix pages** she has already written *or* filled ten pages; **cela a rempli ma journée** it took up my whole day; **cela ne peut r. votre vie entièrement** it can't be the only thing in your life, it can't take up your entire life; **r. qn de joie/colère** to fill sb with joy/anger; **les étrangers remplissaient la ville** the town was filled with *or* full of strangers; **r. l'air de ses cris** to fill the air with one's cries; **comme toujours, il a rempli la salle** as always, he played to a full house *or* he filled the hall; **le corsage est joli mais tu ne le remplis pas** it's a pretty blouse but you're a bit too thin for it **2** *(promesse)* to fulfil, *Am* to fulfill, to carry out; *(condition)* to meet, to satisfy, to fulfil; *(ordre, instructions)* to carry out; *(devoirs, tâche)* to do, to carry out, to perform; *(rôle, contrat)* to fulfil; **r. son office** to do its job

VPR **se remplir** to fill up; **se r. de qch** to fill with sth; **ses yeux se remplirent de larmes** her eyes filled with tears; **la cuve se remplit mal** the tank isn't filling up properly; *Fig* **se r. les poches** to line one's pockets

remplissage [rɑ̃plisaʒ] NM **1** *(d'un tonneau, d'un réservoir)* filling (up); *(d'un trou, d'un espace)* filling (in) **2** *(d'un texte)* padding; **faire du r.** to pad

remplisseuse [rɑ̃plisøz] NF *Ind* bottle-filling machine

remploi [rɑ̃plwa] NM **1** *(réutilisation)* reuse **2** *Fin* reinvestment

remployer [rɑ̃plwaje] VT *(conj like* **employer***)* **1** *(réutiliser)* to reuse **2** *Fin (argent)* to reinvest

remplumer (se) [sərɑ̃plyme] VPR **1** *(d'un oiseau)* to get new feathers *or* new plumage **2** *Fig Fam (financièrement)* to be in funds again **3** *Fig Fam (grossir)* to put on weight again, to fill out again

rempocher [rɑ̃pɔʃe] VT **r. qch** to put sth back in one's pocket

remporter [rɑ̃pɔrte] VT **1** *(reprendre)* to take

back *or* away; **le livreur a remporté la commande** the delivery man took the order away (again) *or* took the order back **2** *(gagner) (prix, titre de champion)* to win, to carry off; *(succès)* to achieve; **r. une victoire** to achieve *or* win a victory, *Fam* to chalk up a win; **c'est lui qui remporte l'avantage** he has gained the advantage

rempotage [rɑ̃pɔtaʒ] NM repotting

rempoter [rɑ̃pɔte] VT *(plante)* to repot

remprunter [rɑ̃prœ̃te] VT to borrow again

remuant [rəmɥɑ̃] ADJ *Péj (personne)* overactive, *Fam* hyper; **elle est très remuante** she can't sit still for a minute

remue-ménage [rəmymenaʒ] NM INV commotion, confusion, hubbub; **faire du r.** *(du bruit)* to make a din; **la nouvelle de sa démission a fait un de ces r.!** the news of his/her resignation caused quite a commotion *or* stir!

remue-méninges [rəmymenɛ̃ʒ] NM INV brainstorming; **un r.** a brainstorming session

remuement [rəmymɑ̃] NM *Litt* movement

remuer [rəmɥe] VT **1** *(bouger) (d'une personne) (tête, jambes, lèvres etc)* to move; *(oreilles)* to waggle; *(mobilier)* to move, to shift; *(du vent) (feuilles)* to move, to stir; **r. la queue** *(d'un chien)* to wag its tail; *Fig* **ne pas r. le petit doigt** not to lift a finger **2** *(mélanger) (sauce, café etc)* to stir; *(sol)* to turn up, to turn over; *Fig (de vieux souvenirs, le passé)* to rake up; **r. la salade** to toss the salad; **r. ciel et terre pour faire qch** to move heaven and earth to do sth **3** *(émouvoir)* **r. qn** *ou* **le cœur de qn** to move sb; **cela m'a profondément remué** it moved me deeply, I found it deeply moving

VI *(d'une personne)* to move, to stir; **ne remue pas tout le temps!** don't fidget!, keep still!; **il est petit, ce garçon, mais qu'est-ce qu'il remue!** he may be just a little boy but gosh he's lively *or* he's got a lot of energy!; **dent qui remue** loose tooth; *Fig* **un pays qui remue et qui se prépare à la révolte** a country stirring in preparation for revolt

VPR **se remuer** *(bouger)* to move, to stir; *Fam (être actif)* to have plenty of get up and go; **il a fallu se r. pour obtenir sa signature** we had to go to great lengths *or* to a lot of trouble to get him to sign; **remue-toi un peu!** get a move on!, shift yourself!, get up off your backside!; **on peut dire qu'il se remue, lui!** he's not just sitting back!

rémunérateur, -trice [remyneratœr, -tris] ADJ *(travail etc)* remunerative, profitable, financially rewarding; *(placement)* interest-bearing

rémunération [remyneraasjɔ̃] NF payment, remuneration (**de** for); *(salaire)* pay; **r. de capital** interest on capital; **r. à la commission** commission only; **r. de départ** starting salary

rémunératoire [remyneratwar] ADJ *Jur* granted as remuneration *or* payment

rémunérer [remynere] VT (**je rémunère, n. rémunérons; je rémunérerai**) *(personne)* to pay, to remunerate; *(travail, services etc)* to pay for; **avoir un emploi rémunéré** to be gainfully employed, to be in gainful employment; **bien/mal rémunéré** well-/poorly *or* badly paid

renâcler [rənakle] VI **1** *(renifler) (d'un animal)* to snort; *(d'une personne)* to sniff, to snort **2** *(rechigner)* to ba(u)lk (**à** at); **r. à la besogne** *ou* **devant le travail** to be workshy; **il a accepté en renâclant** he accepted grudgingly

renaissance [rənɛsɑ̃s] NF **1** *Rel* rebirth **2** *Fig (des lettres, des arts etc)* renaissance, revival; **r. du printemps** reappearance of spring; *Beaux-Arts, Littér* **la R.** the Renaissance

ADJ INV **R.** *(art, château etc)* Renaissance

renaissant [rənɛsɑ̃] ADJ **1** *(force)* reviving; *(économie, industrie)* reviving, *Fml* renascent; *(passion)* reawakening **2** *(de la Renaissance)* (of the) Renaissance

renaître [rənɛtr] VI *(conj like* **naître***, but pp* **rené** *and compound tenses not in use, and p hist* **je renaquis** *rare)* **1** *Rel* to be born again; **ville qui renaît de ses cendres** town that is rising again from its ashes; **r. à la vie** to come back to life, to take on a new lease of life; **c'est ce qui l'a fait r. à la vie** that's what brought him/her back to life; **r. à la joie/au bonheur** to know what it is to feel joy/happiness again **2** *(réapparaître) (d'une industrie, des arts etc)* to revive; *(de l'espoir)* to revive, to be reborn; *Litt (du printemps, des plantes)* to return, to reappear; *(de la nature)* to reawaken; **faire r. les espérances de qn** to revive sb's hopes, to get sb's hopes up again; **faire r. la confiance** to restore confidence

rénal, -ale, -aux, -ales [renal, -o] ADJ *Anat* renal; **calcul r.** kidney stone; **insuffisance rénale** renal insufficiency

renard [rənar] NM **1** *(animal)* fox; **r. argenté** silver fox; **la chasse au r.** fox-hunting; *Fig* **c'est un fin/vieux r.** he's as sly as a fox/he's a sly old devil **2** *(fourrure)* fox (fur) **3** *Tech (dans une chaudière, un barrage etc)* leak, fissure

renarde [rənard] NF vixen

renardeau, -eaux [rənardo] NM fox cub

renardière [rənardjɛr] NF **1** *(tanière)* fox-hole, (fox's) earth **2** *Can (élevage)* fox farm

renauder [rənode] VI *très Fam Vieilli (se plaindre)* to grouse, to grumble

rencaissage [rɑ̃kɛsaʒ] NM replanting *(of container-grown plant)*

rencaissement [rɑ̃kɛsmɑ̃] NM *(d'argent)* putting back (in the till)

rencaisser [rɑ̃kɛse] VT **1** *(plante)* to replant **2** *(de l'argent)* to put back in the till

rencard, rencart [rɑ̃kar] NM **= rancard**

rencarder [rɑ̃karde] VT **= rancarder**

renchérir [rɑ̃ʃerir] VT *(rendre plus cher)* to make dearer, to raise the price of; *(prix)* to raise

VI **1** *(augmenter) (des prix, des loyers)* to go up; *(des marchandises)* to go up, to get dearer **2** *(dire ou faire plus qu'un autre)* to go one better (**sur** than); **'un homme fort aimable', renchérit-elle** 'a most likeable man', she added **3** *(aux enchères)* to make a higher bid

renchérissement [rɑ̃ʃerismɑ̃] NM *(de marchandises)* rise *or* increase in price; *(de prix, loyers)* rise, increase (**de** in)

rencogner [rɑ̃kɔɲe] *Fam Vieilli* VT to push *or* drive into a corner

VPR **se rencogner** to huddle up

rencontre [rɑ̃kɔ̃tr] NF **1** *(de personnes)* meeting, encounter; *(de courants)* meeting; *(de routes)* junction; *(entre deux voitures)* collision; *(de circonstances)* conjunction; **faire la r. de qn** to meet sb; **aller à la r. de qn** to go to meet sb; **faire une mauvaise r.** to have an unpleasant encounter; **point de r.** meeting point; **club de rencontres** dating agency; **des rencontres culturelles** cultural festivals *(intended to encourage cultural cross-fertilization)*; *Pol* **r. au sommet** summit (meeting *or* conference) **2** *(d'adversaires)* encounter, meeting; *Sport* match, meeting, *surtout Am* meet; *Boxe* fight; *Vieilli (duel)* duel; *Mil* **une r. avec l'ennemi** a brush *or* skirmish with the enemy **3** **r. de pétrole** strike *or* striking of oil

rencontrer [rɑ̃kɔ̃tre] VT **1** *(par hasard) (personne)* to meet, to come across, *Fam* to bump *or* run into, *Fml* to encounter; *(thème, plante, arbre)* to come *or* run across, to encounter; *(opposition, difficulté etc)* to encounter, to meet with, to run into, to come up against; *(obstacle)* to encounter, to come up against; **r. qn par hasard** to run *or* come across sb, *Fam* to bump *or* run into sb; **mon travail m'amène à r. beaucoup de gens** I get to meet a lot of people in my job, my job brings me into contact with a lot of people; **r. l'ennemi** to encounter the enemy; **r. les yeux de qn** to meet sb's eyes; **sa main rencontra quelque chose de froid** his/her hand came up against *or* met something cold; **c'est un ami comme on n'en rencontre plus** he's the sort of friend you don't find any more **2** *(avoir un rendez-vous avec)* to meet; *(disputer un match contre)* to meet, to play against; **je vais le r. ce matin** I'll be meeting him *or Am* meeting with him this morning

VPR se rencontrer 1 *(de gens, de rivières), Sport (d'équipes etc)* to meet; **leurs yeux se rencontrèrent** their eyes met **2** *(se heurter)* to collide, to run into each other **3** *(se trouver)* to occur, to be found **4** *(être d'accord) (de personnes)* to agree; *Hum* **les grands esprits se rencontrent** great minds think alike

rendement [rãdmã] **NM 1** *(d'une terre, d'une mine, d'un impôt)* yield; *(d'un investissement)* return, profit, yield; **actions à gros r.** high-yielding shares; **r. réel** inflation-adjusted yield **2** *(de travailleurs)* output; *(d'une usine)* output, production; *(d'un ordinateur)* throughput; **un ouvrier qui a un bon/mauvais r.** a workman whose productivity is good/bad; **travailler à plein r.** *(d'une usine)* to work at full capacity **3** *(d'une machine, d'un moteur)* output, performance, efficiency; **travailler à plein r.** *(d'une machine)* to work at full load; **machine à grand r.** heavy-duty machine; **r. mécanique** mechanical efficiency; **r. thermodynamique** thermodynamic efficiency **4** *Sport* **r. de temps/distance** time/distance handicap

rendez-vous [rãdevu] **NM INV 1** *(rencontre)* appointment; *(d'amoureux)* date, *Hum* rendezvous; *Mil* rendezvous; **votre r. est arrivé** your client/patient/*etc* is here; **donner (un) r. à qn** to arrange to meet sb, to make a date with sb; **prendre r. avec qn/un r. chez le coiffeur** to make an appointment with sb/at the hairdresser's; **j'ai (un) r. à une heure** *(avec un ami)* I'm meeting someone at one o'clock; *(avec un collègue, le médecin, le coiffeur etc)* I have an appointment at *or* for one o'clock; **prendre un r. chez le dentiste** to make an appointment with the dentist; **'ne reçoit que sur r.'** 'by appointment only'; **être en r.** to be in a meeting; **lieu de r.: devant l'église** meet in front of the church; **quel est le lieu du r.?** where are we/they/*etc* meeting?, what's the meeting place?; **le soleil était au r.** the sun was shining **2** *(endroit)* (favourite) meeting place, haunt; **c'est le r. des artistes/musiciens** it's a favourite haunt of artists/musicians
▸▸**r. d'affaires** business meeting *or* appointment; **r. de chasse** meet; **r. citoyen** = short training course due to be introduced following the abolition of the military service in France, emphasizing civic education and defence; **r. social** meeting between employers and unions

rendormir [rãdɔrmir] *(conj like dormir)* **VT** to send to sleep again
VPR se rendormir to fall asleep again, to go (back) (off) to sleep again, to drop (back) off to sleep again

RENDRE [rãdr]

VT to give back **1** ▪ to return **1, 2** ▪ to vomit **3** ▪ to surrender **4** ▪ to give out **8** ▪ to render **10** ▪ to make **11**	
VPR to go **1** ▪ to surrender **2**	
VI to be productive **1** ▪ to vomit **3**	

VT 1 *(restituer, rapporter) (objet emprunté ou pris à qn)* to give back, to return; *(argent)* to repay, to pay back; *(achat)* to take back, to return; *(copies, interrogation, cadeau)* to give back, to return; **elle est venue r. le téléviseur** she brought the television back; **il faut lui r. la** *ou* **sa liberté** he must be given his freedom *or* set free; **l'enfant fut rendu à sa famille** the child was handed back to his family; **les soldes ne peuvent être rendus** sale goods are non-returnable; **r. la vie à qn** to bring sb back to life; **r. le repos à qn,** *Littr* **r. qn au repos** to restore sb's peace of mind; **r. la parole à qn** to hand back over to sb; **r. sa parole à qn** to release sb from his commitment; **r. la vue à qn** to restore sb's sight; **cela m'a rendu des forces** it gave me back my strength; **les médecins sont parvenus à lui r. l'usage de sa main** the doctors managed to give him/her back *or* restore the use of his/her hand; **ce médicament m'a rendu le sommeil** this medicine has made me able to sleep again; **il faut r. à César ce qui est à César** *(reconnaître le mérite de qn)* credit where credit's due
2 *(en retour) (compliment)* to return, to repay; **r. une** *or* **son invitation à qn** to invite sb back, to return sb's invitation; **r. un** *ou* **son baiser/coup/coup de pied à qn** to kiss/hit/kick sb back; **r. son salut/sa visite à qn** to return sb's greeting/visit; **r. coup pour coup** to hit back, to give as good as one gets; **r. le bien pour le mal** to return *or Fml* render good for evil; **il ne m'a pas rendu la monnaie** he didn't give me my change; **r. la monnaie d'un billet de cent euros** to give change for a hundred-euro note; *Fig Fam* **r. à qn la monnaie de sa pièce** to get even with sb; **elle l'aime mais il ne le lui rend pas** she loves him but the feeling isn't mutual, she loves him but he doesn't feel the same way about her; **il me déteste et je le lui rends bien** he hates me and the feeling is mutual, he hates me and I feel the same way about him
3 *(vomir) (nourriture, repas etc)* to bring up; **r. du sang par la bouche** to vomit blood
4 *Mil (armes, forteresse etc)* to give up, to surrender; *Fig* **je rends les armes!** I give up!
5 *(générer) Agr* **terre qui ne rend rien** unproductive land; **placement qui rend 10%** investment that brings in *or* yields 10%; **r. un son aigu** to make a high-pitched sound; *Fam* **ça n'a rien rendu** it didn't work out, it didn't come to anything; **j'ai pris un arc-en-ciel en photo mais ça n'a rien rendu** I took a photo of a rainbow but it didn't come out
6 *(livrer)* to deliver; **r. des marchandises à destination** to deliver goods (to their destination); **prix rendu** delivery price
7 *Jur (prononcer) (décret)* to issue, to pronounce; *(jugement)* to deliver; *(verdict)* to bring in, to return; **elle n'a pas encore rendu sa réponse** she hasn't given her answer yet
8 *Culin (de viande, concombre, champignons etc) (jus, eau)* to give out, to release
9 *Sport* **r. du poids/cent mètres** to have a weight/a one-hundred-metre handicap; *Échecs* **r. une pièce** to be a piece behind
10 *(exprimer)* to render, to express; **r. le sens** to convey *or* express the meaning; **c'est un mot difficile à r. en anglais** it's difficult to find an English equivalent for this word; **les couleurs/émotions sont très bien rendues** the colours/emotions are very well portrayed *or* expressed
11 *(+ adj)* **r. qn malade/heureux/intelligent** to make sb ill/happy/intelligent; **r. qch compliqué/simple/ennuyeux** to make sth complicated/simple/boring; **le homard me rend malade** lobster makes me ill; *Fam* **ça me rend malade de voir ces petits enfants dans les orphelinats** it makes me ill *or* sickens me to see those little children in orphanages; **vous me rendez fou!** you're driving me

mad!; **pour te r. les choses plus agréables** to make things more pleasant for you; **r. qn responsable de qch** to hold sb responsible for sth; **elle sait comment faire pour r. un homme amoureux** she knows how to make a man fall in love with her; **r. qn aveugle/sourd/muet** to make sb go blind/deaf/dumb; **le feu l'a rendu aveugle** the fire blinded him, he was blinded in the fire; *Fig* **l'amour l'a rendu aveugle** he was blinded by love; **c'est lui qui a rendu populaire le mythe du bon sauvage** he is responsible for popularizing the myth of the noble savage
12 *(expressions)* **r. hommage à qn** to pay homage to sb; **r. grâce(s) à qn (d'avoir fait qch)** to give thanks to sb (for doing *or* having done sth); **r. service à qn** to do sb a favour; **r. visite à qn** to visit sb; **r. compte de qch** to make a report on sth; **je n'ai pas de comptes à te r.** I don't owe you any explanation; **r. raison de qch** to explain *or* justify sth; **r. la justice** to dispense *or* administer justice; **r. l'âme** *(d'une personne)* to breathe one's last; *Hum (d'une machine)* to give up the ghost; **r. le dernier soupir** to breathe one's last

VPR se rendre 1 *(aller)* **se r. dans un lieu** to go to *or* make one's way to a place; **vous pouvez vous y r. en train/avion/bateau** you can get there by train/plane/boat; **en se rendant au bureau** on the way to the office; **se r. en toute hâte à un endroit** to hurry to a place; **se r. chez qn** to call on sb, to visit sb
2 *(reconnaître défaite, erreur etc)* to surrender, to give (oneself) up; **se r. à la police** *ou* **aux policiers** to give oneself up to the police, to turn oneself in to the police; **se r. à la raison** to see reason, to yield to reason; **se r. compte de qch** to realize sth; **se r. à l'évidence** to face facts; **se r. à l'avis de qn** to come round to sb's way of thinking
3 *(+ adj, + nom) (devenir)* **se r. malade/utile** to make oneself ill/useful; **se r. ridicule** to make a fool of oneself; **il s'est rendu maître de la situation** he took control of the situation

VI 1 *(d'une terre etc)* to be productive; *(de placement)* to yield
2 le moteur rend bien the engine runs *or* performs well
3 *(vomir)* to vomit

rendu [rãdy] **ADJ 1** *(arrivé)* **être r.** to have arrived; **nous voilà rendus à Manchester** here we are in Manchester; **tu seras plus vite r. par le train** you'll get there quicker by train; *Fig Fam* **on n'est pas r.** *(il y a encore beaucoup à faire)* we're not there yet **2** *Vieilli* **r. (de fatigue)** exhausted, tired out **3 r. à domicile** delivered at domicile; **r. franco bord** delivered free on board; **r. à la frontière** delivered at frontier; **r. droits acquittés/non acquittés** delivery duty paid/unpaid
NM 1 *Beaux-Arts, Ordinat (de sujet)* rendering; **r. exact des couleurs** exact reproduction of colour **2** *Com* returned article, return

rêne [rɛn] **NF** rein; **lâcher les rênes** to loosen the reins, to give a/the horse his head; *Fig (abandonner)* to let go; *Fig* **prendre/tenir les rênes** to take over/hold the reins; **passer les rênes du pouvoir** to hand over the reins (à to)

renégat, -ate [rǝnega, -at] **N** renegade, turncoat; *Rel* renegade

renégociation [rǝnegɔsjasjɔ̃] **NF** renegotiation

renégocier [rǝnegɔsje] **VT** to renegotiate

reneiger [rǝneʒe] **V IMPERS** to snow again

renfermé [rãfɛrme] **ADJ** *(personne)* uncommunicative, withdrawn
NM odeur de r. musty smell; **sentir le r.** to smell musty

renfermer [rãfɛrme] **VT 1** *Vieilli (enfermer)* to shut up; *(de nouveau)* to shut up again **2**

(contenir) to contain; **livre qui renferme des idées nouvelles** book that contains new ideas

VPR se renfermer to withdraw into oneself, to shut oneself off from people; **elle se renferma dans un silence d'airain** she withdrew into total silence

renfiler [rãfile] VT (perles etc) to restring; (aiguille) to rethread

renflé [rãfle] ADJ (pilier) bulging; (amphore) rounded

renflement [rãfləmã] NM (d'un pilier etc) bulge

renfler [rãfle] VT **r. qch** to make a bulge in sth
VPR se renfler to swell (out), to bulge

renflouage [rãflua ʒ], **renflouement** [rãflumã] NM (d'un bateau échoué) refloating, floating off; (d'un bateau coulé) raising; Fig (d'une affaire) refloating

renflouer [rãflue] VT (bateau échoué) to float off, to refloat; (bateau coulé) to raise; Fig **r. une entreprise** to refloat a business, to set a business on its feet again, to bail out a company; Fig **r. les caisses de l'État** to swell the government's coffers; Fig **ça m'a permis de r. mes caisses pendant un mois** it swelled the coffers or kept me going or afloat for a month; Fig **r. qn** to keep sb afloat (financially)

renfoncement [rãfõsmã] NM **1** (creux) (dans un mur) recess; (dans un arbre) hollow; **r. d'une porte** doorway **2** Typ (d'une ligne) indentation

renfoncer [rãfõse] (conj like **enfoncer**) VT **1** (clou etc) to drive further in; (chapeau) to pull down; Fig **je voulais lui r. ses paroles dans la gorge** I wanted to shove the words down his throat **2** Constr (façade etc) to recess, to set back; Typ, Ordinat (ligne, paragraphe) to indent; (écriture) to embolden
VPR se renfoncer Beaux-Arts (du fond) to recede

renforçage [rãfɔrsaʒ] NM **1** (d'un mur, d'une couture etc) strengthening, reinforcing **2** Phot intensification

renforcement [rãfɔrsəmã] NM **1** (d'une poutre etc) strengthening, reinforcement; (d'une équipe, armée) strengthening **2** Phot intensification

renforcer [rãfɔrse] (conj like **forcer**) VT **1** (mur, poutre, couture, couverture de livre etc) to strengthen, to reinforce; (armée, équipe) to strengthen; (sécurité) to increase, to tighten up **2** (couleur, éclairage) to intensify; (crainte) to heighten, to intensify; (impression) to strengthen, to heighten; (suspicions, convictions) to heighten; **r. qn dans une opinion** to confirm sb in an opinion; **tout cela ne fait que r. mes convictions** it just makes me more convinced than ever; **suivre des cours d'anglais renforcé** to do extra English (more than the normal baccalauréat syllabus demands); **faire un henné renforcé** to have an extra-red henna rinse done
VPR se renforcer (d'un mouvement, de la pression) to grow stronger, to grow in strength; (d'une tendance) to grow, to increase

renfort [rãfɔr] NM **1 renforts** (hommes) reinforcements; **demander du r.** to ask for help; (d'un policier, d'un pompier etc) to ask for backup; **il faut du r. pour finir le projet** we need extra people to finish the project; **des soldats envoyés en r.** reinforcements; **un stagiaire recruté en r.** a trainee recruited to help out; **de r.** backup, extra; **à grand r. d'épingles/de conseils** with the help of lots of pins/advice **2** (pièce) reinforcement; Aut **r. (anti-impact) latéral** side-impact bar

renfrogné [rãfrɔɲe] ADJ (visage, personne) frowning, scowling; **avec son air r.** with his scowling look

renfrogner (se) [sərãfrɔɲe] VPR to frown, to scowl

rengagé [rãgaʒe] Mil ADJ re-enlisted
NM re-enlisted soldier

rengagement [rãgaʒmã] NM (du personnel) re-engagement; Mil re-enlistment

rengager [rãgaʒe] (conj like **engager**) VT (personnel) to rehire, to take on again; (combat) to renew; (conversation, partie, débat) to pick up, to start again from where one left off
VI Mil to re-enlist
VPR se rengager Mil to re-enlist

rengaine [rãgɛn] NF cliché; (morceau de musique) tune; **vieille r.** old refrain; Fam **c'est toujours la même r.** it's (always) the same old story

rengainer [rãgɛne] VT (épée) to sheathe, to put up; Fig Fam **r. son compliment** to save one's compliments, to keep one's compliments to oneself

rengorger (se) [sərãgɔrʒe] VPR (conj like **engorger**) (d'un oiseau) to strut; (d'une personne) to strut, to swagger

reniement [rənimã] NM (d'un ami etc) disowning; (du Christ, de la foi) denial; (d'opinions, d'une action etc) disavowal

renier [rənje] (conj like **nier**) VT (ami, père, racines etc) to disown; (le Christ) to deny; (foi) to deny, Fml to abjure; (action, opinion, idée) to repudiate
VPR se renier to repudiate one's opinions

reniflard [r(ə)niflar] NM Aut breather

reniflement [rənifləmã] NM **1** (action) sniffing **2** (bruit) sniff

renifler [rənifle] VI **1** to sniff **2** Fam (sentir mauvais) to stink
VT (fleur) to sniff (at), to take a sniff at or of; (tabac à priser) to sniff (up); **il renifla la bonne odeur qui s'échappait de la cuisine** his nose picked up the lovely smell coming from the kitchen; Fig **il sait r. une bonne affaire** he's got a (good) nose for a bargain, he's good at sniffing out bargains; **j'ai reniflé le coup** I cottoned on to or tumbled to the trick

renifleur, -euse [rəniflœr, -øz] ADJ **avion r.** sniffer plane
N sniffer, sniffler

renipper [rənipe] Can VT (rénover) (maison, pièce) to do up, to renovate
VPR se renipper to smarten oneself up, to smarten up one's appearance

renne [rɛn] NM reindeer

renom [rənõ] NM (popularité) fame, renown; **de r.** famous, renowned; **un restaurant de grand r.** an extremely famous restaurant, a restaurant of great renown; **connaître qn de r.** to know sb by reputation; **en r.** famous, renowned, celebrated

renommé [rənɔme] ADJ renowned, famous, celebrated (**pour** for)

renommée [rənɔme] NF **1** (popularité) fame, renown; **connaître qn de r.** to know sb by reputation or repute; **être de r. internationale** to be internationally famous; **être de r. mondiale** to be world-famous **2** Jur (preuve par) commune r. hearsay evidence

renommer [rənɔme] VT to reappoint; Ordinat (fichier) to rename

renonce [rənõs] NF Cartes **1** renounce, inability to follow suit; **avoir une r. à cœur** to be short of hearts **2 fausse r.** revoke; **faire une fausse r.** to revoke

renoncement [rənõsmã] NM renunciation, renouncement (**à** of); **vie de r.** life of renunciation or sacrifice

renoncer [rənõse] (**je renonçai(s); n. renon-**

çons) VI **1 r. à** (un projet, une carrière) to abandon, to give or throw up; (des vacances) to sacrifice, to forgo; (la couronne, la succession, une réclamation) to relinquish; (la violence, sa foi) to renounce; (le chocolat, la boisson, son indépendance) to give up; **r. à un droit** to waive or relinquish a right; **r. à un voyage** to give up all thoughts of a trip; **r. à la lutte** to give up or relinquish the struggle; **r. au monde** to renounce the world; **r. à faire qch** to give up doing sth; (projet) to give up or drop the idea of doing sth; **je renonce à la convaincre** I've given up trying to convince her; **deux des coureurs ont renoncé** two of the runners dropped out; **j'y renonce!, je renonce!** I give up!; **il est hors de question que j'y renonce** there's no question of me giving up; **r. à qn** (fiancé) to let sb go **2** Cartes to renounce, to fail to follow suit; (faire une fausse renonce) to revoke
VT 1 Arch (personne) to disown; Litt **r. sa foi** to renounce one's faith **2** Belg (résilier) (bail) to cancel

renonciation [rənõsjasjõ] NF **r. à** (la couronne, une réclamation, la violence etc) renunciation of; (à une carrière) sacrifice or renunciation of; (à un projet) abandonment of; (à une lutte) relinquishment of; Jur **r. à un droit** waiver or waiving of a right

renoncule [rənõkyl] NF Bot ranunculus; (sauvage) (wild) buttercup; **fausse r.** lesser celandine

renouée [rənwe] NF Bot knotgrass, polygonum

renouer [rənwe] VT **1** (ruban, lacet etc) to tie (up) again; (cravate) to do up or knot again **2** Fig (conversation, relations) to renew, to resume; (amitié) to renew
VI r. avec qn to make friends with sb again, to make it up with sb; **un auteur qui renoue avec la tradition de la littérature courtoise** an author who is reviving the tradition of courtly literature; **r. avec le succès** to enjoy renewed success

renouveau [rənuvo] NM **1** Litt (printemps) springtide, springtime (of the year) **2** Fig (renaissance) (religieux, des arts) revival; **un r. de succès** renewed success; **connaître un r.** to enjoy or experience a revival

renouvelable [rənuvlabl] ADJ **1** (contrat, énergie etc) renewable; (expérience) repeatable **2** Pol **le comité est r. tous les ans** the committee must stand or Am run for office each year; **mon mandat est r.** I am eligible to stand or Am run (for office) again

renouveler [rənuvle] (**je renouvelle, n. renouvelons; je renouvellerai**) VT **1** (stock, équipement, mobilier, garde-robe etc) to renew, to replace; **r. ses pneus** to get a new set of tyres, to replace one's tyres; **r. l'air d'une salle** to air a room
2 (équipe, personnel, méthode, style) to change completely; **une découverte qui renouvelle totalement notre conception du temps** a discovery which radically alters our conception of time
3 (alliance, contrat, passeport, abonnement, querelle) to renew; (promesse, proposition, offre, ordonnance) to repeat, to renew; (expérience, exploit, Com (commande) to repeat; (usage, tradition, enthousiasme) to revive; Com **r. la commande de qch** to reorder sth; **r. sa demande** to renew or repeat one's request; (pour un emploi) to apply again, to reapply; **r. le prêt d'un livre de bibliothèque** to renew a library book; **r. une traite** to renew a bill of exchange; Rel **ses vœux** to renew one's vows; **le pays a renouvelé sa confiance au parti au pouvoir** the country has renewed confidence in the governing party; **je vous renouvelle mes re-**

merciements pour votre joli cadeau *(dans une lettre)* thanking you once again for the lovely present

VI r. de zèle to act with renewed zeal

VPR se renouveler 1 *(se reformer) (de l'épiderme)* to be renewed

2 *(se produire)* to recur, to happen again; **que cela ne se renouvelle pas!** don't let it happen again!

3 *(changer)* to change; **il ne se renouvelle pas** it's always the same old thing, he never does anything new; **un artiste qui ne se renouvelle pas** an artist who doesn't bring anything new to his work

4 *(être remplacé)* to be replaced

renouvellement [rənuvɛlmɑ̃] **NM 1** *(du stock, de l'équipement)* replacement, renewal; **activer le r. cellulaire** *(d'un produit de beauté)* to encourage the cells to renew themselves **2** *(d'un système)* reform; *(d'une tradition etc)* revival; *(d'une méthode, d'un style)* change **3** *(d'un traité, d'un contrat, d'une offre etc)* renewal

rénovateur, -trice [renɔvatœr, -tris] **ADJ** reforming

N *(personne)* *(d'une méthode etc)* reformer; *(d'un genre artistique)* reviver

rénovation [renɔvasjɔ̃] **NF 1** *(d'un bâtiment, du mobilier etc)* renovation; **la maison est en (cours de) r.** the house is being renovated *or* is undergoing renovation; **projet/travaux de r.** renovation project/work **2** *Fig (d'une institution)* updating, reform

rénover [renɔve] **VT 1** *(bâtiment, mobilier etc)* to renovate **2** *Fig (genre artistique)* to revive; *(méthode, institution etc)* to update, to reform

renseigné [rɑ̃seɲe] **ADJ bien/mal r.** well-/ill-informed (**sur** about)

renseignement [rɑ̃seɲ(ə)mɑ̃] **NM** (piece of) information; *Mil etc* (piece of) intelligence; *Tél* **renseignements** directory enquiries, *Am* information; **pour tout r., veuillez appeler ce numéro** for information *or* if you have any queries, please call this number; **pardon Monsieur, c'est pour un r.** excuse me, could you give me some information?; **nous avons beaucoup de mal à obtenir ce r.** we're having a lot of trouble getting the information; **renseignements complémentaires** further information; *Fin* **renseignements de crédit** status *or* credit enquiry; **demander/donner des renseignements sur qn/qch** to ask for/to give (some) information on *or* about sb/sth; **prendre des renseignements sur qn/qch** to make enquiries *or* to enquire about sb/sth; **aller aux renseignements** to go to find out *or* to make enquiries; **bureau de renseignements** information bureau *or* office; **renseignements (techniques)** data; **service de r.** intelligence branch *or* service *or* department; **organes de renseignements et de sécurité** security; **les renseignements généraux** = the security branch of the French police force, *Br* ≃ the Special Branch, *Am* ≃ the FBI; **agent de** *ou* **du r.** (intelligence) agent

renseigner [rɑ̃seɲe] **VT r. qn** to give sb some information; **on vous a (fort) mal renseigné** you have been (badly) misinformed; **l'office du tourisme nous a très bien/très mal renseignés** the tourist board gave us excellent information/totally the wrong information; **r. qn sur qch** to tell sb about sth, to give sb information *or* inform sb about sth; **r. qn sur un cours/le fonctionnement d'un ordinateur** to tell sb about *or Fam* to fill *or* clue sb in on a course/how a computer works; **être bien renseigné sur qch** to be well informed about sth; **je vais vous r. sur lui** I'll tell you something about him

VPR se renseigner to ask, to make enquiries,

to enquire; *(obtenir des renseignements)* to find out, to get information (**sur** about); **essaie de te r. pour savoir combien coûterait un billet** try to find out how much a ticket would cost

rentabilisation [rɑ̃tabilizasjɔ̃] **NF** making profitable; *(de projet, opération)* making cost-effective

rentabiliser [rɑ̃tabilize] **VT** *(projet, opération)* to make cost-effective; *(société, placement etc)* to make profitable; **r. des investissements** to obtain a return on investments

VPR se rentabiliser *(d'un projet, d'une opération)* to become cost-effective; *(d'un placement, d'une société)* to become profitable

rentabilité [rɑ̃tabilite] **NF** *(d'un projet, d'une opération)* cost-effectiveness; *(d'un placement, d'une société)* profitability; *(d'un investissement)* rate of return; **r. du capital** return on capital; **r. nette d'exploitation** net operating profit

rentable [rɑ̃tabl] **ADJ** *(projet, opération)* cost-effective; *(placement, société)* profitable; **ce n'est pas r.** it doesn't pay; **d'accord, si c'est r.** OK, if there's any money in it *or* any money to be made out of it, OK, if it's financially worthwhile; **ses investigations sont peu rentables** his/her investigations aren't proving very profitable; **loyer r./peu r.** economic/uneconomic rent

rente [rɑ̃t] **NF 1 rentes** *(revenu)* unearned *or* private income; **vivre de ses rentes** to live off one's private income; **je n'ai qu'un rêve: vivre de mes rentes** I dream of having a private income **2** *(pension)* annuity, pension; **faire une r. à qn** to make sb an (annual) allowance; **on lui a fait une r.** he has been pensioned off **3 rentes (sur l'État)** (government) stocks *or* funds *or* bonds

▸▸**r. annuelle** annuity; **r. à paiement différé** deferred annuity; **Fin r. de situation** guaranteed income; **r. viagère** life annuity

rentier, -ière [rɑ̃tje, -jɛr] **N** person of private means *or* with a private income; **petit r.** person with a small private income; **mener une vie de r.** to lead a life of leisure, to be a lady/gentleman of leisure; **avoir une mentalité de r.** to think one is above earning a living

rentrant, -ante [rɑ̃trɑ̃, -ɑ̃t] **ADJ 1** *Math* **angle r.** reflex *or* re-entrant angle; *Phot* **monture rentrante** sunken mount **2** *Aviat* **train d'atterrissage r.** retractable undercarriage

N *Cartes* new player, cutter-in

rentré [rɑ̃tre] **ADJ 1** *(joues)* hollow, sunken; *(yeux)* sunken **2** *(rire, rage etc)* suppressed

rentre-dedans [rɑ̃trədədɑ̃] **NM INV** *Fam* **faire du r. à qn** to come on to sb, to chat sb up, *Am* to hit on sb

rentrée [rɑ̃tre] **NF 1** *(des vacanciers, des automobilistes etc)* return, return home; *Mus (d'un motif, instrument)* re-entry; **les embouteillages causés par les rentrées sur Paris** the traffic jams caused by Parisians returning home; *Astronaut* **r. atmosphérique** re-entry into the atmosphere

2 *(des tribunaux, des théâtres)* reopening; **r. (parlementaire)** reassembly, reopening (of Parliament); *Scol* **la r. (des classes)/(scolaire)** the beginning of term/the new school year; **on se reverra à la r.!** see you next term!, see you after the holidays!; **la préparation de la r.** preparation for the new term/the new school year; **on s'occupera de cela à la r.** we'll worry about that when the new term starts *or* when term starts again; **le jour de la r.** the first day of the (new) term; **la r. des élèves/des professeurs** the day the pupils/teachers go back; **la r. sociale** the start of the social calendar; **faire sa r. politique** *(après les vacances)* to resume one's political

activities; *(après une longue absence)* to make one's political comeback; **la r. littéraire** this autumn's new books

3 *(d'argent)* receipt; **rentrées fiscales** tax revenue; **rentrées journalières** daily takings; *Compta* **rentrées et sorties de caisse** cash receipts and payments; **j'attends une r. d'argent** I'm expecting some money; **il n'y a pas assez de rentrées d'argent** there isn't enough money coming in

4 *(de la récolte)* getting in

5 *Ftbl* **r. en touche** throw-in

La rentrée

The time of the year when children go back to school – in September – has considerable cultural significance in France. Coming after the long summer break or "grandes vacances", it is the time when academic, political, social and commercial activity begins again in earnest.

RENTRER [rɑ̃tre]

| **VI** to come in **1, 5** ▪ to go in **1** ▪ to come home **2** ▪ to go home **2** ▪ to fit in **4** ▪ to collide with **6** |
| **VT** to bring in **1** ▪ to hold back **2** |

VI *(aux être)* **1** *(entrer de nouveau)* to re-enter; *(vers le point de référence choisi)* to come in again; *(en s'éloignant du point de référence choisi)* to go in again; **r. dans sa chambre** to go back into one's room; **lorsqu'il rentra en France/à Paris** when he returned to France/Paris; **r. dans son pays** to go back home, to go back to one's own country; *Astronaut* **r. dans l'atmosphère** to re-enter the atmosphere; **r. au port** to return to port, to put back to port; **r. dans les bonnes grâces de qn** to regain favour with sb, to get back into sb's good books; **r. en correspondance avec qn** to resume correspondence with sb; **r. en relation avec qn** to get in touch with *or* contact sb again; **r. dans le droit chemin** to mend one's ways, to turn over a new leaf; **faire r. qn dans le droit chemin** to get sb back on the straight and narrow; **r. en scène** *(d'un acteur)* to come on again

2 *(à la maison)* to return home; *(vers le point de référence)* to come (back) home; *(en s'éloignant du point de référence)* to go (back) home; **r. d'un voyage/de vacances** to come back from a trip/holiday; **elle rentre de Paris** she is just home *or* back from Paris, she has just got home *or* back from Paris; **je serai rentré à cette date** I'll be (back) home by then; **il est rentré très tard** he was very late back, he came home *or* got in very late; **c'est à cette heure-ci que tu rentres?** what kind of time do you call this (to come home at)?; **il est l'heure de r.** it's time we went home, it's time to go home; **nous allons r.** we're going home; **je rentre chez moi** I'm going home; **je l'ai vu en rentrant chez moi** I saw him/it on my way home; **en rentrant de l'école** on my/his/*etc* way home from school; **je rentre de chez ma voisine et il paraît que ...** I've just come (back) from *or* got back from my neighbour's and it seems that ...; **r. dîner** to go home to dinner *or* for dinner; **tu rentreras dîner, ce soir?** will you be home for dinner this evening?; **voilà deux jours qu'elle n'est pas rentrée dormir ici** she hasn't slept here for the past two nights

3 *(reprendre ses occupations) (d'une école, des tribunaux etc)* to reopen; *(du Parlement)* to reassemble, to reopen; *(d'un élève, d'un professeur)* to go back to school; **les enfants rentrent le 15 septembre** the children go back to school *or* school starts again on the 15th of September

4 *(d'objets)* to go in, to fit (in); **cela ne pourra pas r. dans mon sac** it won't go in *or* fit in my bag; **cela rentre mal dans mon sac** there's not enough room for it in my bag; **ça rentre parfaitement dans mon cartable** it's just the right size for my school bag; **j'ai réussi à tout faire r.** I managed to get everything in; **faire r. qch dans sa boîte** to get sth back into its box; **des tubes qui rentrent les uns dans les autres** tubes that fit into one another

5 *(d'argent etc)* to come in; **faire r. ses fonds** to call in one's money; **r. dans ses fonds** to recoup one's investment; **r. dans ses frais** to recover one's expenses

6 *(forme emphatique d'entrer)* to enter, to come/go in; *Cartes* to cut in; **je t'en prie, rentre!** do come in!; **r. dans l'administration** to join the Civil Service, to become a civil servant; **je n'aurais jamais dû r. dans cette boutique** I should never have gone into *or* set foot inside the shop; *Fig* **r. en soi-même** to retire *or* withdraw into oneself; **r. dans un mur** *(d'une voiture)* to collide with *or* smash into *or* plough into a wall; **r. dans un réverbère/qn** *(d'un piéton)* to walk into *or* bang into *or* collide with a lamppost/sb; **ils se sont rentrés en plein dedans** they ran *or* went slap (bang) into each other; *Fam* **elle m'est rentrée dedans** *ou* **dans le chou** she ran into *or* banged into *or* collided with me; **je ne rentre plus dans mon pantalon** I can't get into my trousers any more!, my trousers don't fit me any more!; **r. dans une catégorie** to fall into a category

7 *Typ* **faire r. une ligne** to indent a line

vt *(aux* avoir*)* **1** *(le linge, les vaches etc)* to take/bring in; *Naut (cordage)* to heave in, to haul in; *(les couleurs)* to haul down, to strike; *Pêche (filet)* to pull in, to haul in; *Aviat (train d'atterrissage)* to retract, to raise; **veux-tu r. le linge?** *(je suis à la maison)* will you bring the washing in?; *(je suis dans le jardin)* will you take the washing in?; **tu peux r. la voiture dans le garage** you can put the car in the garage; **rentre-le dans son étui maintenant** now put it back in its case; **r. ses griffes** *(d'un chat)* to retract *or* sheathe its claws; *Fig* to draw in one's claws; **rentre ton** *ou* **le ventre!** don't stick your stomach out!; *(tiens-toi droit)* straighten your back!; **r. son pull (dans son pantalon)** to tuck one's sweater in(to one's trousers); **r. la récolte** to get in *or* gather in the harvest; **à l'époque où l'on rentre la moisson** at harvest time

2 *(réprimer)* *(désir, colère)* to repress, to stifle; *(larmes)* to stifle, to hold back; **r. sa déception/sa souffrance** not to let one's disappointment/pain show

vpr se rentrer *Fam* to go home

renumérotation [rənymerɔtasjɔ̃] **nf** *Tél* redial

renuméroter [rənymerɔte] **vi** *Tél* to redial

renversant [rɑ̃vɛrsɑ̃] **adj** *Fam (nouvelles, spectacle etc)* astounding, staggering; *(personne)* astounding, amazing; **elle est renversante de bêtise** her stupidity is staggering *or* mind-blowing

renverse [rɑ̃vɛrs] **nf 1** *(du courant)* shift, turn; *(du vent)* shift, change **2 tomber** *ou* **partir à la r.** to fall (over) backwards *or* on one's back; **il y a de quoi tomber à la r.** it's staggering *or* *Fam* mind-boggling

renversé [rɑ̃vɛrse] **adj 1** *(à l'envers)* *(image)* reversed; *(arche, pyramide)* inverted; **écriture renversée** backhanded writing, writing that slopes backwards **2** *(tombé)* *(chaise, statue, bouteille etc)* overturned, upset **3** *Fam (déconcerté)* staggered

nm *Suisse (café crème)* latte

renversement [rɑ̃vɛrsəmɑ̃] **nm 1** *(de tendances, d'alliances, d'une image)* reversal; *(des opinions)* (dramatic) change *or* shift;

Mus (d'un intervalle, d'un accord) inversion; **r. des valeurs** inversion of values; **r. de situation** reversal of the situation; **quel r. de situation!** how the tables have turned!; **r. des rôles** role reversal; **il y a un r. des rôles entre mère et fille** mother and daughter are switching roles **2** *(de la marée)* turn(ing); *(du vent)* shift(ing), backing; **r. de la vapeur** *(d'une locomotive)* reversing; **attendre le r. de la marée** to wait for the tide to turn **3** *(à l'envers)* turning upside down; **charrette à r.** tip-up cart **4** *(d'un cabinet, ministère)* toppling; *(par la violence)* *(d'un régime, gouvernement)* overthrow

renverser [rɑ̃vɛrse] **vt 1** *(tendance, rôles etc)* to reverse; *(lettres d'un mot, proposition)* to invert; **r. la tête** to tip *or* tilt one's head back; **garde-lui la tête renversée** keep his/her head (tilted) back *or* tilted backwards; **r. la marche** to reverse (the engine); *Fig* **r. la vapeur** to change tack; **r. la situation** to reverse the situation

2 *(mettre à l'envers)* *(chaise, vase, assiette)* to turn upside down, to upturn; *(gâteau)* to turn upside down; **'ne pas r.'** 'this side up'

3 *(faire tomber)* *(personne, chaise, vase)* to knock over *or* down; *(verre, seau)* to knock *or* tip over, to overturn, to upset; *(bateau)* to capsize, to overturn; *(liquide)* to spill; *(adversaire)* to knock down; **r. qch d'un coup de pied** to kick sth over; **r. son chargement** *(d'un camion)* to shed its load; **le vent a renversé la table** the wind knocked *or* blew the table over; **être renversé** *ou* **se faire r. par une voiture** to be knocked over *or* down by a car; *Fig* **cela renverse tous mes projets** that disrupts *or* upsets all my plans

4 *Pol (cabinet, ministère)* to bring down, to topple, to vote out of office; *(par la violence)* *(régime, gouvernement)* to overthrow; *Fig (obstacle)* to overcome, to surmount

5 *Fam (bouleverser)* *(personne)* to stagger, to knock sideways; **cela me renverse!** well I'm blowed *or* damned *or* jiggered!; **être renversé par la beauté de qn** to be bowled over by sb's beauty

vi *(de la marée)* to turn

vpr se renverser *(d'une chaise, d'un vase, verre)* to fall over *or* down, to overbalance, to tip over; *(d'un véhicule)* to overturn *(dans on)*; *(d'un bateau)* to capsize, to overturn; **se r. sur sa chaise** to lean back on one's chair, to tilt one's chair back

renvoi [rɑ̃vwa] **nm 1** *(de marchandises etc)* return, sending back

2 *(des employés)* dismissal, *Br Fam* sacking; *(des troupes)* expulsion; *(d'un élève)* expulsion; **signifier à qn son r.** *(employé)* to inform sb that he has been dismissed *or* sacked; *(élève)* to inform sb that he has been expelled; **au bout de trois avertissements, c'est le r. définitif** *(d'un employé)* after three warnings it's dismissal; *(d'un élève)* after three warnings it's expulsion

3 *(ajournement)* postponement, putting off, deferral; *Jur* adjournment; *Jur* **r. à huitaine** week's adjournment

4 *(à une commission etc)* reference, referral; *Jur (d'une affaire à un autre tribunal)* transfer **5** *Typ, Ordinat (dans un texte, une base de données)* cross-reference; **r. en fin de document** endnote

6 *Tech* **levier de r.** reversing lever; **engrenage de r.** reversing gear

7 *(éructation)* burp, belch; **avoir un r./des renvois** to burp, to belch; **le concombre me donne des renvois** cucumber repeats on me **8** *Sport* clearance; *Tennis etc* return; **r. de Zidane** Zidane clears (the ball); **... r. de la tête de Petit** ... Petit heads the ball clear

renvoyer [rɑ̃vwaje] **vt** *(conj like* envoyer*)* **1** *(faire retourner)* *(cadeau, lettre etc)* to send back, to return; *(personne)* to send back;

(son) to throw back, to echo; *(chaleur, lumière)* to reflect; **r. à l'expéditeur** to return to sender; **r. qn au lit** to send sb back to bed; *Fig* **r. l'ascenseur** to return the favour; **je le leur ai proposé pour leur r. l'ascenseur** I suggested it to them as a way of returning the favour they had done me; **elle attend que tu lui renvoies l'ascenseur** she expects you to return the favour, *Fam* she feels you owe her one

2 *(faire partir)* *(visiteur)* to send *or* turn away; *Jur (accusé)* to discharge; **r. qn en cour d'assises** to send sb before the Crown Court; **r. des troupes dans leurs foyers** to discharge *or* dismiss troops

3 *(licencier)* *(employé)* to dismiss, *Br Fam* to sack; *(élève)* to expel; **se faire r.** *(du collège)* to get expelled; *(du travail)* to get sacked, to get the sack

4 *(différer)* *(affaire, débat)* to put off, to postpone, to defer; *Jur* **r. une affaire à huitaine** to adjourn a case for a week; *Jur* **r. le prévenu à une autre audience** to remand the accused

5 *(reporter)* *(affaire)* to refer *(à* to); *Ordinat* to cross-refer; *Pol* **r. un projet à une commission** to send a bill to a committee; **les numéros renvoient (le lecteur) aux notes** the numbers refer to the notes; **cet article renvoie à un autre** *(dans un dictionnaire)* this entry is cross-referred to another

6 *Sport (ballon)* to clear; *Tennis etc* to return; **Boli renvoie le ballon de la tête** Boli heads the ball clear

réoccupation [reɔkypasjɔ̃] **nf** *(d'un territoire, d'une usine etc)* reoccupation

réoccuper [reɔkype] **vt** *(territoire, usine etc)* to reoccupy

réorganisateur, -trice [reɔrganizatœr, -tris] **n** reorganizer

réorganisation [reɔrganizasjɔ̃] **nf** reorganization

réorganiser [reɔrganize] **vt** to reorganize
vpr se réorganiser to be reorganized

réorientation [reɔrjɑ̃tasjɔ̃] **nf** reorientation

réorienter [reɔrjɑ̃te] **vt** to reorient(ate)

réouverture [reuvɛrtyr] **nf** *(d'un théâtre, magasin, de la frontière etc)* reopening; **r. des débats** resumption of proceedings

repaire [rəpɛr] **nm** *(de lions)*, *Fig (de voleurs)* den, lair; *(de pirates)* nest; *(de criminels)* haunt

repaître [rəpɛtr] *(prp* repaissant; *pp* repu; *pr ind* je repais, n. repaissons; *pr sub* je repaisse*)* **vt** *Littt* **r. ses yeux de qch** to feast one's eyes on sth
vpr se repaître 1 *(d'un animal)* to eat its fill **2** *Fig Litt* **se r. de sang** to wallow in blood; **se r. de chimères** to indulge in vain imaginings; **se r. de commérages** to revel in gossip

répandre [repɑ̃dr] **vt 1** *(renverser)* *(sel, liquide etc)* to spill

2 *(parsemer)* *(sable)* to spread, to sprinkle, to scatter; *(liquide)* to pour; *(larmes, sang)* to shed; *(fleurs)* to scatter, to strew; *(lumière)* to shed; *(odeur)* to give off; *(chaleur)* to give *or* throw out; *(rumeur)* to spread (about), to circulate; *(nouvelle)* to spread, to broadcast; *(terreur, usage, doctrine)* to spread; **r. du sable sur le plancher** to sprinkle sand on the floor *or* the floor with sand; **r. du sel sur une tache de vin** to pour salt on a wine stain; **ce poêle répand une douce chaleur dans la maison** the stove spreads a gentle warmth throughout the house; **r. le produit uniformément sur le carrelage** spread the product evenly on the floor; **cette nouvelle répandit la tristesse dans la ville** the news cast a gloom over *or* spread gloom throughout the town; **cette nouvelle répandit le bonheur dans toute la maison** the news brought a general air of happiness to the house

3 *(bénéfices etc)* to lavish; *Litt* **alors que le soleil répandait ses bienfaits ...** as the sun was pouring out its blessings ...

VPR se répandre 1 *(d'un liquide)* to spill; *(d'une odeur, nouvelle, algue, maladie, de la panique, la fumée)* to spread; *(d'une rumeur, opinion, pratique, d'idées)* to spread, to gain ground; **les métastases se sont répandues dans tout le corps** the tumours have spread throughout the body; **la foule se répandit dans la rue** the crowd spilled into the street; **les touristes se répandent dans la ville** tourists are invading or overrunning the town; **l'usage de ce mot s'est répandu** this word is now widely used or in wide use

2 se r. en explications to launch forth into explanations; **se r. en excuses** to apologize profusely, to be full of apologies; **se r. en compliments** to be full of compliments, to be very complimentary

3 *Vieilli* **se r. dans le monde** to lead a sociable life

répandu [repɑ̃dy] ADJ **1** *(méthode, préjugé, idée etc)* widespread, prevalent; *(fleur, animal, oiseau)* widespread, common; *(opinion)* widely held; **un objet d'un usage très peu r.** an object that is in limited use **2** *Vieilli* *(personne)* widely known; **il est très r. dans les milieux politiques** he is extremely well known in political circles

réparabilité [reparabilite] NF repairability

réparable [reparabl] ADJ **1** *(chaussure, machine etc)* repairable; **c'est facilement/difficilement r.** it's easy/difficult to repair; **ce n'est pas r.** it can't be repaired, it's beyond repair **2** *(erreur)* for which amends can be made, *Fml* retrievable; *(perte financière)* which can be made up, *Fml* retrievable; **c'est facilement r.** *(erreur)* it can be easily put right; **c'est difficilement r.** *(erreur)* it won't be easy to put matters right or to make amends

reparaître [rəparɛtr] VI *(conj like* **paraître***; aux often* **avoir***)* *(d'une personne, maladie)* to reappear, to appear again; *(de la lune, du soleil)* to reappear, to appear again, to come out again, to re-emerge

réparateur, -trice [reparatœr, -tris] ADJ *(sommeil)* refreshing; **chirurgie réparatrice** reconstructive surgery

N *(de vélos, d'appareil électroménager)* repairman, f repairwoman; *(d'horloge)* mender

réparation [reparasjɔ̃] NF **1** *(d'une chaussure, d'un vélo, d'une horloge)* repair(ing), mending; *(d'une maison, machine, route etc)* repair(ing); *(d'un bateau)* refit; **les réparations de l'appartement/de la toiture** the repairs to the flat/the roof; **nécessiter des réparations** to need repair; **réparations d'entretien** maintenance; **être en r.** *(d'une route)* to be under repair; *(d'un yacht)* to be under refit, to be refitting; **l'ascenseur/la machine à laver est en r.** the lift/washing machine is being repaired; **route en r.** road up for repairs; **faire des réparations** to make repairs (**sur** to) **2** *(dédommagement)* reparation, amends, redress; *Arch (par les armes)* satisfaction *(by duel)*; **assigner une somme d'argent en r. des dégâts causés** to allocate a sum of money to make good the damage; **en r. d'un tort** to make up for or *Fml* in reparation of or in atonement for a wrong; **demander r.** to seek redress (**de** for); *Ftbl* **coup de pied de r.** penalty kick; *Ftbl* **surface de r.** penalty area

▸▸ *Jur* **r. civile** compensation; *Jur* **r. légale** legal redress; **réparations de guerre** war reparations

réparer [repare] VT **1** *(toit, vélo, machine à laver etc)* to repair, *Fam* to fix; *(chaussure)* to repair, to mend; *(maison)* to repair; *(bateau)*

to refit; *(déchirure, accroc)* to mend; **donner ses chaussures à r.** to take one's shoes to the mender's; **r. ses forces** to get one's strength back, to build up one's strength; **r. le talon d'une chaussure** to re-heel a shoe; **r. ses pertes** to repair or make good one's losses; **la maison a besoin d'être réparée** the house is in need of repair or needs to be repaired **2** *(remédier à)* *(méfait)* to make amends for, *Fml* to atone or make atonement for; *(erreur)* to put right, to rectify; *(omission)* to make good, to rectify; *(tort)* to redress; *(dommage)* to make good

reparler [rəparle] VI *(après un accident)* to speak or talk again; **r. de qch** to speak about sth again; **nous en reparlerons plus tard** we'll talk about or discuss it later; **il ne faut plus en r.** it must not be mentioned again; **r. à qn** to speak to sb again; **elle ne lui a pas reparlé depuis** she hasn't spoken to him/her since; **si je vous surprends à r. ensemble** if I catch you two talking again

VPR se reparler to speak or talk to each other again; **ils se sont remis à se r.** they're talking again, they're on speaking terms again

repartie, répartie [rəparti, re-] NF retort, rejoinder; **avoir l'esprit de r., avoir la r. prompte, avoir de la r.** to be good or quick at repartee

repartir [rəpartir] VI *(conj like* **partir***, aux* **être***)* *(d'un voyageur, train etc)* to set or start off again; *(d'une machine etc)* to start (up) again; **je repars pour Paris** I'm off to Paris again; **r. à zéro** *(dans une tâche)* to start all over or from scratch again, to go back to square one; *(dans une relation)* to make a fresh start, to start all over again; **il est reparti d'un éclat de rire** he burst out laughing again; *Fam* **c'est reparti, ils se disputent encore!** they're at it again!, they're off again!; *Fam* **c'est reparti, ils ont encore mis la musique à fond!** there they go again, putting their music on full blast!

> Do not confuse with **répartir**.

repartir², répartir¹ [repartir] VT *(aux* **avoir***)* *(répondre)* to retort, to reply

répartir² [repartir] (**je répartis, n. répartissons**) VT *(partager)* *(tâches, argent, vivres)* to distribute, to divide (up), to share (out) (**entre** among); *(poids, charge, dividende)* to distribute; *(cours, paiements etc)* to spread (out) (**sur** over); *(dépenses, responsabilités etc)* to allocate, to apportion; *(impôts)* to assess; *Bourse (titres)* to allot, to allocate; **r. des objets selon leur couleur** to divide objects up by colour; **r. une ville en zones/un pays en régions** to divide a town up into areas/a country up into regions; **charge uniformément répartie** evenly distributed load; **tâche de bien r. les cartons** try to distribute the boxes evenly; **r. les frais** to share the costs; **r. les risques** to share the risks; **r. un produit** to distribute a product; *Fin* **r. une avarie** to adjust an average; *Couture* **r. le surplus du col** to ease the collar (onto the neckband)

VPR se répartir to split or divide (up); **ils se répartissent le travail** they divide or split (up) or share (out) the work among themselves; **on se répartit les tâches ménagères** we share the housework; **les sommes se répartissent ainsi** the amounts break down as follows

> Do not confuse with **repartir**.

répartiteur [repartitœr] NM **1** *(personne)* distributor; **(commissaire) r.** tax assessor **2** *Aut* proportioner

répartition [repartisjɔ̃] NF *(de la population, du poids, du travail etc)* distribution; *(des dépenses, des responsabilités etc)* apportion-

ment, allocation; *(des impôts)* assessment; *Bourse (de titres)* allotment, allocation; *(dividende)* dividend; *(des paiements, cours)* spreading (**sur** over); **r. de la population par groupes d'âge** breakdown of the population according to age group; **la r. des richesses est très inégale** the distribution of wealth is very unequal; **la r. des portefeuilles ministériels** the distribution of ministerial posts; **r. des risques** risk spreading; **r. du bénéfice** distribution of profits; **r. du dividende** distribution of the dividend; **r. d'avarie** *(en assurance)* adjustment of average; *Bourse* **première et unique r.** first and final dividend; *Bourse* **dernière r.** final dividend; **r. des votes** voting pattern

repas [rəpa] NM meal; *(d'animal)* feed; **faire trois r. par jour** to have three meals a day; **le bébé fait six r. par jour** the baby has six feeds a day; **ne pas manger entre les r.** don't eat between meals; **r. à 18 h** *(au zoo)* the animals will be fed at 6 p.m., feeding time at 6 p.m.; **r. de noce** ≃ wedding breakfast; **r. chaud** hot meal; **r. d'affaires** business lunch; **r. enfant** children's meal, children's portion; **r. de substitution, substitut de r.** meal replacement; **faire un r.** to have a meal; **r. léger, petit r.** light meal, snack; **aux heures de r.** at meal times; **prendre ses r. chez qn/ chez soi** to have one's meals with sb/to eat at home; **ticket-r., chèque-r.** luncheon voucher, LV

repassage [rəpasaʒ] NM *(des vêtements)* ironing; **faire du r.** to do some ironing; **c'est d'un r. facile** it irons easily, it's easy to iron; **n'exigeant aucun r.** non-iron; **table de r.** ironing board

repasser [rəpase] VI *(aux* **être***)* **1** *(devant qch ou un lieu)* to pass (by) again, to go/come by again; **elle n'est pas là, repassez demain** she's not here, come back tomorrow or call again or call back tomorrow; **je repasserai le prendre** I'll call or come back for it; **r. chez qn** to visit or drop in on or call on sb again; **je dois r. chez Denise** I have to go over to Denise's again; *Fam* **il peut toujours r.!** he's got another think coming!

2 *Ordinat* to rerun; **faites r. la dernière phrase** *(de bande magnétique)* play back the last sentence; **ce film repasse au Royal** the film is showing again or is on again at the Royal; *TV* **ça repassera** it'll be on again, they'll show it again

VT *(aux* **avoir***)* **1** *(franchir)* *(montagne, frontière)* to go across again, to cross (over) again; *(mer)* to cross again

2 *(répéter)* *(cassette, disque)* to play again; *(enregistrement)* to play back; *TV, Cin* to show again, to rerun; *(leçon, rôle)* to look over, to go over; **elle nous a repassé le même disque toute la soirée** she played the same record over and over again the entire evening; **r. une annonce** to put an ad in again, to readvertise; **r. qch dans son esprit** to go over sth in one's mind; **r. un examen** to resit or retake an exam, to take or sit an exam again

3 *(transporter)* to take across again

4 *(donner à nouveau)* **r. un plat à qn** to pass sb a dish again; **si tu as fini avec le dictionnaire, tu peux me le r.?** if you've finished with the dictionary can I have it back?; *Fam* **r. une fausse pièce à qn** to palm off or foist a counterfeit coin on sb

5 *(aiguiser)* *(couteau, outil)* to sharpen, to grind, to whet; **r. un rasoir sur le cuir** to strop a razor

6 *(avec un fer)* *(vêtements)* to iron; **fer à r.** iron; **table** ou **planche à r.** ironing board

repasseur, -euse [rəpasœr, -øz] NM (knife) grinder

NF **repasseuse** *(personne)* presser; *(machine)* ironing machine

repayer [rəpɛje] VT *(conj like* **payer***)* *(facture)* to pay again; *Fam* **j'ai dû lui r. une veste** I had to pay for another jacket for him/her

repêchage [rəpɛʃaʒ] NM **1** *(dans l'eau)* fishing out **2** *Scol Fig* **épreuve conçue pour permettre le r. des candidats** test designed to give candidates another chance; **épreuve de r.** *Scol (pour les élèves qui ont échoué)* resit; *Sport (pour les coureurs qui suivent le gagnant)* extra heat; *Can (pour sélectionner de jeunes concurrents)* selectors' meeting

repêcher [rəpeʃe] VT **1** *(retirer de l'eau)* to fish out **2** *Fig (personne en difficulté)* to rescue, to help (out); *Scol* **r. un candidat à l'oral** to let a candidate scrape through at the oral; **se faire r. à l'oral** to scrape through the oral; **ceux qui ont échoué au mois de juillet peuvent être repêchés en octobre** those who failed in July may sit the exam again in October; *Sport* **r. un concurrent** to let a competitor go through

repeindre [rəpɛdr] VT *(conj like* **peindre***)* to repaint

repeint [rəpɛ̃] NM *Beaux-Arts* touched-up area

repenser [rəpãse] VI to think again (**à** about); **r. à des événements passés** to think back on past events; **quand j'y repense** when I think back (on it); **j'y repenserai** I'll think it over *or* think about it again *or* give it some more thought; **je n'y ai pas repensé** I haven't given it another thought *or* thought about it again
    VT *(problème, projet, concept etc)* to rethink; **r. la question des transports** to rethink the whole question of transport; **le projet doit être complètement repensé** the plan needs to be completely rethought *or* needs a complete rethink

repentant [rəpãtã] ADJ repentant, penitent; **d'un air r.** repentantly, penitently

repenti, -ie [rəpãti] ADJ repentant, penitent; *Vieilli* **fille repentie** reformed prostitute *(who has entered a convent)*
    NF *Vieilli* **repentie** reformed prostitute *(who has entered a convent)*
    N *(ancien terroriste)* = former terrorist who now collaborates with the police

repentir¹ [rəpãtir] NM *Rel* repentance, penitence; *Fig* regret; *(d'un tableau)* touching up; *(d'un manuscrit)* correction

repentir² (se) [sərəpãtir] VPR *(prp* **se repentant**; *pp* **repenti**; *pr ind* **je me repens**, **il se repent**; *pr sub* **je me repente**; *p hist* **je me repentis***) Rel* to repent; **se r. de qch/d'avoir fait qch** to repent (of) sth/doing sth; *Fig* to be sorry for *or* regret sth/doing sth; **je me repens de mon mensonge** I'm sorry I lied; **je me repens de lui avoir prêté mon appartement** I'm sorry I loaned him my flat; **elle s'en repentira** she'll be sorry, she'll rue the day

repérage [rəpɛraʒ] NM **1** *(action de marquer, jalonnement)* marking off *or* out; *Ordinat* marking, flagging **2** *(action de trouver) (d'un défaut, d'une cible etc)* location, locating; *(d'un avion ennemi)* identification, identifying, *Fam* spotting; *TV, Cin* **recce**; **r. radio** radio location, radio fix; **faire des repérages avant de faire un film** to check out the location(s) before making a film; **partir en r.** to go to check out the location(s)

répercussion [rɛpɛrkysjɔ̃] NF **1** *(du son)* reverberation **2** *Fig* repercussion (**sur** on); **r. de l'impôt** impact of taxation

répercuter [rɛpɛrkyte] VT **1** *(son)* to reflect, to reverberate; *(lumière)* to reflect **2** *(ordre, augmentation de prix etc)* to pass on; **r. une augmentation sur les consommateurs** to pass an increase on to the consumer; **r. l'augmentation des salaires sur les prix** to pass the wage increase on to prices
    VPR **se répercuter** *(du son)* to reflect, to be

reflected, to reverberate; *(de la lumière)* to reflect, to be reflected; *Fig* to have repercussions (**sur** on)

repère [rəpɛr] NM *(point de référence)* reference mark, marker; *(fait exprès)* mark; *(pour s'orienter)* landmark; *(en arpentage)* bench mark; *(balise, jalon)* marker; *Ordinat* marker, flag; *Ordinat* **r. de saisie de commandes** dot prompt; *Tech* **r. de montage/d'ajustage** assembly/line-up mark; **r. de niveau** contour line; **il faut le remplir de liquide jusqu'au r.** you have to fill it with liquid up to the mark; *Fig* **la date de son mariage me sert de r.** I use the date of his/her wedding as a reference-point; **point de r.** landmark; *Fig* **tout le monde devrait avoir quelques points de r. dans la vie** everyone should have some landmarks *or* milestones in their lives; **je manquais de points de r.** I had nothing to go by *or* to guide me

repérer [rəpere] *(* **je repère**, *n.* **repérons**; **je repérerai***)* VT **1** *(marquer, jalonner) (terrain, chemin)* to mark off *or* out **2** *(trouver) (défaut, cible, endroit etc)* to locate, to spot; *Fam (robe, coiffeur, personne)* to spot; *TV, Cin (lieu de tournage)* to recce; **r. qn dans la foule** to pick sb out in the crowd; *Courses de chevaux* **r. les gagnants** to pick (out) *or* spot the winners; *Fam* **se faire r.** to attract attention; **attention, tu vas nous faire r. par le prof!** watch out or you'll get us noticed by the teacher!
    VPR **se repérer** to get one's bearings, to find one's way about; *Fig* **je n'arrive pas à me r. dans son galimatias** I can't make head (n)or tail of his/her mumbo jumbo

répertoire [repɛrtwar] NM **1** *(liste)* index, list; *Ordinat* directory; **r. à onglets** thumb index; **r. d'adresses** directory; *(carnet)* address book; *(dans un fichier)* list of adresses; **r. des rues** street directory; **r. des métiers** trade directory; *Ordinat* **r. central** *ou* **principal** main directory; *Ordinat* **r. racine** root directory **2** *Théâtre* repertory; *Mus (de chansons etc)* repertoire; *Fig (de plaisanteries, injures etc)* repertoire; *Théâtre* **pièce de** *ou* **du r.** classic; **le r. classique** the classical repertoire *or* repertory; **il a un r. de trois discours** he has three stock speeches *or* a repertoire of three speeches

répertorier [repɛrtɔrje] VT *(impf, pr sub* **n. répertoriions***) (article, informations)* to list

répéter [repete] *(* **je répète**, *n.* **répétons**; **je répéterai***)* VT **1** *(mots, secret, action, expérience),* *Mus (motif etc)* to repeat; **tu répètes toujours la même chose!** you're constantly repeating yourself!; **r. que ...** to repeat that ...; **je vous répète que ce n'est pas possible!** it's not possible, I tell you!, I repeat, it's not possible!; **répète-moi exactement ce qu'il a dit** tell me (again) exactly what he said; **je t'ai répété cent fois de ne pas le faire** I've told you a hundred times not to do it; **il répète à qui veut l'entendre qu'il a démissionné** he's telling anyone who'll listen that he's resigned; **pourriez-vous me r. votre nom?** could you tell me your name again?; **je ne veux pas avoir à le r.** I don't want to have to say it again *or* to repeat it; **inutile de me le r. deux fois** I don't need to be told twice; **j'ai l'impression de r. toujours le même genre de situations** I feel as if I get involved in the same kind of situation time and time again
    2 *(pièce de théâtre, rôle, morceau de musique)* to rehearse; *(leçon)* to learn; **faire r. son rôle à qn** to help sb rehearse his/her lines, to go over sb's lines with him/her; **faire r. ses leçons à un enfant** to go over a child's lessons with him
    VI *Théâtre, Mus* to rehearse; **faire r. qn** to coach sb, to rehearse sb
    VPR **se répéter** *(d'une personne)* to repeat

oneself; *(d'un événement)* to recur, to happen again; *(d'un motif)* to be repeated; **l'histoire se répète** history repeats itself; **les mêmes situations se répètent toujours** the same situations keep recurring

répéteur [repetœr] NM *TV, Cin* transmitter; *Aut* **r. de clignotant** repeater lamp

répétiteur, -trice [repetitœr, -tris] N *Scol* (private) tutor, coach

répétitif, -ive [repetitif, -iv] ADJ repetitive

répétition [repetisjɔ̃] NF **1** *(d'un mot, d'une action etc)* repetition; *Fig (d'un désastre)* repetition; *Fam* rerun, repeat; *Ordinat* **fonction de r.** repeat function; **fusil à r.** repeating rifle; **montre à r.** repeater (watch); **des laryngites à r.** repeated bouts of laryngitis; **avoir des rhumes à r.** to have one cold after another **2** *Théâtre, Mus* rehearsal; **r. générale** *ou* **en costume** dress rehearsal; **mettre une pièce en r.** to put a play into rehearsal; **nous commençons les répétitions la semaine prochaine** rehearsals start next week, we start rehearsing next week; **r. en studio** studio rehearsal; **r. hors caméra** dry-run; **r. technique** technical run, technical walk-through

repeuplement [rəpœpləmã] NM *(d'un pays etc)* repopulation; *(d'un étang)* restocking; *(d'une forêt)* replanting

repeupler [rəpœple] VT *(pays etc)* to repopulate; *(étang)* to restock; *(forêt)* to replant
    VPR **se repeupler** *(d'un pays)* to be repopulated; *(d'un étang)* to be restocked; *(d'une forêt)* to be replanted; **la ville se repeuple** the population of the town is increasing again; **la forêt s'est repeuplée d'écureuils** squirrels have returned to the forest, the forest has a squirrel population again

repincer [rəpɛ̃se] VT *(conj like* **pincer***)* to pinch again; *Fig Fam* to catch again

repiquage [rəpikaʒ] NM **1** *Couture* restitching **2** *(de la chaussée)* mending, repairing **3** *(de jeunes plants)* pricking out, planting out **4** *(de bactéries)* subculturing **5** *(d'un disque)* re-recording **6** *Phot* retouching **7** *TV, Cin* overprinting; *(de son)* transfer, dub

repiquer [rəpike] VT **1** *(percer)* **l'acupuncteur m'a repiqué** the acupuncturist repeated the treatment; *Couture* **r. l'aiguille au même endroit** take the needle back through in the same place
    2 *(chaussée)* to mend, to repair
    3 *(jeunes plants)* to prick out, to plant out; **plant à r.** bedding plant
    4 *(bactéries)* to subculture
    5 *(disque, air)* to re-record
    6 *Phot* to retouch
    7 *Fam (reprendre)* to catch again; **et que je ne te repique pas à faire ça!** don't let me catch you doing that again!
    VI *Fam* **1 r. au plat** to have a second helping; **r. au truc** to be at it again **2** *(redoubler une classe)* to repeat a year *or Am* grade

répit [repi] NM respite, breathing space; *Com* **jours de r.** days of grace; **ne laisser aucun r. à qn** to give sb no rest *or* respite; **la douleur ne lui laisse aucun r.** he is in constant pain, the pain is always there, he has no respite from the pain; **laisser un moment de r. à qn** to give sb a moment's respite; **sans r.** *(travailler)* without a break, continuously; *(harceler qn)* constantly

replacement [rəplasmã] NM **1** *(de capitaux)* reinvestment **2** **des mesures pour permettre le r. des licenciés** steps to find alternative employment for workers made redundant

replacer [rəplase] VT *(conj like* **placer***)* VT **1 r. un objet** *(remettre en place)* to replace an object, to put an object back in its place *or* where it belongs; *Fig* **r. un événement dans son contexte** to look at *or* put an event in context; **il faut r. la scène à l'époque où elle a eu lieu** you have to bear in mind what things were like then **2** *(capitaux)* to reinvest **3** *(licencié)* to find alternative employment *or* a new job for **4** *Can (reconnaître)* to recognize; **je ne l'avais pas vue depuis si longtemps que je n'arrivais pas à la r.** I hadn't seen her for so long that I was unable to recognize her

VPR se replacer *(dans un emploi)* to find (oneself) a new job; **il faut se r. dans l'époque pour comprendre ce qui s'est passé** in order to understand what happened, you have to remember what things were like then *or* you have to think yourself into the mentality of the period

replanter [rəplãte] **VT** to replant; **r. une forêt en sapins** to replant a forest with firs

replat [rəpla] **NM** *(de versant)* shelf

replâtrage [rəplatraʒ] **NM 1** *(d'un mur)* replastering **2** *Fig* patching up; *(réparation)* makeshift repair; **c'est du r.** *(réparation)* it's a bit rough and ready; **ils ont décidé de reprendre la vie commune, à mon avis, c'est du r.** they've decided to move back in together but I think they're just papering over the cracks

replâtrer [rəplatre] **VT 1** *(mur)* to replaster **2** *Fig (réparer de façon sommaire)* to patch up

replet, -ète [rəplɛ, -ɛt] **ADJ** *(personne)* podgy, dumpy; *(visage)* chubby; **un petit au visage r.** a chubby-faced little boy

réplétion [replesjɔ̃] **NF** repletion

repleuvoir [rəplœvwar] **V IMPERS** to rain again

repli [rəpli] **NM 1** *(d'un vêtement, de la peau)* fold; **replis du terrain** folds in the land; *Fig* **les plis et les replis du cœur** the innermost recesses of the heart **2** *(d'une rivière)* bend, meander; *(d'une corde, des intestins)* coil; **faire des replis** *(d'une rivière)* to wind, to meander; *(d'un serpent)* to slither **3** *Mil* retreat, withdrawal; *Psy* withdrawal; *Mil* **r. stratégique** strategic withdrawal; **une attitude de r. (sur soi)** a withdrawn attitude **4** *(de monnaie, prix)* *Bourse* fall

repliable [rəplijabl] **ADJ** folding, fold-up; *(tablette d'avion)* foldaway; *(antenne)* retractable; **couteau à lame r.** knife with a folding blade

repliement [rəplimã] **NF 1** *Mil* retreat, withdrawal **2** *(sur soi-même)* withdrawal

replier [rəplije] *(conj like* **plier***)* **VT 1** *(journal, drap etc)* to fold up; *(lame de couteau)* to fold away; *(bord, coin) (de papier, tissu)* to turn *or* fold down; *(de métal)* to bend down; *(d'une personne) (jambes)* to tuck up; *(d'un oiseau) (ailes)* to fold; **r. les draps** to turn back *or* fold down the sheets; **l'oiseau a replié sa tête sous son aile** the bird tucked its head under its wing **2** *Mil (troupes)* to withdraw, to pull back **VPR se replier 1** *(d'un objet)* to fold up; *(d'un serpent)* to coil up; **la lame se replie dans le manche** the blade folds away into the handle **2 se r. sur soi-même** to withdraw into oneself; **je la trouve trop repliée sur elle-même** I find her too withdrawn **3** *(des troupes)* to retreat, to withdraw **4** *Bourse* to fall back, to drop

réplique [replik] **NF 1** *(réponse)* retort, rejoinder; **lancer une r.** to make a retort; **avoir la r. prompte** *ou* **facile** to be always ready with an answer; **preuve qui ne souffre aucune r.** incontrovertible *or* irrefutable proof; **prouver qch sans r.** to prove sth incontrovertibly *or* irrefutably; **argument sans r.** unanswerable argument; **obéir sans r.** to obey without a word *or* murmur; **la r. ne s'est pas fait attendre** his retort wasn't long in coming; *Fam* **et pas de r.!** don't answer (me) back! **2** *Théâtre* line(s); **apprendre une r.** to

learn one's lines; **lancer sa r.** to say one's lines, to come in on cue; **manquer sa r.** to miss one's cue; **donner la r. à un acteur** to play opposite an actor **3** *(copie)* replica; *(sosie)* double; **c'est la r. de sa mère** she's her mother's double

répliquer [replike] **VT r. qch à qn** to say sth in answer to sb; **je n'ai pas entendu ce qu'il lui a répliqué** I didn't hear what his reply was *or* what he said to him/her; **'pas de danger!', répliqua-t-il** 'not likely!', he retorted; **que veux-tu r. à ce genre d'arguments?** there's no answer to *or* you can't argue with reasoning like that!

VI *(répondre)* to retort; *(avec impertinence)* to answer back; **r. à qn** to answer sb back; **je ne supporte pas qu'on me réplique** I won't be answered back; **il répliqua par un coup de pied** he answered with a kick; **c'est ainsi qu'il répliquait aux critiques** that was his response to the criticisms

VPR se répliquer to replicate

replonger [rəplɔ̃ʒe] *(conj like* **plonger***)* **VT** *(avec force)* to plunge back (**dans** into); *(doucement)* to dip back (**dans** into); *Fig* **cette nouvelle me replongea dans l'angoisse** the news plunged me back into a state of anxiety; *Fig* **le film nous replonge dans l'atmosphère étrange du Berlin des années vingt** the film takes us back into the strange atmosphere of 1920's Berlin

VI to dive (in) again; *Fam (récidiver)* to commit another crime; *Fam (dans l'alcoolisme)* to fall back into; **r. dans l'eau** to dive back into the water

VPR se replonger se r. dans l'étude to become immersed again in study

repolir [rəpɔlir] **VT** to repolish; *Fig (style)* to polish up

répondant, -ante [repɔ̃dã, -ãt] **N 1** *(responsable, garant)* surety, security, guarantor; *(d'un questionnaire)* respondent; **être le r. de qn** to stand surety for sb; *Fam* **avoir du r.** to have plenty of money stashed away **2** *Rel (à la messe)* server

répondeur, -euse [repɔ̃dœr, -øz] **ADJ** given to answering back, impertinent

NM r. (téléphonique), r. enregistreur (telephone) answering machine, answerphone

RÉPONDRE [repɔ̃dr]

> **VT** to answer **1** ▪ to reply **1**
> **VI** to answer **1** ▪ to reply **1** ▪ to answer back **1** ▪ to respond **2** ▪ to write back **1** ▪ to meet *(répondre à)* **3** ▪ to answer for *(répondre de)* **4**

VT 1 to answer, to reply; *(remarque)* to answer *or* reply with; *(lettre)* to send in reply; **il m'a répondu une sottise** he answered me with something stupid; **essaie de r. quelque chose!** *(pour encourager qn)* try to say something!; *(en s'énervant)* say something!; **r. que ...** to answer *or* reply that ...; *Fml* **il s'est vu r. que ...** he obtained the response that ...; **qu'est-ce qu'elle vous a répondu?** what was her answer *or* reply?, what did she say in reply?; **je n'ai rien répondu** I made no reply, I gave no answer *or* reply; **il répondit n'en rien savoir** he answered *or* replied that he knew nothing about it; **il m'a répondu d'en parler au médecin** he answered *or* replied that I should talk to the doctor about it; **il répond ne pas être au courant** he says he doesn't know; *Pol* **Londres a immédiatement répondu présent** London immediately signalled its readiness to help

2 *Rel* **r. la messe** to make the responses at Mass

VI 1 to answer, to reply; **r. à** *(personne, lettre, invitation etc)* to answer, to reply to; *(salut)* to return, to acknowledge; *(accusation)* to answer; **pour r. à votre invitation** in answer to

your invitation; **elle ne m'a pas encore répondu** she hasn't answered me *or* replied to me yet, I haven't had an answer *or* a reply from her yet; **r. par écrit** to reply in writing, to write back; **r. par un signe de la tête** *(pour dire oui)* to nod in reply, to nod one's reply; *(pour dire non)* to shake one's head in reply; **r. par un haussement d'épaules** to shrug (one's shoulders) in reply; **r. par une mimique** to make a face in reply; **r. par un sourire** to reply with a smile; **est-ce qu'elle a répondu?** *(à la lettre)* has she written back?, did she reply?; *Scol, Mil* **r. à l'appel** to answer the roll *or* to one's name; **r. à un coup de sonnette/au téléphone** to answer the bell/the phone; **laisse, je vais r.!** *(au téléphone, à la porte)* leave it, I'll get it!; *(à une question embarrassante)* leave it, I'll answer it!; **je te défends de me r.!** don't you dare answer me back *or* talk back to me!; **vous devrez r. de plusieurs chefs d'accusation** you'll have to answer several charges; *Tél* **ça ne répond pas** there's no answer; **répondez, s'il vous plaît** *(pour établir un contact radio)* come in, please

2 *(réagir)* *(d'une personne, des freins, d'une voiture)* to respond (**à** to); **la voiture répond très bien** the car responds very well, the car is very responsive; **r. à l'amour/l'affection de qn** to return sb's love/affection; **on a répondu généreusement à l'appel** the appeal met with a generous response; **le chien répond à son nom** the dog responds *or* answers to his name; **il n'a pas répondu à mon appel** he didn't do what I asked him to

3 *(correspondre)* **r. à** *(besoin)* to meet, to fulfil, *Am* to fulfill; *(but)* to fulfil; *(description)* to fit, to match; *(critères)* to meet; **ne pas r. à l'attente** not to come up to expectations, to fall short of expectations

4 *(être garant de)* **r. de qn/qch** to answer for sb/sth, to be answerable *or* accountable *or* responsible for sb/sth; **répondez-vous d'elle pour ce travail?** will you take responsibility *or* be accountable for her work?; **r. de l'innocence de qn** to answer for sb's innocence; **il va revenir, je vous en réponds** he'll come back, take my word for it, I guarantee he'll come back; **je ne réponds de rien** I'm promising nothing, I'm making no promises

VPR se répondre to answer each other; **les deux parties du livre se répondent** the two parts of the book echo each other

> Il faut noter que le verbe anglais **to respond** est un faux ami. Il signifie le plus souvent **réagir**.

répons [repɔ̃] **NM** *Rel* response

réponse [repɔ̃s] **NF 1** answer, reply; **elle a** *ou* **trouve r. à tout** she has an answer for everything, she's never at a loss for an answer; **donner** *ou* **rendre r. à qn** to give sb an answer, to reply to sb; **faire une r. de Normand** to give a non-committal *or* an evasive reply; **argument sans r.** unanswerable argument; **rester sans r.** *(d'une question, une lettre)* to go unanswered; **elle fait toujours les questions et les réponses** she does all the talking; **pour toute r., il éclata en sanglots** his only answer was to burst out sobbing; **il a souri en guise de r.** he answered with a smile; *Fam* **j'ai sonné plusieurs fois, mais pas de r.** I've rung several times, but there's no answer; **en r. à votre lettre** in reply *or* answer to your letter; **bulletin-/carte-r.** reply coupon/card; **r. payée** reply paid; *Jur* **droit de r.** *(dans la presse)* right to reply; *Tél* **r. en retour** answerback; **r. d'attente** holding reply

2 *(réaction)* *(à un appel de fonds, d'aide)*, *Physiol (à un stimulus, d'un moteur, des freins etc)* response; *(à une offre d'emploi)* reply;

Aut r. à mi-régime mid-range response

3 *Ordinat* answering; **r. automatique** unattended answering; **temps de r.** response time

4 *Fig (solution)* answer (à to); **je n'ai pas la r. (à ton problème)** I don't have the answer, I don't know what the answer is; **ce problème est resté sans r.** a solution still hasn't been found to the problem

repopulation [rəpɔpylasjɔ̃] **NF** *(d'une région etc)* repopulation, repopulating

report [rəpɔr] **NM 1** *Compta (du total)* carrying forward, bringing forward; *(somme)* amount carried forward, carry forward, carry over; **'r.'** carried forward; **r. de l'exercice précédent** carried forward from the previous financial year; **r. à l'exercice suivant** carried forward to the next financial year; **r. à nouveau** carried forward; **reports et avances sur titres** collateral loans **2** *(de corrections), Pol (de voix), Phot* transfer; *Phot* **papier (à) r.** transfer paper **3** *(d'un rendez-vous)* postponement **4** *Radio* plot(ting); **table de r.** plotting board

Il faut noter que le nom anglais **report** est un faux ami. Il signifie **rapport**.

reportage [rəpɔrtaʒ] **NM** *Journ, Radio, TV* **1** *(article, émission)* report; **c'est France 2 qui en assurera le r.** France 2 will bring you the report; **r. filmé/télévisé** film/TV report; **r. en direct** live coverage; **r. en exclusivité** scoop, exclusive (report); **r. photographique** photo-reportage; **r. publicitaire** editorial advertisement; *Radio, TV* **r. électronique** electronic news gathering, ENG **2** *(activité)* reporting; **faire du r.** to do some reporting; *(métier)* to be a reporter

reporté [rəpɔrte] **ADJ** postponed, deferred

reporter¹ [rəpɔrtɛr] **NM** *Journ, Radio, TV* reporter; **r. photographe** photojournalist; **r.-cameraman** film reporter

reporter² [rəpɔrte] **VT 1** *(pour rendre) (objet)* to take back, to return

2 *(transférer) (affection), Pol (voix), Phot* to transfer (**sur** to)

3 *(dans le temps) (personne)* to take or carry back, to transport; **cela nous reporte à l'époque où …** that takes us back to the time when …

4 *(différer)* **r. qch à plus tard** to postpone or *Fml* defer sth, to put sth off until later

5 *Compta (total)* to carry forward, to bring forward, to carry over; **à r.** carried forward; **r. une somme** to carry a sum forward

6 *(transcrire) (notes)* to transfer (**sur** to)

VPR se reporter 1 *(se référer)* **se r. à** *(un document, une interview)* to refer to; **se r. à …** *(dans un livre etc)* the reader is referred to …, see …

2 se r. au passé/à la période de l'après-guerre to look back or think back to the past/to the post-war period

3 *(se déplacer) (de colère, d'une affection), Pol (de voix)* to be transferred (**sur** to)

Il faut noter que le verbe anglais **to report** est un faux ami. Il ne correspond jamais au verbe français **reporter**.

reporteur [rəpɔrtœr] **NM** reporter

repos [rəpo] **NM 1** rest, *Fml* repose; **c'est mon seul r.** it's my only (form of) relaxation; **il vous faut le r. complet** you need a complete rest; **avoir besoin de (prendre du) r.** to need to rest, to need a rest; **chercher le r.** to try to rest; **ces enfants ne lui laissent aucun r.** those children give her no rest; **se donner ou prendre du r.** to take a rest; **r. compensateur** time off in lieu; *Mil* **r.!** (stand) at ease!; **au r.** at rest; **soldat au r.** soldier standing at ease; **maison de r.** rest home, convalescent home; *(de personnes âgées)* rest home; **cure**

de r. rest cure; **le dimanche est mon unique jour de r.** Sunday is my only day off or day of rest; **après un mois de r.** after a month's rest; **le r. éternel** eternal rest; **terre au r.** fallow land

2 *Tech* **au r.** *(fusil)* at half cock; *(mécanisme)* in neutral (position); *(muscle)* relaxed

3 *Littér (dans un vers)* pause, rest

4 *(quiétude)* peace; **trouver le r.** to relax; **troubler le r. de qn** to disturb sb, to upset sb; **troubler le r. de la nature** to break the stillness, to disturb the quietness; **être en r. au sujet de qn** to feel easy in one's mind about sb; **je n'aurai de r. que lorsque je me serai vengé** I won't rest until I've had my revenge; **laisser qn en r.** to leave sb alone or in peace; **valeur de tout r.** safe investment, gilt-edged security; **vivre avec lui, ce n'est pas de tout r.!** living with him is no bed of roses!

reposant [rəpozɑ̃] **ADJ** *(vacances, week-end etc)* restful, relaxing; *(sommeil)* refreshing; *(couleur)* soothing

reposé [rəpoze] **ADJ 1** *(personne, esprit)* rested, refreshed; **s'éveiller bien r.** to awake refreshed; **elle a le visage vraiment r.** *(après repos, nuit de sommeil)* she looks really rested or refreshed **2** **je le ferai à tête reposée** I'll do it when my mind's clearer; **laissez-moi y réfléchir à tête reposée** give me time to think it over quietly

repose-bras [rəpozbra] **NM INV** armrest

repose-pied, *pl* **repose-pieds** [rəpozpje] **NM** *Aut* tread plate; *(d'une moto, d'une chaise)* footrest

repose-poignet, *pl* **repose-poignets** [rəpozpwaɲe] **NM** wrist rest

reposer [rəpoze] **VT 1** *(à sa place)* to put back (down), to replace; **merci de le r. là où tu l'as trouvé** please put it back where you found it; *Mil* **reposez arme!** order arms!

2 *(rectifier la pose de) (moquette)* to re-lay

3 *(détendre)* to rest; **r. sa tête contre l'appuie-tête** to lean back against the headrest; **ça le reposera** it'll be a rest for him; **r. l'esprit** *(d'une activité)* to be relaxing; **écouter de la musique me repose l'esprit** listening to music gives my mind a rest; **couleur qui repose les yeux** colour that is restful or soothing to the eyes

4 *(question)* to ask again; **r. un problème** *(au cours d'une réunion)* to bring up a problem again; **je voudrais r. les grandes lignes de notre action** I'd like to outline once again what we'll be doing

VI 1 *(d'une personne)* to rest; *(être étendu)* to lie; **le corps reposait sur son lit de parade** the body was lying in state; **ici repose …** here lies …; **qu'elle repose en paix!** may she rest in peace!; *Fam* **ça repose bien, le sauna** a sauna is very relaxing

2 *r. sur (rocher etc)* to rest on; *Fig* to be based on; *(dépendre de)* to depend on; **le sort de notre association repose sur lui** the fate of our association rests with him

3 *(d'un liquide)* to settle; *Culin (d'une pâte)* to rest; **faire r. ses chevaux** to rest one's horses; **laisser r. la terre** to let the ground rest or lie fallow

VPR se reposer 1 *(se relaxer)* to rest, to take a rest; **avoir besoin de se r.** to need to rest, to need a rest; **se r. les yeux/les jambes** to rest one's eyes/legs, to give one's eyes/legs a rest; **j'ai besoin de me r. les yeux** my eyes need a rest; **je pars me r. en Corse** I'm going to Corsica to rest or for a rest; **vous devriez vous r. davantage** you must get more rest, you must rest more

2 *(compter sur)* **se r. sur qn/qch** to rely on sb/sth; **se r. sur qn du soin de qch** to rely on sb to look after sth; **il se repose sur le travail de ses collègues** he relies on or leaves it up to his colleagues to do the work

3 *(d'une question)* to be asked or put again; **il s'est souvent reposé la question** he asked himself the question time after time

repose-tête [rəpoztɛt] **NM INV** headrest

repositionnement [rəpozisjɔnmɑ̃] **NM** *Mktg (d'un produit)* repositioning

repositionner [rəpozisjɔne] *Mktg* **VT** *(produit)* to reposition

VPR se repositionner se r. à la baisse to move down-market; **se r. à la hausse** to move up-market

reposoir [rəpozwar] **NM** *(en plein air)* wayside altar; *(dans l'église)* temporary altar

repourvoir [rəpurvwar] **VT** *Suisse (poste)* to fill

repoussage [rəpusaʒ] **NM** embossing, repoussé work

repoussant [rəpusɑ̃] **ADJ** *(apparence etc)* repulsive, repellent; **d'une laideur repoussante** repulsively ugly

repousse [rəpus] **NF** *(des cheveux, des plantes, de la pelouse etc)* regrowth, regrowing; **pour activer la r.** to encourage new growth

repoussé [rəpuse] *Tech* **ADJ** embossed, repoussé

NM embossing, repoussé

repoussement [rəpusmɑ̃] **NM** *(d'une arme à feu)* recoil, kick

repousse-peaux [rəpuspo] **NM INV** orange stick

repousser [rəpuse] **VT 1** *(objet) (écarter)* to push aside or away; *(en arrière)* to push back; *(volets)* to push or throw back; *(ennemi, attaque)* to repel, to beat or fight off, to beat back; *(les avances de qn)* to repel; *(offre, proposition, idée, demande)* to reject, to turn down; *(conseils)* to reject, to brush aside; **r. qch de la main** to push sth away or aside; **r. qch du pied** to push sth away with one's foot; **r. qn** to push or thrust sb aside; *Fig (rabrouer)* to rebuff sb; **elle a repoussé mes conseils avec mépris** she pooh-poohed my advice

2 *(différer) (événement, rendez-vous etc)* to postpone, to put off (à until); **r. les délais de livraison du travail** to push back the deadline for completion of the work

3 *(dégoûter) (personne)* to be repellent to, to repel; **cette odeur me repousse** I find the smell repellent

4 *(métal, cuir)* to emboss, to work in repoussé

VI *(d'un arbre, d'une plante)* to shoot (up) again, to spring up again; *(des cheveux, de l'herbe, des feuilles)* to grow again; **elle se laisse r. les cheveux** she's letting her hair grow again

repoussoir [rəpuswar] **NM 1** *(de manucure)* cuticle pen; *Tech (ciseau)* embossing punch **2** *Fig* foil; **servir de r. à la beauté de qn** to set off sb's beauty, to serve as a foil to sb's beauty **3** *Fam (personne laide)* ugly duckling; **c'est un vrai r.** he/she is really ugly

répréhensible [repreɑ̃sibl] **ADJ** reprehensible; **de façon r.** *(se conduire, agir)* reprehensibly, in a reprehensible way

---

REPRENDRE [rəprɑ̃dr] *(conj like* **prendre***)*

VT to retake **1** ▪ to recapture **1** ▪ to have more **2** ▪ to get back **3** ▪ to take back **5** ▪ to resume **6** ▪ to take up again **6** ▪ to repeat **6** ▪ to alter **7** ▪ to correct **7, 8** ▪ to reprimand **8**
VI to start again **1**
VPR to recover **1** ▪ to correct oneself **2**

VT 1 *(ville)* to retake, to recapture; *(fugitif)* to recapture; *(territoire), Sport (titre)* to win back, to recapture (à from)

2 r. du pain/vin to take or have some more

bread/wine; **vous reprendrez bien un peu de thé?** would you like some more tea?

3 *(récupérer) (objet prêté)* to get back; **je suis allé r. mon parapluie** I went to get my umbrella back *or* to recover *or* retrieve my umbrella; **r. ses chaussures chez le cordonnier** to get one's shoes (back) *or* pick up one's shoes from the mender's; **je peux r. ma machine à coudre?** can I have my sewing machine back?; **il est passé r. tous ses meubles** he came and took away all his furniture; **je passerai les r. dans la semaine** I'll come back for them *or* I'll pick them up sometime this week; **je vous reprendrai en passant** I'll pick you up (again) as I go by; **r. sa place** *(s'asseoir)* to take one's seat again; *(dans une entreprise)* to take one's place again; **r. connaissance** to recover *or* regain consciousness, to come to; **r. possession de qch** to regain possession of sth; **r. ses esprits** to collect *or* gather one's thoughts; **r. haleine** to get one's breath back, to recover one's breath; **r. contact avec qn** to get in touch with sb again; **r. contact avec l'actualité** to catch up on the news; **r. goût à la vie** to find life worth living again, to recover one's zest for life; **r. la route** to take to the road again; **r. des forces** to get one's strength back; **r. courage** to summon up one's courage again; **elle reprend espoir** she's starting to hope *or* be hopeful again; **r. la parole** to resume, to go on (talking *or* speaking); **r. les choses/qn en main** to take things/sb in hand again

4 *Fig* **la fièvre l'a repris** he has had another bout of fever; **ça le reprend!** it's starting all over again!; **ça ne va pas te r., tout de même, cette habitude de douter de tout!** you're not going to get back into that habit of doubting everything, are you?; *Fam* **on ne m'y reprendra plus** I won't be had *or* caught again *or* another time; **que je ne vous y reprenne plus!** don't let me catch you at it again!; **et que je ne te reprenne pas à écouter aux portes!** don't let me catch you listening at doors again!

5 *(cadeau, marchandise invendue, article en solde etc)* to take back; *(employé)* to take on again, to re-engage; *(promesse, offre)* to go back on, *Fml* to retract; **les articles ne seront ni repris ni échangés** goods may not be returned or exchanged; **le garagiste me l'a reprise à l'achat de la nouvelle** the man at the garage took it off me in part exchange *or* as a trade-in for the new one

6 *(recommencer) (conversation, fonctions)* to resume, to take up again; *(pourparlers, hostilités, relations)* to reopen, to resume; *Mus (thème)* to restate, to recapitulate; **r. le travail** *(après une grève)* to return to work; *(après une maladie)* to go back to work; **r. son travail** to get back to work, to start work again; **reprenons les faits** let's go over the facts again, let's recapitulate (the facts); **r. les choses au début** to start all over again, to go back to the beginning; **je vais r. toute l'histoire à ses origines** I'll go right back to the beginning *or* to how it all started; **r. son cours** to continue as before, to carry on as before; **r. la lutte/le combat** to continue the *or* carry on the struggle/the fight; *Théâtre* **r. une pièce** to revive a play; **r. un refrain en chœur** to take up a chorus, to join in a chorus; **reprenez après moi ces paroles** repeat these words after me; **'oui', reprit-il** 'yes', he replied

7 *(réparer) (tableau)* to retouch; *(texte)* *(modifier)* to correct; *(refaire)* to redo; *Couture* to alter (**à la taille** at the waist)

8 *(personne) (corriger)* to correct; *(réprimander)* to reprimand; *Fam* to tell off, *Fml* to reprove (**de** for); **il trouve toujours quelque chose à r.** he always finds something to criticize

VI 1 *(recommencer)* to start *or* begin again;

(de pourparlers, hostilités) to resume, to reopen; *(d'une mode)* to return, to be revived; *(des affaires)* to recover, to pick up (again); **les cours reprennent à quatorze heures** classes start *or* begin again at two o'clock; **le froid a repris** the cold weather has set in again

2 *(d'une plante)* to pick up

VPR se reprendre 1 *(se ressaisir)* to recover, to pull oneself together; **reprends-toi!** pull yourself together!, get a grip on yourself!; **donnez-moi le temps de me r.** give me time to collect myself *or* my thoughts

2 *(se corriger)* to correct oneself *(in speaking)*; *(réciproquement)* to correct each other

3 **se r. à faire qch** to begin *or* start doing *or* to do sth again

4 **s'y r. à plusieurs fois pour faire qch** to make several attempts *or* have several goes at doing sth; **j'ai dû m'y r. à trois fois** I had to have three goes at it

repreneur [rəprənœr] **NM** purchaser; *Fin* buyer; **le nom du r. de l'entreprise** the name of the person who took over the company

représailles [rəprezaj] **NFPL** reprisals, retaliation; **par peur des r.** for fear of reprisals; **en r. de qch** in reprisal for sth; **par r.** in reprisal, as a reprisal; **expédition de r.** punitive expedition; **des mesures de r.** reprisals (**contre** against); **user de r.** to take reprisals

représentable [rəprezãtabl] **ADJ** which can be represented

représentant, -ante [rəprezãtã, -ãt] **N 1** *Pol, Ind* representative; **r. syndical** (trade-) union representative; **la Chambre des représentants** the House of Representatives; **être le r. de l'opinion publique** to represent public opinion; **r. du personnel** employees' representative **2** *Com* **r. (de commerce *ou* commercial)** (sales) representative, *Fam* (sales) rep (**en** for); **notre r. au Japon** our agent in Japan; **r. exclusif** sole agent; **r. multicarte** rep for several companies

représentatif, -ive [rəprezãtatif, -iv] **ADJ** *(échantillon, gouvernement)* representative; *(personne)* typical, representative; **symbole r. du pouvoir** symbol representative of *or* representing power; **ceci est tout à fait r. de son état d'esprit** it's quite indicative *or* typical of his state of mind; **voilà des photos, mais elles ne sont pas très représentatives** here are some photos but they don't really give you the right idea

représentation [rəprezãtasjɔ̃] **NF 1** *Pol, Jur etc* representation; *(représentants)* representatives; *Pol* **r. proportionnelle** proportional representation

2 *Com* representation; *(agence)* agency; **faire de la r., être dans la r.** to be a (sales) representative *or Fam* (sales) rep; **r. exclusive** sole agency

3 *(de concept, de faits, d'objet, en peinture etc)* representation; **c'est sa r. de la situation** that's his/her idea *or* reading of the situation, that's how he/she sees *or* reads the situation; **c'est une r. possible de la situation** that's one possible view *or* reading of the situation; *Psy* **faculté de la r. spatiale** spatial perception

4 *Jur (de documents etc)* production

5 *Théâtre* performance; **troupe en r.** touring company; **droits de r.** performing rights

6 frais de r. entertainment allowance; *Fam* **être en r.** to be trying to impress

représentativité [rəprezãtativite] **NF** representativeness; **si vous acceptez la r. de notre échantillon** if you accept that our sample is representative

représenter [rəprezãte] **VT 1** *(présenter de nouveau)* to present again, to re-present; **je voudrais r. ce candidat (au concours)** I

would like to re-enter this candidate (for the exam); **r. une traite à l'acceptation** to re-present a bill for acceptance

2 *Jur (documents etc)* to produce

3 *(figurer)* to represent; **le pronom représente le nom** the pronoun stands for *or* replaces the noun; **on représente souvent Hugo comme un vieil homme barbu** Hugo is often depicted as an old man with a beard; **il représente l'esprit soixante-huitard** he represents *or* typifies the spirit of May 1968; **r. fidèlement/avec réalisme qch** to render sth faithfully/realistically; **il a représenté son modèle avec humour** he has painted his model with great humour; **un croquis qui me représentait à la terrasse d'un café** a sketch of me *or* that showed me sitting outside a cafe; *Théâtre* **la scène représente un patio** the scene is a patio

4 *(être le porte-parole de) (personne, pays, entreprise,* Pol *(circonscription)* to represent; **se faire r.** to be represented; **il représente la France aux Jeux olympiques** he's representing France in the Olympic Games; **je représente les produits Avon®** I'm an Avon® representative; *Jur* **r. qn en justice** to appear for sb

5 *(correspondre à) (somme, chiffre etc)* to represent; **cela ne représente pas une grosse somme *ou* beaucoup pour lui** it's not much to him, it's not a large amount as far as he's concerned; **cela représente une privation financière importante pour eux** that constitutes a major financial sacrifice for them

6 *Théâtre (pièce de théâtre)* to perform, to put on

VI *(en imposer)* **r. (bien)** to impress people, to be impressive; **il ne représente pas au physique** he's not very impressive physically

VPR se représenter 1 se r. à *(examen)* to resit, to sit *or* take again; *(poste, emploi)* to apply for again; **se r. en septembre** to resit in September; **se r. aux élections** to stand for *or Am* to run for election again; *Fam* **se r. au permis de conduire** to take one's driving test again

2 *(d'une occasion)* to arise again; **si ces difficultés se représentent, dis-le moi** let me know if these problems come up again

3 *(s'imaginer)* to imagine; **représentez-vous mon étonnement** (just) imagine my astonishment; **çe n'est pas ainsi que je me le représentais, je me le représentais différemment** that's not how I imagined it

répressif, -ive [represif, -iv] **ADJ** *(loi, parents, tendance etc)* repressive

répression [represjɔ̃] **NF** repression; *(d'une émeute, d'un abus)* suppression; **mesures de r.** repressive measures; **mesures de r. de la fraude fiscale** measures to suppress tax evasion; **r. des fraudes** suppression of fraud, *(service gouvernemental)* consumer protection office

réprimandable [reprimãdabl] **ADJ** reproachable, blameworthy

réprimande [reprimãd] **NF** reprimand, rebuke, *Fml* reproof; **faire des réprimandes à qn** to reprimand *or* rebuke sb, *Fml* to reprove sb; **air/ton de r.** reproving look/tone, look/tone of rebuke

réprimander [reprimãde] **VT** *(personne)* to reprimand, to rebuke, *Fml* to reprove; **se faire r.** to be reprimanded

réprimer [reprime] **VT** *(crime)* to suppress; *(désir, colère, instinct)* to repress, to suppress; *(rire, sanglots, larmes, éternuement)* to suppress, to hold back; *(juron)* to suppress, to smother; *(révolte)* to suppress, to quell, to put down

reprint [rəprint] **NM** *(livre)* reprint

repris [rəpri] **NM r. de justice** ex-prisoner

reprisage [rəprizaʒ] **NM** *(d'un vêtement)* mending; *(de chaussettes)* darning

reprise [rəpriz] NF **1** *Mil (d'une place forte, ville etc)* retaking, recapture **2** *Com (de marchandises invendues, d'articles en solde etc)* taking back; **nous ne faisons pas de r. des articles en solde** sales goods may not be returned; **r. jusqu'à 5000 euros** part exchange *or* trade-in (allowance) up to 5,000 euros; **r. de l'entreprise par ses salariés** employee buy-out; *Compta* **reprises sur provisions** recovery of provisions, write-back of provisions **3** *(du travail, d'un débat, des essais nucléaires)* resumption; *(des négociations, des pourparlers)* renewal, resumption, reopening; *(des hostilités, de la violence)* renewal, resumption; *(de la mode)* return, revival; *Théâtre (d'une pièce de théâtre)* revival; *Cin (d'un film)* reissue; *Radio, TV* repeat; *TV, Cin (d'un but, essai etc)* replay, rerun; *Ordinat (d'un programme)* restart **4** *(de l'activité)* renewal; *(du froid)* return; *(de la fièvre)* fresh bout; **r. des affaires** business recovery *or* revival; **mouvement de r.** *(dans l'économie)* upward movement; **r. économique** economic recovery, upswing *or* upturn in the economy; **les premiers indices de la r. économique** the first signs of economic recovery **5 r. (de vitesse)** *(d'un moteur)* pick-up, acceleration; **cette voiture a de bonnes reprises** the car accelerates quickly *or* has good acceleration **6** *Boxe* round; *Escrime* bout; *Ftbl (du jeu)* second half; *Équitation* lesson; *(groupe de cavaliers)* riders **7 faire qch à plusieurs reprises** to do sth several times *or* on several occasions; **à trois reprises** three times, on three occasions **8** *Mus* repeat; *(d'un thème, des instruments)* re-entry **9** *Couture (raccord)* darn, mend; **r. perdue** invisible mend **10** *(somme payée à un locataire)* = (money paid for) fixtures and fittings *(paid to outgoing tenant)*

repriser [rəprize] VT *(vêtement)* to mend; *(chaussette)* to darn, to mend; **aiguille/coton/œuf à r.** darning needle/cotton/egg *or* mushroom

réprobateur, -trice [reprɔbatœr, -tris] ADJ *(air, ton)* reproving; **dire qch d'un ton r.** to say sth reprovingly *or* in a tone of reproof

réprobation [reprɔbasjɔ̃] NF reproof; **ton/regard de r.** reproving tone/look, tone/look of reproof

reproche [rəprɔʃ] NM **1** *(remontrance)* reproach; **un regard plein de r.** a reproachful look, a look of reproach; **regarder qn d'un air plein de r.** to look at sb reproachfully; **faire des reproches à qn** to reproach sb *(pour avoir fait qch for doing sth)*; **je ne vous fais pas de reproches** I'm not reproaching *or* blaming you; **ton de r.** tone of reproach, reproachful tone; **sans r.** *(vie, personne)* beyond *or* above reproach, blameless; **le seul r. qu'on puisse faire à ce roman, c'est ...** the only criticism one can make about *or* the only thing wrong with the novel is ...; **c'est le seul r. que je trouve à lui faire** it's the only criticism I have to make of him **2** *Jur* **r. de témoin** barring of a witness

reprocher [rəprɔʃe] VT **1** *(blâmer)* to reproach; **r. qch à qn** to blame *or* reproach sb for sth; **r. à qn de faire qch** to blame *or* reproach sb for doing sth; **r. à qn d'avoir fait qch** to blame *or* reproach sb for doing *or* having done sth; **je ne vous reproche rien** I'm not blaming you for anything; **il n'y a absolument rien à lui r.** he's totally blameless **2** *(critiquer)* *(impatience, négligence)* to criticize; **qu'est-ce que vous reprochez à ce livre?** what have you got against the book?; **on lui reproche sa naissance** they've never

forgiven him his background **3** *Jur (témoin, témoignage)* to bar

VPR **se reprocher se r. qch** to blame oneself for sth, to reproach oneself with *or* for sth; **je me reproche de lui avoir fait confiance** I blame *or* reproach myself for trusting him; **ils se reprochent (mutuellement) d'avoir pris cette décision** they're blaming each other for the decision

reproducteur, -trice [rəprɔdyktœr, -tris] ADJ **1** *(organe, cellule etc)* reproductive **2** *(animal)* kept for breeding; *(cheval)* stud NM *(animal)* breeder; **reproducteurs** breeding stock, breeders; **r. d'élite** pedigree sire

reproductibilité [rəprɔdyktibilite] NF reproducibility

reproductible [rəprɔdyktibl] ADJ reproducible

reproductif, -ive [rəprɔdyktif, -iv] ADJ reproductive

reproduction [rəprɔdyksjɔ̃] NF **1** *(génération)* reproduction; **les organes de la r.** the reproductive organs; **animaux élevés en vue de la r.** animals reared for breeding, breeding stock; **r. sexuée/asexuée** sexual/asexual reproduction; **l'époque de la r.** the breeding season **2** *(d'un document, d'une image, du son etc)* reproduction, reproducing; *(image, copie)* reproduction; **cela se prêtera bien à la r.** it will reproduce well; **droits de r.** reproduction rights; **droits de r. en feuilleton** serial *or* serialization rights; **tous droits de r. réservés pour tous pays** all rights of reproduction reserved for all countries; **r. interdite** *(sur disque, cassette)* all rights reserved

reproduire [rəprɔdɥir] *(conj like* **produire***)* VT *(copier)* *(son, image, tableau, document etc)* to reproduce; *Journ (article)* to reprint; *(imiter)* to imitate, to mimic; **ce tableau a été reproduit à des milliers d'exemplaires** thousands of reproductions have been made of this picture; **tu as reproduit les mêmes erreurs** you've made exactly the same mistakes as before

VPR **se reproduire 1** *(des animaux etc)* to breed, to reproduce, to multiply; **ils se reproduisent comme des lapins** they breed like rabbits **2** *(des événements)* to recur, to happen again; **et que cela ne se reproduise plus!** don't let it happen again!

reprogrammable [rəprɔgramabl] ADJ *Ordinat (touche)* reprogrammable

reprogrammer [rəprɔgrame] VT *Ordinat* to reprogram; **r. une livraison** to reschedule a delivery

reprographie [rəprɔgrafi] NF *(de documents)* duplicating, *Spéc* reprography

reprographier [rəprɔgrafje] VT *(document)* to duplicate

réprouvé, -ée [repruve] N outcast; *Rel* reprobate

réprouver [repruve] VT **1** *(crime, attitude, méthode, geste)* to condemn **2** *Rel* to damn

reps [rɛps] NM *Tex* rep(p)

reptation [rɛptasjɔ̃] NF crawling

reptile [rɛptil] NM *Zool, Fig Fam* reptile

repu [rəpy] ADJ satiated, full; *Fig* **être r. de qch** to have had one's fill of sth

républicain, -aine [repyblikɛ̃, -ɛn] ADJ, N republican

républicanisme [repyblikanism] NM republicanism

république [repyblik] NF *Pol* republic; *Hum* **on est en r.** it's a free country; *Fam* **r. bananière** banana republic; **la R. de Saint-Marin** the Republic of San Marino; **la R. française** the French Republic; **la R. populaire de Chine** the People's Republic of China; *Anciennement* **R. démocratique allemande** German Democratic Republic; *Fig* **la r. des lettres** the world of letters

répudiation [repydjasjɔ̃] NF **1** *(d'une épouse, d'une opinion)* repudiation **2** *Jur (d'une succession, d'une nationalité)* renunciation

répudier [repydje] VT *(impf, pr sub n. répudiions)* **1** *(épouse, opinion)* to repudiate **2** *Jur (succession, nationalité)* to renounce, to relinquish

répugnance [repyɲɑ̃s] NF **1** *(dégoût)* repugnance *(pour* for), aversion *(pour* to), loathing *(pour* of, for); **avoir de la r. pour qn/qch** to loathe sb/sth; **éprouver de la r. à faire qch** to do sth with repugnance *or* loathing; **je me souviens de la r. avec laquelle elle en parlait** I remember her repugnance in talking about it; **avec r.** with repugnance *or* loathing **2** *(réticence)* reluctance, unwillingness; **r. à faire qch** reluctance *or* unwillingness to do sth; **avec r.** reluctantly, unwillingly; **faire qch avec r.** to do sth reluctantly *or* with reluctance, to be reluctant to do sth

répugnant [repyɲɑ̃] ADJ *(dégoûtant)* *(personne, odeur)* repulsive, revolting, repugnant; *(lieu)* repulsive, unsavoury; *(acte, comportement)* loathsome, repulsive; **de façon répugnante** disgustingly, repulsively; **il s'est conduit de façon répugnante avec la veuve** he behaved repulsively towards the widow

répugner [repyɲe] VI **1** *(ressentir du dégoût)* **r. à qch** to feel repelled by sth, to find sth repellent, to feel repugnance for sth; **r. à faire qch** to be reluctant *or* lo(a)th to do sth **2** *(dégoûter)* **r. à qn** to be repugnant *or* repellent to sb; **elle/cette idée me répugne** I find her/the idea quite repugnant *or* repellent, she/the idea is quite repugnant *or* repellent to me V IMPERS **il me répugne de le faire** I am reluctant *or* lo(a)th to do it VT *Litt (personne)* to be repugnant to

répulsif, -ive [repylsif, -iv] ADJ *Phys, Fig* repulsive

répulsion [repylsjɔ̃] NF *Phys, Fig* repulsion; **éprouver de la r. pour qn** to be repelled by sb, to feel repulsion for sb

réputation [repytasjɔ̃] NF reputation; **avoir (une) bonne/mauvaise r.** to have a good/bad reputation; **jouir d'une bonne r.** to have a good reputation, to be well spoken of; **se faire une r.** to make a reputation *or* name for oneself; **cela a fait sa r.** it made his/her name; **sa r. de chirurgien** his reputation as a surgeon; **connaître qn de r.** to know sb by reputation *or Fml* repute; **elle a la r. d'être généreuse** she has a reputation for being generous *or* for generosity; **ils ont la r. d'être très chaleureux** they are said *or* reputed to be very kind-hearted; **établissement de mauvaise r.** disreputable establishment; **athlète de r. internationale** world-famous athlete

réputé [repyte] ADJ *(expert, restaurant, vin etc)* well-known, famous, renowned *(pour* for); **c'est un écrivain très r. dans son pays** he's a very well-known *or* renowned writer in his country; **r. intelligent** reputed *or* considered to be intelligent; **il est r. ne rien ignorer de cette science** he is reputed to know everything about the science; **malgré ses qualités réputées extraordinaires, il s'est montré incapable de finir à temps** despite his reportedly extraordinary talents, he proved unable to finish on time

réputer [repyte] VT *Vieilli* to consider, to think, *Fml* to deem; **on le répute bienveillant** he is considered *or* thought *or* deemed (to be) benevolent

requérant, -ante [rəkerɑ̃, -ɑ̃t] *Jur* ADJ **partie requérante** applicant, claimant N applicant, claimant

requérir [rəkerir] **VT** (*conj like* **acquérir**) **1** (*faveur*) to ask for, to seek, *Fml* to solicit; (*la présence ou l'aide de qn*) to request; (*explication, soin, de la patience, des mains habiles etc*) to require, to call for; (*l'attention de qn*) to demand, to require **2** *Hist, Mil* **r. des civils** to conscript civilians (*for a public service*) **3** *Jur* (*sentence*) to demand, to call for

requête [rəkɛt] **NF1** (*demande*) request; *Ordinat* query; **adresser une r. à qn** to make a request to sb, *Fml* to petition sb; **à** *ou* **sur la r. de qn** at sb's request **2** *Jur* petition; **r. en cassation** appeal

requiem [rekɥijɛm] **NM INV** *Rel, Mus* requiem; **messe de r.** requiem (mass)

requin [rəkɛ̃] **NM** *Zool, Fig* shark; **peau de r.** shagreen; **r. de la (haute) finance** financial shark

requinquer [rəkɛ̃ke] *Fam* **VT r. qn** to pick *or* perk sb up; **le voilà requinqué** he's (back to) his old self again
VPR se requinquer to pick *or* perk up

requis [rəki] **ADJ** requisite, required; **les conditions requises** the requirements
NM *Hist* (*civil*) labour conscript

réquisition [rekizisjɔ̃] **NF 1** *Admin* (*de vivres, de véhicules etc*) requisitioning, commandeering; *Hist* **r. civile** (*de personne*) conscription for a public service; **mettre en r.** to requisition, to commander **2** *Jur* (*plaidoirie*) prosecution address

réquisitionner [rekizisjɔne] **VT** (*vivres, véhicules etc*) to requisition, to commander; *Hist* (*civils*) to conscript; *Fam* **elle nous a réquisitionnés pour faire la vaisselle** she requisitioned *or* conscripted us to do the washing-up

réquisitoire [rekizitwar] **NM** *Jur* prosecution address; *Fig* indictment (**contre** of)

RER [ɛraɛr] **NM** *Rail* (*abrév* **Réseau express régional**) = express rail network serving Paris and its suburbs

re-recording [ririkɔrdiŋ] **NM** *TV, Radio* re-recording

RES [ɛraɛs] **NF** *Fin* (*abrév* **reprise de l'entreprise par ses salariés**) employee buy-out

RESA [reza] **NF** (*abrév* **réservation**) = TGV seat reservation ticket

résa [reza] **NF** (*abrév* **réservation**) reservation, booking, bkg

resaler [rəsale] **VT** *Culin* to put more salt in, to add more salt to

resalir [rəsalir] **VT** to (get) dirty again
VPR se resalir to get oneself dirty again, to dirty oneself again

rescapé, -ée [rɛskape] **ADJ** (*personne*) surviving
N (*d'un désastre, d'un naufrage etc*) survivor

rescinder [rɛsɛ̃de] **VT** *Jur* to rescind, to annul

rescision [resizjɔ̃] **NF** *Jur* rescission, annulment

rescousse [rɛskus] **NF aller/venir à la r. de qn** to go/come to the rescue of sb; **arriver à la r.** to come to the rescue; **appeler qn à la r.** to call on sb for help *or* assistance, to call sb to the rescue

réseau, -eaux [rezo] **NM 1** (*de fils etc*) network; *Archit* tracery; *Phys, Nucl* (*de réacteur*) lattice; *Mil* **r. de barbelés** barbed wire entanglement **2** (*de routes, de voies ferrées, de rivières etc*), *Tél* network, system; *Radio, TV* network **3** *Fig* (*d'amis, de contacts etc*) network, circle; **r. d'espionnage** spy ring *or* network; **r. de résistance** resistance network; **un r. de drogue** a drug ring **4** *Ordinat* network; **mise en r.** networking
▸ ▸ *Ordinat* **r. en anneau à jeton** token ring network; **r. d'apport** (*pour aéroport*) feeder network; **r. autoroutier** motorway network;

Ordinat **r. en bus** bus network; **r. câblé** cable(d) network; **r. de commercialisation** marketing network; **r. de communication** communication network; *Tél* **r. à commutation par paquets** packet-switching network; **r. commuté** switched network; *Ordinat* **r. connecté en étoile** star network; **r. de distribution** distribution network; *Élec* **r. de distribution urbain** town mains; *Ordinat* **r. de données** data network; *Rail* **Réseau express régional** = suburban train network in Paris; **r. ferroviaire** rail network; **r. informatique** computer network; *Tél* **r. interurbain** long distance network; *Ordinat* **r. local** local area network; *Ordinat* **r. longue distance** wide area network, WAN; *Élec* **r. national** national grid (system); *Ordinat* **r. numérique à intégration de services** integrated services digital network; *Ordinat* **r. de télématique** *ou* **de communication de données** datacomms network; **r. télévisuel** television network; *Tél* **r. urbain** local area network; *Ordinat* **r. d'utilisateurs** user network; *Ordinat* **r. à valeur ajouté** value-added network, VAN; **r. de vente** sales network

réséda [rezeda] **NM** *Bot* reseda; **r. odorant** mignonette
ADJ INV, NM (*couleur*) reseda, mignonette

réservataire [rezɛrvatɛr] **NM** (*dans un hôtel*) party making a reservation

réservation [rezɛrvasjɔ̃] **NF 1** (*de place, à l'hôtel etc*) reservation, booking; **bureau de r.** booking office; **la r. est obligatoire** reservations are necessary; **billet de train avec r.** train ticket with seat reservation; **faire une r.** to make a reservation; **j'ai fait une r. dans un petit hôtel** I booked *or* reserved a room in a little hotel; **r. d'avion** flight reservation; **r. de groupe** group booking; **r. de place** seat reservation; **r. en bloc** block-booking; **r. ferme** firm reservation *or* booking; **r. par téléphone** *ou* **téléphonique** telephone reservation *or* booking; **r. électronique** electronic reservation **2** *Jur* reservation; **r. faite de tous mes droits** without prejudice to my rights

réserve [rezɛrv] **NF 1** (*restriction*) reservation; **faire des réserves** to have reservations (**sur** about); **je voudrais faire quelques réserves concernant ce contrat** I would like to express some reservations about the contract; *Vieilli* **à la r. de ...** except for ...; **sous r. de qch** subject to sth; *Jur* **sous r.** without prejudice; **donné sous toutes réserves** (*horaires de cinéma etc*) subject to alteration; **je te le dis, mais sous toutes réserves** I can tell you this now, but it will be officially confirmed later; **sans r.** (*éloges, admiration*) unqualified; (*affirmer qch*) without reservation

2 (*discrétion*) reserve; **se tenir** *ou* **demeurer sur la r.** to refuse to commit oneself; **être sur la r.** to be on one's guard; **son attitude manque de r.** his attitude is lacking in caution *or* restraint; **parler avec r.** to speak with restraint; **quand il sort de sa r.** when he breaks through his reserve; **il est un peu sorti de sa r.** he was a little less reserved than usual; **je vous rappelle votre devoir de r.** ≃ may I remind you that you have signed the Official Secrets Act

3 (*de vivres, d'équipement, d'argent etc*) stock, reserve; (*de troupes*) reserve; *Physiol* (*de l'organisme*) reserves, stores (**en** of); *Fin* reserve; **réserves mondiales** (*de pétrole etc*) world reserves; **réserves bancaires** bank reserves; **puiser dans les réserves** to draw on the reserves; **en r.** in reserve, set aside; *Fin* **sans r. de retour** non-returnable, no-return; *Com* **avec r. de retour** on a sale or return basis; **avoir beaucoup d'énergie en r.** to have great reserves of energy; **mettre qch en r.** to put sth aside *or* by, to reserve sth; **tenir**

qch en r. to keep sth in reserve; **fonds de r.** reserve fund; **vivres de r.** emergency rations, iron rations
4 *Mil* reserve; **r. de l'armée active** reserve of the regular army; **officier de r.** reserve officer
5 (*parc*) reserve; (*pour gibier*) preserve hunting/fishing reserve; **réserves (indiennes)** (Indian) reservation
6 (*local*) (*de magasin*) stockroom, storeroom; (*de bibliothèque, musée*) reserve (collection)
7 *TV, Cin* **en r.** white-on-black
▸ ▸ *Aut* **r. d'air** air chest; **r. d'animaux sauvages** safari park; **r. de chasse** hunting reserve; *Fin* **r. contractuelle** contractual reserve; *Fin* **r. facultative** optional reserve; **r. de gibier** game reserve; **r. légale** *Fin* legal reserve; *Jur* (*d'héritage*) legal share; **r. liquide** liquid assets, cash reserve; **r. métallique** bullion reserve; **r. naturelle** nature reserve; **r. de pêche** fishing reserve; **r. de prévoyance** contingency reserve; *Fin* **r. réglementée** regulatory reserve; *Fin* **réserves statuaires** statutory reserves; **r. zoologique** wild life sanctuary

réservé [rezɛrve] **ADJ 1** (*chambre, siège etc*) reserved, booked; **place réservée aux personnes âgées** seat reserved for the elderly; **salle réservée aux réunions** room reserved *or* kept for meetings, meeting room **2** *Typ* **tous droits réservés** all rights reserved **3** (*personne, attitude*) reserved; **elle a un caractère plutôt r.** she's rather reserved; **avis r.** qualified opinion

réserver [rezɛrve] **VT** (*louer*) (*chambre, place etc*) to reserve, to book; (*marchandises, argent etc*) to set aside, to put by, to save (**à, pour** for); **r. une place à qn** to keep *or* save a seat for sb; (*d'une agence de voyages etc*) to reserve a seat for sb; **je vous ai réservé une place sur le prochain vol** I've booked *or* reserved a seat for you *or* I've booked you on the next flight; **place réservée** reserved seat; **r. du bois pour l'hiver** to store wood for the winter; **r. son jugement** to reserve judgement; **r. le meilleur pour la fin** to keep *or* save the best till last; *Journ* **r. la une** to hold the front page; **r. une surprise à qn** to have a surprise in store for sb; **nous ignorons le sort qui lui sera réservé** we do not know what fate is in store for him/her; **ils me réservent toujours un excellent accueil** they always welcome me with open arms; **nous attendons de connaître le sort qui nous est réservé** we are waiting to find out what fate has in store for us; *Litt* **il lui était réservé de grands succès** he was destined for great things; **'chasse/pêche réservée'** 'private hunting/fishing'; *Admin Vieilli* **quartier réservé** red-light district

VI (*au théâtre, à l'hôtel*) to book, to reserve, to make a booking *or* a reservation; (*au restaurant*) to reserve, to make a reservation; **bonsoir madame, vous avez réservé?** good evening, madam, do you have a reservation?; **j'ai réservé au nom de Roux** I have a reservation in the name of Roux; **pour r., appeler ...** for reservations, call ...

VPR se réserver se r. le droit de faire qch to reserve the right to do sth; **je me réserve pour le match de ce soir** I'm saving my strength for this evening's match; **elle s'est réservé une portion du gâteau** she saved a piece of cake for herself; **celui-là, je me le réserve!** I'm keeping that one for myself!; **je préfère me r. pour le dessert** I'd rather save myself *or* keep my appetite *or* leave some room for the dessert

réserviste [rezɛrvist] **NM** *Mil* reservist

réservoir [rezɛrvwar] **NM 1** (*bassin*) reservoir; **r. de barrage** storage basin **2** (*pour poissons*) fish pond **3** (*cuve*) tank; (*de toilet-*

tes) cistern; **r. à gaz** gasholder, gasometer; **r. à mazout** fuel-oil tank; **r. d'encre** ink reservoir; *Aut* **r. d'essence** petrol *or Am* gas tank; *Aut* **r. d'expansion** expansion tank; *Aut* **r. de lave-glace** windscreen washer reservoir; *(en plastique)* windscreen washer bottle; *Aut* **r. de liquide de frein** brake fluid reservoir; *Aut* **r. en charge** header tank; *Aut* **r. à carburant** fuel tank; *Aut* **r. à dépression** vacuum tank *or* reservoir

résidant [rezidɑ̃] ADJ resident; **r. à** resident *or* living in

résidence [rezidɑ̃s] NF **1** *(séjour)* residence; **certificat de r.** residence permit; **avoir sa r. à Lyon** to be resident *or* to live in Lyons; *Jur* **en r. surveillée** under house arrest **2** *(demeure)* residence, home; *(de diplomate)* residency; **changer de r.** to change one's residence, to move (house) **3** *(immeuble)* block of luxury flats, *Am* luxury apartment building
▸ ▸ **r. hôtelière** apartment hotel; **r. médicalisée (pour personnes âgées)** nursing home; **r. principale** main residence *or* home; **r. secondaire** second home, holiday home, *Am* vacation home; **r. de tourisme** apartment hotel

résident, -ente [rezidɑ̃, -ɑ̃t] N **1** *(diplomate)* resident **2** *(étranger)* (foreign) resident; **tous les résidents français en Grande-Bretagne** all French nationals resident in Great Britain
ADJ *Ordinat* **r. en mémoire** memory-resident

résidentiel, -ielle [rezidɑ̃sjɛl] ADJ residential

résider [rezide] VI **1** *(vivre)* to live, *Fml* to reside (**à, dans, en** in); **dans la ville où l'on réside** in the town where one is resident **2** *Fig* to lie, to reside; **toute la difficulté réside en ceci que …** the whole difficulty rests *or* lies in the fact that …

résidu [rezidy] NM **1** residue; **résidus** *Chimie* residue; *(déchets)* waste; **résidus urbains** town refuse; **résidus de fission** radioactive waste **2** *Math* remainder

résiduaire [rezidɥɛr] ADJ waste; *Ind* **eaux résiduaires** waste water, process water

résiduel, -elle [rezidɥɛl] ADJ residual; *Géog* **relief r.** residual relief

résignation [reziɲasjɔ̃] NF *(soumission)* resignation; **avec r.** *(dire qch)* with resignation, resignedly; *(supporter qch)* with resignation

Il faut noter que le terme anglais **resignation** signifie également **démission**.

résigné [reziɲe] ADJ resigned (**à** to); **je suis r.** I've resigned myself

résigner [reziɲe] VT *Litt (fonction, biens)* to resign, to give up; **r. sa charge** *ou* **ses fonctions** to give up *or* relinquish one's appointment, to resign
VPR **se résigner** **se r. à qch/à faire qch** to resign oneself to sth/to doing sth; **se r. à une situation** to resign oneself to a situation; **il faut se r.** you have to resign yourself

résiliable [reziljabl] ADJ which may be terminated *or* cancelled *or* annulled

résiliation [reziljasjɔ̃] NF *(d'un contrat)* termination, cancellation, annulment

résilience [reziljɑ̃s] NF resilience

résilient [reziljɑ̃] ADJ resilient

résilier [rezilje] VT *(accord, contrat etc)* to terminate, to cancel, to annul

résille [rezij] NF **1** *(pour cheveux)* snood; **bas r.** fishnet stockings **2** *(de vitrail)* lattice

résine [rezin] NF resin; **r. vinylique** vinyl resin; **r. époxyde** epoxy resin

résiné [rezine] ADJ, NM **(vin)** r. retsina

résiner [rezine] VT **1** *(enduire de résine)* to coat with resin **2** *(extraire la résine de)* **r. un arbre** to tap a tree *(for resin)*

résineux, -euse [rezinø, -øz] ADJ resinous; *(odeur)* of resin; *(arbre, forêt)* coniferous
NM conifer

résistance [rezistɑ̃s] NF **1** resistance, opposition (**à** to); *Méd (à un virus etc)*, *Pol* resistance; **n'offrir aucune r.** to put up *or* offer no resistance; **opposer une r. à qn/qch** to resist sb/sth; **je sens une r. de sa part quand j'essaie de lui en parler** I can feel a reluctance on his part to talk about it; **je n'ose pas tirer, je sens comme une petite r.** *(c'est collé)* I don't want to pull, it seems to be stuck; **r. passive** passive resistance; **faire de la r. passive** to engage in passive resistance; *Hist* **la R.** the Resistance (movement)
2 *Phys* resistance; **r. de l'air** air resistance; **r. à l'avancement** drag
3 *Élec* resistance; *(conducteur)* *(d'un appareil)* element; *(composant)* resistor; **unité de r.** unit of resistance
4 *Tech (des matériaux)* resistance, strength, toughness; **r. à la flexion** bending strength; **r. à la traction** tensile strength; **r. au choc** impact resistance; **limite de la r.** yield point; **acier à haute r.** high-resistance *or* high-tensile steel; **tissu qui n'a pas de r.** flimsy material; **r. à l'usure** *(d'un tissu)* ability to stand up to wear and tear, durability
5 *(endurance)* stamina, endurance, staying power; **il a une bonne r. à la fatigue** he doesn't tire easily, he's got good stamina
6 pièce de r. *Culin* main course *or* dish, pièce de résistance; *Fig (d'un spectacle etc)* main item (on the programme), pièce de résistance

résistant, -ante [rezistɑ̃, -ɑ̃t] ADJ **1** *(matériau)* hard-wearing, strong, tough; *(couleur)* fast; **r. à -proof; r. à l'acide** acid-proof; **r. à la chaleur** heatproof, heat-resistant; **r. aux chocs** shockproof; **r. à l'usure** hard-wearing **2** *(robuste) (personne)* strong, tough, hardy; *(plante)* hardy
N freedom fighter; *Hist* member of the Resistance movement

résister [reziste] VI *(se débattre, s'opposer)* to resist; **il n'a pas résisté à la pneumonie** he succumbed to pneumonia; **je n'ai pas pu r., je les ai achetées** I couldn't resist them so I bought them; **r. à** *(tentation, influence, personne)* to resist; *(attaque)* to hold out against, to resist; *(douleur, pression etc)* to withstand, to stand up to; *(mauvais traitement, fatigue)* to stand up to; *(maladie, épidémie)* to overcome; *(vent, froid)* to withstand; **il n'a pas pu r. au courant** he couldn't fight against the current; **r. à l'analyse** *(d'un argument, d'une explication etc)* to stand up to analysis; *Tech* **r. à la chaleur/aux acides** to be heatproof/acid-proof; **ce pull a bien résisté au lavage** this jumper washed well; **r. au temps, r. à l'épreuve du temps** *(d'une amitié, d'un amour etc)* to stand the test of time; **ces couleurs ne résistent pas** these colours are not fast; *Fig* **on ne peut pas lui r.** he's irresistible, you can refuse him nothing; **personne n'ose lui r.** nobody dares stand up to him/her

résistivité [rezistivite] NF *Élec* resistivity

resituer [rəsitɥe] VT to place; **r. qch dans son contexte** to put *or* place sth in its context

résolu [rezɔly] ADJ *(personne)* determined, resolute; **un air r.** an air of determination; **d'un air r.** determinedly, with an air of determination, resolutely; **elle est (bien) résolue à le faire** she is (quite) determined to do it

résoluble [rezɔlybl] ADJ **1** *(problème)* solvable **2** *Jur (contrat)* which may be terminated *or* cancelled *or* annulled

résolument [rezɔlymɑ̃] ADV determinedly, resolutely; **être r. contre qch** to be resolutely *or* strongly opposed to sth

résolution [rezɔlysjɔ̃] NF **1** *Tech (d'une sub-*

stance, d'un écran de télévision etc) resolution; **écran à haute r.** high-resolution screen **2** *(d'un problème)* solving, *Fml* resolution **3** *Jur (d'un contrat)* termination, cancellation, annulment **4** *(décision)* resolution; **prendre la r. de faire qch** to make a resolution to do sth, to resolve *or* determine to do sth; **ma r. est prise** I've made my decision; *Pol* **prendre une r.** to pass a resolution; **prendre des résolutions** to make resolutions; **mes bonnes résolutions de début d'année** my New Year's resolutions **5** *(détermination) (d'une personne)* determination, single-mindedness, strength of will; **sa r. est remarquable** he is remarkably determined *or* single-minded

résolutoire [rezɔlytwar] ADJ **clause r.** termination clause

résonance [rezɔnɑ̃s] NF **1** resonance; **la r. est bonne/mauvaise dans cette salle** the acoustics in the hall are good/bad; *Mus* **caisse de r.** sound box; *Méd* **r. magnétique nucléaire** nuclear magnetic resonance, NMR **2** *Fig (effet)* response, echo; **cela n'est pas sans r. sur sa vie affective** it is not without its effects on his/her emotional life; **ce mot prend une r. toute particulière dans ce contexte** in this context, the word has particular connotations

résonateur [rezɔnatœr] NM *Élec* resonator

résonnant, résonant [rezɔnɑ̃] ADJ **1** *(voix)* resonant, resounding, sonorous; **r. de cris** resounding *or* echoing *or* resonant with cries **2** *Phys* resonant

résonner [rezɔne] VI *(d'un son, de pas etc)* to resound, to resonate, to echo; *(d'une voix, d'une pièce)* to echo; **sa voix résonnait dans les haut-parleurs** his/her voice blared out *or* boomed out over the loudspeakers; **ça résonne!** there's an echo!, it echoes!; **faire r. la trompette/le tambour** to sound the trumpet/the drum; **l'air résonnait de leurs cris** the air rang *or* resounded *or* echoed with their cries

résorber [rezɔrbe] VT **1** *Méd* to resorb **2** *(surplus, déficit)* to absorb, to bring down; *(chômage)* to absorb, to curb; *(dettes)* to wipe out, to clear; **r. la crise économique** to solve the economic crisis
VPR **se résorber** **1** *Méd* to be resorbed **2** *(d'un surplus, déficit)* to be absorbed, to be brought down; *(du chômage)* to be absorbed *or* curbed

résorption [rezɔrpsjɔ̃] NF **1** *Méd* resorption **2** *(d'un surplus, déficit)* absorption, bringing down; *(du chômage)* absorption, curbing; *(de dettes)* clearing, wiping out

résoudre [rezudr] *(prp résolvant; pp résolu, parfois résous, -oute; pr ind je résous, il résout, n. résolvons; impf je résolvais; p hist je résolus; fu je résoudrai)* VT **1** *(difficulté)* to resolve, to clear up; *(équation, énigme, problème)* to solve; *(question, conflit)* to resolve, to settle; *(crise)* to solve, to resolve **2** *Chimie (transformer)* to break up; **r. qch en qch** to solve sth into sth, to break up sth into sth **3** *Jur (contrat, accord etc)* to terminate, to cancel, to annul **4** *(décider)* **r. qn à faire qch** to prevail upon *or* persuade *or* induce sb to do sth; **r. de faire qch** to decide *or* make up one's mind to do sth
VPR **se résoudre** **1** **se r. à faire qch** to decide *or* make up one's mind *or* resolve to do sth; **je ne peux pas me r. à la quitter** I can't bring myself to leave her **2** *Chimie* to resolve itself; **se r. en qch** to resolve into sth, to break up into sth

respect [rɛspɛ] NM respect (**pour** for); **le r. de la nature/des morts** respect for nature/the dead; **inspirer le r.** to inspire respect; **montrer** *ou* **faire preuve de r. pour qn/qch** to show sb/sth (some) respect; **avoir du r. pour qn** to respect sb, to have respect for sb; **il n'a aucun r. pour les autres** he has no respect for other people; **avoir le r. des lois/ des convenances** to respect or have respect for or have regard for the law/the conventions; **son courage suscite le r.** his/her courage commands respect; **parler avec r.** to speak respectfully or with respect; **r. de soi** self-respect; *Vieilli* **r. humain** fear of other people's judgement (of one's actions); **faire qch par r. pour qn** to do sth out of respect or regard for sb; **manquer de r. envers qn** to be disrespectful to sb, to show sb a lack of respect; **il t'a manqué de r.** he was disrespectful to you, he did not show you any respect; **tenir qn en r.** to fend sb off, to keep sb at a distance; **j'ai réussi à le tenir en r. en le menaçant d'un couteau** I managed to fend him off with a knife; *Fig* **son autorité naturelle lui permet de tenir en r. les élèves les plus indisciplinés** his/her innate authority enables him to keep the most undisciplined pupils at bay; *Fml* **sauf le r. que je vous dois, sauf votre r.** with all due respect; **en signe de r.** as a mark of respect; *Fml* **rendre** ou **présenter ses respects à qn** to pay one's respects to sb; **(je vous présente) mes respects, chère madame** my respects, madam

respectabilité [rɛspɛktabilite] NF respectability

respectable [rɛspɛktabl] ADJ **1** (digne de respect) (famille, air, femme etc) respectable **2** (digne de considération) (somme) respectable, fairly large; **un appartement de dimensions respectables** a fair-sized flat; **un nombre r. de spectateurs** a respectable or fairly large or fair number of spectators

respecter [rɛspɛkte] VT (personne, chose) to respect, to have respect or regard for; (calme d'un endroit, désir ou opinion de qn, limitation de vitesse) to respect; (la loi) to abide by, to obey, to respect; **r. les délais de livraison** to meet delivery schedules; **il ne respecte rien** he has no respect for anything; **faire r. la loi** to enforce the law; **se faire r.** to command respect; **r. le code de la route** to respect or obey or follow the Highway Code; **vous n'avez pas respecté la priorité** you didn't give way

VPR se respecter to respect oneself; (réciproque) to respect each other; **comme tout homme qui se respecte** like any self-respecting man; **un professeur qui se respecte ne ferait pas cela** no self-respecting teacher would do that; **il se respecte trop pour faire cela** he has too much self-respect to do that

respectif, -ive [rɛspɛktif, -iv] ADJ respective

respectivement [rɛspɛktivmɑ̃] ADV respectively; **ils ont r. deux et trois enfants** they have two and three children respectively

respectueusement [rɛspɛktɥøzmɑ̃] ADV respectfully

respectueux, -euse [rɛspɛktɥø, -øz] ADJ respectful (**de** of; **envers** to, towards); **il ne se montre guère r. envers ses parents** he shows little respect for his parents; **d'un ton r.** in a respectful tone, in a tone of respect; **être r. des autres comme de soi** to respect other people as much as one does oneself; **être r. de qch** to respect sth, to show respect for sth; **r. des lois** respectful of the law, law-abiding; **se tenir à distance respectueuse** to keep at a respectful distance; **je vous prie d'agréer, Monsieur, mes salutations respectueuses** (dans une lettre) yours faithfully; (quand la formule de salutation comprend le nom du destinataire) yours sincerely

respirable [rɛspirabl] ADJ breathable; *Fig* **l'atmosphère n'était plus r.** the atmosphere had become oppressive or suffocating

respirateur [rɛspiratœr] NM respirator, ventilator

respiration [rɛspirasjɔ̃] NF breathing, *Spéc* respiration; (de plante) respiration; **r. artificielle** artificial respiration; **pratiquer la r. artificielle sur qn** to give sb artificial respiration; *Méd* **r. contrôlée/assistée** controlled/assisted respiration; **avoir la r. difficile** ou **des difficultés de r.** to have trouble or difficulty breathing; **s'arrêter pour prendre sa r.** to pause for breath; **retenir sa r.** to hold one's breath; *Fig* **tous retenaient leur r. en attendant le verdict** everyone waited for the verdict with bated breath; **couper la r. à qn** to wind sb; *Fig* to take sb's breath away, to flabbergast sb

respiratoire [rɛspiratwar] ADJ (organe etc) respiratory; (appareil, exercice, problème) breathing; **défaillance r.** respiratory failure; **quotient r.** respiratory quotient; **voies respiratoires** respiratory tract; **troubles respiratoires** breathing or respiratory problems; **difficultés respiratoires** difficulty in breathing

respirer [rɛspire] VI (d'une personne, d'un vin, d'une plante) to breathe; **r. longuement** to take or draw a long breath; **r. par le nez/ la bouche** to breathe through the nose/ mouth; *Fam* **laissez-moi r.!** let me get my breath (back)!, let me catch my breath!; *Fam* **ouf! je respire!** (de soulagement) thank goodness for that!, that's a load off my mind!

VT 1 to breathe (in), to inhale; **aller r. un peu d'air** to go for a breath of air; **r. une fleur** to smell a flower **2** *Fig* **r. la vengeance/la paix/ la confiance** to breathe vengeance/peace/ confidence; **r. la santé/l'honnêteté** to radiate health/honesty; **cela respire l'ennui le plus profond** it is profoundly boring

resplendir [rɛsplɑ̃dir] VI (d'une personne) to be radiant; (briller) to shine, to glitter, to gleam; **r. de joie/santé** (d'un visage) to be shining with joy/glowing with health; (d'une personne) to radiate joy/health; **sa beauté resplendissait** she was radiantly beautiful

resplendissant [rɛsplɑ̃disɑ̃] ADJ (personne, beauté) glowing, radiant; (voiture etc) shining, gleaming; (cuivres) gleaming; **r. de joie/santé** (mine) shining with joy/glowing with health; (personne) radiant with joy/ health; **femme d'une beauté resplendissante** radiantly beautiful woman; **il a une mine resplendissante** he looks wonderfully well

responsabiliser [rɛspɔ̃sabilize] VT **r. qn** (le rendre responsable) to give sb a sense of responsibility

responsabilité [rɛspɔ̃sabilite] NF responsibility; (légale) liability (**de** for); **r. de l'employeur** employer's liability; **r. du fabricant** manufacturer's liability; **accepter une r.** to take on or assume or accept a responsibility; **élever des enfants est une grande r.** bringing up children is quite a responsibility; **c'est ta r. de répondre au téléphone, pas la mienne** answering the phone is your responsibility, not mine; **avoir la r. de qn/qch** to be responsible for sb/sth; **donner à qn la r. de qch** to give sb responsibility or make sb responsible for sth; **partager la r. d'un projet** to share the responsibility or be jointly responsible for a project; **assumer ses responsabilités** to face up to one's responsibilities; **décliner toute r.** to deny all responsibility; **nous déclinons toute r. pour les objets perdus ou volés** we accept no liability for lost or stolen items; **fuir les responsabilités** to evade or avoid responsibility; **être appelé à de hautes responsabilités** to be given important responsibilities; **avoir un poste à responsabilité** to have a responsible job; **je cherche un poste à responsabilités** I want a job with responsibilities; **faire qch sous sa (propre) r.** to do sth on one's own responsibility

▸▸ **r. civile** public liability; *Fin* **être assuré r. civile** to have personal liability insurance; **r. contractuelle** contractual liability; **r. illimitée** unlimited liability; **r. limitée** limited liability; *Pol* **r. ministérielle** ministerial accountability; **r. patronale** employer's liability; **r. solidaire et indivise** joint and several liability; **r. au tiers** third-party liability; **être assuré r. au tiers** to carry third-party insurance

responsable [rɛspɔ̃sabl] ADJ responsible (**de** for); (légalement) liable (**de** for); **elle n'est pas r. de ton échec** she's not responsible or not to blame for your failure; **r. de ses enfants** responsible or answerable for one's children; **le ministre est r. devant** ou **envers les Chambres** the Minister is responsible or answerable or accountable to Parliament; **tenir qn/qch pour r. d'un malheur** to hold sb/sth responsible for a misfortune, to blame sb/sth for a misfortune; **il faut les rendre responsables** they have to be given a sense of responsibility

N **1** (coupable) person responsible (**de** for), culprit; **qui est le r. de cette plaisanterie idiote?** who's responsible or to blame for this silly prank? **2** (personne en charge) person in charge; (dirigeant élu) official; **les responsables du Parti socialiste** Socialist Party officials

▸▸ **r. des achats** buyer; **r. administratif** executive manager; **r. des banquets** banqueting manager; **r. du budget** account executive; **r. client** account manager; **r. des comptes-clients** account executive; **r. des études de marché** market research manager; **r. de la formation** training officer; **r. de groupe** group leader; **r. de magasin** warehouse manager; **r. de marché** market manager; **r. (du) marketing** marketing manager or executive; *TV, Cin* **r. point** focus puller; **r. politique** political leader; **r. produit** product manager; **r. de projet** project leader; *Culin* **r. des sauces** (dans un restaurant) sauce chef, saucier; **r. du service commercial** sales and marketing manager; *Pol* **r. syndical** union leader; **r. de la vente** sales manager; **r. des ventes** sales manager; **r. du vestiaire** cloakroom attendant

resquillage [rɛskijaʒ] NM, **resquille** [rɛskij] NF (au théâtre etc) sneaking in without paying; (dans le cinéma, le métro etc) fare-dodging; (dans une queue) queue-jumping; **faire de la r.** to dodge paying

resquiller [rɛskije] VI (au théâtre, au concert etc) to sneak in without paying; (dans l'autobus, le métro etc) to dodge paying one's fare; (dans une queue) to jump the queue; **entrer dans un cinéma en resquillant** to sneak into a cinema (without paying)

VT **r. une place de théâtre** to sneak into a theatre (without paying); **r. un ticket de métro** to dodge paying one's fare on the metro

resquilleur, -euse [rɛskijœr, -øz] N (au théâtre etc) person who has sneaked in without paying; (dans l'autobus, le métro etc) fare-dodger; (dans une queue) queue-jumper

ressac [rəsak] NM *Naut* undertow

ressaisir [rəsezir] VT (fugitif) to recapture; (biens) to recover (possession of); (pouvoir) to seize again; **la peur l'a ressaisi** fear gripped him again

VPR **se ressaisir** to regain one's self-control, to pull oneself together; **ressaisissez-vous!** pull yourself together!; *Scol* **se r. au second**

trimestre to improve *or* to make more of an effort in the second term

ressasser [rəsase] **VT** *(en esprit)* to brood over; *(répéter)* to keep coming out with; *(d'un professeur) (cours)* to rehash; **plaisanterie ressassée** (old) chestnut; **un thème ressassé** a hackneyed theme, a theme that's been done to death

ressaut [rəso] **NM** *Archit, Géol (d'une corniche, d'une paroi d'escalade)* projection

ressauter [rəsote] **VI** to jump again; **il n'a jamais ressauté en parachute** he never made another parachute jump
VT to jump (over) again

ressemblance [rəsãblãs] **NF** resemblance, likeness; **la r. est grande** there's a great resemblance; **il y a quelques ressemblances entre eux** they resemble each other in a few respects, there are a few points of similarity *or* likeness between them; **il y a une r. frappante entre la mère et la fille** there is a striking resemblance between mother and daughter; **il n'y a aucune r. entre lui et sa sœur** he and his sister do not resemble each other at all; **il y a aussi une r. dans leurs façons de s'exprimer** there is also a similarity in the way they express themselves, they express themselves in a similar way too; **un tableau peint sans aucun souci de r.** a painting done with no concern for rendering a true likeness; *Cin* **toute r. avec des personnes existant ou ayant existé ne peut être que fortuite** any resemblance to persons living or dead is purely coincidental

ressemblant [rəsãblã] **ADJ portrait bien r.** lifelike portrait, good likeness; **elle est très ressemblante** *(sur un portrait)* it is very like her; **ce tableau n'est pas très r.** it's not a very good likeness, it doesn't look much like you/him/*etc*

ressembler [rəsãble] **VI r. à qn** *(physiquement)* to resemble sb, to be like *or* look like sb; *(moralement)* to resemble *or* be like sb; **r. à qch** to resemble *or* be like *or* look like sth; **elle ne ressemble pas beaucoup à ses parents** she doesn't look like *or* resemble her parents very much; **tu ressembles vraiment à ton père, toi!** you're just like your father!; **il te ressemble comme un frère** he's so like you, you'd think he was your brother; **à quoi ressemble-t-elle?** what's she like?, what does she look like?; *Fam* **cela ne ressemble à rien** it looks like nothing on earth; *(ça ne veut rien dire)* it just doesn't make sense; **cela lui ressemble tout à fait!** that's just like him!, that's him all over!; **cela ne lui ressemble pas de se plaindre** it's not like him/her to complain
VPR se ressembler to be alike, to resemble each other; **il n'y en a pas deux qui se ressemblent** no two are alike; **les bébés se ressemblent tous** babies all look alike; **ils se ressemblent comme deux gouttes d'eau** they're as like as two peas in a pod; *Prov* **qui se ressemble s'assemble** birds of a feather flock together; **les jours se suivent et ne se ressemblent pas** day follows day and you never know what to expect; **tu ne te ressembles plus!** you're not your usual self!

ressemelage [rəsəmlaʒ] **NM** resoling

ressemeler [rəsəmle] **VT** *(conj like* **semeler**) *(chaussures)* to resole

ressentiment [rəsãtimã] **NM** resentment (**de** at; **contre** against); **avec r.** resentfully; **éprouver du r.** to feel resentful

ressentir [rəsãtir] *(conj like* **sentir**) **VT** *(douleur, colère, sympathie, effet, insulte etc)* to feel; *(choc, sensation)* to experience; **je me demande comment il a pu r. cette trahison** I wonder how he felt about being betrayed like that; **r. de l'affection pour qn** to be fond of sb; **je ne ressens aucune ten-**

dresse pour elle I don't feel any affection for her, I'm not fond of her; **je ne ressens plus rien pour toi** I don't feel anything for you any more; **r. vivement la perte de qn** to feel the loss of sb deeply, to be deeply affected by the loss of sb; **il a durement ressenti les privations** the effects of the hardships he suffered have gone deep
VPR se ressentir 1 se r. de to feel the effects of **2** *très Fam* **s'en r. pour qch** to feel fit for sth, to feel up to sth

> Il faut noter que le verbe anglais **to resent** est un faux ami. Il signifie **ne pas aimer du tout**.

resserre [rəser] **NF** *(pour outils)* tool shed; *(pour stocker)* storeroom

resserrement [rəsermã] **NM 1** *(contraction) (d'une vallée, route etc)* narrowing; **r. du crédit** credit squeeze, tightening of credit **2** *(d'un nœud, d'un écrou etc)* tightening; *Fig (d'une amitié, de liens)* strengthening

resserrer [rəsere] **VT** *(livres sur étagère)* to push closer together; *(nœud, ceinture, pores)* to tighten; *(écrou)* to tighten (up); *Fig (amitié, liens)* to strengthen; *(récit)* to condense; *(discipline)* to tighten (up); *(crédit)* to squeeze, to tighten
VPR se resserrer 1 *(d'une vallée, route etc)* to narrow, to become narrower; *(des pores)* to tighten **2** *(d'un nœud)* to tighten; *Fig (des liens)* to strengthen, to grow stronger

resservir [rəservir] *(conj like* **servir**) **VT 1** *(servir de nouveau)* to serve again; **tu ne vas pas nous r. ta quiche d'hier?** you're not going to dish up yesterday's quiche again, are you?; **r. un plat** to serve up a dish again **2** *(servir en plus) (poisson etc)* to serve another helping of; **tu nous ressers un peu de ta quiche?** can we have a bit more of your quiche?
VI to be used again; **cette robe pourra r. l'été prochain** the dress will do another summer; **ça peut toujours r.** it might come in handy *or* useful
VPR se resservir reservez-vous de riz help yourself to *or* have some more rice *or* another helping of rice; **tu peux te r., si tu veux** you can have some more if you like

ressort [rəsor] **NM 1** *(élasticité)* elasticity, springiness; **faire r.** to spring back, to fly back; *Fig* **avoir du r.** to be resilient; **elle ne manque pas de r.** she's resilient
2 *(pièce)* spring; **r. de sommier** bed spring; **r. de montre** watch spring; **r. à boudin** *ou* **en spirale** coil *or* spiral spring; **r. à feuilles** *ou* **à lames** leaf *or* laminated spring; *Aut* **r. d'expansion** expansion *or* expander spring; **r. hélicoïdal** helical *or* coil spring; **r. moteur, grand r.** mainspring; **à r.** spring-loaded; **actionné** *ou* **mû par r.** spring-driven; **suspendu à ressort(s)** *(chariot etc)* sprung; **sans ressort(s)** unsprung
3 *Fig (motivation)* motive; **l'intérêt est un puissant r.** self-interest is a powerful motive *or* driving force
4 *Jur (compétence)* province, scope, competence; *(étendue de juridiction)* jurisdiction; **être du r. de la cour** to be *or* fall within the competence of the court; **cela n'est pas de son r.** that's not his/her responsibility, that doesn't fall within his/her province
5 en dernier r. *Jur* without appeal; *Fig* as a *or* in the last resort

ressortir¹ [rəsortir] *(conj like* **sortir**) **VI** *(aux être)* **1** *(d'un lieu) (d'une personne)* to come/go out again, to re-emerge; **elle est ressortie** *(je suis à l'intérieur)* she went out again; *(je suis à l'extérieur)* she came out again; **elle est ressortie de chez elle** she came/went out of her house again; **je n'ai pas envie de r. ce soir** I don't want to go out again this

evening; **la lame est ressortie ensanglantée** the blade came out covered in blood; **la balle est ressortie par l'épaule** the bullet came out *or* exited through the shoulder
2 *(se détacher)* to stand out; **faire r.** *(couleur)* to bring out, to set off; *(fait, importance de qch)* to emphasize, to accentuate, to stress; *(sens de qch)* to bring out; **pour faire r. tes yeux** to highlight *or* emphasize your eyes; **cela ressort d'autant plus que …** it stands out all the more since …
3 *(résulter)* to emerge, to be evident (**de** from); **il en ressort que nous …** it emerges *or* is evident from this that we …
VT *(aux avoir) (parapluie, vêtements etc)* to get out again; *Fig* **elle ressort toujours le même genre d'histoires** she always comes out with the same old stories; **elle nous a encore ressorti son histoire de …** she trotted out her story about …

ressortir² **VI** *Jur* **r. à** to come under the jurisdiction of; *Fig Litt* **concepts qui ressortissent à la géométrie** concepts that belong to geometry *or* that come within the province of geometry

ressortissant, -ante [rəsortisã, -ãt] **ADJ** *Jur* **r. à** under the jurisdiction of
N national, citizen; **r. d'un pays de l'Union européenne** EU national

ressouder [rəsude] **VT** to resolder; *(par la soudure autogène)* to reweld
VPR se ressouder *(d'un os, d'une fracture)* to knit (again)

ressource [rəsurs] **NF 1** *(habileté)* resourcefulness; **personne de r.** resourceful person, person of resource; **elle a de la r.** she is resourceful; **la situation est grave mais tu n'es pas sans r.** the situation is serious but there are things you can do *or* there are ways out of it
2 *(moyen)* expedient; **avoir mille ressources, être plein de ressources** to be very resourceful; **être à bout de ressources** to have exhausted all one's possibilities; **exploiter les ressources d'une situation/d'un scénario** to exploit the possibilities of a situation/a script; **je n'avais d'autre r. que la fuite** I had no choice but to run away, there was no course open to me but flight; **c'est ma seule r.** it's the only course of action open to me; **en dernière r.** as a last resort
3 ressources *(argent)* resources, means; *(agricoles, pétrolières etc)* resources; **ressources d'appoint** additional sources of income; **ressources financières** financial resources; **les ressources en hommes et en matériel** manpower and material resources; **ressources humaines** human resources; **ressources personnelles** private means
4 *Aviat* flattening out, pull-out

ressourcer (se) [sərəsurse] **VPR** *Fam (revenir aux sources)* to go back to one's roots; *(reprendre des forces morales)* to get back in touch with one's inner self

ressusciter [resysite] **VT 1 r. les morts** to raise *or* resurrect the dead; *Fig* **r. qn** to put new life into sb; **ce vin me ressuscite** this wine is putting new life into me *or* reviving me; **tes larmes ne vont pas le r.** crying won't bring him back (to life) **2** *Fig (querelle, mode, traditions etc)* to revive, to resurrect; *(souvenir, commerce)* to revive
VI to revive, to come to life again; *Rel* to rise from the dead; **ressuscité d'entre les morts** risen from the dead, resurrected

> Il faut noter que le verbe anglais **to resuscitate** est un faux ami et ne correspond jamais au français **ressusciter**. Il signifie le plus souvent **ranimer**.

restant [rəstã] **ADJ 1** remaining; left; **les vingt euros restants** the remaining twenty euros, the twenty euros remaining *or* left (over) **2 poste restante** poste restante, *Am* general delivery

NM remainder, rest; **le r. de sa vie** the rest of one's life; **un r. d'étoffe** a leftover piece of material; *Com* **r. en caisse** cash surplus; **r. d'un compte** balance of an account, account balance

restau [rɛsto] **NM** *Fam* restaurant; **r. U** university canteen *or* refectory

restaurant [rɛstɔrɑ̃] **NM** restaurant; **et si on allait au r. ce soir?** how about eating out *or* going to a restaurant this evening?; **ils vont souvent au r.** they often eat out *or* eat in restaurants; **manger au r.** to eat out
▸▸ **r. gastronomique** gourmet restaurant; **r. libre-service** self-service restaurant; **r. de poissons** seafood restaurant; **r. routier** transport café, *Am* truck stop; **r. self-service** self-service restaurant; **r. de spécialités** speciality restaurant; **r. à thème** theme restaurant; **r. universitaire** university canteen *or* refectory

restaurateur, -trice [rɛstɔratœr, -tris] **N 1** *(de bâtiments, de tableaux)* restorer; *Litt (d'un régime, d'une dynastie etc)* restorer **2** *(de restaurant)* restaurateur, restaurant owner/manager

restauration [rɛstɔrasjɔ̃] **NF 1** *(de bâtiment, d'une dynastie, de finances publiques, discipline etc)* restoration; *Ordinat* restore; **faire de la r. de tableaux** *(comme métier)* to work in art restoration; *Hist* **la R.** the Restoration **2** *(métier)* catering; **la r. collective** institutional catering; **r. rapide** fast food; **chaîne de r. rapide** fast-food chain; **être dans la r.** to be in catering, to work in the catering trade; **r. aérienne** in-flight catering, airline catering **3** *Suisse (restaurant)* restaurant

restaurer [rɛstɔre] **VT 1** *(rétablir, réparer)*, *Ordinat* to restore; *Fig (discipline, autorité)* to restore, to re-establish **2** *(faire manger)* **r. qn** to give sb something to eat
VPR se restaurer *(manger)* to eat something

restauroute [rɛstorut] **NM** *(de route)* roadside restaurant; *(d'autoroute)* motorway *or Am* freeway restaurant

reste [rɛst] **NM 1** *(de travail, d'argent, de vin etc)* rest, remainder; *Math* remainder; **le r. du temps** the rest of the time; **commence par ceci et je te dirai quoi faire le r. du temps** start with this and I'll tell you what to do for the rest *or* remainder of the time; **le r. (des gens)** the rest, the others; **il y avait un r. de beurre/lait** there was a bit of butter/milk left (over); **accommoder un r. de viande** to use up the leftover meat; **faire un chemisier avec un r. de tissu** to make a shirt out of a remnant of material; **elle a de beaux restes** *(elle est encore belle)* she still has some of her beauty; *(elle travaille encore très bien, c'est encore une très bonne athlète)* she's still on the ball; *Fig* **il n'a pas demandé son r.** he didn't say another word; **partir sans demander son r.** to leave without another word, to leave without further ado; **finis le r.** *(du repas)* finish it off, finish *or* take what's left; **(et) pour le r., on verra plus tard** as for the rest, we'll see about it later; **il sait parler aux clients, mais pour le r., c'est un incapable** he knows how to talk to the customers but otherwise he's quite incapable; **et (tout) le r.** and so on, and so forth; **être** *ou* **demeurer en r.** to be indebted (**avec qn** to sb), to remain under an obligation to sb; *Fig* **pour ne pas être en r.** so as not to be left out; **vous auriez du pain de r.?** do you have any bread left (over)?, do you have any spare bread?, do you have any bread to spare?; **quand j'ai du temps de r.** when I have some spare time *or* time to spare; **avoir de l'argent de r.** to

have more than enough money; **du** *ou* **au r.** besides, moreover
2 restes *(de repas)* leftovers, scraps; *(d'une ancienne ville, d'une fortune etc)* remains; *(d'une armée)* remnant; **restes humains** human remains; *Litt* **restes mortels** mortal remains

RESTER [rɛste]

| to remain **1-3** ▪ to be left **1** ▪ to stay **2,** |
| **3** ▪ to keep **3** ▪ to last **4** |

VI *(aux* **être)** **1** *(subsister)* to remain, to be left; **les quelques jours qui restent** the few days that are left, the few remaining days; **les cinq euros qui restent** the remaining five euros, the five euros left (over); **dix-neuf divisé par cinq, je pose trois, reste quatre** nineteen divided by five makes three, and four over *or* remainder four; **la vie n'est pas facile pour ceux qui restent** life isn't easy for those left behind
2 *(demeurer)* to stay, to remain; **je pars – non, reste!** I'm going – no, stay!; **il est resté à** *ou* **pour travailler** he stayed (behind) to work; **mon sac a dû r. sur le comptoir** I must have left my bag on the counter; **les mots lui restèrent dans la gorge** the words stuck in his throat; **il restait là à me regarder** he sat/stood there looking at me; **restez où vous êtes** stay where you are; **r. assis** to remain *or* stay seated *or* sitting; **r. debout** to stand; *(ne pas aller se coucher)* to stay up; *(pour attendre)* to wait up; **je ne peux plus r. debout** I can't stay on my feet a minute longer; **je n'en peux plus de r. debout toute la journée** I'm fed up being on my feet all day; **r. au lit** to stay *or* remain in bed; **r. (à) dîner** to stay to *or* for dinner; **qu'est-ce qui reste à faire?** what still has to be done?, what's left to do?; **le plus dur reste à faire** the hardest part remains *or* is still to be done; **r. sur place** to stay where one is, to stay put; *Fam* **j'y suis, j'y reste** here I am and here I stay; *Fam* **y r.** *(mourir)* to kick the bucket, to snuff it; **j'ai bien cru que j'allais y r.** I really thought I'd had it, I really thought my time *or* number was up; **il a bien failli y r.** he nearly didn't make it; **en r. là** to proceed no further; **j'aime autant en r. là** *(dans une conversation, relation)* I'd rather not go any further, I'd rather leave it at that; **restons-en là pour aujourd'hui** let's leave it there *or* at that for today; **les choses en sont restées là** there the matter rested *or* remained; **ne reste donc pas là planté comme un imbécile!** don't just stand there!; **où en sommes-nous restés?** where did we get to?, where did we leave off *or* stop (**de notre lecture** in our reading)?; *TV* **où en es-tu resté?** *(du feuilleton)* what point did you see up to?; **ils en sont restés à l'encre et au papier** *(ils n'utilisent pas encore d'ordinateurs)* they're still stuck in the pen-and-paper era, they haven't progressed beyond the pen-and-paper stage; **que cela reste entre nous** this is strictly between ourselves, this must go no further; **r. sur une impression** to be left with an impression; **cela m'est resté sur l'estomac** *(d'un plat)* it's lying heavy on my stomach; *Fig* it still rankles (with me), *Fam* it still bugs me; *Fig* **cela me reste en travers de la gorge** it still sticks in my throat
3 *(dans un état)* to keep, to stay, to remain; **r. tranquille/calme** to stay *or* keep *or* remain still/calm; **c'est resté collé** it's stuck; **r. en bonne santé** to remain *or* keep in good health, to keep well; **il est resté très en forme** he's kept in very good shape; **je suis resté longtemps fatigué après l'opération** I was tired for a long time after the operation; **la cuisinière est restée allumée** the cooker stayed *or* remained lit; **r. ouvert** *(d'un magasin)* to stay open; **le robinet est resté ouvert toute la journée** the tap was (left) on all day;

la maison est restée ouverte the house wasn't locked up; **r. en bons termes avec qn**, *Fam* **r. bien avec qn** to stay *or* remain on good terms with sb
4 *(durer)* to last, to endure; **le nom lui est resté** the name stayed with him/her, *Fam* the name stuck; **un match qui restera dans les mémoires** a match which will live on in people's memories; **il restera dans l'histoire comme l'un de nos plus grands présidents** he'll live on in history as one of our greatest presidents
5 *Belg* **r. faire qch** *(continuer à faire qch)* to go on *or* continue doing sth
V IMPERS **il me reste cinq euros** I have *or* I've got five euros left; **il me reste à peine de quoi payer le loyer** I barely have enough left to pay the rent; **il ne me reste qu'à vous remercier** it only remains for me to thank you, all that remains is for me to thank you; **(il) reste à savoir s'il a raison** it remains to be seen whether he's right; **il n'en reste pas moins que ...** it is nevertheless the case that ...; **il ne nous restait plus que cinq cents mètres à parcourir** we only had another five hundred metres to go, we only had five hundred metres left to go; **dis-leur ce qui ne va pas, il en restera toujours quelque chose** tell them what's wrong, some of it is bound to sink in; **que reste-t-il de tes belles promesses?** what remains of your wonderful promises?

restituable [rɛstituabl] **ADJ** *(prêt, somme d'argent)* repayable, returnable; *(dépense)* refundable

restituer [rɛstitɥe] **VT 1** *(reconstituer) (inscription, texte)* to restore; **le film restitue parfaitement l'ambiance du Paris d'après-guerre** the film recreates perfectly the atmosphere of post-war Paris **2** *(rendre) (marchandises volées etc)* to restore, to return; *(argent, prêt)* to repay, to pay back; **r. de l'argent à qn** to repay sb **3** *(énergie)* to release; *(son)* to reproduce; **cette chaîne restitue un son plus pur** this system gives a better sound, the sound reproduction on this system is better

restitution [rɛstitysjɔ̃] **NF 1** *(reconstitution) (d'un texte, d'un monument)* restoration; *(d'une ambiance)* recreation **2** *(fait de rendre) (de marchandises volées etc)* return, *Fml* restitution; *(d'argent, prêt)* repayment; **r. d'impôts** tax refund; **r. d'indu** return of payment made in error **3** *(de l'énergie)* release; *(du son)* reproduction

resto [rɛsto] **NM** *Fam* = restau

Restoroute® [rɛstorut] **NM** = restauroute

restreindre [rɛstrɛ̃dr] *(prp* restreignant; *pp* restreint; *pr ind* je restreins, il restreint, n. restreignons; *p hist* je restreignis; *fu* je restreindrai)* **VT** *(ambition, nombre de personnes etc)* to restrict (**à** to), to curb; *(production, sorties, achats, dépenses)* to cut back (on), to restrict, to limit; *(autorité)* to limit; **une offre restreinte aux abonnés** an offer limited *or* restricted to subscribers; *Fin* **r. le crédit** to restrict credit
VPR se restreindre 1 *(réduire ses dépenses)* to cut down; **se r. dans ses achats/dépenses** to buy/spend less **2** *(d'un domaine de recherche etc)* to become narrower *or* restricted; **votre choix de montres s'est restreint** you don't have such a large selection of watches as you used to

restreint [rɛstrɛ̃] **ADJ** *(production, nombre de personnes, vocabulaire etc)* restricted, limited (**à** to); *(gamme, service)* limited; *(espace)* confined, limited; *(limites)* narrow; **édition à tirage r.** limited edition

restrictif, -ive [rɛstriktif, -iv] **ADJ** *(terme, clause, pratique etc)* restrictive

restriction [rɛstriksjɔ̃] **NF 1** *(diminution)* restriction; **restrictions budgétaires** budget restrictions **2** *(réserve)* reservation; **faire des restrictions** to express (some) reservations; **restrictions aux exportations** export restrictions; **restrictions gouvernementales** government restrictions; **restrictions journalistiques** reporting restrictions; **r. mentale** mental reservation; **sans r.** *(accord)* unconditional; *(approuver)* unconditionally, unreservedly, without reservation; *Ordinat* **r. d'accès** access restriction

restructuration [rəstryktyrasjɔ̃] NF **1** *(d'une industrie, d'une entreprise)* restructuring **2** *(de dette)* rescheduling

restructurer [rəstryktyre] VT **1** *(industrie, entreprise)* to restructure **2** *(dette)* to reschedule
   VPR **se restructurer** to be restructured

resucée [rəsyse] NF *très Fam* **1** *(de vin, de café etc)* drop; **je vous en verse une r.?** would you like a drop more? **2** *Péj (répétition) (d'une pièce de théâtre, d'un livre etc)* rehash

résultant, -ante [rezyltɑ̃, -ɑ̃t] ADJ resultant, resulting, consequent
   NF **résultante** consequence, result; *Math* resultant

résultat [rezylta] NM **1** *(de calculs)* result; *(d'une action, d'une enquête etc)* result, outcome; *(d'un traitement)* result, effect; **on arrive à d'excellents résultats avec ce médicament** we're getting excellent results with this drug; **résultats** *(d'examen, de concours)* results; **les résultats de ses recherches** the results of his/her research, his/her findings; **donner des résultats** to give results; **sans r.** without result *or* success; *(expérience)* inconclusive; *(remède)* ineffective; **j'ai essayé de le lui faire comprendre, sans r.** I tried unsuccessfully to make him understand; *Mktg* **résultats antérieurs** past performance; *Mktg* **résultats perçus** perceived performance; **ces révélations eurent pour r. la chute du gouvernement** these revelations led to *or* resulted in the fall of the Government; **ça a eu pour r. de le mettre en colère** it made him angry, he got angry as a result; **attendre le r. des courses** to wait for the racing results; *Fig* to wait and see what happens; *Fam* **r. ou r. des courses: il a été licencié** as a result he was dismissed, the upshot of it all was that he was dismissed **2** *Compta* result, profit *or* loss; **r. brut** gross return; **résultats d'exercice** *ou* **d'exploitation** trading results; **r. courant** profit before tax and extraordinary items; **r. d'exploitation** operating profit or loss; **r. de l'exercice** profit or loss for the financial year; **r. de la période** profit or loss for the financial period; **r. exceptionnel** extraordinary profit or loss; **r. financier** financial profit or loss; **r. net** net return; **résultats prévisionnels** earnings forecast

résulter [rezylte] VI *(used only in the inf, third person and prp; aux often* **être***)* to result, to arise (**de** from); **les avantages économiques qui en résultent** the resulting *or Fml* resultant economic benefits; **qu'en a-t-il résulté?** what was the result (of it)?, what came of it?, what was the outcome?; **ce qui résulte de ses propos, c'est que …** what emerges from *or* comes out of what he said is that …; **il en résulte que …** the result of this is that …; **il résulte de cette discussion que …** the outcome *or* result of the discussion is that …

résumé [rezyme] NM summary, résumé; *(d'un article scientifique)* abstract; *(d'un film, d'un livre)* synopsis; *Scol (livre)* study guide; **faire le r. de** *(texte)* to summarize, to give a summary *or* résumé of; *(histoire, situation)* to sum up, to summarize; *Jur* **r. des débats** summing up; **r. managérial** management summary; **en r.** *(en peu de mots)* in short, in brief; *(à tout prendre)* to sum up

résumer [rezyme] VT *(article, idées etc)* to summarize, to give a summary of; *(situation, argumentation, histoire)* to sum up; *Jur* **r. les débats** to sum up; **pour r. les faits** to sum up; **voilà toute l'affaire résumée en un mot** that's the whole thing in a nutshell
   VPR **se résumer** *(d'une personne)* to sum up; **pour me r.** to sum up; **voilà à quoi tout cela se résume** that's what it all amounts to *or Fam* boils down to; **tout cela se résume en un seul mot/à peu de choses** it can all be summed up in one word/in a few words

> Il faut noter que le verbe anglais **to resume** est un faux ami. Il signifie **reprendre, recommencer.**

résurgence [rezyrʒɑ̃s] NF *(du racisme, d'une doctrine etc)* resurgence, reappearance; *(d'un courant sous-terrain)* resurgence

résurgent [rezyrʒɑ̃] ADJ *(courant)* resurgent

resurgir [rəsyrʒir] VI to reappear suddenly; **cette idée resurgit dans mon esprit** the idea suddenly came back to me

résurrection [rezyrɛksjɔ̃] NF **1** *Rel* resurrection **2** *Fig (des arts, du passé etc)* resurrection, revival

retable [rətabl] NM reredos, altarpiece

rétabli [retabli] ADJ *(après une maladie)* recovered

rétablir [retablir] VT **1** *(ordre, dynastie, paix etc)* to restore, to bring back; *(communications, relations, réputation)* to restore, to re-establish; **le gaz/l'eau a été rétabli(e)** the gas/water has been reconnected *or* restored *or Fam* is back on; **r. qn** *(d'un traitement etc)* to restore sb to health; **r. sa santé** to recover one's health **2** *(texte, finances)* to restore; **r. les faits** *ou* **la vérité** to set the record straight **3 r. qn (dans ses fonctions)** *(fonctionnaire etc)* to reinstate sb; **r. un officier dans son commandement** to restore an officer to his command; **r. qn dans ses droits** to restore sb's rights
   VPR **se rétablir 1** *(après une maladie)* to recover, to get well again; *(après un saut)* to recover **2 l'ordre se rétablit** order is being restored; **le silence s'est rétabli** silence returned **3 se r. dans les bonnes grâces de qn** to get back into sb's good books **4** *Gym* to push oneself up

rétablissement [retablismɑ̃] NM **1** *(de l'ordre, de la paix, d'une dynastie etc)* restoration; *(des communications, des relations)* re-establishment, restoration; *(d'un fonctionnaire etc)* reinstatement; **le r. du téléphone est prévu pour demain** the telephone should be reconnected by tomorrow; **r. de la religion** religious revival **2** *(après une maladie, après un saut)* recovery; **nous vous souhaitons un prompt r.** all our good wishes for a speedy recovery; **faire un mauvais r.** *(après un saut)* to land *or* recover badly **3** *Gym* push-up; **faire un r.** to push oneself up

rétamage [retamaʒ] NM *(d'une casserole etc)* retinning; *(d'un miroir)* resilvering

rétamé [retame] ADJ *Fam (ivre)* canned; *(fatigué)* whacked, dead on one's feet; *(financièrement)* broke

rétamer [retame] VT **1** *(casserole etc)* to retin **2** *(miroir)* to resilver **3** *Fam (enivrer)* to get canned; *(fatiguer)* to wear out; *(au jeu)* to clean out; **se faire r.** *(perdre un match)* to get hammered, to get slaughtered; **je me suis fait r. en anglais** I got a lousy mark in *or Am* I really flunked the English test
   VPR **se rétamer** *Fam (tomber)* to tumble; *(échouer)* to fail, *Am* to flunk; **elle s'est rétamée à l'oral** she failed *or Am* she flunked the oral

rétameur [retamœr] NM *(de casserole etc)* tinsmith

retapage [rətapaʒ] NM *Fam (d'une vieille maison, d'une voiture etc)* doing up; *(d'un lit)* straightening

retape [rətap] NF *très Fam* **faire (de) la r.** *(d'une prostituée, d'un représentant)* to tout for business *or* custom; *(d'un parti politique)* to tout for new members

retaper [rətape] VT **1** *Fam (vieille maison, voiture etc)* to do up; *(lit)* to straighten; **r. qn** to pick sb up **2** *(à la machine) (lettre etc)* to retype, to type again
   VPR **se retaper** *Fam* **1** *(après une maladie)* to get back on one's feet **2 on se retape une belote?** how about another game of belote?

retapisser [rətapise] VT **1** *(pièce etc)* to repaper; *(fauteuil)* to re-cover, to reupholster **2** *Arg (reconnaître)* to clock

retard [rətar] NM **1** *(dans le temps)* delay; *(de personne attendue)* lateness; **il y aura une heure de r.** there will be an hour's delay; **j'ai une heure de r.** I'm an hour late; **son bébé est né avec cinq jours de r.** her baby was born five days late; **je vous prie de m'excuser pour mon** *ou* **ce r.** please excuse me for being late; **et comment expliquez-vous votre r.?** how do you explain your being late *or* your lateness?; **cinq retards par semestre et c'est la porte** if you're late five times per term you're out; **sans r.** immediately, without delay; **avoir du r.** to be late; **le train a du r.** the train is (running) late; **le train a dix minutes de r.** *ou* **est en r. de dix minutes** the train is ten minutes late; **prendre du r.** to fall behind; *(d'un train)* to be running late; **mettre qn en r.** to make sb late, to delay sb; **arriver en r.** to arrive late; **être en r.** to be late; *(sur un programme)* to be behind; *(d'une horloge, d'une montre)* to be slow; **je suis en r. pour la réunion** I'm late for the meeting; **je suis en r. pour le paiement des remboursements** I'm behind with my repayments; **rattraper** *ou* **combler son r.** to catch up; **combler** *ou* **refaire son r. avec le peloton de tête** *(d'un athlète)* to close the gap with *or* to catch up on the front pack; *Com* **compte en r.** account outstanding *or* overdue; **r. de paiement** delay in payment, late payment **2** *(dans un développement)* backwardness; **le r. dont souffre le pays** the backwardness *or* backward state of the country; **r. mental** backwardness, mental retardation; **ils ont une génération de r.** they're a generation behind; **pays en r. sur les autres** backward country, country lagging behind the others; **cet enfant est en r. pour son âge** this child is backward *or* behind for his age; **élève en r. sur les autres** pupil lagging behind the others; **être en r. de dix ans sur les autres pays industrialisés** to be (lagging) ten years behind other industrialized countries; **en r. sur son temps** behind the times; **cet enfant aura du mal à combler son r.** this child will have trouble catching up; **nous voulons aider les pays en voie de développement à combler leur r.** we want to help developing countries to catch up *or* to close the gap; **être en r. pour** *ou* **dans qch** to be *or* lag behind in sth **3** *Aut* **r. à l'allumage** ignition lag, retarded ignition; *Élec* **r. d'aimantation** magnetic lag
   ADJ INV *Pharm (médicament)* slow-release

retardataire [rətardatɛr] ADJ **1** *(qui arrive en retard) (personne)* late **2** *(dans son développement) (pays)* backward; *(enfant)* slow, backward; *(idées, entreprise)* behind the times, out-of-date
   N latecomer

retardateur, -trice [rətardatœr, -tris] ADJ retarding; *(tactiques)* delaying
   NM *Phot* self-timer

retardé [rətarde] ADJ **1** *(départ)* delayed, late; *(arrivée)* late **2** *(mentalement) (élève)* lagging behind, slow; **enfant r.** backward *or* retarded child

retardement [rətardəmɑ̃] **NM** delay; *Mil* **action de r.** delaying action; **bombe à r.** time bomb; *Fig* **faire qch à r.** to be slow to do *or* in doing sth; **j'ai compris à r.** I was slow on the uptake; **comprendre une allusion à r.** to be slow in taking *or* to take a hint

retarder [rətarde] **VT 1** *(faire arriver en retard) (personne, train etc)* to delay, to hold up; **vous êtes sûr que cela ne vous retardera pas?** are you sure that it won't delay you *or* hold you up?; **les absences répétées retardent les progrès** repeated absences will delay progress; **la tuberculose l'a retardé dans ses études** having tuberculosis has held *or* kept him back in his studies **2** *(différer) (événement, départ, voyage etc)* to delay, to postpone, to put off; *(paiement)* to defer, to delay; **l'intervention du Président a été retardée d'une heure** the President's address has been moved forward one hour; *Aut* **r. l'allumage** to retard the ignition **3** *(montre, horloge)* to put back (**de** by)
VI 1 **l'horloge retarde** the clock is slow; **ma montre retarde** *ou Fam* **je retarde de dix minutes** my watch is *or* I'm ten minutes slow; **pendule qui retarde de dix minutes par jour** clock that loses ten minutes a day; **il retarde sur son temps** *ou* **époque** he's behind the times; *Fam* **vous retardez** *(vous n'êtes pas au courant)* you're behind the times **2** *Tech* to lag
VPR se retarder to make oneself late

retâter [rətɑte] **VT r. qch** to feel sth again
VI *Fam* **r. de qch** to have another go at sth; **r. de la prison** to do another stretch

reteindre [rətɛ̃dr] **VT** *(conj like* **teindre***)* to redye, to dye again

retéléphoner [rətelefɔne] **VI** to ring *or* call back *or* again; **r. à qn** to ring sb up *or* call sb (up) again, to ring *or* call sb back
VPR se retéléphoner to call each other again, to speak to each other on the phone again; **allez, on se retéléphone demain, d'accord?** talk to you again tomorrow, OK?

retendre [rətɑ̃dr] **VT 1** *(cordes)* to retighten; *(raquette)* to retension; *(piège)* to reset **2 r. la main** to hold out one's hand again

RETENIR [rət(ə)nir] *(conj like* **tenir***)*

VT to hold back **1** ▪ to hold **2** ▪ to withhold **3** ▪ to remember **4** ▪ to book **5** ▪ to restrain **8**	
VPR to hold on **1** ▪ to restrain oneself **2**	

VT 1 *(faire rester) (personne)* to hold back, to detain, to delay; *(chien)* to hold back, to restrain; **je ne vous retiens pas** I mustn't keep you (back), I mustn't hold you back; **ils nous ont retenus trois quarts d'heure** they kept us three quarters of an hour; **r. qn à dîner** to invite sb to stay for dinner; **elle m'a retenu par le bras** she held me back by the arm; **la grippe m'a retenue au lit pendant dix jours** the flu kept me in bed for ten days; **rien ne me retenait en France** there was nothing to keep me in France; **cette question ne nous retiendra pas** this question need not detain us; **r. l'attention de qn** *(d'un projet, d'une candidature)* to catch sb's attention; **elle a réussi à r. leur attention pendant trois heures** she managed to hold their attention for three hours; **r. la foule** to keep back *or* hold back *or* contain the crowd; **r. qn prisonnier/en otage** to keep *or* hold sb prisoner/hostage; **r. des marchandises en douane** to hold goods up at customs; *Naut* **retenu par les glaces** ice-bound
2 *(maintenir)* to hold in position, to secure, to retain; **r. l'eau** to hold water; *(d'une personne)* to retain water
3 *(garder) (argent)* to withhold; *(cotisation,*

impôt) to deduct (**sur** from); **retenu à la source** deducted at source; **r. 500 euros sur le salaire de qn** to keep back *or* deduct 500 euros from sb's wages; **la plainte a été retenue contre lui** he was charged; **aucune charge n'a été retenue contre vous** all charges against you have been dropped
4 *(se souvenir de) (leçon, nom etc)* to remember; **retenez ce numéro** remember *or* don't forget the number; **je n'ai pas retenu les chiffres** I don't *or* can't remember the figures; **qu'en avez-vous retenu?** how much of it can you remember?; **je le retiens, ton ami!** I won't forget your friend in a hurry!, I'll remember your friend all right!
5 *(réserver) (place, chambre, table etc)* to reserve, to book; *(chambre d'hôtel)* to hold, *Spéc* to block; *(personnel)* to engage; **nous pouvons r. une chambre pour vous jusqu'à demain** we can hold a room for you until tomorrow
6 *(accepter) (projet, suggestion)* to adopt; **deux candidats ont été retenus** *(ont réussi)* two applicants were successful; *(sont admis à l'épreuve suivante)* two applicants have been short-listed; **votre candidature n'a pas été retenue** your application was unsuccessful
7 *Math* **je pose 2 et je retiens 5** put down 2 and carry 5
8 *(contrôler) (colère)* to restrain, to contain, to curb; *(joie, enthousiasme)* to restrain, to contain; *(larmes)* to keep back, to hold back; *(cri)* to stifle, to smother; *(personne)* to restrain, to hold back; **la peur/la modestie m'a retenu** fear/modesty held me back; **r. qn de faire qch** to restrain sb *or* to hold sb back from doing sth; **qu'est-ce qui vous retient?** what's holding you back?; **qu'est-ce qui te retient de le lui dire?** what's stopping *or* preventing you telling him/her?; **retenez-moi ou je fais un scandale** hold me back or I'm going to make a scene; **r. son souffle** *ou* **sa respiration** to hold one's breath; **nous retenions notre souffle comme il allait annoncer les résultats** we waited with bated breath for him to announce the results
VPR se retenir 1 se r. à qch to hold on to sth; *Fig Hum* **se r. aux branches** to back-pedal; **c'est ça, retiens-toi aux branches!** that's it, start back-pedalling!
2 *(se contenir)* to restrain *or* control *or* contain oneself; *(contrôler un besoin naturel)* to hold on; **se r. de faire qch** to stop oneself (from) doing sth, *Fml* to refrain from doing sth; **je n'ai pas pu me r. de pleurer/rire** I couldn't help crying/laughing; **il faut que tu te retiennes, il n'y a pas de toilettes ici** you're going to have to hold it in, there are no toilets here
3 **une comptine qui se retient facilement** a counting rhyme that is easy to remember

rétenteur, -trice [retɑ̃tœr, -tris] **ADJ** *(force)* retaining; *Anat* **muscle r.** retentor (muscle)

rétention [retɑ̃sjɔ̃] **NF** holding back; *Méd (d'eau etc)* retention; *Méd* **faire de la r. d'eau** to be retaining water; *Méd* **r. d'urine** urine retention; **faire de la r. d'information** to hold back *or* withhold information; *Jur* **droit de r.** lien (**de** on); *Psy* **r. sélective** selective retention, selective recall; *Jur* **r. administrative** = detention of illegal immigrants or of asylum-seekers due to be deported

retentir [rətɑ̃tir] **VI 1** to (re)sound, to echo, to ring; *(d'un Klaxon®)* to sound, to honk; *(du tonnerre, du canon)* to crash; *(d'une alarme)* to ring, to sound; *(d'un coup de feu, cri)* to ring out; **le champ retentit de leurs cris** the field resounded *or* echoed *or* rang with their shouts; **la salle retentissait d'acclamations** the hall rang out with applause; **l'explosion retentit dans toute la ville** the explosion was heard right across the city;

leurs cris retentissaient à mes oreilles their cries were ringing in my ears **2** *Fig* **r. sur** to have an effect *or* impact on

retentissant [rətɑ̃tisɑ̃] **ADJ** *(voix)* resounding, ringing, booming; *(succès)* resounding; *(échec)* resounding, dismal; **discours r.** speech that arouses wide interest; **un bruit r.** an earth-shattering noise; **un scandale r.** a sensational scandal

retentissement [rətɑ̃tismɑ̃] **NM 1** *Litt (bruit)* resounding *or* echoing sound *or* noise **2** *Fig (d'un événement etc)* impact, repercussions; **procès qui a eu un grand r.** lawsuit that aroused wide interest *or* that made a great stir; **cela a eu un grand r. sur sa carrière politique** it had a considerable impact on his political career

retenu [rət(ə)ny] **ADJ 1** *(réservé)* reserved; **s'exprimer de façon retenue** to express oneself in restrained terms, to be restrained **2** *Scol* **élève r.** pupil in detention; **vous êtes r. samedi matin** you'll do detention *or* be kept in on Saturday morning

retenue [rət(ə)ny] **NF 1** *(sur salaire etc)* deduction, stoppage; **r. sur salaire** wage deduction; *(mensuel)* salary deduction; **faire une r. de 5% sur les salaires** to stop *or* deduct 5% from the wages; **r. à la source** deduction at source; **retenues patronales** employer's contributions; **retenues salariales** wage deductions, employee's contributions
2 *Math* carry over; **n'oublie pas la r.** don't forget the number you carried over; **n'oublie pas les retenues quand tu fais des additions** don't forget to carry over when you're doing sums
3 *Scol* detention; **mettre un élève en r.** to keep a pupil in, to give a pupil detention
4 *(discrétion)* reserve, restraint; **il manque de r. avec les gens** he's a bit too forthcoming with people; **manger avec r.** to eat sparingly; **s'exprimer sans r.** to express oneself without restraint *or* in unrestrained terms
5 *(eau) (dans un barrage)* impounded water, reservoir water; **lac de r.** impoundment, dam reservoir; **clapet de r.** back-pressure *or* non-return valve
6 *(barrage)* dam
7 *(fait de garder) (de biens par la douane)* holding
8 *Naut (d'un cordage)* stay, guy

réticence [retisɑ̃s] **NF 1** *(hésitation)* hesitation, unwillingness; **sans r.** unhesitatingly, without reservation, unreservedly; **après bien des réticences, il a dit oui** after much hesitation, he said yes; **non sans r.** not without reservations **2** *(omission)* omission

réticent [retisɑ̃] **ADJ** *(hésitant)* hesitant, unwilling (**à faire qch** to do sth)

> Il faut noter que l'adjectif anglais **reticent** est un faux ami. Il signifie **réservé**, **discret**.

réticulaire [retikylɛr] **ADJ** reticular

réticule [retikyl] **NM 1** *(sac)* (small) ladies' handbag **2** *Opt* reticle, cross wires

réticulé [retikyle] **ADJ** reticulate(d)

rétif, -ive [retif, -iv] **ADJ** *(cheval)* stubborn; *(personne)* recalcitrant

rétine [retin] **NF** *Anat* retina

rétinien, -ienne [retinjɛ̃, -jɛn] **ADJ** *Anat* retinal

retirable [rətirabl] **ADJ** withdrawable; **votre argent est r. à tout moment** you can withdraw money at any time

retirage [rətiraʒ] **NM** *(d'un livre, d'une photo etc)* reprinting

retiré [rətire] **ADJ 1** *(lieu)* secluded, remote; *(vie)* solitary; **vivre r. (de la société)** to live in seclusion, to live a solitary life **2** *(à la retraite)* retired; **être r. des affaires** to have retired from business

RETIRER [rətire]

VT to take out **1** ▪ to take off **1, 4** ▪ to remove **1, 4** ▪ to withdraw **1, 5** ▪ to extract **3** ▪ to take back **5** VPR to retire **1, 2** ▪ to withdraw **1** ▪ to subside **3** ▪ to recede **3**

VT **1** (faire sortir) to take out; (aller chercher) to take or get out; (quelque chose d'encastré) to get out; (argent de son compte) to withdraw, to take out (**de** from); (bagages) to reclaim, to collect (**de** from); (billet) to collect, to pick up (**de** from); (bouchon, épine) to pull or get out (**de** of), to remove (**de** from); **r. un enfant du collège** to remove a child from school, to take a child away from school; **r. un athlète d'une course** to withdraw an athlete from a race; **r. des pièces de la circulation** to withdraw coins from circulation; **r. des marchandises de la douane** to take goods out of bond, to clear goods; **r. des marchandises de la circulation** to withdraw goods from circulation; **r. du marché** to take off the market, to demarket; **r. progressivement** (produit) to phase out; **r. sa participation d'une société** to sell one's shares in a company, to sell out; **retire tous ces papiers de (sur) la table** get or clear all those papers off the table; **r. les mains de ses poches** to take one's hands out of one's pockets; **on ne lui retirera pas de l'idée qu'il mérite mieux** he won't be persuaded or convinced that he doesn't deserve better

2 (se procurer) **r. un profit de qch** to make a profit out of sth, to profit from sth; Fig to benefit from sth, to profit from sth; **combien en avez-vous retiré?** how much did you get for it?; **quel plaisir peut-il en r.?** what pleasure can he get or derive from it?; **elle dit n'avoir retiré que des ennuis de cet accord** she says she got nothing but trouble out of the agreement

3 (extraire) (huile de schiste etc) to extract **4** (enlever) (gants, lunettes) to take off, to remove; (manteau, pull etc) to take off; **on me retire mon plâtre la semaine prochaine** I'm having the plaster removed or off next week; **r. sa main** to draw back or pull back one's hand; **retire ta main immédiatement ou je crie** get your hand off me immediately or I'll scream; **r. qch à qn** to withdraw sth from sb, to take away sth from sb; **r. son manteau à qn** (pour le déshabiller) to take off sb's coat; (pour le débarrasser) to take sb's coat; **on ne va pas lui r. le droit de garde** they're not going to take the custody of his children away from him; **personne n'a l'intention de te r. ton emploi** no one intends to take your job away from you; **r. le permis de conduire à qn** to disqualify or ban sb from driving, to take away or Fml revoke sb's driving licence; **on lui a retiré le ou son permis** he's been banned (from driving)

5 (revenir sur) (remarque, promesse) to withdraw, to take back; (offre), Jur (plainte) to withdraw; **r. sa candidature** (à une élection) to withdraw one's candidacy; (pour un travail) to withdraw one's application; **je retire ce que j'ai dit** I take it all back, forget what I said

6 (tirer de nouveau) **r. des coups de feu** to fire more shots; **r. une flèche** to shoot another arrow; Typ **r. un livre** to reprint a book VPR **se retirer 1** (s'en aller) to retire, to withdraw; (d'une foule) to move back or away; Mil to retire, to withdraw, to pull out; **se r. d'un consortium** to back or pull out of a consortium; **se r. dans sa chambre** to retire to one's room; **vous pouvez vous r.** that will be all, you may go; **se r. de la lutte** to retire from the field; **se r. (en faveur de qn)** (d'un candidat) to stand down (in favour of sb)

2 (d'un employé) to retire (**de** from); **se r.**

des affaires to retire from business

3 (des eaux) to subside; (de la mer) to recede; (de la marée) to ebb; **les eaux de la rivière se retirent** the level of the river is dropping

retombée [rətɔ̃be] NF **1** retombées radioactives radioactive fallout **2** Fig (répercussion) retombées repercussions; **l'une des retombées du programme spatial fut la mise au point de nouveaux matériaux** new materials were one of the spin-offs of the space programme; **la grève aura des retombées sur les prix** the strike will have repercussions or a knock-on effect on prices

retomber [rətɔ̃be] VI (aux often être) **1** (tomber de nouveau) to fall (down) again; (de la pluie, des bombes etc), Fig (d'une monnaie) to fall again; **r. dans son fauteuil** to fall back or sink back into one's armchair; **faire r. un store** to let down or pull down a blind; **laisser r. ses bras** to drop one's arms; **r. dans l'erreur** to lapse back into one's old ways; **r. dans le péché** to fall or sink back into one's sinful ways; **r. dans l'oubli** to sink back into obscurity or oblivion; **elle est retombée dans l'anonymat** she faded out of the limelight; **r. dans le désespoir** to fall back into despair; **le pays risque de r. dans la guerre civile** the country may lapse back into a state of civil war; **r. dans le vice** to relapse into vice; **r. en enfance** to lapse into one's second childhood; **r. malade** to fall or become ill again; Fam **r. sur qn** to bump into sb again

2 (tomber) (d'une personne, d'un ballon) to land; **r. sur ses pattes** (d'un chat) to land on its feet; Fig **r. sur ses pieds** ou Fam **ses pattes** to land on one's feet; **r. toujours dans la même situation** always to end up or land in the same situation; **pour éviter que la conversation ne retombe sur le même sujet** to prevent the conversation from coming round to the same subject again; **r. sur qch** (trouver) to come across or stumble on sth; **tu ne retomberas jamais sur une occasion pareille** you'll never come across an opportunity like it again; **le blâme/la responsabilité retombera sur lui** the blame/responsibility will fall on him; **faire r. le blâme sur qn** to put or lay the blame on sb; **tout retombe toujours sur moi!** it's always my fault!, I always get the blame for everything!; Fam **tout ça va me r. dessus** it'll all come back on me

3 (diminuer) (de l'enthousiasme, de l'intérêt) to fall off, to wane; (de l'attention) to fall off, to slacken

4 (des cheveux, des rideaux) to hang (down) (**sur** over); **ses cheveux lui retombent dans le dos** her hair hangs down her back; **laisser ses cheveux r.** to let or take one's hair down

retordre [rətɔrdr] VT **1** (linge) to wring out again **2** Tex (fil) to twist; Fam **il vous donnera du fil à r.** he'll give you trouble

rétorquer [retɔrke] VT **1 r. que ...** to retort that ... **2** (accusation) to cast back, to hurl back; **r. un argument contre qn** to turn sb's argument against him/her

retors [rətɔr] ADJ **1** Tex (fil, corde) twisted **2** (bec) curved **3** (personne) crafty, wily, devious

rétorsion [retɔrsjɔ̃] NF Jur, Pol retaliation; **mesures de r.** retaliatory measures

retouche [rətuʃ] NF (action) (d'un tableau, d'une photo etc) touching up, retouching; (d'un texte, d'un vêtement) altering; (résultat) (d'un tableau, d'une photo etc) retouch; (d'un texte, d'un vêtement) alteration; **faire des retouches à** (un vêtement) to make alterations to; (un tableau, une photo) to retouch; (un texte) to alter; **il faudra faire une r. dans le dos** it will have to be altered at the back; TV, Cin, Ordinat **r. d'image(s)** image editing

or retouching; TV, Cin **r. numérique** digital retouching

retoucher [rətuʃe] VT (tableau, photo etc) to touch up, to retouch; (texte) to touch up, to alter; (vêtement) to alter, to make alterations to VI **votre article est bien, n'y retouchez pas** your article is good, leave it alone or don't change a word of it; **je n'ai jamais retouché à la drogue** I've never touched drugs again

retoucheur, -euse [rətuʃœr, -øz] N **1** Beaux-Arts, Phot retoucher **2** (en confection) alteration hand

RETOUR [rətur] NM **1** (de voyage, après une absence) return; **être de r.** to be back (again); **être de r. de vacances** to be back from holiday; **un journaliste de r. de Paris** a reporter (just) back from Paris; **de r. chez moi, je lui écrivis** I wrote to him when I got home or on my return home; **à mon r.** on my return; **on en parlera à mon r.** we'll talk about it on my return or when I get back; **partir sans espoir de r.** to leave without any hope of returning; **être perdu sans r.** to be irretrievably lost; **point de non-r.** point of no return; **voyage/vol de r.** return journey or trip/flight; **pour le voyage de r., je passerai par Lyon** I'll be coming through Lyons on my way back; **billet aller r.** return ticket, Am round-trip ticket; **coupon de r.** return half; Fam **cheval de r.** (vieux criminel) old offender, old lag; **par r. (du courrier)** by return (of post); **r. à l'envoyeur** return to sender; **le r. de l'hiver/d'une maladie** the return of winter/recurrence of a disease; **faire un r. sur le passé** to look back on the past; **faire un r. sur soi** to take a good hard look at oneself; **r. à la nature/au calme** return to nature/a state of calm; **par un juste r. des choses, celui qui l'a fait a été puni** the one who did it was punished, as was only fair or as was only right and proper; Fam **être sur le r.** (d'une personne) to be past middle age or past one's prime; **beauté sur le r.** beauty on the wane

2 (changement) (de fortune) reversal; **un r. d'opinion** a backlash; **r. de conscience** qualms of conscience

3 **course de r.** (d'un piston) back stroke; **r. de carburateur** backfire; **avoir des retours** to backfire; **r. automatique de ruban** automatic ribbon reverse; Ordinat **r. d'information** feedback

4 TV, Radio (de son) foldback; Élec **r. à la terre** ou **à la masse** earth connection, earthing, Am grounding; **fil de r.** earth or Am ground wire

5 (de marchandises, de lettre) return; **marchandises de r.**, **retours** returns; **vendu avec faculté de r.** sold on a sale or return basis

6 Tennis **r. de service** return of serve

7 (sur clavier) return; **touche r.** return key; **appuyez sur la touche r.** press return; **r. arrière** backspace

8 (locutions) **payer qn de r.** to repay sb in kind; **payer de r. l'affection de qn** to return sb's affection; **il ne semblait pas payer de r. ma curiosité pour lui** he didn't seem to be as curious about me as I was about him; **en r.** in return (**de** for); **aimer qn en r.** to return sb's love, to love sb back or in return; Sport **match r.** return match

▶▶ **r. d'âge** (d'une femme) change of life; Cin **r. en arrière** flashback; **faire un r. en arrière** to flash back; **r. de chariot** (de machine à écrire) carriage return; Ordinat **r. chariot obligatoire** hard carriage return; Aut **r. de flamme** blowback; Ordinat **r. ligne** line feed; Ordinat **r. ligne obligatoire** hard return; Aut **r. de manivelle** backfire kick; Fig **il y a eu un r. de manivelle** it backfired; **il faut s'attendre à des retours de manivelle** we'll have to expect a certain amount of backlash; Fin **r. net** net return; Ordinat **r. obligatoire** hard return; *Mil* **r. offensif** counter attack, counter stroke; *Com* **r. sans frais** return free of charge; **r. sur investissement** return on investment, ROI; **r. sur ventes** return on sales; *Biol* **r. à un type** reversion to type

retourne [rəturn] NF 1 *(aux cartes)* **la r. est à cœur** hearts are trumps 2 *Fam* **les avoir à la r.** to be bone idle

retournement [rəturnəmã] NM *(de situation)* turnaround, reversal; *(d'opinion)* about-turn (**de** in)

RETOURNER [rəturne]

> VT to turn inside out 1 ▪ to turn 2 ▪ to turn over 2 ▪ to turn up 2 ▪ to turn round 3 ▪ to return 4
> VI to go back 1 ▪ to return 1
> VPR to turn over 1 ▪ to turn round 2 ▪ to turn against *(se retourner contre)* 3

VT 1 *(en mettant la face intérieure à l'extérieur) (parapluie, gant, vêtement)* to turn inside out; **retournez vos poches** turn out your pockets

2 *(verticalement)* to turn over; *(terre)* to turn over or up; *(matelas, omelette, steak, foin)* to turn; *(carte)* to turn up; *Fig (idée, projet)* to turn over in one's mind, to mull over; **r. une salade** to toss a salad; **tourner et r. qch** to turn sth over and over (again); *Fig* **r. une question dans tous les sens** to look at or consider a question from every angle; *Fam* **on avait retourné tout le bureau pour trouver la lettre** they had turned the office upside down to find the letter; *Fam* **r. qn** *(le bouleverser)* to upset sb

3 *(horizontalement)* to turn round; **r. la tête** to turn one's head, to look round; **il retourna l'arme contre moi et tira** he turned the gun on me and fired; **r. un argument contre qn** to turn an argument against sb; **r. qn contre qn** to turn sb against sb; **r. une situation** to reverse a situation; *Fam* **elle l'a retourné comme un gant** she very quickly got him to change his mind; *Fam* **on le retourne comme un gant** he is easily swayed

4 *(renvoyer, rapporter)* to return; **r. qch à qn** to return sth to sb, to send sth back to sb; *Com* **r. un effet** to return a bill; **r. à l'expéditeur** to return to sender; **r. le compliment** to return the compliment; **je me permets de vous r. le compliment** the same to you

VI *(aux être)* 1 to go back, to return (**à** to); **r. chez soi** to go back home; **je retourne chez ma mère** I'm going back to my mother; **r. déjeuner chez soi** to go home for lunch; **je ne retournerai pas la voir** I won't go back and see her; **sa fortune retourne à sa famille** his fortune reverts to his family; **r. à l'état sauvage** to revert to the wild; **r. à ses premières amours** to return or go back to one's first love

2 **de quoi retourne-t-il?** *Cartes* what are trumps?; *Fig Fam* what's it all about?, what's up?; **si quelqu'un voulait bien me dire de quoi il retourne!** would someone please tell me what's going on!

VPR **se retourner** 1 *(d'un dormeur)* to turn over; *(d'une voiture)* to turn or *Fam* flip over; *Fig Fam* **ne pas avoir le temps de se r.** not to have time to draw breath; **laisse-lui le temps de se r.** give him time to sort himself out

2 *(tourner la tête)* to turn (round); **partir sans se r.** to leave without looking back; **on se retourne sur leur passage** they make heads turn, all heads turn when they go by

3 **se r. contre qn** *(d'une personne)* to turn against sb; *(verbalement)* to round or turn on sb; *(d'un chien)* to turn on sb; **cela finira par se r. contre lui** it'll eventually backfire on him

4 **s'en r. à un endroit** to return to or go back to a place; **s'en r. à un endroit/chez soi** to return or go back to a place/home

retracer [rətrase] VT *(conj like tracer)* 1 *(trait)* to draw again, to redraw, to retrace; *(sentier)* to mark out again 2 *Fig (raconter) (événement, vie etc)* to recount

rétractable [retraktabl] ADJ *(antenne)* retractable; *Aut (volant)* collapsible

rétractation [retraktasjɔ̃] NF retraction; *Jur (d'une sentence)* rescinding

rétracter [retrakte] VT *(griffes, antennes)* to retract, to draw in
  VPR **se rétracter** *(se contracter) (d'un muscle)* to retract

rétracter [retrakte] VT *(paroles)* to retract, to withdraw, to take back; *(aveu)* to retract; *Jur (arrêt)* to rescind
  VPR **se rétracter** *(se dédire)* to retract

rétracteur [retraktœr] ADJ, NM **(muscle) r.** retractor (muscle)

rétractile [retraktil] ADJ which can be retracted or pulled back, *Spéc* retractile; *Aut (volant)* collapsible

rétraction [retraksjɔ̃] NF retraction

retrait [rətrɛ] NM 1 *(du ciment etc)* shrinkage, shrinking 2 *(des eaux)* subsiding; *(d'un glacier)* retreat 3 *(d'argent, d'un ordre, d'une candidature, un permis etc)* withdrawal; *(de troupes)* withdrawal, pull-back; *(d'un cheval dans une course)* scratching; **r. des bagages** baggage (re)claim; **r. de marchandises** withdrawal of goods; **r. d'espèces** cash withdrawal; **faire un r.** to withdraw money; **r. automatique** automated withdrawal; **r. du permis de conduire** disqualification from driving, driving ban; **un r. de l'ordre de grève est hors de question** calling off the strike is out of the question 4 *(dans un mur)* recess; **en r.** *(étagères etc)* recessed; **maison en r.** house standing back or set back from the road; **en r. de la route** set back from the road; **être/rester en r.** *(d'une personne)* to be/stay in the background 5 *Typ* indent; **mettre en r.** to indent; **en r.** indented; **en r. négatif** hanging; **r. en sommaire** hanging indent; **r. inversé** reverse indent

retraite [rətrɛt] NF 1 *Mil etc* retreat, withdrawal; **battre en r.** to retreat, to beat a retreat, to retire; *Fig* to beat a retreat; **battre/sonner la r.** to beat/sound the retreat

2 *(fanfare)* tattoo; **r. aux flambeaux** torchlight tattoo or procession

3 *(de la vie active)* retirement; **caisse de r.** superannuation fund, pension fund; **être à la** ou **en r.** to be or to have retired; *(d'un officier)* to be on the retired list; **militaire en r.** army pensioner; **quand je serai à la r.** when I retire, when I've retired; **un médecin/policier à la r.** a retired doctor/police officer; **prendre sa r.** to retire; **quand j'ai pris ma r.** when I retired, on my retirement; **prendre sa r. anticipée** to take early retirement; **on parle d'une centaine de mises à la r. anticipée** there's talk of making about a hundred people take early retirement; **mettre qn à la r.** to retire sb, to pension sb off

4 *(pension)* retirement pension; **jouir d'une petite r.** to have a small pension; **r. par capitalisation** loanback pension; **r. complémentaire** supplementary pension; **prendre une r. complémentaire** to take out an extra pension scheme

5 **maison de r. (pour vieillards)** old people's home

6 *(isolement)* retreat; **faire une r.** to go into retreat

7 *(abri)* retreat, refuge; *(de bêtes sauvages)* lair, haunt; *(de voleurs)* hideout

8 *Archit (d'un mur, entre des étages)* offset; *(d'un mur)* recess

retraité, -ée [rətrete] ADJ *(à la retraite)* retired; *(officier)* on the retired list
  N *(personne du troisième âge)* senior citi-

zen, pensioner, *Br* OAP; **les retraités** retired people, senior citizens

retraitement [rətrɛtmã] NM *(de déchets nucléaires, combustible)* reprocessing; **usine de r.** reprocessing plant

retraiter [rətrete] VT 1 *Nucl (déchets, combustible)* to reprocess 2 *Méd (malade)* to treat again

retranchement [rətrãʃmã] NM *Mil* entrenchment; *Fig* **forcer qn dans ses (derniers) retranchements** to drive sb to the wall

retrancher [rətrãʃe] VT 1 *(ôter)* **r. un passage d'un livre** to cut or remove a passage from a book; **r. un nombre d'un autre** to take away or subtract one number from another; **r. qch sur une somme** to deduct sth from a sum of money; **r. qch à qn** to dock sb sth, to dock sth from sb; **r. un nom d'une liste** to remove or delete a name from a list 2 *Mil (position)* to entrench; *Fig* **être retranché** to be entrenched (**derrière ses croyances** in one's beliefs); *Fam* **vivre retranché dans son petit monde** to live in one's own little world or a world of one's own
  VPR **se retrancher** *Mil* to entrench oneself, to dig in; *Fig* **se r. dans le silence** ou **le mutisme** to take refuge in silence; **se r. derrière qn** to hide behind sb

retranscription [rətrãskripsjɔ̃] NF retranscription

retranscrire [rətrãskrir] VT to retranscribe

retransmetteur [rətrãsmɛtœr] NM *Radio (appareil)* relay

retransmettre [rətrãsmɛtr] VT *(conj like transmettre)* to transmit, to broadcast; *(relayer)* to retransmit, to relay

retransmission [rətrãsmisjɔ̃] NF transmission, broadcast(ing); *(par relai)* retransmission, relay; **r. en direct de Cardiff** (broadcast or relayed) live from Cardiff; **r. en différé de Cardiff** in a recorded relay from Cardiff, recorded live at Cardiff earlier; **la r. du match est prévue pour 14 heures 45** and you can see the match at 2. 45 pm

retravailler [rətravaje] VT *(discours, texte etc)* to rework, to work on again; *(exercice de gym, muscle)* to work on again; *(argile, pâte etc)* to work again; **votre thèse a besoin d'être retravaillée** your thesis needs reworking
  VI to go back to work; **après une longue période de chômage, il retravaille enfin** after being unemployed for a long time, he's finally working again

rétréci [retresi] ADJ *(route etc)*, *Fig Péj (esprit, vues)* narrow; *(vêtement)* shrunken

rétrécir [retresir] VT 1 *(rendre plus étroit) (route)* to narrow; *(vêtement)* to take in 2 *(au lavage) (vêtement)* to shrink
  VI *(de vêtement, de tissu)* to shrink; *Fig* **son univers** ou **son horizon a beaucoup rétréci** his world has become much narrower
  VPR **se rétrécir** to narrow, to become narrower; **le chemin continue en se rétrécissant** the path gets narrower and narrower

rétrécissement [retresismã] NM 1 *(action) (d'une route)* narrowing; *(d'un vêtement, un tissu)* shrinking 2 *Méd* narrowing, constriction, *Spéc* stricture 3 *(partie) (d'un tuyau, une route etc)* narrow part

retrempe [rətrãp] NF *(de l'acier)* retempering

retremper [rətrãpe] VT 1 *(linge)* to soak or steep again 2 *(acier)* to retemper
  VPR **se retremper** 1 *(dans l'eau)* to have another quick dip 2 *Fig Fam* **se r. dans un milieu sympathique/le milieu familial** to plunge back into a congenial atmosphere/the family atmosphere

rétribuer [retribɥe] VT *(employé)* to pay; *(travail, service)* to pay for; **travail rétribué**

paid work; **être bien/mal rétribué** to be well/badly paid

rétribution [retribysjɔ̃] NF *(paie) (pour des services)* payment, remuneration; **fonctions sans r.** honorary duties

---

Il faut noter que le terme anglais **retribution** est un faux ami. Il signifie **châtiment**.

---

retriever [retrivœr] NM *(chien)* retriever

rétro [retro] NM **1** *Billard* pull-back, screwback (stroke) **2** = **rétroviseur 3** *(style)* retro ◆ ADJ INV *(film, robe, mode, musique etc)* retro ◆ ADV **s'habiller r.** to wear retro clothes; **leur appartement est meublé r.** their flat is furnished in retro style

rétroactif, -ive [retroaktif, -iv] ADJ *(loi etc)* retroactive; **augmentation avec effet r. au 1er juillet** increase backdated *or* retroactive to 1 July

rétroaction [retroaksjɔ̃] NF *Radio, Électron* feedback; **r. acoustique** acoustic feedback; **r. d'une augmentation de salaire** backdating of a rise, making a rise retroactive

rétroactivement [retroaktivmɑ̃] ADV retroactively

rétroactivité [retroaktivite] NF retroactive nature

rétrocéder [retrosede] *(conj like* **céder***)* VT *(revendre)* to resell; *(droit etc)* to cede back, to release back, to retrocede

rétrocession [retrosesjɔ̃] NF *(d'un droit, un don)* releasing back, retrocession

rétroéclairage [retroeklera3] NM *Ordinat* backlighting

rétroéclairé [retroeklere] ADJ *Ordinat* backlit

rétroflexe [retrofleks] ADJ *Ling* retroflex

rétrofusée [retrofyze] NF retrorocket

rétrogradage [retrograda3] NM *Aut* downchange, downshift, changing down

rétrogradation [retrogradasjɔ̃] NF **1** *Litt (dans un développement)* regression, retrogression **2** *(d'un sous-officier)* reduction in rank, demotion; *(d'un fonctionnaire)* demotion, downgrading

rétrograde [retrograd] ADJ *(mouvement)* retrograde, backward; *Fig (idée)* reactionary; *Pol (mesure, politique)* retrograde, reactionary; *Billard* **effet r.** pull-back, screwback; **phrase r.** palindrome ◆ N *Pol* reactionary

rétrograder [retrograde] VI **1** to move backwards; *Mil* to fall back, to retreat; *Fig (dans son développement)* to regress, to retrogress; *Sport* **il a rétrogradé en cinquième position** he's fallen back to fifth place **2** *Aut* to change *or* shift down; **r. de troisième en seconde** to change down from third to second ◆ VT *(sous-officier)* to reduce in rank, to demote, *Am Fam* to bust; *(fonctionnaire)* to demote, to downgrade

rétrogression [retrogresjɔ̃] NF *(mouvement)* retrogression

rétropédalage [retropedala3] NM *Cyclisme* back-pedalling

rétropédaler [retropedale] VI *Cyclisme* to back-pedal

rétroprojecteur [retroprojɛktœr] NM overhead projector

rétropropulsion [retropropylsjɔ̃] NF *Astronaut* reverse thrust

rétrospectif, -ive [retrospɛktif, -iv] ADJ retrospective; **j'ai eu une peur/jalousie rétrospective** I was frightened/jealous in retrospect ◆ NF **rétrospective 1** *Beaux-Arts etc, Fig* retrospective; *Can Cin* flashback; **une rétrospective de l'année 1944** a look back at the events of 1944; *Cin* **rétrospective René Clair** René Clair retrospective **2** *Fin* review

rétrospectivement [retrospɛktivmɑ̃] ADV retrospectively, in retrospect; **ça me fait peur r.** it frightens me in retrospect *or* looking back on it

retroussé [rɔtruse] ADJ *(manches)* rolled-up; **nez r.** snub *or* turned-up *or Litt* retroussé nose

retroussement [rɔtrusmɑ̃] NM **avec un r. des lèvres** with a curl of the lip

retrousser [rɔtruse] VT *(manches, pantalon)* to turn up, to roll up; *(jupe)* to tuck up; *(lèvres)* to curl (up); *Fig* **r. ses manches** to roll up one's sleeves ◆ VPR **se retrousser** *(d'une femme)* to tuck up one's skirt(s); *(d'une jupe)* to bunch up

retroussis [rɔtrusi] NM *(de vêtement)* turned-back facings; **bottes à r.** topboots

retrouvable [rɔtruvabl] ADJ recoverable, retrievable; **facilement r.** easy to find, easily found

retrouvailles [rɔtruvaj] NFPL reunion

RETROUVER [rɔtruve]

| VT to find **1** ■ to recover **1** ■ to regain **1** ■ to get back **1** ■ to meet up with **2** | VPR to end up **1** ■ to find one's way **2** ■ to meet **3** ■ to exist **5** |

VT **1** to find again; *(objet perdu)* to find; *(personne)* to track down; *Fig (santé, forces, enthousiasme etc)* to recover, to regain; *(sa voix)* to get back; *(son appétit)* to get back, to recover; **r. son chemin** to find one's way again; **je n'arrive pas à r. son adresse** I can't find his address; *Prov* **un(e) de perdu(e), dix de retrouvé(e)s** there are (plenty) more fish in the sea; **la clef a été retrouvée, on a retrouvé la clé** the key has been found; **elle ne parvint jamais à le r.** she never found any trace of him; **la r. après tant d'années, à quoi bon?** what's the point of seeing her again after all this time?; **on retrouve chez lui la curiosité de sa grand-mère** he has his grandmother's curiosity; **on ne retrouve plus cet auteur dans son dernier roman** we don't recognize the author in his last novel, the author's last novel is uncharacteristic; **on retrouve souvent cette image dans le cinéma de Renoir** you often encounter *or* come across this image in Renoir's films; **tu ne retrouveras jamais une telle occasion** you'll never come across an opportunity like it again; **elle a retrouvé toute sa jeunesse en voyant ce film** the film took her back to her youth; **tu as retrouvé le sourire** you're looking more cheerful, you've discovered how to smile again; **tu as retrouvé la parole** *ou Fam* **ta langue, toi!** you've found your tongue again!

2 *(rejoindre)* **il doit r. ses parents à Venise** he's to join up *or* meet up with his parents in Venice; **je vous retrouverai devant le cinéma** I'll meet you outside the cinema; **je vous retrouve dans une heure au pub** I'll join you at the pub in an hour's time ◆ VPR **se retrouver 1 se r. dans la même position** to find oneself *or* to be in the same position again; **se r. à Paris** to be back in Paris; **je me retrouve donc à Paris** so here I am back in Paris; **finir par se r. au poste/à l'hôpital** to end up in the police station/hospital; *Fam* **tu vas te r. sans un sou** you're going to find yourself without a penny; *Fam* **et c'est comme ça que je me suis retrouvé à travailler ici** and that's how I found myself *or* came to be working here

2 *(retrouver son chemin)* to get *or* find one's bearings; **elle se retrouve très bien, dans Londres** she can find her way round London without any difficulty; *Fig* **je ne m'y retrouve plus!** I'm hopelessly confused *or* lost!; *Fam* **vous vous y retrouverez** *(financièrement)*

you'll get your money back soon enough

3 *(entre personnes)* to meet; **nous devons nous r. au restaurant** we're meeting at the restaurant; **ils se retrouvent tous les mardis** they meet every Tuesday, they get together every Tuesday; **nous voulions nous r. seuls pour parler** we wanted to be alone so we could talk; **on se retrouvera!** I'll get even (with you)!, you haven't heard the last of this!; **comme on se retrouve!** fancy meeting you!, it's a small world!

4 *(en soi-même)* to find oneself; **ce couple a besoin de se r.** they need to find each other again as a couple

5 *(exister)* to exist; **ce mot se retrouve dans de nombreuses langues** this word exists *or* can be found in numerous languages; *Fam* **ça se retrouve, des verres comme ça** glasses like that are easy to find *or* are easy to come by

rétroversion [retroversjɔ̃] NF *Méd* retroversion

rétrovirus [retrovirys] NM *Méd* retrovirus

rétroviseur [retrovizœr] NM *Aut* **r.** *(intérieur)* (rear-view) mirror; **r. extérieur** wing mirror, *Am* outside mirror; **r. jour/nuit** anti-glare rear-view mirror; **r. à double miroir** split-view mirror; **r. à position nuit** dipping rear-view mirror

rets [rɛ] NM *Litt* net; **prendre qn dans ses r.** to catch sb in one's toils

réuni [reyni] ADJ **1** *(rassemblé)* put together; **plus forts que nous et les Anglais réunis** stronger than us and the English put together *or* combined; **il s'est adressé à l'ensemble des élèves réunis** he addressed the assembled schoolchildren; **nous sommes réunis aujourd'hui pour ...** we are gathered together today to ... **2** *Com (laiteries etc)* amalgamated, united

réunification [reynifikasjɔ̃] NF *Pol* reunification

réunifier [reynifje] VT *Pol* to reunify

Réunion [reynjɔ̃] NF Réunion

réunion [reynjɔ̃] NF **1** *(action de rassembler)* *(de deux services)* merger, amalgamation; *(de faits, de renseignements etc)* gathering (together); *(de gens, de famille etc)* bringing together; *(à nouveau) (de famille, de parti politique etc)* reunion; *(action de joindre)* joining together; **r. d'une province à la France** union of a province with France; **cette r. de faits** this assemblage of facts; *Math* **r. de deux ensembles** union of two sets **2** *(action de se rassembler)* coming *or* gathering together; **droit de r.** right of assembly; **salle de r.** conference room **3** *(assemblée)* meeting; *(d'un comité)* session, sitting; *(réception dans un hôtel etc)* function; **le directeur est en r.** the manager is in a meeting; **r. de famille** family gathering *or* get-together; **r. électorale** election meeting; **r. publique** public meeting; **r. d'actionnaires** shareholders' meeting; **r. de comité** committee meeting; **r. du conseil** board meeting; **r. du conseil d'administration** board meeting; **r. des créanciers** creditors' meeting; *Mktg* **r. de groupe** *(pour enquête)* group meeting, focus-group session; *Mktg* **r. de remue-méninges** brainstorming session; *Mktg* **r. de représentants** sales meeting; *Pol* **r. au sommet** summit (meeting *or* conference)

Réunion [reynjɔ̃] NF Réunion

réunionite [reynjɔnit] NF *Fam Hum* mania for meetings, *Hum* meetingitis

réunionnais, -aise [reynjɔnɛ, -ɛz] ADJ of/from Réunion ◆ N **R.** *(natif)* native of Réunion; *(habitant)* inhabitant of Réunion

réunir [reynir] VT **1** *(rassembler) (d'une exposition) (objets d'art, toiles)* to bring *or* put together; *(faits, renseignements, documents,* *preuves etc)* to gather (together), to collect; *(somme d'argent, fonds)* to get together, to raise; *(personnes, famille etc)* to bring *or* get together; *(d'un colloque) (scientifiques etc)* to bring together; *(à nouveau) (famille, parti politique etc)* to reunite; *(services, classes)* to combine, to merge; **r. qch à qch** to join sth to sth; **r. une armée** to raise an army; **r. un comité** to convene a committee, to call a committee together **2** *(comporter) (qualités, avantages)* to have, to possess

VPR se réunir 1 *(de personnes)* to meet, to get *or* gather together; *(de routes)* to join up, to meet; **l'assemblée se réunit une fois par semaine** the assembly meets once a week; **se r. autour de qn/qch** to gather *or* congregate around sb/sth **2** *(de banques etc)* to amalgamate; *(d'églises, d'États etc)* to unite

réussi [reysi] ADJ successful; **être r.** *(d'un spectacle, une pièce, un plat)* to be successful *or* a success; *Iron* **c'est r.!, la voilà en larmes!** well done *or* very clever!, she's in tears now!; **mal r.** unsuccessful; **c'est à demi r.** it's partially successful

réussir [reysir] VI **1** to be successful, to be a success, to succeed; *(d'une plante)* to thrive; **c'est un garçon qui réussira** he's a boy who will do well *or* succeed *or* be successful; **le projet avait mal réussi** the plan had proved a failure; **ce truc-là ne réussira pas** that trick won't work, that trick won't come off; **tout lui réussit** he's successful in everything he does, everything he does turns out well; **r. dans qch** to succeed *or* be successful in sth; **il a réussi dans la vie** he's made a success of things; **une femme d'affaires qui a réussi** a successful businesswoman; **r. à un examen** to pass an examination; *Scol* **r. de justesse** to scrape through, to only just pass; **r. à faire qch** to succeed in doing sth, to manage to do sth; **tu as réussi (à finir/à l'ouvrir)?** did you manage (to finish/open it)?; *Iron* **elle a réussi à déranger tout le monde** she managed to disturb everybody; **ne pas r. à faire qch** not to have any success in doing sth, to fail to do sth; **je n'ai pas réussi à la convaincre** I didn't manage *or* I failed to persuade her, I didn't have any success in persuading her **2** *Fam* **le homard ne me réussit pas** lobster doesn't agree with me

VT *(quelque chose)* to make a success of, to be successful with; **elle réussit (bien) les omelettes** she makes very good omelettes; **c'est ta dissertation qui t'a permis de r. l'examen** it was your essay that got you through the exam; *Fam* **r. son coup** to do the trick, to bring it off; *Iron* **tu as bien réussi ton coup** well done, very clever

réussite [reysit] NF **1** *(succès)* success; **fêter sa r. à un examen** to celebrate passing an exam *or* getting through an exam; **cette soirée est une belle r.!** the party is a great success!; **l'une des plus belles réussites industrielles françaises** one of France's biggest industrial successes *or* success stories; **r. sociale** social success; **présenter tous les signes de la r.** to show every sign of succeeding *or* of being successful **2** *Cartes* patience, *Am* solitaire; **faire une r.** to play patience

réutilisation [reytilizasjɔ̃] NF reuse
réutiliser [reytilize] VT to reuse
revaccination [rəvaksinasjɔ̃] NF revaccination
revacciner [rəvaksine] VT to revaccinate
revaloir [rəvalwar] VT *(conj like* **valoir**; *used chiefly in the fu)* **je vous le revaudrai!, je vous revaudrai cela!** *(menace)* I'll get *or* pay you back for that!; *(reconnaissance)* I'll do the same for you some time!

revalorisation [rəvalɔrizasjɔ̃] NF **1** *(d'une monnaie)* revaluation; *(des salaires, du SMIC, des retraites)* upgrade, upgrading; *(de prix)* increasing **2** *(d'une image, d'une profession)* upgrade, upgrading; **cela doit aboutir à une r. de la fonction d'enseignant** this should have as an objective an upgrading of the role of the teacher

revaloriser [rəvalɔrize] VT **1** *(monnaie)* to revalue; *(salaire, SMIC, retraite)* to upgrade, to increase; *(prix)* to increase **2** *(image, profession etc)* to upgrade

revanchard, -arde [rəvɑ̃ʃar, -ard] ADJ, N *Pol Péj* revanchist

revanche [rəvɑ̃ʃ] NF **1** *(vengeance)* revenge; **prendre sa r.** to get one's revenge; **prendre sa r. sur qn** to take one's revenge on sb, to get one's own back on sb, to get even with sb; **je prendrai ma r. un jour** I'll get my revenge *or* get even one day; **vouloir prendre sa r.** to want revenge, to want to get even *or* to get one's own back **2** *Sport* return match *or* game; **je te laisserai prendre ta r. la semaine prochaine** I'll give you your revenge next week **3** *Fig* **en r.** *(en compensation)* in return, in compensation; *(au contraire)* on the other hand; **à charge de r.** on condition that I do the same for you

revanchisme [rəvɑ̃ʃism] NM *Pol* revanchism

revanchiste [rəvɑ̃ʃist] ADJ, N *Pol* revanchist

rêvasser [rɛvase] VI to daydream, to let one's mind wander

rêvasserie [rɛvasri] NF daydreaming; **rêvasseries** daydreams

rêvasseur, -euse [rɛvasœr, -øz] ADJ daydreaming
N (day)dreamer

rêve [rɛv] NM **1** *(de dormeur)* dream; **faire un r.** to (have a) dream; **voir qch en r.** to see sth in a dream *or* in one's dreams; **ça s'est passé comme dans un r.** it happened as if in a dream; **faites de beaux rêves!** pleasant *or* sweet dreams!; **la psychologie du r.** the psychology of dreams *or* of dreaming **2** *(idéal)* dream; **rêves de gloire/célébrité** dreams of glory/fame; **un r. devenu réalité** a dream come true; **maison/voiture de r.** dream house/car; **la maison de nos rêves** the house of our dreams, our dream house; **avoir une silhouette de r.** to have a gorgeous figure; **c'est le r.!** it's/he's/*etc* a dream *or* everything you ever dreamed of!

rêvé [rɛve] ADJ perfect, ideal

revêche [rəvɛʃ] ADJ **1** *(hargneux)* badtempered, cantankerous **2** *Vieilli (vêtement etc)* harsh, rough

réveil [revɛj] NM **1** waking, awakening; *Fig* awakening; **à mon r., au r.** on waking; **le r. de la nature** the awakening of Nature; **le r. d'un volcan** the renewed rumblings *or* the awakening of a volcano **2** *Mil* reveille; **sonner le r.** to sound reveille **3** *(pendulette)* alarm (clock); **mettre le r.** to set the alarm (**à six heures** for six o'clock); **radio-r.** radio alarm, clock radio; **r. automatique** automatic alarm; **r. de voyage** travel alarm clock; **r. téléphonique** *(dans un hôtel)* wake-up call

réveillé [reveje] ADJ awake; **je suis mal r.** I haven't woken up (properly) yet, I'm still half asleep

réveille-matin [revɛjmatɛ̃] NM INV alarm clock

réveiller [reveje] VT **1** *(tirer du sommeil)* to wake (up), to (a)waken; **réveillez-moi à sept heures** wake me (up) *or* waken me at seven o'clock; **Docteur, je n'arrive pas à la r.** I can't waken *or* rouse her, Doctor; **un bruit à r. les morts** a noise to wake the dead; *Prov* **ne réveillez pas le chat qui dort** let sleeping dogs lie **2** *Fig (classe ouvrière, pays)* to stir up, to rouse; *(souvenirs)* to awaken, to revive; *(courage, douleur)* to revive; **r. les consciences** to stir people's consciences

VPR **se réveiller 1** *(d'un dormeur)* to wake (up), to awake; *(de toute nouvelle)* to wake from a troubled sleep; *Fig* **c'est un pays qui est en train de se r.** the country is beginning to stir itself *or* shake itself *or* waken up **2** *(de sentiments)* to be awakened *or* roused *or* stirred (up) **3** *(de la nature, la végétation, l'économie)* to revive

réveillon [revɛjɔ̃] NM *(repas)* midnight supper; *(réjouissances)* midnight party *(after midnight Mass on Christmas Eve or New Year's Eve)*

> ### Réveillons
> Christmas is traditionally a family celebration. In Catholic families, the "crèche" or miniature nativity scene is decorated and everyone goes to midnight mass on Christmas Eve, after which the long and copious Christmas dinner is served: this includes oysters and, for dessert, the traditional "bûche de Noël" or yule log. The presents under the Christmas tree are opened either on Christmas Eve or on Christmas Day morning. The "réveillon de la Saint-Sylvestre" on New Year's Eve is usually celebrated among friends, either at home or in a restaurant. Champagne is drunk at midnight and everybody embraces and wishes each other a happy New Year. New Year greeting cards can, in theory, be sent up until the end of January.

réveillonner [revɛjɔne] VI to see Christmas/the New Year in *(with a midnight supper and party)*

réveillonneur, -euse [revɛjɔnœr, -øz] N (Christmas Eve/New Year's Eve) party-goer *or* reveller

révélateur, -trice [revelatœr, -tris] ADJ *(signe, attitude, silence etc)* revealing, telltale; *(remarque)* revealing, telling; *Chimie (substance)* tracer; **signe r. d'un changement** sign pointing to a change, tell-tale sign of a change; **c'est très r.** it is very revealing; **c'est r. de son manque de confiance en lui** it reveals *or* shows his lack of confidence
NM **1** *(d'une crise etc)* sign, indication **2** *Phot* developer

révélation [revelasjɔ̃] NF **1** *(action) (d'un secret, d'intentions etc)* revelation, disclosure; *Journ (d'un scandale etc)* exposé **2** *(découverte)* **ce fut une r.!** it was a revelation *or* an eye-opener!; **ce jeune musicien est la r. des années 90** this young musician is the discovery *or* find of the 90s *Rel* revelation; **la r. divine** divine revelation

révélé [revele] ADJ *(religion, vérité)* revealed

révéler [revele] (**je révèle, n. révélons; je révélerai**) VT **1** *(dévoiler) (secret, intention, projets etc)* to reveal, to disclose; *Journ* **r. ses sources** to reveal one's sources; **il révéla, sans le faire exprès, la vérité** he unwittingly let out the truth; **somme dont le montant n'a pas été révélé** undisclosed amount; **l'enquête révèle que …** the survey reveals that … **2** *(témoigner de) (talent, technique)* to show; *(gentillesse, humour)* to show, to reveal; *(défauts, ignorance, manque de confiance)* to show, to reveal, to betray **3** *Phot* to develop

VPR **se révéler 1** *(d'une personne)* to reveal oneself *or* one's character; **se r. difficile** to prove difficult; **il s'est révélé un bon ami** he proved (to be) *or* showed himself (to be) a good friend **2** **cela s'est révélé exact** it turned out *or* proved to be true

revenant, -ante [rəvnɑ̃, -ɑ̃t] ADJ *Vieilli (avenant)* pleasing, prepossessing
N ghost; **histoire de revenants** ghost story;

Fam Hum **voilà une revenante!** hello stranger!

revendable [rəvɑ̃dabl] ADJ resaleable

revendeur, -euse [rəvɑ̃dœr, -øz] N *Com* retailer; *(d'articles d'occasion)* second-hand dealer; *(de drogue)* dealer

revendicateur, -trice [rəvɑ̃dikatœr, -tris] ADJ *(discours, lettre etc)* setting forth one's claims *or* demands
▪ N person making demands; **je ne veux pas être mis dans le même sac que tous ces revendicateurs** I don't want to be classed as a troublemaker

revendicatif, -ive [rəvɑ̃dikatif, -iv] ADJ *(mouvement etc)* protest; **journée revendicative** day of protest

revendication [rəvɑ̃dikasjɔ̃] NF **1** *(action)* claiming **2** *(demande)* demand (**sur** on), claim; **les revendications ouvrières** labour demands; **r. salariale** wage demand, pay claim; **revendications syndicales** union demands; *Jur* **(action en) r.** action for recovery of property

revendiquer [rəvɑ̃dike] VT **1** *(demander)* to claim, to demand; *(droits)* to assert, to insist on; *(territoire, succession)* to lay claim to; **r. le droit de faire qch** to claim the right to do sth **2** *(assumer)* *(responsabilité)* to claim; **l'attentat n'a pas été revendiqué** nobody has claimed responsibility for the attack

revendre [rəvɑ̃dr] VT *(après achat)* to resell; *(vendre de nouveau)* to sell again; *Fig* **avoir des jouets/des CD à r.** to have more than enough toys/CDs; *Fig* **avoir du temps à r.** to have time to spare; *Fig* **avoir de la bonne humeur à r.** to be extremely good-natured; *Fig* **avoir de l'énergie à r.** to be bubbling over with energy

revenez-y [rəvnezi] NM INV *Fam* **ce gâteau a un goût de r.** this cake is very moreish; **ce voyage a un goût de r.** I wouldn't mind doing this trip again

REVENIR [rəv(ə)nir]

| to come back **1–3** ▪ to return **1, 2** ▪ to recur **1** ▪ to go back to *(revenir à)* **1** ▪ to go back on *(revenir sur)* **1** ▪ to get over *(revenir de)* **5** ▪ to cost *(revenir à)* **7** ▪ to amount to **8** |

VI *(conj like* **venir***; aux* **être***)* **1** *(rentrer)* to come back, to return; **il n'était jamais revenu en France** he had never been back to France; **je reviens tout de suite** I'll be back in a minute; **le temps passé ne revient plus** time that is past will never come again; **l'herbe reviendra** the grass will grow again *or* back; **ce nom/sujet revient souvent dans la conversation** this name/subject often turns up *or* crops up in conversation; **c'est un problème qui revient souvent chez les adolescents** it's a problem that often occurs with teenagers, it's a common problem with teenagers; **fête qui revient tous les dix ans** festival that occurs *or* recurs that comes round every ten years; **r. à la hâte** to hurry back; **r. en courant** to come running back, to run back; **r. à ses premières amours** to go back *or* return to one's first love; **vous y reviendrez!** *(à une méthode etc)* you'll go/come back to it!; **je suis revenu au régime lacté** I've gone back to a milk diet; **r. à la surface** *(d'un sous-marin)* to resurface; **en r. à qch** to come/go back *or* revert to sth; **pour en r. à la question/à ce que je disais** to come back to our subject/to what I was saying; **il n'y a pas à r. là-dessus** there is no going back on it; **r. de** to come back *or* return from; **r. de l'étranger** to come back from abroad; **je l'ai rencontré en revenant de l'église** I met him on my way back from church; **r. sur** *(ses aveux)* to retract; *(une promesse, une déci-*

sion) to go back on; *(son opinion)* to reconsider; *(un sujet)* to bring up again; *(le passé)* to rake up; **r. sur ses pas** to retrace one's steps, to turn back, to backtrack

2 *(de la force, du courage etc)* to return, to come back (**à qn** to sb); **l'appétit devrait lui r.** he should get his appetite back, his appetite should return; **il ne faudrait pas que ces paroles lui reviennent** don't let this get back to him; **la mémoire me revient** my memory is coming back; **c'est un honneur qui vous revient** the honour is yours by rights; **à chacun ce qui lui revient** to each his due

3 **cela me revient à la mémoire** it's coming back to me; *Fam* **ça me revient maintenant** I have it *or* I've got it now; **votre nom ne me revient pas** your name escapes me *or* has slipped my memory, I can't think of your name

4 *Fam* **il a une tête qui ne me revient pas** there's something about him I don't like; **si ta tête ne lui revient pas …** if he/she doesn't like the look of you …

5 **r. de sa surprise/d'une maladie** to recover from *or* get over one's surprise/an illness; **r. d'une théorie** to abandon a theory; **r. d'une erreur** to realize one's mistake; **je suis revenu de toutes mes illusions** I have lost all my illusions; **j'en suis revenu, de l'homéopathie!** I've had my fill of homeopathy!; **je n'en reviens pas!** *(étonnement)* I can't get over it!; **r. à la santé** to recover *or* regain one's health; **il revient de loin** *(il a failli mourir)* he has been at death's door; **r. à soi** to recover consciousness, to come round, to come to

6 *Culin* **faire r.** to brown

7 *(d'un prix)* **ça nous est revenu à cent euros par personne** it worked out at a hundred euros each; **ça me revient à deux cents euros par mois** it costs me *or* it works out at two hundred euros a month; **sa maison lui est revenue à plusieurs millions** his house cost him several million; **r. cher** to work out expensive, to cost a lot

8 *Fig* **cela revient au même** it amounts to the same thing, it comes (down) *or Fam* boils down to the same thing; **cela revient à dire que …** that amounts to saying that …
▪ VPR **se revenir** *Litt* **s'en r.** to return, to make one's way back; **comme il s'en revenait de l'école …** as he was coming *or* was on his way home from school …
▪ V IMPERS **il me revient encore 100 euros** I still have 100 euros coming *or* owing to me; **c'est à elle qu'il revient de faire la demande** it's up to her *or* down to her to ask; **il m'est revenu que …** it has come to my attention that …

revente [rəvɑ̃t] NF resale; **objet de r.** second-hand article; **r. à perte** selling at a loss

revenu [rəv(ə)ny] NM **1** *(d'une personne)* income; *(de l'État)* revenue; *(d'une entreprise)* revenue, income; **avoir un faible r.** to be on a low income; **impôt sur le r.** income tax; **politique des revenus** incomes policy; **à double r.** *(foyer, ménage)* double-income **2** *(d'un investissement, d'un capital)* income, yield
▸▸ **revenus accessoires** incidental income; **revenus actuels** current earnings; **r. annuel** annual income; *Mktg* **r. cannibalisé** cannibalized income; **r. cumulé** cumulative revenue; **r. dépensable** spendable income; **r. disponible** disposable income; **r. d'entreprise** corporate income, company earnings; **revenus de l'exportation** export revenue; **r. fictif** notional income; **r. fixe** fixed income; **r. généré par les ventes** sales revenue; **r. imposable** taxable income; **r. minimum d'insertion** income support, *Am* welfare; **r. national brut/net** gross/net national income; **r. personnel disponible** disposable personal income; **r. du travail** earned income

rêver [reve] VI **1** *(d'un dormeur)* to dream; **r. de qn/qch** to dream *or* have a dream about sb/sth; **on croit r.!** it can't be true!, I can't believe it!; **non, mais je rêve!** I must be dreaming!; *Fig* **j'en rêve la nuit** I dream about it at night **2** *(rêvasser)* to daydream *(à* about), to dream *(à* of); **je ne rêve pas, il l'a bien dit!** I'm not dreaming *or* I'm not imagining things, he did say it! **3** *(souhaiter)* **r. de** to dream of; **r. de faire** to dream of doing; **elle rêve de partir vivre là-bas** she dreams of going to live there, it is her dream to go and live there
▪ VT *(d'un dormeur)* *(quelque chose)* to dream of; **vous l'avez rêvé!** you must have imagined *or* dreamt it!, you must have been dreaming!; **j'ai rêvé que …** I dreamt (that) …; **r. sa vie au lieu de la vivre** to dream one's life away; **j'ai rêvé la même chose que toi** I dreamt the same thing as you; *Fig* **r. mariage** to dream of marriage

réverbération [reverberasjɔ̃] NF *(de la lumière, de la chaleur)* reflection; *(du son)* reverberation, echo

réverbère [reverber] NM **1** *(lampe)* street light *or* lamp; *(poteau)* lamppost **2** *(réflecteur)* (heat) reflector

réverbérer [reverbere] VT (**il réverbère; il réverbérera**) *(chaleur, lumière)* to reflect, to throw back; *(son)* to reverberate

reverdir [rəverdir] VI to grow *or* turn green again

révérence [reverɑ̃s] NF **1** *(déférence)* reverence (**envers, pour** for); *Fml Vieilli* **r. parler** with all due respect **2 Votre R.** Your Reverence **3** *(salut)* *(d'un homme)* bow; *(d'une femme)* curtsey; **faire la r. à qn** *(d'un homme)* to bow to sb; *(d'une femme)* to curtsey to sb; *Fig* **tirer sa r.** to leave; *Hum* **je vous tire ma r.** I'm off; **la société s'est automatisée, alors il a décidé de leur tirer sa r.** when the company automated, he decided to bow out

révérenciel, -ielle [reverɑ̃sjɛl] ADJ *Litt* **il m'inspire une crainte révérencielle** I stand in awe of him, I find him awe-inspiring

révérencieusement [reverɑ̃sjøzmɑ̃] ADV *Litt* reverently

révérencieux, -ieuse [reverɑ̃sjø, -jøz] ADJ *Litt* reverent; **peu r.** irreverent

révérend [reverɑ̃] *Rel* ADJ reverend; **le r. père Martin** Reverend Father Martin; **la révérende mère supérieure** the Reverend Mother Superior
▪ NM reverend; **oui, mon R.** yes, Reverend

révérer [revere] VT (**je révère, n. révérons; je révérerai**) to revere

rêverie [revri] NF *(activité)* dreaming, reverie, musing; *(moment)* daydream, reverie; *Litt* **elle est toujours plongée** *ou* **perdue dans de vagues rêveries** she's always daydreaming; **être dans une douce r.** to be starry-eyed; **il faut qu'elle cesse ses rêveries** she must stop this daydreaming

revernir [rəvernir] VT to revarnish

revers [rəver] NM **1** *(de pièce, de médaille etc)* reverse (side), back; *(de matériel)* wrong side; *(de page)* other side, back; **r. de la main** back of the hand; *Tennis* **(coup de) r.** backhand (stroke); *Mil* **prendre une position à r.** to capture a position in the rear; *Fig* **c'est le r. de la médaille** that's the other side of the coin **2** *(de manteau)* lapel; *(de chaussette)* turnover; *(de botte)* top; *(de manche)* cuff; **r. de pantalon** trouser turn-up *or Am* pant cuff; **habit à r. de velours** coat faced with velvet *or* with velvet facings; **bottes à r.** top boots **3** *(de fortune)* reversal (of fortune), setback; **les succès et les r. de la vie** the ups and downs of life

reversement [rəversəmɑ̃] NM additional payment

reverser [rəvɛrse] VT 1 (servir de nouveau) to pour out again; **je vous reverse un verre?** shall I pour you another glass? 2 (remettre) to pour back 3 Fin (somme) to transfer (**à, sur** to); (impôt) to pay

réverser [revɛrse] VT Typ (texte) to reverse out

réversibilité [revɛrsibilite] NF reversibility; Jur (d'une pension etc) revertibility; Aut (de la direction) kickback

réversible [revɛrsibl] ADJ 1 (processus, vêtement etc) reversible; Fig **l'histoire n'est pas r.** you can't put the clock back 2 Jur (pension etc) revertible

réversion [revɛrsjɔ̃] NF Jur, Biol reversion

revêtement [rəvɛtmɑ̃] NM 1 surface, overlay; Tech cladding, sheathing, covering; (enduit) coating; (à l'intérieur) lining; Aviat (du fuselage) skin; Menuis veneer; **r. de sol/mur** floor/wall covering; **câble à r. en caoutchouc** rubber-sheathed or-covered cable; **r. calorifuge** (d'une chaudière etc) lagging 2 Constr (d'un mur) facing; (d'un talus) revetment; (de chaussée) surface (material); (action) surfacing

revêtir [rəvɛtir] (conj like vêtir) VT 1 (habiller) to clothe, to dress; **r. qn de qch** to dress sb in sth; **r. qn d'une robe de cérémonie** to robe sb, to dress sb in a ceremonial robe; Fig **r. qn d'une dignité/d'une autorité** to invest sb with a dignity/an authority; **pièce revêtue de votre signature** document bearing your signature; Litt **revêtu de verdure** clothed in greenery, verdure-clad 2 Tech (couvrir) to clad, to sheathe, to cover; (enduire) to coat; (à l'intérieur) to line (**de** with); (chaudière) to lag; Constr (mur) to face; (chaussée) to surface; **r. une route de bitume** to tarmac a road; **murs revêtus de boiseries** panelled walls; **route non revêtue** unsurfaced road 3 (endosser) (uniforme, vêtement de cérémonie etc) to don, to put on; Fig **r. la forme humaine/un caractère particulier** to assume human shape/take on a particular character; **fait qui revêt de l'importance** fact that takes on importance

▪ VPR **se revêtir se r. de** (uniforme, vêtement de cérémonie etc) to don, to put on, to dress oneself in; (dignité) to assume

rêveur, -euse [rɛvœr, -øz] ADJ dreamy; **ces résultats me laissent r.** these results are bewildering

▪ N dreamer

rêveusement [rɛvøzmɑ̃] ADV dreamily

revient [rəvjɛ̃] NM (prix de) **r.** cost price

revigorant [rəvigɔrɑ̃] ADJ (vent, bain) invigorating; (boisson) reviving

revigorer [rəvigɔre] VT 1 (d'un vent, un bain) to invigorate; (d'une boisson, un aliment) to revive 2 (économie) to boost, to give a boost to; **les subventions ont revigoré l'entreprise** the subsidies gave the company a new lease of life

revirement [rəvirmɑ̃] NM 1 Naut tacking about, going about 2 (de fortune) sudden change; (de sentiments) (complete) change, about-turn; (changement d'avis) about-turn, U-turn, about-face; **r. d'opinion** (sudden) change in public opinion

révisable [revizabl] ADJ Jur (procès) reviewable

réviser [revize] VT 1 (texte, loi etc) to revise; (épreuves) to revise, to check; (situation, contrat, salaire) to review; Ordinat (texte, document etc) to edit; Jur (procès) to review, to reconsider; **r. une estimation à la hausse/baisse** to revise an estimate upwards/downwards; **r. son jugement** to revise one's judgement; **les salaires doivent être révisés janvier prochain** salaries come up for review next January 2 Scol to revise; **il faut r.**

you'll/I'll/etc have to do some revision 3 Tech (voiture, moteur etc) to service

réviseur, -euse [revizœr, -øz] N reviser; Typ (correcteur) proofreader; TV, Cin rewriter, rewrite sub; Fin **r. (comptable)** auditor; Fin **r. externe/interne** external/internal auditor

révision [revizjɔ̃] NF 1 (d'un texte, une loi etc) revision; (d'une politique, des salaires) review; Typ proofreading; Ordinat edit; (activité) editing; **être en cours de r.** to be under review; **faire l'objet d'une r.** to be reviewed; **les prix peuvent faire l'objet d'une r.** prices are subject to review 2 Scol revision, Am review; **faire des révisions** to revise 3 (d'un procès) review, reconsideration, reappraisal; (d'une opinion) change 4 Tech (d'une voiture, d'un moteur etc) service, servicing; **la r. des 5000 km** the 5,000 km service

révisionnisme [revizjɔnism] NM Pol revisionism

révisionniste [revizjɔnist] ADJ, N Pol revisionist

revisiter [rəvizite] VT 1 (visiter à nouveau) to revisit 2 (voir sous un jour nouveau) to reinterpret; **r. un auteur/une époque** to reinterpret a writer/an era; **Racine revisité par le célèbre metteur en scène** a new angle or a new take on Racine by the famous director

réviso [revizo] N Pol Fam Péj revisionist

revisser [rəvise] VT to screw back (again)

revitalisant [rəvitalizɑ̃] ADJ (shampooing etc) revitalizing

revitalisation [rəvitalizasjɔ̃] NF (de la peau, une région) revitalization

revitaliser [rəvitalize] VT (peau, région etc) to revitalize

revival [rivajvœl] NM revival

revivifier [rəvivifje] VT (impf, pr sub n. revivifiions, v. revivifiiez) (sentiment, souvenir) to revive

revivre [rəvivr] (conj like vivre) VI (recouvrer son énergie) to revive, to come alive again; **r. dans sa fille/son œuvre** to live on in one's daughter/work; **se sentir r.** to feel revived, to feel alive again; **faire r.** (personne) to revive, to bring to life again; (coutume, tradition etc) to revive

▪ VT (passé, sa vie) to relive; (expérience etc) to relive, to live through or go through again

révocabilité [revɔkabilite] NF 1 Jur (d'un contrat etc) revocability 2 Admin (d'un fonctionnaire) dismissibility 3 Pol (d'un élu) recallability

révocable [revɔkabl] ADJ 1 Jur (contrat etc) revocable; (crédit) revocable, callable 2 Admin (fonctionnaire) dismissible 3 Pol (élu) recallable, subject to recall

révocation [revɔkasjɔ̃] NF 1 Jur (d'un testament, un édit, un contrat etc) revocation; 2 Admin (d'un fonctionnaire) removal, dismissal 3 Pol (d'un élu) recall

révocatoire [revɔkatwar] ADJ Jur revocatory

revoici [rəvwasi] PRÉP Fam **me r.!** here I am again!, it's me again!; **nous r. à Paris** here we are in Paris again or back in Paris; **nous r. à notre point de départ** we're back where we started; **le r. au travail** he's back at work; **la r. qui pleure** she's crying again

revoilà [rəvwala] PRÉP Fam = revoici

revoir[1] [rəvwar] (conj like voir) VT 1 (voir de nouveau) (quelqu'un, quelque chose) to see again; (rencontrer) (quelqu'un) to see or meet again; **je revois encore la maison de mon enfance** (en souvenir) I can see my childhood home again; **je la revois petite** I can see her in my mind's eye when she was little 2 (examiner) (leçon) to revise, to go over; (comptes, manuscrit, texte) to go over or look over again; (épreuves) to read; **je voudrais r. quel-**

ques points avec toi I'd like to go over a few points with you; **r. à la baisse** to revise downwards; **r. à la hausse** to revise upwards

▪ VPR **se revoir 1** (se rencontrer) to see each other again, to meet again **2** (en souvenir) to see oneself (in one's mind's eye); **je me revois petite** I can see myself when I was a little girl

revoir[2] **(au)** [rəvwar] INT goodbye

▪ NM INV goodbye; **des au r. sans fin** endless goodbyes; **dis au r. au monsieur** say goodbye to the gentleman; **ce n'est qu'un au r.** it's only au revoir

révoltant [revɔltɑ̃] ADJ (vision, procédure) revolting, sickening, shocking; (odeur) revolting, sickening; (comportement) revolting, outrageous, appalling; (injustice) appalling, revolting

révolte [revɔlt] NF (émeute, indignation) revolt; (dans une prison) riot; **en r.** in revolt (**contre** against); **esprit de r.** spirit of revolt or rebellion; **sentiment de r.** feeling of revolt, rebellious feeling; **mouvement de r.** movement of revolt

révolté, -ée [revɔlte] ADJ 1 (indigné) outraged, appalled (**de voir** to see) 2 (en révolte) rebellious; **r. contre** in revolt against

▪ N rebel; **c'est un r. de nature** he's a natural rebel

révolter [revɔlte] VT 1 (indigner) to revolt, to appal, to shock; **de telles pratiques me révoltent** I'm appalled by that type of thing; **ça me révolte d'entendre ça!** I'm appalled!, that's appalling! 2 (inciter à la révolte) **r. qn** to induce sb to revolt

▪ VPR **se révolter** to revolt, to rebel (**contre** against); **se r. devant des injustices** to rebel against injustice; **se r. à l'idée que ...** to get indignant at the thought of ...; **ça me donne envie de me r.** I'm tempted to rebel; **le bon sens se révolte contre une telle supposition** common sense revolts against such a supposition

révolu [revɔly] ADJ (jours, époque etc) past, bygone; **ces jours sont révolus, c'est une époque révolue** those days are gone; **avoir quarante ans révolus** to be over forty years of age; **après trois mois révolus ...** after a full three months ...

révolution [revɔlysjɔ̃] NF 1 (rotation) (de la terre, d'une roue) revolution 2 Pol etc revolution; Hist **la R.** the French Revolution; **c'est une r. dans la vie du couple** there has been a revolution in sexual relationships; **toute la ville est en r.** the whole town is in revolt or up in arms; **faire la r.** to cause a revolution; **il veut faire la r. en introduisant ...** he wants to cause a revolution or revolutionize things by introducing ...

▸▸ **r. culturelle** cultural revolution; Hist **la R. française** the French Revolution; **r. industrielle** industrial revolution; **la R. d'octobre** the October Revolution; **r. de palais** palace revolution; **r. verte** green revolution

révolutionnaire [revɔlysjɔner] ADJ, N revolutionary

révolutionnarisme [revɔlysjɔnarism] NM revolutionism

révolutionner [revɔlysjɔne] VT 1 (transformer) (industrie, théorie, vie familiale etc) to revolutionize 2 (mettre en émoi) (village etc) to cause a stir in

revolver [revɔlvɛr] NM 1 revolver; (n'importe quel pistolet) gun; **r. à six coups** six-shooter 2 Tech (porte-outils) revolving tool holder; **tour (à) r.** turret lathe, capstan lathe

revolvériser [revɔlverize] VT Fam Hum to gun down

révoquer [revɔke] VT 1 (fonctionnaire) to dismiss, to remove from office 2 (décret) to revoke, to repeal, to rescind; (contrat) to revoke **3** *Litt* **r. qch en doute** to call sth into question

revoter [rǝvɔte] **VT** *(personne, parti)* to vote again for; **la loi a été revotée** the law has been passed *or* adopted again
VI to vote again

revouloir [rǝvulwar] *(conj like* **vouloir)** **VT** *Fam (quelque chose)* to want again; **en re-veux-tu?** would you like some more?

revoyure (à la) [alarvwajyr] **INT** *Fam* see you!, bye!

revue [rǝvy] **NF 1** *(examen)* review; *Mil (des troupes)* review, inspection; *(de caserne-ment)* inspection; **r. de presse** review of the papers *or* the press; **faire la r. des troupes** to review *or* inspect the troops; **passer en r.** *(problèmes, possibilités etc)* to review, to go over; *Mil (troupes)* to review, to inspect; *Fam* **je suis encore de la r.** I'm left high and dry again **2** *(magazine)* magazine; *(scientifique, littéraire)* review, journal; **r. d'entreprise** company *or* in-house magazine; **r. profes-sionnelle** trade journal *or* magazine **3** *Théâ-tre* revue **4** *Fam Vieilli* **nous sommes (des gens) de r.** we'll meet again

révulsé [revylse] **ADJ** **yeux révulsés** eyes with the whites showing

révulser [revylse] **VT 1** *Fam (dégoûter)* to re-volt, to disgust **2** *Méd* to counter-irritate
VPR se révulser *(d'un visage)* to contort; **ses yeux se révulsèrent** his/her eyes rolled up

révulsif, -ive [revylsif, -iv] **ADJ, NM** *Méd* re-vulsive, counter-irritant

révulsion [revylsjɔ̃] **NF** *Méd* revulsion, counter-irritation; *Fig* revulsion; **éprouver une r. à la vue de qn/qch** to feel revolted at the sight of sb/sth

rewriter [rirajtœr, rǝrajtœr] **NM** rewriter, re-write man

rewriter [rirajte, rǝrajte] **VT** to rewrite

rewriting [rirajtiŋ, rǝrajtiŋ] **NM** rewriting

Reykjavik [rekjavik] **N** Reykjavik

rez-de-chaussée [redʃose] **NM INV 1** *(ni-veau)* ground floor, *Am* first floor; **au r.** on the ground *or* *Am* first floor **2 (appartement en) r.** ground-floor flat, *Am* first-floor apartment

rez-de-jardin [redʒardɛ̃] **NM INV** *(niveau)* garden level; **appartement en r.** garden flat *or* *Am* apartment

RF [ɛrɛf] **NF** *abrév* **République française**

RFA [ɛrɛfa] **NF** *Anciennement (abrév* **Répu-blique fédérale d'Allemagne)** FRG

RG [ɛrʒe] **NMPL** *(abrév* **renseignements géné-raux)** security branch of the French police force, *Br* ≃ Special Branch, *Am* ≃ FBI

rg *abrév* **rive gauche**

Rh **NM** *Méd (abrév* **facteur Rhésus)** Rh; **Rh-négatif** Rh negative; **Rh-positif** Rh positive

rhabillage [rabijaʒ] **NM 1** *(d'une montre)* re-pair, overhaul **2** *(d'un enfant)* dressing again; *(de soi-même)* getting dressed again

rhabiller [rabije] **VT 1** *(réparer) (montre)* to repair **2** *(habiller)* **r. qn** to dress sb again, to put sb's clothes on again; *(acheter de nou-veaux vêtements pour)* to buy new clothes for sb; **je n'ai plus rien pour la r.!** I don't have a thing to put on her *or* to dress her in! **3** *Fig (bâtiment, vieille idée etc)* to give a new look to
VPR se rhabiller *(mettre ses vêtements)* to put one's clothes on again, to get dressed again; *Fam* **il peut aller se r.** *(d'un athlète)* he might as well give up and go home; *Fam* **va te r.!** get off!; **avec vos 12 000 livres par an vous pou-vez aller vous r.!** you can get lost with your £12,000 a year!, you can take your £12,000 and stuff it!

rhabilleur, -euse [rabijœr, -øz] **N** *(de mon-tres)* repairer

rhapsode [rapsɔd] **NM** *Antiq (chanteur)* rhap-sode, rhapsodist

rhapsodie [rapsɔdi] **NF** rhapsody

rhapsodique [rapsɔdik] **ADJ** rhapsodic

rhénan, -ane [renɑ̃, -an] **ADJ** *(industrie, économie)* (of/from the) Rhineland
N R. Rhinelander

Rhénanie [renani] **NF la R.** the Rhineland; **R.-Palatinat** Rhineland-Palatinate

rhénium [renjɔm] **NM** *Chimie* rhenium

rhéostat [reɔsta] **NM** *Élec* rheostat; **r. de dé-marrage** *(d'un moteur électrique)* rheostatic starter

rhésus [rezys] **NM 1** *Zool* rhesus monkey **2** *Physiol* **(facteur) r.** rhesus *or* Rh factor; **r. positif/négatif** rhesus *or* Rh positive/nega-tive; **incompatibilité r.** rhesus *or* Rh incom-patibility

rhéteur [retœr] **NM 1** *(orateur)* rhetorician **2** *Antiq (professeur)* rhetor

rhétoricien, -ienne [retɔrisjɛ̃, -jɛn] **N** rhetorician

rhétorique [retɔrik] **NF 1** *Littér* rhetoric; **fi-gure de r.** figure of speech **2** *Scol Arch* **(classe de) r.** *Br* ≃ lower sixth form, *Am* ≃ eleventh grade **3** *(emphase)* rhetoric
ADJ *(effet etc)* rhetorical

rhéto-roman, -ane, *pl* **rhéto-romans, -anes** [retɔrɔmɑ̃, -an] **ADJ, NM** *Ling* Rhaeto-Romanic

Rhin [rɛ̃] **NM le R.** the (river) Rhine

rhinite [rinit] **NF** *Méd* rhinitis

rhinocéros [rinɔserɔs] **NM** rhinoceros, *Fam* rhino

rhinologie [rinɔlɔʒi] **NF** *Méd* rhinology

rhinopharyngé [rinofarɛ̃ʒe], **rhinopha-ryngien, -ienne** [rinofarɛ̃ʒjɛ̃, -jɛn] **ADJ** *Méd* nose-and-throat, *Spéc* rhinopharyngeal

rhinopharyngite [rinofarɛ̃ʒit] **NF** *Méd* in-flammation of the nose and throat, *Spéc* rhinopharyngitis

rhinopharynx [rinofarɛ̃ks] **NM** *Anat* nose and throat, *Spéc* rhinopharynx

rhinoplastie [rinoplasti] **NF** *Chir* rhino-plasty

rhinoscopie [rinoskɔpi] **NF** *Méd* rhinoscopy

rhizome [rizom] **NM** *Bot* rhizome

rhodanien, -ienne [rɔdanjɛ̃, -jɛn] **ADJ** of the Rhone; *Géog* **couloir r.** Rhone corridor

Rhodes [rɔd] **NF** Rhodes

Rhodésie [rɔdezi] **NF** *Anciennement* Rhodesia

rhodésien, -ienne [rɔdezjɛ̃, -jɛn] **ADJ** *Ancien-nement* Rhodesian
N R. Rhodesian

rhodium [rɔdjɔm] **NM** *Chimie* rhodium

rhododendron [rɔdɔdɛ̃drɔ̃] **NM** *Bot* rhododendron

rhombique [rɔ̃bik] **ADJ** rhombic

rhomboïdal, -ale, -aux, -ales [rɔ̃bɔidal, -o] **ADJ** rhomboid

rhomboïde [rɔ̃bɔid] **NM** rhomboid

Rhône [ron] **NM le R.** the (river) Rhone

rhubarbe [rybarb] **NF** rhubarb; **confiture/tarte à la r.** rhubarb jam/tart

rhum [rɔm] **NM** rum; **r. blanc** white rum

rhumatisant, -ante [rymatizɑ̃, -ɑ̃t] **ADJ, N** *Méd* rheumatic

rhumatismal, -ale, -aux, -ales [ryma-tismal, -o] **ADJ** *Méd* rheumatic

rhumatisme [rymatism] **NM** *Méd* rheuma-tism, *Fam* rheumatics; **avoir des rhumatis-mes** to have rheumatism *or* *Fam* rheumatics; **être perclus de rhumatismes** to be crippled with rheumatism; **mes rhuma-tismes me font souffrir** my rheumatism is playing me up

▸ ▸ *Méd* **r. articulaire** rheumatic fever; *Méd* **r. déformant** polyarthritis

rhumatoïde [rymatɔid] **ADJ** *Méd* rheu-matoid

rhumatologie [rymatɔlɔʒi] **NF** *Méd* rheu-matology

rhumatologue [rymatɔlɔg] **N** *Méd* rheu-matologist

rhume [rym] **NM** *Méd* cold; **gros r.** bad *or* heavy cold; **prendre** *ou* **attraper un r.,** *Fam* **attraper le r.** to catch a cold, to catch cold; **avoir un r.** to have a cold

▸ ▸ **r. de cerveau** head cold; **r. des foins** hay fever

rhumerie [rɔmri] **NF** rum distillery

ria [rija] **NF** *Géog* ria

riant [rijɑ̃] **ADJ 1** *(visage)* smiling, cheerful; *(yeux)* laughing, merry **2** *Fig (ambiance)* merry, cheerful; *(paysage, campagne)* cheerful, sunny, bright

RIB [rib] **NM** *(abrév* **relevé d'identité bancaire)** = document giving details of one's bank account, bank details

ribambelle [ribɑ̃bɛl] **NF** *(d'insultes, de noms etc)* long string; *(de visiteurs)* string, crowd; *Fam* pile; **r. d'enfants** swarm of children

ribaud, -aude [ribo, -od] *Arch Litt* **ADJ** *(per-sonne)* debauched
N debauchee

riboflavine [riboflavin] **NF** riboflavin

ribonucléique [ribonykleik] **ADJ** *(acide)* ribonucleic

ribote [ribɔt] **NF** *Fam Vieilli* spree; **être en r.** to be tipsy *or* tight

ribouldingue [ribuldɛ̃g] **NF** *Fam* spree, binge; **faire la r.** to go on a spree *or* binge

ricain, -aine [rikɛ̃, -ɛn] *Fam* **ADJ** Yank
N R. Yank

ricanement [rikanmɑ̃] **NM** *(rire) (sarcas-tique, de mépris)* sneer, snigger; *(bête)* snig-ger, giggle; **je veux savoir d'où venait ce r.** I want to know who sniggered; **je ne supporte plus tes ricanements** I've had enough of your sniggering/giggling/sneering

ricaner [rikane] **VI** *(sarcastiquement)* to sneer, to snigger; *(bêtement)* to snigger, to giggle

ricaneur, -euse [rikanœr, -øz] **ADJ** *(sarcas-tique)* sneering, sniggering; *(bête)* sniggering, giggling; **air r.** sneering look
N *(sarcastique)* sneerer, sniggerer; *(bête)* sniggerer, giggler

Richard [riʃar] **N R. Cœur de Lion** Richard the Lionheart

richard, -arde [riʃar, -ard] **N** *Fam Péj (per-sonne riche)* **un r.** a moneybags

RICHE [riʃ]

ADJ	rich **1–3** ▪ wealthy **1** ▪ elaborate **2** ▪ lush **2** ▪ fertile **2** ▪ rich in *(riche en)* **3** ▪ full of *(riche de)* **4**

ADJ 1 *(fortuné)* rich, wealthy, well-off; **l'un des hommes les plus riches du monde** one of the richest *or* wealthiest men in the world; **les pays riches** (the) rich *or* wealthy countries; **faire un r. mariage** to marry into a wealthy family, *Fam* to marry money; **être r. à millions** to be worth millions; *Fam* **ça fait r.** that looks very grand *or* posh

2 *(qui abonde en qch)* *(cuisine, fromage, re-pas, aliment)* rich; *(vocabulaire)* extensive; *(style)* elaborate; *(description)* detailed; *(imagination)* vivid, lively; *(végétation)* luxu-riant, lush; *(moisson)* rich, abundant; *(terre)* fertile; *Aut* **mélange r.** rich mixture; **votre analyse est r.** your analysis is full of good things *or* very interesting; **évitez de manger trop r. le soir** don't eat too much rich food in the evening; **une r. nature** a person full of vitality; **il a une très r. personnalité** he's got a lot of personality, he's full of personality; **une r. idée** a splendid idea

3 r. en qch rich in sth; **r. en protéine** rich or high in protein, protein-rich, with a high protein content; **aliment r. en fibres** high-fibre food; **r. en calories** high in calories; **terre r. en minerais** earth rich in minerals; **r. en tableaux/édifices du XIᵉ siècle** with an abundance or wealth of paintings/eleventh-century buildings; **la journée a été r. en événements** it's been an action-packed or exciting day; **mon voyage a été r. en expériences** I learned a lot from my trip, I got a lot out of my trip; **je ne suis pas très r. en produits de beauté** (d'un commerçant) I don't have many cosmetics in stock

4 r. de (espérances etc) full of; **r. de possibilités** (avenir) with lots of potential, full of hope; **livre/expérience r. d'enseignements** very instructive book/experience; **... le cœur gros mais r. de tant d'aventures ...** heavy-hearted but rejoicing in my/his/etc adventures

N rich or wealthy person; **les riches** the rich, the wealthy; **nouveau r.** nouveau riche; Péj **fils ou gosse de riche(s)** rich kid; **tu es vraiment un fils de riche(s)!** you really have no idea how the other half lives, have you?

richelieu, pl **richelieus, richelieux** [riʃəljø] NM lace-up (shoe), Oxford (shoe)

richement [riʃmɑ̃] ADV **1** richly; **pourvoir r. ses enfants** to make abundant provision for one's children; **marier r. sa fille** to marry one's daughter into a wealthy family **2** (luxueusement) (décoré, vêtu, illustré) sumptuously, richly; **être r. logé** to live in sumptuous surroundings

richesse [riʃɛs] NF **1** (d'une personne, d'un pays) wealth; **la r. publique** public wealth; **vivre dans la r.** to be wealthy; **r. en matières premières** (d'un pays) wealth of raw materials; **le tourisme, c'est la seule r. de la région** tourism is the country's only resource or only source of income; **ce tableau fait la r. du musée** this painting is the prize item in the museum's collection; **richesses** riches, wealth; **voilà toutes mes richesses** this is everything I've got; **musée plein de richesses** gallery full of treasures or valuable objects **2** (du sol, d'un gisement, du vocabulaire) richness; (de la végétation) luxuriance, lushness; (de l'imagination) vividness, liveliness; (d'une description) detailed nature; (de rencontres) abundance

richissime [riʃisim] ADJ extremely wealthy, Fam loaded

ricin [risɛ̃] NM Bot castor-oil plant; **huile de r.** castor oil

ricocher [rikɔʃe] VI (d'une balle, un caillou) to ricochet (sur off); (sur l'eau) to bounce (sur off); **faire r. des pierres sur l'eau** = to play (at) ducks and drakes

ricochet [rikɔʃɛ] NM (d'une balle) ricochet; (sur l'eau) bounce; **faire des ricochets (sur l'eau)** = to play (at) ducks and drakes; Fig Fam **apprendre qch par r.** to hear of sth indirectly or in a roundabout way

ric-rac [rikrak] ADV Fam **je suis r. ce mois-ci** money's pretty tight this month; **je pense me débrouiller jusqu'à la fin du mois, mais ça va être r.** I think I'll make it to the end of the month but only just; **il a réussi le bac r.** (de justesse) he only just scraped through the bac; **elle m'a remboursé r.** she paid me back to the very last penny

rictus [riktys] NM grimace, Fml rictus; **prendre/avoir un r.** to grimace

ride [rid] NF **1** (sur le visage) wrinkle, line; (sur un fruit) wrinkle; **crème anti-rides** anti-ageing cream; **front creusé de rides profon-**des deeply lined or furrowed brow; Fig Fam **cela n'a pas pris une r. en trente ans** it's still just as good as it was thirty years ago **2** (sur l'eau, le sable) ripple; (de sable) ridge

ridé [ride] ADJ (visage) wrinkled, lined; (pomme) wrinkled, shrivelled

rideau, -eaux [rido] NM **1** (d'intérieur) curtain, Am drape; **lit garni de rideaux** curtained bed; **rideaux de lit** bed hangings; **tirer les rideaux** to draw the curtains; Fig Fam **tirer le r. sur qch** to draw a veil over sth; **on ne peut pas tirer le r. sur le passé** you can't forget the past, you can't put the past behind you **2** Théâtre curtain; **r. à huit heures précises** the curtain rises at eight sharp; Fig Fam **r.!** let's call it a day!; **allez, r., je ne veux plus en parler!** drop it or that's enough, I don't want to talk about it any more! **3** Fig (d'arbres) wall, screen, curtain; (de feu, fumée) wall; (de pluie) curtain **4** (d'un bureau) roll top; **classeur à r.** tambour-door filing cabinet, roll-shutter cabinet

▸▸ **r. bonne femme** tie-back curtain; **r. à enrouleur** roller blind; **r. d'entr'acte** act drop; **r. de fer** Théâtre safety curtain; (de boutique) metal shutter; Hist, Pol Iron Curtain; TV, Cin **r. de fond** backdrop; TV, Cin **r. de fond scénique** scenic cloth; Aut **r. de radiateur** radiator blind or shutter

ridelle [ridɛl] NF Aut side panel

rider [ride] VT **1** (front) to wrinkle, to line; (peau, fruit) to wrinkle, to shrivel **2** (eau, sable etc) to ripple
VPR **se rider 1** (du front, de la peau) to become wrinkled or lined; (d'une pomme) to shrivel up **2** (de l'eau) to ripple

ridicule [ridikyl] ADJ ridiculous, ludicrous (de faire qch to do sth); (prix) ridiculously low; **tu es vraiment r. dans cette tenue** you look really ridiculous in that get-up; **se rendre r.** to make a fool of oneself, to make oneself look ridiculous
NM **1** (absurdité) ridiculousness; **c'est d'un r. achevé** it is perfectly ridiculous or the height of absurdity; **tomber dans le r.** to make oneself ridiculous; **se couvrir de r.** to make a fool of oneself, to make oneself look ridiculous, to cover oneself in ridicule **2** (dérision) ridicule; **craindre le r.** to fear ridicule; **tourner qn/qch en r.** to ridicule or make fun of sb/sth, to hold sb/sth up to ridicule **3** (chose ridicule) **les ridicules de notre époque** the absurdities of our time

ridiculement [ridikylmɑ̃] ADV ridiculously, ludicrously

ridiculiser [ridikylize] VT to ridicule, to make fun of, to hold up to ridicule
VPR **se ridiculiser** to make oneself look ridiculous, to make a fool of oneself

ridule [ridyl] NF (little) wrinkle

RIEN [rjɛ̃] PRON INDÉF SEE GRAMMAR B16 **1** (quelque chose) (in questions **rien** is preferred to **quelque chose** when a negative answer is expected) anything; **y a-t-il r. de plus triste?** is there anything more depressing?

2 (with **ne** expressed) nothing, not anything; **r. ne l'intéresse** nothing interests him; **r. ne va plus!** (au casino) rien ne va plus!, no more bets!; **je n'ai r. à faire** I have nothing to do, I don't have anything to do; **il n'y a r. à faire** it can't be helped; Fam **r. à faire, ça ne marche pas** it's no good, it's not working; **je n'en sais trop r.** I don't know too much about it; **il n'a plus r.** (plus d'argent) he doesn't have a penny left; (il n'est plus malade) there's nothing wrong or there isn't anything wrong with him now; **tu n'as plus r. à attendre de lui** now you know just or exactly what to expect from him; **il n'y a plus r. à en dire** there is nothing more to be said, there isn't anything more to be said; **je n'ai r. vu** I didn't see anything, I saw nothing; **je n'ai jamais r. vu d'aussi grand** I've never seen anything quite as big; **il n'a r. mangé depuis hier** he has eaten nothing or he hasn't eaten anything since yesterday; **il ne faut r. lui dire** he mustn't be told anything, he must be told nothing; **on ne peut jamais r. lui dire** you can't say a word or Fam open your mouth to him; **personne n'osa r. dire** nobody dared say anything; **n'en dites r.** don't say anything or a word about it, say nothing about it; **il n'y a r. de tel qu'un bon bain chaud** there's nothing like a good hot bath; **je n'ai r. de nouveau à vous dire** I have nothing or I don't have anything new to tell you; **alors, r. de nouveau?** (en attendant des résultats etc) have you heard anything yet?; **sinon? r. de nouveau?** so there's nothing new?, so nothing's been happening?; **r. d'autre** nothing else; **il ne vous fallait r. d'autre?** (is there) anything else?, will that be all?; **elle veut ça et r. d'autre** she wants that and nothing else; **ce n'est r.** it's nothing; **pour elle 10 km à pied, ce n'est r.** she thinks nothing of walking 10 km, a 10 km walk is nothing to her; **ce n'est r. de le dire!** you can say that again!; **ça ne fait r.** it doesn't matter, it makes no difference or Fam no odds; **si cela ne vous fait r.** if you don't mind; **comme si de r. n'était** as if nothing had happened; **elle ne ressemble en r. à sa sœur** she's nothing like her sister; Litt **il n'en est r.!** such is not the case!; **je n'en ferai r.** I'll do nothing of the kind or sort; **après vous – je n'en ferai r.** after you – not at all or I wouldn't dream of it; **elle n'est r. pour moi** she is or means nothing to me; **elle n'est plus r. pour lui** she doesn't mean anything to him any more; **sa fille n'a r. de lui** his daughter doesn't take after him in any way; **je n'ai r. d'un psychiatre, pourtant!** I'm no psychiatrist!; **la nouvelle perceuse X n'a r. d'une perceuse traditionnelle!** the new X drill is nothing like a traditional drill!; **il n'y était pour r.** he had nothing to do with it or had no hand in it; **je n'y suis pour r.** it's nothing to do with me, I've got nothing to do with it; Fam **il ne sait r. de r.** he knows nothing at all or nothing about anything or Fam zilch about anything; **que t'a-t-il donné? – r. de r.!** what did he give you? – zilch! or not a sausage!
SEE GRAMMAR B62–3

3 (with **ne** not expressed) **que faites-vous? – r./presque r.** what do you do? – nothing/hardly anything; **elle lit? – jamais r.** does she read? – not a thing; **r. du tout** nothing at all; **c'est tout ou r.** it's all or nothing; **pour r.** for nothing; **avoir qch pour r.** to get sth for (next to) nothing; **parler pour r.** to waste one's breath; **jouer pour r.** to play for fun; **pourquoi demandez-vous cela? – pour r.** why do you ask? – no reason or I just wondered; **se fâcher de r.** to get angry about or for nothing; **merci, monsieur – de r.** thank you – it's a pleasure or you're welcome or (please) don't mention it; **en moins de r.** in less than no time, in no time at all; **une affaire de r. (du tout)** an insignificant matter; Vieilli Fam **femme de r.** loose woman; **une petite pièce de r. du tout** a wretched little room; **un homme de r. du tout** a man of no account, a nobody; **un/une r.(-)du(-)tout** a (mere) nobody; **c'est une coupure de r. du tout** it's just a scratch; Fam **un moins que r.** (personne) a loser; **pour trois fois r.** (acheter, vendre qch) for next to nothing, for a song; **il possède trois fois r.** he has absolutely nothing; **faire qch comme (un) r.** to do sth easily or without any trouble at all or Fam as easy as winking; Tennis **quinze à r.** fifteen love SEE GRAMMAR B62–3

4 (the negation is expressed or implied elsewhere in the sentence) **il est inutile de r. dire** you needn't say anything; **avant qu'elle ait r. dit** before she said anything; **sans r. faire**

without doing anything; **sans nous gêner en r.** without troubling us at all *or* in the slightest
5 r. que nothing but, only, merely; **r. que la vérité** nothing but the truth; **je frémis r. que d'y songer** the mere thought (of it) *or* just thinking about it makes me shudder; **r. que pour aller à un bal** for the sake of going *or* just to go to a dance; **r. que pour aller à Paris, ça coûte 60 euros** it costs 60 euros just to go to Paris; **je te le dis, r. qu'à toi** I'm telling you and only you *or* and you alone; **c'est à moi, r. qu'à moi** it's mine, all mine; **r. que cela?** is that all?
6 (*with ne … pas*) **on ne peut pas vivre de r.** you can't live on nothing; **ce n'est pas r.!** that's something!; **vingt euros de l'heure, ce n'est pas r.!** twenty euros an hour is something at least!; **élever quatre enfants, ce n'est pas r.!** it's quite something raising four kids!
ADV *Arg Vieilli* really, *Br* not half, *Am* real; **elle est r. chic!** she's really smart!, *Br* she isn't half smart!
NM 1 (*bagatelle*) trifle, (mere) nothing; **un r. l'habille** she looks good (dressed) in anything; **un r. suffit pour le fâcher** he gets upset over the least little thing; **se piquer d'un r.** to take offence at nothing *or* the slightest thing; **perdre son temps à des riens** to waste one's time with trifles; **se disputer pour des riens** to argue over nothing; **il court 400 mètres comme un r.** he runs 400 metres just like that *or* with no trouble (at all), running 400 metres is nothing to him
2 un r. de (*un petit peu de*) (just) a little; **un r. d'huile** the merest drop of oil; **en un r. de temps** in no time (at all), in less than no time; **un r. de femme** a tiny little woman
3 un r. (*un peu*) a bit, a trifle, a touch; **il est un r. pénible en ce moment** he's being a bit of a pain at the moment

riesling [rislin] NM (*vin*) Riesling

rieur, -euse [rijœr, -øz] ADJ (*air, visage*) cheerful, bright; (*yeux*) laughing, merry; **c'est un garçon très r.** he laughs a lot; **mouette rieuse** black-headed gull
▸ N laugher; **mettre les rieurs de son côté** *ou* **avec soi** to have the last laugh

rififi [rififi] NM *Arg* brawl, free-for-all, punch-up; **il va y avoir du r.** there's going to be trouble *or* a punch-up

riflard [riflar] NM *Fam* (*parapluie*) umbrella, *Br* brolly

riflette [riflet] NF *Fam* (*guerre*) war

rift [rift] NM *Géol* rift valley

Riga [riga] N Riga

rigide [riʒid] ADJ **1** (*matériau*) rigid; (*essieu*) fixed; **couverture r.** (*d'un livre*) stiff cover **2** *Fig* (*personne, règlement, système etc*) rigid, inflexible, unbending; **ne sois pas trop r. avec eux** don't be too strict with them

rigidement [riʒidmã] ADV rigidly

rigidifier [riʒidifje] VT to rigidify, to make rigid

rigidité [riʒidite] NF **1** (*d'un matériau*) rigidity; **r. cadavérique** rigor mortis **2** *Fig* (*d'une personne, d'un règlement, d'un système etc*) rigidity, inflexibility

rigolade [rigɔlad] NF *Fam* **ça n'est pas de la r.** it's no laughing matter *or* no joke; **prendre qch à la r.** to treat sth as a joke, to make a joke out of sth; **j'essaie de le prendre à la r.** I'm trying not to take it too seriously; **ah, la r.!** what a hoot *or* scream!

rigolard, -arde [rigɔlar, -ard] *Fam* ADJ (*personne*) fond of a joke *or* a laugh; **il a toujours un air r.** he's always got a grin on his face, something always seems to be amusing him
▸ N **c'est un r./une rigolarde** he's/she's fond of a joke *or* a laugh

rigole [rigɔl] NF (*caniveau*) channel; (*filet d'eau*) rivulet

rigoler [rigɔle] VI *Fam* **1** (*rire*) to laugh; *Iron* **tu me fais r., tiens!** you make me laugh! **2** (*s'amuser*) to have some fun *or* a laugh, to enjoy oneself **3** (*plaisanter*) to joke (**avec** about); **il ne faut pas r. avec le fisc** you shouldn't mess about with the tax man; **ils rigolent pas avec la sécurité dans cet aéroport** they don't mess about *or* take any chances with security at this airport; **tu rigoles?** are you kidding?, are you joking?

rigolo, -ote [rigɔlo, -ɔt] *Fam* ADJ **1** (*drôle*) funny; **ce n'est pas r.** it's no laughing matter *or* joke; **il est r., ton sac** what a fun bag! **2** (*curieux*) funny, queer, odd
▸ N (*personne amusante, fumiste*) joker, comedian; (*incompétent*) cowboy, joker; **quel petit r. a débranché la prise?** what joker pulled the plug out?
▸ NM *Arg Vieilli* (*revolver*) revolver

rigorisme [rigɔrism] NM strictness

rigoriste [rigɔrist] ADJ (*morale, principe, attitude etc*) strict, rigorous
▸ N strict moralist

rigoureusement [riguʀøzmã] ADV **1** (*strictement*) strictly; **il est r. interdit de marcher sur les pelouses** it is strictly forbidden to walk on the grass; **r. exact** absolutely correct; **suivre r. les consignes** to follow the instructions to the letter; **je l'ai r. vérifié** I checked it thoroughly **2** (*avec dureté*) rigorously, severely, harshly; **être r. opposé à qch** to be rigorously opposed to sth

rigoureux, -euse [riguʀø, -øz] ADJ **1** (*dur*) (*punition, mesures, conditions etc*) severe, harsh, rigorous; (*hiver*) hard; (*climat*) harsh **2** (*strict*) strict; (*analyse*) rigorous; (*entraînement*) rigorous, strict; (*discipline*) severe; **observer une neutralité rigoureuse** to observe strict neutrality; **sois plus r.** be more rigorous

rigueur [rigœr] NF **1** (*dureté*) harshness, severity, rigour, *Am* rigor; (*du temps*) harshness, severity; **prendre des mesures de r.** to take rigorous *or* harsh *or* severe measures; **la r. de la loi** the rigour of the law; **les rigueurs de la vie en prison/du climat écossais** the rigours of prison life/the Scottish climate; **un climat de r. économique** a harsh economic climate; **user de r. avec qn** to be severe with *or* hard on sb; **tenir r. à qn** not to forgive sb; **je ne lui en tiens pas r.** I don't hold it against him, I'm not holding a grudge **2** (*du règlement*) strictness; (*d'une analyse*) rigour, *Am* rigor; **manquer de r.** (*d'un style*) to be sloppy; (*d'une personne*) (*dans son travail*) to be sloppy, to lack self-discipline; **manquer de r. dans son analyse** not to be rigorous enough in one's analysis; **apprendre la r.** to learn self-discipline; **être de r.** to be compulsory *or* obligatory; **la cravate est de r.** ties must be worn; **l'habit n'est pas de r.** evening dress is optional; **délai de r.** deadline; **à la r.** (*si nécessaire*) if need be, if really necessary; (*à la limite*) just about, at a pinch

rillettes [rijɛt] NFPL *Culin* potted meat (*made from pork, goose etc*)

rimailler [rimaje] VI *Péj Vieilli* to versify

rimailleur, -euse [rimajœr, -øz] N *Péj Vieilli* versifier, rhymester, poetaster

rimbaldien, -ienne [rɛ̃baldjɛ̃, -jɛn] ADJ **la poésie rimbaldienne** Rimbaud's poetry, the poetry of Rimbaud; **avoir des accents rimbaldiens** to be reminiscent of Rimbaud, to have Rimbaud-like overtones; **ce film a un côté r.** the film has a touch of Rimbaud about it

rime [rim] NF rhyme; **r. pauvre/riche** poor/ rich rhyme; **r. féminine/masculine** feminine/masculine rhyme; **rimes croisées** *ou* **alternées** alternate rhymes; **rimes plates** *ou*

suivies couplet rhymes; *Fam* **sans r. ni raison** without rhyme or reason

rimer [rime] VT (*conte etc*) to put into verse, to versify; **poésie rimée** rhyming verse
▸ VI **1** (*d'un mot etc*) to rhyme (**avec** with); *Fam* **à quoi cela rime-t-il?** what's the sense of that?, what sense is there in that?; **cela ne rime à rien** it doesn't make sense, there's no sense in it, there's neither rhyme nor reason in it; **cela ne rimerait à rien** it wouldn't make sense **2** (*faire des vers*) to write verse *or* poetry

rimeur, -euse [rimœr, -øz] N *Péj* rhymer, rhymester

Rimmel® [rimɛl] NM mascara

rinçage [rɛ̃saʒ] NM (*action*) rinsing; (*opération*) rinse; (*pour les cheveux*) (colour *or Am* color) rinse; **cycle de r.** (*d'une machine à laver*) rinse cycle; **produit de r.** (*pour lave-vaisselle*) rinsing agent *or* aid

rince-bouteilles [rɛ̃sbutɛj] NM INV bottle-washing machine

rince-doigts [rɛ̃sdwa] NM INV finger bowl

rincée [rɛ̃se] NF **1** *Fam* (*averse*) downpour; **on a pris une sacrée r. sur le dos** we got soaked through, we were drenched **2** *Arg* (*défaite*) walloping, pounding; *Fam Vieilli* (*coups*) thrashing

rincer [rɛ̃se] (*je rinçai(s); n. rinçons*) VT (*vêtements, vaisselle, cheveux*) to rinse; (*verre, tasse*) to rinse (out); **se faire r.** *Arg* (*au jeu*) to get cleaned out; *Fam* (*par la pluie*) to get soaked (to the skin) *or* drenched
▸ VI *Fam* (*offrir à boire*) to buy the drinks; **c'est moi qui rince!** I'm buying the drinks!, the drinks are on me!; **c'est le patron qui rince!** the drinks are on the house!
▸ VPR **se rincer se r. les mains** to rinse one's hands; **se r. la bouche** to rinse one's mouth (out); *Arg* **se r. le gosier** *ou* **la dalle** (*boire*) to have a drink; *Fam* **se r. l'œil** to get an eyeful

rincette [rɛ̃sɛt] NF *Fam* nip of brandy/*etc* (*put into emptied cup or glass*)

rinceur, -euse [rɛ̃sœr, -øz] N (*personne*) rinser
▸ NF **rinceuse** (*machine*) bottle-washing machine

ring [riŋ] NM *Boxe* ring; **le r.** (*la boxe*) boxing; **monter sur le r.** to go into the ring; (*faire de la boxe*) to take up boxing

ringard[1] [rɛ̃gar] NM (*tisonnier*) poker

ringard[2]**, -arde** [rɛ̃gar, -ard] *Fam* ADJ **1** (*démodé*) (*personne, chanson*) old-fashioned, *Arg* uncool **2** (*voyant*) (*style, couleur, décor etc*) tacky
▸ N square, nerd

ringardise [rɛ̃gardiz] NF *Fam* tackiness, *Br* naffness; **la déco était d'une r., je te dis pas!** the decor was unbelievably tacky *or Br* naff!

ringuette [rɛ̃gɛt] NF *Can* = type of ice hockey

RIP [ɛripe] NM (*abrév* **relevé d'identité postale**) = document giving details of one's Post Office account

ripage [ripaʒ] NM (*glissement*) slipping; (*de véhicule*) skidding; *Aut* **r. des pneus** tyre scrub

ripaille [ripaj] NF *Fam* feast, blow-out; **faire r.** to have a feast *or* blow-out

ripailler [ripaje] VI *Fam* to feast, to have a (good) blow-out

ripailleur, -euse [ripajœr, -øz] N *Fam* reveller

ripaton [ripatɔ̃] NM *Arg* (*pied*) foot, *Br* plate

riper [ripe] VT (*faire glisser*) (*chargement etc*) to slide along
▸ VI to slip; (*des roues*) to skid; (*d'un chargement*) to shift; *très Fam* (*s'en aller*) to split

Ripolin® [ripolɛ̃] NM enamel (paint)

ripoliner [ripoline] **VT** to enamel, to paint with enamel

riposte [ripɔst] **NF1** *(réponse)* riposte, retort **2** *Boxe, Escrime (coup)* riposte, counter **3** *(représailles)* counterattack

riposter [ripɔste] **VI1** *(répondre)* to retort, to riposte **2** *Boxe, Escrime* to riposte, to counter **3** *(user de représailles)* to counterattack, to mount a counterattack; **les annonceurs ont riposté au procès en …** advertisers responded to the trial by …

ripou [ripu] *Fam* **ADJ** *(policier)* bent, *Am* bad **NM** bent *or Am* bad cop

riquiqui [rikiki] **ADJ INV** *Fam (tout petit)* teeny-weeny; *(mesquin) (portion, cadeau etc)* stingy, mean; *(maillot de bain)* skimpy; **ça fait r.** *(mesquin)* it looks a bit stingy *or* mean

rire¹ [rir] **NM** laughter, laughing; **un r.** a laugh; **il a un gros r.** he has a loud laugh, he guffaws; **il eut un gros r.** he roared with laughter; **éclat de r.** burst of laughter; **des éclats de r.** screams *or* hoots of laughter; **avoir le fou r.** to have a fit of the giggles, to laugh uncontrollably; *(sur scène)* to corpse; **se tenir les côtes de r.** to split one's sides laughing; **provoquer** *ou* **exciter les rires** to cause laughter; **r. moqueur** sneer; **avoir un r. moqueur** to sneer; **il eut un r. d'incrédulité** he laughed incredulously

rire² *(prp* **riant;** *pp* **ri;** *pr ind* **je ris, n. rions, ils rient;** *pr sub* **je rie;** *p hist* **je ris;** *fu* **je rirai)** **VI1** to laugh; *Prov* **rira bien qui rira le dernier** he who laughs last laughs longest; **r. jaune** to force a laugh, to give a forced laugh; **r. comme un bossu** to laugh like a hyena, to split one's sides laughing; **r. aux éclats** to scream *or* roar with laughter; **éclater de r.** to burst out laughing; **r. bruyamment** to guffaw; **r. en soi-même, r. tout bas** to laugh to oneself, to chuckle; **r. en dedans** to laugh up one's sleeve; **r. bêtement** to giggle, to titter; **dire qch en riant** to say sth laughingly *or* with a laugh; **il a ri (jusqu')aux larmes** he laughed till he cried; **ne pas avoir le cœur à r.** not to be in a laughing mood; **il y a de quoi r.** it's laughable, it's enough to make a horse laugh; **il n'y a pas de quoi r.!** it's no laughing matter!, it's no joke!; **cela nous a souvent fait r.** we've often laughed about it, we've had many a laugh over it; **c'était à mourir** *ou Fam* **à crever de r.** we nearly died laughing; **c'est à mourir de r., cette histoire/cette situation** it's a hysterically funny story/situation; **il nous faisait tordre** *ou* **mourir de r.** he had us splitting our sides; **tu me fais mourir** *ou* **tordre de r.** you crack me up; *Iron* **tu me fais (mourir de) r. avec tes grandes idées** you really make me laugh, you and your big ideas; *Fam* **j'étais mort de r.** I was killing myself laughing; **r. de qn** to laugh at sb, to make fun of sb; **r. d'une histoire** to laugh over *or* at a story; **il rit de vos menaces** he laughs at *or* scoffs at *or* makes light of your threats; **je ris de leurs insultes** I don't care about their insults; **il vaut mieux en r.** it's best to laugh, you might as well laugh; **il prête à r.** he makes himself a laughing stock; **tout cela ne prête guère à r.** it's not exactly funny *or* a laughing matter; **il faut dire que la situation prêtait à r.** admittedly the situation was funny; **vous me faites r.!** you make me laugh!, nonsense!, you must be joking!; **laissez-moi r.!, ne me faites pas r.!** don't make me laugh!

2 *(s'amuser)* to have (some) fun, to have a laugh *or* a few laughs; **vous voulez r.!** you're joking!; **prendre qch en riant** to laugh sth off; **pour r.** for fun, for a laugh *or* a joke; **je te le disais en riant** it was a joke, I was pulling your leg; **non mais sans r.!** no, but seriously!; **sans r., c'est vrai** honestly *or* seriously, it's true; *Fam* **c'était pour r.** it was only for fun; **je l'ai fait histoire de r.** I did it for

a laugh *or* a joke *or* for fun

3 *Fig (des yeux)* to dance

VPR se rire se r. de qn to laugh at sb, to make fun of sb; **se r. de qch** to laugh at sth, to make light of sth

ris¹ [ri] **NM** *Litt (rire)* laughter

ris² **NM** *Naut (dans la voile)* reef; **prendre un r.** to take in a reef; **larguer un r.** to shake out a reef

ris³ **NM** *Culin* **r. (de veau)** (calf's) sweetbread

risée [rize] **NF1** *(moquerie)* mockery, derision; **s'exposer à la r. publique** to expose oneself to public scorn *or* derision **2** *(objet de moquerie)* laughing stock; **nous étions la r. de tous** we were a public laughing stock *or* the butt of everyone's jokes **3** *Naut (brise)* light squall, flurry (of wind)

risette [rizɛt] **NF** *(d'enfant)* (little) laugh, smile; **fais (la) r. à papa!** smile for daddy!, give daddy a smile!

risible [rizibl] **ADJ** *(erreur, conduite, demande etc)* laughable, ridiculous, ludicrous; *(personne)* ridiculous; **la situation n'avait rien de r.** the situation was not at all funny, there was nothing to laugh at in the situation

risiblement [rizibləmɑ̃] **ADV** ridiculously, ludicrously

risotto [rizɔto] **NM** *Culin* risotto

risque [risk] **NM** risk; **est-ce qu'il y a un r. que cela se produise?** is there any risk of that happening?; **courir un r.** to run a risk; **c'est un r. à courir** it's a risk I/we/*etc* have to take; **courir le r. de qch** to risk sth; **courir le r. de faire qch** to risk doing sth; **prendre un r./des risques** to take a risk *or* chance/risks *or* chances; **j'en prends le r.** I'll take that risk; **groupe à haut r.** high-risk group; **il est parti à ses risques et périls** he went at his own risk; **vous le faites à vos risques et périls** you do it at your own risk, on your head be it; **cela n'est pas sans r.** it is not without its risks *or* dangers; **sans aucun r., sans courir le moindre r.** without (running) any risk; **avoir le goût du r.** to like taking risks *or* chances, to like living dangerously; **au r. de sa vie** at the risk *or* peril of his life; **les risques d'erreur sont moindres** there's less risk *or* chance of making a mistake; **les risques d'aggravation sont importants** there is a significant risk that things will get worse; *Méd* **r. infectieux** risk of infection; **risques de guerre** *(en assurances)* war risks; **au r. de manquer le train** at the risk of missing the train; **c'est un des risques du métier** it's an occupational hazard; **assurance tous risques** comprehensive *or* all-risks insurance; **risques d'incendie/d'inondations** risk of fire/flooding; **cela constitue un r. pour la santé/la sécurité** it's a health/safety hazard; *Fin* **souscrire un r.** to underwrite a risk; *Fin* **r. de change** exchange risk; *Fin* **r. de contrepartie** credit risk; *Fin* **r. de marché** market risk; **r.-pays** country risk

risqué [riske] **ADJ1** *(dangereux) (entreprise etc)* risky, hazardous **2** *(osé) (plaisanterie etc)* risqué, *Fam* near the knuckle

risquer [riske] **VT1** *(mettre en danger) (vie, réputation etc)* to risk; **il faut r. le combat** we must risk a battle, we must take a chance and fight; **j'ai risqué ma carrière à cause de toi** I risked my career for you, I put my career on the line for you; **après tout, qu'est-ce que tu risques?** what have you got to lose after all?; *Fig* **r. sa tête** to put one's head on the block; *Prov* **qui ne risque rien n'a rien** nothing ventured, nothing gained; **je ne veux rien r.** I'm not taking any risks *or* any chances; **le tout pour le tout** to go for broke; **le coup** to risk *or* chance it, to chance one's luck; **r. gros** to play for big stakes; **il risquait de tout perdre** he risked *or* ran the risk of losing everything; **la grève risque de durer**

longtemps the strike may (well) go on for a long time, there's a chance that the strike will go on for a long time; *Fam* **il risque de gagner** he has *or* stands a good chance of winning, he might well win; *Fam* **il ne risque pas de te le dire** fat chance of him telling you **2** *(avancer)* **r. un œil** to peep out; **r. un œil dans une pièce** to peep into a room; **r. sa tête à la fenêtre** to take a hurried look out of the window; **il risqua une main derrière les assiettes** he put a hand gingerly behind the plates

VPR se risquer to take risks/a risk; **je ne m'y risquerais pas** I wouldn't risk it; **se r. à faire qch** to venture to do sth; **se r. dans une maison abandonnée** to venture into an abandoned house

risque-tout [riskətu] **N INV** daredevil **ADJ INV il est r.** he's a daredevil, he's constantly risking his neck; **un enfant r.** a real little daredevil of a child

rissole [risɔl] **NF** *Culin* rissole

rissoler [risɔle] **VT & VI** *Culin* to brown; **pommes (de terre) rissolées** sauté potatoes

ristourne [risturn] **NF** *Com (rabais)* discount; **faire une r. à qn** to give sb a discount; **r. de droits de douane** customs drawback; **r. de fidélité** regular customer discount *or* rebate; **r. de prime** premium rebate

ristourner [risturne] **VT** *(faire une ristourne de)* to give a discount of; **il nous a ristourné vingt pour cent du prix** he gave us a twenty per cent discount *or* twenty per cent off

ristrette [ristrɛt] **NM** *Suisse (petit café serré)* = very strong small black coffee

Rital, -ale, -als, -ales [rital] **N** *Fam Péj (Italien)* wop, *Br* Eyetie

rite [rit] **NM** rite; *Fig (habitude)* ritual; **les rites de la vie quotidienne** the rituals of everyday life; **rites d'initiation** initiation rites; **rites de passage** *ou* **initiatiques** rites of passage

ritournelle [riturnɛl] **NF** *Mus* ritornello; *Fig Fam* **c'est toujours la même r.** it's (always) the same old story

ritualiser [ritɥalize] **VT** to ritualize, to turn into a ritual

ritualisme [ritɥalism] **NM** *Rel* ritualism

ritualiste [ritɥalist] **ADJ** ritualistic **N** ritualist

rituel, -elle [ritɥɛl] **ADJ** ritual **NM** *Rel, Fig (rites)* ritual; **selon le r.** according to ritual; *Fig* **il a verrouillé les portes selon son r.** he went through his ritual of locking the doors; **r. d'initiation** initiation rites *or* ritual

rituellement [ritɥɛlmɑ̃] **ADV1** *(habituellement)* invariably; **ils y vont r. chaque année** they go every year without fail **2** *(en sociologie)* according to ritual, ritually

rivage [rivaʒ] **NM** *(de mer, lac)* shore; *Litt (de rivière)* bank

Do not confuse with **rive**.

rival, -ale, -aux, -ales [rival, -o] **ADJ, N** rival; **sans r.** unrivalled, unparalleled; **ce boulanger est sans r. pour …** there is no one to equal this baker when it comes to …

rivaliser [rivalize] **VI** **r. avec qn** to compete *or* vie with sb; **r. d'adresse/de générosité/d'élégance avec qn** to try to outdo sb in skill/generosity/elegance

rivalité [rivalite] **NF** rivalry

rive [riv] **NF** *(de rivière)* bank; *(de lac, de mer)* shore; **la R. gauche** *(de la Seine)* the Left Bank; *Can* **la R. sud** *(du Saint-Laurent)* the South Shore

Do not confuse with **rivage**.

Rive droite, rive gauche

The Right (north) Bank of the Seine is traditionally associated with business and trade, and has a reputation for being more conservative than the Left Bank. The Left (south) Bank includes districts traditionally favoured by artists, students and intellectuals, and has a reputation for being Bohemian and unconventional.

river [rive] VT **1** (attacher) to rivet; Fig **le matin, je suis rivé au lit** (je ne peux pas me lever) I just can't get out of bed in the morning; **il est rivé au lit** (il refuse de se lever) he just won't get out of bed; **impossible de bouger, j'étais rivé sur place** I couldn't move, I was rooted to the spot; **être rivé à son bureau** to be glued to or stuck at one's desk; **il a les yeux rivés sur elle** he can't take his eyes off her, his eyes are glued to her **2** Fam **r. son clou à qn** to shut sb up

riverain, -aine [rivrɛ̃, -ɛn] ADJ (de rivière) riverside, waterside; (de lac) (propriété, propriétaire) lakeside, waterside; (de route) (propriété etc) roadside, bordering (on) the road; **propriétaire r.** owner of lakeside/roadside property

N (de rivière) riverside resident; (de lac) lakeside resident; **les riverains de cette rue** the people who live in or along this street; **'route interdite sauf aux riverains'** 'residents only','no entry except for access'

rivet [rivɛ] NM rivet

rivetage [rivtaʒ] NM riveting

riveter [rivte] VT (pr ind **je rivette,** n. **rivetons**) to rivet

riveteuse [rivtøz] NF riveting machine

rivière [rivjɛr] NF **1** river; **pêche en r.** river fishing **2** Équitation water jump **3** Fig (de lave, boue) river; **r. de diamants** diamond necklace, Spéc diamond rivière

rivoir [rivwar] NM (marteau) riveting hammer; (machine) riveting machine

rivure [rivyr] NF (action) riveting; (joint) rivet(ed) joint; (tête) rivet head

rixe [riks] NF brawl; **r. au couteau** knife fight

riz [ri] NM rice; **eau/papier de r.** rice water/paper; **poudre de r.** face powder

▸▸ **r. blanc** white rice; **r. brun** ou **complet** brown rice; **r. créole** boiled rice; **r. au curry** curried rice; **r. décortiqué** husked rice; **r. étuvé** ou **incollable** non-stick rice; **r. jaune** ou **au safran** saffron rice; **r. au lait** rice pudding; **r. long** long-grain rice; **r. rond** short-grain rice; (pour le riz au lait) pudding rice; **r. sauvage** wild rice

riziculteur, -trice [rizikyltœr, -tris] N rice grower

riziculture [rizikyltyr] NF rice growing

rizière [rizjɛr] NF rice field, paddy field

riz-pain-sel NM INV Mil Arg commissariat

RMI [ɛrɛmi] NM abrév **revenu minimum d'insertion**

RMiste [ɛrɛmist] N Br ≃ person on income support, Am ≃ person on Welfare

RMN [ɛrɛmɛn] NF (abrév **résonance magnétique nucléaire**) NMR

RN [ɛrɛn] NF abrév **route nationale**

RNIS [ɛrɛnis] NM Ordinat (abrév **réseau numérique à intégration de services**) ISDN; **envoyer qch par RNIS** to ISDN sth, to send sth by ISDN

robe [rɔb] NF **1** (de femme) dress **2** (d'un avocat) robe, gown; (d'un prêtre, un cardinal etc) robe; **les gens de r., la r.** the legal profession **3** (d'oignon) skin; (de fève) husk; (d'un cigare) wrapper (leaf) **4** (pelage) (de cheval etc) coat **5** (du vin) colour, Am color

▸▸ **r. de baptême** christening robe; **r. de chambre** dressing gown, Am robe; **en r. de chambre** in one's or a dressing gown; **pommes de terre en r. de chambre** ou **en r. des champs** jacket potatoes, baked potatoes; **r. chasuble** pinafore dress, Am jumper; **r. de grossesse** maternity dress; **r. d'intérieur** housecoat; **r. de mariée** wedding dress; **r. du soir** evening gown or dress

Il faut noter que le terme anglais **robe** ne désigne jamais un vêtement de femme.

robert [rɔbɛr] NM très Fam (sein) tit, boob

robe-tablier [rɔb-] pl **robes-tabliers** NF pinafore dress, Am jumper

robin [rɔbɛ̃] NM Péj Vieilli lawyer

robine [rɔbin] NF Can Arg methylated spirits, Br meths

robinet [rɔbinɛ] NM (de l'évier, du lavabo) tap, Am faucet; (de tonneau) spigot; **ouvrir/fermer le r.** to turn the tap on/off; **eau du r.** tap water; **r. d'eau froide/chaude** cold-/hot-water tap; Fig **c'est un r. d'eau tiède** he drones or Br Fam rabbits or witters on; **r. mélangeur** mixer tap; **r. du gaz** gas tap; Tech **r. d'arrêt** ou **de fermeture** stopcock, shut-off (valve); **r. de vidange** ou **de purge** drain cock or tap; **r. à flotteur** ballcock; Naut **r. de prise d'eau à la mer** seacock; Hum **problèmes de robinets** sums about filling baths and tanks

robinetterie [rɔbinɛtri] NF (robinets) (system of) taps

robineux [rɔbinø] NM Can Arg tramp, Am hobo

robot [rɔbo] NM Tech, Fig robot; **r. (ménager)** food processor; **avion r.** drone

robotique [rɔbɔtik] NF robotics

ADJ robotic

robotisation [rɔbɔtizasjɔ̃] NF automation, roboticization

robotiser [rɔbɔtize] VT Tech (chaîne de montage etc) to automate, to roboticize; Fig **r. qn** to turn sb into a robot

robre [rɔbr] NM Cartes rubber

robusta [rɔbysta] NM (café) robusta

robuste [rɔbyst] ADJ (personne, santé, foi) robust; (appétit, confiance en soi) robust, healthy; (plante) hardy; (bicyclette, machine etc) sturdy

robustesse [rɔbystɛs] NF (d'une personne) robustness; (d'une plante) hardiness; (d'une bicyclette, une machine etc) sturdiness

ROC [ɛrose] NF Ordinat (abrév **reconnaissance optique des caractères**) OCR

roc [rɔk] NM rock; **creusé dans le r.** hollowed out of the rock; **bâti sur le r.** built on rock; Fig **bâtir sur du r.** to build on solid foundations; **solide comme un** ou **le r.** rock-solid; **Jules, c'est un r.** Jules is as solid as a rock

rocade [rɔkad] NF (route) bypass; Mil communications line

rocaille [rɔkaj] NF **1** (arrangement) (jardin de) **r.** rockery, rock garden **2** (pierraille) (loose) stones or rocks; **grotte en r.** grotto **3** (terrain) stony or rocky ground

ADJ INV Beaux-Arts (style, table etc) rocaille

rocailleux, -euse [rɔkajø, -øz] ADJ **1** (pierreux) stony, rocky **2** Fig (voix) harsh, rough

rocambole [rɔkɑ̃bɔl] NF Bot Spanish garlic

rocambolesque [rɔkɑ̃bɔlɛsk] ADJ (aventures, histoire etc) fantastic, incredible

roche [rɔʃ] NF (matière, rocher) rock; Géol **roches ignées/sédimentaires/métamorphiques** igneous/sedimentary/metamorphic rocks; **percé dans la r.** drilled in the rock; **r. de fond** bedrock; **eau de r.** clear spring water; Fig **clair comme de l'eau de r.** as clear as crystal, crystal-clear

rocher [rɔʃe] NM **1** (masse de pierre) rock; (escarpé) crag; **r. branlant** rocking stone, logan(stone); **côte hérissée de rochers** rock-bound coast; **le R. de Gibraltar** the Rock of Gibraltar, Fam the Rock **2** (paroi) rock face; **pousser à flanc de r.** to grow out of the bare rock, to cling to the side of the rock; **faire du r.** to go rock climbing **3** (bouchée de chocolat) chocolate (containing nuts) **4** (dans l'oreille) petrous bone

rochet [rɔʃɛ] NM Tech ratchet; **roue à r.** ratchet wheel

rocheux, -euse [rɔʃø, -øz] ADJ (paysage, région) rocky; **masse/paroi rocheuse** rock mass/face; **les (montagnes) Rocheuses** the Rocky Mountains, the Rockies

rock, rock and roll [rɔk(ɛnrɔl)] Mus NM rock (and roll); (danse) rock (and roll), jive; **danser le r.** to rock (and roll), to jive; **un groupe/chanteur de r.** a rock group/singer

ADJ INV (concert, groupe, chanteur etc) rock

rocker [rɔkœr] N (musicien) rock musician; (enthousiaste) rock (music) fan

rocking-chair, pl **rocking-chairs** [rɔkiɲtʃer] NM rocking chair

rococo [rɔkoko] NM Beaux-Arts rococo

ADJ INV **1** Beaux-Arts rococo **2** (démodé) old-fashioned

rodage [rɔdaʒ] NM (d'un moteur, d'une voiture) running in; **période de r.** (d'une structure) running-in or breaking-in period; Aut **en r.** running in; **voiture en r.** car that is being run in

rodéo, rodéo [rɔdeo] NM rodeo; **faire du r.** (métier) to be a rodeo rider; (prendre part à un rodéo) to take part in a rodeo; **finalement, ils se sont livrés à un véritable r. dans les rues du quartier** (en voiture) they ended up having a car chase in the streets; **r. de voitures volées** joyriding

roder [rɔde] VT (moteur, voiture) to run in; Fig (entreprise), Théâtre (spectacle) to get into its stride; (équipe, structure) to break in; **être rodé** (d'une entreprise etc), Théâtre (d'un spectacle) to be into its stride, to have settled down or shaken down; (d'un employé) to have got the hang of things

VPR **se roder** Fam to break oneself in

rôder [rɔde] VI to prowl, to be on the prowl; **r. dans les rues** to prowl about or hang about the streets; **un pauvre chien qui rôde** a poor dog roaming around; Fig Fam **il rôde autour de moi depuis quelques jours** he's been hanging around me for a few days

rôdeur, -euse [rɔdœr, -øz] ADJ prowling

N prowler

rodomontade [rɔdɔmɔ̃tad] NF rodomontade(s) boasting, bragging; **faire des rodomontades** to boast, to brag

rœsti [røʃti] NMPL Suisse Culin rosti, potato cake

Rogations [rɔgasjɔ̃] NFPL Rel Rogations

rogatoire [rɔgatwar] ADJ Jur rogatory; **commission r.** letters of request, Spéc letters rogatory

rogatons [rɔgatɔ̃] NMPL Fam (de nourriture) leftovers, scraps

rognage [rɔɲaʒ] NM (action) (du cuir, du métal etc) trimming, paring; Ordinat (d'image) cropping

rogne [rɔɲ] NF Fam bad temper; **être en r.** to be cross (contre qn with sb); **mettre qn en r.** to make sb cross; **se mettre** ou Fam **se ficher en r.** to get angry, to see red

rogner [rɔɲe] VT (griffes, ongles) to clip, to trim; (cuir, métal etc) to trim, to pare; Ordinat (image) to crop; Fig (de l'inflation) (économies etc) to eat or nibble away at, to whittle away; **r. les tranches d'un livre** to cut or trim the edges of a book; Fig **les patrons ro-**

gnaient (sur) les salaires the bosses were paring wages to the bone; *Fig* **r. sur les dépenses** to cut down on *or* curtail expenses; *Fig* **r. les ailes à qn** to clip sb's wings

rognon [rɔɲɔ̃] NM *Culin* kidney

rognonner [rɔɲɔne] VI *Fam* to grumble, to grouse

rognures [rɔɲyr] NFPL *(déchets) (de griffes, d'ongles)* clippings; *(de cuir, de métal etc)* trimmings, parings; *(de viande)* scraps

rogomme [rɔgɔm] NM *Fam* **voix de r.** (drunkard's) husky voice

rogue [rɔg] ADJ arrogant, haughty

roi [rwa] NM **1** *(souverain)* king; **le r. Louis XIII** (King) Louis XIII; *Bible* **les Rois mages** the Three Wise Men, the Three Kings, the Magi; **le R.-Soleil** the Sun King; **jour** *ou* **fête des Rois** Twelfth Night; *Rel* Epiphany; **tirer les rois** = to celebrate Twelfth Night; **plat de r.** dish fit for a king; **heureux comme un r.** as happy as a sandboy; *Fig* **le r. n'est pas son cousin** he's got a very high opinion of himself; *Fig* **le choix du r.** a boy followed by a girl **2** *Fig* king; **le r. des animaux** *(lion)* the king of the beasts; **le r. du plastique/des pizzas** the plastics/pizza king; **l'un des rois du pétrole** one of the oil barons; *Hum* **r. de la resquille** *(dans une queue)* champion queue-jumper; *(dans le métro etc)* champion fare-dodger; *(au cinéma, au stade)* champion at sneaking in for nothing; **c'est le r. des imbéciles** he's a prize *or* first-class idiot; *très Fam* **c'est le r. des cons** he's a complete arsehole *or Am* asshole **3** *Cartes, Échecs* king
ADJ INV **bleu r.** royal blue

Tirer les rois
The French traditionally celebrate Epiphany with a round, almond-flavoured pastry ("la galette des Rois") containing a small porcelain figurine ("la fève" – originally a dried bean). The pastry is shared out and the person who finds the "fève" is appointed "king" or "queen" and given a cardboard crown to wear. This tradition is called "tirer les Rois".

roide [rwad], **roideur** [rwadœr], **roidir** [rwadir] *Arch* = raide, raideur, raidir

roille [rɔj] NF *Suisse Fam* downpour; **pleuvoir à (la) r.** to bucket down, *Br* to chuck it down

roillé [rɔje] ADJ *Suisse Fam (fou, cinglé)* crazy

roiller [rɔje] VI *Suisse Fam (pleuvoir)* to bucket down, *Br* to chuck it down

roitelet [rwatlɛ] NM **1** *Péj* petty king **2** *(oiseau)* wren; **r. huppé** goldcrest

rôle [rol] NM **1** *Théâtre, Fig* part, role; **r.-titre** title role; **premier r.** leading role, lead; **c'est elle qui a le premier r.** she has the leading role, she is the lead *or* the leading lady; **second r.** supporting part *or* role; **Mme Oldani dans le r. de la Tosca** Mme Oldani as Tosca; **il est toujours excellent dans les rôles de jeune premier** he is always excellent as the romantic lead; **jouer le r. de Macbeth** to play (the part of) Macbeth; **on lui fait jouer le r. d'Ophélia** she's been given the role *or* part of Ophelia, she's been cast as Ophelia; **distribution des rôles** *(action)* casting; *(liste)* cast (list); **répéter/connaître son r.** to learn/know one's part *or* lines; *Fig* **assigner un r. à qn** to assign a role to sb; *Fam* **jouer un r. secondaire** *(d'une personne)* to play second fiddle; **cet élément joue un r. secondaire dans ...** this element plays a secondary role in ...; **tu as le beau r.** it's easy *or* all right for you, you've got the easy job; **il n'a pas le beau r.** he doesn't have it easy; **les femmes n'ont pas toujours un r. facile** a woman's role

---

is not always easy, women do not always have it easy; **le r. du médecin** the doctor's role *or* function *or* job; **il avait, en quelque sorte, le r. de confesseur** he acted as a kind of confessor; **le r. du sport dans l'éducation** the role *or* function of sport in education; **un r. de premier plan** a leading role; **jeu de rôles** role playing; **ce n'est pas son r. de te conseiller** it's not his/her job to advise you **2** *(liste)* list, register; **à tour de r.** in turn, by turns, in rotation; **faire qch à tour de r.** to take turns (in) doing sth, to do sth turn and turn about *or* in turns; **nous sommes entrés dans son bureau à tour de r.** we went into his office in turn; **les rôles de l'armée active** the active list; *Naut* **r. de l'équipage** list of the crew, muster roll; *Admin* **r. des impôts** *ou* **d'impôt** assessment book; *Admin* **r. des contributions** tax roll

roller [rɔlœr] NM roller skate

rolleur, -euse [rɔlœr, -øz] N roller skater

rollier [rɔlje] NM *(oiseau)* roller

rollmops [rɔlmɔps] NM INV *Culin* rollmop

roll on-roll off [rɔlɔnrɔlɔf] ADJ INV, NM INV *(navire)* **r.** roll-on/roll-off ship, RO-RO ship

ROM [rɔm] NF INV *Ordinat* ROM

romain, -aine[1] [rɔmɛ̃, -ɛn] ADJ Roman; **l'Empire r.** the Roman Empire; **l'Église romaine** the Church of Rome; **chiffres romains** Roman numerals; *Typ* **caractère r.** roman character; **en caractères romains** in roman
N **R.** Roman
NM *Typ* roman

romaine[2] ADJ, NF *(balance)* **r.** steelyard

romaine[3] NF *(laitue)* cos (lettuce), *Am* romaine; *Fig Fam* **être bon comme la r.** *(bienveillant)* to be extremely kind; *(destiné à être victime)* to be sure to get it in the neck

roman[1] [rɔmɑ̃] NM **1** *(en prose)* novel; **r. cycle, r.-fleuve** saga, roman fleuve; **sa vie est un véritable r.** his life is like something out of a novel; **le nouveau r.** the antinovel, the nouveau roman **2** *Hist (poème)* romance; **le R. de la Rose** the Romance of the Rose
►► **r. d'amour** love story, romance; **r. d'apprentissage** Bildungsroman; **r. de cape et d'épée** swashbuckler; **r. à clés** roman à clef; **r. de gare** airport novel; **r. noir** thriller; **r. policier** detective novel; *Fam* whodunnit

roman[2] ADJ **1** *Ling* Romance **2** *Archit* Romanesque; *(en Angleterre)* Norman
NM **1** *Ling* Romance **2** *Archit* Romanesque style; *(en Angleterre)* Norman style

> Il faut noter que le terme anglais **Roman** est un faux ami. Il signifie **romain**.

romance [rɔmɑ̃s] NF *(chanson)* (sentimental) song, drawing-room ballad

romancer [rɔmɑ̃se] VT *(biographie)* to fictionalize; *(événement, histoire)* to romanticize

romanche [rɔmɑ̃ʃ] ADJ, NM *Ling* Romans(c)h

romancier, -ière [rɔmɑ̃sje, -jɛr] N novelist

romand [rɔmɑ̃] ADJ **la Suisse romande** French(-speaking) Switzerland
NMPL **les Romands** the French(-speaking) Swiss

romanesque [rɔmanɛsk] ADJ **1** *(personnage, aventure etc)* romantic; **un personnage r.** a romantic figure; **une situation r.** a situation worthy of a novel **2** *Littér (technique etc)* novelistic; **l'œuvre r. de Sartre** Sartre's fiction *or* novels

> Do not confuse with **romantique**.

roman-feuilleton, *pl* **romans-feuilletons** NM serial

romanichel, -elle [rɔmaniʃɛl] N *Péj (tsigane)* gipsy, romany **2** *(vagabond)* tramp, vagrant

---

romaniser [rɔmanize] VT *Hist* to Romanize

romaniste [rɔmanist] N **1** *Ling* student of the Romance languages **2** *Rel, Jur* Romanist

romano [rɔmano] N *Fam Péj (tsigane)* gippo, *Br* pikey

roman-photo, *pl* **romans-photos** NM photo-story, picture story; *(sentimental)* photoromance, picture romance

romantique [rɔmɑ̃tik] ADJ **1** *Beaux-Arts, Littér* Romantic **2** *(personne, idées, film etc)* romantic
N **1** *Beaux-Arts, Littér* Romantic(ist) **2** *(sentimental)* romantic

> Do not confuse with **romanesque**.

romantisme [rɔmɑ̃tism] NM **1** *Beaux-Arts, Littér* Romanticism **2** *(d'une personne)* romanticism; **ça ne manque pas de r.** it's quite romantic; **paysage plein de r.** romantic countryside

romarin [rɔmarɛ̃] NM *Bot, Culin* rosemary

rombière [rɔ̃bjɛr] NF *Arg* **(vieille) r.** old biddy

Rome [rɔm] N Rome; *Prov* **tous les chemins mènent à R.** all roads lead to Rome

rompre [rɔ̃pr] (**je romps, il rompt, ils rompent**) VT **1** *(casser)* to break; *(en deux parties)* to break in two; *(bâton, fil)* to snap; *(en plusieurs parties)* to break (up); **r. ses digues** *(d'un fleuve etc)* to burst its banks; **r. le silence** to break the silence; **le silence de la nuit était rompu par ...** the silence of the night was shattered by ...; **r. une promesse** to break a promise; **r. le pain** to break bread; *Théâtre* **applaudir à tout r.** to applaud wildly; *Mil* **r. les rangs** to fall out, to dismiss, to break ranks **2** *(interrompre) (conversation, fiançailles, relations diplomatiques, amitié)* to break off; *(contrat), Élec (circuit)* to break; **le charme est rompu** the spell is broken; **cela rompt un peu la monotonie** it helps to break *or* relieve the monotony; **il ne faut pas r. le rythme** keep up the rhythm; **r. le rythme quotidien** to provide a distraction from the daily routine; **r. un tête-à-tête** to interrupt a *or* break in on a private conversation; **la France a rompu les relations avec la Chine** France has broken off *or* severed relations with China; **r. l'équilibre** to upset the balance; **r. les chiens** to call off the hounds; *Fig* to change the subject
VI **1** *(casser)* to break; *(d'un bâton, d'un fil)* to break, to snap; *Fig (de deux amants)* to split up, to break it off; **r. avec** *(amant)* to break it off with, to finish with; *(tradition, passé)* to break with; **r. avec sa famille** to break off relations with one's family; **r. avec une habitude** to break (oneself of) a habit **2** *Mil* **r. devant l'ennemi** to break before the enemy **3** *Boxe, Escrime* to break
VPR **se rompre** *(se casser)* to break; *(d'un bâton, d'un fil)* to break, to snap; *(de la glace)* to break (up); *Méd (d'un vaisseau sanguin)* to rupture; **son cœur battait à se r.** his heart was throbbing violently *or* fit to burst; *Fig* **se r. le cou** to break one's neck

rompu [rɔ̃py] ADJ **1** broken; *Méd (vaisseau sanguin)* ruptured; **fiançailles rompues** broken engagement; **chemin r.** road full of potholes; **être r. (de fatigue)** to be worn out *or* tired out; **r. de travail** worn out *or* tired out by work; **couleur rompue** colour with a shot effect **2** **r. à** used to; **être r. aux affaires** to be experienced in business

romsteck [rɔmstɛk] NM rump steak

ronce [rɔ̃s] NF **1** *(arbuste)* bramble (bush), blackberry bush; *(branche)* bramble **2** **ronce(s) artificielle(s)** barbed wire **3** *(nœud de certains bois)* **r. de noyer** bur(r) walnut

ronceraie [rɔ̃srɛ] NF bramble patch

ronchon, -onne [rɔ̃ʃɔ̃, -ɔn] *Fam* ADJ grouchy, grumpy
 N grumbler, grouser

ronchonnement [rɔ̃ʃɔnmɑ̃] NM *Fam* grumbling, grousing, bellyaching; **j'en ai assez de tes ronchonnements** I've had enough of your grumbling *or* grousing *or* bellyaching

ronchonner [rɔ̃ʃɔne] VI *Fam* to grumble, to grouse, to grouch

ronchonneur, -euse [rɔ̃ʃɔnœr, -øz] ADJ, N *Fam* = ronchon

roncier [rɔ̃sje] NM, **roncière** [rɔ̃sjɛr] NF (thick) bramble bush

rond, ronde [rɔ̃, rɔ̃d] ADJ 1 *(balle, table, nappe etc)* round; *(ventre)* rounded; *(poitrine de femme)* full; *(personne, joues, silhouette)* plump; **écriture ronde** round hand(writing); **avoir le dos r.** to be round-shouldered; **avoir le ventre r.** to have a bit of a stomach; **tuiles rondes** curved *or* rounded tiles; **le ballon r.** (association) football, *Br* soccer; **faire des yeux ronds** to goggle, to gape; **avoir des yeux ronds** to be wide-eyed (with astonishment)
 2 *Fig* **voix ronde** full voice; **en chiffres ronds** in round figures; **deux cents euros en chiffres ronds** a round two hundred euros; **compte r.** round sum; *Fam* **homme tout r.** straightforward man; **r. en affaires** businesslike; **être r. en affaires** to be straightforward where business is concerned
 3 *Fam (ivre)* wasted, *Br* ratted; **r. comme une queue de pelle** completely wasted *or Br* ratted
 ADV **tourner r.** *(d'une roue)* to run true; *(d'un moteur), Fig (d'une entreprise, d'une affaire etc)* to run smoothly; **ça fera 100 euros tout r.** that makes it a hundred euros exactly; **avaler qch tout r.** to swallow sth whole; *Fam* **cela ne tourne pas r.** there's something not right, there's something the matter; *Fam* **elle ne tourne pas r.** there's something up *or* the matter with her
 NM 1 *(figure)* circle; **le chat se met en r.** the cat curls (itself) up; **danser/s'asseoir en r.** to dance/sit in a circle *or* a ring; **tourner en r.** to go round in a circle *or* ring; *Fig* to go round in circles; *Fam* **en baver des ronds de chapeau** to be having a helluva time; **il m'en fait baver des ronds de chapeau** he's making my life hell
 2 *(rondelle) (de saucisson, carotte)* slice; *(de beurre)* pat; *Fam* **il n'a pas un r.** he hasn't a penny, he hasn't a brass farthing
 NF **ronde 1** *(danse)* round (dance); *(chanson)* round, roundelay
 2 *Mil etc (visite de surveillance)* round(s); *(de policier)* beat; **faire une/sa ronde** to patrol; *(de policier)* to be on the beat; *Arch* **la ronde de nuit** *(hommes, veille)* the night watch; **chemin de ronde** parapet walk, rampart walk
 3 *(écriture)* round hand(writing)
 4 *Mus (note)* semibreve, *Am* whole note
 5 **à la ronde** around; **visible à dix kilomètres à la ronde** visible for ten kilometres around; **il n'y avait personne à dix kilomètres à la ronde** there was nobody within a radius of ten kilometres; **(faire) passer le vin à la ronde** to pass the wine round, to hand round the wine; **boire à la ronde** to drink in turn
 ▶▶ **r. de cuir** *(coussin)* (round leather) chair cushion; *(figure de danse)* **r. de jambe** rond de jambe; *Fam* **faire des ronds de jambe** to bow and scrape; **r. de serviette** napkin ring

rond-de-cuir, *pl* **ronds-de-cuir** [rɔ̃dkɥir] NM *Fam Péj* penpusher, clerk

rondeau, -eaux [rɔ̃do] NM 1 *Littér* rondeau
 2 *Mus* rondo

ronde-bosse, *pl* **rondes-bosses** NF *Beaux-Arts* sculpture in the round; **en r.** in the round

rondelet, -ette [rɔ̃dlɛ, -ɛt] ADJ *(personne, doigts)* plump, chubby, podgy; **somme rondelette** good (round) sum, tidy sum

rondelle [rɔ̃dɛl] NF 1 *(de carton etc)* disc; *(de citron, de saucisson, de cornichon etc)* slice; *Can* **r. (de hockey)** puck; **couper les légumes en rondelles** to slice the vegetables 2 *(de vis, d'écrou etc)* washer; *Aut* **r. butée** thrust washer; *Aut* **r. de blocage** lock washer

rondement [rɔ̃dmɑ̃] ADV 1 *(promptement)* briskly, promptly, smartly; **mener r. les choses** to make short work of things, to deal with things promptly 2 *(carrément)* bluntly, frankly; **il nous a dit r. qu'il n'était pas d'accord** he told us straight (out) *or* bluntly *or* frankly that he didn't agree

rondeur [rɔ̃dœr] NF 1 roundness; *(d'une personne, des joues etc)* plumpness; **rondeurs** rounded forms *or* lines; *(d'une femme)* curves; **avoir des rondeurs** to be curvy *or* curvaceous 2 *(franchise)* straightforwardness, plain dealing; **avec r.** bluntly, frankly

rondin [rɔ̃dɛ̃] NM log; **cabane en rondins** log cabin; **chemin de rondins** corduroy road

rondo [rɔ̃do] NM *Mus* rondo

rondouillard [rɔ̃dujar] ADJ *Fam (personne)* plump, chubby, podgy

rond-point, *pl* **ronds-points** NM *(sens giratoire)* roundabout, *Am* traffic circle

Ronéo® [rɔneo] NF Roneo®

ronéotyper [rɔneɔtipe] VT to roneo

ronflant [rɔ̃flɑ̃] ADJ *(vent, feu)* roaring; *(moteur)* whirring, purring; *(poêle)* purring; *Fig Péj (titre, promesse, discours, style etc)* high-flown, high-sounding

ronflement [rɔ̃fləmɑ̃] NM 1 *(de dormeur)* snoring 2 *Fig (du vent, d'un feu)* roaring; *(de moteur, machine)* whirring, purring; *(du poêle)* purring

ronfler [rɔ̃fle] VI 1 *(de dormeur)* to snore 2 *Fig (du vent, d'un feu)* to roar; *(d'un moteur)* to whirr, to purr; *(d'un poêle)* to purr; **faire r. le moteur** to rev the engine

ronflette [rɔ̃flɛt] NF *Fam* snooze; **piquer une r.** to have a nap *or* a snooze

ronfleur, -euse [rɔ̃flœr, -øz] N *(personne)* snorer
 NM *Tél* buzzer

ronger [rɔ̃ʒe] **(je rongeai(s); n. rongeons)** VT 1 *(d'une souris etc)* to gnaw (at), to nibble (at); **r. un os** *(d'un chien)* to gnaw (on) a bone; **rongé par les vers** wormeaten 2 *(d'un acide, de la rouille) (métal etc)* to eat away *or* into; *(de la mer) (falaises)* to erode; *Fig* **être rongé de chagrin** to be consumed *or* tormented with grief; **être rongé de remords/par la jalousie/par l'anxiété** to be eaten up with remorse/jealousy/anxiety; **rongé par la maladie** wasted by illness; **rongé par un cancer** riddled with cancer; **c'est quelque chose qui finit par la r.** it's eating away at her
 VPR **se ronger 1** to worry, to fret; **se r. de chagrin, se r. le cœur** *ou* **les sangs** to eat one's heart out 2 **se r. les ongles** to bite one's nails

rongeur, -euse [rɔ̃ʒœr, -øz] ADJ *(mammifère)* rodent-like
 NM rodent

ronron [rɔ̃rɔ̃] NM *Fam (d'un chat)* purr(ing); *(d'un moteur)* purr, purring (noise), whirr, whirring (noise); *(d'un avion, une voix, un discours, de la musique)* drone, droning (noise); *(d'une machine)* whirr, whirring (noise); **faire r.** *(d'un chat)* to purr; *Fig* **le r. de la vie quotidienne** the monotony of everyday life, humdrum routine

ronronnement [rɔ̃rɔnmɑ̃] NM *(d'un chat)* purring; *(d'un moteur)* purr, purring, whirr, whirring, drone; *(d'un avion)* drone, droning (noise); *(d'une machine)* whirr, whirring (noise)

ronronner [rɔ̃rɔne] VI *(d'un chat)* to purr; *(d'un moteur)* to purr, to whirr; *(d'un avion)* to drone; *(d'une machine)* to whirr; *Fig* to be in a rut; **r. de plaisir** to purr with pleasure

room-service [rumsɛrvis] NM room service

roque [rɔk] NM *Échecs* castling; **petit/grand r.** castling on the king's/queen's side

roquefort [rɔkfɔr] NM *(fromage)* Roquefort

roquer [rɔke] VI 1 *Échecs* to castle 2 *(au croquet)* to croquet the ball

roquet [rɔkɛ] NM *Péj (chien)* yapper; *Fam (personne)* little squirt

roquette¹ [rɔkɛt] NF *Bot* rocket

roquette² NF *Mil (projectile)* rocket; **r. antichar** anti-tank rocket

rorqual [rɔrkwal] NM rorqual, finback (whale)

rosace [rozas] NF *Archit* 1 rose (window) 2 **r. de plafond** ceiling rose

rosacé [rozase] ADJ *Bot* rose-like, *Spéc* rosaceous

rosaire [rozɛr] NM *Rel* rosary; **dire** *ou* **réciter son r.** to tell one's beads, to say the rosary

rosâtre [rozɑtr] ADJ pinkish

rosbif [rɔzbif] NM 1 *Culin (rôti)* roast beef; *(à rôtir)* roasting beef 2 *très Fam (terme injurieux) (Britannique)* Brit

rose [roz] NF 1 *(fleur)* rose; **bouton de r.** rosebud; **eau de r.** rosewater; *Fam* **roman à l'eau de r.** soppy love story, soppy romance; **essence de roses** attar *or* otto of roses; **teint de r.** rosy complexion; **frais comme une r.** fresh as a daisy; *Fam* **ça ne sent pas la r.!** it's a bit whiffy!; *Fam* **envoyer qn sur les roses** to send sb packing, to send sb off with a flea in his/her ear; *Prov* **(il n'est) pas de r. sans épines** there's no rose without a thorn 2 **bois de r.** rosewood 3 *Archit* rose (window) 4 *(diamant)* rose (diamond), rose-cut diamond
 ADJ 1 *(robe etc)* pink; *(teint)* rosy; **des rubans r. pivoine** peony-red ribbons; **tout n'est pas r. dans ce monde** life is not a bed of roses; **ce n'est pas bien r., cette histoire-là** it's a pretty grim story 2 *Fam (socialiste)* left-wing *(relating to the French Socialist Party)*
 NM pink; **voir la vie** *ou* **tout en r.** to see everything through rose-coloured glasses *or* spectacles
 ▶▶ *Bot* **r. incarnate** damask rose; **r. mousseuse** moss rose; *Géol* **r. des sables** desert rose; **r. sauvage** wild rose, dog rose; *Naut* **r. des vents** compass card

rosé [roze] ADJ pinkish; **vin r.** rosé
 NM *(vin)* rosé

roseau, -eaux [rozo] NM reed

rose-croix NM INV Rosicrucian
 NF Rosicrucianism

rosée [roze] NF dew; **goutte de r.** dewdrop; *Phys* **point de r.** dew point

roselet [rozlɛ] NM *(fourrure)* ermine

roselier, -ière [rozəlje, -jɛr] ADJ **marais r.** reed marsh
 NF **roselière** reed bed

roséole [rozeɔl] NF *Méd* roseola

roser [roze] VT *Littr* **r. qch** to make *or* turn sth pink

roseraie [rozrɛ] NF rose garden

rose-thé, *pl* **roses-thé** NF INV, ADJ INV tea rose

Rosette [rozɛt] N **la pierre de R.** the Rosetta stone

rosette [rozɛt] NF 1 *(nœud)* bow; *(ornement)* rosette 2 *(insigne)* rosette *(esp of the Legion of Honour)*; **recevoir la r.** to be awarded the Legion of Honour 3 **r. de Lyon** = sort of slicing sausage

rosicrucien, -ienne [rozikrysjɛ̃, -jɛn] ADJ, N Rosicrucian

rosier [rozje] NM rose tree, rose bush; **r.**

ruisseau, -eaux [rɥiso] NM **1** (cours d'eau) brook, (small) stream; Prov **les petits ruisseaux font les grandes rivières** great oaks from little acorns grow **2** Fig (de sang, de lave) stream; (de larmes) flood; **il coulait des ruisseaux de lave/de boue/de sang** the lava/mud/blood was flowing in streams **3** (le long du trottoir) gutter; Fig **ramasser qn dans le r.** to pick sb up out of the gutter; Fig **sortir qn du r.** to pull sb out of the gutter; Fig **pousser qn au r.** to throw sb into the gutter; Fig **tomber dans le r.** to end up in the gutter

ruisselant [rɥislã] ADJ streaming, dripping (wet) (**de** with); **eaux ruisselantes** running water; (en filets) trickling water; **r. de sueur** dripping with sweat; **il était r. de sueur** he was dripping with sweat, the sweat was pouring off him

ruisseler [rɥisle] VI (**il ruisselle; il ruissellera**) **1** (d'un liquide) to stream, to run; (en filets) to trickle; **l'eau ruisselait par la porte** the water was streaming or pouring in/out the door **2** (d'une surface) to run, to drip, to stream (**de** with); **le parquet ruisselait** the floor was running with water; **front ruisselant de sueur** forehead dripping or pouring with sweat; **ses joues ruisselaient de larmes** tears were streaming down his/her cheeks, his/her cheeks were streaming with tears; **r. de lumière** to be ablaze with light

ruisselet [rɥislɛ] NM brooklet, rivulet, rill

ruissellement [rɥisɛlmã] NM **1** (de l'eau) streaming, running; (en filets) trickling; Géog runoff; **eaux de r.** runoff **2** (de bijoux, de lumière etc) shimmer

rumba [rumba] NF (danse, musique) rumba

rumen [rymɛn] NM INV (de ruminant) rumen

rumeur [rymœr] NF **1** (bruit confus) distant murmur; (de la circulation) hum; **la r. lointaine de la ville/de l'usine** the distant sound of the city/the factory; **des rumeurs de mécontentement s'élevèrent de la foule** rumblings of discontent rose from the crowd **2** (on-dit) rumour, Am rumor; **victime de la r. publique, elle dut quitter la ville** a victim of local gossip, she had to leave town; **il démissionna, contraint par la r. publique** he was forced to resign because of rumours going around; **la r. court qu'il est ruiné** rumour has it that or there's a rumour going round that he's ruined; **j'ai entendu des rumeurs selon lesquelles ...** I've heard rumours or whispers or a whisper that ...

ruminant [ryminã] ADJ, NM Zool ruminant

rumination [ryminasjɔ̃] NF Zool rumination, ruminating

ruminer [rymine] VI (d'un animal) to ruminate, to chew the cud
▪ VT **1** (d'un animal) to ruminate, to chew **2** Fig (idée, projet etc) to ponder, to mull or chew over, to ruminate on

rumsteck [rɔmstɛk] NM rump steak

runabout [rœnabawt] NM Naut runabout, speedboat

rune [ryn] NF Ling rune

runique [rynik] ADJ runic

rupestre [rypɛstr] ADJ **dessins rupestres** rock drawings; **peintures rupestres** cave paintings; **plantes rupestres** rock plants

rupin, -ine [rypɛ̃, -in] Fam ADJ (riche) (personne) loaded; (logement) plush
N **c'est un r.** he's loaded, he's rolling in it; **les rupins** the rich, the well-off

rupiner [rypine] VI Arg **r. à un examen** to do well in an exam

rupteur [ryptœr] NM Élec contact breaker, circuit breaker; Aut **r. (d'allumage)** make-and-break

rupture [ryptyr] NF **1** (d'une corde, d'une poutre etc) breaking; (d'un barrage) bursting; (d'un vaisseau sanguin, un ligament) rupture; (d'un os) fracture **2** (d'une surface etc) breaking up; Mil **obus de r.** armour-piercing shell **3** Fig (de négociations) breaking off (**de** of), breakdown (**de** in); (de relations diplomatiques) severance, breaking off; (d'un marché) calling off; **la r. de ses fiançailles** the breaking off of his/her engagement; Jur **r. de contrat/de promesse de mariage** breach of contract/of promise; **r. abusive** (de contrat) breach; Pol **être en r. avec le parti** to be at odds with or in disagreement with the party; **en r. avec la tradition** in a break with tradition; **il y a eu r. entre eux** they've quarrelled, there's been a split between them, there is a rift between them; **scène de r.** break-up scene; **la r. de la princesse et de son époux** the break-up of the princess and her husband; **lors de leur r.** when they broke up or split up; Élec **r. du circuit** breaking of or break in the circuit; **r. de l'alimentation** power outage
▸ ▸ Méd **r. d'anévrisme** ruptured aneurism; Com **r. de charge** transhipment of cargo; **r. de stock** stock outage; **ce magasin est en r. de stock** this shop is out of stock

Il faut noter que le nom anglais **rupture** signifie également **hernie**.

rural, -ale, -aux, -ales [ryral, -o] ADJ (région) rural; (vie) country, rural; **chemin r.** country lane
N country person; **les ruraux** country people

ruse [ryz] NF ruse, trick; **une r. pour faire qch** a trick for doing sth; **la r.** (habileté) cunning; **gagner par la r.** to win by trickery or a trick; **obtenir qch par r.** to obtain sth by a ruse or a trick or by cunning; **r. de guerre** stratagem (of war); Fig crafty trick; **c'est une de mes ruses de guerre pour ne pas payer** it's one of my dodges to get out of paying; Fig **r. d'Indien** crafty or cunning trick

rusé, -ée [ryze] ADJ cunning, crafty, wily; **r. comme un renard** cunning as a fox
N **c'est une (petite) rusée** she's a crafty or cunning little thing

ruser [ryze] VI to use trickery or cunning

rush [rœʃ] NM **1** Sport (à la fin d'une course) sprint, spurt **2** Fam (de la foule) rush **3** Cin **rushes** rushes, dailies

russe [rys] ADJ Russian
NM Ling Russian
N **R.** Russian

Russie [rysi] NF Russia; **R. blanche** White Russia

russification [rysifikasjɔ̃] NF Russification, Russianization

russifier [rysifje] VT (impf, pr sub n. **russifiions**) to Russify, to Russianize

rustaud, -aude [rysto, -od] ADJ uncouth
N (country) bumpkin, Am hick

rusticité [rystisite] NF **1** rusticity, Péj uncouthness **2** Agr (d'une plante) hardiness

Rustine® [rystin] NF repair patch (for mending inner tube of bicycle); **mettre une R.** to mend a puncture; **boîte à Rustines®** repair kit

rustique [rystik] ADJ **1** (manières, vie, maison etc) rustic; **mobilier r.** rustic(-style) or country-style furniture; **petit pont de bois r.** little rustic bridge **2** Constr **ouvrage r.** rustic (stone)work **3** Agr (plante) hardy
NM rustic or country look

rustre [rystr] Péj ADJ uncouth, oafish
NM oaf, boor, lout

rut [ryt] NM Zool (de mâle) rut(ting); (de femelle) heat; **en r.** rutting; (femelle) in or on heat

rutabaga [rytabaga] NM swede, Am rutabaga

ruthénium [rytenjɔm] NM Chimie ruthenium

rutilance [rytilãs] NF gleam; (rouge) red glow

rutilant [rytilã] ADJ gleaming; (rouge) glowing red

rutilement [rytilmã] NM gleam; (rouge) red glow

rutiler [rytile] VI to gleam; (rouge) to glow red

Rwanda [rwãda] NM Rwanda

rwandais, -aise [rwãdɛ, -ɛz] ADJ Rwandan
N **R.** Rwandan

rythme [ritm] NM Mus, Littér rhythm; **r. cardiaque/respiratoire** heart/breathing rate; **le r. de la vie moderne** the tempo or pace of modern life; **il te faudra changer de r.** you'll need to change pace or Fam to move up/down a gear; **travailler à un r. régulier** to work at a steady rhythm or pace; Mus **marquer le r.** to beat time; **suivre le r.** to follow the beat; Fig to keep up with the times; **avoir le sens du r.** to have a sense of rhythm; **avoir le r. dans la peau** to have a natural sense of rhythm, to have rhythm; **ce film manque de r.** the film is a bit slow or lacks pace; Com **r. des livraisons** delivery rate; **r. de production** rate of production; **à quel r. dois-je te les envoyer?** what rate should I send them to you at?; **au r. de trois par semaine** at the rate of three a week; **à ce r., nous n'aurons pas fini ce soir** at this rate, we won't have finished by this evening; **r. biologique** biorhythm; **les rythmes scolaires** the way in which the school year is organized

rythmé [ritme] ADJ rhythmic, rhythmical

rythmer [ritme] VT (mouvement, phrase etc) to put rhythm into, to give rhythm to; **le prof a rythmé la chanson avec une baguette** the teacher tapped out the beat of the song with a stick; **je n'ai pas pu m'empêcher de r. la chanson du pied** I couldn't help tapping my foot to the song

rythmique [ritmik] ADJ rhythmic(al); **section r.** (dans un orchestre de jazz) rhythm section
NF rhythmics

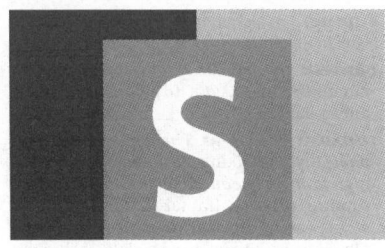

S¹, s [ɛs] NM *(lettre)* S, s; **faire des s to zigzag; la route fait des s sur plusieurs kilomètres** the road zigzags for several kilometres; **en S** S-shaped; **sentier/route en s** winding *or* zigzagging path/road

S² 1 *(abrév* **Sud)** S **2** *(abrév* **seconde)** sec

S.A. [ɛsa] NF *(abrév* **Société Anonyme)** plc

sa [sa] ADJ POSS *voir* **son¹**

Saba [saba] N **la reine de S.** the Queen of Sheba

sabaye [sabɛj] NF *Naut* mooring rope; *(pour remorquer)* towline

sabayon [sabajɔ̃] NM *Culin* zabaglione

sabbat [saba] NM **1** (Jewish) Sabbath; **jour du s.** Sabbath (day); **observer/violer le s.** to keep/break the Sabbath **2** *(assemblée nocturne) (de sorcières)* sabbath; *Litt* **il s'éleva dans la nuit un s. de miaulements et de feulements** a caterwauling sound rent the night air

sabbatique [sabatik] ADJ **1** *Rel (repos)* sabbatical **2** *(d'universitaire) (année, congé)* sabbatical; **prendre un an de congé s., prendre un congé s. d'un an** to take a year's sabbatical, to take a sabbatical year

sabin, -ine [sabɛ̃, -in] *Antiq* ADJ Sabine N **S.** Sabine; **l'enlèvement des Sabines** the rape of the Sabine women

sabir [sabir] NM *Ling* lingua franca, *Fam* gibberish; *Fam* **parler dans un drôle de s.** to talk gibberish

sablage [sablaʒ] NM **1** *Ind (de bâtiment)* sandblasting **2** *(de routes)* sanding, gritting

sable¹ [sabl] NM sand; **plage de s.** sandy beach; **dune de s.** sand dune; **tempête de s.** sandstorm; *Naut* **fond de s.** sandy bottom; **bac à s.** *(pour enfants)* sandpit, *Am* sandbox; *Constr* **s. liant** *ou* **mordant** sharp sand; *Tech* **s. de fer** fine iron filings; *Fig* **bâtir sur du s.** to build on sand; *Fig* **ce fut le grain de s. dans l'engrenage** that threw a spanner in the works; *Fig Fam* **être sur le s.** *(sans travail)* to be out of work *or* a job; *(démuni)* to be down and out; *Fam* **mettre qn sur le s.** to ruin sb
ADJ INV sand-coloured, sandy
▸▸ **sables mouvants** quicksands

sable² NM *Hér* sable

sablé [sable] *Culin* ADJ **pâte sablée** sweet shortcrust pastry
NM shortbread (biscuit *or Am* cookie)

sabler [sable] VT **1** *(chemin etc)* to sand; *(route verglacée)* to grit **2** *(bâtiment)* to sandblast **3** *Fam* **s. le champagne** to break open a bottle of champagne

sableuse [sabløz] NF sandblaster, sand jet

sableux, -euse [sablø, -øz] ADJ sandy

sablier [sablije] NM hourglass; *Culin* egg timer

sablière [sablijer] NF **1** *(carrière)* sand quarry **2** *(de locomotive)* sand box **3** *Constr etc* (lengthwise) beam, stringer

sablonneux, -euse [sablɔnø, -øz] ADJ sandy

sablonnière [sablɔnjer] NF sand quarry

sabord [sabɔr] NM *Naut* porthole; **s. de charge** cargo door; *Fam Vieilli* **mille sabords!** shiver my timbers!

sabordage [sabɔrdaʒ] NM, **sabordement** [sabɔrdəmɑ̃] NM *Naut* scuttling; *Fig (d'entreprise)* scuppering

saborder [sabɔrde] VT *(navire)* to scuttle; *Fig (détruire) (projet, entreprise etc)* to scupper
VPR **se saborder** *Naut* to scuttle one's ship; *Fig (se ruiner)* to bring about one's own downfall; **ce n'est pas possible, il est en train de se s.** *(d'un étudiant, postulant)* it's unbelievable the way he's scuppering his chances

sabot [sabo] NM **1** clog; *Fam* **je vous vois venir avec vos gros sabots** I can see what you're after, I can see you coming a mile off; *Fam* **elle a les deux pieds dans le même s.** she just sits back and waits for things to happen; **elle n'a pas les deux pieds dans le même s.** she doesn't let the grass grow under her feet
2 *Fam Vieilli* old *or* useless article; *(navire)* old tub; *(voiture)* old crock *or* banger; **il joue/chante/danse comme un s.** he can't play/ sing/dance to save his life; **elle travaille comme un s.** she makes a botch of everything
3 *(d'un cheval etc)* hoof
4 *Tech (de meuble)* caster socket; **s. d'arrêt** chock; **s. de frein** brake shoe; **s. de Denver** Denver boot, wheel clamp; **mettre un s. de Denver à une voiture** to (wheel-)clamp a car; *Aut* **s. (de pare-chocs)** overrider; *Phot* **s.-contact** hot shoe
5 *(toupie)* (whipping) top
6 *Bot* **s. de Vénus** lady's slipper

sabotage [sabotaʒ] NM sabotage; **un s., un acte de s.** an act of sabotage; **l'accident était dû à un s.** the accident was caused by (an act of) sabotage; **le s. d'un plan de paix** the sabotage *or* sabotaging of a peace plan; **c'est du s.!** *(d'un travail)* it's sabotage!

saboter [sabote] VT *(voiture, entreprise, plan de paix etc)* to sabotage; *Fam (travail)* to botch (up), to make a mess of

saboteur, -euse [sabotœr, -øz] N *(d'une voiture, un train etc)* saboteur; *(d'un travail)* botcher

sabre [sabr] NM sabre, *Am* saber; **s. d'abordage** cutlass; **s. au clair** with drawn sword; *Fig* **le s. et le goupillon** the Army and the Church

sabrer [sabre] VT **1** *Fam (texte)* to make drastic cuts in; *(paragraphe, phrases)* to cut, to axe; **s. tout un passage dans un chapitre** to slash *or* to hack a whole section out of a chapter; **je vais devoir s.** I'll have to do some drastic editing
2 *Fam (noter sévèrement) (étudiant)* to give a lousy mark to; *(recaler)* to flunk
3 *Fam (renvoyer) (employé)* to fire, to sack, *Am* to can; **se faire s.** to get the chop *or* sack *or Br* boot
4 *(marquer vigoureusement)* to slash; **la toile avait été sabrée à coups de crayon** great pencil slashes marked the canvas
5 *Fam (bâcler) (travail)* to botch, to bungle
6 *(ouvrir)* **s. le champagne** to break open a bottle of champagne *(originally, using a sabre)*

sabreur [sabrœr] NM swordsman; *Sport* fencer

sac¹ [sak] NM **1** bag; *(plus grand)* sack; **s. de** *ou* **en papier** paper bag *or Am* sack; *(grand)* paper *or Am* grocery bag; **s. en plastique** plastic *or Br Fam* poly bag; **s. à blé** grain sack; **contre trois sacs de blé** for three sacks of wheat; **s. à bandoulière** shoulder bag; **porter un s. en bandoulière** to wear a bag slung over *or* across one's shoulder; **s. à dos, s. de campeur** rucksack, backpack; **partir s. au dos** to set off with one's rucksack on one's back *or* with one's backpack; **s. de sable** *ou* **de terre** sandbag; **course en s.** sack race; *Fam* **un s. de nœuds** *ou* **d'embrouilles** a muddle; **c'est un vrai s. de nœuds, cette histoire** I can't make head (n)or tail of this affair; *Fig* **prendre qn la main dans le s.** to catch sb red-handed; *Boxe Fam* **travailler au s.** to practise with the punchbag *or Am* punching bag; *Fam* **habillé comme un s.** dressed like a tramp; *Fam* **je les mets tous dans le même s.** they're as bad as each other, they're all tarred with the same brush; *Fam* **vider son s.** to get it off one's chest; *(avouer)* to come clean; *Fam* **l'affaire est dans le s.** it's in the bag; *Vieilli* **remplir son s.** to fill one's belly; *Arg* **ils ont le s., il y a le s.** they're loaded, they're rolling in it; *Arg* **faire** *ou* **gagner son s.** to make one's pile; *Arg* **épouser le (gros) s.** to marry money
2 *Anciennement Arg* ten francs; **dix sacs** a hundred francs
3 *Anat, Bot* sac
4 *(d'un marsupial)* pouch
5 *Tex (jute)* sackcloth; **sous le s. et la cendre** in sackcloth and ashes
6 *Can Ftbl* quarterback sack
▸▸ **s. de blanchisserie** laundry bag; **s. de couchage** sleeping bag; **s. d'écolier** schoolbag; *Mil* **s. de fantassin** pack, knapsack; **s. à fourrages** nosebag; **s. à main** handbag, *Am* purse; **s. à malices** bag of tricks; *Naut* **s. (de) marin** kitbag; *Mil* **s. à munitions** cartridge pouch; *Vieilli* **s. de nuit** travel *or* overnight bag; *Fam* **s. d'os** bag of bones; **ce n'est plus qu'un s. d'os** he's nothing but skin and bones; **s. à ouvrage** work bag; **s. de plage** beach bag; **s. poubelle** *(petit)* bin liner; *(grand)* bin bag, *Am* garbage bag, **s. à poussière** *(d'un aspirateur)* dust bag; **s. à provisions** shopping bag; *Mil* **s. de soldat** pack, knapsack; *Aviat* **s. à vent** windsock; *Fam* **s. à viande** sleeping bag; *Fam* **s. à vin** boozer, drunk; **s. de voyage** travel *or* overnight bag

sac² NM sacking, pillage; **mettre une ville à s.** to sack or plunder a town; **mettre une maison à s.** to ransack a house; **mise à s. d'une maison** ransacking of a house

saccade [sakad] NF jerk, jolt; **par saccades** in or by fits and starts; **parler par saccades** to speak jerkily or in short bursts, to have a staccato style of delivery

saccadé [sakade] ADJ (mouvement, progression) jerky; (style, voix, débit) jerky, staccato; **respiration saccadée** irregular breathing

saccader [sakade] VT Équitation (cheval) to jerk

saccage [sakaʒ] NM havoc, devastation; **ils se livrèrent à un s. systématique du centre-ville** they engaged in the systematic destruction of the town centre

saccager [sakaʒe] VT (je saccageai(s); n. saccageons) **1** (ville) to wreak havoc in, to devastate; (pour piller) to sack; (maison etc) to ransack; (vandaliser) to vandalize **2** to wreak havoc in, to turn upside down; **ils ont tout saccagé dans la maison** (mis en désordre) they turned the whole house upside down; **les cultures furent saccagées par l'orage** the crops were devastated by the storm

saccageur, -euse [sakaʒœr, -øz] N looter, plunderer

saccharin [sakarɛ̃] ADJ saccharine

saccharine [sakarin] NF Chimie etc saccharin(e)

saccharose [sakaroz] NM Chimie saccharose

sacerdoce [saserdɔs] NM Rel priesthood, ministry; Fig vocation; Fig **l'enseignement est un s.** teaching is a real vocation or calling

sacerdotal, -ale, -aux, -ales [saserdotal, -o] ADJ priestly

sachem [saʃɛm] NM (chef indien d'Amérique) sachem, sagamore

sachet [saʃɛ] NM **1** (de levure, café instantané, lait en poudre) sachet; **s. de lavande** lavender bag or sachet; **s. de thé** teabag; **thé en sachets** teabags; **je n'achète jamais mon thé en sachets** I never buy teabags; **s. pour garniture périodique** sanitary disposal bag **2** Belg (sac) bag; **s. poubelle** dustbin or Am garbage can liner, bin bag

sachet-cuisson, pl **sachets-cuissons** NM **en s.** boil-in-the-bag

sacoche [sakɔʃ] NF **1** (de vélo etc) saddlebag **2** (besace) bag; (pour ordinateur portable) carrier; **s. du facteur** postman's bag; **s. à outils** tool bag; **s. à courrier** mail bag **3** Belg, Can handbag, Am purse

sacquer [sake] VT très Fam **1** (renvoyer) (personne) to sack; **se faire s.** to be sacked, to get the sack **2** Scol (noter sévèrement) (élève) to mark strictly; **je me suis encore fait s. par le prof!** I got another rotten mark from the teacher! **3** (supporter) **je ne peux pas les s.** I can't stomach them, I hate their guts
VI Scol to be a tough marker

sacral, -ale, -aux, -ales [sakral, -o] ADJ sacred

sacraliser [sakralize] VT to consider sacred; **s. la liberté** to consider freedom to be sacred, to consider freedom as something sacred

sacramentel, -elle [sakramɑ̃tɛl] ADJ Rel sacramental; Fig solemn, binding

sacrant [sakrɑ̃] ADJ Can Arg **au plus s.** as fast as possible

sacre [sakr] NM (d'un roi) coronation; (d'un prêtre) consecration; Fig rite; **recevoir le prix Goncourt, c'est le s. pour un écrivain** being awarded the prix Goncourt is the crowning achievement of a writer's career

sacré¹ [sakre] ADJ **1** Rel (vase, lieu, art, musique etc), Fig sacred; **les ordres sacrés** holy orders; Fig **pour lui, rien n'est s.** nothing is sacred to him; **elle a le feu s.** she is truly inspired; Fam **il lui faut son cigare après le dîner, c'est s.!** he has to have his cigar after dinner, it's sacred! **2** Fam (maudit) damn(ed), bloody; **j'en ai assez de ce s. voisin** I've had enough of that bloody man next door; **il a un s. culot!** he's got a bloody cheek!; **s. nom de Dieu** ou **d'un chien** ou **d'une pipe!** damn and blast it!; **s. Paul, qu'est-ce qu'il va encore inventer?** whatever is that Paul going to come up with next?; **s. Paul, qu'est-ce qu'on ferait sans lui?** good old Paul, what would we do without him?; **il a une sacrée chance** he's damn(ed) or bloody lucky; **elle a eu une sacrée vie** she's had quite a life
NM **le s.** the sacred

sacré² ADJ Anat sacral

Sacré-Cœur [sakrekœr] NM Rel Sacred Heart (of Jesus)

sacredieu [sakrədjø], **sacrebleu** [sakrəblø], **sacredié** [sakrədje] INT Vieilli good God!

sacrement [sakramɑ̃] NM Rel sacrament; **le saint S.** the Blessed Sacrament; **recevoir les sacrements** to receive the sacraments; Fig Fam **elle le promène comme le saint S.** she shows it off as if it was the crown jewels

sacrément [sakremɑ̃] ADV Fam damn(ed), bloody; **il fait s. chaud** it's damn(ed) or bloody hot; **elle a s. bien répondu** she gave a damn(ed) or bloody good answer

sacrer [sakre] VT (roi) to crown; (prêtre) to consecrate; **s. qn roi/empereur** to crown sb king/emperor; Fig **il a été sacré meilleur acteur de l'année 2002** he was acclaimed or hailed as the best actor of 2002; **il a été sacré champion de France en 1999** he won the French championship in 1999, he was crowned French champion in 1999
VI Fam Vieilli to curse and swear

sacrifiable [sakrifjabl] ADJ expendable

sacrificateur, -trice [sakrifikatœr, -tris] N sacrificer; **grand s.** (Jewish) High Priest

sacrifice [sakrifis] NM sacrifice; Rel **le saint s.** mass; **ça a dû être un s.** that must have been a sacrifice; **offrir qch en s.** to offer up sth as a sacrifice; **faire à qn le s. de sa vie** to sacrifice one's life for sb; **s'il a réussi, c'est au s. de sa santé** he succeeded, but it was at the cost of his health or it cost him his health; **faire des sacrifices** to make sacrifices; **esprit de s.** spirit of self-sacrifice; **je n'ai pas le goût du s.** I have no desire for self-sacrifice

sacrifier [sakrifje] (impf, pr sub n. **sacrifiions,** v. **sacrifiiez**) VT (victime) to sacrifice; (temps, argent, carrière etc) to sacrifice, to give up (à for, to); Com **s. des marchandises** to sell goods at rock-bottom prices; **sacrifié** (prix) rock-bottom; (article) at a rock-bottom price; **il a réussi en sacrifiant sa santé** he succeeded at the cost of his health; **s. sa vie pour son pays** to sacrifice or lay down one's life for one's country; **s. sa vie à une cause** to devote one's (entire) life to a cause
VI **s. aux idoles** to sacrifice to idols; **s. à la mode** to be a slave to fashion
VPR **se sacrifier** to sacrifice oneself (pour for); **se s. pour la bonne cause** to sacrifice oneself in a good cause; **allez, d'accord, je me sacrifie et je vais les chercher à la gare!** OK, I'll be the martyr and pick them up from the station!

sacrilège¹ [sakrilɛʒ] NM sacrilege; **ce serait un s. que de ...** it would be sacrilege to ...

sacrilège² ADJ (action, pensée etc) sacrilegious
N sacrilegious person

sacristain [sakristɛ̃] NM **1** Rel sacristan **2** Culin = small flaky pastry

sacristi [sakristi] INT Arch good Lord!

sacristie [sakristi] NF Rel sacristy, vestry

sacro-saint [sakrosɛ̃] ADJ sacrosanct; Iron sacrosanct, precious

sacrum [sakrɔm] NM Anat sacrum

sadique [sadik] ADJ sadistic
N sadist

sadisme [sadism] NM sadism

sado-maso [sadomazo] Fam ADJ INV sadomasochistic; **il a des tendances s.** he's into S & M, he has S & M tendencies
N INV sadomasochist; **c'est un s.** he's into S & M

sadomasochisme [sadomazɔʃism] NM Psy sadomasochism

sadomasochiste [sadomazɔʃist] Psy ADJ sadomasochistic
N sadomasochist

saducéen, -enne [sadyseɛ̃, -ɛn] N Sadducee

safari [safari] NM safari; **en s.** on safari; **s.-photo** photographic safari

safran¹ [safrɑ̃] NM **1** Bot saffron, crocus **2** Culin etc saffron
ADJ INV **(jaune) s.** saffron (yellow)

safran² NM Naut rudder blade

safrané [safrane] ADJ saffron(-coloured or Am -colored); Culin (riz) saffron(-flavoured or Am -flavored)

safraner [safrane] VT Culin to flavour or Am flavor with saffron

saga [saga] NF Littér, Fig saga

sagace [sagas] ADJ astute, shrewd

sagacité [sagasite] NF shrewdness, astuteness; **avec s.** shrewdly, astutely; **faire preuve de s.** to be shrewd; **pour une fois, il a fait preuve de s.** for once, he behaved shrewdly

sagaie [sagɛ] NF assegai

sage [saʒ] ADJ **1** (avisé) (politique, personne, décision etc) wise, sensible; **une politique peu s.** an unwise policy, not a very sensible policy; **il serait plus s. de faire ceci** it would be wiser or more sensible to do this **2** (enfant) good, well-behaved; (animal) quiet, docile; (tenue, conduite) sober; (robe) demure; **quand tu seras plus s.** when you're better behaved, once you start behaving yourself; **l'école l'a rendu s.** school has quietened him down; **sois s.!** be good!, behave yourself!; **s. comme une image** as good as gold; **il n'est pas s. du tout, ce petit** that child is very badly behaved; **il porte toujours des tenues très sages** he always dresses very soberly or conservatively; **la mode de cette année est très s.** the demure look is in this year **3** (chaste) good; **j'étais très s. pendant ma jeunesse** I was a very good girl when I was young; **elle n'était pas très s. à cette époque-là!** she was a bit wild then!
NM wise man; Phil sage; **un vieux s.** a wise old man; Pol **comité des sages** committee of wise men

sage-femme, pl **sages-femmes** NF midwife

sagement [saʒmɑ̃] ADV **1** (raisonnablement) wisely, sensibly **2** (tranquillement) quietly

sagesse [saʒɛs] NF **1** (prudence, connaissance) wisdom; **elle a eu la s. de ne pas en parler** she was wise or sensible enough not to mention it; **plein de s.** (remarque) very sensible; (décision) very sensible or wise; **agir avec s.** to act wisely or sensibly; Fig **la voix de la s.** the voice of reason **2** (calme) good behaviour or Am behavior; **la maîtresse lui reproche sa trop grande s.** the teacher says he's too well behaved; **ma grand-mère était d'une s. exemplaire pendant sa**

jeunesse my grandmother was very well-behaved *or* a model of good behaviour when she was a girl; **on le disait d'une très grande s.** he was said to be very well behaved

Sagittaire [saʒiter] NM *Astron, Astrol* **le S.** Sagittarius, the Archer; **être (du signe du) S.** to be (a) Sagittarius *or* (a) Sagittarian

sagou [sagu] NM sago

sagouin [sagwɛ̃] NM **1** *(singe)* squirrel monkey **2** *Fam* slovenly *or* dirty individual; **travailler comme un s.** to be a sloppy worker; **manger comme un s.** to eat like a pig; **vieux s.** revolting old man

Sahara [saara] NM Sahara (Desert)

saharien, -ienne [saarjɛ̃, -jɛn] ADJ Saharan; *(troupes)* desert; **température saharienne** scorching *or* sizzling temperature
N **S.** Saharan
NF **saharienne** safari jacket

Sahel [sael] NM Sahel

sahib [saib] NM sahib

sahraoui, -ie [sarawi] ADJ of the Western Sahara
N **S.** native of the Western Sahara

saignant [sɛɲɑ̃] ADJ **1** *(blessure)* bleeding **2** *Culin (viande)* rare

saignée [sɛɲe] NF **1** *Méd Arch* blood-letting; *Fig* drain; **la guerre fut une véritable s. pour le pays** the country suffered great losses in the war; *Méd Arch* **faire une s. à qn** to bleed sb; **faire une s. dans un arbre** *(pour récolter du caoutchouc etc)* to tap a tree **2** *Anat (pli)* bend of the arm *or* the knee **3** *(rigole)* (drainage) trench, ditch; *Tech (pour l'huile etc)* groove; *Constr (dans un mur, pour un tuyau, un câble etc)* hole

saignement [sɛɲ(ə)mɑ̃] NM bleeding; **s. de nez** nosebleed; **elle souffre de saignements de nez** she suffers from nosebleeds

saigner [sɛɲe] VI *(d'une personne, d'une blessure etc)* to bleed; **mon doigt saigne** my finger is bleeding; **je saigne du nez** my nose is bleeding, I have a nosebleed; **elle a tendance à s. du nez** she tends to get nosebleeds; **la chaleur le fait s. du nez** heat makes his nose bleed *or* gives him nosebleeds; *Fig* **c'est une plaie qui saigne encore** it's an open wound, it still rankles; *Fig Litt* **mon cœur saigne, le cœur m'en saigne** it makes my heart bleed; *Fam* **ça va s.** there's going to be trouble
VT *Agr (poulet), Méd Arch (personne)* to bleed; *Fam (tuer à l'arme blanche)* to stab to death; **s. un porc** to stick a pig; **s. à blanc** *(animal)* to bleed white; **s. un arbre** to tap a tree; **s. un fossé** to drain a ditch; *Fig* **s. qn/un pays (à blanc)** to bleed sb/a country white *or* dry
VPR se saigner *Fig* **se s. aux quatre membres** *ou* **aux quatre veines** to make enormous sacrifices, to bleed oneself white *or* dry

saigneur [sɛɲœr] NM **1** *(d'animaux)* slaughterer, slaughterman **2** *(de caoutchouc)* tree tapper, collector of rubber

saillant [sajɑ̃] ADJ *(toit, corniche etc)* projecting, jutting out; *(pommettes)* prominent, high; *(muscles)* bulging; *Fig (trait, caractéristique etc)* striking, outstanding, salient; **angle s.** *(d'une fortification)* salient angle; **les faits saillants de sa vie** the notable *or* noteworthy events of his life; **les faits saillants de l'année** the highlights of the year
NM *Mil* salient

saillie [saji] NF **1** *(partie en avant)* protrusion; *Archit, Constr* projection; **en s.** projecting, jutting out; **s. du mollet** swell of the calf; **faire s.** to project, to jut out **2** *(dans l'élevage) (par un mâle)* covering **3** *Litt* sally, flash of wit

saillir [sajir] VT *(prp saillissant; pp sailli; pr ind je saillis, n. saillissons; fu je saillirai)* *(dans l'élevage) (femelle)* to cover

VI *(used only in prp* **saillant;** *pp* **sailli;** *pr ind* **il saille, ils saillent;** *fu* **il saillera)** to project, to jut out *(sur over)*; **la poutre saille de 25 cm** the beam projects 25 cm

sain, saine [sɛ̃, sɛn] ADJ **1** *(personne, climat, exercice, maison, relations)* healthy; *(cheval, fruit, bois, gestion etc)* sound; *(nourriture)* healthy, wholesome; *(économie, affaire)* healthy, sound; **un esprit s. dans un corps s.** a healthy mind in a healthy body; **s. de corps et d'esprit** sound in mind and body; **s. et sauf** safe and sound **2** *Naut (côte, ancrage)* safe

saindoux [sɛ̃du] NM *Culin* lard

sainement [sɛnmɑ̃] ADV **1** *(salubrement)* healthily **2** *(raisonnablement) (juger)* sensibly

saint, sainte [sɛ̃, sɛ̃t] ADJ **1** *Rel (lieu, guerre etc)* holy; *(personne, vie)* saintly, holy; **la Sainte Église** the Holy Church; **semaine sainte** Holy Week; **le Vendredi s.** Good Friday; **une sainte action** a pious deed; **faire œuvre sainte** to do good works; **la Terre sainte** the Holy Land; **la Sainte Vierge** the Blessed Virgin; **une petite sainte vierge en ivoire** an ivory miniature of the Blessed Virgin; **le s. patron des horlogers** the patron saint of watch-makers; *Fig* **être saisi ou pris d'une sainte colère/indignation** to be seething with righteous anger/indignation; *Fam* **j'en ai une sainte horreur!** I hate *or* loathe it!; *Fam* **elle ne fait rien de toute la sainte journée** she doesn't do a thing the whole blessed day **2** **s. Pierre** St Peter; **sainte Catherine** St Catherine; **l'église S.-Pierre de Rome** St Peter's (church); **la S. Georges** St George's day; *Can Fam* **du mouvement, Sainte Bénite!** get a move on, for Pete's sake!
N *Rel, Fig* saint; **s. d'une ville** patron saint of a town; **il lasserait la patience d'un s.** he would try the patience of a saint; **elle prêche pour son s.** she has an axe to grind; **ne savoir plus à quel s. se vouer** to be at one's wits' end, not to know which way to turn; *Hum* **il vaut mieux s'adresser à Dieu qu'à ses saints** it's best to go right to the top; *Fig Fam* **c'est un petit s.** he's a prig; *Fam* **arrête de faire ton petit s.!** stop being such a prig!; *Rel* **les Saints du dernier jour** the Latter-day Saints
NM **le S. des Saints** the Holy of Holies; *Fig* the inner sanctum; *Hum* the holy of holies, the sanctum sanctorum

saint-bernard [sɛ̃bernar] NM INV *(chien)* St Bernard; *Fam* **c'est un vrai s.** he's a good Samaritan

Saint-Cyr [sɛ̃sir] N Saint-Cyr military academy

saint-cyrien, -ienne, *pl* **saint-cyriens, -iennes** [sɛ̃sirjɛ̃, -jɛn] N cadet training at Saint-Cyr

Saint-Domingue [sɛ̃dɔmɛ̃g] NM Santo Domingo

Sainte-Croix N **l'île S.** Santa Cruz island

Sainte-Hélène N St Helena

Saint-Elme [sɛ̃ɛlm] NM **feu S.** St Elmo's fire

Sainte-Lucie [sɛ̃lysi] N St Lucia

saintement [sɛ̃tmɑ̃] ADV in a saintly way; **vivre s.** to lead a saintly life, to live like a saint; **mourir s.** to die a saintly death, to die like a saint; **elle s'est toujours conduite très s.** she has always behaved like a saint

sainte-nitouche, *pl* **saintes-nitouches** [sɛ̃nituʃ] NF *Fam* little hypocrite; **prendre des airs de s.** to look as if butter wouldn't melt in one's mouth; **avec des airs de s.** looking as if butter wouldn't melt in his/her/*etc* mouth

Saint-Esprit [sɛ̃tɛspri] NM **le S.** the Holy Ghost, the Holy Spirit; *Hum* **par l'opération du S.** by magic

sainteté [sɛ̃t(ə)te] NF *(d'une personne)* holi-

ness, saintliness; *(de la loi, d'un serment)* sanctity; *(d'un lieu)* holiness, sanctity; *Rel* **sa S. (le pape)** His Holiness (the Pope)

saint-frusquin [sɛ̃fryskɛ̃] NM *(no pl) Fam* **tout le s.** the whole caboodle; **il s'est pointé avec ses disquettes, ses livres et tout son s.** he turned up with his disks, his books and all the rest of his gear; *Litt* **boire (tout) son s.** to waste one's substance with riotous living

saint-glinglin (à la) [alasɛ̃glɛ̃glɛ̃] ADV *Fam* **jusqu'à la s.** till the cows come home, till doomsday; **on sera payé à la s.** we'll be paid when pigs fly; **repoussé à la s.** postponed indefinitely

Saint-Graal (le) NM *Littér* the (Holy) Grail

saint-honoré, *pl* **saint-honoré(s)** NM Saint-Honoré *(choux pastry ring filled with confectioner's custard)*

Saint-Jean (le) [sɛ̃ʒɑ̃] NF **1 la S.** Midsummer Day **2** *Can* **la Saint-Jean-Baptiste** Saint-Jean-Baptiste Day *(24th of July)*

Saint-Laurent (le) [sɛ̃lɔrɑ̃] NM *Géog* the St Lawrence (river); **la Voie maritime du S.** the St Lawrence Seaway

saint-marcellin, *pl* **saint-marcellins** [sɛ̃marsəlɛ̃] NM = type of small, round cheese produced in the Lyons area

Saint-Marin N San Marino

Saint-Martin (la) [lasɛ̃martɛ̃] NF St Martin's day, Martinmas; **l'été de la S.** Indian summer, St Martin's summer

Saint-Michel (la) [lasɛ̃miʃɛl] NF Michaelmas

saint-nectaire, *pl* **saint-nectaires** NM = Saint-Nectaire (cheese)

Saint-Office NM **le S.** *Cathol* the Holy Office; *Hist (l'Inquisition)* the Inquisition

Saint-Père (le) NM *Cathol* the Holy Father

Saint-Pétersbourg [sɛ̃petɛrsbur] N St Petersburg

saint-pierre NM INV *(poisson)* John Dory

Saint-Pierre-et-Miquelon [sɛ̃pjeremiklɔ̃] N St Pierre and Miquelon

Saint-Siège (le) NM *Cathol* the Holy See

Saint-Simonisme [sɛ̃simɔnism] NM *Écon* Saint Simonianism, Saint-Simonism

Saint-Sylvestre (la) NF New Year's Eve, *Scot* Hogmanay; **faire la veillée de la S.** to see the New Year in

saisi, -ie [sezi] N *Jur* distrainee

saisie [sezi] NF *(de marchandises de contrebande etc)* seizure; *Jur* seizure, *Spéc* distraint, distress; *(d'une hypothèque)* foreclosure; *Naut* embargo; **s. conservatoire** seizure of goods *(to prevent sale)*; **procès-verbal de s.** warrant (for seizure of property); *Ordinat* **s. de données** data capture, keyboarding; *Ordinat* **s. automatique/manuelle** automatic/manual input

saisie-arrêt, *pl* **saisies-arrêts** NF *Jur* attachment, garnishment

saisie-exécution, *pl* **saisies-exécutions** NF *Jur* distraint *(for sale by court order)*

saisine [sezin] NF *Jur* referral to a court

saisir [sezir] VT **1** *(attraper) (personne, objet)* to take hold of, to grab, to seize; **s. qn par le bras/au collet** to grab *or* catch *or* seize sb by the arm/by the collar; **s. qn à bras-le-corps** to seize *or Fam* grab sb around the waist; **s. l'occasion de faire qch** to seize *or* grasp the opportunity to do sth; **s. un prétexte pour faire qch** to seize on a pretext to do something; **s. la balle au bond** to catch the ball on the rebound; *Fig* to seize the opportunity; **la peur le saisit** fear seized *or* took hold of *or* gripped him; **être saisi d'étonnement** to be startled *or* staggered; **être saisi par le froid/la peur** to be struck by the cold/to

be gripped by *or* overcome by *or* stricken with fear; **être saisi de panique** to be panic-stricken; **l'artiste a bien saisi la ressemblance** the artist has really caught *or* captured the likeness
2 *(comprendre) (vérité, signification donnée par qn)* to grasp, to get; **elle a tout de suite saisi de quoi il s'agissait** she immediately grasped *or* got what it was about; **je n'ai pas saisi son nom** I didn't catch *or* get his/her name
3 *Ordinat (données)* to capture, to keyboard, to key
4 *Jur (navire, biens immobiliers)* to seize, to attach; *(marchandises)* to seize, *Spéc* to distrain upon; **s. une hypothèque** to foreclose on a mortgage
5 *Jur.* **s. un tribunal d'une affaire** to refer a matter to a court, to lay a matter before a court; **nous sommes saisis de deux questions** we have two questions before us
6 *Culin (viande)* to seal
7 *Naut (ancres, bateaux)* to stow, to secure
VI *(comprendre)* **je ne saisis pas bien** I don't quite get it; **il saisit vite** he's quick (on the uptake); **alors, tu saisis?** do you get it?
VPR se saisir se s. de qn/qch to seize *or* grab sb/sth, to take hold of sb/sth; **se s. d'un marché** to corner a market

saisissable [sezisabl] **ADJ 1** *(distinction)* perceptible **2** *Jur* distrainable, attachable

saisissant, -ante [sezisɑ̃, -ɑ̃t] **ADJ 1** *(froid)* biting; *(ressemblance)* striking; *(spectacle, scène, paroles)* gripping **2** *Jur (partie)* distraining
N *Jur* distrainer

saisissement [sezismɑ̃] **NM 1** *(sensation de froid)* sudden chill **2** *(émotion)* shock, rush of emotion; **pâle de s.** pale with emotion

saison [sɛzɔ̃] **NF** season; **très tôt en s.** very early in the season; **en cette s.** at this time of year; **en toute(s) saison(s)** all (the) year round; **la s. nouvelle** spring(time); **la mauvaise/la belle s.** the winter/summer months; **moyenne s.** shoulder period; **la s. sèche/des pluies** the dry/rainy season; **la s. des semailles** sowing time; **la haute/basse s.** the high/low season; **faire une bonne/mauvaise s.** to have a good/bad season; **la s. bat son plein** the season is in full swing *or* at its height, it is the height of the busy season; **le fort de la s.** the busy season *or* time (of the year); **la s. creuse, la morte s.** the off season, the slack season, the low season; **prendre ses vacances à la s. creuse** to take one's holidays off season; **voyager pendant la s. creuse** to travel off season; **la s. touristique** the tourist season; **la s. sportive/de la chasse** the sporting/hunting season; **la s. des amours** the mating season; **la s. des framboises** the raspberry season, the season *or* time for raspberries; **des fraises! mais ce n'est pas la s.!** strawberries! but it isn't the right time of year *or* it isn't the season for them; **être de s.** *(des fruits)* to be in season *or* seasonal; **le pull est de s.** it's the right kind of weather for sweaters; **c'est un temps de s.** it's seasonal weather, it's typical weather for the time of year; **hors de s.** *(légumes etc)* out of season; *Fig* **décidément, ses plaisanteries ne sont pas de s.** his/her jokes are really quite out of place; **faire une s.** *(dans une station thermale)* to take a cure; **cette robe ne me fera pas la s.** this dress won't last me the season; **travailler en s.**, *Fam* **faire les saisons** *(dans les lieux de vacances)* to do seasonal work SEE GRAMMAR A7; A81; B4; B61

saisonnier, -ière [sɛzɔnje, -jɛr] **ADJ** seasonal
N seasonal worker

sajou [saʒu] **NM** *Zool* capuchin (monkey)

saké [sake], **saki¹** [saki] **NM** *(boisson)* sake, saké, saki

saki² **NM** *Zool* saki (monkey)

salade [salad] **NF 1** *Bot, Culin (plante)* lettuce **2** *(plat)* salad; **faire une s.** to make a salad; **s. verte** green salad; **s. de pommes de terre/de tomates/de riz** potato/tomato/rice salad; **s. composée** mixed salad; **s. niçoise** salade niçoise; **s. russe** Russian salad; **haricots verts en s.** green bean salad; **s. de fruits** fruit salad; *Belg* **s. de blé** lamb's lettuce, corn salad; **3** *Fam (désordre)* mess, shambles; **quelle s.!** what a mess *or* shambles! **4** *Fam* **salades** *(mensonges)* whoppers, fibs; *(absurdités)* nonsense **5** *Fam* **vendre sa s.** to make a pitch, to try to sell an idea

saladier [saladje] **NM** salad bowl

salage [salaʒ] **NM** salting

salaire [salɛr] **NM 1** *(mensuel)* salary, pay; *(hebdomadaire, journalier)* wage(s), pay; *Prov* **toute peine mérite s.** the labourer *or Am* laborer is worthy of his hire VOIR GRAMMAIRE A10-11 **2** *(récompense)* reward, recompense *(de* for); *(punition)* retribution *(de* for); **le s. du péché/de la peur** the wages of sin/of fear
▸▸ **s. annuel garanti** annual guaranteed wage/salary; **s. d'appoint** second salary; **s. de base** basic pay, basic wage/salary; **s. brut** gross pay; **s. de départ** starting salary; **s. fixe** fixed salary; **s. fixe plus commission** salary plus commission; **s. à forfait** job wage; **s. horaire** hourly wage; **s. indexé** index-linked pay; **s. légal** legal wage; **s. indirect** fringe benefits, benefit in kind; **s. minimum interprofessionnel de croissance =** guaranteed minimum wage; **s. net** net pay; **s. plafond** maximum wage/salary; **s. plafonné** wage/salary ceiling; **s. réel** real wage/salary, wage/salary in real terms; **s. au rendement** incentive pay; **s. à la tâche** *ou* **aux pièces** piece wage

salaison [salɛzɔ̃] **NF** *(action)* salting; **les salaisons** salted meats

salamalecs [salamalɛk] **NMPL** *Fam* bowing and scraping; **faire des s. à qn** to bow and scrape to sb

salamandre [salamɑ̃dr] **NF 1** *Zool* salamander; **s. aquatique** newt **2** *(poêle)* salamander (stove), slow-burning *or* slow-combustion stove

salami [salami] **NM** salami

salant [salɑ̃] **ADJ** **marais s.** salt marsh

salarial, -iale, -iaux, -iales [salarjal, -jo] **ADJ** wage; *(mensuel)* salary; **masse salariale** wage(s) bill, payroll; **politique salariale** pay *or* wage(s) policy

salariat [salarja] **NM 1** *(état)* wage-earning; **je préfère le s. au travail free-lance** I'd rather be on a salary *or* have a nine-to-five job than do freelance work **2** *(employés)* wage earners

salarié, -ée [salarje] **ADJ 1** *(travailleur) (payé mensuellement)* salaried; *(payé hebdomadairement)* wage-earning **2** *(travail)* paid
N *(payé mensuellement)* salaried employee; *(payé hebdomadairement)* wage earner; **salariés** *(de société)* employees

salarier [salarje] **VT** *(tous les mois)* to pay a salary to; *(toutes les semaines)* to pay a wage to

salaud [salo] *Vulg* **NM** bastard; **alors là mon s., tu m'en bouches un coin!** you've gobsmacked me this time, you old bastard!
ADJ shitty; **un mec s.** a bastard; **ce qu'il est s.!** what a bastard he is!; **il a été très s. avec elle** he was a real bastard to her; **c'est vraiment s. de faire ça** it's a really shitty thing to do

sale [sal] **ADJ 1** *(maison, vaisselle, mains, eau etc)* dirty; *(répugnant)* filthy; *Fig (paroles, histoire)* dirty, filthy, coarse; *Nucl* **bombe s.** dirty bomb; **industrie s.** dirty industry; **très**

Fam **c'était pas s.!** it was pretty good!, it was quite something! **2** *Fam (always before the noun) (méchant) (grippe, situation)* nasty; **s. gosse** little brat; **c'est un s. boulot!** it's a rotten *or* lousy job!; **faire le s. boulot** to do the dirty work; **être dans une s. affaire** to be caught up in a dirty business; **il a une s. tête** *ou* **gueule** *(antipathique)* he looks really nasty; *(malade)* he looks awful; **s. individu, s. type** nasty character, louse; **s. fasciste!** filthy Fascist!; **s. coup** dirty *or* rotten trick; **s. temps** filthy weather; **ah la s. bête!** *(cet animal)* bloody animal!; *(cette personne)* the beast!, the swine!
NM *Fam* **mettre du linge au s.** to put dirty clothes in the wash

salé [sale] **ADJ 1** *(conservé au sel) (poisson, viande etc)* salt; *(additionné de sel) (beurre, amandes etc)* salted; **eau salée** salt water; **le Grand Lac S.** the Great Salt Lake; **le potage est trop s.** the soup is too salty; **prés salés** saltings, salt meadows **2** *Fig (histoire, plaisanterie)* spicy, risqué; *Fam (condamnation)* stiff; *Fam (addition, prix)* steep
NM **le s. et le sucré** savoury food and sweet food; **petit s.** = type of streaky bacon

salement [salmɑ̃] **ADV 1** *(parler, manger, boire)* in a disgusting manner **2** *Fam (blessé, touché, atteint)* (very) badly; **s. difficile/douloureux** damn(ed) *or Br* bloody difficult/painful; **j'ai s. besoin d'argent** I'm badly in need of money; **ça m'aiderait s.** it would be a big *or* great help; **je suis s. fatigué** I'm dog-tired, *Br* I'm knackered; **elle a s. vieilli** she's aged a hell of a lot; **il est s. amoureux** he's got it bad

saler [sale] **VT 1** *(assaisonner)* to salt, to put salt in, to season with salt **2** *(pour conserver) (bacon etc)* to salt **3** *(route)* to salt **4** *Fam (client)* to rip off, to fleece; **s. la note** to bump up the bill; **on s'est fait s.** *(au restaurant)* we were ripped off *or* done; **il s'est fait s.** *(sanctionné)* he got a stiff *or* tough sentence

saleté [salte] **NF 1** *(d'une personne, d'une rue, de vêtements etc)* dirtiness, filthiness; *(crasse)* dirt, filth; **la maison est d'une s. incroyable** the house is incredibly dirty *or* filthy; **le chat a fait ses saletés par terre** the cat made a mess on the floor **2** *(camelote)* trash, rubbish, junk; **manger des saletés** to eat junk food; **quelle s., cette grippe!** this flu is a real pain *or* nuisance! **3** *(chose obscène)* obscenity; *(remarque)* obscenity, obscene remark; *(blague)* obscene joke; **il m'a dit des saletés** he said dirty *or* filthy things to me **4** *Fam (personne)* bastard; **quelle s.!, il m'a roulé!** the bastard, he's conned me!

saleur, -euse [salœr, -øz] **N** salter

salicoque [salikɔk] **NF** prawn

salicorne [salikɔrn] **NF** *Bot* glasswort, saltwort

salicylate [salisilat] **NM** *Chimie* salicylate

salicylique [salisilik] **ADJ** *Chimie (acide)* salicylic

salière [saljɛr] **NF 1** *Culin* salt cellar **2** *Fam (des clavicules)* salt cellar

saligaud, -aude [saligo, -od] **N** *très Fam (personne sale)* filthy swine, *f* slut; *(ignoble individu)* bastard, *f* bitch

salin, -ine [salɛ̃, -in] **ADJ** *(solution, roches)* saline
NM 1 *(marais)* salt marsh **2** *Chimie, Ind* saline
NF saline 1 *(entreprise)* salt works **2** *(marais)* salt marsh

salinage [salinaʒ] **NM 1** *(entreprise)* salt works **2** *(solution)* saturated solution of salt; *(concentration)* concentrating of the brine

salinier, -ière [salinje, -jɛr] **ADJ** *(industrie etc)* salt
NM salt producer

salinité [salinite] NF *(de l'eau de mer etc)* salinity, saltness

salique [salik] ADJ *Hist (loi)* Salic

salir [salir] VT *(mains, vêtements etc)* to get or make dirty, to dirty, *Fml* to soil; **attention, ça salit les mains** careful, it gets or makes your hands dirty; **s. sa réputation** to tarnish or sully one's reputation; **s. le nom/la mémoire de qn** to sully or besmirch sb's name/memory; **s. l'idée de l'amour** to debase the idea of love

VPR **se salir** to get dirty; **ça se salit facilement** it's easily dirtied, it dirties easily; *Fig* **elle n'aime pas se s. les mains** she doesn't like to get her hands dirty

salissant [salisɑ̃] ADJ **1** *(travail)* dirty, messy **2** *(tissu, vêtement, moquette etc)* easily soiled; *(couleur)* that shows the dirt

salissure [salisyr] NF dirty mark

salivaire [saliver] ADJ *(glande etc)* salivary

salivation [salivasjɔ̃] NF salivation

salive [saliv] NF saliva; *Fam* **pas la peine de dépenser ta s.** don't waste your breath, save your breath

saliver [salive] VI to salivate; **s. devant qch** to drool at the sight of sth

salle [sal] NF **1** *(pièce)* room; *Sport* **partie en s.** indoor game; **travailler en s.** *(d'un restaurant)* to work in the dining room, to be a member of the dining-room staff; **personnel de s.** *(d'un restaurant)* dining-room staff; **les salles du Louvre** the galleries of the Louvre **2** *Théâtre, Cin (auditorium)* auditorium; *(spectateurs)* audience; **faire s. comble** ou **pleine** to have a full house; **toute la s. applaudit** the whole audience applauded; **combien de salles y a-t-il dans ce nouveau cinéma?** how many screens are there in the new cinema?; **sa dernière production sort en s. en septembre** her latest production will be released in September

▸▸**s. d'arrivée** *(à un aéroport)* arrivals lounge; *Cin* **s. d'art et d'essai** art cinema or *Am* movie theater; **s. d'attente** waiting room; **s. de bain(s)** bathroom; **s. de bain(s) particulière** private bathroom, en-suite bathroom; **s. de bal** ballroom; **s. de billard** billiards room, pool room; *Ordinat* **s. blanche** clean room; **s. des chaudières** boiler room; **s. de cinéma** cinema, *Am* movie theater; *Scol* **s. de classe** classroom; *Banque* **s. des coffres** vaults; **s. de composition** *(atelier)* composing room; **s. de conférences** conference room; **s. du conseil** council room or chamber; *Ind* **s.** etc boardroom; **s. de contrôle** *(d'un engin spatial)* control room; **s. de contrôle de production** production control room; **s. de cours** lecture room; **s. des dactylos** typing pool; *Ind* **s. de dessin** drawing office; **s. de détente** common room; *TV, Théâtre* green room; *Can* **s. à dîner** dining room; **s. de douches** shower room; **s. d'eau** shower room; **s. d'embarquement** *(d'aéroport)* gate lounge; **s. d'exploitation radar** radar operations room; *Com* **s. d'exposition** showroom; *(pour une foire)* exhibition hall; **s. d'exposition du revendeur** dealer display room; **s. des fêtes** = community hall; *(d'un village)* village hall; *Mil* **s. de garde** guardroom; *Banque* **s. des guichets** banking hall, front office; **s. d'hôpital** *(hospital)* ward; *Journ* **s. d'impression** publishing room; **s. de jeux** games room; **s. de lecture** *(de bibliothèque)* reading room; **s. des machines** engine room; *Ind* machine room; **s. à manger** dining room; *(meubles)* dining-room suite; **s. de maquillage** make-up room; *Bourse* **s. des marchés** trading floor; **s. de montage** edit suite, cutting room; **s. de musculation** fitness room, gym; **les salles obscures** the movies, *Br* the cinema; *Méd* **s. d'opération** operating theatre or *Am* room; **s. des opéra-**tions operations room; **s. des pas perdus** *(dans une gare etc)* concourse; *(au Parlement, dans les tribunaux)* lobby; **s. de petit déjeuner** breakfast room; **s. de presse** newsroom; **s. des professeurs** staff room, common room; *Cin* **s. de projection** viewing or projection or screening room; **s. de réception** function room; **s. de rédaction** *(d'un journal)* newsroom; *Cin, TV* **s. de régie** control room; **s. de restaurant** dining room; **s. de réunion** meeting room; **s. de réveil** recovery room; **s. de séjour** living room; **s. de service** orderly rooom; **s. de télévision** TV lounge, television room; **s. du trône** throne-room; **s. des** ou **de ventes** saleroom, auction rooms; *Cin* **s. de vision** viewing or projection or screening room; *TV, Cin* **s. de visionnage** looking room

salmigondis [salmigɔ̃di] NM hotchpotch, *Am* hodgepodge

salmis [salmi] NM *Culin* salmi *(game part-cooked by roasting then stewed in a wine sauce)*

salmonella [salmɔnela] NF INV, **salmonelle** [salmɔnɛl] NF *Méd* salmonella

salmonellose [salmɔneloz] NF *Méd* salmonellosis, salmonella poisoning

salmoniculteur, -trice [salmɔnikyltœr, -tris] N salmon farmer

salmoniculture [salmɔnikyltyr] NF salmon farming

saloir [salwar] NM **1** *(pour salaisons) (pièce)* salting room; *(bac)* salting tub **2** *Vieilli Fam (salière)* salt pot

Salomon [salɔmɔ̃] N **le roi S.** King Solomon; **les îles S.** the Solomon Islands

salon [salɔ̃] NM **1** *(de maison)* living room, sitting room, *Br* lounge; **petit s.** morning room; **s. réservé** *(dans un hôtel etc)* private room; **s.** *(dans une gare)* parlour or *Am* parlor games; **s. VIP** VIP lounge; **s. de bridge** card room; *Fig* **un révolutionnaire de s.** an armchair revolutionary

2 *(meuble)* suite

3 *(dans un bateau)* saloon; *(dans un train)* saloon car

4 *Com* **s. de thé** tea room(s), tea shop; **s. de coiffure** hairdressing salon; **s. de beauté** beauty salon

5 *(exposition), Beaux-Arts* exhibition; *(du bateau, des arts ménagers etc)* show; **s.-exposition**, *pl* **salons-expositions** trade fair; **s. d'exposition du distributeur** distributor display room; **s. professionnel** trade show or fair; **s. spécialisé** specialized trade fair

6 *Hist, Littér* salon; **tenir s.** to hold a salon

▸▸**le S. des Arts ménagers** ≃ the Ideal Home Exhibition; **le S. de l'Automobile** ou **de l'auto** the Motor Show; **le S. de l'Informatique** = information technology trade fair; **le S. du Livre** the Book Fair; **le S. nautique** the Boat Show

saloon [salun] NM saloon *(in the Wild West)*; **porte de s.** saloon door

salop [salo] NM = **salaud**

salopard [salɔpar] NM *très Fam* bastard

salope [salɔp] *Vulg* ADJ F bitchy; **qu'est-ce qu'elle a été s. avec moi!** she was really bitchy or a real bitch to me!

NF **1** *(femme méprisable)* bitch **2** *(homme méprisable)* bastard; **c'est vraiment une s., ce type!** he's a real bastard, that guy! **3** *(femme de mauvaise vie)* slut

saloper [salɔpe] VT *Fam* **1** *(salir)* to dirty, to mess up **2** *(mal exécuter)* to make a dog's breakfast or *Br* a pig's ear of

saloperie [salɔpri] NF *Vulg* **1** *(camelote)* trash, rubbish, junk; **s. de montre!** what a trashy watch!; **s. de temps!** what filthy weather!; **tu ne vas pas manger cette s.!** you're not going to eat that rubbish or junk!; **cette grippe est une s.** this flu is a bloody pain in the neck; **il y avait toutes sortes de saloperies par terre** there was a load of trash or crap on the floor **2** *(coup bas)* dirty or rotten trick; **il nous a fait une belle s.** he played a really dirty or rotten trick on us, he really did the dirty on us **3** *dire des saloperies* to talk filth, to talk dirty; **elle a encore dit des saloperies sur moi** she made some more bitchy remarks about me

salopette [salɔpɛt] NF dungarees, *Am* overalls

salpêtrage [salpɛtraʒ] NM **1** *(formation)* manufacture or formation of saltpetre or *Am* saltpeter **2** *(traitement)* treatment with saltpetre or *Am* saltpeter

salpêtre [salpɛtr] NM **1** *Chimie* saltpetre, *Am* saltpeter **2** *(sur les murs)* saltpetre or *Am* saltpetre rot

salpêtrer [salpɛtre] VT **1** *(sol)* to cover or treat with saltpetre or *Am* saltpeter **2** *(murs)* to rot

salpicon [salpikɔ̃] NM *Culin* salpicon *(diced meat, poultry, vegetables etc in sauce, used as a filling for vol-au-vents etc)*

salpingite [salpɛ̃ʒit] NF *Méd* salpingitis

salsa [salsa] NF *Mus* salsa

salsepareille [salsəparɛj] NF *Bot, Pharm* sarsaparilla

salsifis [salsifi] NM *Bot, Culin* salsify

saltimbanque [saltɛ̃bɑ̃k] N *(de cirque)* circus performer; *(comédien)* entertainer

salto [salto] NM *Gym* salto

salubre [salybr] ADJ *(climat, air, appartement)* healthy, *Fml* salubrious

salubrité [salybrite] NF *(du climat, de l'air, d'un appartement)* healthiness, *Fml* salubriousness; **s. publique** public health

saluer [salɥe] VT **1** *(personne) (en arrivant)* to greet; *(en partant)* to take one's leave of; *(faire la révérence à) (d'un homme)* to bow to; *(d'une femme)* to curts(e)y to; **s. qn (d'un geste) de la main** to wave to sb; **s. qn d'une inclination de la tête** to nod to sb; **il est passé sans me s.** he walked past me without saying hello; **s. qn bien bas** to take one's hat off to sb; *Hum* **au revoir/bonjour, mes amis, je vous salue bien bas** goodbye/hello, my friends, and a very good day to you; *Théâtre* **s. le public** to bow to the audience; **s. qn par un vivat** to greet sb with a cheer; **la loi a été froidement saluée par l'opposition** the bill got a cool reception from the opposition or was coolly received by the opposition; **saluez-le de ma part** give him my regards; *Bible* **Je vous salue, Marie** hail, Mary; **s. qn comme ...** to hail sb as ...; **je salue en lui notre sauveur** I salute him as our saviour; *Billard* **s. la bille** to miss **2** *Naut* **s. un grain** to reduce sail for a squall

VI **s. en se découvrant** to raise one's hat in greeting; *Mil etc* **s. du drapeau** to lower the colours; *Naut* **s. (du pavillon)** to dip (the flag); **s. de vingt coups** to fire a twenty-gun salute

VPR **se saluer** *(en arrivant)* to greet each other; *(en partant)* to take leave of each other

salure [salyr] NF saltiness

salut [saly] NM **1** *(sauvegarde)* safety; *Rel* salvation; **chercher son s. dans la fuite** to flee for one's life, to seek safety in flight; **travailler à son s.** to work out one's own salvation; **pour le s. de vos âmes** for the salvation of your souls; **l'Armée du S.** the Salvation Army **2** *(salutation)* greeting, *Fml* salutation; **faire** ou **adresser un s. à qn** *(de la main)* to wave to sb, to give sb a wave; *(en se découvrant)* to raise one's hat to sb; *Fam* **s. (à tous)!** hello or hi(, everybody)!; *(en partant)* so long (everybody)! **3** *Mil etc* salute; **faire un s. to**

give a salute; **faire le s. militaire** to salute; **s. au drapeau** saluting the colours; *Naut* **s. du pavillon** dipping of the flag **4** *Cathol* Benediction (of the Holy Sacrament)

salutaire [salytɛr] ADJ *(decision, mesure etc)* salutary, beneficial; *(remède)* beneficial; **être s. à qn** to do sb good, to be beneficial to sb; **un goût très s. pour les sports de plein air** a healthy liking for outdoor sports

salutation [salytasjɔ̃] NF salutation, greeting; **Je vous prie d'agréer, Monsieur, l'expression de mes salutations distinguées** yours faithfully; *(quand la formule de salutation comprend le nom du destinataire)* yours sincerely

salutiste [salytist] N Salvationist

Salvador [salvadɔr] NM El Salvador

salvadorien, -ienne [salvadɔrjɛ̃, -jɛn] ADJ Salvadorean
■ N **S.** Salvadorean

salvateur, -trice [salvatœr, -tris] ADJ *Litt* saving; **la mort salvatrice** the blessed release of death

salve [salv] NF *Mil* salvo, volley; **tirer une s. (d'honneur)** to fire a salute; **s. d'applaudissements** burst of applause

samare [samar] NF *Bot* key

samaritain, -aine [samaritɛ̃, -ɛn] *Bible* ADJ Samaritan
■ N **S.** Samaritan; **le bon S.** the Good Samaritan; *Fig* **faire le bon S.** to be a Good Samaritan

samba [sɑ̃mba] NF samba

samedi [samdi] NM Saturday; **s. prochain/dernier** next/last Saturday; **s. matin** Saturday morning; **s. soir** Saturday night *or* evening; **dans la soirée de s.** on Saturday evening; **dans la nuit de s. (à dimanche)** on Saturday night; **s. 11 mai 2004** Saturday 11 May 2004; **nous sommes s. aujourd'hui** today's Saturday; **je commence s.** I'm starting on Saturday; **il vient le s./tous les samedis** he comes on Saturdays/every Saturday; **un s. sur deux** every second *or* other Saturday; **s. en huit/quinze** a week/fortnight on Saturday; **passer tout son s. à faire qch** to spend one's whole Saturday doing sth SEE GRAMMAR A81; B61

samizdat [samizdat] NM samizdat

Samoa [samɔa] NFPL **les S. occidentales** Western Samoa

samossa [samɔsa] NM *Culin* samosa

samouraï, samurai [samuraj] NM samurai

samovar [samɔvar] NM samovar

sampan(g) [sɑ̃pɑ̃] NM sampan

sampler¹ [sɑ̃plœr] NM *Mus* sampler

sampler² [sɑ̃ple] VT *Mus* to sample

SAMU [samy] NM *(abrév* **service d'aide médicale d'urgence)** ambulance service; **appelez le S.!** ≃ call an ambulance!; **le S. social =** mobile medical and support service for homeless people

sana [sana] NM *Fam* sanatorium

sanatorium [sanatɔrjɔm] NM sanatorium

sanctificateur, -trice [sɑ̃ktifikatœr, -tris] ADJ sanctifying
■ N sanctifier; **le S.** the Holy Ghost

sanctification [sɑ̃ktifikasjɔ̃] NF sanctification

sanctifier [sɑ̃ktifje] VT *(impf, pr sub* n. **sanctifiions, v. sanctifiiez)** to sanctify, to make holy; **que Ton nom soit sanctifié** hallowed be Thy Name

sanction [sɑ̃ksjɔ̃] NF **1** *(approbation)* sanction, approval **2 s. (pénale)** sanction, penalty; **sanctions diplomatiques** diplomatic sanctions; **sanctions économiques** economic sanctions; *Pol* **prendre des sanctions contre un pays/contre des grévistes** to im-

pose sanctions on a country/take action against strikers; **la s. de la paresse** the price *or* consequence of laziness; **c'est la s. du succès** that's the price of success

sanctionner [sɑ̃ksjɔne] VT **1** *(approuver)* to sanction, to approve; **sanctionné par l'usage** sanctioned by custom **2** *(punir)* *(faute, personne)* to punish, to penalize

sanctuaire [sɑ̃ktɥɛr] NM *Rel, Fig* sanctuary; *Pol, Mil* = territory under the nuclear umbrella

sanctuariser [sɑ̃ktɥarize] NF *(territoire, région)* to sanctuarize

sanctus [sɑ̃ktys] NM *Rel, Mus* sanctus

sandale [sɑ̃dal] NF sandal

sandalette [sɑ̃dalɛt] NF (light) sandal

sandow® [sɑ̃do] NM **1** *Gym* chest expander **2** *(pour bagages)* elastic strap *or Am* bungee; *Aviat* catapult

sandre [sɑ̃dr] NM OU F pikeperch

sandwich, *pl* **sandwich(e)s** [sɑ̃dwi(t)ʃ] NM sandwich; **s. au jambon** ham sandwich; **verre s.** laminated glass; *Fam* **pris en s.** sandwiched (**entre** between)

sandwicherie [sɑ̃dwi(t)ʃəri] NF sandwich bar

sang [sɑ̃] NM **1** blood; **animaux à s. chaud/froid** warm-blooded/cold-blooded animals; **yeux injectés de s.** bloodshot eyes; **faire couler** *ou* **répandre** *ou* **verser le s.** to shed *or* spill blood; **verser son s. pour la patrie** to shed one's blood for one's country; **pincer/fouetter qn jusqu'au s.** to pinch/whip sb till he/she bleeds *or* till one draws blood; **victoire sans effusion de s.** bloodless victory; **le pays fut mis à feu et à s.** the country was put to fire and sword; **laver un outrage par le s.** to avenge an insult with blood; **écoulement de s.** bleeding, haemorrhage, *Am* hemorrhage; **je n'arrive pas à arrêter le s.** I can't stop the bleeding; **donner son s.** to give blood; **donneur de s.** blood donor; **il était tout en s.** he was covered with blood; *aussi Fig* **avoir du s. sur les mains** to have blood on one's hands; **taché de s.** bloodstained; *Méd Vieilli* **coup de s.** stroke; *Fig Fam* **il a eu un coup de s.** he nearly had a heart attack; *Fig* **avoir le s. chaud** to be hot-blooded; *Fig* **avoir le rythme dans le s.** to have an innate sense of rhythm, to have rhythm; **elle a la musique dans le s.** she has music in her blood; **il a ça dans le s.** it's in his blood; **des êtres de chair et de s.** creatures of flesh and blood; **le s. lui monta au visage** the blood rushed to his face; **cela me glace le s.** it makes my blood run cold; **il n'a pas de s. dans les veines** he's got no guts, he's gutless; *Fam* **avoir du s. de navet** to be spineless, to be a yellow-belly; *Fam* **se faire du mauvais s.** to worry, *Fam* to get all worked up; *Fam* **se ronger les sangs, se faire un s. d'encre** to worry oneself sick; **conte à tourner les sangs** bloodcurdling tale; **mon s. n'a fait qu'un tour** *(de peur)* my heart missed a beat; *(de colère)* I saw red; **dans cette famille, il faudrait un apport de s. frais** the family needs some *or* an infusion of new blood; *très Fam* **bon s. (de bonsoir)!, bon s. de bon Dieu!** damn and blast it!
2 *(race, lignée)* blood; **cheval de s.** blood horse; **cheval pur s.** thoroughbred; **liens du s.** blood ties; **ils ont ça dans le s.** it's in their blood; **son propre s.** one's own flesh and blood; **nous ne sommes pas du même s.** we're not of the same flesh and blood; **droit du s.** birthright
▶▶ **s. bleu** blue blood; **c'est un s. bleu** he has blue blood (in his veins)

sang-froid NM INV composure, calm, *Litt* sang-froid; **garder** *ou* **conserver son s.** to keep calm *or* one's head *or Fam* (one's) cool, to maintain one's composure; **perdre son s.**

to lose one's head *or Fam* one's cool, to lose one's composure; **faire qch de s.** to do sth calmly *or* coolly; **tuer qn de s.** to kill sb in cold blood

sanglant [sɑ̃glɑ̃] ADJ **1** *(blessure, bataille, histoire, mort)* bloody; *(vêtement, mouchoir etc)* bloodstained, bloody **2** *Fig (reproche)* bitter; *(affront)* deadly; *(critique)* scathing

sangle [sɑ̃gl] NF strap; *(de selle)* girth; *(de meuble)* webbing; **lit de s.** camp bed

sangler [sɑ̃gle] VT *(cheval)* to girth; **sanglé dans son uniforme** buttoned up tight in his uniform
■ VPR **se sangler** *(dans un vêtement très étroit)* to do oneself up tight

sanglier [sɑ̃glije] NM (wild) boar

sanglot [sɑ̃glo] NM sob; **éclater en sanglots** to burst out sobbing, to burst into tears; **il pleurait à gros sanglots** he was sobbing his heart out; **avec des sanglots dans la voix** with a sob in one's voice, in a tearful voice

sangloter [sɑ̃glɔte] VI to sob

sang-mêlé [sɑ̃mele] N INV half-caste

sangria [sɑ̃grija] NF sangria

sangsue [sɑ̃sy] NF *Zool, Fig* leech

sanguin, -ine [sɑ̃gɛ̃, -in] ADJ **1** *Anat* blood; **groupe/vaisseau s.** blood group/vessel; **produits sanguins** blood products; **transfusion sanguine** blood transfusion; **circulation sanguine** circulation (of the blood) **2** *(tempérament)* impulsive; *(teint, visage)* ruddy **3** **orange sanguine** blood orange
■ NM **1** *(personne)* fiery person **2** *Bot* dogwood
■ NF **sanguine 1** *(craie)* red chalk, sanguine **2** *Minér* bloodstone **3** *(orange)* blood orange

> Il faut noter que l'adjectif anglais **sanguine** est un faux ami. Il signifie **optimiste**.
> Do not confuse with **sanguinaire**.

sanguinaire [sɑ̃ginɛr] ADJ *(homme)* bloodthirsty; *(combat)* bloody

> Do not confuse with **sanguin**.

sanguinolent [sɑ̃ginɔlɑ̃] ADJ **1** *(teinté de sang)* spotted with blood; **sa lèvre sanguinolente** his/her bleeding lip; **une plaie sanguinolente** a wound oozing blood **2** *(rouge)* blood-red

sanie [sani] NF *Méd* pus and blood, *Spéc* sanies

sanitaire [sanitɛr] ADJ **1** *Méd (personnel)* medical, health; *(équipement)* medical; *(mesures)* health; *Mil etc* **voiture s.** ambulance **2** *Constr etc (équipement, installation)* sanitary; **bloc s.** *(dans un camping)* toilet *or* sanitary block; **système s.** sanitation (system)
■ NM **les sanitaires** *(toilettes)* toilet; *(salle de bains et W.-C.)* bathroom and toilet; **sanitaires privatifs** en-suite *or* private facilities
■ NF *Mil etc* ambulance

sans [sɑ̃] PRÉP **1** *(absence, privation, exclusion)* without; **partez s. moi** go without me; **il est revenu s. argent** *ou* **s. un sou** *ou* **s. le sou** he came back without any money *or* without a penny; **elle arriva s. argent ni bagages** she arrived without any *or* without either money or luggage; **elle est s. emploi depuis deux mois** she's been unemployed *or* without work for two months; **couple s. enfants** childless couple; **pain/régime s. sel** salt-free bread/diet; **faire qch s. faute** to do sth without fail; **demain s. faute** tomorrow without fail; **suffisant, s. plus** adequate but no more (than that); **plaintes s. fin** endless complaints; **se plaindre s. fin** to complain endlessly; **baignade s. danger** safe bathing; **s. parler/travailler** without speaking/working; **s. mot dire, s. dire un mot** without saying a word; **s. hésiter** without hesitating *or* hesitation, unhesitatingly; **cela va s. dire** it goes without saying; **il va s. dire que c'est une réussite** it's a success, needless to say, it goes without saying that it's a success; **s. plus attendre** without further delay, immediately; **non s. difficulté** not without difficulty; *Fml* **vous n'êtes pas s. le connaître** you must know him; *Fml* **tu n'es pas s. savoir que …** you are quite well aware that …; *Fml* **ces questions n'étaient pas s. m'embarrasser** these questions were naturally somewhat embarrassing; *Typ* **s. patte** *ou* **serif** sans serif SEE GRAMMAR A73; B57

2 *(condition)* but for; **s. vous je ne l'aurais jamais fait** but for you *or* if it hadn't been for you, I would never have done it; **s. cela, s. quoi** otherwise; *Fam* **sois sage, s. ça tu seras puni!** be good or (else) you'll be punished!

conj s. que + *sub* without + *gerund*; **s. que nous le sachions,** *Rare* **s. que nous ne le sachions** without our knowing, unbeknownst to us; **il ne parlait jamais s. qu'on lui parlât** he never spoke unless he was spoken to

adv *Fam* **que ferais-tu s.?** how would you manage without?; **est-ce que tu pourrais vivre s.?** could you live without it/them?; **la télévision, je ne pourrais pas vivre s.** I couldn't live without television

sans-abri [sɑ̃zabri] **n inv** homeless person; **les s.** the homeless

sans-cœur *Fam* **adj inv** heartless **n inv** heartless person

sanscrit [sɑ̃skri] **adj, nm** = **sanskrit**

sans-culotte, *pl* **sans-culottes nm** *Hist* sans culotte *(person with extreme republican sympathies during the French Revolution)*

sans-dessein [sɑ̃desɛ̃] *Can Fam Péj* **adj inv** clueless, gormless **n inv** clueless person

sans-emploi [sɑ̃zɑ̃plwa] **n inv** unemployed *or* jobless person; **les s.** the unemployed, the jobless; **le nombre des s. augmente** the unemployment *or* jobless figure is rising

sans-façon nm inv *(naturel)* informality **adj inv** *(naturel)* informal

sans-faute nm inv *Sport* clear round; **accomplir** *ou* **faire un s.** *(d'un cheval)* to have a clear round; *Fig (d'un candidat)* not to put a foot wrong, to turn in a faultless performance

sans-fil nf inv *Vieilli* wireless (telegraphy) **nm inv** cordless telephone

sans-gêne *Péj* **nm inv** impudence, brazenness **n inv** *(personne)* impudent *or* brazen person **adj inv** *(personne)* impudent, brazen; **qu'est-ce qu'il est s.!** he's got a cheek!; **des manières s.** brazen ways

sanskrit [sɑ̃skri] **adj, nm** *Ling* Sanskrit

sans-le-sou n inv *Fam* penniless person; **c'est un s.** he doesn't have a penny to his name

sans-logis n inv homeless person; **les s.** the homeless

sansonnet [sɑ̃sɔnɛ] **nm** starling

sans-papiers n inv illegal immigrant *(who does not possess the required work or residence permit)*

sans-parti n inv *Pol* independent member *(of an assembly or a Parliament); (dans un système de parti unique)* non-party member

sans-patrie n inv stateless person

sans-souci adj inv carefree, happy-go-lucky

santal, -als [sɑ̃tal] **nm (bois de) s.** sandalwood

santé [sɑ̃te] **nf** health; **être en bonne s.** to be well, to be in good health; **s. de fer** iron constitution; **avoir une bonne/mauvaise s.** to be healthy/unhealthy; **ne pas avoir de s., avoir une s. fragile** *ou* **délicate,** *Fam* **avoir une petite s.** to be in poor health, to be delicate; *Fig Fam* **avoir de la s.** *(avoir de l'audace)* to have a nerve *or Br* a brass neck; **c'est bon/mauvais pour la s.** it's good/bad for your health; *Fam* **comment va la s.?** how's things?, how are you doing?; **perdre/recouvrer la s.** to lose/recover one's health; **elle respire la s.** she looks *or* is the picture of health, she radiates health; **être plein de s.** to be full of life; **absent pour raison de s.** absent for health reasons *or* on medical grounds; **boire à la s. de qn** to drink sb's health; **à votre s.!** your health!, *Fam* cheers!; **buvons à la s. des mariés** let's drink to the married couple; *Suisse Fam* **s.!** *(à vos souhaits)* bless you!; *Admin* **Ministère de la S. et de la Sécurité sociale** *Br* ≃ Department of Social Security, *Am* ≃ Department of Health and Human Services; *Naut* **agent de (la) s.** quarantine officer; **s. publique** public health

santiag [sɑ̃tjag] **nf** *Fam* cowboy boot

santon [sɑ̃tɔ̃] **nm** *(de crèche)* Christmas crib figure

saoudien, -ienne [saudjɛ̃, -jɛn] **adj** Saudi (Arabian) **n S.** Saudi (Arabian)

saoul [su], **saoulard** [sular], **saouler** [sule] = **soûl, soûlard, soûler**

sapajou [sapaʒu] **nm** *Zool* capuchin (monkey), sapajou

sape [sap] **nf 1** *(d'un mur, d'une tour etc)* undermining; *Mil* sapping; *Fig* **travaux de s.** undermining **2** *(tranchée)* sap, trench **3** *(outil)* mattock **4** *Arg* **sapes** *(vêtements)* gear, togs, *Br* clobber

saper [sape] **vt 1** *Mil etc, Fig* to undermine; **s. le moral de qn** to sap sb's morale **2** *Arg (habiller)* to tog out, to dress; **être bien sapé** to be all togged up **vpr se saper** *Arg* to get dressed; *(s'habiller chic)* to get all dressed up

saperlipopette [sapɛrlipɔpɛt], **saperlotte** [saperlɔt] **int** *Arch, Hum* gad(zooks)!

sapeur [sapœr] **nm** *Mil* sapper; *Fam* **fumer comme un s.** to smoke like a chimney

sapeur-pompier nm *Admin* fireman, fire fighter; **les sapeurs-pompiers** *(service)* the fire brigade *or Am* department

saphique [safik] **adj** Sapphic

saphir [safir] **nm** sapphire

saphisme [safism] **nm** sapphism

sapin [sapɛ̃] **nm 1** *(arbre)* fir (tree); *Com* **(bois de) s.** deal **2** *Fam* **ça sent le s.** that sounds bad, that sounds as if you're heading for an early grave; **il sent le s.** he's done for, he's had it **3** *Can* **se faire passer un s.** *(se faire avoir)* to be taken for a ride

sapine [sapin] **nf 1** *(planche)* deal board **2** *Constr* crane tower **3** *(en viticulture)* deal tub

sapinière [sapinjɛr] **nf** fir plantation

saponaire [sapɔnɛr] **nf** *Bot* soapwort

saponifiant [sapɔnifjɑ̃] *Chimie* **adj** saponifying **nm** saponifier, saponifying agent

saponification [sapɔnifikasjɔ̃] **nf** saponification

saponifier [sapɔnifje] **vt** *(impf, pr sub* **n. saponifiions, v. saponifiiez***)* to saponify

sapristi [sapristi] **int** *Fam Vieilli, Hum* good heavens!

saprophage [saprɔfaʒ] **adj** *Entom* saprophagous

saprophyte [saprɔfit] **nm** *Biol* saprophyte

saquebute [sakbyt] **nf** *Hist, Mus* sackbut

saquer [sake] **vt** *Fam* = **sacquer**

sarabande [sarabɑ̃d] **nf** *(danse), Mus* saraband; *Fam (tapage)* racket, row; **ils ont fait la s. toute la nuit** they made a racket *or* row all night long

Sarajevo [saraʒevo] **n** Sarajevo

sarbacane [sarbakan] **nf** blowpipe; *(jouet)* peashooter

sarcasme [sarkasm] **nm** sarcasm; *(remarque)* sarcastic remark

sarcastique [sarkastik] **adj** sarcastic

sarcastiquement [sarkastikmɑ̃] **adv** sarcastically

sarcelle [sarsɛl] **nf** teal

sarclage [sarklaʒ] **nm** weeding

sarcler [sarkle] **vt 1** *(jardin, plates-bandes)* to weed; *(sol)* to hoe; *(champ)* to clean **2** *(mauvaises herbes)* to hoe up *or* out

sarclette [sarklɛt] **nf** (weeding) hoe

sarcloir [sarklwar] **nm** (weeding) hoe

sarcome [sarkom] **nm** *Méd* sarcoma; **s. de Kaposi** Kaposi's sarcoma

sarcophage [sarkɔfaʒ] **nm** *Antiq, Nucl* sarcophagus **nf** *Entom* bluebottle

Sardaigne [sardɛɲ] **nf** Sardinia

sarde [sard] **adj** Sardinian **n S.** Sardinian **nm** *Ling* Sardinian

sardine [sardin] **nf 1** *(poisson)* sardine; **sardines à l'huile/à la tomate** sardines in oil/in tomato sauce; *Fam* **serrés comme des sardines** packed together like sardines **2** *Mil Fam* stripe **3** *(de tente)* tent peg

sardinerie [sardinri] **nf** sardine cannery

sardinier, -ière [sardinje, -jɛr] **n** *(pêcheur)* sardine fisher; *(ouvrier)* sardine canner **nm** *(filet)* sardine net; *(bateau)* sardine boat

sardonique [sardɔnik] **adj** sardonic

sardonyx [sardɔniks] **nf** *Minér* sardonyx

sargasse [sargas] **nf** sargasso, gulfweed; **la mer des Sargasses** the Sargasso Sea

sari [sari] **nm** sari

sarigue [sarig] **nf** opossum, possum

sarin [sarɛ̃] **nm** sarin

SARL [ɛsaɛrɛl] **nf** *(abrév* **société anonyme à responsabilité limitée***)* = limited liability company, *Br* ≃ Ltd, *Am* ≃ Inc

sarment [sarmɑ̃] **nm** *(tige)* bine; *(de vigne)* vine shoot

sarmenteux, -euse [sarmɑ̃tø, -øz] **adj** *(plante)* climbing

sarong [sarɔ̃] **nm** sarong

saroual [sarwal], **sarouel** [sarwɛl] **nm** = baggy trousers worn by North Africans

sarrasin, -ine [sarazɛ̃, -in] **adj** *Hist* Saracen **n** *Hist* **S.** Saracen **nm** *Agr* buckwheat **nf** **sarrasine** portcullis

sarrau [saro] **nm** smock

Sarre [sar] **nf** **la S.** *(région)* Saarland, the Saar; *(rivière)* the Saar

sarriette [sarjɛt] **nf** *Bot, Culin* savory

sarrois, -oise [sarwa, -waz] **adj** of/from Saarland *or* the Saar **n S.** Saarlander

sas [sɑ(s)] **nm 1** *(crible)* sieve; **passer qch au s.** to sift *or* sieve sth **2** *Tech* lock chamber, coffer **3** *Constr, Naut, Astronaut* airlock

sassafras [sasafrɑ] **nm** *Bot* sassafras

sassage [sasaʒ], **sassement** [sasmɑ̃] **nm 1** *(criblage)* sifting, sieving **2** *(d'un bateau)* passing through a lock

sasser [sase] **vt 1** *(farine, plâtre)* to sift, to sieve; *(grain)* to winnow **2** *(bateau)* to pass through a lock

sasseur, -euse [sasœr, -øz] N sifter

Satan [satã] N Satan

satané [satane] ADJ *Fam* confounded; **s. temps!** what filthy weather!

satanique [satanik] ADJ satanic; *Fig (cruauté, idée, sourire etc)* fiendish

satanisme [satanism] NM satanism

sataniste [satanist] N satanist

satellisation [satelizasjɔ̃] NF **1** *Astronaut (d'un satellite, d'un engin spatial)* putting into orbit; **programme de s.** space programme **2** *Pol (d'un pays, d'une région)* satellization

satelliser [satelize] VT **1** *Astronaut (satellite, engin spatial)* to put into orbit **2** *Pol (pays, région)* to satellize
  VPR se satelliser 1 *Astronaut* to go into orbit **2** *Pol (d'un pays, d'une région)* to become a satellite

satellitaire [sateliter] ADJ *(diffusion, chaîne, téléphone)* satellite; **imagerie s.** satellite pictures

satellite [satelit] NM **1** *Astron* satellite; **s. artificiel** artificial satellite; **s. géostationnaire** geostationary satellite; **s. terrestre/lunaire** earth-orbiting/moon-orbiting satellite; **s. de télécommunications** (tele)communications satellite, *Fam* comsat; **s. météorologique** weather *or* meteorological satellite; *TV* retransmis par **s.** transmitted by satellite; émission retransmise par **s.** satellite broadcast; **télévision par s.** satellite television, *Fam* metsat; **s. de diffusion directe** direct broadcast satellite, DBS; **s. de télédiffusion** broadcast satellite; **s. de télédiffusion directe** direct-broadcast satellite; **s. de télédétection** remote-sensing satellite; **s. météo** weather satellite; **s. terrestre** earth satellite **2** *Pol* satellite; **les satellites du bloc socialiste** the satellite countries of the socialist bloc; *Péj (homme)* satellite, hanger-on **3** *Tech* planet wheel, bevel gear; **engrenage à satellites** (sun-and-)planet gear; *Aut* **s. sur colonne de direction** steering column satellite
  ADJ **1** *Anat* **veines satellites** companion veins **2** *Pol* **pays s.** satellite state; **agglomération s.** satellite town

satiété [sasjete] NF satiety; **manger/boire à s.** to eat/drink one's fill; **répéter qch à s.** to repeat sth ad nauseam

satin [satɛ̃] NM **1** *Tex* satin **2** **bois de s.** satinwood **3** *Bot* **s. blanc** honesty

satiné [satine] ADJ *(tissu)* satiny, satin-like; *(cuir, papier)* glazed; *(papier)* calendered; *(peau)* satin-smooth; **peinture satinée** satin-finish paint
  NM satin finish; *(de la peau)* satin smoothness

satiner [satine] VT *(tissu etc)* to give a satin finish to, to satin; *(cuir)* to glaze; *(papier)* to calender

satinette [satinet] NF *Tex (en coton)* sateen; *(en soie et coton)* satinet(te)

satire [satir] NF satire *(contre on; de of)*; **faire la s. de son époque** to satirize one's times

satirique [satirik] ADJ satirical, satiric

satiriquement [satirikmã] ADV satirically

satiriser [satirize] VT to satirize

satiriste [satirist] N satirist

satisfaction [satisfaksjɔ̃] NF **1** satisfaction; **la s. du travail bien fait** the satisfaction of a job well done; **donner (toute** *ou* **entière) s. à qn** to give sb (complete) satisfaction; **donner s. aux vœux de qn** to satisfy *or* gratify sb's wishes; **avoir la s. de faire qch** to have the satisfaction of doing sth; **nous avons la s. de pouvoir dire que …** it gives us great satisfaction to be able to say that …; **j'éprouve une profonde s.** I feel (a) great satisfaction; **à la s. générale** to everyone's satisfaction;

j'ai eu une s. aujourd'hui a good thing happened today; **ils ne m'ont donné que des satisfactions** they've given me nothing but satisfaction; **s. de la clientèle** *ou* **du client** customer satisfaction **2** *(réparation)* satisfaction *(pour, de* for*)*; *Rel* atonement; **donner s. à qn** to give sb satisfaction; **obtenir s.** to obtain satisfaction

satisfaire [satisfɛr] *(conj like faire)* VT *(personne, besoin, demandes)* to satisfy; *(curiosité)* to satisfy, to gratify; *(sexuellement)* to satisfy; **s. le désir de qn** *(l'accomplir)* to carry out sb's wish; **s. l'attente de qn** to come up to sb's expectations; *Euph* **s. un besoin naturel** to answer a call of nature, to relieve oneself; **de manière à vous s.** to your satisfaction; **s. sa faim** to satisfy *or* appease one's hunger; **s. une commande** to fulfill an order
  VPR **se satisfaire 1 se s. de peu** to be content with very little, *Péj* to be easily satisfied **2** *(uriner)* to relieve oneself **3** *(sexuellement)* to achieve satisfaction
  VI **1 s. à** *(demande, exigence, condition, besoins)* to satisfy, to meet; *(souhaits)* to satisfy, to fulfil, to carry out; *(règlement, normes de sécurité)* to comply with; *(contrat, obligations)* to fulfil; **s. à son devoir** to carry out *or* fulfil one's duty; **s. à un examen** to pass an exam **2** *Arch* **s. à qn** *(dans un duel)* to give sb satisfaction

satisfaisant [satisfəzã] ADJ *(convenable) (réponse, travail etc)* satisfactory; *(qui contente) (repas, occupation)* satisfying

> Attention: ne pas confondre **satisfying** et **satisfactory** lorsqu'on traduit **satisfaisant**.

satisfait [satisfɛ] ADJ *(heureux)* satisfied; *(suffisant)* satisfied, smug; *(désir, vœu)* fulfilled; *Iron* **vous voilà s.!** well, you asked for it!; **je n'en suis pas s.** I'm not satisfied *or* pleased *or* happy with it; *Com* **j'espère que vous en serez entièrement s.** I trust it will give you complete satisfaction; **s. ou remboursé** satisfaction or your money back, money-back guarantee

satisfecit [satisfesit] NM INV *Litt (approbation)* recognition, credit; *Scol Vieilli* = certificate of satisfactory progress; **décerner un s. à qn** to congratulate sb on a job well done

saton [satɔ̃] NM *Fam* **coup de s.** kick, boot; **donner des coups de s. à qn/dans qch** to boot sb/sth, to give sb/sth a kicking

satonner [satone] VT *Fam* **s. qn/qch** to boot sb/sth, to give sb/sth a kicking

saturable [satyrabl] ADJ saturable

saturant [satyrã] ADJ saturating; **vapeur saturante** saturated vapour

saturateur [satyratœr] NM *Chimie, Ind* saturator; *(humidificateur)* humidifier

saturation [satyrasjɔ̃] NF *aussi Fig* saturation; *(du réseau routier)* gridlock; **arriver à s.** to reach saturation point; *Ordinat (d'une disquette)* to become full; **campagne de s.** *(en publicité)* saturation campaign; **s. du marché** saturation of the market; *TV, Radio* **s. acoustique** popping

saturé [satyre] ADJ *(solution)*, *Fig* saturated; *Ordinat (disque)* full; **l'éponge est saturée d'eau** the sponge is saturated; *Com* **le marché est s.** the market is saturated *or* has reached saturation point; **ville saturée** overcrowded city; **j'en suis s.** I'm sick of it/them; **j'étais s. de soleil** I'd had enough sun

saturer [satyre] VT to saturate *(de* with*)*; *TV, Radio* to overload; *Fig* **on nous sature de publicité** we are swamped with advertising; **le professeur nous sature de travail** the teacher is overloading us with work; **les appels de nos téléspectateurs ont saturé le standard** our viewers' calls have jammed the switchboards

VI **1** *(radio, chaîne hi-fi)* to distort **2** *Fam* **je sature** I've had it up to here

saturnales [satyrnal] NFPL *Antiq, Fig* saturnalia

Saturne [satyrn] N *Myth* Saturn
  NF *Astron* Saturn

saturnie [satyrni] NF emperor moth

saturnien, -ienne [satyrnjɛ̃, -jɛn] ADJ saturnine

saturnin, -ine [satyrnɛ̃, -in] ADJ *Méd* intoxication saturnine lead poisoning

saturnisme [satyrnism] NM *Méd* lead poisoning, *Spéc* saturnism

satyre [satir] NM **1** *Myth, Entom* satyr **2** *Fam (obsédé sexuel)* sex maniac

satyrique [satirik] ADJ *Antiq* satyric

sauce [sos] NF **1** *Culin* sauce; **s. hollandaise/béchamel/béarnaise** hollandaise/béchamel/béarnaise sauce; **s. aux champignons** mushroom sauce; **s. (à) salade** salad dressing; **(r)allonger la s.** to water down the sauce; *Fig Fam* to pad things out; *Fam* **accommoder un même sujet à toutes les sauces** to dish up the same subject in every shape and form; *Fam* **mettre qch à toutes les sauces** to use sth in every way imaginable; *Fig* **à quelle s. sera-t-il mangé?** how shall we deal with it/him? **2** *Beaux-Arts (craie noire)* soft black crayon **3** *Fig Fam (pluie)* **prendre la s.** to get soaked *or* drenched, to get a soaking **4** *Fam* **mettre la s.** to pull out all the stops, to go all out

saucée [sose] NF *Fam (pluie)* downpour; **recevoir une s.** to get soaked *or* drenched, to get a soaking

saucer [sose] VT (**je sauçai(s); n. sauçons**) **1** *(assiette)* to mop up the sauce from **2** *Fam* **se faire s.** to get soaked *or* drenched, to get a soaking

saucette [soset] NF *Can Fam* **faire une s.** to have a quickie; **faire une s. à Québec** to make a quick trip to Quebec City, to pop over to Quebec City

saucier [sosje] NM sauce cook *or* chef

saucière [sosjɛr] NF sauce boat

sauciflard [sosiflar] NM *très Fam* sausage

saucisse [sosis] NF **1** *Culin* sausage; **s. de Francfort** frankfurter; **s. de Strasbourg** knackwurst; **s. de Toulouse** = type of pork sausage; *Fam* **il n'attache pas son chien avec des saucisses** he's tight with his money, he's tight-fisted **2** *Mil Fam* barrage balloon **3** *Fam* **grande s.** beanpole; **s. à pattes** sausage dog

saucisson [sosisɔ̃] NM *Culin* sausage; **s. (sec)** (salami-type) sausage; **s. à l'ail** garlic sausage; **s. pur porc** 100% pork sausage; *Fam* **elle est toujours ficelée comme un s.** she's always bulging *or* bursting out of her clothes; *Hum* **s. à pattes** sausage dog

saucissonnage [sosisɔnaʒ] NM *Fam* **1** *(division en petites parties)* breaking up; **le désavantage avec cette chaîne, c'est le s. des films par les publicités** a drawback with this channel is the way films are constantly interrupted by commercial breaks **2** *(fait de ficeler)* trussing up

saucissonné [sosisone] ADJ *Fam* trussed up; **s. dans son collant/sa robe** poured into her tights/dress

saucissonner [sosisone] *Fam* VT *(attacher)* to truss up; *Fig* **film saucissonné de publicités** film broken up by adverts
  VI to picnic, to eat a snack

saucissonneur, -euse [sosisɔnœr, -øz] N *Fam* picnicker

sauf¹, sauve [sof, sov] ADJ *(personne)* safe, unhurt, unharmed; **sain et s.** safe and sound; **avoir la vie sauve** to escape with one's life; **ils lui ont laissé la vie sauve** they spared his life *or* him; **l'honneur est s.** honour is saved; **sa réputation est sauve** his/her reputation is intact or saved

sauf² PRÉP except (for), apart from; **elle n'a rien s. son salaire** she has nothing except (for) or apart from or but her wages; **il est indemne s. une écorchure au bras** he is unhurt except for or apart from a grazed arm; **s. avis contraire, s. contrordre** unless you/I/etc hear to the contrary, unless otherwise advised; **s. bonne fin** under usual reserve; **s. indication contraire** unless otherwise stated or specified; **s. de rares exceptions** with very few exceptions; **s. accidents, s. imprévu** barring accidents, unless anything unforeseen happens; **s. erreur ou omission** errors and omissions excepted; **s. erreur de ma part, je vous dois encore 500 euros** if I'm not mistaken or unless I'm mistaken, I still owe you 500 euros; **s. cas de force majeure** unless anything happens to prevent it; Jur except in cases of force majeure; Litt **je consens, s. à revenir sur ma décision** I consent, but I reserve the right to reconsider my decision; **s. le respect que je vous dois, s. votre respect** with all due respect; **s. s'il pleut** unless it rains, if it doesn't rain; Fam **je n'ai rien fait, s. d'écrire des lettres** I've done nothing except write or apart from writing some letters; Fam **s. que** + ind except that, apart from the fact that

sauf-conduit, pl **sauf-conduits** NM safe conduct, pass

sauge [soʒ] NF **1** Bot, Culin sage **2** Bot (plante ornementale) salvia

saugrenu [sogrəny] ADJ absurd, preposterous

saule [sol] NM willow; **s. pleureur** weeping willow

saumâtre [somɑtr] ADJ **1** (goût, eau) brackish, briny **2** Fig bitter; Fam **je la trouve s.** I'm not amused or impressed, I think it's a bit much

saumon [somɔ̃] NM **1** (poisson) salmon; **darne de s.** salmon steak; Am **lox** VOIR GRAMMAIRE A12 **2** Métal (de plomb, d'étain etc) pig
     ADJ INV salmon-pink; **rose s.** salmon pink

saumoné [somɔne] ADJ **truite saumonée** salmon trout

saumure [somyr] NF brine

saumuré [somyre] ADJ (harengs etc) pickled (in brine)

saumurer [somyre] VT to pickle (in brine)

sauna [sona] NM sauna

saupiquet [sopikɛ] NM Culin = spicy stew

saupoudrage [sopudraʒ] NM **1** Culin sprinkling, dusting **2** Fin, Pol (de crédits) = allocation of small amounts of funding to various beneficiaries

saupoudrer [sopudre] VT **1** Culin to dust, to sprinkle (**de** with); **s. des fraises de sucre** to sprinkle or dust strawberries with sugar **2** Fin, Pol **s. des crédits** = to allocate small amounts of funding to various beneficiaries **3** Fig Litt (parsemer) to scatter, to sprinkle (**de** with); **s. un texte de références/de citations** to pepper or sprinkle a text with references/quotations
     VPR **se saupoudrer se s. les mains de talc** to dust one's hands with talcum powder

saupoudreuse [sopudrøz] NF, **saupoudroir** [sopudrwar] NM Culin dredger, caster

saur [sɔr] ADJ M **hareng s.** kipper, smoked herring

saurer [sɔre] VT (harengs) to kipper, to smoke; (poisson, jambon) to smoke

saurien [sɔrjɛ̃] NM Zool saurian

saut [so] NM **1** (bond) jump, leap; **faire un s.** to jump, to leap, to take a leap; **la voiture a fait un s. de 50 mètres dans la mer** the car

---

plunged 50 metres into the sea; Fig **faire un s. à Paris/chez le boulanger/en ville** to pop or Br nip over to Paris/round to the baker's/into town; **entrer d'un s.** to dash or rush in; **au s. du lit** first thing in the morning; **il m'a trouvé au s. du lit** he caught me when I'd only just got up; **faire un s. dans l'inconnu** to take a leap in the dark or into the unknown; Fig **faire le (grand) s.** (faire qch de très important) to take the plunge; (mourir) to pass on (to the other side); Fig **le héros fit un s. de plusieurs années et se retrouva en l'an 2055** the hero skipped several years and found himself in the year 2055; Arch **par sauts et par bonds** in fits and starts; **il n'y a qu'un s. d'ici là** it's only a stone's throw away **2** Mus skip
3 Ordinat jump; Typ **s. de ligne** line break; Typ **s. de ligne manuel** hard return; Typ **s. de page** page break; Typ **s. de page imposé** hard page break
4 (en élevage) covering
5 (de cours d'eau) waterfall
▸▸ **Natation s. de l'ange** swallow dive, Am swan dive; Gym **s. de carpe** flip; **faire des sauts de carpe** to bounce around; Natation **s. carpé** pike; **s. à la corde** skipping; **s. à l'élastique** bungee jumping; Sport **s. en hauteur** high jump; Sport **s. en longueur** long or Am broad jump; **s. en parachute** parachute jump; (activité) parachute jumping; **faire du s. en parachute** to go parachute jumping; Sport **s. à la perche** pole vault(ing); **s. périlleux** somersault; **s. en** ou **à skis** ski jump; (activité) ski jumping; **faire du s. à skis** to go ski jumping

saut-de-lit NM INV (light) dressing gown

saut-de-loup, pl **sauts-de-loup** NM sunken fence, ha-ha

saut-de-mouton, pl **sauts-de-mouton** NM flyover, Am overpass

saute [sot] NF **s. de vent** change in the wind direction; **sautes de température** sudden changes in temperature; **sautes d'humeur** mood swings

sauté [sote] Culin ADJ sautéed, sauté
     NM sauté; **s. de lièvre** sauté of hare

saute-mouton NM INV leapfrog; **jouer à s.** to play leapfrog

---

SAUTER [sote] (aux **avoir**)	
VI to jump **1** • to skip **1** • to blow up **2** • to fall **2**	
VT to leap over **1** • to skip **2** • to miss out **2**	

VI **1** (bondir) to jump; **s. hors du lit/sur son cheval** to jump or leap out of bed/on to one's horse; **s. par la fenêtre/du pont** to jump out (of) the window/from the bridge; **s. sur un pied** to hop; **s. à la perche** to pole-vault; **s. à la corde** to skip, Am to jump rope; **s. à terre** to jump down; Équitation **le cheval refuse de s.** the horse is refusing (the jump or fence); Fam **et que ça saute!** and make it snappy!, and step on it!, chop! chop!; Fig **s. du coq à l'âne** to jump or skip from one subject to another; **nous allons s. directement à la page 5** we're going to jump straight to page 5; **s. à la gorge de qn** to pounce or jump on sb, to go for sb; (d'un chien) to fly at sb or at sb's throat; **cela saute aux yeux** it's obvious, it's staring you in the face; **s. au cou de qn** to fling one's arms round sb's neck; **s. au plafond** (du bouchon de champagne etc) to hit the ceiling; (de surprise) to jump out of one's skin; (de joie) to jump for joy, to be overjoyed; (de colère) to hit the roof or the ceiling; **s. de joie** to jump for joy; **s. sur qn** to pounce on or fly at or fling oneself at sb; Fig Fam to pounce on sb; **s. sur une offre/sur l'occasion** to jump at an offer/at the opportu-

---

nity; **il faut s. dessus, jamais tu ne trouveras un vélo à ce prix-là** you'll never find another bike at that price, snap it up!
2 (exploser) to blow up, to explode; (d'un bouton) to come off, to fly off; Élec (d'un fusible) to blow, Fam to go; Fig (du gouvernement) to fall; (d'une entreprise) to collapse; (d'un poste) to be axed; Ordinat (d'un réseau) to crash; **faire s.** (rocher) to blast; (pont etc) to blow up; (mine) to explode; (chaudière) to burst; Fig (projet etc) to wreck, to ruin; (gouvernement etc) to bring down; (fonctionnaire) to fire, Br to sack; Culin (pommes de terre) to sauté; Culin (crêpe) to toss; (serrure) to force; (piège) to spring; **faire s. le bouchon** (d'une bouteille) to pop the cork; **j'ai eu du mal à faire s. la partie scellée** I had trouble breaking open the sealed part; Fam **faire s. la banque** to break the bank; Élec **faire s. les plombs** to blow the fuses; **faire s. un enfant sur ses genoux/en l'air** to bounce a child on one's knees/to throw a child up in the air; **se faire s. la cervelle** to blow one's brains out
     VT **1** (fossé, barrière etc) to jump (over), to leap over, to clear; Fig **s. le pas** to take the plunge
2 (omettre) (page, ligne etc) to skip, to miss out; (repas) to skip; Tricot (maille) to drop; Scol **s. une classe** to skip a year; Fam Vieilli **je la saute** I'm starving, I'm ravenous
3 (d'un étalon) (jument) to cover; Vulg (femme) to shag, to screw; **se faire s.** (d'une femme) to get laid

sauterelle [sotrɛl] NF **1** Entom grasshopper; (nuisible) locust; **grande s. d'Orient** locust; **invasion de sauterelles** invasion of locusts **2** Fig Fam (fille, femme) chick, Br bird; (fille maigre) beanpole

sauterie [sotri] NF Vieilli, Hum party, Fam hop

saute-ruisseau NM INV Fam Arch errand boy

sauteur, -euse [sotœr, -øz] ADJ (insecte etc) jumping; **scie sauteuse** jigsaw
     N **1** Sport jumper; **s. en longueur** long jumper; **s. en hauteur** high jumper; **s. à la perche** pole vaulter **2** Fig Fam (homme sans sérieux) unreliable sort
     NF **sauteuse 1** (casserole) frying pan **2** Arg Vieilli (femme de mœurs légères) slut

sautillant [sotijɑ̃] ADJ (rythme, musique) bouncy; **avancer d'un pas s.** to bounce along

sautillement [sotijmɑ̃] NM hopping or skipping (about); **il avançait par sautillements** he was skipping along; (sur un pied) he was hopping along

sautiller [sotije] VI (des oiseaux) to hop (about); (des enfants) to skip or hop about; **s. d'un pied sur l'autre** to hop from one foot to the other; **marcher/courir en sautillant** to skip along

sautoir [sotwar] NM **1** Hér saltire **2** (collier) chain; **s. de perles** string of pearls; **porté en s.** worn round the neck **3** Sport jumping area

sauvage [sovaʒ] ADJ **1** (à l'état de nature) (plante, animal) wild; **chat s.** wildcat; Can raccoon; **lieu s.** wild spot; **la côte ouest est restée très s.** the west coast has remained very wild; **redevenir s.** (d'un animal apprivoisé) to revert to the wild; **à l'état s.** wild
2 Vieilli (peuple, tribu) savage, primitive; **retourner à la vie s.** to go back to the wild
3 (violent) (personne, agression) savage, brutal; (mœurs) uncivilized
4 (peu sociable) unsociable; (enfant) shy
5 (non autorisé) unauthorized; **grève s.** wildcat strike; **camping s.** unauthorized camping; **urbanisation s.** uncontrolled urbanization; **immigration s.** illegal immigration; **psychanalyse s.** amateur psychoanalysis
     N (f parfois **sauvagesse**) **1** Vieilli (indigène) savage; Can Péj (Amérindien) (American) In-

dian; *Fam Hum* **on n'est pas des sauvages!** we're not savages!; *Fam Hum* **bande de sauvages!** you bunch of savages!

2 *(personne peu sociable)* unsociable person; **c'est un vrai s.** he's a real recluse

sauvagement [sovaʒmɑ̃] ADV savagely

sauvageon, -onne [sovaʒɔ̃, -ɔn] NM *(pour greffer)* wild stock
N *(enfant)* little savage

sauvagerie [sovaʒri] NF **1** *(cruauté)* savagery, brutality, barbarity **2** *(insociabilité)* unsociability

sauvagin, -ine [sovaʒɛ̃, -in] ADJ *(goût, odeur)* of wildfowl
NF **chasse à la sauvagine** wildfowling

sauvegarde [sovgard] NF **1** *(protection)* safeguard (**contre** against); **sous la s. de qn** under sb's protection; **la s. des forêts/du patrimoine national** the safeguarding or protection of the forests/the nation's heritage **2** *Ordinat* saving, backup; **faire la s. d'un fichier** to save a file; **s. automatique** automatic backup; **s. en ligne** on-line backup; **s. externe** off-line backup; **s. rapide** fast save; **s. sur bande** tape backup; **copie de s.** backup (copy)

sauvegarder [sovgarde] VT **1** *(protéger)* to safeguard (**contre** against) **2** *Ordinat (fichier)* to save, to back up; **s. un fichier sur disque** to save a file to disk; **s. automatiquement** to autosave

sauve-qui-peut [sovkipø] NM INV *(débandade)* stampede; *(cri)* every man for himself, run for your life

sauver [sove] VT **1** *(personne)* to save, to rescue (**de** from); *Rel (personne, âme)* to save; **le malade est sauvé** the patient is out of danger; **s. la vie à** ou **de qn** to save sb's life; *Fig* **tu me sauves!** you're a lifesaver!; *Fam* **il n'y a que la foi qui sauve!** faith can work miracles!

2 *(préserver) (navire, marchandises)* to salvage; **s. les apparences** to keep up appearances; **s. la face** to save face; *Fig Fam* **s. les meubles** to save or salvage something from the wreckage; *Fam* **s. sa peau** ou **sa tête** to save one's skin; *Fig* **ce qui le sauve, c'est que ...** his saving grace is that ...; **la fin sauve le film** it's the end that saves or rescues the film; **s. la situation** to save the day
VPR **se sauver 1** *(s'échapper)* to escape (**de** from); **sauve qui peut!** every man for himself!, run for your life!

2 *(s'enfuir)* to run away; **se s. à toutes jambes** to take to one's heels, to beat a hasty retreat, *Br Fam* to scarper; *Fam* **il se fait tard, je me sauve** it's getting late, I'm off or I must fly; *Fam* **sauve-toi maintenant, tu vas être en retard** be off or get going now, you'll be late **3** *(du lait, de préparation culinaire etc)* to boil over

sauvetage [sovtaʒ] NM **1** *(d'un accidenté)* rescue; **s. aérien en mer** air-sea rescue; **il a fait plusieurs sauvetages en mer** he has been involved in several sea rescues; **appareil de s.** life-saving or rescue apparatus; **ceinture de s.** life belt; **gilet de s.** life jacket; **bouée de s.** life buoy; **canot** ou **embarcation de s.** lifeboat; **échelle de s.** fire escape; *Fig* **le s. d'une entreprise** the rescue of a company **2** *(d'un navire, de marchandises)* salvage

sauveteur [sovtœr] NM rescuer
ADJ M **bateau s.** lifeboat; **chien s.** rescue dog

sauvette (à la) [alasovɛt] ADV *(pour ne pas être vu)* furtively, on the sly; *(à la hâte)* in a hurry ou rush; **vendre à la s.** *(illégalement)* to peddle (illicitly) on the streets; **marchand à la s.** (illicit) street vendor

sauveur [sovœr] NM saviour, *Am* savior

SAV [ɛsave] NM *(abrév service après-vente)* after-sales service

savamment [savamɑ̃] ADV **1** *(avec érudition)* learnedly; **elle expose s. ses connaissances** she presents her knowledge in a learned manner **2** *(en connaissance de cause)* knowingly; **j'en parle s.** I know what I'm talking about **3** *(habilement)* cleverly, skilfully, *Am* skillfully; **elle sait s. convaincre son monde** she's quite adept at convincing people

savane [savan] NF **1** *Géog* savanna(h) **2** *Can (marécage)* swamp

savant, -ante [savɑ̃, -ɑ̃t] ADJ **1** *(érudit) (personne)* learned (**en** in), erudite, scholarly; *(bien informé)* knowledgeable (**en** about); *(texte)* scholarly, learned; *(mot, terme)* specialist, technical **2** *(habile)* clever, skilful, *Am* skillful; **s. calcul** clever calculation **3** **chien s.** performing dog
N *(scientifique)* scientist; *(érudit)* scholar

savarin [savarɛ̃] NM *Culin* savarin

savate [savat] NF **1** *Fam (pantoufle)* slipper; **être en savates** to be in one's slippers; *Vieilli* **traîner la s.** *(être pauvre)* to be down at heel **2** *Fam (maladroit)* clumsy oaf; **comme une s.** abominably, atrociously **3** *Sport* kick boxing **4** *Tech* sole (plate)

savater [savate] VT *Fam* to kick, to boot

saveur [savœr] NF **1** *(de vin, fruit etc)* taste, flavour, *Am* flavor; **sans s.** tasteless, insipid **2** *Fig (de remarque, récit etc)* spice, pungency

Savoie [savwa] NF Savoy; *Culin* **biscuit de S.** sponge cake

SAVOIR¹ [savwar] *(prp* **sachant;** *pp* **su;** *pr ind* **je sais, il sait, n. savons, ils savent;** *pr sub* **je sache, n. sachions, ils sachent;** *imp* **sache, sachons, sachez;** *impf* **je savais;** *p hist* **je sus;** *fu* **je saurai)** VTI **1** *(avoir connaissance de)* to know; **s. qch par cœur** to know sth by heart; **s. l'anglais** to know English; *Litt* **s. le chemin** to know the way; **tu sais la nouvelle?** have you heard the news ou the latest?; **je n'en sais rien** I don't know anything about it, I know nothing about it; *(je n'y connais rien)* I don't know; **je n'en sais trop rien** I'm not (very) sure; **en s. trop** to know too much; **qu'est-ce j'en sais?** what do I know?; **comment le saurais-je?** how should I know?; **il paraît que tu as des projets, peut-on s.?** it seems you have plans, may one know what they are?; **tu crois qu'il viendra? – va (donc) s.** do you think he'll come? – who knows?; **saura-t-on jamais?** will we ever know?; **qu'en savez-vous?** what do you know about it?; **il sera peut-être là, qui sait?** perhaps he'll be there, who knows?; *Fam* **est-ce que je sais(, moi)?** I haven't a clue!, don't ask me!; **je ne veux pas (le) s.** I don't want to know; **je voudrais bien s. pourquoi** I'd like to know why, I wonder why; **il n'a rien voulu s.** he wouldn't listen, he didn't want to know; *Litt* **je ne sais** I do not know; **il en sait des choses** ou **plus d'une** he knows a thing or two; **reste à s. si ...** it remains to be seen whether or if ...; **la question est de s. si elle viendra** the question is whether she will come; **je crois s. qu'il est ici** I understand or believe he is here; **faire s. qch à qn** to tell sb sth, to let sb know about sth, to inform sb of sth; **vous auriez dû le lui faire s.** you should have told him, you should have let him know; **je ne suis pas content, et je vais le lui faire s.** I'm not happy and I'll tell him so or I'll let him know it; **je le sais par ma sœur** I heard about it from my sister; **(à) s.** that is (to say), namely, i.e.; **pas que je sache** not to my knowledge, not that I know of; **(à ce) que je sache** as or so far as I know; **(pour) autant que je sache** as far as I know; **pour autant que je sache, il pourrait très bien être au Canada** he could be in Canada for all I know; **on ne sait jamais** you never know, you never can tell; **si jeunesse savait!** youth is wasted on the young; **si**

j'avais su if I had known, had I known; **des parents que je sais venir de Londres** relatives who I know come from London; **je ne sais (pas) où les trouver** I don't know where to find them; **je ne sais qui de ses amis** some friend or other of his/hers; **elle a mangé je ne sais quoi et ça l'a rendue malade** she's eaten something or other that's made her ill; **je ne sais quelle maladie/quel problème** some illness/problem or other; **il y a je ne sais combien de temps** ages ago, goodness knows how long ago; **des robes, des chapeaux, des gants, que sais-je (encore)?** dresses, hats, gloves, and what have you or and goodness knows what else

2 *(être conscient de)* to know; **je ne savais pas cela** I didn't know that, I wasn't aware of that; **je le sais bien!** I know!, I realize that!; **elle est jolie et elle le sait bien** she's pretty, and she knows it or and doesn't she know it!; **je ne le savais pas malade** I didn't know he was ill; **ce n'est pas facile, tu sais!** it isn't easy, you know!; **sans le s.** without realizing or knowing it, without being aware of it; *Litt (in first person only)* **je ne sache pas qu'on vous ait invité** I am not aware that you have been invited

3 *Litt (connaître) (personne)* to know (of); **je sais un bon horloger** I know (of) a good watchmaker; *Péj* **avec la fille que vous savez** with you know who; *Péj* **c'est encore une lettre de qui vous savez** it's another letter from you know who

4 *(être certain de)* to know; **il sait ce qu'il veut** he knows what he wants; **ne s. que faire/que dire** not to know or to be at a loss what to do/to say; **je ne sais que penser** I don't know what to think; **sachez que ...** be advised that ..., please note that ...; **ne pas s. où se mettre** not to know where to put oneself

5 *(être capable de)* **s. faire qch** to be able to do sth, to know how to do sth; **savez-vous nager?** can you swim?, do you know how to swim?; **s. écouter** to be a good listener; **il faut s. être patient** you have to learn to be patient; **je ne saurais (pas) vous conseiller** I wouldn't know what advice to give you, I wouldn't know how to advise you; **on ne saurait se souvenir de tout** one cannot expect to remember everything; **on ne saurait trop insister sur ce point** this point cannot be emphasized enough; **je sais y aller** I know how to get there; **je crois que je saurai le faire** I think I can manage it; *Fam* **elle sait y faire avec les enfants** she's good with children; *Fam* **s. s'y prendre avec qn** to know how to handle sb; **je ne saurais guère vous le dire** I'm afraid I couldn't really tell you SEE
GRAMMAR A58; B40

6 *(locutions)* **un je ne sais quoi de déplaisant** something vaguely unpleasant; **c'est Monsieur/Madame je sais tout** he's/she's a real know-all or know-it-all; **arrête de faire ton Monsieur je sais tout** stop being such a know-all or know-it-all; **il a des amis, Dieu sait** Lord ou God knows, he has plenty of friends; **Dieu sait comment** Lord ou God (only) knows how; **Dieu sait si je le lui ai répété** God (only) knows how often I've told him
VPR **se savoir je me savais très malade** I knew I was very ill; **ça se saura vite** it'll soon get out, everyone will know about it soon; **ça se saurait si c'était possible** if it was possible, everyone would know about it

savoir² NM knowledge, learning; **homme d'un grand s.** very knowledgeable or learned man, man of great learning

savoir-faire NM INV expertise, know-how

savoir-vivre NM INV savoir-vivre, good manners; **manquer de s.** to have no manners

savon [savɔ̃] NM soap; **(pain de) s.** bar or cake of soap; **s. de toilette** toilet soap; **s. liquide/doux** liquid/mild soap; **s. en paillettes** soap flakes; **pierre de s.** soapstone, *Spéc* steatite; **tu devrais mettre cette nappe au s.** you should rub the stains on this tablecloth with soap (before putting it into the washing machine); **ça partira avec du s.** it will come off or out with soap, soap will take it off or out; *Fam* **passer un s. à qn** to give sb a telling-off, to give somebody a roasting ▸▸ **s. à barbe** shaving soap; **s. de Marseille** = household soap, used for washing and laundry

savonnage [savɔnaʒ] NM *(de vêtements, mains etc)* soaping

savonner [savɔne] VT **1** *(mains, vêtement etc)* to soap; *(en faisant mousser)* to lather; **s. le dos à qn** to soap sb's back; *Fig* **s. la planche à qn** to make things difficult for sb; *Fam Vieilli* **s. la tête à qn** to give sb a dressing-down; *Aut* **piste savonnée** skidpan **2** *Tech (verre)* to rub, to grind ▪ VPR **se savonner** to soap oneself; **se s. les mains** to soap one's hands

savonnerie [savɔnri] NF *(usine)* soap factory; *(fabrication)* soap manufacture

savonnette [savɔnɛt] NF bar of (toilet) soap

savonneux, -euse [savɔnø, -øz] ADJ soapy

savourer [savure] VT *(plat, moment, vengeance etc)* to savour or Am to savor, to relish, to enjoy

savoureusement [savurøzmɑ̃] ADV with relish

savoureux, -euse [savurø, -øz] ADJ *(plat)* tasty; *(vin)* full-flavoured, Am full-flavored; *Fig (récit, détails)* spicy, juicy

savoyard, -arde [savwajar, -ard] ADJ Savoyard ▪ N S. Savoyard

Saxe [saks] NF Saxony; **porcelaine de S.** Dresden china

saxe [saks] NM *(matière)* Dresden china; *(objet)* piece of Dresden china

saxhorn [saksɔrn] NM *Mus* saxhorn; **s. basse** euphonium

saxifrage [saksifraʒ] NF saxifrage

saxo [sakso] *Fam* NM *(instrument)* sax ▪ N *(musicien)* sax player

saxon, -onne [saksɔ̃, -ɔn] ADJ Saxon ▪ NM *Ling* Saxon ▪ N S. Saxon

saxophone [saksɔfɔn] NM *Mus* saxophone

saxophoniste [saksɔfɔnist] N *Mus* saxophonist

saynète [sɛnɛt] NF *Théâtre* playlet, comic sketch

SBF [ɛsbeɛf] NF *(abrév* **Société des bourses françaises)** = company which runs the Paris Stock Exchange, *Br* ≃ LSE, *Am* ≃ NYSE; **le S.120** = broad-based French stock exchange index

sbire [sbir] NM *Péj (homme de main)* henchman

SCA [ɛssea] NF *(abrév* **société en commandite par actions)** partnership limited by shares

scabieux, -ieuse [skabjø, -jøz] ADJ scabby ▪ NF *Bot* **scabieuse** scabious

scabreux, -euse [skabrø, -øz] ADJ **1** *(indécent)* obscene, indecent; *Litt* scabrous **2** *Litt (dangereux)* risky, tricky

scalaire[1] [skalɛr] NM *(poisson)* angel fish

scalaire[2] ADJ, NM *Math* scalar

scalène [skalɛn] ADJ *Géom, Anat* scalene

scalp [skalp] NM *(trophée)* scalp; *(action de scalper)* scalping

scalpel [skalpɛl] NM *Chir* scalpel

scalper [skalpe] VT to scalp

scandale [skɑ̃dal] NM *(politique, financier etc)* scandal; **faire (un) s., causer un s.** to create or cause a scandal; **il a fait (tout) un s. parce que ...** he made a (tremendous) scene or kicked up a (tremendous) fuss because ...; **crier au s.** to make or create a great fuss; **au grand s. de ses parents** to the great indignation of his/her parents; **c'est un s.!** it's a scandal!, it's scandalous!

scandaleusement [skɑ̃daløzmɑ̃] ADV scandalously, outrageously; **vivre s.** to lead a scandalous life

scandaleux, -euse [skɑ̃daløx, -øz] ADJ scandalous, outrageous

scandaliser [skɑ̃dalize] VT to scandalize, to shock ▪ VPR **se scandaliser** to be scandalized or shocked (**de** by); **il ne se scandalise de rien** nothing shocks him

scander [skɑ̃de] VT *(vers)* to scan; *(slogan)* to chant; *Mus (phrase musicale)* to mark, to stress

scandinave [skɑ̃dinav] ADJ Scandinavian ▪ N S. Scandinavian

Scandinavie [skɑ̃dinavi] NF Scandinavia

scandium [skɑ̃djɔm] NM *Chimie* scandium

scanner[1] [skaner] NM **1** *Ordinat* scanner; insérer qch par s., capturer qch au s.** to scan sth in; **passer qch au s.** to scan sth; **s. à main** hand-held scanner; **s. optique** optical scanner; **s. à plat** flatbed scanner **2** *Méd* scanner; **faire un s.** *(d'un médecin)* to carry out or do a scan; *(d'un patient)* to have a scan; **on lui a fait un s.** he was given a scan

scanner[2] [skane] VT *Ordinat* to scan

scannérisation [skanerizasjɔ̃] NF *Ordinat* scanning

scanneur [skanœr] NM *Ordinat, TV* scanner; *Ordinat* **s. optique** optical scanner; *Ordinat* **s. à main** handheld scanner; *Ordinat* **s. à plat** flatbed scanner

scanographie [skanɔgrafi] NF *Méd* **1** *(science)* scanning **2** *(cliché)* scan

scansion [skɑ̃sjɔ̃] NF *Littér* scansion, scanning

scaphandre [skafɑ̃dr] NM **1** *Naut* diving suit; **s. autonome** aqualung, scuba **2** *Astronaut* space suit

scaphandrier [skafɑ̃drije] NM diver

scaphoïde [skafɔid] ADJ, NM *Anat, Biol* scaphoid

scapulaire [skapylɛr] NM *Rel* scapular ▪ ADJ scapular

scarabée [skarabe] NM scarab

scare [skar] NM *(poisson)* parrot fish, scar

scarificateur [skarifikatœr] NM *Agr* scarifier; *Chir* scarificator

scarifier [skarifje] VT *(impf, pr sub* n. **scarifiions,** v. **scarifiiez)** *Agr, Chir* to scarify

scarlatine [skarlatin] NF *Méd* scarlet fever, *Spéc* scarlatina; **avoir la s.** to have scarlet fever

scarole [skarɔl] NF *Bot* endive

scat [skat] NM *Mus* scat

scato [skato] ADJ INV *Fam* dirty; **plaisanterie s.** dirty joke; **humour s.** lavatorial humour

scatologie [skatɔlɔʒi] NF scatology

scatologique [skatɔlɔʒik] ADJ *(littérature, plaisanterie)* scatological

scatophage [skatɔfaʒ] ADJ *(poisson, insecte)* scatophagous ▪ NM dung fly, *Spéc* scatophage

sceau, *pl* **sceaux** [so] NM seal; **S. de l'État** State seal; **s. privé** private seal; **mettre** ou **apposer son s. à un document** to affix one's seal to or put one's seal on a document; *Fig* **le s. du génie** the mark or stamp of genius; **sous le s. du secret** under the seal of secrecy; *Bot* **s. de Salomon** Solomon's seal

scélérat, -ate [selera, -at] *Arch, Litt* ADJ villainous, wicked ▪ N villain, scoundrel

scellé [sele] ADJ sealed ▪ NM *Jur* (official) seal; **mettre** ou **apposer/lever les scellés** to put on/remove the seals; **sous scellés** under seal

scellement [sɛlmɑ̃] NM *Constr (d'un poteau etc dans la pierre, le béton)* bedding, fixing

sceller [sele] VT **1** *(document, sac etc)* to seal; *(ratifier)* to ratify, to confirm; **s. un pacte** to set the seal on an agreement **2** *Constr* to bed, to fix (in); **faire s. une porte/fenêtre** to seal a door/a window

scénarimage [senarimaʒ] NM story-board

scénario [senarjo] NM *Cin, TV* scenario; *(script)* script, screenplay; **s. d'auteur** writer's script; *Psy* **s. à compléter** story completion; *TV, Cin* **s.-maquette** storyboard; **s. de répétition** rehearsal script; *Fig* scenario

scénariser [senarize] VT **1** *(écrire le scénario de)* to script, write the screenplay for **2** *(donner la forme d'un scénario à)* to adapt for the screen

scénariste [senarist] N *Cin, TV* scriptwriter, screenwriter; **s. (de réécriture)** script editor

scène [sɛn] NF **1** *Théâtre (plateau)* stage; **la s.** *(le théâtre)* the stage, the theatre or Am the theater; **entrer en s.** *(d'un acteur)* to appear, to come on; *Fig* to appear on the scene; **être en s.** *(d'un acteur)* to be on (stage); **en s. pour le un!** on stage for act one!, beginners please!; **porter qch à la s.** to adapt sth for the stage; **quitter la s.** to retire from the stage or from acting; **faire ses adieux à la s.** to make one's final appearance on stage; *Fig* **la s. politique/internationale** the political/international scene; *Fig* **le devant de la s.** the foreground; **occuper le devant de la s.** to hold centre stage; **s. tournante** revolving stage

2 *(décor, action)* scene; **changement de s.** change of scene; **le tableau représente une s. de chasse** the painting represents a hunting scene; **s. d'intérieur** interior scene; **s. de genre** genre painting; **une s. d'amour** a love scene; **acte II, s. trois** act two, scene three; *Fig Hum* **il m'a fait la grande s. du II** he put on an Oscar-winning performance; **la s. se passe au Moyen Âge** the action takes place in the Middle Ages, the scene or the action is set in the Middle Ages

3 *(événement)* scene; **revoir les scènes de sa jeunesse** to revisit the scenes of one's youth; **ce fut une s. pénible** it was a painful scene; **imagine la s.!** imagine or picture the scene!, just imagine or picture it!

4 *Fam (dispute)* scene; **il m'a fait une s.** he made a scene ▸▸ **s. de ménage** domestic squabble; *Psy* **s. primitive** primal scene

scénique [senik] ADJ theatrical; **éclairage s.** stage or theatrical lighting; **indications scéniques** stage directions

scéniquement [senikmɑ̃] ADV theatrically

scénographe [senɔgraf] N **1** *Beaux-Arts etc* scenographer **2** *Théâtre* stage or theatre designer

scénographie [senɔgrafi] NF **1** *Beaux-Arts etc* scenography **2** *Théâtre* stage or theatre design

scepticisme [sɛptisism] NM scepticism, *Am* skepticism

sceptique [sɛptik] ADJ sceptical, sceptic, *Am* skeptic(al) ▪ N sceptic, *Am* skeptic

sceptiquement [sɛptikmɑ̃] ADV *Rare* sceptically, *Am* skeptically

sceptre [sɛptr] NM sceptre, *Am* scepter; *Fig* **s. de fer** rod of iron

schako [ʃako] NM *Mil* shako

scheik [ʃɛk] NM sheik

schelem [ʃlɛm] NM *Cartes* slam; **petit / grand s.** little/grand slam

schéma [ʃema] NM **1** *(graphique) (d'un moteur, d'une structure hiérarchique etc)* diagram, plan **2** *(esquisse) (d'un livre etc)* plan, outline; **s. directeur** master plan; **s. d'entreprise** organization chart; *Ordinat* **s. de clavier** keyboard map; **s. logique** logic diagram

schématique [ʃematik] ADJ **1** *(sous forme de dessin)* diagrammatic **2** *(sous forme de résumé)* schematic, simplified; *Péj* oversimplified

schématiquement [ʃematikmɑ̃] ADV schematically, diagrammatically; *(en gros)* in outline, in a simplified manner; **très s., voici ce que nous vous proposons** in very broad terms or very broadly speaking, this is what we propose

schématisation [ʃematizasjɔ̃] NF schematization, *Péj* over-simplification

schématiser [ʃematize] VT to schematize, *Péj* to oversimplify

schématisme [ʃematism] NM *Péj* oversimplification; *Phil* schematism

schème [ʃɛm] NM *Phil, Psy* schema; *Beaux-Arts etc* design

scherzando [skɛrtsando, skɛrdz-] ADV *Mus* scherzando

scherzo [skɛrtso, -dzo] *Mus* NM scherzo ADV scherzando

schibboleth [ʃibɔlɛt] NM *Rare* shibboleth

schilling [ʃiliŋ] NM *Anciennement (monnaie autrichienne)* schilling

schismatique [ʃismatik] ADJ, N schismatic

schisme [ʃism] NM schism; **faire s.** to break away

schiste [ʃist] NM *Géol* schist, shale

schisteux, -euse [ʃistø, -øz] ADJ *Géol* schistose

schistosomiase [ʃistozomjaz] NF *Méd* bilharzia, schistosomiasis

schizogamie [skizɔgami] NF *Biol* schizogenesis

schizoïde [skizɔid] ADJ, N *Psy* schizoid

schizoïdie [skizɔidi] NF *Psy* schizoidism

schizoïdique [skizɔidik] ADJ *Psy* schizoid

schizophrène [skizɔfrɛn] ADJ, N *Psy* schizophrenic

schizophrénie [skizɔfreni] NF *Psy* schizophrenia

schizophrénique [skizɔfrenik] ADJ, N *Psy* schizophrenic

schizothymie [skizɔtimi] NF *Psy* schizothymia

schizothymique [skizɔtimik] ADJ *Psy* schizothymic

schlague [ʃlag] NF *Hist, Mil* flogging; *Fig Fam* **mener qn à la s.** to rule sb with a rod of iron

schlass¹ [ʃlas] ADJ INV *très Fam (épuisé)* knackered, shattered; *(soûl)* pissed, *Br* ratarsed

schlass² NM *très Fam (couteau)* blade

schlinguer [ʃlɛ̃ge] VI *Vulg* to stink, *Br* to pong

schlittage [ʃlita3] NM *(timber)* sledging

schlitte [ʃlit] NF *(pour transporter le bois)* (timber) sledge

schlitter [ʃlite] VT *(bois)* to sledge

schlof [ʃlɔf] NM *Fam* bed, *Br* pit; **se mettre au s.** to hit the sack or the hay or Am the rack

schmilblick [ʃmilblik] NM *Fam* **faire avancer le s.** to make progress, to get somewhere; **tout ça, ça fait pas avancer le s.** that's not getting us any further forward

schnaps [ʃnaps] NM schnapps

schnauzer [ʃnawzɛr] NM *(chien)* schnauzer

schnock, schnoque [ʃnɔk] *Fam* ADJ *(fou)* crazy, bonkers; *(bête)* moronic
NM cretin, moron; **un vieux s.** an old fogey; **eh, du s.!** hey, you cretin or moron!

schnorchel, schnorkel [ʃnɔrkɛl] NM *(de sous-marin)* snorkel

schnouff [ʃnuf] NF *Arg (drogue)* dope, junk

schofar [ʃɔfar] NM *Rel* shofar, shophar

schuss [ʃus] NM *Ski* schuss; **descendre la piste en s.** ou **tout s.** to schuss down the slope

Schweppes® [ʃwɛps] NM tonic

SCI [ɛssei] NF *(abrév société de commerce international)* international trading corporation

sciage [sja3] NM sawing

sciatique [sjatik] ADJ *Anat (nerf)* sciatic
NM sciatic nerve
NF *Méd* sciatica

scie [si] NF **1** *(outil)* saw; **s. à bois** wood saw; **s. à métaux** hacksaw; **s. mécanique** ou **à main** hand saw; **s. circulaire** circular saw, *Am* buzz saw; **s. articulée, s. à chaîne(tte)** chain saw; **s. à chantourner** *(manuelle)* bowsaw, turning saw; *(mécanique)* jigsaw, scroll saw; **s. à découper, s. anglaise** *(manuelle)* fret saw; *(mécanique)* jigsaw; **en dents de s.** serrated; *Fig (évolution, progrès)* uneven; *Méd* **bruit de s.** rasping murmur **2** *Mus* **s. musicale** musical saw **3** *(poisson)* **s.** sawfish **4** *Fam Vieilli (personne ennuyeuse)* bore

sciemment [sjamɑ̃] ADV knowingly, on purpose, wittingly

science [sjɑ̃s] NF **1** *(savoir)* knowledge, learning; *Fig* **il croit avoir la s. infuse** you can't tell him anything; **je n'ai pas la s. infuse** I can't be expected to know everything; *Fam* **étaler sa s.** to show off one's knowledge **2** *(domaine spécifique)* science; **la s. n'a pas de patrie** science knows no frontiers; **préparer une licence ès sciences** to be studying for a science degree; **homme de s.** scientist; **s. dure/molle** hard/soft science; **les sciences exactes** ou **pures** the exact sciences; **sciences physiques/naturelles/appliquées** physical/natural/applied science; **sciences économiques** economics; **sciences expérimentales** experimental science; **sciences humaines** ≃ social sciences; **les sciences occultes** the occult sciences; **sciences politiques** politics, political science; **sciences sociales** social sciences

science-fiction NF science fiction; **roman/film de s.** science fiction novel/film; *Fig Hum* **c'est de la s.!** it's unbelievable!

Sciences-Po [sjɑ̃spo] NF = grande école for political sciences

scientificité [sjɑ̃tifisite] NF scientific character

scientifique [sjɑ̃tifik] ADJ scientific
N scientist; **ce n'est pas un s.** he's not very scientifically-minded

scientifiquement [sjɑ̃tifikmɑ̃] ADV scientifically

scientisme [sjɑ̃tism] NM **1** *Phil* scientism **2** *Rel* Christian Science

scientiste [sjɑ̃tist] ADJ scientistic
N **1** *Phil* adept of scientism **2** *Rel* **s. chrétien(ne)** Christian Scientist

scientologie [sjɑ̃tɔlɔ3i] NF Scientology®

scientologue [sjɑ̃tɔlɔg] N Scientologist

scier¹ [sje] VT *(pr sub, impf n. sciions, v. sciiez) (bois, métal)* to saw; *(enlever) (branche etc)* to saw off; *Fam* **s. qn** *(étonner)* to dumbfound or Br Fam to gobsmack sb; *Fam* **j'étais scié de rire** I was doubled up with laughter; *Suisse Fam* **s. du bois** to snore like a pig

scier² VI *(à l'aviron)* to back water, to back the oars

scierie [siri] NF sawmill

scieur [sjœr] NM sawyer

scieuse [sjøz] NF mechanical saw

scille [sil] NF *Bot* scilla, squill; **s. maritime** sea onion

scinder [sɛ̃de] VT to divide, to split up *(en* into); *Fin* **s. une société** to break up a company, to split a company
VPR **se scinder** to split up *(en* into)

scinque [sɛ̃k] NM *Zool* skink

scintigramme [sɛ̃tigram] NM *Méd* scintigram

scintigraphie [sɛ̃tigrafi] NF *Méd* scintigraphy

scintillant [sɛ̃tijɑ̃] ADJ *(bijoux, lumières etc)* sparkling, glittering; *(étoile)* twinkling; *(yeux)* sparkling, twinkling; *Fig (esprit, personnalité)* sparkling, scintillating
NM tinsel decoration(s)

scintillation [sɛ̃tijasjɔ̃] NF *Phys, Astron* scintillation

scintillement [sɛ̃tijmɑ̃] NM *(de bijou, lumière etc)* sparkling, glittering; *(d'étoile)* twinkling; *(des yeux)* sparkling; *Cin, TV* flicker(ing), shimmer

scintiller [sɛ̃tije] VI *(d'un bijou, d'une lumière etc)* to sparkle, to glitter; *(d'une étoile)* to twinkle; *(des yeux)* to sparkle; *Électron, TV, Cin* to flicker

scion [sjɔ̃] NM **1** *(pousse)* shoot; *(à greffer)* scion **2** *(d'une canne à pêche)* tip

scirpe [sirp] NM *Bot* bulrush

scissile [sisil] ADJ *Nucl (matériau)* fissionable

scission [sisjɔ̃] NF **1** *Pol etc* split, division; **faire s.** to split away or off, to secede; *Fin* **s. d'actifs** divestment of assets, hive-off of assets; **s. d'une entreprise** break-up of a company **2** *Chimie* scission, cleavage; *Nucl* fission, splitting; **s. nucléaire** nuclear fission

scissionniste [sisjɔnist] ADJ, N secessionist

scissipare [sisipar] ADJ *Biol* fissiparous

scissiparité [sisiparite] NF *Biol* schizogenesis, fissiparity

scissure [sisyr] NF *Anat* fissure

sciure [sjyr] NF **s. (de bois)** sawdust; **s. de marbre** marble dust

scléral, -ale, -aux, -ales [skleral, -o] ADJ *Anat* sclerotic

scléreux, -euse [sklerø, -øz] ADJ *Méd* sclerosed

sclérifié [sklerifje] ADJ *Biol (tégument etc)* sclerosed, hardened

sclérodermie [sklerɔdɛrmi] NF *Méd* scleroderma

sclérogène [sklerɔ3ɛn] ADJ *Méd* sclerogenic

scléroprotéine [sklerɔprɔtein] NF scleroprotein

sclérosant [sklerɔzɑ̃] ADJ *Méd* sclerosing; *Fig* ossifying

sclérose [skleroz] NF *Méd* sclerosis; *Fig* ossification; **s. vasculaire** ou **des artères** arteriosclerosis, hardening of the arteries; **s. en plaques** multiple sclerosis, MS

sclérosé [skleroze] ADJ *Méd* sclerosed; *Fig* hidebound, fossilized

scléroser [skleroze] VT *Méd* to sclerose
VPR **se scléroser 1** *Méd* to become sclerotic **2** *Fig* to become fossilized

sclérotique [sklerɔtik] NF *Anat (de l'œil)* sclerotic, sclera

scolaire [skɔlɛr] ADJ **1** *(résultats, réussite)* academic, scholastic; *(réforme, organisation)* educational; **vie s.** school life; **année s.** school or academic year; **enfant d'âge s.** child of school age; **frais scolaires** school fees; **livres scolaires** school books, text books **2** *Péj (esprit, mentalité)* bookish;

(style, discours) academic, schoolmasterish; *(peinture)* laboured, *Am* labored

scolairement [skɔlɛrmɑ̃] ADV *Péj (réciter, écrire)* in an academic *or* schoolmasterish way

scolarisable [skɔlarizabl] ADJ of school age

scolarisation [skɔlarizasjɔ̃] NF prolongation de la s. raising of the school-leaving age; **je suis pour la s. des enfants à partir de l'âge de cinq ans** I'm in favour of children going to *or* starting school at the age of five; **la s. d'une région** equipping *or* providing an area with schools; **la s. des enfants** providing education for children; **taux de s.** percentage of children in full-time education

scolariser [skɔlarize] VT **s. des enfants** to provide education for children; **s. une région** to equip *or* provide an area with schools; **enfant scolarisé** child attending school

scolarité [skɔlarite] NF **s. obligatoire** compulsory schooling; **prolongation de la s.** raising of the school-leaving age; **j'ai eu une s. difficile** I had a difficult time at school; **s. à temps partiel** = day-release classes; **certificat de s.** = certificate of attendance *(at school or university)*; **frais de s.** school fees

scolasticat [skɔlastika] NM theological training; *(établissement)* theological college

scolastique [skɔlastik] ADJ *(philosophie etc)* scholastic
  NM scholastic
  NF scholasticism

scoliaste [skɔljast] NM scholiast

scoliose [skɔljoz] NF *Méd* scoliosis, lateral curvature of the spine

scolopendre¹ [skɔlɔpɑ̃dr] NF *Zool* centipede, *Spéc* scolopendrid

scolopendre² NF *Bot* hart's-tongue, *Spéc* scolopendrium

sconse [skɔs] NM skunk; *(fourrure)* skunk (fur)

scoop [skup] NM **1** *Journ* scoop **2** *Fig Fam* **c'est un s.!** it's hot news!; *Iron* well I never!; **j'ai un s.!** I've got some hot news!; **ce n'est pas un s.** it's not exactly headline news!

scooter [skutɛr] NM (motor) scooter; **s. des mers** jet-ski

scootériste [skuterist] N (motor) scooter rider, (motor) scooterist

scopie [skɔpi] NF *Méd Arg* radioscopy

scopolamine [skɔpɔlamin] NF *Chimie, Pharm* scopolamine, hyoscine

scorbut [skɔrbyt] NM *Méd* scurvy, *Spéc* scorbutus

scorbutique [skɔrbytik] ADJ, N *Méd* scorbutic

score [skɔr] NM *Sport* score; **s. électoral** share of the vote; **faire un bon/mauvais s.** to turn in a good/bad performance

scoriacé [skɔrjase] ADJ *Métal, Géol etc* slaggy

scorie [skɔri] NF **1** *Métal* **scories** slag, cinders, scoria; *(de fer)* (iron) dross; *(de charbon)* clinker **2** *Géol* **scories (volcaniques)** scoria, volcanic slag **3** *Fig* **scories** dregs; **débarrasser une philosophie de ses scories** to rid a philosophy of its dross

scorpène [skɔrpɛn] NF scorpion fish

scorpion [skɔrpjɔ̃] NM **1** *Zool* scorpion; **s. aquatique** *ou* **d'eau** water scorpion; **s. de mer** scorpion fish **2** *Astron, Astrol* **le S.** Scorpio; **être (du signe du) S.** to be (a) Scorpio

scorsonère [skɔrsɔnɛr], **scorzonère** [skɔrzɔnɛr] NF *Bot* black salsify, *Spéc* scorzonera

Scotch® [skɔtʃ] NM self-adhesive tape, *Br* ≃ Sellotape®, *Am* ≃ Scotchtape®

scotch *pl* **scotchs** *ou* **scotches** [skɔtʃ] NM scotch (whisky); **un double s.** a double scotch

scotché [skɔtʃe] ADJ *Fam* **1** *(stupéfait)* **je suis resté s.** I was staggered *or Br* gobsmacked **2** **être s. devant la télé** to be glued to the TV

scotcher [skɔtʃe] VT **1** *(avec du ruban adhésif)* to tape, *Br* to sellotape, *Am* to scotch-tape; *Fig Fam* **il est toujours scotché devant la télé** he's always glued to the television **2** *Fam (stupéfaire)* to flabbergast, to knock sideways; **ça m'a vraiment scotché!** I was staggered *or Br* gobsmacked!

scotch-terrier, *pl* **scotch-terriers** NM Scotch terrier

scottish-terrier, *pl* **scottish-terriers** [skɔtiʃterje] NM Scotch terrier

scoumoune [skumun] NF *Arg* persistent bad luck; **avoir la s.** to be jinxed

scout [skut] NM (boy) scout
  ADJ **groupe/mouvement s.** scout group/movement; *Péj* **il a des côtés un peu scouts** he's a bit of a boy scout at heart

scoutisme [skutism] NM *(activité)* scouting; *(mouvement)* scout movement

SCPI [ɛssepei] NF *(abrév* **société civile de placement immobilier***)* property investment company

Scrabble® [skrabl] NM Scrabble®; **jouer au S.** to play Scrabble®

scratch, *pl* **scratches** [skratʃ] *Sp* NM *(course)* scratch race; *(joueur)* scratch (player); **partir s.** to start (at) scratch
  ADJ **course s.** scratch race; **joueur s.** scratch (player)

scratcher [skratʃe] VT *Sport* to scratch
  VPR **se scratcher** *Fam* to go off the road; **il s'est scratché avec la moto de son frère à 150** he went off the road doing 150 on his brother's motorbike

scribe [skrib] NM *Antiq* scribe; *Vieilli Péj* pen-pusher

scribouillard, -arde [skribujar, -ard] N *Fam Péj* pen-pusher

script¹ [skript] NM *Fin* scrip

script² NM **1** *(écriture)* printing; **écrire en s.** to print (one's letters); **écriture s.** printing **2** *Cin* (film) script

scripte [skript] N *Cin* continuity man, *f* continuity girl, script girl

script-girl, *pl* **script-girls** [skriptgœrl] NF *Cin* continuity girl

scriptural, -ale, -aux, -ales [skriptyral, -o] ADJ scriptural; *Banque* **monnaie scripturale** bank money

scrofulaire [skrɔfylɛr] NF *Bot* figwort

scrofule [skrɔfyl] NF *Méd* scrofula; *Arch* **les scrofules** scrofula; *Arch* **the king's evil**

scrofuleux, -euse [skrɔfylø, -øz] *Méd* ADJ scrofulous
  N scrofulous person

scrotum [skrɔtɔm] NM *Anat* scrotum

scrupule [skrypyl] NM **1** scruple *(sur* about*)*; **sans scrupules** *(adj)* unscrupulous; *(adv)* unscrupulously; **je n'aurai aucun s. à le lui dire** I'll have no scruples about telling him/her so; **se faire (un) s. de faire qch, avoir des scrupules à faire qch** to have scruples about doing sth; **il ne se fait pas s. d'emprunter à la caisse** he has no scruples about borrowing from the till; **exact jusqu'au s.** scrupulously exact **2** *Arch (unité de poids)* scruple

scrupuleusement [skrypyløzmɑ̃] ADV scrupulously

scrupuleux, -euse [skrypylø, -øz] ADJ scrupulous *(sur* about*)*; **à faire qch** in doing sth*)*; **peu s.** unscrupulous

scrutateur, -trice [skrytatœr, -tris] ADJ *Litt (esprit, regard)* searching
  N *(d'un scrutin)* teller

scruter [skryte] VT to examine, to scrutinize; *(horizon, paysage)* to scan

scrutin [skrytɛ̃] NM **1** *(élection)* poll; **s. d'arrondissement** = constituency poll; **s. majoritaire** first-past-the-post system; **s. majoritaire uninominal** first-past-the-post system *(voting for a single candidate)*; **s. majoritaire plurinominal** first-past-the-post system *(voting for as many candidates/parties as there are seats)*; **s. secret** secret vote *or* ballot; **s. plurinominal** = system of voting for more than one candidate; **s. proportionnel** *ou* **de liste** = system of voting by proportional representation *or* by lists; **s. uninominal** = system of voting for a single candidate **2** *(vote)* ballot; **tour de s.** ballot, round (of voting); **il a été élu au premier tour de s.** he was elected in the first round of voting *or* in the first ballot; **s. de ballotage** second ballot; **dépouiller le s.** to count the votes *or* ballots **3** *(dans une assemblée)* voting; *Br Parl* division; **procéder au s.** to take the vote; *Br Parl* to divide; **demander le s.** to ask for a count; **projet adopté sans s.** bill passed without a vote

SCS [ɛsseɛs] NF *(abrév* **société en commandite simple***)* limited partnership

SCSI [ɛsseɛsi] NF *(abrév* **small computer systems interface***)* SCSI; **adresse S.** SCSI address; **carte S.** SCSI card; **chaîne S.** SCSI chain

SCT [ɛssete] NM *(abrév* **syndrome de choc toxique***)* TSS

scull [skyl, skœl] NM *Sport, Naut* scull; *(activité)* sculling

sculpter [skylte] VT to sculpt, to sculpture; *(dans du bois)* to carve *(* **dans** in, out of*)*; **bois sculpté** carved wood
  VI to sculpt, to (do) sculpture

sculpteur [skyltœr] NM sculptor; **femme s.** woman sculptor, sculptress; **s. sur bois** woodcarver

sculptural, -ale, -aux, -ales [skyltyral, -o] ADJ *(art)* sculptural; *(silhouette, beauté)* statuesque

sculpture [skyltyr] NF **1** *(œuvre, art)* sculpture; **s. sur bois** woodcarving; **faire de la s.** to sculpt, to (do) sculpture **2** *(d'un pneu)* tread

scutellaire [skytelɛr] NF *Bot* skull cap, *Spéc* scutellaria

scythe [sit] ADJ Scythian
  N **S.** Scythian

Scythie [siti] NF Scythia

SDF [ɛsdeɛf] N *Admin (abrév* **sans domicile fixe***)* of no fixed abode; **un S.** a person of no fixed abode; *(sans abri)* a homeless person; **les S.** *(sans abri)* the homeless

SDN [ɛsdeɛn] NF *abrév* **Société des Nations**

SE [s(ə)] PRON **(s'** before vowel or mute *h)* **1** *(réfléchi) (complément direct)* himself; *(sujet féminin)* herself; *(non humain)* itself; *(indéfini)* oneself, *Am* himself; *(pl)* themselves; *(complément indirect)* to himself/herself/itself/oneself/themselves; **se flatter** to flatter oneself; **il se rase** he is shaving; **elle s'est coupée au doigt** *ou* **s'est coupé le doigt** she has cut her finger; **il se parle (à lui-même)** he's talking to himself; **il s'est fait mal** he hurt himself; **il se couche tard** he goes to bed late; **fais se laver les mains à cet enfant** make that child wash his hands SEE GRAMMAR A29–30; B28–9

2 *(réciproque) (complément direct)* each other, one another; *(complément indirect)* to each other, to one another; **se nuire (l'un à l'autre)** to hurt each other *or* one another; **ils/elles se parlent** they talk to each other *or* one another; **il est dur de se quitter** it is hard to part

3 *(passif)* **cet article se vend partout** this article is sold *or* is on sale everywhere; **la porte s'est ouverte** the door opened; **ça ne**

se fait pas you don't do that, it's not the done thing; **ça se mange froid** it's eaten cold, you eat it cold
4 *(avec v impers)* **il se peut qu'elle vienne** (it's possible that) she might come; **comment se fait-il que …?** how is it that …?

séance [seɑ̃s] NF **1** *(réunion) (d'une assemblée etc)* sitting, session, meeting; **être en s., tenir s.** to be sitting *or* in session; **la s. s'ouvrira/sera levée à huit heures** the meeting will open/adjourn at eight o'clock; **je déclare la s. ouverte** I declare the meeting open; **en s. publique** at an open meeting; *Jur* in open court; *Bourse* **s. boursière** trading session; **s. de concertation** policy meeting; **s. d'information** briefing (session); **s. plénière** plenary (session); **s. de spiritisme** seance
2 *Cin* performance, showing; **s. à 19h10, film à 19h30** programme 7.10, film starts 7.30; **s. privée** private showing
3 *(période)* session; **faire une longue s. à table** to sit a long time over one's meal; *Méd* **traitement de trois séances** course of three treatments; **s. de travail/d'entraînement** working/training session; **s. de photo** photocall, photo opportunity; **s. de pose** sitting; *Méd* **s. de rééducation** physiotherapy session; *TV* **à la s.** *(film, programme)* pay-per-view **4 s. tenante** straight away, at once **5** *Fam Péj (scène)* performance; **il nous a fait une s. de larmes** he turned on the waterworks

séancier [seɑ̃sje] NM *(parlementaire)* parliamentary reporter

séant [seɑ̃] ADJ *Arch, Litt (flatteur)* becoming (**à** to); *(convenable)* fitting; **il ne serait pas s. de se contredire** it would not be fitting to contradict each other
NM *Litt, Hum* **se mettre sur son s.** *(au lit etc)* to sit up; **être sur son s.** to be in a sitting position; **tomber sur son s.** to sit down with a bump

seau, *pl* **seaux** [so] NM bucket, pail; *(contenu)* bucket(ful), pail(ful); **s. à glace** *ou* **à rafraîchir** ice bucket; **s. à incendie** fire bucket; **s. à charbon** coal scuttle; **s. à champagne** champagne bucket; *Fam* **il pleut à seaux** it's pouring down, *Br* it's bucketing down

sébacé [sebase] ADJ *(glande)* sebaceous

sébile [sebil] NF *(begging)* bowl

séborrhée [sebɔre] NF *Méd* seborrhoea, *Am* seborrhea

sébum [sebɔm] NM *Anat* sebum

SEC, SÈCHE [sɛk, sɛʃ]

ADJ	dry **1, 3** ▪ dried **1** ▪ lean **2** ▪ sharp **3** ▪ curt **3**
ADV	a lot **1** ▪ sharply **2**

ADJ **1** *(temps, saison, sol, gorge, peau, vin, toux etc)* dry; *(morue, fruit etc)* dried; *(bois, cigare)* seasoned, matured; **regarder d'un œil s.** to look on dry-eyed; **il avait la gorge sèche** *(il avait soif)* his throat was dry, he was dry *or* parched; *(il avait peur)* his throat was dry; **mettre qn au pain s. et à l'eau** to put sb on bread and water; **mur de pierres sèches** drystone wall; *Aut* **être en panne sèche** to have run out of petrol *or Am* gas; **traverser un torrent à pied s.** to cross a torrent without getting one's feet *or* shoes wet; **s. comme une allumette** bone dry; **ne plus avoir un fil de s.** to be soaked to the skin; **régime s.** *(sans boisson)* alcohol-free diet; **pays secs** *(sans boisson)* dry countries, prohibitionist countries; **perte sèche** dead loss; *Fam* **en cinq s.** in no time at all, in two shakes (of a lamb's tail); *Fam* **je l'ai s.!** *(j'ai soif)* I'm dry *or* parched!; *Fig* am I annoyed!
2 *(maigre) (personne)* spare, lean; *(cheval,*

lean; **s. et nerveux** wiry; **s. comme un coup de trique** as thin as a rake
3 *(sans tendresse) (remarque, réponse)* sharp, curt; *(ton)* incisive; *(coup)* sharp; *(cœur)* cold, unfeeling; *(récit, style)* dry, bald; **il est très s. au téléphone** he's very curt on the phone; **casser qch d'un coup s.** to snap sth; **frapper à la porte d'un coup s.** to rap on the door; **arracher un pansement d'un coup s.** to rip a plaster off; **faire un accueil très s. à qn** to give sb a very cool reception
ADV **1** **boire s.** *(beaucoup)* to drink a lot, to be a heavy drinker; **il boit toujours son whisky s.** he always drinks his whisky neat *or* straight
2 *(rudement)* hard, sharply; **la voiture a viré très s.** the car swung round sharply; *Aut* **démarrer s.** to shoot off, to tear off; *Fam* **ils ont dérouillé s. pendant la guerre** they went through total hell during the war
3 à s. dry; *(asséché)* dried up; *Fam (sans argent)* hard up, broke; **mettre à s.** *(marais etc)* to drain; *Fig (personne)* to clean out; **nettoyage à s.** dry cleaning; **navire à s.** *ou* **au s.** ship aground *or* high and dry; **filer** *ou* **courir** *ou* **fuir à s. (de toile)** *(d'un bateau)* to run under bare poles
4 *Fam* **aussi s.** straight away, right away, at once
NM dryness; **tenir au s.** keep in a dry place
NF *Arg* **sèche** *(cigarette)* fag, *Am* butt

sécable [sekabl] ADJ divisible

SECAM [sekam] ADJ, NM *TV (abrév* **séquentiel couleur à mémoire**) SECAM

sécant, -ante [sekɑ̃, -ɑ̃t] *Math* ADJ *(ligne, surface)* secant, cutting
NF **sécante** secant

sécateur [sekatœr] NM pruning shears, *Br* secateurs

sécession [sesesjɔ̃] NF secession; **faire s.** to secede (**de** from)

sécessionniste [sesesjɔnist] ADJ, N secessionist

séchage [seʃaʒ] NM *(du foin, des vêtements, d'une surface peinte etc)* drying; *(du bois)* seasoning

sèche-cheveux [sɛʃʃəvø] NM INV hair dryer

sèche-linge [sɛʃlɛ̃ʒ] NM INV *(appareil)* tumble dryer; *(armoire)* airing cupboard

sèche-mains [sɛʃmɛ̃] NM INV (hot-air) hand dryer

sèchement [sɛʃmɑ̃] ADV **1** *(avec dureté) (parler, répondre etc)* curtly, sharply; *(taper)* sharply **2** *(sans fioritures) (écrire, traiter un sujet etc)* drily, baldly

sécher [seʃe] (**je sèche, n. séchons; je sécherai**) VT *(vêtements, sol, mains, encre, poisson, etc)* to dry; *(rivière etc)* to dry up; **le vent sèche la peau** wind dries (out) the skin; **s. ses larmes** to dry one's tears; *Fam* **s. un verre** *(le vider)* to drain a glass; *Scol etc Fam* **s. un cours** to skip *or* cut a class
VI **1** *(de vêtements, de sols, de surfaces etc)* to dry; **faire s. du bois** to dry *or* season wood; **faire s. du linge** to dry clothes; **mettre du linge à s.** to put clothes out to dry; **laisser s. les peintures** to leave the paintwork to dry; *Bot, Fig* **s. sur pied** to wilt; *Litt* **s. d'impatience/d'ennui** to be consumed with impatience/boredom **2** *Fam (ne pas aller en classe)* to bunk off, *Am* to play hookey **3** *Fam (ne pas connaître la réponse)* to be stumped; *(ne plus savoir quoi dire)* to dry up
VPR **se sécher** to dry oneself

sécheresse [seʃrɛs, se-] NF **1** *(de l'air, du sol, de la peau, de la gorge etc)* dryness **2** *(absence de pluie)* drought **3** *(des manières etc)* curtness; *(du cœur)* coldness, unfeelingness; *(du style)* dryness, baldness; **parler avec s.** to speak curtly

sécherie [seʃri, se-] NF *(appareil)* drying machine, dryer; *(lieu)* drying area

sécheur [seʃœr] NM *Tech* drying machine, dryer

séchoir [seʃwar] NM **1** *(appareil)* dryer; **s. (à cheveux)** hair dryer; *Ind* **s. à vapeur** steam dryer **2** *(dispositif pliant)* **s. (à linge)** clothes-horse **3** *Tech (lieu)* drying area; **s. à houblon** oast house

second, -onde [səgɔ̃, -ɔ̃d] ADJ **1** second; *Théâtre (rôle)* supporting, minor; **au s. étage** on the second *or Am* third floor; **une seconde fois** a second time; **en s. lieu** in the second place, secondly; **seconde nature** second nature *(chez qn* with sb); **de seconde main** secondhand; **de s. ordre** *ou* **choix** second-rate; *Fam* **ça passe en s.** that comes second, that takes second place; **votre ami est un s. Sherlock Holmes** your friend is another *or* a second Sherlock Holmes; **donner un s. souffle à l'économie** to give a new lease of life to *or* to revitalize the economy; *Sport, Fig* **trouver son s. souffle** to get one's second wind; **le don de seconde vue** the gift of second sight; *Mus* **les seconds violons** the second violins; *Gram* **la seconde personne du singulier** the second person singular; *Rail* **seconde classe** second class; **voyager en seconde classe** to travel second-class; *Jur* **signer en s.** *(d'un notaire)* to countersign; *Sport* **prendre la seconde place** to come second, to take second place; *Phil etc* **causes secondes** second causes; *Bourse* **s. marché** unlisted securities market, USM; *TV, Cin* **s. passage** repeat
2 *Méd* **état s.** *(d'un somnambule)* semi-conscious state; *Fig* **être dans un état s.** to be in a trance *or* a daze
3 *Naut* **commandant** *ou* **officier en s.** executive officer; **commander en s.** to be second in command
NM **1** *(assistant)* principal assistant; *Mil Fam* second in command; *Naut* first mate; *(de duelliste)* second; **s. (de cuisine)** second cook, sous chef; *TV, Cin* **s. assistant** best boy **2** *(étage)* second *or Am* third floor; **habiter au s.** to live on the second *or Am* third floor; **les voisins du s.** the neighbours on the second *or Am* third floor
NF **seconde** *Typ* second proof; *Aut* second (gear); *Aut* **passer en seconde** to change *or* go (up/down) into second; *Rail etc* **voyager en seconde** to travel second-class; **billet de seconde** second-class ticket; *Scol* **(classe de) seconde** ≃ fifth form, *Am* ≃ tenth grade; **élève de seconde** ≃ fifth-former, *Am* ≃ tenth-grader; *Mus* **seconde majeure/mineure** major/minor second
N second; *Sport* **finir bon s.** to finish a good second; **la seconde est française** *(dans une compétition)* the competitor in second place is French; **mon s.** *(enfant)* my second child

secondaire [səgɔ̃dɛr] ADJ **1** *Scol* secondary; **établissement d'enseignement s.** secondary school **2** *(peu important)* secondary; **il faut en parler, mais c'est s.** we must talk about it, but it's of secondary importance; **effets secondaires d'un médicament** side effects of a medicine; *Rail* **voie s.** side track; *Ling* **accent s.** secondary accent, secondary stress; *Mus* **temps s.** off-beat; *Théâtre, Littér* **intrigue s.** sub-plot; **personnage/rôle s.** minor character/part **3** *Écon (secteur)* secondary; *Géol* **l'ère s.** the secondary era
NM **1** *Élec* secondary winding; *Radio (du transformateur)* secondary **2** **le s.** *Géol* the secondary era; *Écon* the secondary sector

secondairement [səgɔ̃dɛrmɑ̃] ADV secondarily

seconde [səgɔ̃d] NF *(du temps, d'un arc de cercle, d'un angle)* second; **aiguille des secondes** *(d'une montre)* second hand; **j'en ai pour une s.** I'll only be a second *or* moment;

je reviens dans une s.! I'll be back in a second!, I'll be right back!; **(attendez) une s.!** just a second!, just a moment!; **en un quart** *ou* **une fraction de s., en moins d'une s.** in no time at all

secondement [səgɔ̃dmɑ̃] ADV secondly, in the second place

seconder [səgɔ̃de] VT **1** *(personne)* to second, to back up, to support, to assist **2** *(intérêts, projets etc)* to forward, to further, to promote

secoué [səkwe] ADJ *Fam (fou)* off one's nut *or* rocker

secouement [səkumɑ̃] NM shaking

secouer [səkwe] VT **1** *(arbre, tête etc)* to shake; *(coussin, oreiller)* to plump up, to shake up; *(vêtements, tapis)* to shake (out); *(d'un choc, d'une maladie, de nouvelles etc) (personne)* to shake (up); *(du vent) (bateau)* to buffet; **de grands spasmes secouaient son corps tout entier** violent spasms shook his/her whole body; **nous avons été secoués pendant la traversée** we were shaken about during the crossing, we had a rough crossing; **il faut la s.** *(elle est déprimée)* we have to shake her out of it; *Fam* **s. (les puces à) qn** *(réprimander)* to tell sb off; *(pousser à agir)* to shake sb up; **s. qn/qch comme un prunier** to shake sb/sth vigorously **2** *très Fam* **j'en ai rien à s.** I don't give a damn *or Br* toss **3** *(se débarrasser de) (poussière, joug etc)* to shake off

VI **voiture qui secoue** bumpy car; **ça secoue** *(dans un avion/train etc)* it's bumpy; *(dans un bateau)* it's rough

VPR **se secouer** *(agir)* to shake oneself *or* snap out of it, to pull oneself together

secourable [səkurabl] ADJ helpful, willing to help; **main s.** helping hand; **peu s.** unhelpful

secourir [səkurir] VT *(conj like courir)* to help, to assist, to aid

secourisme [səkurism] NM *Méd* first aid; **brevet de s.** first-aid certificate

secouriste [səkurist] N first-aid worker

secours [səkur] NM help, assistance, aid; *(financier, matériel)* aid; *Mil* relief; **crier au s.** to call for help; **appel au s.** call for help; **au s.!** help!; *Méd* **premiers s.** first aid; **s. en montagne** mountain rescue; **les s. vont arriver** help will arrive; *Mil* relief will arrive; **porter** *ou* **prêter (du) s. à qn** to give sb help *or* assistance, to help *or* assist sb; **demander (du) s.** to ask for help *or* assistance; **aller** *ou* **se porter au s. de qn** to go to sb's assistance; *Mil* **se porter au s. d'un bataillon** to go in support of a battalion; **cela m'a été d'un grand s.** it has been a great help (to me); **puis-je vous être d'aucun s.?** can I be of (some) help *or* (some) assistance?; **sa présence ne m'a été d'aucun s.** his/her presence was of no help to me; *Ordinat* **de s.** *(copie, fichier etc)* backup; **boîte/trousse de s.** first-aid box/kit; **poste de s.** first-aid post; **caisse de s.** relief fund; **société de s. mutuels** friendly *or Am* benefit society; **sortie** *ou* **porte de s.** emergency exit; *Fig* **c'est sa seule porte de s.** it's his only way out; *Aut* **roue de s.** spare wheel; **éclairage de s.** emergency lighting (system); *Mil* **troupes de s., des s.** relief troops, relieving force; *Rail* **locomotive/train de s.** relief engine/train

secousse [səkus] NF shake; *(cahot)* jolt, bump; *Fig (morale)* shock; **se dégager d'une s.** to jerk *or* wrench oneself *or* shake oneself free; *Fig* **se remettre d'une s.** to recover from a shock; **les secousses que faisait la voiture** the jolting of the car; **sans s.** smoothly; **par secousses** *(avancer etc)* jerkily; *(respirer)* in gasps; **s. politique** political upheaval; **s. (sismique** *ou* **tellurique)** (earth) tremor; **s. (électrique)** electric shock

secret¹, -ète [səkrɛ, -ɛt] ADJ *(ordres, signal, traité, porte etc)* secret; *(sentiments, pensées)* secret, hidden; *(réservé) (personne)* reticent, reserved; **ses fantasmes les plus secrets** his/her innermost fantasies; **la raison secrète d'un acte** the secret *or* real reason for an action; **la police secrète** the secret police; *Admin* **très secret, ultra-secret** top secret

NF **secrète 1 la secrète** *(police)* the secret police **2** *Rel (oraison)* secret

secret² NM **1** *(confidence, mystère)* secret; **garder un s.** to keep a secret; **trahir un s.** to betray a secret, to give away a secret; **mettre qn dans le s.** to let sb into *or* in on the secret; **être du s.** *ou* **dans le s.** to be in on the secret, *Fam* to be in the know; **n'avoir point de s. pour qn** *(d'une personne)* to have no secrets from sb; **les ordinateurs n'ont pas de secrets pour elle** computers hold no secrets for her; **ce n'est un s. pour personne** it's no secret; **le s. du bonheur/de la réussite** the secret of happiness/of success; **trouver le s. de qch** to find the secret of sth; **trouver le s. pour faire qch** to find the knack of doing sth; **elle a le s. des soirées réussies** she knows the secret for giving successful parties; **bureau à s.** desk with a secret compartment **2** *(discrétion)* secrecy; **dire qch à qn sous le sceau du s.** to tell sb sth under pledge of secrecy; **je vous demande le (plus grand) s.** I'm asking you to keep this (strictly) secret; **en s.** *(en cachette)* in secret, secretly; *(intérieurement)* secretly **3** **mettre qn au s.** *(l'enfermer)* to put sb in solitary confinement

▸▸ **s. bancaire** banking secrecy; *Rel* **le s. de la confession** the secrecy of the confessional; **s. d'État** state secret; *Fig* **ce n'est pas un s. d'État!** it's not a state secret!; **s. de fabrication** trade secret; **le s. professionnel** professional secrecy; *Journ* obligation to respect the confidentiality of sources; **abuser du** *ou* **trahir le s. professionnel** to commit a breach of confidence

secrétaire [səkretɛr] N secretary; **s. bilingue/trilingue** bilingual/trilingual secretary; **s. particulier** private secretary; **s. médicale** medical secretary; *(de dentiste)* dentist's secretary; **s. d'État** *(en France)* junior minister; *(en Grande-Bretagne)* Secretary of State; *(aux États-Unis)* State Secretary; **s. d'ambassade** secretary; *Journ* **s. de rédaction** sub-editor, copyreader; **s. de séance** meetings secretary; **s. général** secretary general; *Com* company secretary; **s. général de l'Assemblée** *Br* ≃ Clerk of the House; **s. général de l'ONU** UN Secretary-General; **s. général du Sénat** *Br* ≃ Clerk of the Parliaments; **s. de direction** executive secretary, personal assistant; **s. d'administration** *(fonctionnaire) Br* ≃ assistant principal; **s. de mairie** ≃ town clerk; *(de village)* = mayor's secretarial assistant

NM **1** *Orn* secretary bird **2** *(meuble)* writing desk, secretaire

secrétariat [səkretarja] NM **1** *(fonction)* secretaryship **2** *(bureau)* secretariat **3** *(métier)* secretarial work **4** *Pol* **s. d'État** *(fonction en France)* post of Junior Minister; *(ministère français)* Junior Minister's Office; *(fonction en Grande-Bretagne)* post of Secretary of State; *(ministère britannique)* Secretary of State's Office; *(fonction aux États-Unis)* post of State Secretary; **s. général de l'ONU** UN Secretary-Generalship

secrètement [səkrɛtmɑ̃] ADV secretly

sécréter [sekrete] VT *(il sécrète; il sécrétera)* *(d'une glande etc)* to secrete; *Fig* **s. l'ennui** to exude boredom

sécréteur, -trice *ou* **-euse** [sekretœr, -tris, -øz] ADJ *(glande etc)* secretory

sécrétion [sekresjɔ̃] NF *Physiol* secretion; **glande à s. externe/interne** exocrine/endocrine gland

sécrétoire [sekretwar] ADJ *Physiol* secretory

sectaire [sɛktɛr] ADJ **1** *(caractérisé par un esprit d'intolérance)* narrow-minded **2** *(relatif aux sectes religieuses)* sectarian, relating to a sect

N *(personne intolérante)* narrow-minded person

> Il faut noter qu'en anglais britannique, le terme **sectarian** fait le plus souvent référence à l'hostilité et à l'intolérance qui caractérisent les relations entre catholiques et protestants en Irlande du Nord et en Écosse.

sectarisme [sɛktarism] NM sectarianism

> Il faut noter qu'en anglais britannique, le terme **sectarianism** fait le plus souvent référence à l'hostilité et à l'intolérance qui caractérisent les relations entre catholiques et protestants en Irlande du Nord et en Écosse.

secte [sɛkt] NF sect

secteur [sɛktœr] NM **1** *(zone)* area, district; *(d'un magasin)* section; *Mil (de responsabilité, d'attaque etc)* sector, area; **s. français de Berlin** French sector of Berlin; *Com* **s. de vente** sales area; **s. de surveillance** *Radio etc* surveillance sector *or* area; *(de policier)* beat; *Fam* **changer de s.** to move (somewhere else) **2** *Élec* **s. (de distribution électrique)** mains; **branché sur le s.** plugged into the mains; **ça se branche sur le s.** it runs off the mains; **panne de s.** mains failure **3** *Écon (d'une activité)* sector; **le s. privé** the private sector; **s. privé à but non lucratif** private nonprofit sector; **le s. public** the public sector; **s. sanitaire** health sector; **s. primaire** primary sector; **s. secondaire** secondary sector; **s. tertiaire** tertiary sector; *Mktg* **s. de la grande distribution** mass distribution sector; *Mktg* **s. de vente** sales territory; **s. industriel** industrial sector; **s. des services** service sector; **s. du marché** market sector, sector of the market; **un s. en expansion** a growth sector; *Fam* **ce n'est pas mon s.** that's not my line **4** *Astron, Géom, Ordinat* sector; *Tech* sector, quadrant; **graphique à secteurs** pie chart; *Ordinat* **s. d'initialisation** boot sector; *Ordinat* **s. endommagé** bad sector; *Aut etc* **s. de direction** steering sector; *Aut* **s. de frein** handbrake quadrant *or* ratchet; *Naut* **s. dangereux** *(d'un orage)* dangerous quadrant

section [sɛksjɔ̃] NF **1** *(action de couper)* cutting, *Spéc* section; *Vét (de la queue)* docking; **s. des tendons** cutting of the tendons; **l'accident entraîna la s. d'un doigt** a finger was cut off *or* severed in the accident; **la s. du doigt est nécessaire** the finger must be amputated **2** *(division) (d'un livre, d'un bâtiment etc)*, *Admin (d'un département etc)*, *Biol* section; *(d'un parti politique)* branch; *Mil (de l'infanterie)* platoon; *(de l'artillerie)* section; *Naut (de la flotte)* sub-division; **s. syndicale d'entreprise** union branch; *Mus* **la s. rythmique** the rhythm section; **s. (électorale)** ward; **s. de vote** ward; *(bureau)* polling station; **chef de s.** *Mil* platoon commander; *Mil, Aviat* flight commander; *Mil, Aviat* **s. de bombardiers** bomber flight **3** *Géom* section; *(intersection)* intersection; *Archit, Tech (dessin)* section, profile; **point de s.** point of intersection; **ça doit faire cinq centimètres de s.** it must have a section of five centimetres; *Élec* **s. morte** idle coil; *Nucl* **s. efficace** cross section

4 *(d'autoroute)* section; *(sur un trajet de bus etc)* stage; **changement de s.** *Br* ≃ fare stage; *Rail* **s. de block** block section
5 *Scol* = one of the groups into which baccalaureat students are divided, depending on their chosen area of specialization; **il enseigne en s. scientifique** he teaches in the science department; **à l'école, j'étais en s. économique** my main subject at school was economics

sectionnement [sɛksjɔnmā] NM **1** *(d'un département, d'une circonscription etc)* division into sections **2** *(coupe)* severing

sectionner [sɛksjɔne] VT **1** *(fractionner) (service, circonscription etc)* to divide (up) into sections **2** *(couper)* to sever
▸ **VPR se sectionner** *(être coupé)* to be severed

sectionneur [sɛksjɔnœr] NM *Élec* disconnecting switch, isolating switch

sectoriel, -ielle [sɛktɔrjɛl] ADJ sectorial

sectorisation [sɛktɔrizasjɔ̃] NF division into sectors

sectoriser [sɛktɔrize] VT to divide into sectors

Sécu [seky] NF *Fam abrév* **sécurité sociale**

séculaire [sekylɛr] ADJ **1** *(très ancien) (arbre, tradition etc)* centuries-old, age-old **2** *(qui existe depuis un siècle)* a hundred years old; **un arbre plusieurs fois s.** a tree several hundred years old **3** *(événement)* centennial; *Astron* secular; **année s.** last year of the century

Do not confuse with **séculier**.

sécularisation [sekylarizasjɔ̃] NF secularization

séculariser [sekylarize] VT to secularize; *(église)* to deconsecrate

séculier, -ière [sekylje, -jɛr] ADJ *(clergé, juridiction etc)* secular; *(laïque)* lay; **le bras s.** the secular arm
▸ N secular

Do not confuse with **séculaire**.

secundo [sɔgɔ̃do, sek-] ADV secondly, in the second place

sécurisant [sekyrizā] ADJ reassuring

sécuriser [sekyrize] VT **s. qn** to reassure sb, to make sb feel secure; **s. l'accès à l'ordinateur central** to securitize mainframe access; *Fin* **s. un financement** to guarantee a loan; **s. un paiement** *(sur l'Internet)* to guarantee or ensure the security of a payment

sécurit® [sekyrit] NM safety glass

sécuritaire [sekyritɛr] ADJ **mesures sécuritaires** *(pour la protection des informations etc)* security measures; *(pour la protection des personnes)* safety measures; **ce parti tient un discours s.** this party emphasizes law and order

sécurité [sekyrite] NF **1** *(ordre, stabilité)* security; *(sentiment)* (feeling of) security; **être/se sentir en s.** to be/feel safe or secure; **je veille à sa s.** I'm making sure he's safe; **s. matérielle/affective** material/emotional security; **s. de l'emploi** security of employment, job security
2 *(absence de danger)* safety; **s. de la route** road safety; *Admin* **s. publique** public safety; **s. incendie** fire safety; **s. informatique** computer security; *(des données)* data security; **services de s.** *Mil* security forces; *(dans des manifestations etc)* stewards; *(dans une usine etc)* security officers; **s. intérieure** national security; **s. nationale/internationale** national/international security; *Naut* **officier de s.** officer in charge of fire precautions; *Tech, Constr, Ind* **marge de s.** safety margin; **règles de s.** safety rules or code; **dispositif de s.** safety device; **verre de s.** safety glass, splinterproof glass; *Élec* **éclairage de s.** emergency lighting
3 *(dispositif)* safety catch; **porte munie d'une s.-enfants** door with a childproof lock
▸ ▸ *Ordinat* **s. des données** data security; **s. routière** road safety; **S. Routière** = road safety organization; *Admin* **S. sociale** Social Security, *Am* Welfare

Attention: ne pas confondre **security** et **safety** lorsqu'on traduit **sécurité**.

Sécurité sociale
The "Sécu", as it is popularly known, was created in 1945 and provides services such as public health benefits, pensions and maternity benefit. These benefits are paid for by obligatory insurance contributions ("cotisations") made by employers ("cotisations patronales") and employees ("cotisations salariales"). Many French people have complementary health insurance provided by a "mutuelle" which guarantees payment of all or part of the expenses not covered by the "Sécurité sociale".

sédatif, -ive [sedatif, -iv] ADJ, NM *Méd* sedative

sédation [sedasjɔ̃] NF *Méd* sedation

sédentaire [sedɑ̃tɛr] ADJ *(occupation, vie, travail, personne)* sedentary; *(population)* settled; *(troupes)* garrison(ed); *(oiseau)* non-migrant

sédentairement [sedɑ̃tɛrmɑ̃] ADV **vivre s.** to live a sedentary life

sédentarisation [sedɑ̃tarizasjɔ̃] NF settling

sédentariser [sedɑ̃tarize] VT *(population etc)* to settle
▸ **VPR se sédentariser** to settle

sédentarité [sedɑ̃tarite] NF sedentary lifestyle

sédiment [sedimɑ̃] NM sediment, deposit

sédimentaire [sedimɑ̃tɛr] ADJ *Géol etc* sedimentary

sédimentation [sedimɑ̃tasjɔ̃] NF sedimentation

séditieux, -ieuse [sedisjø, -jøz] ADJ *(discours, écrit, assemblée etc)* seditious; *(troupes, groupe etc)* seditious, rebellious; **tenir des propos s.** to talk treason
▸ N rebel, insurgent

sédition [sedisjɔ̃] NF sedition, insurrection

séducteur, -trice [sedyktœr, -tris] N seducer, f seductress
▸ ADJ seductive

séduction [sedyksjɔ̃] NF **1** *(action) (physique)* seduction; *(par le charme)* charming **2** *(moyen de séduire)* attraction; **pouvoir de s.** power of attraction; **exercer une s. mystérieuse/irrésistible sur qn** to exercise a mysterious/an irresistible attraction over sb; **la s. des richesses** the lure or attraction of wealth

séduire [seduir] *(conj like* **conduire***)* VT **1** *(sexuellement)* to seduce **2** *(gagner par son charme) (d'une personne)* to charm; *(d'un projet, d'une proposition etc)* to appeal to; **j'ai été séduite du premier coup** it took my fancy or attracted me or appealed to me right away
▸ VI to charm people

Il faut noter que le verbe anglais **to seduce** ne signifie pas **charmer**.

séduisant [seduizā] ADJ *(idée, proposition etc)* appealing, attractive; *(personne)* attractive

séfarade [sefarad] ADJ Sephardic
▸ N Sephardi; **les séfarades** the Sephardim

segment [sɛgmā] NM segment; *Mktg* **s. démographique** demographic segment; *Aut* **s. de frein** brake shoe; *Aut* **frein à segments** segmented brake; *Mktg* **s. de marché** market segment; *Tech* **s. de piston** piston or packing ring; *Aut* **s. primaire** primary or leading shoe; *Aut* **s. secondaire** secondary shoe, trailing shoe

segmentation [sɛgmɑ̃tasjɔ̃] NF segmentation, segmenting; *Mktg* **s. démographique** demographic segmentation; *Mktg* **s. du marché** market segmentation; *Mktg* **s. en niches** niching; *Mktg* **s. stratégique** strategic segmentation

segmenter [sɛgmɑ̃te] VT to segment, to divide into segments; *Ordinat* to partition, to section, to segment; **s. un marché** to segment a market
▸ **VPR se segmenter** to segment, to split into segments

ségrégation [segregasjɔ̃] NF segregation

ségrégationnisme [segregasjɔnism] NM *Pol* racial segregation

ségrégationniste [segregasjɔnist] ADJ, N *Pol* segregationist

séguedille [segɔdij] NF *(danse, musique)* seguidilla

seiche [sɛʃ] NF *(mollusque)* cuttlefish; **os de s.** cuttlebone

séide [seid] NM henchman

seigle [sɛgl] NM rye; **pain de s.** rye bread

seigneur [sɛɲœr] NM **1** *(maître)* lord; *(d'un manoir)* lord of the manor, *Br* ≃ squire; *Hist (homme noble)* nobleman, noble; *Hum* **mon s. et maître** my lord and master; **le s. de Sercq** the seigneur of Sark; *(femme)* the dame of Sark; *Hist* **les seigneurs** the nobility; **à tout s. tout honneur** honour where honour is due; **mener une vie de grand s.** to live like a lord; **ne faites pas le grand s.** don't try and lord it over us, stop behaving like the lord of the manor; **en grand s.** in grand style **2** *Rel* **le S.** the Lord; **Notre-S.** our Lord; **le jour du S.** the Lord's day; *Fam* **S.!, S. Dieu!** good Lord!

seigneurial, -iale, -iaux, -iales [sɛɲœrjal, -jo] ADJ *(magnifique)* stately, lordly; *Hist (droits, domaine etc)* manorial, seigneurial

seigneurie [sɛɲœri] NF **1** *Hist (terre, pouvoir)* seigneury; **votre S.** *(titre)* your Lordship; *Iron* **sa S.** his lordship, *Arg* his nibs **2** *Belg (maison de retraite)* retirement home, old people's home

sein [sɛ̃] NM *(de femme)* breast; *Litt (d'homme)* breast, bosom; **serrer** ou **presser qn sur son s.** to press sb to one's bosom or heart; **donner le s. à un enfant** to breast-feed a child; **enfant nourri au s.** breast-fed child; **danseuse aux seins nus** topless dancer; **se baigner les seins nus** to swim topless; **le s. de l'Église** the bosom of the Church; **au s. de la famille** in the bosom of the family; **au s. de la commission** within the committee; *Litt* **enfant que j'ai porté dans mon s.** child that I carried in my womb; **le s. de la terre** the bowels of the earth

Seine [sɛn] NF **la S.** the Seine

seine [sɛn] NF *Pêche* seine, draw net

seing [sɛ̃] NM *Jur* **sous s. privé** under private seal; **acte sous s. privé** private agreement *(without legal certification)*

séisme [seism] NM earthquake; *Fig Litt* upheaval

séismique [seismik] ADJ seismic

seize [sɛz] ADJ INV sixteen; **Louis S.** Louis the Sixteenth; **numéro s.** number sixteen
▸ NM INV sixteen; **le s. mai** (on) the sixteenth of May, (on) May the sixteenth, *Am* (on) May sixteenth; **habiter au s.** to live at number sixteen

seizième [sɛzjɛm] ADJ sixteenth
N sixteenth; **ils habitent dans le s.** they live
in the sixteenth arrondissement *(in Paris)*
NM *(fraction)* sixteenth

> ### Seizième
> This term often refers to the upper-class social background, lifestyle, way of dressing etc associated with the sixteenth arrondissement in Paris: "elle est très seizième".

séjour [seʒur] NM **1** stay; **carte** *ou* **permis de s.** residence permit; **droit de s.** right of residence *or* abode; **taxe de s.** tourist tax; **s. discompté** bargain break; **s. éducatif** educational trip *or* holiday; **s. linguistique** language-learning trip *or* holiday; **s. de quinze jours** two week(s') *or Br* fortnight's stay; **je te souhaite un bon s. en Grèce** enjoy your stay in Greece **2** (salle de) s. living room **3** *Litt (lieu)* abode

séjourner [seʒurne] VI *(d'une personne)* to stay; *(de la neige, de l'eau etc)* to lie

sel [sɛl] NM **1** *Chimie, Culin etc* salt; **gros s.** coarse salt; **régime sans s.** salt-free diet; **s. de cuisine** cooking salt; **s. fin** fine salt; **s. marin** sea salt; **s. de céleri** celery salt; *Pharm* **s. d'Angleterre** *ou* **d'Epsom** Epsom salts; **sels de** *ou* **pour le bain** bath salts; **sels (à respirer)** (smelling) salts; *Chimie* **s. double** double salt; *Fam* **mettre** *ou* **ajouter son grain de s.** to put *or* stick one's oar in; *Fig* **le s. de la terre** the salt of the earth **2** *Fig (esprit)* piquancy, wit

select, sélect [selɛkt] ADJ *Fam (soirée, clientèle etc)* select; **le monde s.** high society

sélecteur [selɛktœr] NM *Ordinat, Élec etc* selector; *(de motocyclette)* gear(-change) pedal; **s. automatique** automatic switch; *Aut* **s. de vitesses** gear lever

sélectif, -ive [selɛktif, -iv] ADJ selective; *Radio* **récepteur s.** selective receiver; *Ordinat* **en mode s.** in veto mode

sélection [selɛksjɔ̃] NF **1** *(fait de choisir)* selection; **faire** *ou* **opérer une s. parmi …** to make a selection from among …; *Mktg* **s. au hasard** random selection; *Biol* **s. naturelle** natural selection; **s. professionnelle** professional recruitment; **épreuve de s.** selection trial; *Sport* **match de s.** trial game; **Gavin Hastings a 51 sélections en équipe nationale** Gavin Hastings has been capped 51 times, Gavin Hastings has 51 caps **2** *(choses choisies)* selection

sélectionné, -ée [selɛksjone] ADJ *(joueur, produit etc)* selected; **s. en équipe nationale** capped
N *Sport* selected player

sélectionner [selɛksjone] VT **1** *(choisir)* to select **2** *Ordinat (texte)* to block, to select; **s. qch par défaut** to default to sth; **s. et copier** to block and copy

sélectionneur, -euse [selɛksjonœr, -øz] N selector

sélectivement [selɛktivmɑ̃] ADV selectively

sélectivité [selɛktivite] NF *Radio* selectivity

sélénieux [selenjø] ADJ M *Chimie (acide)* selenious

sélénite [selenit] N *(habitant de la lune)* moon-dweller
ADJ of the moon

sélénium [selenjɔm] NM *Chimie* selenium

sélénographie [selenografi] NF selenography

sélénographique [selenografik] ADJ *(carte etc)* selenographic(al)

self [sɛlf] NM *Fam (restaurant)* self-service restaurant

NF *Élec* self-induction; **(bobine de) s.** self-induction coil

self-control [sɛlfkɔ̃trɔl] NM self-control

self-défense NF self-defence, *Am* self-defense

self-inductance, *pl* **self-inductances** NF *Élec* self-inductance

self-induction, *pl* **self-inductions** NF *Élec* self-induction

self-made-man, *pl* **self-made-men** [selfmedman, selfmedmɛn] NM self-made man

self-service, *pl* **self-services** NM *(restaurant)* self-service restaurant; *(magasin)* self-service shop

selle [sɛl] NF **1** *(de cheval, bicyclette, moto etc)* saddle; **se mettre en s.** to mount; **être bien en s.** to have a good seat; *Fig* to be firmly in the saddle; **aider qn à monter en s.** to help sb into the saddle; *Fig Fam* to give sb a leg up *or* a helping hand; **se remettre en s.** to get back into the saddle; *Fig* to get back in harness; **monter sans s.** to ride bareback **2** *Physiol* stool; **aller à la s.** *(déféquer)* to pass *or* have a motion; **les selles du bébé** the baby's stools *or* motions **3** *Culin* **s. de mouton/d'agneau** saddle of mutton/lamb; **s. de bœuf** baron of beef **4** *(de sculpteur)* turntable

seller [sele] VT *(cheval)* to saddle

sellerie [sɛlri] NF **1** *(selles, métier)* saddlery **2** *(salle)* harness room, tack room **3** *Aut* seating

sellette [sɛlet] NF **1** *Fam* **mettre qn/être sur la s.** to put sb/to be in the hot seat **2** *(d'ouvrier de bâtiment)* cradle; *Aut* trailer coupling, fifth wheel **3** *(de sculpteur)* turntable **4** *(de cheval de trait)* saddle

sellier [selje] NM saddler; **façon s.** hand-stitched

selon [s(ə)lɔ̃] PRÉP **1** according to; **s. lui** according to him; **s. moi** in my opinion *or* view, as I see it; **s. facture** as per invoice; **s. vos instructions** in accordance with your instructions, as per your instructions; **s. toute vraisemblance** in all likelihood *or* probability; **s. les cas** on a case by case basis; **varier s. les cas/les saisons** to vary from case to case/season to season; *Fam* **c'est s.** it all depends; **l'Évangile s. saint Jean** the Gospel according to Saint John **2 s. que** + *ind* depending on whether

Seltz [sɛls] NM **eau de S.** soda water, Seltzer (water)

SEM [sɛm] NF *(abrév* **société d'économie mixte)** = company financed by state and private capital

semailles [səmaj] NFPL **1** *(action)* sowing; **(temps des) s.** sowing time **2** *(graines)* seeds

semaine [s(ə)mɛn] NF **1** *(sept jours)* week; **deux fois par s.** twice a week; **s. de cinq jours** five-day week; **s. de trente-cinq heures** thirty-five-hour week; **une s. de vacances** a week's holiday; **fin de s.** *(jeudi, vendredi)* end of the week; *(week-end)* weekend; *Can* **bonne fin de s.!** have a good weekend!, enjoy your weekend!; **je suis de s.** I'm on duty this week *or* for the week; *Scol* **pensionnaire à la s.** weekly boarder; *Fam* **politique à la petite s.** shortsighted policy; **vivre à la petite s.** to live from day to day; *Fam* **la s. des quatre jeudis!** that'll never happen (in a month of Sundays)!; *Com* **la promotion de la s.** this week's special offer; **s. commerciale** week-long special promotion; **jour de s.** weekday; **en s.** during the week, on weekdays
2 *(salaire)* week's pay *or* wages; *(argent de poche)* pocket money (for the week)
3 *Mil etc (tour de service)* week's duty; **officier de s.** duty officer for the week
4 *(bague/bracelet)* seven-band ring/bracelet

▸▸ **s. anglaise** five-day week; **faire la s. anglaise** to work a five-day week; **la s. sainte** Holy Week

semainier, -ière [s(ə)menje, -jɛr] N *(personne)* person on duty for the week; *Mil* duty officer for the week
NM **1** *(meuble)* chest of seven drawers **2** *(agenda)* desk diary *(with sections for each day of the week)*

sémantème [semɑ̃tɛm] NM *Ling* semanteme

sémanticien, -ienne [semɑ̃tisjɛ̃, -jɛn] N semanticist

sémantique [semɑ̃tik] *Ling* ADJ semantic
NF semantics

sémaphore [semafɔr] NM *Rail* semaphore signal; *Naut (à terre)* signal station

semblable [sɑ̃blabl] ADJ **1** *(pareil)* similar; **être semblables** to be similar *or* alike; **deux cas tout à fait semblables** two quite similar cases; **triangles semblables** similar triangles; **s. à qch** similar to sth, like sth; **s. à son père** like his/her father; **je n'ai rien dit de s.** I said nothing of the sort, I said no such thing **2** *(tel)* **de semblables projets/propos** such plans/remarks, plans/remarks like that
N **1** *(personne semblable)* **vous et vos semblables** you and people like you, you and your kind *or* sort; **il n'a pas son s. dans l'art occidental** there's no one like him in western art **2** *(être humain)* fellow man *or* creature; **nos semblables** our fellow men, our fellow creatures

semblant [sɑ̃blɑ̃] NM semblance (**de** of); **elle portait un s. de jupe** she was wearing an apology for a skirt; **montrer un s. de résistance** to make a show of resistance; **opposer un s. d'indignation** to put up a show of indignation; **faire s. de faire qch** to pretend to do sth; **tu fais s.?** are you pretending?; **sans faire s. de rien** without seeming to take any notice; **elle fit s. de rien** she pretended not to notice

sembler [sɑ̃ble] *(aux avoir)* VI to seem; **elle semblait malade** she seemed (to be) ill; **s. être/faire** to seem to be/do; **le vent semble tomber** the wind seems to be dying down
V IMPERS **il me semblait rêver** it seemed to me (that) *or* I thought (that) I was dreaming; **il me semble avoir entendu son nom** I seem to have heard his/her name; **il me semble idiot d'attendre encore plus longtemps** it seems stupid to me to wait any longer; **à ce qu'il me semble** it seems to me; **faites comme bon vous semble(ra)** do as you think best; **il le fera si bon lui semble** he'll do it if he wants to; **il semble que …** + *ind or sub* it seems that …, it looks as if …; **il me semble que …** + *ind* it seems to me that …; **me semble-t-il** it seems to me SEE GRAMMAR B29

semé [s(ə)me] ADJ **s. de** scattered with; *(rochers etc)* strewn with; *(fleurs etc)* dotted with; *(diamants etc)* studded with; *(citations etc)* sprinkled with; **s. d'embûches** *ou* **de pièges** full of traps

sème [sɛm] NM *Ling* sememe

semelle [s(ə)mɛl] NF **1** *(d'une chaussure)* sole; *(d'un bas, d'une chaussette)* foot; **s. (intérieure)** insole, inner sole; **chaussures à semelles de caoutchouc/de cuir** rubber-/leather-soled shoes; **remettre une s. à une chaussure** to resole a shoe; **ne pas avancer d'une s.** to make no progress; **il ne reculera pas d'une s.** he won't give an inch; **il ne me quitte pas d'une s.** he's always at my heels; **ce n'est pas de la viande, c'est de la s.!** this isn't meat, it's like shoe leather! **2** *Tech (d'une machine, d'un tour)* bed plate; *(d'une ancre, d'un traîneau)* shoe; **s. de poutre** girder flange **3** *Naut* **s. de dérive** leeboard

semence [s(ə)mɑ̃s] **NF 1** *Agr* seed; *Physiol* semen; *Fig* **semences** seeds (**de** of); *Agr* **blé de s.** seed corn; **s. de perles** seed pearls; **s. de diamants** diamond sparks **2** *(clou)* tack; **s. de tapissier** upholstery tack

semer [s(ə)me] **VT** (**je sème, n. semons; je sèmerai**) **1** *(graines, champ)* to sow **2** *(fleurs etc)* to scatter, to strew; *(nouvelles, discorde)* to spread; *Prov* **qui sème le vent récolte la tempête** he who sows the wind shall reap the whirlwind **3** *Fam* **s. qn** *(le distancer)* to shake sb off, to get rid of sb; **s. qch** *(le laisser tomber)* to drop sth, to lose sth

semestre [s(ə)mɛstr] **NM 1** *(six mois)* half-year, six months; **le premier s.** the first half of the year **2** *(paiement)* half-yearly *or* six-monthly payment **3** *Scol, Univ* semester

semestriel, -ielle [səmɛstrijɛl] **ADJ** half-yearly, six-monthly

semestriellement [səmɛstrijɛlmɑ̃] **ADV** half-yearly, every six months; *Scol, Univ* every semester

semeur, -euse [s(ə)mœr, -øz] **N** *Agr* sower; *Fig (de nouvelles etc)* spreader, *Litt* disseminator; *(de discorde)* sower; *Fam* **semeur de zizanie**, *très Fam* **s. de merde** troublemaker

semi- [səmi] **PRÉF** semi- (**NOTE** *in the plural of compound words prefixed by* **semi-**, *semi-* *remains invariable and the following noun or adj takes the pl form*)

semi-automatique **ADJ** semiautomatic

semi-auxiliaire **ADJ** *Gram* semiauxiliary

semi-chenillé **ADJ, NM** **(véhicule) s.** half-track (vehicle)

semi-circulaire **ADJ** semicircular

semi-conducteur, -trice *Élec* **ADJ** semiconducting
  NM semiconductor

semi-conserve **NF** = foodstuff which has a limited life and must be refrigerated

semi-consonne **NF** semivowel

semi-duplex **NM INV** half duplex

semi-fini **ADJ** *Écon (produit)* semifinished

semi-fixe **ADJ** semifixed

semi-grossiste **N** retail wholesaler

semi-illettré **ADJ** semi-illiterate

semi-liberté **NF** *Jur* partial release; *Fig* state of partial freedom

sémillant [semijɑ̃] **ADJ** *(personne, esprit)* sparkling; *(regard)* bright, engaging

semi-lunaire **ADJ** half-moon-shaped

semi-mensuel, -elle **ADJ** *(périodique etc)* bi-monthly, *Br* fortnightly

semi-métal **NM** *Chimie* metalloid

séminaire [seminɛr] **NM 1** *Univ* seminar; *(conférence)* seminar, conference **2** *Rel* **(grand) s.** seminary; **petit s.** secondary school *(staffed by priests)*

séminal, -ale, -aux, -ales [seminal, -o] **ADJ** *Biol* seminal

séminariste [seminarist] **NM** *Rel* seminarist

semi-nomade **ADJ** seminomadic
  N seminomad

semi-nomadisme **NM** seminomadism

semi-occlusif, -ive **ADJ** *Ling* semi-occlusive

semi-officiel, -ielle **ADJ** semiofficial

sémiologie [semjɔlɔʒi] **NF** *Méd, Ling* semiology

sémiologique [semjɔlɔʒik] **ADJ** *Méd, Ling* semiological

semiologue [semjɔlɔg] **N** *Méd, Ling* semiologist

sémiotique [semjɔtik] **ADJ** semiotic
  NF semiotics

semi-ouvré **ADJ** *Écon (produit)* semifinished

semi-perméable **ADJ** semipermeable

semi-précieux, -ieuse **ADJ** *(pierre)* semiprecious

semi-présidentiel, -ielle **ADJ** *Pol* semipresidential

semi-produit **NM** semi-manufactured product

semi-professionnel, -elle **ADJ** semiprofessional

semi-public, -ique **ADJ** *Jur* semipublic

sémique [semik] **ADJ** *Ling* semic

semi-remorque **NF** *(remorque)* semitrailer, *Am Fam* semi
  NM *(poids lourd)* articulated truck *or Br* lorry, *Br Fam* artic

semi-rigide **ADJ** *(dirigeable)* semirigid

semis [səmi] **NM** *Agr* **1** *(action)* sowing **2** *(terrain)* seedbed **3** *(jeune plante)* seedling

sémite [semit] **ADJ** Semitic
  N S. Semite

sémitique [semitik] **ADJ** Semitic

sémitisant, -ante [semitizɑ̃, -ɑ̃t], **sémitiste** [semitist] **N** Semitist

sémitisme [semitism] **NM** Semitism

semi-ton **NM** *Mus* semitone

semi-voyelle **NF** *Ling* semivowel

semoir [s(ə)mwar] **NM** *Agr* **1** *(sac)* seed bag **2** *(machine)* sowing machine, seeder

semonce [səmɔ̃s] **NF 1** *(réprimande)* reprimand, scolding; **une verte s.** a good telling-off **2** *Naut* **coup de s.** warning shot

semoule [səmul] **NF** semolina; **sucre s.** caster *or Am* powdered sugar; **s. de blé dur** semolina

sempiternel, -elle [sɛ̃piternɛl] **ADJ** never-ending, endless, *Fml* sempiternel

sempiternellement [sɛ̃piternɛlmɑ̃] **ADV** eternally, endlessly

sénat [sena] **NM** senate; *(édifice)* senate (house)

Sénat

The "Sénat" is the upper house of the French Parliament. Its members are elected for a nine-year mandate by the Deputies of the "Assemblée nationale" and certain other government officals. The President of the Senate may deputize for the President of the Republic in the case of incapacity or death. The powers of the Senate are almost as extensive as those of the "Assemblée nationale", although the latter is empowered to override the decisions of the Senate in cases where the two houses disagree.

sénateur [senatœr] **NM** senator

sénatorial, -iale, -iaux, -iales [senatɔrjal, -jo] **ADJ** senatorial
  NFPL **sénatoriales** senatorial elections

séné [sene] **NM** *Bot, Pharm* senna

sénéchal, -aux [seneʃal, -o] **NM** *Hist* seneschal

sénéchaussée [seneʃose] **NF** *Hist (juridiction)* seneschalsy; *(tribunal)* seneschal's court

sénecon [senesɔ̃] **NM** *Bot* groundsel

Sénégal [senegal] **NM** Senegal

sénégalais, -aise [senegalɛ, -ɛz] **ADJ** Senegalese
  N S. Senegalese

Sénégambie [senegɑ̃bi] **NF** Senegambia

Sénèque [senɛk] **N** Seneca

sénescence [senesɑ̃s] **NF** *Biol* senescence, ageing, aging

sénescent [senesɑ̃] **ADJ** *Biol* senescent

sénevé [senve] **NM 1** *Bot* mustard **2** *(graine)* mustard seed

sénile [senil] **ADJ** *Méd, Fam Péj* senile

sénilité [senilite] **NF** senility

senior [senjɔr] **ADJ, N** *Sport* senior

senne [sɛn] **NF** *Pêche* seine, draw net

señorita [senjorita] **NM** cigarillo, whiff

SENS [sɑ̃s]

sense **1, 3, 4**	▪ meaning **4**
▪ direction **5**	

NM 1 *(du toucher, de la vue, de la beauté, du rythme etc)* sense; **les cinq s.** the five senses; **le sixième s.** the sixth sense; **s. moral** moral sense, conscience; **avoir le s. de l'humour/du ridicule/de la famille** to have a sense of humour/of the ridiculous/of family; **avoir le s. des affaires** to have good business sense; **j'ai un très bon s. de l'orientation** I have a very good sense of direction; **s. pratique** practical (common) sense; **il n'a aucun s. pratique** he's completely unpractical, he's not practically minded at all; **reprendre ses s.** to regain consciousness

2 *(sensualité)* **plaisir des s.** sensual pleasures; **éveiller/exciter les s.** to excite/arouse the senses

3 *(jugement)* sense; **s. commun** common sense; **bon s.** good sense; **un homme de bon s.** a sensible man; **tu t'es encore coiffé en dépit du bon s.** what possessed you to do your hair like that?; **agir en dépit du bon s.** to act in a way that defies common sense; **le bon s. veut que ...** it stands to reason that ...; **gros** *ou* **robuste bon s.** elementary common sense; **à mon s.** to my mind, in my view *or* opinion; **j'abonde dans votre s.** I entirely agree with you; **cela tombe sous le s.** it's perfectly obvious

4 *(signification) (d'un mot etc)* meaning, sense; **s. propre/figuré** literal/figurative meaning *or* sense; **au s. propre/figuré** in the literal/figurative sense, literally/figuratively; **au s. ordinaire du mot** in the ordinary meaning *or* sense of the word; **mot à double s.** word with a double meaning; **faire un faux s.** to make a mistranslation; **ça n'a aucun s.** it doesn't make (any) sense; **cela n'a pas de s.** it's crazy, there's no sense to it; **trouver un s. à sa vie** to find a meaning to one's life; **en ce s. que ...** in the sense that ...

5 *(direction)* direction; **accident sur la voie express dans le s. Brest-Quimper** accident on the Brest-Quimper expressway; **il tenait son livre dans le mauvais s.** he was holding his book the wrong way up; **tu as mis la cassette dans le mauvais s.** you put the tape in the wrong way round; **il a pris l'autoroute dans le mauvais s.** he drove the wrong way up the motorway; **fais demi-tour, on n'est pas dans le bon s.** turn round, we're going the wrong way *or* in the wrong direction; **en s. inverse** in the opposite direction; **dans le s. des aiguilles d'une montre** clockwise; **dans le s. inverse des aiguilles d'une montre** anticlockwise, *Am* counterclockwise; **dans le s. du courant** with the current, with the stream; **dans le s. de la longueur** lengthwise, lengthways; **dans le s. de la largeur** widthwise, breadthwise, across; **tailler dans le s. du bois** to cut in the direction of the grain *or* along the grain; **dans le s. inverse du grain** against *or* across the grain; **courir dans tous les s.** to run in all directions; **s. dessus dessous** [sɑ̃dsydsu] upside down, the wrong way up; *(en désordre)* upside down, in a mess, in a state of confusion; **s. devant derrière** back to front, the wrong way round; **dans les deux s.** both ways; *Fig* **ces mesures vont toutes dans le même s.** these measures are all directed at the same object; **son action allait aussi dans ce s.** his/her action was also directed to this end; **le s. de l'histoire** the course of history; **s. de la circulation** direction of the traffic; **rue à double s.** two-way street; **rue en s. unique** one-way street; **s. unique** *(sur panneau)* one-way (street); **s. interdit** *(sur panneau)* no entry; **prendre une rue en s. interdit** to go the wrong way along a street; *Aut* **s. giratoire** roundabout, *Am* traffic circle; *Rail* **voyager dans le s. de la marche** to travel facing the engine; *Math* **s. direct/rétrograde** positive/negative direction; *Ordinat* **s. de déroulement** flow direction

sensas(s) [sãsas] ADJ INV *Fam* fantastic, great

sensation [sãsasjõ] NF **1** *(impression)* feeling; *Physiol* sensation; **une s. de fatigue** a feeling of tiredness, a tired feeling; **avoir la s. que ...** to have a *or* the feeling that ...; **cela donne la s. de ...** it feels like ... **2** *(scandale)* **à s.** *(article, titre)* sensationalist; **presse à s.** gutter press, tabloid press; **roman à s.** sensational novel; **titres à s.** sensationalist headlines; **faire s.** to create a sensation

sensationnel, -elle [sãsasjɔnɛl] ADJ *(nouvelles, roman etc)* sensational; *Fam (remarquable)* fantastic, great

  NM journaliste à la recherche du s. journalist in search of a sensational story

sensé [sãse] ADJ *(personne, action, remarque etc)* sensible

senseur [sãsœr] NM *Électron* sensor, sensing device

sensibilisateur, -trice [sãsibilizatœr, -tris] ADJ *Phot etc* sensitizing; **lancer une campagne sensibilisatrice pour qch** to launch a campaign to heighten *or* increase public awareness of sth

  NM *Phot* sensitizer

  NF *Biol* **sensibilisatrice** sensitizer

sensibilisation [sãsibilizasjõ] NF *Phot, Méd* sensitization; *Fig* growing awareness **(à** of); **la s. de l'opinion** *(action)* heightening *or* increasing public awareness; *(résultat)* heightened *or* increased public awareness; **campagne de s. à qch** campaign to heighten *or* increase public awareness of sth

sensibiliser [sãsibilize] VT *Phot, Méd etc* to sensitize; *Fig* **s. qn à qch** to heighten *or* increase sb's awareness of sth; **s. l'opinion** to heighten *or* increase public awareness (**à** of)

  VPR **se sensibiliser se s. à qch** to become aware of sth

sensibilité [sãsibilite] NF sensitivity; **s. à fleur de peau** hypersensitivity; **avoir une s. à fleur de peau** to be hypersensitive; **enfant d'une grande s.** extremely sensitive child; **la s. romantique/wagnérienne** the Romantic/Wagnerian sensibility; **avoir de la s.** to be sensitive; *Mktg* **s. aux prix** price sensitivity

sensible [sãsibl] ADJ **1** *(personne)* sensitive; **cœur s.** tender *or* compassionate heart; **ce programme est déconseillé aux personnes sensibles** this programme is not recommended for people of a sensitive disposition; **s. à** *(ridicule, charme, injustice, douleur etc)* sensitive to; *(influence)* susceptible to; **être s. aux bontés de qn** to appreciate sb's kindness; **peu s.** insensitive; **être peu s. au froid/à la critique** to be impervious to the cold/to criticism; **être s. au froid** to feel the cold, to be sensitive to the cold; *(d'une plante)* to be tender; *Mktg* **s. au prix** price-sensitive; **les plantes sont sensibles à la musique** plants are sensitive to music; **cet enfant est très s. à la musique** this child has a great feeling for music; *Fig* **avoir l'épiderme s.** to be thin-skinned; *Fig* **toucher la note** *ou* **la corde s.** to appeal to the emotions

  2 *(physiquement fragile ou douloureux)*

(pieds etc) tender; *(dent, peau)* sensitive; **s. au toucher** tender *or* painful to the touch; **toucher qn à un endroit s.** to touch sb on a tender spot; *Fig* **blesser qn au point s.** to tread on sb's corns; *Fig* **vous avez touché un point s.** you've touched on a sore point, you've touched a raw nerve

  3 *(balance, thermomètre, plaque etc)* sensitive; **papier s. à la lumière** light-sensitive paper

  4 *(apte à percevoir)* *Phil* sentient; **avoir l'oreille s.** to have a keen sense of hearing; **ouïe peu s.** dull hearing

  5 *(perceptible)* *(son etc)* perceptible; **le monde s.** the tangible world

  6 *(différence, progrès etc)* noticeable, appreciable; **d'une manière s.** noticeably; **un vide s.** a noticeable gap; **éprouver un plaisir s.** to feel a keen pleasure

  7 *Mus* **la note s.** the leading note

> Il faut noter que l'adjectif anglais **sensible** est un faux ami. Il signifie **sensé**.

sensiblement [sãsibləmã] ADV **1** *(notablement)* noticeably, appreciably **2** *(à peu près)* approximately, roughly, more or less

sensiblerie [sãsibləri] NF *Péj* sentimentality

sensitif, -ive [sãsitif, -iv] ADJ **1** *Litt* oversensitive **2** *Physiol* sensory

  NF *Bot* **sensitive** sensitive plant, mimosa pudica

sensoriel, -ielle [sãsɔrjɛl] ADJ sensorial, sensory

sensorimoteur, -trice [sãsɔrimɔtœr, -tris] ADJ *Méd, Psy* sensorimotor

sensualisme [sãsɥalism] NM *Phil* sensualism, sensationalism

sensualiste [sãsɥalist] ADJ, N *Phil* sensualist, sensationalist

sensualité [sãsɥalite] NF sensuality

sensuel, -elle [sãsɥel] ADJ *(personne, plaisir etc)* sensual; *(lèvres, voix etc)* sensual, sensuous

sentant [sãtã] ADJ sentient

sente [sãt] NF *(sentier)* (foot)path

sentence [sãtãs] NF **1** *(jugement)* sentence **2** *(maxime)* maxim

sentencieusement [sãtãsjøzmã] ADV sententiously

sentencieux, -ieuse [sãtãsjø, -jøz] ADJ sententious

senteur, -euse [sãtœr, -øz] ADJ *Can Péj (indiscret)* nosy, prying

  NF *Litt* scent

senti [sãti] ADJ heartfelt

  NM *Phil* sense datum

sentier [sãtje] NM (foot)path; *Fig* path; **s. pour cavaliers** bridle path; **s. balisé** signposted footpath; **s. de grande randonnée** long-distance footpath; **s. battu** beaten track; *Fig* **sortir des sentiers battus** to venture off the beaten track; *Fig* **sur le s. de la guerre** on the warpath

sentiment [sãtimã] NM **1** *(sensation)* *(de joie, de soulagement etc)* feeling, sensation; **avoir le s. que ...** to have a *or* the feeling that ...; **privé de s.** *(membre)* devoid of feeling, numb; **il avait le s. de sa mort prochaine** he sensed he would die soon

  2 *(émotion)* feeling; *Mus* **jouer avec s.** to play with feeling; **avoir le s. de la nature** to have a feeling for nature; **avoir le s. de l'honneur/de la beauté** to have a sense of honour/of the aesthetic; **avoir du s. pour qn** to feel attracted to sb, to be drawn to sb; **ses sentiments vis-à-vis de moi** his/her feelings towards me; **je ne doute pas de ses sentiments pour moi** I have no doubt that he loves me; **faire appel aux bons sentiments de qn** to appeal to sb's finer feelings; **prendre**

qn par les sentiments to appeal to sb's softer side; *Fam* **c'est parti d'un bon s.** it was well meant, the intention was good; **faire du s.** to sentimentalize; **je ne fais pas de s. en affaires** I don't let sentiment interfere with business; **allons! pas de s.!** come on, don't be sentimental!; **avoir qn au s.** to win sb over by appealing to his/her softer side; **privé de s.** *(personne)* *(sans réaction)* numb; *(insensible)* devoid of feeling; **s. national** sense of nationhood; **je n'ai aucun s. religieux** I'm not the slightest bit religious; **veuillez agréer, Madame, l'expression de mes sentiments distingués** yours faithfully; **veuillez recevoir, Monsieur, l'expression de mes sentiments les meilleurs** yours sincerely

  3 *Litt (opinion)* feeling; **quel est votre s. sur la question?** what is your feeling about the matter?

sentimental, -ale, -aux, -ales [sãtimãtal, -o] ADJ **1** **vie sentimentale** love life; *Cin, Théâtre etc* **intrigue sentimentale** love affair **2** *(romantique)* *(personne, attachement, chanson etc)* sentimental, *Fam* soppy

  N **c'est un s./une sentimentale** he's/she's a romantic

sentimentalement [sãtimãtalmã] ADV sentimentally

sentimentalisme [sãtimãtalism] NM sentimentalism; **faire du s.** to be sentimental

sentimentaliste [sãtimãtalist] ADJ, N sentimentalist

sentimentalité [sãtimãtalite] NF sentimentality

sentine [sãtin] NF *Naut (d'un navire)* bilge; *Litt* **s. de tous les vices** sink of iniquity

sentinelle [sãtinɛl] NF *Mil (soldat)* guard, sentry, *Vieilli* sentinel; **nous disposerons des sentinelles le long des quais** we shall be posting guards along the quays; **en s.** on guard, on sentry duty; *Fig* **se mettre en s.** to stand guard, to keep (a) watch

◼SENTIR◼ [sãtir] *(prp* **sentant;** *pp* **senti;** *pr ind* **je sens, il sent, n. sentons, ils sentent;** *pr sub* **je sente;** *impf* **je sentais;** *p hist* **je sentis;** *fu* **je sentirai)**

> | | |
> | --- | --- |
> | **VT** to feel **1, 2** ▪ to be aware of **2** ▪ to be conscious of **2** ▪ to smell **3** ▪ to taste **4** ▪ to smell of **5** ▪ to reek of **5** ▪ to smack of **5** | |
> | **VI** to smell **1, 2** | |
> | **VPR** to feel **2** | |

VT **SEE GRAMMAR A41; B35 1** *(douleur, faim, froid, joie, peine etc)* to feel; *(par le toucher)* to feel; **je sentais trembler le plancher** I could feel the floor trembling; *Fam* **je sens mes bras/mes jambes** my arms/legs are aching; **je ne sens plus mes jambes/mes pieds** my legs/my feet are killing me; *(devenu insensible)* my legs/my feet have gone numb; **je sens l'hiver qui vient** I can feel winter coming; **on ne sent pas la différence** you can't feel the difference; *Fam* **je l'ai senti passer!** *(à propos d'une douleur, d'une facture, d'une réprimande)* I knew all about it!

  2 *(être conscient de)* *(injure, force, pouvoir etc)* to be conscious of, to feel; *(danger)* to be aware of *or* conscious of; **elle ne sentait pas tout le ridicule de la situation** she wasn't fully aware *or* conscious of the ridiculousness of the situation; **s. grandir son influence** to feel one's influence growing; **je sens que vous avez raison** I have a *or* the feeling that you are right; **ce sont des choses que l'on sent** you can sense *or* feel these things; **il m'a fait s. que ...** he gave me to understand that ...; **fais-lui s. qu'il se trompe** make him understand that he's mistaken; **faire s. son autorité** to make one's authority felt; **l'effet se fera s.** the effect will be felt; **je**

sentis la peur me gagner peu à peu I felt more and more frightened or I felt a growing fear; **je sentis sa colère monter peu à peu** I sensed his/her growing anger; **s. qch de loin** to feel sth coming; **s. qn de loin** to see through sb; **s. la barre** *(d'un navire)* to answer to the helm

3 *(par l'odorat) (odeur, fleur etc)* to smell; **je ne sens rien** I can't smell anything; **faire s. qch à qn** to let sb smell sth; *Fam* **je ne peux pas le s.** *(supporter)* I can't stand (the sight of) him, *Br* I can't stick him; *Fam* **je le sens pas bien, ce mec-là** *(il me déplaît)* I don't take to that guy, there's something about that guy I don't like; *Vieilli Fig* **s. le cadavre** to sense impending disaster

4 *(par le goût)* to taste

5 *(avoir l'odeur de)* to smell of; *(avoir un goût de)* to taste of; **cela sent le brûlé** *(dans une pièce)* there's a smell of burning; *(devant un mets etc)* it smells burnt; **ça sent le bébé/le linge frais** it smells of or there's a smell of babies/clean washing; **ça sent bon le pain frais** there's a delicious smell of fresh bread; **vin qui sent le bouchon** corked wine; **la pièce sent l'humidité** the room smells damp; **la salle sentait le tabac à plein nez** the room reeked of tobacco; *Fig* **ça sentait le piège à plein nez** I/he/*etc* could smell a trap; **il sentait l'acteur à plein nez** he had actor written all over him; *Péj* **ce livre sent l'effort** this book is very laboured; **cet article sent le plagiat** this article smacks of plagiarism; *Fam* **il sent le cadavre** he looks as if he's on his last legs

VI 1 s. bon/mauvais to smell good/bad; **fleurs qui sentent bon** sweet-smelling flowers; **ça sent fort** it has a strong smell

2 *Fam (puer)* to smell; **il sent des pieds** his feet smell, he has smelly feet

VPR se sentir 1 cela se sent it is something that you feel or sense

2 se s. bien/fatigué to feel well/tired; **se s. dix ans de moins** to feel ten years younger; **elle se sentait mourir/revivre** she felt she was dying/coming alive again; **se s. le courage de faire qch** to feel up to doing sth; **je ne m'en sens pas le courage** I don't feel equal or up to it; **tu t'en sens capable?** do you think you can manage it?, do you feel capable of it?

3 il ne se sent pas de joie he is beside himself with joy; *Fam* **ne plus se s.** *(agir comme un fou)* to have taken leave of one's senses; *(agir avec vanité)* to be very full of oneself

4 *Fam (se supporter)* **ils ne peuvent pas se s.** they can't stand (the sight of) each other, *Br* they can't stick each other

---

SEO [ɛsəo] *Compta (abrév* **sauf erreur ou omission)** E & OE

seoir [swar] **VI** *Litt (used only in prp* **seyant, séant;** *pr ind* **il sied, ils siéent;** *pr sub* **il siée, ils siéent;** *impf* **il seyait, ils seyaient;** *fu* **il siéra, ils siéront) s. à** to suit; **cette robe vous sied** that dress suits you or is very becoming **V IMPERS il lui sied de/lui sied mal de ...** it becomes him to/ill becomes him to ...; **comme il sied** as is fitting (**à** for)

Séoul [seul] **N** Seoul

sépale [sepal] **NM** *Bot* sepal

séparable [separabl] **ADJ** separable (**de** from); **deux théories difficilement séparables** two theories which are difficult to separate

séparateur, -trice [separatœr, -tris] **ADJ** separating, separative; *Opt (pouvoir)* resolving

NM *Tech* separator; *Ordinat* delimiter; *Ordinat* **s. de champs** field delimiter or separator; *TV* **s. de faisceau** beam splitter

séparation [separasjɔ̃] **NF 1** separation; **s. d'avec qn** separation from sb; **il n'a pas supporté la s. d'avec son épouse** he could not

bear to be parted or separated from his wife; **s. de la tête et du corps** severance of the head from the body; *Ordinat* **s. automatique des pages** automatic pagination; *Typ* **s. des couleurs** colour separation; **s. quadrichromique** four-colour separation

2 *Jur* **s. de corps** *(entre époux)* legal separation; **s. de fait, s. amiable** voluntary separation; **s. de biens** = marriage settlement under which husband and wife administer their separate properties

3 *Pol* **la s. des pouvoirs** the separation of powers; **s. de l'Église et de l'État** separation of Church and State

4 *(cloison)* partition, division; **mur de s.** dividing wall; **s. en bois** wooden partition; *Fig* boundary, dividing line

séparatisme [separatism] **NM** *Pol* separatism

séparatiste [separatist] **ADJ, N** *Pol* separatist

séparé [separe] **ADJ 1** *(distinct) (notions, chambres etc)* separate **2** *(désuni)* separated; **nous vivons s. l'un de l'autre** we've separated, we live apart; **il vit s. de sa femme** he's separated (from his wife)

séparément [separemɑ̃] **ADV** separately

séparer [separe] **VT 1** *(éloigner)* to separate (**de** from); **s. deux combattants** to part or separate two fighters; *Boxe* **séparez!** break!; **personne ne peut nous s.** no one can separate us or come between us; **la guerre sépare les familles** war separates families or keeps families apart; **des milliers de kilomètres nous séparent** we are thousands of miles apart, we are separated by thousands of miles

2 *(partager)* to divide; **le fleuve sépare la ville en deux** the river divides the town in two; **mur qui sépare deux champs** wall separating two fields; **s. une chambre en trois** to divide a room into three; **s. les cheveux en faisant une raie sur le côté** to part one's hair on the side

3 *(diviser)* to divide; **leurs opinions politiques les séparent** their political opinions divide them; **tout les sépare** they are poles apart; **jusqu'à ce que la mort nous sépare** till death do us part

4 *(isoler)* **s. les bons d'avec les mauvais** to separate the good from the bad; **s. la substance active de la substance inerte** to separate the active substance from the inert substances; **il faut savoir s. l'amour de la luxure** you must be able to distinguish between love and lust

VPR se séparer *(d'époux)* to separate, to part, *Fam* to split up; *(de la foule, d'une assemblée etc)* to break up, to disperse; *(d'une rivière, d'une route etc)* to divide, to branch off; **nous devons nous s. maintenant** we'll have to say goodbye now; **c'est ici que nos chemins se séparent** this is where we go our separate ways or where our paths diverge; **nous ne nous séparerons jamais** we shall never part; **l'armée se sépara** the army disbanded; **se s. de** ou **d'avec sa femme/son mari** to separate or part from one's wife/one's husband; **elle a dû se s. de son vieux chat/sa voiture** she had to part with her old cat/her car; *Chimie* **se s. à l'état cristallin** *(du sel)* to crystallize out

sépia [sepja] **NF** *(couleur, matière colorante)* sepia; **dessin à la s.** sepia drawing **ADJ INV** sepia

sept [sɛt] **ADJ INV 1** seven; **à s. heures** at seven o'clock; **les S. Merveilles du monde** the Seven Wonders of the World **2** *(dans des séries)* seventh; **page/numéro s.** page/number seven; **Édouard S.** Edward the Seventh **NM INV** seven; **le s. mai** (on) the seventh of May, (on) May (the) seventh, *Am* (on) May seventh; *Cartes* **le s. de cœur** the seven of hearts; **habiter au s.** to live at number seven

septain [sɛtɛ̃] **NM** *Littér* seven-line stanza

septantaine [sɛptɑ̃tɛn] **NF** *Belg, Suisse* **1** *(quantité)* **une s.** around or about seventy, seventy or so; **une s. de voitures** around or about seventy cars **2** *(âge)* **avoir la s.** to be around or about seventy

septante [sɛptɑ̃t] **ADJ INV** *Belg, Suisse* seventy **NM INV** *Bible* **la version des S.** the Septuagint

septantième [sɛptɑ̃tjɛm] *Belg, Suisse* **ADJ** seventieth **N** seventieth (one)

septembre [sɛptɑ̃br] **NM** September; **en s., au mois de s.** in September SEE GRAMMAR A81–2; B60–2

septennal, -ale, -aux, -ales [sɛptenal, -o] **ADJ** *(période, parlement etc)* seven-year, *Fml* septennial

septennat [sɛptena] **NM** *(d'un président etc)* (seven-year) term

septentrion [sɛptɑ̃trijɔ̃] **NM** *Litt* north

septentrional, -ale, -aux, -ales [sɛptɑ̃trijonal, -o] **ADJ** northern

septicémie [sɛptisemi] **NF** *Méd* blood poisoning, septicaemia, *Am* septicemia

septicémique [sɛptisemik] **ADJ** *Méd* septicaemic, *Am* septicemic

septième [sɛtjɛm] **ADJ** seventh; **être au s. ciel** to be in seventh heaven; **s. étage** seventh or *Am* eighth floor; **le s. art** the cinema **N** *(personne, objet, événement etc)* seventh; **habiter au s.** to live on the seventh or *Am* eighth floor **NM** *(fraction)* seventh; **trois septièmes** three sevenths **NF 1** *Mus* seventh **2** *Scol Anciennement* = top class or *Am* grade of primary school

septièmement [sɛtjɛmmɑ̃] **ADV** seventhly, in the seventh place

septique [sɛptik] **ADJ** septic; **fosse s.** septic tank

septuagénaire [sɛptɥaʒener] **ADJ, N** septuagenarian, seventy-year-old

septuagésime [sɛptɥaʒezim] **NF** *Rel* Septuagesima

septum [sɛptɔm] **NM** *Anat, Bot* septum

septuor [sɛptɥɔr] **NM** *Mus* septet(te)

septuple [sɛptɥpl] **ADJ** sevenfold, *Fml* septuple **NM** **au s.** sevenfold; **le s. de deux** seven times two; **payer le s.** to pay seven times as much

septupler [sɛptɥple] **VTI** to increase sevenfold

sépulcral, -ale, -aux, -ales [sepylkral, -o] **ADJ** sepulchral

sépulcre [sepylkr] **NM** sepulchre; **le saint s.** the Holy Sepulchre; *Fig* **s. blanchi** whited sepulchre

sépulture [sepyltyr] **NF 1** *Litt (inhumation)* burial; **refuser la s. à qn** to refuse burial to sb; **être privé de s.** to be refused burial **2** *(lieu)* burial place; **sépultures militaires** war cemeteries; **violation de s.** desecration of graves

séquelles [sekɛl] **NFPL** *(de maladie, d'accident)* aftereffects; *(de guerre, catastrophe etc)* aftermath; **une des s. de la guerre** one of the consequences or aftereffects of the war

séquençage [sekɑ̃saʒ] **NM** *Biol* sequencing

séquence [sekɑ̃s] **NF** sequence; *Cartes* run; *Ordinat* **s. de caractères** character string, sequence of characters; *Biol* **s. génétique** gene sequence; *Aut* **s. de combustion** firing order; **s. vidéo** video sequence

séquencer [sekɑ̃se] **VT** *(en génétique)* to sequence

séquenceur [sekɑ̃sœr] **NM** *Ordinat* sequencer

séquentiel, -ielle [sekɑ̃sjɛl] ADJ sequential; *Ordinat* **accès s.** sequential *or* serial access

séquentiellement [sekɑ̃sjɛlmɑ̃] ADV sequentially

séquestration [sekɛstrasjɔ̃] NF *Jur* **1** *(de biens)* sequestration **2** *(de personne)* illegal confinement

séquestre [sekɛstr] NM *Jur* **1** *(action)* sequestration; *Naut* embargo; **mettre qch sous s.** to sequester *or* seize sth **2** *(personne)* depository, trustee, administrator

séquestrer [sekɛstre] VT **1** *(biens)* to sequester, to sequestrate; *Naut (navire)* to lay an embargo upon **2 s. qn** to keep sb locked up; *Jur* to confine sb illegally
▪ **VPR se séquestrer** to cut oneself off from the world

séquoia [sekɔja] NM *(arbre)* sequoia

sérac [serak] NM *Géol* serac

sérail [seraj] NM seraglio; *Fig* **c'est normal qu'il soit un financier international, il est né** *ou* **a été élevé dans le s.** it's not surprising he's an international financier, he grew up in that world

séraphin [serafɛ̃] NM seraph ▪ VOIR GRAMMAIRE A14

séraphique [serafik] ADJ seraphic

serbe [sɛrb] ADJ Serb, Serbian
▪ N **S.** Serb, Serbian

Serbie [sɛrbi] NF Serbia

serbo-croate [sɛrbokrɔat] ADJ Serbo-Croat(ian)
▪ NM *Ling* Serbo-Croat

Sercq [sɛrk] NM Sark

séré [sere] NM *Suisse* fromage frais

serein¹ [sərɛ̃] ADJ *(personne, visage, esprit, jour etc)* serene, calm; *(ciel, nuit)* clear; **jugement s.** calm *or* impartial judgement

serein² NM evening dew

sereinement [sərɛnmɑ̃] ADV serenely, calmly

sérénade [serenad] NF **1** *Mus* serenade; **donner la s. à qn** to serenade sb **2** *Fam (tapage)* racket; **le bébé nous a fait une drôle de s. toute la nuit** the baby treated us to a demonstration of his vocal power all night; **il nous a fait sa s. habituelle** he treated us to one of his usual scenes

sérénissime [serenisim] ADJ **son Altesse s.** His/Her Most Serene Highness

sérénité [serenite] NF serenity, calmness; **avec s.** serenely, calmly

séreuse¹ [serøz] NF *Anat* serous membrane

séreux, -euse² [serø, -øz] ADJ *Anat, Méd* serous

serf, serve [sɛrf, sɛrv] *Hist* N serf
▪ ADJ **condition serve** serfdom; **terre serve** land in bondage *or* in villein tenure

serfouette [sɛrfwɛt] NF combined hoe and fork

serge [sɛrʒ] NF *Tex* serge

sergent [sɛrʒɑ̃] NM **1** *Mil* sergeant; **s. fourrier, s. comptable** quartermaster sergeant; **s. instructeur** drill sergeant; *Can* **s. d'armes** sergeant at arms; *Arch* **s. de ville** policeman **2** *Tech* cramp, clamp

sergent-chef, *pl* **sergents-chefs** NM *Mil* staff sergeant

séricicole [serisikɔl] ADJ silkworm-breeding, *Spéc* sericultural

sériciculteur, -trice [serisikyltœr, -tris] N silkworm breeder, *Spéc* sericulturist

sériciculture [serisikyltyr] NF silkworm breeding, *Spéc* sericulture

série [seri] NF VOIR GRAMMAIRE A13 **1** *(d'événements, de changements, de dates etc)* series, succession; *Sport (épreuve)* heat; *Billard* break; *Billard (de canons)* run; **s. de catastrophes, s. noire** series *or* catalogue of disasters, run of bad luck; **livre de s. noire** (crime) thriller; **s. de conférences** series *or* course of lectures; *Radio, TV* **s. (télévisée/radiophonique)** (television/radio) series; *TV* **s. AB** popular television; **s. dramatique** drama series; **s. policière** crime series, *Fam* cop show; *Sport* **s. éliminatoire** qualifying heat
2 *(d'articles de presse, de timbres etc)* series; *(de documents, d'outils etc)* set; *(d'échantillons etc)* range; *Ind, Com (de marchandises)* range, line; *Math, Chimie, Phys, Nucl* series; **s. complète de connaissances** full set of bills of lading; *Admin etc* **s. de prix** *(pour travaux publics etc)* list of charges; **s. de produits** product line; *Fam* **elle en a toute une s.** she has a whole collection of them; **en** *ou* **par série(s)** in series, serially; *Élec* **en s.** in series; **fabrication** *ou* **production en s.** mass production; **fabriquer qch en s.** to mass-produce sth; **chaîne de fabrication en s.** production line; **voiture de s.** standard car; *Com* **fins de séries** ends of lines, oddments, remnants; *(livres invendus)* remainders; **article hors s.** custom-made *or* custom-built article; **numéro hors s.** *(magazine)* special issue; *Fig* **c'est tout à fait hors s.** it's quite exceptional; **une personnalité hors s.** an exceptional personality
3 *(groupe)* group, category; *Sport* rank; *Boxe* **s. poids plume** featherweight rating; *Cin* **s. B** B-movie *or* film; *Péj* **film de s. Z** real bummer of a film
4 *Scol* specialization; **choisir une s.** to choose a specialization, to decide what one is going to specialize in
▪ ADJ INV *Ordinat* serial

sériel, -ielle [serjɛl] ADJ serial; *Mus* serial, twelve-tone, dodecaphonic

sérier [serje] VT *(impf, pr sub* **n. sériions,** *v.* **sériiez)** to arrange (in series), to classify

sérieusement [serjøzmɑ̃] ADV **1** *(avec sérieux)* seriously; *(sincèrement)* seriously, genuinely; **parlez-vous s.?** are you serious?, do you really mean it? **2** *(gravement) (malade, blessé, handicapé)* seriously; **il en a s. besoin** he's seriously in need of it

sérieux, -ieuse [serjø, -jøz] ADJ **1** *(qui ne plaisante pas)* serious; *(sincère) (offre, acheteur etc)* serious, genuine; *(information)* reliable; *(employé, entreprise etc)* responsible, reliable, serious; **des lectures sérieuses** serious reading; *Fam* **s. comme un pape** as solemn as a judge; **êtes-vous s.?** are you serious *or* in earnest?, do you mean it?; **d'un ton** *ou* **d'un air s.** seriously; **peu s.** *(personne)* unreliable; **voyons, ce n'est pas s.** come on, you're not serious *or* you don't mean it; **pas s. s'abstenir** *(dans une petite annonce)* genuine replies only; *Com* **client s.** good customer
2 *(important) (maladie, blessure, affaire, situation etc)* serious; **il a fait de s. progrès** he has made good *or* considerable progress; **si seulement tu avais des raisons sérieuses de refuser** if only you had good reasons to refuse
▪ NM seriousness; **garder son s.** to keep a straight face; **se prendre au s.** to take oneself seriously; **je vous ai pris au s.** I took you seriously, I thought you were serious, I thought you meant it; **on ne peut pas la prendre au s.** you can't take her seriously; **manque de s.** unreliability; **avec s.** seriously
▪ ADV *Fam (sérieusement)* seriously; **ils se sont foutus sur la gueule s.** they seriously went for each other; **s.?** seriously?

serif [serif] NM *Typ* serif

sérigraphie [serigrafi] NF silk-screen printing

sérigraphié [serigrafje] ADJ silk-screen(-printed)

serin, -ine [sərɛ̃, -in] NM *Orn* canary
▪ ADJ INV **jaune s.** canary yellow
▪ ADJ *Fam (personne)* silly, stupid, idiotic
▪ N *Fam (idiot)* nitwit

seriner [sərine] VT **1** *Péj* **s. qch à qn** to go on and on at sb about sth; **s. à qn que …** to tell sb time after time that … **2 s. un air à un oiseau** to teach a bird to sing by using a bird organ

seringa(t) [sərɛ̃ga] NM *Bot* seringa

seringue [sərɛ̃g] NF syringe; *Méd* **s. à injections** hypodermic syringe; **s. jetable** disposable syringe; *Aut* **s. à graisse** grease gun

serment [sɛrmɑ̃] NM *(parole solennelle)* oath; *(promesse)* pledge; *(d'amoureux)* vow, pledge; **prêter s.** to take an oath; *(d'un jury)* to be sworn in; **faire prêter s. à qn** to administer the oath to sb; **déclarer sous s.** to state *or* declare under oath; **déclaration sous s.** sworn statement, statement under oath; **certifier qch sous s.** to declare sth on oath; **violer un s.** to break an oath; **être sous la foi du s.** to be on oath; **faire le s. de faire qch** to swear *or* vow *or* pledge to do sth; **faire un faux s.** to commit perjury
▪▪ **s. d'allégeance** oath of allegiance; *Méd* **s. d'Hippocrate** Hippocratic oath; **s. d'ivrogne** empty promise; *Pol* **s. politique** oath of allegiance; *Admin* **s. professionnel** *(des magistrats, des avocats, de la police etc)* oath of office

sermon [sɛrmɔ̃] NM *Rel* sermon (**sur** on); *Fam Péj (remontrance)* sermon, lecture; *Bible* **le S. sur la Montagne** the Sermon on the Mount

sermonner [sɛrmɔne] VT *Fam Péj* **s. qn** to lecture sb, to give sb a lecture *or* talking-to

sermonneur, -euse [sɛrmɔnœr, -øz] *Fam Péj* ADJ sermonizing
▪ N sermonizer

séroconversion [serɔkɔ̃vɛrsjɔ̃] NF *Méd* seroconversion

sérodiagnostic [serɔdjagnɔstik] NM *Méd* serodiagnosis

sérologie [serɔlɔʒi] NF serology; **faire une s.** to be screened for antibodies

séronégatif, -ive [serɔnegatif, -iv] *Méd* ADJ HIV negative
▪ N person who is HIV negative

séronégativité [serɔnegativite] NF *Méd* the state of being HIV negative; **prouver sa s.** to prove that one is HIV negative

séropo [seropo] ADJ, N *Fam abrév* séropositif

séropositif, -ive [serɔpozitif, -iv] *Méd* ADJ HIV positive
▪ N person who is HIV positive; **séropositifs non-évoluteurs** long-term survivors, LTS

séropositivité [serɔpozitivite] NF *Méd* the state of being HIV positive; **taux de s.** HIV positive rate; **il a été renvoyé à cause de sa s.** he was dismissed for being HIV positive

sérosité [serozite] NF serous fluid

serpe [sɛrp] NF billhook; **visage taillé à coups de s.** rugged face

serpent [sɛrpɑ̃] NM **1** *(reptile)* snake; *UE, Fin* (currency) snake; *Bible* **le s.** the serpent; **s. à coiffe** *ou* **à lunettes** (Indian) cobra; **s. d'eau** water snake; **s. de mer** *Myth* sea serpent; *(poisson)* pipe fish; *Journ* stock story; **s. à sonnettes** rattlesnake, *Am Fam* rattler; **s. à sonnettes cornu** horned rattlesnake, *Am Fam* sidewinder; **s. de verre** slow-worm; *Fig* **s. de fumée** wreath *or* coil of smoke; *Écon* **s. monétaire européen** European currency snake; *Journ* **s. de mer** silly-season story **2** *Hist, Mus* serpent

serpentaire [sɛrpɑ̃tɛr] NF **1** *Bot* serpentaria;

s. de Virginie snakeroot **2** *Orn* serpent eater, secretary bird

serpentant [sɛrpɑ̃tɑ̃] **ADJ** *(courant, route etc)* winding, snaking, meandering

serpenteau, -eaux [sɛrpɑ̃to] **NM 1** *Zool* young snake **2** *(fusée volante)* serpent

serpenter [sɛrpɑ̃te] **VI** *(d'une rivière, d'une route etc)* to wind, to snake, to meander; **le chemin monte/descend en serpentant** the road winds *or* snakes *or* meanders up/down

serpentin, -ine [sɛrpɑ̃tɛ̃, -in] **ADJ** serpentine
NM 1 *Tech* coil **2** *(ruban pour les fêtes)* paper streamer
NF *Minér* **serpentine** serpentine, ophite

serpette [sɛrpɛt] **NF** pruning knife

serpillière [sɛrpijɛr] **NF** floorcloth; **passer la s. dans la cuisine** to mop the kitchen floor

serpolet [sɛrpɔle] **NM** *Bot* wild thyme

serrage [sɛraʒ] **NM** *Tech (d'une vis, d'un écrou, d'un nœud etc)* tightening; *(d'un joint)* clamping; **s. des freins** application of the brakes, braking; **vis de s.** set screw, locking screw

serre [sɛr] **NF 1** *(construction)* greenhouse; *(qui fait partie d'une maison)* conservatory; **s. chaude** hothouse; **s. de palmiers** palm house; **plante de s. chaude** hothouse plant; **plantes sous s.** plants under glass; *Écol* **effet de s.** greenhouse effect; *Écol* **gaz à effet de s.** greenhouse gas **2** *(action) (des raisins etc)* pressing, squeezing **3** **serres** *(des oiseaux de proie)* claws, talons

serré [sɛre] **ADJ** *(bottes, vêtements, nœud, vis etc)* tight; *(texture)* close; *(formation)* dense; *(discussion)* closely argued; *(argumentation)* closely reasoned; *(programme)* tight; *Géog (col)* narrow; **budget s.** tight budget; **surveillance serrée** close supervision; **étude serrée** *(d'un texte)* close *or* intensive study; **style s.** concise style; **on était vraiment serrés dans cette voiture** we were really (tightly) packed in that car; **une robe serrée à la taille** a dress with a fitted waist; **un café noir bien s.** a strong black coffee; **pluie serrée** teeming rain; **deux pages d'une écriture serrée** two closely written pages; **les dents serrées** with clenched teeth; **elle était pâle, les lèvres serrées** she was pale, her lips pressed tightly together; **maisons serrées** houses huddled together; **serrés comme des harengs** *ou* **des sardines** packed like sardines; **rangs serrés** serried *or* closed ranks; **avoir le cœur s.** to be sad at heart, to have a heavy heart; **la gorge serrée** with a lump in one's throat; *Sport* **la partie va être serrée** it's going to be a tight *or* close game; *Sport etc* **arrivée serrée** close finish
ADV **écrire s.** to have cramped handwriting; **tricoter s.** to knit tightly; *Fig* **jouer s.** to play a cautious game, to take no chances

serre-fils **NM INV** *Élec* wire-retaining screw

serre-frein(s) **NM INV** *Rail* brakeman

serre-joint(s) **NM INV** *(outil)* clamp

serre-livres **NM INV** book end

serrement [sɛrmɑ̃] **NM** **s. de main** handshake; **avoir un s. de cœur** to feel a pang; **elles se dirent au revoir avec un s. de cœur** they both felt a pang as they said their goodbyes; **il comprit dans un s. de cœur que la maladie serait fatale** his heart sank as he realized the illness was fatal

serre-patte, *pl* **serre-pattes** [sɛrpat] **NM** *Fam* sergeant

SERRER [sɛre] **VT 1** *(saisir, tenir)* to grip, to clasp; *(presser)* to squeeze, to press; **s. la main à** *ou* **de qn** to shake hands with sb, to shake sb's hand; **tenir qch sans s.** to hold sth loosely; **s. qn entre ses bras** to clasp sb in one's arms, to hug sb; **s. qn/qch contre soi** to

hold sb/sth tightly to one; **s. le cou à qn** to wring sb's neck; **cela me serre le cœur** it wrings my heart; **le chagrin lui serrait la gorge** he felt choked with grief
2 *(d'un vêtement, des chaussures etc) (personne)* to be too tight for; **s. les pieds à qn** to pinch sb's feet; **cette jupe me serre (à) la taille** this skirt is too tight round the waist
3 *(nœud, écrou, ceinture etc)* to tighten; *(joint)* to clamp; *(voiles)* to furl, to take in; *(poings)* to clench; **s. les dents** to clench one's teeth; *Fig* to grit one's teeth; **s. les freins** to put on *or* apply the brakes; *Mus* **en serrant** stringendo
4 *(rapprocher)* to close up, to put close together; *Mil, Fig* **s. les rangs** to close ranks; **s. son style** to condense one's style; *Typ* **s. une ligne** to close up a line
5 *(être près de) (personne, chose)* to keep close to; *Naut (côte, Aut (trottoir)* to hug; **s. qn de près** to follow sb closely; *Fig* **s. une femme de près** to be all over a woman; **s. un adversaire dans un coin** to corner an enemy; **s. une question de près** to focus narrowly on a question; **s. le vent** to sail close to the wind
6 *(ranger) Can, Litt* **s. des bijoux dans une cassette** to stow one's jewels in a case
7 *Fam (emprisonner) Br* to nick, to lift, *Am* to bust
VI serrez à droite! keep to the right!
VPR se serrer 1 *(se rapprocher)* to squeeze up *or* together; **se s. les uns contre les autres** to huddle together; **se s. contre qn** to snuggle up to sb; *(pour être protégé)* to cling to sb; **se s. contre un mur** to hug a wall
2 **mon cœur se serra** my heart sank; **ma gorge se serra** I had a lump in my throat; **nous nous serrâmes la main** we shook hands
3 *Fig* **se s. (la ceinture)** to tighten one's belt; *Fam* **se s. les coudes** to back one another up, to support one another

serre-tête **NM INV 1** *(bandeau)* headband **2** *Sport (bonnet)* cap; *Aviat* helmet

serriculture [sɛrikyltyr] **NF** hothouse growing

serrure [sɛryr] **NF** lock; **trou de la s.** keyhole; **s. de capot** bonnet lock; **s. à carte perforée** card-operated lock; **s. électronique** electronic lock, computer-coded lock; **s. magnétique** magnetic lock; **s. de sûreté** safety lock

serrurerie [sɛryrri] **NF 1** *(métier)* locksmith's trade; *(magasin)* locksmith's (shop) **2** *(travail, ouvrages)* ironwork, metal work; **s. d'art** ornamental ironwork; **grosse s.** heavy ironwork

serrurier [sɛryrje] **NM 1** *(de serrures)* locksmith **2** *(de métaux)* ironsmith

sertir [sɛrtir] **VT** *(pierre précieuse)* to set; *(cartouche, boîte de conserve etc)* to crimp

sertissage [sɛrtisaʒ] **NM** *(d'une pierre précieuse)* setting; *(d'une cartouche, d'une boîte de conserve etc)* crimping

sertisseur, -euse [sɛrtisœr, -øz] **N** *(ouvrier) (de pierres précieuses)* setter; *(de cartouches, de boîtes de conserve etc)* crimper
NM *(appareil) (pour boîtes de conserves etc)* crimper

sertissure [sɛrtisyr] **NF** *(action, manière) (de pierre précieuse)* setting; *(partie de chaton)* bezel

sérum [serɔm] **NM 1** *Physiol, Méd* serum; **s. physiologique** saline solution, saline; **s. sanguin** blood serum; **s. de vérité** truth serum; *Fam* truth drug **2** **s. (lactique)** whey

servage [sɛrvaʒ] **NM** *Hist* serfdom, bondage; *Fig* bondage

serval, -als [sɛrval] **NM** *Zool* serval

servant, -ante [sɛrvɑ̃, -ɑ̃t] **ADJ** **frère s.** lay brother; **cavalier** *ou* **chevalier s.** faithful admirer
NM 1 *Mil* gunner **2** *Rel* **s. (de messe)** server

NF servante 1 *(domestique)* (maid)servant **2** *(table)* side table **3** *Tech* (adjustable) support

serve [sɛrv] **ADJ, N** *voir* **serf**

serveur, -euse [sɛrvœr, -øz] **N 1** *(dans un bar)* barman, *surtout Am* bartender, f barmaid; *(dans un restaurant)* waiter, f waitress **2** *Cartes* dealer **3** *Tennis* server
NM *Ordinat* server; **s. de fichiers** file server; **s. FTP** FTP server; **s. mandataire** proxy server; **s. Minitel®** Minitel® service provider; **s. de réseau** network server; **s. sécurisé** secure server; **s. télématique** bulletin board (system); **s. Web** HTTP server

serviabilité [sɛrvjabilite] **NF** obligingness, helpfulness

serviable [sɛrvjabl] **ADJ** obliging, helpful

SERVICE [sɛrvis]

service **1–3, 5, 7, 9** ▪ duty **4** ▪ department **5** ▪ operation **6** ▪ favour **8** ▪ sitting **10** ▪ set **11**

NM 1 *(pour un client, un maître)* service; **le s. est désastreux** *(dans ce restaurant)* the service here is appalling; **faire le s.** to serve; **s. (non) compris** service (not) included; **libre s.** *(dans un magasin)* self-service; *Écon* **services** services; **les biens et les services** goods and services; **le secteur des services** the service sector; **société de services** service company; **entrer en s. (chez qn)** to go into (sb's) service, to go into service (with sb); **gens de s.** domestic staff; **être au s. de qn** to be in sb's service; **se passer des services d'un employé** to dispense with an employee's services; **mourir au s. du roi** to die in the king's service; **escalier de s.** backstairs; **porte de s.** tradesmen's entrance; *Admin, Mil* **états de s.** service record; *Com* **s. après vente** after-sales service; **s. clients** customer service; **s. à l'américaine** *(dans un restaurant)* American service; **s. à l'anglaise** *(dans un restaurant)* English service; **s. à la française** *(dans un restaurant)* French service; **s. à la russe** *(dans un restaurant)* Russian service; **s. à l'assiette** *(dans un restaurant)* plate service, American service; **s. au guéridon** *(dans un restaurant)* gueridon service, French service; **s. à table** table service, waiter service, waitress service; **services bancaires** banking services; *Banque* **services de caisse** counter services; **s. dans les chambres** *ou* **en chambre** room service; **services à la clientèle** customer services, customer-support services; **s. du contentieux** *(département)* legal department; *(personnes)* legal experts; *Admin* **s. contractuel** contract service; *Fin* **s. d'un emprunt** servicing a loan; *Fin* **s. des intérêts** interest charges

2 *Mil* **s. militaire (obligatoire)** (compulsory) military service; **faire son s.** to do one's military service; **en s. actif, en activité de s.** on the active list; **service(s) de guerre** active service; **en s. aux armées** on active service; **(in)apte au s.** (un)fit for service; **bon pour le s.** *(jeune appelé)* fit for service; *Fig (appareil)* in working order; **être libéré du s.** to be discharged; **libération du s.** discharge

3 *Tennis* service; **faire un** *ou* **le s.** to serve; **au s., Martin** Martin to serve

4 *(travail)* duty; **s. de jour** day duty; **s. de nuit** night duty; *Naut* night watch; **être de s./ne pas être de s.** to be on/off duty; **à quelle heure prenez-vous/quittez-vous votre s.?** at what time do you go on/off duty?; **avoir dix ans de s. dans une entreprise** to have completed ten years' service with a company; **reprendre du s.** *(personne)* to return to work; *(machine)* to be brought back into operation *or* service; **après des années d'inactivité, le chanteur a repris du s.** after years of silence, the singer has made a come-back; *Mil etc* **mort en s. commandé** killed on active service; **s. de corvée** *Mil* fatigue duty; *Naut* duty; **s. de garde** guard duty; **planton de s.** duty orderly; **tableau de s.** duty chart *or* list *or* roster; **officier/sous-officier de s.** duty/non-commissioned officer; *Fam* **le crétin/pigeon de s.** the usual *or* inevitable cretin/sucker; *Fam* **être s. s.** to be a stickler for rules and regulations

5 *(département)*, *Admin, Com* department; *Mil* corps, service; *Méd etc* department, service; **chef de s.** head of department; **correspondance de s.** official correspondence; **s. central** headquarters; **s. clientèle** customer service (department); **s. d'études** research department; **s. de relation avec la clientèle** customer service department; **services commerciaux** marketing services; **services financiers** financial services; **s. informatique** computer department

6 *(d'une machine etc)* operation; **s. à bras** *ou* **manuel** hand *or* manual operation; **en s.** *(machine)* in service, in use, in operation; *(avion, navire)* in commission; **aptitude au s.** serviceability; **en (bon) état de s.**, **propre au s.** in (good) working order, serviceable; **hors (de) s.** *(machine, mécanisme)* out of order; *(canon)* out of action; *(navire)* disabled; **mettre en s.** *(machine etc)* to bring *or* put into service; *(avion, navire)* to bring *or* put into commission; **retirer du s.** to withdraw from service *or* from use; *(avion, navire)* to decommission; **retirer graduellement du s.** to phase out

7 *(transport)* service; **assurer** *ou* **faire le s. entre ... et ...** to operate between ... and ...; **s. assuré toute l'année** year-round service; **s. de marchandises** *ou* freight service; **s. de voyageurs** passenger service

8 *(aide)* favour, *Am* favor, service; **rendre (un) s. à qn** *(d'une personne)* to do sb a favour *or* a service; **si ça peut te rendre s.**, **prends-le** if it's of any use to you, take it; **rendre un bon/un mauvais s. à qn** to do sb a good/a bad turn; **demander un s. à qn** to ask sb a favour; **les services qu'il a rendus à l'enseignement** his services to education; **ce livre m'a rendu grand s.** I found this book very useful; **à votre s.** at your service; **qu'y a-t-il pour votre s.?** what can I do for you?

9 *(en élevage)* *(d'un étalon)* service

10 *(ensemble de repas)* sitting; *Rail etc* **dernier s. à deux heures** last sitting (for lunch) at two o'clock

11 *(d'ustensiles de cuisine, de linge de table etc)* set; **s. (de table)** *(assiettes etc)* dinner service; *(linge)* set of table linen; **s. à découper** carving knife and fork

  INT *Suisse (je vous en prie)* don't mention it!, you're welcome!

  NMPL *Suisse* **services** *(couverts)* knifes and forks *(for laying table)*

▸▸ **s. des achats** purchasing (department); *(plus grand)* procurement (department); **s. d'action commerciale** marketing department; **s. administratif** administration (department), *Fam* admin; **s. après-vente** aftersales (department); **services autoroutiers** motorway services; **s. babyphone** baby-listening service; *Méd* **s. de cardiologie** cardiology department; **s. des commandes** order department; **s. commercial export** export department; **s. comptable** *ou* **de comptabilité** accounts (department); **s. de conseil** consulting service; **s. consommateurs** customer service (department); *Méd* **s. des contagieux** isolation ward; **s. contrôle qualité**, **s. de contrôle de qualité** quality control (department); **s. du courrier** mail room; **s. de dépannage** repair service; *Aut* recovery service; *Fin* **s. de la dette** debt servicing; **s. des eaux** = water board; **s. d'écoute** monitoring service; **s. d'étude mer-**

catique marketing research department; **s. de l'expédition** shipping (department); **s. export** export (department); **s. export intégré** integrated export service; **services extérieurs** external services; **s. de facturation** invoicing department; **s. financier** finance (department); **s. de fixation des prix** pricing department; **s. gouvernemental** government agency *or* department; **s. de l'immigration** immigration department; **services industriels** industrial services; **s. informations** enquiries; *Journ* **s. des informations** information service; **s. informatique** EDP-department, computer department; **s. juridique** legal department; **s. lancement** product launch department; *Ordinat* **s. en ligne** on-line service; **s. marketing** marketing department; **s. marketing-vente** sales and marketing department; **s. mercatique** marketing department; **s. d'ordre** *(police)* police contingent; *(dans une manifestation etc)* team of stewards; **s. du personnel** personnel (department); **s. des postes** *ou* **postal** postal service, *surtout Am* mail service; **s. de presse** press office; **s. (de) production** production department; **s. de la prospection** sales and marketing (department), new business department; **s. public** civil service; *TV* public-service broadcasting (network); **s. de la publicité** publicity *or* advertising department; **services publics** (public) utilities; **s. de recherche** research department; **s. de recouvrement** collection department; **Service régional de la police judiciaire** *Br* ≃ regional crime squad; **s. de relations publiques** public relations department; **s. de remorquage et de dépannage** breakdown and recovery service; **s. de renseignements** information office; *Tél* directory enquiries, *Am* information; *Mil* military intelligence (department); *Com* **s. des renseignements commerciaux** status enquiry department; **s. de santé** health services; **services du secteur tertiaire** business services; **services de soutien** support services; **s. de stylique** design department; *(plus grand)* procurement (department); **services supplémentaires** service backup; **s. technique** engineering department, technical branch; *Ordinat* **s. télématique** bulletin board service; *Arg* **s. trois-pièces** wedding tackle; **s. d'urgence** emergency service; **s. vente** *ou* **des ventes** sales department; **s. de voiturier** valet parking

---

Service militaire

Military service (for a period of ten months) used to be compulsory for French men aged between 18 and 26 unless they were declared unfit for service ("réformé"). As an alternative to military service, some chose to work overseas, often in developing countries, as part of a voluntary aid scheme known as "la coopération". However, following the "loi de programmation" 1997–2002, a reform was introduced in order to gradually abolish military service and move towards an exclusively professional army.

---

serviette [sɛrvjɛt] **NF 1 s. (de table)** (table) napkin, serviette; **s. d'enfant** feeder, bib **2** towel; **s. de toilette** hand towel; **s. de plage** beach towel; **s. sans fin** roller towel **3** *(sac)* briefcase

▸▸ **s. hygiénique** sanitary towel *or Am* napkin

serviette-éponge, *pl* **serviettes-éponges** **NF** terry towel

servile [sɛrvil] **ADJ** servile; *(imitation, traduction, traducteur)* slavish

servilement [sɛrvilmã] **ADV** servilely; *(imiter, traduire)* slavishly

servilité [sɛrvilite] **NF** servility; *(d'imitation, de traduction)* slavishness

SERVIR [sɛrvir] *(prp* **servant;** *pp* **servi;** *pr ind* **je sers, il sert, n. servons;** *pr sub* **je serve;** *impf* **je servais;** *p hist* **je servis;** *fu* **je servirai)**

> **VI** to be useful **1** ▪ to be used for *(servir à)* **2** ▪ to be used as *(servir de)* **3** ▪ to serve **4, 5**
> **VT** to serve **1–4, 6** ▪ to wait on **1**
> **VPR** to help oneself **1** ▪ to be served **2** ▪ to use *(se servir de)* **4**

  VI 1 *(être utile)* to be useful *or* of use (**à qn** to sb); **la machine peut encore s.** the machine can still be used *or* is still fit for use; **la voiture peut encore s. quelques années** the car has still got a few years' use left in it; **cela peut s. un de ces jours** it may come in handy *or* be of use one day; **toujours prêt à s.** always ready for use

  2 s. à qch/à faire qch *(être destiné à)* to be used for sth/for doing sth; **ne s. à rien** to be (of) no use, to be useless; **je vais le lui dire, mais je sais que ça ne servira à rien** I'm going to tell him but I know it won't do any good *or* it'll be pointless; **ça ne servira pas à grand-chose** that won't be much good *or* much use; **cela ne sert qu'à l'irriter** it only irritates him *or Fml* serves to irritate him; **à quoi cela sert-il?, à quoi ça sert?** what's the good *or* the use *or* the point of that?; **à quoi sert ce truc-là?** what's that gadget (used) for?; **je ne vois pas à quoi sert d'y aller** I don't see the point *or* good of going; **à quoi sert qu'on l'attende?** what's the point *or* use of waiting for him/her?

  3 s. de *(d'un objet)* to serve as, to be used as; *(d'une personne)* to act as; **les pupitres servent de tables** the desks serve *or* are used as tables; **s. de prétexte** to serve as a pretext; **elle lui a servi de mère** she has been (like) a mother to him; **tu vas me s. de conseiller** you'll act as *or* be my adviser

  4 *Tennis* to serve; *Cartes* **à vous de s.** (it's) your deal

  5 *(dans l'armée, dans le gouvernement etc)* to serve (**sous** under); *Mil* **en âge de s.** of military age; **s. à table** to wait at table, *Am* wait (on) table

  V IMPERS il ne sert à rien de pleurer it's no good *or* use crying, there's no point in crying; **rien ne sert de courir, il faut partir à point** slow and steady wins the race

  VT 1 *(consommateur, dîner, poisson etc)* to serve; *(dîneur)* to wait on, to serve; *(client)* to serve, to attend to; **s. qn en marchandises** to supply sb with goods; **s. Dieu/le roi** to serve God/the king; *Vieilli* **Comte de Monte-Cristo, pour vous s.** the Count of Monte-Cristo, at your service; **est-ce qu'on vous sert?** are you being served *or* attended to?; **tout le monde est servi?** has everybody got a drink/something to eat?; *(dans un magasin)* is anybody waiting to be served?; **madame est servie** dinner is served, madam; **vous pouvez nous s., Nestor** you may serve dinner, Nestor; **à s. frais** best (served) chilled; **puis-je vous s. de gratin?** can I serve you with *or* help you to some gratin?; **s. à boire à qn** to give sb a drink *or* something to drink; **nous sommes très bien servis** we have very good domestic help; **on est très bien servi dans ce restaurant** the service in this restaurant is very good; **on n'est jamais si bien servi que par soi-même** if you want something done, do it yourself; *Fam* **en fait de pluie, nous sommes servis** as far as rain goes, we get more than our share; **ce cours d'eau sert le moulin** this stream drives the mill; **s. une rente à qn** to pay an annuity to sb

2 *(aider)* *(personne)* to help, to assist, to be of service to; *(intérêts)* to serve, to further; *(patrie, cause)* to serve; **en quoi puis-je vous s.?** what can I do for you?, how can I help you *or Fml* be of service to you?; **les choses l'ont bien servi** things have worked in his favour; **sa mémoire l'a mal servi** his memory served him badly; **mes études m'ont peu servi** my studies haven't been of much use to me *or* haven't got me anywhere much; **cela m'a peu servi pour obtenir un emploi** that wasn't much use to me in getting a job **3** *Tennis (balle)* to serve **4** *(d'un étalon) (jument)* to serve, to cover **5** *(à la chasse) (animal)* to dispatch **6** *Rel* **s. la messe** to serve at mass **7** *Suisse (utiliser)* to use; **c'est un manteau que je ne sers plus** I don't wear this coat any more

VPR se servir 1 *(d'une personne)* **se s. d'un plat** to help oneself to a dish; **servez-vous!** help yourself!; **je me suis déjà servie deux fois** I've already had two helpings **2** *(d'un plat, d'un vin etc)* to be served; **le champagne se sert frappé** champagne should be *or* is best served chilled **3** *Com* **se s. chez Martin** to shop at Martin's **4** **se s. de qch/qn** *(utiliser)* to use sth/sb; **se s. d'un parapluie comme d'un pare-soleil** to use an umbrella as a sunshade; **il sait se s. de ses poings** he knows how to use his fists, he's good with his fists

serviteur [sɛrvitœr] NM servant; **s. de l'État** civil servant; *Arch* **votre s.** *(dans une lettre)* your obedient servant; *Arch, Hum* **personne ne le sait mieux que votre s.** no one knows it better than yours truly

servitude [sɛrvityd] NF **1** *(asservissement)* servitude; *(contrainte)* constraint; **réduire un pays en s.** to reduce a country to servitude; **la s. de la mode** the tyranny *or* constraints of fashion **2** *Jur* easement; **s. de passage** right of way

servo [sɛrvo] NM *Aut etc* **s. à air comprimé** compressed-air servo

servocommande [sɛrvokomãd] NF *Aviat, Aut etc* servo(control)

servodirection [sɛrvodirɛksjɔ̃] NF *Aut etc* servo steering, power steering

servofrein [sɛrvofrɛ̃] NM *Aut etc* servo-brake, servo-assisted brake

servomécanisme [sɛrvomekanism] NM *Tech* servomechanism, servo system

servomoteur [sɛrvomotœr] NM *Tech* servomotor

ses [se] ADJ POSS *voir* **son**[1]

sésame [sezam] NM **1** *Bot* sesame **2 s., ouvre-toi!** open, sesame!; **ce diplôme lui a servi de s.** the diploma opened doors for him/her

session [sesjɔ̃] NF **1** *Parl, Jur* session, sitting **2** *Univ (examens)* (exam) session; **la s. de juin** the June exams; **il a eu son bac à la deuxième s.** he passed his baccalauréat the second time round *or Br* at the resits; **s. de rattrapage** repeat exams, *Br* resits

sesterce [sɛstɛrs] NM *Antiq (monnaie)* sestertius, sesterce

SET [ɛsœte] NF *Ordinat (abrév* **secure electronic transaction)** SET®

set [sɛt] NM **1** *Tennis* set; **gagner en deux sets** to win in two sets **2 s. (de table)** *(ensemble de napperons)* set of table mats; *(napperon)* table mat

sétacé [setase] ADJ *Biol* bristly, *Spéc* setaceous

setter [setɛr] NM *(chien)* setter; **s. irlandais** Irish setter

seuil [sœj] NM **1** *(entrée)* doorway, threshold; *(dalle etc)* doorstep; *Phys, Psy, Fig* threshold;

franchir le s. to cross the threshold; **sur le s.** in the doorway; **un inconnu se tenait sur le s.** there was a stranger standing on the doorstep *or* in the doorway; *Bourse* **s. d'annonce obligatoire** disclosure threshold; **s. d'émissions** *(des gaz d'échappement)* emissions limit; **s. d'imposition** tax threshold; *Écon* **s. de pauvreté** poverty line; **s. de prix** price threshold; *Écon* **s. de rentabilité** break-even point; *Physiol* **s. de sensibilité** threshold of sensitivity *or* of response; *Psy* **s. de la conscience** threshold of consciousness **2** *Géog* **s. continental** continental shelf **3** *(d'une vanne, d'une cale sèche)* sill

SEUL, SEULE [sœl]

> **ADJ** only **1, 3** ▪ alone **2, 3** ▪ by oneself **2** ▪ on one's own **2**
> **N** only one

ADJ SEE GRAMMAR B10 **1** *(preceding the noun)* *(unique)* only, sole; **un s. homme** *(pas plus qu'un)* a single man; *(d'entre tous les autres)* just *or* only one man; **ils se sont tous avancés comme un s. homme** they moved forward as one man; **un s. être vous manque et tout est dépeuplé** there's just one person missing in your life and the entire world seems like a desert; **son s. exécuteur testamentaire** his/her sole executor; **son s. souci** his only *or* sole worry; **c'est la seule chose qui me retient** it's the one *or* the only thing keeping me here; **il ne suffit pas d'un s. exemple** a single example *or* one example alone will not suffice; **il suffit d'une seule fois** once is enough; **mon s. et unique ami/ stylo** my one and only friend/pen; **un s. mot, et je pars** one word (from you) and I'll go; **la seule pensée de sa venue m'effraie** the mere *or* very thought of him/her coming frightens me

2 *(following the noun or used predicatively)* *(séparé des autres)* alone, by oneself, on one's own; **je suis s., tu peux venir** you can come over, I'm on my own; **se sentir très s.** to feel very lonely *or* alone; **tu es trop s.** you're on your own *or* by yourself too much; **être s. au monde** to be alone in the world; **enfin seuls!** alone at last!; **une femme seule** an unattached woman; **il peut marcher tout s. maintenant** he can walk by himself now; **faire cavalier s.** to go it alone; **parler s. à s. à qn** to speak to sb in private, to have a private conversation with sb; **s. (à s.) avec soi-même** alone with one's thoughts; **l'œuvre seule de ...** the sole *or* exclusive work of ...; **j'ai une cachette que moi s. connais** I have a hiding place which no-one else knows about *or Fml* which I alone know; **je l'ai fait tout s. ou à moi s.** I did it (by) myself *or* all on my own *or* single-handed; **cela va tout s.** it's plain sailing, it's straightforward; **cela n'a pas été tout s.** it wasn't all that easy, it wasn't plain sailing; **ça se mange tout s.** it doesn't need anything else; *(se mange facilement)* it's very light; **parler/chanter tout s.** to talk/ sing to oneself; *Mus* **passage pour violon s.** passage for unaccompanied *or* solo violin

3 *(following the noun or preceding the article or poss adj) (seulement)* only, alone; **la violence seule** *ou* **seule la violence le contraindrait** only violence *or* violence alone *or* nothing short of violence would compel him; **seule la chasse les fait vivre** hunting is their only *or* sole source of food; **s. un expert pourrait nous conseiller** only an expert could advise us; **réservé aux seuls adultes** for adults only; **nous sommes seuls à le savoir** we are the only ones *or* people who know about it

N un s. *(pas plus qu'un)* a single person; *(chose)* a single one; *(d'entre tous les autres)* only one person; *(chose)* only one; **le gou-**

vernement d'un s. absolute rule; **pas un s.** *(chose)* not (a single) one; *(personne)* not a single person; **vous êtes le s. qui puissiez m'aider** you're the only one *or* person who can help me, *Fml* you alone can help me; **ne t'en fais pas, tu n'es pas le s.!** don't worry, you're not the only one!

> Attention: ne pas confondre **alone** et **lonely** lorsqu'on traduit **seul**. Contrairement à l'adjectif **alone**, **lonely** suggère toujours un sentiment de solitude. Par ailleurs **alone** est toujours utilisé comme attribut.

seule [sœl] NF *Com* **s. de change** sola of exchange

seulement [sœlmɑ̃] ADV **1** *(juste)* only; **nous sommes s. deux** there are only *or* just two of us; **elle m'a donné s. les plus mûres** she gave me only *or* she only gave me the ripest ones; **je te demande s. un peu de patience** I'm just asking you to be a bit patient; **je viens s. d'arriver/de terminer** I've only just arrived/finished, I've just this minute arrived/finished; **et c'est s. maintenant que tu me le dis!** and you're only telling me about it now!, and you haven't told me before this!; **non s. ..., mais aussi ...** *ou* **mais encore ...** not only ..., but also ... VOIR GRAMMAIRE A22

2 *(uniquement)* only, solely, merely; **il y a s. pour vous faire plaisir** he is only going to please you, he is going just *or* merely *or* solely to please you; *Fam* **entrez s.** do come in; *Fam* **essaie s.!** just (you) try!

3 *(même)* even; **sans s. me regarder** without even looking at me, without so much as looking at me; **si s. ...!** if only ...!

4 *(with conj force)* **je viendrais bien, s. ...** I'd like to come, but ... *or* only ...; **elle est gentille, s. elle est un peu sotte** she's kind, but she's a bit silly

sève [sɛv] NF *Bot (d'une plante)* sap; *Fig Litt* vitality, vigour, *Am* vigor; *Bot, Fig* **la s. monte** the sap is rising

sévère [sevɛr] ADJ **1** *(dur) (juge, critique, peine, paroles etc)* severe, harsh; *(visage, regard, air)* stern, severe; **climat s.** severe *or* hard climate; **être s. envers** *ou* **pour** *ou* **avec qn/pour les fautes de qn** to be severe *or* hard on sb/on sb's failings; **mener un train s.** to set a gruelling pace **2** *(discipline, principes moraux)* strict, rigid; **morale peu s.** lax morals **3** *(sans ornements) (architecture, style, beauté)* severe **4** *(grave) (pertes, dégâts)* severe, serious

ADV *Fam (gravement)* something rotten; **je déprime s. en ce moment** I'm depressed something rotten at the moment

sévèrement [sevɛrmɑ̃] ADV **1** *(durement)* severely, harshly **2** *(strictement)* strictly, rigidly **3** *(gravement)* severely; **s. atteint** severely affected

sévérité [severite] NF **1** *(d'un juge, de mesures, d'une critique, d'une peine etc)* severity, harshness; *(d'un visage, d'un regard)* sternness, severity; *(d'une discipline, d'une éducation)* strictness; **avec s.** with severity, severely **2** *(d'une architecture, du style etc)* severity

sévices [sevis] NMPL brutality, cruelty; **s. (sexuels) à enfant** child abuse

Séville [sevil, sevij] N Seville

sévir [sevir] VI **1** *(agir avec rigueur)* to act ruthlessly; **s. contre qn/qch** to deal ruthlessly with *or Fam* to clamp down on sb/sth **2** *(d'une épidémie, de la guerre etc)* to rage; *(de vandales)* to wreak havoc; **la crise qui sévit actuellement** the present crisis

sevrage [səvraʒ] NM **1** *(de nourrisson)* weaning; *(de drogué)* detoxification; *Méd* **symptômes de s.** withdrawal symptoms **2** *Bot (d'une marcotte, d'un greffon)* separating

sevrer [səvre] VT (je **sèvre**, n. **sevrons**; je **sèvrerai**) **1** *(enfant, agneau, drogué etc)* to wean; *Litt* **s. qn de qch** to deprive sb of sth **2** *Bot (marcotte, greffon)* to separate

sèvres [sɛvr] NM *(porcelaine)* Sèvres (porcelain)

sexage [sɛksaʒ] NM *(de la volaille)* sexing

sexagénaire [sɛgzaʒenɛ, sɛksa-] ADJ, N sixty-year-old; *Litt* sexagenarian

sex-appeal, *pl* **sex-appeals** [sɛksapil] NM *Fam* sex appeal

sexe [sɛks] NM **1** *(classement)* sex; **le (beau) s.** the fair sex; **le deuxième s.** the weaker sex; **changer de s.** to have a sex-change; **changement de s.** sex-change operation **2** *(parties sexuelles)* genitals **3** *(sexualité)* sex; **problèmes de s.** sexual problems
▸▸ **le s. faible** the weaker sex; **le s. fort** the stronger sex

sexisme [sɛksism] NM sexism; **faire du s.** to be sexist

sexiste [sɛksist] ADJ, N sexist

sexologie [sɛksɔlɔʒi] NF sexology

sexologique [sɛksɔlɔʒik] ADJ sexological

sexologue [sɛksɔlɔg] N sexologist

sex-shop, *pl* **sex-shops** [sɛksʃɔp] NM sex shop

sextant [sɛkstɑ̃] NM *Naut, Math* sextant

sextuor [sɛkstɥɔr] NM *Mus* sextet(te)

sextuple [sɛkstypl] ADJ sixfold, *Fml* sextuple NM **au s.** sixfold; **le s. de deux** six times two; **payer le s.** to pay six times as much

sextuplé, -ée [sɛkstyple] N sextuplet

sextupler [sɛkstyple] VTI to increase sixfold

sexualisation [sɛksɥalizasjɔ̃] NF sexualization

sexualiser [sɛksɥalize] VT to sexualize

sexualité [sɛksɥalite] NF sexuality

sexué [sɛksɥe] ADJ *(plante, animal)* sexed; *(reproduction)* sexual

sexuel, -elle [sɛksɥɛl] ADJ sexual; **vie sexuelle** sex life; **acte s.** sex act; **organes** *ou* **parties sexuel(le)s** sex organs; **éducation sexuelle** sex education; **rapports sexuels** sexual relations, *Fam* **nos rapports sexuels se sont détériorés** the sex isn't as good as it used to be; **un obsédé s.** a sex maniac

sexuellement [sɛksɥɛlmɑ̃] ADV sexually; **maladie s. transmissible** sexually transmitted disease; **être attiré s. par qn** to be sexually attracted to sb

sexy [sɛksi] ADJ INV *Fam* sexy

seyant [sejɑ̃] ADJ *(vêtement)* becoming

Seychelles [seʃɛl] NFPL **les S.** the Seychelles

SF [ɛsɛf] NF *Fam (abrév* **science fiction)** sci-fi, SF

SFIO [ɛsɛfio] NF *(abrév* **Section française de l'Internationale ouvrière)** = French Socialist Party 1905–1969

SGAO [ɛsʒeao] NM *Ordinat (abrév* **système de gestion assisté par ordinateur)** computer-assisted management system

SGBD [ɛsʒebede] NM *Ordinat (abrév* **système de gestion de base de données)** DBMS

SGBDR [ɛsʒebedeɛr] NM *Ordinat (abrév* **système de gestion de bases de données relationnelles)** RDBMS

SGDG [ɛsʒedeʒe] *(abrév* **sans garantie du gouvernement)** without government guarantee

shah [ʃa] NM shah

shake-hand [ʃɛkɑ̃d] NM INV *Arch, Hum* handshake

shaker [ʃɛkœr] NM cocktail shaker

shakespearien, -ienne [ʃɛkspirjɛ̃, -jɛn] ADJ Shakespearian, Shakespearean

shako [ʃako] NM *Mil* shako

shampoing [ʃɑ̃pwɛ̃] N = **shampooing**

shampooiner [ʃɑ̃pwine] VT to shampoo

shampooineur, -euse [ʃɑ̃pwinœr, -øz] N *(employé)* shampooer
NF **shampooineuse** *(à moquette)* carpet shampooer

shampooing [ʃɑ̃pwɛ̃] NM **1** *(action)* shampoo; **faire** *ou* **donner un s. à qn** to shampoo sb('s hair), to give sb a shampoo **2** *(produit)* shampoo; **s. sec** dry shampoo; **s. pour cheveux secs/gras** shampoo for dry/greasy hair; **s. antipelliculaire** anti-dandruff shampoo; **s. aux œufs** egg shampoo; **s. à moquettes** carpet shampoo

shampouiner [ʃɑ̃pwine] VT to shampoo

shampouineur, -euse [ʃɑ̃pwinœr, -øz] N = **shampooineur**

shant(o)ung [ʃɑ̃tuŋ] NM *Tex* shantung

shareware [ʃɛrwɛr] NM *Ordinat* shareware

sharia [ʃarja] NF *(loi islamique)* sharia

sheik [ʃɛk] NM sheik

shekel [ʃɛkɛl] NM shekel

shérif [ʃerif] NM sheriff

sherpa [ʃɛrpa] N Sherpa

sherry [ʃɛri] NM sherry

shetland [ʃɛtlɑ̃d] NFPL **les (îles) S.** the Shetland Islands, the Shetlands
NM *Tex* Shetland wool; **(pull en) s.** Shetland sweater

shilling [ʃiliŋ] NM shilling

shimmy [ʃimi] NM *Aut* shimmy

shinto [ʃɛ̃to], **shintoïsme** [ʃɛ̃tɔism] NM *Rel* Shinto, Shintoism

shintoïste [ʃɛ̃tɔist] ADJ, N *Rel* Shintoist

shipchandler [ʃipʃɑ̃dlœr] NM ship's chandler

shit [ʃit] NM *Fam* hash, *Br* blow, draw

shocking [ʃɔkiŋ] ADJ INV *Hum, Vieilli* shocking

shog(o)un [ʃɔgun] NM *Hist* shogun

shoot [ʃut] NM **1** *Ftbl* shot **2** *Arg (de drogue)* shot; **se faire un s. (d'héroïne)** to give oneself a shot (of heroin), to shoot up (heroin)

shooter [ʃute] VI *Ftbl* to shoot
VT **1** *Ftbl* **s. un pénalty** to take a penalty (kick) **2** *Arg (avec de la drogue)* **s. qn** to shoot sb up
VPR **se shooter** *Arg* to shoot (up); **se s. à l'héroïne** to shoot (up) heroin

shopping [ʃɔpiŋ] NM shopping; **faire du s.** to go shopping

short [ʃɔrt] NM (pair of) shorts; **être en s.** to be in shorts, to be wearing shorts VOIR GRAMMAIRE A10

show [ʃo] NM show; **s. aérien** air show

show-biz [ʃobiz] NM INV *Fam* show biz

show-business [ʃobiznɛs] NM INV show business

showroom [ʃorum] NM showroom

shrapnell [ʃrapnɛl] NM *Mil* shrapnel

shunt [ʃœ̃t] NM *Élec, Chir* shunt

shunter [ʃœ̃te] VT **1** *Élec* to shunt **2** *TV, Cin* to fade

SI¹ [si]

if **1–3** ▪ whether **3** ▪ how **4** ▪ what if **5** ▪ what about **5**

CONJ *(by elision* **s'** *before* **il, ils)* **1** *(hypothèse, condition)* if; **je ne sortirai pas s'il pleut** I won't go out if it rains; **s'il n'avait pas plu, nous serions partis** if it hadn't rained we would have gone; *Fml* had it not rained we would have gone; **si on ne le surveille pas, il s'échappera** he will escape unless he is watched *or* if he is not watched; **j'aurais été**

soldat, si je n'étais poète I would have been a soldier if I were not a poet, I would have been a soldier were I not a poet; **si j'avais su** if I'd known, had I (but) known; **si tu veux la paix, prépare la guerre** if you want peace, prepare for war; **qui le fera si ce n'est moi?** who'll do it if I don't *or* unless I do?; **si ce n'était que je l'ai vu moi-même** if I hadn't seen it (for) myself; **un des plus grands, si ce n'est le plus grand** one of the biggest, if not the biggest; **tout va bien, si ce n'est mon dos qui me fait souffrir** everything's fine apart from my sore back *or* apart from the fact that my back is hurting me; **s'il fait beau et si je suis libre, je sortirai** if it's fine and (if) I'm free, I'll go out; **oui, si on veut** yes, if you like; **un artiste, si on veut** an artist, so to speak; **si je ne m'abuse, si je ne me trompe** if I'm not mistaken; **si j'ose dire** if I may make so bold; **si seulement j'étais à Paris!** if only I were *or* was in Paris!; *Fml* **si tant est que ...** + *sub* provided that ..., so long as ... SEE GRAMMAR A52–3; B34

2 *(concession)* if; **si je me plains, c'est que j'en ai sujet** if I complain, it's with good reason; **s'il est malheureux et s'il a des ennuis, c'est bien de sa faute** if he is unhappy and in trouble, it is entirely his own fault; **s'il fut sévère, il fut juste** he was fair though severe, he might have been severe but he was fair; **ce fut à peine s'il put distinguer l'heure à sa montre** he could scarcely see the hands of his watch; **c'est tout au plus si l'on peut compter jusqu'à vingt femmes dans la salle** at (the) most there are only about twenty women in the hall; **le père Martin, (un) brave homme s'il en fut** old Martin, a good chap if ever there was one

3 *(question indirecte)* if, whether; **je me demande si c'est vrai/s'il viendra** I wonder if *or* whether it's true/he'll come; **je lui ai demandé s'il était marié** I asked him if *or* whether he was married; *Fam* **si je connais Paris?** do I know Paris?; *Fam* **si c'est pas malheureux (de voir ça)!** isn't it just dreadful (to see that)!

4 *(combien)* how; **pensez si j'étais furieux!** (you can) imagine how angry I was!

5 *(supposition)* what if, suppose; **et si elle l'apprend?** what if she finds out?, and suppose she finds out?; **si nous changions de sujet?** suppose we change the subject?, how about changing the subject?; **si on faisait une partie de bridge?** what about *or* how about a game of bridge?

NM **tes si et tes mais** your ifs and buts; **tu mets toujours des si à tout!** you're always iffing and butting; *Prov* **avec des si, on mettrait Paris dans une bouteille** if ifs and ands were pots and pans there'd be no need for tinkers

SI²

so **1** ▪ as **2** ▪ so that *(si bien que)* **4** ▪ yes **6**

ADV 1 *(tellement)* so; **ne courez pas si vite** don't run so fast; **il est si faible que ...** he is so weak that ...; **un si bon dîner** such a good dinner; **de si bons dîners** such good dinners; **il n'est pas si à plaindre que cela** he is not to be as pitied as all that; **ce n'est pas si facile** it's not so *or* that easy VOIR GRAMMAIRE A5

2 *(= 'aussi' dans une proposition négative)* il n'est pas si beau que vous he is not as handsome *or* not so handsome as you

3 donnez-m'en si peu que vous voudrez *ou* **si peu que rien** give me just a (very) little

4 si bien que ... so that ..., with the result that ...; **il dépensa sans regarder, si bien qu'en fin de compte il fut ruiné** he spent recklessly, so that *or* with the result that he was ruined

5 *(concession)* **si ... que** + *sub* however; **si jeune qu'il soit** however young he may be, young as he is; **aucun médecin, si habile soit-il** no doctor, however capable (he may be); **si peu que ce soit** however little (it may be)

6 *(réponse à une question négative)* yes; **si fait** yes indeed; **ça ne fait rien – si, ça fait quelque chose** it doesn't matter – yes, it does (matter); **il n'est pas parti? – si/je crois que si** he hasn't gone? – yes, he has/yes, I think he has *or* I think so; **j'ai l'impression qu'il ne pleut pas – il me semble que si** I have the impression it's not raining – it seems to me it is; **tu crois qu'il ne va pas venir? – il m'a assuré que si** do you think he won't come? – he assured me that he would; **mais si, je l'ai vue** I <u>did</u> see her; **il ne s'en remettra pas – que si!** he won't get over it – yes, he will!; **tu ne t'en souviens plus, je pense? – si, si** you probably don't remember, do you? – yes, I do; **vous en voulez? – non merci – mais si!** would you like some? – no, thank you – oh go on! SEE GRAMMAR B64

si³ NM INV *Mus (note)* B; *(en chantant la gamme)* te, ti; **morceau en si** piece in B; **en si bémol** in B flat

Siam [sjam] NM Siam

siamois, -oise [sjamwa, -waz] ADJ Siamese; **chat s.** Siamese cat; **frères s., sœurs siamoises** Siamese twins
▸ N S. Siamese
▸ NM **1** *(chat)* Siamese (cat) **2** *Ling* Siamese

siau [sjo] NM *Can Fam* bucket, pail

Sibérie [siberi] NF Siberia

sibérien, -ienne [siberjɛ̃, -jɛn] ADJ Siberian; *Fig* **il fait un froid s.** it's bitterly cold
▸ N S. Siberian

sibilance [sibilɑ̃s] NF *Méd* **s. respiratoire** wheezing

sibilant [sibilɑ̃] ADJ *Méd* sibilant, hissing

sibylle [sibil] NF *Antiq* sibyl

sibyllin [sibilɛ̃] ADJ **1** *Antiq* sibylline **2** *Litt (énigmatique)* cryptic, enigmatic

sic [sik] ADV sic

SICAF [sikaf] NF *Fin (abrév* **société d'investissement à capital fixe)** closed-end investment company

SICAV [sikav] NF *Fin (abrév* **société d'investissement à capital variable)** *Br* ≃ unit trust, *Am* ≃ mutual fund; *Bourse* **S. actions** equity-based unit trust; *Bourse* **S. monétaires** money unit trust; *Bourse* **S. obligataire** bond-based unit trust

siccatif, -ive [sikatif, -iv] ADJ, NM siccative

Sicile [sisil] NF Sicily

sicilien, -ienne [sisiljɛ̃, -jɛn] ADJ Sicilian
▸ N S. Sicilian

sicle [sikl] NM *Hist (monnaie, poids)* shekel

sida, SIDA [sida] NM *Méd* AIDS, Aids; **avoir le s.** to have AIDS; **s. avéré** full-blown AIDS

sidatique [sidatik] ADJ, N *Péj* = sidéen

side-car, *pl* **side-cars** [sajdkar, sidkar] NM *(habitacle)* sidecar; *(véhicule)* motorcycle and sidecar, *Br* combination

sidéen, -enne [sideɛ̃, -ɛn] *Méd* ADJ suffering from AIDS
▸ N AIDS sufferer

sidéral, -ale, -aux, -ales [sideral, -o] ADJ sidereal

sidérant [siderɑ̃] ADJ *Fam (nouvelles, histoire etc)* staggering

sidéré [sidere] ADJ **1** *Fam* flabbergasted, staggered (**de faire** to do), thunderstruck **2** *Vieilli (par la foudre, par une crise d'apoplexie)* struck down

sidérer [sidere] VT (**il sidère; il sidérera) 1** *Fam (personne)* to flabbergast, to stagger **2** *Vieilli (de la foudre, d'une crise d'apoplexie etc)* to strike down

sidérose [sideroz] NF **1** *Minér* siderite **2** *Méd* siderosis

sidérurgie [sideryrʒi] NF iron and steel metallurgy; *(industrie)* iron and steel industry

sidérurgique [sideryrʒik] ADJ **industrie s.** iron and steel industry; **usine s.** iron and steel works

sidérurgiste [sideryrʒist] N iron and steel worker

siècle [sjɛkl] NM **1** *(cent ans)* century; **au vingtième s.** in the twentieth century; **cette maison a au moins un s./deux siècles** this house is at least a hundred/two hundred years old; **un lit vieux d'un bon s.** a bed at least a hundred *or* a good hundred years old **2** *(époque)* age; **le s. de Louis XIV, le grand s.** the age of Louis XIV; **le s. des Lumières** the Age of Enlightenment; **notre s.** our age *or* century, the age *or* times we live in; **c'est un homme de son s./d'un autre s.** he's a man of his time(s)/he belongs to another age *or* another century; **vivre dans** *ou* **avec son s.** to be in tune with one's age *or* time(s); **jusqu'à la fin des siècles** to the end of time; *Rel* **pour les siècles des siècles** world without end; *Fam* **il y a un s.** *ou* **ça fait des siècles que je ne vous ai vu** I haven't seen you for ages, it's ages since I saw you **3** *Rel* **le s.** the world, worldly life; **vivre dans le s.** to live in the world

siège [sjɛʒ] NM **1** *(centre)* seat, centre, *Am* center; *(d'une douleur)* seat; **s. administratif** administrative headquarters; **s. épiscopal** see; **s. d'exploitation** *(d'une entreprise)* operational headquarters; **s. principal** *(d'une entreprise)* head office; **s. social** *(d'une entreprise)* head office, registered office; **avoir son s. à Londres** *(d'une société etc)* to have its head office *or* headquarters in London, to be headquartered in London

2 *Mil* siege; **mettre le s. devant une ville, faire le s. d'une ville** to lay siege to *or* besiege a town; **lever le s.** to raise the siege; *Fam (partir)* to make tracks; **état de s.** state of siege

3 *(meuble)* seat; *(de cocher)* box; *Parl* seat; *Aut* **s. avant/arrière** front/back seat; *Aut* **s. baquet** bucket seat; *Aut* **s. basculant** tilting seat; **s. de camping** folding chair; **s. chauffant** heated seat; *Aut* **s.-club** armchair; *Aviat* **s. éjectable** ejector seat; *Aut* **s. pour enfant** baby/child seat; **s. inclinable** reclining seat; *Aut* **s. rehausseur** child booster seat; **s. sport** sports seat; **offrir un s. à qn** to offer sb a seat; **prenez un s.** take a seat, do sit down; **s. à pourvoir au conseil d'administration** vacancy on the board

4 *(de chaise, de W.-C., de personne)* seat; **bain de s.** sitz bath, hip bath; *Obst* **(accouchement par le) s.** breech delivery/birth; **le bébé se présente par le s.** the baby is in the breech position

5 *(fonction) Pol* **s. à la Chambre** seat in Parliament; **s. parlementaire** seat in Parliament; *Jur* **le s. du juge** the judge's bench; **elle occupe un s. important** she holds an important position

6 *Tech (d'une valve etc)* seating

siéger [sjeʒe] VI (**je siège, n. siégeons; je siégeai(s); je siégerai) 1 s. à Londres** *(d'une entreprise etc)* to have its head office *or* headquarters in London, to be headquartered in London; **s. au conseil d'administration** to have a seat on the board, to be on the board; **après avoir siégé à Bayeux pendant dix ans** *(d'un évêque)* having held the see of Bayeux for ten years; *Méd, Fig* **c'est là que siège le mal** that is the root of the problem **2** *(d'un tribunal de justice, d'un juge, d'une assemblée etc)* to sit **3 s. à la Chambre/au Parle-**

Vieilli *(de la foudre, d'une crise d'apoplexie etc)* to strike down

ment to have a seat *or* to sit in Parliament; *Jur* **s. au tribunal** to be on the bench

sien, sienne [sjɛ̃, sjɛn] PRON POSS *(d'homme etc)* his; *(de femme etc)* hers; *(de bébé, d'animal domestique)* his, hers; *(d'animal, de nation, de chose etc)* its; *(après un sujet indéfini)* one's own; **il te prête le s.** you can borrow his; **tu n'as qu'à prendre la sienne** you can just take his/hers; **de toutes ces solutions, il préfère la sienne** out of those possible solutions, he prefers his own; **elle n'en a pas besoin, elle a le s.** she doesn't need it, she has her own; **je n'en ai pas besoin, j'ai le s.** I don't need it, I've got his/hers; **les deux siens** his/her two, the two *or* both of his/hers; *(en insistant)* his/her own two; **elle t'a laissé deux des siens** she gave you two of hers; **on doit acheter la sienne** everyone must buy their own, *Fml* one must buy one's own; **au total, il y a plus de deux cents drapeaux car chaque pays a le s.** in total there are more than two hundred flags, each country having its own; *très Fam* **le s. de bébé est plus intelligent** his/her baby is more intelligent; *Fam* **à la sienne!** *(en buvant)* let's drink to him/her SEE GRAMMAR A30; B21–2
▸ NM **le s.** *(ce qui lui appartient)* his/hers; **il devrait y mettre du s.** he should do his share
▸ NMPL **les siens** *(sa famille)* his/her family *or Am* folks; *(ses partisans)* his/her followers; *(ses coéquipiers)* his/her team-mates; *(après un sujet indéfini)* one's family/followers/team-mates
▸ NFPL **il a encore fait des siennes** he's been up to his old tricks again
▸ ADJ POSS *Litt* his/hers; **un s. cousin** a cousin of his/hers; **il fera siens tes principes** he will adopt your principles as his own; **fera-t-il siennes les félicitations qu'ils m'adresseront?** will he join them in congratulating me?

Sienne [sjɛn] N Siena; *Com* **terre de S. naturelle/brûlée** raw/burnt sienna

sierra [sjera] NF *Géog* sierra

Sierra Leone [sjeralɛɔn] NF Sierra Leone

sieste [sjɛst] NF *(après le repas)* siesta, nap; **faire la s.** to take *or* have a siesta *or* nap

sieur [sjœr] NM **le s. Martin** *Jur, Arch* Mr Martin, *Péj* old Martin

sifflant, -ante [siflɑ̃, -ɑ̃t] ADJ *(bruit)* hissing; *(note)* whistling; *(respiration, toux)* wheezing, wheezy; *(consonne)* sibilant
▸ NF **sifflante 1** *Ling* sibilant **2** *Radio* sibilance

sifflard [siflar] NM *Fam* (salami-type) sausage

sifflement [sifləmɑ̃] NM **1** *(d'une personne, du vent etc)* whistling, whistle; *(d'un serpent, d'une oie, de la vapeur)* hiss(ing); *(du fouet)* swish(ing); *(d'une balle, d'une flèche)* whizz; *(d'un asthmatique)* wheezing; *(de la friture, d'une lampe à arc)* sizzling; **un s.** a whistle/hiss **2** *Théâtre etc* hiss(ing), boo(ing), catcall **3 s. d'oreilles** buzzing *or* ringing in the ears

siffler [sifle] VI **1** *(d'une personne, d'un oiseau, d'un train, d'une bouilloire, du vent etc)* to whistle; *(d'un serpent, d'une oie, de la vapeur)* to hiss; *(d'un asthmatique)* to wheeze; *(de la friture, d'une lampe à arc)* to sizzle; *Fam* **ça me siffle dans les oreilles** I've got a buzzing *or* ringing in my ears **2** *(avec un sifflet)* to blow a/the whistle; *(chien)* to whistle for, to whistle up; *(chien)* to whistle for; *Aut Fam* **je me suis fait s. (par la police)** I've been pulled up (by the police); **s. une fille** to (wolf-)whistle at a girl **3** *Théâtre etc (acteur, pièce etc)* to hiss, to boo **4** *Fam (boire) (verre, bouteille etc)* to knock back
▸ VT **1** *(air)* to whistle; *Naut (ordre)* to pipe; *Sport* **s. une faute/la mi-temps** to blow (the whistle) for a foul/for half time **2** *(taxi etc)* to whistle for, to whistle up; *(chien)* to whistle for;

sifflet [siflɛ] **NM 1** *(instrument)* whistle; *Naut* pipe; **coup de s.** blow *or* blast of a/the whistle; *Naut* pipe; **donner un coup de s.** to blow the whistle; **j'ai entendu un coup de s.** I heard a whistle (blowing); **démarrez au coup de s.** start when you hear the whistle *or* when the whistle blows; *Sport* **coup de s. final** final whistle; **s. à vapeur** steam whistle; *Naut* **s. de brume** fog whistle; *Arg* **ça lui a coupé le s.** that shut him up; *Arg* **serrer le s. à qn** to throttle *or* strangle sb; **attaquer en s.** *(de rameur)* to catch a crab **2** *(sifflement)* whistle; *Théâtre etc* hiss, boo, catcall

siffleur, -euse [siflœr, -øz] **N** *(personne)* whistler; *Théâtre* hisser, booer
NM *(oiseau)* widgeon
ADJ *(oiseau)* whistling; *(serpent)* hissing; *(asthmatique)* wheezy; **canard s.** widgeon

siffleux [siflø] **NM** *Can Zool* groundhog, woodchuck

sifflotement [siflɔtmã] **NM** whistling (to oneself *or* under one's breath)

siffloter [siflɔte] **VTI** to whistle (to oneself *or* under one's breath)

sigillaire [siʒilɛr] **ADJ anneau s.** signet ring

sigillé [siʒile] **ADJ** *Bot, Cér etc* sigillate(d)

sigisbée [siʒisbe] **NM** *Hum, Litt* gallant

sigle [sigl] **NM** acronym; *(d'une entreprise)* logo

sigma [sigma] **NM** *(lettre grecque)* sigma

signal, -aux [siɲal, -o] **NM 1** *(signe)* signal; *(indice)* sign; *Psy* **réagir à un s.** to react to a signal; **faire des signaux** to signal; **envoyer** *ou* **lancer un s.** to send a signal; **donner le s. de qch** to give the signal for sth; *Fig (d'un événement etc)* to be the signal for sth; **s. de départ** *(d'un train, d'une course etc)* starting signal; **au s., tous se levèrent** on the given signal *or* when the signal was given they all stood up; **le s. d'une crise sociale** the sign of a social crisis **2** *Électron, Radio* signal
▸▸**s. d'alarme** alarm (signal); **s. d'alerte** warning (signal); *Mil, Aviat* air-raid warning; *Tél* **s. d'appel** call(ing) signal; *Rail* **s. à l'arrêt** signal at danger; *Rail* **s. d'arrêt** danger signal; *Rail* **s. d'arrêt absolu** stop signal; *Rail* **s. avancé** distant (block) signal; **s. d'avertissement** *ou* **avertisseur** warning signal; *Ordinat* **s. d'avertissement de réception** acknowledge; *Ordinat* **s. de baisse de tension des piles** battery low warning; **s. de baisse du toner** toner low warning; **s. à bras** semaphore signal; *Naut* **s. de brume** fog signal; *TV, Cin* **s. caméra** camera cue; **s. de chemin de fer** railway *or* Am railroad signal; **s. de danger** warning sign; **s. de détresse** distress *or* S.O.S. signal; *Rail* **s. à distance** distant (block) signal; *Rail* **s. d'entrée** home signal; *Mil* **s. par fanions** flag signal; *Mil, Aviat etc* **s. de fin d'alerte** all-clear; *Naut, Radio* **s. horaire** time signal; *Ordinat* **s. horodateur** time and date signal; *TV* **s. d'image** picture signal; **s. d'incendie** fire alarm; *Ordinat* **s. d'invitation à transmettre** proceed-to-send signal, *Am* start-dialing signal; **s. lumineux** light signal; *TV, Cin* light cue; *Aut* beacon; *Ordinat* indicator light, warning light; *Admin* **signaux lumineux** traffic lights; **s. optique** visible *or* visual signal; **signaux parasites** clutter; *Naut* **s. à pavillons** flag signal; **s. de priorité** give way sign, *Am* yield sign; *Rail* **s. rapproché** home signal; *Aut* **signaux routiers** *(écriteaux)* road signs; **s. sonore** beep; *(pour avertir)* warning beep; **s. de (sortie)** lecture sense signal; **s. vidéo** video signal; **s. à vue** visible *or* visual signal

signalé [siɲale] **ADJ** *Litt (service, récompense)* signal

signalement [siɲalmã] **NM 1** *(d'une personne)* description, particulars **2** *Jur* reporting

signaler [siɲale] **VT 1** *(faire remarquer) (erreur, fait etc)* to point out, to indicate (**à qn** to sb); **un sifflement signale que l'eau est à la bonne température** a whistling indicates that the water is at the right temperature; **s. à qn que** to point out to sb that; **s. un livre/un restaurant à qn** to recommend a book/a restaurant to sb; **Libération a signalé cet artiste** Libération drew attention to this artist; **c'est cette première pièce qui l'a signalé au monde du spectacle** it was this first play that brought him to the attention of the theatrical world
2 *(reporter) (retard, changement, vol etc)* to report, to notify (**à qn** to sb); **on nous signale que l'autoroute est bouchée** we have reports that the motorway is blocked, the motorway is reported to be blocked; **rien à s.** nothing to report; *Naut* **date à laquelle un navire a été signalé pour la dernière fois** date when a ship was last contacted *or Spéc* spoken
3 *(par un signal) (train, navire etc)* to signal; *Aviat (piste)* to indicate the position of; **l'entrée de l'autoroute est très mal signalée** the entry onto the motorway is very badly indicated *or* signposted; **c'est signalé par des pancartes lumineuses** it's indicated by illuminated signs
4 *Ordinat (marquer)* to flag up
5 *Vieilli (rendre remarquable)* to make conspicuous
VPR se signaler to distinguish oneself (**par** by); **se s. dans les sciences** to have a reputation as a scientist; **se s. à l'attention de qn** to catch sb's eye; *Fam* **se s. par son absence** to be conspicuous by one's absence

signalétique [siɲaletik] **ADJ** *Admin* descriptive *(of a person)*; **fiche s.** *(dans les rapports de police)* description

signaleur [siɲalœr] **NM** *Mil etc* signaller; *Rail* signalman

signalisation [siɲalizasjɔ̃] **NF 1** *Aut (action)* signposting and marking; *(signaux)* signs and markings; **s. routière internationale** international (system of) road signs; **panneau de s.** roadsign; **feux de s.** traffic lights **2** *Rail (action)* installation of signals (**de** on); *(signaux)* signals **3** *Aviat (action)* installation of lights and markings (**de** on)

signaliser [siɲalize] **VT** *Aut (route)* to signpost and mark; *Rail (voie)* to install signals on; *Aviat (piste)* to install lights and markings on

signataire [siɲatɛr] **ADJ, N** signatory

signature [siɲatyr] **NF 1** signature; *(acte)* signing; **s. électronique** *ou* **numérique** digital signature, signature line; **apposer sa s. à un acte** to sign a document; **pour s.** for signature; **document porté à la s. du directeur** document given to the director for his signature; **présenter le courrier à la s.** to present the mail for signature; **avoir la s.** *(pour une entreprise etc)* to be authorized to sign; *Fig* **les plus grandes signatures de la littérature française** the greatest names in French literature; **s. d'un contrat** signing of a contract; **s. légalisée** authenticated signature; **s. par procuration** per pro signature, pp, signature by proxy; **s. sociale** company signature (and stamp) **2** *Typ (lettre, chiffre)* signature; *Journ* by-line

signe [siɲ] **NM 1** *(indice) (de pluie, d'impatience etc)* sign, indication; *(de maladie)* sign; *(d'amitié, d'amour)* sign, mark, token; **il t'a offert des fleurs? c'est un s.** he gave you flowers? that must mean something; **ne donner aucun s. de vie, ne pas donner s. de vie** to show no sign of life; *Fig* **elle ne nous a pas donné s. de vie depuis un mois** we haven't heard from her for a month; **en s. de désapprobation/solidarité** as a sign of dis-

approval/solidarity; **porter du noir en s. de deuil** to wear black as a sign of mourning; **un s. des temps** a sign of the times; **signes extérieurs de richesses** trappings *or* outward signs of wealth; **la réunion a eu lieu sous le s. de la cordialité** cordiality was the keynote of the meeting; **politique conduite sous le s. de la rigueur** policy in which austerity is the keynote; **signes d'usure/de vieillesse** signs of wear/age; **c'est bon/mauvais s.** it's a good/bad sign; **c'est s. que quelque chose ne va pas** it's a sign that there's something wrong
2 *(symbole)* sign, symbol; **s. algébrique** algebraical sign; **s. de classification** number of section or paragraph; **signes de ponctuation** punctuation marks; *Typ* **signes de correction** proof correction marks; *Mus* **signes constitutifs** key signature; **s. du zodiaque** sign of the zodiac; **être né sous le s. du Capricorne/de la Balance/des Poissons** to be born under the sign of Capricorn/Libra/Pisces; **s. de chance** lucky sign; *Typ* **s. différent de** not equals sign; *Typ* **s. dollar** dollar sign; **s. du marché** market signal; *Typ* **s. inférieur à** *ou* **plus petit que** less than sign; *Typ* **s. livre** pound sign; *Typ* **s. moins** minus sign; *Typ* **s. multiplié** multiplication sign; *Typ* **s. plus** plus sign; *Typ* **s. pour cent** percent sign; *Typ* **s. supérieur à** *ou* **plus grand que** greater than sign; *Typ* **s. égal** equals sign
3 *(trait physique) (de personne)* (distinctive) mark; *Admin* **signes particuliers: néant** distinguishing marks: none
4 *(geste)* sign, gesture; **il me faisait des signes** he was making signs *or* he was gesturing to me; **parler par signes** to use sign language; *(d'un sourd)* to use sign language, to sign; **langage par signes** sign language; **apprendre le langage par signes** to learn sign language, to learn how to sign; **s. d'adieu** farewell wave (of the hand); **il me fit un s. d'adieu** he waved me goodbye; **faire s. à qn** to make a sign to sb; *(contacter)* to get in touch with sb; **faire s. à qn de faire qch** to signal to sb to do sth; **je lui ai fait s. de venir** I beckoned him to come over; **il fit s. de se taire** he gave a signal *or* signalled for silence, he made a shushing gesture; **s. de la main** hand signal; **faire s. à qn (de la main) de reculer/de s'écarter/de partir** to wave sb back/aside/away; **faire s. que oui** to nod (in agreement); **faire s. que non** *(de la tête)* to shake one's head; *(du doigt)* to wag one's finger
5 *Rel* **s. de (la) croix** sign of the cross; **faire le s. de la croix** *ou* **un s. de croix** to make the sign of the cross, to cross oneself

signer [siɲe] **VT 1** *(contrat, lettre, tableau etc)* to sign; *Can Sport (joueur)* to sign (up); **s. son nom** to sign one's name; **s. par procuration** to sign by proxy, to pp; *Naut* **s. l'engagement** to sign on; *Fig Fam* **c'est signé** it's easy to guess who did that; *Fig Fam* **c'est signé Paul** it has Paul written all over it, it's just like *or* typical of Paul **2** *Tech (bijoux)* to hallmark
VI to sign; **s. de son nom** to sign one's name
VPR se signer *Rel* to cross oneself

signet [siɲɛ] **NM** *aussi Ordinat* bookmark; *Ordinat* **créer un s. sur une page** to bookmark a page

signifiant [siɲifjã] **ADJ** *Litt (plein de sens)* meaningful
NM *Ling* signifier

significatif, -ive [siɲifikatif, -iv] **ADJ** significant; **s. de** indicative of

signification [siɲifikasjɔ̃] **NF 1** *(d'un mot, d'un symbole etc)* meaning, sense; *(d'un événement, d'un fait etc)* significance **2** *Jur (d'une décision)* notification; *(d'un acte judiciaire)* serving

signifié [siɲifje] **NM** *Ling* signified

signifier [siɲifje] VT (impf, pr sub n. **signifiions**, v. **signifiiez**) **1** (vouloir dire) (d'un mot) to mean; (d'une attitude) to mean, to signify; **que signifie ce mot?** what does this word mean?, what is the meaning of this word?; **s. que** (d'une action etc) to show or mean that; **cela ne signifie rien** it doesn't mean anything; **des remarques qui ne signifient rien** meaningless remarks; **qu'est-ce que cela signifie?** (indignation) what is the meaning of this?; **la moindre imprudence signifierait la mort pour eux** the slightest imprudence would mean death for them **2** (notifier) to notify (**qch à qn** sb of sth); **s. son congé à qn** (d'un propriétaire, d'un employé) to give sb notice; Jur **s. un jugement à qn** to notify sb of a decision; Fig **son visage signifiait bien sa douleur** his grief was written on his face for all to see

signofil(e) [siɲofil] NM Suisse Aut (clignotant) indicator, Am turn signal; **mettre son s. (à droite/gauche)** to indicate (to the right/left), Am to put on one's turn signal (to turn right/left)

sikh, sikhe [sik] ADJ Sikh
▶ N S. Sikh

silence [silɑ̃s] NM **1** silence; (pause) pause; **il se fit un s. subit** there was a sudden silence; **écrire à qn après un s. de deux ans** to write to sb after a silence of two years; **un s. de mort** a deathly silence or hush; **s. ému** breathless silence; **observer une minute de s.** to observe a minute's silence; **dans le s. de la nuit** in the silence or Litt still of the night; **réduire qn au s.** to reduce sb to silence, to silence sb; **rompre le s.** to break the silence; **garder** ou **observer le s.** to keep silent (**sur** about); **(du) s.!** silence!, be quiet!; **souffrir en s.** to suffer in silence; **passer qch sous s.** to keep quiet about sth, to pass over sth in silence; (par diplomatie) not to mention sth; **la loi du s.** the law of silence (preventing criminals from informing on their fellows); (dans la mafia) omerta; **préparer qch dans le s.** to prepare sth in secrecy; **faire jurer le s. à qn** to swear sb to secrecy; Aviat **cône de s.** cone of silence; Électron **zone de s.** silent zone; **s. radio** Tech radio silence; (silence total) total silence; **j'ai reçu quelques cartes postales peu après mon départ, mais depuis, c'est le s. radio** I got a few postcards shortly after I left, but since then there's been total silence or I haven't heard a word **2** Mus rest

silencieusement [silɑ̃sjøzmɑ̃] ADV silently

silencieux, -ieuse [silɑ̃sjø, -jøz] ADJ (personne, pas etc) silent; (rue, jardin etc) silent, quiet; (moteur, lave-vaisselle etc) quiet, silent; (soirée) quiet, peaceful; **après la dispute, la reste de la soirée fut s.** (plus personne ne parla) after the quarrel the rest of the evening passed in silence
▶ NM Aut silencer, Am muffler; (d'arme) silencer; Radio squelch

Silène [silɛn] N Myth Silenus

silène [silɛn] NM Bot campion

siler [sile] VI Can **1** (siffler) to whistle; Fig **j'ai les oreilles qui me silent** my ears are ringing **2** (gémir) to whine **3** (respirer avec difficulté) to wheeze

Silésie [silezi] NF Silesia

silex [silɛks] NM INV (roche) flint; **des s.** (outils, armes) flints

silhouette [silwɛt] NF (contours) silhouette, outline; (ligne générale du corps) figure; Mil (cible) figure target; **en s.** silhouetted

silhouetter [silwete] VT (dessiner) to outline; Phot to block out
▶ VPR **se silhouetter** to be silhouetted, to be outlined (**sur** against)

silicate [silikat] NM Chimie silicate

silice [silis] NF Chimie silica, silicon dioxide; **verre de s., s. fondue** silica (glass)

siliceux, -euse [silisø, -øz] ADJ siliceous

silicium [silisjɔm] NM Chimie silicon

silicone [silikɔn] NF Chimie silicone

siliconer [silikɔne] VT to coat with silicone; Hum **elle a les seins siliconés** she's got silicone implants

silicose [silikoz] NF Méd silicosis

silicosé [silikoze] ADJ Méd silicotic

silique [silik] NF Bot siliqua, silique

sillage [sijaʒ] NM (d'un navire) wake; Aviat etc slipstream; Aviat **s. aérodynamique** aerodynamic drag; Fig **marcher dans le s. de qn** to follow in sb's wake

sillon [sijɔ̃] NM **1** Agr furrow; Fig (sur le front) furrow, line; Litt **sillons** (champs) fields, country; Fig **creuser** ou **tracer son s.** to plough or Am plow one's furrow **2** (d'une roue) track; (d'un navire) wake; (d'un projectile) path; **s. de lumière/feu** (d'une fusée etc) streak of light/fire **3** (de disque) groove

sillonner [sijɔne] VT **1** (creuser) to furrow; (traverser) to cross; **la police sillonne la région** police are combing the area; **les touristes sillonnent le sud de la France** there's a non-stop flow of tourists through the south of France; **flanc de montagne sillonné par les torrents** mountainside grooved or scored by torrents; **forêt sillonnée de nombreux sentiers** forest criss-crossed by many paths; **front sillonné de rides** furrowed brow **2** (d'une lumière, de la foudre etc) (ciel) to streak

silo [silo] NM (fosse, tour) silo; **mettre en s.** to silo; **s. à blé** grain silo; **s. à ciment** cement silo; Mil **s. (de lancement)** (launching) silo

silotage [silɔtaʒ] NM Agr etc (action) ensilage

silure [silyr] NM (poisson) silurid

silurien, -ienne [silyrjɛ̃, -jɛn] Géol ADJ Silurian
▶ NM Silurian; **s. inférieur** Ordovician

SIM [sim] NM (abrév **système d'information marketing**) MIS

simagrées [simagre] NFPL airs and graces, affectation; **ne fais pas tant de s.** don't make so much fuss

simien, -ienne [simjɛ̃, -jɛn] Zool ADJ simian
▶ NMPL **simiens** simians, Spéc Simiidae

simiesque [simjɛsk] ADJ (visage, grimace etc) monkey-like, ape-like, Spéc, Litt simian

similaire [similɛr] ADJ similar (**à** to), of the same kind

similairement [similɛrmɑ̃] ADV similarly

similarité [similarite] NF similarity

simili [simili] PRÉF imitation, artificial
▶ NM Fam Vieilli imitation; Phot half-tone; **bijoux en s.** imitation or costume jewellery
▶ NF Fam = **similigravure**

similicuir [similikɥir] NM imitation leather, leatherette

similigravure [similigravyr] NF half-tone engraving

similitude [similityd] NF similarity

simoniaque [simɔnjak] Rel ADJ simoniacal
▶ NM simoniac, simonist

simonie [simɔni] NF Rel simony

simoun [simun] NM Météo simoom, simoon

simple [sɛ̃pl] ADJ SEE GRAMMAR B10–11 **1** (direct) (personne) simple, unaffected; (tenue, nourriture, cérémonie etc) simple; **réduit à sa plus s. expression** reduced to its simplest form; **dans le plus s. appareil** (nu) in the altogether, in one's birthday suit
 2 (facile) (calcul, méthode etc) simple, easy, straightforward; **c'est bien s., il accepte ou**

on part it's quite simple, either he accepts or we go; **c'est simple comme bonjour** it's as easy as pie or as falling off a log
 3 (crédule) simple; **s. d'esprit** simple-minded
 4 (pur) condamner qn sur un s. soupçon to condemn sb on a mere suspicion; **c'est une s. question de temps** it is simply a matter of time; **c'est de la folie pure et s.** it's sheer madness; **c'est la vérité pure et s.** it's the pure and simple truth; **croire qn sur sa s. parole** to believe sb on his/her word alone; **la s. prudence veut que …** ordinary or elementary prudence demands that …
 5 (commun) ordinary; **un s. particulier** an ordinary citizen; **s. soldat** private (soldier); **s. matelot** ordinary seaman; **je ne suis qu'une s. secrétaire** I'm merely a secretary, I'm just a or a mere secretary; **une s. enveloppe ira parfaitement** an ordinary or a plain envelope will do perfectly
 6 (non multiple) (fleur, nœud etc) single; **un cornet s. ou double?** (de glace) one scoop or two?; **un aller s.** a single, Am a one-way ticket; Ordinat **s. densité** single density
 7 (non composé), Courses de chevaux **faire un pari s.** to back a horse to win; Gram **passé s.** past historic (tense), simple past; Gram **les temps simples d'un verbe** the simple tenses of a verb SEE GRAMMAR B30; Chimie **corps s.** simple body; Math **équation s.** simple equation
▶ NM **1** Tennis **jouer un s.** to play a singles (match); **s. messieurs/dames** men's/ladies' singles **2** **varier du s. au double** to vary by twice as much **3** **un s. d'esprit** a simpleton, a simple-minded person
▶ NMPL Bot **simples** medicinal herbs

simplement [sɛ̃pləmɑ̃] ADV **1** (vivre) simply; habillé **s.** simply or plainly dressed; **elle se maquille s.** she doesn't wear much make-up **2** (avec naturel) simply, naturally, unaffectedly; **le plus s. du monde** without any fuss; **il faut prendre les choses s.** you have to take things as they come **3** (uniquement) simply, just, merely; **purement et s.** purely and simply; **je voulais s. te dire que …** I simply or just or merely wanted to tell you that …

simplet, -ette [sɛ̃plɛ, -ɛt] ADJ (personne) simple; (idée, théorie, livre etc) simplistic

simplex [sɛ̃plɛks] NM Ordinat simplex

simplicité [sɛ̃plisite] NF **1** (d'une tenue, des manières etc) simplicity; **elle manque de s.** she is pretentious or affected; **la s. de ses manières** his/her lack of affectation, his/her unaffected ways; **elle l'a avoué en toute s.** she admitted it without making a big thing of it; **nous ferons un repas en toute s.** we'll have a very simple meal; **ils se sont mariés en toute s.** they had a very quiet wedding; **venez en toute s.** come as you are; (pour manger) come and take pot luck; **vivre avec s.** to live simply **2** Phys (des atomes etc) elementary nature **3** (facilité) simplicity; **c'est d'une s. enfantine** it's child's play, a child could do it

simplifiable [sɛ̃plifjabl] ADJ that can be simplified, capable of simplification; Math (fraction) reducible

simplificateur, -trice [sɛ̃plifikatœr, -tris] ADJ (méthode etc) simplifying

simplification [sɛ̃plifikasjɔ̃] NF simplification; Math simplification, reduction

simplifier [sɛ̃plifje] VT (impf, pr sub n. **simplifiions**, v. **simplifiiez**) VT to simplify; Math (fraction) to simplify, to reduce; **cela me simplifie la vie** that simplifies my life, that makes life or things easier for me; **trop s.** to oversimplify
▶ VPR **se simplifier** to become simpler, to become simplified

simplisme [sɛ̃plism] NM simplism

simpliste [sɛ̃plist] *Péj* **ADJ** *(théorie, explication etc)* simplistic; *(esprit)* simplistic, superficial

N simplistic person

simulacre [simylakr] **NM** semblance, show, pretence, *Am* pretense; **s. de résistance** semblance *or* show of resistance; *Mil* **s. de combat** sham fight; **s. de justice** travesty of justice; **son procès ne fut qu'un s.** his/her trial was a travesty of justice *or* a mere mockery

simulateur, -trice [simylatœr, -tris] **N** pretender; *Méd* malingerer; **c'est un habile s.** he's good at pretending *or Fam* faking

NM *Tech* simulator; *Ordinat* **s. de réalité virtuelle** virtual reality simulator; *Aviat* **s. de vol** flight simulator

simulation [simylasjɔ̃] **NF 1** *(action)* simulation, feigning; *Méd* malingering **2** *Aviat, Électron, Ordinat etc* simulation; *Compta (prévision)* forecast; **formation en s. de vol** simulated flight training; **s. par ordinateur** computer simulation

simulé [simyle] **ADJ** *(maladie)* feigned, simulated; *(combat)* sham; *(sentiment, colère, sérieux etc)* feigned, sham, bogus, simulated; *(vente)* bogus; *Tech (situation, conditions etc)* simulated

simuler [simyle] **VT** *(sentiment, colère etc)* to feign, to simulate, to sham; *Tech (situation, conditions, vol etc)* to simulate; **s. une maladie** to pretend to be ill, to feign (an) illness, to malinger; **s. la folie** to pretend to be mad, to feign madness; **la porte simule un rideau** the door is made to look like a curtain

simultané [simyltane] **ADJ** simultaneous

simultanéité [simyltaneite] **NF** simultaneousness, simultaneity

simultanément [simyltanemã] **ADV** simultaneously

Sinaï [sinai] **NM** Sinai; **le mont S.** Mount Sinai

sinapisé [sinapize] **ADJ** **bain/cataplasme s.** mustard bath/poultice *or* plaster

sinapisme [sinapism] **NM** *Méd* mustard poultice *or* plaster, *Spéc* sinapism

sincère [sɛ̃sɛr] **ADJ 1** *(franc) (personne)* sincere, genuine; *(opinion)* honest, candid; **être s. avec soi-même** to be honest with oneself **2** *(véritable) (joie, amour, effort etc)* genuine, sincere; **ses paroles étaient sincères** he was being sincere, he meant it; **vœux/remerciements sincères** sincere *or* heartfelt wishes/thanks; **agréez mes sincères salutations** yours sincerely **3** *(authentique) (document etc)* genuine, authentic

sincèrement [sɛ̃sɛrmã] **ADV 1** *(franchement)* sincerely, frankly; **s., je ne crois pas que ce soit une bonne idée** frankly, I don't think it's a good idea **2** *(vraiment) (heureux etc)* genuinely, sincerely

sincérité [sɛ̃serite] **NF 1** *(franchise)* sincerity, frankness; **en toute s.** in all sincerity **2** *(des regrets, de l'amour etc)* sincerity, genuineness; **je ne mets pas en doute la s. de vos paroles** I'm not questioning your sincerity

sinécure [sinekyr] **NF** sinecure; *Fam* **ce n'est pas une s.** it's not exactly a rest cure

sine die [sinedje] **ADV** indefinitely, sine die

sine qua non [sinekwanɔn] **ADJ** *Phil* **condition s.** sine qua non; **c'est la condition s. pour avoir un emploi bien rémunéré** it's essential in order to get a well-paid job, it's a prerequisite for a well-paid job

Singapour [sɛ̃gapur] **NM** Singapore

singapourien, -ienne [sɛ̃gapurjɛ̃, -jen] **ADJ** Singaporean

N S. Singaporean

singe [sɛ̃ʒ] **NM 1** *(animal)* monkey; *Fam (imitateur)* mimic; **grand s.** ape; *Fam* **c'est un s., il est laid comme un s.** he's as ugly as sin; **faire**

le s. to clown around; **malin/adroit comme un s.** as crafty/clever as a monkey; **payer qn en monnaie de s.** *(en fausse monnaie)* to pay sb with counterfeit money; *(ne pas payer qn)* to make false promises to pay sb; *Prov* **on n'apprend pas à un vieux s. à faire des grimaces** don't teach your grandmother to suck eggs **2** *Culin Arg* **du s.** corned beef **3** *Arg* **le s.** *(patron)* the boss **4** *Ordinat* monkey

singer [sɛ̃ʒe] **VT** *(je singeai(s); n. singeons)* *(quelqu'un)* to ape, to mimic, *Fam* to take off; *(sentiment)* to feign, *Fam* to fake

singerie [sɛ̃ʒri] **NF 1** singeries *(grimaces, gestes)* antics; **il fait tout le temps des singeries** he's always clowning aound **2** *(imitation)* (grotesque) imitation **3** *(cage)* monkey *or* ape house

single [siŋɡəl] **NM 1** *Tennis* singles (game) **2** *Rail* single-berth compartment **3** *(dans un hôtel)* single room

singulariser [sɛ̃gylarize] **VT s. qn** to set sb apart, to make sb stand out (**de** from)

VPR se singulariser to attract attention, to make oneself conspicuous; **il se singularise par sa curiosité** his curiosity sets him apart from the others *or* makes him stand out

singularité [sɛ̃gylarite] **NF 1** *(particularité)* peculiarity; **cette maison a la s. d'être solaire** the house is unusual in that it is solar-heated **2** *(caractère étrange)* strangeness, oddness, peculiarity; **c'est une des singularités de son caractère** it's one of the strange *or* odd things about him; **esprit de s.** desire to be different

singulier, -ière [sɛ̃gylje, -jer] **ADJ 1** *Gram* singular **2** **combat s.** single combat **3** *(remarquable)* remarkable, *Fml* singular; *(étrange)* strange, odd, peculiar, *Fml* singular; **il est s. qu'il ne soit pas encore arrivé** it is strange *or* odd *or* peculiar that he has not arrived yet

NM *Gram* singular; **au s.** in the singular VOIR GRAMMAIRE A14-15

singulièrement [sɛ̃gyljermã] **ADV 1** *(étrangement)* oddly, strangely, *Fml* singularly **2** *(en particulier)* especially, particularly **3** *(très beaucoup)* remarkably, extremely, *Fml* singularly

sinistre [sinistr] **ADJ 1** *(effrayant) (lieu, atmosphère, personne, expression)* sinister; **c'est s. ici!** it's spooky here! **2** *(déprimant) (paysage)* bleak; *(soirée, repas)* dismal, grim; **on a passé un jour de l'an s.** we spent a dismal *or* a miserable New Year's Day **3** *(emploi intensif)* awful, terrible; **un s. menteur** an awful *or* a terrible liar

NM *(catastrophe)* disaster, catastrophe; *Jur (dommage) (après des dégâts)* damage; *(réclamation)* claim; **bonification pour non-s.** no-claims bonus

sinistré, -ée [sinistre] **ADJ** **population sinistrée** stricken population; **bâtiment s.** damaged building; **région** *ou* **zone sinistrée** disaster area

N disaster victim

sinistrement [sinistrəmã] **ADV** sinisterly

sinistrose [sinistroz] **NF** *Psy* post-traumatic stress disorder; *Fam (mélancolie)* pessimism, gloom; *Fam* **atteint de s.** gloomy, depressed; *Fam* **la s. progresse dans les milieux bourgeois** the middle classes are becoming increasingly pessimistic *or* gloomy

sino- [sino] **PRÉF** Sino-; **s.-japonais** Sino-Japanese

sinologue [sinolɔg] **N** sinologist, sinologue

sinon [sinɔ̃] **CONJ 1** *(autrement)* otherwise, or else; **donne-moi la clef, s. je me fâche** give me the key otherwise *or* or (else) I'll get angry; **un jus d'orange, s. rien** an orange juice,

otherwise nothing, an orange juice or, failing that, nothing **2** *(excepté)* except, but; **il ne fait rien s. manger et boire** he does nothing except *or* but eat and drink; *Vieilli* **s. que** except that **3** *(si ce n'est)* if not; **c'est un des meilleurs, s. le meilleur** it's one of the best, if not the best

sinoque [sinɔk] **ADJ** *Arg (fou)* crackers, crazy

sinuer [sinɥe] **VI** *Litt* to wind, to meander

sinueux, -euse [sinɥø, -øz] **ADJ** *(ligne)* sinuous; *(chemin, courant etc)* winding, meandering; *Fig (raisonnement)* tortuous

sinuosité [sinɥozite] **NF** *(d'un chemin, d'une rivière etc)* bend, curve; *Fig (d'un raisonnement)* tortuousness

sinus ¹ [sinys] **NM** *Anat* sinus

sinus ² **NM** *Math* sine

sinusite [sinyzit] **NF** *Méd* sinusitis; **avoir de la s.** to have sinusitis

sinusoïdal, -ale, -aux, -ales [sinyzɔidal, -o] **ADJ** *Math* sinusoidal

sinusoïde [sinyzɔid] **NF** *Math* sinusoid, sine curve

Sion [sjɔ̃] **N** Zion

sionisme [sjɔnism] **NM** Zionism

sioniste [sjɔnist] **ADJ, N** Zionist

sioux [sju] **ADJ INV** Sioux

N INV S. Sioux; *Fig* **ruses de S.** crafty *or* cunning tricks

siphon [sifɔ̃] **NM 1** *Phys etc (tube)* siphon **2** *(bouteille)* (soda) siphon **3** *Constr etc (d'un évier, d'une canalisation etc)* U-bend, trap **4** *Géol* siphon **5** *Zool* siphon

siphonné [sifɔne] **ADJ** *Fam (fou)* crackers, crazy

siphonner [sifɔne] **VT** to siphon

sire [sir] **NM 1** sir; **beau s.** fair sir; *Péj* **un triste s.** an unsavoury character **2 S.** *(à un souverain)* Sire

sirène [siren] **NF 1** *Myth* siren, mermaid; *Fig (femme)* siren; **chant de s.** siren song **2** *(appareil)* siren; *(d'usine)* hooter, siren; *(de brume)* foghorn; **s. d'alarme** fire alarm; *(en temps de guerre)* air-raid siren

SIRET [siret] **NM N° S.** company registration number

siroc(c)o [sirɔko] **NM** *(vent)* sirocco

sirop [siro] **NM** syrup, (fruit) cordial; *Pharm* syrup; **s. d'érable** maple syrup; **s. de fraise** ≃ strawberry cordial; **s. de menthe** ≃ mint cordial; **s. d'orgeat** barley water; **s. de sucre** golden syrup; **s. contre la toux** cough mixture *or* syrup

siroter [sirɔte] **VT** *Fam (vin, café etc)* to sip

sirupeux, -euse [sirypø, -øz] **ADJ** *(liquide)*, *Péj (musique, ton)* syrupy

sis [si] **ADJ** *Jur, Litt* situated, located; **maison sise rue Saint-Honoré** house situated *or* located in the rue Saint-Honoré

sisal [sizal] **NM** *Bot* sisal

sismal, -ale, -aux, -ales [sismal, -o] **ADJ** **ligne sismale** line of an *or* the earthquake

sismicité [sismisite] **NF** seismicity

sismique [sismik] **ADJ** seismic

sismogramme [sismogram] **NM** seismogram

sismographe [sismograf] **NM** seismograph

sismographie [sismografi] **NF** seismography

sismologie [sismɔlɔʒi] **NF** seismology

sismomètre [sismɔmetr] **NM** seismometer

Sisyphe [sizif] **N** Sisyphus; **le rocher de S.** the rock of Sisyphus

Sit [sit] **NM** *(abrév* **système interbancaire de télépaiement)** *Br* ≃ CHAPS, *Am* ≃ CHIPS

sitar [sitar] **NM** *Mus* sitar

sitcom [sitkɔm] NM OU F TVsitcom, situation comedy

site [sit] NM **1** (pittoresque) beauty spot; **s. (touristique)** (monument etc) place of interest, tourist attraction; **s. classé** conservation area; **s. historique** historic site **2** Archéol, Ind (lieu) site; Mktg **s.-témoin** test site **3** (configuration d'un lieu) setting, site; **s. d'enfouissement des déchets nucléaires** nuclear dump **4** Mil etc **ligne de s.** line of sight **5** Ordinat **s. Web** ou **Internet** Web site, Internet site; **s. de bavardage** chat room; **s. marchand** e-commerce site

sit-in [sitin] NM INV sit-in; **faire un s.** to have or hold a sit-in

sitôt [sito] ADV **1** (aussitôt) **s. le soleil couché** (dans le présent ou le futur) as soon as the sun sets; (dans le passé) as soon as the sun had set; **s. dit s. fait** no sooner said than done; **s. que** + ind as soon as; **s. après** immediately after **2** (with nég) **vous ne la reverrez pas de s.** it will be some time or a good while before you see her again; **je ne reviendrai pas ici de s.** I won't come back here in a hurry

sittelle [sitɛl] NF (oiseau) nuthatch

situation [situasjɔ̃] NF **1** (emplacement) (d'une ville, d'un bâtiment etc) situation, position, location; Naut bearing; **l'hôtel jouit d'une excellente s.** the hotel is excellently situated

2 (circonstances) situation; **s. du marché** market situation; **quelle est votre s. de famille?** what is your marital status?; **quelle est votre s. financière?** what is your financial situation or position or status?; **je lui ai exposé ma s.** I explained my situation or position to him; **être en s. de faire qch** to be in a position to do sth; **se trouver devant une s. de fait** to be faced with a fait accompli; Fam **elle est dans une s. intéressante** (enceinte) she's in the family way, Vieilli Euph she's in an interesting condition; **l'homme de la s.** the right man for the job; **mettre qn en s.** to give sb experience of a real-life situation; Compta **s. nette** net worth; **s. de la banque** bank balance; **s. de caisse** cash position or balance; **s. de compte** account position or balance

3 Admin, Mil etc report, return

4 (emploi) job, position; **il a une belle s.** he has a good position; **se faire une belle s.** to work one's way up into a good position; Journ **situations vacantes** (job) vacancies, Br situations vacant

situé [situe] ADJ situated, located; **bien/mal s.** well/badly situated or located

situer [situe] VT (maison etc) to situate, to locate; Fig (qch dans son contexte) to place; Fam **s. qn** to size sb up; **je situerais plutôt ce groupe dans le courant be-bop** I would describe the band as being more be-bop
VPR se situer to stand; **je ne sais pas comment il se situe sur ce point** I don't know where he stands on this point; Théâtre etc **l'action se situe à Rome en 1516** the action takes place in Rome in 1516; Pol **se s. à droite** to be on the right, to be right-wing; **elle se situe plutôt à droite** she's rather to the right

six (before noun beginning with consonant [si]; before noun beginning with vowel sound [siz]; otherwise [sis]) ADJ INV six; Aut **une s. chevaux** a six-horsepower car; **les s. jours** (course cycliste) = six-day cycle race **2** (dans des séries) sixth; **page/numéro s.** page/number six; **Charles S.** Charles the Sixth
NM INV six; **le s. mai** (on) the sixth of May, (on) May the sixth, Am (on) May sixth; Cartes **le s. de cœur** the six of hearts; **habiter au s.** to live at number six

sixain [sizɛ̃] NM = sizain

six-huit [sisɥit] NM INV Mus six-eight time

sixième [sizjɛm] ADJ NUM sixth; **au s. étage** on the sixth or Am seventh floor
N (personne, objet, événement etc) sixth (one); **habiter au s.** to live on the sixth or Am seventh floor; Sport etc **arriver le/la s.** to come (in) sixth
NM sixth (part); **cinq sixièmes** five sixths
NF Scol (enseignement secondaire) Br ≃ first year of secondary school, Am ≃ sixth grade

sixièmement [sizjɛmmɑ̃] ADV in the sixth place, sixthly

six-quatre-deux (à la) [alasiskatdø] ADV Fam Vieilli **faire qch à la s.** to do sth in a slapdash manner

sixte [sikst] NF **1** Mus sixth **2** Escrime sixte

Sixtine [sikstin] ADJ F **la chapelle S.** the Sistine Chapel

sizain [sizɛ̃] NM **1** Littér six-line stanza **2** Cartes set of six packs or Am decks of playing cards

Skaï® [skaj] NM leatherette, imitation leather

skate(-board), pl **skate-boards, skates** [skɛtbɔrd] NM skateboard; **faire du s.(-b.)** to skateboard, to go skateboarding

sketch, pl **sketches** [skɛtʃ] NM Théâtre sketch

ski [ski] NM **1** (planche) ski; **descendre à** ou **en skis** to ski down; **skis de fond** cross-country skis; **skis paraboliques** parabolic skis, carving skis **2** (activité) skiing; **s. alpin** downhill (skiing); **s. de piste** on-piste skiing; **s. de fond, s. de randonnée** cross-country (skiing), langlauf; **faire du s.** to ski; Fam **aller au s.** to go skiing; **chaussures de s.** ski boots; **station de s.** ski resort; **vacances de s.** skiing holiday **3** **s. nautique** water-skiing; **faire du s. nautique** to water-ski

skiable [skjabl] ADJ skiable, fit for skiing

ski-bob, pl **ski-bobs** [skibɔb] NM skibob

skier [skje] VI to ski

skieur, -euse [skjœr, -øz] N skier; **s. nautique** water-skier; **s. de fond** cross-country or langlauf skier; Mil **éclaireurs skieurs** ski troops

skif(f) [skif] NM Naut skiff

skin(head) [skin(ɛd)] NM skin(head)

skip [skip] NM Ind skip

skippé [skipe] ADJ Naut **s. par** skippered by

skipper [skipœr] NM Naut (barreur) skipper

slacker [slake] VI Can (relâcher) to ease up; **s. d'une coche** to ease up a bit

slalom [slalɔm] NM Ski slalom; **descente en s.** slalom descent; **s. géant** giant slalom; **s. spécial** special slalom; Fig **faire du s. entre les voitures** to dodge in and out among the cars

slalomer [slalɔme] VI Ski to slalom; Fig to dodge in and out

slalomeur, -euse [slalɔmœr, -øz] N Ski slalom skier

slave [slav] ADJ Slav(onic)
NM Ling Slavonic
N S. Slav

slavisant, -ante [slavizɑ̃, -ɑ̃t], **slaviste** [slavist] N Slavist

sleeping [slipiŋ] NM Rail Fam Vieilli (wagon) sleeping car; (couchette) berth

slibar(d) [slibar] NM très Fam underpants

slip [slip] NM **1** (d'homme) briefs, underpants; (de femme) briefs, panties, pants; **s. de bain** (d'homme) swimming trunks; (de femme) bikini bottoms; **s. kangourou** Y-fronts; **s. de soutien (pour sportifs)** athletic support, Fam jockstrap VOIR GRAMMAIRE A10 **2** Naut slipway

Il faut noter que le terme anglais **slip** est un faux ami; il ne signifie jamais **culotte**.

sloche [slɔʃ] NF Can slush

slogan [slɔgɑ̃] NM Com, Pol slogan; **s. publicitaire** advertising slogan

sloop [slup] NM Naut sloop; **s. à tape-cul** yawl

sloughi [slugi] NM (chien) Saluki

slovaque [slɔvak] ADJ Slovak
NM Ling Slovak
N S. Slovak

Slovaquie [slɔvaki] NF Slovakia

slovène [slɔvɛn] ADJ Slovene, Slovenian
NM Ling Slovene, Slovenian
N S. Slovene, Slovenian

Slovénie [slɔveni] NF Slovenia

slow [slo] NM (danse, musique) slow dance; **danser un s.** to have a slow dance

SM¹ [ɛsɛm] (abrév **Sa Majesté**) HM

SM² NM (abrév **sadomasochisme**) S & M

smala(h) [smala] NF (de chef arabe) retinue; Fam (famille etc) tribe; Fam **toute la s.** the whole tribe

smart [smart] ADJ INV Fam Vieilli (élégant) smart

smash [smaʃ] NM Tennis etc smash; **faire un s.** to smash the ball

smasher [smaʃe] Tennis VT (balle) to smash
VI to smash (the ball)

SME [ɛsɛmə] NM UE (abrév **Système monétaire européen**) EMS

smectique [smɛktik] ADJ **argile s.** fuller's earth

SMIC [smik] NM (abrév **salaire minimum interprofessionnel de croissance**) = guaranteed minimum wage

smicard, -arde [smikar, -ard] N Fam worker on minimum wage, minimum wage earner

smocks [smɔk] NMPL Couture smocking

smog [smɔg] NM smog

smoking [smɔkiŋ] NM (veston) dinner jacket, Am tuxedo, Fam tux; (costume) dinner or evening suit

SMS [ɛsɛmɛs] NM (abrév **short message service**) SMS

smurf [smœrf] NM break dance; **danser le s.** to break-dance

snack(-bar), pl **snack-bars, snacks** [snak(-bar)] NM Fam snack bar

SNC [ɛsɛnse] NF (abrév **société en nom collectif**) commercial/industrial partnership

SNCB [ɛsɛnsebe] NF Belg (abrév **Société nationale des chemins de fer belges**) = Belgian national railway company

SNCF [ɛsɛnseɛf] NF (abrév **Société nationale des chemins de fer français**) = French national railway company

snif [snif] INT Fam sniff; **s., s. il me l'a pris!** boo-hoo, he's taken it from me!

sniffer [snife] VT Arg (colle, cocaïne) to sniff

snob [snob] N snob
ADJ (inv in f sing) (personne, restaurant etc) snobbish, snobby; **elle est un peu s.** she's a bit of a snob

snober [snobe] VT (mépriser) to look down on; (éviter) to snub

snobinard, -arde [snobinar, -ard] Fam Péj ADJ stuck-up, snobbish
N stuck-up or snobbish type

snobisme [snobism] NM snobbery, snobbishness; **s. à rebours** inverted snobbery

snowboard [snobɔrd] NM (sport) snowboarding; (planche) snowboard

snow-boot, pl **snow-boots** [snobut] NM snow boot

sobre [sɔbr] ADJ **1** (personne) (qui n'a pas bu) sober; (qui boit ou mange peu) abstemious; (repas, vie) simple; **s. comme un chameau** as sober as a judge **2** (de paroles/louanges) sparing in one's words/praise **3** *(style, lignes, dessin)* sober, restrained

sobrement [sɔbrəmã] ADV **1** *(manger, boire)* in moderation **2** *(s'exprimer)* soberly **3** *(s'habiller etc)* soberly

sobriété [sɔbrijete] NF **1** *(concernant l'alimentation, la boisson)* temperance, sobriety; **manger et boire avec s.** to eat and drink in moderation **2** *(des paroles)* soberness; **s'exprimer avec s.** to speak soberly **3** *(du style)* soberness, sobriety, restraint; *(des lignes)* soberness

sobriquet [sɔbrikɛ] NM nickname

soc [sɔk] NM ploughshare, *Am* plowshare

sociabilité [sɔsjabilite] NF sociability

sociable [sɔsjabl] ADJ sociable; **peu s.** unsociable

social, -ale, -aux, -ales [sɔsjal, -o] ADJ **1** social; **aide sociale** social welfare; *Zool* **animal s.** social animal; **l'homme est un animal s.** man is a social animal; **assistant s.** social worker; **conflit s.** industrial dispute; **couche sociale** social stratum; **l'échelle sociale** the social ladder; **guerre sociale** class war; **œuvres sociales** welfare activities; **l'ordre s.** the social order; **politique sociale** social policy; **réforme sociale** social reform; **science sociale** social science; **vie sociale** social life **2** *Com* **nom s., raison sociale** company name; **capital s.** share capital
▪ NM *Pol* social questions; *Fam* **faire du s.** to do one's good turn for the day

social-chrétien, *pl* **sociaux-chrétiens** ADJ, N *Belg Pol* Christian Socialist

social-démocrate, *pl* **sociaux-démocrates** ADJ, N *Pol* social democrat

social-démocratie, *pl* **social-démocraties** NF *Pol* social democracy

socialement [sɔsjalmã] ADV socially

socialisant, -ante [sɔsjalizã, -ãt] *Pol* ADJ with socialist sympathies *or* tendencies ▪ N socialist sympathizer

socialisation [sɔsjalizasjɔ̃] NF **1** *Écon (du capital, des industries)* socialization, collectivization **2** *(de personne)* socialization

socialiser [sɔsjalize] VT **1** *Écon (biens etc)* to socialize, to collectivize **2** *(personne)* to socialize

socialisme [sɔsjalism] NM socialism; **s. chrétien** Christian socialism; **s. d'État** State socialism

socialiste [sɔsjalist] ADJ, N socialist

socialo [sɔsjalo] ADJ, N *Fam* socialist

social-révolutionnaire, *pl* **sociaux-révolutionnaires** ADJ, N social-revolutionary

sociétaire [sɔsjetɛr] N **1** *(membre)* member **2** *(actionnaire)* Br shareholder, *Am* stockholder

SOCIÉTÉ [sɔsjete]

society **1, 2, 5** ▪ association **2** ▪ company **3, 4** ▪ companionship **4**

NF **1** *(communauté)* society; **dans notre s.** in our society; **ça ne se fait pas dans la bonne s.** that is not done in polite society; **devoirs envers la s.** civic duty; **valeurs de la s.** social values; **vie en s.** life in society; **animaux qui vivent en s.** social animals; **problème de s.** social problem

2 *(association)* society, association; *Sport* club; **s. de secours aux blessés** first-aid association; **s. secrète** secret society

3 *Com, Ind* company, firm; **se monter en s.** to set up in business; **la S. Martin** Martin's

4 *(compagnie)* company, companionship, *Fml* society; **il aime la s.** he likes company; **la s. des personnes de son âge** the company *or Fml* society of people his/her own age

5 *(beau monde) (à la mode)* society; **la**

haute **s.** high society; **femmes de s.** society women; **faire ses débuts dans la s.** to make one's debut in society

6 jeux de s. board games, *Vieilli* parlour *or Am* parlor games

▸▸**s. d'abondance** affluent society; **s. par actions** joint-stock *or Am* incorporated company; **s. d'affacturage** factoring company; **s. affiliée** affiliated company; **s. anonyme** public limited company, *Am* corporation; **s. d'assurance** insurance company; **s. d'autoroutes** private company which maintains motorways; **s. de Bourse** stockbroker, stockbroking firm; **s. de capital-risque** venture capital company; **s. civile** non-trading company; **s. en commandite** limited partnership; **s. en commandite par actions** partnership limited by shares; **s. en commandite simple** limited partnership; **s. de commerce international** international trading corporation; **s. commerciale** business firm; **s. commune** joint venture; **s. de conseil en investissement** investment consultancy; **s. de conseil en mercatique** marketing consultancy (firm); **s. de consommation** consumer society; **s. de crédit immobilier** *Br* ≃ building society, *Am* ≃ savings and loan company; **s. de crédit mutuel** friendly society; **s. d'économie mixte** semi-public company; **s. d'édition** publishing company *or* firm; **s. d'entrepôts** warehousing company; **s. d'épargne** savings society; **s. d'État** state-owned *or* public company; **s. d'études** research company *or* firm; **s. d'études de marché** market research company *or* firm; **s. d'études mercatiques** marketing research company *or* firm; **s. d'exploitation en commun** joint venture; **s. d'exportation** export company *or* house; **s. fictive** dummy company; **s. fiduciaire** trust company; **s. financière** finance company; **s. de gestion** holding company; **s. immobilière** real-estate company; **s. de location** rental firm; **s. de location de voitures** car hire company; **s. de mercatique** marketing company *or* firm; **s. mère** parent company; **s. multinationale** multinational company *or* corporation, multinational; **s. nationale** state-owned *or* public company; *Hist* **la S. des Nations** the League of Nations; **s. de négoce** trading company; **s. en nom collectif** ≃ general partnership, commercial/industrial partnership; **s. de panels** = market research company specializing in consumer panels; **s. en participation** joint venture; **s. de personnes** partnership; **s. de placement** investment trust; **s. de portage** export management company; **s. à portefeuille** holding company; **s. de prévisions** forecasting firm; **s. de prévoyance** provident society; **s. privée** private company; *TV, Cin* **s. de production** production company; **S. protectrice des animaux** *Br* ≃ RSPCA, *Am* ≃ ASPCA; **s. de radiodiffusion** broadcasting company; **s. à responsabilité limitée** ≃ limited (liability) company; **s. de services** service business; **s. sœur** sister company; *Ordinat* **s. spécialisée dans l'hébergement** host company; **s. de télédiffusion** broadcasting company; **s. de transport** transport company; **s. d'utilité publique** public utility company, *Am* utility; **s. de vente par correspondance** mail order company *or* firm

société-écran, *pl* **sociétés-écrans** NF shield company

socio [sɔsjo] NF *Fam* = **sociologie**

socio- [sɔsjo] PRÉF socio-

socioculturel, -elle [sɔsjokyltyrɛl] ADJ sociocultural; **centre s.** social and cultural centre

sociodrame [sɔsjodram] NM *Psy* sociodrama

socio-économique, *pl* **socio-économiques** ADJ socio-economic

socio-éducatif, -ive, *pl* **socio-éducatifs, socio-éducatives** ADJ socioeducational

sociogramme [sɔsjogram] NM *Psy* sociogram

sociolinguistique [sɔsjolɛ̃gɥistik] ADJ sociolinguistic ▪ NF sociolinguistics

sociologie [sɔsjolɔʒi] NF sociology

sociologique [sɔsjolɔʒik] ADJ sociological

sociologiquement [sɔsjolɔʒikmã] ADV sociologically

sociologue [sɔsjolɔg] N sociologist

socioprofessionnel, -elle [sɔsjoprɔfesjonɛl] ADJ socio-professional

socio-style, *pl* **socio-styles** NM *Mktg* lifestyle

socle [sɔkl] NM **1** *(pour une statue, une colonne)* base, pedestal; *(pour un vase, une horloge)* base; *(pour un appareil)* stand; *(pour un mât etc)* base, socket; *(pour un moteur)* bed plate; *Ordinat* **s. orientable** *ou* **pivotant** *(d'un moniteur)* swivel base **2** *Géol* insular shelf **3** *Constr* **s. de lambris** skirting board, *Am* baseboard **4** *Ordinat* **s. d'extension** expansion socket

socque [sɔk] NM *(sabot)* clog; *Théâtre, Antiq* sock

socquette [sɔkɛt] NF ankle sock, *Am* bobby sock

Socrate [sɔkrat] N Socrates

socratique [sɔkratik] ADJ Socratic

soda [sɔda] NM fizzy drink, *Am* soda (pop); **s. à l'orange** orangeade; **whisky s.** whisky and soda

sodique [sɔdik] ADJ *Chimie* sodic

sodium [sɔdjɔm] NM *Chimie* sodium

Sodome [sɔdom] N Sodom

sodomie [sɔdomi] NF sodomy, buggery

sodomiser [sɔdomize] VT to sodomize, to bugger

sodomite [sɔdomit] NM sodomite

sœur [sœr] NF **1** sister; **ma s. cadette/aînée** my younger/older sister; **s. jumelle** twin sister; *Litt* **sœurs d'infortune** sisters in misfortune; *Fam* **et ta s.!** get lost!, mind your own business!; *Fig* **ces deux théories sont sœurs** these two theories go hand in hand; *Fig* **rencontrer l'âme s.** to find a soul mate **2** *Rel* sister, nun; **entrez, ma s.** come in, sister; **bonne s.** nun; **S. Thérèse** Sister Theresa
▸▸**s. de lait** foster sister

sœurette [sœrɛt] NF *Fam* little sister

sofa [sɔfa] NM sofa, settee

soffite [sɔfit] NM *Archit* soffit

SOFI [sɔfi] NM *(abrév* **système d'ordinateurs pour le fret international**) = computerized system for international freight

Sofia [sɔfja] N Sofia

SOFININDEX [sɔfinɛ̃dɛks] *(abrév* **Société pour le financement des industries exportatrices**) = independent agency providing funding for export industries

SOFRES [sɔfrɛs] NF *(abrév* **Société française d'enquêtes et de sondages**) *Br* ≃ MORI

soft [sɔft] ADJ **1** *Fam (édulcoré) (débat, discussion)* soft **2** *Fam (film, roman)* softporn ▪ NM **1** *Ordinat* software **2** *Fam (genre cinématographique)* soft porn

software [sɔftwɛr] NM *Ordinat* software

soi [swa] PRON PERS *(stressed referring to an indef subject)* **1** *(réflexif ou exprimant la réciprocité) (personne)* oneself, one; *(referring to 'il', 'elle')* himself/herself/itself; **malgré s.** in spite of oneself; **parler de s.** to talk about oneself; **conscience de s.** awareness of self, self-awareness; **confiance en s.** self-confidence; **avoir confiance en s.** to be self-confident; **être sûr de s.** to be sure of oneself; **content/fier de s.** pleased with/proud of oneself; **avoir de l'argent/ses papiers sur s.** to have some money/one's papers on one; **prendre sur s.** to exercise self-control; **prendre qch sur s.** to take sth upon oneself; **chacun pour s.** every man for himself; **chez s.** at home; **rentrer chez s.** to go home; **avoir la loi pour s.** to have the law on one's side; **il n'est plus maître de s.** he is no longer in control of himself; **quand on marche, il faut regarder devant s.** you must keep looking in front of you when you walk; **petits services qu'on se rend entre s.** small mutual favours

2 (emphatic) **se parler à s.-même** to talk to oneself; **rester s.-même** to remain (true to) oneself; **faire tout par s.-même** to do everything oneself; **aimer son prochain comme s.-même** to love one's neighbour as oneself; **on n'est jamais si bien servi que par s.-même** if you want something done, do it yourself

3 (chose, idée) **en s.** in itself, per se; **il va de s. que …** it goes without saying that …; *Fam* **ça va de s.!** it goes without saying!, of course!; **ça paraît pourtant aller de s.** it seems obvious

4 *Phil* self; **le sens du s.** the sense of self

5 *Psy* self

6 il a trouvé en ce camarade un autre s.-même he's found a soul-mate in this friend

soi-disant [swadizɑ̃] **ADJ INV 1** (qui se prétend) (romancier, artiste etc) self-styled, would-be; **une s. comtesse** a self-styled countess **2** (appelé) so-called; **les arts s. libéraux** the so-called liberal arts

ADV supposedly; **il est parti s. pour réfléchir** he's gone, supposedly to think it over; *Fam* **s. qu'il serait parti** he's gone, apparently or so they say

soie [swa] **NF 1** *Tex* silk; **s. grège/naturelle/sauvage** raw/natural/wild silk; **robe de s.** silk dress; **papier de s.** tissue paper; **la route de la s.** the silk road **2** (d'un sanglier, d'une chenille etc) bristle; **brosse à cheveux en soies** bristle hairbrush; **couvert de soies** bristly, covered with bristles **3** *Tech* (d'une lame, d'une lime etc) tang

soierie [swari] **NF** (tissu) silk; (commerce) silk trade

soif [swaf] **NF** thirst; *Fig* (désir) thirst, craving (de for; de faire to do); **avoir s.** to be thirsty; **étancher sa s.** to quench one's thirst; **boire à sa s.**, *Fam* **boire jusqu'à plus s.** to drink one's fill; *Fam* **il fait s.** I'd kill for a drink, *Br* I could murder a drink; **cela me donne s.** it makes me thirsty; *Fig* **rester sur sa s.** to remain unsatisfied; **cette émission m'a laissé sur ma s.** the program didn't come up to my expectations or left me unsatisfied; **lire jusqu'à plus s.** to read until; **nous avons ri jusqu'à plus s.** we laughed till we could laugh no more; *Fig* **avoir s. de** to be thirsty or to thirst for; **avoir s. de sang** to be thirsting for blood

soiffard, -arde [swafar, -ard] *Arg* **ADJ** (personne) boozy

N boozer

soignant [swaɲɑ̃] **ADJ** *Méd* **aide soignant(e)** nursing auxiliary, auxiliary nurse; **personnel s.** auxiliary nursing staff

soigné [swaɲe] **ADJ 1** (personne, apparence) neat, well-groomed; (travail) careful; (repas) carefully prepared; (vêtement) neat, tidy; (style) polished; (cheval) groomed; (mains, ongles, jardin) well-kept; **elle est très soignée (de sa personne)** she is very careful or particular about her appearance; **peu s.** (personne, apparence, tenue, travail) untidy **2** *Fam* **une raclée soignée** a sound thrashing; **un rhume s.** a hell or a stinker of a cold; **l'addition était soignée** the *Br* bill or *Am* check was huge

soigner [swaɲe] **VT 1** (maintenir en bon état) (meubles, livre, apparence etc) to look after, to take care of; (apporter du soin à) (travail, repas, détails etc) to take care over; **s. le moindre détail** to take care over every detail; **s. sa ligne** to watch one's figure; **s. son image** to be careful of one's image; **s. sa popularité** to nurse one's public; *Fam* **s. l'addition** (dans un restaurant etc) to bump up the bill

2 (maladie) to treat; **on soigne cette maladie avec des antibiotiques** the illness is treated with antibiotics

3 (personne) (d'un hôte, d'une infirmière etc) to look after, to take care of; (d'un médecin) to treat; *Fam* **s. qn aux petits oignons** to give sb first-class treatment; **se faire s.** to be treated; **il faut te faire s.** *Méd* you should have (medical) treatment or see a doctor; *Fam* (tu es fou) you need your head examined; *Fam* **ils nous ont soignés** (dans un restaurant etc) they've ripped us off

VPR se soigner (d'une personne) (médicalement) to treat oneself; (faire attention à soi) to take care of or look after oneself; **elle refuse de se s., elle dit que ça va passer tout seul** she won't take anything, she says it'll go away on its own; **cette maladie ne se soigne pas bien** the disease is difficult to treat; **ça se soigne très bien** it's easily treated; *Fam* **ça se soigne!** you need your head examined!

soigneur [swaɲœr] **NM** *Sport* trainer; *Boxe* second

soigneusement [swaɲøzmɑ̃] **ADV** carefully

soigneux, -euse [swaɲø, -øz] **ADJ** careful (de with); (propre) (personne, travail etc) tidy, neat

soi-même PRON PERS voir **soi, même**

soin [swɛ̃] **NM 1** (charge) care; **le s. des enfants** the care of children, looking after children; **c'est à lui que revient le s. des enfants** he's in charge of or looks after or takes care of the children; **les soins du ménage** housekeeping; **avoir** ou **prendre s. de qn/de qch** to look after or take care of sb/sth; **confier qch aux soins de qn** to place sth in sb's care, to entrust sb with sth; **aux (bons) soins de …** (sur une lettre etc) care of …, c/o …; **par les soins de …** by courtesy of …, thanks to …

2 (effort) care; **avoir (grand) s. de faire qch** to take (particular) care to do sth, to make a (particular) point of doing sth; **elle prend grand s. de son jardin/de son apparence** she takes great care of her garden/over her appearance; **il prend peu de s. de sa personne** he is very careless or slovenly about his appearance; **elle a pris s. de lui envoyer tous les documents** she made sure she sent him/her all the documents; **avoir s. que qch ne s'ébruite pas/soit fait** to take care that sth does not leak out/is done; **mettre tous ses soins à faire qch/à ce que qch soit fait** to go to a great deal of trouble or take great pains to do sth/to see that sth is done

3 (tâche) care; **on lui a confié le s. de les recevoir** he was entrusted with the task or job of receiving them; **je vous laisse le s. de décider** I leave it to you to decide

4 **avoir beaucoup de s.** to be very tidy or orderly; **avec s.** carefully, with care; **avec beaucoup de s.** very carefully, with great care; **manquer de s.** to be careless; **manque de s.** carelessness; **sans s.** (utilisé adjectivement) careless; (pas propre) untidy; (utilisé adverbialement) carelessly; (pas proprement) untidily

5 soins (attention) care, attention; **soins de beauté** beauty care or treatment; **soins médicaux** medical care; **premiers soins, soins d'urgence** first aid; **rien ne peut remplacer les soins d'une mère** nothing can take the place of a mother; **les soins dont il entoure sa femme/son jardin** the care or attention

he lavishes on his wife/his garden; **être aux petits soins pour** ou **avec qn** to fuss over sb, to wait hand and foot on sb; **soins esthétiques** beauty treatment; *Méd* **soins intensifs** intensive care; *Méd* **soins à domicile** home care or nursing; *Méd* **soins palliatifs** terminal care

6 *Arch* (souci) anxiety, worry

soir [swar] **NM** evening; **ce s.** this evening, tonight; **à ce s.!** see you tonight or this evening!; **le s. tombe** night is falling; *Fig* **le s. de la vie** the evening of one's life; **il fait frais le s.** it's cool in the evening; **que faites-vous le s.?** what do you do in the evening(s)?; **à dix heures du s.** at ten (o'clock) in the evening or at night; **lundi/demain/hier (au) s.** Monday/tomorrow/yesterday evening; **tous les lundis s.** every Monday evening; **le lendemain s.** the next evening; **la veille au s.** the evening before, the previous evening; **travailler du matin au s.** to work from morning till night; **être du s.** to be a night owl; **journal du s.** evening newspaper; *TV* evening news; **presse du s.** evening newspapers; **robe du s.** evening dress

soirée [sware] **NF 1** (durée du soir) evening; **passer la s. chez un ami** to spend the evening at a friend's house; **passer ses soirées à lire** to spend one's evenings reading; **toute la s.** all evening, the whole evening; **les longues soirées d'hiver** the long winter evenings or nights; **en fin de s.** late in the evening, towards the end of the evening; **tard dans la s.** late in the evening; **bonne s.!** have a good evening (out)!, enjoy your evening!; *Fam* **faire une s. télévision** to spend an evening in front of the television; **s. étape** stopover at a hotel; **s. à thème** theme evening; *TV* **s. thématique** themed evening

2 (fête) party; **s. dansante** dance; **s. musicale** musical evening; **tenue de s.** evening dress SEE GRAMMAR B61

3 *Théâtre, Cin etc* (représentation de) **s.**, représentation donnée en s. evening performance; **projeter un film en s.** to show a film in the evening, to have an evening showing of a film

soit [swa] before a vowel or as adv [swat] (third person of pr sub of **être**) **ADV** all right!, *Fml* so be it!; **s., tu peux t'en aller** all right then, go

CONJ 1 (supposons) **s. trois multiplié par six** if three is multiplied by six; **s. ABC un triangle** let ABC be a triangle, given a triangle ABC

2 (à savoir) that is to say; **trois objets à dix euros, s. trente euros** three articles at ten euros, that is to say thirty euros

3 s. … s. … either … or …, whether … or …; **s. l'un s. l'autre** (either) one or the other; **j'ai cet article s. en rouge, s. en bleu, s. en vert** I have this item (either) in red, blue or green; **s. tu le fais maintenant ou alors je m'en occupe demain** either you do it now or I'll take care of it tomorrow; **elle va trancher, s. dans un sens, s. dans l'autre** she'll decide (either) one way or the other; **il faut que tu te décides, s. que tu restes, s. que tu partes** you'll have to decide whether you're staying or going; **s. modestie, s. paresse, il n'a jamais rien écrit** whether from modesty or laziness, he has never written anything

soixantaine [swasɑ̃tɛn] **NF 1** (nombre) **une s.** about sixty; **une s. de personnes** about sixty people, sixty or so people; **la s. de livres qu'elle a** the sixty (or so) books she has **2** (âge) **la s.** (the age of) sixty; **elle approche de la s.** she's getting on for sixty; **avoir dépassé la s.** to be in one's sixties, to be over sixty

soixante [swasɑ̃t] **ADJ INV** sixty; **page s.** page sixty; **s. et un** sixty-one; **s. et onze**

seventy-one; **s. et onzième** seventy-first **NM INV** sixty; **habiter au s.** to live at number sixty

soixante-dix ADJ INV, NM INV seventy

soixante-dixième ADJ seventieth **N** seventieth **NM** *(fraction)* seventieth (part)

soixante-huitard, -arde [swasãtɥitar, -ard] *Pol* ADJ relating to the events of May 1968 **N** = person involved in the events of May 1968

soixante-neuf [swasãtnœf] NM *Fam (position sexuelle)* sixty-nine

soixantième [swasãtjɛm] ADJ sixtieth **N** sixtieth **NM** *(fraction)* sixtieth (part)

soja [sɔʒa] NM *(plante)* soya (bean); *Culin* **lait de s.** soya milk; **sauce de s.** soy sauce; **germes de s.** bean sprouts

sol¹ [sɔl] NM **1** *(surface de la terre)* ground; *(territoire)* soil; **le s. natal** one's native soil or *Hum, Litt* heath; **au s.** at ground level; **interdit sur le s. français** prohibited on French soil; *Élec* **relier un fil au s.** to earth *or Am* ground a wire; **conducteur au s.** earthed *or Am* grounded conductor; **cloué au s.** *Aviat* grounded; *Fig* rooted to the spot; **position s.** ground position; *Aviat* **personnel au s.** ground staff **2** *Géol, Agr (matière)* soil; **s. fertile/argileux** fertile/clay soil **3** *(plancher)* floor; **revêtement de s.** floor covering; **dormir sur** ou **à même le s.** to sleep on the floor; *Sport* **faire de la gymnastique au s.** to do floor exercises

> Attention: ne pas confondre **floor** et **ground** lorsqu'on traduit **sol**. **Floor** désigne toujours le sol à l'intérieur d'un bâtiment, alors que **ground** s'utilise uniquement pour l'extérieur.

sol² NM INV *Mus (note)* G; *(en chantant la gamme)* so(h), sol; **morceau en s.** piece in G

sol-air ADJ INV *(missile)* ground-to-air

solaire [sɔlɛr] ADJ *(chauffage, moteur, four etc)* solar; **cadran s.** sundial; **crème s.** sun lotion; **heure s.** solar time; **maison s.** solar-heated house; *Anat* **plexus s.** solar plexus; **système s.** solar system; *Astron* **taches solaires** sunspots; *Méd* **traitement s.** sunray treatment

solarisation [sɔlarizasjõ] NF solarization

solarium [sɔlarjɔm] NM **1** *Méd (établissment) (pour bronzer)* solarium **2** *(terrasse)* sun terrace

soldat, -ate [sɔlda, -at] NM soldier; **s. du génie** sapper; **s. de marine** marine; **s. Dubois!** Private Dubois!; *Aviat* **s. de 2ᵉ classe/de première classe** aircraftman second-class/first-class; **s. de 2ᵉ classe, simple s.** private; **les simples soldats** the rank and file; **se faire s.** to go into *or* join the army; *Fig* **c'est un vrai petit s.** he's a real trooper **NF soldate** (woman *or* female) soldier; **à la soldate** in a soldierly *or* soldier-like way *or* fashion ▸▸ **s. des bois** soldier (ant); **s. de fortune** soldier of fortune; **le S. inconnu** the Unknown Soldier *or* Warrior; **s. marin** *(crustacé)* soldier (crab); **s. de plomb** tin soldier

soldatesque [sɔldatɛsk] *Péj* ADJ *(langage, manières etc)* barrackroom **NF** army rabble

solde¹ [sɔld] NF *Mil etc (rémunération)* pay; *Mil, Ind* **feuille de s.** payroll; **soldes et indemnités** ordinary pay and allowances; **officier en demi-s.** officer on half pay; **cahier de s.** ledger; *Péj* **être à la s. de l'ennemi** to be in the pay of the enemy; *Péj* **avoir qn à sa s.** to have sb in one's pay

solde² NM *Com* **1** *(somme)* balance; **paie-**

ment pour s. payment of balance; **pour s. (de tout compte)** in (full *or* final) settlement; **s. actif** credit balance; **s. bancaire, s. en banque** bank balance; **s. bénéficiaire** credit balance; **s. en caisse** cash balance; **s. de compte** balance of account; **s. créditeur** credit balance, balance in hand; **s. cumulé** cumulative balance; **s. débiteur** ou **déficitaire** debit balance, balance owed; **s. disponible** available balance; **s. passif** debit balance **2 soldes** *(articles)* sale goods; *(vente au rabais)* sale; **courir** ou **faire les soldes** to go round the sales; **ce magasin fait des soldes** this shop is having a sale; **saison** ou **période des soldes** sales season; **s. d'édition** *(livre)* remainder; **(en) s.** to clear; **je l'ai acheté en s.** I got it in *or* at a sale *or* the sales; **prix de s.** bargain prices

solder [sɔlde] VT **1** *Fin (arrêter) (compte)* to balance, to close; *(pour acquitter)* to settle, to pay (off); **s. l'arriéré** to make up back payments **2** *Com (stock)* to sell off, to clear; *(livres)* to remainder **VPR se solder 1** *Fin* **les comptes se soldent par un bénéfice net de …** the accounts show a net profit of … **2** *Fig* **se s. par** *(échec etc)* to end in; **tout ça va se s. par une catastrophe financière** it's going to end in financial disaster

soldeur, -euse [sɔldœr, -øz] N *Com* discount trader

sole¹ [sɔl] NF **1** *Tech, Métal* bed plate **2** *Naut (d'un navire)* flat bottom **3** *Agr (de l'assolement des cultures)* field

sole² NF *(poisson)* sole

solécisme [sɔlesism] NM *Ling* solecism

soleil [sɔlɛj] NM **1** *(astre)* sun; **lever/coucher du s.** sunrise/sunset; **se lever avec le s.** to get up with the sun; **il n'y a rien de nouveau sous le s.** there is nothing new under the sun; *Hist* **le Roi S.** the Sun King; *Couture* **plissé s.** sunray pleats **2** *(lumière, chaleur)* sun, sunshine; **il y a** ou **il fait du s.** the sun is shining, it's sunny; **il y fait un s. de plomb** the sun is scorching hot there; **se protéger du s.** to protect oneself from the sun; **au (grand) s.** in the sun(shine); **jour de s.** sunny day; *Fam* **cette petite est mon rayon de s.!** that little girl is my ray of sunshine!; **sans s.** sunless; **coup de s.** sunburn; *(plus fort)* touch of sunstroke; *Fam* **piquer un s.** to blush; **ôte-toi de mon s.!** get out of here!; *Fig* **avoir sa/se faire une place au s.** to have one's/find oneself a place in the sun; **avoir des biens** ou **du bien au s.** to own property **3** *Bot* sunflower **4** *Gym* **grand s.** grand circle **5** *(feu d'artifice)* Catherine wheel, pinwheel ▸▸ **s. de minuit** midnight sun

solennel, -elle [sɔlanɛl] ADJ **1** *(serment, déclaration etc)* solemn; *(occasion etc)* solemn, formal **2** *(ton, silence)* solemn, grave; **prendre des airs solennels** to adopt a solemn air **3** *Rel* **communion solennelle** solemn communion

solennellement [sɔlanɛlmã] ADV solemnly; *(inaugurer etc)* formally; **je le jure s.** I solemnly swear

solenniser [sɔlanize] VT to solemnize

solennité [sɔlanite] NF **1** *(caractère)* solemnity; **avec s.** solemnly **2** *(fête)* solemn ceremony

solénoïde [sɔlenɔid] NM *Élec* solenoid

solex® [sɔlɛks] NM moped

solfatare [sɔlfatar] NF *Géol* solfatara, sulphur spring

solfège [sɔlfɛʒ] NM *Mus* (tonic) sol-fa, music theory; **apprendre le s.** to learn music theory; **(livre de) s.** (music) primer

solfier [sɔlfje] VT *Mus (ton)* to sol-fa

solidaire [sɔlidɛr] ADJ **1** *(personnes)* **être s. de qn** to stand by sb, to support sb; **se sentir s. de qn** to feel a sense of solidarity with sb; **nous sommes tous solidaires (les uns des autres)** we all stand *or* stick together; **dans leur famille, ils sont très solidaires** they're a very close-knit family; **ses intérêts sont solidaires des nôtres** his/her interests are bound up with ours **2** *Tech (roue d'engrenage etc)* interdependent; **roue s. d'une autre** wheel integral with another **3** *Jur* jointly liable *or* responsible (**de** for); **obligation s.** obligation binding on all parties

solidairement [sɔlidɛrmã] ADV jointly

solidariser [sɔlidarize] VT **1** *Jur* to render jointly liable *or* responsible **2** *Tech* **mécanisme à action solidarisée** interlocking gear **VPR se solidariser** to make common cause, to show solidarity (**avec** with)

solidarité [sɔlidarite] NF **1** *(entre personnes)* solidarity; **en signe de s., nous portons ce badge** we wear this badge as a sign of solidarity; **faire appel à la s. nationale** to call for national solidarity; **grève de s.** sympathy strike; **débrayer par s. (avec)** to come out (on strike) in sympathy (with) **2** *Tech (des pièces)* interdependence **3** *Jur* joint liability *or* responsibility

solide [sɔlid] ADJ **1** *(non liquide) (corps, aliment, terre)* solid; *Math* **angle s.** solid angle **2** *(résistant) (mur, fondation)* solid, strong; *(tissu)* strong; *(personne)* strong, sturdy; *(repas)* solid, hearty; *(appétit)* hearty; *(preuve)* solid, sound; *(raisonnement, éducation)* sound; *(amitié)* strong; *Com (personne)* sound, solvent; *(position, affaire)* sound, strong, well-established; **s. sur ses jambes** steady on one's feet; **peu s. (personne)** weak; *(meuble)* flimsy; **solides qualités** solid *or* sterling qualities; **garantie s.** solid *or* reliable guarantee; **ami s.** staunch *or* reliable *or* trusty friend; **de solides liens nous unissent** strong *or* close ties unite us; **une s. poignée de main** a firm handshake; **avoir la tête s.** to be level-headed; **il faut avoir les nerfs solides** you need nerves of steel (**pour faire qch** to do sth); **j'ai de solides raisons de croire que …** I have good *or* sound reasons for believing that …; *Fig* **être s. au poste** to be extremely reliable *or* dependable; *Fig* **ça ne repose sur rien de s.** there is no sound *or* solid basis for that; **être encore s. (comme un chêne** ou **un roc)** to be still hale and hearty **NM 1** *Géom, Phys* solid (body); *Géom* **s. de révolution** solid of revolution **2** *Fam* **ça, c'est du s.!** that's pretty solid!

solidement [sɔlidmã] ADV *(construire etc)* solidly; *(attacher, tenir, établir etc)* firmly, securely; **homme s. bâti** solidly *or* sturdily built man; *Fam* **elle s'est fait s. reprendre** she got a good telling-off

solidification [sɔlidifikasjõ] NF solidification

solidifier [sɔlidifje] *(impf, pr sub* n. **solidifiions, v. solidifiiez)** VT to solidify **VPR se solidifier** to solidify

solidité [sɔlidite] NF solidity; *(d'un édifice, d'un matériau)* strength; *(d'une société, d'un jugement)* soundness; *(d'une amitié)* strength, staunchness; *(d'une couleur)* fastness; **c'est d'une s. à toute épreuve** it stands up to anything

soliloque [sɔlilɔk] NM soliloquy

soliloquer [sɔlilɔke] VI to soliloquize

solin [sɔlɛ̃] NM *Constr (espace)* space; *(enduit)* plaster filling

solipsisme [sɔlipsism] NM *Phil* solipsism

soliste [sɔlist] N soloist

solitaire [sɔlitɛr] ADJ **1** *(qui vit seul)* solitary;

(involontairement) (personne) lonely, *Am Fam* lonesome; **passer des vacances solitaires** to spend one's holidays on one's own; **vivre s.** to live a solitary life; **avoir l'humeur s.** to like to be on one's own *or* alone, to like one's own company; **plaisir/vice s.** masturbation/self-abuse **2** *(séparé des autres) (voyageur, arbre, maison etc)* solitary, lone **3** *(désert) (route, lieu etc)* lonely, deserted **4** **ver s.** tapeworm
N *(personne)* loner, lone wolf; *(ermite)* hermit, recluse; **en s.** on one's own, alone; *Naut* **croisière en s.** solo cruise
NM 1 *(jeu)* solitaire **2** *(diamant)* solitaire **3** *(sanglier)* rogue boar; *(éléphant)* rogue elephant

solitairement [sɔlitɛrmɑ̃] **ADV** on one's own, alone

solitude [sɔlityd] **NF 1** *(de personne)* solitude; *(involontaire)* loneliness; **rechercher la s.** to seek solitude; **j'aime la s.** I like being alone *or* on my own, I like my own company; **vivre dans la s.** to live alone *or* on one's own **2** *(de lieu)* loneliness; **dans la s. de la nuit/campagne** in the loneliness *or* solitude of the night/countryside **3** *Litt (endroit)* lonely spot

solive [sɔliv] **NF** *Constr* joist

sollicitation [sɔ(l)lisitasjɔ̃] **NF 1** *(demande)* request; *(avec instance)* entreaty; **céder aux sollicitations de qn** to give in to sb's pleas **2** **les sollicitations de la faim/de l'ambition** gnawing hunger/ambition

solliciter [sɔ(l)lisite] **VT 1** *(entretien, audience etc)* to request; **s. qn (de faire qch)** to appeal to sb (to do sth); **j'ai l'honneur de s. votre bienveillance** I appeal to your kindness; **s. un emploi (de qn)** to apply (to sb) for a job; **s. des voix** to canvass for votes; **ils nous ont souvent sollicités par téléphone** they often made telephone appeals to us; **il est sollicité de toutes parts** he is very much in demand **2** *(attention, regards)* to attract; *(curiosité)* to arouse

solliciteur, -euse [sɔ(l)lisitœr, -øz] **N** petitioner, supplicant (**de** for)

sollicitude [sɔ(l)lisityd] **NF** *(soin)* solicitude; *(inquiétude)* solicitude, concern, anxiety (**pour** for); **ton plein de s.** solicitous *or* concerned tone

solo [sɔlo] **NM** solo; **s. de violon** violin solo; **faire un s.** *(en danse)* to do a solo, to dance a solo; *(en musique)* to do a solo, to play a solo; **jouer en s.** to play solo
ADJ INV solo; **violon s.** solo violin

sol-sol **ADJ INV** *(missile)* ground-to-ground

solstice [sɔlstis] **NM** solstice; **s. d'été/d'hiver** summer/winter solstice

solubiliser [sɔlybilize] **VT** **s. qch** to make sth soluble

solubilité [sɔlybilite] **NF** *(d'un corps)* solubility

soluble [sɔlybl] **ADJ 1** *(produit)* soluble; **café s.** instant coffee **2** *(problème)* solvable

soluté [sɔlyte] **NM** *Pharm, Chimie* solution, serum

solution [sɔlysjɔ̃] **NF 1** *(de problème, situation, d'équation etc)* solution, answer (**de** to); **s. de paresse** *ou* **de facilité** easy way out; **ce n'est pas une s.!** that's no answer *or* solution! **2** *Chimie, Phys etc (liquide, dissolution)* solution; **sel en s. (dans l'eau)** salt in solution (in water); **s. détergente** cleaning solution *or* fluid **3** **s. de continuité** solution of continuity; *Élec etc* break of continuity
▸▸ *Hist* **la s. finale** the Final Solution

solutionner [sɔlysjɔne] **VT** *(problème, difficulté)* to solve

solvabilité [sɔlvabilite] **NF** solvency; *(en vue d'un emprunt)* credit rating

solvable [sɔlvabl] **ADJ** *(financially)* solvent

> Il faut noter que l'adjectif anglais **solvable** est un faux ami. Il signifie **soluble, résoluble**.

solvant [sɔlvɑ̃] **NM** *Chimie* solvent

soma [sɔma] **NM** *Biol* soma

somali, -ie [sɔmali] **ADJ** Somali
NM *Ling* Somali
N S. Somali; **les Somalis** the Somali(s)

Somalie [sɔmali] **NF** Somalia; *Hist* **S. britannique/italienne** British/Italian Somaliland

somalien, -enne [sɔmaljɛ̃, -ɛn] **ADJ** Somalian
N S. Somalian

somatique [sɔmatik] **ADJ** *Biol, Psy* somatic

somatisation [sɔmatizasjɔ̃] **NF** *Biol, Psy* psychosomatic reaction, *Spéc* somatization

somatiser [sɔmatize] **VT** *Biol, Psy* to react psychosomatically to, *Spéc* to somatize

sombre [sɔ̃br] **ADJ 1** *(foncé) (couleur)* dark; **des robes bleu s.** dark blue dresses **2** *(obscur) (forêt, pièce etc)* dark, dim; *(ciel)* dull, overcast; **il fait s.** *(temps)* it is dull (weather); **il faisait très s. dans la pièce** it was very dark in the room **3** *(triste) (visage, pensées, caractère, avenir etc)* gloomy, *Fml* sombre, *Am* somber; **ils sont fâchés pour une s. histoire d'argent** they quarrelled over some sordid little business of money; **une s. histoire d'assassinat** a sinister tale of murder **4** *Fam* **un s. imbécile** a total imbecile *or* idiot

sombrement [sɔ̃brəmɑ̃] **ADV** *(tristement)* gloomily, sombrely, *Am* somberly; **s'habiller s.** to wear dark clothes

sombrer [sɔ̃bre] **VI** *(d'un navire)* to sink, to founder; *(d'un empire)* to fall, to collapse; *(d'une affaire)* to come to grief, to fail; **s. dans l'alcool/la misère/la folie** to sink into alcoholism/poverty/madness; **il vit s. sa fortune** he saw his fortune swallowed up; **elle vit s. ses espérances** she saw her hopes dashed; **sa raison sombra** he lost his mind *or* his reason; **le bateau a sombré corps et biens** the boat went down with all hands

sombrero [sɔ̃brero] **NM** sombrero

sommaire [sɔ(m)mɛr] **ADJ 1** *(récit)* brief, succinct, concise **2** *(rudimentaire) (repas)* scanty, skimpy; *(examen)* hasty, cursory; **porter une tenue s.** to be scantily *or* skimpily dressed; **faire une toilette s.** to have a quick wash; **avoir des vues sommaires sur qch** to have superficial views on sth **3** *Jur (procédure, exécution)* summary
NM summary, synopsis

sommairement [sɔ(m)mɛrmɑ̃] **ADV 1** *(expliquer, raconter etc)* briefly, in summary **2** *(de façon rudimentaire)* **vêtu s.** scantily *or* skimpily clad *or* dressed; **l'appartement est s. meublé** the furniture in the flat is very basic, the flat is meagrely furnished; **s. organisé** improvised, hastily organized **3** *Jur (juger)* summarily

sommation [sɔ(m)masjɔ̃] **NF 1** *Jur (injonction)* notice, demand; *(de paraître en justice)* summons; **avoir s. de payer une dette** to receive notice *or* a demand to pay a debt **2** *Mil (de sentinelle)* challenge

sommation [sɔ(m)masjɔ̃] **NF** *Math (d'une série)* summation

somme [sɔm] **NF** **bête de s.** beast of burden; *Fig* drudge; **travailler comme une bête de s.** to work like a slave, to slave away

somme **NF 1** *Math* sum, total; **faire la s. de dix nombres** to add (up) ten numbers; **s. générale/totale** overall total/total sum; **la s. des trois angles d'un triangle** the sum of the three angles of a triangle
2 *(quantité) (d'objets)* number; *(des pertes etc)* amount; **la s. des efforts** the amount of

effort; **en s.** *(tout compte fait)* on the whole, all things considered; *(en bref)* in short; **en s., j'ai été plutôt agréablement surpris** on the whole, I was rather pleasantly surprised; **en s. il s'agit d'un travail commercial** in short, it's a sales job; **s. toute** when all is said and done
3 s. (d'argent) sum (of money); **payer la s. de 500 euros** to pay 500 euros; **être mis à l'amende pour la s. de 500 euros** to be fined (a total of) 500 euros; **dépenser des sommes folles** to spend vast sums *or* amounts (of money); **un million! c'est une s.!** a million! that's a lot of money!; **s. due** amount due, total due; **s. nette** net (amount); *Compta* **sommes payables** payables, sums payable
4 *(d'une œuvre)* outline, survey

somme **NM** nap, snooze; **faire un (petit) s.** to have *or* take a nap *or* a snooze, *Fam* to have forty winks

sommeil [sɔmɛj] **NM 1** *(de dormeur)* sleep, *Litt* slumber; **avoir besoin de très peu de s.** to need very little sleep; **s. réparateur/profond** refreshing/deep sleep; **s. de mort** *ou* **de plomb** heavy *or* deep sleep; **dormir d'un s. de plomb** to sleep like a log; **avoir le s. léger/profond** to be a light/a heavy sleeper; **dormir du s. du juste** to sleep the sleep of the just; **chercher le s.** to try to sleep; **faire une cure de s.** to undergo sleep therapy; **j'en perds le s.** I'm losing sleep over it; *Fig* **s. éternel** eternal rest; *Bot* **en s.** (lying) dormant; *Fig* **laisser une affaire en s.** to put a matter aside *or* on the back burner *or* on ice, *Fml* to leave a matter in abeyance; *Zool* **s. hivernal** winter sleep
2 *(somnolence)* sleepiness, drowsiness; **avoir s.** to be *or* feel sleepy *or* drowsy; **ça risque de te donner s.** it might make you sleepy; **le s. me gagne** I'm beginning to fall asleep; **je tombe** *ou* **je meurs de s.** I can't keep awake, I can't keep my eyes open; **maladie du s.** sleeping sickness
▸▸ **s. paradoxal** REM sleep

sommeiller [sɔmeje] **VI 1** to doze **2** *Fig* to lie dormant, to be latent (**en qn** in sb)

sommelier [sɔməlje] **NM** cellarman; *(serveur)* wine waiter, sommelier

sommellerie [sɔmɛlri] **NF 1** wine waiter's job **2** *(cave)* wine cellar

sommer [sɔme] **VT** *Math* to sum

sommer [sɔme] **VT** *aussi Jur* to summon (**de faire qch** to do sth); **s. qn de payer** to require sb to pay

sommet [sɔmɛ] **NM** *(d'une montagne, d'une colline)* top, summit, peak; *(d'un arbre, d'un toit, d'une hiérarchie)* top; *(d'un angle, d'une courbe, d'une trajectoire, d'un cône)* vertex; *(d'une vague)* crest; *(d'une arche, de la tête)* crown; *Fig (du pouvoir, de la renommée)* summit, pinnacle, height; *Fig* **atteindre des sommets vertigineux** to reach the dizzy heights; *Fig* **être au s. de l'échelle** to be at the top of the ladder; **atteindre le s. de la gloire/du succès** to reach the height *or* pinnacle of fame/success; *Pol* **conférence** *ou* **réunion au s.** summit (meeting *or* conference); **un s. franco-américain** a Franco-American summit; *Obst* **présentation d'un bébé par le s.** head presentation of a baby

sommier [sɔmje] **NM 1** *(de lit)* base; **s. à ressorts/lattes** sprung/slatted base **2** *Tech (d'arche)* springer; *(de porte etc)* lintel; *(du sol)* cross beam; *(de pont)* stringer; *(de balance)* beam; *(de machine)* bed **3** *Admin etc* register; *Jur* **sommiers judiciaires** criminal records; **il n'y a rien sur lui au s.** he's got a clean record **4** *Com* cash book

sommier-divan, *pl* **sommiers-divans** **NM** divan base

sommité [sɔ(m)mite] **NF 1** *Bot* head **2** *Fig*

(personnage) leading figure *or* light; **sommités de l'art** leading figures *or* lights in the art world; **les sommités du monde scientifique** leading experts in the scientific field

somnambule [sɔmnɑ̃byl] ADJ sómnambulistic, somnambulant; **il est s.** he's a sleepwalker, he sleepwalks, he walks in his sleep N sleepwalker, *Spéc* somnambulist; **c'est un s.** he's a sleepwalker, he sleepwalks, he walks in his sleep; **travailler/parler comme un s.** to work/speak like a zombie *or Fml* as if in a trance; **ses gestes de s.** his/her zombie-like movements

somnambulisme [sɔmnɑ̃bylism] NM sleepwalking, *Spéc* somnambulism; **s. provoqué** hypnotic state

somnifère [sɔmnifɛr] *Méd* ADJ sleep-inducing, soporific; **comprimé s.** sleeping tablet *or* pill
NM sleeping tablet *or* pill

somnolence [sɔmnɔlɑ̃s] NF sleepiness, drowsiness, *Litt* somnolence; **ce médicament peut provoquer des états de s.** this medicine may cause drowsiness; **la chaleur nous plonge dans un état de s.** the heat makes us drowsy *or* lethargic

somnolent [sɔmnɔlɑ̃] ADJ sleepy, drowsy, *Litt* somnolent

somnoler [sɔmnɔle] VI to doze

somptuaire [sɔ̃ptɥɛr] ADJ **1** *Jur (loi)* sumptuary **2** *Fin* **taxes somptuaires** tax on luxury articles; **dépenses somptuaires** expenditure on luxuries

somptueusement [sɔ̃ptɥøzmɑ̃] ADV sumptuously, magnificently

somptueux, -euse [sɔ̃ptɥø, -øz] ADJ sumptuous, magnificent

somptuosité [sɔ̃ptɥozite] NF sumptuousness, magnificence

son¹, sa, ses [sɔ̃, sa, se] ADJ POSS SEE GRAMMAR A30; B21 (**son** *is used instead of* **sa** *before* f *nouns beginning with a vowel or mute* h) *(d'homme etc)* his; *(de femme etc)* her; *(de chose, d'idée, d'animal etc)* its; *(de bébé)* his/her, its; *(d'animal domestique)* its, his/her; *(après un sujet indéfini)* one's; *(après 'tout le monde', 'personne', 'chacun' etc)* their, *Fml* his/her; **s. ami/amie** his/her friend; **s. meilleur ami/sa meilleure amie** his/her best friend; **s. oncle et sa tante** his/her aunt and (his/her) uncle; **s. père et sa mère,** *Litt* **ses père et mère** his/her mother and father; **il a mis s. chapeau et ses gants** he put on his hat and (his) gloves; **un(e) de ses ami(e)s** one of his/her friends, a friend of his/hers; **un professeur de ses amis** a teacher friend of his/hers; **chacun a pris s. sac** *(chacun a un sac)* everybody took their bags; *(le sac de Pierre)* everybody took his bag; **un bébé peut reconnaître sa mère peu de temps après sa naissance** a baby can recognize its mother shortly after it's born; **perdre s. temps** to waste one's time; **ici, on passe s. temps à bavarder** everybody spends their time chatting here; **en Alsace, on prend s. café en même temps que le dessert** in Alsace, they have their coffee along with their desert; *Fam* **elle aura sa chambre à elle** she'll have her own room; *Fam* **s. imbécile de frère** his/her idiot of a brother; *Fam* **s. artiste de mari** her artist husband; *Fam* **alors, tu veux bien le rencontrer, s. artiste?** so, do you want to meet this artist of his/hers?; *Fam* **il a eu s. vendredi** he got Friday off; *Fam* **alors, c'était ça ses vacances de rêve!** so much for his/her dream holiday!

son² NM **1** *(de voix, d'instrument etc)* sound; *(volume)* sound, volume; **baisser/monter le s.** to turn the sound up/down; **le s. profond de la cloche** the deep sound *or* tone of the bell; *Fig* **c'est un autre s. de cloche** that's

(quite) another story; **j'ai entendu plusieurs sons de cloche** I've heard several variants *ou* versions of that story; **s. du tambour/de la trompette** beat of the drum/blare of the trumpet; **danser au s. des accordéons** to dance to the sound of accordions; **annoncer une nouvelle à s. de trompe** to shout a piece of news from the rooftops; *Naut* **s. de sirène** *ou* **de sifflet** siren blast

2 *Phys, Mus* sound; **s. pur** pure tone; **niveau du s.** sound level; **vitesse du s.** speed of sound; *Aviat* **mur du s.** sound barrier; *Cin etc* **enregistrement du s.** sound recording; **prise de s.** sound pick-up; **la prise de s. est bonne** the recording is good; *Cin etc* **ingénieur du s.** sound engineer; **(spectacle) s. et lumière** son et lumière; **s. d'ambiance** ambient sound; *TV* **s. sur image** sound over vision, SOV; **s. numérique** digital sound; **s. stéréo** stereo sound; **s. témoin** cue track; *TV, Radio* **s. de transition** bridging sound; **s. 3D** surround sound

son³ NM *(de grains)* bran; **céréales à base de s.** bran cereal; **pain de s.** bran loaf; **tache de s.** freckle; **poupée de s.** stuffed doll

sonal, -als [sɔnal] NM *Radio, TV* (advertising) jingle

sonar [sɔnar] NM *Naut* sonar

sonate [sɔnat] NF *Mus* sonata; **s. pour violon** violin sonata

sonatine [sɔnatin] NF *Mus* sonatina

sondage [sɔ̃daʒ] NM **1** poll, survey; **s. Gallup** Gallup poll; **faire** *ou* **pratiquer un s.** to carry out a poll; **enquête par s., s. (d'opinion)** opinion poll *or* survey; **faire un s. auprès d'un groupe** to poll a group, to carry out a survey among a group; **s. aléatoire** random sampling; **s. aréolaire** cluster sampling; **sondages de paix** peace feelers; **s. probabiliste** probability survey; **s. par quotas** quotas survey; **s. par téléphone** telephone interviewing

2 *Naut, Aviat etc* sounding, probe; **faire des sondages** to take soundings; **ballon de s.** pilot balloon, sounding balloon

3 *Min* boring; **appareil de s.** drilling rig

4 *Métal* **essai de s.** probe test

5 *Méd (de blessure)* probing

sonde [sɔ̃d] NF **1** *Naut* (sounding) lead, sounding line, plummet; **naviguer à la s.** to navigate by soundings; **être sur la s.** to be in soundings, to have struck soundings

2 *(de pompe, de puits etc)* sounding rod

3 *faire la s. (d'une baleine)* to sound

4 *Météo, Aviat* **s. aérienne** sounding balloon; **s. spatiale** space probe; *Aviat* **s. de réservoir** tank probe; **s. à fil chaud** hot-wire anemometer

5 *Méd* probe, tube, catheter; **s. (creuse)** catheter; **nourri à la s.** tube-fed

6 *(à fromage etc)* taster

7 *Min* borer, drill

sondé [sɔ̃de] NM *Mktg* respondent, person polled

sonder [sɔ̃de] VT **1** *Naut* to sound; *Fig (mystère)* to fathom

2 *Aviat, Météo* **s. l'atmosphère** to make soundings in the atmosphere

3 *Min* **s. un terrain** to make borings

4 *(examiner) (fromage)* to taste; *(poutre)* to examine; *(horizon)* to scan; **s. le cœur/les intentions de qn** to sound out sb's heart/intentions; **s. qn** to sound sb out; **je l'ai sondée là-dessus** I sounded her out on the matter; **il la sonda du regard** he looked intently at her; **s. l'opinion** to sound out public opinion, to make a survey of public opinion; **10% de la population sondée** 10% of those polled; *Fig* **s. le terrain** to see how the land lies

5 *Méd (blessure)* to probe; *(patient)* to sound; *(avec une sonde creuse)* to catheterize

VI **1** *(d'une baleine)* to sound
2 *Min* to make borings

sondeur, -euse [sɔ̃dœr, -øz] NM **1** *Naut (personne)* leadsman; *(machine)* sounder **2** *Min (personne)* borer, driller
NF *Min* **sondeuse** borer, drill

songe [sɔ̃ʒ] NM *Litt* dream; **faire un s.** to have a dream; **en s.** in a dream

songe-creux NM INV *Litt* dreamer

songer [sɔ̃ʒe] VI *(je songeai(s); n. songeons)* **1 s. à qch** *(penser à)* to think about sth; *(considérer)* to consider sth, to think sth over; **s. à l'avenir** to think about the future; **songez à ce que vous faites!** think about what you're doing!; **il ne faut pas y s.** that's quite out of the question; **on ne peut pas ne pas s. à elle** you can't help but think about her; **s. au mariage** to consider *or* to contemplate marriage; **sans y s.** without thinking; **sans s. à mal** without meaning any harm; **s. à faire qch** to think of doing sth, to contemplate doing sth; **il ne songe qu'à gagner de l'argent** making money is all he thinks about

2 *(imaginer)* to imagine (**que** that); **songez si j'étais furieux** you can imagine how angry I was; **je ne songeais guère que ...** little did I think *or* imagine that ...; **songez donc!** just think!, just imagine!

3 s. à *(se souvenir de)* to remember; **songez à lui** keep *or* bear him in mind, remember him; **songez que ...** remember *or* bear in mind that ...; **je ne songeais pas que ...** I had forgotten that ...; **cela m'a fait s. que ...** that reminded me that ...

4 *Arch (rêver)* to dream

songerie [sɔ̃ʒri] NF *Litt* reverie, daydreaming

songeur, -euse [sɔ̃ʒœr, -øz] ADJ *(rêveur)* *(personne, nature)* dreamy; *(pensif) (personne)* pensive, thoughtful

sonique [sɔnik] ADJ sonic; **bang s.** sonic boom

sonnaille [sɔnaj] NF (cow)bell

sonnant [sɔnɑ̃] ADJ *(horloge)* striking; **arriver à dix heures sonnant(es)** to arrive on the stroke of ten *or* at ten (o'clock) sharp; *Fig* **espèces sonnantes et trébuchantes** hard cash

sonné [sɔne] ADJ **1** **il est dix heures sonnées** it's past *or* gone ten; **il a quarante ans (bien) sonnés** he's well over forty, *Fam* he's on the wrong side of forty, he won't see forty again **2** *Boxe etc Fam (groggy)* groggy, punch-drunk; *(fou)* crazy, cracked

sonner [sɔne] VI *(d'une horloge)* to strike; *(de cloches, du téléphone)* to ring; **le glas sonne** the bell is tolling; **s. creux** to sound hollow; *Fig* to ring hollow; **sa réponse a sonné faux** his/her answer did not ring true; **quand elle rit, ça sonne faux** when she laughs it rings false; *Fig* **s. bien/mal** to sound good/bad; **l'italien sonne bien à l'oreille** Italian is a pleasant-sounding language; **adresse qui sonne bien** good address; **faire s. les consonnes** to sound the consonants; **faire s. un mot** to emphasize a word; **faire s. son argent/ses clefs** to jingle one's money/one's keys; *Fam* **il va se faire s.!** he'll catch it!; **six heures sonnèrent** the clock struck six; **midi vient de s.** it has just struck twelve; **le réveil vient de s.** the alarm (clock) has just gone off; **faire s. le réveil à 6 heures** to set the alarm for 6 o'clock; **les vêpres sonnent** the bells are ringing for vespers; **on sonne** there's a ring at the door; **on a sonné** that was the doorbell, there's someone at the door; **j'ai sonné chez eux, mais personne ne m'a répondu** I rang their doorbell, but nobody answered; **s. avant d'entrer** *(sur panneau)* ring before entering; **entrez sans s.** go (straight) in; **s. du clairon** to sound the bugle; **son heure** *ou* **sa dernière heure a sonné** his last hour has come; **la trompette sonne** the trumpet sounds; **les oreilles lui sonnaient** his ears were buzzing

VT 1 *(trompettes etc)* to sound; **s. la cloche** to ring the bell; *Fam* **il va se faire s. les cloches!** he'll catch it!; **horloge qui sonne les heures** clock that strikes the hours; **l'horloge a sonné dix heures** the clock struck ten; **il a sonné deux coups à la porte** he rang the doorbell twice; **s. la messe/l'office** to ring the bell for mass/for church; **s. le dîner** to ring the dinner bell; *Mil* **s. la charge/la retraite** to sound the charge/the retreat **2** *(appeler) (domestique, infirmière etc)* to ring for; *très Fam* **on ne vous a pas sonné, vous!** mind your own business!, nobody asked you! **3** *très Fam (assommer)* **s. qn** to knock sb out **4** *Belg (appeler au téléphone)* to telephone, to call

sonnerie [sɔnri] **NF 1** *(son) (des cloches, du téléphone)* ringing; *(cloches)* (set of) bells or chimes; **c'est la s. du téléphone qui m'a réveillé** it was the telephone (ringing) that woke me up **2** *(mécanisme) (d'une horloge)* striking mechanism; *(sonnette)* bell; **pendule à s.** striking clock; **bouton de s.** bell push; **fil à s.** bell wire **3** *Mil (de clairon etc)* call

sonnet [sɔnɛ] **NM** sonnet

sonnette [sɔnɛt] **NF 1** *(de porte)* doorbell; *(clochette)* (small) bell; *(de vélo, pour serviteurs)* bell; **appuyer sur la s.** to ring the bell; **personne ne répondit à mon coup de s.** no one answered the bell; **as-tu entendu la s.?** did you hear the bell?; **cordon de s.** bell pull; **s. d'alarme** alarm bell; **coup de s.** ring **2** *Constr* pile driver **3** **serpent à s.** rattlesnake

sonneur, -euse [sɔnœr, -øz] **N** bellringer; *Fam* **dormir comme un s.** to sleep like a log **NM** *Constr* pile-driver operator

sono [sɔno] **NF** *abrév Fam* = **sonorisation 2, sonorisation 3**

sonore [sɔnɔr] **ADJ 1** *(relatif au son)* sound; **onde s.** soundwave; *Cin* **film s.** sound film; **effets sonores** sound effects; **bande** *ou* **piste s.** sound track; **bip s.** beep; **pollution s.** noise pollution; **église s.** church with good acoustics; **vibrations sonores** acoustic resonance **2** *(voix)* ringing, loud, sonorous; *(cloche)* clear-toned; *(rire)* resounding; *(voûte, couloir etc)* echoing; *Ling* **consonne s.** voiced consonant; **niveau (d'intensité) s.** sound (intensity) level

NF *Ling* voiced consonant

Il faut noter que l'adjectif anglais **sonorous** signifie souvent **grandiloquent**.

sonorisation [sɔnorizasjɔ̃] **NF 1** *Ling (d'une consonne)* voicing **2** *Cin* addition of the soundtrack (**de** to), dubbing **3** *(d'une pièce)* fitting of a PA system; *(équipement)* public address system, PA system; *(de discothèque etc)* sound system

sonoriser [sɔnorize] **VT 1** *Ling (consonne)* to voice **2** *TV, Cin* to dub; *(présentation)* to add sound to; **s. un film** to add the soundtrack to a film **3** **s. une salle** to fit a room with a PA system

VPR se sonoriser *Ling (de consonne)* to be voiced

sonorité [sɔnorite] **NF 1** *(qualité de son)* tone **2** *(résonance)* resonance; *(de salle etc)* acoustics; **ce piano a une belle s.** this piano has a beautiful tone

sonothèque [sɔnotɛk] **NF** sound effects or audio library

sonotone® [sɔnoton] **NM** miniature hearing aid

sont [sɔ̃] *voir* **être²**

sopalin® [sɔpalɛ̃] **NM** kitchen paper

sophisme [sɔfism] **NM** sophism

sophiste [sɔfist] **N** sophist

sophistication [sɔfistikasjɔ̃] **NF 1** *(d'une personne, d'un équipement)* sophistication **2** *Vieilli (du vin etc)* adulteration

sophistique [sɔfistik] **ADJ** sophistic(al)

NF sophistry

sophistiqué [sɔfistike] **ADJ 1** *(personne)* sophisticated; *(équipement etc)* sophisticated, advanced **2** *Vieilli (frelaté) (vin etc)* adulterated

Sophocle [sɔfɔkl] **N** Sophocles

sophrologie [sɔfrɔlɔʒi] **NF** sophrology

sophrologue [sɔfrɔlɔg] **N** sophrologist

soporifique [sɔpɔrifik] **ADJ** *(drogue)* soporific, sleep-inducing; *Fam (ennuyeux)* boring, soporific

NM *(drogue)* sleeping drug, soporific; *Fam (livre)* boring book, book that sends you to sleep

soprane [sɔpran] **N** *Mus* = **soprano**

sopraniste [sɔpranist] **NM** *Mus* male soprano

soprano [sɔprano] *Mus* **NM** soprano (voice) **N** *(personne)* soprano **ADJ** **saxophone s.** soprano saxophone

sorbe [sɔrb] **NF** *Bot* sorb (apple)

sorbet [sɔrbɛ] **NM** *Culin* sorbet; **s. au cassis** blackcurrant sorbet

sorbetière [sɔrbətjɛr] **NF** ice-cream maker

sorbier [sɔrbje] **NM** *Bot* sorb (tree), service (tree)

sorbique [sɔrbik] **ADJ** *Chimie (acide)* sorbic

sorbonnard, -arde [sɔrbɔnar, -ard] *Fam* **N** *(étudiant)* student at the Sorbonne; *(professeur)* teacher at the Sorbonne **ADJ** *Péj* pedantic

sorcellerie [sɔrsɛlri] **NF** witchcraft, sorcery, magic; **c'est de la s.!** it's magic!

sorcier [sɔrsje] **NM** sorcerer, wizard; **il ne faut pas être s. pour faire ça** you don't need to be a genius to do that, that doesn't take much intelligence; *Can Fam* **être en s.** to be fuming, to be hopping mad

ADJ M *Fam* **ce n'est pas s.** it's simple enough, there's no magic about that

sorcière [sɔrsjɛr] **NF** sorceress, witch; *Fam Péj* **vieille s.** old hag, old witch; **chasse aux sorcières** witch hunt; **cercle** *ou* **rond de sorcières** fairy ring

sordide [sɔrdid] **ADJ 1** *(vêtements)* filthy; *(pièce, quartier etc)* squalid, sordid **2** *(crime, détails, avarice etc)* sordid

sordidement [sɔrdidmɑ̃] **ADV** sordidly; **vivre s.** to live in squalor

sordidité [sɔrdidite] **NF** sordidness

sorgho [sɔrgo] **NM** *Bot* sorghum

Sorlingues [sɔrlɛ̃g] **NFPL** **les S.** the Isles of Scilly, the Scilly Isles

sornettes [sɔrnɛt] **NFPL** twaddle, rubbish

sort [sɔr] **NM 1** *(situation)* **être satisfait de son s.** to be satisfied with one's lot; **faire un s. à** *(choses inutiles, encombrantes)* to dispose of; *Fam (ne rien laisser de) (bouteille, poulet rôti etc)* to polish off, to finish off **2** *(destin)* fate, destiny; **notre s. est décidé** our fate is sealed; **abandonner qn à son triste s.** to abandon sb to his/her fate; **l'artillerie fit le s. de la bataille** the artillery decided the battle; **coup/ironie du s.** stroke/irony of fate; **et alors, ironie du s., qui vois-je en face de moi? lui!** and as fate would have it, who do I see in front of me? him! **3** *(hasard)* chance, fortune; **tirer (qch) au s.** to draw lots (for something); *(jouer à pile ou face)* to toss a coin; **tirer une place au s.** to draw lots for a place; **tirage au s.** drawing of lots; *Ftbl etc* toss; **le s. en est jeté** the die is cast

4 *(magique)* spell, charm; **jeter un s. à qn** to cast a spell on *or* over sb; **conjurer le mauvais s.** to ward off bad luck

sortable [sɔrtabl] **ADJ** *Fam (personne)* presentable; **tu n'es pas s.!** I can't take you anywhere!

sortant, -ante [sɔrtɑ̃, -ɑ̃t] **ADJ** *(numéro à la loterie)* winning; *(membres d'un comité etc)* outgoing, retiring; **élèves sortants** pupils in their last term; *Mil* cadets passing out; **les députés sortants** the outgoing members of parliament

N **les sortants** those going/coming out

sorte [sɔrt] **NF 1** *(manière)* way; **ne parlez pas de la s.** don't talk like that *or* in that way; **en quelque s.** as it were, in a way; **il sort très peu habillé, de s. qu'il tombe malade** he doesn't dress warmly when he goes out and so he falls ill *or* with the result that he falls ill; **de s. à faire** so as to do; **je lui en ai parlé de s. qu'il ne soit pas pris au dépourvu** I told him about it so that he wouldn't be caught unawares; SEE GRAMMAR B33 **faites en s. que tout soit prêt à temps** see to it that everything is ready in time; **fais en s. de tout préparer à l'avance** try to prepare everything in advance

2 *(genre)* sort, kind; **toute(s) sorte(s) de choses, des choses de toute(s) sorte(s)** all sorts *or* kinds of things; **des gens de toute(s) sorte(s)** all sorts *or* kinds of people; **un homme de s.** a man of that sort *or* kind; **une s. de ragoût** a *or* some sort *or* kind of stew; **je n'ai rien dit/rien fait de la s.** I said/did no such thing, I said/did nothing of the kind *or* sort VOIR GRAMMAIRE A13

sorteur, -euse [sɔrtœr, -øz] *Belg* **ADJ** *(noceur)* **ils sont très sorteurs** they like to party *or* to live it up **N** *(noceur)* reveller, partygoer **NM** *(videur)* bouncer

sorteux, -euse [sɔrtø, -øz] *Can Fam* **ADJ** *(qui aime sortir)* sociable, who likes going out **N** *(personne sociable)* sociable person

SORTIE [sɔrti]

leaving **1** ▪ exit **1, 5, 12** ▪ way out **12** ▪ publication **2** ▪ release **2** ▪ output **4, 5** ▪ outflow **3, 8** ▪ export **7** ▪ sortie **10** ▪ outburst **11** ▪ outlet **13**

NF 1 *(action de quitter un lieu)* going out, coming out, leaving; *Théâtre* exit; **préparer sa s.** to prepare one's exit; **faire une fausse s.** to make a false exit; **c'était ma première s. depuis mon accident** it was the first time I had been out since my accident, it was my first outing after my accident; **à la s. du théâtre/du cinéma** at the end of the performance/of the film; **à la s. des classes** when school comes out; **à (l'heure de) la s. des bureaux** when the offices come out

2 *Com (d'un livre, d'un journal)* publication; *(d'un film, d'un disque)* release; *(d'un modèle)* launch(ing); **s. en salle** *(d'un film)* (cinema) release

3 *(écoulement) (de liquide)* outflow, flowing out; **tuyaux de s.** outlet pipes

4 *Élec, Électron* output

5 *Ordinat* exit; *(information)* output; **s. d'imprimante** printer output; **dispositif de s.** output device; **signal de s.** output signal

6 *Tech (de feuilles de la presse d'imprimerie etc)* delivery; **table de s.** delivery table

7 *Com (de marchandises)* export

8 *Fin* **les sorties** *or* the gold withdrawals; **s. de devises/de capitaux** currency/capital outflow

9 *(excursion)* trip, excursion, outing; *(congé)* leave; **organiser une s. entre élèves** to organize a school trip; **priver qn de s.** to stop sb from going out; **faire une s. en mer**

to go for a short sea trip; **jour de s.** day out; **avoir un jour de s. par semaine** to have one free day a week; **nous sommes de s. aujourd'hui** we're going out today; **j'étais de s. mardi** I was out on Tuesday; **quelles sont vos sorties?** where do you go when you go out?; *Naut* **s. à terre** shore leave; **l'année dernière les canots de sauvetage ont fait cinquante sorties** last year the lifeboats went out fifty times

10 *Mil* sally, sortie; **faire une s.** *Ftbl (de gardien de but)* to leave the penalty box

11 *Fam (verbale)* outburst, tirade; **faire une s. à** *ou* **contre qn** to lash out at sb; **je le sais capable de n'importe quelle s. devant eux** I know he's capable of saying anything in front of them

12 *(issue)* exit, way out; **porte de s.** exit door; *Fig* **se ménager une porte de s.** to make sure one has a way out *or* an escape route; **il y a une s. sur la ruelle** there is a way out into the lane; **à la s. de la gare** at the station exit; **par ici la s.** this way out; **s. d'autoroute** motorway exit

13 *(pour l'eau, la vapeur)* outlet

14 *TV, Cin (fin de séquence)* out

▸▸ **s. de bain** bathrobe; *Vieilli* **s. de bal** evening wrap, opera cloak; **sorties de caisse** cash payments; *Ordinat* **s. écran** screen output; **sorties de fonds** outgoings, expenses; *Ordinat* **s. (sur) imprimante** printout; *Ordinat* **s. imprimée** printed output; *Ordinat* **s. jeux** games port; *Ordinat* **s. parallèle** parallel output; **s. de secours** emergency exit; *Ordinat* **s. série** serial output; **sorties de trésorerie** cash outflow *or* outgoings

sortilège [sɔrtilɛʒ] **NM** spell, charm

SORTIR[1] [sɔrtir] *(prp* **sortant;** *pp* **sorti;** *pr ind* **je sors, il sort, n. sortons, ils sortent;** *pr sub* **je sorte;** *impf* **je sortais;** *p hist* **je sortis;** *fu* **je sortirai)**

> **VI** to go out **1, 8** ▪ to come out **1, 5** ▪ to leave **1, 5** ▪ to come up **4** ▪ to get out **1, 5** ▪ to stand out **12** ▪ to stick out **12, 13** ▪ to exit **14**
> **VT** to take out **1, 2** ▪ to bring out **3** ▪ to release **3** ▪ to output **5**
> **VPR** to get out of *(se sortir de)*

VI *(aux* **être) 1** *(à pied) (aller)* to go out, to leave; *(venir)* to come out, to leave; *(d'un magazine, d'un livre)* to come out, to be published; *(d'un film)* to come out, to be released; **le livre sort chez Gallimard le mois prochain** the book will be published by Gallimard next month; **s. sur le marché** to come onto the market; **je n'arrivais pas à s.** I couldn't get out; *Scol* **est-ce que je peux s.?** may I be excused?; **entrer par une porte et s. par l'autre** to go in one door and out the other; **faire s. qn** *(en promenade etc)* to take sb out; *(mettre à la porte)* to make sb leave, to put sb out; **fais s. les enfants, nous avons à parler** send the children out of the room, we have to talk; **sortez (d'ici)!** get out (of here)!; **je sors d'une mauvaise grippe** I'm just recovering from *or* getting over a bad dose of flu; **s. vainqueur d'un tournoi** to come out on top *or* emerge the winner in a tournament; **tu sors à quelle heure, ce soir?** *(du bureau, du lycée etc)* what time do you finish tonight?; *Fig Fam* **nous ne sommes pas sortis de l'auberge!** we're not out of the wood(s) yet; **cela ne doit pas s. d'ici** *(cela doit rester secret)* it mustn't go any further; *Fam* **d'où sors-tu?** *(tu n'es pas au courant)* what planet have you been on?; *(tu es mal élevé)* where did they find you?; **cela m'est sorti de la mémoire** *ou* **de la tête** it has slipped my mind *or* gone out of my head; **il ne sortira pas grand-chose de tout cela** not much will come of all this; *Ind* **s. de la chaîne de fabrication** to come off the production line;

Théâtre **Macbeth sort** exit Macbeth; *Fin* **s. au tirage** *(d'obligations)* to be drawn; *Scol* **cette question est sortie (à l'examen)** this question came up (in the examination); *Cartes* **le dix de carreau est sorti** the ten of diamonds turned up

2 *(d'un cavalier)* to ride out; *(d'un conducteur, d'un véhicule)* to drive out; *(d'un capitaine de navire)* to sail out; **nous ne sommes pas beaucoup sortis en mer cet été** we didn't get out on the boat much this summer

3 *(avec complément de manière)* **s. en courant/en dansant** to run/dance out; **s. précipitamment** *ou* **à la hâte** *ou* **en toute hâte** to hurry out; **s. furtivement** *ou* **à pas de loup** to steal *or* creep out

4 *(des fleurs)* to come out; *(d'une plante)* to come up, to spring up; **ses dents commencent à s.** *(d'un bébé)* his/her teeth are beginning to come through

5 **s. de** *(quitter) (collège, port, bureau, emploi etc)* to leave; *(voiture)* to get out of; *(enfance, brume, obscurité)* to emerge from; **je sors du collège/de table** I have just left school/the table; **il sort d'ici** he has just left; **je sortais de chez toi quand …** I was just leaving your house when …; **je ne savais pas comment le faire s. du bureau** I didn't know how to get him out of the office; **on sortait de l'hiver** winter was just over; **s. de la salle** to go/come out of the room, to leave the room; **s. de son lit** to get out of bed; *Méd* to leave one's bed; *(d'une rivière)* to overflow its banks; *Fig* **s. du bois** *(se révéler tel qu'on est)* to show one's true colours; **il est à peine sorti de l'enfance** he's little more than a child; **s. indemne d'un accident** to come out of an accident unscathed; **sortira-t-elle blanchie de ce scandale?** will she come out of this scandal with her name cleared?; **s. de sa froideur habituelle** to show unusual warmth; **cela lui a permis de s. de soi** it brought him out of himself

6 *Arch, Fam* **s. de faire qch** to have just done sth; *Fam* **merci bien! je sors d'en prendre** no thank you! once is enough

7 *(quitter la maison)* to go out; **Madame Dupont est sortie** Mrs Dupont is out *or* has gone out; **elle est sortie à trois heures** she went out at three o'clock; **il ne sort pas de chez moi** he practically lives at my place; **je ne sors pas de chez moi** I don't go out, I don't leave the house; **tu devrais s. un peu plus** you should get out (of the house) a bit more; **s. faire des courses** to go out shopping; **s. acheter du pain** to go out to buy bread; **s. à cheval/à pied** to go out riding/walking; **faire s. le chien** to let the dog out

8 *(pour s'amuser)* **ils sortent tous les samedis soir** they go out every Saturday evening; **s. avec qn** *(en amis)* to go out with sb; *(avoir une relation amoureuse avec)* to be going out with sb; **ils sortent ensemble depuis deux ans** they've been going out together *or* with each other for two years; *Fig* **tu n'as pas entendu parler de ce film? mais il faut s. un peu!** you haven't heard of this film? what planet have you been on?

9 **s. de** *(s'écarter de) (son devoir etc)* to swerve *or* deviate from; **s. de son sujet** to deviate *or* wander from one's subject; **cela sort de ma compétence** that doesn't come within my scope; **s. des bornes de la bienséance** to overstep the bounds of decency; **s. d'une règle** to ignore *or* depart from a rule; *(transgresser)* to break a rule; **s. des rails** *(d'un train)* to jump the rails; **la voiture est sortie de la route** the car left the road; *Fig* **il ne sort pas de là, il n'en sort pas** he is sticking to his guns; **ça sort de l'ordinaire** that's out of the ordinary; **s. de cadence** *(d'un danseur)* to be *or* get out of step; *Mus* **s. de mesure** to be *or* get out of time; **s. du ton** to be *or* get out of tune

10 s. de *(échapper à) (difficulté, danger)* to get out of, to extricate oneself from; **aider qn à s. d'une difficulté** to help sb out (of a difficulty); **s. d'affaire** to get out of trouble; **soyez plus précis ou nous n'en sortirons pas** be more precise or we shall never get to the end of it; **j'ai trop à faire, je n'en sors pas** I've too much to do, I shall never get through it *or* to the end of it

11 s. de *(être issu de) (bonne famille etc)* to come from; **ce livre sort de ma plume** this book is one of mine; **s. de l'université** to graduate (from university); **cheval sorti d'un bon haras** horse (that comes) from a good stud *or* stable

12 *(dépasser, être en relief)* to stand out, to stick out, to protrude (**de** from); **yeux qui sortent de la tête** protruding *or* bulging eyes; **les yeux lui sortaient de la tête** his eyes were popping out of his head; **son portefeuille sortait de sa poche** his wallet was sticking out of his pocket

13 *(d'une silhouette sur une photo, d'une pensée, d'une caractéristique etc)* to stand out, to be prominent; **faire s. un trait de caractère/un rôle** to emphasize a characteristic/a part

14 *Ordinat* **s. (d'un système)** to exit (from a system); **s. d'un programme** to exit a program; **s. sans sauvegarder** to exit without saving

VT *(aux* **avoir) 1** *(mener dehors) (enfant, chien etc)* to take out; **s. la voiture** to get the car out; **sortez-la!** get her out (of here)!; **cela nous sortira de l'ordinaire** that will make a change; **il faut le s. d'affaire/de ce mauvais pas** I/we'll *etc* have to get him out of this mess/fix

2 *(tirer) (objet)* to take out; **s. les mains de ses poches** to take one's hands out of one's pockets; **et si tu sortais ton bon whisky/tes photos de mariage?** how about getting out your good whisky/your wedding photographs?; **il sortit sa pipe** he brought out *or* took out *or* got out his pipe; **s. ses griffes** to unsheathe its claws; **s. ses cornes** *(d'un escargot)* to put out its horns; **s. un livre de la bibliothèque** to take a book out of the library; *Typ* **s. une ligne** *(dans la marge)* to run out a line

3 *(mettre sur le marché) (livre)* to bring out, to publish; *(journal)* to bring out; *(film, disque)* to bring out, to release; *esp Ordinat* **s. sur le marché** to ship

4 *Fam (raconter)* **il nous en a sorti une bien bonne** he came out with a good one; **tu sais ce qu'il m'a sorti?** do you know what he came out with?; **elle m'a sorti qu'elle y avait pensé avant moi!** she had the cheek to tell me she'd thought of it before me!

5 *Ordinat* to output

VPR **se sortir** **se s. d'une situation difficile** to get out of *or* extricate oneself from a difficult situation; **elle aura du mal à se s. de là toute seule** she'll have trouble getting out of that on her own; **le malade s'en sortira** the patient will pull through; **je crois que je ne vais pas m'en s.** I don't think I'll be able to cope *or* manage; **je ne m'en serais jamais sorti sans toi** I'd never have done it *or* managed without you; **tu t'en es bien sorti, pour une première tentative** you did very well considering it was your first attempt

sortir[2] **NM** **au s. du cinéma** on coming out of the cinema; **au s. de l'école** when they/we/ *etc* come/came out of school; *(pour toujours)* on leaving school; **au s. de la table** at the end of the meal, when we/they/*etc* get up *or* get up from the table; **au s. de l'hiver/de la réunion** at the end of the winter/the meeting

sortir[3] **VT** *(conj like* **finir)** *(used only in third* *person) Jur* **cette sentence sortira son plein (et entier) effet** this decision shall have full effect

S.O.S. [ɛsoɛs] NM *Aviat, Naut, Fig* SOS; **envoyer** *ou* **lancer un S.** to send (out) an SOS (à to); **S. Amitié** = helpline for people in need of emotional support, *Br* ≃ Samaritans; **S. médecins** emergency medical service; **S.-Racisme** = anti-racist movement

sosie [sɔzi] NM *(personne)* double; **on dirait ton s.** he/she is your double; **c'est vraiment le s. de son père** he really is the double of *or* the spitting image of his father

sot, sotte [so, sɔt] ADJ *(personne, réponse, projet etc)* silly, stupid, foolish
  N fool, idiot; *Hist, Théâtre* fool

> Il faut noter que le nom anglais **sot** est un faux ami. Il signifie **ivrogne**.

sotie [sɔti] NF *Hist, Théâtre* (medieval) farce

sot-l'y-laisse [soliɛs] NM INV *Culin (du poulet)* oyster

sotte [sɔt] ADJ *voir* **sot**

sottement [sɔtmɑ̃] ADV stupidly, foolishly

sottise [sɔtiz] NF **1** *(stupidité)* stupidity, silliness, foolishness; **cette fille est d'une s. rare** that girl is exceptionally stupid; **je n'ai jamais rencontré une telle s. chez quiconque** I've never met anyone so stupid **2** *(action stupide)* foolish *or* stupid act; *(parole stupide)* foolish *or* stupid remark; **faire des sottises** to do foolish *or* stupid things; *(d'un enfant)* to be naughty; **dire des sottises** to say foolish *or* stupid things, to talk nonsense; **ai-je dit une s.?** have I said something stupid? **3** *Vieilli (parole injurieuse)* offensive remark, insult; **dire des sottises à qn** to abuse sb

sottisier [sɔtizje] NM collection of howlers

sou [su] NM **1** **amasser une fortune s. par s.** to scrape a fortune together; **un s. est un s.** every penny counts; **payer s. à s.** to pay in small instalments; **donne un s. au petit** give the lad some coppers; **ne pas avoir** *ou* **être sans le s.** to be penniless; **je n'ai pas le s.** I don't have a penny; *Vieilli* **cela vaut vingt mille euros comme un s.** it's worth a twenty thousand euros if it's worth a penny; **affaire de quatre sous** *Br* twopenny-halfpenny business, *Am* nickel-and-dime business; **il n'est pas ambitieux pour deux sous** *ou* **pour un s.** he hasn't an ounce of ambition, he's not in the least ambitious; **il n'a pas pour deux sous de courage** he hasn't an ounce of courage; **elle n'est pas méchante pour deux sous** *ou* **pour un s.** she hasn't got a nasty bone in her body; *Fam* **s'ennuyer à cent sous de l'heure** to be bored stiff *or* bored out of one's mind; **il est toujours en train de compter ses sous** he watches every last penny, he's always counting every penny; **je te l'achèterais si j'avais des sous** I'd buy it for you if I had the money; **c'est une affaire de gros sous** there's big money involved; **être près de ses sous** to be a penny-pincher; **ils veulent des sous, toujours des sous!** all they want is money for this and money for that!; **appareil** *ou* **machine à sous** slot machine; *(jeu)* one-armed bandit, *Br* fruit machine
  2 *Can (cent)* cent
  3 *Hist (pièce de cinq centimes)* sou; *Arch* **pièce de cent sous** five-franc piece

souahéli [swaheli], **souahili** [swahili] ADJ Swahili
  NM *Ling* Swahili

soubassement [subasmɑ̃] NM **1** *Archit (d'un bâtiment)* base, basement; *Fig* **le s. social** the social substructure **2** *Tech (d'une machine-outil etc)* base (plate) **3** *Géol* bedrock **4** *Aut* sub-frame, under-structure, underbody frame; **s. de châssis** underframe

soubresaut [subrəso] NM *(d'un véhicule)* jolt; *(d'une personne)* start, jerk; **avoir un s.** to jump, to give a start

soubrette [subrɛt] NF *Théâtre* soubrette, maidservant; *Fam (servante coquette)* soubrette

souche [suʃ] NF **1** *(d'un arbre)* stump; *(du vin)* stock; *Fam* **rester comme une s.** to be rooted to the spot; **dormir comme une s.** to sleep like a log
  2 *(de famille)* founder; **faire s.** to found a line; **il vient de bonne s.** he comes from good stock; **famille de vieille s.** an old family
  3 *(d'un virus etc)* strain
  4 *Com (de chèques, de tickets etc)* counterfoil, stub; **carnet de tickets à s.** book of tickets with counterfoils
  5 *(d'une cheminée)* stack
  6 *Ling* root; **mot s.** root word
  7 *Belg (ticket de caisse, reçu)* receipt

souci¹ [susi] NM *Bot* marigold; **s. d'eau** marsh marigold

souci² NM **1** *(soin)* concern (**de** for); **avoir le s. de plaire** to be anxious to please; **avoir le s. de la vérité/de l'exactitude** to be meticulously truthful/accurate; **je me suis limité à deux auteurs dans un s. de clarté** I limited myself to two authors in order to keep things clear; **c'est le moindre** *ou* **le dernier** *ou* **le cadet de mes soucis** that's the least of my worries
  2 *(inquiétude)* worry, anxiety; **elle doit avoir des soucis** she must have problems; **sans s., libre de soucis** carefree, free from worry *or* anxiety; **cet enfant est un perpétuel s.** this child is a perpetual (source of) worry; *Fam* **il nous fait bien du s.** he worries us a lot, he gives us a lot of worry; **se faire du s.** to worry (**pour qch** about sth); **inutile de te faire du s. pour ça, ce n'est rien** there's no point worrying about it, it's not important; **soucis d'argent** *ou* **financiers** money *or* financial troubles *or* worries; *Fam* **il n'y a pas de soucis!** no worries!

soucier [susje] *(impf, pr sub* **n. souciions, v. souciiez)** VT *Arch (d'une chose) (personne)* to trouble, to worry
  VPR **se soucier se s. de qn/de qch/de faire qch** to worry *or* be concerned about sb/sth/doing sth; **il se soucie toujours des autres** he is always worrying about other people; **ne se s. de rien** not to worry about anything; **pars en vacances et ne te soucie de rien** go on holiday and don't worry about a thing; *Fam* **je m'en soucie comme de l'an quarante** *ou* **de ma première chemise** I don't give a damn (about it)

soucieux, -ieuse [susjø, -jøz] ADJ **1** *(attentif)* anxious, concerned (**de** about); **être s. de faire qch** to be anxious to do sth; **elle a toujours été soucieuse de ne pas les décevoir** she has always been anxious not to let them down; **peu s.** unconcerned (**de** about); **peu s. de la rencontrer** unconcerned about meeting her **2** *(inquiète)* anxious, worried, concerned; **avoir un air s.** to look anxious *or* worried *or* concerned

soucoupe [sukup] NF saucer; *Fig Fam* **elle a ouvert** *ou* **fait des yeux comme des soucoupes** her eyes were as big as saucers
  ▸▸ **s. volante** flying saucer

soudage [sudaʒ] NM soldering; **s. (autogène)** *(de pièces en métal etc)* welding

soudain [sudɛ̃] ADJ sudden
  ADV suddenly, all of a sudden; **s. elle se mit à hurler** all of a sudden, she started to scream, she suddenly started to scream

soudainement [sudɛnmɑ̃] ADV suddenly

soudaineté [sudɛnte] NF suddenness

Soudan [sudɑ̃] NM **le S.** the Sudan

soudanais, -aise [sudanɛ, -ɛz] ADJ Sudanese
  N **S.** Sudanese

soudant [sudɑ̃] ADJ *Métal* **blanc s.** welding heat

soudard [sudar] NM *Litt Péj* brutish soldier

soude [sud] NF **1** *Bot* saltwort, (prickly) glasswort **2** *Chimie, Ind* soda; **(carbonate de) s., cristaux de s., s. ordinaire** washing *or* common soda; **bicarbonate de s.** bicarbonate of soda; **s. caustique** caustic soda

souder [sude] VT **1** *(avec alliage fusible)* to solder; **s. au cuivre** *ou* **au laiton** to braze; **s. à l'étain** to soft-solder **2** *(autogène)* to weld; **s. à l'arc (électrique)** to arc-weld; **machine à s.** welding machine, welder; **s. par points** to spot-weld **3** *(unir) (os fracturé)* to knit, to join; *Fig (groupes etc)* to unite; **cette épreuve nous a soudés** this hardship united us *or* brought us together
  VPR **se souder** *(des os)* to knit (together), to join; *Fig (d'un groupe)* to unite

soudeur, -euse [sudœr, -øz] N *(personne) (employant la soudure par alliage)* solderer; *(employant la soudure autogène)* welder; **s. par points** spot-welder; **s. au chalumeau** lamp *or* torch welder
  NF **soudeuse** *(machine)* welder, welding machine; **s. par points** spot-welder

soudoyer [sudwaje] VT (**je soudoie, n. soudoyons; je soudoierai**) **1** *Péj (personne)* to bribe; **s. qn pour qu'il fasse qch** to bribe sb into doing sth; **il n'accepterait jamais de se faire s.** he would never accept a bribe; **s. un assassin** to hire a killer **2** *Mil Arch (mercenaire)* to pay

soudure [sudyr] NF **1** *(opération) (par alliage)* soldering; *(autogène)* welding; **s. au cuivre** *ou* **au laiton** brazing; **s. à l'étain** soft-soldering; **s. par points** spot weld
  2 *(lieu)* soldered joint; *(autogène)* weld; **s. à nœud** wipe(d) joint; **sans soudure(s)** seamless; **la s. ne se voit pas du tout** you can't see the join *or* weld at all
  3 *(alliage)* solder
  4 *(d'os)* join
  5 *Écon* **faire la s.** to bridge the gap; *Fig* **faire la s. entre deux directeurs/systèmes** to bridge the gap between two directors/systems; **c'est moi qui fait la s.** I'm filling in (in the meantime); **elle fera la s. entre les deux directeurs** she'll be acting manager

soufflage [suflaʒ] NM **1** *(de verre)* glass blowing **2** *Métal* blowing

soufflant, -ante [suflɑ̃, -ɑ̃t] ADJ **1** *Tech* blowing; **machine soufflante** blowing *or* blast engine **2** *Fam (étonnant)* breathtaking
  NF *Tech* **soufflante** blower, fan; **soufflante de sustentation** *(d'un aéroglisseur)* lift fan; *Aut etc* **soufflante de suralimentation** supercharger

soufflard [suflar] NM *Géol* fumarole

souffle [sufl] NM **1** *(d'air, de vent)* breath, puff; **pas un s.** not a breath of air
  2 *(respiration)* breathing; *(de coureur etc)* breath, wind; *(air respiré)* breath; *(air expiré)* blow, puff; **retenir son s.** to hold one's breath; **éteindre une chandelle d'un (seul) s.** to blow out a candle; **on la renverserait d'un s.** you could knock her over with a feather; **couper le s. à qn** to take sb's breath away; **le s. vital** *ou* **de la vie** the breath of life; **être à bout de s.** to be out of breath *or* winded; *Fig* to be unable to go on, *Fam* to have run out of steam; **l'économie est à bout de s.** the economy is running out of steam *or* is on its last legs; **manquer de s., avoir le s. court** to be short of breath *or* short-winded; **reprendre son s.** to get one's breath back; **exhaler son dernier s.** to breathe one's last; **n'avoir plus de s.** to be out of breath; **sa vie ne tient qu'à un s.** his/her life hangs by a

thread; *Fig* **second s. de l'économie** new lease of life for the economy; *Fam* **c'est à vous couper le s.** it's breathtaking; *Fam* **il ne manque pas de s.!** *(culot)* he's got a cheek *or* a nerve!

3 *(d'une explosion)* blast

4 *Aviat (d'hélices)* slipstream, wash

5 *Méd* **(bruit de) s.** murmur; **s. au cœur** *ou* **cardiaque** heart murmur

6 *(force créatrice)* inspiration; **s. poétique** poetic inspiration

soufflé [sufle] **ADJ** *(visage)* puffy, puffed up; *Culin (omelette, pommes de terre etc)* soufflé; *Fam (ahuri)* amazed, taken aback

NM *Culin* soufflé; **s. au fromage/au chocolat** cheese/chocolate soufflé; **moule à soufflés** soufflé dish

soufflement [sufləmã] **NM** blowing

souffler [sufle] **VI 1** *(en expulsant de l'air)* to blow; *(d'un taureau, d'un buffle)* to snort; **s. dans ses doigts** to blow on one's fingers; **si la soupe est trop chaude, souffle!** if the soup's too hot, blow on it!; **s. dans une trompette** to blow a trumpet; *Fig Fam* **tu peux s. dessus!** you haven't a chance!; *Fig Fam* **si tu crois que ça va marcher en soufflant dessus, tu te trompes** if you think it's going to work just like that, you're mistaken; *Fam* **s. dans les bronches à qn** to bawl sb out

2 *(reprendre son souffle)* to get one's breath back; **laisser s. un cheval** to let a horse get its wind, to give a horse a breather; **elle ne nous a pas laissé s.** *(entre deux tâches etc)* she didn't give us time to get our breath back; *(de toute la journée)* she didn't give us time to draw breath *or* to catch our breath

3 *(respirer avec peine)* to pant, to puff; **suant et soufflant** huffing and puffing, puffing and blowing; *Fig Fam* **s. comme un bœuf** to puff and pant

4 *(du vent etc)* to blow; **le vent va s. fort cette nuit** it will be very windy tonight; *Fig* **regarder** *ou* **voir d'où vient** *ou* **de quel côté souffle le vent** to see which way the wind is blowing, to see which way the land lies; *Fig* **un vent de révolte soufflait** there was a spirit of revolt in the air

5 *surtout Scol (à ses camarades)* to prompt; **on ne souffle pas!** no prompting!

6 *(aux dames)* to take; **s. n'est pas jouer** taking a piece doesn't count as a go

VT 1 *(verre)* to blow; *(ballon etc)* to blow up

2 *(fumée, poussière etc)* to blow (**dans** into); *(orgue)* to blow; *(bougie)* to blow out

3 *(chuchoter)* to whisper (**à qn** to sb); **s. qch à l'oreille de qn** to whisper sth in sb's ear; **ne pas s. (un) mot** not to breathe a word; **s. (son rôle à) un acteur** to prompt an actor; **quelqu'un a dû lui s. l'idée** someone must have given him/her the idea

4 *Fam (prendre) (peine)* to pinch (**à qn** from sb); **se faire s. sa place** to have one's seat pinched; **s. un pion** *(aux dames)* to huff a man

5 *(d'une explosion) (bâtiment etc)* to blast

6 *Fam (ahurir)* **s. qn** to amaze sb, to take sb aback; **son culot nous a soufflés** his/her cheek took our breath away

soufflerie [sufləri] **NF 1** *(d'un orgue, d'une forge)* bellows **2** *Ind* blower **3** *Aviat, Phys* wind tunnel; **essais en s.** wind-tunnel tests

soufflet [sufle] **NM 1** *(instrument)* (pair of) bellows **VOIR GRAMMAIRE A10 2 valise à soufflets** expanding suitcase **3** *Rail (entre les voitures)* concertina vestibule **4** *Couture* gusset **5** *Mus (d'un orgue)* swell **6** *Litt (gifle)* slap (in the face); *(insulte)* insult **7** *Aut* gaiter

souffleter [suflate] **VT** *(je soufflette, n. souffletons; je souffletterai)* *Litt Vieilli* **s. qn** *(le gifler)* to slap sb's face; *(l'insulter)* to insult sb

soufflette [suflɛt] **NF** *Belg (ampoule)* blister; *(boursouflure)* swelling

souffleur, -euse [suflœr, -øz] **N s. de verre** glass blower

NF souffleuse 1 *Can (chasse-neige)* snowblower **2** *Agr (pour les graines etc)* blower container

N *Théâtre* prompter

souffrure [suflyr] **NF** *(dans la peinture, le verre, le métal)* blister, bubble; *(dans un pneu)* bulge

souffrance [sufrãs] **NF 1 en s.** *(travail)* pending; *(candidats)* on the waiting list; *(factures)* overdue, outstanding; *(colis)* held up in transit, awaiting delivery **2** *(douleur)* suffering, pain; **s. physique/morale** physical/mental suffering *or* pain; **rien ne pouvait apaiser ses souffrances** nothing could alleviate his/her suffering

souffrant [sufrã] **ADJ 1** *(un peu malade)* unwell, poorly; **il a l'air s.** he doesn't look well **2** *Litt (qui souffre)* suffering; **l'humanité souffrante** suffering humanity

souffre-douleur **NM INV** laughing stock, butt (of the joke); **c'est le s. du lycée** he's the laughing stock of the school

souffreteux, -euse [sufrətø, -øz] **ADJ** *(enfant etc)* sickly

souffrir [sufrir] *(prp* **souffrant**; *pp* **souffert**; *pr ind* **je souffre, il souffre, n. souffrons, ils souffrent**; *impf* **je souffrais**; *p hist* **je souffris**; *fu* **je souffrirai**) **VT 1** *(supporter) (douleur, fatigue, froid, perte, insulte etc)* to suffer, to endure; **s. le martyre** to go through torture *or* agonies; **je ne peux pas s. qu'on vienne me déranger** I cannot bear to be disturbed, I cannot permit *or* allow that; *Fam* **je ne peux pas s. cet homme/cette odeur** I can't bear *or* stand that man/smell

2 *(permettre)* to permit, to allow; **je ne saurais s. cela** I cannot permit *or* allow that; **souffrez que je vous dise la vérité** allow *or* permit me to tell you the truth; **situation qui ne souffre aucun retard** situation that admits of no delay; **s. l'étalon** *(d'une jument)* to take the stallion

VI 1 *(physiquement)* to be in pain, to suffer; *(moralement)* to suffer; **mon bras me fait s.** my arm is hurting (me) *or* giving me pain; **il m'a fait s.** *(physiquement, sentimentalement)* he hurt me; **s. du froid/des maux de tête** to suffer from the cold/from headaches; **s. de la jambe** to have trouble with one's leg; **je souffre de le voir si changé** it pains *or* upsets me to see him so changed; **je souffre à marcher** I find walking painful; **avoir cessé de s.** to be out of pain

2 *(pâtir)* to suffer (**de** from); **les vignes ont souffert de la gelée** the vines have suffered from the frost; **nous avons beaucoup souffert de la guerre** we suffered a lot in the war, we were hard hit by the war

VPR se souffrir *Fam (se supporter)* **ils ne peuvent pas se s.** they can't stand each other

soufi [sufi] *Rel* **ADJ INV** Sufic

NM Sufi

soufisme [sufism] **NM** *Rel* Sufism

soufrage [sufraʒ] **NF** *(des allumettes, des plantes etc)* sulphuring, *Am* sulfuring; *Tex* sulphuration, *Am* sulfuration

soufre [sufr] **NM** sulphur, *Am* sulfur; *Fig* **ces écrits sentent le s.** these writings smack *or* reek of heresy

ADJ INV s. (jaune) sulphur *or* *Am* sulfur yellow

soufré [sufre] **NM** *(papillon)* brimstone

soufrer [sufre] **VT** *(allumettes, plantes etc)* to sulphur, *Am* to sulfur; *Tex* to sulphurate, *Am* to sulfurate

souhait [swɛ] **NM** wish; **faire** *ou* **formuler un s.** to make a wish; **présenter ses souhaits à qn** to offer sb one's good wishes; **présenter**

ses souhaits de bonne année to wish sb a Happy New Year; **à s.** perfectly; **doré/ensoleillé à s.** beautifully golden/sunny; **j'ai fini par trouver une pièce silencieuse à s.** I finally found a room that was as quiet as I could wish; **à vos souhaits!** *(à qn qui éternue)* bless you! SEE GRAMMAR A60; B40

souhaitable [swɛtabl] **ADJ** desirable; **il est s. que ... +** *sub* it is to be hoped that ...; **ce n'est guère s.** one can hardly wish for that; **il serait s. que ...** it would be desirable if ...

souhaiter [swɛte] **VT** *(succès etc)* to wish for; **je vous souhaite d'être pleinement heureux** I wish you every happiness; **je souhaite qu'on me tienne au courant** I wish to be kept informed; **je souhaite que vous réussissiez, je vous souhaite de réussir** I hope you will succeed; **s. la réussite/bon voyage à qn** to wish sb success/bon voyage; **je vous souhaite une bonne année/un joyeux anniversaire** best wishes for a happy New Year/a happy birthday; **s. bonne chance à qn** to wish sb (good) luck; *Fam Iron* **je vous souhaite bien du plaisir!, je vous en souhaite!** I wish you joy of it!; **cela n'est pas à s.** that is not very desirable; **il est à s. que ... +** *sub* it is to be hoped that ...; **je ne le souhaite à personne** I wouldn't wish that on anyone

souiller [suje] **VT 1** *(vêtements etc)* to soil, to dirty (**de** with); **vêtements souillés de boue** mudstained clothes **2** *Fig (contaminer)* to taint; **s. ses mains de sang** to stain one's hands with blood **3** *Litt (réputation, souvenir de qn etc)* to tarnish

souillon [sujɔ̃] **NF** *Litt* slut, sloven; *(servante)* slovenly maid

souillure [sujyr] **NF** *(sur un vêtement etc)* stain, *Litt* blot, blemish

souk [suk] **NM 1** *(marché)* souk **2** *Fam (lieu ou désordre)* shambles; **c'est le s., dans cette chambre!** what a shambles this bedroom is!; **foutre le s. (dans)** *(mettre en désordre)* to make a mess (of); **il fout le s. en classe** he creates havoc in the classroom

soul [sul] **ADJ INV, NF** *Mus* soul

soûl [su] **ADJ 1** *Fam (ivre)* drunk; **s. comme un Polonais** *ou* **comme un cochon** *ou* **comme une bourrique** drunk as a lord; **s. perdu** blind drunk **2** *Arch (rassasié)* replete, *Litt* **être s. de plaisir/de musique** to have had a surfeit of pleasure/music, to be sated with pleasure/music

NM rire/chanter/fumer tout son s. to laugh/sing/smoke to one's heart's content; **manger/boire tout son s.** to eat/drink one's fill *or* to one's heart's content

soulagement [sulaʒmã] **NM** relief; **éprouver un sentiment de s.** to feel relieved; **son départ sera un s. pour tous** his/her departure will come as a relief to all; **pousser un soupir de s.** to heave a sigh of relief

soulager [sulaʒe] *(je soulageai(s); n. soulageons)* **VT** *(pression, douleur)* to ease, to relieve; *(esprit, chagrin)* to soothe, to comfort; *(quelqu'un)* to relieve; **je vais vous faire une piqûre, ça va vous s.** I'm going to give you an injection which will bring you relief *or* make you feel better; **traitement qui soulage les douleurs** treatment for pain relief; **si ça peut te s., sache que je suis dans la même situation** if it makes you feel any better, I'm in the same situation; **s. les pauvres** to relieve the poor; **je suis soulagé de l'apprendre** I'm relieved to hear it; **on soulage ses maux à les raconter** it is a relief *or* a comfort *or* it helps to talk about one's troubles; **s. une poutre** to ease the strain on a beam; **s. les soupapes** to let off steam; **cela me soulage l'esprit d'un grand poids** that's a great weight off my mind; *Fam* **s. qn de son portefeuille** to relieve sb of his/her wallet

VPR se soulager 1 *(en parlant etc)* to ease

spationef [spasjɔnɛf] NM spaceship, spacecraft

spatio-temporel, -elle [spasjotɑ̃pɔrɛl] ADJ space-time, spatiotemporal

spatule [spatyl] NF 1 spatula; **en s.** spatulate 2 *(de ski)* (ski) tip 3 *(oiseau)* spoonbill

spatulé [spatyle] ADJ spatulate

speaker [spikœr] NM 1 *Radio, TV* announcer; *(qui donne les informations)* newsreader 2 *Pol (en Grande-Bretagne, aux États-Unis)* **le s.** the Speaker

speakerine [spikrin] NF *Radio, TV* (female) announcer; *(qui donne les informations)* (female) newsreader

spécial, -ale, -aux, -ales [spesjal, -o] ADJ 1 *(d'une catégorie particulière)* special, specific, distinctive; **une clé spéciale** a special key; **rien de s.** nothing special; *Journ* **envoyé s.** special correspondent; **édition spéciale** special edition; **privilège s. aux militaires** privilege reserved for *or* restricted to military men; **savon s. peaux grasses** soap for greasy skin 2 *(bizarre)* peculiar, odd; **c'est/il est un peu s.** it's/he's rather odd *or* peculiar; **c'est s., il faut aimer** *(d'un plat curieux etc)* not everybody likes it, it's not to everybody's taste
▪ NM *Can* 1 *(plat du jour)* special 2 **en s.** *(en solde)* on special

> Il faut noter qu'en anglais l'adjectif **special** ne s'emploie jamais à propos de quelque chose d'inhabituel ou d'étrange.

spécialement [spesjalmɑ̃] ADV (e)specially, particularly; *(exprès)* specially; **pas s.** not especially *or* particularly

spécialisation [spesjalizasjɔ̃] NF specialization

spécialisé [spesjalize] ADJ *(travail, matériaux etc)* specialized; **ouvrier s.** semi-skilled worker; **école/hôpital spécialisé(e)** special school/hospital; **enseignement s.** specialized teaching; **aciers spécialisés** speciality *or Am* specialty steels; **ils sont spécialisés dans les déménagements internationaux** they specialize in international relocations, they're international relocation specialists

spécialiser [spesjalize] VT **s. qn** to make *or* turn sb into a specialist
▪ VPR **se spécialiser se s. dans** *ou* **en qch** to specialize in sth

spécialiste [spesjalist] N specialist (**de, en** in); *Méd* **s. du cœur** heart specialist; *Mktg* **s. produit** product specialist; **s. du vol à voile** gliding specialist *or* expert; *Hum* **c'est un s. des rendez-vous manqués** missing appointments is his speciality, he specializes in missing appointments
▪ ADJ specialist; **médecin s.** specialist (doctor); *Hum* **elle est s. de ce genre de gaffes** she specializes in that sort of blunder

spécialité [spesjalite] NF 1 speciality, *Am* specialty; *Culin* **s. de la maison** speciality of the house; **faire sa s. de qch** to specialize in *or* make a special study of sth; **s. budgétaire** budgetary restriction; **s. médicale** specialized area of medicine; *Hum* **elle sera en retard, c'est sa s.** she'll be late, it's her speciality 2 **spécialités pharmaceutiques** patent medicines

spécieusement [spesjøzmɑ̃] ADV *Litt* speciously

spécieux, -euse [spesjø, -øz] ADJ *Litt* specious

spécification [spesifikasjɔ̃] NF *(action, définition)* specification; **s. de la fonction** job description; **s. du produit** product specification

spécificité [spesifisite] NF *Méd etc* specificity

spécifier [spesifje] VT *(impf, pr sub* **n. spéci-** *fiions, v.* **spécifiiez)** to specify, to state (**que** that); **compte spécifié** detailed *or* itemized account; **nous le lui avions pourtant spécifié par écrit** we had specifically informed him in writing; **je l'avais pourtant bien spécifié** I was quite specific about it

spécifique [spesifik] ADJ specific

spécifiquement [spesifikmɑ̃] ADV specifically

spécimen [spesimɛn] NM specimen; *(livre, fascicule)* specimen *or* sample copy; **page s.** specimen page; **s. gratuit** *(de livre)* presentation copy; **s. de signature** specimen signature

spectacle [spɛktakl] NM 1 *(choses vues)* sight, scene; **au s. de** at the sight of; **se donner en s.** to make an exhibition *or* a spectacle of oneself 2 *Théâtre, Cin etc (représentation)* show; **le s.** *(industrie)* show business; **monter un s.** to put on a show; **s. de variétés** variety show; **s. folklorique** performance of national/regional music/dancing; **s. solo** one-man show; **aller au s.** to go to a show; **salle de s.** hall; *Théâtre* theatre, *Am* theater; *Cin* cinema, *Am* movie theater; *Théâtre* **pièce à grand s.** lavish production; *Cin* **film à grand s.** epic (film)

spectaculaire [spɛktakylɛr] ADJ spectacular

spectateur, -trice [spɛktatœr, -tris] N 1 *(témoin)* spectator, onlooker; *(d'accident)* witness 2 *Sport* spectator; *Théâtre* member of the audience; *Théâtre* **spectateurs** audience

spectral, -ale, -aux, -ales [spɛktral, -o] ADJ 1 *(de fantôme)* ghostly, spectral 2 *Opt* spectral

spectre [spɛktr] NM 1 *(fantôme)* ghost, phantom; *Fig (de la guerre, de la misère etc)* spectre, *Am* specter 2 *Phys etc* spectrum; **s. solaire** solar spectrum; *Pharm* **s. d'action** *(d'un antibiotique)* spectrum

spectrogramme [spɛktrɔgram] NM spectrogram

spectrographe [spɛktrɔgraf] NM spectrograph

spectromètre [spɛktrɔmɛtr] NM spectrometer

spectrométrie [spɛktrɔmetri] NF spectrometry

spectroscope [spɛktrɔskɔp] NM *Opt* spectroscope

spectroscopie [spɛktrɔskɔpi] NF spectroscopy

spéculaire [spekylɛr] ADJ 1 *(minéral)* specular 2 *Méd* **écriture s.** mirror writing

spéculateur, -trice [spekylatœr, -tris] N *Fin* speculator; **s. sur devises** currency speculator; *Bourse* **s. à la baisse** bear; *Bourse* **s. à la hausse** bull; **s. à la journée** day to day trader, scalper; **s. sur plusieurs positions** position trader

spéculatif, -ive [spekylatif, -iv] ADJ *Phil, Fin* speculative
▪ NF **spéculative** *(publicité)* pitch

spéculation [spekylasjɔ̃] NF 1 *Phil* speculation (**sur** on) 2 *Fin* speculation; **s. à la baisse** bear operations; **s. à la hausse** bull operations; **s. immobilière** property speculation

spéculer [spekyle] VI 1 *Phil* to speculate (**sur** on, about) 2 *Fin* to speculate (**sur** in; **à** for); *Bourse* **s. en Bourse** to speculate on the Stock Market; **s. à la baisse** to go a bear, to be bearish; *Bourse* **s. à la hausse** to go a bull, to be bullish; *Fig* **s. sur qch** to count *or* bank on sth

speculum, spéculum [spekylɔm] NM *Méd* speculum

speech, pl speeches [spitʃ] NM speech; **il nous a fait tout un s. sur la ponctualité** he gave us a long speech about punctuality

speed [spid] *Fam* ADJ *(nerveux)* hyper
▪ NM *(amphétamine)* speed

speedé [spide] ADJ *Fam* 1 *(hyperactif)* hyped up, hyper 2 *(drogué)* high

speeder [spide] *Fam* VT to rush
▪ VI to get a move on; **je n'aime pas s. le lundi matin** I don't like rushing on Monday mornings; **j'ai speedé toute la journée** I've been running around like a headless chicken all day

spéléologie [speleɔlɔʒi] NF caving, potholing, *Am* spelunking; *(étude)* speleology

spéléologique [speleɔlɔʒik] ADJ speleological

spéléologue [speleɔlɔg] N caver, potholer, *Am* spelunker; *(étudiant)* speleologist

spencer [spɛnsœr] NM 1 *(d'homme), Naut* monkey jacket; *Mil* mess jacket 2 *(de femme)* short jacket, *Arch* spencer

spermaceti [spɛrmaseti] NM spermaceti

spermatique [spɛrmatik] ADJ *Anat* spermatic

spermatogénèse [spɛrmatɔʒenɛz] NF *Biol* spermatogenesis

spermatozoïde [spɛrmatɔzɔid] NM *Biol* spermatozoon

sperme [spɛrm] NM 1 *Physiol* sperm, semen 2 **s. de baleine** spermaceti

spermicide [spɛrmisid] *Méd* ADJ spermicidal
▪ NM spermicide

spermophile [spɛrmɔfil] NM *Zool* gopher, *Spéc* spermophile

sphaigne [sfɛɲ] NF *Bot* sphagnum (moss), peat moss

sphénoïde [sfenɔid] ADJ, NM *Anat* sphenoid

sphère [sfɛr] NF 1 *Astron* sphere; *Géog* **s. terrestre** globe; **s. céleste** celestial sphere 2 *Fig (d'activité, d'influence etc)* sphere; **la s. des finances** the sphere *or* field of finance, financial circles; **nous ne sommes pas dans les mêmes sphères** we're not in the same field; **les hautes sphères de la politique** the higher reaches *or* realms of politics

sphéricité [sferisite] NF sphericity

sphérique [sferik] ADJ spherical

sphéroïde [sferɔid] NM spheroid

sphéromètre [sferɔmɛtr] NM spherometer

sphincter [sfɛ̃ktɛr] NM *Anat* sphincter

sphinx [sfɛ̃ks] NM 1 *Myth, Fig* sphinx; **sourire de s.** sphinx-like smile 2 *Entom* hawk *or Am* sphinx moth

sphygmomanomètre [sfigmomanɔmɛtr] NM *Méd* sphygmo-manometer

spi [spi] NM *Naut Fam* = **spinnaker**

spic [spik] NM *Bot* spike lavender

spider [spidɛr] NM *Aut* dick(e)y, *Am* rumble seat

spin [spin] NM *Nucl* spin

spina-bifida [spinabifida] NM *Méd* spina bifida

spinal, -ale, -aux, -ales [spinal, -o] ADJ *Anat* spinal

spinelle [spinɛl] NM *Minér* spinel

spinnaker [spinakə, -kɛr] NM *Naut* spinnaker

spiral, -ale, -aux, -ales [spiral, -o] ADJ spiral
▪ NM *(de montre)* hair-spring
▪ NF **spirale** spiral, *Spéc* helix; **la spirale inflationniste** the inflationary spiral; **spirale des prix et des salaires** wage and price spiral; **en spirale** *(utilisé adverbialement)* in a spiral, spirally; *(utilisé adjectivement)* spiral; **descendre/monter en spirale** to spiral down/up, to go down/up in a spiral

spirant, -ante [spirɑ̃, -ɑ̃t] *Ling* ADJ spirant
▪ NF **spirante** spirant

spire [spir] NF *(d'une spirale)*, Élec *(d'une bobine)* (single) turn; *(d'un coquillage)* whorl

spirée [spire] NF *Bot* spiraea

spirille [spirij] NM *Biol* spirillum

spirite [spirit] ADJ, N spiritualist

spiritisme [spiritism] NM spiritualism

spiritualiser [spiritɥalize] VT to spiritualize

spiritualisme [spiritɥalism] NM *Phil* spiritualism

spiritualiste [spiritɥalist] *Phil* ADJ spiritualist(ic)
N spiritualist

spiritualité [spiritɥalite] NF *Phil* spirituality

spirituel, -elle [spiritɥɛl] ADJ 1 *Phil, Rel etc (être, pouvoir, vie etc)* spiritual; *(musique)* sacred; **père s.** spiritual father 2 *(fin) (personne, réponse etc)* witty; *Iron* **que c'est s.!** very witty *or* droll!
NM **le s.** things spiritual; *(pouvoir)* spiritual power

spirituellement [spiritɥɛlmɑ̃] ADV 1 *(de l'esprit)* spiritually 2 *(finement)* wittily

spiritueux, -euse [spiritɥø, -øz] ADJ *(boisson)* alcoholic
NM *(liqueur)* spirit

spiroïdal, -ale, -aux, -ales [spirɔidal, -o] ADJ spiroid

spitant [spitɑ̃] *Belg* ADJ 1 *(personne)* lively 2 *(gazeux)* **eau spitante** carbonated water

spleen [splin] NM *Litt (mélancolie)* spleen, melancholy; **avoir le s.** to be melancholic

spleenétique [splinetik] ADJ *Litt* splenetic, melancholy

splendeur [splɑ̃dœr] NF 1 *(somptuosité)* splendour, *Am* splendor, magnificence; *Litt (éclat)* radiance, brightness; *(gloire)* splendour, grandeur, glory; **dans toute sa s.** in all his/her/its splendour 2 *(chose)* **splendeurs** splendours, *Am* splendors; **c'est une s.** it's splendid

splendide [splɑ̃did] ADJ *(journée, temps)* splendid; *(soleil)* brilliant; *(palais, victoire, repas)* splendid, magnificent; *(personne)* splendid-looking

splendidement [splɑ̃didmɑ̃] ADV splendidly

splénectomie [splenɛktɔmi] NF *Chir* splenectomy

splénique [splenik] ADJ *(artère, maladie)* splenic

spoiler [spɔjlœr] NM *Aut* spoiler

spoliateur, -trice [spɔljatœr, -tris] *Litt* N despoiler
ADJ *(loi, mesure etc)* spoliatory

spoliation [spɔljasjɔ̃] NF *Litt (d'une personne)* despoiling, robbing

spolier [spɔlje] VT *(impf, pr sub* n. **spoliions,** v. **spoliiez)** *Litt* to despoil, to rob (**de** of)

spondée [spɔ̃de] NM *Littér* spondee

spondylarthrite [spɔ̃dilartrit] NF *Méd* spondylarthritis; **s. ankylosante** ankylosing spondylitis

spondylite [spɔ̃dilit] NF *Méd* spondylitis

spongieux, -ieuse [spɔ̃ʒjø, -jøz] ADJ spongy

sponsor [spɔ̃sɔr] NM sponsor

sponsoring [spɔ̃sɔriŋ] NM sponsorship

sponsorisation [spɔ̃sɔrizasjɔ̃] NF sponsoring

sponsoriser [spɔ̃sɔrize] VT to sponsor

spontané [spɔ̃tane] ADJ *(action, personne, combustion)*, *Biol (génération etc)* spontaneous; *(aveux)* unprompted; *(candidature)* unsolicited

spontanéité [spɔ̃taneite] NF spontaneity

spontanément [spɔ̃tanemɑ̃] ADV spontaneously

sporadique [spɔradik] ADJ sporadic

sporadiquement [spɔradikmɑ̃] ADV sporadically

sporange [spɔrɑ̃ʒ] NM *Bot* sporangium, spore case

spore [spɔr] NF *Bot* spore

sport [spɔr] NM sport; **faire du s.** to do sport; **elle ne pratique aucun s.** she doesn't do any sport; **chaussures/terrain/salle/voiture de s.** sports shoes/ground/arena/car; *Fig Fam* **vous allez voir du s.** now you're going to see some fun; *Fam* **il va y avoir du s.!** there's going to be some fun!
ADJ INV 1 **vêtements s., costume s.** casual clothes; **habillé s.** casually dressed; *Aut* **coupé s.** sports coupé 2 *(personne)* sporting, fair
▸ ▸ *Fam* **s. en chambre** bedroom sports; **s. de combat** combat sport; **s. d'équipe** team sport; **sports d'hiver** winter sports; **aller aux sports d'hiver** to go skiing; **s. individuel** individual sport; **sports nautiques** water sports

sportif, -ive [spɔrtif, -iv] ADJ 1 *(résultats, édition, club etc)* sports; **réunion sportive** sports *or* athletics meeting 2 *(fair-play) (personne)* sporting, fair; **esprit s.** sporting spirit, sportsmanship 3 *(amateur de sport)* sporty, athletic; **allure sportive** sporty *or* athletic look
N sportsman, *f* sportswoman

sportivement [spɔrtivmɑ̃] ADV sportingly, in a sporting spirit; **il prit les choses très s.** he was very sporting about things

sportivité [spɔrtivite] NF sportsmanship; **elle eut la s. de …** she was sporting enough to …

sport(s)wear [spɔrt(s)wɛr] NM sportswear, casual wear
ADJ *(style etc)* casual

sporuler [spɔryle] VI *Biol* to sporulate

spot [spɔt] NM 1 *TV, Électron etc (point)* spot; *Radio* blip 2 *Théâtre (lampe)* spot(light); *TV, Cin* **s. à pinces** clip lamp 3 *Radio, TV* **s. (publicitaire)** commercial, advertisement; **un s. de trente secondes** a thirty-second spot

spouler [spule] VT *Ordinat* to spool

spouleur [spulœr] NM *Ordinat* spooler; **s. d'imprimante** printer spooler

spoutnik [sputnik] NM sputnik

sprat [sprat] NM *(poisson)* sprat

spray [sprɛ] NM spray, aerosol (spray); **peinture/déodorant en s.** spray(-on) *or* aerosol paint/deodorant

spread [spred] NM *Bourse* **s. baissier** bear spread; **s. haussier** bull spread; **s. papillon** butterfly spread

springbok [spriŋbɔk] NM springbok

springer [spriŋœr] NM *(chien)* springer (spaniel)

sprint [sprint] NM *Sport* (final) sprint; *(course)* sprint; *Fam* **piquer un s.** to sprint; **être bon au s.** to have a good sprint finish

sprinter[1] [sprintœr] NM *Sport* sprinter

sprinter[2] [sprinte] VI *Sport* to sprint

squale [skwal] NM *(roussette)* dogfish; *(requin)* shark

squame [skwam] NF *Méd* scale, *Spéc* squama

squameux, -euse [skwamø, -øz] ADJ *Méd* scaly, *Spéc* squamous

square [skwar] NM *(jardin public)* public garden

squash [skwaʃ] NM *Sport* squash; **jouer au s.** to play squash

squat [skwat] NM *(action, lieu)* squat

squatter[1] [skwatœr] NM squatter

squatter[2] [skwate], **squatteriser** [skwate-rize] VT *(occuper)* to squat in; *Fam* **il squatte toujours la télécommande quand on regarde un film** he always takes over the remote control when we're watching a film; *Fam* **arrête de s. le joint, fais tourner!** stop bogarting that joint, pass it round!; *Fam* **tous les matins elle squatte la salle de bain pendant une heure** every morning she takes over *or* hogs the bathroom for an hour
VI to squat; *Fam* **ça fait trois semaines qu'il squatte chez moi** he's been squatting *or* camping out at mine for three weeks now

squatteur [skwatœr] NM squatter

squaw [skwo] NF (Indian) squaw

squeeze [skwiz] NM *(au bridge)* squeeze

squelette [skəlɛt] NM 1 skeleton; **c'est un vrai s.** *ou* **un s. ambulant** he's/she's a bag of bones *or* a walking skeleton 2 *Fig (d'un navire, d'un roman etc)* skeleton, framework; *Typ* rough layout

squelettique [skəletik] ADJ 1 *Anat* skeletal 2 *(maigre) (personne, bras etc)* skeleton-like; **il est devenu s.** he's turned into a walking skeleton 3 *(réduit) (personnel, armée etc)* skeleton

squille [skij] NF *(crustacé)* squill

SRAS [sras] NM *(abrév* **syndrome respiratoire aigu sévère)** SARS

Sri Lanka [srilɑ̃ka] NF Sri Lanka

sri lankais, -aise [srilɑ̃kɛ, -ɛz] ADJ Sri Lankan
N S. Sri Lankan

SRPJ [ɛsɛrpeʒi] NM *(abrév* **Service régional de la police judiciaire)** = regional crime unit

SS [ɛsɛs] NM *Hist* member of the SS; **les SS** the SS
NF *Admin abrév* **Sécurité sociale**

SSR [ɛsɛsɛr] NF *Suisse TV (abrév* **Société suisse de Radiodiffusion et de Télévision**) = French-speaking Swiss broadcasting company

stabilisant [stabilizɑ̃] NM *Chimie* stabilizing agent

stabilisateur, -trice [stabilizatœr, -tris] ADJ stabilizing; **appareil s.** stabilizing device
NM 1 *(de vélo)*, *Naut* stabilizer; *Aviat* tailplane, *Am* horizontal stabilizer; *(vertical)* fin, *Am* vertical stabilizer 2 *Chimie* stabilizer

stabilisation [stabilizasjɔ̃] NF stabilization

stabilisé [stabilize] ADJ *Chimie, Écon etc* stabilized; *Biol* balanced

stabiliser [stabilize] VT to stabilize, to steady
VPR **se stabiliser** *(d'une voiture, d'une monnaie)* to stabilize, to steady; *(d'une personne) (dans la vie)* to settle down; **quand la situation se sera stabilisée** once the situation settles down *or* stabilizes

stabilité [stabilite] NF stability; **s. des changes** exchange rate stability; **s. des prix** price stability; **s. en courbe** cornering stability

stable [stabl] ADJ *(substance, équilibre, échelle, tempérament etc)* stable, steady; *(paix)* stable, lasting

stabulation [stabylasjɔ̃] NF *(du bétail)* keeping in sheds; *(des chevaux)* stabling

staccato [stakato] ADV, NM *Mus* staccato

stade [stad] NM 1 *(de sport)* stadium 2 *(étape) (d'évolution, de développement, de maladie etc)* stage; *Psy* **s. anal/oral/génital** anal/oral/genital stage 3 *Entom (des chenilles etc)* instar

stadier [stadje] NM steward *(at sports stadium)*

staff [staf] NM 1 *Constr (matériau)* staff 2 *(personnel)* staff; **s. de direction** managerial staff

stage [staʒ] NM *(période)* period of instruction *or* training; *(cours)* training course;

(pédagogique) teaching practice; **s. de formation** training period; **s. professionnel** *ou* **en entreprise** work placement, *Am* internship; **faire un s. de musique/de poterie** *(en vacances)* to do a music/pottery course; **être en s.** to be undergoing training *or* under instruction; **s. de perfectionnement** advanced training course

> Il faut noter que le terme anglais **stage** est un faux ami.

stagflation [stagflasjɔ̃] NF *Écon* stagflation

stagiaire [staʒjɛr] ADJ trainee; **interprète s.** trainee interpreter
▪ N trainee; *TV, Cin* runner, best boy

stagnant [stagnɑ̃] ADJ *(eau)*, *Fig (ventes etc)* stagnant

stagnation [stagnasjɔ̃] NF *(de l'eau)*, *Fig (des ventes etc)* stagnation; *Fig* **en s.** at a standstill, stagnant

stagner [stagne] VI *(de l'eau)*, *Fig (du commerce etc)* to stagnate

stakhanovisme [stakanɔvism] NM Stakhanovism

stalactite [stalaktit] NF *Géol* stalactite

stalag [stalag] NM stalag

stalagmite [stalagmit] NF *Géol* stalagmite

stalinien, -ienne [stalinjɛ̃, -jɛn] ADJ, N Stalinist

stalinisme [stalinism] NM Stalinism

stalle [stal] NF **1** *(dans une cathédrale)* stall **2** *(dans une étable)* stall, box

stance [stɑ̃s] NF *(strophe)* stanza

stand [stɑ̃d] NM **1** *(dans une course, une exposition etc)* stand, *Am* booth; *(dans une kermesse)* stall; **s. d'exposition** exhibition stand; *Sport, Aut* **les stands de ravitaillement** the pits **2 s. (de tir)** rifle range **3** *(de machine à écrire etc)* stand, rest

standard [stɑ̃dar] NM **1** *(norme)* standard; **s. de vie** standard of living **2** *Tél* switchboard
▪ ADJ INV standard; *Péj* **sourire s.** fixed smile

standardisation [stɑ̃dardizasjɔ̃] NF standardization

standardiser [stɑ̃dardize] VT to standardize

standardiste [stɑ̃dardist] N *Tél* (switchboard) operator

stand-by [stɑ̃dbaj] *Aviat* ADJ INV stand-by
▪ NM **(ticket/passager en) s.** stand-by (ticket/passenger)

standing [stɑ̃diŋ] NM *Fam* status; *(social)* (social) standing; **avoir un bon s.** to have a good standard of living; **appartement de grand s.** luxury flat *or Am* apartment; **quartier de grand s.** select district

staphylocoque [stafilɔkɔk] NM *(bactérie)* staphylococcus

star [star] NF *(vedette de cinéma, chanteur, sportif etc)*, *Mktg (produit)* star; **faire la s.** to act the star

stariser [starize] VT *Fam* **s. qn** to turn sb into a star

starlette [starlɛt] NF *Cin* starlet

star-system, *pl* **star-systems** [starsistɛm] NM *Cin, Théâtre etc* star system

starter [startɛr] NM **1** *Sport (qui donne le signal)* starter **2** *Aut* choke; **mettre/enlever le s.** to pull out/push in the choke; **rouler avec le s.** to drive with the choke out

> Il faut noter que le terme anglais **starter** est un faux ami: il ne désigne jamais le dispositif servant à faciliter le démarrage d'un moteur.

starting-block, *pl* **starting-blocks** [startiŋblɔk] NM *Sport* starting block

starting-gate, *pl* **starting-gates** [startiŋget] NM *Courses de chevaux* starting gate

start-up [startœp] NF *Com* start-up

stase [staz] NF *Méd* stasis

station [stasjɔ̃] NF **1** *(position)* position, posture; **s. debout** standing position; **la s. debout lui est décommandée** he has been advised not to stand for any length of time; **je me fatigue vite en s. debout** standing tires me quickly; **s. horizontale/verticale** horizontal/vertical position; **mise en s.** *(d'un instrument etc)* setting up
2 *(halte)* stop, pause; **faire une s. à … to** stop *or* pause at …; **faire de longues stations devant les magasins** to stop for long periods in front of shops
3 *Rel (de la Croix)* station
4 *(lieu d'arrêt)* *(d'autobus)* (bus) stop; *(de métro)* station; *(de train)* halt; *(de taxis)* (taxi) rank; *Belg (gare)* station
5 *(lieu de séjour)* resort
6 *(centre de recherches)* station
7 *Ordinat (d'un réseau)* station, node
▸▸ *Ordinat* **s. d'accueil** docking station; **s. balnéaire** seaside *or* coastal resort; *TV, Radio* **s. de base** base station; *Élec* **s. centrale** power station; **s. climatique** health resort; *Aut* **s. diagnostic** diagnostics bay; **s. émettrice** broadcasting station; *Aut* **s. d'essence** petrol *or Am* gas station; *TV, Radio* **s. généraliste** general-interest station; **s. hydrominérale** spa resort; *Ordinat* **s. individuelle** stand-alone workstation; *Aut* **s. de lavage** car wash; **s. météorologique** weather *or* meteorological station; **s. de métro** tube *or* underground *or Am* subway station; **s. de montagne** mountain resort; **s. orbitale** orbiting station; *Pétr* **s. de pompage** pumping station; **s. de radio** radio station; *Ordinat* **s. réseau** network station; *TV, Radio* **s. satellite** satellite station; **s. de ski** winter sports *or* ski resort; **s. spatiale** space station; **s. de sports d'hiver** winter sports *or* ski resort; **s. de télévision** television station; *TV* **s. terrestre** ground *or* earth station; *TV* **s. thématique** themed channel; **s. thermale** spa; **s. de travail** workstation; **s. verte** = well-preserved, picturesque French rural town or village

stationnaire [stasjɔnɛr] ADJ stationary; *(baromètre)* steady; **l'état du malade est s.** the patient('s condition) is stable
▪ NM *Naut* guardship, station ship

stationné [stasjɔne] ADJ **1** *(véhicule)* parked **2** *Mil* **les troupes stationnées en Allemagne** troops stationed in Germany

stationnement [stasjɔnmɑ̃] NM **1** *(de voitures etc)* parking; **en s.** parked; **parc de s.** car park; **s. interdit** *(sur panneau)* no parking; *(devant la gare etc)* no waiting; **s. gênant** no parking **2** *Can (parking)* car park, *Am* parking lot **3** *Aviat* **aire de s.** apron

stationner [stasjɔne] VI *(d'une voiture, d'un conducteur etc)* to park; **défense de s.** *(sur panneau)* no parking; *(devant la gare etc)* no waiting

station-service, *pl* **stations-service(s)** NF *Aut* service *or* filling *or* petrol *or Am* gas station

statique [statik] ADJ *(électricité, personnage etc)* static
▪ NF statics

statiquement [statikmɑ̃] ADV statically

statisticien, -ienne [statistisjɛ̃, -jɛn] N statistician

statistique [statistik] ADJ statistical
▪ NF **1** *(science)* statistics **2** *(donnée)* statistic; **statistiques démographiques** demographics; **statistiques de natalité** birth statistics; **statistiques sociales** social statistics; **statistiques syndicales** trade statistics

statistiquement [statistikmɑ̃] ADV statistically

stator [statɔr] NM stator

statoréacteur [statoreaktœr] NM *Aviat* ramjet

statuaire [statɥɛr] ADJ *(art, marbre etc)* statuary
▪ N sculptor, f sculptress
▪ NF (art of) statuary

statue [staty] NF statue; **la s. de la Liberté** the Statue of Liberty; **immobile comme une s.** stock-still; **s. de sel** pillar of salt

statuer [statɥe] VI to give a decision *or* a ruling (**sur** on)

statuette [statɥɛt] NF statuette

statufier [statyfje] VT *(impf, pr sub* n. **statufiions,** v. **statufiiez)** *Fam (quelqu'un)* to erect a statue to

statu quo [statykwo] NM status quo

stature [statyr] NF stature; **de haute s.** very tall; *Fig* of (great) stature; **elle a une s. de basketteuse** she's very tall; *Fig* **ils ne sont pas de la même s.** they're not in the same league

statut [staty] NM *(état)* status; **avoir un s. privilégié** to have privileged status; **s. social** social status; **s. juridique** *or* **légal** legal status; **avoir le s. de cadre/de fonctionnaire** to have executive/civil servant status; **il réclame le s. de réfugié politique** he is asking for political refugee status
▪ NMPL **statuts** *(de sociétés, d'associations)* statutes, memorandum and articles of association, *Am* bylaws; **statuts et règlements** rules and regulations

statutaire [statytɛr] ADJ statutory

statutairement [statytɛrmɑ̃] ADV in accordance with the statutes *or* regulations

stayer [stejœr] NM *Cyclisme (derrière une moto)* long-distance cyclist; *Courses de chevaux* stayer

St, Ste *(abrév* **Saint(e))** St

Sté *(abrév* **Société)** Co

steak [stɛk] NM *Culin* steak; **s. tartare** steak tartare; **s. au poivre** peppered steak, steak au poivre; **s. frites** steak and chips

stéarine [stearin] NF *Chimie* stearin

stéarique [stearik] ADJ *Chimie* stearic (acid)

stéatite [steatit] NF *Minér* steatite, soapstone

stéatopyge [steatɔpiʒ] ADJ steatopygic

stéatose [steatoz] NF *Méd* steatosis

steeple [stipl], **steeple-chase,** *pl* **steeple-chases** [stipəlʃɛz] NM *Sport* steeplechase

stèle [stɛl] NF stele

stellage [stelaʒ] NM *Bourse* double option, put and call (option)

stellaire [stelɛr] ADJ *(lumière etc)* stellar
▪ NF *Bot* starwort

stem(m) [stɛm] NM *Ski* stem turn

stencil [stɛnsil] NM *(à polycopier)* stencil

sténo [steno] NF *(abrév* **sténographie)** shorthand, stenography; **prendre une lettre en s.** to take down a letter in shorthand
▪ N *(abrév* **sténographe)** stenographer

sténodactylo [stenodaktilo] N shorthand typist, *Am* stenographer
▪ NF *(abrév* **sténodactylographie)** shorthand typing

sténodactylographie [stenodaktilɔgrafi] NF shorthand typing

sténographe [stenɔgraf] N stenographer, shorthand writer; **s. de presse** press stenographer

sténographie [stenɔgrafi] NF shorthand, stenography

sténographier [stenɔgrafje] VT *(pr sub, impf* n. **sténographiions,** v. **sténographiiez)** **s. une lettre** to take a letter down in shorthand

sténographique [stenɔgrafik] ADJ *(écriture etc)* shorthand

sténopé [stenɔpe] NM pinhole

sténotype [stenɔtip] NF stenotype, stenotyper

sténotyper [stenɔtipe] VT to stenotype

sténotypie [stenɔtipi] NF stenotypy

sténotypiste [stenɔtipist] N stenotypist

stentor [stɑ̃tɔr] NM **1** voix de s. stentorian voice **2** *Zool* stentor

step [stɛp] NM step aerobics

stéphanois, -oise [stefanwa, -waz] ADJ of *or* from Saint-Étienne
■ N S. *(natif)* native of Saint-Étienne; *(habitant)* inhabitant of Saint-Étienne

steppe [stɛp] NF *Géog* steppe

stercoraire [stɛrkɔrɛr] ADJ *Méd* stercoraceous
■ NM *(oiseau)* skua

stère [stɛr] NM *(unité de mesure)* stere

stéréo [stereo] ADJ INV *(abrév* **stéréophonique)** stereo
■ NF **1** *(abrév* **stéréophonie)** stereo; **en s.** in stereo; **s. VHF** stereo VHF **2** *(radio)* stereo radio

stéréogramme [stereɔgram] NM *Opt, Phot* stereogram, stereograph

stéréographie [stereɔgrafi] NF *Opt* stereography

stéréométrie [stereɔmetri] NF stereometry

stéréophonie [stereɔfɔni] NF stereophony

stéréophonique [stereɔfɔnik] ADJ stereophonic

stéréoscope [stereɔskɔp] NM *Opt* stereoscope

stéréoscopie [stereɔskɔpi] NF stereoscopy

stéréoscopique [stereɔskɔpik] ADJ stereoscopic

stéréotype [stereotip] NM *Typ, Fig* stereotype

stéréotypé [stereotipe] ADJ *(idées, phrases etc)* stereotype(d)

stéréotypie [stereotipi] NF *Typ, Psy* stereotypy

stérile [steril] ADJ *(homme, femme, animal)* sterile; *(mariage)* childless; *(terre)* sterile, barren, unproductive; *(travail)* unprofitable; *(discussion, efforts etc)* sterile, vain, fruitless; *Méd etc* **instruments stériles** sterile *or* sterilized instruments

stérilement [sterilmɑ̃] ADV *(vainement)* fruitlessly

stérilet [sterilɛ] NM *(contraceptif)* coil, IUD; **se faire poser un s.** to have a coil *or* an IUD fitted

stérilisant [sterilizɑ̃] ADJ *(agent etc)* sterilizing; *Fig* mind-numbing

stérilisateur [sterilizatœr] NM sterilizer

stérilisation [sterilizasjɔ̃] NF sterilization

stériliser [sterilize] VT *(lait, instrument, personne etc)* to sterilize; *Fig* to stifle, to suffocate

stérilité [sterilite] NF *(d'une personne)* sterility; *(d'une terre)* barrenness; *Fig (d'une discussion, d'efforts etc)* fruitlessness, futility

sterling [sterliŋ] ADJ INV sterling; **dix livres s.** ten pounds sterling
■ NM INV sterling; **payé en s.** paid in sterling

sterne [stɛrn] NF *(oiseau)* tern

sternum [stɛrnɔm] NM *Anat* breastbone, *Spéc* sternum

sternutatoire [stɛrnytatwar] ADJ sternutatory; **poudre s.** sneezing powder

stéroïde [sterɔid] NM *Biol, Méd* steroid; **stéroïdes anabolisants** anabolic steroids

stérol [sterɔl] NM *Chimie, Physiol* sterol

stertoreux, -euse [stɛrtɔrø, -øz] ADJ *Méd (respiration)* stertorous

stéthoscope [stetɔskɔp] NM *Méd* stethoscope

steward [stjuwart, stiwart] NM *Naut* steward; *Aviat* flight *or* cabin attendant

stick [stik] NM **1** *Mil, Sp, Aviat etc* stick; *(de cavalier)* riding whip *or* crop **2** *(de colle etc)* stick; **un s. de rouge à lèvres** a lipstick; **déodorant en s.** stick deodorant **3** *Fam (de marijuana)* (thin) joint *or* spliff

stigmate [stigmat] NM **1** *Méd* mark, stigma; *Fig (du vice etc)* mark **2** *Hist (châtiment)* brand **3** *Hist, Rel* **stigmates** stigmata **4** *Bot, Entom* stigma

stigmatisation [stigmatizasjɔ̃] NF *(condamnation), Rel* stigmatization

stigmatisé, -ée [stigmatize] ADJ stigmatized
■ N *Hist, Rel* stigmatist, stigmatic

stigmatiser [stigmatize] VT **1** *(condamner) (quelqu'un)* to stigmatize, to condemn **2** *Hist (marquer) (détenu)* to brand

stillation [stilasjɔ̃] NF *(en sciences)* dripping

stim [stim] NF *Mktg (abrév* **stimulation)** incentive, stimulus

stimulant [stimylɑ̃] ADJ stimulating; *(résultats)* encouraging
■ NM **1** *Méd etc* stimulant **2** *Fig* stimulus, spur, incentive; *Mktg* **stimulants** stimuli

stimulateur [stimylatœr] NM *Méd* **s. cardiaque** pacemaker; **on lui a mis un s. cardiaque** he was fitted with a pacemaker

stimulation [stimylasjɔ̃] NF stimulation, incentive, stimulus; **s. de la demande** demand stimulation; **s. financière** cash incentive; **s. à l'achat** incentive to buy; **s. à la consommation** consumer incentive

stimuler [stimyle] VT **1** *(personne)* to stimulate; *(encourager)* to spur on; **il faut le s. sans arrêt** you have to keep prodding him; **cela ne me stimule pas vraiment de travailler avec elle** I don't find working with her very stimulating **2** *(enthousiasme, digestion, économie etc)* to stimulate; *(appétit)* to stimulate, to whet; *(amitié, commerce etc)* to stimulate, to encourage; **s. la demande** to stimulate demand

stimulus [stimylys], *pl* **stimulus** *ou* **stimuli** [stimyli] NM stimulus

stipendiaire [stipɑ̃djɛr], **stipendié, -ée** [stipɑ̃dje] *Litt Péj* ADJ *(soldat etc)* hired
■ N hireling

stipendier [stipɑ̃dje] VT *(pr sub, impf* n. **stipendiions,** v. **stipendiiez)** *Litt Péj (soldats, politiciens etc)* to hire

stipulation [stipylasjɔ̃] NF stipulation, condition

stipuler [stipyle] VT to stipulate; **il est stipulé dans le contrat que …** it is stipulated in the contract that …

stochastique [stɔkastik] ADJ stochastic

stock [stɔk] NM *Com (des biens)* stock; **stocks** *(en comptabilité)* stock, *Am* inventory; **en s.** in stock; **nous n'avons plus ce modèle en s.** we no longer have this model in stock, this model is out of stock; **rupture de s.** stock outage; **être en rupture de s.** to be out of stock; *Fam* **tout un s., un vrai s.** a whole stock *or* collection; **dans la limite des stocks disponibles** while stocks last, subject to availability; **c'est là qu'elle cache son s. de biscuits** that's where she hides her stock of biscuits; **elle a mis tout son s. de chaussures dans ce tiroir** she put her whole stock of shoes in this drawer; **s. d'alerte** minimum stock level; **stocks excédentaires** surplus stock; **s. final** closing stock; **s. d'ouverture** opening stock; **s. de sécurité** safety stock; **s. stratégique** perpetual inventory; **s. tampon** buffer stock

stockage [stɔkaʒ] NM **1** *(des marchandises)* stocking; *Ordinat* storage; *Ordinat* **s. de don-** **nées** data storage; *Ordinat* **s. en mémoire tampon** buffering; **s. excessif** overstocking **2** *(en grande quantité)* stockpiling, building up of stocks

stock-car, *pl* **stock-cars** NM *Sport (voiture)* stock car; *(sport)* stock-car racing

stocker [stɔke] VT **1** *(marchandises)* to stock **2** *(en grande quantité)* to stockpile **3** *Ordinat (informations)* to store

stockfish [stɔkfiʃ] NM INV stockfish

Stockholm [stɔkɔlm] N Stockholm

stockiste [stɔkist] N *Com* stockist, *Am* dealer; *Aut* dealer, agent

stoeffer [stufe] VI *Belg (se vanter)* to show off

stoïcien, -ienne [stɔisjɛ̃, -jɛn] ADJ stoical, stoic; *Hist, Phil* Stoic
■ N stoic; *Hist, Phil* Stoic

stoïcisme [stɔisism] NM stoicism; *Hist, Phil* Stoicism; **avec s.** stoically, with stoicism

stoïque [stɔik] ADJ stoic, stoical
■ N stoic

stoïquement [stɔikmɑ̃] ADV stoically

stolon [stɔlɔ̃] NM *Bot* stolon, runner

stomacal, -ale, -aux, -ales [stɔmakal, -o] ADJ *(spasme etc)* stomach

stomachique [stɔmaʃik] ADJ, NM *Pharm* stomachic

stomatite [stɔmatit] NF *Méd* stomatitis

stomatologie [stɔmatɔlɔʒi] NF stomatology

stomatologiste [stɔmatɔlɔʒist], **stomatologue** [stɔmatɔlɔg] N stomatologist

stomie [stɔmi] NF *Méd* stoma

stop [stɔp] INT stop!; *(dans un télégramme)* stop; **il faut savoir dire s.** you have to learn to say enough is enough; **alors je dis 's.!', j'arrête de travailler avec vous** I'm telling you that's enough, I'm not working with you any more
■ NM **1** *Aut (feu arrière)* brake light; *(panneau)* stop sign **2** *Fam (abrév* **auto-stop)** hitchhiking; **faire du s.** to hitch(hike); **aller à Paris en s.** to hitch(hike) to Paris

stoppage [stɔpaʒ] NM *Couture (d'un vêtement)* invisible mending

stopper [stɔpe] VTI to stop; **il faut le s. quand il est dans cet état** he has to be stopped when he's in this state
■ VT *Couture* to repair by invisible mending

stoppeur, -euse [stɔpœr, -øz] N *Fam* **1** *(abrév* **auto-stoppeur)** hitcher, hitchhiker **2** *Sport* fullback

store [stɔr] NM blind; *(devant un magasin)* awning; **s. vénitien** Venetian blind

story-board, *pl* **story-boards** [stɔribɔrd] NM *TV, Cin* storyboard

strabisme [strabism] NM strabismus, squint(ing); **s. convergent/divergent** esotropia *or* convergent strabismus/exotropia *or* divergent strabismus; **yeux atteints d'un léger/fort s.** eyes with a slight/severe squint

stradivarius [stradivarjys] NM *Mus (instrument)* Stradivarius

strangulation [strɑ̃gylasjɔ̃] NF strangulation

strapontin [strapɔ̃tɛ̃] NM **1** *Aut, Théâtre etc* folding seat, tip-up seat **2** *Fig (fonction secondaire)* minor role

strasbourgeois, -oise [strazburʒwa, -waz] ADJ of *or* from Strasbourg
■ N S. *(natif)* native of Strasbourg; *(habitant)* inhabitant of Strasbourg

stras(s) [stras] NM *(clinquant)* paste, strass; *Fig* **robe en s.** sequined dress

stratagème [strataʒɛm] NM stratagem

strate [strat] NF *Géol, Fig* stratum, layer

stratège [strateʒ] NM strategist

stratégie [strateʒi] NF strategy; **s. commerciale** business strategy; **s. concurrentielle** competitive strategy; *Mktg* **s. de créneau unique** single niching; *Mktg* **s. de créneaux multiples** multiple-niche strategy; **s. électorale** election strategy; *Mktg* **s. d'encerclement** encirclement strategy; **s. de l'entreprise** corporate strategy; **s. globale de l'entreprise** overall business strategy; *Mktg* **s. d'imitation** imitation *or* me-too strategy; *Mktg* **s. de marque** brand strategy; **s. (de) mercatique** game plan, marketing strategy; *Mktg* **s. de niche unique** single-niche strategy; *Mktg* **s. poussée** *ou* **'pousser'** push strategy; *Mktg* **s. du prétendant** challenger strategy; *Mktg* **s. du suiveur** follower strategy; *Mktg* **s. tirée** *ou* **'tirer'** pull strategy

stratégique [strateʒik] ADJ strategic

stratégiquement [strateʒikmã] ADV strategically

stratification [stratifikasjɔ̃] NF stratification; **s. sociale** social stratification

stratifié [stratifje] ADJ stratified; *Tech (papier, tissu etc)* laminated ▪ NM laminate

stratifier [stratifje] VT to stratify

strato-cumulus [stratokymylys] NM INV *Météo* stratocumulus

stratosphère [stratosfɛr] NF *Météo* stratosphere

stratosphérique [stratosferik] ADJ stratospheric

stratus [stratys] NM INV *Météo* stratus

streamer [strimœr] NM *Ordinat* tape streamer

streptocoque [strɛptɔkɔk] NM *(bactérie)* streptococcus

streptomycine [strɛptɔmisin] NF *Méd* streptomycin

stress [strɛs] NM stress; **être en proie au s.** to be under stress; **maladie due au s.** stress-related illness

stressant [strɛsã] ADJ stressful

stresser [strɛse] VT **s. qn** *(d'un travail, d'une activité)* to put sb under stress, *Fam* to stress sb out; **être stressé** to be under stress, *Fam* to be stressed out; **elle/vivre à Paris me stresse** I find her/living in Paris very stressful

stretch® [strɛtʃ] NM *(tissu)* stretch material; **jupe en s.** stretch skirt

striation [strijasjɔ̃] NF striation

strict [strikt] ADJ **1** *(obligation, principes etc)* strict; *(essentiel, minimum)* bare; **au sens s.** in the strict sense; **dans la plus stricte intimité** strictly in private; **c'est la stricte vérité** it's the simple or absolute truth; **c'est son droit le plus s.** it's his absolute right **2** *(personne)* strict *(sur* about*)*; **ils sont très stricts sur la politesse** they're very strict about politeness **3** *(costume, coupe de cheveux)* severe

strictement [striktəmã] ADV **1** *(rigoureusement)* strictly; **s. interdit** *ou* **défendu** strictly forbidden; **s. confidentiel** strictly confidential; **je ne comprends s. rien** I don't understand a (single) thing **2** *(sévèrement)* (habillé *etc)* severely

striction [striksjɔ̃] NF *Méd* constriction

stricto sensu [striktosɛ̃sy] ADV strictly speaking

strident [stridã] ADJ strident, shrill

stridulation [stridylasjɔ̃] NF stridulation

strie [stri] NF **1** *(sillon)* groove; *(en relief)* ridge; *Anat, Bot, Géol* stria **2** *(de couleur)* streak

strié [strije] ADJ **1** *(sillonné)* grooved; *(en relief)* ridged; *Anat, Bot, Géol* striated **2** *(rayé)* (marbre *etc)* streaked

strier [strije] VT *(impf, pr sub* n. **striions**, v. **striiez**) **1** *(sillonner)* to groove; *(en relief)* to ridge **2** *(rayer)* to streak

string [striŋ] NM *(maillot de bain)* tanga; *(slip)* G-string

stringer [striŋœr] NM *Journ* stringer

stringman [striŋman] NM *Journ* stringer

strioscopie [strijɔskɔpi] NF *Opt* schlieren photography

stripper [stripœr] NM *Chir (instrument)* stripper

stripping [stripiŋ] NM *Méd, Pétr etc* stripping

strip-tease, *pl* **strip-teases** [striptiz] NM striptease; **faire un s.** to do a striptease *or* strip

strip-teaseur [striptizœr] NM male stripper

strip-teaseuse, *pl* **strip-teaseuses** [striptizøz] NF stripper, striptease artist(e)

striure [strijyr] NF striation

stroboscope [strɔbɔskɔp] NM *Opt* stroboscope

stroboscopique [strɔbɔskɔpik] ADJ stroboscopic, strobe

strombolien [strɔ̃bɔljɛ̃] ADJ *Géog* Strombolian

strontium [strɔ̃sjɔm] NM *Chimie* strontium

strophe [strɔf] NF *Littér* stanza

structural, -ale, -aux, -ales [stryktyral, -o] ADJ structural; *Ling* **analyse structurale** structural analysis

structuralement [stryktyralmã] ADV structurally

structuralisme [stryktyralism] NM structuralism

structuraliste [stryktyralist] ADJ, N structuralist

structurant [stryktyrã] ADJ structuring

structuration [stryktyrasjɔ̃] NF structuring

structure [stryktyr] NF structure; **fauteuil à s. métallique** metal-framed armchair ▸▸ **s. d'accueil** *(pour minorités)* reception facilities; **s. administrative** administrative structure; *Ordinat* **s. en anneau** ring structure; *Ordinat* **s. arborescente** directory *or* tree structure; *Ordinat* **s. en arbre** tree structure; *Ordinat* **s. de bloc** block structure; *Ordinat* **s. en bus** bus structure; **s. de l'entreprise** company *or* corporate structure; *Ordinat* **s. en étoile** star structure; *Ordinat* **s. de fichier** file structure; **s. hiérarchique** line organization; **s. du marché** market structure; **s. des prix** price structure; **s. des salaires** wage structure

structuré [stryktyre] ADJ structured; *Ordinat* **fichier non s.** flat file

structurel, -elle [stryktyrɛl] ADJ structural; **chômage s.** structural unemployment

structurellement [stryktyrɛlmã] ADV structurally

structurer [stryktyre] VT to structure

strume [strym] NF *Méd, Arch* **1** *(goitre)* goitre **2** *(scrofule)* scrofula

strychnine [striknin] NF *Chimie, Pharm* strychnine

stuc [styk] NM *Constr* stucco; **décoration en s.** stucco decoration

stucage [stykaʒ] NM *Constr* stucco work

stucateur [stykatœr] NM stucco worker

studieusement [stydjøzmã] ADV studiously

studieux, -ieuse [stydjø, -jøz] ADJ *(personne)* studious; *(vacances etc)* study

studio [stydjo] NM **1** *Cin, Phot, TV, Beaux-Arts etc* studio; **tourné en s.** shot in studio **2** *(logement)* studio *or* one-roomed flat, *Am* studio apartment ▸▸ *TV, Radio* **s. d'annonceur** announcer studio; **s. de cinéma** film studio; **s. de danse** dance studio; **s. de doublage** dubbing suite; **s. d'enregistrement** recording *or* sound studio; **s. de peintre** artist's studio; **s. de photographe** photographer's studio; *TV, Cin* **s. de postproduction** postproduction studio; *TV, Cin* **s. de reportage** self-op studio; **s. de télévision** television studio

stupéfaction [stypefaksjɔ̃] NF stupefaction, amazement; **je constate avec s. que ...** I am amazed to note that ...

stupéfait [stypefɛ] ADJ stupefied, stunned, amazed *(de* by*)*

stupéfiant [stypefjã] ADJ **1** *Méd (substance)* stupefying, *Spéc* stupefacient **2** *(nouvelles)* astounding, amazing ▪ NM *Méd* drug, narcotic, *Spéc* stupefacient; **brigade des stupéfiants** drug squad

stupéfier [stypefje] VT *(impf, pr sub* n. **stupéfiions**, v. **stupéfiiez**) to stupefy, to stun, to amaze

stupeur [stypœr] NF **1** *Méd* stupor **2** *(étonnement)* amazement; **muet de s.** dumbfounded; **je constate avec s. que ...** I am amazed to note that ...

stupide [stypid] ADJ **1** *(idiot)* stupid, silly; **c'est s., mais je n'ai pas pu m'empêcher de le lui dire** it was stupid, but I couldn't stop myself telling him; **accident/mort s.** stupid *or* silly accident/death **2** *Litt (stupéfait)* stunned

stupidement [stypidmã] ADV stupidly; **rire s.** to give a stupid laugh; **mourir s.** to die a stupid death; **il m'a regardé faire s.** he stood there like an idiot and watched me

stupidité [stypidite] NF **1** *(caractère)* stupidity, foolishness **2** *(parole, acte)* stupid thing (to say/do *etc)*; **dire/faire des stupidités** to say/do stupid things; **répondre par une s.** to give a silly answer

stupre [stypr] NM *Litt* debauchery

stups [styp] NMPL *Fam (abrév* **stupéfiants)** **la Brigade des s., les s.** the Drug Squad

stuquer [styke] VT *Constr* to stucco

style [stil] NM **1** *Littér, Archit, Gram etc* style; **j'ai envie de changer de s.** I want to change my style; **elle a beaucoup de s.** she has a lot of style, she's very stylish; **tourner ses phrases avec s.** to have a stylish turn of phrase; **s. de vie** lifestyle; **ce skieur a un beau s.** this skier has (a) good style; **ce chapeau est tout à fait ton s.** this hat is just your style; *Fam Péj* **ça serait bien son s.!** that would be just like him *or* just his style!; **dans le s. de** in the style of; **une veste un peu dans le s. de la tienne** a jacket in the same sort of style as yours; **meubles de s.** period furniture; **meubles s. Louis XIII/Régence** Louis XIII-/Regency-style furniture **2** *Antiq (pour écrire)* stylus, style **3** *(pour enregistrer un disque)* record cutter; *(d'appareil enregistreur)* (recording) needle **4** *(de cadran solaire)* style, pin, gnomon; *(de baromètre)* hand **5** *Bot* style

stylé¹ [stile] ADJ *Biol* stylate

stylé² ADJ *(domestique etc)* trained

styler [stile] VT *(domestique etc)* to train

stylet [stile] NM **1** *(poignard)* stiletto **2** *Chir* stylet, probe **3** *Zool* stylet **4** *Ordinat* **s. lumineux** light pen

stylicien [stilisjɛ̃] NM designer

stylique [stilik] NF design

stylisation [stilizasjɔ̃] NF stylization

styliser [stilize] VT *Beaux-Arts etc* to stylize

stylisme [stilism] NM **1** *Littér* attention to style **2** *Com, Ind* designing

styliste [stilist] N **1** *Littér* stylist **2** *Com, Ind* designer

stylisticien, -ienne [stilistisjɛ̃, -jɛn] **N** expert in stylistics

stylistique [stilistik] **ADJ** stylistic
NF stylistics

stylite [stilit] **NM** *Hist, Rel* stylite

stylo [stilo] **NM** pen; **s. à encre** *ou* **à plume** fountain pen; **s. bille, s. bic**® ballpoint (pen), *Br* Biro®; *Ordinat* **s. électronique** electronic pen; **s. optique** light pen

stylo-feutre, *pl* **stylos-feutres NM** felt-tip (pen)

stylographe [stilɔgraf] **NM** *Arch* fountain pen

Stylomine® [stilomin] **NM** propelling pencil

stylo-surligneur, *pl* **stylo-surligneurs NM** highlighter

styptique [stiptik] **ADJ, NM** *Méd* styptic

styrax [stiraks] **NM** *Bot* styrax

styrène [stirɛn] **NM** *Chimie* styrene

Styx [stiks] **NM le S.** the Styx

su [sy] **PP** *voir* **savoir¹**
  NM au su de to the knowledge of; **au vu et au su de qn** right in front of sb; **elle l'a fait au vu et au su de tout le monde** she did it quite openly *or* for all the world to see

suage¹ [sɥaʒ] **NM** *(du bois etc)* sweating, oozing

suage² **NM** *(d'un bougeoir, d'un plat en étain etc)* fillet (border)

suaire [sɥɛr] **NM 1** *Litt (linceul)* winding sheet, shroud **2** *Rel* **le saint s.** the holy shroud

suant [sɥɑ̃] **ADJ 1** *Fam* sweating, sweaty **2** *Arg (ennuyeux)* boring

suave [sɥav] **ADJ 1** *(musique, odeur, goût etc)* sweet **2** *Fig (ton, manières)* suave, smooth

> Il faut noter que le terme anglais **suave** ne se rapporte pas aux sens et a le plus souvent une connotation péjorative.

suavement [sɥavmɑ̃] **ADV** *(parler)* suavely

suavité [sɥavite] **NF 1** *(d'un parfum, d'une mélodie)* sweetness **2** *(des manières)* suavity

subaigu, -uë [sybegy] **ADJ** *Méd* subacute

subalpin [sybalpɛ̃] **ADJ** subalpine

subalterne [sybaltɛrn] **ADJ** *(officier, position, rôle)* subordinate, minor; *(esprit)* inferior; *(employé)* junior
  NM subordinate; *Mil (grade)* subaltern

subaquatique [sybakwatik] **ADJ** subaquatic, underwater

subatomique [sybatɔmik] **ADJ** subatomic

subconscient [sybkɔ̃sjɑ̃] **ADJ, NM** subconscious

subdiviser [sybdivize] **VT** to subdivide
  VPR se subdiviser to be subdivided

subdivision [sybdivizjɔ̃] **NF** subdivision

subéquatorial, -ale, -aux, -ales [sybekwatɔrjal, -o] **ADJ** *Géog* subequatorial

subéreux, -euse [syberø, -øz] **ADJ** *Bot* suberose, corky

subir [sybir] **VT** *(procès, examen, opération, torture, changement etc)* to undergo; *(mort, violence, conséquences)* to suffer; *(sentence)* to serve; *(influence)* to be under; *(défaite, pertes)* to suffer, to sustain; **s. une majoration** to increase, to rise; **il commence à s. les contrecoups de la crise économique** he's starting to suffer the effects of the economic crisis; **s. qn** to put up with sb; **je ne veux pas avoir à le s. tout le week end!** I don't want to have to put up with *or* suffer him all weekend!; **faire s. qch à qn** to subject sb to sth

subit [sybi] **ADJ** *(mort, changement)* sudden, unexpected

subitement [sybitmɑ̃] **ADV** suddenly, all of a sudden

subito [sybito] **ADV** *Fam* all of a sudden; *(immédiatement)* at once; **s. presto** at once

subjectif, -ive [sybʒɛktif, -iv] **ADJ** subjective; *Gram* **cas s.** nominative case

subjectivement [sybʒɛktivmɑ̃] **ADV** subjectively

subjectivisme [sybʒɛktivism] **NM** *Phil* subjectivism

subjectivité [sybʒɛktivite] **NF** subjectivity; **propos pleins de s.** subjective remarks

subjonctif, -ive [sybʒɔ̃ktif, -iv] SEE GRAMMAR A53–4; B32-4 *Gram* **ADJ** *(mode)* subjunctive **NM** subjunctive; **au s.** in the subjunctive

subjugation [sybʒygasjɔ̃] **NF** subjugation

subjuguer [sybʒyge] **VT** *(personnes, nation)* to subjugate, to subdue; *(cheval)* to subdue, to master; *Fig (audience, cœurs etc)* to captivate, to enthral

sublimation [syblimasjɔ̃] **NF** *Chimie, Psy* sublimation

sublimatoire [syblimatwar] **ADJ** sublimatory

sublime [syblim] **ADJ** sublime; *Fam* **ça n'a rien de s.** it's nothing to write home about **NM le s.** the sublime

sublimé [syblime] **ADJ** sublimated
  NM *Chimie* sublimate

sublimement [syblimmɑ̃] **ADV** sublimely

sublimer [syblime] **VT** *Chimie, Psy* to sublimate

subliminaire [sybliminɛr], **subliminal, -ale, -aux, -ales** [sybliminal, -o] **ADJ** subliminal; **publicité s.** *ou* **subliminale** subliminal advertising

sublimité [syblimite] **NF** *Litt* sublimeness

sublingual, -ale, -aux, -ales [syblɛ̃gwal, -o] **ADJ** *Anat (glande etc)* sublingual; *Pharm* **comprimé s.** tablet to be placed under the tongue

submerger [sybmɛrʒe] **VT** (**je submergeai(s); n. submergeons**) **1** *(pré etc)* to submerge, to flood; *(bateau)* to submerge, to swamp; *(objet)* to submerge; *Fig* **ville submergée par les touristes** town inundated with *or* overrun by tourists **2** *Fig (quelqu'un)* to overwhelm; **être submergé de travail** to be snowed under *or* overwhelmed with work; **depuis que son troisième enfant est né, elle est submergée** she's been snowed under since the birth of her third child

submersible [sybmɛrsibl] **ADJ 1** *(bateau)* submersible **2** *Bot (plante)* submerged **3** *(sol)* liable to flooding
  NM *Naut* submarine

submersion [sybmɛrsjɔ̃] **NF** submersion, flooding; **mort par s.** death by drowning

subodorer [sybɔdɔre] **VT** *Fam (danger, complot etc)* to suspect; **il a subodoré quelque chose** he smelt a rat

subordination [sybɔrdinasjɔ̃] **NF** subordination; **complément/conjonction de s.** subordinating complement/conjunction

subordonnant [sybɔrdɔnɑ̃] **ADJ** *Gram (conjonction etc)* subordinating SEE GRAMMAR A74–6; B58

subordonné, -ée [sybɔrdɔne] **ADJ 1** *Gram (proposition)* subordinate **2** *(dépendant)* subordinate (à to); **c'est s. aux revenus de l'année précédente** it is subject to the previous year's income
  N *(personne)* subordinate
  NF *Gram* **subordonnée** subordinate clause

subordonner [sybɔrdɔne] **VT** to subordinate (à to); *Fig* **s. ses dépenses à ses revenus** to cut one's coat according to one's cloth, to live within one's means; **le service est subordonné au nombre des voyageurs** the service depends on the number of travellers
  VPR se subordonner se s. à qn to subordinate oneself to sb

subornation [sybɔrnasjɔ̃] **NF** *Jur* subornation, bribing

suborner [sybɔrne] **VT 1** *Jur (témoin)* to suborn, to bribe **2** *Litt (séduire) (femme)* to seduce

suborneur, -euse [sybɔrnœr, -øz] **N** *Jur (d'un témoin)* suborner, briber
  NM *Litt (séducteur)* seducer

subreptice [sybrɛptis] **ADJ** surreptitious

subrepticement [sybrɛptismɑ̃] **ADV** surreptitiously

subrogation [sybrɔgasjɔ̃] **NF** *Jur* subrogation, substitution

subrogé, -ée [sybrɔʒe] **ADJ** subrogated; *(gardien)* deputy, surrogate
  N *Rel, Jur* surrogate, deputy

subroger [sybrɔʒe] **VT** (**je subrogeai(s); n. subrogeons**) *Jur* to subrogate, to substitute

subséquemment [sypsekamɑ̃, sybs-] **ADV** *Jur, Litt* subsequently

subséquent [sypsekɑ̃, sybs-] **ADJ** *Jur, Géog, Litt* subsequent

subside [sypsid, sybz-] **NM** subsidy, grant; **vivre des subsides de l'État** to live on state grants *or* subsidies

subsidence [sypsidɑ̃s, sybz-] **NF** *Géol* subsidence

subsidiaire [sypsidjɛr, sybz-] **ADJ** subsidiary; **question s.** tie-breaker

subsidiairement [sypsidjɛrmɑ̃, sybz-] **ADV** subsidiarily; **s. à** in addition to

subsidiarité [sypsidjarite, sybz-] **NF** *UE* subsidiarity

subsistance [sybzistɑ̃s] **NF 1** *(survie)* subsistence; **pourvoir à la s. de sa famille** to keep *or* support one's family; **moyen de s.** means of support **2 subsistances** *(vivres)* provisions; *Mil* supplies

subsistant [sybzistɑ̃] **ADJ** remaining, existing

subsister [sybziste] **VI 1** *(d'une chose)* to survive, to remain **2** *(d'une personne)* to live, *Fml* to subsist (**de** on); **moyens de s.** means of support; **cela lui suffit à peine à s.** it's barely enough for him to live on

subsonique [sypsɔnik, sybs-] **ADJ** *Aviat* subsonic

substance [sybstɑ̃s] **NF 1** *(essentiel) (d'un article etc)* substance, gist; **sans s.** *(arguments etc)* insubstantial; **en s.** in substance; **voici en s. de quoi nous avons parlé** this is the gist of what we were talking about **2** *(matière)* substance, matter; **s. étrangère** extraneous substance; **plaie avec perte de s.** wound with loss of tissue; *Anat* **s. grise** grey matter

substantialité [sybstɑ̃sjalite] **NF** *Phil* substantiality

substantiel, -ielle [sybstɑ̃sjɛl] **ADJ** substantial

substantiellement [sybstɑ̃sjɛlmɑ̃] **ADV** substantially

substantif, -ive [sybstɑ̃tif, -iv] *Gram* **ADJ** nominal
  NM noun, substantive

substantifique [sybstɑ̃tifik] **ADJ la s. moelle** *(d'un texte etc)* the essence, the pith

substantivement [sybstɑ̃tivmɑ̃] **ADV** *Gram* as a noun, substantively

substantiver [sybstɑ̃tive] *Gram* **VT s. un verbe/un adjectif** to use a verb/an adjective as a noun *or* substantively
  VPR se substantiver to be used as a noun *or* substantively

substituer [sypstitɥe] **VT 1** *(remplacer)* to substitute (à for); **s. un objet à un autre** to substitute one object for another, to replace one object by another **2** *Jur* **s. un héritier** to appoint an heir in succession to another *or* failing another; **s. un héritage** to entail an estate

VPR **se substituer se s. à qn/à qch** to substitute for sb/sth, to take the place of sb/sth; **tu ne peux tout de même pas te s. à son père!** you can't take the place of his/her father!

substitut [sypstity] NM substitute (**de** for); *Jur* deputy public prosecutor; **un s. de père** a surrogate father; **s. de repas** meal substitute; *Mktg* **s. rapproché** close substitute

substitution [sypstitysjɔ̃] NF **1** (*remplacement*) substitution (**à** for); **son père de s.** his/her surrogate father **2** *Jur* **s. d'enfant** switching round of babies

substrat [sypstra] NM *Géol, Ling, Phil* substratum; *Phot, Biol, Ordinat* substrate

subterfuge [syptɛrfyʒ] NM subterfuge; **user de s.** to resort to subterfuge

subtil [syptil] ADJ **1** (*fin*) (*plaisanterie, remarque*) subtle; (*esprit, humour etc*) subtle, discerning **2** (*ténu*) (*distinction, différence etc*) subtle, fine **3** *Arch* (*fluide*) tenuous, thin; (*poussière*) fine **4** (*qui pénètre*) (*poison, odeur etc*) pervasive

subtilement [syptilmɑ̃] ADV subtly

subtiliser [syptilize] VT **1** *Fam* (*dérober*) to pinch, *Br* to nick (**à** from); **on lui a subtilisé son portefeuille** he's had his wallet pinched **2** *Arch* (*substance*) to refine
VI (*en raisonnant*) to split hairs, to be oversubtle

subtilité [syptilite] NF **1** (*de l'esprit, d'une manœuvre etc*) subtlety **2** (*d'une distinction*) subtlety, fineness **3** (*d'un argument etc*) subtlety; **les subtilités de la langue** the subtleties of the language

subtropical, -ale, -aux, -ales [syptrɔpikal, -o] ADJ subtropical

suburbain [sybyrbɛ̃] ADJ suburban

subvenir [sybvənir] (*conj like* **venir**; *aux* **avoir**) VI **s. à** (*besoins*) to provide for; (*dépenses*) to meet; **s. aux dépenses de sa famille** to provide for one's family

subvention [sybvɑ̃sjɔ̃] NF subsidy, grant; **subventions en capital** capital grants; **s. aux entreprises** development grant; **recevoir** *ou* **toucher des subventions** to get a subsidy, to be subsidized; **s. d'exploitation** operating subsidy; **s. à l'exportation** export subsidy

subventionner [sybvɑ̃sjɔne] VT (*entreprise, institution etc*) to subsidize, to grant (financial) aid to; **subventionné** (*industrie, théâtre etc*) subsidized; (*école*) maintained, grant-aided

subversif, -ive [sybvɛrsif, -iv] ADJ subversive

subversion [sybvɛrsjɔ̃] NF subversion

subversivement [sybvɛrsivmɑ̃] ADV subversively

subvertir [sybvɛrtir] VT *Litt* to subvert

suc [syk] NM **1** (*de fruit, viande*), *Physiol* juice; *Bot* sap; **s. gastrique** gastric juice **2** *Fig Litt* (*de texte etc*) essence

succédané [syksedane] ADJ, NM *aussi Méd* substitute (**de** for); **s. de café** coffee substitute; *Fig* **un s. de Truffaut** a second-rate Truffaut

succéder [syksede] (**je succède, n. succédons; je succéderai**) VI **s. à qn/qch** to succeed sb/sth, to take over from sb/sth; **un sentiment de pitié succéda à sa rage** his/her anger gave way to a feeling of pity; **les champs succèdent aux bois** (the) fields give way to woods; **s. au trône** to succeed to the throne; **s. à une fortune** to inherit a fortune
VPR **se succéder les révolutions se succédèrent** revolution followed revolution, there was a succession of revolutions; **les générations qui se sont succédé** the generations

that followed each other; **les journées se succédaient** day followed day, the days followed each other

succès [syksɛ] NM success; **avoir du s.** to be successful *or* a success; **ne pas avoir de s.** to be unsuccessful; **elle a un grand s. auprès des hommes** she is very successful *or* has great success with men; **se vanter de ses s.** to boast about one's success; **remporter un beau/de grands s.** to have *or* achieve great success; **passer un examen avec s.** to pass an exam; **sans s.** (*utilisé adjectivement*) unsuccessful; (*utilisé adverbialement*) unsuccessfully; **j'ai essayé de le convaincre, mais sans s.** I tried to convince him, but without success *or* I was unsuccessful; **une seconde tentative n'eut pas plus de s.** a second attempt met with no more success *or* was no more successful; **je n'ai pas eu de s. avec ma proposition** I was unsuccessful *or* had no success with my proposal; *Sport* **le plus beau s. de l'équipe** the team's greatest success; **livre à s., s. de librairie** bestseller; **auteur à s.** bestselling author; **chanteur/acteur à s.** successful singer/actor; **pièce/chanson à s.** hit play/song; **remporter un ou avoir grand s.** (*d'une pièce de théâtre etc*) to be a great *or* a huge success; **le public a fait un s. à ce livre/cette pièce/ce film** the book/play/film has been well received (by the public); **s. fou** great success; **s. d'audience** ratings success, *Fam* big *or* smash hit (**auprès de, parmi** with); **les casquettes de baseball ont un s. fou auprès des jeunes** baseball caps are big *or* a big hit with young people

successeur [syksesœr] NM successor (**de** to, of)

successif, -ive [syksesif, -iv] ADJ successive

succession [syksesjɔ̃] NF **1** (*série*) (*d'idées, de sons, de jours etc*) succession, series; (*de personnes, d'admirateurs etc*) stream, succession; **s. de catastrophes** series *or* catalogue of disasters **2** (*au trône, au pouvoir etc*) succession (**à** to); **la s. du poste sera assurée par M. Dupont** Mr Dupont will take over the post; **prendre la s. d'une maison de commerce** to take over a business **3** *Jur* (*par héritage*) succession; (*biens*) inheritance; **droits de s.** death duties

successivement [syksesivmɑ̃] ADV successively

succinct [syksɛ̃] ADJ succinct, brief, concise; *Fam* **repas s.** frugal meal; **sois s.** be brief, keep it brief

succinctement [syksɛ̃tmɑ̃] ADV succinctly, briefly; *Fam* (*manger*) frugally

succion [sy(k)sjɔ̃] NF suction; **bruit de s.** sucking noise

succomber [sykɔ̃be] VI **1** (*tomber*) to succumb, to collapse; **s. sous le poids de qch** to collapse under the weight of sth; **s. sous le nombre** to yield to greater numbers; *Fig* **s. sous les soucis/les problèmes financiers** to be overwhelmed by worries/financial problems; **s. devant un adversaire** (*dans un combat*), *Fig* to yield to an opponent **2** **s. à** (*peine, tentation etc*) to succumb to, to yield to; (*émotion*) to be overcome by; **j'ai succombé à la fatigue** I succumbed to fatigue **3** (*mourir*) to die, to succumb

succube [sykyb] NM succubus, succuba

succulence [sykylɑ̃s] NF *Litt* succulence

succulent [sykylɑ̃] ADJ (*nourriture*) succulent; *Bot* (*feuille*) fleshy; **plante succulente** succulent

succursale [sykyrsal] NF *Com* branch; **magasin à succursales** chain store

sucer [syse] (**je suçai(s); n. suçons**) VT **1** (*lait, orange, os etc*) to suck; **comprimés à s.** (*sur boîte*) to be sucked; **s. son pouce** to suck

one's thumb; *Vieilli* **s. qch avec le lait** to take sth in with one's mother's milk; *Fig Fam* **s. qn jusqu'au dernier sou** *ou* **jusqu'à la moelle des os** to suck sb dry, to bleed sb white; *Arg* **s. la poire à qn** to French-kiss sb; **ils sont tout le temps à se s. la poire** they're always snogging; *Fam* **il ne suce pas que de la glace** he drinks like a fish **2** *Vulg* (*sexuellement*) **s. qn** (*fellation*) to go down on sb, to give sb head; (*cunnilinctus*) to go down on sb
VPR **se sucer 1 se s. les doigts** to suck one's fingers; *Arg* **se s. la poire** to snog **2 ces cachets se sucent** these tablets are (meant) to be sucked *or* are for sucking

sucette [sysɛt] NF **1** (*de bébé*) dummy, *Am* pacifier **2** (*confiserie*) lollipop, *Fam* lolly **3** *Fam* **partir en s.** to go down the tubes *or* pan

suceur, -euse [sysœr, -øz] N *Péj* **s. de sang** (*personne*) bloodsucker
NM **1** (*poisson*) sucker, sucking fish **2** (*d'aspirateur*) nozzle
NF **suceuse** (*drague*) suction dredger

suçon [sysɔ̃] NM *Fam* lovebite, *Am* hickey; **faire un s. à qn** to give sb a lovebite *or Am* hickey

suçoter [sysɔte] VT *Fam* to suck (at)

sucrage [sykraʒ] NM (*du vin*) sugaring

sucrant [sykrɑ̃] ADJ sweetening; **avoir un grand pouvoir s.** to be a strong sweetener; **produit s.** sweetener

sucrase [sykraz] NF *Chimie* sucrase

sucre [sykr] NM **1** (*substance*) sugar; **s. en pains** loaf sugar; **pain de s.** sugar loaf; **montagne en pain de s.** sugar-loaf mountain; **un s. dans mon café** one sugar in my coffee; **vous le prenez avec ou sans s., votre café?** do you take sugar in your coffee or not?; **fruit au s.** fruit sprinkled with sugar; **décorations en s.** sugar decorations; *Fig Fam* **il a été tout s. tout miel** he was all sweetness and light; *Fig* **elle n'est pas en s.!** she's not made of glass!; *Fam* **mon bébé en s.** my sweetie pie; *Fam* **c'est un vrai s.** he's a honey; *Can* **partie de s.** sugaring-off party; *Fam* **casser du s. sur le dos de qn** to bad-mouth sb, *Br* to slag sb off **2** (*monnaie*) sucre
▸▸ **s. de betterave** beet sugar; **s. brut** unrefined sugar; **s. de canne** cane sugar; **s. cristallisé** granulated sugar; **s. de fruit** fructose; **s. glace** icing *or Am* confectioner's sugar; *Chimie* **s. de lait** lactose; **s. en morceaux** lump sugar, sugar lumps; **s. d'orge** barley sugar; *Can* **s. du pays** maple sugar; **s. en poudre** caster sugar; **s. roux** brown sugar; **s. semoule** caster sugar

sucré, -ée [sykre] ADJ **1** (*naturellement*) (*aliment, substance, goût etc*) sweet **2** (*additionné de sucre*) (*à la fabrication*) sweetened; (*café etc*) sugared, sweetened; **boisson non sucrée** unsweetened drink; **eau sucrée** sugar and water; **mon thé est trop s.** my tea is too sweet, there's too much sugar in my tea **3** *Fig* (*paroles, manières, sourire*) sugary; **prendre un ton s.** to speak in a smarmy tone
N **faire le/la sucré(e)** to be all sweetness and light

sucrer [sykre] VT **1** to sugar, to sweeten; **s. son café** to sugar one's coffee; **je ne sucre pas mes yaourts** I don't put sugar in my yoghurt; *Fig Fam* **s. les fraises** (*trembler*) to shake; (*être gâteux*) to be an old dodderer **2** *Fig Fam* (*supprimer*) (*passage, émission etc*) to cut; **on lui a sucré sa prime** he has had his bonus taken away; **on ne va pas me s. mes vacances!** I'm not going to have my holidays cancelled!
VI (*du miel etc*) to sweeten
VPR **se sucrer 1** *Fam* (*prendre du sucre*) to help oneself to sugar **2** *Arg* (*faire des bénéfices*) to line one's pockets

sucrerie [sykrəri] NF **1** (*usine*) sugar refinery

2 sucreries *(friandises)* confectionery, sweets, *surtout Am* candy; **dans votre condition il faut éviter les sucreries** you must avoid eating sweet things in your condition; **aimer les sucreries** to have a sweet tooth **3** *Can (forêt)* maple tree grove

sucrette [sykʁɛt] NF artificial sweetener

sucrier, -ière [sykʁije, -jɛʁ] ADJ sugar; **industrie sucrière** sugar industry
  N *(fabricant)* sugar manufacturer
  NM *(récipient)* sugar bowl *or* basin; **s. verseur** sugar shaker

sud [syd] NM *(no pl)* **1** *(point cardinal)* south; **au s., dans le s.** in the south; **où est le s.?** which way is south?; **la partie la plus au s. de l'île** the southernmost part of the island; **le vent vient du s.** it's a south *or* southerly wind, the wind is coming from the south; **un vent du s.** a southerly wind; **le vent du s.** the south wind; **aller au** *ou* **vers le s.** to go south *or* southwards; **les trains qui vont vers le s.** trains going south, southbound trains; **rouler vers le s.** to drive south *or* southwards; **aller droit vers le s.** to head due south; **la cuisine est plein s.** *ou* **exposée au s.** the kitchen faces due south
  2 *(partie d'un pays, d'un continent)* south, southern area *or* regions; *(partie d'une ville)* south; **le s. de l'Italie** southern Italy, the south of Italy; **dans le s. de l'Espagne** in southern Spain, in the south of Spain; **elle habite dans le s.** she lives in the South; **il habite dans le s. de Paris** he lives in the south of Paris; **elle est du s.** she's from the south; **les gens du s.** people who live in the south
  ADJ INV *(côté, face)* south; *(banlieue, partie, région)* southern; **le pôle S.** the South Pole **le Pacifique S.** South Pacific; **la façade s. d'un immeuble** the south-facing wall of a building; **la chambre est côté s.** the bedroom faces south; **dans la partie s. de la France** in the South of France, in southern France; **suivre la direction s.** to head *or* to go southward

sud-africain, -aine, *pl* **sud-africain(e)s** ADJ South African; **la République sud-africaine** the Republic of South Africa
  N S. South African

sud-américain, -aine, *pl* **sud-américain(e)s** ADJ South American
  N S. South American

sudation [sydasjɔ̃] NF *Méd etc* sudation, sweating

sud-coréen, -enne, *pl* **sud-coréen(ne)s** ADJ South Korean
  N S. South Korean

sud-est [sydɛst] NM INV **1** *(point cardinal)* south-east; **au s. de Paris** south-east of Paris **2** *Géog* **le S. asiatique** South East Asia
  ADJ INV south-east

sudiste [sydist] *Hist* N *(de la guerre de Sécession)* Confederate
  ADJ Southern

sudorifère [sydoʁifɛʁ] ADJ = **sudoripare**

sudorifique [sydoʁifik] ADJ, NM *Pharm* sudorific

sudoripare [sydoʁipaʁ] ADJ *Anat* sudoriferous; **glande s.** sweat gland

sud-ouest NM INV *(point cardinal)* south-west **2** *(vent)* south-west *or* south-westerly wind
  ADJ INV south-west

Sud-Ouest africain NM *Hist* South West Africa

sud-sud-est NM INV south-south-east
  ADJ INV south-south-east

sud-sud-ouest NM INV south-south-west
  ADJ INV south-south-west

sud-vietnamien, -ienne, *pl* **sud-vietnamien(ne)s** ADJ South Vietnamese
  N S. South Vietnamese

Suède [sɥɛd] NF Sweden

suédé [sɥede] ADJ, NM suede

suédine [sɥedin] NF *Tex* suedette

suédois, -oise [sɥedwa, -waz] VOIR GRAMMAIRE A19 ADJ Swedish; *Gym* **la gymnastique suédoise** Swedish gymnastics *or* exercises
  NM *Ling* Swedish
  N S. Swede

suée [sɥe] NF *Fam (transpiration)* sweat; *(sous l'effet de la peur)* (cold) sweat; **prendre une s.** to get up *or* work up a sweat; **cela m'a donné une sacrée s.** *(d'un travail)* I sweated blood over it; *(d'une expérience effrayante)* it brought me out in a cold sweat; **j'en ai encore des suées** I still break out in a cold sweat when I think about it

suer [sɥe] VI **1** *(d'une personne)* to sweat; **s. à grosses gouttes** to be pouring with sweat, to be sweating buckets; *Fam* **faire s. qn** *(embêter)* to annoy sb; **ça me fait s. d'aller à cette soirée** it's a drag having to go to that party; **ce que j'ai pu me faire s. pendant les vacances** I was bored stiff during the holidays, the holidays were a real drag; **tu me fais s. à la fin avec tes devoirs!** you're getting on my nerves with your homework!
  2 *(des murs etc)* to ooze
  3 *(travailler)* to labour, *Am* to labor, to sweat; *Fam* **faire s. le burnous** to use sweated labour
  VT to sweat; *Fig (piété, ennui, hypocrisie etc)* to ooze; *Fig* **s. sang et eau** to sweat blood and tears; **cette banlieue sue la tristesse** this suburb positively exudes dreariness

sueur [sɥœʁ] NF sweat; **son visage ruissellait de s.** his/her face was streaming with sweat; **être en s.** to be sweating *or* in a sweat; **avoir des sueurs froides** to be in a cold sweat; **j'en ai encore des sueurs froides, rien que d'y penser** I get in a cold sweat just thinking about it; **à la s. de son front** by the sweat of one's brow; **le fruit de mes sueurs** the fruits of my labour *or Am* labor

Suez [sɥɛz] N Suez; **le canal de S.** the Suez Canal

suffire [syfiʁ] *(prp* **suffisant;** *pp* **suffi;** *pr ind* **je suffis, n. suffisons, ils suffisent;** *pr sub* **je suffise;** *impf* **je suffisais;** *p hist* **je suffis;** *fu* **je suffirai)** VI to be enough, to be sufficient; **cela ne me suffit pas (pour vivre)** that is not enough for me (to live on); **votre promesse me suffit** your promise is enough for me; *Prov* **à chaque jour suffit sa peine** sufficient unto the day is the evil thereof; **s. à qch/à faire qch** to be up to sth/to doing sth; **s. à la tâche** to be up to *or* equal to the job; **cela suffit à mes besoins** that's enough for my needs; **je n'y suffis plus** it's too much for me, I can't cope
  VPR se suffire il s'est toujours suffi he has always supported himself *or* earned his own living; **pays qui se suffisent (à eux-mêmes)** self-supporting countries
  V IMPERS il a suffi de quelques mots pour le persuader a few words were enough to persuade him; **il suffit de l'écouter pour …** one only has to *or* one need only listen to him to …; **il suffit qu'il le dise** all he has to do is say so; **ça ne lui suffit pas** that's not enough for him; **il te l'a promis, ça ne te suffit pas?** he's promised you, is that not enough?; **il suffisait que tu passes un coup de téléphone** all you had to do was phone; **ça suffit!, (il) suffit!** that's enough!, that'll do!; **il suffit d'une heure pour …** it only takes an hour to … SEE GRAMMAR B29–30

suffisamment [syfizamɑ̃] ADV enough, sufficiently; **agir sans avoir s. réfléchi** to act without sufficient thought; **s. de** enough, sufficient; **j'ai pris s. de temps à le lui expliquer** I took the time to explain it to him/her; **j'ai s. souffert pour savoir que …** I've suffered enough to know that …

suffisance [syfizɑ̃s] NF **1 avoir s. de** to have sufficient *or* enough; **manger à sa s.** to eat one's fill; **avoir de qch à s.** *ou* **en s.** to have sth in abundance, to have plenty of sth **2** *(vanité)* arrogance, self-importance; **il est d'une s. insupportable** he is unbearably conceited **3** *Arch (capacité)* competence; **homme de s.** competent man

suffisant, -ante [syfizɑ̃, -ɑ̃t] ADJ **1** sufficient, enough; **c'est plus que s.** that is more than sufficient *or* enough **2** *(vaniteux) (air, ton)* self-important, conceited
  N faire le s. to give oneself airs

suffixe [syfiks] NM *Gram, Ordinat* suffix

suffixer [syfikse] VT *Gram, Ordinat* to suffix, to add a suffix to; **mot suffixé** word with *or* that has a suffix

suffocant [syfɔkɑ̃] ADJ **1** *(chaleur etc)* suffocating, stifling **2** *Fig (nouvelle, réponse etc)* staggering, astounding

suffocation [syfɔkasjɔ̃] NF suffocation; *(crise)* choking fit

suffoquer [syfɔke] VT **1** *(d'une odeur, de la fumée etc)* to suffocate, to stifle; *Fig (de nouvelles)* to stagger, to astound; **les sanglots la suffoquaient** she was choking with sobs **2** *Arch (tuer)* to suffocate
  VI to suffocate, to choke; **s. de colère/d'indignation** to choke with anger/indignation

suffragant [syfʁagɑ̃] *Rel* ADJ *(évêque)* suffragan
  NM suffragan (bishop)

suffrage [syfʁaʒ] NM *Pol (voix)* vote; *(système)* suffrage; **dix mille suffrages** ten thousand votes; **recueillir de nombreux suffrages** to win numerous votes; **s. universel** universal franchise *or* suffrage, one-man-one-vote; **s. direct/indirect** direct/indirect suffrage; *Fig* **ce nouveau modèle remporte tous les suffrages** this new model wins everyone's approval *or* is universally liked

suffragette [syfʁaʒɛt] NF *Hist, Pol* suffragette

suffusion [syfyzjɔ̃] NF *Méd* suffusion

suggérer [syɡʒeʁe] VT *(* **je suggère, n. suggérons; je suggérerai)** to suggest (à to); **s. de faire qch** to suggest doing sth; **s. à qn de faire qch** to suggest to sb that he should do sth; **cette expression suggère la lumière/la vitesse** this expression suggests light/speed

suggestibilité [syɡʒɛstibilite] NF suggestibility

suggestible [syɡʒɛstibl] ADJ suggestible

suggestif, -ive [syɡʒɛstif, -iv] ADJ **1** *(évocateur)* evocative, suggestive **2** *(érotique) (plaisanterie, geste etc)* suggestive; *(tenue, décolleté)* revealing

suggestion [syɡʒɛs(t)jɔ̃] NF suggestion; **agir sur la s. de qn** to act on sb's suggestion; **pas la moindre s. de …** not the slightest hint *or* suggestion of … VOIR GRAMMAIRE A59–60

suggestionner [syɡʒɛstjɔne] VT **s. qn** to put an idea *or* ideas into sb's head; **se laisser s.** to allow ideas to be put into one's head (**par** by)

suicidaire [sɥisidɛʁ] ADJ *(tendances, personne)* suicidal; *Fig (entreprise etc)* suicidal
  N suicidal person

suicide [sɥisid] NM *(acte)* suicide; **tentative de s.** suicide attempt; *Fig* **le s. économique d'un pays** the economic suicide of a country; **s. politique** political suicide; **attentat-s.** suicide attack; **avion-s.** suicide plane

suicidé, -ée [sɥiside] ADJ who has committed suicide
  N *(personne)* suicide

suicider (se) [səsɥiside] VPR to commit sui-

2 *(digne de confiance) (personne, mémoire)* trustworthy, reliable; *(ami)* trusty, true; *(information, entreprise)* reliable; **savoir qch de source sûre** to learn sth from a reliable source; **avoir le coup d'œil s.** to have a keen eye; **goût s.** discerning taste; **avoir la main sûre/le pied s.** to have a steady hand/to be surefooted; **ne pas avoir le pied s.** to be unsteady on one's feet; **frapper un coup s.** *ou* à **coup s.** to strike an unerring blow; **mettre son argent en mains sûres** to put one's money into safe hands

3 *(certain)* certain, sure; **il l'a oublié, c'est s.** he has forgotten it, that's for certain *or* sure; **c'est une affaire sûre** it's a certainty *or* a sure thing *or Fam* a dead cert; **être s. de réussir** to be sure of success; **être s. de qch** to be sure *or* certain of sth; **je ne suis pas s. de la réussite de ce projet** I'm not sure that this plan will succeed; **je suis s. de lui** I can depend on him; **être s. de son fait** to be positive; **elle n'était pas vraiment sûre de son coup** she wasn't really sure of success; **je suis s. de ce que je te dis** I'm sure about what I'm saying; **s. de soi** self-assured; *Fam* **j'en suis s. et certain** I'm absolutely certain *or* sure of it; **mais oui ça va marcher, c'est s. et certain!** of course it'll work, it's absolutely certain!; **parier à coup s.** to bet on a certainty; **à coup s.** for certain, definitely

NM jouer au plus s. to play for safety; **le plus s. serait de ...** the safest thing would be to ...
ADV *Fam* surely; **s.!** of course!; *Am* sure!; **pas s.!** perhaps not; *Fam* **bien s.!, pour s.!** of course!, *Am* sure!; *Fam* **bien s.?** you really mean it?; **bien s. que non!** of course not!; **bien s. que je viendrai aussi** of course I'll come too

surabondance [syrabɔ̃dɑ̃s] **NF** overabundance; *Com* glut; **s. de richesses/de détails** wealth of riches/details

surabondant [syrabɔ̃dɑ̃] **ADJ** overabundant

surabonder [syrabɔ̃de] **VI** to be overabundant; **s. de** *ou* **en qch** to have an overabundance of sth

suraccumulation [syrakymylasjɔ̃] **NF s. de capital** over-accumulation of capital

suractivé [syraktive] **ADJ** superactivated

suractivité [syraktivite] **NF** *Physiol* overactivity

surah [syra] **NM** *Tex* syrah

suraigu, -uë [syregy] **ADJ 1** *(voix, son)* high-pitched **2** *Méd (inflammation)* acute

surajouter [syraʒute] **VT** to add (on)
VPR se surajouter to be added (on)

suralimentation [syralimɑ̃tasjɔ̃] **NF 1** *(de personne)* overfeeding; *Méd* feeding up **2** *Aut (de moteur)* supercharging; **s. par turbocompresseur** turbocharging

suralimenter [syralimɑ̃te] **VT 1** to overfeed; *Méd (personne)* to feed up **2** *(moteur)* to supercharge; **suralimenté** *(moteur)* supercharged; **suralimenté refroidi** charge-cooled

suranné [syrane] **ADJ 1** *(vieilli)* outdated, old-fashioned; **beauté surannée** faded beauty **2** *Arch (qui a expiré) (passeport etc)* expired

surarmement [syrarmɑ̃mɑ̃] **NM** *Mil* excessive arms build-up

surbaissé [syrbese] **ADJ 1** *Archit (arche, voûte)* lowered, depressed **2** *Aut etc (essieu, carrosserie etc)* dropped; *(châssis)* (extra-)low, underslung; **taille surbaissée** *(d'une robe)* drop waist

surbaissement [syrbɛsmɑ̃] **NM** *Archit* surbasement

surbaisser [syrbese] **VT 1** *Archit (arche, voûte)* to lower, to depress **2** *Aut etc (carrosserie etc)* to drop, to undersling

surbook [syrbuk] **NM** *(d'une chambre d'hô-*

---

tel, de billets d'avion) overbooking; *(en double)* double booking

surbooker [syrbuke] **VT** to overbook; *(en double)* to double book

surbooking [syrbukiŋ] **NM** overbooking; *(en double)* double booking

surboum [syrbum] **NF** *Fam Vieilli* party; **faire une s.** to have *or* throw a party

surbrillance [syrbrijɑ̃s] **NF** *Typ* highlighting; **apparaître en s.** to be highlighted

surcapacité [syrkapasite] **NF** *Ind etc* overcapacity

surcapitalisation [syrkapitalizasjɔ̃] **NF** overcapitalization

surcapitaliser [syrkapitalize] **VI** to overcapitalize

surcharge [syrʃarʒ] **NF 1** *Tech* overload; *Élec (d'un accumulateur)* overcharge; *Fig* **une s. de travail/de responsabilités/de soucis** extra work/responsibilities/worries; **la s. d'un programme d'études** a heavy syllabus
2 *(dans un véhicule)* excess load; *(de bagages)* excess weight; **prendre des passagers en s.** to take on excess passengers; **rouler en s.** to drive an overloaded vehicle; *Méd* **s. pondérale** excess weight
3 *(d'une course de chevaux)* weight handicap
4 *(à payer)* surcharge
5 *Typ* correction, alteration; *(dans un contrat etc)* alteration; *(imprimée sur une timbre-poste)* surcharge

surcharger [syrʃarʒe] **VT** (**je surchargeai(s); n. surchargeons**) **1** *(véhicule, cheval, estomac etc)* to overload; *Élec (accumulateur)* to overcharge; *Fig* **s. ses employés de travail** to overwork one's employees; **je suis surchargée de travail depuis deux mois** I've been overburdened with work for two months; **s. d'impôts** to overburden with taxes; *Fin* **s. le marché** to overload the market **2** *Typ (caractères)* to write over with corrections; *(timbre)* to surcharge, to overprint

surchauffe [syrʃof] **NF** *(d'un four, d'un moteur)*, *Fig (de l'économie)* overheating

surchauffer [syrʃofe] **VT 1** *(four etc)* to overheat; **salle surchauffée** overheated room **2** *(vapeur)* to superheat

surchoix [syrʃwa] *Com* **NM** finest quality
ADJ INV *(produit)* top-quality

surclassement [syrklasmɑ̃] **NM** *(de titre de transport)* upgrade

surclasser [syrklase] **VT** to outclass; *(titre de transport)* to upgrade

surcompensation [syrkɔ̃pɑ̃sasjɔ̃] **NF** *Psy* overcompensation

surcomposé [syrkɔ̃poze] **ADJ** *Gram (temps)* double-compound

surcompression [syrkɔ̃presjɔ̃] **NF** *Tech* supercharging

surcomprimer [syrkɔ̃prime] **VT** *Tech* to supercharge; **moteur surcomprimé** supercharged engine

surconsommation [syrkɔ̃sɔmasjɔ̃] **NF** *Écon* overconsumption

surcontrer [syrkɔ̃tre] **VT** *Cartes* to redouble

sur-correction **NF** *Aut* over-correction

surcouper [syrkupe] **VT** *Cartes* to overtrump

surcoût [syrku] **NM** cost overrun

surcroît [syrkrwa] **NM un s. de** extra; **un s. d'effort** an extra effort; **pour donner un s. d'effet à ...** to give an added effect to ...; **par s., de s.** in addition, moreover; **par s. de besogne** to add to my work; **pour s. de malheur** to make matters worse; **s. de dépenses** additional expenditure

surdéveloppé [syrdevlɔpe] **ADJ** *Écon* highly developed; *(excessivement)* overdeveloped

surdéveloppement [syrdevlɔpmɑ̃] **NM**

Écon high state of development; *(excessif)* overdevelopment

surdimensionné [syrdimɑ̃sjɔne] **ADJ** oversized

surdi-mutité [syrdimytite] **NF** deaf-muteness

surdiplômé [syrdiplome] **ADJ** overqualified

surdité [syrdite] **NF** deafness; **s. musicale** tone deafness

surdon [syrdɔ̃] **NM 1** *(compensation)* = compensation allowable to purchaser for damage to goods **2** *(droit)* = right to non-acceptance of damaged goods

surdosage [syrdozaʒ] **NM** *Méd* overdosage

surdose [syrdoz] **NF** overdose

surdoué, -ée [syrdwe] **N** gifted child
ADJ exceptionally gifted

sureau, -eaux [syro] **NM** elder (tree); **baie de s.** elderberry

sureffectif [syrefɛktif] **NM** excessive numbers, overmanning; **en s.** surplus; **personnel en s.** excessive (numbers of) staff

surélévation [syrelevasjɔ̃] **NF** *(action)* raising; *(augmentation de hauteur)* increase in height

surélevé [syrelve] **ADJ 1** *(voie ferrée)* elevated **2** *Archit (arche, rez-de-chaussée etc)* raised

surélever [syrelve] **VT** *(conj like* **élever**) *Constr etc* to heighten, to raise; **s. un malade dans son lit** to prop a patient up in his bed

suremballage [syrɑ̃balaʒ] **NM** over-packaging

sûrement [syrmɑ̃] **ADV 1** *(sans doute)* surely; **s.!** certainly!, more than likely!; **s. pas!** certainly not!; **elle est s. tombée en panne** she must have broken down; **il va s. y avoir des changements** there are surely going to be some changes **2** *(de manière confiante)* confidently, with confidence **3** *(sans risque)* safely **4** *(immanquablement)* **frapper s.** to strike with accuracy; **lentement mais s.** slowly but surely

surémission [syremisjɔ̃] **NF** *Fin* overissue

suremploi [syrɑ̃plwa] **NM** overemployment

surenchère [syrɑ̃ʃɛr] **NF 1** *Com* higher bid, overbid; **faire une s. sur qn** to outbid sb **2** *Fig* **une s. de violence** an increase in violence; **faire de la s.** to try to go one better than one's rivals, to try to outdo one's rivals; **faire de la s. électorale** to make more extravagant promises to obtain votes

surenchérir [syrɑ̃ʃerir] **VI 1** *Com* to bid higher; *Fig* to try to outdo each other; **s. sur qn** to outbid sb, to bid higher than sb; *Fig* to try to outdo sb *or* go one better than sb **2** *(devenir plus cher)* to rise in price

surenchérisseur [syrɑ̃ʃerisœr] **NM** highest bidder

surencombré [syrɑ̃kɔ̃bre] **ADJ** *(rue etc)* (severely) congested (**de** with)

surencombrement [syrɑ̃kɔ̃brəmɑ̃] **NM** (severe) congestion

surendetté [syrɑ̃dete] **ADJ** *Écon* excessively in debt

surendettement [syrɑ̃dɛtmɑ̃] **NM** *Écon* excessive debt (burden), overindebtedness, over-gearing; **courir un risque de s.** to run a risk of getting into excessive debt

surentraînement [syrɑ̃trɛnmɑ̃] **NM** *Sport* overtraining

surentraîner [syrɑ̃trɛne] **VT** *Sport* to overtrain

suréquipement [syrekipmɑ̃] **NM** *Écon* overequipment

suréquiper [syrekipe] **VT** *Écon* to over-equip

surestarie [syrɛstari] **NF** *Com* demurrage

surestimation [syrɛstimasjɔ̃] NF *(de l'importance, la capacité)* overestimation; *(d'une œuvre d'art etc)* overvaluation

surestimer [syrɛstime] VT **1** *(importance, capacité, nombre, difficulté etc)* to overestimate; *(person)* to overrate, to overestimate **2** *(en valeur) (œuvre d'art etc)* to overvalue
VPR **se surestimer** to overrate oneself, to overestimate oneself; **j'ai peur que tu te surestimes si tu penses pouvoir ...** I'm afraid you're being a bit optimistic if you think you can ...

suret, -ette [syrɛ, -ɛt] ADJ *(fruit, goût etc)* sour(ish), tart

sûreté [syrte] NF **1** *(absence de danger)* safety; **lieu de s.** place of safety; **être en s.** to be safe *or* out of harm's way; **mettre qn en (lieu de) s.** *(en prison)* to put sb in prison; *(à l'abri)* to put sb in a safe place *or* out of harm's way; **pour plus de s.** for greater safety; **rasoir/serrure/soupape de s.** safety razor/lock/valve; **épingle de s.** safety pin; *Aut* **à s. intégrée** failsafe
2 *Pol etc* security; **la s. de l'État** state *or* national security; **la S. (nationale)** = the (French) criminal investigation department, *Br* ≃ the CID, *Am* ≃ the FBI; **agent de la S.** detective
3 *(de la main, du pied)* sureness, steadiness; *(de la vision, du goût, du jugement)* soundness; *(d'un coup)* accuracy; **s. de soi** self-confidence, self-assurance
4 *Com (garantie)* surety, guarantee; **s. en garantie d'une créance** surety for a loan

surévaluation [syrevalɥasjɔ̃] NF overvaluation

surévaluer [syrevalɥe] VT *(objet, antiquité)* to overvalue; *(efficacité, capacités etc)* to overestimate

surexcitable [syrɛksitabl] ADJ overexcitable, easily excited

surexcitation [syrɛksitasjɔ̃] NF overexcitement

surexciter [syrɛksite] VT to overexcite; **des adolescentes surexcitées** hysterical teenage girls

surexploitation [syrɛksplwatasjɔ̃] NF overexploitation

surexploiter [syrɛksplwate] VT *(terre, travailleurs etc)* to overexploit

surexposer [syrɛkspoze] VT *Phot* to overexpose

surexposition [syrɛkspozisjɔ̃] NF *Phot* overexposure

surf [sœrf] NM *Sport* **1** *(sport)* surfing; **faire du s.** to go surfing, to surf **2** *(planche)* surfboard

surface [syrfas] NF **1** surface; **eau de s.** surface water; *Phys* **tension de s.** *(d'un liquide)* surface tension; **bruit de s.** surface noise; **vitesse en s.** *(de sous-marin)* surface speed; **nager en s.** to swim near the surface; **remonter à la s.** to rise to the surface, to surface; **faire s.,** **revenir en s.** *(d'un sous-marin)* to surface; *Fig Fam* **faire s.** *(se réveiller)* to surface; *Fig* **refaire s.** *(après une période difficile)* to get back on one's feet; **en s.** *(de l'eau)* on the surface; *Fig* superficially; **tout en s.** superficial; **il reste à la s. des choses** he doesn't go into things in any depth
2 *Géom* surface; **s. de révolution** *ou* **de rotation** surface of revolution; **s. plane** plane surface
3 *(étendue etc)* (surface) area; **quelle est la s. de l'appartement** how big is the flat?; *Fam* **avoir de la s.** to have influence; **(magasin à) grande s.** hypermarket; **grande s. de bricolage** DIY centre
▸▸ *Ordinat* **s. d'affichage** display area; **s. d'appui** bearing area *or* surface; *Constr* **s. couverte** floor area; *Ordinat* **s. d'enregistre-**

ment read-write surface; *Mktg* **s. d'exposition** display space; *Fin* **s. financière** financial situation; **il présente une s. financière suffisante** his financial situation is sound; **s. portante** *ou* **de portée** bearing area *or* surface; *Ftbl* **s. de réparation** penalty area *or* box; **s. au sol** floor area; **s. utile** floor space; **s. de vente** sales area *or* floor; **s. de voilure** sail area

surfaceuse [syrfasøz] NF *Tech* surfacer, planing machine

surfacturation [syrfaktyrasjɔ̃] NF overbilling

surfaire [syrfɛr] VT *(conj like* **faire***)* *Litt* **1** *(marchandises etc)* to overprice **2** *(personne, talent etc)* to overestimate, to overrate

surfait [syrfɛ] ADJ *(prix)* excessive; *(personne, réputation etc)* overrated

surfer [sœrfe] VI to surf; **s. sur l'Internet** *ou* **le Net** to surf the Net *or* the Internet

surfeur, -euse [sœrfœr, -øz] N surfer; **s. des neiges** snowboarder

surfilage [syrfilaʒ] NM *Couture* overcasting, oversewing

surfiler [syrfile] VT **1** *Couture* to overcast, to oversew **2** *Tex (fil)* to give an extra twist to

surfin [syrfɛ̃] ADJ *Com (produit)* superior, top-quality

surfrappe [syrfrap] NF *Ordinat* double strike, overstrike

surfréquentation [syrfrekɑ̃tasjɔ̃] NF *(d'un lieu)* overfrequentation

surgé [syrʒe] N *Fam (abrév* **surveillant(e) général(e)***)* head supervisor *(in charge of school discipline)*

surgélateur [syrʒelatœr] NM deep-freeze, freezer

surgélation [syrʒelasjɔ̃] NF deep *or* quick freezing

surgelé [syrʒəle] ADJ deep- *or* quick-frozen
NMPL **surgelés** frozen foods

surgeler [syrʒəle] VT *(conj like* **geler***)* to deep- *or* quick-freeze

surgénérateur [syrʒeneratœr] ADJ, NM *Nucl* **(réacteur) s.** breeder reactor

surgeon [syrʒɔ̃] NM *(de plante)* sucker

surgir [syrʒir] VI *(aux* **avoir***, parfois* **être***)* to appear suddenly; *(d'une plante)* to spring up; *(d'une difficulté)* to crop up; **faire s. de nouveaux problèmes** to create new problems

surgissement [syrʒismɑ̃] NM *Litt* sudden appearance

surglacé [syrglase] ADJ *(papier)* calendered

surhaussé [syrose] ADJ *Archit* raised

surhaussement [syrosmɑ̃] NM *Archit* raising; *(différence de hauteur)* increase in height

surhausser [syrose] VT *Archit (mur etc)* to raise

surhomme [syrɔm] NM superman

surhumain [syrymɛ̃] ADJ superhuman

surimi [syrimi] NM *Culin* crab stick

surimposer [syrɛ̃poze] VT *(par l'impôt)* to overtax

surimposition [syrɛ̃pozisjɔ̃] NF **1** *(par l'impôt)* overtaxation **2** *Géol* pseudomorphism

surimpression [syrɛ̃presjɔ̃] NF *Phot, Cin* superimposition; *Ordinat* overprinting, overstrike; **en s.** superimposed; *Fig* **une foule d'émotions me sont venues en s.** I experienced a whole range of emotions in quick succession

surimprimer [syrɛ̃prime] VT *Ordinat* to overprint

surin [syrɛ̃] NM *Fam Vieilli* knife, dagger

Surinam(e) [syrinam] NM Surinam

surindustrialisation [syrɛ̃dystrijalizasjɔ̃] NF overindustrialization

suriner [syrine] VT *Fam Vieilli (personne)* to knife

surinfection [syrɛ̃fɛksjɔ̃] NF *Méd* secondary infection

surinformation [syrɛ̃fɔrmasjɔ̃] NF information overload

surinformé [syrɛ̃fɔrme] ADJ overinformed; **les gens sont surinformés** people are bombarded with too much information

surintendance [syrɛ̃tɑ̃dɑ̃s] NF *Hist* superintendence

surintendant [syrɛ̃tɑ̃dɑ̃] NM *Hist* superintendent

surinvestissement [syrɛ̃vɛstismɑ̃] NM *Fin, Psy* overinvestment

surir [syrir] VI *(du vin, de la soupe etc)* to turn sour

surjet [syrʒɛ] NM *Couture* overcasting, whipping

surjeter [syrʒəte] VT *(conj like* **jeter***)* *Couture* to overcast, to whip

sur-le-champ ADV at once, immediately

surlendemain [syrlɑ̃dmɛ̃] NM **le s.** the day after the next, two days later; **le s. de leur départ** two days after their departure

surligner [syrliɲe] VT to highlight

surligneur [syrliɲœr] NM highlighter (pen)

surlocation [syrlɔkasjɔ̃] NF overbooking, *Am* oversale; *(en double)* double booking

surlouer [syrlwe] VT to overbook; *(en double)* to double book

surmarquage [syrmarkaʒ] NM overpricing, overcharging

surmarquer [syrmarke] to overprice

surmédiatisation [syrmedjatizasjɔ̃] NF excessive media coverage

surmédiatisé [syrmedjatize] ADJ *(événement)* that receives/has received too much media coverage

surmédicaliser [syrmedikalize] VT to overmedicalize

surmédication [syrmedikasjɔ̃] NF overmedication

surmenage [syrmənaʒ] NM **1** *(état)* overwork, overtiredness; **s. intellectuel** mental strain; **élève en état de s.** overworked pupil **2** *(action)* overworking

surmenant [syrmənɑ̃] ADJ *(travail etc)* exhausting

surmené [syrməne] ADJ overworked

surmener [syrməne] *(conj like* **mener***)* VT *(employés, élèves etc)* to overwork, to work too hard
VPR **se surmener** to overwork, to work too hard, *Fam* to overdo it

sur-moi NM *(no pl)* *Psy* superego

surmontable [syrmɔ̃tabl] ADJ surmountable

surmonter [syrmɔ̃te] VT **1** *(être placé sur)* to surmount; **colonne surmontée d'une croix** column surmounted *or* topped by a cross **2** *Fig (obstacle, difficulté)* to overcome, to surmount; *(faim, peine)* to conquer, to get over; *Litt (ennemis)* to overcome
VPR **se surmonter** to master *or* control one's feelings

surmortalité [syrmɔrtalite] NF excessively high death rate

surmultiplication [syrmyltiplikasjɔ̃] NF *Aut* overdrive (system)

surmultiplié, -ée [syrmyltiplije] ADJ, NF *Aut* **(vitesse) surmultipliée** overdrive

surnager [syrnaʒe] VI *(je* **surnageai(s)***; n.* **surnageons***)* **1** to float (on the surface) **2** *Fig* to survive, to remain

surnatalité [syrnatalite] NF excessively high birth rate

surnaturel, -elle [syrnatyrɛl] ADJ supernatural
NM le s. the supernatural

surnom [syrnɔ̃] NM nickname; **on lui a donné le s. de Rick** he was given the nickname of Rick, he was nicknamed Rick

---
Il faut noter que le terme anglais **surname** est un faux ami. Il signifie **nom de famille**.

---

surnombre [syrnɔ̃br] NM en s. too many; **les exemplaires/passagers en s.** the excess copies/passengers; **ils étaient en s.** there were too many of them

surnommer [syrnɔme] VT to nickname; **s. qn 'le Tigre'** to nickname sb 'The Tiger'

surnuméraire [syrnymerɛr] ADJ, N supernumerary

suroffre [syrɔfr] NF **1** (offre plus avantageuse) better offer or bid **2** (surabondance par rapport à la demande) excess supply

suroît [syrwa] NM (vent, chapeau) sou'wester

suroxygéner [syrɔksiʒene] VT (je suroxygène, n. suroxygénons; je suroxygénerai) Chimie to superoxygenate

surpaie [syrpɛj, -pɛ] NF overpaying, overpayment

surpasser [syrpase] VT (espoirs) to surpass, to exceed; (rival) to surpass, to outdo; **dépense qui surpasse mes moyens** expense beyond my means; **s. qn en éclat** to outshine sb; **s. une armée en nombre** to outnumber an army
VPR **se surpasser** to surpass or excel oneself

surpatte [syrpat] NF Fam Vieilli (surprise-party) party

surpaye [syrpɛj, -pɛ] NF overpaying, overpayment

surpayer [syrpeje] VT (conj like **payer**) (personne) to overpay; (quelque chose) to pay too much for

surpeuplé [syrpœple] ADJ (pays, région etc) overpopulated; (maison, plage etc) overcrowded

surpeuplement [syrpœpləmɑ̃] NM (de pays etc) overpopulation; (de maison, plage etc) overcrowding

surplace [syrplas] NM (d'un cycliste avant la course) track stand; **faire du s.** Aut Fam to crawl; (d'un cycliste) to do a track stand; Fig **j'ai l'impression de faire du s. depuis deux ou trois ans** I feel like I've been getting nowhere for the last two or three years

surplis [syrpli] NM Rel surplice

surplomb [syrplɔ̃] NM overhang; **en s.** overhanging

surplombant [syrplɔ̃bɑ̃] ADJ overhanging

surplomber [syrplɔ̃be] VTI to overhang

surplus [syrply] NM surplus; **le s.** the surplus, what is left (over); **le s. de marchandises** the surplus goods, the goods that are left (over); **payer le s.** to pay the difference; **au s.** besides, what is more; **les s. du gouvernement** government surplus (stock); Fin **s. monétaire** monetary surplus; **s. américain** US army surplus

surpopulation [syrpɔpylasjɔ̃] NF overpopulation

surpositionnement [syrpozisjɔnmɑ̃] NM Mktg over-positioning

surprenant [syrprənɑ̃] ADJ surprising, amazing; **chose surprenante** strange to say; **rien de s. si ...** I shouldn't be surprised if ...; **il est s. que vous le sachiez** it is surprising that you should know of it

surprendre [syrprɑ̃dr] (conj like **prendre**) VT **1** (prendre par surprise) (quelqu'un) to surprise; **aller s. un ami chez lui** to pay a friend a surprise visit; **la nuit nous surprit** night overtook us; **être surpris par la pluie** to be caught in the rain; **s. qn à faire qch** to catch sb (in the act of) doing sth; **s. un voleur en flagrant délit** to catch a thief in the act
2 (découvrir) (lettre, regard) to intercept; (conversation etc) to overhear; **s. le secret de qn** to find out sb's secret
3 (étonner) to surprise, to astonish; **ce qui me surprend, c'est que ...** what surprises or astonishes me is that ...; **cela me surprendrait qu'il revienne ou s'il revenait** I should be surprised or astonished if he came back; **ça a l'air de vous s.** you seem surprised; **ce n'est pas pour me s.** it doesn't surprise me in the least
VPR **se surprendre se s. à faire qch** to find oneself doing sth

surpression [syrpresjɔ̃] NF Tech overpressure, excessive pressure

surprime [syrprim] NF (d'assurance) extra or additional premium

surpris [syrpri] ADJ surprised (de at); **je suis s. de te voir ici** I'm surprised to see you here; **je m'arrêtai, s.** I paused in surprise; **s., je les regardais** I watched them in surprise; **s. que + sub/si + ind** surprised that/if; **je ne serais pas s. qu'il revienne ou s'il revenait** I shouldn't be surprised if he came back

surprise [syrpriz] NF (étonnement, cadeau) surprise; **ça m'a fait une s. agréable** it came as a pleasant surprise to me; **à sa grande s.** to his great surprise, much to his surprise; **à la s. générale** to everyone's surprise; **s'emparer d'une ville par s. ou par un coup de s.** to capture a town by surprise; **il m'a fait sa demande par s.** he surprised me with his request, he sprang his request on me; **expédition/voyage sans s.** uneventful expedition/journey; **il est bon ce bordeaux? – sans s.** is this Bordeaux good? – nothing special; **craindre une s.** to fear a sudden attack; **quelle bonne s.!** what a pleasant surprise!; **attendez-vous à une drôle de s.** be prepared for a shock; **boîte à s.** Jack-in-the-box; **pochette s.** lucky bag; **grève-s.** lightning strike

surprise-partie, pl **surprises-parties** NF party

surprix [syrpri] NM excess price

surproducteur, -trice [syrprɔdyktœr] ADJ overproducing

surproduction [syrprɔdyksjɔ̃] NF overproduction

surproduire [syrprɔdɥir] VTI to overproduce

surprofit [syrprɔfi] NM excess profit

surprotection [syrprɔtɛksjɔ̃] NF (d'un enfant) over-protection, coddling

surpuissant [syrpɥisɑ̃] ADJ (moteur, pays etc) extremely powerful

surqualifié [syrkalifje] ADJ overqualified

surréalisme [syrrealism] NM surrealism

surréaliste [syrrealist] ADJ, N surrealist

surréel, -elle [syrreɛl] ADJ surreal(istic)
NM le s. the surreal

surrégénérateur, -trice [syrreʒeneratœr, -tris] ADJ, NM Nucl (réacteur) s. breeder reactor

sur-régime NM Aut etc overspeeding

surrénal, -ale, -aux, -ales [syrrenal, -o] ADJ Anat (artère, ganglion) suprarenal; (glande) adrenal

surréservation [syrrezɛrvasjɔ̃] NF overbooking; (en double) double booking

surréserver [syrrezɛrve] VT to overbook; (en double) to double book

sursalaire [syrsalɛr] NM bonus

sursaturation [syrsatyrasjɔ̃] NF **1** Écon oversaturation **2** Phys supersaturation

sursaturé [syrsatyre] ADJ Phys (solution) supersaturated; Fig **s. de** overwhelmed with

sursaturer [syrsatyre] VT **1** Écon to oversaturate **2** Phys to supersaturate

sursaut [syrso] NM start, jump; **avoir ou faire un s.** to (give a) start, to (give a) jump; **en s.** with a start; **se lever en s.** to jump up with a start; **dans un s. d'énergie** with a (sudden) burst of energy; **un s. de terrorisme** a new outbreak of terrorism

sursauter [syrsote] VI to (give a) start, to (give a) jump; **faire s. qn** to startle sb; **s. d'indignation** to leap up in indignation

surseoir [syrswar] VI (prp sursoyant; pp sursis; pr ind je sursois, n. sursoyons; pr sub je sursoie; impf je sursoyais; p hist je sursis; fut je surseoirai) Jur **s. à un jugement** to suspend a judgement; **s. à l'exécution d'un condamné** to reprieve a condemned man; **ordonnance de s. (à un jugement)** stay of execution

sursis [syrsi] NM Jur (de condamné à mort) stay of execution; Fig reprieve; **condamné à un an de prison avec s.** given a suspended (prison) sentence of one year; Mil **s. d'appel** deferment (of call-up); Fig **mort en s.** condemned man; **s. de paiement** extra time to pay

sursitaire [syrsitɛr] Mil ADJ provisionally exempted
NM provisionally exempted conscript

sursouscription [syrsuskripsjɔ̃] NF Fin oversubscription

sursouscrire [syrsuskrir] VT Fin to oversubscribe

sursouscrit [syrsuskrit] ADJ Fin oversubscribed

surtaux [syrto] NM overassessment

surtaxe [syrtaks] NF **1** surtax, surcharge; (de lettre etc) surcharge; **s. à l'importation** import surcharge **2** (excessive) excessive tax

surtaxer [syrtakse] VT **1** Admin to surtax, to surcharge **2** (lettre etc) to surcharge

surtension [syrtɑ̃sjɔ̃] NF Élec overvoltage

surtitre [syrtitr] NM Journ strapline

surtout¹ [syrtu] ADV particularly, especially; (avant tout) above all; **ayez s. soin de ...** be especially or particularly careful to ...; **s. n'oubliez pas de ...** do not forget to ...; **non, s. pas!** no, certainly not!; Fam **s. que ...** especially as ...

surtout² NM **1** (sur une table) centrepiece, Am centerpiece **2** Arch (manteau) overcoat

survaleur [syrvalœr] NF Compta goodwill

surveillance [syrvɛjɑ̃s] NF (contrôle) supervision; Scol invigilation; Mil observation, surveillance; Radio monitoring; (en prenant soin de qn ou qch) watch; **exercer une s. discrète sur qn/qch** to keep a discreet watch on sb/sth; **être sous la s. de la police** to be under police observation or surveillance; Mil **avion/navire de s.** surveillance plane/ship; **s. médicale** medical supervision; **s. électronique** electronic surveillance; Écon **s. des prix** price monitoring

surveillant, -ante [syrvɛjɑ̃, -ɑ̃t] N Ind, Admin etc supervisor; (de prison) warder, Am guard; Rail inspector; Scol (d'examen) invigilator; (chargé de la discipline) supervisor
NF Méd **surveillante** head nurse, Br ≃ (ward) sister

Il faut noter que le terme anglais **surveyor** est un faux ami. Il signifie le plus souvent **expert** ou **géomètre**.

---

surveiller [syrveje] VT **1** (contrôler) (travail, employés etc) to supervise; (prix) to monitor;

(machine) to man; *Scol (examen)* to invigilate; *Mil* to observe

2 *(prendre soin de) (personne)* to watch (over); **s. les enfants** to watch (over) *or* keep an eye on the children; **s. la situation de près** to keep a close eye on the situation; **s. son langage** to watch *or* mind one's language; **s. sa ligne** to watch one's figure; *Jur* **en liberté surveillée** on probation

3 *Radio* to monitor

VPR se surveiller to keep a watch on oneself

Il faut noter que le verbe anglais **to survey** est un faux ami. Il ne signifie jamais **surveiller**.

---

survendre [syrvãdr] **VT** *Com* to overcharge for

survenir [syrvənir] *(conj like* **venir***; aux* être) **VI** *(d'événements)* to happen, to occur; *(d'une crise, d'une difficulté)* to arise; *(d'une personne)* to arrive unexpectedly

V IMPERS s'il ne survient pas de complications if no complications arise *or* occur; **s'il survient un visiteur** if a visitor happens to come

survenue [syrvəny] **NF** *Litt* unexpected arrival

survêt [syrvɛt] **NM** *Fam* = **survêtement**

survêtement [syrvɛtmã] **NM** tracksuit; *(tenue relaxe)* shellsuit

survie [syrvi] **NF** survival; *Rel* afterlife; **croire à la s. de l'homme** to believe in the afterlife; *Astronaut etc* **équipement de s.** life support equipment; **couverture de s.** survival blanket; **une s. de quelques jours, quelques jours de s.** a few more days of life

survirage [syrviraʒ] **NM** *Aut* oversteer

survirer [syrvire] **VI** *Aut* to oversteer

survireur, -euse [syrvirœr, -øz] **ADJ** **une voiture survireuse** a car that oversteers

survivance [syrvivãs] **NF 1** *(de l'âme)* survival **2** *(vestige) (du passé etc)* survival, relic

survivant, -ante [syrvivã, -ãt] **ADJ** surviving

N survivor

survivre [syrvivr] *(conj like* **vivre***; aux* avoir) **VI** to survive; **s. à** *(personne)* to survive, to outlive; *(période, théorie etc)* to outlive; *(accident, maladie etc)* to survive; **va-t-il s.?** will he live *or* survive?

VPR se survivre 1 *(dans ses enfants, son œuvre etc)* to live on **2** *Péj (d'une personne qui est devenu médiocre)* to have had one's day

survol [syrvɔl] **NM 1** *Aviat* **le s. d'un lieu** flying over a place **2** *Fig (d'un problème etc)* cursory glance (**de** at)

survoler [syrvɔle] **VT 1** *Aviat (montagne, localité etc)* to fly over **2** *Ordinat* to browse through **3** *Fig (problème etc)* to get a general view of

survoltage [syrvɔltaʒ] **NM** *Élec* boosting

survolté [syrvɔlte] **ADJ 1** *Élec* boosted **2** *Fam (surexcité)* (over)excited, worked up

survolteur [syrvɔltœr] **NM** *Élec* booster

sus [sy(s)] **ADV 1** *Arch* **courir s. à son adversaire** to rush upon *or* at one's opponent, to charge one's opponent **2 s. de** *(somme d'argent)* in addition to, over and above

INT *Arch* **s. à l'ennemi!** at them!

susceptibilité [syseptibilite] **NF 1** *(sensibilité)* touchiness, sensitivity; **il est d'une grande s.** he's very touchy *or* sensitive; **ménager la s. de qn** to tread carefully where sb is concerned; **blesser la s. de qn** to wound sb's feelings **2** *(en magnétisme)* susceptibility

susceptible [syseptibl] **ADJ 1** *(qui s'offense facilement)* touchy, sensitive **2 s. de** *(interprétations, critiques etc)* open to, *Fml* susceptible of; **être s. de faire qch** to be liable *or* likely to do sth

susciter [sysite] **VT** *(difficultés, commentaires)* to give rise to; *(étonnement)* to cause; *(hostilité, admiration, intérêt etc)* to arouse; **des ennuis à qn** to cause *or* create trouble for sb

suscription [syskripsjõ] **NF** *Admin (sur une lettre)* address

sus-dénommé [sysdenɔme] **ADJ** aforementioned

susdit, -ite [sysdi, -it] **ADJ, N** *Jur* aforesaid, above-mentioned

sus-dominante, *pl* **sus-dominantes NF** *Mus* submediant

susmentionné, -ée [sysmãsjɔne] **ADJ, N** *Jur* above-mentioned, aforesaid

susnommé, -ée [sysnɔme] **ADJ, N** *Jur* above-named

suspect, -e [syspɛ, -ɛkt] **ADJ** *(personne, action etc)* suspicious, suspect; *(idées, preuve etc)* dubious, suspect; **des individus suspects rôdaient autour de la maison** suspicious-looking types were hanging around the house; **une viande tout à fait suspecte** meat which seems decidedly doubtful; **s. de** suspected of, under suspicion of; **cela m'est s.** it looks suspicious *or* suspect to me, I don't like the look of it; **tenir qn pour s.** to be suspicious of sb; **devenir s. (à qn)** to arouse (sb's) suspicion

N suspect

suspecter [syspɛkte] **VT** *(personne)* to suspect (**de qch** of sth; **de faire** of doing); *(bonne foi de qn etc)* to suspect, to question, to doubt; **je le suspecte de ne pas me dire la vérité** I suspect he's not telling me the truth, I suspect him of not telling me the truth

suspendre [syspãdr] **VT 1** *(vêtements, tableau, lampe etc)* to hang (up); *(hamac)* to hang up, to sling; **s. qch à un clou/au mur/à ou par un crochet** to hang sth on *or* from a nail/on the wall/on *or* from a hook

2 *(hostilités, enquête, émission)* to suspend; *(paiement, travail)* to suspend, to stop; *(séance)* to adjourn; **la séance est suspendue** we will now adjourn; **s. le paiement d'un chèque** to stop a cheque; *Ordinat* **s. l'exécution d'un programme** to abort a program; **s. son jugement** to suspend judgement

3 *(fonctionnaire etc)* to suspend

VPR se suspendre to hang (**à** from; **par** by); **il est toujours en train de se s. aux jupes de sa mère** he's very clingy, he never leaves his mother's side

suspendu [syspãdy] **ADJ 1** *(pendu)* hanging, suspended; **s. au plafond** hanging from the ceiling; **s. dans le vide** hanging *or* suspended in mid-air; **les jardins suspendus de Babylone** the hanging gardens of Babylon; **pont s.** suspension bridge; *Aut* **voiture bien suspendue** car with good suspension; *Fig* **enfant toujours s. aux jupes de sa mère** clingy child, child who never leaves his mother's side; **être s. aux lèvres de qn** to be hanging on sb's every word

2 *(arrêté, interrompu)* suspended; *(séance)* adjourned; *Jur (jugement)* postponed

3 *Aut (freins)* inboard

suspens [syspã] **NM 1 en s.** *(personne)* in suspense; *(travail)* unfinished, *Fml* in abeyance; *(affaire etc)* outstanding, *Fml* in abeyance; *(problème)* outstanding, unresolved; *(fumée, poussière etc)* hanging in the air; **tenir qn en s.** to keep sb in suspense **2** *Litt (suspense)* suspense

suspense [syspɛns] **NM** *Cin, Littér etc* suspense; **film à s.** thriller; **je le saurai demain, quel s.!** I'll know tomorrow, the suspense is killing me!

suspensif, -ive [syspãsif, -iv] **ADJ** *Jur (veto etc)* suspensive

suspension [syspãsjõ] **NF 1** *(en haut)* suspension, hanging (up)

2 *Chimie* **en s.** in suspension, suspended; *Méd* **s. buvable** oral suspension

3 *(des hostilités, d'un travail, d'une enquête, d'un paiement etc)* suspension; *(de la circulation)* stoppage; *(de la loi)* abeyance; *(d'une séance)* adjournment; *Mil* **s. d'armes** suspension of fighting; **s. d'un paiement** stopping of a payment; **s. de paiements** moratorium on payment; *Ordinat* **s. d'exécution** *(d'un programme)* abort, aborting; *Gram* **points de s.** suspension points, dots; *Aut* **s. pour un an du permis de conduire** a year's driving ban; *Jur* **arrêt de s.** injunction

4 *(de fonctionnaire etc)* suspension

5 *(lampe)* light pendant, ceiling lamp

6 *Aut* suspension; **s. avant à roues indépendantes** independent front suspension; **s. compound** hydrolastic suspension; **s. hydragas** hydragas suspension; **s. hydraulique** hydraulic suspension; **s. hydro-élastique** hydrolastic suspension; **s. hydropneumatique** hydropneumatic suspension; **s. à roues indépendantes** independent suspension; **s. triangulée** wishbone suspension

suspicieux, -euse [syspisjø, -øz] **ADJ** suspicious

suspicion [syspisjõ] **NF** suspicion; **avoir de la s. ou des suspicions à l'égard de qn** to have one's suspicions about sb; **s. légitime** reasonable suspicion

sustentateur, -trice [systãtatœr, -tris] *Aviat* **ADJ** *(force etc)* lifting; **effort s.** lift; **surface sustentatrice** aerofoil, *Am* airfoil

NM s. rotatif *(d'un hélicoptère)* rotor

sustentation [systãtasjõ] **NF 1** *Géom* base *ou* **polygone de s.** basis of support **2** *Aviat* lift

sustenter [systãte] **VT** *Arch (nourrir)* to sustain, to nourish

VPR se sustenter *Arch, Hum* to take sustenance, to keep up one's strength

sus-tonique, *pl* **sus-toniques NF** *Mus* supertonic

susurrement [sysyrmã] **NM** *Litt* whispering, murmuring

susurrer [sysyre] **VTI** *Litt* to whisper, to murmur; **s. des mots doux à l'oreille de qn** to whisper sweet nothings in sb's ear

suture [sytyr] **NF** *Anat, Chir* suture; **(point de) s.** stitch

suturer [sytyre] **VT** *Chir* to stitch, to suture

suzerain, -aine [syzrɛ̃, -ɛn] **ADJ, N** suzerain

suzeraineté [syzrɛnte] **NF** suzerainty

svastika [svastika] **NM** swastika

svelte [svɛlt] **ADJ** *(personne, corps etc)* slender, svelte

sveltesse [svɛltes] **NF** slenderness, slimness

SVP [esvepe] *(abrév* **s'il vous plaît)** please

swahili [swaili] **ADJ, N** *Ling* Swahili

swap [swap] **NM** *Bourse* swap; **s. d'actifs** asset swap; **s. de change** exchange rate swap; **s. vanilla** vanilla swap

swaper [swape] **VT** *Bourse* to swap

Swaziland [swazilãd] **NM** Swaziland

sweater [switœr, swɛ-] **NM** sweater

sweat-shirt, *pl* **sweat-shirts** [switʃœrt, swɛt-] **NM** sweat shirt

sweepstake [swipstɛk] **NM** *Courses de chevaux* sweepstake

swing [swiŋ] **NM 1** *Boxe, Golf* swing **2** *Mus* swing

swinguer [swiŋge] **VI** *Mus Fam* to swing; **ça swingue, ce soir!** it's really swinging tonight!

sybarite [sibarit] **ADJ, N** sybarite

sybaritique [sibaritik] **ADJ** sybaritic

sybaritisme [sibaritism] **NM** sybaritism

sycomore [sikɔmɔr] **NM** sycamore (tree)

sycophante [sikɔfãt] **NM** informer

syllabaire [silabɛr] **NM** spelling-book

tailles exceptionnelles, pour les grandes tailles outsize; de petite t. small; une lettre de la t. d'une affiche a letter the size of a poster, a poster-sized letter; des avocats de la t. du poing avocados the size of your fist; une erreur de belle t. a huge mistake; *Ordinat* t. de disque dur hard disk size; *Ordinat* t. de mémoire memory size; *Ordinat* t. de champ field size; *Typ* t. de corps body size; *Typ* t. de fonte font size; *Typ* t. des caractères type size; t. du papier paper size **3** *Fig (mesure)* trouver un adversaire à sa t. to meet one's match; trouver un collaborateur à sa t. to find a colleague who is one's equal *or* who has an equal level of skills; il est de t. à vous battre he is big enough *or* strong enough to beat you; il n'est pas de t. à être chef he's not cut out to be a leader, he's not the stuff that leaders are made of; je ne suis pas de t. à vous prouver le contraire I'm not in a position to prove you wrong; il n'est pas de t. à lutter contre vous he is no match for you, he stands no chance against you; rien à craindre, il n'est pas de t. have no fear, he's not up to it; un mensonge de t. a whopper; le mensonge était de t. it was a thumping great lie **4** *(partie du corps)* waist; *(de vêtement)* waist, waistline; tour de t. waist (measurement); avoir la t. fine to have a trim waist *or* a good waistline; retrouver une t. fine to get one's waistline back; elle a une t. de guêpe she is wasp-waisted; tu as la t. bien prise dans cette jupe the skirt is a perfect fit at the waist; prendre qn par la t. *(d'un bras)* to put an arm round sb's waist; *(des deux mains)* to take sb by the waist, to seize sb round the waist; pantalon à t. haute/basse trousers with a high/low waist(line), high-/ low-waisted trousers; pardessus à t. fitted overcoat **5** *(action) (de pierre, de pierres précieuses, de vêtements, de cheveux etc)* cutting; *(d'arbuste)* pruning, trimming; *(de haie)* trimming, clipping; *(de roue d'engrenage)* milling **6** *(tranchant) (d'une épée etc)* edge **7** *(taillis)* jeune t. coppice **8** *Min* gallery **9** *Hist (redevance)* tallage
▸ ▸ t. basse *(d'un pneu)* low profile; *Bourse* t. boursière market size; *Couture* t. normale natural waistline

taillé [tɑje] ADJ bien t. *(personne)* well-built; bien/mal t. *(ongles, moustaches)* well-/badly trimmed; *(vêtement)* well-/badly cut; *Fig* t. pour commander/pour un métier cut out to be a leader/for a job; cheveux taillés en brosse crew cut; crayon t. en pointe sharp pencil; t. dans le roc carved out of the rock

taille-crayon, *pl* **taille-crayon(s)** NM pencil sharpener

taille-douce, *pl* **tailles-douces** NF *(technique, estampe)* copper-plate engraving

tailler [tɑje] VT **1** *(pierre, diamant, herbe, cheveux, bifteck etc)* to cut; *(arbre)* to prune, to trim; *(haie, barbe etc)* to trim, to clip; *(vigne)* to dress; *(crayon)* to sharpen; t. qch en biseau to bevel sth; *Fig* t. une armée en pièces to cut an army to pieces; *Fig Fam* t. une bavette to have a chat *or Br* natter; *Fam* t. la route *(parcourir beaucoup de chemin)* to eat up the miles; *(partir)* to beat it, *Br* to scarper, *Am* to book it **2** *Couture* t. un vêtement to cut out a garment; t. une robe d'après *ou* sur un patron to cut out a dress from a pattern; *Fig Fam* t. un costard *ou* une veste à qn to slag sb off; *Fam* il a failli se faire t. un short en traversant la rue he almost got run over crossing the street
VI *Chir* to make an incision; t. dans la chair *ou* dans le vif to cut into the flesh
VPR se tailler **1** *(se couper)* se t. la barbe to trim one's beard; se t. un chemin à travers

... to carve one's way through ...; *Fig* se t. un beau succès to be very successful **2** *Fam (partir)* to beat it, to scram; je me taille! I'm off!

tailleur [tɑjœr] NM **1** *(de pierres, de diamants, d'arbres etc)* cutter **2** *Couture* tailor; s'asseoir en t. to sit cross-legged **3** *(costume)* suit

tailleur-pantalon, *pl* **tailleurs-pantalons** NM trouser *or Am* pant suit

taillis [tɑji] NM copse, coppice; dans les t. in the copse *or* coppice
ADJ bois t. copsewood, brushwood

tain [tɛ̃] NM *(de glace)* silvering; refaire le t. d'une glace to resilver a mirror; glace *ou* miroir sans t. two-way mirror

taire [tɛr] *(prp* taisant; *pp* tu; *pr ind* je tais, il tait, n. taisons, ils taisent; *pr sub* je taise; *impf* je taisais; *p hist* je tus; *fu* je tairai) VT *(quelque chose)* to say nothing about, not to mention; *(cacher)* to suppress, to hush up; une dame dont je tairai le nom a lady who shall be nameless; t. qch à qn to keep *or* hide *or* conceal sth from sb
VPR se taire *(être silencieux)* to be quiet *or* silent; *(cesser de parler)* to stop talking, to be *or Fml* fall silent; *(décider de ne rien dire)* to keep quiet *or* silent; *(d'un son)* to stop, to cease; tu ne vas pas te t. jusqu'à la fin du dîner! you're surely going to open your mouth and say something before the end of the dinner!; tais-toi! be quiet!, *Fam* shut up!; faire t. *(bavard, opposition, critiques)* to silence, to reduce to silence, *Fam* to shut up; *(conscience)* to silence; *(enfant)* to keep quiet, *Fam* to shut up; faire t. sa douleur to stifle one's grief; savoir se t. to know how to keep quiet *or* to keep one's mouth shut; elle a perdu une occasion de se t. she would have done better to say nothing *or* to keep her mouth shut

taiseux, -euse [tɛzø, -øz] *Belg* ADJ *(taciturne)* taciturn
N *(personne taciturne)* taciturn person

Taiwan [tajwan] N Taiwan

taiwanais, -aise [tajwanɛ, -ɛz] ADJ Taiwanese
N T. Taiwanese

tajine [taʒin] NM *Culin* tajine

take-off [tɛkɔf] NM INV *Écon* takeoff

talc [talk] NM *Minér* talc; *(produit)* talc, talcum powder

talé [tale] ADJ *(fruit)* bruised

talent [talɑ̃] NM **1** *(don)* talent; son t. de pianiste his talent as a pianist; avoir du t. to be talented; homme/musicien de t. talented man/musician; sans t. untalented; elle n'a aucun t. pour faire la cuisine she has no talent for cooking, she's a hopeless cook; avoir le t. de faire qch to have a knack *or* gift for doing sth; exploiter ses talents to make use of one's talents *(de cuisinier* as a cook); faire appel à tous les talents to call in the best talent *or* brains; éditeur à la recherche de nouveaux talents publisher in search of new talent **2** *Antiq (monnaie)* talent

talentueusement [talɑ̃tɥøzmɑ̃] ADV with talent

talentueux, -euse [talɑ̃tɥø, -øz] ADJ talented

taler [tale] VT *(fruit etc)* to bruise

taleth [talɛt] NM *Rel* tallith

talion [taljɔ̃] NM la loi du t. an eye for an eye (and a tooth for a tooth); appliquer la loi du t. to demand an eye for an eye

talisman [talismɑ̃] NM talisman

talitre [talitr] NM *(crustacé)* sand flea *or* hopper

talkie-walkie, *pl* **talkies-walkies** [tokiwoki] NM walkie-talkie

talk-show, *pl* **talk-shows** [tokʃo] NM *TV* talk *or Br* chat show

Tallinn [talin] N Tallin

Talmud [talmyd] NM *Rel* le T. the Talmud

talmudique [talmydik] ADJ Talmudic(al)

talmudiste [talmydist] NM Talmudist

taloche [talɔʃ] NF **1** *Fam (gifle)* clout, cuff **2** *Constr* (plasterer's) hawk

talocher [talɔʃe] VT *Fam (personne)* to clout, to cuff

talon [talɔ̃] NM **1** *(de pied, de chaussure, de bas etc)* heel; marcher sur les talons de qn to tread on sb's heels, to follow close *or* hard on sb's heels; être toujours sur les talons de qn to dog sb's footsteps; la police est sur ses talons depuis quinze jours the police have been on his heels for two weeks; donner du t. à son cheval to give one's horse the spur; montrer *ou* tourner les talons to turn on one's heel **2** *Tech (d'outil, de mât, de club de golf, de crosse de fusil)* heel; *Mus (d'archet)* heel, nut; *(de queue de billard)* butt; *(de lame d'épée, de baïonnette, de palan, d'essieu)* shoulder **3** *Cartes* stock, reserve, talon **4** *(bout) (de pain, de fromage, de jambon etc)* heel **5** *(de chèque etc)* stub, *Br* counterfoil; t. à retourner reply slip; t. et volant *(de chèque)* counterfoil and leaf **6** *Archit* ogee (moulding), talon
▸ ▸ t. d'Achille Achilles' heel; talons aiguilles stiletto heels; *(chaussures)* stilettos; talons compensés built-up heels; talons hauts high heels; chaussures à talons hauts high-heeled shoes, high heels; t. minute heel bar; talons plats flat heels; chaussures à talons plats flat-heeled shoes, flats

talonnage [talɔnaʒ] NM *Rugby* heeling

talonnement [talɔnmɑ̃] NM *(de cheval)* spurring on; *Fig (harcèlement) (de qn)* hounding

talonner [talɔne] VT **1** *(suivre) (personne)* to follow on the heels of, to follow close behind **2** *(harceler) (d'une personne)* to hound; *(de la faim)* to dog; être talonné par la mort to be pursued by death; se faire t. par le fisc to be hounded by the tax man, to have the tax man breathing down one's neck **3** *(presser du talon) (cheval)* to spur on **4** *Rugby* to heel
VI **1** *Naut (d'un navire)* to touch, to bump **2** *Rugby* to heel

talonnette [talɔnɛt] NF **1** *(d'une chaussure)* counter; *(à l'intérieur de la chaussure)* heel pad **2** *(à l'intérieur d'un pantalon)* binding

talonneur [talɔnœr] NM *Rugby* hooker

talquer [talke] VT to sprinkle with talc *or* talcum powder

talure [talyr] NF *(sur un fruit)* bruise

talus [taly] NM **1** *(pente)* slope; en t. sloping; la voiture est tombée dans le t. the car fell down the slope **2** *(construit)* embankment, slope, ramp **3** *Géol* talus, scree

talweg [talvɛg] NM *Géog* t(h)alweg

tamanoir [tamanwar] NM *Zool* great anteater, ant bear

tamarin[1] [tamarɛ̃] NM **1** *(fruit)* tamarind **2** *(tamaris)* tamarisk

tamarin[2] NM *Zool* tamarin

tamarinier [tamarinje] NM tamarind (tree)

tamaris [tamaris] NM *Bot* tamarisk

tambouille [tɑ̃buj] NF *Arg* **1** *(cuisine)* cooking; faire la t. to do the cooking **2** *(plat etc)* grub, nosh; on s'est fait une bonne petite t. we made ourselves some great grub *or* nosh

tambour [tɑ̃bur] NM **1** *(instrument de musique)* drum; battre du t. to play the drum, to drum; entendre un bruit de t. to hear the sound of drums; peau de t. drum-head; *Fam* raisonner comme un t. to talk through one's hat; sans t. ni trompette quietly, without (any) fuss, *Fam* without a song and dance **2** *(personne)* drummer **3** *Tech (d'une turbine, d'une machine à laver etc)*, *Naut (d'un*

tambourin   878   tant

cabestan) drum; *Élec (d'une bobine)* cylinder; **freins à t.** drum brakes **4** *(entrée) (d'église etc)* vestibule; *(tourniquet)* revolving door **5** *(à broder)* (embroidery) frame, tambour **6** *Archit (d'une colonne etc)* drum

▸▸ **t. de basque** tambourine; **t. de câble** cable drum; **t. de frein** brake drum; *Typ* **t. d'impression** print drum; **t. de photocopie** photocopier drum; **t. photosensible** photosensitive drum; *Hist* **t. de ville** town crier

tambourin [tɑ̃buʀɛ̃] NM **1** *(en Provence)* = small drum used in Provençal folk music **2** *(tambour de basque)* tambourine

tambourinage [tɑ̃buʀinaʒ] NM drumming

tambourinaire [tɑ̃buʀinɛʀ] NM **1** *(musicien)* tambourin player **2** *Hist (annonceur)* town crier

tambourinement [tɑ̃buʀinmɑ̃] NM drumming

tambouriner [tɑ̃buʀine] VI *(avec ses doigts, des objets etc)* to drum; **la pluie tambourine sur le toit** the rain is drumming on the roof ▪ VT **1** *(rythme, air etc)* to drum out; *(avec les doigts)* to tap out **2** *(nouvelle)* Arch to announce; *Fam* to shout from the rooftops

tambour-major, *pl* **tambours-majors** NM *Mil* drum major

Tamerlan [tamɛʀlɑ̃] NM Tamburlaine

tamil, -ile [tamil] ADJ Tamil
▪ NM *Ling* Tamil
▪ N **T.** Tamil

tamis [tami] NM sieve; *(pour le sable etc)* sifter; *(pour les liquides)* strainer; *Ind* riddle, screen; **passer au t.** *(farine etc)* to sieve; *(sable etc)* to sift; *(liquide)* to strain; *Ind* to riddle, to screen; *Fig (témoignage, information, candidats etc)* to sift through

tamisage [tamizaʒ] NM *(de farine etc)* sieving; *(de sable etc)* sifting; *(de liquide)* straining; *Ind* riddling, screening

Tamise [tamiz] NF la **T.** the Thames

tamiser [tamize] VT *(farine etc)* to sieve; *(sable etc)* to sift; *(liquide)* to strain; *Ind* to riddle, to screen; **rideaux qui tamisent la lumière** curtains that filter the light; **lumière tamisée** subdued light ▪ VI *(de la poussière, de la lumière etc)* to filter through

tamoul, -oule [tamul] ADJ Tamil
▪ NM *Ling* Tamil
▪ N **T.** Tamil

tampon [tɑ̃pɔ̃] NM **1** *(bouchon)* plug, stopper; *(d'un tonneau)* bung **2** *Constr* wall plug **3** *Méd* swab; *Chir* pad, plug, tampon; *(hygiénique)* tampon **4** *(cachet, instrument)* stamp; *(de la poste)* postmark; **coup de t.** stamp **5** *(pour polir)* pad **6** **t. (de choc)** *(de train)* buffer; **coup de t.** collision *(between buffers)*; *Pol* **État/zone t.** buffer state/zone; *Fig Fam* **servir de t.** *(entre deux personnes)* to act as a buffer *(between two people)*

▸▸ **t. buvard** blotter; **t. dateur** date stamp; **t. encreur** ink pad; **t. hygiénique** ou **périodique** tampon; **t. à récurer** scourer, scouring pad

tamponnage [tɑ̃pɔnaʒ] NM *Chimie* neutralizing

tamponne [tɑ̃pɔn] NF *Belg Fam* (drinking) binge; **prendre une t.** to get plastered or *Br* ratted

tamponnement [tɑ̃pɔnmɑ̃] NM **1** *(bouchage) (de blessure etc)* plugging **2** *(essuyage) (avec un tampon)* swabbing, dabbing **3** *Aut, Rail* collision

tamponner [tɑ̃pɔne] VT **1** *(essuyer)* to swab, to dab; *Typ (caractères, plaque de métal)* to ink up **2** *(timbrer) (document etc)* to stamp; **t. une lettre** to frank a letter **3** *(polir) (meuble)* to French-polish **4** *Chimie* to neutralize **5** *(voiture, train etc)* to run into, to collide

with **6** *Vieilli (boucher)* to plug, to stop (up); *Méd (blessure)* to put a wad over, to plug; *Constr (mur)* to plug
▪ VPR **se tamponner 1** *(de voitures, de trains etc)* to run into each other, to collide **2 se t. le front** to mop one's brow; **se t. les yeux** to dab one's eyes; *Arg* **il s'en tamponne (le coquillard)** he doesn't give a damn or a monkey's

tamponneur, -euse [tɑ̃pɔnœʀ, -øz] ADJ **autos tamponneuses** Dodgems®, bumper cars

tamponnoir [tɑ̃pɔnwaʀ] NM wall drill

tam-tam, *pl* **tam-tams** [tamtam] NM **1** *(tambour)* tom-tom **2** *Fam Péj (tapage)* fuss, ballyhoo; **faire du t. autour de qch** to make a great fuss or great ballyhoo about sth **3** *(gong)* gong

tan [tɑ̃] NM tan, (tanner's) bark

tancer [tɑ̃se] VT **(je tançai(s); n. tançons)** *Litt* to berate, to scold

tanche [tɑ̃ʃ] NF **1** *(poisson)* tench **2** *Fam (imbécile)* pillock, plonker, *Am* meathead

tandem [tɑ̃dɛm] NM **1 chevaux attelés en t.** horses driven tandem **2** *(bicyclette)* tandem **3** *(deux personnes)* twosome, duo; **travailler en t.** to work in tandem; **un t. de comédiens** a comic duo **4** *Tech* **cylindres en t.** tandem cylinders **5** *Ordinat* **central t.** tandem exchange, tandem central office

tandis que [tɑ̃di(s)kə] CONJ **1** *(alors que)* while, whereas **2** *(pendant que)* while, *Fml* whilst

tangage [tɑ̃gaʒ] NM *Naut, Aviat* pitching; *Fig* reeling, swaying; **pour supprimer le t. du bateau** to stop the boat pitching

tangara [tɑ̃gaʀa] NM *Orn* tanager

tangence [tɑ̃ʒɑ̃s] NF *Géom* tangency; **point de t.** point of contact

tangent, -ente [tɑ̃ʒɑ̃, -ɑ̃t] ADJ *Géom* tangential, tangent (**à** to); *Fam* **c'est t.** it's touch and go; **c'était t.** it was touch and go, it was a near thing
▪ NF **tangente** tangent; *Fam* **prendre la tangente** to dodge the question; *(partir)* to slip away

tangentiel, -ielle [tɑ̃ʒɑ̃sjɛl] ADJ *Géom* tangential

tangentiellement [tɑ̃ʒɑ̃sjɛlmɑ̃] ADV tangentially

Tanger [tɑ̃ʒe] N Tangier(s)

tangible [tɑ̃ʒibl] ADJ tangible

tangiblement [tɑ̃ʒibləmɑ̃] ADV tangibly

tango [tɑ̃go] NM *(danse, musique)* tango; **danser le t.** to tango
▪ ADJ INV *(couleur)* tangerine

tangon [tɑ̃gɔ̃] NM *Naut (mobile)* swinging boom; *(de spi)* spinnaker boom

tanguer [tɑ̃ge] VI *Aviat, Naut* to pitch; *Fig* to reel, to sway

tanière [tanjɛʀ] NF **1** *(d'animal)* den, lair **2** *(habitation sordide)* hovel **3** *(retraite)* retreat

tanin [tanɛ̃] NM *Chimie, Ind* tannin

tank [tɑ̃k] NM *Mil, Naut, Fam (grande voiture)* tank

tanker [tɑ̃kɛʀ] NM *Naut* tanker

tankiste [tɑ̃kist] NM *Mil* soldier with a/the tank unit

tannage [tanaʒ] NM *Tech (des peaux)* tanning

tannant, -ante [tanɑ̃] ADJ **1** *Fam (ennuyeux)* annoying; **il est t.!** he's a drag!; **qu'est-ce que c'est t., ces réunions de famille!** these family get-togethers are a real drag! **2** *Tech* tanning **3** *Can Fam (remuant)* obstreperous, rumbustious

tanne [tan] NF *(sur le cuir)* spot; *(sur le visage)* blackhead

tanné, -ée [tane] ADJ **1** *(peau, visage etc)* weatherbeaten **2** *Can Fam* **être t.** *(en avoir assez)* to be fed up; **je suis t. à faire le ménage** I'm fed up or I've had it up to here doing housework
▪ NM *(couleur)* tan (colour) **2 gants en t.** tan(ned) leather gloves
▪ NF *Fam* **tannée** thrashing, good hiding

tanner [tane] VT **1** *Tech (peaux)* to tan **2** *Arg (ennuyer)* to annoy; *(harceler)* to pester; **elle m'a tanné pour que je le lui dise** she pestered me to tell her **3** *Arg* **t. (le cuir à) un enfant** to thrash a child, to tan a child's hide; **il s'est fait t. le cuir par des voleurs** he was beaten up by thieves

tannerie [tanʀi] NF *(établissement)* tannery; *(industrie)* tanning

tanneur [tanœʀ] NM *(de peaux)* tanner

tannin [tanɛ̃] NM *Chimie, Ind* tannin

tannique [tanik] ADJ *Chimie (acide)* tannic

tanrec [tɑ̃ʀɛk] NM *Zool* tenrec

tan-sad, *pl* **tan-sads** [tɑ̃sad] NM pillion(-seat)

TANT [tɑ̃]

> so much **1** ▪ such **1** ▪ so many **2** ▪ so **3** ▪ as *(en tant que)* **4** ▪ so much the better *(tant mieux)* **6** ▪ as long as *(tant que)* **8**

ADV 1 *(quantité)* so much; **t. de bonté** so much or such kindness; **il a t. bu que ...** he has drunk so much that ...; **ce n'est pas la peine de t. vous presser** you needn't be in such a hurry; **elle s'est donné t. de mal** she went to such (a lot of) or so much trouble; **pour t. faire** ou **à t. faire** ou *Fam* **t. qu'à faire, j'aimerais autant ...** while I'm at it or about it, I would just as soon ...; *Fam* **tu m'en diras t.!** you don't say!, really?; **t. pour cent** so much per cent; **votre lettre du t.** your letter of such and such a date; **il a t. et plus d'argent** he has any amount of money; **ils tiraient t. et plus** they were pulling for all they were worth; **s'inquiéter t. et plus** to be worried to death; **je me suis ennuyé t. et plus** I was bored to tears or to death; **t. et si bien que ...** so much so that ...; **j'ai crié t. et t. qu'il est parti** I shouted so much that he went (away); **on a attendu t. et t. que ...** we waited so long that ...; **t. s'en faut** far from it; **un t. soit peu** a little, somewhat; **s'il était un t. soit peu intelligent** if he had any intelligence, if he was the slightest bit intelligent; **si t. est qu'il soit mort** if he really is dead; **il y en a peu, si t. est qu'il y en ait du tout** there is little/there are few, if any
2 *(nombre)* so many; **t. de fois** so many times, so often; **il a des amis t. et plus** he has plenty of friends; **inutile de faire t. d'histoires pour ça** it's pointless to make such a fuss over that
3 *(tellement, à tel point)* so, to such a degree; **il ne peut pas se lever, t. il est malade** he cannot get up, he is so ill; **elle ne parle plus, t. elle a été choquée** the shock was so great that she has stopped speaking; **t. était grande sa discrétion que ...** so great was his discretion that ...; **t. il est vrai que ...** so much so that ...; **elle est t. aimée** she is loved so much; **elle n'est pas t. sotte que naïve** she's not so much stupid as naive; **n'aimer rien t. que ...** to like nothing more than ...; **elle dit n'aimer rien t. que l'automne** she says there is nothing she likes more than the autumn
4 en t. que *(comme)* as; *(dans la mesure où)* in so far as; **je suis Russe en t. que je suis né en Russie** I am a Russian in so far as I was born in Russia; **l'homme en t. qu'il diffère des animaux** man, as distinct from animals; **en t. que vieil ami de votre père** as a very old friend of your father('s)

5 *(quelque)* however; **t. aimable qu'il soit** however pleasant he may be

6 t. mieux so much the better, that's all to the good; **t. mieux pour toi** good for you; **t. pis!** too bad!, it can't be helped!, what a pity!, never mind!; **c'est t. pis** that's just too bad; **t. pis pour toi** (that's) too bad for you!, that's just too bad!

7 t. que *(autant que)* as much as; **j'ai couru t. que j'ai pu** I ran as hard as I could; *Fam* **il pleut t. qu'il peut** it's raining like anything; **t. aux Indes qu'ailleurs** both in India and elsewhere; **t. les enfants que les adultes** children and adults alike; **un film t. pour les petits que pour les grands** a film for children and adults alike; **t. pour vous que pour moi** for your sake as much as mine, for you as much as for me; **il est sévère t. avec ses enfants qu'avec ses élèves** he is as strict with his children as he is with his pupils; **je suis à l'aise t. avec lui qu'avec elle** I'm at ease with him and her; **t. bien que mal** somehow or other, after a fashion

8 t. que *(aussi longtemps que)* as long as; *(pendant que)* while; **t. que je vivrai** as long as I live; **t. que la vue s'étend** as far as the eye can see; **t. que vous y êtes** while you're about or at it; **rien ne peut être décidé t. qu'il n'a pas donné son avis** nothing can be decided until (such time as) he makes his opinion known [SEE GRAMMAR B31–2]

9 *Arg* **t. qu'à = quant à,** *voir* **quant à**

Tantale [tɑ̃tal] NM Tantalus

tantale [tɑ̃tal] NM *Chimie* tantalum

tante [tɑ̃t] NF **1** aunt **2** *Vulg Péj (homosexuel)* queer, *Br* poof(ter), *Am* faggot **3** *Arg* **ma t.** *(mont-de-piété)* uncle's, the pawnbroker's (shop)

tantième [tɑ̃tjɛm] NM *Com (de bénéfices etc)* percentage, quota; **t. des administrateurs** directors' fee

tantine [tɑ̃tin] NF *Fam* auntie, aunty

tantinet [tɑ̃tinɛ] NM *Fam* tiny bit; **un t. plus long** a tiny bit *or* a shade *or* a fraction longer; **un t. vieillot/ridicule** a tiny bit *or* a touch *or* ever so slightly old-fashioned/ridiculous

tantôt [tɑ̃to] ADV **1** *(parfois)* **t. triste, t. gai** now sad, now gay; **t. je suis à Paris, t. à Londres** sometimes I am in Paris, sometimes in London **2** *Arch, Région (bientôt)* soon, presently; *(il y a peu de temps)* just now, a little while ago; **voici t. deux mois qu'il est parti** it will soon be two months since he left **3** *(cet après-midi)* this afternoon; **il pleuvra/il a plu t.** it will rain/it rained this afternoon; **à t.** see you soon

tantouse [tɑ̃tuz] NF *Vulg Péj (homosexuel)* queer, *Br* poof(ter)

tantrique [tɑ̃trik] ADJ Tantric

tantrisme [tɑ̃trism] NM Tantrism

Tanzanie [tɑ̃zani] NF Tanzania

tanzanien, -ienne [tɑ̃zanjɛ̃, -jɛn] ADJ Tanzanian
N **T.** Tanzanian

Tao [tao] NM Tao

taôisme, taoïsme [taoism] NM *Rel* Taoism

taôiste, taoïste [taoist] ADJ, N *Rel* Taoist

taon [tɑ̃] NM gadfly, horsefly, cleg

tapage [tapaʒ] NM **1** *(bruit)* din, uproar, *Fam* racket, row; **faire du t.** to kick up a din or racket or row **2** *(publicité)* fuss, ballyhoo; **cette nouvelle a fait du t.** the news caused quite a stir; **faire du t. autour de qch** to make a great fuss or a great ballyhoo or a song and dance about sth; **annoncer qch à grand t.** to announce sth with a lot of ballyhoo

▸▸ *Jur* **t. nocturne: faire du t. nocturne** to create a disturbance

tapageur, -euse [tapaʒœr, -øz] ADJ **1** *(enfant, soirée etc)* noisy, rowdy, raucous **2** *(vê-*

tements, couleur) loud, flashy; *(décoration)* flashy; *(publicité)* blatant

tapageusement [tapaʒøzmɑ̃] ADV *(s'habiller etc)* flashily, loudly

tapant [tapɑ̃] ADJ **à sept heures tapant(es)** on the stroke of seven, at seven o'clock sharp or on the dot

tape [tap] NF slap; **il m'a donné une t. sur l'épaule** he slapped me or gave me a slap on the shoulder; **une petite t. sur la joue** a pat on the cheek

tapé [tape] ADJ **1** *(fruit) (séché)* dried; *(abîmé)* damaged **2** *Arg* **réponse tapée** snappy answer **3** *Fam (fou)* nuts, crazy, cracked

tape-à-l'œil ADJ INV loud, gaudy, flashy
NM INV gaudy or flashy rubbish

tape(-)cul, *pl* **tape(-)culs** NM **1** *(bascule)* seesaw **2** *Naut* jigger (sail) **3** *Fam (véhicule)* rattletrap, boneshaker

tapée [tape] NF *Fam* **une t.** *ou* **des tapées de** … masses or heaps or loads of …

taper¹ [tape] VT **1** *(frapper) (enfant)* to hit, to slap; *(cuisse)* to slap; *(table etc)* to bang; *Ordinat* to key; **t. du tambour** to beat the drum; **t. un coup/deux coups à la porte** to knock/knock twice at the door; **t. une lettre (à la machine)** to type a letter; *Ordinat* **tapez entrée ou retour** select enter or return; **t. un air (au piano)** to thump out a tune (on the piano); *Fam* **t. la carte** to play cards

2 *Fam (emprunter)* **t. qch à qn, t. qn de qch** to bum or cadge sth off sb, to hit *or Br* tap sb for sth; **il est encore venu me t.** he came to scrounge off me again; **t. qn de mille euros** to touch *or Br* tap sb for a thousand euros

3 *Fam (atteindre)* **t. le cent/le deux cents** to hit a hundred/two hundred (kilometres an hour)

VI **1** *(frapper)* to bang (**sur** on); **la bôme est venu t. contre le mât** the boom hit the or banged into the mast; *Ordinat* **t. sur une touche** to hit a key; **t. sur le piano** to thump or plonk away on the piano; **t. sur qn** to hit sb; *Fig Fam (critiquer)* to knock sb, to have a go at sb; **t. à la porte** to bang on the door; **t. avec un marteau (contre le mur)** to hammer (the wall); *Fam* **t. sur le ventre à qn** to give sb a dig in the ribs *(as a mark of familiarity)*; **le soleil tapait** the sun was beating down; **le soleil tape dans ma chambre** the sun shines straight into my room; *Fam* **ça tape** *(il fait chaud)* it's scorching; **t. dans** *(nourriture)* to help oneself to, to dig into; *(ses économies, ses réserves)* to break or dig into; *Fam* **t. dans l'œil à qn** to take sb's fancy; **t. dans un ballon** to knock or kick a ball around; **t. du pied** to stamp one's foot; *Mil Fam* **t. sur un objectif** to strafe a target; **t. à côté** to miss the target; *Fig* **alors là, tu as tapé à côté** you're way off beam, *Am* you're way out in left field; **t. à la tête** *(d'un vin)* to go to one's head; **il tape, ce petit vin!** this wine is pretty potent!

2 *(dactylographier)* **t. (à la machine)** to type; **t. au toucher** to touch-type

3 *Vulg (puer)* to stink

VPR **se taper 1** *(se frapper)* to knock each other about; **se t. sur la cuisse** to slap one's thigh; **avec lui, on se tape les cuisses de rire** he makes you split your sides laughing; *Fig* **se t. le derrière par terre** to split one's sides laughing, to fall about laughing; **une situation à se t. le derrière par terre** a hysterically funny situation

2 *très Fam* **se t. qch** *(manger, boire)* to put sth away; *(avoir à supporter)* to let oneself in for sth; **se t. qn** *(sexuellement)* to lay sb; *(avoir à supporter)* to get lumbered with sb; **je me taperais bien une bière** I could murder a beer; **on s'est tapé deux heures d'embouteillages** we got stuck in two hours of traffic jams; **il a fallu que je me tape tout Proust pour l'examen** I had to devour the entire works of Proust for the exam

3 *très Fam (s'en moquer)* **elle s'en tape** she doesn't give a monkey's (**de** about); **si tu savais comme je m'en tape!** I don't give a monkey's!

4 *très Fam (espérer)* **tu peux te t.!** you'll be lucky!, no way!, you can whistle for it!

taper² VT *(boucher) (trou etc)* to plug, to stop up

tapette [tapɛt] NF **1** *(petit marteau)* mallet **2** *(à tapis)* carpet beater; *(à mouches)* fly swatter **3** *(piège)* **t. (à souris)** mousetrap **4** *Arg (langue)* **quelle t.!** what a chatterer or chatterbox!; **il a une fière t.** can he talk! **5** *(petite tape)* (gentle) slap **6** *Vulg (homosexuel)* queer, *Br* poof(ter)

tapeur, -euse [tapœr, -øz] N *Fam* cadger

tapin [tapɛ̃] NM *Arg* **faire le t.** *(se prostituer)* to turn tricks, *surtout Br* to be on the game; **la police a ramassé toutes les filles qui faisaient le t. du côté du port** the police arrested all the girls who were trying to pick up customers on the docks

tapiner [tapine] VI *Arg* to walk the streets, *Br* to be on the game, *Am* to hook

tapineur, -euse [tapinœr, -øz] N *Arg* streetwalker

tapinois (en) [ɑ̃tapinwa] ADV stealthily; **s'approcher en t.** to creep up

tapioca [tapjɔka] NM tapioca; *(soupe)* vegetable soup containing tapioca

tapir¹ [tapir] NM *Zool* tapir

tapir² (se) [sətapir] VPR to crouch; *(se cacher)* to cower, to hide; **maison tapie dans un bois** house nestling in a wood

tapis [tapi] NM **1** *(recouvrant un meuble)* cloth, cover; *Fig* **le t. brûle!** *(au jeu)* put down your stakes!; *Fig* **mettre qch sur le t.** to bring sth up for consideration or for discussion; *Fig* **ce genre de discussion revient toujours sur le t.** this sort of discussion is always coming up

2 *(sur le sol)*, *Fig (de fleurs, neige)* carpet; *(petit)* rug; **t. de haute laine/de laine rase** long-pile/short-pile carpet; **marchand de t.** carpet dealer; **recouvrir le plancher d'un t.** to carpet the floor; **terrain recouvert d'un t. de gazon/de neige** ground carpeted with turf/snow; *Fig* **se prendre les pieds dans le t.** to get into a mess

3 *Boxe etc* canvas; **aller au t.** to go down, to be knocked down; *Fig* **entreprise française mise au t. par la concurrence** French company knocked for six or k.o.'d by the competition; **il est resté au t.** he stayed down, he didn't get up

▸▸ **t. de billiard** billiard cloth; **t. de gym** gym mat; **t. de livraison des bagages** baggage conveyor belt; **t. d'Orient** oriental carpet; **t. de prière** prayer mat; **t. rouge: dérouler le t. rouge pour qn** to roll out the red carpet for sb, to give sb the red carpet treatment; **t. roulant** *Ind etc* conveyor belt; *(pour piétons)* moving walkway, travelator; **t. de salle de bain** bathroom carpet; **t. de selle** saddlecloth; **t. de sol** *(sol de tente)* groundsheet; *(petit matelas)* sleeping mat *(underneath sleeping bag)*; *Ordinat* **t. de souris** mouse mat or pad; **t. de table** table cover; **t. vert** gaming table; *(de conseil)* conference table

tapis-brosse, *pl* **tapis-brosses** NM doormat

tapisser [tapise] VT **1** *(de papier peint) (pièce, appartement etc)* to (wall)paper; **les murs sont tapissés de jaune** the walls are papered in yellow; **mur tapissé d'affiches** wall covered or plastered with posters **2** *(de tentures ou tapisseries) (pièce etc)* to cover with hangings or tapestries **3** *(l'intérieur d'une armoire)* to line, to cover (**de** with); **une membrane tapisse l'estomac** the stomach is lined with a membrane; **mur tapissé de lierre** wall covered with ivy, ivy-clad wall

tapisserie [tapisri] **NF 1** *(papier peint)* wallpaper; **refaire toutes les tapisseries d'un appartement** to repaper a flat **2** *(tissage)* tapestry making *or* weaving; **faire de la t.** to make tapestry **3** *(tenture)* tapestry; **chaise en t.** chair upholstered with tapestry, tapestry chair; *Fig* **faire t.** *(dans une soirée dansante etc)* to be a wallflower **4** *(broderie.)* **t.** *(au ou sur canevas)* tapestry *or* crewel work

tapissier, -ière [tapisje, -jɛr] **N 1** *(décorateur)* (interior) decorator **2** *(tisseur)* tapestry maker **3** *(de meubles)* upholsterer

tapocher [tapɔʃe] **VT** *Can Fam (frapper)* to hit; *(battre)* to beat up

tapon [tapɔ̃] **NM** *Vieilli (de tissu, de papier etc)* ball; **en t.** *(vêtements etc)* in a ball, bundled up; *(cheveux)* screwed up into a bun

tapotement [tapɔtmã] **NM** tapping; *(de piano)* plonking

tapoter [tapɔte] **VT** to tap; *(joue d'un enfant etc)* to pat; **t. un air (au piano)** to thump out a tune (on the piano)
VI t. sur *(porte, fenêtre)* to tap on; *(en signe d'énervement)* to drum on

tapuscrit [tapyskri] **NM** typescript

taquet [takɛ] **NM 1** *Menuis etc (support)* angle block; *(cale)* wedge **2** *(butée)* stop; **t. de sûreté** safety stop **3** *(de machine à écrire)* stop; *Ordinat* **t. de tabulation** tab stop; **poser un t. (de tabulateur)** to set a tab(ulator stop) **4** *(d'arpenteur)*, *Agr* (small) picket, peg **5** *Naut* **t. (de tournage)** (belaying) cleat

taquin, -ine [takɛ̃, -in] **ADJ** *(personne, tempérament)* (given to) teasing; *(sourire)* teasing; **elle est un peu taquine** she's a bit of a tease; **elle est très taquine** she's a great one for teasing
N *(personne)* tease(r)

taquiner [takine] **VT 1** *(d'une personne)* to tease; *Fam* **t. le goujon** to do a bit of fishing; *Fam* **t. la muse** to write the odd bit of verse **2** *(de quelque chose)* to bother, to worry; **une pensée qui revient me t. parfois** a thought that still haunts me sometimes; **j'ai une dent qui me taquine** I've got bother with one of my teeth, one of my teeth is bothering me

taquinerie [takinri] **NF** teasing; **j'en ai assez de tes taquineries** I've had enough of your teasing

tarabiscoté [tarabiskɔte] **ADJ** *(meuble, décor, maison, dessin)* over-elaborate, fussy; *(style)* over-elaborate, convoluted

tarabuster [tarabyste] **VT 1** *(d'une personne)* to pester **2** *(de quelque chose)* to bother, to worry

tarage [taraʒ] **NM** *Com* allowance for tare

tarama [tarama] **NM** *Culin* taramasalata

taratata [taratata] **INTR** rubbish!

taraud [taro] **NM** (screw) tap

taraudage [tarodaʒ] **NM** screw cutting, tapping

tarauder [tarode] **VT 1** *Tech (tige, écrou etc)* to tap, to cut, to screw, to thread **2** *(d'un insecte)* *(bois)* to bore into **3** *Litt Fig (des remords, des scrupules etc) (personne)* to gnaw at

taraudeuse [tarodøz] **NF** *(machine)* tapper, thread cutter

tarbouch(e) [tarbuʃ] **NM** tarboosh

tard [tar] **ADV** late; **plus t.** later, later on; **au plus t.** at the latest; **tôt ou t.** sooner or later; **il est t.** it's late; **il se fait t.** it's getting late; **je ne pensais pas qu'il fût si t.** I didn't think it was so late; **je me suis couché t.** I went to bed late, I was late (in) going to bed; **trop t., il fallait te décider plus vite** (it's) too late, you should have decided sooner; **il se maria t.** he married late (in life); **deux minutes plus**

t. et je manquais le bateau another two minutes and I would have missed the boat; *Prov* **mieux vaut t. que jamais** better late than never; **t. dans la nuit** late at night; **remettre qch à plus t.** to put sth off until later; **je le ferai et pas plus t. que ce soir** I'll do it this very evening; **pas plus t. qu'hier** as recently as yesterday, only yesterday
NM sur le t. *(dans la vie)* late in life

tarder [tarde] **VI** to delay; **pourquoi tarde-t-il?** why is he (taking) so long?; **il ne tardera pas maintenant** he won't be long now; **cela n'a pas tardé** it wasn't long coming; **et cela n'a pas tardé, il s'est cassé le pied** and he broke his ankle before long; **tu vas recevoir une gifle, cela ne va pas t.** you're going to get smacked before long *or* in a minute or two, you've got a smack coming to you; **t. en chemin** to loiter on the way; **t. à faire qch** to take a long time doing sth; **excusez-moi si j'ai tardé à vous répondre** I apologize for not answering sooner; **nous ne tarderons pas à le voir venir** it won't be long before he appears, he'll appear before too long; **nous ne tardâmes pas à avoir de ses nouvelles** it wasn't long before we heard from him, we didn't have to wait too long for news of him; **ça tarde à commencer/venir** it's a long time starting/coming; **sans t.** without delay
V IMPERS il lui tarde de partir/qu'elle revienne he is longing to get away/for her to return

tardif, -ive [tardif, -iv] **ADJ** *(regrets, excuse etc)* belated; *(heure, fruit etc)* late; **c'était un peu t., comme réponse/excuse** the answer/apology was a bit slow in coming

tardivement [tardivmã] **ADV** *(prendre des mesures, s'excuser)* belatedly; *(rentrer, arriver etc)* late; *(se marier, s'établir)* late in life

tare [tar] **NF 1** *(défaut)* defect, flaw; *Méd, Vét* defect; *Hum* **ça n'est pas une t.!** it's not a crime! **2** *Com (pour calculer le poids net)* tare; **faire la t.** to allow for the tare

taré, -ée [tare] **ADJ 1** *Com (fruit etc)* spoilt; *(biens)* damaged **2** *(corrompu) (régime etc)* depraved, corrupt **3** *(dégénéré)* degenerate **4** *Fam (idiot)* crazy; **il faut être t. pour faire cela!** you have to be crazy *or* to have a screw loose to do that!
N *Fam* nutcase, headcase, *Br* nutter

tarentelle [tarãtɛl] **NF** *(danse, musique)* tarantella

tarentule [tarãtyl] **NF** *(araignée)* tarantula

tarer [tare] **VT** *Com (emballage etc)* to tare

targette [tarʒɛt] **NF 1** *(verrou)* bolt **2** *Fam* **targettes** *(pieds)* feet, *Br* plates, *Am* dogs; *(chaussures)* shoes

targuer (se) [sətarge] **VPR se t. de qch/de faire qch** to pride oneself on sth/on doing sth; **se t. de ce que ...** to pride oneself on the fact that ...

targui, -ie [targi], *pl* **touareg** [twarɛg] **ADJ** Tuareg
N T. Tuareg

tarière [tarjɛr] **NF 1** *(pour le bois)* auger **2** *(de forage)* drill; *Min* borer **3** *Entom* ovipositor

tarif [tarif] **NM** *(tableau des prix)* tariff, price list; *(prix)* rate; *Fam* **trois mois de prison, c'est le t.** three months' prison is what it'll cost you; **tarifs aériens/ferroviaires** air/rail fares; **t. adulte** adult fare; **t. affaires** business rate; *(transport)* business fare; **t. aller simple** single *or Am* one-way fare; **t. APEX** APEX fare; **t. de base** basic rate; **t. des chambres** room rate; **t. en chambre double** *(dans un hôtel)* double occupancy rate; *Aviat* **t. commun** common rated fare, joint fare; **t. couplage** *(en publicité)* combination rate; **t. dégressif** tapering *or* declining rate; **t. différentiel** differential rate; **t. discriminatoire** price discrimination; **t. du distributeur**

dealer list price; **t. douanier** customs tariff; **t. économique** economy rate; *(d'un voyage)* economy *or* budget fare; **t. étudiant** rate; *(d'un voyage)* student fare; **t. excursion** excursion fare *or* APEX fare; **t. export** export tariff; **t. famille** family rate; *(d'un voyage)* family fare; **t. de faveur** preferential rate; **t. à forfait** all-in price; **t. forfaitaire** flat rate; *Aviat* **t. hebdomadaire** weekly rate; **t. horaire** hourly rate; **t. intérieur** inland rate; **t. jeune** youth fare; **t. journalier** daily *or* day rate; **t. lettres** letter rate; **plein t.** *(pour passagers)* full fare; *(pour marchandises etc)* full tariff; *Fam (pour un crime etc)* maximum (penalty); **voyager à plein t./à t. réduit** to travel at full/reduced rate *or* fare; **billet (à) plein t.** full-fare ticket; **t. minimum** minimum charge; **tarifs postaux** postal *or* postage rates; **t. préférentiel** special *or* preferential rate; **t. progressif** increasing rate; **t. promotionnel** promotional rate; *(d'un voyage)* promotional fare; **t. réduit** *Cin* concession; *(d'un voyage)* concession fare; **t. de référence** basing fare; **t. social** reduced train fare for the general public; **t. société** commercial *or* corporate rate; **t. standby** standby fare; **t. syndical** trade union tariff; **t. d'urgence** = first-class rate

tarifaire [tarifɛr] **ADJ** *(lois etc)* tariff; *Com* **politique t.** pricing policy

tarifer [tarife] **VT** *(impôts, prix etc)* to fix the rate for, to set the rate of

tarification [tarifikasjɔ̃] **NF** fixing *or* setting of rates (**de** for), pricing; **t. au coût-plus-marge** mark-up pricing; **t. différentielle** differential pricing; **t. discriminatoire** discriminatory pricing; **t. en fonction de la valeur perçue** perceived value pricing; **t. géographique** geographical pricing

tarin [tarɛ̃] **NM 1** *(oiseau)* siskin **2** *Arg (nez)* beak, *Br* conk

tarir [tarir] **VT** *(source, rivière)* to dry up; *(larmes)* to dry; **la source est tarie** the spring is dry; *Fig* **cela a tari sa créativité** it caused his creativity to dry up
VI 1 *(de l'eau)* to dry up, to run dry; **la source a tari** the spring has dried up **2** *Fig (d'une conversation, de l'inspiration etc)* to dry up; *(de larmes)* to dry; **la discussion n'a pas tari pendant deux heures** the discussion has been flowing freely for two hours; **une fois lancé sur ce sujet, il ne tarit pas** once he's started on the subject he never shuts up *or* stops; **il ne tarit pas sur le sujet** he never stops talking *or* shuts up about the subject; **ne pas t. d'éloges sur qch** to be full of praise for *or* be forever praising sth
VPR se tarir *(d'une rivière, du lait, de l'inspiration etc)* to dry up

tarissement [tarismã] **NM** drying up

tarlatane [tarlatan] **NF** *Tex* tarlatan

tarmacadam [tarmakadam] **NM** *Constr* tarmacadam

tarot [taro] **NM** *Cartes (jeu de)* **tarot(s)** tarot (pack); **faire un t. ou une partie de t.** to have a game of tarot

Tarse [tars] **N** Tarsus

tarse [tars] **NM** *Anat, Zool* tarsus

tarsien, -ienne [tarsjɛ̃, -jɛn] **ADJ** *Anat (os)* tarsal

tartan [tartã] **NM** *(tissu)* tartan

tartane [tartan] **NF** *(bateau)* tartan(e), tartana

tartare [tartar] **ADJ 1** *Hist* Tartar **2** *Culin* **sauce t.** tartar(e) sauce; **steak t.** steak tartare
N *Hist* **T.** Tartar
NM *Culin* steak tartare

tarte [tart] **NF 1** *Culin* tart, *Am* (open) pie; **t. aux pommes** apple tart *or Am* pie; *Fig Fam* **ce n'est pas de la t.** it's no picnic **2** *Fam (gifle)* slap

10 *(argile etc)* clay; **pipe en t.** clay pipe; **cruche de** *ou* **en t.** earthenware *or* terracotta jar ▸▸ **t. battue:** *Tennis* **jouer sur t. battue** to play on clay; *Tennis* **jouer bien/mal sur t. battue** to be good/bad on clay, to be a good/bad clay court player; *Tennis* **court en t. battue** clay court; **sol en t. battue** mud floor; **t. de Chine** kaolin; **t. cuite** earthenware, terracotta; *Beaux-Arts* terracotta; *Beaux-Arts* **une t. cuite** a terracotta; **t. ferme** (dry) land, terra firma; *(opposé à l'espace)* earth, terra firma; **la T. de Feu** Tierra del Fuego; **t. d'ombre** umber; **t. de pipe** pipeclay; **t. à poêle** fireclay; **t. à porcelaine** kaolin; **t. à potier** potter's clay; *Chimie* **terres rares** rare earths; **la T. Sainte** the Holy Land; **t. de Sienne** sienna

terreau, -eaux [tɛro] NM compost

Terre-Neuve NF Newfoundland
NM INV **t.** Newfoundland (dog)

terre-neuvien, -ienne, *pl* **terre-neuvien(ne)s** [tɛrnœvjɛ̃, -jɛn] ADJ Newfoundland N **T.** Newfoundlander

terre-neuvier, -ière, *pl* **terre-neuviers, -ières** [tɛrnœvje, -jɛr] ADJ *(pêcheur etc)* Newfoundland
NM **1** *(pêcheur)* Newfoundland fisherman **2** *(bateau)* banker, Newfoundland fishing vessel

terre-plein, *pl* **terre-pleins** NM **1** *Constr* earth platform, raised strip **2** *Aut* **t. central** central reservation, *Am* median strip; **t. circulaire** *(dans un rond-point)* central island

terrer [tɛre] VT **1** *(arbre, plante)* to earth up **2** *(couvrir de terre)* to spread earth over
VPR **se terrer** *(d'un animal)* to go to earth; *Mil* to entrench oneself, to dig oneself in; *Fig* to go to earth, to hole up; **être terré dans** *(d'un animal)* to have gone to earth in; *Mil* to be entrenched in; *Fig* to have gone to earth in, to be holed up in

terrestre [tɛrɛstr] ADJ **1** *(plante)* ground; *(animal)* land; **transports terrestres** surface transport; *Mil* **effectifs terrestres** land forces **2** *(magnétisme, attraction)* of the earth; **la croûte t.** the earth's crust **3** *Fig (pensées)* worldly; *(plaisirs)* earthly, worldly; **paradis t.** earthly paradise; **c'est un vrai paradis t.** it's heaven on earth

terreur [tɛrœr] NF **1** *(effroi)* terror, dread; **fou de t.** wild with fear; **glacé de t.** terror-stricken; **vivre dans la t.** to be terrified *or* in (a state of) terror **2** *(emploi de la violence etc)* terror; **gouverner par la t.** to rule by terror; **faire régner la t.** to instil terror; **semer la t.** to sow terror; **un régime de t.** a reign of terror; *Hist* **la T.** the Reign of Terror **3** *Fig (personne) (d'une ville, d'une école etc)* terror; **jouer les terreurs** to play the tough guy

terreux, -euse [tɛrø, -øz] ADJ *(goût, odeur)* earthy **2** *(mains)* grubby; *(teint, ciel, gris etc)* muddy; *(visage)* sickly; *(laitue)* gritty

terrible [tɛribl] ADJ **1** *(catastrophe, accident, blessure etc)* terrible, appalling; *(froid, bruit)* dreadful, terrible; *(orage, chaleur)* terrific, terrible; *(temps, caractère)* awful, terrible; **ce n'est qu'une coupure, rien de t.** it's just a cut, nothing serious *or* major; **d'une humeur t.** in an awful *or* a terrible mood; **il est t. quand il s'énerve** he's awful *or* terrible when he loses his temper; **enfant t.** enfant terrible **2** *Fam (formidable) (personne, film, effet etc)* terrific, great; **ce/il n'est pas t.** it's/he's nothing special; **rien de t.** nothing much, nothing to write home about **3** *(impossible)* incredible; **vous êtes t.!** you really are the limit!
ADV *Fam* **ça marche t.!** it's going great!

terriblement [tɛribləmɑ̃] ADV *(extrêmement) (gêné, égoïste)* terribly, dreadfully, awfully

terrien, -ienne [tɛrjɛ̃, -jɛn] ADJ **1** *(proprié-*taire etc)* landed **2** *(rural)* country, rural **3** *(de la Terre)* of the Earth
N **1** *(propriétaire)* landowner, landed proprietor **2** *Naut* landlubber **3** *(paysan)* countryman, *f* countrywoman **4** *(habitant de la Terre)* earthling, earthman, *f* earthwoman

terrier [tɛrje] NM **1** *(d'un lapin)* burrow, hole; *(d'une taupe)* hole; *(d'un renard)* earth; *(d'un blaireau)* sett **2** *(chien)* terrier

terrifiant [tɛrifjɑ̃] ADJ **1** *(effrayant) (description, situation)* terrifying **2** *(extraordinaire)* incredible

terrifier [tɛrifje] VT *(impf, pr sub* n. **terrifiions, v. terrifiiez)** to terrify

terril [tɛril] NM *Min* slag heap

terrine [tɛrin] NF *Culin (pâté, récipient)* terrine; **t. de canard/de foie de volaille** duck/chicken-liver pâté

terrir [tɛrir] VI *Pêche* **poissons qui terrissent** fish living in coastal waters

territoire [tɛritwar] NM *(d'un État, d'un oiseau, d'un animal)* territory; *(de juge, d'évêque)* jurisdiction; *(de commune, d'arrondissement etc)* area; **marquer son t.** *(d'un animal)* *Fig (d'une personne)* to mark out one's territory; *Pol* **territoires occupés** occupied territories; **t. d'outre-mer** overseas territory; **aménagement du t.** regional planning *or* development

territorial, -iale, -iaux, -iales [tɛritɔrjal, -jo] ADJ *(impôt, eaux)* territorial
NM *Hist, Mil* territorial (soldier)
NF *Hist, Mil* **la territoriale** the territorial army

territorialité [tɛritɔrjalite] NF territoriality; *(d'un impôt)* territoriality

terroir [tɛrwar] NM *Agr* soil; **goût de t.** *(d'un vin)* tang of the soil, native tang; **du t.** *(accent, expression)* local

terrorisant [tɛrɔrizɑ̃] ADJ *(expérience, souvenir etc)* terrifying

terroriser [tɛrɔrize] VT *(d'une personne)* to terrorize; *(d'une expérience, d'un souvenir)* to terrify

terrorisme [tɛrɔrism] NM terrorism; **un acte de t.** an act of terrorism; **t. d'État** government-sponsored terrorism

terroriste [tɛrɔrist] ADJ, N terrorist

tertiaire [tɛrsjɛr] ADJ tertiary; *Écon* **secteur t.** tertiary sector
NM **1** *Écon* tertiary sector **2** *Géol* Tertiary N *Cathol* tertiary

tertiairisation [tɛrsjɛrizasjɔ̃], **tertiarisation** [tɛrsjarizasjɔ̃] NF *Écon* tertiarization, growth of the tertiary sector *or* service industries; **la t. de l'économie** the tertiarization of the economy

tertio [tɛrsjo] ADV thirdly

tertre [tɛrtr] NM hillock, mound, knoll; *Archéol* **t. funéraire** barrow, tumulus

tes [te] ADJ POSS *voir* **ton**[1]

tessiture [tɛsityr] NF *Mus (de voix)* range, tessitura; *(d'un instrument)* range

tesson [tɛsɔ̃] NM shard; **t. de bouteille** fragment of broken bottle

test [tɛst] NM *(examen)*, *Méd* test **passer/réussir un t.** to take/pass a test; **c'est le t. de sa bonne foi** it is a test of his good faith; **zone/département/semaine t.** test area/department/week; **pendant une période t.** for a trial period; *Méd, Psy, Scol etc* **méthode des tests** testing method; *Mktg* **t. d'acceptabilité auprès des consommateurs** customer-acceptance test; *Mktg* **t. d'acceptation** acceptance test; **t. d'aptitude professionnelle** aptitude test; **t. d'association** association test; **t. aveugle** blind test; *Mktg* **t. de la bande dessinée** *ou* **de la bulle** balloon test; *Aut* **t. de choc** impact test; **t. comparatif** comparative test; **t. de conformité** compliance test; **tests auprès des consommateurs** consumer testing; *Mktg* **tests d'emballage** package testing; *Mktg* **t. d'enquête** enquiry test; *Mktg* **t. de frustration** balloon test; *Mktg* **t. du lendemain** (day-after) recall test; **t. de marché** *(d'un produit)* test marketing, market test; *Mktg* **t. de média** media test; *Mktg* **t. de mémoire** memory *or* recall test; *Mktg* **tests de nom** name testing; **t. de performance** benchmark *or* performance test; **t. de performance du produit** product performance test; *Mktg* **t. de préférence** preference test; **t. de produit** product test; **tests de produit** product testing; *Mktg* **t. de rappel** recall test; *Mktg* **t. de reconnaissance** recognition test; **t. de Rorschach** Rorschach *or* ink blot test; *Aut* **t. de roulage** road testing; **un t. de roulage** a road test; **t. à sec** dry run; *Mktg* **t. de support** media test; **t. technique** engineering test; *Aut* **t. de tonneaux** roll-over test

Testament [tɛstamɑ̃] NM *Bible* **Ancien/Nouveau T.** Old/New Testament

testament [tɛstamɑ̃] NM **1** *Jur* will, testament; **absence de t.** intestacy; **ceci est mon t.** this is my last will and testament; **tu ne seras pas dans mon t.** you'll be cut out of my will; **elle l'a mis** *ou* **couché sur son t.** she put him in her will; **mourir sans t.** to die intestate; **léguer qch par t.** to leave sth in one's will, to bequeath sth **2** *Fig (artistique, politique)* legacy

testamentaire [tɛstamɑ̃tɛr] ADJ **disposition t.** clause *or* provision (of a/the will); **exécuteur/exécutrice t.** executor/executrix; **héritier t.** legal heir, heir as established by a/the will; **succession t.** succession as prescribed by a/the will

testateur, -trice [tɛstatœr, -tris] N *Jur* testator, *f* testatrix

tester[1] [tɛste] VI *Jur* to make one's will

tester[2] VT *(élève, produit etc)* to test; *Mktg* to test, to test-market; **t. sur le marché** to test-market; **t. un questionnaire** to pilot a questionnaire; **testé en laboratoire** laboratory-tested

testiculaire [tɛstikylɛr] ADJ *Anat* testicular

testicule [tɛstikyl] NM *Anat* testicle, *Spéc* testis

testimonial, -iale, -iaux, -iales [tɛstimɔnjal, -jo] ADJ *Jur* **preuve testimoniale** evidence of witnesses

testostérone [tɛstɔsterɔn] NF *Biol, Physiol* testosterone

têt [tɛ] NM *Chimie* **t. à gaz** beehive shelf; **t. à rôtir** roasting crucible

tétanie [tetani] NF *Méd* spasms, *Spéc* tetany; **accès de t.** fit of spasm; **avoir un accès de t.** to go into spasm

tétanique [tetanik] *Méd* ADJ tetanic; **malade t.** person with tetanus
N person with tetanus

tétaniser [tetanize] *Méd* VT *(muscle)* to tetanize, to cause tetanus in; *Fig* **tétanisé de peur** paralysed with fear, petrified; **tétanisé de froid** numb with cold
VPR **se tétaniser** *(d'un muscle)* to become tetanized

tétanos [tetanos, -ɔs] NM *Méd (maladie)* tetanus, *Fam (contraction de muscle)* tetanus; **vaccin contre le t.** tetanus vaccine

têtard [tɛtar] NM **1** *Zool* tadpole **2** *Fam (enfant)* kid **3** *(arbre taillé)* pollard

TÊTE [tɛt]

head **1, 4–10** ■ hair **2** ■ face **3** ■ mind **5** ■ top **7, 10** ■ front **10** ■ in the lead *(en tête)* **10**		

NF **1** *Anat* head; **de la t. aux pieds** from head

to foot, from top to toe; **dépasser qn d'une t.** to be a head taller than sb; **il a une t. de plus que sa mère** he is a head taller than his mother; **t. nue** bare-headed; **vieillard à t. grise** grey-haired old man; **avoir la grosse t.** to have a big head; *Fig Fam* **une grosse t.** *(intellectuel)* a highbrow, an intellectual; *Fam* **faire une (grosse) t. à qn, faire une t. au carré à qn** to smash sb's face in; *Fam* **c'est une t., ce mec-là** that guy is a bit of a genius *or* has got brains; **monstre à deux têtes** two-headed monster; **corps sans t.** headless body; **faire t.** *(d'un animal chassé)* to stand at bay; **faire** *ou* **tenir t. à qn** to stand up to sb; **je t'interdis de me faire** *ou* **tenir t.!** I don't you dare defy me!; **faire** *ou* **tenir t. au malheur** to bear up in the face of misfortune; *Naut, Fig* **tenir t. à l'orage** to ride out the storm; **les nuages qui flottent sur nos têtes** the clouds overhead; **endetté par-dessus la t.** up to the eyes in debt; **j'en ai par-dessus la t.** I've had it up to here; **je n'en ai pas encore par-dessus la t., mais ça va arriver** I'm not at screaming pitch yet, but I soon will be; **la t. en bas** head down(wards), upside down; *(objet)* upside down; **se laisser pendre la t. en bas** to hang upside down; **marcher la t. haute** to walk with (one's) head held high; *Fig* **je peux à nouveau marcher la t. haute** I can hold my head up again; **la t. la première** head first; **tomber sur la t.** to fall and hit one's head; *Fam* **tu es tombé sur la t.?** have you got a screw loose?; **je ne sais (pas) où donner de la t.** I don't know which way to turn, I don't know whether I'm coming or going; *Fig* **donner t. baissée dans un piège** to rush headlong into a trap; *Vulg* **avoir la t. dans le cul** to be out of it; **par t.,** *Fam* **par t. de pipe** a head; **t. à t. = tête-à-tête; je te le jure sur la t. de mes enfants** I swear on my children's lives; **j'en réponds sur ma t.** I'd stake my life on it; **il y va de votre t.** your life is at stake; **ça va lui en coûter la t.** it is going to cost him his life; **je donnerais ma t. à couper que …** I'll bet anything you like *or* I'd stake my life that …; **signe de t.** nod (of the head); **faire un signe de t. à qn** to nod to sb, to give sb a nod; **mal de t.** headache; **avoir (très) mal à la t.** to have a (bad) headache; **la t. lui tourne, il a la t. qui tourne** his head is spinning; **t. chauve** bald head; **t. ronde** bullet *or* round head; *Hist* Roundhead; **à t. ronde** bullet- *or* round-headed; *Ftbl* **faire une t.** to head the ball; **piquer une t.** *(tomber)* to take a header; *Natation* to dive; **je piquerais bien une t.** I'd really like to dive in; *Gym, Mil* **t. (à droite!** eyes right!; **t. d'une médaille** obverse of a medal; *Arch* **t. ou pile?** heads or tails?

  2 *(cheveux)* hair; **une t. rousse/blonde** a red-head/blonde; **se laver la t.** to wash one's hair

  3 *(visage)* face; **il a une très belle t.** he's very good-looking; **elle a une jolie t.** she's pretty; **elle a une bonne t.** she looks nice; **il a une t. vraiment bizarre** he looks very strange, he's very strange-looking; *Arg* **il a une t. de con** he looks like a total prat *or Am* jackass; *Théâtre* **se faire la t. d'un rôle** to make up for a part; *Fam* **faire une t. d'imbécile** to look like an idiot; **je ne sais pas quelle t. il fera** I don't know how he'll take it *or* react; **il fait une de ces têtes** *(de colère)* he's got a face like thunder; *(de surprise)* he looks stunned *or* thunderstruck; *(de tristesse)* he looks grief-stricken; **faire sa t. des mauvais jours** to look like thunder; **il me fait une de ces têtes!** he keeps glowering at me!; *Fam* **faire la t.** to be in a huff, to sulk; **faire la t. à qn** to be sulky with sb; *Fam* **faire une t. de six pieds de long** to have a face like a wet weekend; *Fam* **faire sa mauvaise t.** to look like thunder; **faire une t. de circonstance** to look grim; *(hypocritement)* to look suitably upset; **je connais cette t.-là** I know that face; **sa t. ne**

me revient pas I don't like the look of him

  4 *(d'un animal, d'un poisson, d'un oiseau etc)* head; **d'une courte t.** *(gagner une course)* by a short head; **têtes** *(de bétail)* head of cattle

  5 *(esprit)* mind; *(cerveau)* brains; **il n'a rien dans la t.** he's stupid; **petite t.!** idiot!; **une pareille idée ne me serait jamais passée par la t.** such an idea would never have entered my mind *or* head; **si une idée te passe par la t., dis-le-moi** let me know if you have any ideas; **se creuser la t.** to rack one's brains; **c'est une femme de t.** she's a capable woman; **elle n'a pas de t.** she's very forgetful; **avoir la t. légère** to be irresponsible *or* featherbrained; **avoir la t. dure** to be stupid *or Br Fam* thick; *(têtu)* to be pig-headed; **mettre qch dans la t. de qn** to get sth into sb's head; **je me demande qui lui a mis ça dans la t.** I wonder who put that idea in his head; **il s'est mis en t. d'écrire un roman** he's got *or* taken it into his head to write a novel; **je me suis mis dans la t. qu'il fallait que je déménage** I got it into my head that I had to move; **n'avoir qu'une idée en t.** to have a one-track mind; **quand il a une idée en t.** once he gets an idea in his head; **il n'a que ça en t.** he's got it on the brain, that's all he thinks about; **avoir toutes les informations en t.** to have all the information in one's head; **je n'ai plus son nom en t.** his name has slipped my mind; **ça m'est sorti de la t.** it went clean out of my head *or* mind; **il a quelque chose en t.** he's planning something, *Fam* he's up to something; **s'endormir des souvenirs plein la t.** to fall asleep with nice memories going through one's head; **des idées plein la t.** full of ideas; **forte t.** *(personne)* strong-minded person; **calculer de t.** to do mental arithmetic; **faire un rapide calcul de t.** to do a quick bit of mental arithmetic; **n'en faire qu'à sa t.** to do exactly as one pleases; **avoir une idée derrière la t.** to have an ulterior motive; *Litt* **idée de derrière la t.** preposterous *or* ludicrous idea; **où ai-je la t.!** what am I thinking of!; **monter à la t.** to go to sb's head; **garder la t. froide** to stay calm, to keep cool *or* a cool head; **essaie de garder la t. froide** try to stay calm, *Fam* try not to lose your cool; **est-ce que vous perdez la t.?** have you taken leave of your senses?; **ne perdez pas la t.!** keep *or* don't lose your head!, keep calm!; **faire perdre la t. à qn** to make sb lose his/her head; **c'était à perdre la t.** it was bewildering; **avoir toute sa t.** to be all there; **il n'a plus toute sa t.** he's not quite all there; **se monter la t.** to imagine things; **ne va pas te monter la t.** don't start imagining things, don't go getting ideas; **j'y penserai à t. reposée** I'll think about it later (when I've got some peace and quiet); *Fam* **prendre la t. à qn** to get up sb's nose, to get on sb's wick, *Am* to tick sb off; *Fam* **quelle prise de t.!** what a pain (in the neck)!

  6 *(chef)* *(d'une société, d'un organisme)* head

  7 *(du chapitre d'un livre)* top; *Typ* **blanc de t.** margin at the head of a book; **ligne de t.** headline; **t. de lettre** letterhead; *Journ* **article de t.** feature (article), *Am* leading article; *Journ* **t. de colonne** lead (story), top

  8 *(de chou, d'ail, d'artichaut)* head; *(d'un arbre)* top, crown; *Anat (du fémur)* apophysis; *(de l'humérus)* head

  9 *Tech (d'un violon, d'un mât, d'un marteau, d'un clou etc)* head; *(de fusée)* warhead; **t. inclinable** *(d'une machine-outil, d'un support pour appareil photo ou instrument)* tilting head; *Aut* **soupapes en t.** overhead valves

  10 *(d'une procession, d'une colonne, d'une entreprise, d'un régiment etc)* head; *(d'un train)* front; *Sport etc* **prendre la t.** to take the lead; **prendre la t. d'une entreprise** to take over as the head of a company; **être à la t. de** *(une entreprise, une fortune)* to be (at) the head of, to head; *(une conjuration,*

une insurrection) to be the leader of; **être à la t. de la classe** to be (at the) top of the class; **colonne de t.** front column; *Sport* **arriver en t.** to come in first; **être en t.** to be in the lead; **les joueurs en t.** the leaders, the front runners; **marcher en t.** to lead the way; **marcher à la t.** *ou* **en t. du cortège** to walk at the head of the procession, to lead *or* head the procession; **arriver en t. du scrutin** to head *or* come first in the poll; **taxi en t. de file** taxi at the head of the rank; *Rail* **voiture de t.** front carriage *or Am* car; **en t. du train** at the front of the train; **en t. de liste** at the top of the list; **candidats en t. de liste** candidates at the top of *or* heading the list

  ▸▸ *Théâtre, Cin* **t. d'affiche** top of the bill (de in); **être t. d'affiche** to be top of the bill, to top the bill; *Aut* **t. d'allumeur** distributor cap; **t. de benne** grab head; **t. blonde: nos chères têtes blondes** *(enfants)* our little darlings; **t. brûlée** hothead; **t. de cabestan** drum head; **t. de câble** cable terminal; *TV, Cin* **t. de caméra** camera head; **t. de chapitre** chapter heading; **t. chercheuse** *(d'un missile etc)* homing device; *Fam* **t. à claques: c'est une t. à claques** he just asks for it; *Fam* **t. de cochon: c'est une t. de cochon** he's pig-headed, he's as stubborn as a mule; **t. couronnée** *(souverain)* crowned head; *Aut* **t. de distribution** distributor cap; *Ordinat* **t. d'écriture** writing *or* write head; *Électron, Ordinat* **t. d'effacement** *(d'un magnétophone etc)* erase head; **t. d'électrode** electrode tip; **t. d'enregistrement, t. enregistreuse** *(d'un ordinateur, d'un magnétophone)* record(ing) head; **t. de flèche** *(d'une grue)* jib head; **t. de fraisage** cutter head, milling head; **t. de fusée** warhead; *Fam* **t. à gifles: c'est une t. à gifles** he just asks for it; *Com* **t. de gondole** end of gondola, aisle end display; **t. d'impression** print head; *Pétr* **t. d'injection** swivel; *Fam* **t. de lard: c'est une t. de lard** he's pig-headed, he's as stubborn as a mule; **t. de lecture** *Cin* sound head; *Ordinat* read(ing) head; *(de magnétophone)* tape reader, play-back head; *(de tourne-disque)* pick-up (head); *Ordinat* **t. de lecture-écriture** read-write head; *Rail etc* **t. de ligne** starting point, terminus; **t. de linotte** bird-brain; **être une t. de linotte** to be bird-brained, to be a bird-brain; *Pol* **t. de liste** leading candidate, *Am* head of the ticket; **t. de lit** bed head; **t. magnétique** magnetic head; **t. de mule: c'est une t. de mule** he's pig-headed, he's as stubborn as a mule; *Vulg* **t. de nœud!** dickhead!, *Am* asshole!; **t. nucléaire** nuclear warhead; *Ordinat* **t. à palpeur** sensor head; **t. de perçage** drill(ing) head; *Fam* **c'est une t. de pioche** he's pig-headed, he's as stubborn as a mule; *Aut* **t. de piston** piston head *or* crown; *Mil* **t. de pont** bridgehead; **t. porte-foret** drill(ing) head; **t. porte-fraise** cutter head, milling head; **t. porte-outil** tool head; *Tennis* **t. de série** seeded player, seed; **t. sonore** sound head; **t. de Turc** target, butt; **c'est la t. de Turc de toute la classe** the whole class picks on him/her; *Culin* **t. de veau vinaigrette** calf's head in vinaigrette

---

tête-à-queue NM INV *Aut* spin; *Équitation* (sudden) turn; **faire (un) t.** *Aut* to spin *or* slew round; *(d'un cheval)* to whip round; **la voiture a fait plusieurs t.** the car spun round several times

tête-à-tête NM INV **1** *(à deux)* private interview, tête-à-tête; **en t.** in private; **un dîner en t.** a private dinner; **voir qn en t.** to see sb in private *or* privately; **en t. avec** alone with **2** *(canapé)* (two-seater) sofa, *surtout Am* love seat **3** *(service)* tea/coffee/breakfast set (for two)

tête-bêche ADV **dormir t.** to sleep head to foot; **ranger des bouteilles t.** to store bottles alternate ways up

tonnant [tɔnɑ̃] ADJ thundering; **voix tonnante** voice of thunder, thunderous voice

tonne [tɔn] NF **1** *(unité de poids)* (metric) ton, tonne *(1000 kg)*; **un camion de 8 tonnes, un 8 tonnes** an 8-ton lorry, an 8-tonner; *Fig Fam* **des tonnes (et des tonnes) de** tons (and tons) of **2** *(récipient)* tun, (large) cask
▸▸**t. d'arrimage** measurement ton; **t. courte** short ton *(907.185 kg)*; *Naut* **t. de déplacement** ton of displacement, displacement ton; **t. d'encombrement** measurement ton; **t. équivalent charbon** ton coal equivalent; **t. équivalent pétrole** ton oil equivalent; **t. forte** long *or* gross ton *(1016.06 kg)*; *Naut* **t. de jauge** gross *or* register ton; **t. kilométrique** ton kilometre *or Am* kilometer

tonneau, -eaux [tɔno] NM **1** barrel, cask; **mettre du vin en t.** to put wine into barrels *or* casks; **bière au t.** draught *or Am* draft beer; *Fig* **ils sont tous du même t.** they're all the same; *Fig* **des remarques du même t.** remarks in the same vein; **petit t.** keg; **t. à mortier** mortar mixer; *Hist* **le t. de Diogène** Diogenes' tub; **t. de fret** freight ton; *Fig* **c'est le t. des Danaïdes** it's a never-ending task, it's no sooner finished than you have to start all over again; **t. d'arrosage** water cart **2** *Naut (unité de volume)* ton; **navire de 500 tonneaux** 500-tonner, ship of 500 tons burden **3** *Hist (voiture à cheval)* governess cart **4** *Aviat, Aut* roll, roll-over; **faire un t.** *Aviat* to do a barrel roll; *Aviat, Aut (par accident)* to flip *or* roll over; **la voiture a fait trois tonneaux** the car flipped *or* rolled over three times

tonnelet [tɔnlɛ] NM (small) cask, keg

tonnelier [tɔnəlje] NM cooper

tonnelle [tɔnɛl] NF **1** *(charmille)* arbour, *Am* arbor, *Br* bower **2** *Archit* barrel *or* tunnel vault

tonnellerie [tɔnɛlri] NF cooperage

tonner [tɔne] VI **1** *(de canons etc)* to thunder, to boom **2** *(fulminer)* to rage (**contre** about), to thunder (**contre** against)
V IMPERS **il tonne** it is thundering; **le chien a peur quand il tonne** the dog is frightened of thunder

tonnerre [tɔnɛr] NM **1** *(bruit)* thunder; **coup de t.** clap *or* peal of thunder, thunderclap; *Fig* bombshell; **roulement de t.** roll of thunder; **sous un t. d'applaudissements** to thunderous applause; **accueilli par un t. d'applaudissements** welcomed by thunderous applause; **voix de t.** voice of *or* like thunder; **un bruit/fracas de t.** a racket, a din **2** *Fam* **du t.** *(film, personne)* wonderful, terrific; **t. (de Dieu ou de Brest)!** heavens above!, good grief!; *Vieilli* **il fera un marin du t. de Dieu** he'll make a thundering good *or* a hell of a good sailor

tonométrie [tɔnɔmetri] NF tonometry

tonsure [tɔ̃syr] NF **1** *Rel* tonsure **2** *Fam (calvitie)* bald patch

tonsuré [tɔ̃syre] *Rel* ADJ tonsured; **tête tonsurée** shaven head
NM cleric

tonsurer [tɔ̃syre] VT *(clerc)* to tonsure

tonte [tɔ̃t] NF **1** *(des moutons)* shearing; *(laine)* clip; *(saison)* shearing time **2** *(du gazon)* mowing

tontine [tɔ̃tin] NF **1** *Jur* tontine **2** *(pour protéger un arbuste)* protective covering

tonton [tɔ̃tɔ̃] NM *Fam* uncle; **T. Jules** Uncle Jules; **les tontons Macoute** *(en Haïti)* the Tonton Macoutes *(militia of the Duvalier regime)*

tonus [tɔnys] NM **1** *Méd (d'un muscle)* tone, *Spéc* tonus, tonicity **2** *Fig (énergie)* energy, dynamism; **je manque de t.** I don't have any

energy; **elle a un sacré t.** she's got an incredible amount of energy, she's incredibly energetic; **un peu de nerf les gars, ça manque de t., tout ça!** put your backs into it, lads, you're like a bunch of old women!; **ce slogan manque de t.** the slogan doesn't have any punch *or* pizzazz

top [tɔp] NM **1** *(son)* Radio, TV time signal, cue; **les tops** the pips; **au quatrième t., il sera exactement dix heures** at the fourth stroke, it will be ten o'clock precisely; *Électron* **t. d'écho** blip; *Am* pip; *Électron* **t. de synchronisation** synchronizing signal; **donner le t. départ** to give the starting signal **2** *Fam* **c'est le t. (du t.)!** it's the best of stuff!, *Br* it's the business!
ADJ *Fam* great, *Br* fab, *Am* awesome

topaze [tɔpaz] NF topaz

toper [tɔpe] VI *Fam* to agree (**à qch** to sth); **tope (là)!** done!, agreed!, put it there!

topette [tɔpɛt] NF *Région* small bottle

topinambour [tɔpinɑ̃bur] NM *Bot, Culin* Jerusalem artichoke

topique [tɔpik] ADJ **1** *Méd (remède)* local, topical **2** *(argument)* apposite, to the point
NM *Méd* topical *or* local remedy
NF *Phil* **la t.** topics

top-modèle, *pl* **top-modèles** NM supermodel

top niveau NM *Fam* top level; **être au t.** to be at the top, to be top-notch; **arriver au t.** to get to the top; **des scientifiques au t.** top-level *or* top-notch scientists

topo [tɔpo] NM *Fam* **1** *Journ* article **2** *(discours)* lecture; *(exposé)* rundown; **faire le t. de la situation** to give a rundown on the situation; **c'est toujours le même t.** it's always the same old story

topographe [tɔpɔgraf] N topographer

topographie [tɔpɔgrafi] NF **1** *(technique, relief)* topography **2** *(représentation)* map, plan

topographique [tɔpɔgrafik] ADJ topographical

topographiquement [tɔpɔgrafikmɑ̃] ADV topographically

topologie [tɔpɔlɔʒi] NF topology

topologique [tɔpɔlɔʒik] ADJ topologic(al)

toponyme [tɔpɔnim] NM place name, *Spéc* toponym

toponymie [tɔpɔnimi] NF study of place names, *Spéc* toponymy

toponymique [tɔpɔnimik] ADJ *(étude)* of place names, *Spéc* toponymic(al)

top secret ADJ INV top secret

toquade [tɔkad] NF *Fam* craze (**pour qch** for sth); infatuation (**pour qn** with sb); **avoir une t. pour qn** to be infatuated with sb; **ça lui passera, ce n'est qu'une t.** he'll get over it, it's just a passing fancy

toquante [tɔkɑ̃t] NF *Fam (montre)* watch

toquard, -arde [tɔkar, -ard] = **tocard**

toque [tɔk] NF **1** *(chapeau) (de fourrure)* fur hat; *(de jockey, juge)* cap; **t. (blanche)** *(de cuisinier)* hat, toque **2** *(cuisinier dans un restaurant)* chef

toqué, -ée [tɔke] *Fam* ADJ **1** *(fou)* crazy, nuts **2** *(amoureux)* infatuated, madly in love (**de** with) **3** *(têtu)* stubborn, pigheaded
N **1** *(fou)* nut, *Br* nutter; **il doit me prendre pour une toquée** he must think I'm nuts **2** *Can (personne têtue)* **c'est un t.** he's as stubborn as they come

toquer [tɔke] VI *Fam (à la porte etc)* to knock
VPR **se toquer** *Fam* **se t. de qn** to fall for sb, to go crazy over sb

Torah [tɔra] NF *Rel* Torah

torailler [tɔraje] VI *Suisse (fumer beaucoup)* to smoke like a chimney

torche [tɔrʃ] NF **1** *(flambeau)* torch; **ils furent transformés en torches vivantes** they were turned into human torches; **procession à la t.** torchlight procession; **t. électrique** (electric) torch, *Am* flashlight **2** *Aviat* **parachute en t.** unopened parachute

torché [tɔrʃe] ADJ *Fam* **1 bien t.** *(réponse, devoir, travail etc)* pretty good **2** *(bâclé) (travail etc)* botched

torche-cul NM INV *Vulg (papier)* toilet paper, *Br* loo paper; *Vulg Péj (texte)* (piece of) trash; *(journal)* rag

torchée [tɔrʃe] NF *Arg (coups)* (good) beating *or* thrashing

torcher [tɔrʃe] VT **1** *Fam (nettoyer) (assiette)* to wipe clean; *(derrière d'un enfant, enfant)* to wipe **2** *Fam (bâcler) (travail etc)* to botch, to do in a hurry
VPR **se torcher 1** *Arg* **se t. (le derrière** *ou Vulg* **le cul)** to wipe one's backside *or Vulg* arse *or Am* ass; *Fig* **je m'en torche (de tes problèmes)!** I don't give a damn (about your problems)! **2** *très Fam (s'enivrer)* to get shitfaced *or Br* pissed *or* rat-arsed

torchère [tɔrʃɛr] NF *(candélabre)* candelabra

torchis [tɔrʃi] NM *Constr* cob, daub

torchon [tɔrʃɔ̃] NM **1** cloth; *(pour essuyer la vaisselle)* dish *or* tea towel; *(pour épousseter)* duster; **donner un coup de t. à qch** *(verre, table)* to give sth a wipe; *Fig* **coup de t.** *(querelle)* dust-up; *(épuration)* shake-up; *Fam* **le t. brûle entre** *ou* **chez eux** they've had a serious falling out; *Fig* **il ne faut pas mélanger les torchons et les serviettes** you can't compare apples and oranges **2** *Fig Fam (copie peu soignée)* mess; *(texte sans valeur)* trash; *(journal)* rag
ADJ INV *Beaux-Arts* **papier t.** torchon paper

torchonner [tɔrʃɔne] VT **1** *Fam (travail etc)* to botch **2** *Belg (passer la serpillière)* to mop, to clean (with a floorcloth)

torcol [tɔrkɔl] NM *Orn* **t. (fourmilier)** wryneck

tordant [tɔrdɑ̃] ADJ *Fam* screamingly funny, hilarious, side-splitting

tord-boyaux [tɔrbwajo] NM INV *Arg Péj (eau-de-vie)* rotgut

tordeuse [tɔrdøz] NF *Entom (papillon)* leaf roller

tordre [tɔrdr] VT *(barre de fer)* to bend, to twist; *(fil de fer, laine etc)* to twist; *(métal)* to buckle, to bend; *(vêtements etc) (pour essorer)* to wring; *(cheveux en chignon)* to twist; *(de la douleur) (visage)* to contort, to distort, to twist; **t. le cou à un poulet/** *Fam* **à qn** to wring a chicken's/sb's neck; **t. le bras à qn** to twist sb's arm; **t. l'estomac à qn** *(de la peur etc)* to churn up sb's insides; *Fam* **t. les boyaux à qn** *(d'un alcool etc)* to rot sb's insides; **t. la bouche** to pull a face, to grimace, to make a wry face; **un rictus de douleur tordait sa bouche** his mouth was twisted *or* contorted in a grimace of pain; **tordu par la douleur** contorted by pain
VPR **se tordre** *(de douleur)* to writhe, to twist; *(de branches)* to become gnarled; **se t. les mains** to wring one's hands; **se t. sur son siège** to squirm in one's seat; **se t. le pied** to twist one's ankle; *Fam* **se t. (de rire), rire à se t.** to split one's sides laughing; **c'était à se t. de rire, il y avait de quoi se t.** it was a scream, it was hilarious; **il n'y a vraiment pas de quoi se t.** there's really nothing to laugh about; **le film est amusant, mais il n'y a pas de quoi se t.** the film is funny, but not all that funny

tordu, -ue [tɔrdy] ADJ **1** *(membres, traits)* twisted, distorted; *(châssis, couverts etc)* bent, buckled; *(branche)* twisted, gnarled; *Arg* **avoir la gueule tordue** to be as ugly as sin **2** *(esprit)* warped, twisted; **avoir l'esprit t.** to be warped *or* twisted, to have a warped *or* twisted mind **3** *Fam (fou)* cracked, nutty *N Fam (fou)* nut, *Br* nutter; **avance eh t.!** move, you stupid bastard!

tore [tɔr] NM *Archit, Géom* torus; *Ordinat* (magnetic) core

toréador [tɔreadɔr] NM toreador, bullfighter

toréer [tɔree] VI to fight (in the bullring)

torero [tɔrero] NM bullfighter, torero

torgnole [tɔrɲɔl] NF *Arg (coup)* clout; **je vais lui filer** *ou* **flanquer une t.** I'll clout *or* land him one; **recevoir** *ou* **prendre une t.** to get clouted

toril [tɔril] NM bull pen

torique [tɔrik] ADJ *Géom, Opt etc* toric

tornade [tɔrnad] NF tornado, *Fam* twister; **entrer comme une t.** to come in like a whirlwind

toron [tɔrɔ̃] NM *(d'une corde)* strand

Toronto [tɔrɔ̃to] N Toronto

torpédo [tɔrpedo] NF *Aut* (open) tourer, *Am* touring car

torpeur [tɔrpœr] NF torpor; **je voulus le faire sortir de sa t.** I tried to rouse him from his torpor

torpide [tɔrpid] ADJ *Méd* torpid

torpillage [tɔrpijaʒ] NM *Naut, Mil, Fig (de négociations, d'un plan de paix)* torpedoing

torpille [tɔrpij] NF ╎VOIR GRAMMAIRE A12╎ **1** *(poisson)* torpedo (ray), electric ray **2** *Naut, Mil* torpedo; **t. d'avion** aerial torpedo

torpiller [tɔrpije] VT *aussi Fig* to torpedo

torpilleur [tɔrpijœr] NM torpedo boat

torque [tɔrk] NM *(collier)* torque
NF *Tech* coil of wire

torréfacteur [tɔrefaktœr] NM **1** *(appareil)* roaster; **t. à café** coffee roaster **2** *(marchand)* = purveyor of coffee which is roasted on the premises

torréfaction [tɔrefaksjɔ̃] NF *(du café, du tabac)* roasting

torréfier [tɔrefje] VT *(impf, pr sub n. torréfiions, v. torréfiiez)* *(café, maïs etc)* to roast

torrent [tɔrɑ̃] NM *(cours d'eau)* torrent; *Fig (de larmes, lumière)* flood; *(d'injures)* torrent, barrage, spate; *(de questions)* barrage; **il pleut à torrents** it's raining in torrents, *Fam* it's bucketing down

torrentiel, -ielle [tɔrɑ̃sjɛl] ADJ torrential

torrentueux, -euse [tɔrɑ̃tɥø, -øz] ADJ *Litt (rivière etc)* torrent-like; *Fig (vie etc)* stormy, tempestuous

torride [tɔrid] ADJ *(zone, climat etc)*, *Fig (érotisme)* torrid; *(chaleur)* torrid, scorching; *(été)* scorching (hot); **il fait une chaleur t.** it's scorching; **une journée t.** a scorching (hot) day, a scorcher

torrieu [tɔrjø] INT *Can Fam* hell!

tors [tɔr] ADJ *(fil, jambe)* twisted; *Archit (colonne)* barley-sugar
NM *(torsion) (de corde etc)* twist

torsade [tɔrsad] NF **1** twisted cord; *Tricot* cable; **t. de cheveux** twist *or* coil of hair; *Tricot* **(point) t.** cable stitch; *Tricot* **aiguille à t.** cable needle **2** *Archit* rope *or* cable moulding *or Am* molding

torsadé [tɔrsade] ADJ *(cheveux)* coiled; *Archit* **colonne torsadée** cabled column; *Élec, Tél* **paire torsadée** twisted pair; **raccord t.** twist joint

torsader [tɔrsade] VT **1** *(corde, fil de fer etc)* to twist; *(cheveux)* to twist, to coil **2** *(mettre ensemble)* to twist together

torse [tɔrs] NM *(poitrine)* chest, torso, trunk; *Beaux-Arts* torso; **le t. pris dans une veste très serrée** wearing a very tight jacket; **le t.**

nu stripped to the waist; **se mettre t. nu to strip to the waist; **bomber le t.** to stick out one's chest; *Fig* to be swollen with pride; **il bombe le t. sous le coup de la fierté** he's puffed up with pride

torseur [tɔrsœr] NM *Phys* torque

torsion [tɔrsjɔ̃] NF twisting; *(des traits, de la bouche)* distortion; *Tech, Phys* torsion; **faire une t. à droite** to twist to the right

tort [tɔr] NM **1** *(faute)* fault; **c'est son seul t.** it's his only fault; **son seul t. a été d'être trop franc** his only mistake was being too frank; **il a eu le t. de ne pas demander de reçu** he made the mistake of not asking for a receipt; **reconnaître ses torts** to acknowledge one's faults; **il a tous les torts** he is entirely to blame, it's all his fault; **c'est un t. de le lui avoir dit** it was wrong *or* a mistake to tell him; **avoir des torts envers qn** to have treated sb badly; **avoir t.** to be wrong (**de** faire to do); **c'est elle qui a t., pas toi** she's the one who's wrong *or* (who's) in the wrong, not you; **il n'est pas d'accord, et il n'a pas t.** he doesn't agree, and he's right (not to); **donner t. à qn** to blame sb, to lay the blame on sb; *(d'un résultat, d'une preuve etc)* to prove sb wrong; **elle donne toujours t. à l'aîné de ses fils** she always blames the elder boy, the elder boy is always in the wrong as far as she's concerned; **être en t.** *ou* **dans son t.** to be in the wrong *or* at fault; **se mettre en t.** *ou* **dans son t.** to put oneself in the wrong; **à t.** wrongly; **à t. ou à raison** rightly or wrongly; **à t. et à travers** at random, without rhyme or reason; **dépenser son argent à t. et travers** to spend one's money thoughtlessly *or* recklessly; **il parle à t. et travers** he talks wildly; *Jur* **prononcer un jugement au t. d'une partie** to find against one of the parties
2 *(dommage)* harm; **un t.** a wrong; **faire du t. à qn** to wrong sb, to do sb wrong; **tu lui as fait beaucoup de t. en l'accusant** you did him/her great wrong in accusing her; **quel t. cela peut-il vous faire?** what harm can it do you?; **cette loi a fait beaucoup de t. aux petits épargnants** this law penalizes the small saver heavily

torticolis [tɔrtikɔli] NM *Méd* stiff neck, *Spéc* torticollis; **avoir/attraper un t.** to have/get a stiff neck

tortillard [tɔrtijar] NM local train

tortillement [tɔrtijmɑ̃] NM wriggling, squirming; *(des hanches)* wiggling

tortiller [tɔrtije] VT *(tordre) (papier, ruban, cheveux etc)* to twist; *(moustache)* to twirl; *(tripoter)* to twiddle (with)
VI **1 t. des hanches** to wiggle one's hips; **marcher en tortillant du postérieur** to walk with a wiggle; **elle avança vers la porte en tortillant du postérieur** she wiggled her way to the door **2** *Fam* **il n'y a pas à t.** it's no good trying to wriggle *or* wiggle out of it
VPR **se tortiller** *(d'un ver, d'une personne sur sa chaise)* to wriggle, to squirm, to wiggle; *(en dansant)* to wriggle about; *(des hanches)* to wiggle

tortillon [tɔrtijɔ̃] NM **1** *(de papier)* twist **2** *(sur la tête) (pour porter une charge)* pad

tortillonner [tɔrtijɔne] VT to twist and turn
VI *Fam* to quibble, to hedge

tortionnaire [tɔrsjɔner] NM torturer
ADJ **policier t.** police torturer

tortore [tɔrtɔr] NF *Fam* cooking; **elle fait de la vachement bonne t.** she makes really great food *or Br* scran

tortorer [tɔrtɔre] VT *Fam (manger)* to wolf down, to gobble up

tortu [tɔrty] ADJ *Litt (nez)* crooked; *(esprit)* warped

tortue [tɔrty] NF **1** *(reptile)* tortoise; *Fig (personne lente)* slowcoach, *Am* slowpoke; **t.**

d'eau douce terrapin; **t. de mer** turtle; **à pas de t.** at a snail's pace **2** *(papillon)* tortoiseshell (butterfly) **3** *Hist, Mil* testudo, tortoise

tortueusement [tɔrtɥøzmɑ̃] ADV tortuously; *(se conduire, manœuvrer etc)* deviously; **la route se déroule t. jusqu'au col** the road winds *or* twists its way (tortuously) up to the col

tortueux, -euse [tɔrtɥø, -øz] ADJ *(rivière)* winding, meandering; *(rue, sentier)* winding, twisting, twisty; *(attitude, personne, esprit, manœuvres)* devious; *(argumentation, discours etc)* tortuous

torturant [tɔrtyrɑ̃] ADJ *(situation, regret, sentiments, pensées etc)* agonizing

torture [tɔrtyr] NF torture; *Fig* torment, torture; **instrument de t.** instrument of torture; **chambre de t.** torture chamber; **victime de la t.** *ou* **de tortures** victim of torture, torture victim; *Fig* **cette séparation est une vraie t. morale pour moi** it's torture being separated; **mettre qn à la t.** to torment *or* torture sb; **je ne souhaite pas vous mettre à la t.** I hate to keep you on tenterhooks; **mettre son esprit à la t.** to rack one's brains

torturer [tɔrtyre] VT *(prisonnier)* to torture; *Fig* to torment (**sur** about); **cette situation la torture** the situation is torture *or* torment for her; **la jalousie le torturait** he was tortured *or* tormented by jealousy, he suffered torments of jealousy
VPR **se torturer** to torture oneself; **se t. l'esprit** to rack one's brains

torve [tɔrv] ADJ *(regard)* grim, menacing

tory [tɔri] ADJ, N Tory

toscan, -ane [tɔskɑ̃, -an] ADJ Tuscan
NM *Ling* Tuscan
N **T.** Tuscan

Toscane [tɔskan] NF Tuscany

tôt [to] ADV **1** *(bientôt, vite)* soon, early; **vous faut-il partir si t.?** must you leave so soon?; **plus t. tu commenceras, plus vite tu auras fini** the sooner you begin, the sooner you'll finish; **vous auriez dû me le dire plus t.** you should have told me sooner *or* earlier *or* before this; **nous n'étions pas plus t. rentrés que …** we had no sooner returned than …; **le plus t. sera le mieux** the sooner *or* earlier the better; **le plus t. possible** as soon *or* as early as possible; **revenez au plus t.** come back as soon *or* quick(ly) as possible; **mardi au plus t.** (on) Tuesday at the earliest; *Fam* **c'est pas trop t.!** and about time too!, and not before time either!; **on ne le reverra pas de si t.** we won't see him for a long time; *(il est parti fâché, ruiné etc)* we won't see him again in a hurry; **je ne pensais pas les revoir de si t.** I didn't think I would see them again so soon; **elle a eu t. fait de changer d'avis** she soon changed her mind, it wasn't long before she changed her mind; **t. après** soon after; **t. ou tard** sooner or later
2 *(de bonne heure)* early; **t. dans l'après-midi/dans l'année/dans sa vie** early in the afternoon/in the year/in his life; **il est trop t. pour manger** it's too early to eat; **il est trop t. pour le dire** it's too soon to say, it's early days yet

total, -ale, -aux, -ales [tɔtal, -o] ADJ *(somme, guerre, destruction, éclipse, silence etc)* total; *(obscurité)* total, complete; *(confiance, liberté)* complete; *(hauteur, largeur)* overall; *Méd (hystérectomie)* complete, *Spéc* radical; **c'était une surprise totale** it was a complete surprise; **un échec t.** a complete (and utter) *or* a total failure
NM total; **le t. de la population** the total population; **faire le t.** to work out the total; **faire le t. de** to add up, to total; **au t.** in all, in total; *(tout compte fait)* all in all; *Compta* **t. des recettes** total receipts; **t. général** grand total; **t. à payer** total payable; *Fam* **et t.** to

sum it all up, in short, in sum; **et t., on l'a renvoyé** and, to cut a long story short, he got the sack; **tu voulais faire ton indépendante, et t., tu es toute seule maintenant** you wanted to be independent, and the sum total of that is that you're all alone now

NF totale 1 *Chir Fam* hysterectomy **2** *Fam* (*ensemble de problèmes*) **on a eu droit à la totale: verglas, embouteillages, barrages de routiers** black ice, traffic jams, lorry drivers' road blocks, you name it, we had it; **quand il m'a demandée en mariage, il m'a fait la totale** when he proposed to me, he really went all out

totalement [tɔtalmɑ̃] **ADV** totally, completely

totalisateur, -trice [tɔtalizatœr, -tris] **ADJ** (*machine*) adding

NM adding machine; *Ordinat* accumulator; *Courses de chevaux* totalizer, *Fam* tote, *Am* pari-mutuel; *Aut* **t. kilométrique journalier** trip recorder

totalisation [tɔtalizasjɔ̃] **NF** totalling, adding up

totaliser [tɔtalize] **VT 1** (*additionner*) to total, to add up **2** (*compter en tout*) to total, to have a total of

totalitaire [tɔtaliter] **ADJ** *Pol* totalitarian

totalitarisme [tɔtalitarism] **NM** *Pol* totalitarianism

totalité [tɔtalite] **NF la t. de** all of; **l'entreprise exporte la t. de sa production** the company exports its entire production; **payer qch en t.** to pay sth in full; **la presque t. de** almost *or* virtually all (of); (**pris**) **dans sa/leur t.** (taken) as a whole; **en t.** in full

totem [tɔtɛm] **NM** totem

totémique [tɔtemik] **ADJ** totemic

totémisme [tɔtemism] **NM** totemism

toto [toto] **NM** *Arg* (*pou*) louse

toton [tɔtɔ̃] **NM** (*toupie*) teetotum

touareg [twarɛg] **ADJ** Tuareg
NM *Ling* Tuareg
N T. Tuareg

toubib [tubib] **NM** *Fam* doctor, quack

toucan [tukɑ̃] **NM** (*oiseau*) toucan

touchant [tuʃɑ̃] **ADJ** (*spectacle, discours, geste etc*) touching, moving; (*reconnaissance*) touching; **d'une manière touchante** touchingly, movingly; **elle est touchante d'humilité** she is touchingly humble
PRÉP *Litt* (*au sujet de*) touching, concerning, about

touche [tuʃ] **NF 1** (*style*) (*d'un peintre*) brushwork, style; (*d'un écrivain*) style
2 (*d'un piano, d'un clavier*) key
3 pierre de t. touchstone
4 *Billard, Escrime* hit
5 *Pêche* bite, nibble; *Fam* **avoir** *ou* **faire une t. avec qn** to make a hit with sb; **tu as fait une t.!** you've made a hit there!
6 *Sport* (*ligne*) touchline; (*remise en jeu*) *Ftbl* throw-in; *Rugby* line-out; (*au hockey*) roll-in; **t. longue** long throw-in; **envoi de t.** kick into touch; **jouer la t.** to take the throw-in; *Rugby* **trouver la t.** to find touch; **sortir en t.** to go into touch; **rester sur la t.** to stay on the sidelines *or* touchlines; *Fig* to stay on the sidelines
7 *Arg* (*aspect*) appearance, look; **avoir une drôle de t.** to be weird-looking; **t'as vu la t. qu'il a!** get a load of him!
8 *Arg* (*de drogue etc*) shot, jab
9 *Beaux-Arts* (*tache de couleur*) touch; *Fig* **une t. romantique** a touch of romance, a romantic touch; **pour apporter une t. locale** for a bit of local colour; **mettre la t. finale à qch** to put the finishing touches to sth; **procéder par petites touches** to proceed step by step
10 *Mus* (*de violon*) finger board; **touches** (*de guitare etc*) frets

▸▸ *Ordinat* **t. d'alimentation** power-on key; **t. alt** alt (key); **t. d'arrêt de défilement** scroll lock key; **t. à auto-maintien** sticky key; **t. à bascule** toggle key; **t. contrôle** control key; **t. de curseur** cursor key; **t. début** home key; **t. de défilement** scroll key; **t. de déplacement du curseur** cursor movement key; **t. de direction** arrow key; **t. d'échappement** escape key; **t. d'effacement** delete key; **t. d'effacement arrière** backspace delete key; **t. à effleurement** touch-sensitive key; **t. (d')entrée** enter key; **t. d'espacement arrière** backspace key; **t. fin** end key; **t. fléchée** *ou* (**à**) **flèche** arrow key; **t. flèche vers la droite/la gauche** right/left arrow key; **t. flèche vers le bas/le haut** down/up arrow key; **t. (de) fonction** function key; **t. d'impression d'écran** print screen key; **t. d'insertion** insert key; **t. d'interruption** break key; **t. majuscule** shift key; **t. morte** dead key; **t. multifonction** multifunctional key; **t. numérique** number key; **t. de raccourci** shortcut key; **t. de répétition** repeat-action key; **t. retour** return *or* enter key; **t. de retour arrière** backspace key; **t. de verrouillage des majuscules du clavier numérique** caps/num(-bers) lock key

touche-à-tout *Fam* **ADJ INV 1 il est t.** (*adulte*) he can't keep his hands off anything; (*bébé*) he's into everything **2** *Fig* **j'ai toujours été un peu t.** I've always dabbled in this and that
N INV 1 c'est un t. (*adulte*) he can't keep his hands off anything; (*bébé*) he's into everything **2** (*personne qui a plusieurs occupations*) dabbler; **il écrit, il peint, c'est un peu un t.** he writes, he paints, he does a bit of everything

touche-pipi **NM** *Fam* **jouer à t.** to play at doctors and nurses

toucher¹ [tuʃe] **NM 1** (*sens, action*) touch; (*qualité*) feel; **sens du t.** sense of touch; **au t.** to the touch *or* feel; **le mur était chaud au t.** the wall was hot to the touch *or* felt hot; **reconnaître qch au t.** to recognize sth by touch *or* by the feel of it **2** *Méd* examination; **t. vaginal** vaginal examination **3** *Mus* (*d'un pianiste*) touch

TOUCHER²

VT to touch **1, 3, 5** ▪ to hit **1, 2** ▪ to damage **2** ▪ to move **3** ▪ to affect **4** ▪ to reach **7** ▪ to receive **8** ▪ to adjoin **9**	
VI to touch **2, 3** ▪ to tamper with **2** ▪ to touch on **3** ▪ to concern **4**	
VPR to touch	

VT 1 (*du doigt, avec un objet etc*) (*quelque chose, quelqu'un sur l'épaule etc*) to touch; *Ftbl* (*balle*) to handle; (*cible*), *Billard* (*boule*), *Escrime* (*adversaire*) to hit; **t. qch avec des gants** to handle sth with gloves on, to wear gloves when handling sth; **la voiture a failli t. le mur** the car almost hit *or* clipped the wall; *Fam* **touchons du bois!** touch wood!; *Fam* **pas touche!** (*à un enfant*) don't touch!; *Rugby* **t. dans les buts** to touch down
2 (*maison etc*) (*d'un incendie*) to damage; (*d'une explosion*) to damage, to hit; (*personne*) (*d'un éclat d'obus etc*) to hit (**à la jambe** in the leg); **le soldat a été gravement touché** the soldier was seriously injured
3 (*émouvoir*) to move, to touch; **t. qn jusqu'aux larmes** to move sb to tears; **être touché au vif** to be cut *or* stung to the quick
4 (*concerner, affecter*) to concern, to affect; **le chômage touche particulièrement les jeunes** the young are particularly affected *or* hard hit by unemployment
5 *Naut* (*terre*) to touch; **t. le port** to put in at *or* touch port; **t. le fond** *Naut* to strike, to touch (bottom); (*être à sec*) to be aground; *Fig* (*déprimer*) to touch (rock) bottom

6 *Min* **t. le pétrole** to strike oil
7 (*contacter*) to get in touch with, to get hold of, to reach; (*d'une lettre*) to reach; **t. qn par téléphone** to reach sb by telephone
8 (*recevoir*) (*argent*) to get, to receive; (*chèque*) to cash; **t. ses appointements/sa paie** to draw *or* receive one's salary/one's pay; **t. un intérêt** to receive interest; **elle doit bien t. dans les 2 000 euros par mois** she must be making *or* getting about 2,000 euros a month; **je pense t. 500 euros le 15 juin** I think I've got 500 euros coming to me on the 15th of June; **t. le tiercé** = to win the pools, to hit the jackpot
9 (*être tout proche de*) to adjoin; **la bibliothèque touche l'église** the library adjoins the church; **la maison qui touche la nôtre** the house adjoining ours
10 je lui en toucherai un mot *ou* **deux mots** I'll mention it to him, I'll speak to him about it

VI 1 t. à un port (*d'un navire*) to put in *or* call at a port, to touch a port
2 t. à (*entrer en contact avec*) to touch; *Fig* (*en modifiant*) to touch, to meddle with, to tamper with; **palmes qui touchent au plafond** palms that touch *or* reach the ceiling; **t. à terre** to touch the ground; **si tu touches au chat, je te quitte!** if you touch *or* lay a finger on the cat, I'll leave you!; **n'y touchez pas!** (keep your) hands off!; **on ne touche pas!** hands off!; **je n'ai pas touché à l'héroïne/l'alcool depuis** I haven't touched heroin/alcohol since; **il n'avait pas touché à la nourriture** he hadn't touched the food, he had left the food untouched; **t. à ses économies** to touch *or* break into one's savings; *Fig* **avec son air de ne pas y t.** looking as if butter wouldn't melt in his mouth, with an ever so innocent look on his face
3 t. à (*être en contact avec*) (*quelque chose*) to touch; (*pays*) to border on; (*maison, jardin etc*) to adjoin; *Fig* (*problème, question*) to touch on; **t. au but** to near one's goal; **l'année/le projet touche à sa fin** the year/the project is drawing to a close *or* nearing its end; **il touche à la quarantaine** he is getting on for *or* nearing forty
4 t. à (*concerner*) to concern; **tout ce qui touche à l'écologie** everything to do with *or* touching on *or* concerning ecology
VPR se toucher 1 (*de lignes etc*) to touch; **nos deux maisons se touchent** our two houses adjoin *or* are adjoining
2 (*se masturber*) to touch oneself

touche-touche (à) **ADV** *Aut* nose-to-tail, bumper to bumper

touchette [tuʃɛt] **NF** (*d'une guitare, d'une mandoline*) fret

toucheur, -euse [tuʃœr, -øz] **N** (cattle) drover

touée [twe] **NF** *Naut* **1** (*câble*) warp, (warping) cable **2** (*longueur*) scope

touer [twe] **VT 1** *Naut* (*avec point fixe*) to warp **2** (*avec ancre*) to kedge

toueur [twœr] **NM** *Naut* tug

touffe [tuf] **NF 1** (*de cheveux, d'herbe, de poils etc*) tuft; (*de végétation*) clump **2** *Vulg* (*toison pubienne*) bush, pubes; **une jupe ras la t.** a bum-freezer

touffeur [tufœr] **NF** *Arch, Litt* suffocating heat

touffu [tufy] **ADJ** (*bois, végétation*) thick, dense; (*barbe, cheveux etc*) bushy; *Fig* (*livre*) dense

touillage [tujaʒ] **NM** *Fam* (*de liquide*) stirring; (*de salade*) tossing; (*de cartes*) shuffling

touiller [tuje] **VT** *Fam* (*liquide, soupe etc*) to stir; (*salade*) to toss; (*cartes*) to shuffle

toujours [tuʒur] **ADV 1** (*répétition*) always; **c'est ce que j'ai t. dit, et dirai t.** that's what

I've always said and will keep on saying; **t. plus nombreux** more and more numerous; **influence t. plus étendue** ever-increasing influence; **comme t.** as always, as ever; **optimiste comme t., il ...** ever the optimist, he ...; **presque t.** almost or nearly always; **un ami de t.** a lifelong friend; **pour t.** for ever; **depuis t.** always; **je t'aime depuis t.** I've always loved you, I've been in love with you for as long as I can remember VOIR GRAMMAIRE A21

2 (encore) still; **il fait t. aussi chaud** it is as hot as ever (it was); **cherchez t.** go on looking; **elle ne le lui a t. pas dit** she still hasn't told him; **alors, il est rentré? – t. pas** he's back then? – not yet

3 (concession) always, anyhow; **je peux t. essayer** I can always or at least try; **essaie/entrez t.** try/come in anyway; **t. est-il que ...** the fact remains that ..., anyhow, ...; **elle peut t. attendre!** she'll be lucky!, she'll have a long wait!, in her dreams!; **il peut t. me redemander ma voiture, il ne l'aura pas** he can always ask me for my car again, but he won't get it; **c'est t. ça (de pris)** (at any rate) it's better than nothing, at least it's something; **allez-y t., je vous rejoindrai plus tard** you go on anyhow, I'll catch you up later

Attention: ne pas confondre **still** et **always** lorsqu'on traduit **toujours**. **Still** exprime l'idée de continuité, alors que **always** exprime l'idée de répétition.

toulousain, -aine [tuluzɛ̃, -ɛn] ADJ of or from Toulouse
  N **T.** (natif) native of Toulouse; (habitant) inhabitant of Toulouse

toundra [tundra] NF Géog tundra

toupet [tupɛ] NM **1** (de cheveux) tuft of hair, Br quiff; (faux) **t.** toupee **2** Fam (culot) cheek, nerve; **quel t.!** what a cheek or a nerve!; **il faut un sacré t. pour le faire!** it takes a helluva nerve or cheek!; **avoir du t.** to have a cheek or the nerve; **il a eu le t. de ...** he had the cheek or the nerve to ...; **elle ne manque pas de t.!** she's got a cheek or a nerve!

toupie [tupi] NF **1** (jouet) (spinning) top **2** Menuis etc moulding or Am molding machine **3** (de meuble) moulded or Am molded foot (Louis XVI style) **4** Fam **vieille t.** (femme) old trout

tour¹ [tur] NF **1** (bâtiment, d'une cathédrale, d'un château etc) tower; (d'habitation) highrise building; Ordinat tower; TV, Cin camera tower; **(immeuble) t., grande t.** tower block, high-rise **2** Fam (personne) hulk **3** Échecs castle, rook
  ▸▸ **la t. de Babel** the Tower of Babel; Aviat **t. de contrôle** control tower; **la t. Eiffel** the Eiffel Tower; **t. de forage** derrick, rig; Ind, Chimie **t. de fractionnement** fractionating tower; Fig **t. d'ivoire** ivory tower; **t. de lancement** launch tower; **la t. de Londres** the Tower of London; **t. d'observation** watchtower, observation tower; **la t. (penchée) de Pise** the Leaning Tower of Pisa; **t. de réfrigération** cooling tower; **t. de remplissage** (pour fusée) umbilical tower; **t. de sondage** derrick, rig

TOUR²

circumference **1**	measurement **1**
turn **2–5, 8, 12**	to go round (faire le tour de) **1**
revolution **5**	stroll **6**
ride **6**	trip **7**
lathe **9**	wheel **10**
round **11**	ballot **13**
trick **14, 15**	

NM **1** (circonférence) circumference; (de partie du corps) size, measurement; **arbre qui a deux mètres de t.** tree two metres in circumference, tree with a girth of two metres; **faire le t.** to go round; **faire tout le t.** to go all the way round; **le chemin fait le t. de la propriété** the path runs right round the estate; Fig **faire le t. de** (situation, problème) to review sth; **faire le t. du monde** to go round the world; **faire le t. du monde à la voile/à pied** to sail/walk round the world; **c'est son deuxième t. du monde à la voile** this is the second time he's sailed round the world; Sport **t. de piste** ou **de circuit** lap; **en être au troisième t.** to be on the third lap; **prendre un t. d'avance sur qn** to lap sb; **faire un t. de piste pour s'échauffer** to do a warm-up lap; **faire le t. du cadran** to sleep round the clock; **t. de cou** (mesure) collar size or measurement; Vieilli **quel est votre t. de cou?** what (size) neck are you?; **t. de tête** (mesure) hat size; **t. de taille** (measurement); **quel est votre t. de taille?** what waist are you?; **avoir 75 cm de t. de taille** to have a waist measurement of 75 cm, to measure 75 cm round the waist, to be a 75 cm waist; **perdre cinq centimètres de t. de taille** to lose five centimetres round the waist; **quel est votre t. de hanche?** what hip size are you?

2 Naut (autour de la bitte d'amarrage) turn; **avoir des tours** to have a foul hawse

3 tours et détours d'un chemin twists and turns of a road

4 (tournure) (de phrase, d'une situation) turn; **prendre un mauvais t./un t. dramatique** to take a bad/a dramatic turn; **tout cela est en train de prendre un tout autre t. que ce que j'avais prévu** it's all turning out quite differently from what I expected; **cette affaire prend un t. qui ne me plaît guère** this matter is developing in a way I don't like; **donner un autre t. à la conversation** (rendre sérieuse) to raise the tone of the conversation; (rendre légère) to lower the tone of the conversation; **t. d'esprit** turn of mind; Suisse **donner le t.** (maladie) to take a turn for the better; (personne) to wrap up

5 (rotation) (de clé, tournevis, vis) turn; (de roue, moteur) revolution, turn; (de manivelle) turn, swing; **donner un t. de clé à la porte** to turn the key in the door; **fermer qch à double t.** to double-lock sth; Aut **tours de volant** steering wheel turns; (de butée à butée) turns lock to lock; **à t. de bras** (frapper) with all one's might; Fig **vendre/distribuer qch à t. de bras** to sell/distribute loads or masses of sth; **tours par minute, tours/minute** revolutions per minute, Fam revs; **(disque à) 45/33 tours** single/LP

6 (balade) stroll; (à bicyclette, en voiture) ride; **faire un t.** to go for a stroll/ride; **elle aime bien faire un t. en ville** she likes going into town; **faire un t. de** ou **dans le jardin** to have or take a turn or a stroll round the garden; Euph **elle est allée faire un petit t.** she's gone to spend a penny

7 (petit voyage) trip, tour; **ils sont allés faire un t. en Bretagne** they've gone touring in Brittany

8 (de participation) turn; **à qui le t.?** whose turn is it?; **t. de service** spell of duty; **chacun (à) son t.** each in (his) turn; **chacun son t.!** (dans une queue) wait your turn!; **hier c'est moi qui l'ai fait, aujourd'hui c'est toi, chacun son t.!** I did it yesterday, now it's your turn!; **ils s'occupent des enfants chacun leur t.** they look after the children in turn or turn and turn about, they take turns looking after the children; **à t. de rôle** in turns; **nous le faisons à t. de rôle** we do it in turns, we take turns doing it; **les membres assurent la présidence à t. de rôle tous les deux ans** the presidency rotates among members every two years; **t. à t.** by turns, in turn; **s'emporter et se calmer à t.** to flare up one moment and calm down the next

9 Tech (machine-outil) (turning) lathe; **fait**

au **t.** machine-turned; Fam Vieilli (jambe, taille etc) shapely; **atelier des tours** turning shop
  10 Cér (potter's) wheel
  11 Cartes (manche) round
  12 Théâtre etc turn, number
  13 Pol **t.** (de scrutin) ballot
  14 (sale coup) trick; **faire** ou **jouer un (mauvais) t. à qn** to play a (nasty) trick on sb, to play sb a (nasty) trick; **mes yeux ont dû me jouer des tours** my eyes must have been playing tricks on me; **cela te jouera des tours** you'll (live to) regret it; Fam **avoir plus d'un t. dans son sac** to have more than one trick up one's sleeve
  15 (manipulation) feat; (de prestidigitateur, chien) trick; **t. d'adresse** feat of skill; **t. de cartes** card trick; Fam **en un t. de main** in two minutes flat, in the twinkling of an eye; **je n'ai pas le t. de main** I haven't the knack or hang of it; **c'est un t. à prendre** there's a knack to it
  ▸▸ **t. de chant** song recital; Fam **t. de cochon** lousy or rotten trick; **t. de cou** (ruban) choker; (en fourrure, écharpe) scarf; **t. de force** feat, achievement; **il a réalisé un véritable t. de force en organisant la fête** organizing the festival was quite a feat or an achievement on his part; **T. de France** (cycliste) Tour de France (cycle race); **faire son t. de France** (d'un compagnon) to do one's journeymanship; **t. d'honneur** lap of honour; Fig **t. d'horizon: faire un t. d'horizon** to review matters; **t. de lit** bed valance; **t. de reins: se faire un t. de reins** to strain or rick one's back; Fin **t. de table** backers; **faire un t. de table** (pendant un débat) to go round the table

Touraine [turɛn] NF Touraine

tourangeau, -elle, -eaux, -elles [turɑ̃-ʒo, -ɛl] ADJ (de la région) of/from Touraine; (de la ville) of/from Tours
  N **T.** (natif) (de la région/la ville) native of Touraine/Tours; (habitant) (de la région/la ville) inhabitant of Touraine/Tours

tourbe [turb] NF peat, turf

tourbeux, -euse [turbø, -øz] ADJ (sol etc) peaty

tourbière [turbjɛr] NF peat bog

tourbillon [turbijɔ̃] NM **1** (vent) whirlwind; (de poussière, de sable, de cendres, de fumée) swirl, cloud; (de neige) flurry; **monter en tourbillons** (de la poussière, du sable etc) to swirl or whirl up **2** (remous) whirlpool **3** Phys, Astron, Phil vortex VOIR GRAMMAIRE A14 **4** Aut (dans un moteur) rotary or barrel swirl, swirl **5** Fig (des plaisirs etc) whirl; **dans le t. de la vie** in the hurly-burly of life; **le t. de la vie mondaine** the social whirl

tourbillonnaire [turbijɔnɛr] ADJ swirling

tourbillonnant [turbijɔnɑ̃] ADJ (feuilles, jupes etc) whirling

tourbillonnement [turbijɔnmɑ̃] NM whirling

tourbillonner [turbijɔne] VI Fig (d'idées etc) to whirl (round); (de feuilles, d'un danseur) to whirl (round), to spin round and round

tourelle [turɛl] NF **1** Archit turret; **à tourelles** turreted **2** Mil, Naut (gun) turret **3** Opt, Phot **t. à objectifs** lens turret

tourière [turjer] ADJ, NF Rel extern

tourillon [turijɔ̃] NM **1** (d'axe) journal; (axe) (wheel) spindle **2** Mil (de canon etc) trunnion **3** (pivot) pivot (pin)

Touring Club de France [turiŋklœbdəfrɑ̃s] NM = French motoring organization

tourismatique [turismatik] NF computerized reservation systems

tourisme [turism] NM tourism; (industrie) tourism, tourist trade; **faire du t.** to do some volved in some mysterious game with their toys **2** (circulation) traffic; **le t. est ralenti sur la nationale 7** traffic is moving slowly on route 7 **3** Électron traffic **4** (de site Internet) traffic **5** Vieilli (commerce) trading, trade ▸▸ **t. aérien** air traffic; **t. commercial** commercial trade; **t. d'influence** influence peddling; **il a obtenu ce marché grâce à un véritable t. d'influence** he landed the deal thanks to a fair amount of string-pulling; **t. des marchandises** goods traffic; Ordinat **t. de réseau** network traffic; **t. routier** road traffic

traficoter [trafikɔte] Fam VI Péj to tinker VT (manigancer) **je me demande ce qu'il traficote** I wonder what he's up to

trafiquant, -ante [trafikɑ̃, -ɑ̃t] N Péj trafficker; **t. de** ou **en stupéfiants** ou **de drogues** drug trafficker; **t. d'armes** arms dealer, gunrunner; **t. du marché noir** black marketeer

trafiquer [trafike] VI Péj to traffic (**de** in) VT Fam **1** (modifier) (moteur de voiture, Mobylette® etc) to tinker with; (freins, compteur) to tamper with; (chèque) to falsify, to tamper with; (vin) to doctor, to tamper with; **t. les comptes** to fiddle the accounts **2** (manigancer) **qu'est-ce qu'il trafique?** what's he up to?

trafiqueur, -euse [trafikœr, -øz] N Péj trafficker (**de, en** in)

tragédie [traʒedi] NF Théâtre, Fig tragedy; Fig **c'est une véritable t.** it's a real tragedy, it's really tragic; Fam Fig **ce n'est pas une t.!** it's not the end of the world!

tragédien, -ienne [traʒedjɛ̃, -jɛn] N tragic actor, f tragic actress, tragedian, f tragedienne

tragi-comédie, pl **tragi-comédies** [traʒikɔmedi] NF Théâtre, Fig tragi-comedy

tragi-comique, pl **tragi-comiques** [traʒikɔmik] ADJ Théâtre, Fig tragi-comic

tragique [traʒik] ADJ (auteur, pièce, rôle), Fig (événement, conséquences etc) tragic; **... dit-elle d'un accent t. ...** she said in a tragic tone of voice; **ce qu'il y avait de vraiment t., c'est que ...** what was really tragic or the real tragedy was that ...; Littér **le genre t.** tragedy NM **1** (d'un événement) tragedy, tragic side; **cela tourne au t.** it's turning into a tragedy; Fig **prendre qch au t.** to make a tragedy or a big thing out of sth **2** Théâtre **le t.** tragedy N (auteur) tragic author, writer of tragedies

tragiquement [traʒikmɑ̃] ADV tragically; **finir t.** to end tragically or in tragedy

trahir [trair] VT **1** (divulguer) (secret) to betray, to reveal, to give away; (de paroles, silence) (gêne, ignorance etc) to betray, to reveal; (d'un accent) (personne) to give away; **je fus trahi par les aboiements d'un chien** I was betrayed or given away by a dog barking **2** (cesser d'être fidèle à) (personne, pays, confiance, intérêts) to betray; (serment, promesse etc) to break; Fig (de jambes, forces, traducteur) (personne, auteur) to fail; Fig **la traduction trahit le texte** the translation fails or is not faithful to the text; **son mari la trahit pour une femme plus âgée** her husband is being unfaithful to or deceiving her with an older woman; **se sentir trahi** to feel betrayed **3** Arch **t. qn/qch à qn** to betray sb/ sth to sb

VPR **se trahir** (d'une personne) to give oneself away; (d'un sentiment etc) to betray itself, to be revealed

trahison [traizɔ̃] NF **1** (fait de trahir) (d'un ami, de son pays etc) betrayal **2** (faute) treachery; Pol treason; **haute t.** high treason; **une t.** an act of treachery

traille [traj] NF **1** (câble) ferry cable **2** (bac) ferry

train [trɛ̃] NM **1** Rail train; **je prends le t. de cinq heures** I'm catching the five o'clock

(train); **je préfère le t. à la route** I'd rather go by train than by road; **voyager en t.** ou **par le t.** to travel by train; **voyage en t.** train journey; **être dans un t.** to be on a train; **monter dans le t.** to get on the train; **prendre le t. en marche** to jump on (a/the train while it's moving); Fig to jump or climb on the bandwagon; **comme une vache qui regarde passer un t.** like a cow at a five-bar gate **2** Mil **le t.** ≃ transport branch of the Army Service Corps **3** (file) (de véhicules, de péniches, d'animaux transhumants etc) string, line; (de roues etc) set; (de réformes, décrets) series, string **4** Arch (escorte) suite, attendants; (de serviteurs etc) train **5** (de cheval) quarters; (derrière) (de chien) rump; **t. de derrière/de devant** hindquarters/forequarters **6** Arg (derrière) (d'une personne) backside, rear (end), Am butt; **se manier le t.** to get a move on, to shift oneself, Arg to get one's arse in gear; **filer le t. à qn** to shadow or tail sb **7** (allure) pace; **aller bon t.** to go at a good pace; **aller son petit t.** to jog along; **les choses vont leur t.** things are going along as usual; Vieilli **dans le t.** up to date; Fam **à fond de t.** at top or full speed, Fam at a rate of knots; **rouler à un t. d'enfer** to go hell for leather; **au t. où il va/où vont les choses** at the rate he's/things are going; **à ce t.-là** at this rate; Sport **meneur de t.** pacemaker; **mener le t.** to set the pace; **mener grand t.** to live it up; **avec le salaire que je gagne, je ne risque pas de mener grand t.** I'm not likely to paint the town red on what I make **8 en t.** (projet, affaire) under way, in progress; Fam **ils ont un petit en t.** they've got a baby on the way, they're expecting; Fam **il était un peu en t.** (ivre) he'd had a drop (too much); **être en bon t.** to be making good progress; **mettre qch en t.** (projet etc) to set sth in train or motion, to start sth, to set sth going; (tricot) to start sth; **c'est lui qui a tout mis en t.** he got everything started or under way; **mise en t.** shakedown; **être en t. de faire qch** to be doing sth; **il était en t. de travailler** he was (busy) working; **elle est toujours en t. de crier** she's always shouting

SEE GRAMMAR B30

9 Fam (tapage) noise, row; **faire du t., faire un t. de tous les diables** to kick up (a hell of) a row **10** (humeur) **être en t.** to be in good spirits or in good form; **il n'était pas en t. ce jour-là** he wasn't at his best that day; **être mal en t.** to be out of sorts, to feel unwell; **je ne suis pas en t. pour travailler** I don't feel like working, I'm not in the mood for work; **mettre qn en t.** to get sb into a good mood **11** Aviat landing gear, undercarriage ▸▸ Aviat **t. d'atterrissage** landing gear, undercarriage; T. **Auto et Moto Accompagnées**, T. **Automobile Accompagnée** Br ≃ Motorail, Am ≃ AutoTrain; **t. autos-couchettes** car-sleeper train; **t. avant** Aviat nose gear or wheel; Aut front axle (assembly); **t. de bois** timber raft, float; **t. de croisière** luxury train; **t. direct** through train; **t. électrique** electric train; **t. d'engrenages** gear train; **t. express** express (train); **t. (de) grandes lignes** inter-city (train); Rail **t. à grande vitesse** high-speed train; Vieilli **t. de maison** style of living; **t. de marchandises** goods or Am freight train; **t. militaire** troop train; **t. de neige** = train carrying holidaymakers to ski resorts; **t. omnibus** local or slow or stopping train; Phys **t. d'ondes** wavetrain; **t. postal** mail train; Tech **t. de roulement** (d'un véhicule à roues) undercarriage; (d'un véhicule chenillé) suspension and tracks; **t. routier** road train; **t. spatial** space train; **t. supplémentaire** relief train; **t. de vie** lifestyle, way of life; **t. de voyageurs** passenger train

traînage [trɛnaʒ] NM **1** dragging; Rail (de trains) haulage; **câble de t.** haulage rope **2** (transport par traîneaux) sleigh transport

traînailler [trɛnaje] VI Fam = **traînasser**

traînant [trɛnɑ̃] ADJ **1** (robe etc) trailing **2** (lent) (voix) drawling; (démarche, pas) shuffling, dragging

traînard, -arde [trɛnar, -ard] N Fam (en arrière d'un groupe) straggler; (dans son travail) dawdler, slowcoach, Am slowpoke

traînasser [trɛnase] VI Fam **1** (errer) to loaf or slouch about or around **2** (être lent) to dawdle, to drag one's feet; (n'avoir aucune énergie) to drag oneself around

train-couchettes NM INV sleeper

traîne [trɛn] NF **1** Naut à la t. in tow; Fig Fam **être à la t.** to lag behind **2** (d'une robe) train **3** Pêche seine (net), drag net **4** Can **t. sauvage** toboggan

traîneau, -eaux [trɛno] NM **1** (tiré par des chevaux) sleigh; (tiré par des chiens) sledge, Am sled; **faire une promenade en t.** to go for a sleigh ride; **chien de t.** sledge dog, husky; **attelage de chiens de t.** dog team **2** Pêche seine (net), drag net

traîne-bûches NM INV Pêche Fam bait, Spéc caddis worm

traîne-buisson, pl **traîne-buissons** NM Orn dunnock, hedge sparrow

traînée [trɛne] NF **1** (de fumée, de sang, de lumière etc) trail; (de saleté) streak; (de poudre) train; (d'un escargot) trail; Aviat vapour or Am vapor trail, Spéc contrail; Fig **se répandre comme une t. de poudre** to spread like wildfire **2** Phys (force) drag **3** Arg (prostituée), Péj (femme) tart

traînement [trɛnmɑ̃] NM (des pieds) dragging; (de la voix) drawling

traîne-misère N INV Fam down-and-out

traîner [trɛne] VT (quelqu'un, quelque chose) to drag; Rail (wagons etc) to pull, to haul; (péniches) to tow; Fig (sa vie) to drag out; (discours, affaire etc) to spin out, to drag out; (paroles) to drawl; **faire t. qch en longueur** to spin or drag sth out; **elle traînait cinq enfants après elle** she was trailing or dragging five children after her; **elle traîne sa sœur partout** she drags her sister everywhere with her; **t. la jambe** to limp; **t. les pieds** to drag one's feet; Fig to drag one's feet; **elle entra dans la pièce en traînant les pieds** she shuffled into the room; **la perdrix traînait (de) l'aile** the partridge was dragging a wing; **t. qn en prison** to drag sb off to prison; Fig **elle traîne un rhume depuis quinze jours** she's had a cold for two weeks that she can't get rid of or shake off; Fig **t. qn dans la boue** to drag sb or sb's name through the mud; Fam **il doit bien t. ses guêtres** ou **bottes quelque part!** he must be somewhere around!; **j'ai traîné mes bottes dans tous les pays d'Afrique** I've kicked around every country in Africa; **t. son ennui** to be constantly bored

VI **1** (dans la poussière, la boue etc) to trail, to drag; **votre robe traîne (par terre)** your dress is trailing **2** (rester en arrière) to lag or trail (behind); **t. derrière qn** to lag or trail behind sb; **une voix qui traîne** a drawling voice **3** (errer) (dans un endroit) to hang or kick or knock around or about; **t. dans la rue** ou **par les rues** to hang or kick or knock around or about the streets; **où est-ce qu'il traîne d'habitude?** where does he usually hang out?; **t. avec qn** to hang about with sb; **il y a un virus qui traîne** there's a virus going around or doing the rounds **4** (être lent) (d'une personne) to dawdle; (de la conversation), Théâtre etc (d'une intrigue) to drag

5 *(en désordre)* to lie *or* kick around *or* about; **laisser t. son argent** to leave one's money lying around *or* about; **tes vêtements traînent partout dans la maison** your clothes are scattered all over the house

6 *(durer longtemps)* *(d'une maladie, d'une conversation etc)* to drag on; **t. en longueur** *(d'un procès etc)* to drag (on); **les choses ne traînent pas avec vous** you're a fast worker, you don't hang about, you don't let the grass grow under your feet; *Fam* **... et que ça ne traîne pas!** ... and don't take forever about it!, ... and be quick about it!; **laisser t. un compte** to leave an account unpaid

VPR se traîner 1 *(d'une personne)* to drag oneself; **il se traînait à peine** he could hardly drag himself along; **il se traîna jusqu'au fossé** he dragged himself *or* crawled to the ditch; **se t. aux pieds de qn** to go on one's knees to sb; **je me suis traîné cette sale grippe tout l'hiver** I've had this rotten cold hanging around all winter; **je me suis traîné ces vieilles chaussures tout l'hiver** I've had to wear *or* put up with these old shoes all winter **2** *(d'une conversation, d'une soirée etc)* to drag on; **les heures se traînent lourdement** time drags, time hangs heavy

traînerie [trɛnri] NF *Can Fam* **1 ramasse les traîneries dans ta chambre!** *(objets en désordre)* clear away all the junk lying around your bedroom! **2 pas de traînerie!** *(dépêche-toi)* look sharp!, be quick about it!

traîne-savates N INV *Fam* layabout, loafer

traîneux, -euse [trɛnø, -øz] NM *Can Fam* slob

training [trɛniŋ] NM **1** *Sport (entraînement)* training **2** *Psy* **t. autogène** relaxation by autosuggestion **3** *(survêtement)* tracksuit **4** *(chaussure)* trainer

train-poste, *pl* **trains-poste** NM mail train

train-train NM INV *Fam* routine, daily round; **le t. quotidien** the daily routine *or* grind; **rien qui sort du t. des événements ordinaires** nothing out of the ordinary

traire [trɛr] VT *(prp* trayant; *pp* trait; *pr ind* je trais, n. trayons, ils traient; *impf* je trayais; *fu* je trairai; *no p hist) (vache, chèvre etc)* to milk; *(lait)* to draw; **machine à t.** milking machine

trait [trɛ] NM **1** *(ligne etc)* stroke, line; *Typ* long dash; **d'un t. de plume** with a stroke of the pen; **signer d'un t. de plume** to sign with a flourish; **t. plein/discontinu** continuous/broken line; **dessin au t.** outline drawing; **copier qch t. pour t.** to copy sth line by line; *Fig* **c'est sa sœur t. pour t.** she is her sister to a T; **gravure au t.** line engraving; **les grands traits de qch** the main features of sth; *Tél* **points et traits** dots and dashes; *Fig* **tirer un t. sur le passé** to forget the past, to draw a line under the past; **tirer un t. sur ses vacances** to say goodbye to one's holidays, to kiss one's holidays goodbye; **j'ai tiré un t. sur lui/notre relation** I've crossed him/our relationship off; **t. de scie** cut(ting) line

2 *(du visage)* feature; **traits réguliers/fins/grossiers** regular/fine/coarse features; **elle avait les traits tirés** she looked drawn, her face was drawn

3 *(caractéristique) (d'une personne)* trait; *(d'un écrivain etc)* characteristic touch; **t. de caractère** character trait, trait of character; **c'est l'un de ses traits distinctifs** it's one of his peculiarities *or* distinctive traits

4 *(flèche)* arrow; *Fig* **partir comme un t.** *(d'une personne)* to be off like a shot; *Fig* **les traits de la médisance/la satire** slanders/shafts of satire; *Fig* **un t. mordant/méchant** a sarcastic/nasty remark; *Fig* **envoyer** *ou* **lancer un t. à qn** to get a dig in at sb

5 avoir t. à qch to be connected with sth, to relate to sth; **tout ce qui a t. à la psychana-**

lyse everything connected *or* to do with psychoanalysis

6 *(de lumière)* beam, shaft

7 *Mus* fast passage

8 *(de boisson)* gulp, *Litt* draught, *Am* draft; **boire à longs traits** *(bière etc)* to gulp down; **d'un (seul) t.** *(boire qch)* at one gulp, *Fam* at one go, in a oner; *(raconter qch)* without stopping, in one fell swoop; *(lire qch)* without stopping, at a single sitting

9 *(de cordes, de poids)* pulling; **cheval de (gros) t.** (heavy) draught *or Am* draft horse

10 *(d'un harnais)* trace

11 *Échecs etc* **avoir le t.** to have first move

12 *(acte) (de courage)* act, deed; *(de génie)* stroke

▸▸ *Typ* **t. double** double line; *Fig* **t. d'esprit** flash *or* stroke of wit, witticism; *Typ* **t. en pointillé** dotted underline; *Typ* **t. simple** single line; **t. d'union** hyphen; *Fig (entre deux personnes, deux villes etc)* link; *Ordinat* **t. d'union conditionnel** soft hyphen; *Ordinat* **t. d'union insécable** hard hyphen

traitable [trɛtabl] ADJ **1** *Litt (personne)* tractable, accommodating **2** *(sujet etc)* treatable, manageable

traitant [trɛtɑ̃] ADJ **1** *(shampoing, crème de beauté etc)* medicated **2 mon médecin t.** my (usual) doctor; **nom du médecin t.** name of the doctor in attendance *or* of the consulting physician

traite [trɛt] NF **1** *(d'une route etc)* stretch; **j'ai fait une longue t.** I've come a long way; **(tout) d'une t., d'une seule t.** in one go; **faire le chemin d'une t.** to do the journey nonstop *or* without stopping *or Fam* in a oner **2** *Fin (billet)* (banker's) draft, bill (of exchange); **présenter une t. à l'acceptation** to present a bill for acceptance **3** *(des vaches)* milking

▸▸ **t. bancaire** bank draft; **t. des Blanches** white slave trade; *Fin* **t. de complaisance** accommodation bill; *Fin* **t. contre acceptation** acceptance bill; *Fin* **t. à courte échéance** short-dated bill; *Fin* **t. à date fixe** time bill; *Fin* **t. documentaire** documentary bill; *Fin* **t. libre** clean bill; *Fin* **t. à longue échéance** long-dated bill; **t. des Noirs** slave trade; *Fin* **t. pro forma** pro forma bill; *Fin* **t. 'sans frais'** bill 'without protest'; *Fin* **t. à terme** term draft; *Fin* **t. à vue** sight draft

traité [trɛte] NM **1** *(ouvrage)* treatise (**de, sur on) 2** *Pol (accord)* treaty; *UE* **t. d'adhésion** membership treaty; **t. d'alliance** treaty of alliance; **t. de commerce** commercial treaty; *UE* **t. de Maastricht** Maastricht Treaty; **t. de non-prolifération nucléaire** Nuclear Non-Proliferation Treaty; **t. de paix** peace treaty; *UE* **t. sur l'Union européenne** Treaty on European Union

traitement [trɛtmɑ̃] NM **1** *(comportement à l'égard de qn), Méd* treatment; *(d'un sujet par un auteur)* treatment, handling; **mauvais t.** ill-treatment, maltreatment; *Méd* **prescrire un t.** to prescribe treatment; **premier t.** initial treatment; **t. chirurgical** surgery; **malade en t.** patient under(going) treatment; **t. de choc/de fond** shock/long-term treatment **2** *Tech (de matières premières)* processing, treatment; *(de l'eau)* treatment; *Constr* **t. superficiel** *(des routes etc)* surfacing; *Ind* **capacité de t.** processing *or* handling capacity **3** *Ordinat* processing; **données en t., capacité** *ou* **débit de t.** throughput; **machine à** *ou* **de t. de texte** word processor; **logiciel de t. de texte** word processor, word processing software; **unité de t.** task, job **4** *(rémunération)* pay, salary; **t. de base** basic pay *or* salary; **t. fixe** fixed salary; **t. initial** starting salary; **sans t.** *(secrétaire)* honorary; *(magistrat)* unsalaried

▸▸ *Ordinat* **t. automatique de l'information** *ou* **des informations** automatic data pro-

cessing; *Com* **t. des commandes** order processing; *Ordinat* **t. différé par lots** batch processing; **t. à distance** teleprocessing; **t. des données** data processing, DP; **t. électronique de l'information** electronic data processing, EDP; **t. de faveur** preferential treatment, red carpet treatment; **t. d'images** image processing; **t. de l'information** *ou* **des informations** data processing, DP, information processing; **t. par lots** batch processing; **t. multitâche** multitasking processing; *Ordinat* **t. en temps réel** real time processing; **t. de texte** word processing, WP; *(logiciel)* word processor, word processing software; *(machine)* word processor; **réaliser qch par t. de texte** to word process sth; *Ordinat* **t. de texte à balises** word processing with embedded visible commands; **t. vectoriel** vector processing

traiter [trɛte] VT **1** *(se conduire envers)* to treat; **t. qn en ami/enfant** to treat sb like *or* as a friend/a child; **t. qn d'égal (à égal)** to treat sb as an *or* one's equal; **t. qn avec douceur** to treat *or* handle sb gently; **t. qn avec condescendance** to be condescending towards sb, to patronize sb; **je ne supporterai pas plus longtemps de me faire t. comme cela!** I won't take much more of being treated like this!, I won't take much more of this treatment!

2 *(qualifier)* to call; **t. qn de lâche** to call sb a coward; **se faire t. de lâche** to be called a coward; **elle l'a traité de tous les noms** she called him all the names under the sun

3 *Méd (patient, maladie)* to treat; **elle se fait t. pour un cancer** she's being treated for cancer, she is having *or* undergoing treatment for cancer; **tu devrais faire t. ça** you ought to get it treated

4 *Tech (matière première, minerai)* to process; *(bois)* to treat; *Agr (vignobles, cultures etc)* to treat, to spray; **oranges non traitées** unsprayed oranges

5 *Ordinat (informations)* to process; **données non traitées** raw data

6 *Litt Vieilli (régaler)* to entertain

7 *Com (marché etc)* to negotiate; *(affaire)* to handle

8 *(s'occuper de) (sujet, problème, question etc) (d'un auteur, un artiste, un élève, un article)* to deal with; *(demande d'emploi, dossier de bourse etc)* to process; **l'auteur traite bien le sujet** the author handles the subject well; **comment Paris-Match traite-t-il cet événement?** how does Paris-Match deal with *or* handle *or* cover the event?; **t. une accusation avec mépris** to treat an accusation with scorn

VI 1 *(négocier)* **t. avec** to deal with; *(créanciers)* to negotiate with **2 t. de** *(d'un livre, un écrivain etc) (sujet, problème etc)* to deal with

VPR se traiter 1 *(réciproque)* to treat each other; **elles se traitent de tous les noms** they call each other all the names under the sun **2** *(se négocier)* to be dealt with **3** *(d'un sujet, d'un écrivain etc)* to be dealt with; **cela se traite facilement** that can be easily dealt with **4** *(d'une maladie)* to be treated; **cela se traite très bien, maintenant** it can be treated now, there's treatment for it now

traiteur [trɛtœr] NM **1** *Com* caterer **2** *Arch (restaurateur)* restaurateur

traître, traîtresse [trɛtr, trɛtrɛs] ADJ *(personne)* treacherous; *(escalier, crevasse etc)* dangerous, treacherous; *(soleil)* treacherous, strong; *(vin)* deceptively strong; *Fam* **pas un t. mot** not a single word

N 1 traitor, *f* traitress; *Iron, Hum* **ah, le t., il ne nous disait rien!** the sly devil, he didn't tell us!; **être t. à sa patrie** to be a traitor to one's country, to commit treason; **prendre qn en t.** to set out to trap sb, to set a trap for sb; **agir en t.** to be underhanded **2** *Théâtre* **le t.** the villain

traîtreusement [tretrøzmã] ADV *(agir)* treacherously; **se venger t.** to take a traitor's revenge

traîtrise [tretriz] NF **1** *(comportement)* treachery, treacherousness **2** *(action)* (piece of) treachery

trajectoire [traʒɛktwar] NF *(d'une étoile, une comète, un avion, un électron, une balle etc)* path, trajectory; *Météo* depression; *Aviat* **t. de vol** flight path; **t. de collision** collision course

trajet [traʒɛ] NM **1** *(voyage)* journey; *(distance)* distance; *(itinéraire)* route; **j'ai fait une partie du t. en avion** I flew part of the way; **faire le t. en voiture** to do the journey by car; **j'ai dû faire le t. à pied** I had to walk all the way; **j'ai dû faire le t. dans l'autre sens pour le chercher** I had to come/go all the way back to get it; **un t. en voiture/autobus** a car/bus journey or ride; **il y a bien deux heures de t.** it takes a good two hours; **il a deux heures de t. pour aller au bureau** he has a two-hour journey to the office **2** *(d'une artère, d'un nerf etc)* course; *Mil (d'un projectile), Élec (d'un courant)* path; **t. de papier** *(dans une imprimante)* paper path

tralala [tralala] NM INV *Fam* **en grand t.** *(se marier)* with a lot of fuss; **pas la peine d'en faire tout un t.** there's no point making a great fuss about it; **... et tout le t.** ... et cetera, et cetera, ... and all the rest of it ▸ INT **j'ai gagné, t.!** ha-ha, I've won!

tram [tram] NM *Fam* = **tramway**

tramage [tramaʒ] NM *Ordinat* rastering

tramail, -ails [tramaj] NM *Pêche* trammel (net)

trame [tram] NF **1** *Tex* woof, weft; *Fig (de la vie)* fabric; **usé jusqu'à la t.** *(pull, tapis)* threadbare; *Fig* **la t. du récit** the framework of the story; *Fig* **la t. de l'histoire** the storyline **2** *Arch (complot)* plot, conspiracy **3** *Phot, Typ (écran)* (half-tone) screen **4** *TV* raster; **t. (double)** frame **5** *Typ* **t. de maquette** layout sheet

tramer [trame] VT **1** *Tex, Fig (intrigue d'un roman)* to weave **2** *(combiner) (complot)* to devise, *Fam* to hatch; **je me demande ce qu'il est en train de t.** I wonder what he's up to **3** *Phot* **t. un cliché** to take a negative through a screen
▸ VPR **se tramer il se trame quelque chose** there's something going on, there's something in the wind or afoot

traminot [tramino] NM tram or *Am* streetcar worker

tramontane [tramõtan] NF **1** *(vent)* tramontana **2** *Arch (étoile)* north star; *Fig* **perdre la t.** to lose one's bearings; *(devenir fou)* to go off one's head

tramp [trãp] NM *Naut* tramp (steamer)

trampoline [trãpɔlin] NM *(toile)* trampoline; *(sport)* trampolining; **faire du t.** to go or do trampolining

tramway [tramwɛ] NM tram, *Am* streetcar; **voyager en t.** to travel by tram

tranchant [trãʃã] ADJ **1** *(outil, épée, bord etc)* sharp **2** *Fig (paroles, ton)* trenchant, peremptory, decisive; *(personne)* assertive, peremptory
▸ NM **1** *(d'un couteau, d'une épée etc)* (cutting) edge; *(d'une cale)* thin end; *(de la main)* edge; **à deux tranchants, à double t.** *(épée, couteau etc)* two-edged; *Fig* **argument à double t.** argument that cuts both ways; *Fig* **cette décision est à double t.** the decision is a two-edged sword **2** *(de tanneur)* fleshing knife

tranche [trãʃ] NF **1** *(morceau coupé) (de pain, de melon, de viande etc)* slice; *(de bacon)* rasher; **en tranches** in slices, sliced; **vous le voulez en tranches?** would you like

it sliced?; *Culin* **t. napolitaine** Neapolitan ice (cream); *Culin* **t. grasse** *(morceau de bœuf)* round, top rump; **morceau dans la t.** = piece of topside; *Fam* **s'en payer une t.** to have the time of one's life **2** *(de marbre, de pierre)* slab **3** *(bord, côté)* (d'une pièce de monnaie, d'une cale, d'une planche) edge; *(d'un livre)* (cut) edge; **doré sur t.** *(livre)* with gilt edges, gilt-edged **4** *(série, section)* (de chiffres) group, block; *(d'actions)* block, portion; *(d'un crédit)* instalment, *Am* instalment; *(d'assistance financière internationale)* tranche; *(d'un programme immobilier)* stage, portion; *Rail* **t. de voitures** portion; **t. des salariés moyens** middle-income bracket **5** *Tech (coupe)* section; **t. verticale** vertical section **6** *Ordinat* wafer; **microprocesseur en tranches** bit slice microprocessor
▸▸ **t. d'âge** age bracket or group or band; *Radio, TV* **t. horaire** (time) slot; **t. d'imposition** tax band or bracket; **t. de paiement** instalment, *Am* installment; **t. de prix** price bracket; **t. de revenu** income group; **les gens dans les tranches de revenus les plus élevées** people in the upper income brackets; *Fig* **t. de vie** slice or cross-section of life

tranché [trãʃe] ADJ *Fig (couleur, motif etc)* definite, distinct; *(opinion)* definite, clear-cut; *(refus)* blunt; **les avis sont très tranchés** opinions are very clear-cut, people are very definite in their opinion

tranchée [trãʃe] NF **1** *(fossé)* trench; *Agr* drain; *Rail* cutting; *Mil* **guerre de tranchées** trench warfare **2** *(dans une forêt)* cutting; **t. garde-feu** firebreak **3** *Méd* **tranchées** colic

tranchée-abri, *pl* **tranchées-abris** NF *Mil* dugout

tranchefile [trãʃfil] NF *(d'un livre relié)* headband

trancher [trãʃe] VT **1** *(cordage, câble etc)* to cut; *(bras, membre, tête)* to sever; **t. la gorge à qn** to slit or cut sb's throat; **t. la tête à qn** to cut off or chop off sb's head; **qu'on lui tranche la tête!** off with his/her head! **2** *(discussion)* to cut short; *(question, différend)* to settle (once and for all); *(problème, difficulté)* to resolve, to make short work of; **voilà qui tranche la question!** that settles it!; **tranchons là** let's stop there
▸ VI **1** *(décider)* to decide, to reach a decision; **t. dans le vif** *Chir* to cut into healthy tissue; *Fig* to adopt drastic measures; **il tranche sur tout** he's always laying down the law **2** *(de couleurs etc)* to contrast strongly (**sur** with), to stand out (**sur** against)
▸ VPR **se trancher se t. le doigt** to sever one's finger

tranchet [trãʃɛ] NM **1** *(de serrurier etc)* anvil cutter **2** *(de tanneur)* paring knife

trancheur, -euse [trãʃœr, -øz] NM *Tech, Min* cutter; *Pêche* cod gutter
▸ NF **trancheuse** stone saw

tranchoir [trãʃwar] NM *(planche)* chopping board

tranquille [trãkil] ADJ **1** *(calme, paisible)* (personne, vie etc), Com (marché) quiet; *(soirée)* still, peaceful, quiet; *(mer)* calm, still, *Litt* tranquil; *(conscience, esprit etc)* easy, untroubled; *(sommeil)* untroubled, peaceful; *(boussole)* steady; *Fam* **un père t.** (homme, bébé) a quiet one; **se tenir t.** to keep still; **j'adore cet endroit, je m'y sens vraiment t.** I love this place, I really feel at peace here; **travailler t.** to work in peace; **vous pouvez dormir t.** you can sleep in peace or rest easy; **laissez-moi t.** leave me alone or in peace, let me be; *Fam* **laisse ce vase t.!** leave that vase alone!; **laisse ça t., je m'en occuperai** don't bother with that, I'll take care of it; **soyez t.** don't worry, set your mind at rest or at ease; **soyez t., il reviendra!** he'll come back, don't you worry!; **avec ce**

plan d'épargne/ces chaussures en cuir, je suis t. with this savings plan/these leather shoes I don't need to worry; **elle ne m'a pas rappelé, je ne suis pas t.** she hasn't phoned me back, I'm anxious or worried or not easy in my mind; **je ne suis pas t. dans cette grande maison** I get nervous in this big house; *Fam* **tu peux être t. que ...** you can be sure that ...; **je n'ai pas la conscience t.** my conscience is bothering me; **moi, j'ai la conscience t.** my conscience is clear; **faire qch la conscience t.** to do sth with a clear conscience
2 *(sans bruit) (ville, quartier)* quiet, peaceful; **est-ce que nous pouvons aller dans un endroit t.?** can we go somewhere quiet?; **se tenir t.** *(ne rien dire)* to keep quiet

tranquillement [trãkilmã] ADV *(répondre, examiner, travailler etc)* calmly, quietly; *(vivre)* quietly, peacefully; *(dormir)* peacefully; *(partir)* with an easy mind, with a clear conscience, without worrying

tranquillisant [trãkilizã] ADJ *(nouvelles)* reassuring; *(paroles, voix)* reassuring, soothing, calming; *(effet)* soothing, calming; *Pharm* tranquillizing; *Pharm* **avoir un effet t.** to act as a sedative; **cela n'est pas très t.** that's not very reassuring
▸ NM *Pharm* tranquillizer

tranquilliser [trãkilize] VT **t. qn** to reassure sb, to set sb's mind at rest; **ça te tranquillisera** it will set your mind at rest or give you peace of mind
▸ VPR **se tranquilliser** to stop worrying; **tranquillisez-vous** don't worry, set your mind at rest

tranquillité [trãkilite] NF **1** *(calme) (de la mer)* calmness, stillness; *(de la campagne)* stillness, quietness, peace; *(de la nature)* tranquillity; *(du sommeil)* peacefulness; **j'ai besoin de t.** I need some peace and quiet; **c'est un enfant d'une grande t.** he's a very quiet or placid child; **t. d'esprit** peace of mind; **troubler la t. publique** to disturb the peace; **en toute t.** without being disturbed; *(sans souci)* with an easy mind, without worrying, with a clear conscience; **je vais pouvoir travailler en toute t.** I'll be able to work in peace (and quiet) **2** *(absence de bruit) (d'une ville)* quietness

tranquillos [trãkilos] ADV *Fam (tranquillement)* vas-y **t.**, inutile de faire des excès de vitesse take your time, there's no need to break the speed limit; **ils étaient dans le canapé en train de siroter mon whisky, t.** they were on the sofa sipping away at my whisky, without a care in the world

trans- [trãs, trãz] PRÉF trans-

transaction [trãzaksjõ] NF **1** *Com, Fin* transaction; **transactions** transactions, dealings; **transactions bancaires** bank transactions; **transactions boursières** Stock Exchange transactions; **transactions commerciales** business transactions; *Bourse* **t. au comptant** spot transaction; *Bourse* **t. de clôture** closing trade; *Banque* **t. par carte** card transaction; *Bourse* **transactions hors bourse** after-hours dealings, street dealing; *Bourse* **transactions à terme** futures; *Banque* **t. valeur jour** value today trade **2** *(arrangement)* compromise

transactionnel, -elle [trãzaksjɔnɛl] ADJ **solution transactionnelle** compromise; *Psy* **analyse transactionnelle** transactional analysis

transafricain [trãzafrikɛ̃] ADJ transafrican, cross-Africa

transalpin [trãzalpɛ̃] ADJ transalpine

transaméricain [trãzamerikɛ̃] ADJ transamerican

transat [trãzat] NM *Fam* deck chair

transatlantique [trãzatlãtik] ADJ transatlantic
 NM **1** *(paquebot)* (transatlantic) liner **2** *(chaise longue)* deck chair

transbahuter [trãsbayte] *Fam* VT *(affaires, enfants)* to cart, to lug
 VPR se transbahuter to shift

transbordement [trãsbɔrdəmã] NM *Naut* transhipment; *Rail* transfer

transborder [trãsbɔrde] VT *Naut* to tranship; *Rail (passagers, marchandises)* to transfer

transbordeur, -euse [trãsbɔrdœr] ADJ, NM (pont) t. transporter bridge

transcanadien, -ienne [trãskanadjɛ̃, -jɛn] ADJ trans-Canada
 NF la Transcanadienne *(autoroute)* the Trans-Canada Highway

transcendance [trãsãdãs] NF *Phil, Rel etc* transcendence, transcendency

transcendant [trãsãdã] ADJ **1** *Phil, Rel etc* transcendent; *Fam* ce/il n'est pas t. it's/he's not much to write home about, it's/he's nothing great **2** *Math* transcendental

transcendantal, -ale, -aux, -ales [trãsãdãtal, -o] ADJ *Phil* transcendental

transcendantalisme [trãsãdãtalism] NM *Phil* transcendentalism

transcender [trãsãde] VT to transcend
 VPR se transcender to surpass oneself

transcodage [trãskɔdaʒ] NM *Ordinat* transcribing, transcoding; *TV* standards conversion

transcoder [trãskɔde] VT *Ordinat* to transcribe

transcodeur [trãskɔdœr] NM *TV* transcoder, standards converter; *Ordinat* transcoder

transconteneur [trãskɔ̃t(ə)nœr] NM transcontainer; *(navire)* transcontainer ship

transcontinental, -ale, -aux, -ales [trãskɔ̃tinãtal, -o] ADJ transcontinental

transcriptase [trãskriptaz] NF t. inverse *ou* reverse t. reverse transcriptase

transcripteur [trãskriptœr] NM transcriber

transcription [trãskripsjɔ̃] NF **1** *(action)* transcription, transcribing; *(dans un autre alphabet)* transliteration; t. phonétique phonetic transcription; t. génétique (genetic) transcription **2** *(texte)* transcript; *Mus* transcription; t. à l'état civil = certified copy of registry office document

transcrire [trãskrir] VT *(conj like* écrire*)* **1** *(recopier) (manuscrit), Mus (morceau)* to transcribe; t. une lettre à la machine to type a letter **2** *Jur (divorce etc)* to register; *Com* to post **3** *(dans un autre alphabet) (texte etc)* to transcribe, to transliterate; t. un livre en braille to copy a book in Braille

transculturel, -elle [trãskyltyrɛl] ADJ cross-cultural

transcutané [trãskytane] ADJ transcutaneous

transdermique [trãsdɛrmik] ADJ transdermal; timbre t. skin patch, transdermal patch

transdisciplinaire [trãsdisiplinɛr] ADJ interdisciplinary

transducteur [trãsdyktœr] NM *Phys, Électron* transducer

transe [trãs] NF **1** transes *(anxiété)* fear; *Vieilli* être dans les transes to be sick with worry, to be out of one's mind with anxiety **2** *(hypnose)* (hypnotic) trance; en t. *(médium), Fig (fans)* in a trance; entrer en t. to go into a trance; *Fig Fam (se mettre en colère)* to hit the ceiling

transept [trãsɛpt] NM *Archit* transept

transférable [trãsferabl] ADJ transferable

transfèrement [trãsfɛrmã] NM *(de prisonnier etc)* transfer; t. cellulaire transfer by police van

transférer [trãsfere] VT (je transfère, n. transférons; je transférerai) **1** *(dans un autre lieu) (détenu, siège social etc)* to transfer (à to); *Rel (évêque)* to translate; t. de l'argent d'un compte à un autre to transfer money from one account to another **2** *(céder) (marchandises etc)* to transfer, to make over, to assign (à to); *(propriété)* to convey (à to) **3** *Psy (affection etc)* to transfer (sur to) **4** *Ordinat (données)* to transfer

transfériste [trãsferist] N *(dans l'industrie du tourisme)* transferist

transfert [trãsfɛr] NM **1** *(d'un prisonnier, d'un siège social), Sport (d'un footballeur etc)* transfer; *(de population)* resettlement (dans in) **2** *(cession) (du stock, de droits etc)* transfer, assignment, making over; *(d'un domaine)* conveyance **3** *Psy* transference; faire un t. sur qn to use sb as an object of transference; cela fait partie du t. it's part of the transference process
 ▸▸ t. d'actions transfer of shares; *Tél* t. d'appel call transfer; t. de capitaux transfer of capital, capital transfer; *Banque* t. par CCP giro transfer; *Compta* t. de charges expense transfer, transfer of charges; *Compta* t. de créances assignment of accounts receivable *or* of debts; t. de devises currency transfer; *Ordinat* t. de données data transfer; *Ordinat* t. de fichiers file transfer; t. de fonds électronique, t. électronique de fonds electronic funds transfer, EFT

transfiguration [trãsfigyrasjɔ̃] NF transfiguration

transfigurer [trãsfigyre] VT to transfigure

transfiler [trãsfile] VT *Naut* **1** *(voiles etc)* to lace **2** *(cordage)* to snub

transfo [trãsfo] NM *Élec Fam* transformer

transformable [trãsfɔrmabl] ADJ *(canapé, fauteuil etc)* convertible

transformateur, -trice [trãsfɔrmatœr, -tris] *Élec* ADJ transforming; *(station)* transformer
 NM transformer

transformation [trãsfɔrmasjɔ̃] NF **1** *(changement)* change; *(radicale)* transformation; *(d'un local)* conversion; la t. de l'eau en glace the transformation of water to ice; acteur à transformations quick-change artist(e); industrie de t. processing industry; *Math* t. algébrique algebraic transformation **2** *Élec* rapport de t. transformer ratio; *Électron* t. de signaux signal transformation **3** *Rugby (d'un essai)* conversion; faire une t. to convert (a try)

transformer [trãsfɔrme] VT **1** *(personne, rapports etc)* to change; *(radicalement)* to transform; *(local, maison)* to convert, to remodel; ils ont transformé l'appartement en l'agrandissant they've transformed the flat by making it bigger; cette expérience l'a profondément transformé the experience has caused a profound change in him *or* has transformed him; t. en to turn *or* change *or* transform into; l'école fut transformée en cinéma the school was turned *or* converted into a cinema; la sorcière l'a transformé en souris the witch turned him into a mouse **2** *Math (équation)* to transform **3** *Rugby (essai)* to convert **4** *Électron* to transform, to map **5** *(en logique) (proposition)* to convert
 VPR se transformer to be transformed, to change; tout se transforme everything changes; se t. en to turn into; se t. en monstre/papillon to turn *or* change *or* be transformed into a monster/butterfly; se t. en haine/en cauchemar to turn into hate/a nightmare

transformisme [trãsfɔrmism] NM *Phil etc* transformism

transformiste [trãsfɔrmist] ADJ *Phil etc* transformist

N *Phil etc* transformist; *(qui s'habille en femme)* drag queen; *(dans cabaret)* drag artist; spectacle de transformistes drag show

transfrontalier, -ière [trãsfrɔ̃talje, -jɛr] ADJ cross-border

transfuge [trãsfyʒ] N *Pol, Mil, Fig* defector

transfusé, -ée [trãsfyze] ADJ sang t. transfused blood
 N le nombre des transfusés the number of people receiving (blood) transfusions

transfuser [trãsfyze] VT *(sang)* to transfuse; *(malade)* to give a (blood) transfusion to, to transfuse

transfusion [trãsfyzjɔ̃] NF (blood) transfusion; faire une t. à un malade to give a patient a transfusion; t. sanguine blood transfusion; centre de t. sanguine blood transfusion centre; t. d'échange exchange transfusion

transgène [trãsʒɛn] NM transgene

transgenèse [trãsʒənɛz] NF transgenesis

transgénique [trãsʒenik] ADJ transgenic

transgresser [trãsgrese] VT *(règlement, loi)* to infringe, to contravene, *Fml* to transgress; *(interdit)* to infringe; *(ordres)* to disobey

transgresseur [trãsgresœr] NM *Litt* transgressor

transgression [trãsgresjɔ̃] NF *(du règlement, de la loi)* infringement, contravention, *Fml* transgression; *(d'ordres)* disobeying

transhumance [trãzymãs] NF move from/to summer pastures, *Spéc* transhumance

transhumant [trãzymã] ADJ moving from/to summer pastures, *Spéc* transhumant

transhumer [trãzyme] VTI to move from/to summer pastures

transi [trãzi] ADJ paralysed (de peur with fear); t. (de froid) freezing, chilled to the bone; *Iron* un amoureux t. a bashful lover

transiger [trãziʒe] VI (je transigeai(s); n. transigeons) **1** to compromise (avec with; sur on); t. sur ses principes/avec sa conscience to compromise one's principles/ one's conscience; je ne transigerai pas avec mon devoir/le règlement I refuse to compromise *or* I am intransigent when it comes to my duty/the rules; je ne transigerai pas sur l'honnêteté I refuse to be anything less than totally honest; il ne transige pas sur l'honnêteté he is uncompromisingly honest, he makes no compromises when it comes to a question of honesty **2** *Can (négocier)* to negotiate

Transilvanie [trãsilvani] NF Transylvania

transir [trãzir] VT *(du vent etc)* to chill to the bone; *(de la peur)* to paralyse
 VI *Arch (de froid)* to be chilled to the bone; *(de peur)* to be paralysed with fear

transistor [trãzistɔr] NM **1** *Électron (dispositif)* transistor; à transistors transistorized; t. en couche mince thin film transistor, TFT **2** *(poste de radio)* transistor (radio)

transistorisé [trãzistɔrize] ADJ *Électron* transistorized

transistoriser [trãzistɔrize] VT *Électron* to transistorize

transit [trãzit] NM **1** transit; en t. in transit; passagers en t. *(dans un aéroport)* passengers in transit, transfer passengers; *Aviat* salle de t. transit *or* transfer lounge; *Com* t. communautaire Community transit; marchandises de t. goods for transit; maison de t. forwarding agency **2** *Électron* t. par bande perforée tape relay
 ▸▸ *Com* t. douanier Customs transit; *Méd* t. intestinal intestinal transit; favoriser le t. intestinal to encourage regular bowel movements; favorise le t. intestinal keeps you regular

troisièmement [trwazjɛmmɑ̃] ADV thirdly, in the third place

trois-mâts NM INV *Naut* three-masted ship, three-master

trois-pièces NM INV 1 *(appartement)* three-room(ed) flat *or Am* apartment 2 *(costume)* three-piece suit

trois-quarts NM INV 1 *Rugby* three-quarter; **t. aile/centre** wing/centre three-quarter; **t. arrière** three-quarter back 2 *(manteau)* three-quarter-length coat

trois-quatre NM INV *Mus* three-four time

troll [trɔl] NM *Myth* troll

trolley [trɔle] NM 1 *(caténaire)* trolley pole and wheel; **perche de t.** trolley pole 2 *(véhicule)* trolleybus

trolleybus [trɔlebys] NM trolleybus

trombe [trɔ̃b] NF 1 *(cyclone)* waterspout 2 **t. de vent** whirlwind; **t. d'eau** cloudburst; *Fig Fam* **entrer/sortir en t.** to tear *or* hurtle in/out, to burst in/out (like a whirlwind); **il est passé/parti en t.** he tore *or* hurtled past/off, he went past/left in a cloud of dust

trombine [trɔ̃bin] NF *Arg (visage)* mug

trombinoscope [trɔ̃binɔskɔp] NM *Fam (d'une association, d'un groupe etc)* rogues' gallery

tromblon [trɔ̃blɔ̃] NM *(fusil)* blunderbuss

trombone [trɔ̃bɔn] NM 1 *Mus (instrument)* trombone; *(instrumentiste)* trombone (player), trombonist; **t. à coulisse/à pistons** slide/valve trombone 2 *(agrafe)* paper clip

trompe [trɔ̃p] NF 1 *Mus* horn; **t. de brume/chasse** fog/hunting horn; *Fig* **publier qch à son de t.** to trumpet sth abroad 2 *Zool (d'un animal, d'un insecte)* proboscis; *(d'un éléphant)* trunk 3 *Anat* **t. d'Eustache/de Fallope** Eustachian/Fallopian tube 4 *Archit* pendentive, squinch 5 *Tech* pump; *Métal* blast pump, trompe

trompe-la-mort N INV *Fam (volontaire)* daredevil

trompe-l'œil NM INV 1 *Beaux-Arts* trompe l'œil *(painting)*; **en t.** *(peinture, scène etc)* trompe l'œil; **peindre en t.** to do a trompe l'œil painting, to use trompe l'œil techniques 2 *Fig Péj* bluff, window-dressing

tromper [trɔ̃pe] VT 1 *(abuser)* to deceive, to (deliberately) mislead, to take in; **cela ne trompe personne** nobody's taken in, nobody's fooled; **t. qn sur qn/qch** to deceive *or* mislead sb about sb/sth; **il est incapable de t. qui que ce soit** he is totally incapable of deceit

2 *(être infidèle à) (femme, mari)* to deceive, to be unfaithful to, *Fam* to cheat on, to two-time; **il trompe sa femme avec sa secrétaire** he's having an affair with his secretary

3 *(induire en erreur)* to mislead (**sur** as, to); *(decevoir) (espoirs de qn)* to disappoint; **son air de s'y connaître m'a trompé** I was misled *or* fooled *or* taken in by the fact that he seemed to know what he was doing; **ne vous laissez pas t.** don't be misled, don't be fooled, don't be taken in; **ça a l'air lourd, mais c'est ce qui vous trompe** it looks heavy, that's what's so misleading; **je ne voulais pas t. son attente** I didn't want to disappoint him; **se laisser t. par les apparences** to be taken in by appearances

4 *(échapper à) (contrôle, surveillance, vigilance)* to elude, to escape

5 *Fig (ennui)* to relieve; *(temps)* to while away; **t. la faim** to stave off (one's) hunger

VPR **se tromper 1** *(commettre une erreur)* to be mistaken, to be wrong, to make a mistake; **c'est justement en ça en quoi tu te trompes** that's just where you're wrong; **je dois me t.** I must be mistaken, I must be wrong; **j'ai dû me t.** I must have made a mistake; **si/à**

moins que je ne me trompe if I'm not/unless I'm mistaken; **ou je me trompe** or I'm much mistaken; **tout le monde peut se t.** anybody can make a mistake, we all make mistakes; **se t. dans les dates/les proportions** to get the dates/the proportions wrong; **se t. dans son calcul** to get one's sums wrong, *Fml* to be out in one's reckoning; *Tél* **vous devez vous t. de numéro** you must have the wrong number; **je me suis trompé de direction/de maison** I went the wrong way/to the wrong house; **je me suis trompé de Laurent!** I got the wrong Laurent!; **se t. d'heure/de jour** to mistake the time/day, to get the time/day wrong; **je ne m'y trompe pas, du reste** I'm not fooled *or* taken in; **elle ressemble à sa sœur à s'y t.** you can't tell her and her sister apart; **il n'y a pas à s'y t.** there's no mistake about it; **que l'on ne s'y trompe pas** make no mistake about it; **vous m'avez fait me t.** you made me make a mistake; **tu es en train de la faire se t.** you're confusing her 2 *(entre époux)* **se t. (mutuellement)** to be unfaithful to *or Fam* to cheat on each other

tromperie [trɔ̃pri] NF deceit, deception; *(en affaires)* fraud; **j'en ai assez de tes tromperies** I've had enough of your deceit *or* deceitfulness; **il y a t. sur la marchandise** this isn't what it was said to be

trompeter [trɔ̃pete] VT (**je trompette**; **je trompetterai**) *(nouvelles)* to shout from the rooftops

trompette [trɔ̃pet] NF 1 *Mus* trumpet; *Mil* **jouer/sonner de la t.** to play/sound the trumpet; **t. de jazz** jazz trumpet; **à la t., Louis Armstrong!** on (the) trumpet, Louis Armstrong!; *Litt* **la t. du jugement dernier** the last trump; *Fig* **nez en t.** turned-up nose 2 *(coquillage)* trumpet shell

▶ NM trumpet (player), trumpeter

▶ ▶ **t. bouchée** muted trumpet; **t. de cavalerie** bugle

trompette-de-la-mort, *pl* **trompettes-de-la-mort** NF *(champignon)* horn of plenty

trompettiste [trɔ̃petist] N *Mus* trumpet (player), trumpeter

trompeur, -euse [trɔ̃pœr, -øz] ADJ 1 *(volontairement) (personne, paroles etc)* deceitful 2 *(symptôme, apparences etc)* deceptive, misleading; *(publicité)* misleading

▶ N deceiver, cheat; *Prov* **à t., t. et demi** = cheats never win

trompeusement [trɔ̃pøzmɑ̃] ADV deceptively

tronc [trɔ̃] NM 1 *(d'un arbre, d'un corps)* trunk; **homme-/femme-t.** armless and legless man/woman 2 *(d'une famille)* parent stock 3 *Rel* poor box 4 **Fam se casser le t.** to strain oneself; **il ne s'est pas cassé le t.** he didn't kill himself, he didn't overexert himself 5 *Math* **t. de cône/pyramide** truncated cone/pyramid

▶ ▶ *Univ etc* **t. commun** core syllabus

troncature [trɔ̃katyr] NF *Ordinat* truncation

tronche [trɔ̃ʃ] NF 1 *Fam (tête)* nut, bonce; *(visage)* mug, kisser; **sa t. ne me revient pas** I don't like the look of him; **il a une sale t.** he's an ugly-looking customer; *Fam* **faire la t.** to sulk 2 *(personne intelligente)* brain, brainy person; **ce mec-là, c'est une t.!** that guy's a real brain *or* so brainy!

troncher [trɔ̃ʃe] VT *Vulg* to fuck, to screw

tronçon [trɔ̃sɔ̃] NM *(de chemin de fer, d'autoroute)* section; *(d'une canalisation)* section, length; *(de phrase, de texte etc)* part, portion; *(d'épée, de lance, de mât etc)* (broken) stump; **t. de bois** log

tronconique [trɔ̃kɔnik] ADJ segment t. truncated segment

tronçonnage [trɔ̃sɔnaʒ], **tronçonnement** [trɔ̃sɔnmɑ̃] NM cutting into lengths *or* pieces

tronçonner [trɔ̃sɔne] VT to cut up (into lengths *or* pieces)

tronçonneuse [trɔ̃sɔnøz] NF *(à chaîne)* chain saw; *(circulaire)* circular saw

trône [tron] NM 1 *(de roi, pape etc)* throne; **monter sur le t.** to come to the throne; **placer** *ou* **mettre qn sur le t.** to put sb on the throne 2 *Fam Hum (siège des cabinets)* **être sur le t.** to be on the throne

trôner [trone] VI 1 *(d'un monarque)*, *Fig (d'une personne)* to sit enthroned 2 *(d'objets)* to occupy a place of honour *or Am* honor; **son diplôme trône sur la cheminée** his diploma occupies a place of honour on the mantelpiece; **toutes ses décorations trônaient dans son bureau** all his decorations were prominently displayed in his office 3 *Péj (faire l'important)* to lord it

tronqué [trɔ̃ke] ADJ *(colonne, pyramide)* truncated; *(mât)* stub; *(texte)* cut, truncated

tronquer [trɔ̃ke] VT *(arbre)* to pollard; *Fig (roman, scène etc)* to cut, to shorten, to truncate

trop [tro] ADV 1 *(devant un adj)* too, over-; *(devant un adv)* too; **c'est t. difficile** it's too difficult; **un travail t. difficile** too difficult a job; **t. aimable** [trɔpɛmabl] too *or* extremely kind; **aliments t. riches** over-rich food; **t. attaché à** too attached to, overfond of; **t. cuit** overcooked; **être t. habillé** to have too many clothes on; **vous n'êtes que t. généreux** you are much too *or* far too *or* overly generous; **t. fatigué** too tired (**pour faire** to do), over-tired; *Litt* **par t. généreux** far too generous; **t. beau pour être vrai** too good to be true; **vous n'êtes pas t. en avance** you're none too early; **je ne me sens pas t. à l'aise** I'm not overly comfortable, I'm none too comfortable; **ça va? – pas t. mal** how are things? – not bad at all *or* not too bad; **ça te plaît/c'est bien fait? – pas t. mal** do you like it/is it good? – it's not bad at all; **c'était t. drôle** it was too funny for words *or* just too funny; **le trou était t. étroit pour qu'un rat entrât par là** the hole was too narrow for a rat to get in by; **c'est t. grand pour qu'on puisse le mettre dans la voiture** it's too big to go in the car; *Fam* **il est vraiment t.!** he's too much! VOIR GRAMMAIRE A5

2 *(avec un verbe)* too much, over-; **t. travailler** to overwork, to work too much *or* too hard; **t. manger** to overeat, to eat too much; **boire t., t. boire** to drink to excess *or* too much; **t. simplifier** to oversimplify; **je ne l'ai que t. dit** I've said it time and time again; **je ne la connais que t.** I know her all *or* only too well; **je l'ai t. aimé** [trɔpeme] I loved him too much; **il n'y tient pas t.** he's not too bothered (about it); *Fam* **ça te plaît? – pas t.** do you like it? – not (very) much; **ne vous y fiez pas t., il ne faut pas t. vous y fier** don't count on it too much; **je ne le croirais pas t.** I wouldn't put too much faith in what he says, I wouldn't be too ready to believe him; **on ne saurait t. le répéter** it cannot be repeated too often; **je ne sais pas t.** I'm not too sure; **je ne sais t. que dire/penser** I hardly know *or* I don't quite know what to say/think

3 *(emploi nominal) (quantité)* too much; *(nombre)* too many; **t. de** *(bruit, sel, travail etc)* too much; *(amis, choses, problèmes etc)* too many; **je n'aurai pas t. d'une heure pour le faire** it will take me a good hour; **il a t. d'expérience pour se tromper** he is too experienced to make a mistake; **elle n'a fait preuve que de t. de patience** she has shown far too much patience; **j'ai une carte de t.** *ou* **en t.** I have one card too many; **payer 100 euros de t.** *ou* **en t.** to pay 100 euros too much; **c'est une fois de t.** that's once too often; **quand j'ai du temps de t.** when I have time to spare; **être/se sentir de t.** to be/feel in the way *or* unwelcome *or* de trop; *Fam* **tra-**

vailler de t. to work too hard *or* too much, to overwork; *Fam* **boire de t.** to drink too much, *Fam* to overdo the drink; **t., c'est t.!** enough is enough!; **c'en est t.!** this really is the limit!; **il allait t. en dire** *ou* **en dire t.** he was going to say too much

trope [trɔp] NM *Littér* trope

trophée [trɔfe] NM trophy

tropical, -ale, -aux, -ales [trɔpikal, -o] ADJ *(plante, climat, température etc)* tropical; *(vêtement)* for wear in the tropics

tropique [trɔpik] NM *Astron, Géog (cercle)* tropic; **le t. du Cancer/du Capricorne** the tropic of Cancer/of Capricorn
▪ NMPL **les tropiques** *(région)* the tropics; **sous les tropiques** in the tropics

tropisme [trɔpism] NM *Biol* tropism

troposphère [trɔpɔsfɛr] NF *Météo* troposphere

trop-perçu, *pl* **trop-perçus** [trɔpɛrsy] NM *Fin (d'impôts)* over-payment, excess payment

trop-plein, *pl* **trop-pleins** NM *(réservoir, excédent)* overflow; **(tuyau de) t.** waste pipe, overflow pipe; **t. d'énergie/de tendresse** overabundance of energy/affection; **laisser déborder le t. de son cœur** to give vent to one's overflowing emotions

troquer [trɔke] VT **1** *Com* to exchange, to barter **2** *(faire l'échange)* to exchange, *Fam* to swap (**contre qch** for sth)

troquet [trɔkɛ] NM *Fam* (small) café

trot [tro] NM *(de cheval)* trot; **t. assis** sitting trot; **t. enlevé** rising trot, *Am* posting trot; **au petit/grand t.** at a gentle/brisk trot; **prendre le t.** to break into a trot; **aller le t.** *ou* **au t.** to trot; *Fig Fam* **allez-y, et au t.!** go on, and be quick about it!; **t. attelé** harness race; **monté** = type of race in which the horse is ridden instead of being harnessed to the sulky; **course de t.** trotting *or* harness race

Trotski [trɔtski] N Trotsky

trotskisme, trotskysme [trɔtskism] NM Trotskyism

trotskiste, trotskyste [trɔtskist] ADJ, N Trotskyist, Trotskyite

trotte [trɔt] NF *Fam (longue distance)* (long) stretch; **il y a une bonne t. d'ici au château** it's a good way *or* hike from here to the castle; **tout d'une t.** without stopping

trotte-menu ADJ INV **la gent t.** mice

trotter [trɔte] VI *(d'un cheval, d'un cavalier)* to trot; *(d'une personne)* to trot (around/along); *(d'une souris)* to scamper; *Fam* **toujours à t.** always on the go; **on entendrait t. une souris** you could have heard a pin drop; *Fig* **cette chanson me trotte dans la tête** that song keeps running through my head; **ça me trotte dans la tête depuis** I haven't been able to stop thinking about it since

trotteur, -euse [trɔtœr, -øz] ADJ **talons trotteurs** flat *or* low heels
▪ N *(cheval)* trotter
▪ NM **1** *(chaussure)* flat(-heeled) *or* low-heeled shoe **2** *(pour bébé)* baby-walker
▪ NF **trotteuse 1** *(de montre)* second hand **2** *Can (pour bébés)* babywalker

trottinement [trɔtinmɑ̃] NM *(d'une souris)* scampering; *(d'une personne)* trotting about

trottiner [trɔtine] VI **1** *(de cheval, mule)* to jog-trot **2** *(de souris)* to scamper (around/along), to patter about; *(de personne)* to trot about

trottinette [trɔtinɛt] NF **1** *(jouet)* scooter; **faire de la t.** to ride one's scooter **2** *Fam (petite voiture)* small car, runabout

trottoir [trɔtwar] NM pavement, *Am* sidewalk; *Aut* **heurter le t.** to hit the kerb; **artiste de t.** pavement artist; *Fam* **faire le t.** to walk the streets, to be on the game; **t. roulant**

travelator, moving pavement *or Am* sidewalk

trou [tru] NM **1** *(ouverture)* hole; *(d'aiguille)* eye; **avoir des trous à ses chaussettes** to have holes in one's socks; **t. de clef** *(d'horloge, de montre)* keyhole; **t. de serrure** keyhole; **le t. de la couche d'ozone** the hole in the ozone layer; *Fig* **faire son t.** to find one's niche; *Aviat Arg* **il a fait un t. dans l'eau** he's gone for a Burton; *Fam* **boire comme un t.** to drink like a fish; *Fam* **s'en mettre jusqu'aux trous de nez** to stuff one's face
2 *(dans une haie)*, *Fig (dans un emploi du temps)* gap, opening; *Fig (de mémoire, dans une explication, un CV etc)* gap; *(dans ses économies, son budget)* hole, dent; **j'ai un t. de cinq à sept** I'm free *or* I'm not doing anything between five and seven; **il est parti en laissant un t. de 50 000 euros** he went off leaving us/the company/etc 50,000 euros worse off; **j'ai eu un t. (de mémoire)** my mind went blank *or* was a blank; **j'ai un t.** my mind has gone blank *or* is a blank; *Sport* **faire le t.** to break away from the field
3 *Anat Fam* **je n'ai pas les yeux en face des trous** I haven't come to yet, I'm still fast asleep, my brain's still not in gear; *Méd Fam* **t. dans le cœur** hole in the heart
4 *(creusé etc)* hole; *Aut* (pot)hole; **t. de souris** mouse-hole; *Agr* **t. au fumier** manure pit
5 *Fam Péj (village etc)* hole; **elle n'est jamais sortie de son t.** she has never been out of her own backyard; **habiter un petit t. (perdu)** to live at the back of beyond
6 *Golf* hole; **envoyer la balle dans le t.** to hole out; **partie par trous** match play
7 *Arg (tombe)* grave; *(prison)* prison; **on l'a mis dans le t. (au tombeau)** they put him six feet under; **on l'a mis au t. (en prison)** he was sent down
8 *Tech* **t. de graissage** oil hole; **t. d'aération** air vent; *Min* **t. de mine** blast *or* drill hole; *Min, Constr* **t. de sondage** *ou* **de sonde** borehole
▶▶ *Aviat* **t. d'air** air pocket; *Aut* **t. d'alimentation** supply port; *Fam* **t. de balle** arsehole, *Am* asshole; *Naut* **t. du chat** lubber's hole; *Vulg* **t. du cul** arsehole, *Am* asshole; **espèce de t. du cul!** you arsehole *or Am* asshole!; *Aut* **t. d'évacuation** drain hole; **t. d'homme** manhole; *Fam* **trous de nez** nostrils; *Fig Fam* **il me sort par les trous de nez** I can't stand the sight of him; *Astron* **t. noir** black hole; *Fig* **c'est le t. noir** I am/he is/*etc* extremely depressed *or Fam* really down; **t. normand: faire le t. normand** to have a (glass of) Calvados *(in the middle of a meal)*; *Théâtre* **t. du souffleur** prompter's box

troubadour [trubadur] NM *Hist, Littér* troubadour

troublant [trublɑ̃] ADJ **1** *(qui dérange)* disturbing, unsettling; *(qui déconcerte)* disconcerting **2** *(sensuel)* disturbing, provocative; *(parfum)* heady

trouble¹ [trubl] ADJ **1** *(liquide, eau)* cloudy; *(lumière, yeux)* dim; *(ciel)* murky, overcast; *(image, photographe)* blurred, fuzzy; **avoir la vue t.** to have blurred vision; **aux yeux troubles** bleary-eyed **2** *(qui manque de clarté)* *(situation, motivations)* confused, unclear; *(émotion)* mixed, uneasy; *Péj (comportement, affaire etc)* shady, fishy, suspicious; **période t. de l'histoire** murky period of history; **il y a quelque chose de t. dans cette affaire** there's something shady *or* fishy *or* not kosher about this business
▪ ADV **voir t.** to have blurred vision, to see things through a mist *or* haze; **tu ne me reconnais pas? tu vois t.?** is there something wrong with your eyes that you don't recognize me?; **je commence à voir t.** things are beginning to look fuzzy

trouble² NM **1** *(confusion)* confusion, disorder; **jeter le t. dans une famille** to cause

trouble in a family; **c'est une cause de t. dans notre couple** it causes trouble between us, it's a bone of contention between us **2** *(agitation)* agitation, uneasiness; *(gêne)* confusion, embarrassment; *(amoureux)* agitation; **semer** *ou* **jeter le t. dans l'esprit de qn** to perturb sb **3** *troubles* (public) disturbances, unrest; **fauteur de troubles** agitator, troublemaker; **période de troubles** period of unrest; **troubles sociaux** social unrest **4** *Méd* **troubles** disorder; **troubles de digestion/de vision/respiratoires** digestive/eye/respiratory disorder *or Fam* problems; **troubles affectifs** emotional disturbance **5** *Jur* **t. de jouissance** disturbance of possession

trouble-fête NM INV spoilsport, killjoy, party-pooper; **jouer les t.** to be a spoilsport *or* wet blanket, to spoil the fun

troubler [truble] VT **1** *(liquide)* to make cloudy; *Fig (esprit)* to cloud; *(yeux, horizon)* to dim **2** *(sommeil, silence etc)* to disturb; *(réunion, soirée)* to disrupt; *(opération, projets, activités)* to interfere with, to disrupt; *(progrès)* to impede; *(bonheur)* to spoil, to mar; *(digestion)* to upset; **période troublée par la guerre** period disrupted by war; **un vent léger troubla l'eau** a slight wind ruffled the water; **t. le repos** *ou* **l'ordre public** to create a disturbance; *Jur* to disturb the peace, to create a disturbance; **l'ordre public n'a été nullement troublé** there has been no breach of the peace; **imagination troublée** disturbed imagination **3** *(personne)* to disturb, to make uneasy; *(gêner)* to confuse; **ce qui me trouble dans cette affaire** what bothers *or* disturbs me about this matter **4** *(sensuellement) (personne)* to disturb, to excite, to thrill; *(sens, émotions)* to stir **5** *(émouvoir)* to move **6** *Jur* **t. qn dans la jouissance d'un bien** to disturb sb's enjoyment of possession
▪ VPR **se troubler 1** *(du vin etc)* to get cloudy; *(du ciel)* to become overcast; *(d'une vision)* to become blurred; *(de la voix)* to break (with emotion) **2** *(se déconcerter)* to become confused *or* flustered; **sans se t.** *(répondre etc)* unruffled, without turning a hair; **elle se trouble facilement** she is easily flustered, she gets flustered easily

trouée [true] NF gap, opening; (**de** in); **une t. de ciel bleu** a patch of blue sky

trouer [true] VT *(mur etc)* to make a hole/holes in; *(lignes ennemies etc)* to breach; *(vêtement)* to wear *or* make a hole in; *Tech (zinc etc)* to perforate; **avoir les bas troués** to have holes in one's stockings; **être troué** *(de la coque d'un navire)* to be holed; **t. les nuages** *(du soleil)* to break through (the clouds); **des immeubles troués par des bombes** buildings pockmarked with shell holes; *Arg* **se faire t. la peau** to get shot, to be pumped full of lead
▪ VPR **se trouer** *(d'une chaussette etc)* to get a hole/holes

troufignon [trufiɲɔ̃] NM *Arg (anus)* arsehole, *Am* asshole; *(derrière)* arse, *Am* ass

troufion [trufjɔ̃] NM *Arg* soldier, private, *Am* grunt

trouillard, -arde [trujar, -ard] *Arg* ADJ yellow-bellied, chicken, cowardly; **je n'aime pas les types trouillards** I don't like yellow-bellies *or* cowards
▪ N yellow-belly, chicken, coward

trouille [truj] NF *Fam (peur)* **avoir la t.** to be petrified, to be scared stiff; **je n'ai jamais eu une telle t. de ma vie** I've never been so petrified in my life; **au dernier moment, j'ai eu la t.** I got the wind up at the last minute; **donner** *ou* **ficher** *ou* **flanquer la t. à qn** to put the wind up sb; **tu n'as pas la t.!** you've got a nerve!

trouillomètre [trujɔmɛtr] NM *Arg* **avoir le t. à zéro** to be scared stiff *or* witless, to be petrified

trouilloter [trujɔte] vi très Fam **1** (avoir peur) to be scared shitless, to be shit-scared **2** (sentir mauvais) to stink, Br to pong

troupe [trup] nf **1** (de personnes) troop, band, group; (de brigands etc) gang, set; (de scouts) troop **2** Théâtre **t.** (de théâtre ou de comédiens) company, troupe; **t. d'amateurs** amateur company or troupe **3** (d'éléphants) herd; (de lions) pride; (d'oiseaux) flock; **ces animaux vivent en t.** these animals live in herds or are gregarious **4** Mil troop; **troupes** (armée) troops, forces; **officier de t.** regimental officer; **officiers et t.** officers and men or and other ranks; Vieilli **enfant de t.** army child or Fam brat; **cigarettes de t.** army issue cigarettes; Fam **en route, mauvaise t.!** come on, let's get moving!

troupeau, -eaux [trupo] nm (de bétail, de girafes etc) herd; (de moutons) flock; (d'oies) gaggle, flock; (de gens) flock, Péj horde, gaggle, herd

troupier, -ière [trupje, -jɛr] adj **comique t.** (chanson, blague) music-hall; **du comique t.** music-hall comedy
▪ nm Mil Fam private, soldier; **jurer comme un t.** to swear like a trooper, Br Arg to eff and blind

troussage [trusaʒ] nm Culin (de volaille) trussing

trousse [trus] nf **1 être aux trousses de qn** to be after or chasing sb, to be (hot) on sb's heels; **il avait la police aux trousses** he had the police after him or chasing him or (hot) on his heels; **comme s'il avait le feu aux trousses** ou **le diable à ses trousses** like a bat out of hell **2** (étui) kit; (de médecin) instrument case; **t. de toilette** toilet or sponge bag; **t. d'écolier** pencil case; **t. à ongles** manicure kit; **t. de premiers soins** ou **de secours** first-aid kit; **t. à outils** tool kit

troussé [truse] adj Fam **bien t.** (objet, compliment) neat

trousseau, -eaux [truso] nm **1** (de clés) bunch **2** (de fiancée) trousseau, bottom drawer, Am hope chest **3** (de pensionnaire) clothes, outfit

trousser [truse] vt **1** Culin (volaille) to truss **2** Fam (faire rapidement) (travail, repas, affaire) to polish off, to make short work of; **t. un compliment à qn** to pay sb a neat compliment **3** Vieilli (retrousser) (jupe etc) to tuck up; Fam **t. une fille** to tumble a girl

trousseur [trusœr] nm Fam Vieilli **t. de jupons** womanizer, skirt chaser

trouvaille [truvaj] nf **1** (chose trouvée) (lucky) find; **une excellente t.** a great find **2** (bonne idée) brainwave

�b **TROUVER** [truve]

| vt | to find **1–5** ▪ to come up with **2** ▪ to discover **2, 3** ▪ to come across **3** ▪ to think **4** |
| vpr | to find oneself **1, 3** ▪ to be **1** ▪ to feel **1** ▪ to happen **2** |

vt **1** (en cherchant) (personne, objet) to find; **je ne trouve pas mes clefs** I can't find my keys; **il ne trouve plus ses lunettes** he can't find his glasses, he's lost his glasses; **où est-ce qu'on trouve cela?** where can you get it?; **on le trouve au bar, à cette heure-là** you can find him in the bar at this time; **aller t. qn** to go and see sb; **je n'ai pas trouvé le temps de le faire** I didn't find time to do it, I didn't get round to it; **il n'a pas trouvé les mots pour le dire** he couldn't find the words; Ordinat **t. et remplacer** to find and replace; **il trouve du plaisir à lire** he takes or finds pleasure in reading, he enjoys reading; **elle trouve un malin plaisir à me faire attendre** she takes malicious pleasure in making me wait; **il va bien t. quelque chose à redire** he's sure to have something to say

2 (découvrir, inventer) (solution, moyen, compromis, arrangement) to find, to come up with; (procédé) to discover, to invent, to come up with; (erreur) to find; **c'est bien trouvé!** good idea!; **exemple bien/mal trouvé** well-/badly chosen example; **je me demande où il est allé t.** ça I wonder where he got that idea from; Iron **tu as trouvé ça tout seul?** did you think of that all on your own?

3 t. (par hasard) to find (by chance), to discover, to come upon, to come across; (idée, méthode) to hit on; **on l'a trouvé mort** he was found dead; **t. qn en faute** to catch sb out; **t. porte close** to find nobody home; **que je ne te trouve pas en train de fouiller dans mes affaires** don't let me find or catch you rummaging about in my things; **bureau des objets trouvés** lost-property office; Fig **il a trouvé à qui parler** he has met his match; **il trouva la mort à l'âge de 35 ans/dans un accident de voiture** he died or Fml met his death at the age of 35/in a car accident; **il trouva la mort bêtement** he died a stupid death

4 (juger) to find; (penser) to think; **je la trouve jolie** I think she's pretty, I find or consider her pretty; **vous trouvez?** do you think so?; **comment as-tu trouvé ce livre?** how did you find or like the book?; **je la trouve mauvaise** ou **saumâtre** (action) I think it's a bit much or a bit thick; **il trouve bon/mauvais de vous en parler** he thinks it's a good/bad idea to talk to you about it; **je trouve mieux de ne pas ...** I think it's better not to ...; **je lui trouve du charme/mauvaise mine** I think he has charm/looks ill; **je ne trouve aucun intérêt à le refaire** I don't think there's any point in doing it again; **qu'est-ce qu'elle lui trouve?** what does she see in him?; **je trouve que ...** I think (that) ...; **t. le temps long** to find or feel that the time is dragging

5 (obtenir) (travail, mari, maison etc) to find, to get; **t. le sommeil** to get to sleep
▪ vpr **se trouver 1** (dans une situation) to be, to find oneself; (d'un objet) to be; (sentir) to feel; **ces plantes se trouvent partout** these plants can be found everywhere; **ça ne se trouve pas partout** you can't get it just anywhere; **je me trouve très bien ici** I'm very comfortable here; **comment vous êtes-vous trouvé de ce traitement?** how did the treatment work?; **à ce moment-là, je me suis trouvé bien bête** at that moment I felt really stupid; **je me trouve trop grosse** I think I'm too fat; **se t. bien de qch/ d'avoir fait qch** to feel all the better for sth/for having done sth; **je me trouve mieux** I feel better; **elle se trouve mal** she feels faint

2 (arriver) to happen, to turn up; **je me trouve avoir** ou **il se trouve que j'ai une heure de libre** I happen to have or it so happens or it turns out that I have an hour to spare; **la dame se trouva être sa propre femme** the lady turned out to be his own wife; Fam **si cela** ou **ça se trouve, il est déjà rentré** maybe he's back, with a bit of luck he might be back

3 (se réaliser) to find oneself

trouvère [truvɛr] nm Hist, Littér trouvère

troyen¹, -enne¹ [trwajɛ̃, -ɛn] adj (de Troie) Trojan
▪ **N T.** Trojan

troyen², -enne² adj (de Troyes) of/from Troyes
▪ **N T.** (natif) native of Troyes; (habitant) inhabitant of Troyes

truand, -ande [tryã, -ãd] n **1** Fam (escroc) crook; (gangster) gangster, hood **2** Arch (mendiant) beggar

Il faut noter que le terme anglais **truant** est un faux ami. Il désigne un élève qui fait l'école buissonnière.

truander [tryãde] Fam vt (quelqu'un) to swindle, to do; (faire payer trop cher) to rip off; **se faire t.** to be swindled or done; (payer trop cher) to get ripped off
▪ vi to cheat (**à un examen** in an exam)

trublion [tryblijɔ̃] nm troublemaker

truc¹ [tryk] nm Fam **1** (moyen) trick; **il y a un t.!** there's a trick in it!; **un t. pour enlever les taches** a trick for or a clever way of removing stains; **connaître les trucs du métier** to know the tricks of the trade; **c'est un t. qu'il faut connaître** there's a trick or a knack to it; Théâtre **pièce à trucs** play with elaborate stage effects

2 (personne) **machin t. (chouette)** thingumajig, what's-his-name, f what's-her-name

3 (chose) thing; (machin) thingumajig, thingummy, thingy; **qu'est-ce que c'est que t.-là?** what's that (thingumajig)?; **des trucs comme ça** things like that; **elle a encore acheté des trucs** she's been shopping again; **je voudrais lui offrir un petit t.** I'd like to give him a little something; **il faudrait que tu me dises un t. ...** tell me something ...

4 la montagne/la cuisine/le droit, c'est vraiment son t. he's/she's really into mountain climbing/cooking/the law; **ce n'est pas son t.** it's not his/her thing or bag, he's/she's not into that

truc² nm Rail truck, Am freight car

trucage [trykaʒ] nm **1** Cin special effect; **c'est du t.** it's all faked **2** (d'une photographie) faking; (d'un match, une élection etc) fixing, rigging; (de comptes) window-dressing

truchement [tryʃmã] nm **1** (intermédiaire) **par le t. de ...** through ... **2** Arch (interprète) interpreter

trucider [tryside] vt Fam (tuer) to bump off; **je vais me faire t. s'il l'apprend** I'm going to end up dead if he finds out

truck [tryk] nm Rail truck, Am freight car

truckman [trykman], pl **truckmen** [trykmɛn] nm TV, Cin special effects person or engineer

trucmuche [trykmyʃ] nm Fam **1** (chose) thingumajig, thingummy, thingy **2 T.** (personne) thingumajig, what's-his-name, f what's-her-name

truculence [trykylãs] nf (pittoresque) (d'un personnage, du langage) colourfulness, Am colorfulness; (verdeur) raciness

truculent [trykylã] adj (pittoresque) (personnage) colourful, Am colorful, larger than life; (cru) (langage, personnage) racy

Il faut noter que l'adjectif anglais **truculent** est un faux ami. Il signifie **agressif**.

truelle [tryɛl] nf **1** (outil) trowel **2** Culin **t. à poisson** fish slice

truffe [tryf] nf **1** (champignon) truffle; **omelette aux truffes** truffle omelette **2** (au chocolat) truffle **3** (nez) (d'un chien) nose; Fam (d'une personne) conk **4** Fam (imbécile) divvy, Am schmuck

truffer [tryfe] vt **1** Culin (dinde) to garnish with truffles; **poularde truffée** truffled chicken **2** Fig **truffé de** (balles, fautes, inexactitudes) riddled with; (citations) peppered with

truffier, -ière [tryfje, -jɛr] adj (sol) truffle(-producing); **chien t.** truffle hound

truie [trɥi] nf sow

truisme [trɥism] nm truism

truite [trɥit] nf trout; **t. de rivière** brown trout; **t. arc-en-ciel** rainbow trout; Culin **t.**

meunière = trout sautéed in butter and served with parsley and lemon juice; **t. au bleu** = trout poached in a vinegar-flavoured broth VOIR GRAMMAIRE A12

truité [tryite] ADJ speckled; *(chien, cheval)* spotted; *(poterie)* crackled

trumeau, -eaux [trymo] NM **1** *Archit* pier **2** *(miroir)* pier glass **3** *Culin* leg of beef **4** *Fam (femme laide)* dog, *Br* boot, *Am* beast

truquage [trykaʒ] NM = **trucage**

truquer [tryke] VT **1** *(photographie, expérience, données etc)* to fake, to rig; *(match, combat, élection etc)* to fix, to rig; *Fam* **t. les comptes** to cook the books, to window-dress the accounts; **t. les dés** to load the dice **2** *Cin* **scène truquée** scene with special effects **3** *Min (mine, minerai, échantillon)* to salt

truqueur, -euse [trykœr, -øz] N **1** *(qui triche)* cheat **2** *Cin* special effects person or engineer

truquiste [trykist] N *Cin* special effects person or engineer

trust [trœst] NM *Fin, Com* trust; **t. de l'acier/du pétrole** steel/oil cartel; **t. commercial** commercial monopoly; **t. industriel** industrial monopoly; **t. de valeurs** holding company

truster [trœste] VT **1** *Fin, Com,* to monopolize, to form into a monopoly **2** *Fam (monopoliser)* to monopolize, to hog; **il truste tous les premiers rôles du cinéma français** he gets all the leading roles in French cinema **VI** *Com* to form a monopoly

tsar [tsar, dzar] NM tsar, czar

tsarévitch [tsarevitʃ, dz-] NM tsarevitch, czarevitch

tsarine [tsarin, dz-] NF tsarina, czarina

tsarisme [tsarism, dz-] NM *Hist* tsarism

tsariste [tsarist, dz-] ADJ, N *Hist* tsarist

tsé-tsé [tsetse] NF INV *Entom* tsetse (fly); *Hum* **tu t'es fait piquer par la mouche t.?** have you got sleeping sickness?

TSF [teesef] NF *Vieilli (abrév* **télégraphie sans fil) (poste de) T.** wireless (set)

T-shirt, *pl* **T-shirts** [tiʃœrt] NM T-shirt, tee shirt

tsigane [tsigan] ADJ, N tzigane, Hungarian gypsy

tsunami [tsynami] NM tidal wave, tsunami

TSVP [teesvepe] *(abrév* **tournez s'il vous plaît)** PTO

TTC [tetese] *(abrév* **toutes taxes comprises)** inclusive of tax

TU [tey] NM *(abrév* **temps universel)** GMT

tu [ty] PRON PERS **1** you *(usual form of address to relations, close friends, children and animals)*; **tu as raison** you are right; **qui es-tu?** who are you?; **être à tu et à toi** to be very friendly (**avec qn** with sb); **être à tu et à toi avec tout le monde** to be on first-name terms with everybody; **elle lui dit 'tu'** she calls him 'tu'; **crois-tu?** do you think so?; *Arg (elided to* **t'** *before vowel or* **h** *mute)* **qu'est-ce que t'as?** what's up (with you)? SEE GRAMMAR A27; B18; B67 **2** *Rel* thou; *(à Dieu)* Thou; *Bible* **tu ne tueras point** thou shalt not kill

Tuamotu [twamotu] NFPL **les T.** the Tuamotu Archipelago

tuant [tɥɑ̃] ADJ *Fam* **1** *(fatigant) (travail)* killing, back-breaking, exhausting; **elle fait un travail t.** she has an exhausting job **2** *(insupportable)* exasperating; **c'est t., ce bruit** this noise is sending me up the wall; **les enfants sont vraiment tuants aujourd'hui** the kids are being a real pain today

tub [tœb] NM *Vieilli (cuvette)* tub, bath; *(bain)* bath; **prendre un t.** to take or have a bath

tuba [tyba] NM **1** *Mus* tuba **2** *(de plongée)* snorkel

tubage [tybaʒ] NM *Constr, Min, Chir, Vét* tubing

tubaire [tybɛr] ADJ *Méd* tubal

tubard, -arde [tybar, -ard] N *Méd Fam* TB case

tube [tyb] NM **1** *(tuyau)* tube; *(de canalisation)* pipe; *Constr* **bâti en tubes d'acier** tubular-steel-frame; *Fig Fam* **à pleins tubes** at full blast; *Fig Fam* **il déconne à pleins tubes** he's off his rocker; **chaudière à tubes** tubular boiler **2** *(de canon)* barrel **3** *Chir, Vét* tube **4** *Anat* tube, duct **5** *Bot (de la corolle, du calice)* tube **6** *Courses de chevaux Arg (indication)* tip **7** *Fam (chanson, disque)* hit; *Théâtre* (smash) hit, smash; **le t. de l'été** this summer's smash hit **8** *(emballage) (de dentifrice, de peinture etc)* tube; **t. d'aspirine** = packet of aspirin; **t. de rouge à lèvres** (stick of) lipstick; **en t.** in a tube; **acheter de la mayonnaise en t.** to buy a tube of mayonnaise **9** *Élec, Électron* tube
▸▸ **t. d'alimentation** feed pipe; **t. amplificateur** amplifier tube or valve; *Anat* **t. bronchique** bronchial tube; *Anat, Phys* **t. capillaire** capillary tube; *Min* **t. carottier** core bar rel; *Électron, Radio* **t. cathodique** cathode-ray tube; **t. de chaudière** boiler tube; **t. de condenseur** ou **à condensation** condenser tube; *Anat* **t. digestif** digestive tract, alimentary canal; *Aut* **t. de direction** steering column; *Chimie* **t. pour dosage, t. doseur** measuring tube; *Aut* **t. d'échappement** exhaust pipe; **t. électronique** electron tube; *Chimie* **t. à essai** test tube; **tubes d'exploitation** tubing; **t. à flamme** *(d'un moteur à réaction)* flame tube; **t. fluorescent** fluorescent tube; **t. à gaz** gas-filled tube or valve; **t. de graissage** oil duct or way; *Élec* **t. guide-fils** *(sur un édifice)* race track, race way; *Naut* **t. lance-torpille(s)** torpedo tube; *Élec* **t. au néon** neon tube; **t. de niveau d'eau** water-gauge column; **t. de Pitot** Pitot tube; **tubes de pompage** tubing; **t. raccord** pipe connection; **t. à vide** vacuum tube or valve

tubeless [tybles] ADJ INV *(pneu)* tubeless

tuber [tybe] VT **1** *Constr (puits de mine, puits)* to tube, to case; *(conduit d'air, puits)* to case *Fam (téléphoner à)* **t. qn** to give sb a buzz or *Br* a bell

tubercule [tyberkyl] NM **1** *Bot* tuber **2** *Méd* tubercle

tuberculeux, -euse [tyberkylø, -øz] ADJ **1** *Bot (racine)* tubercular **2** *Méd* tubercular **N** tubercular patient, TB case

tuberculine [tyberkylin] NF *Méd* tuberculin

tuberculose [tyberkyloz] NF *Méd* tuberculosis, TB; **t. pulmonaire** pulmonary tuberculosis

tubéreux, -euse [tyberø, -øz] *Bot* ADJ tuberous
NF tubéreuse tuberose

tubérosité [tyberozite] NF tuberosity

tubulaire [tybylɛr] ADJ tubular

tubulé [tybyle] ADJ *(cornue, fleur)* tubular

tubuleux, -euse [tybylø, -øz] ADJ tubulous

tubulure [tybylyr] NF **1** *Tech (ouverture)* tubulure, pipe(-run), neck; *Aut* manifold; **t. d'alimentation** ou **d'admission** intake manifold; *Aut* **t. d'admission** inlet pipe; *Aut* **t. d'échappement** exhaust pipe **2** *(tube)* pipe; *(ensemble de tubes)* piping, pipes

TUC [tyk] NMPL *(abrév* **travaux d'utilité collective)** = community work for unemployed young people
N *Fam (employé)* = person doing community work on a 'TUC' scheme

tue-mouches [tymyʃ] NM INV **1** *(champignon)* fly agaric **2** *(tapette)* fly swatter; *(insecticide)* fly spray
ADJ INV papier ou **ruban t.** fly paper

tuer [tɥe] VT **1** *(personne, animal, cultures), Tennis (balle), Fig (l'amour)* to kill; **t. qn d'un coup de couteau** ou **de poignard** to stab sb to death; **t. qn d'un coup de revolver** to shoot and kill sb (with a revolver); **c'est la solitude/le chagrin qui l'a tué** he died of loneliness/grief; **un coup à t. un bœuf** a blow to fell an ox; **il a reçu une gifle à t. un bœuf** he got an almighty slap, he got a slap that made his ears ring; **la route tue tous les ans** people die on the roads every year; **les tués et les blessés** the dead and wounded; **se faire t.** to get killed; **ils se firent t. en braves** they died like heroes; *Fig* **tu veux te faire t.!** you're asking for it!, you're taking your life in your hands!; *Fig* **cette musique va t. l'ambiance** that music is going to kill the atmosphere, stone dead or totally destroy the atmosphere; *Fig* **t. le temps** to kill time; *Fig* **l'habitude tue la passion** familiarity breeds contempt; *Fig* **t. qch dans l'œuf** to nip sth in the bud
2 *Fig (épuiser)* **tous ces déplacements m'ont tué** I'm dead or done for after all that travelling; **ces escaliers me tuent** these stairs will be the death of me
3 *Fig Fam (révolter)* **ça me tue d'entendre des conneries pareilles!** it really gets me when I hear such nonsense!; **ça m'a tué d'apprendre qu'il se remariait** *(sidéré)* I was staggered to hear that he was getting married again
4 *Fam (être remarquable)* **écoute cette chanson; ça tue!** listen to this song, it's a killer!
VPR se tuer 1 *(se suicider)* to kill oneself, to commit suicide, *Br Fam* to top oneself **2** *(mourir dans un accident etc)* to die, to get killed **3** *(s'entre-tuer)* to kill one another **4** *Fig* **se t. au travail** ou **à travailler/à force de boire** to work/drink oneself to death; **je me tue à vous le dire** I'm sick and tired of or sick to death telling you; **c'est ce que je me tue à vous dire** that's what I've been trying to tell you

tuerie [tyri] NF slaughter, butchery

tue-tête (à) [atytet] ADV at the top of one's voice

tueur, -euse [tɥœr, -øz] ADJ *(fauves, cellule)* killer
N *(assassin)* killer
NM *(dans un abattoir)* slaughterman
▸▸ **t. à gages** hired killer or assassin; **t. en série** serial killer

tuf [tyf] NM **1** *Géol* **t. volcanique** tuff; *(calcaire)* tufa **2** *Fig Litt* bedrock, foundation

tuile [tɥil] NF **1** *Constr* (roof) tile; **toit en tuiles** tiled roof **2** *Culin* **tuiles aux amandes** almond biscuits **3** *Fam (malchance)* (piece of) bad luck, blow; **il lui est arrivé une (sale) t.** he's had a terrible blow or piece of bad luck; **j'ai peur qu'il lui arrive une t.** I'm worried that something will happen to him; **la t.!** what bad or rotten luck!

tuilerie [tɥilri] NF **1** *(fabrique)* tile works; *(four)* tile kiln **2** **les Tuileries** = a former royal residence in Paris, now the site of the Tuileries gardens, near the Louvre

tulipe [tylip] NF **1** *Bot* tulip **2** *(lampe)* tulip-shaped lamp; *(verre)* tulip glass **3** *Tech (d'une imprimante)* thimble

tulipier [tylipje] NM *Bot* tulip tree

tulle [tyl] NM *Tex* tulle, net (fabric); **t. de soie/de coton** silk/cotton tulle; **robe de t.** tulle dress; *Méd* **t. gras** = material used for dressing burns and wounds

tuméfaction [tymefaksjɔ̃] NF *Méd* swelling, *Spéc* tumefaction

tuméfier [tymefje] VT *(articulations etc)* to cause to swell, *Spéc* to tumefy; **visage tuméfié** swollen face
VPR se tuméfier to swell (up)

tumescence [tymesɑ̃s] NF swelling, *Spéc* tumescence

tumescent [tymesɑ̃] ADJ swelling, *Spéc* tumescent

tumeur [tymœr] NF *Méd* tumour, *Am* tumor, growth; **t. bénigne/maligne** benign/malignant tumour; **une t. au cerveau** a brain tumour

tumoral, -ale, -aux, -ales [tymɔral, -o] ADJ tumorous, tumoral

tumulaire [tymylɛr] ADJ **pierre t.** tombstone

tumulte [tymylt] NM uproar, commotion, hubbub, *Fml* tumult; *(d'applaudissements)* thunder; *(d'armes)* clash; *(de la politique, des passions)* turmoil; *(des affaires, de la ville)* hustle and bustle; **le t. au sujet de** the uproar *or* commotion about, the furore over; **provoquer un t.** to cause an uproar *or* a commotion; **dans le t.** in an uproar, in confusion; **il y eut des tumultes** there were riots

tumultueusement [tymyltɥøzmɑ̃] ADV tumultuously

tumultueux, -euse [tymyltɥø, -øz] ADJ *(réunion, débat, séance, accueil etc)* noisy, tumultuous; *(rues)* noisy; *(vie, période etc)* tumultuous

tumulus, *pl* **tumulus** *ou* **tumuli** [tymylys, -li] NM barrow, *Spéc* tumulus

tuner [tynœr, tyner] NM *Radio* tuner

tungstène [tœ̃ksten, tœ̃g-] NM *Métal* tungsten

tungstène-halogène NM tungsten-halogen

tunique [tynik] NF **1** *(vêtement)* tunic **2** *Biol (d'un organe)* tunic, envelope, membrane; *Bot (d'un bulbe)* coat

Tunis [tynis] N Tunis

Tunisie [tynizi] NF Tunisia

tunisien, -ienne [tynizjɛ̃, -jɛn] ADJ Tunisian
N **T.** Tunisian

tunnel [tynɛl] NM tunnel; **t. routier** road tunnel; **le t. sous la Manche** the Channel Tunnel; *Fig* **voir le bout du t.** to see the light at the end of the tunnel
▸▸ *Aviat* **t. aérodynamique** wind tunnel; **t. de publicités** extended commercial break

TUP [typ] NM *(abrév* **titre universel de paiement)** universal payment order

tuque [tyk] NF *Can* tuque, *Fam* pompom hat, bobble cap

turban [tyrbɑ̃] NM *(coiffure)* turban

turbide [tyrbid] ADJ *(liquide etc)* cloudy, turbid

turbidité [tyrbidite] NF cloudiness, *Fml* turbidity

turbin [tyrbɛ̃] NM *Fam (travail)* grind, slog; *(emploi)* job; **toujours au t.?** still slogging away?

turbine [tyrbin] NF turbine; *(d'une pompe à eau)* impeller; **à t.** turbine-powered; **t. à air** air *or* wind turbine; **t. à eau, t. hydraulique** water turbine *or* wheel; **t. à gaz/à vapeur** gas/steam turbine; *Tech* **t. centrifuge** centrifugal blower; *Tech* **t. de ventilation** blower; *Tech* **t. moteur** power turbine

turbiner [tyrbine] VI *Arg (travailler)* to slog (away); *Scol* to swot

turbo [tyrbo] ADJ INV turbine-driven, turbo
NM **1** *Aut* turbo; *Fam* **mettre le t.** to get a move on **2** *Ordinat* turbo
NF turbo

turboalternateur [tyrboalternatœr] NM *Élec* turbo-alternator

turbocompresseur [tyrbokɔ̃presœr] NM *Tech, Aviat* turbocompressor; *Aut* turbo-supercharger, turbocharger

turbodiesel [tyrbodjezɛl] NM *(moteur)* turbo diesel
NF *(voiture)* turbo diesel

turbomarketing NM turbomarketing

turbomoteur [tyrbomɔtœr] NM turbomotor, turboshaft engine

turbopompe [tyrbopɔ̃p] NF turbo pump, turbine pump

turbopropulseur [tyrbopropylsœr] NM turboprop(eller); **avion à t.** turboprop aircraft

turboréacteur [tyrboreaktœr] NM turbojet (engine)

turbot [tyrbo] NM *(poisson)* turbot

turbotière [tyrbotjɛr] NF *Culin (récipient)* fish kettle *(especially for cooking turbot)*

turbotrain [tyrbotrɛ̃] NM *Rail* turbotrain

turbulence [tyrbylɑ̃s] NF *Aviat* turbulence; *(d'un enfant)* boisterousness, noisiness; *(de la mer)* storminess, turbulence; *Aviat* **il y aura des turbulences** there will be some turbulence

turbulent [tyrbylɑ̃] ADJ **1** *Vieilli (population)* restless, unruly **2** *(enfant, classe)* boisterous, noisy; *(mer)*, *Fig (relation, période)* stormy, turbulent **3** *Phys* **régime t.** turbulent flow

turc, turque [tyrk] ADJ Turkish; **café t.** Turkish coffee; **être assis à la turque** to be sitting cross-legged; **W.-C.** *ou* **cabinets à la turque** hole in the ground
NM *Ling* Turkish
N **T.** Turk; *Pol* **jeune T.** Young Turk; *Fam* **fort comme un T.** as strong as an ox; *Fig* **tête de T.** whipping-boy

turf [tœrf, tyrf] NM **1** *(terrain)* racecourse **2** **le t.** *(activité)* racing; **habitué du t.** racegoer **3** *Fam Vieilli (travail)* work; *(lieu de travail)* workplace **4** *Fam Vieilli (prostitution)* prostitution; **faire le t.** to turn tricks, *Br* to be on the game

turfiste [tœrfist, tyr-] N racegoer

turgescence [tyrʒesɑ̃s] NF *Méd, Bot* turgescence

turgescent [tyrʒesɑ̃] ADJ turgescent

turgide [tyrʒid] ADJ *Litt* turgid, swollen

turista [turista] NF *Fam* **la t.** Montezuma's revenge, Delhi belly, Spanish tummy

turkmène [tyrkmɛn] ADJ Turkoman
NM *Ling* Turkmen
N **T.** Turkoman

Turkménistan [tyrkmenistɑ̃] NM Turkmenistan

turlupiner [tyrlypine] VT *Fam* to worry, to bother

turlute [tyrlyt] NF *très Fam* blow-job; **faire une t. à qn** to give sb a blow-job, to go down on sb, to give sb head

turluter [tyrlyte] VI *Can Fam* to trill, to sing tra-la-la

turlututu [tyrlytyty] INT *(pour refuser, se moquer gentiment, interrompre)* fiddlesticks!; **t. chapeau pointu!** yah boo, sucks to you!

turne [tyrn] NF **1** *Fam Péj (chambre, maison)* dump, hole **2** *Scol Arg (student's)* room

turnep(s) [tyrnɛp(s)] NM *Agr* kohlrabi

turnover [tœrnɔvœr, -œr] NM turnover

turpitude [tyrpityd] NF **1** *(caractère)* vileness, moral turpitude **2** *(action)* vile act **3** *(parole)* vile remark

turque [turk] ADJ F, NF *voir* turc

turquerie [tyrk(ə)ri] NF work of art in an Oriental style

Turquie [tyrki] NF Turkey; **tapis de T.** Turkish carpet

turquoise [tyrkwaz] NF *(pierre)* turquoise
ADJ INV, NM INV *(couleur)* turquoise (blue)

tussor(e) [tysɔr] NM *Tex* tussore (silk)

tutélaire [tytelɛr] ADJ *(divinité)* tutelary; *Jur* **gestion t.** guardianship; **puissance t.** power of guardianship

tutelle [tytɛl] NF **1** *Jur* guardianship; **enfant en t.** child under guardianship; **t. administrative** administrative supervision *(established over mismanaged public body)*; *Pol* **territoires sous t.** trust territories **2** *(protection)* protection; **sous la t. de** *(famille, loi etc)* under the protection of; **prendre qn sous sa t.** to take sb under one's wing

tuteur, -trice [tytœr, -tris] N **1** *Jur* guardian; **t. légal** legal guardian **2** *(protecteur)* protector
NM *(pour plante)* support, stake; **mettre un t. à une plante** to stake a plant

tutoiement [tytwamɑ̃] NM use of the familiar 'tu' *(instead of the more formal 'vous')*; **le t. est de rigueur** everybody addresses each other as *or* calls each other 'tu'

Tutoiement et vouvoiement

Traditionally, non-native French speakers waited until they were addressed using the informal "tu" form before using it themselves, except when speaking to young children. However in the past twenty or thirty years people in France have become much more casual about using "tu", and it is now commonly used among colleagues in the workplace, while the "vous" form tends to be used when talking to people from an older generation or to hierarchical superiors (see also entries **tu** and **vous**).

---

tutoyer [tytwaje] (**je tutoie, n. tutoyons; je tutoierai**) VT **1 t. qn** to address sb as 'tu', = to be on familiar terms with sb **2** *Équitation* **t. l'obstacle** to brush against the fence *(without knocking it)* **3** *Fig (être proche de)* to come close to; **il a tutoyé la mort plus d'une fois** he's had more than one brush with death
VPR **se tutoyer** to address each other as 'tu', = to be on familiar terms (with each other)

tutti [tuti] NM INV *Mus* tutti

tutti frutti [tutifruti] NM INV *(glace)* tutti-frutti

tutti quanti [tutikwɑ̃ti] NMPL **et t.** et cetera, et cetera

tutu [tyty] NM tutu

tuyau, -aux [tɥijo] NM **1** *(canalisation etc)* pipe; *(flexible)* tube; **t. d'eau/de gaz** water/gas pipe; **t. vertical, t. de chute** standpipe; **t. flexible** *ou* **en caoutchouc** rubber tube *or* tubing; **t. acoustique** speaking tube; *Fam Vieilli* **dire qch à qn dans le t. de l'oreille** to whisper sth in sb's ear **2** *(d'une pipe)* stem **3** *(du maïs, de l'herbe etc)* stalk **4** *(pli)* flute, goffer, quill **5** *Fam (conseil)* tip; *(donné à la police, un journaliste)* tip-off; **je vais te filer un t.** I'll give you a tip; **qui est-ce qui t'a donné le t.?** who tipped you off?, who put you on to it?; **un t. percé** a rotten tip; **c'est un t. increvable** it's straight from the horse's mouth; **quelques tuyaux pour économiser l'énergie** a few tips *or* pointers on how to save energy; **avoir des tuyaux** to know the ropes
▸▸ **t. d'arrosage** garden hose; **t. de cheminée** (chimney) flue; *Aut* **t. d'échappement** exhaust (pipe), tailpipe; *Aut* **t. d'essence** petrol pipe; **t. d'incendie** fire hose; *Mus* **t. d'orgue** organ pipe; **t. de poêle** stove *or* flue pipe; **en t. de poêle** *(pantalon)* drainpipe; *(chapeau)* stove pipe; *Fam* **la famille t. de poêle** = family whose members have an incestuous relationship; *Aut* **t. de pression** pressure hose; *Aut* **t. de reniflard** breather pipe; *Aut* **t. de trop-plein** overflow pipe

tuyautage [tɥijotaʒ] NM **1** *(d'un tissu)* fluting, goffering **2** *Fam (action de donner des conseils)* giving of tips

tuyauter [tɥijote] VT **1** *(un tissu)* to flute, to goffer; **fer à t.** goffering tongs **2** *Fam (conseiller)* **t. qn** to give sb a tip; *(le mettre au courant)* to tip sb off, to put sb in the know (**sur** about)

tuyauterie [tɥijotri] NF *(tuyaux)* piping, pipes; *Aut* **t. de carburant** fuel pipe *or* line; *Aut* **t. de frein** brake pipe *or* line

tuyauteur, -euse [tɥijotœr, -øz] N *Fam* tipster

tuyère [tɥijɛr] NF *Tech, Métal* nozzle; *Aviat etc* **t. d'échappement** jet pipe; **t. de propulsion** thrust nozzle

TV [teve] NF *(abrév* **télévision**) TV

TVA [tevea] NF *(abrév* **taxe à la valeur ajoutée**) *Br* ≃ VAT, *Am* ≃ sales tax; **exempt de T.** zero-rated; **soumis à la T.** subject to *Br* VAT *or Am* sales tax; **T. encaissée** output tax; **T. récupérée** input tax

TVHD [teveaʃde] NF *(abrév* **télévision haute définition**) HDTV

TVP [tevepe] NF *(abrév* **thrombose veineuse profonde**) DVT

tweed [twid] NM *Tex* tweed; **veste de t.** tweed jacket

twin-set, *pl* **twin-sets** [twinsɛt] NM matching sweater and cardigan, *Br* twinset

twist [twist] NM *(danse)* twist

twister [twiste] VI to twist

tympan [tɛ̃pɑ̃] NM **1** *Anat* eardrum, *Spéc* tympanum; **bruit à briser** *ou* **crever** *ou* **déchirer** *ou* **rompre les tympans** ear-splitting noise **2** *Archit* tympanum **3** *Tech (mounted on shaft)* pinion

tympanal, -ale, -aux, -ales [tɛ̃panal, -o] ADJ, NM *Anat* **(os) t.** tympanic bone

tympanique [tɛ̃panik] ADJ *Anat* of the ear, *Spéc* tympanic

tympanon [tɛ̃panɔ̃] NM *Mus* dulcimer

type [tip] NM **1** *(modèle) (de travail, intervention etc)* type; *(chose ou personne typique)* classic example (**de** of); *Zool* type, *Spéc* phylum; *Biol* **genre t.** type genus; **arbre t.** sample tree; **t. de la beauté italienne** typical Italian beauty; **avoir le t. latin/nordique** to have Latin/Nordic looks; **elle est très sensible au t. italien** she really goes for Italian-looking men; **ce n'est pas du tout mon t.** *(il ne m'attire pas)* he's not at all my type; **c'est tout à fait mon t.** he's just my type (of man) *or* my sort of man, he's exactly the kind of man I find attractive; **c'est un problème t.** it's a typical problem, it's a standard type of problem; **c'est vraiment l'avare t.** he's a typical miser; **c'est vraiment l'Italienne t.** she's your typical Italian woman, she's typically Italian; **maison t.** show house; **motocyclette t.** motorbike of standard design; **c'est le t. même de la femme d'affaires** she is the classic example of a businesswoman, she is a *or* the typical businesswoman; **des ennuis techniques (du) t. (de la) panne** breakdown problems VOIR GRAMMAIRE A13

2 *Fam (bonhomme)* guy, man, *Br* bloke; **t'es un chic t.!** you're a good sort!; **un sale t.** a bastard; **un pauvre t.** a loser; **pauvre t.!** you're pathetic! **3** *Typ* type; **t. de caractères** typeface

typé [tipe] ADJ typical; **il est bien** *ou* **très t.** he has all the characteristic features; **c'est un Portugais mais il n'est pas très t.** he's Portuguese but you wouldn't think so to look at him

typer [tipe] VT *Tech* to stamp, to mark

typesse [tipɛs] NF *Arg Péj Vieilli (femme, fille)* female

typhique [tifik] *Méd* ADJ *(du typhus)* typhus; *(de la typhoïde)* typhoid
N typhus/typhoid sufferer

typhoïde [tifɔid] ADJ, NF *Méd* **(fièvre) t.** typhoid (fever)

typhoïdique [tifɔidik] ADJ typhoid, typhoidal; **bacille t.** typhoid bacillus

typhon [tifɔ̃] NM *Météo* typhoon

typhus [tifys] NM *Méd* typhus (fever); *Vét* **t. du chat** (infectious) feline gastroenteritis

typique [tipik] ADJ typical; **il a encore oublié, c'est t.** he's forgotten again, (it's) typical!

typiquement [tipikmɑ̃] ADV typically

typo [tipo] *Fam* NF = **typographie**
NM = **typographe**

typographe [tipɔɡraf] N typographer

typographie [tipɔɡrafi] NF *(art, procédé)* typography, letterpress printing; *(présentation d'un texte)* typography

typographique [tipɔɡrafik] ADJ typographic(al); **erreur t.** typographic(al) error, misprint, *Fam* typo

typographiquement [tipɔɡrafikmɑ̃] ADV typographically

typologie [tipɔlɔʒi] NF typology

typologique [tipɔlɔʒik] ADJ typological

typote [tipɔt] NF *Fam* = **typographe**

typothèque [tipɔtɛk] NF *Ordinat* type library

Tyr [tir] N Tyre

tyran [tirɑ̃] NM *Pol, Fig* tyrant; **se conduire en t.** to act like a tyrant *or* tyrannically; **arrête de jouer les tyrans** stop acting like a tyrant; **il est le t. de sa famille** he tyrannizes his family

tyranneau, -eaux [tirano] NM *Litt* petty tyrant

tyrannie [tirani] NF *Pol, Fig* tyranny; **exercer sa t. sur qn** to tyrannize sb; *(frère, sœur)* to bully sb

tyrannique [tiranik] ADJ tyrannical; **ne sois pas si t.** don't be such a tyrant; **il est t. avec elle** he bullies her

tyranniquement [tiranikmɑ̃] ADV tyrannically, like a tyrant

tyranniser [tiranize] VT *(quelqu'un)* to tyrannize; *(frère, sœur)* to bully

tyrannosaure [tiranozɔr] NM tyrannosaurus

Tyrol [tirɔl] NM **le T.** the Tyrol

tyrolien, -ienne [tirɔljɛ̃, -jɛn] ADJ Tyrolean
N **T.** Tyrolean, Tyrolese
NF *Mus* **tyrolienne** Tyrolienne

tzar [tsar, dzar] NM tsar, czar

tzarévitch [tsarevitʃ, dz-] NM tsarevitch, czarevitch

tzarine [tsarin, dz-] NF tsarina, czarina

tzigane [tsigan, dz-] ADJ, N tzigane, Hungarian gypsy

U, u [y] NM **1** *(lettre)* U, u; **fer en U** channel iron; *Géog* **vallée (à profil) en U** U-shaped valley; **tables (disposées) en U** tables arranged in a horseshoe **2** *Univ Fam (abrév* **universitaire) resto U** student refectory; **cité U** student residence, hall(s) of residence

UAS [yaɛs] NF *Com (abrév* **unité d'activité stratégique)** SBU

ubac [ybak] NM = shady side of an Alpine mountain, *Spéc* ubac

ubiquité [ybikɥite] NF ubiquity; **avoir le don d'u.** to have the ability to be in several places at the same time; **je n'ai pas le don d'u.** I can't be in two places at the same time

ubuesque [ybyɛsk] ADJ Ubuesque

UDF [ydeɛf] NF *(abrév* **Union pour la démocratie française)** = right-of-centre French political party

UE [yə] NF *(abrév* **Union européenne)** EU

UEM [yəɛm] NF *(abrév* **Union économique et monétaire)** EMU

UEO [yəo] NF *(abrév* **Union de l'Europe occidentale)** WEU

UER [yəɛr] NF *Univ Anciennement (abrév* **unité d'enseignement et de recherche)** = university department

ufologie [yfɔlɔʒi] NF ufology

UFR [yɛfɛr] NF *Univ (abrév* **unité de formation et de recherche)** = university department

UHF [yaʃɛf] *Radio (abrév* **ultra-haute fréquence)** UHF

UHT [yaʃte] *(abrév* **ultra-haute température)** UHT

ukase [ykɑz] NM *Hist* ukase; *Fig* **u. paternel** paternal fiat

Ukraine [ykrɛn] NF **l'U.** the Ukraine

ukrainien, -ienne [ykrɛnjɛ̃, -jɛn] ADJ Ukranian
  NM *Ling* Ukranian
  N **U.** Ukranian

ukulélé [jukulele] NM ukulele

ulcération [ylserasjɔ̃] NF *Méd* ulceration

ulcère [ylsɛr] NM ulcer; **avoir un u. à l'estomac** to have a stomach ulcer

ulcéré [ylsere] ADJ **1** *Méd* ulcerated **2** *Fig* **elle en était ulcérée** it rankled with her

ulcérer [ylsere] *(pr ind* **il ulcère;** *fu* **il ulcérera)** VT **1** *Méd* to ulcerate **2** *Fig* **u. qn** to cause resentment in sb, to embitter sb; **sa réaction m'a ulcéré** I resented his reaction, his reaction rankled with me
  VPR **s'ulcérer** *Méd* to ulcerate, to fester

ulcéreux, -euse [ylserø, -øz] ADJ *Méd* ulcerous; *(plaie)* ulcerated, festering

ULM [yɛlɛm] NM INV *Aviat (abrév* **ultraléger motorisé)** microlight

ulmaire [ylmɛr] NF *Bot* meadowsweet

ulnaire [ylnɛr] ADJ *Anat* ulnar

ultérieur [ylterjœr] ADJ later, subsequent (à

to); *(nouvelles, date etc)* later; *(dans le futur)* future; **notre voyage est remis à une date ultérieure** our trip has been postponed; **la parution de ce livre est ultérieure à celle du vôtre** this book came out after yours did

ultérieurement [ylterjœrmɑ̃] ADV later (on), subsequently

ultimatum [yltimatɔm] NM ultimatum; **adresser un u. à un pays** to present a country with an ultimatum

ultime [yltim] ADJ *(paroles, moment, phénomène)* (very) last; *(préparatifs)* final; **l'u. sacrifice** the ultimate sacrifice

ultimo [yltimo] ADV lastly, finally

ultra [yltra] N *Pol* extremist

ultra-chic ADJ *Fam* ultra-fashionable

ultracompétitif, -ive [yltrakɔ̃petitif, -iv] ADJ *(société, prix)* very highly competitive

ultraconfidentiel, -ielle ADJ top-secret

ultraconservateur, -trice ADJ *Pol* ultraconservative, far right

ultracourt ADJ *(jupe)* ultra-short, microscopic; *Phys* **ondes ultracourtes** ultra-short waves

ultrafin [yltrafɛ̃] ADJ *(filament, aiguille)* extra-fine

ultra-haute fréquence NF *Phys* ultrahigh frequency

ultraléger, -ère [yltraleʒe, -ɛr] ADJ ultralight
  NM microlight
  NF **ultralégère** *(cigarette)* superlight, ultra low

ultralibéralisme [yltraliberalism] NM extreme liberalism

ultramicroscope [yltramikrɔskɔp] NM ultra-microscope

ultramoderne [yltramɔdɛrn] ADJ *(équipement, voiture, intérieur)* ultramodern, state-of-the-art, high-tech; *(appartement)* ultra-modern, high-tech

ultramontain, -aine [yltramɔ̃tɛ̃, -ɛn] ADJ **1** *Rel, Pol* ultramontane **2** *(par rapport à la France)* beyond the Alps
  N *Rel, Pol* ultramontanist

ultraportatif [yltrapɔrtatif] NM notebook computer

ultrarapide [yltrarapid] ADJ *(avion, train, voiture)* ultrafast

ultraroyaliste ADJ, N *Hist* ultraroyalist

ultrasensible ADJ ultra-sensitive; **pellicule/film u.** ultra-sensitive *or* high-speed film; *Fam* **elle est u.** she's hypersensitive

ultrason NM *Phys* ultrasound; **ultrasons** ultrasonic waves; **science des ultrasons** ultrasonics

ultrasonique [yltrasɔnik], **ultrasonore** [yltrasɔnɔr] ADJ ultrasonic, supersonic

ultraviolet, -ette ADJ, NM ultraviolet; **faire une séance d'ultraviolets** to have a sunbed session

ululation [ylylasjɔ̃] NF, **ululement** [ylylmɑ̃] NM ululation; *(des oiseaux de nuit)* hooting

ululer [ylyle] VI to ululate; *(des oiseaux de nuit)* to hoot

Ulysse [ylis] NM Ulysses

UME [yɛmə] NF *(abrév* **Union monétaire européenne)** EMU

UMP [yɛmpe] NF **1** *(abrév* **Union pour la majorité présidentielle)** = former centre-right coalition, now renamed "Union pour un Mouvement Populaire" **2** *(abrév* **Union pour un mouvement populaire)** = centre-right French political party, formed mainly from members from the former RPR party

UMTS [yɛmteɛs] NM *Tél (abrév* **universal mobile telecommunications system)** UMTS

un, une [œ̃, yn] ADJ **1** one; **pourrais-tu me prêter un euro?** could you lend me a euro?; **tu n'aurais pas une pièce d'un euro?** you wouldn't happen to have a one-euro piece?; **deux brioches et un pain** two buns and a loaf (of bread); **il n'en reste qu'un** there's only one left; **il vient un jour sur deux** he comes every other *or* second day; **une personne/une maison sur cent** one person/house in a hundred; **un à un** [œ̃aœ̃], **un par un** one by one, one at a time; **il est une heure** it's one o'clock; **page un(e)** page one, the first page; **numéro un** number one
  2 *(uni)* one; **Dieu est un** God is one; **c'est tout un** [sɛtutœ̃] it's the same thing *or* all one *or* all the same; **ils ne font qu'un** *(ils sont très proches)* they are as one; **la maison et l'atelier ne font qu'un** the house and workshop are one and the same
  N **1** *(chiffre)* one; **un et un** [œ̃eœ̃] **font deux** one and one are two; **un(e), deux, trois, partez!** one, two, three, go!; **il n'a fait ni une ni deux** he didn't hesitate (for a moment); **et d'un(e) tu es toujours en retard, et de deux tu mens** for one thing you're always late, and for another you're lying, one, you're always late, and two, you're lying; *Fam* **en savoir plus d'une** to know a thing or two; *Fam* **il était moins une** it was a close thing *or* a close shave; **heureusement que je suis arrivé, il était moins une** it was lucky I arrived when I did, another minute and it would have been too late
  2 *(première page)* *Journ* **la une** [layn] *(d'un journal)* the front page, page one; **faire la une** *(d'un magazine)* to appear on *or* make the front cover; *(d'un journal)* to make the headlines; *Fig (faire parler de soi)* to make *or* hit the headlines; **la guerre fait la une** the war is front-page news *or* in the headlines; **tu es à la une des journaux** you've made the front page, you're front-page news *or* in the headlines
  PRON one; **un de ces jours** one of these days; **un qui a de la chance** a lucky one, a lucky man; **un qui a de la chance, c'est Pierre, il est parti à la Réunion** Pierre's one of the

lucky ones, he's gone off to Réunion; **en voilà une qui sait ce qu'elle veut!** there's somebody who knows what she wants!; **un que je plains, c'est ...** one person I do feel sorry for is ...; **il n'y en a pas un qui parle anglais** not one of them speaks English; *Fam* **pas un n'était au courant** not a (single solitary) soul *or* absolutely nobody knew about it; *Fam* **être menteur/hypocrite comme pas un** to be a dreadful liar/hypocrite; *Fam* **il fait du bruit comme pas un** he's unbelievably noisy; *Fam* **il danse comme pas un** he's a great dancer; **(l')un de nous, (l')un d'entre nous** one of us; **ni l'un ni l'autre** neither (of them), neither one nor the other; **ni l'un ni l'autre ne me plaît** I don't like either of them; **l'un dans l'autre** all in all, by and large; **(l')un des danseurs les plus célèbres du monde** one of the most famous dancers in the world; **l'une des voitures les plus vendues d'Europe** one of the biggest-selling cars in Europe; **les uns disent que ...** some say that ...; **les uns et les autres** people, everybody

ART INDÉF SEE GRAMMAR A5–6; B4–5 (*pl* **des**, *see* **de**) **1** a; *(devant voyelle ou h muet)* an; *(pl some)* **un jour/une pomme/une heure** a day/an apple/an hour; **un père et une mère** a father and mother; **un père de famille** the father of a family; **il est là pour un certain temps** he is here for some time; **cela ne durera qu'un temps** it won't last for long; **venez me voir un lundi** come and see me one Monday *or* some Monday; **cela tombe un mardi** it falls on a Tuesday; **un jour de la semaine dernière** one day last week; *Fam* **un de ces quatre** one of these days; **pour une raison ou pour une autre** for some reason or other
2 *(introduisant un nom propre)* a; *(devant voyelle ou h muet)* an; **c'est une Martin** she's a Martin, she's one of the Martins; **ce sera un Einstein** he'll be another Einstein
3 *(intensif)* **j'ai eu un monde aujourd'hui!** I've had such a lot of visitors today!; **il y a un de ces mondes en ville!** the town is incredibly busy, there are an incredible lot of people in town; **elle parle avec une élégance!** she has such an elegant way of putting things!; **il est d'une bêtise!** he is incredibly *or* so stupid!; **il a fait une de ces têtes!** you should have seen his face!; **elle a poussé un de ces cris** she gave such a shout; **tu m'as fait une peur!** you gave me such a fright!, you did give me a fright!

unanime [ynanim] ADJ *(approbation, vote etc)* unanimous; **ils sont unanimes à vous accuser** they are unanimous in accusing you

unanimement [ynanimmɑ̃] ADV unanimously

unanimité [ynanimite] NF *(d'une réponse, une réaction etc)* unanimity; **à l'u.** unanimously; **faire l'u.** *(d'une proposition, une invitation etc)* to be accepted unanimously

underground [œndœrgrawnd] ADJ, NM underground

une [yn] *voir* **un**

UNEF [ynɛf] NF *Univ (abrév* **Union nationale des étudiants de France***)* = French students' union, *Br* ≃ NUS

Unesco [ynɛsko] NF Unesco

unguéal, -ale, -aux, -ales [ɔ̃gɥeal, -o] ADJ (of the) nail; **infection unguéale** nail infection, infection of the nail

uni, -ie [yni] ADJ **1** *(famille, couple etc)* united; **ils sont très unis** they are very close **2** *(sans irrégularité) (sol, surface etc)* smooth, level, even; *(mer etc)* smooth, calm, unruffled **3** *(couleur)* plain; *(tissu, robe)* self-coloured, *Am* self-colored
NM *Tex* self-coloured *or Am* self-colored material
NF *Belg, Suisse Fam (abrév* **université***) Br* uni, *Am* school

uniate [ynjat] ADJ, N *Rel* Uniat(e)

Unicef [ynisɛf] NM OU F *(abrév* **United Nations International Children's Emergency Fund***)* **l'U.** Unicef

unicellulaire [yniselylɛr] ADJ *Biol* unicellular

unicité [ynisite] NF *Phil etc* uniqueness

unicolore [ynikɔlɔr] ADJ *(tissu etc)* self-coloured, *Am* self-colored, plain

unicorne [ynikɔrn] NM *Myth* unicorn
ADJ one-horned, single-horned

unidimensionnel, -elle [ynidimɑ̃sjɔnɛl] ADJ one-dimensional

unidirectionnel, -elle [ynidirɛksjɔnɛl] ADJ unidirectional

unidose [ynidoz] NF single-dose sachet; **ce médicament est disponible en u.** this medicine is available in single-dose sachets

unième [ynjɛm] ADJ *(used only in compounds)* **trente et u.** thirty-first

unièmement [ynjɛmmɑ̃] ADV *(used only in compounds)* **vingt et u.** in twenty-first place

unificateur, -trice [ynifikatœr, -tris] ADJ unifying

unification [ynifikasjɔ̃] NF *(d'un pays etc)* unification; *(des crédits)*, Pol *(de la législation)* consolidation; *(des poids et mesures etc)* standardization

unifier [ynifje] VT *(impf, pr sub n.* **unifiions**, *v.* **unifiiez***) (parti politique, pays etc)* to unify; *(crédits, législation)* to consolidate; *(poids et mesures etc)* to standardize

uniforme [ynifɔrm] ADJ *(opinions, expression)* uniform; *(vie)* unchanging; *(allure, surface)* even; *(mouvement)* regular; **taux u.** *(d'un intérêt etc)* flat rate
NM *Mil* **grand u.** full-dress uniform; **endosser l'u.** to join the forces; **le prestige de l'u.** the appeal of the uniform; **elle est sensible au prestige de l'u.** she has a thing about men in uniform; **quitter l'u.** to leave the service

uniformément [ynifɔrmemɑ̃] ADV *(réparti)* uniformly, evenly; *(avancer)* smoothly

uniformisation [ynifɔrmizasjɔ̃] NF standardization

uniformiser [ynifɔrmize] VT to standardize

uniformité [ynifɔrmite] NF *(d'un paysage)* sameness, uniformity; *(des habitudes, coutumes, de la vie etc)* monotony; *(de couleur, teinte)* uniformity

unijambiste [yniʒɑ̃bist] ADJ one-legged
N one-legged person

unilatéral, -ale, -aux, -ales [ynilateral, -o] ADJ *(décision, désarmement etc)* unilateral; *(contrat, accord)* one-sided; **stationnement u.** parking on one side only

unilatéralisme [ynilateralism] NM unilateralism

unilingue [ynilɛ̃g] ADJ *(dictionnaire, pays etc)* unilingual, monolingual

uniment [ynimɑ̃] ADV evenly; *Litt* **tout u.** *(simplement)* plainly, simply

uninominal, -ale, -aux, -ales [yninɔminal, -o] ADJ *Pol* **scrutin u.** voting for a single member *or* for one member only

union [ynjɔ̃] NF **1** *(alliance)* union; **l'u. du corps et de l'esprit** the union of mind and body **2** *(association) (de partis, consommateurs etc)* union, society, association **3** *(mariage)* marriage; **u. conjugale** marriage **4** *(accord, entente)* unity, agreement; *(entre les membres d'une famille, un groupe d'amis)* closeness, unity; **resserrer l'u. entre deux personnes** to strengthen the links *or* bond between two people; *Prov* **l'u. fait la force** unity is strength, strength through unity
▸ **u. douanière** customs union; **u. économique** economic union; **U. économique et** monétaire Economic and Monetary Union; **U. européenne** European Union; **u. libre** *(pour un couple non marié)* cohabitation; **vivre en u. libre** to live together, *surtout Jur* to cohabit; **u. monétaire** monetary union; **u. monétaire à deux vitesses** two-speed monetary union; **U. nationale des étudiants de France** French National Union of Students; **u. patronale** employers' organization; *Anciennement* **l'U. des républiques socialistes soviétiques** the Union of Soviet Socialist Republics; *Hist* **U. sacrée** = unity of all Frenchmen in the face of the enemy *(called for by Poincaré on the outbreak of the First World War)*; *Anciennement* **l'U. soviétique** the Soviet Union

unionisme [ynjɔnism] NM *Pol* unionist movement

unioniste [ynjɔnist] ADJ, N unionist

unipare [ynipar] ADJ *Biol* uniparous

unipersonnel, -elle [ynipɛrsɔnɛl] ADJ *Gram (verbe)* impersonal

unipolaire [ynipɔlɛr] ADJ *Élec (interrupteur etc)* unipolar, single-pole; *Biol (cellule, neurone etc)* unipolar

unique [ynik] ADJ **1** *(seul) (fils, tasse)* only; *(parti)* single; *(talent, savoir-faire, occasion, cas)* unique; **d'un même et u. problème** of one and the same problem; **c'est loin d'être un cas u.** it's far from being an isolated case; **il se croit u.** he thinks he's unique; **c'est vendu à un prix u. dans toute la France** it sells for the same price throughout France; **taille u.** one size; **c'est une taille u.** it only comes in the one size; **j'étais enfant u.** I was an only child; **(rue à) sens u.** one-way street; **c'est à sens u.** it's (a) one-way; **voie u.** single lane; **je possède l'exemplaire u.** I have the sole copy; **c'est un exemplaire u.** it's the only copy there is; **c'est une pièce de collection u. au monde** it's the only piece like it in the world; **c'est son u. souci** this is his sole *or* only concern; **c'est son u. sujet de conversation** it's all he ever talks about; **u. en son genre** one of a kind; **ce sont des gens uniques en leur genre** there's nobody like them; **ce fut une soirée u. en son genre** there's never been and there'll never be another party like it; **u. au monde** unlike anything else in the world; **c'est son seul et u. défaut** it's his one and only fault; **je ne ferai qu'une seule et u. critique** I have one and only one criticism to make; **la seule et l'u.** Arletty the one and only Arletty **2** *(incomparable)* unparalleled, unrivalled, unique; *Fam* **il est u.!** he's priceless!

uniquement [ynikmɑ̃] ADV just, only; **elle mange u. des légumes** she eats just *or* only vegetables, she eats nothing but vegetables; **je viens u. pour vous voir** I've come just to see you, the only reason I've come is to see you; **vous faites des dictionnaires? – pas u., nous faisons aussi des traductions** you compile dictionaries, don't you? – not just that, we do translations as well

unir [ynir] VT **1** *(relier) (personnes, territoires)* to unite; *(d'un pont, d'une autoroute)* to join, to link; **u. un territoire à un autre** to unite one territory with another; **le tunnel sous la Manche unit Londres à Paris** the Channel Tunnel links London and Paris; **être uni par le mariage à ...** to be joined in matrimony *or* marriage to ...; **vous voilà unis par les liens du mariage** ≃ I now pronounce you man and wife; **le Père Patrick les unira** Father Patrick will marry them *or* will officiate at their wedding; **l'amitié qui nous a toujours unis** the friendship there has always been between us; **un homme qui unit des qualités de décideur à un sens de l'humour** a man who combines decision-making abilities with a sense of humour **2** *(sol, surface etc)* to smooth, to level

vertèbre [vɛrtɛbr] NF *Anat* vertebra; **v. cervicale/dorsale/lombaire** cervical/dorsal/lumbar vertebra; **se déplacer une v.** to slip a disc

vertébré [vɛrtebre] ADJ, NM *Zool* vertebrate

vertement [vɛrtəmɑ̃] ADV **réprimander v. qn** to reprimand sb sharply *or* severely, *Fam* to give sb a good telling off *or* ticking off; **il le tança v.** he gave him a good dressing-down; **répondre v. à qn** to answer sb sharply, to give sb a sharp reply

vertical, -ale, -aux, -ales [vɛrtikal, -o] ADJ vertical, upright; *(organisation, structuration)* vertical; **en position verticale** *(objet)* in a vertical position, upright; *(personne)* in a standing position; **elle se sent mal en station verticale** she doesn't feel well when she stands up; **éclairage v.** overhead lighting; *Ordinat* **boîtier v.** tower; *Écon* **concentration verticale** vertical integration ▪ NF **verticale** vertical; *Tech* plumb-line; **à la verticale** vertically; *(monter)* vertically, straight up; *(tomber, descendre)* vertically, straight down; **la falaise tombe à la verticale dans la mer** there is a sheer drop from the cliff to the sea; **falaise à la verticale** sheer cliff

verticalement [vɛrtikalmɑ̃] ADV vertically; *(avec mouvement vers le haut)* straight up; *(avec mouvement vers le bas)* straight down; *(dans les mots croisés)* down

verticalité [vɛrtikalite] NF verticality

verticille [vɛrtisil] NM *Bot* whorl

vertige [vɛrtiʒ] NM vertigo, fear of heights; *(étourdissement)* dizziness, giddiness, dizzy spell; **cela me donne le v.** it gives me vertigo, it makes me feel dizzy *or* giddy, it makes my head swim; **des salaires à vous donner le v.** salaries that make your head spin; **je n'ai pas le v.** I'm not scared of heights; **avoir facilement le v.** to have a bad head for heights; **avoir des vertiges** to get dizzy *or* giddy, to have fits of giddiness, to have dizzy spells; *Fig* **les vertiges du succès** the feeling of intoxication that success brings

vertigineusement [vɛrtiʒinøzmɑ̃] ADV dizzily, *Fml* vertiginously; **une route v. escarpée** a breathtakingly steep road

vertigineux, -euse [vɛrtiʒinø, -øz] ADJ *(hauteur etc)* dizzy, giddy; *(vitesse)* breakneck, breathtaking; *(somme)* staggering; **hausse vertigineuse des prix** staggering increase in prices

vertigo [vɛrtigo] NM *Vét* (blind) staggers

vertiport [vɛrtipɔr] NM *Aviat* heliport

vertu [vɛrty] NF **1** *(de remède etc)* quality, property, virtue; **v. sédative/calmante** sedative/calming property; **plantes aux vertus curatives** plants that have healing properties; **en v. de** by virtue of; *Jur* in pursuance of; **en v. de quoi est-il intervenu?** what gave him the right to intervene?; **et en v. de ce contrat, vous nous devez ...** under the terms of this contract, you owe us ...; **vous avez signé ce contrat, en v. de quoi vous nous devez une certaine prestation** you signed this contract, under the terms of which *or* in accordance with which you owe us a certain sum of money; **en v. de cet arrangement** under (the terms of) this agreement **2** *(morale)* virtue; **faire de nécessité v.** to make a virtue (out) of necessity; **l'honnêteté est une v.** honesty is a virtue; **il a de la v. à la supporter** I admire his courage in putting up with her; **je n'ai aucune v. à ne pas fumer, je n'aime pas ça** I can't claim any credit for not smoking *or Fml* there is nothing admirable in my not smoking, I just don't like it; **elle le pare de toutes les vertus** she's forever singing his praises; **femme de petite v.** woman of easy virtue

vertueusement [vɛrtɥøzmɑ̃] ADV virtuously

vertueux, -euse [vɛrtɥø, -øz] ADJ virtuous; **intentions vertueuses** honourable intentions; *Arch* **femme vertueuse** virtuous *or* chaste woman

vertugadin [vɛrtygadɛ̃] NM *Hist* farthingale

verve [vɛrv] NF verve, vigour, *Am* vigor, *Fam* go; **être v.** to be in top form; **jouer avec v.** to give a spirited performance

verveine [vɛrvɛn] NF *Bot* vervain, verbena; **(tisane de) v.** verbena tea; **(liqueur de) v. =** verbena flavoured liqueur

verveux ¹, -euse [vɛrvø, -øz] ADJ *Litt* animated, lively, spirited

verveux ² NM *(filet)* hoop net

vesce [vɛs] NF *Bot* vetch, tare

vésical, -ale, -aux, -ales [vezikal, -o] ADJ *Anat* vesical

vésicant [vezikɑ̃] ADJ, NM *Méd* vesicatory; **gaz v.** blister gas

vésicatoire [vezikatwar] ADJ, NM *Méd* vesicatory; **appliquer un v. à qn** to blister sb

vésicule [vezikyl] NF **1** *Anat* vesicle; *Bot* air cell; *Anat* **v. biliaire** gall bladder **2** *(sur la peau)* blister

vespasienne [vɛspazjɛn] NF street urinal

vespéral, -ale, -aux, -ales [vɛsperal, -o] ADJ evening

vesse-de-loup, *pl* **vesses-de-loup** [vɛsdəlu] NF puffball

vessie [vesi] NF *Anat etc* bladder; **v. natatoire** *(de poisson)* air bladder, swim bladder; *Méd* **v. à ou de glace** ice bag *or* pack; *Fig* **prendre des vessies pour des lanternes** to believe that the moon is made of green cheese

vestale [vɛstal] NF *Antiq* vestal (virgin)

veste [vɛst] NF jacket; **v. d'intérieur** smoking jacket; **v. croisée** double-breasted jacket; *Fam* **tomber la v.** to take off one's jacket; *Fig* **retourner sa v.** to be a turncoat; *Fig Fam* **ramasser** *ou* **prendre une v.** *(échouer)* to come unstuck; *(être rejeté)* to get turned down, *Br* to get a knockback

> Il faut noter que le terme anglais **vest** est un faux ami. Il signifie **maillot de corps** en anglais britannique et **gilet** en anglais américain.

vestiaire [vɛstjɛr] NM **1** *(dans un théâtre etc)* cloakroom; *Sport etc* changing room, locker room; *Jur* robing room; *Théâtre Fam* **au v.!** off! off! **2** *(vêtements)* **renouveler son v.** to renew one's wardrobe; *Fam* **mon v., s'il vous plaît** could I have my coat/hat and coat, please?; **récupérer son v.** to collect one's things from the cloakroom; *Fig* **laisser sa fierté/ses principes au v.** to forget one's pride/principles **3** *(meuble) (dans une usine etc)* locker

vestibule [vɛstibyl] NM vestibule, (entrance) hall, lobby

vestige [vɛstiʒ] NM *(d'anciennes habitations etc)* vestige, trace; **derniers vestiges de ...** last remnants of ...; **vestiges du passé** relics of the past

vestimentaire [vɛstimɑ̃tɛr] ADJ *(commerce)* clothing; **détails vestimentaires** accessories

veston [vɛstɔ̃] NM *(d'homme)* jacket; *Naut* monkey jacket; **complet v.** lounge suit

Vésuve [vezyv] NM Vesuvius

vêtement [vɛtmɑ̃] NM garment, article *or* item of clothing; **vêtements** clothes, clothing; **mon budget vêtements** my clothes *or* clothing budget; **industrie du v.** clothing *or Fam* rag trade; **tissus pour vêtements** dress material; **mettre ses vêtements du dimanche** to put on one's Sunday best; **vêtements de plage/de pluie** beachwear/rainwear; *Rel* **vêtements sacerdotaux** vestments; **tu devrais mettre** *ou* **passer un v.** you should put something on

vétéran [veterɑ̃] NM *Mil etc* veteran, old campaigner; *Sport* veteran; *Fig* old hand; *Pol* elder statesman

vétérinaire [veterinɛr] ADJ veterinary ▪ N vet, *Br Fml* veterinary surgeon, *Am* veterinarian

vétille [vetij] NF (mere) trifle, triviality; **vétilles** trivia; **se disputer pour des vétilles** to argue over trivialities *or* trivial details

vétilleux, -euse [vetijø, -øz] ADJ *Litt* captious

vêtir [vetir] (*prp* **vêtant**; *pp* **vêtu**; *pr ind* **je vêts, n. vêtons**; *impf* **je vêtais**; *p hist* **je vêtis**; *fu* **je vêtirai**) VT *(quelqu'un)* to clothe, to dress (**de** in); **tout de noir vêtu** dressed *or Fml* clad all in black ▪ VPR **se vêtir** to dress (oneself) (**de** in)

vétiver [vetivɛr] NM vetiver

veto [veto] NM veto; **opposer son v. à qch** to veto sth, to exercise one's veto over sth; **mettre son v. à qch** to veto sth; **droit de v.** right of veto

véto [veto] N *Fam* (*abrév* **vétérinaire**) vet, *Am* veterinarian

vêtu [vety] ADJ dressed; **v. de blanc/de lin** dressed in white/in linen; **être v. chaudement** *ou* **chaudement v.** to be warmly dressed; **professeurs vêtus de leurs toges** professors wearing *or* in their gowns; **à demi-v.** half-dressed; *Litt* **mur v. de lierre** ivy-clad wall, wall covered in ivy

vétuste [vetyst] ADJ decayed, decrepit

vétusté [vetyste] NF decay, decrepitude

veuf, veuve [vœf, vœv] ADJ *(homme, femme)* widowed; *Fig* **v. de qch** bereft of sth ▪ N **widower,** *f* **widow** ▪ NF **veuve 1** *Typ* widow **2** *Fam Arch* **la Veuve** the guillotine **3** *très Fam* **la veuve Poignet** masturbation; **fréquenter la veuve Poignet** to bang *or Br* bash the bishop

veule [vøl] ADJ *(personne etc)* weak, feeble; **un air v.** a listless look

veulerie [vølri] NF inertia, listlessness

veuvage [vœvaʒ] NM widowhood

vexant [vɛksɑ̃] ADJ **1** *(remarque, personne etc)* hurtful **2** *Vieilli (contrariant)* vexing, provoking, annoying; **nous nous sommes manquées de peu, c'est v.!** how annoying that we just missed each other!

vexation [vɛksasjɔ̃] NF **1** *(humiliation)* mortification; **essuyer** *ou* **subir des vexations** to be snubbed *or* put down; **elle ne supporte pas les vexations** she can't stand being snubbed *or* put down; **être en proie aux vexations de qn** to be constantly being snubbed *or* put down by sb **2** *Vieilli (mauvais traitement)* vexation

vexatoire [vɛksatwar] ADJ vexatious

vexer [vɛkse] VT **v. qn** to hurt sb *or* sb's feelings ▪ VPR **se vexer** to get upset *or* offended; **elle se vexe facilement** she gets upset very easily, she's easily offended; **se v. de qch** to feel hurt *or* to be upset by sth; **il se vexe de tout/pour un rien** he gets upset over everything/the slightest thing

> Il faut noter que le verbe anglais **to vex** est un faux ami. Il signifie **fâcher, chagriner.**

VF [veɛf] NF (*abrév* **version française**) French version

VHF [veaʃɛf] NF VHF

VHS [veaʃɛs] NM (*abrév* **video home system**) VHS

VI [vei] NF *Compta* (*abrév* **valeur d'in-**

ventaire) balance sheet value, break-up value

via [vja] PRÉP via, by way of; **Paris, v. Calais** Paris, via Calais

viabilisé [vjabilize] ADJ Admin **terrain v.** serviced site, site with services

viabiliser [vjabilize] VT to service; **v. un terrain** to service a site; **v. une entreprise** to make a business viable

viabilité¹ [vjabilite] NF (d'un fœtus) viability, survival potential; (d'un projet etc) viability

viabilité² NF 1 (de chemin etc) practicability 2 Constr (d'un site de construction) development

viable [vjabl] ADJ (fœtus, projet etc) viable

viaduc [vjadyk] NM viaduct

viager, -ère [vjaʒe, -ɛr] ADJ (for) life; **rente viagère** life annuity
NM life interest; **placer son argent en v.** to invest one's money in or to buy an annuity; **acheter une propriété en v.** = to acquire a property by paying predetermined instalments until the death of the owner(s)

viande [vjɑ̃d] NF 1 meat; **v. de boucherie** butcher meat, fresh meat; **v. blanche/rouge** white/red meat; **jus de v.** meat juices, gravy; **v. hachée** minced or Am ground meat, Br mince; **v. de cheval** horsemeat, horseflesh 2 Arg **amène ta v.!** come on, move your carcass!; **il y a de la v. soûle dans les rues** the streets are full of drunken bodies; **de la v. froide** (un cadavre) a stiff; (des cadavres) stiffs

viander (se) [səvjɑ̃de] VPR Fam to get smashed up; **ils se sont viandés contre un mur** they smashed into a wall

viatique [vjatik] NM 1 Vieilli (argent) money; (provisions) provisions for a journey; **on lui a donné un v. de 200 livres pour son voyage** we gave him £200 for his trip; Fig Litt **il n'a que ce diplôme pour v.** this diploma is his sole asset; **j'avais pour seul v. cette lettre de recommandation** this letter was all I had to recommend me 2 Rel last sacrament

vibrant [vibrɑ̃] ADJ 1 (corde etc) vibrating; **consonne vibrante** vibrant consonant 2 (voix) resonant, vibrant; (discours) rousing, stirring; (personnalité etc) vibrant; **v. et réceptif** (personne) eager and receptive; **c'est une nature vibrante** he is very sensitive or highly strung

vibraphone [vibrafɔn] NM Mus vibraphone

vibraphoniste [vibrafɔnist] N Mus vibraphone player

vibrateur [vibratœr] NM vibrator

vibration [vibrasjɔ̃] NF 1 vibration; (de la voix) resonance; Phys **v. de la lumière** vibration of light 2 Tél (de téléphone portable) vibrating alert

vibrato [vibrato] NM Mus vibrato

vibratoire [vibratwar] ADJ vibratory

vibrer [vibre] VI to vibrate; Fig **v. d'enthousiasme** to be quivering with excitement; Fig **faire v. le cœur de qn** to make sb's heart pound; Fig **c'est la seule chose qui le fait v.** it's the only thing that gets him going

vibreur [vibrœr] NM Tech vibrator; (d'une sonnette) buzzer

vibrion [vibrijɔ̃] NM 1 (bactérie) vibrio(n); Méd **v. septique** gas bacillus 2 (personne agitée) fidget

vibromasseur [vibromasœr] NM (électrique) (pour massage) vibrator

vicaire [vikɛr] NM Rel 1 **v. apostolique** vicar apostolic; **grand v., v. général** vicar-general 2 Rel (dans l'église anglicaine) curate; Cathol (assistant) priest

vicariat [vikarja] NM Rel curacy

vice [vis] NM 1 (défaut moral) vice; **il a tous**

les vices he has all the vices; **il a le v. de la boisson** drinking is his vice; Fig **mais c'est un v.!** it's an obsession!, he/she/they etc is/are totally obsessed! 2 (défaut) fault, defect, flaw 3 (corruption etc) vice; **vivre dans le v.** to lead a life of vice
▸▸ Com **v. apparent** obvious defect; **v. caché** hidden or latent defect; Vét etc **v. de conformation** (congenital) malformation, physical defect; **v. de construction** structural fault or defect or flaw; **v. de fabrication** manufacturing defect; Jur **v. de forme** legal technicality; (dans un contrat etc) flaw; Com **v. inhérent** inherent vice; **v. contre nature** unnatural vice; **v. de prononciation** faulty pronunciation; **v. propre** inherent defect; Com **v. rédhibitoire** material defect; **v. solitaire** masturbation, self-abuse

vice-amiral, pl **vice-amiraux** NM vice admiral

vice-chancelier, pl **vice-chanceliers** NM vice chancellor

vice-consul, pl **vice-consuls** NM vice-consul

vice-consulat, pl **vice-consulats** NM vice-consulate

vice-gérant, -ante, pl **vice-gérant(e)s** N deputy manager

vicelard, -arde [vislar, -ard] Fam ADJ 1 (dépravé) dirty 2 (perfide) vicious
N lecher, pervert; **un vieux v.** a dirty old man; **c'est une petite vicelarde!** she's a little tramp!

vicennal, -ale, -aux, -ales [visenal, -o] ADJ (qui dure vingt ans) twenty-year, Fml vicennial; (qui a lieu tous les vingt ans) occurring every twenty years, Fml vicennial

vice-présidence, pl **vice-présidences** NF (d'État, d'organisation) vice-presidency; (d'entreprise) vice-chairmanship

vice-président, -ente, pl **vice-président(e)s** N (d'État, d'organisation) vice-president; (d'entreprise) vice-chairman

vice-roi, pl **vice-rois** NM viceroy

vice versa [vis(e)vɛrsa] ADV vice versa

vichy [viʃi] NM 1 Tex gingham; **jupe en v. rouge et blanc** red and white checked cotton skirt, red and white gingham skirt 2 (eau minérale) vichy water; **v. fraise** = strawberry syrup in vichy water 3 V. Vichy; Hist **la France de V.** Vichy France

viciateur, -trice [visjatœr, -tris] ADJ contaminating, Fml vitiating

viciation [visjasjɔ̃] NF (de principes, moraux etc) corruption, Fml vitiation; (de l'air etc) pollution, contamination; (du sang) thinness; Jur (d'un contrat) invalidation, vitiation

vicié [visje] ADJ corrupt, Fml vitiated; (sang) poor, thin; **air v.** (par des émanations) stale or foul air

vicier [visje] VT (impf, pr sub n. viciions, vous viciiez) 1 to corrupt, Fml to vitiate; (air) to pollute, to contaminate; Fig (jugement, goût) to corrupt 2 Jur (contrat) to invalidate, to vitiate

vicieusement [visjøzmɑ̃] ADV 1 (avec dépravation) lecherously 2 (perfidement) viciously

vicieux, -ieuse [visjø, -jøz] ADJ 1 (corrompu) (personne) depraved 2 (perfide) (personne, coup) underhand, sly; **cercle v.** vicious circle 3 (incorrecte) (prononciation) wrong, incorrect 4 (rétif) (cheval) bad-tempered

---

Il faut noter que l'adjectif anglais **vicious** est un faux ami. Il signifie **méchant, agressif**.

---

vicinal, -ale, -aux, -ales [visinal, -o] ADJ **chemin v.** local road

NM Belg (tramway de banlieue) suburban tram

vicissitude [visisityd] NF vicissitude; **les vicissitudes de la vie** ou **de l'existence** the ups and downs or trials and tribulations of life

vicomte, -esse [vikɔ̃t, -ɛs] N viscount, f viscountess

vicomté [vikɔ̃te] NF 1 (titre) viscountcy 2 (terrain) viscounty

victime [viktim] NF 1 victim; **les victimes du désastre/de la guerre** the victims or casualties of the disaster/of war; **les victimes de la route** road accident victims; **être (la) v. d'un système d'imposition** to be badly hit by a system of taxation; **être (la) v. d'une illusion/d'un malentendu** to labour or Am labor under an illusion/a misconception; **j'ai été (la) v. d'un escroc** I've been had by a conman; **se prendre pour une v.** to think oneself a victim, to feel victimized; **j'ai dû être v. d'une hallucination** I must have been hallucinating; **être v. de la fourberie/négligence de qn** to be the victim of sb's deceit/negligence 2 (de sacrifice) victim

victimologie [viktimɔlɔʒi] NF victimology

victoire [viktwar] NF 1 victory; Sport win, victory; **remporter la v.** to gain a victory (sur over), to carry or win the day; **remporter une v. sur soi-même** to triumph over oneself; **chanter** ou **crier v.** to claim victory; **v. à la Pyrrhus** Pyrrhic victory 2 (déesse) V. Victory, Victoria

Victoria [viktɔrja] NF 1 **la reine V.** Queen Victoria 2 **v.** (voiture) victoria

victorien, -ienne [viktɔrjɛ̃, -jɛn] ADJ Victorian

victorieusement [viktɔrjøzmɑ̃] ADV victoriously

victorieux, -ieuse [viktɔrjø, -jøz] ADJ victorious; (air, sourire etc) triumphant; Sport **sortir v. d'une épreuve/d'un match** to emerge the winner of a heat/a match; **être v.** to win (the day), to be victorious

victuailles [viktɥaj] NFPL Vieilli food, provisions, Fml victuals

vidage [vidaʒ] NM 1 (de poissons) gutting, cleaning; (de volailles) drawing 2 Fam (d'un bar etc) throwing out, chucking out 3 Ordinat dump

vidange [vidɑ̃ʒ] NF 1 Aut oil change; **faire la v.** to change the oil; **v.-graissage** oil change and lubrication; **bouchon de v.** sump plug; (de radiateur) draining plug; **robinet de v.** draincock; **tuyau de v.** waste pipe; **tonneau en v.** broached cask 2 (d'un carter à huile, d'une fosse d'aisances etc) draining, emptying; (d'une chaudière) blowing off 3 Belg (bouteille vide consignée) returnable empty
NFPL **vidanges** sewage

vidanger [vidɑ̃ʒe] VT (je vidangeai(s); n. vidangeons) (fosse d'aisances, radiateur, carter à huile etc) to empty, to drain; (chaudière) to blow off; (huile, eaux résidentielles) to empty out, to drain off

vidangeur [vidɑ̃ʒœr] NM 1 (de fosses septiques) cesspit clearer or emptier 2 Can Fam (éboueur) dustman, Am garbage collector

vide [vid] ADJ (verre, pièce etc) empty; (case dans un document etc) blank; (siège, place) empty, unoccupied, vacant; **la ville est v. de ses habitants** the town is empty (of its inhabitants); **l'appartement est encore très v.** (peu meublé) the flat is still very bare; **bouteilles vides** empty bottles, Fam empties; **arriver les mains vides** to arrive empty-handed; **je suis rentré de vacances les poches vides** I came back from holiday penniless; **avoir l'estomac v.** to have an empty stomach; **j'ai l'estomac v.** my stomach is empty; **j'ai la tête v.** my mind's a blank; **ma vie est v.** my life is empty; **v. de sens** devoid

X, x [iks] NM INV **1** *(lettre)* X, x **2** *(nombre inconnu, personne inconnue)* X, x; **Monsieur X** Mr X; **je vous l'ai dit x fois** I've told you umpteen times *or* a thousand times; **dans x années** in X number of years; **plainte contre X** suit against person or persons unknown **3** *Méd* **rayons X** X-rays **4** *Univ Fam* **l'X** the École polytechnique; **un X** a student at the École polytechnique **5** *Cin* **film classé X** adults-only *or* X-rated film **6** *Jur* **accoucher sous X** to give birth anonymously; **naître sous X** to be born to an unidentified mother **7** *Fam (ecstasy)* X, E

xanthome [gzɑ̃tom] NM *Méd* fatty lump, *Spéc* xanthoma

xanthophylle [gzɑ̃tɔfil] NF *Bot* xanthophyll

xénon [gzenɔ̃] NM *Chimie* xenon

xénophobe [gzenɔfɔb] ADJ xenophobic N xenophobe

xénophobie [gzenɔfɔbi] NF xenophobia

Xénophon [gzenɔfɔ̃] NM Xenophon

xérès [keres, gzeres] NM *(vin)* sherry N **X.** *(ville)* Jerez

xérophile [gzerɔfil] ADJ *Bot* xerophilous

xérophyte [gzerɔfit] NF *Bot* xerophyte

Xerxès [gzerses] NM Xerxes

xiphoïde [gzifɔid] ADJ *Anat* **appendice x.** xiphoid process

xiphophore [gzifɔfɔr] NM *(poisson)* swordtail

xylène [gzilɛn] NM *Chimie* xylene

xylographe [gzilɔgraf] N wood-engraver, *Spéc* xylographer

xylographie [gzilɔgrafi] NF **1** *(technique)* wood-engraving, *Spéc* xylography **2** *(gravure)* woodcut, *Spéc* xylograph

xylophage [gzilɔfaʒ] *Zool* ADJ wood-eating NM wood-eater

xylophone [gsilɔfɔn, gz-] NM *Mus* xylophone

xylophoniste [gzilɔfɔnist] N xylophone player

Y, y¹ [igrek] **NM INV** (*lettre*) Y, y

y² [i] [SEE GRAMMAR B20] **ADV** (*lieu*) there; **est-il à Paris? – oui, il y est** is he in Paris? – yes, he is (there); **je ne m'y sentais pas très bien, dans cette ville** I didn't feel very happy in that town; **j'y suis, j'y reste!** here I am and here I stay!; **je n'y suis pour personne** I'm not at home to anybody; *Fam* **ah, j'y suis!** ah, now I've got *or* I get it; **excusez-moi, je n'y étais pas du tout** I'm sorry, I didn't get that at all; **vous n'y êtes pas du tout** you're way off the mark; **pendant que vous y êtes** while you're at *or* about it; *Iron* **non mais fouille dans mes affaires pendant que tu y es!** just rummage through my things, why don't you!

PRON INV 1 j'y pense sans cesse I think about it constantly; **l'aider? tu n'y penses pas!** help him? what are you thinking of?; **vous y avez tout intérêt** you'd be well advised to; **je n'y comprends rien** I can't make head nor tail of it; **tu as l'air de t'y connaître en informatique** you seem to know quite a bit about computers *or* what you're doing when it comes to computers; **je ne m'y connais pas du tout** I don't know the slightest thing about it/them; **tu peux lui faire confiance, il s'y connaît** you can trust him, he knows what he's doing; **j'y gagnerai** I'll gain by it; **n'y compte pas** don't count on it; **je m'y attendais** I expected as much; **ça, on pouvait s'y attendre** it was to be expected; **venez nous voir – je n'y manquerai pas** come and see us – I certainly shall *or* I'll do that

2 (*standing for person just mentioned*) **pensez-vous encore à lui? – oui, j'y pense sans cesse** do you still think of him? – yes I do, all the time; **les femmes? je n'y comprends rien** women? I don't understand them

3 (*indeterminate uses*) **je vous y prends!** caught you!; **ça y est, on peut manger/elle est prête** OK, we can eat/she's ready; **ça y est, j'ai une idée!** I've had an idea!; **alors ça y est, tu as fini?** have you finished?; **ça y est, la vitre est cassée!** I knew it, they've broken the window!; **ça y est, j'ai trouvé!** (*solution*)

I've got it!; **ça y est enfin, je l'ai retrouvé!** I've found it at last!; **j'y suis pour un tiers** I'm in for a third; **elle n'y est pour rien** she's got nothing to do with it; **il y est pour quelque chose** he's got a hand in it, he's got something to do with it; **il doit y être pour une bonne part** (*dans une décision*) he must have had a lot to do with it; **j'ai tout mangé, y compris les légumes** I've eaten everything, including the vegetables

4 (*imperative form preceding y takes s for liaison*) **vas-y** [vazi] go there; (*agis*) go on!, get on with it!; **penses-y** [pɑ̃szi] think about it

y³ **PRON PERS** *Fam* = **il**

*****yacht** [jɔt] **NM** yacht; **croisière en y.** yachting cruise; **y. de croisière** cabin cruiser

*****yacht-club,** *pl* **yacht-clubs NM** yacht club

*****yachting** [jɔtiŋ] **NM** yachting; **faire du y.** to go yachting

*****yacht(s)man,** *pl* **yacht(s)men** [jɔtman, -mɛn] **NM** yachtsman

*****ya(c)k** [jak] **NM** *Zool* yak

*****yang** [jɑ̃g] **NM** yang

*****yankee** [jɑ̃ki] **ADJ** Yankee
N Y. Yankee

*****yaourt** [jaur(t)] **NM** yog(h)urt; **y. nature/aux fruits/aromatisé** plain/fruit/flavoured *or Am* flavored yog(h)urt; **y. maigre** low-fat yog(h)urt

*****yaourtière** [jaurtjɛr] **NF** (*appareil*) yog(h)urt maker

*****yatagan** [jatagɑ̃] **NM** (*sabre*) yataghan

*****yearling** [jœrliŋ] **NM** yearling (colt)

*****Yémen** [jemɛn] **NM** Yemen

*****yéménite** [jemenit] **ADJ** Yemeni
N Y. Yemeni

*****yen** [jɛn] **NM** (*monnaie japonaise*) yen

*****yeti** [jeti] **NM** yeti

yeuse [jøz] **NF** *Bot* ilex, holm-oak, holly-oak

yeux [jœ] **NMPL** *voir* **œil**

*****yé-yé** [jeje] *Vieilli* **ADJ INV** (*chanteur, groupe*)

(60s style) pop; (*style, mode*) 60s
N INV pop fan

*****yiddish** [jidiʃ] **ADJ INV, NM** Yiddish

*****yi-king** [jikiŋ] **NM** I Ching

*****yin** [jin] **NM** yin

*****yoga** [jɔga] **NM** yoga; **faire du y.** to do yoga; **cours/prof/posture de y.** yoga class/teacher/position

*****yoghourt** [jogurt] **NM** = **yaourt**

*****yogi** [jɔgi] **NM** yogi

*****yogourt** [jogurt] **NM** = **yaourt**

*****yole** [jɔl] **NF** *Naut* gig, skiff

*****Yom Kippour** [jɔmkipur] **NM** *Rel* Yom Kippur

*****yorkshire** [jɔrkʃœr] **NM** Yorkshire terrier

*****yougoslave** [jugoslav] *Anciennement* **ADJ** Yugoslav, Yugoslavian
N Y. Yugoslav, Yugoslavian

*****Yougoslavie** [jugoslavi] **NF** *Anciennement* Yugoslavia; **l'ex-Y.** the former Yugoslavia

youp [jup] **INT** hup!

*****youpala** [jupala] **NM** baby bouncer

youpi [jupi] **INT** yippee!

*****youpin, -ine** [jupɛ̃, -in] **N** *Fam* (*terme injurieux*) (*juif*) Yid, *Am* hebe

*****youyou** [juju] **NM** *Naut* dinghy

*****Yo-Yo**® [jojo] **NM INV** yo-yo

yoyoter [jɔjɔte] **VI** *Fam* **1** (*mal fonctionner*) to be on the blink, *Am* to be on the fritz **2** (*déraisonner*) to have a screw *or Br* a slate loose, to be off one's trolley

ypérite [iperit] **NF** *Mil* mustard gas, *Spéc* yperite

ypréau, -aux [ipreo] **NM** *Bot* **1** (*orme*) wych-elm **2** (*peuplier blanc*) white poplar

ytterbium [itɛrbjɔm] **NM** *Chimie* ytterbium

yttrium [itrijɔm] **NM** *Chimie* yttrium

*****yuan** [juan] **NM** yuan

*****yucca** [juka] **NM** *Bot* yucca

*****Yukon** [jukɔ] **NM le Y.** the Yukon

*****yuppie** [jœpi, jupi] **N** yuppie

An asterisk before a noun indicates that the definite article is **le** *or* **la**, *not* **l'**